Volume 1 / **Fundamental Algorithms**

MW01194184

THE ART OF
COMPUTER PROGRAMMING

THIRD EDITION

Upper Saddle River, NJ · Boston · Indianapolis · San Francisco
New York · Toronto · Montréal · London · Munich · Paris · Madrid
Capetown · Sydney · Tokyo · Singapore · Mexico City

TeX is a trademark of the American Mathematical Society

METAFONT is a trademark of Addison–Wesley

The publisher offers excellent discounts on this book when ordered in quantity for bulk purposes or special sales, which may include electronic versions and/or custom covers and content particular to your business, training goals, marketing focus, and branding interests. For more information, please contact:

    U.S. Corporate and Government Sales   (800) 382–3419
    corpsales@pearsontechgroup.com

For sales outside the U.S., please contact:

    International Sales   international@pearsoned.com

Visit us on the Web: informit.com/aw

Library of Congress Cataloging-in-Publication Data

```
Knuth, Donald Ervin, 1938-
  The art of computer programming / Donald Ervin Knuth.
  xx,652 p.  24 cm.
  Includes bibliographical references and index.
  Contents: v. 1. Fundamental algorithms. -- v. 2. Seminumerical
algorithms. -- v. 3. Sorting and searching. -- v. 4a. Combinatorial
algorithms, part 1.
  Contents: v. 1. Fundamental algorithms. -- 3rd ed.
  ISBN 978-0-201-89683-1 (v. 1, 3rd ed.)
  ISBN 978-0-201-89684-8 (v. 2, 3rd ed.)
  ISBN 978-0-201-89685-5 (v. 3, 2nd ed.)
  ISBN 978-0-201-03804-0 (v. 4a)
  1. Electronic digital computers--Programming.  2. Computer
algorithms.   I. Title.
QA76.6.K64  1997
005.1--DC21                                            97-2147
```

Internet page http://www-cs-faculty.stanford.edu/~knuth/taocp.html contains current information about this book and related books.

ISBN-13 978-0-201-89683-1
ISBN-10   0-201-89683-4

Text printed in the United States at Courier Westford in Westford, Massachusetts.
Twenty-ninth printing, January 2012

*This series of books is affectionately dedicated
to the Type 650 computer once installed at
Case Institute of Technology,
in remembrance of many pleasant evenings.*

DONALD E. KNUTH *Stanford University*

ADDISON–WESLEY

PREFACE

Here is your book, the one your thousands of letters have asked us
to publish. It has taken us years to do, checking and rechecking countless
recipes to bring you only the best, only the interesting, only the perfect.
Now we can say, without a shadow of a doubt, that every single one of them,
if you follow the directions to the letter, will work for you exactly as well
as it did for us, even if you have never cooked before.

— *McCall's Cookbook* (1963)

THE PROCESS of preparing programs for a digital computer is especially attractive, not only because it can be economically and scientifically rewarding, but also because it can be an aesthetic experience much like composing poetry or music. This book is the first volume of a multi-volume set of books that has been designed to train the reader in various skills that go into a programmer's craft.

The following chapters are *not* meant to serve as an introduction to computer programming; the reader is supposed to have had some previous experience. The prerequisites are actually very simple, but a beginner requires time and practice in order to understand the concept of a digital computer. The reader should possess:

a) Some idea of how a stored-program digital computer works; not necessarily the electronics, rather the manner in which instructions can be kept in the machine's memory and successively executed.

b) An ability to put the solutions to problems into such explicit terms that a computer can "understand" them. (These machines have no common sense; they do exactly as they are told, no more and no less. This fact is the hardest concept to grasp when one first tries to use a computer.)

c) Some knowledge of the most elementary computer techniques, such as looping (performing a set of instructions repeatedly), the use of subroutines, and the use of indexed variables.

d) A little knowledge of common computer jargon — "memory," "registers," "bits," "floating point," "overflow," "software." Most words not defined in the text are given brief definitions in the index at the close of each volume.

These four prerequisites can perhaps be summed up into the single requirement that the reader should have already written and tested at least, say, four programs for at least one computer.

I have tried to write this set of books in such a way that it will fill several needs. In the first place, these books are reference works that summarize the knowledge that has been acquired in several important fields. In the second place, they can be used as textbooks for self-study or for college courses in the computer and information sciences. To meet both of these objectives, I have incorporated a large number of exercises into the text and have furnished answers for most of them. I have also made an effort to fill the pages with facts rather than with vague, general commentary.

This set of books is intended for people who will be more than just casually interested in computers, yet it is by no means only for the computer specialist. Indeed, one of my main goals has been to make these programming techniques more accessible to the many people working in other fields who can make fruitful use of computers, yet who cannot afford the time to locate all of the necessary information that is buried in technical journals.

We might call the subject of these books "nonnumerical analysis." Computers have traditionally been associated with the solution of numerical problems such as the calculation of the roots of an equation, numerical interpolation and integration, etc., but such topics are not treated here except in passing. Numerical computer programming is an extremely interesting and rapidly expanding field, and many books have been written about it. Since the early 1960s, however, computers have been used even more often for problems in which numbers occur only by coincidence; the computer's decision-making capabilities are being used, rather than its ability to do arithmetic. We have some use for addition and subtraction in nonnumerical problems, but we rarely feel any need for multiplication and division. Of course, even a person who is primarily concerned with numerical computer programming will benefit from a study of the nonnumerical techniques, for they are present in the background of numerical programs as well.

The results of research in nonnumerical analysis are scattered throughout numerous technical journals. My approach has been to try to distill this vast literature by studying the techniques that are most basic, in the sense that they can be applied to many types of programming situations. I have attempted to coordinate the ideas into more or less of a "theory," as well as to show how the theory applies to a wide variety of practical problems.

Of course, "nonnumerical analysis" is a terribly negative name for this field of study; it is much better to have a positive, descriptive term that characterizes the subject. "Information processing" is too broad a designation for the material I am considering, and "programming techniques" is too narrow. Therefore I wish to propose *analysis of algorithms* as an appropriate name for the subject matter covered in these books. This name is meant to imply "the theory of the properties of particular computer algorithms."

The complete set of books, entitled *The Art of Computer Programming*, has the following general outline:

Volume 1. Fundamental Algorithms

Chapter 1. Basic Concepts
Chapter 2. Information Structures

Volume 2. Seminumerical Algorithms

    Chapter 3. Random Numbers
    Chapter 4. Arithmetic

Volume 3. Sorting and Searching

    Chapter 5. Sorting
    Chapter 6. Searching

Volume 4. Combinatorial Algorithms

    Chapter 7. Combinatorial Searching
    Chapter 8. Recursion

Volume 5. Syntactical Algorithms

    Chapter 9. Lexical Scanning
    Chapter 10. Parsing

Volume 4 deals with such a large topic, it actually represents several separate books (Volumes 4A, 4B, and so on). Two additional volumes on more specialized topics are also planned: Volume 6, *The Theory of Languages* (Chapter 11); Volume 7, *Compilers* (Chapter 12).

I started out in 1962 to write a single book with this sequence of chapters, but I soon found that it was more important to treat the subjects in depth rather than to skim over them lightly. The resulting length of the text has meant that each chapter by itself contains more than enough material for a one-semester college course; so it has become sensible to publish the series in separate volumes. I know that it is strange to have only one or two chapters in an entire book, but I have decided to retain the original chapter numbering in order to facilitate cross references. A shorter version of Volumes 1 through 5 is planned, intended specifically to serve as a more general reference and/or text for undergraduate computer courses; its contents will be a subset of the material in these books, with the more specialized information omitted. The same chapter numbering will be used in the abridged edition as in the complete work.

The present volume may be considered as the "intersection" of the entire set, in the sense that it contains basic material that is used in all the other books. Volumes 2 through 5, on the other hand, may be read independently of each other. Volume 1 is not only a reference book to be used in connection with the remaining volumes; it may also be used in college courses or for self-study as a text on the subject of *data structures* (emphasizing the material of Chapter 2), or as a text on the subject of *discrete mathematics* (emphasizing the material of Sections 1.1, 1.2, 1.3.3, and 2.3.4), or as a text on the subject of *machine-language programming* (emphasizing the material of Sections 1.3 and 1.4).

The point of view I have adopted while writing these chapters differs from that taken in most contemporary books about computer programming in that I am not trying to teach the reader how to use somebody else's software. I am concerned rather with teaching people how to write better software themselves.

My original goal was to bring readers to the frontiers of knowledge in every subject that was treated. But it is extremely difficult to keep up with a field that is economically profitable, and the rapid rise of computer science has made such a dream impossible. The subject has become a vast tapestry with tens of thousands of subtle results contributed by tens of thousands of talented people all over the world. Therefore my new goal has been to concentrate on "classic" techniques that are likely to remain important for many more decades, and to describe them as well as I can. In particular, I have tried to trace the history of each subject, and to provide a solid foundation for future progress. I have attempted to choose terminology that is concise and consistent with current usage. I have tried to include all of the known ideas about sequential computer programming that are both beautiful and easy to state.

A few words are in order about the mathematical content of this set of books. The material has been organized so that persons with no more than a knowledge of high-school algebra may read it, skimming briefly over the more mathematical portions; yet a reader who is mathematically inclined will learn about many interesting mathematical techniques related to discrete mathematics. This dual level of presentation has been achieved in part by assigning ratings to each of the exercises so that the primarily mathematical ones are marked specifically as such, and also by arranging most sections so that the main mathematical results are stated *before* their proofs. The proofs are either left as exercises (with answers to be found in a separate section) or they are given at the end of a section.

A reader who is interested primarily in programming rather than in the associated mathematics may stop reading most sections as soon as the mathematics becomes recognizably difficult. On the other hand, a mathematically oriented reader will find a wealth of interesting material collected here. Much of the published mathematics about computer programming has been faulty, and one of the purposes of this book is to instruct readers in proper mathematical approaches to this subject. Since I profess to be a mathematician, it is my duty to maintain mathematical integrity as well as I can.

A knowledge of elementary calculus will suffice for most of the mathematics in these books, since most of the other theory that is needed is developed herein. However, I do need to use deeper theorems of complex variable theory, probability theory, number theory, etc., at times, and in such cases I refer to appropriate textbooks where those subjects are developed.

The hardest decision that I had to make while preparing these books concerned the manner in which to present the various techniques. The advantages of flow charts and of an informal step-by-step description of an algorithm are well known; for a discussion of this, see the article "Computer-Drawn Flowcharts" in the ACM *Communications*, Vol. 6 (September 1963), pages 555–563. Yet a formal, precise language is also necessary to specify any computer algorithm, and I needed to decide whether to use an algebraic language, such as ALGOL or FORTRAN, or to use a machine-oriented language for this purpose. Perhaps many of today's computer experts will disagree with my decision to use a machine-oriented language, but I have become convinced that it was definitely the correct choice, for the following reasons:

a) A programmer is greatly influenced by the language in which programs are written; there is an overwhelming tendency to prefer constructions that are simplest in that language, rather than those that are best for the machine. By understanding a machine-oriented language, the programmer will tend to use a much more efficient method; it is much closer to reality.

b) The programs we require are, with a few exceptions, all rather short, so with a suitable computer there will be no trouble understanding the programs.

c) High-level languages are inadequate for discussing important low-level details such as coroutine linkage, random number generation, multi-precision arithmetic, and many problems involving the efficient usage of memory.

d) A person who is more than casually interested in computers should be well schooled in machine language, since it is a fundamental part of a computer.

e) Some machine language would be necessary anyway as output of the software programs described in many of the examples.

f) New algebraic languages go in and out of fashion every five years or so, while I am trying to emphasize concepts that are timeless.

From the other point of view, I admit that it is somewhat easier to write programs in higher-level programming languages, and it is considerably easier to debug the programs. Indeed, I have rarely used low-level machine language for my own programs since 1970, now that computers are so large and so fast. Many of the problems of interest to us in this book, however, are those for which the programmer's art is most important. For example, some combinatorial calculations need to be repeated a trillion times, and we save about 11.6 days of computation for every microsecond we can squeeze out of their inner loop. Similarly, it is worthwhile to put an additional effort into the writing of software that will be used many times each day in many computer installations, since the software needs to be written only once.

Given the decision to use a machine-oriented language, which language should be used? I could have chosen the language of a particular machine X, but then those people who do not possess machine X would think this book is only for X-people. Furthermore, machine X probably has a lot of idiosyncrasies that are completely irrelevant to the material in this book yet which must be explained; and in two years the manufacturer of machine X will put out machine $X + 1$ or machine $10X$, and machine X will no longer be of interest to anyone.

To avoid this dilemma, I have attempted to design an "ideal" computer with very simple rules of operation (requiring, say, only an hour to learn), which also resembles actual machines very closely. There is no reason why a student should be afraid of learning the characteristics of more than one computer; once one machine language has been mastered, others are easily assimilated. Indeed, serious programmers may expect to meet many different machine languages in the course of their careers. So the only remaining disadvantage of a mythical machine is the difficulty of executing any programs written for it. Fortunately, that is not really a problem, because many volunteers have come forward to write simulators for the hypothetical machine. Such simulators are ideal for instructional purposes, since they are even easier to use than a real computer would be.

I have attempted to cite the best early papers in each subject, together with a sampling of more recent work. When referring to the literature, I use standard abbreviations for the names of periodicals, except that the most commonly cited journals are abbreviated as follows:

CACM = Communications of the Association for Computing Machinery

JACM = Journal of the Association for Computing Machinery

Comp. J. = The Computer Journal (British Computer Society)

Math. Comp. = Mathematics of Computation

AMM = American Mathematical Monthly

SICOMP = SIAM Journal on Computing

FOCS = IEEE Symposium on Foundations of Computer Science

SODA = ACM–SIAM Symposium on Discrete Algorithms

STOC = ACM Symposium on Theory of Computing

Crelle = Journal für die reine und angewandte Mathematik

As an example, "*CACM* **6** (1963), 555–563" stands for the reference given in a preceding paragraph of this preface. I also use "*CMath*" to stand for the book *Concrete Mathematics*, which is cited in the introduction to Section 1.2.

Much of the technical content of these books appears in the exercises. When the idea behind a nontrivial exercise is not my own, I have attempted to give credit to the person who originated that idea. Corresponding references to the literature are usually given in the accompanying text of that section, or in the answer to that exercise, but in many cases the exercises are based on unpublished material for which no further reference can be given.

I have, of course, received assistance from a great many people during the years I have been preparing these books, and for this I am extremely thankful. Acknowledgments are due, first, to my wife, Jill, for her infinite patience, for preparing several of the illustrations, and for untold further assistance of all kinds; secondly, to Robert W. Floyd, who contributed a great deal of his time towards the enhancement of this material during the 1960s. Thousands of other people have also provided significant help — it would take another book just to list their names! Many of them have kindly allowed me to make use of hitherto unpublished work. My research at Caltech and Stanford was generously supported for many years by the National Science Foundation and the Office of Naval Research. Addison–Wesley has provided excellent assistance and cooperation ever since I began this project in 1962. The best way I know how to thank everyone is to demonstrate by this publication that their input has led to books that resemble what I think they wanted me to write.

Preface to the Third Edition

After having spent ten years developing the TEX and METAFONT systems for computer typesetting, I am now able to fulfill the dream that I had when I began that work, by applying those systems to *The Art of Computer Programming*. At last the entire text of this book has been captured inside my personal computer, in an electronic form that will make it readily adaptable to future changes in printing and display technology. The new setup has allowed me to make literally thousands of improvements that I have been wanting to incorporate for a long time.

In this new edition I have gone over every word of the text, trying to retain the youthful exuberance of my original sentences while perhaps adding some more mature judgment. Dozens of new exercises have been added; dozens of old exercises have been given new and improved answers.

The Art of Computer Programming is, however, still a work in progress. Therefore some parts of this book are headed by an "under construction" icon, to apologize for the fact that the material is not up-to-date. My files are bursting with important material that I plan to include in the final, glorious, fourth edition of Volume 1, perhaps 15 years from now; but I must finish Volumes 4 and 5 first, and I do not want to delay their publication any more than absolutely necessary.

Most of the hard work of preparing the new edition was accomplished by Phyllis Winkler and Silvio Levy, who expertly keyboarded and edited the text of the second edition, and by Jeffrey Oldham, who converted nearly all of the original illustrations to METAPOST format. I have corrected every error that alert readers detected in the second edition (as well as some mistakes that, alas, nobody noticed); and I have tried to avoid introducing new errors in the new material. However, I suppose some defects still remain, and I want to fix them as soon as possible. Therefore I will cheerfully award \$2.56 to the first finder of each technical, typographical, or historical error. The webpage cited on page iv contains a current listing of all corrections that have been reported to me.

Stanford, California   D. E. K.
April 1997

> *Things have changed in the past two decades.*
> — BILL GATES (1995)

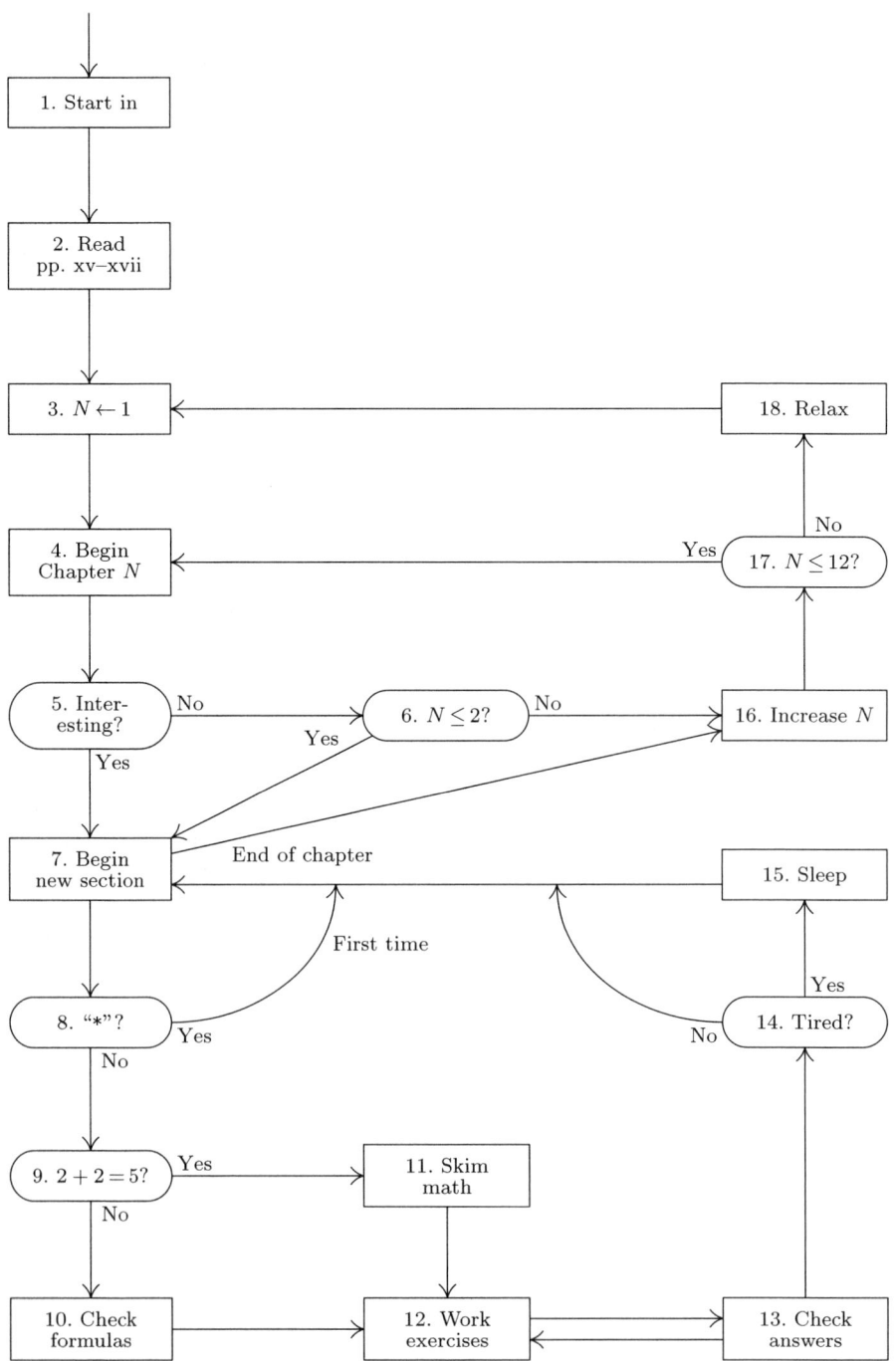

Flow chart for reading this set of books.

Procedure for Reading
This Set of Books

1. Begin reading this procedure, unless you have already begun to read it. *Continue to follow the steps faithfully.* (The general form of this procedure and its accompanying flow chart will be used throughout this book.)

2. Read the Notes on the Exercises, on pages xv–xvii.

3. Set N equal to 1.

4. Begin reading Chapter N. Do *not* read the quotations that appear at the beginning of the chapter.

5. Is the subject of the chapter interesting to you? If so, go to step 7; if not, go to step 6.

6. Is $N \leq 2$? If not, go to step 16; if so, scan through the chapter anyway. (Chapters 1 and 2 contain important introductory material and also a review of basic programming techniques. You should at least skim over the sections on notation and about MIX.)

7. Begin reading the next section of the chapter; if you have already reached the end of the chapter, however, go to step 16.

8. Is section number marked with "*"? If so, you may omit this section on first reading (it covers a rather specialized topic that is interesting but not essential); go back to step 7.

9. Are you mathematically inclined? If math is all Greek to you, go to step 11; otherwise proceed to step 10.

10. Check the mathematical derivations made in this section (and report errors to the author). Go to step 12.

11. If the current section is full of mathematical computations, you had better omit reading the derivations. However, you should become familiar with the basic results of the section; they are usually stated near the beginning, or in *slanted type* right at the very end of the hard parts.

12. Work the recommended exercises in this section in accordance with the hints given in the Notes on the Exercises (which you read in step 2).

13. After you have worked on the exercises to your satisfaction, check your answers with the answer printed in the corresponding answer section at the

rear of the book (if any answer appears for that problem). Also read the answers to the exercises you did not have time to work. *Note:* In most cases it is reasonable to read the answer to exercise n before working on exercise $n + 1$, so steps 12–13 are usually done simultaneously.

14. Are you tired? If not, go back to step 7.

15. Go to sleep. Then, wake up, and go back to step 7.

16. Increase N by one. If $N = 3, 5, 7, 9, 11$, or 12, begin the next volume of this set of books.

17. If N is less than or equal to 12, go back to step 4.

18. Congratulations. Now try to get your friends to purchase a copy of Volume 1 and to start reading it. Also, go back to step 3.

Woe be to him that reads but one book.
— GEORGE HERBERT, *Jacula Prudentum*, 1144 (1640)

Le défaut unique de tous les ouvrages
c'est d'être trop longs.
— VAUVENARGUES, *Réflexions*, 628 (1746)

Books are a triviality. Life alone is great.
— THOMAS CARLYLE, *Journal* (1839)

NOTES ON THE EXERCISES

THE EXERCISES in this set of books have been designed for self-study as well as for classroom study. It is difficult, if not impossible, for anyone to learn a subject purely by reading about it, without applying the information to specific problems and thereby being encouraged to think about what has been read. Furthermore, we all learn best the things that we have discovered for ourselves. Therefore the exercises form a major part of this work; a definite attempt has been made to keep them as informative as possible and to select problems that are enjoyable as well as instructive.

In many books, easy exercises are found mixed randomly among extremely difficult ones. A motley mixture is, however, often unfortunate because readers like to know in advance how long a problem ought to take—otherwise they may just skip over all the problems. A classic example of such a situation is the book *Dynamic Programming* by Richard Bellman; this is an important, pioneering work in which a group of problems is collected together at the end of some chapters under the heading "Exercises and Research Problems," with extremely trivial questions appearing in the midst of deep, unsolved problems. It is rumored that someone once asked Dr. Bellman how to tell the exercises apart from the research problems, and he replied, "If you can solve it, it is an exercise; otherwise it's a research problem."

Good arguments can be made for including both research problems and very easy exercises in a book of this kind; therefore, to save the reader from the possible dilemma of determining which are which, *rating numbers* have been provided to indicate the level of difficulty. These numbers have the following general significance:

Rating   Interpretation

00 An extremely easy exercise that can be answered immediately if the material of the text has been understood; such an exercise can almost always be worked "in your head."

10 A simple problem that makes you think over the material just read, but is by no means difficult. You should be able to do this in one minute at most; pencil and paper may be useful in obtaining the solution.

20 An average problem that tests basic understanding of the text material, but you may need about fifteen or twenty minutes to answer it completely.

    30 A problem of moderate difficulty and/or complexity; this one may involve more than two hours' work to solve satisfactorily, or even more if the TV is on.

    40 Quite a difficult or lengthy problem that would be suitable for a term project in classroom situations. A student should be able to solve the problem in a reasonable amount of time, but the solution is not trivial.

    50 A research problem that has not yet been solved satisfactorily, as far as the author knew at the time of writing, although many people have tried. If you have found an answer to such a problem, you ought to write it up for publication; furthermore, the author of this book would appreciate hearing about the solution as soon as possible (provided that it is correct).

By interpolation in this "logarithmic" scale, the significance of other rating numbers becomes clear. For example, a rating of *17* would indicate an exercise that is a bit simpler than average. Problems with a rating of *50* that are subsequently solved by some reader may appear with a *40* rating in later editions of the book, and in the errata posted on the Internet (see page iv).

The remainder of the rating number divided by 5 indicates the amount of detailed work required. Thus, an exercise rated *24* may take longer to solve than an exercise that is rated *25*, but the latter will require more creativity.

The author has tried earnestly to assign accurate rating numbers, but it is difficult for the person who makes up a problem to know just how formidable it will be for someone else to find a solution; and everyone has more aptitude for certain types of problems than for others. It is hoped that the rating numbers represent a good guess at the level of difficulty, but they should be taken as general guidelines, not as absolute indicators.

This book has been written for readers with varying degrees of mathematical training and sophistication; as a result, some of the exercises are intended only for the use of more mathematically inclined readers. The rating is preceded by an *M* if the exercise involves mathematical concepts or motivation to a greater extent than necessary for someone who is primarily interested only in programming the algorithms themselves. An exercise is marked with the letters "*HM*" if its solution necessarily involves a knowledge of calculus or other higher mathematics not developed in this book. An "*HM*" designation does *not* necessarily imply difficulty.

Some exercises are preceded by an arrowhead, "▶"; this designates problems that are especially instructive and especially recommended. Of course, no reader/student is expected to work *all* of the exercises, so those that seem to be the most valuable have been singled out. (This distinction is not meant to detract from the other exercises!) Each reader should at least make an attempt to solve all of the problems whose rating is *10* or less; and the arrows may help to indicate which of the problems with a higher rating should be given priority.

Solutions to most of the exercises appear in the answer section. Please use them wisely; do not turn to the answer until you have made a genuine effort to

solve the problem by yourself, or unless you absolutely do not have time to work this particular problem. *After* getting your own solution or giving the problem a decent try, you may find the answer instructive and helpful. The solution given will often be quite short, and it will sketch the details under the assumption that you have earnestly tried to solve it by your own means first. Sometimes the solution gives less information than was asked; often it gives more. It is quite possible that you may have a better answer than the one published here, or you may have found an error in the published solution; in such a case, the author will be pleased to know the details. Later printings of this book will give the improved solutions together with the solver's name where appropriate.

When working an exercise you may generally use the answers to previous exercises, unless specifically forbidden from doing so. The rating numbers have been assigned with this in mind; thus it is possible for exercise $n + 1$ to have a lower rating than exercise n, even though it includes the result of exercise n as a special case.

Summary of codes:	*00* Immediate
	10 Simple (one minute)
	20 Medium (quarter hour)
▶ Recommended	*30* Moderately hard
M Mathematically oriented	*40* Term project
HM Requiring "higher math"	*50* Research problem

EXERCISES

▶ **1.** [*00*] What does the rating "*M20*" mean?

2. [*10*] Of what value can the exercises in a textbook be to the reader?

3. [*14*] Prove that $13^3 = 2197$. Generalize your answer. [This is an example of a horrible kind of problem that the author has tried to avoid.]

4. [*HM45*] Prove that when n is an integer, $n > 2$, the equation $x^n + y^n = z^n$ has no solution in positive integers x, y, z.

We can face our problem.
We can arrange such facts as we have
with order and method.
— HERCULE POIROT, in *Murder on the Orient Express* (1934)

CONTENTS

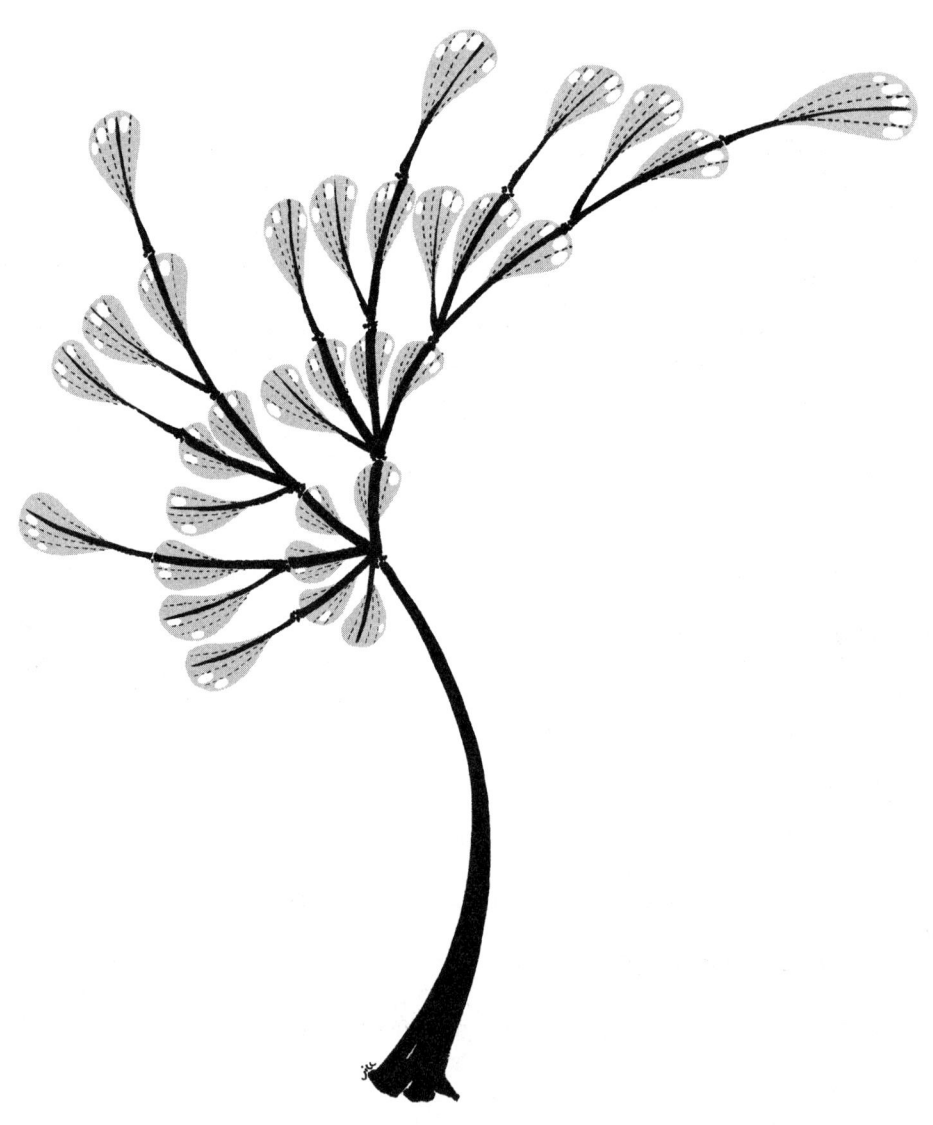

CHAPTER ONE

BASIC CONCEPTS

*Many persons who are not conversant with mathematical studies
imagine that because the business of [Babbage's Analytical Engine] is to
give its results in numerical notation, the nature of its processes must
consequently be arithmetical and numerical, rather than algebraical and
analytical. This is an error. The engine can arrange and combine its
numerical quantities exactly as if they were letters or any other general
symbols; and in fact it might bring out its results in algebraical notation,
were provisions made accordingly.*

— AUGUSTA ADA, Countess of Lovelace (1843)

*Practice yourself, for heaven's sake, in little things;
and thence proceed to greater.*

— EPICTETUS (*Discourses* IV.i)

1.1. ALGORITHMS

THE NOTION of an *algorithm* is basic to all of computer programming, so we
should begin with a careful analysis of this concept.

The word "algorithm" itself is quite interesting; at first glance it may look
as though someone intended to write "logarithm" but jumbled up the first four
letters. The word did not appear in *Webster's New World Dictionary* as late as
1957; we find only the older form "algorism" with its ancient meaning, the process
of doing arithmetic using Arabic numerals. During the Middle Ages, abacists
computed on the abacus and algorists computed by algorism. By the time of the
Renaissance, the origin of this word was in doubt, and early linguists attempted
to guess at its derivation by making combinations like *algiros* [painful]+*arithmos*
[number]; others said no, the word comes from "King Algor of Castile." Finally,
historians of mathematics found the true origin of the word algorism: It comes
from the name of a famous Persian textbook author, Abū 'Abd Allāh Muḥammad
ibn Mūsā al-Khwārizmī (c. 825) — literally, "Father of Abdullah, Mohammed,
son of Moses, native of Khwārizm." The Aral Sea in Central Asia was once
known as Lake Khwārizm, and the Khwārizm region is located in the Amu River
basin just south of that sea. Al-Khwārizmī wrote the celebrated Arabic text
Kitāb al-jabr wa'l-muqābala ("Rules of restoring and equating"); another word,
"algebra," stems from the title of that book, which was a systematic study of the
solution of linear and quadratic equations. [For notes on al-Khwārizmī's life and
work, see H. Zemanek, *Lecture Notes in Computer Science* **122** (1981), 1–81.]

1

Gradually the form and meaning of *algorism* became corrupted; as explained by the *Oxford English Dictionary*, the word "passed through many pseudo-etymological perversions, including a recent *algorithm*, in which it is learnedly confused" with the Greek root of the word *arithmetic*. This change from "algorism" to "algorithm" is not hard to understand in view of the fact that people had forgotten the original derivation of the word. An early German mathematical dictionary, *Vollständiges mathematisches Lexicon* (Leipzig: 1747), gave the following definition for the word *Algorithmus*: "Under this designation are combined the notions of the four types of arithmetic calculations, namely addition, multiplication, subtraction, and division." The Latin phrase *algorithmus infinitesimalis* was at that time used to denote "ways of calculation with infinitely small quantities, as invented by Leibniz."

By 1950, the word algorithm was most frequently associated with Euclid's algorithm, a process for finding the greatest common divisor of two numbers that appears in Euclid's *Elements* (Book 7, Propositions 1 and 2). It will be instructive to exhibit Euclid's algorithm here:

Algorithm E (*Euclid's algorithm*). Given two positive integers m and n, find their *greatest common divisor*, that is, the largest positive integer that evenly divides both m and n.

E1. [Find remainder.] Divide m by n and let r be the remainder. (We will have $0 \leq r < n$.)

E2. [Is it zero?] If $r = 0$, the algorithm terminates; n is the answer.

E3. [Reduce.] Set $m \leftarrow n$, $n \leftarrow r$, and go back to step E1. ∎

Of course, Euclid did not present his algorithm in just this manner. The format above illustrates the style in which all of the algorithms throughout this book will be presented.

Each algorithm we consider has been given an identifying letter (E in the preceding example), and the steps of the algorithm are identified by this letter followed by a number (E1, E2, E3). The chapters are divided into numbered sections; within a section the algorithms are designated by letter only, but when algorithms are referred to in other sections, the appropriate section number is attached. For example, we are now in Section 1.1; within this section Euclid's algorithm is called Algorithm E, while in later sections it is referred to as Algorithm 1.1E.

Each step of an algorithm, such as step E1 above, begins with a phrase in brackets that sums up as briefly as possible the principal content of that step. This phrase also usually appears in an accompanying *flow chart*, such as Fig. 1, so that the reader will be able to picture the algorithm more readily.

After the summarizing phrase comes a description in words and symbols of some *action* to be performed or some decision to be made. Parenthesized *comments*, like the second sentence in step E1, may also appear. Comments are included as explanatory information about that step, often indicating certain invariant characteristics of the variables or the current goals. They do not specify

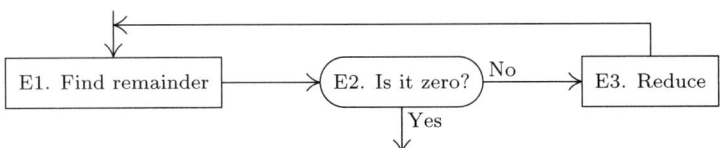

Fig. 1. Flow chart for Algorithm E.

actions that belong to the algorithm, but are meant only for the reader's benefit
as possible aids to comprehension.

The arrow " ← " in step E3 is the all-important *replacement* operation, sometimes called *assignment* or *substitution*: "$m \leftarrow n$" means that the value of
variable m is to be replaced by the current value of variable n. When Algorithm E
begins, the values of m and n are the originally given numbers; but when it
ends, those variables will have, in general, different values. An arrow is used
to distinguish the replacement operation from the equality relation: We will
not say, "Set $m = n$," but we will perhaps ask, "Does $m = n$?" The " $=$ "
sign denotes a condition that can be tested, the " ← " sign denotes an action
that can be performed. The operation of *increasing n by one* is denoted by
"$n \leftarrow n + 1$" (read "n is replaced by $n + 1$" or "n gets $n + 1$"). In general,
"variable ← formula" means that the formula is to be computed using the present
values of any variables appearing within it; then the result should replace the
previous value of the variable at the left of the arrow. Persons untrained in
computer work sometimes have a tendency to say "n becomes $n + 1$" and to
write "$n \rightarrow n + 1$" for the operation of increasing n by one; this symbolism can
only lead to confusion because of its conflict with standard conventions, and it
should be avoided.

Notice that the order of actions in step E3 is important: "Set $m \leftarrow n$,
$n \leftarrow r$" is quite different from "Set $n \leftarrow r$, $m \leftarrow n$," since the latter would imply
that the previous value of n is lost before it can be used to set m. Thus the
latter sequence is equivalent to "Set $n \leftarrow r$, $m \leftarrow r$." When several variables
are all to be set equal to the same quantity, we can use multiple arrows; for
example, "$n \leftarrow r$, $m \leftarrow r$" may be written "$n \leftarrow m \leftarrow r$." To interchange the
values of two variables, we can write "Exchange $m \leftrightarrow n$"; this action could also
be specified by using a new variable t and writing "Set $t \leftarrow m$, $m \leftarrow n$, $n \leftarrow t$."

An algorithm starts at the lowest-numbered step, usually step 1, and it
performs subsequent steps in sequential order unless otherwise specified. In step
E3, the imperative "go back to step E1" specifies the computational order in an
obvious fashion. In step E2, the action is prefaced by the condition "If $r = 0$";
so if $r \neq 0$, the rest of that sentence does not apply and no action is specified.
We might have added the redundant sentence, "If $r \neq 0$, go on to step E3."

The heavy vertical line " $\blacksquare$ " appearing at the end of step E3 is used to
indicate the end of an algorithm and the resumption of text.

We have now discussed virtually all the notational conventions used in the
algorithms of this book, except for a notation used to denote "subscripted" or

"indexed" items that are elements of an ordered array. Suppose we have n quantities, $v_1, v_2, \ldots, v_n$; instead of writing v_j for the jth element, the notation $v[j]$ is often used. Similarly, $a[i, j]$ is sometimes used in preference to a doubly subscripted notation like a_{ij}. Sometimes multiple-letter names are used for variables, usually set in capital letters; thus TEMP might be the name of a variable used for temporarily holding a computed value, PRIME[K] might denote the Kth prime number, and so on.

So much for the *form* of algorithms; now let us *perform* one. It should be mentioned immediately that the reader should *not* expect to read an algorithm as if it were part of a novel; such an attempt would make it pretty difficult to understand what is going on. An algorithm must be seen to be believed, and the best way to learn what an algorithm is all about is to try it. The reader should always take pencil and paper and work through an example of each algorithm immediately upon encountering it in the text. Usually the outline of a worked example will be given, or else the reader can easily conjure one up. This is a simple and painless way to gain an understanding of a given algorithm, and all other approaches are generally unsuccessful.

Let us therefore work out an example of Algorithm E. Suppose that we are given $m = 119$ and $n = 544$; we are ready to begin, at step E1. (The reader should now follow the algorithm as we give a play-by-play account.) Dividing m by n in this case is quite simple, almost too simple, since the quotient is zero and the remainder is 119. Thus, $r \leftarrow 119$. We proceed to step E2, and since $r \neq 0$ no action occurs. In step E3 we set $m \leftarrow 544$, $n \leftarrow 119$. It is clear that if $m < n$ originally, the quotient in step E1 will always be zero and the algorithm will always proceed to interchange m and n in this rather cumbersome fashion. We could insert a new step at the beginning:

E0. [Ensure $m \geq n$.] If $m < n$, exchange $m \leftrightarrow n$.

This would make no essential change in the algorithm, except to increase its length slightly, and to decrease its running time in about one half of all cases.

Back at step E1, we find that $544/119 = 4 + 68/119$, so $r \leftarrow 68$. Again E2 is inapplicable, and at E3 we set $m \leftarrow 119$, $n \leftarrow 68$. The next round sets $r \leftarrow 51$, and ultimately $m \leftarrow 68$, $n \leftarrow 51$. Next $r \leftarrow 17$, and $m \leftarrow 51$, $n \leftarrow 17$. Finally, when 51 is divided by 17, we set $r \leftarrow 0$, so at step E2 the algorithm terminates. The greatest common divisor of 119 and 544 is 17.

So this is an algorithm. The modern meaning for algorithm is quite similar to that of *recipe, process, method, technique, procedure, routine, rigmarole*, except that the word "algorithm" connotes something just a little different. Besides merely being a finite set of rules that gives a sequence of operations for solving a specific type of problem, an algorithm has five important features:

1) *Finiteness.* An algorithm must always terminate after a finite number of steps. Algorithm E satisfies this condition, because after step E1 the value of r is *less* than n; so if $r \neq 0$, the value of n *decreases* the next time step E1 is encountered. A decreasing sequence of positive integers must eventually terminate, so step E1 is executed only a finite number of times for any given original

value of n. Note, however, that the number of steps can become arbitrarily large; certain huge choices of m and n will cause step E1 to be executed more than a million times.

(A procedure that has all of the characteristics of an algorithm except that it possibly lacks finiteness may be called a *computational method*. Euclid originally presented not only an algorithm for the greatest common divisor of numbers, but also a very similar geometrical construction for the "greatest common measure" of the lengths of two line segments; this is a computational method that does not terminate if the given lengths are incommensurable. Another example of a nonterminating computational method is a *reactive process*, which continually interacts with its environment.)

2) *Definiteness.* Each step of an algorithm must be precisely defined; the actions to be carried out must be rigorously and unambiguously specified for each case. The algorithms of this book will hopefully meet this criterion, but they are specified in the English language, so there is a possibility that the reader might not understand exactly what the author intended. To get around this difficulty, formally defined *programming languages* or *computer languages* are designed for specifying algorithms, in which every statement has a very definite meaning. Many of the algorithms of this book will be given both in English and in a computer language. An expression of a computational method in a computer language is called a *program*.

In Algorithm E, the criterion of definiteness as applied to step E1 means that the reader is supposed to understand exactly what it means to divide m by n and what the remainder is. In actual fact, there is no universal agreement about what this means if m and n are not positive integers; what is the remainder of -8 divided by $-\pi$? What is the remainder of $59/13$ divided by zero? Therefore the criterion of definiteness means we must make sure that the values of m and n are always positive integers whenever step E1 is to be executed. This is initially true, by hypothesis; and after step E1, r is a nonnegative integer that must be nonzero if we get to step E3. So m and n are indeed positive integers as required.

3) *Input.* An algorithm has zero or more *inputs*: quantities that are given to it initially before the algorithm begins, or dynamically as the algorithm runs. These inputs are taken from specified sets of objects. In Algorithm E, for example, there are two inputs, namely m and n, both taken from the set of *positive integers*.

4) *Output.* An algorithm has one or more *outputs*: quantities that have a specified relation to the inputs. Algorithm E has one output, namely n in step E2, the greatest common divisor of the two inputs.

(We can easily *prove* that this number is indeed the greatest common divisor, as follows. After step E1, we have

$$m = qn + r,$$

for some integer q. If $r = 0$, then m is a multiple of n, and clearly in such a case n is the greatest common divisor of m and n. If $r \neq 0$, note that any number that divides both m and n must divide $m - qn = r$, and any number that divides both n and r must divide $qn + r = m$; so the set of common divisors of $\{m, n\}$ is the same as the set of common divisors of $\{n, r\}$. In particular, the *greatest* common divisor of $\{m, n\}$ is the same as the greatest common divisor of $\{n, r\}$. Therefore step E3 does not change the answer to the original problem.)

5) *Effectiveness.* An algorithm is also generally expected to be *effective*, in the sense that its operations must all be sufficiently basic that they can in principle be done exactly and in a finite length of time by someone using pencil and paper. Algorithm E uses only the operations of dividing one positive integer by another, testing if an integer is zero, and setting the value of one variable equal to the value of another. These operations are effective, because integers can be represented on paper in a finite manner, and because there is at least one method (the "division algorithm") for dividing one by another. But the same operations would *not* be effective if the values involved were arbitrary real numbers specified by an infinite decimal expansion, nor if the values were the lengths of physical line segments (which cannot be specified exactly). Another example of a noneffective step is, "If 4 is the largest integer n for which there is a solution to the equation $w^n + x^n + y^n = z^n$ in positive integers w, x, y, and z, then go to step E4." Such a statement would not be an effective operation until someone successfully constructs an algorithm to determine whether 4 is or is not the largest integer with the stated property.

Let us try to compare the concept of an algorithm with that of a cookbook recipe. A recipe presumably has the qualities of finiteness (although it is said that a watched pot never boils), input (eggs, flour, etc.), and output (TV dinner, etc.), but it notoriously lacks definiteness. There are frequent cases in which a cook's instructions are indefinite: "Add a dash of salt." A "dash" is defined to be "less than $\frac{1}{8}$ teaspoon," and salt is perhaps well enough defined; but where should the salt be added—on top? on the side? Instructions like "toss lightly until mixture is crumbly" or "warm cognac in small saucepan" are quite adequate as explanations to a trained chef, but an algorithm must be specified to such a degree that even a computer can follow the directions. Nevertheless, a computer programmer can learn much by studying a good recipe book. (The author has in fact barely resisted the temptation to name the present volume "The Programmer's Cookbook." Perhaps someday he will attempt a book called "Algorithms for the Kitchen.")

We should remark that the finiteness restriction is not really strong enough for practical use. A useful algorithm should require not only a finite number of steps, but a *very* finite number, a reasonable number. For example, there is an algorithm that determines whether or not the game of chess can always be won by White if no mistakes are made (see exercise 2.2.3–28). That algorithm can solve a problem of intense interest to thousands of people, yet it is a safe bet that we will never in our lifetimes know the answer; the algorithm requires fantastically large amounts of time for its execution, even though it is finite. See also Chapter 8 for a discussion of some finite numbers that are so large as to actually be beyond comprehension.

In practice we not only want algorithms, we want algorithms that are *good* in some loosely defined aesthetic sense. One criterion of goodness is the length of time taken to perform the algorithm; this can be expressed in terms of the number of times each step is executed. Other criteria are the adaptability of the algorithm to different kinds of computers, its simplicity and elegance, etc.

We often are faced with several algorithms for the same problem, and we must decide which is best. This leads us to the extremely interesting and all-important field of *algorithmic analysis*: Given an algorithm, we want to determine its performance characteristics.

For example, let's consider Euclid's algorithm from this point of view. Suppose we ask the question, "Assuming that the value of n is known but m is allowed to range over all positive integers, what is the *average* number of times, T_n, that step E1 of Algorithm E will be performed?" In the first place, we need to check that this question does have a meaningful answer, since we are trying to take an average over infinitely many choices for m. But it is evident that after the first execution of step E1 only the remainder of m after division by n is relevant. So all we must do to find T_n is to try the algorithm for $m = 1$, $m = 2$, ..., $m = n$, count the total number of times step E1 has been executed, and divide by n.

Now the important question is to determine the *nature* of T_n; is it approximately equal to $\frac{1}{3}n$, or $\sqrt{n}$, for instance? As a matter of fact, the answer to this question is an extremely difficult and fascinating mathematical problem, not yet completely resolved, which is examined in more detail in Section 4.5.3. For large values of n it is possible to prove that T_n is approximately $\bigl(12(\ln 2)/\pi^2\bigr)\ln n$, that is, proportional to the *natural logarithm* of n, with a constant of proportionality that might not have been guessed offhand! For further details about Euclid's algorithm, and other ways to calculate the greatest common divisor, see Section 4.5.2.

Analysis of algorithms is the name the author likes to use to describe investigations such as this. The general idea is to take a particular algorithm and to determine its quantitative behavior; occasionally we also study whether or not an algorithm is optimal in some sense. The *theory of algorithms* is another subject entirely, dealing primarily with the existence or nonexistence of effective algorithms to compute particular quantities.

So far our discussion of algorithms has been rather imprecise, and a mathematically oriented reader is justified in thinking that the preceding commentary makes a very shaky foundation on which to erect any theory about algorithms. We therefore close this section with a brief indication of one method by which the concept of algorithm can be firmly grounded in terms of mathematical set theory. Let us formally define a *computational method* to be a quadruple (Q, I, Ω, f), in which Q is a set containing subsets I and Ω, and f is a function from Q into itself. Furthermore f should leave Ω pointwise fixed; that is, $f(q)$ should equal q for all elements q of Ω. The four quantities Q, I, Ω, f are intended to represent respectively the states of the computation, the input, the output, and the computational rule. Each input x in the set I defines a *computational sequence,* $x_0, x_1, x_2, \ldots,$ as follows:

$$x_0 = x \qquad \text{and} \qquad x_{k+1} = f(x_k) \quad \text{for} \quad k \ge 0. \tag{1}$$

The computational sequence is said to *terminate in k steps* if k is the smallest integer for which x_k is in Ω, and in this case it is said to produce the output x_k from x. (Note that if x_k is in Ω, so is x_{k+1}, because $x_{k+1} = x_k$ in such a case.) Some computational sequences may never terminate; an *algorithm* is a computational method that terminates in finitely many steps for all x in I.

Algorithm E may, for example, be formalized in these terms as follows: Let Q be the set of all singletons (n), all ordered pairs (m, n), and all ordered quadruples $(m, n, r, 1)$, $(m, n, r, 2)$, and $(m, n, p, 3)$, where m, n, and p are positive integers and r is a nonnegative integer. Let I be the subset of all pairs (m, n) and let Ω be the subset of all singletons (n). Let f be defined as follows:

$$\begin{aligned} &f\big((m, n)\big) = (m, n, 0, 1); \qquad f\big((n)\big) = (n); \\ &f\big((m, n, r, 1)\big) = (m,\ n,\ \text{remainder of } m \text{ divided by } n,\ 2); \\ &f\big((m, n, r, 2)\big) = (n) \quad \text{if} \quad r = 0, \qquad (m, n, r, 3) \quad \text{otherwise;} \\ &f\big((m, n, p, 3)\big) = (n, p, p, 1). \end{aligned} \tag{2}$$

The correspondence between this notation and Algorithm E is evident.

This formulation of the concept of an algorithm does not include the restriction of effectiveness mentioned earlier. For example, Q might denote infinite sequences that are not computable by pencil and paper methods, or f might involve operations that mere mortals cannot always perform. If we wish to restrict the notion of algorithm so that only elementary operations are involved, we can place restrictions on Q, I, Ω, and f, for example as follows: Let A be a finite set of letters, and let A^* be the set of all strings on A (the set of all ordered sequences $x_1 x_2 \ldots x_n$, where $n \ge 0$ and x_j is in A for $1 \le j \le n$). The idea is to encode the states of the computation so that they are represented by strings of A^*. Now let N be a nonnegative integer and let Q be the set of all (σ, j), where σ is in A^* and j is an integer, $0 \le j \le N$; let I be the subset of Q with $j = 0$ and let Ω be the subset with $j = N$. If θ and σ are strings in A^*, we say that θ *occurs in* σ if σ has the form $\alpha\theta\omega$ for strings α and ω. To complete our definition, let f be a function of the following type, defined by the strings θ_j, ϕ_j and the integers a_j, b_j for $0 \le j < N$:

$$f\big((\sigma, j)\big) = (\sigma, a_j) \qquad \text{if } \theta_j \text{ does not occur in } \sigma;$$

$$f\big((\sigma, j)\big) = (\alpha\phi_j\omega, b_j) \quad \text{if } \alpha \text{ is the shortest possible string for which } \sigma = \alpha\theta_j\omega;$$

$$f\big((\sigma, N)\big) = (\sigma, N). \tag{3}$$

Such a computational method is clearly effective, and experience shows that it is also powerful enough to do anything we can do by hand. There are many other essentially equivalent ways to formulate the concept of an effective computational method (for example, using Turing machines). The formulation above is virtually the same as that given by A. A. Markov in his book *The*

Theory of Algorithms [*Trudy Mat. Inst. Akad. Nauk* **42** (1954), 1–376], later revised and enlarged by N. M. Nagorny (Moscow: Nauka, 1984; English edition, Dordrecht: Kluwer, 1988).

EXERCISES

1. [*10*] The text showed how to interchange the values of variables m and n, using the replacement notation, by setting $t \leftarrow m$, $m \leftarrow n$, $n \leftarrow t$. Show how the values of *four* variables (a, b, c, d) can be rearranged to (b, c, d, a) by a sequence of replacements. In other words, the new value of a is to be the original value of b, etc. Try to use the minimum number of replacements.

2. [*15*] Prove that m is always greater than n at the beginning of step E1, except possibly the first time this step occurs.

3. [*20*] Change Algorithm E (for the sake of efficiency) so that all trivial replacement operations such as "$m \leftarrow n$" are avoided. Write this new algorithm in the style of Algorithm E, and call it Algorithm F.

4. [*16*] What is the greatest common divisor of 2166 and 6099?

▶ **5.** [*12*] Show that the "Procedure for Reading This Set of Books" that appears after the preface actually fails to be a genuine algorithm on at least three of our five counts! Also mention some differences in format between it and Algorithm E.

6. [*20*] What is T_5, the average number of times step E1 is performed when $n = 5$?

▶ **7.** [*M21*] Suppose that m is known and n is allowed to range over all positive integers; let U_m be the average number of times that step E1 is executed in Algorithm E. Show that U_m is well defined. Is U_m in any way related to T_m?

8. [*M25*] Give an "effective" formal algorithm for computing the greatest common divisor of positive integers m and n, by specifying θ_j, ϕ_j, a_j, b_j as in Eqs. (3). Let the input be represented by the string $a^m b^n$, that is, m a's followed by n b's. Try to make your solution as simple as possible. [*Hint:* Use Algorithm E, but instead of division in step E1, set $r \leftarrow |m - n|$, $n \leftarrow \min(m, n)$.]

▶ **9.** [*M30*] Suppose that $C_1 = (Q_1, I_1, \Omega_1, f_1)$ and $C_2 = (Q_2, I_2, \Omega_2, f_2)$ are computational methods. For example, C_1 might stand for Algorithm E as in Eqs. (2), except that m and n are restricted in magnitude, and C_2 might stand for a computer program implementation of Algorithm E. (Thus Q_2 might be the set of all states of the machine, i.e., all possible configurations of its memory and registers; f_2 might be the definition of single machine actions; and I_2 might be the set of initial states, each including the program that determines the greatest common divisor as well as the particular values of m and n.)

Formulate a set-theoretic definition for the concept "C_2 is a representation of C_1" or "C_2 simulates C_1." This is to mean intuitively that any computation sequence of C_1 is mimicked by C_2, except that C_2 might take more steps in which to do the computation and it might retain more information in its states. (We thereby obtain a rigorous interpretation of the statement, "Program X is an implementation of Algorithm Y.")

1.2. MATHEMATICAL PRELIMINARIES

IN THIS SECTION we shall investigate the mathematical notations that occur throughout *The Art of Computer Programming*, and we'll derive several basic formulas that will be used repeatedly. Even a reader not concerned with the more complex mathematical derivations should at least become familiar with the *meanings* of the various formulas, so as to be able to use the results of the derivations.

Mathematical notation is used for two main purposes in this book: to describe portions of an algorithm, and to analyze the performance character-istics of an algorithm. The notation used in descriptions of algorithms is quite simple, as explained in the previous section. When analyzing the performance of algorithms, we need to use other more specialized notations.

Most of the algorithms we will discuss are accompanied by mathematical calculations that determine the speed at which the algorithm may be expected to run. These calculations draw on nearly every branch of mathematics, and a separate book would be necessary to develop all of the mathematical concepts that are used in one place or another. However, the majority of the calculations can be carried out with a knowledge of college algebra, and the reader with a knowledge of elementary calculus will be able to understand nearly all of the mathematics that appears. Sometimes we will need to use deeper results of complex variable theory, group theory, number theory, probability theory, etc.; in such cases the topic will be explained in an elementary manner, if possible, or a reference to other sources of information will be given.

The mathematical techniques involved in the analysis of algorithms usually have a distinctive flavor. For example, we will quite often find ourselves working with finite summations of rational numbers, or with the solutions to recurrence relations. Such topics are traditionally given only a light treatment in mathe-matics courses, and so the following subsections are designed not only to give a thorough drilling in the use of the notations to be defined but also to illustrate in depth the types of calculations and techniques that will be most useful to us.

Important note: Although the following subsections provide a rather extensive training in the mathematical skills needed in connection with the study of com-puter algorithms, most readers will not see at first any very strong connections between this material and computer programming (except in Section 1.2.1). The reader may choose to read the following subsections carefully, with implicit faith in the author's assertion that the topics treated here are indeed very relevant; but it is probably preferable, for motivation, to *skim over this section lightly at first, and* (after seeing numerous applications of the techniques in future chapters) *return to it later for more intensive study.* If too much time is spent studying this material when first reading the book, a person might never get on to the computer programming topics! However, each reader should at least become familiar with the general contents of these subsections, and should try to solve a few of the exercises, even on first reading. Section 1.2.10 should receive particular attention, since it is the point of departure for most of the theoretical material

developed later. Section 1.3, which follows 1.2, abruptly leaves the realm of
"pure mathematics" and enters into "pure computer programming."

An expansion and more leisurely presentation of much of the following
material can be found in the book *Concrete Mathematics* by Graham, Knuth,
and Patashnik, second edition (Reading, Mass.: Addison–Wesley, 1994). That
book will be called simply *CMath* when we need to refer to it later.

1.2.1. Mathematical Induction

Let $P(n)$ be some statement about the integer n; for example, $P(n)$ might be
"n times $(n + 3)$ is an even number," or "if $n \geq 10$, then $2^n > n^3$." Suppose we
want *to prove that $P(n)$ is true for all positive integers n.* An important way to
do this is:

a) Give a proof that $P(1)$ is true.

b) Give a proof that "if all of $P(1), P(2), \ldots, P(n)$ are true, then $P(n + 1)$ is
also true"; this proof should be valid for any positive integer n.

As an example, consider the following series of equations, which many people
have discovered independently since ancient times:

$$1 = 1^2,$$
$$1 + 3 = 2^2,$$
$$1 + 3 + 5 = 3^2,$$
$$1 + 3 + 5 + 7 = 4^2,$$
$$1 + 3 + 5 + 7 + 9 = 5^2. \tag{1}$$

We can formulate the general property as follows:

$$1 + 3 + \cdots + (2n - 1) = n^2. \tag{2}$$

Let us, for the moment, call this equation $P(n)$; we wish to prove that $P(n)$ is
true for all positive n. Following the procedure outlined above, we have:

a) "$P(1)$ is true, since $1 = 1^2$."

b) "If all of $P(1), \ldots, P(n)$ are true, then, in particular, $P(n)$ is true, so Eq. (2)
holds; adding $2n + 1$ to both sides we obtain

$$1 + 3 + \cdots + (2n - 1) + (2n + 1) = n^2 + 2n + 1 = (n + 1)^2,$$

which proves that $P(n + 1)$ is also true."

We can regard this method as an *algorithmic proof procedure.* In fact, the
following algorithm produces a proof of $P(n)$ for any positive integer n, assuming
that steps (a) and (b) above have been worked out:

Algorithm I (*Construct a proof*). Given a positive integer n, this algorithm
will output a proof that $P(n)$ is true.

I1. [Prove $P(1)$.] Set $k \leftarrow 1$, and, according to (a), output a proof of $P(1)$.

I2. $[k = n?]$ If $k = n$, terminate the algorithm; the required proof has been output.

I3. [Prove $P(k + 1)$.] According to (b), output a proof that "If all of $P(1), \ldots, P(k)$ are true, then $P(k + 1)$ is true." Also output "We have already proved $P(1), \ldots, P(k)$; hence $P(k + 1)$ is true."

I4. [Increase k.] Increase k by 1 and go to step I2.   ∎

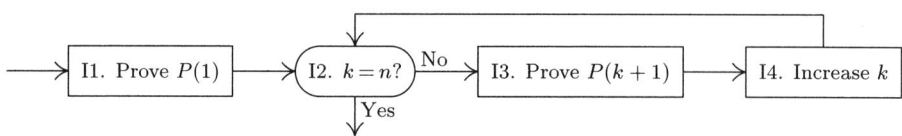

Fig. 2. Algorithm I: Mathematical induction.

Since this algorithm clearly presents a proof of $P(n)$, for any given n, the proof technique consisting of steps (a) and (b) is logically valid. It is called *proof by mathematical induction*.

The concept of mathematical induction should be distinguished from what is usually called inductive reasoning in science. A scientist takes specific observations and creates, by "induction," a general theory or hypothesis that accounts for these facts; for example, we might observe the five relations in (1), above, and formulate (2). In this sense, induction is no more than our best guess about the situation; mathematicians would call it an empirical result or a conjecture.

Another example will be helpful. Let $p(n)$ denote the number of *partitions* of n, that is, the number of different ways to write n as a sum of positive integers, disregarding order. Since 5 can be partitioned in exactly seven ways,

$$1+1+1+1+1 = 2+1+1+1 = 2+2+1 = 3+1+1 = 3+2 = 4+1 = 5,$$

we have $p(5) = 7$. In fact, it is easy to establish the first few values,

$$p(1) = 1, \quad p(2) = 2, \quad p(3) = 3, \quad p(4) = 5, \quad p(5) = 7.$$

At this point we might tentatively formulate, by induction, the hypothesis that the sequence $p(2)$, $p(3)$, ... runs through the *prime numbers*. To test this hypothesis, we proceed to calculate $p(6)$ and behold! $p(6) = 11$, confirming our conjecture.

[Unfortunately, $p(7)$ turns out to be 15, spoiling everything, and we must try again. The numbers $p(n)$ are known to be quite complicated, although S. Ramanujan succeeded in guessing and proving many remarkable things about them. For further information, see G. H. Hardy, *Ramanujan* (London: Cambridge University Press, 1940), Chapters 6 and 8. See also Section 7.2.1.4.]

Mathematical induction is quite different from induction in the sense just explained. It is not just guesswork, but a conclusive proof of a statement; indeed, it is a proof of infinitely many statements, one for each n. It has been called "induction" only because one must first decide somehow *what* is to be proved, *before* one can apply the technique of mathematical induction. Henceforth in this book we shall use the word induction only when we wish to imply proof by mathematical induction.

There is a geometrical way to prove Eq. (2). Figure 3 shows, for $n = 6$, n^2 cells broken into groups of $1 + 3 + \cdots + (2n - 1)$ cells. However, in the final analysis, this picture can be regarded as a "proof" only if we show that the construction can be carried out for all n, and such a demonstration is essentially the same as a proof by induction.

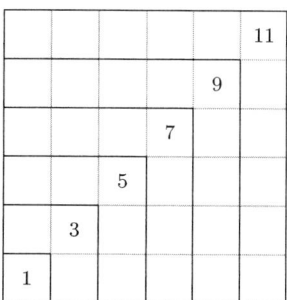

Our proof of Eq. (2) used only a special case of (b); we merely showed that the truth of $P(n)$ implies the truth of $P(n+1)$. This is an important simple case that arises frequently, but our next example illustrates the power of the method a little

Fig. 3. The sum of odd numbers is a square.

more. We define the *Fibonacci sequence* F_0, F_1, F_2, ... by the rule that $F_0 = 0$, $F_1 = 1$, and every further term is the sum of the preceding two. Thus the sequence begins 0, 1, 1, 2, 3, 5, 8, 13, ...; we will investigate it in detail in Section 1.2.8. We will now prove that if ϕ is the number $(1 + \sqrt{5})/2$ we have

$$F_n \leq \phi^{n-1} \tag{3}$$

for all positive integers n. Call this formula $P(n)$.

If $n = 1$, then $F_1 = 1 = \phi^0 = \phi^{n-1}$, so step (a) has been done. For step (b) we notice first that $P(2)$ is also true, since $F_2 = 1 < 1.6 < \phi^1 = \phi^{2-1}$. Now, if all of $P(1)$, $P(2)$, ..., $P(n)$ are true and $n > 1$, we know in particular that $P(n-1)$ and $P(n)$ are true; so $F_{n-1} \leq \phi^{n-2}$ and $F_n \leq \phi^{n-1}$. Adding these inequalities, we get

$$F_{n+1} = F_{n-1} + F_n \leq \phi^{n-2} + \phi^{n-1} = \phi^{n-2}(1 + \phi). \tag{4}$$

The important property of the number ϕ, indeed the reason we chose this number for this problem in the first place, is that

$$1 + \phi = \phi^2. \tag{5}$$

Plugging (5) into (4) gives $F_{n+1} \leq \phi^n$, which is $P(n + 1)$. So step (b) has been done, and (3) has been proved by mathematical induction. Notice that we approached step (b) in two different ways here: We proved $P(n+1)$ *directly* when $n = 1$, and we used an inductive method when $n > 1$. This was necessary, since when $n = 1$ our reference to $P(n - 1) = P(0)$ would not have been legitimate.

Mathematical induction can also be used to prove things about *algorithms*. Consider the following generalization of Euclid's algorithm.

Algorithm E (*Extended Euclid's algorithm*). Given two positive integers m and n, we compute their greatest common divisor d, and we also compute two not-necessarily-positive integers a and b such that $am + bn = d$.

E1. [Initialize.] Set $a' \leftarrow b \leftarrow 1$, $a \leftarrow b' \leftarrow 0$, $c \leftarrow m$, $d \leftarrow n$.

E2. [Divide.]   Let q and r be the quotient and remainder, respectively, of c divided by d. (We have $c = qd + r$ and $0 \leq r < d$.)

E3. [Remainder zero?] If $r = 0$, the algorithm terminates; we have in this case $am + bn = d$ as desired.

E4. [Recycle.] Set $c \leftarrow d$, $d \leftarrow r$, $t \leftarrow a'$, $a' \leftarrow a$, $a \leftarrow t - qa$, $t \leftarrow b'$, $b' \leftarrow b$, $b \leftarrow t - qb$, and go back to E2. ∎

If we suppress the variables a, b, a', and b' from this algorithm and use m and n for the auxiliary variables c and d, we have our old algorithm, 1.1E. The new version does a little more, by determining the coefficients a and b. Suppose that $m = 1769$ and $n = 551$; we have successively (after step E2):

a'	a	b'	b	c	d	q	r
1	0	0	1	1769	551	3	116
0	1	1	-3	551	116	4	87
1	-4	-3	13	116	87	1	29
-4	5	13	-16	87	29	3	0

The answer is correct: $5 \times 1769 - 16 \times 551 = 8845 - 8816 = 29$, the greatest common divisor of 1769 and 551.

The problem is to *prove* that this algorithm works properly, for all m and n. We can try to apply the method of mathematical induction by letting $P(n)$ be the statement "Algorithm E works for n and all integers m." However, that approach doesn't work out so easily, and we need to prove some extra facts. After a little study, we find that something must be proved about a, b, a', and b', and the appropriate fact is that the equalities

$$a'm + b'n = c, \qquad am + bn = d \qquad (6)$$

always hold whenever step E2 is executed. We may prove these equalities directly by observing that they are certainly true the first time we get to E2, and that step E4 does not change their validity. (See exercise 6.)

Now we are ready to show that Algorithm E is valid, by induction on n: If m is a multiple of n, the algorithm obviously works properly, since we are done immediately at E3 the first time. This case always occurs when $n = 1$. The only case remaining is when $n > 1$ and m is not a multiple of n. In such a case, the algorithm proceeds to set $c \leftarrow n$, $d \leftarrow r$ after the first execution, and since $r < n$, *we may assume by induction* that the final value of d is the gcd of n and r. By the argument given in Section 1.1, the pairs $\{m, n\}$ and $\{n, r\}$ have the same common divisors, and, in particular, they have the same greatest common divisor. Hence d is the gcd of m and n, and $am + bn = d$ by (6).

The italicized phrase in the proof above illustrates the conventional language that is so often used in an inductive proof: When doing part (b) of the construction, rather than saying "We will now assume $P(1), P(2), \ldots, P(n)$, and with this assumption we will prove $P(n+1)$," we often say simply "We will now prove $P(n)$; *we may assume by induction* that $P(k)$ is true whenever $1 \leq k < n$."

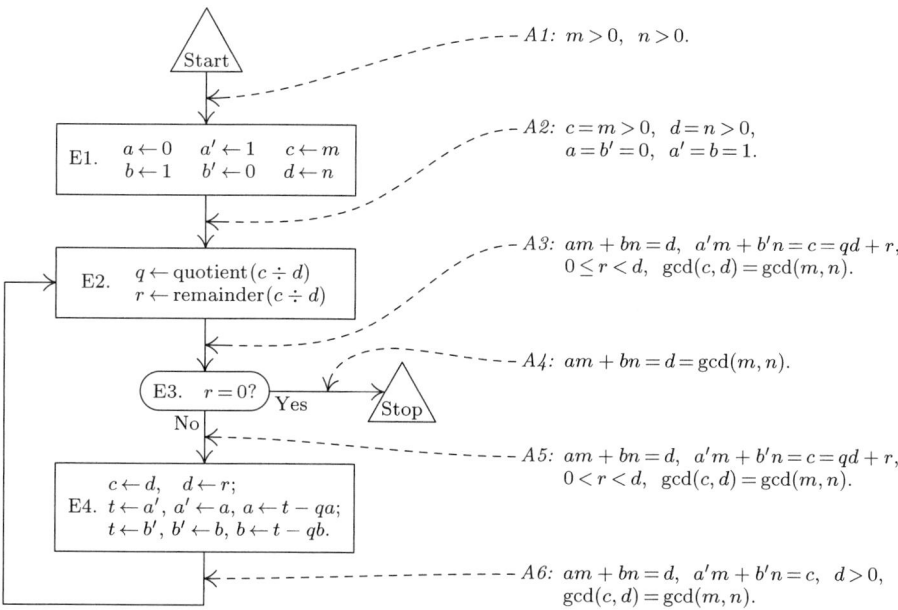

Fig. 4. Flow chart for Algorithm E, labeled with assertions that prove the validity of the algorithm.

If we examine this argument very closely and change our viewpoint slightly, we can envision a general method applicable to proving the validity of *any* algorithm. The idea is to take a flow chart for some algorithm and to label each of the arrows with an assertion about the current state of affairs at the time the computation traverses that arrow. See Fig. 4, where the assertions have been labeled $A1, A2, \ldots, A6$. (All of these assertions have the additional stipulation that the variables are integers; this stipulation has been omitted to save space.) $A1$ gives the initial assumptions upon entry to the algorithm, and $A4$ states what we hope to prove about the output values a, b, and d.

The general method consists of proving, for each box in the flow chart, that

> *if an assertion attached to any arrow leading into the box is true before the operation in that box is performed, then all of the assertions on relevant arrows leading away from the box are true after the operation.* $\qquad(7)$

Thus, for example, we must prove that either $A2$ or $A6$ before E2 implies $A3$ after E2. (In this case $A2$ is a stronger statement than $A6$; that is, $A2$ implies $A6$. So we need only prove that $A6$ before E2 implies $A3$ after. Notice that the condition $d > 0$ is necessary in $A6$ just to prove that operation E2 even makes sense.) It is also necessary to show that $A3$ and $r = 0$ implies $A4$; that $A3$ and $r \neq 0$ implies $A5$; etc. Each of the required proofs is very straightforward.

Once statement (7) *has been proved for each box, it follows that all assertions are true during any execution of the algorithm.* For we can now use induction on the number of steps of the computation, in the sense of the number of arrows traversed in the flow chart. While traversing the first arrow, the one leading from "Start", the assertion $A1$ is true since we always assume that our input values meet the specifications; so the assertion on the first arrow traversed is correct. If the assertion that labels the nth arrow is true, then by (7) the assertion that labels the $(n + 1)$st arrow is also true.

Using this general method, the problem of proving that a given algorithm is valid evidently consists mostly of inventing the right assertions to put in the flow chart. Once this inductive leap has been made, it is pretty much routine to carry out the proofs that each assertion leading into a box logically implies each assertion leading out. In fact, it is pretty much routine to invent the assertions themselves, once a few of the difficult ones have been discovered; thus it is very simple in our example to write out essentially what $A2$, $A3$, and $A5$ must be, if only $A1$, $A4$, and $A6$ are given. In our example, assertion $A6$ is the creative part of the proof; all the rest could, in principle, be supplied mechanically. Hence no attempt has been made to give detailed formal proofs of the algorithms that follow in this book, at the level of detail found in Fig. 4. It suffices to state the key inductive assertions. Those assertions either appear in the discussion following an algorithm or they are given as parenthetical remarks in the text of the algorithm itself.

This approach to proving the correctness of algorithms has another aspect that is even more important: *It mirrors the way we understand an algorithm.* Recall that in Section 1.1 the reader was cautioned not to expect to read an algorithm like part of a novel; one or two trials of the algorithm on some sample data were recommended. This was done expressly because an example run-through of the algorithm helps a person formulate the various assertions mentally. It is the contention of the author that we really understand why an algorithm is valid only when we reach the point that our minds have implicitly filled in all the assertions, as was done in Fig. 4. This point of view has important psychological consequences for the proper communication of algorithms from one person to another: It implies that the key assertions, those that cannot easily be derived by an automaton, should always be stated explicitly when an algorithm is being explained to someone else. When Algorithm E is being put forward, assertion $A6$ should be mentioned too.

An alert reader will have noticed a gaping hole in our last proof of Algorithm E, however. We never showed that the algorithm terminates; all we have proved is that *if* it terminates, it gives the right answer!

(Notice, for example, that Algorithm E still makes sense if we allow its variables m, n, c, d, and r to assume values of the form $u + v\sqrt{2}$, where u and v are integers. The variables q, a, b, a', b' are to remain integer-valued. If we start the method with $m = 12 - 6\sqrt{2}$ and $n = 20 - 10\sqrt{2}$, say, it will compute a "greatest common divisor" $d = 4 - 2\sqrt{2}$ with $a = +2$, $b = -1$. Even under this extension of the assumptions, the proofs of assertions $A1$ through $A6$ remain valid; therefore all assertions are true throughout any execution of the procedure. But if we start out with $m = 1$ and $n = \sqrt{2}$, the computation never terminates (see exercise 12). Hence a proof of assertions *A1* through *A6* does *not* logically prove that the algorithm is finite.)

Proofs of termination are usually handled separately. But exercise 13 shows that it *is* possible to extend the method above in many important cases so that a proof of termination is included as a by-product.

We have now twice proved the validity of Algorithm E. To be strictly logical, we should also try to prove that the first algorithm in this section, Algorithm I, is valid; in fact, we have used Algorithm I to establish the correctness of any proof by induction. If we attempt to *prove* that Algorithm I works properly, however, we are confronted with a dilemma — we can't really prove it without using induction again! The argument would be circular.

In the last analysis, *every* property of the integers must be proved using induction somewhere along the line, because if we get down to basic concepts, the integers are essentially *defined* by induction. Therefore we may take as axiomatic the idea that any positive integer n either equals 1 or can be reached by starting with 1 and repetitively adding 1; this suffices to prove that Algorithm I is valid. [For a rigorous study of fundamental concepts about the integers, see the article "On Mathematical Induction" by Leon Henkin, *AMM* **67** (1960), 323–338.]

The idea behind mathematical induction is thus intimately related to the concept of number. The first European to apply mathematical induction to rigorous proofs was the Italian scientist Francesco Maurolico, in 1575. Pierre de Fermat made further improvements, in the early 17th century; he called it the "method of infinite descent." The notion also appears clearly in the later writings of Blaise Pascal (1653). The phrase "mathematical induction" apparently was coined by A. De Morgan in the early nineteenth century. [See *The Penny Cyclopædia* **11** (1838), 465–466; *AMM* **24** (1917), 199–207; **25** (1918), 197–201; *Arch. Hist. Exact Sci.* **9** (1972), 1–21.] Further discussion of mathematical induction can be found in G. Pólya's book *Induction and Analogy in Mathematics* (Princeton, N.J.: Princeton University Press, 1954), Chapter 7.

The formulation of algorithm-proving in terms of assertions and induction, as given above, is essentially due to R. W. Floyd. He pointed out that a semantic definition of each operation in a programming language can be formulated as a logical rule that tells exactly what assertions can be proved after the operation, based on what assertions are true beforehand [see "Assigning Meanings to Programs," *Proc. Symp. Appl. Math.*, Amer. Math. Soc., **19** (1967), 19–32]. Similar ideas were voiced independently by Peter Naur, *BIT* **6** (1966), 310–316, who called the assertions "general snapshots." An important refinement, the notion of "invariants," was introduced by C. A. R. Hoare; see, for example, *CACM* **14** (1971), 39–45. Later authors found it advantageous to reverse Floyd's direction, going from an assertion that should hold *after* an operation to the "weakest precondition" that must hold *before* the operation is done; such an approach makes it possible to discover new algorithms that are guaranteed to be correct, if we start from the specifications of the desired output and work backwards. [See E. W. Dijkstra, *CACM* **18** (1975), 453–457; *A Discipline of Programming* (Prentice–Hall, 1976).]

The concept of inductive assertions actually appeared in embryonic form in 1946, at the same time as flow charts were introduced by H. H. Goldstine and J. von Neumann. Their original flow charts included "assertion boxes" that are in close analogy with the assertions in Fig. 4. [See John von Neumann, *Collected Works* **5** (New York: Macmillan, 1963), 91–99. See also A. M. Turing's early comments about verification in *Report of a Conference on High Speed Automatic Calculating Machines* (Cambridge Univ., 1949), 67–68 and figures; reprinted with commentary by F. L. Morris and C. B. Jones in *Annals of the History of Computing* **6** (1984), 139–143.]

> *The understanding of the theory of a routine*
> *may be greatly aided by providing, at the time of construction*
> *one or two statements concerning the state of the machine*
> *at well chosen points. ...*
> *In the extreme form of the theoretical method*
> *a watertight mathematical proof is provided for the assertions.*
> *In the extreme form of the experimental method*
> *the routine is tried out on the machine with a variety of initial*
> *conditions and is pronounced fit if the assertions hold in each case.*
> *Both methods have their weaknesses.*
>
> — A. M. TURING, Ferranti Mark I Programming Manual (1950)

EXERCISES

1. [*05*] Explain how to modify the idea of proof by mathematical induction, in case we want to prove some statement $P(n)$ for all *nonnegative* integers — that is, for $n = 0$, 1, 2, ... instead of for $n = 1, 2, 3, \ldots$.

▶ **2.** [*15*] There must be something wrong with the following proof. What is it? "**Theorem.** Let a be any positive number. For all positive integers n we have $a^{n-1} = 1$. *Proof.* If $n = 1$, $a^{n-1} = a^{1-1} = a^0 = 1$. And by induction, assuming that the theorem is true for $1, 2, \ldots, n$, we have

$$a^{(n+1)-1} = a^n = \frac{a^{n-1} \times a^{n-1}}{a^{(n-1)-1}} = \frac{1 \times 1}{1} = 1;$$

so the theorem is true for $n + 1$ as well."

3. [*18*] The following proof by induction seems correct, but for some reason the equation for $n = 6$ gives $\frac{1}{2} + \frac{1}{6} + \frac{1}{12} + \frac{1}{20} + \frac{1}{30} = \frac{5}{6}$ on the left-hand side, and $\frac{3}{2} - \frac{1}{6} = \frac{4}{3}$ on the right-hand side. Can you find a mistake? "**Theorem.**

$$\frac{1}{1 \times 2} + \frac{1}{2 \times 3} + \cdots + \frac{1}{(n-1) \times n} = \frac{3}{2} - \frac{1}{n}.$$

Proof. We use induction on n. For $n = 1$, clearly $3/2 - 1/n = 1/(1 \times 2)$; and, assuming that the theorem is true for n,

$$\frac{1}{1 \times 2} + \cdots + \frac{1}{(n-1) \times n} + \frac{1}{n \times (n+1)}$$
$$= \frac{3}{2} - \frac{1}{n} + \frac{1}{n(n+1)} = \frac{3}{2} - \frac{1}{n} + \left(\frac{1}{n} - \frac{1}{n+1}\right) = \frac{3}{2} - \frac{1}{n+1}.\text{"}$$

4. [*20*] Prove that, in addition to Eq. (3), Fibonacci numbers satisfy $F_n \geq \phi^{n-2}$.

5. [*21*] A *prime number* is an integer > 1 that has no exact divisors other than 1 and itself. Using this definition and mathematical induction, prove that every integer > 1 may be written as a product of one or more prime numbers. (A prime number is considered to be the "product" of a single prime, namely itself.)

6. [*20*] Prove that if Eqs. (6) hold just before step E4, they hold afterwards also.

7. [*23*] Formulate and prove by induction a rule for the sums 1^2, $2^2 - 1^2$, $3^2 - 2^2 + 1^2$, $4^2 - 3^2 + 2^2 - 1^2$, $5^2 - 4^2 + 3^2 - 2^2 + 1^2$, etc.

▶ **8.** [*25*] (a) Prove the following theorem of Nicomachus (A.D. c. 100) by induction: $1^3 = 1$, $2^3 = 3 + 5$, $3^3 = 7 + 9 + 11$, $4^3 = 13 + 15 + 17 + 19$, etc. (b) Use this result to prove the remarkable formula $1^3 + 2^3 + \cdots + n^3 = (1 + 2 + \cdots + n)^2$.

[*Note:* An attractive geometric interpretation of this formula, suggested by Warren Lushbaugh, is shown in Fig. 5; see *Math. Gazette* **49** (1965), 200. The idea is related to Nicomachus's theorem and Fig. 3. Other "look-see" proofs can be found in books by Martin Gardner, *Knotted Doughnuts* (New York: Freeman, 1986), Chapter 16; J. H. Conway and R. K. Guy, *The Book of Numbers* (New York: Copernicus, 1996), Chapter 2.]

Side $= 5+5+5+5+5+5 = 5 \cdot (5+1)$

Side $= 5+4+3+2+1+1+2+3+4+5$
$\qquad = 2 \cdot (1+2+ \cdots +5)$

Area $= 4 \cdot 1^2 + 4 \cdot 2 \cdot 2^2 + 4 \cdot 3 \cdot 3^2 + 4 \cdot 4 \cdot 4^2 + 4 \cdot 5 \cdot 5^2$
$\qquad = 4 \cdot (1^3 + 2^3 + \cdots + 5^3)$

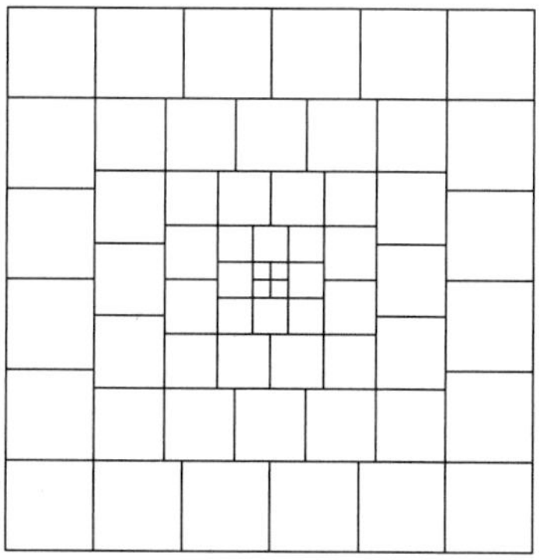

Fig. 5. Geometric version of exercise 8(b).

9. [*20*] Prove by induction that if $0 < a < 1$, then $(1-a)^n \geq 1 - na$.

10. [*M22*] Prove by induction that if $n \geq 10$, then $2^n > n^3$.

11. [*M30*] Find and prove a simple formula for the sum

$$\frac{1^3}{1^4 + 4} - \frac{3^3}{3^4 + 4} + \frac{5^3}{5^4 + 4} - \cdots + \frac{(-1)^n (2n+1)^3}{(2n+1)^4 + 4}.$$

12. [*M25*] Show how Algorithm E can be generalized as stated in the text so that it will accept input values of the form $u + v\sqrt{2}$, where u and v are integers, and the computations can still be done in an elementary way (that is, without using the infinite decimal expansion of $\sqrt{2}$). Prove that the computation will not terminate, however, if $m = 1$ and $n = \sqrt{2}$.

▶ **13.** [*M23*] Extend Algorithm E by adding a new variable T and adding the operation "$T \leftarrow T+1$" at the beginning of each step. (Thus, T is like a clock, counting the number of steps executed.) Assume that T is initially zero, so that assertion *A1* in Fig. 4 becomes "$m > 0$, $n > 0$, $T = 0$." The additional condition "$T = 1$" should similarly be appended to *A2*. Show how to append additional conditions to the assertions in such a way that any one of *A1*, *A2*, ..., *A6* implies $T \leq 3n$, and such that the inductive proof can still be carried out. (Hence the computation must terminate in at most $3n$ steps.)

14. [50] (R. W. Floyd.) Prepare a computer program that accepts, as input, programs in some programming language together with optional assertions, and that attempts to fill in the remaining assertions necessary to make a proof that the computer program is valid. (For example, strive to get a program that is able to prove the validity of Algorithm E, given only assertions *A1*, *A4*, and *A6*. See the papers by R. W. Floyd and J. C. King in the IFIP Congress proceedings, 1971, for further discussion.)

▶ **15.** [HM28] (*Generalized induction.*) The text shows how to prove statements $P(n)$ that depend on a single integer n, but it does not describe how to prove statements $P(m, n)$ depending on two integers. In these circumstances a proof is often given by some sort of "double induction," which frequently seems confusing. Actually, there is an important principle more general than simple induction that applies not only to this case but also to situations in which statements are to be proved about uncountable sets — for example, $P(x)$ for all real x. This general principle is called *well-ordering*.

Let "$\prec$" be a relation on a set S, satisfying the following properties:

   i) Given x, y, and z in S, if $x \prec y$ and $y \prec z$, then $x \prec z$.

  ii) Given x and y in S, exactly one of the following three possibilities is true: $x \prec y$, $x = y$, or $y \prec x$.

 iii) If A is any nonempty subset of S, there is an element x in A with $x \preceq y$ (that is, $x \prec y$ or $x = y$) for all y in A.

This relation is said to be a well-ordering of S. For example, it is clear that the positive integers are well-ordered by the ordinary "less than" relation, $<$.

  a) Show that the set of *all* integers is not well-ordered by $<$.

  b) Define a well-ordering relation on the set of all integers.

  c) Is the set of all nonnegative real numbers well-ordered by $<$?

  d) (*Lexicographic order.*) Let S be well-ordered by $\prec$, and for $n > 0$ let T_n be the set of all n-tuples $(x_1, x_2, \ldots, x_n)$ of elements x_j in S. Define $(x_1, x_2, \ldots, x_n) \prec (y_1, y_2, \ldots, y_n)$ if there is some k, $1 \le k \le n$, such that $x_j = y_j$ for $1 \le j < k$, but $x_k \prec y_k$ in S. Is $\prec$ a well-ordering of T_n?

  e) Continuing part (d), let $T = \bigcup_{n \ge 1} T_n$; define $(x_1, x_2, \ldots, x_m) \prec (y_1, y_2, \ldots, y_n)$ if $x_j = y_j$ for $1 \le j < k$ and $x_k \prec y_k$, for some $k \le \min(m, n)$, or if $m < n$ and $x_j = y_j$ for $1 \le j \le m$. Is $\prec$ a well-ordering of T?

  f) Show that $\prec$ is a well-ordering of S if and only if it satisfies (i) and (ii) above and there is no infinite sequence x_1, x_2, x_3, ... with $x_{j+1} \prec x_j$ for all $j \ge 1$.

  g) Let S be well-ordered by $\prec$, and let $P(x)$ be a statement about the element x of S. Show that if $P(x)$ can be proved under the assumption that $P(y)$ is true for all $y \prec x$, then $P(x)$ is true for *all* x in S.

[*Notes:* Part (g) is the generalization of simple induction that was promised; in the case $S = $ positive integers, it is just the simple case of mathematical induction treated in the text. In that case we are asked to prove that $P(1)$ is true if $P(y)$ is true for all positive integers $y < 1$; this is the same as saying we should prove $P(1)$, since $P(y)$ certainly is (vacuously) true for all such y. Consequently, one finds that in many situations $P(1)$ need not be proved using a special argument.

    Part (d), in connection with part (g), gives us a powerful method of n-tuple induction for proving statements $P(m_1, \ldots, m_n)$ about n positive integers m_1, ..., m_n.

    Part (f) has further application to computer algorithms: If we can map each state x of a computation into an element $f(x)$ belonging to a well-ordered set S, in such a way that every step of the computation takes a state x into a state y with $f(y) \prec f(x)$, then

the algorithm must terminate. This principle generalizes the argument about strictly
decreasing values of n, by which we proved the termination of Algorithm 1.1E.]

1.2.2. Numbers, Powers, and Logarithms

Let us now begin our study of numerical mathematics by taking a good look at
the numbers we are dealing with. The *integers* are the whole numbers

$$\ldots, -3, -2, -1, 0, 1, 2, 3, \ldots$$

(negative, zero, or positive). A *rational number* is the ratio (quotient) of two
integers, p/q, where q is positive. A *real number* is a quantity x that has a
decimal expansion

$$x = n + 0.d_1 d_2 d_3 \ldots, \tag{1}$$

where n is an integer, each d_i is a digit between 0 and 9, and the sequence of
digits doesn't end with infinitely many 9s. The representation (1) means that

$$n + \frac{d_1}{10} + \frac{d_2}{100} + \cdots + \frac{d_k}{10^k} \le x < n + \frac{d_1}{10} + \frac{d_2}{100} + \cdots + \frac{d_k}{10^k} + \frac{1}{10^k}, \tag{2}$$

for all positive integers k. Examples of real numbers that are not rational are

$\pi = 3.14159265358979\ldots,$ the ratio of circumference to diameter in a circle;

$\phi = 1.61803398874989\ldots,$ the *golden ratio* $(1 + \sqrt{5})/2$ (see Section 1.2.8).

A table of important constants, to forty decimal places of accuracy, appears in
Appendix A. We need not discuss the familiar properties of addition, subtraction, multiplication, division, and comparison of real numbers.

Difficult problems about integers are often solved by working with real
numbers, and difficult problems about real numbers are often solved by working
with a still more general class of values called complex numbers. A *complex
number* is a quantity z of the form $z = x + iy$, where x and y are real and i is
a special quantity that satisfies the equation $i^2 = -1$. We call x and y the *real
part* and *imaginary part* of z, and we define the absolute value of z to be

$$|z| = \sqrt{x^2 + y^2}. \tag{3}$$

The *complex conjugate* of z is $\bar{z} = x - iy$, and we have $z\bar{z} = x^2 + y^2 = |z|^2$. The
theory of complex numbers is in many ways simpler and more beautiful than
the theory of real numbers, but it is usually considered to be an advanced topic.
Therefore we shall concentrate on real numbers in this book, except when real
numbers turn out to be unnecessarily complicated.

If u and v are real numbers with $u \le v$, the *closed interval* $[u\,..\,v]$ is the set
of real numbers x such that $u \le x \le v$. The *open interval* $(u\,..\,v)$ is, similarly,
the set of x such that $u < x < v$. And *half-open intervals* $[u\,..\,v)$ or $(u\,..\,v]$ are
defined in an analogous way. We also allow u to be $-\infty$ or v to be ∞ at an
open endpoint, meaning that there is no lower or upper bound; thus $(-\infty\,..\,\infty)$
stands for the set of all real numbers, and $[0\,..\,\infty)$ denotes the nonnegative reals.

Throughout this section, let the letter b stand for a positive real number. If n is an integer, then b^n is defined by the familiar rules

$$b^0 = 1, \qquad b^n = b^{n-1}b \quad \text{if} \quad n > 0, \qquad b^n = b^{n+1}/b \quad \text{if} \quad n < 0. \qquad (4)$$

It is easy to prove by induction that the *laws of exponents* are valid:

$$b^{x+y} = b^x b^y, \qquad (b^x)^y = b^{xy}, \qquad\qquad (5)$$

whenever x and y are integers.

If u is a positive real number and if m is a positive integer, there is always a unique positive real number v such that $v^m = u$; it is called the *mth root* of u, and denoted $v = \sqrt[m]{u}$.

We now define b^r for rational numbers $r = p/q$ as follows:

$$b^{p/q} = \sqrt[q]{b^p}. \qquad\qquad (6)$$

This definition, due to Oresme (c. 1360), is a good one, since $b^{ap/aq} = b^{p/q}$, and since the laws of exponents are still correct even when x and y are arbitrary rational numbers (see exercise 9).

Finally, we define b^x for all real values of x. Suppose first that $b > 1$; if x is given by Eq. (1), we want

$$b^{n+d_1/10+\cdots+d_k/10^k} \le b^x < b^{n+d_1/10+\cdots+d_k/10^k+1/10^k}. \qquad (7)$$

This *defines* b^x as a unique positive real number, since the difference between the right and left extremes in Eq. (7) is $b^{n+d_1/10+\cdots+d_k/10^k}(b^{1/10^k} - 1)$; by exercise 13 below, this difference is less than $b^{n+1}(b-1)/10^k$, and if we take k large enough, we can therefore get any desired accuracy for b^x.

For example, we find that

$$10^{0.30102999} = 1.9999999739\ldots, \qquad 10^{0.30103000} = 2.0000000199\ldots; \qquad (8)$$

therefore if $b = 10$ and $x = 0.30102999\ldots$, we know the value of 10^x with an accuracy of better than one part in 10 million (although we still don't even know whether the decimal expansion of 10^x is $1.999\ldots$ or $2.000\ldots$).

When $b < 1$, we define $b^x = (1/b)^{-x}$; and when $b = 1$, $b^x = 1$. With these definitions, it can be proved that the laws of exponents (5) hold for any *real* values of x and y. These ideas for defining b^x were first formulated by John Wallis (1655) and Isaac Newton (1669).

Now we come to an important question. Suppose that a positive real number y is given; can we find a real number x such that $y = b^x$? The answer is "yes" (provided that $b \ne 1$), for we simply use Eq. (7) *in reverse* to determine n and $d_1, d_2, \ldots$ when $b^x = y$ is given. The resulting number x is called the *logarithm* of y to the base b, and we write this as $x = \log_b y$. By this definition we have

$$x = b^{\log_b x} = \log_b(b^x). \qquad\qquad (9)$$

As an example, Eqs. (8) show that

$$\log_{10} 2 = 0.30102999\ldots. \qquad\qquad (10)$$

From the laws of exponents it follows that

$$\log_b(xy) = \log_b x + \log_b y, \quad \text{if} \quad x > 0, \ y > 0 \tag{11}$$

and

$$\log_b(c^y) = y \log_b c, \quad \text{if} \quad c > 0. \tag{12}$$

Equation (10) illustrates the so-called *common logarithms*, which we get when the base is 10. One might expect that in computer work *binary logarithms* (to the base 2) would be more useful, since most computers do binary arithmetic. Actually, we will see that binary logarithms are indeed very useful, but not only for that reason; the reason is primarily that a computer algorithm often makes two-way branches. Binary logarithms arise so frequently, it is wise to have a shorter notation for them. Therefore we shall write

$$\lg x = \log_2 x, \tag{13}$$

following a suggestion of Edward M. Reingold.

The question now arises as to whether or not there is any relationship between $\lg x$ and $\log_{10} x$; fortunately there is,

$$\log_{10} x = \log_{10}(2^{\lg x}) = (\lg x)(\log_{10} 2),$$

by Eqs. (9) and (12). Hence $\lg x = \log_{10} x / \log_{10} 2$, and in general we find that

$$\log_c x = \frac{\log_b x}{\log_b c}. \tag{14}$$

Equations (11), (12), and (14) are the fundamental rules for manipulating logarithms.

It turns out that neither base 10 nor base 2 is really the most convenient base to work with in most cases. There is a real number, denoted by $e = 2.718281828459045\ldots$, for which the logarithms have simpler properties. Logarithms to the base e are conventionally called *natural logarithms*, and we write

$$\ln x = \log_e x. \tag{15}$$

This rather arbitrary definition (in fact, we haven't really defined e) probably doesn't strike the reader as being a very "natural" logarithm; yet we'll find that $\ln x$ seems more and more natural, the more we work with it. John Napier actually discovered natural logarithms (with slight modifications, and without connecting them with powers) before the year 1590, many years before any other kind of logarithm was known. The following two examples, proved in every calculus text, shed some light on why Napier's logarithms deserve to be called "natural": (a) In Fig. 6 the area of the shaded portion is $\ln x$. (b) If a bank pays compound interest at rate r, compounded semiannually, the annual return on each dollar is

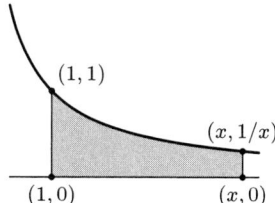

Fig. 6. Natural logarithm.

$(1 + r/2)^2$ dollars; if it is compounded quarterly, you get $(1 + r/4)^4$ dollars; and if it is compounded daily you probably get $(1 + r/365)^{365}$ dollars. Now if the interest were compounded *continuously*, you would get exactly e^r dollars for every dollar (ignoring roundoff error). In this age of computers, many bankers have now actually reached the limiting formula.

The interesting history of the concepts of logarithm and exponential has been told in a series of articles by F. Cajori, *AMM* **20** (1913), 5–14, 35–47, 75–84, 107–117, 148–151, 173–182, 205–210.

We conclude this section by considering how to *compute* logarithms. One method is suggested immediately by Eq. (7): If we let $b^x = y$ and raise all parts of that equation to the 10^k-th power, we find that

$$b^m \leq y^{10^k} < b^{m+1}, \tag{16}$$

for some integer m. All we have to do to get the logarithm of y is to raise y to this huge power and find which powers $(m, m + 1)$ of b the result lies between; then $m/10^k$ is the answer to k decimal places.

A slight modification of this apparently impractical method leads to a simple and reasonable procedure. We will show how to calculate $\log_{10} x$ and to express the answer in the *binary* system, as

$$\log_{10} x = n + b_1/2 + b_2/4 + b_3/8 + \cdots. \tag{17}$$

First we shift the decimal point of x to the left or to the right so that we have $1 \leq x/10^n < 10$; this determines the integer part, n. To obtain $b_1, b_2, \ldots$, we now set $x_0 = x/10^n$ and, for $k \geq 1$,

$$\begin{aligned} b_k = 0, \quad & x_k = x_{k-1}^2, \quad && \text{if} \quad x_{k-1}^2 < 10; \\ b_k = 1, \quad & x_k = x_{k-1}^2/10, \quad && \text{if} \quad x_{k-1}^2 \geq 10. \end{aligned} \tag{18}$$

The validity of this procedure follows from the fact that

$$1 \leq x_k = x^{2^k}/10^{2^k(n+b_1/2+\cdots+b_k/2^k)} < 10, \tag{19}$$

for $k = 0, 1, 2, \ldots$, as is easily proved by induction.

In practice, of course, we must work with only finite accuracy, so we cannot set $x_k = x_{k-1}^2$ exactly. Instead, we set $x_k = x_{k-1}^2$ *rounded* or *truncated* to a certain number of decimal places. For example, here is the evaluation of $\log_{10} 2$ rounded to four significant figures:

x_0	= 2.000;				
x_1	= 4.000,	$b_1 = 0$;	x_6	= 1.845,	$b_6 = 1$;
x_2	= 1.600,	$b_2 = 1$;	x_7	= 3.404,	$b_7 = 0$;
x_3	= 2.560,	$b_3 = 0$;	x_8	= 1.159,	$b_8 = 1$;
x_4	= 6.554,	$b_4 = 0$;	x_9	= 1.343,	$b_9 = 0$;
x_5	= 4.295,	$b_5 = 1$;	x_{10}	= 1.804,	$b_{10} = 0$; etc.

Computational error has caused errors to propagate; the true rounded value of x_{10} is 1.798. This will eventually cause b_{19} to be computed incorrectly, and we get the binary value $(0.0100110100010000011\ldots)_2$, which corresponds to the decimal equivalent $0.301031\ldots$ rather than the true value given in Eq. (10).

With any method such as this it is necessary to examine the amount of computational error due to the limitations imposed. Exercise 27 derives an upper bound for the error; working to four figures as above, we find that the error in the value of the logarithm is guaranteed to be less than 0.00044. Our answer above was more accurate than this primarily because x_0, x_1, x_2, and x_3 were obtained *exactly*.

This method is simple and quite interesting, but it is probably not the best way to calculate logarithms on a computer. Another method is given in exercise 25.

EXERCISES

1. [*00*] What is the smallest positive rational number?

2. [*00*] Is $1 + 0.239999999\ldots$ a decimal expansion?

3. [*02*] What is $(-3)^{-3}$?

▶ **4.** [*05*] What is $(0.125)^{-2/3}$?

5. [*05*] We defined real numbers in terms of a decimal expansion. Discuss how we could have defined them in terms of a binary expansion instead, and give a definition to replace Eq. (2).

6. [*10*] Let $x = m + 0.d_1d_2\ldots$ and $y = n + 0.e_1e_2\ldots$ be real numbers. Give a rule for determining whether $x = y$, $x < y$, or $x > y$, based on the decimal representation.

7. [*M23*] Given that x and y are integers, prove the laws of exponents, starting from the definition given by Eq. (4).

8. [*25*] Let m be a positive integer. *Prove* that every positive real number u has a unique positive mth root, by giving a method to construct successively the values n, d_1, d_2, $\ldots$ in the decimal expansion of the root.

9. [*M23*] Given that x and y are rational, prove the laws of exponents under the assumption that the laws hold when x and y are integers.

10. [*18*] Prove that $\log_{10} 2$ is not a rational number.

▶ **11.** [*10*] If $b = 10$ and $x \approx \log_{10} 2$, to how many decimal places of accuracy will we need to know the value of x in order to determine the first three decimal places of the decimal expansion of b^x? [*Note:* You may use the result of exercise 10 in your discussion.]

12. [*02*] Explain why Eq. (10) follows from Eqs. (8).

▶ **13.** [*M23*] (a) Given that x is a positive real number and n is a positive integer, prove the inequality $\sqrt[n]{1+x} - 1 \le x/n$. (b) Use this fact to justify the remarks following (7).

14. [*15*] Prove Eq. (12).

15. [*10*] Prove or disprove:

$$\log_b x/y = \log_b x - \log_b y, \quad \text{if} \quad x, y > 0.$$

16. [*00*] How can $\log_{10} x$ be expressed in terms of $\ln x$ and $\ln 10$?

▶ **17.** [*05*] What is $\lg 32$? $\log_\pi \pi$? $\ln e$? $\log_b 1$? $\log_b(-1)$?

18. [*10*] Prove or disprove: $\log_8 x = \frac{1}{2} \lg x$.

▶ **19.** [*20*] If n is an integer whose decimal representation is 14 digits long, will the value of n fit in a computer word with a capacity of 47 bits and a sign bit?

20. [*10*] Is there any simple relation between $\log_{10} 2$ and $\log_2 10$?

21. [*15*] (*Logs of logs.*) Express $\log_b \log_b x$ in terms of $\ln \ln x$, $\ln \ln b$, and $\ln b$.

▶ **22.** [*20*] (R. W. Hamming.) Prove that

$$\lg x \approx \ln x + \log_{10} x,$$

with less than 1% error! (Thus a table of natural logarithms and of common logarithms can be used to get approximate values of binary logarithms as well.)

23. [*M25*] Give a *geometric* proof that $\ln xy = \ln x + \ln y$, based on Fig. 6.

24. [*15*] Explain how the method used for calculating logarithms to the base 10 at the end of this section can be modified to produce logarithms to base 2.

25. [*22*] Suppose that we have a binary computer and a number x, $1 \le x < 2$. Show that the following algorithm, which uses only shifting, addition, and subtraction operations proportional to the number of places of accuracy desired, may be used to calculate an approximation to $y = \log_b x$:

L1. [Initialize.] Set $y \leftarrow 0$, $z \leftarrow x$ shifted right 1, $k \leftarrow 1$.

L2. [Test for end.] If $x = 1$, stop.

L3. [Compare.] If $x - z < 1$, set $z \leftarrow z$ shifted right 1, $k \leftarrow k + 1$, and repeat this step.

L4. [Reduce values.] Set $x \leftarrow x - z$, $z \leftarrow x$ shifted right k, $y \leftarrow y + \log_b(2^k/(2^k - 1))$, and go to L2. ▮

[*Notes:* This method is very similar to the method used for division in computer hardware. The idea goes back in essence to Henry Briggs, who used it (in decimal rather than binary form) to compute logarithm tables, published in 1624. We need an auxiliary table of the constants $\log_b 2$, $\log_b(4/3)$, $\log_b(8/7)$, etc., to as many values as the precision of the computer. The algorithm involves intentional computational errors, as numbers are shifted to the right, so that eventually x will be reduced to 1 and the algorithm will terminate. The purpose of this exercise is to explain why it will terminate and why it computes an approximation to $\log_b x$.]

26. [*M27*] Find a rigorous upper bound on the error made by the algorithm in the previous exercise, based on the precision used in the arithmetic operations.

▶ **27.** [*M25*] Consider the method for calculating $\log_{10} x$ discussed in the text. Let x'_k denote the computed approximation to x_k, determined as follows: $x(1 - \delta) \le 10^n x'_0 \le x(1 + \epsilon)$; and in the determination of x'_k by Eqs. (18), the quantity y_k is used in place of $(x'_{k-1})^2$, where $(x'_{k-1})^2(1 - \delta) \le y_k \le (x'_{k-1})^2(1 + \epsilon)$ and $1 \le y_k < 100$. Here δ and ϵ are small constants that reflect the upper and lower errors due to rounding or truncation. If $\log' x$ denotes the result of the calculations, show that after k steps we have

$$\log_{10} x + 2 \log_{10}(1 - \delta) - 1/2^k < \log' x \le \log_{10} x + 2 \log_{10}(1 + \epsilon).$$

28. [*M30*] (R. Feynman.) Develop a method for computing b^x when $0 \le x < 1$, using only shifting, addition, and subtraction (similar to the algorithm in exercise 25), and analyze its accuracy.

29. [*HM20*] Let x be a real number greater than 1. (a) For what real number $b > 1$ is $b \log_b x$ a minimum? (b) For what *integer* $b > 1$ is it a minimum? (c) For what integer $b > 1$ is $(b + 1) \log_b x$ a minimum?

30. [*12*] Simplify the expression $(\ln x)^{\ln x / \ln \ln x}$, assuming that $x > 1$ and $x \neq e$.

1.2.3. Sums and Products

Let $a_1, a_2, \ldots$ be any sequence of numbers. We are often interested in sums such as $a_1 + a_2 + \cdots + a_n$, and this sum is more compactly written using either of the following equivalent notations:

$$\sum_{j=1}^{n} a_j \qquad \text{or} \qquad \sum_{1 \leq j \leq n} a_j. \tag{1}$$

If n is zero, the value of $a_1 + a_2 + \cdots + a_n = \sum_{j=1}^{n} a_j = \sum_{1 \leq j \leq n} a_j$ is defined to be zero. Our convention of using "three dots" in sums such as $a_1 + a_2 + \cdots + a_n$ therefore has some slightly peculiar, but sensible, behavior in borderline cases (see exercise 1).

In general, if $R(j)$ is any relation involving j, the symbol

$$\sum_{R(j)} a_j \tag{2}$$

means the sum of all a_j where j is an integer satisfying the condition $R(j)$. If no such integers exist, notation (2) denotes zero. The letter j in (1) and (2) is a *dummy index* or *index variable*, introduced just for the purposes of the notation. Symbols used as index variables are usually the letters i, j, k, m, n, r, s, t (occasionally with subscripts or accent marks). Large summation signs like those in (1) and (2) can also be rendered more compactly as $\sum_{j=1}^{n} a_j$ or $\sum_{R(j)} a_j$. The use of a $\sum$ and index variables to indicate summation with definite limits was introduced by J. Fourier in 1820.

Strictly speaking, the notation $\sum_{1 \leq j \leq n} a_j$ is ambiguous, since it does not clarify whether the summation is taken with respect to j or to n. In this particular case it would be rather silly to interpret it as a sum on values of $n \geq j$; but meaningful examples can be constructed in which the index variable is not clearly specified, as in $\sum_{j \leq k} \binom{j+k}{2j-k}$. In such cases the context must make clear which variable is a dummy variable and which variable has a significance that extends beyond its appearance in the sum. A sum such as $\sum_{j \leq k} \binom{j+k}{2j-k}$ would presumably be used only if either j or k (not both) has exterior significance.

In most cases we will use notation (2) only when the sum is *finite* — that is, when only a finite number of values j satisfy $R(j)$ and have $a_j \neq 0$. If an infinite sum is required, for example

$$\sum_{j=1}^{\infty} a_j = \sum_{j \geq 1} a_j = a_1 + a_2 + a_3 + \cdots$$

with infinitely many nonzero terms, the techniques of calculus must be employed; the precise meaning of (2) is then

$$\sum_{R(j)} a_j = \left(\lim_{n \to \infty} \sum_{\substack{R(j) \\ 0 \leq j < n}} a_j \right) + \left(\lim_{n \to \infty} \sum_{\substack{R(j) \\ -n \leq j < 0}} a_j \right), \tag{3}$$

provided that both limits exist. If either limit fails to exist, the infinite sum is *divergent*; it does not exist. Otherwise it is *convergent*.

When two or more conditions are placed under the $\sum$ sign, as in (3), we mean that *all* conditions must hold.

Four simple algebraic operations on sums are very important, and familiarity with them makes the solution of many problems possible. We shall now discuss these four operations.

a) *The distributive law*, for products of sums:

$$\left(\sum_{R(i)} a_i\right)\left(\sum_{S(j)} b_j\right) = \sum_{R(i)}\left(\sum_{S(j)} a_i b_j\right). \tag{4}$$

To understand this law, consider for example the special case

$$\left(\sum_{i=1}^{2} a_i\right)\left(\sum_{j=1}^{3} b_j\right) = (a_1 + a_2)(b_1 + b_2 + b_3)$$

$$= (a_1 b_1 + a_1 b_2 + a_1 b_3) + (a_2 b_1 + a_2 b_2 + a_2 b_3)$$

$$= \sum_{i=1}^{2}\left(\sum_{j=1}^{3} a_i b_j\right).$$

It is customary to drop the parentheses on the right-hand side of (4); a double summation such as $\sum_{R(i)}\left(\sum_{S(j)} a_{ij}\right)$ is written simply $\sum_{R(i)}\sum_{S(j)} a_{ij}$.

b) *Change of variable:*

$$\sum_{R(i)} a_i = \sum_{R(j)} a_j = \sum_{R(p(j))} a_{p(j)}. \tag{5}$$

This equation represents two kinds of transformations. In the first case we are simply changing the name of the index variable from i to j. The second case is more interesting: Here $p(j)$ is a function of j that represents a *permutation* of the relevant values; more precisely, for each integer i satisfying the relation $R(i)$, there must be exactly one integer j satisfying the relation $p(j) = i$. This condition is always satisfied in the important cases $p(j) = c + j$ and $p(j) = c - j$, where c is an integer not depending on j, and these are the cases used most frequently in applications. For example,

$$\sum_{1 \le j \le n} a_j = \sum_{1 \le j-1 \le n} a_{j-1} = \sum_{2 \le j \le n+1} a_{j-1}. \tag{6}$$

The reader should study this example carefully.

The replacement of j by $p(j)$ cannot be done for all *infinite* sums. The operation is always valid if $p(j) = c \pm j$, as above, but in other cases some care must be used. [For example, see T. M. Apostol, *Mathematical Analysis* (Reading, Mass.: Addison–Wesley, 1957), Chapter 12. A sufficient condition to guarantee the validity of (5) for any permutation of the integers, $p(j)$, is that $\sum_{R(j)} |a_j|$ exists.]

   c) *Interchanging order of summation:*

$$\sum_{R(i)} \sum_{S(j)} a_{ij} = \sum_{S(j)} \sum_{R(i)} a_{ij}. \tag{7}$$

Let us consider a very simple special case of this equation:

$$\sum_{R(i)} \sum_{j=1}^{2} a_{ij} = \sum_{R(i)} (a_{i1} + a_{i2}),$$

$$\sum_{j=1}^{2} \sum_{R(i)} a_{ij} = \sum_{R(i)} a_{i1} + \sum_{R(i)} a_{i2}.$$

By Eq. (7), these two are equal; this says no more than

$$\sum_{R(i)} (b_i + c_i) = \sum_{R(i)} b_i + \sum_{R(i)} c_i, \tag{8}$$

where we let $b_i = a_{i1}$ and $c_i = a_{i2}$.

   The operation of interchanging the order of summation is extremely useful, since it often happens that we know a simple form for $\sum_{R(i)} a_{ij}$, but not for $\sum_{S(j)} a_{ij}$. We frequently need to interchange the summation order also in a more general situation, where the relation $S(j)$ depends on i as well as j. In such a case we can denote the relation by "$S(i,j)$." The interchange of summation can always be carried out, in theory at least, as follows:

$$\sum_{R(i)} \sum_{S(i,j)} a_{ij} = \sum_{S'(j)} \sum_{R'(i,j)} a_{ij}, \tag{9}$$

where $S'(j)$ is the relation "there is an integer i such that both $R(i)$ and $S(i,j)$ are true"; and $R'(i,j)$ is the relation "both $R(i)$ and $S(i,j)$ are true." For example, if the summation is $\sum_{i=1}^{n} \sum_{j=1}^{i} a_{ij}$, then $S'(j)$ is the relation "there is an integer i such that $1 \le i \le n$ and $1 \le j \le i$," that is, $1 \le j \le n$; and $R'(i,j)$ is the relation "$1 \le i \le n$ and $1 \le j \le i$," that is, $j \le i \le n$. Thus,

$$\sum_{i=1}^{n} \sum_{j=1}^{i} a_{ij} = \sum_{j=1}^{n} \sum_{i=j}^{n} a_{ij}. \tag{10}$$

[*Note:* As in case (b), the operation of interchanging order of summation is *not always valid for infinite series.* If the series is *absolutely convergent* — that is, if $\sum_{R(i)} \sum_{S(j)} |a_{ij}|$ exists — it can be shown that Eqs. (7) and (9) are valid. Also if *either one* of $R(i)$ or $S(j)$ specifies a *finite* sum in Eq. (7), and if each infinite sum that appears is convergent, then the interchange is justified. In particular, Eq. (8) is always true for convergent infinite sums.]

d) *Manipulating the domain.* If $R(j)$ and $S(j)$ are arbitrary relations, we have

$$\sum_{R(j)} a_j + \sum_{S(j)} a_j = \sum_{R(j) \text{ or } S(j)} a_j + \sum_{R(j) \text{ and } S(j)} a_j. \qquad (11)$$

For example,

$$\sum_{1 \le j \le m} a_j + \sum_{m \le j \le n} a_j = \left(\sum_{1 \le j \le n} a_j \right) + a_m, \qquad (12)$$

assuming that $1 \le m \le n$. In this case "$R(j)$ and $S(j)$" is simply "$j = m$," so we have reduced the second sum to simply "a_m." In most applications of Eq. (11), either $R(j)$ and $S(j)$ are simultaneously satisfied for only one or two values of j, or else it is impossible to have both $R(j)$ and $S(j)$ true for the same j. In the latter case, the second sum on the right-hand side of Eq. (11) simply disappears.

Now that we have seen the four basic rules for manipulating sums, let's study some further illustrations of how to apply these techniques.

Example 1.

$$\sum_{\substack{0 \le j \le n \\ j \text{ even}}} a_j = \sum_{\substack{0 \le j \le n \\ j \text{ even}}} a_j + \sum_{\substack{0 \le j \le n \\ j \text{ odd}}} a_j \qquad \text{by rule (d)}$$

$$= \sum_{\substack{0 \le 2j \le n \\ 2j \text{ even}}} a_{2j} + \sum_{\substack{0 \le 2j+1 \le n \\ 2j+1 \text{ odd}}} a_{2j+1} \qquad \text{by rule (b)}$$

$$= \sum_{0 \le j \le n/2} a_{2j} + \sum_{0 \le j < n/2} a_{2j+1}.$$

The last step merely consists of simplifying the relations below the $\sum$'s.

Example 2. Let

$$S_1 = \sum_{i=0}^{n} \sum_{j=0}^{i} a_i a_j = \sum_{j=0}^{n} \sum_{i=j}^{n} a_i a_j \qquad \text{by rule (c) [see Eq. (10)]}$$

$$= \sum_{i=0}^{n} \sum_{j=i}^{n} a_i a_j \qquad \text{by rule (b),}$$

interchanging the names i and j and recognizing that $a_j a_i = a_i a_j$. If we denote the latter sum by S_2, we have

$$2S_1 = S_1 + S_2 = \sum_{i=0}^{n} \left(\sum_{j=0}^{i} a_i a_j + \sum_{j=i}^{n} a_i a_j \right) \qquad \text{by Eq. (8)}$$

$$= \sum_{i=0}^{n} \left(\left(\sum_{j=0}^{n} a_i a_j \right) + a_i a_i \right) \qquad \begin{array}{l} \text{by rule (d)} \\ \text{[see Eq. (12)]} \end{array}$$

$$= \sum_{i=0}^{n} \sum_{j=0}^{n} a_i a_j + \sum_{i=0}^{n} a_i a_i \qquad \text{by Eq. (8)}$$

$$= \left(\sum_{i=0}^{n} a_i \right) \left(\sum_{j=0}^{n} a_j \right) + \left(\sum_{i=0}^{n} a_i^2 \right) \quad \text{by rule (a)}$$

$$= \left(\sum_{i=0}^{n} a_i \right)^2 + \left(\sum_{i=0}^{n} a_i^2 \right) \qquad \text{by rule (b).}$$

Thus we have derived the important identity

$$\sum_{i=0}^{n} \sum_{j=0}^{i} a_i a_j = \frac{1}{2} \left(\left(\sum_{i=0}^{n} a_i \right)^2 + \left(\sum_{i=0}^{n} a_i^2 \right) \right). \qquad (13)$$

Example 3 (*The sum of a geometric progression*). Assume that $x \neq 1$, $n \geq 0$. Then

$$a + ax + \cdots + ax^n = \sum_{0 \leq j \leq n} ax^j \qquad \text{by definition (2)}$$

$$= a + \sum_{1 \leq j \leq n} ax^j \qquad \text{by rule (d)}$$

$$= a + x \sum_{1 \leq j \leq n} ax^{j-1} \qquad \text{by a very special case of (a)}$$

$$= a + x \sum_{0 \leq j \leq n-1} ax^j \qquad \text{by rule (b) [see Eq. (6)]}$$

$$= a + x \sum_{0 \leq j \leq n} ax^j - ax^{n+1} \quad \text{by rule (d).}$$

Comparing the first relation with the last, we have

$$(1 - x) \sum_{0 \leq j \leq n} ax^j = a - ax^{n+1};$$

hence we obtain the basic formula

$$\sum_{0 \leq j \leq n} ax^j = a \left(\frac{1 - x^{n+1}}{1 - x} \right). \qquad (14)$$

Example 4 (*The sum of an arithmetic progression*). Assume that $n \geq 0$. Then

$$a + (a+b) + \cdots + (a + nb)$$

$$= \sum_{0 \leq j \leq n} (a + bj) \qquad \text{by definition (2)}$$

$$= \sum_{0 \le n-j \le n} \bigl(a + b(n - j)\bigr) \qquad \text{by rule (b)}$$

$$= \sum_{0 \le j \le n} (a + bn - bj) \qquad \text{by simplification}$$

$$= \sum_{0 \le j \le n} (2a + bn) - \sum_{0 \le j \le n} (a + bj) \qquad \text{by Eq. (8)}$$

$$= (n + 1)(2a + bn) - \sum_{0 \le j \le n} (a + bj),$$

since the first sum simply adds together $(n + 1)$ terms that do not depend on j. Now by equating the first and last expressions and dividing by 2, we obtain

$$\sum_{0 \le j \le n} (a + bj) = a(n + 1) + \tfrac{1}{2}bn(n + 1). \tag{15}$$

This is $n + 1$ times $\tfrac{1}{2}\bigl(a + (a + bn)\bigr)$, which can be understood as the number of terms times the average of the first and last terms.

Notice that we have derived the important equations (13), (14), and (15) purely by using simple manipulations of sums. Most textbooks would simply *state* those formulas, and prove them by *induction*. Induction is, of course, a perfectly valid procedure; but it does not give any insight into how on earth a person would ever have dreamed the formula up in the first place, except by some lucky guess. In the analysis of algorithms we are confronted with hundreds of sums that do not conform to any apparent pattern; by manipulating those sums, as above, we can often get the answer without the need for ingenious guesses.

Many manipulations of sums and other formulas become considerably simpler if we adopt the following *bracket notation*:

$$[\text{statement}] = \begin{cases} 1, & \text{if the statement is true;} \\ 0, & \text{if the statement is false.} \end{cases} \tag{16}$$

Then we can write, for example,

$$\sum_{R(j)} a_j = \sum_j a_j \bigl[R(j)\bigr], \tag{17}$$

where the sum on the right is over *all* integers j, because the terms of that infinite sum are zero when $R(j)$ is false. (We assume that a_j is defined for all j.)

With bracket notation we can derive rule (b) from rules (a) and (c) in an interesting way:

$$\sum_{R(p(j))} a_{p(j)} = \sum_j a_{p(j)} \bigl[R(p(j))\bigr]$$

$$= \sum_j \sum_i a_i \bigl[R(i)\bigr] \bigl[i = p(j)\bigr]$$

$$= \sum_i a_i \left[R(i) \right] \sum_j [i = p(j)] . \tag{18}$$

The remaining sum on j is equal to 1 when $R(i)$ is true, if we assume that p is a permutation of the relevant values as required in (5); hence we are left with $\sum_i a_i[R(i)]$, which is $\sum_{R(i)} a_i$. This proves (5). If p is *not* such a permutation, (18) tells us the true value of $\sum_{R(p(j))} a_{p(j)}$.

The most famous special case of bracket notation is the so-called *Kronecker delta* symbol,

$$\delta_{ij} = [i = j] = \begin{cases} 1, & \text{if } i = j, \\ 0, & \text{if } i \neq j, \end{cases} \tag{19}$$

introduced by Leopold Kronecker in 1868. More general notations such as (16) were introduced by K. E. Iverson in 1962; therefore (16) is often called *Iverson's convention.* [See D. E. Knuth, *AMM* **99** (1992), 403–422.]

There is a notation for products, analogous to our notation for sums: The symbols

$$\prod_{R(j)} a_j \tag{20}$$

stand for the product of all a_j for which the integer j satisfies $R(j)$. If no such integer j exists, the product is defined to have the value 1 (*not* 0).

Operations (b), (c), and (d) are valid for the $\prod$-notation as well as for the $\sum$-notation, with suitable simple modifications. The exercises at the end of this section give a number of examples of product notation in use.

We conclude this section by mentioning another notation for multiple summation that is often convenient: A single $\sum$-sign may be used with one or more relations in *several* index variables, meaning that the sum is taken over all combinations of variables that meet the conditions. For example,

$$\sum_{0 \leq i \leq n} \sum_{0 \leq j \leq n} a_{ij} = \sum_{0 \leq i,j \leq n} a_{ij}; \quad \sum_{0 \leq i \leq n} \sum_{0 \leq j \leq i} a_{ij} = \sum_{0 \leq j \leq i \leq n} a_{ij}.$$

This notation gives no preference to one index of summation over any other, so it allows us to derive (10) in a new way:

$$\sum_{i=1}^{n} \sum_{j=1}^{i} a_{ij} = \sum_{i,j} a_{ij}[1 \leq i \leq n][1 \leq j \leq i] = \sum_{i,j} a_{ij}[1 \leq j \leq n][j \leq i \leq n]$$

$$= \sum_{j=1}^{n} \sum_{i=j}^{n} a_{ij} ,$$

using the fact that $[1 \leq i \leq n][1 \leq j \leq i] = [1 \leq j \leq i \leq n] = [1 \leq j \leq n][j \leq i \leq n]$. The more general equation (9) follows in a similar way from the identity

$$[R(i)] [S(i,j)] = [R(i) \text{ and } S(i,j)] = [S'(j)] [R'(i,j)] . \tag{21}$$

A further example that demonstrates the usefulness of summation with several indices is

$$\sum_{\substack{j_1+\cdots+j_n=n \\ j_1\geq\cdots\geq j_n\geq 0}} a_{j_1\ldots j_n},\tag{22}$$

where a is an n-tuply subscripted variable; for example, if $n = 5$ this notation stands for

$$a_{11111} + a_{21110} + a_{22100} + a_{31100} + a_{32000} + a_{41000} + a_{50000}.$$

(See the remarks on partitions of a number in Section 1.2.1.)

EXERCISES — First Set

▶ **1.** [10] The text says that $a_1 + a_2 + \cdots + a_0 = 0$. What, then, is $a_2 + \cdots + a_0$?

2. [01] What does the notation $\sum_{1\leq j\leq n} a_j$ mean, if $n = 3.14$?

▶ **3.** [13] Without using the $\sum$-notation, write out the equivalent of

$$\sum_{0\leq n\leq 5} \frac{1}{2n+1},$$

and also the equivalent of

$$\sum_{0\leq n^2\leq 5} \frac{1}{2n^2+1}.$$

Explain why the two results are different, in spite of rule (b).

4. [10] Without using the $\sum$-notation, write out the equivalent of each side of Eq. (10) as a sum of sums for the case $n = 3$.

▶ **5.** [HM20] Prove that rule (a) is valid for arbitrary infinite series, provided that the series converge.

6. [HM20] Prove that rule (d) is valid for an arbitrary infinite series, provided that any three of the four sums exist.

7. [HM23] Given that c is an integer, show that $\sum_{R(j)} a_j = \sum_{R(c-j)} a_{c-j}$, even if both series are infinite.

8. [HM25] Find an example of infinite series in which Eq. (7) is false.

▶ **9.** [05] Is the derivation of Eq. (14) valid even if $n = -1$?

10. [05] Is the derivation of Eq. (14) valid even if $n = -2$?

11. [03] What should the right-hand side of Eq. (14) be if $x = 1$?

12. [10] What is $1 + \frac{1}{7} + \frac{1}{49} + \frac{1}{343} + \cdots + \left(\frac{1}{7}\right)^n$?

13. [10] Using Eq. (15) and assuming that $m \leq n$, evaluate $\sum_{j=m}^{n} j$.

14. [11] Using the result of the previous exercise, evaluate $\sum_{j=m}^{n} \sum_{k=r}^{s} jk$.

▶ **15.** [M22] Compute the sum $1\times 2 + 2\times 2^2 + 3\times 2^3 + \cdots + n\times 2^n$ for small values of n. Do you see the pattern developing in these numbers? If not, discover it by manipulations similar to those leading up to Eq. (14).

16. [*M22*] Prove that

$$\sum_{j=0}^{n} j x^j = \frac{nx^{n+2} - (n+1)x^{n+1} + x}{(x-1)^2},$$

if $x \neq 1$, without using mathematical induction.

▸ **17.** [*M00*] Let S be a set of integers. What is $\sum_{j \in S} 1$?

18. [*M20*] Show how to interchange the order of summation as in Eq. (9) given that $R(i)$ is the relation "n is a multiple of i" and $S(i, j)$ is the relation "$1 \leq j < i$."

19. [*20*] What is $\sum_{j=m}^{n}(a_j - a_{j-1})$?

▸ **20.** [*25*] Dr. I. J. Matrix has observed a remarkable sequence of formulas:

$$9 \times 1 + 2 = 11, \; 9 \times 12 + 3 = 111, \; 9 \times 123 + 4 = 1111, \; 9 \times 1234 + 5 = 11111.$$

a) Write the good doctor's great discovery in terms of the $\sum$-notation.

b) Your answer to part (a) undoubtedly involves the number 10 as base of the decimal system; generalize this formula so that you get a formula that will perhaps work in any base b.

c) Prove your formula from part (b) by using formulas derived in the text or in exercise 16 above.

▸ **21.** [*M25*] Derive rule (d) from (8) and (17).

▸ **22.** [*20*] State the appropriate analogs of Eqs. (5), (7), (8), and (11) for *products* instead of sums.

23. [*10*] Explain why it is a good idea to define $\sum_{R(j)} a_j$ and $\prod_{R(j)} a_j$ as zero and one, respectively, when no integers satisfy $R(j)$.

24. [*20*] Suppose that $R(j)$ is true for only finitely many j. By induction on the number of integers satisfying $R(j)$, prove that $\log_b \prod_{R(j)} a_j = \sum_{R(j)} (\log_b a_j)$, assuming that all $a_j > 0$.

▸ **25.** [*15*] Consider the following derivation; is anything amiss?

$$\left(\sum_{i=1}^{n} a_i \right) \left(\sum_{j=1}^{n} \frac{1}{a_j} \right) = \sum_{1 \leq i \leq n} \sum_{1 \leq j \leq n} \frac{a_i}{a_j} = \sum_{1 \leq i \leq n} \sum_{1 \leq i \leq n} \frac{a_i}{a_i} = \sum_{i=1}^{n} 1 = n.$$

26. [*25*] Show that $\prod_{i=0}^{n} \prod_{j=0}^{i} a_i a_j$ may be expressed in terms of $\prod_{i=0}^{n} a_i$ by manipulating the $\prod$-notation as stated in exercise 22.

27. [*M20*] Generalize the result of exercise 1.2.1–9 by proving that

$$\prod_{j=1}^{n}(1 - a_j) \geq 1 - \sum_{j=1}^{n} a_j,$$

assuming that $0 < a_j < 1$.

28. [*M22*] Find a simple formula for $\prod_{j=2}^{n}(1 - 1/j^2)$.

▸ **29.** [*M30*] (a) Express $\sum_{i=0}^{n} \sum_{j=0}^{i} \sum_{k=0}^{j} a_i a_j a_k$ in terms of the multiple-sum notation explained at the end of the section. (b) Express the same sum in terms of $\sum_{i=0}^{n} a_i$, $\sum_{i=0}^{n} a_i^2$, and $\sum_{i=0}^{n} a_i^3$ [see Eq. (13)].

▶ **30.** [*M23*] (J. Binet, 1812.) Without using induction, prove the identity

$$\left(\sum_{j=1}^{n} a_j x_j\right)\left(\sum_{j=1}^{n} b_j y_j\right) = \left(\sum_{j=1}^{n} a_j y_j\right)\left(\sum_{j=1}^{n} b_j x_j\right) + \sum_{1\le j<k\le n} (a_j b_k - a_k b_j)(x_j y_k - x_k y_j).$$

[An important special case arises when $w_1, \ldots, w_n, z_1, \ldots, z_n$ are arbitrary complex numbers and we set $a_j = w_j$, $b_j = \bar{z}_j$, $x_j = \bar{w}_j$, $y_j = z_j$:

$$\left(\sum_{j=1}^{n} |w_j|^2\right)\left(\sum_{j=1}^{n} |z_j|^2\right) = \left|\sum_{j=1}^{n} w_j z_j\right|^2 + \sum_{1\le j<k\le n} |w_j \bar{z}_k - w_k \bar{z}_j|^2.$$

The terms $|w_j \bar{z}_k - w_k \bar{z}_j|^2$ are nonnegative, so the famous *Cauchy–Schwarz inequality*

$$\left(\sum_{j=1}^{n} |w_j|^2\right)\left(\sum_{j=1}^{n} |z_j|^2\right) \ge \left|\sum_{j=1}^{n} w_j z_j\right|^2$$

is a consequence of Binet's formula.]

31. [*M20*] Use Binet's formula to express the sum $\sum_{1\le j<k\le n}(u_j - u_k)(v_j - v_k)$ in terms of $\sum_{j=1}^{n} u_j v_j$, $\sum_{j=1}^{n} u_j$, and $\sum_{j=1}^{n} v_j$.

32. [*M20*] Prove that

$$\prod_{j=1}^{n} \sum_{i=1}^{m} a_{ij} = \sum_{1\le i_1,\ldots,i_n\le m} a_{i_1 1}\ldots a_{i_n n}.$$

▶ **33.** [*M30*] One evening Dr. Matrix discovered some formulas that might even be classed as more remarkable than those of exercise 20:

$$\frac{1}{(a-b)(a-c)} + \frac{1}{(b-a)(b-c)} + \frac{1}{(c-a)(c-b)} = 0,$$

$$\frac{a}{(a-b)(a-c)} + \frac{b}{(b-a)(b-c)} + \frac{c}{(c-a)(c-b)} = 0,$$

$$\frac{a^2}{(a-b)(a-c)} + \frac{b^2}{(b-a)(b-c)} + \frac{c^2}{(c-a)(c-b)} = 1,$$

$$\frac{a^3}{(a-b)(a-c)} + \frac{b^3}{(b-a)(b-c)} + \frac{c^3}{(c-a)(c-b)} = a+b+c.$$

Prove that these formulas are a special case of a general law; let $x_1, x_2, \ldots, x_n$ be distinct numbers, and show that

$$\sum_{j=1}^{n}\left(x_j^r \Big/ \prod_{\substack{1\le k\le n\\k\ne j}} (x_j - x_k)\right) = \begin{cases} 0, & \text{if } 0\le r<n-1; \\ 1, & \text{if } r=n-1; \\ \sum_{j=1}^{n} x_j, & \text{if } r=n. \end{cases}$$

34. [*M25*] Prove that

$$\sum_{k=1}^{n} \frac{\prod_{1\le r\le n,\, r\ne m}(x+k-r)}{\prod_{1\le r\le n,\, r\ne k}(k-r)} = 1,$$

provided that $1 \le m \le n$ and x is arbitrary. For example, if $n = 4$ and $m = 2$, then

$$\frac{x(x-2)(x-3)}{(-1)(-2)(-3)} + \frac{(x+1)(x-1)(x-2)}{(1)(-1)(-2)} + \frac{(x+2)x(x-1)}{(2)(1)(-1)} + \frac{(x+3)(x+1)x}{(3)(2)(1)} = 1.$$

35. [*HM20*] The notation $\sup_{R(j)} a_j$ is used to denote the least upper bound of the elements a_j, in a manner exactly analogous to the $\sum$- and $\prod$-notations. (When $R(j)$ is satisfied for only finitely many j, the notation $\max_{R(j)} a_j$ is often used to denote the same quantity.) Show how rules (a), (b), (c), and (d) can be adapted for manipulation of *this* notation. In particular discuss the following analog of rule (a):

$$(\sup_{R(i)} a_i) + (\sup_{S(j)} b_j) = \sup_{R(i)}(\sup_{S(j)}(a_i + b_j)),$$

and give a suitable definition for the notation when $R(j)$ is satisfied for *no j*.

EXERCISES — Second Set

Determinants and matrices. The following interesting problems are for the reader who has experienced at least an introduction to determinants and elementary matrix theory. A determinant may be evaluated by astutely combining the operations of: (a) factoring a quantity out of a row or column; (b) adding a multiple of one row (or column) to another row (or column); (c) expanding by cofactors. The simplest and most often used version of operation (c) is to simply delete the entire first row and column, provided that the element in the upper left corner is $+1$ and the remaining elements in either the entire first row or the entire first column are zero; then evaluate the resulting smaller determinant. In general, the cofactor of an element a_{ij} in an $n \times n$ determinant is $(-1)^{i+j}$ times the $(n-1) \times (n-1)$ determinant obtained by deleting the row and column in which a_{ij} appeared. The value of a determinant is equal to $\sum a_{ij} \cdot \mathrm{cofactor}(a_{ij})$ summed with either i or j held constant and with the other subscript varying from 1 to n.

If (b_{ij}) is the *inverse* of matrix (a_{ij}), then b_{ij} equals the cofactor of a_{ji} (*not* a_{ij}), divided by the determinant of the whole matrix.

The following types of matrices are of special importance:

Vandermonde's matrix,   *Combinatorial matrix,*

$$a_{ij} = x_j^i \qquad\qquad\qquad\qquad\qquad a_{ij} = y + \delta_{ij} x$$

$$\begin{pmatrix} x_1 & x_2 & \cdots & x_n \\ x_1^2 & x_2^2 & \cdots & x_n^2 \\ \vdots & & & \vdots \\ x_1^n & x_2^n & \cdots & x_n^n \end{pmatrix} \qquad \begin{pmatrix} x+y & y & \cdots & y \\ y & x+y & \cdots & y \\ \vdots & & & \vdots \\ y & y & \cdots & x+y \end{pmatrix}$$

Cauchy's matrix,

$$a_{ij} = 1/(x_i + y_j)$$

$$\begin{pmatrix} 1/(x_1+y_1) & 1/(x_1+y_2) & \cdots & 1/(x_1+y_n) \\ 1/(x_2+y_1) & 1/(x_2+y_2) & \cdots & 1/(x_2+y_n) \\ \vdots & & & \vdots \\ 1/(x_n+y_1) & 1/(x_n+y_2) & \cdots & 1/(x_n+y_n) \end{pmatrix}$$

36. [*M23*] Show that the determinant of the combinatorial matrix is $x^{n-1}(x+ny)$.

▶ **37.** [*M24*] Show that the determinant of Vandermonde's matrix is

$$\prod_{1\le j\le n} x_j \prod_{1\le i<j\le n} (x_j - x_i).$$

▶ **38.** [*M25*] Show that the determinant of Cauchy's matrix is

$$\prod_{1\le i<j\le n} (x_j - x_i)(y_j - y_i) \bigg/ \prod_{1\le i,j\le n} (x_i + y_j).$$

39. [*M23*] Show that the inverse of a combinatorial matrix is a combinatorial matrix with the entries $b_{ij} = (-y + \delta_{ij}(x+ny))/x(x+ny)$.

40. [*M24*] Show that the inverse of Vandermonde's matrix is given by

$$b_{ij} = \left(\sum_{\substack{1\le k_1<\cdots<k_{n-j}\le n \\ k_1,\ldots,k_{n-j}\ne i}} (-1)^{j-1} x_{k_1}\ldots x_{k_{n-j}} \right) \bigg/ x_i \prod_{\substack{1\le k\le n \\ k\ne i}} (x_k - x_i).$$

Don't be dismayed by the complicated sum in the numerator — it is just the coefficient of x^{j-1} in the polynomial $(x_1 - x)\ldots(x_n - x)/(x_i - x)$.

41. [*M26*] Show that the inverse of Cauchy's matrix is given by

$$b_{ij} = \left(\prod_{1\le k\le n} (x_j + y_k)(x_k + y_i) \right) \bigg/ (x_j + y_i)\left(\prod_{\substack{1\le k\le n \\ k\ne j}} (x_j - x_k) \right)\left(\prod_{\substack{1\le k\le n \\ k\ne i}} (y_i - y_k) \right).$$

42. [*M18*] What is the sum of all n^2 elements in the inverse of the combinatorial matrix?

43. [*M24*] What is the sum of all n^2 elements in the inverse of Vandermonde's matrix? [*Hint:* Use exercise 33.]

▶ **44.** [*M26*] What is the sum of all n^2 elements in the inverse of Cauchy's matrix?

▶ **45.** [*M25*] A *Hilbert matrix*, sometimes called an $n\times n$ segment of *the* (infinite) Hilbert matrix, is a matrix for which $a_{ij} = 1/(i+j-1)$. Show that this is a special case of Cauchy's matrix, find its inverse, show that each element of the inverse is an integer, and show that the sum of all elements of the inverse is n^2. [*Note:* Hilbert matrices have often been used to test various matrix manipulation algorithms, because they are numerically unstable, and they have known inverses. However, it is a mistake to compare the *known* inverse, given in this exercise, to the *computed* inverse of a Hilbert matrix, since the matrix to be inverted must be expressed in rounded numbers beforehand; the inverse of an approximate Hilbert matrix will be somewhat different from the inverse of an exact one, due to the instability present. Since the elements of the inverse are integers, and since the inverse matrix is just as unstable as the original, the inverse can be specified exactly, and one could try to invert the inverse. The integers that appear in the inverse are, however, quite large.] The solution to this problem requires an elementary knowledge of factorials and binomial coefficients, which are discussed in Sections 1.2.5 and 1.2.6.

▶ **46.** [*M30*] Let A be an $m \times n$ matrix, and let B be an $n \times m$ matrix. Given that $1 \le j_1, j_2, \ldots, j_m \le n$, let $A_{j_1 j_2 \ldots j_m}$ denote the $m \times m$ matrix consisting of columns

$j_1, \ldots, j_m$ of A, and let $B_{j_1 j_2 \ldots j_m}$ denote the $m \times m$ matrix consisting of rows $j_1, \ldots, j_m$ of B. Prove the *Binet–Cauchy identity*

$$\det(AB) = \sum_{1 \le j_1 < j_2 < \cdots < j_m \le n} \det(A_{j_1 j_2 \ldots j_m}) \det(B_{j_1 j_2 \ldots j_m}).$$

(Note the special cases: (i) $m = n$, (ii) $m = 1$, (iii) $B = A^T$, (iv) $m > n$, (v) $m = 2$.)

47. [*M27*] (C. Krattenthaler.) Prove that

$$\det \begin{pmatrix} (x+q_2)(x+q_3) & (x+p_1)(x+q_3) & (x+p_1)(x+p_2) \\ (y+q_2)(y+q_3) & (y+p_1)(y+q_3) & (y+p_1)(y+p_2) \\ (z+q_2)(z+q_3) & (z+p_1)(z+q_3) & (z+p_1)(z+p_2) \end{pmatrix}$$
$$= (x-y)(x-z)(y-z)(p_1-q_2)(p_1-q_3)(p_2-q_3),$$

and generalize this equation to an identity for an $n \times n$ determinant in $3n-2$ variables $x_1, \ldots, x_n, p_1, \ldots, p_{n-1}, q_2, \ldots, q_n$. Compare your formula to the result of exercise 38.

1.2.4. Integer Functions and Elementary Number Theory

If x is any real number, we write

$\lfloor x \rfloor$ = the greatest integer less than or equal to x (the *floor* of x);

$\lceil x \rceil$ = the least integer greater than or equal to x (the *ceiling* of x).

The notation $[x]$ was often used before 1970 for one or the other of these functions, usually the former; but the notations above, introduced by K. E. Iverson in the 1960s, are more useful, because $\lfloor x \rfloor$ and $\lceil x \rceil$ occur about equally often in practice. The function $\lfloor x \rfloor$ is sometimes called the *entier* function, from the French word for "integer."

The following formulas and examples are easily verified:

$$\lfloor \sqrt{2} \rfloor = 1, \quad \lceil \sqrt{2} \rceil = 2, \quad \lfloor +\tfrac{1}{2} \rfloor = 0, \quad \lceil -\tfrac{1}{2} \rceil = 0, \quad \lfloor -\tfrac{1}{2} \rfloor = -1 \ (\textit{not} \ \text{zero!});$$

$$\lceil x \rceil = \lfloor x \rfloor \qquad \text{if and only if } x \text{ is an integer,}$$
$$\lceil x \rceil = \lfloor x \rfloor + 1 \quad \text{if and only if } x \text{ is not an integer;}$$

$$\lfloor -x \rfloor = -\lceil x \rceil; \qquad x - 1 < \lfloor x \rfloor \le x \le \lceil x \rceil < x + 1.$$

Exercises at the end of this section list other important formulas involving the floor and ceiling operations.

If x and y are any real numbers, we define the following binary operation:

$$x \bmod y = x - y\lfloor x/y \rfloor, \quad \text{if } y \ne 0; \qquad x \bmod 0 = x. \tag{1}$$

From this definition we can see that, when $y \ne 0$,

$$0 \le \frac{x}{y} - \left\lfloor \frac{x}{y} \right\rfloor = \frac{x \bmod y}{y} < 1. \tag{2}$$

Consequently

a) if $y > 0$, then $0 \le x \bmod y < y$;

b) if $y < 0$, then $0 \ge x \bmod y > y$;

c) the quantity $x - (x \bmod y)$ is an integral multiple of y.

We call $x \bmod y$ the *remainder* when x is divided by y; similarly, we call $\lfloor x/y \rfloor$ the *quotient*.

When x and y are integers, "mod" is therefore a familiar operation:

$$5 \bmod 3 = 2, \qquad 18 \bmod 3 = 0, \qquad -2 \bmod 3 = 1. \tag{3}$$

We have $x \bmod y = 0$ if and only if x is a multiple of y, that is, if and only if x is divisible by y. The notation $y \backslash x$, read "y divides x," means that y is a positive integer and $x \bmod y = 0$.

The "mod" operation is useful also when x and y take arbitrary real values. For example, with trigonometric functions we can write

$$\tan x = \tan (x \bmod \pi).$$

The quantity $x \bmod 1$ is the *fractional part* of x; we have, by Eq. (1),

$$x = \lfloor x \rfloor + (x \bmod 1). \tag{4}$$

Writers on number theory often use the abbreviation "mod" in a different but closely related sense. We will use the following form to express the number-theoretical concept of *congruence*: The statement

$$x \equiv y \pmod{z} \tag{5}$$

means that $x \bmod z = y \bmod z$; it is the same as saying that $x - y$ is an integral multiple of z. Expression (5) is read, "x is congruent to y modulo z."

Let's turn now to the basic elementary properties of congruences that will be used in the number-theoretical arguments of this book. All variables in the following formulas are assumed to be integers. Two integers x and y are said to be *relatively prime* if they have no common factor, that is, if their greatest common divisor is 1; in such a case we write $x \perp y$. The concept of relatively prime integers is a familiar one, since it is customary to say that a fraction is in "lowest terms" when the numerator is relatively prime to the denominator.

Law A. If $a \equiv b$ and $x \equiv y$, then $a \pm x \equiv b \pm y$ and $ax \equiv by \pmod{m}$.

Law B. If $ax \equiv by$ and $a \equiv b$, and if $a \perp m$, then $x \equiv y \pmod{m}$.

Law C. $a \equiv b \pmod{m}$ if and only if $an \equiv bn \pmod{mn}$, when $n \neq 0$.

Law D. If $r \perp s$, then $a \equiv b \pmod{rs}$ if and only if $a \equiv b \pmod{r}$ and $a \equiv b \pmod{s}$.

Law A states that we can do addition, subtraction, and multiplication modulo m just as we do ordinary addition, subtraction, and multiplication. Law B considers the operation of division and shows that, when the divisor is relatively prime to the modulus, we can also divide out common factors. Laws C and D consider what happens when the modulus is changed. These laws are proved in the exercises below.

The following important theorem is a consequence of Laws A and B.

Theorem F (*Fermat's theorem*, 1640). *If p is a prime number, then $a^p \equiv a$ (modulo p) for all integers a.*

Proof. If a is a multiple of p, obviously $a^p \equiv 0 \equiv a$ (modulo p). So we need only consider the case $a \bmod p \neq 0$. Since p is a prime number, this means that $a \perp p$. Consider the numbers

$$0 \bmod p, \quad a \bmod p, \quad 2a \bmod p, \quad \ldots, \quad (p-1)a \bmod p. \qquad (6)$$

These p numbers are all *distinct*, for if $ax \bmod p = ay \bmod p$, then by definition (5) $ax \equiv ay$ (modulo p); hence by Law B, $x \equiv y$ (modulo p).

Since (6) gives p distinct numbers, all nonnegative and less than p, we see that the first number is zero and the rest are the integers $1, 2, \ldots, p-1$ in some order. Therefore by Law A,

$$(a)(2a) \ldots ((p-1)a) \equiv 1 \cdot 2 \ldots (p-1) \pmod{p}. \qquad (7)$$

Multiplying each side of this congruence by a, we obtain

$$a^p (1 \cdot 2 \ldots (p-1)) \equiv a(1 \cdot 2 \ldots (p-1)) \pmod{p}; \qquad (8)$$

and this proves the theorem, since each of the factors $1, 2, \ldots, p-1$ is relatively prime to p and can be canceled by Law B. ∎

EXERCISES

1. [*00*] What are $\lfloor 1.1 \rfloor$, $\lfloor -1.1 \rfloor$, $\lceil -1.1 \rceil$, $\lfloor 0.99999 \rfloor$, and $\lfloor \lg 35 \rfloor$?

▸ **2.** [*01*] What is $\lceil \lfloor x \rfloor \rceil$?

3. [*M10*] Let n be an integer, and let x be a real number. Prove that
a) $\lfloor x \rfloor < n$ if and only if $x < n$; b) $n \leq \lfloor x \rfloor$ if and only if $n \leq x$;
c) $\lceil x \rceil \leq n$ if and only if $x \leq n$; d) $n < \lceil x \rceil$ if and only if $n < x$;
e) $\lfloor x \rfloor = n$ if and only if $x - 1 < n \leq x$, and if and only if $n \leq x < n + 1$;
f) $\lceil x \rceil = n$ if and only if $x \leq n < x + 1$, and if and only if $n - 1 < x \leq n$.

[*These formulas are the most important tools for proving facts about* $\lfloor x \rfloor$ *and* $\lceil x \rceil$.]

▸ **4.** [*M10*] Using the previous exercise, prove that $\lfloor -x \rfloor = -\lceil x \rceil$.

5. [*16*] Given that x is a positive real number, state a simple formula that expresses x *rounded to the nearest integer*. The desired rounding rule is to produce $\lfloor x \rfloor$ when $x \bmod 1 < \frac{1}{2}$, and to produce $\lceil x \rceil$ when $x \bmod 1 \geq \frac{1}{2}$. Your answer should be a single formula that covers both cases. Discuss the rounding that would be obtained by your formula when x is negative.

▸ **6.** [*20*] Which of the following equations are true for all positive real numbers x?
(a) $\lfloor \sqrt{\lfloor x \rfloor} \rfloor = \lfloor \sqrt{x} \rfloor$; (b) $\lceil \sqrt{\lceil x \rceil} \rceil = \lceil \sqrt{x} \rceil$; (c) $\lceil \sqrt{\lfloor x \rfloor} \rceil = \lceil \sqrt{x} \rceil$.

7. [*M15*] Show that $\lfloor x \rfloor + \lfloor y \rfloor \leq \lfloor x + y \rfloor$ and that equality holds if and only if $x \bmod 1 + y \bmod 1 < 1$. Does a similar formula hold for ceilings?

8. [*00*] What are 100 mod 3, 100 mod 7, -100 mod 7, -100 mod 0?

9. [*05*] What are 5 mod -3, 18 mod -3, -2 mod -3?

▸ **10.** [*10*] What are 1.1 mod 1, 0.11 mod .1, 0.11 mod $-.1$?

11. [*00*] What does "$x \equiv y$ (modulo 0)" mean by our conventions?

12. [*00*] What integers are relatively prime to 1?

13. [*M00*] By convention, we say that the greatest common divisor of 0 and n is $|n|$. What integers are relatively prime to 0?

▶ **14.** [*12*] If $x \bmod 3 = 2$ and $x \bmod 5 = 3$, what is $x \bmod 15$?

15. [*10*] Prove that $z(x \bmod y) = (zx) \bmod (zy)$. [Law C is an immediate consequence of this distributive law.]

16. [*M10*] Assume that $y > 0$. Show that if $(x - z)/y$ is an integer and if $0 \le z < y$, then $z = x \bmod y$.

17. [*M15*] Prove Law A directly from the definition of congruence, and also prove half of Law D: If $a \equiv b$ (modulo rs), then $a \equiv b$ (modulo r) and $a \equiv b$ (modulo s). (Here r and s are arbitrary integers.)

18. [*M15*] Using Law B, prove the other half of Law D: If $a \equiv b$ (modulo r) and $a \equiv b$ (modulo s), then $a \equiv b$ (modulo rs), provided that $r \perp s$.

▶ **19.** [*M10*] (*Law of inverses.*) If $n \perp m$, there is an integer n' such that $nn' \equiv 1$ (modulo m). Prove this, using the extension of Euclid's algorithm (Algorithm 1.2.1E).

20. [*M15*] Use the law of inverses and Law A to prove Law B.

21. [*M22*] (*Fundamental theorem of arithmetic.*) Use Law B and exercise 1.2.1–5 to prove that every integer $n > 1$ has a *unique* representation as a product of primes (except for the order of the factors). In other words, show that there is exactly one way to write $n = p_1 p_2 \ldots p_k$, where each p_j is prime and $p_1 \le p_2 \le \cdots \le p_k$.

▶ **22.** [*M10*] Give an example to show that Law B is not always true if a is not relatively prime to m.

23. [*M10*] Give an example to show that Law D is not always true if r is not relatively prime to s.

▶ **24.** [*M20*] To what extent can Laws A, B, C, and D be generalized to apply to arbitrary real numbers instead of integers?

25. [*M02*] Show that, according to Theorem F, $a^{p-1} \bmod p = [a$ is not a multiple of $p]$, whenever p is a prime number.

26. [*M15*] Let p be an odd prime number, let a be any integer, and let $b = a^{(p-1)/2}$. Show that $b \bmod p$ is either 0 or 1 or $p - 1$. [*Hint:* Consider $(b+1)(b-1)$.]

27. [*M15*] Given that n is a positive integer, let $\varphi(n)$ be the number of values among $\{0, 1, \ldots, n - 1\}$ that are relatively prime to n. Thus $\varphi(1) = 1$, $\varphi(2) = 1$, $\varphi(3) = 2$, $\varphi(4) = 2$, etc. Show that $\varphi(p) = p - 1$ if p is a prime number; and evaluate $\varphi(p^e)$, when e is a positive integer.

▶ **28.** [*M25*] Show that the method used to prove Theorem F can be used to prove the following extension, called *Euler's theorem*: $a^{\varphi(m)} \equiv 1$ (modulo m), for *any* positive integer m, when $a \perp m$. (In particular, the number n' in exercise 19 may be taken to be $n^{\varphi(m)-1} \bmod m$.)

29. [*M22*] A function $f(n)$ of positive integers n is called *multiplicative* if $f(rs) = f(r)f(s)$ whenever $r \perp s$. Show that each of the following functions is multiplicative: (a) $f(n) = n^c$, where c is any constant; (b) $f(n) = [n$ is not divisible by k^2 for any integer $k > 1]$; (c) $f(n) = c^k$, where k is the number of distinct primes that divide n; (d) the product of any two multiplicative functions.

30. [*M30*] Prove that the function $\varphi(n)$ of exercise 27 is multiplicative. Using this fact, evaluate $\varphi(1000000)$, and give a method for evaluating $\varphi(n)$ in a simple way once n has been factored into primes.

31. [*M22*] Prove that if $f(n)$ is multiplicative, so is $g(n) = \sum_{d\backslash n} f(d)$.

32. [*M18*] Prove the double-summation identity
$$\sum_{d\backslash n}\sum_{c\backslash d} f(c,d) = \sum_{c\backslash n}\sum_{d\backslash(n/c)} f(c,cd),$$
for any function $f(x,y)$.

33. [*M18*] Given that m and n are integers, evaluate (a) $\lfloor\frac{1}{2}(n+m)\rfloor + \lfloor\frac{1}{2}(n-m+1)\rfloor$; (b) $\lceil\frac{1}{2}(n+m)\rceil + \lceil\frac{1}{2}(n-m+1)\rceil$. (The special case $m=0$ is worth noting.)

▶ **34.** [*M21*] What conditions on the real number $b > 1$ are necessary and sufficient to guarantee that $\lfloor\log_b x\rfloor = \lfloor\log_b\lfloor x\rfloor\rfloor$ for all real $x \geq 1$?

▶ **35.** [*M20*] Given that m and n are integers and $n > 0$, prove that
$$\lfloor(x+m)/n\rfloor = \lfloor(\lfloor x\rfloor+m)/n\rfloor$$
for all real x. (When $m = 0$, we have an important special case.) Does an analogous result hold for the ceiling function?

36. [*M23*] Prove that $\sum_{k=1}^{n}\lfloor k/2\rfloor = \lfloor n^2/4\rfloor$; also evaluate $\sum_{k=1}^{n}\lceil k/2\rceil$.

▶ **37.** [*M30*] Let m and n be integers, $n > 0$. Show that
$$\sum_{0\leq k<n}\left\lfloor\frac{mk+x}{n}\right\rfloor = \frac{(m-1)(n-1)}{2} + \frac{d-1}{2} + d\lfloor x/d\rfloor,$$
where d is the greatest common divisor of m and n, and x is any real number.

38. [*M26*] (E. Busche, 1909.) Prove that, for all real x and y with $y > 0$,
$$\sum_{0\leq k<y}\left\lfloor x+\frac{k}{y}\right\rfloor = \lfloor xy + \lfloor x+1\rfloor(\lceil y\rceil - y)\rfloor.$$

In particular, when y is a positive integer n, we have the important formula
$$\lfloor x\rfloor + \left\lfloor x+\frac{1}{n}\right\rfloor + \cdots + \left\lfloor x+\frac{n-1}{n}\right\rfloor = \lfloor nx\rfloor.$$

39. [*HM35*] A function f for which $f(x) + f(x+\frac{1}{n}) + \cdots + f(x+\frac{n-1}{n}) = f(nx)$, whenever n is a positive integer, is called a *replicative function*. The previous exercise establishes the fact that $\lfloor x\rfloor$ is replicative. Show that the following functions are replicative:

a) $f(x) = x - \frac{1}{2}$;
b) $f(x) = [x$ is an integer$]$;
c) $f(x) = [x$ is a positive integer$]$;
d) $f(x) = [$there exists a rational number r and an integer m such that $x = r\pi + m]$;
e) three other functions like the one in (d), with r and/or m restricted to positive values;
f) $f(x) = \log|2\sin\pi x|$, if the value $f(x) = -\infty$ is allowed;
g) the sum of any two replicative functions;
h) a constant multiple of a replicative function;
i) the function $g(x) = f(x - \lfloor x\rfloor)$, where $f(x)$ is replicative.

40. [*HM46*] Study the class of replicative functions; determine all replicative functions of a special type. For example, is the function in (a) of exercise 39 the only continuous replicative function? It may be interesting to study also the more general class of functions for which

$$f(x) + f\left(x + \frac{1}{n}\right) + \cdots + f\left(x + \frac{n-1}{n}\right) = a_n f(nx) + b_n.$$

Here a_n and b_n are numbers that depend on n but not on x. Derivatives and (if $b_n = 0$) integrals of these functions are of the same type. If we require that $b_n = 0$, we have, for example, the Bernoulli polynomials, the trigonometric functions $\cot \pi x$ and $\csc^2 \pi x$, as well as Hurwitz's generalized zeta function $\zeta(s, x) = \sum_{k \geq 0} 1/(k + x)^s$ for fixed s. With $b_n \neq 0$ we have still other well-known functions, such as the psi function.

41. [*M23*] Let a_1, a_2, a_3, ... be the sequence 1, 2, 2, 3, 3, 3, 4, 4, 4, 4, ...; find an expression for a_n in terms of n, using the floor and/or ceiling function.

42. [*M24*] (a) Prove that

$$\sum_{k=1}^{n} a_k = na_n - \sum_{k=1}^{n-1} k(a_{k+1} - a_k), \qquad \text{if } n > 0.$$

(b) The preceding formula is useful for evaluating certain sums involving the floor function. Prove that, if b is an integer ≥ 2,

$$\sum_{k=1}^{n} \lfloor \log_b k \rfloor = (n + 1)\lfloor \log_b n \rfloor - \left(b^{\lfloor \log_b n \rfloor + 1} - b\right)/(b - 1).$$

43. [*M23*] Evaluate $\sum_{k=1}^{n} \lfloor \sqrt{k} \rfloor$.

44. [*M24*] Show that $\sum_{k \geq 0} \sum_{1 \leq j < b} \lfloor (n + jb^k)/b^{k+1} \rfloor = n$, if b and n are integers, $n \geq 0$, and $b \geq 2$. What is the value of this sum when $n < 0$?

▶ **45.** [*M28*] The result of exercise 37 is somewhat surprising, since it implies that

$$\sum_{0 \leq k < n} \left\lfloor \frac{mk + x}{n} \right\rfloor = \sum_{0 \leq k < m} \left\lfloor \frac{nk + x}{m} \right\rfloor.$$

This "reciprocity relationship" is one of many similar formulas (see Section 3.3.3). Show that for any function f, we have

$$\sum_{0 \leq j < n} f\left(\left\lfloor \frac{mj}{n} \right\rfloor\right) = \sum_{0 \leq r < m} \left\lceil \frac{rn}{m} \right\rceil (f(r - 1) - f(r)) + nf(m - 1).$$

In particular, prove that

$$\sum_{0 \leq j < n} \binom{\lfloor mj/n \rfloor + 1}{k} + \sum_{0 \leq j < m} \left\lceil \frac{jn}{m} \right\rceil \binom{j}{k - 1} = n\binom{m}{k}.$$

[*Hint:* Consider the change of variable $r = \lfloor mj/n \rfloor$. Binomial coefficients $\binom{m}{k}$ are discussed in Section 1.2.6.]

46. [*M29*] (*General reciprocity law.*) Extend the formula of exercise 45 to obtain an expression for $\sum_{0 \leq j < \alpha n} f(\lfloor mj/n \rfloor)$, where α is *any* positive real number.

▶ **47.** [*M31*] When p is an odd prime number, the *Legendre symbol* $\left(\frac{q}{p}\right)$ is defined to be $+1$, 0, or -1, depending on whether $q^{(p-1)/2} \bmod p$ is 1, 0, or $p-1$. (Exercise 26 proves that these are the only possible values.)

a) Given that q is not a multiple of p, show that the numbers

$$(-1)^{\lfloor 2kq/p \rfloor}(2kq \bmod p), \qquad 0 < k < p/2,$$

are congruent in some order to the numbers 2, 4, ..., $p-1$ (modulo p). Hence $\left(\frac{q}{p}\right) = (-1)^\sigma$ where $\sigma = \sum_{0 \le k < p/2} \lfloor 2kq/p \rfloor$.

b) Use the result of (a) to calculate $\left(\frac{2}{p}\right)$.

c) Given that q is odd, show that $\sum_{0 \le k < p/2} \lfloor 2kq/p \rfloor \equiv \sum_{0 \le k < p/2} \lfloor kq/p \rfloor$ (modulo 2), unless q is a multiple of p. [*Hint:* Consider the quantity $\lfloor (p-1-2k)q/p \rfloor$.]

d) Use the general reciprocity formula of exercise 46 to obtain the *law of quadratic reciprocity*, $\left(\frac{q}{p}\right)\left(\frac{p}{q}\right) = (-1)^{(p-1)(q-1)/4}$, given that p and q are distinct odd primes.

48. [*M26*] Prove or disprove the following identities, for integers m and n:

(a) $\left\lfloor \dfrac{m+n-1}{n} \right\rfloor = \left\lceil \dfrac{m}{n} \right\rceil$; (b) $\left\lfloor \dfrac{n+2-\lfloor n/25 \rfloor}{3} \right\rfloor = \left\lfloor \dfrac{8n+24}{25} \right\rfloor$.

49. [*M30*] Suppose the integer-valued function $f(x)$ satisfies the two simple laws (i) $f(x+1) = f(x) + 1$; (ii) $f(x) = f(f(nx)/n)$ for all positive integers n. Prove that either $f(x) = \lfloor x \rfloor$ for all rational x, or $f(x) = \lceil x \rceil$ for all rational x.

1.2.5. Permutations and Factorials

A *permutation of n objects* is an arrangement of n distinct objects in a row. There are six permutations of three objects $\{a, b, c\}$:

$$a\,b\,c, \qquad a\,c\,b, \qquad b\,a\,c, \qquad b\,c\,a, \qquad c\,a\,b, \qquad c\,b\,a. \qquad (1)$$

The properties of permutations are of great importance in the analysis of algorithms, and we will deduce many interesting facts about them later in this book.* Our first task is simply to *count* them: How many permutations of n objects are possible? There are n ways to choose the leftmost object, and once this choice has been made there are $n-1$ ways to select a different object to place next to it; this gives us $n(n-1)$ choices for the first two positions. Similarly, we find that there are $n-2$ choices for the third object distinct from the first two, and a total of $n(n-1)(n-2)$ possible ways to choose the first three objects. In general, if p_{nk} denotes the number of ways to choose k objects out of n and to arrange them in a row, we see that

$$p_{nk} = n(n-1)\ldots(n-k+1). \qquad (2)$$

The total number of permutations is therefore $p_{nn} = n(n-1) \ldots (1)$.

The process of *constructing* all permutations of n objects in an inductive manner, assuming that all permutations of $n-1$ objects have been constructed,

---

* In fact, permutations are so important, Vaughan Pratt has suggested calling them "perms." As soon as Pratt's convention is established, textbooks of computer science will be somewhat shorter (and perhaps less expensive).

is very important in our applications. Let us rewrite (1) using the numbers $\{1, 2, 3\}$ instead of the letters $\{a, b, c\}$; the permutations are then

$$1\,2\,3, \qquad 1\,3\,2, \qquad 2\,1\,3, \qquad 2\,3\,1, \qquad 3\,1\,2, \qquad 3\,2\,1. \qquad (3)$$

Consider how to get from this array to the permutations of $\{1, 2, 3, 4\}$. There are two principal ways to go from $n - 1$ objects to n objects.

Method 1. For each permutation $a_1 a_2 \ldots a_{n-1}$ of $\{1, 2, \ldots, n-1\}$, form n others by inserting the number n in all possible places, obtaining

$$n\,a_1 a_2 \ldots a_{n-1}, \quad a_1\,n\,a_2 \ldots a_{n-1}, \quad \ldots, \quad a_1 a_2 \ldots n\,a_{n-1}, \quad a_1 a_2 \ldots a_{n-1}\,n.$$

For example, from the permutation 2 3 1 in (3), we get 4 2 3 1, 2 4 3 1, 2 3 4 1, 2 3 1 4. It is clear that all permutations of n objects are obtained in this manner and that no permutation is obtained more than once.

Method 2. For each permutation $a_1 a_2 \ldots a_{n-1}$ of $\{1, 2, \ldots, n-1\}$, form n others as follows: First construct the array

$$a_1 a_2 \ldots a_{n-1} \tfrac{1}{2}, \quad a_1 a_2 \ldots a_{n-1} \tfrac{3}{2}, \quad \ldots, \quad a_1 a_2 \ldots a_{n-1} \left(n - \tfrac{1}{2}\right).$$

Then rename the elements of each permutation using the numbers $\{1, 2, \ldots, n\}$, *preserving order*. For example, from the permutation 2 3 1 in (3) we get

$$2\,3\,1\,\tfrac{1}{2}, \quad 2\,3\,1\,\tfrac{3}{2}, \quad 2\,3\,1\,\tfrac{5}{2}, \quad 2\,3\,1\,\tfrac{7}{2}$$

and, renaming, we get

$$3\,4\,2\,1, \qquad 3\,4\,1\,2, \qquad 2\,4\,1\,3, \qquad 2\,3\,1\,4.$$

Another way to describe this process is to take the permutation $a_1 a_2 \ldots a_{n-1}$ and a number k, $1 \le k \le n$; add one to each a_j whose value is $\ge k$, thus obtaining a permutation $b_1 b_2 \ldots b_{n-1}$ of the elements $\{1, \ldots, k-1, k+1, \ldots, n\}$; then $b_1 b_2 \ldots b_{n-1} k$ is a permutation of $\{1, \ldots, n\}$.

Again it is clear that we obtain each permutation of n elements exactly once by this construction. Putting k at the left instead of the right, or putting k in any other fixed position, would obviously work just as well.

If p_n is the number of permutations of n objects, both of these methods show that $p_n = n p_{n-1}$; this offers us two further proofs that $p_n = n(n-1) \ldots (1)$, as we already established in Eq. (2).

The important quantity p_n is called n *factorial* and it is written

$$n! = 1 \cdot 2 \cdot \ldots \cdot n = \prod_{k=1}^{n} k. \qquad (4)$$

Our convention for vacuous products (Section 1.2.3) gives us the value

$$0! = 1, \qquad (5)$$

and with this convention the basic identity

$$n! = (n-1)!\,n \qquad (6)$$

is valid for all positive integers n.

Factorials come up sufficiently often in computer work that the reader is advised to memorize the values of the first few:

$$0! = 1, \quad 1! = 1, \quad 2! = 2, \quad 3! = 6, \quad 4! = 24, \quad 5! = 120.$$

The factorials increase very rapidly; for example, 1000! is an integer with over 2500 decimal digits.

It is helpful to keep the value $10! = 3{,}628{,}800$ in mind; one should remember that 10! is about $3\frac{1}{2}$ million. In a sense, this number represents an approximate dividing line between things that are practical to compute and things that are not. If an algorithm requires the testing of more than 10! cases, it may consume too much computer time to be practical. On the other hand, if we decide to test 10! cases and each case requires, say, one millisecond of computer time, then the entire run will take about an hour. These comments are very vague, of course, but they can be useful to give an intuitive idea of what is computationally feasible.

It is only natural to wonder what relation $n!$ bears to other quantities in mathematics. Is there any way to tell how large 1000! is, without laboriously carrying out the multiplications implied in Eq. (4)? The answer was found by James Stirling in his famous work *Methodus Differentialis* (1730), page 137; we have

$$n! \approx \sqrt{2\pi n}\left(\frac{n}{e}\right)^n. \tag{7}$$

The "$\approx$" sign that appears here denotes "approximately equal," and "e" is the base of natural logarithms introduced in Section 1.2.2. We will prove Stirling's approximation (7) in Section 1.2.11.2. Exercise 24 gives a simple proof of a less precise result.

As an example of the use of this formula, we may compute

$$40320 = 8! \approx 4\sqrt{\pi}\left(\frac{8}{e}\right)^8 = 2^{26}\sqrt{\pi}\,e^{-8} \approx 67108864 \cdot 1.77245 \cdot 0.00033546 \approx 39902.$$

In this case the error is about 1%; we will see later that the relative error is approximately $1/(12n)$.

In addition to the approximate value given by Eq. (7), we can also rather easily obtain the exact value of $n!$ factored into primes. In fact, the prime p is a divisor of $n!$ with the multiplicity

$$\mu = \left\lfloor\frac{n}{p}\right\rfloor + \left\lfloor\frac{n}{p^2}\right\rfloor + \left\lfloor\frac{n}{p^3}\right\rfloor + \cdots = \sum_{k>0}\left\lfloor\frac{n}{p^k}\right\rfloor. \tag{8}$$

For example, if $n = 1000$ and $p = 3$, we have

$$\mu = \left\lfloor\frac{1000}{3}\right\rfloor + \left\lfloor\frac{1000}{9}\right\rfloor + \left\lfloor\frac{1000}{27}\right\rfloor + \left\lfloor\frac{1000}{81}\right\rfloor + \left\lfloor\frac{1000}{243}\right\rfloor + \left\lfloor\frac{1000}{729}\right\rfloor$$

$$= 333 + 111 + 37 + 12 + 4 + 1 = 498,$$

so 1000! is divisible by 3^{498} but not by 3^{499}. Although formula (8) is written as an infinite sum, it is really finite for any particular values of n and p, because all of the terms are eventually zero. It follows from exercise 1.2.4–35 that $\lfloor n/p^{k+1} \rfloor = \lfloor \lfloor n/p^k \rfloor/p \rfloor$; this fact facilitates the calculation in Eq. (8), since we can just divide the value of the previous term by p and discard the remainder.

Equation (8) follows from the fact that $\lfloor n/p^k \rfloor$ is the number of integers among $\{1, 2, \ldots, n\}$ that are multiples of p^k. If we study the integers in the product (4), any integer that is divisible by p^j but not by p^{j+1} is counted exactly j times: once in $\lfloor n/p \rfloor$, once in $\lfloor n/p^2 \rfloor$, $\ldots$, once in $\lfloor n/p^j \rfloor$. This accounts for all occurrences of p as a factor of $n!$. [See A. M. Legendre, *Essai sur la Théorie des Nombres*, second edition (Paris: 1808), page 8.]

Another natural question arises: Now that we have defined $n!$ for nonnegative integers n, perhaps the factorial function is meaningful also for rational values of n, and even for real values. What is $(\frac{1}{2})!$, for example? Let us illustrate this point by introducing the "termial" function

$$n? = 1 + 2 + \cdots + n = \sum_{k=1}^{n} k, \tag{9}$$

which is analogous to the factorial function except that we are adding instead of multiplying. We already know the sum of this arithmetic progression from Eq. 1.2.3–(15):

$$n? = \tfrac{1}{2} n(n+1). \tag{10}$$

This suggests a good way to generalize the "termial" function to arbitrary n, by using (10) instead of (9). We have $(\frac{1}{2})? = \frac{3}{8}$.

Stirling himself made several attempts to generalize $n!$ to noninteger n. He extended the approximation (7) into an infinite sum, but unfortunately the sum did not converge for any value of n; his method gave extremely good approximations, but it couldn't be extended to give an *exact* value. [For a discussion of this somewhat unusual situation, see K. Knopp, *Theory and Application of Infinite Series*, 2nd ed. (Glasgow: Blackie, 1951), 518–520, 527, 534.]

Stirling tried again, by noticing that

$$n! = 1 + \left(1 - \frac{1}{1!}\right)n + \left(1 - \frac{1}{1!} + \frac{1}{2!}\right)n(n-1)$$

$$+ \left(1 - \frac{1}{1!} + \frac{1}{2!} - \frac{1}{3!}\right)n(n-1)(n-2) + \cdots. \tag{11}$$

(We will prove this formula in the next section.) The apparently infinite sum in Eq. (11) is in reality finite for any nonnegative integer n; however, it does not provide the desired generalization of $n!$, since the infinite sum does not exist *except* when n is a nonnegative integer. (See exercise 16.)

Still undaunted, Stirling found a sequence $a_1, a_2, \ldots$ such that

$$\ln n! = a_1 n + a_2 n(n-1) + \cdots = \sum_{k \geq 0} a_{k+1} \prod_{0 \leq j \leq k} (n-j). \tag{12}$$

He was unable to *prove* that this sum defined $n!$ for all fractional values of n, although he was able to deduce the value of $(\frac{1}{2})! = \sqrt{\pi}/2$.

At about the same time, Leonhard Euler considered the same problem, and he was the first to find the appropriate generalization:

$$n! = \lim_{m \to \infty} \frac{m^n m!}{(n+1)(n+2)\dots(n+m)}. \tag{13}$$

Euler communicated this idea in a letter to Christian Goldbach on October 13, 1729. His formula defines $n!$ for any value of n except negative integers (when the denominator becomes zero); in such cases $n!$ is taken to be infinite. Exercises 8 and 22 explain why Eq. (13) is a reasonable definition.

Nearly two centuries later, in 1900, C. Hermite proved that Stirling's idea (12) actually does define $n!$ successfully for nonintegers n, and that in fact Euler's and Stirling's generalizations are identical.

Many notations were used for factorials in the early days. Euler actually wrote $[n]$, Gauss wrote $\Pi\, n$, and the symbols $\lfloor n$ and $n\rfloor$ were popular in England and Italy. The notation $n!$, which is universally used today when n is an integer, was introduced by a comparatively little known mathematician, Christian Kramp, in an algebra text [*Élémens d'Arithmétique Universelle* (Cologne: 1808), page 219].

When n is *not* an integer, however, the notation $n!$ is less common; instead we customarily employ a notation due to A. M. Legendre:

$$n! = \Gamma(n+1) = n\Gamma(n). \tag{14}$$

This function $\Gamma(x)$ is called the *gamma function*, and by Eq. (13) we have the definition

$$\Gamma(x) = \frac{x!}{x} = \lim_{m \to \infty} \frac{m^x m!}{x(x+1)(x+2)\dots(x+m)}. \tag{15}$$

A graph of $\Gamma(x)$ is shown in Fig. 7.

Equations (13) and (15) define factorials and the gamma function for complex values as well as real values; but we generally use the letter z, instead of n or x, when thinking of a variable that has both real and imaginary parts. The factorial and gamma functions are related not only by the rule $z! = \Gamma(z+1)$ but also by

$$(-z)!\,\Gamma(z) = \frac{\pi}{\sin \pi z}, \tag{16}$$

which holds whenever z is not an integer. (See exercise 23.)

Although $\Gamma(z)$ is infinite when z is zero or a negative integer, the function $1/\Gamma(z)$ is well defined for all complex z. (See exercise 1.2.7–24.) Advanced applications of the gamma function often make use of an important contour integral formula due to Hermann Hankel:

$$\frac{1}{\Gamma(z)} = \frac{1}{2\pi i} \oint \frac{e^t\, dt}{t^z}; \tag{17}$$

the path of complex integration starts at $-\infty$, then circles the origin in a counterclockwise direction and returns to $-\infty$. [*Zeitschrift für Math. und Physik* **9** (1864), 1–21.]

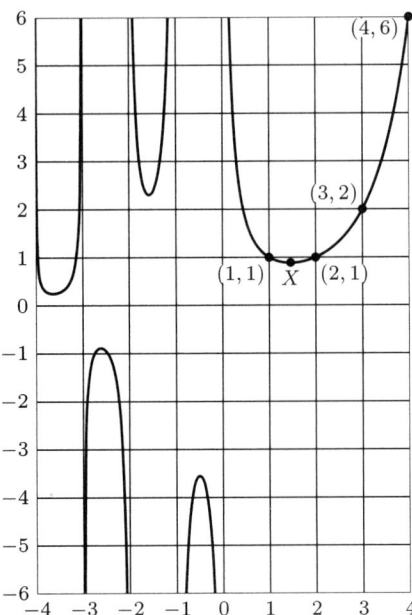

Fig. 7. The function $\Gamma(x) = (x-1)!$. The local minimum at X has the coordinates (1.46163 21449 68362 34126 26595, 0.88560 31944 10888 70027 88159).

Many formulas of discrete mathematics involve factorial-like products known as *factorial powers*. The quantities $x^{\underline{k}}$ and $x^{\overline{k}}$ (read, "x to the k falling" and "x to the k rising") are defined as follows, when k is a positive integer:

$$x^{\underline{k}} = x(x-1)\ldots(x-k+1) = \prod_{j=0}^{k-1}(x-j); \qquad (18)$$

$$x^{\overline{k}} = x(x+1)\ldots(x+k-1) = \prod_{j=0}^{k-1}(x+j). \qquad (19)$$

Thus, for example, the number p_{nk} of (2) is just $n^{\underline{k}}$. Notice that we have

$$x^{\overline{k}} = (x+k-1)^{\underline{k}} = (-1)^k(-x)^{\underline{k}}. \qquad (20)$$

The general formulas

$$x^{\underline{k}} = \frac{x!}{(x-k)!}\,, \qquad\qquad x^{\overline{k}} = \frac{\Gamma(x+k)}{\Gamma(x)} \qquad (21)$$

can be used to define factorial powers for other values of k. [The notations $x^{\overline{k}}$ and $x^{\underline{k}}$ are due respectively to A. Capelli, *Giornale di Mat. di Battaglini* **31** (1893), 291–313, and L. Toscano, *Comment. Accademia della Scienze* **3** (1939), 721–757.]

The interesting history of factorials from the time of Stirling to the present day is traced in an article by P. J. Davis, "Leonhard Euler's integral: A historical profile of the gamma function," *AMM* **66** (1959), 849–869. See also J. Dutka, *Archive for History of Exact Sciences* **31** (1984), 15–34.

EXERCISES

1. [00] How many ways are there to shuffle a 52-card deck?

2. [10] In the notation of Eq. (2), show that $p_{n(n-1)} = p_{nn}$, and explain why this happens.

3. [10] What permutations of $\{1, 2, 3, 4, 5\}$ would be constructed from the permutation 3 1 2 4 using Methods 1 and 2, respectively?

▶ **4.** [13] Given the fact that $\log_{10} 1000! = 2567.60464\ldots$, determine exactly how many decimal digits are present in the number 1000!. What is the *most significant* digit? What is the *least significant* digit?

5. [15] Estimate 8! using the following more exact version of Stirling's approximation:

$$n! \approx \sqrt{2\pi n} \left(\frac{n}{e}\right)^n \left(1 + \frac{1}{12n}\right).$$

▶ **6.** [17] Using Eq. (8), write 20! as a product of prime factors.

7. [M10] Show that the "generalized termial" function in Eq. (10) satisfies the identity $x? = x + (x - 1)?$ for all real numbers x.

8. [HM15] Show that the limit in Eq. (13) does equal $n!$ when n is a nonnegative integer.

9. [M10] Determine the values of $\Gamma(\frac{1}{2})$ and $\Gamma(-\frac{1}{2})$, given that $(\frac{1}{2})! = \sqrt{\pi}/2$.

▶ **10.** [HM20] Does the identity $\Gamma(x + 1) = x\Gamma(x)$ hold for all real numbers x? (See exercise 7.)

11. [M15] Let the representation of n in the binary system be $n = 2^{e_1} + 2^{e_2} + \cdots + 2^{e_r}$, where $e_1 > e_2 > \cdots > e_r \geq 0$. Show that $n!$ is divisible by 2^{n-r} but not by 2^{n-r+1}.

▶ **12.** [M22] (A. Legendre, 1808.) Generalizing the result of the previous exercise, let p be a prime number, and let the representation of n in the p-ary number system be $n = a_k p^k + a_{k-1} p^{k-1} + \cdots + a_1 p + a_0$. Express the number μ of Eq. (8) in a simple formula involving n, p, and a's.

13. [M23] (*Wilson's theorem*, actually due to Leibniz, 1682.) If p is prime, then $(p - 1)! \bmod p = p - 1$. Prove this, by pairing off numbers among $\{1, 2, \ldots, p - 1\}$ whose product modulo p is 1.

▶ **14.** [M28] (L. Stickelberger, 1890.) In the notation of exercise 12, we can determine $n! \bmod p$ in terms of the p-ary representation, for *any* positive integer n, thus generalizing Wilson's theorem. In fact, prove that $n!/p^\mu \equiv (-1)^\mu a_0! \, a_1! \ldots a_k! \pmod{p}$.

15. [HM15] The *permanent* of a square matrix is defined by the same expansion as the determinant except that each term of the permanent is given a plus sign while the determinant alternates between plus and minus. Thus the permanent of

$$\begin{pmatrix} a & b & c \\ d & e & f \\ g & h & i \end{pmatrix}$$

is $aei + bfg + cdh + gec + hfa + idb$. What is the permanent of

$$\begin{pmatrix} 1 \times 1 & 1 \times 2 & \cdots & 1 \times n \\ 2 \times 1 & 2 \times 2 & \cdots & 2 \times n \\ \vdots & \vdots & \ddots & \vdots \\ n \times 1 & n \times 2 & \cdots & n \times n \end{pmatrix}?$$

16. [*HM15*] Show that the infinite sum in Eq. (11) does not converge unless n is a nonnegative integer.

17. [*HM20*] Prove that the infinite product

$$\prod_{n \geq 1} \frac{(n + \alpha_1) \, \dots \, (n + \alpha_k)}{(n + \beta_1) \, \dots \, (n + \beta_k)}$$

equals $\Gamma(1 + \beta_1) \, \dots \, \Gamma(1 + \beta_k)/\Gamma(1 + \alpha_1) \, \dots \, \Gamma(1 + \alpha_k)$, if $\alpha_1 + \dots + \alpha_k = \beta_1 + \dots + \beta_k$ and if none of the β's is a negative integer.

18. [*M20*] Assume that $\pi/2 = \frac{2}{1} \cdot \frac{2}{3} \cdot \frac{4}{3} \cdot \frac{4}{5} \cdot \frac{6}{5} \cdot \frac{6}{7} \cdot \dots$. (This is "Wallis's product," obtained by J. Wallis in 1655, and we will prove it in exercise 1.2.6–43.) Using the previous exercise, prove that $(\frac{1}{2})! = \sqrt{\pi}/2$.

19. [*HM22*] Denote the quantity appearing after "$\lim_{m \to \infty}$" in Eq. (15) by $\Gamma_m(x)$. Show that

$$\Gamma_m(x) = \int_0^m \left(1 - \frac{t}{m}\right)^m t^{x-1} \, dt = m^x \int_0^1 (1 - t)^m t^{x-1} \, dt, \quad \text{if } x > 0.$$

20. [*HM21*] Using the fact that $0 \leq e^{-t} - (1 - t/m)^m \leq t^2 e^{-t}/m$, if $0 \leq t \leq m$, and the previous exercise, show that $\Gamma(x) = \int_0^\infty e^{-t} t^{x-1} \, dt$, if $x > 0$.

21. [*HM25*] (L. F. A. Arbogast, 1800.) Let $D_x^k u$ represent the kth derivative of a function u with respect to x. The chain rule states that $D_x^1 w = D_u^1 w \, D_x^1 u$. If we apply this to second derivatives, we find $D_x^2 w = D_u^2 w (D_x^1 u)^2 + D_u^1 w \, D_x^2 u$. Show that the *general formula* is

$$D_x^n w = \sum_{j=0}^{n} \sum_{\substack{k_1 + k_2 + \dots + k_n = j \\ k_1 + 2k_2 + \dots + nk_n = n \\ k_1, k_2, \dots, k_n \geq 0}} D_u^j w \, \frac{n!}{k_1! \, (1!)^{k_1} \dots k_n! \, (n!)^{k_n}} (D_x^1 u)^{k_1} \dots (D_x^n u)^{k_n}.$$

▶ **22.** [*HM20*] Try to put yourself in Euler's place, looking for a way to generalize $n!$ to noninteger values of n. Since $(n + \frac{1}{2})!/n!$ times $((n + \frac{1}{2}) + \frac{1}{2})!/(n + \frac{1}{2})!$ equals $(n + 1)!/n! = n + 1$, it seems natural that $(n + \frac{1}{2})!/n!$ should be approximately $\sqrt{n}$. Similarly, $(n + \frac{1}{3})!/n!$ should be $\approx \sqrt[3]{n}$. Invent a hypothesis about the ratio $(n + x)!/n!$ as n approaches infinity. Is your hypothesis correct when x is an integer? Does it tell anything about the appropriate value of $x!$ when x is not an integer?

23. [*HM20*] Prove (16), given that $\pi z \prod_{n=1}^{\infty}(1 - z^2/n^2) = \sin \pi z$.

▶ **24.** [*HM21*] Prove the handy inequalities

$$\frac{n^n}{e^{n-1}} \leq n! \leq \frac{n^{n+1}}{e^{n-1}}, \qquad \text{integer } n \geq 1.$$

[*Hint:* $1 + x \leq e^x$ for all real x; hence $(k + 1)/k \leq e^{1/k} \leq k/(k - 1)$.]

25. [*M20*] Do factorial powers satisfy a law analogous to the ordinary law of exponents, $x^{m+n} = x^m x^n$?

1.2.6. Binomial Coefficients

The *combinations of n objects taken k at a time* are the possible choices of k different elements from a collection of n objects, disregarding order. The combinations of the five objects $\{a, b, c, d, e\}$ taken three at a time are

$$abc, \quad abd, \quad abe, \quad acd, \quad ace, \quad ade, \quad bcd, \quad bce, \quad bde, \quad cde. \qquad (1)$$

It is a simple matter to count the total number of k-combinations of n objects: Equation (2) of the previous section told us that there are $n(n-1)\ldots(n-k+1)$ ways to choose the first k objects for a permutation; and every k-combination appears exactly $k!$ times in these arrangements, since each combination appears in all its permutations. Therefore the number of combinations, which we denote by $\binom{n}{k}$, is

$$\binom{n}{k} = \frac{n(n-1)\ldots(n-k+1)}{k(k-1)\ldots(1)}. \qquad (2)$$

For example,

$$\binom{5}{3} = \frac{5 \cdot 4 \cdot 3}{3 \cdot 2 \cdot 1} = 10,$$

which is the number of combinations we found in (1).

The quantity $\binom{n}{k}$, read "n choose k," is called a *binomial coefficient*; these numbers have an extraordinary number of applications. They are probably the most important quantities entering into the analysis of algorithms, so the reader is urged to become familiar with them.

Equation (2) may be used to define $\binom{n}{k}$ even when n is not an integer. To be precise, we define the symbol $\binom{r}{k}$ for all real numbers r and all integers k as follows:

$$\binom{r}{k} = \frac{r(r-1)\ldots(r-k+1)}{k(k-1)\ldots(1)} = \frac{r^{\underline{k}}}{k!} = \prod_{j=1}^{k} \frac{r+1-j}{j}, \qquad \text{integer } k \geq 0;$$

$$\binom{r}{k} = 0, \qquad \text{integer } k < 0.$$

$$(3)$$

In particular cases we have

$$\binom{r}{0} = 1, \qquad \binom{r}{1} = r, \qquad \binom{r}{2} = \frac{r(r-1)}{2}. \qquad (4)$$

Table 1 gives values of the binomial coefficients for small integer values of r and k; the values for $0 \leq r \leq 4$ should be memorized.

Binomial coefficients have a long and interesting history. Table 1 is called "Pascal's triangle" because it appeared in Blaise Pascal's *Traité du Triangle Arithmétique* in 1653. This treatise was significant because it was one of the first works on probability theory, but Pascal did not invent the binomial coefficients (which were well-known in Europe at that time). Table 1 also appeared in the treatise *Szu-yüan Yü-chien* ("The Precious Mirror of the Four Elements") by the Chinese mathematician Chu Shih-Chieh in 1303, where they were said to be an old invention. Yang Hui, in 1261, credited them to Chia Hsien (c. 1100), whose work is now lost. The earliest known detailed discussion of binomial coefficients is in a tenth-century commentary, due to Halāyudha, on an ancient Hindu classic, Piṅgala's *Chandaḥśāstra*. [See G. Chakravarti, *Bull.*

Table 1

TABLE OF BINOMIAL COEFFICIENTS (PASCAL'S TRIANGLE)

r	$\binom{r}{0}$	$\binom{r}{1}$	$\binom{r}{2}$	$\binom{r}{3}$	$\binom{r}{4}$	$\binom{r}{5}$	$\binom{r}{6}$	$\binom{r}{7}$	$\binom{r}{8}$	$\binom{r}{9}$
0	1	0	0	0	0	0	0	0	0	0
1	1	1	0	0	0	0	0	0	0	0
2	1	2	1	0	0	0	0	0	0	0
3	1	3	3	1	0	0	0	0	0	0
4	1	4	6	4	1	0	0	0	0	0
5	1	5	10	10	5	1	0	0	0	0
6	1	6	15	20	15	6	1	0	0	0
7	1	7	21	35	35	21	7	1	0	0
8	1	8	28	56	70	56	28	8	1	0
9	1	9	36	84	126	126	84	36	9	1

Calcutta Math. Soc. **24** (1932), 79–88.] Another Indian mathematician, Mahāvīra, had previously explained rule (3) for computing $\binom{r}{k}$ in Chapter 6 of his *Ganita Sāra Saṅgraha*, written about 850; and in 1150 Bhāskara repeated Mahāvīra's rule near the end of his famous book *Līlāvatī*. For small values of k, binomial coefficients were known much earlier; they appeared in Greek and Roman writings with a geometric interpretation (see Fig. 8). The notation $\binom{r}{k}$ was introduced by Andreas von Ettingshausen in §31 of his book *Die combinatorische Analysis* (Vienna: 1826).

The reader has probably noticed several interesting patterns in Table 1. Binomial coefficients satisfy literally thousands of identities, and for centuries their amazing properties have been continually explored. In fact, there are so many relations present that when someone finds a new identity, not many people get excited about it any more, except the discoverer. In order to manipu-

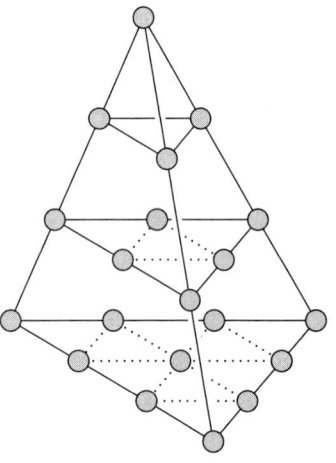

Fig. 8. Geometric interpretation of $\binom{n+2}{3}$, $n = 4$.

late the formulas that arise in the analysis of algorithms, a facility for handling binomial coefficients is a must, and so an attempt has been made in this section to explain in a simple way how to maneuver with these numbers. Mark Twain once tried to reduce all jokes to a dozen or so primitive kinds (farmer's daughter, mother-in-law, etc.); we will try to condense the thousands of identities into a small set of basic operations with which we can solve nearly every problem involving binomial coefficients that we will meet.

In most applications, both of the numbers r and k that appear in $\binom{r}{k}$ will be integers, and some of the techniques we will describe are applicable only in such cases. Therefore we will be careful to list, at the right of each numbered equation, any restrictions on the variables that appear. For example, Eq. (3) mentions the requirement that k is an integer; there is no restriction on r. The identities with fewest restrictions are the most useful.

Now let us study the basic techniques for operating on binomial coefficients:

A. Representation by factorials. From Eq. (3) we have immediately

$$\binom{n}{k} = \frac{n!}{k!\,(n-k)!}, \qquad \text{integer } n \geq \text{integer } k \geq 0. \tag{5}$$

This allows combinations of factorials to be represented as binomial coefficients and conversely.

B. Symmetry condition. From Eqs. (3) and (5), we have

$$\binom{n}{k} = \binom{n}{n-k}, \qquad \text{integer } n \geq 0, \text{ integer } k. \tag{6}$$

This formula holds for all integers k. *When k is negative or greater than n, the binomial coefficient is zero* (provided that n is a nonnegative integer).

C. Moving in and out of parentheses. From the definition (3), we have

$$\binom{r}{k} = \frac{r}{k}\binom{r-1}{k-1}, \qquad \text{integer } k \neq 0. \tag{7}$$

This formula is very useful for combining a binomial coefficient with other parts of an expression. By elementary transformation we have the rules

$$k\binom{r}{k} = r\binom{r-1}{k-1}, \qquad \frac{1}{r}\binom{r}{k} = \frac{1}{k}\binom{r-1}{k-1},$$

the first of which is valid for all integers k, and the second when no division by zero has been performed. We also have a similar relation:

$$\binom{r}{k} = \frac{r}{r-k}\binom{r-1}{k}, \qquad \text{integer } k \neq r. \tag{8}$$

Let us illustrate these transformations, by proving Eq. (8) using Eqs. (6) and (7) alternately:

$$\binom{r}{k} = \binom{r}{r-k} = \frac{r}{r-k}\binom{r-1}{r-1-k} = \frac{r}{r-k}\binom{r-1}{k}.$$

[*Note:* This derivation is valid only when r is a positive integer $\neq k$, because of the constraints involved in Eqs. (6) and (7); yet Eq. (8) claims to be valid for *arbitrary* $r \neq k$. This can be proved in a simple and important manner: We have verified that

$$r\binom{r-1}{k} = (r-k)\binom{r}{k}$$

for *infinitely many values of r*. Both sides of this equation are *polynomials* in r. A nonzero polynomial of degree n can have at most n distinct zeros; so (by subtraction) *if two polynomials of degree $\leq n$ agree at $n+1$ or more different points, the polynomials are identically equal.* This principle may be used to extend the validity of many identities from integers to all real numbers.]

D. Addition formula. The basic relation

$$\binom{r}{k} = \binom{r-1}{k} + \binom{r-1}{k-1}, \quad \text{integer } k, \tag{9}$$

is clearly valid in Table 1 (every value is the sum of the two values above and to the left) and we may easily verify it in general from Eq. (3). Alternatively, Eqs. (7) and (8) tell us that

$$r\binom{r-1}{k} + r\binom{r-1}{k-1} = (r-k)\binom{r}{k} + k\binom{r}{k} = r\binom{r}{k}.$$

Equation (9) is often useful in obtaining proofs by induction on r, when r is an integer.

E. Summation formulas. Repeated application of (9) gives

$$\binom{r}{k} = \binom{r-1}{k} + \binom{r-1}{k-1} = \binom{r-1}{k} + \binom{r-2}{k-1} + \binom{r-2}{k-2} = \cdots;$$

or

$$\binom{r}{k} = \binom{r-1}{k-1} + \binom{r-1}{k} = \binom{r-1}{k-1} + \binom{r-2}{k-1} + \binom{r-2}{k} = \cdots.$$

Thus we are led to two important summation formulas that can be expressed as follows:

$$\sum_{k=0}^{n} \binom{r+k}{k} = \binom{r}{0} + \binom{r+1}{1} + \cdots + \binom{r+n}{n} = \binom{r+n+1}{n},$$

$$\text{integer } n \geq 0. \tag{10}$$

$$\sum_{k=0}^{n} \binom{k}{m} = \binom{0}{m} + \binom{1}{m} + \cdots + \binom{n}{m} = \binom{n+1}{m+1},$$

$$\text{integer } m \geq 0, \text{ integer } n \geq 0. \tag{11}$$

Equation (11) can easily be proved by induction on n, but it is interesting to see how it can also be derived from Eq. (10) with two applications of Eq. (6):

$$\sum_{0 \leq k \leq n} \binom{k}{m} = \sum_{0 \leq m+k \leq n} \binom{m+k}{m} = \sum_{-m \leq k < 0} \binom{m+k}{m} + \sum_{0 \leq k \leq n-m} \binom{m+k}{k}$$

$$= 0 + \binom{m+(n-m)+1}{n-m} = \binom{n+1}{m+1},$$

assuming that $n \geq m$. If $n < m$, Eq. (11) is obvious.

Equation (11) occurs very frequently in applications; in fact, we have already derived special cases of it in previous sections. For example, when $m = 1$, we have our old friend, the sum of an arithmetic progression:

$$\binom{0}{1} + \binom{1}{1} + \cdots + \binom{n}{1} = 0 + 1 + \cdots + n = \binom{n+1}{2} = \frac{(n+1)n}{2}.$$

Suppose that we want a simple formula for the sum $1^2 + 2^2 + \cdots + n^2$. This can be obtained by observing that $k^2 = 2\binom{k}{2} + \binom{k}{1}$; hence

$$\sum_{k=0}^{n} k^2 = \sum_{k=0}^{n} \left(2\binom{k}{2} + \binom{k}{1} \right) = 2\binom{n+1}{3} + \binom{n+1}{2}.$$

And this answer, obtained in terms of binomial coefficients, can be put back into polynomial notation if desired:

$$1^2 + 2^2 + \cdots + n^2 = 2\frac{(n+1)n(n-1)}{6} + \frac{(n+1)n}{2} = \tfrac{1}{3}n(n+\tfrac{1}{2})(n+1). \quad (12)$$

The sum $1^3 + 2^3 + \cdots + n^3$ can be obtained in a similar way; *any* polynomial $a_0 + a_1 k + a_2 k^2 + \cdots + a_m k^m$ can be expressed as $b_0 \binom{k}{0} + b_1 \binom{k}{1} + \cdots + b_m \binom{k}{m}$ for suitably chosen coefficients $b_0, \ldots, b_m$. We will return to this subject later.

F. The binomial theorem. Of course, the binomial theorem is one of our principal tools:

$$(x + y)^r = \sum_k \binom{r}{k} x^k y^{r-k}, \quad \text{integer } r \geq 0. \quad (13)$$

For example, $(x + y)^4 = x^4 + 4x^3 y + 6x^2 y^2 + 4xy^3 + y^4$. $\big($At last we are able to justify the name "binomial coefficient" for the numbers $\binom{r}{k}$.$\big)$

It is important to notice that we have written $\sum_k$ in Eq. (13), rather than $\sum_{k=0}^{r}$ as might have been expected. If no restriction is placed on k, we are summing over *all* integers, $-\infty < k < +\infty$; but the two notations are exactly equivalent in this case, since the terms in Eq. (13) are zero when $k < 0$ or $k > r$. The simpler form $\sum_k$ is to be preferred, since all manipulations with sums are simpler when the conditions of summation are simpler. We save a good deal of tedious effort if we do not need to keep track of the lower and/or upper limits of summation, so the limits should be left unspecified whenever possible. Our notation has another advantage also: If r is not a nonnegative integer, Eq. (13) becomes an *infinite* sum, and the *binomial theorem* of calculus states that *Eq. (13) is valid for all* r, if $|x/y| < 1$.

It should be noted that formula (13) gives

$$0^0 = 1. \quad (14)$$

We will use this convention consistently.

The special case $y = 1$ in Eq. (13) is so important, we state it specially:

$$\sum_k \binom{r}{k} x^k = (1 + x)^r, \quad \text{integer } r \geq 0 \text{ or } |x| < 1. \quad (15)$$

The discovery of the binomial theorem was announced by Isaac Newton in letters to Oldenburg on June 13, 1676 and October 24, 1676. [See D. Struik, *Source Book in Mathematics* (Harvard Univ. Press, 1969), 284–291.] But he apparently had no real proof of the formula; at that time the necessity for rigorous proof was not fully realized. The first attempted proof was given by L. Euler in 1774, although his effort was incomplete. Finally, C. F. Gauss gave the first actual proof in 1812. In fact, Gauss's work represented the first time *anything* about infinite sums was proved satisfactorily.

Early in the nineteenth century, N. H. Abel found a surprising generalization of the binomial formula (13):

$$(x+y)^n = \sum_k \binom{n}{k} x(x-kz)^{k-1}(y+kz)^{n-k}, \quad \text{integer } n \geq 0, \ x \neq 0. \quad (16)$$

This is an identity in *three* variables, x, y, and z (see exercises 50 through 52). Abel published and proved this formula in Volume 1 of A. L. Crelle's soon-to-be-famous *Journal für die reine und angewandte Mathematik* (1826), pages 159–160. It is interesting to note that Abel contributed many other papers to the same Volume 1, including his famous memoirs on the unsolvability of algebraic equations of degree 5 or more by radicals, and on the binomial theorem. See H. W. Gould, *AMM* **69** (1962), 572, for a number of references to Eq. (16).

G. Negating the upper index. The basic identity

$$\binom{r}{k} = (-1)^k \binom{k-r-1}{k}, \quad \text{integer } k, \quad (17)$$

follows immediately from the definition (3) when each term of the numerator is negated. This is often a useful transformation on the upper index.

One easy consequence of Eq. (17) is the summation formula

$$\sum_{k \leq n} \binom{r}{k}(-1)^k = \binom{r}{0} - \binom{r}{1} + \cdots + (-1)^n \binom{r}{n} = (-1)^n \binom{r-1}{n}, \quad \text{integer } n. \quad (18)$$

This identity could be proved by induction using Eq. (9), but we can use Eqs. (17) and (10) directly:

$$\sum_{k \leq n} \binom{r}{k}(-1)^k = \sum_{k \leq n} \binom{k-r-1}{k} = \binom{-r+n}{n} = (-1)^n \binom{r-1}{n}.$$

Another important application of Eq. (17) can be made when r is an integer:

$$\binom{n}{m} = (-1)^{n-m} \binom{-(m+1)}{n-m}, \quad \text{integer } n \geq 0, \text{ integer } m. \quad (19)$$

(Set $r = n$ and $k = n - m$ in Eq. (17) and use (6).) We have moved n from the upper position to the lower.

H. Simplifying products. When products of binomial coefficients appear, they can usually be reexpressed in several different ways by expanding into factorials and out again using Eq. (5). For example,

$$\binom{r}{m}\binom{m}{k} = \binom{r}{k}\binom{r-k}{m-k}, \quad \text{integer } m, \quad \text{integer } k. \quad (20)$$

It suffices to prove Eq. (20) when r is an integer $\geq m$ (see the remarks after Eq. (8)), and when $0 \leq k \leq m$. Then

$$\binom{r}{m}\binom{m}{k} = \frac{r!\,m!}{m!\,(r-m)!\,k!\,(m-k)!} = \frac{r!\,(r-k)!}{k!\,(r-k)!\,(m-k)!\,(r-m)!} = \binom{r}{k}\binom{r-k}{m-k}.$$

Equation (20) is very useful when an index (namely m) appears in both the upper and the lower position, and we wish to have it appear in one place rather than two. Notice that Eq. (7) is the special case of Eq. (20) when $k = 1$.

I. Sums of products. To complete our set of binomial-coefficient manipulations, we present the following very general identities, which are proved in the exercises at the end of this section. These formulas show how to sum over a product of two binomial coefficients, considering various places where the running variable k might appear:

$$\sum_k \binom{r}{k}\binom{s}{n-k} = \binom{r+s}{n}, \quad \text{integer } n. \tag{21}$$

$$\sum_k \binom{r}{m+k}\binom{s}{n+k} = \binom{r+s}{r-m+n}, \tag{22}$$
$$\text{integer } m, \text{ integer } n, \text{ integer } r \geq 0.$$

$$\sum_k \binom{r}{k}\binom{s+k}{n}(-1)^{r-k} = \binom{s}{n-r}, \quad \text{integer } n, \text{ integer } r \geq 0. \tag{23}$$

$$\sum_{k=0}^r \binom{r-k}{m}\binom{s}{k-t}(-1)^{k-t} = \binom{r-t-s}{r-t-m}, \tag{24}$$
$$\text{integer } t \geq 0, \text{ integer } r \geq 0, \text{ integer } m \geq 0.$$

$$\sum_{k=0}^r \binom{r-k}{m}\binom{s+k}{n} = \binom{r+s+1}{m+n+1}, \tag{25}$$
$$\text{integer } n \geq \text{integer } s \geq 0, \text{ integer } m \geq 0, \text{ integer } r \geq 0.$$

$$\sum_{k\geq 0} \binom{r-tk}{k}\binom{s-t(n-k)}{n-k}\frac{r}{r-tk} = \binom{r+s-tn}{n}, \quad \text{integer } n. \tag{26}$$

Of these identities, Eq. (21) is by far the most important, and it should be memorized. One way to remember it is to interpret the right-hand side as the number of ways to select n people from among r men and s women; each term on the left is the number of ways to choose k of the men and $n - k$ of the women. Equation (21) is commonly called Vandermonde's convolution, since A. Vandermonde published it in *Mém. Acad. Roy. Sciences* (Paris, 1772), part 1, 489–498. However, it had appeared already in Chu Shih-Chieh's 1303 treatise mentioned earlier [see J. Needham, *Science and Civilisation in China* **3** (Cambridge University Press, 1959), 138–139].

If $r = tk$ in Eq. (26), we avoid the zero denominator by canceling with a factor in the numerator; therefore Eq. (26) is a polynomial identity in the variables r, s, t. Obviously Eq. (21) is a special case of Eq. (26) with $t = 0$.

We should point out a nonobvious use of Eqs. (23) and (25): It is often helpful to replace the simple binomial coefficient on the right-hand side by the more complicated expression on the left, interchange the order of summation, and simplify. We may regard the left-hand sides as expansions of

$$\binom{s}{n+a} \quad \text{in terms of} \quad \binom{s+k}{n}.$$

Formula (23) is used for negative a, formula (25) for positive a.

This completes our study of binomial-coefficientology. The reader is advised to learn especially Eqs. (5), (6), (7), (9), (13), (17), (20), and (21) — frame them with your favorite highlighter pen!

With all these methods at our disposal, we should be able to solve almost any problem that comes along, in at least three different ways. The following examples illustrate the techniques.

Example 1. When r is a positive integer, what is the value of $\sum_k \binom{r}{k}\binom{s}{k} k$?

Solution. Formula (7) is useful for disposing of the outside k:

$$\sum_k \binom{r}{k}\binom{s}{k} k = \sum_k \binom{r}{k}\binom{s-1}{k-1} s = s\sum_k \binom{r}{k}\binom{s-1}{k-1}.$$

Now formula (22) applies, with $m = 0$ and $n = -1$. The answer is therefore

$$\sum_k \binom{r}{k}\binom{s}{k} k = \binom{r+s-1}{r-1} s, \quad \text{integer } r \geq 0.$$

Example 2. What is the value of $\sum_k \binom{n+k}{2k}\binom{2k}{k}\frac{(-1)^k}{k+1}$, if n is a nonnegative integer?

Solution. This problem is tougher; the summation index k appears in six places! First we apply Eq. (20), and we obtain

$$\sum_k \binom{n+k}{k}\binom{n}{k}\frac{(-1)^k}{k+1}.$$

We can now breathe more easily, since several of the menacing characteristics of the original formula have disappeared. The next step should be obvious; we apply Eq. (7) in a manner similar to the technique used in Example 1:

$$\sum_k \binom{n+k}{k}\binom{n+1}{k+1}\frac{(-1)^k}{n+1}. \tag{27}$$

Good, another k has vanished. At this point there are two equally promising lines of attack. We can replace the $\binom{n+k}{k}$ by $\binom{n+k}{n}$, assuming that $k \geq 0$, and evaluate the sum with Eq. (23):

$$\sum_{k \geq 0} \binom{n+k}{n}\binom{n+1}{k+1}\frac{(-1)^k}{n+1}$$

$$= -\frac{1}{n+1}\sum_{k \geq 1}\binom{n-1+k}{n}\binom{n+1}{k}(-1)^k$$

$$= -\frac{1}{n+1}\sum_{k \geq 0}\binom{n-1+k}{n}\binom{n+1}{k}(-1)^k + \frac{1}{n+1}\binom{n-1}{n}$$

$$= -\frac{1}{n+1}(-1)^{n+1}\binom{n-1}{-1} + \frac{1}{n+1}\binom{n-1}{n} = \frac{1}{n+1}\binom{n-1}{n}.$$

The binomial coefficient $\binom{n-1}{n}$ equals zero except when $n = 0$, in which case it equals one. So we can conveniently state the answer to our problem as $[n=0]$, using Iverson's convention (Eq. 1.2.3–(16)), or as δ_{n0}, using the Kronecker delta (Eq. 1.2.3–(19)).

Another way to proceed from Eq. (27) is to use Eq. (17), obtaining

$$\sum_{k}\binom{-(n+1)}{k}\binom{n+1}{k+1}\frac{1}{n+1}.$$

We can now apply Eq. (22), which yields the sum

$$\binom{n+1-(n+1)}{n+1-1+0}\frac{1}{n+1} = \binom{0}{n}\frac{1}{n+1}.$$

Once again we have derived the answer:

$$\sum_{k}\binom{n+k}{2k}\binom{2k}{k}\frac{(-1)^k}{k+1} = \delta_{n0}, \qquad \text{integer } n \geq 0. \tag{28}$$

Example 3. What is the value of $\displaystyle\sum_{k}\binom{n+k}{m+2k}\binom{2k}{k}\frac{(-1)^k}{k+1}$, for positive integers m and n?

Solution. If m were zero, we would have the same formula to work with that we had in Example 2. However, the presence of m means that we cannot even begin to use the method of the previous solution, since the first step there was to use Eq. (20) — which no longer applies. In this situation it pays to complicate things even more by replacing the unwanted $\binom{n+k}{m+2k}$ by a sum of terms of the form $\binom{x+k}{2k}$, since our problem will then become a sum of problems that we know how to solve. Accordingly, we use Eq. (25) with

$$r = n+k-1, \quad m = 2k, \quad s = 0, \quad n = m-1,$$

and we have

$$\sum_{k}\sum_{0 \leq j \leq n+k-1}\binom{n+k-1-j}{2k}\binom{2k}{k}\binom{j}{m-1}\frac{(-1)^k}{k+1}. \tag{29}$$

We wish to perform the summation on k first; but interchanging the order of summation demands that we sum on the values of k that are ≥ 0 and $\geq j-n+1$. Unfortunately, the latter condition raises problems, because we do *not* know the desired sum if $j \geq n$. Let us save the situation, however, by observing the terms of (29) are zero when $n \leq j \leq n+k-1$. This condition implies that $k \geq 1$; thus $0 \leq n+k-1-j \leq k-1 < 2k$, and the first binomial coefficient in (29) will vanish. We may therefore replace the condition on the second sum by $0 \leq j < n$, and the interchange of summation is routine. Summing on k by Eq. (28) now gives

$$\sum_{0 \leq j < n} \binom{j}{m-1} \delta_{(n-1-j)0},$$

and all terms are zero except when $j = n-1$. Hence our final answer is

$$\binom{n-1}{m-1}.$$

The solution to this problem was fairly complicated, but not really mysterious; there was a good reason for each step. The derivation should be studied closely because it illustrates some delicate maneuvering with the conditions in our equations. There is actually a better way to attack this problem, however; it is left to the reader to figure out a way to transform the given sum so that Eq. (26) applies (see exercise 30).

Example 4. Prove that

$$\sum_{k} A_k(r,t) A_{n-k}(s,t) = A_n(r+s,t), \quad \text{integer } n \geq 0, \tag{30}$$

where $A_n(x,t)$ is the nth degree polynomial in x that satisfies

$$A_n(x,t) = \binom{x-nt}{n} \frac{x}{x-nt}, \quad \text{for } x \neq nt.$$

Solution. We may assume that $r \neq kt \neq s$ for $0 \leq k \leq n$, since both sides of (30) are polynomials in r, s, t. Our problem is to evaluate

$$\sum_{k} \binom{r-kt}{k} \binom{s-(n-k)t}{n-k} \frac{r}{r-kt} \frac{s}{s-(n-k)t},$$

which, if anything, looks much worse than our previous horrible problems! Notice the strong similarity to Eq. (26), however, and also note the case $t = 0$.

We are tempted to change

$$\binom{r-kt}{k} \frac{r}{r-kt} \qquad \text{to} \qquad \binom{r-kt-1}{k-1} \frac{r}{k},$$

except that the latter tends to lose the analogy with Eq. (26) and it fails when $k = 0$. A better way to proceed is to use the technique of *partial fractions*, whereby a fraction with a complicated denominator can often be replaced by a sum of fractions with simpler denominators. Indeed, we have

$$\frac{1}{r-kt}\frac{1}{s-(n-k)t} = \frac{1}{r+s-nt}\left(\frac{1}{r-kt}+\frac{1}{s-(n-k)t}\right).$$

Putting this into our sum we get

$$\frac{s}{r+s-nt}\sum_k\binom{r-kt}{k}\binom{s-(n-k)t}{n-k}\frac{r}{r-kt}$$

$$+\frac{r}{r+s-nt}\sum_k\binom{r-kt}{k}\binom{s-(n-k)t}{n-k}\frac{s}{s-(n-k)t},$$

and Eq. (26) evaluates both of these formulas if we change k to $n-k$ in the second; the desired result follows immediately. Identities (26) and (30) are due to H. A. Rothe, *Formulæ de Serierum Reversione* (Leipzig: 1793); special cases of these formulas are still being "discovered" frequently. For the interesting history of these identities and some generalizations, see H. W. Gould and J. Kaucký, *Journal of Combinatorial Theory* **1** (1966), 233–247.

Example 5. Determine the values of $a_0, a_1, a_2, \ldots$ such that

$$n! = a_0 + a_1 n + a_2 n(n-1) + a_3 n(n-1)(n-2) + \cdots \tag{31}$$

for all nonnegative integers n.

Solution. Equation 1.2.5–(11), which was presented without proof in the previous section, gives the answer. Let us pretend that we don't know it yet. It is clear that the problem does have a solution, since we can set $n = 0$ and determine a_0, then set $n = 1$ and determine a_1, etc.

First we would like to write Eq. (31) in terms of binomial coefficients:

$$n! = \sum_k \binom{n}{k} k!\, a_k. \tag{32}$$

The problem of solving implicit equations like this for a_k is called the *inversion problem*, and the technique we shall use applies to similar problems as well.

The idea is based on the special case $s = 0$ of Eq. (23):

$$\sum_k \binom{r}{k}\binom{k}{n}(-1)^{r-k} = \binom{0}{n-r} = \delta_{nr}, \quad \text{integer } n, \text{ integer } r \geq 0. \tag{33}$$

The importance of this formula is that when $n \neq r$, the sum is zero; this enables us to solve our problem since a lot of terms cancel out as they did in Example 3:

$$\sum_n n!\binom{m}{n}(-1)^{m-n} = \sum_n\sum_k\binom{n}{k}k!\,a_k\binom{m}{n}(-1)^{m-n}$$

$$= \sum_k k!\,a_k\sum_n\binom{n}{k}\binom{m}{n}(-1)^{m-n}$$

$$= \sum_k k!\,a_k\delta_{km} = m!\,a_m.$$

Notice how we were able to get an equation in which only one value a_m appears, by adding together suitable multiples of Eq. (32) for $n = 0, 1, \ldots$. We have now

$$a_m = \sum_{n \geq 0} (-1)^{m-n} \frac{n!}{m!} \binom{m}{n} = \sum_{0 \leq n \leq m} \frac{(-1)^{m-n}}{(m-n)!} = \sum_{0 \leq n \leq m} \frac{(-1)^n}{n!}.$$

This completes the solution to Example 5. Let us now take a closer look at the implications of Eq. (33): When r and m are nonnegative integers we have

$$\sum_k \binom{r}{k} (-1)^{r-k} \left(c_0 \binom{k}{0} + c_1 \binom{k}{1} + \cdots + c_m \binom{k}{m} \right) = c_r,$$

since the other terms vanish after summation. By properly choosing the coefficients c_i, we can represent *any* polynomial in k as a sum of binomial coefficients with upper index k. We find therefore that

$$\sum_k \binom{r}{k} (-1)^{r-k} (b_0 + b_1 k + \cdots + b_r k^r) = r! \, b_r, \quad \text{integer } r \geq 0, \qquad (34)$$

where $b_0 + \cdots + b_r k^r$ represents any polynomial whatever of degree r or less. (This formula will be of no great surprise to students of numerical analysis, since $\sum_k \binom{r}{k} (-1)^{r-k} f(x+k)$ is the "rth difference" of the function $f(x)$.)

Using Eq. (34), we can immediately obtain many other relations that appear complicated at first and that are often given very lengthy proofs, such as

$$\sum_k \binom{r}{k} \binom{s - kt}{r} (-1)^k = t^r, \quad \text{integer } r \geq 0. \qquad (35)$$

It is customary in textbooks such as this to give a lot of impressive examples of neat tricks, etc., but never to mention simple-looking problems where the techniques fail. The examples above may have given the impression that all things are possible with binomial coefficients; it should be mentioned, however, that in spite of Eqs. (10), (11), and (18), there seems to be no simple formula for the analogous sum

$$\sum_{k=0}^n \binom{m}{k} = \binom{m}{0} + \binom{m}{1} + \cdots + \binom{m}{n}, \qquad (36)$$

when $n < m$. (For $n = m$ the answer is simple; what is it? See exercise 36.) On the other hand this sum does have a closed form as a function of n when m is an explicit negative integer; for example,

$$\sum_{k=0}^n \binom{-2}{k} = (-1)^n \left\lceil \frac{n+1}{2} \right\rceil. \qquad (37)$$

There is also a simple formula

$$\sum_{k=0}^n \binom{m}{k} \left(k - \frac{m}{2} \right) = -\frac{m}{2} \binom{m-1}{n} \qquad (38)$$

for a sum that looks as though it should be harder, not easier.

How can we decide when to stop working on a sum that resists simplification? Fortunately, there is now a good way to answer that question in many important cases: An algorithm due to R. W. Gosper and D. Zeilberger will discover closed forms in binomial coefficients when they exist, and will prove the impossibility when they do not exist. The Gosper–Zeilberger algorithm is beyond the scope of this book, but it is explained in *CMath* §5.8. See also the book $A = B$ by Petkovšek, Wilf, and Zeilberger (Wellesley, Mass.: A. K. Peters, 1996).

The principal tool for dealing with sums of binomial coefficients in a systematic, mechanical way is to exploit the properties of *hypergeometric functions*, which are infinite series defined as follows in terms of rising factorial powers:

$$F\left(\begin{matrix}a_1, \ldots, a_m \\ b_1, \ldots, b_n\end{matrix} \,\middle|\, z\right) = \sum_{k \geq 0} \frac{a_1^{\bar{k}} \ldots a_m^{\bar{k}}}{b_1^{\bar{k}} \ldots b_n^{\bar{k}}} \frac{z^k}{k!}. \tag{39}$$

An introduction to these important functions can be found in Sections 5.5 and 5.6 of *CMath*. See also J. Dutka, *Archive for History of Exact Sciences* **31** (1984), 15–34, for historical references.

The concept of binomial coefficients has several significant generalizations, which we should discuss briefly. First, we can consider arbitrary real values of the lower index k in $\binom{r}{k}$; see exercises 40 through 45. We also have the generalization

$$\binom{r}{k}_q = \frac{(1 - q^r)(1 - q^{r-1}) \ldots (1 - q^{r-k+1})}{(1 - q^k)(1 - q^{k-1}) \ldots (1 - q^1)}, \tag{40}$$

which becomes the ordinary binomial coefficient $\binom{r}{k}_1 = \binom{r}{k}$ when q approaches the limiting value 1; this can be seen by dividing each term in numerator and denominator by $1 - q$. The basic properties of such "q-nomial coefficients" are discussed in exercise 58.

However, for our purposes the most important generalization is the *multinomial coefficient*

$$\binom{k_1 + k_2 + \cdots + k_m}{k_1, k_2, \ldots, k_m} = \frac{(k_1 + k_2 + \cdots + k_m)!}{k_1! \, k_2! \ldots k_m!}, \quad \text{integer } k_i \geq 0. \tag{41}$$

The chief property of multinomial coefficients is the generalization of Eq. (13):

$$(x_1 + x_2 + \cdots + x_m)^n = \sum_{k_1 + k_2 + \cdots + k_m = n} \binom{n}{k_1, k_2, \ldots, k_m} x_1^{k_1} x_2^{k_2} \ldots x_m^{k_m}. \tag{42}$$

It is important to observe that any multinomial coefficient can be expressed in terms of binomial coefficients:

$$\binom{k_1 + k_2 + \cdots + k_m}{k_1, k_2, \ldots, k_m} = \binom{k_1 + k_2}{k_1}\binom{k_1 + k_2 + k_3}{k_1 + k_2} \cdots \binom{k_1 + k_2 + \cdots + k_m}{k_1 + \cdots + k_{m-1}}, \tag{43}$$

so we may apply the techniques that we already know for manipulating binomial coefficients. Both sides of Eq. (20) are the trinomial coefficient

$$\binom{r}{k, \, m - k, \, r - m}.$$

Table 2
STIRLING NUMBERS OF BOTH KINDS

n	$\left[{n\atop 0}\right]$	$\left[{n\atop 1}\right]$	$\left[{n\atop 2}\right]$	$\left[{n\atop 3}\right]$	$\left[{n\atop 4}\right]$	$\left[{n\atop 5}\right]$	$\left[{n\atop 6}\right]$	$\left[{n\atop 7}\right]$	$\left[{n\atop 8}\right]$
0	1	0	0	0	0	0	0	0	0
1	0	1	0	0	0	0	0	0	0
2	0	1	1	0	0	0	0	0	0
3	0	2	3	1	0	0	0	0	0
4	0	6	11	6	1	0	0	0	0
5	0	24	50	35	10	1	0	0	0
6	0	120	274	225	85	15	1	0	0
7	0	720	1764	1624	735	175	21	1	0
8	0	5040	13068	13132	6769	1960	322	28	1

n	$\left\{{n\atop 0}\right\}$	$\left\{{n\atop 1}\right\}$	$\left\{{n\atop 2}\right\}$	$\left\{{n\atop 3}\right\}$	$\left\{{n\atop 4}\right\}$	$\left\{{n\atop 5}\right\}$	$\left\{{n\atop 6}\right\}$	$\left\{{n\atop 7}\right\}$	$\left\{{n\atop 8}\right\}$
0	1	0	0	0	0	0	0	0	0
1	0	1	0	0	0	0	0	0	0
2	0	1	1	0	0	0	0	0	0
3	0	1	3	1	0	0	0	0	0
4	0	1	7	6	1	0	0	0	0
5	0	1	15	25	10	1	0	0	0
6	0	1	31	90	65	15	1	0	0
7	0	1	63	301	350	140	21	1	0
8	0	1	127	966	1701	1050	266	28	1

For approximations valid when n is large, see L. Moser and M. Wyman, *J. London Math. Soc.* **33** (1958), 133–146; *Duke Math. J.* **25** (1958), 29–43; D. E. Barton, F. N. David, and M. Merrington, *Biometrika* **47** (1960), 439–445; **50** (1963), 169–176; N. M. Temme, *Studies in Applied Math.* **89** (1993), 233–243; H. S. Wilf, *J. Combinatorial Theory* **A64** (1993), 344–349; H.-K. Hwang, *J. Combinatorial Theory* **A71** (1995), 343–351.

We conclude this section with a brief analysis of the transformation from a polynomial expressed in powers of x to a polynomial expressed in binomial coefficients. The coefficients involved in this transformation are called *Stirling numbers*, and these numbers arise in the study of numerous algorithms.

Stirling numbers come in two flavors: We denote Stirling numbers of the first kind by $\left[{n\atop k}\right]$, and those of the second kind by $\left\{{n\atop k}\right\}$. These notations, due to Jovan Karamata [*Mathematica* (Cluj) **9** (1935), 164–178], have compelling advantages over the many other symbolisms that have been tried [see D. E. Knuth, *AMM* **99** (1992), 403–422]. We can remember the curly braces in $\left\{{n\atop k}\right\}$ because curly braces denote sets, and $\left\{{n\atop k}\right\}$ is the number of ways to partition a set of n elements into k disjoint subsets (exercise 64). The other Stirling numbers $\left[{n\atop k}\right]$ also have a combinatorial interpretation, which we will study in Section 1.3.3: $\left[{n\atop k}\right]$ is the number of permutations on n letters having k cycles.

Table 2 displays Stirling's triangles, which are in some ways analogous to Pascal's triangle.

Stirling numbers of the first kind are used to convert from factorial powers to ordinary powers:

$$x^{\underline{n}} = x(x-1)\ldots(x-n+1)$$

$$= \begin{bmatrix} n \\ n \end{bmatrix} x^n - \begin{bmatrix} n \\ n-1 \end{bmatrix} x^{n-1} + \cdots + (-1)^n \begin{bmatrix} n \\ 0 \end{bmatrix}$$

$$= \sum_k (-1)^{n-k} \begin{bmatrix} n \\ k \end{bmatrix} x^k. \tag{44}$$

For example, from Table 2,

$$\binom{x}{5} = \frac{x^{\underline{5}}}{5!} = \frac{1}{120}(x^5 - 10x^4 + 35x^3 - 50x^2 + 24x).$$

Stirling numbers of the second kind are used to convert from ordinary powers to factorial powers:

$$x^n = \begin{Bmatrix} n \\ n \end{Bmatrix} x^{\underline{n}} + \cdots + \begin{Bmatrix} n \\ 1 \end{Bmatrix} x^{\underline{1}} + \begin{Bmatrix} n \\ 0 \end{Bmatrix} x^{\underline{0}} = \sum_k \begin{Bmatrix} n \\ k \end{Bmatrix} x^{\underline{k}}. \tag{45}$$

This formula was, in fact, Stirling's original reason for studying the numbers $\begin{Bmatrix} n \\ k \end{Bmatrix}$ in his *Methodus Differentialis* (London: 1730). From Table 2 we have, for example,

$$x^5 = x^{\underline{5}} + 10x^{\underline{4}} + 25x^{\underline{3}} + 15x^{\underline{2}} + x^{\underline{1}}$$

$$= 120\binom{x}{5} + 240\binom{x}{4} + 150\binom{x}{3} + 30\binom{x}{2} + \binom{x}{1}.$$

We shall now list the most important identities involving Stirling numbers. In these equations, the variables m and n always denote nonnegative integers.

Addition formulas:

$$\begin{bmatrix} n+1 \\ m \end{bmatrix} = n\begin{bmatrix} n \\ m \end{bmatrix} + \begin{bmatrix} n \\ m-1 \end{bmatrix};$$

$$\begin{Bmatrix} n+1 \\ m \end{Bmatrix} = m\begin{Bmatrix} n \\ m \end{Bmatrix} + \begin{Bmatrix} n \\ m-1 \end{Bmatrix}. \tag{46}$$

Inversion formulas (compare with Eq. (33)):

$$\sum_k \begin{bmatrix} n \\ k \end{bmatrix}\begin{Bmatrix} k \\ m \end{Bmatrix}(-1)^{n-k} = \delta_{mn}, \quad \sum_k \begin{Bmatrix} n \\ k \end{Bmatrix}\begin{bmatrix} k \\ m \end{bmatrix}(-1)^{n-k} = \delta_{mn}. \tag{47}$$

Special values:

$$\binom{0}{n} = \begin{bmatrix} 0 \\ n \end{bmatrix} = \begin{Bmatrix} 0 \\ n \end{Bmatrix} = \delta_{n0}, \quad \binom{n}{n} = \begin{bmatrix} n \\ n \end{bmatrix} = \begin{Bmatrix} n \\ n \end{Bmatrix} = 1; \tag{48}$$

$$\begin{bmatrix} n \\ n-1 \end{bmatrix} = \begin{Bmatrix} n \\ n-1 \end{Bmatrix} = \binom{n}{2}; \tag{49}$$

$$\begin{bmatrix} n+1 \\ 0 \end{bmatrix} = \left\{ \begin{matrix} n+1 \\ 0 \end{matrix} \right\} = 0, \quad \begin{bmatrix} n+1 \\ 1 \end{bmatrix} = n!, \quad \left\{ \begin{matrix} n+1 \\ 1 \end{matrix} \right\} = 1, \quad \left\{ \begin{matrix} n+1 \\ 2 \end{matrix} \right\} = 2^n - 1.$$
$$(50)$$

Expansion formulas:

$$\sum_k \begin{bmatrix} n \\ k \end{bmatrix} \binom{k}{m} = \begin{bmatrix} n+1 \\ m+1 \end{bmatrix}, \quad \sum_k \begin{bmatrix} n+1 \\ k+1 \end{bmatrix} \binom{k}{m} (-1)^{k-m} = \begin{bmatrix} n \\ m \end{bmatrix}; \quad (51)$$

$$\sum_k \left\{ \begin{matrix} k \\ m \end{matrix} \right\} \binom{n}{k} = \left\{ \begin{matrix} n+1 \\ m+1 \end{matrix} \right\}, \quad \sum_k \left\{ \begin{matrix} k+1 \\ m+1 \end{matrix} \right\} \binom{n}{k} (-1)^{n-k} = \left\{ \begin{matrix} n \\ m \end{matrix} \right\}; \quad (52)$$

$$\sum_k \binom{m}{k} (-1)^{m-k} k^n = m! \left\{ \begin{matrix} n \\ m \end{matrix} \right\}; \quad (53)$$

$$\sum_k \binom{m-n}{m+k} \binom{m+n}{n+k} \left\{ \begin{matrix} m+k \\ k \end{matrix} \right\} = \begin{bmatrix} n \\ n-m \end{bmatrix},$$
$$\sum_k \binom{m-n}{m+k} \binom{m+n}{n+k} \begin{bmatrix} m+k \\ k \end{bmatrix} = \left\{ \begin{matrix} n \\ n-m \end{matrix} \right\}; \quad (54)$$

$$\sum_k \left\{ \begin{matrix} n+1 \\ k+1 \end{matrix} \right\} \begin{bmatrix} k \\ m \end{bmatrix} (-1)^{k-m} = \binom{n}{m}; \quad (55)$$

$$\sum_{k \le n} \begin{bmatrix} k \\ m \end{bmatrix} \frac{n!}{k!} = \begin{bmatrix} n+1 \\ m+1 \end{bmatrix}, \quad \sum_{k \le n} \left\{ \begin{matrix} k \\ m \end{matrix} \right\} (m+1)^{n-k} = \left\{ \begin{matrix} n+1 \\ m+1 \end{matrix} \right\}. \quad (56)$$

Some other fundamental Stirling number identities appear in exercises 1.2.6–61 and 1.2.7–6, and in Eqs. (23), (26), (27), and (28) of Section 1.2.9.

Eq. (49) is just one instance of a general phenomenon: Both kinds of Stirling numbers $\begin{bmatrix} n \\ n-m \end{bmatrix}$ and $\left\{ \begin{matrix} n \\ n-m \end{matrix} \right\}$ are polynomials in n of degree $2m$, whenever m is a nonnegative integer. For example, the formulas for $m = 2$ and $m = 3$ are

$$\begin{bmatrix} n \\ n-2 \end{bmatrix} = \binom{n}{4} + 2\binom{n+1}{4}, \qquad \left\{ \begin{matrix} n \\ n-2 \end{matrix} \right\} = \binom{n+1}{4} + 2\binom{n}{4};$$
$$\begin{bmatrix} n \\ n-3 \end{bmatrix} = \binom{n}{6} + 8\binom{n+1}{6} + 6\binom{n+2}{6}, \quad \left\{ \begin{matrix} n \\ n-3 \end{matrix} \right\} = \binom{n+2}{6} + 8\binom{n+1}{6} + 6\binom{n}{6}.$$
$$(57)$$

Therefore it makes sense to define the numbers $\begin{bmatrix} r \\ r-m \end{bmatrix}$ and $\left\{ \begin{matrix} r \\ r-m \end{matrix} \right\}$ for arbitrary real (or complex) values of r. With this generalization, the two kinds of Stirling numbers are united by an interesting duality law

$$\left\{ \begin{matrix} n \\ m \end{matrix} \right\} = \begin{bmatrix} -m \\ -n \end{bmatrix}, \quad (58)$$

which was implicit in Stirling's original discussion. Moreover, Eq. (45) remains true in general, in the sense that the infinite series

$$z^r = \sum_k \left\{ \begin{matrix} r \\ r-k \end{matrix} \right\} z^{\underline{r-k}} \tag{59}$$

converges whenever the real part of z is positive. The companion formula, Eq. (44), generalizes in a similar way to an asymptotic (but not convergent) series:

$$z^{\underline{r}} = \sum_{k=0}^{m} \left[\begin{matrix} r \\ r-k \end{matrix} \right] (-1)^k z^{r-k} + O(z^{r-m-1}). \tag{60}$$

(See exercise 65.) Sections 6.1, 6.2, and 6.5 of *CMath* contain additional information about Stirling numbers and how to manipulate them in formulas. See also exercise 4.7–21 for a general family of triangles that includes Stirling numbers as a very special case.

EXERCISES

1. [*00*] How many combinations of n things taken $n-1$ at a time are possible?

2. [*00*] What is $\binom{0}{0}$?

3. [*00*] How many bridge hands (13 cards out of a 52-card deck) are possible?

4. [*10*] Give the answer to exercise 3 as a product of prime numbers.

▶ **5.** [*05*] Use Pascal's triangle to explain the fact that $11^4 = 14641$.

▶ **6.** [*10*] Pascal's triangle (Table 1) can be extended in all directions by use of the addition formula, Eq. (9). Find the three rows that go on *top* of Table 1 (i.e., for $r = -1, -2$, and -3).

7. [*12*] If n is a fixed positive integer, what value of k makes $\binom{n}{k}$ a maximum?

8. [*00*] What property of Pascal's triangle is reflected in the "symmetry condition," Eq. (6)?

9. [*01*] What is the value of $\binom{n}{n}$? (Consider all integers n.)

▶ **10.** [*M25*] If p is prime, show that:

a) $\binom{n}{p} \equiv \left\lfloor \dfrac{n}{p} \right\rfloor$ (modulo p).

b) $\binom{p}{k} \equiv 0$ (modulo p), for $1 \le k \le p-1$.

c) $\binom{p-1}{k} \equiv (-1)^k$ (modulo p), for $0 \le k \le p-1$.

d) $\binom{p+1}{k} \equiv 0$ (modulo p), for $2 \le k \le p-1$.

e) (É. Lucas, 1877.)

$$\binom{n}{k} \equiv \binom{\lfloor n/p \rfloor}{\lfloor k/p \rfloor} \binom{n \bmod p}{k \bmod p} \quad \text{(modulo } p\text{)}.$$

f) If the p-ary number system representations of n and k are

$$\begin{matrix} n = a_r p^r + \cdots + a_1 p + a_0, \\ k = b_r p^r + \cdots + b_1 p + b_0, \end{matrix} \quad \text{then} \quad \binom{n}{k} \equiv \binom{a_r}{b_r} \cdots \binom{a_1}{b_1} \binom{a_0}{b_0} \quad \text{(modulo } p\text{)}.$$

▶ **11.** [*M20*] (E. Kummer, 1852.) Let p be prime. Show that if p^n divides

$$\binom{a+b}{a}$$

but p^{n+1} does not, then n is equal to the number of *carries* that occur when a is added to b in the p-ary number system. [*Hint:* See exercise 1.2.5–12.]

12. [*M22*] Are there any positive integers n for which all the nonzero entries in the nth row of Pascal's triangle are *odd*? If so, find all such n.

13. [*M13*] Prove the summation formula, Eq. (10).

14. [*M21*] Evaluate $\sum_{k=0}^{n} k^4$.

15. [*M15*] Prove the binomial formula, Eq. (13).

16. [*M15*] Given that n and k are positive integers, prove the symmetrical identity

$$(-1)^n \binom{-n}{k-1} = (-1)^k \binom{-k}{n-1}.$$

▶ **17.** [*M18*] Prove the Chu–Vandermonde formula (21) from Eq. (15), using the idea that $(1+x)^{r+s} = (1+x)^r (1+x)^s$.

18. [*M15*] Prove Eq. (22) using Eqs. (21) and (6).

19. [*M18*] Prove Eq. (23) by induction.

20. [*M20*] Prove Eq. (24) by using Eqs. (21) and (19), then show that another use of Eq. (19) yields Eq. (25).

▶ **21.** [*M05*] Both sides of Eq. (25) are polynomials in s; why isn't that equation an identity in s?

22. [*M20*] Prove Eq. (26) for the special case $s = n - 1 - r + nt$.

23. [*M13*] Assuming that Eq. (26) holds for (r, s, t, n) and $(r, s - t, t, n - 1)$, prove it for $(r, s + 1, t, n)$.

24. [*M15*] Explain why the results of the previous two exercises combine to give a proof of Eq. (26).

25. [*HM30*] Let the polynomial $A_n(x, t)$ be defined as in Eq. (30). Let $z = x^{t+1} - x^t$. Prove that $\sum_k A_k(r, t) z^k = x^r$, provided z is small enough. [*Note:* If $t = 0$, this result is essentially the binomial theorem, and this equation is an important generalization of the binomial theorem. The binomial theorem (15) may be assumed in the proof.] *Hint:* Start with the identity

$$\sum_j (-1)^j \binom{k}{j} \binom{r - jt}{k} \frac{r}{r - jt} = \delta_{k0}.$$

26. [*HM25*] Using the assumptions of the previous exercise, prove that

$$\sum_k \binom{r - tk}{k} z^k = \frac{x^{r+1}}{(t+1)x - t}.$$

27. [*HM21*] Solve Example 4 in the text by using the result of exercise 25; and prove Eq. (26) from the preceding two exercises. [*Hint:* See exercise 17.]

28. [*M25*] Prove that

$$\sum_k \binom{r+tk}{k}\binom{s-tk}{n-k} = \sum_{k \geq 0}\binom{r+s-k}{n-k}t^k,$$

if n is a nonnegative integer.

29. [*M20*] Show that Eq. (34) is just a special case of the general identity proved in exercise 1.2.3–33.

▶ **30.** [*M24*] Show that there is a better way to solve Example 3 than the way used in the text, by manipulating the sum so that Eq. (26) applies.

▶ **31.** [*M20*] Evaluate

$$\sum_k \binom{m-r+s}{k}\binom{n+r-s}{n-k}\binom{r+k}{m+n}$$

in terms of r, s, m, and n, given that m and n are integers. Begin by replacing

$$\binom{r+k}{m+n} \quad \text{by} \quad \sum_j \binom{r}{m+n-j}\binom{k}{j}.$$

32. [*M20*] Show that $\sum_k \genfrac{[}{]}{0pt}{}{n}{k}x^k = x^{\bar{n}}$, where $x^{\bar{n}}$ is the rising factorial power defined in Eq. 1.2.5–(19).

33. [*M20*] (A. Vandermonde, 1772.) Show that the binomial formula is valid also when it involves factorial powers instead of the ordinary powers. In other words, prove that

$$(x+y)^{\underline{n}} = \sum_k \binom{n}{k}x^{\underline{k}}y^{\underline{n-k}}; \qquad (x+y)^{\bar{n}} = \sum_k \binom{n}{k}x^{\bar{k}}y^{\overline{n-k}}.$$

34. [*M23*] (*Torelli's sum.*) In the light of the previous exercise, show that Abel's generalization, Eq. (16), of the binomial formula is true also for rising powers:

$$(x+y)^{\bar{n}} = \sum_k \binom{n}{k}x(x-kz+1)^{\overline{k-1}}(y+kz)^{\overline{n-k}}.$$

35. [*M23*] Prove the addition formulas (46) for Stirling numbers directly from the definitions, Eqs. (44) and (45).

36. [*M10*] What is the sum $\sum_k \binom{n}{k}$ of the numbers in each row of Pascal's triangle? What is the sum of these numbers with alternating signs, $\sum_k \binom{n}{k}(-1)^k$?

37. [*M10*] From the answers to the preceding exercise, deduce the value of the sum of every other entry in a row, $\binom{n}{0} + \binom{n}{2} + \binom{n}{4} + \cdots$.

38. [*HM30*] (C. Ramus, 1834.) Generalizing the result of the preceding exercise, show that we have the following formula, given that $0 \leq k < m$:

$$\binom{n}{k} + \binom{n}{m+k} + \binom{n}{2m+k} + \cdots = \frac{1}{m}\sum_{0 \leq j < m}\left(2\cos\frac{j\pi}{m}\right)^n \cos\frac{j(n-2k)\pi}{m}.$$

For example,

$$\binom{n}{1} + \binom{n}{4} + \binom{n}{7} + \cdots = \frac{1}{3}\left(2^n + 2\cos\frac{(n-2)\pi}{3}\right).$$

[*Hint:* Find the right combinations of these coefficients multiplied by mth roots of unity.] This identity is particularly remarkable when $m \geq n$.

39. [*M10*] What is the sum $\sum_k \left[{n \atop k}\right]$ of the numbers in each row of Stirling's first triangle? What is the sum of these numbers with alternating signs? (See exercise 36.)

40. [*HM17*] The *beta function* $B(x, y)$ is defined for positive real numbers x, y by the formula $B(x, y) = \int_0^1 t^{x-1}(1-t)^{y-1}\, dt$.

a) Show that $B(x, 1) = B(1, x) = 1/x$.

b) Show that $B(x + 1, y) + B(x, y + 1) = B(x, y)$.

c) Show that $B(x, y) = ((x + y)/y)\, B(x, y + 1)$.

41. [*HM22*] We proved a relation between the gamma function and the beta function in exercise 1.2.5–19, by showing that $\Gamma_m(x) = m^x B(x, m+1)$, if m is a positive integer.

a) Prove that

$$B(x, y) = \frac{\Gamma_m(y)m^x}{\Gamma_m(x+y)} B(x,\ y + m + 1).$$

b) Show that

$$B(x, y) = \frac{\Gamma(x)\Gamma(y)}{\Gamma(x+y)}.$$

42. [*HM10*] Express the binomial coefficient $\binom{r}{k}$ in terms of the beta function defined above. (This gives us a way to extend the definition to all real values of k.)

43. [*HM20*] Show that $B(1/2, 1/2) = \pi$. (From exercise 41 we may now conclude that $\Gamma(1/2) = \sqrt{\pi}$.)

44. [*HM20*] Using the generalized binomial coefficient suggested in exercise 42, show that

$$\binom{r}{1/2} = 2^{2r+1} \bigg/ \binom{2r}{r}\ \pi.$$

45. [*HM21*] Using the generalized binomial coefficient suggested in exercise 42, find $\lim_{r\to\infty} \binom{r}{k}/r^k$.

▶ **46.** [*M21*] Using Stirling's approximation, Eq. 1.2.5–(7), find an approximate value of $\binom{x+y}{y}$, assuming that both x and y are large. In particular, find the approximate size of $\binom{2n}{n}$ when n is large.

47. [*M21*] Given that k is an integer, show that

$$\binom{r}{k}\binom{r - 1/2}{k} = \binom{2r}{k}\binom{2r - k}{k}\bigg/4^k = \binom{2r}{2k}\binom{2k}{k}\bigg/4^k.$$

Give a simpler formula for the special case $r = -1/2$.

▶ **48.** [*M25*] Show that

$$\sum_{k\geq 0}\binom{n}{k}\frac{(-1)^k}{k + x} = \frac{n!}{x(x + 1)\dots(x + n)} = \frac{1}{x\binom{n+x}{n}},$$

if the denominators are not zero. [Note that this formula gives us the reciprocal of a binomial coefficient, as well as the partial fraction expansion of $1/x(x + 1)\dots(x + n)$.]

49. [*M20*] Show that the identity $(1 + x)^r = (1 - x^2)^r(1 - x)^{-r}$ implies a relation on binomial coefficients.

50. [*M20*] Prove Abel's formula, Eq. (16), in the special case $x + y = 0$.

51. [*M21*] Prove Abel's formula, Eq. (16), by writing $y = (x + y) - x$, expanding the right-hand side in powers of $(x + y)$, and applying the result of the previous exercise.

52. [*HM11*] Prove that Abel's binomial formula (16) is not always valid when n is not a nonnegative integer, by evaluating the right-hand side when $n = x = -1$, $y = z = 1$.

53. [*M25*] (a) Prove the following identity by induction on m, where m and n are integers:

$$\sum_{k=0}^{m} \binom{r}{k}\binom{s}{n-k}(nr-(r+s)k) = (m+1)(n-m)\binom{r}{m+1}\binom{s}{n-m}.$$

(b) Making use of important relations from exercise 47,

$$\binom{-1/2}{n} = \frac{(-1)^n}{2^{2n}}\binom{2n}{n}, \quad \binom{1/2}{n} = \frac{(-1)^{n-1}}{2^{2n}(2n-1)}\binom{2n}{n} = \frac{(-1)^{n-1}}{2^{2n-1}(2n-1)}\binom{2n-1}{n} - \delta_{n0},$$

show that the following formula can be obtained as a special case of the identity in part (a):

$$\sum_{k=0}^{m} \binom{2k-1}{k}\binom{2n-2k}{n-k}\frac{-1}{2k-1} = \frac{n-m}{2n}\binom{2m}{m}\binom{2n-2m}{n-m} + \frac{1}{2}\binom{2n}{n}.$$

(This result is considerably more general than Eq. (26) in the case $r = -1$, $s = 0$, $t = -2$.)

54. [*M21*] Consider Pascal's triangle (as shown in Table 1) as a matrix. What is the *inverse* of that matrix?

55. [*M21*] Considering each of Stirling's triangles (Table 2) as matrices, determine their inverses.

56. [*20*] (*The combinatorial number system.*) For each integer $n = 0, 1, 2, \ldots, 20$, find three integers a, b, c for which $n = \binom{a}{3} + \binom{b}{2} + \binom{c}{1}$ and $a > b > c \geq 0$. Can you see how this pattern can be continued for higher values of n?

▶ **57.** [*M22*] Show that the coefficient a_m in Stirling's attempt at generalizing the factorial function, Eq. 1.2.5–(12), is

$$\frac{(-1)^m}{m!}\sum_{k\geq 1}(-1)^k\binom{m-1}{k-1}\ln k.$$

58. [*M23*] (H. A. Rothe, 1811.) In the notation of Eq. (40), prove the "q-nomial theorem":

$$(1+x)(1+qx)\ldots(1+q^{n-1}x) = \sum_{k}\binom{n}{k}_q q^{k(k-1)/2}x^k.$$

Also find q-nomial generalizations of the fundamental identities (17) and (21).

59. [*M25*] A sequence of numbers A_{nk}, $n \geq 0$, $k \geq 0$, satisfies the relations $A_{n0} = 1$, $A_{0k} = \delta_{0k}$, $A_{nk} = A_{(n-1)k} + A_{(n-1)(k-1)} + \binom{n}{k}$ for $nk > 0$. Find A_{nk}.

▶ **60.** [*M23*] We have seen that $\binom{n}{k}$ is the number of combinations of n things, k at a time, namely the number of ways to choose k different things out of a set of n. The *combinations with repetitions* are similar to ordinary combinations, except that we may choose each object any number of times. Thus, the list (1) would be extended to include also *aaa, aab, aac, aad, aae, abb*, etc., if we were considering combinations with repetition. How many k-combinations of n objects are there, if repetition is allowed?

61. [*M25*] Evaluate the sum

$$\sum_k \begin{bmatrix} n+1 \\ k+1 \end{bmatrix} \begin{Bmatrix} k \\ m \end{Bmatrix} (-1)^{k-m},$$

thereby obtaining a companion formula for Eq. (55).

▶ **62.** [*M23*] The text gives formulas for sums involving a product of two binomial coefficients. Of the sums involving a product of three binomial coefficients, the following one and the identity of exercise 31 seem to be most useful:

$$\sum_k (-1)^k \binom{l+m}{l+k} \binom{m+n}{m+k} \binom{n+l}{n+k} = \frac{(l+m+n)!}{l!\,m!\,n!}, \quad \text{integer } l,m,n \geq 0.$$

(The sum includes both positive and negative values of k.) Prove this identity. [*Hint:* There is a very short proof, which begins by applying the result of exercise 31.]

63. [*M30*] If l, m, and n are integers and $n \geq 0$, prove that

$$\sum_{j,k} (-1)^{j+k} \binom{j+k}{k+l} \binom{r}{j} \binom{n}{k} \binom{s+n-j-k}{m-j} = (-1)^l \binom{n+r}{n+l} \binom{s-r}{m-n-l}.$$

▶ **64.** [*M20*] Show that $\begin{Bmatrix} n \\ m \end{Bmatrix}$ is the number of ways to partition a set of n elements into m nonempty disjoint subsets. For example, the set $\{1, 2, 3, 4\}$ can be partitioned into two subsets in $\begin{Bmatrix} 4 \\ 2 \end{Bmatrix} = 7$ ways: $\{1,2,3\}\{4\}$; $\{1,2,4\}\{3\}$; $\{1,3,4\}\{2\}$; $\{2,3,4\}\{1\}$; $\{1,2\}\{3,4\}$; $\{1,3\}\{2,4\}$; $\{1,4\}\{2,3\}$. *Hint:* Use Eq. (46).

65. [*HM35*] (B. F. Logan.) Prove Eqs. (59) and (60).

66. [*HM30*] Suppose x, y, and z are real numbers satisfying

$$\binom{x}{n} = \binom{y}{n} + \binom{z}{n-1},$$

where $x \geq n-1$, $y \geq n-1$, $z > n-2$, and n is an integer ≥ 2. Prove that

$$\binom{x}{n-1} \leq \binom{y}{n-1} + \binom{z}{n-2} \quad \text{if and only if} \quad y \geq z;$$
$$\binom{x}{n+1} \leq \binom{y}{n+1} + \binom{z}{n} \quad \text{if and only if} \quad y \leq z.$$

▶ **67.** [*M20*] We often need to know that binomial coefficients aren't too large. Prove the easy-to-remember upper bound

$$\binom{n}{k} \leq \left(\frac{ne}{k}\right)^k, \quad \text{when } n \geq k \geq 0.$$

68. [*M25*] (A. de Moivre.) Prove that, if n is a nonnegative integer,

$$\sum_k \binom{n}{k} p^k (1-p)^{n-k} |k - np| = 2\lceil np \rceil \binom{n}{\lceil np \rceil} p^{\lceil np \rceil} (1-p)^{n+1-\lceil np \rceil}.$$

1.2.7. Harmonic Numbers

The following sum will be of great importance in our later work:

$$H_n = 1 + \frac{1}{2} + \frac{1}{3} + \cdots + \frac{1}{n} = \sum_{k=1}^{n} \frac{1}{k}, \quad n \geq 0. \tag{1}$$

This sum does not occur very frequently in classical mathematics, and there is no standard notation for it; but in the analysis of algorithms it pops up nearly every time we turn around, and we will consistently call it H_n. Besides H_n, the notations h_n and S_n and $\psi(n+1) + \gamma$ are found in mathematical literature. The letter H stands for "harmonic," and we speak of H_n as a *harmonic number* because (1) is customarily called the harmonic series. Chinese bamboo strips written before 186 B.C. already explained how to compute $H_{10} = 7381/2520$, as an exercise in arithmetic. [See C. Cullen, *Historia Math.* **34** (2007), 10–44.]

It may seem at first that H_n does not get too large when n has a large value, since we are always adding smaller and smaller numbers. But actually it is not hard to see that H_n will get as large as we please if we take n to be big enough, because

$$H_{2^m} \geq 1 + \frac{m}{2}. \tag{2}$$

This lower bound follows from the observation that, for $m \geq 0$, we have

$$H_{2^{m+1}} = H_{2^m} + \frac{1}{2^m + 1} + \frac{1}{2^m + 2} + \cdots + \frac{1}{2^{m+1}}$$

$$\geq H_{2^m} + \frac{1}{2^{m+1}} + \frac{1}{2^{m+1}} + \cdots + \frac{1}{2^{m+1}} = H_{2^m} + \tfrac{1}{2}.$$

So as m increases by 1, the left-hand side of (2) increases by at least $\tfrac{1}{2}$.

It is important to have more detailed information about the value of H_n than is given in Eq. (2). The approximate size of H_n is a well-known quantity (at least in mathematical circles) that may be expressed as follows:

$$H_n = \ln n + \gamma + \frac{1}{2n} - \frac{1}{12n^2} + \frac{1}{120n^4} - \epsilon, \quad 0 < \epsilon < \frac{1}{252n^6}. \tag{3}$$

Here $\gamma = 0.5772156649\ldots$ is *Euler's constant*, introduced by Leonhard Euler in *Commentarii Acad. Sci. Imp. Pet.* **7** (1734), 150–161. Exact values of H_n for small n, and a 40-place value for γ, are given in the tables in Appendix A. We shall derive Eq. (3) in Section 1.2.11.2.

Thus H_n is reasonably close to the natural logarithm of n. Exercise 7(a) demonstrates in a simple way that H_n has a somewhat logarithmic behavior.

In a sense, H_n just barely goes to infinity as n gets large, because the similar sum

$$1 + \frac{1}{2^r} + \frac{1}{3^r} + \cdots + \frac{1}{n^r} \tag{4}$$

stays bounded for all n, when r is any real-valued exponent *greater* than unity. (See exercise 3.) We denote the sum in Eq. (4) by $H_n^{(r)}$.

When the exponent r in Eq. (4) is at least 2, the value of $H_n^{(r)}$ is fairly close to its maximum value $H_\infty^{(r)}$, except for very small n. The quantity $H_\infty^{(r)}$ is very well known in mathematics as *Riemann's zeta function*:

$$H_\infty^{(r)} = \zeta(r) = \sum_{k \geq 1} \frac{1}{k^r}. \tag{5}$$

If r is an even integer, the value of $\zeta(r)$ is known to be equal to

$$H_\infty^{(r)} = \frac{1}{2} |B_r| \frac{(2\pi)^r}{r!}, \qquad \text{integer } r/2 \geq 1, \tag{6}$$

where B_r is a Bernoulli number (see Section 1.2.11.2 and Appendix A). In particular,

$$H_\infty^{(2)} = \frac{\pi^2}{6}, \quad H_\infty^{(4)} = \frac{\pi^4}{90}, \quad H_\infty^{(6)} = \frac{\pi^6}{945}, \quad H_\infty^{(8)} = \frac{\pi^8}{9450}. \tag{7}$$

These results are due to Euler; for discussion and proof, see *CMath*, §6.5.

Now we will consider a few important sums that involve harmonic numbers. First,

$$\sum_{k=1}^{n} H_k = (n+1)H_n - n. \tag{8}$$

This follows from a simple interchange of summation:

$$\sum_{k=1}^{n} \sum_{j=1}^{k} \frac{1}{j} = \sum_{j=1}^{n} \sum_{k=j}^{n} \frac{1}{j} = \sum_{j=1}^{n} \frac{n+1-j}{j}.$$

Formula (8) is a special case of the sum $\sum_{k=1}^{n} \binom{k}{m} H_k$, which we will now determine using an important technique called *summation by parts* (see exercise 10). Summation by parts is a useful way to evaluate $\sum a_k b_k$ whenever the quantities $\sum a_k$ and $(b_{k+1} - b_k)$ have simple forms. We observe in this case that

$$\binom{k}{m} = \binom{k+1}{m+1} - \binom{k}{m+1},$$

and therefore

$$\binom{k}{m} H_k = \binom{k+1}{m+1} \left(H_{k+1} - \frac{1}{k+1} \right) - \binom{k}{m+1} H_k;$$

hence

$$\sum_{k=1}^{n} \binom{k}{m} H_k = \left(\binom{2}{m+1} H_2 - \binom{1}{m+1} H_1 \right) + \cdots$$

$$+ \left(\binom{n+1}{m+1} H_{n+1} - \binom{n}{m+1} H_n \right) - \sum_{k=1}^{n} \binom{k+1}{m+1} \frac{1}{k+1}$$

$$= \binom{n+1}{m+1} H_{n+1} - \binom{1}{m+1} H_1 - \frac{1}{m+1} \sum_{k=0}^{n} \binom{k}{m} + \frac{1}{m+1} \binom{0}{m}.$$

Applying Eq. 1.2.6–(11) yields the desired formula:

$$\sum_{k=1}^{n}\binom{k}{m}H_k = \binom{n+1}{m+1}\left(H_{n+1}-\frac{1}{m+1}\right). \tag{9}$$

(This derivation and its final result are analogous to the evaluation of

$$\int_{1}^{n} x^m \ln x \, dx = \frac{n^{m+1}}{m+1}\left(\ln n - \frac{1}{m+1}\right) + \frac{1}{(m+1)^2}$$

using what calculus books call integration by parts.)

We conclude this section by considering a different kind of sum, $\sum_k \binom{n}{k}x^k H_k$, which we will temporarily denote by S_n for brevity. We find that

$$S_{n+1} = \sum_{k}\left(\binom{n}{k}+\binom{n}{k-1}\right)x^k H_k = S_n + x\sum_{k\geq 1}\binom{n}{k-1}x^{k-1}\left(H_{k-1}+\frac{1}{k}\right)$$

$$= S_n + x\,S_n + \frac{1}{n+1}\sum_{k\geq 1}\binom{n+1}{k}x^k.$$

Hence $S_{n+1} = (x+1)S_n + \big((x+1)^{n+1}-1\big)/(n+1)$, and we have

$$\frac{S_{n+1}}{(x+1)^{n+1}} = \frac{S_n}{(x+1)^n} + \frac{1}{n+1} - \frac{1}{(n+1)(x+1)^{n+1}}.$$

This equation, together with the fact that $S_1 = x$, shows us that

$$\frac{S_n}{(x+1)^n} = H_n - \sum_{k=1}^{n}\frac{1}{k(x+1)^k}. \tag{10}$$

The new sum is part of the infinite series 1.2.9–(17) for $\ln\big(1/(1-1/(x+1))\big) = \ln(1+1/x)$, and when $x > 0$, the series is convergent; the difference is

$$\sum_{k>n}\frac{1}{k(x+1)^k} < \frac{1}{(n+1)(x+1)^{n+1}}\sum_{k\geq 0}\frac{1}{(x+1)^k} = \frac{1}{(n+1)(x+1)^n x}.$$

This proves the following theorem:

Theorem A. If $x > 0$, then

$$\sum_{k=1}^{n}\binom{n}{k}x^k H_k = (x+1)^n\left(H_n - \ln\left(1+\frac{1}{x}\right)\right) + \epsilon,$$

where $0 < \epsilon < 1/\big(x(n+1)\big)$. ∎

EXERCISES

1. [01] What are H_0, H_1, and H_2?

2. [13] Show that the simple argument used in the text to prove that $H_{2m} \geq 1+m/2$ can be slightly modified to prove that $H_{2m} \leq 1+m$.

3. [*M21*] Generalize the argument used in the previous exercise to show that, for $r > 1$, the sum $H_n^{(r)}$ remains bounded for all n. Find an upper bound.

▶ **4.** [*10*] Decide which of the following statements are true for all positive integers n:
(a) $H_n < \ln n$. (b) $H_n > \ln n$. (c) $H_n > \ln n + \gamma$.

5. [*15*] Give the value of H_{10000} to 15 decimal places, using the tables in Appendix A.

6. [*M15*] Prove that the harmonic numbers are directly related to Stirling's numbers, which were introduced in the previous section; in fact,

$$H_n = \begin{bmatrix} n+1 \\ 2 \end{bmatrix} \Big/ n!.$$

7. [*M21*] Let $T(m,n) = H_m + H_n - H_{mn}$. (a) Show that when m or n increases, $T(m,n)$ never increases (assuming that m and n are positive). (b) Compute the minimum and maximum values of $T(m,n)$ for $m, n > 0$.

8. [*HM18*] Compare Eq. (8) with $\sum_{k=1}^{n} \ln k$; estimate the difference as a function of n.

▶ **9.** [*M18*] Theorem A applies only when $x > 0$; what is the value of the sum considered when $x = -1$?

10. [*M20*] (*Summation by parts.*) We have used special cases of the general method of summation by parts in exercise 1.2.4–42 and in the derivation of Eq. (9). Prove the general formula

$$\sum_{1 \le k < n} (a_{k+1} - a_k) b_k = a_n b_n - a_1 b_1 - \sum_{1 \le k < n} a_{k+1}(b_{k+1} - b_k).$$

▶ **11.** [*M21*] Using summation by parts, evaluate

$$\sum_{1 < k \le n} \frac{1}{k(k-1)} H_k.$$

▶ **12.** [*M10*] Evaluate $H_\infty^{(1000)}$ correct to at least 100 decimal places.

13. [*M22*] Prove the identity

$$\sum_{k=1}^{n} \frac{x^k}{k} = H_n + \sum_{k=1}^{n} \binom{n}{k} \frac{(x-1)^k}{k}.$$

(Note in particular the special case $x = 0$, which gives us an identity related to exercise 1.2.6–48.)

14. [*M22*] Show that $\sum_{k=1}^{n} H_k/k = \frac{1}{2}(H_n^2 + H_n^{(2)})$, and evaluate $\sum_{k=1}^{n} H_k/(k+1)$.

▶ **15.** [*M23*] Express $\sum_{k=1}^{n} H_k^2$ in terms of n and H_n.

16. [*18*] Express the sum $1 + \frac{1}{3} + \cdots + \frac{1}{2n-1}$ in terms of harmonic numbers.

17. [*M24*] (E. Waring, 1782.) Let p be an odd prime. Show that the numerator of H_{p-1} is divisible by p.

18. [*M33*] (J. Selfridge.) What is the highest power of 2 that divides the numerator of $1 + \frac{1}{3} + \cdots + \frac{1}{2n-1}$?

▶ **19.** [*M30*] List all nonnegative integers n for which H_n is an integer. [*Hint:* If H_n has odd numerator and even denominator, it cannot be an integer.]

20. [*HM22*] There is an analytic way to approach summation problems such as the one leading to Theorem A in this section: If $f(x) = \sum_{k \geq 0} a_k x^k$, and this series converges for $x = x_0$, prove that

$$\sum_{k \geq 0} a_k x_0^k H_k = \int_0^1 \frac{f(x_0) - f(x_0 y)}{1 - y} \, dy.$$

21. [*M24*] Evaluate $\sum_{k=1}^n H_k/(n + 1 - k)$.

22. [*M28*] Evaluate $\sum_{k=0}^n H_k H_{n-k}$.

▶ **23.** [*HM20*] By considering the function $\Gamma'(x)/\Gamma(x)$, show how we can get a natural generalization of H_n to noninteger values of n. You may use the fact that $\Gamma'(1) = -\gamma$, anticipating the next exercise.

24. [*HM21*] Show that

$$xe^{\gamma x} \prod_{k \geq 1} \left(\left(1 + \frac{x}{k} \right) e^{-x/k} \right) = \frac{1}{\Gamma(x)}.$$

(Consider the partial products of this infinite product.)

1.2.8. Fibonacci Numbers

The sequence

$$0, \ 1, \ 1, \ 2, \ 3, \ 5, \ 8, \ 13, \ 21, \ 34, \ \ldots, \tag{1}$$

in which each number is the sum of the preceding two, plays an important role in at least a dozen seemingly unrelated algorithms that we will study later. The numbers in the sequence are denoted by F_n, and we formally define them as

$$F_0 = 0; \qquad F_1 = 1; \qquad F_{n+2} = F_{n+1} + F_n, \quad n \geq 0. \tag{2}$$

This famous sequence was published in 1202 by Leonardo Pisano (Leonardo of Pisa), who is sometimes called Leonardo Fibonacci (*Filius Bonaccii*, son of Bonaccio). His *Liber Abaci* (Book of the Abacus) contains the following exercise: "How many pairs of rabbits can be produced from a single pair in a year's time?" To solve this problem, we are told to assume that each pair produces a new pair of offspring every month, and that each new pair becomes fertile at the age of one month. Furthermore, the rabbits never die. After one month there will be 2 pairs of rabbits; after two months, there will be 3; the following month the original pair and the pair born during the first month will both usher in a new pair and there will be 5 in all; and so on.

Fibonacci was by far the greatest European mathematician of the Middle Ages. He studied the work of al-Khwārizmī (after whom "algorithm" is named, see Section 1.1) and he added numerous original contributions to arithmetic and geometry. The writings of Fibonacci were reprinted in 1857 [B. Boncompagni, *Scritti di Leonardo Pisano* (Rome, 1857–1862), 2 vols.; F_n appears in Vol. 1, 283–285]. His rabbit problem was, of course, not posed as a practical application to biology and the population explosion; it was an exercise in addition. In fact, it still makes a rather good computer exercise about addition (see exercise 3);

Fibonacci wrote: "It is possible to do [the addition] in this order for an infinite number of months."

Before Fibonacci wrote his work, the sequence $\langle F_n \rangle$ had already been discussed by Indian scholars, who had long been interested in rhythmic patterns that are formed from one-beat and two-beat notes or syllables. The number of such rhythms having n beats altogether is F_{n+1}; therefore both Gopāla (before 1135) and Hemacandra (c. 1150) mentioned the numbers 1, 2, 3, 5, 8, 13, 21, 34, ... explicitly. [See P. Singh, *Historia Math.* **12** (1985), 229–244; see also exercise 4.5.3–32.]

The same sequence also appears in the work of Johannes Kepler, 1611, who was musing about the numbers he saw around him [J. Kepler, *The Six-Cornered Snowflake* (Oxford: Clarendon Press, 1966), 21]. Kepler was presumably unaware of Fibonacci's brief mention of the sequence. Fibonacci numbers have often been observed in nature, probably for reasons similar to the original assumptions of the rabbit problem. [See Conway and Guy, *The Book of Numbers* (New York: Copernicus, 1996), 113–126, for an especially lucid explanation.]

A first indication of the intimate connections between F_n and algorithms came to light in 1837, when É. Léger used Fibonacci's sequence to study the efficiency of Euclid's algorithm. He observed that if the numbers m and n in Algorithm 1.1E are not greater than F_k, step E2 will be executed at most $k-1$ times. This was the first practical application of Fibonacci's sequence. (See Theorem 4.5.3F.) During the 1870s the mathematician É. Lucas obtained very profound results about the Fibonacci numbers, and in particular he used them to prove that the 39-digit number $2^{127}-1$ is prime. Lucas gave the name "Fibonacci numbers" to the sequence $\langle F_n \rangle$, and that name has been used ever since.

We already have examined the Fibonacci sequence briefly in Section 1.2.1 (Eq. (3) and exercise 4), where we found that $\phi^{n-2} \leq F_n \leq \phi^{n-1}$ if n is a positive integer and if

$$\phi = \tfrac{1}{2}(1 + \sqrt{5}\,). \tag{3}$$

We will see shortly that this quantity, ϕ, is intimately connected with the Fibonacci numbers.

The number ϕ itself has a very interesting history. Euclid called it the "extreme and mean ratio"; the ratio of A to B is the ratio of $A+B$ to A, if the ratio of A to B is ϕ. Renaissance writers called it the "divine proportion"; and in the last century it has commonly been called the "golden ratio." Many artists and writers have said that the ratio of ϕ to 1 is the most aesthetically pleasing proportion, and their opinion is confirmed from the standpoint of computer programming aesthetics as well. For the story of ϕ, see the excellent article "The Golden Section, Phyllotaxis, and Wythoff's Game," by H. S. M. Coxeter, *Scripta Math.* **19** (1953), 135–143; see also Chapter 8 of *The 2nd Scientific American Book of Mathematical Puzzles and Diversions*, by Martin Gardner (New York: Simon and Schuster, 1961). Several popular myths about ϕ have been debunked by George Markowsky in *College Math. J.* **23** (1992), 2–19. The fact that the ratio

F_{n+1}/F_n approaches ϕ was known to the early European reckoning master Simon Jacob, who died in 1564 [see P. Schreiber, *Historia Math.* **22** (1995), 422–424].

The notations we are using in this section are a little undignified. In much of the sophisticated mathematical literature, F_n is called u_n instead, and ϕ is called τ. Our notations are almost universally used in recreational mathematics (and some crank literature!) and they are rapidly coming into wider use. The designation ϕ comes from the name of the Greek artist Phidias who is said to have used the golden ratio in his sculpture. [See T. A. Cook, *The Curves of Life* (1914), 420.] The notation F_n is in accordance with that used in the *Fibonacci Quarterly*, where the reader may find numerous facts about the Fibonacci sequence. A good reference to the classical literature about F_n is Chapter 17 of L. E. Dickson's *History of the Theory of Numbers* **1** (Carnegie Inst. of Washington, 1919).

The Fibonacci numbers satisfy many interesting identities, some of which appear in the exercises at the end of this section. One of the most commonly discovered relations, mentioned by Kepler in a letter he wrote in 1608 but first published by J. D. Cassini [*Histoire Acad. Roy. Paris* **1** (1680), 201], is

$$F_{n+1}F_{n-1} - F_n^2 = (-1)^n, \tag{4}$$

which is easily proved by induction. A more esoteric way to prove the same formula starts with a simple inductive proof of the matrix identity

$$\begin{pmatrix} F_{n+1} & F_n \\ F_n & F_{n-1} \end{pmatrix} = \begin{pmatrix} 1 & 1 \\ 1 & 0 \end{pmatrix}^n. \tag{5}$$

We can then take the determinant of both sides of this equation.

Relation (4) shows that F_n and F_{n+1} are relatively prime, since any common divisor would have to be a divisor of $(-1)^n$.

From the definition (2) we find immediately that

$$F_{n+3} = F_{n+2} + F_{n+1} = 2F_{n+1} + F_n; \quad F_{n+4} = 3F_{n+1} + 2F_n;$$

and, in general, by induction that

$$F_{n+m} = F_m F_{n+1} + F_{m-1} F_n \tag{6}$$

for any positive integer m.

If we take m to be a multiple of n in Eq. (6), we find inductively that

$$F_{nk} \text{ is a multiple of } F_n.$$

Thus every third number is even, every fourth number is a multiple of 3, every fifth is a multiple of 5, and so on.

In fact, much more than this is true. If we write $\gcd(m, n)$ to stand for the greatest common divisor of m and n, a rather surprising theorem emerges:

Theorem A (É. Lucas, 1876). *A number divides both F_m and F_n if and only if it is a divisor of F_d, where $d = \gcd(m, n)$; in particular,*

$$\gcd(F_m, F_n) = F_{\gcd(m,n)}. \tag{7}$$

Proof. This result is proved by using Euclid's algorithm. We observe that because of Eq. (6) any common divisor of F_m and F_n is also a divisor of F_{n+m}; and, conversely, any common divisor of F_{n+m} and F_n is a divisor of $F_m F_{n+1}$. Since F_{n+1} is relatively prime to F_n, a common divisor of F_{n+m} and F_n also divides F_m. Thus we have proved that, for any number d,

$$d \text{ divides } F_m \text{ and } F_n \text{ if and only if } d \text{ divides } F_{m+n} \text{ and } F_n. \qquad (8)$$

We will now show that *any* sequence $\langle F_n \rangle$ for which statement (8) holds, and for which $F_0 = 0$, satisfies Theorem A.

First it is clear that statement (8) may be extended by induction on k to the rule

$$d \text{ divides } F_m \text{ and } F_n \text{ if and only if } d \text{ divides } F_{m+kn} \text{ and } F_n,$$

where k is any nonnegative integer. This result may be stated more succinctly:

$$d \text{ divides } F_{m \bmod n} \text{ and } F_n \text{ if and only if } d \text{ divides } F_m \text{ and } F_n. \qquad (9)$$

Now if r is the remainder after division of m by n, that is, if $r = m \bmod n$, then the common divisors of $\{F_m, F_n\}$ are the common divisors of $\{F_n, F_r\}$. It follows that throughout the manipulations of Algorithm 1.1E the set of common divisors of $\{F_m, F_n\}$ remains unchanged as m and n change; finally, when $r = 0$, the common divisors are simply the divisors of $F_0 = 0$ and $F_{\gcd(m,n)}$. ∎

Most of the important results involving Fibonacci numbers can be deduced from the representation of F_n in terms of ϕ, which we now proceed to derive. The method we shall use in the following derivation is extremely important, and the mathematically oriented reader should study it carefully; we will study the same method in detail in the next section.

We start by setting up the infinite series

$$\begin{aligned} G(z) &= F_0 + F_1 z + F_2 z^2 + F_3 z^3 + F_4 z^4 + \cdots \\ &= z + z^2 + 2z^3 + 3z^4 + \cdots. \end{aligned} \qquad (10)$$

We have no *a priori* reason to expect that this infinite sum exists or that the function $G(z)$ is at all interesting — but let us be optimistic and see what we can conclude about the function $G(z)$ if it does exist. The advantage of such a procedure is that $G(z)$ is a single quantity that represents the *entire* Fibonacci sequence at once; and if we find out that $G(z)$ is a "known" function, its coefficients can be determined. We call $G(z)$ the *generating function* for the sequence $\langle F_n \rangle$.

We can now proceed to investigate $G(z)$ as follows:

$$\begin{aligned} zG(z) &= F_0 z + F_1 z^2 + F_2 z^3 + F_3 z^4 + \cdots, \\ z^2 G(z) &= \qquad\quad F_0 z^2 + F_1 z^3 + F_2 z^4 + \cdots; \end{aligned}$$

by subtraction, therefore,

$$\begin{aligned} (1 - z - z^2)G(z) = F_0 &+ (F_1 - F_0)z + (F_2 - F_1 - F_0)z^2 \\ &+ (F_3 - F_2 - F_1)z^3 + (F_4 - F_3 - F_2)z^4 + \cdots. \end{aligned}$$

All terms but the second vanish because of the definition of F_n, so this expression equals z. Therefore we see that, if $G(z)$ exists,

$$G(z) = z/(1 - z - z^2).\tag{11}$$

In fact, this function *can* be expanded in an infinite series in z (a Taylor series); working backwards we find that the coefficients of the power series expansion of Eq. (11) must be the Fibonacci numbers.

We can now manipulate $G(z)$ and find out more about the Fibonacci sequence. The denominator $1 - z - z^2$ is a quadratic equation with the two roots $\frac{1}{2}(-1 \pm \sqrt{5})$; after a little calculation we find that $G(z)$ can be expanded by the method of partial fractions into the form

$$G(z) = \frac{1}{\sqrt{5}} \left(\frac{1}{1 - \phi z} - \frac{1}{1 - \hat{\phi} z} \right),\tag{12}$$

where

$$\hat{\phi} = 1 - \phi = \tfrac{1}{2}(1 - \sqrt{5}).\tag{13}$$

The quantity $1/(1 - \phi z)$ is the sum of the infinite geometric series $1 + \phi z + \phi^2 z^2 + \cdots$, so we have

$$G(z) = \frac{1}{\sqrt{5}} (1 + \phi z + \phi^2 z^2 + \cdots - 1 - \hat{\phi} z - \hat{\phi}^2 z^2 - \cdots).$$

We now look at the coefficient of z^n, which must be equal to F_n; hence

$$F_n = \frac{1}{\sqrt{5}} (\phi^n - \hat{\phi}^n).\tag{14}$$

This is an important closed form expression for the Fibonacci numbers, first discovered early in the eighteenth century. (See D. Bernoulli, *Comment. Acad. Sci. Petrop.* **3** (1728), 85–100, §7; see also A. de Moivre, *Philos. Trans.* **32** (1722), 162–178, who showed how to solve general linear recurrences in essentially the way we have derived (14).)

We could have merely stated Eq. (14) and proved it by induction. However, the point of the rather long derivation above was to show how it would be possible to *discover* the equation in the first place, using the important method of generating functions, which is a valuable technique for solving a wide variety of problems.

Many things can be proved from Eq. (14). First we observe that $\hat{\phi}$ is a *negative* number ($-0.61803\ldots$) whose magnitude is less than unity, so $\hat{\phi}^n$ gets very small as n gets large. In fact, the quantity $\hat{\phi}^n/\sqrt{5}$ is always small enough so that we have

$$F_n = \phi^n/\sqrt{5} \text{ rounded to the nearest integer.}\tag{15}$$

Other results can be obtained directly from $G(z)$; for example,

$$G(z)^2 = \frac{1}{5} \left(\frac{1}{(1 - \phi z)^2} + \frac{1}{(1 - \hat{\phi} z)^2} - \frac{2}{1 - z - z^2} \right),\tag{16}$$

and the coefficient of z^n in $G(z)^2$ is $\sum_{k=0}^{n} F_k F_{n-k}$. We deduce therefore that

$$\sum_{k=0}^{n} F_k F_{n-k} = \tfrac{1}{5}\big((n+1)(\phi^n + \hat{\phi}^n) - 2F_{n+1}\big)$$

$$= \tfrac{1}{5}\big((n+1)(F_n + 2F_{n-1}) - 2F_{n+1}\big)$$

$$= \tfrac{1}{5}(n-1)F_n + \tfrac{2}{5}nF_{n-1}. \tag{17}$$

(The second step in this derivation follows from the result of exercise 11.)

EXERCISES

1. [10] What is the answer to Leonardo Fibonacci's original problem: How many pairs of rabbits are present after a year?

▶ **2.** [20] In view of Eq. (15), what is the approximate value of F_{1000}? (Use logarithms found in Appendix A.)

3. [25] Write a computer program that calculates and prints F_1 through F_{1000} in decimal notation. (The previous exercise determines the size of numbers that must be handled.)

▶ **4.** [14] Find all n for which $F_n = n$.

5. [20] Find all n for which $F_n = n^2$.

6. [HM10] Prove Eq. (5).

▶ **7.** [15] If n is not a prime number, F_n is not a prime number (with one exception). Prove this and find the exception.

8. [15] In many cases it is convenient to define F_n for *negative* n, by assuming that $F_{n+2} = F_{n+1} + F_n$ for *all* integers n. Explore this possibility: What is F_{-1}? What is F_{-2}? Can F_{-n} be expressed in a simple way in terms of F_n?

9. [M20] Using the conventions of exercise 8, determine whether Eqs. (4), (6), (14), and (15) still hold when the subscripts are allowed to be *any* integers.

10. [15] Is $\phi^n/\sqrt{5}$ greater than F_n or less than F_n?

11. [M20] Show that $\phi^n = F_n\phi + F_{n-1}$ and $\hat{\phi}^n = F_n\hat{\phi} + F_{n-1}$, for *all* integers n.

▶ **12.** [M26] The "second order" Fibonacci sequence is defined by the rule

$$\mathcal{F}_0 = 0, \quad \mathcal{F}_1 = 1, \quad \mathcal{F}_{n+2} = \mathcal{F}_{n+1} + \mathcal{F}_n + F_n.$$

Express $\mathcal{F}_n$ in terms of F_n and F_{n+1}. [*Hint:* Use generating functions.]

▶ **13.** [M22] Express the following sequences in terms of the Fibonacci numbers, when r, s, and c are given constants:

a) $a_0 = r$, $a_1 = s$; $a_{n+2} = a_{n+1} + a_n$, for $n \geq 0$.
b) $b_0 = 0$, $b_1 = 1$; $b_{n+2} = b_{n+1} + b_n + c$, for $n \geq 0$.

14. [M28] Let m be a fixed positive integer. Find a_n, given that

$$a_0 = 0, \quad a_1 = 1; \quad a_{n+2} = a_{n+1} + a_n + \binom{n}{m}, \quad \text{for } n \geq 0.$$

15. [M22] Let $f(n)$ and $g(n)$ be arbitrary functions, and for $n \geq 0$ let

$$a_0 = 0, \quad a_1 = 1, \quad a_{n+2} = a_{n+1} + a_n + f(n);$$
$$b_0 = 0, \quad b_1 = 1, \quad b_{n+2} = b_{n+1} + b_n + g(n);$$
$$c_0 = 0, \quad c_1 = 1, \quad c_{n+2} = c_{n+1} + c_n + xf(n) + yg(n).$$

Express c_n in terms of x, y, a_n, b_n, and F_n.

▶ **16.** [*M20*] Fibonacci numbers appear implicitly in Pascal's triangle if it is viewed from
the right angle. Show that the following sum of binomial coefficients is a Fibonacci
number:
$$\sum_{k=0}^{n}\binom{n-k}{k}.$$

17. [*M24*] Using the conventions of exercise 8, prove the following generalization of
Eq. (4): $F_{n+k}F_{m-k} - F_n F_m = (-1)^n F_{m-n-k}F_k$.

18. [*20*] Is $F_n^2 + F_{n+1}^2$ always a Fibonacci number?

▶ **19.** [*M27*] What is $\cos 36°$?

20. [*M16*] Express $\sum_{k=0}^{n} F_k$ in terms of Fibonacci numbers.

21. [*M25*] What is $\sum_{k=0}^{n} F_k x^k$?

▶ **22.** [*M20*] Show that $\sum_k \binom{n}{k} F_{m+k}$ is a Fibonacci number.

23. [*M23*] Generalizing the preceding exercise, show that $\sum_k \binom{n}{k} F_t^k F_{t-1}^{n-k} F_{m+k}$ is
always a Fibonacci number.

24. [*HM20*] Evaluate the $n \times n$ determinant
$$\begin{pmatrix} 1 & -1 & 0 & 0 & \cdots & 0 & 0 & 0 \\ 1 & 1 & -1 & 0 & \cdots & 0 & 0 & 0 \\ 0 & 1 & 1 & -1 & \cdots & 0 & 0 & 0 \\ \vdots & \vdots & \vdots & \vdots & \ddots & \vdots & \vdots & \vdots \\ 0 & 0 & 0 & 0 & \cdots & 1 & 1 & -1 \\ 0 & 0 & 0 & 0 & \cdots & 0 & 1 & 1 \end{pmatrix}.$$

25. [*M21*] Show that
$$2^n F_n = 2\sum_{k\ \text{odd}}\binom{n}{k} 5^{(k-1)/2}.$$

▶ **26.** [*M20*] Using the previous exercise, show that $F_p \equiv 5^{(p-1)/2}$ (modulo p) if p is an
odd prime.

27. [*M20*] Using the previous exercise, show that if p is a prime different from 5, then
either F_{p-1} or F_{p+1} (not both) is a multiple of p.

28. [*M21*] What is $F_{n+1} - \phi F_n$?

▶ **29.** [*M23*] (*Fibonomial coefficients.*) Édouard Lucas defined the quantities
$$\binom{n}{k}_{\mathcal{F}} = \frac{F_n F_{n-1}\ldots F_{n-k+1}}{F_k F_{k-1}\ldots F_1} = \prod_{j=1}^{k}\left(\frac{F_{n-k+j}}{F_j}\right)$$

in a manner analogous to binomial coefficients. (a) Make a table of $\binom{n}{k}_{\mathcal{F}}$ for $0 \le k \le n \le 6$. (b) Show that $\binom{n}{k}_{\mathcal{F}}$ is always an integer because we have
$$\binom{n}{k}_{\mathcal{F}} = F_{k-1}\binom{n-1}{k}_{\mathcal{F}} + F_{n-k+1}\binom{n-1}{k-1}_{\mathcal{F}}.$$

▶ **30.** [*M38*] (D. Jarden, T. Motzkin.) The sequence of mth powers of Fibonacci numbers satisfies a recurrence relation in which each term depends on the preceding $m+1$
terms. Show that
$$\sum_k \binom{m}{k}_{\mathcal{F}}(-1)^{\lceil(m-k)/2\rceil} F_{n+k}^{m-1} = 0, \quad \text{if } m > 0.$$

For example, when $m = 3$ we get the identity $F_n^2 - 2F_{n+1}^2 - 2F_{n+2}^2 + F_{n+3}^2 = 0$.

31. [*M20*] Show that $F_{2n}\phi \bmod 1 = 1 - \phi^{-2n}$ and $F_{2n+1}\phi \bmod 1 = \phi^{-2n-1}$.

32. [*M24*] The remainder of one Fibonacci number divided by another is $\pm$ a Fibonacci number: Show that, modulo F_n,

$$F_{mn+r} \equiv \begin{cases} F_r, & \text{if } m \bmod 4 = 0; \\ (-1)^{r+1}F_{n-r}, & \text{if } m \bmod 4 = 1; \\ (-1)^n F_r, & \text{if } m \bmod 4 = 2; \\ (-1)^{r+1+n}F_{n-r}, & \text{if } m \bmod 4 = 3. \end{cases}$$

33. [*HM24*] Given that $z = \pi/2 + i \ln \phi$, show that $\sin nz/\sin z = i^{1-n}F_n$.

▶ **34.** [*M24*] (*The Fibonacci number system.*) Let the notation $k \gg m$ mean that $k \geq m + 2$. Show that every positive integer n has a *unique* representation $n = F_{k_1} + F_{k_2} + \cdots + F_{k_r}$, where $k_1 \gg k_2 \gg \cdots \gg k_r \gg 0$.

35. [*M24*] (*A phi number system.*) Consider real numbers written with the digits 0 and 1 using base ϕ; thus $(100.1)_\phi = \phi^2 + \phi^{-1}$. Show that there are infinitely many ways to represent the number 1; for example, $1 = (.11)_\phi = (.011111\ldots)_\phi$. But if we require that no two adjacent 1s occur and that the representation does not end with the infinite sequence $01010101\ldots$, then every nonnegative number has a unique representation. What are the representations of integers?

▶ **36.** [*M32*] (*Fibonacci strings.*) Let $S_1 = $ "a", $S_2 = $ "b", and $S_{n+2} = S_{n+1}S_n$, $n > 0$; in other words, S_{n+2} is formed by placing S_n at the right of S_{n+1}. We have $S_3 = $ "ba", $S_4 = $ "bab", $S_5 = $ "$babba$", etc. Clearly S_n has F_n letters. Explore the properties of S_n. (Where do double letters occur? Can you predict the value of the kth letter of S_n? What is the density of the b's? And so on.)

▶ **37.** [*M35*] (R. E. Gaskell, M. J. Whinihan.) Two players compete in the following game: There is a pile containing n chips; the first player removes any number of chips except that he cannot take the whole pile. From then on, the players alternate moves, each person removing one or more chips but *not more than twice as many chips as the preceding player has taken.* The player who removes the last chip wins. (For example, suppose that $n = 11$; player A removes 3 chips; player B may remove up to 6 chips, and he takes 1. There remain 7 chips; player A may take 1 or 2 chips, and he takes 2; player B may remove up to 4, and he picks up 1. There remain 4 chips; player A now takes 1; player B must take at least one chip and player A wins in the following turn.)

What is the best move for the first player to make if there are initially 1000 chips?

38. [*35*] Write a computer program that plays the game described in the previous exercise and that plays optimally.

39. [*M24*] Find a closed form expression for a_n, given that $a_0 = 0$, $a_1 = 1$, and $a_{n+2} = a_{n+1} + 6a_n$ for $n \geq 0$.

40. [*M25*] Solve the recurrence

$$f(1) = 0; \quad f(n) = \min_{0<k<n} \max(1 + f(k), 2 + f(n - k)), \quad \text{for } n > 1.$$

▶ **41.** [*M25*] (Yuri Matiyasevich, 1990.) Let $f(x) = \lfloor x + \phi^{-1} \rfloor$. Prove that if $n = F_{k_1} + \cdots + F_{k_r}$ is the representation of n in the Fibonacci number system of exercise 34, then $F_{k_1+1} + \cdots + F_{k_r+1} = f(\phi n)$. Find a similar formula for $F_{k_1-1} + \cdots + F_{k_r-1}$.

42. [*M26*] (D. A. Klarner.) Show that if m and n are nonnegative integers, there is a unique sequence of indices $k_1 \gg k_2 \gg \cdots \gg k_r$ such that

$$m = F_{k_1} + F_{k_2} + \cdots + F_{k_r}, \quad n = F_{k_1+1} + F_{k_2+1} + \cdots + F_{k_r+1}.$$

(See exercise 34. The k's may be negative, and r may be zero.)

1.2.9. Generating Functions

Whenever we want to obtain information about a sequence of numbers $\langle a_n \rangle = a_0, a_1, a_2, \ldots$, we can set up an infinite sum in terms of a "parameter" z,

$$G(z) = a_0 + a_1 z + a_2 z^2 + \cdots = \sum_{n \geq 0} a_n z^n. \qquad (1)$$

We can then try to obtain information about the function G. This function is a single quantity that represents the whole sequence; if the sequence $\langle a_n \rangle$ has been defined inductively (that is, if a_n has been defined in terms of $a_0, a_1, \ldots, a_{n-1}$) this is an important advantage. Furthermore, we can recover the individual values of a_0, a_1, ... from the function $G(z)$, assuming that the infinite sum in Eq. (1) exists for some nonzero value of z, by using techniques of differential calculus.

We call $G(z)$ the *generating function* for the sequence a_0, a_1, a_2, ... The use of generating functions opens up a whole new range of techniques, and it broadly increases our capacity for problem solving. As mentioned in the previous section, A. de Moivre introduced generating functions in order to solve the general linear recurrence problem. De Moivre's theory was extended to slightly more complicated recurrences by James Stirling, who showed how to apply differentiation and integration as well as arithmetic operations [*Methodus Differentialis* (London: 1730), Proposition 15]. A few years later, L. Euler began to use generating functions in several new ways, for example in his papers on partitions [*Commentarii Acad. Sci. Pet.* **13** (1741), 64–93; *Novi Comment. Acad. Sci. Pet.* **3** (1750), 125–169]. Pierre S. Laplace developed the techniques further in his classic work *Théorie Analytique des Probabilités* (Paris: 1812).

The question of convergence of the infinite sum (1) is of some importance. Any textbook about the theory of infinite series will prove that:

a) If the series converges for a particular value of $z = z_0$, then it converges for all values of z with $|z| < |z_0|$.

b) The series converges for some $z \neq 0$ if and only if the sequence $\langle \sqrt[n]{|a_n|} \rangle$ is bounded. (If this condition is not satisfied, we may be able to get a convergent series for the sequence $\langle a_n/n! \rangle$ or for some other related sequence.)

On the other hand, it often does not pay to worry about convergence of the series when we work with generating functions, since we are only exploring possible approaches to the solution of some problem. When we discover the solution by *any* means, however sloppy, we may be able to justify the solution independently. For example, in the previous section we used a generating function to deduce Eq. (14); yet once such an equation has been found, it is a simple matter to prove it by induction, and we need not even mention that we used generating functions to discover it. Furthermore one can show that most (if not all) of the operations we do with generating functions can be rigorously justified without regard to the convergence of the series. See, for example, E. T. Bell, *Trans. Amer. Math. Soc.* **25** (1923), 135–154; Ivan Niven, *AMM* **76** (1969),

871–889; Peter Henrici, *Applied and Computational Complex Analysis* **1** (Wiley, 1974), Chapter 1.

Let us now study the principal techniques used with generating functions.

A. Addition. If $G(z)$ is the generating function for $\langle a_n \rangle = a_0, a_1, \ldots$ and $H(z)$ is the generating function for $\langle b_n \rangle = b_0, b_1, \ldots$, then $\alpha G(z) + \beta H(z)$ is the generating function for $\langle \alpha a_n + \beta b_n \rangle = \alpha a_0 + \beta b_0, \alpha a_1 + \beta b_1, \ldots$:

$$\alpha \sum_{n \geq 0} a_n z^n + \beta \sum_{n \geq 0} b_n z^n = \sum_{n \geq 0} (\alpha a_n + \beta b_n) z^n. \tag{2}$$

B. Shifting. If $G(z)$ is the generating function for $\langle a_n \rangle = a_0, a_1, \ldots$ then $z^m G(z)$ is the generating function for $\langle a_{n-m} \rangle = 0, \ldots, 0, a_0, a_1, \ldots$:

$$z^m \sum_{n \geq 0} a_n z^n = \sum_{n \geq m} a_{n-m} z^n. \tag{3}$$

The last summation may be extended over all $n \geq 0$ if we regard $a_n = 0$ for any negative value of n.

Similarly, $\bigl(G(z) - a_0 - a_1 z - \cdots - a_{m-1} z^{m-1}\bigr)/z^m$ is the generating function for $\langle a_{n+m} \rangle = a_m, a_{m+1}, \ldots$:

$$z^{-m} \sum_{n \geq m} a_n z^n = \sum_{n \geq 0} a_{n+m} z^n. \tag{4}$$

We combined operations A and B to solve the Fibonacci problem in the previous section: $G(z)$ was the generating function for $\langle F_n \rangle$, $zG(z)$ for $\langle F_{n-1} \rangle$, $z^2 G(z)$ for $\langle F_{n-2} \rangle$, and $(1 - z - z^2)G(z)$ for $\langle F_n - F_{n-1} - F_{n-2} \rangle$. Then, since $F_n - F_{n-1} - F_{n-2}$ is zero when $n \geq 2$, we found that $(1 - z - z^2)G(z)$ is a polynomial. Similarly, given any *linearly recurrent* sequence, that is, a sequence where $a_n = c_1 a_{n-1} + \cdots + c_m a_{n-m}$, the generating function will be a polynomial divided by $(1 - c_1 z - \cdots - c_m z^m)$.

Let us consider the simplest example of all: If $G(z)$ is the generating function for the *constant* sequence $1, 1, 1, \ldots$, then $zG(z)$ generates $0, 1, 1, \ldots$, so $(1 - z)G(z) = 1$. This gives us the simple but very important formula

$$\frac{1}{1 - z} = 1 + z + z^2 + \cdots. \tag{5}$$

C. Multiplication. If $G(z)$ is the generating function for $a_0, a_1, \ldots$ and $H(z)$ is the generating function for $b_0, b_1, \ldots$, then

$$G(z)H(z) = (a_0 + a_1 z + a_2 z^2 + \cdots)(b_0 + b_1 z + b_2 z^2 + \cdots)$$
$$= (a_0 b_0) + (a_0 b_1 + a_1 b_0)z + (a_0 b_2 + a_1 b_1 + a_2 b_0)z^2 + \cdots;$$

thus $G(z)H(z)$ is the generating function for the sequence $c_0, c_1, \ldots$, where

$$c_n = \sum_{k=0}^{n} a_k b_{n-k}. \tag{6}$$

Equation (3) is a very special case of this. Another important special case occurs when each b_n is equal to unity:

$$\frac{1}{1-z}G(z) = a_0 + (a_0 + a_1)z + (a_0 + a_1 + a_2)z^2 + \cdots. \qquad (7)$$

Here we have the generating function for the sums of the original sequence.

The rule for a product of *three* functions follows from (6); $F(z)G(z)H(z)$ generates $d_0, d_1, d_2, \ldots$, where

$$d_n = \sum_{\substack{i,j,k \geq 0 \\ i+j+k=n}} a_i b_j c_k. \qquad (8)$$

The general rule for products of *any number* of functions (whenever this is meaningful) is

$$\prod_{j \geq 0} \sum_{k \geq 0} a_{jk} z^k = \sum_{n \geq 0} z^n \sum_{\substack{k_0, k_1, \ldots \geq 0 \\ k_0 + k_1 + \cdots = n}} a_{0k_0} a_{1k_1} \cdots. \qquad (9)$$

When the recurrence relation for some sequence involves binomial coefficients, we often want to get a generating function for a sequence $c_0, c_1, \ldots$ defined by

$$c_n = \sum_k \binom{n}{k} a_k b_{n-k}. \qquad (10)$$

In this case it is usually better to use generating functions for the sequences $\langle a_n/n! \rangle$, $\langle b_n/n! \rangle$, $\langle c_n/n! \rangle$, since we have

$$\left(\frac{a_0}{0!} + \frac{a_1}{1!}z + \frac{a_2}{2!}z^2 + \cdots \right) \left(\frac{b_0}{0!} + \frac{b_1}{1!}z + \frac{b_2}{2!}z^2 + \cdots \right) = \left(\frac{c_0}{0!} + \frac{c_1}{1!}z + \frac{c_2}{2!}z^2 + \cdots \right), \qquad (11)$$

where c_n is given by Eq. (10).

D. Change of z. Clearly $G(cz)$ is the generating function for the sequence $a_0, ca_1, c^2 a_2, \ldots$. As a particular case, the generating function for $1, c, c^2, c^3, \ldots$ is $1/(1-cz)$.

There is a familiar trick for extracting alternate terms of a series:

$$\begin{aligned}
\tfrac{1}{2}\big(G(z) + G(-z)\big) &= a_0 \; + \; a_2 z^2 \; + \; a_4 z^4 \; + \; \cdots, \\
\tfrac{1}{2}\big(G(z) - G(-z)\big) &= \quad\; a_1 z \; + \; a_3 z^3 \; + \; a_5 z^5 \; + \; \cdots.
\end{aligned} \qquad (12)$$

Using complex roots of unity, we can extend this idea and extract every mth term: Let $\omega = e^{2\pi i/m} = \cos(2\pi/m) + i\sin(2\pi/m)$; we have

$$\sum_{n \bmod m = r} a_n z^n = \frac{1}{m} \sum_{0 \leq k < m} \omega^{-kr} G(\omega^k z), \quad 0 \leq r < m. \qquad (13)$$

(See exercise 14.) For example, if $m = 3$ and $r = 1$, we have $\omega = -\frac{1}{2} + \frac{\sqrt{3}}{2}i$, a complex cube root of unity; it follows that

$$a_1 z + a_4 z^4 + a_7 z^7 + \cdots = \tfrac{1}{3}\big(G(z) + \omega^{-1}G(\omega z) + \omega^{-2}G(\omega^2 z)\big).$$

E. Differentiation and integration. The techniques of calculus give us further operations. If $G(z)$ is given by Eq. (1), the derivative is

$$G'(z) = a_1 + 2a_2 z + 3a_3 z^2 + \cdots = \sum_{k \geq 0} (k+1) a_{k+1} z^k. \tag{14}$$

The generating function for the sequence $\langle na_n \rangle$ is $zG'(z)$. Hence we can combine the nth term of a sequence with polynomials in n by manipulating the generating function.

Reversing the process, integration gives another useful operation:

$$\int_0^z G(t)\, dt = a_0 z + \frac{1}{2} a_1 z^2 + \frac{1}{3} a_2 z^3 + \cdots = \sum_{k \geq 1} \frac{1}{k} a_{k-1} z^k. \tag{15}$$

As special cases, we have the derivative and integral of (5):

$$\frac{1}{(1-z)^2} = 1 + 2z + 3z^2 + \cdots = \sum_{k \geq 0} (k+1) z^k. \tag{16}$$

$$\ln \frac{1}{1-z} = z + \frac{1}{2} z^2 + \frac{1}{3} z^3 + \cdots = \sum_{k \geq 1} \frac{1}{k} z^k. \tag{17}$$

We can combine the second formula with Eq. (7) to get the generating function for the harmonic numbers:

$$\frac{1}{1-z} \ln \frac{1}{1-z} = z + \frac{3}{2} z^2 + \frac{11}{6} z^3 + \cdots = \sum_{k \geq 0} H_k z^k. \tag{18}$$

F. Known generating functions. Whenever it is possible to determine the power series expansion of a function, we have implicitly found the generating function for a particular sequence. These special functions can be quite useful in conjunction with the operations described above. The most important power series expansions are given in the following list.

  i) *Binomial theorem.*

$$(1+z)^r = 1 + rz + \frac{r(r-1)}{2} z^2 + \cdots = \sum_{k \geq 0} \binom{r}{k} z^k. \tag{19}$$

When r is a negative integer, we get a special case already reflected in Eqs. (5) and (16):

$$\frac{1}{(1-z)^{n+1}} = \sum_{k \geq 0} \binom{-n-1}{k} (-z)^k = \sum_{k \geq 0} \binom{n+k}{n} z^k. \tag{20}$$

There is also a generalization, which was proved in exercise 1.2.6–25:

$$x^r = 1 + rz + \frac{r(r-2t-1)}{2} z^2 + \cdots = \sum_{k \geq 0} \binom{r-kt}{k} \frac{r}{r-kt} z^k, \tag{21}$$

if x is the continuous function of z that solves the equation $x^{t+1} = x^t + z$, where $x = 1$ when $z = 0$.

ii) *Exponential series.*

$$\exp z = e^z = 1 + z + \frac{1}{2!}z^2 + \cdots = \sum_{k \geq 0} \frac{1}{k!}z^k. \tag{22}$$

In general, we have the following formula involving Stirling numbers:

$$(e^z - 1)^n = z^n + \frac{1}{n+1}\left\{{n+1 \atop n}\right\}z^{n+1} + \cdots = n!\sum_k \left\{{k \atop n}\right\}\frac{z^k}{k!}. \tag{23}$$

iii) *Logarithm series* (see (17) and (18)).

$$\ln(1+z) = z - \frac{1}{2}z^2 + \frac{1}{3}z^3 - \cdots = \sum_{k \geq 1} \frac{(-1)^{k+1}}{k}z^k, \tag{24}$$

$$\frac{1}{(1-z)^{m+1}}\ln\left(\frac{1}{1-z}\right) = \sum_{k \geq 1}(H_{m+k} - H_m)\binom{m+k}{k}z^k. \tag{25}$$

Stirling numbers, as in (23), give us a more general equation:

$$\left(\ln\frac{1}{1-z}\right)^n = z^n + \frac{1}{n+1}\left[{n+1 \atop n}\right]z^{n+1} + \cdots = n!\sum_k \left[{k \atop n}\right]\frac{z^k}{k!}. \tag{26}$$

Further generalizations, including many sums of harmonic numbers, appear in papers by D. A. Zave, *Inf. Proc. Letters* **5** (1976), 75–77; J. Spieß, *Math. Comp.* **55** (1990), 839–863.

iv) *Miscellaneous.*

$$z(z+1)\ldots(z+n-1) = \sum_k \left[{n \atop k}\right]z^k, \tag{27}$$

$$\frac{z^n}{(1-z)(1-2z)\ldots(1-nz)} = \sum_k \left\{{k \atop n}\right\}z^k, \tag{28}$$

$$\frac{z}{e^z - 1} = 1 - \frac{1}{2}z + \frac{1}{12}z^2 + \cdots = \sum_{k \geq 0}\frac{B_k z^k}{k!}. \tag{29}$$

The coefficients B_k that appear in the last formula are the *Bernoulli numbers*; they will be examined further in Section 1.2.11.2. A table of Bernoulli numbers appears in Appendix A.

The next identity, analogous to (21), will be proved in exercise 2.3.4.4–29:

$$x^r = 1 + rz + \frac{r(r+2t)}{2}z^2 + \cdots = \sum_{k \geq 0}\frac{r(r+kt)^{k-1}}{k!}z^k, \tag{30}$$

if x is the continuous function of z that solves the equation $x = e^{zx^t}$, where $x = 1$ when $z = 0$. Significant generalizations of (21) and (30) are discussed in exercise 4.7–22.

G. Extracting a coefficient. It is often convenient to use the notation

$$[z^n] \, G(z) \tag{31}$$

for the coefficient of z^n in $G(z)$. For example, if $G(z)$ is the generating function in (1) we have $[z^n] \, G(z) = a_n$ and $[z^n] \, G(z)/(1 - z) = \sum_{k=0}^n a_k$. One of the most fundamental results in the theory of complex variables is a formula of A. L. Cauchy [*Exercices de Math.* **1** (1826), 95–113 = Œuvres (2) **6**, 124–145, Eq. (11)], by which we can extract any desired coefficient with the help of a contour integral:

$$[z^n] \, G(z) = \frac{1}{2\pi i} \oint_{|z|=r} \frac{G(z) \, dz}{z^{n+1}}, \tag{32}$$

if $G(z)$ converges for $z = z_0$ and $0 < r < |z_0|$. The basic idea is that $\oint_{|z|=r} z^m \, dz$ is zero for all integers m except $m = -1$, when the integral is

$$\int_{-\pi}^{\pi} (re^{i\theta})^{-1} d(re^{i\theta}) = i \int_{-\pi}^{\pi} d\theta = 2\pi i.$$

Equation (32) is of importance primarily when we want to study the approximate value of a coefficient.

We conclude this section by returning to a problem that was only partially solved in Section 1.2.3. We saw in Eq. 1.2.3–(13) and exercise 1.2.3–29 that

$$\sum_{1 \le i \le j \le n} x_i x_j = \frac{1}{2} \left(\sum_{k=1}^n x_k \right)^2 + \frac{1}{2} \left(\sum_{k=1}^n x_k^2 \right);$$

$$\sum_{1 \le i \le j \le k \le n} x_i x_j x_k = \frac{1}{6} \left(\sum_{k=1}^n x_k \right)^3 + \frac{1}{2} \left(\sum_{k=1}^n x_k \right) \left(\sum_{k=1}^n x_k^2 \right) + \frac{1}{3} \left(\sum_{k=1}^n x_k^3 \right).$$

In general, suppose that we have n numbers $x_1, x_2, \ldots, x_n$ and we want the sum

$$h_m = \sum_{1 \le j_1 \le \cdots \le j_m \le n} x_{j_1} \cdots x_{j_m}. \tag{33}$$

If possible, this sum should be expressed in terms of $S_1, S_2, \ldots, S_m$, where

$$S_j = \sum_{k=1}^n x_k^j, \tag{34}$$

the sum of jth powers. Using this more compact notation, the formulas above become $h_2 = \frac{1}{2} S_1^2 + \frac{1}{2} S_2$; $h_3 = \frac{1}{6} S_1^3 + \frac{1}{2} S_1 S_2 + \frac{1}{3} S_3$.

We can attack this problem by setting up the generating function

$$G(z) = 1 + h_1 z + h_2 z^2 + \cdots = \sum_{k \ge 0} h_k z^k. \tag{35}$$

By our rules for multiplying series, we find that

$$G(z) = (1 + x_1 z + x_1^2 z^2 + \cdots)(1 + x_2 z + x_2^2 z^2 + \cdots) \ldots (1 + x_n z + x_n^2 z^2 + \cdots)$$

$$= \frac{1}{(1 - x_1 z)(1 - x_2 z) \ldots (1 - x_n z)}. \tag{36}$$

So $G(z)$ is the reciprocal of a polynomial. It often helps to take the logarithm of a product, and we find from (17) that

$$\ln G(z) = \ln \frac{1}{1 - x_1 z} + \cdots + \ln \frac{1}{1 - x_n z}$$

$$= \left(\sum_{k \geq 1} \frac{x_1^k z^k}{k} \right) + \cdots + \left(\sum_{k \geq 1} \frac{x_n^k z^k}{k} \right) = \sum_{k \geq 1} \frac{S_k z^k}{k}. \tag{37}$$

Now $\ln G(z)$ has been expressed in terms of the S's; so all we must do to obtain the answer to our problem is to compute the power series expansion of $G(z)$ again, with the help of (22) and (9):

$$G(z) = e^{\ln G(z)} = \exp\left(\sum_{k \geq 1} \frac{S_k z^k}{k} \right) = \prod_{k \geq 1} e^{S_k z^k / k}$$

$$= \left(1 + S_1 z + \frac{S_1^2 z^2}{2!} + \cdots \right) \left(1 + \frac{S_2 z^2}{2} + \frac{S_2^2 z^4}{2^2 \cdot 2!} + \cdots \right) \cdots$$

$$= \sum_{m \geq 0} \left(\sum_{\substack{k_1, k_2, \ldots, k_m \geq 0 \\ k_1 + 2k_2 + \cdots + mk_m = m}} \frac{S_1^{k_1}}{1^{k_1} k_1!} \frac{S_2^{k_2}}{2^{k_2} k_2!} \cdots \frac{S_m^{k_m}}{m^{k_m} k_m!} \right) z^m. \tag{38}$$

The parenthesized quantity is h_m. This rather imposing sum is really not complicated when it is examined carefully. The number of terms for a particular value of m is $p(m)$, the number of partitions of m (Section 1.2.1). For example, one partition of 12 is

$$12 = 5 + 2 + 2 + 2 + 1;$$

this corresponds to a solution of the equation $k_1 + 2k_2 + \cdots + 12k_{12} = 12$, where k_j is the number of j's in the partition. In our example $k_1 = 1$, $k_2 = 3$, $k_5 = 1$, and the other k's are zero; so we get the term

$$\frac{S_1}{1^1 1!} \frac{S_2^3}{2^3 3!} \frac{S_5}{5^1 1!} = \frac{1}{240} S_1 S_2^3 S_5$$

as part of the expression for h_{12}. By differentiating (37) it is not difficult to derive the recurrence

$$h_n = \frac{1}{n}(S_1 h_{n-1} + S_2 h_{n-2} + \cdots + S_n h_0), \qquad n \geq 1. \tag{39}$$

An enjoyable introduction to the applications of generating functions has been given by G. Pólya, "On picture writing," *AMM* **63** (1956), 689–697; his approach is continued in *CMath*, Chapter 7. See also the book *generatingfunctionology* by H. S. Wilf, second edition (Academic Press, 1994).

A generating function is a clothesline
on which we hang up a sequence of numbers for display.
— H. S. WILF (1989)

EXERCISES

1. [*M12*] What is the generating function for the sequence $2, 5, 13, 35, \ldots = \langle 2^n + 3^n \rangle$?

▶ **2.** [*M13*] Prove Eq. (11).

3. [*HM21*] Differentiate the generating function (18) for $\langle H_n \rangle$, and compare this with the generating function for $\langle \sum_{k=0}^{n} H_k \rangle$. What relation can you deduce?

4. [*M01*] Explain why Eq. (19) is a special case of Eq. (21).

5. [*M20*] Prove Eq. (23) by induction on n.

▶ **6.** [*HM15*] Find the generating function for

$$\left\langle \sum_{0 < k < n} \frac{1}{k(n-k)} \right\rangle ;$$

differentiate it and express the coefficients in terms of harmonic numbers.

7. [*M15*] Verify all the steps leading to Eq. (38).

8. [*M23*] Find the generating function for $p(n)$, the number of partitions of n.

9. [*M11*] In the notation of Eqs. (34) and (35), what is h_4 in terms of S_1, S_2, S_3, and S_4?

▶ **10.** [*M25*] An *elementary symmetric function* is defined by the formula

$$e_m = \sum_{1 \le j_1 < \cdots < j_m \le n} x_{j_1} \ldots x_{j_m}.$$

(This is the same as h_m of Eq. (33), except that equal subscripts are not allowed.) Find the generating function for e_m, and express e_m in terms of the S_j in Eq. (34). Write out the formulas for e_1, e_2, e_3, and e_4.

▶ **11.** [*M25*] Equation (39) can also be used to express the S's in terms of the h's: We find $S_1 = h_1$, $S_2 = 2h_2 - h_1^2$, $S_3 = 3h_3 - 3h_1 h_2 + h_1^3$, etc. What is the coefficient of $h_1^{k_1} h_2^{k_2} \ldots h_m^{k_m}$ in this representation of S_m, when $k_1 + 2k_2 + \cdots + mk_m = m$?

▶ **12.** [*M20*] Suppose we have a doubly subscripted sequence $\langle a_{mn} \rangle$ for $m, n = 0, 1, \ldots$; show how this double sequence can be represented by a *single* generating function of two variables, and determine the generating function for $\langle \binom{n}{m} \rangle$.

13. [*HM22*] The *Laplace transform* of a function $f(x)$ is the function

$$\mathbf{L}f(s) = \int_0^\infty e^{-st} f(t) \, dt.$$

Given that $a_0, a_1, a_2, \ldots$ is an infinite sequence having a convergent generating function, let $f(x)$ be the step function $\sum_k a_k$ $[0 \le k \le x]$. Express the Laplace transform of $f(x)$ in terms of the generating function G for this sequence.

14. [*HM21*] Prove Eq. (13).

15. [*M28*] By considering $H(w) = \sum_{n \geq 0} G_n(z) w^n$, find a closed form for the generating function

$$G_n(z) = \sum_{k=0}^{n} \binom{n-k}{k} z^k = \sum_{k=0}^{n} \binom{2k-n-1}{k} (-z)^k.$$

16. [*M22*] Give a simple formula for the generating function $G_{nr}(z) = \sum_k a_{nkr} z^k$, where a_{nkr} is the number of ways to choose k out of n objects, subject to the condition that each object may be chosen at most r times. (If $r = 1$, we have $\binom{n}{k}$ ways, and if $r \geq k$, we have the number of combinations with repetitions as in exercise 1.2.6–60.)

17. [*M25*] What are the coefficients of $1/(1-z)^w$ if this function is expanded into a *double* power series in terms of both z and w?

▶ **18.** [*M25*] Given positive integers n and r, find a simple formula for the value of the following sums: (a) $\sum_{1 \leq k_1 < k_2 < \cdots < k_r \leq n} k_1 k_2 \ldots k_r$; (b) $\sum_{1 \leq k_1 \leq k_2 \leq \cdots \leq k_r \leq n} k_1 k_2 \ldots k_r$. (For example, when $n = 3$ and $r = 2$ the sums are, respectively, $1 \cdot 2 + 1 \cdot 3 + 2 \cdot 3$ and $1 \cdot 1 + 1 \cdot 2 + 1 \cdot 3 + 2 \cdot 2 + 2 \cdot 3 + 3 \cdot 3$.)

19. [*HM32*] (C. F. Gauss, 1812.) The sums of the following infinite series are well known:

$$1 - \frac{1}{2} + \frac{1}{3} - \frac{1}{4} + \cdots = \ln 2; \quad 1 - \frac{1}{3} + \frac{1}{5} - \frac{1}{7} + \cdots = \frac{\pi}{4};$$

$$1 - \frac{1}{4} + \frac{1}{7} - \frac{1}{10} + \cdots = \frac{\pi\sqrt{3}}{9} + \frac{1}{3}\ln 2.$$

Using the definition

$$H_x = \sum_{n \geq 1} \left(\frac{1}{n} - \frac{1}{n+x} \right)$$

found in the answer to exercise 1.2.7–24, these series may be written respectively as

$$1 - \frac{1}{2}H_{1/2}; \quad \frac{2}{3} - \frac{1}{4}H_{1/4} + \frac{1}{4}H_{3/4}; \quad \frac{3}{4} - \frac{1}{6}H_{1/6} + \frac{1}{6}H_{2/3}.$$

Prove that, in general, $H_{p/q}$ has the value

$$\frac{q}{p} - \frac{\pi}{2}\cot\frac{p}{q}\pi - \ln 2q + 2 \sum_{0 < k < q/2} \cos\frac{2pk}{q}\pi \cdot \ln\sin\frac{k}{q}\pi,$$

when p and q are integers with $0 < p < q$. [*Hint:* By Abel's limit theorem the sum is

$$\lim_{x \to 1-} \sum_{n \geq 1} \left(\frac{1}{n} - \frac{1}{n+p/q} \right) x^{p+nq}.$$

Use Eq. (13) to express this power series in such a way that the limit can be evaluated.]

20. [*M21*] For what coefficients c_{mk} is $\sum_{n \geq 0} n^m z^n = \sum_{k=0}^{m} c_{mk} z^k / (1-z)^{k+1}$?

21. [*HM30*] Set up the generating function for the sequence $\langle n! \rangle$ and study properties of this function.

22. [*M21*] Find a generating function $G(z)$ for which

$$[z^n] G(z) = \sum_{k_0 + 2k_1 + 4k_2 + 8k_3 + \cdots = n} \binom{r}{k_0}\binom{r}{k_1}\binom{r}{k_2}\binom{r}{k_3} \cdots .$$

23. [*M33*] (L. Carlitz.) (a) Prove that for all integers $m \geq 1$ there are polynomials $f_m(z_1, \ldots, z_m)$ and $g_m(z_1, \ldots, z_m)$ such that the formula

$$\sum_{k_1, \ldots, k_m \geq 0} \binom{r}{n - k_1} \binom{k_1}{n - k_2} \cdots \binom{k_{m-1}}{n - k_m} z_1^{k_1} \ldots z_m^{k_m}$$

$$= f_m(z_1, \ldots, z_m)^{n-r} g_m(z_1, \ldots, z_m)^{r}$$

is an identity for all integers $n \geq r \geq 0$.

(b) Generalizing exercise 15, find a closed form for the sum

$$S_n(z_1, \ldots, z_m) = \sum_{k_1, \ldots, k_m \geq 0} \binom{k_1}{n - k_2} \binom{k_2}{n - k_3} \cdots \binom{k_m}{n - k_1} z_1^{k_1} \ldots z_m^{k_m}$$

in terms of the functions f_m and g_m in part (a).

(c) Find a simple expression for $S_n(z_1, \ldots, z_m)$ when $z_1 = \cdots = z_m = z$.

24. [*M22*] Prove that, if $G(z)$ is any generating function, we have

$$\sum_k \binom{m}{k} [z^{n-k}] G(z)^k = [z^n] (1 + zG(z))^m.$$

Evaluate both sides of this identity when $G(z)$ is (a) $1/(1 - z)$; (b) $(e^z - 1)/z$.

▶ **25.** [*M23*] Evaluate the sum $\sum_k \binom{n}{k} \binom{2n-2k}{n-k} (-2)^k$ by simplifying the equivalent formula $\sum_k [w^k] (1 - 2w)^n [z^{n-k}] (1 + z)^{2n-2k}$.

26. [*M40*] Explore a generalization of the notation (31) according to which we might write, for example, $[z^2 - 2z^5] G(z) = a_2 - 2a_5$ when $G(z)$ is given by (1).

1.2.10. Analysis of an Algorithm

Let us now apply some of the techniques of the preceding sections to the study of a typical algorithm.

Algorithm M (*Find the maximum*). Given n elements $X[1], X[2], \ldots, X[n]$, we will find m and j such that $m = X[j] = \max_{1 \leq i \leq n} X[i]$, where j is the largest index that satisfies this relation.

M1. [Initialize.] Set $j \leftarrow n$, $k \leftarrow n - 1$, $m \leftarrow X[n]$. (During this algorithm we will have $m = X[j] = \max_{k < i \leq n} X[i]$.)

M2. [All tested?] If $k = 0$, the algorithm terminates.

M3. [Compare.] If $X[k] \leq m$, go to M5.

M4. [Change m.] Set $j \leftarrow k$, $m \leftarrow X[k]$. (This value of m is a new current maximum.)

M5. [Decrease k.] Decrease k by one and return to M2. ▮

This rather obvious algorithm may seem so trivial that we shouldn't bother to analyze it in detail; but it actually makes a good demonstration of the way in which more complicated algorithms may be studied. Analysis of algorithms is quite important in computer programming, because there are usually several algorithms available for a particular application and we would like to know which is best.

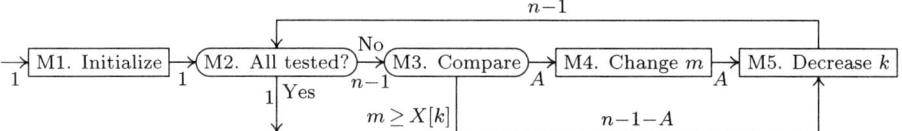

Fig. 9. Algorithm M. Labels on the arrows indicate the number of times each path is taken. Note that "Kirchhoff's first law" must be satisfied: The amount of flow into each node must equal the amount of flow going out.

Algorithm M requires a fixed amount of storage, so we will analyze only the time required to perform it. To do this, we will count the number of times each step is executed (see Fig. 9):

Step number	Number of times
M1	1
M2	n
M3	$n - 1$
M4	A
M5	$n - 1$

Knowing the number of times each step is executed gives us the information necessary to determine the running time on a particular computer.

In the table above we know everything except the quantity A, which is the number of times we must change the value of the current maximum. To complete the analysis, we shall study this interesting quantity A.

The analysis usually consists of finding the *minimum* value of A (for optimistic people), the *maximum* value of A (for pessimistic people), the *average* value of A (for probabilistic people), and the *standard deviation* of A (a quantitative indication of how close to the average we may expect the value to be).

The *minimum* value of A is zero; this happens if

$$X[n] = \max_{1 \le k \le n} X[k].$$

The *maximum* value is $n - 1$; this happens in case

$$X[1] > X[2] > \cdots > X[n].$$

Thus the average value lies between 0 and $n - 1$. Is it $\frac{1}{2}n$? Is it $\sqrt{n}$? To answer this question we need to define what we mean by the average; and to define the average properly, we must make some assumptions about the characteristics of the input data $X[1], X[2], \ldots, X[n]$. *We will assume that the $X[k]$ are distinct values, and that each of the $n!$ permutations of these values is equally likely.* (This is a reasonable assumption to make in most situations, but the analysis can be carried out under other assumptions, as shown in the exercises at the end of this section.)

The performance of Algorithm M does not depend on the precise values of the $X[k]$; only the relative order is involved. For example, if $n = 3$ we are assuming that each of the following six possibilities is equally probable:

Situation	Value of A	Situation	Value of A
$X[1] < X[2] < X[3]$	0	$X[2] < X[3] < X[1]$	1
$X[1] < X[3] < X[2]$	1	$X[3] < X[1] < X[2]$	1
$X[2] < X[1] < X[3]$	0	$X[3] < X[2] < X[1]$	2

The average value of A when $n = 3$ comes to $(0 + 1 + 0 + 1 + 1 + 2)/6 = 5/6$.

It is clear that we may take $X[1], X[2], \ldots, X[n]$ to be the numbers $1, 2, \ldots, n$ in some order; under our assumption we regard each of the $n!$ permutations as equally likely. The *probability* that A has the value k will be

$$p_{nk} = (\text{number of permutations of } n \text{ objects for which } A = k)/n!. \qquad (1)$$

For example, from our table above, $p_{30} = \frac{1}{3}$, $p_{31} = \frac{1}{2}$, $p_{32} = \frac{1}{6}$.

The *average* ("mean" or "expected") value is defined, as usual, to be

$$A_n = \sum_k k p_{nk}. \qquad (2)$$

The *variance* V_n is defined to be the average value of $(A - A_n)^2$; we have therefore

$$V_n = \sum_k (k - A_n)^2 p_{nk} = \sum_k k^2 p_{nk} - 2A_n \sum_k k p_{nk} + A_n^2 \sum_k p_{nk}$$

$$= \sum_k k^2 p_{nk} - 2A_n A_n + A_n^2 = \sum_k k^2 p_{nk} - A_n^2. \qquad (3)$$

Finally, the *standard deviation* σ_n is defined to be $\sqrt{V_n}$.

The significance of σ_n can perhaps best be understood by noting that, for all $r \geq 1$, the probability that A fails to lie within $r\sigma_n$ of its average value is less than $1/r^2$. For example, $|A - A_n| > 2\sigma_n$ with probability $< 1/4$. (*Proof:* Let p be the stated probability. Then if $p > 0$, the average value of $(A - A_n)^2$ is more than $p \cdot (r\sigma_n)^2 + (1 - p) \cdot 0$; that is, $V_n > pr^2 V_n$.) This is usually called *Chebyshev's inequality*, although it was actually discovered first by J. Bienaymé [*Comptes Rendus Acad. Sci.* **37** (Paris, 1853), 320–321].

We can determine the behavior of A by determining the probabilities p_{nk}. It is not hard to do this inductively: By Eq. (1) we want to count the number of permutations on n elements that have $A = k$. Let this number be $P_{nk} = n! \, p_{nk}$.

Consider the permutations $x_1 x_2 \ldots x_n$ on $\{1, 2, \ldots, n\}$, as in Section 1.2.5. If $x_1 = n$, the value of A is *one higher* than the value obtained on $x_2 \ldots x_n$; if $x_1 \neq n$, the value of A is *exactly the same* as its value on $x_2 \ldots x_n$. Therefore we find that $P_{nk} = P_{(n-1)(k-1)} + (n-1)P_{(n-1)k}$, or equivalently

$$p_{nk} = \frac{1}{n} p_{(n-1)(k-1)} + \frac{n-1}{n} p_{(n-1)k}. \qquad (4)$$

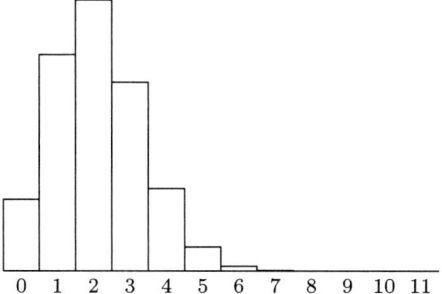

Fig. 10. Probability distribution for step M4, when $n = 12$. The mean is $58301/27720$, or approximately 2.10. The variance is approximately 1.54.

This equation will determine p_{nk} if we provide the initial conditions

$$p_{1k} = \delta_{0k}; \qquad p_{nk} = 0 \quad \text{if } k < 0. \tag{5}$$

We can now get information about the quantities p_{nk} by using generating functions. Let

$$G_n(z) = p_{n0} + p_{n1}z + \cdots = \sum_k p_{nk}z^k. \tag{6}$$

We know that $A \leq n - 1$, so $p_{nk} = 0$ for large values of k; thus $G_n(z)$ is actually a polynomial, even though an infinite sum has been specified for convenience.

From Eq. (5) we have $G_1(z) = 1$; and from Eq. (4) we have

$$G_n(z) = \frac{z}{n} G_{n-1}(z) + \frac{n-1}{n} G_{n-1}(z) = \frac{z+n-1}{n} G_{n-1}(z). \tag{7}$$

(The reader should study the relation between Eqs. (4) and (7) carefully.) We can now see that

$$G_n(z) = \frac{z+n-1}{n} G_{n-1}(z) = \frac{z+n-1}{n} \frac{z+n-2}{n-1} G_{n-2}(z) = \cdots$$

$$= \frac{1}{n!}(z+n-1)(z+n-2)\dots(z+1)$$

$$= \frac{1}{z+n}\binom{z+n}{n}. \tag{8}$$

So $G_n(z)$ is essentially a binomial coefficient!

This function appears in the previous section, Eq. 1.2.9–(27), where we have

$$G_n(z) = \frac{1}{n!}\sum_k \begin{bmatrix} n \\ k \end{bmatrix} z^{k-1}.$$

Therefore p_{nk} can be expressed in terms of Stirling numbers:

$$p_{nk} = \begin{bmatrix} n \\ k+1 \end{bmatrix} \bigg/ n!. \tag{9}$$

Figure 10 shows the approximate sizes of p_{nk} when $n = 12$.

Now all we must do is plug this value of p_{nk} into Eqs. (2) and (3) and we have the desired average value. But this is easier said than done. It is, in fact, unusual to be able to determine the probabilities p_{nk} explicitly; in most problems we will know the generating function $G_n(z)$, but we will not have any special knowledge about the actual probabilities. The important fact is that *we can determine the mean and variance easily from the generating function itself.*

To see this, let's suppose that we have a generating function whose coefficients represent probabilities:

$$G(z) = p_0 + p_1 z + p_2 z^2 + \cdots.$$

Here p_k is the probability that some event has a value k. We wish to calculate the quantities

$$\text{mean}(G) = \sum_k k p_k, \quad \text{var}(G) = \sum_k k^2 p_k - \big(\text{mean}(G)\big)^2. \tag{10}$$

Using differentiation, it is not hard to discover how to do this. Note that

$$G(1) = 1, \tag{11}$$

since $G(1) = p_0 + p_1 + p_2 + \cdots$ is the sum of all possible probabilities. Similarly, since $G'(z) = \sum_k k p_k z^{k-1}$, we have

$$\text{mean}(G) = \sum_k k p_k = G'(1). \tag{12}$$

Finally, we apply differentiation again and we obtain (see exercise 2)

$$\text{var}(G) = G''(1) + G'(1) - G'(1)^2. \tag{13}$$

Equations (12) and (13) give the desired expressions of the mean and variance in terms of the generating function.

In our case, we wish to calculate $G_n'(1) = A_n$. From Eq. (7) we have

$$G_n'(z) = \frac{1}{n} G_{n-1}(z) + \frac{z+n-1}{n} G_{n-1}'(z);$$

$$G_n'(1) = \frac{1}{n} + G_{n-1}'(1).$$

From the initial condition $G_1'(1) = 0$, we find therefore

$$A_n = G_n'(1) = H_n - 1. \tag{14}$$

This is the desired average number of times step M4 is executed; it is approximately $\ln n$ when n is large. [*Note:* The rth moment of $A+1$, namely the quantity $\sum_k (k+1)^r p_{nk}$, is $[z^n] (1-z)^{-1} \sum_k \left\{{r \atop k}\right\} (\ln \frac{1}{1-z})^k$, and it has the approximate value $(\ln n)^r$; see P. B. M. Roes *CACM* **9** (1966), 342. The distribution of A was first studied by F. G. Foster and A. Stuart, *J. Roy. Stat. Soc.* **B16** (1954), 1–22.]

We can proceed similarly to calculate the variance V_n. Before doing this, let us state an important simplification:

Theorem A. *Let G and H be two generating functions with $G(1) = H(1) = 1$. If the quantities $\mathrm{mean}(G)$ and $\mathrm{var}(G)$ are defined by Eqs. (12) and (13), we have*

$$\mathrm{mean}(GH) = \mathrm{mean}(G) + \mathrm{mean}(H); \qquad \mathrm{var}(GH) = \mathrm{var}(G) + \mathrm{var}(H). \quad (15)$$

We will prove this theorem later. It tells us that the mean and variance of a product of generating functions may be reduced to a sum. ∎

Letting $Q_n(z) = (z + n - 1)/n$, we have $Q'_n(1) = 1/n$, $Q''_n(1) = 0$; hence

$$\mathrm{mean}(Q_n) = \frac{1}{n}, \quad \mathrm{var}(Q_n) = \frac{1}{n} - \frac{1}{n^2}.$$

Finally, since $G_n(z) = \prod_{k=2}^{n} Q_k(z)$, it follows that

$$\mathrm{mean}(G_n) = \sum_{k=2}^{n} \mathrm{mean}(Q_k) = \sum_{k=2}^{n} \frac{1}{k} = H_n - 1;$$

$$\mathrm{var}(G_n) = \sum_{k=2}^{n} \mathrm{var}(Q_k) = \sum_{k=1}^{n} \left(\frac{1}{k} - \frac{1}{k^2} \right) = H_n - H_n^{(2)}.$$

Summing up, we have found the desired statistics related to quantity A:

$$A = \left(\min\ 0, \quad \mathrm{ave}\ H_n - 1, \quad \max\ n - 1, \quad \mathrm{dev}\ \sqrt{H_n - H_n^{(2)}} \right). \quad (16)$$

The notation used in Eq. (16) will be used to describe the statistical characteristics of other probabilistic quantities throughout this book.

We have completed the analysis of Algorithm M; the new feature that has appeared in this analysis is the introduction of probability theory. Elementary probability theory is sufficient for most of the applications in this book: The simple counting techniques and the definitions of mean, variance, and standard deviation already given will answer most of the questions we want to ask. More complicated algorithms will help us develop an ability to reason fluently about probabilities.

Let us consider some simple probability problems, to get a little more practice using these methods. In all probability the first question that comes to mind is a coin-tossing problem: Suppose we flip a coin n times and there is a probability p that heads turns up after any particular toss; what is the average number of heads that will occur? What is the standard deviation?

We will consider our coin to be biased; that is, we will not assume that $p = \frac{1}{2}$. This makes the problem more interesting, and, furthermore, every real coin is biased (or we could not tell one side from the other).

Proceeding as before, we let p_{nk} be the probability that k heads will occur, and let $G_n(z)$ be the corresponding generating function. We have clearly

$$p_{nk} = p\, p_{(n-1)(k-1)} + q\, p_{(n-1)k}, \qquad (17)$$

where $q = 1 - p$ is the probability that tails turns up. As before, we argue from Eq. (17) that $G_n(z) = (q + pz)G_{n-1}(z)$; and from the obvious initial condition

$G_1(z) = q + pz$ we have

$$G_n(z) = (q + pz)^n. \tag{18}$$

Hence, by Theorem A,

$$\text{mean}(G_n) = n \ \text{mean}(G_1) = pn;$$
$$\text{var}(G_n) = n \ \text{var}(G_1) = (p - p^2)n = pqn.$$

For the number of heads, we have therefore

$$(\text{min } 0, \quad \text{ave } pn, \quad \text{max } n, \quad \text{dev } \sqrt{pqn}). \tag{19}$$

Figure 11 shows the values of p_{nk} when $p = \frac{3}{5}$, $n = 12$. When the standard deviation is proportional to $\sqrt{n}$ and the difference between maximum and minimum is proportional to n, we may consider the situation "stable" about the average.

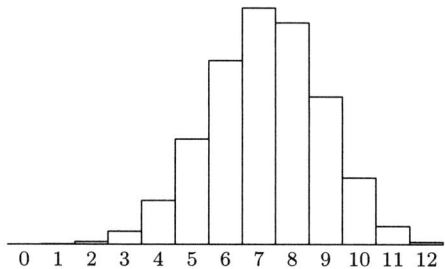

0 1 2 3 4 5 6 7 8 9 10 11 12

Fig. 11. Probability distribution for coin-tossing: 12 independent tosses with a chance of success equal to 3/5 at each toss.

Let us work one more simple problem. Suppose that in some process there is *equal* probability of obtaining the values $1, 2, \ldots, n$. The generating function for this situation is

$$G(z) = \frac{1}{n}z + \frac{1}{n}z^2 + \cdots + \frac{1}{n}z^n = \frac{1}{n}\frac{z^{n+1} - z}{z - 1}. \tag{20}$$

We find after some rather laborious calculation that

$$G'(z) = \frac{nz^{n+1} - (n+1)z^n + 1}{n(z-1)^2};$$

$$G''(z) = \frac{n(n-1)z^{n+1} - 2(n+1)(n-1)z^n + n(n+1)z^{n-1} - 2}{n(z-1)^3}.$$

Now to calculate the mean and variance, we need to know $G'(1)$ and $G''(1)$; but the form in which we have expressed these equations reduces to $0/0$ when we substitute $z = 1$. This makes it necessary to find the limit as z approaches unity, and that is a nontrivial task.

Fortunately there is a much simpler way to proceed. By Taylor's theorem we have

$$G(1 + z) = G(1) + G'(1)z + \frac{G''(1)}{2!}z^2 + \cdots; \tag{21}$$

therefore we merely have to replace z by $z+1$ in (20) and read off the coefficients:

$$G(1+z) = \frac{1}{n}\frac{(1+z)^{n+1}-1-z}{z} = 1 + \frac{n+1}{2}z + \frac{(n+1)(n-1)}{6}z^2 + \cdots.$$

It follows that $G'(1) = \frac{1}{2}(n+1)$, $G''(1) = \frac{1}{3}(n+1)(n-1)$, and the statistics for the uniform distribution are

$$\left(\min 1, \quad \text{ave}\ \frac{n+1}{2}, \quad \max n, \quad \text{dev}\ \sqrt{\frac{(n+1)(n-1)}{12}}\right). \tag{22}$$

In this case the deviation of approximately $0.289n$ gives us a recognizably *unstable* situation.

We conclude this section by proving Theorem A and relating our notions to classical probability theory. Suppose X is a random variable that takes on only nonnegative integer values, where $X = k$ with probability p_k. Then $G(z) = p_0 + p_1 z + p_2 z^2 + \cdots$ is called the *probability generating function* for X, and the quantity $G(e^{it}) = p_0 + p_1 e^{it} + p_2 e^{2it} + \cdots$ is conventionally called the *characteristic function* of this distribution. The distribution given by the product of two such generating functions is called the *convolution* of the two distributions, and it represents the sum of two independent random variables belonging to those respective distributions.

The mean or average value of a random quantity X is often called its *expected value*, and denoted by $\mathrm{E}\,X$. The variance of X is then $\mathrm{E}\,X^2 - (\mathrm{E}\,X)^2$. Using this notation, the probability generating function for X is $G(z) = \mathrm{E}\,z^X$, the expected value of z^X, in cases when X takes only nonnegative integer values. Similarly, if X is a statement that is either true or false, the probability that X is true is $\Pr(X) = \mathrm{E}[X]$, using Iverson's convention $\bigl(\mathrm{Eq.}\ 1.2.3\text{--}(16)\bigr)$.

The mean and variance are just two of the so-called *semi-invariants* or *cumulants* introduced by T. N. Thiele in 1889 [see A. Hald, *International Statistical Review* **68** (2000), 137–153]. The semi-invariants $\kappa_1, \kappa_2, \kappa_3, \ldots$ are defined by the rule

$$\frac{\kappa_1 t}{1!} + \frac{\kappa_2 t^2}{2!} + \frac{\kappa_3 t^3}{3!} + \cdots = \ln G(e^t). \tag{23}$$

We have

$$\kappa_n = \frac{d^n}{dt^n}\ln G(e^t)\bigg|_{t=0};$$

in particular,

$$\kappa_1 = \frac{e^t G'(e^t)}{G(e^t)}\bigg|_{t=0} = G'(1)$$

because $G(1) = \sum_k p_k = 1$, and

$$\kappa_2 = \frac{e^{2t}G''(e^t)}{G(e^t)} + \frac{e^t G'(e^t)}{G(e^t)} - \frac{e^{2t}G'(e^t)^2}{G(e^t)^2}\bigg|_{t=0} = G''(1) + G'(1) - G'(1)^2.$$

Since the semi-invariants are defined in terms of the *logarithm* of a generating function, Theorem A is obvious, and, in fact, it can be generalized to apply to all of the semi-invariants.

A *normal distribution* is one for which all semi-invariants are zero except the mean and variance. In a normal distribution, we can improve significantly on Chebyshev's inequality: The probability that a normally distributed random value differs from the mean by less than the standard deviation is

$$\frac{1}{\sqrt{2\pi}} \int_{-1}^{+1} e^{-t^2/2}\, dt,$$

that is, about 68.268949213709% of the time. The difference is less than twice the standard deviation about 95.449973610364% of the time, and it is less than three times the standard deviation about 99.730020393674% of the time. The distributions specified by Eqs. (8) and (18) are *approximately* normal when n is large (see exercises 13 and 14).

We often need to know that a random variable is unlikely to be much larger or smaller than its mean value. Two extremely simple yet powerful formulas, called the *tail inequalities*, provide convenient estimates of such probabilities. If X has the probability generating function $G(z)$, then

$$\Pr(X \le r) \le x^{-r}G(x) \qquad \text{for } 0 < x \le 1; \tag{24}$$
$$\Pr(X \ge r) \le x^{-r}G(x) \qquad \text{for } x \ge 1. \tag{25}$$

The proofs are easy: If $G(z) = p_0 + p_1 z + p_2 z^2 + \cdots$, we have

$$\Pr(X \le r) = p_0 + p_1 + \cdots + p_{\lfloor r \rfloor} \le x^{-r}p_0 + x^{1-r}p_1 + \cdots + x^{\lfloor r \rfloor - r}p_{\lfloor r \rfloor} \le x^{-r}G(x)$$

when $0 < x \le 1$, and

$$\Pr(X \ge r) = p_{\lceil r \rceil} + p_{\lceil r \rceil + 1} + \cdots \le x^{\lceil r \rceil - r}p_{\lceil r \rceil} + x^{\lceil r \rceil + 1 - r}p_{\lceil r \rceil + 1} + \cdots \le x^{-r}G(x)$$

when $x \ge 1$. By choosing values of x that minimize or approximately minimize the right-hand sides of (24) and (25), we often obtain upper bounds that are fairly close to the true tail probabilities on the left-hand sides.

Exercises 21–23 illustrate the tail inequalities in several important cases. These inequalities are special cases of a more general principle first pointed out by A. N. Kolmogorov in his book *Grundbegriffe der Wahrscheinlichkeitsrechnung* (Springer, 1933): If $f(t) \ge s > 0$ for all $t \ge r$, then $\Pr(X \ge r) \le s^{-1} \mathrm{E} f(X)$ whenever $\mathrm{E} f(X)$ exists. We obtain (25) when $f(t) = x^t$ and $s = x^r$.

EXERCISES

1. [10] Determine the value of p_{n0} from Eqs. (4) and (5) and interpret this result from the standpoint of Algorithm M.

2. [HM16] Derive Eq. (13) from Eq. (10).

3. [M15] What are the minimum, maximum, average, and standard deviation of the number of times step M4 is executed, if we are using Algorithm M to find the maximum of 1000 randomly ordered, distinct items? (Give your answer as decimal approximations to these quantities.)

4. [M10] Give an explicit, closed formula for the values of p_{nk} in the coin-tossing experiment, Eq. (17).

5. [M13] What are the mean and standard deviation of the distribution in Fig. 11?

6. [*HM27*] We have computed the mean and the variance of the important probability distributions (8), (18), (20). What is the *third* semi-invariant, κ_3, in each of those cases?

▶ **7.** [*M27*] In our analysis of Algorithm M, we assumed that all the $X[k]$ were distinct. Suppose, instead, that we make only the weaker assumption that $X[1], X[2], \ldots, X[n]$ contain precisely m distinct values; the values are otherwise random, subject to this constraint. What is the probability distribution of A in this case?

▶ **8.** [*M20*] Suppose that each $X[k]$ is taken at random from a set of M distinct elements, so that each of the M^n possible choices for $X[1], X[2], \ldots, X[n]$ is considered equally likely. What is the probability that all the $X[k]$ will be distinct?

9. [*M25*] Generalize the result of the preceding exercise to find a formula for the probability that exactly m distinct values occur among the X's. Express your answer in terms of Stirling numbers.

10. [*M20*] Combine the results of the preceding three exercises to obtain a formula for the probability that $A = k$ under the assumption that each X is selected at random from a set of M objects.

▶ **11.** [*M15*] What happens to the semi-invariants of a distribution if we change $G(z)$ to $F(z) = z^n G(z)$?

12. [*HM21*] When $G(z) = p_0 + p_1 z + p_2 z^2 + \cdots$ represents a probability distribution, the quantities $M_n = \sum_k k^n p_k$ and $m_n = \sum_k (k - M_1)^n p_k$ are called the "nth moment" and "nth central moment," respectively. Show that $G(e^t) = 1 + M_1 t + M_2 t^2/2! + \cdots$; then use Arbogast's formula (exercise 1.2.5–21) to show that

$$\kappa_n = \sum_{\substack{k_1, k_2, \ldots, k_n \geq 0 \\ k_1 + 2k_2 + \cdots = n}} \frac{(-1)^{k_1 + k_2 + \cdots + k_n - 1} n! \, (k_1 + k_2 + \cdots + k_n - 1)!}{k_1! \, 1!^{k_1} k_2! \, 2!^{k_2} \ldots k_n! \, n!^{k_n}} M_1^{k_1} M_2^{k_2} \ldots M_n^{k_n}.$$

In particular, $\kappa_1 = M_1$, $\kappa_2 = M_2 - M_1^2$ (as we already knew), $\kappa_3 = M_3 - 3M_1 M_2 + 2M_1^3$, and $\kappa_4 = M_4 - 4M_1 M_3 + 12M_1^2 M_2 - 3M_2^2 - 6M_1^4$. What are the analogous expressions for κ_n in terms of the central moments $m_2, m_3, \ldots$, when $n \geq 2$?

13. [*HM38*] A sequence of probability generating functions $G_n(z)$ with means μ_n and deviations σ_n is said to *approach a normal distribution* if

$$\lim_{n \to \infty} e^{-it\mu_n/\sigma_n} G_n(e^{it/\sigma_n}) = e^{-t^2/2}$$

for all real values of t. Using $G_n(z)$ as given by Eq. (8), show that $G_n(z)$ approaches a normal distribution.

Note: "Approaching the normal distribution," as defined here, can be shown to be equivalent to the fact that

$$\lim_{n \to \infty} \Pr\left(\frac{X_n - \mu_n}{\sigma_n} \leq x\right) = \frac{1}{\sqrt{2\pi}} \int_{-\infty}^{x} e^{-t^2/2} \, dt,$$

where X_n is a random quantity whose probabilities are specified by $G_n(z)$. This is a special case of P. Lévy's important "continuity theorem," a basic result in mathematical probability theory. A proof of Lévy's theorem would take us rather far afield, although it is not extremely difficult [for example, see *Limit Distributions for Sums of Independent Random Variables* by B. V. Gnedenko and A. N. Kolmogorov, tr. by K. L. Chung (Reading, Mass.: Addison–Wesley, 1954)].

14. [*HM30*] (A. de Moivre.) Using the conventions of the previous exercise, show that the binomial distribution $G_n(z)$ given by Eq. (18) approaches the normal distribution.

15. [*HM23*] When the probability that some quantity has the value k is $e^{-\mu}(\mu^k/k!)$, it is said to have the *Poisson distribution with mean* μ.

   a) What is the generating function for this set of probabilities?

   b) What are the values of the semi-invariants?

   c) Show that as $n \to \infty$ the Poisson distribution with mean np approaches the normal distribution in the sense of exercise 13.

16. [*M25*] Suppose X is a random variable whose values are a *mixture* of the probability distributions generated by $g_1(z)$, $g_2(z)$, $\ldots$, $g_r(z)$, in the sense that it uses $g_k(z)$ with probability p_k, where $p_1 + p_2 + \cdots + p_r = 1$. What is the generating function for X? Express the mean and variance of X in terms of the means and variances of g_1, g_2, $\ldots$, g_r.

▶ **17.** [*M27*] Let $f(z)$ and $g(z)$ be generating functions that represent probability distributions.

   a) Show that $h(z) = g(f(z))$ is also a generating function representing a probability distribution.

   b) Interpret the significance of $h(z)$ in terms of $f(z)$ and $g(z)$. (What is the *meaning* of the probabilities represented by the coefficients of $h(z)$?)

   c) Give formulas for the mean and variance of h in terms of those for f and g.

18. [*M28*] Suppose that the values taken on by $X[1]$, $X[2]$, $\ldots$, $X[n]$ in Algorithm M include exactly k_1 ones, k_2 twos, $\ldots$, k_n n's, arranged in random order. (Here

$$k_1 + k_2 + \cdots + k_n = n.$$

The assumption in the text is that $k_1 = k_2 = \cdots = k_n = 1$.) Show that in this generalized situation, the generating function (8) becomes

$$\left(\frac{k_n z}{k_n}\right)\left(\frac{k_{n-1}z + k_n}{k_{n-1} + k_n}\right)\left(\frac{k_{n-2}z + k_{n-1} + k_n}{k_{n-2} + k_{n-1} + k_n}\right) \cdots \left(\frac{k_1 z + k_2 + \cdots + k_n}{k_1 + k_2 + \cdots + k_n}\right) \Big/ z,$$

using the convention $0/0 = 1$.

19. [*M21*] If $a_k > a_j$ for $1 \le j < k$, we say that a_k is a *left-to-right maximum* of the sequence $a_1 a_2 \ldots a_n$. Suppose $a_1 a_2 \ldots a_n$ is a permutation of $\{1, 2, \ldots, n\}$, and let $b_1 b_2 \ldots b_n$ be the inverse permutation, so that $a_k = l$ if and only if $b_l = k$. Show that a_k is a left-to-right maximum of $a_1 a_2 \ldots a_n$ if and only if k is a right-to-left minimum of $b_1 b_2 \ldots b_n$.

▶ **20.** [*M22*] Suppose we want to calculate $\max\{|a_1 - b_1|, |a_2 - b_2|, \ldots, |a_n - b_n|\}$ when $b_1 \le b_2 \le \cdots \le b_n$. Show that it is sufficient to calculate $\max\{m_L, m_R\}$, where

$$m_L = \max\{a_k - b_k \mid a_k \text{ is a left-to-right maximum of } a_1 a_2 \ldots a_n\},$$
$$m_R = \max\{b_k - a_k \mid a_k \text{ is a right-to-left minimum of } a_1 a_2 \ldots a_n\}.$$

(Thus, if the a's are in random order, the number of k's for which a subtraction must be performed is only about $2 \ln n$.)

▶ **21.** [*HM21*] Let X be the number of heads that occur when a random coin is flipped n times, with generating function (18). Use (25) to prove that

$$\Pr(X \ge n(p + \epsilon)) \le e^{-\epsilon^2 n/(2q)}$$

when $\epsilon \ge 0$, and obtain a similar estimate for $\Pr(X \le n(p - \epsilon))$.

▶ **22.** [*HM22*] Suppose X has the generating function $(q_1+p_1z)(q_2+p_2z)\ldots(q_n+p_nz)$, where $p_k + q_k = 1$ for $1 \le k \le n$. Let $\mu = \mathrm{E}\,X = p_1 + p_2 + \cdots + p_n$. (a) Prove that

$$\Pr(X \le \mu r) \le (r^{-r}e^{r-1})^\mu, \quad \text{when } 0 < r \le 1;$$
$$\Pr(X \ge \mu r) \le (r^{-r}e^{r-1})^\mu, \quad \text{when } r \ge 1.$$

(b) Express the right-hand sides of these estimates in convenient form when $r \approx 1$.
(c) Show that if r is sufficiently large we have $\Pr(X \ge \mu r) \le 2^{-\mu r}$.

23. [*HM23*] Estimate the tail probabilities for a random variable that has the *negative binomial distribution* generated by $(q - pz)^{-n}$, where $q = p + 1$.

*1.2.11. Asymptotic Representations

We often want to know a quantity approximately, instead of exactly, in order to compare it to another. For example, Stirling's approximation to $n!$ is a useful representation of this type, when n is large, and we have also made use of the fact that $H_n \approx \ln n + \gamma$. The derivations of such *asymptotic formulas* generally involve higher mathematics, although in the following subsections we will use nothing more than elementary calculus to get the results we need.

*1.2.11.1. The O-notation.

Paul Bachmann introduced a very convenient notation for approximations in his book *Analytische Zahlentheorie* (1894). It is the O-notation, which allows us to replace the "$\approx$" sign by "$=$" and to quantify the degree of accuracy; for example,

$$H_n = \ln n + \gamma + O\left(\frac{1}{n}\right). \tag{1}$$

(Read, "H sub n equals the natural log of n plus Euler's constant [pronounced 'Oiler's constant'] plus big-oh of one over n.")

In general, the notation $O\big(f(n)\big)$ may be used whenever $f(n)$ is a function of the positive integer n; it stands for a *quantity that is not explicitly known*, except that its magnitude isn't too large. Every appearance of $O\big(f(n)\big)$ means precisely this: There are positive constants M and n_0 such that the number x_n represented by $O\big(f(n)\big)$ satisfies the condition $|x_n| \le M\,|f(n)|$, for all integers $n \ge n_0$. We do not say *what* the constants M and n_0 are, and indeed those constants are usually different for each appearance of O.

For example, Eq. (1) means that $|H_n - \ln n - \gamma| \le M/n$ when $n \ge n_0$. Although the constants M and n_0 are not stated, we can be sure that the quantity $O(1/n)$ will be arbitrarily small if n is large enough.

Let's look at some more examples. We know that

$$1^2 + 2^2 + \cdots + n^2 = \tfrac{1}{3}n(n + \tfrac{1}{2})(n + 1) = \tfrac{1}{3}n^3 + \tfrac{1}{2}n^2 + \tfrac{1}{6}n;$$

so it follows that

$$1^2 + 2^2 + \cdots + n^2 = O(n^4), \tag{2}$$
$$1^2 + 2^2 + \cdots + n^2 = O(n^3), \tag{3}$$
$$1^2 + 2^2 + \cdots + n^2 = \tfrac{1}{3}n^3 + O(n^2). \tag{4}$$

Equation (2) is rather crude, but not incorrect; Eq. (3) is a stronger statement; and Eq. (4) is stronger yet. To justify these equations we shall prove that *if $P(n) = a_0 + a_1 n + \cdots + a_m n^m$ is any polynomial of degree m or less, then we have $P(n) = O(n^m)$.* This follows because

$$|P(n)| \le |a_0| + |a_1|\, n + \cdots + |a_m|\, n^m = \left(|a_0|\,/n^m + |a_1|\,/n^{m-1} + \cdots + |a_m|\right)n^m$$

$$\le \left(|a_0| + |a_1| + \cdots + |a_m|\right)n^m,$$

when $n \ge 1$. So we may take $M = |a_0| + |a_1| + \cdots + |a_m|$ and $n_0 = 1$. Or we could take, say, $M = |a_0|/2^m + |a_1|/2^{m-1} + \cdots + |a_m|$ and $n_0 = 2$.

The O-notation is a big help in approximation work, since it describes briefly a concept that occurs often and it suppresses detailed information that is usually irrelevant. Furthermore, it can be manipulated algebraically in familiar ways, although certain important differences need to be kept in mind. The most important consideration is the idea of *one-way equalities*: We write $\frac{1}{2}n^2 + n = O(n^2)$, but we *never* write $O(n^2) = \frac{1}{2}n^2 + n$. (Or else, since $\frac{1}{4}n^2 = O(n^2)$, we might come up with the absurd relation $\frac{1}{4}n^2 = \frac{1}{2}n^2 + n$.) We always use the convention that *the right-hand side of an equation does not give more information than the left-hand side*; the right-hand side is a "crudification" of the left.

This convention about the use of "=" may be stated more precisely as follows: Formulas that involve the $O\big(f(n)\big)$-notation may be regarded as sets of functions of n. The symbol $O\big(f(n)\big)$ stands for the set of all functions g of integers such that there exist constants M and n_0 with $|g(n)| \le M\,|f(n)|$ for all integers $n \ge n_0$. If S and T are sets of functions, then $S + T$ denotes the set $\{g + h \mid g \in S \text{ and } h \in T\}$; we define $S + c$, $S - T$, $S \cdot T$, $\log S$, etc., in a similar way. If $\alpha(n)$ and $\beta(n)$ are formulas that involve the O-notation, then the notation $\alpha(n) = \beta(n)$ means that the set of functions denoted by $\alpha(n)$ is *contained in* the set denoted by $\beta(n)$.

Consequently we may perform most of the operations we are accustomed to doing with the "=" sign: If $\alpha(n) = \beta(n)$ and $\beta(n) = \gamma(n)$, then $\alpha(n) = \gamma(n)$. Also, if $\alpha(n) = \beta(n)$ and if $\delta(n)$ is a formula resulting from the substitution of $\beta(n)$ for some occurrence of $\alpha(n)$ in a formula $\gamma(n)$, then $\gamma(n) = \delta(n)$. These two statements imply, for example, that if $g(x_1, x_2, \ldots, x_m)$ is any real function whatever, and if $\alpha_k(n) = \beta_k(n)$ for $1 \le k \le m$, then $g\big(\alpha_1(n), \alpha_2(n), \ldots, \alpha_m(n)\big) = g\big(\beta_1(n), \beta_2(n), \ldots, \beta_m(n)\big)$.

Here are some of the simple operations we can do with the O-notation:

$$f(n) = O\big(f(n)\big), \tag{5}$$

$$c \cdot O\big(f(n)\big) = O\big(f(n)\big), \qquad \text{if } c \text{ is a constant,} \tag{6}$$

$$O\big(f(n)\big) + O\big(f(n)\big) = O\big(f(n)\big), \tag{7}$$

$$O\big(O(f(n))\big) = O\big(f(n)\big), \tag{8}$$

$$O\big(f(n)\big)O\big(g(n)\big) = O\big(f(n)g(n)\big), \tag{9}$$

$$O\big(f(n)g(n)\big) = f(n)O\big(g(n)\big). \tag{10}$$

The O-notation is also frequently used with functions of a complex variable z, in the neighborhood of $z = 0$. We write $O(f(z))$ to stand for any quantity $g(z)$ such that $|g(z)| \le M |f(z)|$ whenever $|z| < r$. (As before, M and r are unspecified constants, although we could specify them if we wanted to.) The context of O-notation should always identify the variable that is involved and the range of that variable. When the variable is called n, we implicitly assume that $O(f(n))$ refers to functions of a large integer n; when the variable is called z, we implicitly assume that $O(f(z))$ refers to functions of a small complex number z.

Suppose that $g(z)$ is a function given by an infinite power series

$$g(z) = \sum_{k \ge 0} a_k z^k$$

that converges for $z = z_0$. Then the sum of absolute values $\sum_{k \ge 0} |a_k z^k|$ also converges whenever $|z| < |z_0|$. If $z_0 \ne 0$, we can therefore always write

$$g(z) = a_0 + a_1 z + \cdots + a_m z^m + O(z^{m+1}). \tag{11}$$

For we have $g(z) = a_0 + a_1 z + \cdots + a_m z^m + z^{m+1}(a_{m+1} + a_{m+2}z + \cdots)$; we need only show that the parenthesized quantity is bounded when $|z| \le r$, for some positive r, and it is easy to see that $|a_{m+1}| + |a_{m+2}| r + |a_{m+3}| r^2 + \cdots$ is an upper bound whenever $|z| \le r < |z_0|$.

For example, the generating functions listed in Section 1.2.9 give us many important asymptotic formulas valid when z is sufficiently small, including

$$e^z = 1 + z + \frac{1}{2!}z^2 + \cdots + \frac{1}{m!}z^m + O(z^{m+1}), \tag{12}$$

$$\ln(1 + z) = z - \frac{1}{2}z^2 + \cdots + \frac{(-1)^{m+1}}{m}z^m + O(z^{m+1}), \tag{13}$$

$$(1 + z)^\alpha = 1 + \alpha z + \binom{\alpha}{2}z^2 + \cdots + \binom{\alpha}{m}z^m + O(z^{m+1}), \tag{14}$$

$$\frac{1}{1 - z}\ln\frac{1}{1 - z} = z + H_2 z^2 + \cdots + H_m z^m + O(z^{m+1}), \tag{15}$$

for all nonnegative integers m. It is important to note that the hidden constants M and r implied by any particular O are related to each other. For example, the function e^z is obviously $O(1)$ when $|z| \le r$, for any fixed r, since $|e^z| \le e^{|z|}$; but there is no constant M such that $|e^z| \le M$ for all values of z. Therefore we need to use larger and larger bounds M as the range r increases.

Sometimes an asymptotic series is correct although it does not correspond to a convergent infinite series. For example, the basic formulas that express factorial powers in terms of ordinary powers,

$$n^{\bar{r}} = \sum_{k=0}^{m} \left[\begin{matrix} r \\ r-k \end{matrix}\right] n^{r-k} + O(n^{r-m-1}), \tag{16}$$

$$n^{\underline{r}} = \sum_{k=0}^{m} (-1)^k \left[\begin{matrix} r \\ r-k \end{matrix}\right] n^{r-k} + O(n^{r-m-1}), \tag{17}$$

are asymptotically valid for any real r and any fixed integer $m \geq 0$, yet the sum

$$\sum_{k=0}^{\infty} \begin{bmatrix} 1/2 \\ 1/2 - k \end{bmatrix} n^{1/2-k}$$

diverges for all n. (See exercise 12.) Of course, when r is a nonnegative integer, $n^{\bar{r}}$ and $n^{\underline{r}}$ are simply polynomials of degree r, and (17) is essentially the same as 1.2.6–(44). When r is a negative integer and $|n| > |r|$, the infinite sum $\sum_{k=0}^{\infty} \begin{bmatrix} r \\ r-k \end{bmatrix} n^{r-k}$ does converge to $n^{\bar{r}} = 1/(n-1)^{\underline{-r}}$; this sum can also be written in the more natural form $\sum_{k=0}^{\infty} \left\{ {k-r \atop -r} \right\} n^{r-k}$, using Eq. 1.2.6–(58).

Let us give one simple example of the concepts we have introduced so far. Consider the quantity $\sqrt[n]{n}$; as n gets large, the operation of taking an nth root tends to decrease the value, but it is not immediately obvious whether $\sqrt[n]{n}$ decreases or increases. It turns out that $\sqrt[n]{n}$ decreases to unity. Let us consider the slightly more complicated quantity $n(\sqrt[n]{n} - 1)$. Now $(\sqrt[n]{n} - 1)$ gets smaller as n gets bigger; what happens to $n(\sqrt[n]{n} - 1)$?

This problem is easily solved by applying the formulas above. We have

$$\sqrt[n]{n} = e^{\ln n / n} = 1 + (\ln n / n) + O\big((\ln n / n)^2\big), \tag{18}$$

because $\ln n / n \to 0$ as $n \to \infty$; see exercises 8 and 11. This equation proves our previous contention that $\sqrt[n]{n} \to 1$. Furthermore, it tells us that

$$n(\sqrt[n]{n} - 1) = n\big(\ln n / n + O((\ln n / n)^2)\big) = \ln n + O\big((\ln n)^2 / n\big). \tag{19}$$

In other words, $n(\sqrt[n]{n} - 1)$ is approximately equal to $\ln n$; the difference is $O\big((\ln n)^2 / n\big)$, which approaches zero as n approaches infinity.

People often abuse O-notation by assuming that it gives an exact order of growth; they use it as if it specifies a lower bound as well as an upper bound. For example, an algorithm to sort n numbers might be called inefficient "because its running time is $O(n^2)$." But a running time of $O(n^2)$ does not necessarily imply that the running time is not also $O(n)$. There's another notation, Big Omega, for lower bounds: The statement

$$g(n) = \Omega\big(f(n)\big) \tag{20}$$

means that there are positive constants L and n_0 such that

$$\big|g(n)\big| \geq L\big|f(n)\big| \quad \text{for all } n \geq n_0.$$

Using this notation we can correctly conclude that a sorting algorithm whose running time is $\Omega(n^2)$ will not be as efficient as one whose running time is $O(n \log n)$, if n is large enough. However, without knowing the constant factors implied by O and Ω, we cannot say anything about how large n must be before the $O(n \log n)$ method will begin to win.

Finally, if we want to state an exact order of growth without being precise about constant factors, we can use Big Theta:

$$g(n) = \Theta\big(f(n)\big) \quad \Longleftrightarrow \quad g(n) = O\big(f(n)\big) \text{ and } g(n) = \Omega\big(f(n)\big). \tag{21}$$

EXERCISES

1. [*HM01*] What is $\lim_{n\to\infty} O(n^{-1/3})$?

▶ **2.** [*M10*] Mr. B. C. Dull obtained astonishing results by using the "self-evident" formula $O(f(n)) - O(f(n)) = 0$. What was his mistake, and what should the right-hand side of his formula have been?

3. [*M15*] Multiply $(\ln n + \gamma + O(1/n))$ by $(n + O(\sqrt{n}))$, and express your answer in O-notation.

▶ **4.** [*M15*] Give an asymptotic expansion of $n(\sqrt[n]{a} - 1)$, if $a > 0$, to terms $O(1/n^3)$.

5. [*M20*] Prove or disprove: $O(f(n) + g(n)) = f(n) + O(g(n))$, if $f(n)$ and $g(n)$ are positive for all n. (Compare with (10).)

▶ **6.** [*M20*] What is wrong with the following argument? "Since $n = O(n)$, and $2n = O(n)$, $\ldots$, we have

$$\sum_{k=1}^{n} kn = \sum_{k=1}^{n} O(n) = O(n^2)."$$

7. [*HM15*] Prove that if m is any integer, there is no M such that $e^x \le M x^m$ for arbitrarily large values of x.

8. [*HM20*] Prove that as $n \to \infty$, $(\ln n)^m/n \to 0$.

9. [*HM20*] Show that $e^{O(z^m)} = 1 + O(z^m)$, for all fixed $m \ge 0$.

10. [*HM22*] Make a statement similar to that in exercise 9 about $\ln(1 + O(z^m))$.

▶ **11.** [*M11*] Explain why Eq. (18) is true.

12. [*HM25*] Prove that $\left[\begin{smallmatrix} 1/2 \\ 1/2-k \end{smallmatrix}\right] n^{-k}$ does not approach zero as $k \to \infty$ for any integer n, using the fact that $\left[\begin{smallmatrix} 1/2 \\ 1/2-k \end{smallmatrix}\right] = (-\tfrac{1}{2})^k [z^k] \left(ze^z/(e^z - 1)\right)^{1/2}$.

▶ **13.** [*M10*] Prove or disprove: $g(n) = \Omega(f(n))$ if and only if $f(n) = O(g(n))$.

*1.2.11.2. Euler's summation formula. One of the most useful ways to obtain good approximations to a sum is an approach due to Leonhard Euler. His method approximates a finite sum by an integral, and gives us a means to get better and better approximations in many cases. [*Commentarii Academiæ Scientiarum Petropolitanæ* **6** (1732), 68–97.]

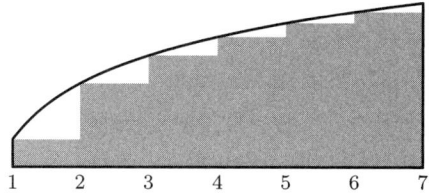

Fig. 12. Comparing a sum with an integral.

Figure 12 shows a comparison of $\int_1^n f(x)\,dx$ and $\sum_{k=1}^{n-1} f(k)$, when $n = 7$. Euler's strategy leads to a useful formula for the difference between these two quantities, assuming that $f(x)$ is a differentiable function.

For convenience we shall use the notation

$$\{x\} = x \bmod 1 = x - \lfloor x \rfloor. \tag{1}$$

Our derivation starts with the following identity:

$$\int_k^{k+1} \left(\{x\} - \tfrac{1}{2}\right) f'(x)\, dx = (x - k - \tfrac{1}{2}) f(x) \Big|_k^{k+1} - \int_k^{k+1} f(x)\, dx$$

$$= \tfrac{1}{2}\big(f(k+1) + f(k)\big) - \int_k^{k+1} f(x)\, dx. \tag{2}$$

(This follows from integration by parts.) Adding both sides of this equation for $1 \le k < n$, we find that

$$\int_1^n \left(\{x\} - \tfrac{1}{2}\right) f'(x)\, dx = \sum_{1 \le k < n} f(k) + \tfrac{1}{2}\big(f(n) - f(1)\big) - \int_1^n f(x)\, dx;$$

that is,

$$\sum_{1 \le k < n} f(k) = \int_1^n f(x)\, dx - \tfrac{1}{2}\big(f(n) - f(1)\big) + \int_1^n B_1(\{x\}) f'(x)\, dx, \tag{3}$$

where $B_1(x)$ is the polynomial $x - \tfrac{1}{2}$. This is the desired connection between the sum and the integral.

The approximation can be carried further if we continue to integrate by parts. Before doing this, however, we shall discuss the *Bernoulli numbers*, which are the coefficients in the following infinite series:

$$\frac{z}{e^z - 1} = B_0 + B_1 z + \frac{B_2 z^2}{2!} + \cdots = \sum_{k \ge 0} \frac{B_k z^k}{k!}. \tag{4}$$

The coefficients of this series, which occur in a wide variety of problems, were introduced to European mathematicians in James Bernoulli's *Ars Conjectandi*, published posthumously in 1713. Curiously, they were also discovered at about the same time by Takakazu Seki in Japan — and first published in 1712, shortly after *his* death. [See *Takakazu Seki's Collected Works* (Osaka: 1974), 39–42.]

We have

$$B_0 = 1, \quad B_1 = -\tfrac{1}{2}, \quad B_2 = \tfrac{1}{6}, \quad B_3 = 0, \quad B_4 = -\tfrac{1}{30}; \tag{5}$$

further values appear in Appendix A. Since

$$\frac{z}{e^z - 1} + \frac{z}{2} = \frac{z}{2} \frac{e^z + 1}{e^z - 1} = -\frac{z}{2} \frac{e^{-z} + 1}{e^{-z} - 1}$$

is an even function, we see that

$$B_3 = B_5 = B_7 = B_9 = \cdots = 0. \tag{6}$$

If we multiply both sides of the defining equation (4) by $e^z - 1$, and equate coefficients of equal powers of z, we obtain the formula

$$\sum_k \binom{n}{k} B_k = B_n + \delta_{n1}. \tag{7}$$

(See exercise 1.) We now define the *Bernoulli polynomial*

$$B_m(x) = \sum_k \binom{m}{k} B_k x^{m-k}. \tag{8}$$

If $m = 1$, then $B_1(x) = B_0 x + B_1 = x - \frac{1}{2}$, corresponding to the polynomial used above in Eq. (3). If $m > 1$, we have $B_m(1) = B_m = B_m(0)$, by (7); in other words, $B_m(\{x\})$ has no discontinuities at integer points x.

The relevance of Bernoulli polynomials and Bernoulli numbers to our problem will soon be clear. We find by differentiating Eq. (8) that

$$B_m'(x) = \sum_k \binom{m}{k}(m-k) B_k x^{m-k-1}$$

$$= m \sum_k \binom{m-1}{k} B_k x^{m-1-k}$$

$$= m B_{m-1}(x), \tag{9}$$

and therefore when $m \geq 1$, we can integrate by parts as follows:

$$\frac{1}{m!}\int_1^n B_m(\{x\}) f^{(m)}(x)\, dx = \frac{1}{(m+1)!}\left(B_{m+1}(1) f^{(m)}(n) - B_{m+1}(0) f^{(m)}(1)\right)$$

$$- \frac{1}{(m+1)!}\int_1^n B_{m+1}(\{x\}) f^{(m+1)}(x)\, dx.$$

From this result we can continue to improve the approximation, Eq. (3), and we obtain Euler's general formula:

$$\sum_{1\leq k<n} f(k) = \int_1^n f(x)\, dx - \frac{1}{2}\left(f(n) - f(1)\right) + \frac{B_2}{2!}\left(f'(n) - f'(1)\right) + \cdots$$

$$+ \frac{(-1)^m B_m}{m!}\left(f^{(m-1)}(n) - f^{(m-1)}(1)\right) + R_{mn}$$

$$= \int_1^n f(x)\, dx + \sum_{k=1}^m \frac{B_k}{k!}\left(f^{(k-1)}(n) - f^{(k-1)}(1)\right) + R_{mn}, \tag{10}$$

using (6), where

$$R_{mn} = \frac{(-1)^{m+1}}{m!}\int_1^n B_m(\{x\}) f^{(m)}(x)\, dx. \tag{11}$$

The remainder R_{mn} will be small when $B_m(\{x\}) f^{(m)}(x)/m!$ is very small, and in fact, one can show that

$$\left|\frac{B_m(\{x\})}{m!}\right| \leq \frac{|B_m|}{m!} < \frac{4}{(2\pi)^m} \tag{12}$$

when m is even. [See *CMath*, §9.5.] On the other hand, it usually turns out that the magnitude of $f^{(m)}(x)$ gets large as m increases, so there is a "best" value of m at which $|R_{mn}|$ has its least value when n is given.

It is known that, when m is even, there is a number θ such that

$$R_{mn} = \theta \frac{B_{m+2}}{(m+2)!} \left(f^{(m+1)}(n) - f^{(m+1)}(1) \right), \quad 0 < \theta < 1, \tag{13}$$

provided that $f^{(m+2)}(x) \, f^{(m+4)}(x) > 0$ for $1 < x < n$. So in these circumstances the remainder has the same sign as, and is less than, the first discarded term. A simpler version of this result is proved in exercise 3.

Let us now apply Euler's formula to some important examples. First, we set $f(x) = 1/x$. The derivatives are $f^{(m)}(x) = (-1)^m m!/x^{m+1}$, so we have, by Eq. (10),

$$H_{n-1} = \ln n + \sum_{k=1}^{m} \frac{B_k}{k} (-1)^{k-1} \left(\frac{1}{n^k} - 1 \right) + R_{mn}. \tag{14}$$

Now we find

$$\gamma = \lim_{n \to \infty} \left(H_{n-1} - \ln n \right) = \sum_{k=1}^{m} \frac{B_k}{k} (-1)^k + \lim_{n \to \infty} R_{mn}. \tag{15}$$

The fact that $\lim_{n \to \infty} R_{mn} = -\int_1^\infty B_m(\{x\}) \, dx / x^{m+1}$ exists proves that the constant γ does in fact exist. We can therefore put Eqs. (14) and (15) together, to deduce a general approximation for the harmonic numbers:

$$H_{n-1} = \ln n + \gamma + \sum_{k=1}^{m} \frac{(-1)^{k-1} B_k}{kn^k} + \int_n^\infty \frac{B_m(\{x\}) \, dx}{x^{m+1}}$$

$$= \ln n + \gamma + \sum_{k=1}^{m-1} \frac{(-1)^{k-1} B_k}{kn^k} + O\left(\frac{1}{n^m} \right).$$

Replacing m by $m+1$ yields

$$H_{n-1} = \ln n + \gamma + \sum_{k=1}^{m} \frac{(-1)^{k-1} B_k}{kn^k} + O\left(\frac{1}{n^{m+1}} \right). \tag{16}$$

Furthermore, by Eq. (13) we see that the error is less than the first term discarded. As a particular case we have (adding $1/n$ to both sides)

$$H_n = \ln n + \gamma + \frac{1}{2n} - \frac{1}{12n^2} + \frac{1}{120n^4} - \epsilon, \quad 0 < \epsilon < \frac{B_6}{6n^6} = \frac{1}{252n^6}.$$

This is Eq. 1.2.7–(3). The Bernoulli numbers B_k for large k get very large (approximately $(-1)^{1+k/2} 2 \left(k!/(2\pi)^k \right)$ when k is even), so Eq. (16) cannot be extended to a convergent infinite series for any fixed value of n.

The same technique can be applied to deduce Stirling's approximation. This time we set $f(x) = \ln x$, and Eq. (10) yields

$$\ln(n-1)! = n\ln n - n + 1 - \tfrac{1}{2}\ln n + \sum_{1<k\leq m} \frac{B_k(-1)^k}{k(k-1)}\left(\frac{1}{n^{k-1}} - 1\right) + R_{mn}. \quad (17)$$

Proceeding as above, we find that the limit

$$\lim_{n\to\infty}\left(\ln n! - n\ln n + n - \tfrac{1}{2}\ln n\right) = 1 + \sum_{1<k\leq m}\frac{B_k(-1)^{k+1}}{k(k-1)} + \lim_{n\to\infty} R_{mn}$$

exists; let it be called σ ("Stirling's constant") temporarily. We get Stirling's result

$$\ln n! = (n+\tfrac{1}{2})\ln n - n + \sigma + \sum_{1<k\leq m}\frac{B_k(-1)^k}{k(k-1)n^{k-1}} + O\left(\frac{1}{n^m}\right). \quad (18)$$

In particular, let $m = 5$; we have

$$\ln n! = (n+\tfrac{1}{2})\ln n - n + \sigma + \frac{1}{12n} - \frac{1}{360n^3} + O\left(\frac{1}{n^5}\right).$$

Now we can take the exponential of both sides:

$$n! = e^\sigma \sqrt{n}\left(\frac{n}{e}\right)^n \exp\left(\frac{1}{12n} - \frac{1}{360n^3} + O\left(\frac{1}{n^5}\right)\right).$$

Using the fact that $e^\sigma = \sqrt{2\pi}$ (see exercise 5), and expanding the exponential, we get our final result:

$$n! = \sqrt{2\pi n}\left(\frac{n}{e}\right)^n\left(1 + \frac{1}{12n} + \frac{1}{288n^2} - \frac{139}{51840n^3} - \frac{571}{2488320n^4} + O\left(\frac{1}{n^5}\right)\right). \quad (19)$$

EXERCISES

1. [M18] Prove Eq. (7).

2. [HM20] Note that Eq. (9) follows from Eq. (8) for *any* sequence B_n, not only for the sequence defined by Eq. (4). Explain why the latter sequence is necessary for the validity of Eq. (10).

3. [HM20] Let $C_{mn} = (B_m/m!)(f^{(m-1)}(n) - f^{(m-1)}(1))$ be the mth correction term in Euler's summation formula. Assuming that $f^{(m)}(x)$ has a constant sign for all x in the range $1 \leq x \leq n$, prove that $|R_{mn}| \leq |C_{mn}|$ when $m = 2k > 0$; in other words, show that the remainder is not larger in absolute value than the last term computed.

▶ **4.** [HM20] (*Sums of powers.*) When $f(x) = x^m$, the high-order derivatives of f are all zero, so Euler's summation formula gives an *exact* value for the sum

$$S_m(n) = \sum_{0\leq k<n} k^m$$

in terms of Bernoulli numbers. (It was the study of $S_m(n)$ for $m = 1, 2, 3, \ldots$ that led Bernoulli and Seki to discover those numbers in the first place.) Express $S_m(n)$ in terms of Bernoulli *polynomials*. Check your answer for $m = 0, 1,$ and 2. (Note that the desired sum is performed for $0 \leq k < n$ instead of $1 \leq k < n$; Euler's summation formula may be applied with 0 replacing 1 throughout.)

5. [*HM30*] Given that

$$n! = \kappa \sqrt{n} \left(\frac{n}{e}\right)^n \left(1 + O\left(\frac{1}{n}\right)\right),$$

show that $\kappa = \sqrt{2\pi}$ by using Wallis's product (exercise 1.2.5–18). [*Hint:* Consider $\binom{2n}{n}$ for large values of n.]

▶ 6. [*HM30*] Show that Stirling's approximation holds for noninteger n as well:

$$\Gamma(x+1) = \sqrt{2\pi x} \left(\frac{x}{e}\right)^x \left(1 + O\left(\frac{1}{x}\right)\right), \qquad x \geq a > 0.$$

[*Hint:* Let $f(x) = \ln(x+c)$ in Euler's summation formula, and apply the definition of $\Gamma(x)$ given in Section 1.2.5.]

▶ 7. [*HM32*] What is the approximate value of $1^1 2^2 3^3 \ldots n^n$?

8. [*M23*] Find the asymptotic value of $\ln(an^2+bn)!$ with absolute error $O(n^{-2})$. Use it to compute the asymptotic value of $\binom{cn^2}{n}/c^n \binom{n^2}{n}$ with relative error $O(n^{-2})$, when c is a positive constant. Here *absolute error* ϵ means that (truth) $=$ (approximation) $+ \epsilon$; *relative error* ϵ means that (truth) $=$ (approximation)$(1 + \epsilon)$.

▶ 9. [*M25*] Find the asymptotic value of $\binom{2n}{n}$ with a relative error of $O(n^{-3})$, in two ways: (a) via Stirling's approximation; (b) via exercise 1.2.6–47 and Eq. 1.2.11.1–(16).

*1.2.11.3. Some asymptotic calculations. In this subsection we shall investigate the following three intriguing sums, in order to deduce their approximate values:

$$P(n) = 1 + \frac{n-1}{n} + \frac{n-2}{n}\frac{n-2}{n-1} + \cdots = \sum_{k=0}^{n} \frac{(n-k)^k (n-k)!}{n!}, \qquad (1)$$

$$Q(n) = 1 + \frac{n-1}{n} + \frac{n-1}{n}\frac{n-2}{n} + \cdots = \sum_{k=1}^{n} \frac{n!}{(n-k)!\, n^k}, \qquad (2)$$

$$R(n) = 1 + \frac{n}{n+1} + \frac{n}{n+1}\frac{n}{n+2} + \cdots = \sum_{k \geq 0} \frac{n!\, n^k}{(n+k)!}. \qquad (3)$$

These functions, which are similar in appearance yet intrinsically different, arise in several algorithms that we shall encounter later. Both $P(n)$ and $Q(n)$ are finite sums, while $R(n)$ is an infinite sum. It seems that when n is large, all three sums will be nearly equal, although it is not obvious what the approximate value of *any* of them will be. Our quest for approximate values of these functions will lead us through a number of very instructive side results. (You may wish to stop reading temporarily and try your hand at studying these functions before going on to see how they are attacked here.)

First, we observe an important connection between $Q(n)$ and $R(n)$:

$$Q(n) + R(n) = \frac{n!}{n^n}\left(\left(1 + n + \cdots + \frac{n^{n-1}}{(n-1)!}\right) + \left(\frac{n^n}{n!} + \frac{n^{n+1}}{(n+1)!} + \cdots\right)\right)$$

$$= \frac{n!\, e^n}{n^n}. \qquad (4)$$

Stirling's formula tells us that $n!\, e^n/n^n$ is approximately $\sqrt{2\pi n}$, so we can guess that $Q(n)$ and $R(n)$ will each turn out to be roughly equal to $\sqrt{\pi n/2}$.

To get any further we must consider the partial sums of the series for e^n. By using Taylor's formula with remainder,

$$f(x) = f(0) + f'(0)x + \cdots + \frac{f^{(n)}(0)x^n}{n!} + \int_0^x \frac{t^n}{n!} f^{(n+1)}(x-t)\, dt, \qquad (5)$$

we are soon led to an important function known as the *incomplete gamma function:*

$$\gamma(a, x) = \int_0^x e^{-t} t^{a-1}\, dt. \qquad (6)$$

We shall assume that $a > 0$. By exercise 1.2.5–20, we have $\gamma(a, \infty) = \Gamma(a)$; this accounts for the name "incomplete gamma function." It has two useful series expansions in powers of x (see exercises 2 and 3):

$$\gamma(a, x) = \frac{x^a}{a} - \frac{x^{a+1}}{a+1} + \frac{x^{a+2}}{2!\,(a+2)} - \cdots \quad = \sum_{k \geq 0} \frac{(-1)^k x^{k+a}}{k!\,(k+a)}, \qquad (7)$$

$$e^x \gamma(a, x) = \frac{x^a}{a} + \frac{x^{a+1}}{a(a+1)} + \frac{x^{a+2}}{a(a+1)(a+2)} + \cdots = \sum_{k \geq 0} \frac{x^{k+a}}{a(a+1)\ldots(a+k)}. \qquad (8)$$

From the second formula we see the connection with $R(n)$:

$$R(n) = \frac{n!\, e^n}{n^n} \left(\frac{\gamma(n, n)}{(n-1)!} \right). \qquad (9)$$

This equation has purposely been written in a more complicated form than necessary, since $\gamma(n, n)$ is a fraction of $\gamma(n, \infty) = \Gamma(n) = (n-1)!$, and $n!\, e^n/n^n$ is the quantity in (4).

The problem boils down to getting good estimates of $\gamma(n, n)/(n-1)!$. We shall now determine the approximate value of $\gamma(x+1, x+y)/\Gamma(x+1)$, when y is fixed and x is large. The methods to be used here are more important than the results, so the reader should study the following derivation carefully.

By definition, we have

$$\frac{\gamma(x+1, x+y)}{\Gamma(x+1)} = \frac{1}{\Gamma(x+1)} \int_0^{x+y} e^{-t} t^x\, dt$$

$$= 1 - \frac{1}{\Gamma(x+1)} \int_x^\infty e^{-t} t^x\, dt + \frac{1}{\Gamma(x+1)} \int_x^{x+y} e^{-t} t^x\, dt. \qquad (10)$$

Let us set

$$I_1 = \int_x^\infty e^{-t} t^x\, dt,$$

$$I_2 = \int_x^{x+y} e^{-t} t^x\, dt,$$

and consider each integral in turn.

Estimate of I_1: We convert I_1 to an integral from 0 to infinity by substituting $t = x(1 + u)$; we further substitute $v = u - \ln(1 + u)$, $dv = \left(1 - 1/(1 + u)\right) du$, which is legitimate since v is a monotone function of u:

$$I_1 = e^{-x} x^x \int_0^\infty x e^{-xu} (1 + u)^x\, du = e^{-x} x^x \int_0^\infty x e^{-xv} \left(1 + \frac{1}{u}\right) dv. \qquad (11)$$

In the last integral we will replace $1 + 1/u$ by a power series in v. We have

$$v = \tfrac{1}{2} u^2 - \tfrac{1}{3} u^3 + \tfrac{1}{4} u^4 - \tfrac{1}{5} u^5 + \cdots = (u^2/2)(1 - \tfrac{2}{3} u + \tfrac{1}{2} u^2 - \tfrac{2}{5} u^3 + \cdots).$$

Setting $w = \sqrt{2v}$, we have therefore

$$w = u(1 - \tfrac{2}{3} u + \tfrac{1}{2} u^2 - \tfrac{2}{5} u^3 + \cdots)^{1/2} = u - \tfrac{1}{3} u^2 + \tfrac{7}{36} u^3 - \tfrac{73}{540} u^4 + \tfrac{1331}{12960} u^5 + O(u^6).$$

(This expansion may be obtained by the binomial theorem; efficient methods for performing such transformations, and for doing the other power series manipulations needed below, are considered in Section 4.7.) We can now solve for u as a power series in w:

$$u = w + \frac{1}{3} w^2 + \frac{1}{36} w^3 - \frac{1}{270} w^4 + \frac{1}{4320} w^5 + O(w^6);$$

$$1 + \frac{1}{u} = 1 + \frac{1}{w} - \frac{1}{3} + \frac{1}{12} w - \frac{2}{135} w^2 + \frac{1}{864} w^3 + O(w^4)$$

$$= \frac{1}{\sqrt{2}} v^{-1/2} + \frac{2}{3} + \frac{\sqrt{2}}{12} v^{1/2} - \frac{4}{135} v + \frac{\sqrt{2}}{432} v^{3/2} + O(v^2). \qquad (12)$$

In all of these formulas, the O-notation refers to small values of the argument, that is, $|u| \le r$, $|v| \le r$, $|w| \le r$ for sufficiently small positive r. Is this good enough? The substitution of $1 + 1/u$ in terms of v in Eq. (11) is supposed to be valid for $0 \le v < \infty$, not only for $|v| \le r$. Fortunately, it turns out that the value of the integral from 0 to ∞ depends almost entirely on the values of the integrand near zero. In fact, we have (see exercise 4)

$$\int_r^\infty x e^{-xv} \left(1 + \frac{1}{u}\right) dv = O(e^{-rx}) \qquad (13)$$

for any fixed $r > 0$ and for large x. We are interested in an approximation up to terms $O(x^{-m})$, and since $O\left((1/e^r)^x\right)$ is much smaller than $O(x^{-m})$ for any positive r and m, we need integrate only from 0 to r, for any fixed positive r. We therefore take r to be small enough so that all the power series manipulations done above are justified $\bigl($see Eqs. 1.2.11.1–(11) and 1.2.11.3–(13)$\bigr)$.

Now

$$\int_0^\infty x e^{-xv} v^\alpha\, dv = \frac{1}{x^\alpha} \int_0^\infty e^{-q} q^\alpha\, dq = \frac{1}{x^\alpha} \Gamma(\alpha + 1), \quad \text{if } \alpha > -1; \qquad (14)$$

so by plugging the series (12) into the integral (11) we have finally

$$I_1 = e^{-x} x^x \left(\sqrt{\frac{\pi}{2}} x^{1/2} + \frac{2}{3} + \frac{\sqrt{2\pi}}{24} x^{-1/2} - \frac{4}{135} x^{-1} + \frac{\sqrt{2\pi}}{576} x^{-3/2} + O(x^{-2}) \right). \qquad (15)$$

Estimate of I_2: In the integral I_2, we substitute $t = u + x$ and obtain

$$I_2 = e^{-x}x^x \int_0^y e^{-u}\left(1 + \frac{u}{x}\right)^x du. \tag{16}$$

Now

$$e^{-u}\left(1 + \frac{u}{x}\right)^x = \exp\left(-u + x\ln\left(1 + \frac{u}{x}\right)\right) = \exp\left(\frac{-u^2}{2x} + \frac{u^3}{3x^2} + O(x^{-3})\right)$$

$$= 1 - \frac{u^2}{2x} + \frac{u^4}{8x^2} + \frac{u^3}{3x^2} + O(x^{-3})$$

for $0 \le u \le y$ and large x. Therefore we find that

$$I_2 = e^{-x}x^x\left(y - \frac{y^3}{6}x^{-1} + \left(\frac{y^4}{12} + \frac{y^5}{40}\right)x^{-2} + O(x^{-3})\right). \tag{17}$$

Finally, we analyze the coefficient $e^{-x}x^x/\Gamma(x+1)$ that appears when we multiply Eqs. (15) and (17) by the factor $1/\Gamma(x+1)$ in (10). By Stirling's approximation, which is valid for the gamma function by exercise 1.2.11.2–6, we have

$$\frac{e^{-x}x^x}{\Gamma(x+1)} = \frac{e^{-1/12x+O(x^{-3})}}{\sqrt{2\pi x}}$$

$$= \frac{1}{\sqrt{2\pi}}x^{-1/2} - \frac{1}{12\sqrt{2\pi}}x^{-3/2} + \frac{1}{288\sqrt{2\pi}}x^{-5/2} + O(x^{-7/2}). \tag{18}$$

And now the grand summing up: Equations (10), (15), (17), and (18) yield

Theorem A. *For large values of x, and fixed y,*

$$\frac{\gamma(x+1, x+y)}{\Gamma(x+1)} = \frac{1}{2} + \left(\frac{y - 2/3}{\sqrt{2\pi}}\right)x^{-1/2} + \frac{1}{\sqrt{2\pi}}\left(\frac{23}{270} - \frac{y}{12} - \frac{y^3}{6}\right)x^{-3/2}$$

$$+ O(x^{-5/2}). \quad\blacksquare \tag{19}$$

The method we have used shows how this approximation could be extended to further powers of x as far as we please.

Theorem A can be used to obtain the approximate values of $R(n)$ and $Q(n)$, by using Eqs. (4) and (9), but we shall defer that calculation until later. Let us now turn to $P(n)$, for which somewhat different methods seem to be required. We have

$$P(n) = \sum_{k=0}^n \frac{k^{n-k}k!}{n!} = \frac{\sqrt{2\pi}}{n!}\sum_{k=0}^n k^{n+1/2}e^{-k}\left(1 + \frac{1}{12k} + O(k^{-2})\right). \tag{20}$$

Thus to get the values of $P(n)$, we must study sums of the form

$$\sum_{k=0}^n k^{n+1/2}e^{-k}.$$

Let $f(x) = x^{n+1/2}e^{-x}$ and apply Euler's summation formula:

$$\sum_{k=0}^{n} k^{n+1/2}e^{-k} = \int_0^n x^{n+1/2}e^{-x}\,dx + \tfrac{1}{2}n^{n+1/2}e^{-n} + \tfrac{1}{24}n^{n-1/2}e^{-n} - R. \quad (21)$$

A crude analysis of the remainder (see exercise 5) shows that $R = O(n^n e^{-n})$; and since the integral is an incomplete gamma function, we have

$$\sum_{k=0}^{n} k^{n+1/2}e^{-k} = \gamma\left(n + \tfrac{3}{2}, n\right) + \tfrac{1}{2}n^{n+1/2}e^{-n} + O(n^n e^{-n}). \quad (22)$$

Our formula, Eq. (20), also requires an estimate of the sum

$$\sum_{k=0}^{n} k^{n-1/2}e^{-k} = \sum_{0 \le k \le n-1} k^{(n-1)+1/2}e^{-k} + n^{n-1/2}e^{-n},$$

and this can also be obtained by Eq. (22).

We now have enough formulas at our disposal to determine the approximate values of $P(n)$, $Q(n)$, and $R(n)$, and it is only a matter of substituting and multiplying, etc. In this process we shall have occasion to use the expansion

$$(n+\alpha)^{n+\beta} = n^{n+\beta}e^{\alpha}\left(1 + \alpha\left(\beta - \frac{\alpha}{2}\right)\frac{1}{n} + O(n^{-2})\right), \quad (23)$$

which is proved in exercise 6. The method of (21) yields only the first two terms in the asymptotic series for $P(n)$; further terms can be obtained by using the instructive technique described in exercise 14.

The result of all these calculations gives us the desired asymptotic formulas:

$$P(n) = \sqrt{\frac{\pi n}{2}} - \frac{2}{3} + \frac{11}{24}\sqrt{\frac{\pi}{2n}} + \frac{4}{135n} - \frac{71}{1152}\sqrt{\frac{\pi}{2n^3}} + O(n^{-2}), \quad (24)$$

$$Q(n) = \sqrt{\frac{\pi n}{2}} - \frac{1}{3} + \frac{1}{12}\sqrt{\frac{\pi}{2n}} - \frac{4}{135n} + \frac{1}{288}\sqrt{\frac{\pi}{2n^3}} + O(n^{-2}), \quad (25)$$

$$R(n) = \sqrt{\frac{\pi n}{2}} + \frac{1}{3} + \frac{1}{12}\sqrt{\frac{\pi}{2n}} + \frac{4}{135n} + \frac{1}{288}\sqrt{\frac{\pi}{2n^3}} + O(n^{-2}). \quad (26)$$

The functions studied here have received only light treatment in the published literature. The first term $\sqrt{\pi n/2}$ in the expansion of $P(n)$ was given by H. B. Demuth [Ph.D. thesis (Stanford University, October 1956), 67–68]. Using this result, a table of $P(n)$ for $n \le 2000$, and a good slide rule, the author proceeded in 1963 to deduce the empirical estimate $P(n) \approx \sqrt{\pi n/2} - 0.6667 + 0.575/\sqrt{n}$. It was natural to conjecture that 0.6667 was really an approximation to $2/3$, and that 0.575 would perhaps turn out to be an approximation to $\gamma = 0.57721\ldots$ (why not be optimistic?). Later, as this section was being written, the correct expansion of $P(n)$ was developed, and the conjecture $2/3$ was verified; for the other coefficient 0.575 we have not γ but $\frac{11}{24}\sqrt{\pi/2} \approx 0.5744$. This nicely confirms both the theory and the empirical estimates.

Formulas equivalent to the asymptotic values of $Q(n)$ and $R(n)$ were first determined by the brilliant self-taught Indian mathematician S. Ramanujan, who posed the problem of estimating $n!\,e^n/2n^n - Q(n)$ in *J. Indian Math. Soc.* **3** (1911), 128; **4** (1912), 151–152. In his answer to the problem, he gave the asymptotic series $\frac{1}{3} + \frac{4}{135}n^{-1} - \frac{8}{2835}n^{-2} - \frac{16}{8505}n^{-3} + \cdots$, which goes considerably beyond Eq. (25). His derivation was somewhat more elegant than the method described above; to estimate I_1, he substituted $t = x + u\sqrt{2x}$, and expressed the integrand as a sum of terms of the form $c_{jk}\int_0^\infty \exp(-u^2)u^j x^{-k/2}\,du$. The integral I_2 can be avoided completely, since $a\gamma(a,x) = x^a e^{-x} + \gamma(a+1,\,x)$ when $a > 0$; see (8). An even simpler approach to the asymptotics of $Q(n)$, perhaps the simplest possible, appears in exercise 20. The derivation we have used, which is instructive in spite of its unnecessary complications, is due to R. Furch [*Zeitschrift für Physik* **112** (1939), 92–95], who was primarily interested in the value of y that makes $\gamma(x+1,\,x+y) = \Gamma(x+1)/2$. The asymptotic properties of the incomplete gamma function were later extended to complex arguments by F. G. Tricomi [*Math. Zeitschrift* **53** (1950), 136–148]. See also N. M. Temme, *Math. Comp.* **29** (1975), 1109–1114; *SIAM J. Math. Anal.* **10** (1979), 757–766. H. W. Gould has listed references to several other investigations of $Q(n)$ in *AMM* **75** (1968), 1019–1021.

Our derivations of the asymptotic series for $P(n)$, $Q(n)$, and $R(n)$ use only simple techniques of elementary calculus; notice that we have used different methods for each function! Actually we could have solved all three problems using the techniques of exercise 14, which are explained further in Sections 5.1.4 and 5.2.2. That would have been more elegant but less instructive.

For additional information, interested readers should consult the beautiful book *Asymptotic Methods in Analysis* by N. G. de Bruijn (Amsterdam: North-Holland, 1958). See also the more recent survey by A. M. Odlyzko [*Handbook of Combinatorics* **2** (MIT Press, 1995), 1063–1229], which includes 65 detailed examples and an extensive bibliography.

EXERCISES

1. [*HM20*] Prove Eq. (5) by induction on n.

2. [*HM20*] Obtain Eq. (7) from Eq. (6).

3. [*M20*] Derive Eq. (8) from Eq. (7).

▶ **4.** [*HM10*] Prove Eq. (13).

5. [*HM24*] Show that R in Eq. (21) is $O(n^n e^{-n})$.

▶ **6.** [*HM20*] Prove Eq. (23).

▶ **7.** [*HM30*] In the evaluation of I_2, we had to consider $\int_0^y e^{-u}\left(1 + \frac{u}{x}\right)^x du$. Give an asymptotic representation of

$$\int_0^{yx^{1/4}} e^{-u}\left(1 + \frac{u}{x}\right)^x du$$

to terms of order $O(x^{-2})$, when y is fixed and x is large.

8. [*HM30*] If $f(x) = O(x^r)$ as $x \to \infty$ and $0 \le r < 1$, show that

$$\int_0^{f(x)} e^{-u} \left(1 + \frac{u}{x} \right)^x du = \int_0^{f(x)} \exp\left(\frac{-u^2}{2x} + \frac{u^3}{3x^2} - \cdots + \frac{(-1)^{m-1} u^m}{m x^{m-1}} \right) du + O(x^{-s})$$

if $m = \lceil (s + 2r)/(1 - r) \rceil$. [This proves in particular a result due to Tricomi: If $f(x) = O(\sqrt{x})$, then

$$\int_0^{f(x)} e^{-u} \left(1 + \frac{u}{x} \right)^x du = \sqrt{2x} \int_0^{f(x)/\sqrt{2x}} e^{-t^2} dt + O(1).]$$

▶ **9.** [*HM36*] What is the behavior of $\gamma(x + 1, px)/\Gamma(x + 1)$ for large x? (Here p is a real constant; and if $p < 0$, we assume that x is an integer, so that t^x is well defined for negative t.) Obtain at least two terms of the asymptotic expansion, before resorting to O-terms.

10. [*HM34*] Under the assumptions of the preceding problem, with $p \ne 1$, obtain the asymptotic expansion of $\gamma(x + 1, px + py/(p-1)) - \gamma(x + 1, px)$, for fixed y, to terms of the same order as obtained in the previous exercise.

▶ **11.** [*HM35*] Let us generalize the functions $Q(n)$ and $R(n)$ by introducing a parameter x:

$$Q_x(n) = 1 + \frac{n-1}{n} x + \frac{n-1}{n} \frac{n-2}{n} x^2 + \cdots,$$

$$R_x(n) = 1 + \frac{n}{n+1} x + \frac{n}{n+1} \frac{n}{n+2} x^2 + \cdots.$$

Explore this situation and find asymptotic formulas when $x \ne 1$.

12. [*HM20*] The function $\int_0^x e^{-t^2/2} dt$ that appeared in connection with the normal distribution (see Section 1.2.10) can be expressed as a special case of the incomplete gamma function. Find values of a, b, and y such that $b\gamma(a, y)$ equals $\int_0^x e^{-t^2/2} dt$.

13. [*HM42*] (S. Ramanujan.) Prove that $R(n) - Q(n) = \frac{2}{3} + 8/(135(n + \theta(n)))$, where $\frac{2}{21} \le \theta(n) \le \frac{8}{45}$. (This implies the much weaker result $R(n+1) - Q(n+1) < R(n) - Q(n)$.)

▶ **14.** [*HM39*] (N. G. de Bruijn.) The purpose of this exercise is to find the asymptotic expansion of $\sum_{k=0}^n k^{n+\alpha} e^{-k}$ for fixed α, as $n \to \infty$.

a) Replacing k by $n-k$, show that the given sum equals $n^{n+\alpha} e^{-n} \sum_{k=0}^n e^{-k^2/2n} f(k, n)$, where

$$f(k, n) = \left(1 - \frac{k}{n} \right)^\alpha \exp\left(-\frac{k^3}{3n^2} - \frac{k^4}{4n^3} - \cdots \right).$$

b) Show that for all $m \ge 0$ and $\epsilon > 0$, the quantity $f(k, n)$ can be written in the form

$$\sum_{0 \le i \le j \le m} c_{ij} k^{2i+j} n^{-i-j} + O(n^{(m+1)(-1/2+3\epsilon)}), \quad \text{if } 0 \le k \le n^{1/2+\epsilon}.$$

c) Prove that as a consequence of (b), we have

$$\sum_{k=0}^n e^{-k^2/2n} f(k, n) = \sum_{0 \le i \le j \le m} c_{ij} n^{-i-j} \sum_{k \ge 0} k^{2i+j} e^{-k^2/2n} + O(n^{-m/2+\delta}),$$

for all $\delta > 0$. [*Hint:* The sums over the range $n^{1/2+\epsilon} < k < \infty$ are $O(n^{-r})$ for all r.]

d) Show that the asymptotic expansion of $\sum_{k \geq 0} k^t e^{-k^2/2n}$ for fixed $t \geq 0$ can be obtained by Euler's summation formula.

e) Finally therefore

$$\sum_{k=0}^{n} k^{n+\alpha} e^{-k} = n^{n+\alpha} e^{-n} \left(\sqrt{\frac{\pi n}{2}} - \frac{1}{6} - \alpha + \left(\frac{1}{12} + \frac{1}{2}\alpha + \frac{1}{2}\alpha^2 \right) \sqrt{\frac{\pi}{2n}} + O(n^{-1}) \right);$$

this computation can in principle be extended to $O(n^{-r})$ for any desired r.

15. [*HM20*] Show that the following integral is related to $Q(n)$:

$$\int_0^\infty \left(1 + \frac{z}{n}\right)^n e^{-z}\, dz.$$

16. [*M24*] Prove the identity

$$\sum_k (-1)^k \binom{n}{k} k^{n-1} Q(k) = (-1)^n (n-1)!, \quad \text{when } n > 0.$$

17. [*HM29*] (K. W. Miller.) Symmetry demands that we consider also a fourth series, which is to $P(n)$ as $R(n)$ is to $Q(n)$:

$$S(n) = 1 + \frac{n}{n+1} + \frac{n}{n+2}\frac{n+1}{n+2} + \cdots = \sum_{k \geq 0} \frac{(n+k-1)!}{(n-1)!\,(n+k)^k}.$$

What is the asymptotic behavior of this function?

18. [*M25*] Show that the sums $\sum \binom{n}{k} k^k (n-k)^{n-k}$ and $\sum \binom{n}{k} (k+1)^k (n-k)^{n-k}$ can be expressed very simply in terms of the Q function.

19. [*HM30*] (*Watson's lemma.*) Show that if the integral $C_n = \int_0^\infty e^{-nx} f(x)\, dx$ exists for all large n, and if $f(x) = O(x^\alpha)$ for $0 \leq x \leq r$, where $r > 0$ and $\alpha > -1$, then $C_n = O(n^{-1-\alpha})$.

▶ **20.** [*HM30*] Let $u = w + \frac{1}{3}w^2 + \frac{1}{36}w^3 - \frac{1}{270}w^4 + \cdots = \sum_{k=1}^{\infty} c_k w^k$ be the power series solution to the equation $w = (u^2 - \frac{2}{3}u^3 + \frac{2}{4}u^4 - \frac{2}{5}u^5 + \cdots)^{1/2}$, as in (12). Show that

$$Q(n) + 1 = \sum_{k=1}^{m-1} k c_k \Gamma(k/2) \left(\frac{n}{2}\right)^{1-k/2} + O(n^{1-m/2})$$

for all $m \geq 1$. [*Hint:* Apply Watson's lemma to the identity of exercise 15.]

I feel as if I should succeed in doing something in mathematics,
although I cannot see why it is so very important.

— HELEN KELLER (1898)

1.3. MIX

IN MANY PLACES throughout this book we will have occasion to refer to a computer's internal machine language. The machine we use is a mythical computer called "MIX." MIX is very much like nearly every computer of the 1960s and 1970s, except that it is, perhaps, nicer. The language of MIX has been designed to be powerful enough to allow brief programs to be written for most algorithms, yet simple enough so that its operations are easily learned.

The reader is urged to study this section carefully, since MIX language appears in so many parts of this book. There should be no hesitation about learning a machine language; indeed, the author once found it not uncommon to be writing programs in a half dozen different machine languages during the same week! Everyone with more than a casual interest in computers will probably get to know at least one machine language sooner or later. MIX has been specially designed to preserve the simplest aspects of historic computers, so that its characteristics are easy to assimilate.

However, it must be admitted that MIX is now quite obsolete. Therefore MIX will be replaced in subsequent editions of this book by a new machine called MMIX, the 2009. MMIX will be a so-called reduced instruction set computer (RISC), which will do arithmetic on 64-bit words. It will be even nicer than MIX, and it will be similar to machines that have become dominant during the 1990s.

The task of converting everything in this book from MIX to MMIX will take a long time; volunteers are solicited to help with that conversion process. Meanwhile, the author hopes that people will be content to live for a few more years with the old-fashioned MIX architecture — which is still worth knowing, because it helps to provide a context for subsequent developments.

1.3.1. Description of MIX

MIX is the world's first polyunsaturated computer. Like most machines, it has an identifying number — the 1009. This number was found by taking 16 actual computers very similar to MIX and on which MIX could easily be simulated, then averaging their numbers with equal weight:

$$\lfloor (360 + 650 + 709 + 7070 + \text{U3} + \text{SS80} + 1107 + 1604 + \text{G20} + \text{B220}$$
$$+ \text{S2000} + 920 + 601 + \text{H800} + \text{PDP-4} + \text{II})/16 \rfloor = 1009. \quad (1)$$

The same number may also be obtained in a simpler way by taking Roman numerals.

MIX has a peculiar property in that it is both binary and decimal at the same time. *MIX programmers don't actually know whether they are programming a machine with base 2 or base 10 arithmetic.* Therefore algorithms written in MIX can be used on either type of machine with little change, and MIX can be simulated easily on either type of machine. Programmers who are accustomed to a binary machine can think of MIX as binary; those accustomed to decimal may regard MIX as decimal. Programmers from another planet might choose to think of MIX as a ternary computer.

Words. The basic unit of MIX data is a *byte*. Each byte contains an *unspecified* amount of information, but it must be capable of holding at least 64 distinct values. That is, we know that any number between 0 and 63, inclusive, can be contained in one byte. Furthermore, each byte contains *at most* 100 distinct values. On a binary computer a byte must therefore be composed of six bits; on a decimal computer we have two digits per byte.*

Programs expressed in MIX's language should be written so that no more than sixty-four values are ever assumed for a byte. If we wish to treat the number 80, we should always leave two adjacent bytes for expressing it, even though one byte is sufficient on a decimal computer. *An algorithm in MIX should work properly regardless of how big a byte is.* Although it is quite possible to write programs that depend on the byte size, such actions are anathema to the spirit of this book; the only legitimate programs are those that would give correct results with all byte sizes. It is usually not hard to abide by this ground rule, and we will thereby find that programming a decimal computer isn't so different from programming a binary one after all.

Two adjacent bytes can express the numbers 0 through 4,095.

Three adjacent bytes can express the numbers 0 through 262,143.

Four adjacent bytes can express the numbers 0 through 16,777,215.

Five adjacent bytes can express the numbers 0 through 1,073,741,823.

A computer word consists of five bytes and a sign. The sign portion has only two possible values, + and −.

Registers. There are nine registers in MIX (see Fig. 13):

The A-register (Accumulator) consists of five bytes and a sign.

The X-register (Extension), likewise, comprises five bytes and a sign.

The I-registers (Index registers) I1, I2, I3, I4, I5, and I6 each hold two bytes together with a sign.

The J-register (Jump address) holds two bytes; it behaves as if its sign is always +.

We shall use a small letter "r", prefixed to the name, to identify a MIX register. Thus, "rA" means "register A."

The A-register has many uses, especially for arithmetic and for operating on data. The X-register is an extension on the "right-hand side" of rA, and it is used in connection with rA to hold ten bytes of a product or dividend, or it can be used to hold information shifted to the right out of rA. The index registers rI1, rI2, rI3, rI4, rI5, and rI6 are used primarily for counting and for referencing variable memory addresses. The J-register always holds the address of the instruction following the most recent "jump" operation, and it is primarily used in connection with subroutines.

---

* Since 1975 or so, the word "byte" has come to mean a sequence of precisely eight binary digits, capable of representing the numbers 0 to 255. Real-world bytes are therefore larger than the bytes of the hypothetical MIX machine; indeed, MIX's old-style bytes are just barely bigger than nybbles. When we speak of bytes in connection with MIX we shall confine ourselves to the former sense of the word, harking back to the days when bytes were not yet standardized.

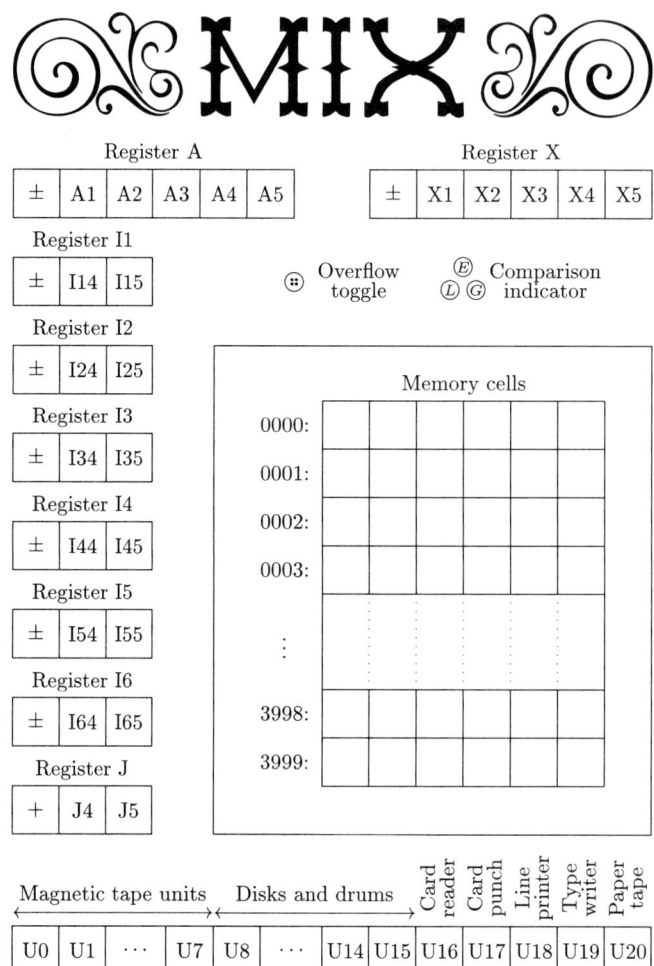

Fig. 13. The MIX computer.

Besides its registers, MIX contains

an *overflow toggle* (a single bit that is either "on" or "off");
a *comparison indicator* (having three values: LESS, EQUAL, or GREATER);
memory (4000 words of storage, each word with five bytes and a sign);
and *input-output devices* (cards, tapes, disks, etc.).

Partial fields of words. The five bytes and sign of a computer word are numbered as follows:

0	1	2	3	4	5
±	Byte	Byte	Byte	Byte	Byte

$$(2)$$

Most of the instructions allow a programmer to use only part of a word if desired. In such cases a nonstandard "field specification" can be given. The allowable fields are those that are adjacent in a computer word, and they are represented by (L:R), where L is the number of the left-hand part and R is the number of the right-hand part of the field. Examples of field specifications are:

(0:0), the sign only.
(0:2), the sign and the first two bytes.
(0:5), the whole word; this is the most common field specification.
(1:5), the whole word except for the sign.
(4:4), the fourth byte only.
(4:5), the two least significant bytes.

The use of field specifications varies slightly from instruction to instruction, and it will be explained in detail for each instruction where it applies. Each field specification (L:R) is actually represented inside the machine by the single number 8L + R; notice that this number fits easily in one byte.

Instruction format. Computer words used for instructions have the following form:

0	1	2	3	4	5
±	A	A	I	F	C

$$. \tag{3}$$

The rightmost byte, C, is the *operation code* telling what operation is to be performed. For example, C = 8 specifies the operation LDA, "load the A-register."

The F-byte holds a *modification* of the operation code. It is usually a field specification (L:R) = 8L + R; for example, if C = 8 and F = 11, the operation is "load the A-register with the (1:3) field." Sometimes F is used for other purposes; on input-output instructions, for example, F is the number of the relevant input or output unit.

The left-hand portion of the instruction, ±AA, is the *address*. (Notice that the sign is part of the address.) The I-field, which comes next to the address, is the *index specification*, which may be used to modify the effective address. If I = 0, the address ±AA is used without change; otherwise I should contain a number i between 1 and 6, and the contents of index register Ii are added algebraically to ±AA before the instruction is carried out; the result is used as the address. This indexing process takes place on *every* instruction. We will use the letter M to indicate the address after any specified indexing has occurred. (If the addition of the index register to the address ±AA yields a result that does not fit in two bytes, the value of M is undefined.)

In most instructions, M will refer to a memory cell. The terms "memory cell" and "memory location" are used almost interchangeably in this book. We assume that there are 4000 memory cells, numbered from 0 to 3999; hence every memory location can be addressed with two bytes. For every instruction in which M refers to a memory cell we must have $0 \le M \le 3999$, and in this case we will write CONTENTS(M) to denote the value stored in memory location M.

On certain instructions, the "address" M has another significance, and it may even be negative. Thus, one instruction adds M to an index register, and such an operation takes account of the sign of M.

Notation. To discuss instructions in a readable manner, we will use the notation

$$\text{OP} \quad \text{ADDRESS,I(F)} \tag{4}$$

to denote an instruction like (3). Here OP is a symbolic name given to the operation code (the C-part) of the instruction; ADDRESS is the $\pm$AA portion; I and F represent the I- and F-fields, respectively.

If I is zero, the ",I" is omitted. If F is the *normal* F-specification for this particular operator, the "(F)" need not be written. The normal F-specification for almost all operators is (0:5), representing a whole word. If a different F is normal, it will be mentioned explicitly when we discuss a particular operator.

For example, the instruction to load a number into the accumulator is called LDA and it is operation code number 8. We have

Conventional representation   Actual numeric instruction

LDA	2000,2(0:3)	+	2000	2	3	8
LDA	2000,2(1:3)	+	2000	2	11	8
LDA	2000(1:3)	+	2000	0	11	8
LDA	2000	+	2000	0	5	8
LDA	-2000,4	−	2000	4	5	8

$$\tag{5}$$

The instruction "LDA 2000,2(0:3)" may be read "Load A with the contents of location 2000 indexed by 2, the zero-three field."

To represent the numerical contents of a MIX word, we will always use a box notation like that above. Notice that in the word

+	2000	2	3	8

the number +2000 is shown filling two adjacent bytes and sign; the actual contents of byte (1:1) and of byte (2:2) will vary from one MIX computer to another, since byte size is variable. As a further example of this notation for MIX words, the diagram

−	10000	3000

represents a word with two fields, a three-byte-plus-sign field containing −10000 and a two-byte field containing 3000. When a word is split into more than one field, it is said to be "packed."

Rules for each instruction. The remarks following (3) above have defined the quantities M, F, and C for every word used as an instruction. We will now define the actions corresponding to each instruction.

Loading operators.

• LDA (load A). C = 8; F = field.

The specified field of CONTENTS(M) replaces the previous contents of register A.

On all operations where a partial field is used as an input, the sign is used if it is a part of the field, otherwise the sign + is understood. The field is shifted over to the right-hand part of the register as it is loaded.

Examples: If F is the normal field specification (0:5), everything in location M is copied into rA. If F is (1:5), the absolute value of CONTENTS(M) is loaded with a plus sign. If M contains an *instruction* word and if F is (0:2), the "±AA" field is loaded as

| ± | 0 | 0 | 0 | A | A | .

Suppose location 2000 contains the word

| − | 80 | 3 | 5 | 4 | ;   (6)

then we get the following results from loading various partial fields:

Instruction	Contents of rA afterwards
LDA 2000	− | 80 | 3 | 5 | 4
LDA 2000(1:5)	+ | 80 | 3 | 5 | 4
LDA 2000(3:5)	+ | 0 | 0 | 3 | 5 | 4
LDA 2000(0:3)	− | 0 | 0 | 80 | 3
LDA 2000(4:4)	+ | 0 | 0 | 0 | 0 | 5
LDA 2000(0:0)	− | 0 | 0 | 0 | 0 | 0
LDA 2000(1:1)	+ | 0 | 0 | 0 | 0 | ?

(The last example has a partially unknown effect, since byte size is variable.)

• LDX (load X). C = 15; F = field.

This is the same as LDA, except that rX is loaded instead of rA.

• LDi (load i). C = 8 + i; F = field.

This is the same as LDA, except that rIi is loaded instead of rA. An index register contains only two bytes (not five) and a sign; bytes 1, 2, 3 are always assumed to be zero. The LDi instruction is undefined if it would result in setting bytes 1, 2, or 3 to anything but zero.

In the description of all instructions, "i" stands for an integer, $1 \le i \le 6$. Thus, LDi stands for six different instructions: LD1, LD2, ..., LD6.

• LDAN (load A negative). C = 16; F = field.
• LDXN (load X negative). C = 23; F = field.
• LDiN (load i negative). C = 16 + i; F = field.

These eight instructions are the same as LDA, LDX, LDi, respectively, except that the *opposite* sign is loaded.

Storing operators.

• STA (store A). C = 24; F = field.
A portion of the contents of rA replaces the field of CONTENTS(M) specified by F.
The other parts of CONTENTS(M) are unchanged.

On a *store* operation the field F has the opposite significance from the *load*
operation: The number of bytes in the field is taken from the right-hand portion
of the register and shifted *left* if necessary to be inserted in the proper field of
CONTENTS(M). The sign is not altered unless it is part of the field. The contents
of the register are not affected.

Examples: Suppose that location 2000 contains

$$ - \boxed{1} \boxed{2} \boxed{3} \boxed{4} \boxed{5} $$

and register A contains

$$ + \boxed{6} \boxed{7} \boxed{8} \boxed{9} \boxed{0} \; . $$

Then:

Instruction	Contents of location 2000 afterwards
STA 2000	+ 6 7 8 9 0
STA 2000(1:5)	− 6 7 8 9 0
STA 2000(5:5)	− 1 2 3 4 0
STA 2000(2:2)	− 1 0 3 4 5
STA 2000(2:3)	− 1 9 0 4 5
STA 2000(0:1)	+ 0 2 3 4 5

• STX (store X). C = 31; F = field.
Same as STA, except that rX is stored rather than rA.

• STi (store i). C = 24 + i; F = field.
Same as STA, except that rIi is stored rather than rA. Bytes 1, 2, 3 of an index
register are zero; thus if rI1 contains

$$ \boxed{\pm} \boxed{m} \boxed{n} \; , $$

it behaves as though it were

$$ \boxed{\pm} \boxed{0} \boxed{0} \boxed{0} \boxed{m} \boxed{n} \; . $$

• STJ (store J). C = 32; F = field.
Same as STi, except that rJ is stored and its sign is always +.

With STJ the normal field specification for F is (0:2), not (0:5). This is
natural, since STJ is almost always done into the address field of an instruction.

• STZ (store zero). C = 33; F = field.
Same as STA, except that plus zero is stored. In other words, the specified field
of CONTENTS(M) is cleared to zero.

Arithmetic operators. On the add, subtract, multiply, and divide operations, a field specification is allowed. A field specification of "(0:6)" can be used to indicate a "floating point" operation (see Section 4.2), but few of the programs we will write for MIX will use this feature, since we will primarily be concerned with algorithms on integers.

The standard field specification is, as usual, (0:5). Other fields are treated as in LDA. We will use the letter V to indicate the specified field of CONTENTS(M); thus, V is the value that would have been loaded into register A if the operation code were LDA.

• ADD. C = 1; F = field.

V is added to rA. If the magnitude of the result is too large for register A, the overflow toggle is set on, and the remainder of the addition appearing in rA is as though a "1" had been carried into another register to the left of rA. (Otherwise the setting of the overflow toggle is unchanged.) If the result is zero, the sign of rA is unchanged.

Example: The sequence of instructions below computes the sum of the five bytes of register A.

```
              STA    2000
              LDA    2000(5:5)
              ADD    2000(4:4)
              ADD    2000(3:3)
              ADD    2000(2:2)
              ADD    2000(1:1)
```

This is sometimes called "sideways addition."

Overflow will occur in some MIX computers when it would not occur in others, because of the variable definition of byte size. We have not said that overflow will occur definitely if the value is greater than 1073741823; overflow occurs when the magnitude of the result is greater than the contents of five bytes, depending on the byte size. One can still write programs that work properly and that give the same final answers, regardless of the byte size.

• SUB (subtract). C = 2; F = field.

V is subtracted from rA. (Equivalent to ADD but with −V in place of V.)

• MUL (multiply). C = 3; F = field.

The 10-byte product, V times rA, replaces registers A and X. The signs of rA and rX are both set to the algebraic sign of the product (namely, + if the signs of V and rA were the same, − if they were different).

• DIV (divide). C = 4; F = field.

The value of rA and rX, treated as a 10-byte number rAX with the sign of rA, is divided by the value V. If V = 0 or if the quotient is more than five bytes in magnitude (this is equivalent to the condition that $|rA| \geq |V|$), registers A and X are filled with undefined information and the overflow toggle is set on. Otherwise the quotient $\pm\lfloor|rAX/V|\rfloor$ is placed in rA and the remainder $\pm(|rAX| \bmod |V|)$ is placed in rX. The sign of rA afterwards is the algebraic sign of the quotient (namely, $+$ if the signs of V and rA were the same, $-$ if they were different). The sign of rX afterwards is the previous sign of rA.

Examples of arithmetic instructions: In most cases, arithmetic is done only with MIX words that are single five-byte numbers, not packed with several fields. It is, however, possible to operate arithmetically on packed MIX words, if some caution is used. The following examples should be studied carefully. (As before, ? designates an unknown value.)

		+	1234	1	150	rA before
		+	100	5	50	Cell 1000
ADD	1000	+	1334	6	200	rA after

		$-$	1234	0	0	9	rA before
		$-$	2000	150	0		Cell 1000
SUB	1000	+	766	149	?		rA after

		+	1	1	1	1	1	rA before
		+	1	1	1	1	1	Cell 1000
MUL	1000	+	0	1	2	3	4	rA after
		+	5	4	3	2	1	rX after

		$-$					112	rA before
		?	2	?	?	?	?	Cell 1000
MUL	1000(1:1)	$-$					0	rA after
		$-$					224	rX after

		$-$	50	0	112	4	rA before
		$-$	2	0	0	0	0	Cell 1000
MUL	1000	+	100	0	224		rA after
		+	8	0	0	0	0	rX after

		+					0	rA before
		?					17	rX before
		+					3	Cell 1000
DIV	1000	+					5	rA after
		+					2	rX after

−				0	rA before
+	1235	0	3	1	rX before
−	0	0	0	2	0

−	0	0	0	2	0	Cell 1000

DIV   1000

+	0	617	?	?	rA after
−	0	0	?	1	rX after

(These examples have been prepared with the philosophy that it is better to give a complete, baffling description than an incomplete, straightforward one.)

Address transfer operators. In the following operations, the (possibly in-dexed) "address" M is used as a signed number, not as the address of a cell in memory.

• **ENTA** (enter A). C = 48; F = 2.
The quantity M is loaded into rA. The action is equivalent to "**LDA**" from a memory word containing the signed value of M. If M = 0, the sign of the instruction is loaded.

   Examples: "**ENTA 0**" sets rA to zeros, with a + sign. "**ENTA 0,1**" sets rA to the current contents of index register 1, except that −0 is changed to +0. "**ENTA -0,1**" is similar, except that +0 is changed to −0.

• **ENTX** (enter X). C = 55; F = 2.
• **ENTi** (enter i). C = 48 + i; F = 2.
Analogous to **ENTA**, loading the appropriate register.

• **ENNA** (enter negative A). C = 48; F = 3.
• **ENNX** (enter negative X). C = 55; F = 3.
• **ENNi** (enter negative i). C = 48 + i; F = 3.
Same as **ENTA**, **ENTX**, and **ENTi**, except that the opposite sign is loaded.

   Example: "**ENN3 0,3**" replaces rI3 by its negative, although −0 remains −0.

• **INCA** (increase A). C = 48; F = 0.
The quantity M is added to rA; the action is equivalent to "**ADD**" from a memory word containing the value of M. Overflow is possible and it is treated just as in **ADD**.

   Example: "**INCA 1**" increases the value of rA by one.

• **INCX** (increase X). C = 55; F = 0.
The quantity M is added to rX. If overflow occurs, the action is equivalent to **ADD**, except that rX is used instead of rA. Register A is never affected by this instruction.

• **INCi** (increase i). C = 48 + i; F = 0.
Add M to rIi. Overflow must not occur; if M + rIi doesn't fit in two bytes, the result of this instruction is undefined.

- DECA (decrease A). C = 48; F = 1.
- DECX (decrease X). C = 55; F = 1.
- DEC*i* (decrease *i*). C = 48 + *i*; F = 1.

These eight instructions are the same as INCA, INCX, and INC*i*, respectively, except that M is subtracted from the register rather than added.

Notice that the operation code C is the same for ENTA, ENNA, INCA, and DECA; the F-field is used to distinguish the various operations from each other.

Comparison operators. MIX's comparison operators all compare the value contained in a register with a value contained in memory. The comparison indicator is then set to LESS, EQUAL, or GREATER according to whether the value of the register is less than, equal to, or greater than the value of the memory cell. A minus zero is *equal to* a plus zero.

- CMPA (compare A). C = 56; F = field.

The specified field of rA is compared with the *same* field of CONTENTS(M). If F does not include the sign position, the fields are both considered nonnegative; otherwise the sign is taken into account in the comparison. (An equal comparison always occurs when F is (0:0), since minus zero equals plus zero.)

- CMPX (compare X). C = 63; F = field.

This is analogous to CMPA.

- CMP*i* (compare *i*). C = 56 + *i*; F = field.

Analogous to CMPA. Bytes 1, 2, and 3 of the index register are treated as zero in the comparison. (Thus if F = (1:2), the result cannot be GREATER.)

Jump operators. Instructions are ordinarily executed in sequential order; in other words, the command that is performed after the command in location P is usually the one found in location P + 1. But several "jump" instructions allow this sequence to be interrupted. When a typical jump takes place, the J-register is set to the address of the next instruction (that is, to the address of the instruction that would have been next if we hadn't jumped). A "store J" instruction then can be used by the programmer, if desired, to set the address field of another command that will later be used to return to the original place in the program. The J-register is changed whenever a jump actually occurs in a program, except when the jump operator is JSJ, and it is never changed by non-jumps.

- JMP (jump). C = 39; F = 0.

Unconditional jump: The next instruction is taken from location M.

- JSJ (jump, save J). C = 39; F = 1.

Same as JMP except that the contents of rJ are unchanged.

- JOV (jump on overflow). C = 39; F = 2.

If the overflow toggle is on, it is turned off and a JMP occurs; otherwise nothing happens.

- JNOV (jump on no overflow). C = 39; F = 3.

If the overflow toggle is off, a JMP occurs; otherwise it is turned off.

• JL, JE, JG, JGE, JNE, JLE (jump on less, equal, greater, greater-or-equal, unequal, less-or-equal). C = 39; F = 4, 5, 6, 7, 8, 9, respectively.

Jump if the comparison indicator is set to the condition indicated. For example, JNE will jump if the comparison indicator is LESS or GREATER. The comparison indicator is not changed by these instructions.

• JAN, JAZ, JAP, JANN, JANZ, JANP (jump A negative, zero, positive, nonnegative, nonzero, nonpositive). C = 40; F = 0, 1, 2, 3, 4, 5, respectively.

If the contents of rA satisfy the stated condition, a JMP occurs, otherwise nothing happens. "Positive" means *greater* than zero (not zero); "nonpositive" means the opposite, namely zero or negative.

• JXN, JXZ, JXP, JXNN, JXNZ, JXNP (jump X negative, zero, positive, nonnegative, nonzero, nonpositive). C = 47; F = 0, 1, 2, 3, 4, 5, respectively.

• JiN, JiZ, JiP, JiNN, JiNZ, JiNP (jump i negative, zero, positive, nonnegative, nonzero, nonpositive). C = $40 + i$; F = 0, 1, 2, 3, 4, 5, respectively. These 42 instructions are analogous to the corresponding operations for rA.

Miscellaneous operators.

• SLA, SRA, SLAX, SRAX, SLC, SRC (shift left A, shift right A, shift left AX, shift right AX, shift left AX circularly, shift right AX circularly). C = 6; F = 0, 1, 2, 3, 4, 5, respectively.

These six are the "shift" commands, in which M specifies a number of MIX bytes to be shifted left or right; M must be nonnegative. SLA and SRA do not affect rX; the other shifts affect both registers A and X as though they were a single 10-byte register. With SLA, SRA, SLAX, and SRAX, zeros are shifted into the register at one side, and bytes disappear at the other side. The instructions SLC and SRC call for a "circulating" shift, in which the bytes that leave one end enter in at the other end. Both rA and rX participate in a circulating shift. The signs of registers A and X are not affected in any way by any of the shift commands.

Examples:			Register A								Register X			
Initial contents	+	1	2	3	4	5		−	6	7	8	9	10
SRAX 1	+	0	1	2	3	4		−	5	6	7	8	9
SLA 2	+	2	3	4	0	0		−	5	6	7	8	9
SRC 4	+	6	7	8	9	2		−	3	4	0	0	5
SRA 2	+	0	0	6	7	8		−	3	4	0	0	5
SLC 501	+	0	6	7	8	3		−	4	0	0	5	0

• MOVE. C = 7; F = number, normally 1.

The number of words specified by F is moved, starting from location M to the location specified by the contents of index register 1. The transfer occurs one word at a time, and rI1 is increased by the value of F at the end of the operation. If F = 0, nothing happens.

Care must be taken when there's overlap between the locations involved; for example, suppose that F = 3 and M = 1000. Then if rI1 = 999, we transfer

CONTENTS(1000) to CONTENTS(999), CONTENTS(1001) to CONTENTS(1000), and CONTENTS(1002) to CONTENTS(1001); nothing unusual occurred here. But if rI1 were 1001 instead, we would move CONTENTS(1000) to CONTENTS(1001), then CONTENTS(1001) to CONTENTS(1002), then CONTENTS(1002) to CONTENTS(1003), so we would have moved the *same* word CONTENTS(1000) into three places.

• NOP (no operation). C = 0.

No operation occurs, and this instruction is bypassed. F and M are ignored.

• HLT (halt). C = 5; F = 2.

The machine stops. When the computer operator restarts it, the net effect is equivalent to NOP.

Input-output operators. MIX has a fair amount of input-output equipment (all of which is optional at extra cost). Each device is given a number as follows:

Unit number	Peripheral device	Block size
t	Tape unit number t $(0 \leq t \leq 7)$	100 words
d	Disk or drum unit number d $(8 \leq d \leq 15)$	100 words
16	Card reader	16 words
17	Card punch	16 words
18	Line printer	24 words
19	Typewriter terminal	14 words
20	Paper tape	14 words

Not every MIX installation will have all of this equipment available; we will occasionally make appropriate assumptions about the presence of certain devices. Some devices may not be used both for input and for output. The number of words mentioned in the table above is a fixed block size associated with each unit.

Input or output with magnetic tape, disk, or drum units reads or writes full words (five bytes and a sign). Input or output with units 16 through 20, however, is always done in a *character code* where each byte represents one alphameric character. Thus, five characters per MIX word are transmitted. The character code is given at the top of Table 1, which appears at the close of this section and on the end papers of this book. The code 00 corresponds to "␣", which denotes a *blank space*. Codes 01–29 are for the letters A through Z with a few Greek letters thrown in; codes 30–39 represent the digits 0, 1, ..., 9; and further codes 40, 41, ... represent punctuation marks and other special characters. (MIX's character set harks back to the days before computers could cope with lowercase letters.) We cannot use character code to read in or write out all possible values that a byte may have, since certain combinations are undefined. Moreover, some input-output devices may be unable to handle all the symbols in the character set; for example, the symbols Σ and Π that appear amid the letters will perhaps not be acceptable to the card reader. When character-code input is being done, the signs of all words are set to +; on output, signs are ignored. If a typewriter is used for input, the "carriage return" that is typed at the end of each line causes the remainder of that line to be filled with blanks.

The disk and drum units are external memory devices each containing 100-word blocks. On every IN, OUT, or IOC instruction as defined below, the particular 100-word block referred to by the instruction is specified by the current contents of rX, which should not exceed the capacity of the disk or drum involved.

• IN (input). C = 36; F = unit.
This instruction initiates the transfer of information from the input unit specified into consecutive locations starting with M. The number of locations transferred is the block size for this unit (see the table above). The machine will wait at this point if a preceding operation for the same unit is not yet complete. The transfer of information that starts with this instruction will not be complete until an unknown future time, depending on the speed of the input device, so a program must not refer to the information in memory until then. It is improper to attempt to read any block from magnetic tape that follows the latest block written on that tape.

• OUT (output). C = 37; F = unit.
This instruction starts the transfer of information from memory locations starting at M to the output unit specified. The machine waits until the unit is ready, if it is not initially ready. The transfer will not be complete until an unknown future time, depending on the speed of the output device, so a program must not alter the information in memory until then.

• IOC (input-output control). C = 35; F = unit.
The machine waits, if necessary, until the specified unit is not busy. Then a control operation is performed, depending on the particular device being used. The following examples are used in various parts of this book:

Magnetic tape: If M = 0, the tape is rewound. If M < 0 the tape is skipped backward −M blocks, or to the beginning of the tape, whichever comes first. If M > 0, the tape is skipped forward; it is improper to skip forward over any blocks following the one last written on that tape.

For example, the sequence "OUT 1000(3); IOC -1(3); IN 2000(3)" writes out one hundred words onto tape 3, then reads it back in again. Unless the tape reliability is questioned, the last two instructions of that sequence are only a slow way to move words 1000–1099 to locations 2000–2099. The sequence "OUT 1000(3); IOC +1(3)" is improper.

Disk or drum: M should be zero. The effect is to position the device according to rX so that the next IN or OUT operation on this unit will take less time if it uses the same rX setting.

Line printer: M should be zero. "IOC 0(18)" skips the printer to the top of the following page.

Paper tape: M should be zero. "IOC 0(20)" rewinds the tape.

• JRED (jump ready). C = 38; F = unit.
A jump occurs if the specified unit is ready, that is, finished with the preceding operation initiated by IN, OUT, or IOC.

• JBUS (jump busy). C = 34; F = unit.
Analogous to JRED, but the jump occurs when the specified unit is *not* ready.

Example: In location 1000, the instruction "JBUS 1000(16)" will be executed repeatedly until unit 16 is ready.

The simple operations above complete MIX's repertoire of input-output instructions. There is no "tape check" indicator, etc., to cover exceptional conditions on the peripheral devices. Any such condition (e.g., paper jam, unit turned off, out of tape, etc.) causes the unit to remain busy, a bell rings, and the skilled computer operator fixes things manually using ordinary maintenance procedures. Some more complicated peripheral units, which are more expensive and more representative of contemporary equipment than the fixed-block-size tapes, drums, and disks described here, are discussed in Sections 5.4.6 and 5.4.9.

Conversion Operators.

• NUM (convert to numeric). C = 5; F = 0.

This operation is used to change the character code into numeric code. M is ignored. Registers A and X are assumed to contain a 10-byte number in character code; the NUM instruction sets the magnitude of rA equal to the numerical value of this number (treated as a decimal number). The value of rX and the sign of rA are unchanged. Bytes 00, 10, 20, 30, 40, ... convert to the digit zero; bytes 01, 11, 21, ... convert to the digit one; etc. Overflow is possible, and in this case the remainder modulo b^5 is retained, where b is the byte size.

• CHAR (convert to characters). C = 5; F = 1.

This operation is used to change numeric code into character code suitable for output to punched cards or tape or the line printer. The value in rA is converted into a 10-byte decimal number that is put into registers A and X in character code. The signs of rA and rX are unchanged. M is ignored.

Examples:

	Register A						Register X				
Initial contents	–	00	00	31	32	39	+	37	57	47	30	30
NUM 0	–			12977700			+	37	57	47	30	30
INCA 1	–			12977699			+	37	57	47	30	30
CHAR 0	–	30	30	31	32	39	+	37	37	36	39	39

Timing. To give quantitative information about the efficiency of MIX programs, each of MIX's operations is assigned an *execution time* typical of vintage-1970 computers.

ADD, SUB, all LOAD operations, all STORE operations (including STZ), all shift commands, and all comparison operations take *two units* of time. MOVE requires one unit plus two for each word moved. MUL, NUM, CHAR each require 10 units and DIV requires 12. The execution time for floating point operations is specified in Section 4.2.1. All remaining operations take one unit of time, plus the time the computer may be idle on the IN, OUT, IOC, or HLT instructions.

Notice in particular that ENTA takes one unit of time, while LDA takes two units. The timing rules are easily remembered because of the fact that, except for shifts, conversions, MUL, and DIV, the number of time units equals the number of references to memory (including the reference to the instruction itself).

MIX's basic unit of time is a relative measure that we will denote simply by u. It may be regarded as, say, 10 microseconds (for a relatively inexpensive computer) or as 10 nanoseconds (for a relatively high-priced machine).

Example: The sequence LDA 1000; INCA 1; STA 1000 takes exactly $5u$.

> And now I see with eye serene
> The very pulse of the machine.
> — WILLIAM WORDSWORTH,
> *She Was a Phantom of Delight* (1804)

Summary. We have now discussed all the features of MIX, except for its "GO button," which is discussed in exercise 26. Although MIX has nearly 150 different operations, they fit into a few simple patterns so that they can easily be remembered. Table 1 summarizes the operations for each C-setting. The name of each operator is followed in parentheses by its default F-field.

The following exercises give a quick review of the material in this section. They are mostly quite simple, and the reader should try to do nearly all of them.

EXERCISES

1. [*00*] If MIX were a ternary (base 3) computer, how many "trits" would there be per byte?

2. [*02*] If a value to be represented within MIX may get as large as 99999999, how many adjacent bytes should be used to contain this quantity?

3. [*02*] Give the partial field specifications, (L:R), for the (a) address field, (b) index field, (c) field field, and (d) operation code field of a MIX instruction.

4. [*00*] The last example in (5) is "LDA -2000,4". How can this be legitimate, in view of the fact that memory addresses should not be negative?

5. [*10*] What symbolic notation, analogous to (4), corresponds to (6) if (6) is regarded as a MIX instruction?

▶ **6.** [*10*] Assume that location 3000 contains

$$\boxed{+\ \vert\ 5\ \vert\ 1\ \vert\ 200\ \vert 15}\ .$$

What is the result of the following instructions? (State if any of them are undefined or only partially defined.) (a) LDAN 3000; (b) LD2N 3000(3:4); (c) LDX 3000(1:3); (d) LD6 3000; (e) LDXN 3000(0:0).

7. [*M15*] Give a precise definition of the results of the DIV instruction for all cases in which overflow does not occur, using the algebraic operations $X \bmod Y$ and $\lfloor X/Y \rfloor$.

8. [*15*] The last example of the DIV instruction that appears on page 133 has "rX before" equal to $\boxed{+\ \vert\ 1235\ \vert\ 0\ \vert\ 3\ \vert\ 1}$. If this were $\boxed{-\ \vert\ 1234\ \vert\ 0\ \vert\ 3\ \vert\ 1}$ instead, but other parts of that example were unchanged, what would registers A and X contain after the DIV instruction?

Table 1

Character code:	00 01 02 03 04 05 06 07 08 09 10 11 12 13 14 15 16 17 18 19 20 21 22 23 24
	␣ A B C D E F G H I Δ J K L M N O P Q R Σ Π S T U

00	*1*	01	*2*	02	*2*	03	*10*
No operation		rA ← rA + V		rA ← rA − V		rAX ← rA × V	
NOP(0)		ADD(0:5) FADD(6)		SUB(0:5) FSUB(6)		MUL(0:5) FMUL(6)	
08	*2*	**09**	*2*	**10**	*2*	**11**	*2*
rA ← V		rI1 ← V		rI2 ← V		rI3 ← V	
LDA(0:5)		LD1(0:5)		LD2(0:5)		LD3(0:5)	
16	*2*	**17**	*2*	**18**	*2*	**19**	*2*
rA ← −V		rI1 ← −V		rI2 ← −V		rI3 ← −V	
LDAN(0:5)		LD1N(0:5)		LD2N(0:5)		LD3N(0:5)	
24	*2*	**25**	*2*	**26**	*2*	**27**	*2*
M(F) ← rA		M(F) ← rI1		M(F) ← rI2		M(F) ← rI3	
STA(0:5)		ST1(0:5)		ST2(0:5)		ST3(0:5)	
32	*2*	**33**	*2*	**34**	*1*	**35**	*1 + T*
M(F) ← rJ		M(F) ← 0		Unit F busy?		Control, unit F	
STJ(0:2)		STZ(0:5)		JBUS(0)		IOC(0)	
40	*1*	**41**	*1*	**42**	*1*	**43**	*1*
rA : 0, jump		rI1 : 0, jump		rI2 : 0, jump		rI3 : 0, jump	
JA[+]		J1[+]		J2[+]		J3[+]	
48	*1*	**49**	*1*	**50**	*1*	**51**	*1*
rA ← [rA]? ± M		rI1 ← [rI1]? ± M		rI2 ← [rI2]? ± M		rI3 ← [rI3]? ± M	
INCA(0) DECA(1) ENTA(2) ENNA(3)		INC1(0) DEC1(1) ENT1(2) ENN1(3)		INC2(0) DEC2(1) ENT2(2) ENN2(3)		INC3(0) DEC3(1) ENT3(2) ENN3(3)	
56	*2*	**57**	*2*	**58**	*2*	**59**	*2*
CI ← rA(F) : V		CI ← rI1(F) : V		CI ← rI2(F) : V		CI ← rI3(F) : V	
CMPA(0:5) FCMP(6)		CMP1(0:5)		CMP2(0:5)		CMP3(0:5)	

General form:

C	*t*
Description	
OP(F)	

C = operation code, $(5:5)$ field of instruction
F = op variant, $(4:4)$ field of instruction
M = address of instruction after indexing
V = M(F) = contents of F field of location M
OP = symbolic name for operation
(F) = normal F setting
t = execution time; T = interlock time

25 26 27 28 29 30 31 32 33 34 35 36 37 38 39 40 41 42 43 44 45 46 47 48 49 50 51 52 53 54 55
V W X Y Z 0 1 2 3 4 5 6 7 8 9 . , ( ) + - * / = $ < > @ ; : '

04	*12*	**05**	*10*	**06**	*2*	**07**	*1 + 2F*
rA ← rAX/V rX ← remainder DIV(0:5) FDIV(6)		Special NUM(0) CHAR(1) HLT(2)		Shift M bytes SLA(0)　SRA(1) SLAX(2)　SRAX(3) SLC(4)　SRC(5)		Move F words from M to rI1 MOVE(1)	
12	*2*	**13**	*2*	**14**	*2*	**15**	*2*
rI4 ← V LD4(0:5)		rI5 ← V LD5(0:5)		rI6 ← V LD6(0:5)		rX ← V LDX(0:5)	
20	*2*	**21**	*2*	**22**	*2*	**23**	*2*
rI4 ← −V LD4N(0:5)		rI5 ← −V LD5N(0:5)		rI6 ← −V LD6N(0:5)		rX ← −V LDXN(0:5)	
28	*2*	**29**	*2*	**30**	*2*	**31**	*2*
M(F) ← rI4 ST4(0:5)		M(F) ← rI5 ST5(0:5)		M(F) ← rI6 ST6(0:5)		M(F) ← rX STX(0:5)	
36	*1 + T*	**37**	*1 + T*	**38**	*1*	**39**	*1*
Input, unit F IN(0)		Output, unit F OUT(0)		Unit F ready? JRED(0)		Jumps JMP(0)　JSJ(1) JOV(2)　JNOV(3) also [*] below	
44	*1*	**45**	*1*	**46**	*1*	**47**	*1*
rI4 : 0, jump J4[+]		rI5 : 0, jump J5[+]		rI6 : 0, jump J6[+]		rX : 0, jump JX[+]	
52	*1*	**53**	*1*	**54**	*1*	**55**	*1*
rI4 ← [rI4]? ± M INC4(0) DEC4(1) ENT4(2) ENN4(3)		rI5 ← [rI5]? ± M INC5(0) DEC5(1) ENT5(2) ENN5(3)		rI6 ← [rI6]? ± M INC6(0) DEC6(1) ENT6(2) ENN6(3)		rX ← [rX]? ± M INCX(0) DECX(1) ENTX(2) ENNX(3)	
60	*2*	**61**	*2*	**62**	*2*	**63**	*2*
CI ← rI4(F) : V CMP4(0:5)		CI ← rI5(F) : V CMP5(0:5)		CI ← rI6(F) : V CMP6(0:5)		CI ← rX(F) : V CMPX(0:5)	

rA = register A
rX = register X
rAX = registers A and X as one
rIi = index register i, $1 \leq i \leq 6$
rJ = register J
CI = comparison indicator

[*]:
JL(4)　<
JE(5)　=
JG(6)　>
JGE(7)　≥
JNE(8)　≠
JLE(9)　≤

[+]:
N(0)
Z(1)
P(2)
NN(3)
NZ(4)
NP(5)

▶ **9.** [*15*] List all the MIX operators that can possibly affect the setting of the overflow toggle. (Do not include floating point operators.)

10. [*15*] List all the MIX operators that can possibly affect the setting of the comparison indicator.

▶ **11.** [*15*] List all the MIX operators that can possibly affect the setting of rI1.

12. [*10*] Find a single instruction that has the effect of multiplying the current contents of rI3 by two and leaving the result in rI3.

▶ **13.** [*10*] Suppose location 1000 contains the instruction "JOV 1001". This instruction turns off the overflow toggle if it is on (and the next instruction executed will be in location 1001, in any case). If this instruction were changed to "JNOV 1001", would there be any difference? What if it were changed to "JOV 1000" or "JNOV 1000"?

14. [*20*] For each MIX operation, consider whether there is a way to set the $\pm$AA, I, and F portions so that the result of the instruction is precisely equivalent to NOP (except that the execution time may be longer). Assume that nothing is known about the contents of any registers or any memory locations. Whenever it is possible to produce a NOP, state how it can be done. *Examples:* INCA is a no-op if the address and index parts are zero. JMP can never be a no-op, since it affects rJ.

15. [*10*] How many *alphameric characters* are there in a typewriter or paper-tape block? in a card-reader or card-punch block? in a line-printer block?

16. [*20*] Write a program that sets memory cells 0000–0099 all to zero and is (a) as short a program as possible; (b) as fast a program as possible. [*Hint:* Consider using the MOVE command.]

17. [*26*] This is the same as the previous exercise, except that locations 0000 through N, inclusive, are to be set to zero, where N is the current contents of rI2. Your programs (a) and (b) should work for any value $0 \leq N \leq 2999$; they should start in location 3000.

▶ **18.** [*22*] After the following "number one" program has been executed, what changes to registers, toggles, and memory have taken place? (For example, what is the final setting of rI1? of rX? of the overflow and comparison indicators?)

```
STZ   1
ENNX  1
STX   1(0:1)
SLAX  1
ENNA  1
INCX  1
ENT1  1
SRC   1
ADD   1
DEC1  -1
STZ   1
CMPA  1
MOVE  -1,1(1)
NUM   1
CHAR  1
HLT   1  ▮
```

▶ **19.** [*14*] What is the execution time of the program in the preceding exercise, not counting the HLT instruction?

20. [*20*] Write a program that sets *all* 4000 memory cells equal to a "HLT" instruction, and then stops.

▶ **21.** [*24*] (a) Can the J-register ever be zero? (b) Write a program that, given a number N in rI4, sets register J equal to N, assuming that $0 < N \le 3000$. Your program should start in location 3000. When your program has finished its execution, the contents of all memory cells must be unchanged.

▶ **22.** [*28*] Location 2000 contains an integer number, X. Write two programs that compute X^{13} and halt with the result in register A. One program should use the minimum number of MIX memory locations; the other should require the minimum execution time possible. Assume that X^{13} fits into a single word.

23. [*27*] Location 0200 contains a word

$$\boxed{+\;|\;a\;|\;b\;|\;c\;|\;d\;|\;e\;}\;;$$

write two programs that compute the "reflected" word

$$\boxed{+\;|\;e\;|\;d\;|\;c\;|\;b\;|\;a\;}$$

and halt with the result in register A. One program should do this without using MIX's ability to load and store partial fields of words. Both programs should take the minimum possible number of memory locations under the stated conditions (including all locations used for the program and for temporary storage of intermediate results).

24. [*21*] Assuming that registers A and X contain

$$\boxed{+\;|\;0\;|\;a\;|\;b\;|\;c\;|\;d\;}\quad\text{and}\quad\boxed{+\;|\;e\;|\;f\;|\;g\;|\;h\;|\;i\;}\;,$$

respectively, write two programs that change the contents of these registers to

$$\boxed{+\;|\;a\;|\;b\;|\;c\;|\;d\;|\;e\;}\quad\text{and}\quad\boxed{+\;|\;0\;|\;f\;|\;g\;|\;h\;|\;i\;}\;,$$

respectively, using (a) minimum memory space and (b) minimum execution time.

▶ **25.** [*30*] Suppose that the manufacturer of MIX wishes to come out with a more powerful computer ("Mixmaster"?), and he wants to convince as many as possible of those people now owning a MIX computer to invest in the more expensive machine. He wants to design this new hardware to be an *extension* of MIX, in the sense that all programs correctly written for MIX will work on the new machines without change. Suggest desirable things that could be incorporated in this extension. (For example, can you make better use of the I-field of an instruction?)

▶ **26.** [*32*] This problem is to write a card-loading routine. Every computer has its own peculiar "bootstrapping" problems for getting information initially into the machine and for starting a job correctly. In MIX's case, the contents of a card can be read only in character code, and the cards that contain the loading program itself must meet this restriction. Not all possible byte values can be read from a card, and each word read in from cards is positive.

MIX has one feature that has not been explained in the text: There is a "GO button," which is used to get the computer started from scratch when its memory contains arbitrary information. When this button is pushed by the computer operator, the following actions take place:

1) A single card is read into locations 0000–0015; this is essentially equivalent to the instruction "IN 0(16)".

2) When the card has been completely read and the card reader is no longer busy, a JMP to location 0000 occurs. The J-register is also set to zero, and the overflow toggle is cleared.

3) The machine now begins to execute the program it has read from the card.

Note: MIX computers without card readers have their GO-button attached to another input device. But in this problem we will assume the presence of a card reader, unit 16.

The loading routine to be written must satisfy the following conditions:

i) The input deck should begin with the loading routine, followed by information cards containing the numbers to be loaded, followed by a "transfer card" that shuts down the loading routine and jumps to the beginning of the program. The loading routine should fit onto two cards.

ii) The information cards have the following format:

> Columns 1–5, ignored by the loading routine.
> Column 6, the number of consecutive words to be loaded on this card (a number between 1 and 7, inclusive).
> Columns 7–10, the location of word 1, which is always greater than 100 (so that it does not overlay the loading routine).
> Columns 11–20, word 1.
> Columns 21–30, word 2 (if column $6 \geq 2$).
> ...
> Columns 71–80, word 7 (if column $6 = 7$).

The contents of words 1, 2, ... are punched numerically as decimal numbers. If a word is to be negative, a minus ("11-punch") is *overpunched* over the least significant digit, e.g., in column 20. Assume that this causes the character code input to be 10, 11, 12, ..., 19 rather than 30, 31, 32, ..., 39. For example, a card that has

$$\text{ABCDE31000012345678900000000010000000010}\overline{0}$$

punched in columns 1–40 should cause the following data to be loaded:

> 1000:   +0123456789;   1001:   +0000000001;   1002:   −0000000100.

iii) The transfer card has the format TRANSOnnnn in columns 1–10, where nnnn is the place where execution should start.

iv) The loading routine should work for all byte sizes without any changes to the cards bearing the loading routine. No card should contain any of the characters corresponding to bytes 20, 21, 48, 49, 50, ... (namely, the characters Σ, Π, =, $, <, ...), since these characters cannot be read by all card readers. In particular, the ENT, INC, and CMP instructions cannot be used; they can't necessarily be punched on a card.

1.3.2. The MIX Assembly Language

A symbolic language is used to make MIX programs considerably easier to read and to write, and to save the programmer from worrying about tedious clerical details that often lead to unnecessary errors. This language, MIXAL ("MIX Assembly Language"), is an extension of the notation used for instructions in the previous section. Its main features are the optional use of alphabetic names to stand for numbers, and a location field to associate names with memory locations.

MIXAL can readily be comprehended if we consider first a simple example. The following code is part of a larger program; it is a subroutine to find the maximum of n elements $X[1], \ldots, X[n]$, according to Algorithm 1.2.10M.

Program M (*Find the maximum*). Register assignments: rA $\equiv m$, rI1 $\equiv n$, rI2 $\equiv j$, rI3 $\equiv k$, $X[i] \equiv$ CONTENTS(X + i).

Assembled instructions	Line no.	LOC	OP	ADDRESS	Times	Remarks
	01	X	EQU	1000		
	02		ORIG	3000		
3000: + 3009 0 2 32	03	MAXIMUM	STJ	EXIT	1	Subroutine linkage
3001: + 0 1 2 51	04	INIT	ENT3	0,1	1	*M1. Initialize.* $k \leftarrow n$.
3002: + 3005 0 0 39	05		JMP	CHANGEM	1	$j \leftarrow n, m \leftarrow X[n], k \leftarrow n-1$.
3003: + 1000 3 5 56	06	LOOP	CMPA	X,3	$n-1$	*M3. Compare.*
3004: + 3007 0 7 39	07		JGE	*+3	$n-1$	To M5 if $m \geq X[k]$.
3005: + 0 3 2 50	08	CHANGEM	ENT2	0,3	$A+1$	*M4. Change m.* $j \leftarrow k$.
3006: + 1000 3 5 08	09		LDA	X,3	$A+1$	$m \leftarrow X[k]$.
3007: + 1 0 1 51	10		DEC3	1	n	*M5. Decrease k.*
3008: + 3003 0 2 43	11		J3P	LOOP	n	*M2. All tested?* To M3 if $k>0$.
3009: + 3009 0 0 39	12	EXIT	JMP	*	1	Return to main program. ∎

This program is an example of several things simultaneously:

a) The columns headed "LOC", "OP", and "ADDRESS" are of principal interest; they contain a program in the MIXAL symbolic machine language, and we shall explain the details of this program below.

b) The column headed "Assembled instructions" shows the actual numeric machine language that corresponds to the MIXAL program. MIXAL has been designed so that any MIXAL program can easily be translated into numeric machine language; the translation is usually carried out by another computer program called an *assembly program* or *assembler*. Thus, programmers may do all of their machine language programming in MIXAL, never bothering to determine the equivalent numeric codes by hand. Virtually all MIX programs in this book are written in MIXAL.

c) The column headed "Line no." is not an essential part of the MIXAL program; it is merely included with MIXAL examples in this book so that we can readily refer to parts of the program.

d) The column headed "Remarks" gives explanatory information about the program, and it is cross-referenced to the steps of Algorithm 1.2.10M. The reader should compare that algorithm (page 96) with the program above. Notice that a little "programmer's license" was used during the transcription into MIX code; for example, step M2 has been put last. The "register assignments" stated at the beginning of Program M show what components of MIX correspond to the variables in the algorithm.

e) The column headed "Times" will be instructive in many of the MIX programs we will be studying in this book; it represents the *profile*, the number of times the instruction on that line will be executed during the course of the program. Thus, line 06 will be performed $n-1$ times, etc. From this information we can determine the length of time required to perform the subroutine; it is $(5+5n+3A)u$, where A is the quantity that was carefully analyzed in Section 1.2.10.

Now let's discuss the MIXAL part of Program M. Line 01,

$$\text{X EQU 1000},$$

says that symbol X is to be *equivalent* to the number 1000. The effect of this may be seen on line 06, where the numeric equivalent of the instruction "CMPA X,3" appears as

| + | 1000 | 3 | 5 | 56 |

that is, "CMPA 1000,3".

Line 02 says that the locations for succeeding lines should be chosen sequentially, originating with 3000. Therefore the symbol MAXIMUM that appears in the LOC field of line 03 becomes equivalent to the number 3000, INIT is equivalent to 3001, LOOP is equivalent to 3003, etc.

On lines 03 through 12 the OP field contains the symbolic names of MIX instructions: STJ, ENT3, etc. But the symbolic names EQU and ORIG, which appear in the OP column of lines 01 and 02, are somewhat different; EQU and ORIG are called *pseudo-operations*, because they are operators of MIXAL but not of MIX. Pseudo-operations provide special information about a symbolic program, without being instructions of the program itself. Thus the line

$$\text{X EQU 1000}$$

only talks *about* Program M, it does not signify that any variable is to be set equal to 1000 when the program is run. Notice that no instructions are assembled for lines 01 and 02.

Line 03 is a "store J" instruction that stores the contents of register J into the (0:2) field of location EXIT. In other words, it stores rJ into the address part of the instruction found on line 12.

As mentioned earlier, Program M is intended to be part of a larger program; elsewhere the sequence

```
ENT1 100
JMP  MAXIMUM
STA  MAX
```

would, for example, jump to Program M with n set to 100. Program M would then find the largest of the elements $X[1],\ldots,X[100]$ and would return to the instruction "STA MAX" with the maximum value in rA and with its position, j, in rI2. (See exercise 3.)

Line 05 jumps the control to line 08. Lines 04, 05, 06 need no further explanation. Line 07 introduces a new notation: An asterisk (read "self") refers to the location of the line on which it appears; "*+3" ("self plus three") therefore refers to three locations past the current line. Since line 07 is an instruction that corresponds to location 3004, the "*+3" appearing there refers to location 3007.

The rest of the symbolic code is self-explanatory. Notice the appearance of an asterisk again on line 12 (see exercise 2).

Our next example introduces a few more features of the assembly language. The object is to compute and print a table of the first 500 prime numbers, with 10 columns of 50 numbers each. The table should appear as follows on the line printer:

```
FIRST FIVE HUNDRED PRIMES
        0002 0233 0547 0877 1229 1597 1993 2371 2749 3187
        0003 0239 0557 0881 1231 1601 1997 2377 2753 3191
        0005 0241 0563 0883 1237 1607 1999 2381 2767 3203
        0007 0251 0569 0887 1249 1609 2003 2383 2777 3209
        0011 0257 0571 0907 1259 1613 2011 2389 2789 3217
          ⋮                                          ⋮
        0229 0541 0863 1223 1583 1987 2357 2741 3181 3571
```

We will use the following method.

Algorithm P (*Print table of 500 primes*). This algorithm has two distinct parts: Steps P1–P8 prepare an internal table of 500 primes, and steps P9–P11 print the answer in the form shown above. The latter part uses two "buffers," in which line images are formed; while one buffer is being printed, the other one is being filled.

P1. [Start table.] Set PRIME[1] ← 2, N ← 3, J ← 1. (In the following steps, N will run through the odd numbers that are candidates for primes; J will keep track of how many primes have been found so far.)

P2. [N is prime.] Set J ← J + 1, PRIME[J] ← N.

P3. [500 found?] If J = 500, go to step P9.

P4. [Advance N.] Set N ← N + 2.

P5. [K ← 2.] Set K ← 2. (PRIME[K] will run through the possible prime divisors of N.)

P6. [PRIME[K]\N?] Divide N by PRIME[K]; let Q be the quotient and R the remainder. If R = 0 (hence N is not prime), go to P4.

P7. [PRIME[K] large?] If Q ≤ PRIME[K], go to P2. (In such a case, N must be prime; the proof of this fact is interesting and a little unusual — see exercise 6.)

P8. [Advance K.] Increase K by 1, and go to P6.

P9. [Print title.] Now we are ready to print the table. Advance the printer to the next page. Set BUFFER[0] to the title line and print this line. Set B ← 1, M ← 1.

P10. [Set up line.] Put PRIME[M], PRIME[50 + M], ..., PRIME[450 + M] into BUFFER[B] in the proper format.

P11. [Print line.] Print BUFFER[B]; set B ← 1 − B (thereby switching to the other buffer); and increase M by 1. If M ≤ 50, return to P10; otherwise the algorithm terminates. ∎

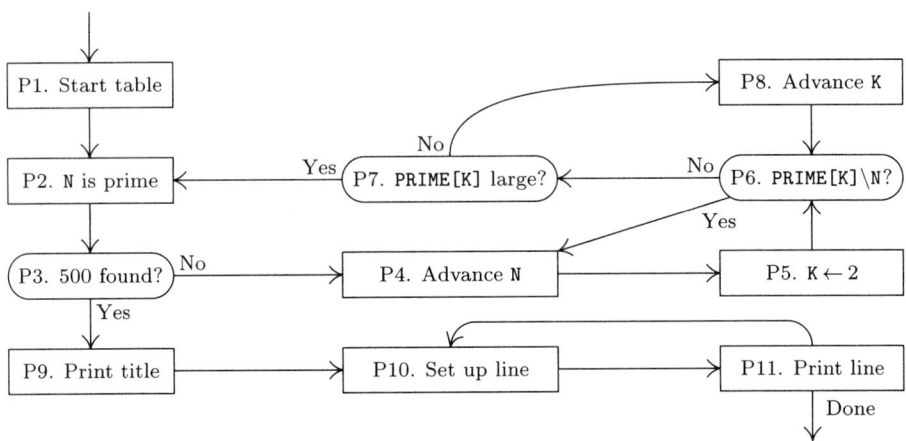

Fig. 14. Algorithm P.

Program P (*Print table of 500 primes*). This program has deliberately been
written in a slightly clumsy fashion in order to illustrate most of the features of
MIXAL in a single program. rI1 ≡ J − 500; rI2 ≡ N; rI3 ≡ K; rI4 indicates B; rI5
is M plus multiples of 50.

```
01  * EXAMPLE PROGRAM   ...   TABLE OF PRIMES
02  *
03  L       EQU  500            The number of primes to find
04  PRINTER EQU  18             Unit number of the line printer
05  PRIME   EQU  -1             Memory area for table of primes
06  BUF0    EQU  2000           Memory area for BUFFER[0]
07  BUF1    EQU  BUF0+25        Memory area for BUFFER[1]
08          ORIG 3000
09  START   IOC  0(PRINTER)     Skip to new page.
10          LD1  =1-L=          P1. Start table. J ← 1.
11          LD2  =3=                N ← 3.
12  2H      INC1 1              P2. N is prime. J ← J + 1.
13          ST2  PRIME+L,1          PRIME[J] ← N.
14          J1Z  2F             P3. 500 found?
15  4H      INC2 2              P4. Advance N.
16          ENT3 2              P5. K ← 2.
17  6H      ENTA 0              P6. PRIME[K]\N?
18          ENTX 0,2               rAX ← N.
19          DIV  PRIME,3           rA ← Q, rX ← R.
20          JXZ  4B                To P4 if R = 0.
21          CMPA PRIME,3        P7. PRIME[K] large?
22          INC3 1              P8. Advance K.
23          JG   6B                To P6 if Q > PRIME[K].
24          JMP  2B                Otherwise N is prime.
```

25	2H	OUT	TITLE(PRINTER)	*P9. Print title.*
26		ENT4	BUF1+10	Set B ← 1.
27		ENT5	-50	Set M ← 0.
28	2H	INC5	L+1	Advance M.
29	4H	LDA	PRIME,5	*P10. Set up line.* (Right to left)
30		CHAR		Convert PRIME[M] to decimal.
31		STX	0,4(1:4)	
32		DEC4	1	
33		DEC5	50	(rI5 goes down by 50 until
34		J5P	4B	it becomes nonpositive)
35		OUT	0,4(PRINTER)	*P11. Print line.*
36		LD4	24,4	Switch buffers.
37		J5N	2B	If rI5 = 0, we are done.
38		HLT		
39	* INITIAL CONTENTS OF TABLES AND BUFFERS			
40		ORIG	PRIME+1	
41		CON	2	The first prime is 2.
42		ORIG	BUF0-5	
43	TITLE	ALF	FIRST	Alphabetic information for
44		ALF	FIVE	title line
45		ALF	HUND	
46		ALF	RED P	
47		ALF	RIMES	
48		ORIG	BUF0+24	
49		CON	BUF1+10	Each buffer refers to the other.
50		ORIG	BUF1+24	
51		CON	BUF0+10	
52		END	START	End of routine. ∎

The following points of interest should be noted about this program:

1. Lines 01, 02, and 39 begin with an asterisk: This signifies a "comment" line that is merely explanatory, having no actual effect on the assembled program.

2. As in Program M, the pseudo-operation EQU in line 03 sets the equivalent of a symbol; in this case, the equivalent of L is set to 500. (In the program of lines 10–24, L represents the number of primes to be computed.) Notice that in line 05 the symbol PRIME gets a *negative* equivalent; the equivalent of a symbol may be any signed five-byte number. In line 07 the equivalent of BUF1 is calculated as BUF0+25, namely 2025. MIXAL provides a limited amount of arithmetic on numbers; another example appears on line 13, where the value of PRIME+L (in this case, 499) is calculated by the assembly program.

3. The symbol PRINTER has been used in the F-part on lines 09, 25, and 35. The F-part, which is always enclosed in parentheses, may be numeric or symbolic, just as the other portions of the ADDRESS field are. Line 31 illustrates the partial field specification "(1:4)", using a colon.

4. MIXAL provides several ways to specify non-instruction words. Line 41 uses the pseudo-operation CON to specify an ordinary constant, "2"; the result

of line 41 is to assemble the word

 .

Line 49 shows a slightly more complicated constant, "BUF1+10", which assembles as the word

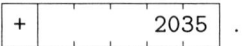 .

A constant may be enclosed in equal signs, in which case we call it a *literal constant* (see lines 10 and 11). The assembler automatically creates internal names and inserts "CON" lines for literal constants. For example, lines 10 and 11 of Program P are effectively changed to

> *10*   LD1   con1
> *11*   LD2   con2

and then at the end of the program, between lines 51 and 52, the lines

> *51a*   con1   CON   1-L
> *51b*   con2   CON   3

are effectively inserted as part of the assembly procedure (possibly with con2 first). Line 51a will assemble into the word

$$\boxed{-\quad\quad\quad 499}\ .$$

The use of literal constants is a decided convenience, because it means that programmers do not have to invent symbolic names for trivial constants, nor do they have to remember to insert constants at the end of each program. Programmers can keep their minds on the central problems and not worry about such routine details. (However, the literal constants in Program P aren't especially good examples, because we would have had a slightly better program if we had replaced lines 10 and 11 by the more efficient commands "ENT1 1-L" and "ENT2 3".)

5. A good assembly language should mimic the way a programmer *thinks* about machine programs. One example of this philosophy is the use of literal constants, as we have just mentioned; another example is the use of "*", which was explained in Program M. A third example is the idea of *local symbols* such as the symbol 2H, which appears in the location field of lines 12, 25, and 28.

Local symbols are special symbols whose equivalents can be *redefined* as many times as desired. A global symbol like PRIME has but one significance throughout a program, and if it were to appear in the location field of more than one line an error would be indicated by the assembler. But local symbols have a different nature; we write, for example, 2H ("2 here") in the location field, and 2F ("2 forward") or 2B ("2 backward") in the address field of a MIXAL line:

> 2B means the closest *previous* location 2H;
> 2F means the closest *following* location 2H.

Thus the "2F" in line 14 refers to line 25; the "2B" in line 24 refers back to line 12; and the "2B" in line 37 refers to line 28. An address of 2F or 2B never refers to its *own* line; for example, the three lines of MIXAL code

```
2H    EQU    10
2H    MOVE   2F(2B)
2H    EQU    2B-3
```

are virtually equivalent to the single line

```
MOVE *-3(10).
```

The symbols 2F and 2B should never be used in the location field; the symbol 2H should never be used in the address field. There are ten local symbols, which can be obtained by replacing "2" in these examples by any digit from 0 to 9.

The idea of local symbols was introduced by M. E. Conway in 1958, in connection with an assembly program for the UNIVAC I. Local symbols relieve programmers from the necessity of choosing symbolic names for every address, when all they want to do is refer to an instruction a few lines away. There often is no appropriate name for nearby locations, so programmers have tended to introduce meaningless symbols like X1, X2, X3, etc., with the potential danger of duplication. Local symbols are therefore quite useful and natural in an assembly language.

6. The address part of lines 30 and 38 is blank. This means that the assembled address will be zero. We could have left the address blank in line 17 as well, but the program would have been less readable without the redundant 0.

7. Lines 43–47 use the pseudo-operation ALF, which creates a five-byte constant in MIX alphameric character code. For example, line 45 causes the word

+	00	08	24	15	04

to be assembled, representing "⊔HUND" — part of the title line in Program P's output.

All locations whose contents are not specified in the MIXAL program are ordinarily set to positive zero (except the locations that are used by the loading routine, usually 3700–3999). Thus there is no need to set the other words of the title line to blanks, after line 47.

8. Arithmetic may be used together with ORIG: See lines 40, 42, 48, and 50.

9. The last line of a complete MIXAL program always has the OP-code "END". The address on this line is the location at which the program is to begin, once it has been loaded into memory.

10. As a final note about Program P, we can observe that the instructions have been organized so that index registers are counted towards zero, and tested against zero, whenever possible. For example, the quantity J–500, not J, is kept in rI1. Lines 26–34 are particularly noteworthy, although perhaps a bit tricky.

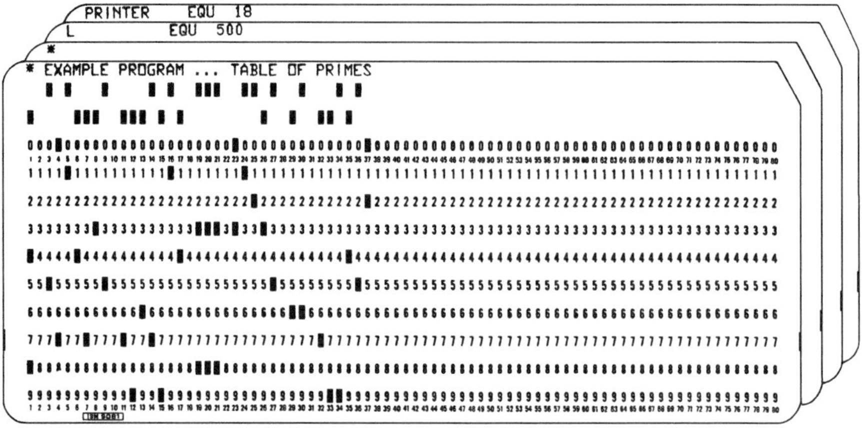

```
* EXAMPLE PROGRAM ...  TABLE OF PRIMES
*
L EQU 500
PRINTER EQU 18
PRIME EQU -1
BUF0 EQU 2000
BUF1 EQU BUF0+25
 ORIG 3000
START IOC 0(PRINTER)
 LD1 =1-L=
```

Fig. 15. The first lines of Program P punched onto cards, or typed on a terminal.

It may be of interest to note a few of the statistics observed when Program P was actually run. The division instruction in line 19 was executed 9538 times; the time to perform lines 10–24 was $182144u$.

MIXAL programs can be punched onto cards or typed on a computer terminal, as shown in Fig. 15. The following format is used in the case of punched cards:

Columns 1–10	LOC (location) field;
Columns 12–15	OP field;
Columns 17–80	ADDRESS field and optional remarks;
Columns 11, 16	blank.

However, if column 1 contains an asterisk, the entire card is treated as a comment. The ADDRESS field ends with the first blank column following column 16; any explanatory information may be punched to the right of this first blank column with no effect on the assembled program. (*Exception:* When the OP field is ALF, the remarks always start in column 22.)

When the input comes from a terminal, a less restrictive format is used: The LOC field ends with the first blank space, while the OP and ADDRESS fields (if present) begin with a nonblank character and continue to the next blank; the special OP-code ALF is, however, followed either by two blank spaces and five characters of alphameric data, or by a single blank space and five alphameric characters, the first of which is nonblank. The remainder of each line contains optional remarks.

The MIX assembly program accepts input files prepared in this manner and converts them to machine language programs in loadable form. Under favorable circumstances the reader will have access to a MIX assembler and MIX simulator, on which various exercises in this book can be worked out.

Now we have seen what can be done in MIXAL. We conclude this section by describing the rules more carefully, and in particular we shall observe what is *not* allowed in MIXAL. The following comparatively few rules define the language.

1. A *symbol* is a string of one to ten letters and/or digits, containing at least one letter. *Examples:* PRIME, TEMP, 20BY20. The special symbols dH, dF, and dB, where d is a single digit, will for the purposes of this definition be replaced by other unique symbols according to the "local symbol" convention described earlier.

2. A *number* is a string of one to ten digits. *Example:* 00052.

3. Each appearance of a symbol in a MIXAL program is said to be either a "defined symbol" or a "future reference." A *defined symbol* is a symbol that has appeared in the LOC field of a preceding line of this MIXAL program. A *future reference* is a symbol that has not yet been defined in this way.

4. An *atomic expression* is either

a) a number, or

b) a defined symbol (denoting the numerical equivalent of that symbol, see rule 13), or

c) an asterisk (denoting the value of ⊛; see rules 10 and 11).

5. An *expression* is either

a) an atomic expression, or

b) a plus or minus sign followed by an atomic expression, or

c) an expression followed by a binary operation followed by an atomic expression.

The six admissible binary operations are +, -, *, /, //, and : . They are defined on numeric MIX words as follows:

```
C = A+B     LDA AA; ADD BB; STA CC.
C = A-B     LDA AA; SUB BB; STA CC.
C = A*B     LDA AA; MUL BB; STX CC.
C = A/B     LDA AA; SRAX 5; DIV BB; STA CC.
C = A//B    LDA AA; ENTX 0; DIV BB; STA CC.
C = A:B     LDA AA; MUL =8=; SLAX 5; ADD BB; STA CC.
```

Here AA, BB, and CC denote locations containing the respective values of the symbols A, B, and C. Operations within an expression are carried out from left to right. *Examples:*

    -1+5   equals 4.
    -1+5*20/6   equals 4*20/6 equals 80/6 equals 13 (going from left to right).
    1//3   equals a MIX word whose value is approximately $b^5/3$ where
                b is the byte size; that is, a word representing the fraction $\frac{1}{3}$
                with an assumed radix point at the left.
    1:3   equals 11 (usually used in partial field specification).
    *-3   equals ⊛ minus three.
    ***   equals ⊛ times ⊛.

6. An *A-part* (which is used to describe the address field of a MIX instruction)
is either

a) vacuous (denoting the value zero), or

b) an expression, or

c) a future reference (denoting the eventual equivalent of the symbol; see
   rule 13), or

d) a literal constant (denoting a reference to an internally created symbol; see
   rule 12).

7. An *index part* (which is used to describe the index field of a MIX instruction) is either

a) vacuous (denoting the value zero), or

b) a comma followed by an expression (denoting the value of that expression).

8. An *F-part* (which is used to describe the F-field of a MIX instruction) is
either

a) vacuous (denoting the normal F-setting, based on the OP field as shown in
   Table 1.3.1–1), or

b) a left parenthesis followed by an expression followed by a right parenthesis
   (denoting the value of the expression).

9. A *W-value* (which is used to describe a *full-word* MIX constant) is either

a) an expression followed by an F-part (in which case a vacuous F-part denotes
   $(0\!:\!5)$), or

b) a W-value followed by a comma followed by a W-value of the form (a).

A W-value denotes the value of a numeric MIX word determined as follows:
Let the W-value have the form "$E_1(F_1), E_2(F_2), \ldots, E_n(F_n)$", where $n \geq 1$,
the E's are expressions, and the F's are fields. The desired result is the final
value that would appear in memory location WVAL if the following hypothetical
program were executed:

    STZ WVAL; LDA C_1; STA WVAL(F_1); ...; LDA C_n; STA WVAL(F_n).

Here C_1, ..., C_n denote locations containing the values of expressions E_1, ...,
E_n. Each F_i must have the form $8L_i + R_i$ where $0 \leq L_i \leq R_i \leq 5$. *Examples:*

1	is the word	+ 1
1,-1000(0:2)	is the word	− 1000 1
-1000(0:2),1	is the word	+ 1

10. The assembly process makes use of a value denoted by ⊛ (called the
location counter), which is initially zero. The value of ⊛ should always be a
nonnegative number that can fit in two bytes. When the location field of a line
is not blank, it must contain a symbol that has not been previously defined. The
equivalent of that symbol is then defined to be the current value of ⊛.

11. After processing the LOC field as described in rule 10, the assembly
process depends on the value of the OP field. There are six possibilities for OP:

a) OP is a symbolic MIX operator (see Table 1 at the end of the previous section).
   The chart defines the normal C and F values for each MIX operator. In this
   case the ADDRESS should be an A-part (rule 6), followed by an index part
   (rule 7), followed by an F-part (rule 8). We thereby obtain four values: C,
   F, A, and I. The effect is to assemble the word determined by the sequence
   "LDA C; STA WORD; LDA F; STA WORD(4:4); LDA I; STA WORD(3:3); LDA A;
   STA WORD(0:2)" into the location specified by ⊛, and to advance ⊛ by 1.

b) OP is "EQU". The ADDRESS should be a W-value (see rule 9). If the LOC field
   is nonblank, the equivalent of the symbol appearing there is set equal to the
   value specified in ADDRESS. This rule takes precedence over rule 10. The
   value of ⊛ is unchanged. (As a nontrivial example, consider the line

   BYTESIZE   EQU   1(4:4)

   which allows the programmer to have a symbol whose value depends on the
   byte size. This is an acceptable situation so long as the resulting program
   is meaningful with each possible byte size.)

c) OP is "ORIG". The ADDRESS should be a W-value (see rule 9); the location
   counter, ⊛, is set to this value. (Notice that because of rule 10, a symbol
   appearing in the LOC field of an ORIG line gets as its equivalent the value of
   ⊛ *before* it has changed. For example,

   TABLE   ORIG   *+100

   sets the equivalent of TABLE to the *first* of 100 locations.)

d) OP is "CON". The ADDRESS should be a W-value; the effect is to assemble a
   word, having this value, into the location specified by ⊛, and to advance ⊛
   by 1.

e) OP is "ALF". The effect is to assemble the word of character codes formed
   by the first five characters of the address field, otherwise behaving like CON.

f) OP is "END". The ADDRESS should be a W-value, which specifies in its (4:5) field the location of the instruction at which the program begins. The END line signals the end of a MIXAL program. The assembler effectively inserts additional lines just before the END line, in arbitrary order, corresponding to all undefined symbols and literal constants (see rules 12 and 13). Thus a symbol in the LOC field of the END line will denote the first location following the inserted words.

12. Literal constants: A W-value that is less than 10 characters long may be enclosed between "=" signs and used as a future reference. The effect is to create a new symbol internally and to insert a CON line defining that symbol, just before the END line (see remark 4 following Program P).

13. Every symbol has one and only one equivalent value; this is a full-word MIX number that is normally determined by the symbol's appearance in LOC according to rule 10 or rule 11(b). If the symbol never appears in LOC, a new line is effectively inserted before the END line, having OP = "CON" and ADDRESS = "0" and the name of the symbol in LOC.

Note: The most significant consequence of the rules above is the restriction on future references. A symbol that has not yet been defined in the LOC field of a previous line may not be used except as the A-part of an instruction. In particular, it may not be used (a) in connection with arithmetic operations; or (b) in the ADDRESS field of EQU, ORIG, or CON. For example,

                            LDA   2F+1

and

                            CON   3F

are both illegal. This restriction has been imposed in order to allow more efficient assembly of programs, and the experience gained in writing this set of books has shown that it is a mild limitation that rarely makes much difference.

Actually MIX has two symbolic languages for low-level programming: MIXAL,* a machine-oriented language that is designed to facilitate one-pass translation by a very simple assembly program; and PL/MIX, which more adequately reflects data and control structures and which looks rather like the Remarks field of MIXAL programs.

EXERCISES — First set

1. [*00*] The text remarked that "X EQU 1000" does not assemble any instruction that sets the value of a variable. Suppose that you are writing a MIX program in which the algorithm is supposed to set the value contained in a certain memory cell (whose symbolic name is X) equal to 1000. How could you express this in MIXAL?

▶ 2. [*10*] Line 12 of Program M says "JMP *", where * denotes the location of that line. Why doesn't the program go into an infinite loop, endlessly repeating this instruction?

---

   * The author was astonished to learn in 1971 that MIXAL is also the name of a laundry detergent in Yugoslavia, developed for use with *avtomate* [automatics].

▶ **3.** [*23*] What is the effect of the following program, if it is used in conjunction with Program M?

```
START IN   X+1(0)
      JBUS *(0)
      ENT1 100
1H    JMP  MAXIMUM
      LDX  X,1
      STA  X,1
      STX  X,2
      DEC1 1
      J1P  1B
      OUT  X+1(1)
      HLT
      END  START
```

▶ **4.** [*25*] Assemble Program P by hand. (It won't take as long as you think.) What are the actual numerical contents of memory, corresponding to that symbolic program?

5. [*11*] Why doesn't Program P need a JBUS instruction to determine when the line printer is ready?

6. [*HM20*] (a) Show that if n is not prime, n has a divisor d with $1 < d \le \sqrt{n}$. (b) Use this fact to show that the test in step P7 of Algorithm P proves that N is prime.

7. [*10*] (a) What is the meaning of "4B" in line 34 of Program P? (b) What effect, if any, would be caused if the location of line 15 were changed to "2H" and the address of line 20 were changed to "2B"?

▶ **8.** [*24*] What does the following program do? (Do not run it on a computer, figure it out by hand!)

```
* MYSTERY PROGRAM
BUF ORIG *+3000
1H  ENT1 1
    ENT2 0
    LDX  4F
2H  ENT3 0,1
3H  STZ  BUF,2
    INC2 1
    DEC3 1
    J3P  3B
    STX  BUF,2
    INC2 1
    INC1 1
    CMP1 =75=
    JL   2B
    ENN2 2400
    OUT  BUF+2400,2(18)
    INC2 24
    J2N  *-2
    HLT
4H  ALF  AAAAA
    END  1B
```

EXERCISES — Second set

These exercises are short programming problems, representing typical computer applications and covering a wide range of techniques. Every reader is encouraged to choose a few of these problems, in order to get some experience using MIX as well as a good review of basic programming skills. If desired, these exercises may be worked concurrently as the rest of Chapter 1 is being read.

The following list indicates the types of programming techniques that are involved:

The use of switching tables for multiway decisions: exercises 9, 13, and 23.

The use of index registers with two-dimensional arrays: exercises 10, 21, and 23.

Unpacking characters: exercises 13 and 23.

Integer and scaled decimal arithmetic: exercises 14, 16, and 18.

The use of subroutines: exercises 14 and 20.

Input buffering: exercise 13.

Output buffering: exercises 21 and 23.

List processing: exercise 22.

Real-time control: exercise 20.

Graphical display: exercise 23.

Whenever an exercise in this book says, "write a MIX program" or "write a MIX subroutine," you need only write symbolic MIXAL code for what is asked. This code will not be complete in itself, it will merely be a fragment of a (hypothetical) complete program. No input or output need be done in a code fragment, if the data is to be supplied externally; one need write only LOC, OP, and ADDRESS fields of MIXAL lines, together with appropriate remarks. The numeric machine language, line number, and "times" columns (see Program M) are not required unless specifically requested, nor will there be an END line.

On the other hand, if an exercise says, "write a *complete* MIX program," it implies that an executable program should be written in MIXAL, including in particular the final END line. Assemblers and MIX simulators on which such complete programs can be tested are widely available.

▶ **9.** [*25*] Location INST contains a MIX word that purportedly is a MIX instruction. Write a MIX program that jumps to location GOOD if the word has a valid C-field, valid ±AA-field, valid I-field, and valid F-field, according to Table 1.3.1–1; your program should jump to location BAD otherwise. Remember that the test for a valid F-field depends on the C-field; for example, if C = 7 (MOVE), any F-field is acceptable, but if C = 8 (LDA), the F-field must have the form 8L + R where $0 \le L \le R \le 5$. The "±AA"-field is to be considered valid *unless* C specifies an instruction requiring a memory address and I = 0 and ±AA is not a valid memory address.

Note: Inexperienced programmers tend to tackle a problem like this by writing a long series of tests on the C-field, such as "LDA C; JAZ 1F; DECA 5; JAN 2F; JAZ 3F; DECA 2; JAN 4F; ...". This is *not* good practice! The best way to make multiway decisions is to prepare an auxiliary *table* containing information that encapsulates the desired logic. If there were, for example, a table of 64 entries, we could write "LD1 C; LD1 TABLE,1; JMP 0,1" — thereby jumping very speedily to the desired routine. Other useful information can also be kept in such a table. A tabular approach to the present problem makes the program only a little bit longer (including the table) and greatly increases its speed and flexibility.

▶ **10.** [*31*] Assume that we have a 9×8 matrix

$$\begin{pmatrix} a_{11} & a_{12} & a_{13} & \cdots & a_{18} \\ a_{21} & a_{22} & a_{23} & \cdots & a_{28} \\ \vdots & & & & \vdots \\ a_{91} & a_{92} & a_{93} & \cdots & a_{98} \end{pmatrix}$$

stored in memory so that a_{ij} is in location $1000+8i+j$. In memory the matrix therefore appears as follows:

$$\begin{pmatrix} (1009) & (1010) & (1011) & \cdots & (1016) \\ (1017) & (1018) & (1019) & \cdots & (1024) \\ \vdots & & & & \vdots \\ (1073) & (1074) & (1075) & \cdots & (1080) \end{pmatrix}.$$

A matrix is said to have a "saddle point" if some position is the smallest value in its row and the largest value in its column. In symbols, a_{ij} is a saddle point if

$$a_{ij} = \min_{1 \le k \le 8} a_{ik} = \max_{1 \le k \le 9} a_{kj}.$$

Write a MIX program that computes the location of a saddle point (if there is at least one) or zero (if there is no saddle point), and stops with this value in rI1.

11. [*M29*] What is the *probability* that the matrix in the preceding exercise has a saddle point, assuming that the 72 elements are distinct and assuming that all 72! arrangements are equally probable? What is the corresponding probability if we assume instead that the elements of the matrix are zeros and ones, and that all 2^{72} such matrices are equally probable?

12. [*HM42*] Two solutions are given for exercise 10 (see page 512), and a third is suggested; it is not clear which of them is better. Analyze the algorithms, using each of the assumptions of exercise 11, and decide which is the better method.

13. [*28*] A cryptanalyst wants a frequency count of the letters in a certain code. The code has been punched on paper tape; the end is signaled by an asterisk. Write a complete MIX program that reads in the tape, counts the frequency of each character up to the first asterisk, and then types out the results in the form

A	0010257
B	0000179
D	0794301

etc., one character per line. The number of blanks should not be counted, nor should characters for which the count is zero (like C in the above) be printed. For efficiency, "buffer" the input: While reading a block into one area of memory you can be counting characters from another area. You may assume that an extra block (following the one that contains the terminating asterisk) is present on the input tape.

▶ **14.** [*31*] The following algorithm, due to the Neapolitan astronomer Aloysius Lilius and the German Jesuit mathematician Christopher Clavius in the late 16th century, is used by most Western churches to determine the date of Easter Sunday for any year after 1582.

Algorithm E (*Date of Easter*). Let Y be the year for which the date of Easter is desired.

    E1. [Golden number.] Set $G \leftarrow (Y \bmod 19) + 1$. ($G$ is the so-called "golden number" of the year in the 19-year Metonic cycle.)

    E2. [Century.] Set $C \leftarrow \lfloor Y/100 \rfloor + 1$. (When Y is not a multiple of 100, C is the century number; for example, 1984 is in the twentieth century.)

    E3. [Corrections.] Set $X \leftarrow \lfloor 3C/4 \rfloor - 12$, $Z \leftarrow \lfloor (8C + 5)/25 \rfloor - 5$. (Here X is the number of years, such as 1900, in which leap year was dropped in order to keep in step with the sun; Z is a special correction designed to synchronize Easter with the moon's orbit.)

    E4. [Find Sunday.] Set $D \leftarrow \lfloor 5Y/4 \rfloor - X - 10$. (March $((-D) \bmod 7)$ will actually be a Sunday.)

    E5. [Epact.] Set $E \leftarrow (11G + 20 + Z - X) \bmod 30$. If $E = 25$ and the golden number G is greater than 11, or if $E = 24$, then increase E by 1. (This number E is the *epact*, which specifies when a full moon occurs.)

    E6. [Find full moon.] Set $N \leftarrow 44 - E$. If $N < 21$ then set $N \leftarrow N + 30$. (Easter is supposedly the first Sunday following the first full moon that occurs on or after March 21. Actually perturbations in the moon's orbit do not make this strictly true, but we are concerned here with the "calendar moon" rather than the actual moon. The Nth of March is a calendar full moon.)

    E7. [Advance to Sunday.] Set $N \leftarrow N + 7 - ((D + N) \bmod 7)$.

    E8. [Get month.] If $N > 31$, the date is $(N - 31)$ `APRIL`; otherwise the date is N `MARCH`. ∎

    Write a subroutine to calculate and print Easter date given the year, assuming that the year is less than 100000. The output should have the form "*dd* `MONTH`, *yyyyy*" where *dd* is the day and *yyyyy* is the year. Write a complete `MIX` program that uses this subroutine to prepare a table of the dates of Easter from 1950 through 2000.

15. [*M30*] A fairly common error in the coding of the previous exercise is to fail to realize that the quantity $(11G + 20 + Z - X)$ in step E5 may be negative; therefore the positive remainder mod 30 might not be computed properly. (See *CACM* **5** (1962), 556.) For example, in the year 14250 we would find $G = 1$, $X = 95$, $Z = 40$; so if we had $E = -24$ instead of $E = +6$ we would get the ridiculous answer "`42 APRIL`". Write a complete `MIX` program that finds the *earliest* year for which this error would actually cause the wrong date to be calculated for Easter.

16. [*31*] We showed in Section 1.2.7 that the sum $1 + \frac{1}{2} + \frac{1}{3} + \cdots$ becomes infinitely large. But if it is calculated with finite accuracy by a computer, the sum actually exists, in some sense, because the terms eventually get so small that they contribute nothing to the sum if added one by one. For example, suppose we calculate the sum by rounding to one decimal place; then we have $1 + 0.5 + 0.3 + 0.3 + 0.2 + 0.2 + 0.1 + 0.1 + 0.1 + 0.1 + 0.1 + 0.1 + 0.1 + 0.1 + 0.1 + 0.1 + 0.1 + 0.1 + 0.1 = 3.9$.

    More precisely, let $r_n(x)$ be the number x rounded to n decimal places; we define $r_n(x) = \lfloor 10^n x + \frac{1}{2} \rfloor / 10^n$. Then we wish to find

$$S_n = r_n(1) + r_n(\tfrac{1}{2}) + r_n(\tfrac{1}{3}) + \cdots ;$$

we know that $S_1 = 3.9$, and the problem is to write a complete `MIX` program that calculates and prints S_n for $n = 2, 3, 4,$ and 5.

Note: There is a much faster way to do this than the simple procedure of adding $r_n(1/m)$, one number at a time, until $r_n(1/m)$ becomes zero. For example, we have $r_5(1/m) = 0.00001$ for all values of m from 66667 to 200000; it's wise to avoid calculating $1/m$ all 133334 times! An algorithm along the following lines should rather be used:

A. Start with $m_h = 1$, $S = 1$.

B. Set $m_e = m_h + 1$ and calculate $r_n(1/m_e) = r$.

C. Find m_h, the largest m for which $r_n(1/m) = r$.

D. Add $(m_h - m_e + 1)r$ to S and return to Step B.

17. [*HM30*] Using the notation of the preceding exercise, prove or disprove the formula

$$\lim_{n\to\infty}(S_{n+1} - S_n) = \ln 10.$$

18. [*25*] The ascending sequence of all reduced fractions between 0 and 1 that have denominators $\leq n$ is called the "Farey series of order n." For example, the Farey series of order 7 is

$$\frac{0}{1}, \frac{1}{7}, \frac{1}{6}, \frac{1}{5}, \frac{1}{4}, \frac{2}{7}, \frac{1}{3}, \frac{2}{5}, \frac{3}{7}, \frac{1}{2}, \frac{4}{7}, \frac{3}{5}, \frac{2}{3}, \frac{5}{7}, \frac{3}{4}, \frac{4}{5}, \frac{5}{6}, \frac{6}{7}, \frac{1}{1}.$$

If we denote this series by x_0/y_0, x_1/y_1, x_2/y_2, $\ldots$, exercise 19 proves that

$$x_0 = 0, \quad y_0 = 1; \qquad x_1 = 1, \quad y_1 = n;$$
$$x_{k+2} = \lfloor (y_k + n)/y_{k+1} \rfloor x_{k+1} - x_k;$$
$$y_{k+2} = \lfloor (y_k + n)/y_{k+1} \rfloor y_{k+1} - y_k.$$

Write a MIX subroutine that computes the Farey series of order n, by storing the values of x_k and y_k in locations $X + k$, $Y + k$, respectively. (The total number of terms in the series is approximately $3n^2/\pi^2$, so you may assume that n is rather small.)

19. [*M30*] (a) Show that the numbers x_k and y_k defined by the recurrence in the preceding exercise satisfy the relation $x_{k+1}y_k - x_k y_{k+1} = 1$. (b) Show that the fractions x_k/y_k are indeed the Farey series of order n, using the fact proved in (a).

▶ **20.** [*33*] Assume that MIX's overflow toggle and X-register have been wired up to the traffic signals at the corner of Del Mar Boulevard and Berkeley Avenue, as follows:

$$\left.\begin{array}{l} \text{rX(2:2)} = \text{Del Mar traffic light} \\ \text{rX(3:3)} = \text{Berkeley traffic light} \end{array}\right\} \text{ 0 off, 1 green, 2 amber, 3 red;}$$

$$\left.\begin{array}{l} \text{rX(4:4)} = \text{Del Mar pedestrian light} \\ \text{rX(5:5)} = \text{Berkeley pedestrian light} \end{array}\right\} \text{ 0 off, 1 "WALK", 2 "DON'T WALK".}$$

Cars or pedestrians wishing to travel on Berkeley across the boulevard must trip a switch that causes the overflow toggle of MIX to go on. If this condition never occurs, the light for Del Mar should remain green.

Cycle times are as follows:

Del Mar traffic light is green $\geq$ 30 sec, amber 8 sec;
Berkeley traffic light is green 20 sec, amber 5 sec.

When a traffic light is green or amber for one direction, the other direction has a red light. When the traffic light is green, the corresponding WALK light is on, except that

22	47	16	41	10	35	04
05	23	48	17	42	11	29
30	06	24	49	18	36	12
13	31	07	25	43	19	37
38	14	32	01	26	44	20
21	39	08	33	02	27	45
46	15	40	09	34	03	28

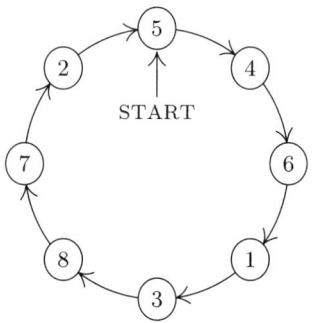

Fig. 16. A magic square.   **Fig. 17.** Josephus's problem, $n = 8$, $m = 4$.

DON'T WALK flashes for 12 sec just before a green light turns to amber, as follows:

$$\left.\begin{array}{ll} \text{DON'T WALK} & \tfrac{1}{2} \text{ sec} \\ \text{off} & \tfrac{1}{2} \text{ sec} \end{array}\right\} \text{repeat 8 times;}$$

DON'T WALK   4 sec (and remains on through amber and red cycles).

If the overflow is tripped while the Berkeley light is green, the car or pedestrian will pass on that cycle, but if it is tripped during the amber or red portions, another cycle will be necessary after the Del Mar traffic has passed.

Assume that one MIX time unit equals 10 μsec. Write a complete MIX program that controls these lights by manipulating rX, according to the input given by the overflow toggle. The stated times are to be followed exactly unless it is impossible to do so. *Note:* The setting of rX changes precisely at the *completion* of a LDX or INCX instruction.

21. [*28*] A *magic square of order* n is an arrangement of the numbers 1 through n^2 in a square array in such a way that the sum of each row and column is $n(n^2+1)/2$, and so is the sum of the two main diagonals. Figure 16 shows a magic square of order 7. The rule for generating it is easily seen: Start with 1 just below the middle square, then go down and to the right diagonally — when running off the edge imagine an entire plane tiled with squares — until reaching a filled square; then drop down two spaces from the most-recently-filled square and continue. This method works whenever n is odd.

Using memory allocated in a fashion like that of exercise 10, write a complete MIX program to generate the 23×23 magic square by the method above, and to print the result. [This algorithm is due to Ibn al-Haytham, who was born in Basra about 965 and died in Cairo about 1040. Many other magic square constructions make good programming exercises; see W. W. Rouse Ball, *Mathematical Recreations and Essays*, revised by H. S. M. Coxeter (New York: Macmillan, 1939), Chapter 7.]

22. [*31*] (*The Josephus problem.*) There are n men arranged in a circle. Beginning at a particular position, we count around the circle and brutally execute every mth man; the circle closes as men die. For example, the execution order when $n = 8$ and $m = 4$ is 54613872, as shown in Fig. 17: The first man is fifth to go, the second man is fourth, etc. Write a complete MIX program that prints out the order of execution when $n = 24$, $m = 11$. Try to design a clever algorithm that works at high speed when n and m are large (it may save your life). *Reference:* W. Ahrens, *Mathematische Unterhaltungen und Spiele* **2** (Leipzig: Teubner, 1918), Chapter 15.

23. [*37*] This is an exercise designed to give some experience in the many applications of computers for which the output is to be displayed graphically rather than in the usual tabular form. In this case, the object is to "draw" a crossword puzzle diagram.

You are given as input a matrix of zeros and ones. An entry of zero indicates a white square; a one indicates a black square. The output should be a diagram of the puzzle, with the appropriate squares numbered for words across and down.

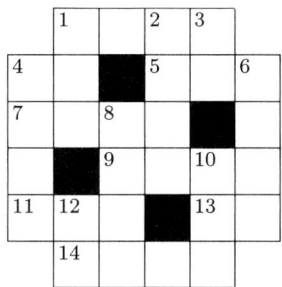

For example, given the matrix

$$\begin{pmatrix} 1 & 0 & 0 & 0 & 0 & 1 \\ 0 & 0 & 1 & 0 & 0 & 0 \\ 0 & 0 & 0 & 0 & 1 & 0 \\ 0 & 1 & 0 & 0 & 0 & 0 \\ 0 & 0 & 0 & 1 & 0 & 0 \\ 1 & 0 & 0 & 0 & 0 & 1 \end{pmatrix},$$

Fig. 18. Diagram corresponding to the matrix in exercise 23.

the corresponding puzzle diagram would be as shown in Fig. 18. A square is numbered if it is a white square and either (a) the square below it is white and there is no white square immediately above, or (b) the square to its right is white and there is no white square immediately to its left. If black squares occur at the edges, they should be removed from the diagram. This is illustrated in Fig. 18, where the black squares at the corners were dropped. A simple way to accomplish this is to artificially insert rows and columns of -1's at the top, bottom, and sides of the given input matrix, then to change every $+1$ that is adjacent to a -1 into a -1 until no $+1$ remains next to any -1.

The following method should be used to print the final diagram on a line printer: Each box of the puzzle should correspond to 5 columns and 3 rows of the output page, where the 15 positions are filled as follows:

Unnumbered white squares:	Number **nn** white squares:	Black squares:
⊔⊔⊔⊔+	**nn**⊔+	+++++
⊔⊔⊔⊔+	⊔⊔⊔⊔+	+++++
+++++	+++++	+++++

"-1" squares, depending on whether there are -1's to the right or below:

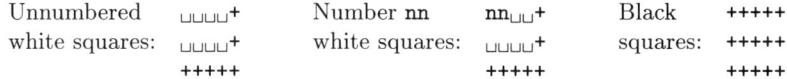

The diagram shown in Fig. 18 would then be printed as shown in Fig. 19.

The width of a printer line — 120 characters — is enough to allow up to 23 columns in the crossword puzzle. The data supplied as input will be a 23×23 matrix of zeros and ones, each row punched in columns 1–23 of an input card. For example, the card corresponding to the matrix above would be punched "10000111111111111111111". The diagram will not necessarily be symmetrical, and it might have long paths of black squares that are connected to the outside in strange ways.

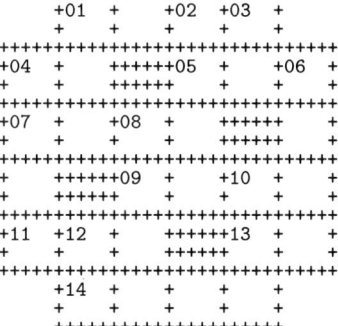

Fig. 19. Representation of Fig. 18 on a line printer.

1.3.3. Applications to Permutations

In this section we shall give several more examples of MIX programs, and at the same time introduce some important properties of permutations. These investigations will also bring out some interesting aspects of computer programming in general.

Permutations were discussed earlier in Section 1.2.5; we treated the permutation $c\,d\,f\,b\,e\,a$ as an *arrangement* of the six objects a, b, c, d, e, f in a straight line. Another viewpoint is also possible: We may think of a permutation as a *rearrangement* or renaming of the objects. With this interpretation it is customary to use a two-line notation, for example,

$$\begin{pmatrix} a & b & c & d & e & f \\ c & d & f & b & e & a \end{pmatrix}, \tag{1}$$

to mean "a becomes c, b becomes d, c becomes f, d becomes b, e becomes e, f becomes a." Considered as a rearrangement, this means that object c moves to the place formerly occupied by object a; considered as a renaming, it means that object a is renamed c. The two-line notation is unaffected by changes in the order of the columns; for example, the permutation (1) could also be written

$$\begin{pmatrix} c & d & f & b & a & e \\ f & b & a & d & c & e \end{pmatrix}$$

and in 718 other ways.

A *cycle notation* is often used in connection with this interpretation. Permutation (1) could be written

$$(a\,c\,f)\,(b\,d), \tag{2}$$

again meaning "a becomes c, c becomes f, f becomes a, b becomes d, d becomes b." A cycle $(x_1\,x_2\,\ldots\,x_n)$ means "x_1 becomes x_2, $\ldots$, x_{n-1} becomes x_n, x_n becomes x_1." Since e is fixed under the permutation, it does not appear in the cycle notation; that is, singleton cycles like "(e)" are conventionally not written. If a permutation fixes *all* elements, so that there are only singleton cycles present, it is called the *identity permutation*, and we denote it by "$()$".

The cycle notation is not unique. For example,

$$(b\,d)\,(a\,c\,f), \qquad (c\,f\,a)\,(b\,d), \qquad (d\,b)\,(f\,a\,c), \tag{3}$$

etc., are all equivalent to (2). However, "$(a\,f\,c)\,(b\,d)$" is not the same, since it says that a goes to f.

It is easy to see why the cycle notation is always possible. Starting with any element x_1, the permutation takes x_1 into x_2, say, and x_2 into x_3, etc., until finally (since there are only finitely many elements) we get to some element x_{n+1} that has already appeared among $x_1, \ldots, x_n$. Now x_{n+1} must equal x_1. For if it were equal to, say, x_3, we already know that x_2 goes into x_3; but by assumption, $x_n \neq x_2$ goes to x_{n+1}. So $x_{n+1} = x_1$, and we have a cycle $(x_1\,x_2\,\ldots\,x_n)$ as part of our permutation, for some $n \geq 1$. If this does not account for the entire permutation, we can find another element y_1 and get another cycle $(y_1\,y_2\,\ldots\,y_m)$

in the same way. None of the y's can equal any of the x's, since $x_i = y_j$ implies that $x_{i+1} = y_{j+1}$, etc., and we would ultimately find $x_k = y_1$ for some k, contradicting the choice of y_1. All cycles will eventually be found.

One application of these concepts to programming comes up whenever some set of n objects is to be put into a different order. If we want to rearrange the objects without moving them elsewhere, we must essentially follow the cycle structure. For example, to do the rearrangement (1), namely to set

$$(a, b, c, d, e, f) \leftarrow (c, d, f, b, e, a),$$

we would essentially follow the cycle structure (2) and successively set

$$t \leftarrow a, \quad a \leftarrow c, \quad c \leftarrow f, \quad f \leftarrow t; \quad t \leftarrow b, \quad b \leftarrow d, \quad d \leftarrow t.$$

It is frequently useful to realize that any such transformation takes place in disjoint cycles.

Products of permutations. We can multiply two permutations together, with the understanding that multiplication means the application of one permutation after the other. For example, if permutation (1) is followed by the permutation

$$\begin{pmatrix} a & b & c & d & e & f \\ b & d & c & a & f & e \end{pmatrix},$$

we have a becomes c, which then becomes c; b becomes d, which becomes a; etc.:

$$\begin{pmatrix} a & b & c & d & e & f \\ c & d & f & b & e & a \end{pmatrix} \times \begin{pmatrix} a & b & c & d & e & f \\ b & d & c & a & f & e \end{pmatrix}$$
$$= \begin{pmatrix} a & b & c & d & e & f \\ c & d & f & b & e & a \end{pmatrix} \times \begin{pmatrix} c & d & f & b & e & a \\ c & a & e & d & f & b \end{pmatrix}$$
$$= \begin{pmatrix} a & b & c & d & e & f \\ c & a & e & d & f & b \end{pmatrix}. \tag{4}$$

It should be clear that multiplication of permutations is not commutative; in other words, $\pi_1 \times \pi_2$ is not necessarily equal to $\pi_2 \times \pi_1$ when π_1 and π_2 are permutations. The reader may verify that the product in (4) gives a different result if the two factors are interchanged (see exercise 3).

Some people multiply permutations from right to left rather than the somewhat more natural left-to-right order shown in (4). In fact, mathematicians are divided into two camps in this regard; should the result of applying transformation T_1, then T_2, be denoted by $T_1 T_2$ or by $T_2 T_1$? Here we use $T_1 T_2$.

Equation (4) would be written as follows, using the cycle notation:

$$(a\,c\,f)\,(b\,d)\,(a\,b\,d)\,(e\,f) = (a\,c\,e\,f\,b). \tag{5}$$

Note that the multiplication sign "$\times$" is conventionally dropped; this does not conflict with the cycle notation since it is easy to see that the permutation $(a\,c\,f)(b\,d)$ is really the product of the permutations $(a\,c\,f)$ and $(b\,d)$.

Multiplication of permutations can be done directly in terms of the cycle notation. For example, to compute the product of several permutations

$$(a\,c\,f\,g)\,(b\,c\,d)\,(a\,e\,d)\,(f\,a\,d\,e)\,(b\,g\,f\,a\,e),\qquad\qquad (6)$$

we find (proceeding from left to right) that "a goes to c, then c goes to d, then d goes to a, then a goes to d, then d is unchanged"; so the net result is that a goes to d under (6), and we write down "$(a\,d$" as the partial answer. Now we consider the effect on d: "d goes to b goes to g"; we have the partial result "$(a\,d\,g$". Considering g, we find that "g goes to a, to e, to f, to a", and so the first cycle is closed: "$(a\,d\,g)$". Now we pick a new element that hasn't appeared yet, say c; we find that c goes to e, and the reader may verify that ultimately the answer "$(a\,d\,g)(c\,e\,b)$" is obtained for (6).

Let us now try to do this process by computer. The following algorithm formalizes the method described in the preceding paragraph, in a way that is amenable to machine calculation.

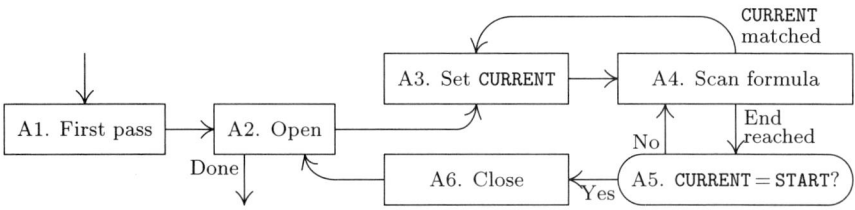

Fig. 20. Algorithm A for multiplying permutations.

Algorithm A (*Multiply permutations in cycle form*). This algorithm takes a product of cycles, such as (6), and computes the resulting permutation in the form of a product of disjoint cycles. For simplicity, the removal of singleton cycles is not described here; that would be a fairly simple extension of the algorithm. As this algorithm is performed, we successively "tag" the elements of the input formula; that is, we mark somehow those symbols of the input formula that have been processed.

A1. [First pass.] Tag all left parentheses, and replace each right parenthesis by a tagged copy of the input symbol that follows its matching left parenthesis. (See the example in Table 1.)

A2. [Open.] Searching from left to right, find the first untagged element of the input. (If all elements are tagged, the algorithm terminates.) Set START equal to it; output a left parenthesis; output the element; and tag it.

A3. [Set CURRENT.] Set CURRENT equal to the next element of the formula.

A4. [Scan formula.] Proceed to the right until either reaching the end of the formula, or finding an element equal to CURRENT; in the latter case, tag it and go back to step A3.

Table 1

ALGORITHM A APPLIED TO (6)

After step	START	CURRENT	$(acfg)(bcd)(aed)(fade)(bgfae)$	Output
A1			$(acfga(bcdb(aeda(fadef(bgfaeb$	
A2	a		$(a\rceil cfga(bcdb(aeda(fadef(bgfaeb$	$(a$
A3	a	c	$(ac\rceil fga(bcdb(aeda(fadef(bgfaeb$	
A4 ...	a	c	$(acfga(bc\rceil db(aeda(fadef(bgfaeb$	
A4 ...	a	d	$(acfga(bcdb(aed\rceil a(fadef(bgfaeb$	
A4 ...	a	a	$(acfga(bcdb(aeda(fa\rceil def(bgfaeb$	
A5 ...	a	d	$(acfga(bcdb(aeda(fadef(bgfaeb\lceil$	d
A5 ...	a	g	$(acfga(bcdb(aeda(fadef(bgfaeb\lceil$	g
A5	a	a	$(acfga(bcdb(aeda(fadef(bgfaeb\lceil$	
A6 ...	a	a	$(acfga(bcdb(aeda(fadef(bgfaeb\lceil$	$)$
A2 ...	c	a	$(ac\rceil fga(bcdb(aeda(fadef(bgfaeb$	$(c$
A5 ...	c	e	$(acfga(bcdb(aeda(fadef(bgfueb\lceil$	e
A5 ...	c	b	$(acfga(bcdb(aeda(fadef(bgfacb\lceil$	b
A6 ...	c	c	$(acfga(bcdb(aeda(fadef(bgfaeb\lceil$	$)$
A6	f	f	$(acfga(bcdb(aeda(fadef(bgfaeb\lceil$	(f)

Here $\lceil$ represents a cursor following the element just scanned; tagged elements are light gray.

A5. [CURRENT = START?] If CURRENT ≠ START, output CURRENT and go back to step A4 starting again at the left of the formula (thereby continuing the development of a cycle in the output).

A6. [Close.] (A complete cycle in the output has been found.) Output a right parenthesis, and go back to step A2. ∎

For example, consider formula (6); Table 1 shows successive stages in its processing. The first line of that table shows the formula after right parentheses have been replaced by the leading element of the corresponding cycle; succeeding lines show the progress that is made as more and more elements are tagged. A cursor shows the current point of interest in the formula. The output is "$(adg)(ceb)(f)$"; notice that singleton cycles will appear in the output.

A MIX program. To implement this algorithm for MIX, the "tagging" can be done by using the sign of a word. Suppose our input is punched onto cards in the following format: An 80-column card is divided into 16 five-character fields. Each field is either (a) "␣␣␣␣(", representing the left parenthesis beginning a cycle; (b) ")␣␣␣␣", representing the right parenthesis ending a cycle; (c) "␣␣␣␣␣", all blanks, which may be inserted anywhere to fill space; or (d) anything else, representing an element to be permuted. The last card of the input is recognized by having columns 76–80 equal to "␣␣␣␣=". For example, (6) might be punched on two cards as follows:

(	A	C	F	G	)		(	B	C	D	)		(	A	E	D	)	
(	F	A	D	E	)		(	B	G	F	A	E	)					=

The output of our program will consist of a verbatim copy of the input, followed
by the answer in essentially the same format.

Program A (*Multiply permutations in cycle form*). This program implements
Algorithm A, and it also includes provision for input, output, and the removing
of singleton cycles. But it doesn't catch errors in the input.

```
01 MAXWDS   EQU  1200                          Maximum length of input
02 PERM     ORIG *+MAXWDS                       The input permutation
03 ANS      ORIG *+MAXWDS                       Place for answer
04 OUTBUF   ORIG *+24                           Place for printing
05 CARDS    EQU  16                             Unit number for card reader
06 PRINTER  EQU  18                             Unit number for printer
07 BEGIN    IN   PERM(CARDS)                    Read first card.
08          ENT2 0
09          LDA  EQUALS
10 1H       JBUS *(CARDS)                       Wait for cycle complete.
11          CMPA PERM+15,2
12          JE   *+2                            Is it the last card?
13          IN   PERM+16,2(CARDS)              No, read another.
14          ENT1 OUTBUF
15          JBUS *(PRINTER)                     Print a copy of
16          MOVE PERM,2(16)                         the input card.
17          OUT  OUTBUF(PRINTER)
18          JE   1F
19          INC2 16
20          CMP2 =MAXWDS-16=
21          JLE  1B                             Repeat until input is complete.
22          HLT  666                            Too much input!
23 1H       INC2 15                       1     At this point, rI2 words of
24          ST2  SIZE                     1       input are in PERM, PERM + 1, ...
25          ENT3 0                        1     A1. First pass.
26 2H       LDAN PERM,3                    A    Get next element of input.
27          CMPA LPREN(1:5)                A    Is it "("?
28          JNE  1F                        A
29          STA  PERM,3                    B    If so, tag it.
30          INC3 1                         B    Put the next nonblank input symbol
31          LDXN PERM,3                    B       into rX.
32          JXZ  *-2                       B
33 1H       CMPA RPREN(1:5)                C
34          JNE  *+2                       C
35          STX  PERM,3                    D    Replace ")" by tagged rX.
36          INC3 1                         C
37          CMP3 SIZE                      C    Have all elements been processed?
38          JL   2B                        C
```

39		LDA	LPREN	1	Prepare for main program.
40		ENT1	ANS	1	rI1 = place to store next answer
41	OPEN	ENT3	0	E	*A2. Open.*
42	1H	LDXN	PERM,3	F	Look for untagged element.
43		JXN	GO	F	
44		INC3	1	G	
45		CMP3	SIZE	G	
46		JL	1B	G	
47	*				All are tagged. Now comes the output.
48	DONE	CMP1	=ANS=		
49		JNE	*+2		Is answer the identity permutation?
50		MOVE	LPREN(2)		If so, change to "()".
51		MOVE	=0=		Put 23 words of blanks after answer.
52		MOVE	-1,1(22)		
53		ENT3	0		
54		OUT	ANS,3(PRINTER)		
55		INC3	24		
56		LDX	ANS,3		Print as many lines as necessary.
57		JXNZ	*-3		
58		HLT			
59	*				
60	LPREN	ALF	(		Constants used in the program
61	RPREN	ALF	)		
62	EQUALS	ALF	=		
63	*				
64	GO	MOVE	LPREN	H	Open a cycle in the output.
65		MOVE	PERM,3	H	
66		STX	START	H	
67	SUCC	STX	PERM,3	J	Tag an element.
68		INC3	1	J	Move one step to the right.
69		LDXN	PERM,3(1:5)	J	*A3. Set* CURRENT (namely rX).
70		JXN	1F	J	Skip past blanks.
71		JMP	*-3	0	
72	5H	STX	0,1	Q	Output CURRENT.
73		INC1	1	Q	
74		ENT3	0	Q	Scan formula again.
75	4H	CMPX	PERM,3(1:5)	K	*A4. Scan formula.*
76		JE	SUCC	K	Element = CURRENT?
77	1H	INC3	1	L	Move to right.
78		CMP3	SIZE	L	End of formula?
79		JL	4B	L	
80		CMPX	START(1:5)	P	*A5.* CURRENT = START?
81		JNE	5B	P	
82	CLOSE	MOVE	RPREN	R	*A6. Close.*
83		CMPA	-3,1	R	Note: rA = "(".
84		JNE	OPEN	R	
85		INC1	-3	S	Suppress singleton cycles.
86		JMP	OPEN	S	
87		END	BEGIN		

This program of approximately 75 instructions is quite a bit longer than the programs of the previous section, and indeed it is longer than most of the programs we will meet in this book. Its length is not formidable, however, since it divides into several small parts that are fairly independent. Lines 07–22 read in the input cards and print a copy of each card; lines 23–38 accomplish step A1 of the algorithm, the preconditioning of the input; lines 39–46 and 64–86 do the main business of Algorithm A; and lines 48–57 output the answer.

The reader will find it instructive to study as many of the MIX programs given in this book as possible. An ability to read and to understand computer programs that you haven't written yourself is exceedingly important; yet such training has been sadly neglected in too many computer courses, and some horribly inefficient uses of computing machinery have arisen as a result.

Timing. The parts of Program A that are not concerned with input-output have been decorated with frequency counts, as we did for Program 1.3.2M. Thus, for example, line 30 is supposedly executed B times. For convenience we shall assume that no blank words appear in the input except at the extreme right end; under this assumption, line 71 is never executed and the jump in line 32 never occurs.

By simple addition the total time to execute the program is

$$(7 + 5A + 6B + 7C + 2D + E + 3F + 4G + 8H + 6J$$
$$+ 3K + 4L + 3P + 4Q + 6R + 2S)u, \quad (7)$$

plus the time for input and output. In order to understand the meaning of formula (7), we need to examine the fifteen unknowns A, B, C, D, E, F, G, H, J, K, L, P, Q, R, S and we must relate them to pertinent characteristics of the input. Let's look at some general principles of attack for problems of this kind.

First we can apply "Kirchhoff's first law" of electrical circuit theory: The number of times an instruction is executed must equal the number of times we transfer to that instruction. This seemingly obvious rule often relates several quantities in a nonobvious way. Analyzing the flow of Program A, we get the following equations.

From lines	*We deduce*
26, 38, 39	$A = 1 + (C - 1)$
33, 28, 29	$C = B + (A - B)$
41, 84, 86	$E = 1 + R$
42, 46, 48	$F = E + (G - 1)$
64, 43, 44	$H = F - G$
67, 70, 76	$J = H + (K - (L - J))$
75, 79, 80	$K = Q + (L - P)$
82, 72, 81	$R = P - Q$

The equations given by Kirchhoff's law will not all be independent; in the present case, for example, we see that the first and second equations are obviously equivalent. Furthermore, the last equation can be deduced from the others, since the third, fourth, and fifth imply that $H = R$; hence the sixth says that $K = L - R$. At any rate we have already eliminated six of our fifteen unknowns:

$$A = C, \quad E = R + 1, \quad F = R + G, \quad H = R, \quad K = L - R, \quad Q = P - R. \quad (8)$$

Kirchhoff's first law is an effective tool that is analyzed more closely in Section 2.3.4.1.

The next step is to try to match up the variables with important character-istics of the data. We find from lines 24, 25, 30, and 36 that

$$B + C = \text{number of words of input} = 16X - 1, \quad (9)$$

where X is the number of input cards. From line 28,

$$B = \text{number of "(" in input} = \text{number of cycles in input.} \quad (10)$$

Similarly, from line 34,

$$D = \text{number of ")" in input} = \text{number of cycles in input.} \quad (11)$$

Now (10) and (11) give us a fact that could not be deduced by Kirchhoff's law:

$$B = D. \quad (12)$$

From line 64,

$$H = \text{number of cycles in output (including singletons).} \quad (13)$$

Line 82 says R is equal to this same quantity; the fact that $H = R$ *was* in this case deducible from Kirchhoff's law, since it already appears in (8).

Using the fact that each nonblank word is ultimately tagged, and lines 29, 35, and 67, we find that

$$J = Y - 2B, \quad (14)$$

where Y is the number of nonblank words appearing in the input permutations. From the fact that every *distinct* element appearing in the input permutation is written into the output just once, either at line 65 or line 72, we have

$$P = H + Q = \text{number of distinct elements in input.} \quad (15)$$

$\big($See Eqs. (8).$\big)$ A moment's reflection makes this clear from line 80 as well. Finally, we see from line 85 that

$$S = \text{number of singleton cycles in output.} \quad (16)$$

Clearly the quantities B, C, H, J, P, and S that we have now interpreted are essentially independent parameters that may be expected to enter into the timing of Program A.

The results we have obtained so far leave us with only the unknowns G and L to be analyzed. For these we must use a little more ingenuity. The scans of the input that start at lines 41 and 74 always terminate either at line 47 (the last time) or at line 80. During each one of these $P + 1$ loops, the instruction

"INC3 1" is performed $B+C$ times; this takes place only at lines 44, 68, and 77, so we get the nontrivial relation

$$G + J + L = (B + C)(P + 1) \tag{17}$$

connecting our unknowns G and L. Fortunately, the running time (7) is a function of $G+L$ (it involves $\cdots+3F+4G+\cdots+3K+4L+\cdots = \cdots+7G+7L+\cdots$), so we need not try to analyze the individual quantities G and L any further.

Summing up all these results, we find that the total time exclusive of input-output comes to

$$(112NX + 304X - 2M - Y + 11U + 2V - 11)u; \tag{18}$$

in this formula, new names for the data characteristics have been used as follows:

$$
\begin{aligned}
X &= \text{number of cards of input,}\\
Y &= \text{number of nonblank fields in input (excluding final ``='')},\\
M &= \text{number of cycles in input,}\\
N &= \text{number of distinct element names in input,}\\
U &= \text{number of cycles in output (including singletons),}\\
V &= \text{number of singleton cycles in output.}
\end{aligned}
\tag{19}
$$

In this way we have found that analysis of a program like Program A is in many respects like solving an amusing puzzle.

We will show below that, if the output permutation is assumed to be random, the quantities U and V will be H_N and 1, respectively, on the average.

Another approach. Algorithm A multiplies permutations together much as people ordinarily do the same job. Quite often we find that problems to be solved by computer are very similar to problems that have confronted humans for many years; therefore time-honored methods of solution, which have evolved for use by mortals such as we, are also appropriate procedures for computer algorithms.

Just as often, however, we encounter new methods that turn out to be superior for computers, although they are quite unsuitable for human use. The central reason is that a computer "thinks" differently; it has a different kind of memory for facts. An instance of this difference may be seen in our permutation-multiplication problem: Using the algorithm below, a computer can do the multiplication in one sweep over the formula, remembering the entire current state of the permutation as its cycles are being multiplied. The human-oriented Algorithm A scans the formula many times, once for each element of the output, but the new algorithm handles everything in one scan. This is a feat that could not be done reliably by *Homo sapiens*.

What is this computer-oriented method for permutation multiplication? Table 2 illustrates the basic idea. The column below each character of the cycle form in that table says what permutation is represented by the partial cycles *to the right*; for example, the fragmentary formula "… *d e*)(*b g f a e*)" represents

Table 2

MULTIPLYING PERMUTATIONS IN ONE PASS

$$(a\ c\ f\ g)\ (b\ c\ d)\ (a\ e\ d)\ (f\ a\ d\ e)\ (b\ g\ f\ a\ e)$$

$a \to d\ d\ a\ a\ a\ a\ a\ a\ a\ a\ a\ a\ a\ d\ d\ d\ d\ d\ d\ e\ e\ e\ e\ e\ e\ e\ e\ a\ a$

$b \to c\ c\ c\ c\ c\ c\ c\ c\ g\ g\ g\ g\ g\ g\ g\ g\ g\ g\ g\ g\ g\ g\ g\ g\ b\ b\ b\ b\ b$

$c \to e\ e\ e\ d\ d\ d\ d\ d\ d\ c\ c\ c\ c\ c\ c\ c\ c\ c\ c\ c\ c\ c\ c\ c\ c\ c\ c\ c\ c$

$d \to g\ g\ g\ g\ g\ g\ g\ )\ )\ )\ d\ d\ )\ )\ )\ b\ b\ b\ b\ b\ d\ d\ d\ d\ d\ d\ d\ d\ d$

$e \to b\ b\ b\ b\ b\ b\ b\ b\ b\ b\ b\ b\ b\ b\ a\ a\ a\ )\ )\ )\ )\ b\ b\ )\ )\ )\ )\ )\ e$

$f \to f\ f\ f\ f\ e\ e\ e\ e\ e\ e\ e\ e\ e\ e\ e\ e\ e\ e\ e\ a\ a\ a\ a\ a\ a\ a\ a\ f\ f\ f$

$g \to a\ )\ )\ )\ )\ f\ f\ f\ f\ f\ f\ f\ f\ f\ f\ f\ f\ f\ f\ f\ f\ f\ f\ f\ f\ f\ g\ g\ g\ g$

the permutation

$$\begin{pmatrix} a & b & c & d & e & f & g \\ e & g & c & b & ? & a & f \end{pmatrix},$$

which appears under the rightmost d of the table.

Inspection of Table 2 shows that it can be created systematically, if we start with the identity permutation on the right and work backward from right to left. The column below letter x differs from the column to its right (which records the previous status) only in row x; and the new value in row x is the one that disappeared in the preceding change. More precisely, we have the following algorithm:

Algorithm B (*Multiply permutations in cycle form*). This algorithm accomplishes essentially the same result as Algorithm A. Assume that the elements permuted are named $x_1, x_2, \ldots, x_n$. We use an auxiliary table $T[1], T[2], \ldots, T[n]$; upon termination of this algorithm, x_i goes to x_j under the input permutation if and only if $T[i] = j$.

B1. [Initialize.] Set $T[k] \leftarrow k$ for $1 \le k \le n$. Also, prepare to scan the input from right to left.

B2. [Next element.] Examine the next element of the input (right to left). If the input has been exhausted, the algorithm terminates. If the element is a ")", set $Z \leftarrow 0$ and repeat step B2; if it is a "(", go to B4. Otherwise the element is x_i for some i; go on to B3.

B3. [Change $T[i]$.] Exchange $Z \leftrightarrow T[i]$. If this makes $T[i] = 0$, set $j \leftarrow i$. Return to step B2.

B4. [Change $T[j]$.] Set $T[j] \leftarrow Z$. (At this point, j is the row that shows a ")" entry in the notation of Table 2, corresponding to the right parenthesis that matches the left parenthesis just scanned.) Return to step B2. ∎

Of course, after this algorithm has been performed, we still must output the contents of table T in cycle form; this is easily done by a "tagging" method, as we shall see below.

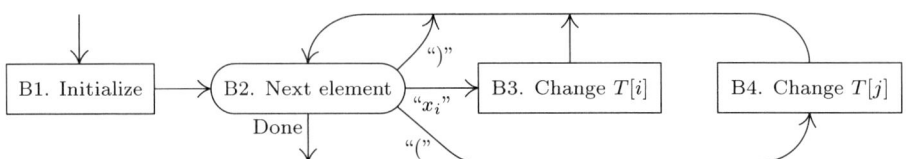

Fig. 21. Algorithm B for multiplying permutations.

Let us now write a MIX program based on the new algorithm. We wish to use the same ground rules as those in Program A, with input and output in the same format as before. A slight problem presents itself; namely, how can we implement Algorithm B without knowing in advance what the elements $x_1, x_2, \ldots, x_n$ are? We don't know n, and we don't know whether the element named b is to be x_1, or x_2, etc. A simple way to solve this problem is to maintain a table of the element names that have been encountered so far, and to search for the current name each time (see lines 35–44 in the program below).

Program B (*Same effect as Program A*). $rX \equiv Z$; $rI4 \equiv i$; $rI1 \equiv j$; $rI3 = n$, the number of distinct names seen.

01	MAXWDS	EQU	1200		Maximum length of input
02	X	ORIG	*+MAXWDS		The table of names
03	T	ORIG	*+MAXWDS		The auxiliary state table
04	PERM	ORIG	*+MAXWDS		The input permutation
05	ANS	EQU	PERM		Place for answer
06	OUTBUF	ORIG	*+24		Place for printing
07	CARDS	EQU	16		
	...				Same as lines 05–22 of Program A
24		HLT	666		At this point, rI2 words of
25	1H	INC2	15	1	input are in PERM, PERM + 1, ...
26		ENT3	0	1	and we haven't seen any names yet.
27	RIGHT	ENTX	0	A	Set $Z \leftarrow 0$.
28	SCAN	DEC2	1	B	*B2. Next element.*
29		LDA	PERM,2	B	
30		JAZ	CYCLE	B	Skip over blanks.
31		CMPA	RPREN	C	
32		JE	RIGHT	C	Is the next element ")"?
33		CMPA	LPREN	D	
34		JE	LEFT	D	Is it "("?
35		ENT4	1,3	E	Prepare for the search.
36		STA	X	E	Store at beginning of table.
37	2H	DEC4	1	F	Search through names table.
38		CMPA	X,4	F	
39		JNE	2B	F	Repeat until match found.
40		J4P	FOUND	G	Has the name appeared before?
41		INC3	1	H	No; increase the table size.
42		STA	X,3	H	Insert the new name x_n.

```
43           ST3   T,3      H   Set T[n] ← n,
44           ENT4  0,3      H     i ← n.
45  FOUND    LDA   T,4      J   B3. Change T[i].
46           STX   T,4      J   Store Z.
47           SRC   5        J   Set Z.
48           JANZ  SCAN     J
49           ENT1  0,4      K   If Z was zero, set j ← i.
50           JMP   SCAN     K
51  LEFT     STX   T,1      L   B4. Change T[j].
52  CYCLE    J2P   SCAN     P   Return to B2, unless finished.
53  *
54  OUTPUT   ENT1  ANS      1   All input has been scanned.
55           J3Z   DONE     1   The x and T tables contain the answer.
56  1H       LDAN  X,3      Q   Now we construct cycle notation.
57           JAP   SKIP     Q   Has name been tagged?
58           CMP3  T,3      R   Is there a singleton cycle?
59           JE    SKIP     R
60           MOVE  LPREN    S   Open a cycle.
61  2H       MOVE  X,3      T
62           STA   X,3      T   Tag the name.
63           LD3   T,3      T   Find successor of element.
64           LDAN  X,3      T
65           JAN   2B       T   Is it already tagged?
66           MOVE  RPREN    W   Yes, cycle closes.
67  SKIP     DEC3  1        Z   Move to next name.
68           J3P   1B       Z
69  *
70  DONE     CMP1  =ANS=    ⎫
    · · ·                   ⎬  Same as lines 48–62 of Program A
84  EQUALS   ALF   =        ⎭
85           END   BEGIN    ▮
```

Lines 54–68, which construct the cycle notation from the T table and the table of names, make a rather pretty little algorithm that merits some study. The quantities $A, B, \ldots, R, S, T, W, Z$ that enter into the timing of this program are, of course, different from the quantities of the same name in the analysis of Program A. The reader will find it an interesting exercise to analyze these times (see exercise 10).

Experience shows that the main portion of the execution time of Program B will be spent in searching the names table — this is quantity F in the timing. Much better algorithms for searching and building dictionaries of names are available; they are called *symbol table algorithms*, and they are of great importance in computer applications. Chapter 6 contains a thorough discussion of efficient symbol table algorithms.

Inverses. The inverse π^- of a permutation π is the rearrangement that undoes the effect of π; if i goes to j under π, then j goes to i under π^-. Thus the product $\pi\pi^-$ equals the identity permutation, and so does the product $\pi^-\pi$.

People often denote the inverse by π^{-1} instead of π^-, but the superscript 1 is redundant (for the same reason that $x^1 = x$).

Every permutation has an inverse. For example, the inverse of

$$\begin{pmatrix} a & b & c & d & e & f \\ c & d & f & b & e & a \end{pmatrix} \quad \text{is} \quad \begin{pmatrix} c & d & f & b & e & a \\ a & b & c & d & e & f \end{pmatrix} = \begin{pmatrix} a & b & c & d & e & f \\ f & d & a & b & e & c \end{pmatrix}.$$

We will now consider some simple algorithms for computing the inverse of a permutation.

In the rest of this section, let us assume that we are dealing with permutations of the numbers $\{1, 2, \ldots, n\}$. If $X[1]\,X[2]\ldots X[n]$ is such a permutation, there is a simple method to compute its inverse: Set $Y[X[k]] \leftarrow k$ for $1 \leq k \leq n$. Then $Y[1]\,Y[2]\ldots Y[n]$ is the desired inverse. This method uses $2n$ memory cells, namely n for X and n for Y.

Just for fun, however, let's suppose that n is very large and suppose also that we wish to compute the inverse of $X[1]\,X[2]\ldots X[n]$ without using much additional memory space. We want to compute the inverse "in place," so that after our algorithm is finished the array $X[1]\,X[2]\ldots X[n]$ will be the inverse of the original permutation. Merely setting $X[X[k]] \leftarrow k$ for $1 \leq k \leq n$ will certainly fail, but by considering the cycle structure we can derive the following simple algorithm:

Algorithm I (*Inverse in place*). Replace $X[1]X[2]\ldots X[n]$, a permutation of $\{1, 2, \ldots, n\}$, by its inverse. This algorithm is due to Bing-Chao Huang [*Inf. Proc. Letters* **12** (1981), 237–238].

I1. [Initialize.] Set $m \leftarrow n$, $j \leftarrow -1$.

I2. [Next element.] Set $i \leftarrow X[m]$. If $i < 0$, go to step I5 (the element has already been processed).

I3. [Invert one.] (At this point $j < 0$ and $i = X[m]$. If m is not the largest element of its cycle, the original permutation had $X[-j] = m$.) Set $X[m] \leftarrow j$, $j \leftarrow -m$, $m \leftarrow i$, $i \leftarrow X[m]$.

I4. [End of cycle?] If $i > 0$, go back to I3 (the cycle has not ended); otherwise set $i \leftarrow j$. (In the latter case, the original permutation had $X[-j] = m$, and m is largest in its cycle.)

I5. [Store final value.] Set $X[m] \leftarrow -i$. (Originally $X[-i]$ was equal to m.)

I6. [Loop on m.] Decrease m by 1. If $m > 0$, go back to I2; otherwise the algorithm terminates. ∎

See Table 3 for an example of this algorithm. The method is based on inversion of successive cycles of the permutation, tagging the inverted elements by making them negative, afterwards restoring the correct sign.

Algorithm I resembles parts of Algorithm A, and it very strongly resembles the cycle-finding algorithm in Program B (lines 54–68). Thus it is typical of a number of algorithms involving rearrangements. When preparing a MIX implementation, we find that it is most convenient to keep the value of $-i$ in a register instead of i itself:

Table 3

COMPUTING THE INVERSE OF 6 2 1 5 4 3 BY ALGORITHM I

After step:	I2	I3	I3	I3	I5*	I2	I3	I3	I5	I2	I5	I5	I3	I5	I5
$X[1]$	6	6	6	-3	-3	-3	-3	-3	-3	-3	-3	-3	-3	-3	3
$X[2]$	2	2	2	2	2	2	2	2	2	2	2	2	-4	2	2
$X[3]$	1	1	-6	-6	-6	-6	-6	-6	-6	-6	-6	6	6	6	6
$X[4]$	5	5	5	5	5	5	5	-5	-5	-5	5	5	5	5	5
$X[5]$	4	4	4	4	4	4	-1	-1	4	4	4	4	4	4	4
$X[6]$	3	-1	-1	-1	1	1	1	1	1	1	1	1	1	1	1
m	6	3	1	6	6	5	4	5	5	4	4	3	2	2	1
j	-1	-6	-3	-1	-1	-1	-5	-4	-4	-4	-4	-4	-2	-2	-2
i	3	1	6	-1	-1	4	5	-1	-4	-5	-5	-6	-4	-2	-3

Read the columns from left to right. At point *, the cycle (1 6 3) has been inverted.

Program I (*Inverse in place*). rI1 ≡ m; rI2 ≡ $-i$; rI3 ≡ j; and n = N, a symbol to be defined when this program is assembled as part of a larger routine.

01	INVERT	ENT1	N	1	*I1. Initialize.* $m \leftarrow n$.
02		ENT3	-1	1	$j \leftarrow -1$.
03	2H	LD2N	X,1	N	*I2. Next element.* $i \leftarrow X[m]$.
04		J2P	5F	N	To I5 if $i < 0$.
05	3H	ST3	X,1	N	*I3. Invert one.* $X[m] \leftarrow j$.
06		ENN3	0,1	N	$j \leftarrow -m$.
07		ENN1	0,2	N	$m \leftarrow i$.
08		LD2N	X,1	N	$i \leftarrow X[m]$.
09	4H	J2N	3B	N	*I4. End of cycle?* To I3 if $i > 0$.
10		ENN2	0,3	C	Otherwise set $i \leftarrow j$.
11	5H	ST2	X,1	N	*I5. Store final value.* $X[m] \leftarrow -i$.
12	6H	DEC1	1	N	*I6. Loop on m.*
13		J1P	2B	N	To I2 if $m > 0$. ∎

The timing for this program is easily worked out in the manner shown earlier; every element $X[m]$ is set first to a negative value in step I3 and later to a positive value in step I5. The total time comes to $(14N + C + 2)u$, where N is the size of the array and C is the total number of cycles. The behavior of C in a random permutation is analyzed below.

There is almost always more than one algorithm to do any given task, so we would expect that there may be another way to invert a permutation. The following ingenious algorithm is due to J. Boothroyd:

Algorithm J (*Inverse in place*). This algorithm has the same effect as Algorithm I but uses a different method.

J1. [Negate all.] Set $X[k] \leftarrow -X[k]$, for $1 \leq k \leq n$. Also set $m \leftarrow n$.

J2. [Initialize j.] Set $j \leftarrow m$.

J3. [Find negative entry.] Set $i \leftarrow X[j]$. If $i > 0$, set $j \leftarrow i$ and repeat this step.

J4. [Invert.] Set $X[j] \leftarrow X[-i]$, $X[-i] \leftarrow m$.

J5. [Loop on m.] Decrease m by 1; if $m > 0$, go back to J2. Otherwise the algorithm terminates. ∎

Table 4

COMPUTING THE INVERSE OF 621543 BY ALGORITHM J

After step:	J2	J3	J5	J3	J5	J3	J5	J3	J5	J3	J5	J3	J5
$X[1]$	-6	-6	-6	-6	-6	-6	-6	-6	3	3	3	3	3
$X[2]$	-2	-2	-2	-2	-2	-2	-2	-2	-2	-2	2	2	2
$X[3]$	-1	-1	6	6	6	6	6	6	6	6	6	6	6
$X[4]$	-5	-5	-5	-5	5	5	5	5	5	5	5	5	5
$X[5]$	-4	-4	-4	-4	-5	-5	4	4	4	4	4	4	4
$X[6]$	-3	-3	-1	-1	-1	-1	-1	-1	-6	-6	-6	-6	1
m	6	6	5	5	4	4	3	3	2	2	1	1	0
i		-3	-3	-4	-4	-5	-5	-1	-1	-2	-2	-6	-6
j	6	6	6	5	5	5	5	6	6	2	2	6	6

See Table 4 for an example of Boothroyd's algorithm. Again the method is essentially based on the cycle structure, but this time it is less obvious that the algorithm really works! Verification is left to the reader (see exercise 13).

Program J (*Analogous to Program I*). rI1 $\equiv m$; rI2 $\equiv j$; rI3 $\equiv -i$.

01	INVERT	ENN1 N	1	*J1. Negate all.*
02		ST1	X+N+1,1(0:0)	N Set sign negative.
03		INC1 1	N	
04		J1N *-2	N	More?
05		ENT1 N	1	$m \leftarrow n$.
06	2H	ENN3 0,1	N	*J2. Initialize j.* $i \leftarrow m$.
07		ENN2 0,3	A	$j \leftarrow i$.
08		LD3N X,2	A	*J3. Find negative entry.*
09		J3N *-2	A	$i > 0$?
10		LDA X,3	N	*J4. Invert.*
11		STA X,2	N	$X[j] \leftarrow X[-i]$.
12		ST1 X,3	N	$X[-i] \leftarrow m$.
13		DEC1 1	N	*J5. Loop on m.*
14		J1P 2B	N	To J2 if $m > 0$. ∎

To decide how fast this program runs, we need to know the quantity A; this quantity is so interesting and instructive, it has been left as an exercise (see exercise 14).

Although Algorithm J is deucedly clever, analysis shows that Algorithm I is definitely superior. In fact, the average running time of Algorithm J turns out to be essentially proportional to $n \ln n$, while that of Algorithm I is essentially proportional to n. Maybe some day someone will find a use for Algorithm J (or some related modification); it is a bit too pretty to be forgotten altogether.

An unusual correspondence. We have already remarked that the cycle notation for a permutation is not unique; the six-element permutation $(1\ 6\ 3)(4\ 5)$ may be written $(5\ 4)(3\ 1\ 6)$, etc. It will be useful to consider a *canonical form* for the cyclic notation; the canonical form *is* unique. To get the canonical form, proceed as follows:

a) Write all singleton cycles explicitly.

b) Within each cycle, put the smallest number first.

c) Order the cycles in *decreasing* order of the first number in the cycle.

For example, starting with (3 1 6)(5 4) we would get

$$\text{(a): } (3\ 1\ 6)\,(5\ 4)\,(2); \quad \text{(b): } (1\ 6\ 3)\,(4\ 5)\,(2); \quad \text{(c): } (4\ 5)\,(2)\,(1\ 6\ 3). \tag{20}$$

The important property of this canonical form is that the parentheses may be dropped and uniquely reconstructed again. Thus there is only one way to insert parentheses in "4 5 2 1 6 3" to get a canonical cycle form: One must insert a left parenthesis just before each *left-to-right minimum* (namely, just before each element that is preceded by no smaller elements).

This insertion and removal of parentheses gives us an unusual one-to-one correspondence between the set of all permutations expressed in cycle form and the set of all permutations expressed in linear form. For example, the permutation 6 2 1 5 4 3 in canonical cycle form is (4 5) (2) (1 6 3); remove parentheses to get 4 5 2 1 6 3, which in cycle form is (2 5 6 3) (1 4); remove parentheses to get 2 5 6 3 1 4, which in cycle form is (3 6 4) (1 2 5); etc.

This correspondence has numerous applications to the study of permutations of different types. For example, let us ask "How many cycles does a permutation of n elements have, on the average?" To answer this question we consider the set of all $n!$ permutations expressed in canonical form, and drop the parentheses; we are left with the set of all $n!$ permutations in some order. Our original question is therefore equivalent to, "How many left-to-right minima does a permutation of n elements have, on the average?" We have already answered the latter question in Section 1.2.10; this was the quantity $(A + 1)$ in the analysis of Algorithm 1.2.10M, for which we found the statistics

$$\min 1, \quad \text{ave } H_n, \quad \max n, \quad \text{dev } \sqrt{H_n - H_n^{(2)}}. \tag{21}$$

(Actually, we discussed the average number of right-to-left maxima, but that's clearly the same as the number of left-to-right minima.) Furthermore, we proved in essence that a permutation of n objects has k left-to-right minima with probability $\left[\begin{smallmatrix} n \\ k \end{smallmatrix}\right]/n!$; therefore *a permutation of n objects has k cycles with probability* $\left[\begin{smallmatrix} n \\ k \end{smallmatrix}\right]/n!$.

We can also ask about the average distance *between* left-to-right minima, which becomes equivalent to the average length of a cycle. By (21), the *total* number of cycles among all the $n!$ permutations is $n!\, H_n$, since it is $n!$ times the *average* number of cycles. If we pick one of these cycles at random, what is its average length?

Imagine all $n!$ permutations of $\{1, 2, \ldots, n\}$ written down in cycle notation; how many three-cycles are present? To answer this question, let us consider how many times a particular three-cycle $(x\ y\ z)$ appears: It clearly appears in exactly $(n - 3)!$ of the permutations, since this is the number of ways the remaining $n - 3$ elements may be permuted. Now the number of different possible three-cycles $(x\ y\ z)$ is $n(n-1)(n-2)/3$, since there are n choices for x, $(n - 1)$ for y, $(n - 2)$ for z, and among these $n(n-1)(n-2)$ choices each different three-cycle has appeared in three forms $(x\,y\,z)$, $(y\,z\,x)$, $(z\,x\,y)$. Therefore the total number of three-cycles among all $n!$ permutations is $n(n-1)(n-2)/3$ times $(n-3)!$, namely $n!/3$. Similarly, the total number of m-cycles is $n!/m$, for $1 \le m \le n$. (This provides another simple proof of the fact that the total number of cycles is $n!\,H_n$; hence the average number of cycles in a random permutation is H_n, as we already knew.) Exercise 17 shows that the average length of a randomly chosen cycle is n/H_n, if we consider the $n!\,H_n$ *cycles* to be equally probable; but if we choose an *element* at random in a random permutation, the average length of the cycle containing that element is somewhat greater than n/H_n.

To complete our analyses of Algorithms A and B, we would like to know the average number of *singleton cycles* in a random permutation. This is an interesting problem. Suppose we write down the $n!$ permutations, listing first those with no singleton cycles, then those with just one, etc.; for example, if $n = 4$,

no fixed elements: 2143 2341 2413 3142 3412 3421 4123 4312 4321

one fixed element: $\overline{1}$342 $\overline{1}$423 3$\overline{2}$41 4$\overline{2}$13 24$\overline{3}$1 41$\overline{3}$2 231$\overline{4}$ 312$\overline{4}$

two fixed elements: $\overline{1}$2$\overline{4}$3 $\overline{1}$4$\overline{3}$2 $\overline{1}$32$\overline{4}$ 4$\overline{2}$3$\overline{1}$ 3$\overline{2}$1$\overline{4}$ 21$\overline{3}\overline{4}$

three fixed elements:

four fixed elements: $\overline{1}\overline{2}\overline{3}\overline{4}$

(Singleton cycles, which are the elements that remain fixed by a permutation, have been specially marked in this list.) Permutations with no fixed elements are called *derangements*; the number of derangements is the number of ways to put n letters into n envelopes, getting them all wrong.

Let P_{nk} be the number of permutations of n objects having exactly k fixed elements, so that for example,

$$P_{40} = 9, \quad P_{41} = 8, \quad P_{42} = 6, \quad P_{43} = 0, \quad P_{44} = 1.$$

An examination of the list above reveals the principal relationship between these numbers: We can get all permutations with k fixed elements by first choosing the k that are to be fixed $\left(\text{this can be done in } \binom{n}{k} \text{ ways}\right)$ and then permuting the remaining $n - k$ elements in all $P_{(n-k)0}$ ways that leave no further elements fixed. Hence

$$P_{nk} = \binom{n}{k} P_{(n-k)0}. \tag{22}$$

We also have the rule that "the whole is the sum of its parts":

$$n! = P_{nn} + P_{n(n-1)} + P_{n(n-2)} + P_{n(n-3)} + \cdots. \tag{23}$$

Combining Eqs. (22) and (23) and rewriting the result slightly, we find that

$$n! = \frac{P_{00}}{0!} + n\frac{P_{10}}{1!} + n(n-1)\frac{P_{20}}{2!} + n(n-1)(n-2)\frac{P_{30}}{3!} + \cdots, \tag{24}$$

an equation that must be true for all positive integers n. This equation has already confronted us before — it appears in Section 1.2.5 in connection with

Stirling's attempt to generalize the factorial function — and we found a simple derivation of its coefficients in Section 1.2.6 (Example 5). We conclude that

$$\frac{P_{m0}}{m!} = 1 - \frac{1}{1!} + \frac{1}{2!} - \cdots + (-1)^m \frac{1}{m!}. \tag{25}$$

Now let p_{nk} be the probability that a permutation of n objects has exactly k singleton cycles. Since $p_{nk} = P_{nk}/n!$, we have from Eqs. (22) and (25)

$$p_{nk} = \frac{1}{k!}\left(1 - \frac{1}{1!} + \frac{1}{2!} - \cdots + (-1)^{n-k}\frac{1}{(n-k)!}\right). \tag{26}$$

The generating function $G_n(z) = p_{n0} + p_{n1}z + p_{n2}z^2 + \cdots$ is therefore

$$G_n(z) = 1 + \frac{1}{1!}(z-1) + \cdots + \frac{1}{n!}(z-1)^n = \sum_{0 \le j \le n} \frac{1}{j!}(z-1)^j. \tag{27}$$

From this formula it follows that $G'_n(z) = G_{n-1}(z)$, and with the methods of Section 1.2.10 we obtain the following statistics on the number of singleton cycles:

$$(\text{min } 0, \quad \text{ave } 1, \quad \text{max } n, \quad \text{dev } 1), \qquad \text{if} \quad n \ge 2. \tag{28}$$

A somewhat more direct way to count the number of permutations having no singleton cycles follows from the *principle of inclusion and exclusion,* which is an important method for many enumeration problems. The general principle of inclusion and exclusion may be formulated as follows: We are given N elements, and M subsets, $S_1, S_2, \ldots, S_M$, of these elements; and our goal is to count how many of the elements lie in none of the subsets. Let $|S|$ denote the number of elements in a set S; then the desired number of objects in none of the sets S_j is

$$N - \sum_{1 \le j \le M} |S_j| + \sum_{1 \le j < k \le M} |S_j \cap S_k| - \sum_{1 \le i < j < k \le M} |S_i \cap S_j \cap S_k| + \cdots$$
$$+ (-1)^M |S_1 \cap \cdots \cap S_M|. \tag{29}$$

(Thus we first subtract the number of elements in $S_1, \ldots, S_M$ from the total number, N; but this underestimates the desired total. So we add back the number of elements that are common to pairs of sets, $S_j \cap S_k$, for each pair S_j and S_k; this, however, gives an overestimate. So we subtract the elements common to triples of sets, etc.) There are several ways to prove this formula, and the reader is invited to discover one of them. (See exercise 25.)

To count the number of permutations on n elements having no singleton cycles, we consider the $N = n!$ permutations and let S_j be the set of permutations in which element j forms a singleton cycle. If $1 \le j_1 < j_2 < \cdots < j_k \le n$, the number of elements in $S_{j_1} \cap S_{j_2} \cap \cdots \cap S_{j_k}$ is the number of permutations in which $j_1, \ldots, j_k$ are singleton cycles, and this is clearly $(n-k)!$. Thus formula (29) becomes

$$n! - \binom{n}{1}(n-1)! + \binom{n}{2}(n-2)! - \binom{n}{3}(n-3)! + \cdots + (-1)^n \binom{n}{n}0!,$$

in agreement with (25).

The principle of inclusion and exclusion is due to A. de Moivre [see his *Doctrine of Chances* (London: 1718), 61–63; 3rd ed. (1756, reprinted by Chelsea, 1957), 110–112], but its significance was not generally appreciated until it was popularized and developed further by I. Todhunter in his *Algebra* (second edition, 1860), §762, and by W. A. Whitworth in the well-known book *Choice and Chance* (Cambridge: 1867).

Combinatorial properties of permutations are explored further in Section 5.1.

EXERCISES

1. [*02*] Consider the transformation of $\{0, 1, 2, 3, 4, 5, 6\}$ that replaces x by $2x$ mod 7. Show that this transformation is a permutation, and write it in cycle form.

2. [*10*] The text shows how we might set $(a, b, c, d, e, f) \leftarrow (c, d, f, b, e, a)$ by using a series of replacement operations $(x \leftarrow y)$ and one auxiliary variable t. Show how to do the job by using a series of *exchange* operations $(x \leftrightarrow y)$ and no auxiliary variables.

3. [*03*] Compute the product $\left(\begin{smallmatrix} a & b & c & d & e & f \\ b & d & c & a & f & e \end{smallmatrix}\right) \times \left(\begin{smallmatrix} a & b & c & d & e & f \\ c & d & f & b & e & a \end{smallmatrix}\right)$, and express the answer in two-line notation. (Compare with Eq. (4).)

4. [*10*] Express $(a\,b\,d)(e\,f)(a\,c\,f)(b\,d)$ as a product of disjoint cycles.

▶ **5.** [*M10*] Equation (3) shows several equivalent ways to express the same permutation in cycle form. How many different ways of writing that permutation are possible, if all singleton cycles are suppressed?

6. [*M28*] What changes are made to the timing of Program A if we remove the assumption that all blank words occur at the extreme right?

7. [*10*] If Program A is presented with the input (6), what are the quantities X, Y, M, N, U, and V of (19)? What is the time required by Program A, excluding input-output?

▶ **8.** [*23*] Would it be feasible to modify Algorithm B to go from left to right instead of from right to left through the input?

9. [*10*] Both Programs A and B accept the same input and give the answer in essentially the same form. Is the output *exactly* the same under both programs?

▶ **10.** [*M28*] Examine the timing characteristics of Program B, namely, the quantities A, B, ..., Z shown there; express the total time in terms of the quantities X, Y, M, N, U, V defined in (19), and of F. Compare the total time for Program B with the total time for Program A on the input (6), as computed in exercise 7.

11. [*15*] Find a simple rule for writing π^- in cycle form, if the permutation π is given in cycle form.

12. [*M27*] (*Transposing a rectangular matrix.*) Suppose an $m \times n$ matrix (a_{ij}), $m \neq n$, is stored in memory in a fashion like that of exercise 1.3.2–10, so that the value of a_{ij} appears in location $L + n(i-1) + (j-1)$, where L is the location of a_{11}. The problem is to find a way to *transpose* this matrix, obtaining an $n \times m$ matrix (b_{ij}), where $b_{ij} = a_{ji}$ is stored in location $L + m(i-1) + (j-1)$. Thus the matrix is to be transposed "on itself." (a) Show that the transposition transformation moves the value that appears in cell $L + x$ to cell $L + (mx \bmod N)$, for all x in the range $0 \leq x < N = mn - 1$. (b) Discuss methods for doing this transposition by computer.

▶ **13.** [*M24*] Prove that Algorithm J is valid.

▶ **14.** [*M34*] Find the average value of the quantity A in the timing of Algorithm J.

15. [*M12*] Is there a permutation that represents exactly the same transformation both in the canonical cycle form without parentheses and in the linear form?

16. [*M15*] Start with the permutation 1324 in linear notation; convert it to canonical cycle form and then remove the parentheses; repeat this process until arriving at the original permutation. What permutations occur during this process?

17. [*M24*] (a) The text demonstrates that there are $n! H_n$ cycles altogether, among all the permutations on n elements. If these cycles (including singleton cycles) are individually written on $n! H_n$ slips of paper, and if one of these slips of paper is chosen at random, what is the average length of the cycle that is thereby picked? (b) If we write the $n!$ permutations on $n!$ slips of paper, and if we choose a number k at random and also choose one of the slips of paper, what is the probability that the cycle containing k on that slip is an m-cycle? What is the average length of the cycle containing k?

▶ **18.** [*M27*] What is p_{nkm}, the probability that a permutation of n objects has exactly k cycles of length m? What is the corresponding generating function $G_{nm}(z)$? What is the average number of m-cycles and what is the standard deviation? (The text considers only the case $m = 1$.)

19. [*HM21*] Show that, in the notation of Eq. (25), the number P_{n0} of derangements is exactly equal to $n!/e$ *rounded to the nearest integer*, for all $n \geq 1$.

20. [*M20*] Given that all singleton cycles are written out explicitly, how many different ways are there to write the cycle notation of a permutation that has α_1 one-cycles, α_2 two-cycles, ...? (See exercise 5.)

21. [*M22*] What is the probability $P(n; \alpha_1, \alpha_2, \dots)$ that a permutation of n objects has exactly α_1 one-cycles, α_2 two-cycles, etc.?

▶ **22.** [*HM34*] (The following approach, due to L. Shepp and S. P. Lloyd, gives a convenient and powerful method for solving problems related to the cycle structure of random permutations.) Instead of regarding the number, n, of objects as fixed, and the permutation variable, let us assume instead that we independently choose the quantities $\alpha_1, \alpha_2, \alpha_3, \dots$ appearing in exercises 20 and 21 according to some probability distribution. Let w be any real number between 0 and 1.

   a) Suppose that we choose the random variables $\alpha_1, \alpha_2, \alpha_3, \dots$ according to the rule that "the probability that $\alpha_m = k$ is $f(w, m, k)$," for some function $f(w, m, k)$. Determine the value of $f(w, m, k)$ so that the following two conditions hold: (i) $\sum_{k \geq 0} f(w, m, k) = 1$, for $0 < w < 1$ and $m \geq 1$; (ii) the probability that $\alpha_1 + 2\alpha_2 + 3\alpha_3 + \dots = n$ *and* that $\alpha_1 = k_1$, $\alpha_2 = k_2$, $\alpha_3 = k_3$, ... equals $(1 - w)w^n P(n; k_1, k_2, k_3, \dots)$, where $P(n; k_1, k_2, k_3, \dots)$ is defined in exercise 21.

   b) A permutation whose cycle structure is $\alpha_1, \alpha_2, \alpha_3, \dots$ clearly permutes exactly $\alpha_1 + 2\alpha_2 + 3\alpha_3 + \dots$ objects. Show that if the α's are randomly chosen according to the probability distribution in part (a), the probability that $\alpha_1 + 2\alpha_2 + 3\alpha_3 + \dots = n$ is $(1 - w)w^n$; the probability that $\alpha_1 + 2\alpha_2 + 3\alpha_3 + \dots$ is *infinite* is zero.

   c) Let $\phi(\alpha_1, \alpha_2, \dots)$ be any function of the infinitely many numbers $\alpha_1, \alpha_2, \dots$. Show that if the α's are chosen according to the probability distribution in (a), the average value of ϕ is $(1 - w) \sum_{n \geq 0} w^n \phi_n$; here ϕ_n denotes the average value of ϕ taken over all permutations of n objects, where the variable α_j represents the number of j-cycles of a permutation. [For example, if $\phi(\alpha_1, \alpha_2, \dots) = \alpha_1$, the value of ϕ_n is the average number of singleton cycles in a random permutation of n objects; we showed in (28) that $\phi_n = 1$ for all n.]

   d) Use this method to find the average number of cycles of *even* length in a random permutation of n objects.

   e) Use this method to solve exercise 18.

23. [*HM42*] (Golomb, Shepp, Lloyd.) If l_n denotes the average length of the *longest* cycle in a permutation of n objects, show that $l_n \approx \lambda n + \frac{1}{2}\lambda$, where $\lambda \approx 0.62433$ is a constant. Prove in fact that $\lim_{n\to\infty}(l_n - \lambda n - \frac{1}{2}\lambda) = 0$.

24. [*M41*] Find the variance of the quantity A that enters into the timing of Algorithm J. (See exercise 14.)

25. [*M22*] Prove Eq. (29).

▶ **26.** [*M24*] Extend the principle of inclusion and exclusion to obtain a formula for the number of elements that are in exactly r of the subsets $S_1, S_2, \ldots, S_M$. (The text considers only the case $r = 0$.)

27. [*M20*] Use the principle of inclusion and exclusion to count the number of integers n in the range $0 \le n < am_1m_2\ldots m_t$ that are not divisible by any of $m_1, m_2, \ldots, m_t$. Here $m_1, m_2, \ldots, m_t$, and a are positive integers, with $m_j \perp m_k$ when $j \ne k$.

28. [*M21*] (I. Kaplansky.) If the "Josephus permutation" defined in exercise 1.3.2–22 is expressed in cycle form, we obtain $(1\ 5\ 3\ 6\ 8\ 2\ 4)(7)$ when $n = 8$ and $m = 4$. Show that this permutation in the general case is the product $(n\ n{-}1\ \ldots\ 2\ 1)^{m-1} \times (n\ n{-}1\ \ldots\ 2)^{m-1} \ldots (n\ n{-}1)^{m-1}$.

29. [*M25*] Prove that the cycle form of the Josephus permutation when $m = 2$ can be obtained by first expressing the "perfect shuffle" permutation of $\{1, 2, \ldots, 2n\}$, which takes $(1, 2, \ldots, 2n)$ into $(2, 4, \ldots, 2n, 1, 3, \ldots, 2n{-}1)$, in cycle form, then reversing left and right and erasing all the numbers greater than n. For example, when $n = 11$ the perfect shuffle is $(1\ 2\ 4\ 8\ 16\ 9\ 18\ 13\ 3\ 6\ 12)(5\ 10\ 20\ 17\ 11\ 22\ 21\ 19\ 15\ 7\ 14)$ and the Josephus permutation is $(7\ 11\ 10\ 5)(6\ 3\ 9\ 8\ 4\ 2\ 1)$.

30. [*M24*] Use exercise 29 to show that the fixed elements of the Josephus permutation when $m = 2$ are precisely the numbers $(2^d - 1)(2n + 1)/(2^{d+1} - 1)$ for all positive integers d such that this is an integer.

31. [*HM38*] Generalizing exercises 29 and 30, prove that the jth man to be executed, for general m and n, is in position x, where x may be computed as follows: Set $x \leftarrow jm$; then, while $x > n$, set $x \leftarrow \lfloor (m(x - n) - 1)/(m - 1) \rfloor$. Consequently the average number of fixed elements, for $1 \le n \le N$ and fixed $m > 1$ as $N \to \infty$, approaches $\sum_{k\ge 1}(m-1)^k/(m^{k+1} - (m-1)^k)$. [Since this value lies between $(m-1)/m$ and 1, the Josephus permutations have slightly fewer fixed elements than random ones do.]

32. [*M25*] (a) Prove that any permutation $\pi = \pi_1\pi_2\ldots\pi_{2m+1}$ of the form

$$\pi = (2\ 3)^{e_2}(4\ 5)^{e_4}\ldots(2m\ 2m{+}1)^{e_{2m}}(1\ 2)^{e_1}(3\ 4)^{e_3}\ldots(2m{-}1\ 2m)^{e_{2m-1}},$$

where each e_k is 0 or 1, has $|\pi_k - k| \le 2$ for $1 \le k \le 2m + 1$.

(b) Given any permutation ρ of $\{1, 2, \ldots, n\}$, construct a permutation π of the stated form such that $\rho\pi$ is a single cycle. Thus every permutation is "near" a cycle.

33. [*M33*] If $m = 2^{2^l}$ and $n = 2^{2l+1}$, show how to construct sequences of permutations $(\alpha_{j1}, \alpha_{j2}, \ldots, \alpha_{jn}; \beta_{j1}, \beta_{j2}, \ldots, \beta_{jn})$ for $0 \le j < m$ with the following "orthogonality" property:

$$\alpha_{i1}\beta_{j1}\alpha_{i2}\beta_{j2}\ldots\alpha_{in}\beta_{jn} = \begin{cases} (1\ 2\ 3\ 4\ 5), & \text{if } i = j; \\ (), & \text{if } i \ne j. \end{cases}$$

Each α_{jk} and β_{jk} should be a permutation of $\{1, 2, 3, 4, 5\}$.

▶ **34.** [*M25*] (*Transposing blocks of data.*) One of the most common permutations needed in practice is the change from $\alpha\beta$ to $\beta\alpha$, where α and β are substrings of an array.

In other words, if $x_0 x_1 \ldots x_{m-1} = \alpha$ and $x_m x_{m+1} \ldots x_{m+n-1} = \beta$, we want to change the array $x_0 x_1 \ldots x_{m+n-1} = \alpha\beta$ to the array $x_m x_{m+1} \ldots x_{m+n-1} x_0 x_1 \ldots x_{m-1} = \beta\alpha$; each element x_k should be replaced by $x_{p(k)}$ for $0 \leq k < m + n$, where $p(k) = (k + m) \bmod (m + n)$. Show that every such "cyclic-shift" permutation has a simple cycle structure, and exploit that structure to devise a simple algorithm for the desired rearrangement.

35. [*M30*] Continuing the previous exercise, let $x_0 x_1 \ldots x_{l+m+n-1} = \alpha\beta\gamma$ where α, β, and γ are strings of respective lengths l, m, and n, and suppose that we want to change $\alpha\beta\gamma$ to $\gamma\beta\alpha$. Show that the corresponding permutation has a convenient cycle structure that leads to an efficient algorithm. [Exercise 34 considered the special case $m = 0$.] *Hint:* Consider changing $(\alpha\beta)(\gamma\beta)$ to $(\gamma\beta)(\alpha\beta)$.

36. [*27*] Write a MIX subroutine for the algorithm in the answer to exercise 35, and analyze its running time. Compare it with the simpler method that goes from $\alpha\beta\gamma$ to $(\alpha\beta\gamma)^R = \gamma^R \beta^R \alpha^R$ to $\gamma\beta\alpha$, where σ^R denotes the left-right reversal of the string σ.

37. [*M26*] (*Even permutations.*) Let π be a permutation of $\{1, \ldots, n\}$. Prove that π can be written as the product of an even number of 2-cycles if and only if π can be written as the product of exactly two n-cycles.

1.4. SOME FUNDAMENTAL PROGRAMMING TECHNIQUES

1.4.1. Subroutines

WHEN A CERTAIN task is to be performed at several different places in a program, it is usually undesirable to repeat the coding in each place. To avoid this situation, the coding (called a *subroutine*) can be put into one place only, and a few extra instructions can be added to restart the outer program properly after the subroutine is finished. Transfer of control between subroutines and main programs is called *subroutine linkage*.

Each machine has its own peculiar manner for achieving efficient subroutine linkage, usually involving special instructions. In MIX, the J-register is used for this purpose; our discussion will be based on MIX machine language, but similar remarks will apply to subroutine linkage on other computers.

Subroutines are used to save space in a program; they do not save any time, other than the time implicitly saved by occupying less space — for example, less time to load the program, or fewer passes necessary in the program, or better use of high-speed memory on machines with several grades of memory. The extra time taken to enter and leave a subroutine is usually negligible.

Subroutines have several other advantages. They make it easier to visualize the structure of a large and complex program; they form a logical segmentation of the entire problem, and this usually makes debugging of the program easier. Many subroutines have additional value because they can be used by people other than the programmer of the subroutine.

Most computer installations have built up a large library of useful subroutines, and such a library greatly facilitates the programming of standard computer applications that arise. A programmer should not think of this as the *only* purpose of subroutines, however; subroutines should not always be regarded as general-purpose programs to be used by the community. Special-purpose subroutines are just as important, even when they are intended to appear in only one program. Section 1.4.3.1 contains several typical examples.

The simplest subroutines are those that have only one entrance and one exit, such as the MAXIMUM subroutine we have already considered (see Section 1.3.2, Program M). For reference, we will recopy that program here, changing it so that a fixed number of cells, 100, is searched for the maximum:

```
* MAXIMUM OF X[1..100]
MAX100  STJ   EXIT   Subroutine linkage
        ENT3  100    M1. Initialize.
        JMP   2F
1H      CMPA  X,3    M3. Compare.
        JGE   *+3
2H      ENT2  0,3    M4. Change m.
        LDA   X,3    New maximum found
        DEC3  1      M5. Decrease k.
        J3P   1B     M2. All tested?
EXIT    JMP   *      Return to main program.
```

$$(1)$$

In a larger program containing this coding as a subroutine, the single instruction "JMP MAX100" would cause register A to be set to the current maximum value of locations X + 1 through X + 100, and the position of the maximum would appear in rI2. Subroutine linkage in this case is achieved by the instructions "MAX100 STJ EXIT" and, later, "EXIT JMP *". Because of the way the J-register operates, the exit instruction will then jump to the location following the place where the original reference to MAX100 was made.

> *Newer computers, such as the machine MMIX that is destined to replace MIX, have better ways to remember return addresses. The main difference is that program instructions are no longer modified in memory; the relevant information is kept in registers or in a special array, not within the program itself. (See exercise 7.) The next edition of this book will adopt the modern view, but for now we will stick to the old-time practice of self-modifying code.*

It is not hard to obtain *quantitative* statements about the amount of code saved and the amount of time lost when subroutines are used. Suppose that a piece of coding requires k locations and that it appears in m places in the program. Rewriting this as a subroutine, we need an extra instruction STJ and an exit line for the subroutine, plus a single JMP instruction in each of the m places where the subroutine is called. This gives a total of $m + k + 2$ locations, rather than mk, so the amount saved is

$$(m - 1)(k - 1) - 3. \tag{2}$$

If k is 1 or m is 1 we cannot possibly save any space by using subroutines; this, of course, is obvious. If k is 2, m must be greater than 4 in order to gain, etc.

The amount of time lost is the time taken for the extra JMP, STJ, and JMP instructions, which are not present if the subroutine is not used; therefore if the subroutine is used t times during a run of the program, $4t$ extra cycles of time are required.

These estimates must be taken with a grain of salt, because they were given for an idealized situation. Many subroutines cannot be called simply with a single JMP instruction. Furthermore, if the coding is repeated in many parts of a program, without using a subroutine approach, the coding for each part can be customized to take advantage of special characteristics of the particular part of the program in which it lies. With a subroutine, on the other hand, the coding must be written for the most general case, not a specific case, and this will often add several additional instructions.

When a subroutine is written to handle a general case, it is expressed in terms of *parameters*. Parameters are values that govern the subroutine's actions; they are subject to change from one call of the subroutine to another.

The coding in the outside program that transfers control to the subroutine and gets it properly started is known as the *calling sequence*. Particular values of parameters, supplied when the subroutine is called, are known as *arguments*. With our MAX100 subroutine, the calling sequence is simply "JMP MAX100", but a longer calling sequence is generally necessary when arguments must be supplied. For example, Program 1.3.2M is a generalization of MAX100 that finds the maximum of the first n elements of the table. The parameter n appears in index register 1, and its calling sequence

$$\begin{array}{ccc} \texttt{LD1} \quad \texttt{=}n\texttt{=} & & \texttt{ENT1} \quad n \\ & \text{or} & \\ \texttt{JMP} \quad \texttt{MAXIMUM} & & \texttt{JMP} \quad \texttt{MAXIMUM} \end{array}$$

involves two steps.

If the calling sequence takes c memory locations, formula (2) for the amount of space saved changes to

$$(m - 1)\,(k - c) - \text{constant} \tag{3}$$

and the time lost for subroutine linkage is slightly increased.

A further correction to the formulas above can be necessary because certain registers might need to be saved and restored. For example, in the MAX100 subroutine, we must remember that by writing "JMP MAX100" we are not only getting the maximum value in register A and its position in register I2; we are also setting register I3 to zero. A subroutine may destroy register contents, and this must be kept in mind. In order to prevent MAX100 from changing the setting of rI3, it would be necessary to include additional instructions. The shortest and fastest way to do this with MIX would be to insert the instruction "ST3 3F(0:2)" just after MAX100 and then "3H ENT3 *" just before EXIT. The net cost would be an extra two lines of code, plus three machine cycles on every call of the subroutine.

A subroutine may be regarded as an *extension* of the computer's machine language. With the MAX100 subroutine in memory, we now have a single instruction (namely, "JMP MAX100") that is a maximum-finder. It is important to define the effect of each subroutine just as carefully as the machine language operators themselves have been defined; a programmer should therefore be sure to write down the characteristics of each subroutine, even though nobody else will be making use of the routine or its specification. In the case of MAXIMUM as given in Section 1.3.2, the characteristics are as follows:

$$\left.\begin{array}{l} \text{Calling sequence: JMP MAXIMUM.} \\ \text{Entry conditions: rI1} = n; \quad \text{assume that } n \geq 1. \\ \text{Exit conditions: } \quad \text{rA} = \max_{1 \leq k \leq n} \texttt{CONTENTS}(\texttt{X} + k) = \texttt{CONTENTS}(\texttt{X} + \text{rI2}); \\ \text{rI3} = 0; \text{ rJ and CI are also affected.} \end{array}\right\} \quad (4)$$

(We will customarily omit mention of the fact that register J and the comparison indicator are affected by a subroutine; it has been mentioned here only for completeness.) Note that rX and rI1 are unaffected by the action of the subroutine, for otherwise these registers would have been mentioned in the exit conditions. A specification should also mention all memory locations external to the subroutine that might be affected; in this case the specification allows us to conclude that nothing has been stored, since (4) doesn't say anything about changes to memory.

Now let's consider *multiple entrances* to subroutines. Suppose we have a program that requires the general subroutine MAXIMUM, but it usually wants to use the special case MAX100 in which $n = 100$. The two can be combined as follows:

```
MAX100 ENT3 100    First entrance
MAXN   STJ  EXIT   Second entrance
       JMP  2F     Continue as in (1).                        (5)
...
EXIT   JMP  *      Return to main program.  ▌
```

Subroutine (5) is essentially the same as (1), with the first two instructions interchanged; we have used the fact that "ENT3" does not change the setting of the J-register. If we wanted to add a *third* entrance, MAX50, to this subroutine, we could insert the code

```
MAX50  ENT3 50
       JSJ  MAXN                                              (6)
```

at the beginning. (Recall that "JSJ" means jump without changing register J.)

When the number of parameters is small, it is often desirable to transmit them to a subroutine either by having them in convenient registers (as we have used rI3 to hold the parameter n in MAXN and as we used rI1 to hold the parameter n in MAXIMUM), or by storing them in fixed memory cells.

Another convenient way to supply arguments is simply to list them *after* the JMP instruction; the subroutine can refer to its parameters because it knows the J-register setting. For example, if we wanted to make the calling sequence for MAXN be

```
        JMP   MAXN
        CON   n                                               (7)
```

then the subroutine could be written as follows:

```
MAXN    STJ   *+1
        ENT1  *      rI1 ← rJ.
        LD3   0,1    rI3 ← n.
        JMP   2F     Continue as in (1).                      (8)
...
        J3P   1B
        JMP   1,1    Return.  ▌
```

On machines like System/360, for which linkage is ordinarily done by putting the exit location in an index register, a convention like this is particularly convenient. It is also useful when a subroutine needs many arguments, or when a program has been written by a compiler. The technique of multiple entrances that we used above often fails in this case, however. We could "fake it" by writing

```
MAX100 STJ   1F
       JMP   MAXN
       CON   100
1H     JMP   *      ▌
```

but this is not as attractive as (5).

A technique similar to that of listing arguments after the jump is normally used for subroutines with *multiple exits*. Multiple exit means that we want the subroutine to return to one of several different locations, depending on conditions detected by the subroutine. In the strictest sense, the location to which a subroutine exits is a parameter; so if there are several places to which it might exit, depending on the circumstances, they should be supplied as arguments. Our final example of the "maximum" subroutine will have two entrances and two exits. The calling sequence is:

<table>
<tr><td>For general n</td><td>For $n = 100$</td></tr>
</table>

```
ENT3  n
JMP   MAXN                          JMP   MAX100
Exit here if max ≤ 0 or max ≥ rX.   Exit here if max ≤ 0 or max ≥ rX.
Exit here if 0 < max < rX.          Exit here if 0 < max < rX.
```

(In other words, exit is made to the location *two* past the jump when the maximum value is positive and less than the contents of register X.) The subroutine for these conditions is easily written:

```
MAX100 ENT3 100    Entrance for n = 100
MAXN   STJ  EXIT   Entrance for general n
       JMP  2F     Continue as in (1).
...
       J3P  1B
       JANP EXIT   Take normal exit if the max is ≤ 0.          (9)
       STX  TEMP
       CMPA TEMP
       JGE  EXIT   Take normal exit if the max is ≥ rX.
       ENT3 1      Otherwise take the second exit.
EXIT   JMP  *,3    Return to proper place. ▮
```

Subroutines may call on other subroutines; in complicated programs it is not unusual to have subroutine calls nested more than five deep. The only restriction that must be followed when using linkage as described here is that no subroutine may call on any other subroutine that is (directly or indirectly) calling on it. For example, consider the following scenario:

[Main program]	[Subroutine A]	[Subroutine B]	[Subroutine C]
	A STJ EXITA	B STJ EXITB	C STJ EXITC
⋮	⋮	⋮	⋮
JMP A	JMP B	JMP C	JMP A
⋮	⋮	⋮	⋮
	EXITA JMP *	EXITB JMP *	EXITC JMP * (10)

If the main program calls on A, which calls B, which calls C, and then C calls on A, the address in EXITA referring to the main program is destroyed, and there is no way to return to that program. A similar remark applies to all temporary storage cells and registers used by each subroutine. It is not difficult to devise subroutine linkage conventions that will handle such recursive situations properly; Chapter 8 considers recursion in detail.

We conclude this section by discussing briefly how we might go about writing a complex and lengthy program. How can we decide what kind of subroutines we will need, and what calling sequences should be used? One successful way to determine this is to use an iterative procedure:

Step 0 (Initial idea). First we decide vaguely upon the general plan of attack that the program will use.

Step 1 (A rough sketch of the program). We start now by writing the "outer levels" of the program, in any convenient language. A somewhat systematic way to go about this has been described very nicely by E. W. Dijkstra, *Structured Programming* (Academic Press, 1972), Chapter 1, and by N. Wirth, *CACM* **14** (1971), 221–227. We may begin by breaking the whole program into a small number of pieces, which might be thought of temporarily as subroutines, although they are called only once. These pieces are successively refined into smaller and smaller parts, having correspondingly simpler jobs to do. Whenever some computational task arises that seems likely to occur elsewhere or that has already occurred elsewhere, we define a subroutine (a real one) to do that job. We do not write the subroutine at this point; we continue writing the main program, assuming that the subroutine has performed its task. Finally, when the main program has been sketched, we tackle the subroutines in turn, trying to take the most complex subroutines first and then their sub-subroutines, etc. In this manner we will come up with a list of subroutines. The actual function of each subroutine has probably already changed several times, so that the first parts of our sketch will by now be incorrect; but that is no problem, it is merely a sketch. For each subroutine we now have a reasonably good idea about how it will be called and how general-purpose it should be. It usually pays to extend the generality of each subroutine a little.

Step 2 (First working program). This step goes in the opposite direction from step 1. We now write in computer language, say MIXAL or PL/MIX or a higher-level language; we start this time with the lowest level subroutines, and do the main program last. As far as possible, we try never to write any instructions that call a subroutine before the subroutine itself has been coded. (In step 1, we tried the opposite, never considering a subroutine until all of its calls had been written.)

As more and more subroutines are written during this process, our confidence gradually grows, since we are continually extending the power of the machine we are programming. After an individual subroutine is coded, we should immediately prepare a complete description of what it does, and what its calling sequences are, as in (4). It is also important not to overlay temporary storage cells; it may very well be disastrous if every subroutine refers to location TEMP, although when preparing the sketch in step 1, it was convenient not to worry about such problems. An obvious way to overcome overlay worries is to have each subroutine use only its own temporary storage, but if this is too wasteful of space, another scheme that does fairly well is to name the cells TEMP1, TEMP2, etc.; the numbering within a subroutine starts with TEMPj, where j is one higher than the greatest number used by any of the sub-subroutines of this subroutine.

Step 3 (Reexamination). The result of step 2 should be very nearly a working program, but it may be possible to improve on it. A good way is to reverse direction again, studying for each subroutine *all* of the calls made on it. It may well be that the subroutine should be enlarged to do some of the more common things that are always done by the outside routine just before or after it uses the subroutine. Perhaps several subroutines should be merged into one; or perhaps a subroutine is called only once and should not be a subroutine at all. (Perhaps a subroutine is never called and can be dispensed with entirely.)

At this point, it is often a good idea to scrap everything and start over again at step 1! This is not intended to be a facetious remark; the time spent in getting this far has not been wasted, for we have learned a great deal about the problem. With hindsight, we will probably have discovered several improvements that could be made to the program's overall organization. There's no reason to be afraid to go back to step 1 — it will be much easier to go through steps 2 and 3 again, now that a similar program has been done already. Moreover, we will quite probably save as much debugging time later on as it will take to rewrite everything. Some of the best computer programs ever written owe much of their success to the fact that all the work was unintentionally lost, at about this stage, and the authors had to begin again.

On the other hand, there is probably never a point when a complex computer program cannot be improved somehow, so steps 1 and 2 should not be repeated indefinitely. When significant improvement can clearly be made, it is well worth the additional time required to start over, but eventually a point of diminishing returns is reached.

Step 4 (Debugging). After a final polishing of the program, including perhaps the allocation of storage and other last-minute details, it is time to look at it in still another direction from the three that were used in steps 1, 2, and 3 — now we study the program in the order in which the computer will *perform* it. This may be done by hand or, of course, by machine. The author has found it quite helpful at this point to make use of system routines that trace each instruction the first two times it is executed; it is important to rethink the ideas underlying the program and to check that everything is actually taking place as expected.

Debugging is an art that needs much further study, and the way to approach it is highly dependent on the facilities available at each computer installation. A good start towards effective debugging is often the preparation of appropriate test data. The most effective debugging techniques seem to be those that are designed and built into the program itself — many of today's best programmers will devote nearly half of their programs to facilitating the debugging process in the other half; the first half, which usually consists of fairly straightforward routines that display relevant information in a readable format, will eventually be thrown away, but the net result is a surprising gain in productivity.

Another good debugging practice is to keep a record of every mistake made. Even though this will probably be quite embarrassing, such information is invaluable to anyone doing research on the debugging problem, and it will also help you learn how to reduce the number of future errors.

Note: The author wrote most of the preceding comments in 1964, after he had successfully completed several medium-sized software projects but before he had developed a mature programming style. Later, during the 1980s, he learned that an additional technique, called *structured documentation* or *literate programming*, is probably even more important. A summary of his current beliefs about the best way to write programs of all kinds appears in the book *Literate Programming* (Cambridge Univ. Press, first published in 1992). Incidentally, Chapter 11 of that book contains a detailed record of all bugs removed from the TeX program during the period 1978–1991.

> *Up to a point it is better to let the snags [bugs] be there*
> *than to spend such time in design that there are none*
> *(how many decades would this course take?).*
> — A. M. TURING, Proposals for ACE (1945)

EXERCISES

1. [*10*] State the characteristics of subroutine (5), just as (4) gives the characteristics of Subroutine 1.3.2M.

2. [*10*] Suggest code to substitute for (6) without using the JSJ instruction.

3. [*M15*] Complete the information in (4) by stating precisely what happens to register J and the comparison indicator as a result of the subroutine; state also what happens if register I1 is not positive.

▶ **4.** [*21*] Write a subroutine that generalizes MAXN by finding the maximum value of $X[a], X[a+r], X[a+2r], \ldots, X[n]$, where r and n are parameters and a is the smallest positive number with $a \equiv n$ (modulo r), namely $a = 1 + (n-1) \bmod r$. Give a special entrance for the case $r = 1$. List the characteristics of your subroutine, as in (4).

5. [*21*] Suppose MIX did not have a J-register. Invent a means for subroutine linkage that does not use register J, and give an example of your invention by writing a MAX100 subroutine effectively equivalent to (1). State the characteristics of this subroutine in a fashion similar to (4). (Retain MIX's conventions of self-modifying code.)

▶ **6.** [*26*] Suppose MIX did not have a MOVE operator. Write a subroutine entitled MOVE such that the calling sequence "JMP MOVE; NOP A,I(F)" has an effect just the same as "MOVE A,I(F)" if the latter were admissible. The only differences should be the effect on register J and the fact that a subroutine naturally consumes more time and space than a hardware instruction does.

▶ **7.** [*20*] Why is self-modifying code now frowned on?

1.4.2. Coroutines

Subroutines are special cases of more general program components, called *coroutines*. In contrast to the unsymmetric relationship between a main routine and a subroutine, there is complete symmetry between coroutines, which *call on each other*.

To understand the coroutine concept, let us consider another way of thinking about subroutines. The viewpoint adopted in the previous section was that a subroutine merely was an extension of the computer hardware, introduced to save lines of coding. This may be true, but another point of view is possible: We may consider the main program and the subroutine as a *team* of programs, each member of the team having a certain job to do. The main program, in the course of doing its job, will activate the subprogram; the subprogram will perform its own function and then activate the main program. We might stretch our imagination to believe that, from the subroutine's point of view, when it exits *it* is calling the *main* routine; the main routine continues to perform its duty, then "exits" to the subroutine. The subroutine acts, then calls the main routine again.

This somewhat far-fetched philosophy actually takes place with coroutines, for which it is impossible to distinguish which is a subroutine of the other. Suppose we have coroutines A and B; when programming A, we may think of B as our subroutine, but when programming B, we may think of A as our subroutine. That is, in coroutine A, the instruction "JMP B" is used to activate coroutine B. In coroutine B the instruction "JMP A" is used to activate coroutine A again. Whenever a coroutine is activated, it resumes execution of its program at the point where the action was last suspended.

The coroutines A and B might, for example, be two programs that play chess. We can combine them so that they will play against each other.

With MIX, such linkage between coroutines A and B is done by including the following four instructions in the program:

$$
\begin{array}{llll}
\texttt{A} & \texttt{STJ} & \texttt{BX} \qquad\qquad\qquad \texttt{B} & \texttt{STJ} \quad \texttt{AX} \\
\texttt{AX} & \texttt{JMP} & \texttt{A1} \qquad\qquad\qquad \texttt{BX} & \texttt{JMP} \quad \texttt{B1}
\end{array} \qquad (1)
$$

This requires four machine cycles for transfer of control each way. Initially AX and BX are set to jump to the starting places of each coroutine, A1 and B1. Suppose we start up coroutine A first, at location A1. When it executes "JMP B" from location A2, say, the instruction in location B stores rJ in AX, which then says "JMP A2+1". The instruction in BX gets us to location B1, and after coroutine B begins its execution, it will eventually get to an instruction "JMP A" in location B2, say. We store rJ in BX and jump to location A2+1, continuing the execution of coroutine A until it again jumps to B, which stores rJ in AX and jumps to B2+1, etc.

The essential difference between routine-subroutine and coroutine-coroutine linkage, as can be seen by studying the example above, is that a subroutine is always initiated *at its beginning*, which is usually a fixed place; the main routine or a coroutine is always initiated *at the place following* where it last terminated.

Coroutines arise most naturally in practice when they are connected with algorithms for input and output. For example, suppose it is the duty of coroutine A to read cards and to perform some transformation on the input, reducing it to a sequence of items. Another coroutine, which we will call B, does further processing of these items, and prints the answers; B will periodically call for the successive input items found by A. Thus, coroutine B jumps to A whenever it wants the next input item, and coroutine A jumps to B whenever an input item has been found. The reader may say, "Well, B is the main program and A is merely a *subroutine* for doing the input." This, however, becomes less true when the process A is very complicated; indeed, we can imagine A as the main routine and B as a subroutine for doing the output, and the above description remains valid. The usefulness of the coroutine idea emerges midway between these two extremes, when both A and B are complicated and each one calls the other in numerous places. It is rather difficult to find short, simple examples of coroutines that illustrate the importance of the idea; the most useful coroutine applications are generally quite lengthy.

In order to study coroutines in action, let us consider a contrived example. Suppose we want to write a program that translates one code into another. The input code to be translated is a sequence of alphameric characters terminated by a period, such as

$$\text{A2B5E3426FG0ZYW3210PQ89R.} \tag{2}$$

This has been punched onto cards; blank columns appearing on these cards are to be ignored. The input is to be understood as follows, from left to right: If the next character is a digit $0, 1, \ldots, 9$, say n, it indicates $(n+1)$ repetitions of the following character, whether the following character is a digit or not. A nondigit simply denotes itself. The output of our program is to consist of the sequence indicated in this manner and separated into groups of three characters each, until a period appears; the last group may have fewer than three characters. For example, (2) should be translated by our program into

$$\text{ABB BEE EEE E44 446 66F GZY W22 220 0PQ 999 999 999 R.} \tag{3}$$

Note that 3426F does not mean 3427 repetitions of the letter F; it means 4 fours and 3 sixes followed by F. If the input sequence is '1.', the output is simply '.', not '..', because the first period terminates the output. Our program should punch the output onto cards, with sixteen groups of three on each card except possibly the last.

To accomplish this translation, we will write two coroutines and a subroutine. The subroutine, called NEXTCHAR, is designed to find nonblank characters of the input, and to put the next such character into register A:

```
01   * SUBROUTINE FOR CHARACTER INPUT
02   READER   EQU  16                   Unit number of card reader
03   INPUT    ORIG *+16                  Place for input cards
04   NEXTCHAR STJ  9F                    Entrance to subroutine
05            JXNZ 3F                     Initially rX = 0
06   1H       J6N  2F                     Initially rI6 = 0
07            IN   INPUT(READER)         Read next card.
08            JBUS *(READER)             Wait for completion.
09            ENN6 16                     Let rI6 point to the first word.
10   2H       LDX  INPUT+16,6            Get the next word of input.
11            INC6 1                      Advance pointer.
```

```
12   3H        ENTA  0
13             SLAX  1                    Next character → rA.
14   9H        JANZ  *                    Skip blanks.
15             JMP   NEXTCHAR+1           ▮
```

This subroutine has the following characteristics:

Calling sequence: JMP NEXTCHAR.
Entry conditions: rX = characters yet to be used; rI6 points to next word, or
              rI6 = 0 indicating that a new card must be read.
Exit conditions: rA = next nonblank character of input; rX and rI6 are set for
              next entry to NEXTCHAR.

Our first coroutine, called IN, finds the characters of the input code with
the proper replication. It begins initially at location IN1:

```
16   * FIRST COROUTINE
17   2H        INCA  30            Nondigit found
18             JMP   OUT           Send it to OUT coroutine.
19   IN1       JMP   NEXTCHAR      Get character.
20             DECA  30
21             JAN   2B            Is it a letter?
22             CMPA  =10=
23             JGE   2B            Is it a special character?
24             STA   *+1(0:2)      Digit n found
25             ENT5  *             rI5 ← n.
26             JMP   NEXTCHAR      Get next character.
27             JMP   OUT           Send it to OUT coroutine.
28             DEC5  1             Decrease n by 1.
29             J5NN  *-2           Repeat if necessary.
30             JMP   IN1           Begin new cycle.   ▮
```

(Recall that in MIX's character code, the digits 0–9 have codes 30–39.) This
coroutine has the following characteristics:

Calling sequence: JMP IN.
Exit conditions (when
    jumping to OUT):   rA = next character of input with proper replication; rI4
                    unchanged from its value at entry.
Entry conditions
    (upon return):   rA, rX, rI5, rI6 should be unchanged from their values
                    at the last exit.

The other coroutine, called OUT, puts the code into three-character groups
and punches the cards. It begins initially at OUT1:

```
31   * SECOND COROUTINE
32             ALF                 Constant used for blanking
33   OUTPUT    ORIG  *+16          Buffer area for answers
34   PUNCH     EQU   17            Unit number for card punch
35   OUT1      ENT4  -16           Start new output card.
```

36		ENT1	OUTPUT	
37		MOVE	-1,1(16)	Set output area to blanks.
38	1H	JMP	IN	Get next translated character.
39		STA	OUTPUT+16,4(1:1)	Store it in the (1:1) field.
40		CMPA	PERIOD	Is it "."?
41		JE	9F	
42		JMP	IN	If not, get another character.
43		STA	OUTPUT+16,4(2:2)	Store it in the (2:2) field.
44		CMPA	PERIOD	Is it "."?
45		JE	9F	
46		JMP	IN	If not, get another character.
47		STA	OUTPUT+16,4(3:3)	Store it in the (3:3) field.
48		CMPA	PERIOD	Is it "."?
49		JE	9F	
50		INC4	1	Move to next word in output buffer.
51		J4N	1B	End of card?
52	9H	OUT	OUTPUT(PUNCH)	If so, punch it.
53		JBUS	*(PUNCH)	Wait for completion.
54		JNE	OUT1	Return for more, unless
55		HLT		"." was sensed.
56	PERIOD	ALF	␣␣␣␣.	▌

This coroutine has the following characteristics:

Calling sequence: JMP OUT.

Exit conditions (when

 jumping to IN): rA, rX, rI5, rI6 unchanged from their value at entry; rI1 possibly affected; previous character recorded in output.

Entry conditions

 (upon return):   rA = next character of input with proper replication; rI4 unchanged from its value at the last exit.

To complete the program, we need to write the coroutine linkage (see (1)) and to provide the proper initialization. Initialization of coroutines tends to be a little tricky, although not really difficult.

57	* INITIALIZATION AND LINKAGE			
58	START	ENT6	0	Initialize rI6 for NEXTCHAR.
59		ENTX	0	Initialize rX for NEXTCHAR.
60		JMP	OUT1	Start with OUT (see exercise 2).
61	OUT	STJ	INX	Coroutine linkage
62	OUTX	JMP	OUT1	
63	IN	STJ	OUTX	
64	INX	JMP	IN1	
65		END	START	▌

This completes the program. The reader should study it carefully, noting in particular how each coroutine can be written independently as though the other coroutine were its subroutine.

The entry and exit conditions for the IN and OUT coroutines mesh perfectly in the program above. In general, we would not be so fortunate, and the coroutine linkage would also include instructions for loading and storing appropriate registers. For example, if OUT would destroy the contents of register A, the coroutine linkage would become

```
OUT   STJ   INX
      STA   HOLDA    Store A when leaving IN.
OUTX  JMP   OUT1
IN    STJ   OUTX                                          (4)
      LDA   HOLDA    Restore A when leaving OUT.
INX   JMP   IN1     ∎
```

There is an important relation between coroutines and *multipass algorithms*. For example, the translation process we have just described could have been done in two distinct passes: We could first have done just the IN coroutine, applying it to the entire input and writing each character with the proper amount of replication onto magnetic tape. After this was finished, we could rewind the tape and then do just the OUT coroutine, taking the characters from tape in groups of three. This would be called a "two-pass" process. (Intuitively, a "pass" denotes a complete scan of the input. This definition is not precise, and in many algorithms the number of passes taken is not at all clear; but the intuitive concept of "pass" is useful in spite of its vagueness.)

Figure 22(a) illustrates a four-pass process. Quite often we will find that the same process can be done in just one pass, as shown in part (b) of the figure, if we substitute four coroutines A, B, C, D for the respective passes A, B, C, D. Coroutine A will jump to B when pass A would have written an item of output on tape 1; coroutine B will jump to A when pass B would have read an item of input from tape 1, and B will jump to C when pass B would have written an item of output on tape 2; etc. UNIX® users will recognize this as a "pipe," denoted by "PassA | PassB | PassC | PassD". The programs for passes B, C, and D are sometimes referred to as "filters."

Conversely, a process done by n coroutines can often be transformed into an n-pass process. Due to this correspondence it is worthwhile to compare multipass algorithms with one-pass algorithms.

a) *Psychological difference.* A multipass algorithm is generally easier to create and to understand than a one-pass algorithm for the same problem. Breaking a process down into a sequence of small steps that happen one after the other is easier to comprehend than an involved process in which many transformations take place simultaneously.

Also, if a very large problem is being tackled and if many people are to co-operate in producing a computer program, a multipass algorithm provides a natural way to divide up the job.

These advantages of a multipass algorithm are present in coroutines as well, since each coroutine can be written essentially separate from the others, and the linkage makes an apparently multipass algorithm into a single-pass process.

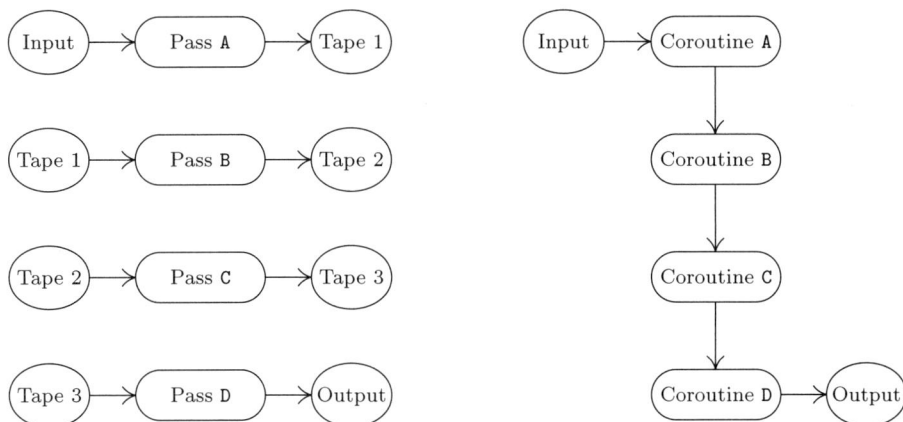

Fig. 22. Passes: (a) a four-pass algorithm, and (b) a one-pass algorithm.

b) *Time difference.* The time required to pack, write, read, and unpack the intermediate data that flows between passes (for example, the information on tapes in Fig. 22) is avoided in a one-pass algorithm. For this reason, a one-pass algorithm will be faster.

c) *Space difference.* The one-pass algorithm requires space to hold all the programs in memory simultaneously, while a multipass algorithm requires space for only one at a time. This requirement may affect the speed, even to a greater extent than indicated in statement (b). For example, many computers have a limited amount of "fast memory" and a larger amount of slower memory; if each pass just barely fits into the fast memory, the result will be considerably faster than if we use coroutines in a single pass (since the use of coroutines would presumably force most of the program to appear in the slower memory or to be repeatedly swapped in and out of fast memory).

Occasionally there is a need to design algorithms for several computer configurations at once, some of which have larger memory capacity than others. In such cases it is possible to write the program in terms of coroutines, and to let the memory size govern the number of passes: Load together as many coroutines as feasible, and supply input or output subroutines for the missing links.

Although this relationship between coroutines and passes is important, we should keep in mind that coroutine applications cannot always be split into multipass algorithms. If coroutine B gets input from A and also sends back crucial information to A, as in the example of chess play mentioned earlier, the sequence of actions can't be converted into pass A followed by pass B.

Conversely, it is clear that some multipass algorithms cannot be converted to coroutines. Some algorithms are inherently multipass; for example, the second pass may require cumulative information from the first pass (like the total number of occurrences of a certain word in the input). There is an old joke worth noting in this regard:

> *Little old lady, riding a bus.* "Little boy, can you tell me how to get off at Pasadena Street?"
>
> *Little boy.* "Just watch me, and get off two stops before I do."

(The joke is that the little boy gives a two-pass algorithm.)

So much for multipass algorithms. We will see further examples of coroutines in numerous places throughout this book, for example, as part of the buffering schemes in Section 1.4.4. Coroutines also play an important role in discrete system simulation; see Section 2.2.5. The important idea of *replicated coroutines* is discussed in Chapter 8, and some interesting applications of this idea may be found in Chapter 10.

EXERCISES

1. [*10*] Explain why short, simple examples of coroutines are hard for the author of a textbook to find.

▶ **2.** [*20*] The program in the text starts up the OUT coroutine first. What would happen if IN were the first to be executed — that is, if line 60 were changed from "JMP OUT1" to "JMP IN1"?

3. [*20*] True or false: The three "CMPA PERIOD" instructions within OUT may all be omitted, and the program would still work. (Look carefully.)

4. [*20*] Show how coroutine linkage analogous to (1) can be given for real-life computers you are familiar with.

5. [*15*] Suppose both coroutines IN and OUT want the contents of register A to remain untouched between exit and entry; in other words, assume that wherever the instruction "JMP IN" occurs within OUT, the contents of register A are to be unchanged when control returns to the next line, and make a similar assumption about "JMP OUT" within IN. What coroutine linkage is needed? (Compare with (4).)

▶ **6.** [*22*] Give coroutine linkage analogous to (1) for the case of *three* coroutines, A, B, and C, each of which can jump to either of the other two. (Whenever a coroutine is activated, it begins where it last left off.)

▶ **7.** [*30*] Write a MIX program that *reverses* the translation done by the program in the text; that is, your program should convert cards punched like (3) into cards punched like (2). The output should be as short a string of characters as possible, so that the zero before the Z in (2) would not really be produced from (3).

1.4.3. Interpretive Routines

In this section we will investigate a common type of computer program, the *interpretive routine* (which will be called *interpreter* for short). An interpretive routine is a computer program that performs the instructions of another program, where the other program is written in some machine-like language. By a machine-like language, we mean a way of representing instructions, where the instructions typically have operation codes, addresses, etc. (This definition, like most definitions of today's computer terms, is not precise, nor should it be; we cannot draw the line exactly and say just which programs are interpreters and which are not.)

Historically, the first interpreters were built around machine-like languages designed specially for simple programming; such languages were easier to use than a real machine language. The rise of symbolic languages for programming soon eliminated the need for interpretive routines of that kind, but interpreters have by no means begun to die out. On the contrary, their use has continued to grow, to the extent that an effective use of interpretive routines may be regarded as one of the essential characteristics of modern programming. The new applications of interpreters are made chiefly for the following reasons:

a) a machine-like language is able to represent a complicated sequence of decisions and actions in a compact, efficient manner; and

b) such a representation provides an excellent way to communicate between passes of a multipass process.

In such cases, special purpose machine-like languages are developed for use in a particular program, and programs in those languages are often generated only by computers. (Today's expert programmers are also good machine designers, as they not only create an interpretive routine, they also define a *virtual machine* whose language is to be interpreted.)

The interpretive technique has the further advantage of being relatively machine-independent — only the interpreter must be rewritten when changing computers. Furthermore, helpful debugging aids can readily be built into an interpretive system.

Examples of interpreters of type (a) appear in several places later in this series of books; see, for example, the recursive interpreter in Chapter 8 and the "Parsing Machine" in Chapter 10. We typically need to deal with a situation in which a great many special cases arise, all similar, but having no really simple pattern.

For example, consider writing an algebraic compiler in which we want to generate efficient machine-language instructions that add two quantities together. There might be ten classes of quantities (constants, simple variables, temporary storage locations, subscripted variables, the contents of an accumulator or index register, fixed or floating point, etc.) and the combination of all pairs yields 100 different cases. A long program would be required to do the proper thing in each case. The interpretive solution to this problem is to make up an ad hoc language whose "instructions" fit in one byte. Then we simply prepare a table of 100 "programs" in this language, where each program ideally fits in a single word. The idea is then to pick out the appropriate table entry and to perform the program found there. This technique is simple and efficient.

An example interpreter of type (b) appears in the article "Computer-Drawn Flowcharts" by D. E. Knuth, *CACM* **6** (1963), 555–563. In a multipass program, the earlier passes must transmit information to the later passes. This information is often transmitted most efficiently in a machine-like language, as a set of instructions for the later pass; the later pass is then nothing but a special purpose interpretive routine, and the earlier pass is a special purpose "compiler." This philosophy of multipass operation may be characterized as *telling* the later pass what to do, whenever possible, rather than simply presenting it with a lot of facts and asking it to *figure out* what to do.

Another example of a type-(b) interpreter occurs in connection with compilers for special languages. If the language includes many features that are not easily done on the machine except by subroutine, the resulting object programs will be very long sequences of subroutine calls. This would happen, for example, if the language were concerned primarily with multiple-precision arithmetic. In such a case the object program would be considerably shorter if it were expressed in an interpretive language. See, for example, the book *ALGOL 60 Implementation*, by B. Randell and L. J. Russell (New York: Academic Press, 1964), which describes a compiler to translate from ALGOL 60 into an interpretive language, and which also describes the interpreter for that language; and see "An ALGOL 60 Compiler," by Arthur Evans, Jr., *Ann. Rev. Auto. Programming* **4** (1964), 87–124, for examples of interpretive routines used *within* a compiler. The rise of microprogrammed machines and of special-purpose integrated circuit chips has made this interpretive approach even more valuable.

The TEX program, which produced the pages of the book you are now reading, converted a file that contained the text of this section into an interpretive language called DVI format, designed by D. R. Fuchs in 1979. [See D. E. Knuth, *TEX: The Program* (Reading, Mass.: Addison–Wesley, 1986), Part 31.] The DVI file that TEX produced was then processed by an interpreter called dvips, written by T. G. Rokicki, and converted to a file of instructions in another interpretive language called PostScript® [Adobe Systems Inc., *PostScript Language Reference Manual*, 2nd edition (Reading, Mass.: Addison–Wesley, 1990)]. The PostScript file was sent to the publisher, who sent it to a commercial printer, who used a PostScript interpreter to produce printing plates. This three-pass operation illustrates interpreters of type (b); TEX itself also includes a small interpreter of type (a) to process the so-called ligature and kerning information for characters of each font of type [*TEX: The Program*, §545].

There is another way to look at a program written in interpretive language: It may be regarded as a series of subroutine calls, one after another. Such a program may in fact be expanded into a long sequence of calls on subroutines, and, conversely, such a sequence can usually be packed into a coded form that is readily interpreted. The advantages of interpretive techniques are the compactness of representation, the machine independence, and the increased diagnostic capability. An interpreter can often be written so that the amount of time spent in interpretation of the code itself and branching to the appropriate routine is negligible.

1.4.3.1. A MIX simulator. When the language presented to an interpretive routine is the machine language of another computer, the interpreter is often called a *simulator* (or sometimes an *emulator*).

In the author's opinion, entirely too much programmers' time has been spent in writing such simulators and entirely too much computer time has been wasted in using them. The motivation for simulators is simple: A computer installation buys a new machine and still wants to run programs written for the old machine (rather than rewriting the programs). However, this usually costs more and gives poorer results than if a special task force of programmers were given temporary employment to do the reprogramming. For example, the author once participated in such a reprogramming project, and a serious error was discovered in the original program, which had been in use for several years; the new program worked at five times the speed of the old, besides giving the right answers for a change! (Not all simulators are bad; for example, it is usually advantageous for a computer manufacturer to simulate a new machine before it has been built, so that software for the new machine may be developed as soon as possible. But that is a very specialized application.) An extreme example of the inefficient use of computer simulators is the true story of machine A simulating machine B running a program that simulates machine C! This is the way to make a large, expensive computer give poorer results than its cheaper cousin.

In view of all this, why should such a simulator rear its ugly head in this book? There are two reasons:

a) The simulator we will describe below is a good example of a typical interpretive routine; the basic techniques employed in interpreters are illustrated here. It also illustrates the use of subroutines in a moderately long program.

b) We will describe a simulator of the MIX computer, written in (of all things) the MIX language. This will facilitate the writing of MIX simulators for most computers, which are similar; the coding of our program intentionally avoids making heavy use of MIX-oriented features. A MIX simulator will be of advantage as a teaching aid in conjunction with this book and possibly others.

Computer simulators as described in this section should be distinguished from *discrete system simulators*. Discrete system simulators are important programs that will be discussed in Section 2.2.5.

Now let's turn to the task of writing a MIX simulator. The input to our program will be a sequence of MIX instructions and data, stored in locations 0000–3499. We want to mimic the precise behavior of MIX's hardware, pretending that MIX itself is interpreting those instructions; thus, we want to implement the specifications that were laid down in Section 1.3.1. Our program will, for example, maintain a variable called AREG that will hold the magnitude of the simulated A-register; another variable, SIGNA, will hold the corresponding sign. A variable called CLOCK will record how many MIX units of simulated time have elapsed during the simulated program execution.

The numbering of MIX's instructions LDA, LD1, ..., LDX and other similar commands suggests that we keep the simulated contents of these registers in consecutive locations, as follows:

AREG, I1REG, I2REG, I3REG, I4REG, I5REG, I6REG, XREG, JREG, ZERO.

Here ZERO is a "register" filled with zeros at all times. The positions of JREG and ZERO are suggested by the op-code numbers of the instructions STJ and STZ.

In keeping with our philosophy of writing the simulator as though it were not really done with MIX hardware, we will treat the signs as independent parts of a register. For example, many computers cannot represent the number "minus zero", while MIX definitely can; therefore we will always treat signs specially in this program. The locations AREG, I1REG, ..., ZERO will always contain the absolute values of the corresponding register contents; another set of locations in our program, called SIGNA, SIGN1, ..., SIGNZ will contain +1 or −1, depending on whether the sign of the corresponding register is plus or minus.

An interpretive routine generally has a central control section that is called into action between interpreted instructions. In our case, the program transfers to location CYCLE at the end of each simulated instruction.

The control routine does the things common to all instructions, unpacks the instruction into its various parts, and puts the parts into convenient places for later use. The program below sets

> rI6 = location of the next instruction;
> rI5 = M (address of the present instruction, plus indexing);
> rI4 = operation code of the present instruction;
> rI3 = F-field of the present instruction;
> INST = the present instruction.

Program M.

```
001  * MIX SIMULATOR
002          ORIG 3500          Simulated memory is in locations 0000 up.
003  BEGIN   STZ  TIME(0:2)
004          STZ  OVTOG          OVTOG is the simulated overflow toggle.
005          STZ  COMPI          COMPI, ±1 or 0, is comparison indicator.
006          ENT6 0              Take first instruction from location zero.
007  CYCLE   LDA  CLOCK         Beginning of control routine:
008  TIME    INCA 0              This address is set to the execution time
009          STA  CLOCK             of the previous instruction (see line 033).
010          LDA  0,6            rA ← instruction to simulate.
011          STA  INST
012          INC6 1              Advance the location counter.
013          LDX  INST(1:2)      Get absolute value of the address.
014          SLAX 5              Attach sign to the address.
015          STA  M
016          LD2  INST(3:3)      Examine the index field.
017          J2Z  1F             Is it zero?
018          DEC2 6
019          J2P  INDEXERROR     Illegal index specified?
020          LDA  SIGN6,2        Get sign of the index register.
021          LDX  I6REG,2        Get magnitude of the index register.
022          SLAX 5              Attach the sign.
023          ADD  M              Do signed addition for indexing.
024          CMPA ZERO(1:3)      Is the result too large?
025          JNE  ADDRERROR      If so, simulate an error.
026          STA  M              Otherwise the address has been found.
```

027	1H	LD3	INST(4:4)	rI3 ← F-field.
028		LD5	M	rI5 ← M.
029		LD4	INST(5:5)	rI4 ← C-field.
030		DEC4	63	
031		J4P	OPERROR	Is the op code ≥ 64?
032		LDA	OPTABLE,4(4:4)	Get execution time from the table.
033		STA	TIME(0:2)	
034		LD2	OPTABLE,4(0:2)	Get address of the proper routine.
035		JNOV	0,2	Jump to operator.
036		JMP	0,2	(Protect against overflows.) ▌

The reader's attention is called particularly to lines 034–036: A "switching table" of the 64 operators is part of the simulator, allowing it to jump rapidly to the correct routine for the current instruction. This is an important time-saving technique (see exercise 1.3.2–9).

The 64-word switching table, called OPTABLE, gives also the execution time for the various operators; the following lines indicate the contents of that table:

037		NOP	CYCLE(1)	Operation code table;
038		ADD	ADD(2)	typical entry is
039		SUB	SUB(2)	"OP routine(time)"
040		MUL	MUL(10)	
041		DIV	DIV(12)	
042		HLT	SPEC(10)	
043		SLA	SHIFT(2)	
044		MOVE	MOVE(1)	
045		LDA	LOAD(2)	
046		LD1	LOAD,1(2)	
			. . .	
051		LD6	LOAD,1(2)	
052		LDX	LOAD(2)	
053		LDAN	LOADN(2)	
054		LD1N	LOADN,1(2)	
			. . .	
060		LDXN	LOADN(2)	
061		STA	STORE(2)	
			. . .	
069		STJ	STORE(2)	
070		STZ	STORE(2)	
071		JBUS	JBUS(1)	
072		IOC	IOC(1)	
073		IN	IN(1)	
074		OUT	OUT(1)	
075		JRED	JRED(1)	
076		JMP	JUMP(1)	
077		JAP	REGJUMP(1)	
			. . .	
084		JXP	REGJUMP(1)	
085		INCA	ADDROP(1)	

```
086              INC1 ADDROP,1(1)
                 ...
092              INCX ADDROP(1)
093              CMPA COMPARE(2)
                 ...
100  OPTABLE     CMPX COMPARE(2)    ▌
```

(The entries for operators LD*i*, LD*i*N, and INC*i* have an additional ",1" to set the (3:3) field nonzero; this is used below in lines 289–290 to indicate the fact that the size of the quantity within the corresponding index register must be checked after simulating these operations.)

The next part of our simulator program merely lists the locations used to contain the contents of the simulated registers:

```
101  AREG    CON   0    Magnitude of A-register
102  I1REG   CON   0    Magnitude of index registers
              ...
107  I6REG   CON   0
108  XREG    CON   0    Magnitude of X-register
109  JREG    CON   0    Magnitude of J-register
110  ZERO    CON   0    Constant zero, for "STZ"
111  SIGNA   CON   1    Sign of A-register
112  SIGN1   CON   1    Sign of index registers
              ...
117  SIGN6   CON   1
118  SIGNX   CON   1    Sign of X-register
119  SIGNJ   CON   1    Sign of J-register
120  SIGNZ   CON   1    Sign stored by "STZ"
121  INST    CON   0    Instruction being simulated
122  COMPI   CON   0    Comparison indicator
123  OVTOG   CON   0    Overflow toggle
124  CLOCK   CON   0    Simulated execution time    ▌
```

Now we will consider three subroutines used by the simulator. First comes the MEMORY subroutine:

Calling sequence: JMP MEMORY.

Entry conditions: rI5 = valid memory address (otherwise the subroutine will jump to MEMERROR).

Exit conditions: rX = sign of word in memory location rI5; rA = magnitude of word in memory location rI5.

```
125  * SUBROUTINES
126  MEMORY  STJ   9F          Memory fetch subroutine:
127          J5N   MEMERROR
128          CMP5  =BEGIN=      The simulated memory is in
129          JGE   MEMERROR       locations 0000 to BEGIN − 1.
130          LDX   0,5
131          ENTA  1
132          SRAX  5            rX ← sign of word.
```

```
133                 LDA   0,5(1:5)    rA ← magnitude of word.
134   9H            JMP   *           Exit.  ▮
```

The FCHECK subroutine processes a partial field specification, making sure that it has the form 8L + R with L ≤ R ≤ 5.

Calling sequence: JMP FCHECK.
Entry conditions: rI3 = valid field specification (otherwise the subroutine will jump to FERROR).
Exit conditions: rA = rI1 = L, rX = R.

```
135   FCHECK    STJ   9F             Field check subroutine:
136             ENTA  0
137             ENTX  0,3            rAX ← field specification.
138             DIV   =8=            rA ← L, rX ← R.
139             CMPX  =5=            Is R > 5?
140             JG    FERROR
141             STX   R
142             STA   L
143             LD1   L              rI1 ← L.
144             CMPA  R
145   9H        JLE   *              Exit unless L > R.
146             JMP   FERROR  ▮
```

The last subroutine, GETV, finds the quantity V (namely, the appropriate field of location M) used in various MIX operators, as defined in Section 1.3.1.

Calling sequence: JMP GETV.
Entry conditions: rI5 = valid memory address; rI3 = valid field. (If invalid, an error will be detected as above.)
Exit conditions: rA = magnitude of V; rX = sign of V; rI1 = L; rI2 = −R.
Second entrance: JMP GETAV, used only in comparison operators to extract a field from a register.

```
147   GETAV     STJ   9F             Special entrance, see line 300.
148             JMP   1F
149   GETV      STJ   9F             Subroutine to find V:
150             JMP   FCHECK         Process the field and set rI1 ← L.
151             JMP   MEMORY         rA ← memory magnitude, rX ← sign.
152   1H        J1Z   2F             Is the sign included in the field?
153             ENTX  1              If not, set the sign positive.
154             SLA   -1,1           Zero out all bytes to the left
155             SRA   -1,1               of the field.
156   2H        LD2N  R              Shift right into the
157             SRA   5,2                proper position.
158   9H        JMP   *              Exit.  ▮
```

Now we come to the routines for each individual operator. These routines are given here for completeness, but the reader should study only a few of them unless there's a compelling reason to look closer; the SUB and JUMP operators are recommended as typical examples for study. Notice the way in which routines

for similar operations can be neatly combined, and notice how the JUMP routine
uses another switching table to govern the type of jump.

```
159  * INDIVIDUAL OPERATORS
160  ADD     JMP   GETV          Get the value of V in rA and rX.
161          ENT1  0             rI1 ← index of simulated rA.
162          JMP   INC           Go to the "increase" routine.
163  SUB     JMP   GETV          Get the value of V in rA and rX.
164          ENT1  0             rI1 ← index of simulated rA.
165          JMP   DEC           Go to the "decrease" routine.
166  *
167  MUL     JMP   GETV          Get the value of V in rA and rX.
168          CMPX  SIGNA         Are signs the same?
169          ENTX  1
170          JE    *+2           Set rX to the result sign.
171          ENNX  1
172          STX   SIGNA         Put it in both simulated registers.
173          STX   SIGNX
174          MUL   AREG          Multiply the operands.
175          JMP   STOREAX       Store the magnitudes.
176  *
177  DIV     LDA   SIGNA         Set the sign of the remainder.
178          STA   SIGNX
179          JMP   GETV          Get the value of V in rA and rX.
180          CMPX  SIGNA         Are signs the same?
181          ENTX  1
182          JE    *+2           Set rX to the result sign.
183          ENNX  1
184          STX   SIGNA         Put it in the simulated rA.
185          STA   TEMP
186          LDA   AREG          Divide the operands.
187          LDX   XREG
188          DIV   TEMP
189  STOREAX STA   AREG          Store the magnitudes.
190          STX   XREG
191  OVCHECK JNOV  CYCLE         Did overflow just occur?
192          ENTX  1             If so, set the simulated
193          STX   OVTOG            overflow toggle on.
194          JMP   CYCLE         Return to control routine.
195  *
196  LOADN   JMP   GETV          Get the value of V in rA and rX.
197          ENT1  47,4          rI1 ← C − 16; indicates register.
198  LOADN1  STX   TEMP          Negate the sign.
199          LDXN  TEMP
200          JMP   LOAD1         Change LOADN to LOAD.
201  LOAD    JMP   GETV          Get the value of V in rA and rX.
202          ENT1  55,4          rI1 ← C − 8, indicates register.
203  LOAD1   STA   AREG,1        Store the magnitude.
204          STX   SIGNA,1       Store the sign.
```

205		JMP	SIZECHK	Check if the magnitude is too large.
206	*			
207	STORE	JMP	FCHECK	rI1 ← L.
208		JMP	MEMORY	Get contents of memory location.
209		J1P	1F	Is the sign included in the field?
210		ENT1	1	If so, change L to 1
211		LDX	SIGNA+39,4	and "store" the register's sign.
212	1H	LD2N	R	rI2 ← −R.
213		SRAX	5,2	Save the area to the field's right.
214		LDA	AREG+39,4	Insert register in the field.
215		SLAX	5,2	
216		ENN2	0,1	rI2 ← −L.
217		SRAX	6,2	
218		LDA	0,5	Restore the area to the field's left.
219		SRA	6,2	
220		SRAX	-1,1	Attach the sign.
221		STX	0,5	Store in memory.
222		JMP	CYCLE	Return to control routine.
223	*			
224	JUMP	DEC3	9	Jump operators:
225		J3P	FERROR	Is F too large?
226		LDA	COMPI	rA ← comparison indicator.
227		JMP	JTABLE,3	Jump to appropriate routine.
228	JMP	ST6	JREG	Set the simulated J-register.
229		JMP	JSJ	
230		JMP	JOV	
231		JMP	JNOV	
232		JMP	LS	
233		JMP	EQ	
234		JMP	GR	
235		JMP	GE	
236		JMP	NE	
237	JTABLE	JMP	LE	End of the jump table
238	JOV	LDX	OVTOG	Check whether to jump on
239		JMP	*+3	overflow.
240	JNOV	LDX	OVTOG	
241		DECX	1	Get complement of overflow toggle.
242		STZ	OVTOG	Shut off overflow toggle.
243		JXNZ	JMP	Jump.
244		JMP	CYCLE	Don't jump.
245	LE	JAZ	JMP	Jump if rA zero or negative.
246	LS	JAN	JMP	Jump if rA negative.
247		JMP	CYCLE	Don't jump.
248	NE	JAN	JMP	Jump if rA negative or positive.
249	GR	JAP	JMP	Jump if rA positive.
250		JMP	CYCLE	Don't jump.
251	GE	JAP	JMP	Jump if rA positive or zero.
252	EQ	JAZ	JMP	Jump if rA zero.
253		JMP	CYCLE	Don't jump.

254	JSJ	JMP	MEMORY	Check for valid memory address.
255		ENT6	0,5	Simulate a jump.
256		JMP	CYCLE	Return to main control routine.
257	*			
258	REGJUMP	LDA	AREG+23,4	Register jumps:
259		JAZ	*+2	Is register zero?
260		LDA	SIGNA+23,4	If not, put sign into rA.
261		DEC3	5	
262		J3NP	JTABLE,3	Change to a conditional JMP, unless
263		JMP	FERROR	the F-specification is too large.
264	*			
265	ADDROP	DEC3	3	Address transfer operators:
266		J3P	FERROR	Is F too large?
267		ENTX	0,5	
268		JXNZ	*+2	Find the sign of M.
269		LDX	INST	
270		ENTA	1	
271		SRAX	5	rX ← sign of M.
272		LDA	M(1:5)	rA ← magnitude of M.
273		ENT1	15,4	rI1 indicates the register.
274		JMP	1F,3	Four-way jump.
275		JMP	INC	Increase.
276		JMP	DEC	Decrease.
277		JMP	LOAD1	Enter.
278	1H	JMP	LOADN1	Enter negative.
279	DEC	STX	TEMP	Reverse the sign.
280		LDXN	TEMP	Reduce DEC to INC.
281	INC	CMPX	SIGNA,1	Addition routine:
282		JE	1F	Are signs the same?
283		SUB	AREG,1	No; subtract magnitudes.
284		JANP	2F	Sign change needed?
285		STX	SIGNA,1	Change the register's sign.
286		JMP	2F	
287	1H	ADD	AREG,1	Add magnitudes.
288	2H	STA	AREG,1(1:5)	Store magnitude of the result.
289	SIZECHK	LD1	OPTABLE,4(3:3)	Have we just loaded an
290		J1Z	OVCHECK	index register?
291		CMPA	ZERO(1:3)	If so, make sure that the result
292		JE	CYCLE	fits in two bytes.
293		JMP	SIZEERROR	
294	*			
295	COMPARE	JMP	GETV	Get the value of V in rA and rX.
296		SRAX	5	Attach the sign.
297		STX	V	
298		LDA	XREG,4	Get field F of the appropriate register.
299		LDX	SIGNX,4	
300		JMP	GETAV	
301		SRAX	5	Attach the sign.
302		CMPX	V	Compare (note that $-0 = +0$).

303		STZ	COMPI	Set comparison indicator to
304		JE	CYCLE	either zero, plus one,
305		ENTA	1	or minus one.
306		JG	*+2	
307		ENNA	1	
308		STA	COMPI	
309		JMP	CYCLE	Return to control routine.
310	*			
311		END	BEGIN ▌	

The code above adheres to a subtle rule that was stated in Section 1.3.1:
The instruction "ENTA -0" loads minus zero into register A, as does "ENTA -5,1"
when index register 1 contains +5. In general, when M is zero, ENTA loads the
sign of the instruction and ENNA loads the opposite sign. The need to specify this
condition was overlooked when the author prepared his first draft of Section 1.3.1;
such questions usually come to light only when a computer program is being
written to follow the rules.

In spite of its length, the program above is incomplete in several respects:

a) It does not recognize floating point operations.
b) The coding for operation codes 5, 6, and 7 has been left as an exercise.
c) The coding for input-output operators has been left as an exercise.
d) No provision has been made for loading simulated programs (see exercise 4).
e) The error routines

    INDEXERROR, ADDRERROR, OPERROR, MEMERROR, FERROR, SIZEERROR

have not been included; they handle error conditions that are detected in
the simulated program.
f) There is no provision for diagnostic facilities. (A useful simulator should,
for example, make it possible to print out the register contents as a program
is being executed.)

EXERCISES

1. [*14*] Study all the uses of the FCHECK subroutine in the simulator program. Can
you suggest a better way to organize the code? (See step 3 in the discussion at the end
of Section 1.4.1.)

2. [*20*] Write the SHIFT routine, which is missing from the program in the text
(operation code 6).

▶ **3.** [*22*] Write the MOVE routine, which is missing from the program in the text
(operation code 7).

4. [*14*] Change the program in the text so that it begins as though MIX's "GO button"
had been pushed (see exercise 1.3.1–26).

▶ **5.** [*24*] Determine the time required to simulate the LDA and ENTA operators, compared with the actual time for MIX to execute these operators directly.

6. [*28*] Write programs for the input-output operators JBUS, IOC, IN, OUT, and JRED,
which are missing from the program in the text, allowing only units 16 and 18. Assume

that the operations "read-card" and "skip-to-new-page" take $T = 10000u$, while "print-line" takes $T = 7500u$. [*Note:* Experience shows that the JBUS instruction should be simulated by treating "JBUS *" as a special case; otherwise the simulator seems to stop!]

▶ **7.** [*32*] Modify the solutions of the previous exercise in such a way that execution of IN or OUT does not cause I/O transmission immediately; the transmission should take place after approximately half of the time required by the simulated devices has elapsed. (This will prevent a frequent student error, in which IN and OUT are used improperly.)

8. [*20*] True or false: Whenever line 010 of the simulator program is executed, we have $0 \le rI6 < \text{BEGIN}$.

*1.4.3.2. Trace routines. When a machine is being simulated on itself (as MIX was simulated on MIX in the previous section) we have the special case of a simulator called a *trace* or *monitor* routine. Such programs are occasionally used to help in debugging, since they print out a step-by-step account of how the simulated program behaves.

The program in the preceding section was written as though another computer were simulating MIX. A quite different approach is used for trace programs; we generally let registers represent themselves and let the operators perform themselves. In fact, we usually contrive to let the machine execute most of the instructions by itself. The chief exception is a jump or conditional jump instruction, which must not be executed without modification, since the trace program must remain in control. Each machine also has idiosyncratic features that make tracing more of a challenge; in MIX's case, the J-register presents the most interesting problem.

The trace routine given below is initiated when the main program jumps to location ENTER, with register J set to the address for *starting* to trace and register X set to the address where tracing should *stop*. The program is interesting and merits careful study.

```
01   * TRACE ROUTINE
02   ENTER  STX   TEST(0:2)        Set the exit location.
03          STX   LEAVEX(0:2)
04          STA   AREG             Save the contents of rA.
05          STJ   JREG             Save the contents of rJ.
06          LDA   JREG(0:2)        Get the start location for tracing.
07   CYCLE  STA   PREG(0:2)        Store the location of the next instruction.
08   TEST   DECA  *                Is it the exit location?
09          JAZ   LEAVE
10   PREG   LDA   *                Get the next instruction.
11          STA   INST             Copy it.
12          SRA   2
13          STA   INST1(0:3)       Store the address and index parts.
14          LDA   INST(5:5)        Get the operation code, C.
15          DECA  38
16          JANN  1F               Is C ≥ 38 (JRED)?
```

17		INCA	6	
18		JANZ	2F	Is C $\neq$ 32 (STJ)?
19		LDA	INST(0:4)	
20		STA	*+2(0:4)	Change STJ to STA.
21	JREG	ENTA	*	rA ← simulated rJ contents.
22		STA	*	
23		JMP	INCP	
24	2H	DECA	2	
25		JANZ	2F	Is C $\neq$ 34 (JBUS)?
26		JMP	3F	
27	1H	DECA	9	Test for jump instructions.
28		JAP	2F	Is C $>$ 47 (JXNP)?
29	3H	LDA	8F(0:3)	We detected a jump instruction;
30		STA	INST(0:3)	change its address to "JUMP".
31	2H	LDA	AREG	Restore register A.
32	*			All registers except J now have proper
33	*			values with respect to the external program.
34	INST	NOP	*	The instruction is executed.
35		STA	AREG	Store register A again.
36	INCP	LDA	PREG(0:2)	Move to the next instruction.
37		INCA	1	
38		JMP	CYCLE	
39	8H	JSJ	JUMP	Constant for lines 29 and 40
40	JUMP	LDA	8B(4:5)	A jump has occurred.
41		SUB	INST(4:5)	Was it JSJ?
42		JAZ	*+4	
43		LDA	PREG(0:2)	If not, update the simulated
44		INCA	1	J-register.
45		STA	JREG(0:2)	
46	INST1	ENTA	*	
47		JMP	CYCLE	Move to the address of the jump.
48	LEAVE	LDA	AREG	Restore register A.
49	LEAVEX	JMP	*	Stop tracing.
50	AREG	CON	0	Simulated rA contents

The following things should be noted about trace routines in general and this one in particular.

1) We have presented only the most interesting part of a trace program, the part that retains control while executing another program. For a trace to be useful, there must also be a routine for writing out the contents of registers, and this has not been included. Such a routine distracts from the more subtle features of a trace program, although it certainly is important; the necessary modifications are left as an exercise (see exercise 2).

2) Space is generally more important than time; that is, the program should be written to be as short as possible. Then the trace routine will be able to coexist with extremely large programs. The running time is consumed by output anyway.

3) Care was taken to avoid destroying the contents of most registers; in fact, the program uses only MIX's A-register. Neither the comparison indicator nor

the overflow toggle are affected by the trace routine. (The less we use, the less we need to restore.)

4) When a jump to location JUMP occurs, it is not necessary to "STA AREG", since rA cannot have changed.

5) After leaving the trace routine, the J-register is not reset properly. Exercise 1 shows how to remedy this.

6) The program being traced is subject to only three restrictions:

    a) It must not store anything into the locations used by the trace program.

    b) It must not use the output device on which tracing information is being recorded (for example, JBUS would give an improper indication).

    c) It will run at a slower speed while being traced.

EXERCISES

1. [*22*] Modify the trace routine of the text so that it restores register J when leaving. (You may assume that register J is not zero.)

2. [*26*] Modify the trace routine of the text so that before executing each program step it writes the following information on tape unit 0.

Word 1, (0:2) field: location.
Word 1, (4:5) field: register J (before execution).
Word 1, (3:3) field: 2 if comparison is greater, 1 if equal, 0 if less; plus 8 if overflow
    is not on before execution.
Word 2: instruction.
Word 3: register A (before execution).
Words 4–9: registers I1–I6 (before execution).
Word 10: register X (before execution).

Words 11–100 of each 100-word tape block should contain nine more ten-word groups, in the same format.

3. [*10*] The previous exercise suggests having the trace program write its output onto tape. Discuss why this would be preferable to printing directly.

▶ **4.** [*25*] What would happen if the trace routine were tracing *itself*? Specifically, consider the behavior if the two instructions ENTX LEAVEX; JMP *+1 were placed just before ENTER.

5. [*28*] In a manner similar to that used to solve the previous exercise, consider the situation in which two copies of the trace routine are placed in different places in memory, and each is set up to trace the other. What would happen?

▶ **6.** [*40*] Write a trace routine that is capable of tracing itself, in the sense of exercise 4: It should print out the steps of its own program at slower speed, and *that* program will be tracing itself at still *slower* speed, ad infinitum, until memory capacity is exceeded.

▶ **7.** [*25*] Discuss how to write an efficient *jump trace* routine, which emits much less output than a normal trace. Instead of displaying the register contents, a jump trace simply records the jumps that occur. It outputs a sequence of pairs (x_1, y_1), (x_2, y_2), ..., meaning that the program jumped from location x_1 to y_1, then (after performing the instructions in locations $y_1, y_1 + 1, \ldots, x_2$) it jumped from x_2 to y_2, etc. [From this information it is possible for a subsequent routine to reconstruct the flow of the program and to deduce how frequently each instruction was performed.]

1.4.4. Input and Output

Perhaps the most outstanding differences between one computer and the next are the facilities available for doing input and output, and the computer instructions that govern those peripheral devices. We cannot hope to discuss in a single book all of the problems and techniques that arise in this area, so we will confine ourselves to a study of typical input-output methods that apply to most computers. The input-output operators of MIX represent a compromise between the widely varying facilities available in actual machines; to give an example of how to think about input-output, let us discuss in this section the problem of getting the best MIX input-output.

Once again the reader is asked to be indulgent about the anachronistic MIX computer with its punched cards, etc. Although such old-fashioned devices are now quite obsolete, they still can teach important lessons. The MMIX computer, when it comes, will of course teach those lessons even better.

Many computer users feel that input and output are not actually part of "real" programming; input and output are considered to be tedious tasks that people must perform only because they need to get information in and out of a machine. For this reason, the input and output facilities of a computer are usually not learned until after all other features have been examined, and it frequently happens that only a small fraction of the programmers of a particular machine ever know much about the details of input and output. This attitude is somewhat natural, because the input-output facilities of machines have never been especially pretty. However, the situation cannot be expected to improve until more people give serious thought to the subject. We shall see in this section and elsewhere (for example, in Section 5.4.6) that some very interesting issues arise in connection with input-output, and some pleasant algorithms do exist.

A brief digression about terminology is perhaps appropriate here. Although dictionaries of English formerly listed the words "input" and "output" only as nouns ("What kind of input are we getting?"), it is now customary to use them grammatically as adjectives ("Don't drop the input tape.") and as transitive verbs ("Why did the program output this garbage?"). The combined term "input-output" is most frequently referred to by the abbreviation "I/O". Inputting is often called *reading*, and outputting is, similarly, called *writing*. The stuff that is input or output is generally known as "data" — this word is, strictly speaking, a plural form of the word "datum," but it is used collectively as if it were singular ("The data has not been read."), just as the word "information" is both singular and plural. This completes today's English lesson.

Suppose now that we wish to read from magnetic tape. The IN operator of MIX, as defined in Section 1.3.1, merely *initiates* the input process, and the computer continues to execute further instructions while the input is taking place. Thus the instruction "IN 1000(5)" will begin to read 100 words from tape unit number 5 into memory cells 1000–1099, but the ensuing program must not refer to these memory cells until later. The program can assume that input is complete only after (a) another I/O operation (IN, OUT, or IOC) referring

to unit 5 has been initiated, or (b) a conditional jump instruction JBUS(5) or
JRED(5) indicates that unit 5 is no longer "busy."

The simplest way to read a tape block into locations 1000–1099 and to have
the information present is therefore the sequence of two instructions

$$\text{IN } 1000(5); \text{ JBUS } *(5). \tag{1}$$

We have used this rudimentary method in the program of Section 1.4.2 (see lines
07–08 and 52–53). The method is generally wasteful of computer time, however,
because a very large amount of potentially useful calculating time, say $1000u$ or
even $10000u$, is consumed by repeated execution of the "JBUS" instruction. The
program's running speed can be as much as doubled if this additional time is
utilized for calculation. (See exercises 4 and 5.)

One way to avoid such a "busy wait" is to use two areas of memory for the
input: We can read into one area while computing with the data in the other.
For example, we could begin our program with the instruction

$$\text{IN} \quad 2000(5) \quad \text{Begin reading first block.} \tag{2}$$

Subsequently, we may give the following five commands whenever a tape block
is desired:

$$
\begin{array}{lll}
\text{ENT1} & 1000 & \text{Prepare for MOVE operator.} \\
\text{JBUS} & *(5) & \text{Wait until unit 5 is ready.} \\
\text{MOVE} & 2000(50) & (2000\text{–}2049) \to (1000\text{–}1049). \\
\text{MOVE} & 2050(50) & (2050\text{–}2099) \to (1050\text{–}1099). \\
\text{IN} & 2000(5) & \text{Begin reading next block.}
\end{array}
\tag{3}
$$

This has the same overall effect as (1), but it keeps the input tape busy while
the program works on the data in locations 1000–1099.

The last instruction of (3) begins to read a tape block into locations 2000–
2099 before the preceding block has been examined. This is called "reading
ahead" or *anticipated input* — it is done on faith that the block will eventually be
needed. In fact, however, we might discover that no more input is really required,
after we begin to examine the block in 1000–1099. For example, consider the
analogous situation in the coroutine program of Section 1.4.2, where the input
was coming from punched cards instead of tape: A "." appearing anywhere in
the card meant that it was the final card of the deck. Such a situation would
make anticipated input impossible, unless we could assume that either (a) a
blank card or special trailer card of some other sort would follow the input deck,
or (b) an identifying mark (e.g., ".") would appear in, say, column 80 of the final
card of the deck. Some means for terminating the input properly at the end of
the program must always be provided whenever input has been anticipated.

The technique of overlapping computation time and I/O time is known as
buffering, while the rudimentary method (1) is called *unbuffered* input. The
area of memory 2000–2099 used to hold the anticipated input in (3), as well as
the area 1000–1099 to which the input was moved, is called a *buffer*. Webster's
New World Dictionary defines "buffer" as "any person or thing that serves to
lessen shock," and the term is appropriate because buffering tends to keep I/O

devices running smoothly. (Computer engineers often use the word "buffer" in another sense, to denote a part of the I/O device that stores information during the transmission. In this book, however, "buffer" will signify an area of *memory* used by a programmer to hold I/O data.)

The sequence (3) is not always superior to (1), although the exceptions are rare. Let us compare the execution times: Suppose T is the time required to input 100 words, and suppose C is the computation time that intervenes between input requests. Method (1) requires a time of essentially $T + C$ per tape block, while method (3) takes essentially $\max(C, T) + 202u$. (The quantity $202u$ is the time required by the two MOVE instructions.) One way to look at this running time is to consider "critical path time" — in this case, the amount of time the I/O unit is idle between uses. Method (1) keeps the unit idle for C units of time, while method (3) keeps it idle for 202 units (assuming that $C < T$).

The relatively slow MOVE commands of (3) are undesirable, particularly because they take up critical path time when the tape unit must be inactive. An almost obvious improvement of the method allows us to avoid these MOVE instructions: The outside program can be revised so that it refers alternately to locations 1000–1099 and 2000–2099. While we are reading into one buffer area, we can be computing with the information in the other; then we can begin reading into the second buffer while computing with the information in the first. This is the important technique known as *buffer swapping*. The location of the current buffer of interest will be kept in an index register (or, if no index registers are available, in a memory location). We have already seen an example of buffer swapping applied to output in Algorithm 1.3.2P (see steps P9–P11) and the accompanying program.

As an example of buffer swapping on input, suppose that we have a computer application in which each tape block consists of 100 separate one-word items. The following program is a subroutine that gets the next word of input and begins to read in a new block if the current one is exhausted.

01	WORDIN	STJ	1F	Store the exit location.
02		INC6	1	Advance to the next word.
03	2H	LDA	0,6	Is it the end of the
04		CMPA	=SENTINEL=	buffer?
05	1H	JNE	*	If not, exit.
06		IN	-100,6(U)	Refill this buffer.
07		LD6	1,6	Switch to the other
08		JMP	2B	buffer and return.
09	INBUF1	ORIG	*+100	First buffer
10		CON	SENTINEL	Sentinel at end of buffer
11		CON	*+1	Address of other buffer
12	INBUF2	ORIG	*+100	Second buffer
13		CON	SENTINEL	Sentinel at end of buffer
14		CON	INBUF1	Address of other buffer

$$(4)$$

In this routine, index register 6 is used to address the last word of input; we assume that the calling program does not affect this register. The symbol U refers to a tape unit, and the symbol SENTINEL refers to a value that is known (from characteristics of the program) to be *absent* from all tape blocks.

Several things about this subroutine should be noted:

1) The sentinel constant appears as the 101st word of each buffer, and it makes a convenient test for the end of the buffer. In many applications, however, the sentinel technique will not be reliable, since any word may appear on tape. If we were doing card input, a similar method (with the 17th word of the buffer equal to a sentinel) could always be used without fear of failure; in that case, any negative word could serve as a sentinel, since MIX input from cards always gives nonnegative words.

2) Each buffer contains the address of the other buffer (see lines 07, 11, and 14). This "linking together" facilitates the swapping process.

3) No JBUS instruction was necessary, since the next input was initiated before any word of the previous block was accessed. If the quantities C and T refer as before to computation time and tape time, the execution time per tape block is now $\max(C, T)$; it is therefore possible to keep the tape going at full speed if $C \leq T$. (*Note:* MIX is an idealized computer in this regard, however, since no I/O errors must be treated by the program. On most machines some instructions to test the successful completion of the previous operation would be necessary just before the "IN" instruction here.)

4) To make subroutine (4) work properly, it will be necessary to get things started out right when the program begins. Details are left to the reader (see exercise 6).

5) The WORDIN subroutine makes the tape unit appear to have a block length of 1 rather than 100 as far as the rest of the program is concerned. The idea of having several program-oriented records filling a single actual tape block is called *blocking of records*.

The techniques that we have illustrated for input apply, with minor changes, to output as well (see exercises 2 and 3).

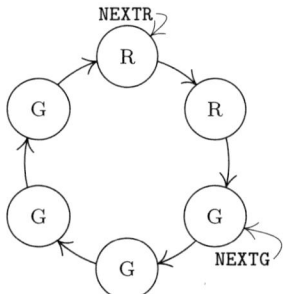

Fig. 23. A circle of buffers ($N = 6$).

Multiple buffers. Buffer swapping is just the special case $N = 2$ of a general method involving N buffers. In some applications it is desirable to have more than two buffers; for example, consider the following type of algorithm:

Step 1. Read five blocks in rapid succession.

Step 2. Perform a fairly long calculation based on this data.

Step 3. Return to step 1.

Here five or six buffers would be desirable, so that the next batch of five blocks could be read during step 2. This tendency for I/O activity to be "bunched" makes multiple buffering an improvement over buffer swapping.

Suppose we have N buffers for some input or output process using a single I/O device; we will imagine that the buffers are arranged in a circle, as in Fig. 23. The program external to the buffering process can be assumed to have the following general form with respect to the I/O unit of interest:

$$\vdots$$

ASSIGN

$$\vdots$$

RELEASE

$$\vdots$$

ASSIGN

$$\vdots$$

RELEASE

$$\vdots$$

in other words, we can assume that the program alternates between an action called "ASSIGN" and an action called "RELEASE", separated by other computations that do not affect the allocation of buffers.

ASSIGN   means that the program acquires the address of the next buffer area; this address is assigned as the value of some program variable.

RELEASE   means that the program is done with the current buffer area.

Between ASSIGN and RELEASE the program is communicating with one of the buffers, called the *current* buffer area; between RELEASE and ASSIGN, the program makes no reference to any buffer area.

Conceivably, ASSIGN could immediately follow RELEASE, and discussions of buffering have often been based on this assumption. However, if RELEASE is done as soon as possible, the buffering process has more freedom and will be more effective; by separating the two essentially different functions of ASSIGN and RELEASE we will find that the buffering technique remains easy to understand, and our discussion will be meaningful even if $N = 1$.

To be more explicit, let us consider the cases of input and output separately. For input, suppose we are dealing with a card reader. The action ASSIGN means that the program needs to see information from a new card; we would like to set an index register to the memory address at which the next card image is located. The action RELEASE occurs when the information in the current card image is no longer needed — it has somehow been digested by the program, perhaps copied to another part of memory, etc. The current buffer area may therefore be filled with further anticipated input.

For output, consider the case of a line printer. The action ASSIGN occurs when a free buffer area is needed, into which a line image is to be placed for printing. We wish to set an index register equal to the memory address of such an area. The action RELEASE occurs when this line image has been fully set up in the buffer area, in a form ready to be printed.

Example: To print the contents of locations 0800–0823, we might write

$$
\begin{array}{lll}
\texttt{JMP} & \texttt{ASSIGNP} & \text{(Sets rI5 to buffer location)} \\
\texttt{ENT1} & \texttt{0,5} & \\
\texttt{MOVE} & \texttt{800(24)} & \text{Move 24 words into the output buffer.} \\
\texttt{JMP} & \texttt{RELEASEP} &
\end{array}
\tag{5}
$$

where ASSIGNP and RELEASEP represent subroutines to do the two buffering functions for the line printer.

In an optimal situation, from the standpoint of the computer, the ASSIGN operation will require virtually no execution time. This means, on input, that each card image will have been anticipated, so that the data is available when the program is ready for it; and on output, it means that there will always be a free place in memory to record the line image. In either case, no time will be spent waiting for the I/O device.

To help describe the buffering algorithm, and to make it more colorful, we will say that buffer areas are either green, yellow, or red (shown as G, Y, and R in Fig. 24).

Green means that the area is ready to be ASSIGNed; this means that it has been filled with anticipated information (in an input situation), or that it is a free area (in an output situation).

Yellow means that the area has been ASSIGNed, not RELEASEd; this means that it is the current buffer, and the program is communicating with it.

Red means that the area has been RELEASEd; thus it is a free area (in an input situation) or it has been filled with information (in an output situation).

Figure 23 shows two "pointers" associated with the circle of buffers. These are, conceptually, index registers in the program. NEXTG and NEXTR point to the "next green" and "next red" buffer, respectively. A third pointer, CURRENT (shown in Fig. 24), indicates the yellow buffer when one is present.

The algorithms below apply equally well to input or output, but for definiteness we will consider first the case of input from a card reader. Suppose that a program has reached the state shown in Fig. 23. This means that four card images have been anticipated by the buffering process, and they reside in the green buffers. At this moment, two things are happening *simultaneously*: (a) The program is computing, following a RELEASE operation; (b) a card is being read into the buffer indicated by NEXTR. This state of affairs will continue until the input cycle is completed (the unit will then go from "busy" to "ready"), or until the program does an ASSIGN operation. Suppose the latter occurs first; then the buffer indicated by NEXTG changes to yellow (it is assigned as the current buffer),

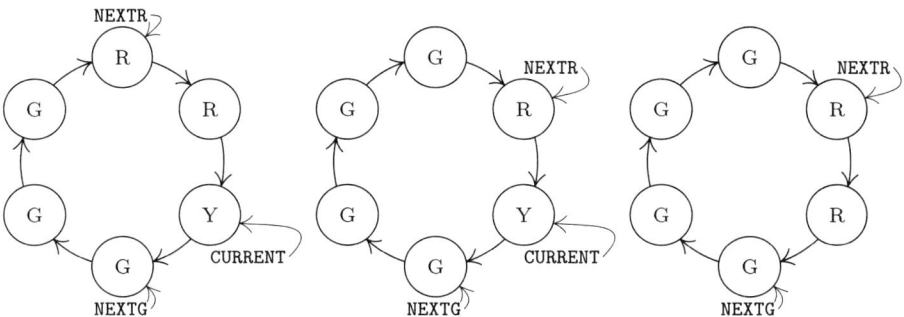

Fig. 24. Buffer transitions, (a) after `ASSIGN`, (b) after I/O complete, and (c) after `RELEASE`.

`NEXTG` moves clockwise, and we arrive at the position shown in Fig. 24(a). If now the input is completed, another anticipated block is present; so the buffer changes from red to green, and `NEXTR` moves over as shown in Fig. 24(b). If the `RELEASE` operation follows next, we obtain Fig. 24(c).

For an example concerning output, see Fig. 27 on page 226. That illustration shows the "colors" of buffer areas as a function of time, in a program that opens with four quick outputs, then produces four at a slow pace, and finally issues two in rapid succession as the program ends. Three buffers appear in that example.

The pointers `NEXTR` and `NEXTG` proceed merrily around the circle, each at an independent rate of speed, moving clockwise. It is a race between the program (which turns buffers from green to red) and the I/O buffering process (which turns them from red to green). Two situations of conflict can occur:

a) if `NEXTG` tries to pass `NEXTR`, the program has gotten ahead of the I/O device and it must wait until the device is ready.

b) if `NEXTR` tries to pass `NEXTG`, the I/O device has gotten ahead of the program and we must shut it down until the next `RELEASE` is given.

Both of these situations are depicted in Fig. 27. (See exercise 9.)

Fortunately, in spite of the rather lengthy explanation just given of the ideas behind a circle of buffers, the actual algorithms for handling the situation are quite simple. In the following description,

$$N = \text{total number of buffers};$$
$$n = \text{current number of red buffers}. \tag{6}$$

The variable n is used in the algorithm below to avoid interference between `NEXTG` and `NEXTR`.

Algorithm A (`ASSIGN`). This algorithm includes the steps implied by `ASSIGN` within a computational program, as described above.

A1. [Wait for $n < N$.] If $n = N$, stall the program until $n < N$. (If $n = N$, no buffers are ready to be assigned; but Algorithm B below, which runs in parallel with this one, will eventually succeed in producing a green buffer.)

A2. [CURRENT ← NEXTG.] Set CURRENT ← NEXTG (thereby assigning the current buffer).

A3. [Advance NEXTG.] Advance NEXTG to the next clockwise buffer. ▮

Algorithm R (RELEASE). This algorithm includes the steps implied by RELEASE within a computational program, as described above.

R1. [Increase n.] Increase n by one. ▮

Algorithm B (*Buffer control*). This algorithm performs the actual initiation of I/O operators in the machine; it is to be executed "simultaneously" with the main program, in the sense described below.

B1. [Compute.] Let the main program compute for a short period of time; step B2 will be executed after a certain time delay, at a time when the I/O device is ready for another operation.

B2. [$n = 0$?] If $n = 0$, go to B1. (Thus, if no buffers are red, no I/O action can be performed.)

B3. [Initiate I/O.] Initiate transmission between the buffer area designated by NEXTR and the I/O device.

B4. [Compute.] Let the main program run for a period of time; then go to step B5 when the I/O operation is completed.

B5. [Advance NEXTR.] Advance NEXTR to the next clockwise buffer.

B6. [Decrease n.] Decrease n by one, and go to B2. ▮

In these algorithms, we have two independent processes going on "simultaneously," the buffering control program and the computation program. These processes are, in fact, *coroutines*, which we will call CONTROL and COMPUTE. Coroutine CONTROL jumps to COMPUTE in steps B1 and B4; coroutine COMPUTE jumps to CONTROL by interspersing "jump ready" instructions at sporadic intervals in its program.

Coding this algorithm for MIX is extremely simple. For convenience, assume that the buffers are linked so that the word *preceding* each one is the address of the next; for example, with $N = 3$ buffers we have CONTENTS(BUF1 − 1) = BUF2, CONTENTS(BUF2 − 1) = BUF3, and CONTENTS(BUF3 − 1) = BUF1.

Program A (ASSIGN, *a subroutine within the* COMPUTE *coroutine*). rI4 ≡ CURRENT; rI6 ≡ n; calling sequence is JMP ASSIGN; on exit, rX contains NEXTG.

```
ASSIGN STJ  9F               Subroutine linkage
1H     JRED CONTROL(U)        A1. Wait for n < N.
       CMP6 =N=
       JE   1B
       LD4  NEXTG             A2. CURRENT ← NEXTG.
       LDX  -1,4              A3. Advance NEXTG.
       STX  NEXTG
9H     JMP  *                 Exit. ▮
```

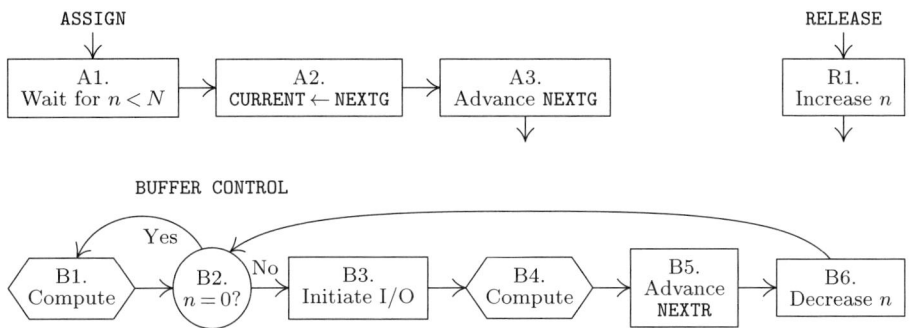

Fig. 25. Algorithms for multiple buffering.

Program R (RELEASE, *code used within the* COMPUTE *coroutine*). rI6 $\equiv n$. This short code is to be inserted wherever RELEASE is desired.

```
INC6  1              R1. Increase n.
JRED  CONTROL(U)     Possible jump to CONTROL coroutine  ▌
```

Program B (*The* CONTROL *coroutine*). rI6 $\equiv n$, rI5 $\equiv$ NEXTR.

```
CONT1  JMP   COMPUTE   B1. Compute.
1H     J6Z   *-1       B2. n = 0?
       IN    0,5(U)    B3. Initiate I/O.
       JMP   COMPUTE   B4. Compute.
       LD5   -1,5      B5. Advance NEXTR.
       DEC6  1         B6. Decrease n.
       JMP   1B  ▌
```

Besides the code above, we also have the usual coroutine linkage

```
CONTROL   STJ  COMPUTEX      COMPUTE   STJ  CONTROLX
CONTROLX  JMP  CONT1         COMPUTEX  JMP  COMP1
```

and the instruction "JRED CONTROL(U)" should be placed within COMPUTE about once in every fifty instructions.

Thus the programs for multiple buffering essentially amount to only seven instructions for CONTROL, eight for ASSIGN, and two for RELEASE.

It is perhaps remarkable that *exactly* the same algorithm will work for both input and output. What is the difference — how does the control routine know whether to anticipate (for input) or to lag behind (for output)? The answer lies in the initial conditions: For input we start out with $n = N$ (all buffers red) and for output we start out with $n = 0$ (all buffers green). Once the routine has been started properly, it continues to behave as either an input process or an output process, respectively. The other initial condition is that NEXTR = NEXTG, both pointing at one of the buffers.

At the conclusion of the program, it is necessary to stop the I/O process (if it is input) or to wait until it is completed (for output); details are left to the reader (see exercises 12 and 13).

It is important to ask what is the best value of N to use. Certainly as N gets larger, the speed of the program will not decrease, but it will not increase indefinitely either and so we come to a point of diminishing returns. Let us refer again to the quantities C and T, representing computation time between I/O operators and the I/O time itself. More precisely, let C be the amount of time between successive ASSIGNs, and let T be the amount of time needed to transmit one block. If C is always *greater* than T, then $N = 2$ is adequate, for it is not hard to see that with two buffers we keep the computer busy at all times. If C is always *less* than T, then again $N = 2$ is adequate, for we keep the I/O device busy at all times (except when the device has special timing constraints as in exercise 19). Larger values of N are therefore useful chiefly when C varies between small values and large values; the average number of consecutive small values, plus 1, may be right for N, if the large values of C are significantly longer than T. (However, the advantage of buffering is virtually nullified if all input occurs at the beginning of the program and if all output occurs at the end.) If the time between ASSIGN and RELEASE is always quite small, the value of N may be decreased by 1 throughout the discussion above, with little effect on running time.

This approach to buffering can be adapted in many ways, and we will mention a few of them briefly. So far we have assumed that only one I/O device was being used; in practice, of course, several devices will be in use at the same time.

There are several ways to approach the subject of multiple units. In the simplest case, we can have a separate circle of buffers for each device. Each unit will have its own values of n, N, NEXTR, NEXTG, and CURRENT, and its own CONTROL coroutine. This will give efficient buffering action simultaneously on every I/O device.

It is also possible to "pool" buffer areas that are of the same size, so that two or more devices share buffers from a common list. This can be handled by using the linked memory techniques of Chapter 2, with all red input buffers linked together in one list and all green output buffers linked together in another. It becomes necessary to distinguish between input and output in this case, and to rewrite the algorithms without using n and N. The algorithm may get irrevocably stuck, if all buffers in the pool are filled with anticipated input; so a check should be made that there is always at least one buffer (preferably one for each device) that is not input-green; only if the COMPUTE routine is stalled at step A1 for some input device should we allow input into the final buffer of the pool from that device.

Some machines have additional constraints on the use of input-output units, so that it is impossible to be transmitting data from certain pairs of devices at the same time. (For example, several units might be attached to the computer by means of a single "channel.") This constraint also affects our buffering routine; when we must choose which I/O unit to initiate next, how is the choice to be made? This is called the problem of "forecasting." The best forecasting rule for the general case would seem to give preference to the unit whose buffer circle

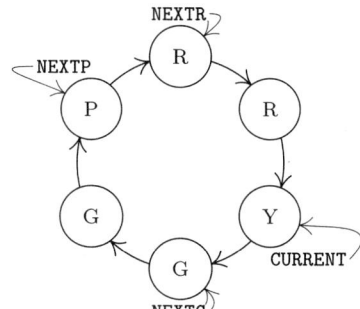

Fig. 26. Input and output from the same circle.

has the largest value of n/N, assuming that the number of buffers in the circles has been chosen wisely.

Let's conclude this discussion by taking note of a useful method for doing both input and output from the *same* buffer circle, under certain conditions. Figure 26 introduces a new kind of buffer, which has the color purple. In this situation, green buffers represent anticipated *input*; the program ASSIGNs and a green buffer becomes yellow, then upon RELEASE it turns red and represents a block to be *output*. The input and output processes follow around the circle independently as before, except that now we turn red buffers to purple after the output is done, and convert purple to green on input. It is necessary to ensure that none of the pointers NEXTG, NEXTR, NEXTP pass each other. At the instant shown in Fig. 26, the program is computing between ASSIGN and RELEASE, while accessing the yellow buffer; simultaneously, input is going into the buffer indicated by NEXTP; and output is coming from the buffer indicated by NEXTR.

EXERCISES

1. [05] (a) Would sequence (3) still be correct if the MOVE instructions were placed before the JBUS instruction instead of after it? (b) What if the MOVE instructions were placed after the IN command?

2. [10] The instructions "OUT 1000(6); JBUS *(6)" may be used to output a tape block in an unbuffered fashion, just as the instructions (1) did this for input. Give a method analogous to (2) and (3) that buffers this output, by using MOVE instructions and an auxiliary buffer in locations 2000–2099.

▶ **3.** [22] Write a buffer-swapping output subroutine analogous to (4). The subroutine, called WORDOUT, should store the word in rA as the next word of output, and if a buffer is full it should write 100 words onto tape unit V. Index register 5 should be used to refer to the current buffer position. Show the layout of buffer areas and explain what instructions (if any) are necessary at the beginning and end of the program to ensure that the first and last blocks are properly written. The final block should be filled out with zeros if necessary.

4. [M20] Show that if a program refers to a single I/O device, we might be able to cut the running time in half by buffering the I/O, in favorable circumstances; but we can never decrease the running time by more than a factor of two, with respect to the time taken by unbuffered I/O.

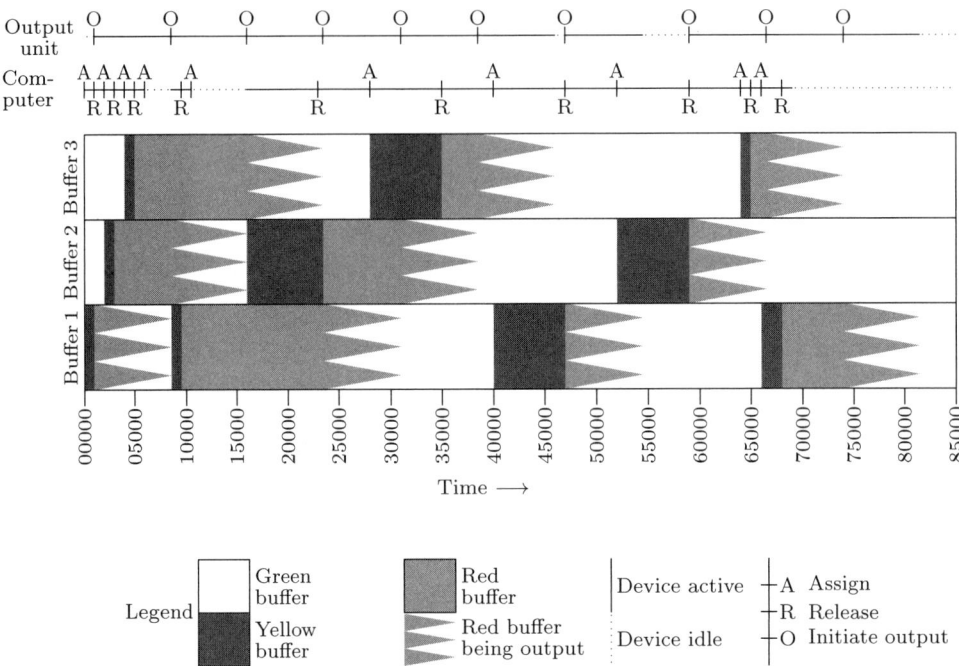

Fig. 27. Output with three buffers (see exercise 9).

▶ **5.** [*M21*] Generalize the situation of the preceding exercise to the case when the program refers to n I/O devices instead of just one.

6. [*12*] What instructions should be placed at the beginning of a program so that the WORDIN subroutine (4) gets off to the right start? (For example, index register 6 must be set to *something*.)

7. [*22*] Write a subroutine called WORDIN that is essentially like (4) except that it does not make use of a sentinel.

8. [*11*] The text describes a hypothetical input scenario that leads from Fig. 23 through parts (a), (b), and (c) of Fig. 24. Interpret the same scenario under the assumption that output to the line printer is being done, instead of input from cards. (For example, what things are happening at the time shown in Fig. 23?)

▶ **9.** [*21*] A program that leads to the buffer contents shown in Fig. 27 may be characterized by the following list of times:

A, 1000, R, 1000, A, 1000, R, 1000, A, 1000, R, 1000, A, 1000, R, 1000,
A, 7000, R, 5000, A, 7000, R, 5000, A, 7000, R, 5000, A, 7000, R, 5000,
A, 1000, R, 1000, A, 2000, R, 1000.

This list means "assign, compute for $1000u$, release, compute for $1000u$, assign, …, compute for $2000u$, release, compute for $1000u$." The computation times given do not include any intervals during which the computer might have to wait for the output device to catch up (as at the fourth "assign" in Fig. 27). The output device operates at a speed of $7500u$ per block.

The following chart specifies the actions shown in Fig. 27 as time passes:

Time	Action	Time	Action
0	ASSIGN(BUF1)	38500	OUT BUF3
1000	RELEASE, OUT BUF1	40000	ASSIGN(BUF1)
2000	ASSIGN(BUF2)	46000	Output stops.
3000	RELEASE	47000	RELEASE, OUT BUF1
4000	ASSIGN(BUF3)	52000	ASSIGN(BUF2)
5000	RELEASE	54500	Output stops.
6000	ASSIGN (wait)	59000	RELEASE, OUT BUF2
8500	BUF1 assigned, OUT BUF2	64000	ASSIGN(BUF3)
9500	RELEASE	65000	RELEASE
10500	ASSIGN (wait)	66000	ASSIGN(BUF1)
16000	BUF2 assigned, OUT BUF3	66500	OUT BUF3
23000	RELEASE	68000	RELEASE
23500	OUT BUF1	69000	Computation stops.
28000	ASSIGN(BUF3)	74000	OUT BUF1
31000	OUT BUF2	81500	Output stops.
35000	RELEASE		

The total time required was therefore $81500u$; the computer was idle from 6000–8500, 10500–16000, and 69000–81500, or $20500u$ altogether; the output unit was idle from 0–1000, 46000–47000, and 54500–59000, or $6500u$.

Make a time-action chart like the above for the same program, assuming that there are only *two* buffers.

10. [*21*] Repeat exercise 9, except with *four* buffers.

11. [*21*] Repeat exercise 9, except with just *one* buffer.

12. [*24*] Suppose that the multiple buffering algorithm in the text is being used for card input, and suppose the input is to terminate as soon as a card with "." in column 80 has been read. Show how the CONTROL coroutine (Algorithm B and Program B) should be changed so that input is shut off in this way.

13. [*20*] What instructions should be included at the end of the COMPUTE coroutine in the text, if the buffering algorithms are being applied to output, to ensure that all information has been output from the buffers?

▶ **14.** [*20*] Suppose the computational program does not alternate between ASSIGN and RELEASE, but instead gives the sequence of actions ... ASSIGN ... ASSIGN ... RELEASE ... RELEASE. What effect does this have on the algorithms described in the text? Is it possibly useful?

▶ **15.** [*22*] Write a complete MIX program that copies 100 blocks from tape unit 0 to tape unit 1, using just three buffers. The program should be as fast as possible.

16. [*29*] Formulate the "green-yellow-red-purple" algorithm, suggested by Fig. 26, in the manner of the algorithms for multiple buffering given in the text, using three coroutines (one to control the input device, one for the output device, and one for the computation).

17. [*40*] Adapt the multiple-buffer algorithm to pooled buffers; build in methods that keep the process from slowing down, due to too much anticipated input. Try to make the algorithm as elegant as possible. Compare your method to nonpooling methods, applied to real-life problems.

▶ **18.** [*30*] A proposed extension of MIX allows its computations to be interrupted, as explained below. Your task in this exercise is to modify Algorithms and Programs A, R, and B of the text so that they use these interrupt facilities instead of the "JRED" instructions.

The new MIX features include an additional 3999 memory cells, locations −3999 through −0001. The machine has two internal "states," *normal state* and *control state*. In normal state, locations −3999 through −0001 are not admissible memory locations and the MIX computer behaves as usual. When an "interrupt" occurs, due to conditions explained later, locations −0009 through −0001 are set equal to the contents of MIX's registers: rA in −0009; rI1 through rI6 in −0008 through −0003; rX in −0002; and rJ, the overflow toggle, the comparison indicator, and the location of the next instruction are stored in −0001 as

$$\boxed{\begin{array}{c|c|c|c} + & \begin{array}{c} \text{next} \\ \text{inst.} \end{array} & \begin{array}{c} \text{OV,} \\ \text{CI} \end{array} & \text{rJ} \end{array}} \quad ;$$

the machine enters control state, at a location depending on the type of interrupt.

Location −0010 acts as a "clock": Every 1000u of time, the number appearing in this location is decreased by one, and if the result is zero an interrupt to location −0011 occurs.

The new MIX instruction "INT" (C = 5, F = 9) works as follows: (a) In normal state, an interrupt occurs to location −0012. (Thus a programmer may force an interrupt, to communicate with a control routine; the address of INT has no effect, although the control routine may use it for information to distinguish between types of interrupt.) (b) In control state, all MIX registers are loaded from locations −0009 to −0001, the computer goes into normal state, and it resumes execution. The execution time for INT is 2u in each case.

An IN, OUT, or IOC instruction given in *control* state will cause an interrupt to occur as soon as the I/O operation is completed. The interrupt goes to location −(0020+ unit number).

No interrupts occur while in control state; any interrupt conditions are "saved" until after the next INT operation, and interrupt will occur after one instruction of the normal state program has been performed.

▶ **19.** [*M28*] Special considerations arise when input or output involves short blocks on a rotating device like a magnetic disk. Suppose a program works with $n \geq 2$ consecutive blocks of information in the following way: Block k begins to be input at time t_k, where $t_1 = 0$. It is assigned for processing at time $u_k \geq t_k + T$ and released from its buffer at time $v_k = u_k + C$. The disk rotates once every P units of time, and its reading head passes the start of a new block every L units; so we must have $t_k \equiv (k-1)L$ (modulo P). Since the processing is sequential, we must also have $u_k \geq v_{k-1}$ for $1 < k \leq n$. There are N buffers, hence $t_k \geq v_{k-N}$ for $N < k \leq n$.

How large does N have to be so that the finishing time v_n has its minimum possible value, $T + C + (n - 1) \max(L, C)$? Give a general rule for determining the smallest such N. Illustrate your rule when $L = 1$, $P = 100$, $T = .5$, $n = 100$, and (a) $C = .5$; (b) $C = 1.0$; (c) $C = 1.01$; (d) $C = 1.5$; (e) $C = 2.0$; (f) $C = 2.5$; (g) $C = 10.0$; (h) $C = 50.0$; (i) $C = 200.0$.

1.4.5. History and Bibliography

Most of the fundamental techniques described in Section 1.4 have been developed independently by a number of different people, and the exact history of the ideas will probably never be known. An attempt has been made to record here the most important contributions to the history, and to put them in perspective.

Subroutines were the first labor-saving devices invented for programmers. In the 19th century, Charles Babbage envisioned a library of routines for his Analytical Engine [see *Charles Babbage and His Calculating Engines*, edited by Philip and Emily Morrison (Dover, 1961), 56]; and we might say that his dream came true in 1944 when Grace M. Hopper wrote a subroutine for computing sin x on the Harvard Mark I calculator [see *Mechanisation of Thought Processes* (London: Nat. Phys. Lab., 1959), 164]. However, these were essentially "open subroutines," meant to be inserted into a program where needed instead of being linked up dynamically. Babbage's planned machine was controlled by sequences of punched cards, as on the Jacquard loom; the Mark I was controlled by a number of paper tapes. Thus they were quite different from today's stored-program computers.

Subroutine linkage appropriate to stored-program machines, with the return address supplied as a parameter, was discussed by Herman H. Goldstine and John von Neumann in their widely circulated monograph on programming, written during 1946 and 1947; see von Neumann's *Collected Works* **5** (New York: Macmillan, 1963), 215–235. The main routine of their programs was responsible for storing parameters into the body of the subroutine, instead of passing the necessary information in registers. In England, A. M. Turing had designed hardware and software for subroutine linkage as early as 1945; see *Proceedings of a Second Symposium on Large-Scale Digital Calculating Machinery* (Cambridge, Mass.: Harvard University, 1949), 87–90; B. E. Carpenter and R. W. Doran, editors, *A. M. Turing's ACE Report of 1946 and Other Papers* (Cambridge, Mass.: MIT Press, 1986), 35–36, 76, 78–79. The use and construction of a very versatile subroutine library is the principal topic of the first textbook of computer programming, *The Preparation of Programs for an Electronic Digital Computer*, by M. V. Wilkes, D. J. Wheeler, and S. Gill, 1st ed. (Reading, Mass.: Addison–Wesley, 1951).

The word "coroutine" was coined by M. E. Conway in 1958, after he had developed the concept, and he first applied it to the construction of an assembly program. Coroutines were independently studied by J. Erdwinn and J. Merner, at about the same time; they wrote a paper entitled "Bilateral Linkage," which was not then considered sufficiently interesting to merit publication, and unfortunately no copies of that paper seem to exist today. The first published explanation of the coroutine concept appeared much later in Conway's article "Design of a Separable Transition-Diagram Compiler," *CACM* **6** (1963), 396–408. Actually a primitive form of coroutine linkage had already been noted briefly as a "programming tip" in an early UNIVAC publication [*The Programmer* **1**, 2 (February 1954), 4]. A suitable notation for coroutines in ALGOL-like languages was introduced in Dahl and Nygaard's SIMULA I [*CACM* **9** (1966), 671–678], and several excellent examples of coroutines (including replicated coroutines) appear in the book *Structured Programming* by O.-J. Dahl, E. W. Dijkstra, and C. A. R. Hoare, Chapter 3.

The first interpretive routine may be said to be the "Universal Turing Machine," a Turing machine capable of simulating any other Turing machines. Turing machines are not actual computers; they are theoretical constructions used to prove that certain problems are unsolvable by algorithms. Interpretive routines in the conventional sense were mentioned by John Mauchly in his lectures at the Moore School in 1946. The most notable early interpreters, chiefly intended to provide a convenient means of doing floating point arithmetic, were certain routines for the Whirlwind I (by C. W. Adams and others) and for the ILLIAC I (by D. J. Wheeler and others). Turing took a part in this development also; interpretive systems for the Pilot ACE computer were written under his direction. For references to the state of interpreters in the early fifties, see the article "Interpretative Sub-routines" by J. M. Bennett, D. G. Prinz, and M. L. Woods, *Proc. ACM* (Toronto: 1952), 81–87; see also various papers in the *Proceedings of the Symposium on Automatic Programming for Digital Computers* (1954), published by the Office of Naval Research, Washington, D.C.

The most extensively used early interpretive routine was probably John Backus's "IBM 701 Speedcoding system" [see *JACM* **1** (1954), 4–6]. This interpreter was slightly modified and skillfully rewritten for the IBM 650 by V. M. Wolontis and others of the Bell Telephone Laboratories; their routine, called the "Bell Interpretive System," became extremely popular. The IPL interpretive systems, which were designed beginning in 1956 by A. Newell, J. C. Shaw, and H. A. Simon for applications to quite different problems (see Section 2.6), were used extensively for list processing. Modern uses of interpreters, as mentioned in the introduction to Section 1.4.3, are often mentioned in passing in the computer literature; see the references listed in that section for articles that discuss interpreters in somewhat more detail.

The first tracing routine was developed by Stanley Gill in 1950; see his interesting article in *Proceedings of the Royal Society of London*, series A, **206** (1951), 538–554. The text by Wilkes, Wheeler, and Gill mentioned above includes several programs for tracing. Perhaps the most interesting of them is subroutine C-10 by D. J. Wheeler, which includes a provision for suppressing the trace upon entry to a library subroutine, executing the subroutine at full speed, then continuing the trace. Published information about trace routines is quite rare in the general computer literature, primarily because the methods are inherently oriented to a particular machine. The only other early reference known to the author is H. V. Meek, "An Experimental Monitoring Routine for the IBM 705," *Proc. Western Joint Computer Conf.* (1956), 68–70, which discusses a trace routine for a machine on which the problem was particularly difficult. See also the trace routine for IBM's System/360 architecture, presented in *A Compiler Generator* by W. M. McKeeman, J. J. Horning, and D. B. Wortman (Prentice-Hall, 1970), 305–363. Nowadays the emphasis on trace routines has shifted to software that provides selective symbolic output and measurements of program performance; one of the best such systems was developed by E. Satterthwaite, and described in *Software Practice & Experience* **2** (1972), 197–217.

Buffering was originally performed by computer hardware, in a manner analogous to the code 1.4.4–(3); an internal buffer area inaccessible to the programmer played the role of locations 2000–2099, and the instructions 1.4.4–(3) were implicitly performed behind the scenes when an input command was given. During the late 1940s, software buffering techniques that are especially useful for sorting were developed by early programmers of the UNIVAC (see Section 5.5). For a good survey of the prevailing philosophy towards I/O in 1952, see the proceedings of the Eastern Joint Computer Conference held in that year.

The DYSEAC computer [Alan L. Leiner, *JACM* **1** (1954), 57–81] introduced the idea of input-output devices communicating directly with memory while a program is running, then interrupting the program upon completion. Such a system implies that buffering algorithms had been developed, but the details went unpublished. The first published reference to buffering techniques in the sense we have described gives a highly sophisticated approach; see O. Mock and C. J. Swift, "Programmed Input-Output Buffering," *Proc. ACM Nat. Meeting* **13** (1958), paper 19, and *JACM* **6** (1959), 145–151. (The reader is cautioned that both articles contain a good deal of local jargon, which may take some time to understand, but neighboring articles in *JACM* **6** will help.) An interrupt system that enabled buffering of input and output was independently developed by E. W. Dijkstra in 1957 and 1958, in connection with B. J. Loopstra's and C. S. Scholten's X1 computer [see *Comp. J.* **2** (1959), 39–43]. Dijkstra's doctoral thesis, "Communication with an Automatic Computer" (1959), discussed primitive synchronization operations by which users could create long chains of buffers with respect to paper tape and typewriter I/O; each buffer contained either a single character or a single number. He later developed the ideas into the important general notion of *semaphores*, which are basic to the control of all sorts of concurrent processes, not just input-output [see *Programming Languages*, ed. by F. Genuys (Academic Press, 1968), 43–112; *BIT* **8** (1968), 174–186; *Acta Informatica* **1** (1971), 115–138]. The paper "Input-Output Buffering and FORTRAN" by David E. Ferguson, *JACM* **7** (1960), 1–9, describes buffer circles and gives a detailed description of simple buffering with many units at once.

> *About 1,000 instructions is a reasonable upper limit*
> *for the complexity of problems now envisioned.*
> — HERMAN GOLDSTINE and JOHN VON NEUMANN (1946)

CHAPTER TWO

INFORMATION STRUCTURES

I think that I shall never see
A poem lovely as a tree.
— JOYCE KILMER (1913)

Yea, from the table of my memory
I'll wipe away all trivial fond records.
— HAMLET (Act I, Scene 5, Line 98)

2.1. INTRODUCTION

COMPUTER PROGRAMS usually operate on tables of information. In most cases these tables are not simply amorphous masses of numerical values; they involve important *structural relationships* between the data elements.

In its simplest form, a table might be a linear list of elements, when its relevant structural properties might include the answers to such questions as: Which element is first in the list? Which is last? Which elements precede and follow a given one? How many elements are in the list? A lot can be said about structure even in this apparently simple case (see Section 2.2).

In more complicated situations, the table might be a two-dimensional array (a matrix or grid, having both a row and a column structure), or it might be an *n*-dimensional array for higher values of *n*; it might be a tree structure, representing hierarchical or branching relationships; or it might be a complex multilinked structure with a great many interconnections, such as we may find in a human brain.

In order to use a computer properly, we need to understand the structural relationships present within data, as well as the basic techniques for representing and manipulating such structure within a computer.

The present chapter summarizes the most important facts about information structures: the static and dynamic properties of different kinds of structure; means for storage allocation and representation of structured data; and efficient algorithms for creating, altering, accessing, and destroying structural information. In the course of this study, we will also work out several important examples that illustrate the application of such methods to a wide variety of problems. The examples include topological sorting, polynomial arithmetic, discrete system simulation, sparse matrix transformation, algebraic formula manipulation, and applications to the writing of compilers and operating systems. Our concern will be almost entirely with structure as represented *inside* a computer; the

232

conversion from external to internal representations is the subject of Chapters 9 and 10.

Much of the material we will discuss is often called "List processing," since a number of programming systems such as LISP have been designed to facilitate working with general kinds of structures called *Lists*. (When the word "list" is capitalized in this chapter, it is being used in a technical sense to denote a particular type of structure that is highlighted in Section 2.3.5.) Although List processing systems are useful in a large number of situations, they impose constraints on the programmer that are often unnecessary; it is usually better to use the methods of this chapter directly in one's own programs, tailoring the data format and the processing algorithms to the particular application. Many people unfortunately still feel that List processing techniques are quite complicated (so that it is necessary to use someone else's carefully written interpretive system or a prefabricated set of subroutines), and that List processing must be done only in a certain fixed way. We will see that there is nothing magic, mysterious, or difficult about the methods for dealing with complex structures; these techniques are an important part of every programmer's repertoire, and we can use them easily whether we are writing a program in assembly language or in an algebraic language like FORTRAN, C, or Java.

We will illustrate methods of dealing with information structures in terms of the MIX computer. A reader who does not care to look through detailed MIX programs should at least study the ways in which structural information is represented in MIX's memory.

It is important at this point to define several terms and notations that we will be using frequently from now on. The information in a table consists of a set of *nodes* (called "records," "entities," or "beads" by some authors); we will occasionally say "item" or "element" instead of "node." Each node consists of one or more consecutive words of the computer memory, divided into named parts called *fields*. In the simplest case, a node is just one word of memory, and it has just one field comprising that whole word. As a more interesting example, suppose the elements of our table are intended to represent playing cards; we might have two-word nodes broken into five fields, TAG, SUIT, RANK, NEXT, and TITLE:

+	TAG	SUIT	RANK	NEXT
+		TITLE		

(1)

(This format reflects the contents of two MIX words. Recall that a MIX word consists of five bytes and a sign; see Section 1.3.1. In this example we assume that the signs are + in each word.) The *address* of a node, also called a *link*, *pointer*, or *reference* to that node, is the memory location of its first word. The address is often taken relative to some base location, but in this chapter for simplicity we will take the address to be an absolute memory location.

The contents of any field within a node may represent numbers, alphabetic characters, links, or anything else the programmer may desire. In connection with the example above, we might wish to represent a pile of cards that might appear in a game of solitaire: TAG = 1 means that the card is face down, TAG = 0 means that it is face up; SUIT = 1, 2, 3, or 4 for clubs, diamonds, hearts, or spades, respectively; RANK = 1, 2, ..., 13 for ace, deuce, ..., king; NEXT is a *link* to the card *below* this one in the pile; and TITLE is a five-character alphabetic name of this card, for use in printouts. A typical pile might look like this:

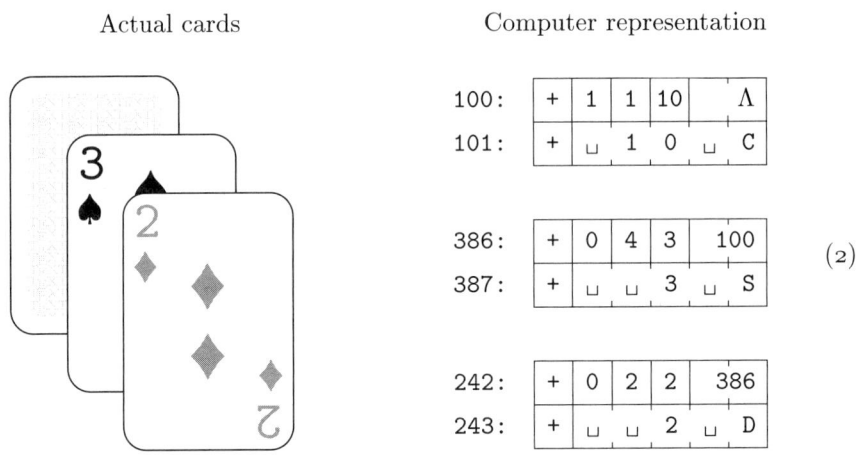

The memory locations in the computer representation are shown here as 100, 386, and 242; they could have been any other numbers as far as this example is concerned, since each card links to the one below it. Notice the special link "Λ" in node 100; *we use the capital Greek letter Lambda to denote the null link,* the link to no node. The null link Λ appears in node 100 since the 10 of clubs is the bottom card of the pile. Within the machine, Λ is represented by some easily recognizable value that cannot be the address of a node. We will generally assume that no node appears in location 0; consequently, Λ will almost always be represented as the link value 0 in MIX programs.

The introduction of links to other elements of data is an extremely important idea in computer programming; links are the key to the representation of complex structures. When displaying computer representations of nodes it is usually convenient to represent links by arrows, so that example (2) would appear thus:

$$
\text{TOP} \longrightarrow \boxed{\begin{array}{|c|c|c|c|}\hline + & 0 & 2 & 2 & \bullet \\\hline + & \sqcup & \sqcup & 2 & \sqcup & D \\\hline\end{array}} \longrightarrow \boxed{\begin{array}{|c|c|c|c|}\hline + & 0 & 4 & 3 & \bullet \\\hline + & \sqcup & \sqcup & 3 & \sqcup & S \\\hline\end{array}} \longrightarrow \boxed{\begin{array}{|c|c|c|c|}\hline + & 1 & 1 & 10 & \bullet \\\hline + & \sqcup & 1 & 0 & \sqcup & C \\\hline\end{array}} \quad (3)
$$

The actual locations 242, 386, and 100 (which are irrelevant anyway) no longer appear in representation (3). Electrical circuit notation for a "grounded" wire is used to indicate a null link, shown here at the right of the diagram. Notice also that (3) indicates the top card by an arrow from "TOP"; here TOP is a *link variable,* often called a pointer variable, namely a variable whose value is a link. All references to nodes in a program are made directly through link variables (or link constants), or indirectly through link fields in other nodes.

Now we come to the most important part of the notation, the means of referring to fields within nodes. This is done simply by giving the name of the field followed by a link to the desired node in parentheses; for example, in (2) and (3) with the fields of (1) we have

$$\begin{aligned} & \texttt{RANK(100)} = 10; \qquad \texttt{SUIT(TOP)} = 2; \\ & \texttt{TITLE(TOP)} = \text{``}\texttt{\textvisiblespace\textvisiblespace 2\textvisiblespace D}\text{''}; \qquad \texttt{RANK(NEXT(TOP))} = 3. \end{aligned} \qquad (4)$$

The reader should study these examples carefully, since such field notations will be used in many algorithms of this chapter and the following chapters. To make the ideas clearer, we will now state a simple algorithm for placing a new card face up on top of the pile, assuming that NEWCARD is a link variable whose value is a link to the new card:

A1. Set NEXT(NEWCARD) ← TOP. (This puts the appropriate link into the new card node.)

A2. Set TOP ← NEWCARD. (This keeps TOP pointing to the top of the pile.)

A3. Set TAG(TOP) ← 0. (This marks the card as "face up.") ∎

Another example is the following algorithm, which counts the number of cards currently in the pile:

B1. Set N ← 0, X ← TOP. (Here N is an integer variable, X is a link variable.)

B2. If X = Λ, stop; N is the number of cards in the pile.

B3. Set N ← N + 1, X ← NEXT(X), and go back to step B2. ∎

Notice that we are using symbolic names for two quite different things in these algorithms: as names of *variables* (TOP, NEWCARD, N, X) and as names of *fields* (TAG, NEXT). These two usages must not be confused. If F is a field name and L ≠ Λ is a link, then F(L) is a variable; but F itself is not a variable — it does not possess a value unless it is qualified by a nonnull link.

Two further notations are used, to convert between addresses and the values stored there, when we are discussing low-level machine details:

a) CONTENTS always denotes a full-word field of a one-word node. Thus CONTENTS(1000) denotes the value stored in memory location 1000; it is a variable having this value. If V is a link variable, CONTENTS(V) denotes the value pointed to by V (not the value V itself).

b) If V is the name of some value held in a memory cell, LOC(V) denotes the address of that cell. Consequently, if V is a variable whose value is stored in a full word of memory, we have CONTENTS(LOC(V)) = V.

It is easy to transform this notation into MIXAL assembly language code, although MIXAL's notation is somewhat backwards. The values of link variables are put into index registers, and the partial-field capability of MIX is used to refer to the desired field. For example, Algorithm A above could be written thus:

```
NEXT EQU  4:5        Definition of the NEXT
TAG  EQU  1:1            and TAG fields for the assembler
     LD1  NEWCARD     A1. rI1 ← NEWCARD.
     LDA  TOP             rA ← TOP.
     STA  0,1(NEXT)       NEXT(rI1) ← rA.
     ST1  TOP         A2. TOP ← rI1.
     STZ  0,1(TAG)    A3. TAG(rI1) ← 0. ∎
```

$$(5)$$

The ease and efficiency with which these operations can be carried out in a computer is the primary reason for the importance of the "linked memory" concept.

Sometimes we have a single variable that denotes a whole node; its value is a sequence of fields instead of just one field. Thus we might write

$$\text{CARD} \leftarrow \text{NODE(TOP)}, \tag{6}$$

where NODE is a field specification just like CONTENTS, except that it refers to an entire node, and where CARD is a variable that assumes structured values like those in (1). If there are c words in a node, the notation (6) is an abbreviation for the c low-level assignments

$$\text{CONTENTS(LOC(CARD)} + j) \leftarrow \text{CONTENTS(TOP} + j), \quad 0 \le j < c. \tag{7}$$

There is an important distinction between assembly language and the notation used in algorithms. Since assembly language is close to the machine's internal language, the symbols used in MIXAL programs stand for addresses instead of values. Thus in the left-hand columns of (5), the symbol TOP actually denotes the *address* where the pointer to the top card appears in memory; but in (6) and (7) and in the remarks at the right of (5), it denotes the *value* of TOP, namely the address of the top card node. This difference between assembly language and higher-level language is a frequent source of confusion for beginning programmers, so the reader is urged to work exercise 7. The other exercises also provide useful drills on the notational conventions introduced in this section.

EXERCISES

1. [*04*] In the situation depicted in (3), what is the value of (a) SUIT(NEXT(TOP)); (b) NEXT(NEXT(NEXT(TOP)))?

2. [*10*] The text points out that in many cases CONTENTS(LOC(V)) = V. Under what conditions do we have LOC(CONTENTS(V)) = V?

3. [*11*] Give an algorithm that essentially undoes the effect of Algorithm A: It removes the top card of the pile (if the pile is not empty) and sets NEWCARD to the address of this card.

4. [*18*] Give an algorithm analogous to Algorithm A, except that it puts the new card *face down* at the *bottom* of the pile. (The pile may be empty.)

▶ **5.** [*21*] Give an algorithm that essentially undoes the effect of exercise 4: Assuming that the pile is not empty and that its bottom card is face down, your algorithm should remove the bottom card and make `NEWCARD` link to it. (This algorithm is sometimes called "cheating" in solitaire games.)

6. [*06*] In the playing card example, suppose that `CARD` is the name of a variable whose value is an entire node as in (6). The operation `CARD ← NODE(TOP)` sets the fields of `CARD` respectively equal to those of the top of the pile. After this operation, which of the following notations stands for the suit of the top card? (a) `SUIT(CARD)`; (b) `SUIT(LOC(CARD))`; (c) `SUIT(CONTENTS(CARD))`; (d) `SUIT(TOP)`?

▶ **7.** [*04*] In the text's example `MIX` program, (5), the link variable `TOP` is stored in the `MIX` computer word whose assembly language name is `TOP`. Given the field structure (1), which of the following sequences of code brings the quantity `NEXT(TOP)` into register A? Explain why the other sequence is incorrect.

a) `LDA  TOP(NEXT)`   b) `LD1  TOP`
                                      `LDA  0,1(NEXT)`

▶ **8.** [*18*] Write a `MIX` program corresponding to steps B1–B3.

9. [*23*] Write a `MIX` program that prints out the alphabetic names of the current contents of the card pile, starting at the top card, with one card per line, and with parentheses around cards that are face down.

2.2. LINEAR LISTS

2.2.1. Stacks, Queues, and Deques

DATA USUALLY HAS much more structural information than we actually want to represent directly in a computer. For example, each "playing card" node in the preceding section had a NEXT field to specify what card was beneath it in the pile, but we provided no direct way to find what card, if any, was *above* a given card, or to find what pile a given card was in. And of course we totally suppressed most of the characteristic features of *real* playing cards: the details of the design on the back, the relation to other objects in the room where the game was being played, the individual molecules within the cards, etc. It is conceivable that such structural information would be relevant in certain computer applications, but obviously we never want to store *all* of the structure that is present in every situation. Indeed, for most card-playing situations we would not need all of the facts retained in the earlier example; the TAG field, which tells whether a card is face up or face down, will often be unnecessary.

We must decide in each case how much structure to represent in our tables, and how accessible to make each piece of information. To make such decisions, we need to know what operations are to be performed on the data. For each problem considered in this chapter, therefore, *we consider not only the data structure but also the class of operations to be done on the data*; the design of computer representations depends on the desired function of the data as well as on its intrinsic properties. Indeed, an emphasis on function as well as form is basic to design problems in general.

In order to illustrate this point further, let's consider a related aspect of computer hardware design. A computer memory is often classified as a "random access memory," like MIX's main memory; or as a "read-only memory," which is supposed to contain essentially constant information; or a "secondary bulk memory," like MIX's disk units, which cannot be accessed at high speed although large quantities of information can be stored; or an "associative memory," more properly called a "content-addressed memory," for which information is addressed by its value rather than by its location; and so on. The intended function of each kind of memory is so important that it enters into the name of the particular memory type; all of these devices are "memory" units, but the purposes to which they are put profoundly influence their design and their cost.

A *linear list* is a sequence of $n \geq 0$ nodes X[1], X[2], ..., X[n] whose essential structural properties involve only the relative positions between items as they appear in a line. The only things we care about in such structures are the facts that, if $n > 0$, X[1] is the first node and X[n] is the last; and if $1 < k < n$, the kth node X[k] is preceded by X[$k-1$] and followed by X[$k+1$].

The operations we might want to perform on linear lists include, for example, the following.

i) Gain access to the kth node of the list to examine and/or to change the contents of its fields.

 ii) Insert a new node just before or after the kth node.

iii) Delete the kth node.

iv) Combine two or more linear lists into a single list.

 v) Split a linear list into two or more lists.

vi) Make a copy of a linear list.

vii) Determine the number of nodes in a list.

viii) Sort the nodes of the list into ascending order based on certain fields of the nodes.

 ix) Search the list for the occurrence of a node with a particular value in some field.

In operations (i), (ii), and (iii) the special cases $k = 1$ and $k = n$ are of principal importance, since the first and last items of a linear list may be easier to get at than a general element is. We will not discuss operations (viii) and (ix) in this chapter, since those topics are the subjects of Chapters 5 and 6, respectively.

A computer application rarely calls for all nine of these operations in their full generality, so we find that there are many ways to represent linear lists depending on the class of operations that are to be done most frequently. It is difficult to design a single representation method for linear lists in which all of these operations are efficient; for example, the ability to gain access to the kth node of a long list for random k is comparatively hard to do if at the same time we are inserting and deleting items in the middle of the list. Therefore we distinguish between types of linear lists depending on the principal operations to be performed, just as we have noted that computer memories are distinguished by their intended applications.

Linear lists in which insertions, deletions, and accesses to values occur almost always at the first or the last node are very frequently encountered, and we give them special names:

> A *stack* is a linear list for which all insertions and deletions (and usually all accesses) are made at one end of the list.

> A *queue* is a linear list for which all insertions are made at one end of the list; all deletions (and usually all accesses) are made at the other end.

> A *deque* ("double-ended queue") is a linear list for which all insertions and deletions (and usually all accesses) are made at the ends of the list.

A deque is therefore more general than a stack or a queue; it has some properties in common with a deck of cards, and it is pronounced the same way. We also distinguish *output-restricted* or *input-restricted* deques, in which deletions or insertions, respectively, are allowed to take place at only one end.

In some disciplines the word "queue" has been used in a much broader sense, to describe any kind of list that is subject to insertions and deletions; the special cases identified above are then called various "queuing disciplines." Only the restricted use of the term "queue" is intended in this book, however, by analogy with orderly queues of people waiting in line for service.

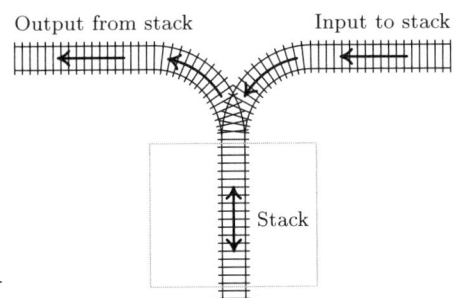

Fig. 1. A stack represented as a railway switching network.

Sometimes it helps to understand the mechanism of a stack in terms of an analogy from the switching of railroad cars, as suggested by E. W. Dijkstra (see Fig. 1). A corresponding picture for deques is shown in Fig. 2.

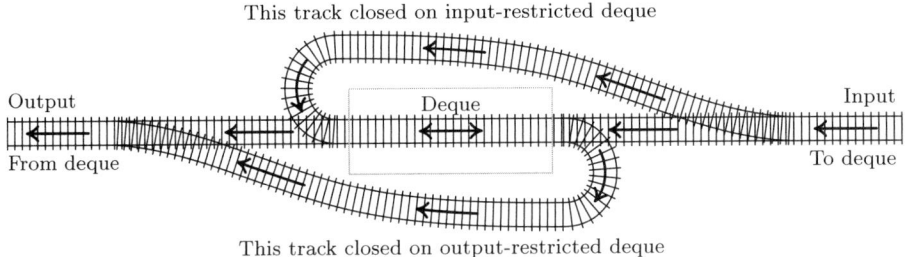

Fig. 2. A deque represented as a railway switching network.

With a stack we always remove the "youngest" item currently in the list, namely the one that has been inserted more recently than any other. With a queue just the opposite is true: The "oldest" item is always removed; the nodes leave the list in the same order as they entered it.

Many people who have independently realized the importance of stacks and queues have given them other names: Stacks have been called push-down lists, reversion storages, cellars, nesting stores, piles, last-in-first-out ("LIFO") lists, and even yo-yo lists. Queues are sometimes called circular stores or first-in-first-out ("FIFO") lists. The terms LIFO and FIFO have been used for many years by accountants, as names of methods for pricing inventories. Still another term, "shelf," has been applied to output-restricted deques, and input-restricted deques have been called "scrolls" or "rolls." This multiplicity of names is interesting in itself, since it is evidence for the importance of the concepts. The words stack and queue are gradually becoming standard terminology; of all the other words listed above, only "push-down list" is still reasonably common, particularly in connection with automata theory.

Stacks arise quite frequently in practice. We might, for example, go through a set of data and keep a list of exceptional conditions or things to do later; after we're done with the original set, we can then do the rest of the processing by coming back to the list, removing entries until it becomes empty. (The "saddle point" problem, exercise 1.3.2–10, is an instance of this situation.) Either a stack or a queue will be suitable for such a list, but a stack is generally more convenient. We all have "stacks" in our minds when we are solving problems: One problem leads to another and this leads to another; we stack up problems and subproblems and remove them as they are solved. Similarly, the process of entering and leaving subroutines during the execution of a computer program has a stack-like behavior. Stacks are particularly useful for the processing of languages with a nested structure, like programming languages, arithmetic expressions, and the literary German "Schachtelsätze." In general, stacks occur most frequently in connection with explicitly or implicitly recursive algorithms, and we will discuss this connection thoroughly in Chapter 8.

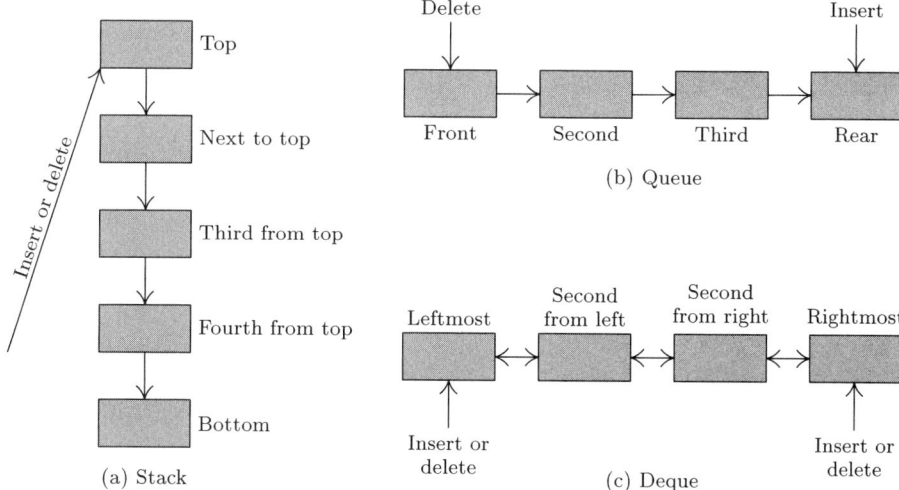

Fig. 3. Three important classes of linear lists.

Special terminology is generally used when algorithms refer to these structures: We put an item onto the *top* of a stack, or take the top item off (see Fig. 3a). The *bottom* of the stack is the least accessible item, and it will not be removed until all other items have been deleted. (People often say that they *push* an item *down* onto a stack, and *pop* the stack *up* when the top item is deleted. This terminology comes from an analogy with the stacks of plates often found in cafeterias. The brevity of the words "push" and "pop" has its advantages, but these terms falsely imply a motion of the whole list within computer memory. Nothing is physically pushed down; items are added onto the top, as in haystacks or stacks of boxes.) With queues, we speak of the *front* and the *rear* of the queue; things enter at the rear and are removed when they ultimately reach the front position (see Fig. 3b). When referring to deques, we speak of the *left* and *right* ends (Fig. 3c). The concepts of top, bottom, front, and rear are sometimes applied to deques that are being used as stacks or queues, with no standard conventions as to whether top, front, and rear should appear at the left or the right.

Thus we find it easy to use a rich variety of descriptive words from English in our algorithms: "up-down" terminology for stacks, "waiting in line" terminology for queues, and "left-right" terminology for deques.

A little bit of additional notation has proved to be convenient for dealing with stacks and queues: We write

$$A \Leftarrow x \tag{1}$$

(when A is a stack) to mean that the value x is *inserted* on top of stack A, or (when A is a queue) to mean that x is *inserted* at the rear of the queue. Similarly, the notation

$$x \Leftarrow A \tag{2}$$

is used to mean that the variable x is set equal to the value at the top of stack A or at the front of queue A, and this value is *deleted* from A. Notation (2) is meaningless when A is empty — that is, when A contains no values.

If A is a nonempty stack, we may write

$$\text{top}(A) \tag{3}$$

to denote its top element.

EXERCISES

1. [*06*] An input-restricted deque is a linear list in which items may be inserted at one end but removed from either end; clearly an input-restricted deque can operate either as a stack or as a queue, if we consistently remove all items from one of the two ends. Can an output-restricted deque also be operated either as a stack or as a queue?

▶ **2.** [*15*] Imagine four railroad cars positioned on the input side of the track in Fig. 1, numbered 1, 2, 3, and 4, from left to right. Suppose we perform the following sequence of operations (which is compatible with the direction of the arrows in the diagram and does not require cars to "jump over" other cars): (i) move car 1 into the stack; (ii) move car 2 into the stack; (iii) move car 2 into the output; (iv) move car 3 into the stack; (v) move car 4 into the stack; (vi) move car 4 into the output; (vii) move car 3 into the output; (viii) move car 1 into the output.

As a result of these operations the original order of the cars, 1234, has been changed into 2431. *It is the purpose of this exercise and the following exercises to examine what permutations are obtainable in such a manner from stacks, queues, or deques.*

If there are six railroad cars numbered 123456, can they be permuted into the order 325641? Can they be permuted into the order 154623? (In case it is possible, show how to do it.)

3. [*25*] The operations (i) through (viii) in the previous exercise can be much more concisely described by the code SSXSSXXX, where S stands for "move a car from the input into the stack," and X stands for "move a car from the stack into the output." Some sequences of S's and X's specify meaningless operations, since there may be no cars available on the specified track; for example, the sequence SXXSSXXS cannot be carried out, since we assume that the stack is initially empty.

Let us call a sequence of S's and X's *admissible* if it contains n S's and n X's, and if it specifies no operations that cannot be performed. Formulate a rule by which it is easy to distinguish between admissible and inadmissible sequences; show furthermore that no two different admissible sequences give the same output permutation.

4. [*M34*] Find a simple formula for a_n, the number of permutations on n elements that can be obtained with a stack like that in exercise 2.

▶ **5.** [*M28*] Show that it is possible to obtain a permutation $p_1 p_2 \ldots p_n$ from $12 \ldots n$ using a stack if and only if there are no indices $i < j < k$ such that $p_j < p_k < p_i$.

6. [*00*] Consider the problem of exercise 2, with a queue substituted for a stack. What permutations of $12 \ldots n$ can be obtained with use of a queue?

▶ **7.** [*25*] Consider the problem of exercise 2, with a deque substituted for a stack. (a) Find a permutation of 1234 that can be obtained with an input-restricted deque, but it cannot be obtained with an output-restricted deque. (b) Find a permutation of 1234 that can be obtained with an output-restricted deque but not with an input-restricted deque. [As a consequence of (a) and (b), there is definitely a difference between input-restricted and output-restricted deques.] (c) Find a permutation of 1234 that cannot be obtained with either an input-restricted or an output-restricted deque.

8. [*22*] Are there any permutations of $12 \ldots n$ that cannot be obtained with the use of a deque that is neither input- nor output-restricted?

9. [*M20*] Let b_n be the number of permutations on n elements obtainable by the use of an input-restricted deque. (Note that $b_4 = 22$, as shown in exercise 7.) Show that b_n is also the number of permutations on n elements with an *output*-restricted deque.

10. [*M25*] (See exercise 3.) Let S, Q, and X denote respectively the operations of inserting an element at the left, inserting an element at the right, and emitting an element from the left, of an output-restricted deque. For example, the sequence QQXSXSXX will transform the input sequence 1234 into 1342. The sequence SXQSXSXX gives the same transformation.

Find a way to define the concept of an *admissible* sequence of the symbols S, Q, and X, so that the following property holds: Every permutation of n elements that is attainable with an output-restricted deque corresponds to precisely one admissible sequence.

▶ **11.** [*M40*] As a consequence of exercises 9 and 10, the number b_n is the number of admissible sequences of length $2n$. Find a closed form for the generating function $\sum_{n \geq 0} b_n z^n$.

12. [*HM34*] Compute the asymptotic values of the quantities a_n and b_n in exercises 4 and 11.

13. [*M48*] How many permutations of n elements are obtainable with the use of a general deque? [See Rosenstiehl and Tarjan, *J. Algorithms* **5** (1984), 389–390, for an algorithm that decides in $O(n)$ steps whether or not a given permutation is obtainable.]

▶ **14.** [*26*] Suppose you are allowed to use only stacks as data structures. How can you implement a queue efficiently with two stacks?

2.2.2. Sequential Allocation

The simplest and most natural way to keep a linear list inside a computer is to put the list items in consecutive locations, one node after the other. Then we will have

$$\text{LOC}(X[j+1]) = \text{LOC}(X[j]) + c,$$

where c is the number of words per node. (Usually $c = 1$. When $c > 1$, it is sometimes more convenient to split a single list into c "parallel" lists, so that the kth word of node $X[j]$ is stored a fixed distance from the location of the first word of $X[j]$, depending on k. We will continually assume, however, that adjacent groups of c words form a single node.) In general,

$$\text{LOC}(X[j]) = L_0 + cj, \tag{1}$$

where L_0 is a constant called the *base address*, the location of an artificially assumed node $X[0]$.

This technique for representing a linear list is so obvious and well-known that there seems to be no need to dwell on it at any length. But we will be seeing many other "more sophisticated" methods of representation later on in this chapter, and it is a good idea to examine the simple case first to see just how far we can go with it. It is important to understand the limitations as well as the power of the use of sequential allocation.

Sequential allocation is quite convenient for dealing with a *stack*. We simply have a variable T called the *stack pointer*. When the stack is empty, we let $T = 0$. To place a new element Y on top of the stack, we set

$$T \leftarrow T + 1; \qquad X[T] \leftarrow Y. \tag{2}$$

And when the stack is not empty, we can set Y equal to the top node and delete that node by reversing the actions of (2):

$$Y \leftarrow X[T]; \qquad T \leftarrow T - 1. \tag{3}$$

(Inside a computer it is usually most efficient to maintain the value cT instead of T, because of (1). Such modifications are easily made, so we will continue our discussion as though $c = 1$.)

The representation of a *queue* or a more general *deque* is a little trickier. An obvious solution is to keep two pointers, say F and R (for the front and rear of the queue), with $F = R = 0$ when the queue is empty. Then inserting an element at the rear of the queue would be

$$R \leftarrow R + 1; \qquad X[R] \leftarrow Y. \tag{4}$$

Removing the front node (F points just below the front) would be

$$F \leftarrow F + 1; \qquad Y \leftarrow X[F]; \qquad \text{if } F = R, \text{ then set } F \leftarrow R \leftarrow 0. \tag{5}$$

But note what can happen: If R always stays ahead of F (so that there is always at least one node in the queue) the table entries used are $X[1]$, $X[2]$, ..., $X[1000]$, ..., ad infinitum, and this is terribly wasteful of storage space. The simple method of (4) and (5) should therefore be used only in the situation when F is known to catch up to R quite regularly — for example, if all deletions come in spurts that empty the queue.

To circumvent the problem of the queue overrunning memory, we can set aside M nodes X[1], ..., X[M] arranged implicitly in a circle with X[1] following X[M]. Then processes (4) and (5) above become

$$\text{if } R = M \text{ then } R \leftarrow 1, \quad \text{otherwise } R \leftarrow R + 1; \quad X[R] \leftarrow Y. \qquad (6)$$

$$\text{if } F = M \text{ then } F \leftarrow 1, \quad \text{otherwise } F \leftarrow F + 1; \quad Y \leftarrow X[F]. \qquad (7)$$

We have, in fact, already seen circular queuing action like this, when we looked at input-output buffering in Section 1.4.4.

Our discussion so far has been very unrealistic, because we have tacitly assumed that nothing could go wrong. When we deleted a node from a stack or queue, we assumed that there was at least one node present. When we inserted a node into a stack or queue, we assumed that there was room for it in memory. But clearly the method of (6) and (7) allows at most M nodes in the entire queue, and methods (2), (3), (4), (5) allow T and R to reach only a certain maximum amount within any given computer program. The following specifications show how the actions should be rewritten for the common case where we do not assume that these restrictions are automatically satisfied:

$$X \Leftarrow Y \text{ (insert into stack): } \begin{cases} T \leftarrow T + 1; \\ \text{if } T > M, \text{ then OVERFLOW}; \\ X[T] \leftarrow Y. \end{cases} \qquad (2a)$$

$$Y \Leftarrow X \text{ (delete from stack): } \begin{cases} \text{if } T = 0, \text{ then UNDERFLOW}; \\ Y \leftarrow X[T]; \\ T \leftarrow T - 1. \end{cases} \qquad (3a)$$

$$X \Leftarrow Y \text{ (insert into queue): } \begin{cases} \text{if } R = M, \text{ then } R \leftarrow 1, \text{ otherwise } R \leftarrow R + 1; \\ \text{if } R = F, \text{ then OVERFLOW}; \\ X[R] \leftarrow Y. \end{cases} \qquad (6a)$$

$$Y \Leftarrow X \text{ (delete from queue): } \begin{cases} \text{if } F = R, \text{ then UNDERFLOW}; \\ \text{if } F = M, \text{ then } F \leftarrow 1, \text{ otherwise } F \leftarrow F + 1; \\ Y \leftarrow X[F]. \end{cases} \qquad (7a)$$

Here we assume that X[1], ..., X[M] is the total amount of space allowed for the list; OVERFLOW and UNDERFLOW mean an excess or deficiency of items. The initial setting F = R = 0 for the queue pointers is no longer valid when we use (6a) and (7a), because overflow will not be detected when F = 0; we should start with F = R = 1, say.

The reader is urged to work exercise 1, which discusses a nontrivial aspect of this simple queuing mechanism.

The next question is, "What do we do when UNDERFLOW or OVERFLOW occurs?" In the case of UNDERFLOW, we have tried to remove a nonexistent item; this is usually a meaningful condition — not an error situation — that can be used to govern the flow of a program. For example, we might want to delete items repeatedly until UNDERFLOW occurs. An OVERFLOW situation, however, is

usually an error; it means that the table is full already, yet there is still more
information waiting to be put in. The usual policy in case of OVERFLOW is to
report reluctantly that the program cannot go on because its storage capacity
has been exceeded; then the program terminates.

Of course we hate to give up in an OVERFLOW situation when only one list
has gotten too large, while other lists of the same program may very well have
plenty of room remaining. In the discussion above we were primarily thinking of
a program with only one list. However, we frequently encounter programs that
involve several stacks, each of which has a dynamically varying size. In such a
situation we don't want to impose a maximum size on each stack, since the size
is usually unpredictable; and even if a maximum size has been determined for
each stack, we will rarely find *all* stacks simultaneously filling their maximum
capacity.

When there are just two variable-size lists, they can coexist together very
nicely if we let the lists grow toward each other:

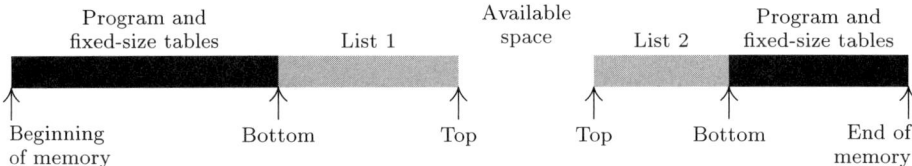

Here list 1 expands to the right, and list 2 (stored in reverse order) expands to
the left. OVERFLOW will not occur unless the total size of both lists exhausts all
memory space. The lists may independently expand and contract so that the
effective maximum size of each one could be significantly more than half of the
available space. This layout of memory space is used very frequently.

We can easily convince ourselves, however, that there is no way to store three
or more variable-size sequential lists in memory so that (a) OVERFLOW will occur
only when the total size of all lists exceeds the total space, and (b) each list has
a fixed location for its "bottom" element. When there are, say, ten or more
variable-size lists — and this is not unusual — the storage allocation problem
becomes very significant. If we wish to satisfy condition (a), we must give up
condition (b); that is, we must allow the "bottom" elements of the lists to change
their positions. This means that the location L_0 of Eq. (1) is not constant any
longer; no reference to the table may be made to an absolute memory address,
since all references must be relative to the base address L_0. In the case of MIX,
the coding to bring the Ith one-word node into register A is changed from

$$
\begin{array}{lll}
&& \texttt{LD1 \quad I} \\
\texttt{LD1 \quad I} && \texttt{LDA \quad BASE(0:2)} \\
\texttt{LDA \quad } L_0\texttt{,1} & \text{to, for example,} & \texttt{STA \quad *+1(0:2)} \\
&& \texttt{LDA \quad *,1}
\end{array}
\qquad (8)
$$

where BASE contains $\boxed{\ \ L_0\ \ |\ 0\ |\ 0\ |\ 0\ }$. Such relative addressing evidently
takes longer than fixed-base addressing, although it would be only slightly slower
if MIX had an "indirect addressing" feature (see exercise 3).

An important special case occurs when each of the variable-size lists is a stack. Then, since only the top element of each stack is relevant at any time, we can proceed almost as efficiently as before. Suppose that we have n stacks; the insertion and deletion algorithms above become the following, if BASE$[i]$ and TOP$[i]$ are link variables for the ith stack, and if each node is one word long:

Insertion: TOP$[i] \leftarrow$ TOP$[i] + 1$; if TOP$[i] >$ BASE$[i + 1]$, then
$\qquad$ OVERFLOW; otherwise set CONTENTS(TOP$[i]) \leftarrow$ Y.   (9)

Deletion: if TOP$[i] =$ BASE$[i]$, then UNDERFLOW; otherwise
$\qquad$ set Y $\leftarrow$ CONTENTS(TOP$[i]$), TOP$[i] \leftarrow$ TOP$[i] - 1$.   (10)

Here BASE$[i + 1]$ is the base location of the $(i + 1)$st stack. The condition TOP$[i] =$ BASE$[i]$ means that stack i is empty.

In (9), OVERFLOW is no longer such a crisis as it was before; we can "repack memory," making room for the table that overflowed by taking some away from tables that aren't yet filled. Several ways to do the repacking suggest themselves; we will now consider some of them in detail, since they can be quite important when linear lists are allocated sequentially. We will start by giving the simplest of the methods, and will then consider some of the alternatives.

Assume that there are n stacks, and that the values BASE$[i]$ and TOP$[i]$ are to be treated as in (9) and (10). These stacks are all supposed to share a common memory area consisting of all locations L with $L_0 < L \leq L_\infty$. (Here L_0 and L_∞ are constants that specify the total number of words available for use.) We might start out with all stacks empty, and

$$\text{BASE}[j] = \text{TOP}[j] = L_0 \qquad \text{for } 1 \leq j \leq n. \tag{11}$$

We also set BASE$[n + 1] = L_\infty$ so that (9) will work properly for $i = n$.

When OVERFLOW occurs with respect to stack i, there are three possibilities:

a) We find the smallest k for which $i < k \leq n$ and TOP$[k] <$ BASE$[k + 1]$, if any such k exist. Now move things *up* one notch:

$\qquad$ Set CONTENTS(L $+ 1) \leftarrow$ CONTENTS(L),   for TOP$[k] \geq$ L $>$ BASE$[i + 1]$.

(This must be done for decreasing, not increasing, values of L to avoid losing information. It is possible that TOP$[k] =$ BASE$[i + 1]$, in which case nothing needs to be moved.) Finally we set BASE$[j] \leftarrow$ BASE$[j] + 1$ and TOP$[j] \leftarrow$ TOP$[j] + 1$, for $i < j \leq k$.

b) No k can be found as in (a), but we find the largest k for which $1 \leq k < i$ and TOP$[k] <$ BASE$[k + 1]$. Now move things *down* one notch:

$\qquad$ Set CONTENTS(L $- 1) \leftarrow$ CONTENTS(L),   for BASE$[k + 1] <$ L $<$ TOP$[i]$.

(This must be done for increasing values of L.)   Then set BASE$[j] \leftarrow$ BASE$[j] - 1$ and TOP$[j] \leftarrow$ TOP$[j] - 1$, for $k < j \leq i$.

c) We have TOP$[k] =$ BASE$[k + 1]$ for all $k \neq i$. Then obviously we cannot find room for the new stack entry, and we must give up.

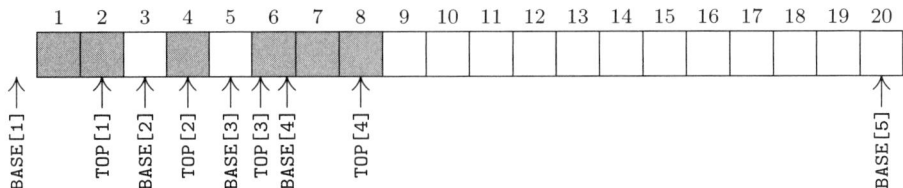

Fig. 4. Example of memory configuration after several insertions and deletions.

Figure 4 illustrates the configuration of memory for the case $n = 4$, $L_0 = 0$, $L_\infty = 20$, after the successive actions

$$ I_1^* \; I_1^* \; I_4 \; I_2^* \; D_1 \; I_3^* \; I_1 \; I_1^* \; I_2^* \; I_4 \; D_2 \; D_1. \qquad (12)$$

(Here I_j and D_j refer to insertion and deletion in stack j, and an asterisk refers to an occurrence of OVERFLOW, assuming that no space is initially allocated to stacks 1, 2, and 3.)

It is clear that many of the first stack overflows that occur with this method could be eliminated if we chose our initial conditions wisely, instead of allocating all space initially to the nth stack as suggested in (11). For example, if we expect each stack to be of the same size, we can start out with

$$ \mathtt{BASE}[j] = \mathtt{TOP}[j] = \left\lfloor \left(\frac{j-1}{n} \right)(L_\infty - L_0) \right\rfloor + L_0, \qquad \text{for } 1 \le j \le n. \qquad (13)$$

Operating experience with a particular program may suggest better starting values; however, no matter how well the initial allocation is set up, it can save at most a fixed number of overflows, and the effect is noticeable only in the early stages of a program run. (See exercise 17.)

Another possible way to improve the method above would be to make room for more than one new entry each time memory is repacked. This idea has been exploited by J. Garwick, who suggests a complete repacking of memory when overflow occurs, based on the change in size of each stack since the last repacking. His algorithm uses an additional array, called OLDTOP$[j]$, $1 \le j \le n$, which retains the value that TOP$[j]$ had just after the previous allocation of memory. Initially, the tables are set as before, with OLDTOP$[j]$ = TOP$[j]$. The algorithm proceeds as follows:

Algorithm G (*Reallocate sequential tables*). Assume that OVERFLOW has occurred in stack i, according to (9). After Algorithm G has been performed, either we will find the memory capacity exceeded or the memory will have been rearranged so that the action CONTENTS(TOP$[i]$) ← Y may be done. (Notice that TOP$[i]$ has already been increased in (9) before Algorithm G takes place.)

G1. [Initialize.] Set SUM ← $L_\infty - L_0$, INC ← 0. Then do step G2 for $1 \le j \le n$. (The effect will be to make SUM equal to the total amount of memory space left, and INC equal to the total amount of increases in table sizes since the last allocation.) After this has been done, go on to step G3.

G2. [Gather statistics.] Set SUM ← SUM − (TOP[j] − BASE[j]). If TOP[j] > OLDTOP[j], set D[j] ← TOP[j] − OLDTOP[j] and INC ← INC + D[j]; otherwise set D[j] ← 0.

G3. [Is memory full?] If SUM < 0, we cannot proceed.

G4. [Compute allocation factors.] Set α ← 0.1 × SUM/n, β ← 0.9 × SUM/INC. (Here α and β are fractions, not integers, which are to be computed to reasonable accuracy. The following step awards the available space to individual lists as follows: Approximately 10 percent of the memory presently available will be shared equally among the n lists, and the other 90 percent will be divided proportionally to the amount of increase in table size since the previous allocation.)

G5. [Compute new base addresses.] Set NEWBASE[1] ← BASE[1] and σ ← 0; then for j = 2, 3, ..., n set τ ← σ + α + D[j − 1]β, NEWBASE[j] ← NEWBASE[j − 1] + TOP[j − 1] − BASE[j − 1] + $\lfloor \tau \rfloor$ − $\lfloor \sigma \rfloor$, and σ ← τ.

G6. [Repack.] Set TOP[i] ← TOP[i] − 1. (This reflects the true size of the ith list, so that no attempt will be made to move information from beyond the list boundary.) Perform Algorithm R below, and then reset TOP[i] ← TOP[i] + 1. Finally set OLDTOP[j] ← TOP[j] for 1 ≤ j ≤ n. ▌

Perhaps the most interesting part of this whole algorithm is the general repacking process, which we shall now describe. Repacking is not trivial, since some portions of memory shift up and others shift down; it is obviously important not to overwrite any of the good information in memory while it is being moved.

Algorithm R (*Relocate sequential tables*). For 1 ≤ j ≤ n, the information specified by BASE[j] and TOP[j] in accord with the conventions stated above is moved to new positions specified by NEWBASE[j], and the values of BASE[j] and TOP[j] are suitably adjusted. This algorithm is based on the easily verified fact that the data to be moved downward cannot overlap with any data that is to be moved upward, nor with any data that is supposed to stay put.

R1. [Initialize.] Set j ← 1.

R2. [Find start of shift.] (Now all lists from 1 to j that were to be moved down have been shifted into the desired position.) Increase j in steps of 1 until finding either

a) NEWBASE[j] < BASE[j]: Go to R3; or

b) j > n: Go to R4.

R3. [Shift list down.] Set δ ← BASE[j] − NEWBASE[j]. Set CONTENTS(L − δ) ← CONTENTS(L), for L = BASE[j] + 1, BASE[j] + 2, ..., TOP[j]. (It is possible for BASE[j] to equal TOP[j], in which case no action is required.) Set BASE[j] ← NEWBASE[j], TOP[j] ← TOP[j] − δ. Go back to R2.

R4. [Find start of shift.] (Now all lists from j to n that were to be moved up have been shifted into the desired position.) Decrease j in steps of 1 until finding either

a) NEWBASE[j] > BASE[j]: Go to R5; or

b) j = 1: The algorithm terminates.

R5. [Shift list up.] Set $\delta \leftarrow$ NEWBASE[j] $-$ BASE[j]. Set CONTENTS(L $+ \delta$) $\leftarrow$ CONTENTS(L), for L = TOP[j], TOP[j] $- 1, \ldots,$ BASE[j] $+ 1$. (As in step R3, no action may actually be needed here.) Set BASE[j] $\leftarrow$ NEWBASE[j], TOP[j] $\leftarrow$ TOP[j] $+ \delta$. Go back to R4. ∎

Notice that stack 1 never needs to be moved. Therefore we should put the largest stack first, if we know which one will be largest.

In Algorithms G and R we have purposely made it possible to have

$$\text{OLDTOP}[j] \equiv \text{D}[j] \equiv \text{NEWBASE}[j+1]$$

for $1 \le j \le n$; that is, these three tables can share common memory locations since their values are never needed at conflicting times.

We have described these repacking algorithms for stacks, but it is clear that they can be adapted to any relatively addressed tables in which the current information is contained between BASE[j] and TOP[j]. Other pointers (for example, FRONT[j] and REAR[j]) could also be attached to the lists, making them serve as a queue or deque. See exercise 8, which considers the case of a queue in detail.

The mathematical analysis of dynamic storage-allocation algorithms like those above is extremely difficult. Some interesting results appear in the exercises below, although they only begin to scratch the surface as far as the general behavior is concerned.

As an example of the theory that *can* be derived, suppose we consider the case when the tables grow only by insertion; deletions and subsequent insertions that cancel their effect are ignored. Let us assume further that each table is expected to fill at the same rate. This situation can be modeled by imagining a sequence of m insertion operations $a_1, a_2, \ldots, a_m$, where each a_i is an integer between 1 and n (representing an insertion on top of stack a_i). For example, the sequence 1, 1, 2, 2, 1 means two insertions to stack 1, followed by two to stack 2, followed by another onto stack 1. We can regard each of the n^m possible specifications $a_1, a_2, \ldots, a_m$ as equally likely, and then we can ask for the average number of times it is necessary to move a word from one location to another during the repacking operations as the entire table is built. For the first algorithm, starting with all available space given to the nth stack, this question is analyzed in exercise 9. We find that the average number of move operations required is

$$\frac{1}{2}\left(1 - \frac{1}{n}\right)\binom{m}{2}. \tag{14}$$

Thus, as we might expect, the number of moves is essentially proportional to the *square* of the number of times the tables grow. The same is true if the individual stacks aren't equally likely (see exercise 10).

The moral of the story seems to be that a very large number of moves will be made if a reasonably large number of items is put into the tables. This is the price we must pay for the ability to pack a large number of sequential tables together tightly. No theory has been developed to analyze the average behavior of Algorithm G, and it is unlikely that any simple model will be able to describe the characteristics of real-life tables in such an environment. However, exercise 18 provides a worst-case guarantee that the running time will not be too bad if the memory doesn't get too full.

Experience shows that when memory is only half loaded (that is, when the available space equals half the total space), we need very little rearranging of the tables with Algorithm G. The important thing is perhaps that the algorithm behaves well in the half-full case and that it at least delivers the right answers in the almost-full case.

But let us think about the almost-full case more carefully. When the tables nearly fill memory, Algorithm R takes rather long to perform its job. And to make matters worse, OVERFLOW is much more frequent just before the memory space is used up. There are very few programs that will come *close* to filling memory without soon thereafter completely overflowing it; and those that do overflow memory will probably waste enormous amounts of time in Algorithms G and R just before memory is overrun. Unfortunately, undebugged programs will frequently overflow memory capacity. To avoid wasting all this time, a possible suggestion would be to stop Algorithm G in step G3 if SUM is less than $S_{\min}$, where the latter is chosen by the programmer to prevent excessive repacking. When there are many variable-size sequential tables, we should *not* expect to make use of 100 percent of the memory space before storage is exceeded.

Further study of Algorithm G has been made by D. S. Wise and D. C. Watson, *BIT* **16** (1976), 442–450. See also A. S. Fraenkel, *Inf. Proc. Letters* **8** (1979), 9–10, who suggests working with pairs of stacks that grow towards each other.

EXERCISES

▶ **1.** [15] In the queue operations given by (6a) and (7a), how many items can be in the queue at one time without OVERFLOW occurring?

▶ **2.** [22] Generalize the method of (6a) and (7a) so that it will apply to any deque with fewer than M elements. In other words, give specifications for the other two operations, "delete from rear" and "insert at front."

3. [21] Suppose that MIX is extended as follows: The I-field of each instruction is to have the form $8I_1 + I_2$, where $0 \le I_1 < 8$, $0 \le I_2 < 8$. In assembly language one writes "OP ADDRESS,I_1:I_2" or (as presently) "OP ADDRESS,I_2" if $I_1 = 0$. The meaning is to perform first the "address modification" I_1 on ADDRESS, then to perform the "address modification" I_2 on the resulting address, and finally to perform the OP with the new address. The address modifications are defined as follows:

0: M = A
1: M = A + rI1
2: M = A + rI2

. . .

6: M = A + rI6
7: M = resulting address defined from the "ADDRESS,I_1:I_2" fields found in location A. The case $I_1 = I_2 = 7$ in location A is not allowed. (The reason for the latter restriction is discussed in exercise 5.)

Here A denotes the address before the operation, and M denotes the resulting address after the address modification. In all cases the result is undefined if the value of M does not fit in two bytes and a sign. The execution time is increased by one unit for each "indirect-addressing" (modification 7) operation performed.

As a nontrivial example, suppose that location 1000 contains "NOP 1000,1:7"; location 1001 contains "NOP 1000,2"; and index registers 1 and 2 respectively contain 1 and 2. Then the command "LDA 1000,7:2" is equivalent to "LDA 1004", because

$$1000,7:2 = (1000,1:7),2 = (1001,7),2 = (1000,2),2 = 1002,2 = 1004.$$

a) Using this indirect addressing feature (if necessary), show how to simplify the coding on the right-hand side of (8) so that two instructions are saved per reference to the table. How much faster is your code than (8)?

b) Suppose there are several tables whose base addresses are stored in locations BASE + 1, BASE + 2, BASE + 3, ...; how can the indirect addressing feature be used to bring the Ith element of the Jth table into register A in one instruction, assuming that I is in rI1 and J is in rI2?

c) What is the effect of the instruction "ENT4 X,7", assuming that the (3:3)-field in location X is zero?

4. [25] Assume that MIX has been extended as in exercise 3. Show how to give a *single instruction* (plus auxiliary constants) for each of the following actions:

a) To loop indefinitely because indirect addressing never terminates.

b) To bring into register A the value LINK(LINK(x)), where the value of link variable x is stored in the (0:2) field of the location whose symbolic address is X, the value of LINK(x) is stored in the (0:2) field of location x, etc., assuming that the (3:3) fields in these locations are zero.

c) To bring into register A the value LINK(LINK(LINK(x))), under assumptions like those in (b).

d) To bring into register A the contents of location rI1 + rI2 + rI3 + rI4 + rI5 + rI6.

e) To quadruple the current value of rI6.

▶ **5.** [35] The extension of MIX suggested in exercise 3 has an unfortunate restriction that "7:7" is not allowed in an indirectly addressed location.

a) Give an example to indicate that, without this restriction, it would probably be necessary for the MIX hardware to be capable of maintaining a long internal stack of three-bit items. (This would be prohibitively expensive hardware, even for a mythical computer like MIX.)

b) Explain why such a stack is not needed under the present restriction; in other words, design an algorithm with which the hardware of a computer could perform the desired address modifications without much additional register capacity.

c) Give a milder restriction than that of exercise 3 on the use of 7:7 that alleviates the difficulties of exercise 4(c), yet can be cheaply implemented in computer hardware.

6. [10] Starting with the memory configuration shown in Fig. 4, determine which of the following sequences of operations causes overflow or underflow:

(a) I_1; (b) I_2; (c) I_3; (d) $I_4I_4I_4I_4I_4$; (e) $D_2D_2I_2I_2I_2$.

7. [12] Step G4 of Algorithm G indicates a division by the quantity INC. Can INC ever be zero at that point in the algorithm?

▶ **8.** [26] Explain how to modify (9), (10), and the repacking algorithms for the case that one or more of the lists is a queue being handled circularly as in (6a) and (7a).

▶ **9.** [*M27*] Using the mathematical model described near the end of the text, prove that Eq. (14) is the expected number of moves. (Note that the sequence 1, 1, 4, 2, 3, 1, 2, 4, 2, 1 specifies $0 + 0 + 0 + 1 + 1 + 3 + 2 + 0 + 3 + 6 = 16$ moves.)

10. [*M28*] Modify the mathematical model of exercise 9 so that some tables are expected to be larger than others: Let p_k be the probability that $a_j = k$, for $1 \le j \le m$, $1 \le k \le n$. Thus $p_1 + p_2 + \cdots + p_n = 1$; the previous exercise considered the special case $p_k = 1/n$ for all k. Determine the expected number of moves, as in Eq. (14), for this more general case. It is possible to rearrange the relative order of the n lists so that the lists expected to be longer are put to the right (or to the left) of the lists that are expected to be shorter; what relative order for the n lists will minimize the expected number of moves, based on $p_1, p_2, \ldots, p_n$?

11. [*M30*] Generalize the argument of exercise 9 so that the first t insertions in any stack cause no movement, while subsequent insertions are unaffected. Thus if $t = 2$, the sequence in exercise 9 specifies $0+0+0+0+0+3+0+0+3+6 = 12$ moves. What is the average total number of moves under this assumption? [This is an approximation to the behavior of the algorithm when each stack starts with t available spaces.]

12. [*M28*] The advantage of having two tables coexist in memory by growing towards each other, rather than by having them kept in separate independently bounded areas, may be quantitatively estimated (to a certain extent) as follows. Use the model of exercise 9 with $n = 2$; for each of the 2^m equally probable sequences $a_1, a_2, \ldots, a_m$, let there be k_1 1s and k_2 2s. (Here k_1 and k_2 are the respective sizes of the two tables after the memory is full. We are able to run the algorithm with $m = k_1 + k_2$ locations when the tables are adjacent, instead of $2 \max(k_1, k_2)$ locations to get the same effect with separate tables.)

What is the average value of $\max(k_1, k_2)$?

13. [*HM42*] The value $\max(k_1, k_2)$ investigated in exercise 12 will be even greater if larger fluctuations in the tables are introduced by allowing random *deletions* as well as random insertions. Suppose we alter the model so that with probability p the sequence value a_j is interpreted as a deletion instead of an insertion; the process continues until $k_1 + k_2$ (the total number of table locations in use) equals m. A deletion from an empty list causes no effect.

For example, if $m = 4$ it can be shown that we get the following probability distribution when the process stops:

$(k_1, k_2) =$	$(0, 4)$	$(1, 3)$	$(2, 2)$	$(3, 1)$	$(4, 0)$
with probability	$\dfrac{1}{16 - 12p + 4p^2}$,	$\dfrac{1}{4}$,	$\dfrac{6 - 6p + 2p^2}{16 - 12p + 4p^2}$,	$\dfrac{1}{4}$,	$\dfrac{1}{16 - 12p + 4p^2}$.

Thus as p increases, the difference between k_1 and k_2 tends to increase. It is not difficult to show that in the limit as p approaches unity, the distribution of k_1 becomes essentially uniform, and the limiting expected value of $\max(k_1, k_2)$ is exactly $\frac{3}{4}m + \frac{1}{4m}[m \text{ odd}]$. This behavior is quite different from that in the previous exercise (when $p = 0$); however, it may not be extremely significant, since when p approaches unity, the amount of time taken to terminate the process rapidly approaches infinity. The problem posed in this exercise is to examine the dependence of $\max(k_1, k_2)$ on p and m, and to determine asymptotic formulas for fixed p (like $p = \frac{1}{3}$) as m approaches infinity. The case $p = \frac{1}{2}$ is particularly interesting.

14. [*HM43*] Generalize the result of exercise 12 to arbitrary $n \geq 2$, by showing that, when n is fixed and m approaches infinity, the quantity

$$\frac{m!}{n^m} \sum_{\substack{k_1+k_2+\cdots+k_n=m \\ k_1,k_2,\ldots,k_n \geq 0}} \frac{\max(k_1,k_2,\ldots,k_n)}{k_1!\,k_2!\ldots k_n!}$$

has the asymptotic form $m/n + c_n\sqrt{m} + O(1)$. Determine the constants c_2, c_3, c_4, and c_5.

15. [*40*] Using a Monte Carlo method, simulate the behavior of Algorithm G under varying distributions of insertions and deletions. What do your experiments imply about the efficiency of Algorithm G? Compare its performance with the algorithm given earlier that shifts up and down one node at a time.

16. [*20*] The text illustrates how two stacks can be located so they grow towards each other, thereby making efficient use of a common memory area. Can two *queues*, or a stack and a queue, make use of a common memory area with the same efficiency?

17. [*30*] If σ is any sequence of insertions and deletions such as (12), let $s_0(\sigma)$ be the number of stack overflows that occur when the simple method of Fig. 4 is applied to σ with initial conditions (11), and let $s_1(\sigma)$ be the corresponding number of overflows with respect to other initial conditions such as (13). Prove that $s_0(\sigma) \leq s_1(\sigma) + L_\infty - L_0$.

▶ **18.** [*M30*] Show that the total running time for any sequence of m insertions and/or deletions by Algorithms G and R is $O(m + n \sum_{k=1}^{m} \alpha_k/(1-\alpha_k))$, where α_k is the fraction of memory occupied on the most recent repacking previous to the kth operation; $\alpha_k = 0$ before the first repacking. (Therefore if the memory never gets more than, say, 90% full, each operation takes at most $O(n)$ units of time in an amortized sense, regardless of the total memory size.) Assume that $L_\infty - L_0 \geq n^2$.

▶ **19.** [*16*] (*0-origin indexing.*) Experienced programmers learn that it is generally wise to denote the elements of a linear list by X[0], X[1], ..., X[$n-1$], instead of using the more traditional notation X[1], X[2], ..., X[n]. Then, for example, the base address L_0 in (1) points to the smallest cell of the array.

Revise the insertion and deletion methods (2a), (3a), (6a), and (7a) for stacks and queues so that they conform to this convention. In other words, change them so that the list elements will appear in the array X[0], X[1], ..., X[$M-1$], instead of X[1], X[2], ..., X[M].

2.2.3. Linked Allocation

Instead of keeping a linear list in sequential memory locations, we can make use of a much more flexible scheme in which each node contains a link to the next node of the list.

Sequential allocation:			Linked allocation:		
Address	Contents		Address	Contents	
$L_0 + c$:	Item 1		A:	Item 1	B
$L_0 + 2c$:	Item 2		B:	Item 2	C
$L_0 + 3c$:	Item 3		C:	Item 3	D
$L_0 + 4c$:	Item 4		D:	Item 4	E
$L_0 + 5c$:	Item 5		E:	Item 5	Λ

Here A, B, C, D, and E are arbitrary locations in the memory, and Λ is the null link (see Section 2.1). The program that uses this table in the case of sequential allocation would have an additional variable or constant whose value indicates that the table is five items in length, or else this information would be specified by a sentinel code within item 5 or in the following location. A program for linked allocation would have a link variable or link constant that points to A; all the other items of the list can be found from address A.

Recall from Section 2.1 that links are often shown simply by arrows, since the actual memory locations occupied are usually irrelevant. The linked table above might therefore be shown as follows:

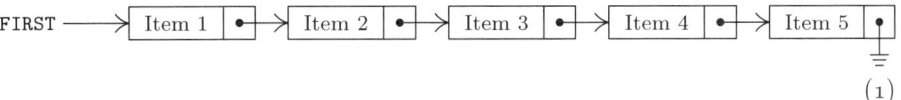

$$(1)$$

Here FIRST is a link variable pointing to the first node of the list.

We can make several obvious comparisons between these two basic forms of storage:

1) Linked allocation takes up additional memory space for the links. This can be the dominating factor in some situations. However, we frequently find that the information in a node does not take up a whole word anyway, so there is already space for a link field present. Also, it is possible in many applications to combine several items into one node so that there is only one link for several items of information (see exercise 2.5–2). But even more importantly, there is often an implicit *gain* in storage by the linked memory approach, since tables can overlap, sharing common parts; and in many cases, sequential allocation will not be as efficient as linked allocation unless a rather large number of additional memory locations are left vacant anyway. For example, the discussion at the end of the previous section explains why the systems described there are necessarily inefficient when memory is densely loaded.

2) It is easy to delete an item from within a linked list. For example, to delete item 3 we need only change the link associated with item 2. But with sequential allocation such a deletion generally implies moving a large part of the list up into different locations.

3) It is easy to insert an item into the midst of a list when the linked scheme is being used. For example, to insert an item $2\frac{1}{2}$ into (1) we need to change only two links:

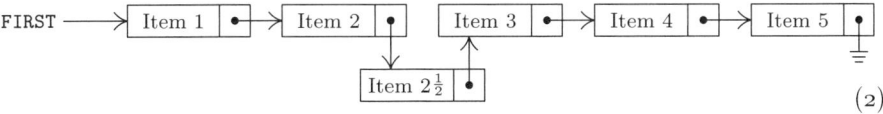

$$(2)$$

By comparison, this operation would be extremely time-consuming in a long sequential table.

4) References to random parts of the list are much faster in the sequential case. To gain access to the kth item in the list, when k is a variable, takes a fixed time in the sequential case, but we need k iterations to march down to the right

place in the linked case. Thus the usefulness of linked memory is predicated on the fact that in the large majority of applications we want to walk through lists sequentially, not randomly; if items in the middle or at the bottom of the list are needed, we try to keep an additional link variable or list of link variables pointing to the proper places.

5) The linked scheme makes it easier to join two lists together, or to break one apart into two that will grow independently.

6) The linked scheme lends itself immediately to more intricate structures than simple linear lists. We can have a variable number of variable-size lists; any node of the list may be a starting point for another list; the nodes may simultaneously be linked together in several orders corresponding to different lists; and so on.

7) Simple operations, like proceeding sequentially through a list, are slightly faster for sequential lists on many computers. For MIX, the comparison is between "INC1 c" and "LD1 0,1(LINK)", which is only one cycle different, but many machines do not enjoy the property of being able to load an index register from an indexed location. If the elements of a linked list belong to different pages in a bulk memory, the memory accesses might take significantly longer.

Thus we see that the linking technique, which frees us from any constraints imposed by the consecutive nature of computer memory, gives us a good deal more efficiency in some operations, while we lose some capabilities in other cases. It is usually clear which allocation technique will be most appropriate in a given situation, and both methods are often used in different lists of the same program.

In the next few examples we will assume for convenience that a node has one word and that it is broken into the two fields INFO and LINK:

$$\boxed{\text{INFO} \mid \text{LINK}} \ . \tag{3}$$

The use of linked allocation generally implies the existence of some mechanism for finding empty space available for a new node, when we wish to insert some newly created information onto a list. This is usually done by having a special list called the *list of available space*. We will call it the AVAIL list (or the AVAIL stack, since it is usually treated in a last-in-first-out manner). The set of all nodes not currently in use is linked together in a list just like any other list; the link variable AVAIL refers to the top element of this list. Thus, if we want to set link variable X to the address of a new node, and to reserve that node for future use, we can proceed as follows:

$$\text{X} \leftarrow \text{AVAIL}, \quad \text{AVAIL} \leftarrow \text{LINK(AVAIL)}. \tag{4}$$

This effectively removes the top of the AVAIL stack and makes X point to the node just removed. *Operation* (4) *occurs so often that we have a special notation for it:* "X $\Leftarrow$ AVAIL" will mean X is set to point to a new node.

When a node is deleted and no longer needed, process (4) can be reversed:

$$\text{LINK(X)} \leftarrow \text{AVAIL}, \quad \text{AVAIL} \leftarrow \text{X}. \tag{5}$$

This operation puts the node addressed by X back onto the list of raw material; we denote (5) by "AVAIL ⇐ X".

Several important things have been omitted from this discussion of the AVAIL stack. We did not say how to set it up at the beginning of a program; clearly this can be done by (a) linking together all nodes that are to be used for linked memory, (b) setting AVAIL to the address of the first of these nodes, and (c) making the last node link to Λ. The set of all nodes that can be allocated is called the *storage pool*.

A more important omission in our discussion was the test for overflow: We neglected to check in (4) if all available memory space has been taken. The operation X ⇐ AVAIL should really be defined as follows:

$$\text{if AVAIL} = \Lambda, \text{ then OVERFLOW};$$

$$\text{otherwise X} \leftarrow \text{AVAIL, AVAIL} \leftarrow \text{LINK(AVAIL).} \qquad (6)$$

The possibility of overflow must always be considered. Here OVERFLOW generally means that we terminate the program with regrets; or else we can go into a "garbage collection" routine that attempts to find more available space. Garbage collection is discussed in Section 2.3.5.

There is another important technique for handling the AVAIL stack: We often do not know in advance how much memory space should be used for the storage pool. There may be a sequential table of variable size that wants to coexist in memory with the linked tables; in such a case we do not want the linked memory area to take any more space than is absolutely necessary. So suppose that we wish to place the linked memory area in ascending locations beginning with L_0 and that this area is never to extend past the value of variable SEQMIN (which represents the current lower bound of the sequential table). Then we can proceed as follows, using a new variable POOLMAX:

a) Initially set AVAIL ← Λ and POOLMAX ← L_0.

b) The operation X ⇐ AVAIL becomes the following:

"If AVAIL ≠ Λ, then X ← AVAIL, AVAIL ← LINK(AVAIL).
Otherwise set X ← POOLMAX and POOLMAX ← X + c, where c is the   (7)
     node size; OVERFLOW now occurs if POOLMAX > SEQMIN."

c) When other parts of the program attempt to decrease the value of SEQMIN, they should sound the OVERFLOW alarm if SEQMIN < POOLMAX.

d) The operation AVAIL ⇐ X is unchanged from (5).

This idea actually represents little more than the previous method with a special recovery procedure substituted for the OVERFLOW situation in (6). The net effect is to keep the storage pool as small as possible. Many people like to use this idea even when *all* lists occupy the storage pool area (so that SEQMIN is constant), since it avoids the rather time-consuming operation of initially linking all available cells together and it facilitates debugging. We could, of course, put the sequential list on the bottom and the pool on the top, having POOLMIN and SEQMAX instead of POOLMAX and SEQMIN.

Thus it is quite easy to maintain a pool of available nodes, in such a way that free nodes can efficiently be found and later returned. These methods give us a source of raw material to use in linked tables. Our discussion was predicated on the implicit assumption that all nodes have a fixed size, c; the cases that arise when different sizes of nodes are present are very important, but we will defer that discussion until Section 2.5. Now we will consider a few of the most common list operations in the special case where stacks and queues are involved.

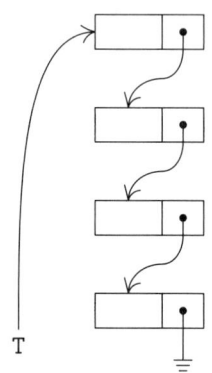

The simplest kind of linked list is a stack. Figure 5 shows a typical stack, with a pointer T to the top of the stack. When the stack is empty, this pointer will have the value Λ.

Fig. 5. A linked stack.

It is clear how to insert ("push down") new information Y onto the top of such a stack, using an auxiliary pointer variable P.

$$P \Leftarrow \text{AVAIL}, \qquad \text{INFO}(P) \leftarrow Y, \qquad \text{LINK}(P) \leftarrow T, \qquad T \leftarrow P. \qquad (8)$$

Conversely, to set Y equal to the information at the top of the stack and to "pop up" the stack:

If $T = \Lambda$, then UNDERFLOW;

otherwise set $P \leftarrow T$, $T \leftarrow \text{LINK}(P)$, $Y \leftarrow \text{INFO}(P)$, $\text{AVAIL} \Leftarrow P$. $\quad (9)$

These operations should be compared with the analogous mechanisms for sequentially allocated stacks, (2a) and (3a) in Section 2.2.2. The reader should study (8) and (9) carefully, since they are extremely important operations.

Before looking at the case of queues, let us see how the stack operations can be expressed conveniently in programs for MIX. A program for insertion, with $P \equiv \text{rI1}$, can be written as follows:

```
INFO EQU  0:3          Definition of the INFO field
LINK EQU  4:5          Definition of the LINK field
     LD1  AVAIL        P ← AVAIL.          ⎫
     J1Z  OVERFLOW     Is AVAIL = Λ?       ⎬ P ⇐ AVAIL
     LDA  0,1(LINK)                        ⎪
     STA  AVAIL        AVAIL ← LINK(P).    ⎭          (10)
     LDA  Y
     STA  0,1(INFO)    INFO(P) ← Y.
     LDA  T
     STA  0,1(LINK)    LINK(P) ← T.
     ST1  T            T ← P.          ▮
```

This takes 17 units of time, compared to 12 units for the comparable operation with a sequential table (although OVERFLOW in the sequential case would in many cases take considerably longer). In this program, as in others to follow in this chapter, OVERFLOW denotes either an ending routine or a subroutine that finds more space and returns to location rJ $-$ 2.

A program for deletion is equally simple:

```
LD1  T              P ← T.
J1Z  UNDERFLOW      Is T = Λ?
LDA  0,1(LINK)
STA  T              T ← LINK(P).
LDA  0,1(INFO)
STA  Y              Y ← INFO(P).
LDA  AVAIL
STA  0,1(LINK)      LINK(P) ← AVAIL.  ⎫ AVAIL ⇐ P
ST1  AVAIL          AVAIL ← P.        ⎭   ▮
```
(11)

It is interesting to observe that each of these operations involves a cyclic
permutation of three links. For example, in the insertion operation let P be the
value of AVAIL before the insertion; if P ≠ Λ, we find that after the operation

the value of AVAIL has become the previous value of LINK(P),

the value of LINK(P) has become the previous value of T, and

the value of T has become the previous value of AVAIL.

So the insertion process (except for setting INFO(P) ← Y) is the cyclic permutation

Similarly in the case of deletion, where P has the value of T before the operation
and we assume that P ≠ Λ, we have Y ← INFO(P) and

The fact that the permutation is cyclic is not really a relevant issue, since *any*
permutation of three elements that moves every element is cyclic. The important
point is rather that precisely three links are permuted in these operations.

The insertion and deletion algorithms of (8) and (9) have been described
for stacks, but they apply much more generally to insertion and deletion in *any*
linear list. Insertion, for example, is performed just before the node pointed to
by link variable T. The insertion of item $2\frac{1}{2}$ in (2) above would be done by using
operation (8) with T = LINK(LINK(FIRST)).

Linked allocation applies in a particularly convenient way to queues. In this
case it is easy to see that the links should run from the front of the queue towards
the rear, so that when a node is removed from the front, the new front node is
directly specified. We will make use of pointers F and R, to the front and rear:

$$F \longrightarrow \boxed{\ \ |\bullet\!\rightarrow} \boxed{\ \ |\bullet\!\rightarrow} \boxed{\ \ |\bullet\!\rightarrow} \boxed{\ \ |\bullet} \!\leftarrow\! R$$
(12)

Except for R, this diagram is abstractly identical to Fig. 5 on page 258.

Whenever the layout of a list is designed, it is important to specify all conditions carefully, particularly for the case when the list is empty. One of the most common programming errors connected with linked allocation is the failure to handle empty lists properly; the other common error is to forget about changing some of the links when a structure is being manipulated. In order to avoid the first type of error, we should always examine the "boundary conditions" carefully. To avoid making the second type of error, it is helpful to draw "before and after" diagrams and to compare them, in order to see which links must change.

Let's illustrate the remarks of the preceding paragraph by applying them to the case of queues. First consider the insertion operation: If (12) is the situation before insertion, the picture after insertion at the rear of the queue should be

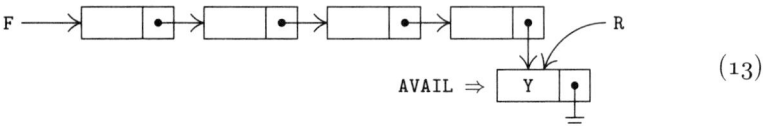

$$(13)$$

(The notation used here implies that a new node has been obtained from the AVAIL list.) Comparing (12) and (13) shows us how to proceed when inserting the information Y at the rear of the queue:

$$\text{P} \Leftarrow \text{AVAIL}, \quad \text{INFO(P)} \leftarrow \text{Y}, \quad \text{LINK(P)} \leftarrow \Lambda, \quad \text{LINK(R)} \leftarrow \text{P}, \quad \text{R} \leftarrow \text{P}. \quad (14)$$

Let us now consider the "boundary" situation when the queue is empty: In this case the situation before insertion is yet to be determined, and the situation "after" is

$$\text{F} \longrightarrow \boxed{\text{Y} \mid \bullet} \leftarrow \text{R} \qquad (15)$$
$$\text{AVAIL}$$

It is desirable to have operations (14) apply in this case also, even if insertion into an empty queue means that we must change *both* F and R, not only R. We find that (14) will work properly if $\text{R} = \text{LOC(F)}$ when the queue is empty, *assuming that* $\text{F} \equiv \text{LINK(LOC(F))}$; the value of variable F must be *stored in the* LINK *field of its location* if this idea is to work. In order to make the testing for an empty queue as efficient as possible, we will let $\text{F} = \Lambda$ in this case. Our policy is therefore that

an empty queue is represented by $\text{F} = \Lambda$ and $\text{R} = \text{LOC(F)}$.

If the operations (14) are applied under these circumstances, we obtain (15).

The deletion operation for queues is derived in a similar fashion. If (12) is the situation before deletion, the situation afterwards is

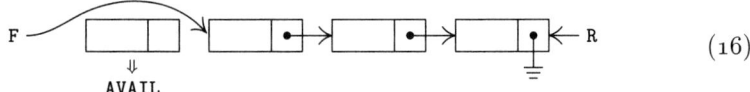

$$(16)$$

For the boundary conditions we must make sure that the deletion operation works when the queue is empty either before or after the operation. These considerations lead us to the following way to do queue deletion in general:

> If F = Λ, then UNDERFLOW;
> otherwise set P ← F, F ← LINK(P), Y ← INFO(P), AVAIL ⇐ P,   (17)
> and if F = Λ, then set R ← LOC(F).

Notice that R must be changed when the queue becomes empty; this is precisely the type of "boundary condition" we should always be watching for.

These suggestions are not the only way to represent queues in a linearly linked fashion; exercise 30 describes a somewhat more natural alternative, and we will give other methods later in this chapter. Indeed, none of the operations above are meant to be prescribed as the only way to do something; they are intended as examples of the basic means of operating with linked lists. The reader who has had only a little previous experience with such techniques will find it helpful to reread the present section up to this point before going on.

So far in this chapter we have discussed how to perform certain operations on tables, but our discussions have always been "abstract," in the sense that we never exhibited actual programs in which the particular techniques were useful. People aren't generally motivated to study abstractions of a problem until they've seen enough special instances of the problem to arouse their interest. The operations discussed so far — manipulations of variable-size lists of information by insertion and deletion, and the use of tables as stacks or queues — are of such wide application, it is hoped that the reader will have encountered them often enough already to grant their importance. But now we will leave the realm of the abstract as we begin to study a series of significant practical examples of the techniques of this chapter.

Our first example is a problem called *topological sorting*, which is an important process needed in connection with network problems, with so-called PERT charts, and even with linguistics; in fact, it is of potential use whenever we have a problem involving a *partial ordering*. A partial ordering of a set S is a relation between the objects of S, which we may denote by the symbol "$\preceq$", satisfying the following properties for any objects x, y, and z (not necessarily distinct) in S:

i) If $x \preceq y$ and $y \preceq z$, then $x \preceq z$. (Transitivity.)

ii) If $x \preceq y$ and $y \preceq x$, then $x = y$. (Antisymmetry.)

iii) $x \preceq x$. (Reflexivity.)

The notation $x \preceq y$ may be read "x precedes or equals y." If $x \preceq y$ and $x \neq y$, we write $x \prec y$ and say "x precedes y." It is easy to see from (i), (ii), and (iii) that we always have

i′) If $x \prec y$ and $y \prec z$, then $x \prec z$. (Transitivity.)

ii′) If $x \prec y$, then $y \not\prec x$. (Asymmetry.)

iii′) $x \not\prec x$. (Irreflexivity.)

The relation denoted by $y \not\prec x$ means "y does not precede x." If we start with a relation $\prec$ satisfying properties (i$'$), (ii$'$), and (iii$'$), we can reverse the process above and define $x \preceq y$ if $x \prec y$ or $x = y$; then properties (i), (ii), and (iii) are true. Therefore we may regard either properties (i), (ii), (iii) or properties (i$'$), (ii$'$), (iii$'$) as the definition of partial order. Notice that property (ii$'$) is actually a consequence of (i$'$) and (iii$'$), although (ii) does not follow from (i) and (iii).

Partial orderings occur quite frequently in everyday life as well as in mathematics. As examples from mathematics we can mention the relation $x \leq y$ between real numbers x and y; the relation $x \subseteq y$ between sets of objects; the relation $x \backslash y$ (x divides y) between positive integers. In the case of PERT networks, S is a set of jobs that must be done, and the relation "$x \prec y$" means "x must be done before y."

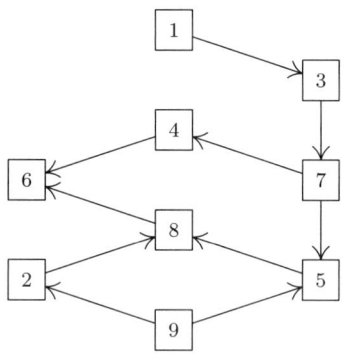

Fig. 6. A partial ordering.

We will naturally assume that S is a finite set, since we want to work with S inside a computer. A partial ordering on a finite set can always be illustrated by drawing a diagram such as Fig. 6, in which the objects are represented by small boxes and the relation is represented by arrows between these boxes; $x \prec y$ means there is a path from the box labeled x to box y that follows the direction of the arrows. Property (ii) of partial ordering means there are *no closed loops* (no paths that close on themselves) in the diagram. If an arrow were drawn from 4 to 1 in Fig. 6, we would no longer have a partial ordering.

The problem of topological sorting is to *embed the partial order in a linear order*; that is, to arrange the objects into a linear sequence $a_1 a_2 \ldots a_n$ such that whenever $a_j \prec a_k$, we have $j < k$. Graphically, this means that the boxes are to be rearranged into a line so that all arrows go towards the right (see Fig. 7). It is not immediately obvious that such a rearrangement is possible in every case, although such a rearrangement certainly could not be done if any loops were present. Therefore the algorithm we will give is interesting not only because it does a useful operation, but also because it proves that this operation is *possible* for every partial ordering.

As an example of topological sorting, imagine a large glossary containing definitions of technical terms. We can write $w_2 \prec w_1$ if the definition of word w_1

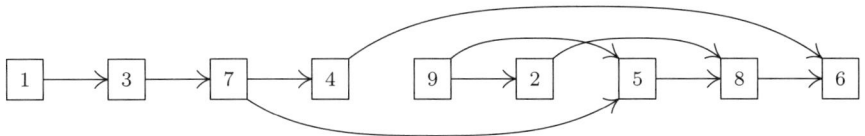

Fig. 7. The ordering relation of Fig. 6 after topological sorting.

depends directly or indirectly on that of word w_2. This relation is a partial ordering provided that there are no "circular" definitions. The problem of topological sorting in this case is to *find a way to arrange the words in the glossary so that no term is used before it has been defined.* Analogous problems arise in writing programs to process the declarations in certain assembly and compiler languages; they also arise in writing a user's manual describing a computer language or in writing textbooks about information structures.

There is a very simple way to do topological sorting: We start by taking an object that is not preceded by any other object in the ordering. This object may be placed first in the output. Now we remove this object from the set S; the resulting set is again partially ordered, and the process can be repeated until the whole set has been sorted. For example, in Fig. 6 we could start by removing 1 or 9; after 1 has been removed, 3 can be taken, and so on. The only way in which this algorithm could fail would be if there were a nonempty partially ordered set in which every element was preceded by another; for in such a case the algorithm would find nothing to do. But if every element is preceded by another, we could construct an arbitrarily long sequence $b_1, b_2, b_3, \ldots$ in which $b_{j+1} \prec b_j$. Since S is finite, we must have $b_j = b_k$ for some $j < k$; but $j < k$ implies that $b_k \preceq b_{j+1}$, hence $b_j = b_k$ contradicts (ii).

In order to implement this process efficiently by computer, we need to be ready to perform the actions described above, namely to locate objects that are not preceded by any others, and to remove them from the set. Our implementation is also influenced by the desired input and output characteristics. The most general program would accept alphabetic names for the objects and would allow gigantic sets of objects to be sorted — more than could possibly fit in the computer memory at once. Such complications would obscure the main points we are trying to make here, however; the handling of alphabetic data can be done efficiently by using the methods of Chapter 6, and the handling of large networks is left as an interesting project for the reader.

Therefore we will assume that the objects to be sorted are numbered from 1 to n in any order. The input of the program will be on tape unit 1: Each tape record contains 50 pairs of numbers, where the pair (j, k) means that object j precedes object k. The first pair, however, is $(0, n)$, where n is the number of objects. The pair $(0, 0)$ terminates the input. We shall assume that n plus the number of relation pairs will fit comfortably in memory; and we shall assume that it is not necessary to check the input for validity. The output is to be the numbers of the objects in sorted order, followed by the number 0, on tape unit 2.

As an example of the input, we might have the relations

$$9 \prec 2, \ 3 \prec 7, \ 7 \prec 5, \ 5 \prec 8, \ 8 \prec 6, \ 4 \prec 6, \ 1 \prec 3, \ 7 \prec 4, \ 9 \prec 5, \ 2 \prec 8. \quad (18)$$

It is not necessary to give any more relations than are needed to characterize the desired partial ordering. Thus, additional relations like $9 \prec 8$ (which can be deduced from $9 \prec 5$ and $5 \prec 8$) may be omitted from or added to the input without harm. In general, it is necessary to give only the relations corresponding to arrows on a diagram such as Fig. 6.

The algorithm that follows uses a sequential table X[1], X[2], ..., X[n], and each node X[k] has the form

| + | 0 | COUNT[k] | TOP[k] | .

Here COUNT[k] is the *number of direct predecessors* of object k (the number of relations $j \prec k$ that have appeared in the input), and TOP[k] is a link to the beginning of the *list of direct successors* of object k. The latter list contains entries in the format

| + | 0 | SUC | NEXT | ,

where SUC is a direct successor of k and NEXT is the next item of the list. As an example of these conventions, Fig. 8 shows the schematic contents of memory corresponding to the input (18).

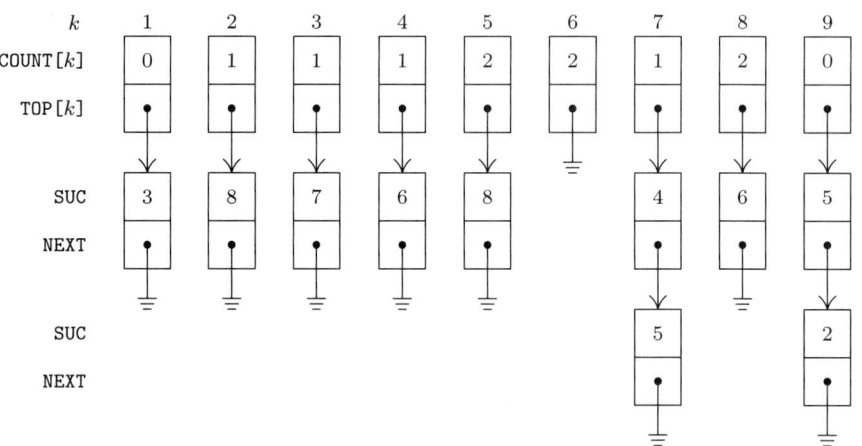

Fig. 8. Computer representation of Fig. 6 corresponding to the relations (18).

Using this memory layout, it is not difficult to work out the algorithm. We want to output the nodes whose COUNT field is zero, then to decrease the COUNT fields of all successors of those nodes by one. The trick is to avoid doing any "searching" for nodes whose COUNT field is zero, and this can be done by maintaining a queue containing those nodes. The links for this queue are kept in the COUNT field, which by now has served its previous purpose; for clarity in the algorithm below, we use the notation QLINK[k] to stand for COUNT[k] when that field is no longer being used to keep a count.

Algorithm T (*Topological sort*). This algorithm inputs a sequence of relations $j \prec k$, indicating that object j precedes object k in a certain partial ordering, assuming that $1 \leq j, k \leq n$. The output is the set of n objects embedded in a linear order. The internal tables used are: QLINK[0], COUNT[1] = QLINK[1], COUNT[2] = QLINK[2], ..., COUNT[n] = QLINK[n]; TOP[1], TOP[2], ..., TOP[n]; a storage pool with one node for each input relation and with SUC and NEXT fields as shown above; P, a link variable used to refer to the nodes in the storage pool; F and R, integer-valued variables used to refer to the front and rear of a queue whose links are in the QLINK table; and N, a variable that counts how many objects have yet to be output.

T1. [Initialize.] Input the value of n. Set COUNT[k] $\leftarrow$ 0 and TOP[k] $\leftarrow \Lambda$ for $1 \leq k \leq n$. Set N $\leftarrow n$.

T2. [Next relation.] Get the next relation "$j \prec k$" from the input; if the input has been exhausted, however, go to T4.

T3. [Record the relation.] Increase COUNT[k] by one. Set

$$\text{P} \Leftarrow \text{AVAIL}, \ \text{SUC(P)} \leftarrow k, \ \text{NEXT(P)} \leftarrow \text{TOP}[j], \ \text{TOP}[j] \leftarrow \text{P}.$$

(This is operation (8).) Go back to T2.

T4. [Scan for zeros.] (At this point we have completed the input phase; the input (18) would now have been transformed into the computer representation shown in Fig. 8. The next job is to initialize the queue of output, which is linked together in the QLINK field.) Set R $\leftarrow$ 0 and QLINK[0] $\leftarrow$ 0. For $1 \leq k \leq n$ examine COUNT[k], and if it is zero, set QLINK[R] $\leftarrow k$ and R $\leftarrow k$. After this has been done for all k, set F $\leftarrow$ QLINK[0] (which will contain the first value k encountered for which COUNT[k] was zero).

T5. [Output front of queue.] Output the value of F. If F = 0, go to T8; otherwise, set N $\leftarrow$ N $-$ 1, and set P $\leftarrow$ TOP[F]. (Since the QLINK and COUNT tables overlap, we have QLINK[R] = 0; therefore the condition F = 0 occurs when the queue is empty.)

T6. [Erase relations.] If P = Λ, go to T7. Otherwise decrease COUNT[SUC(P)] by one, and if it has thereby gone down to zero, set QLINK[R] $\leftarrow$ SUC(P) and R $\leftarrow$ SUC(P). Set P $\leftarrow$ NEXT(P) and repeat this step. (We are removing all relations of the form "F $\prec k$" for some k from the system, and putting new nodes into the queue when all their predecessors have been output.)

T7. [Remove from queue.] Set F $\leftarrow$ QLINK[F] and go back to T5.

T8. [End of process.] The algorithm terminates. If N = 0, we have output all of the object numbers in the desired "topological order," followed by a zero. Otherwise the N object numbers not yet output contain a loop, in violation of the hypothesis of partial order. (See exercise 23 for an algorithm that prints out the contents of one such loop.) ∎

The reader will find it helpful to try this algorithm by hand on the input (18). Algorithm T shows a nice interplay between sequential memory and linked

memory techniques. Sequential memory is used for the main table X[1], ...,
X[n], which contains the COUNT[k] and TOP[k] entries, because we want to
make references to "random" parts of this table in step T3. (If the input were
alphabetic, however, another type of table would be used for speedier search, as
in Chapter 6.) Linked memory is used for the tables of "immediate successors,"
since those table entries have no particular order in the input. The queue of
nodes waiting to be output is kept in the midst of the sequential table by linking
the nodes together in output order. This linking is done by table index instead
of by address; in other words, when the front of the queue is X[k], we have
F = k instead of F = LOC(X[k]). The queue operations used in steps T4, T6,
and T7 are not identical to those in (14) and (17), since we are taking advantage
of special properties of the queue in this system; no nodes need to be created or
returned to available space during this part of the algorithm.

The coding of Algorithm T in MIX assembly language has a few additional
points of interest. Since no deletion from tables is made in the algorithm (because
no storage must be freed for later use), the operation P $\Leftarrow$ AVAIL can be done
in an extremely simple way, as shown in lines 19 and 32 below; we need not
keep any linked pool of memory, and we can choose new nodes consecutively.
The program includes complete input and output with magnetic tape, according
to the conventions mentioned above, but buffering is omitted for the sake of
simplicity. The reader should not find it very difficult to follow the details of
the coding in this program, since it corresponds directly to Algorithm T but
with slight changes for efficiency. The efficient use of index registers, which is an
important aspect of linked memory processing, is illustrated here.

Program T (*Topological sort*). In this program, the following equivalences
should be noted: rI6 $\equiv$ N, rI5 $\equiv$ buffer pointer, rI4 $\equiv$ k, rI3 $\equiv$ j and R, rI2 $\equiv$
AVAIL and P, rI1 $\equiv$ F, TOP[j] $\equiv$ X + j(4:5), COUNT[k] $\equiv$ QLINK[k] $\equiv$ X + k(2:3).

```
01  *  BUFFER AREA AND FIELD DEFINITIONS
02  COUNT    EQU   2:3                      Definition of symbolic
03  QLINK    EQU   2:3                         names of fields
04  TOP      EQU   4:5
05  SUC      EQU   2:3
06  NEXT     EQU   4:5
07  TAPEIN   EQU   1                        Input is on tape unit 1
08  TAPEOUT  EQU   2                        Output is on tape unit 2
09  BUFFER   ORIG  *+100                    Tape buffer area
10           CON   -1                       Sentinel at end of buffer
11  *  INPUT PHASE
12  TOPSORT  IN    BUFFER(TAPEIN)    1       T1. Initialize. Read in the first
13           JBUS  *(TAPEIN)                    tape block; wait for completion.
14  1H       LD6   BUFFER+1         1        N ← n.
15           ENT4  0,6              1
16           STZ   X,4              n + 1    Set COUNT[k] ← 0 and TOP[k] ← Λ,
17           DEC4  1                n + 1        for 0 ≤ k ≤ n.
18           J4NN  *-2              n + 1    (Anticipate QLINK[0] ← 0 in step T4.)
19           ENT2  X,6              1        Available storage starts after X[n].
```

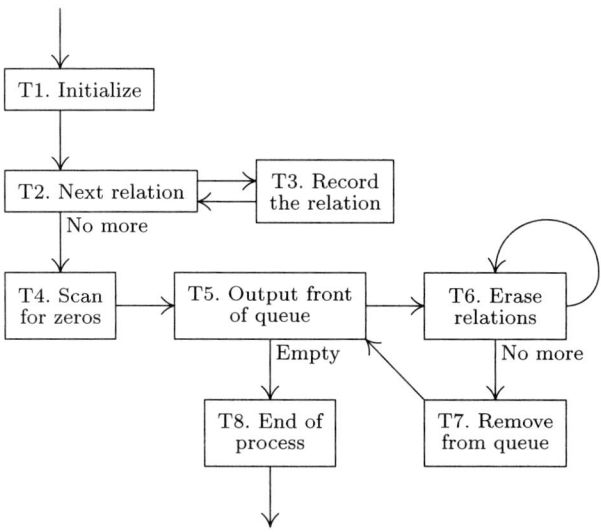

Fig. 9. Topological sorting.

20		ENT5 BUFFER+2	1	Prepare to read the first pair (j, k).
21	2H	LD3 0,5	$m + b$	*T2. Next relation.*
22		J3P 3F	$m + b$	Is $j > 0$?
23		J3Z 4F	b	Is input exhausted?
24		IN BUFFER(TAPEIN)	$b - 1$	Sentinel sensed; read another
25		JBUS *(TAPEIN)		tape block, wait for completion.
26		ENT5 BUFFER	$b - 1$	Reset the buffer pointer.
27		JMP 2B	$b - 1$	
28	3H	LD4 1,5	m	*T3. Record the relation.*
29		LDA X,4(COUNT)	m	COUNT[k]
30		INCA 1	m	+1
31		STA X,4(COUNT)	m	$\to$ COUNT[k].
32		INC2 1	m	AVAIL $\leftarrow$ AVAIL $+ 1$.
33		LDA X,3(TOP)	m	TOP[j]
34		STA 0,2(NEXT)	m	$\to$ NEXT(P).
35		ST4 0,2(SUC)	m	$k \to$ SUC(P).
36		ST2 X,3(TOP)	m	P $\to$ TOP[j].
37		INC5 2	m	Increase buffer pointer.
38		JMP 2B	m	
39	4H	IOC 0(TAPEIN)	1	Rewind the input tape.
40		ENT4 0,6	1	*T4. Scan for zeros.* $k \leftarrow n$.
41		ENT5 -100	1	Reset buffer pointer for output.
42		ENT3 0	1	R $\leftarrow 0$.
43	4H	LDA X,4(COUNT)	n	Examine COUNT[k].
44		JAP *+3	n	Is it nonzero?
45		ST4 X,3(QLINK)	a	QLINK[R] $\leftarrow k$.
46		ENT3 0,4	a	R $\leftarrow k$.
47		DEC4 1	n	
48		J4P 4B	n	$n \geq k \geq 1$.

```
49   *   SORTING PHASE
50           LD1   X(QLINK)              1       F ← QLINK[0].
51   5H      JBUS  *(TAPEOUT)                    T5. Output front of queue.
52           ST1   BUFFER+100,5          n + 1   Store F in buffer area.
53           J1Z   8F                    n + 1   Is F zero?
54           INC5  1                     n       Advance buffer pointer.
55           J5N   *+3                   n       Test if buffer is full.
56           OUT   BUFFER(TAPEOUT)       c − 1   If so, output a tape block.
57           ENT5  -100                  c − 1   Reset the buffer pointer.
58           DEC6  1                     n       N ← N − 1.
59           LD2   X,1(TOP)              n       P ← TOP[F].
60           J2Z   7F                    n       T6. Erase relations.
61   6H      LD4   0,2(SUC)              m       rI4 ← SUC(P).
62           LDA   X,4(COUNT)            m       COUNT[rI4]
63           DECA  1                     m       −1
64           STA   X,4(COUNT)            m       → COUNT[rI4].
65           JAP   *+3                   m       Has zero been reached?
66           ST4   X,3(QLINK)            n − a   If so, set QLINK[R] ← rI4.
67           ENT3  0,4                   n − a   R ← rI4.
68           LD2   0,2(NEXT)             m       P ← NEXT(P).
69           J2P   6B                    m       If P ≠ Λ, repeat.
70   7H      LD1   X,1(QLINK)            n       T7. Remove from queue.
71           JMP   5B                    n       F ← QLINK(F), go to T5.
72   8H      OUT   BUFFER(TAPEOUT)       1       T8. End of process.
73           IOC   0(TAPEOUT)            1       Output last block and rewind.
74           HLT   0,6                   1       Stop, displaying N on console.
75   X       END   TOPSORT                       Beginning of table area   ∎
```

The analysis of Algorithm T is quite simple with the aid of Kirchhoff's law; the execution time has the approximate form $c_1 m + c_2 n$, where m is the number of input relations, n is the number of objects, and c_1 and c_2 are constants. It is hard to imagine a faster algorithm for this problem! The exact quantities in the analysis are given with Program T above, where $a =$ number of objects with no predecessor, $b =$ number of tape records in input $= \lceil(m + 2)/50\rceil$, and $c =$ number of tape records in output $= \lceil(n + 1)/100\rceil$. Exclusive of input-output operations, the total running time in this case is only $(32m + 24n + 7b + 2c + 16)u$.

A topological sorting technique similar to Algorithm T (but without the important feature of the queue links) was first published by A. B. Kahn, *CACM* **5** (1962), 558–562. The fact that topological sorting of a partial ordering is always possible was first proved in print by E. Szpilrajn, *Fundamenta Mathematica* **16** (1930), 386–389; he proved it for infinite sets as well as finite sets, and mentioned that the result was already known to several of his colleagues.

In spite of the fact that Algorithm T is so efficient, we will study an even better algorithm for topological sorting in Section 7.4.1.

EXERCISES

▶ **1.** [*10*] Operation (9) for popping up a stack mentions the possibility of UNDERFLOW; why doesn't operation (8), pushing down a stack, mention the possibility of OVERFLOW?

2. [22] Write a "general purpose" MIX subroutine to do the insertion operation, (10). This subroutine should have the following specifications (as in Section 1.4.1):

Calling sequence: JMP INSERT   Jump to subroutine.
                  NOP T   Location of pointer variable
Entry conditions: rA = information to be put into the INFO field of a new node.
Exit conditions: The stack whose pointer is the link variable T has the new node on top; rI1 = T; rI2, rI3 are altered.

3. [22] Write a "general purpose" MIX subroutine to do the deletion operation, (11). This subroutine should have the following specifications:

Calling sequence: JMP DELETE   Jump to subroutine.
                  NOP T   Location of pointer variable
                  JMP UNDERFLOW First exit, if UNDERFLOW sensed
Entry conditions: None
Exit conditions: If the stack whose pointer is the link variable T is empty, the first exit is taken; otherwise the top node of that stack is deleted, and exit is made to the third location following "JMP DELETE". In the latter case, rI1 = T and rA is the contents of the INFO field of the deleted node. In either case, rI2 and rI3 are used by this subroutine.

4. [22] The program in (10) is based on the operation P ⇐ AVAIL, as given in (6). Show how to write an OVERFLOW subroutine so that, without *any* change in the coding (10), the operation P ⇐ AVAIL makes use of SEQMIN, as given by (7). For general-purpose use, your subroutine should not change the contents of any registers, except rJ and possibly the comparison indicator. It should exit to location rJ − 2, instead of the usual rJ.

▸ **5.** [24] Operations (14) and (17) give the effect of a queue; show how to define the further operation "insert at front" so as to obtain all the actions of an output-restricted deque. How could the operation "delete from rear" be defined (so that we would have a general deque)?

6. [21] In operation (14) we set LINK(P) ← Λ, while the very next insertion at the rear of the queue will change the value of this same link field. Show how the setting of LINK(P) in (14) could be avoided if we make a change to the testing of "F = Λ" in (17).

▸ **7.** [23] Design an algorithm to "invert" a linked linear list such as (1), that is, to change its links so that the items appear in the opposite order. [If, for example, the list (1) were inverted, we would have FIRST linking to the node containing item 5; that node would link to the one containing item 4; etc.] Assume that the nodes have the form (3).

8. [24] Write a MIX program for the problem of exercise 7, attempting to design your program to operate as fast as possible.

9. [20] Which of the following relations is a partial ordering on the specified set S? [*Note:* If the relation "$x \prec y$" is defined below, the intent is to define the relation "$x \preceq y \equiv (x \prec y \text{ or } x = y),$" and then to determine whether $\preceq$ is a partial ordering.] (a) S = all rational numbers, $x \prec y$ means $x > y$. (b) S = all people, $x \prec y$ means x is an ancestor of y. (c) S = all integers, $x \preceq y$ means x is a multiple of y (that is, $x \bmod y = 0$). (d) S = all the mathematical results proved in this book, $x \prec y$ means the proof of y depends upon the truth of x. (e) S = all positive integers, $x \preceq y$ means $x + y$ is even. (f) S = a set of subroutines, $x \prec y$ means "x calls y," that is, y may be in operation while x is in operation, with recursion not allowed.

10. [*M21*] Given that "⊂" is a relation that satisfies properties (i) and (ii) of a partial ordering, prove that the relation "≼", defined by the rule "$x \preceq y$ if and only if $x = y$ or $x \subset y$," satisfies all three properties of a partial ordering.

▶ **11.** [*24*] The result of topological sorting is not always completely determined, since there may be several ways to arrange the nodes and to satisfy the conditions of topological order. Find all possible ways to arrange the nodes of Fig. 6 into topological order.

12. [*M20*] There are 2^n subsets of a set of n elements, and these subsets are partially ordered by the set-inclusion relation. Give two interesting ways to arrange these subsets in topological order.

13. [*M48*] How many ways are there to arrange the 2^n subsets described in exercise 12 into topological order? (Give the answer as a function of n.)

14. [*M21*] A *linear ordering* of a set S, also called a *total ordering*, is a partial ordering that satisfies the additional "comparability" condition

> (iv)   For any two objects x, y in S, either $x \preceq y$ or $y \preceq x$.

Prove directly from the definitions given that a topological sort can result in only one possible output if and only if the relation $\preceq$ is a linear ordering. (You may assume that the set S is finite.)

15. [*M25*] Show that for any partial ordering on a finite set S there is a *unique* set of irredundant relations that characterizes this ordering, as in (18) and Fig. 6. Is the same fact true also when S is an infinite set?

16. [*M22*] Given any partial ordering on a set $S = \{x_1, \dots, x_n\}$, we can construct its *incidence matrix* (a_{ij}), where $a_{ij} = 1$ if $x_i \preceq x_j$, and $a_{ij} = 0$ otherwise. Show that there is a way to permute the rows and columns of this matrix so that all entries below the diagonal are zero.

▶ **17.** [*21*] What output does Algorithm T produce if it is presented with the input (18)?

18. [*20*] What, if anything, is the significance of the values of QLINK[0], QLINK[1], ..., QLINK[n] when Algorithm T terminates?

19. [*18*] In Algorithm T we examine the front position of the queue in step T5, but do not remove that element from the queue until step T7. What would happen if we set F ← QLINK[F] at the conclusion of step T5, instead of in T7?

▶ **20.** [*24*] Algorithm T uses F, R, and the QLINK table to obtain the effect of a queue that contains those nodes whose COUNT field has become zero but whose successor relations have not yet been removed. Could a stack be used for this purpose instead of a queue? If so, compare the resulting algorithm with Algorithm T.

21. [*21*] Would Algorithm T still perform a valid topological sort if one of the relations "$j \prec k$" were repeated several times in the input? What if the input contained a relation of the form "$j \prec j$"?

22. [*23*] Program T assumes that its input tape contains valid information, but a program that is intended for general use should always make careful tests on its input so that clerical errors can be detected, and so that the program cannot "destroy itself." For example, if one of the input relations for k were negative, Program T may erroneously change one of its own instructions when storing into X[k]. Suggest ways to modify Program T so that it is suitable for general use.

▶ **23.** [*27*] When the topological sort algorithm cannot proceed because it has detected a loop in the input (see step T8), it is usually of no use to stop and say, "There was a loop." It is helpful to print out one of the loops, thereby showing part of the input that was in error. Extend Algorithm T so that it will do this additional printing of a loop when necessary. [*Hint:* The text gives a proof for the existence of a loop when $N > 0$ in step T8; that proof suggests an algorithm.]

24. [*24*] Incorporate the extensions of Algorithm T made in exercise 23 into Program T.

25. [*47*] Design as efficient an algorithm as possible for doing a topological sort of very large sets S having considerably more nodes than the computer memory can contain. Assume that the input, output, and temporary working space are done with magnetic tape. [*Possible hint:* A conventional sort of the input allows us to assume that all relations for a given node appear together. But then what can be done? In particular, we must consider the worst case in which the given ordering is already a linear ordering that has been wildly permuted; exercise 24 in the introduction to Chapter 5 explains how to handle this case with $O(\log n)^2$ passes over the data.]

26. [*29*] (*Subroutine allocation.*) Suppose that we have a tape containing the main subroutine library in relocatable form, for a 1960s-style computer installation. The loading routine wants to determine the amount of relocation for each subroutine used, so that it can make one pass through the tape to load the necessary routines. The problem is that some subroutines require others to be present in memory. Infrequently used subroutines (which appear toward the end of the tape) may call on frequently used subroutines (which appear toward the beginning of the tape), and we want to know all of the subroutines that are required, before passing through the tape.

One way to tackle this problem is to have a "tape directory" that fits in memory. The loading routine has access to two tables:

a) The tape directory. This table is composed of variable-length nodes having the form

B	SPACE	LINK		B	SPACE	LINK
B	SUB1	SUB2		B	SUB1	SUB2
⋮			or	⋮		
B	SUBn	0		B	SUB$(n-1)$	SUBn

where SPACE is the number of words of memory required by the subroutine; LINK is a link to the directory entry for the subroutine that appears on the tape following this subroutine; SUB1, SUB2, ..., SUBn ($n \geq 0$) are links to the directory entries for any other subroutines required by this one; B = 0 on all words except the last, B = −1 on the last word of a node. The address of the directory entry for the first subroutine on the library tape is specified by the link variable FIRST.

b) The list of subroutines directly referred to by the program to be loaded. This is stored in consecutive locations X[1], X[2], ..., X[N], where $N \geq 0$ is a variable known to the loading routine. Each entry in this list is a link to the directory entry for the subroutine desired.

The loading routine also knows MLOC, the amount of relocation to be used for the first subroutine loaded.

As a small example, consider the following configuration:

	Tape directory			List of subroutines needed
	B	SPACE	LINK	X[1] = 1003
1000:	0	20	1005	X[2] = 1010
1001:	−1	1002	0	
1002:	−1	30	1010	N = 2
1003:	0	200	1007	FIRST = 1002
1004:	−1	1000	1006	MLOC = 2400
1005:	−1	100	1003	
1006:	−1	60	1000	
1007:	0	200	0	
1008:	0	1005	1002	
1009:	−1	1006	0	
1010:	−1	20	1006	

The tape directory in this case shows that the subroutines on tape are 1002, 1010, 1006, 1000, 1005, 1003, and 1007 in that order. Subroutine 1007 takes 200 locations and implies the use of subroutines 1005, 1002, and 1006; etc. The program to be loaded requires subroutines 1003 and 1010, which are to be placed into locations ≥ 2400. These subroutines in turn imply that 1000, 1006, and 1002 must also be loaded.

The subroutine allocator is to change the X-table so that each entry X[1], X[2], X[3], ... has the form

+	0	BASE	SUB

(except the last entry, which is explained below), where SUB is a subroutine to be loaded, and BASE is the amount of relocation. These entries are to be in the order in which the subroutines appear on tape. One possible answer for the example above would be

	BASE	SUB		BASE	SUB
X[1]:	2400	1002	X[4]:	2510	1000
X[2]:	2430	1010	X[5]:	2530	1003
X[3]:	2450	1006	X[6]:	2730	0

The last entry contains the first unused memory address.

(Clearly, this is not the only way to treat a library of subroutines. The proper way to design a library is heavily dependent upon the computer used and the applications to be handled. Large modern computers require an entirely different approach to subroutine libraries. But this is a nice exercise anyway, because it involves interesting manipulations on both sequential and linked data.)

The problem in this exercise is to design an algorithm for the stated task. Your allocator may transform the tape directory in any way as it prepares its answer, since the tape directory can be read in anew by the subroutine allocator on its next assignment, and the tape directory is not needed by other parts of the loading routine.

27. [*25*] Write a MIX program for the subroutine allocation algorithm of exercise 26.

28. [*40*] The following construction shows how to "solve" a fairly general type of two-person game, including chess, nim, and many simpler games: Consider a finite set of nodes, each of which represents a possible position in the game. For each position there are zero or more moves that transform that position into some other position. We say that position x is a predecessor of position y (and y is a successor of x) if there is a move from x to y. Certain positions that have no successors are classified as *won* or *lost* positions. The player to move in position x is the opponent of the player to move in the successors of position x.

Given such a configuration of positions, we can compute the complete set of won positions (those in which the next player to move can force a victory) and the complete set of lost positions (those in which the player must lose against an expert opponent) by repeatedly doing the following operation until it yields no change: Mark a position "lost" if all its successors are marked "won"; mark a position "won" if at least one of its successors is marked "lost."

After this operation has been repeated as many times as possible, there may be some positions that have not been marked at all; a player in such a position can neither force a victory nor be compelled to lose.

This procedure for obtaining the complete set of won and lost positions can be adapted to an efficient algorithm for computers that closely resembles Algorithm T. We may keep with each position a count of the number of its successors that have not been marked "won," and a list of all its predecessors.

The problem in this exercise is to work out the details of the algorithm that has just been so vaguely described, and to apply it to some interesting games that do not involve too many possible positions [like the "military game": É. Lucas, *Récréations Mathématiques* **3** (Paris: 1893) 105–116; E. R. Berlekamp, J. H. Conway, and R. K. Guy, *Winning Ways* **3** (A. K. Peters, 2003), Chapter 21].

▶ **29.** [*21*] (a) Give an algorithm to "erase" an entire list like (1), by putting all of its nodes on the AVAIL stack, given only the value of FIRST. The algorithm should operate as fast as possible. (b) Repeat part (a) for a list like (12), given the values of F and R.

30. [*17*] Suppose that queues are represented as in (12), but with an empty queue represented by $F = \Lambda$ and R *undefined*. What insertion and deletion procedures should replace (14) and (17)?

2.2.4. Circular Lists

A slight change in the manner of linking furnishes us with an important alternative to the methods of the preceding section.

A *circularly linked list* (briefly: a circular list) has the property that its last node links back to the first instead of to Λ. It is then possible to access all of the list starting at any given point; we also achieve an extra degree of symmetry, and if we choose we need not think of the list as having a last or first node.

The following situation is typical:

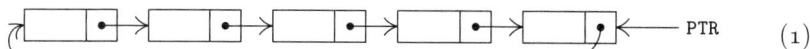

$$(1)$$

Assume that the nodes have two fields, INFO and LINK, as in the preceding section. There is a link variable PTR that points to the rightmost node of the list, and LINK(PTR) is the address of the leftmost node. The following primitive operations are most important:

a) Insert Y at left: P $\Leftarrow$ AVAIL, INFO(P) $\leftarrow$ Y, LINK(P) $\leftarrow$ LINK(PTR),
LINK(PTR) $\leftarrow$ P.
b) Insert Y at right: Insert Y at left, then PTR $\leftarrow$ P.
c) Set Y to left node and delete: P $\leftarrow$ LINK(PTR), Y $\leftarrow$ INFO(P), LINK(PTR) $\leftarrow$
LINK(P), AVAIL $\Leftarrow$ P.

Operation (b) is a little surprising at first glance; the operation PTR ← LINK(PTR)
effectively moves the leftmost node to the right in the diagram (1), and this is
quite easy to understand if the list is regarded as a circle instead of as a straight
line with connected ends.

The alert reader will observe that we have made a serious mistake in operations (a), (b), and (c). What is it? *Answer:* We have forgotten to consider the
possibility of an *empty* list. If, for example, operation (c) is applied five times
to the list (1), we will have PTR pointing to a node in the AVAIL list, and this
can lead to serious difficulties; for example, imagine applying operation (c) once
more! If we take the position that PTR will equal Λ in the case of an empty
list, we could remedy the operations by inserting the additional instructions "if
PTR = Λ, then PTR ← LINK(P) ← P; otherwise ..." after "INFO(P) ← Y" in (a);
preceding (c) by the test "if PTR = Λ, then UNDERFLOW"; and following (c) by "if
PTR = P, then PTR ← Λ".

Notice that operations (a), (b), and (c) give us the actions of an output-
restricted deque, in the sense of Section 2.2.1. Therefore we find in particular
that a circular list can be used as either a stack or a queue. Operations (a)
and (c) combined give us a stack; operations (b) and (c) give us a queue. These
operations are only slightly less direct than their counterparts in the previous
section, where we saw that operations (a), (b), and (c) can be performed on
linear lists using two pointers F and R.

Other important operations become efficient with circular lists. For example,
it is very convenient to "erase" a list, that is, to put an entire circular list onto
the AVAIL stack at once:

$$\text{If PTR} \neq \Lambda, \text{ then AVAIL} \leftrightarrow \text{LINK(PTR)}. \tag{2}$$

[Recall that the "↔" operation denotes interchange: P ← AVAIL, AVAIL ←
LINK(PTR), LINK(PTR) ← P.] Operation (2) is clearly valid if PTR points *anywhere* in the circular list. Afterwards we should of course set PTR ← Λ.

Using a similar technique, if PTR₁ and PTR₂ point to disjoint circular lists L₁
and L₂, respectively, we can insert the entire list L₂ at the right of L₁:

$$\text{If PTR}_2 \neq \Lambda, \text{ then}$$
$$(\text{if PTR}_1 \neq \Lambda, \text{ then LINK(PTR}_1) \leftrightarrow \text{LINK(PTR}_2); \tag{3}$$
$$\text{set PTR}_1 \leftarrow \text{PTR}_2, \text{PTR}_2 \leftarrow \Lambda).$$

Splitting one circular list into two, in various ways, is another simple operation that can be done. These operations correspond to the concatenation and
deconcatenation of strings.

Thus we see that a circular list can be used not only to represent inherently
circular structures, but also to represent linear structures; a circular list with one
pointer to the rear node is essentially equivalent to a straight linear list with two
pointers to the front and rear. The natural question to ask, in connection with
this observation, is "How do we find the end of the list, when there is circular
symmetry?" There is no Λ link to signal the end! The answer is that when we

are operating on an entire list, moving from one node to the next, we should stop when we get back to our starting place (assuming, of course, that the starting place is still present in the list).

An alternative solution to the problem just posed is to put a special, recognizable node into each circular list, as a convenient stopping place. This special node is called the *list head,* and in applications we often find it is quite convenient to insist that every circular list have exactly one node that is its list head. One advantage is that the circular list will then never be empty. With a list head, diagram (1) becomes

List head

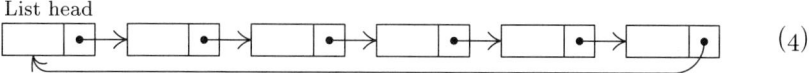
$$(4)$$

References to lists like (4) are usually made via the list head, which is often in a fixed memory location. The disadvantage of list heads is that there is no pointer to the right end, so we must sacrifice operation (b) stated above.

Diagram (4) may be compared with 2.2.3–(1) at the beginning of the previous section, in which the link associated with "item 5" now points to LOC(FIRST) instead of to Λ; the variable FIRST is now thought of as a link within a node, namely the link that is in NODE(LOC(FIRST)). The principal difference between (4) and 2.2.3–(1) is that (4) makes it possible (though not necessarily efficient) to get to any point of the list from any other point.

As an example of the use of circular lists, we will discuss *arithmetic on polynomials* in the variables x, y, and z, with integer coefficients. There are many problems in which a scientist wants to manipulate polynomials instead of just numbers; we are thinking of operations like the multiplication of

$$(x^4 + 2x^3y + 3x^2y^2 + 4xy^3 + 5y^4) \qquad \text{by} \qquad (x^2 - 2xy + y^2)$$

to get

$$(x^6 - 6xy^5 + 5y^6).$$

Linked allocation is a natural tool for this purpose, since polynomials can grow to unpredictable sizes and we may want to represent many polynomials in memory at the same time.

We will consider here the two operations of addition and multiplication. Let us suppose that a polynomial is represented as a list in which each node stands for one nonzero term, and has the two-word form

COEF			
± A	B	C	LINK

$$(5)$$

Here COEF is the coefficient of the term in $x^A y^B z^C$. We will assume that the coefficients and exponents will always lie in the range allowed by this format, and that it is not necessary to check the ranges during our calculations. The notation ABC will be used to stand for the ± A B C fields of the node (5), treated as a single unit. The sign of ABC, namely the sign of the second word in (5), will always be

plus, except that there is a *special node* at the end of every polynomial that has
$ABC = -1$ and $COEF = 0$. This special node is a great convenience, analogous to
our discussion of a list head above, because it provides a convenient sentinel and
it avoids the problem of an empty list (corresponding to the polynomial 0). The
nodes of the list always appear in *decreasing order* of the ABC field, if we follow
the direction of the links, except that the special node (which has $ABC = -1$)
links to the largest value of ABC. For example, the polynomial $x^6 - 6xy^5 + 5y^6$
would be represented thus:

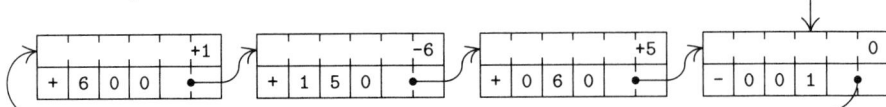

Algorithm A (*Addition of polynomials*). This algorithm adds polynomial(P)
to polynomial(Q), assuming that P and Q are pointer variables pointing to
polynomials having the form above. The list P will be unchanged; the list Q
will retain the sum. Pointer variables P and Q return to their starting points
at the conclusion of this algorithm; auxiliary pointer variables Q1 and Q2 are
also used.

A1. [Initialize.] Set $P \leftarrow LINK(P)$, $Q1 \leftarrow Q$, $Q \leftarrow LINK(Q)$. (Now both P and Q
point to the leading terms of their polynomials. Throughout most of this
algorithm the variable Q1 will be one step behind Q, in the sense that Q =
LINK(Q1).)

A2. [ABC(P):ABC(Q).] If $ABC(P) < ABC(Q)$, set $Q1 \leftarrow Q$ and $Q \leftarrow LINK(Q)$ and
repeat this step. If $ABC(P) = ABC(Q)$, go to step A3. If $ABC(P) > ABC(Q)$,
go to step A5.

A3. [Add coefficients.] (We've found terms with equal exponents.) If $ABC(P) < 0$,
the algorithm terminates. Otherwise set $COEF(Q) \leftarrow COEF(Q) + COEF(P)$.
Now if $COEF(Q) = 0$, go to A4; otherwise, set $P \leftarrow LINK(P)$, $Q1 \leftarrow Q$,
$Q \leftarrow LINK(Q)$, and go to A2. (Curiously the latter operations are identical
to step A1.)

A4. [Delete zero term.] Set $Q2 \leftarrow Q$, $LINK(Q1) \leftarrow Q \leftarrow LINK(Q)$, and $AVAIL \Leftarrow$
Q2. (A zero term created in step A3 has been removed from polynomial(Q).)
Set $P \leftarrow LINK(P)$ and go back to A2.

A5. [Insert new term.] (Polynomial(P) contains a term that is not present
in polynomial(Q), so we insert it in polynomial(Q).) Set $Q2 \Leftarrow AVAIL$,
$COEF(Q2) \leftarrow COEF(P)$, $ABC(Q2) \leftarrow ABC(P)$, $LINK(Q2) \leftarrow Q$, $LINK(Q1) \leftarrow Q2$,
$Q1 \leftarrow Q2$, $P \leftarrow LINK(P)$, and return to step A2. ∎

One of the most noteworthy features of Algorithm A is the manner in which
the pointer variable Q1 follows the pointer Q around the list. This is very typical
of list processing algorithms, and we will see a dozen more algorithms with the
same characteristic. Can the reader see why this idea was used in Algorithm A?

A reader who has little prior experience with linked lists will find it very
instructive to study Algorithm A carefully; as a test case, try adding $x + y + z$
to $x^2 - 2y - z$.

Given Algorithm A, the multiplication operation is surprisingly easy:

Algorithm M (*Multiplication of polynomials*). This algorithm, analogous to Algorithm A, replaces polynomial(Q) by

$$\text{polynomial(Q)} + \text{polynomial(M)} \times \text{polynomial(P)}.$$

M1. [Next multiplier.] Set M ← LINK(M). If ABC(M) < 0, the algorithm terminates.

M2. [Multiply cycle.] Perform Algorithm A, except that wherever the notation "ABC(P)" appears in that algorithm, replace it by "(if ABC(P) < 0 then −1, otherwise ABC(P) + ABC(M))"; wherever "COEF(P)" appears in that algorithm replace it by "COEF(P) × COEF(M)". Then go back to step M1. ∎

The programming of Algorithm A in MIX language shows again the ease with which linked lists are manipulated in a computer. In the following code we assume that OVERFLOW is a subroutine that either terminates the program (due to lack of memory space) or finds further available space and exits to rJ − 2.

Program A (*Addition of polynomials*). This is a subroutine written so that it can be used in conjunction with a multiplication subroutine (see exercise 15).

Calling sequence: JMP   ADD
Entry conditions: rI1 = P, rI2 = Q.
Exit conditions: polynomial(Q) has been replaced by polynomial(Q) + polynomial(P); rI1 and rI2 are unchanged; all other registers have undefined contents.

In the coding below, P ≡ rI1, Q ≡ rI2, Q1 ≡ rI3, and Q2 ≡ rI6, in the notation of Algorithm A.

01	LINK	EQU	4:5		Definition of LINK field
02	ABC	EQU	0:3		Definition of ABC field
03	ADD	STJ	3F	1	Entrance to subroutine
04	1H	ENT3	0,2	$1 + m''$	*A1. Initialize.* Set Q1 ← Q.
05		LD2	1,3(LINK)	$1 + m''$	Q ← LINK(Q1).
06	0H	LD1	1,1(LINK)	$1 + p$	P ← LINK(P).
07	SW1	LDA	1,1	$1 + p$	rA(0:3) ← ABC(P).
08	2H	CMPA	1,2(ABC)	x	*A2. ABC(P):ABC(Q).*
09		JE	3F	x	If equal, go to A3.
10		JG	5F	$p' + q'$	If greater, go to A5.
11		ENT3	0,2	q'	If less, set Q1 ← Q.
12		LD2	1,3(LINK)	q'	Q ← LINK(Q1).
13		JMP	2B	q'	Repeat.
14	3H	JAN	*	$m + 1$	*A3. Add coefficients.*
15	SW2	LDA	0,1	m	COEF(P)
16		ADD	0,2	m	+ COEF(Q)
17		STA	0,2	m	→ COEF(Q).
18		JANZ	1B	m	Jump if nonzero.

19		ENT6	0,2	m'	*A4. Delete zero term.* Q2 ← Q.
20		LD2	1,2(LINK)	m'	Q ← LINK(Q).
21		LDX	AVAIL	m'	⎫
22		STX	1,6(LINK)	m'	⎬ AVAIL ⇐ Q2.
23		ST6	AVAIL	m'	⎭
24		ST2	1,3(LINK)	m'	LINK(Q1) ← Q.
25		JMP	0B	m'	Go to advance P.
26	5H	LD6	AVAIL	p'	⎫ *A5. Insert new term.*
27		J6Z	OVERFLOW	p'	⎬ Q2 ⇐ AVAIL.
28		LDX	1,6(LINK)	p'	⎪
29		STX	AVAIL	p'	⎭
30		STA	1,6	p'	ABC(Q2) ← ABC(P).
31	SW3	LDA	0,1	p'	rA ← COEF(P).
32		STA	0,6	p'	COEF(Q2) ← rA.
33		ST2	1,6(LINK)	p'	LINK(Q2) ← Q.
34		ST6	1,3(LINK)	p'	LINK(Q1) ← Q2.
35		ENT3	0,6	p'	Q1 ← Q2.
36		JMP	0B	p'	Go to advance P. ∎

Note that Algorithm A traverses each of the two lists just once; it is not necessary to loop around several times. Using Kirchhoff's law, we find that an analysis of the instruction counts presents no difficulties; the execution time depends on four quantities

m' = number of matching terms that cancel with each other;
m'' = number of matching terms that do not cancel;
p' = number of unmatched terms in polynomial(P);
q' = number of unmatched terms in polynomial(Q).

The analysis given with Program A uses the abbreviations

$$m = m' + m'', \quad p = m + p', \quad q = m + q', \quad x = 1 + m + p' + q';$$

the running time for MIX is $(27m' + 18m'' + 27p' + 8q' + 13)u$. The total number of nodes in the storage pool needed during the execution of the algorithm is at least $2 + p + q$, and at most $2 + p + q + p'$.

EXERCISES

1. [*21*] The text suggests at the beginning of this section that an empty circular list could be represented by PTR = Λ. It might be more consistent with the philosophy of circular lists to have PTR = LOC(PTR) indicate an empty list. Does this convention facilitate operations (a), (b), or (c) described at the beginning of this section?

2. [*20*] Draw "before and after" diagrams illustrating the effect of the concatenation operation (3), assuming that PTR₁ and PTR₂ are ≠ Λ.

▶ **3.** [*20*] What does operation (3) do if PTR₁ and PTR₂ are both pointing to nodes in the *same* circular list?

4. [*20*] State insertion and deletion operations that give the effect of a *stack*, using representation (4).

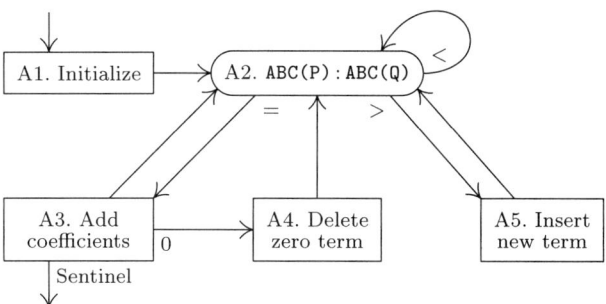

Fig. 10. Addition of polynomials.

▶ **5.** [*21*] Design an algorithm that takes a circular list such as (1) and reverses the direction of all the arrows.

6. [*18*] Give diagrams of the list representation for the polynomials (a) $xz - 3$; (b) 0.

7. [*10*] Why is it useful to assume that the ABC fields of a polynomial list appear in decreasing order?

▶ **8.** [*10*] Why is it useful to have Q1 trailing one step behind Q in Algorithm A?

▶ **9.** [*23*] Would Algorithm A work properly if P = Q (i.e., both pointer variables point at the same polynomial)? Would Algorithm M work properly if P = M, if P = Q, or if M = Q?

▶ **10.** [*20*] The algorithms in this section assume that we are using three variables x, y, and z in the polynomials, and that their exponents individually never exceed $b - 1$ (where b is the byte size in MIX's case). Suppose instead that we want to do addition and multiplication of polynomials in only one variable, x, and to let its exponent take on values up to $b^3 - 1$. What changes should be made to Algorithms A and M?

11. [*24*] (The purpose of this exercise and many of those following is to create a package of subroutines useful for polynomial arithmetic, in conjunction with Program A.) Since Algorithms A and M change the value of polynomial(Q), it is sometimes desirable to have a subroutine that makes a copy of a given polynomial. Write a MIX subroutine with the following specifications:

Calling sequence: JMP   COPY
Entry conditions: rI1 = P
Exit conditions: rI2 points to a newly created polynomial equal to polynomial(P);
                   rI1 is unchanged; other registers are undefined.

12. [*21*] Compare the running time of the program in exercise 11 with that of Program A when polynomial(Q) = 0.

13. [*20*] Write a MIX subroutine with the following specifications:

Calling sequence: JMP   ERASE
Entry conditions: rI1 = P
Exit conditions: polynomial(P) has been added to the AVAIL list; all register contents
                   are undefined.

[*Note:* This subroutine can be used in conjunction with the subroutine of exercise 11 in the sequence "LD1 Q; JMP ERASE; LD1 P; JMP COPY; ST2 Q" to achieve the effect "polynomial(Q) ← polynomial(P)".]

14. [*22*] Write a MIX subroutine with the following specifications:

Calling sequence: JMP   ZERO
Entry conditions: None
Exit conditions: rI2 points to a newly created polynomial equal to 0; other register
                   contents are undefined.

15. [*24*] Write a MIX subroutine to perform Algorithm M, having the following specifications:

Calling sequence: JMP   MULT
Entry conditions: rI1 = P, rI2 = Q, rI4 = M.
Exit conditions: polynomial(Q) ← polynomial(Q) + polynomial(M) × polynomial(P);
                   rI1, rI2, rI4 are unchanged; other registers undefined.

[*Note:* Use Program A as a subroutine, changing the settings of SW1, SW2, and SW3.]

16. [*M28*] Estimate the running time of the subroutine in exercise 15 in terms of some
relevant parameters.

▶ **17.** [*22*] What advantage is there in representing polynomials with a circular list as
in this section, instead of with a straight linear linked list terminated by Λ as in the
previous section?

▶ **18.** [*25*] Devise a way to represent circular lists inside a computer in such a way that
the list can be traversed efficiently in both directions, yet only one link field is used
per node. [*Hint:* If we are given two pointers, to two successive nodes x_{i-1} and x_i, it
should be possible to locate both x_{i+1} and x_{i-2}.]

2.2.5. Doubly Linked Lists

For even greater flexibility in the manipulation of linear lists, we can include two
links in each node, pointing to the items on either side of that node:

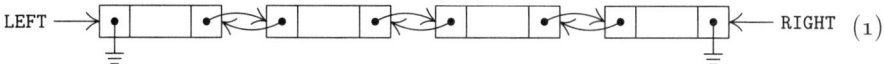

Here LEFT and RIGHT are pointer variables to the left and right of the list. Each
node of the list includes two links, called, for example, LLINK and RLINK. The
operations of a general deque are readily performed with such a representation;
see exercise 1. However, manipulations of doubly linked lists almost always
become much easier if a *list head* node is part of each list, as described in the
preceding section. When a list head is present, we have the following typical
diagram of a doubly linked list:

List head

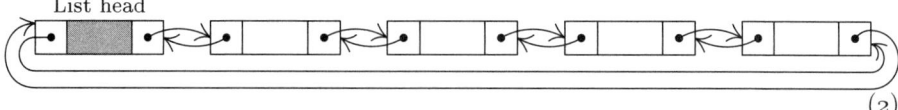

$$(2)$$

The RLINK and LLINK fields of the list head take the place of LEFT and RIGHT
in (1). There is complete symmetry between left and right; the list head could
equally well have been shown at the right of (2). If the list is empty, both link
fields of the list head point to the head itself.

The list representation (2) clearly satisfies the condition

$$\text{RLINK(LLINK(X))} = \text{LLINK(RLINK(X))} = \text{X} \qquad (3)$$

if X is the location of any node in the list (including the head). This fact is the principal reason that representation (2) is preferable to (1).

A doubly linked list usually takes more memory space than a singly linked one does (although there is sometimes room for another link in a node that doesn't fill a complete computer word). But the additional operations that can be performed efficiently with two-way links are often more than ample compensation for the extra space requirement. Besides the obvious advantage of being able to go back and forth at will when examining a doubly linked list, one of the principal new abilities is the fact that *we can delete* NODE(X) *from the list it is in, given only the value of* X. This deletion operation is easy to derive from a "before and after" diagram (Fig. 11) and it is very simple:

$$\text{RLINK(LLINK(X))} \leftarrow \text{RLINK(X)}, \qquad \text{LLINK(RLINK(X))} \leftarrow \text{LLINK(X)},$$
$$\text{AVAIL} \Leftarrow \text{X}. \tag{4}$$

In a list that has only one-way links, we cannot delete NODE(X) without knowing which node precedes it in the chain, since the preceding node needs to have its link altered when NODE(X) is deleted. In all the algorithms considered in Sections 2.2.3 and 2.2.4 this additional knowledge was present whenever a node was to be deleted; see, in particular, Algorithm 2.2.4A, where we had pointer Q1 following pointer Q for just this purpose. But we will meet several algorithms that require removing random nodes from the middle of a list, and doubly linked lists are frequently used just for this reason. (We should point out that in a circular list it is possible to delete NODE(X), given X, if we go around the entire circle to find the predecessor of X. But this operation is clearly inefficient when the list is long, so it is rarely an acceptable substitute for doubly linking the list. See also the answer to exercise 2.2.4–8.)

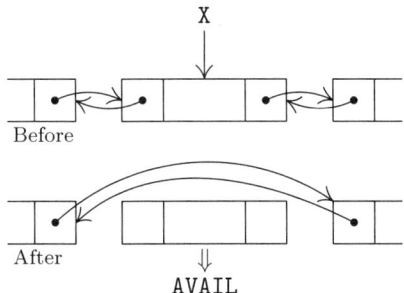

Fig. 11. Deletion from a doubly linked list.

Similarly, a doubly linked list permits the easy insertion of a node adjacent to NODE(X) at either the left or the right. The steps

$$\text{P} \Leftarrow \text{AVAIL}, \qquad \text{LLINK(P)} \leftarrow \text{X}, \qquad \text{RLINK(P)} \leftarrow \text{RLINK(X)},$$
$$\text{LLINK(RLINK(X))} \leftarrow \text{P}, \qquad \text{RLINK(X)} \leftarrow \text{P} \tag{5}$$

do such an insertion to the right of NODE(X); and by interchanging left and right we get the corresponding algorithm for insertion to the left. Operation (5) changes the settings of five links, so it is a little slower than an insertion operation in a one-way list where only three links need to be changed.

As an example of the use of doubly linked lists, we will now consider the writing of a *discrete simulation* program. "Discrete simulation" means the simulation of a system in which all changes in the state of the system may be assumed to happen at certain discrete instants of time. The "system" being simulated is usually a set of individual activities that are largely independent although they interact with each other; examples are customers at a store, ships in a harbor, people in a corporation. In a discrete simulation, we proceed by doing whatever is to be done at a certain instant of simulated time, then advance the simulated clock to the next time when some action is scheduled to occur.

By contrast, a "continuous simulation" would be simulation of activities that are under continuous changes, such as traffic moving on a highway, spaceships traveling to other planets, etc. Continuous simulation can often be satisfactorily approximated by discrete simulation with very small time intervals between steps; however, in such a case we usually have "synchronous" discrete simulation, in which many parts of the system are slightly altered at each discrete time interval, and such an application generally calls for a somewhat different type of program organization than the kind considered here.

The program developed below simulates the elevator system in the Mathematics building of the California Institute of Technology. The results of such a simulation will perhaps be of use only to people who make reasonably frequent visits to Caltech; and even for them, it may be simpler just to try using the elevator several times instead of writing a computer program. But, as is usual with simulation studies, the methods we will use are of much more interest than the answers given by the program. The methods to be discussed below illustrate typical implementation techniques used with discrete simulation programs.

The Mathematics building has five floors: sub-basement, basement, first, second, and third. There is a single elevator, which has automatic controls and can stop at each floor. For convenience we will renumber the floors 0, 1, 2, 3, and 4.

On each floor there are two call buttons, one for UP and one for DOWN. (Actually floor 0 has only UP and floor 4 has only DOWN, but we may ignore that anomaly since the excess buttons will never be used.) Corresponding to these buttons, there are ten variables CALLUP[j] and CALLDOWN[j], $0 \le j \le 4$. There are also variables CALLCAR[j], $0 \le j \le 4$, representing buttons within the elevator car, which direct it to a destination floor. When a person presses a button, the appropriate variable is set to 1; the elevator clears the variable to 0 after the request has been fulfilled.

So far we have described the elevator from a user's point of view; the situation is more interesting as viewed by the elevator. The elevator is in one of three states: GOINGUP, GOINGDOWN, or NEUTRAL. (The current state is indicated to passengers by lighted arrows inside the elevator.) If it is in NEUTRAL state and not on floor 2, the machine will close its doors and (if no command is given by the time its doors are shut) it will change to GOINGUP or GOINGDOWN, heading for floor 2. (This is the "home floor," since most passengers get in there.) On floor 2 in NEUTRAL state, the doors will eventually close and the machine will wait silently for another command. The first command received for another floor sets the machine GOINGUP or GOINGDOWN as appropriate; it stays in this state until there are no commands waiting in the same direction, and then it switches direction or switches to NEUTRAL just before opening the doors, depending on what other commands are in the CALL variables. The elevator takes a certain amount of time to open and close its doors, to accelerate and decelerate, and to get from one floor to another. All of these quantities are indicated in the algorithm below, which is much more precise than an informal description can be. The algorithm we will now study may not reflect the elevator's true principles of operation, but it is believed to be the simplest set of rules that explain all the phenomena observed during several hours of experimentation by the author during the writing of this section.

The elevator system is simulated by using two coroutines, one for the passengers and one for the elevator; these routines specify all the actions to be performed, as well as various time delays that are to be used in the simulation. In the following description, the variable TIME represents the current value of the simulated time clock. All units of time are given in *tenths of seconds*. There are also several other variables:

> FLOOR, the current position of the elevator;
> D1, a variable that is zero except during the time people are getting in or out of the elevator;
> D2, a variable that becomes zero if the elevator has sat on one floor without moving for 30 sec or more;
> D3, a variable that is zero except when the doors are open but nobody is getting in or out of the elevator;
> STATE, the current state of the elevator (GOINGUP, GOINGDOWN, or NEUTRAL).

Initially FLOOR = 2, D1 = D2 = D3 = 0, and STATE = NEUTRAL.

Coroutine U (*Users*). Everyone who enters the system begins to perform the actions specified below, starting at step U1.

U1. [Enter, prepare for successor.] The following quantities are determined in some manner that will not be specified here:

> IN, the floor on which the new user has entered the system;
> OUT, the floor to which this user wants to go (OUT ≠ IN);
> GIVEUPTIME, the amount of time this user will wait for the elevator before running out of patience and deciding to walk;
> INTERTIME, the amount of time before another user will enter the system.

After these quantities have been computed, the simulation program sets things up so that another user enters the system at TIME + INTERTIME.

U2. [Signal and wait.] (The purpose of this step is to call for the elevator; some special cases arise if the elevator is already on the right floor.) If FLOOR = IN and if the elevator's next action is step E6 below (that is, if the elevator doors are now closing), send the elevator immediately to its step E3 and cancel its activity E6. (This means that the doors will open again before the elevator moves.) If FLOOR = IN and if D3 ≠ 0, set D3 ← 0, set D1 to a nonzero value, and start up the elevator's activity E4 again. (This means that the elevator doors are open on this floor, but everyone else has already gotten on or off. Elevator step E4 is a sequencing step that grants people permission to enter the elevator according to normal laws of courtesy; therefore, restarting E4 gives this user a chance to get in before the doors close.) In all other cases, the user sets CALLUP[IN] ← 1 or CALLDOWN[IN] ← 1, according as OUT > IN or OUT < IN; and if D2 = 0 or the elevator is in its "dormant" position E1, the DECISION subroutine specified below is performed. (The DECISION subroutine is used to take the elevator out of NEUTRAL state at certain critical times.)

U3. [Enter queue.] Insert this user at the rear of QUEUE[IN], which is a linear list representing the people waiting on this floor. Now the user waits patiently for GIVEUPTIME units of time, unless the elevator arrives first — more precisely, unless step E4 of the elevator routine below sends this user to U5 and cancels the scheduled activity U4.

U4. [Give up.] If FLOOR ≠ IN or D1 = 0, delete this user from QUEUE[IN] and from the simulated system. (The user has decided that the elevator is too slow, or that a bit of exercise will be better than an elevator ride.) If FLOOR = IN and D1 ≠ 0, the user stays and waits (knowing that the wait won't be long).

U5. [Get in.] This user now leaves QUEUE[IN] and enters ELEVATOR, which is a stack-like list representing the people now on board the elevator. Set CALLCAR[OUT] ← 1.

Now if STATE = NEUTRAL, set STATE ← GOINGUP or GOINGDOWN as appropriate, and set the elevator's activity E5 to be executed after 25 units of time. (This is a special feature of the elevator, allowing the doors to close faster than usual if the elevator is in NEUTRAL state when the user selects a destination floor. The 25-unit time interval gives step E4 the opportunity to make sure that D1 is properly set up by the time step E5, the door-closing action, occurs.)

Now the user waits until being sent to step U6 by step E4 below, when the elevator has reached the desired floor.

U6. [Get out.] Delete this user from the ELEVATOR list and from the simulated system.   ∎

Coroutine E (*Elevator*). This coroutine represents the actions of the elevator; step E4 also handles the control of when people get in and out.

E1. [Wait for call.] (At this point the elevator is sitting at floor 2 with the doors closed, waiting for something to happen.) If someone presses a button, the DECISION subroutine will take us to step E3 or E6. Meanwhile, wait.

E2. [Change of state?] If STATE = GOINGUP and CALLUP[j] = CALLDOWN[j] = CALLCAR[j] = 0 for all j > FLOOR, then set STATE ← NEUTRAL or STATE ←

GOINGDOWN, according as CALLCAR[j] = 0 for all $j <$ FLOOR or not, and set all CALL variables for the current floor to zero. If STATE = GOINGDOWN, do similar actions with directions reversed.

E3. [Open doors.] Set D1 and D2 to any nonzero values. Set elevator activity E9 to start up independently after 300 units of time. (This activity may be canceled in step E6 below before it occurs. If it has already been scheduled and not canceled, we cancel it and reschedule it.) Also set elevator activity E5 to start up independently after 76 units of time. Then wait 20 units of time (to simulate opening of the doors) and go to E4.

E4. [Let people out, in.] If anyone in the ELEVATOR list has OUT = FLOOR, send the user of this type who has most recently entered immediately to step U6, wait 25 units, and repeat step E4. If no such users exist, but QUEUE[FLOOR] is not empty, send the front person of that queue immediately to step U5 instead of U4, wait 25 units, and repeat step E4. But if QUEUE[FLOOR] is empty, set D1 ← 0, make D3 nonzero, and wait for some other activity to initiate further action. (Step E5 will send us to E6, or step U2 will restart E4.)

E5. [Close doors.] If D1 ≠ 0, wait 40 units and repeat this step (the doors flutter a little, but they spring open again, since someone is still getting out or in). Otherwise set D3 ← 0 and set the elevator to start at step E6 after 20 units of time. (This simulates closing the doors after people have finished getting in or out; but if a new user enters on this floor while the doors are closing, they will open again as stated in step U2.)

E6. [Prepare to move.] Set CALLCAR[FLOOR] to zero; also set CALLUP[FLOOR] to zero if STATE ≠ GOINGDOWN, and also set CALLDOWN[FLOOR] to zero if STATE ≠ GOINGUP. (*Note:* If STATE = GOINGUP, the elevator does not clear out CALLDOWN, since it assumes that people who are going down will not have entered; but see exercise 6.) Now perform the DECISION subroutine.

If STATE = NEUTRAL even after the DECISION subroutine has acted, go to E1. Otherwise, if D2 ≠ 0, cancel the elevator activity E9. Finally, if STATE = GOINGUP, wait 15 units of time (for the elevator to build up speed) and go to E7; if STATE = GOINGDOWN, wait 15 units and go to E8.

E7. [Go up a floor.] Set FLOOR ← FLOOR + 1 and wait 51 units of time. If now CALLCAR[FLOOR] = 1 or CALLUP[FLOOR] = 1, or if ((FLOOR = 2 or CALLDOWN[FLOOR] = 1) and CALLUP[j] = CALLDOWN[j] = CALLCAR[j] = 0 for all $j >$ FLOOR), wait 14 units (for deceleration) and go to E2. Otherwise, repeat this step.

E8. [Go down a floor.] This step is like E7 with directions reversed, and also the times 51 and 14 are changed to 61 and 23, respectively. (It takes the elevator longer to go down than up.)

E9. [Set inaction indicator.] Set D2 ← 0 and perform the DECISION subroutine. (This independent action is initiated in step E3 but it is almost always canceled in step E6. See exercise 4.) ∎

Table 1

SOME ACTIONS OF THE ELEVATOR SYSTEM

TIME	STATE	FLOOR	D1	D2	D3	step	action
0000	N	2	0	0	0	U1	User 1 arrives at floor 0, destination is 2.
0035	D	2	0	0	0	E8	Elevator moving down
0038	D	1	0	0	0	U1	User 2 arrives at floor 4, destination is 1.
0096	D	1	0	0	0	E8	Elevator moving down
0136	D	0	0	0	0	U1	User 3 arrives at floor 2, destination is 1.
0141	D	0	0	0	0	U4	User 4 arrives at floor 2, destination is 1.
0152	D	0	0	0	0	U4	User 1 decides to give up, leaves the system.
0180	D	0	0	0	0	E2	Elevator stops.
0180	N	0	X	X	0	E4	Doors open, nobody is there.
0200	N	0	X	X	0	E5	Elevator doors start to close.
0256	N	0	X	X	X	E5	Elevator doors start to close.
0291	U	0	0	X	0	U1	User 5 arrives at floor 3, destination is 1.
0291	U	0	0	X	0	E7	Elevator moving up
0342	U	1	0	X	0	E7	Elevator moving up
0364	U	2	0	X	0	U1	User 6 arrives at floor 2, destination is 1.
0393	U	2	0	X	0	E7	Elevator moving up
0444	U	3	0	X	0	E7	Elevator moving up
0509	U	4	0	X	0	E2	Elevator stops.
0509	N	4	0	X	0	E3	Elevator doors start to open.
0529	N	4	X	X	0	U5	User 2 gets in.
0540	D	4	X	X	X	U4	User 6 decides to give up, leaves the system.
0554	D	4	0	X	X	E5	Elevator doors start to close.
0589	D	4	0	X	0	E8	Elevator moving down
0602	D	3	0	X	0	U1	User 7 arrives at floor 1, destination is 2.
0673	D	3	0	X	0	E2	Elevator stops.
0673	D	3	0	X	0	E3	Elevator doors start to open.
0693	D	3	X	X	0	U5	User 5 gets in.
0749	D	3	0	X	X	E5	Elevator doors start to close.
0784	D	3	0	X	0	E8	Elevator moving down
0827	D	2	0	X	0	U1	User 8 arrives at floor 1, destination is 0.
0868	D	2	0	X	0	E2	Elevator stops.
0868	D	2	0	X	0	E3	Elevator doors start to open.
0876	D	2	X	X	0	U1	User 9 arrives at floor 1, destination is 3.
0888	D	2	X	X	0	U5	User 3 gets in.
0913	D	2	X	X	0	U5	User 4 gets in.
0944	D	2	0	X	X	E5	Elevator doors start to close.
0979	D	2	0	X	0	E8	Elevator moving down
1048	D	1	0	X	0	U1	User 10 arrives at floor 0, destination is 4.
1063	D	1	0	X	0	E2	Elevator stops.
1063	D	1	0	X	0	E3	Elevator doors start to open.
1083	D	1	X	X	0	U6	User 4 gets out, leaves the system.
1108	D	1	X	X	0	U6	User 3 gets out, leaves the system.
1133	D	1	X	X	0	U6	User 5 gets out, leaves the system.
1139	D	1	X	X	0	E5	Doors flutter.
1158	D	1	X	X	0	U6	User 2 gets out, leaves the system.
1179	D	1	X	X	0	E5	Doors flutter.
1183	D	1	X	X	0	U5	User 7 gets in.
1208	D	1	X	X	0	U5	User 8 gets in.
1219	D	1	X	X	0	E5	Doors flutter.
1233	D	1	X	X	0	U5	User 9 gets in.
1259	D	1	0	X	X	E5	Elevator doors start to close.
1294	D	0	0	X	0	E8	Elevator moving down
1378	D	0	0	X	0	E2	Elevator stops.
1378	U	0	0	X	0	E3	Elevator doors start to open.
1398	U	0	X	X	0	U6	User 8 gets out, leaves the system.
1423	U	0	0	X	0	U5	User 10 gets in.
1454	U	0	0	X	X	E5	Elevator doors start to close.
1489	U	1	0	X	0	E7	Elevator moving up
1554	U	1	0	X	0	E2	Elevator stops.
1554	N	1	0	X	0	E3	Elevator doors start to open.
1630	D	1	0	X	X	E5	Elevator doors start to close.
1665	U	1	0	X	0	E7	Elevator moving up
...							
4257	N	2	0	X	0	E1	Elevator dormant
4384	N	2	0	X	0	U1	User 17 arrives at floor 2, destination is 3.
4404	N	2	0	X	0	E3	Elevator doors start to open.
4424	N	2	X	X	0	U5	User 17 gets in.
4449	U	2	0	X	X	E5	Elevator doors start to close.
4484	U	2	0	X	0	E7	Elevator moving up
4549	U	3	0	X	0	E2	Elevator stops.
4549	N	3	0	X	0	E2	Elevator stops.
4569	N	3	X	X	0	E3	Elevator doors start to open.
4625	N	3	0	X	X	U6	User 17 gets out, leaves the system.
4660	D	3	0	X	0	E5	Elevator doors start to close.
4744	D	2	0	X	0	E8	Elevator moving down
4744	N	2	0	X	0	E2	Elevator stops.
4764	N	2	X	X	0	E4	Doors open, nobody is there.
4820	N	2	0	X	X	E5	Elevator doors start to close.
4840	N	2	0	X	0	E1	Elevator dormant
...							

Subroutine D (DECISION *subroutine*). This subroutine is performed at certain critical times, as specified in the coroutines above, when a decision about the elevator's next direction is to be made.

D1. [Decision necessary?] If STATE ≠ NEUTRAL, exit from this subroutine.

D2. [Should doors open?] If the elevator is positioned at E1 and if CALLUP[2], CALLCAR[2], and CALLDOWN[2] are not all zero, cause the elevator to start its activity E3 after 20 units of time, and exit from this subroutine. (If the DECISION subroutine is currently being invoked by the independent activity E9, it is possible for the elevator coroutine to be positioned at E1.)

D3. [Any calls?] Find the smallest $j \neq$ FLOOR for which CALLUP[j], CALLCAR[j], or CALLDOWN[j] is nonzero, and go on to step D4. But if no such j exists, then set $j \leftarrow 2$ if the DECISION subroutine is currently being invoked by step E6; otherwise exit from this subroutine.

D4. [Set STATE.] If FLOOR $> j$, set STATE ← GOINGDOWN; if FLOOR $< j$, set STATE ← GOINGUP.

D5. [Elevator dormant?] If the elevator coroutine is positioned at step E1, and if $j \neq 2$, set the elevator to perform step E6 after 20 units of time. Exit from the subroutine. ∎

The elevator system described above is quite complicated by comparison with other algorithms we have seen in this book, but the choice of a real-life system is more typical of a simulation problem than any cooked-up "textbook example" would ever be.

To help understand the system, consider Table 1, which gives part of the history of one simulation. It is perhaps best to start by examining the simple case starting at time 4257: The elevator is sitting idly at floor 2 with its doors shut, when a user arrives (time 4384); let's say the user's name is Don. Two seconds later, the doors open, and Don gets in after two more seconds. By pushing button "3" he starts the elevator moving up; ultimately he gets off at floor 3 and the elevator returns to floor 2.

The first entries in Table 1 show a much more dramatic scenario: A user calls the elevator to floor 0, but loses patience and gives up after 15.2 sec. The elevator stops at floor 0 but finds nobody there; then it heads to floor 4, since there are several calls wanting to go downward; etc.

The programming of this system for a computer (in our case, MIX) merits careful study. At any given time during the simulation, we may have many simulated users in the system (in various queues and ready to "give up" at various times), and there is also the possibility of essentially simultaneous execution of steps E4, E5, and E9 if many people are trying to get out as the elevator is trying to close its doors. The passing of simulated time and the handling of "simultaneity" may be programmed by having each entity represented by a node that includes a **NEXTTIME** field (denoting the time when the next action for this entity is to take place) and a **NEXTINST** field (denoting the memory address where this entity is to start executing instructions, analogous to ordinary coroutine

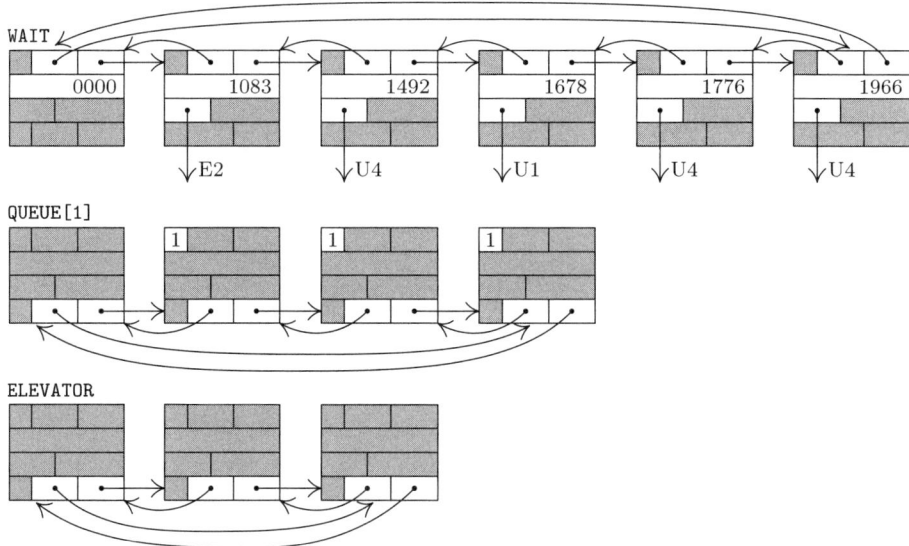

Fig. 12. Some lists used in the elevator simulation program. (List heads appear at the left.)

linkage). Each entity waiting for time to pass is placed in a doubly linked list called the WAIT list; this "agenda" is sorted on the NEXTTIME fields of its nodes, so that the actions may be processed in the correct sequence of simulated times. The program also uses doubly linked lists for the ELEVATOR and for the QUEUE lists.

Each node representing an activity (whether a user or an elevator action) has the form

+	IN	LLINK1	RLINK1
+	NEXTTIME		
+	NEXTINST	0	0	39
+	OUT	LLINK2	RLINK2

$$. \tag{6}$$

Here LLINK1 and RLINK1 are the links for the WAIT list; LLINK2 and RLINK2 are used as links in the QUEUE lists or the ELEVATOR. The latter two fields and the IN and OUT field are relevant when node (6) represents a user, but they are not relevant for nodes that represent elevator actions. The third word of the node is actually a MIX "JMP" instruction.

Figure 12 shows typical contents of the WAIT list, ELEVATOR list, and one of the QUEUE lists; each node in the QUEUE list is simultaneously in the WAIT list with NEXTINST = U4, but this has not been indicated in the figure, since the complexity of the linking would obscure the basic idea.

Now let us consider the program itself. It is quite long, although (as with all long programs) it divides into small parts each of which is quite simple in itself.

First comes a number of lines of code that just serve to define the initial contents of the tables. There are several points of interest here: We have list heads for the WAIT list (lines 010–011), the QUEUE lists (lines 026–031), and the ELEVATOR list (lines 032–033). Each of them is a node of the form (6), but with unimportant words deleted; the WAIT list head contains only the first two words of a node, and the QUEUE and ELEVATOR list heads require only the last word of a node. We also have four nodes that are always present in the system (lines 012–023): USER1, a node that is always positioned at step U1 ready to enter a new user into the system; ELEV1, a node that governs the main actions of the elevator at steps E1, E2, E3, E4, E6, E7, and E8; and ELEV2 and ELEV3, nodes that are used for the elevator actions E5 and E9, which take place independently of other elevator actions with respect to simulated time. Each of these four nodes contains only three words, since they never appear in the QUEUE or ELEVATOR lists. The nodes representing each actual user in the system will appear in a storage pool following the main program.

```
001  * THE ELEVATOR SIMULATION
002  IN        EQU  1:1                          Definition of fields
003  LLINK1    EQU  2:3                             within nodes
004  RLINK1    EQU  4:5
005  NEXTINST  EQU  0:2
006  OUT       EQU  1:1
007  LLINK2    EQU  2:3
008  RLINK2    EQU  4:5

009  * FIXED-SIZE TABLES AND LIST HEADS
010  WAIT      CON  *+2(LLINK1),*+2(RLINK1)      List head for WAIT list
011            CON  0                            NEXTTIME = 0 always
012  USER1     CON  *-2(LLINK1),*-2(RLINK1)      This node represents action
013            CON  0                            U1 and it is initially the
014            JMP  U1                           sole entry in the WAIT list.
015  ELEV1     CON  0                            This node represents the
016            CON  0                            elevator actions, except
017            JMP  E1                           for E5 and E9.
018  ELEV2     CON  0                            This node represents the
019            CON  0                            independent elevator
020            JMP  E5                           action at E5.
021  ELEV3     CON  0                            This node represents the
022            CON  0                            independent elevator
023            JMP  E9                           action at E9.
024  AVAIL     CON  0                            Link to available nodes
025  TIME      CON  0                            Current simulated time
026  QUEUE     EQU  *-3
027            CON  *-3(LLINK2),*-3(RLINK2)      List head for QUEUE[0]
028            CON  *-3(LLINK2),*-3(RLINK2)      List head for QUEUE[1]
029            CON  *-3(LLINK2),*-3(RLINK2)      All queues initially
030            CON  *-3(LLINK2),*-3(RLINK2)        are empty
031            CON  *-3(LLINK2),*-3(RLINK2)      List head for QUEUE[4]
```

```
032  ELEVATOR  EQU  *-3
033            CON  *-3(LLINK2),*-3(RLINK2)   List head for ELEVATOR
034            CON  0          ⎫
035            CON  0          ⎪  "Padding" for CALL table
036            CON  0          ⎬      (see lines 183–186)
037            CON  0          ⎭
038  CALL      CON  0             CALLUP[0], CALLCAR[0], CALLDOWN[0]
039            CON  0             CALLUP[1], CALLCAR[1], CALLDOWN[1]
040            CON  0             CALLUP[2], CALLCAR[2], CALLDOWN[2]
041            CON  0             CALLUP[3], CALLCAR[3], CALLDOWN[3]
042            CON  0             CALLUP[4], CALLCAR[4], CALLDOWN[4]
043            CON  0          ⎫
044            CON  0          ⎪  "Padding" for CALL table
045            CON  0          ⎬      (see lines 178–181)
046            CON  0          ⎭
047  D1        CON  0             Indicates doors open, activity
048  D2        CON  0             Indicates no prolonged standstill
049  D3        CON  0             Indicates doors open, inactivity  ∎
```

The next part of the program coding contains basic subroutines and the main control routines for the simulation process. Subroutines INSERT and DELETE perform typical manipulations on doubly linked lists; they put the current node into or take it out of a QUEUE or ELEVATOR list. (In the program, the "current node" C is always represented by index register 6.) There are also subroutines for the WAIT list: Subroutine SORTIN adds the current node to the WAIT list, sorting it into the right place based on its NEXTTIME field. Subroutine IMMED inserts the current node at the front of the WAIT list. Subroutine HOLD puts the current node into the WAIT list, with NEXTTIME equal to the current time plus the amount in register A. Subroutine DELETEW deletes the current node from the WAIT list.

The routine CYCLE is the heart of the simulation control: It decides which activity is to act next (namely, the first element of the WAIT list, which we know is nonempty), and jumps to it. There are two special entrances to CYCLE: CYCLE1 first sets NEXTINST in the current node, and HOLDC is the same with an additional call on the HOLD subroutine. Thus, the effect of the instruction "JMP HOLDC" with amount t in register A is to suspend activity for t units of simulated time and then to return to the following location.

```
050  * SUBROUTINES AND CONTROL ROUTINE
051  INSERT  STJ  9F                Insert NODE(C) to left of NODE(rI1):
052          LD2  3,1(LLINK2)       rI2 ← LLINK2(rI1).
053          ST2  3,6(LLINK2)       LLINK2(C) ← rI2.
054          ST6  3,1(LLINK2)       LLINK2(rI1) ← C.
055          ST6  3,2(RLINK2)       RLINK2(rI2) ← C.
056          ST1  3,6(RLINK2)       RLINK2(C) ← rI1.
057  9H      JMP  *                 Exit from subroutine.
058  DELETE  STJ  9F                Delete NODE(C) from its list:
059          LD1  3,6(LLINK2)       P ← LLINK2(C).
060          LD2  3,6(RLINK2)       Q ← RLINK2(C).
```

061		ST1	3,2(LLINK2)	LLINK2(Q) ← P.
062		ST2	3,1(RLINK2)	RLINK2(P) ← Q.
063	9H	JMP	*	Exit from subroutine.
064	IMMED	STJ	9F	Insert NODE(C) first in WAIT list:
065		LDA	TIME	
066		STA	1,6	Set NEXTTIME(C) ← TIME.
067		ENT1	WAIT	P ← LOC(WAIT).
068		JMP	2F	Insert NODE(C) to right of NODE(P).
069	HOLD	ADD	TIME	rA ← TIME + rA.
070	SORTIN	STJ	9F	Sort NODE(C) into WAIT list:
071		STA	1,6	Set NEXTTIME(C) ← rA.
072		ENT1	WAIT	P ← LOC(WAIT).
073		LD1	0,1(LLINK1)	P ← LLINK1(P).
074		CMPA	1,1	Compare NEXTTIME fields, right to left.
075		JL	*-2	Repeat until NEXTTIME(C) ≥ NEXTTIME(P).
076	2H	LD2	0,1(RLINK1)	Q ← RLINK1(P).
077		ST2	0,6(RLINK1)	RLINK1(C) ← Q.
078		ST1	0,6(LLINK1)	LLINK1(C) ← P.
079		ST6	0,1(RLINK1)	RLINK1(P) ← C.
080		ST6	0,2(LLINK1)	LLINK1(Q) ← C.
081	9H	JMP	*	Exit from subroutine.
082	DELETEW	STJ	9F	Delete NODE(C) from WAIT list:
083		LD1	0,6(LLINK1)	(This is same as lines 058–063
084		LD2	0,6(RLINK1)	except LLINK1, RLINK1 are used
085		ST1	0,2(LLINK1)	instead of LLINK2, RLINK2.)
086		ST2	0,1(RLINK1)	
087	9H	JMP	*	
088	CYCLE1	STJ	2,6(NEXTINST)	Set NEXTINST(C) ← rJ.
089		JMP	CYCLE	
090	HOLDC	STJ	2,6(NEXTINST)	Set NEXTINST(C) ← rJ.
091		JMP	HOLD	Insert NODE(C) in WAIT, delay rA.
092	CYCLE	LD6	WAIT(RLINK1)	Set current node C ← RLINK1(LOC(WAIT)).
093		LDA	1,6	
094		STA	TIME	TIME ← NEXTTIME(C).
095		JMP	DELETEW	Remove NODE(C) from WAIT list.
096		JMP	2,6	Jump to NEXTINST(C). ∎

Now comes the program for Coroutine U. At the beginning of step U1, the current node C is USER1 (see lines 012–014 above), and lines 099–100 of the program cause USER1 to be reinserted into the WAIT list so that the next user will be generated after INTERTIME units of simulated time. The following lines 101–114 take care of setting up a node for the newly generated user; the IN and OUT floors are recorded in this node position. The AVAIL stack is singly linked in the RLINK1 field of each node. Note that lines 101–108 perform the action "C ⇐ AVAIL" using the POOLMAX technique, 2.2.3–(7); no test for OVERFLOW is necessary here, since the total size of the storage pool (the number of users in the system at any one time) rarely exceeds 10 nodes (40 words). The return of a node to the AVAIL stack appears in lines 156–158.

Throughout the program, index register 4 equals the variable FLOOR, and index register 5 is positive, negative, or zero, depending on whether STATE = GOINGUP, GOINGDOWN, or NEUTRAL. The variables CALLUP[j], CALLCAR[j], and CALLDOWN[j] occupy the respective fields (1:1), (3:3), and (5:5) of location CALL + j.

097	*	COROUTINE U		*U1. Enter, prepare for successor.*
098	U1	JMP	VALUES	Set INFLOOR, OUTFLOOR, GIVEUPTIME, INTERTIME.
099		LDA	INTERTIME	INTERTIME is computed by VALUES subroutine.
100		JMP	HOLD	Put NODE(C) in WAIT, delay INTERTIME.
101		LD6	AVAIL	C ← AVAIL.
102		J6P	1F	If AVAIL ≠ Λ, jump.
103		LD6	POOLMAX(0:2)	
104		INC6	4	C ← POOLMAX + 4.
105		ST6	POOLMAX(0:2)	POOLMAX ← C.
106		JMP	*+3	Assume that memory overflow won't happen.
107	1H	LDA	0,6(RLINK1)	
108		STA	AVAIL	AVAIL ← RLINK1(AVAIL).
109		LD1	INFLOOR	rI1 ← INFLOOR (computed by VALUES above).
110		ST1	0,6(IN)	IN(C) ← rI1.
111		LD2	OUTFLOOR	rI2 ← OUTFLOOR (computed by VALUES).
112		ST2	3,6(OUT)	OUT(C) ← rI2.
113		ENTA	39	Put constant 39 (JMP operation code)
114		STA	2,6	into third word of node format (6).
115	U2	ENTA	0,4	*U2. Signal and wait.* Set rA ← FLOOR.
116		DECA	0,1	FLOOR − IN.
117		ST6	TEMP	Save value of C.
118		JANZ	2F	Jump if FLOOR ≠ IN.
119		ENT6	ELEV1	Set C ← LOC(ELEV1).
120		LDA	2,6(NEXTINST)	Is elevator positioned at E6?
121		DECA	E6	
122		JANZ	3F	
123		ENTA	E3	If so, reposition it at E3.
124		STA	2,6(NEXTINST)	
125		JMP	DELETEW	Remove it from WAIT list
126		JMP	4F	and reinsert it at front of WAIT.
127	3H	LDA	D3	
128		JAZ	2F	Jump if D3 = 0.
129		ST6	D1	Otherwise make D1 nonzero.
130		STZ	D3	Set D3 ← 0.
131	4H	JMP	IMMED	Insert ELEV1 at front of WAIT list.
132		JMP	U3	(rI1 and rI2 have changed.)
133	2H	DEC2	0,1	rI2 ← OUT − IN.
134		ENTA	1	
135		J2P	*+3	Jump if going up.
136		STA	CALL,1(5:5)	Set CALLDOWN[IN] ← 1.
137		JMP	*+2	
138		STA	CALL,1(1:1)	Set CALLUP[IN] ← 1.
139		LDA	D2	

140		JAZ	*+3	If D2 = 0, call the DECISION subroutine.
141		LDA	ELEV1+2(NEXTINST)	
142		DECA	E1	If the elevator is at E1, call
143		JAZ	DECISION	the DECISION subroutine.
144	U3	LD6	TEMP	*U3. Enter queue.*
145		LD1	0,6(IN)	
146		ENT1	QUEUE,1	rI1 ← LOC(QUEUE[IN]).
147		JMP	INSERT	Insert NODE(C) at right end of QUEUE[IN].
148	U4A	LDA	GIVEUPTIME	
149		JMP	HOLDC	Wait GIVEUPTIME units.
150	U4	LDA	0,6(IN)	*U4. Give up.*
151		DECA	0,4	IN(C) − FLOOR.
152		JANZ	*+3	
153		LDA	D1	FLOOR = IN(C).
154		JANZ	U4A	See exercise 7.
155	U6	JMP	DELETE	*U6. Get out.* NODE(C) is deleted
156		LDA	AVAIL	from QUEUE or ELEVATOR.
157		STA	0,6(RLINK1)	AVAIL ⇐ C.
158		ST6	AVAIL	
159		JMP	CYCLE	Continue simulation.
160	U5	JMP	DELETE	*U5. Get in.* NODE(C) is deleted
161		ENT1	ELEVATOR	from QUEUE.
162		JMP	INSERT	Insert it at right of ELEVATOR.
163		ENTA	1	
164		LD2	3,6(OUT)	
165		STA	CALL,2(3:3)	Set CALLCAR[OUT(C)] ← 1.
166		J5NZ	CYCLE	Jump if STATE ≠ NEUTRAL.
167		DEC2	0,4	rI2 ← OUT(C) − FLOOR.
168		ENT5	0,2	Set STATE to proper direction.
169		ENT6	ELEV2	Set C ← LOC(ELEV2).
170		JMP	DELETEW	Remove E5 action from WAIT list.
171		ENTA	25	
172		JMP	E5A	Restart E5 action 25 units from now. ▌

The program for Coroutine E is a rather straightforward rendition of the semiformal description given earlier. Perhaps the most interesting portion is the preparation for the elevator's independent actions in step E3, and the searching of the ELEVATOR and QUEUE lists in step E4.

173	* COROUTINE E		
174	E1A	JMP	CYCLE1	Set NEXTINST ← E1, go to CYCLE.
175	E1	EQU	*	*E1. Wait for call.* (no action)
176	E2A	JMP	HOLDC	
177	E2	J5N	1F	*E2. Change of state?*
178		LDA	CALL+1,4	State is GOINGUP.
179		ADD	CALL+2,4	
180		ADD	CALL+3,4	
181		ADD	CALL+4,4	
182		JAP	E3	Are there calls for higher floors?

183		LDA	CALL-1,4(3:3)	If not, have passengers in the
184		ADD	CALL-2,4(3:3)	elevator called for lower floors?
185		ADD	CALL-3,4(3:3)	
186		ADD	CALL-4,4(3:3)	
187		JMP	2F	
188	1H	LDA	CALL-1,4	State is GOINGDOWN.
189		ADD	CALL-2,4	Actions are like lines 178–186.

⋮

196		ADD	CALL+4,4(3:3)	
197	2H	ENN5	0,5	Reverse direction of STATE.
198		STZ	CALL,4	Set CALL variables to zero.
199		JANZ	E3	Jump if called to the opposite direction;
200		ENT5	0	otherwise set STATE ← NEUTRAL.
201	E3	ENT6	ELEV3	*E3. Open doors.*
202		LDA	0,6	If activity E9 is already scheduled,
203		JANZ	DELETEW	remove it from the WAIT list.
204		ENTA	300	
205		JMP	HOLD	Schedule activity E9 after 300 units.
206		ENT6	ELEV2	
207		ENTA	76	
208		JMP	HOLD	Schedule activity E5 after 76 units.
209		ST6	D2	Set D2 nonzero.
210		ST6	D1	Set D1 nonzero.
211		ENTA	20	
212	E4A	ENT6	ELEV1	
213		JMP	HOLDC	
214	E4	ENTA	0,4	*E4. Let people out, in.*
215		SLA	4	Set OUT field of rA to FLOOR.
216		ENT6	ELEVATOR	C ← LOC(ELEVATOR).
217	1H	LD6	3,6(LLINK2)	C ← LLINK2(C).
218		CMP6	=ELEVATOR=	Search ELEVATOR list, right to left.
219		JE	1F	If C = LOC(ELEVATOR), search is complete.
220		CMPA	3,6(OUT)	Compare OUT(C) with FLOOR.
221		JNE	1B	If not equal, continue searching;
222		ENTA	U6	otherwise prepare to send user to U6.
223		JMP	2F	
224	1H	LD6	QUEUE+3,4(RLINK2)	Set C ← RLINK2(LOC(QUEUE[FLOOR])).
225		CMP6	3,6(RLINK2)	Is C = RLINK2(C)?
226		JE	1F	If so, the queue is empty.
227		JMP	DELETEW	If not, cancel action U4 for this user.
228		ENTA	U5	Prepare to replace U4 by U5.
229	2H	STA	2,6(NEXTINST)	Set NEXTINST(C).
230		JMP	IMMED	Put user at the front of the WAIT list.
231		ENTA	25	
232		JMP	E4A	Wait 25 units and repeat E4.
233	1H	STZ	D1	Set D1 ← 0.
234		ST6	D3	Set D3 nonzero.
235		JMP	CYCLE	Return to simulate other events.

236	E5A	JMP	HOLDC	
237	E5	LDA	D1	*E5. Close doors.*
238		JAZ	*+3	Is D1 = 0?
239		ENTA	40	If not, people are still getting in or out.
240		JMP	E5A	Wait 40 units, repeat E5.
241		STZ	D3	If D1 = 0, set D3 ← 0.
242		ENT6	ELEV1	
243		ENTA	20	
244		JMP	HOLDC	Wait 20 units, then go to E6.
245	E6	J5N	*+2	*E6. Prepare to move.*
246		STZ	CALL,4(1:3)	If STATE ≠ GOINGDOWN, CALLUP and CALLCAR
247		J5P	*+2	on this floor are reset.
248		STZ	CALL,4(3:5)	If ≠ GOINGUP, reset CALLCAR and CALLDOWN.
249		J5Z	DECISION	Perform DECISION subroutine.
250	E6B	J5Z	E1A	If STATE = NEUTRAL, go to E1 and wait.
251		LDA	D2	
252		JAZ	*+4	
253		ENT6	ELEV3	Otherwise, if D2 ≠ 0,
254		JMP	DELETEW	cancel activity E9
255		STZ	ELEV3	(see line 202).
256		ENT6	ELEV1	
257		ENTA	15	Wait 15 units of time.
258		J5N	E8A	If STATE = GOINGDOWN, go to E8.
259	E7A	JMP	HOLDC	
260	E7	INC4	1	*E7. Go up a floor.*
261		ENTA	51	
262		JMP	HOLDC	Wait 51 units.
263		LDA	CALL,4(1:3)	Is CALLCAR[FLOOR] or CALLUP[FLOOR] ≠ 0?
264		JAP	1F	
265		ENT1	-2,4	If not,
266		J1Z	2F	is FLOOR = 2?
267		LDA	CALL,4(5:5)	If not, is CALLDOWN[FLOOR] ≠ 0?
268		JAZ	E7	If not, repeat step E7.
269	2H	LDA	CALL+1,4	
270		ADD	CALL+2,4	
271		ADD	CALL+3,4	
272		ADD	CALL+4,4	
273		JANZ	E7	Are there calls for higher floors?
274	1H	ENTA	14	It is time to stop the elevator.
275		JMP	E2A	Wait 14 units and go to E2.
276	E8A	JMP	HOLDC	
⋮				(See exercise 8.)
292		JMP	E2A	
293	E9	STZ	0,6	*E9. Set inaction indicator.* (See line 202.)
294		STZ	D2	D2 ← 0.
295		JMP	DECISION	Perform DECISION subroutine.
296		JMP	CYCLE	Return to simulation of other events. ▌

We will not consider here the DECISION subroutine (see exercise 9), nor the VALUES subroutine that is used to specify the demands on the elevator. At the very end of the program comes the code

```
BEGIN     ENT4 2        Start with FLOOR = 2
          ENT5 0              and STATE = NEUTRAL.
          JMP  CYCLE     Begin simulation.
POOLMAX NOP  POOL
POOL      END  BEGIN     Storage pool follows literals, temp storage.   ▌
```

The program above does a fine job of simulating the elevator system, as it goes through its paces. But it would be useless to run this program, since there is no output! Actually, the author added a PRINT subroutine that was called at most of the critical steps in the program above, and this was used to prepare Table 1; the details have been omitted, since they are very straightforward but they only clutter up the code.

Several programming languages have been devised that make it quite easy to specify the actions in a discrete simulation, and to use a compiler to translate these specifications into machine language. Assembly language was used in this section, of course, since we are concerned here with the basic techniques of linked list manipulation, and we want to see the details of how discrete simulations can actually be performed by a computer that has a one-track mind. The technique of using a WAIT list or agenda to control the sequencing of coroutines, as we have done in this section, is called *quasiparallel processing*.

It is quite difficult to give a precise analysis of the running time of such a long program, because of the complex interactions involved; but large programs often spend most of their time in comparatively short routines doing comparatively simple things. Therefore we can usually get a good indication of the overall efficiency by using a special trace routine called a *profiler*, which executes the program and records how often each instruction is performed. This identifies the "bottlenecks," the places that should be given special attention. [See exercise 1.4.3.2–7. See also *Software Practice & Experience* **1** (1971), 105–133, for examples of such studies on randomly selected FORTRAN programs found in wastebaskets at the Stanford Computer Center.] The author made such an experiment with the elevator program above, running it for 10000 units of simulated elevator time; 26 users entered the simulated system. The instructions in the SORTIN loop, lines 073–075, were executed by far the most often, 1432 times, while the SORTIN subroutine itself was called 437 times. The CYCLE routine was performed 407 times; so we could gain a little speed by not calling the DELETEW subroutine at line 095: The four lines of that subroutine could be written out in full (to save $4u$ each time CYCLE is used). The profiler also showed that the DECISION subroutine was called only 32 times and the loop in E4 (lines 217–219) was executed only 142 times.

It is hoped that some reader will learn as much about simulation from the example above as the author learned about elevators while the example was being prepared.

EXERCISES

1. [21] Give specifications for the insertion and deletion of information at the left end of a doubly linked list represented as in (1). (With the dual operations at the right end, which are obtained by symmetry, we therefore have all the actions of a general deque.)

▶ **2.** [22] Explain why a list that is singly linked cannot allow efficient operation as a general deque; the deletion of items can be done efficiently at only one end of a singly linked list.

▶ **3.** [22] The elevator system described in the text uses three call variables, CALLUP, CALLCAR, and CALLDOWN, for each floor, representing buttons that have been pushed by the users in the system. It is conceivable that the elevator actually needs only one or two binary variables for the call buttons on each floor, instead of three. Explain how an experimenter could push buttons in a certain sequence with this elevator system to *prove* that there are three independent binary variables for each floor (except the top and bottom floors).

4. [24] Activity E9 in the elevator coroutine is usually canceled by step E6; and even when it hasn't been canceled, it doesn't do very much. Explain under what circumstances the elevator would behave differently if activity E9 were deleted from the system. Would it, for example, sometimes visit floors in a different order?

5. [20] In Table 1, user 10 arrived on floor 0 at time 1048. Show that if user 10 had arrived on floor 2 instead of floor 0, the elevator would have gone *up* after receiving its passengers on floor 1, instead of down, in spite of the fact that user 8 wants to go down to floor 0.

6. [23] During the time period 1183–1233 in Table 1, users 7, 8, and 9 all get in the elevator on floor 1; then the elevator goes down to floor 0 and only user 8 gets out. Now the elevator stops again on floor 1, presumably to pick up users 7 and 9 who are already aboard; nobody is actually on floor 1 waiting to get in. (This situation occurs not infrequently at Caltech; if you get on the elevator going the wrong way, you must wait for an extra stop as you go by your original floor again.) In many elevator systems, users 7 and 9 would not have boarded the elevator at time 1183, since lights outside the elevator would show that it was going down, not up; those users would have waited until the elevator came back up and stopped for them. On the system described, there are no such lights and it is impossible to tell which way the elevator is going to go until you are in it; hence Table 1 reflects the actual situation.

What changes should be made to coroutines U and E if we were to simulate the same elevator system, but with indicator lights, so that people do not get on the elevator when its state is contrary to their desired direction?

7. [25] Although bugs in programs are often embarrassing to a programmer, if we are to learn from our mistakes we should record them and tell other people about them instead of forgetting them. The following error (among others) was made by the author when he first wrote the program in this section: Line 154 said "JANZ CYCLE" instead of "JANZ U4A". The reasoning was that if indeed the elevator had arrived at this user's floor, there was no need to perform the "give up" activity U4 any more, so we could simply go to CYCLE and continue simulating other activities. What was the error?

8. [21] Write the code for step E8, lines 277–292, which has been omitted from the program in the text.

9. [*23*] Write the code for the DECISION subroutine, which has been omitted from the program in the text.

10. [*40*] It is perhaps significant to note that although the author had used the elevator system for years and thought he knew it well, it wasn't until he attempted to write this section that he realized there were quite a few facts about the elevator's system of choosing directions that he did not know. He went back to experiment with the elevator six separate times, each time believing he had finally achieved a complete understanding of its *modus operandi*. (Now he is reluctant to ride it for fear that some new facet of its operation will appear, contradicting the algorithms given.) We often fail to realize how little we know about a thing until we attempt to simulate it on a computer.

Try to specify the actions of some elevator you are familiar with. Check the algorithm by experiments with the elevator itself (looking at its circuitry is not fair!); then design a discrete simulator for the system and run it on a computer.

▶ **11.** [*21*] (*A sparse-update memory.*) The following problem often arises in *synchronous* simulations: The system has n variables $V[1]$, ..., $V[n]$, and at every simulated step new values for some of them are calculated from the old values. These calculations are assumed done "simultaneously" in the sense that the variables do not change to their new values until after all assignments have been made. Thus, the two statements

$$V[1] \leftarrow V[2] \qquad \text{and} \qquad V[2] \leftarrow V[1]$$

appearing at the same simulated time would interchange the values of $V[1]$ and $V[2]$; this is quite different from what would happen in a sequential calculation.

The desired action can of course be simulated by keeping an additional table $NEWV[1]$, ..., $NEWV[n]$. Before each simulated step, we could set $NEWV[k] \leftarrow V[k]$ for $1 \le k \le n$, then record all changes of $V[k]$ in $NEWV[k]$, and finally, after the step we could set $V[k] \leftarrow NEWV[k]$, $1 \le k \le n$. But this "brute force" approach is not completely satisfactory, for the following reasons: (1) Often n is very large, but the number of variables changed per step is rather small. (2) The variables are often not arranged in a nice table $V[1]$, ..., $V[n]$, but are scattered throughout memory in a rather chaotic fashion. (3) This method does not detect the situation (usually an error in the model) when one variable is given two values in the same simulated step.

Assuming that the number of variables changed per step is rather small, design an efficient algorithm that simulates the desired actions, using two auxiliary tables $NEWV[k]$ and $LINK[k]$, $1 \le k \le n$. If possible, your algorithm should give an error stop if the same variable is being given two different values in the same step.

▶ **12.** [*22*] Why is it a good idea to use doubly linked lists instead of singly linked or sequential lists in the simulation program of this section?

2.2.6. Arrays and Orthogonal Lists

One of the simplest generalizations of a linear list is a two-dimensional or higher-dimensional array of information. For example, consider the case of an $m \times n$ matrix

$$\begin{pmatrix} A[1,1] & A[1,2] & \dots & A[1,n] \\ A[2,1] & A[2,2] & \dots & A[2,n] \\ \vdots & \vdots & & \vdots \\ A[m,1] & A[m,2] & \dots & A[m,n] \end{pmatrix}. \qquad (1)$$

In this two-dimensional array, each node $A[j,k]$ belongs to two linear lists: the "row j" list $A[j,1]$, $A[j,2]$, ..., $A[j,n]$ and the "column k" list $A[1,k]$, $A[2,k]$, ..., $A[m,k]$. These orthogonal row and column lists essentially account for the two-dimensional structure of a matrix. Similar remarks apply to higher-dimensional arrays of information.

Sequential Allocation. When an array like (1) is stored in *sequential* memory locations, storage is usually allocated so that

$$\text{LOC}(A[J,K]) = a_0 + a_1 J + a_2 K, \tag{2}$$

where a_0, a_1, and a_2 are constants. Let us consider a more general case: Suppose we have a four-dimensional array with one-word elements $Q[I,J,K,L]$ for $0 \le I \le 2$, $0 \le J \le 4$, $0 \le K \le 10$, $0 \le L \le 2$. We would like to allocate storage so that

$$\text{LOC}(Q[I,J,K,L]) = a_0 + a_1 I + a_2 J + a_3 K + a_4 L. \tag{3}$$

This means that a change in I, J, K, or L leads to a readily calculated change in the location of $Q[I,J,K,L]$. The most natural (and most commonly used) way to allocate storage is to arrange the array elements according to the lexicographic order of their indices $\big(\text{exercise 1.2.1–15(d)}\big)$, sometimes called "row major order":

$$Q[0,0,0,0],\ Q[0,0,0,1],\ Q[0,0,0,2],\ Q[0,0,1,0],\ Q[0,0,1,1],\ \ldots,$$
$$Q[0,0,10,2],\ Q[0,1,0,0],\ \ldots,\ Q[0,4,10,2],\ Q[1,0,0,0],\ \ldots,$$
$$Q[2,4,10,2].$$

It is easy to see that this order satisfies the requirements of (3), and we have

$$\text{LOC}(Q[I,J,K,L]) = \text{LOC}(Q[0,0,0,0]) + 165 I + 33 J + 3K + L. \tag{4}$$

In general, given a k-dimensional array with c-word elements $A[I_1, I_2, \ldots, I_k]$ for

$$0 \le I_1 \le d_1, \quad 0 \le I_2 \le d_2, \quad \ldots, \quad 0 \le I_k \le d_k,$$

we can store it in memory as

$$\begin{aligned}
&\text{LOC}(A[I_1, I_2, \ldots, I_k])\\
&\quad = \text{LOC}(A[0,0,\ldots,0]) + c\,(d_2+1)\ldots(d_k+1)I_1 + \cdots + c\,(d_k+1)I_{k-1} + cI_k\\
&\quad = \text{LOC}(A[0,0,\ldots,0]) + \sum_{1 \le r \le k} a_r I_r,
\end{aligned} \tag{5}$$

where

$$a_r = c \prod_{r < s \le k} (d_s + 1). \tag{6}$$

To see why this formula works, observe that a_r is the amount of memory needed to store the subarray $A[I_1, \ldots, I_r, J_{r+1}, \ldots, J_k]$ if $I_1, \ldots, I_r$ are constant and $J_{r+1}, \ldots, J_k$ vary through all values $0 \le J_{r+1} \le d_{r+1}$, ..., $0 \le J_k \le d_k$; hence by the nature of lexicographic order the address of $A[I_1, \ldots, I_k]$ should change by precisely this amount when I_r changes by 1.

Formulas (5) and (6) correspond to the value of the number $I_1 I_2 \ldots I_k$ in a mixed-radix number system. For example, if we had the array TIME[W,D,H,M,S] with $0 \leq$ W < 4, $0 \leq$ D < 7, $0 \leq$ H < 24, $0 \leq$ M < 60, and $0 \leq$ S < 60, the location of TIME[W,D,H,M,S] would be the location of TIME[0,0,0,0,0] plus the quantity "W weeks + D days + H hours + M minutes + S seconds" converted to seconds. Of course, it takes a pretty fancy application to make use of an array that has 2,419,200 elements.

The normal method for storing arrays is generally suitable when the array has a complete rectangular structure, so that all elements $A[I_1, I_2, \ldots, I_k]$ are present for indices in the independent ranges $l_1 \leq I_1 \leq u_1$, $l_2 \leq I_2 \leq u_2$, ..., $l_k \leq I_k \leq u_k$. Exercise 2 shows how to adapt (5) and (6) to the case when the lower bounds $(l_1, l_2, \ldots, l_k)$ are not $(0, 0, \ldots, 0)$.

But there are many situations in which an array is not perfectly rectangular. Most common is the *triangular matrix*, where we want to store only the entries $A[j,k]$ for, say, $0 \leq k \leq j \leq n$:

$$\begin{pmatrix} A[0,0] & & & \\ A[1,0] & A[1,1] & & \\ \vdots & \vdots & \ddots & \\ A[n,0] & A[n,1] & \cdots & A[n,n] \end{pmatrix}. \tag{7}$$

We may know that all other entries are zero, or that $A[j,k] = A[k,j]$, so that only half of the values need to be stored. If we want to store the lower triangular matrix (7) in $\frac{1}{2}(n+1)(n+2)$ consecutive memory positions, we are forced to give up the possibility of linear allocation as in Eq. (2), but we can ask instead for an allocation arrangement of the form

$$\text{LOC}(A[J,K]) = a_0 + f_1(J) + f_2(K) \tag{8}$$

where f_1 and f_2 are functions of one variable. (The constant a_0 may be absorbed into either f_1 or f_2 if desired.) When the addressing has the form (8), a random element $A[j,k]$ can be quickly accessed if we keep two (rather short) auxiliary tables of the values of f_1 and f_2; therefore these functions need to be calculated only once.

It turns out that lexicographic order of indices for the array (7) satisfies condition (8), and with one-word entries we have in fact the simple formula

$$\text{LOC}(A[J,K]) = \text{LOC}(A[0,0]) + \frac{J(J+1)}{2} + K. \tag{9}$$

But there is actually a far better way to store triangular matrices, if we are fortunate enough to have two of them with the same size. Suppose that we want to store both $A[j,k]$ and $B[j,k]$ for $0 \leq k \leq j \leq n$. Then we can fit them both into a single matrix $C[j,k]$ for $0 \leq j \leq n$, $0 \leq k \leq n+1$, using the convention

$$A[j,k] = C[j,k], \qquad B[j,k] = C[k,j+1]. \tag{10}$$

Thus

$$\begin{pmatrix} C[0,0] & C[0,1] & C[0,2] & \dots C[0,n+1] \\ C[1,0] & C[1,1] & C[1,2] & \dots C[1,n+1] \\ \vdots & & & \vdots \\ C[n,0] & C[n,1] & C[n,2] & \dots C[n,n+1] \end{pmatrix} \equiv \begin{pmatrix} A[0,0] & B[0,0] & B[1,0] & \dots B[n,0] \\ A[1,0] & A[1,1] & B[1,1] & \dots B[n,1] \\ \vdots & & & \vdots \\ A[n,0] & A[n,1] & A[n,2] & \dots B[n,n] \end{pmatrix}.$$

The two triangular matrices are packed together tightly within the space of $(n+1)(n+2)$ locations, and we have linear addressing as in (2).

The generalization of triangular matrices to higher dimensions is called a *tetrahedral array*. This interesting topic is the subject of exercises 6 through 8.

As an example of typical programming techniques for use with sequentially stored arrays, see exercise 1.3.2–10 and the two answers given for that exercise. The fundamental techniques for efficient traversal of rows and columns, as well as the uses of sequential stacks, are of particular interest within those programs.

Linked Allocation. Linked memory allocation also applies to higher-dimensional arrays of information in a natural way. In general, our nodes can contain k link fields, one for each list the node belongs to. The use of linked memory is generally for cases in which the arrays are not strictly rectangular in character.

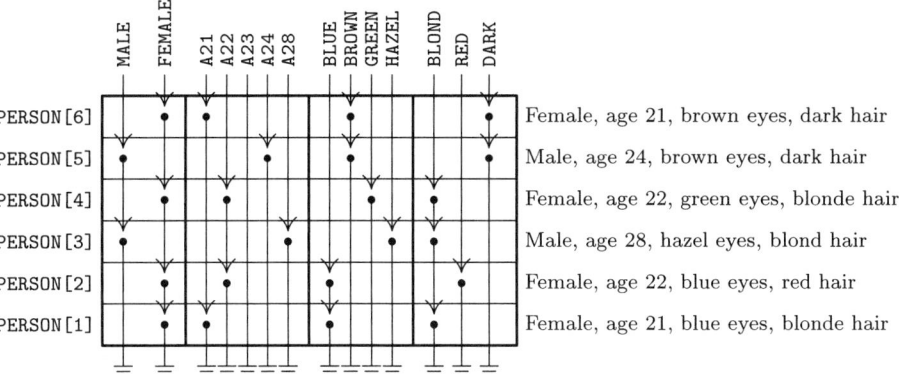

Fig. 13. Each node in four different lists.

As an example, we might have a list in which every node represents a person, with four link fields: SEX, AGE, EYES, and HAIR. In the EYES field we link together all nodes with the same eye color, etc. (See Fig. 13.) It is easy to visualize efficient algorithms for inserting new people into the list; deletion would, however, be much slower, unless we used double linking. We can also conceive of algorithms of varying degrees of efficiency for doing things like "Find all blue-eyed blonde women of ages 21 through 23"; see exercises 9 and 10. Problems in which each node of a list is to reside in several kinds of other lists at once arise rather frequently; indeed, the elevator system simulation described in the preceding section has nodes that are in both the QUEUE and WAIT lists simultaneously.

As a detailed example of the use of linked allocation for orthogonal lists, we will consider the case of *sparse matrices* (that is, matrices of large order in which most of the elements are zero). The goal is to operate on these matrices as though the entire matrix were present, but to save great amounts of time and space because the zero entries need not be represented. One way to do this, intended for random references to elements of the matrix, would be to use the storage and retrieval methods of Chapter 6, to find $A[j,k]$ from the key "$[j,k]$"; however, there is another way to deal with sparse matrices that is often preferable because it reflects the matrix structure more appropriately, and this is the method we will discuss here.

The representation we will discuss consists of circularly linked lists for each row and column. Every node of the matrix contains three words and five fields:

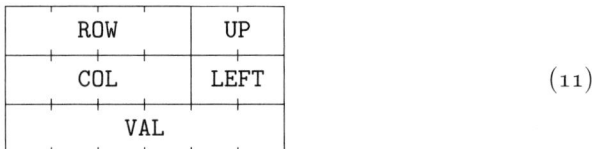

ROW	UP
COL	LEFT
VAL	

(11)

Here ROW and COL are the row and column indices of the node; VAL is the value stored at that part of the matrix; LEFT and UP are links to the next nonzero entry to the left in the row, or upward in the column, respectively. There are special list head nodes, BASEROW[i] and BASECOL[j], for every row and column. These nodes are identified by

$$\text{COL(LOC(BASEROW}[i])) < 0 \qquad \text{and} \qquad \text{ROW(LOC(BASECOL}[j])) < 0.$$

As usual in a circular list, the LEFT link in BASEROW[i] is the location of the rightmost value in that row, and UP in BASECOL[j] points to the bottom-most value in that column. For example, the matrix

$$\begin{pmatrix} 50 & 0 & 0 & 0 \\ 10 & 0 & 20 & 0 \\ 0 & 0 & 0 & 0 \\ -30 & 0 & -60 & 5 \end{pmatrix}$$

(12)

would be represented as shown in Fig. 14.

Using sequential allocation of storage, a 200×200 matrix would take 40000 words, and this is more memory than many computers used to have; but a suitably sparse 200×200 matrix can be represented as above even in MIX's 4000-word memory. (See exercise 11.) The amount of time taken to access a random element $A[j,k]$ is also quite reasonable, *if* there are but few elements in each row or column; and since most matrix algorithms proceed by walking sequentially through a matrix, instead of accessing elements at random, this linked representation often works faster than a sequential one.

As a typical example of a nontrivial algorithm dealing with sparse matrices in this form, we will consider the *pivot step* operation, which is an important part of algorithms for solving linear equations, for inverting matrices, and for

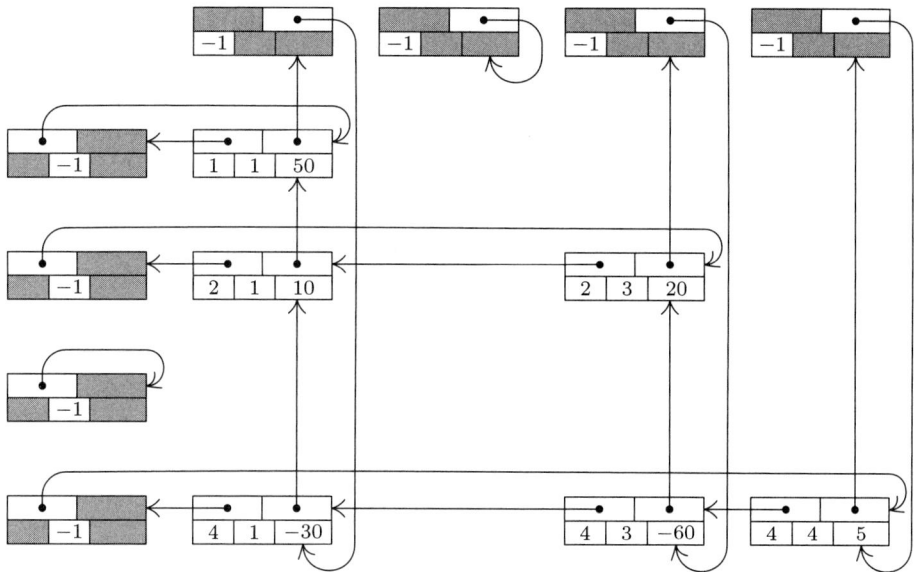

Fig. 14. Representation of matrix (12), with nodes in the format

LEFT		UP
ROW	COL	VAL

List heads appear at the left and at the top.

linear programming problems by the simplex method. A pivot step is the follow-ing matrix transformation (see M. H. Doolittle, *Report of the Superintendent of the U. S. Coast and Geodetic Survey* (1878), 115–120):

$$
\text{Before pivot step} \qquad\qquad \text{After pivot step}
$$

$$
\begin{array}{c}
 \\
\text{Pivot row} \\
 \\
\text{Any other row} \\
 \\
\end{array}
\begin{pmatrix}
\vdots & & \vdots & \\
\cdots & a & \cdots & b & \cdots \\
\vdots & & \vdots & \\
\cdots & c & \cdots & d & \cdots \\
\vdots & & \vdots & \\
\end{pmatrix},
\begin{pmatrix}
\vdots & & \vdots & \\
\cdots & 1/a & \cdots & b/a & \cdots \\
\vdots & & \vdots & \\
\cdots & -c/a & \cdots & d-bc/a & \cdots \\
\vdots & & \vdots & \\
\end{pmatrix}
\tag{13}
$$

It is assumed that the *pivot element*, a, is nonzero. For example, a pivot step applied to matrix (12), with the element 10 in row 2 column 1 as pivot, leads to

$$
\begin{pmatrix}
-5 & 0 & -100 & 0 \\
0.1 & 0 & 2 & 0 \\
0 & 0 & 0 & 0 \\
3 & 0 & 0 & 5 \\
\end{pmatrix}.
\tag{14}
$$

Our goal is to design an algorithm that performs this pivot operation on sparse matrices that are represented as in Fig. 14. It is clear that the transformation (13) affects only those rows of a matrix for which there is a nonzero element in the pivot column, and it affects only those columns for which there is a nonzero entry in the pivot row.

The pivoting algorithm is in many ways a straightforward application of linking techniques we have already discussed; in particular, it bears strong resemblances to Algorithm 2.2.4A for addition of polynomials. There are two things, however, that make the problem a little tricky: If in (13) we have $b \neq 0$ and $c \neq 0$ but $d = 0$, the sparse matrix representation has no entry for d and we must insert a new entry; and if $b \neq 0$, $c \neq 0$, $d \neq 0$, but $d - bc/a = 0$, we must delete the entry that was formerly there. These insertion and deletion operations are more interesting in a two-dimensional array than in the one-dimensional case; to do them we must know what links are affected. Our algorithm processes the matrix rows successively from bottom to top. The efficient ability to insert and delete involves the introduction of a set of pointer variables PTR[j], one for each column considered; these variables traverse the columns upwards, giving us the ability to update the proper links in both dimensions.

Algorithm S (*Pivot step in a sparse matrix*). Given a matrix represented as in Fig. 14, we perform the pivot operation (13). Assume that PIVOT is a link variable pointing to the pivot element. The algorithm makes use of an auxiliary table of link variables PTR[j], one for each column of the matrix. The variable ALPHA and the VAL field of each node are assumed to be floating point or rational quantities, while everything else in this algorithm has integer values.

S1. [Initialize.] Set ALPHA $\leftarrow$ 1.0/VAL(PIVOT), VAL(PIVOT) $\leftarrow$ 1.0, and

$$I0 \leftarrow \text{ROW(PIVOT)}, \quad P0 \leftarrow \text{LOC(BASEROW[I0])};$$
$$J0 \leftarrow \text{COL(PIVOT)}, \quad Q0 \leftarrow \text{LOC(BASECOL[J0])}.$$

S2. [Process pivot row.] Set P0 $\leftarrow$ LEFT(P0), J $\leftarrow$ COL(P0). If J $<$ 0, go on to step S3 (the pivot row has been traversed). Otherwise set PTR[J] $\leftarrow$ LOC(BASECOL[J]) and VAL(P0) $\leftarrow$ ALPHA $\times$ VAL(P0), and repeat step S2.

S3. [Find new row.] Set Q0 $\leftarrow$ UP(Q0). (The remainder of the algorithm deals successively with each row, from bottom to top, for which there is an entry in the pivot column.) Set I $\leftarrow$ ROW(Q0). If I $<$ 0, the algorithm terminates. If I $=$ I0, repeat step S3 (we have already done the pivot row). Otherwise set P $\leftarrow$ LOC(BASEROW[I]), P1 $\leftarrow$ LEFT(P). (The pointers P and P1 will now proceed across row I from right to left, as P0 goes in synchronization across row I0; Algorithm 2.2.4A is analogous. We have P0 $=$ LOC(BASEROW[I0]) at this point.)

S4. [Find new column.] Set P0 $\leftarrow$ LEFT(P0), J $\leftarrow$ COL(P0). If J $<$ 0, set VAL(Q0) $\leftarrow$ $-$ALPHA $\times$ VAL(Q0) and return to S3. If J $=$ J0, repeat step S4. (Thus we process the pivot column entry in row I *after* all other column entries have been processed; the reason is that VAL(Q0) is needed in step S7.)

S5. [Find I, J element.] If COL(P1) > J, set P ← P1, P1 ← LEFT(P), and repeat step S5. If COL(P1) = J, go to step S7. Otherwise go to step S6 (we need to insert a new element in column J of row I).

S6. [Insert I, J element.] If ROW(UP(PTR[J])) > I, set PTR[J] ← UP(PTR[J]), and repeat step S6. (Otherwise, we will have ROW(UP(PTR[J])) < I; the new element is to be inserted just above NODE(PTR[J]) in the vertical dimension, and just left of NODE(P) in the horizontal dimension.) Otherwise set X ⇐ AVAIL, VAL(X) ← 0, ROW(X) ← I, COL(X) ← J, LEFT(X) ← P1, UP(X) ← UP(PTR[J]), LEFT(P) ← X, UP(PTR[J]) ← X, P1 ← X.

S7. [Pivot.] Set VAL(P1) ← VAL(P1) − VAL(Q0) × VAL(P0). If now VAL(P1) = 0, go to S8. (*Note:* When floating point arithmetic is being used, this test "VAL(P1) = 0" should be replaced by "|VAL(P1)| < EPSILON" or better yet by the condition "most of the significant figures of VAL(P1) were lost in the subtraction.") Otherwise, set PTR[J] ← P1, P ← P1, P1 ← LEFT(P), and go back to S4.

S8. [Delete I, J element.] If UP(PTR[J]) ≠ P1 (or, what is essentially the same thing, if ROW(UP(PTR[J])) > I), set PTR[J] ← UP(PTR[J]) and repeat step S8; otherwise, set UP(PTR[J]) ← UP(P1), LEFT(P) ← LEFT(P1), AVAIL ⇐ P1, P1 ← LEFT(P). Go back to S4. ∎

The programming of this algorithm is left as a very instructive exercise for the reader (see exercise 15). It is worth pointing out here that it is necessary to allocate only one word of memory to each of the nodes BASEROW[i], BASECOL[j], since most of their fields are irrelevant. (See the shaded areas in Fig. 14, and see the program of Section 2.2.5.) Furthermore, the value −PTR[j] can be stored as ROW(LOC(BASECOL[j])) for additional storage space economy. The running time of Algorithm S is very roughly proportional to the number of matrix elements affected by the pivot operation.

This representation of sparse matrices via orthogonal circular lists is instructive, but numerical analysts have developed better methods. See Fred G. Gustavson, *ACM Trans. on Math. Software* **4** (1978), 250–269; see also the graph and network algorithms in Chapter 7 (for example, Algorithm 7B).

EXERCISES

1. [*17*] Give a formula for LOC(A[J,K]) if A is the matrix of (1), and if each node of the array is two words long, assuming that the nodes are stored consecutively in lexicographic order of the indices.

▶ **2.** [*21*] Formulas (5) and (6) have been derived from the assumption that $0 \le I_r \le d_r$ for $1 \le r \le k$. Give a general formula that applies to the case $l_r \le I_r \le u_r$, where l_r and u_r are any lower and upper bounds on the dimensionality.

3. [*21*] The text considers lower triangular matrices A[j,k] for $0 \le k \le j \le n$. How can the discussion of such matrices readily be modified for the case that subscripts start at 1 instead of 0, so that $1 \le k \le j \le n$?

4. [*22*] Show that if we store the *upper* triangular array A[j,k] for $0 \le j \le k \le n$ in lexicographic order of the indices, the allocation satisfies the condition of Eq. (8). Find a formula for LOC(A[J,K]) in this sense.

5. [*20*] Show that it is possible to bring the value of A[J,K] into register A in one MIX instruction, using the indirect addressing feature of exercise 2.2.2–3, even when A is a *triangular* matrix as in (9). (Assume that the values of J and K are in index registers.)

▸ **6.** [*M24*] Consider the "tetrahedral arrays" A[i,j,k], B[i,j,k], where $0 \leq k \leq j \leq i \leq n$ in A, and $0 \leq i \leq j \leq k \leq n$ in B. Suppose that both of these arrays are stored in consecutive memory locations in lexicographic order of the indices; show that LOC(A[I,J,K]) $= a_0 + f_1(\text{I}) + f_2(\text{J}) + f_3(\text{K})$ for certain functions f_1, f_2, f_3. Can LOC(B[I,J,K]) be expressed in a similar manner?

7. [*M23*] Find a general formula to allocate storage for the k-dimensional tetrahedral array A[$i_1,i_2,\ldots,i_k$], where $0 \leq i_k \leq \cdots \leq i_2 \leq i_1 \leq n$.

8. [*33*] (P. Wegner.) Suppose we have six tetrahedral arrays A[I,J,K], B[I,J,K], C[I,J,K], D[I,J,K], E[I,J,K], and F[I,J,K] to store in memory, where $0 \leq \text{K} \leq \text{J} \leq \text{I} \leq n$. Is there a neat way to accomplish this, analogous to (10) in the two-dimensional case?

9. [*22*] Suppose a table, like that indicated in Fig. 13 but much larger, has been set up so that all links go in the same direction as shown there (namely, LINK(X) $<$ X for all nodes and links). Design an algorithm that finds the addresses of all blue-eyed blonde women of ages 21 through 23, by going through the various link fields in such a way that upon completion of the algorithm at most one pass has been made through each of the lists FEMALE, A21, A22, A23, BLOND, and BLUE.

10. [*26*] Can you think of a better way to organize a personnel table so that searches as described in the previous exercise would be more efficient? (The answer to this exercise is *not* merely "yes" or "no.")

11. [*11*] Suppose that we have a 200×200 matrix in which there are at most four nonzero entries per row. How much storage is required to represent this matrix as in Fig. 14, if we use three words per node except for list heads, which will use one word?

▸ **12.** [*20*] What are VAL(Q0), VAL(P0), and VAL(P1) at the beginning of step S7, in terms of the notation a, b, c, d used in (13)?

▸ **13.** [*22*] Why were circular lists used in Fig. 14 instead of straight linear lists? Could Algorithm S be rewritten so that it does not make use of the circular linkage?

14. [*22*] Algorithm S actually saves pivoting time in a sparse matrix, since it avoids consideration of those columns in which the pivot row has a zero entry. Show that this savings in running time can be achieved in a large sparse matrix that is stored sequentially, with the help of an auxiliary table LINK[j], $1 \leq j \leq n$.

▸ **15.** [*29*] Write a MIXAL program for Algorithm S. Assume that the VAL field is a floating point number, and that MIX's floating point arithmetic operators FADD, FSUB, FMUL, and FDIV can be used for operations on this field. Assume for simplicity that FADD and FSUB return the answer zero when the operands added or subtracted cancel most of the significance, so that the test "VAL(P1) $= 0$" may safely be used in step S7. The floating point operations use only rA, not rX.

16. [*25*] Design an algorithm to *copy* a sparse matrix. (In other words, the algorithm is to yield two distinct representations of a matrix in memory, having the form of Fig. 14, given just one such representation initially.)

17. [*26*] Design an algorithm to *multiply* two sparse matrices; given matrices A and B, form a new matrix C, where C[i,j] $= \sum_k$ A[i,k]B[k,j]. The two input matrices and the output matrix should be represented as in Fig. 14.

18. [*22*] The following algorithm replaces a matrix by the inverse of that matrix, assuming that the entries are A[i,j], for $1 \le i, j \le n$:

i) For $k = 1, 2, \ldots, n$ do the following: Search row k in all columns not yet used as a pivot column, to find an entry with the greatest absolute value; set C[k] equal to the column in which this entry was found, and do a pivot step with this entry as pivot. (If all such entries are zero, the matrix is singular and has no inverse.)

ii) Permute rows and columns so that what was row k becomes row C[k], and what was column C[k] becomes column k.

The problem in this exercise is to use the stated algorithm to invert the matrix

$$\begin{pmatrix} 1 & 2 & 3 \\ 0 & 1 & 2 \\ 0 & 0 & 1 \end{pmatrix}$$

by hand calculation.

19. [*31*] Modify the algorithm described in exercise 18 so that it obtains the inverse of a sparse matrix that is represented in the form of Fig. 14. Pay special attention to making the row- and column-permutation operations of step (ii) efficient.

20. [*20*] A *tridiagonal matrix* has entries a_{ij} that are zero except when $|i - j| \le 1$, for $1 \le i, j \le n$. Show that there is an allocation function of the form

$$\text{LOC(A[I,J])} = a_0 + a_1 I + a_2 J, \quad |I - J| \le 1,$$

which represents all of the relevant elements of a tridiagonal matrix in $(3n - 2)$ consecutive locations.

21. [*20*] Suggest a storage allocation function for $n \times n$ matrices where n is variable. The elements A[I,J] for $1 \le I, J \le n$ should occupy n^2 consecutive locations, regardless of the value of n.

22. [*M25*] (P. Chowla, 1961.) Find a polynomial $p(i_1, \ldots, i_k)$ that assumes each nonnegative integer value exactly once as the indices $(i_1, \ldots, i_k)$ run through all k-dimensional nonnegative integer vectors, with the additional property that $i_1 + \cdots + i_k < j_1 + \cdots + j_k$ implies $p(i_1, \ldots, i_k) < p(j_1, \ldots, j_k)$.

23. [*23*] An *extendible matrix* is initially 1×1, then it grows from size $m \times n$ either to size $(m + 1) \times n$ or to size $m \times (n + 1)$ by adding either a new row or a new column. Show that such a matrix can be given a simple allocation function in which the elements A[I,J] occupy mn consecutive locations, for $0 \le I < m$ and $0 \le J < n$; no elements change location when the matrix grows.

▶ **24.** [*25*] (*The sparse array trick.*) Suppose you want to use a large array for random access, although you won't actually be referring to very many of its entries. You want A[k] to be zero the first time you access it, yet you don't want to spend the time to set every location to zero. Explain how it is possible to read and write any desired elements A[k] reliably, given k, without assuming anything about the actual initial memory contents, by doing only a small fixed number of additional operations per array access.

2.3. TREES

WE NOW TURN to a study of trees, the most important nonlinear structures
that arise in computer algorithms. Generally speaking, tree structure means a
"branching" relationship between nodes, much like that found in the trees of
nature.

Let us define a *tree* formally as a finite set T of one or more nodes such that

a) there is one specially designated node called the *root* of the tree, $\text{root}(T)$;
   and

b) the remaining nodes (excluding the root) are partitioned into $m \geq 0$ disjoint
   sets $T_1, \ldots, T_m$, and each of these sets in turn is a tree. The trees $T_1, \ldots, T_m$
   are called the *subtrees* of the root.

The definition just given is recursive: We have defined a tree in terms of
trees. Of course, there is no problem of circularity involved here, since trees
with one node must consist of only the root, and trees with $n > 1$ nodes are
defined in terms of trees with fewer than n nodes; hence the concept of a tree
with two nodes, three nodes, or ultimately any number of nodes, is determined
by the definition given. There are nonrecursive ways to define trees (for example,
see exercises 10, 12, and 14, and Section 2.3.4), but a recursive definition seems
most appropriate since recursion is an innate characteristic of tree structures.
The recursive character of trees is present also in nature, since buds on young
trees eventually grow into subtrees with buds of their own, and so on. Exercise 3
illustrates how to give rigorous proofs of important facts about trees based on a
recursive definition such as the one above, by using induction on the number of
nodes in a tree.

It follows from our definition that every node of a tree is the root of some
subtree contained in the whole tree. The number of subtrees of a node is called
the *degree* of that node. A node of degree zero is called a *terminal node*, or
sometimes a *leaf*. A nonterminal node is often called a *branch node*. The *level*
of a node with respect to T is defined recursively: The level of $\text{root}(T)$ is zero,
and the level of any other node is one higher than that node's level with respect
to the subtree of $\text{root}(T)$ containing it.

These concepts are illustrated in Fig. 15, which shows a tree with seven
nodes. The root is A, and it has the two subtrees $\{B\}$ and $\{C, D, E, F, G\}$. The
tree $\{C, D, E, F, G\}$ has node C as its root. Node C is on level 1 with respect to
the whole tree, and it has three subtrees $\{D\}$, $\{E\}$, and $\{F, G\}$; therefore C has
degree 3. The terminal nodes in Fig. 15 are B, D, E, and G; F is the only node
with degree 1; G is the only node with level 3.

If the relative order of the subtrees $T_1, \ldots, T_m$ in (b) of the definition is
important, we say that the tree is an *ordered tree*; when $m \geq 2$ in an ordered
tree, it makes sense to call T_2 the "second subtree" of the root, etc. Ordered trees
are also called "plane trees" by some authors, since the manner of embedding
the tree in a plane is relevant. If we do not care to regard two trees as different
when they differ only in the respective ordering of subtrees of nodes, the tree
is said to be *oriented*, since only the relative orientation of the nodes, not their

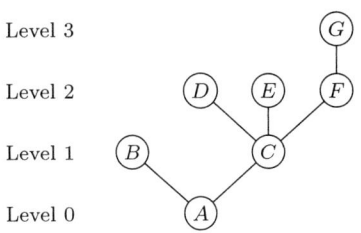

Level 3

Level 2

Level 1

Level 0

Fig. 15. A tree.

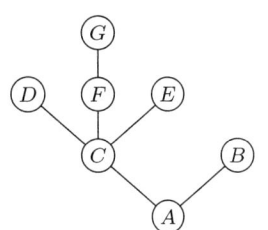

Fig. 16. Another tree.

order, is being considered. The very nature of computer representation defines an implicit ordering for any tree, so in most cases ordered trees are of greatest interest to us. We will therefore tacitly assume that *all trees we discuss are ordered, unless explicitly stated otherwise.* Accordingly, the trees of Figs. 15 and 16 will generally be considered to be different, although they would be the same as oriented trees.

A *forest* is a set (usually an ordered set) of zero or more disjoint trees. Another way to phrase part (b) of the definition of tree would be to say that *the nodes of a tree excluding the root form a forest.*

There is very little distinction between abstract forests and trees. If we delete the root of a tree, we have a forest; conversely, if we add just one node to any forest and regard the trees of the forest as subtrees of the new node, we get a tree. Therefore the words tree and forest are often used almost interchangeably during informal discussions about data structures.

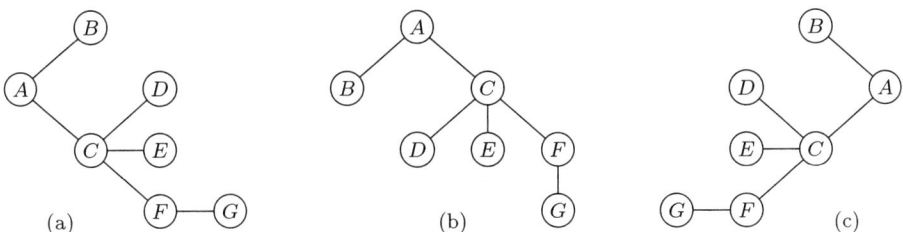

(a)   (b)   (c)

Fig. 17. How shall we draw a tree?

Trees can be drawn in many ways. Besides the diagram of Fig. 15, three of the principal alternatives are shown in Fig. 17, depending on where the root is placed. It is not a frivolous joke to worry about how tree structures are drawn in diagrams, since there are many occasions in which we want to say that one node is "above" or "higher than" another node, or to refer to the "rightmost" element, etc. Certain algorithms for dealing with tree structures have become known as "top down" methods, as opposed to "bottom up." Such terminology leads to confusion unless we adhere to a uniform convention for drawing trees.

It may seem that the form of Fig. 15 would be preferable simply because that is how trees grow in nature; in the absence of any compelling reason to adopt any of the other three forms, we might as well adopt nature's time-honored

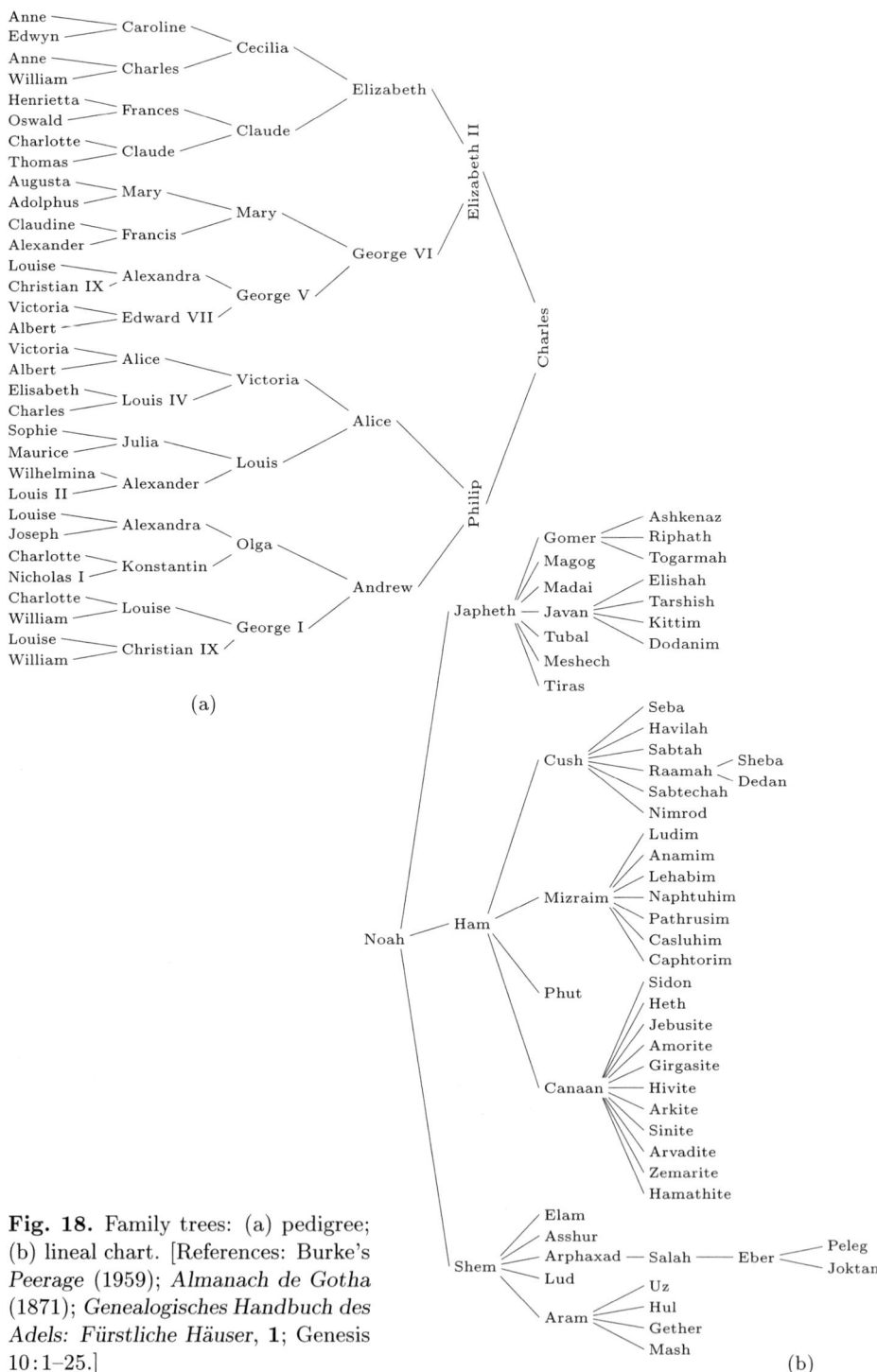

Fig. 18. Family trees: (a) pedigree; (b) lineal chart. [References: Burke's *Peerage* (1959); *Almanach de Gotha* (1871); *Genealogisches Handbuch des Adels: Fürstliche Häuser*, **1**; Genesis 10:1–25.]

tradition. With real trees in mind, the author consistently followed a root-at-the-bottom convention as the present set of books was first being prepared, but after two years of trial it was found to be a mistake: Observations of the computer literature and numerous informal discussions with computer scientists about a wide variety of algorithms showed that trees were drawn with the *root at the top* in more than 80 percent of the cases examined. There is an overwhelming tendency to make hand-drawn charts grow downwards instead of upwards (and this is easy to understand in view of the way we write); even the word "subtree," as opposed to "supertree," tends to connote a downward relationship. From these considerations we conclude that *Fig. 15 is upside down.* Henceforth we will almost always draw trees as in Fig. 17(b), with the root at the top and leaves at the bottom. Corresponding to this orientation, we should perhaps call the root node the *apex* of the tree, and speak of nodes at *shallow* and *deep* levels.

It is necessary to have good descriptive terminology for talking about trees. Instead of making somewhat ambiguous references to "above" and "below," we generally use genealogical words taken from the terminology of *family trees.* Figure 18 shows two common types of family trees. The two types are quite different: A *pedigree* shows the ancestors of a given individual, while a *lineal chart* shows the descendants.

If "cross-breeding" occurs, a pedigree is not really a tree, because different branches of a tree (as we have defined it) can never be joined together. To compensate for this discrepancy, Fig. 18(a) mentions Queen Victoria and Prince Albert twice in the sixth generation; King Christian IX and Queen Louise actually appear in both the fifth and sixth generations. A pedigree can be regarded as a true tree if each of its nodes represents "a person in the role of mother or father of so-and-so," not simply a person as an individual.

Standard terminology for tree structures is taken from the *second* form of family tree, the lineal chart: Each root is said to be the *parent* of the roots of its subtrees, and the latter are said to be *siblings*; they are *children* of their parent. The root of the entire tree has no parent. For example, in Fig. 19, C has three children, D, E, and F; E is the parent of G; B and C are siblings. Extension of this terminology — for example, A is the great-grandparent of G; B is an aunt or uncle of F; H and F are first cousins — is clearly possible. Some authors use the masculine designations "father, son, brother" instead of "parent, child, sibling"; others use "mother, daughter, sister." In any case a node has at most one parent or progenitor. We use the words *ancestor* and *descendant* to denote a relationship that may span several levels of the tree: The descendants of C in Fig. 19 are D, E, F, and G; the ancestors of G are E, C, and A. Sometimes, especially when talking

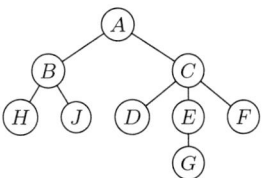

Fig. 19. Conventional tree diagram.

about "nearest common ancestors," we consider a node to be an ancestor of itself (and a descendant of itself); the *inclusive ancestors* of G are G, E, C, and A, while its *proper ancestors* are just E, C, and A.

The pedigree in Figure 18(a) is an example of a *binary tree*, which is another important type of tree structure. The reader has undoubtedly seen binary trees in connection with tennis tournaments or other sporting events. In a binary tree each node has at most two subtrees; and when only one subtree is present, we distinguish between the left and right subtree. More formally, let us define a binary tree as *a finite set of nodes that either is empty, or consists of a root and the elements of two disjoint binary trees* called the left and right subtrees of the root.

This recursive definition of binary tree should be studied carefully. Notice that a binary tree is *not* a special case of a tree; it is another concept entirely (although we will see many relations between the two concepts). For example, the binary trees

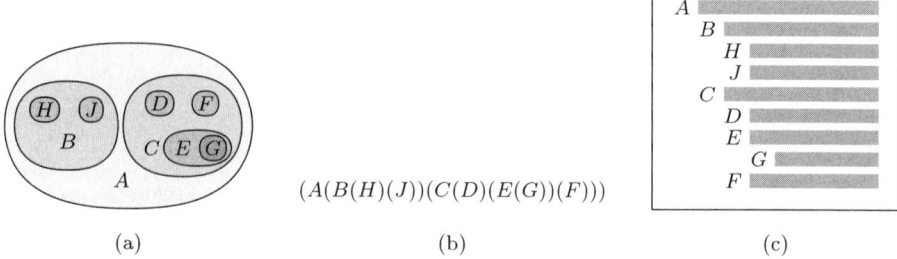

$$\text{and} \tag{1}$$

are distinct — the root has an empty right subtree in one case and a nonempty right subtree in the other — although as trees these diagrams would represent identical structures. A binary tree can be empty; a tree cannot. Therefore we will always be careful to use the word "binary" to distinguish between binary trees and ordinary trees. Some authors define binary trees in a slightly different manner (see exercise 20).

Tree structure can be represented graphically in several other ways bearing no resemblance to actual trees. Figure 20 shows three diagrams that reflect the structure of Fig. 19: Figure 20(a) essentially represents Fig. 19 as an *oriented tree*; this diagram is a special case of the general idea of *nested sets*, namely a collection of sets in which any pair of sets is either disjoint or one contains the other. (See exercise 10.) Part (b) of the figure shows nested sets in a line, much as part (a) shows them in a plane; in part (b) the ordering of the tree is also indicated. Part (b) may also be regarded as an outline of an algebraic formula involving nested parentheses. Part (c) shows still another common way to represent tree structure, using *indentation*. The number of different representation methods in itself is ample evidence for the importance of tree structures in everyday life as well as in computer programming. Any hierarchical classification scheme leads to a tree structure.

$$(A(B(H)(J))(C(D)(E(G))(F)))$$

(a)   (b)   (c)

Fig. 20. Further ways to show tree structure: (a) nested sets; (b) nested parentheses; (c) indentation.

An algebraic formula defines an implicit tree structure that is often conveyed by other means instead of, or in addition to, the use of parentheses. For example, Figure 21 shows a tree corresponding to the arithmetic expression

$$a - b(c/d + e/f). \tag{2}$$

Standard mathematical conventions, according to which multiplication and division take precedence over addition and subtraction, allow us to use a simplified form like (2) instead of the fully parenthesized form "$a - \big(b \times \big((c/d) + (e/f)\big)\big)$". This connection between formulas and trees is very important in applications.

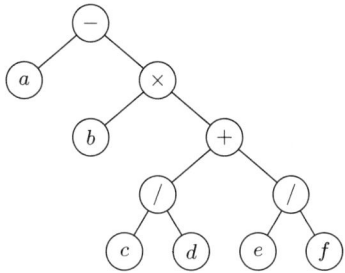

Fig. 21. Tree representation of formula (2).

Notice that the indented list in Fig. 20(c) looks very much like the table of contents in a book. Indeed, this book itself has a tree structure; the tree structure of Chapter 2 is shown in Fig. 22. Here we notice a significant idea: *The method used to number sections in this book is another way to specify tree structure.* Such a method is often called "Dewey decimal notation" for trees, by analogy with the similar classification scheme of this name used in libraries. The Dewey decimal notation for the tree of Fig. 19 is

1 *A*;　1.1 *B*;　1.1.1 *H*;　1.1.2 *J*;　1.2 *C*;
1.2.1 *D*;　1.2.2 *E*;　1.2.2.1 *G*;　1.2.3 *F*.

Dewey decimal notation applies to any forest: The root of the kth tree in the forest is given number k; and if α is the number of any node of degree m, its children are numbered $\alpha.1, \alpha.2, \ldots, \alpha.m$. The Dewey decimal notation satisfies many simple mathematical properties, and it is a useful tool in the analysis of trees. One example of this is the natural sequential ordering it gives to the nodes of an arbitrary tree, analogous to the ordering of sections within this book. Section 2.3 precedes Section 2.3.1, and follows Section 2.2.6.

There is an intimate relation between Dewey decimal notation and the notation for indexed variables that we have already been using extensively. If F is a forest of trees, we may let $F[1]$ denote the subtrees of the first tree, so that $F[1][2] \equiv F[1, 2]$ stands for the subtrees of the second subtree of $F[1]$, and $F[1, 2, 1]$ stands for the first subforest of the latter, and so on. Node $a.b.c.d$ in Dewey decimal notation is the parent of $F[a, b, c, d]$. This notation is an extension of ordinary index notation, because the admissible range of each index depends on the values in the preceding index positions.

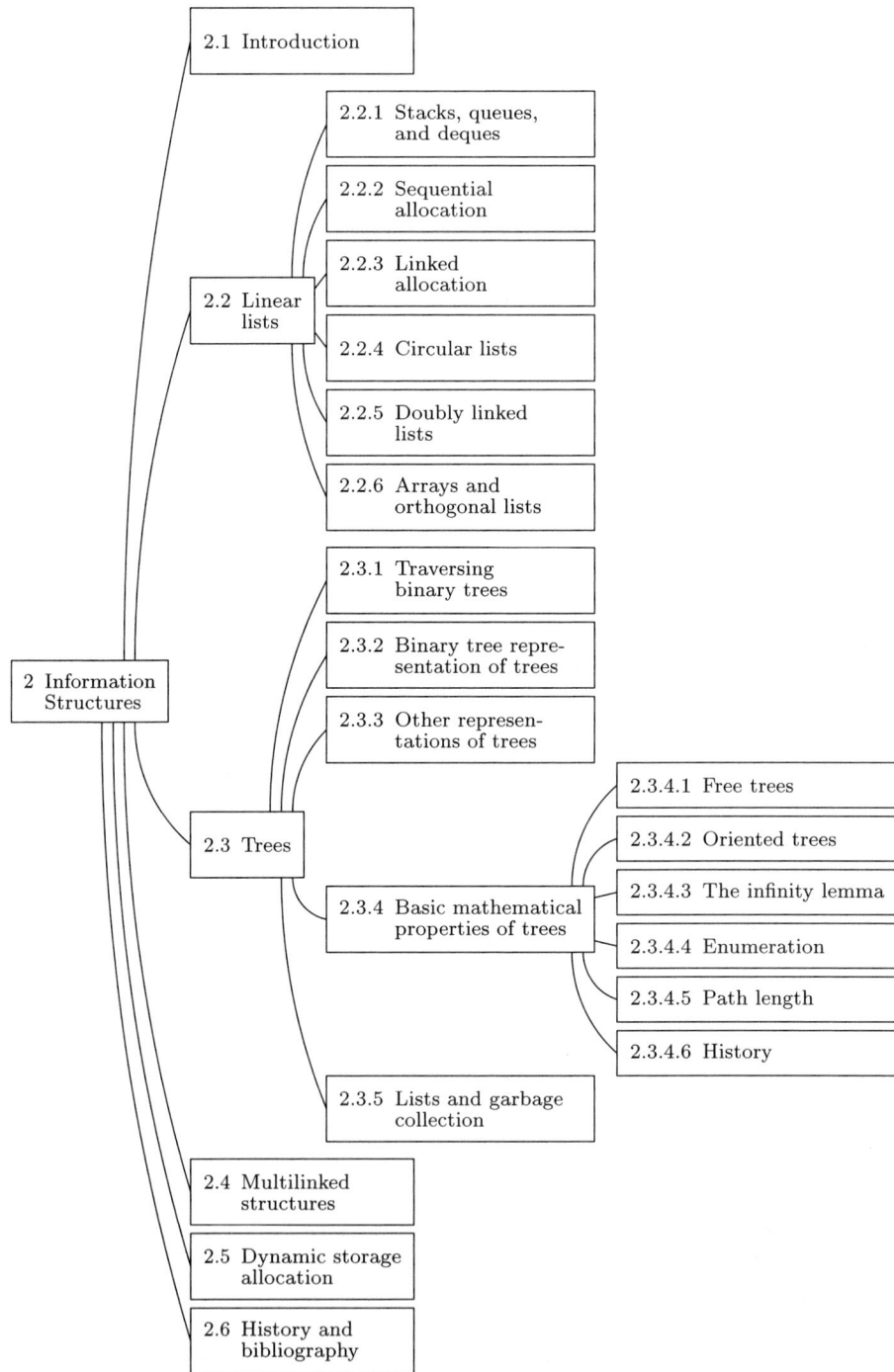

Fig. 22. The structure of Chapter 2.

Thus, in particular, we see that any rectangular array can be thought of as a special case of a tree or forest structure. For example, here are two representations of a 3×4 matrix:

$$\begin{pmatrix} A[1,1] & A[1,2] & A[1,3] & A[1,4] \\ A[2,1] & A[2,2] & A[2,3] & A[2,4] \\ A[3,1] & A[3,2] & A[3,3] & A[3,4] \end{pmatrix}$$

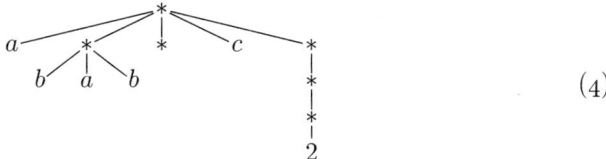

It is important to observe, however, that this tree structure does not faithfully reflect all of the matrix structure; the row relationships appear explicitly in the tree but the column relationships do not.

A forest can, in turn, be regarded as a special case of what is commonly called a *list structure*. The word "list" is being used here in a very technical sense, and to distinguish the technical use of the word we will always capitalize it: "List." A List is defined (recursively) as *a finite sequence of zero or more atoms or Lists.* Here "atom" is an undefined concept referring to elements from any universe of objects that might be desired, so long as it is possible to distinguish an atom from a List. By means of an obvious notational convention involving commas and parentheses, we can distinguish between atoms and Lists and we can conveniently display the ordering within a List. As an example, consider

$$L = (a, \ (b,a,b), \ (\ ), \ c, \ (((2)))), \tag{3}$$

which is a List with five elements: first the atom a, then the List (b, a, b), then the empty List ( ), then the atom c, and finally the List $(((2)))$. The latter List consists of the List $((2))$, which consists of the List (2), which consists of the atom 2.

The following tree structure corresponds to L:

$$\tag{4}$$

The asterisks in this diagram indicate the definition and appearance of a List, as opposed to the appearance of an atom. Index notation applies to Lists as it does to forests; for example, $L[2] = (b, a, b)$, and $L[2, 2] = a$.

No data is carried in the nodes for the Lists in (4) other than the fact that they are Lists. But it is possible to label the nonatomic elements of Lists with information, as we have done for trees and other structures; thus

$$A = (a\!:\!(b,c), \ d\!:\!(\ ))$$

would correspond to a tree that we can draw as follows:

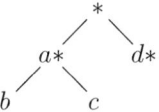

The big difference between Lists and trees is that Lists may overlap (that is, sub-Lists need not be disjoint) and they may even be recursive (may contain themselves). The List

$$M = (M) \tag{5}$$

corresponds to no tree structure, nor does the List

$$N = (a\!:\!M, b\!:\!M, c, N). \tag{6}$$

(In these examples, capital letters refer to Lists, lowercase letters to labels and atoms.) We might diagram (5) and (6) as follows, using an asterisk to denote each place where a List is defined:

$$\tag{7}$$

Actually, Lists are not so complicated as the examples above might indicate. They are, in essence, a rather simple generalization of the linear lists that we have considered in Section 2.2, with the additional proviso that the elements of linear Lists may be link variables that point to other linear Lists (and possibly to themselves).

Summary: Four closely related kinds of information structures — trees, forests, binary trees, and Lists — arise from many sources, and they are therefore important in computer algorithms. We have seen various ways to diagram these structures, and we have considered some terminology and notations that are useful in talking about them. The following sections develop these ideas in greater detail.

EXERCISES

1. [*18*] How many different trees are there with three nodes, A, B, and C?

2. [*20*] How many different *oriented* trees are there with three nodes, A, B, and C?

3. [*M20*] Prove rigorously from the definitions that for every node X in a tree there is a unique path up to the root, namely a unique sequence of $k \geq 1$ nodes $X_1, X_2, \ldots, X_k$ such that X_1 is the root of the tree, $X_k = X$, and X_j is the parent of X_{j+1} for $1 \leq j < k$. (This proof will be typical of the proofs of nearly all the elementary facts about tree structures.) *Hint:* Use induction on the number of nodes in the tree.

4. [*01*] True or false: In a conventional tree diagram (root at the top), if node X has a *higher* level number than node Y, then node X appears *lower* in the diagram than node Y.

5. [*02*] If node A has three siblings and B is the parent of A, what is the degree of B?

▶ **6.** [*21*] Define the statement "X is an mth cousin of Y, n times removed" as a meaningful relation between nodes X and Y of a tree, by analogy with family trees, if $m > 0$ and $n \geq 0$. (See a dictionary for the meaning of these terms in regard to family trees.)

7. [*23*] Extend the definition given in the previous exercise to all $m \geq -1$ and to all integers $n \geq -(m+1)$ in such a way that for any two nodes X and Y of a tree there are unique m and n such that X is an mth cousin of Y, n times removed.

▶ **8.** [*03*] What binary tree is not a tree?

9. [*00*] In the two binary trees of (1), which node is the root (B or A)?

10. [*M20*] A collection of nonempty sets is said to be *nested* if, given any pair X, Y of the sets, either $X \subseteq Y$ or $X \supseteq Y$ or X and Y are disjoint. (In other words, $X \cap Y$ is either X, Y, or $\emptyset$.) Figure 20(a) indicates that any tree corresponds to a collection of nested sets; conversely, does every such collection correspond to a tree?

▶ **11.** [*HM32*] Extend the definition of tree to infinite trees by considering collections of nested sets as in exercise 10. Can the concepts of level, degree, parent, and child be defined for each node of an infinite tree? Give examples of nested sets of real numbers that correspond to a tree in which
   a) every node has uncountable degree and there are infinitely many levels;
   b) there are nodes with uncountable level;
   c) every node has degree at least 2 and there are uncountably many levels.

12. [*M23*] Under what conditions does a partially ordered set correspond to an unordered tree or forest? (Partially ordered sets are defined in Section 2.2.3.)

13. [*10*] Suppose that node X is numbered $a_1.a_2. \cdots .a_k$ in the Dewey decimal system; what are the Dewey numbers of the nodes in the path from X to the root (see exercise 3)?

14. [*M22*] Let S be any nonempty set of elements having the form "$1.a_1. \cdots .a_k$", where $k \geq 0$ and $a_1, \ldots, a_k$ are positive integers. Show that S specifies a tree when it is finite and satisfies the following condition: "If $\alpha.m$ is in the set, then so is $\alpha.(m-1)$ if $m > 1$, or α if $m = 1$." (This condition is clearly satisfied in the Dewey decimal notation for a tree; therefore it is another way to characterize tree structure.)

▶ **15.** [*20*] Invent a notation for the nodes of binary trees, analogous to the Dewey decimal notation for nodes of trees.

16. [*20*] Draw trees analogous to Fig. 21 corresponding to the arithmetic expressions (a) $2(a - b/c)$; (b) $a + b + 5c$.

17. [*01*] If Z stands for Fig. 19 regarded as a forest, what node is parent($Z[1, 2, 2]$)?

18. [*08*] In List (3), what is $L[5, 1, 1]$? What is $L[3, 1]$?

19. [*15*] Draw a List diagram analogous to (7) for the List $L = (a, (L))$. What is $L[2]$ in this List? What is $L[2, 1, 1]$?

▶ **20.** [*M21*] Define a *0-2-tree* as a tree in which each node has exactly zero or two children. (Formally, a 0-2-tree consists of a single node, called its root, plus 0 or 2 disjoint 0-2-trees.) Show that every 0-2-tree has an odd number of nodes; and give a one-to-one correspondence between binary trees with n nodes and (ordered) 0-2-trees with $2n + 1$ nodes.

21. [*M22*] If a tree has n_1 nodes of degree 1, n_2 nodes of degree 2, ..., and n_m nodes of degree m, how many terminal nodes does it have?

▸ **22.** [*21*] Standard European paper sizes A0, A1, A2, ..., An, ... are rectangles whose sides are in the ratio $\sqrt{2}$ to 1 and whose areas are 2^{-n} square meters. Therefore if we cut a sheet of An paper in half, we get two sheets of A($n+1$) paper. Use this principle to design a graphic representation of binary trees, and illustrate your idea by drawing the representation of 2.3.1–(1) below.

2.3.1. Traversing Binary Trees

It is important to acquire a good understanding of the properties of binary trees before making further investigations of trees, since general trees are usually represented in terms of some equivalent binary tree inside a computer.

We have defined a binary tree as a finite set of nodes that either is empty, or consists of a root together with two binary trees. This definition suggests a natural way to represent binary trees within a computer: We can have two links, LLINK and RLINK, within each node, and a link variable T that is a "pointer to the tree." If the tree is empty, T = Λ; otherwise T is the address of the root node of the tree, and LLINK(T), RLINK(T) are pointers to the left and right subtrees of the root, respectively. These rules recursively define the memory representation of any binary tree; for example,

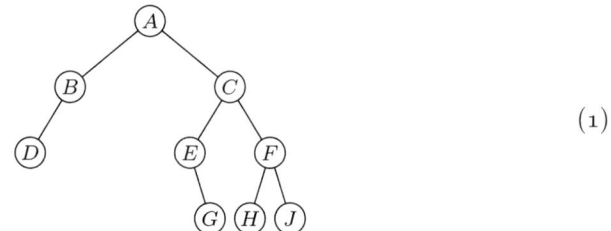

$$(1)$$

is represented by

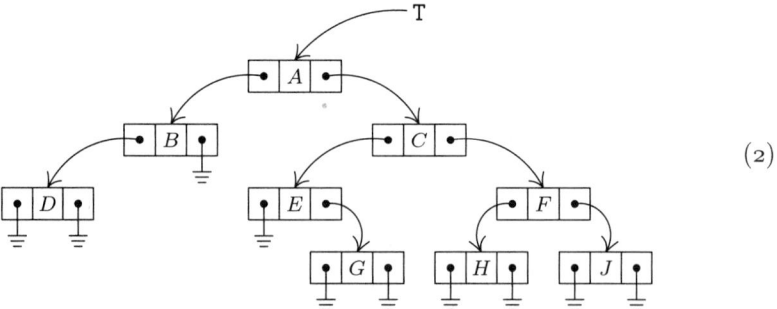

$$(2)$$

This simple and natural memory representation accounts for the special importance of binary tree structures. We will see in Section 2.3.2 that general trees can conveniently be represented as binary trees. Moreover, many trees that arise in applications are themselves inherently binary, so binary trees are of interest in their own right.

There are many algorithms for manipulation of tree structures, and one idea that occurs repeatedly in these algorithms is the notion of *traversing* or "walking through" a tree. This is a method of examining the nodes of the tree systematically so that each node is visited exactly once. A complete traversal of the tree gives us a linear arrangement of the nodes, and many algorithms are facilitated if we can talk about the "next" node following or preceding a given node in such a sequence.

Three principal ways may be used to traverse a binary tree: We can visit the nodes in *preorder*, *inorder*, or *postorder*. These three methods are defined recursively. When the binary tree is empty, it is "traversed" by doing nothing; otherwise the traversal proceeds in three steps:

Preorder traversal	Inorder traversal
Visit the root	Traverse the left subtree
Traverse the left subtree	Visit the root
Traverse the right subtree	Traverse the right subtree

Postorder traversal
Traverse the left subtree
Traverse the right subtree
Visit the root

If we apply these definitions to the binary tree of (1) and (2), we find that the nodes in preorder are

$$A \quad B \quad D \quad C \quad E \quad G \quad F \quad H \quad J. \tag{3}$$

(First comes the root A, then comes the left subtree

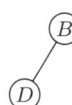

in preorder, and finally we traverse the right subtree in preorder.) For inorder we visit the root between visits to the nodes of each subtree, essentially as though the nodes were "projected" down onto a single horizontal line, and this gives the sequence

$$D \quad B \quad A \quad E \quad G \quad C \quad H \quad F \quad J. \tag{4}$$

The postorder for the nodes of this binary tree is, similarly,

$$D \quad B \quad G \quad E \quad H \quad J \quad F \quad C \quad A. \tag{5}$$

We will see that these three ways of arranging the nodes of a binary tree into a sequence are extremely important, as they are intimately connected with most of the computer methods for dealing with trees. The names *preorder*, *inorder*, and *postorder* come, of course, from the relative position of the root with respect to its subtrees. In many applications of binary trees, there is symmetry between the meanings of left subtrees and right subtrees, and in such cases the term *symmetric order* is used as a synonym for inorder. Inorder, which puts the root

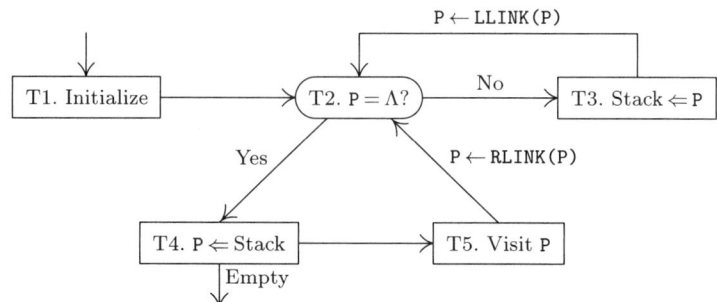

Fig. 23. Algorithm T for inorder traversal.

in the middle, is essentially symmetric between left and right: If the binary tree is reflected about a vertical axis, the symmetric order is simply reversed.

A recursively stated definition, such as the one just given for the three basic orders, must be reworked in order to make it directly applicable to computer implementation. General methods for doing this are discussed in Chapter 8; we usually make use of an auxiliary stack, as in the following algorithm:

Algorithm T (*Traverse binary tree in inorder*). Let T be a pointer to a binary tree having a representation as in (2); this algorithm visits all the nodes of the binary tree in inorder, making use of an auxiliary stack A.

T1. [Initialize.] Set stack A empty, and set the link variable P ← T.

T2. [P = Λ?] If P = Λ, go to step T4.

T3. [Stack ⇐ P.] (Now P points to a nonempty binary tree that is to be traversed.) Set A ⇐ P; that is, push the value of P onto stack A. (See Section 2.2.1.) Then set P ← LLINK(P) and return to step T2.

T4. [P ⇐ Stack.] If stack A is empty, the algorithm terminates; otherwise set P ⇐ A.

T5. [Visit P.] Visit NODE(P). Then set P ← RLINK(P) and return to step T2. ▮

In the final step of this algorithm, the word "visit" means that we do whatever activity is intended as the tree is being traversed. Algorithm T runs like a coroutine with respect to this other activity: The main program activates the coroutine whenever it wants P to move from one node to its inorder successor. Of course, since this coroutine calls the main routine in only one place, it is not much different from a subroutine (see Section 1.4.2). Algorithm T assumes that the external activity deletes neither NODE(P) nor any of its ancestors from the tree.

The reader should now attempt to play through Algorithm T using the binary tree (2) as a test case, in order to see the reasons behind the procedure. When we get to step T3, we want to traverse the binary tree whose root is indicated by pointer P. The idea is to save P on a stack and then to traverse the left subtree; when this has been done, we will get to step T4 and will find the old value of P on the stack again. After visiting the root, NODE(P), in step T5, the remaining job is to traverse the right subtree.

Algorithm T is typical of many other algorithms that we will see later, so it is instructive to look at a formal proof of the remarks made in the preceding paragraph. Let us now attempt to *prove* that Algorithm T traverses a binary tree of n nodes in inorder, by using induction on n. Our goal is readily established if we can prove a slightly more general result:

> *Starting at step T2 with* P *a pointer to a binary tree of n nodes and with the stack* A *containing* A[1] ... A[m] *for some $m \geq 0$, the procedure of steps T2–T5 will traverse the binary tree in question, in inorder, and will then arrive at step T4 with stack* A *returned to its original value* A[1] ... A[m].

This statement is obviously true when $n = 0$, because of step T2. If $n > 0$, let P_0 be the value of P upon entry to step T2. Since $P_0 \neq \Lambda$, we will perform step T3, which means that stack A is changed to A[1] ... A[m] P_0 and P is set to LLINK(P_0). Now the left subtree has fewer than n nodes, so by induction we will traverse the left subtree in inorder and will ultimately arrive at step T4 with A[1] ... A[m] P_0 on the stack. Step T4 returns the stack to A[1] ... A[m] and sets P $\leftarrow$ P_0. Step T5 now visits NODE(P_0) and sets P $\leftarrow$ RLINK(P_0). Now the right subtree has fewer than n nodes, so by induction we will traverse the right subtree in inorder and arrive at step T4 as required. The tree has been traversed in inorder, by the definition of that order. This completes the proof.

An almost identical algorithm may be formulated that traverses binary trees in preorder (see exercise 12). It is slightly more difficult to achieve the traversal in postorder (see exercise 13), and for this reason postorder is not as important for binary trees as the others are.

It is convenient to define a new notation for the successors and predecessors of nodes in these various orders. If P points to a node of a binary tree, let

$$
\begin{aligned}
\text{P*} &= \text{ address of successor of NODE(P) in preorder;} \\
\text{P\$} &= \text{ address of successor of NODE(P) in inorder;} \\
\text{P\sharp} &= \text{ address of successor of NODE(P) in postorder;} \\
\text{*P} &= \text{ address of predecessor of NODE(P) in preorder;} \\
\text{\$P} &= \text{ address of predecessor of NODE(P) in inorder;} \\
\text{\sharp P} &= \text{ address of predecessor of NODE(P) in postorder.}
\end{aligned}
\tag{6}
$$

If there is no such successor or predecessor of NODE(P), the value LOC(T) is generally used, where T is an external pointer to the tree in question. We have *(P*) = (*P)* = P, \$(P\$) = (\$P)\$ = P, and \sharp(P\sharp) = (\sharp P)\sharp = P. As an example of this notation, let INFO(P) be the letter shown in NODE(P) in the tree (2); then if P points to the root, we have INFO(P) = A, INFO(P*) = B, INFO(P\$) = E, INFO(\$P) = B, INFO(\sharp P) = C, and P\sharp = *P = LOC(T).

At this point the reader will perhaps experience a feeling of insecurity about the intuitive meanings of P*, P\$, etc. As we proceed further, the ideas will gradually become clearer; exercise 16 at the end of this section may also be of help. The "\$" in "P\$" is meant to suggest the letter S, for "symmetric order."

There is an important alternative to the memory representation of binary trees given in (2), which is somewhat analogous to the difference between circular lists and straight one-way lists. Notice that there are more null links than other pointers in the tree (2), and indeed this is true of any binary tree represented by the conventional method (see exercise 14). But we don't really need to waste all that memory space. For example, we could store two "tag" indicators with each node, which would tell in just two bits of memory whether or not the LLINK or RLINK, or both, are null; the memory space for terminal links could then be used for other purposes.

An ingenious use of this extra space has been suggested by A. J. Perlis and C. Thornton, who devised the so-called *threaded* tree representation. In this method, terminal links are replaced by "threads" to other parts of the tree, as an aid to traversal. The threaded tree equivalent to (2) is

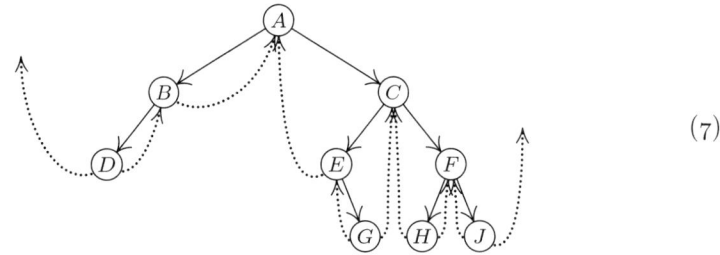

(7)

Here dotted lines represent the "threads," which always go to a higher node of the tree. *Every* node now has two links: Some nodes, like C, have two ordinary links to left and right subtrees; other nodes, like H, have two thread links; and some nodes have one link of each type. The special threads emanating from D and J will be explained later. They appear in the "leftmost" and "rightmost" nodes.

In the memory representation of a threaded binary tree it is necessary to distinguish between the dotted and solid links; this can be done as suggested above by two additional one-bit fields in each node, LTAG and RTAG. The threaded representation may be defined precisely as follows:

Unthreaded representation	Threaded representation
LLINK(P) = Λ	LTAG(P) = 1, LLINK(P) = \$P
LLINK(P) = Q ≠ Λ	LTAG(P) = 0, LLINK(P) = Q
RLINK(P) = Λ	RTAG(P) = 1, RLINK(P) = P\$
RLINK(P) = Q ≠ Λ	RTAG(P) = 0, RLINK(P) = Q

According to this definition, each new thread link points directly to the predecessor or successor of the node in question, in symmetric order (inorder). Figure 24 illustrates the general orientation of thread links in any binary tree.

In some algorithms it can be guaranteed that the root of any subtree always will appear in a lower memory location than the other nodes of the subtree. Then LTAG(P) will be 1 if and only if LLINK(P) < P, so LTAG will be redundant. The RTAG bit will be redundant for the same reason.

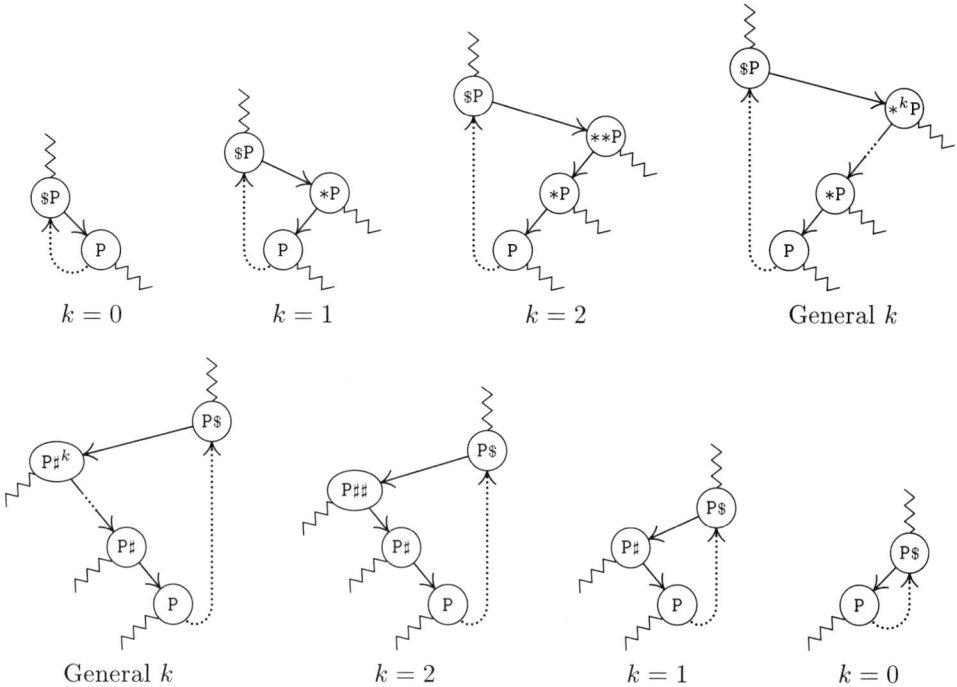

$k = 0$ $k = 1$ $k = 2$ General k

General k $k = 2$ $k = 1$ $k = 0$

Fig. 24. General orientation of left and right thread links in a threaded binary tree. Wavy lines indicate links or threads to other parts of the tree.

The great advantage of threaded trees is that traversal algorithms become simpler. For example, the following algorithm calculates P$, given P:

Algorithm S (*Symmetric (inorder) successor in a threaded binary tree*). If P points to a node of a threaded binary tree, this algorithm sets Q ← P$.

S1. [RLINK(P) a thread?] Set Q ← RLINK(P). If RTAG(P) = 1, terminate the algorithm.

S2. [Search to left.] If LTAG(Q) = 0, set Q ← LLINK(Q) and repeat this step. Otherwise the algorithm terminates. ∎

Notice that no stack is needed here to accomplish what was done using a stack in Algorithm T. In fact, the ordinary representation (2) makes it impossible to find P$ efficiently, given only the address of a random point P in the tree. Since no links point upward in an unthreaded representation, there is no clue to what nodes are above a given node, unless we retain a history of how we reached that point. The stack in Algorithm T provides the necessary history when threads are absent.

We claim that Algorithm S is "efficient," although this property is not immediately obvious, since step S2 can be executed any number of times. In view of the loop in step S2, would it perhaps be faster to use a stack after all,

as Algorithm T does? To investigate this question, we will consider the average
number of times that step S2 must be performed if P is a "random" point in
the tree; or what is the same, we will determine the total number of times that
step S2 is performed if Algorithm S is used repeatedly to traverse an entire tree.

At the same time as this analysis is being carried out, it will be instructive
to study complete programs for both Algorithms S and T. As usual, we should
be careful to set all of our algorithms up so that they work properly with empty
binary trees; and if T is the pointer to the tree, we would like to have LOC(T)*
and LOC(T)$ be the *first* nodes in preorder or symmetric order, respectively. For
threaded trees, it turns out that things will work nicely if NODE(LOC(T)) is made
into a "list head" for the tree, with

$$
\begin{aligned}
\text{LLINK(HEAD)} &= \text{T}, & \text{LTAG(HEAD)} &= 0, \\
\text{RLINK(HEAD)} &= \text{HEAD}, & \text{RTAG(HEAD)} &= 0.
\end{aligned}
\tag{8}
$$

(Here HEAD denotes LOC(T), the address of the list head.) An empty threaded
tree will satisfy the conditions

$$
\text{LLINK(HEAD)} = \text{HEAD}, \quad \text{LTAG(HEAD)} = 1.
\tag{9}
$$

The tree grows by having nodes inserted to the *left* of the list head. (These
initial conditions are primarily dictated by the algorithm to compute P*, which
appears in exercise 17.) In accordance with these conventions, the computer
representation for the binary tree (1), as a threaded tree, is

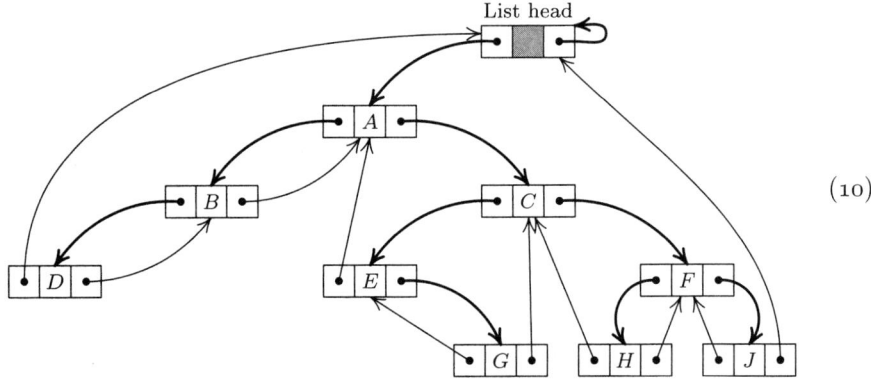

$$\tag{10}$$

With these preliminaries out of the way, we are now ready to consider MIX
versions of Algorithms S and T. The following programs assume that binary tree
nodes have the two-word form

LTAG	LLINK	INFO1
RTAG	RLINK	INFO2

In an unthreaded tree, LTAG and RTAG will always be "+" and terminal links will
be represented by zero. In a threaded tree, we will use "+" for tags that are 0
and "−" for tags that are 1. The abbreviations LLINKT and RLINKT will be used
to stand for the combined LTAG-LLINK and RTAG-RLINK fields, respectively.

The two tag bits occupy otherwise-unused sign positions of a MIX word, so they cost nothing in memory space. Similarly, with the MMIX computer we will be able to use the *least significant* bits of link fields as tag bits that come "for free," because pointer values will generally be even, and because MMIX will make it easy to ignore the low-order bits when addressing memory.

The following two programs traverse a binary tree in symmetric order (that is, inorder), jumping to location VISIT periodically with index register 5 pointing to the node that is currently of interest.

Program T. In this implementation of Algorithm T, the stack is kept in locations $A + 1$, $A + 2$, ..., $A + MAX$; rI6 is the stack pointer and $rI5 \equiv P$. OVERFLOW occurs if the stack grows too large. The program has been rearranged slightly from Algorithm T (step T2 appears thrice), so that the test for an empty stack need not be made when going directly from T3 to T2 to T4.

```
01 LLINK EQU  1:2
02 RLINK EQU  1:2
03 T1    LD5  HEAD(LLINK)    1    T1. Initialize. Set P ← T.
04 T2A   J5Z  DONE           1    Stop if P = Λ.
05       ENT6 0              1
06 T3    DEC6 MAX            n    T3. Stack ⇐ P.
07       J6NN OVERFLOW       n    Has that stack reached capacity?
08       INC6 MAX+1          n    If not, increase the stack pointer.
09       ST5  A,6            n    Store P in the stack.
10       LD5  0,5(LLINK)     n    P ← LLINK(P).
11 T2B   J5NZ T3             n    To T3 if P ≠ Λ.
12 T4    LD5  A,6            n    T4. P ⇐ Stack.
13       DEC6 1              n    Decrease the stack pointer.
14 T5    JMP  VISIT          n    T5. Visit P.
15       LD5  1,5(RLINK)     n    P ← RLINK(P).
16 T2C   J5NZ T3             n    T2. P = Λ?
17       J6NZ T4             a    Test if the stack is empty.
18 DONE  ...                      ▌
```

Program S. Algorithm S has been augmented with initialization and termination conditions to make this program comparable to Program T.

```
01 LLINKT EQU  0:2
02 RLINKT EQU  0:2
03 S0     ENT5 HEAD           1      S0. Initialize. Set P ← HEAD.
04        JMP  2F             1
05 S3     JMP  VISIT          n      S3. Visit P.
06 S1     LD5N 1,5(RLINKT)    n      S1. RLINK(P) a thread?
07        J5NN 1F             n      Jump if RTAG(P) = 1.
08        ENN6 0,5          n - a    Otherwise set Q ← RLINK(P).
09 S2     ENT5 0,6            n      S2. Search to left. Set P ← Q.
10 2H     LD6  0,5(LLINKT)   n + 1   Q ← LLINK(P).
11        J6P  S2            n + 1   If LTAG(P) = 0, repeat.
12 1H     ENT6 -HEAD,5       n + 1
13        J6NZ S3            n + 1   Visit unless P = HEAD.   ▌
```

An analysis of the running time appears with the code above. These quantities are easy to determine, using Kirchhoff's law and the facts that

i) in Program T, the number of insertions onto the stack must equal the number of deletions;

ii) in Program S, the LLINK and RLINK of each node are examined precisely once;

iii) the number of "visits" is the number of nodes in the tree.

The analysis tells us Program T takes $15n + a + 4$ units of time, and Program S takes $11n - a + 7$ units, where n is the number of nodes in the tree and a is the number of terminal right links (nodes with no right subtree). The quantity a can be as low as 1, assuming that $n \neq 0$, and it can be as high as n. If left and right are symmetrical, the average value of a is $(n + 1)/2$, as a consequence of facts proved in exercise 14.

The principal conclusions we may reach on the basis of this analysis are:

i) Step S2 of Algorithm S is performed only *once* on the average per execution of that algorithm, if P is a random node of the tree.

ii) Traversal is slightly faster for threaded trees, because it requires no stack manipulation.

iii) Algorithm T needs more memory space than Algorithm S because of the auxiliary stack required. In Program T we kept the stack in consecutive memory locations; therefore we needed to put an arbitrary bound on its size. It would be very embarrassing if this bound were exceeded, so it must be set reasonably large (see exercise 10); thus the memory requirement of Program T is significantly more than Program S. Not infrequently a complex computer application will be independently traversing several trees at once, and a separate stack will be needed for each tree under Program T. This suggests that Program T might use linked allocation for its stack (see exercise 20); its execution time then becomes $30n + a + 4$ units, roughly twice as slow as before, although the traversal speed may not be terribly important when the execution time for the other coroutine is added in. Still another alternative is to keep the stack links within the tree itself in a tricky way, as discussed in exercise 21.

iv) Algorithm S is, of course, more general than Algorithm T, since it allows us to go from P to P$ when we are not necessarily traversing the entire binary tree.

So a threaded binary tree is decidedly superior to an unthreaded one, with respect to traversal. These advantages are offset in some applications by the slightly increased time needed to insert and delete nodes in a threaded tree. It is also sometimes possible to save memory space by "sharing" common subtrees with an unthreaded representation, while threaded trees require adherence to a strict tree structure with no overlapping of subtrees.

Thread links can also be used to compute P*, $P, and ♯P with efficiency comparable to that of Algorithm S. The functions *P and P♯ are slightly harder to compute, just as they are for unthreaded tree representations. The reader is urged to work exercise 17.

Most of the usefulness of threaded trees would disappear if it were hard to set up the thread links in the first place. What makes the idea really work is that threaded trees grow almost as easily as ordinary ones do. We have the following algorithm:

Algorithm I (*Insertion into a threaded binary tree*). This algorithm attaches a single node, NODE(Q), as the right subtree of NODE(P), if the right subtree is empty (that is, if RTAG(P) = 1); otherwise it inserts NODE(Q) between NODE(P) and NODE(RLINK(P)), making the latter node the right child of NODE(Q). The binary tree in which the insertion takes place is assumed to be threaded as in (10); for a modification, see exercise 23.

I1. [Adjust tags and links.] Set RLINK(Q) ← RLINK(P), RTAG(Q) ← RTAG(P), RLINK(P) ← Q, RTAG(P) ← 0, LLINK(Q) ← P, LTAG(Q) ← 1.

I2. [Was RLINK(P) a thread?] If RTAG(Q) = 0, set LLINK(Q$) ← Q. (Here Q$ is determined by Algorithm S, which will work properly even though LLINK(Q$) now points to NODE(P) instead of NODE(Q). This step is necessary only when inserting into the midst of a threaded tree instead of merely inserting a new leaf.) ∎

By reversing the roles of left and right (in particular, by replacing Q$ by $Q in step I2), we obtain an algorithm that inserts to the left in a similar way.

Our discussion of threaded binary trees so far has made use of thread links both to the left and to the right. There is an important middle ground between the completely unthreaded and completely threaded methods of representation: A *right-threaded binary tree* combines the two approaches by making use of threaded RLINKs, while representing empty left subtrees by LLINK = Λ. (Similarly, a left-threaded binary tree threads only the null LLINKs.) Algorithm S does not make essential use of threaded LLINKs; if we change the test "LTAG = 0" in step S2 to "LLINK ≠ Λ", we obtain an algorithm for traversing right-threaded binary trees in symmetric order. Program S works without change in the right-threaded case. A great many applications of binary tree structures require only a left-to-right traversal of trees using the functions P$ and/or P∗, and for these applications there is no need to thread the LLINKs. We have described threading in both the left and right directions in order to indicate the symmetry and possibilities of the situation, but in practice one-sided threading is much more common.

Let us now consider an important property of binary trees, and its connection to traversal. Two binary trees T and T' are said to be *similar* if they have the same structure; formally, this means that (a) they are both empty, or (b) they are both nonempty and their left and right subtrees are respectively similar. Similarity means, informally, that the diagrams of T and T' have the same "shape." Another way to phrase similarity is to say that there is a one-to-one correspondence between the nodes of T and T' that preserves the structure:

If nodes u_1 and u_2 in T correspond respectively to u_1' and u_2' in T', then u_1 is in the left subtree of u_2 if and only if u_1' is in the left subtree of u_2', and the same is true for right subtrees.

The binary trees T and T' are said to be *equivalent* if they are similar and if corresponding nodes contain the same information. Formally, let $\text{info}(u)$ denote the information contained in a node u; the trees are equivalent if and only if (a) they are both empty, or (b) they are both nonempty and $\text{info}(\text{root}(T)) = \text{info}(\text{root}(T'))$ and their left and right subtrees are respectively equivalent.

As examples of these definitions, consider the four binary trees

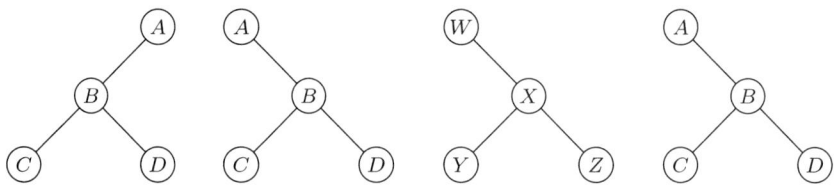

in which the first two are dissimilar. The second, third, and fourth are similar and, in fact, the second and fourth are equivalent.

Some computer applications involving tree structures require an algorithm to decide whether two binary trees are similar or equivalent. The following theorem is useful in this regard:

Theorem A. *Let the nodes of binary trees T and T' be respectively*

$$u_1, u_2, \ldots, u_n \qquad \text{and} \qquad u_1', u_2', \ldots, u_{n'}'$$

in preorder. For any node u let

$$
\begin{aligned}
l(u) &= 1 \quad \text{if } u \text{ has a nonempty left subtree,} & l(u) &= 0 \quad \text{otherwise;} \\
r(u) &= 1 \quad \text{if } u \text{ has a nonempty right subtree,} & r(u) &= 0 \quad \text{otherwise.}
\end{aligned}
\tag{11}
$$

Then T and T' are similar if and only if $n = n'$ and

$$l(u_j) = l(u_j'), \qquad r(u_j) = r(u_j') \qquad \text{for } 1 \le j \le n. \tag{12}$$

Moreover, T and T' are equivalent if and only if in addition we have

$$\text{info}(u_j) = \text{info}(u_j') \qquad \text{for } 1 \le j \le n. \tag{13}$$

Notice that l and r are the complements of the LTAG and RTAG bits in a threaded tree. This theorem characterizes any binary tree structure in terms of two sequences of 0s and 1s.

Proof. It is clear that the condition for equivalence of binary trees will follow immediately if we prove the condition for similarity; furthermore the conditions $n = n'$ and (12) are certainly necessary, since corresponding nodes of similar trees must have the same position in preorder. Therefore it suffices to prove that the conditions (12) and $n = n'$ are sufficient to guarantee the similarity of T and T'. The proof is by induction on n, using the following auxiliary result:

Lemma P. *Let the nodes of a nonempty binary tree be $u_1, u_2, \ldots, u_n$ in preorder, and let $f(u) = l(u) + r(u) - 1$. Then*

$$f(u_1) + f(u_2) + \cdots + f(u_n) = -1, \quad \text{and} \quad f(u_1) + \cdots + f(u_k) \geq 0, \quad 1 \leq k < n. \quad (14)$$

Proof. The result is clear for $n = 1$. If $n > 1$, the binary tree consists of its root u_1 and further nodes. If $f(u_1) = 0$, then either the left subtree or the right subtree is empty, so the condition is obviously true by induction. If $f(u_1) = 1$, let the left subtree have n_l nodes; by induction we have

$$f(u_1) + \cdots + f(u_k) > 0 \quad \text{for } 1 \leq k \leq n_l, \quad f(u_1) + \cdots + f(u_{n_l+1}) = 0, \quad (15)$$

and the condition (14) is again evident. ∎

(For other theorems analogous to Lemma P, see the discussion of Polish notation in Chapter 10.)

To complete the proof of Theorem A, we note that the theorem is clearly true when $n = 0$. If $n > 0$, the definition of preorder implies that u_1 and u_1' are the respective roots of their trees, and there are integers n_l and n_l' (the sizes of the left subtrees) such that

$u_2, \ldots, u_{n_l+1}$ and $u_2', \ldots, u_{n_l'+1}'$ are the left subtrees of T and T';

$u_{n_l+2}, \ldots, u_n$ and $u_{n_l'+2}', \ldots, u_n'$ are the right subtrees of T and T'.

The proof by induction will be complete if we can show $n_l = n_l'$. There are three cases:

   if $l(u_1) = 0$, then $n_l = 0 = n_l'$;
   if $l(u_1) = 1$, $r(u_1) = 0$, then $n_l = n - 1 = n_l'$;
   if $l(u_1) = r(u_1) = 1$, then by Lemma P we can find the least $k > 0$ such that $f(u_1) + \cdots + f(u_k) = 0$; and $n_l = k - 1 = n_l'$ $\bigl($see $(15)\bigr)$. ∎

As a consequence of Theorem A, we can test two threaded binary trees for equivalence or similarity by simply traversing them in preorder and checking the INFO and TAG fields. Some interesting extensions of Theorem A have been obtained by A. J. Blikle, *Bull. de l'Acad. Polonaise des Sciences*, Série des Sciences Math., Astr., Phys., **14** (1966), 203–208; he considered an infinite class of possible traversal orders, only six of which (including preorder) were called "addressless" because of their simple properties.

We conclude this section by giving a typical, yet basic, algorithm for binary trees, one that makes a copy of a binary tree into different memory locations.

Algorithm C (*Copy a binary tree*). Let HEAD be the address of the list head of a binary tree T; thus, T is the left subtree of HEAD, reached via LLINK(HEAD). Let NODE(U) be a node with an empty left subtree. This algorithm makes a copy of T and the copy becomes the left subtree of NODE(U). In particular, if NODE(U) is the list head of an empty binary tree, this algorithm changes the empty tree into a copy of T.

C1. [Initialize.] Set P ← HEAD, Q ← U. Go to C4.

C2. [Anything to right?] If NODE(P) has a nonempty right subtree, set R $\Leftarrow$ AVAIL, and attach NODE(R) to the right of NODE(Q). (At the beginning of step C2, the right subtree of NODE(Q) was empty.)

C3. [Copy INFO.] Set INFO(Q) $\leftarrow$ INFO(P). (Here INFO denotes all parts of the node that are to be copied, except for the links.)

C4. [Anything to left?] If NODE(P) has a nonempty left subtree, set R $\Leftarrow$ AVAIL, and attach NODE(R) to the left of NODE(Q). (At the beginning of step C4, the left subtree of NODE(Q) was empty.)

C5. [Advance.] Set P $\leftarrow$ P$*$, Q $\leftarrow$ Q$*$.

C6. [Test if complete.] If P = HEAD (or equivalently if Q = RLINK(U), assuming that NODE(U) has a nonempty right subtree), the algorithm terminates; otherwise go to step C2. ∎

This simple algorithm shows a typical application of tree traversal. The description here applies to threaded, unthreaded, or partially threaded trees. Step C5 requires the calculation of preorder successors P$*$ and Q$*$; for unthreaded trees, this generally is done with an auxiliary stack. A proof of the validity of Algorithm C appears in exercise 29; a MIX program corresponding to this algorithm in the case of a right-threaded binary tree appears in exercise 2.3.2–13. For threaded trees, the "attaching" in steps C2 and C4 is done using Algorithm I.

The exercises that follow include quite a few topics of interest relating to the material of this section.

> *Binary or dichotomous systems, although regulated by a principle,*
> *are among the most artificial arrangements*
> *that have ever been invented.*
>
> — WILLIAM SWAINSON, *A Treatise on the Geography and*
> *Classification of Animals* (1835)

EXERCISES

1. [*01*] In the binary tree (2), let INFO(P) denote the letter stored in NODE(P). What is INFO(LLINK(RLINK(RLINK(T))))?

2. [*11*] List the nodes of the binary tree   in (a) preorder; (b) symmetric order; (c) postorder.

3. [*20*] Is the following statement true or false? "The terminal nodes of a binary tree occur in the same relative position in preorder, inorder, and postorder."

▶ **4.** [*20*] The text defines three basic orders for traversing a binary tree; another alternative would be to proceed in three steps as follows:

a) Visit the root,
b) traverse the right subtree,
c) traverse the left subtree,

using the same rule recursively on all nonempty subtrees. Does this new order bear any simple relation to the three orders already discussed?

5. [*22*] The nodes of a binary tree may be identified by a sequence of zeros and ones, in a notation analogous to "Dewey decimal notation" for trees, as follows: The root (if present) is represented by the sequence "1". Roots (if present) of the left and right subtrees of the node represented by α are respectively represented by $\alpha 0$ and $\alpha 1$. For example, the node H in (1) would have the representation "1110". (See exercise 2.3–15.)

Show that preorder, inorder, and postorder can be described conveniently in terms of this notation.

6. [*M22*] Suppose that a binary tree has n nodes that are $u_1 u_2 \ldots u_n$ in preorder and $u_{p_1} u_{p_2} \ldots u_{p_n}$ in inorder. Show that the permutation $p_1 p_2 \ldots p_n$ can be obtained by passing $12 \ldots n$ through a stack, in the sense of exercise 2.2.1–2. Conversely, show that any permutation $p_1 p_2 \ldots p_n$ obtainable with a stack corresponds to some binary tree in this way.

7. [*22*] Show that if we are given the preorder and the inorder of the nodes of a binary tree, the binary tree structure may be constructed. (Assume that the nodes are distinct.) Does the same result hold true if we are given the preorder and postorder, instead of preorder and inorder? Or if we are given the inorder and postorder?

8. [*20*] Find all binary trees whose nodes appear in exactly the same sequence in both (a) preorder and inorder; (b) preorder and postorder; (c) inorder and postorder. (As in the previous exercise, we assume that the nodes have distinct labels.)

9. [*M20*] When a binary tree having n nodes is traversed using Algorithm T, state how many times each of steps T1, T2, T3, T4, and T5 is performed (as a function of n).

▶ **10.** [*20*] What is the largest number of entries that can be in the stack at once, during the execution of Algorithm T, if the binary tree has n nodes? (The answer to this question is very important for storage allocation, if the stack is being stored consecutively.)

11. [*HM41*] Analyze the *average* value of the largest stack size occurring during the execution of Algorithm T as a function of n, given that all binary trees with n nodes are considered equally probable.

12. [*22*] Design an algorithm analogous to Algorithm T that traverses a binary tree in *preorder*, and prove that your algorithm is correct.

▶ **13.** [*24*] Design an algorithm analogous to Algorithm T that traverses a binary tree in *postorder*.

14. [*22*] Show that if a binary tree with n nodes is represented as in (2), the total number of Λ links in the representation can be expressed as a simple function of n; this quantity does not depend on the shape of the tree.

15. [*15*] In a threaded-tree representation like (10), each node except the list head has exactly one link pointing to it from above, namely the link from its parent. Some of the nodes also have links pointing to them from below; for example, the node containing C has two pointers coming up from below, while node E has just one. Is there any simple connection between the number of links pointing to a node and some other basic property of that node? (We need to know how many links point to a given node when we are changing the tree structure.)

▶ **16.** [*22*] The diagrams in Fig. 24 help to provide an intuitive characterization of the position of NODE(Q$) in a binary tree, in terms of the structure near NODE(Q): If NODE(Q) has a nonempty right subtree, consider Q = P, Q = P in the upper diagrams; NODE(Q$)

is the "leftmost" node of that right subtree. If NODE(Q) has an empty right subtree, consider Q = P in the lower diagrams; NODE(Q$) is located by proceeding upward in the tree until after the first upward step to the right.

Give a similar "intuitive" rule for finding the position of NODE(Q*) in a binary tree in terms of the structure near NODE(Q).

▶ **17.** [*22*] Give an algorithm analogous to Algorithm S for determining P* in a threaded binary tree. Assume that the tree has a list head as in (8), (9), and (10).

18. [*24*] Many algorithms dealing with trees like to visit each node *twice* instead of once, using a combination of preorder and inorder that we might call *double order*. Traversal of a binary tree in double order is defined as follows: If the binary tree is empty, do nothing; otherwise

a) visit the root, for the first time;
b) traverse the left subtree, in double order;
c) visit the root, for the second time;
d) traverse the right subtree, in double order.

For example, traversal of (1) in double order gives the sequence

$$A_1 B_1 D_1 D_2 B_2 A_2 C_1 E_1 E_2 G_1 G_2 C_2 F_1 H_1 H_2 F_2 J_1 J_2,$$

where A_1 means that A is being visited for the first time.

If P points to a node of the tree and if $d = 1$ or 2, define $(P, d)^\Delta = (Q, e)$ if the next step in double order after visiting NODE(P) the dth time is to visit NODE(Q) the eth time; or, if (P, d) is the last step in double order, we write $(P, d)^\Delta = (HEAD, 2)$, where HEAD is the address of the list head. We also define $(HEAD, 1)^\Delta$ as the first step in double order.

Design an algorithm analogous to Algorithm T that traverses a binary tree in double order, and also design an algorithm analogous to Algorithm S that computes $(P, d)^\Delta$. Discuss the relation between these algorithms and exercises 12 and 17.

▶ **19.** [*27*] Design an algorithm analogous to Algorithm S for the calculation of P♯ in (a) a right-threaded binary tree; (b) a fully threaded binary tree. If possible, the average running time of your algorithm should be at most a small constant, when P is a random node of the tree.

20. [*23*] Modify Program T so that it keeps the stack in a linked list, not in consecutive memory locations.

▶ **21.** [*33*] Design an algorithm that traverses an unthreaded binary tree in inorder *without using any auxiliary stack.* It is permissible to alter the LLINK and RLINK fields of the tree nodes in any manner whatsoever during the traversal, subject only to the condition that the binary tree should have the conventional representation illustrated in (2) both before and after your algorithm has traversed the tree. No other bits in the tree nodes are available for temporary storage.

22. [*25*] Write a MIX program for the algorithm given in exercise 21 and compare its execution time to Programs S and T.

23. [*22*] Design algorithms analogous to Algorithm I for insertion to the right and insertion to the left in a *right-threaded* binary tree. Assume that the nodes have the fields LLINK, RLINK, and RTAG.

24. [*M20*] Is Theorem A still valid if the nodes of T and T' are given in symmetric order instead of preorder?

25. [*M24*] Let $\mathcal{T}$ be a set of binary trees in which the value of each info field belongs to a given set S, where S is linearly ordered by a relation "$\preceq$" (see exercise 2.2.3–14). Given any trees T, T' in $\mathcal{T}$, let us now define $T \preceq T'$ if and only if

  i) T is empty; or

 ii) T and T' are not empty, and $\mathrm{info}(\mathrm{root}(T)) \prec \mathrm{info}(\mathrm{root}(T'))$; or

iii) T and T' are not empty, $\mathrm{info}(\mathrm{root}(T)) = \mathrm{info}(\mathrm{root}(T'))$, $\mathrm{left}(T) \preceq \mathrm{left}(T')$, and $\mathrm{left}(T)$ is not equivalent to $\mathrm{left}(T')$; or

 iv) T and T' are not empty, $\mathrm{info}(\mathrm{root}(T)) = \mathrm{info}(\mathrm{root}(T'))$, $\mathrm{left}(T)$ is equivalent to $\mathrm{left}(T')$, and $\mathrm{right}(T) \preceq \mathrm{right}(T')$.

Here $\mathrm{left}(T)$ and $\mathrm{right}(T)$ denote the left and right subtrees of T. Prove that (a) $T \preceq T'$ and $T' \preceq T''$ implies $T \preceq T''$; (b) T is equivalent to T' if and only if $T \preceq T'$ and $T' \preceq T$; (c) for any T, T' in $\mathcal{T}$ we have either $T \preceq T'$ or $T' \preceq T$. [Thus, if equivalent trees in $\mathcal{T}$ are regarded as equal, the relation $\preceq$ induces a linear ordering on $\mathcal{T}$. This ordering has many applications (for example, in the simplification of algebraic expressions). When S has only one element, so that the "info" of each node is the same, we have the special case that equivalence is the same as similarity.]

26. [*M24*] Consider the ordering $T \preceq T'$ defined in the preceding exercise. Prove a theorem analogous to Theorem A, giving a necessary and sufficient condition that $T \preceq T'$, and making use of double order as defined in exercise 18.

▶ **27.** [*28*] Design an algorithm that tests two given trees T and T' to see whether $T \prec T'$, $T \succ T'$, or T is equivalent to T', in terms of the relation defined in exercise 25, assuming that both binary trees are right-threaded. Assume that each node has the fields LLINK, RLINK, RTAG, INFO; use no auxiliary stack.

28. [*00*] After Algorithm C has been used to make a copy of a tree, is the new binary tree *equivalent* to the original, or *similar* to it?

29. [*M25*] Prove as rigorously as possible that Algorithm C is valid.

▶ **30.** [*22*] Design an algorithm that threads an unthreaded tree; for example, it should transform (2) into (10). *Note:* Always use notations like P* and P$ when possible, instead of repeating the steps for traversal algorithms like Algorithm T.

31. [*23*] Design an algorithm that "erases" a right-threaded binary tree. Your algorithm should return all of the tree nodes except the list head to the AVAIL list, and it should make the list head signify an empty binary tree. Assume that each node has the fields LLINK, RLINK, RTAG; use no auxiliary stack.

32. [*21*] Suppose that each node of a binary tree has four link fields: LLINK and RLINK, which point to left and right subtrees or Λ, as in an unthreaded tree; SUC and PRED, which point to the successor and predecessor of the node in symmetric order. (Thus SUC(P) = P$ and PRED(P) = $P. Such a tree contains more information than a threaded tree.) Design an algorithm like Algorithm I for insertion into such a tree.

▶ **33.** [*30*] There is more than one way to thread a tree! Consider the following representation, using three fields LTAG, LLINK, RLINK in each node:

LTAG(P): defined the same as in a threaded binary tree;

LLINK(P): always equal to P*;

RLINK(P): defined the same as in an unthreaded binary tree.

Discuss insertion algorithms for such a representation, and write out the copying algorithm, Algorithm C, in detail for this representation.

34. [*22*] Let P point to a node in some binary tree, and let HEAD point to the list head of an empty binary tree. Give an algorithm that (i) removes NODE(P) and all of its subtrees from whatever tree it was in, and then (ii) attaches NODE(P) and its subtrees to NODE(HEAD). Assume that all the binary trees in question are right-threaded, with fields LLINK, RTAG, RLINK in each node.

35. [*40*] Define a *ternary tree* (and, more generally, a *t-ary tree* for any $t \geq 2$) in a manner analogous to our definition of a binary tree, and explore the topics discussed in this section (including topics found in the exercises above) that can be generalized to *t*-ary trees in a meaningful way.

36. [*M23*] Exercise 1.2.1–15 shows that lexicographic order extends a well-ordering of a set S to a well-ordering of the n-tuples of elements of S. Exercise 25 above shows that a linear ordering of the information in tree nodes can be extended to a linear ordering of trees, using a similar definition. If the relation $\prec$ well-orders S, is the extended relation of exercise 25 a well-ordering of $\mathcal{T}$?

▶ **37.** [*24*] (D. Ferguson.) If two computer words are necessary to contain two link fields and an INFO field, representation (2) requires $2n$ words of memory for a tree with n nodes. Design a representation scheme for binary trees that uses less space, assuming that *one* link and an INFO field will fit in a single computer word.

2.3.2. Binary Tree Representation of Trees

We turn now from binary trees to just plain trees. Let us recall the basic differences between trees and binary trees as we have defined them:

1) A tree always has a root node, so it is never empty; each node of a tree can have 0, 1, 2, 3, … children.
2) A binary tree can be empty, and each of its nodes can have 0, 1, or 2 children; we distinguish between a "left" child and a "right" child.

Recall also that a forest is an ordered set of zero or more trees. The subtrees immediately below any node of a tree form a forest.

There is a natural way to represent any forest as a binary tree. Consider the following forest of two trees:

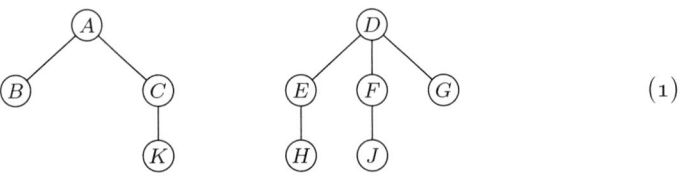

(1)

The corresponding binary tree is obtained by linking together the children of each family and removing vertical links except from a parent to a first child:

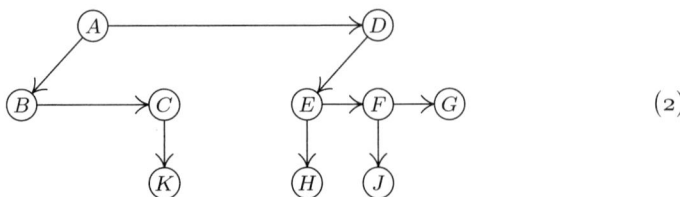

(2)

Then, tilt the diagram 45° clockwise and tweak it slightly, obtaining a binary tree:

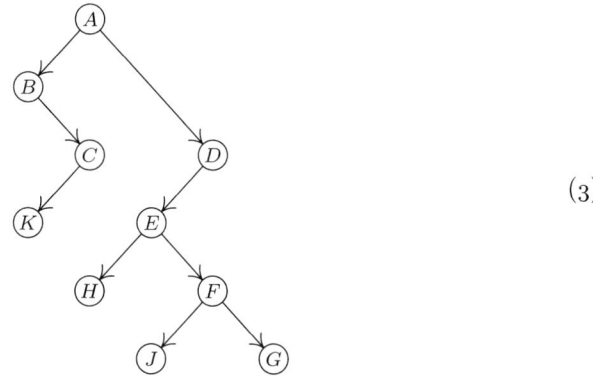

$$(3)$$

Conversely, it is easy to see that any binary tree corresponds to a unique forest of trees by reversing the process.

The transformation from (1) to (3) is extremely important; it is called the *natural correspondence* between forests and binary trees. In particular, it gives a correspondence between trees and a special class of binary trees, namely the binary trees that have a root but no right subtree. (We might also change our viewpoint slightly and let the root of a tree correspond to the list head of a binary tree, thus obtaining a one-to-one correspondence between trees with $n+1$ nodes and binary trees with n nodes.)

Let $F = (T_1, T_2, \ldots, T_n)$ be a forest of trees. The binary tree $B(F)$ corresponding to F can be defined rigorously as follows:

a) If $n = 0$, $B(F)$ is empty.

b) If $n > 0$, the root of $B(F)$ is root(T_1); the left subtree of $B(F)$ is $B(T_{11}, T_{12}, \ldots, T_{1m})$, where $T_{11}, T_{12}, \ldots, T_{1m}$ are the subtrees of root(T_1); and the right subtree of $B(F)$ is $B(T_2, \ldots, T_n)$.

These rules specify the transformation from (1) to (3) precisely.

It will occasionally be convenient to draw our binary tree diagram as in (2), without the 45° rotation. The *threaded* binary tree corresponding to (1) is

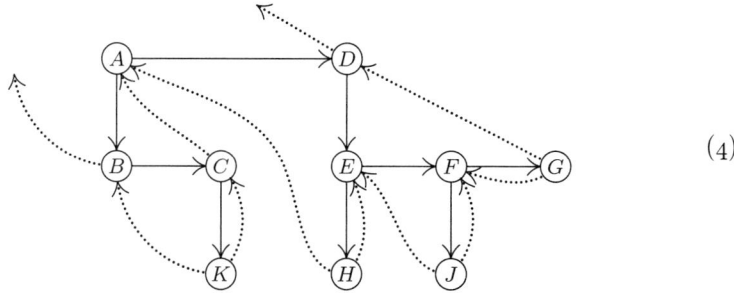

$$(4)$$

(compare with Fig. 24, giving the latter a 45° change in orientation). Notice that *right thread links go from the rightmost child of a family to the parent.*

Left thread links do not have such a natural interpretation, due to the lack of symmetry between left and right.

The ideas about traversal explored in the previous section can be recast in terms of forests (and, therefore, trees). There is no simple analog of the inorder sequence, since there is no obvious place to insert a root among its descendants; but preorder and postorder carry over in an obvious manner. Given any nonempty forest, the two basic ways to traverse it may be defined as follows:

Preorder traversal	Postorder traversal
Visit the root of the first tree	Traverse the subtrees of the first tree
Traverse the subtrees of the first tree	Visit the root of the first tree
Traverse the remaining trees	Traverse the remaining trees

In order to understand the significance of these two methods of traversal, consider the following notation for expressing tree structure by nested parentheses:

$$\big(A(B, C(K)), \, D(E(H), \, F(J), \, G)\big). \tag{5}$$

This notation corresponds to the forest (1): We represent a tree by the information written in its root, followed by a representation of its subtrees; we represent a nonempty forest by a parenthesized list of the representations of its trees, separated by commas.

If (1) is traversed in preorder, we visit the nodes in the sequence $A\,B\,C\,K\,D\,E\,H\,F\,J\,G$; this is simply (5) with the parentheses and commas removed. Preorder is a natural way to list the nodes of a tree: We list the root first, then the descendants. If a tree structure is represented by indentation as in Fig. 20(c), the rows appear in preorder. The section numbers of this book itself (see Fig. 22) appear in preorder; thus, for example, Section 2.3 is followed by Section 2.3.1, then come Sections 2.3.2, 2.3.3, 2.3.4, 2.3.4.1, ..., 2.3.4.6, 2.3.5, 2.4, etc.

It is interesting to note that preorder is a time-honored concept that might meaningfully be called *dynastic order*. At the death of a king, duke, or earl, the title passes to the first son, then to descendants of the first son, and finally if these all die out it passes to other sons of the family in the same way. (English custom also includes daughters in a family on the same basis as sons, except that they come after all the sons.) In theory, we could take a lineal chart of all the aristocracy and write out the nodes in preorder; then if we consider only the people presently living, we would obtain the *order of succession to the throne* (except as modified by Acts of Abdication).

Postorder for the nodes in (1) is $B\,K\,C\,A\,H\,E\,J\,F\,G\,D$; this is analogous to preorder, except that it corresponds to the similar parenthesis notation

$$\big((B, \, (K)C)A, \, ((H)E, \, (J)F, \, G)D\big), \tag{6}$$

in which a node appears just *after* its descendants instead of just before.

The definitions of preorder and postorder mesh very nicely with the natural correspondence between trees and binary trees, since the subtrees of the first tree correspond to the left binary subtree, and the remaining trees correspond to the right binary subtree. By comparing these definitions with the corresponding definitions on page 319, we find that traversing a forest in preorder is *exactly the same* as traversing the corresponding binary tree in preorder. Traversing a forest in postorder is exactly the same as traversing the corresponding binary tree in *inorder*. The algorithms developed in Section 2.3.1 may therefore be used without change. (Note that postorder for trees corresponds to inorder, *not* postorder, for binary trees. This is fortunate, since we have seen that it is comparatively hard to traverse binary trees in postorder.) Because of this equivalence, we use the notation P$ for the *postorder* successor of node P in a tree or forest, while it denotes the *inorder* successor in a binary tree.

As an example of the application of these methods to a practical problem, we will consider the manipulation of algebraic formulas. Such formulas are most properly regarded as representations of tree structures, not as one- or two-dimensional configurations of symbols, nor even as binary trees. For example, the formula $y = 3\ln(x+1) - a/x^2$ has the tree representation

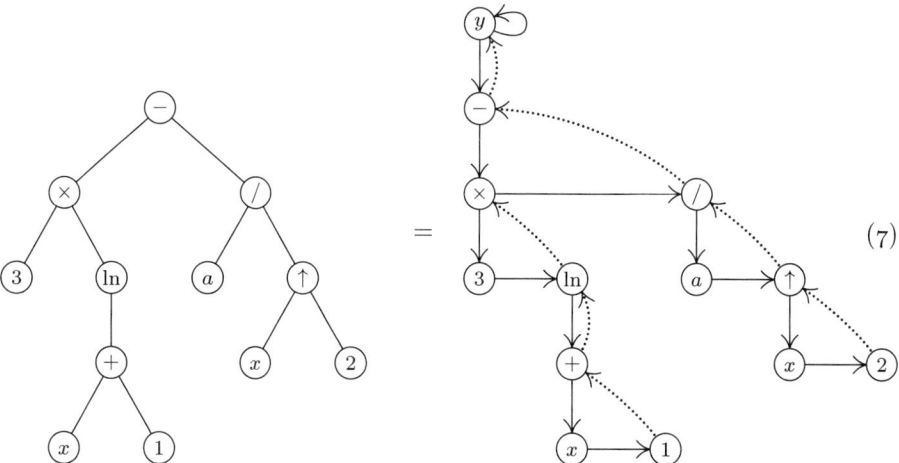

$$(7)$$

Here the illustration on the left is a conventional tree diagram like Fig. 21, in which the binary operators $+$, $-$, $\times$, $/$, and $\uparrow$ (the latter denotes exponentiation) have two subtrees corresponding to their operands; the unary operator "ln" has one subtree; variables and constants are terminal nodes. The illustration on the right shows the equivalent right-threaded binary tree, including an additional node y that is a list head for the tree. The list head has the form described in 2.3.1–(8).

It is important to note that, even though the left-hand tree in (7) bears a superficial resemblance to a binary tree, we are treating it here as a *tree*, and representing it by a quite different binary tree, shown at the right in (7). Although we could develop routines for algebraic manipulations based directly on binary tree structures — the so-called "three-address code" representations of algebraic formulas — several simplifications occur in practice if we use the general tree representation of algebraic formulas, as in (7), because postorder traversal is easier in a tree.

The nodes of the left-hand tree in (7) are

$$- \quad \times \quad 3 \quad \ln \quad + \quad x \quad 1 \quad / \quad a \quad \uparrow \quad x \quad 2 \qquad \text{in preorder;} \quad (8)$$

$$3 \quad x \quad 1 \quad + \quad \ln \quad \times \quad a \quad x \quad 2 \quad \uparrow \quad / \quad - \qquad \text{in postorder.} \quad (9)$$

Algebraic expressions like (8) and (9) are very important, and they are known as "Polish notations" because form (8) was introduced by the Polish logician, Jan Łukasiewicz. Expression (8) is the *prefix notation* for formula (7), and (9) is the corresponding *postfix notation*. We will return to the interesting topic of Polish notation in later chapters; for now let us be content with the knowledge that Polish notation is directly related to the basic orders of tree traversal.

We shall assume that tree structures for the algebraic formulas with which we will be dealing have nodes of the following form in MIX programs:

$$
\begin{array}{|c|c|c|c|}
\hline
\text{RTAG} & \text{RLINK} & \text{TYPE} & \text{LLINK} \\
\hline
\multicolumn{4}{|c|}{\text{INFO}} \\
\hline
\end{array}
\qquad (10)
$$

Here RLINK and LLINK have the usual significance, and RTAG is negative for thread links (corresponding to RTAG = 1 in the statements of algorithms). The TYPE field is used to distinguish different kinds of nodes: TYPE = 0 means that the node represents a constant, and INFO is the value of the constant. TYPE = 1 means that the node represents a variable, and INFO is the five-letter alphabetic name of this variable. TYPE $\geq$ 2 means that the node represents an operator; INFO is the alphabetic name of the operator and the value TYPE = 2, 3, 4, ... is used to distinguish the different operators $+$, $-$, $\times$, $/$, etc. We will not concern ourselves here with how the tree structure has been set up inside the computer memory in the first place, since this topic is analyzed in great detail in Chapter 10; let us merely assume that the tree already appears in our computer memory, deferring questions of input and output until later.

We shall now discuss the classical example of algebraic manipulation, finding the *derivative* of a formula with respect to the variable x. Programs for algebraic differentiation were among the first symbol-manipulation routines ever written for computers; they were used as early as 1952. The process of differentiation illustrates many of the techniques of algebraic manipulation, and it is of significant practical value in scientific applications.

Readers who are not familiar with mathematical calculus may consider this problem as an abstract exercise in formula manipulation, defined by the following rules:

$$
\begin{aligned}
D(x) &= 1 & (11) \\
D(a) &= 0, \quad \text{if } a \text{ is a constant or a variable} \neq x & (12) \\
D(\ln u) &= D(u)/u, \quad \text{if } u \text{ is any formula} & (13) \\
D(-u) &= -D(u) & (14) \\
D(u+v) &= D(u) + D(v) & (15) \\
D(u-v) &= D(u) - D(v) & (16) \\
D(u \times v) &= D(u) \times v + u \times D(v) & (17)
\end{aligned}
$$

$$D(u \,/\, v) = D(u)/v - \big(u \times D(v)\big)/(v \uparrow 2) \tag{18}$$

$$D(u \uparrow v) = D(u) \times \big(v \times (u \uparrow (v-1))\big) + \big((\ln u) \times D(v)\big) \times (u \uparrow v) \tag{19}$$

These rules allow us to evaluate the derivative $D(y)$ for any formula y composed of the operators listed. The "$-$" sign in rule (14) is a unary operator, which is different from the binary "$-$" in (16); we will use "neg" to stand for unary negation in the tree nodes below.

Unfortunately rules (11)–(19) don't tell the whole story. If we apply them blindly to a rather simple formula like

$$y = 3\ln(x+1) - a/x^2,$$

we get

$$D(y) = 0 \cdot \ln(x+1) + 3\big((1+0)/(x+1)\big)$$
$$- \big(0/x^2 - \big(a(1(2x^{2-1}) + ((\ln x) \cdot 0)x^2)\big)/(x^2)^2\big), \tag{20}$$

which is correct but totally unsatisfactory. To avoid so many redundant operations in the answer, we must recognize the special cases of adding or multiplying by zero, multiplying by one, or raising to the first power. These simplifications reduce (20) to

$$D(y) = 3\big(1/(x+1)\big) - \big(-(a(2x))/(x^2)^2\big), \tag{21}$$

which is more acceptable but still not ideal. The concept of a really satisfactory answer is not well-defined, because different mathematicians will prefer formulas to be expressed in different ways; however, it is clear that (21) is not as simple as it could be. In order to make substantial progress over formula (21), it is necessary to develop algebraic simplification routines (see exercise 17), which would reduce (21) to, for example,

$$D(y) = 3(x+1)^{-1} + 2ax^{-3}. \tag{22}$$

We will content ourselves here with routines that can produce (21), not (22).

Our main interest in this algorithm is, as usual, in the details of how the process is carried out inside a computer. Many higher-level languages and special routines are available at most computer installations, with built-in facilities to simplify algebraic manipulations like these; but the purpose of the present example is to gain more experience in fundamental tree operations.

The idea behind the following algorithm is to traverse the tree in postorder, forming the derivative of each node as we go, until eventually the entire derivative has been calculated. Using postorder means that we will arrive at an operator node (like "+") *after* its operands have been differentiated. Rules (11) through (19) imply that every subformula of the original formula will have to be differentiated, sooner or later, so we might as well do the differentiations in postorder.

By using a right-threaded tree, we avoid the need for a stack during the operation of the algorithm. On the other hand, a threaded tree representation has the disadvantage that we will need to make copies of subtrees; for example, in the rule for $D(u \uparrow v)$ we might need to copy u and v three times each. If we had chosen to use a List representation as in Section 2.3.5 instead of a tree, we could have avoided such copying.

Algorithm D (*Differentiation*). If Y is the address of a list head that points to a formula represented as described above, and if DY is the address of the list head for an empty tree, this algorithm makes NODE(DY) point to a tree representing the analytic derivative of Y with respect to the variable "X".

D1. [Initialize.] Set P ← Y$ (namely, the first node of the tree, in postorder, which is the first node of the corresponding binary tree in inorder).

D2. [Differentiate.] Set P1 ← LLINK(P); and if P1 ≠ Λ, also set Q1 ← RLINK(P1). Then perform the routine DIFF[TYPE(P)], described below. (The routines DIFF[0], DIFF[1], etc., will form the derivative of the tree with root P, and will set pointer variable Q to the address of the root of the derivative. The variables P1 and Q1 are set up first, in order to simplify the specification of the DIFF routines.)

D3. [Restore link.] If TYPE(P) denotes a binary operator, set RLINK(P1) ← P2. (See the next step for an explanation.)

D4. [Advance to P$.] Set P2 ← P, P ← P$. Now if RTAG(P2) = 0 (that is, if NODE(P2) has a sibling to the right), set RLINK(P2) ← Q. (This is the tricky part of the algorithm: We temporarily destroy the structure of tree Y, so that a link to the derivative of P2 is saved for future use. The missing link will be restored later in step D3. See exercise 21 for further discussion of this trick.)

D5. [Done?] If P ≠ Y, return to step D2. Otherwise set LLINK(DY) ← Q and RLINK(Q) ← DY, RTAG(Q) ← 1. ▮

The procedure described in Algorithm D is just the background routine for the differentiation operations that are performed by the processing routines DIFF[0], DIFF[1], ..., called in step D2. In many ways, Algorithm D is like the control routine for an interpretive system or machine simulator, as discussed in Section 1.4.3, but it traverses a tree instead of a simple sequence of instructions.

To complete Algorithm D we must define the routines that do the actual differentiation. In the following discussion, the statement "P points to a tree" means that NODE(P) is the root of a tree stored as a right-threaded binary tree, although both RLINK(P) and RTAG(P) will be meaningless so far as this tree is concerned. We will make use of a *tree construction function* that makes new trees by joining smaller ones together: Let x denote some kind of node, either a constant, variable, or operator, and let U and V denote pointers to trees; then

   TREE(x,U,V) makes a new tree with x in its root node and with U and V the subtrees of the root: W ⟸ AVAIL, INFO(W) ← x, LLINK(W) ← U, RLINK(U) ← V, RTAG(U) ← 0, RLINK(V) ← W, RTAG(V) ← 1.

   TREE(x,U) similarly makes a new tree with only one subtree: W ⟸ AVAIL, INFO(W) ← x, LLINK(W) ← U, RLINK(U) ← W, RTAG(U) ← 1.

   TREE(x) makes a new tree with x as a terminal root node: W ⟸ AVAIL, INFO(W) ← x, LLINK(W) ← Λ.

Furthermore TYPE(W) is set appropriately, depending on x. In all cases, the value of TREE is W, that is, a pointer to the tree just constructed. The reader should study these three definitions carefully, since they illustrate the binary tree representation of trees. Another function, COPY(U), makes a copy of the tree pointed to by U and has as its value a pointer to the tree thereby created. The basic functions TREE and COPY make it easy to build up a tree for the derivative of a formula, step by step.

Nullary operators (*constants and variables*). For these operations, NODE(P) is a terminal node, and the values of P1, P2, Q1, and Q before the operation are irrelevant.

DIFF[0]: (NODE(P) is a constant.) Set Q ← TREE(0).

DIFF[1]: (NODE(P) is a variable.) If INFO(P) = "X", set Q ← TREE(1); otherwise set Q ← TREE(0).

Unary operators (*logarithm and negation*). For these operations, NODE(P) has one child, U, pointed to by P1, and Q points to $D(U)$. The values of P2 and Q1 before the operation are irrelevant.

DIFF[2]: (NODE(P) is "ln".) If INFO(Q) $\neq 0$, set Q ← TREE("/",Q,COPY(P1)).

DIFF[3]: (NODE(P) is "neg".) If INFO(Q) $\neq 0$, set Q ← TREE("neg",Q).

Binary operators (*addition, subtraction, multiplication, division, exponentiation*). For these operations, NODE(P) has two children, U and V, pointed to respectively by P1 and P2; Q1 and Q point respectively to $D(U)$, $D(V)$.

DIFF[4]: ("+" operation.) If INFO(Q1) = 0, set AVAIL ⇐ Q1. Otherwise if INFO(Q) = 0, set AVAIL ⇐ Q and Q ← Q1; otherwise set Q ← TREE("+",Q1,Q).

DIFF[5]: ("−" operation.) If INFO(Q) = 0, set AVAIL ⇐ Q and Q ← Q1. Otherwise if INFO(Q1) = 0, set AVAIL ⇐ Q1 and set Q ← TREE("neg",Q); otherwise set Q ← TREE("−",Q1,Q).

DIFF[6]: ("×" operation.) If INFO(Q1) $\neq 0$, set Q1 ← MULT(Q1,COPY(P2)). Then if INFO(Q) $\neq 0$, set Q ← MULT(COPY(P1),Q). Then go to DIFF[4].

Here MULT(U,V) is a new function that constructs a tree for U × V but also makes a test to see if U or V is equal to 1:

if INFO(U) = 1 and TYPE(U) = 0, set AVAIL ⇐ U and MULT(U,V) ← V;
if INFO(V) = 1 and TYPE(V) = 0, set AVAIL ⇐ V and MULT(U,V) ← U;
   otherwise set MULT(U,V) ← TREE("×",U,V).

DIFF[7]: ("/" operation.) If INFO(Q1) $\neq 0$, set

$$Q1 ← \text{TREE}("/",Q1,\text{COPY}(P2)).$$

Then if INFO(Q) $\neq 0$, set

$$Q ← \text{TREE}("/",\text{MULT}(\text{COPY}(P1),Q),\text{TREE}("\uparrow",\text{COPY}(P2),\text{TREE}(2))).$$

Then go to DIFF[5].

DIFF[8]: ("↑" operation.) See exercise 12.

We conclude this section by showing how all of the operations above are readily transformed into a computer program, starting "from scratch" with only MIX machine language as a basis.

Program D (*Differentiation*). The following MIXAL program performs Algorithm D, with rI2 ≡ P, rI3 ≡ P2, rI4 ≡ P1, rI5 ≡ Q, rI6 ≡ Q1. The order of computations has been rearranged a little, for convenience.

```
001  * DIFFERENTIATION IN A RIGHT-THREADED TREE
002  LLINK  EQU  4:5           Definition of fields, see (10)
003  RLINK  EQU  1:2
004  RLINKT EQU  0:2
005  TYPE   EQU  3:3
006  * MAIN CONTROL ROUTINE    D1. Initialize.
007  D1     STJ  9F            Treat the whole procedure as a subroutine.
008         LD4  Y(LLINK)      P1 ← LLINK(Y), prepare to find Y$.
009  1H     ENT2 0,4           P ← P1.
010  2H     LD4  0,2(LLINK)    P1 ← LLINK(P).
011         J4NZ 1B            If P1 ≠ Λ, repeat.
012  D2     LD1  0,2(TYPE)     D2. Differentiate.
013         JMP  *+1,1         Jump to DIFF[TYPE(P)].
014         JMP  CONSTANT      Switch to table entry for DIFF[0].
015         JMP  VARIABLE                             DIFF[1].
016         JMP  LN                                   DIFF[2].
017         JMP  NEG                                  DIFF[3].
018         JMP  ADD                                  DIFF[4].
019         JMP  SUB                                  DIFF[5].
020         JMP  MUL                                  DIFF[6].
021         JMP  DIV                                  DIFF[7].
022         JMP  PWR                                  DIFF[8].
023  D3     ST3  0,4(RLINK)    D3. Restore link. RLINK(P1) ← P2.
024  D4     ENT3 0,2           D4. Advance to P$. P2 ← P.
025         LD2  0,2(RLINKT)   P ← RLINKT(P).
026         J2N  1F            Jump if RTAG(P) = 1;
027         ST5  0,3(RLINK)      otherwise set RLINK(P2) ← Q.
028         JMP  2B            Note that NODE(P$) will be terminal.
029  1H     ENN2 0,2
030  D5     ENT1 -Y,2          D5. Done?
031         LD4  0,2(LLINK)    P1 ← LLINK(P), prepare for step D2.
032         LD6  0,4(RLINK)    Q1 ← RLINK(P1).
033         J1NZ D2            Jump to D2 if P ≠ Y;
034         ST5  DY(LLINK)       otherwise set LLINK(DY) ← Q.
035         ENNA DY
036         STA  0,5(RLINKT)   RLINK(Q) ← DY, RTAG(Q) ← 1.
037  9H     JMP  *             Exit from differentiation subroutine.  ▮
```

The next part of the program contains the basic subroutines TREE and COPY. The former has three entrances TREE0, TREE1, and TREE2, according to the number of subtrees of the tree being constructed. Regardless of which entrance to the subroutine is used, rA will contain the address of a special constant indicating what type of node forms the root of the tree being constructed; these special constants appear in lines 105–124.

```
038  * BASIC SUBROUTINES FOR TREE CONSTRUCTION
039  TREE0      STJ  9F              TREE(rA) function:
040             JMP  2F
041  TREE1      ST1  3F(0:2)         TREE(rA,rI1) function:
042             JSJ  1F
043  TREE2      STX  3F(0:2)         TREE(rA,rX,rI1) function:
044  3H         ST1  *(RLINKT)       RLINK(rX) ← rI1, RTAG(rX) ← 0.
045  1H         STJ  9F
046             LDXN AVAIL
047             JXZ  OVERFLOW
048             STX  0,1(RLINKT)     RLINK(rI1) ← AVAIL, RTAG(rI1) ← 1.
049             LDX  3B(0:2)
050             STA  *+1(0:2)
051             STX  *(LLINK)        Set LLINK of next root node.
052  2H         LD1  AVAIL           rI1 ⇐ AVAIL.
053             J1Z  OVERFLOW
054             LDX  0,1(LLINK)
055             STX  AVAIL
056             STA  *+1(0:2)        Copy root info to new node.
057             MOVE *(2)
058             DEC1 2               Reset rI1 to point to the new root.
059  9H         JMP  *               Exit from TREE, rI1 points to new tree.
060  COPYP1     ENT1 0,4             COPY(P1), special entrance to COPY
061             JSJ  COPY
062  COPYP2     ENT1 0,3             COPY(P2), special entrance to COPY
063  COPY       STJ  9F              COPY(rI1) function:
  ⋮              ⋮                   (see exercise 13)
104  9H         JMP  *               Exit from COPY, rI1 points to new tree.
105  CON0       CON  0               Node representing the constant "0"
106             CON  0
107  CON1       CON  0               Node representing "1"
108             CON  1
109  CON2       CON  0               Node representing "2"
110             CON  2
111  LOG        CON  2(TYPE)         Node representing "ln"
112             ALF     LN
113  NEGOP      CON  3(TYPE)         Node representing "neg"
114             ALF    NEG
115  PLUS       CON  4(TYPE)         Node representing "+"
116             ALF      +
117  MINUS      CON  5(TYPE)         Node representing "−"
118             ALF      −
119  TIMES      CON  6(TYPE)         Node representing "×"
120             ALF      *
121  SLASH      CON  7(TYPE)         Node representing "/"
122             ALF      /
```

123	UPARROW	CON 8(TYPE)	Node representing "↑"
124		ALF **	

The remaining portion of the program corresponds to the differentiation routines DIFF[0], DIFF[1], ...; these routines are written to return control to step D3 after processing a binary operator, otherwise they return to step D4.

125	* DIFFERENTIATION ROUTINES		
126	VARIABLE	LDX 1,2	
127		ENTA CON1	
128		CMPX 2F	Is INFO(P) = "X"?
129		JE *+2	If so, call TREE(1).
130	CONSTANT	ENTA CON0	Call TREE(0).
131		JMP TREE0	
132	1H	ENT5 0,1	Q ← location of new tree.
133		JMP D4	Return to control routine.
134	2H	ALF X	
135	LN	LDA 1,5	
136		JAZ D4	Return to control routine if INFO(Q) = 0;
137		JMP COPYP1	otherwise set rI1 ← COPY(P1).
138		ENTX 0,5	
139		ENTA SLASH	
140		JMP TREE2	rI1 ← TREE("/",Q,rI1).
141		JMP 1B	Q ← rI1, return to control.
142	NEG	LDA 1,5	
143		JAZ D4	Return if INFO(Q) = 0.
144		ENTA NEGOP	
145		ENT1 0,5	
146		JMP TREE1	rI1 ← TREE("neg",Q).
147		JMP 1B	Q ← rI1, return to control.
148	ADD	LDA 1,6	
149		JANZ 1F	Jump unless INFO(Q1) = 0.
150	3H	LDA AVAIL	AVAIL ⇐ Q1.
151		STA 0,6(LLINK)	
152		ST6 AVAIL	
153		JMP D3	Return to control, binary operator.
154	1H	LDA 1,5	
155		JANZ 1F	Jump unless INFO(Q) = 0.
156	2H	LDA AVAIL	AVAIL ⇐ Q.
157		STA 0,5(LLINK)	
158		ST5 AVAIL	
159		ENT5 0,6	Q ← Q1.
160		JMP D3	Return to control.
161	1H	ENTA PLUS	Prepare to call TREE("+",Q1,Q).
162	4H	ENTX 0,6	
163		ENT1 0,5	
164		JMP TREE2	
165		ENT5 0,1	Q ← TREE("±",Q1,Q).
166		JMP D3	Return to control.
167	SUB	LDA 1,5	
168		JAZ 2B	Jump if INFO(Q) = 0.

169		LDA	1,6
170		JANZ	1F	Jump unless INFO(Q1) = 0.
171		ENTA	NEGOP
172		ENT1	0,5
173		JMP	TREE1
174		ENT5	0,1	Q ← TREE("neg",Q).
175		JMP	3B	AVAIL ⇐ Q1 and return.
176	1H	ENTA	MINUS	Prepare to call TREE("−",Q1,Q).
177		JMP	4B
178	MUL	LDA	1,6
179		JAZ	1F	Jump if INFO(Q1) = 0;
180		JMP	COPYP2	otherwise set rI1 ← COPY(P2).
181		ENTA	0,6
182		JMP	MULT	rI1 ← MULT(Q1,COPY(P2)).
183		ENT6	0,1	Q1 ← rI1.
184	1H	LDA	1,5
185		JAZ	ADD	Jump if INFO(Q) = 0;
186		JMP	COPYP1	otherwise set rI1 ← COPY(P1).
187		ENTA	0,1
188		ENT1	0,5
189		JMP	MULT	rI1 ← MULT(COPY(P1),Q).
190		ENT5	0,1	Q ← rI1.
191		JMP	ADD
192	MULT	STJ	9F	MULT(rA,rI1) subroutine:
193		STA	1F(0:2)	Let rA ≡ U, rI1 ≡ V.
194		ST2	8F(0:2)	Save rI2.
195	1H	ENT2	*	rI2 ← U.
196		LDA	1,2	Test if INFO(U) = 1
197		DECA	1
198		JANZ	1F
199		LDA	0,2(TYPE)	and if TYPE(U) = 0.
200		JAZ	2F
201	1H	LDA	1,1	If not, test if INFO(V) = 1
202		DECA	1
203		JANZ	1F
204		LDA	0,1(TYPE)	and if TYPE(V) = 0.
205		JANZ	1F
206		ST1	*+2(0:2)	If so, interchange U ↔ V.
207		ENT1	0,2
208		ENT2	*
209	2H	LDA	AVAIL	AVAIL ⇐ U.
210		STA	0,2(LLINK)
211		ST2	AVAIL
212		JMP	8F	Result is V.
213	1H	ENTA	TIMES
214		ENTX	0,2
215		JMP	TREE2	Result is TREE("×",U,V).
216	8H	ENT2	*	Restore rI2 setting.
217	9H	JMP	*	Exit MULT with result in rI1. ∎

The other two routines DIV and PWR are similar and they have been left as exercises (see exercises 15 and 16).

EXERCISES

▶ **1.** [20] The text gives a formal definition of $B(F)$, the binary tree corresponding to a forest F. Give a formal definition that reverses the process; in other words, define $F(B)$, the forest corresponding to a binary tree B.

▶ **2.** [20] We defined Dewey decimal notation for forests in Section 2.3, and for binary trees in exercise 2.3.1–5. Thus the node "J" in (1) is represented by "2.2.1", and in the equivalent binary tree (3) it is represented by "11010". If possible, give a rule that directly expresses the natural correspondence between trees and binary trees as a correspondence between the Dewey decimal notations.

3. [22] What is the relation between Dewey decimal notation for the nodes of a forest and the preorder and postorder of those nodes?

4. [19] Is the following statement true or false? "The terminal nodes of a tree occur in the same relative position in preorder and postorder."

5. [23] Another correspondence between forests and binary trees could be defined by letting RLINK(P) point to the rightmost child of NODE(P), and LLINK(P) to the nearest sibling on the left. Let F be a forest that corresponds in this way to a binary tree B. What order, on the nodes of B, corresponds to (a) preorder (b) postorder on F?

6. [25] Let T be a nonempty binary tree in which each node has 0 or 2 children. If we regard T as an ordinary tree, it corresponds (via the natural correspondence) to *another* binary tree T'. Is there any simple relation between preorder, inorder, and postorder of the nodes of T (as defined for binary trees) and the same three orders for the nodes of T'?

7. [M20] A forest may be regarded as a partial ordering, if we say that each node precedes its descendants in the tree. Are the nodes topologically sorted (as defined in Section 2.2.3) when they are listed in (a) preorder? (b) postorder? (c) reverse preorder? (d) reverse postorder?

8. [M20] Exercise 2.3.1–25 shows how an ordering between the information stored in the individual nodes of a binary tree may be extended to a linear ordering of all binary trees. The same construction leads to an ordering of all trees, under the natural correspondence. Reformulate the definition of that exercise, in terms of trees.

9. [M21] Show that the total number of nonterminal nodes in a forest has a simple relation to the total number of right links equal to Λ in the corresponding unthreaded binary tree.

10. [M23] Let F be a forest of trees whose nodes in preorder are $u_1, u_2, \ldots, u_n$, and let F' be a forest whose nodes in preorder are $u'_1, u'_2, \ldots, u'_{n'}$. Let $d(u)$ denote the degree (the number of children) of node u. In terms of these ideas, formulate and prove a theorem analogous to Theorem 2.3.1A.

11. [15] Draw trees analogous to those shown in (7), corresponding to the formula $y = e^{-x^2}$.

12. [M21] Give specifications for the routine DIFF[8] (the "↑" operation), which was omitted from the algorithm in the text.

▸ **13.** [*26*] Write a MIX program for the COPY subroutine (which fits in the program of the text between lines 063–104). [*Hint:* Adapt Algorithm 2.3.1C to the case of right-threaded binary trees, with suitable initial conditions.]

▸ **14.** [*M21*] How long does it take the program of exercise 13 to copy a tree with n nodes?

15. [*23*] Write a MIX program for the DIV routine, corresponding to DIFF[7] as specified in the text. (This routine should be added to the program in the text after line 217.)

16. [*24*] Write a MIX program for the PWR routine, corresponding to DIFF[8] as specified in exercise 12. (This routine should be added to the program in the text after the solution to exercise 15.)

17. [*M40*] Write a program to do algebraic simplification capable of reducing, for example, (20) or (21) to (22). [*Hints:* Include a new field with each node, representing its coefficient (for summands) or its exponent (for factors in a product). Apply algebraic identities, like replacing $\ln(u \uparrow v)$ by $v \ln u$; remove the operations $-$, $/$, $\uparrow$, and neg when possible by using equivalent addition or multiplication operations. Make $+$ and $\times$ into n-ary instead of binary operators; collect like terms by sorting their operands in tree order (exercise 8); some sums and products will now reduce to zero or unity, presenting perhaps further simplifications. Other adjustments, like replacing a sum of logarithms by the logarithm of a product, also suggest themselves.]

▸ **18.** [*25*] An oriented tree specified by n links PARENT[j] for $1 \leq j \leq n$ implicitly defines an ordered tree if the nodes in each family are ordered by their location. Design an efficient algorithm that constructs a doubly linked circular list containing the nodes of this ordered tree in preorder. For example, given

$$j = 1\ 2\ 3\ 4\ 5\ 6\ 7\ 8$$
$$\text{PARENT}[j] = 3\ 8\ 4\ 0\ 4\ 8\ 3\ 4$$

your algorithm should produce

$$\text{LLINK}[j] = 3\ 8\ 4\ 6\ 7\ 2\ 1\ 5$$
$$\text{RLINK}[j] = 7\ 6\ 1\ 3\ 8\ 4\ 5\ 2$$

and it should also report that the root node is 4.

19. [*M35*] A *free lattice* is a mathematical system, which (for the purposes of this exercise) can be simply defined as the set of all formulas composed of variables and two abstract binary operators "$\vee$" and "$\wedge$". A relation "$X \succeq Y$" is defined between certain formulas X and Y in the free lattice by the following rules:

   i) $X \vee Y \succeq W \wedge Z$ if and only if $X \vee Y \succeq W$ or $X \vee Y \succeq Z$ or $X \succeq W \wedge Z$ or $Y \succeq W \wedge Z$;

   ii) $X \wedge Y \succeq Z$ if and only if $X \succeq Z$ and $Y \succeq Z$;

   iii) $X \succeq Y \vee Z$ if and only if $X \succeq Y$ and $X \succeq Z$;

   iv) $x \succeq Y \wedge Z$ if and only if $x \succeq Y$ or $x \succeq Z$, when x is a variable;

   v) $X \vee Y \succeq z$ if and only if $X \succeq z$ or $Y \succeq z$, when z is a variable;

   vi) $x \succeq y$ if and only if $x = y$, when x and y are variables.

For example, we find $a \wedge (b \vee c) \succeq (a \wedge b) \vee (a \wedge c) \not\succeq a \wedge (b \vee c)$.

   Design an algorithm that tests whether or not $X \succeq Y$, given two formulas X and Y in the free lattice.

▶ **20.** [*M22*] Prove that if u and v are nodes of a forest, u is a proper ancestor of v if and only if u precedes v in preorder and u follows v in postorder.

21. [*25*] Algorithm D controls the differentiation activity for binary operators, unary operators, and nullary operators, thus for trees whose nodes have degree 2, 1, and 0; but it does not indicate explicitly how the control would be handled for ternary operators and nodes of higher degree. (For example, exercise 17 suggests making addition and multiplication into operators with any number of operands.) Is it possible to extend Algorithm D in a simple way so that it will handle operators of degree more than 2?

▶ **22.** [*M26*] If T and T' are trees, let us say T *can be embedded in* T', written $T \subseteq T'$, if there is a one-to-one function f from the nodes of T into the nodes of T' such that f preserves both preorder and postorder. (In other words, u precedes v in preorder for T if and only if $f(u)$ precedes $f(v)$ in preorder for T', and the same holds for postorder. See Fig. 25.)

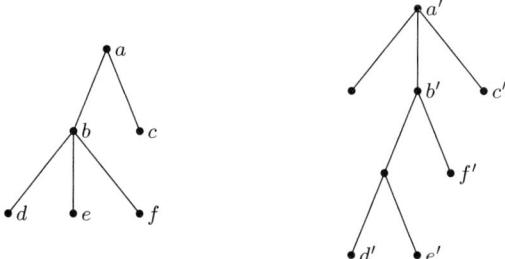

Fig. 25. One tree embedded in another (see exercise 22).

If T has more than one node, let $l(T)$ be the leftmost subtree of root(T) and let $r(T)$ be the rest of T, that is, T with $l(T)$ deleted. Prove that T can be embedded in T' if (i) T has just one node, or (ii) both T and T' have more than one node and either $T \subseteq l(T')$, or $T \subseteq r(T')$, or $\bigl(l(T) \subseteq l(T')$ and $r(T) \subseteq r(T')\bigr)$. Does the converse hold?

2.3.3. Other Representations of Trees

There are many ways to represent tree structures inside a computer besides the LLINK-RLINK (left child–right sibling) method given in the previous section. As usual, the proper choice of representation depends heavily on what kind of operations we want to perform on the trees. In this section we will consider a few of the tree representation methods that have proved to be especially useful.

First we can use *sequential* memory techniques. As in the case of linear lists, this mode of allocation is most suitable when we want a compact representation of a tree structure that is not going to be subject to radical dynamic changes in size or shape during program execution. There are many situations in which we need essentially constant tables of tree structures for reference within a program, and the desired form of these trees in memory depends on the way in which the tables are to be examined.

The most common sequential representation of trees (and forests) corresponds essentially to the omission of LLINK fields, by using consecutive addressing instead. For example, let us look again at the forest

$$\bigl(A(B,C(K)),\ D(E(H),F(J),G)\bigr) \qquad (1)$$

considered in the previous section, which has the tree diagrams

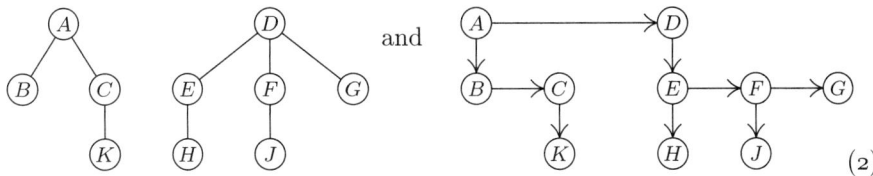

$$(2)$$

The *preorder sequential representation* has the nodes appearing in preorder, with the fields INFO, RLINK, and LTAG in each node:

$$
\begin{array}{l}
\text{RLINK} \\
\text{INFO} \qquad A \ B \ C \ K \ D \ E \ H \ F \ J \ G \\
\text{LTAG}
\end{array} \qquad (3)
$$

Here nonnull RLINKs have been indicated by arrows, and LTAG = 1 (for terminal nodes) is indicated by "⌋". LLINK is unnecessary, since it would either be null or it would point to the next item in sequence. It is instructive to compare (1) with (3).

This representation has several interesting properties. In the first place, all subtrees of a node appear immediately after that node, so that all subtrees within the original forest appear in consecutive blocks. [Compare this with the "nested parentheses" in (1) and in Fig. 20(b).] In the second place, notice that the RLINK arrows never cross each other in (3); this will be true in general, for in a binary tree all nodes between X and RLINK(X) in preorder lie in the left subtree of X, hence no outward arrows will emerge from that part of the tree. In the third place, we may observe that the LTAG field, which indicates whether a node is terminal or not, is redundant, since "⌋" occurs only at the end of the forest and just *preceding* every downward pointing arrow.

Indeed, these remarks show that the RLINK field itself is almost redundant; all we really need to represent the structure is RTAG and LTAG. Thus it is possible to deduce (3) from much less data:

$$
\begin{array}{l}
\text{RTAG} \\
\text{INFO} \qquad A \ B \ C \ K \ D \ E \ H \ F \ J \ G \\
\text{LTAG}
\end{array} \qquad (4)
$$

As we scan (4) from left to right, the positions with RTAG ≠ "⌉" correspond to nonnull RLINKs that must be filled in. Each time we pass an item with LTAG = "⌋", we should complete the most recent instance of an incomplete RLINK. (The locations of incomplete RLINKs can therefore be kept on a stack.) We have essentially proved Theorem 2.3.1A again.

The fact that RLINK or LTAG is redundant in (3) is of little or no help to us unless we are scanning the entire forest sequentially, since extra computation is required to deduce the missing information. Therefore we often need all of the data in (3). However, there is evidently some wasted space, since more than half of the RLINK fields are equal to Λ for this particular forest. There are two common ways to make use of the wasted space:

1) Fill the RLINK of each node with the address following the subtree below that node. The field is now often called "SCOPE" instead of RLINK, since it indicates the right boundary of the "influence" (descendants) of each node. Instead of (3), we would have

$$
\begin{array}{l}
\text{SCOPE} \\
\text{INFO} \quad A \quad B \quad C \quad K \quad D \quad E \quad H \quad F \quad J \quad G
\end{array} \tag{5}
$$

The arrows still do not cross each other. Furthermore, LTAG(X) = "$|$" is characterized by the condition SCOPE(X) = X$+c$, where c is the number of words per node. One example of the use of this SCOPE idea appears in exercise 2.4–12.

2) Decrease the size of each node by removing the RLINK field, and add special "link" nodes just before nodes that formerly had a nonnull RLINK:

$$
\begin{array}{l}
\text{INFO} \quad * \quad A \quad * \quad B \quad C \quad K \quad D \quad * \quad E \quad H \quad * \quad F \quad J \quad G \\
\text{LTAG}
\end{array} \tag{6}
$$

Here "$*$" indicates the special link nodes, whose INFO somehow characterizes them as links pointing as shown by the arrows. If the INFO and RLINK fields of (3) occupy roughly the same amount of space, the net effect of the change to (6) is to consume less memory, since the number of "$*$" nodes is always less than the number of non-"$*$" nodes. Representation (6) is somewhat analogous to a sequence of instructions in a one-address computer like MIX, with the "$*$" nodes corresponding to conditional jump instructions.

Another sequential representation analogous to (3) may be devised by omitting RLINKs instead of LLINKs. In this case we list the nodes of the forest in a new order that may be called *family order* since the members of each family appear together. Family order for any forest may be defined recursively as follows:

Visit the root of the first tree.

Traverse the remaining trees (in family order).

Traverse the subtrees of the root of the first tree (in family order).

(Compare this with the definitions of preorder and postorder in the previous section. Family order is identical with the reverse of postorder in the corresponding binary tree.)

The *family order sequential representation* of the trees (2) is

$$
\begin{array}{l}
\text{LLINK} \\
\text{INFO} \quad A \quad D \quad E \quad F \quad G \quad J \quad H \quad B \quad C \quad K \\
\text{RTAG}
\end{array} \tag{7}
$$

In this case the RTAG entries serve to delimit the families. Family order begins by listing the roots of all trees in the forest, then continues by listing individual families, successively choosing the family of the most recently appearing node whose family has not yet been listed. It follows that the LLINK arrows will never cross; and the other properties of preorder representation carry over in a similar way.

Instead of using family order, we could also simply list the nodes from left to right, one level at a time. This is called "level order" [see G. Salton, *CACM* **5** (1962), 103–114], and the *level order sequential representation* of (2) is

$$
\begin{array}{l}
\text{LLINK} \\
\text{INFO} \qquad A \quad D \quad B \quad C \quad E \quad F \quad G \quad K \quad H \quad J \\
\text{RTAG}
\end{array}
\tag{8}
$$

This is like (7), but the families are chosen in first-in-first-out fashion rather than last-in-first-out. Either (7) or (8) may be regarded as a natural analog, for trees, of the sequential representation of linear lists.

The reader will easily see how to design algorithms that traverse and analyze trees represented sequentially as above, since the LLINK and RLINK information is essentially available just as though we had a fully linked tree structure.

Another sequential method, called *postorder with degrees*, is somewhat different from the techniques above. We list the nodes in postorder and give the degree of each node instead of links:

$$
\begin{array}{l}
\text{DEGREE} \quad 0 \quad 0 \quad 1 \quad 2 \quad 0 \quad 1 \quad 0 \quad 1 \quad 0 \quad 3 \\
\text{INFO} \qquad B \quad K \quad C \quad A \quad H \quad E \quad J \quad F \quad G \quad D
\end{array}
\tag{9}
$$

For a proof that this is sufficient to characterize the tree structure, see exercise 2.3.2–10. This order is useful for the "bottom-up" evaluation of functions defined on the nodes of a tree, as in the following algorithm.

Algorithm F (*Evaluate a locally defined function in a tree*). Suppose f is a function of the nodes of a tree, such that the value of f at a node x depends only on x and the values of f on the children of x. The following algorithm, using an auxiliary stack, evaluates f at each node of a nonempty forest.

F1. [Initialize.] Set the stack empty, and let P point to the first node of the forest in postorder.

F2. [Evaluate f.] Set $d \leftarrow$ DEGREE(P). (The first time this step is reached, d will be zero. In general, when we get to this point, it will always be true that the top d items of the stack are $f(x_d)$, ..., $f(x_1)$ — from the top of the stack downward — where x_1, ..., x_d are the children of NODE(P) from left to right.) Evaluate $f\big(\text{NODE(P)}\big)$, using the values of $f(x_d)$, ..., $f(x_1)$ found on the stack.

F3. [Update the stack.] Remove the top d items of the stack; then put the value $f\big(\text{NODE(P)}\big)$ on top of the stack.

F4. [Advance.] If P is the last node in postorder, terminate the algorithm. (The stack will then contain $f\big(\text{root}(T_m)\big)$, ..., $f\big(\text{root}(T_1)\big)$, from top to bottom, where T_1, ..., T_m are the trees of the given forest.) Otherwise set P to its successor in postorder (this would be simply $P \leftarrow P + c$ in the representation (9)), and return to step F2. ∎

The validity of Algorithm F follows by induction on the size of the trees processed (see exercise 16). This algorithm bears a striking similarity to the differentiation procedure of the previous section (Algorithm 2.3.2D), which evaluates a function of a closely related type; see exercise 3. The same idea is used in many interpretive routines in connection with the evaluation of arithmetic expressions in postfix notation; we will return to this topic in Chapter 8. See also exercise 17, which gives another important procedure similar to Algorithm F.

Thus we have seen various sequential representations of trees and forests. There are also a number of *linked* forms of representation, which we shall now consider.

The first idea is related to the transformation that takes (3) into (6): We remove the INFO fields from all nonterminal nodes and put this information as a new terminal node below the previous node. For example, the trees (2) would become

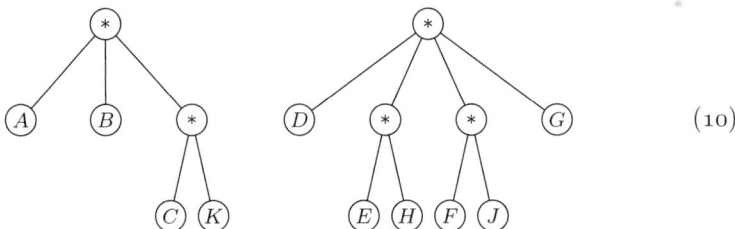

$$(10)$$

This new form shows that we may assume (without loss of generality) that all INFO in a tree structure appears in its terminal nodes. Therefore in the natural binary tree representation of Section 2.3.2, the LLINK and INFO fields are mutually exclusive and they can share the same field in each node. A node might have the fields

LTAG	LLINK or INFO	RLINK

where the sign LTAG tells whether the second field is a link or not. (Compare this representation with, for example, the two-word format of (10) in Section 2.3.2.) By cutting INFO down from 5 bytes to 3, we can fit each node into one word. However, notice that there are now 15 nodes instead of 10; the forest (10) takes 15 words of memory while (2) takes 20, yet the latter has 50 bytes of INFO compared to 30 in the other. There is no real gain in memory space in (10) unless the excess INFO space was going to waste; the LLINKs replaced in (10) are removed at the expense of about the same number of new RLINKs in the added nodes. Precise details of the differences between the two representations are discussed in exercise 4.

In the standard binary tree representation of a tree, the LLINK field might be more accurately called the LCHILD field, since it points from a parent node to its leftmost child. The leftmost child is usually the "youngest" of the children in the tree, since it is easier to insert a node at the left of a family than at the right; so the abbreviation LCHILD may also be thought of as the "last child" or "least child."

Many applications of tree structures require rather frequent references upward in the tree as well as downward. A threaded tree gives us the ability to go upward, but not with great speed; we can sometimes do better if we have a third link, PARENT, in each node. This leads to a *triply linked tree*, where each node has LCHILD, RLINK, and PARENT links. Figure 26 shows a triply linked tree representation of (2). For an example of the use of triply linked trees, see Section 2.4.

INFO	PARENT
LCHILD	RLINK

Fig. 26. A triply linked tree.

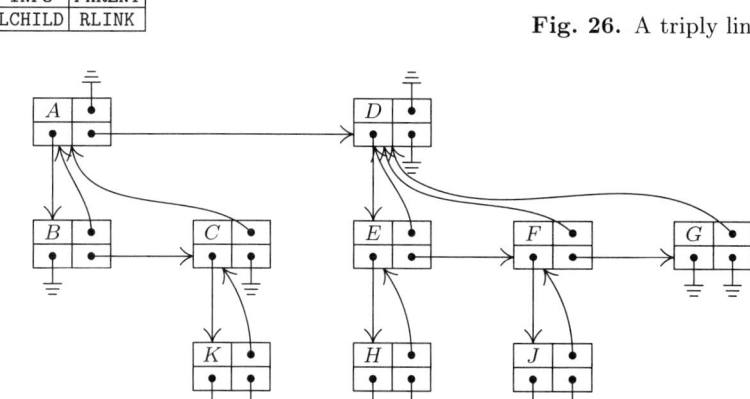

It is clear that the PARENT link all by itself is enough to specify any *oriented* tree (or forest) completely. For we can draw the diagram of the tree if we know all the upward links. Every node except the root has just one parent, but there may be several children; so it is simpler to give upward links than downward ones. Why then haven't we considered upward links much earlier in our discussion? The answer, of course, is that upward links by themselves are hardly adequate in most situations, since it is very difficult to tell quickly if a node is terminal or not, or to locate any of its children, etc. There is, however, a very important application in which upward links are sufficient by themselves: We now turn to a brief study of an elegant algorithm for dealing with equivalence relations, due to M. J. Fischer and B. A. Galler.

An *equivalence relation* "≡" is a relation between the elements of a set of objects S satisfying the following three properties for any objects x, y, and z (not necessarily distinct) in S:

i) If $x \equiv y$ and $y \equiv z$, then $x \equiv z$. (Transitivity.)
ii) If $x \equiv y$, then $y \equiv x$. (Symmetry.)
iii) $x \equiv x$. (Reflexivity.)

(Compare this with the definition of a partial ordering relation in Section 2.2.3; equivalence relations are quite different from partial orderings, in spite of the fact that two of the three defining properties are the same.) Examples of equivalence relations are the relation "=", the relation of congruence (modulo m) for integers, the relation of similarity between trees as defined in Section 2.3.1, etc.

The equivalence problem is to read in pairs of equivalent elements and to determine later whether two particular elements can be proved equivalent or not on the basis of the given pairs. For example, suppose that S is the set $\{1, 2, 3, 4, 5, 6, 7, 8, 9\}$ and suppose that we are given the pairs

$$1 \equiv 5, \quad 6 \equiv 8, \quad 7 \equiv 2, \quad 9 \equiv 8, \quad 3 \equiv 7, \quad 4 \equiv 2, \quad 9 \equiv 3. \qquad (11)$$

It follows that, for example, $2 \equiv 6$, since $2 \equiv 7 \equiv 3 \equiv 9 \equiv 8 \equiv 6$. But we cannot show that $1 \equiv 6$. In fact, the pairs (11) divide S into two classes

$$\{1, 5\} \quad \text{and} \quad \{2, 3, 4, 6, 7, 8, 9\}, \qquad (12)$$

such that two elements are equivalent if and only if they belong to the same class. It is not difficult to prove that *any* equivalence relation partitions its set S into disjoint classes (called the *equivalence classes*), such that two elements are equivalent if and only if they belong to the same class.

Therefore a solution to the equivalence problem is a matter of keeping track of equivalence classes like (12). We may start with each element alone in its class, thus:

$$\{1\} \ \{2\} \ \{3\} \ \{4\} \ \{5\} \ \{6\} \ \{7\} \ \{8\} \ \{9\} \qquad (13)$$

Now if we are given the relation $1 \equiv 5$, we put $\{1, 5\}$ together in a class. After processing the first three relations $1 \equiv 5$, $6 \equiv 8$, and $7 \equiv 2$, we will have changed (13) to

$$\{1, 5\} \ \{2, 7\} \ \{3\} \ \{4\} \ \{6, 8\} \ \{9\}. \qquad (14)$$

Now the pair $9 \equiv 8$ puts $\{6, 8, 9\}$ together, etc.

The problem is to find a good way to represent situations like (12), (13), and (14) within a computer so that we can efficiently perform the operations of merging classes together and of testing whether two given elements are in the same class. The algorithm below uses oriented tree structures for this purpose: The elements of S become nodes of an oriented forest; and two nodes are equivalent, as a consequence of the equivalent pairs read so far, *if and only if they belong to the same tree.* This test is easy to make, since two elements are in the same tree if and only if they are below the same root element. Furthermore, it is easy to merge two oriented trees together, by simply attaching one as a new subtree of the other's root.

Algorithm E (*Process equivalence relations*). Let S be the set of numbers $\{1, 2, \ldots, n\}$, and let PARENT[1], PARENT[2], $\ldots$, PARENT[n] be integer variables. This algorithm inputs a set of relations such as (11) and adjusts the PARENT table to represent a set of oriented trees, so that two elements are equivalent as a consequence of the given relations if and only if they belong to the same tree. (*Note:* In a more general situation, the elements of S would be symbolic names instead of simply the numbers from 1 to n; then a search routine, as in Chapter 6, would locate nodes corresponding to the elements of S, and PARENT would be a field in each node. The modifications for this more general case are straightforward.)

E1. [Initialize.] Set PARENT[k] ← 0 for $1 \le k \le n$. (This means that all trees initially consist of a root alone, as in (13).)

E2. [Input new pair.] Get the next pair of equivalent elements "$j \equiv k$" from the input. If the input is exhausted, the algorithm terminates.

E3. [Find roots.] If PARENT[j] > 0, set j ← PARENT[j] and repeat this step. If PARENT[k] > 0, set k ← PARENT[k] and repeat this step. (After this operation, j and k have moved up to the roots of two trees that are to be made equivalent. The input relation $j \equiv k$ was redundant if and only if we now have $j = k$.)

E4. [Merge trees.] If $j \ne k$, set PARENT[j] ← k. Go back to step E2. ∎

The reader should try this algorithm on the input (11). After processing $1 \equiv 5$, $6 \equiv 8$, $7 \equiv 2$, and $9 \equiv 8$, we will have

$$
\begin{array}{lccccccccc}
\text{PARENT}[k]: & 5 & 0 & 0 & 0 & 0 & 8 & 2 & 0 & 8 \\
k\ : & 1 & 2 & 3 & 4 & 5 & 6 & 7 & 8 & 9
\end{array}
\tag{15}
$$

which represents the trees

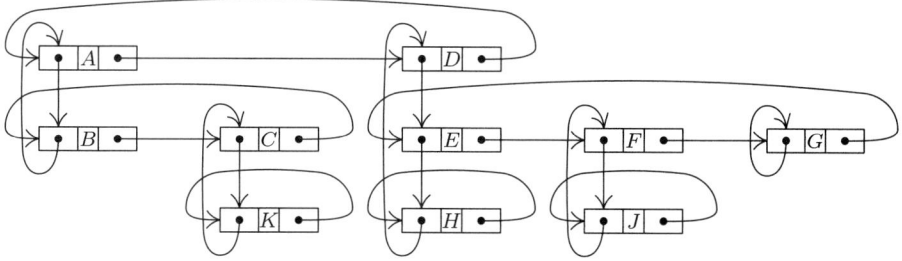

(16)

After this point, the remaining relations of (11) are somewhat more interesting; see exercise 9.

This equivalence problem arises in many applications. We will discuss significant refinements of Algorithm E in Section 7.4.1, when we study the connectivity of graphs. A more general version of the problem, which arises when a compiler processes "equivalence declarations" in languages like FORTRAN, is discussed in exercise 11.

Fig. 27. A ring structure.

There are still more ways to represent trees in computer memory. Recall that we discussed three principal methods for representing linear lists in Section 2.2: the straight representation with terminal link Λ, the circularly linked lists, and the doubly linked lists. The representation of unthreaded binary trees described in Section 2.3.1 corresponds to a straight representation in both LLINKs and

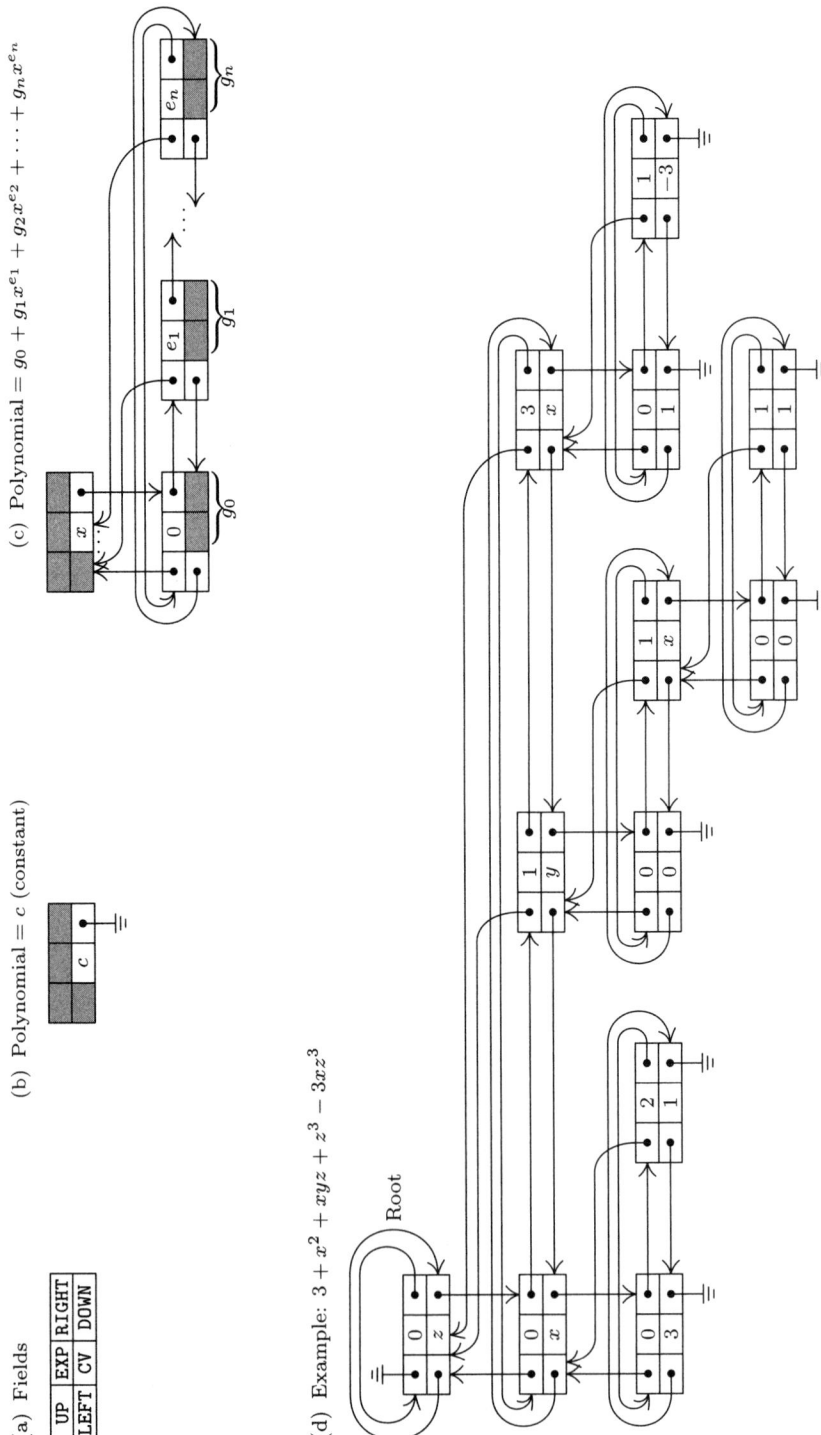

(a) Fields

(b) Polynomial $= c$ (constant)

(c) Polynomial $= g_0 + g_1 x^{e_1} + g_2 x^{e_2} + \cdots + g_n x^{e_n}$

(d) Example: $3 + x^2 + xyz + z^3 - 3xz^3$

Fig. 28. Representation of polynomials using four-directional links. Shaded areas of nodes indicate information that is irrelevant in the context considered.

RLINKs. It is possible to get eight other binary tree representations by independently using any of these three methods in the LLINK and RLINK directions. For example, Fig. 27 shows what we get if circular linking is used in both directions. If circular links are used throughout as in the figure, we have what is called a *ring structure*; ring structures have proved to be quite flexible in a number of applications. The proper choice of representation depends, as always, on the types of insertions, deletions, and traversals that are needed in the algorithms that manipulate these structures. A reader who has looked over the examples given so far in this chapter should have no difficulty understanding how to deal with any of these memory representations.

We close this section with an example of modified doubly linked ring structures applied to a problem we have considered before: arithmetic on polynomials. Algorithm 2.2.4A performs the addition of one polynomial to another, given that the two polynomials are expressed as circular lists; various other algorithms in that section give other operations on polynomials. However, the polynomials of Section 2.2.4 are restricted to at most three variables. When multi-variable polynomials are involved, it is usually more appropriate to use a tree structure instead of a linear list.

A polynomial either is a constant or has the form

$$\sum_{0 \le j \le n} g_j x^{e_j},$$

where x is a variable, $n > 0$, $0 = e_0 < e_1 < \cdots < e_n$, and $g_0, \ldots, g_n$ are polynomials involving only variables alphabetically less than x; $g_1, \ldots, g_n$ are not zero. This recursive definition of polynomials lends itself to tree representation as indicated in Fig. 28. Nodes have six fields, which in the case of MIX might fit in three words:

+	0	LEFT	RIGHT
+	EXP	UP	DOWN
CV			

(17)

Here LEFT, RIGHT, UP, and DOWN are links; EXP is an integer representing an exponent; and CV is either a constant (coefficient) or the alphabetic name of a variable. The root node has UP $= \Lambda$, EXP $= 0$, LEFT $=$ RIGHT $= *$ (self).

The following algorithm illustrates traversal, insertion, and deletion in such a four-way-linked tree, so it bears careful study.

Algorithm A (*Addition of polynomials*). This algorithm adds polynomial(P) to polynomial(Q), assuming that P and Q are pointer variables that link to the roots of distinct polynomial trees having the form shown in Fig. 28. At the conclusion of the algorithm, polynomial(P) will be unchanged, and polynomial(Q) will contain the sum.

A1. [Test type of polynomial.] If DOWN(P) $= \Lambda$ (that is, if P points to a constant), then set Q $\leftarrow$ DOWN(Q) zero or more times until DOWN(Q) $= \Lambda$

and go to A3. If DOWN(P) $\neq \Lambda$, then if DOWN(Q) $= \Lambda$ or if CV(Q) $<$ CV(P),
go to A2. Otherwise if CV(Q) $=$ CV(P), set P $\leftarrow$ DOWN(P), Q $\leftarrow$ DOWN(Q)
and repeat this step; if CV(Q) $>$ CV(P), set Q $\leftarrow$ DOWN(Q) and repeat this
step. (Step A1 either finds two matching terms of the polynomials or
else determines that an insertion of a new variable must be made into the
current part of polynomial(Q).)

A2. [Downward insertion.] Set R $\Leftarrow$ AVAIL, S $\leftarrow$ DOWN(Q). If S $\neq \Lambda$, set
UP(S) $\leftarrow$ R, S $\leftarrow$ RIGHT(S) and if EXP(S) $\neq$ 0, repeat this operation
until ultimately EXP(S) $=$ 0. Set UP(R) $\leftarrow$ Q, DOWN(R) $\leftarrow$ DOWN(Q),
LEFT(R) $\leftarrow$ R, RIGHT(R) $\leftarrow$ R, CV(R) $\leftarrow$ CV(Q) and EXP(R) $\leftarrow$ 0. Finally,
set CV(Q) $\leftarrow$ CV(P) and DOWN(Q) $\leftarrow$ R, and return to A1. (We have inserted
a "dummy" zero polynomial just below NODE(Q), to obtain a match with
a corresponding polynomial found within P's tree. The link manipulations
done in this step are straightforward and may be derived easily using
"before-and-after" diagrams, as explained in Section 2.2.3.)

A3. [Match found.] (At this point, P and Q point to corresponding terms of
the given polynomials, so addition is ready to proceed.) Set CV(Q) $\leftarrow$
CV(Q) $+$ CV(P). If this sum is zero and if EXP(Q) $\neq$ 0, go to step A8. If
EXP(Q) $=$ 0, go to A7.

A4. [Advance to left.] (After successfully adding a term, we look for the next
term to add.) Set P $\leftarrow$ LEFT(P). If EXP(P) $=$ 0, go to A6. Otherwise
set Q $\leftarrow$ LEFT(Q) one or more times until EXP(Q) $\leq$ EXP(P). If then
EXP(Q) $=$ EXP(P), return to step A1.

A5. [Insert to right.] Set R $\Leftarrow$ AVAIL. Set UP(R) $\leftarrow$ UP(Q), DOWN(R) $\leftarrow \Lambda$,
CV(R) $\leftarrow$ 0, LEFT(R) $\leftarrow$ Q, RIGHT(R) $\leftarrow$ RIGHT(Q), LEFT(RIGHT(R)) $\leftarrow$ R,
RIGHT(Q) $\leftarrow$ R, EXP(R) $\leftarrow$ EXP(P), and Q $\leftarrow$ R. Return to step A1. (We
needed to insert a new term in the current row, just to the right of NODE(Q),
in order to match a corresponding exponent in polynomial(P). As in
step A2, a "before-and-after" diagram makes the operations clear.)

A6. [Return upward.] (A row of polynomial(P) has now been completely traversed.) Set P $\leftarrow$ UP(P).

A7. [Move Q up to right level.] If UP(P) $= \Lambda$, go to A11; otherwise set
Q $\leftarrow$ UP(Q) zero or more times until CV(UP(Q)) $=$ CV(UP(P)). Return
to step A4.

A8. [Delete zero term.] Set R $\leftarrow$ Q, Q $\leftarrow$ RIGHT(R), S $\leftarrow$ LEFT(R), LEFT(Q) $\leftarrow$ S,
RIGHT(S) $\leftarrow$ Q, and AVAIL $\Leftarrow$ R. (Cancellation occurred, so a row element
of polynomial(Q) is deleted.) If now EXP(LEFT(P)) $=$ 0 and Q $=$ S, go
to A9; otherwise return to A4.

A9. [Delete constant polynomial.] (Cancellation has caused a polynomial to
reduce to a constant, so a row of polynomial(Q) is deleted.) Set R $\leftarrow$ Q,
Q $\leftarrow$ UP(Q), DOWN(Q) $\leftarrow$ DOWN(R), CV(Q) $\leftarrow$ CV(R), and AVAIL $\Leftarrow$ R. Set
S $\leftarrow$ DOWN(Q); if S $\neq \Lambda$, set UP(S) $\leftarrow$ Q, S $\leftarrow$ RIGHT(S), and if EXP(S) $\neq$ 0,
repeat this operation until ultimately EXP(S) $=$ 0.

A10. [Zero detected?] If `DOWN(Q)` = Λ, `CV(Q)` = 0, and `EXP(Q)` $\neq$ 0, set P $\leftarrow$ `UP(P)` and go to A8; otherwise go to A6.

A11. [Terminate.] Set Q $\leftarrow$ `UP(Q)` zero or more times until `UP(Q)` = Λ (thus bringing Q to the root of the tree). $\blacksquare$

This algorithm will actually run much faster than Algorithm 2.2.4A if polynomial(P) has few terms and polynomial(Q) has many, since it is not necessary to pass over all of polynomial(Q) during the addition process. The reader will find it instructive to simulate Algorithm A by hand, adding the polynomial $xy - x^2 - xyz - z^3 + 3xz^3$ to the polynomial shown in Fig. 28. (This case does not demonstrate the efficiency of the algorithm, but it makes the algorithm go through all of its paces by showing the difficult situations that must be handled.) For further commentary on Algorithm A, see exercises 12 and 13.

No claim is being made here that the representation shown in Fig. 28 is the "best" for polynomials in several variables; in Chapter 8 we will consider another format for polynomial representation, together with arithmetic algorithms using an auxiliary stack, with significant advantages of conceptual simplicity when compared to Algorithm A. Our main interest in Algorithm A is the way it typifies manipulations on trees with many links.

EXERCISES

▶ **1.** [*20*] If we had only `LTAG`, `INFO`, and `RTAG` fields (not `LLINK`) in a level order sequential representation like (8), would it be possible to reconstruct the `LLINK`s? (In other words, are the `LLINK`s redundant in (8), as the `RLINK`s are in (3)?)

2. [*22*] (Burks, Warren, and Wright, *Math. Comp.* **8** (1954), 53–57.) The trees (2) stored in *preorder* with degrees would be

DEGREE	2	0	1	0	3	1	0	1	0	0
INFO	*A*	*B*	*C*	*K*	*D*	*E*	*H*	*F*	*J*	*G*

[compare with (9), where postorder was used]. Design an algorithm analogous to Algorithm F to evaluate a locally defined function of the nodes by going from right to left in this representation.

▶ **3.** [*24*] Modify Algorithm 2.3.2D so that it follows the ideas of Algorithm F, placing the derivatives it computes as intermediate results on a stack, instead of recording their locations in an anomalous fashion as is done in step D3. (See exercise 2.3.2–21.) The stack may be maintained by using the `RLINK` field in the root of each derivative.

4. [*18*] The trees (2) contain 10 nodes, five of which are terminal. Representation of these trees in the normal binary-tree fashion involves 10 `LLINK` fields and 10 `RLINK` fields (one for each node). Representation of these trees in the form (10), where `LLINK` and `INFO` share the same space in a node, requires 5 `LLINK`s and 15 `RLINK`s. There are 10 `INFO` fields in each case.

Given a forest with n nodes, m of which are terminal, compare the total number of `LLINK`s and `RLINK`s that must be stored using these two methods of tree representation.

5. [*16*] A triply linked tree, as shown in Fig. 26, contains `PARENT`, `LCHILD`, and `RLINK` fields in each node, with liberal use of Λ-links when there is no appropriate node to mention in the `PARENT`, `LCHILD`, or `RLINK` field. Would it be a good idea to extend this representation to a *threaded* tree, by putting "thread" links in place of the null LCHILD and RLINK entries, as we did in Section 2.3.1?

▶ **6.** [*24*] Suppose that the nodes of an *oriented* forest have three link fields, PARENT, LCHILD, and RLINK, but only the PARENT link has been set up to indicate the tree structure. The LCHILD field of each node is Λ and the RLINK fields are set as a linear list that simply links the nodes together in some order. The link variable FIRST points to the first node, and the last node has RLINK $= \Lambda$.

Design an algorithm that goes through these nodes and fills in the LCHILD and RLINK fields compatible with the PARENT links, so that a triply linked tree representation like that in Fig. 26 is obtained. Also, reset FIRST so that it now points to the root of · the first tree in this representation.

7. [*15*] What classes would appear in (12) if the relation $9 \equiv 3$ had not been given in (11)?

8. [*15*] Algorithm E sets up a tree structure that represents the given pairs of equivalent elements, but the text does not mention explicitly how the result of Algorithm E can be used. Design an algorithm that answers the question, "Is $j \equiv k$?", assuming that $1 \le j \le n$, $1 \le k \le n$, and that Algorithm E has set up the PARENT table for some set of equivalences.

9. [*20*] Give a table analogous to (15) and a diagram analogous to (16) that shows the trees present after Algorithm E has processed all of the equivalences in (11) from left to right.

10. [*28*] In the worst case, Algorithm E may take order n^2 steps to process n equivalences. Show how to modify the algorithm so that the worst case is not this bad.

▶ **11.** [*24*] (*Equivalence declarations.*) Several compiler languages, notably FORTRAN, provide a facility for overlapping the memory locations assigned to sequentially stored tables. The programmer gives the compiler a set of relations of the form $X[j] \equiv Y[k]$, which means that variable $X[j + s]$ is to be assigned to the same location as variable $Y[k + s]$ for all s. Each variable is also given a range of allowable subscripts: "ARRAY $X[l{:}u]$" means that space is to be set aside in memory for the table entries $X[l], X[l + 1], \ldots, X[u]$. For each equivalence class of variables, the compiler reserves as small a block of consecutive memory locations as possible, to contain all the table entries for the allowable subscript values of these variables.

For example, suppose we have ARRAY $X[0{:}10]$, ARRAY $Y[3{:}10]$, ARRAY $A[1{:}1]$, and ARRAY $Z[-2{:}0]$, plus the equivalences $X[7] \equiv Y[3]$, $Z[0] \equiv A[0]$, and $Y[1] \equiv A[8]$. We must set aside 20 consecutive locations

$$X_0 \quad X_1 \quad X_2 \quad X_3 \quad X_4 \quad X_5 \quad X_6 \quad X_7 \quad X_8 \quad X_9 \, X_{10}$$

$$\bullet \;\; \bullet \;\; \bullet \;\; \bullet \;\; \bullet \;\; \bullet \;\; \bullet \;\; \bullet \;\; \bullet \;\; \bullet \;\; \bullet \;\; \bullet \;\; \bullet \;\; \bullet \;\; \bullet \;\; \bullet \;\; \bullet \;\; \bullet \;\; \bullet \;\; \bullet$$

$$Z_{-2} \, Z_{-1} \;\; Z_0 \quad A_1 \qquad\qquad\qquad\qquad Y_3 \quad Y_4 \quad Y_5 \quad Y_6 \quad Y_7 \quad Y_8 \quad Y_9 \, Y_{10}$$

for these variables. (The location following $A[1]$ is not an allowable subscript value for any of the arrays, but it must be reserved anyway.)

The object of this exercise is to modify Algorithm E so that it applies to the more general situation just described. Assume that we are writing a compiler for such a language, and the tables inside our compiler program itself have one node for each array, containing the fields NAME, PARENT, DELTA, LBD, and UBD. Assume that the compiler program has previously processed all the ARRAY declarations, so that if

ARRAY X[l:u] has appeared and if P points to the node for X, then

$$\text{NAME}(P) = \text{``X''}, \quad \text{PARENT}(P) = \Lambda, \quad \text{DELTA}(P) = 0,$$
$$\text{LBD}(P) = l, \quad \text{UBD}(P) = u.$$

The problem is to design an algorithm that processes the equivalence declarations, so that, after this algorithm has been performed,

PARENT(P) $= \Lambda$ means that locations X[LBD(P)]$,\ldots,$X[UBD(P)] are to be reserved in memory for this equivalence class;

PARENT(P) $= Q \neq \Lambda$ means that location X[k] equals location Y[$k +$ DELTA(P)], where NAME(Q) $=$ "Y".

For example, before the equivalences listed above we might have the nodes

P	NAME(P)	PARENT(P)	DELTA(P)	LBD(P)	UBD(P)
α	X	Λ	0	0	10
β	Y	Λ	0	3	10
γ	A	Λ	0	1	1
δ	Z	Λ	0	-2	0

After the equivalences are processed, the nodes might appear thus:

α	X	Λ	*	-5	14
β	Y	α	4	*	*
γ	A	δ	0	*	*
δ	Z	α	-3	*	*

("*" denotes irrelevant information.)

Design an algorithm that makes this transformation. Assume that inputs to your algorithm have the form (P, j, Q, k), denoting X[j] $\equiv$ Y[k], where NAME(P) $=$ "X" and NAME(Q) $=$ "Y". Be sure to check whether the equivalences are contradictory; for example, X[1] $\equiv$ Y[2] contradicts X[2] $\equiv$ Y[1].

12. [*21*] At the beginning of Algorithm A, the variables P and Q point to the roots of two trees. Let P_0 and Q_0 denote the values of P and Q before execution of Algorithm A. (a) After the algorithm terminates, is Q_0 always the address of the root of the sum of the two given polynomials? (b) After the algorithm terminates, have P and Q returned to their original values P_0 and Q_0?

▶ **13.** [*M29*] Give an informal proof that at the beginning of step A8 of Algorithm A we always have EXP(P) $=$ EXP(Q) and CV(UP(P)) $=$ CV(UP(Q)). (This fact is important to the proper understanding of that algorithm.)

14. [*40*] Give a formal proof (or disproof) of the validity of Algorithm A.

15. [*40*] Design an algorithm to compute the product of two polynomials represented as in Fig. 28.

16. [*M24*] Prove the validity of Algorithm F.

▶ **17.** [*25*] Algorithm F evaluates a "bottom-up" locally defined function, namely, one that should be evaluated at the children of a node before it is evaluated at the node. A "top-down" locally defined function f is one in which the value of f at a node x depends only on x and the value of f at the *parent* of x. Using an auxiliary stack, design an algorithm analogous to Algorithm F that evaluates a "top-down" function f at each node of a tree. (Like Algorithm F, your algorithm should work efficiently on trees that have been stored in *postorder* with degrees, as in (9).)

▶ **18.** [*28*] Design an algorithm that, given the two tables INFO1[*j*] and RLINK[*j*] for $1 \le j \le n$ corresponding to preorder sequential representation, forms tables INFO2[*j*] and DEGREE[*j*] for $1 \le j \le n$, corresponding to postorder with degrees. For example, according to (3) and (9), your algorithm should transform

j	1	2	3	4	5	6	7	8	9	10
INFO1[j]	A	B	C	K	D	E	H	F	J	G
RLINK[j]	5	3	0	0	0	8	0	10	0	0

into

INFO2[j]	B	K	C	A	H	E	J	F	G	D
DEGREE[j]	0	0	1	2	0	1	0	1	0	3

19. [*M27*] Instead of using SCOPE links in (5), we could simply list the number of descendants of each node, in preorder:

DESC	3	0	1	0	5	1	0	1	0	0
INFO	A	B	C	K	D	E	H	F	J	G

Let $d_1 d_2 \ldots d_n$ be the sequence of descendant numbers of a forest, obtained in this way.
   a) Show that $k+d_k \le n$ for $1 \le k \le n$, and that $k \le j \le k+d_k$ implies $j+d_j \le k+d_k$.
   b) Conversely, prove that if $d_1 d_2 \ldots d_n$ is a sequence of nonnegative integers satisfying the conditions of (a), it is the sequence of descendant numbers of a forest.
   c) Suppose $d_1 d_2 \ldots d_n$ and $d'_1 d'_2 \ldots d'_n$ are the descendant number sequences for two forests. Prove that there is a third forest whose descendant numbers are

$$\min(d_1, d'_1) \min(d_2, d'_2) \ldots \min(d_n, d'_n).$$

2.3.4. Basic Mathematical Properties of Trees

Tree structures have been the object of extensive mathematical investigations for many years, long before the advent of computers, and many interesting facts have been discovered about them. In this section we will survey the mathematical theory of trees, which not only gives us more insight into the nature of tree structures but also has important applications to computer algorithms.

Nonmathematical readers are advised to skip to subsection 2.3.4.5, which discusses several topics that arise frequently in the applications we shall study later.

The material that follows comes mostly from a larger area of mathematics known as the theory of graphs. Unfortunately, there will probably never be a standard terminology in this field, and so the author has followed the usual practice of contemporary books on graph theory, namely to use words that are similar but not identical to the terms used in any *other* books on graph theory. An attempt has been made in the following subsections (and, indeed, throughout this book) to choose short, descriptive words for the important concepts, selected from those that are in reasonably common use and that do not sharply conflict with other common terminology. The nomenclature used here is also biased towards computer applications. Thus, an electrical engineer may prefer to call a "tree" what we call a "free tree"; but we want the shorter term "tree" to stand for the concept that is generally used in the computer literature and that is so much

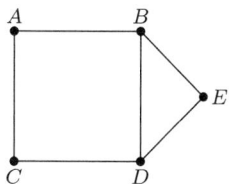

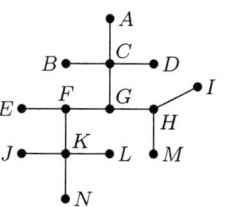

Fig. 29. A graph.   **Fig. 30.** A free tree.

more important in computer applications. If we were to follow the terminology of some authors on graph theory, we would have to say "finite labeled rooted ordered tree" instead of just "tree," and "topological bifurcating arborescence" instead of "binary tree"!

2.3.4.1. Free trees. A *graph* is generally defined to be a set of points (called *vertices*) together with a set of lines (called *edges*) joining certain pairs of distinct vertices. There is at most one edge joining any pair of vertices. Two vertices are called *adjacent* if there is an edge joining them. If V and V' are vertices and if $n \geq 0$, we say that $(V_0, V_1, \ldots, V_n)$ is a *walk* of length n from V to V' if $V = V_0$, V_k is adjacent to V_{k+1} for $0 \leq k < n$, and $V_n = V'$. The walk is a *path* if vertices $V_0, V_1, \ldots, V_n$ are distinct; it is a *cycle* if V_0 through V_{n-1} are distinct, $V_n = V_0$, and $n \geq 3$. Sometimes we are less precise, and refer to a cycle as "a path from a vertex to itself." We often speak of a "simple path" to emphasize the fact that we're talking about a path instead of an arbitrary walk. A graph is *connected* if there is a path between any two vertices of the graph.

These definitions are illustrated in Fig. 29, which shows a connected graph with five vertices and six edges. Vertex C is adjacent to A but not to B; there are two paths of length two from B to C, namely (B, A, C) and (B, D, C). There are several cycles, including (B, D, E, B).

A *free tree* or "unrooted tree" (Fig. 30) is defined to be a connected graph with no cycles. This definition applies to infinite graphs as well as to finite ones, although for computer applications we naturally are most concerned with finite trees. There are many equivalent ways to define a free tree; some of them appear in the following well-known theorem:

Theorem A. *If G is a graph, the following statements are equivalent:*

a) G *is a free tree.*

b) G *is connected, but if any edge is deleted, the resulting graph is no longer connected.*

c) *If V and V' are distinct vertices of G, there is exactly one simple path from V to V'.*

Furthermore, if G is finite, containing exactly $n > 0$ vertices, the following statements are also equivalent to (a), (b), *and* (c):

d) G *contains no cycles and has $n - 1$ edges.*

e) G *is connected and has $n - 1$ edges.*

Proof. (a) implies (b), for if the edge $V - V'$ is deleted but G is still connected, there must be a simple path $(V, V_1, \ldots, V')$ of length two or more — see exercise 2 — and then $(V, V_1, \ldots, V', V)$ would be a cycle in G.

(b) implies (c), for there is at least one simple path from V to V'. And if there were two such paths $(V, V_1, \ldots, V')$ and $(V, V_1', \ldots, V')$, we could find the smallest k for which $V_k \neq V_k'$; deleting the edge $V_{k-1} - V_k$ would not disconnect the graph, since there would still be a path $(V_{k-1}, V_k', \ldots, V', \ldots, V_k)$ from V_{k-1} to V_k that does not use the deleted edge.

(c) implies (a), for if G contains a cycle $(V, V_1, \ldots, V)$, there are two simple paths from V to V_1.

To show that (d) and (e) are also equivalent to (a), (b), and (c), let us first prove an auxiliary result: If G is any finite graph that has no cycles and at least one edge, then there is at least one vertex that is adjacent to exactly one other vertex. This follows because we can find some vertex V_1 and an adjacent vertex V_2; for $k \geq 2$ either V_k is adjacent to V_{k-1} and no other, or it is adjacent to a vertex that we may call $V_{k+1} \neq V_{k-1}$. Since there are no cycles, $V_1, V_2, \ldots, V_{k+1}$ must be distinct vertices, so this process must ultimately terminate.

Now assume that G is a tree with $n > 1$ vertices, and let V_n be a vertex that is adjacent to only one other vertex, namely V_{n-1}. If we delete V_n and the edge $V_{n-1} - V_n$, the remaining graph G' is a tree, since V_n appears in no simple path of G except as the first or the last element. This argument proves (by induction on n) that G has $n - 1$ edges; hence (a) implies (d).

Assume that G satisfies (d) and let V_n, V_{n-1}, G' be as in the preceding paragraph. Then the graph G is connected, since V_n is connected to V_{n-1}, which (by induction on n) is connected to all other vertices of G'. Thus (d) implies (e).

Finally assume that G satisfies (e). If G contains a cycle, we can delete any edge appearing in that cycle and G would still be connected. We can therefore continue deleting edges in this way until we obtain a connected graph G' with $n - 1 - k$ edges and no cycles. But since (a) implies (d), we must have $k = 0$, that is, $G = G'$. ∎

The idea of a free tree can be applied directly to the analysis of computer algorithms. In Section 1.3.3, we discussed the application of Kirchhoff's first law to the problem of counting the number of times each step of an algorithm is performed; we found that Kirchhoff's law does not completely determine the number of times each step is executed, but it reduces the number of unknowns that must be specially interpreted. The theory of trees tells us how many independent unknowns will remain, and it gives us a systematic way to find them.

It is easier to understand the method that follows if an example is studied, so we will work an example as the theory is being developed. Figure 31 shows an abstracted flow chart for Program 1.3.3A, which was subjected to a "Kirchhoff's law" analysis in Section 1.3.3. Each box in Fig. 31 represents part of the computation, and the letter or number inside the box denotes the number of times that computation will be performed during one run of the program, using

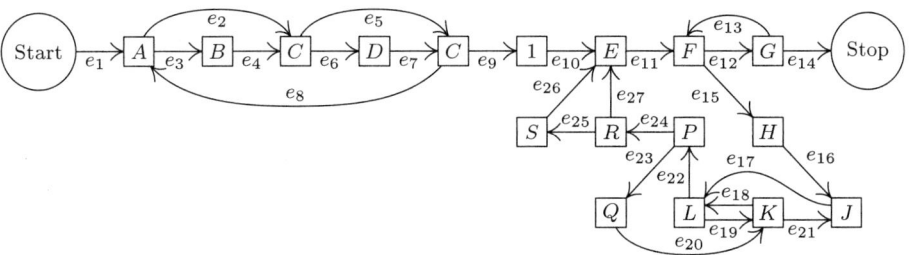

Fig. 31. Abstracted flow chart of Program 1.3.3A.

the notation of Section 1.3.3. An arrow between boxes represents a possible jump in the program. The arrows have been labeled $e_1, e_2, \ldots, e_{27}$. Our goal is to find all relations between the quantities A, B, C, D, E, F, G, H, J, K, L, P, Q, R, and S that are implied by Kirchhoff's law, and at the same time we hope to gain some insight into the general problem. (*Note:* Some simplifications have already been made in Fig. 31; for example, the box between C and E has been labeled "1", and this in fact is a consequence of Kirchhoff's law.)

Let E_j denote the number of times branch e_j is taken during the execution of the program being studied; Kirchhoff's law is

$$\text{sum of } E\text{'s into box} = \text{value in box} = \text{sum of } E\text{'s leaving box}; \qquad (1)$$

for example, in the case of the box marked K we have

$$E_{19} + E_{20} = K = E_{18} + E_{21}. \qquad (2)$$

In the discussion that follows, we will regard $E_1, E_2, \ldots, E_{27}$ as the unknowns, instead of $A, B, \ldots, S$.

The flow chart in Fig. 31 may be abstracted further so that it becomes a graph G as in Fig. 32. The boxes have shrunk to vertices, and the arrows $e_1, e_2, \ldots$ now represent edges of the graph. (A graph, strictly speaking, has no implied direction in its edges, and the direction of the arrows should be ignored when we refer to graph-theoretical properties of G. Our application to Kirchhoff's law, however, makes use of the arrows, as we will see shortly.) For convenience an extra edge e_0 has been drawn from the Stop vertex to the Start vertex, so that Kirchhoff's law applies uniformly to all parts of the graph. Figure 32 also includes some other minor changes from Fig. 31: An extra vertex and edge have been added to divide e_{13} into two parts e'_{13} and e''_{13}, so that the basic definition of a graph (no two edges join the same two vertices) is valid; e_{19} has also been split up in this way. A similar modification would have been made if we had any vertex with an arrow leading back to itself.

Some of the edges in Fig. 32 have been drawn much heavier than the others. These edges form a *free subtree* of the graph, connecting all the vertices. It is always possible to find a free subtree of the graphs arising from flow charts, because the graphs must be connected and, by part (b) of Theorem A, if G is connected and not a free tree, we can delete some edge and still have the resulting

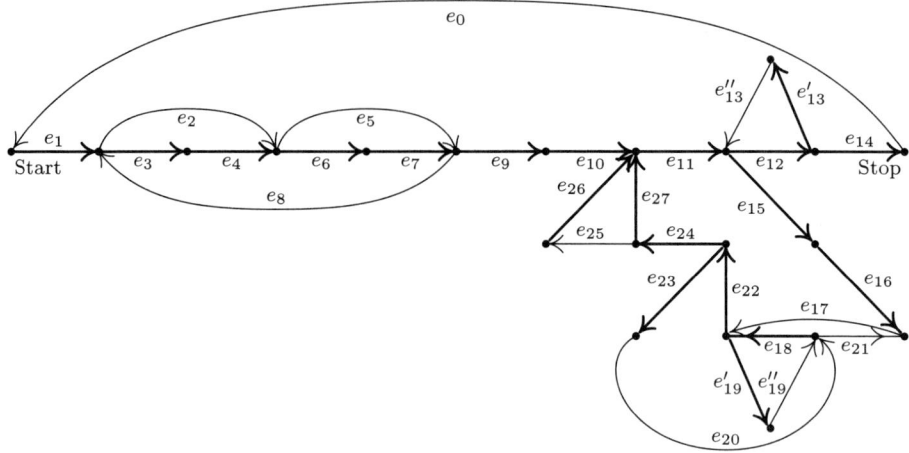

Fig. 32. Graph corresponding to Fig. 31, including a free subtree.

graph connected; this process can be iterated until we reach a subtree. Another algorithm for finding a free subtree appears in exercise 6. We can in fact always discard the edge e_0 (which went from the Stop to the Start vertex) first; thus we may assume that e_0 does not appear in the subtree chosen.

Let G' be a free subtree of the graph G found in this way, and consider any edge V — V' of G that is *not* in G'. We may now note an important consequence of Theorem A: G' plus this new edge V — V' contains a cycle; and in fact there is *exactly one* cycle, having the form $(V, V', \ldots, V)$, since there is a unique simple path from V' to V in G'. For example, if G' is the free subtree shown in Fig. 32, and if we add the edge e_2, we obtain a cycle that goes along e_2 and then (in the direction opposite to the arrows) along e_4 and e_3. This cycle may be written algebraically as "$e_2 - e_4 - e_3$", using plus signs and minus signs to indicate whether the cycle goes in the direction of the arrows or not.

If we carry out this process for each edge not in the free subtree, we obtain the so-called *fundamental cycles*, which in the case of Fig. 32 are

$$
\begin{aligned}
&C_0: \ e_0 + e_1 + e_3 + e_4 + e_6 + e_7 + e_9 + e_{10} + e_{11} + e_{12} + e_{14}, \\
&C_2: \ e_2 - e_4 - e_3, \\
&C_5: \ e_5 - e_7 - e_6, \\
&C_8: \ e_8 + e_3 + e_4 + e_6 + e_7, \\
&C_{13}'': e_{13}'' + e_{12} + e_{13}', \\
&C_{17}: e_{17} + e_{22} + e_{24} + e_{27} + e_{11} + e_{15} + e_{16}, \\
&C_{19}'': e_{19}'' + e_{18} + e_{19}', \\
&C_{20}: e_{20} + e_{18} + e_{22} + e_{23}, \\
&C_{21}: e_{21} - e_{16} - e_{15} - e_{11} - e_{27} - e_{24} - e_{22} - e_{18}, \\
&C_{25}: e_{25} + e_{26} - e_{27}.
\end{aligned}
\qquad (3)
$$

Obviously an edge e_j that is not in the free subtree will appear in only one of the fundamental cycles, namely C_j.

We are now approaching the climax of this construction. Each fundamental cycle represents a solution to Kirchhoff's equations; for example, the solution corresponding to C_2 is to let $E_2 = +1$, $E_4 = -1$, $E_3 = -1$, and all other E's $= 0$. It is clear that flow around a cycle in a graph always satisfies the condition (1) of Kirchhoff's law. Moreover, Kirchhoff's equations are "homogeneous," so the sum or difference of solutions to (1) yields another solution. Therefore we may conclude that the values of $E_0, E_2, E_5, \ldots, E_{25}$ are *independent* in the following sense:

> If $x_0, x_2, \ldots, x_{25}$ are any real numbers (one x_j for each e_j not in the free subtree G'), there is a solution to Kirchhoff's equations (1) such that $\qquad$ (4) $E_0 = x_0$, $E_2 = x_2$, ..., $E_{25} = x_{25}$.

Such a solution is found by going x_0 times around the cycle C_0, x_2 times around cycle C_2, etc. Furthermore, we find that the values of the remaining variables $E_1, E_3, E_4, \ldots$ are completely *dependent* on the values $E_0, E_2, \ldots, E_{25}$:

> *The solution mentioned in statement* (4) *is unique.* $\qquad$ (5)

For if there are two solutions to Kirchhoff's equations such that $E_0 = x_0, \ldots,$ $E_{25} = x_{25}$, we can subtract one from the other and we thereby obtain a solution in which $E_0 = E_2 = E_5 = \cdots = E_{25} = 0$. But now *all* E_j must be zero, for it is easy to see that a nonzero solution to Kirchhoff's equations is impossible when the graph is a free tree (see exercise 4). Therefore the two assumed solutions must be identical. We have now proved that all solutions of Kirchhoff's equations may be obtained as sums of multiples of the fundamental cycles.

When these remarks are applied to the graph in Fig. 32, we obtain the following general solution of Kirchhoff's equations in terms of the independent variables $E_0, E_2, \ldots, E_{25}$:

$$
\begin{aligned}
E_1 &= E_0, & E_{14} &= E_0, \\
E_3 &= E_0 - E_2 + E_8, & E_{15} &= E_{17} - E_{21}, \\
E_4 &= E_0 - E_2 + E_8, & E_{16} &= E_{17} - E_{21}, \\
E_6 &= E_0 - E_5 + E_8, & E_{18} &= E''_{19} + E_{20} - E_{21}, \\
E_7 &= E_0 - E_5 + E_8, & E'_{19} &= E''_{19}, \\
E_9 &= E_0, & E_{22} &= E_{17} + E_{20} - E_{21}, \\
E_{10} &= E_0, & E_{23} &= E_{20}, \\
E_{11} &= E_0 + E_{17} - E_{21}, & E_{24} &= E_{17} - E_{21}, \\
E_{12} &= E_0 + E''_{13}, & E_{26} &= E_{25}, \\
E'_{13} &= E''_{13}, & E_{27} &= E_{17} - E_{21} - E_{25}.
\end{aligned}
$$

(6)

To obtain these equations, we merely list, for each edge e_j in the subtree, all E_k for which e_j appears in cycle C_k, with the appropriate sign. [Thus, the matrix of coefficients in (6) is just the transpose of the matrix of coefficients in (3).]

Strictly speaking, C_0 should not be called a fundamental cycle, since it involves the special edge e_0. We may call C_0 minus the edge e_0 a *fundamental path from Start to Stop*. Our boundary condition, that the Start and Stop boxes in the flow chart are performed exactly once, is equivalent to the relation

$$E_0 = 1. \tag{7}$$

The preceding discussion shows how to obtain all solutions to Kirchhoff's law; the same method may be applied (as Kirchhoff himself applied it) to electrical circuits instead of program flow charts. It is natural to ask at this point whether Kirchhoff's law is the strongest possible set of equations that can be given for the case of program flow charts, or whether more can be said: Any execution of a computer program that goes from Start to Stop gives us a set of values $E_1, E_2, \ldots, E_{27}$ for the number of times each edge is traversed, and these values obey Kirchhoff's law; but are there solutions to Kirchhoff's equations that do not correspond to any computer program execution? (In this question, we do not assume that we know anything about the given computer program, except its flow chart.) If there are solutions that meet Kirchhoff's conditions but do not correspond to actual program execution, we can give stronger conditions than Kirchhoff's law. For the case of electrical circuits Kirchhoff himself gave a second law [*Ann. Physik und Chemie* **64** (1845), 497–514]: The sum of the voltage drops around a fundamental cycle must be zero. This second law does not apply to our problem.

There is indeed an obvious further condition that the E's must satisfy, if they are to correspond to some actual walk in the flow chart from Start to Stop; they must be integers, and in fact they must be *nonnegative integers*. This is not a trivial condition, since we cannot simply assign any arbitrary nonnegative integer values to the independent variables $E_2, E_5, \ldots, E_{25}$; for example, if we take $E_2 = 2$ and $E_8 = 0$, we find from (6) and (7) that $E_3 = -1$. (Thus, no execution of the flow chart in Fig. 31 will take branch e_2 twice without taking branch e_8 at least once.) The condition that all the E's be nonnegative integers is not enough either; for example, consider the solution in which $E''_{19} = 1$, $E_2 = E_5 = \cdots = E_{17} = E_{20} = E_{21} = E_{25} = 0$; there is no way to get to e_{18} except via e_{15}. The following condition is a necessary and sufficient condition that answers the problem raised in the previous paragraph: Let $E_2, E_5, \ldots, E_{25}$ be any given values, and determine $E_1, E_3, \ldots, E_{27}$ according to (6), (7). Assume that all the E's are nonnegative integers, and assume that the graph whose edges are those e_j for which $E_j > 0$, and whose vertices are those that touch such e_j, is *connected*. Then there is a walk from Start to Stop in which edge e_j is traversed exactly E_j times. This fact is proved in the next section (see exercise 2.3.4.2–24).

Let us now summarize the preceding discussion:

Theorem K. *If a flow chart (such as Fig. 31) contains n boxes (including Start and Stop) and m arrows, it is possible to find $m - n + 1$ fundamental cycles and a fundamental path from Start to Stop, such that any walk from Start to Stop is equivalent (in terms of the number of times each edge is traversed)*

to one traversal of the fundamental path plus a uniquely determined number
of traversals of each of the fundamental cycles. (The fundamental path and
fundamental cycles may include some edges that are to be traversed in a direction
opposite that shown by the arrow on the edge; we conventionally say that such
edges are being traversed -1 times.)

Conversely, for any traversal of the fundamental path and the fundamental
cycles in which the total number of times each edge is traversed is nonnegative,
and in which the vertices and edges corresponding to a positive number of
traversals form a connected graph, there is at least one equivalent walk from
Start to Stop. ∎

The fundamental cycles are found by picking a free subtree as in Fig. 32; if
we choose a different subtree we get, in general, a different set of fundamental
cycles. The fact that there are $m - n + 1$ fundamental cycles follows from
Theorem A. The modifications we made to get from Fig. 31 to Fig. 32, after
adding e_0, do not change the value of $m - n + 1$, although they may increase
both m and n; the construction could have been generalized so as to avoid these
trivial modifications entirely (see exercise 9).

Theorem K is encouraging because it says that Kirchhoff's law (which consists of n equations in the m unknowns $E_1, E_2, \ldots, E_m$) has just one "redundancy": These n equations allow us to eliminate $n - 1$ unknowns. However, the
unknown variables throughout this discussion have been the number of times the
edges have been traversed, not the number of times each *box* of the flow chart
has been entered. Exercise 8 shows how to construct another graph whose edges
correspond to the boxes of the flow chart, so that the theory above can be used
to deduce the true number of redundancies between the variables of interest.

Applications of Theorem K to software for measuring the performance of
programs in high-level languages are discussed by Thomas Ball and James R.
Larus in *ACM Trans. Prog. Languages and Systems* **16** (1994), 1319–1360.

EXERCISES

1. [*14*] List all cycles from B to B that are present in the graph of Fig. 29.

2. [*M20*] Prove that if V and V' are vertices of a graph and if there is a walk from
V to V', then there is a (simple) path from V to V'.

3. [*15*] What walk from Start to Stop is equivalent (in the sense of Theorem K) to
one traversal of the fundamental path plus one traversal of cycle C_2 in Fig. 32?

▶ **4.** [*M20*] Let G' be a finite free tree in which arrows have been drawn on its edges
$e_1, \ldots, e_{n-1}$; let $E_1, \ldots, E_{n-1}$ be numbers satisfying Kirchhoff's law (1) in G'. Show
that $E_1 = \cdots = E_{n-1} = 0$.

5. [*20*] Using Eqs. (6), express the quantities $A, B, \ldots, S$ that appear inside the
boxes of Fig. 31 in terms of the independent variables $E_2, E_5, \ldots, E_{25}$.

▶ **6.** [*M27*] Suppose a graph has n vertices $V_1, \ldots, V_n$ and m edges $e_1, \ldots, e_m$. Each
edge e is represented by a pair of integers (a, b) if it joins V_a to V_b. Design an algorithm
that takes the input pairs $(a_1, b_1), \ldots, (a_m, b_m)$ and prints out a subset of edges that
forms a free tree; the algorithm reports failure if this is impossible. Strive for an efficient
algorithm.

7. [*22*] Carry out the construction in the text for the flow chart

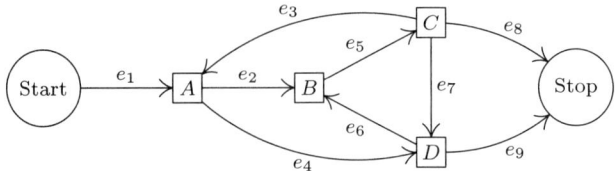

using the free subtree consisting of edges e_1, e_2, e_3, e_4, e_9. What are the fundamental cycles? Express E_1, E_2, E_3, E_4, E_9 in terms of E_5, E_6, E_7, and E_8.

▶ **8.** [*M25*] When applying Kirchhoff's first law to program flow charts, we usually are interested only in the *vertex flows* (the number of times each box of the flow chart is performed), not the edge flows analyzed in the text. For example, in the graph of exercise 7, the vertex flows are $A = E_2 + E_4$, $B = E_5$, $C = E_3 + E_7 + E_8$, $D = E_6 + E_9$.

If we group some vertices together, treating them as one "supervertex," we can combine edge flows that correspond to the same vertex flow. For example, edges e_2 and e_4 can be combined in the flow chart above if we also put B with D:

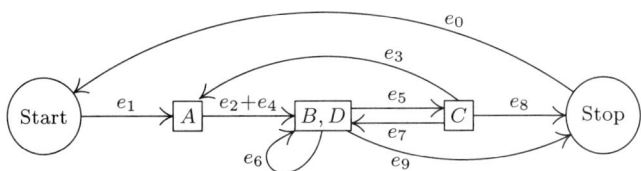

(Here e_0 has also been added from Stop to Start, as in the text.) Continuing this procedure, we can combine $e_3 + e_7$, then $(e_3 + e_7) + e_8$, then $e_6 + e_9$, until we obtain the *reduced flow chart* having edges $s = e_1$, $a = e_2 + e_4$, $b = e_5$, $c = e_3 + e_7 + e_8$, $d = e_6 + e_9$, $t = e_0$, precisely one edge for each vertex in the original flow chart:

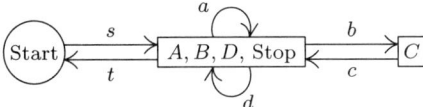

By construction, Kirchhoff's law holds in this reduced flow chart. The new edge flows are the vertex flows of the original; hence the analysis in the text, applied to the reduced flow chart, shows how the original vertex flows depend on each other.

Prove that this reduction process can be reversed, in the sense that any set of flows $\{a, b, \ldots\}$ satisfying Kirchhoff's law in the reduced flow chart can be "split up" into a set of edge flows $\{e_0, e_1, \ldots\}$ in the original flow chart. These flows e_j satisfy Kirchhoff's law and combine to yield the given flows $\{a, b, \ldots\}$; some of them might, however, be negative. (Although the reduction procedure has been illustrated here for only one particular flow chart, your proof should be valid in general.)

9. [*M22*] Edges e_{13} and e_{19} were split into two parts in Fig. 32, since a graph is not supposed to have two edges joining the same two vertices. However, if we look at the final result of the construction, this splitting into two parts seems quite artificial since $E'_{13} = E''_{13}$ and $E'_{19} = E''_{19}$ are two of the relations found in (6), while E''_{13} and E''_{19} are two of the independent variables. Explain how the construction could be generalized so that an artificial splitting of edges may be avoided.

10. [*16*] An electrical engineer, designing the circuitry for a computer, has n terminals $T_1, T_2, \ldots, T_n$ that should be at essentially the same voltage at all times. To achieve this, the engineer can solder wires between any pairs of terminals; the idea is to make enough wire connections so that there is a path through the wires from any terminal to any other. Show that the minimum number of wires needed to connect all the terminals is $n - 1$, and $n - 1$ wires achieve the desired connection if and only if they form a free tree (with terminals and wires standing for vertices and edges).

11. [*M27*] (R. C. Prim, *Bell System Tech. J.* **36** (1957), 1389–1401.) Consider the wire connection problem of exercise 10 with the additional proviso that a cost $c(i, j)$ is given for each $i < j$, denoting the expense of wiring terminal T_i to terminal T_j. Show that the following algorithm gives a connection tree of minimum cost: "If $n = 1$, do nothing. Otherwise, renumber terminals $\{1, \ldots, n-1\}$ and the associated costs so that $c(n - 1, n) = \min_{1 \le i < n} c(i, n)$; connect terminal T_{n-1} to T_n; then change $c(j, n - 1)$ to $\min(c(j, n - 1), c(j, n))$ for $1 \le j < n - 1$, and repeat the algorithm for $n - 1$ terminals $T_1, \ldots, T_{n-1}$ using these new costs. (The algorithm is to be repeated with the understanding that whenever a connection is subsequently requested between the terminals now called T_j and T_{n-1}, the connection is actually made between terminals now called T_j and T_n if it is cheaper; thus T_{n-1} and T_n are being regarded as though they were one terminal in the remainder of the algorithm.)" This algorithm may also be stated as follows: "Choose a particular terminal to start with; then repeatedly make the cheapest possible connection from an unchosen terminal to a chosen one, until all have been chosen."

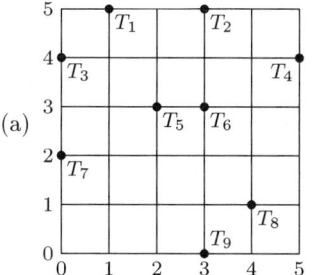
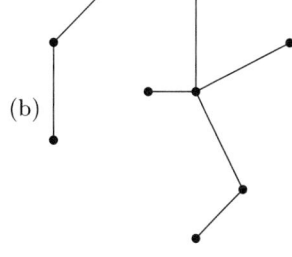

(a)

(b)

Fig. 33. Free tree of minimum cost. (See exercise 11.)

For example, consider Fig. 33(a), which shows nine terminals on a grid; let the cost of connecting two terminals be the wire length, namely the distance between them. (The reader may wish to try to find a minimal cost tree by hand, using intuition instead of the suggested algorithm.) The algorithm would first connect T_8 to T_9, then T_6 to T_8, T_5 to T_6, T_2 to T_6, T_1 to T_2, T_3 to T_1, T_7 to T_3, and finally T_4 to either T_2 or T_6. A minimum cost tree (wire length $7 + 2\sqrt{2} + 2\sqrt{5}$) is shown in Fig. 33(b).

▶ **12.** [*29*] The algorithm of exercise 11 is not stated in a fashion suitable for direct computer implementation. Reformulate that algorithm, specifying in more detail the operations that are to be done, in such a way that a computer program can carry out the process with reasonable efficiency.

13. [*M24*] Consider a graph with n vertices and m edges, in the notation of exercise 6. Show that it is possible to write any permutation of the integers $\{1, 2, \ldots, n\}$ as a product of transpositions $(a_{k_1} b_{k_1})(a_{k_2} b_{k_2}) \ldots (a_{k_t} b_{k_t})$ if and only if the graph is connected. (Hence there are sets of $n - 1$ transpositions that generate all permutations on n elements, but no set of $n - 2$ will do so.)

2.3.4.2. Oriented trees. In the previous section, we saw that an abstracted flow chart may be regarded as a graph, if we ignore the direction of the arrows on its edges; the graph-theoretic ideas of cycle, free subtree, etc., were shown to be relevant in the study of flow charts. There is a good deal more that can be said when the direction of each edge is given more significance, and in this case we have what is called a "directed graph" or "digraph."

Let us define a *directed graph* formally as a set of vertices and a set of *arcs*, each arc leading from a vertex V to a vertex V'. If e is an arc from V to V' we say V is the *initial* vertex of e, and V' is the *final* vertex, and we write $V = \text{init}(e)$, $V' = \text{fin}(e)$. The case that $\text{init}(e) = \text{fin}(e)$ is not excluded (although it was excluded from the definition of edge in an ordinary graph), and several different arcs may have the same initial and final vertices. The *out-degree* of a vertex V is the number of arcs leading out from it, namely the number of arcs e such that $\text{init}(e) = V$; similarly, the *in-degree* of V is defined to be the number of arcs with $\text{fin}(e) = V$.

The concepts of paths and cycles are defined for directed graphs in a manner similar to the corresponding definitions for ordinary graphs, but some important new technicalities must be considered. If $e_1, e_2, \ldots, e_n$ are arcs (with $n \geq 1$), we say that $(e_1, e_2, \ldots, e_n)$ is an *oriented walk* of length n from V to V' if $V = \text{init}(e_1)$, $V' = \text{fin}(e_n)$, and $\text{fin}(e_k) = \text{init}(e_{k+1})$ for $1 \leq k < n$. An oriented walk $(e_1, e_2, \ldots, e_n)$ is called *simple* if $\text{init}(e_1)$, $\ldots$, $\text{init}(e_n)$ are distinct and $\text{fin}(e_1)$, $\ldots$, $\text{fin}(e_n)$ are distinct; such a walk is an *oriented cycle* if $\text{fin}(e_n) = \text{init}(e_1)$, otherwise it's an *oriented path*. (An oriented cycle can have length 1 or 2, but such short cycles were excluded from our definition of "cycle" in the previous section. Can the reader see why this makes sense?)

As examples of these straightforward definitions, we may refer to Fig. 31 in the previous section. The box labeled "J" is a vertex with in-degree 2 (because of the arcs e_{16}, e_{21}) and out-degree 1. The sequence $(e_{17}, e_{19}, e_{18}, e_{22})$ is an oriented walk of length 4 from J to P; this walk is not simple since, for example, $\text{init}(e_{19}) = L = \text{init}(e_{22})$. The diagram contains no oriented cycles of length 1, but (e_{18}, e_{19}) is an oriented cycle of length 2.

A directed graph is said to be *strongly connected* if there is an oriented path from V to V' for any two vertices $V \neq V'$. It is said to be *rooted* if there is at least one *root*, that is, at least one vertex R such that there is an oriented path from V to R for all $V \neq R$. "Strongly connected" always implies "rooted," but the converse does not hold. A flow chart such as Fig. 31 in the previous section is an example of a rooted digraph, with R the Stop vertex; with the additional arc from Stop to Start (Fig. 32) it becomes strongly connected.

Every directed graph G corresponds in an obvious manner to an ordinary graph G_0, if we ignore orientations and discard duplicate edges or loops. Formally speaking, G_0 has an edge from V to V' if and only if $V \neq V'$ and G has an arc from V to V' or from V' to V. We can speak of (unoriented) *paths* and *cycles* in G with the understanding that these are paths and cycles of G_0; we can say that G is *connected* — this is a much weaker property than "strongly connected," even weaker than "rooted" — if the corresponding graph G_0 is connected.

An *oriented tree* (see Fig. 34), sometimes called a "rooted tree" by other authors, is a directed graph with a specified vertex R such that:

a) Each vertex $V \neq R$ is the initial vertex of exactly one arc, denoted by $e[V]$.

b) R is the initial vertex of no arc;

c) R is a root in the sense defined above (that is, for each vertex $V \neq R$ there is an oriented path from V to R).

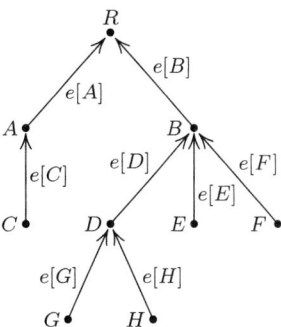

Fig. 34. An oriented tree.

It follows immediately that for each vertex $V \neq R$ there is a *unique* oriented path from V to R; and hence there are no oriented cycles.

Our previous definition of "oriented tree" (at the beginning of Section 2.3) is easily seen to be compatible with the new definition just given, when there are finitely many vertices. The vertices correspond to nodes, and the arc $e[V]$ is the link from V to PARENT[V].

The (undirected) graph corresponding to an oriented tree is connected, because of property (c). Furthermore, it has no cycles. For if $(V_0, V_1, \ldots, V_n)$ is an undirected cycle with $n \geq 3$, and if the edge between V_0 and V_1 is $e[V_1]$, then the edge between V_1 and V_2 must be $e[V_2]$, and similarly the edge between V_{k-1} and V_k must be $e[V_k]$ for $1 \leq k \leq n$, contradicting the absence of oriented cycles. If the edge between V_0 and V_1 is not $e[V_1]$, it must be $e[V_0]$, and the same argument applies to the cycle

$$(V_1, V_0, V_{n-1}, \ldots, V_1),$$

because $V_n = V_0$. Therefore *an oriented tree is a free tree when the direction of the arcs is neglected.*

Conversely, it is important to note that we can reverse the process just described. If we start with any nonempty free tree, such as that in Fig. 30, we can choose *any* vertex as the root R, and assign directions to the edges. The intuitive idea is to "pick up" the graph at vertex R and shake it; then assign upward-pointing arrows. More formally, the rule is this:

Change the edge $V \mathbin{\text{---}} V'$ to an arc from V to V' if and only if the simple path from V to R leads through V', that is, if it has the form $(V_0, V_1, \ldots, V_n)$, where $n > 0$, $V_0 = V$, $V_1 = V'$, $V_n = R$.

To verify that such a construction is valid, we need to prove that each edge $V \mathbin{\text{---}} V'$ is assigned the direction $V \longleftarrow V'$ or the direction $V \longrightarrow V'$; and this is easy to prove, for if $(V, V_1, \ldots, R)$ and $(V', V'_1, \ldots, R)$ are simple paths, there is a cycle unless $V = V'_1$ or $V_1 = V'$. This construction demonstrates that the directions of the arcs in an oriented tree are completely determined if we know which vertex is the root, so they need not be shown in diagrams when the root is explicitly indicated.

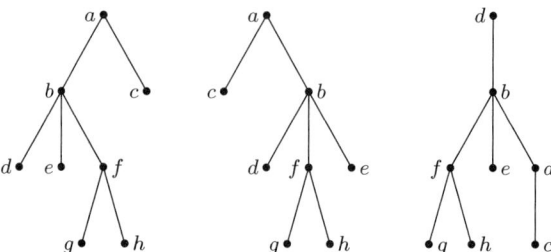

Fig. 35. Three tree structures.

We now see the relation between three types of trees: the (ordered) tree, which is of principal importance in computer programs, as defined at the beginning of Section 2.3; the oriented tree (or unordered tree); and the free tree. Both of the latter two types arise in the study of computer algorithms, but not as often as the first type. *The essential distinction between these types of tree structure is merely the amount of information that is taken to be relevant.* For example, Fig. 35 shows three trees that are distinct if they are considered as ordered trees (with root at the top). As oriented trees, the first and second are identical, since the left-to-right order of subtrees is immaterial; as free trees, all three graphs in Fig. 35 are identical, since the root is immaterial.

An *Eulerian trail* in a directed graph is an oriented walk $(e_1, e_2, \ldots, e_m)$ such that *every* arc in the directed graph occurs exactly once, and $\text{fin}(e_m) = \text{init}(e_1)$. This is a "complete traversal" of the arcs of the digraph. (Eulerian trails get their name from Leonhard Euler's famous discussion in 1736 of the impossibility of traversing each of the seven bridges in the city of Königsberg exactly once during a Sunday stroll. He treated the analogous problem for undirected graphs. Eulerian trails should be distinguished from "Hamiltonian cycles," which are oriented cycles that encounter each *vertex* exactly once; see Chapter 7.)

A directed graph is said to be *balanced* (see Fig. 36) if every vertex V has the same in-degree as its out-degree, that is, if there are just as many edges with V as their initial vertex as there are with V as their final vertex. This condition is closely related to Kirchhoff's law (see exercise 24). If a directed graph has an Eulerian trail, it must obviously be connected and balanced — unless it has *isolated vertices*, which are vertices with in-degree and out-degree both equal to zero.

So far in this section we've looked at quite a few definitions (directed graph, arc, initial vertex, final vertex, out-degree, in-degree, oriented walk, oriented path, oriented cycle, oriented tree, Eulerian trail, isolated vertex, and the properties of being strongly connected, rooted, and balanced), but there has been a scarcity of important results connecting these concepts. Now we are ready for meatier material. The first basic result is a theorem due to I. J. Good [*J. London Math. Soc.* **21** (1947), 167–169], who showed that Eulerian trails are always possible unless they are obviously impossible:

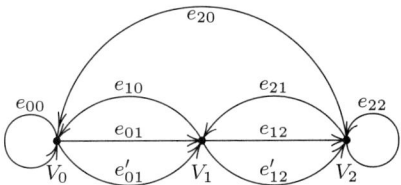

Fig. 36. A balanced directed graph.

Theorem G. *A finite, directed graph with no isolated vertices possesses an Eulerian trail if and only if it is connected and balanced.*

Proof. Assume that G is balanced, and let

$$P = (e_1, \ldots, e_m)$$

be an oriented walk of longest possible length that uses no arc twice. Then if $V = \mathrm{fin}(e_m)$, and if k is the out-degree of V, all k arcs e with $\mathrm{init}(e) = V$ must already appear in P; otherwise we could add e and get a longer walk. But if $\mathrm{init}(e_j) = V$ and $j > 1$, then $\mathrm{fin}(e_{j-1}) = V$. Hence, since G is balanced, we must have

$$\mathrm{init}(e_1) = V = \mathrm{fin}(e_m),$$

otherwise the in-degree of V would be at least $k + 1$.

Now by the cyclic permutation of P it follows that any arc e not in the walk has neither initial nor final vertex in common with any arc in the walk. So if P is not an Eulerian trail, G is not connected. ∎

There is an important connection between Eulerian trails and oriented trees:

Lemma E. *Let $(e_1, \ldots, e_m)$ be an Eulerian trail of a directed graph G having no isolated vertices. Let $R = \mathrm{fin}(e_m) = \mathrm{init}(e_1)$. For each vertex $V \neq R$ let $e[V]$ be the last exit from V in the trail; that is,*

$$e[V] = e_j \qquad \text{if } \mathrm{init}(e_j) = V \quad \text{and} \quad \mathrm{init}(e_k) \neq V \quad \text{for } j < k \leq m. \qquad (1)$$

Then the vertices of G with the arcs $e[V]$ form an oriented tree with root R.

Proof. Properties (a) and (b) of the definition of oriented tree are evidently satisfied. By exercise 7 we need only show that there are no oriented cycles among the $e[V]$; but this is immediate, since if $\mathrm{fin}(e[V]) = V' = \mathrm{init}(e[V'])$, where $e[V] = e_j$ and $e[V'] = e_{j'}$, then $j < j'$. ∎

This lemma can perhaps be better understood if we turn things around and consider the "first entrances" to each vertex; the first entrances form an unordered tree with all arcs pointing *away* from R. Lemma E has a surprising and important converse, proved by T. van Aardenne-Ehrenfest and N. G. de Bruijn [*Simon Stevin* **28** (1951), 203–217]:

Theorem D. *Let G be a finite, balanced, directed graph, and let G' be an oriented tree consisting of the vertices of G plus some of the arcs of G. Let R be the root of G' and let $e[V]$ be the arc of G' with initial vertex V. Let e_1 be any arc of G with $\mathrm{init}(e_1) = R$. Then $P = (e_1, e_2, \ldots, e_m)$ is an Eulerian trail if it is an oriented walk for which*

i) *no arc is used more than once; that is, $e_j \neq e_k$ when $j \neq k$.*

ii) *$e[V]$ is not used in P unless it is the only choice consistent with rule (i); that is, if $e_j = e[V]$ and if e is an arc with $\mathrm{init}(e) = V$, then $e = e_k$ for some $k \leq j$.*

iii) *P terminates only when it cannot be continued by rule (i); that is, if $\mathrm{init}(e) = \mathrm{fin}(e_m)$, then $e = e_k$ for some k.*

Proof. By (iii) and the argument in the proof of Theorem G, we must have $\mathrm{fin}(e_m) = \mathrm{init}(e_1) = R$. Now if e is an arc not appearing in P, let $V = \mathrm{fin}(e)$. Since G is balanced, it follows that V is the initial vertex of some arc not in P; and if $V \neq R$, condition (ii) tells us that $e[V]$ is not in P. Now use the same argument with $e = e[V]$, and we ultimately find that R is the initial vertex of some arc not in the walk, contradicting (iii). ∎

The essence of Theorem D is that it shows us a simple way to construct an Eulerian trail in a balanced directed graph, given any oriented subtree of the graph. (See the example in exercise 14.) In fact, Theorem D allows us to count the exact number of Eulerian trails in a directed graph; this result and many other important consequences of the ideas developed in this section appear in the exercises that follow.

EXERCISES

1. [*M20*] Prove that if V and V' are vertices of a directed graph and if there is an oriented walk from V to V', then there is a simple oriented path from V to V'.

2. [*15*] Which of the ten "fundamental cycles" listed in (3) of Section 2.3.4.1 are *oriented* cycles in the directed graph (Fig. 32) of that section?

3. [*16*] Draw the diagram for a directed graph that is connected but not rooted.

▶ **4.** [*M20*] The concept of *topological sorting* can be defined for any finite directed graph G as a linear arrangement of the vertices $V_1 V_2 \ldots V_n$ such that $\mathrm{init}(e)$ precedes $\mathrm{fin}(e)$ in the ordering for all arcs e of G. (See Section 2.2.3, Figs. 6 and 7.) Not all finite directed graphs can be topologically sorted; which ones can be? (Use the terminology of this section to give the answer.)

5. [*M16*] Let G be a directed graph that contains an oriented walk $(e_1, \ldots, e_n)$ with $\mathrm{fin}(e_n) = \mathrm{init}(e_1)$. Give a proof that G is not an oriented tree, using the terminology defined in this section.

6. [*M21*] True or false: A directed graph that is rooted and contains no cycles and no oriented cycles is an oriented tree.

▶ **7.** [*M22*] True or false: A directed graph satisfying properties (a) and (b) of the definition of oriented tree, and having no oriented cycles, is an oriented tree.

8. [*HM40*] Study the properties of *automorphism groups* of oriented trees, namely the groups consisting of all permutations π of the vertices and arcs for which we have $\text{init}(e\pi) = \text{init}(e)\pi$, $\text{fin}(e\pi) = \text{fin}(e)\pi$.

9. [*18*] By assigning directions to the edges, draw the oriented tree corresponding to the free tree in Fig. 30 on page 363, with G as the root.

10. [*22*] An oriented tree with vertices $V_1, \ldots, V_n$ can be represented inside a computer by using a table $P[1], \ldots, P[n]$ as follows: If V_j is the root, $P[j] = 0$; otherwise $P[j] = k$, if the arc $e[V_j]$ goes from V_j to V_k. (Thus $P[1], \ldots, P[n]$ is the same as the "parent" table used in Algorithm 2.3.3E.)

The text shows how a free tree can be converted into an oriented tree by choosing any desired vertex to be the root. Consequently, it is possible to start with an oriented tree that has root R, then to convert this into a free tree by neglecting the orientation of the arcs, and finally to assign new orientations, obtaining an oriented tree with any specified vertex as the root. Design an algorithm that performs this transformation: Starting with a table $P[1], \ldots, P[n]$, representing an oriented tree, and given an integer j, $1 \leq j \leq n$, design the algorithm to transform the P table so that it represents the same free tree but with V_j as the root.

▶ **11.** [*28*] Using the assumptions of exercise 2.3.4.1–6, but with (a_k, b_k) representing an arc from V_{a_k} to V_{b_k}, design an algorithm that not only prints out a free subtree as in that algorithm, but also prints out the fundamental cycles. [*Hint:* The algorithm given in the solution to exercise 2.3.4.1–6 can be combined with the algorithm in the preceding exercise.]

12. [*M10*] In the correspondence between oriented trees as defined here and oriented trees as defined at the beginning of Section 2.3, is the *degree* of a tree node equal to the *in-degree* or the *out-degree* of the corresponding vertex?

▶ **13.** [*M24*] Prove that if R is a root of a (possibly infinite) directed graph G, then G contains an oriented subtree with the same vertices as G and with root R. (As a consequence, it is always possible to choose the free subtree in flow charts like Fig. 32 of Section 2.3.4.1 so that it is actually an *oriented* subtree; this would be the case in that diagram if we had selected e_{13}'', e_{19}'', e_{20}, and e_{17} instead of e_{13}', e_{19}', e_{23}, and e_{15}.)

14. [*21*] Let G be the balanced digraph shown in Fig. 36, and let G' be the oriented subtree with vertices V_0, V_1, V_2 and arcs e_{01}, e_{21}. Find all oriented walks P that meet the conditions of Theorem D, starting with arc e_{12}.

15. [*M20*] True or false: A directed graph that is connected and balanced is strongly connected.

▶ **16.** [*M24*] In a popular solitaire game called "clock," the 52 cards of an ordinary deck of playing cards are dealt face down into 13 piles of four each; 12 piles are arranged in a circle like the 12 hours of a clock and the thirteenth pile goes in the center. The solitaire game now proceeds by turning up the top card of the center pile, and then if its face value is k, by placing it next to the kth pile. (The numbers $1, 2, \ldots, 13$ are equivalent to A, 2, $\ldots$, 10, J, Q, K.) Play continues by turning up the top card of the kth pile and putting it next to *its* pile, etc., until we reach a point where we cannot continue since there are no more cards to turn up on the designated pile. (The player has no choice in the game, since the rules completely specify what to do.) The game is won if all cards are face up when play terminates. [*Reference:* E. D. Cheney, *Patience* (Boston: Lee & Shepard, 1870), 62–65; the game was called "Travellers' Patience" in

England, according to M. Whitmore Jones, *Games of Patience* (London: L. Upcott Gill, 1900), Chapter 7.]

Show that the game will be won if and only if the following directed graph is an oriented tree: The vertices are $V_1, V_2, \ldots, V_{13}$; the arcs are $e_1, e_2, \ldots, e_{12}$, where e_j goes from V_j to V_k if k is the *bottom* card in pile j after the deal.

(In particular, if the bottom card of pile j is a "j", for $j \neq 13$, it is easy to see that the game is certainly lost, since this card could never be turned up. The result proved in this exercise gives a much faster way to play the game!)

17. [*M32*] What is the probability of winning the solitaire game of clock (described in exercise 16), assuming the deck is randomly shuffled? What is the probability that exactly k cards are still face down when the game is over?

18. [*M30*] Let G be a graph with $n+1$ vertices $V_0, V_1, \ldots, V_n$ and m edges $e_1, \ldots, e_m$. Make G into a directed graph by assigning an arbitrary orientation to each edge; then construct the $m \times (n+1)$ matrix A with

$$a_{ij} = \begin{cases} +1, & \text{if init}(e_i) = V_j\,; \\ -1, & \text{if fin}(e_i) = V_j\,; \\ 0, & \text{otherwise.} \end{cases}$$

Let A_0 be the $m \times n$ matrix A with column 0 deleted.

a) If $m = n$, show that the determinant of A_0 is equal to 0 if G is not a free tree, and equal to ± 1 if G *is* a free tree.

b) Show that for general m the determinant of $A_0^T A_0$ is the number of free subtrees of G (namely the number of ways to choose n of the m edges so that the resulting graph is a free tree). [*Hint:* Use (a) and the result of exercise 1.2.3–46.]

19. [*M31*] (*The matrix tree theorem.*) Let G be a directed graph with $n+1$ vertices $V_0, V_1, \ldots, V_n$. Let A be the $(n+1) \times (n+1)$ matrix with

$$a_{ij} = \begin{cases} -k, & \text{if } i \neq j \text{ and there are } k \text{ arcs from } V_i \text{ to } V_j; \\ t, & \text{if } i = j \text{ and there are } t \text{ arcs from } V_j \text{ to other vertices.} \end{cases}$$

(It follows that $a_{i0} + a_{i1} + \cdots + a_{in} = 0$ for $0 \leq i \leq n$.) Let A_0 be the same matrix with row 0 and column 0 deleted. For example, if G is the directed graph of Fig. 36, we have

$$A = \begin{pmatrix} 2 & -2 & 0 \\ -1 & 3 & -2 \\ -1 & -1 & 2 \end{pmatrix}, \qquad A_0 = \begin{pmatrix} 3 & -2 \\ -1 & 2 \end{pmatrix}.$$

a) Show that if $a_{00} = 0$ and $a_{jj} = 1$ for $1 \leq j \leq n$, and if G contains no arcs from a vertex to itself, then $\det A_0 = [G$ is an oriented tree with root $V_0]$.

b) Show that in general, $\det A_0$ is the number of oriented subtrees of G rooted at V_0 (namely the number of ways to select n of the arcs of G so that the resulting directed graph is an oriented tree, with V_0 as the root). [*Hint:* Use induction on the number of arcs.]

20. [*M21*] If G is an undirected graph on $n+1$ vertices $V_0, \ldots, V_n$, let B be the $n \times n$ matrix defined as follows for $1 \leq i, j \leq n$:

$$b_{ij} = \begin{cases} t, & \text{if } i = j \text{ and there are } t \text{ edges touching } V_j; \\ -1, & \text{if } i \neq j \text{ and } V_i \text{ is adjacent to } V_j; \\ 0, & \text{otherwise.} \end{cases}$$

For example, if G is the graph of Fig. 29 on page 363, with $(V_0, V_1, V_2, V_3, V_4) = (A, B, C, D, E)$, we find that

$$
B = \begin{pmatrix}
3 & 0 & -1 & -1 \\
0 & 2 & -1 & 0 \\
-1 & -1 & 3 & -1 \\
-1 & 0 & -1 & 2
\end{pmatrix}.
$$

Show that the number of free subtrees of G is $\det B$. [*Hint:* Use exercise 18 or 19.]

21. [*HM38*] (T. van Aardenne-Ehrenfest and N. G. de Bruijn.) Figure 36 is an example of a directed graph that is not only balanced, it is *regular*, which means that every vertex has the same in-degree and out-degree as every other vertex. Let G be a regular digraph with n vertices $V_0, V_1, \ldots, V_{n-1}$, in which every vertex has in-degree and out-degree equal to m. (Hence there are mn arcs in all.) Let G^* be the digraph with mn vertices corresponding to the arcs of G; let a vertex of G^* corresponding to an arc from V_j to V_k in G be denoted by V_{jk}. An arc goes from V_{jk} to $V_{j'k'}$ in G^* if and only if $k = j'$. For example, if G is the directed graph of Fig. 36, G^* is shown in Fig. 37. An Eulerian trail in G is a Hamiltonian cycle in G^* and conversely.

Prove that the number of oriented subtrees of G^* is $m^{(m-1)n}$ times the number of oriented subtrees of G. [*Hint:* Use exercise 19.]

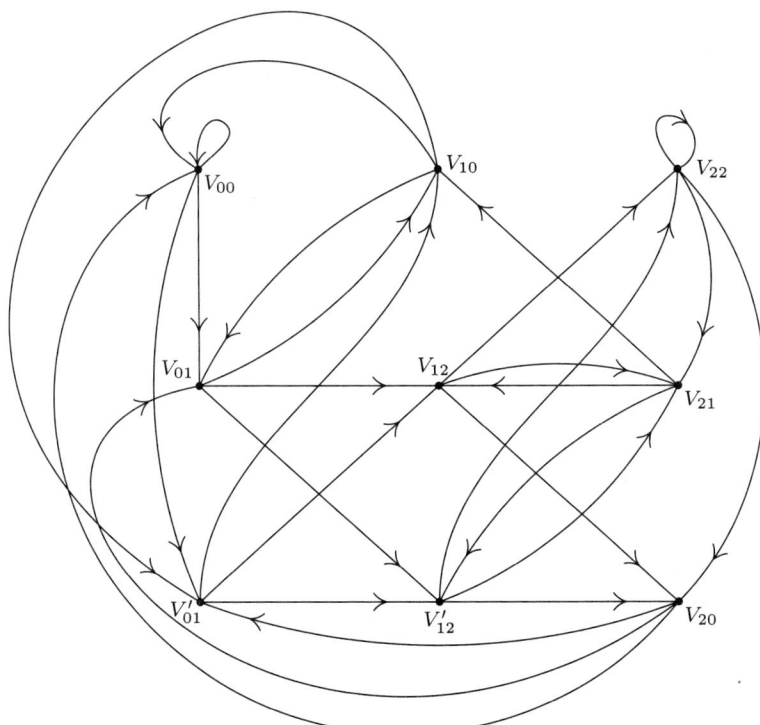

Fig. 37. Arc digraph corresponding to Fig. 36. (See exercise 21.)

▶ **22.** [*M26*] Let G be a balanced, directed graph with vertices $V_1, V_2, \ldots, V_n$ and no isolated vertices. Let σ_j be the out-degree of V_j. Show that the number of Eulerian trails of G is

$$(\sigma_1 + \sigma_2 + \cdots + \sigma_n)\, T \prod_{j=1}^{n} (\sigma_j - 1)!,$$

where T is the number of oriented subtrees of G with root V_1. [*Note:* The factor $(\sigma_1 + \cdots + \sigma_n)$, which is the number of arcs of G, may be omitted if the Eulerian trail $(e_1, \ldots, e_m)$ is regarded as equal to $(e_k, \ldots, e_m, e_1, \ldots, e_{k-1})$.]

▶ **23.** [*M33*] (N. G. de Bruijn.) For each sequence of nonnegative integers $x_1, \ldots, x_k$ less than m, let $f(x_1, \ldots, x_k)$ be a nonnegative integer less than m. Define an infinite sequence as follows: $X_1 = X_2 = \cdots = X_k = 0$; $X_{n+k+1} = f(X_{n+k}, \ldots, X_{n+1})$ when $n \geq 0$. For how many of the m^{m^k} possible functions f is this sequence periodic with a period of the maximum length m^k? [*Hint:* Construct a directed graph with vertices $(x_1, \ldots, x_{k-1})$ for all $0 \leq x_j < m$, and with arcs from $(x_1, x_2, \ldots, x_{k-1})$ to $(x_2, \ldots, x_{k-1}, x_k)$; apply exercises 21 and 22.]

▶ **24.** [*M20*] Let G be a connected digraph with arcs $e_0, e_1, \ldots, e_m$. Let $E_0, E_1, \ldots, E_m$ be a set of positive integers that satisfy Kirchhoff's law for G; that is, for each vertex V,

$$\sum_{\mathrm{init}(e_j)=V} E_j = \sum_{\mathrm{fin}(e_j)=V} E_j.$$

Assume further that $E_0 = 1$. Prove that there is an oriented walk in G from $\mathrm{fin}(e_0)$ to $\mathrm{init}(e_0)$ such that edge e_j appears exactly E_j times, for $1 \leq j \leq m$, while edge e_0 does not appear. [*Hint:* Apply Theorem G to a suitable directed graph.]

25. [*26*] Design a computer representation for directed graphs that generalizes the right-threaded binary tree representation of a tree. Use two link fields `ALINK`, `BLINK` and two one-bit fields `ATAG`, `BTAG`; and design the representation so that: (i) there is one node for each *arc* of the directed graph (*not* for each vertex); (ii) if the directed graph is an oriented tree with root R, and if we add an arc from R to a new vertex H, then the representation of this directed graph is essentially the same as a right-threaded representation of this oriented tree (with some order imposed on the children in each family), in the sense that `ALINK`, `BLINK`, `BTAG` are respectively the same as `LLINK`, `RLINK`, `RTAG` in Section 2.3.2; and (iii) the representation is symmetric in the sense that interchanging `ALINK`, `ATAG`, with `BLINK`, `BTAG` is equivalent to changing the direction on all the arcs of the directed graph.

▶ **26.** [*HM39*] (*Analysis of a random algorithm.*) Let G be a directed graph on the vertices $V_1, V_2, \ldots, V_n$. Assume that G represents the flow chart for an algorithm, where V_1 is the Start vertex and V_n is the Stop vertex. (Therefore V_n is a root of G.) Suppose each arc e of G has been assigned a probability $p(e)$, where the probabilities satisfy the conditions

$$0 < p(e) \leq 1; \qquad \sum_{\mathrm{init}(e)=V_j} p(e) = 1 \quad \text{for } 1 \leq j < n.$$

Consider a random walk, which starts at V_1 and subsequently chooses branch e of G with probability $p(e)$, until V_n is reached; the choice of branch taken at each step is to be independent of all previous choices.

For example, consider the graph of exercise 2.3.4.1–7, and assign the respective probabilities $1, \frac{1}{2}, \frac{1}{2}, \frac{1}{2}, 1, \frac{3}{4}, \frac{1}{4}, \frac{1}{4}, \frac{1}{4}$ to arcs $e_1, e_2, \ldots, e_9$. Then the walk "Start–A–B–C–A–D–B–C–Stop" is chosen with probability $1 \cdot \frac{1}{2} \cdot 1 \cdot \frac{1}{2} \cdot \frac{1}{2} \cdot \frac{3}{4} \cdot 1 \cdot \frac{1}{4} = \frac{3}{128}$.

Such random walks are called *Markov chains*, after the Russian mathematician Andrei A. Markov, who first made extensive studies of stochastic processes of this kind. The situation serves as a model for certain algorithms, although our requirement that each choice must be independent of the others is a very strong assumption. The purpose of this exercise is to analyze the computation time for algorithms of this kind.

The analysis is facilitated by considering the $n \times n$ matrix $A = (a_{ij})$, where $a_{ij} = \sum p(e)$ summed over all arcs e that go from V_i to V_j. If there is no such arc, $a_{ij} = 0$. The matrix A for the example considered above is

$$\begin{pmatrix} 0 & 1 & 0 & 0 & 0 & 0 \\ 0 & 0 & \frac{1}{2} & 0 & \frac{1}{2} & 0 \\ 0 & 0 & 0 & 1 & 0 & 0 \\ 0 & \frac{1}{2} & 0 & 0 & \frac{1}{4} & \frac{1}{4} \\ 0 & 0 & \frac{3}{4} & 0 & 0 & \frac{1}{4} \\ 0 & 0 & 0 & 0 & 0 & 0 \end{pmatrix}.$$

It follows easily that $(A^k)_{ij}$ is the probability that a walk starting at V_i will be at V_j after k steps.

Prove the following facts, for an arbitrary directed graph G of the stated type:

a) The matrix $(I - A)$ is nonsingular. [*Hint:* Show that there is no nonzero vector x with $xA^n = x$.]

b) The average number of times that vertex V_j appears in the walk is

$$(I - A)_{1j}^{-1} = \text{cofactor}_{j1}(I - A)/\det(I - A), \qquad \text{for } 1 \le j \le n.$$

[Thus in the example considered we find that the vertices A, B, C, D are traversed respectively $\frac{13}{6}, \frac{7}{3}, \frac{7}{3}, \frac{5}{3}$ times, on the average.]

c) The probability that V_j occurs in the walk is

$$a_j = \text{cofactor}_{j1}(I - A)/\text{cofactor}_{jj}(I - A);$$

furthermore, $a_n = 1$, so the walk terminates in a finite number of steps with probability one.

d) The probability that a random walk starting at V_j will never return to V_j is $b_j = \det(I - A)/\text{cofactor}_{jj}(I - A)$.

e) The probability that V_j occurs exactly k times in the walk is $a_j(1 - b_j)^{k-1}b_j$, for $k \ge 1$, $1 \le j \le n$.

27. [*M30*] (*Steady states.*) Let G be a directed graph on vertices $V_1, \ldots, V_n$, whose arcs have been assigned probabilities $p(e)$ as in exercise 26. Instead of having Start and Stop vertices, however, assume that G is strongly connected; thus each vertex V_j is a root, and we assume that the probabilities $p(e)$ are positive and satisfy $\sum_{\text{init}(e)=V_j} p(e) = 1$ for all j. A random process of the kind described in exercise 26 is said to have a "steady state" $(x_1, \ldots, x_n)$ if

$$x_j = \sum_{\substack{\text{init}(e)=V_i \\ \text{fin}(e)=V_j}} p(e)\, x_i, \qquad \text{for } 1 \le j \le n.$$

Let t_j be the sum, over all oriented subtrees T_j of G that are rooted at V_j, of the products $\prod_{e \in T_j} p(e)$. Prove that $(t_1, \ldots, t_n)$ is a steady state of the random process.

▶ **28.** [*M35*] Consider the $(m+n) \times (m+n)$ determinant illustrated here for $m = 2$ and $n = 3$:

$$\det \begin{pmatrix} a_{10} + a_{11} + a_{12} + a_{13} & 0 & a_{11} & a_{12} & a_{13} \\ 0 & a_{20} + a_{21} + a_{22} + a_{23} & a_{21} & a_{22} & a_{23} \\ b_{11} & b_{12} & b_{10} + b_{11} + b_{12} & 0 & 0 \\ b_{21} & b_{22} & 0 & b_{20} + b_{21} + b_{22} & 0 \\ b_{31} & b_{32} & 0 & 0 & b_{30} + b_{31} + b_{32} \end{pmatrix}.$$

Show that when this determinant is expanded as a polynomial in the a's and b's, each nonzero term has coefficient $+1$. How many terms appear in the expansion? Give a rule, related to oriented trees, that characterizes exactly which terms are present.

*2.3.4.3. The "infinity lemma." Until now we have concentrated mainly on trees that have only finitely many vertices (nodes), but the definitions we have given for free trees and oriented trees apply to infinite graphs as well. Infinite *ordered* trees can be defined in several ways; we can, for example, extend the concept of "Dewey decimal notation" to infinite collections of numbers, as in exercise 2.3–14. Even in the study of computer algorithms there is occasionally a need to know the properties of infinite trees — for example, to prove by contradiction that a certain tree is *not* infinite. One of the most fundamental properties of infinite trees, first stated in its full generality by D. Kőnig, is the following:

Theorem K. (*The "infinity lemma."*) *Every infinite oriented tree in which every vertex has finite degree has an infinite path to the root, that is, an infinite sequence of vertices $V_0, V_1, V_2, \ldots$ in which V_0 is the root and* $\mathrm{fin}(e[V_{j+1}]) = V_j$ *for all $j \geq 0$.*

Proof. We define the path by starting with V_0, the root of the oriented tree. Assume that $j \geq 0$ and that V_j has been chosen having infinitely many descendants. The degree of V_j is finite by hypothesis, so V_j has finitely many children $U_1, \ldots, U_n$. At least one of these children must possess infinitely many descendants, so we take V_{j+1} to be such a child of V_j.

Now $V_0, V_1, V_2, \ldots$ is an infinite path to the root. ∎

Students of calculus may recognize that the argument used here is essentially like that used to prove the classical Bolzano–Weierstrass theorem, "A bounded infinite set of real numbers has an accumulation point." One way of stating Theorem K, as Kőnig observed, is this: "If the human race never dies out, somebody now living has a line of descendants that will never die out."

Most people think that Theorem K is completely obvious when they first encounter it, but after more thought and a consideration of further examples they realize that there is something profound about it. Although the degree of each node of the tree is finite, we have not assumed that the degrees are *bounded* (less than some number N for all vertices), so there may be nodes with higher and higher degrees. It is at least conceivable that everyone's descendants will ultimately die out although there will be some families that go on a million generations, others a billion, and so on. In fact, H. W. Watson once published a "proof" that under certain laws of biological probability carried out indefinitely, there will be infinitely many people born in the future but each family line will die out with probability one. His paper [*J. Anthropological Inst. Gt. Britain and Ireland* **4** (1874), 138–144] contains important and far-reaching theorems in spite of the minor slip that caused him to make this statement, and it is significant that he did not find his conclusions to be logically inconsistent.

The contrapositive of Theorem K is directly applicable to computer algorithms: *If we have an algorithm that periodically divides itself up into finitely many subalgorithms, and if each chain of subalgorithms ultimately terminates, then the algorithm itself terminates.*

Phrased yet another way, suppose we have a set S, finite or infinite, such that each element of S is a sequence $(x_1, x_2, \ldots, x_n)$ of positive integers of finite length $n \geq 0$. If we impose the conditions that

i) if $(x_1, \ldots, x_n)$ is in S, so is $(x_1, \ldots, x_k)$ for $0 \leq k \leq n$;
ii) if $(x_1, \ldots, x_n)$ is in S, only finitely many x_{n+1} exist for which $(x_1, \ldots, x_n, x_{n+1})$ is also in S;
iii) there is no infinite sequence $(x_1, x_2, \ldots)$ all of whose initial subsequences $(x_1, x_2, \ldots, x_n)$ lie in S;

then S is essentially an oriented tree, specified essentially in a Dewey decimal notation, and Theorem K tells us that S is *finite*.

One of the most convincing examples of the potency of Theorem K arises in connection with a family of interesting tiling problems introduced by Hao Wang. A *tetrad type* is a square divided into four parts, each part having a specified number in it, such as

$$\begin{array}{c}
\boxed{\begin{matrix} & 3 & \\ 10 & \times & 2 \\ & 5 & \end{matrix}}
\end{array} \qquad (1)$$

The problem of *tiling the plane* is to take a finite set of tetrad types, with an infinite supply of tetrads of each type, and to show how to place one in each square of an infinite plane (without rotating or reflecting the tetrad types) in such a way that two tetrads are adjacent only if they have equal numbers where they touch. For example, we can tile the plane using the six tetrad types

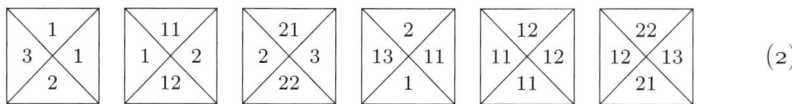

$$(2)$$

in essentially only one way, by repeating the rectangle

$$(3)$$

over and over. The reader may easily verify that there is no way to tile the plane
with the three tetrad types

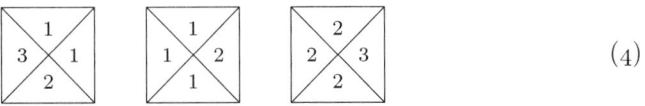

(4)

Wang's observation [*Scientific American* **213**, 5 (November 1965), 98–106] is
that *if it is possible to tile the upper right quadrant of the plane, it is possible to
tile the whole plane.* This is certainly unexpected, because a method for tiling
the upper right quadrant involves a "boundary" along the x and y axes, and it
would seem to give no hint as to how to tile the upper *left* quadrant of the plane
(since tetrad types may not be rotated or reflected). We cannot get rid of the
boundary merely by shifting the upper-quadrant solution down and to the left,
since it does not make sense to shift the solution by more than a finite amount.
But Wang's proof runs as follows: The existence of an upper-right-quadrant
solution implies that there is a way to tile a $2n \times 2n$ square, for all n. The set
of all solutions to the problem of tiling squares with an even number of cells on
each side forms an oriented tree, if the children of each $2n \times 2n$ solution x are
the possible $(2n + 2) \times (2n + 2)$ solutions that can be obtained by bordering x.
The root of this oriented tree is the 0×0 solution; its children are the 2×2
solutions, etc. Each node has only finitely many children, since the problem of
tiling the plane assumes that only finitely many tetrad types are given; hence by
the infinity lemma there is an infinite path to the root. This means that there
is a way to tile the whole plane (although we may be at a loss to find it)!

For later developments in tetrad tiling, see the beautiful book *Tilings and
Patterns* by B. Grünbaum and G. C. Shephard (Freeman, 1987), Chapter 11.

EXERCISES

1. [*M10*] The text refers to a set S containing finite sequences of positive integers,
and states that this set is "essentially an oriented tree." What is the root of this
oriented tree, and what are the arcs?

2. [*20*] Show that if rotation of tetrad types is allowed, it is always possible to tile
the plane.

▶ **3.** [*M23*] If it is possible to tile the upper right quadrant of the plane when given an
infinite set of tetrad types, is it always possible to tile the whole plane?

4. [*M25*] (H. Wang.) The six tetrad types (2) lead to a toroidal solution to the
tiling problem, that is, a solution in which some rectangular pattern — namely (3) —
is replicated throughout the entire plane.

Assume without proof that whenever it is possible to tile the plane with a finite
set of tetrad types, there is a toroidal solution using those tetrad types. Use this
assumption together with the infinity lemma to design an algorithm that, given the
specifications of any finite set of tetrad types, determines in a finite number of steps
whether or not there exists a way to tile the plane with these types.

5. [*M40*] Show that using the following 92 tetrad types it is possible to tile the plane,
but that there is no toroidal solution in the sense of exercise 4.

To simplify the specification of the 92 types, let us first introduce some notation. Define the following "basic codes":

$\alpha = (\,1,\ 2,\ 1,\ 2)$ $\beta = (\,3,\ 4,\ 2,\ 1)$ $\gamma = (\,2,\ 1,\ 3,\ 4)$ $\delta = (\,4,\ 3,\ 4,\ 3)$
$a = (Q, D,\ P, R)$ $b = (\ ,\ \ , L, P)$ $c = (U, Q, T, S)$ $d = (\ ,\ \ , S, T)$
$N = (Y,\ \ , X,\ \ )$ $J = (D, U,\ \ , X)$ $K = (\ \ , Y, R, L)$ $B = (\ ,\ \ ,\ \ ,\ \ )$
$R = (\ ,\ \ , R, R)$ $L = (\ \ ,\ \ , L, L)$ $P = (\ \ ,\ \ , P, P)$ $S = (\ \ ,\ \ , S, S)$
 $T = (\ \ ,\ \ , T, T)$ $X = (\ \ ,\ \ , X, X)$
$Y = (Y, Y,\ \ ,\ \ )$ $U = (U, U,\ \ ,\ \ )$ $D = (D, D,\ \ ,\ \ )$ $Q = (Q, Q,\ \ ,\ \ )$

The tetrad types are now

$\alpha\{a, b, c, d\}$ [4 types]
$\beta\{Y\{B, U, Q\}\{P, T\}, \{B, U, D, Q\}\{P, S, T\}, K\{B, U, Q\}\}$ [21 types]
$\gamma\{\{\{X, B\}\{L, P, S, T\}, R\}\{B, Q\}, J\{L, P, S, T\}\}$ [22 types]
$\delta\{X\{L, P, S, T\}\{B, Q\}, Y\{B, U, Q\}\{P, T\}, N\{a, b, c, d\},$
$\qquad J\{L, P, S, T\}, K\{B, U, Q\}, \{R, L, P, S, T\}\{B, U, D, Q\}\}$ [45 types]

These abbreviations mean that the basic codes are to be put together component by component and sorted into alphabetic order in each component; thus

$$\beta Y\{B, U, Q\}\{P, T\}$$

stands for six types βYBP, βYUP, βYQP, βYBT, βYUT, βYQT. The type βYQT is

$$(3, 4, 2, 1)(Y, Y,\ \ ,\ \ )(Q, Q,\ \ ,\ \ )(\ ,\ \ , T, T) = (3QY, 4QY, 2T, 1T)$$

after multiplying corresponding components and sorting into order. This is intended to correspond to the tetrad type shown on the right, where we use strings of symbols instead of numbers in the four quarters of the type. Two tetrad types can be placed next to each other only if they have the same string of symbols at the place they touch.

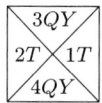

A β-tetrad is one that has a β in its specification as given above. To get started on the solution to this exercise, note that any β-tetrad must have an α-tetrad to its left and to its right, and a δ-tetrad above and below. An αa-tetrad must have βKB or βKU or βKQ to its right, and then must come an αb-tetrad, etc.

(This construction is a simplified version of a similar one given by Robert Berger, who went on to prove that the general problem in exercise 4, without the invalid assumption, cannot be solved. See *Memoirs Amer. Math. Soc.* **66** (1966).)

▶ **6.** [*M23*] (Otto Schreier.) In a famous paper [*Nieuw Archief voor Wiskunde* (2) **15** (1927), 212–216], B. L. van der Waerden proved the following theorem:

> If k and m are positive integers, and if we have k sets $S_1, \ldots, S_k$ of positive integers with every positive integer included in at least one of these sets, then at least one of the sets S_j contains an arithmetic progression of length m.

(The latter statement means there exist integers a and $\delta > 0$ such that $a + \delta$, $a + 2\delta$, $\ldots$, $a + m\delta$ are all in S_j.) If possible, use this result and the infinity lemma to prove the following stronger statement:

> If k and m are positive integers, there is a number N such that if we have k sets $S_1, \ldots, S_k$ of integers with every integer between 1 and N included in at least one of these sets, then at least one of the sets S_j contains an arithmetic progression of length m.

▶ **7.** [*M30*] If possible, use van der Waerden's theorem of exercise 6 and the infinity lemma to prove the following stronger statement:

> If k is a positive integer, and if we have k sets $S_1, \ldots, S_k$ of integers with every positive integer included in at least one of these sets, then at least one of the sets S_j contains an infinitely long arithmetic progression.

▶ **8.** [*M39*] (J. B. Kruskal.) If T and T' are (finite, ordered) trees, let the notation $T \subseteq T'$ signify that T can be embedded in T', as in exercise 2.3.2–22. Prove that if $T_1, T_2, T_3, \ldots$ is any infinite sequence of trees, there exist integers $j < k$ such that $T_j \subseteq T_k$. (In other words, it is impossible to construct an infinite sequence of trees in which no tree contains any of the earlier trees of the sequence. This fact can be used to prove that certain algorithms must terminate.)

*2.3.4.4. Enumeration of trees. Some of the most instructive applications of the mathematical theory of trees to the analysis of algorithms are connected with formulas for counting how many different trees there are of various kinds. For example, if we want to know how many different oriented trees can be constructed having four indistinguishable vertices, we find that there are just 4 possibilities:

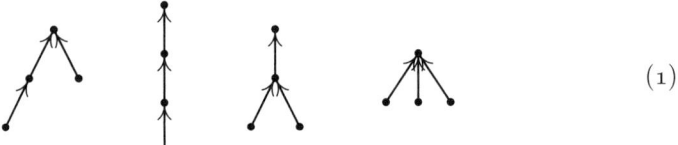

$$(1)$$

For our first enumeration problem, let us determine the number a_n of structurally different oriented trees with n vertices. Obviously, $a_1 = 1$. If $n > 1$, the tree has a root and various subtrees; suppose there are j_1 subtrees with 1 vertex, j_2 with 2 vertices, etc. Then we may choose j_k of the a_k possible k-vertex trees in

$$\binom{a_k + j_k - 1}{j_k}$$

ways, since repetitions are allowed (exercise 1.2.6–60), and so we see that

$$a_n = \sum_{j_1 + 2j_2 + \cdots = n-1} \binom{a_1 + j_1 - 1}{j_1} \cdots \binom{a_{n-1} + j_{n-1} - 1}{j_{n-1}}, \quad \text{for } n > 1. \quad (2)$$

If we consider the generating function $A(z) = \sum_n a_n z^n$, with $a_0 = 0$, we find that the identity

$$\frac{1}{(1 - z^r)^a} = \sum_j \binom{a + j - 1}{j} z^{rj}$$

together with (2) implies

$$A(z) = \frac{z}{(1 - z)^{a_1}(1 - z^2)^{a_2}(1 - z^3)^{a_3} \cdots}. \quad (3)$$

This is not an especially nice form for $A(z)$, since it involves an infinite product and the coefficients $a_1, a_2, \ldots$ appear on the right-hand side. A somewhat more aesthetic way to represent $A(z)$ is given in exercise 1; it leads to a reasonably efficient formula for calculating the values a_n (see exercise 2) and, in fact, it also can be used to deduce the asymptotic behavior of a_n for large n (see exercise 4). We find that

$$A(z) = z + z^2 + 2z^3 + 4z^4 + 9z^5 + 20z^6 + 48z^7 + 115z^8$$
$$+ 286z^9 + 719z^{10} + 1842z^{11} + \cdots. \quad (4)$$

Now that we have essentially found the number of oriented trees, it is quite interesting to determine the number of structurally different *free trees* with n vertices. There are just two distinct free trees with four vertices, namely

and $\qquad (5)$

because the first two and last two oriented trees of (1) become identical when the orientation is dropped.

We have seen that it is possible to select any vertex X of a free tree and to assign directions to the edges in a unique way so that it becomes an oriented tree with X as root. Once this has been done, for a given vertex X, suppose there are k subtrees of the root X, with $s_1, s_2, \ldots, s_k$ vertices in these respective subtrees. Clearly, k is the number of arcs touching X, and $s_1 + s_2 + \cdots + s_k = n - 1$. In these circumstances we say that the *weight* of X is $\max(s_1, s_2, \ldots, s_k)$. Thus in the tree

$\qquad (6)$

the vertex D has weight 3 (each of the subtrees leading from D has three of the nine remaining vertices), and vertex E has weight $\max(7, 2) = 7$. A vertex with minimum weight is called a *centroid* of the free tree.

Let X and $s_1, s_2, \ldots, s_k$ be as above, and let $Y_1, Y_2, \ldots, Y_k$ be the roots of the subtrees emanating from X. If Y is any node in the Y_1 subtree, its weight must be at least $n - s_1 = 1 + s_2 + \cdots + s_k$, since when Y is the assumed root there are at least $n - s_1$ vertices in its subtree containing X. Thus if Y is a centroid we have

$$\text{weight}\,(X) = \max\,(s_1, s_2, \ldots, s_k) \geq \text{weight}\,(Y) \geq 1 + s_2 + \cdots + s_k,$$

and this is possible only if $s_1 > s_2 + \cdots + s_k$. A similar result may be derived if we replace Y_1 by Y_j in this discussion. So *at most one of the subtrees at a vertex can contain a centroid.*

This is a strong condition, for it implies that *there are at most two centroids in a free tree, and if two centroids exist, they are adjacent.* (See exercise 9.)

Conversely, if $s_1 > s_2 + \cdots + s_k$, there *is* a centroid in the Y_1 subtree, since

$$\text{weight}\,(Y_1) \leq \max\,(s_1 - 1, 1 + s_2 + \cdots + s_k) \leq s_1 = \text{weight}\,(X),$$

and the weight of all nodes in the $Y_2, \ldots, Y_k$ subtrees is at least $s_1 + 1$. We have proved that *the vertex X is the only centroid of a free tree if and only if*

$$s_j \leq s_1 + \cdots + s_k - s_j, \qquad \text{for } 1 \leq j \leq k. \tag{7}$$

Therefore the number of free trees with n vertices, having only one centroid, is the number of oriented trees with n vertices minus the number of such oriented trees violating condition (7); the latter consist essentially of an oriented tree with s_j vertices and another oriented tree with $n - s_j \leq s_j$ vertices. The number with one centroid therefore comes to

$$a_n - a_1 a_{n-1} - a_2 a_{n-2} - \cdots - a_{\lfloor n/2 \rfloor} a_{\lceil n/2 \rceil}. \tag{8}$$

A free tree with two centroids has an even number of vertices, and the weight of each centroid is $n/2$ (see exercise 10). So if $n = 2m$, the number of bicentroidal free trees is the number of choices of 2 things out of a_m with repetition, namely

$$\binom{a_m + 1}{2}.$$

To get the total number of free trees, we therefore add $\frac{1}{2} a_{n/2}(a_{n/2} + 1)$ to (8) when n is even. The form of Eq. (8) suggests a simple generating function, and indeed, we find without difficulty that *the generating function for the number of structurally different free trees is*

$$F(z) = A(z) - \frac{1}{2} A(z)^2 + \frac{1}{2} A(z^2)$$

$$= z + z^2 + z^3 + 2z^4 + 3z^5 + 6z^6 + 11z^7 + 23z^8$$

$$\qquad\qquad + 47z^9 + 106z^{10} + 235z^{11} + \cdots. \tag{9}$$

This simple relation between $F(z)$ and $A(z)$ is due primarily to C. Jordan, who considered the problem in 1869.

Now let us turn to the question of enumerating *ordered trees*, which are our principal concern with respect to computer programming algorithms. There are five structurally different ordered trees with four vertices:

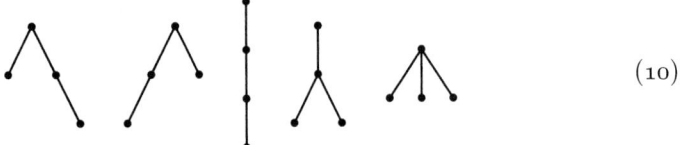

$$(10)$$

The first two are identical as oriented trees, so only one of them appeared in (1) above.

Before we examine the number of different ordered tree structures, let us first consider the case of *binary trees*, since this is closer to the actual computer representation and it is easier to study. Let b_n be the number of different binary trees with n nodes. From the definition of binary tree it is apparent that $b_0 = 1$, and for $n > 0$ the number of possibilities is the number of ways to put a binary tree with k nodes to the left of the root and another with $n - 1 - k$ nodes to the right. So

$$b_n = b_0 b_{n-1} + b_1 b_{n-2} + \cdots + b_{n-1} b_0, \qquad n \geq 1. \tag{11}$$

From this relation it is clear that the generating function

$$B(z) = b_0 + b_1 z + b_2 z^2 + \cdots$$

satisfies the equation

$$z B(z)^2 = B(z) - 1. \tag{12}$$

Solving this quadratic equation and using the fact that $B(0) = 1$, we obtain

$$B(z) = \frac{1}{2z}\left(1 - \sqrt{1 - 4z}\right) = \frac{1}{2z}\left(1 - \sum_{k \geq 0}\binom{\frac{1}{2}}{k}(-4z)^k\right)$$

$$= 2\sum_{n \geq 0}\binom{\frac{1}{2}}{n+1}(-4z)^n = \sum_{n \geq 0}\binom{-\frac{1}{2}}{n}\frac{(-4z)^n}{n+1}$$

$$= \sum_{n \geq 0}\binom{2n}{n}\frac{z^n}{n+1}$$

$$= 1 + z + 2z^2 + 5z^3 + 14z^4 + 42z^5 + 132z^6 + 429z^7$$
$$+ 1430z^8 + 4862z^9 + 16796z^{10} + \cdots. \tag{13}$$

(See exercise 1.2.6–47.) The desired answer is therefore

$$b_n = \frac{1}{n+1}\binom{2n}{n}. \tag{14}$$

By Stirling's formula, this is asymptotically $4^n/n\sqrt{\pi n} + O(4^n n^{-5/2})$. Some important generalizations of Eq. (14) appear in exercises 11 and 32.

Returning to our question about ordered trees with n nodes, we can see that this is essentially the same question as the number of binary trees, since we have a natural correspondence between binary trees and forests, and a tree minus its root is a forest. Hence *the number of (ordered) trees with n vertices is b_{n-1}, the number of binary trees with $n - 1$ vertices.*

The enumerations performed above assume that the vertices are indistinguishable points. If we label the vertices 1, 2, 3, 4 in (1) and insist that 1 is to be the root, we now get 16 different oriented trees:

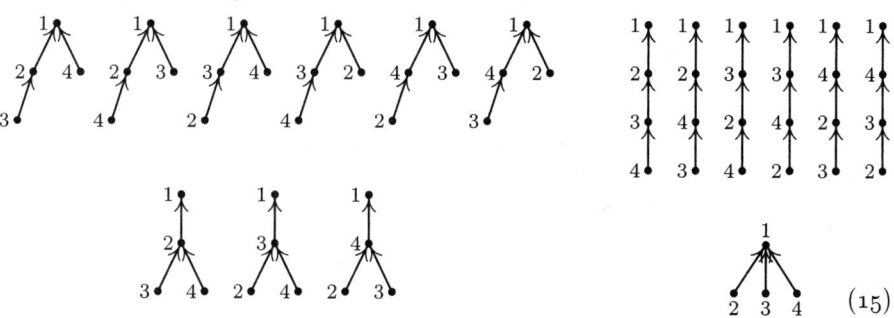

$$\tag{15}$$

The question of enumeration for labeled trees is clearly quite different from the
one solved above. In this case it can be rephrased as follows: "Consider drawing
three lines, pointing from each of the vertices 2, 3, and 4 to another vertex;
there are three choices of lines emanating from each vertex, so there are $3^3 = 27$
possibilities in all. How many of these 27 ways will yield oriented trees with 1
as the root?" The answer, as we have seen, is 16. A similar reformulation of the
same problem, this time for the case of n vertices, is the following: "Let $f(x)$ be
an integer-valued function such that $f(1) = 1$ and $1 \le f(x) \le n$ for all integers
$1 \le x \le n$. We call f a *tree mapping* if $f^{[n]}(x)$, that is, $f\big(f(\cdots(f(x))\cdots)\big)$
iterated n times, equals 1, for all x. How many tree mappings are there?" This
problem comes up, for example, in connection with random number generation.
We will find, rather surprisingly, that on the average exactly one out of every n
such functions f is a tree mapping.

The solution to this enumeration problem can readily be derived using the
general formulas for counting subtrees of graphs that have been developed in
previous sections (see exercise 12). But there is a much more informative way
to solve the problem, one that gives us a new and compact manner to represent
oriented tree structure.

Suppose that we've been given an oriented tree with vertices $\{1, 2, \ldots, n\}$
and with $n - 1$ arcs, where the arcs go from j to $f(j)$ for all j except the root.
There is at least one terminal (leaf) vertex; let V_1 be the smallest number of a
leaf. If $n > 1$, write down $f(V_1)$ and delete both V_1 and the arc $V_1 \to f(V_1)$
from the tree; then let V_2 be the smallest number whose vertex is terminal in
the resulting tree. If $n > 2$, write down $f(V_2)$ and delete both V_2 and the arc
$V_2 \to f(V_2)$ from the tree; and proceed in this way until all vertices have been
deleted except the root. The resulting sequence of $n - 1$ numbers,

$$ f(V_1), \; f(V_2), \; \ldots, \; f(V_{n-1}), \qquad 1 \le f(V_j) \le n, \tag{16} $$

is called the *canonical representation* of the original oriented tree.

For example, the oriented tree

$$ \tag{17} $$

with 10 vertices has the canonical representation 1, 3, 10, 5, 10, 1, 3, 5, 3.

The important point here is that we can reverse this process and go from
any sequence of $n - 1$ numbers (16) back to the oriented tree that produced it.
For if we have any sequence $x_1, x_2, \ldots, x_{n-1}$ of numbers between 1 and n, let
V_1 be the smallest number that does not appear in the sequence $x_1, \ldots, x_{n-1}$;
then let V_2 be the smallest number $\ne V_1$ that does not appear in the sequence
$x_2, \ldots, x_{n-1}$; and so on. After obtaining a permutation $V_1 V_2 \ldots V_n$ of the integers
$\{1, 2, \ldots, n\}$ in this way, draw arcs from vertex V_j to vertex x_j, for $1 \le j < n$.
This gives a construction of a directed graph with no oriented cycles, and by

exercise 2.3.4.2–7 it is an oriented tree. Clearly, the sequence $x_1, x_2, \ldots, x_{n-1}$ is the same as the sequence (16) for this oriented tree.

Since the process is reversible, we have obtained a one-to-one correspondence between $(n - 1)$-tuples of numbers $\{1, 2, \ldots, n\}$ and oriented trees on these vertices. Hence *there are n^{n-1} distinct oriented trees with n labeled vertices.* If we specify that one vertex is to be the root, there is clearly no difference between one vertex and another, so there are n^{n-2} distinct oriented trees on $\{1, 2, \ldots, n\}$ having a given root. This accounts for the $16 = 4^{4-2}$ trees in (15). From this information it is easy to determine the number of *free trees* with labeled vertices (see exercise 22). The number of *ordered trees* with labeled vertices is also easy to determine, once we know the answer to that problem when no labels are involved (see exercise 23). So we have essentially solved the problems of enumerating the three fundamental classes of trees, with both labeled and unlabeled vertices.

It is interesting to see what would happen if we were to apply our usual method of generating functions to the problem of enumerating labeled oriented trees. For this purpose we would probably find it easiest to consider the quantity $r(n, q)$, the number of labeled directed graphs with n vertices, with no oriented cycles, and with one arc emanating from each of q designated vertices. The number of labeled oriented trees with a specified root is therefore $r(n, n-1)$. In this notation we find by simple counting arguments that, for any fixed integer m,

$$r(n, q) = \sum_k \binom{q}{k} r(m+k, k) r(n-m-k, q-k), \quad \text{if } 0 \le m \le n-q, \quad (18)$$

$$r(n, q) = \sum_k \binom{q}{k} r(n-1, q-k), \quad \text{if } q = n-1. \quad (19)$$

The first of these relations is obtained if we partition the undesignated vertices into two groups A and B, with m vertices in A and $n - q - m$ vertices in B; then the q designated vertices are partitioned into k vertices that begin paths leading into A, and $q - k$ vertices that begin paths leading into B. Relation (19) is obtained by considering oriented trees in which the root has degree k.

The form of these relations indicates that we can work profitably with the generating function

$$G_m(z) = r(m, 0) + r(m+1, 1)z + \frac{r(m+2, 2)z^2}{2!} + \cdots = \sum_k \frac{r(k+m, k)z^k}{k!}.$$

In these terms Eq. (18) says that $G_{n-q}(z) = G_m(z)G_{n-q-m}(z)$, and therefore by induction on m, we find that $G_m(z) = G_1(z)^m$. Now from Eq. (19), we obtain

$$G_1(z) = \sum_{n \ge 1} \frac{r(n, n-1)z^{n-1}}{(n-1)!} = \sum_{k \ge 0} \sum_{n \ge 1} \frac{r(n-1, n-1-k)z^{n-1}}{k!\,(n-1-k)!}$$

$$= \sum_{k \ge 0} \frac{z^k}{k!} G_k(z) = \sum_{k \ge 0} \frac{(zG_1(z))^k}{k!} = e^{zG_1(z)}.$$

In other words, putting $G_1(z) = w$, the solution to our problem comes from the coefficients of the solution to the transcendental equation

$$w = e^{zw}. \tag{20}$$

This equation can be solved with the use of Lagrange's inversion formula: $z = \zeta/f(\zeta)$ implies that

$$\zeta = \sum_{n \geq 1} \frac{z^n}{n!} g_n^{(n-1)}(0), \tag{21}$$

where $g_n(\zeta) = f(\zeta)^n$, when f is analytic in the neighborhood of the origin, and $f(0) \neq 0$ (see exercise 4.7–16). In this case, we may set $\zeta = zw$, $f(\zeta) = e^\zeta$, and we deduce the solution

$$w = \sum_{n \geq 0} \frac{(n+1)^{n-1}}{n!} z^n, \tag{22}$$

in agreement with the answer obtained above.

G. N. Raney has shown that we can extend this method in an important way to obtain an explicit power series for the solution to the considerably more general equation

$$w = y_1 e^{z_1 w} + y_2 e^{z_2 w} + \cdots + y_s e^{z_s w},$$

solving for w in terms of a power series in $y_1, \ldots, y_s$ and $z_1, \ldots, z_s$. For this generalization, let us consider s-dimensional vectors of integers

$$\mathbf{n} = (n_1, n_2, \ldots, n_s),$$

and let us write for convenience

$$\Sigma \mathbf{n} = n_1 + n_2 + \cdots + n_s.$$

Suppose that we have s colors $C_1, C_2, \ldots, C_s$, and consider directed graphs in which each vertex is assigned a color; for example,

(23)

Let $r(\mathbf{n}, \mathbf{q})$ be the number of ways to draw arcs and to assign colors to the vertices $\{1, 2, \ldots, n\}$, such that

i) for $1 \leq i \leq s$ there are exactly n_i vertices of color C_i (hence $n = \Sigma \mathbf{n}$);

ii) there are q arcs, one leading from each of the vertices $\{1, 2, \ldots, q\}$;

iii) for $1 \leq i \leq s$ there are exactly q_i arcs leading to vertices of color C_i (hence $q = \Sigma \mathbf{q}$);

iv) there are no oriented cycles (hence $q < n$, unless $q = n = 0$).

Let us call this an $(\mathbf{n}, \mathbf{q})$-construction.

For example, if C_1 = red, C_2 = yellow, and C_3 = blue, then (23) shows a $((3,2,2),(1,2,2))$-construction. When there is only one color, we have the oriented tree problem that we have already solved. Raney's idea is to generalize the one-dimension construction to s dimensions.

Let $\mathbf{n}$ and $\mathbf{q}$ be fixed s-place vectors of nonnegative integers, and let $n = \sum \mathbf{n}$, $q = \sum \mathbf{q}$. For each $(\mathbf{n},\mathbf{q})$-construction and each number k, $1 \le k \le n$, we will define a *canonical representation* consisting of four things:

a) a number t, with $q < t \le n$;
b) a sequence of n colors, with n_i of color C_i;
c) a sequence of q colors, with q_i of color C_i;
d) for $1 \le i \le s$, a sequence of q_i elements of the set $\{1, 2, \ldots, n_i\}$.

The canonical representation is defined thus: First list the vertices $\{1, 2, \ldots, q\}$ in the order $V_1, V_2, \ldots, V_q$ of the canonical representation of oriented trees (as given above), and then write below vertex V_j the number $f(V_j)$ of the vertex on the arc leading from V_j. Let $t = f(V_q)$; and let the sequence (c) of colors be the respective colors of the vertices $f(V_1), \ldots, f(V_q)$. Let the sequence (b) of colors be the respective colors of the vertices k, $k+1$, $\ldots$, n, 1, $\ldots$, $k-1$. Finally, let the ith sequence in (d) be $x_{i1}, x_{i2}, \ldots, x_{iq_i}$, where $x_{ij} = m$ if the jth C_i-colored element of the sequence $f(V_1), \ldots, f(V_q)$ is the mth C_i-colored element of the sequence k, $k+1$, $\ldots$, n, 1, $\ldots$, $k-1$.

For example, consider construction (23) and let $k = 3$. We start by listing $V_1, \ldots, V_5$ and $f(V_1), \ldots, f(V_5)$ below them as follows:

$$1 \quad 2 \quad 4 \quad 5 \quad 3$$
$$7 \quad 6 \quad 3 \quad 3 \quad 6$$

Hence $t = 6$, and sequence (c) represents the respective colors of 7, 6, 3, 3, 6, namely red, yellow, blue, blue, yellow. Sequence (b) represents the respective colors of 3, 4, 5, 6, 7, 1, 2, namely blue, yellow, red, yellow, red, blue, red. Finally, to get the sequences in (d), proceed as follows:

color	elements this color in $3, 4, 5, 6, 7, 1, 2$	elements this color in $7, 6, 3, 3, 6$	encode column 3 by column 2
red	$5, 7, 2$	7	2
yellow	$4, 6$	$6, 6$	$2, 2$
blue	$3, 1$	$3, 3$	$1, 1$

Hence the (d) sequences are 2; 2, 2; and 1, 1.

From the canonical representation, we can recover both the original $(\mathbf{n},\mathbf{q})$-construction and the number k as follows: From (a) and (c) we know the color of vertex t. The last element of the (d) sequence for this color tells us, in conjunction with (b), the position of t in the sequence $k, \ldots, n, 1, \ldots, k-1$; hence we know k and the colors of all vertices. Then the subsequences in (d) together with (b) and (c) determine $f(V_1), f(V_2), \ldots, f(V_q)$, and finally the directed graph is reconstructed by locating $V_1, \ldots, V_q$ as we did for oriented trees.

The reversibility of this canonical representation allows us to count the number of possible $(\mathbf{n}, \mathbf{q})$-constructions, since there are $n - q$ choices for (a), and the multinomial coefficient

$$\binom{n}{n_1, \ldots, n_s}$$

choices for (b), and

$$\binom{q}{q_1, \ldots, q_s}$$

choices for (c), and $n_1^{q_1} n_2^{q_2} \ldots n_s^{q_s}$ choices for (d). Dividing by the n choices for k, we have the general result

$$r(\mathbf{n}, \mathbf{q}) = \frac{n - q}{n} \frac{n!}{n_1! \ldots n_s!} \frac{q!}{q_1! \ldots q_s!} n_1^{q_1} n_2^{q_2} \ldots n_s^{q_s}. \qquad (24)$$

Furthermore, we can derive analogs of Eqs. (18) and (19):

$$r(\mathbf{n}, \mathbf{q}) = \sum_{\substack{\mathbf{k}, \mathbf{t} \\ \sum(\mathbf{t} - \mathbf{k}) = m}} \binom{\sum \mathbf{q}}{\sum \mathbf{k}} r(\mathbf{t}, \mathbf{k}) \, r(\mathbf{n} - \mathbf{t}, \mathbf{q} - \mathbf{k}) \quad \text{if } 0 \le m \le \sum(\mathbf{n} - \mathbf{q}), \quad (25)$$

with the convention that $r(\mathbf{0}, \mathbf{0}) = 1$, and $r(\mathbf{n}, \mathbf{q}) = 0$ if any n_i or q_i is negative or if $q > n$;

$$r(\mathbf{n}, \mathbf{q}) = \sum_{i=1}^{s} \sum_{k} \binom{\sum \mathbf{q}}{k} r(\mathbf{n} - \mathbf{e}_i, \mathbf{q} - k\mathbf{e}_i) \quad \text{if } \sum \mathbf{n} = 1 + \sum \mathbf{q}, \qquad (26)$$

where $\mathbf{e}_i$ is the vector with 1 in position i and zeros elsewhere. Relation (25) is based on breaking the vertices $\{q + 1, \ldots, n\}$ into two parts having m and $n - q - m$ elements, respectively; the second relation is derived by removing the unique root and considering the remaining structure. We now obtain the following result:

Theorem R. [George N. Raney, *Canadian J. Math.* **16** (1964), 755–762.] *Let*

$$w = \sum_{\substack{\mathbf{n}, \mathbf{q} \\ \sum(\mathbf{n} - \mathbf{q}) = 1}} \frac{r(\mathbf{n}, \mathbf{q})}{(\sum \mathbf{q})!} y_1^{n_1} \ldots y_s^{n_s} z_1^{q_1} \ldots z_s^{q_s}, \qquad (27)$$

where $r(\mathbf{n}, \mathbf{q})$ is defined by (24), *and where $\mathbf{n}, \mathbf{q}$ are s-dimensional integer vectors. Then w satisfies the identity*

$$w = y_1 e^{z_1 w} + y_2 e^{z_2 w} + \cdots + y_s e^{z_s w}. \qquad (28)$$

Proof. By (25) and induction on m, we find that

$$w^m = \sum_{\substack{\mathbf{n}, \mathbf{q} \\ \sum(\mathbf{n} - \mathbf{q}) = m}} \frac{r(\mathbf{n}, \mathbf{q})}{(\sum \mathbf{q})!} y_1^{n_1} \ldots y_s^{n_s} z_1^{q_1} \ldots z_s^{q_s}. \qquad (29)$$

Now by (26),

$$w = \sum_{i=1}^{s} \sum_{k} \sum_{\substack{\mathbf{n},\mathbf{q} \\ \sum(\mathbf{n}-\mathbf{q})=1}} \frac{r(\mathbf{n}-\mathbf{e}_i, \mathbf{q}-k\mathbf{e}_i)}{k!\,(\sum\mathbf{q}-k)!}\, y_1^{n_1}\dots y_s^{n_s}\, z_1^{q_1}\dots z_s^{q_s}$$

$$= \sum_{i=1}^{s} \sum_{k} \frac{1}{k!}\, y_i z_i^{k} \sum_{\substack{\mathbf{n},\mathbf{q} \\ \sum(\mathbf{n}-\mathbf{q})=k}} \frac{r(\mathbf{n},\mathbf{q})}{(\sum\mathbf{q})!}\, y_1^{n_1}\dots y_s^{n_s}\, z_1^{q_1}\dots z_s^{q_s}$$

$$= \sum_{i=1}^{s} \sum_{k} \frac{1}{k!}\, y_i z_i^{k} w^{k}. \quad\blacksquare$$

The special case where $s = 1$ and $z_1 = 1$ in (27) and (28) is especially important in applications, so it has become known as the "tree function"

$$T(y) = \sum_{n\geq 1} \frac{n^{n-1}}{n!}\, y^n = y e^{T(y)}. \tag{30}$$

See Corless, Gonnet, Hare, Jeffrey, and Knuth, *Advances in Computational Math.* **5** (1996), 329–359, for a discussion of this function's history and some of its remarkable properties.

A survey of enumeration formulas for trees, based on skillful manipulations of generating functions, has been given by I. J. Good [*Proc. Cambridge Philos. Soc.* **61** (1965), 499–517; **64** (1968), 489]. More recently, a mathematical *theory of species* developed by André Joyal [*Advances in Math.* **42** (1981), 1–82] has led to a high-level viewpoint in which algebraic operations on generating functions correspond directly to combinatorial properties of structures. The book *Combinatorial Species and Tree-like Structures* by F. Bergeron, G. Labelle, and P. Leroux (Cambridge Univ. Press, 1998), presents numerous examples of this beautiful and instructive theory, generalizing many of the formulas derived above.

EXERCISES

1. [*M20*] (G. Pólya.) Show that

$$A(z) = z \cdot \exp\left(A(z) + \tfrac{1}{2}A(z^2) + \tfrac{1}{3}A(z^3) + \cdots\right).$$

[*Hint:* Take logarithms of (3).]

2. [*HM24*] (R. Otter.) Show that the numbers a_n satisfy the following condition:

$$n a_{n+1} = a_1 s_{n1} + 2 a_2 s_{n2} + \cdots + n a_n s_{nn},$$

where

$$s_{nk} = \sum_{1 \leq j \leq n/k} a_{n+1-jk}.$$

(These formulas are useful for the calculation of the a_n, since $s_{nk} = s_{(n-k)k} + a_{n+1-k}$.)

3. [*M40*] Write a computer program that determines the number of (unlabeled) free trees and of oriented trees with n vertices, for $n \leq 100$. (Use the result of exercise 2.) Explore arithmetical properties of these numbers; can anything be said about their prime factors, or their residues modulo p?

▶ **4.** [*HM39*] (G. Pólya, 1937.) Using complex variable theory, determine the asymptotic value of the number of oriented trees as follows:

a) Show that there is a real number α between 0 and 1 for which $A(z)$ has radius of convergence α and $A(z)$ converges absolutely for all complex z such that $|z| \leq \alpha$, having maximum value $A(\alpha) = a < \infty$. [*Hint:* When a power series has nonnegative coefficients, it either is entire or has a positive real singularity; and show that $A(z)/z$ is bounded as $z \to \alpha-$, by using the identity in exercise 1.]

b) Let
$$ F(z, w) = \exp\left(zw + \tfrac{1}{2}A(z^2) + \tfrac{1}{3}A(z^3) + \cdots\right) - w. $$
Show that in a neighborhood of $(z, w) = (\alpha, a/\alpha)$, $F(z, w)$ is analytic in each variable separately.

c) Show that at the point $(z, w) = (\alpha, a/\alpha)$, we have $\partial F/\partial w = 0$; hence $a = 1$.

d) At the point $(z, w) = (\alpha, 1/\alpha)$ show that
$$ \frac{\partial F}{\partial z} = \beta = \alpha^{-2} + \sum_{k \geq 2} \alpha^{k-2} A'(\alpha^k), \quad \text{and} \quad \frac{\partial^2 F}{\partial w^2} = \alpha. $$

e) When $|z| = \alpha$ and $z \neq \alpha$, show that $\partial F/\partial w \neq 0$; hence $A(z)$ has only one singularity on $|z| = \alpha$.

f) Prove that there is a region larger than $|z| < \alpha$ in which
$$ \frac{1}{z} A(z) = \frac{1}{\alpha} - \sqrt{2\beta(1 - z/\alpha)} + (1 - z/\alpha)R(z), $$
where $R(z)$ is an analytic function of $\sqrt{z - \alpha}$.

g) Prove that consequently
$$ a_n = \frac{1}{\alpha^{n-1}n}\sqrt{\beta/2\pi n} + O(n^{-5/2}\alpha^{-n}). $$

[*Note:* $1/\alpha \approx 2.955765285652$, and $\alpha\sqrt{\beta/2\pi} \approx 0.439924012571$.]

▶ **5.** [*M25*] (A. Cayley.) Let c_n be the number of (unlabeled) oriented trees having n leaves (namely, vertices with in-degree zero) and having at least two subtrees at every other vertex. Thus $c_3 = 2$, by virtue of the two trees

Find a formula analogous to (3) for the generating function
$$ C(z) = \sum_n c_n z^n. $$

6. [*M25*] Let an "oriented binary tree" be an oriented tree in which each vertex has in-degree two or less. Find a reasonably simple relation that defines the generating function $G(z)$ for the number of distinct oriented binary trees with n vertices, and find the first few values.

7. [*HM40*] Obtain asymptotic values for the numbers of exercise 6. (See exercise 4.)

8. [*20*] According to Eq. (9), there are six free trees with six vertices. Draw them, and indicate their centroids.

9. [*M20*] From the fact that at most one subtree of a vertex in a free tree can contain a centroid, prove that there are at most two centroids in a free tree; furthermore if there are two, then they must be adjacent.

▶ **10.** [*M22*] Prove that a free tree with n vertices and two centroids consists of two free trees with $n/2$ vertices, joined by an edge. Conversely, if two free trees with m vertices are joined by an edge, we obtain a free tree with $2m$ vertices and two centroids.

▶ **11.** [*M28*] The text derives the number of different binary trees with n nodes (14). Generalize this to find the number of different t-ary trees with n nodes. (See exercise 2.3.1–35; a t-ary tree is either empty or consists of a root and t disjoint t-ary trees.) *Hint:* Use Eq. (21) of Section 1.2.9.

12. [*M20*] Find the number of labeled oriented trees with n vertices by using determinants and the result of exercise 2.3.4.2–19. (See also exercise 1.2.3–36.)

13. [*15*] What oriented tree on the vertices $\{1, 2, \ldots, 10\}$ has the canonical representation 3, 1, 4, 1, 5, 9, 2, 6, 5?

14. [*10*] True or false: The last entry, $f(V_{n-1})$, in the canonical representation of an oriented tree is always the root of that tree.

15. [*21*] Discuss the relationships that exist (if any) between the topological sort algorithm of Section 2.2.3 and the canonical representation of an oriented tree.

16. [*25*] Design an algorithm (as efficient as possible) that converts from the canonical representation of an oriented tree to a conventional computer representation using PARENT links.

▶ **17.** [*M26*] Let $f(x)$ be an integer-valued function, where $1 \le f(x) \le m$ for all integers $1 \le x \le m$. Define $x \equiv y$ if $f^{[r]}(x) = f^{[s]}(y)$ for some $r, s \ge 0$, where $f^{[0]}(x) = x$ and $f^{[r+1]}(x) = f(f^{[r]}(x))$. By using methods of enumeration like those in this section, show that the number of functions such that $x \equiv y$ for all x and y is $m^{m-1}Q(m)$, where $Q(m)$ is the function defined in Section 1.2.11.3.

18. [*24*] Show that the following method is another way to define a one-to-one correspondence between $(n - 1)$-tuples of numbers from 1 to n and oriented trees with n labeled vertices: Let the leaves of the tree be $V_1, \ldots, V_k$ in ascending order. Let $(V_1, V_{k+1}, V_{k+2}, \ldots, V_q)$ be the path from V_1 to the root, and write down the vertices $V_q, \ldots, V_{k+2}, V_{k+1}$. Then let $(V_2, V_{q+1}, V_{q+2}, \ldots, V_r)$ be the shortest oriented path from V_2 such that V_r has already been written down, and write down $V_r, \ldots, V_{q+2}, V_{q+1}$. Then let $(V_3, V_{r+1}, \ldots, V_s)$ be the shortest oriented path from V_3 such that V_s has already been written, and write $V_s, \ldots, V_{r+1}$; and so on. For example, the tree (17) would be encoded as 3, 1, 3, 3, 5, 10, 5, 10, 1. Show that this process is reversible, and in particular, draw the oriented tree with vertices $\{1, 2, \ldots, 10\}$ and representation 3, 1, 4, 1, 5, 9, 2, 6, 5.

19. [*M24*] How many different labeled, oriented trees are there having n vertices, k of which are leaves (have in-degree zero)?

20. [*M24*] (J. Riordan.) How many different labeled, oriented trees are there having n vertices, k_0 of which have in-degree 0, k_1 have in-degree 1, k_2 have in-degree 2, ...? (Note that necessarily $k_0 + k_1 + k_2 + \cdots = n$, and $k_1 + 2k_2 + 3k_3 + \cdots = n - 1$.)

▶ **21.** [*M21*] Enumerate the number of labeled oriented trees in which each vertex has in-degree zero or two. (See exercise 20 and exercise 2.3–20.)

22. [*M20*] How many *labeled* free trees are possible with n vertices? (In other words, if we are given n vertices, there are $2^{\binom{n}{2}}$ possible graphs having these vertices, depending on which of the $\binom{n}{2}$ possible edges are incorporated into the graph; how many of these graphs are free trees?)

23. [*M21*] How many ordered trees are possible with n labeled vertices? (Give a simple formula involving factorials.)

24. [*M16*] All labeled oriented trees with vertices 1, 2, 3, 4 and with root 1 are shown in (15). How many would there be if we listed all labeled *ordered* trees with these vertices and this root?

25. [*M20*] What is the value of the quantity $r(n, q)$ that appears in Eqs. (18) and (19)? (Give an explicit formula; the text only mentions that $r(n, \, n - 1) = n^{n-2}$.)

26. [*20*] In terms of the notation at the end of this section, draw the $((3, 2, 4), (1, 4, 2))$-construction, analogous to (23), and find the number k that corresponds to the canonical representation having $t = 8$, the sequences of colors "red, yellow, blue, red, yellow, blue, red, blue, blue" and "red, yellow, blue, yellow, yellow, blue, yellow", and the index sequences 3; 1, 2, 2, 1; 2, 4.

▶ **27.** [*M28*] Let $U_1, U_2, \ldots, U_p, \ldots, U_q$; $V_1, V_2, \ldots, V_r$ be vertices of a directed graph, where $1 \leq p \leq q$. Let f be any function from the set $\{p+1, \ldots, q\}$ into the set $\{1, 2, \ldots, r\}$, and let the directed graph contain exactly $q - p$ arcs, from U_k to $V_{f(k)}$ for $p < k \leq q$. Show that the number of ways to add r additional arcs, one from each of the V's to one of the U's, such that the resulting directed graph contains no oriented cycles, is $q^{r-1}p$. Prove this by generalizing the canonical representation method; that is, set up a one-to-one correspondence between all such ways of adding r further arcs and the set of all sequences of integers $a_1, a_2, \ldots, a_r$, where $1 \leq a_k \leq q$ for $1 \leq k < r$, and $1 \leq a_r \leq p$.

28. [*M22*] (*Bipartite trees.*) Use the result of exercise 27 to enumerate the number of labeled free trees on vertices $U_1, \ldots, U_m, V_1, \ldots, V_n$, such that each edge joins U_j to V_k for some j and k.

29. [*HM26*] Prove that if $E_k(r, t) = r(r + kt)^{k-1}/k!$, and if $zx^t = \ln x$, then

$$x^r = \sum_{k \geq 0} E_k(r, t) z^k$$

for fixed t and for sufficiently small $|z|$ and $|x - 1|$. [Use the fact that $G_m(z) = G_1(z)^m$ in the discussion following Eq. (19).] In this formula, r stands for an arbitrary real number. [*Note:* As a consequence of this formula we have the identity

$$\sum_{k=0}^{n} E_k(r, t) E_{n-k}(s, t) = E_n(r + s, \, t);$$

this implies Abel's binomial theorem, Eq. (16) of Section 1.2.6. Compare also Eq. (30) of that section.]

30. [*M23*] Let $n, x, y, z_1, \ldots, z_n$ be positive integers. Consider a set of $x + y + z_1 + \cdots + z_n + n$ vertices r_i, s_{jk}, t_j ($1 \leq i \leq x + y$, $1 \leq j \leq n$, $1 \leq k \leq z_j$), in which arcs have been drawn from s_{jk} to t_j for all j and k. According to exercise 27, there are $(x + y)(x + y + z_1 + \cdots + z_n)^{n-1}$ ways to draw one arc from each of $t_1, \ldots, t_n$ to other vertices such that the resulting directed graph contains no oriented cycles. Use this fact to prove Hurwitz's generalization of the binomial theorem:

$$\sum x(x+\epsilon_1 z_1 + \cdots + \epsilon_n z_n)^{\epsilon_1 + \cdots + \epsilon_n - 1} y(y + (1-\epsilon_1)z_1 + \cdots + (1-\epsilon_n)z_n)^{n-1-\epsilon_1 - \cdots - \epsilon_n}$$
$$= (x+y)(x+y+z_1 + \cdots + z_n)^{n-1},$$

where the sum is over all 2^n choices of $\epsilon_1, \ldots, \epsilon_n$ equal to 0 or 1.

31. [*M24*] Solve exercise 5 for ordered trees; that is, derive the generating function for the number of unlabeled ordered trees with n terminal nodes and no nodes of degree 1.

32. [*M37*] (A. Erdélyi and I. M. H. Etherington, *Edinburgh Math. Notes* **32** (1941), 7–12.) How many (ordered, unlabeled) trees are there with n_0 nodes of degree 0, n_1 of degree 1, $\ldots$, n_m of degree m, and none of degree higher than m? (An explicit solution to this problem can be given in terms of factorials, thereby considerably generalizing the result of exercise 11.)

▸ **33.** [*M28*] The text gives an explicit power series solution for the equation $w = y_1 e^{z_1 w} + \cdots + y_r e^{z_r w}$, based on enumeration formulas for certain oriented forests. Similarly, show that the enumeration formula of exercise 32 leads to an explicit power series solution to the equation

$$w = z_1 w^{e_1} + z_2 w^{e_2} + \cdots + z_r w^{e_r},$$

expressing w as a power series in $z_1, \ldots, z_r$. (Here $e_1, \ldots, e_r$ are fixed nonnegative integers, at least one of which is zero.)

2.3.4.5. Path length. The concept of the "path length" of a tree is of great importance in the analysis of algorithms, since this quantity is often directly related to the execution time. Our primary concern is with binary trees, since they are so close to actual computer representations.

In the following discussion we will extend each binary tree diagram by adding special nodes wherever a null subtree was present in the original tree, so that

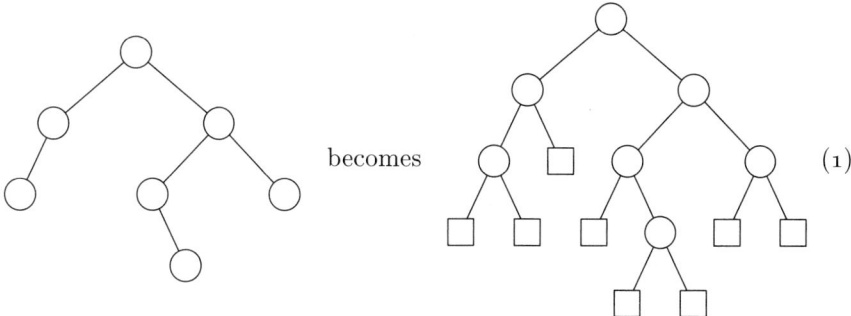

becomes   (1)

The latter is called an *extended binary tree*. After the square-shaped nodes have been added in this way, the structure is sometimes more convenient to deal with, and we shall therefore meet extended binary trees frequently in later chapters. It is clear that every circular node has two children and every square node has none. (Compare with exercise 2.3–20.) If there are n circular nodes and s square nodes, we have $n + s - 1$ edges (since the diagram is a free tree); counting another way, by the number of children, we see that there are $2n$ edges. Hence it is clear that

$$s = n + 1; \qquad (2)$$

in other words, the number of "external" nodes just added is one more than the number of "internal" nodes we had originally. (For another proof, see exercise 2.3.1–14.) Formula (2) is correct even when $n = 0$.

Assume that a binary tree has been extended in this way. The *external path length of the tree*, E, is defined to be the sum — taken over all external (square) nodes — of the lengths of the paths from the root to each node. The *internal path length*, I, is the same quantity summed over the internal (circular) nodes. In (1) the external path length is

$$E = 3 + 3 + 2 + 3 + 4 + 4 + 3 + 3 = 25,$$

and the internal path length is

$$I = 2 + 1 + 0 + 2 + 3 + 1 + 2 = 11.$$

These two quantities are always related by the formula

$$E = I + 2n, \qquad (3)$$

where n is the number of internal nodes.

To prove formula (3), consider deleting an internal node V at a distance k from the root, where both children of V are external. The quantity E goes down by $2(k + 1)$, since the children of V are removed, then it goes up by k, since V becomes external; so the net change in E is $-k - 2$. The net change in I is $-k$, so (3) follows by induction.

It is not hard to see that the internal path length (and hence the external path length also) is greatest when we have a degenerate tree with linear structure; in that case the internal path length is

$$(n - 1) + (n - 2) + \cdots + 1 + 0 = \frac{n^2 - n}{2}.$$

It can be shown that the "average" path length over all binary trees is essentially proportional to $n\sqrt{n}$ (see exercise 5).

Consider now the problem of constructing a binary tree with n nodes that has *minimum* path length. Such a tree will be important, since it will minimize the computation time for various algorithms. Clearly, only one node (the root) can be at zero distance from the root; at most two nodes can be at distance 1 from the root, at most four can be 2 away, and so on. Therefore *the internal path length is always at least as big as the sum of the first n terms of the series*

$$0,\ 1,\ 1,\ 2,\ 2,\ 2,\ 2,\ 3,\ 3,\ 3,\ 3,\ 3,\ 3,\ 3,\ 3,\ 4,\ 4,\ 4,\ 4, \ldots .$$

This is the sum $\sum_{k=1}^{n} \lfloor \lg k \rfloor$, which we know from exercise 1.2.4–42 is

$$(n + 1)q - 2^{q+1} + 2, \qquad q = \lfloor \lg(n + 1) \rfloor. \qquad (4)$$

The optimum value (4) is $n \lg n + O(n)$, since $q = \lg n + O(1)$; it is clearly achieved in a tree that looks like this (illustrated for $n = 12$):

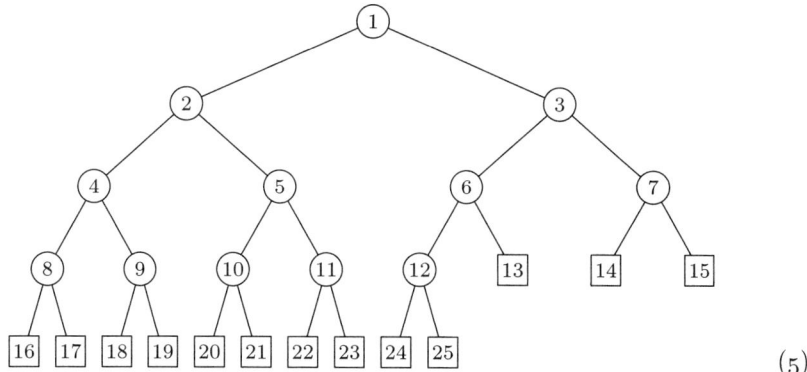

$$(5)$$

A tree such as (5) is called the *complete binary tree* with n internal nodes. In the general case we can number the internal nodes $1, 2, \ldots, n$; this numbering has the useful property that the parent of node k is node $\lfloor k/2 \rfloor$, and the children of node k are nodes $2k$ and $2k + 1$. The external nodes are numbered $n + 1$ through $2n + 1$, inclusive.

It follows that a complete binary tree may simply be represented in sequential memory locations, with the structure implicit in the locations of the nodes (not in links). The complete binary tree appears explicitly or implicitly in many important computer algorithms, so the reader should give it special attention.

These concepts have important generalizations to ternary, quaternary, and higher-order trees. We define a *t-ary tree* as a set of nodes that is either empty or consists of a root and t ordered, disjoint t-ary trees. (This generalizes the definition of binary tree in Section 2.3.) The *complete ternary tree* with 12 internal nodes is

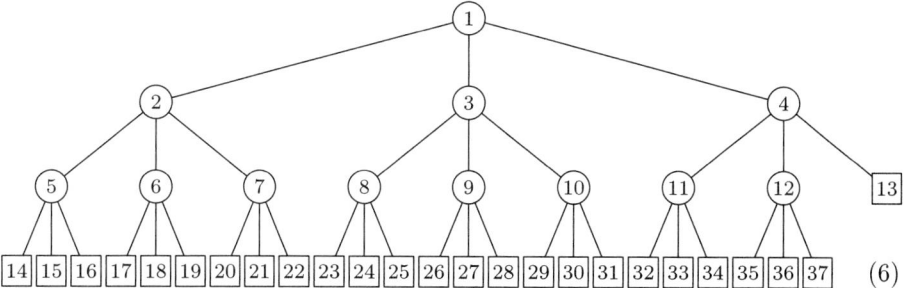

$$(6)$$

It is easy to see that the same construction works for any $t \geq 2$. In the complete t-ary tree with internal nodes $\{1, 2, \ldots, n\}$, the parent of node k is node

$$\lfloor (k + t - 2)/t \rfloor = \lceil (k - 1)/t \rceil,$$

and the children of node k are

$$t(k - 1) + 2, \quad t(k - 1) + 3, \quad \ldots, \quad tk + 1.$$

This tree has the minimum internal path length among all t-ary trees with n internal nodes; exercise 8 proves that its internal path length is

$$\left(n + \frac{1}{t-1}\right)q - \frac{(t^{q+1} - t)}{(t-1)^2}, \qquad q = \lfloor \log_t((t-1)n + 1) \rfloor. \tag{7}$$

These results have another important generalization if we shift our point of view slightly. Suppose that we are given m real numbers $w_1, w_2, \ldots, w_m$; the problem is to find an extended binary tree with m external nodes, and to associate the numbers $w_1, \ldots, w_m$ with these nodes in such a way that the sum $\sum w_j l_j$ is minimized, where l_j is the length of path from the root and the sum is taken over all external nodes. For example, if the given numbers are 2, 3, 4, 11, we can form extended binary trees such as these three:

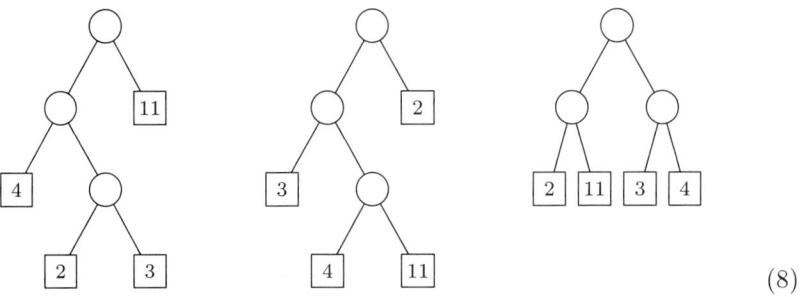

$$\tag{8}$$

Here the "weighted" path lengths $\sum w_j l_j$ are 34, 53, and 40, respectively. (Therefore a perfectly balanced tree does *not* give the minimum weighted path length when the weights are 2, 3, 4, and 11, although we have seen that it does give the minimum in the special case $w_1 = w_2 = \cdots = w_m = 1$.)

Several interpretations of weighted path length arise in connection with different computer algorithms; for example, we can apply it to the merging of sorted sequences of respective lengths $w_1, w_2, \ldots, w_m$ (see Chapter 5). One of the most straightforward applications of this idea is to consider a binary tree as a general search procedure, where we start at the root and then make some test; the outcome of the test sends us to one of the two branches, where we may make further tests, etc. For example, if we want to decide which of four different alternatives is true, and if these possibilities will be true with the respective probabilities $\frac{2}{20}$, $\frac{3}{20}$, $\frac{4}{20}$, and $\frac{11}{20}$, a tree that minimizes the weighted path length will constitute an *optimal search procedure*. [These are the weights shown in (8), times a scale factor.]

An elegant algorithm for finding a tree with minimum weighted path length was discovered by D. Huffman [*Proc. IRE* **40** (1952), 1098–1101]: First find the two w's of lowest value, say w_1 and w_2. Then solve the problem for $m - 1$ weights $w_1 + w_2, w_3, \ldots, w_m$, and replace the node

$$\boxed{w_1 + w_2} \tag{9}$$

in this solution by

$$\begin{array}{c} \bigcirc \\ \diagup \quad \diagdown \\ \boxed{w_1} \quad \boxed{w_2} \end{array} \qquad (10)$$

As an example of Huffman's method, let us find the optimal tree for the weights 2, 3, 5, 7, 11, 13, 17, 19, 23, 29, 31, 37, 41. First we combine $2 + 3$, and look for the solution to $5, 5, 7, \ldots, 41$; then we combine $5 + 5$, etc. The computation is summarized as follows:

2	3	5	7	11	13	17	19	23	29	31	37	41
	5	5	7	11	13	17	19	23	29	31	37	41
		10	7	11	13	17	19	23	29	31	37	41
			17	11	13	17	19	23	29	31	37	41
			17		24	17	19	23	29	31	37	41
					24	34	19	23	29	31	37	41
					24	34		42	29	31	37	41
						34		42	53	31	37	41
								42	53	65	37	41
								42	53	65		78
									95	65		78
									95			143
												238

Therefore the following tree corresponds to Huffman's construction:

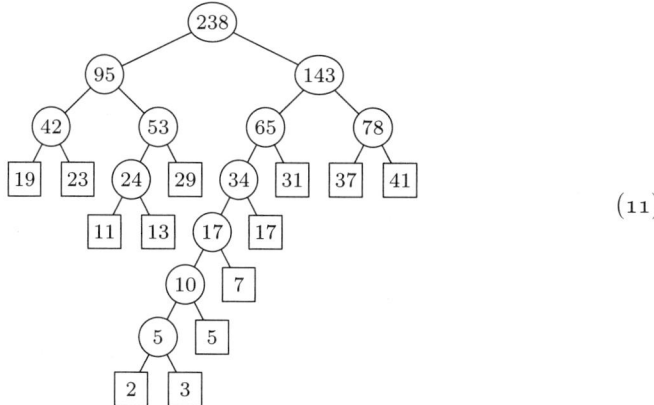

$$(11)$$

(The numbers inside the circular nodes show the correspondence between this tree and our computation; see also exercise 9.)

It is not hard to prove that this method does in fact minimize the weighted path length, by induction on m. Suppose we have $w_1 \le w_2 \le w_3 \le \cdots \le w_m$, where $m \ge 2$, and suppose that we are given a tree that minimizes the weighted path length. (Such a tree certainly exists, since only finitely many binary trees with m terminal nodes are possible.) Let V be an internal node of maximum distance from the root. If w_1 and w_2 are not the weights already attached to the children of V, we can interchange them with the values that are already there;

such an interchange does not increase the weighted path length. Thus there is a tree that minimizes the weighted path length and contains the subtree (10). Now it is easy to prove that the weighted path length of a tree for the weights $w_1, \ldots, w_m$ that contains (10) as a subtree is minimized if and only if that tree with (10) replaced by (9) has minimum path length for the weights $w_1 + w_2, w_3, \ldots, w_m$. (See exercise 9.)

Every time this construction combines two weights, they are at least as big as the weights previously combined, if the given w_i were nonnegative. This means that there is a neat way to find Huffman's tree, provided that the given weights have been sorted into nondecreasing order: We simply maintain two queues, one containing the original weights and the other containing the combined weights. At each step the smallest unused weight will appear at the front of one of the queues, so we never have to search for it. See exercise 13, which shows that the same idea works even when the weights might be negative.

In general, there are many trees that minimize $\sum w_j l_j$. If the algorithm sketched in the preceding paragraph always uses an original weight instead of a combined weight in case of ties, then the tree it constructs has the smallest value of $\max l_j$ and of $\sum l_j$ among all trees that minimize $\sum w_j l_j$. If the weights are positive, this tree actually minimizes $\sum w_j f(l_j)$ for *any* convex function f, over all such trees. [See E. S. Schwartz, *Information and Control* **7** (1964), 37–44; G. Markowsky, *Acta Informatica* **16** (1981), 363–370.]

Huffman's method can be generalized to t-ary trees as well as binary trees. (See exercise 10.) Another important generalization of Huffman's method is discussed in Section 6.2.2. Further discussion of path length appears in Sections 5.3.1, 5.4.9, and 6.3.

EXERCISES

1. [*12*] Are there any other binary trees with 12 internal nodes and minimum path length, besides the complete binary tree (5)?

2. [*17*] Draw an extended binary tree with terminal nodes containing the weights 1, 4, 9, 16, 25, 36, 49, 64, 81, 100, having minimum weighted path length.

▶ **3.** [*M24*] An extended binary tree with m external nodes determines a set of path lengths $l_1, l_2, \ldots, l_m$ that describe the lengths of paths from the root to the respective external nodes. Conversely, if we are given a set of numbers $l_1, l_2, \ldots, l_m$, is it always possible to construct an extended binary tree in which these numbers are the path lengths in some order? Show that this is possible if and only if $\sum_{j=1}^{m} 2^{-l_j} = 1$.

▶ **4.** [*M25*] (E. S. Schwartz and B. Kallick.) Assume that $w_1 \le w_2 \le \cdots \le w_m$. Show that there is an extended binary tree that minimizes $\sum w_j l_j$ and for which the terminal nodes in left to right order contain the respective values $w_1, w_2, \ldots, w_m$. [For example, tree (11) does *not* meet this condition since the weights appear in the order 19, 23, 11, 13, 29, 2, 3, 5, 7, 17, 31, 37, 41. We seek a tree for which the weights appear in ascending order, and this does not always happen with Huffman's construction.]

5. [*HM26*] Let

$$B(w, z) = \sum_{n, p \ge 0} b_{np} w^p z^n,$$

where b_{np} is the number of binary trees with n nodes and internal path length p. [Thus,

$$B(w,z) = 1 + z + 2wz^2 + (w^2 + 4w^3)z^3 + (4w^4 + 2w^5 + 8w^6)z^4 + \cdots;$$

$B(1,z)$ is the function $B(z)$ of Eq. (13) in Section 2.3.4.4.]

  a) Find a functional relation that characterizes $B(w,z)$, generalizing 2.3.4.4–(12).

  b) Use the result of (a) to determine the *average internal path length* of a binary tree with n nodes, assuming that each of the $\frac{1}{n+1}\binom{2n}{n}$ trees is equally probable.

  c) Find the asymptotic value of this quantity.

6. [*16*] If a t-ary tree is extended with square nodes as in (1), what is the relation between the number of square and circular nodes corresponding to Eq. (2)?

7. [*M21*] What is the relation between external and internal path length in a t-ary tree? (See exercise 6; a generalization of Eq. (3) is desired.)

8. [*M23*] Prove Eq. (7).

9. [*M21*] The numbers that appear in the circular nodes of (11) are equal to the sums of the weights in the external nodes of the corresponding subtree. Show that the sum of all values in the circular nodes is equal to the weighted path length.

▶ **10.** [*M26*] (D. Huffman.) Show how to construct a t-ary tree with minimum weighted path length, given nonnegative weights $w_1, w_2, \ldots, w_m$. Construct an optimal ternary tree for weights 1, 4, 9, 16, 25, 36, 49, 64, 81, 100.

11. [*16*] Is there any connection between the complete binary tree (5) and the "Dewey decimal notation" for binary trees described in exercise 2.3.1–5?

▶ **12.** [*M20*] Suppose that a node has been chosen at random in a binary tree, with each node equally likely. Show that the average size of the subtree rooted at that node is related to the path length of the tree.

13. [*22*] Design an algorithm that begins with m weights $w_1 \le w_2 \le \cdots \le w_m$ and constructs an extended binary tree having minimum weighted path length. Represent the final tree in three arrays

$$A[1]\ldots A[2m-1], \quad L[1]\ldots L[m-1], \quad R[1]\ldots R[m-1];$$

here $L[i]$ and $R[i]$ point to the left and right children of internal node i, the root is node 1, and $A[i]$ is the weight of node i. The original weights should appear as the external node weights $A[m], \ldots, A[2m-1]$. Your algorithm should make fewer than $2m$ weight-comparisons. *Caution:* Some or all of the given weights may be negative!

14. [*25*] (T. C. Hu and A. C. Tucker.) After k steps of Huffman's algorithm, the nodes combined so far form a forest of $m-k$ extended binary trees. Prove that this forest has the smallest total weighted path length, among all forests of $m-k$ extended binary trees that have the given weights.

15. [*M25*] Show that a Huffman-like algorithm will find an extended binary tree that minimizes (a) $\max(w_1 + l_1, \ldots, w_m + l_m)$; (b) $w_1 x^{l_1} + \cdots + w_m x^{l_m}$, given $x > 1$.

16. [*M25*] (F. K. Hwang.) Let $w_1 \le \cdots \le w_m$ and $w'_1 \le \cdots \le w'_m$ be two sets of weights with

$$\sum_{j=1}^{k} w_j \le \sum_{j=1}^{k} w'_j \qquad \text{for } 1 \le k \le m.$$

Prove that the minimum weighted path lengths satisfy $\sum_{j=1}^{m} w_j l_j \le \sum_{j=1}^{m} w'_j l'_j$.

17. [*HM30*] (C. R. Glassey and R. M. Karp.) Let $s_1, \ldots, s_{m-1}$ be the numbers inside the internal (circular) nodes of an extended binary tree formed by Huffman's algorithm, in the order of construction. Let $s'_1, \ldots, s'_{m-1}$ be the internal node weights of any extended binary tree on the same set of weights $\{w_1, \ldots, w_m\}$, listed in any order such that each nonroot internal node appears before its parent. (a) Prove that $\sum_{j=1}^k s_j \leq \sum_{j=1}^k s'_j$ for $1 \leq k < m$. (b) The result of (a) is equivalent to

$$\sum_{j=1}^{m-1} f(s_j) \leq \sum_{j=1}^{m-1} f(s'_j)$$

for every nondecreasing concave function f, namely every function f with $f'(x) \geq 0$ and $f''(x) \leq 0$. [See Hardy, Littlewood, and Pólya, *Messenger of Math.* **58** (1929), 145–152.] Use this fact to show that the minimum value in the recurrence

$$F(n) = f(n) + \min_{1 \leq k < n} \left(F(k) + F(n-k) \right), \qquad F(1) = 0$$

always occurs when $k = 2^{\lceil \lg(n/3) \rceil}$, given any function $f(n)$ with the property that $\Delta f(n) = f(n+1) - f(n) \geq 0$ and $\Delta^2 f(n) = \Delta f(n+1) - \Delta f(n) \leq 0$.

*2.3.4.6. History and bibliography. Trees have of course been in existence since the third day of creation, and through the ages tree structures (especially *family* trees) have been in common use. The concept of tree as a formally defined *mathematical* entity seems to have appeared first in the work of G. Kirchhoff [*Annalen der Physik und Chemie* **72** (1847), 497–508, English translation in *IRE Transactions* **CT-5** (1958), 4–7]; Kirchhoff used free trees to find a set of fundamental cycles in an electrical network in connection with the law that bears his name, essentially as we did in Section 2.3.4.1. The concept also appeared at about the same time in the book *Geometrie der Lage* (pages 20–21) by K. G. Chr. von Staudt. The name "tree" and many results dealing mostly with enumeration of trees began to appear ten years later in a series of papers by Arthur Cayley [see *Collected Mathematical Papers of A. Cayley* **3** (1857), 242–246; **4** (1859), 112–115; **9** (1874), 202–204; **9** (1875), 427–460; **10** (1877), 598–600; **11** (1881), 365–367; **13** (1889), 26–28]. Cayley was unaware of the previous work of Kirchhoff and von Staudt; his investigations began with studies of the structure of algebraic formulas, and they were later inspired chiefly by applications to the problem of isomers in chemistry. Tree structures were also studied independently by C. W. Borchardt [*Crelle* **57** (1860), 111–121]; J. B. Listing [*Göttinger Abhandlungen, Math. Classe,* **10** (1862), 137–139]; and C. Jordan [*Crelle* **70** (1869), 185–190].

The "infinity lemma" was formulated first by Dénes Kőnig [*Fundamenta Math.* **8** (1926), 114–134], and he gave it a prominent place in his classic book *Theorie der endlichen und unendlichen Graphen* (Leipzig: 1936), Chapter 6. A similar result called the "fan theorem" occurred slightly earlier in the work of L. E. J. Brouwer [*Verhandelingen Akad. Amsterdam* **12** (1919), 7], but this involved much stronger hypotheses; see A. Heyting, *Intuitionism* (1956), Section 3.4, for a discussion of Brouwer's work.

Formula (3) of Section 2.3.4.4 for enumerating unlabeled oriented trees was given by Cayley in his first paper on trees. In his second paper he enumerated unlabeled ordered trees; an equivalent problem in geometry (see exercise 1) had already been proposed and solved by L. Euler, who mentioned his results in a letter to C. Goldbach on 4 September 1751 [see J. von Segner and L. Euler, *Novi Commentarii Academiæ Scientiarum Petropolitanæ* **7** (1758–1759), summary 13–15, 203–210]. Euler's problem was the subject of seven papers by G. Lamé, E. Catalan, O. Rodrigues, and J. Binet in *Journal de mathématiques* **3, 4** (1838, 1839); additional references appear in the answer to exercise 2.2.1–4. The corresponding numbers are now commonly called "Catalan numbers." A Mongolian Chinese mathematician, An-T'u Ming, had encountered the Catalan numbers before 1750 in his study of infinite series, but he did not relate them to trees or other combinatorial objects [see J. Luo, *Acta Scientiarum Naturalium Universitatis Intramongolicæ* **19** (1988), 239–245; *Combinatorics and Graph Theory* (World Scientific Publishing, 1993), 68–70]. Catalan numbers occur in an enormous number of different contexts; Richard Stanley explains more than 60 of them in his magnificent book *Enumerative Combinatorics* **2** (Cambridge Univ. Press, 1999), Chapter 6. Perhaps most surprising of all is the Catalan connection to certain arrangements of numbers that H. S. M. Coxeter has called "frieze patterns" because of their symmetry; see exercise 4.

The formula n^{n-2} for the number of *labeled* free trees was discovered by J. J. Sylvester [*Quart. J. Pure and Applied Math.* **1** (1857), 55–56], as a byproduct of his evaluation of a certain determinant (exercise 2.3.4.2–28). Cayley gave an independent derivation of the formula in 1889 [see the reference above]; his discussion, which was extremely vague, hinted at a connection between labeled oriented trees and $(n-1)$-tuples of numbers. An explicit correspondence demonstrating such a connection was first published by Heinz Prüfer [*Arch. Math. und Phys.* **27** (1918), 142–144], quite independently of Cayley's prior work. A large literature on this subject has developed, and the classical results are surveyed beautifully in J. W. Moon's book, *Counting Labelled Trees* (Montreal: Canadian Math. Congress, 1970).

A very important paper on the enumeration of trees and many other kinds of combinatorial structures was published by G. Pólya in *Acta Math.* **68** (1937), 145–253. For a discussion of enumeration problems for graphs and an excellent bibliography of the early literature, see the survey by Frank Harary in *Graph Theory and Theoretical Physics* (London: Academic Press, 1967), 1–41.

The principle of minimizing weighted path length by repeatedly combining the smallest weights was discovered by D. Huffman [*Proc. IRE* **40** (1952), 1098–1101], in connection with the design of codes for minimizing message lengths. The same idea was independently published by Seth Zimmerman [*AMM* **66** (1959), 690–693].

Several other noteworthy papers about the theory of tree structures have been cited in Sections 2.3.4.1 through 2.3.4.5 in connection with particular topics.

EXERCISES

▶ **1.** [*21*] Find a simple one-to-one correspondence between binary trees with n nodes and dissections of an $(n+2)$-sided convex polygon into n triangles, assuming that the sides of the polygon are distinct.

▶ **2.** [*M26*] T. P. Kirkman conjectured in 1857 that the number of ways to draw k non-overlapping diagonals in an r-sided polygon is $\binom{r+k}{k+1}\binom{r-3}{k}/(r+k)$.

    a) Extend the correspondence of exercise 1 to obtain an equivalent problem about the enumeration of trees.

    b) Prove Kirkman's conjecture by using the methods of exercise 2.3.4.4–32.

▶ **3.** [*M30*] Consider all ways of partitioning the vertices of a convex n-gon into k non-empty parts, in such a way that no diagonal between two vertices of one part crosses a diagonal between two vertices of another part.

    a) Find a one-to-one correspondence between noncrossing partitions and an interesting class of tree structures.

    b) Given n and k, how many ways are there to make such a partition?

▶ **4.** [*M38*] (Conway and Coxeter.) A *frieze pattern* is an infinite array such as

```
1 1 1 1 1 1 1 1 1 1 1 1 1 1 1 1 1 1 1 ...
 3 1 3 1 4 1 2 3 1 3 1 4 1 2 3 1 3 1 4 ...
5 2 2 2 3 3 1 5 2 2 2 3 3 1 5 2 2 2 3 ...
 3 3 1 5 2 2 2 3 3 1 5 2 2 2 3 3 1 5 2 ...
1 4 1 2 3 1 3 1 4 1 2 3 1 3 1 4 1 2 3 ...
 1 1 1 1 1 1 1 1 1 1 1 1 1 1 1 1 1 1 1 ...
```

in which the top and bottom rows consist entirely of 1s, and each diamond of adjacent values $a \ {}^{b}_{c} \ d$ satisfies $ad - bc = 1$. Find a one-to-one correspondence between n-node binary trees and $(n+1)$-rowed frieze patterns of positive integers.

2.3.5. Lists and Garbage Collection

Near the beginning of Section 2.3 we defined a List informally as "a finite sequence of zero or more atoms or Lists."

    Any forest is a List; for example,

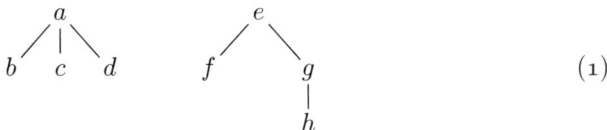

$$(1)$$

may be regarded as the List

$$\bigl(a\colon (b, c, d), e\colon (f, g\colon (h))\bigr), \qquad (2)$$

and the corresponding List diagram would be

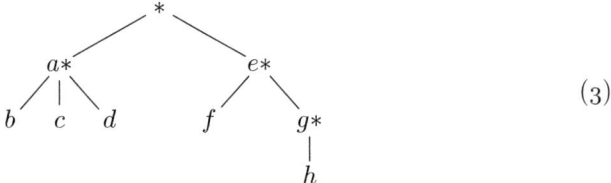

$$(3)$$

    The reader should review at this point the introduction to Lists given earlier, in particular (3), (4), (5), (6), (7) in the opening pages of Section 2.3. Recall that, in (2) above, the notation "$a\colon (b, c, d)$" means that (b, c, d) is a List of three atoms, which has been labeled with the attribute "a". This convention is compatible

with our general policy that each node of a tree may contain information besides
its structural connections. However, as was discussed for trees in Section 2.3.3,
it is quite possible and sometimes desirable to insist that all Lists be unlabeled,
so that all the information appears in the atoms.

Although any forest may be regarded as a List, the converse is not true.
The following List is perhaps more typical than (2) and (3) since it shows how
the restrictions of tree structure might be violated:

$$L = \big(a\colon N, b, c\colon (d\colon N), e\colon L\big), \qquad N = \big(f\colon (\,), g\colon (h\colon L, j\colon N)\big) \tag{4}$$

which may be diagrammed as

$$\tag{5}$$

[Compare with the example in 2.3–(7). The form of these diagrams need not be
taken too seriously.]

As we might expect, there are many ways to represent List structures within
a computer memory. These methods are usually variations on the same basic
theme by which we have used binary trees to represent general forests of trees:
One field, say RLINK, is used to point to the next element of a List, and another
field DLINK may be used to point to the first element of a sub-List. By a natural
extension of the memory representation described in Section 2.3.2, we would
represent the List (5) as follows:

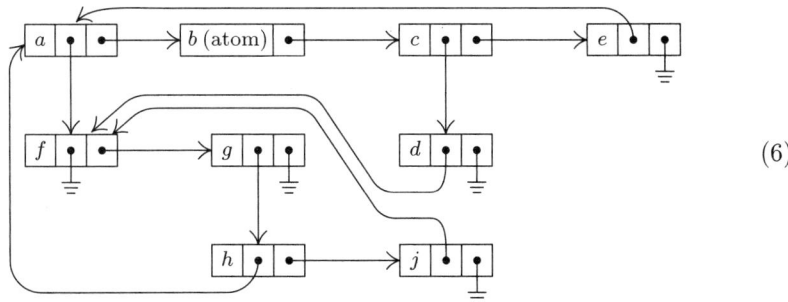

$$\tag{6}$$

Unfortunately, this simple idea is *not* quite adequate for the most common
List processing applications. For example, suppose that we have the List $L =
\big(A, a, (A, A)\big)$, which contains three references to another List $A = (b, c, d)$. One
of the typical List processing operations is to remove the leftmost element of A,
so that A becomes (c, d); but this requires *three* changes to the representation
of L, if we are to use the technique shown in (6), since each pointer to A points

to the element b that is being deleted. A moment's reflection will convince the reader that it is extremely undesirable to change the pointers in every reference to A just because the first element of A is being deleted. (In this example we could try to be tricky, assuming that there are no pointers to the element c, by copying the entire element c into the location formerly occupied by b and then deleting the old element c. But this trick fails to work when A loses its last element and becomes empty.)

For this reason the representation scheme (6) is generally replaced by another scheme that is similar, but uses a *List head* to begin each List, as was introduced in Section 2.2.4. Each List contains an additional node called its List head, so that the configuration (6) would, for example, be represented thus:

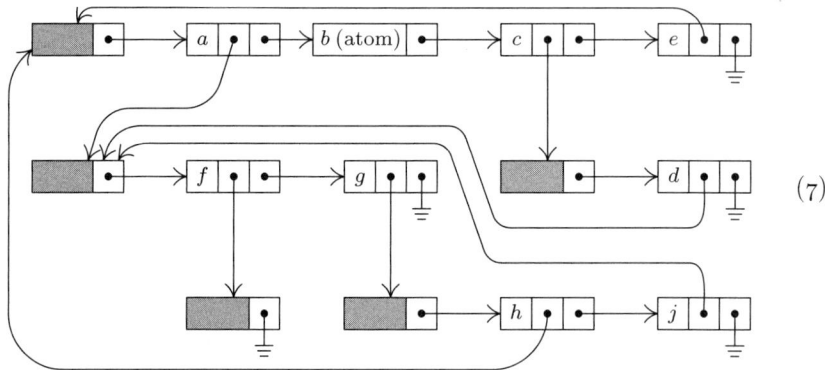

$$(7)$$

The introduction of such header nodes is not really a waste of memory space in practice, since many uses for the apparently unused fields — the shaded areas in diagram (7) — generally present themselves. For example, there is room for a reference count, or a pointer to the right end of the List, or an alphabetic name, or a "scratch" field that aids traversal algorithms, etc.

In our original diagram (6), the node containing b is an atom while the node containing f specifies an empty List. These two things are structurally identical, so the reader would be quite justified in asking why we bother to talk about "atoms" at all; with no loss of generality we could have defined Lists as merely "a finite sequence of zero or more Lists," with our usual convention that each node of a List may contain data besides its structural information. This point of view is certainly defensible and it makes the concept of an "atom" seem very artificial. There is, however, a good reason for singling out atoms as we have done, when efficient use of computer memory is taken into consideration, since atoms are not subject to the same sort of general-purpose manipulation that is desired for Lists. The memory representation (6) shows there is probably more room for information in an atomic node, b, than in a List node, f; and when List head nodes are also present as in (7), there is a dramatic difference between the storage requirements for the nodes b and f. Thus the concept of atoms is introduced primarily to aid in the effective use of computer memory. Typical

Lists contain many more atoms than our example would indicate; the example of (4)–(7) is intended to show the complexities that are possible, not the simplicities that are usual.

A List is in essence nothing more than a linear list whose elements may contain pointers to other Lists. The common operations we wish to perform on Lists are the usual ones desired for linear lists (creation, destruction, insertion, deletion, splitting, concatenation), plus further operations that are primarily of interest for tree structures (copying, traversal, input and output of nested information). For these purposes any of the three basic techniques for representing linked linear lists in memory — namely straight, circular, or double linkage — can be used, with varying degrees of efficiency depending on the algorithms being employed. For these three types of representation, diagram (7) might appear in memory as follows:

Memory location	Straight linkage INFO	DLINK	RLINK	Circular linkage INFO	DLINK	RLINK	Double linkage INFO	DLINK	LLINK	RLINK	
010:	—	head	020	—	head	020	—	head	050	020	
020:	a	060	030	a	060	030	a	060	010	030	
030:	b	atom	040	b	atom	040	b	atom	020	040	
040:	c	090	050	c	090	050	c	090	030	050	
050:	e	010	Λ	e	010	010	e	010	040	010	
060:	—	head	070	—	head	070	—	head	080	070	(8)
070:	f	110	080	f	110	080	f	110	060	080	
080:	g	120	Λ	g	120	060	g	120	070	060	
090:	—	head	100	—	head	100	—	head	100	100	
100:	d	060	Λ	d	060	090	d	060	090	090	
110:	—	head	Λ	—	head	110	—	head	110	110	
120:	—	head	130	—	head	130	—	head	140	130	
130:	h	010	140	h	010	140	h	010	120	140	
140:	j	060	Λ	j	060	120	j	060	130	120	

Here "LLINK" is used for a pointer to the left in a doubly linked representation. The INFO and DLINK fields are identical in all three forms.

There is no need to repeat here the algorithms for List manipulation in any of these three forms, since we have already discussed the ideas many times. The following important points about Lists, which distinguish them from the simpler special cases treated earlier, should however be noted:

1) It is implicit in the memory representation above that atomic nodes are distinguishable from nonatomic nodes; furthermore, when circular or doubly linked Lists are being used, it is desirable to distinguish header nodes from the other types, as an aid in traversing the Lists. Therefore each node generally contains a TYPE field that tells what kind of information the node represents. This TYPE field is often used also to distinguish between various types of atoms (for example, between alphabetic, integer, or floating point quantities, for use when manipulating or displaying the data).

2) The format of nodes for general List manipulation with the MIX computer might be designed in one of the following two ways.

a) Possible one-word format, assuming that all INFO appears in atoms:

$$\boxed{\text{S} \mid \text{T} \mid \text{REF} \mid \text{RLINK}} \tag{9}$$

S (sign): Mark bit used in garbage collection (see below).

T (type): T $= 0$ for List head; T $= 1$ for sub-List element; T > 1 for atoms.

REF: When T $= 0$, REF is a reference count (see below); when T $= 1$, REF points to the List head of the sub-List in question; when T > 1, REF points to a node containing a mark bit and five bytes of atomic information.

RLINK: Pointer for straight or circular linkage as in (8).

b) Possible two-word format:

$$\boxed{\begin{array}{c} \text{S} \mid \text{T} \mid \text{LLINK} \mid \text{RLINK} \\ \hline \text{INFO} \end{array}} \tag{10}$$

S, T: As in (9).

LLINK, RLINK: The usual pointers for double linkage as in (8).

INFO: A full word of information associated with this node; for a header node this may include a reference count, a running pointer to the interior of the List to facilitate linear traversal, an alphabetic name, etc. When T $= 1$ this information includes DLINK.

3) It is clear that Lists are very general structures; indeed, it seems fair to state that any structure whatsoever can be represented as a List when appropriate conventions are made. Because of this universality of Lists, a large number of programming systems have been designed to facilitate List manipulation, and there are usually several such systems available at any computer installation. Such systems are based on a general-purpose format for nodes such as (9) or (10) above, designed for flexibility in List operations. Actually, it is clear that this general-purpose format is usually not the best format suited to a *particular* application, and the processing time using the general-purpose routines is noticeably slower than a person would achieve by hand-tailoring the system to a particular problem. For example, it is easy to see that nearly all of the applications we have worked out so far in this chapter would be encumbered by a general-List representation as in (9) or (10) instead of the node format that was given in each case. A List manipulation routine must often examine the T-field when it processes nodes, and that was not needed in any of our programs so far. This loss of efficiency is repaid in many instances by the comparative ease of programming and the reduction of debugging time when a general-purpose system is used.

4) There is also an extremely significant difference between algorithms for List processing and the algorithms given previously in this chapter. Since a single

List may be contained in many other Lists, it is by no means clear exactly when a List should be returned to the pool of available storage. Our algorithms so far have always said "AVAIL ⇐ X", whenever NODE(X) was no longer needed. But since general Lists can grow and die in a completely unpredictable manner, it is often quite difficult to tell just when a particular node is superfluous. Therefore the problem of maintaining the list of available space is considerably more difficult with Lists than it was in the simple cases considered previously. We will devote the rest of this section to a discussion of the storage reclamation problem.

Let us imagine that we are designing a general-purpose List processing system that will be used by hundreds of other programmers. Two principal methods have been suggested for maintaining the available space list: the use of *reference counters*, and *garbage collection*. The reference-counter technique makes use of a new field in each node, which contains a count of how many arrows point to this node. Such a count is rather easy to maintain as a program runs, and whenever it drops to zero, the node in question becomes available. The garbage-collection technique, on the other hand, requires a new one-bit field in each node called the *mark bit*. The idea in this case is to write nearly all the algorithms so that they do not return any nodes to free storage, and to let the program run merrily along until all of the available storage is gone; then a "recycling" algorithm makes use of the mark bits to identify all nodes that are not currently accessible and to return them to available storage, after which the program can continue.

Neither of these two methods is completely satisfactory. The principal drawback of the reference-counter method is that it does not always free all the nodes that are available. It works fine for overlapped Lists (Lists that contain common sub-Lists); but recursive Lists, like our examples L and N in (4), will *never* be returned to storage by the reference-counter technique. Their counts will be nonzero (since they refer to themselves) even when no other List accessible to the running program points to them. Furthermore, the reference-counter method uses a good chunk of space in each node (although this space is sometimes available anyway due to the computer word size).

The difficulty with the garbage-collection technique, besides the annoying loss of a bit in each node, is that it runs very slowly when nearly all the memory space is in use; and in such cases the number of free storage cells found by the reclamation process is not worth the effort. Programs that exceed the capacity of storage (and many undebugged programs do!) often waste a good deal of time calling the garbage collector several almost fruitless times just before storage is finally exhausted. A partial solution to this problem is to let the programmer specify a number k, signifying that processing should not continue after a garbage collection run has found k or fewer free nodes.

Another problem is the occasional difficulty of determining exactly what Lists are not garbage at a given stage. If the programmer has been using any nonstandard techniques or keeping any pointer values in unusual places, chances are good that the garbage collector will go awry. Some of the greatest mysteries in the history of debugging have been caused by the fact that garbage collection suddenly took place at an unexpected time during the running of programs that had worked many times before. Garbage collection also requires that programmers keep valid information in all pointer fields at all times, although we often find it convenient to leave meaningless information in fields that the program doesn't use — for example, the link in the rear node of a queue; see exercise 2.2.3–6.

Although garbage collection requires one mark bit for each node, we could keep a separate table of all the mark bits packed together in another memory area, with a suitable correspondence between the location of a node and its mark bit. On some computers this idea can lead to a method of handling garbage collection that is more attractive than giving up a bit in each node.

J. Weizenbaum has suggested an interesting modification of the reference-counter technique. Using doubly linked List structures, he puts a reference counter only in the header of each List. Thus, when pointer variables traverse a List, they are not included in the reference counts for the individual nodes. If we know the rules by which reference counts are maintained for entire Lists, we know (in theory) how to avoid referring to any List that has a reference count of zero. We also have complete freedom to explicitly override reference counts and to return particular Lists to available storage. These ideas require careful handling; they prove to be somewhat dangerous in the hands of inexperienced programmers, and they've tended to make program debugging more difficult due to the consequences of referring to nodes that have been erased. The nicest part of Weizenbaum's approach is his treatment of Lists whose reference count has just gone to zero: Such a List is appended at the *end* of the current available list — this is easy to do with doubly linked Lists — and it is considered for available space only after all previously available cells are used up. Eventually, as the individual nodes of this List do become available, the reference counters of Lists *they* refer to are decreased by one. This delayed action of erasing Lists is quite efficient with respect to running time; but it tends to make incorrect programs run correctly for awhile! For further details see *CACM* **6** (1963), 524–544.

Algorithms for garbage collection are quite interesting for several reasons. In the first place, such algorithms are useful in other situations when we want to mark all nodes that are directly or indirectly referred to by a given node. (For example, we might want to find all subroutines called directly or indirectly by a certain subroutine, as in exercise 2.2.3–26.)

Garbage collection generally proceeds in two phases. We assume that the mark bits of all nodes are initially zero (or we set them all to zero). Now the first phase marks all the nongarbage nodes, starting from those that are immediately accessible to the main program. The second phase makes a sequential pass over the entire memory pool area, putting all unmarked nodes onto the list of free space. The marking phase is the most interesting, so we will concentrate our attention on it. Certain variations on the second phase can, however, make it nontrivial; see exercise 9.

When a garbage collection algorithm is running, only a very limited amount of storage is available to control the marking procedure. This intriguing problem will become clear in the following discussion; it is a difficulty that is not appreciated by most people when they first hear about the idea of garbage collection, and for several years there was no good solution to it.

The following marking algorithm is perhaps the most obvious.

Algorithm A (*Marking*). Let the entire memory used for List storage be NODE(1), NODE(2), ..., NODE(M), and suppose that these words either are atoms or contain two link fields ALINK and BLINK. Assume that all nodes are initially *unmarked*. The purpose of this algorithm is to *mark* all of the nodes that can be reached by a chain of ALINK and/or BLINK pointers in nonatomic nodes, starting from a set of "immediately accessible" nodes, that is, nodes pointed to by certain fixed locations in the main program; these fixed pointers are used as a source for all memory accesses.

A1. [Initialize.] Mark all nodes that are immediately accessible. Set $K \leftarrow 1$.

A2. [Does NODE(K) imply another?] Set $K1 \leftarrow K + 1$. If NODE(K) is an atom or unmarked, go to step A3. Otherwise, if NODE(ALINK(K)) is unmarked: Mark it and, if it is not an atom, set $K1 \leftarrow \min(K1, ALINK(K))$. Similarly, if NODE(BLINK(K)) is unmarked: Mark it and, if it is not an atom, set $K1 \leftarrow \min(K1, BLINK(K))$.

A3. [Done?] Set $K \leftarrow K1$. If $K \leq M$, return to step A2; otherwise the algorithm terminates. ∎

Throughout this algorithm and the ones that follow in this section, we will assume for convenience that the nonexistent node "NODE(Λ)" *is marked.* (For example, ALINK(K) or BLINK(K) may equal Λ in step A2.)

A variant of Algorithm A sets $K1 \leftarrow M + 1$ in step A1, removes the operation "$K1 \leftarrow K + 1$" from step A2, and instead changes step A3 to

A3′. [Done?] Set $K \leftarrow K + 1$. If $K \leq M$, return to step A2. Otherwise if $K1 \leq M$, set $K \leftarrow K1$ and $K1 \leftarrow M + 1$ and return to step A2. Otherwise the algorithm terminates. ∎

It is very difficult to give a precise analysis of Algorithm A, or to determine whether it is better or worse than the variant just described, since no meaningful way to describe the probability distribution of the input presents itself. We can say that it takes up time proportional to nM in the worst case, where n is the number of cells it marks; and, in general, we can be sure that it is very slow when n is large. Algorithm A is too slow to make garbage collection a usable technique.

Another fairly evident marking algorithm is to follow all paths and to record branch points on a stack as we go:

Algorithm B (*Marking*). This algorithm achieves the same effect as Algorithm A, using STACK[1], STACK[2], ... as auxiliary storage to keep track of all paths that have not yet been pursued to completion.

B1. [Initialize.] Let T be the number of immediately accessible nodes; mark them and place pointers to them in STACK[1], ..., STACK[T].

B2. [Stack empty?] If T = 0, the algorithm terminates.

B3. [Remove top entry.] Set K ← STACK[T], T ← T − 1.

B4. [Examine links.] If NODE(K) is an atom, return to step B2. Otherwise, if
NODE(ALINK(K)) is unmarked, mark it and set T ← T + 1, STACK[T] ←
ALINK(K); if NODE(BLINK(K)) is unmarked, mark it and set T ← T + 1,
STACK[T] ← BLINK(K). Return to B2. ∎

Algorithm B clearly has an execution time essentially proportional to the
number of cells it marks, and this is as good as we could possibly expect; but it
is not really usable for garbage collection because there is no place to keep the
stack! It does not seem unreasonable to assume that the stack in Algorithm B
might grow up to, say, five percent of the size of memory; but when garbage
collection is called, and all available space has been used up, there is only a
fixed (rather small) number of cells to use for such a stack. Most of the early
garbage collection procedures were essentially based on this algorithm. If the
special stack space was used up, the entire program had to be terminated.

A somewhat better alternative is possible, using a fixed stack size, by combining Algorithms A and B:

Algorithm C (*Marking*). This algorithm achieves the same effect as Algorithms A and B, using an auxiliary table of H cells, STACK[0], STACK[1], ...,
STACK[H − 1].

In this algorithm, the action "insert X on the stack" means the following:
"Set T ← (T + 1) mod H, and STACK[T] ← X. If T = B, set B ← (B + 1) mod H and
K1 ← min(K1, STACK[B])." (Note that T points to the current top of the stack,
and B points one place below the current bottom; STACK essentially operates as
an input-restricted deque.)

C1. [Initialize.] Set T ← H − 1, B ← H − 1, K1 ← M + 1. Mark all the immediately
accessible nodes, and successively insert their locations onto the stack (as
just described above).

C2. [Stack empty?] If T = B, go to C5.

C3. [Remove top entry.] Set K ← STACK[T], T ← (T − 1) mod H.

C4. [Examine links.] If NODE(K) is an atom, return to step C2. Otherwise, if
NODE(ALINK(K)) is unmarked, mark it and insert ALINK(K) on the stack.
Similarly, if NODE(BLINK(K)) is unmarked, mark it and insert BLINK(K) on
the stack. Return to C2.

C5. [Sweep.] If K1 > M, the algorithm terminates. (The variable K1 represents
the smallest location where there is a possibility of a new lead to a node
that should be marked.) Otherwise, if NODE(K1) is an atom or unmarked,
increase K1 by 1 and repeat this step. If NODE(K1) is marked, set K ← K1,
increase K1 by 1, and go to C4. ∎

This algorithm and Algorithm B can be improved if X is never put on the
stack when NODE(X) is an atom; moreover, steps B4 and C4 need not put items
on the stack when they know that the items will immediately be removed. Such

modifications are straightforward and they have been left out to avoid making the algorithms unnecessarily complicated.

Algorithm C is essentially equivalent to Algorithm A when H = 1, and to Algorithm B when H = M; it gradually becomes more efficient as H becomes larger. Unfortunately, Algorithm C defies a precise analysis for the same reason as Algorithm A, and we have no good idea how large H should be to make this method fast enough. It is plausible but uncomfortable to say that a value like H = 50 is sufficient to make Algorithm C usable for garbage collection in most applications.

Algorithms B and C use a stack kept in sequential memory locations; but we have seen earlier in this chapter that linked memory techniques are well suited to maintaining stacks that are not consecutive in memory. This suggests the idea that we might keep the stack of Algorithm B somehow scattered *through the same memory area in which we are collecting garbage*. This could be done easily if we were to give the garbage collection routine a little more room in which to breathe. Suppose, for example, we assume that all Lists are represented as in (9), except that the REF fields of List head nodes are used for garbage collection purposes instead of as reference counts. We can then redesign Algorithm B so that the stack is maintained in the REF fields of the header nodes:

Algorithm D (*Marking*). This algorithm achieves the same effect as Algorithms A, B, and C, but it assumes that the nodes have S, T, REF, and RLINK fields as described above, instead of ALINKs and BLINKs. The S field is used as the mark bit, so that S(P) = 1 means that NODE(P) is marked.

D1. [Initialize.] Set TOP ← Λ. Then for each pointer P to the head of an immediately accessible List (see step A1 of Algorithm A), if S(P) = 0, set S(P) ← 1, REF(P) ← TOP, TOP ← P.

D2. [Stack empty?] If TOP = Λ, the algorithm terminates.

D3. [Remove top entry.] Set P ← TOP, TOP ← REF(P).

D4. [Move through List.] Set P ← RLINK(P); then if P = Λ, or if T(P) = 0, go to D2. Otherwise set S(P) ← 1. If T(P) > 1, set S(REF(P)) ← 1 (thereby marking the atomic information). Otherwise (T(P) = 1), set Q ← REF(P); if Q ≠ Λ and S(Q) = 0, set S(Q) ← 1, REF(Q) ← TOP, TOP ← Q. Repeat step D4. ∎

Algorithm D may be compared to Algorithm B, which is quite similar, and its running time is essentially proportional to the number of nodes marked. However, Algorithm D is *not* recommended without qualification, because its seemingly rather mild restrictions are often too stringent for a general List-processing system. This algorithm essentially requires that all List structures be well-formed, as in (7), whenever garbage collection is called into action. But algorithms for List manipulations *momentarily* leave the List structures malformed, and a garbage collector such as Algorithm D must not be used during those momentary periods. Moreover, care must be taken in step D1 when the program contains pointers to the middle of a List.

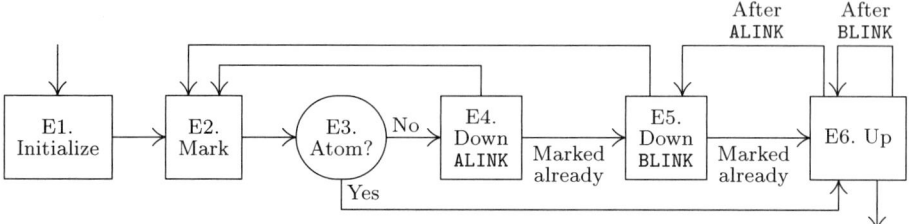

Fig. 38. Algorithm E for marking with no auxiliary stack space.

These considerations bring us to Algorithm E, which is an elegant marking method discovered independently by Peter Deutsch and by Herbert Schorr and W. M. Waite in 1965. The assumptions used in this algorithm are just a little different from those of Algorithms A through D.

Algorithm E (*Marking*). Assume that a collection of nodes is given having the following fields:

MARK (a one-bit field),
ATOM (another one-bit field),
ALINK (a pointer field),
BLINK (a pointer field).

When ATOM = 0, the ALINK and BLINK fields may contain Λ or a pointer to another node of the same format; when ATOM = 1, the contents of the ALINK and BLINK fields are irrelevant to this algorithm.

Given a nonnull pointer P0, this algorithm sets the MARK field equal to 1 in NODE(P0) and in every other node that can be reached from NODE(P0) by a chain of ALINK and BLINK pointers in nodes with ATOM = MARK = 0. The algorithm uses three pointer variables, T, Q, and P. It modifies the links and control bits in such a way that all ATOM, ALINK, and BLINK fields are restored to their original settings after completion, although they may be changed temporarily.

E1. [Initialize.] Set T ← Λ, P ← P0. (Throughout the remainder of this algorithm, the variable T has a dual significance: When T ≠ Λ, it points to the top of what is essentially a stack as in Algorithm D; and the node that T points to once contained a link equal to P in place of the "artificial" stack link that currently occupies NODE(T).)

E2. [Mark.] Set MARK(P) ← 1.

E3. [Atom?] If ATOM(P) = 1, go to E6.

E4. [Down ALINK.] Set Q ← ALINK(P). If Q ≠ Λ and MARK(Q) = 0, set ATOM(P) ← 1, ALINK(P) ← T, T ← P, P ← Q, and go to E2. (Here the ATOM field and ALINK fields are temporarily being altered, so that the List structure in certain marked nodes has been rather drastically changed. But these changes will be restored in step E6.)

E5. [Down BLINK.] Set Q ← BLINK(P). If Q ≠ Λ and MARK(Q) = 0, set BLINK(P) ← T, T ← P, P ← Q, and go to E2.

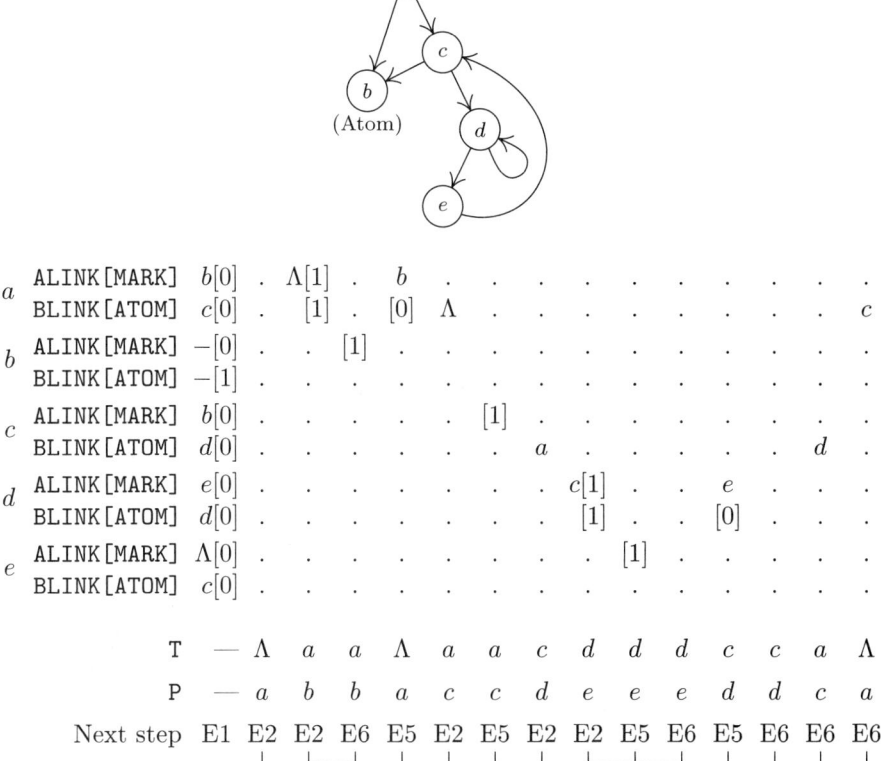

a	ALINK[MARK]	$b[0]$	.	$\Lambda[1]$	.	b	.	.	.	.	.	.	.	.	.	.
	BLINK[ATOM]	$c[0]$	.	$[1]$	.	$[0]$	Λ	.	.	.	.	.	.	.	.	c
b	ALINK[MARK]	$-[0]$	.	.	$[1]$	.	.	.	.	.	.	.	.	.	.	.
	BLINK[ATOM]	$-[1]$	.	.	.	.	.	.	.	.	.	.	.	.	.	.
c	ALINK[MARK]	$b[0]$	.	.	.	.	.	$[1]$	.	.	.	.	.	.	.	.
	BLINK[ATOM]	$d[0]$	.	.	.	.	.	.	a	.	.	.	.	.	d	.
d	ALINK[MARK]	$e[0]$	.	.	.	.	.	.	.	$c[1]$	.	.	e	.	.	.
	BLINK[ATOM]	$d[0]$	.	.	.	.	.	.	.	$[1]$	.	.	$[0]$	.	.	.
e	ALINK[MARK]	$\Lambda[0]$	.	.	.	.	.	.	.	.	$[1]$	.	.	.	.	.
	BLINK[ATOM]	$c[0]$	.	.	.	.	.	.	.	.	.	.	.	.	.	.

$$\text{T} \quad - \quad \Lambda \quad a \quad a \quad \Lambda \quad a \quad a \quad c \quad d \quad d \quad d \quad c \quad c \quad a \quad \Lambda$$

$$\text{P} \quad - \quad a \quad b \quad b \quad a \quad c \quad c \quad d \quad e \quad e \quad e \quad d \quad d \quad c \quad a$$

Next step   E1 E2 E2 E6 E5 E2 E5 E2 E2 E5 E6 E5 E6 E6 E6

Nesting

Fig. 39. A structure marked by Algorithm E. (The table shows only changes that have occurred since the previous step.)

E6. [Up.] (This step undoes the link switching made in step E4 or E5; the setting of ATOM(T) tells whether ALINK(T) or BLINK(T) is to be restored.) If T = Λ, the algorithm terminates. Otherwise set Q ← T. If ATOM(Q) = 1, set ATOM(Q) ← 0, T ← ALINK(Q), ALINK(Q) ← P, P ← Q, and return to E5. If ATOM(Q) = 0, set T ← BLINK(Q), BLINK(Q) ← P, P ← Q, and repeat E6. ∎

An example of this algorithm in action appears in Fig. 39, which shows the successive steps encountered for a simple List structure. The reader will find it worthwhile to study Algorithm E very carefully; notice how the linking structure is artificially changed in steps E4 and E5, in order to maintain a stack analogous to the stack in Algorithm D. When we return to a previous state, the ATOM field is used to tell whether ALINK or BLINK contains the artificial address. The "nesting" shown at the bottom of Fig. 39 illustrates how each nonatomic node is visited three times during Algorithm E: The same configuration (T,P) occurs at the beginning of steps E2, E5, and E6.

A proof that Algorithm E is valid can be formulated by induction on the number of nodes that are to be marked. We prove at the same time that P returns to its initial value P0 at the conclusion of the algorithm; for details, see exercise 3. Algorithm E will run faster if step E3 is deleted and if special tests for "ATOM(Q) = 1" and appropriate actions are made in steps E4 and E5, as well as a test "ATOM(P0) = 1" in step E1. We have stated the algorithm in its present form for simplicity; the modifications just stated appear in the answer to exercise 4.

The idea used in Algorithm E can be applied to problems other than garbage collection; in fact, its use for tree traversal has already been mentioned in exercise 2.3.1–21. The reader may also find it useful to compare Algorithm E with the simpler problem solved in exercise 2.2.3–7.

Of all the marking algorithms we have discussed, only Algorithm D is directly applicable to Lists represented as in (9). The other algorithms all test whether or not a given node P is an atom, and the conventions of (9) are incompatible with such tests because they allow atomic information to fill an entire word except for the mark bit. However, each of the other algorithms can be modified so that they will work when atomic data is distinguished from pointer data in the word that links to it instead of by looking at the word itself. In Algorithms A or C we can simply avoid marking atomic words until all nonatomic words have been properly marked; then one further pass over all the data suffices to mark all the atomic words. Algorithm B is even easier to modify, since we need merely keep atomic words off the stack. The adaptation of Algorithm E is almost as simple, although if both ALINK and BLINK are allowed to point to atomic data it will be necessary to introduce another 1-bit field in nonatomic nodes. This is generally not hard to do. (For example, when there are two words per node, the least significant bit of each link field may be used to store temporary information.)

Although Algorithm E requires a time proportional to the number of nodes it marks, this constant of proportionality is not as small as in Algorithm B; the fastest garbage collection method known combines Algorithms B and E, as discussed in exercise 5.

Let us now try to make some quantitative estimates of the efficiency of garbage collection, as opposed to the philosophy of "AVAIL ⇐ X" that was used in most of the previous examples in this chapter. In each of the previous cases we could have omitted all specific mention of returning nodes to free space and we could have substituted a garbage collector instead. (In a special-purpose application, as opposed to a set of general-purpose List manipulation subroutines, the programming and debugging of a garbage collector is more difficult than the methods we have used, and, of course, garbage collection requires an extra bit reserved in each node; but we are interested here in the relative speed of the programs once they have been written and debugged.)

The best garbage collection routines known have an execution time essentially of the form $c_1 N + c_2 M$, where c_1 and c_2 are constants, N is the number of nodes marked, and M is the total number of nodes in the memory. Thus $M - N$ is the number of free nodes found, and the amount of time required to return these nodes to free storage is $(c_1 N + c_2 M)/(M - N)$ per node. Let $N = \rho M$; this figure becomes $(c_1 \rho + c_2)/(1 - \rho)$. So if $\rho = \frac{3}{4}$, that is, if the memory is three-fourths full, we spend $3c_1 + 4c_2$ units of time per free node returned to storage; when $\rho = \frac{1}{4}$, the corresponding cost is only $\frac{1}{3}c_1 + \frac{4}{3}c_2$. If we do not use the garbage collection technique, the amount of time per node returned is essentially a constant, c_3, and it is doubtful that c_3/c_1 will be very large. Hence we can see to what extent garbage collection is inefficient when the memory becomes full, and how it is correspondingly efficient when the demand on memory is light.

Many programs have the property that the ratio $\rho = N/M$ of good nodes to total memory is quite small. When the pool of memory becomes full in such cases, it might be best to move all the active List data to another memory pool of equal size, using a copying technique (see exercise 10) but without bothering to preserve the contents of the nodes being copied. Then when the second memory pool fills up, we can move the data back to the first one again. With this method more data can be kept in high-speed memory at once, because link fields tend to point to nearby nodes. Moreover, there's no need for a marking phase, and storage allocation is simply sequential.

It is possible to combine garbage collection with some of the other methods of returning cells to free storage; these ideas are not mutually exclusive, and some systems employ both the reference counter and the garbage collection schemes, besides allowing the programmer to erase nodes explicitly. The idea is to employ garbage collection only as a "last resort" whenever all other methods of returning cells have failed. An elaborate system, which implements this idea and also includes a mechanism for postponing operations on reference counts in order to achieve further efficiency, has been described by L. P. Deutsch and D. G. Bobrow in *CACM* **19** (1976), 522–526.

A sequential representation of Lists, which saves many of the link fields at the expense of more complicated storage management, is also possible. See N. E. Wiseman and J. O. Hiles, *Comp. J.* **10** (1968), 338–343; W. J. Hansen, *CACM* **12** (1969), 499–507; and C. J. Cheney, *CACM* **13** (1970), 677–678.

Daniel P. Friedman and David S. Wise have observed that the reference counter method can be employed satisfactorily in many cases even when Lists point to themselves, if certain link fields are not included in the counts [*Inf. Proc. Letters* **8** (1979), 41–45].

A great many variants and refinements of garbage collection algorithms have been proposed. Jacques Cohen, in *Computing Surveys* **13** (1981), 341–367, presents a detailed review of the literature prior to 1981, with important comments about the extra cost of memory accesses when pages of data are shuttled between slow memory and fast memory.

Garbage collection as we have described it is unsuitable for "real time" applications, where each basic List operation must be quick; even if the garbage collector goes into action infrequently, it requires large chunks of computer time on those occasions. Exercise 12 discusses some approaches by which real-time garbage collection is possible.

> *It is a very sad thing nowadays*
> *that there is so little useless information.*
> — OSCAR WILDE (1894)

EXERCISES

▶ **1.** [*M21*] In Section 2.3.4 we saw that trees are special cases of the "classical" mathematical concept of a directed graph. Can Lists be described in graph-theoretic terminology?

2. [*20*] In Section 2.3.1 we saw that tree traversal can be facilitated using a threaded representation inside the computer. Can List structures be threaded in an analogous way?

3. [*M26*] Prove the validity of Algorithm E. [*Hint:* See the proof of Algorithm 2.3.1T.]

4. [*28*] Write a MIX program for Algorithm E, assuming that nodes are represented as one MIX word, with MARK the (0:0) field ["+" = 0, "−" = 1], ATOM the (1:1) field, ALINK the (2:3) field, BLINK the (4:5) field, and $\Lambda = 0$. Also determine the execution time of your program in terms of relevant parameters. (In the MIX computer the problem of determining whether a memory location contains −0 or +0 is not quite trivial, and this can be a factor in your program.)

5. [*25*] (Schorr and Waite.) Give a marking algorithm that combines Algorithms B and E as follows: The assumptions of Algorithm E with regard to fields within the nodes, etc., are retained; but an auxiliary stack STACK[1], STACK[2], ..., STACK[N] is used as in Algorithm B, and the mechanism of Algorithm E is employed only when the stack is full.

6. [*00*] The quantitative discussion at the end of this section says that the cost of garbage collection is approximately $c_1 N + c_2 M$ units of time; where does the "$c_2 M$" term come from?

7. [*24*] (R. W. Floyd.) Design a marking algorithm that is similar to Algorithm E in using no auxiliary stack, except that (i) it has a more difficult task to do, because each node contains only MARK, ALINK, and BLINK fields — there is no ATOM field to provide additional control; yet (ii) it has a simpler task to do, because it marks only a binary tree instead of a general List. Here ALINK and BLINK are the usual LLINK and RLINK in a binary tree.

▶ **8.** [*27*] (L. P. Deutsch.) Design a marking algorithm similar to Algorithms D and E in that it uses no auxiliary memory for a stack, but modify the method so that it works with nodes of variable size and with a variable number of pointers having the following format: The first word of a node has two fields MARK and SIZE; the MARK field is to be treated as in Algorithm E, and the SIZE field contains a number $n \geq 0$. This means that there are n consecutive words after the first word, each containing two fields MARK (which is zero and should remain so) and LINK (which is Λ or points to the first word of another node). For example, a node with three pointers would comprise four consecutive words:

First word	MARK = 0 (will be set to 1)	SIZE = 3
Second word	MARK = 0	LINK = first pointer
Third word	MARK = 0	LINK = second pointer
Fourth word	MARK = 0	LINK = third pointer.

Your algorithm should mark all nodes reachable from a given node P0.

▶ **9.** [*28*] (D. Edwards.) Design an algorithm for the second phase of garbage collection that "compacts storage" in the following sense: Let NODE(1), ..., NODE(M) be one-word nodes with fields MARK, ATOM, ALINK, and BLINK, as described in Algorithm E. Assume that MARK = 1 in all nodes that are not garbage. The desired algorithm should relocate the marked nodes, if necessary, so that they all appear in consecutive locations NODE(1), ..., NODE(K), and at the same time the ALINK and BLINK fields of nonatomic nodes should be altered if necessary so that the List structure is preserved.

▶ **10.** [*28*] Design an algorithm that copies a List structure, assuming that an internal representation like that in (7) is being used. (Thus, if your procedure is asked to copy the List whose head is the node at the upper left corner of (7), a new set of Lists having 14 nodes, and with structure and information identical to that shown in (7), should be created.)

Assume that the List structure is stored in memory using S, T, REF, and RLINK fields as in (9), and that NODE(PO) is the head of the List to be copied. Assume further that the REF field in each List head node is Λ; to avoid the need for additional memory space, your copying procedure should make use of the REF fields (and reset them to Λ again afterwards).

11. [*M30*] Any List structure can be "fully expanded" into a tree structure by repeating all overlapping elements until none are left; when the List is recursive, this gives an infinite tree. For example, the List (5) would expand into an infinite tree whose first four levels are

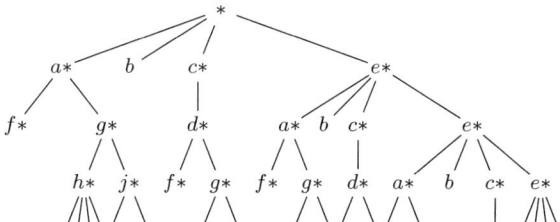

Design an algorithm to test the *equivalence* of two List structures, in the sense that they have the same diagram when fully expanded. For example, Lists A and B are equivalent in this sense, if

$$A = \big(a\!:\!C, b, a\!:\!(b\!:\!D)\big)$$
$$B = \big(a\!:\!(b\!:\!D), b, a\!:\!E\big)$$
$$C = \big(b\!:\!(a\!:\!C)\big)$$
$$D = \big(a\!:\!(b\!:\!D)\big)$$
$$E = \big(b\!:\!(a\!:\!C)\big).$$

12. [*30*] (M. Minsky.) Show that it is possible to use a garbage collection method reliably in a "real time" application, for example when a computer is controlling some physical device, even when stringent upper bounds are placed on the maximum execution time required for each List operation performed. [*Hint:* Garbage collection can be arranged to work in parallel with the List operations, if appropriate care is taken.]

2.4. MULTILINKED STRUCTURES

NOW THAT WE have examined linear lists and tree structures in detail, the principles of representing structural information within a computer should be evident. In this section we will look at another application of these techniques, this time for the typical case in which the structural information is slightly more complicated: In higher-level applications, several types of structure are usually present simultaneously.

A "multilinked structure" involves nodes with several link fields in each node, not just one or two as in most of our previous examples. We have already seen some examples of multiple linkage, such as the simulated elevator system in Section 2.2.5 and the multivariate polynomials in Section 2.3.3.

We shall see that the presence of many different kinds of links per node does *not* necessarily make the accompanying algorithms any more difficult to write or to understand than the algorithms already studied. We will also discuss the important question, *"How much structural information ought to be explicitly recorded in memory?"*

The problem we will consider arises in connection with writing a compiler program for the translation of COBOL and related languages. A programmer who uses COBOL may give alphabetic names to program variables on several levels; for example, the program might refer to files of data for sales and purchases, having the following structure:

```
1 SALES                 1 PURCHASES
   2 DATE                   2 DATE
      3 MONTH                  3 DAY
      3 DAY                    3 MONTH
      3 YEAR                   3 YEAR
   2 TRANSACTION            2 TRANSACTION
      3 ITEM                   3 ITEM                  (1)
      3 QUANTITY               3 QUANTITY
      3 PRICE                  3 PRICE
      3 TAX                    3 TAX
      3 BUYER                  3 SHIPPER
         4 NAME                   4 NAME
         4 ADDRESS                4 ADDRESS
```

This configuration indicates that each item in SALES consists of two parts, the DATE and the TRANSACTION; the DATE is further divided into three parts, and the TRANSACTION likewise has five subdivisions. Similar remarks apply to PURCHASES. The relative order of these names indicates the order in which the quantities appear in external representations of the file (for example, magnetic tape or printed forms); notice that in this example "DAY" and "MONTH" appear in opposite order in the two files. The programmer also gives further information, not shown in this illustration, that tells how much space each item of information occupies and in what format it appears; such considerations are not relevant to us in this section, so they will not be mentioned further.

A COBOL programmer first describes the file layout and the other program variables, then specifies the algorithms that manipulate those quantities. To refer to an individual variable in the example above, it would not be sufficient merely to give the name DAY, since there is no way of telling if the variable called DAY is in the SALES file or in the PURCHASES file. Therefore a COBOL programmer is given the ability to write "DAY OF SALES" to refer to the DAY part of a SALES item. The programmer could also write, more completely,

$$\text{``DAY OF DATE OF SALES''},$$

but in general there is no need to give more qualification than necessary to avoid ambiguity. Thus,

$$\text{``NAME OF SHIPPER OF TRANSACTION OF PURCHASES''}$$

may be abbreviated to

$$\text{``NAME OF SHIPPER''}$$

since only one part of the data has been called SHIPPER.

These rules of COBOL may be stated more precisely as follows:

a) Each name is immediately preceded by an associated positive integer called its *level number*. A name either refers to an *elementary item* or it is the name of a *group* of one or more items whose names follow. In the latter case, each item of the group must have the same level number, which must be greater than the level number of the group name. (For example, DATE and TRANSACTION above have level number 2, which is greater than the level number 1 of SALES.)

b) To refer to an elementary item or group of items named A_0, the general form is

$$A_0 \text{ OF } A_1 \text{ OF } \ldots \text{ OF } A_n,$$

where $n \geq 0$ and where, for $0 \leq j < n$, A_j is the name of some item contained directly or indirectly within a group named A_{j+1}. There must be exactly one item A_0 satisfying this condition.

c) If the same name A_0 appears in several places, there must be a way to refer to each use of the name by using qualification.

As an example of rule (c), the data configuration

$$
\begin{array}{ll}
\text{1 AA} & \\
\quad \text{2 BB} & \\
\quad\quad \text{3 CC} & \qquad\qquad (2)\\
\quad\quad \text{3 DD} & \\
\quad \text{2 CC} &
\end{array}
$$

would not be allowed, since there is no unambiguous way to refer to the second appearance of CC. (See exercise 4.)

COBOL has another feature that affects compiler writing and the application we are considering, namely an option in the language that makes it possible to refer to many items at once. A COBOL programmer may write

$$\text{MOVE CORRESPONDING } \alpha \text{ TO } \beta$$

which moves all items with corresponding names from data area α to data area β. For example, the COBOL statement

MOVE CORRESPONDING DATE OF SALES TO DATE OF PURCHASES

would mean that the values of MONTH, DAY, and YEAR from the SALES file are to be moved to the variables MONTH, DAY, and YEAR in the PURCHASES file. (The relative order of DAY and MONTH is thereby interchanged.)

The problem we will investigate in this section is to design three algorithms suitable for use in a COBOL compiler, which are to do the following things:

Operation 1. To process a description of names and level numbers such as (1), putting the relevant information into tables within the compiler for use in operations 2 and 3.

Operation 2. To determine if a given qualified reference, as in rule (b), is valid, and when it is valid to locate the corresponding data item.

Operation 3. To find all corresponding pairs of items indicated by a given CORRESPONDING statement.

We will assume that our compiler already has a "symbol table subroutine" that will convert an alphabetic name into a link that points to a table entry for that name. (Methods for constructing symbol table algorithms are discussed in detail in Chapter 6.) In addition to the Symbol Table, there is a larger table that contains one entry for each item of data in the COBOL source program that is being compiled; we will call this the *Data Table*.

Clearly, we cannot design an algorithm for operation 1 until we know what kind of information is to be stored in the Data Table, and the form of the Data Table depends on what information we need in order to perform operations 2 and 3; thus we look first at operations 2 and 3.

In order to determine the meaning of the COBOL reference

$$A_0 \text{ OF } A_1 \text{ OF } \ldots \text{ OF } A_n, \qquad n \geq 0, \tag{3}$$

we should first look up the name A_0 in the Symbol Table. There ought to be a series of links from the Symbol Table entry to all Data Table entries for this name. Then for each Data Table entry we will want a link to the entry for the group item that contains it. Now if there is a further link field from the Data Table items back to the Symbol Table, it is not hard to see how a reference like (3) can be processed. Furthermore, we will want some sort of links from the Data Table entries for group items to the items in the group, in order to locate the pairs indicated by "MOVE CORRESPONDING".

We have thereby found a potential need for five link fields in each Data Table entry:

PREV (a link to the previous entry with the same name, if any);
PARENT (a link to the smallest group, if any, containing this item);
NAME (a link to the Symbol Table entry for this item);
CHILD (a link to the first subitem of a group);
SIB (a link to the next subitem in the group containing this item).

It is clear that COBOL data structures like those for SALES and PURCHASES above are essentially trees; and the PARENT, CHILD, and SIB links that appear here are familiar from our previous study. (The conventional binary tree representation of a tree consists of the CHILD and SIB links; adding the PARENT link gives what we have called a "triply linked tree." The five links above consist of these three tree links together with PREV and NAME, which superimpose further information on the tree structure.)

Perhaps not all five of these links will turn out to be necessary, or sufficient, but we will try first to design our algorithms under the tentative assumption that Data Table entries will involve these five link fields (plus further information irrelevant to our problems). As an example of the multiple linking used, consider the two COBOL data structures

$$
\begin{array}{ll}
\begin{array}{ll}
1 & A \\
3 & B \\
7 & C \\
7 & D \\
3 & E \\
3 & F \\
4 & G \\
\end{array}
&
\begin{array}{ll}
1 & H \\
5 & F \\
8 & G \\
5 & B \\
5 & C \\
9 & E \\
9 & D \\
9 & G \\
\end{array}
\end{array} \tag{4}
$$

They would be represented as shown in (5) (with links indicated symbolically). The LINK field of each Symbol Table entry points to the most recently encountered Data Table entry for the symbolic name in question.

The first algorithm we require is one that builds the Data Table in such a form. Note the flexibility in choice of level numbers that is allowed by the COBOL rules; the left structure in (4) is completely equivalent to

$$
\begin{array}{ll}
1 & A \\
2 & B \\
3 & C \\
3 & D \\
2 & E \\
2 & F \\
3 & G \\
\end{array}
$$

because level numbers do not have to be sequential.

Symbol Table

	LINK
A:	A1
B:	B5
C:	C5
D:	D9
E:	E9
F:	F5
G:	G9
H:	H1

Empty boxes indicate additional information not relevant here

Data Table

	PREV	PARENT	NAME	CHILD	SIB	
A1:	Λ	Λ	A	B3	H1	
B3:	Λ	A1	B	C7	E3	
C7:	Λ	B3	C	Λ	D7	
D7:	Λ	B3	D	Λ	Λ	
E3:	Λ	A1	E	Λ	F3	
F3:	Λ	A1	F	G4	Λ	
G4:	Λ	F3	G	Λ	Λ	
H1:	Λ	Λ	H	F5	Λ	
F5:	F3	H1	F	G8	B5	
G8:	G4	F5	G	Λ	Λ	
B5:	B3	H1	B	Λ	C5	
C5:	C7	H1	C	E9	Λ	
E9:	E3	C5	E	Λ	D9	
D9:	D7	C5	D	Λ	G9	
G9:	G8	C5	G	Λ	Λ	

$$(5)$$

Some sequences of level numbers are illegal, however; for example, if the level number of D in (4) were changed to "6" (in either place) we would have a meaningless data configuration, violating the rule that all items of a group must have the same number. The following algorithm therefore makes sure that COBOL's rule (a) has not been broken.

Algorithm A (*Build Data Table*). This algorithm is given a sequence of pairs (L, P), where L is a positive integer "level number" and P points to a Symbol Table entry, corresponding to COBOL data structures such as (4) above. The algorithm builds a Data Table as in the example (5) above. When P points to a Symbol Table entry that has not appeared before, LINK(P) will equal Λ. This algorithm uses an auxiliary stack that is treated as usual (using either sequential memory allocation, as in Section 2.2.2, or linked allocation, as in Section 2.2.3).

A1. [Initialize.] Set the stack contents to the single entry (0, Λ). (The stack entries throughout this algorithm are pairs (L, P), where L is an integer and P a pointer; as this algorithm proceeds, the stack contains the level number and pointers to the most recent data entries on all levels higher in the tree than the current level. For example, just before encountering the pair "3 F" in the example above, the stack would contain

$$(0, \Lambda) \qquad (1, A1) \qquad (3, E3)$$

from bottom to top.)

A2. [Next item.] Let (L, P) be the next data item from the input. If the input is exhausted, however, the algorithm terminates. Set $Q \Leftarrow$ AVAIL (that is, let Q be the location of a new node in which we can put the next Data Table entry).

A3. [Set name links.] Set

$$\text{PREV(Q)} \leftarrow \text{LINK(P)}, \qquad \text{LINK(P)} \leftarrow \text{Q}, \qquad \text{NAME(Q)} \leftarrow \text{P}.$$

(This properly sets two of the five links in NODE(Q). We now want to set PARENT, CHILD, and SIB appropriately.)

A4. [Compare levels.] Let the top entry of the stack be $(L1, P1)$. If $L1 < L$, set CHILD(P1) $\leftarrow$ Q (or, if P1 $= \Lambda$, set FIRST $\leftarrow$ Q, where FIRST is a variable that will point to the first Data Table entry) and go to A6.

A5. [Remove top level.] If $L1 > L$, remove the top stack entry, let $(L1, P1)$ be the new entry that has just come to the top of the stack, and repeat step A5. If $L1 < L$, signal an error (mixed numbers have occurred on the same level). Otherwise, namely when $L1 = L$, set SIB(P1) $\leftarrow$ Q, remove the top stack entry, and let $(L1, P1)$ be the pair that has just come to the top of the stack.

A6. [Set family links.] Set PARENT(Q) $\leftarrow$ P1, CHILD(Q) $\leftarrow \Lambda$, SIB(Q) $\leftarrow \Lambda$.

A7. [Add to stack.] Place (L, Q) on top of the stack, and return to step A2. ∎

The introduction of an auxiliary stack, as explained in step A1, makes this algorithm so transparent that it needs no further explanation.

The next problem is to locate the Data Table entry corresponding to a reference

$$A_0 \text{ OF } A_1 \text{ OF } \dots \text{ OF } A_n, \qquad n \geq 0. \tag{6}$$

A good compiler will also check to ensure that such a reference is unambiguous. In this case, a suitable algorithm suggests itself immediately: All we need to do is to run through the list of Data Table entries for the name A_0 and make sure that exactly one of these entries matches the stated qualification $A_1, \dots, A_n$.

Algorithm B (*Check a qualified reference*). Corresponding to reference (6), a Symbol Table subroutine will find pointers $P_0, P_1, \dots, P_n$ to the Symbol Table entries for $A_0, A_1, \dots, A_n$, respectively.

The purpose of this algorithm is to examine $P_0, P_1, \dots, P_n$ and either to determine that reference (6) is in error, or to set variable Q to the address of the Data Table entry for the item referred to by (6).

B1. [Initialize.] Set Q $\leftarrow \Lambda$, P $\leftarrow$ LINK(P_0).

B2. [Done?] If P $= \Lambda$, the algorithm terminates; at this point Q will equal Λ if (6) does not correspond to any Data Table entry. But if P $\neq \Lambda$, set S $\leftarrow$ P and $k \leftarrow 0$. (S is a pointer variable that will run from P up the tree through PARENT links; k is an integer variable that goes from 0 to n. In practice, the pointers $P_0, \dots, P_n$ would often be kept in a linked list, and instead of k, we would substitute a pointer variable that traverses this list; see exercise 5.)

B3. [Match complete?] If $k < n$ go on to B4. Otherwise we have found a matching Data Table entry; if $Q \neq \Lambda$, this is the second entry found, so an error condition is signaled. Set $Q \leftarrow P$, $P \leftarrow \text{PREV}(P)$, and go to B2.

B4. [Increase k.] Set $k \leftarrow k + 1$.

B5. [Move up tree.] Set $S \leftarrow \text{PARENT}(S)$. If $S = \Lambda$, we have failed to find a match; set $P \leftarrow \text{PREV}(P)$ and go to B2.

B6. [A_k match?] If $\text{NAME}(S) = P_k$, go to B3, otherwise go to B5. ∎

Note that the CHILD and SIB links are not needed by this algorithm.

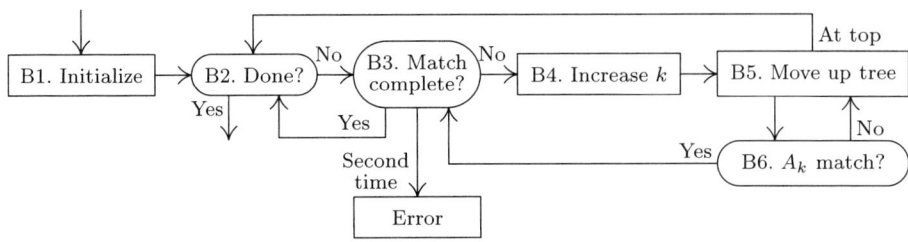

Fig. 40. Algorithm for checking a COBOL reference.

The third and final algorithm that we need concerns "MOVE CORRESPONDING"; before we design such an algorithm, we must have a precise definition of what is required. The COBOL statement

$$\text{MOVE CORRESPONDING } \alpha \text{ TO } \beta \tag{7}$$

where α and β are references such as (6) to data items, is an abbreviation for the set of all statements

$$\text{MOVE } \alpha' \text{ TO } \beta'$$

where there exists an integer $n \geq 0$ and n names $A_0, A_1, \ldots, A_{n-1}$ such that

$$\begin{aligned} \alpha' &= A_0 \text{ OF } A_1 \text{ OF } \ldots \text{ OF } A_{n-1} \text{ OF } \alpha \\ \beta' &= A_0 \text{ OF } A_1 \text{ OF } \ldots \text{ OF } A_{n-1} \text{ OF } \beta \end{aligned} \tag{8}$$

and either α' or β' is an elementary item (not a group item). Furthermore we require that the first levels of (8) show *complete* qualifications, namely that A_{j+1} be the parent of A_j for $0 \leq j < n - 1$ and that α and β are parents of A_{n-1}; α' and β' must be exactly n levels farther down in the tree than α and β are.

With respect to our example (4),

$$\text{MOVE CORRESPONDING A TO H}$$

is therefore an abbreviation for the statements

```
MOVE B OF A TO B OF H
MOVE G OF F OF A TO G OF F OF H
```

The algorithm to recognize all corresponding pairs α', β' is quite interesting although not difficult; we move through the tree whose root is α, in preorder, simultaneously looking in the β tree for matching names, and skipping over subtrees in which no corresponding elements can possibly occur. The names $A_0, \ldots, A_{n-1}$ of (8) are discovered in the opposite order $A_{n-1}, \ldots, A_0$.

Algorithm C (*Find* CORRESPONDING *pairs*). Given P0 and Q0, which point to Data Table entries for α and β, respectively, this algorithm successively finds all pairs (P, Q) of pointers to items (α', β') satisfying the constraints mentioned above.

C1. [Initialize.] Set P $\leftarrow$ P0, Q $\leftarrow$ Q0. (In the remainder of this algorithm, the pointer variables P and Q will walk through trees having the respective roots α and β.)

C2. [Elementary?] If CHILD(P) = Λ or CHILD(Q) = Λ, output (P, Q) as one of the desired pairs and go to C5. Otherwise set P $\leftarrow$ CHILD(P), Q $\leftarrow$ CHILD(Q). (In this step, P and Q point to items α' and β' satisfying (8), and we wish to MOVE α' TO β' if and only if either α' or β' (or both) is an elementary item.)

C3. [Match name.] (Now P and Q point to data items that have respective complete qualifications of the forms

$$A_0 \text{ OF } A_1 \text{ OF } \ldots \text{ OF } A_{n-1} \text{ OF } \alpha$$

and

$$B_0 \text{ OF } A_1 \text{ OF } \ldots \text{ OF } A_{n-1} \text{ OF } \beta.$$

The object is to see if we can make $B_0 = A_0$ by examining all the names of the group $A_1 \text{ OF } \ldots \text{ OF } A_{n-1} \text{ OF } \beta$.) If NAME(P) = NAME(Q), go to C2 (a match has been found). Otherwise, if SIB(Q) $\neq \Lambda$, set Q $\leftarrow$ SIB(Q) and repeat step C3. (If SIB(Q) = Λ, no matching name is present in the group, and we continue on to step C4.)

C4. [Move on.] If SIB(P) $\neq \Lambda$, set P $\leftarrow$ SIB(P) and Q $\leftarrow$ CHILD(PARENT(Q)), and go back to C3. If SIB(P) = Λ, set P $\leftarrow$ PARENT(P) and Q $\leftarrow$ PARENT(Q).

C5. [Done?] If P = P0, the algorithm terminates; otherwise go to C4. ∎

A flow chart for this algorithm is shown in Fig. 41. A proof that this algorithm is valid can readily be constructed by induction on the size of the trees involved (see exercise 9).

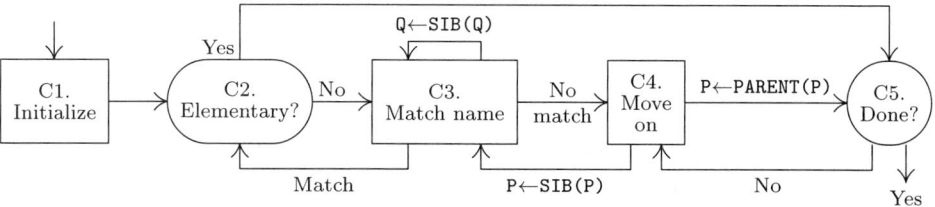

Fig. 41. Algorithm for "MOVE CORRESPONDING".

At this point it is worthwhile to study the ways in which the five link fields PREV, PARENT, NAME, CHILD, and SIB are used by Algorithms B and C. The striking feature is that these five links constitute a "complete set" in the sense that Algorithms B and C do virtually the minimum amount of work as they move through the Data Table. Whenever they need to refer to another Data Table entry, its address is immediately available; there is no need to conduct a search. It would be difficult to imagine how Algorithms B and C could possibly be made any faster if any additional link information were present in the table. (See exercise 11, however.)

Each link field may be viewed as a *clue* to the program, planted there in order to make the algorithms run faster. (Of course, the algorithm that builds the tables, Algorithm A, runs correspondingly slower, since it has more links to fill in. But table-building is done only once.) It is clear, on the other hand, that the Data Table constructed above contains much redundant information. Let us consider what would happen if we were to *delete* certain of the link fields.

The PREV link, while not used in Algorithm C, is extremely important for Algorithm B, and it seems to be an essential part of any COBOL compiler unless lengthy searches are to be carried out. A field that links together all items of the same name therefore seems essential for efficiency. We could perhaps modify the strategy slightly and adopt circular linking instead of terminating each list with Λ, but there is no reason to do this unless other link fields are changed or eliminated.

The PARENT link is used in both Algorithms B and C, although its use in Algorithm C could be avoided if we used an auxiliary stack in that algorithm, or if we augmented SIB so that thread links are included (as in Section 2.3.2). So we see that the PARENT link has been used in an essential way only in Algorithm B. If the SIB link were threaded, so that the items that now have SIB = Λ would have SIB = PARENT instead, it would be possible to locate the parent of any data item by following the SIB links; the added thread links could be distinguished either by having a new TAG field in each node that says whether the SIB link is a thread, or by the condition "SIB(P) < P" if the Data Table entries are kept consecutively in memory in order of appearance. This would mean a short search would be necessary in step B5, and the algorithm would be correspondingly slower.

The NAME link is used by the algorithms only in steps B6 and C3. In both cases we could make the tests "NAME(S) = P_k" and "NAME(P) = NAME(Q)" in other ways if the NAME link were not present (see exercise 10), but this would significantly slow down the inner loops of both Algorithms B and C. Here again we see a trade-off between the space for a link and the speed of the algorithms. (The speed of Algorithm C is not especially significant in COBOL compilers, when typical uses of MOVE CORRESPONDING are considered; but Algorithm B should be fast.) Experience indicates that other important uses are found for the NAME link within a COBOL compiler, especially in printing diagnostic information.

Algorithm A builds the Data Table step by step, and it never has occasion to return a node to the pool of available storage; so we usually find that Data Table entries take consecutive memory locations in the order of appearance of the data items in the COBOL source program. Thus in our example (5), locations A1, B3, ... would follow each other. This sequential nature of the Data Table leads to certain simplifications; for example, the CHILD link of each node is either Λ or it points to the node immediately following, so CHILD can be reduced to a 1-bit field. Alternatively, CHILD could be removed in favor of a test if PARENT(P + c) = P, where c is the node size in the Data Table.

Thus the five link fields are not all essential, although they are helpful from the standpoint of speed in Algorithms B and C. This situation is fairly typical of most multilinked structures.

It is interesting to note that at least half a dozen people writing COBOL compilers in the early 1960s arrived independently at this same way to maintain a Data Table using five links (or four of the five, usually with the CHILD link missing). The first publication of such a technique was by H. W. Lawson, Jr. [*ACM National Conference Digest* (Syracuse, N.Y.: 1962)]. But in 1965 an ingenious technique for achieving the effects of Algorithms B and C, using only two link fields and sequential storage of the Data Table, without a very great decrease in speed, was introduced by David Dahm; see exercises 12 through 14.

EXERCISES

1. [*00*] Considering COBOL data configurations as tree structures, are the data items listed by a COBOL programmer in preorder, postorder, or neither of those orders?

2. [*10*] Comment about the running time of Algorithm A.

3. [*22*] The PL/I language accepts data structures like those in COBOL, except that any sequence of level numbers is possible. For example, the sequence

1 A			1 A	
3 B			2 B	
5 C	is equivalent to		3 C	
4 D			3 D	
2 E			2 E	

In general, rule (a) is modified to read, "The items of a group must have a sequence of nonincreasing level numbers, all of which are greater than the level number of the group name." What modifications to Algorithm A would change it from the COBOL convention to this PL/I convention?

▶ **4.** [*26*] Algorithm A does not detect the error if a COBOL programmer violates rule (c) stated in the text. How should Algorithm A be modified so that only data structures satisfying rule (c) will be accepted?

5. [*20*] In practice, Algorithm B may be given a linked list of Symbol Table references as input, instead of what we called "$P_0, P_1, \ldots, P_n$." Let T be a pointer variable such that

$$\text{INFO}(T) \equiv P_0, \ \text{INFO}(\text{RLINK}(T)) \equiv P_1, \ \ldots, \ \text{INFO}(\text{RLINK}^{[n]}(T)) \equiv P_n, \ \text{RLINK}^{[n+1]}(T) = \Lambda.$$

Show how to modify Algorithm B so that it uses such a linked list as input.

6. [*23*] The PL/I language accepts data structures much like those in COBOL, but does not make the restriction of rule (c); instead, we have the rule that a qualified reference (3) is unambiguous if it shows "complete" qualification—that is, if A_{j+1} is the parent of A_j for $0 \leq j < n$, and if A_n has no parent. Rule (c) is now weakened to the simple condition that no two items of a group may have the same name. The second "CC" in (2) would be referred to as "CC OF AA" without ambiguity; the three data items

$$
\begin{array}{l}
\texttt{1 A} \\
\quad\texttt{2 A} \\
\qquad\texttt{3 A}
\end{array}
$$

would be referred to as "A", "A OF A", "A OF A OF A" with respect to the PL/I convention just stated. [*Note:* Actually the word "OF" is replaced by a period in PL/I, and the order is reversed; "CC OF AA" is really written "AA.CC" in PL/I, but this is not important for the purposes of the present exercise.] Show how to modify Algorithm B so that it follows the PL/I convention.

7. [*15*] Given the data structures in (1), what does the COBOL statement "MOVE CORRESPONDING SALES TO PURCHASES" mean?

8. [*10*] Under what circumstances is "MOVE CORRESPONDING α TO β" exactly the same as "MOVE α TO β", according to the definition in the text?

9. [*M23*] Prove that Algorithm C is correct.

10. [*23*] (a) How could the test "NAME(S) = P_k" in step B6 be performed if there were no NAME link in the Data Table nodes? (b) How could the test "NAME(P) = NAME(Q)" in step C3 be performed if there were no NAME link in the Data Table entries? (Assume that all other links are present as in the text.)

▸ **11.** [*23*] What additional links or changes in the strategy of the algorithms of the text could make Algorithm B or Algorithm C faster?

12. [*25*] (D. M. Dahm.) Consider representing the Data Table in sequential locations with just two links for each item:

        PREV (as in the text);

        SCOPE (a link to the last elementary item in this group).

We have SCOPE(P) = P if and only if NODE(P) represents an elementary item. For example, the Data Table of (5) would be replaced by

	PREV	SCOPE		PREV	SCOPE		PREV	SCOPE
A1:	Λ	G4	F3:	Λ	G4	B5:	B3	B5
B3:	Λ	D7	G4:	Λ	G4	C5:	C7	G9
C7:	Λ	C7	H1:	Λ	G9	E9:	E3	E9
D7:	Λ	D7	F5:	F3	G8	D9:	D7	D9
E3:	Λ	E3	G8:	G4	G8	G9:	G8	G9

(Compare with (5) of Section 2.3.3.) Notice that NODE(P) is part of the tree below NODE(Q) if and only if $Q < P \leq$ SCOPE(Q). Design an algorithm that performs the function of Algorithm B when the Data Table has this format.

▸ **13.** [*24*] Give an algorithm to substitute for Algorithm A when the Data Table is to have the format shown in exercise 12.

▸ **14.** [*28*] Give an algorithm to substitute for Algorithm C when the Data Table has the format shown in exercise 12.

15. [*25*] (David S. Wise.) Reformulate Algorithm A so that no extra storage is used for the stack. [*Hint:* The SIB fields of all nodes pointed to by the stack are Λ in the present formulation.]

2.5. DYNAMIC STORAGE ALLOCATION

WE HAVE SEEN how the use of links implies that data structures need not be sequentially located in memory; a number of tables may independently grow and shrink in a common pooled memory area. However, our discussions have always tacitly assumed that all nodes have the same size — that every node occupies a certain fixed number of memory cells.

For a great many applications, a suitable compromise can be found so that a uniform node size is indeed used for all structures (for example, see exercise 2). Instead of simply taking the maximum size that is needed and wasting space in smaller nodes, it is customary to pick a rather small node size and to employ what may be called the classical *linked-memory philosophy*: "If there isn't room for the information here, let's put it somewhere else and plant a link to it."

For a great many other applications, however, a single node size is not reasonable; we often wish to have nodes of varying sizes sharing a common memory area. Putting this another way, we want algorithms for reserving and freeing variable-size blocks of memory from a larger storage area, where these blocks are to consist of consecutive memory locations. Such techniques are generally called *dynamic storage allocation* algorithms.

Sometimes, often in simulation programs, we want dynamic storage allocation for nodes of rather small sizes (say one to ten words); and at other times, often in operating systems, we are dealing primarily with rather large blocks of information. These two points of view lead to slightly different approaches to dynamic storage allocation, although the methods have much in common. For uniformity in terminology between these two approaches, we will generally use the terms *block* and *area* rather than "node" in this section, to denote a set of contiguous memory locations.

Several authors began about 1975 to call the pool of available memory a "heap." But in the present series of books, we will use that word only in its more traditional sense related to priority queues (see Section 5.2.3).

A. Reservation. Figure 42 shows a typical *memory map* or "checkerboard," a chart showing the current state of some memory pool. In this case the memory is shown partitioned into 53 blocks of storage that are "reserved," or in use, mixed together with 21 "free" or "available" blocks that are not in use. After dynamic storage allocation has been in operation for awhile, the computer memory will perhaps look something like this. Our first problem is to answer two questions:

a) How is this partitioning of available space to be represented inside the computer?

b) Given such a representation of the available spaces, what is a good algorithm for finding a block of n consecutive free spaces and reserving them?

The answer to question (a) is, of course, to keep a *list* of the available space somewhere; this is almost always done best by using the available space *itself* to contain such a list. (An exception is the case when we are allocating storage for a disk file or other memory in which nonuniform access time makes it better to maintain a separate directory of available space.)

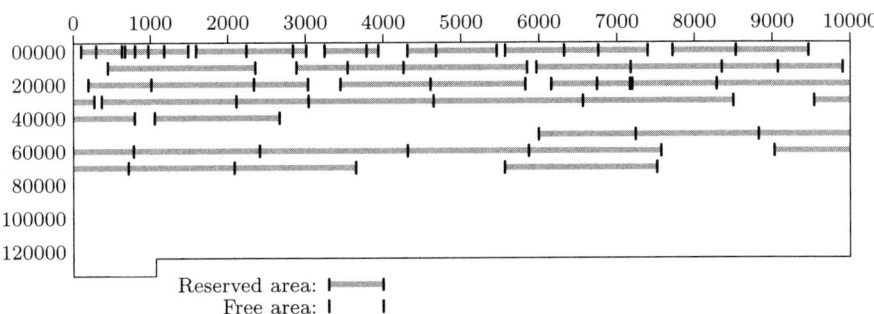

Fig. 42. A memory map.

Thus, we can *link together* the available segments: The first word of each free storage area can contain the size of that block and the address of the next free area. The free blocks can be linked together in increasing or decreasing order of size, or in order of memory address, or in essentially random order.

For example, consider Fig. 42, which illustrates a memory of 131,072 words, addressed from 0 to 131071. If we were to link together the available blocks in order of memory location, we would have one variable AVAIL pointing to the first free block (in this case AVAIL would equal 0), and the other blocks would be represented as follows:

location	SIZE	LINK	
0	101	632	
632	42	1488	
⋮	⋮	⋮	[17 similar entries]
73654	1909	77519	
77519	53553	Λ	[special marker for last link]

Thus locations 0 through 100 form the first available block; after the reserved areas 101–290 and 291–631 shown in Fig. 42, we have more free space in location 632–673; etc.

As for question (b), if we want n consecutive words, clearly we must locate some block of $m \geq n$ available words and reduce its size to $m - n$. (Furthermore, when $m = n$, we must also delete this block from the list.) There may be several blocks with n or more cells, and so the question becomes, *which* area should be chosen?

Two principal answers to this question suggest themselves: We can use the *best-fit method* or the *first-fit method*. In the former case, we decide to choose an area with m cells, where m is the smallest value present that is n or more. This might require searching the entire list of available space before a decision can be made. The first-fit method, on the other hand, simply chooses the first area encountered that has $\geq n$ words.

Historically, the best-fit method was widely used for several years; this naturally appears to be a good policy since it saves the larger available areas for a later time when they might be needed. But several objections to the best-fit technique can be raised: It is rather slow, since it involves a fairly long search; if best-fit is not substantially better than first-fit for other reasons, this extra searching time is not worthwhile. More importantly, the best-fit method tends to increase the number of very small blocks, and proliferation of small blocks is usually undesirable. There are certain situations in which the first-fit technique is demonstrably better than the best-fit method; for example, suppose we are given just two available areas of memory, of sizes 1300 and 1200, and suppose there are subsequent requests for blocks of sizes 1000, 1100, and 250:

memory request	available areas, first-fit	available areas, best-fit	
—	1300, 1200	1300, 1200	(1)
1000	300, 1200	1300, 200	
1100	300, 100	200, 200	
250	50, 100	stuck	

(A contrary example appears in exercise 7.) The point is that neither method clearly dominates the other, hence the simple first-fit method can be recommended.

Algorithm A (*First-fit method*). Let AVAIL point to the first available block of storage, and suppose that each available block with address P has two fields: SIZE(P), the number of words in the block; and LINK(P), a pointer to the next available block. The last pointer is Λ. This algorithm searches for and reserves a block of N words, or reports failure.

A1. [Initialize.] Set Q ← LOC(AVAIL). (Throughout the algorithm we use two pointers, Q and P, which are generally related by the condition P = LINK(Q). We assume that LINK(LOC(AVAIL)) = AVAIL.)

A2. [End of list?] Set P ← LINK(Q). If P = Λ, the algorithm terminates unsuccessfully; there is no room for a block of N consecutive words.

A3. [Is SIZE enough?] If SIZE(P) ≥ N, go to A4; otherwise set Q ← P and return to step A2.

A4. [Reserve N.] Set K ← SIZE(P) − N. If K = 0, set LINK(Q) ← LINK(P) (thereby removing an empty area from the list); otherwise set SIZE(P) ← K. The algorithm terminates successfully, having reserved an area of length N beginning with location P + K. ∎

This algorithm is certainly straightforward enough. However, a significant improvement in its running speed can be made with only a rather slight change in strategy. This improvement is quite important, and the reader will find it a pleasure to discover it without being told the secret (see exercise 6).

Algorithm A may be used whether storage allocation is desired for small N or large N. Let us assume temporarily, however, that we are primarily interested in *large* values of N. Then notice what happens when SIZE(P) is equal to N+1 in that algorithm: We get to step A4 and reduce SIZE(P) to 1. In other words, an available block of size 1 has just been created; this block is so small it is virtually useless, and it just clogs up the system. We would have been better off if we had reserved the whole block of N + 1 words, instead of saving the extra word; it is often better to expend a few words of memory to avoid handling unimportant details. Similar remarks apply to blocks of N + K words when K is very small.

If we allow the possibility of reserving slightly more than N words it will be necessary to remember how many words have been reserved, so that later when this block becomes available again the entire set of N + K words is freed. This added amount of bookkeeping means that we are tying up space in *every* block in order to make the system more efficient only in certain circumstances when a tight fit is found; so the strategy doesn't seem especially attractive. However, a special *control word* as the first word of each variable-size block often turns out to be desirable for other reasons, and so it is usually not unreasonable to expect the SIZE field to be present in the first word of all blocks, whether they are available or reserved.

In accordance with these conventions, we would modify step A4 above to read as follows:

A4′. [Reserve ≥ N.] Set K ← SIZE(P) − N. If K < c (where c is a small positive constant chosen to reflect an amount of storage we are willing to sacrifice in the interests of saving time), set LINK(Q) ← LINK(P) and L ← P. Otherwise set SIZE(P) ← K, L ← P + K, SIZE(L) ← N. The algorithm terminates successfully, having reserved an area of length N or more beginning with location L.

A value for the constant c of about 8 or 10 is suggested, although very little theory or empirical evidence exists to compare this with other choices. When the best-fit method is being used, the test of K < c is even *more* important than it is for the first-fit method, because tighter fits (smaller values of K) are much more likely to occur, and the number of available blocks should be kept as small as possible for that algorithm.

B. Liberation. Now let's consider the inverse problem: How should we return blocks to the available space list when they are no longer needed?

It is perhaps tempting to dismiss this problem by using garbage collection (see Section 2.3.5); we could follow a policy of simply doing nothing until space runs out, then searching for all the areas currently in use and fashioning a new AVAIL list.

The idea of garbage collection is not to be recommended, however, for all applications. In the first place, we need a fairly "disciplined" use of pointers if we are to be able to guarantee that all areas currently in use will be easy to locate, and this amount of discipline is often lacking in the applications considered here. Secondly, as we have seen before, garbage collection tends to be slow when the memory is nearly full.

There is another more important reason why garbage collection is not satisfactory, due to a phenomenon that did not confront us in our previous discussion of the technique: Suppose that there are two adjacent areas of memory, both of which are available, but because of the garbage-collection philosophy one of them (shown shaded) is not in the AVAIL list.

$$(2)$$

In this diagram, the heavily shaded areas at the extreme left and right are unavailable. We may now reserve a section of the area known to be available:

$$(3)$$

If garbage collection occurs at this point, we have two separate free areas,

$$(4)$$

Boundaries between available and reserved areas have a tendency to perpetuate themselves, and as time goes on the situation gets progressively worse. But if we had used a philosophy of returning blocks to the AVAIL list as soon as they become free, *and collapsing adjacent available areas together*, we would have collapsed (2) into

$$(5)$$

and we would have obtained

$$(6)$$

which is much better than (4). This phenomenon causes the garbage-collection technique to leave memory more broken up than it should be.

In order to remove this difficulty, we can use garbage collection together with the process of *compacting memory*, that is, moving all the reserved blocks into consecutive locations, so that all available blocks come together whenever garbage collection is done. The allocation algorithm now becomes completely trivial by contrast with Algorithm A, since there is only one available block at all times. Even though this technique takes time to recopy all the locations that are in use, and to change the value of the link fields therein, it can be applied with reasonable efficiency when there is a disciplined use of pointers, and when there is a spare link field in each block for use by the garbage collection algorithms. (See exercise 33.)

Since many applications do not meet the requirements for the feasibility of garbage collection, we shall now study methods for returning blocks of memory to the available space list. The only difficulty in these methods is the collapsing problem: Two adjacent free areas should be merged into one. In fact, when an area bounded by two available blocks becomes free, all three areas should be merged together into one. *In this way a good balance is obtained in memory even though storage areas are continually reserved and freed over a long period of time.* (For a proof of this fact, see the "fifty-percent rule" below.)

The problem is to determine whether the areas at either side of the returned block are currently available; and if they are, we want to update the AVAIL list properly. The latter operation is a little more difficult than it sounds.

The first solution to these problems is to maintain the AVAIL list in order of increasing memory locations.

Algorithm B (*Liberation with sorted list*). Under the assumptions of Algorithm A, with the additional assumption that the AVAIL list is sorted by memory location (that is, if P points to an available block and LINK(P) $\neq \Lambda$, then LINK(P) $>$ P), this algorithm adds the block of N consecutive cells beginning at location P0 to the AVAIL list. We naturally assume that none of these N cells is already available.

B1. [Initialize.] Set Q $\leftarrow$ LOC(AVAIL). (See the remarks in step A1 above.)

B2. [Advance P.] Set P $\leftarrow$ LINK(Q). If P $= \Lambda$, or if P $>$ P0, go to B3; otherwise set Q $\leftarrow$ P and repeat step B2.

B3. [Check upper bound.] If P0 $+$ N $=$ P and P $\neq \Lambda$, set N $\leftarrow$ N $+$ SIZE(P) and set LINK(P0) $\leftarrow$ LINK(P). Otherwise set LINK(P0) $\leftarrow$ P.

B4. [Check lower bound.] If Q $+$ SIZE(Q) $=$ P0 (we assume that

$$SIZE(LOC(AVAIL)) = 0,$$

so this test always fails when Q $=$ LOC(AVAIL)), set SIZE(Q) $\leftarrow$ SIZE(Q) $+$ N and LINK(Q) $\leftarrow$ LINK(P0). Otherwise set LINK(Q) $\leftarrow$ P0, SIZE(P0) $\leftarrow$ N. ∎

Steps B3 and B4 do the desired collapsing, based on the fact that the pointers Q $<$ P0 $<$ P are the beginning locations of three consecutive available areas.

If the AVAIL list is not maintained in order of locations, the reader can see that a "brute force" approach to the collapsing problem would require a complete search through the entire AVAIL list; Algorithm B reduces this to a search through about *half* of the AVAIL list (in step B2) on the average. Exercise 11 shows how Algorithm B can be modified so that, on the average, only about one-third of the AVAIL list must be searched. But obviously, when the AVAIL list is long, all of these methods are much slower than we want them to be. Isn't there some way to reserve and free storage areas so that we don't need to do extensive searching through the AVAIL list?

We will now consider a method that eliminates all searching when storage is returned and that can be modified, as in exercise 6, to avoid almost all of the searching when storage is reserved. The technique makes use of a TAG field at both ends of each block, and a SIZE field in the first word of each block; this overhead is negligible when reasonably large blocks are being used, although it is perhaps too much of a penalty to pay in situations when the blocks have a very small average size. Another method described in exercise 19 requires only one bit in the first word of each block, at the expense of a little more running time and a slightly more complicated program.

At any rate, let us now assume that we don't mind adding a little bit of control information, in order to save a good deal of time over Algorithm B when the AVAIL list is long. The method we will describe assumes that each block has the following form:

Reserved block (`TAG` = "+") Free block (`TAG` = "−")

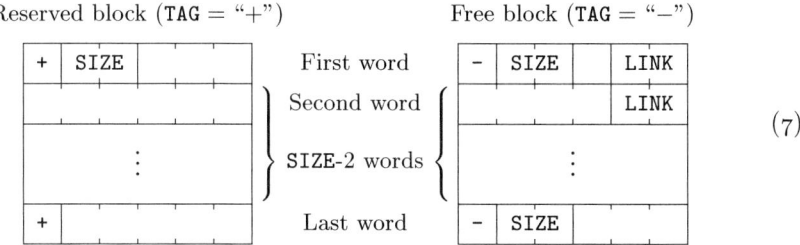

$$(7)$$

The idea in the following algorithm is to maintain a doubly linked `AVAIL` list, so that entries may conveniently be deleted from random parts of the list. The `TAG` field at either end of a block can be used to control the collapsing process, since we can tell easily whether or not both adjacent blocks are available.

Double linking is achieved in a familiar way, by letting the `LINK` in the first word point to the next free block in the list, and letting the `LINK` in the second word point back to the previous block; thus, if `P` is the address of an available block, we always have

$$\texttt{LINK(LINK(P)} + 1) = \texttt{P} = \texttt{LINK(LINK(P} + 1)). \tag{8}$$

To ensure proper "boundary conditions," the list head is set up as follows:

`LOC(AVAIL)`: | − | 0 0 | • → | to first block in available space list
`LOC(AVAIL)+1`: | − | 0 0 | • → | to last block in available space list

$$(9)$$

A first-fit reservation algorithm for this technique may be designed very much like Algorithm A, so we shall not consider it here (see exercise 12). The principal new feature of this method is the way the block can be freed in essentially a fixed amount of time:

Algorithm C (*Liberation with boundary tags*). Assume that blocks of locations have the forms shown in (7), and assume that the `AVAIL` list is doubly linked, as described above. This algorithm puts the block of locations starting with address `P0` into the `AVAIL` list. If the pool of available storage runs from locations m_0 through m_1, inclusive, the algorithm assumes for convenience that

$$\texttt{TAG}(m_0 - 1) = \texttt{TAG}(m_1 + 1) = \text{"+"}.$$

C1. [Check lower bound.] If `TAG(P0 − 1)` = "+", go to C3.

C2. [Delete lower area.] Set `P ← P0−SIZE(P0 − 1)`, and then set `P1 ← LINK(P)`, `P2 ← LINK(P + 1)`, `LINK(P1 + 1) ← P2`, `LINK(P2) ← P1`, `SIZE(P) ← SIZE(P) + SIZE(P0)`, `P0 ← P`.

C3. [Check upper bound.] Set `P ← P0 + SIZE(P0)`. If `TAG(P)` = "+", go to C5.

C4. [Delete upper area.] Set `P1 ← LINK(P)`, `P2 ← LINK(P+1)`, `LINK(P1+1) ← P2`, `LINK(P2) ← P1`, `SIZE(P0) ← SIZE(P0) + SIZE(P)`, `P ← P + SIZE(P)`.

C5. [Add to `AVAIL` list.] Set `SIZE(P − 1)` ← `SIZE(P0)`, `LINK(P0)` ← `AVAIL`, `LINK(P0 + 1)` ← `LOC(AVAIL)`, `LINK(AVAIL + 1)` ← `P0`, `AVAIL` ← `P0`, `TAG(P0)` ← `TAG(P − 1)` ← "−". ∎

The steps of Algorithm C are straightforward consequences of the storage layout (7); a slightly longer algorithm that is a little faster appears in exercise 15. In step C5, `AVAIL` is an abbreviation for `LINK(LOC(AVAIL))`, as shown in (9).

C. The "buddy system." We will now study another approach to dynamic storage allocation, suitable for use with binary computers. This method uses one bit of overhead in each block, and it requires all blocks to be of length 1, 2, 4, 8, or 16, etc. If a block is not 2^k words long for some integer k, the next higher power of 2 is chosen and extra unused space is allocated accordingly.

The idea of this method is to keep separate lists of available blocks of each size 2^k, $0 \leq k \leq m$. The entire pool of memory space under allocation consists of 2^m words, which can be assumed to have the addresses 0 through $2^m − 1$. Originally, the entire block of 2^m words is available. Later, when a block of 2^k words is desired, and if nothing of this size is available, a larger available block is *split* into two equal parts; ultimately, a block of the right size 2^k will appear. When one block splits into two (each of which is half as large as the original), these two blocks are called *buddies*. Later when both buddies are available again, they coalesce back into a single block; thus the process can be maintained indefinitely, unless we run out of space at some point.

The key fact underlying the practical usefulness of this method is that if we know the address of a block (the memory location of its first word), and if we also know the size of that block, we know the address of its buddy. For example, the buddy of the block of size 16 beginning in binary location 101110010110000 is a block starting in binary location 101110010100000. To see why this must be true, we first observe that as the algorithm proceeds, *the address of a block of size 2^k is a multiple of 2^k*. In other words, the address in binary notation has at least k zeros at the right. This observation is easily justified by induction: If it is true for all blocks of size 2^{k+1}, it is certainly true when such a block is halved.

Therefore a block of size, say, 32 has an address of the form $xx \ldots x00000$ (where the x's represent either 0 or 1); if it is split, the newly formed buddy blocks have the addresses $xx \ldots x00000$ and $xx \ldots x10000$. In general, let $\mathrm{buddy}_k(x) =$ address of the buddy of the block of size 2^k whose address is x; we find that

$$\mathrm{buddy}_k(x) = \begin{cases} x + 2^k, & \text{if } x \bmod 2^{k+1} = 0; \\ x - 2^k, & \text{if } x \bmod 2^{k+1} = 2^k. \end{cases} \tag{10}$$

This function is readily computed with the "exclusive or" instruction (sometimes called "selective complement" or "add without carry") usually found on binary computers; see exercise 28.

The buddy system makes use of a one-bit `TAG` field in each block:

$$\begin{aligned} &\texttt{TAG(P)} = 0, &&\text{if the block with address P is reserved;} \\ &\texttt{TAG(P)} = 1, &&\text{if the block with address P is available.} \end{aligned} \tag{11}$$

This TAG field is present in all blocks, and it must not be tampered with by the users who reserve blocks. The *available* blocks also have two link fields, LINKF and LINKB, which are the usual forward and backward links of a doubly linked list; and they also have a KVAL field to specify k when their size is 2^k. The algorithms below make use of the table locations AVAIL[0], AVAIL[1], ..., AVAIL[m], which serve respectively as the heads of the lists of available storage of sizes 1, 2, 4, ..., 2^m. These lists are doubly linked, so as usual the list heads contain two pointers (see Section 2.2.5):

$$\begin{aligned} \text{AVAILF}[k] &= \text{LINKF}(\text{LOC}(\text{AVAIL}[k])) = \text{link to rear of AVAIL}[k] \text{ list};\\ \text{AVAILB}[k] &= \text{LINKB}(\text{LOC}(\text{AVAIL}[k])) = \text{link to front of AVAIL}[k] \text{ list}. \end{aligned} \quad (12)$$

Initially, before any storage has been allocated, we have

$$\begin{aligned} \text{AVAILF}[m] &= \text{AVAILB}[m] = 0,\\ \text{LINKF}(0) &= \text{LINKB}(0) = \text{LOC}(\text{AVAIL}[m]),\\ \text{TAG}(0) &= 1, \quad \text{KVAL}(0) = m \end{aligned} \quad (13)$$

(indicating a single available block of length 2^m, beginning in location 0), and

$$\text{AVAILF}[k] = \text{AVAILB}[k] = \text{LOC}(\text{AVAIL}[k]), \qquad \text{for } 0 \le k < m \quad (14)$$

(indicating empty lists for available blocks of lengths 2^k for all $k < m$).

From this description of the buddy system, the reader may find it enjoyable to design the necessary algorithms for reserving and freeing storage areas before looking at the algorithms given below. Notice the comparative ease with which blocks can be halved in the reservation algorithm.

Algorithm R (*Buddy system reservation*). This algorithm finds and reserves a block of 2^k locations, or reports failure, using the organization of the buddy system as explained above.

R1. [Find block.] Let j be the smallest integer in the range $k \le j \le m$ for which AVAILF[j] $\ne$ LOC(AVAIL[j]), that is, for which the list of available blocks of size 2^j is not empty. If no such j exists, the algorithm terminates unsuccessfully, since there are no known available blocks of sufficient size to meet the request.

R2. [Remove from list.] Set L $\leftarrow$ AVAILB[j], P $\leftarrow$ LINKB(L), AVAILB[j] $\leftarrow$ P, LINKF(P) $\leftarrow$ LOC(AVAIL[j]), and TAG(L) $\leftarrow$ 0.

R3. [Split required?] If $j = k$, the algorithm terminates (we have found and reserved an available block starting at address L).

R4. [Split.] Decrease j by 1. Then set P $\leftarrow$ L $+ 2^j$, TAG(P) $\leftarrow$ 1, KVAL(P) $\leftarrow j$, LINKF(P) $\leftarrow$ LINKB(P) $\leftarrow$ LOC(AVAIL[j]), AVAILF[j] $\leftarrow$ AVAILB[j] $\leftarrow$ P. (This splits a large block and enters the unused half in the AVAIL[j] list, which was empty.) Go back to step R3. ∎

Algorithm S (*Buddy system liberation*). This algorithm returns a block of 2^k locations, starting in address L, to free storage, using the organization of the buddy system as explained above.

S1. [Is buddy available?] Set P $\leftarrow$ buddy$_k$(L). (See Eq. (10).) If $k = m$ or if TAG(P) $= 0$, or if TAG(P) $= 1$ and KVAL(P) $\neq k$, go to S3.

S2. [Combine with buddy.] Set

   LINKF(LINKB(P)) $\leftarrow$ LINKF(P),   LINKB(LINKF(P)) $\leftarrow$ LINKB(P).

(This removes block P from the AVAIL[k] list.) Then set $k \leftarrow k + 1$, and if P $<$ L set L $\leftarrow$ P. Return to S1.

S3. [Put on list.] Set TAG(L) $\leftarrow 1$, P $\leftarrow$ AVAILF[k], LINKF(L) $\leftarrow$ P, LINKB(P) $\leftarrow$ L, KVAL(L) $\leftarrow k$, LINKB(L) $\leftarrow$ LOC(AVAIL[k]), AVAILF[k] $\leftarrow$ L. (This puts block L on the AVAIL[k] list.) ▮

D. Comparison of the methods. The mathematical analysis of these dynamic storage-allocation algorithms has proved to be quite difficult, but there is one interesting phenomenon that is fairly easy to analyze, namely the "fifty-percent rule":

> *If Algorithms A and B are used continually in such a way that the system tends to an equilibrium condition, where there are N reserved blocks in the system, on the average, each equally likely to be the next one freed, and where the quantity K in Algorithm A takes on nonzero values (or, more generally, values $\geq c$ as in step A4') with probability p, then the average number of available blocks tends to approximately $\frac{1}{2}pN$.*

This rule tells us approximately how long the AVAIL list will be. When the quantity p is near 1 — this will happen if c is very small and if the block sizes are infrequently equal to each other — we have about half as many available blocks as unavailable ones; hence the name "fifty-percent rule."

It is not hard to derive this rule. Consider the following memory map:

This shows the reserved blocks divided into three categories:

   A: when freed, the number of available blocks will decrease by one;
   B: when freed, the number of available blocks will not change;
   C: when freed, the number of available blocks will increase by one.

Now let N be the number of reserved blocks, and let M be the number of available ones; let A, B, and C be the number of blocks of the types identified above. We have

$$N = A + B + C$$
$$M = \tfrac{1}{2}(2A + B + \epsilon) \tag{15}$$

where $\epsilon = 0$, 1, or 2 depending on conditions at the lower and upper boundaries.

Let us assume that N is essentially constant, but that A, B, C, and ϵ are random quantities that reach a stationary distribution after a block is freed and a (slightly different) stationary distribution after a block is allocated. The average change in M when a block is freed is the average value of $(C - A)/N$; the average change in M when a block is allocated is $-1 + p$. So the equilibrium assumption tells us that the average value of $C - A - N + pN$ is zero. But then the average value of $2M$ is pN plus the average value of ϵ, since $2M = N + A - C + \epsilon$ by (15). The fifty-percent rule follows.

Our assumption that each deletion applies to a random reserved block will be valid if the lifetime of a block is an exponentially distributed random variable. On the other hand, if all blocks have roughly the same lifetime, this assumption is false; John E. Shore has pointed out that type A blocks tend to be "older" than type C blocks when allocations and liberations tend to have a somewhat first-in-first-out character, since a sequence of adjacent reserved blocks tends to be in order from youngest to oldest and since the most recently allocated block is almost never type A. This tends to produce a smaller number of available blocks, giving even better performance than the fifty-percent rule would predict. [See *CACM* **20** (1977), 812–820.]

For more detailed information about the fifty-percent rule, see D. J. M. Davies, *BIT* **20** (1980), 279–288; C. M. Reeves, *Comp. J.* **26** (1983), 25–35; G. Ch. Pflug, *Comp. J.* **27** (1984), 328–333.

Besides this interesting rule, our knowledge of the performance of dynamic storage allocation algorithms is based almost entirely on Monte Carlo experiments. Readers will find it instructive to conduct their own simulation experiments when they are choosing between storage allocation algorithms for a particular machine and a particular application or class of applications. The author carried out several such experiments just before writing this section (and, indeed, the fifty-percent rule was noticed during those experiments before a proof for it was found); let us briefly examine the methods and results of those experiments here.

The basic simulation program ran as follows, with TIME initially zero and with the memory area initially all available:

P1. [Tick.] Advance TIME by 1.

P2. [Sync.] Free all blocks in the system that are scheduled to be freed at the current value of TIME.

P3. [Get data.] Calculate two quantities S (a random size) and T (a random lifetime), based on some probability distributions, using the methods of Chapter 3.

P4. [Use data.] Reserve a new block of length S, which is due to be freed at (TIME $+ T$). Return to P1. ∎

Whenever TIME was a multiple of 200, detailed statistics about the performance of the reservation and liberation algorithms were printed. The same sequence of values of S and T was used for each pair of algorithms tested. After TIME advanced past 2000, the system usually had reached a more or less steady state that gave every indication of being maintained indefinitely thereafter. However, depending on the total amount of storage available and on the distributions of S and T in step P3, the allocation algorithms would occasionally fail to find enough space and the simulation experiment was then terminated.

Let C be the total number of memory locations available, and let $\bar{S}$ and $\bar{T}$ denote the average values of S and T in step P3. It is easy to see that the expected number of unavailable words of memory at any given time is $\bar{S}\bar{T}$, once TIME is sufficiently large. When $\bar{S}\bar{T}$ was greater than about $\frac{2}{3}C$ in the experiments, memory overflow usually occurred, often before C words of memory were actually needed. The memory was able to become over 90 percent filled when the block size was small compared to C, but when the block sizes were allowed to exceed $\frac{1}{3}C$ (as well as taking on much smaller values) the program tended to regard the memory as "full" when fewer than $\frac{1}{2}C$ locations were actually in use. Empirical evidence suggests strongly that *block sizes larger than $\frac{1}{10}C$ should not be used with dynamic storage allocation* if effective operation is expected.

The reason for this behavior can be understood in terms of the fifty-percent rule: If the system reaches an equilibrium condition in which the size f of an average free block is less than the size r of an average block in use, we can expect to get an unfillable request unless a large free block is available for emergencies. Hence $f \geq r$ in a saturated system that doesn't overflow, and we have $C = fM + rN \geq rM + rN \approx (p/2 + 1)rN$. The total memory in use is therefore $rN \leq C/(p/2+1)$; when $p \approx 1$ we are unable to use more than about $2/3$ of the memory cells.

The experiments were conducted with three size distributions for S:

($S1$) an integer chosen uniformly between 100 and 2000;

($S2$) sizes $(1, 2, 4, 8, 16, 32)$ chosen with respective probabilities $(\frac{1}{2}, \frac{1}{4}, \frac{1}{8}, \frac{1}{16}, \frac{1}{32}, \frac{1}{32})$;

($S3$) sizes $(10, 12, 14, 16, 18, 20, 30, 40, 50, 60, 70, 80, 90, 100, 150, 200, 250, 500, 1000, 2000, 3000, 4000)$ selected with equal probability.

The time distribution T was usually a random integer chosen uniformly between 1 and t, for fixed $t = 10$, 100, or 1000.

Experiments were also made in which T was chosen uniformly between 1 and $\min(\lfloor\frac{5}{4}U\rfloor, 12500)$ in step P3, where U is the number of time units remaining until the next scheduled freeing of some currently reserved block in the system. This time distribution was meant to simulate an "almost-last-in-first-out" behavior: For if T were always chosen $\leq U$, the storage allocation system would degenerate into simply a stack operation requiring no complex algorithms. (See exercise 1.) The stated distribution causes T to be chosen greater than U about 20 percent of the time, so we have almost, but not quite, a stack operation. When this distribution was used, algorithms such as A, B, and C behaved much better than usual; there were rarely, if ever, more than two items in the entire AVAIL list, while there were about 14 reserved blocks. On the other hand, the buddy system algorithms, R and S, were slower when this distribution was used, because they tend to split and coalesce blocks more frequently in a stack-like operation. The theoretical properties of this time distribution appear to be quite difficult to deduce (see exercise 32).

Figure 42, which appeared near the beginning of this section, was the configuration of memory at TIME = 5000, with size distribution ($S1$) and with

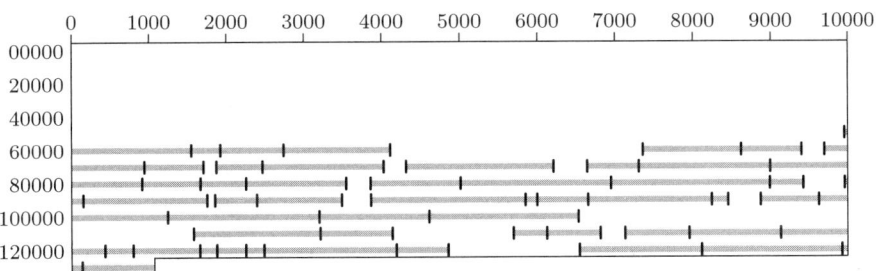

Fig. 43. Memory map obtained with the best-fit method. (Compare this with Fig. 42, which shows the first-fit method, and Fig. 44, which shows the buddy system, for the same sequence of storage requests.)

the times distributed uniformly in $\{1, \ldots, 100\}$, using the first-fit method just as in Algorithms A and B above. For this experiment, the probability p that enters into the "fifty-percent rule" was essentially 1, so we would expect about half as many available blocks as reserved blocks. Actually Fig. 42 shows 21 available and 53 reserved. This does not disprove the fifty-percent rule: For example, at TIME = 4600 there were 25 available and 49 reserved. The configuration in Fig. 42 merely shows how the fifty-percent rule is subject to statistical variations. The number of available blocks generally ranged between 20 and 30, while the number of reserved blocks was generally between 45 and 55.

Figure 43 shows the configuration of memory obtained with *the same data as Fig. 42* but with the best-fit method used instead of the first-fit method. The constant c in step A4′ was set to 16, to eliminate small blocks, and as a result the probability p dropped to about 0.7 and there were fewer available areas.

When the time distribution was changed to vary from 1 to 1000 instead of 1 to 100, situations precisely analogous to those shown in Figs. 42 and 43 were obtained, with all appropriate quantities approximately multiplied by 10. For example, there were 515 reserved blocks; and 240 free blocks in the equivalent of Fig. 42, 176 free blocks in the equivalent of Fig. 43.

In all experiments comparing the best-fit and first-fit methods, the latter always appeared to be superior. When memory size was exhausted, the first-fit method actually stayed in action longer than the best-fit method before memory overflow occurred, in most instances.

The buddy system was also applied to the same data that led to Figs. 42 and 43, and Fig. 44 was the result. Here, all sizes in the range 257 to 512 were treated as 512, those between 513 and 1024 were raised to 1024, etc. On the average this means that more than four thirds as much memory was requested (see exercise 21); the buddy system, of course, works better on size distributions like that of (*S2*) above, instead of (*S1*). Notice that there are available blocks of sizes 2^9, 2^{10}, 2^{11}, 2^{12}, 2^{13}, and 2^{14} in Fig. 44.

Simulation of the buddy system showed that it performs much better than might be expected. It is clear that the buddy system will sometimes allow two adjacent areas of the same size to be available without merging them into one

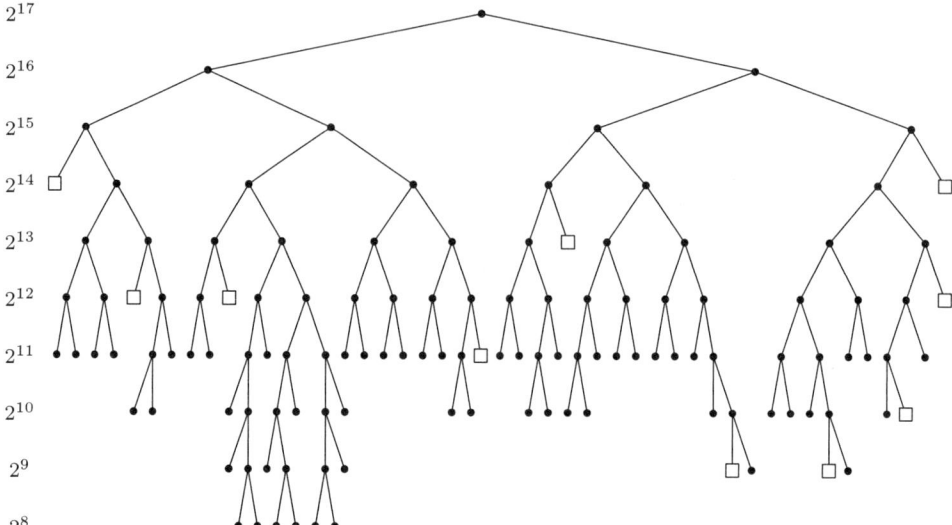

Fig. 44. Memory map obtained with the buddy system. (The tree structure indicates the division of certain large blocks into buddies of half the size. Squares indicate available blocks.)

(if they are not buddies); but this situation is not present in Fig. 44 and, in fact, it is rare in practice. In cases where memory overflow occurred, memory was 95 percent reserved, and this reflects a surprisingly good allocation balance. Furthermore, it was very seldom necessary to split blocks in Algorithm R, or to merge them in Algorithm S; the tree remained much like Fig. 44, with available blocks on the most commonly used levels. Some mathematical results that give insight into this behavior, at the lowest level of the tree, have been obtained by P. W. Purdom, Jr., and S. M. Stigler, *JACM* **17** (1970), 683–697.

Another surprise was the excellent behavior of Algorithm A after the modification described in exercise 6; only 2.8 inspections of available block sizes were necessary on the average (using size distribution (*S1*) and times chosen uniformly between 1 and 1000), and more than half of the time only the minimum value, one iteration, was necessary. This was true in spite of the fact that about 250 available blocks were present. The same experiment with Algorithm A unmodified showed that about 125 iterations were necessary on the average (so about half of the `AVAIL` list was being examined each time); 200 or more iterations were found to be necessary about 20 percent of the time.

This behavior of Algorithm A unmodified can, in fact, be predicted as a consequence of the fifty-percent rule. At equilibrium, the portion of memory containing the last half of the reserved blocks will also contain the last half of the free blocks; that portion will be involved half of the time when a block is freed, and so it must be involved in half of the allocations in order to maintain equilibrium. The same argument holds when one-half is replaced by any other fraction. (These observations are due to J. M. Robson.)

The exercises below include MIX programs for the two principal methods that are recommended as a consequence of the remarks above: (i) the boundary tag system, as modified in exercises 12 and 16; and (ii) the buddy system. Here are the approximate results:

	Time for reservation	Time for liberation
Boundary tag system:	$33 + 7A$	18, 29, 31, or 34
Buddy system:	$19 + 25R$	$27 + 26S$

Here $A \geq 1$ is the number of iterations necessary when searching for an available block that is large enough; $R \geq 0$ is the number of times a block is split in two (the initial difference of $j - k$ in Algorithm R); and $S \geq 0$ is the number of times buddy blocks are reunited during Algorithm S. The simulation experiments indicate that under the stated assumptions with size distribution $(S1)$ and time chosen between 1 and 1000, we may take $A = 2.8$, $R = S = 0.04$ on the average. (The average values $A = 1.3$, $R = S = 0.9$ were observed when the "almost-last-in-first-out" time distribution was substituted as explained above.) This shows that both methods are quite fast, with the buddy system slightly faster in MIX's case. Remember that the buddy system requires about 44 percent more space when block sizes are not constrained to be powers of 2.

A corresponding time estimate for the garbage collection and compacting algorithm of exercise 33 is about 104 units of time to locate a free node, assuming that garbage collection occurs when the memory is approximately half full, and assuming that the nodes have an average length of 5 words with 2 links per node. The pros and cons of garbage collection are discussed in Section 2.3.5. When the memory is not heavily loaded and when the appropriate restrictions are met, garbage collection and compacting is very efficient; for example, on the MIX computer, the garbage collection method is faster than the other two, if the accessible items never occupy more than about one-third of the total memory space, and if the nodes are relatively small.

If the assumptions underlying garbage collection are met, the best strategy may be to divide the pool of memory into two halves and to do all allocation sequentially within one half. Instead of freeing blocks as they become available, we simply wait until the current active half of memory is full; then we can copy all active data to the other half, simultaneously removing all holes between blocks, with a method like that of exercise 33. The size of each half pool might also be adjusted as we switch from one half to the other.

The simulation techniques mentioned above were applied also to some other storage allocation algorithms. The other methods were so poor by comparison with the algorithms of this section that they will be given only brief mention here:

a) Separate AVAIL lists were kept for each size. A single free block was occasionally split into two smaller blocks when necessary, but no attempt was made to put such blocks together again. The memory map became fragmented into finer and finer parts until it was in terrible shape; a simple scheme like this is almost equivalent to doing separate allocation in disjoint areas, one area for each block size.

b) An attempt was made to do two-level allocation: The memory was divided into 32 large sectors. A brute-force allocation method was used to reserve large blocks of 1, 2, or 3 (rarely more) adjacent sectors; each large block such as this was subdivided to meet storage requests until no more room was left within the current large block, and then another large block was reserved for use in subsequent allocations. Each large block was returned to free storage only when *all* space within it became available. This method almost always ran out of storage space very quickly.

Although this particular method of two-level allocation was a failure for the data considered in the author's simulation experiments, there are other circumstances (which occur not infrequently in practice) when a multiple-level allocation strategy can be beneficial. For example, if a rather large program operates in several stages, we might know that certain types of nodes are needed only within a certain subroutine. Some programs might also find it desirable to use quite different allocation strategies for different classes of nodes. The idea of allocating storage by zones, with possibly different strategies employed in each zone and with the ability to free an entire zone at once, is discussed by Douglas T. Ross in *CACM* **10** (1967), 481–492.

For further empirical results about dynamic storage allocation, see the articles by B. Randell, *CACM* **12** (1969), 365–369, 372; P. W. Purdom, S. M. Stigler, and T. O. Cheam, *BIT* **11** (1971), 187–195; B. H. Margolin, R. P. Parmelee, and M. Schatzoff, *IBM Systems J.* **10** (1971), 283–304; J. A. Campbell, *Comp. J.* **14** (1971), 7–9; John E. Shore, *CACM* **18** (1975), 433–440; Norman R. Nielsen, *CACM* **20** (1977), 864–873.

*E. Distributed fit. If the distribution of block sizes is known in advance, and if each block present is equally likely to be the next one freed regardless of when it was allocated, we can use a technique that has substantially better memory utilization than the general-purpose techniques described so far, by following the suggestions of E. G. Coffman, Jr., and F. T. Leighton [*J. Computer and System Sci.* **38** (1989), 2–35]. Their "distributed-fit method" works by partitioning memory into roughly $N + \sqrt{N} \lg N$ slots, where N is the desired maximum number of blocks to be handled in steady state. Each slot has a fixed size, although different slots may have different sizes; the main point is that any given slot has fixed boundaries, and it will either be empty or contain a single allocated block.

The first N slots in Coffman and Leighton's scheme are laid out according to the assumed distribution of sizes, while the last $\sqrt{N} \lg N$ slots all have the maximum size. For example, if we assume that the block sizes will be uniformly distributed between 1 and 256, and if we expect to handle $N = 2^{14}$ such blocks, we would divide the memory into $N/256 = 2^6$ slots of each size 1, 2, ..., 256, followed by an "overflow area" that contains $\sqrt{N} \lg N = 2^7 \cdot 14 = 1792$ blocks of size 256. When the system is operating at full capacity, we expect it to handle N blocks of average size $\frac{257}{2}$, occupying $\frac{257}{2} N = 2^{21} + 2^{13} = 2{,}105{,}344$ locations; this is the amount of space we have allocated to the first N slots. We have also set aside an additional $1792 \cdot 256 = 458{,}752$ locations to handle the effects of random variations; this additional overhead amounts to $O(N^{-1/2} \log N)$ of the total space, rather than a constant multiple of N as in the buddy system, so it becomes a negligible fraction when $N \to \infty$. In our example, however, it still amounts to about 18% of the total allocation.

The slots should be arranged in order so that the smaller slots precede the larger ones. Given this arrangement, we can allocate blocks by using either the first-fit or the best-fit technique. (Both methods are equivalent in this case, because the slot sizes are ordered.) The effect, under our assumptions, is to start searching at an essentially random place among the first N slots whenever a new allocation request comes in, and to continue until we find an empty slot.

If the starting slot for each search is truly random between 1 and N, we will not have to invade the overflow area very often. Indeed, if we insert exactly N items starting at random slots, overflow will occur only $O(\sqrt{N})$ times, on the average. The reason is that we can compare this algorithm to hashing with linear probing (Algorithm 6.4L), which has the same behavior except that the search for an empty cell wraps around from N to 1 instead of going into an overflow area. The analysis of Algorithm 6.4L in Theorem 6.4K shows that, when N items have been inserted, the average displacement of each item from its hash address is $\frac{1}{2}(Q(N) - 1) \sim \sqrt{\pi N/8}$; by circular symmetry this average is easily seen to be the same as the average number of times a search goes from slot k to slot $k + 1$, for each k. Overflows in the distributed-fit method correspond to searches that go from slot N to slot 1, except that our situation is even better because we avoid some congestion by not wrapping around. Therefore fewer than $\sqrt{\pi N/8}$ overflows will occur, on the average. This analysis does not take account of deletions, which preserve the assumptions of Algorithm 6.4L only if we move blocks back when deleting another block that intervened between their starting slots and their allocated slots (see Algorithm 6.4R); again, however, moving them back would only increase the chance of overflow. Our analysis also fails to account for the effect of having more than N blocks present at once; this can happen if we assume only that the arrival time between blocks is about one Nth of the residence time. For the case of more than N blocks we need to extend the analysis of Algorithm 6.4L, but Coffman and Leighton proved that the overflow area will almost never need more than $\sqrt{N} \lg N$ slots; the probability of running off the end is less than $O(N^{-M})$ for all M.

In our example, the starting slot for the search during an allocation is not uniform among slots 1, 2, ..., N; it is, instead, uniform among slots 1, 65, 129, ..., $N - 63$, because there are $N/256 = 64$ slots of each size. But this deviation from the random model considered in the previous paragraph makes overflow even less likely than predicted. All bets are off, of course, if the assumptions about block size distribution and occupancy time are violated.

F. Overflow. What do we do when no more room is available? Suppose there is a request for, say, n consecutive words, when all available blocks are too small. The first time this happens, there usually are more than n available locations present, but they are not consecutive; compacting memory (that is, moving some of the locations that are in use, so that all available locations are brought together) would mean that we could continue processing. But compacting is slow, and it requires a disciplined use of pointers; moreover, the vast majority of cases in which the first-fit method runs out of room will soon thereafter run completely out of space anyway, no matter how much compacting and re-compacting is done. Therefore it is generally not worthwhile to write a compacting program, except under special circumstances in connection with garbage collection, as in exercise 33. If overflow is expected to occur, some method for removing items from memory and storing them on an external memory device can be used, with provision for bringing the information back again when it is needed. This implies that all programs referring to the dynamic memory area must be severely restricted with regard to the allowable references they make to other blocks, and special computer hardware (for example, interrupt on absence of data, or automatic "paging") is generally required for efficient operation under these conditions.

Some decision procedure is necessary to decide which blocks are the most likely candidates for removal. One idea is to maintain a doubly linked list of the reserved blocks, in which a block is moved up to the front of the list each time it is accessed; then the blocks are effectively sorted in order of their last access, and the block at the rear of the list is the one to remove first. A similar effect can be achieved more simply by putting the reserved blocks into a circular list and including a "recently used" bit in each block; the latter is set to 1 whenever the block is accessed. When it is time to remove a block, a pointer moves along the circular list, resetting all "recently used" bits to 0 until finding a block that has not been used since the last time the pointer reached this part of the circle.

J. M. Robson has shown [*JACM* **18** (1971), 416–423] that dynamic storage allocation strategies that never relocate reserved blocks cannot possibly be guaranteed to use memory efficiently; there will always be pathological circumstances in which the method breaks down. For example, even when blocks are restricted to be of sizes 1 and 2, overflow might occur with the memory only about $\frac{2}{3}$ full, no matter what allocation algorithm is used! Robson's interesting results are surveyed in exercises 36–40, and in exercises 42–43 where he has shown that the best-fit method has a very bad worst case by comparison with first-fit.

G. For further reading. A comprehensive survey and critical review of dynamic storage allocation techniques, based on many more years of experience than were available to the author when the material above was written, has been compiled by Paul R. Wilson, Mark S. Johnstone, Michael Neely, and David Boles, *Lecture Notes in Computer Science* **986** (1995), 1–116.

EXERCISES

1. [*20*] What simplifications can be made to the reservation and liberation algorithms of this section, if storage requests always appear in a "last-in-first-out" manner, that is, if no reserved block is freed until after all blocks that were reserved subsequently have already been freed?

2. [*HM23*] (E. Wolman.) Suppose that we want to choose a fixed node size for variable-length items, and suppose also that when each node has length k and when an item has length l, it takes $\lceil l/(k-b) \rceil$ nodes to store this item. (Here b is a constant, signifying that b words of each node contain control information, such as a link to the next node.) If the average length l of an item is L, what choice of k minimizes the average amount of storage space required? (Assume that the average value of $(l/(k-b)) \bmod 1$ is equal to $1/2$, for any fixed k, as l varies.)

3. [*40*] By computer simulation, compare the best-fit, first-fit, and *worst-fit* methods of storage allocation; in the latter method, the largest available block is always chosen. Is there any significant difference in the memory usage?

4. [*22*] Write a MIX program for Algorithm A, paying special attention to making the inner loop fast. Assume that the SIZE field is (4:5), the LINK field is (0:2), and $\Lambda < 0$.

▶ **5.** [*18*] Suppose it is known that N is always 100 or more in Algorithm A. Would it be a good idea to set $c = 100$ in the modified step A4′?

▶ **6.** [*23*] (*Next fit.*) After Algorithm A has been used repeatedly, there will be a strong tendency for blocks of small SIZE to remain at the front of the AVAIL list, so that it will often be necessary to search quite far into the list before finding a block of length N or more. For example, notice how the size of the blocks essentially increases in Fig. 42, for both reserved and free blocks, from the beginning of memory to the end. (The AVAIL list used while Fig. 42 was being prepared was kept sorted by order of location, as required by Algorithm B.) Can you suggest a way to modify Algorithm A so that (a) short blocks won't tend to accumulate in a particular area, and (b) the AVAIL list may still be kept in order of increasing memory locations, for purposes of algorithms like Algorithm B?

7. [*10*] The example (1) shows that first-fit can sometimes be definitely superior to best-fit. Give a similar example that shows a case where best-fit is superior to first-fit.

8. [*21*] Show how to modify Algorithm A in a simple way to obtain an algorithm for the best-fit method, instead of first-fit.

▶ **9.** [*26*] In what ways could a reservation algorithm be designed to use the best-fit method, without searching through the whole AVAIL list? (Try to think of ways that cut down the necessary search as much as possible.)

10. [*22*] Show how to modify Algorithm B so that the block of N consecutive cells beginning at location P0 is made available, without assuming that each of these N cells is currently unavailable; assume, in fact, that the area being freed may actually overlap several blocks that are already free.

11. [*M25*] Show that the improvement to Algorithm A suggested in the answer to exercise 6 can also be used to lead to a slight improvement in Algorithm B, which cuts the average length of search from half the length of the AVAIL list to one-third this length. (Assume that the block being freed will be inserted into a random place within the sorted AVAIL list.)

▶ **12.** [*20*] Modify Algorithm A so that it follows the boundary-tag conventions of (7)–(9), uses the modified step A4′ described in the text, and also incorporates the improvement of exercise 6.

13. [*21*] Write a MIX program for the algorithm of exercise 12.

14. [*21*] What difference would it make to Algorithm C and the algorithm of exercise 12, (a) if the SIZE field were not present in the last word of a free block? or (b) if the SIZE field were not present in the first word of a reserved block?

▶ **15.** [*24*] Show how to speed up Algorithm C at the expense of a slightly longer program, by not changing any more links than absolutely necessary in each of four cases depending on whether TAG(PO − 1), TAG(PO + SIZE(PO)) are plus or minus.

16. [*24*] Write a MIX program for Algorithm C, incorporating the ideas of exercise 15.

17. [*10*] What should the contents of LOC(AVAIL) and LOC(AVAIL) + 1 be in (9) when there are no available blocks present?

▶ **18.** [*20*] Figures 42 and 43 were obtained using the same data, and essentially the same algorithms (Algorithms A and B), except that Fig. 43 was prepared by modifying Algorithm A to choose best-fit instead of first-fit. Why did this cause Fig. 42 to have a large available area in the *higher* locations of memory, while in Fig. 43 there is a large available area in the *lower* locations?

▶ **19.** [*24*] Suppose that blocks of memory have the form of (7), but without the TAG or SIZE fields required in the last word of the block. Suppose further that the following simple algorithm is being used to make a reserved block free again: Q ← AVAIL, LINK(PO) ← Q, LINK(PO + 1) ← LOC(AVAIL), LINK(Q + 1) ← PO, AVAIL ← PO, TAG(PO) ← "−". (This algorithm does nothing about collapsing adjacent areas together.)

Design a reservation algorithm, similar to Algorithm A, that does the necessary collapsing of adjacent free blocks while searching the AVAIL list, and at the same time avoids any unnecessary fragmentation of memory as in (2), (3), and (4).

20. [*00*] Why is it desirable to have the AVAIL[k] lists in the buddy system doubly linked instead of simply having straight linear lists?

21. [*HM25*] Examine the ratio a_n/b_n, where a_n is the sum of the first n terms of $1 + 2 + 4 + 4 + 8 + 8 + 8 + 8 + 16 + 16 + \cdots$, and b_n is the sum of the first n terms of $1 + 2 + 3 + 4 + 5 + 6 + 7 + 8 + 9 + 10 + \cdots$, as n goes to infinity.

▶ **22.** [*21*] The text repeatedly states that the buddy system allows only blocks of size 2^k to be used, and exercise 21 shows this can lead to a substantial increase in the storage required. But if an 11-word block is needed in connection with the buddy system, why couldn't we find a 16-word block and divide it into an 11-word piece together with two free blocks of sizes 4 and 1?

23. [*05*] What is the binary address of the buddy of the block of size 4 whose binary address is 011011110000? What would it be if the block were of size 16 instead of 4?

24. [*20*] According to the algorithm in the text, the largest block (of size 2^m) has no buddy, since it represents all of storage. Would it be correct to define $\text{buddy}_m(0) = 0$ (namely, to make this block its own buddy), and then to avoid testing $k = m$ in step S1?

▶ **25.** [*22*] Criticize the following idea: "Dynamic storage allocation using the buddy system will never reserve a block of size 2^m in practical situations (since this would fill the whole memory), and, in general, there is a maximum size 2^n for which no blocks of greater size will ever be reserved. Therefore it is a waste of time to start with such large blocks available, and to combine buddies in Algorithm S when the combined block has a size larger than 2^n."

▶ **26.** [*21*] Explain how the buddy system could be used for dynamic storage allocation in memory locations 0 through M − 1 even when M does not have the form 2^m as required in the text.

27. [*24*] Write a MIX program for Algorithm R, and determine its running time.

28. [*25*] Assume that MIX is a binary computer, with a new operation code XOR defined as follows (using the notation of Section 1.3.1): "C = 5, F = 5. For each bit position in location M that equals 1, the corresponding bit position in register A is complemented (changed from 0 to 1 or 1 to 0); the sign of rA is unaffected. The execution time is $2u$."

Write a MIX program for Algorithm S, and determine its running time.

29. [*20*] Could the buddy system do without the tag bit in each reserved block?

30. [*M48*] Analyze the average behavior of Algorithms R and S, given reasonable distributions for the sequence of storage requests.

31. [*M40*] Can a storage allocation system analogous to the buddy system be designed using the Fibonacci sequence instead of powers of two? (Thus, we might start with F_m available words, and split an available block of F_k words into two buddies of respective lengths F_{k-1} and F_{k-2}.)

32. [*HM46*] Determine $\lim_{n\to\infty} \alpha_n$, if it exists, where α_n is the mean value of t_n in a random sequence defined as follows: Given the values of t_k for $0 \le k < n$, let t_n be chosen uniformly from $\{1, 2, \ldots, g_n\}$, where

$$g_n = \lfloor \tfrac{5}{4} \min(10000, f(t_{n-1} - 1), f(t_{n-2} - 2), \ldots, f(t_0 - n)) \rfloor,$$

and $f(x) = x$ if $x > 0$, $f(x) = \infty$ if $x \le 0$. [*Note:* Some limited empirical tests indicate that α_n might be approximately 14, but this is probably not very accurate.]

▶ **33.** [*28*] (*Garbage collection and compacting.*) Assume that memory locations 1, 2, ..., AVAIL − 1 are being used as a storage pool for nodes of varying sizes, having the following form: The first word of NODE(P) contains the fields

SIZE(P) = number of words in NODE(P);
  T(P) = number of link fields in NODE(P); T(P) < SIZE(P);
LINK(P) = special link field for use only during garbage collection.

The node immediately following NODE(P) in memory is NODE(P + SIZE(P)). Assume that the only fields in NODE(P) that are used as links to other nodes are LINK(P + 1), LINK(P + 2), ..., LINK(P + T(P)), and each of these link fields is either Λ or the address of the first word of another node. Finally, assume that there is one further link variable in the program, called USE, and it points to one of the nodes.

Design an algorithm that (i) determines all nodes accessible directly or indirectly from the variable USE, (ii) moves these nodes into memory locations 1 through K − 1, for some K, changing all links so that structural relationships are preserved, and (iii) sets AVAIL ← K.

For example, consider the following contents of memory, where INFO(L) denotes the contents of location L, excluding LINK(L):

1: SIZE = 2, T = 1	6: SIZE = 2, T = 0	AVAIL = 11,
2: LINK = 6, INFO = A	7: CONTENTS = D	USE = 3.
3: SIZE = 3, T = 1	8: SIZE = 3, T = 2	
4: LINK = 8, INFO = B	9: LINK = 8, INFO = E	
5: CONTENTS = C	10: LINK = 3, INFO = F	

Your algorithm should transform this into

1: SIZE = 3, T = 1	4: SIZE = 3, T = 2	AVAIL = 7,
2: LINK = 4, INFO = B	5: LINK = 4, INFO = E	USE = 1.
3: CONTENTS = C	6: LINK = 1, INFO = F	

34. [*29*] Write a MIX program for the algorithm of exercise 33, and determine its running time.

35. [*22*] Contrast the dynamic storage allocation methods of this section with the techniques for variable-size sequential lists discussed at the end of Section 2.2.2.

▶ **36.** [*20*] A certain lunch counter in Hollywood, California, contains 23 seats in a row. Diners enter the shop in groups of one or two, and a glamorous hostess shows them where to sit. Prove that she will always be able to seat people immediately without splitting up any pairs, if no customer who comes alone is assigned to any of the seats numbered 2, 5, 8, ..., 20, provided that there never are more than 16 customers present at a time. (Pairs leave together.)

▶ **37.** [*26*] Continuing exercise 36, prove that the hostess can't always do such a good job when there are only 22 seats at the counter: No matter what strategy she uses, it will be possible to reach a situation where two friends enter and only 14 people are seated, but no two adjacent seats are vacant.

38. [*M21*] (J. M. Robson.) The lunch-counter problem in exercises 36 and 37 can be generalized to establish the worst-case performance of any dynamic storage allocation algorithm that never relocates reserved blocks. Let $N(n, m)$ be the smallest amount of memory such that any series of requests for allocation and liberation can be handled without overflow, provided that all block sizes are $\leq m$ and the total amount of space requested never exceeds n. Exercises 36 and 37 prove that $N(16, 2) = 23$; determine the exact value of $N(n, 2)$ for all n.

39. [*HM23*] (J. M. Robson.) In the notation of exercise 38, show that $N(n_1+n_2, m) \leq N(n_1, m) + N(n_2, m) + N(2m - 2, m)$; hence for fixed m, $\lim_{n \to \infty} N(n, m)/n = N(m)$ exists.

40. [*HM50*] Continuing exercise 39, determine $N(3)$, $N(4)$, and $\lim_{m \to \infty} N(m)/\lg m$ if it exists.

41. [*M27*] The purpose of this exercise is to consider the worst-case memory usage of the buddy system. A particularly bad case occurs, for example, if we start with an empty memory and proceed as follows: First reserve $n = 2^{r+1}$ blocks of length 1, which go into locations 0 through $n - 1$; then for $k = 1, 2, ..., r$, liberate all blocks whose starting location is not divisible by 2^k, and reserve $2^{-k-1}n$ blocks of length 2^k, which go into locations $\frac{1}{2}(1 + k)n$ through $\frac{1}{2}(2 + k)n - 1$. This procedure uses $1 + \frac{1}{2}r$ times as much memory as is ever occupied.

Prove that the worst case cannot be substantially worse than this: When all requests are for block sizes 1, 2, ..., 2^r, and if the total space requested at any time never exceeds n, where n is a multiple of 2^r, the buddy system will never overflow a memory area of size $(r + 1)n$.

42. [*M40*] (J. M. Robson, 1975.) Let $N_{\text{BF}}(n, m)$ be the amount of memory needed to guarantee non-overflow when the best-fit method is used for allocation as in exercise 38. Find an attacking strategy to show that $N_{\text{BF}}(n, m) \geq mn - O(n + m^2)$.

43. [*HM35*] Continuing exercise 42, let $N_{\text{FF}}(n, m)$ be the memory needed when the first-fit method is used. Find a defensive strategy to show that $N_{\text{FF}}(n, m) \leq H_m n/\ln 2$. (Hence the worst case of first-fit is not far from the best possible worst case.)

44. [*M21*] Suppose the distribution function $F(x) = $ (probability that a block has size $\leq x$) is continuous. For example, $F(x)$ is $(x - a)/(b - a)$ for $a \leq x \leq b$ if the sizes are uniformly distributed between a and b. Give a formula that expresses the sizes of the first N slots that should be set up when we use the distributed-fit method.

2.6. HISTORY AND BIBLIOGRAPHY

LINEAR LISTS and rectangular arrays of information kept in consecutive memory locations were widely used from the earliest days of stored-program computers, and the earliest treatises on programming gave the basic algorithms for traversing these structures. [For example, see J. von Neumann, *Collected Works* **5**, 113–116 (written 1946); M. V. Wilkes, D. J. Wheeler, S. Gill, *The Preparation of Programs for an Electronic Digital Computer* (Reading, Mass.: Addison–Wesley, 1951), subroutine V-1; and see especially also the work of Konrad Zuse, *Berichte der Gesellschaft für Mathematik und Datenverarbeitung* **63** (Bonn: 1972), written in 1945. Zuse was the first to develop nontrivial algorithms that worked with lists of dynamically varying lengths.] Before the days of index registers, operations on sequential linear lists were done by performing arithmetic on the machine language instructions themselves, and the need to do such arithmetic was one of the early motivations for having a computer whose programs share memory space with the data they manipulate.

Techniques that permit variable-length linear lists to share sequential locations, in such a way that they shift back and forth when necessary as described in Section 2.2.2, were apparently a much later invention. J. Dunlap of Digitek Corporation developed such techniques before 1963 in connection with the design of a series of compiler programs; about the same time the idea appeared independently in the design of a COBOL compiler at IBM Corporation, and a collection of related subroutines called CITRUS was subsequently used at various installations. The techniques remained unpublished until after they had been developed independently by Jan Garwick of Norway; see *BIT* **4** (1964), 137–140.

The idea of having linear lists in *non*sequential locations seems to have originated in connection with the design of computers with rotating drum memories. After executing the instruction in location n, such a computer was usually not ready to get its next instruction from location $n + 1$, because the drum had already rotated past that point. Depending on the instruction being performed, the most favorable position for the next instruction might be $n + 7$ or $n + 18$, say, and the machine could operate up to six or seven times faster if its instructions were located optimally rather than consecutively. [For a discussion of the interesting problems concerning the best placement of instructions, see the author's article in *JACM* **8** (1961), 119–150.] Therefore an extra address field was provided in each machine language instruction, to serve as a link to the next command. This idea, called "one-plus-one addressing," was discussed by John Mauchly in 1946 [*Theory and Techniques for the Design of Electronic Computers* **4** (U. of Pennsylvania, 1946), Lecture 37]; it contained the notion of linked lists in embryonic form, although the dynamic insertion and deletion operations that we used so frequently in this chapter were still unknown. Another early appearance of links in programs was in H. P. Luhn's 1953 memorandum suggesting the use of "chaining" for external searching; see Section 6.4.

Linked memory techniques were really born when A. Newell, J. C. Shaw, and H. A. Simon began their investigations of heuristic problem-solving by machine. As an aid to writing programs that searched for proofs in mathematical

logic, they designed the first List-processing language, IPL-II, in the spring of
1956. (IPL was an acronym for Information Processing Language.) This was
a system that made use of pointers and included important concepts like the
list of available space, but the concept of stacks was not yet well developed.
IPL-III, designed a year later, included "push down" and "pop up" for stacks as
important basic operations. [For references to IPL-II see *IRE Transactions* **IT-2**
(September 1956), 61–70; *Proc. Western Joint Comp. Conf.* **9** (1957), 218–240.
Material on IPL-III first appeared in course notes given at the University of
Michigan in the summer of 1957.]

The work of Newell, Shaw, and Simon inspired many other people to use
linked memory, which was often referred to as NSS memory at the time, but
mostly for problems dealing with simulation of human thought processes. Gradually, the techniques became recognized as basic computer-programming tools;
the first article describing the usefulness of linked memory for "down-to-earth"
problems was published by J. W. Carr, III, in *CACM* **2**, 2 (February 1959), 4–6.
Carr pointed out in this article that linked lists can readily be manipulated in
ordinary programming languages, without requiring sophisticated subroutines
or interpretive systems. See also G. A. Blaauw, "Indexing and control-word
techniques," *IBM J. Res. and Dev.* **3** (1959), 288–301.

At first, one-word nodes were used for linked tables, but about 1959 the
usefulness of several consecutive words per node and "multilinked" lists was
gradually being discovered by several different groups of people. The first article
dealing specifically with this idea was published by D. T. Ross, *CACM* **4** (1961),
147–150. At that time he used the term "plex" for what has been called a "node"
in this chapter, but he subsequently used the word "plex" in a different sense to
denote a class of nodes combined with associated algorithms for their traversal.

Notations for referring to fields within nodes are generally of two kinds: The
name of the field either precedes or follows the pointer designation. Thus, while
we have written "INFO(P)" in this chapter, some other authors write, for example, "P.INFO". At the time this chapter was prepared, the two notations seemed
to be equally prominent. The notation adopted here has the great advantage
that it translates immediately into FORTRAN, COBOL, or similar languages, if
we define INFO and LINK arrays and use P as the index. Furthermore it seems
natural to use mathematical functional notation to describe attributes of a node.
Note that "INFO(P)" is pronounced "info of P" in conventional mathematical
verbalization, just as $f(x)$ is rendered "f of x." The alternative notation P.INFO
has less of a natural flavor, since it tends to put the emphasis on P, although it
can be read "P's info"; the reason INFO(P) seems preferable is apparently the
fact that P is variable, but INFO has a fixed significance when the notation is
employed. By analogy, we could consider a vector $A = (A[1], A[2], \ldots, A[100])$
to be a node having 100 fields named $1, 2, \ldots, 100$. Now the second field would
be referred to as "2(P)" in our notation, where P points to the vector A; but
if we are referring to the jth element of the vector, we find it more natural to
write $A[j]$, putting the variable quantity "j" second. Similarly it seems most
appropriate to put the variable quantity "P" second in the notation INFO(P).

Perhaps the first people to recognize that the concepts "stack" (last-in-first-out) and "queue" (first-in-first-out) are important objects of study were cost accountants interested in reducing income tax assessments; for a discussion of the "LIFO" and "FIFO" methods of pricing inventories, see any intermediate accounting textbook, e.g., C. F. and W. J. Schlatter, *Cost Accounting* (New York: Wiley, 1957), Chapter 7. In the mid-1940s, A. M. Turing developed a stack mechanism called Reversion Storage for subroutine linkage, local variables, and parameters. His names for "push" and "pop" were "bury" and "disinter/unbury." (See the references in Section 1.4.5.) No doubt simple uses of stacks kept in sequential memory locations were common in computer programming from the earliest days, since a stack is such an intuitive concept. The programming of stacks in linked form appeared first in IPL, as stated above; the name "stack" stems from IPL terminology (although "pushdown list" was the more official IPL wording), and it was also independently introduced by E. W. Dijkstra [*Numer. Math.* **2** (1960), 312–318]. "Deque" is a term coined by E. J. Schweppe in 1966.

The origin of circular and doubly linked lists is obscure; presumably these ideas occurred naturally to many people. A strong factor in the popularization of such techniques was the existence of general List-processing systems based on them [principally the Knotted List Structures, *CACM* **5** (1962), 161–165, and Symmetric List Processor, *CACM* **6** (1963), 524–544, of J. Weizenbaum]. Ivan Sutherland introduced the use of independent doubly linked lists within larger nodes, in his Sketchpad system (Ph.D. thesis, Mass. Inst. of Technology, 1963).

Various methods for addressing and traversing multidimensional arrays of information were developed independently by clever programmers since the earliest days of computers, and thus another part of the unpublished computer folklore was born. This subject was first surveyed in print by H. Hellerman, *CACM* **5** (1962), 205–207. See also J. C. Gower, *Comp. J.* **4** (1962), 280–286.

Tree structures represented explicitly in computer memory were originally used for applications to algebraic formula manipulation. The machine language for several early computers used a three-address code to represent the computation of arithmetic expressions; the latter is equivalent to the INFO, LLINK, and RLINK of a binary tree representation. In 1952, H. G. Kahrimanian developed algorithms for differentiating algebraic formulas represented in an extended three-address code; see *Symposium on Automatic Programming* (Washington, D.C.: Office of Naval Research, May 1954), 6–14.

Since then, tree structures in various guises have been studied independently by many people in connection with numerous computer applications, but the basic techniques for tree manipulation (not general List manipulation) have seldom appeared in print except in detailed description of particular algorithms. The first general survey was made in connection with a more general study of all data structures by K. E. Iverson and L. R. Johnson [IBM Corp. research reports RC-390, RC-603, 1961; see Iverson, *A Programming Language* (New York: Wiley, 1962), Chapter 3]. See also G. Salton, *CACM* **5** (1962), 103–114.

The concept of *threaded* trees is due to A. J. Perlis and C. Thornton, *CACM* **3** (1960), 195–204. Their paper also introduced the important idea of traversing trees in various orders, and gave numerous examples of algebraic manipulation algorithms. Unfortunately, this important paper was prepared hastily and it contains many misprints. The threaded lists of Perlis and Thornton were only "right-threaded trees" in our terminology; binary trees that are threaded in *both* directions were independently discovered by A. W. Holt, *A Mathematical and Applied Investigation of Tree Structures* (Thesis, U. of Pennsylvania, 1963). Postorder and preorder for the nodes of trees were called "normal along order" and "dual along order" by Z. Pawlak [*Colloquium on the Foundation of Mathematics*, Tihany, 1962 (Budapest: Akadémiai Kiadó, 1965), 227–238]. Preorder was called "subtree order" by Iverson and Johnson in the references cited above. Graphical ways to represent the connection between tree structures and corresponding linear notations were described by A. G. Oettinger, *Proc. Harvard Symp. on Digital Computers and their Applications* (April 1961), 203–224. The representation of trees in preorder by degrees, with associated algorithms relating this representation to Dewey decimal notation and other properties of trees, was presented by S. Gorn, *Proc. Symp. Math. Theory of Automata* (Brooklyn: Poly. Inst., 1962), 223–240.

The history of tree structures as mathematical entities, together with a bibliography of the subject, is reviewed in Section 2.3.4.6.

At the time this section was first written in 1966, the most widespread knowledge about information structures was due to programmers' exposure to List processing systems, which played a very important part in this history. The first widely used system was IPL-V (a descendant of IPL-III, developed late in 1959); IPL-V was an interpretive system in which a programmer learned a machine-like language for List operations. At about the same time, FLPL (a set of FORTRAN subroutines for List manipulation, also inspired by IPL but using subroutine calls instead of interpretive language) was developed by H. Gelernter and others. A third system, LISP, was designed by J. McCarthy, also in 1959. LISP was quite different from its predecessors: Its programs were (and still are) expressed in mathematical functional notation combined with "conditional expressions," then converted into a List representation. Many List processing systems came into existence during the 1960s; the most prominent among these from a historical standpoint was J. Weizenbaum's SLIP, a set of subroutines that implemented doubly linked Lists in FORTRAN.

An article by Bobrow and Raphael, *CACM* **7** (1964), 231–240, may be read as a brief introduction to IPL-V, LISP, and SLIP; it gives a comparison of these systems. An excellent early introduction to LISP was published by P. M. Woodward and D. P. Jenkins, *Comp. J.* **4** (1961), 47–53. See also the authors' discussions of their own systems, which are articles of considerable historical importance: "An introduction to IPL-V" by A. Newell and F. M. Tonge, *CACM* **3** (1960), 205–211; "A FORTRAN-compiled List Processing Language" by H. Gelernter, J. R. Hansen, and C. L. Gerberich, *JACM* **7** (1960), 87–101; "Recursive functions of symbolic expressions and their computation by machine, I" by John McCarthy, *CACM* **3** (1960), 184–195; "Symmetric List Processor" by J. Weizenbaum, *CACM* **6** (1963), 524–544. Weizenbaum's article included a complete description of all of the algorithms used in SLIP. Of all these early systems, only LISP had the necessary ingredients to survive the ensuing decades of further progress. McCarthy has described LISP's early history in *History of Programming Languages* (Academic Press, 1981), 173–197.

Several *string manipulation* systems also appeared during the 1960s; they were primarily concerned with operations on variable-length strings of alphabetic information — looking for occurrences of certain substrings and replacing them by others, etc. The most important of these from a historical perspective were COMIT [V. H. Yngve, *CACM* **6** (1963), 83–84] and SNOBOL [D. J. Farber, R. E. Griswold, and I. P. Polonsky, *JACM* **11** (1964), 21–30]. String manipulation systems were used widely, and they were composed primarily of algorithms like the ones we have seen in this chapter, but they played a comparatively small role in the history of the techniques of information structure representation; users of such systems were isolated from the details of the actual internal processes carried on by the computer. For a survey of early string manipulation techniques, see S. E. Madnick, *CACM* **10** (1967), 420–424.

The IPL-V and FLPL systems for List-processing did not use either a garbage collection or a reference count technique for the problem of shared Lists; instead, each List was "owned" by one List and "borrowed" by all other Lists that referred to it, and a List was erased when its "owner" allowed it to disappear. Hence, the programmer was enjoined to make sure that no List was still borrowing any Lists that were being erased. The reference counter technique for Lists was introduced by G. E. Collins, *CACM* **3** (1960), 655–657, and explained further in *CACM* **9** (1966), 578–588. Garbage collection was first described in McCarthy's article of 1960; see also Weizenbaum's remarks in *CACM* **7** (1964), 38, and an article by Cohen and Trilling, *BIT* **7** (1967), 22–30.

An increasing realization of the importance of link manipulations led naturally to their inclusion in algebraic programming languages designed after 1965. The new languages allowed programmers to choose suitable forms of data representation without resorting to assembly language or paying the overhead of completely general List structures. Some of the fundamental steps in this development were the work of N. Wirth and H. Weber [*CACM* **9** (1966), 13–23, 25, 89–99]; H. W. Lawson [*CACM* **10** (1967), 358–367]; C. A. R. Hoare [*Symbol Manipulation Languages and Techniques*, ed. by D. G. Bobrow (Amsterdam: North-Holland, 1968), 262–284]; O.-J. Dahl and K. Nygaard [*CACM* **9** (1966), 671–678]; A. van Wijngaarden, B. J. Mailloux, J. E. L. Peck, and C. H. A. Koster [*Numerische Math.* **14** (1969), 79–218]; Dennis M. Ritchie [*History of Programming Languages — II* (ACM Press, 1996), 671–698].

Dynamic storage allocation algorithms were in use several years before they were ever described in print. A very readable discussion was prepared by W. T. Comfort in 1961 and published in *CACM* **7** (1964), 357–362. The boundary-tag method, introduced in Section 2.5, was designed by the author in 1962 for use in an operating system for the Burroughs B5000 computer. The buddy system was first used by H. Markowitz in connection with the SIMSCRIPT programming system in 1963, and it was independently discovered and published by K. Knowlton, *CACM* **8** (1965), 623–625; see also *CACM* **9** (1966), 616–625. For additional early discussions of dynamic storage allocation, see the articles by Iliffe and Jodeit, *Comp. J.* **5** (1962), 200–209; Bailey, Barnett, and Burleson, *CACM* **7** (1964), 339–346; A. T. Berztiss, *CACM* **8** (1965), 512–513; and D. T. Ross, *CACM* **10** (1967), 481–492.

A general discussion of information structures and their relation to programming was prepared by Mary d'Imperio, "Data Structures and their Representation in Storage," *Annual Review in Automatic Programming* **5** (Oxford: Pergamon Press, 1969). Her paper is a valuable guide to the history of the topic, since it includes a detailed analysis of the structures used in connection with twelve List processing and string manipulation systems. See also the proceedings of two symposia, *CACM* **3** (1960), 183–234 and *CACM* **9** (1966), 567–643, for further historical details. (Several of the individual papers from those proceedings have already been cited above.)

An excellent annotated bibliography of early work on symbol manipulation and algebraic formula manipulation, having numerous connections with the material of this chapter, was compiled by Jean E. Sammet; see *Computing Reviews* **7** (July–August 1966), B1–B31.

In this chapter we have looked at particular types of information structures in great detail, and (lest we fail to see the forest for the trees) it is perhaps wise to take stock of what we have learned and to summarize briefly the general subject of information structures from a broader perspective. Starting with the basic idea of a *node* as an element of data, we have seen many examples that illustrate convenient ways to represent structural relationships either implicitly (based on the relative order in which nodes are stored in computer memory) or explicitly (by means of links in the nodes, which point to other nodes). The amount of structural information that ought to be represented within the tables of a computer program depends on the operations that are to be performed on the nodes.

For pedagogic reasons, we have largely concentrated on the connections between information structures and their machine representations, instead of discussing those issues separately. However, to gain a deeper understanding it is helpful to consider the subject from a more abstract point of view, distilling off several layers of ideas that can be studied by themselves. Several noteworthy approaches of this kind have been developed, and the following thought-provoking papers are especially recommended from the early literature: G. Mealy, "Another look at data," *Proc. AFIPS Fall Joint Computer Conf.* **31** (1967), 525–534; J. Earley, "Toward an understanding of data structures," *CACM* **14** (1971), 617–627; C. A. R. Hoare, "Notes on data structuring," in *Structured Programming* by O.-J. Dahl, E. W. Dijkstra, and C. A. R. Hoare (Academic Press, 1972), 83–174; Robert W. Engles, "A tutorial on data-base organization," *Annual Review in Automatic Programming* **7** (1972), 3–63.

The discussion in this chapter does not cover the entire subject of information structures in full generality; at least three important aspects of the subject have not been treated here:

a) We often want to search through a table to find a node or set of nodes possessing a certain value, and the need for such an operation often has a profound effect on the structure of the table. This situation is explored in detail in Chapter 6.

b) We have primarily been concerned with the internal representation of structure within a computer; but that is obviously only part of the story, since structure must also be represented in the external input and output data. In simple cases, external structure can be treated by essentially the same techniques that we have been considering; but the processes of converting between strings of characters and more complex structures are also very important. Those processes are analyzed in Chapters 9 and 10.

c) We have primarily discussed representations of structures within a high-speed random-access memory. When slower memory devices such as disks or tapes are being used, we find that all of the structural problems are intensified; it becomes much more crucial to have efficient algorithms and efficient schemes for data representation. Nodes that link to each other in such cases ought to go into nearby areas of the memory. Usually the problems are highly dependent on the characteristics of individual machines, so it is difficult to discuss them in general. The simpler examples treated in this chapter should help to prepare the reader for solving the more difficult problems that arise in connection with less ideal memory devices; Chapters 5 and 6 discuss some of these problems in detail.

What are the main implications of the subjects treated in this chapter? Perhaps the most important conclusion we can reach is that the ideas we have encountered are not limited to computer programming alone; they apply more generally to everyday life. A collection of nodes containing fields, some of which point to other nodes, appears to be a very good abstract model for structural relationships of all kinds. This model shows how we can build up complicated structures from simple ones, and we have seen that corresponding algorithms for manipulating the structure can be designed in a natural manner.

Therefore it seems appropriate to develop much more theory about linked sets of nodes than we know at this time. Perhaps the most obvious way to start such a theory is to define a new kind of abstract machine or "automaton" that deals with linked structures. For example, such a device might be defined informally as follows: There are numbers k, l, r, and s, such that the automaton processes nodes containing k link fields and r information fields; it has l link registers and s information registers, which enable it to control the processes it is performing. The information fields and registers may contain any symbols from some given set of information symbols; each of the link fields and link registers either contains Λ or points to a node. The machine can (i) create new nodes (putting a link to the node into a register), (ii) compare information symbols or link values for equality, and (iii) transfer information symbols or link values between registers and nodes. Only nodes pointed to by link registers are immediately accessible. Suitable restrictions on the machine's behavior will make it equivalent to several other species of automata.

A related model of computation was proposed by A. N. Kolmogorov as early as 1952. His machine essentially operates on graphs G, having a specially designated starting vertex v_0. The action at each step depends only on the subgraph G' consisting of all vertices at distance $\leq n$ from v_0 in G, replacing G' in G by another graph $G'' = f(G')$, where G'' includes v_0 and the vertices at distance exactly n from v_0, and possibly other vertices (which are newly created); the remainder of graph G is left unaltered. Here n is a fixed number specified in advance for any particular algorithm, but it can be arbitrarily large. A symbol from a finite alphabet is attached to each vertex, and restrictions are made so that no two vertices with the same symbol can be adjacent to a common vertex. (See A. N. Kolmogorov, *Uspekhi Mat. Nauk* **8**, 4 (1953), 175–176; Kolmogorov and Uspensky, *Uspekhi Mat. Nauk* **13**, 4 (1958), 3–28; *Amer. Math. Soc. Translations*, series 2, **29** (1963), 217–245.)

Linking automata can easily simulate graph machines, taking at most a bounded number of steps per graph step. Conversely, however, it is unlikely that graph machines can simulate arbitrary linking automata without unboundedly increasing the running time, unless the definition is changed from undirected to directed graphs, in view of the restriction to vertices of bounded degree. The linking model is, of course, quite close to the operations available to programmers on real machines, while the graph model is not.

Some of the most interesting problems to solve for such devices would be to determine how fast they can solve certain problems, or how many nodes they need to solve certain problems (for example, to translate certain formal languages). At the time this chapter was first written, several interesting results of this kind had been obtained (notably by J. Hartmanis and R. E. Stearns) but only for special classes of Turing machines having multiple tapes and read/write heads. The Turing machine model is comparatively unrealistic, so these results tended to have little to do with practical problems.

We must admit that, as the number n of nodes created by a linking automaton approaches infinity, we don't know how to build such a device physically, since we want the machine operations to take the same amount of time regardless of the size of n; if linking is represented by using addresses as in a computer memory, it is necessary to put a bound on the number of nodes, since the link fields have a fixed size. A multitape Turing machine is therefore a more realistic model when n approaches infinity. Yet it seems reasonable to believe that a linking automaton as described above leads to a more appropriate theory of the complexity of algorithms than Turing machines do, even when asymptotic formulas for large n are considered, because the theory is more likely to be relevant for practical values of n. Furthermore when n gets bigger than 10^{30} or so, not even a one-tape Turing machine is realistic: It could never be built. Relevance is more important than realism.

Many years have passed since the author wrote most of the comments above, and everybody can be glad that substantial progress has indeed been made on the theory of linking automata (now called *pointer machines*). But of course much still remains to be done.

General rules for programming have been discovered.
Most of them have been used in the
Kansas City freight yards for a long time.
— DERRICK LEHMER (1949)

You will, I am sure, agree with me ... that if page
534 finds us only in the second chapter, the length of
the first one must have been really intolerable.
— SHERLOCK HOLMES, in *The Valley of Fear* (1888)

ANSWERS TO EXERCISES

I am not bound to please thee with my answers.

— SHYLOCK, in *The Merchant of Venice* (Act IV, Scene 1, Line 65)

NOTES ON THE EXERCISES

1. An average problem for a mathematically inclined reader.

4. See W. J. LeVeque, *Topics in Number Theory* **2** (Reading, Mass.: Addison–Wesley, 1956), Chapter 3; P. Ribenboim, *13 Lectures on Fermat's Last Theorem* (New York: Springer-Verlag, 1979); A. Wiles, *Annals of Mathematics* (2) **141** (1995), 443–551.

SECTION 1.1

1. $t \leftarrow a$, $a \leftarrow b$, $b \leftarrow c$, $c \leftarrow d$, $d \leftarrow t$.

2. After the first time, the values of the variables m and n are the previous values of n and r, respectively; and $n > r$.

3. Algorithm F (*Euclid's algorithm*). Given two positive integers m and n, find their greatest common divisor.

> **F1.** [Remainder m/n.] Divide m by n and let m be the remainder.
>
> **F2.** [Is it zero?] If $m = 0$, the algorithm terminates with answer n.
>
> **F3.** [Remainder n/m.] Divide n by m and let n be the remainder.
>
> **F4.** [Is it zero?] If $n = 0$, the algorithm terminates with answer m; otherwise go back to step F1. ∎

4. By Algorithm E, $n = 6099$, 2166, 1767, 399, 171, 57. Answer: 57.

5. Not finite nor definite nor effective, perhaps no output; in format, no letter is given before step numbers, no summary phrase appears, and there is no "∎".

6. Trying Algorithm E with $n = 5$ and $m = 1, 2, 3, 4, 5$, we find that step E1 is executed 2, 3, 4, 3, 1 times, respectively. So the average is $2.6 = T_5$.

7. In all but a finite number of cases, $n > m$. And when $n > m$, the first iteration of Algorithm E merely exchanges these numbers; so $U_m = T_m + 1$.

8. Let $A = \{a, b, c\}$, $N = 5$. The algorithm will terminate with the string $a^{\gcd(m,n)}$.

j	θ_j	ϕ_j	b_j	a_j	
0	ab	(empty)	1	2	Remove one a and one b, or go to 2.
1	(empty)	c	0	0	Add c at extreme left, go back to 0.
2	a	b	2	3	Change all a's to b's.
3	c	a	3	4	Change all c's to a's.
4	b	b	0	5	If b's remain, repeat.

9. For example we can say C_2 represents C_1 if there is a function g from I_1 into I_2, a function h from Q_2 into Q_1, and a function j from Q_2 into the positive integers, satisfying the following conditions:

a) If x is in I_1 then $h(g(x)) = x$.

b) If q is in Q_2 then $f_1(h(q)) = h(f_2^{[j(q)]}(q))$, where $f_2^{[j(q)]}$ means that the function f_2 is to be iterated $j(q)$ times.

c) If q is in Q_2 then $h(q)$ is in Ω_1 if and only if q is in Ω_2.

For example, let C_1 be as in (2) and let C_2 have $I_2 = \{(m, n)\}$, $\Omega_2 = \{(m, n, d)\}$, $Q_2 = I_2 \cup \Omega_2 \cup \{(m, n, a, b, 1)\} \cup \{(m, n, a, b, r, 2)\} \cup \{(m, n, a, b, r, 3)\} \cup \{(m, n, a, b, r, 4)\} \cup \{(m, n, a, b, 5)\}$. Let $f_2((m, n)) = (m, n, m, m, 1)$; $f_2((m, n, d)) = (m, n, d)$; $f_2((m, n, a, b, 1)) = (m, n, a, b, a \bmod b, 2)$; $f_2((m, n, a, b, r, 2)) = (m, n, b)$ if $r = 0$, otherwise $(m, n, a, b, r, 3)$; $f_2((m, n, a, b, r, 3)) = (m, n, b, b, r, 4)$; $f_2((m, n, a, b, r, 4)) = (m, n, a, r, 5)$; $f_2((m, n, a, b, 5)) = f_2((m, n, a, b, 1))$.

Now let $h((m, n)) = g((m, n)) = (m, n)$; $h((m, n, d)) = (d)$; $h((m, n, a, b, 1)) = (a, b, 0, 1)$; $h((m, n, a, b, r, 2)) = (a, b, r, 2)$; $h((m, n, a, b, r, 3)) = (a, b, r, 3)$; $h((m, n, a, b, r, 4)) = h(f_2((m, n, a, b, r, 4)))$; $h((m, n, a, b, 5)) = (a, b, b, 1)$; $j((m, n, a, b, r, 3)) = j((m, n, a, b, r, 4)) = 2$, otherwise $j(q) = 1$. Then C_2 represents C_1.

Notes: It is tempting to try to define things in a more simple way — for example, to let g map Q_1 into Q_2 and to insist only that when $x_0, x_1, \ldots$ is a computational sequence in C_1 then $g(x_0), g(x_1), \ldots$ is a subsequence of the computational sequence in C_2 that begins with $g(x_0)$. But this is inadequate; in the example above, C_1 forgets the original value of m and n but C_2 does not.

If C_2 represents C_1 by means of functions g, h, j, and if C_3 represents C_2 by means of functions g', h', j', then C_3 represents C_1 by means of functions g'', h'', j'', where

$$g''(x) = g'(g(x)), \qquad h''(x) = h(h'(x)), \qquad \text{and} \qquad j''(q) = \sum_{0 \le k < j(h'(q))} j'(q_k),$$

if $q_0 = q$ and $q_{k+1} = f_3^{[j'(q_k)]}(q_k)$. Hence the relation defined above is transitive. We can say C_2 *directly represents* C_1 if the function j is bounded; this relation is also transitive. The relation "C_2 represents C_1" generates an equivalence relation in which two computational methods apparently are equivalent if and only if they compute isomorphic functions of their inputs; the relation "C_2 directly represents C_1" generates a more interesting equivalence relation that perhaps matches the intuitive idea of being "essentially the same algorithm."

For an alternative approach to simulation, see R. W. Floyd and R. Beigel, *The Language of Machines* (Computer Science Press, 1994), Section 3.3.

SECTION 1.2.1

1. (a) Prove $P(0)$. (b) Prove that $P(0), \ldots, P(n)$ implies $P(n+1)$, for all $n \geq 0$.

2. The theorem has not been proved for $n = 2$. In the second part of the proof, take $n = 1$; we assume there that $a^{(n-1)-1} = a^{-1} = 1$. If this condition is true (so that $a = 1$), the theorem is indeed valid.

3. The correct answer is $1 - 1/n$. The mistake occurs in the proof for $n = 1$, when the formula on the left either may be assumed to be meaningless, or it may be assumed to be zero (since there are $n - 1$ terms).

5. If n is prime, it is trivially a product of one or more primes. Otherwise n has factors, so $n = km$ for some k and m with $1 < k, m < n$. Since both k and m are less than n, by induction they can be written as products of primes; hence n is the product of the primes appearing in the representations of k and m.

6. In the notation of Fig. 4, we prove *A5* implies *A6*. This is clear since *A5* implies $(a' - qa)m + (b' - qb)n = (a'm + b'n) - q(am + bn) = c - qd = r$.

7. $n^2 - (n-1)^2 + \cdots - (-1)^n 1^2 = 1 + 2 + \cdots + n = n(n+1)/2$.

8. (a) We must show that $(n^2 - n + 1) + (n^2 - n + 3) + \cdots + (n^2 + n - 1)$ equals n^3: And indeed, the sum is $n(n^2 - n) + (1 + 3 + \cdots + (2n-1)) = n^3 - n^2 + n^2$, by Eq. (2). But an inductive proof was requested, so another approach should be taken! For $n = 1$, the result is obvious. Let $n \geq 1$; we have $(n+1)^2 - (n+1) = n^2 - n + 2n$, so the first terms for $n + 1$ are $2n$ larger; thus the sum for $n + 1$ is the sum for n plus

$$\underbrace{2n + \cdots + 2n}_{n \text{ times}} + (n+1)^2 + (n+1) - 1;$$

this equals $n^3 + 2n^2 + n^2 + 3n + 1 = (n+1)^3$. (b) We have shown that the first term for $(n+1)^3$ is two greater than the last term for n^3. Therefore by Eq. (2), $1^3 + 2^3 + \cdots + n^3 =$ sum of consecutive odd numbers starting with unity $=$ (number of terms)$^2 = (1 + 2 + \cdots + n)^2$.

10. Obvious for $n = 10$. If $n \geq 10$, we have $2^{n+1} = 2 \cdot 2^n > (1 + 1/n)^3 2^n$ and by induction this is greater than $(1 + 1/n)^3 n^3 = (n+1)^3$.

11. $(-1)^n (n+1)/(4(n+1)^2 + 1)$.

12. The only nontrivial part of the extension is the calculation of the integer q in E2. This can be done by repeated subtraction, reducing to the problem of determining whether $u + v\sqrt{2}$ is positive, negative, or zero, and the latter problem is readily solved.

It is easy to show that whenever $u + v\sqrt{2} = u' + v'\sqrt{2}$, we must have $u = u'$ and $v = v'$, since $\sqrt{2}$ is irrational. Now it is clear that 1 and $\sqrt{2}$ have no common divisor, if we define divisor in the sense that $u + v\sqrt{2}$ divides $a(u + v\sqrt{2})$ if and only if a is an integer. The algorithm extended in this way computes the regular continued fraction of the ratio of its inputs; see Section 4.5.3.

[*Note:* However, if we extend the concept of divisor so that $u + v\sqrt{2}$ is said to divide $a(u+v\sqrt{2})$ if and only if a has the form $u' + v'\sqrt{2}$ for integers u' and v', there *is* a way to extend Algorithm E so that it always will terminate: If in step E2 we have $c = u + v\sqrt{2}$ and $d = u' + v'\sqrt{2}$, compute $c/d = c(u' - v'\sqrt{2})/(u'^2 - 2v'^2) = x + y\sqrt{2}$ where x and y are rational. Now let $q = u'' + v''\sqrt{2}$, where u'' and v'' are the nearest integers to x and y; and let $r = c - qd$. If $r = u''' + v'''\sqrt{2}$, it follows that $|u'''^2 - 2v'''^2| < |u'^2 - 2v'^2|$, hence the computation will terminate. For further information, see "quadratic Euclidean domains" in number theory textbooks.]

13. Add "$T \leq 3(n-d)+k$" to assertions $A3$, $A4$, $A5$, $A6$, where k takes the respective values 2, 3, 3, 1. Also add "$d > 0$" to $A4$.

15. (a) Let $A = S$ in (iii); every nonempty well-ordered set has a least element.

(b) Let $x \prec y$ if $|x| < |y|$ or if $|x| = |y|$ and $x < 0 < y$.

(c) No, the subset of all positive reals fails to satisfy (iii). [*Note:* Using the so-called axiom of choice, a rather complicated argument can be given to show that every set can be well-ordered somehow; but nobody has yet been able to define an explicit relation that well-orders the real numbers.]

(d) To prove (iii) for T_n, use induction on n: Let A be a nonempty subset of T_n and consider A_1, the set of first components of A. Since A_1 is a nonempty subset of S, and S is well-ordered, A_1 contains a smallest element x. Now consider A_x, the subset of A in which the first component equals x; A_x may be considered a subset of T_{n-1} if its first component is suppressed, so by induction A_x contains a smallest element $(x, x_2, \ldots, x_n)$ that in fact is the smallest element of A.

(e) No, although properties (i) and (ii) are valid. If S contains at least two distinct elements, $a \prec b$, the set (b), (a, b), (a, a, b), (a, a, a, b), (a, a, a, a, b), ... has no least element. On the other hand T can be well-ordered if we define $(x_1, \ldots, x_m) \prec (y_1, \ldots, y_n)$ whenever $m < n$, or $m = n$ and $(x_1, \ldots, x_n) \prec (y_1, \ldots, y_n)$ in T_n.

(f) Let S be well-ordered by $\prec$. If such an infinite sequence exists, the set A consisting of the members of the sequence fails to satisfy property (iii), for no element of the sequence can be smallest. Conversely if $\prec$ is a relation satisfying (i) and (ii) but not (iii), let A be a nonempty subset of S that has no smallest element. Since A is not empty, we can find x_1 in A; since x_1 is not the smallest element of A, there is x_2 in A for which $x_2 \prec x_1$; since x_2 is not the smallest element either, we can find $x_3 \prec x_2$; etc.

(g) Let A be the set of all x for which $P(x)$ is false. If A is not empty, it contains a smallest element x_0. Hence $P(y)$ is true for all $y \prec x_0$. But this implies $P(x_0)$ is true, so x_0 is not in A (a contradiction). Therefore A must be empty: $P(x)$ is always true.

SECTION 1.2.2

1. There is none; if r is a positive rational, $r/2$ is smaller.

2. Not if infinitely many nines appear in a row; in that case the decimal expansion of the number is $1 + .24000000\ldots$, according to Eq. (2).

3. $-1/27$, but the text hasn't defined it.

4. 4.

6. The decimal expansion of a number is unique, so $x = y$ if and only if $m = n$ and $d_i = e_i$ for all $i \geq 1$. If $x \neq y$, one may compare m vs. n, d_1 vs. e_1, d_2 vs. e_2, etc.; when the first inequality occurs, the larger quantity belongs to the larger of $\{x, y\}$.

7. One may use induction on x, first proving the laws for x positive, and then for x negative. Details are omitted here.

8. By trying $n = 0, 1, 2, \ldots$ we find the value of n for which $n^m \leq u < (n+1)^m$. Assuming inductively that $n, d_1, \ldots, d_{k-1}$ have been determined, d_k is the digit such that

$$\left(n + \frac{d_1}{10} + \cdots + \frac{d_k}{10^k}\right)^m \leq u < \left(n + \frac{d_1}{10} + \cdots + \frac{d_k}{10^k} + \frac{1}{10^k}\right)^m.$$

9. $((b^{p/q})^{u/v})^{qv} = (((b^{p/q})^{u/v})^v)^q = ((b^{p/q})^u)^q = ((b^{p/q})^q)^u = b^{pu}$, hence $(b^{p/q})^{u/v} = b^{pu/qv}$. This proves the second law. We prove the first law using the second: $b^{p/q}b^{u/v} = (b^{1/qv})^{pv}(b^{1/qv})^{qu} = (b^{1/qv})^{pv+qu} = b^{p/q+u/v}$.

10. If $\log_{10} 2 = p/q$, with p and q positive, then $2^q = 10^p$, which is absurd since the right-hand side is divisible by 5 but the left-hand side isn't.

11. Infinitely many! No matter how many digits of x are given, we will not know whether $10^x = 1.99999\ldots$ or $2.00000\ldots$, if x's digits agree with the digits of $\log_{10} 2$. There is nothing mysterious or paradoxical in this; a similar situation occurs in addition, if we are adding $.444444\ldots$ to $.55555\ldots$.

12. They are the only values of $d_1, \ldots, d_8$ that satisfy Eq. (7).

13. (a) First prove by induction that if $y > 0$, $1 + ny \le (1 + y)^n$. Then set $y = x/n$, and take nth roots. (b) $x = b - 1$, $n = 10^k$.

14. Set $x = \log_b c$ in the second equation of (5), then take logarithms of both sides.

15. Prove it, by transposing "$\log_b y$" to the other side of the equation and using (11).

16. $\ln x/\ln 10$, by (14).

17. 5; 1; 1; 0; undefined.

18. No, $\log_8 x = \lg x/\lg 8 = \frac{1}{3}\lg x$.

19. Yes, since $\lg n < (\log_{10} n)/.301 < 14/.301 < 47$.

20. They are reciprocals.

21. $(\ln \ln x - \ln \ln b)/\ln b$.

22. From the tables in Appendix A, $\lg x \approx 1.442695 \ln x$; $\log_{10} x \approx .4342945 \ln x$. The relative error is $\approx (1.442695 - 1.4342945)/1.442695 \approx 0.582\%$.

23. Take the figure of area $\ln y$, and divide its height by x while multiplying its length by x. This deformation preserves its area and makes it congruent to the piece left when $\ln x$ is removed from $\ln xy$, since the height at point $x + xt$ in the diagram for $\ln xy$ is $1/(x + xt) = (1/(1 + t))/x$.

24. Substitute 2 everywhere 10 appears.

25. Note that $z = 2^{-p}\lfloor 2^{p-k}x \rfloor > 0$, when p is the precision (the number of binary digits after the radix point). The quantity $y + \log_b x$ stays approximately constant.

27. Prove by induction on k that

$$x^{2^k}(1 - \delta)^{2^{k+1}-1} \le 10^{2^k(n + b_1/2 + \cdots + b_k/2^k)}x'_k \le x^{2^k}(1 + \epsilon)^{2^{k+1}-1}$$

and take logarithms.

28. The following solution uses the same auxiliary table as before.

> **E1.** [Initialize.] Set $x \leftarrow 1 - \epsilon - x$, $y \leftarrow y_0$, and $k \leftarrow 1$, where $1 - \epsilon$ is the largest possible value of x, and y_0 is the nearest approximation to $b^{1-\epsilon}$. (The quantity yb^{-x} will remain approximately constant in the following steps.)
>
> **E2.** [Test for end.] If $x = 0$, stop.
>
> **E3.** [Compare.] If $x < \log_b(2^k/(2^k - 1))$, increase k by 1 and repeat this step.
>
> **E4.** [Reduce values.] Set $x \leftarrow x - \log_b(2^k/(2^k - 1))$, $y \leftarrow y - (y$ shifted right $k)$, and go to E2. ∎

If y is set to $b^{1-\epsilon}(1 + \epsilon_0)$ in step E1, the subsequent computational error arises when $x \leftarrow x + \log_b(1 - 2^{-k}) + \delta_j$ and $y \leftarrow y(1 - 2^{-k})(1 + \epsilon_j)$ during the jth execution of step E4, for certain small errors δ_j and ϵ_j. When the algorithm terminates we have computed $y = b^{x - \Sigma \delta_j}\prod_j(1 + \epsilon_j)$. Further analysis depends on b and the computer word size. Notice that both in this case and in exercise 26, it is possible to refine the error estimates somewhat if the base is e, since for most values of k the table entry $\ln(2^k/(2^k - 1))$ can be given with high accuracy: It equals $2^{-k} + \frac{1}{2}2^{-2k} + \frac{1}{3}2^{-3k} + \cdots$.

Note: Similar algorithms can be given for trigonometric functions; see J. E. Meggitt, *IBM J. Res. and Dev.* **6** (1962), 210–226; **7** (1963), 237–245. See also T. C. Chen, *IBM J. Res. and Dev.* **16** (1972), 380–388; V. S. Linsky, *Vychisl. Mat.* **2** (1957), 90–119; D. E. Knuth, METAFONT: *The Program* (Reading, Mass.: Addison–Wesley, 1986), §120–§147.

29. e; 3; 4.

30. x.

SECTION 1.2.3

1. $-a_1$; and $a_2 + \cdots + a_1 = 0$. In general, sums with '$\cdots$' are defined so that $(a_p + \cdots + a_q) + (a_{q+1} + \cdots + a_r) = a_p + \cdots + a_r$ for arbitrary integers p, q, and r.

2. $a_1 + a_2 + a_3$.

3. $\frac{1}{1} + \frac{1}{3} + \frac{1}{5} + \frac{1}{7} + \frac{1}{9} + \frac{1}{11}$; $\frac{1}{9} + \frac{1}{3} + \frac{1}{1} + \frac{1}{3} + \frac{1}{9}$. The rule for $p(j)$ is violated: In the first case $n^2 = 3$ occurs for no n, and in the second case $n^2 = 4$ occurs for *two* n. [See Eq. (18).]

4. $(a_{11}) + (a_{21} + a_{22}) + (a_{31} + a_{32} + a_{33}) = (a_{11} + a_{21} + a_{31}) + (a_{22} + a_{32}) + (a_{33})$.

5. It is only necessary to use the rule $a \sum_{R(i)} x_i = \sum_{R(i)} (a x_i)$:

$$\left(\sum_{R(i)} a_i \right) \left(\sum_{S(j)} b_j \right) = \sum_{R(i)} a_i \left(\sum_{S(j)} b_j \right) = \sum_{R(i)} \left(\sum_{S(j)} a_i b_j \right).$$

7. Use Eq. (3); the two limits are interchanged and the terms between a_0 and a_c must be transferred from one limit to the other.

8. Let $a_{(i+1)i} = +1$, and $a_{i(i+1)} = -1$, for all $i \geq 0$, and all other a_{ij} zero; let $R(i) = S(i) = $ "$i \geq 0$". The left-hand side is -1, the right-hand side is $+1$.

9, 10. No; the applications of rule (d) assume that $n \geq 0$. (The result is correct for $n = -1$ but the derivation isn't.)

11. $(n+1)a$.

12. $\frac{7}{6}(1 - 1/7^{n+1})$.

13. $m(n - m + 1) + \frac{1}{2}(n - m)(n - m + 1)$; or, $\frac{1}{2}(n(n+1) - m(m-1))$.

14. $\frac{1}{4}(n(n+1) - m(m-1))(s(s+1) - r(r-1))$, if $m \leq n$ and $r \leq s$.

15, 16. Key steps:

$$\sum_{0 \leq j \leq n} j x^j = x \sum_{1 \leq j \leq n} j x^{j-1} = x \sum_{0 \leq j \leq n-1} (j+1) x^j$$

$$= x \sum_{0 \leq j \leq n} j x^j - n x^{n+1} + x \sum_{0 \leq j \leq n-1} x^j.$$

17. The number of elements in S.

18. $S'(j) = $ "$1 \leq j < n$". $R'(i,j) = $ "n is a multiple of i and $i > j$".

19. $(a_n - a_{m-1})[m \leq n]$.

20. $(b-1) \sum_{k=0}^{n} (n-k) b^k + n + 1 = \sum_{k=0}^{n} b^k$; this formula follows from (14) and the result of exercise 16.

21. $\sum_{R(j)} a_j + \sum_{S(j)} a_j = \sum_j a_j [R(j)] + \sum_j a_j [S(j)] = \sum_j a_j ([R(j)] + [S(j)])$; now use the fact that $[R(j)] + [S(j)] = [R(j) \text{ or } S(j)] + [R(j) \text{ and } S(j)]$. In general, bracket notation gives us the ability to manipulate "on the line" instead of "below the line."

22. For (5) and (7), just change $\sum$ to $\prod$. We also have $\prod_{R(i)} b_i c_i = (\prod_{R(i)} b_i)(\prod_{R(i)} c_i)$ and

$$\left(\prod_{R(j)} a_j\right)\left(\prod_{S(j)} a_j\right) = \left(\prod_{R(j) \text{ or } S(j)} a_j\right)\left(\prod_{R(j) \text{ and } S(j)} a_j\right).$$

23. $0 + x = x$ and $1 \cdot x = x$. This makes many operations and equations simpler, such as rule (d) and its analog in the previous exercise.

25. The first step and last step are OK. The second step uses i for two different purposes at once. The third step should probably be $\sum_{i=1}^{n} n$.

26. Key steps, after transforming the problem as in Example 2:

$$\prod_{i=0}^{n}\left(\prod_{j=0}^{n} a_i a_j\right) = \prod_{i=0}^{n}\left(a_i^{n+1} \prod_{j=0}^{n} a_j\right) = \left(\prod_{i=0}^{n} a_i^{n+1}\right)\left(\prod_{i=0}^{n}\left(\prod_{j=0}^{n} a_j\right)\right) = \left(\prod_{i=0}^{n} a_i\right)^{2n+2}.$$

The answer is $(\prod_{i=0}^{n} a_i)^{n+2}$.

28. $(n+1)/2n$.

29. (a) $\sum_{0 \le k \le j \le i \le n} a_i a_j a_k$. (b) Let $S_r = \sum_{i=0}^{n} a_i^r$. *Solution:* $\frac{1}{3}S_3 + \frac{1}{2}S_1 S_2 + \frac{1}{6}S_1^3$. The general solution to this problem, as the number of indices gets larger, may be found in Section 1.2.9, Eq. (38).

30. Write the left side as $\sum_{1 \le j,k \le n} a_j b_k x_j y_k$, and do a similar thing on the right. (This identity is the special case $m = 2$ of exercise 46.)

31. Set $a_j = u_j$, $b_j = 1$, $x_j = v_j$, and $y_j = 1$, to obtain the answer $n \sum_{j=1}^{n} u_j v_j - (\sum_{j=1}^{n} u_j)(\sum_{j=1}^{n} v_j)$. Consequently we have $(\sum_{j=1}^{n} u_j)(\sum_{j=1}^{n} v_j) \le n \sum_{j=1}^{n} u_j v_j$ when $u_1 \le u_2 \le \cdots \le u_n$ and $v_1 \le v_2 \le \cdots \le v_n$, a result known as *Chebyshev's monotonic inequality*. [See *Soobshch. mat. obshch. Khar,kovskom Univ.* **4**, 2 (1882), 93–98.]

33. This can be proved by induction on n, if we rewrite the formula as

$$\frac{1}{x_n - x_{n-1}}\left(\sum_{j=1}^{n} \frac{x_j^r(x_j - x_{n-1})}{\prod_{1 \le k \le n,\, k \ne j}(x_j - x_k)} - \sum_{j=1}^{n} \frac{x_j^r(x_j - x_n)}{\prod_{1 \le k \le n,\, k \ne j}(x_j - x_k)}\right).$$

Each of these sums now has the form of the original sum, except on $n-1$ elements, and the values turn out nicely by induction when $0 \le r \le n-1$. When $r = n$, consider the identity

$$0 = \sum_{j=1}^{n} \frac{\prod_{k=1}^{n}(x_j - x_k)}{\prod_{1 \le k \le n,\, k \ne j}(x_j - x_k)} = \sum_{j=1}^{n} \frac{x_j^n - (x_1 + \cdots + x_n)x_j^{n-1} + P(x_j)}{\prod_{1 \le k \le n,\, k \ne j}(x_j - x_k)}$$

where $P(x_j)$ is a polynomial of degree $n-2$ in x_j whose coefficients are symmetric functions of $\{x_1, \ldots, x_n\}$ that don't depend on j. (See exercise 1.2.9–10.) We obtain the desired answer from the solutions for $r = 0, 1, \ldots, n-1$.

Notes: Dr. Matrix was anticipated in this discovery by L. Euler, who wrote to Christian Goldbach about it on 9 November 1762. See Euler's *Institutionum Calculi Integralis* **2** (1769), §1169; and E. Waring, *Phil. Trans.* **69** (1779), 64–67. The following alternative method of proof, using complex variable theory, is less elementary but more elegant: By the residue theorem, the value of the given sum is

$$\frac{1}{2\pi i}\int_{|z|=R} \frac{z^r\, dz}{(z - x_1) \ldots (z - x_n)}$$

where $R > |x_1|, \ldots, |x_n|$. The Laurent expansion of the integrand converges uniformly on $|z| = R$; it is

$$z^{r-n} \left(\frac{1}{1 - x_1/z} \right) \cdots \left(\frac{1}{1 - x_n/z} \right)$$
$$= z^{r-n} + (x_1 + \cdots + x_n)z^{r-n-1} + (x_1^2 + x_1 x_2 + \cdots)z^{r-n-2} + \cdots.$$

Integrating term by term, everything vanishes except the coefficient of z^{-1}. This method gives us the *general formula* for an arbitrary integer $r \geq 0$:

$$\sum_{\substack{j_1 + \cdots + j_n = r-n+1 \\ j_1, \ldots, j_n \geq 0}} x_1^{j_1} \ldots x_n^{j_n} = \sum_{1 \leq j_1 \leq \cdots \leq j_{r-n+1} \leq n} x_{j_1} \ldots x_{j_{r-n+1}};$$

see Eq. 1.2.9–(33). [J. J. Sylvester, *Quart. J. Math.* **1** (1857), 141–152.]

34. If the reader has tried earnestly to solve this problem, *without* getting the answer, perhaps its purpose has been achieved. The temptation to regard the numerators as polynomials in x rather than as polynomials in k is almost overwhelming. It would undoubtedly be easier to prove the considerably more general result

$$\sum_{k=1}^{n} \frac{\prod_{1 \leq r \leq n-1}(y_k - z_r)}{\prod_{1 \leq r \leq n, \, r \neq k}(y_k - y_r)} = 1,$$

which is an identity in $2n - 1$ variables!

35. If $R(j)$ never holds, the value should be $-\infty$. The stated analog of rule (a) is based on the identity $a + \max(b, c) = \max(a+b, a+c)$. Similarly if all a_i, b_j are *nonnegative*, we have

$$\sup_{R(i)} a_i \sup_{S(j)} b_j = \sup_{R(i)} \sup_{S(j)} a_i b_j.$$

Rules (b), (c) do not change; for rule (d) we get the simpler form

$$\sup\left(\sup_{R(j)} a_j, \sup_{S(j)} a_j\right) = \sup_{R(j) \text{ or } S(j)} a_j.$$

36. Subtract column one from columns $2, \ldots, n$. Add rows $2, \ldots, n$ to row one. The result is a triangular determinant.

37. Subtract column one from columns $2, \ldots, n$. Then subtract x_1 times row $k - 1$ from row k, for $k = n, n-1, \ldots, 2$ (in that order). Now factor x_1 out of the first column and factor $x_k - x_1$ out of columns $k = 2, \ldots, n$, obtaining $x_1(x_2 - x_1) \ldots (x_n - x_1)$ times a Vandermonde determinant of order $n - 1$. The process continues by induction.

    Alternative proof, using "higher" mathematics: The determinant is a polynomial in the variables $x_1, \ldots, x_n$ of total degree $1+2+\cdots+n$. It vanishes if $x_j = 0$ or if $x_i = x_j$ $(i < j)$, and the coefficient of $x_1^1 x_2^2 \ldots x_n^n$ is $+1$. These facts characterize its value. In general, if two rows of a matrix become equal for $x_i = x_j$, their difference is usually divisible by $x_i - x_j$, and this observation often speeds the evaluation of determinants.

38. Subtract column one from columns $2, \ldots, n$, and factor out

$$(x_1 + y_1)^{-1} \ldots (x_n + y_1)^{-1}(y_1 - y_2) \ldots (y_1 - y_n)$$

from rows and columns. Now subtract row one from rows $2, \ldots, n$ and factor out $(x_1 - x_2) \ldots (x_1 - x_n)(x_1 + y_2)^{-1} \ldots (x_1 + y_n)^{-1}$; we are left with the Cauchy determinant of order $n - 1$.

39. Let I be the identity matrix (δ_{ij}), and J the matrix of all ones. Since $J^2 = nJ$, we have $(xI + yJ)\big((x + ny)I - yJ\big) = x(x + ny)I$.

40. [A. de Moivre, *The Doctrine of Chances*, 2nd edition (London: 1738), 197–199.]
We have

$$\sum_{t=1}^{n} b_{it} x_j^t = x_j \prod_{\substack{1 \le k \le n \\ k \neq i}} (x_k - x_j) \left/ x_i \prod_{\substack{1 \le k \le n \\ k \neq i}} (x_k - x_i) = \delta_{ij}.\right.$$

41. This follows immediately from the relation of an inverse matrix to its cofactors. It may also be interesting to give a direct proof here: We have

$$\sum_{t=1}^{n} \frac{1}{x_i + y_t} b_{tj} = \sum_{t=1}^{n} \frac{\prod_{k \neq t}(x_j + y_k - x) \prod_{k \neq i}(x_k + y_t)}{\prod_{k \neq j}(x_j - x_k) \prod_{k \neq t}(y_t - y_k)}$$

when $x = 0$. This is a polynomial of degree at most $n - 1$ in x. If we set $x = x_j + y_s$, $1 \le s \le n$, the terms are zero except when $s = t$, so the value of this polynomial is

$$\prod_{k \neq i}(-x_k - y_s) \left/ \prod_{k \neq j}(x_j - x_k) = \prod_{k \neq i}(x_j - x_k - x) \left/ \prod_{k \neq j}(x_j - x_k).\right.\right.$$

These polynomials of degree at most $n - 1$ agree at n distinct points x, so they agree also for $x = 0$; hence

$$\sum_{t=1}^{n} \frac{1}{x_i + y_t} b_{tj} = \prod_{k \neq i}(x_j - x_k) \left/ \prod_{k \neq j}(x_j - x_k) = \delta_{ij}.\right.$$

42. $n/(x + ny)$.

43. $1 - \prod_{k=1}^{n}(1 - 1/x_k)$. This is easily verified if any $x_i = 1$, since the inverse of any matrix having a row or column all of ones must have elements whose sum is 1. If none of the x_i equals one, sum the elements of row i by setting $x = 1$ in exercise 40 and obtaining $\prod_{k \neq i}(x_k - 1)/x_i \prod_{k \neq i}(x_k - x_i)$. After multiplying numerator and denominator by $x_i - 1$, we can sum on i by applying exercise 33 with $r = 0$ to the $n + 2$ numbers $\{0, 1, x_1, \ldots, x_n\}$.

44. We find

$$c_j = \sum_{i=1}^{n} b_{ij} = \prod_{k=1}^{n}(x_j + y_k) \left/ \prod_{\substack{1 \le k \le n \\ k \neq j}}(x_j - x_k),\right.$$

after applying exercise 33. And

$$\sum_{j=1}^{n} c_j = \sum_{j=1}^{n} \frac{(x_j^n + (y_1 + \cdots + y_n)x_j^{n-1} + \cdots)}{\prod_{1 \le k \le n,\, k \neq j}(x_j - x_k)}$$

$$= (x_1 + x_2 + \cdots + x_n) + (y_1 + y_2 + \cdots + y_n).$$

45. Let $x_i = i$, $y_j = j - 1$. From exercise 44, the sum of the elements of the inverse is $(1 + 2 + \cdots + n) + ((n - 1) + (n - 2) + \cdots + 0) = n^2$. From exercise 38, the elements of the inverse are

$$b_{ij} = \frac{(-1)^{i+j}(i + n - 1)!\,(j + n - 1)!}{(i + j - 1)(i - 1)!^2(j - 1)!^2(n - i)!\,(n - j)!}.$$

This quantity can be put into several forms involving binomial coefficients, for example

$$\frac{(-1)^{i+j}ij}{i+j-1}\binom{-i}{n}\binom{n}{i}\binom{-j}{n}\binom{n}{j} = (-1)^{i+j}j\binom{i+j-2}{i-1}\binom{i+n-1}{i-1}\binom{j+n-1}{n-i}\binom{n}{j}.$$

From the latter formula we see that b_{ij} is not only an integer, it is divisible by i, j, n, $i + j - 1$, $i + n - 1$, $j + n - 1$, $n - i + 1$, and $n - j + 1$. Perhaps the prettiest formula for b_{ij} is

$$(i + j - 1)\binom{i + j - 2}{i - 1}^2 \binom{-(i+j)}{n - i}\binom{-(i+j)}{n - j}.$$

The solution to this problem would be extremely difficult if we had not realized that a Hilbert matrix is a special case of a Cauchy matrix; the more general problem is much easier to solve than its special case! It is frequently wise to generalize a problem to its "inductive closure," i.e., to the smallest generalization such that all subproblems that arise in an attempted proof by mathematical induction belong to the same class. In this case, we see that cofactors of a Cauchy matrix are determinants of Cauchy matrices, but cofactors of Hilbert matrices are not determinants of Hilbert matrices. [For further information, see J. Todd, *J. Research Nat. Bur. Stand.* **65** (1961), 19–22; A. Cauchy, *Exercices d'analyse et de physique mathématique* **2** (1841), 151–159.]

46. For any integers $k_1, k_2, \ldots, k_m$, let $\epsilon(k_1, \ldots, k_m) = \text{sign}(\prod_{1 \le i < j \le m}(k_j - k_i))$, where $\text{sign } x = [x > 0] - [x < 0]$. If $(l_1, \ldots, l_m)$ is equal to $(k_1, \ldots, k_m)$ except for the fact that k_i and k_j have been interchanged, we have $\epsilon(l_1, \ldots, l_m) = -\epsilon(k_1, \ldots, k_m)$. Therefore we have the equation $\det(B_{k_1 \ldots k_m}) = \epsilon(k_1, \ldots, k_m)\det(B_{j_1 \ldots j_m})$, if $j_1 \le \cdots \le j_m$ are the numbers $k_1, \ldots, k_m$ rearranged into nondecreasing order. Now by definition of the determinant,

$$\det(AB) = \sum_{1 \le l_1, \ldots, l_m \le m} \epsilon(l_1, \ldots, l_m)\left(\sum_{k=1}^n a_{1k}b_{kl_1}\right)\cdots\left(\sum_{k=1}^n a_{mk}b_{kl_m}\right)$$

$$= \sum_{1 \le k_1, \ldots, k_m \le n} a_{1k_1}\ldots a_{mk_m}\sum_{1 \le l_1, \ldots, l_m \le m} \epsilon(l_1, \ldots, l_m)b_{k_1 l_1}\ldots b_{k_m l_m}$$

$$= \sum_{1 \le k_1, \ldots, k_m \le n} a_{1k_1}\ldots a_{mk_m}\det(B_{k_1 \ldots k_m})$$

$$= \sum_{1 \le k_1, \ldots, k_m \le n} \epsilon(k_1, \ldots, k_m)a_{1k_1}\ldots a_{mk_m}\det(B_{j_1 \ldots j_m})$$

$$= \sum_{1 \le j_1 \le \cdots \le j_m \le n} \det(A_{j_1 \ldots j_m})\det(B_{j_1 \ldots j_m}).$$

Finally, if $j_i = j_{i+1}$, $\det(A_{j_1 \ldots j_m}) = 0$. [*J. de l'École Polytechnique* **9** (1813), 280–354; **10** (1815), 29–112. Binet and Cauchy presented their papers on the same day in 1812.]

47. Let $a_{ij} = (\prod_{k=1}^{j-1}(x_i + p_k))(\prod_{k=j+1}^n(x_i + q_k))$. Subtract column $k - 1$ from column k and factor out $p_{k-j} - q_k$, for $k = n$, $n - 1$, $\ldots$, $j + 1$ (in that order), for $j = 1$, 2, $\ldots$, $n - 1$ (in that order). This leaves $\prod_{1 \le i < j \le n}(p_i - q_j)$ times $\det(b_{ij})$ where $b_{ij} = \prod_{k=j+1}^n(x_i + q_k)$. Now subtract q_{k+j} times column $k + 1$ from column k for $k = 1$, $\ldots$, $n - j$, and for $j = 1$, $\ldots$, $n - 1$; this leaves $\det(c_{ij})$, where $c_{ij} = x_i^{n-j}$ essentially defines a Vandermonde matrix. We can now proceed as in exercise 37, operating on rows instead of columns, obtaining

$$\det(a_{ij}) = \prod_{1 \le i < j \le n} (x_i - x_j)(p_i - q_j).$$

When $p_j = q_j = y_j$ for $1 \le j \le n$, the matrix in this exercise is a Cauchy matrix with row i multiplied by $\prod_{j=1}^n(x_i + y_j)$. Therefore this result generalizes exercise 38 by adding $n - 2$ independent parameters. [*Manuscripta Math.* **69** (1990), 177–178.]

SECTION 1.2.4

1. $1, -2, -1, 0, 5$.

2. $\lfloor x \rfloor$.

3. By definition, $\lfloor x \rfloor$ is the greatest integer less than or equal to x; therefore $\lfloor x \rfloor$ is an integer, $\lfloor x \rfloor \leq x$, and $\lfloor x \rfloor + 1 > x$. The latter properties, plus the fact that when m and n are integers we have $m < n$ if and only if $m \leq n - 1$, lead to an easy proof of propositions (a) and (b). Similar arguments prove (c) and (d). Finally, (e) and (f) are just combinations of previous parts of this exercise.

4. $x - 1 < \lfloor x \rfloor \leq x$; so $-x + 1 > -\lfloor x \rfloor \geq -x$; hence the result.

5. $\lfloor x + \frac{1}{2} \rfloor$. The value of $(-x$ rounded) will be the same as $-(x$ rounded), *except* when $x \bmod 1 = \frac{1}{2}$. In the latter case, the negative value is rounded towards zero and the positive value is rounded away from zero.

6. (a) is true: $\lfloor \sqrt{x} \rfloor = n \iff n^2 \leq x < (n+1)^2 \iff n^2 \leq \lfloor x \rfloor < (n+1)^2 \iff \lfloor \sqrt{\lfloor x \rfloor} \rfloor = n$. Similarly, (b) is true. But (c) fails when x is, say, 1.1.

7. $\lfloor x + y \rfloor = \lfloor \lfloor x \rfloor + x \bmod 1 + \lfloor y \rfloor + y \bmod 1 \rfloor = \lfloor x \rfloor + \lfloor y \rfloor + \lfloor x \bmod 1 + y \bmod 1 \rfloor$. The inequality should be $\geq$ for ceilings, and then equality holds if and only if either x or y is an integer or $x \bmod 1 + y \bmod 1 > 1$; that is, if and only if $(-x) \bmod 1 + (-y) \bmod 1 < 1$.

8. $1, 2, 5, -100$.

9. $-1, 0, -2$.

10. $0.1, 0.01, -0.09$.

11. $x = y$.

12. All.

13. $+1, -1$.

14. 8.

15. Multiply both sides of Eq. (1) by z; the result is also easily verified if $y = 0$.

17. As an example, consider the multiplication portion of Law A: We have $a = b + qm$ and $x = y + rm$, for some integers q and r; so $ax = by + (br + yq + qrm)m$.

18. We have $a - b = kr$ for some integer k, and also $kr \equiv 0$ (modulo s). Hence by Law B, $k \equiv 0$ (modulo s), so $a - b = qsr$ for some integer q.

20. Multiply both sides of the congruence by a'.

21. There is at least one such representation, by the previously proved exercise. If there are two representations, $n = p_1 \ldots p_k = q_1 \ldots q_m$, we have $q_1 \ldots q_m \equiv 0$ (modulo p_1); so if none of the q's equals p_1 we could cancel them all by Law B and obtain $1 \equiv 0$ (modulo p_1). The latter is impossible since p_1 is not equal to 1. So some q_j equals p_1, and $n/p_1 = p_2 \ldots p_k = q_1 \ldots q_{j-1} q_{j+1} \ldots q_m$. Either n is prime, when the result is clearly true, or by induction the two factorizations of n/p_1 are the same.

22. Let $m = ax$, where $a > 1$ and $x > 0$. Then $ax \equiv 0$ but $x \not\equiv 0$ (modulo m).

24. Law A is always valid for addition and subtraction; Law C is always valid.

26. If b is not a multiple of p, then $b^2 - 1$ is, so one of the factors must be.

27. A number is relatively prime to p^e if and only if it is not a multiple of p. So we count those that are not multiples of p and get $\varphi(p^e) = p^e - p^{e-1}$.

28. If a and b are relatively prime to m, so is $ab \bmod m$, since any prime dividing the latter and m must divide a or b also. Now simply let $x_1, \ldots, x_{\varphi(m)}$ be the numbers relatively prime to m, and observe that $ax_1 \bmod m, \ldots, ax_{\varphi(m)} \bmod m$ are the same numbers in some order, etc.

29. We prove (b): If $r \perp s$ and if k^2 divides rs, then p^2 divides rs for some prime p, so p divides r (say) and cannot divide s; so p^2 divides r. We see that $f(rs) = 0$ if and only if $f(r) = 0$ or $f(s) = 0$.

30. Suppose $r \perp s$. One idea is to prove that the $\varphi(rs)$ numbers relatively prime to rs are precisely the $\varphi(r)\varphi(s)$ distinct numbers $(sx_i + ry_j) \bmod (rs)$ where $x_1, \ldots, x_{\varphi(r)}$ and $y_1, \ldots, y_{\varphi(s)}$ are the corresponding values for r and s.

Since φ is multiplicative, $\varphi(10^6) = \varphi(2^6)\varphi(5^6) = (2^6 - 2^5)(5^6 - 5^5) = 400000$. And in general when $n = p_1^{e_1} \ldots p_r^{e_r}$, we have $\varphi(n) = (p_1^{e_1} - p_1^{e_1-1}) \ldots (p_r^{e_r} - p_r^{e_r-1}) = n \prod_{p \backslash n, p\,\text{prime}} (1 - 1/p)$. (Another proof appears in exercise 1.3.3–27.)

31. Use the fact that the divisors of rs may be uniquely written in the form cd where c divides r and d divides s. Similarly, if $f(n) \geq 0$, one can show that the function $\max_{d\backslash n} f(d)$ is multiplicative (see exercise 1.2.3–35).

33. Either $n + m$ or $n - m + 1$ is even, so one of the quantities inside the brackets is an integer; so equality holds in exercise 7, and we obtain (a) n; (b) $n + 1$.

34. b must be an integer ≥ 2. (Set $x = b$.) The sufficiency is proved as in exercise 6. The same condition is necessary and sufficient for $\lceil \log_b x \rceil = \lceil \log_b \lceil x \rceil \rceil$.

Note: R. J. McEliece has pointed out the following generalization: Let f be a continuous, strictly increasing function defined on an interval A, and assume that both $\lfloor x \rfloor$ and $\lceil x \rceil$ are in A whenever x is in A. Then the relation $\lfloor f(x) \rfloor = \lfloor f(\lfloor x \rfloor) \rfloor$ holds for all x in A if and only if the relation $\lceil f(x) \rceil = \lceil f(\lceil x \rceil) \rceil$ holds for all x in A, if and only if the following condition is satisfied for all x in A: "$f(x)$ is an integer implies x is an integer." The condition is obviously necessary, for if $f(x)$ is an integer and it equals $\lfloor f(\lfloor x \rfloor) \rfloor$ or $\lceil f(\lceil x \rceil) \rceil$ then x must equal $\lfloor x \rfloor$ or $\lceil x \rceil$. Conversely if, say, $\lfloor f(\lfloor x \rfloor) \rfloor < \lfloor f(x) \rfloor$ then by continuity there is some y with $\lfloor x \rfloor < y \leq x$ for which $f(y)$ is an integer; but y cannot be an integer.

35. $$\frac{x+m}{n} - 1 = \frac{x+m}{n} - \frac{1}{n} - \frac{n-1}{n} < \frac{\lfloor x \rfloor + m}{n} - \frac{n-1}{n} \leq \left\lfloor \frac{\lfloor x \rfloor + m}{n} \right\rfloor \leq \frac{x+m}{n};$$
apply exercise 3. Use of exercise 4 gives a similar result for the ceiling function. Both identities follow as a special case of McEliece's theorem in exercise 34.

36. Assume first that $n = 2t$. Then
$$\sum_{k=1}^{n} \left\lfloor \frac{k}{2} \right\rfloor = \sum_{k=1}^{n} \left\lfloor \frac{n+1-k}{2} \right\rfloor;$$
hence
$$\sum_{k=1}^{n} \left\lfloor \frac{k}{2} \right\rfloor = \frac{1}{2} \sum_{k=1}^{n} \left(\left\lfloor \frac{k}{2} \right\rfloor + \left\lfloor \frac{n+1-k}{2} \right\rfloor \right) = \frac{1}{2} \sum_{k=1}^{n} \left\lfloor \frac{2t+1}{2} \right\rfloor = t^2 = \frac{n^2}{4},$$
by exercise 33. And if $n = 2t + 1$, we have $t^2 + \lfloor n/2 \rfloor = t^2 + t = n^2/4 - 1/4$. For the second sum we get, similarly, $\lceil n(n+2)/4 \rceil$.

37. $\sum_{0\le k<n} \dfrac{mk+x}{n} = \dfrac{m(n-1)}{2} + x$. Let $\{y\}$ denote y mod 1; we must subtract

$$S = \sum_{0\le k<n} \left\{ \frac{mk+x}{n} \right\}.$$

This quantity S consists of d copies of the same sum, since if $t = n/d$ we have

$$\left\{ \frac{mk+x}{n} \right\} = \left\{ \frac{m(k+t)+x}{n} \right\}.$$

Let $u = m/d$; then

$$\sum_{0\le k<t} \left\{ \frac{mk+x}{n} \right\} = \sum_{0\le k<t} \left\{ \frac{x}{n} + \frac{uk}{t} \right\},$$

and since $t \perp u$ this sum may be rearranged to equal

$$\left\{ \frac{x \bmod d}{n} \right\} + \left\{ \frac{x \bmod d}{n} + \frac{1}{t} \right\} + \cdots + \left\{ \frac{x \bmod d}{n} + \frac{t-1}{t} \right\}.$$

Finally, since $(x \bmod d)/n < 1/t$, the braces in this sum may be removed and we have

$$S = d\left(\frac{t(x \bmod d)}{n} + \frac{t-1}{2} \right).$$

An application of exercise 4 yields the similar identity

$$\sum_{0\le k<n} \left\lceil \frac{mk+x}{n} \right\rceil = \frac{(m+1)(n-1)}{2} - \frac{d-1}{2} + d\lceil x/d \rceil.$$

This formula would become symmetric in m and n if it were extended over the range $0 < k \le n$. (The symmetry can be explained by drawing the graph of the summand as a function of k, then reflecting about the line $y = x$.)

38. Both sides increase by $\lceil y \rceil$ when x increases by 1, so we can assume that $0 \le x < 1$. Then both sides are zero when $x = 0$, and both sides increase by 1 when x increases past the values $1 - k/y$ for $y > k \ge 0$. [*Crelle* **136** (1909), 42; the case $y = n$ is due to C. Hermite, *Acta Math.* **5** (1884), 315.]

39. Proof of part (f): Consider the more general identity $\prod_{0\le k<n} 2\sin\pi(x+k/n) = 2\sin\pi nx$, which can be demonstrated as follows: Since $2\sin\theta = (e^{i\theta} - e^{-i\theta})/i = (1 - e^{-2i\theta})e^{i\theta - i\pi/2}$, the identity is a consequence of the two formulas

$$\prod_{0\le k<n} (1 - e^{-2\pi(x+ik/n)}) = 1 - e^{-2\pi nx} \quad \text{and} \quad \prod_{0\le k<n} e^{\pi(x-(1/2)+(k/n))} = e^{\pi(nx-1/2)}.$$

The latter is true since the function $x - \frac{1}{2}$ is replicative; and the former is true because we may set $z = 1$ in the factorization of the polynomial $z^n - \alpha^n = (z - \alpha)(z - \omega\alpha)\cdots (z - \omega^{n-1}\alpha)$, where $\omega = e^{-2\pi i/n}$.

40. (Note by N. G. de Bruijn.) If f is replicative, $f(nx+1) - f(nx) = f(x+1) - f(x)$ for all $n > 0$. Hence if f is continuous, $f(x+1) - f(x) = c$ for all x, and $g(x) = f(x) - c\lfloor x \rfloor$ is replicative and periodic. Now

$$\int_0^1 e^{2\pi inx} g(x)\, dx = \frac{1}{n} \int_0^1 e^{2\pi iy} g(y)\, dy;$$

expanding in Fourier series shows that $g(x) = (x - \frac{1}{2})a$ for $0 < x < 1$. It follows that $f(x) = (x - \frac{1}{2})a$. In general, this argument shows that any replicative locally Riemann-integrable function has the form $(x-\frac{1}{2})a+b\max(\lfloor x \rfloor, 0)+c\min(\lfloor x \rfloor, 0)$ almost everywhere. For further results see L. J. Mordell, *J. London Math. Soc.* **33** (1958), 371–375; M. F. Yoder, *Æquationes Mathematicæ* **13** (1975), 251–261.

41. We want $a_n = k$ when $\frac{1}{2}k(k-1) < n \leq \frac{1}{2}k(k+1)$. Since n is an integer, this is equivalent to

$$\frac{k(k-1)}{2} + \frac{1}{8} < n < \frac{k(k+1)}{2} + \frac{1}{8},$$

i.e., $k - \frac{1}{2} < \sqrt{2n} < k + \frac{1}{2}$. Hence $a_n = \lfloor \sqrt{2n} + \frac{1}{2} \rfloor$, the nearest integer to $\sqrt{2n}$. Other correct answers are $\lceil \sqrt{2n} - \frac{1}{2} \rceil$, $\lceil (\sqrt{8n+1} - 1)/2 \rceil$, $\lfloor (\sqrt{8n-7} + 1)/2 \rfloor$, etc.

42. (a) See exercise 1.2.7–10. (b) The given sum is $n \lfloor \log_b n \rfloor - S$, where

$$S = \sum_{\substack{1 \leq k < n \\ k+1 \text{ is a power of } b}} k = \sum_{1 \leq t \leq \log_b n} (b^t - 1) = (b^{\lfloor \log_b n \rfloor + 1} - b)/(b - 1) - \lfloor \log_b n \rfloor.$$

43. $\lfloor \sqrt{n} \rfloor \left(n - \frac{1}{6}(2\lfloor \sqrt{n} \rfloor + 5)(\lfloor \sqrt{n} \rfloor - 1) \right).$

44. The sum is $n + 1$ when n is negative.

45. $\lfloor mj/n \rfloor = r$ if and only if $\left\lceil \dfrac{rn}{m} \right\rceil \leq j < \left\lceil \dfrac{(r+1)n}{m} \right\rceil$, and we find that the given sum is therefore

$$\sum_{0 \leq r < m} f(r) \left(\left\lceil \frac{(r+1)n}{m} \right\rceil - \left\lceil \frac{rn}{m} \right\rceil \right).$$

The stated result follows by rearranging the latter sum, grouping the terms with a particular value of $\lceil rn/m \rceil$. The second formula is immediate by the substitution

$$f(x) = \binom{x+1}{k}.$$

46. $\sum_{0 \leq j < \alpha n} f(\lfloor mj/n \rfloor) = \sum_{0 \leq r < \alpha m} \lceil rn/m \rceil (f(r-1) - f(r)) + \lceil \alpha n \rceil f(\lceil \alpha m \rceil - 1).$

47. (a) The numbers $2, 4, \ldots, p-1$ are the even residues (modulo p); since $2kq = p\lfloor 2kq/p \rfloor + (2kq) \bmod p$, the number $(-1)^{\lfloor 2kq/p \rfloor}((2kq) \bmod p)$ will be an even residue or an even residue minus p, and each even residue clearly occurs just once. Hence $(-1)^\sigma q^{(p-1)/2} 2 \cdot 4 \ldots (p-1) \equiv 2 \cdot 4 \ldots (p-1)$. (b) Let $q = 2$. If $p = 4n+1$, $\sigma = n$; if $p = 4n+3$, $\sigma = n+1$. Hence $\left(\frac{2}{p}\right) = (1, -1, -1, 1)$ according as $p \bmod 8 = (1, 3, 5, 7)$, respectively. (c) For $k < p/4$, we have

$$\lfloor (p-1-2k)q/p \rfloor = q - \lceil (2k+1)q/p \rceil = q - 1 - \lfloor (2k+1)q/p \rfloor \equiv \lfloor (2k+1)q/p \rfloor \pmod 2.$$

Hence we may replace the last terms $\lfloor (p-1)q/p \rfloor$, $\lfloor (p-3)q/p \rfloor, \ldots$ by $\lfloor q/p \rfloor$, $\lfloor 3q/p \rfloor$, etc. (d) $\sum_{0 \leq k < p/2} \lfloor kq/p \rfloor + \sum_{0 \leq r < q/2} \lceil rp/q \rceil = \lfloor p/2 \rfloor (\lceil q/2 \rceil - 1) = (p+1)(q-1)/4$. Also $\sum_{0 \leq r < q/2} \lceil rp/q \rceil = \sum_{0 \leq r < q/2} \lfloor rp/q \rfloor + (q-1)/2$. The idea of this proof goes back to G. Eisenstein, *Crelle* **28** (1844), 246–248; Eisenstein also gave several other proofs of this and other reciprocity laws in the same volume.

48. (a) This is clearly not always true when $n < 0$; when $n > 0$ it is easy to verify. (b) $\lfloor (n+2-\lfloor n/25 \rfloor)/3 \rfloor = \lceil (n-\lfloor n/25 \rfloor)/3 \rceil = \lceil (n+\lceil -n/25 \rceil)/3 \rceil = \lceil \lceil 24n/25 \rceil/3 \rceil = \lceil 8n/25 \rceil = \lfloor (8n+24)/25 \rfloor$. The penultimate equality is justified by exercise 35.

49. Since $f(0) = f(f(0)) = f(f(0) + 0) = f(0) + f(0)$, we have $f(n) = n$ for all integers n. If $f(\frac{1}{2}) = k \le 0$, we have $k = f(\frac{1}{1-2k} f(\frac{1}{2} - k)) = f(\frac{1}{1-2k}(f(\frac{1}{2}) - k)) = f(0) = 0$. And if $f(\frac{1}{n-1}) = 0$ we have $f(\frac{1}{n}) = f(\frac{1}{n}f(1 + \frac{1}{n-1})) = f(\frac{1}{n-1}) = 0$; furthermore $1 \le m < n$ implies $f(\frac{m}{n}) = f(\frac{1}{a}f(\frac{am}{n})) = f(\frac{1}{a}) = 0$, for $a = \lceil n/m \rceil$, by induction on m. Thus $f(\frac{1}{2}) \le 0$ implies $f(x) = \lfloor x \rfloor$ for all rational x. On the other hand, if $f(\frac{1}{2}) > 0$ the function $g(x) = -f(-x)$ satisfies (i) and (ii) and has $g(\frac{1}{2}) = 1 - f(\frac{1}{2}) \le 0$; hence $f(x) = -g(-x) = -\lfloor -x \rfloor = \lceil x \rceil$ for all rational x. [P. Eisele and K. P. Hadeler, *AMM* **97** (1990), 475–477.]

It does not follow, however, that $f(x) = \lfloor x \rfloor$ or $\lceil x \rceil$ for all *real* values of x. If, for example, $h(x)$ is any function with $h(1) = 1$ and $h(x + y) = h(x) + h(y)$ for all real x and y, then the function $f(x) = \lfloor h(x) \rfloor$ satisfies (i) and (ii); but $h(x)$ may be unbounded and highly erratic when $0 < x < 1$ [G. Hamel, *Math. Annalen* **60** (1905), 459–462].

SECTION 1.2.5

1. 52!. For the curious, this number is 806 58175 17094 38785 71660 63685 64037 66975 28950 54408 83277 82400 00000 00000. (!)

2. $p_{nk} = p_{n(k-1)}(n - k + 1)$. After the first $n - 1$ objects have been placed, there is only one possibility for the last object.

3. $5\,3\,1\,2\,4, 3\,5\,1\,2\,4, 3\,1\,5\,2\,4, 3\,1\,2\,5\,4, 3\,1\,2\,4\,5; 4\,2\,3\,5\,1, 4\,1\,3\,5\,2, 4\,1\,2\,5\,3, 3\,1\,2\,5\,4, 3\,1\,2\,4\,5$.

4. There are 2568 digits. The leading digit is 4 (since $\log_{10} 4 = 2\log_{10} 2 \approx .602$). The least significant digit is zero, and in fact by Eq. (8) the low order 249 digits are all zero. The exact value of 1000! was calculated by H. S. Uhler using a desk calculator and much patience over a period of several years, and appears in *Scripta Mathematica* **21** (1955), 266–267. It begins with 402 38726 00770 .... (The last step in the calculation, to multiply the two numbers 750! and $\prod_{k=751}^{1000} k$, was performed on UNIVAC I by John W. Wrench, Jr., "in the extraordinary time of $2\frac{1}{2}$ minutes." Nowadays, of course, a desktop machine easily produces 1000! in a fraction of a second, and we can confirm that Uhler's value was 100% correct.)

5. $(39902)(97/96) \approx 416 + 39902 = 40318$.

6. $2^{18} \cdot 3^8 \cdot 5^4 \cdot 7^2 \cdot 11 \cdot 13 \cdot 17 \cdot 19$.

8. It is $\lim_{m \to \infty} m^n m!/((n + m)!/n!) = n! \lim_{m \to \infty} m^n/((m + 1) \ldots (m + n)) = n!$, since $m/(m + k) \to 1$.

9. $\sqrt{\pi}$ and $-2\sqrt{\pi}$. (Exercise 10 used.)

10. Yes, except when x is zero or a negative integer. For we have

$$\Gamma(x + 1) = x \lim_{m \to \infty} \frac{m^x m!}{x(x + 1) \ldots (x + m)} \left(\frac{m}{x + m + 1}\right).$$

11, 12. $\mu = (a_k p^{k-1} + \cdots + a_1) + (a_k p^{k-2} + \cdots + a_2) + \cdots + a_k$

$= a_k(p^{k-1} + \cdots + p + 1) + \cdots + a_1 = (a_k(p^k - 1) + \cdots + a_0(p^0 - 1))/(p - 1)$

$= (n - a_k - \cdots - a_1 - a_0)/(p - 1)$.

13. For each n, $1 \le n < p$, determine n' as in exercise 1.2.4–19. There is exactly one such n', by Law 1.2.4B; and $(n')' = n$. Therefore we can pair off the numbers in groups of two, provided that $n' \ne n$. If $n' = n$, we have $n^2 \equiv 1$ (modulo p); hence, as in exercise 1.2.4–26, $n = 1$ or $n = p - 1$. So $(p - 1)! \equiv 1 \cdot 1 \ldots 1 \cdot (-1)$, since 1 and $p - 1$ are the only unpaired elements.

14. Among the numbers $\{1, 2, \ldots, n\}$ that are *not* multiples of p, there are $\lfloor n/p \rfloor$ complete sets of $p - 1$ consecutive elements, each with a product congruent to -1 (modulo p) by Wilson's theorem. There are also a_0 left over, which are congruent to $a_0!$ (modulo p); so the contribution from the factors that are not multiples of p is $(-1)^{\lfloor n/p \rfloor} a_0!$. The contribution from the factors that *are* multiples of p is the same as the contribution in $\lfloor n/p \rfloor!$; this argument can therefore be repeated to get the desired formula.

15. $(n!)^3$. There are $n!$ terms. Each term has one entry from each row and each column, so it has the value $(n!)^2$.

16. The terms do not approach zero, since the coefficients approach $1/e$.

17. Express the gamma functions as limits by Eq. (15).

18. $\displaystyle\prod_{n\geq 1} \frac{n}{n - \frac{1}{2}} \frac{n}{n + \frac{1}{2}} = \frac{\Gamma(\frac{1}{2})\Gamma(\frac{3}{2})}{\Gamma(1)\Gamma(1)} = 2\Gamma(\frac{3}{2})^2.$

[Wallis's own heuristic "proof" can be found in D. J. Struik's *Source Book in Mathematics* (Harvard University Press, 1969), 244–253.]

19. Change of variable $t = mt$, integration by parts, and induction.

20. [For completeness, we prove the stated inequality. Start with the easily verified inequality $1 + x \leq e^x$; set $x = \pm t/n$ and raise to the nth power to get $(1 \pm t/n)^n \leq e^{\pm t}$. Hence $e^{-t} \geq (1-t/n)^n = e^{-t}(1-t/n)^n e^t \geq e^{-t}(1-t/n)^n(1+t/n)^n = e^{-t}(1-t^2/n^2)^n \geq e^{-t}(1 - t^2/n)$ by exercise 1.2.1–9.]

Now the given integral minus $\Gamma_m(x)$ is

$$\int_m^\infty e^{-t} t^{x-1}\, dt + \int_0^m \left(e^{-t} - \left(1 - \frac{t}{m}\right)^m\right) t^{x-1}\, dt.$$

As $m \to \infty$, the first of these integrals approaches zero, since $t^{x-1} < e^{t/2}$ for large t; and the second is less than

$$\frac{1}{m}\int_0^m t^{x+1} e^{-t}\, dt < \frac{1}{m}\int_0^\infty t^{x+1} e^{-t}\, dt \to 0.$$

21. If $c(n, j, k_1, k_2, \ldots)$ denotes the appropriate coefficient, we find

$$c(n+1, j, k_1, \ldots) = c(n, j-1, k_1-1, k_2, \ldots) + (k_1+1)c(n, j, k_1+1, k_2-1, k_3, \ldots)$$
$$+ (k_2+1)c(n, j, k_1, k_2+1, k_3-1, k_4, \ldots) + \cdots,$$

by differentiation. The equations $k_1 + k_2 + \cdots = j$ and $k_1 + 2k_2 + \cdots = n$ are preserved in this induction relationship. We can easily factor $n!/(k_1!(1!)^{k_1} k_2!(2!)^{k_2} \ldots)$ out of each term appearing on the right-hand side of the equation for $c(n + 1, j, k_1, \ldots)$, and we are left with $k_1 + 2k_2 + 3k_3 + \cdots = n + 1$. (In the proof it is convenient to assume that there are infinitely many k's, although clearly $k_{n+1} = k_{n+2} = \cdots = 0$.)

The solution just given makes use of standard techniques, but it doesn't give a satisfactory explanation of *why* the formula has this form, nor how it could have been discovered in the first place. Let us examine this question using a combinatorial argument suggested by H. S. Wall [*Bull. Amer. Math. Soc.* **44** (1938), 395–398]. Write for convenience $w_j = D_u^j w$, $u_k = D_x^k u$. Then $D_x(w_j) = w_{j+1}u_1$ and $D_x(u_k) = u_{k+1}$.

By these two rules and the rule for derivative of a product we find

$$D_x^1 w = w_1 u_1$$
$$D_x^2 w = (w_2 u_1 u_1 + w_1 u_2)$$
$$D_x^3 w = ((w_3 u_1 u_1 u_1 + w_2 u_2 u_1 + w_2 u_1 u_2) + (w_2 u_1 u_2 + w_1 u_3)), \text{ etc.}$$

Analogously we may set up a corresponding tableau of set partitions thus:

$$\mathcal{D}^1 = \{1\}$$
$$\mathcal{D}^2 = (\{2\}\{1\} + \{2,1\})$$
$$\mathcal{D}^3 = ((\{3\}\{2\}\{1\} + \{3,2\}\{1\} + \{2\}\{3,1\}) + (\{3\}\{2,1\} + \{3,2,1\})), \text{ etc.}$$

Formally, if $a_1 a_2 \dots a_j$ is a partition of the set $\{1, 2, \dots, n-1\}$, define

$$\mathcal{D} a_1 a_2 \dots a_j = \{n\} a_1 a_2 \dots a_j + (a_1 \cup \{n\}) a_2 \dots a_j$$
$$+ a_1 (a_2 \cup \{n\}) \dots a_j + \dots + a_1 a_2 \dots (a_j \cup \{n\}).$$

This rule is an exact parallel of the rule

$$D_x(w_j u_{r_1} u_{r_2} \dots u_{r_j}) = w_{j+1} u_1 u_{r_1} u_{r_2} \dots u_{r_j} + w_j u_{r_1+1} u_{r_2} \dots u_{r_j}$$
$$+ w_j u_{r_1} u_{r_2+1} \dots u_{r_j} + \dots + w_j u_{r_1} u_{r_2} \dots u_{r_j+1},$$

if we let the term $w_j u_{r_1} u_{r_2} \dots u_{r_j}$ correspond to a partition $a_1 a_2 \dots a_j$ with r_t elements in a_t, $1 \leq t \leq j$. So there is a natural mapping from $\mathcal{D}^n$ onto $D_x^n w$, and furthermore it is easy to see that $\mathcal{D}^n$ includes each partition of the set $\{1, 2, \dots, n\}$ exactly once. (See exercise 1.2.6–64.)

From these observations we find that if we collect like terms in $D_x^n w$, we obtain a sum of terms $c(k_1, k_2, \dots) w_j u_1^{k_1} u_2^{k_2} \dots$, where $j = k_1 + k_2 + \dots$ and $n = k_1 + 2k_2 + \dots$, and where $c(k_1, k_2, \dots)$ is *the number of partitions of $\{1, 2, \dots, n\}$ into j subsets such that there are k_t subsets having t elements.*

It remains to count these partitions. Consider an array of k_t boxes of capacity t:

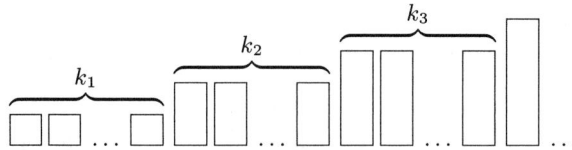

The number of ways to put n different elements into these boxes is the multinomial coefficient

$$\binom{n}{1, 1, \dots, 1, 2, 2, \dots, 2, 3, 3, \dots, 3, 4, \dots} = \frac{n!}{1!^{k_1} 2!^{k_2} 3!^{k_3} \dots}.$$

To get $c(k_1, k_2, k_3, \dots)$ we should divide this by $k_1! \, k_2! \, k_3! \dots$, since the boxes in each group of k_t are indistinguishable from each other; they may be permuted in $k_t!$ ways without affecting the set partition.

Arbogast's original proof [*Du Calcul des Dérivations* (Strasbourg: 1800), §52] was based on the fact that $D_x^k u / k!$ is the coefficient of z^k in $u(x+z)$ and $D_u^j w / j!$ is the coefficient of y^j in $w(u+y)$, hence the coefficient of z^n in $w(u(x+z))$ is

$$\frac{D_x^n w}{n!} = \sum_{j=0}^{n} \frac{D_u^j w}{j!} \sum_{\substack{k_1+k_2+\cdots+k_n=j \\ k_1+2k_2+\cdots+nk_n=n \\ k_1,k_2,\ldots,k_n \geq 0}} \frac{j!}{k_1!\,k_2!\ldots k_n!} \left(\frac{D_x^1 u}{1!}\right)^{k_1} \left(\frac{D_x^2 u}{2!}\right)^{k_2} \cdots \left(\frac{D_x^n u}{n!}\right)^{k_n}.$$

His formula was forgotten for many years, then rediscovered independently by F. Faà di Bruno [*Quarterly J. Math.* **1** (1857), 359–360], who observed that it can also be expressed as a determinant

$$D_x^n = \det \begin{pmatrix} \binom{n-1}{0}u_1 & \binom{n-1}{1}u_2 & \binom{n-1}{2}u_3 & \cdots & \binom{n-1}{n-2}u_{n-1} & \binom{n-1}{n-1}u_n \\ -1 & \binom{n-2}{0}u_1 & \binom{n-2}{1}u_2 & \cdots & \binom{n-2}{n-3}u_{n-2} & \binom{n-2}{n-2}u_{n-1} \\ 0 & -1 & \binom{n-3}{0}u_1 & \cdots & \binom{n-3}{n-4}u_{n-3} & \binom{n-3}{n-3}u_{n-2} \\ \vdots & \vdots & \vdots & \ddots & \vdots & \vdots \\ 0 & 0 & 0 & \cdots & -1 & \binom{0}{0}u_1 \end{pmatrix}$$

where $u_j = (D_x^j u)\, D_u$; both sides of this equation are differential operators to be applied to w. For a generalization of Arbogast's formula to functions of several variables, and a list of references to other related work, see the paper by I. J. Good, *Annals of Mathematical Statistics* **32** (1961), 540–541.

22. The hypothesis that $\lim_{n\to\infty}(n+x)!/(n!\,n^x)=1$ is valid for integers x; for example, if x is positive, the quantity is $(1+1/n)(1+2/n)\ldots(1+x/n)$, which certainly approaches unity. If we also assume that $x! = x(x-1)!$, the hypothesis leads us to conclude immediately that

$$1 = \lim_{n\to\infty} \frac{(n+x)!}{n!\,n^x} = x!\, \lim_{n\to\infty} \frac{(x+1)\ldots(x+n)}{n!\,n^x},$$

which is equivalent to the definition given in the text.

23. $z\,(-z)!\,\Gamma(z) = \lim_{m\to\infty}\prod_{n=1}^{m}(1-z/n)^{-1}(1+z/n)^{-1}$ by (13) and (15).

24. $n^n/n! = \prod_{k=1}^{n-1}(k+1)^k/k^k \leq \prod_{k=1}^{n-1} e; \quad n!/n^{n+1} = \prod_{k=1}^{n-1} k^{k+1}/(k+1)^{k+1} \leq \prod_{k=1}^{n-1} e^{-1}$.

25. $x^{\overline{m+n}} = x^{\overline{m}}(x-m)^{\underline{n}}$; $x^{\overline{m+n}} = x^{\overline{m}}(x+m)^{\overline{n}}$. These laws hold also when m and n are nonintegers, by (21).

SECTION 1.2.6

  1. n, since each combination leaves out one item.

  2. 1. There's exactly one way to choose nothing from the empty set.

  3. $\binom{52}{13}$. The actual number is 635013559600.

  4. $2^4 \cdot 5^2 \cdot 7^2 \cdot 17 \cdot 23 \cdot 41 \cdot 43 \cdot 47$.

  5. $(10+1)^4 = 10000 + 4(1000) + 6(100) + 4(10) + 1$.

  6. $r = -3$:   1 −3   6 −10   15 −21   28 −36 ...
       $r = -2$:   1 −2   3   −4   5   −6   7   −8 ...
       $r = -1$:   1 −1   1   −1   1   −1   1   −1 ...

  7. $\lfloor n/2 \rfloor$; or, alternatively, $\lceil n/2 \rceil$. It is clear from (3) that for smaller values the binomial coefficient is strictly increasing, and afterwards it decreases to zero.

8. The nonzero entries in each row are the same from left to right as from right to left.

9. One if n is positive or zero; zero if n is negative.

10. (a), (b) and (f) follow immediately from (e); (c) and (d) follow from (a), (b), and Eq. (9). Thus it suffices to prove (e). Consider $\binom{n}{k}$ as a fraction, given by Eq. (3) with factors in numerator and denominator. The first $k \bmod p$ factors have no p's in the denominator, and in the numerator and denominator these terms are clearly congruent to the corresponding terms of

$$\binom{n \bmod p}{k \bmod p},$$

which differ by multiples of p. (When dealing with non-multiples of p we may work modulo p in both numerator and denominator, since if $a \equiv c$ and $b \equiv d$ and a/b, c/d are integers, then $a/b \equiv c/d$.) There remain $k - k \bmod p$ factors, which fall into $\lfloor k/p \rfloor$ groups of p consecutive values each. Each group contains exactly one multiple of p; the other $p - 1$ factors in a group are congruent (modulo p) to $(p-1)!$ so they cancel in numerator and denominator. It remains to investigate the $\lfloor k/p \rfloor$ multiples of p in numerator and denominator; we divide each of them by p and are left with the binomial coefficient

$$\binom{\lfloor (n - k \bmod p)/p \rfloor}{\lfloor k/p \rfloor}.$$

If $k \bmod p \le n \bmod p$, this equals

$$\binom{\lfloor n/p \rfloor}{\lfloor k/p \rfloor}$$

as desired; and if $k \bmod p > n \bmod p$, the other factor $\binom{n \bmod p}{k \bmod p}$ is zero, so the formula holds in general. [*American J. Math.* **1** (1878), 229–230; see also L. E. Dickson, *Quart. J. Math.* **33** (1902), 383–384; N. J. Fine, *AMM* **54** (1947), 589–592.]

11. If $a = a_r p^r + \cdots + a_0$, $b = b_r p^r + \cdots + b_0$, and $a + b = c_r p^r + \cdots + c_0$, the value of n (according to exercise 1.2.5–12 and Eq. (5)) is

$$(a_0 + \cdots + a_r + b_0 + \cdots + b_r - c_0 - \cdots - c_r)/(p - 1).$$

A carry decreases c_j by p and increases c_{j+1} by 1, giving a net change of $+1$ in this formula. [Similar results hold for q-nomial and Fibonomial coefficients; see Knuth and Wilf, *Crelle* **396** (1989), 212–219.]

12. By either of the two previous exercises, n must be one less than a power of 2. More generally, $\binom{n}{k}$ is never divisible by the prime p, $0 \le k \le n$, if and only if $n = ap^m - 1$, $1 \le a < p$, $m \ge 0$.

14. $24\binom{n+1}{5} + 36\binom{n+1}{4} + 14\binom{n+1}{3} + \binom{n+1}{2}$

$$= \frac{n^5}{5} + \frac{n^4}{2} + \frac{n^3}{3} - \frac{n}{30} = \frac{n(n+1)(n+\frac{1}{2})(3n^2 + 3n - 1)}{15}.$$

15. Induction and (9).

17. We may assume that r and s are positive integers. Also

$$\sum_n \binom{r+s}{n} x^n = (1+x)^{r+s} = \sum_k \binom{r}{k} x^k \sum_m \binom{s}{m} x^m$$

$$= \sum_k \binom{r}{k} x^k \sum_n \binom{s}{n-k} x^{n-k} = \sum_n \left(\sum_k \binom{r}{k} \binom{s}{n-k} \right) x^n$$

for all x, so the coefficients of x^n must be identical.

21. The left-hand side is a polynomial of degree $\le n$; the right-hand side is a polynomial of degree $m+n+1$. The polynomials agree at $n+1$ points, but that isn't enough to prove them equal. [In fact, the correct formula in general is

$$\sum_{k=0}^{r}\binom{r-k}{m}\binom{s+k}{n} = \binom{r+s+1}{m+n+1} - \sum_{k=0}^{m}\binom{r+1}{k}\binom{s}{m+n+1-k}$$

when m, n, and r are nonnegative integers.]

22. Assume $n > 0$. The kth term is r times

$$\frac{1}{n!}\binom{n}{k} \prod_{0<j<k}(r-tk-j)\prod_{0\le j<n-k}(n-1-r+tk-j)$$

$$= \frac{(-1)^{k-1}}{n!}\binom{n}{k}\prod_{0<j<k}(-r+tk+j)\prod_{k\le j<n}(-r+tk+j)$$

and the two products give a polynomial of degree $n-1$ in k, so the sum over k is zero by Eq. (34).

24. The proof is by induction on n. If $n \le 0$ the identity is obvious. If $n > 0$, we prove it holds for $(r, n-r+nt+m, t, n)$, by induction on the integer $m \ge 0$, using the previous two exercises and the validity for $n-1$. This establishes the identity (r, s, t, n) for infinitely many s, and it holds for all s since both sides are polynomials in s.

25. Using the ratio test and straightforward estimates for large values of k we can prove convergence. (Alternatively using complex variable theory we know that the function is analytic in the neighborhood of $x = 1$.) We have

$$1 = \sum_{k,j}(-1)^j\binom{k}{j}\binom{r-jt}{k}\frac{r}{r-jt}w^k = \sum_j(-1)^j\frac{r}{r-jt}\sum_k\binom{k}{j}\binom{r-jt}{k}w^k$$

$$= \sum_j\frac{(-1)^j r}{r-jt}\sum_k\binom{r-jt}{j}\binom{r-jt-j}{k-j}w^k = \sum_j(-1)^j A_j(r,t)(1+w)^{r-jt-j}w^j.$$

Now let $x = 1/(1+w)$, $z = -w/(1+w)^{1+t}$. This proof is due to H. W. Gould [*AMM* **63** (1956), 84–91]. See also the more general formulas in exercises 2.3.4.4–33 and 4.7–22.

26. We could start with identity (35) in the form

$$\sum_j(-1)^j\binom{k}{j}\binom{r-jt}{k} = t^k$$

and proceed as in exercise 25. Another way is to differentiate the formula of that exercise with respect to z; we get

$$\sum_k kA_k(r,t)z^k = z\frac{d(x^r)}{dz} = \frac{(x^{t+1}-x^t)rx^r}{(t+1)x^{t+1}-tx^t},$$

hence we can obtain the value of

$$\sum_k\left(1-\frac{t}{r}k\right)A_k(r,t)z^k.$$

27. For Eq. (26), multiply the series for $x^{r+1}/((t+1)x-t)$ by the series for x^s, and get a series for $x^{r+s+1}/((t+1)x-t)$ in which coefficients of z may be equated to the coefficients arising from the series for $x^{(r+s)+1}/((t+1)x-t)$.

28. Denoting the left-hand side by $f(r, s, t, n)$, we find

$$\binom{r+s}{n} + t f(r+t-1, \, s-t, \, t, \, n-1) = f(r, s, t, n)$$

by considering the identity

$$\sum_k \binom{r+tk}{k} \binom{s-tk}{n-k} \frac{r}{r+tk} + \sum_k \binom{r+tk}{k}\binom{s-tk}{n-k}\frac{tk}{r+tk} = f(r, s, t, n).$$

29. $(-1)^k \binom{n}{k} \Big/ n! = (-1)^k / (k! \, (n-k)!) = (-1)^n \Big/ \prod_{\substack{0 \le j \le n \\ j \ne k}} (k-j)$.

30. Apply (7), (6), and (19) to get

$$\sum_{k \ge 0} \binom{-m-2k-1}{n-m-k}\binom{2k+1}{k} \frac{(-1)^{n-m}}{2k+1}.$$

Now we can apply Eq. (26) with $(r, s, t, n) = (1, m - 2n - 1, -2, n - m)$, obtaining

$$(-1)^{n-m}\binom{-m}{n-m} = \binom{n-1}{n-m}.$$

This result is the same as our previous formula, when n is positive, but when $n = 0$ the answer we have obtained is correct while $\binom{n-1}{m-1}$ is not. Our derivation has a further bonus, since the answer $\binom{n-1}{n-m}$ is valid for $n \ge 0$ and *all* integers m.

31. [This sum was first obtained in closed form by J. F. Pfaff, *Nova Acta Acad. Scient. Petr.* **11** (1797), 38–57.] We have

$$\sum_k \sum_j \binom{m-r+s}{k}\binom{n+r-s}{n-k}\binom{r}{m+n-j}\binom{k}{j}$$

$$= \sum_j \sum_k \binom{m-r+s}{j}\binom{n+r-s}{n-k}\binom{r}{m+n-j}\binom{m-r+s-j}{k-j}$$

$$= \sum_j \binom{m-r+s}{j}\binom{r}{m+n-j}\binom{m+n-j}{n-j}.$$

Changing $\binom{m+n-j}{n-j}$ to $\binom{m+n-j}{m}$ and applying (20) again, we get

$$\sum_j \binom{m-r+s}{j}\binom{r}{m}\binom{r-m}{n-j} = \binom{r}{m}\binom{s}{n}.$$

32. Replace x by $-x$ in (44).

33, 34. [*Mém. Acad. Roy. Sci.* (Paris, 1772), part 1, 492; C. Kramp, *Élémens d'Arithmétique Universelle* (Cologne: 1808), 359; *Giornale di Mat. Battaglini* **33** (1895), 179–182.] Since $x^{\bar{n}} = n! \binom{x+n-1}{n}$, the equation may be transformed into

$$\binom{x+y+n-1}{n} = \sum_k \binom{x+(1-z)k}{k}\binom{y-1+nz+(n-k)(1-z)}{n-k}\frac{x}{x+(1-z)k},$$

which is a case of (26). Similarly, $(x+y)^n = \sum_k \binom{n}{k} x(x - kz - 1)^{\underline{k-1}}(y + kz)^{\underline{n-k}}$, an equivalent formula of Rothe [*Formulæ de Serierum Reversione* (Leipzig: 1793), 18].

35. For example, we prove the first formula:

$$\sum_k (-1)^{n+1-k}\left(n\left[{n \atop k}\right] + \left[{n \atop k-1}\right]\right) x^k = -nx^n + x x^n = x^{\underline{n+1}}.$$

36. By (13), assuming that n is a nonnegative integer, we get 2^n and δ_{n0}, respectively.

37. When $n > 0$, 2^{n-1}. (The odd and even terms cancel, so each equals half the total sum.)

38. Let $\omega = e^{2\pi i/m}$. Then

$$\sum_{0 \le j < m} (1 + \omega^j)^n \omega^{-jk} = \sum_t \sum_{0 \le j < m} \binom{n}{t} \omega^{j(t-k)}.$$

Now

$$\sum_{0 \le j < m} \omega^{rj} = m\,[r \equiv 0 \pmod{m}]$$

(it is the sum of a geometric progression), so the right-hand sum is $m \sum_{t \bmod m = k} \binom{n}{t}$.

The original sum on the left is

$$\sum_{0 \le j < m} (\omega^{-j/2} + \omega^{j/2})^n \omega^{j(n/2-k)} = \sum_{0 \le j < m} \left(2 \cos \frac{j\pi}{m}\right)^n \omega^{j(n/2-k)}.$$

Since the quantity is known to be real, we may take the real part and obtain the stated formula. [See *Crelle* **11** (1834), 353–355.]

    The cases $m = 3$ and $m = 5$ have special properties discussed in *CMath*, exercises 5.75 and 6.57.

39. $n!$; $\delta_{n0} - \delta_{n1}$. (The row sums in the second triangle are not so simple; we will find (exercise 64) that $\sum_k \{{n \atop k}\}$ is the number of ways to partition a set of n elements into disjoint sets, which is the number of equivalence relations on $\{1, 2, \ldots, n\}$.)

40. Proof of (c): By parts,

$$B(x + 1,\, y) = -\frac{t^x (1 - t)^y}{y}\bigg|_0^1 + \frac{x}{y} \int_0^1 t^{x-1}(1 - t)^y \, dt.$$

Now use (b).

41. $m^x B(x,\, m + 1) \to \Gamma(x)$ as $m \to \infty$, regardless of whether m runs through integer values or not (by monotonicity). Hence, $(m + y)^x B(x,\, m + y + 1) \to \Gamma(x)$, and $(m/(m + y))^x \to 1$.

42. $1/((r + 1)B(k + 1,\, r - k + 1))$, if this is defined according to exercise 41(b). In general when z and w are arbitrary complex numbers we define

$$\binom{z}{w} = \lim_{\zeta \to z} \lim_{\omega \to w} \frac{\zeta!}{\omega!\,(\zeta - \omega)!}, \qquad \text{where } \zeta! = \Gamma(\zeta + 1);$$

the value is infinite when z is a negative integer and w is not an integer.

    With this definition, the symmetry condition (6) holds for all complex n and k, except when n is a negative integer and k is an integer; Eqs. (7), (9), and (20) are never false, although they may occasionally take indeterminate forms such as $0 \cdot \infty$ or $\infty + \infty$. Equation (17) becomes

$$\binom{z}{w} = \frac{\sin \pi (w - z - 1)}{\sin \pi z} \binom{w - z - 1}{w}.$$

We can even extend the binomial theorem (13) and Vandermonde's convolution (21), obtaining $\sum_k \binom{r}{\alpha+k} z^{\alpha+k} = (1 + z)^r$ and $\sum_k \binom{r}{\alpha+k}\binom{s}{\beta-k} = \binom{r+s}{\alpha+\beta}$; these formulas hold for all complex r, s, z, α, and β whenever the series converge, provided that complex powers are suitably defined. [See L. Ramshaw, *Inf. Proc. Letters* **6** (1977), 223–226.]

43. $\int_0^1 dt/(t^{1/2}(1-t)^{1/2}) = 2\int_0^1 du/(1-u^2)^{1/2} = 2 \arcsin u\big|_0^1 = \pi.$

45. For large r, $\dfrac{1}{k\Gamma(k)}\sqrt{\dfrac{r}{r-k}}\,\dfrac{1}{e^k}\,\dfrac{(1-k/r)^k}{(1-k/r)^r} \to \dfrac{1}{\Gamma(k+1)}.$

46. $\sqrt{\dfrac{1}{2\pi}\left(\dfrac{1}{x}+\dfrac{1}{y}\right)}\left(1+\dfrac{y}{x}\right)^x\left(1+\dfrac{x}{y}\right)^y$, and $\dbinom{2n}{n} \approx 4^n/\sqrt{\pi n}.$

47. Each quantity is δ_{k0} when $k \le 0$, and is multiplied by $(r-k)(r-\frac12-k)/(k+1)^2$ when k is replaced by $k+1$. When $r = -\frac12$ this implies $\binom{-1/2}{k} = (-1/4)^k\binom{2k}{k}.$

48. This can be proved by induction, using the fact that

$$0 = \sum_k \binom{n}{k}(-1)^k = \sum_k\binom{n}{k}\frac{(-1)^k k}{k+x} + \sum_k\binom{n}{k}\frac{(-1)^k x}{k+x}$$

when $n > 0$. Alternatively, we have

$$B(x, n+1) = \int_0^1 t^{x-1}(1-t)^n\,dt = \sum_k\binom{n}{k}(-1)^k\int_0^1 t^{x+k-1}\,dt.$$

(In fact, the stated sum equals $B(x, n+1)$ for noninteger n also, when the series converges.)

49. $\dbinom{r}{m} = \sum_k\dbinom{r}{k}\dbinom{-r}{m-2k}(-1)^{m+k}$, integer m. (See exercise 17.)

50. The kth summand is $\binom{n}{k}(-1)^{n-k}(x-kz)^{n-1}x$. Apply Eq. (34).

51. The right-hand side is

$$\sum_k\binom{n}{n-k}x(x-kz)^{k-1}\sum_j\binom{n-k}{j}(x+y)^j(-x+kz)^{n-k-j}$$

$$= \sum_j\binom{n}{j}(x+y)^j\sum_k\binom{n-j}{n-j-k}x(x-kz)^{k-1}(-x+kz)^{n-k-j}$$

$$= \sum_{j\le n}\binom{n}{j}(x+y)^j 0^{n-j} = (x+y)^n.$$

The same device may be used to prove Torelli's sum (exercise 34).

Another neat proof of Abel's formula comes from the fact that it is readily transformed into the more symmetric identity derived in exercise 2.3.4.4–29:

$$\sum_k\binom{n}{k}x(x+kz)^{k-1}y(y+(n-k)z)^{n-k-1} = (x+y)(x+y+nz)^{n-1}.$$

Abel's theorem has been generalized even further by A. Hurwitz [*Acta Mathematica* **26** (1902), 199–203] as follows:

$$\sum x(x+\epsilon_1 z_1+\cdots+\epsilon_n z_n)^{\epsilon_1+\cdots+\epsilon_n-1}(y-\epsilon_1 z_1-\cdots-\epsilon_n z_n)^{n-\epsilon_1-\cdots-\epsilon_n} = (x+y)^n$$

where the sum is over all 2^n choices of $\epsilon_1,\ldots,\epsilon_n = 0$ or 1 independently. This is an identity in $x, y, z_1,\ldots,z_n$, and Abel's formula is the special case $z_1 = z_2 = \cdots = z_n$. Hurwitz's formula follows from the result in exercise 2.3.4.4–30.

52. $\sum_{k\geq 0}(k+1)^{-2} = \pi^2/6$. [M. L. J. Hautus observes that the sum is absolutely convergent for all complex x, y, z, n whenever $z \neq 0$, since the terms for large k are always of order $1/k^2$. This convergence is uniform in bounded regions, so we may differentiate the series term by term. If $f(x, y, n)$ is the value of the sum when $z = 1$, we find $(\partial/\partial y)f(x, y, n) = nf(x, y, n-1)$ and $(\partial/\partial x)f(x, y, n) = nf(x-1, y+1, n-1)$. These formulas are consistent with $f(x, y, n) = (x+y)^n$; but actually the latter equality seems to hold rarely, if ever, unless the sum is finite. Furthermore the derivative with respect to z is almost always nonzero.]

53. For (b), set $r = \frac{1}{2}$ and $s = -\frac{1}{2}$ in the result of (a).

54. Insert minus signs in a checkerboard pattern as shown.

$$\begin{pmatrix} 1 & -0 & 0 & -0 \\ -1 & 1 & -0 & 0 \\ 1 & -2 & 1 & -0 \\ -1 & 3 & -3 & 1 \end{pmatrix}$$

This is equivalent to multiplying a_{ij} by $(-1)^{i+j}$. The result is the desired inverse, by Eq. (33).

55. Insert minus signs in one triangle, as in the previous exercise, to get the inverse of the other. (Eq. (47).)

56. 210 310 320 321 410 420 421 430 431 432 510 520 521 530 531 532 540 541 542 543 610. With a fixed, b and c run through the combinations of a things two at a time; with a and b fixed, c runs through the combinations of b things one at a time.

Similarly, we could express all numbers in the form $n = \binom{a}{4} + \binom{b}{3} + \binom{c}{2} + \binom{d}{1}$ with $a > b > c > d \geq 0$; the sequence begins 3210 4210 4310 4320 4321 5210 5310 5320 .... We can find the combinatorial representation by a "greedy" method, first choosing the largest possible a, then the largest possible b for $n - \binom{a}{4}$, etc. [Section 7.2.1.3 discusses further properties of this representation.]

58. [*Systematisches Lehrbuch der Arithmetik* (Leipzig: 1811), xxix.] Use induction and

$$\binom{n}{k}_q = \binom{n-1}{k}_q + \binom{n-1}{k-1}_q q^{n-k} = \binom{n-1}{k}_q q^k + \binom{n-1}{k-1}_q.$$

Therefore [F. Schweins, *Analysis* (Heidelberg: 1820), §151] the q-generalization of (21) is

$$\sum_k \binom{r}{k}_q \binom{s}{n-k}_q q^{(r-k)(n-k)} = \sum_k \binom{r}{k}_q \binom{s}{n-k}_q q^{(s-n+k)k} = \binom{r+s}{n}_q.$$

And the identity $1 - q^t = -q^t(1 - q^{-t})$ makes it easy to generalize (17) to

$$\binom{r}{k}_q = (-1)^k \binom{k-r-1}{k}_q q^{kr-k(k-1)/2}.$$

The q-nomial coefficients arise in many diverse applications; see, for example, Section 5.1.2, and the author's note in *J. Combinatorial Theory* **A10** (1971), 178–180.

Useful facts: When n is a nonnegative integer, $\binom{n}{k}_q$ is a polynomial of degree $k(n-k)$ in q with nonnegative integer coefficients, and it satisfies the reflective laws

$$\binom{n}{k}_q = \binom{n}{n-k}_q = q^{k(n-k)}\binom{n}{k}_{q^{-1}}.$$

If $|q| < 1$ and $|x| < 1$, the q-nomial theorem holds when n is an arbitrary real number, if we replace the left-hand side by $\prod_{k\geq 0}((1 + q^k x)/(1 + q^{n+k}x))$. Properties of power series make it necessary to verify this only when n is a positive integer, because we can set $q^n = y$; the identity has then been verified for infinitely many values of y. Now we can negate the upper index in the q-nomial theorem, obtaining

$$\prod_{k \geq 0} \frac{(1 - q^{k+r+1}x)}{(1 - q^k x)} = \sum_k \binom{-r-1}{k}_q q^{k(k-1)/2}(-q^{r+1}x)^k = \sum_k \binom{k+r}{k}_q x^k.$$

For further information, see G. Gasper and M. Rahman, *Basic Hypergeometric Series* (Cambridge Univ. Press, 1990). The q-nomial coefficients were introduced by Gauss in *Commentationes societatis regiæ scientiarum Gottingensis recentiores* **1** (1808), 147–186; see also Cauchy [*Comptes Rendus Acad. Sci.* **17** (Paris, 1843), 523–531], Jacobi [*Crelle* **32** (1846), 197–204], Heine [*Crelle* **34** (1847), 285–328], and Section 7.2.1.4.

59. $(n+1)\binom{n}{k} - \binom{n}{k+1}$.

60. $\binom{n+k-1}{k}$. This formula can be remembered easily, since it is

$$\frac{n(n+1)\ldots(n+k-1)}{k(k-1)\ldots 1},$$

like Eq. (2) except that the numbers in the numerator go up instead of down. A slick way to prove it is to note that we want to count the number of integer solutions $(a_1, \ldots, a_k)$ to the relations $1 \leq a_1 \leq a_2 \leq \cdots \leq a_k \leq n$. This is the same as $0 < a_1 < a_2 + 1 < \cdots < a_k + k - 1 < n + k$; and the number of solutions to

$$0 < b_1 < b_2 < \cdots < b_k < n + k$$

is the number of choices of k distinct things from the set $\{1, 2, \ldots, n+k-1\}$. (This trick is due to H. F. Scherk, *Crelle* **3** (1828), 97; curiously it was also given by W. A. Förstemann in the same journal, **13** (1835), 237, who said "One would almost believe this must have been known long ago, but I have found it nowhere, even though I have consulted many works in this regard.")

61. If a_{mn} is the desired quantity, we have $a_{mn} = n a_{m(n-1)} + \delta_{mn}$ by (46) and (47). Hence the answer is $[n \geq m] n!/m!$. The same formula is also easily obtained by inversion of (56).

62. Use the identity of exercise 31, with $(m, n, r, s, k) \leftarrow (m+k, l-k, m+n, n+l, j)$:

$$\sum_k (-1)^k \binom{l+m}{l+k}\binom{m+n}{m+k}\binom{n+l}{n+k}$$

$$= \sum_{j,k} (-1)^k \binom{l+m}{l+k}\binom{l+k}{j}\binom{m-k}{l-k-j}\binom{m+n+j}{m+l}$$

$$= \sum_{j,k} (-1)^k \binom{2l-2j}{l-j+k} \frac{(m+n+j)!}{(2l-2j)!\,j!\,(m-l+j)!\,(n+j-l)!},$$

by rearranging the factorial signs. The sum on k now vanishes unless $j = l$.

The case $l = m = n$ of this identity was published by A. C. Dixon [*Messenger of Math.* **20** (1891), 79–80], who established the general case twelve years later [*Proc. London Math. Soc.* **35** (1903), 285–289]. However, L. J. Rogers had already published a much more general formula in the meantime [*Proc. London Math. Soc.* **26** (1895), 15–32, §8]. See also papers by P. A. MacMahon, *Quarterly Journal of Pure and Applied Math.* **33** (1902), 274–288, and John Dougall, *Proc. Edinburgh Math. Society* **25**

(1907), 114–132. The corresponding q-nomial identities are

$$\sum_k \binom{m-r+s}{k}_q \binom{n+r-s}{n-k}_q \binom{r+k}{m+n}_q q^{(m-r+s-k)(n-k)} = \binom{r}{m}_q \binom{s}{n}_q,$$

$$\sum_k (-1)^k \binom{l+m}{l+k}_q \binom{m+n}{m+k}_q \binom{n+l}{n+k}_q q^{(3k^2-k)/2} = \frac{(l+m+n)!_q}{l!_q\, m!_q\, n!_q},$$

where $n!_q = \prod_{k=1}^n (1+q+\cdots+q^{k-1})$.

63. See *CMath*, exercises 5.83 and 5.106.

64. Let $f(n,m)$ be the number of partitions of $\{1,2,\ldots,n\}$ into m parts. Clearly $f(1,m) = \delta_{1m}$. If $n > 1$, the partitionings are of two varieties: (a) The element n alone forms a set of the partition; there are $f(n-1, m-1)$ ways to construct partitions like this. (b) The element n appears together with another element; there are m ways to insert n into any m-partition of $\{1, 2, \ldots, n-1\}$, hence there are $mf(n-1, m)$ ways to construct partitions like this. We conclude that $f(n,m) = f(n-1, m-1) + mf(n-1, m)$, and $f(n,m) = \left\{{n \atop m}\right\}$ by induction.

65. See *AMM* **99** (1992), 410–422.

66. Let $X = \binom{x}{n}$, $\underline{X} = \binom{x}{n-1} = \frac{n}{x-n+1}X$, $\overline{X} = \binom{x}{n+1} = \frac{x-n}{n+1}X$, with similar notations for Y and Z. We may assume that $y > n-1$ is fixed, so that x is a function of z.

Let $F(z) = \overline{X} - \overline{Y} - \overline{Z}$, and suppose that $F(z) = 0$ for some $z > n-2$. We will prove that $F'(z) < 0$; therefore $z = y$ must be the only root $> n-2$, proving the second inequality. Since $F(z) = \frac{x-n}{n+1}(Y+Z) - \frac{y-n}{n+1}Y - \frac{z-n+1}{n}Z = 0$ and $x > y$ and $Y, Z > 0$, we must have $\frac{x-n}{n+1} < \frac{z-n+1}{n}$. Setting $X' = dX/dx$ and $Z' = dZ/dz = dX/dz$, we have

$$\frac{X'}{X} = \frac{1}{x} + \frac{1}{x-1} + \cdots + \frac{1}{x-n+1} > \frac{n}{n+1}\left(\frac{1}{z} + \cdots + \frac{1}{z-n+2}\right) = \frac{n}{n+1}\frac{Z'}{Z},$$

since $\frac{x-n+1}{n+1} < \frac{z-n+2}{n}, \ldots, \frac{x-1}{n+1} < \frac{z}{n}$. Thus $dx/dz = Z'/X' < \frac{n+1}{n}(Z/X)$, and

$$F'(z) = \frac{X}{n+1}\frac{dx}{dz} + \frac{x-n}{n+1}Z' - \frac{Z}{n} - \frac{z-n+1}{n}Z' < \left(\frac{x-n}{n+1} - \frac{z-n+1}{n}\right)Z' < 0.$$

To prove the first inequality, we may assume that $n > 2$. Then if $\underline{X} = \underline{Y} + \underline{Z}$ for some $z > n-2$, the second inequality tells us that $z = y$.

References: L. Lovász, *Combinatorial Problems and Exercises* (1993), Problem 13.31(a); R. M. Redheffer, *AMM* **103** (1996), 62–64.

67. If $k > 0$, exercise 1.2.5–24 gives the slightly sharper (but less memorable) upper bounds $\binom{n}{k} = n^{\underline{k}}/k! \le n^k/k! \le \frac{1}{e}\left(\frac{ne}{k}\right)^k \le \left(\frac{ne}{k+1}\right)^k$. The corresponding lower bound is $\binom{n}{k} \ge \left(\frac{(n-k)e}{k}\right)^k \frac{1}{ek}$.

68. Let $t_k = k\binom{n}{k}p^k(1-p)^{n+1-k}$; then $t_k - t_{k+1} = \binom{n}{k}p^k(1-p)^{n-k}(k-np)$. So the stated sum is

$$\sum_{k<\lceil np \rceil}(t_{k+1} - t_k) + \sum_{k \ge \lceil np \rceil}(t_k - t_{k+1}) = 2t_{\lceil np \rceil}.$$

[De Moivre stated this identity in *Miscellanea Analytica* (1730), 101, in the case that np is an integer; H. Poincaré proved the general case in his *Calcul des Probabilités* (1896), 56–60. See P. Diaconis and S. Zabell, *Statistical Science* **6** (1991), 284–302, for the interesting history of this identity and for a variety of similar formulas.]

SECTION 1.2.7

1. 0, 1, and 3/2.

2. Replace each term $1/(2^m + k)$ by the upper bound $1/2^m$.

3. $H_{2^m-1}^{(r)} \leq \sum_{0 \leq k < m} 2^k/2^{kr}$; $2^{r-1}/(2^{r-1} - 1)$ is an upper bound.

4. (b) and (c).

5. 9.78760 60360 44382 ...

6. Induction and Eq. 1.2.6–(46).

7. $T(m+1, n) - T(m, n) = 1/(m+1) - 1/(mn+1) - \cdots - 1/(mn+n) \leq 1/(m+1) - (1/(mn + n) + \cdots + 1/(mn + n)) = 1/(m + 1) - n/(mn + n) = 0$. The maximum value occurs at $m = n = 1$, and the minimum is approached when m and n get very large. By Eq. (3) the greatest lower bound is γ, which is never actually attained. A generalization of this result appears in *AMM* **70** (1963), 575–577.

8. By Stirling's approximation, $\ln n!$ is approximately $(n + \frac{1}{2}) \ln n - n + \ln \sqrt{2\pi}$; also $\sum_{k=1}^{n} H_k$ is approximately $(n+1) \ln n - n(1-\gamma) + (\gamma + \frac{1}{2})$; the difference is approximately $\gamma n + \frac{1}{2} \ln n + .158$.

9. $-1/n$.

10. Break the left side into two sums; change k to $k + 1$ in the second sum.

11. $2 - H_n/n - 1/n$, for $n > 0$.

12. $1.000\ldots$ is correct to more than three hundred decimal places.

13. Use induction as in the proof of Theorem A. Or use calculus: Differentiate with respect to x, also evaluate at $x = 1$.

14. See Section 1.2.3, Example 2. The second sum is $\frac{1}{2}(H_{n+1}^2 - H_{n+1}^{(2)})$.

15. $\sum_{j=1}^{n}(1/j) \sum_{k=j}^{n} H_k$ can be summed by formulas in the text; the answer comes to $(n + 1)H_n^2 - (2n + 1)H_n + 2n$.

16. $H_{2n-1} - \frac{1}{2}H_{n-1}$.

17. *First solution* (elementary): Taking the denominator to be $(p - 1)!$, which is a multiple of the true denominator but not a multiple of p, we must show only that the corresponding numerator, $(p - 1)!/1 + (p - 1)!/2 + \cdots + (p - 1)!/(p - 1)$, *is* a multiple of p. Modulo p, $(p - 1)!/k \equiv (p - 1)! \, k'$, where k' can be determined by the relation $kk' \bmod p = 1$. The set $\{1', 2', \ldots, (p - 1)'\}$ is just the set $\{1, 2, \ldots, p - 1\}$; so the numerator is congruent to $(p - 1)! \, (1 + 2 + \cdots + p - 1) \equiv 0$.

Second solution (advanced): By exercise 4.6.2–6, we have $x^{\bar{p}} \equiv x^p - x$ (modulo p); hence $\left[{p \atop k}\right] \equiv \delta_{kp} - \delta_{k1}$, by exercise 1.2.6–32. Now apply exercise 6.

The numerator of H_{p-1} is in fact known to be a multiple of p^2 when $p > 3$; see Hardy and Wright, *An Introduction to the Theory of Numbers*, Section 7.8.

18. If $n = 2^k m$ where m is odd, the sum equals $2^{2k} m_1/m_2$ where m_1 and m_2 are both odd. [*AMM* **67** (1960), 924–925.]

19. Only $n = 0$, $n = 1$. For $n \geq 2$, let $k = \lfloor \lg n \rfloor$. There is precisely one term whose denominator is 2^k, so $2^{k-1} H_n - \frac{1}{2}$ is a sum of terms involving only odd primes in the denominator. If H_n were an integer, $2^{k-1} H_n - \frac{1}{2}$ would have a denominator equal to 2.

20. Expand the integrand term by term. See also *AMM* **69** (1962), 239, and an article by H. W. Gould, *Mathematics Magazine* **34** (1961), 317–321.

21. $H_{n+1}^2 - H_{n+1}^{(2)}$.

22. $(n+1)(H_n^2 - H_n^{(2)}) - 2n(H_n - 1)$.

23. $\Gamma'(n+1)/\Gamma(n+1) = 1/n + \Gamma'(n)/\Gamma(n)$, since $\Gamma(x+1) = x\Gamma(x)$. Hence $H_n = \gamma + \Gamma'(n+1)/\Gamma(n+1)$. The function $\psi(x) = \Gamma'(x)/\Gamma(x) = H_{x-1} - \gamma$ is called the *psi function* or the *digamma function*. Some values for rational x appear in Appendix A.

24. It is

$$x \lim_{n\to\infty} e^{(H_n - \ln n)x} \prod_{k=1}^{n} \left(\left(1 + \frac{x}{k}\right) e^{-x/k} \right) = \lim_{n\to\infty} \frac{x(x+1)\ldots(x+n)}{n^x n!}.$$

Note: The generalization of H_n considered in the previous exercise is therefore equal to $H_x^{(r)} = \sum_{k\geq0}(1/(k+1)^r - 1/(k+1+x)^r)$, when $r = 1$; the same idea can be used for larger values of r. The infinite product converges for all complex x.

SECTION 1.2.8

1. After k months there are F_{k+2} pairs, so the answer is $F_{14} = 377$ pairs.

2. $\ln(\phi^{1000}/\sqrt{5}) = 1000 \ln\phi - \frac{1}{2}\ln 5 = 480.40711$; $\log_{10} F_{1000}$ is $1/(\ln 10)$ times this, or 208.64; F_{1000} is therefore a 209-digit number whose leading digit is 4.

4. 0, 1, 5; afterwards F_n increases too fast.

5. 0, 1, 12.

6. Induction. (The equation holds for *negative* n also; see exercise 8.)

7. If d is a proper divisor of n, F_d divides F_n. Now F_d is greater than one and less than F_n provided d is greater than 2. The only nonprime number that has no proper factor greater than 2 is $n = 4$; $F_4 = 3$ is the only exception.

8. $F_{-1} = 1$; $F_{-2} = -1$; $F_{-n} = (-1)^{n+1} F_n$ by induction on n.

9. Not (15). The others are valid, by an inductive argument that proves something true for $n - 1$ assuming it true for n and greater.

10. When n is even, it is greater; when n is odd, it is less. (See Eq. (14).)

11. Induction; see exercise 9. This is a special case of exercise 13(a).

12. If $\mathcal{G}(z) = \sum \mathcal{F}_n z^n$, $(1 - z - z^2)\mathcal{G}(z) = z + F_0 z^2 + F_1 z^3 + \cdots = z + z^2 G(z)$. Hence $\mathcal{G}(z) = G(z) + zG(z)^2$; from Eq. (17) we find $\mathcal{F}_n = ((3n+3)/5)F_n - (n/5)F_{n+1}$.

13. (a) $a_n = rF_{n-1} + sF_n$. (b) Since $(b_{n+2} + c) = (b_{n+1} + c) + (b_n + c)$, we may consider the new sequence $b_n' = b_n + c$. Applying part (a) to b_n', we obtain the answer $cF_{n-1} + (c+1)F_n - c$.

14. $a_n = F_{m+n+1} + F_n - \binom{n}{m} - \binom{n+1}{m-1} - \cdots - \binom{n+m}{0}$.

15. $c_n = xa_n + yb_n + (1 - x - y)F_n$.

16. F_{n+1}. Induction, and $\binom{n+1-k}{k} = \binom{n-k}{k} + \binom{(n-1)-(k-1)}{k-1}$.

17. In general, the quantity $(x^{n+k} - y^{n+k})(x^{m-k} - y^{m-k}) - (x^n - y^n)(x^m - y^m)$ is equal to $(xy)^n(x^{m-n-k} - y^{m-n-k})(x^k - y^k)$. Set $x = \phi$, $y = \hat{\phi}$, and divide by $(\sqrt{5})^2$.

18. It is F_{2n+1}.

19. Let $u = \cos 72°$, $v = \cos 36°$. We have $u = 2v^2 - 1$; $v = 1 - 2\sin^2 18° = 1 - 2u^2$. Hence $u + v = 2(v^2 - u^2)$, i.e., $1 = 2(v - u) = 2v - 4v^2 + 2$. We conclude that $v = \frac{1}{2}\phi$. (Also $u = \frac{1}{2}\phi^{-1}$, $\sin 36° = \frac{1}{2}5^{1/4}\phi^{-1/2}$, $\sin 72° = \frac{1}{2}5^{1/4}\phi^{1/2}$. Another interesting angle is $\alpha = \arctan\phi = \frac{\pi}{4} + \frac{1}{2}\arctan\frac{1}{2}$, for which we have $\sin\alpha = 5^{-1/4}\phi^{1/2}$, $\cos\alpha = 5^{-1/4}\phi^{-1/2}$.)

20. $F_{n+2} - 1$.

21. Multiply by $x^2 + x - 1$; the solution is $(x^{n+1}F_{n+1} + x^{n+2}F_n - x)/(x^2 + x - 1)$. If the denominator is zero, x is $1/\phi$ or $1/\hat{\phi}$; then the solution is $(n + 1 - x^n F_{n+1})/(2x + 1)$.

22. F_{m+2n}; set $t = 2$ in the next exercise.

23. $\dfrac{1}{\sqrt{5}} \sum_k \binom{n}{k} (\phi^k F_t^k F_{t-1}^{n-k} \phi^m - \hat{\phi}^k F_t^k F_{t-1}^{n-k} \hat{\phi}^m)$

$$= \frac{1}{\sqrt{5}} (\phi^m (\phi F_t + F_{t-1})^n - \hat{\phi}^m (\hat{\phi} F_t + F_{t-1})^n) = F_{m+tn}.$$

24. F_{n+1} (expand by cofactors in the first row).

25. $2^n \sqrt{5} F_n = (1 + \sqrt{5})^n - (1 - \sqrt{5})^n$.

26. By Fermat's theorem, $2^{p-1} \equiv 1$; now apply the previous exercise and exercise 1.2.6–10(b).

27. The statement is true if $p = 2$. Otherwise $F_{p-1}F_{p+1} - F_p^2 = -1$; hence, from the previous exercise and Fermat's theorem, $F_{p-1}F_{p+1} \equiv 0$ (modulo p). Only one of these factors can be a multiple of p, since $F_{p+1} = F_p + F_{p-1}$.

28. $\hat{\phi}^n$. *Note:* The solution to the recurrence $a_{n+1} = Aa_n + B^n$, $a_0 = 0$, is

$$a_n = (A^n - B^n)/(A - B) \text{ if } A \neq B, \qquad a_n = nA^{n-1} \text{ if } A = B.$$

29. (a)

$\binom{n}{0}_{\mathcal{F}}$	$\binom{n}{1}_{\mathcal{F}}$	$\binom{n}{2}_{\mathcal{F}}$	$\binom{n}{3}_{\mathcal{F}}$	$\binom{n}{4}_{\mathcal{F}}$	$\binom{n}{5}_{\mathcal{F}}$	$\binom{n}{6}_{\mathcal{F}}$
1	0	0	0	0	0	0
1	1	0	0	0	0	0
1	1	1	0	0	0	0
1	2	2	1	0	0	0
1	3	6	3	1	0	0
1	5	15	15	5	1	0
1	8	40	60	40	8	1

(b) follows from (6). [É. Lucas, *Amer. J. Math.* **1** (1878), 201–204.]

30. We argue by induction on m, the statement being obvious when $m = 1$:

(a) $\displaystyle\sum_k \binom{m}{k}_{\mathcal{F}} (-1)^{\lceil (m-k)/2 \rceil} F_{n+k}^{m-2} F_k = F_m \sum_k \binom{m-1}{k-1}_{\mathcal{F}} (-1)^{\lceil (m-k)/2 \rceil} F_{n+k}^{m-2} = 0.$

(b) $\displaystyle\sum_k \binom{m}{k}_{\mathcal{F}} (-1)^{\lceil (m-k)/2 \rceil} F_{n+k}^{m-2} (-1)^k F_{m-k}$

$$= (-1)^m F_m \sum_k \binom{m-1}{k}_{\mathcal{F}} (-1)^{\lceil (m-1-k)/2 \rceil} F_{n+k}^{m-2} = 0.$$

(c) Since $(-1)^k F_{m-k} = F_{k-1}F_m - F_k F_{m-1}$ and $F_m \neq 0$, we conclude from (a) and (b) that $\sum_k \binom{m}{k}_{\mathcal{F}} (-1)^{\lceil (m-k)/2 \rceil} F_{n+k}^{m-2} F_{k-1} = 0$.

(d) Since $F_{n+k} = F_{k-1}F_n + F_k F_{n+1}$ the result follows from (a) and (c). This result may also be proved in slightly more general form by using the q-nomial theorem of exercise 1.2.6–58. *References:* Dov Jarden, *Recurring Sequences*, 2nd ed. (Jerusalem, 1966), 30–33; J. Riordan, *Duke Math. J.* **29** (1962), 5–12.

31. Use exercises 8 and 11.

32. Modulo F_n the Fibonacci sequence is $0, 1, \ldots, F_{n-1}, 0, F_{n-1}, -F_{n-2}, \ldots$.

33. Note that $\cos z = \frac{1}{2}(e^{iz} + e^{-iz}) = -i/2$, for this particular z; then use the fact that $\sin(n+1)z + \sin(n-1)z = 2 \sin nz \cos z$, for all z.

34. Prove that the only possible value for F_{k_1} is the largest Fibonacci number less than or equal to n; hence $n - F_{k_1}$ is less than F_{k_1-1}, and by induction there is a unique representation of $n - F_{k_1}$. The outline of this proof is quite similar to the proof of the unique factorization theorem. The Fibonacci number system is due to E. Zeckendorf [see *Simon Stevin* **29** (1952), 190–195; *Bull. Soc. Royale des Sciences de Liège* **41** (1972), 179–182]; but Section 7.2.1.7 points out that it was implicitly known in 14th-century India. Generalizations are discussed in exercise 5.4.2–10 and in Section 7.1.3.

35. See G. M. Bergman, *Mathematics Magazine* **31** (1957), 98–110. To represent $x > 0$, find the largest k with $\phi^k \leq x$ and represent x as ϕ^k plus the representation of $x - \phi^k$.

The representation of nonnegative integers can also be obtained from the following all-integer recursive rules, starting with the trivial representations of 0 and 1: Let $L_n = \phi^n + \hat{\phi}^n = F_{n+1} + F_{n-1}$. The representation of $L_{2n} + m$ for $0 \leq m \leq L_{2n-1}$ and $n \geq 1$ is $\phi^{2n} + \phi^{-2n}$ plus the representation of m. The representation of $L_{2n+1} + m$ for $0 < m < L_{2n}$ and $n \geq 0$ is $\phi^{2n+1} + \phi^{-2n-2}$ plus the representation of $m - \phi^{-2n}$, where the latter is obtained by applying the rule $\phi^k - \phi^{k-2j} = \phi^{k-1} + \phi^{k-3} + \cdots + \phi^{k-2j+1}$. It turns out that all strings α of 0s and 1s, such that α begins with 1 and has no adjacent 1s, occur to the left of the radix point in the representation of exactly one positive integer, except for the strings that end with $10^{2k}1$; the latter strings never occur in such representations.

36. We may consider the infinite string S_∞, since S_n for $n > 1$ consists of the first F_n letters of S_∞. There are no double a's, no triple b's. The string S_n contains F_{n-2} a's and F_{n-1} b's. If we express $m - 1$ in the Fibonacci number system as in exercise 34, the mth letter of S_∞ is a if and only if $k_r = 2$. The kth letter of S_∞ is b if and only if $\lfloor (k+1)\phi^{-1} \rfloor - \lfloor k\phi^{-1} \rfloor = 1$; the number of b's in the first k letters is therefore $\lfloor (k+1)\phi^{-1} \rfloor$. Also, the kth letter is b if and only if $k = \lfloor m\phi \rfloor$ for some positive integer m. This sequence was studied by John Bernoulli III in the 18th century, by A. A. Markov in the 19th, and by many other mathematicians since then; see K. B. Stolarsky, *Canadian Math. Bull.* **19** (1976), 473–482.

37. [*Fibonacci Quart.* **1** (December 1963), 9–12.] Consider the Fibonacci number system of exercise 34; if $n = F_{k_1} + \cdots + F_{k_r} > 0$ in that system, let $\mu(n) = F_{k_r}$. Let $\mu(0) = \infty$. We find that: (A) If $n > 0$, $\mu(n - \mu(n)) > 2\mu(n)$. *Proof:* $\mu(n - \mu(n)) = F_{k_{r-1}} \geq F_{k_r+2} > 2F_{k_r}$ since $k_r \geq 2$. (B) If $0 < m < F_k$, $\mu(m) \leq 2(F_k - m)$. *Proof:* Let $\mu(m) = F_j$; $m \leq F_{k-1} + F_{k-3} + \cdots + F_{j+(k-1-j) \bmod 2} = -F_{j-1+(k-1-j) \bmod 2} + F_k \leq -\frac{1}{2}F_j + F_k$. (C) If $0 < m < \mu(n)$, $\mu(n - \mu(n) + m) \leq 2(\mu(n) - m)$. *Proof:* This follows from (B). (D) If $0 < m < \mu(n)$, $\mu(n - m) \leq 2m$. *Proof:* Set $m = \mu(n) - m$ in (C).

Now we will prove that if there are n chips, and if at most q may be taken in the next turn, there is a winning move if and only if $\mu(n) \leq q$. *Proof:* (a) If $\mu(n) > q$ all moves leave a position n', q' with $\mu(n') \leq q'$. [This follows from (D), above.] (b) If $\mu(n) \leq q$, we can either win on this move (if $q \geq n$) or we can make a move that leaves a position n', q' with $\mu(n') > q'$. [This follows from (A) above: Our move is to take $\mu(n)$ chips.] It can be seen that the set of all winning moves, if $n = F_{k_1} + \cdots + F_{k_r}$, is to remove $F_{k_j} + \cdots + F_{k_r}$, for some j with $1 \leq j \leq r$, provided that $j = 1$ or $F_{k_{j-1}} > 2(F_{k_j} + \cdots + F_{k_r})$.

The Fibonacci representation of 1000 is $987 + 13$; the *only* lucky move to force a victory is to take 13 chips. The first player can always win unless n is a Fibonacci number.

The solution to considerably more general games of this type has been obtained by A. Schwenk [*Fibonacci Quarterly* **8** (1970), 225–234].

39. $(3^n - (-2)^n)/5$.

40. We prove, by induction on m, that $f(n) = m$ for $F_m < n \le F_{m+1}$: First, $f(n) \le \max(1 + f(F_m), 2 + f(n - F_m)) = m$. Second, if $f(n) < m$ there is some $k < n$ with $1 + f(k) < m$ (hence $k \le F_{m-1}$) and $2 + f(n - k) < m$ (hence $n - k \le F_{m-2}$); but then $n \le F_{m-1} + F_{m-2}$. [Thus the Fibonacci trees defined in Section 6.2.1 minimize the maximum root-to-leaf cost when a right branch costs twice as much as a left branch.]

41. $F_{k_1+1} + \cdots + F_{k_r+1} = \phi n + (\hat\phi^{k_1} + \cdots + \hat\phi^{k_r})$ is an integer, and the parenthesized quantity lies between $\hat\phi^3 + \hat\phi^5 + \cdots = \phi^{-1} - 1$ and $\hat\phi^2 + \hat\phi^4 + \cdots = \phi^{-1}$. Similarly, $F_{k_1-1} + \cdots + F_{k_r-1} = \phi^{-1}n + (\hat\phi^{k_1} + \cdots + \hat\phi^{k_r}) = f(\phi^{-1}n)$. [Such Fibonacci shifting is a convenient way to convert mentally between miles and kilometers; see *CMath*, §6.6.]

42. [*Fibonacci Quarterly* **6** (1968), 235–244.] If such a representation exists, we have

$$mF_{N-1} + nF_N = F_{k_1+N} + F_{k_2+N} + \cdots + F_{k_r+N} \tag{$*$}$$

for all integers N; hence two different representations would contradict exercise 34.

Conversely, we can prove the existence of such joint representations for all non-negative m and n by induction. But it is more interesting to use the previous exercise, and to prove that such joint representations exist for possibly negative integers m and n if and only if $m + \phi n \ge 0$: Let N be large enough so that $|m\hat\phi^{N-1} + n\hat\phi^N| < \phi^{-2}$, and represent $mF_{N-1} + nF_N$ as in $(*)$. Then $mF_N + nF_{N+1} = \phi(mF_{N-1} + nF_N) + (m\hat\phi^{N-1} + n\hat\phi^N) = f(\phi(mF_{N-1} + nF_N)) = F_{k_1+N+1} + \cdots + F_{k_r+N+1}$, and it follows that $(*)$ holds for all N. Now set $N = 0$ and $N = 1$.

SECTION 1.2.9

1. $1/(1 - 2z) + 1/(1 - 3z)$.

2. It follows from (6), since $\binom{n}{k} = n!/k!(n - k)!$.

3. $G'(z) = \ln(1/(1 - z))/(1 - z)^2 + 1/(1 - z)^2$. From this and the significance of $G(z)/(1 - z)$, we have $\sum_{k=1}^{n-1} H_k = nH_n - n$; this agrees with Eq. 1.2.7–(8).

4. Put $t = 0$.

5. The coefficient of z^k is, by (11) and (22),

$$\frac{(n - 1)!}{k!} \sum_{0 \le j < k} \left\{ {j \atop n - 1} \right\} \binom{k}{j}.$$

Now apply Eqs. 1.2.6–(46) and 1.2.6–(52). (Or, differentiate and use 1.2.6–(46).)

6. $(\ln(1/(1 - z)))^2$; the derivative is twice the generating function for the harmonic numbers; the sum is therefore $2H_{n-1}/n$.

8. $1/((1 - z)(1 - z^2)(1 - z^3)\ldots)$. [This is historically one of the first applications of generating functions. For an interesting account of L. Euler's eighteenth-century researches concerning this generating function, see G. Pólya, *Induction and Analogy in Mathematics* (Princeton: Princeton University Press, 1954), Chapter 6.]

9. $\frac{1}{24}S_1^4 + \frac{1}{4}S_1^2 S_2 + \frac{1}{8}S_2^2 + \frac{1}{3}S_1 S_3 + \frac{1}{4}S_4$.

10. $G(z) = (1 + x_1 z)\ldots(1 + x_n z)$. Taking logarithms as in the derivation of Eq. (38), we have the same formulas except that (24) replaces (17), and the answer is exactly the same except that $S_2, S_4, S_6, \ldots$ are replaced by $-S_2, -S_4, -S_6, \ldots$. We have $e_1 = S_1$, $e_2 = \frac{1}{2}S_1^2 - \frac{1}{2}S_2$, $e_3 = \frac{1}{6}S_1^3 - \frac{1}{2}S_1 S_2 + \frac{1}{3}S_3$, $e_4 = \frac{1}{24}S_1^4 - \frac{1}{4}S_1^2 S_2 + \frac{1}{8}S_2^2 + \frac{1}{3}S_1 S_3 - \frac{1}{4}S_4$. (See exercise 9.) The recurrence analogous to (39) is $ne_n = S_1 e_{n-1} - S_2 e_{n-2} + \cdots$.

Note: The equations in this recurrence are called *Newton's identities*, since they were first published in Isaac Newton's *Arithmetica Universalis* (1707); see D. J. Struik's *Source Book in Mathematics* (Harvard University Press, 1969), 94–95.

11. Since $\sum_{m \geq 1} S_m z^m/m = \ln G(z) = \sum_{k \geq 1}(-1)^{k-1}(h_1 z + h_2 z^2 + \cdots)^k/k$, the desired coefficient is $(-1)^{k_1+k_2+\cdots+k_m-1} m(k_1 + k_2 + \cdots + k_m - 1)!/k_1! \, k_2! \ldots k_m!$. [Multiply by $(-1)^{m-1}$ to get the coefficient of $e_1^{k_1} e_2^{k_2} \ldots e_m^{k_m}$ when S_m is expressed in terms of the e's of exercise 10. Albert Girard stated the formulas for S_1, S_2, S_3, and S_4 in terms of e_1, e_2, e_3, and e_4 near the end of his *Invention Nouvelle en Algébre* (Amsterdam: 1629); this was the birth of the theory of symmetric functions.]

12. $\displaystyle \sum_{m,n \geq 0} a_{mn} w^m z^n = \sum_{m,n \geq 0} \binom{n}{m} w^m z^n = \sum_{n \geq 0}(1+w)^n z^n = 1/(1 - z - wz)$.

13. $\int_n^{n+1} e^{-st} f(t)\,dt = (a_0 + \cdots + a_n)(e^{-sn} - e^{-s(n+1)})/s$. Adding these expressions together for all n, we find $\mathbf{L}f(s) = G(e^{-s})/s$.

14. See exercise 1.2.6–38.

15. $G_n(z) = G_{n-1}(z) + zG_{n-2}(z) + \delta_{n0}$, so we find $H(w) = 1/(1 - w - zw^2)$. Hence, ultimately, we find

$$G_n(z) = \left(\left(\frac{1 + \sqrt{1+4z}}{2} \right)^{n+1} - \left(\frac{1 - \sqrt{1+4z}}{2} \right)^{n+1} \right) \bigg/ \sqrt{1+4z} \quad \text{when } z \neq -\tfrac{1}{4};$$

$G_n(-\tfrac{1}{4}) = (n+1)/2^n$ for $n \geq 0$.

16. $G_{nr}(z) = (1 + z + \cdots + z^r)^n = \left(\dfrac{1 - z^{r+1}}{1 - z} \right)^n$. [Note the case $r = \infty$.]

17. $\displaystyle \sum_k \binom{-w}{k}(-z)^k = \sum_k \frac{w(w+1)\ldots(w+k-1)}{k(k-1)\ldots 1} z^k = \sum_{n,k} \begin{bmatrix} k \\ n \end{bmatrix} z^k w^n/k!$.

(Alternatively, write it as $e^{w \ln(1/(1-z))}$ and expand first by powers of w.)

18. (a) For fixed n and varying r, the generating function is

$$G_n(z) = (1+z)(1+2z)\ldots(1+nz) = z^{n+1}\left(\frac{1}{z}\right)\left(\frac{1}{z}+1\right)\left(\frac{1}{z}+2\right)\ldots\left(\frac{1}{z}+n\right)$$

$$= \sum_k \begin{bmatrix} n+1 \\ k \end{bmatrix} z^{n+1-k}$$

by Eq. (27). Hence the answer is $\begin{bmatrix} n+1 \\ n+1-r \end{bmatrix}$. (b) Similarly, the generating function is

$$\frac{1}{1-z} \cdot \frac{1}{1-2z} \cdot \cdots \cdot \frac{1}{1-nz} = \sum_k \begin{Bmatrix} k \\ n \end{Bmatrix} z^{k-n}$$

by Eq. (28), so the answer is $\begin{Bmatrix} n+r \\ n \end{Bmatrix}$.

19. $\sum_{n \geq 1}(1/n - 1/(n+p/q))x^{p+nq} = \sum_{k=0}^{q-1} \omega^{-kp} \ln(1 - \omega^k x) - x^p \ln(1 - x^q) + \frac{q}{p}x^p = f(x) + g(x)$, where $\omega = e^{2\pi i/q}$ and

$$f(x) = \sum_{k=1}^{q-1} \omega^{-kp} \ln(1 - \omega^k x), \quad g(x) = (1 - x^p)\ln(1 - x) + \frac{q}{p}x^p - x^p \ln \frac{1 - x^q}{1 - x}.$$

Now $\lim_{x\to 1-} g(x) = q/p - \ln q$. From the identity

$$\ln(1 - e^{i\theta}) = \ln\left(2e^{i(\theta-\pi)/2}\,\frac{e^{i\theta/2} - e^{-i\theta/2}}{2i}\right) = \ln 2 + \tfrac{1}{2}i(\theta - \pi) + \ln\sin\frac{\theta}{2},$$

we may write $\lim_{x\to 1-} f(x) = f(1) = A + B$ where

$$A = \sum_{k=1}^{q-1} \omega^{-kp}\left(\ln 2 - \frac{i\pi}{2} + \frac{ik\pi}{q}\right) = -\ln 2 + \frac{i\pi}{2} + \frac{i\pi}{(\omega^{-p}-1)};$$

$$B = \sum_{k=1}^{q-1} \omega^{-kp}\ln\sin\frac{k}{q}\pi = \sum_{0<k<q/2}\left(\omega^{-kp} + \omega^{-(q-k)p}\right)\ln\sin\frac{k}{q}\pi$$

$$= 2\sum_{0<k<q/2}\cos\frac{2pk}{q}\pi\cdot\ln\sin\frac{k}{q}\pi.$$

Finally,

$$\frac{i}{2} + \frac{i}{(\omega^{-p}-1)} = \frac{i}{2}\left(\frac{1+\omega^p}{1-\omega^p}\right) = -\frac{i}{2}\left(\frac{\omega^{p/2} + \omega^{-p/2}}{\omega^{p/2} - \omega^{-p/2}}\right) = -\frac{1}{2}\cot\frac{p}{q}\pi.$$

[Gauss derived these results in §33 of his monograph on hypergeometric series, Eq. [75], but with insufficient proof; Abel provided a justification in *Crelle* **1** (1826), 314–315.]

20. $c_{mk} = k!\left\{{m\atop k}\right\}$, by Eq. 1.2.6–(45).

21. We find $z^2 G'(z) + zG(z) = G(z) - 1$. The solution to this differential equation is $G(z) = (-1/z)e^{-1/z}(E_1(-1/z) + C)$, where $E_1(z) = \int_z^\infty e^{-t}\,dt/t$ and C is a constant. This function is very ill-behaved in the neighborhood of $z = 0$, and $G(z)$ has no power series expansion. Indeed, since $\sqrt[n]{n!} \approx n/e$ is not bounded, the generating function does not converge in this case; it is, however, an asymptotic expansion for the stated function, when $z < 0$. [See K. Knopp, *Infinite Sequences and Series* (Dover, 1956), Section 66.]

22. $G(z) = (1 + z)^r (1 + z^2)^r (1 + z^4)^r (1 + z^8)^r \ldots = (1 - z)^{-r}$. It follows that the stated sum is $\binom{r+n-1}{n}$.

23. (a) When $m = 1$ this is the binomial theorem, with $f_1(z) = z$ and $g_1(z) = 1 + z$. When $m \geq 1$ we can increase m by 1 if we replace z_m by $z_m(1 + z_{m+1}^{-1})$ and let $f_{m+1}(z_1, \ldots, z_{m+1}) = z_{m+1}f_m(z_1, \ldots, z_{m-1}, z_m(1 + z_{m+1}^{-1}))$, $g_{m+1}(z_1, \ldots, z_{m+1}) = z_{m+1}g_m(z_1, \ldots, z_{m-1}, z_m(1 + z_{m+1}^{-1}))$. Thus $g_2(z_1, z_2) = z_1 + z_2 + z_1 z_2$ and

$$\frac{g_m(z_1, \ldots, z_m)}{f_m(z_1, \ldots, z_m)} = 1 + \cfrac{z_1^{-1}}{1 + \cfrac{z_2^{-1}}{1 + \cfrac{\ddots}{1 + z_m^{-1}}}}.$$

Both polynomials f_m and g_m satisfy the same recurrence $f_m = z_m f_{m-1} + z_{m-1}f_{m-2}$, $g_m = z_m g_{m-1} + z_{m-1}g_{m-2}$, with the initial conditions $f_{-1} = 0$, $f_0 = g_{-1} = g_0 = z_0 = 1$. It follows that g_m is the sum of all terms obtainable by starting with $z_1 \ldots z_m$ and striking out zero or more nonadjacent factors; there are F_{m+2} ways to do this. A similar interpretation applies to f_m, except that z_1 must remain. In part (b) we will encounter the polynomial $h_m = z_m g_{m-1} + z_{m-1}f_{m-2}$; this is the sum of all terms obtained from $z_1 \ldots z_m$ by striking out factors that are not *cyclically* adjacent. For example, $h_3 = z_1 z_2 z_3 + z_1 z_2 + z_1 z_3 + z_2 z_3$.

(b) By part (a), $S_n(z_1, \ldots, z_{m-1}, z) = [z_m^n] \sum_{r=0}^{n} z^r z_m^{n-r} f_m^{n-r} g_m^r$; hence

$$S_n(z_1, \ldots, z_m) = \sum_{0 \le s \le r \le n} \binom{r}{s} \binom{n-r}{s} a^{r-s} b^s c^s d^{n-r-s},$$

where $a = z_m g_{m-1}$, $b = z_{m-1} g_{m-2}$, $c = z_m f_{m-1}$, $d = z_{m-1} f_{m-2}$. Multiplying this equation by z^n and summing first on n, then on r, then on s, yields the closed form

$$S_n(z_1, \ldots, z_m) = [z^n] \frac{1}{(1 - az)(1 - dz) - bcz^2} = \frac{\rho^{n+1} - \sigma^{n+1}}{\rho - \sigma},$$

where $1 - (a + d)z + (ad - bc)z^2 = (1 - \rho z)(1 - \sigma z)$. Here $a + d = h_m$, and $ad - bc$ simplifies to $(-1)^m z_1 \ldots z_m$. [We have, incidentally, established the recurrence $S_n = h_m S_{n-1} - (-1)^m z_1 \ldots z_m S_{n-2}$, a relation that is not easy to derive without the help of generating functions.]

(c) Let $\rho_1 = (z + \sqrt{z^2 + 4z})/2$ and $\sigma_1 = (z - \sqrt{z^2 + 4z})/2$ be the roots when $m = 1$; then $\rho_m = \rho_1^m$ and $\sigma_m = \sigma_1^m$.

Carlitz used this result to deduce a surprising fact: The characteristic polynomial $\det(xI - A)$ of the $n \times n$ matrix

$$A = \begin{pmatrix} 0 & 0 & \cdots & 0 & \binom{0}{0} \\ 0 & 0 & \cdots & \binom{1}{0} & \binom{1}{1} \\ \vdots & \vdots & \ddots & \vdots & \vdots \\ \binom{n-1}{0} & \binom{n-1}{1} & \cdots & \binom{n-1}{n-2} & \binom{n-1}{n-1} \end{pmatrix}$$

of "right justified binomial coefficients" is $\sum_k \binom{n}{k}_{\mathcal{F}} (-1)^{\lceil (n-k)/2 \rceil} x^k$, with Fibonomial coefficients (see exercise 1.2.8–30). He also showed, using similar methods, that

$$\sum_{k_1, \ldots, k_m \ge 0} \binom{k_1 + k_2}{k_1} \binom{k_2 + k_3}{k_2} \cdots \binom{k_m + k_1}{k_m} z_1^{k_1} \ldots z_m^{k_m}$$

$$= \frac{1}{\sqrt{z_1^2 \ldots z_m^2 \, h_m(-z_1^{-1}, \ldots, -z_m^{-1})^2 - 4z_1 \ldots z_m}}.$$

[*Collectanea Math.* **27** (1965), 281–296.]

24. Both sides are equal to $\sum_k \binom{m}{k} [z^n] (zG(z))^k$. When $G(z) = 1/(1-z)$, the identity becomes $\sum_k \binom{m}{k} \binom{n-1}{n-k} = \binom{m+n-1}{n}$, a case of 1.2.6–(21). When $G(z) = (e^z - 1)/z$, it becomes $\sum_k m^{\underline{k}} \{ {n \atop k} \} = m^n$, Eq. 1.2.6–(45).

25. $\sum_k [w^k] (1 - 2w)^n [z^n] z^k (1 + z)^{2n-2k} = [z^n] (1 + z)^{2n} \sum_k [w^k] (1 - 2w)^n (z/(1+z)^2)^k$, which equals $[z^n] (1 + z)^{2n} (1 - 2z/(1 + z)^2)^n = [z^n] (1 + z^2)^n = \binom{n}{n/2} [n \text{ even}]$. Similarly, we find $\sum_k \binom{n}{k} \binom{2n-2k}{n-k} (-4)^k = (-1)^n \binom{2n}{n}$. Many examples of this summation technique can be found in G. P. Egorychev's book *Integral Representation and the Computation of Combinatorial Sums* (Amer. Math. Soc., 1984), translated from the Russian edition of 1977.

26. $[F(z)] G(z)$ denotes the constant term of $F(z^{-1}) G(z)$. See the discussion by D. E. Knuth in *A Classical Mind* (Prentice–Hall, 1994), 247–258.

SECTION 1.2.10

1. $G_n(0) = 1/n$; this is the probability that $X[n]$ is the largest.

2. $G''(1) = \sum_k k(k-1)p_k$, $G'(1) = \sum_k kp_k$.

3. (min 0, ave 6.49, max 999, dev 2.42). Note that $H_n^{(2)}$ is approximately $\pi^2/6$; see Eq. 1.2.7–(7).

4. $\binom{n}{k}p^k q^{n-k}$.

5. The mean is $36/5 = 7.2$; the standard deviation is $6\sqrt{2}/5 \approx 1.697$.

6. For (18), the formula

$$\ln(q + pe^t) = \ln\left(1 + pt + \frac{pt^2}{2} + \frac{pt^3}{6} + \cdots\right) = pt + p(1-p)\frac{t^2}{2} + p(1-p)(1-2p)\frac{t^3}{6} + \cdots$$

tells us that $\kappa_3/n = p(1-p)(1-2p) = pq(q-p)$. (This nice pattern does not continue to the coefficient of t^4.) Setting $p = k^{-1}$ gives us $\kappa_3 = \sum_{k=2}^n k^{-1}(1-k^{-1})(1-2k^{-1}) = H_n - 3H_n^{(2)} + 2H_n^{(3)}$ in the case of distribution (8). And for (20), we have $\ln G(e^t) = t + H(nt) - H(t)$ where $H(t) = \ln((e^t - 1)/t)$. Since $H'(t) = e^t/(e^t - 1) - 1/t$, we have $\kappa_r = (n^r - 1)B_r/r$ for all $r \geq 2$ in this case; in particular, $\kappa_3 = 0$.

7. The probability that $A = k$ is p_{mk}. For we may consider the values to be $1, 2, \ldots, m$. Given any partitioning of the n positions into m disjoint sets, there are $m!$ ways to assign the numbers $1, \ldots, m$ to these sets. Algorithm M treats these values as if only the rightmost element of each set were present; so p_{mk} is the average for any fixed partitioning. For example, if $n = 5$, $m = 3$, one partition is

$$\{X[1], X[4]\} \quad \{X[2], X[5]\} \quad \{X[3]\};$$

the arrangements possible are 12312, 13213, 21321, 23123, 31231, 32132. In every partition we get the same percentage of arrangements with $A = k$.

On the other hand, the probability distribution does change if more information is given. If $n = 3$ and $m = 2$, for example, our argument in the previous paragraph considers the six possibilities 122, 212, 221, 211, 121, 112; if we know that there are two 2s and one 1, then only the first three of these possibilities should be considered. But this interpretation is not consistent with the statement of the exercise.

8. $M^{\underline{n}}/M^n$. The larger M is, the closer this probability gets to one.

9. Let q_{nm} be the probability that exactly m distinct values occur; then from the recurrence

$$q_{nm} = \frac{M - m + 1}{M} q_{(n-1)(m-1)} + \frac{m}{M} q_{(n-1)m}$$

we deduce that

$$q_{nm} = M! \left\{\begin{matrix} n \\ m \end{matrix}\right\} \Big/ (M - m)! \, M^n.$$

See also exercise 1.2.6–64.

10. This is $q_{nm}p_{mk}$ summed over all m, namely $M^{-n}\sum_m \binom{M}{m}\left\{\begin{matrix} n \\ m \end{matrix}\right\}\left[\begin{matrix} m \\ k+1 \end{matrix}\right]$. There does not appear to be a simple formula for the average, which is one less than

$$H_M - \sum_{m=1}^M \left(1 - \frac{m}{M}\right)^n m^{-1} = H_n + \sum_{k=1}^n \left(\binom{n}{k} - 1\right) B_k M^{-k} k^{-1}.$$

11. Since this is a product, we add the semi-invariants of each term. If $H(z) = z^n$, $H(e^t) = e^{nt}$, so we find $\kappa_1 = n$ and all others are zero. Therefore, $\mathrm{mean}(F) = n +$

mean(G), and all other semi-invariants are unchanged. (This accounts for the name "semi-invariant.")

12. The first identity is obvious by writing out the power series for e^{kt}. For the second, let $u = 1 + M_1 t + M_2 t^2/2! + \cdots$; when $t = 0$ we have $u = 1$ and $D_t^k u = M_k$. Also, $D_u^j (\ln u) = (-1)^{j-1}(j-1)!/u^j$. By exercise 11, the same formula applies for central moments except that we leave out all terms with $k_1 > 0$; thus $\kappa_2 = m_2$, $\kappa_3 = m_3$, $\kappa_4 = m_4 - 3m_2^2$.

13. $G_n(z) = \dfrac{\Gamma(n+z)}{\Gamma(z+1)n!} = \dfrac{e^{-z}(n+z)^{z-1}}{\Gamma(z+1)}\left(1+\dfrac{z}{n}\right)^n(1+O(n^{-1})) = \dfrac{n^{z-1}}{\Gamma(z+1)}(1+O(n^{-1}))$.

Let $z_n = e^{it/\sigma_n}$. When $n \to \infty$ and t is fixed, we have $z_n \to 1$; hence $\Gamma(z_n + 1) \to 1$, and

$$\lim_{n\to\infty} z_n^{-\mu_n} G_n(z_n) = \lim_{n\to\infty} \exp\left(\dfrac{-it\mu_n}{\sigma_n} + (e^{it/\sigma_n} - 1)\ln n\right)$$

$$= \lim_{n\to\infty} \exp\left(\dfrac{-t^2 \ln n}{2\sigma_n^2} + O\left(\dfrac{1}{\sqrt{\log n}}\right)\right) = e^{-t^2/2}.$$

Notes: This is a theorem of Goncharov [*Izv. Akad. Nauk SSSR Ser. Math.* **8** (1944), 3–48]. P. Flajolet and M. Soria [*Disc. Math.* **114** (1993), 159–180] have extended the analysis to show that $G_n(z)$ and a large family of related distributions not only are approximately normal near their mean values, they also have uniformly exponential tails, in the sense that

$$\Pr\left(\left|\dfrac{X_n - \mu_n}{\sigma_n}\right| > x\right) < e^{-ax}$$

for some positive constant a and for all n and x.

14. $e^{-itpn/\sqrt{pqn}}(q + pe^{it/\sqrt{pqn}})^n = (qe^{-itp/\sqrt{pqn}} + pe^{itq/\sqrt{pqn}})^n$. Expand the exponentials in power series, to get $(1 - t^2/2n + O(n^{-3/2}))^n = \exp(n\ln(1 - t^2/2n + O(n^{-3/2}))) = \exp(-t^2/2 + O(n^{-1/2})) \to \exp(-t^2/2)$.

15. (a) $\sum_{k\geq0} e^{-\mu}(\mu z)^k/k! = e^{\mu(z-1)}$. (b) $\ln e^{\mu(e^t-1)} = \mu(e^t - 1)$, so all semi-invariants equal μ. (c) $\exp(-itnp/\sqrt{np}) \exp(np(it/\sqrt{np} - t^2/(2np) + O(n^{-3/2}))) = \exp(-t^2/2 + O(n^{-1/2}))$.

16. $g(z) = \sum_k p_k g_k(z)$; $\operatorname{mean}(g) = \sum_k p_k \operatorname{mean}(g_k)$; and $\operatorname{var}(g) = \sum_k p_k \operatorname{var}(g_k) + \sum_{j<k} p_j p_k (\operatorname{mean}(g_j) - \operatorname{mean}(g_k))^2$.

17. (a) The coefficients of $f(z)$ and $g(z)$ are nonnegative, and $f(1) = g(1) = 1$. Clearly $h(z)$ shares these same characteristics, since $h(1) = g(f(1))$, and the coefficients of h are polynomials in those of f and g, with nonnegative coefficients.

(b) Let $f(z) = \sum p_k z^k$ where p_k is the probability that some event yields a "score" of k. Let $g(z) = \sum q_k z^k$ where q_k is the probability that the event described by f happens exactly k times (each occurrence of the event being independent of the others). Then $h(z) = \sum r_k z^k$, where r_k is the probability that the sum of the scores of the events that occurred is equal to k. (This is easy to see if we observe that $f(z)^k = \sum s_t z^t$, where s_t is the probability that a total score t is obtained in k independent occurrences of the event.) *Example:* If f gives the probabilities that a woman has k female offspring, and if g gives the probabilities that there are k females in the nth generation, then h gives the probabilities that there are k females in the $(n + 1)$st generation, assuming independence.

(c) $\operatorname{mean}(h) = \operatorname{mean}(g)\operatorname{mean}(f)$; $\operatorname{var}(h) = \operatorname{var}(g)\operatorname{mean}^2(f) + \operatorname{mean}(g)\operatorname{var}(f)$.

18. Consider the choice of $X[1], \ldots, X[n]$ as a process in which we first place all the n's, then place all the $(n-1)$'s among these n's, $\ldots$, finally place the ones among the rest. As we place the r's among the numbers $\{r+1, \ldots, n\}$, the number of local maxima from right to left increases by one if and only if we put an r at the extreme right. This happens with probability $k_r/(k_r + k_{r+1} + \cdots + k_n)$.

19. Let $a_k = l$. Then a_k is a left-to-right maximum of $a_1 \ldots a_n \iff j < k$ implies $a_j < l$ $\iff a_j > l$ implies $j > k \iff j > l$ implies $b_j > k \iff k$ is a right-to-left minimum of $b_1 \ldots b_n$.

20. We have $m_L = \max\{a_1 - b_1, \ldots, a_n - b_n\}$. *Proof:* If not, let k be the smallest subscript such that $a_k - b_k > m_L$. Then a_k is not a left-to-right maximum, so there is a $j < k$ with $a_j \geq a_k$. But then $a_j - b_j \geq a_k - b_k > m_L$, contradicting the minimality of k. Similarly, $m_R = \max\{b_1 - a_1, \ldots, b_n - a_n\}$.

21. The result is trivial when $\epsilon \geq q$, so we may assume that $\epsilon < q$. Setting $x = \frac{p+\epsilon}{p}\frac{q}{q-\epsilon}$ in (25) gives $\Pr(X \geq n(p + \epsilon)) \leq ((\frac{p}{p+\epsilon})^{p+\epsilon}(\frac{q}{q-\epsilon})^{q-\epsilon})^n$. Now $(\frac{p}{p+\epsilon})^{p+\epsilon} \leq e^{-\epsilon}$ since $t \leq e^{t-1}$ for all real t. And $(q - \epsilon)\ln\frac{q}{q-\epsilon} = \epsilon - \frac{1}{2\cdot1}\epsilon^2 q^{-1} - \frac{1}{3\cdot2}\epsilon^3 q^{-2} - \cdots \leq \epsilon - \frac{1}{2q}\epsilon^2$. (A more detailed analysis yields the slightly stronger estimate $\exp(-\epsilon^2 n/(2pq))$ when $p \geq \frac{1}{2}$; still further work yields the upper bound $\exp(-2\epsilon^2 n)$ for all p.)

By reversing the roles of heads and tails we find

$$\Pr(X \leq n(p - \epsilon)) = \Pr(n - X \geq n(q + \epsilon)) \leq e^{-\epsilon^2 n/(2p)}.$$

(One should not confuse "tails" with the tail of a probability distribution.)

22. (a) Set $x = r$ in (24) and (25), and note that $q_k + p_k r = 1 + (r - 1)p_k \leq e^{(r-1)p_k}$. [See H. Chernoff, *Annals of Math. Stat.* **23** (1952), 493–507.]

(b) Let $r = 1 + \delta$ where $|\delta| \leq 1$. Then $r^{-r}e^{r-1} = \exp(-\frac{1}{2\cdot1}\delta^2 + \frac{1}{3\cdot2}\delta^3 - \cdots)$, which is $\leq e^{-\delta^2/2}$ when $\delta \leq 0$ and $\leq e^{-\delta^2/3}$ when $\delta \geq 0$.

(c) The function $r^{-1}e^{1-r^{-1}}$ decreases from 1 to 0 as r increases from 1 to ∞. If $r \geq 2$ it is $\leq \frac{1}{2}e^{1/2} < .825$; if $r \geq 4.32$ it is $< \frac{1}{2}$.

Incidentally, the tail inequalities with $x = r$ give precisely the same estimate $(r^{-r}e^{r-1})^\mu$ when X has the Poisson distribution of exercise 15.

23. Setting $x = \frac{p-\epsilon}{p}\frac{q}{q-\epsilon}$ in (24) gives $\Pr(X \leq n(p - \epsilon)) \leq ((\frac{p}{p-\epsilon})^{p-\epsilon}(\frac{q-\epsilon}{q})^{q-\epsilon})^n \leq e^{-\epsilon^2 n/(2pq)}$. Similarly, $x = \frac{p+\epsilon}{p}\frac{q}{q+\epsilon}$ yields $\Pr(X \geq n(p + \epsilon)) \leq ((\frac{p}{p+\epsilon})^{p+\epsilon}(\frac{q+\epsilon}{q})^{q+\epsilon})^n$. Let $f(\epsilon) = (q+\epsilon)\ln(1+\frac{\epsilon}{q}) - (p+\epsilon)\ln(1+\frac{\epsilon}{p})$, and note that $f'(\epsilon) = \ln(1+\frac{\epsilon}{q}) - \ln(1+\frac{\epsilon}{p})$. It follows that $f(\epsilon) \leq -\epsilon^2/(6pq)$ if $0 \leq \epsilon \leq p$.

SECTION 1.2.11.1

1. Zero.

2. Each O-symbol represents a different approximate quantity; since the left-hand side might be $f(n) - (-f(n)) = 2f(n)$, the best we can say is $O(f(n)) - O(f(n)) = O(f(n))$, which follows from (6) and (7). To prove (7), note that if $|x_n| \leq M|f(n)|$ for $n \geq n_0$ and $|x'_n| \leq M'|f(n)|$ for $n \geq n'_0$, then $|x_n \pm x'_n| \leq |x_n| + |x'_n| \leq (M + M')|f(n)|$ for $n \geq \max(n_0, n'_0)$. (Signed, J. H. Quick, student.)

3. $n(\ln n) + \gamma n + O(\sqrt{n}\ln n)$.

4. $\ln a + (\ln a)^2/2n + (\ln a)^3/6n^2 + O(n^{-3})$.

5. If $f(n) = n^2$ and $g(n) = 1$, then n belongs to the set $O(f(n) + g(n))$ but not to the set $f(n) + O(g(n))$. So the statement is false.

6. A variable number, n, of O-symbols has been replaced by a single O-symbol, falsely implying that a single value of M will suffice for each term $|kn| \le Mn$. The given sum is actually $\Theta(n^3)$, as we know. The last equality, $\sum_{k=1}^{n} O(n) = O(n^2)$, is perfectly valid.

7. If x is positive, the power series 1.2.9–(22) tells us that $e^x > x^{m+1}/(m+1)!$; hence the ratio of e^x/x^m is unbounded by any M.

8. Replace n by e^n and apply the method of the previous exercise.

9. If $|f(z)| \le M|z|^m$ for $|z| \le r$, then $|e^{f(z)}| \le e^{M|z|^m} = 1 + |z|^m(M + M^2|z|^m/2! + M^3|z|^{2m}/3! + \cdots) \le 1 + |z|^m(M + M^2r^m/2! + M^3r^{2m}/3! + \cdots)$.

10. $\ln(1 + O(z^m)) = O(z^m)$, if m is a positive integer. *Proof:* If $f(z) = O(z^m)$, there exist positive numbers $r < 1$, $r' < 1$, and a constant M such that $|f(z)| \le M|z|^m \le r'$ when $|z| \le r$. Then $|\ln(1 + f(z))| \le |f(z)| + \frac{1}{2}|f(z)|^2 + \cdots \le |z|^m M(1 + \frac{1}{2}r' + \cdots)$.

11. We can apply Eq. (12) with $m = 1$ and $z = \ln n/n$. This is justified since $\ln n/n \le r$ for any given $r > 0$, when n is sufficiently large.

12. Let $f(z) = (ze^z/(e^z - 1))^{1/2}$. If $\left[\begin{smallmatrix}1/2\\1/2-k\end{smallmatrix}\right]$ were $O(n^k)$, the stated identity would show that $[z^k]\,f(z) = O(n^k/(k-1)!)$, so $f(z)$ would converge when $z = 2\pi i$. But $f(2\pi i) = \infty$.

13. *Proof:* We may take $L = 1/M$ in the definitions of O and Ω.

SECTION 1.2.11.2

1. $(B_0 + B_1z + B_2z^2/2! + \cdots)e^z = (B_0 + B_1z + B_2z^2/2! + \cdots) + z$; apply Eq. 1.2.9–(11).

2. The function $B_{m+1}(\{x\})$ must be continuous, for the integration by parts.

3. $|R_{mn}| \le |B_m/(m)!| \int_1^n |f^{(m)}(x)|\,dx$. [*Notes:* We have $B_m(x) = (-1)^m B_m(1-x)$, and $B_m(x)$ is $m!$ times the coefficient of z^m in $ze^{xz}/(e^z - 1)$. In particular, since $e^{z/2}/(e^z - 1) = 1/(e^{z/2} - 1) - 1/(e^z - 1)$ we have $B_m(\frac{1}{2}) = (2^{1-m} - 1)B_m$. It is not difficult to prove that the maximum of $|B_m - B_m(x)|$ for $0 \le x \le 1$ occurs at $x = \frac{1}{2}$ when m is even. Now when $m = 2k \ge 4$, let us write simply R_m and C_m for the quantities R_{mn} and C_{mn}. We have $R_{m-2} = C_m + R_m = \int_1^n (B_m - B_m(\{x\}))f^{(m)}(x)\,dx/m!$, and $B_m - B_m(\{x\})$ is between 0 and $(2 - 2^{1-m})B_m$; hence R_{m-2} lies between 0 and $(2 - 2^{1-m})C_m$. It follows that R_m lies between $-C_m$ and $(1 - 2^{1-m})C_m$, a slightly stronger result. According to this argument we see that if $f^{(m+2)}(x)\,f^{(m+4)}(x) > 0$ for $1 < x < n$, the quantities C_{m+2} and C_{m+4} have opposite signs, while R_m has the sign of C_{m+2} and R_{m+2} has the sign of C_{m+4} and $|R_{m+2}| \le |C_{m+2}|$; this proves (13). See J. F. Steffensen, *Interpolation* (Baltimore: 1937), §14.]

4. $$\sum_{0 \le k < n} k^m = \frac{n^{m+1}}{1+m} + \sum_{k=1}^m \frac{B_k}{k!}\frac{m!}{(m-k+1)!}n^{m-k+1} = \frac{1}{m+1}B_{m+1}(n) - \frac{1}{m+1}B_{m+1}.$$

5. It follows that
$$\kappa = \sqrt{2}\lim_{n\to\infty}\frac{2^{2n}(n!)^2}{\sqrt{n}\,(2n)!};$$
$$\kappa^2 = \lim_{n\to\infty}\frac{2}{n}\frac{n^2(n-1)^2\dots(1)^2}{(n-\frac{1}{2})^2(n-\frac{3}{2})^2\dots(\frac{1}{2})^2} = 4\frac{2\cdot2\cdot4\cdot4\cdots}{1\cdot3\cdot3\cdot5\cdots} = 2\pi.$$

6. Assume that $c > 0$ and consider $\sum_{0 \le k < n} \ln(k + c)$. We find
$$\ln(c(c+1)\dots(c+n-1)) = (n+c)\ln(n+c) - c\ln c - n - \tfrac{1}{2}\ln(n+c) + \tfrac{1}{2}\ln c$$
$$+ \sum_{1 < k \le m}\frac{B_k(-1)^k}{k(k-1)}\left(\frac{1}{(n+c)^{k-1}} - \frac{1}{c^{k-1}}\right) + R_{mn}.$$

Also

$$\ln(n-1)! = (n - \tfrac{1}{2})\ln n - n + \sigma + \sum_{1<k\le m} \frac{B_k(-1)^k}{k(k-1)}\left(\frac{1}{n^{k-1}}\right) - \frac{1}{m}\int_n^\infty \frac{B_m(\{x\})\,dx}{x^m}.$$

Now $\ln\Gamma_{n-1}(c) = c\ln(n-1) + \ln(n-1)! - \ln(c\ldots(c+n-1))$; substituting and letting $n \to \infty$, we get

$$\ln\Gamma(c) = -c + (c - \tfrac{1}{2})\ln c + \sigma + \sum_{1<k\le m} \frac{B_k(-1)^k}{k(k-1)c^{k-1}} - \frac{1}{m}\int_0^\infty \frac{B_m(\{x\})\,dx}{(x+c)^m}.$$

This shows that $\Gamma(c+1) = ce^{\ln\Gamma(c)}$ has the same expansion we derived for $c!$.

7. $A\,n^{n^2/2+n/2+1/12}e^{-n^2/4}$ where A is a constant. To obtain this result, apply Euler's summation formula to $\sum_{k=1}^{n-1} k\ln k$. A more accurate formula is obtained if we multiply the answer above by

$$\exp\bigl(-B_4/(2\cdot 3\cdot 4n^2) - \cdots - B_{2t}/((2t-2)(2t-1)(2t)n^{2t-2}) + O(1/n^{2t})\bigr).$$

In these formulas, A is the "Kinkelin–Glaisher constant" $1.2824271\ldots$ [*Crelle* **57** (1860), 122–158; *Messenger of Math.* **7** (1877), 43–47], which can be shown to equal $e^{1/12-\zeta'(-1)} = (2\pi e^{\gamma-\zeta'(2)/\zeta(2)})^{1/12}$ [de Bruijn, *Asymptotic Methods in Analysis*, §3.7].

8. We have, for example, $\ln(an^2 + bn) = 2\ln n + \ln a + \ln(1 + b/(an))$. Thus the answer to the first question is found to be $2an^2\ln n + a(\ln a - 1)n^2 + 2bn\ln n + bn\ln a + \ln n + b^2/(2a) + \tfrac{1}{2}\ln a + \sigma + (3a-b^2)b/(6a^2 n) + O(n^{-2})$. Massive cancellation occurs when we compute the quantity $\ln(cn^2)! - \ln(cn^2 - n)! - n\ln c - \ln n^2! + \ln(n^2-n)! = (c-1)/(2c) - (c-1)(2c-1)/(6c^2 n) + O(n^{-2})$. The answer is therefore

$$e^{(c-1)/(2c)}\left(1 - \frac{(c-1)(2c-1)}{6c^2 n}\right)(1 + O(n^{-2})).$$

Incidentally, $\binom{cn^2}{n}/c^n\binom{n^2}{n}$ can be written $\prod_{j=1}^{n-1}(1 + \alpha j/(n^2 - j))$ where $\alpha = 1 - 1/c$.

9. (a) We have $\ln(2n)! = (2n + \tfrac{1}{2})\ln 2n - 2n + \sigma + \frac{1}{24n} + O(n^{-3})$, and $\ln(n!)^2 = (2n+1)\ln n - 2n + 2\sigma + \frac{1}{6n} + O(n^{-3})$; hence $\binom{2n}{n} = \exp(2n\ln 2 - \tfrac{1}{2}\ln\pi n - \frac{1}{8n} + O(n^{-3})) = 2^{2n}(\pi n)^{-1/2}(1 - \tfrac{1}{8}n^{-1} + \frac{1}{128}n^{-2} + O(n^{-3}))$. (b) Since $\binom{2n}{n} = 2^{2n}\binom{n-1/2}{n}$ and $\binom{n-1/2}{n} = \Gamma(n+1/2)/(n\Gamma(n)\Gamma(1/2)) = n^{-1}n^{\overline{1/2}}/\sqrt{\pi}$, we obtain the same result from 1.2.11.1–(16) because

$$\begin{bmatrix}1/2\\1/2\end{bmatrix} = 1, \quad \begin{bmatrix}1/2\\-1/2\end{bmatrix} = \binom{1/2}{2} = -\frac{1}{8}, \quad \begin{bmatrix}1/2\\-3/2\end{bmatrix} = \binom{1/2}{4} + 2\binom{3/2}{4} = \frac{1}{128}.$$

Method (b) explains why the denominators in

$$\binom{2n}{n} = \frac{2^{2n}}{\sqrt{\pi n}}\left(1 - \frac{n^{-1}}{8} + \frac{n^{-2}}{128} + \frac{5n^{-3}}{1024} - \frac{21n^{-4}}{32768} - \frac{399n^{-5}}{262144} + \frac{869n^{-6}}{4194304} + O(n^{-7})\right)$$

are all powers of 2 [Knuth and Vardi, *AMM* **97** (1990), 629–630].

SECTION 1.2.11.3

1. Integrate by parts.

2. Substitute the series for e^{-t} in the integral.

3. See Eq. 1.2.9–(11) and exercise 1.2.6–48.

4. $1 + 1/u$ is bounded as a function of v, since it goes to zero as v goes from r to infinity. Replace it by M and the resulting integral is Me^{-rx}.

5. $f''(x) = f(x)((n + 1/2)(n - 1/2)/x^2 - (2n + 1)/x + 1)$ changes sign at the point $r = n + 1/2 - \sqrt{n + 1/2}$, so $|R| = O(\int_0^n |f''(x)| \, dx) = O(\int_0^r f''(x) \, dx - \int_r^n f''(x) \, dx) = O(f'(n) - 2f'(r) + f'(0)) = O(f(n)/\sqrt{n})$.

6. It is $n^{n+\beta} \exp((n + \beta)(\alpha/n - \alpha^2/2n^2 + O(n^{-3})))$, etc.

7. The integrand as a power series in x^{-1} has the coefficient of x^{-n} as $O(u^{2n})$. After integration, terms in x^{-3} are $Cu^7/x^3 = O(x^{-5/4})$, etc. To get $O(x^{-2})$ in the answer, we can discard terms u^n/x^m with $4m - n \geq 9$. Thus, an expansion of the product $\exp(-u^2/2x) \exp(u^3/3x^2) \dots$ leads ultimately to the answer

$$yx^{1/4} - \frac{y^3}{6}x^{-1/4} + \frac{y^5}{40}x^{-3/4} + \frac{y^4}{12}x^{-1} - \frac{y^7}{336}x^{-5/4} - \frac{y^6}{36}x^{-3/2} + \left(\frac{y^9}{3456} - \frac{y^5}{20}\right)x^{-7/4} + O(x^{-2}).$$

8. (Solution by Miklós Simonovits.) We have $|f(x)| < x$ if x is large enough. Let $R(x) = \int_0^{f(x)}(e^{-g(u,x)} - e^{-h(u,x)}) \, du$ be the difference between the two given integrals, where $g(u, x) = u - x \ln(1 + u/x)$ and $h(u, x) = u^2/2x - u^3/3x^2 + \dots + (-1)^m u^m/mx^{m-1}$. Notice that $g(u, x) \geq 0$ and $h(u, x) \geq 0$ when $|u| < x$; also $g(u, x) = h(u, x) + O(u^{m+1}/x^m)$.

According to the mean value theorem, $e^a - e^b = (a - b)e^c$ for some c between a and b. Therefore $|e^a - e^b| \leq |a - b|$ when $a, b \leq 0$. It follows that

$$|R(x)| \leq \int_{-|f(x)|}^{|f(x)|} |g(u, x) - h(u, x)| \, du = O\left(\int_{-Mx^r}^{Mx^r} \frac{u^{m+1} du}{x^m}\right)$$

$$= O(x^{(m+2)r-m}) = O(x^{-s}).$$

9. We may assume that $p \neq 1$, since $p = 1$ is given by Theorem A. We also assume that $p \neq 0$, since the case $p = 0$ is trivial.

Case 1: $p < 1$. Substitute $t = px(1 - u)$ and then $v = -\ln(1 - u) - pu$. We have $dv = ((1 - p + pu)/(1 - u)) \, du$, so the transformation is monotone for $0 \leq u \leq 1$, and we obtain an integral of the form

$$\int_0^\infty xe^{-xv} dv \left(\frac{1 - u}{1 - p + pu}\right).$$

Since the parenthesized quantity is $(1 - p)^{-1}(1 - v(1 - p)^{-2} + \dots)$, the answer is

$$\frac{p}{1 - p}(pe^{1-p})^x \frac{e^{-x}x^x}{\Gamma(x + 1)}\left(1 - \frac{1}{(p - 1)^2x} + O(x^{-2})\right).$$

Case 2: $p > 1$. This is $1 - \int_{px}^\infty(\ )$. In the latter integral, substitute $t = px(1 + u)$, then $v = pu - \ln(1 + u)$, and proceed as in Case 1. The answer turns out to be the same formula as Case 1, plus one. Notice that $pe^{1-p} < 1$, so $(pe^{1-p})^x$ is *very* small.

The answer to exercise 11 gives another way to solve this problem.

10. $\dfrac{p}{p - 1}(pe^{1-p})^x e^{-x}x^x \left(1 - e^{-y} - \dfrac{e^{-y}(e^y - 1 - y - y^2/2)}{x(p - 1)^2} + O(x^{-2})\right).$

11. First, $xQ_x(n) + R_{1/x}(n) = n! \, (x/n)^n e^{n/x}$ generalizes (4). Next, we have $R_x(n) = n! \, (e^x/nx)^n \gamma(n, nx)/(n - 1)!$, generalizing (9). Since $a\gamma(a, x) = \gamma(a + 1, x) + e^{-x}x^a$ we can also write $R_x(n) = 1 + (e^x/nx)^n \gamma(n + 1, nx)$, relating this problem to exercise 9.

Moreover, we can tackle $Q_x(n)$ and $R_x(n)$ directly by using Eqs. 1.2.9–(27) and (28) to derive series expansions involving Stirling numbers:

$$1 + xQ_x(n) = \sum_{k\geq 0} x^k n^{\underline{k}}/n^k = \sum_{k,m\geq 0} \frac{(-1)^m}{n^m}\begin{bmatrix} k \\ k-m \end{bmatrix}x^k;$$

$$R_x(n) = \sum_{k\geq 0} x^k n^k/(n+1)^{\overline{k}} = \sum_{k,m\geq 0} \frac{(-1)^m}{n^m}\begin{Bmatrix} k+m \\ k \end{Bmatrix}x^k.$$

The sums over k are convergent for fixed m when $|x| < 1$, and when $|x| > 1$ we can use the relation between $Q_x(n)$ and $R_{1/x}(n)$; this leads to the formulas

$$Q_x(n) = \frac{1}{1-x} - \frac{x}{(1-x)^3 n} + \cdots + \frac{(-1)^m q_m(x)}{(1-x)^{2m+1}n^m} + O(n^{-1-m}),$$

$$R_x(n) = \frac{1}{1-x} - \frac{x}{(1-x)^3 n} + \cdots + \frac{(-1)^m r_m(x)}{(1-x)^{2m+1}n^m} + O(n^{-1-m}), \quad \text{if } x < 1;$$

$$Q_x(n) = \frac{n!\,x^{n-1}e^{n/x}}{n^n} + \frac{1}{1-x} - \frac{x}{(1-x)^3 n} + \cdots + \frac{(-1)^m q_m(x)}{(1-x)^{2m+1}n^m} + O(n^{-1-m}),$$

$$R_x(n) = \frac{n!\,e^{nx}}{n^n x^n} + \frac{1}{1-x} - \frac{x}{(1-x)^3 n} + \cdots + \frac{(-1)^m r_m(x)}{(1-x)^{2m+1}n^m} + O(n^{-1-m}), \quad \text{if } x > 1.$$

Here

$$q_m(x) = \left\langle\!\!\left\langle \begin{matrix} m \\ 0 \end{matrix} \right\rangle\!\!\right\rangle x^{2m-1} + \left\langle\!\!\left\langle \begin{matrix} m \\ 1 \end{matrix} \right\rangle\!\!\right\rangle x^{2m-2} + \cdots$$

and

$$r_m(x) = \left\langle\!\!\left\langle \begin{matrix} m \\ 0 \end{matrix} \right\rangle\!\!\right\rangle x + \left\langle\!\!\left\langle \begin{matrix} m \\ 1 \end{matrix} \right\rangle\!\!\right\rangle x^2 + \cdots$$

are polynomials whose coefficients are "second-order Eulerian numbers" [*CMath* §6.2; see L. Carlitz, *Proc. Amer. Math. Soc.* **16** (1965), 248–252]. The case $x = -1$ is somewhat delicate, but it can be handled by continuity, because the bound implied by $O(n^{-1-m})$ is independent of x when $x < 0$. It is interesting to note that $R_{-1}(n) - Q_{-1}(n) = (-1)^n n!/(e^n n^n) \approx (-1)^n \sqrt{2\pi n}/e^{2n}$ is extremely small.

12. $\gamma(\frac{1}{2}, \frac{1}{2}x^2)/\sqrt{2}$.

13. See P. Flajolet, P. Grabner, P. Kirschenhofer, and H. Prodinger, *J. Computational and Applied Math.* **58** (1995), 103–116.

15. Expanding the integrand by the binomial theorem, we obtain $1 + Q(n)$.

16. Write $Q(k)$ as a sum, and interchange the order of summation using Eq. 1.2.6–(53).

17. $S(n) = \sqrt{\pi n/2} + \frac{2}{3} - \frac{1}{24}\sqrt{\pi/2n} - \frac{4}{135}n^{-1} + \frac{49}{1152}\sqrt{\pi/2n^3} + O(n^{-2})$. [Note that $S(n+1) + P(n) = \sum_{k\geq 0} k^{n-k}k!/n!$, while $Q(n) + R(n) = \sum_{k\geq 0} n!/k!\,n^{n-k}$.]

18. Let $S_n(x,y) = \sum_k \binom{n}{k}(x+k)^k(y+n-k)^{n-k}$. Then for $n > 0$ we have $S_n(x,y) = x\sum_k \binom{n}{k}(x+k)^{k-1}(y+n-k)^{n-k} + n\sum_k \binom{n-1}{k}(x+1+k)^k(y+n-1-k)^{n-1-k} = (x+y+n)^n + nS_{n-1}(x+1, y)$ by Abel's formula 1.2.6–(16); consequently $S_n(x,y) = \sum_k \binom{n}{k}k!\,(x+y+n)^{n-k}$. [This formula is due to Cauchy, who proved it using the calculus of residues; see his *Œuvres* (2) **6**, 62–73.] The stated sums are therefore equal respectively to $n^n(1 + Q(n))$ and $(n+1)^n Q(n+1)$.

19. Suppose C_n exists for all $n \geq N$ and $|f(x)| \leq Mx^\alpha$ for $0 \leq x \leq r$. Let $F(x) = \int_r^x e^{-Nt} f(t)\, dt$. Then when $n > N$ we have

$$|C_n| \leq \int_0^r e^{-nx} |f(x)|\, dx + \left| \int_r^\infty e^{-(n-N)x} e^{-Nx} f(x)\, dx \right|$$

$$\leq M \int_0^r e^{-nx} x^\alpha\, dx + (n-N)\left| \int_r^\infty e^{-(n-N)x} F(x)\, dx \right|$$

$$\leq M \int_0^\infty e^{-nx} x^\alpha\, dx + (n-N)\sup_{x \geq r}|F(x)| \int_r^\infty e^{-(n-N)x}\, dx$$

$$= M\Gamma(\alpha + 1)n^{-1-\alpha} + \sup_{x \geq r}|F(x)| e^{-(n-N)r} = O(n^{-1-\alpha}).$$

[E. W. Barnes, *Phil. Trans.* **A206** (1906), 249–297; G. N. Watson, *Proc. London Math. Soc.* **17** (1918), 116–148.]

20. [C. C. Rousseau, *Applied Math. Letters* **2** (1989), 159–161.] We have $Q(n) + 1 = n\int_0^\infty e^{-nx}(1+x)^n\, dx = n\int_0^\infty e^{-n(x-\ln(1+x))}\, dx = n\int_0^\infty e^{-nu} g(u)\, du$, by substituting $u = x - \ln(1+x)$ and letting $g(u) = dx/du$. Notice that $x = \sum_{k=1}^\infty c_k(2u)^{k/2}$ when u is sufficiently small. Hence $g(u) = \sum_{k=1}^{m-1} kc_k(2u)^{k/2-1} + O(u^{m/2-1})$, and we can apply Watson's lemma to $Q(n) + 1 - n\int_0^\infty e^{-nu} \sum_{k=1}^{m-1} kc_k(2u)^{k/2-1}\, du$.

SECTION 1.3.1

1. Four; each byte would then contain $3^4 = 81$ different values.

2. Five, since five bytes is always adequate but four is not.

3. $(0\!:\!2)$; $(3\!:\!3)$; $(4\!:\!4)$; $(5\!:\!5)$.

4. Presumably index register 4 contains a value greater than or equal to 2000, so that a valid memory address results after indexing.

5. "DIV -80,3(0:5)" or simply "DIV -80,3".

6. (a) rA ← | − | 5 | 1 | 200 | 15 |. (b) rI2 ← −200. (c) rX ← | + | 0 | 0 | 5 | 1 | ? |.
(d) Undefined; we can't load such a big value into an index register. (e) rX ← | − | 0 | 0 | 0 | 0 | 0 |.

7. Let $n = |\text{rAX}|$ be the magnitude of registers A and X before the operation, and let $d = |V|$ be the magnitude of the divisor. After the operation the magnitude of rA is $\lfloor n/d \rfloor$, and the magnitude of rX is $n \bmod d$. The sign of rX afterwards is the previous sign of rA; the sign of rA afterwards is + if the previous signs of rA and V were the same, otherwise it is −.

Stating this another way: If the signs of rA and V are the same, rA ← $\lfloor \text{rAX}/V \rfloor$ and rX ← rAX mod V. Otherwise rA ← $\lceil \text{rAX}/V \rceil$ and rX ← rAX mod −V.

8. rA ← | + | 0 | 617 | 0 | 1 |; rX ← | − | 0 | 0 | 0 | 1 | 1 |.

9. ADD, SUB, DIV, NUM, JOV, JNOV, INCA, DECA, INCX, DECX.

10. CMPA, CMP1, CMP2, CMP3, CMP4, CMP5, CMP6, CMPX. (Also FCMP, for floating point.)

11. MOVE, LD1, LD1N, INC1, DEC1, ENT1, ENN1.

12. INC3 0,3.

13. "JOV 1000" makes no difference except time. "JNOV 1001" makes a different setting of rJ in most cases. "JNOV 1000" makes an extraordinary difference, since it may lock the computer in an infinite loop.

14. NOP with anything; ADD, SUB with F = (0:0) or with address equal to * (the location of the instruction) and F = (3:3); HLT (depending on how you interpret the statement of the exercise); any shift with address and index zero; SLC or SRC with index 0 and address a multiple of 10; MOVE with F = 0; STJ *(0:0), STZ *(0:0), and STZ *(3:3); JSJ *+1; any of the INC or DEC instructions with address and index zero. But "ENT1 0,1" is not always a no-op, because it might change rI1 from −0 to +0.

15. 70; 80; 120. (The block size times 5.)

16. (a) STZ 0; ENT1 1; MOVE 0(49); MOVE 0(50). If the byte size were known to equal 100, only one MOVE instruction would have been necessary, but we are not allowed to make assumptions about the byte size. (b) Use 100 STZ's.

17. (a) STZ 0,2; DEC2 1; J2NN 3000.

> (b)   STZ   0
>   ENT1 1
>   JMP   3004
>   (3003) MOVE 0(63)
>   (3004) DEC2 63
>   J2P   3003
>   INC2 63
>   ST2   3008(4:4)
>   (3008) MOVE 0   ▮

(A slightly faster, but quite preposterous, program uses 993 STZ's: JMP 3995; STZ 1,2; STZ 2,2; ...; STZ 993,2; J2N 3999; DEC2 993; J2NN 3001; ENN1 0,2; JMP 3000,1.)

18. (If you have correctly followed the instructions, an overflow will occur on the ADD, with minus zero in register A afterwards.) *Answer:* Overflow is set on, comparison is set EQUAL, rA is set to $\boxed{-\ 30\ 30\ 30\ 30\ 30}$, rX is set to $\boxed{-\ 31\ 30\ 30\ 30\ 30}$, rI1 is set to +3, and memory locations 0001, 0002 are set to +0. (Unless the program itself begins in location 0000.)

19. $42u = (2 + 1 + 2 + 2 + 1 + 1 + 1 + 2 + 2 + 1 + 2 + 2 + 3 + 10 + 10)u.$

20. (Solution by H. Fukuoka.)

> (3991) ENT1 0
>   MOVE 3995   (standard F for MOVE is 1)
> (3993) MOVE 0(43)   (3999 = 93 times 43)
>   JMP   3993
> (3995) HLT   0   ▮

21. (a) Not unless it can be set to zero by external means (see the "GO button", exercise 26), since a program can set rJ ← N only by jumping from location N − 1.

> (b)   LDA   -1,4
>   LDX   3004
>   STX   -1,4
>   JMP   -1,4
>   (3004) JMP   3005
>   (3005) STA   -1,4   ▮

22. *Minimum time:* If b is the byte size, the assumption that $\left|X^{13}\right| < b^5$ implies that $X^2 < b$, so X^2 can be contained in one byte. The following ingenious solution due to Y. N. Patt makes use of this fact. The sign of rA is the sign of X.

			rA					rX				
(3000)	LDA	2000										
	MUL	2000(1:5)										
	STX	3500(1:1)										
	SRC	1	X^2	0	0	0	0	0	0	0	0	0
	MUL	3500	X^4		0	0	0	0	0	0	0	0
	STA	3501	X^4		0	0	0	0	0	0	0	0
	ADD	2000	X^4		0	0	X	0	0	0	0	0
	MUL	3501(1:5)	X^8			0	X^5	0	0	0	
	STX	3501	X^8			0	X^5	0	0	0	
	MUL	3501(1:5)	0	X^{13}			0	0	0	0	
	SLAX	1	X^{13}			0	0	0	0	0	
	HLT	0										
(3500)	NOP	0										
(3501)	NOP	0 ∎										

space $= 14$; time $= 54u$, not counting the HLT.

At least five multiplications are "necessary," according to the theory developed in Section 4.6.3, yet this program uses only four! And in fact there is an even better solution below.

Minimum space:

(3000)	ENT4	12	DEC4	1
	LDA	2000	J4P	3002
(3002)	MUL	2000	HLT	0 ∎
	SLAX	5		space $= 7$; time $= 171u$.

True minimum time: As R. W. Floyd points out, the conditions imply that $|X| \leq 5$, so the minimum execution time is achieved by referring to a table:

(3000)	LD1	2000
	LDA	3500,1
	HLT	0
(3495)	$(-5)^{13}$	[This line needed only when $b > 65$.]
(3496)	$(-4)^{13}$	
	$\vdots$	
(3505)	$(+5)^{13}$	[This line needed only when $b > 65$.] ∎

space $= 14$; time $= 4u$.

23. The following solution by R. D. Dixon appears to satisfy all the conditions:

(3000)	ENT1	4	DEC1	1
(3001)	LDA	200	J1NN	3001
	SRA	0,1	SLAX	5
	SRAX	1	HLT	0 ∎

24. (a) DIV 3500, where 3500 $=$ | + | 1 | 0 | 0 | 0 | 0 |.

(b) SRC 4; SRA 1; SLC 5.

25. Some ideas: (a) Obvious things like faster memory, more input-output devices. (b) The I field could be used for J-register indexing, and/or multiple indexing (to specify two different index registers) and/or "indirect addressing" (exercises 2.2.2–3, 4, 5). (c) Index registers and J register could be extended to a full five bytes; therefore locations with higher addresses could be referred to only by indexing, but that would not be so intolerable if multiple indexing were available as in (b). (d) An interrupt capability could be added, using negative memory addresses as in exercise 1.4.4–18. (e) A "real time clock" could be added, in a negative memory address. (f) Bitwise operations, jumps on register even or odd, and binary shifts could be added to binary versions of MIX (see, for example, exercises 2.5–28, 5.2.2–12, and 6.3–9; also Program 4.5.2B, 6.4–(24), and Section 7.1). (g) An "execute" command, meaning to perform the instruction at location M, could be another variant of $C = 5$. (h) Another variant of $C = 48, \ldots, 55$ could set CI ← register : M.

26. It is tempting to use a $(2:5)$ field to get at columns 7–10 of the card, but this cannot be done since $2 \cdot 8 + 5 = 21$. To make the program easier to follow, it is presented here in symbolic language, anticipating Section 1.3.2.

					characters punched on card:
	BUFF	EQU	29	Buffer area is 0029–0044	
		ORIG	0		
00	LOC	IN	16(16)	Read in second card.	␣0␣06
01	READ	IN	BUFF(16)	Read next card.	␣Z␣06
02		LD1	0(0:0)	rI1 ← 0.	␣␣␣␣I
03		JBUS	*(16)	Wait for read to finish.	␣C␣04
04		LDA	BUFF+1	rA ← columns 6–10.	␣0␣EH
05	=1=	SLA	1		␣A␣␣F
06		SRAX	6	rAX ← columns 7–10.	␣F␣CF
07	=30=	NUM	30		␣0␣␣E
08		STA	LOC	LOC ← starting location.	␣␣␣EU
09		LDA	BUFF+1(1:1)		␣0␣IH
10		SUB	=30=(0:2)		␣G␣BB
11	LOOP	LD3	LOC	rI3 ← LOC.	␣␣␣EJ
12		JAZ	0,3	Jump, if transfer card.	␣␣CA.
13		STA	BUFF	BUFF ← count.	␣Z␣EU
14		LDA	LOC		␣␣␣EH
15		ADD	=1=(0:2)		␣E␣BA
16		STA	LOC	LOC ← LOC + 1.	␣␣␣EU
17		LDA	BUFF+3,1(5:5)		␣2A-H
18		SUB	=25=(0:2)		␣S␣BB
19		STA	0,3(0:0)	Store the sign.	␣␣C␣U
20		LDA	BUFF+2,1		␣1AEH
21		LDX	BUFF+3,1		␣2AEN
22	=25=	NUM	25		␣V␣␣E
23		STA	0,3(1:5)	Store the magnitude.	␣␣CLU
24		MOVE	0,1(2)	rI1 ← rI1 + 2. (!)	␣␣ABG
25		LDA	BUFF		␣Z␣EH
26		SUB	=1=(0:2)	Decrease the count.	␣E␣BB
27		JAP	LOOP	Repeat until the count is zero.	␣J␣B.
28		JMP	READ	Now read a new card.	␣A␣␣9

SECTION 1.3.2

1. ENTX 1000; STX X.

2. The STJ instruction in line 03 resets this address. (It is conventional to denote the address of such instructions by "*", both because it is simple to write, and because it provides a recognizable test of an error condition in a program, in case a subroutine has not been entered properly because of some oversight. Some people prefer "*-*".)

3. Read in 100 words from tape unit zero; exchange their maximum with the last of them; exchange the maximum of the remaining 99 with the last of those; etc. Eventually the 100 words will become completely sorted into nondecreasing order. The result is then written onto tape unit one. (Compare with Algorithm 5.2.3S.)

4. Nonzero locations:

3000:	+	0000	00	18	35	3021:	+	0000	00	01	05
3001:	+	2051	00	05	09	3022:	+	0000	04	12	31
3002:	+	2050	00	05	10	3023:	+	0001	00	01	52
3003:	+	0001	00	00	49	3024:	+	0050	00	01	53
3004:	+	0499	01	05	26	3025:	+	3020	00	02	45
3005:	+	3016	00	01	41	3026:	+	0000	04	18	37
3006:	+	0002	00	00	50	3027:	+	0024	04	05	12
3007:	+	0002	00	02	51	3028:	+	3019	00	00	45
3008:	+	0000	00	02	48	3029:	+	0000	00	02	05
3009:	+	0000	02	02	55	0000:	+				2
3010:	−	0001	03	05	04	1995:	+	06	09	19	22	23
3011:	+	3006	00	01	47	1996:	+	00	06	09	25	05
3012:	−	0001	03	05	56	1997:	+	00	08	24	15	04
3013:	+	0001	00	00	51	1998:	+	19	05	04	00	17
3014:	+	3008	00	06	39	1999:	+	19	09	14	05	22
3015:	+	3003	00	00	39	2024:	+				2035
3016:	+	1995	00	18	37	2049:	+				2010
3017:	+	2035	00	02	52	2050:	+				3
3018:	−	0050	00	02	53	2051:	−				499
3019:	+	0501	00	00	53						
3020:	−	0001	05	05	08						

(the latter two may be interchanged, with corresponding changes to 3001 and 3002)

5. Each OUT waits for the previous printer operation to finish (from the other buffer).

6. (a) If n is not prime, by definition n has a divisor d with $1 < d < n$. If $d > \sqrt{n}$, then n/d is a divisor with $1 < n/d < \sqrt{n}$. (b) If N is not prime, N has a *prime* divisor d with $1 < d \le \sqrt{N}$. The algorithm has verified that N has no prime divisors $\le p = $ PRIME[K]; also $N = pQ + R < pQ + p \le p^2 + p < (p+1)^2$. Any prime divisor of N is therefore greater than $p + 1 > \sqrt{N}$.

We must also prove that there will be a sufficiently large prime less than N when N is prime, namely that the $(k+1)$st prime p_{k+1} is less than $p_k^2 + p_k$; otherwise K would exceed J and PRIME[K] would be zero when we needed it to be large. The necessary proof follows from "Bertrand's postulate": If p is prime there is a larger prime less than $2p$.

7. (a) It refers to the location of line 29. (b) The program would then fail; line 14 would refer to line 15 instead of line 25; line 24 would refer to line 15 instead of line 12.

8. It prints 100 lines. If the 12000 characters on these lines were arranged end to end, they would reach quite far and would consist of five blanks followed by five A's followed by ten blanks followed by five A's followed by fifteen blanks ... followed by $5k$ blanks followed by five A's followed by $5(k+1)$ blanks ... until 12000 characters have been printed. The third-from-last line ends with AAAAA and 35 blanks; the final two lines are entirely blank. The total effect is one of OP art.

9. The $(4:4)$ field of each entry in the following table holds the maximum F setting; the $(1:2)$ field is the location of an appropriate validity-check routine.

```
B       EQU  1(4:4)          BEGIN LDA  INST
BMAX    EQU  B-1                   CMPA VALID(3:3)
UMAX    EQU  20                    JG   BAD              I field > 6?
TABLE   NOP  GOOD(BMAX)            LD1  INST(5:5)
        ADD  FLOAT(5:5)            DEC1 64
        SUB  FLOAT(5:5)            J1NN BAD              C field ≥ 64?
        MUL  FLOAT(5:5)            CMPA TABLE+64,1(4:4)
        DIV  FLOAT(5:5)            JG   BAD              F field > F max?
        HLT  GOOD                  LD1  TABLE+64,1(1:2) Jump to special
        SRC  GOOD                  JMP  0,1             routine.
        MOVE MEMORY(BMAX)    FLOAT CMPA VALID(4:4)      F = 6 allowed on
        LDA  FIELD(5:5)            JE   MEMORY          arithmetic op
        ...                  FIELD ENTA 0
        STZ  FIELD(5:5)            LDX  INST(4:4)       This is a tricky
        JBUS MEMORY(UMAX)          DIV  =9=             way to check
        IOC  GOOD(UMAX)            STX  *+1(0:2)        for a valid
        IN   MEMORY(UMAX)          INCA 0               partial field.
        OUT  MEMORY(UMAX)          DECA 5
        JRED MEMORY(UMAX)          JAP  BAD
        JLE  MEMORY          MEMORY LDX INST(3:3)
        JANP MEMORY                JXNZ GOOD            If I = 0,
        ...                        LDX  INST(0:2)       ensure the
        JXNP MEMORY                JXN  BAD             address is a
        ENNA GOOD                  DECX 3999            valid memory
        ...                        JXNP GOOD            location.
        ENNX GOOD                  JMP  BAD
        CMPA FLOAT(5:5)      VALID CMPX 3999,6(6)       ▌
        CMP1 FIELD(5:5)
        ...
        CMPX FIELD(5:5)
```

10. The catch to this problem is that there may be several places in a row or column where the minimum or maximum occurs, and each is a potential saddle point.

Solution 1: In this solution we run through each row in turn, making a list of all columns in which the row minimum occurs and then checking each column on the list to see if the row minimum is also a column maximum. $rX \equiv$ current min; rI1 traces through the matrix, going from 72 down to zero unless a saddle point is found; $rI2 \equiv$ column index of rI1; $rI3 \equiv$ size of list of minima. Notice that in all cases the terminating condition for a loop is that an index register is ≤ 0.

```
* SOLUTION 1
A10      EQU   1008      Location of a₁₀
LIST     EQU   1000

START    ENT1  9*8       Begin at the lower right corner.
ROWMIN   ENT2  8         Now rI1 is at column 8 of its row.
2H       LDX   A10,1     Candidate for row minimum
         ENT3  0         List empty
4H       INC3  1
         ST2   LIST,3    Put column index in list.
1H       DEC1  1         Go left one.
         DEC2  1
         J2Z   COLMAX    Done with row?
3H       CMPX  A10,1
         JL    1B        Is rX still minimum?
         JG    2B        New minimum?
         JMP   4B        Remember another minimum.
COLMAX   LD2   LIST,3    Get column from list.
         INC2  9*8-8
1H       CMPX  A10,2
         JL    NO        Is row min < column element?
         DEC2  8
         J2P   1B        Done with column?
YES      INC1  A10+8,2   Yes; rI1 ← address of saddle.
         HLT
NO       DEC3  1         Is list empty?
         J3P   COLMAX    No; try again.
         J1P   ROWMIN    Have all rows been tried?
         HLT             Yes; rI1 = 0, no saddle.  ∎
```

Solution 2: An infusion of mathematics gives a different algorithm.

Theorem. *Let* $R(i) = \min_j a_{ij}$, $C(j) = \max_i a_{ij}$. *The element* $a_{i_0 j_0}$ *is a saddle point if and only if* $R(i_0) = \max_i R(i) = C(j_0) = \min_j C(j)$.

Proof. If $a_{i_0 j_0}$ is a saddle point, then for any fixed i, $R(i_0) = C(j_0) \geq a_{ij_0} \geq R(i)$; so $R(i_0) = \max_i R(i)$. Similarly $C(j_0) = \min_j C(j)$. Conversely, we have $R(i) \leq a_{ij} \leq C(j)$ for all i and j; hence $R(i_0) = C(j_0)$ implies that $a_{i_0 j_0}$ is a saddle point. ∎

(This proof shows that we always have $\max_i R(i) \leq \min_j C(j)$. So there is no saddle point if and only if all the R's are less than all the C's.)

According to the theorem, it suffices to find the smallest column maximum, then to search for an equal row minimum. During Phase 1, $rI1 \equiv$ column index; rI2 runs through the matrix. During Phase 2, $rI1 \equiv$ possible answer; rI2 runs through the matrix; $rI3 \equiv$ row index times 8; $rI4 \equiv$ column index.

```
* SOLUTION 2
CMAX   EQU   1000
A10    EQU   CMAX+8
PHASE1 ENT1  8              Start at column 8.
3H     ENT2  9*8-8,1
       JMP   2F
1H     CMPX  A10,2          Is rX still maximum?
       JGE   *+2
2H     LDX   A10,2          New maximum in column
       DEC2  8
       J2P   1B
       STX   CMAX+8,2       Store column maximum.
       J2Z   1F             First time?
       CMPA  CMAX+8,2       rA still min max?
       JLE   *+2
1H     LDA   CMAX+8,2
       DEC1  1              Move left a column.
       J1P   3B
PHASE2 ENT3  9*8-8          At this point rA = min_j C(j)
3H     ENT2  8,3            Prepare to search a row.
       ENT4  8
1H     CMPA  A10,2          Is min_j C(j) > a[i,j]?
       JG    NO             No saddle in this row
       JL    2F
       CMPA  CMAX,4         Is a[i,j] = C(j)?
       JNE   2F
       ENT1  A10,2          Remember a possible saddle point.
2H     DEC4  1              Move left in row.
       DEC2  1
       J4P   1B
       HLT                  A saddle point was found.
NO     DEC3  8
       J3P   3B             Try another row.
       ENT1  0
       HLT                  rI1 = 0; no saddle.  ▮
```

We leave it to the reader to invent a still better solution in which Phase 1 records all possible rows that are candidates for the row search in Phase 2. It is not necessary to search all rows, just those i_0 for which $C(j_0) = \min_j C(j)$ implies $a_{i_0 j_0} = C(j_0)$. Usually there is at most one such row.

In some trial runs with elements selected at random from $\{0, 1, 2, 3, 4\}$, solution 1 required approximately $730u$ to run, while solution 2 took about $530u$. Given a matrix of all zeros, solution 1 found a saddle point in $137u$, solution 2 in $524u$.

If an $m \times n$ matrix has *distinct* elements, and $m \geq n$, we can solve the problem by looking at only $O(m + n)$ of them and doing $O(m \log n)$ auxiliary operations. See Bienstock, Chung, Fredman, Schäffer, Shor, and Suri, *AMM* **98** (1991), 418–419.

11. Assume an $m \times n$ matrix. (a) By the theorem in the answer to exercise 10, all saddle points of a matrix have the same value, so (under our assumption of distinct elements) there is at most one saddle point. By symmetry the desired probability is mn times the probability that a_{11} is a saddle point. This latter is $1/(mn)!$ times the number of permutations with $a_{12} > a_{11}, \ldots, a_{1n} > a_{11}, a_{11} > a_{21}, \ldots, a_{11} > a_{m1}$; this is $1/(m+n-1)!$ times the number of permutations of $m+n-1$ elements in which the first is greater than the next $(m-1)$ and less than the remaining $(n-1)$, namely $(m-1)!\,(n-1)!$. The answer is therefore

$$mn(m-1)!\,(n-1)!/(m+n-1)! = (m+n)\Big/\binom{m+n}{n}.$$

In our case this is $17/\binom{17}{8}$, only one chance in 1430. (b) Under the second assumption, an entirely different method must be used. The probability equals the probability that there is a saddle point with value zero plus the probability that there is a saddle point with value one. The former is the probability that there is at least one column of zeros; the latter is the probability that there is at least one row of ones. The answer is $\big(1 - (1 - 2^{-m})^n\big) + \big(1 - (1 - 2^{-n})^m\big)$; in our case it comes to 924744796234036231/ 18446744073709551616, about 1 in 19.9. An approximate answer is $n2^{-m} + m2^{-n}$.

12. M. Hofri and P. Jacquet [*Algorithmica* **22** (1998), 516–528] have analyzed the case when the $m \times n$ matrix entries are distinct and in random order. The running times of the two MIX programs are then respectively $\big(6mn + 5mH_n + 8m + 6 + 5(m+1)/(n-1)\big)u + O\big((m+n)^2/\binom{m+n}{m}\big)$ and $(5mn + 2nH_m + 7m + 7n + 9H_n)u + O(1/n) + O\big((\log n)^2/m\big)$, as $m \to \infty$ and $n \to \infty$, assuming that $(\log n)/m \to 0$.

13.

```
      * CRYPTANALYST PROBLEM (CLASSIFIED)
TAPE  EQU   20          Input unit number
TYPE  EQU   19          Output unit number
SIZE  EQU   14          Input block size
OSIZE EQU   14          Output block size
TABLE EQU   1000        Table of counts
      ORIG  TABLE          (initially zero
      CON   -1             except entries for
      ORIG  TABLE+46       blank space and
      CON   -1             asterisk)
      ORIG  2000
BUF1  ORIG  *+SIZE      First buffer area
      CON   -1          "Sentinel" at end of buffer
      CON   *+1         Reference to second buffer
BUF2  ORIG  *+SIZE      Second buffer
      CON   -1          "Sentinel"
      CON   BUF1        Reference to first buffer
BEGIN IN    BUF1(TAPE)  Input first block.
      ENT6  BUF2
1H    IN    0,6(TAPE)   Input next block.
      LD6   SIZE+1,6    During this input, prepare
      ENT5  0,6            to process the previous one.
      JMP   4F
2H    INCA  1
      STA   TABLE,1     Update table entry.
3H    SLAX  1
      STA   *+1(2:2)    rI1 ← next char.
      ENT1  0
      LDA   TABLE,1
      JANN  2B          Normal character?
```

Update table entry. $\Big\}$ main loop, should run as fast as possible

```
        J1NZ  3F              Asterisk?
        JXP   3B              Skip over a blank.
        INC5  1
4H      LDX   0,5             rX ← five chars.
        JXNN  3B              Jump if not a sentinel.
        JMP   1B              Done with block.
3H      ENT1  1              Begin the endgame: rI1 ← "A".
2H      LDA   TABLE,1
        JANP  1F              Skip zero answers.
        CHAR                  Convert to decimal.
        JBUS  *(TYPE)         Wait till the typewriter is ready.
        ST1   CHAR(1:1)
        STA   CHAR(4:5)
        STX   FREQ
        OUT   ANS(TYPE)       Type one answer.
1H      CMP1  =63=
        INC1  1              Up to 63 character
        JL    2B                codes are counted
        HLT
ANS     ALF                   The output buffer
        ALF
CHAR    ALF   C  NN
FREQ    ALF   NNNNN
        ORIG  ANS+OSIZE       Rest of buffer is blank
        END   BEGIN           The literal constant =63= comes here.  ▌
```

For this problem, buffering of *output* is not desirable since it could save at most $7u$ of time per line output.

14. To make the problem more challenging, the following solution due in part to J. Petolino uses a lot of *trickery* in order to reduce execution time. Can the reader squeeze out any more microseconds?

```
* DATE OF EASTER
EASTER   STJ   EASTX
         STX   Y
         ENTA  0               E1.
         DIV   =19=
         STX   GMINUS1(0:2)
         LDA   Y               E2.
         MUL   =1//100+1=      (see
         INCA  61                below)
         STA   CPLUS60(1:2)
         MUL   =3//4+1=
         STA   XPLUS57(1:2)
CPLUS60  ENTA  *
         MUL   =8//25+1=       rA ← Z + 24.
GMINUS1  ENT2  *               E5.
         ENT1  1,2             rI1 ← G.
         INC2  1,1
         INC2  0,2
```

```
           INC2 0,1
           INC2 0,2
           INC2 773,1         rI2 ← 11G + 773.
XPLUS57    INCA -*,2          rA ← 11G + Z - X + 20 + 24·30 (≥ 0).
           SRAX 5
           DIV  =30=          rX ← E.
           DECX 24
           JXN  4F
           DECX 1
           JXP  2F
           JXN  3F
           DEC1 11
           J1NP 2F
3H         INCX 1
2H         DECX 29                 E6.
4H         STX  20MINUSN(0:2)
           LDA  Y                  E4.
           MUL  =1//4+1=
           ADD  Y
           SUB  XPLUS57(1:2)   rA ← D - 47.
20MINUSN   ENN1 *
           INCA 67,1               E7.
           SRAX 5             rX ← D + N
           DIV  =7=
           SLAX 5
           DECA -4,1          rA ← 31 - N
           JAN  1F                 E8.
           DECA 31
           CHAR
           LDA  MARCH
           JMP  2F
1H         CHAR
           LDA  APRIL
2H         JBUS *(18)
           STA  MONTH
           STX  DAY(1:2)
           LDA  Y
           CHAR
           STX  YEAR
           OUT  ANS(18)       Print
EASTX      JMP  *
MARCH      ALF  MARCH
APRIL      ALF  APRIL
ANS        ALF
DAY        ALF  DD
MONTH      ALF  MMMMM
           ALF  ,
YEAR       ALF  YYYYY
           ORIG *+20
```

```
BEGIN    ENTX 1950          "driver"
         ENT6 1950-2000        routine,
         JMP  EASTER          uses the
         INC6 1               subroutine
         ENTX 2000,6          above.
         J6NP EASTER+1
         HLT
         END  BEGIN          ∎
```

A rigorous justification for the change from division to multiplication in several places can be based on the fact that the number in rA is not too large. The program works with all byte sizes.

[To calculate Easter in years ≤ 1582, see *CACM* **5** (1962), 209–210. The first systematic algorithm for calculating the date of Easter was the *canon paschalis* due to Victorius of Aquitania (A.D. 457). There are many indications that the sole nontrivial application of arithmetic in Europe during the Middle Ages was the calculation of Easter date, hence such algorithms are historically significant. See *Puzzles and Paradoxes* by T. H. O'Beirne (London: Oxford University Press, 1965), Chapter 10, for further commentary; and see the book *Calendrical Calculations* by E. M. Reingold and N. Dershowitz (Cambridge Univ. Press, 2001) for date-oriented algorithms of all kinds.]

15. The first such year is A.D. 10317, although the error *almost* leads to failure in A.D. $10108 + 19k$ for $0 \leq k \leq 10$.

Incidentally, T. H. O'Beirne pointed out that the date of Easter repeats with a period of exactly 5,700,000 years. Calculations by Robert Hill show that the most common date is April 19 (220400 times per period), while the earliest and least common is March 22 (27550 times); the latest, and next-to-least common, is April 25 (42000 times). Hill found a nice explanation for the curious fact that the number of times any particular day occurs in the period is always a multiple of 25.

16. Work with scaled numbers, $R_n = 10^n r_n$. Then $R_n(1/m) = R$ if and only if $10^n/(R + \frac{1}{2}) < m \leq 10^n/(R - \frac{1}{2})$; thus we find $m_h = \lfloor 2 \cdot 10^n/(2R-1) \rfloor$.

```
      * SUM OF HARMONIC SERIES
      BUF    ORIG *+24
      START  ENT2 0
             ENT1 3          5 − n
             ENTA 20
      OUTER  MUL  =10=
             STX  CONST      2 · 10ⁿ
             DIV  =2=
             ENTX 2
             JMP  1F
      INNER  STA  R
             ADD  R
             DECA 1
             STA  TEMP       2R − 1
             LDX  CONST
             ENTA 0
             DIV  TEMP
             INCA 1
             STA  TEMP       mₕ + 1
```

```
         SUB   M
         MUL   R
         SLAX  5
         ADD   S
         LDX   TEMP
1H       STA   S          Partial sum
         STX   M          m = m_e
         LDA   M
         ADD   M
         STA   TEMP
         LDA   CONST
         ADD   M          Compute R = R_n(1/m) =
         SRAX  5            ⌊(2 · 10^n + m)/(2m)⌋.
         DIV   TEMP
         JAP   INNER      R > 0?
         LDA   S          10^n S_n
         CHAR
         SLAX  0,1        Neat formatting
         SLA   1
         INCA  40         Decimal point
         STA   BUF,2
         STX   BUF+1,2
         INC2  3
         DEC1  1
         LDA   CONST
         J1NN  OUTER
         OUT   BUF(18)
         HLT
         END   START      ▮
```

The output is

$$\text{0006.16}\qquad\text{0008.449}\qquad\text{0010.7509}\qquad\text{0013.05363}$$

in $65595u$ plus output time. (It would be faster to calculate $R_n(1/m)$ directly when $m < 10^{n/2}\sqrt{2}$, and then to apply the suggested procedure.)

17. Let $N = \lfloor 2 \cdot 10^n/(2m+1)\rfloor$. Then $S_n = H_N + O(N/10^n) + \sum_{k=1}^m(\lfloor 2 \cdot 10^n/(2k-1)\rfloor - \lfloor 2 \cdot 10^n/(2k+1)\rfloor)k/10^n = H_N + O(m^{-1}) + O(m/10^n) - 1 + 2H_{2m} - H_m = n\ln 10 + 2\gamma - 1 + 2\ln 2 + O(10^{-n/2})$ if we sum by parts and set $m \approx 10^{n/2}$.

Incidentally, the next several values are $S_6 = 15.356262$, $S_7 = 17.6588276$, $S_8 = 19.96140690$, $S_9 = 22.263991779$, and $S_{10} = 24.5665766353$; our approximation to S_{10} is ≈ 24.566576621, which is closer than predicted.

18. FAREY
```
   STJ   9F       Assume that rI1 contains n, where n > 1.
   STZ   X        x_0 ← 0.
   ENTX  1
   STX   Y        y_0 ← 1.
   STX   X+1      x_1 ← 1.
   ST1   Y+1      y_1 ← n.
   ENT2  0        k ← 0.
```

```
1H      LDX   Y,2
        INCX  0,1
        ENTA  0
        DIV   Y+1,2
        STA   TEMP    ⌊(yₖ + n)/yₖ₊₁⌋
        MUL   Y+1,2
        SLAX  5
        SUB   Y,2
        STA   Y+2,2   yₖ₊₂
        LDA   TEMP
        MUL   X+1,2
        SLAX  5
        SUB   X,2
        STA   X+2,2   xₖ₊₂
        CMPA  Y+2,2   Test if xₖ₊₂ < yₖ₊₂.
        INC2  1       k ← k + 1.
        JL    1B      If so, continue.
9H      JMP   *       Exit from subroutine.  ▌
```

19. (a) Induction. (b) Let $k \geq 0$ and $X = ax_{k+1} - x_k$, $Y = ay_{k+1} - y_k$, where $a = \lfloor (y_k + n)/y_{k+1} \rfloor$. By part (a) and the fact that $0 < Y \leq n$, we have $X \perp Y$ and $X/Y > x_{k+1}/y_{k+1}$. So if $X/Y \neq x_{k+2}/y_{k+2}$ we have, by definition, $X/Y > x_{k+2}/y_{k+2}$. But this implies that

$$\frac{1}{Y y_{k+1}} = \frac{X y_{k+1} - Y x_{k+1}}{Y y_{k+1}} = \frac{X}{Y} - \frac{x_{k+1}}{y_{k+1}}$$

$$= \left(\frac{X}{Y} - \frac{x_{k+2}}{y_{k+2}}\right) + \left(\frac{x_{k+2}}{y_{k+2}} - \frac{x_{k+1}}{y_{k+1}}\right)$$

$$\geq \frac{1}{Y y_{k+2}} + \frac{1}{y_{k+1} y_{k+2}} = \frac{y_{k+1} + Y}{Y y_{k+1} y_{k+2}} > \frac{n}{Y y_{k+1} y_{k+2}} \geq \frac{1}{Y y_{k+1}}.$$

Historical notes: C. Haros gave a (more complicated) rule for constructing such sequences, in *J. de l'École Polytechnique* **4**, 11 (1802), 364–368; his method was correct, but his proof was inadequate. Several years later, the geologist John Farey independently conjectured that x_k/y_k is always equal to $(x_{k-1} + x_{k+1})/(y_{k-1} + y_{k+1})$ [*Philos. Magazine and Journal* **47** (1816), 385–386]; a proof was supplied shortly afterwards by A. Cauchy [*Bull. Société Philomathique de Paris* (3) **3** (1816), 133–135], who attached Farey's name to the series. For more of its interesting properties, see G. H. Hardy and E. M. Wright, *An Introduction to the Theory of Numbers*, Chapter 3.

20.
```
      * TRAFFIC SIGNAL PROBLEM
        BSIZE   EQU   1(4:4)      Bytesize
        2BSIZE  EQU   2(4:4)      Twice bytesize
        DELAY   STJ   1F          If rA contains n,
                DECA  6             this subroutine
                DECA  2             waits max(n, 7)u
                JAP   *-1           exactly, not including
                JAN   *+2           the jump to the subroutine
                NOP
        1H      JMP   *
```

```
FLASH   STJ   2F          4   This subroutine flashes the
        ENT2  8           5      appropriate DON'T WALK light
1H      LDA   =49991=     7
        JMP   DELAY       8
        DECX  0,1         9   Turn light off.
        LDA   =49996=     2
        JMP   DELAY       3
        INCX  0,1         4   "DON'T WALK"
        DEC2  1           1
        J2Z   1F          2   Repeat eight times.
        LDA   *           4   Waste 2u of time.
        JMP   1B          5   Get back in synch.
1H      LDA   =399992=    4   Set amber 2u after exit.
        JMP   DELAY       5
2H      JMP   *           6
WAIT    JNOV  *           5   Del Mar green until tripped
TRIP    INCX  BSIZE       6   DON'T WALK on Del Mar
        ENT1  2BSIZE      1
        JMP   FLASH       2   Flash Del Mar.
        LDX   BAMBER      8   Amber on boulevard
        LDA   =799995=    2
        JMP   DELAY       3   Wait 8 seconds.
        LDX   AGREEN      5   Green for avenue
        LDA   =799996=    2
        JMP   DELAY       3   Wait 8 seconds.
        INCX  1           4   DON'T WALK on Berkeley
        ENT1  2           1
        JMP   FLASH       2   Flash Berkeley.
        LDX   AAMBER      8   Amber on avenue
        JOV   *+1         1   Cancel redundant trip.
        LDA   =499994=    3
        JMP   DELAY       4   Wait 5 seconds.
BEGIN   LDX   BGREEN      6   Green on boulevard
        LDA   =1799994=   2
        JMP   DELAY       3   Wait at least 18
        JMP   WAIT        4      seconds.
AGREEN  ALF   CABA            Green for avenue
AAMBER  ALF   CBBB            Amber for avenue
BGREEN  ALF   ACAB            Green for boulevard
BAMBER  ALF   BCBB            Amber for boulevard
        END   BEGIN       ▮
```

22. * JOSEPHUS PROBLEM

```
N   EQU   24
M   EQU   11
X   ORIG  *+N
OH  ENT1  N-1        1       Set each cell to the
    STZ   X+N-1      1          number of the next man
    ST1   X-1,1      N - 1      in the sequence.
    DEC1  1          N - 1
    J1P   *-2        N - 1
```

```
        ENTA 1              1           (Now rI1 = 0)
   1H   ENT2 M-2            N - 1       (Assume M > 2)
        LD1  X,1       (M - 2)(N - 1)   Count around
        DEC2 1         (M - 2)(N - 1)      the circle.
        J2P  *-2       (M - 2)(N - 1)
        LD2  X,1            N - 1       rI1 ≡ lucky man
        LD3  X,2            N - 1       rI2 ≡ doomed man
        CHAR               N - 1        rI3 ≡ next man
        STX  X,2(4:5)      N - 1        Store execution number.
        NUM                N - 1
        INCA 1             N - 1
        ST3  X,1           N - 1        Take man from circle.
        ENT1 0,3           N - 1
        CMPA =N=           N - 1
        JL   1B            N - 1
        CHAR                1           One man left;
        STX  X,1(4:5)       1             he is clobbered too.
        OUT  X(18)          1           Print the answer.
        HLT                 1
        END  0B             ▮
```

The last man is in position 15. The total time before output is $(4(N-1)(M+7.5)+16)u$. Several improvements are possible, such as D. Ingalls's suggestion to have three-word packets of code "DEC2 1; J2P NEXT; JMP OUT", where OUT modifies the NEXT field so as to delete a packet. An asymptotically faster method appears in exercise 5.1.1–5.

SECTION 1.3.3

1. $(1\ 2\ 4)(3\ 6\ 5)$.

2. $a \leftrightarrow c$, $c \leftrightarrow f$; $b \leftrightarrow d$. The generalization to arbitrary permutations is clear.

3. $\begin{pmatrix} a & b & c & d & e & f \\ d & b & f & c & a & e \end{pmatrix}$.

4. $(a\,d\,c\,f\,e)$.

5. 12. (See exercise 20.)

6. The total time decreases by $8u$ for every blank word following a "(", because lines 30–32 cost $4u$ while lines 26–28, 33–34, 36–38 cost $12u$. It decreases by $2u$ for every blank word following a name, because lines 68–71 cost $5u$ while 42–46 or 75–79 cost $7u$. Initial blanks and blanks between cycles do not affect the execution time. The position of blanks has no effect whatever on Program B.

7. $X = 2$, $Y = 29$, $M = 5$, $N = 7$, $U = 3$, $V = 1$. Total, by Eq. (18), $2161u$.

8. Yes; we would then keep the inverse of the permutation, so that x_i goes to x_j if and only if $T[j] = i$. (The final cycle form would then be constructed from right to left, using the T table.)

9. No. For example, given (6) as input, Program A will produce "(ADG)(CEB)" as output, while Program B produces "(CEB)(DGA)". The answers are equivalent but not identical, due to the nonuniqueness of cycle notation. The first element chosen for a cycle is the leftmost available name, in the case of Program A, and the last available distinct name to be encountered from right to left, in Program B.

10. (1) Kirchhoff's law yields $A = 1 + C - D$; $B = A + J + P - 1$; $C = B - (P - L)$; $E = D - L$; $G = E$; $Q = Z$; $W = S$. (2) Interpretations: $B =$ number of words of input $= 16X - 1$; $C =$ number of nonblank words $= Y$; $D = C - M$; $E = D - M$; $F =$ number of comparisons in names table search; $H = N$; $K = M$; $Q = N$; $R = U$; $S = R - V$; $T = N - V$ since each of the other names gets tagged. (3) Summing up, we have $(4F + 16Y + 80X + 21N - 19M + 9U - 16V)u$, which is somewhat better than Program A because F is certainly less than $16NX$. The time in the stated case is $983u$, since $F = 74$.

11. "Reflect" it. For example, the inverse of $(a\,c\,f)(b\,d)$ is $(d\,b)(f\,c\,a)$.

12. (a) The value in cell $L+mn-1$ is fixed by the transposition, so we may omit it from consideration. Otherwise if $x = n(i-1) + (j-1) < mn - 1$, the value in $L + x$ should go to cell $L + mx \bmod N = L + (mn(i-1) + m(j-1)) \bmod N = L + m(j-1) + (i-1)$, since $mn \equiv 1$ (modulo N) and $0 \le m(j-1) + (i-1) < N$. (b) If one bit in each memory cell is available (for example, the sign), we can "tag" elements as we move them, using an algorithm like Algorithm I. [See M. F. Berman, *JACM* **5** (1958), 383–384.] If there is no room for a tag bit, tag bits can be kept in an auxiliary table, or else a list of representatives of all non-singleton cycles can be used: For each divisor d of N, we can transpose those elements that are multiples of d separately, since m is prime to N. The length of the cycle containing x, when $\gcd(x, N) = d$, is the smallest integer $r > 0$ such that $m^r \equiv 1$ (modulo N/d). For each d, we want to find $\varphi(N/d)/r$ representatives, one from each of these cycles. Some number-theoretic methods are available for this purpose, but they are not simple enough to be really satisfactory. An efficient but rather complicated algorithm can be obtained by combining number theory with a small table of tag bits. [See N. Brenner, *CACM* **16** (1973), 692–694.] Finally, there is a method analogous to Algorithm J; it is slower, but needs no auxiliary memory, and it performs *any* desired permutation *in situ*. [See P. F. Windley, *Comp. J.* **2** (1959), 47–48; D. E. Knuth, *Proc. IFIP Congress* (1971), **1**, 19–27; E. G. Cate and D. W. Twigg, *ACM Trans. Math. Software* **3** (1977), 104–110; F. E. Fich, J. I. Munro, and P. V. Poblete, *SICOMP* **24** (1995), 266–278.]

13. Show by induction that, at the beginning of step J2, $X[i] = +j$ if and only if $j > m$ and j goes to i under π; $X[i] = -j$ if and only if i goes to j under π^{k+1}, where k is the smallest nonnegative integer such that π^k takes i into a number $\le m$.

14. Writing the *inverse* of the given permutation in canonical cycle form and dropping parentheses, the quantity $A - N$ is the sum of the number of consecutive elements greater than a given element and immediately to its right. For example, if the original permutation is $(1\,6\,5)(3\,7\,8\,4)$, the canonical form of the inverse is $(3\,4\,8\,7)(2)(1\,5\,6)$; set up the array

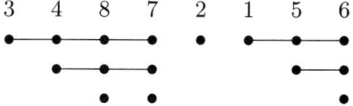

and the quantity A is the number of "dots," 16. The number of dots below the kth element is the number of right-to-left minima in the first k elements (there are 3 dots below 7 in the example above, since there are 3 right-to-left minima in 3487). Hence the average is $H_1 + H_2 + \cdots + H_n = (n+1)H_n - n$.

15. If the first character of the linear representation is 1, the last character of the canonical representation is 1. If the first character of the linear representation is $m > 1$, then "...$1m$..." appears in the canonical representation. So the only solution is the permutation of a single object. (Well, there's also the permutation of *no* objects.)

16. $1324, 4231, 3214, 4213, 2143, 3412, 2413, 1243, 3421, 1324, \ldots$.

17. (a) The probability p_m that the cycle is an m-cycle is $n!/m$ divided by $n! \, H_n$, so $p_m = 1/(mH_n)$. The average length is $p_1 + 2p_2 + 3p_3 + \cdots = \sum_{m=1}^n m/(mH_n) = n/H_n$. (b) Since the total number of m-cycles is $n!/m$, the total number of appearances of elements in m-cycles is $n!$. Each element appears as often as any other, by symmetry, so k appears $n!/n$ times in m-cycles. In *this* case, therefore, $p_m = 1/n$ for all k and m; the average is $\sum_{m=1}^n m/n = (n+1)/2$.

18. See exercise 22(e).

19. $|P_{n0} - n!/e| = n!/(n+1)! - n!/(n+2)! + \cdots$, an alternating series of decreasing magnitudes, which is less than $n!/(n+1)! \le \frac{1}{2}$.

20. There are $\alpha_1 + \alpha_2 + \cdots$ cycles in all, which can be permuted among one another, and each m-cycle can be independently written in m ways. So the answer is

$$(\alpha_1 + \alpha_2 + \cdots)! \, 1^{\alpha_1} 2^{\alpha_2} 3^{\alpha_3} \cdots.$$

21. $1/(\alpha_1! \, 1^{\alpha_1} \alpha_2! \, 2^{\alpha_2} \ldots)$ if $n = \alpha_1 + 2\alpha_2 + \cdots$; zero otherwise.

Proof. Write out α_1 1-cycles, α_2 2-cycles, etc., in a row, with empty positions; for example if $\alpha_1 = 1$, $\alpha_2 = 2$, $\alpha_3 = \alpha_4 = \cdots = 0$, we would have "(-)(--)(--)". Fill the empty positions in all $n!$ possible ways; we obtain each permutation of the desired form exactly $\alpha_1! \, 1^{\alpha_1} \alpha_2! \, 2^{\alpha_2} \ldots$ times.

22. (a) If $k_1 + 2k_2 + \cdots = n$, the probability in (ii) is $\prod_{j>0} f(w, j, k_j)$, which is assumed to equal $(1 - w) w^n/(k_1! \, 1^{k_1} k_2! \, 2^{k_2} \ldots)$; hence

$$\frac{f(w, m, k_m + 1)}{f(w, m, k_m)} = \left(\prod_{j>0} f(w, j, k_j) \right)^{-1} \prod_{j>0} f(w, j, k_j + \delta_{jm}) = \frac{w^m}{m(k_m + 1)}.$$

Therefore by induction $f(w, m, k) = (w^m/m)^k f(w, m, 0)/k!$, and condition (i) implies that $f(w, m, k) = (w^m/m)^k e^{-w^m/m}/k!$. [In other words, α_m is chosen with a Poisson distribution; see exercise 1.2.10–15.]

(b) $\displaystyle \sum_{\substack{k_1 + 2k_2 + \cdots = n \\ k_1, k_2, \ldots \ge 0}} \left(\prod_{j>0} f(w, j, k_j) \right) = (1-w) w^n \sum_{\substack{k_1 + 2k_2 + \cdots = n \\ k_1, k_2, \ldots \ge 0}} P(n; k_1, k_2, \ldots) = (1-w) w^n.$

Hence the probability that $\alpha_1 + 2\alpha_2 + \cdots \le n$ is $(1-w)(1 + w + \cdots + w^n) = 1 - w^{n+1}$.

(c) The average of ϕ is

$$\sum_{n \ge 0} \left(\sum_{k_1 + 2k_2 + \cdots = n} \phi(k_1, k_2, \ldots) \Pr(\alpha_1 = k_1, \alpha_2 = k_2, \ldots) \right)$$

$$= (1 - w) \sum_{n \ge 0} w^n \left(\sum_{k_1 + 2k_2 + \cdots = n} \phi(k_1, k_2, \ldots)/k_1! \, 1^{k_1} k_2! \, 2^{k_2} \ldots \right).$$

(d) Let $\phi(\alpha_1, \alpha_2, \ldots) = \alpha_2 + \alpha_4 + \alpha_6 + \cdots$. The average value of the linear combination ϕ is the sum of the average values of $\alpha_2, \alpha_4, \alpha_6, \ldots$; and the average value of α_m is

$$\sum_{k \ge 0} k f(w, m, k) = \sum_{k \ge 1} \frac{1}{(k-1)!} \left(\frac{w^m}{m} \right)^k e^{-w^m/m} = \frac{w^m}{m}.$$

Therefore the average value of ϕ is

$$\frac{w^2}{2} + \frac{w^4}{4} + \frac{w^6}{6} + \cdots = \frac{1-w}{2}(H_1 w^2 + H_1 w^3 + H_2 w^4 + H_2 w^5 + H_3 w^6 + \cdots).$$

The desired answer is $\frac{1}{2}H_{\lfloor n/2 \rfloor}$.

(e) Set $\phi(\alpha_1, \alpha_2, \dots) = z^{\alpha_m}$, and observe that the average value of ϕ is

$$\sum_{k \geq 0} f(w,m,k) z^k = \sum_{k \geq 0} \frac{1}{k!}\left(\frac{w^m z}{m}\right)^k e^{-w^m/m} = e^{w^m(z-1)/m} = \sum_{j \geq 0} \frac{w^{mj}}{j!}\left(\frac{z-1}{m}\right)^j$$

$$= (1-w) \sum_{n \geq 0} w^n \left(\sum_{0 \leq j \leq n/m} \frac{1}{j!}\left(\frac{z-1}{m}\right)^j \right) = (1-w) \sum_{n \geq 0} w^n G_{nm}(z).$$

Hence

$$G_{nm}(z) = \sum_{0 \leq j \leq n/m} \frac{1}{j!}\left(\frac{z-1}{m}\right)^j ; \qquad p_{nkm} = \frac{1}{m^k k!} \sum_{0 \leq j \leq n/m - k} \frac{(-1/m)^j}{j!} ;$$

the statistics are (min 0, ave $1/m$, max $\lfloor n/m \rfloor$, dev $\sqrt{1/m}$), when $n \geq 2m$.

23. The constant λ is $\int_0^\infty \exp(-t - E_1(t))\, dt$, where $E_1(x) = \int_x^\infty e^{-t} dt/t$. See *Trans. Amer. Math. Soc.* **121** (1966), 340–357, where many other results are proved, in particular that the average length of the *shortest* cycle is approximately $e^{-\gamma} \ln n$. Further terms of the asymptotic representation of l_n have been found by Xavier Gourdon [Ph.D. thesis, École Polytechnique (Paris, 1996)]; the series begins

$$\lambda n + \tfrac{1}{2}\lambda - \tfrac{1}{24}e^\gamma n^{-1} + \left(\tfrac{1}{48}e^\gamma - \tfrac{1}{8}(-1)^n\right)n^{-2} + \left(\tfrac{17}{3840}e^\gamma + \tfrac{1}{8}(-1)^n + \tfrac{1}{6}\omega^{1-n} + \tfrac{1}{6}\omega^{n-1}\right)n^{-3},$$

where $\omega = e^{2\pi i/3}$. William C. Mitchell has calculated a high-precision value of $\lambda = .62432\ 99885\ 43550\ 87099\ 29363\ 83100\ 83724\ 41796+$ [*Math. Comp.* **22** (1968), 411–415]; no relation between λ and classical mathematical constants is known. The same constant had, however, been computed in another context by Karl Dickman in *Arkiv för Mat., Astron. och Fys.* **22A**, 10 (1930), 1–14; the coincidence wasn't noticed until many years later [*Theor. Comp. Sci.* **3** (1976), 373].

24. See D. E. Knuth, *Proc. IFIP Congress* (1971), **1**, 19–27.

25. One proof, by induction on N, is based on the fact that when the Nth element is a member of s of the sets it contributes exactly

$$\binom{s}{0} - \binom{s}{1} + \binom{s}{2} - \cdots = (1-1)^s = \delta_{s0}$$

to the sum. Another proof, by induction on M, is based on the fact that the number of elements that are in S_M but not in $S_1 \cup \cdots \cup S_{M-1}$ is

$$|S_M| - \sum_{1 \leq j < M} |S_j \cap S_M| + \sum_{1 \leq j < k < M} |S_j \cap S_k \cap S_M| - \cdots.$$

26. Let $N_0 = N$ and let $N_k = \sum_{1 \leq j_1 < \cdots < j_k \leq M} |S_{j_1} \cap \cdots \cap S_{j_k}|$. Then

$$N_r - \binom{r+1}{r} N_{r+1} + \binom{r+2}{r} N_{r+2} - \cdots$$

is the desired formula. It can be proved from the principle of inclusion and exclusion itself, or by using the method of exercise 25 together with the fact that

$$\binom{r}{r}\binom{s}{r} - \binom{r+1}{r}\binom{s}{r+1} + \cdots = \binom{s}{r}\binom{s-r}{0} - \binom{s}{r}\binom{s-r}{1} + \cdots = \delta_{sr}.$$

27. Let S_j be the multiples of m_j in the stated range and let $N = am_1 \dots m_t$. Then $|S_j \cap S_k| = N/m_j m_k$, etc., so the answer is

$$N - N \sum_{1 \le j \le t} \frac{1}{m_j} + N \sum_{1 \le j < k \le t} \frac{1}{m_j m_k} - \dots = N \left(1 - \frac{1}{m_1}\right) \dots \left(1 - \frac{1}{m_t}\right).$$

This also solves exercise 1.2.4–30, if we let $m_1, \dots, m_t$ be the primes dividing N.

28. See I. N. Herstein and I. Kaplansky, *Matters Mathematical* (1974), §3.5.

29. When passing over a man, assign him a new number (starting with $n + 1$). Then the kth man executed is number $2k$, and man number j for $j > n$ was previously number $(2j) \bmod (2n + 1)$. Incidentally, the original number of the kth man executed is $2n + 1 - (2n + 1 - 2k)2^{\lfloor \lg(2n/(2n+1-2k)) \rfloor}$. [Armin Shams, *Proc. Nat. Computer Conf. 2002*, English papers section, **2** (Mashhad, Iran: Ferdowsi University, 2002), 29–33.]

31. See *CMath*, Section 3.3. Let $x_0 = jm$ and $x_{i+1} = (m(x_i - n) - d_i)/(m - 1)$, where $1 \le d_i < m$. Then $x_k = j$ if and only if $a_k j = b_k n + t_k$, where $a_k = m^{k+1} - (m-1)^k$, $b_k = m(m^k - (m-1)^k)$, and $t_k = \sum_{i=0}^{k-1} m^{k-1-i}(m-1)^i d_i$. Since $a_k \perp b_k$ and the $(m-1)^k$ possibilities for t_k are distinct, the average number of k-step fixed elements is $(m-1)^k/a_k$.

32. (a) In fact, $k - 1 \le \pi_k \le k + 2$ when k is even; $k - 2 \le \pi_k \le k + 1$ when k is odd. (b) Choose the exponents from left to right, setting $e_k = 1$ if and only if k and $k+1$ are in different cycles of the permutation so far. [Steven Alpern, *J. Combinatorial Theory* **B25** (1978), 62–73.]

33. For $l = 0$, let $(\alpha_{01}, \alpha_{02}; \beta_{01}, \beta_{02}) = (\pi, \rho; \epsilon, \epsilon)$ and $(\alpha_{11}, \alpha_{12}; \beta_{11}, \beta_{12}) = (\epsilon, \epsilon; \pi, \rho)$, where $\pi = (1\,4)(2\,3)$, $\rho = (1\,5)(2\,4)$, and $\epsilon = ()$.

Suppose we have made such a construction for some $l \ge 0$, where $\alpha_{jk}^2 = \beta_{jk}^2 = ()$ for $0 \le j < m$ and $1 \le k \le n$. Then the permutations

$$(A_{(jm+j')1}, \dots, A_{(jm+j')(4n)}; B_{(jm+j')1}, \dots, B_{(jm+j')(4n)}) =$$
$$(\sigma^- \alpha_{j1} \sigma, \dots, \sigma^- \alpha_{jn} \sigma, \tau^- \alpha_{j'1} \tau, \dots, \tau^- \alpha_{j'n} \tau,$$
$$\sigma^- \beta_{jn} \sigma, \dots, \sigma^- \beta_{j1} \sigma, \tau^- \beta_{j'n} \tau, \dots, \tau^- \beta_{j'1} \tau;$$
$$\sigma^- \beta_{j1} \sigma, \dots, \sigma^- \beta_{jn} \sigma, \tau^- \beta_{j'1} \tau, \dots, \tau^- \beta_{j'n} \tau,$$
$$\sigma^- \alpha_{jn} \sigma, \dots, \sigma^- \alpha_{j1} \sigma, \tau^- \alpha_{j'n} \tau, \dots, \tau^- \alpha_{j'1} \tau)$$

have the property that

$$A_{(im+i')1} B_{(jm+j')1} \dots A_{(im+i')(4n)} B_{(jm+j')(4n)} =$$
$$\sigma^- (1\,2\,3\,4\,5) \sigma \tau^- (1\,2\,3\,4\,5) \tau \sigma^- (5\,4\,3\,2\,1) \sigma \tau^- (5\,4\,3\,2\,1) \tau$$

if $i = j$ and $i' = j'$, otherwise the product is $()$. Choosing $\sigma = (2\,3)(4\,5)$ and $\tau = (3\,4\,5)$ will make the product $(1\,2\,3\,4\,5)$ as desired, when $im + i' = jm + j'$.

The construction that leads from l to $l+1$ is due to David A. Barrington [*J. Comp. Syst. Sci.* **38** (1989), 150–164], who proved a general theorem by which any Boolean function can be represented as a product of permutations of $\{1, 2, 3, 4, 5\}$. With a similar construction we can, for example, find sequences of permutations $(\alpha_{j1}, \dots, \alpha_{jn}; \beta_{j1}, \dots, \beta_{jn})$ such that

$$\alpha_{i1} \beta_{j1} \alpha_{i2} \beta_{j2} \dots \alpha_{in} \beta_{jn} = \begin{cases} (1\,2\,3\,4\,5), & \text{if } i < j; \\ (), & \text{if } i \ge j; \end{cases}$$

for $0 \le i, j < m = 2^{2^l}$ when $n = 6^{l+1} - 4^{l+1}$.

34. Let $N = m + n$. If $m \perp n$ there is only one cycle, because every element can be written in the form $am \bmod N$ for some integer a. And in general if $d = \gcd(m, n)$, there are exactly d cycles $C_0, C_1, \ldots, C_{d-1}$, where C_j contains the elements $\{j, j + d, \ldots, j + N - d\}$ in some order. To carry out the permutation, we can therefore proceed as follows for $0 \le j < d$ (in parallel, if convenient): Set $t \leftarrow x_j$ and $k \leftarrow j$; then while $(k + m) \bmod N \ne j$, set $x_k \leftarrow x_{(k+m) \bmod N}$ and $k \leftarrow (k + m) \bmod N$; finally set $x_k \leftarrow t$. In this algorithm the relation $(k + m) \bmod N \ne j$ will hold if and only if $(k + m) \bmod N \ge d$, so we can use whichever test is more efficient. [W. Fletcher and R. Silver, *CACM* **9** (1966), 326.]

35. Let $M = l + m + n$ and $N = l + 2m + n$. The cycles for the desired rearrangement are obtained from the cycles of the permutation on $\{0, 1, \ldots, N - 1\}$ that takes k to $(k + l + m) \bmod N$, by simply striking out all elements of each cycle that are $\ge M$. (Compare this behavior with the similar situation in exercise 29.) *Proof:* When the hinted interchange sets $x_k \leftarrow x_{k'}$ and $x_{k'} \leftarrow x_{k''}$ for some k with $k' = (k + l + m) \bmod N$ and $k'' = (k' + l + m) \bmod N$ and $k' \ge M$, we know that $x_{k'} = x_{k''}$; hence the rearrangement $\alpha\beta\gamma \to \gamma\beta\alpha$ replaces x_k by $x_{k''}$.

It follows that there are exactly $d = \gcd(l + m, m + n)$ cycles, and we can use an algorithm similar to the one in the previous exercise.

A slightly simpler way to reduce this problem to the special case in exercise 34 is also noteworthy, although it makes a few more references to memory: Suppose $\gamma = \gamma'\gamma''$ where $|\gamma''| = |\alpha|$. Then we can change $\alpha\beta\gamma'\gamma''$ to $\gamma''\beta\gamma'\alpha$, and interchange $\gamma''\beta$ with γ'. A similar approach works if $|\alpha| > |\gamma|$. [See J. L. Mohammed and C. S. Subi, *J. Algorithms* **8** (1987), 113–121.]

37. The result is clear when $n \le 2$. Otherwise we can find $a, b < n$ such that π takes a to b. Then $(n\,a)\,\pi\,(b\,n) = (\alpha\,a)(b\,\beta)$ for $(n - 1)$-cycles $(\alpha\,a)$ and $(b\,\beta)$ if and only if $\pi = (n\,\alpha\,a)(b\,\beta\,n)$. [See A. Jacques, C. Lenormand, A. Lentin, and J.-F. Perrot, *Comptes Rendus Acad. Sci.* **266** (Paris, 1968), A446–A448.]

SECTION 1.4.1

1. Calling sequence: `JMP MAXN`; or, `JMP MAX100` if $n = 100$.
    Entry conditions: For the `MAXN` entrance, rI3 $= n$; assume $n \ge 1$.
    Exit conditions: Same as in (4).

2.
```
MAX50 STJ  EXIT
      ENT3 50
      JMP  2F
```

3. Entry conditions: rI1 $= n$.
    Exit conditions: If $n \ge 1$, rA, rI2, and rI3 are as in (4), with rI2 maximal $\le n$;
                      otherwise rA $=$ `CONTENTS(X+n)`, rI2 $= n$, and rI3 $= n - 1$;
                      rJ $=$ `EXIT` $+ 1$; CI is unchanged if $n \le 1$; otherwise CI is greater,
                      equal, or less, according as the maximum is greater than $X[1]$,
                      equal to $X[1]$ with rI2 > 1, or equal to $X[1]$ with rI2 $= 1$.

(The analogous exercise for (9) would of course be somewhat more complicated.)

4.
```
SMAX1 ENT1 1         r = 1
SMAX  STJ  EXIT      general r
      JMP  2F        continue as before
```

```
      . . .
          DEC3  0,1      decrease by r
          J3P   1B
EXIT  JMP   *        exit.
```

Calling sequence: JMP SMAX; or, JMP SMAX1 if $r = 1$.

Entry conditions: rI3 $= n$, assumed positive; for the SMAX entrance, rI1 $= r$, assumed positive.

Exit conditions: rA $= \max_{0 \le k < n/r}$ CONTENTS(X $+ n - kr$) $=$ CONTENTS(X $+$ rI2); and rI3 $= (n - 1) \bmod r + 1 - r = -((-n) \bmod r)$.

   5. Any other register can be used. For example,

Calling sequence: ENTA *+2

                  JMP   MAX100

Entry conditions: None.

Exit conditions: Same as in (4).

The code is like (1), but the first instruction becomes "MAX100 STA EXIT(0:2)".

   6. (Solution by Joel Goldberg and Roger M. Aarons.)

```
MOVE  STJ   3F
      STA   4F          Save rA and rI2.
      ST2   5F(0:2)
      LD2   3F(0:2)     rI2 ← address of "NOP A,I(F)".
      LDA   0,2(0:3)    rA ← "A,I".
      STA   *+2(0:3)
      LD2   5F(0:2)     Restore rI2, because I might be 2.
      ENTA  *           rA ← indexed address.
      LD2   3F(0:2)
      LD2N  0,2(4:4)    rI2 ← −F.
      J2Z   1F
      DECA  0,2
      STA   2F(0:2)
      DEC1  0,2         rI1 ← rI1 + F.
      ST1   6F(0:2)
2H    LDA   *,2
6H    STA   *,2
      INC2  1           Increase rI2 until it becomes zero.
      J2N   2B
1H    LDA   4F          Restore rA and rI2.
5H    ENT2  *
3H    JMP   *           Exit to the NOP instruction.
4H    CON   0    ▮
```

   7. (1) An operating system can allocate high-speed memory more efficiently if program blocks are known to be "read-only." (2) An instruction cache in hardware will be faster and less expensive if instructions cannot change. (3) Same as (2), with "pipeline" in place of "cache." If an instruction is modified after entering a pipeline, the pipeline needs to be flushed; the circuitry needed to check this condition is complex and time-consuming. (4) Self-modifying code cannot be used by more than one process at once. (5) Self-modifying code can defeat a jump-trace routine (exercise 1.4.3.2–7), which is an important diagnostic tool for "profiling" (that is, for computing the number of times each instruction is executed).

SECTION 1.4.2

1. If one coroutine calls the other only once, it is nothing but a subroutine; so we need an application in which each coroutine calls the other in at least two distinct places. Even then, it is often easy to set some sort of switch or to use some property of the data, so that upon entry to a fixed place within one coroutine it is possible to branch to one of two desired places; again, nothing more than a subroutine would be required. Coroutines become correspondingly more useful as the number of references between them grows larger.

2. The first character found by IN would be lost. [We started OUT first because lines 58–59 do the necessary initialization for IN. If we wanted to start IN first, we'd have to initialize OUT by saying "ENT4 -16", and clearing the output buffer if it isn't known to be blank. Then we could make line 62 jump first to line 39.]

3. *Almost* true, since "CMPA =10=" within IN is then the only comparison instruction of the program, and since the code for "." is 40. (!) But the comparison indicator isn't initialized; and if the final period is preceded by a replication digit, it won't be noticed. [*Note:* The most nitpickingly efficient program would probably remove lines 40, 44, and 48, and would insert "CMPA PERIOD" between lines 26 and 27, "CMPX PERIOD" between lines 59 and 60. The state of the comparison indicator should then become part of the coroutine characteristics in the program documentation.]

4. Here are examples from three rather different computers of historic importance: (i) On the IBM 650, using SOAP assembly language, we would have the calling sequences "LDD   A" and "LDD   B", and linkage "A STD BX AX" and "B STD AX BX" (with the two linkage instructions preferably in core). (ii) On the IBM 709, using common assembly languages, the calling sequences would be "TSX A,4" and "TSX B,4"; the linkage instructions would be as follows:

```
A   SXA  BX,4              B   SXA  AX,4
AX  AXT  1-A1,4            BX  AXT  1-B1,4
    TRA  1,4                   TRA  1,4
```

(iii) On the CDC 1604, the calling sequences would be "return jump" (SLJ 4) to A or B, and the linkage would be, for example,

```
A:   SLJ  B1;  ALS  0
B:   SLJ  A1;  SLJ  A
```

in two consecutive 48-bit words.

5. "STA HOLDAIN; LDA HOLDAOUT" between OUT and OUTX, and "STA HOLDAOUT; LDA HOLDAIN" between IN and INX.

6. Within A write "JMP AB" to activate B, "JMP AC" to activate C. Locations BA, BC, CA, and CB would, similarly, be used within B and C. The linkage is:

```
AB   STJ  AX          BC   STJ  BX          CA   STJ  CX
BX   JMP  B1          CX   JMP  C1          AX   JMP  A1
CB   STJ  CX          AC   STJ  AX          BA   STJ  BX
     JMP  BX               JMP  CX               JMP  AX
```

[*Note:* With n coroutines, $2(n-1)n$ cells would be required for this style of linkage. If n is large, a "centralized" routine for linkage could of course be used; a method with $3n+2$ cells is not hard to invent. But in practice the faster method above requires just $2m$ cells, where m is the number of pairs (i, j) such that coroutine i jumps to coroutine j. When there are many coroutines each independently jumping to others, the sequence of control is usually under external influence, as discussed in Section 2.2.5.]

SECTION 1.4.3.1

1. FCHECK is used only twice, both times immediately followed by a call on MEMORY. So it would be slightly more efficient to make FCHECK a special entrance to the MEMORY subroutine, and also to make it put −R in rI2.

2. SHIFT	J5N	ADDRERROR		**3.** MOVE	J3Z	CYCLE
	DEC3	5			JMP	MEMORY
	J3P	FERROR			SRAX	5
	LDA	AREG			LD1	I1REG
	LDX	XREG			LDA	SIGN1
	LD1	1F,3(4:5)			JAP	*+3
	ST1	2F(4:5)			J1NZ	MEMERROR
	J5Z	CYCLE			STZ	SIGN1(0:0)
2H	SLA	1			CMP1	=BEGIN=
	DEC5	1			JGE	MEMERROR
	J5P	2B			STX	0,1
	JMP	STOREAX			LDA	CLOCK
	SLA	1			INCA	2
	SRA	1			STA	CLOCK
	SLAX	1			INC1	1
	SRAX	1			ST1	I1REG
	SLC	1			INC5	1
1H	SRC	1 ∎			DEC3	1
					JMP	MOVE ∎

4. Just insert "IN 0(16)" and "JBUS *(16)" between lines 003 and 004. (Of course on another computer this would be considerably different since it would be necessary to convert to MIX character code.)

5. Central control time is $34u$, plus $15u$ if indexing is required; the GETV subroutine takes $52u$, plus $5u$ if $L \neq 0$; extra time to do the actual loading is $11u$ for LDA or LDX, $13u$ for LDi, $21u$ for ENTA or ENTX, $23u$ for ENTi (add $2u$ to the latter two times if $M = 0$). Summing up, we have a total time of $97u$ for LDA and $55u$ for ENTA, plus $15u$ for indexing, and plus $5u$ or $2u$ in certain other circumstances. It would seem that simulation in this case is causing roughly a 50:1 ratio in speeds. (Results of a test run that involved $178u$ of simulated time required $8422u$ of actual time, a 47:1 ratio.)

7. Execution of IN or OUT sets a variable associated with the appropriate input device to the time when transmission is desired. The "CYCLE" control routine interrogates these variables on each cycle, to see if CLOCK has exceeded either (or both) of them; if so, the transmission is carried out and the variable is set to ∞. (When more than two I/O units must be handled in this way, there might be so many variables that it would be preferable to keep them in a sorted list using linked memory techniques; see Section 2.2.5.) We must be careful to complete the I/O when simulating HLT.

8. False; rI6 can equal BEGIN, if we "fall through" from the location BEGIN − 1. But then a MEMERROR will occur, trying to STZ into TIME! On the other hand, we always do have $0 \leq$ rI6 $\leq$ BEGIN, because of line 254.

SECTION 1.4.3.2

1. Change lines 48 and 49 to the following sequence:

```
XREG  ORIG *+2                          JMP   -1,1
LEAVE STX  XREG            1H           JMP   *+1
      ST1  XREG+1                       STA   -1,1
      LD1  JREG(0:2)                    LD1   XREG+1
      LDA  -1,1                         LDX   XREG
      LDX  1F                           LDA   AREG
      STX  -1,1            LEAVEX       JSJ   *
```

The operator "JSJ" here is, of course, particularly crucial.

2.
```
* TRACE ROUTINE                        STA   BUF+1,1(4:5)
      ORIG *+99                         ENTA  8
BUF   CON  0                            JNOV  1F
.............lines 02–04                ADD   BIG
      ST1  I1REG           1H    JL     1F
.............lines 05–07                INCA  1
PTR   ENT1 -100                         JE    1F
      JBUS *(0)                         INCA  1
      STA  BUF+1,1(0:2)    1H    STA    BUF+1,1(3:3)
.............lines 08–11                INC1  10
      STA  BUF+2,1                      J1N   1F
.............lines 12–13                OUT   BUF-99(0)
      LDA  AREG                         ENT1  -100
      STA  BUF+3,1         1H    ST1    PTR(0:2)
      LDA  I1REG                        LD1   I1REG
      STA  BUF+4,1         .............lines 14–35
      ST2  BUF+5,1                      ST1   I1REG
      ST3  BUF+6,1         .............lines 36–48
      ST4  BUF+7,1                      LD1   I1REG
      ST5  BUF+8,1         .............lines 49–50
      ST6  BUF+9,1         B4    EQU    1(1:1)
      STX  BUF+10,1        BIG   CON    B4-8,B4-1(1:1)  ▌
      LDA  JREG(0:2)
```

A supplementary routine that writes out the final buffer and rewinds tape 0 should be called after all tracing has been performed.

3. Tape is faster; and the editing of this information into characters while tracing would consume far too much space. Furthermore the tape contents can be selectively printed.

4. A true trace, as desired in exercise 6, would not be obtained, since restriction (a) mentioned in the text is violated. The first attempt to trace CYCLE would cause a loop back to tracing ENTER+1, because PREG is clobbered.

6. Suggestion: Keep a table of values of each memory location within the trace area that has been changed by the outer program.

7. The routine should scan the program until finding the first jump (or conditional jump) instruction; after modifying that instruction and the one following, it should restore registers and allow the program to execute all its instructions up to that point, in one burst. [This technique can fail if the program modifies its own jump instructions, or changes non-jumps into jumps. For practical purposes we can outlaw such practices, except for STJ, which we probably ought to handle separately anyway.]

SECTION 1.4.4

1. (a) No; the input operation might not yet be complete. (b) No; the input operation might be going just a little faster than the MOVE. This proposal is much too risky.

2.
```
ENT1 2000
JBUS *(6)
MOVE 1000(50)
MOVE 1050(50)
OUT  2000(6)  ▮
```

3.
```
WORDOUT STJ  1F                          DEC5 100
        STA  0,5                          JMP  2B
        INC5 1                   * BUFFER AREAS
2H      CMP5 BUFMAX              OUTBUF1 ORIG *+100
1H      JNE  *                   ENDBUF1 CON  *+101    (ENDBUF2)
        OUT  -100,5(V)           OUTBUF2 ORIG *+100
        LD5  0,5                 ENDBUF2 CON  ENDBUF1
        ST5  BUFMAX              BUFMAX  CON  ENDBUF1  ▮
```
At the beginning of the program, give the instruction "ENT5 OUTBUF1". At the end of the program, say
```
LDA  BUFMAX                      INC5 1
DECA 100,5                       CMP5 BUFMAX
JAZ  *+6                         JNE  *-3
STZ  0,5                         OUT  -100,5(V)
```

4. If the calculation time exactly equals the I/O time (which is the most favorable situation), both the computer and the peripheral device running simultaneously will take half as long as if they ran separately. Formally, let C be the calculation time for the entire program, and let T be the total I/O time required; then the best possible running time with buffering is $\max(C, T)$, while the running time without buffering is $C + T$; and of course $\frac{1}{2}(C + T) \leq \max(C, T) \leq C + T$.

However, some devices have a "shutdown penalty" that causes an extra amount of time to be lost if too long an interval occurs between references to that unit; in such a case, better than 2:1 ratios are possible. (See, for example, exercise 19.)

5. The best ratio is $(n + 1):1$.

6. $\left\{\begin{array}{l} \text{IN   INBUF1(U)} \\ \text{ENT6 INBUF2+99} \end{array}\right\}$ or $\left\{\begin{array}{l} \text{IN   INBUF2(U)} \\ \text{ENT6 INBUF1+99} \end{array}\right\}$

(possibly preceded by IOC 0(U) to rewind the tape just in case it is necessary).

7. One way is to use coroutines:
```
INBUF1  ORIG *+100                      INC6 1
INBUF2  ORIG *+100                      J6N  2B
1H      LDA  INBUF2+100,6               IN   INBUF1(U)
        JMP  MAIN                       ENN6 100
        INC6 1                          JMP  1B
        J6N  1B                 WORDIN  STJ  MAINX
WORDIN1 IN   INBUF2(U)          WORDINX JMP  WORDIN1
        ENN6 100               MAIN     STJ  WORDINX
2H      LDA  INBUF1+100,6      MAINX    JMP  *  ▮
        JMP  MAIN
```

Adding a few more instructions to take advantage of special cases will actually make this routine faster than (4).

8. At the time shown in Fig. 23, the two red buffers have been filled with line images, and the one indicated by NEXTR is being printed. At the same time, the program is computing between RELEASE and ASSIGN. When the program ASSIGNs, the green buffer indicated by NEXTG becomes yellow; NEXTG moves clockwise and the program begins to fill the yellow buffer. When the output operation is complete, NEXTR moves clockwise, the buffer that has just been printed turns green, and the remaining red buffer begins to be printed. Finally, the program RELEASEs the yellow buffer and it too is ready for subsequent printing.

9, 10, 11.

time	action ($N = 1$)	action ($N = 2$)	action ($N = 4$)
0	ASSIGN(BUF1)	ASSIGN(BUF1)	ASSIGN(BUF1)
1000	RELEASE, OUT BUF1	RELEASE, OUT BUF1	RELEASE, OUT BUF1
2000	ASSIGN (wait)	ASSIGN(BUF2)	ASSIGN(BUF2)
3000		RELEASE	RELEASE
4000		ASSIGN (wait)	ASSIGN(BUF3)
5000			RELEASE
6000			ASSIGN(BUF4)
7000			RELEASE
8000			ASSIGN (wait)
8500	BUF1 assigned, output stops	BUF1 assigned, OUT BUF2	BUF1 assigned, OUT BUF2
9500	RELEASE, OUT BUF1	RELEASE	
10500	ASSIGN (wait)	ASSIGN (wait)	
15500			RELEASE

and so on. Total time when $N = 1$ is $110000u$; when $N = 2$ it is $89000u$; when $N = 3$ it is $81500u$; and when $N \geq 4$ it is $76000u$.

12. Replace the last three lines of Program B by

```
       STA   2F
       LDA   3F
       CMPA  15,5(5:5)
       LDA   2F
       LD5   -1,5
       DEC6  1
       JNE   1B
       JMP   COMPUTE
       JMP   *-1     (or JMP COMPUTEX)
    2H CON   0
    3H ALF   ⊔⊔⊔⊔·    ▮
```

13.
```
       JRED  CONTROL(U)
       J6NZ  *-1     ▮
```

14. If $N = 1$ the algorithm breaks down (possibly referring to the buffer while I/O is in progress); otherwise the construction will have the effect that there are two yellow buffers. This can be useful if the computational program wants to refer to two buffers at once, although it ties up buffer space. In general, the excess of ASSIGNs over RELEASEs should be nonnegative and not greater than N.

15.

```
U        EQU  0              OUT  BUF2(V)
V        EQU  1              IN   BUF1(U)
BUF1     ORIG *+100          OUT  BUF3(V)
BUF2     ORIG *+100          DEC1 3
BUF3     ORIG *+100          J1P  1B
TAPECPY  IN   BUF1(U)        JBUS *(U)
         ENT1 99             OUT  BUF1(V)
1H       IN   BUF2(U)        HLT
         OUT  BUF1(V)        END  TAPECPY  ∎
         IN   BUF3(U)
```

This is a special case of the algorithm indicated in Fig. 26.

18. Partial solution: In the algorithms below, t is a variable that equals 0 when the I/O device is idle, and 1 when it is active.

Algorithm A′ (ASSIGN, *a normal state subroutine*).

   This algorithm is unchanged from Algorithm 1.4.4A.

Algorithm R′ (RELEASE, *a normal state subroutine*).

   R1′. Increase n by one.

   R2′. If $t = 0$, force an interrupt, going to step B3′ (using the INT operator). ∎

Algorithm B′ (*Buffer control routine, which processes interrupts*).

   B1′. Restart the main program.

   B2′. If $n = 0$, set $t \leftarrow 0$ and go to B1′.

   B3′. Set $t \leftarrow 1$, and initiate I/O from the buffer area specified by NEXTR.

   B4′. Restart the main program; an "I/O complete" condition will interrupt it and lead to step B5′.

   B5′. Advance NEXTR to the next clockwise buffer.

   B6′. Decrease n by one, and go to step B2′. ∎

19. If $C \leq L$ we can have $t_k = (k-1)L$, $u_k = t_k + T$, and $v_k = u_k + C$ if and only if $NL \geq T + C$. If $C > L$ the situation is more complex; we can have $u_k = (k-1)C + T$ and $v_k = kC + T$ if and only if there are integers $a_1 \leq a_2 \leq \cdots \leq a_n$ such that $t_k = (k-1)L + a_k P$ satisfies $u_k - T \geq t_k \geq v_{k-N}$ for $N < k \leq n$. An equivalent condition is that $NC \geq b_k$ for $N < k \leq n$, where $b_k = C + T + \big((k-1)(C-L)\big) \bmod P$. Let $c_l = \max\{b_{l+1}, \ldots, b_n, 0\}$; then c_l decreases as l increases, and the smallest value of N that keeps the process going steadily is the minimum l such that $c_l/l \leq C$. Since $c_l < C + T + P$ and $c_l \leq L + T + n(C - L)$, this value of N never exceeds $\lceil \min\{C + T + P, L + T + n(C - L)\}/C \rceil$. [See A. Itai and Y. Raz, *CACM* **31** (1988), 1338–1342.]

   In the stated example we have therefore (a) $N = 1$; (b) $N = 2$; (c) $N = 3$, $c_N = 2.5$; (d) $N = 35$, $c_N = 51.5$; (e) $N = 51$, $c_N = 101.5$; (f) $N = 41$, $c_N = 102$; (g) $N = 11$, $c_N = 109.5$; (h) $N = 3$, $c_N = 149.5$; (i) $N = 2$, $c_N = 298.5$.

SECTION 2.1

1. (a) SUIT(NEXT(TOP)) = SUIT(NEXT(242)) = SUIT(386) = 4. (b) Λ.

2. Whenever V is a link variable (else CONTENTS(V) makes no sense) whose value is not Λ. It is wise to *avoid* using LOC in contexts like this.

3. Set NEWCARD ← TOP, and if TOP ≠ Λ set TOP ← NEXT(TOP).

4. C1. Set X ← LOC(TOP). (For convenience we make the reasonable assumption that TOP ≡ NEXT(LOC(TOP)), namely that the value of TOP appears in the NEXT field of the location where it is stored. This assumption is compatible with program (5), and it saves us the bother of writing a special routine for the case of an empty pile.)

C2. If NEXT(X) ≠ Λ, set X ← NEXT(X) and repeat this step.

C3. Set NEXT(X) ← NEWCARD, NEXT(NEWCARD) ← Λ, TAG(NEWCARD) ← 1. ∎

5. D1. Set X ← LOC(TOP), Y ← TOP. (See step C1 above. By hypothesis, Y ≠ Λ. Throughout the algorithm that follows, X trails one step behind Y in the sense that Y = NEXT(X).)

D2. If NEXT(Y) ≠ Λ, set X ← Y, Y ← NEXT(Y), and repeat this step.

D3. (Now NEXT(Y) = Λ, so Y points to the bottom card; also X points to the next-to-last card.) Set NEXT(X) ← Λ, NEWCARD ← Y. ∎

6. Notations (b) and (d). *Not* (a)! CARD is a node, not a link to a node.

7. Sequence (a) gives NEXT(LOC(TOP)), which in this case is identical to the value of TOP; sequence (b) is correct. There is no need for confusion; consider the analogous example when X is a numeric variable: To bring X into register A, we write LDA X, not ENTA X, since the latter brings LOC(X) into the register.

8. Let rA ≡ N, rI1 ≡ X.

ENTA	0	*B1.* N ← 0.	INCA	1	*B3.* N ← N + 1.
LD1	TOP	X ← TOP.	LD1	0,1(NEXT)	X ← NEXT(X).
J1Z	*+4	*B2.* Is X = Λ?	J1NZ	*-2	∎

9. Let rI2 ≡ X.

PRINTER	EQU	18	Unit number for line printer
TAG	EQU	1:1	
NEXT	EQU	4:5	Definition of fields
NAME	EQU	0:5	
PBUF	ALF	PILE	Message printed in case
	ALF	EMPTY	pile is empty
	ORIG	PBUF+24	
BEGIN	LD2	TOP	Set X ← TOP.
	J2Z	2F	Is the pile empty?
1H	LDA	0,2(TAG)	rA ← TAG(X).
	ENT1	PBUF	Get ready for MOVE instruction.
	JBUS	*(PRINTER)	Wait until printer is ready.
	JAZ	*+3	Is TAG = 0 (is card face up)?
	MOVE	PAREN(3)	No: Copy parentheses.
	JMP	*+2	
	MOVE	BLANKS(3)	Yes: Copy blanks.
	LDA	1,2(NAME)	rA ← NAME(X).
	STA	PBUF+1	
	LD2	0,2(NEXT)	Set X ← NEXT(X).
2H	OUT	PBUF(PRINTER)	Print the line.
	J2NZ	1B	If X ≠ Λ, repeat the print loop.
DONE	HLT		

```
PAREN   ALF      (
BLANKS  ALF
        ALF   )
        ALF              ▌
```

SECTION 2.2.1

1. Yes. (Consistently insert all items at one of the two ends.)

2. To obtain 325641, do SSSXXSSXSXXX (in the notation of the following exercise). The order 154623 cannot be achieved, since 2 can precede 3 only if it is removed from the stack before 3 has been inserted.

3. An admissible sequence is one in which the number of X's never exceeds the number of S's if we read from the left to the right.

Two different admissible sequences must give a different result, since if the two sequences agree up to a point where one has S and the other has X, the latter sequence outputs a symbol that cannot possibly be output before the symbol just inserted by the S of the former sequence.

4. This problem is equivalent to many other interesting problems, such as the enumeration of binary trees, the number of ways to insert parentheses into a formula, and the number of ways to divide a polygon into triangles, and it appeared as early as 1759 in notes by Euler and von Segner (see Section 2.3.4.6).

The following elegant solution uses a "reflection principle" due to J. Aebly and D. Mirimanoff [*L'Enseignement Math.* **23** (1923), 185–189]: There are obviously $\binom{2n}{n}$ sequences of S's and X's that contain n of each. It remains to evaluate the number of *inadmissible* sequences (those that contain the right number of S's and X's but violate the other condition). In any inadmissible sequence, locate the first X for which the X's outnumber the S's. Then in the partial sequence leading up to and including this X, replace each X by S and each S by X. The result is a sequence with $(n+1)$ S's and $(n-1)$ X's. Conversely for every sequence of the latter type we can reverse the process and find the inadmissible sequence of the former type that leads to it. For example, the sequence XXSXSSSXXSSS must have come from SSXSXXXXXSSS. This correspondence shows that the number of inadmissible sequences is $\binom{2n}{n-1}$. Hence $a_n = \binom{2n}{n} - \binom{2n}{n-1}$.

Using the same idea, we can solve the more general "ballot problem" of probability theory, which essentially is the enumeration of all partial admissible sequences with a given number of S's and X's. This problem was actually resolved as early as 1708 by Abraham de Moivre, who showed that the number of sequences containing l A's and m B's, and containing at least one initial substring with n more A's than B's, is $f(l,m,n) = \binom{l+m}{\min(m,l-n)}$. In particular, $a_n = \binom{2n}{n} - f(n,n,1)$ as above. (De Moivre stated this result without proof [*Philos. Trans.* **27** (1711), 262–263]; but it is clear from other passages in his paper that he knew how to prove it, since the formula is obviously true when $l \geq m+n$, and since his generating-function approach to similar problems yields the symmetry condition $f(l,m,n) = f(m+n,l-n,n)$ by simple algebra.) For the later history of the ballot problem and some generalizations, see the comprehensive survey by D. E. Barton and C. L. Mallows, *Annals of Math. Statistics* **36** (1965), 236–260; see also exercise 2.3.4.4–32 and Section 5.1.4.

We present here a new method for solving the ballot problem with the use of double generating functions, since this method lends itself to the solution of more difficult problems such as the question in exercise 11.

Let g_{nm} be the number of sequences of S's and X's of length n, in which the number of X's never exceeds the number of S's if we count from the left, and in which there are m more S's than X's in all. Then $a_n = g_{(2n)0}$. Obviously g_{nm} is zero unless $m + n$ is even. We see easily that these numbers can be defined by the recurrence relations

$$g_{(n+1)m} = g_{n(m-1)} + g_{n(m+1)}, \quad m \geq 0, \quad n \geq 0; \qquad g_{0m} = \delta_{0m}.$$

Consider the double generating function $G(x, z) = \sum_{n,m} g_{nm} x^m z^n$, and let $g(z) = G(0, z)$. The recurrence above is equivalent to the equation

$$\left(x + \frac{1}{x}\right) G(x, z) = \frac{1}{x} g(z) + \frac{1}{z}(G(x, z) - 1), \quad \text{i.e.,} \quad G(x, z) = \frac{zg(z) - x}{z(x^2 + 1) - x}.$$

This equation unfortunately tells us nothing if we set $x = 0$, but we can proceed by factoring the denominator as $z(1 - r_1(z)x)(1 - r_2(z)x)$ where

$$r_1(z) = \frac{1}{2z}(1 + \sqrt{1 - 4z^2}), \quad r_2(z) = \frac{1}{2z}(1 - \sqrt{1 - 4z^2}).$$

(Note that $r_1 + r_2 = 1/z$; $r_1 r_2 = 1$.) We now proceed heuristically; the problem is to find some value of $g(z)$ such that $G(x, z)$ as given by the formula above has an infinite power series expansion in x and z. The function $r_2(z)$ has a power series, and $r_2(0) = 0$; moreover, for fixed z, the value $x = r_2(z)$ causes the denominator of $G(x, z)$ to vanish. This suggests that we should choose $g(z)$ so that the numerator also vanishes when $x = r_2(z)$; in other words, we probably ought to take $zg(z) = r_2(z)$. With this choice, the equation for $G(x, z)$ simplifies to

$$G(x, z) = \frac{r_2(z)}{z(1 - r_2(z)x)} = \sum_{n \geq 0}(r_2(z))^{n+1} x^n z^{-1}.$$

This is a power series expansion that satisfies the original equation, so we must have found the right function $g(z)$.

The coefficients of $g(z)$ are the solution to our problem. Actually we can go further and derive a simple form for all the coefficients of $G(x, z)$: By the binomial theorem,

$$r_2(z) = \sum_{k \geq 0} z^{2k+1} \binom{2k + 1}{k} \frac{1}{2k + 1}.$$

Let $w = z^2$ and $r_2(z) = zf(w)$. Then $f(w) = \sum_{k \geq 0} A_k(1, -2)w^k$ in the notation of exercise 1.2.6–25; hence

$$f(w)^r = \sum_{k \geq 0} A_k(r, -2)w^k.$$

We now have

$$G(x, z) = \sum_{n,m} A_m(n + 1, -2)x^n z^{2m+n},$$

so the general solution is

$$g_{(2n)(2m)} = \binom{2n + 1}{n - m}\frac{2m + 1}{2n + 1} = \binom{2n}{n - m} - \binom{2n}{n - m - 1};$$

$$g_{(2n+1)(2m+1)} = \binom{2n + 2}{n - m}\frac{2m + 2}{2n + 2} = \binom{2n + 1}{n - m} - \binom{2n + 1}{n - m - 1}.$$

5. If $j < k$ and $p_j < p_k$, we must have taken p_j off the stack before p_k was put on; if $p_j > p_k$, we must have left p_k on the stack until after p_j was put on. Combining these two rules, the condition $i < j < k$ and $p_j < p_k < p_i$ is impossible, since it means that p_j must go off before p_k and after p_i, yet p_i appears after p_k.

Conversely, the desired permutation can be obtained by using the following algorithm: "For $j = 1, 2, \ldots, n$, input zero or more items (as many as necessary) until p_j first appears in the stack; then output p_j." This algorithm can fail only if we reach a j for which p_j is not at the top of the stack but it is covered by some element p_k for $k > j$. Since the values on the stack are always monotone increasing, we have $p_j < p_k$. And the element p_k must have gotten there because it was less than p_i for some $i < j$.

P. V. Ramanan [*SICOMP* **13** (1984), 167–169] has shown how to characterize the permutations obtainable when m auxiliary storage locations can be used freely in addition to a stack. (This generalization of the problem is surprisingly difficult.)

6. Only the trivial one, $12 \ldots n$, by the nature of a queue.

7. An input-restricted deque that first outputs n must simply put the values 1, 2, $\ldots, n$ on the deque in order as its first n operations. An output-restricted deque that first outputs n must put the values $p_1 p_2 \ldots p_n$ on its deque as its first n operations. Therefore we find the unique answers (a) 4132, (b) 4213, (c) 4231.

8. When $n \leq 4$, no; when $n = 5$, there are four (see exercise 13).

9. By operating backwards, we can get the reverse of the inverse of the reverse of any input-restricted permutation with an output-restricted deque, and conversely. This rule sets up a one-to-one correspondence between the two sets of permutations.

10. (i) There should be n X's and n combined S's and Q's. (ii) The number of X's must never exceed the combined number of S's and Q's, if we read from the left. (iii) Whenever the number of X's equals the combined number of S's and Q's (reading from the left), the next character must be a Q. (iv) The two operations XQ must never be adjacent in this order.

Clearly rules (i) and (ii) are necessary. The extra rules (iii) and (iv) are added to remove ambiguity, since S is the same as Q when the deque is empty, and since XQ can always be replaced by QX. Thus, any obtainable sequence corresponds to at least one admissible sequence.

To show that two admissible sequences give different permutations, consider sequences that are identical up to a point, and then one sequence has an S while the other has an X or Q. Since by (iii) the deque is not empty, clearly different permutations (relative to the order of the element inserted by S) are obtained by the two sequences. The remaining case is where sequences A, B agree up to a point and then sequence A has Q, sequence B has X. Sequence B may have further X's at this point, and by (iv) they must be followed by an S, so again the permutations are different.

11. Proceeding as in exercise 4, we let g_{nm} be the number of partial admissible sequences of length n, leaving m elements on the deque, *not* ending in the symbol X; h_{nm} is defined analogously, for those sequences that *do* end with X. We have $g_{(n+1)m} = 2g_{n(m-1)} + h_{n(m-1)}[m>1]$, and $h_{(n+1)m} = g_{n(m+1)} + h_{n(m+1)}$. Define $G(x,z)$ and $H(x,z)$ by analogy with the definition in exercise 4; we have

$$G(x, z) = xz + 2x^2 z^2 + 4x^3 z^3 + (8x^4 + 2x^2)z^4 + (16x^5 + 8x^3)z^5 + \cdots;$$
$$H(x, z) = z^2 + 2xz^3 + (4x^2 + 2)z^4 + (8x^3 + 6x)z^5 + \cdots.$$

Setting $h(z) = H(0, z)$, we find $z^{-1}G(x, z) = 2xG(x, z) + x(H(x, z) - h(z)) + x$, and $z^{-1}H(x, z) = x^{-1}G(x, z) + x^{-1}(H(x, z) - h(z))$; consequently

$$G(x, z) = \frac{xz(x - z - xh(z))}{x - z - 2x^2z + xz^2}.$$

As in exercise 4, we try to choose $h(z)$ so that the numerator cancels with a factor of the denominator. We find $G(x, z) = xz/(1 - 2xr_2(z))$ where

$$r_2(z) = \frac{1}{4z}(z^2 + 1 - \sqrt{(z^2 + 1)^2 - 8z^2}).$$

Using the convention $b_0 = 1$, the desired generating function comes to

$$\tfrac{1}{2}(3 - z - \sqrt{1 - 6z + z^2}) = 1 + z + 2z^2 + 6z^3 + 22z^4 + 90z^5 + \cdots.$$

By differentiation we find a recurrence relation that is handy for calculation: $nb_n = 3(2n - 3)b_{n-1} - (n - 3)b_{n-2}$, $n \geq 2$.

Another way to solve this problem, suggested by V. Pratt, is to use context-free grammars for the set of strings (see Chapter 10). The infinite grammar with productions $S \to q^n(Bx)^n$, $B \to sq^n(Bx)^{n+1}B$, for all $n \geq 0$, and $B \to \epsilon$, is unambiguous, and it allows us to count the number of strings with n x's, as in exercise 2.3.4.4–31.

12. We have $a_n = 4^n/\sqrt{\pi n^3} + O(4^n n^{-5/2})$ by Stirling's formula. To analyze b_n, let us first consider the general problem of estimating the coefficient of w^n in the power series for $\sqrt{1 - w}\sqrt{1 - \alpha w}$ when $|\alpha| < 1$. We have, for sufficiently small α,

$$\sqrt{1 - w}\sqrt{1 - \alpha w} = \sqrt{1 - w}\sqrt{1 - \alpha + \alpha(1 - w)} = \sqrt{1 - \alpha}\sum_k \binom{1/2}{k}\beta^k(1 - w)^{k + 1/2},$$

where $\beta = \alpha/(1 - \alpha)$; hence the desired coefficient is $(-1)^n\sqrt{1 - \alpha}\sum_k\binom{1/2}{k}\beta^k\binom{k+1/2}{n}$. Now

$$(-1)^n\binom{k + 1/2}{n} = \binom{n - k - 3/2}{n} = \frac{\Gamma(n - k - 1/2)}{\Gamma(n + 1)\Gamma(-k - 1/2)} = \frac{(-1/2)^{k+1}}{\sqrt{\pi n}}n^{-k-1/2},$$

and $n^{-k-1/2} = \sum_{j=0}^{m}\left[\begin{smallmatrix}-k-1/2\\-k-1/2-j\end{smallmatrix}\right]n^{-k-1/2-j} + O(n^{-k-3/2-m})$ by Eq. 1.2.11.1–(16). Thus we obtain the asymptotic series $[w^n]\sqrt{1 - w}\sqrt{1 - \alpha w} = c_0 n^{-3/2} + c_1 n^{-5/2} + \cdots + c_m n^{-m-3/2} + O(n^{-m-5/2})$ where

$$c_j = \sqrt{\frac{1 - \alpha}{\pi}}\sum_{k=0}^{j}\binom{1/2}{k}(-1/2)^{k+1}\left\{\begin{matrix}j + 1/2\\k + 1/2\end{matrix}\right\}\frac{\alpha^k}{(1 - \alpha)^k}.$$

For b_n, we write $1 - 6z + z^2 = (1 - (3 + \sqrt{8})z)(1 - (3 - \sqrt{8})z)$ and let $w = (3 + \sqrt{8})z$, $\alpha = (3 - \sqrt{8})/(3 + \sqrt{8})$, obtaining the asymptotic formula

$$b_n = \frac{(\sqrt{2} - 1)(3 + \sqrt{8})^n}{2^{3/4}\pi^{1/2}n^{3/2}}(1 + O(n^{-1})) = \frac{(\sqrt{2} + 1)^{2n-1}}{2^{3/4}\pi^{1/2}n^{3/2}}(1 + O(n^{-1})).$$

13. V. Pratt has found that a permutation is unobtainable if and only if it contains a subsequence whose relative magnitudes are respectively

$$5, 2, 7, 4, \ldots, 4k+1, 4k-2, 3, 4k, 1 \quad \text{or} \quad 5, 2, 7, 4, \ldots, 4k+3, 4k, 1, 4k+2, 3$$

for some $k \geq 1$, or the same with the last two elements interchanged, or with the 1 and 2 interchanged, or both. Thus the forbidden patterns for $k = 1$ are 52341, 52314, 51342, 51324, 5274163, 5274136, 5174263, 5174236. [*STOC* **5** (1973), 268–277.]

14. (Solution by R. Melville, 1980.) Let R and S be stacks such that the queue runs from top to bottom of R followed by bottom to top of S. When R is empty, pop the elements of S onto R until S becomes empty. To delete from the front, pop the top of R, which will not be empty unless the entire queue is empty. To insert at the rear, push onto S (unless R is empty). Each element is pushed at most twice and popped at most twice before leaving the queue.

SECTION 2.2.2

1. $M - 1$ (*not* M). If we allowed M items, as (6) and (7) do, it would be impossible to distinguish an empty queue from a full one by examination of R and F, since only M possibilities can be detected. It is better to give up one storage cell than to make the program overly complicated.

2. Delete from rear: If $R = F$ then UNDERFLOW; $Y \leftarrow X[R]$; if $R = 1$ then $R \leftarrow M$, otherwise $R \leftarrow R - 1$. Insert at front: Set $X[F] \leftarrow Y$; if $F = 1$ then $F \leftarrow M$, otherwise $F \leftarrow F - 1$; if $F = R$ then OVERFLOW.

3. (a) LD1 I; LDA BASE,7:1. This takes 5 cycles instead of 4 or 8 as in (8).

(b) *Solution 1:* LDA BASE,2:7 where each base address is stored with $I_1 = 0$, $I_2 = 1$. *Solution 2:* If it is desired to store the base addresses with $I_1 = I_2 = 0$, we could write LDA X2,7:1 where location X2 contains NOP BASE,2:7. The second solution takes one more cycle, but it allows the base table to be used with any index registers.

(c) This is equivalent to "LD4 X(0:2)", and takes the same execution time, except that rI4 will be set to $+0$ when X(0:2) contains -0.

4. (a) NOP *,7. (b) LDA X,7:7(0:2). (c) This is impossible; the code LDA Y,7:7 where location Y contains NOP X,7:7 breaks the restriction on 7:7. (See exercise 5.) (d) LDA X,7:1 with the auxiliary constants

```
X   NOP   *+1,7:2
    NOP   *+1,7:3
    NOP   *+1,7:4
    NOP   0,5:6
```

The execution time is 6 units. (e) INC6 X,7:6 where X contains NOP 0,6:6.

5. (a) Consider the instruction ENTA 1000,7:7 with the memory configuration

location	ADDRESS	I_1	I_2
1000:	1001	7	7
1001:	1004	7	1
1002:	1002	2	2
1003:	1001	1	1
1004:	1005	1	7
1005:	1006	1	7
1006:	1008	7	7
1007:	1002	7	1
1008:	1003	7	2

and with rI1 $= 1$, rI2 $= 2$. We find that 1000,7,7 = 1001,7,7,7 = 1004,7,1,7,7 = 1005,1,7,1,7,7 = 1006,7,1,7,7 = 1008,7,7,1,7,7 = 1003,7,2,7,1,7,7 = 1001,1,1,2,7,1,7,7 = 1002,1,2,7,1,7,7 = 1003,2,7,1,7,7 = 1005,7,1,7,7 = 1006,1,7,1,7,7 = 1007,7,1,7,7 = 1002,7,1,1,7,7 = 1002,2,2,1,1,7,7 = 1004,2,1,1,7,7 = 1006,1,1,7,7 = 1007,1,7,7 = 1008,7,7 = 1003,7,2,7 = 1001,1,1,2,7 = 1002,1,2,7 = 1003,2,7 = 1005,7 = 1006,1,7 = 1007,7 =

$1002,7,1 = 1002,2,2,1 = 1004,2,1 = 1006,1 = 1007$. (A faster way to do this derivation by hand would be to evaluate successively the addresses specified in locations 1002, 1003, 1007, 1008, 1005, 1006, 1004, 1001, 1000, in this order; but a computer evidently needs to go about the evaluation essentially as shown.) The author tried out several fancy schemes for changing the contents of memory while evaluating the address, with everything to be restored again by the time the final address has been obtained. Similar algorithms appear in Section 2.3.5. However, these attempts were unfruitful and it appears that there is just not enough room to store the necessary information.

(b, c) Let H and C be auxiliary registers and let N be a counter. To get the effective address M, for the instruction in location L, do the following:

A1. [Initialize.] Set $H \leftarrow 0$, $C \leftarrow L$, $N \leftarrow 0$. (In this algorithm, C is the "current" location, H is used to add together the contents of various index registers, and N measures the depth of indirect addressing.)

A2. [Examine address.] Set $M \leftarrow$ ADDRESS(C). If $I_1(C) = j$, $1 \le j \le 6$, set $M \leftarrow M + rIj$. If $I_2(C) = j$, $1 \le j \le 6$, set $H \leftarrow H + rIj$. If $I_1(C) = I_2(C) = 7$, set $N \leftarrow N + 1$, $H \leftarrow 0$.

A3. [Indirect?] If either $I_1(C)$ or $I_2(C)$ equals 7, set $C \leftarrow M$ and go to A2. Otherwise set $M \leftarrow M + H$, $H \leftarrow 0$.

A4. [Reduce depth.] If $N > 0$, set $C \leftarrow M$, $N \leftarrow N - 1$, and go to A2. Otherwise M is the desired answer. ∎

This algorithm will handle any situation correctly except those in which $I_1 = 7$ and $1 \le I_2 \le 6$ *and* the evaluation of the address in ADDRESS involves a case with $I_1 = I_2 = 7$. The effect is as if I_2 were zero. To understand the operation of Algorithm A, consider the notation of part (a); the state "L,7,1,2,5,2,7,7,7,7" is represented by C or $M = L$, $N = 4$ (the number of trailing 7s), and $H = rI1 + rI2 + rI5 + rI2$ (the post-indexing). In a solution to part (b) of this exercise, the counter N will always be either 0 or 1.

6. (c) causes OVERFLOW. (e) causes UNDERFLOW, and if the program resumes it causes OVERFLOW on the final I_2.

7. No, since TOP[i] must be greater than OLDTOP[i].

8. With a stack, the useful information appears at one end with the vacant information at the other:

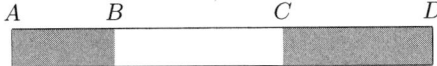

where $A =$ BASE[j], $B =$ TOP[j], $C =$ BASE[$j + 1$]. With a queue or deque, the useful information appears at the ends with the vacant information somewhere in the middle:

or in the middle with the vacant information at the ends:

where $A =$ BASE[j], $B =$ REAR[j], $C =$ FRONT[j], $D =$ BASE[$j + 1$]. The two cases are distinguished by the conditions $B \le C$ and $B > C$, respectively, in a nonempty queue; or, if the queue is known not to have overflowed, the distinguishing conditions are respectively $B < C$ and $B \geq C$. The algorithms should therefore be modified in an obvious way so as to widen or narrow the gaps of vacant information. (Thus in case of overflow, when $B = C$, we make empty space between B and C by moving one part and not the other.) In the calculation of SUM and D[j] in step G2, each queue should be considered to occupy one more cell than it really does (see exercise 1).

9. Given any sequence specification $a_1, a_2, \ldots, a_m$ there is one move operation required for every pair (j, k) such that $j < k$ and $a_j > a_k$. (Such a pair is called an "inversion"; see Section 5.1.1.) The number of such pairs is therefore the number of moves required. Now imagine all n^m specifications written out, and for each of the $\binom{m}{2}$ pairs (j, k) with $j < k$ count how many specifications have $a_j > a_k$. Clearly this equals $\binom{n}{2}$, the number of choices for a_j and a_k, times n^{m-2}, the number of ways to fill in the remaining places. Hence the total number of moves among all specifications is $\binom{m}{2}\binom{n}{2}n^{m-2}$. Divide this by n^m to get the average, Eq. (14).

10. As in exercise 9 we find that the expected value is

$$\binom{m}{2} \sum_{1 \leq j < k \leq n} p_j p_k = \frac{1}{2}\binom{m}{2}\left((p_1 + \cdots + p_n)^2 - (p_1^2 + \cdots + p_n^2)\right)$$

$$= \frac{1}{2}\binom{m}{2}\left(1 - (p_1^2 + \cdots + p_n^2)\right).$$

For this model, it makes *absolutely no difference* what the relative order of the lists is! (A moment's reflection explains why; if we consider all possible permutations of a given sequence $a_1, \ldots, a_m$, we find that the total number of moves summed over all these permutations depends only on the number of pairs of distinct elements $a_j \neq a_k$.)

11. Counting as before, we find that the expected number is

$$E_{mnt} = \frac{1}{n^m}\binom{n}{2}\sum_{k=1}^{m}\sum_{r \geq t}(k-1)\binom{k-2}{r}(n-1)^{k-2-r}n^{m-k};$$

here r is the number of entries in $a_1, a_2, \ldots, a_{k-1}$ that equal a_k. This quantity can also be expressed in the simpler form

$$E_{mnt} = \frac{1}{n^m}\binom{n}{2}\sum_{k>t}\binom{m}{k}(n-1)^{m-k}\left(\binom{k}{2} - \binom{t+1}{2}\right), \quad \text{for } t \geq 0.$$

Is there a simpler way yet to give the answer? Apparently not, since the generating function for given n and t is

$$\sum_{m}E_{mnt}z^m = \frac{n-1}{2n}\frac{z}{(1-z)^3}\left(\frac{z}{n-(n-1)z}\right)^{t+1}(z + (1-z)n(t+1)).$$

12. If $m = 2k$, the average is 2^{-2k} times

$$\binom{2k}{0}2k + \binom{2k}{1}(2k-1) + \cdots + \binom{2k}{k}k + \binom{2k}{k+1}(k+1) + \cdots + \binom{2k}{2k}2k.$$

The latter sum is

$$\binom{2k}{k}k + 2\left(\binom{2k-1}{k}2k + \cdots + \binom{2k-1}{2k-1}2k\right) = \binom{2k}{k}k + 4k \cdot \frac{1}{2} \cdot 2^{2k-1}.$$

A similar argument may be used when $m = 2k + 1$. The answer is

$$\frac{m}{2} + \frac{m}{2^m} \binom{m-1}{\lfloor m/2 \rfloor}.$$

13. A. C. Yao has proved that we have $\mathrm{E}\max(k_1, k_2) = \frac{1}{2}m + (2\pi(1-2p))^{-1/2}\sqrt{m} + O(m^{-1/2}(\log m)^2)$ for large m, when $p < \frac{1}{2}$. [*SICOMP* **10** (1981), 398–403.] And P. Flajolet has extended the analysis, showing in particular that the expected value is asymptotically αm when $p = \frac{1}{2}$, where

$$\alpha = \frac{1}{2} + 8\sum_{n \geq 1} \frac{\sin(n\pi/2)\cosh(n\pi/2)}{n^2\pi^2\sinh n\pi} \approx 0.67531\,44833.$$

Moreover, when $p > \frac{1}{2}$ the final value of k_1 tends to be uniformly distributed as $m \to \infty$, so $\mathrm{E}\max(k_1, k_2) \approx \frac{3}{4}m$. [See *Lecture Notes in Comp. Sci.* **233** (1986), 325–340.]

14. Let $k_j = m/n + \sqrt{m}\,x_j$. (This idea was suggested by N. G. de Bruijn.) Stirling's approximation implies that

$$n^{-m}\frac{m!}{k_1!\dots k_n!}\max(k_1, \dots, k_n)$$

$$= (\sqrt{2\pi m})^{1-n} n^{n/2} \left(\frac{m}{n} + \sqrt{m}\max(x_1, \dots, x_n)\right)$$

$$\times \exp\left(-\frac{n}{2}(x_1^2 + \dots + x_n^2)\right)(\sqrt{m})^{1-n}\left(1 + O\left(\frac{1}{\sqrt{m}}\right)\right),$$

when $k_1 + \dots + k_n = m$ and when the x's are uniformly bounded. The sum of the latter quantity over all nonnegative $k_1, \dots, k_n$ satisfying this condition is an approximation to a Riemann integral; we may deduce that the asymptotic behavior of the sum is $a_n(m/n) + c_n\sqrt{m} + O(1)$, where

$$a_n = (\sqrt{2\pi})^{1-n} n^{n/2} \int_{x_1 + \dots + x_n = 0} \exp\left(-\frac{n}{2}(x_1^2 + \dots + x_n^2)\right) dx_2 \dots dx_n,$$

$$c_n = (\sqrt{2\pi})^{1-n} n^{n/2} \int_{x_1 + \dots + x_n = 0} \max(x_1, \dots, x_n)\exp\left(-\frac{n}{2}(x_1^2 + \dots + x_n^2)\right) dx_2 \dots dx_n,$$

since it is possible to show that the corresponding sums come within ϵ of a_n and c_n for any ϵ.

We know that $a_n = 1$, since the corresponding sum can be evaluated explicitly. The integral that appears in the expression for c_n equals nI_1, where

$$I_1 = \int_{\substack{x_1 + \dots + x_n = 0 \\ x_1 \geq x_2, \dots, x_n}} x_1 \exp\left(-\frac{n}{2}(x_1^2 + \dots + x_n^2)\right) dx_2 \dots dx_n.$$

We may make the substitution

$$x_1 = \frac{1}{n}(y_2 + \dots + y_n), \quad x_2 = x_1 - y_2, \quad x_3 = x_1 - y_3, \quad \dots, \quad x_n = x_1 - y_n;$$

then we find $I_1 = I_2/n^2$, where

$$I_2 = \int_{y_2, \dots, y_n \geq 0} (y_2 + \dots + y_n)\exp\left(-\frac{Q}{2}\right) dy_2 \dots dy_n,$$

and $Q = n(y_2^2 + \cdots + y_n^2) - (y_2 + \cdots + y_n)^2$. Now by symmetry, I_2 is $(n-1)$ times the same integral with $(y_2 + \cdots + y_n)$ replaced by y_2; hence $I_2 = (n-1)I_3$, where

$$I_3 = \int_{y_2,\ldots,y_n \geq 0} (ny_2 - (y_2 + \cdots + y_n)) \exp\left(-\frac{Q}{2}\right) dy_2 \ldots dy_n$$

$$= \int_{y_3,\ldots,y_n \geq 0} \exp\left(-\frac{Q_0}{2}\right) dy_3 \ldots dy_n;$$

here Q_0 is Q with y_2 replaced by zero. [When $n = 2$, let $I_3 = 1$.] Now let $z_j = \sqrt{n}\, y_j - (y_3 + \cdots + y_n)/(\sqrt{2} + \sqrt{n})$, $3 \leq j \leq n$. Then $Q_0 = z_3^2 + \cdots + z_n^2$, and we deduce that $I_3 = I_4/n^{(n-3)/2}\sqrt{2}$, where

$$I_4 = \int_{y_3,\ldots,y_n \geq 0} \exp\left(-\frac{z_3^2 + \cdots + z_n^2}{2}\right) dz_3 \ldots dz_n$$

$$= \alpha_n \int \exp\left(-\frac{z_3^2 + \cdots + z_n^2}{2}\right) dz_3 \ldots dz_n = \alpha_n (\sqrt{2\pi})^{n-2},$$

where α_n is the "solid angle" in $(n-2)$-dimensional space spanned by the vectors $(n+\sqrt{2n}, 0, \ldots, 0) - (1, 1, \ldots, 1)$, $\ldots$, $(0, 0, \ldots, n+\sqrt{2n}) - (1, 1, \ldots, 1)$, divided by the total solid angle of the whole space. Hence

$$c_n = \frac{(n-1)\sqrt{n}}{2\sqrt{\pi}} \alpha_n.$$

We have $\alpha_2 = 1$, $\alpha_3 = \frac{1}{2}$, $\alpha_4 = \pi^{-1} \arctan \sqrt{2} \approx .304$, and

$$\alpha_5 = \frac{1}{8} + \frac{3}{4\pi} \arctan \frac{1}{\sqrt{8}} \approx .206.$$

[The value of c_3 was found by Robert M. Kozelka, *Annals of Math. Stat.* **27** (1956), 507–512, but the solution to this problem for higher values of n has apparently never appeared in the literature.]

16. Not unless the queues meet the restrictions that apply to the primitive method of (4) and (5).

17. First show that $\texttt{BASE}[j]_0 \leq \texttt{BASE}[j]_1$ at all times. Then observe that each overflow for stack i in $s_0(\sigma)$ that does not also overflow in $s_1(\sigma)$ occurs at a time when stack i has gotten larger than ever before, yet its new size is not more than the original size allocated to stack i in $s_1(\sigma)$.

18. Suppose the cost of an insertion is a, plus $bN + cn$ if repacking is needed, where N is the number of occupied cells; let the deletion cost be d. After a repacking that leaves N cells occupied and $S = M - N$ cells vacant, imagine that each insertion until the next repacking costs $a + b + 10c + 10(b + c)nN/S = O(1 + n\alpha/(1-\alpha))$, where $\alpha = N/M$. If p insertions and q deletions occur before that repacking, the imagined cost is $p(a+b+10c+10(b+c)nN/S)+qd$, while the actual cost is $pa + bN' + cn + qd \leq pa + pb + bN + cn + qd$. The latter is less than the imagined cost, because $p > .1S/n$; our assumption that $M \geq n^2$ implies that $cS/n + (b+c)N \geq bN + cn$.

19. We could simply decrease all the subscripts by 1; the following solution is slightly nicer. Initially $\texttt{T} = \texttt{F} = \texttt{R} = 0$.

    Push Y onto stack X: If $\texttt{T} = \texttt{M}$ then $\texttt{OVERFLOW}$; $\texttt{X[T]} \leftarrow \texttt{Y}$; $\texttt{T} \leftarrow \texttt{T}+1$.

    Pop Y from stack X: If $\texttt{T} = 0$ then $\texttt{UNDERFLOW}$; $\texttt{T} \leftarrow \texttt{T}-1$; $\texttt{Y} \leftarrow \texttt{X[T]}$.

Insert Y into queue X: X[R] ← Y; R ← (R + 1) mod M; if R = F then OVERFLOW.

Delete Y from queue X: if F = R then UNDERFLOW; Y ← X[F]; F ← (F + 1) mod M.

As before, T is the number of elements on the stack, and (R − F) mod M is the number of elements on the queue. But the top stack element is now X[T − 1], not X[T].

Even though it is almost always better for computer scientists to start counting at 0, the rest of the world will probably never change to 0-origin indexing. Even Edsger Dijkstra counts "1–2–3–4 | 1–2–3–4" when he plays the piano!

SECTION 2.2.3

1. OVERFLOW is implicit in the operation P ⇐ AVAIL.

2.
INSERT	STJ	1F	Store location of "NOP T".
	STJ	9F	Store exit location.
	LD1	AVAIL	rI1 ⇐ AVAIL.
	J1Z	OVERFLOW	
	LD3	0,1(LINK)	
	ST3	AVAIL	
	STA	0,1(INFO)	INFO(rI1) ← Y.
1H	LD3	*(0:2)	rI3 ← LOC(T).
	LD2	0,3	rI2 ← T.
	ST2	0,1(LINK)	LINK(rI1) ← T.
	ST1	0,3	T ← rI1.
9H	JMP	*	▌

3.
DELETE	STJ	1F	Store location of "NOP T".
	STJ	9F	Store exit location.
1H	LD2	*(0:2)	rI2 ← LOC(T).
	LD3	0,2	rI3 ← T.
	J3Z	9F	Is T = Λ?
	LD1	0,3(LINK)	rI1 ← LINK(T).
	ST1	0,2	T ← rI1.
	LDA	0,3(INFO)	rA ← INFO(rI1).
	LD2	AVAIL	AVAIL ⇐ rI3.
	ST2	0,3(LINK)	
	ST3	AVAIL	
	ENT3	2	Prepare for second exit.
9H	JMP	*,3	▌

4.
OVERFLOW	STJ	9F	Store setting of rJ.
	ST1	8F(0:2)	Save rI1 setting.
	LD1	POOLMAX	
	ST1	AVAIL	Set AVAIL to new location.
	INC1	c	
	ST1	POOLMAX	Increment POOLMAX.
	CMP1	SEQMIN	
	JG	TOOBAD	Has storage been exceeded?
	STZ	-c,1(LINK)	Set LINK(AVAIL) ← Λ.
9H	ENT1	*	Take rJ setting.
	DEC1	2	Subtract 2.
	ST1	*+2(0:2)	Store exit location.
8H	ENT1	*	Restore rI1.
	JMP	*	Return. ▌

5. Inserting at the front is essentially like the basic insertion operation (8), with an additional test for empty queue: P ⇐ AVAIL, INFO(P) ← Y, LINK(P) ← F; if F = Λ then R ← P; F ← P.

To delete from the rear, we would have to find which node links to NODE(R), and that is necessarily inefficient since we have to search all the way from F. This could be done, for example, as follows:

a) If F = Λ then UNDERFLOW, otherwise set P ← LOC(F).

b) If LINK(P) ≠ R then set P ← LINK(P) and repeat this step until LINK(P) = R.

c) Set Y ← INFO(R), AVAIL ⇐ R, R ← P, LINK(P) ← Λ.

6. We could remove the operation LINK(P) ← Λ from (14), if we delete the commands "F ← LINK(P)" and "if F = Λ then set R ← LOC(F)" from (17); the latter are to be replaced by "if F = R then F ← Λ and R ← LOC(F), otherwise set F ← LINK(P)".

The effect of these changes is that the LINK field of the rear node in the queue will contain spurious information that is never interrogated by the program. A trick like this saves execution time and it is quite useful in practice, although it violates one of the basic assumptions of garbage collection (see Section 2.3.5) so it cannot be used in conjunction with such algorithms.

7. (Make sure that your solution works for empty lists.)

I1. Set P ← FIRST, Q ← Λ.

I2. If P ≠ Λ, set R ← Q, Q ← P, P ← LINK(Q), LINK(Q) ← R, and repeat this step.

I3. Set FIRST ← Q. ∎

In essence we are popping nodes off one stack and pushing them onto another.

8.					
	LD1	FIRST	1	_I1._ P ≡ rI1 ← FIRST.	
	ENT2	0	1	Q ≡ rI2 ← Λ.	
	J1Z	2F	1	_I2._ If the list is empty, jump.	
1H	ENTA	0,2	n	R ≡ rA ← Q.	
	ENT2	0,1	n	Q ← P.	
	LD1	0,2(LINK)	n	P ← LINK(Q).	
	STA	0,2(LINK)	n	LINK(Q) ← R.	
	J1NZ	1B	n	Is P ≠ Λ?	
2H	ST2	FIRST	1	_I3._ FIRST ← Q. ∎	

The time is $(7n + 6)u$. Better speed $(5n + \text{constant})u$ is attainable; see exercise 1.1–3.

9. (a) Yes.   (b) Yes, if biological parenthood is considered; no, if legal parenthood is considered (a man's daughter might marry his father, as in the song "I'm My Own Grampa").   (c) No $(-1 \prec 1$ and $1 \prec -1)$.   (d) Let us hope so, or else there is a circular argument.   (e) $1 \prec 3$ and $3 \prec 1$.   (f) The statement is ambiguous. If we take the position that the subroutines called by y are dependent upon which subroutine calls y, we would have to conclude that the transitive law does not necessarily hold. (For example, a general input-output subroutine might call on different processing routines for each I/O device present, but these processing routines are usually not all needed in a single program. This is a problem that plagues many automatic programming systems.)

10. For (i) there are three cases: $x = y$; $x \subset y$ and $y = z$; $x \subset y$ and $y \subset z$. For (ii) there are two cases: $x = y$; $x \neq y$. Each case is handled trivially, as is (iii).

11. "Multiply out" the following to get all 52 solutions: $13749(25 + 52)86 + (1379 + 1397 + 1937 + 9137)(4258 + 4528 + 2458 + 5428 + 2548 + 5248 + 2584 + 5284)6 + (1392 + 1932 + 1923 + 9123 + 9132 + 9213)7(458 + 548 + 584)6$.

12. For example: (a) List all sets with k elements (in any order) before all sets with $k+1$ elements, $0 \leq k < n$. (b) Represent a subset by a sequence of 0s and 1s showing which elements are in the set. This gives a correspondence between all subsets and the integers 0 through $2^n - 1$, via the binary number system. The order of correspondence is a topological sequence.

13. Sha and Kleitman, *Discrete Math.* **63** (1987), 271–278, have proved that the number is at most $\prod_{k=0}^{n} \binom{n}{k}^{\binom{n}{k}}$. This exceeds the obvious lower bound $\prod_{k=0}^{n} \binom{n}{k}! = 2^{2^n(n+O(\log n))}$ by a factor of $e^{2^n + O(n)}$; they conjecture that the lower bound is closer to the truth.

14. If $a_1 a_2 \ldots a_n$ and $b_1 b_2 \ldots b_n$ are two possible topological sorts, let j be minimal such that $a_j \neq b_j$; then $a_k = b_j$ and $a_j = b_m$ for some $k, m > j$. Now $b_j \npreceq a_j$ since $k > j$, and $a_j \npreceq b_j$ since $m > j$, hence (iv) fails. Conversely if there is only one topological sort $a_1 a_2 \ldots a_n$, we must have $a_j \preceq a_{j+1}$ for $1 \leq j < n$, since otherwise a_j and a_{j+1} could be interchanged. This and transitivity imply (iv).

Note: The following alternative proofs work also for infinite sets. (a) Every partial ordering can be embedded in a linear ordering. For if we have two elements with $x_0 \npreceq y_0$ and $y_0 \npreceq x_0$ we can generate another partial ordering by the rule "$x \preceq y$ or ($x \preceq x_0$ and $y_0 \preceq y$)." The latter ordering "includes" the former and has $x_0 \preceq y_0$. Now apply Zorn's lemma or transfinite induction in the usual way to complete the proof. (b) Obviously a linear ordering cannot be embedded in any different linear ordering. (c) A partial ordering that has incomparable elements x_0 and y_0 as in (a) can be extended to two linear orderings in which $x_0 \preceq y_0$ and $y_0 \preceq x_0$, respectively, so at least two linear orderings exist.

15. If S is finite, we can list all relations $a \prec b$ that are true in the given partial ordering. By successively removing, one at a time, any relations that are implied by others, we arrive at an irredundant set. The problem is to show there is just one such set, no matter in what order we go about removing redundant relations. If there were two irredundant sets U and V, in which "$a \prec b$" appears in U but not in V, there are $k+1$ relations $a \prec c_1 \prec \cdots \prec c_k \prec b$ in V for some $k \geq 1$. But it is possible to deduce $a \prec c_1$ and $c_1 \prec b$ from U, *without* using the relation $a \prec b$ (since $b \npreceq c_1$ and $c_1 \npreceq a$), hence the relation $a \prec b$ is redundant in U.

The result is false for infinite sets S, when there is *at most* one irredundant set of relations. For example if S denotes the integers plus the element ∞ and we define $n \prec n+1$ and $n \prec \infty$ for all n, there is no irredundant set of relations that characterizes this partial ordering.

16. Let $x_{p_1} x_{p_2} \ldots x_{p_n}$ be a topological sorting of S; apply the permutation $p_1 p_2 \ldots p_n$ to both rows and columns.

17. If k increases from 1 to n in step T4, the output is 1932745860. If k decreases from n to 1 in step T4, as it does in Program T, the output is 9123745860.

18. They link together the items in sorted order: `QLINK[0]` first, `QLINK[QLINK[0]]` second, and so on; `QLINK[last]` $= 0$.

19. This would fail in certain cases; when the queue contains only one element in step T5, the modified method would set $F = 0$ (thereby emptying the queue), but other entries could be placed in the queue in step T6. The suggested modification would therefore require an additional test of $F = 0$ in step T6.

20. Indeed, a stack *could* be used, in the following way. (Step T7 disappears.)

T4. Set T ← 0. For $1 \leq k \leq n$ if COUNT[k] is zero do the following: Set SLINK[k] ← T, T ← k. (SLINK[k] ≡ QLINK[k].)

T5. Output the value of T. If T = 0, go to T8; otherwise, set N ← N − 1, P ← TOP[T], T ← SLINK[T].

T6. Same as before, except go to T5 instead of T7; and when COUNT[SUC(P)] goes down to zero, set SLINK[SUC(P)] ← T and T ← SUC(P).

21. Repeated relations only make the algorithm a little slower and take up more space in the storage pool. A relation "$j \prec j$" would be treated like a loop (an arrow from a box to itself in the corresponding diagram), which violates partial order.

22. To make the program "fail-safe" we should (a) check that $0 < n <$ some appropriate maximum; (b) check each relation $j \prec k$ for the conditions $0 < j, k \leq n$; (c) make sure that the number of relations doesn't overflow the storage pool area.

23. At the end of step T5, add "TOP[F] ← Λ". (Then at all times TOP[1], ..., TOP[n] point to all the relations not yet canceled.) In step T8, if N > 0, print "LOOP DETECTED IN INPUT:", and set QLINK[k] ← 0 for $1 \leq k \leq n$. Now add the following steps:

T9. For $1 \leq k \leq n$ set P ← TOP[k], TOP[k] ← 0, and perform step T10. (This will set QLINK[j] to one of the predecessors of object j, for each j not yet output.) Then go to T11.

T10. If P ≠ Λ, set QLINK[SUC(P)] ← k, P ← NEXT(P), and repeat this step.

T11. Find a k with QLINK[k] ≠ 0.

T12. Set TOP[k] ← 1 and k ← QLINK[k]. Now if TOP[k] = 0, repeat this step.

T13. (We have found the start of a loop.) Print the value of k, set TOP[k] ← 0, k ← QLINK[k], and if TOP[k] = 1 repeat this step.

T14. Print the value of k (the beginning and end of the loop) and stop. (*Note:* The loop has been printed backwards; if it is desired to print the loop in forward order, an algorithm like that in exercise 7 should be used between steps T12 and T13.) ∎

24. Insert three lines in the program of the text:

```
08a  PRINTER EQU  18
14a          ST6  NO
59a          STZ  X,1(TOP)      TOP[F] ← Λ.
```

Replace lines 74–75 by the following:

```
74          J6Z   DONE
75          OUT   LINE1(PRINTER)   Print indication of loop.
76          LD6   NO
77          STZ   X,6(QLINK)       QLINK[k] ← 0.
78          DEC6  1
79          J6P   *-2              n ≥ k ≥ 1.
80          LD6   NO
81  T9      LD2   X,6(TOP)         P ← TOP[k].
82          STZ   X,6(TOP)         TOP[k] ← 0.
83          J2Z   T9A              Is P = Λ?
84  T10     LD1   0,2(SUC)         rI1 ← SUC(P).
85          ST6   X,1(QLINK)       QLINK[rI1] ← k.
86          LD2   0,2(NEXT)        P ← NEXT(P).
```

87		J2P	T10	Is P $\neq$ Λ?
88	T9A	DEC6	1	
89		J6P	T9	$n \geq k \geq 1$.
90	T11	INC6	1	
91		LDA	X,6(QLINK)	
92		JAZ	*-2	Find k with QLINK$[k] \neq 0$.
93	T12	ST6	X,6(TOP)	TOP$[k] \leftarrow k$.
94		LD6	X,6(QLINK)	$k \leftarrow$ QLINK$[k]$.
95		LD1	X,6(TOP)	
96		J1Z	T12	Is TOP$[k] = 0$?
97	T13	ENTA	0,6	
98		CHAR		Convert k to alphameric.
99		JBUS	*(PRINTER)	
100		STX	VALUE	Print.
101		OUT	LINE2(PRINTER)	
102		J1Z	DONE	Stop when TOP$[k] = 0$.
103		STZ	X,6(TOP)	TOP$[k] \leftarrow 0$.
104		LD6	X,6(QLINK)	$k \leftarrow$ QLINK$[k]$.
105		LD1	X,6(TOP)	
106		JMP	T13	
107	LINE1	ALF	LOOP	Title line
108		ALF	DETEC	
109		ALF	TED I	
110		ALF	N INP	
111		ALF	UT:	
112	LINE2	ALF		Succeeding lines
113	VALUE	EQU	LINE2+3	
114		ORIG	LINE2+24	
115	DONE	HLT		End of computation
116	X	END	TOPSORT	∎

Note: If the relations $9 \prec 1$ and $6 \prec 9$ are added to the data (18), this program will print "9, 6, 8, 5, 9" as the loop.

26. One solution is to proceed in two phases as follows:

Phase 1. (We use the X table as a (sequential) stack as we mark B = 1 or 2 for each subroutine that needs to be used.)

   A0. For $1 \leq J \leq N$ set B(X[J]) $\leftarrow$ B(X[J]) + 2, if B(X[J]) ≤ 0.

   A1. If N = 0, go to phase 2; otherwise set P $\leftarrow$ X[N] and decrease N by 1.

   A2. If $|$B(P)$| = 1$, go to A1, otherwise set P $\leftarrow$ P + 1.

   A3. If B(SUB1(P)) ≤ 0, set N $\leftarrow$ N + 1, B(SUB1(P)) $\leftarrow$ B(SUB1(P)) + 2, X[N] $\leftarrow$ SUB1(P). If SUB2(P) $\neq 0$ and B(SUB2(P)) ≤ 0, do a similar set of actions with SUB2(P). Go to A2. ∎

Phase 2. (We go through the table and allocate memory.)

   B1. Set P $\leftarrow$ FIRST.

   B2. If P = Λ, set N $\leftarrow$ N + 1, BASE(LOC(X[N])) $\leftarrow$ MLOC, SUB(LOC(X[N])) $\leftarrow$ 0, and terminate the algorithm.

B3. If $B(P) > 0$, set $N \leftarrow N + 1$, $\mathtt{BASE(LOC(X[N]))} \leftarrow \mathtt{MLOC}$, $\mathtt{SUB(LOC(X[N]))} \leftarrow \mathtt{P}$, $\mathtt{MLOC} \leftarrow \mathtt{MLOC} + \mathtt{SPACE(P)}$.

B4. Set $\mathtt{P} \leftarrow \mathtt{LINK(P)}$ and return to B2. ∎

27. Comments on the following code are left to the reader.

```
B     EQU  0:1        A1 J1Z  B1              INC1 1
SPACE EQU  2:3           LD2  X,1              INCA 2
LINK  EQU  4:5           DEC1 1               STA  0,3(B)
SUB1  EQU  2:3        A2 LDA  0,2(1:1)        ST3  X,1
SUB2  EQU  4:5           DECA 1               JMP  A2
BASE  EQU  0:3           JAZ  A1           B1 ENT2 FIRST
SUB   EQU  4:5           INC2 1               LDA  MLOC
A0    LD2  N          A3 LD3  0,2(SUB1)        JMP  1F
      J2Z  2F            LDA  0,3(B)        B3 LDX  0,2(B)
1H    LD3  X,2           JAP  9F               JXNP B4
      LDA  0,3(B)        INC1 1               INC1 1
      JAP  *+3           INCA 2               ST2  X,1(SUB)
      INCA 2             STA  0,3(B)           ADD  0,2(SPACE)
      STA  0,3(B)        ST3  X,1          1H STA  X+1,1(BASE)
      DEC2 1          9H LD3  0,2(SUB2)     B4 LD2  0,2(LINK)
      J2P  1B            J3Z  A2           B2 J2NZ B3
2H    LD1  N             LDA  0,3(B)           STZ  X+1,1(SUB) ∎
                         JAP  A2
```

28. We give here only a few comments related to the military game. Let A be the player with three men whose pieces start on nodes A13; let B be the other player. In this game, A must "trap" B, and if B can cause a position to be repeated for a second time we can consider B the winner. To avoid keeping the entire past history of the game as an integral part of the positions, however, we should modify the algorithm in the following way: Start by marking the positions 157–4, 789–B, 359–6 with B to move as "lost" and apply the suggested algorithm. Now the idea is for player A to move only to B's lost positions. But A must also take precautions against repeating prior moves. A good computer game-playing program will use a random number generator to select between several winning moves when more than one is present, so an obvious technique would be to make the computer, playing A, just choose randomly among those moves that lead to a lost position for B. But there are interesting situations that make this plausible procedure fail! For example, consider position 258–7 with A to move; this is a won position. From position 258–7, player A might try moving to 158–7 (which is a lost position for B, according to the algorithm). But then B plays to 158–B, and this forces A to play to 258–B, after which B plays back to 258–7; B has won, since the former position has been repeated! This example shows that the algorithm must be re-invoked after every move has been made, starting with each position that has previously occurred marked "lost" (if A is to move) or "won" (if B is to move). The military game makes a very satisfactory computer demonstration program.

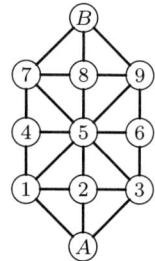

Board for the "military game."

29. (a) If FIRST = Λ, do nothing; otherwise set P ← FIRST, and then repeatedly set P ← LINK(P) zero or more times until LINK(P) = Λ. Finally set LINK(P) ← AVAIL and AVAIL ← FIRST (and probably also FIRST ← Λ).   (b) If F = Λ, do nothing; otherwise set LINK(R) ← AVAIL and AVAIL ← F (and probably also F ← Λ, R ← LOC(F)).

30. To insert, set P ⇐ AVAIL, INFO(P) ← Y, LINK(P) ← Λ, if F = Λ then F ← P else LINK(R) ← P, and R ← P. To delete, do (9) with F replacing T. (Although it is convenient to let R be undefined for an empty queue, this lack of discipline might confuse a garbage collection algorithm, as in exercise 6.)

SECTION 2.2.4

1. No, it does not help; it seems to hinder, if anything. (The stated convention is *not* especially consistent with the circular list philosophy, unless we put NODE(LOC(PTR)) into the list as its list head.)

2. Before:

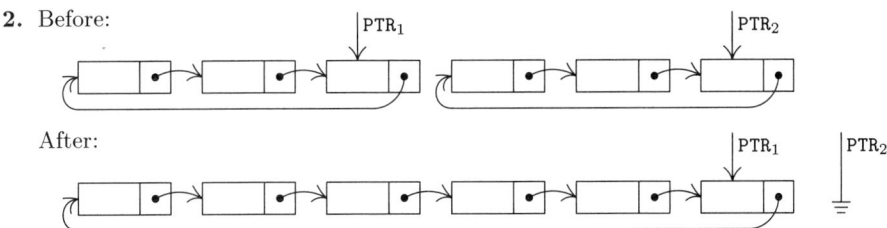

After:

3. If $PTR_1 = PTR_2$, the only effect is $PTR_2 ← Λ$. If $PTR_1 ≠ PTR_2$, the exchange of links breaks the list into two parts, as if a circle had been broken in two by cutting at two points; the second part of the operation then makes PTR_1 point to a circular list that consists of the nodes that would have been traversed if, in the original list, we followed the links from PTR_1 to PTR_2.

4. Let HEAD be the address of the list head. To push down Y onto the stack: Set P ⇐ AVAIL, INFO(P) ← Y, LINK(P) ← LINK(HEAD), LINK(HEAD) ← P. To pop up the stack onto Y: If LINK(HEAD) = HEAD then UNDERFLOW; otherwise set P ← LINK(HEAD), LINK(HEAD) ← LINK(P), Y ← INFO(P), AVAIL ⇐ P.

5. (Compare with exercise 2.2.3–7.) Set Q ← Λ, P ← PTR, and then while P ≠ Λ repeatedly set R ← Q, Q ← P, P ← LINK(Q), LINK(Q) ← R. (Afterwards Q = PTR.)

6.

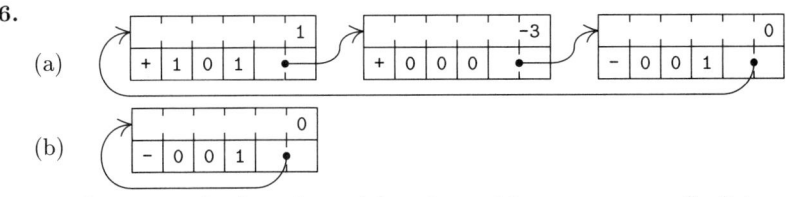

(a)

(b)

7. Matching terms in the polynomial are located in one pass over the list, so repeated random searches are avoided. Also, *increasing* order would be incompatible with the "−1" sentinel.

8. We must know what node points to the current node of interest, if we are going to delete that node or to insert another one ahead of it. There are alternatives, however: We could delete NODE(Q) by setting Q2 ← LINK(Q) and then setting NODE(Q) ← NODE(Q2), AVAIL ⇐ Q2; we could insert a NODE(Q2) in front of NODE(Q) by first interchanging NODE(Q2) ↔ NODE(Q), then setting LINK(Q) ← Q2, Q ← Q2. These clever tricks allow the deletion and insertion *without* knowing which node links to NODE(Q); they were used in early versions of IPL. But they have the disadvantage that the sentinel node at the end of a polynomial will occasionally move, and other link variables may be pointing to this node.

9. Algorithm A with P = Q simply doubles polynomial(Q), as it should — except in the anomalous case that COEF = 0 for some term with ABC $\geq$ 0, when it fails badly. Algorithm M with P = M also gives the expected result. Algorithm M with P = Q sets polynomial(P) $\leftarrow$ polynomial(P) times $(1 + t_1)(1 + t_2)\ldots(1 + t_k)$ if M = $t_1 + t_2 + \cdots + t_k$ (although this is not immediately obvious). When M = Q, Algorithm M surprisingly gives the expected result, polynomial(Q) $\leftarrow$ polynomial(Q) + polynomial(Q) × polynomial(P), except that the computation blows up when the constant term of polynomial(P) is -1.

10. None. (The only possible difference would be in step M2, removing error checks that A, B, or C might individually overflow; these error checks were not specified because we assumed that they were not necessary.) In other words, the algorithms in this section may be regarded as operations on the polynomial $f(x^{b^2}, x^b, x)$ instead of on $f(x, y, z)$.

```
11. COPY STJ  9F        (comments        ST6  1,3(LINK)
         ENT3 9F         are             ENT3 0,6
         LDA  1,1        left            LD1  1,1(LINK)
    1H   LD6  AVAIL      to              LDA  1,1
         J6Z  OVERFLOW   the             JANN 1B
         LDX  1,6(LINK)  reader)         LD2  8F(LINK)
         STX  AVAIL                      ST2  1,3(LINK)
         STA  1,6                   9H JMP  *
         LDA  0,1                   8H CON  0   ▮
         STA  0,6
```

12. Let the polynomial copied have p terms. Program A takes $(29p + 13)u$, and to make it a fair comparison we should add the time to create a zero polynomial, say $18u$ with exercise 14. The program of exercise 11 takes $(21p + 31)u$, about $\frac{3}{4}$ as much.

```
13. ERASE STJ  9F
          LDX  AVAIL
          LDA  1,1(LINK)
          STA  AVAIL
          STX  1,1(LINK)
    9H    JMP  *   ▮
```

```
14. ZERO STJ  9F              MOVE 1F(2)
         LD1  AVAIL           ST2  1,2(LINK)
         J1Z  OVERFLOW   9H JMP  *
         LDX  1,1(LINK)  1H CON  0
         STX  AVAIL         CON  -1(ABC)  ▮
         ENT2 0,1
```

```
15. MULT STJ  9F        Entrance to subroutine
         LDA  5F        Change settings of switches
         STA  SW1
         LDA  6F
         STA  SW2
         STA  SW3
```

```
            JMP   *+2
     2H     JMP   ADD            M2. Multiply cycle.
     1H     LD4   1,4(LINK)      M1. Next multiplier. M ← LINK(M).
            LDA   1,4
            JANN  2B             To M2 if ABC(M) ≥ 0.
     8H     LDA   7F             Restore settings of switches.
            STA   SW1
            LDA   8F
            STA   SW2
            STA   SW3
     9H     JMP   *              Return.
     5H     JMP   *+1            New setting of SW1
            LDA   0,1
            MUL   0,4            rX ← COEF(P) × COEF(M).
            LDA   1,1(ABC)       ABC(P)
            JAN   *+2
            ADD   1,4(ABC)        + ABC(M), if ABC(P) ≥ 0.
            SLA   2              Move into 0:3 field of rA.
            STX   OF             Save rX for use in SW2 and SW3.
            JMP   SW1+1
     6H     LDA   OF             New setting of SW2 and SW3
     7H     LDA   1,1            Usual setting of SW1
     8H     LDA   0,1            Usual setting of SW2 and SW3
     OH     CON   0              Temp storage ▮
```

16. Let r be the number of terms in polynomial(M). The subroutine requires $21pr + 38r + 29 + 27 \sum m' + 18 \sum m'' + 27 \sum p' + 8 \sum q'$ units of time, where the summations refer to the corresponding quantities during the r activations of Program A. The number of terms in polynomial(Q) goes up by $p' - m'$ each activation of Program A. If we make the not unreasonable assumption that $m' = 0$ and $p' = \alpha p$ where $0 < \alpha < 1$, we get the respective sums equal to 0, $(1 - \alpha)pr$, αpr, and $rq_0' + \alpha p(r(r - 1)/2)$, where q_0' is the value of q' in the first iteration. The grand total is $4\alpha pr^2 + 40pr + 4\alpha pr + 8q_0'r + 38r + 29$. This analysis indicates that the multiplier ought to have fewer terms than the multiplicand, since we have to skip over unmatching terms in polynomial(Q) more often. (See exercise 5.2.3–29 for a faster algorithm.)

17. There actually is very little advantage; addition and multiplication routines with either type of list would be virtually the same. The efficiency of the ERASE subroutine (see exercise 13) is apparently the only important difference.

18. Let the link field of node x_i contain LOC$(x_{i+1}) \oplus$ LOC(x_{i-1}), where "$\oplus$" denotes "exclusive or." Other invertible operations, such as addition or subtraction modulo the pointer field size, could also be used. It is convenient to include two adjacent list heads in the circular list, to help get things started properly. (The origin of this ingenious technique is unknown.)

SECTION 2.2.5

1. Insert Y at the left: P $\Leftarrow$ AVAIL; INFO(P) ← Y; LLINK(P) ← Λ; RLINK(P) ← LEFT; if LEFT $\neq$ Λ then LLINK(LEFT) ← P else RIGHT ← P; LEFT ← P. Set Y to leftmost and delete: if LEFT = Λ then UNDERFLOW; P ← LEFT; LEFT ← RLINK(P); if LEFT = Λ then RIGHT ← Λ, else LLINK(LEFT) ← Λ; Y ← INFO(P); AVAIL $\Leftarrow$ P.

2. Consider the case of several deletions (at the same end) in succession. After each deletion we must know what to delete next, so the links in the list must point away from that end of the list. Deletion at both ends therefore implies that the links must go both ways. On the other hand, exercise 2.2.4–18 explains how to represent two links in a single link field; in that way general deque operations *are* possible.

3. To show the independence of CALLUP from CALLDOWN, notice for example that in Table 1 the elevator did not stop at floors 2 or 3 at time 0393–0444 although there were people waiting; these people had pushed CALLDOWN, but if they had pushed CALLUP the elevator would have stopped.

To show the independence of CALLCAR from the others, notice that in Table 1, when the doors start to open at time 1378, the elevator has already decided to be GOINGUP. Its state would have been NEUTRAL at that point if CALLCAR[1] = CALLCAR[2] = CALLCAR[3] = CALLCAR[4] = 0, according to step E2, but in fact CALLCAR[2] and CALLCAR[3] have been set to 1 by users 7 and 9 in the elevator. (If we envision the same situation with all floor numbers increased by 1, the fact that STATE = NEUTRAL or STATE = GOINGUP when the doors open would affect whether the elevator would perhaps continue to go downward or would unconditionally go upward.)

4. If a dozen or more people were getting out at the same floor, STATE might be NEUTRAL all during this time, and when E9 calls the DECISION subroutine this may set a new state before anyone has gotten in on the current floor. It happens very rarely indeed (and it certainly was the most puzzling phenomenon observed by the author during his elevator experiments).

5. The state from the time the doors start to open at time 1063 until user 7 gets in at time 1183 would have been NEUTRAL, since there would have been no calls to floor 0 and nobody on board the elevator. Then user 7 would set CALLCAR[2] ← 1 and the state would correspondingly change to GOINGUP.

6. Add the condition "if OUT < IN then STATE ≠ GOINGUP; if OUT > IN then STATE ≠ GOINGDOWN" to the condition "FLOOR = IN" in steps U2 and U4. In step E4, accept users from QUEUE[FLOOR] only if they are headed in the elevator's direction, unless STATE = NEUTRAL (when we accept all comers).

[Stanford's math department has just such an elevator, but its users don't actually pay much attention to the indicator lights; people tend to get on as soon as they can, regardless of direction. Why didn't the elevator designers realize this, and design the logic accordingly by clearing both CALLUP and CALLDOWN? The whole process would be faster, since the elevator wouldn't have to stop as often.]

7. In line 227 this user is assumed to be in the WAIT list. Jumping to U4A makes sure that this assumption is valid. It is assumed that GIVEUPTIME is positive, and indeed that it is probably 100 or more.

8. Comments are left to the reader.

```
277   E8   DEC4  1
278        ENTA  61
279        JMP   HOLDC
280        LDA   CALL,4(3:5)
281        JAP   1F
282        ENT1  -2,4
283        J1Z   2F
284        LDA   CALL,4(1:1)
```

```
285        JAZ  E8
286  2H    LDA  CALL-1,4
287        ADD  CALL-2,4
288        ADD  CALL-3,4
289        ADD  CALL-4,4
290        JANZ E8
291  1H    ENTA 23
292        JMP  E2A              ▌
```

```
9. 01  DECISION STJ  9F                    Store exit location.
   02           J5NZ 9F                    D1. Decision necessary?
   03           LDX  ELEV1+2(NEXTINST)
   04           DECX E1                    D2. Should doors open?
   05           JXNZ 1F                    Jump if elevator not at E1.
   06           LDA  CALL+2
   07           ENT3 E3                    Prepare to schedule E3,
   08           JANZ 8F                      if there is a call on floor 2.
   09  1H       ENT1 -4                    D3. Any calls?
   10           LDA  CALL+4,1              Search for a nonzero call variable.
   11           JANZ 2F
   12  1H       INC1 1                     rI1 ≡ j − 4
   13           J1NP *-3
   14           LDA  9F(0:2)               All CALL[j], j ≠ FLOOR, are zero.
   15           DECA E6B                   Is exit location = line 250?
   16           JANZ 9F
   17           ENT1 -2                    Set j ← 2.
   18  2H       ENT5 4,1                   D4. Set STATE.
   19           DEC5 0,4                   STATE ← j − FLOOR.
   20           J5NZ *+2
   21           JANZ 1B                    j = FLOOR not allowed in general.
   22           JXNZ 9F                    D5. Elevator dormant?
   23           J5Z  9F                    Jump if not at E1 or if j = 2.
   24           ENT3 E6                    Otherwise schedule E6.
   25  8H       ENTA 20                    Wait 20 units of time.
   26           ST6  8F(0:2)               Save rI6.
   27           ENT6 ELEV1
   28           ST3  2,6(NEXTINST)         Set NEXTINST to E3 or E6.
   29           JMP  HOLD                  Schedule the activity.
   30  8H       ENT6 *                     Restore rI6.
   31  9H       JMP  *                     Exit from subroutine.   ▌
```

11. Initially let LINK[k] = 0, $1 \le k \le n$, and HEAD = −1. During a simulation step that changes V[k], give an error indication if LINK[k] ≠ 0; otherwise set LINK[k] ← HEAD, HEAD ← k and set NEWV[k] to the new value of V[k]. After each simulation step, set k ← HEAD, HEAD ← −1, and do the following operation repeatedly zero or more times until $k < 0$: set V[k] ← NEWV[k], t ← LINK[k], LINK[k] ← 0, k ← t.

Clearly this method is readily adapted to the case of scattered variables, if we include a NEWV and LINK field in each node associated with a variable field V.

12. The WAIT list has deletions from the left to the right, but insertions are sorted in from the right to the left (since the search is likely to be shorter from that side).

Also we delete nodes from all three lists in several places when we do not know the predecessor or successor of the node being deleted. Only the ELEVATOR list could be converted to a one-way list, without much loss of efficiency.

Note: It may be preferable to use a nonlinear list as the WAIT list in a discrete simulator, to reduce the time for sorting in. Section 5.2.3 discusses the general problem of maintaining priority queues, or "smallest in, first out" lists, such as this. Several ways are known in which only $O(\log n)$ operations are needed to insert or delete when there are n elements in the list, although there is of course no need for such a fancy method when n is known to be small.

SECTION 2.2.6

1. (Here the indices run from 1 to n, not from 0 to n as in Eq. (6).) $\text{LOC}(\text{A}[\text{J},\text{K}]) = \text{LOC}(\text{A}[0,0]) + 2n\text{J} + 2\text{K}$, where $\text{A}[0,0]$ is an assumed node that is actually nonexistent. If we set $\text{J} = \text{K} = 1$, we get $\text{LOC}(\text{A}[1,1]) = \text{LOC}(\text{A}[0,0]) + 2n + 2$, so the answer can be expressed in several ways. The fact that $\text{LOC}(\text{A}[0,0])$ might be negative has led to many bugs in compilers and loading routines.

2. $\text{LOC}(\text{A}[\text{I}_1,\ldots,\text{I}_k]) = \text{LOC}(\text{A}[0,\ldots,0]) + \sum_{1 \leq r \leq k} a_r \text{I}_r = \text{LOC}(\text{A}[l_1,\ldots,l_k]) + \sum_{1 \leq r \leq k} a_r \text{I}_r - \sum_{1 \leq r \leq k} a_r l_r$, where $a_r = c \prod_{r < s \leq k}(u_s - l_s + 1)$.

Note: For a generalization to the structures occurring in programming languages such as C, and a simple algorithm to compute the relevant constants, see P. Deuel, *CACM* **9** (1966), 344–347.

3. $1 \leq k \leq j \leq n$ if and only if $0 \leq k - 1 \leq j - 1 \leq n - 1$; so replace k, j, n respectively by $k - 1$, $j - 1$, $n - 1$ in all formulas derived for lower bound zero.

4. $\text{LOC}(\text{A}[\text{J},\text{K}]) = \text{LOC}(\text{A}[0,0]) + n\text{J} - \text{J}(\text{J} - 1)/2 + \text{K}$.

5. Let $\text{A0} = \text{LOC}(\text{A}[0,0])$. There are at least two solutions, assuming that J is in rI1 and K is in rI2. (i) "LDA TA2,1:7", where location TA2+j is "NOP $j+1*j/2+\text{A0},2$"; (ii) "LDA C1,7:2", where location C1 contains "NOP TA,1:7" and location TA+j says "NOP $j+1*j/2+\text{A0}$". The latter takes one more cycle but doesn't tie the table down to index register 2.

6. (a) $\text{LOC}(\text{A}[\text{I},\text{J},\text{K}]) = \text{LOC}(\text{A}[0,0,0]) + \binom{\text{I} + 2}{3} + \binom{\text{J} + 1}{2} + \binom{\text{K}}{1}$.

(b) $\text{LOC}(\text{B}[\text{I},\text{J},\text{K}]) = \text{LOC}(\text{B}[0,0,0])$

$$+ \binom{n + 3}{3} - \binom{n + 3 - \text{I}}{3} + \binom{n + 2 - \text{I}}{2} - \binom{n + 2 - \text{J}}{2} + \text{K} - \text{J},$$

hence the stated form is possible in this case also.

7. $\text{LOC}(\text{A}[\text{I}_1, \ldots, \text{I}_k]) = \text{LOC}(\text{A}[0,\ldots,0]) + \sum_{1 \leq r \leq k} \binom{\text{I}_r + k - r}{1 + k - r}$. See exercise 1.2.6–56.

8. (Solution by P. Nash.) Let $\text{X}[\text{I},\text{J},\text{K}]$ be defined for $0 \leq \text{I} \leq n$, $0 \leq \text{J} \leq n + 1$, $0 \leq \text{K} \leq n + 2$. We can let $\text{A}[\text{I},\text{J},\text{K}] = \text{X}[\text{I},\text{J},\text{K}]$; $\text{B}[\text{I},\text{J},\text{K}] = \text{X}[\text{J},\text{I} + 1,\text{K}]$; $\text{C}[\text{I},\text{J},\text{K}] = \text{X}[\text{I},\text{K},\text{J} + 1]$; $\text{D}[\text{I},\text{J},\text{K}] = \text{X}[\text{J},\text{K},\text{I} + 2]$; $\text{E}[\text{I},\text{J},\text{K}] = \text{X}[\text{K},\text{I} + 1,\text{J} + 1]$; $\text{F}[\text{I},\text{J},\text{K}] = \text{X}[\text{K},\text{J} + 1,\text{I} + 2]$. This scheme is the best possible, since it packs the $(n + 1)(n + 2)(n + 3)$ elements of the six tetrahedral arrays into consecutive locations with no overlap. *Proof:* A and B exhaust all cells $\text{X}[i,j,k]$ with $k = \min(i,j,k)$; C and D exhaust all cells with $j = \min(i,j,k) \neq k$; E and F exhaust all cells with $i = \min(i,j,k) \neq j, k$.

(The construction generalizes to m dimensions, if anybody ever wants to pack the elements of $m!$ generalized tetrahedral arrays into $(n+1)(n+2)\ldots(n+m)$ consecutive locations. Associate a permutation $a_1 a_2 \ldots a_m$ with each array, and store its elements in $X[I_{a_1} + B_1, I_{a_2} + B_2, \ldots, I_{a_m} + B_m]$, where $B_1 B_2 \ldots B_m$ is an inversion table for $a_1 a_2 \ldots a_m$ as defined in exercise 5.1.1–7.)

9. G1. Set pointer variables P1, P2, P3, P4, P5, P6 to the first locations of the lists FEMALE, A21, A22, A23, BLOND, BLUE, respectively. Assume in what follows that the end of each list is given by link Λ, and Λ is smaller than any other link. If P6 = Λ, stop (the list, unfortunately, is empty).

G2. (Many possible orderings of the following actions could be done; we have chosen to examine EYES first, then HAIR, then AGE, then SEX.) Set P5 $\leftarrow$ HAIR(P5) zero or more times until P5 $\leq$ P6. If now P5 $<$ P6, go to step G5.

G3. Set P4 $\leftarrow$ AGE(P4) repeatedly if necessary until P4 $\leq$ P6. Similarly do the same to P3 and P2 until P3 $\leq$ P6 and P2 $\leq$ P6. If now P4, P3, P2 are all smaller than P6, go to G5.

G4. Set P1 $\leftarrow$ SEX(P1) until P1 $\leq$ P6. If P1 = P6, we have found one of the young ladies desired, so output her address, P6. (Her age can be determined from the settings of P2, P3, and P4.)

G5. Set P6 $\leftarrow$ EYES(P6). Now stop if P6 = Λ; otherwise return to G2. ▮

This algorithm is interesting but not the best way to organize a list for such a search.

10. See Section 6.5.

11. At most $200 + 200 + 3 \cdot 4 \cdot 200 = 2800$ words.

12. VAL(Q0) = c, VAL(P0) = b/a, VAL(P1) = d.

13. It is convenient to have at the end of each list a sentinel that "compares low" in some field on which the list is ordered. A straight one-way list *could* have been used, for example by retaining just the LEFT links in BASEROW[i] and the UP links in BASECOL[j], by modifying Algorithm S thus: In S2, test if P0 = Λ before setting J $\leftarrow$ COL(P0); if so, set P0 $\leftarrow$ LOC(BASEROW[I0]) and go to S3. In S3, test if Q0 = Λ; if so, terminate. Step S4 should change by analogy with step S2. In S5, test if P1 = Λ; if so, act as if COL(P1) $<$ 0. In S6, test if UP(PTR[J]) = Λ; if so, act as if its ROW field were negative.

These modifications make the algorithm more complicated and save no storage space except a ROW or COL field in the list heads (which in the case of MIX is no saving at all).

14. One could first link together those columns that have a nonzero element in the pivot row, so that all other columns could be skipped as we pivot on each row. Rows in which the pivot column is zero are skipped over immediately.

15. Let rI1 $\equiv$ PIVOT, J; rI2 $\equiv$ P0; rI3 $\equiv$ Q0; rI4 $\equiv$ P; rI5 $\equiv$ P1, X; LOC(BASEROW[i]) $\equiv$ BROW + i; LOC(BASECOL[j]) $\equiv$ BCOL + j; PTR[j] $\equiv$ BCOL + j(1:3).

```
01  ROW        EQU  0:3
02  UP         EQU  4:5
03  COL        EQU  0:3
04  LEFT       EQU  4:5
05  PTR        EQU  1:3
06  PIVOTSTEP STJ  9F           Subroutine entrance, rI1 = PIVOT
07  S1         LD2  0,1(ROW)     S1. Initialize.
08             ST2  I0           I0 ← ROW(PIVOT).
09             LD3  1,1(COL)
```

```
10              ST3   J0         J0 ← COL(PIVOT).
11              LDA   =1.0=      Floating point constant 1
12              FDIV  2,1
13              STA   ALPHA      ALPHA ← 1/VAL(PIVOT).
14              LDA   =1.0=
15              STA   2,1        VAL(PIVOT) ← 1.
16              ENT2  BROW,2     P0 ← LOC(BASEROW[I0]).
17              ENT3  BCOL,3     Q0 ← LOC(BASECOL[J0]).
18              JMP   S2
19      2H      ENTA  BCOL,1
20              STA   BCOL,1(PTR)  PTR[J] ← LOC(BASECOL[J]).
21              LDA   2,2
22              FMUL  ALPHA
23              STA   2,2        VAL(P0) ← ALPHA × VAL(P0).
24      S2      LD2   1,2(LEFT)  S2. Process pivot row. P0 ← LEFT(P0).
25              LD1   1,2(COL)   J ← COL(P0).
26              J1NN  2B         If J ≥ 0, process J.
27      S3      LD3   0,3(UP)    S3. Find new row. Q0 ← UP(Q0).
28              LD4   0,3(ROW)   rI4 ← ROW(Q0).
29      9H      J4N   *          If rI4 < 0, exit.
30              CMP4  I0
31              JE    S3         If rI4 = I0, repeat.
32              ST4   I(ROW)     I ← rI4.
33              ENT4  BROW,4     P ← LOC(BASEROW[I]).
34      S4A     LD5   1,4(LEFT)  P1 ← LEFT(P).
35      S4      LD2   1,2(LEFT)  S4. Find new column. P0 ← LEFT(P0).
36              LD1   1,2(COL)   J ← COL(P0).
37              CMP1  J0
38              JE    S4         Repeat if J = J0.
39              ENTA  0,1
40              SLA   2          rA(0:3) ← J.
41              J1NN  S5
42              LDAN  2,3        If J < 0,
43              FMUL  ALPHA          set VAL(Q0) ← −ALPHA × VAL(Q0).
44              STA   2,3
45              JMP   S3
46      1H      ENT4  0,5        P ← P1.
47              LD5   1,4(LEFT)  P1 ← LEFT(P).
48      S5      CMPA  1,5(COL)   S5. Find I, J element.
49              JL    1B         Loop until COL(P1) ≤ J.
50              JE    S7         If =, go right to S7.
51      S6      LD5   BCOL,1(PTR)  S6. Insert I, J element. rI5 ← PTR[J].
52              LDA   I          rA(0:3) ← I.
53      2H      ENT6  0,5        rI6 ← rI5.
54              LD5   0,6(UP)    rI5 ← UP(rI6).
55              CMPA  0,5(ROW)
56              JL    2B         Jump if ROW(rI5) > I.
57              LD5   AVAIL      X ⇐ AVAIL.
58              J5Z   OVERFLOW
```

59		LDA	0,5(UP)
60		STA	AVAIL
61		LDA	0,6(UP)
62		STA	0,5(UP)
63		LDA	1,4(LEFT)
64		STA	1,5(LEFT)
65		ST1	1,5(COL)
66		LDA	I(ROW)
67		STA	0,5(ROW)
68		STZ	2,5
69		ST5	1,4(LEFT)
70		ST5	0,6(UP)
71	S7	LDAN	2,3
72		FMUL	2,2
73		FADD	2,5
74		JAZ	S8
75		STA	2,5
76		ST5	BCOL,1(PTR)
77		ENT4	0,5
78		JMP	S4A
79	S8	LD6	BCOL,1(PTR)
80		JMP	*+2
81		LD6	0,6(UP)
82		LDA	0,6(UP)
83		DECA	0,5
84		JANZ	*-3
85		LDA	0,5(UP)
86		STA	0,6(UP)
87		LDA	1,5(LEFT)
88		STA	1,4(LEFT)
89		LDA	AVAIL
90		STA	0,5(UP)
91		ST5	AVAIL
92		JMP	S4A

Annotations:
- line 62: $UP(X) \leftarrow UP(PTR[J])$.
- line 64: $LEFT(X) \leftarrow LEFT(P)$.
- line 65: $COL(X) \leftarrow J$.
- line 67: $ROW(X) \leftarrow I$.
- line 68: $VAL(X) \leftarrow 0$.
- line 69: $LEFT(P) \leftarrow X$.
- line 70: $UP(PTR[J]) \leftarrow X$.
- line 71: *S7. Pivot.* $-VAL(Q0)$
- line 72: $\times VAL(P0)$
- line 73: $+ VAL(P1)$.
- line 74: If significance lost, to S8.
- line 75: Otherwise store in VAL(P1).
- line 76: $PTR[J] \leftarrow P1$.
- line 77: $P \leftarrow P1$.
- line 78: $P1 \leftarrow LEFT(P)$, to S4.
- line 79: *S8. Delete I, J element.* $rI6 \leftarrow PTR[J]$.
- line 81: $rI6 \leftarrow UP(rI6)$.
- line 83: Is $UP(rI6) = P1$?
- line 84: Loop until equal.
- line 86: $UP(rI6) \leftarrow UP(P1)$.
- line 88: $LEFT(P) \leftarrow LEFT(P1)$.
- line 89: $AVAIL \Leftarrow P1$.
- line 92: $P1 \leftarrow LEFT(P)$, to S4. ▮

Note: Using the conventions of Chapter 4, lines 71–74 would actually be coded

LDA 2,3; FMUL 2,2; FCMP 2,5; JE S8; STA TEMP; LDA 2,5; FSUB TEMP;

with a suitable parameter EPSILON in location zero.

17. For each row i and each element $A[i,k] \neq 0$, add $A[i,k]$ times row k of B to row i of C. Maintain only the COL links of C while doing this; the ROW links are easily filled in afterwards. [A. Schoor, *Inf. Proc. Letters* **15** (1982), 87–89.]

18. The three pivot steps, in respective columns 3, 1, 2, yield respectively

$$
\begin{pmatrix} \frac{1}{3} & \frac{2}{3} & \frac{1}{3} \\ -\frac{2}{3} & -\frac{1}{3} & -\frac{2}{3} \\ -\frac{1}{3} & -\frac{2}{3} & -\frac{1}{3} \end{pmatrix},
\quad
\begin{pmatrix} \frac{1}{2} & \frac{1}{2} & 0 \\ -\frac{3}{2} & \frac{1}{2} & 1 \\ -\frac{1}{2} & -\frac{1}{2} & 0 \end{pmatrix},
\quad
\begin{pmatrix} 0 & 1 & 0 \\ -2 & 1 & 1 \\ 1 & -2 & 0 \end{pmatrix};
$$

after the final permutations, we have the answer

$$\begin{pmatrix} 1 & -2 & 1 \\ 0 & 1 & -2 \\ 0 & 0 & 1 \end{pmatrix}.$$

20. $a_0 = \text{LOC}(\text{A}[1,1]) - 3$, $a_1 = 1$ or 2, $a_2 = 3 - a_1$.

21. For example, $\text{M} \leftarrow \max(\text{I},\text{J})$, $\text{LOC}(\text{A}[\text{I},\text{J}]) = \text{LOC}(\text{A}[1,1]) + \text{M}(\text{M}-1) + \text{I} - \text{J}$. (Such formulas have been proposed independently by many people. A. L. Rosenberg and H. R. Strong have suggested the following k-dimensional generalization: $\text{LOC}(\text{A}[\text{I}_1,\ldots,\text{I}_k]) = \text{L}_k$ where $\text{L}_1 = \text{LOC}(\text{A}[1,\ldots,1]) + \text{I}_1 - 1$, $\text{L}_r = \text{L}_{r-1} + (\text{M}_r - 1)^r + (\text{M}_r - \text{I}_r)(\text{M}_r^{r-1} - (\text{M}_r - 1)^{r-1})$, and $\text{M}_r = \max(\text{I}_1,\ldots,\text{I}_r)$ [*IBM Technical Disclosure Bulletin* **14** (1972), 3026–3028]. See *Current Trends in Programming Methodology* **4** (Prentice–Hall, 1978), 263–311, for further results of this kind.)

22. According to the combinatorial number system (exercise 1.2.6–56), we can let

$$p(i_1,\ldots,i_k) = \binom{i_1}{1} + \binom{i_1 + i_2 + 1}{2} + \cdots + \binom{i_1 + i_2 + \cdots + i_k + k - 1}{k}.$$

[*Det Kongelige Norske Videnskabers Selskabs Forhandlinger* **34** (1961), 8–9.]

23. Let $c[\text{J}] = \text{LOC}(\text{A}[0,\text{J}]) = \text{LOC}(\text{A}[0,0]) + m\text{J}$, if there were m rows when the matrix grew from J to J+1 columns; similarly, let $r[\text{I}] = \text{LOC}(\text{A}[\text{I},0]) = \text{LOC}(\text{A}[0,0]) + n\text{I}$, if there were n columns when we created row I. Then we can use the allocation function

$$\text{LOC}(\text{A}[\text{I},\text{J}]) = \begin{cases} \text{I} + c[\text{J}], & \text{if } c[\text{J}] \geq r[\text{I}]; \\ \text{J} + r[\text{I}], & \text{otherwise.} \end{cases}$$

It is not hard to prove that $c[\text{J}] \geq r[\text{I}]$ implies $c[\text{J}] \geq r[\text{I}] + \text{J}$, and $c[\text{J}] \leq r[\text{I}]$ implies $c[\text{J}] + \text{I} \leq r[\text{I}]$; therefore the relation

$$\text{LOC}(\text{A}[\text{I},\text{J}]) = \max(\text{I} + \text{LOC}(\text{A}[0,\text{J}]), \text{J} + \text{LOC}(\text{A}[\text{I},0]))$$

also holds. We need not restrict allocation to mn consecutive locations; the only constraint is that, when the matrix grows, we allocate m or n consecutive new cells in locations greater than those previously used. This construction is due to E. J. Otoo and T. H. Merrett [*Computing* **31** (1983), 1–9], who also generalized it to k dimensions.

24. [Aho, Hopcroft, and Ullman, *The Design and Analysis of Computer Algorithms* (Addison–Wesley, 1974), exercise 2.12.] Besides the array A, maintain also a verification array V of the same size, and a list L of the locations used. Let n be the number of items in L; initially $n = 0$ and the contents of L, A, and V are arbitrary. Whenever you want to access $\text{A}[k]$ for a value of k that you might not have used before, first check whether $0 \leq \text{V}[k] < n$ and $\text{L}[\text{V}[k]] = k$. If not, set $\text{V}[k] \leftarrow n$, $\text{L}[n] \leftarrow k$, $\text{A}[k] \leftarrow 0$, and $n \leftarrow n+1$. Otherwise you can be sure that $\text{A}[k]$ already contains legitimate data. (By a slight extension of this method, it is possible to save and eventually restore the contents of all entries of A and V that change during the computation.)

SECTION 2.3

1. There are three ways to choose the root. Once the root has been chosen, say A, there are three ways to partition the other nodes into subtrees: $\{B\}$, $\{C\}$; $\{C\}$, $\{B\}$; $\{B,C\}$. In the latter case there are two ways to make $\{B,C\}$ into a tree, depending

on which is the root. Hence we get
the four trees shown when A is the
root, and 12 in all. This problem is
solved for any number n of nodes
in exercise 2.3.4.4–23.

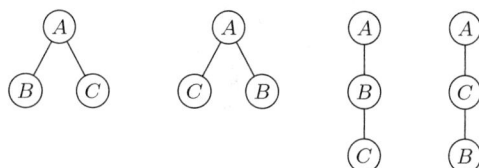

2. The first two trees in the answer to exercise 1 are the same, as oriented trees, so we get only 9 different possibilities in this case. For the general solution, see Section 2.3.4.4, where the formula n^{n-1} is proved.

3. Part 1: To show there is *at least one* such sequence. Let the tree have n nodes. The result is clear when $n = 1$, since X must be the root. If $n > 1$, the definition implies there is a root X_1 and subtrees $T_1, T_2, \ldots, T_m$; either $X = X_1$ or X is a member of a unique T_j. In the latter case, there is by induction a path $X_2, \ldots, X$ where X_2 is the root of T_j, and since X_1 is the parent of X_2 we have a path $X_1, X_2, \ldots, X$.

Part 2: To show there is *at most one* such sequence. We will prove by induction that if X is not the root of the tree, X has a unique parent (so that X_k determines X_{k-1} determines X_{k-2}, etc.) If the tree has one node, there is nothing to prove; otherwise X is in a unique T_j. Either X is the root of T_j, in which case X has a unique parent by definition; or X is not the root of T_j, in which case X has a unique parent in T_j by induction, and no node outside of T_j can be X's parent.

4. True (unfortunately).

5. 4.

6. Let $\mathrm{parent}^{[0]}(X)$ denote X, and let $\mathrm{parent}^{[k+1]}(X) = \mathrm{parent}(\mathrm{parent}^{[k]}(X))$, so that $\mathrm{parent}^{[1]}(X)$ is X's parent, and $\mathrm{parent}^{[2]}(X)$ is X's grandparent; when $k \geq 2$, $\mathrm{parent}^{[k]}(X)$ is X's "(great-)$^{k-2}$grandparent." The requested cousinship condition is that $\mathrm{parent}^{[m+1]}(X) = \mathrm{parent}^{[m+n+1]}(Y)$ but $\mathrm{parent}^{[m]}(X) \neq \mathrm{parent}^{[m+n]}(Y)$. When $n > 0$, this relation is not symmetrical with respect to X and Y, although people usually treat it as symmetrical in everyday conversation.

7. Use the (unsymmetric) condition defined in exercise 6, with the convention that $\mathrm{parent}^{[j]}(X) \neq \mathrm{parent}^{[k]}(Y)$ if either j or k (or both) is -1. To show that this relation is always valid for some unique m and n, consider the Dewey decimal notation for X and Y, namely $1.a_1. \cdots .a_p.b_1. \cdots .b_q$ and $1.a_1. \cdots .a_p.c_1. \cdots .c_r$, where $p \geq 0$, $q \geq 0$, $r \geq 0$ and (if $qr \neq 0$) $b_1 \neq c_1$. The Dewey numbers of any pair of nodes can be written in this form, and clearly we must take $m = q - 1$ and $m + n = r - 1$.

8. *No* binary tree is really a tree; the concepts are quite separate, even though the diagram of a nonempty binary tree may look treelike.

9. A is the root, since we conventionally put the root at the top.

10. Any *finite* collection of nested sets corresponds to a forest as defined in the text, as follows: Let $A_1, \ldots, A_n$ be the sets of the collection that are contained in no other. For fixed j, the sub-collection of all sets contained in A_j is nested; hence we may assume that this sub-collection corresponds to a tree (unordered) with A_j as the root.

11. In a nested collection $\mathcal{C}$ let $X \equiv Y$ if there is some $Z \in \mathcal{C}$ such that $X \cup Y \subseteq Z$. This relation is obviously reflexive and symmetric, and it is in fact an equivalence relation since $W \equiv X$ and $X \equiv Y$ implies that there are Z_1 and Z_2 in $\mathcal{C}$ with $W \subseteq Z_1$, $X \subseteq Z_1 \cap Z_2$, and $Y \subseteq Z_2$. Since $Z_1 \cap Z_2 \neq \emptyset$, either $Z_1 \subseteq Z_2$ or $Z_2 \subseteq Z_1$; hence $W \cup Y \subseteq Z_1 \cup Z_2 \in \mathcal{C}$. Now if $\mathcal{C}$ is a nested collection, define an oriented forest corresponding to $\mathcal{C}$ by the rule "X is an ancestor of Y, and Y is a descendant of X (that is, a *proper* ancestor or descendant), if and only if $X \supset Y$." Each equivalence class of $\mathcal{C}$ corresponds to an oriented tree, which is an oriented forest with $X \equiv Y$ for all X, Y. (We thereby have generalized the definitions of forest and tree that were given for finite collections.) In these terms, we may define the *level* of X as the cardinal number of ancestors(X). Similarly, the *degree* of X is the cardinal number of equivalence classes in the nested collection descendants(X). We say X is the *parent* of Y, and Y is a *child* of X, if X is an ancestor of Y but there is no Z such that $X \supset Z \supset Y$. (It is possible for X to have descendants but no children, ancestors but no parent.) To get *ordered* trees and forests, order the equivalence classes mentioned above in some ad hoc manner, for example by embedding the relation $\subseteq$ into linear order as in exercise 2.2.3–14.

   Example (a): Let $S_{\alpha k} = \{\, x \mid x = .d_1 d_2 d_3 \ldots$ in decimal notation, where $\alpha = .e_1 e_2 e_3 \ldots$ in decimal notation, and $d_j = e_j$ if $j \bmod 2^k \neq 0 \}$. The collection $\mathcal{C} = \{ S_{\alpha k} \mid k \geq 0, 0 < \alpha < 1 \}$ is nested, and gives a tree with infinitely many levels and uncountable degree for each node.

   Example (b), (c): It is convenient to define this set in the plane, instead of in terms of real numbers, and this is sufficient since there is a one-to-one correspondence between the plane and the real numbers. Let $S_{\alpha m n} = \{ (\alpha, y) \mid m/2^n \leq y < (m+1)/2^n \}$, and let $T_\alpha = \{ (x,y) \mid x \leq \alpha \}$. The collection $\mathcal{C} = \{ S_{\alpha m n} \mid 0 < \alpha < 1, n \geq 0, 0 \leq m < 2^n \} \cup \{ T_\alpha \mid 0 < \alpha < 1 \}$ is easily seen to be nested. The children of $S_{\alpha m n}$ are $S_{\alpha(2m)(n+1)}$ and $S_{\alpha(2m+1)(n+1)}$, and T_α has the child $S_{\alpha 00}$ plus the subtree $\{ S_{\beta m n} \mid \beta < \alpha \} \cup \{ T_\beta \mid \beta < \alpha \}$. So each node has degree 2, and each node has uncountably many ancestors of the form T_α. This construction is due to R. Bigelow.

   Note: If we take a suitable well-ordering of the real numbers, and if we define $T_\alpha = \{ (x,y) \mid x \succ \alpha \}$, we can improve this construction slightly, obtaining a nested collection where each node has uncountable level, degree 2, *and* two children.

12. We impose an additional condition on the partial ordering (analogous to that of "nested sets") to ensure that it corresponds to a forest: If $x \preceq y$ and $x \preceq z$ then either $y \preceq z$ or $z \preceq y$. In other words, the elements larger than any given element are linearly ordered. To make a tree, also assert the existence of a largest element r such that $x \preceq r$ for all x. A proof that this gives an unordered tree as defined in the text, when the number of nodes is finite, runs like the proof for nested sets in exercise 10.

13. $a_1.a_2. \cdots .a_k,\ a_1.a_2. \cdots .a_{k-1},\ \ldots,\ a_1.a_2,\ a_1.$

14. Since S is nonempty, it contains an element $1.a_1. \cdots .a_k$ where k is as small as possible; if $k > 0$ we also take a_k as small as possible in S, and we immediately see that k must be 0. In other words, S must contain the element 1. Let 1 be the root. All other elements have $k > 0$, and so the remaining elements of S can be partitioned into sets $S_j = \{ 1.j.a_2. \cdots .a_k \}$, $1 \leq j \leq m$, for some $m \geq 0$. If $m \neq 0$ and S_m is nonempty, we deduce by reasoning as above that $1.j$ is in S_j for each S_j; hence each S_j is nonempty. Then it is easy to see that the sets $S'_j = \{ 1.a_2. \cdots .a_k \mid 1.j.a_2. \cdots .a_k$ is in $S_j \}$ satisfy the same condition as S did. By induction, each of the S_j forms a tree.

15. Let the root be 1, and let the roots of the left and right subtrees of α be $\alpha.0$ and $\alpha.1$, respectively, when such roots exist. For example, King Christian IX appears in two positions of Fig. 18(a), namely 1.0.0.0.0 and 1.1.0.0.1.0. For brevity we may drop the decimal points and write merely 10000 and 110010. *Note:* This notation is due to Francis Galton; see *Natural Inheritance* (Macmillan, 1889), 249. For pedigrees, it is more mnemonic to use F and M in place of 0 and 1 and to drop the initial 1; thus Christian IX is Charles's *MFFMF*, his mother's father's father's mother's father.

The 0 and 1 convention is interesting for another reason: It gives us an important correspondence between nodes in a binary tree and positive integers expressed in the binary system (namely, memory addresses in a computer).

16. (a)

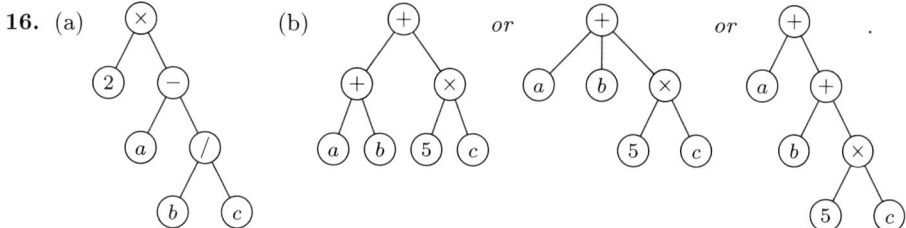

(b)

17. $\mathrm{parent}(Z[1]) = A$; $\mathrm{parent}(Z[1,2]) = C$; $\mathrm{parent}(Z[1,2,2]) = E$.

18. $L[5,1,1] = (2)$. $L[3,1]$ is nonsense, since $L[3]$ is an empty List.

19.

$L[2] = (L)$; $L[2,1,1] = a$.

20. (Intuitively, the correspondence between 0-2-trees and binary trees is obtained by removing all terminal nodes of the 0-2-tree; see the important construction in Section 2.3.4.5.) Let a 0-2-tree with one node correspond to the empty binary tree; and let a 0-2-tree with more than one node, consisting therefore of a root r and 0-2-trees T_1 and T_2, correspond to the binary tree with root r, left subtree T_1', and right subtree T_2', where T_1 and T_2 correspond respectively to T_1' and T_2'.

21. $1 + 0 \cdot n_1 + 1 \cdot n_2 + \cdots + (m-1) \cdot n_m$. *Proof:* The number of nodes in the tree is $n_0 + n_1 + n_2 + \cdots + n_m$, and this also equals $1 +$ (number of children in the tree) $= 1 + 0 \cdot n_0 + 1 \cdot n_1 + 2 \cdot n_2 + \cdots + m \cdot n_m$.

22. The basic idea is to proceed recursively, with the representation of a nonempty binary tree defined to be the representation of its root plus half-size-and-rotated representations of its left and right subtrees. Thus an arbitrarily large binary tree can be represented on a single sheet of paper, if one has a sufficiently powerful magnifying glass.

Many variations on this theme are possible. For example, one idea is to represent the root by a line from the center of a given landscape-oriented page to the top edge, and to rotate the left-subtree representation by 90° clockwise in the left halfpage, the right-subtree representation by 90° counterclockwise in the right halfpage. Each node is then represented by a line. (When this method is applied to a complete binary tree having $2^k - 1$ nodes on k levels, it yields so-called "H-trees," which are the most efficient layouts of such binary trees on a VLSI chip; see R. P. Brent and H. T. Kung, *Inf. Proc. Letters* **11** (1980), 46–48.)

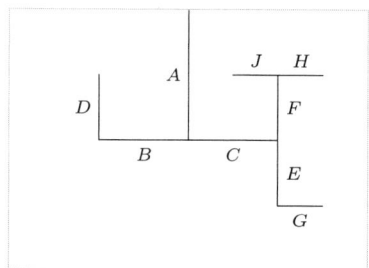

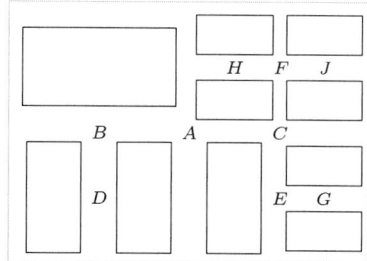

Another idea is to represent an empty binary tree by some sort of box, and to rotate the subtree representations of nonempty binary trees so that left subsubtrees are alternately to the left of or below the corresponding right subsubtrees, depending on whether the depth of recursion is even or odd. Then the boxes correspond to external nodes in an extended binary tree (see Section 2.3.4.5). This representation, which is strongly related to the 2-d trees and quadtrees discussed in Section 6.5, is especially appropriate when the external nodes carry information but the internal nodes do not.

SECTION 2.3.1

1. INFO(T) = A, INFO(RLINK(T)) = C, etc.; the answer is H.

2. Preorder: 1245367; symmetric order: 4251637; postorder: 4526731.

3. The statement is true; notice, for example, that nodes 4, 5, 6, 7 always appear in this order in exercise 2. The result is immediately proved by induction on the size of the binary tree.

4. It is the reverse of postorder. (This is easily proved by induction.)

5. In the tree of exercise 2, for example, preorder is 1, 10, 100, 101, 11, 110, 111, using binary notation (which is in this case equivalent to the Dewey system). The strings of digits have been sorted, like words in a dictionary.

In general, the nodes will be listed in preorder if they are sorted lexicographically from left to right, with "blank" $< 0 < 1$. The nodes will be listed in postorder if they are sorted lexicographically with $0 < 1 <$ "blank". For inorder, use $0 <$ "blank" < 1.

(Moreover, if we imagine the blanks at the left and treat the Dewey labels as ordinary binary numbers, we get *level order*; see 2.3.3–(8).)

6. The fact that $p_1 p_2 \ldots p_n$ is obtainable with a stack is readily proved by induction on n, or in fact we may observe that Algorithm T does precisely what is required in its stack actions. (The corresponding sequence of S's and X's, as in exercise 2.2.1–3, is the same as the sequence of 1s and 2s as subscripts in double order; see exercise 18.)

Conversely, if $p_1 p_2 \ldots p_n$ is obtainable with a stack and if $p_k = 1$, then $p_1 \ldots p_{k-1}$ is a permutation of $\{2, \ldots, k\}$ and $p_{k+1} \ldots p_n$ is a permutation of $\{k+1, \ldots, n\}$; these are the permutations corresponding to the left and right subtrees, and both are obtainable with a stack. The proof now proceeds by induction.

7. From the preorder, the root is known; then from the inorder, we know the left subtree and the right subtree; and in fact we know the preorder and inorder of the nodes in the latter subtrees. Hence the tree is readily constructed (and indeed it is quite amusing to construct a simple algorithm that links the tree together in the normal fashion, starting with the nodes linked together in preorder in LLINK and in inorder in RLINK). Similarly, postorder and inorder together characterize the structure. But preorder and postorder do not; there are two binary trees having AB as preorder and BA as postorder. If all nonterminal nodes of a binary tree have *both* branches nonempty, its structure *is* characterized by preorder and postorder.

8. (a) Binary trees with all LLINKs null. (b) Binary trees with zero or one nodes. (c) Binary trees with all RLINKs null.

9. T1 once, T2 $2n+1$ times, T3 n times, T4 $n+1$ times, T5 n times. These counts can be derived by induction or by Kirchhoff's law, or by examining Program T.

10. A binary tree with all RLINKs null will cause all n node addresses to be put in the stack before any are removed.

11. Let a_{nk} be the number of binary trees with n nodes for which the stack in Algorithm T never contains more than k items. If $g_k(z) = \sum_n a_{nk} z^n$, we find $g_1(z) = 1/(1-z)$, $g_2(z) = 1/(1 - z/(1-z)) = (1-z)/(1-2z)$, ..., $g_k(z) = 1/(1 - zg_{k-1}(z)) = q_{k-1}(z)/q_k(z)$ where $q_{-1}(z) = q_0(z) = 1$, $q_{k+1}(z) = q_k(z) - zq_{k-1}(z)$; hence $g_k(z) = \left(f_1(z)^{k+1} - f_2(z)^{k+1}\right)/\left(f_1(z)^{k+2} - f_2(z)^{k+2}\right)$ where $f_j(z) = \frac{1}{2}(1 \pm \sqrt{1-4z})$. It can now be shown that $a_{nk} = [u^n](1-u)(1+u)^{2n}(1 - u^{k+1})/(1 - u^{k+2})$; hence $s_n = \sum_{k \geq 1} k(a_{nk} - a_{n(k-1)})$ is $[u^{n+1}](1-u)^2(1+u)^{2n}\sum_{j \geq 1} u^j/(1 - u^j)$, minus a_{nn}. The technique of exercise 5.2.2–52 now yields the asymptotic series

$$s_n/a_{nn} = \sqrt{\pi n} - \frac{3}{2} - \frac{13}{24}\sqrt{\frac{\pi}{n}} + \frac{1}{2n} + O(n^{-3/2}).$$

[N. G. de Bruijn, D. E. Knuth, and S. O. Rice, in *Graph Theory and Computing*, ed. by R. C. Read (New York: Academic Press, 1972), 15–22.]

When the binary tree represents a forest as described in Section 2.3.2, the quantity analyzed here is the *height* of that forest (the furthest distance between a node and a root, plus one). Generalizations to many other varieties of trees have been obtained by Flajolet and Odlyzko [*J. Computer and System Sci.* **25** (1982), 171–213]; the asymptotic distribution of heights, both near the mean and far away, was subsequently analyzed by Flajolet, Gao, Odlyzko, and Richmond [*Combinatorics, Probability, and Computing* **2** (1993), 145–156].

12. Visit NODE(P) between steps T2 and T3, instead of in step T5. For the proof, demonstrate the validity of the statement "*Starting at step T2 with ... original value* A[1] ... A[m]," essentially as in the text.

13. (Solution by S. Araújo, 1976.) Let steps T1 through T4 be unchanged, except that a new variable Q is initialized to Λ in step T1′; Q will point to the last node visited, if any. Step T5 becomes two steps:

T5′. [Right branch done?] If RLINK(P) = Λ or RLINK(P) = Q, go on to T6; otherwise set A ⇐ P, P ← RLINK(P) and return to T2′.

T6′. [Visit P.] Visit NODE(P), set Q ← P, and return to T4′.

A similar proof applies. (Steps T4′ and T5′ can be streamlined so that nodes are not taken off the stack and immediately reinserted.)

14. By induction, there are always exactly $n + 1$ Λ links (counting T when it is null). There are n nonnull links, counting T, so the remark in the text about the majority of null links is justified.

15. There is a thread LLINK or RLINK pointing to a node if and only if it has a nonempty right or left subtree, respectively. (See Fig. 24.)

16. If LTAG(Q) = 0, Q* is LLINK(Q); thus Q* is one step down and to the left. Otherwise Q* is obtained by going upwards in the tree (if necessary) repeatedly until the first time it is possible to go down to the right without retracing steps; typical examples are the trips from P to P* and from Q to Q* in the following tree:

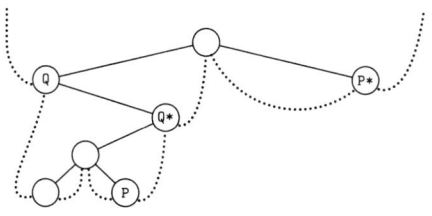

17. If LTAG(P) = 0, set Q ← LLINK(P) and terminate. Otherwise set Q ← P, then set Q ← RLINK(Q) zero or more times until finding RTAG(Q) = 0; finally set Q ← RLINK(Q) once more.

18. Modify Algorithm T by inserting a step T2.5, "Visit NODE(P) the first time"; in step T5, we are visiting NODE(P) the second time.

Given a threaded tree the traversal is extremely simple:

$$(P,1)^\Delta = (\texttt{LLINK(P)},1) \text{ if LTAG(P)} = 0, \text{ otherwise } (P,2);$$
$$(P,2)^\Delta = (\texttt{RLINK(P)},1) \text{ if RTAG(P)} = 0, \text{ otherwise } (\texttt{RLINK(P)},2).$$

In each case, we move at most one step in the tree; in practice, therefore, double order and the values of d and e are embedded in a program and not explicitly mentioned.

Suppressing all the first visits gives us precisely Algorithms T and S; suppressing all the second visits gives us the solutions to exercises 12 and 17.

19. The basic idea is to start by finding the parent Q of P. Then if P ≠ LLINK(Q) we have P♯ = Q; otherwise we can find P♯ by repeatedly setting Q ← Q$ zero or more times until RTAG(Q) = 1. (See, for example, P and P♯ in the tree shown.)

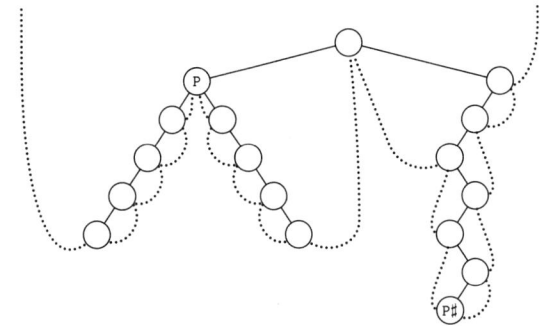

There is no efficient algorithm to find the parent of P in a general right-threaded tree, since a degenerate right-threaded tree in which all left links are null is essentially a circular list in which the links go the wrong way. Therefore we cannot traverse a right-threaded tree in postorder with the same efficiency as the stack method of exercise 13, if we keep no history of how we have reached the current node P.

But if the tree is threaded in both directions, we *can* find P's parent efficiently:

F1. Set Q ← P and R ← P.

F2. If LTAG(Q) = RTAG(R) = 0, set Q ← LLINK(Q) and R ← RLINK(R) and repeat this step. Otherwise go to F4 if RTAG(R) = 1.

F3. Set Q ← LLINK(Q), and terminate if P = RLINK(Q). Otherwise set R ← RLINK(R) zero or more times until RTAG(R) = 1, then set Q ← RLINK(R) and terminate.

F4. Set R ← RLINK(R), and terminate with Q ← R if P = LLINK(R). Otherwise set Q ← LLINK(Q) zero or more times until LTAG(Q) = 1, then set Q ← LLINK(Q) and terminate. ▌

The average running time of Algorithm F is $O(1)$ when P is a random node of the tree. For if we count only the steps Q ← LLINK(Q) when P is a right child, or only the steps R ← RLINK(R) when P is a left child, each link is traversed for exactly one node P.

20. Replace lines 06–09 by: Replace lines 12–13 by:

```
T3  ENT4  0,6                LD4  0,6(LINK)
    LD6   AVAIL              LD5  0,6(INFO)
    J6Z   OVERFLOW           LDX  AVAIL
    LDX   0,6(LINK)          STX  0,6(LINK)
    STX   AVAIL              ST6  AVAIL
    ST5   0,6(INFO)          ENT6 0,4
    ST4   0,6(LINK)
```

If two more lines of code are added at line 06

```
T3  LD3  0,5(LLINK)
    J3Z  T5                  To T5 if LLINK(P) = Λ.
```

with appropriate changes in lines 10 and 11, the running time goes down from $(30n + a + 4)u$ to $(27a + 6n - 22)u$. (This same device would reduce the running time of Program T to $(12a + 6n - 7)u$, which is a slight improvement, if we set $a = (n+1)/2$.)

21. The following solution by Joseph M. Morris [*Inf. Proc. Letters* **9** (1979), 197–200] traverses also in preorder (see exercise 18).

U1. [Initialize.] Set P ← T and R ← Λ.

U2. [Done?] If P = Λ, the algorithm terminates.

U3. [Look left.] Set Q ← LLINK(P). If Q = Λ, visit NODE(P) in preorder and go to U6.

U4. [Search for thread.] Set Q ← RLINK(Q) zero or more times until either Q = R or RLINK(Q) = Λ.

U5. [Insert or remove thread.] If Q ≠ R, set RLINK(Q) ← P and go to U8. Otherwise set RLINK(Q) ← Λ (it had been changed temporarily to P, but we've now traversed P's left subtree).

U6. [Inorder visit.] Visit NODE(P) in inorder.

U7. [Go to right or up.] Set R ← P, P ← RLINK(P), and return to U2.

U8. [Preorder visit.] Visit NODE(P) in preorder.

U9. [Go to left.] Set P ← LLINK(P) and return to step U3. ∎

Morris also suggested a slightly more complicated way to traverse in postorder.

A completely different solution was found by J. M. Robson [*Inf. Proc. Letters* **2** (1973), 12–14]. Let's say that a node is "full" if its LLINK and RLINK are nonnull, "empty" if its LLINK and RLINK are both empty. Robson found a way to maintain a stack of pointers to the full nodes whose right subtrees are being visited, using the link fields in empty nodes!

Yet another way to avoid an auxiliary stack was discovered independently by G. Lindstrom and B. Dwyer, *Inf. Proc. Letters* **2** (1973), 47–51, 143–145. Their algorithm traverses in *triple order* — it visits every node exactly three times, once in each of preorder, inorder, and postorder — but it does not know which of the three is currently being done.

W1. [Initialize.] Set P ← T and Q ← S, where S is a sentinel value — any number that is known to be different from any link in the tree (e.g., −1).

W2. [Bypass null.] If P = Λ, set P ← Q and Q ← Λ.

W3. [Done?] If P = S, terminate the algorithm. (We will have Q = T at termination.)

W4. [Visit.] Visit NODE(P).

W5. [Rotate.] Set R ← LLINK(P), LLINK(P) ← RLINK(P), RLINK(P) ← Q, Q ← P,
P ← R, and return to W2. ∎

Correctness follows from the fact that if we start at W2 with P pointing to the root of
a binary tree T and Q pointing to X, where X is not a link in that tree, the algorithm
will traverse the tree in triple order and reach step W3 with P = X and Q = T.

If $\alpha(T) = x_1 x_2 \ldots x_{3n}$ is the resulting sequence of nodes in triple order, we have
$\alpha(T) = T \ \alpha(\text{LLINK}(T)) \ T \ \alpha(\text{RLINK}(T)) \ T$. Therefore, as Lindstrom observed, the three
subsequences $x_1 x_4 \ldots x_{3n-2}$, $x_2 x_5 \ldots x_{3n-1}$, $x_3 x_6 \ldots x_{3n}$ each include every tree node
just once. (Since x_{j+1} is either the parent or child of x_j, these subsequences visit the
nodes in such a way that each is at most three links away from its predecessor. Section
7.2.1.6 describes a general traversal scheme called *prepostorder* that has this property
not only for binary trees but for trees in general.)

22. This program uses the conventions of Programs T and S, with Q in rI6 and/or rI4.
The old-fashioned MIX computer is not good at comparing index registers for equality,
so variable R is omitted and the test "Q = R" is changed to "RLINK(Q) = P".

01	U1	LD5	HEAD(LLINK)	1	*U1. Initialize.* P ← T.
02	U2A	J5Z	DONE	1	Stop if P = Λ.
03	U3	LD6	0,5(LLINK)	$n+a-1$	*U3. Look left.* Q ← LLINK(P).
04		J6Z	U6	$n+a-1$	To U6 if Q = Λ.
05	U4	CMP5	1,6(RLINK)	$2n-2b$	*U4. Search for thread.*
06		JE	5F	$2n-2b$	Jump if RLINK(Q) = P.
07		ENT4	0,6	$2n-2b-a+1$	rI4 ← Q.
08		LD6	1,6(RLINK)	$2n-2b-a+1$	
09		J6NZ	U4	$2n-2b-a+1$	To U4 with Q ← RLINK(Q) if it's ≠ 0.
10	U5	ST5	1,4(RLINK)	$a-1$	*U5a. Insert thread.* RLINK(Q) ← P.
11	U9	LD5	0,5(LLINK)	$a-1$	*U9. Go to left.* P ← LLINK(P).
12		JMP	U3	$a-1$	To U3.
13	5H	STZ	1,6(RLINK)	$a-1$	*U5b. Remove thread.* RLINK(Q) ← Λ.
14	U6	JMP	VISIT	n	*U6. Inorder visit.*
15	U7	LD5	1,5(RLINK)	n	*U7. Go to right or up.* P ← RLINK(P).
16	U2	J5NZ	U3	n	*U2. Done?* To U3 if P ≠ Λ.
17	DONE	...			∎

The total running time is $21n + 6a - 3 - 14b$, where n is the number of nodes, a is
the number of null RLINKs (hence $a - 1$ is the number of nonnull LLINKs), and b is the
number of nodes on the tree's "right spine" T, RLINK(T), RLINK(RLINK(T)), etc.

23. Insertion to the right: RLINKT(Q) ← RLINKT(P), RLINK(P) ← Q, RTAG(P) ← 0,
LLINK(Q) ← Λ. Insertion to the left, assuming LLINK(P) = Λ: Set LLINK(P) ← Q,
LLINK(Q) ← Λ, RLINK(Q) ← P, RTAG(Q) ← 1. Insertion to the left, between P and
LLINK(P) ≠ Λ: Set R ← LLINK(P), LLINK(Q) ← R, and then set R ← RLINK(R) zero or
more times until RTAG(R) = 1; finally set RLINK(R) ← Q, LLINK(P) ← Q, RLINK(Q) ← P,
RTAG(Q) ← 1.

(A more efficient algorithm for the last case can be used if we know a node F
such that P = LLINK(F) or P = RLINK(F); assuming the latter, for example, we could
set INFO(P) ↔ INFO(Q), RLINK(F) ← Q, LLINK(Q) ← P, RLINKT(Q) ← RLINKT(P),
RLINK(P) ← Q, RTAG(P) ← 1; this takes a fixed amount of time, but it is generally not
recommended because it switches nodes around in memory.)

24. No:

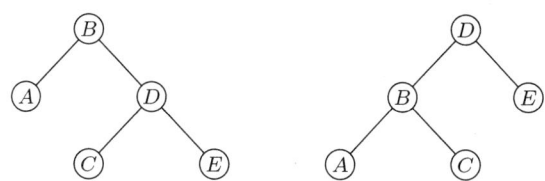

25. We first prove (b), by induction on the number of nodes in T, and similarly (c). Now (a) breaks into several cases; write $T \preceq_1 T'$ if (i) holds, $T \preceq_2 T'$ if (ii) holds, etc. Then $T \preceq_1 T'$ and $T' \preceq T''$ implies $T \preceq_1 T''$; $T \preceq_2 T'$ and $T' \preceq T''$ implies $T \preceq_2 T''$; and the remaining two cases are treated by proving (a) by induction on the number of nodes in T.

26. If the double order of T is $(u_1, d_1), (u_2, d_2), \ldots, (u_{2n}, d_{2n})$ where the u's are nodes and the d's are 1 or 2, form the "trace" of the tree $(v_1, s_1), (v_2, s_2), \ldots, (v_{2n}, s_{2n})$, where $v_j = \mathrm{info}(u_j)$, and $s_j = l(u_j)$ or $r(u_j)$ according as $d_j = 1$ or 2. Now $T \preceq T'$ if and only if the trace of T (as defined here) *lexicographically* precedes or equals the trace of T'. Formally, this means that we have either $n \leq n'$ and $(v_j, s_j) = (v'_j, s'_j)$ for $1 \leq j \leq 2n$, or else there is a k for which $(v_j, s_j) = (v'_j, s'_j)$ for $1 \leq j < k$ and either $v_k \prec v'_k$ or $v_k = v'_k$ and $s_k < s'_k$.

27. R1. [Initialize.] Set $P \leftarrow \mathtt{HEAD}$, $P' \leftarrow \mathtt{HEAD}'$; these are the respective list heads of the given right-threaded binary trees. Go to R3.

    R2. [Check INFO.] If $\mathtt{INFO(P)} \prec \mathtt{INFO(P')}$, terminate $(T \prec T')$; if $\mathtt{INFO(P)} \succ \mathtt{INFO(P')}$, terminate $(T \succ T')$.

    R3. [Go to left.] If $\mathtt{LLINK(P)} = \Lambda = \mathtt{LLINK(P')}$, go to R4; if $\mathtt{LLINK(P)} = \Lambda \neq \mathtt{LLINK(P')}$, terminate $(T \prec T')$; if $\mathtt{LLINK(P)} \neq \Lambda = \mathtt{LLINK(P')}$, terminate $(T \succ T')$; otherwise set $P \leftarrow \mathtt{LLINK(P)}$, $P' \leftarrow \mathtt{LLINK(P')}$, and go to R2.

    R4. [End of tree?] If $P = \mathtt{HEAD}$ (or, equivalently, if $P' = \mathtt{HEAD}'$), terminate (T is equivalent to T').

    R5. [Go to right.] If $\mathtt{RTAG(P)} = 1 = \mathtt{RTAG(P')}$, set $P \leftarrow \mathtt{RLINK(P)}$, $P' \leftarrow \mathtt{RLINK(P')}$, and go to R4. If $\mathtt{RTAG(P)} = 1 \neq \mathtt{RTAG(P')}$, terminate $(T \prec T')$. If $\mathtt{RTAG(P)} \neq 1 = \mathtt{RTAG(P')}$, terminate $(T \succ T')$. Otherwise, set $P \leftarrow \mathtt{RLINK(P)}$, $P' \leftarrow \mathtt{RLINK(P')}$, and go to R2. ∎

    To prove the validity of this algorithm (and therefore to understand how it works), one may show by induction on the size of the tree T_0 that the following statement is valid: *Starting at step R2 with P and P' pointing to the roots of two nonempty right-threaded binary trees T_0 and T'_0, the algorithm will terminate if T_0 and T'_0 are not equivalent, indicating whether $T_0 \prec T'_0$ or $T_0 \succ T'_0$; the algorithm will reach step R4 if T_0 and T'_0 are equivalent, with P and P' then pointing respectively to the successor nodes of T_0 and T'_0 in symmetric order.*

28. Equivalent *and* similar.

29. Prove by induction on the size of T that the following statement is valid: *Starting at step C2 with P pointing to the root of a nonempty binary tree T and with Q pointing to a node that has empty left and right subtrees, the procedure will ultimately arrive at step C6 after setting $\mathtt{INFO(Q)} \leftarrow \mathtt{INFO(P)}$ and attaching copies of the left and right subtrees of $\mathtt{NODE(P)}$ to $\mathtt{NODE(Q)}$, and with P and Q pointing respectively to the preorder successor nodes of the trees T and $\mathtt{NODE(Q)}$.*

30. Assume that the pointer T in (2) is LLINK(HEAD) in (10).

L1. [Initialize.] Set Q ← HEAD, RLINK(Q) ← Q.

L2. [Advance.] Set P ← Q$. (See below.)

L3. [Thread.] If RLINK(Q) = Λ, set RLINK(Q) ← P, RTAG(Q) ← 1; otherwise set RTAG(Q) ← 0. If LLINK(P) = Λ, set LLINK(P) ← Q, LTAG(P) ← 1; otherwise set LTAG(P) ← 0.

L4. [Done?] If P ≠ HEAD, set Q ← P and return to L2. ∎

Step L2 of this algorithm implies the activation of an inorder traversal coroutine like Algorithm T, with the additional proviso that Algorithm T visits HEAD after it has fully traversed the tree. This notation is a convenient simplification in the description of tree algorithms, since we need not repeat the stack mechanisms of Algorithm T over and over again. Of course Algorithm S cannot be used during step L2, since the tree hasn't been threaded yet. But the algorithm of exercise 21 *can* be used in step L2, and this provides us with a very pretty method that threads a tree without using any auxiliary stack.

31. **X1.** Set P ← HEAD.

X2. Set Q ← P$ (using, say, Algorithm S, modified for a right-threaded tree).

X3. If P ≠ HEAD, set AVAIL ⇐ P.

X4. If Q ≠ HEAD, set P ← Q and go back to X2.

X5. Set LLINK(HEAD) ← Λ. ∎

Other solutions that decrease the length of the inner loop are clearly possible, although the order of the basic steps is somewhat critical. The stated procedure works because we never return a node to available storage until after Algorithm S has looked at both its LLINK and its RLINK; as observed in the text, each of these links is used precisely once during a complete tree traversal.

32. RLINK(Q) ← RLINK(P), SUC(Q) ← SUC(P), SUC(P) ← RLINK(P) ← Q, PRED(Q) ← P, PRED(SUC(Q)) ← Q.

33. Inserting NODE(Q) just to the left and below NODE(P) is quite simple: Set LLINKT(Q) ← LLINKT(P), LLINK(P) ← Q, LTAG(P) ← 0, RLINK(Q) ← Λ. Insertion to the right is considerably harder, since it essentially requires finding *Q, which is of comparable difficulty to finding Q♯ (see exercise 19); the node-moving technique discussed in exercise 23 could perhaps be used. So general insertions are more difficult with this type of threading. But the insertions required by Algorithm C are not as difficult as insertions are in general, and in fact the copying process is slightly faster for this kind of threading:

C1. Set P ← HEAD, Q ← U, go to C4. (The assumptions and philosophy of Algorithm C in the text are being used throughout.)

C2. If RLINK(P) ≠ Λ, set R ⇐ AVAIL, LLINK(R) ← LLINK(Q), LTAG(R) ← 1, RLINK(R) ← Λ, RLINK(Q) ← LLINK(Q) ← R.

C3. Set INFO(Q) ← INFO(P).

C4. If LTAG(P) = 0, set R ⇐ AVAIL, LLINK(R) ← LLINK(Q), LTAG(R) ← 1, RLINK(R) ← Λ, LLINK(Q) ← R, LTAG(Q) ← 0.

C5. Set P ← LLINK(P), Q ← LLINK(Q).

C6. If P ≠ HEAD, go to C2. ∎

The algorithm now seems almost too simple to be correct!

Algorithm C for threaded or right-threaded binary trees takes slightly longer due to the extra time to calculate P∗, Q∗ in step C5.

It would be possible to thread RLINKs in the usual way or to put ♯P in RLINK(P), in conjunction with this copying method, by appropriately setting the values of RLINK(R) and RLINKT(Q) in steps C2 and C4.

34. A1. Set Q ← P, and then repeatedly set Q ← RLINK(Q) zero or more times until RTAG(Q) = 1.

A2. Set R ← RLINK(Q). If LLINK(R) = P, set LLINK(R) ← Λ. Otherwise set R ← LLINK(R), then repeatedly set R ← RLINK(R) zero or more times until RLINK(R) = P; then finally set RLINKT(R) ← RLINKT(Q). (This step has removed NODE(P) and its subtrees from the original tree.)

A3. Set RLINK(Q) ← HEAD, LLINK(HEAD) ← P. ∎

(The key to inventing and/or understanding this algorithm is the construction of good "before and after" diagrams.)

36. No; see the answer to exercise 1.2.1–15(e).

37. If LLINK(P) = RLINK(P) = Λ in the representation (2), let LINK(P) = Λ; otherwise let LINK(P) = Q where NODE(Q) corresponds to NODE(LLINK(P)) and NODE(Q + 1) to NODE(RLINK(P)). The condition LLINK(P) or RLINK(P) = Λ is represented by a sentinel in NODE(Q) or NODE(Q + 1) respectively. This representation uses between n and $2n − 1$ memory positions; under the stated assumptions, (2) would require 18 words of memory, compared to 11 in the present scheme. Insertion and deletion operations are approximately of equal efficiency in either representation. But this representation is not quite as versatile in combination with other structures.

SECTION 2.3.2

1. If B is empty, $F(B)$ is an empty forest. Otherwise, $F(B)$ consists of a tree T plus the forest $F\big(\text{right}(B)\big)$, where $\text{root}(T) = \text{root}(B)$ and $\text{subtrees}(T) = F\big(\text{left}(B)\big)$.

2. The number of zeros in the binary notation is the number of decimal points in the decimal notation; the exact formula for the correspondence is

$$a_1.a_2.\cdots.a_k \leftrightarrow 1^{a_1}01^{a_2-1}0\dots01^{a_k-1},$$

where 1^a denotes a ones in a row.

3. Sort the Dewey decimal notations for the nodes lexicographically (from left to right, as in a dictionary), placing a shorter sequence $a_1.\cdots.a_k$ in front of its extensions $a_1.\cdots.a_k.\cdots.a_r$ for preorder, and behind its extensions for postorder. Thus, if we were sorting words instead of sequences of numbers, we would place the words *cat*, *cataract* in the usual dictionary order, to get preorder; we would reverse the order of initial subwords (*cataract*, *cat*), to get postorder. These rules are readily proved by induction on the size of the tree.

4. True, by induction on the number of nodes.

5. (a) Inorder. (b) Postorder. It is interesting to formulate rigorous induction proofs of the equivalence of these traversal algorithms.

6. We have $\text{preorder}(T) = \text{preorder}(T')$, and $\text{postorder}(T) = \text{inorder}(T')$, even if T has nodes with only one child. The remaining two orders are not in any simple relation; for example, the root of T comes at the end in one case and about in the middle in the other.

7. (a) Yes; (b) no; (c) no; (d) yes. Note that reverse preorder of a forest equals postorder of the left-right reversed forest (in the sense of mirror reflection).

8. $T \preceq T'$ means that either $\mathrm{info}(\mathrm{root}(T)) \prec \mathrm{info}(\mathrm{root}(T'))$, or these info's are equal and the following condition holds: Suppose the subtrees of $\mathrm{root}(T)$ are $T_1, \ldots, T_n$ and the subtrees of $\mathrm{root}(T')$ are $T'_1, \ldots, T'_{n'}$, and let $k \geq 0$ be as large as possible such that T_j is equivalent to T'_j for $1 \leq j \leq k$. Then either $k = n$ or $k < n$ and $T_{k+1} \preceq T'_{k+1}$.

9. The number of nonterminal nodes is one less than the number of right links that are Λ, in a nonempty forest, because the null right links correspond to the rightmost child of each nonterminal node, and also to the root of the rightmost tree in the forest. (This fact gives another proof of exercise 2.3.1–14, since the number of null left links is obviously equal to the number of *terminal* nodes.)

10. The forests are similar if and only if $n = n'$ and $d(u_j) = d(u'_j)$, for $1 \leq j \leq n$; they are equivalent if and only if in addition $\mathrm{info}(u_j) = \mathrm{info}(u'_j)$, $1 \leq j \leq n$. The proof is similar to the previous proof, by generalizing Lemma 2.3.1P; let $f(u) = d(u) - 1$.

11.

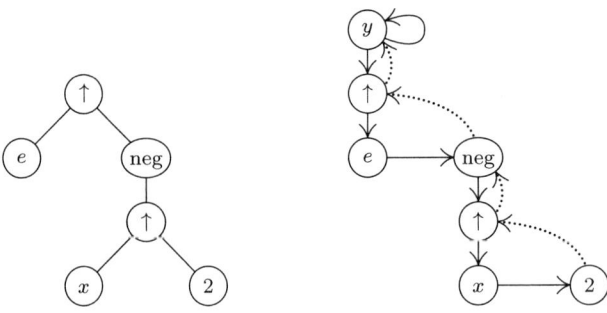

12. If $\mathrm{INFO(Q1)} \neq 0$: Set $\mathrm{R} \leftarrow \mathrm{COPY(P1)}$; then if $\mathrm{TYPE(P2)} = 0$ and $\mathrm{INFO(P2)} \neq 2$, set $\mathrm{R} \leftarrow \mathrm{TREE}(\text{"↑"},\mathrm{R},\mathrm{TREE}(\mathrm{INFO(P2)} - 1))$; if $\mathrm{TYPE(P2)} \neq 0$, set $\mathrm{R} \leftarrow \mathrm{TREE}(\text{"↑"},\mathrm{R}, \mathrm{TREE}(\text{"−"},\mathrm{COPY(P2)},\mathrm{TREE(1)}))$; then set $\mathrm{Q1} \leftarrow \mathrm{MULT(Q1,MULT(COPY(P2),R))}$.

   If $\mathrm{INFO(Q)} \neq 0$: Set $\mathrm{Q} \leftarrow \mathrm{TREE}(\text{"×"},\mathrm{MULT(TREE(\text{"ln"},COPY(P1))},\mathrm{Q}),\mathrm{TREE}(\text{"↑"}, \mathrm{COPY(P1),COPY(P2)}))$.

   Finally go to DIFF[4].

13. The following program implements Algorithm 2.3.1C with $\mathrm{rI1} \equiv \mathrm{P}$, $\mathrm{rI2} \equiv \mathrm{Q}$, $\mathrm{rI3} \equiv \mathrm{R}$, and with appropriate changes to the initialization and termination conditions:

064		ST3	6F(0:2)	Save contents of rI3, rI2.
065		ST2	7F(0:2)	*C1. Initialize.*
066		ENT2	8F	Start by creating NODE(U) with
067		JMP	1F	RLINK(U) = Λ.
068	8H	CON	0	Zero constant for initialization
069	4H	LD1	0,1(LLINK)	Set P $\leftarrow$ LLINK(P) = P*.
070	1H	LD3	AVAIL	R $\Leftarrow$ AVAIL.
071		J3Z	OVERFLOW	
072		LDA	0,3(LLINK)	
073		STA	AVAIL	
074		ST3	0,2(LLINK)	LLINK(Q) $\leftarrow$ R.
075		ENNA	0,2	
076		STA	0,3(RLINKT)	RLINK(R) $\leftarrow$ Q, RTAG(R) $\leftarrow$ 1.

077		INCA	8B	rA ← LOC(init node) − Q.
078		ENT2	0,3	Set Q ← R = Q*.
079		JAZ	C3	To C3, the first time.
080	C2	LDA	0,1	*C2. Anything to right?*
081		JAN	C3	Jump if RTAG(P) = 1.
082		LD3	AVAIL	R ⇐ AVAIL.
083		J3Z	OVERFLOW	
084		LDA	0,3(LLINK)	
085		STA	AVAIL	
086		LDA	0,2(RLINKT)	
087		STA	0,3(RLINKT)	Set RLINKT(R) ← RLINKT(Q).
088		ST3	0,2(RLINKT)	RLINK(Q) ← R, RTAG(Q) ← 0.
089	C3	LDA	1,1	*C3. Copy INFO.*
090		STA	1,2	INFO field copied.
091		LDA	0,1(TYPE)	
092		STA	0,2(TYPE)	TYPE field copied.
093	C4	LDA	0,1(LLINK)	*C4. Anything to left?*
094		JANZ	4B	Jump if LLINK(P) ≠ Λ.
095		STZ	0,2(LLINK)	LLINK(Q) ← Λ.
096	C5	LD2N	0,2(RLINKT)	*C5. Advance.* Q ← −RLINKT(Q).
097		LD1	0,1(RLINK)	P ← RLINK(P).
098		J2P	C5	Jump if RTAG(Q) was 1.
099		ENN2	0,2	Q ← −Q.
100	C6	J2NZ	C2	*C6. Test if complete.*
101		LD1	8B(LLINK)	rI1 ← location of first node created.
102	6H	ENT3	*	Restore index registers.
103	7H	ENT2	*	∎

14. Let a be the number of nonterminal (operator) nodes copied. The number of executions of the various lines in the previous program is as follows: 064–067, 1; 069, a; 070–079, $a + 1$; 080–081, $n − 1$; 082–088, $n − 1 − a$; 089–094, n; 095, $n − a$; 096–098, $n + 1$; 099–100, $n − a$; 101–103, 1. The total time is $(36n + 22)u$; we use about 20% of the time to get available nodes, 40% to traverse, and 40% to copy the INFO and LINK information.

15. Comments are left to the reader.

218	DIV	LDA	1,6
219		JAZ	1F
220		JMP	COPYP2
221		ENTA	SLASH
222		ENTX	0,6
223		JMP	TREE2
224		ENT6	0,1
225	1H	LDA	1,5
226		JAZ	SUB
227		JMP	COPYP2
228		ST1	1F(0:2)
229		ENTA	CON2
230		JMP	TREE0

231		ENTA	UPARROW
232	1H	ENTX	*
233		JMP	TREE2
234		ST1	1F(0:2)
235		JMP	COPYP1
236		ENTA	0,1
237		ENT1	0,5
238		JMP	MULT
239		ENTX	0,1
240	1H	ENT1	*
241		ENTA	SLASH
242		JMP	TREE2
243		ENT5	0,1
244		JMP	SUB ∎

16. Comments are left to the reader.

245	PWR	LDA	1,6	263		JMP	TREE0	281		ENTA	LOG
246		JAZ	4F	264	1H	ENTX	*	282		JMP	TREE1
247		JMP	COPYP1	265		ENTA	MINUS	283		ENTA	0,1
248		ST1	R(0:2)	266		JMP	TREE2	284		ENT1	0,5
249		LDA	0,3(TYPE)	267	5H	LDX	R(0:2)	285		JMP	MULT
250		JANZ	2F	268		ENTA	UPARROW	286		ST1	1F(0:2)
251		LDA	1,3	269		JMP	TREE2	287		JMP	COPYP1
252		DECA	2	270		ST1	R(0:2)	288		ST1	2F(0:2)
253		JAZ	3F	271	3H	JMP	COPYP2	289		JMP	COPYP2
254		INCA	1	272		ENTA	0,1	290	2H	ENTX	*
255		STA	CON0+1	273	R	ENT1	*	291		ENTA	UPARROW
256		ENTA	CON0	274		JMP	MULT	292		JMP	TREE2
257		JMP	TREE0	275		ENTA	0,6	293	1H	ENTX	*
258		STZ	CON0+1	276		JMP	MULT	294		ENTA	TIMES
259		JMP	5F	277		ENT6	0,1	295		JMP	TREE2
260	2H	JMP	COPYP2	278	4H	LDA	1,5	296		ENT5	0,1
261		ST1	1F(0:2)	279		JAZ	ADD	297		JMP	ADD
262		ENTA	CON1	280		JMP	COPYP1				

17. References to early work on such problems can be found in a survey article by
J. Sammet, *CACM* **9** (1966), 555–569.

18. First set LLINK[j] ← RLINK[j] ← j for all j, so that each node is in a circular
list of length 1. Then for $j = n, n - 1, \ldots, 1$ (in this order), if PARENT[j] = 0 set
$r \leftarrow j$, otherwise insert the circular list starting with j into the circular list starting with
PARENT[j] as follows: $k \leftarrow$ PARENT[j], $l \leftarrow$ RLINK[k], $i \leftarrow$ LLINK[j], LLINK[j] ← k,
RLINK[k] ← j, LLINK[l] ← i, RLINK[i] ← l. This works because (a) each nonroot
node is always preceded by its parent or by a descendant of its parent; (b) nodes of
each family appear in their parent's list, in order of location; (c) preorder is the unique
order satisfying (a) and (b).

20. If u is an ancestor of v, it is immediate by induction that u precedes v in preorder
and follows v in postorder. Conversely, suppose u precedes v in preorder and follows
v in postorder; we must show that u is an ancestor of v. This is clear if u is the root
of the first tree. If u is another node of the first tree, v must be also, since u follows v
in postorder; so induction applies. Similarly if u is not in the first tree, v must not be
either, since u precedes v in preorder. (This exercise also follows easily from the result
of exercise 3. It gives us a quick test for ancestorhood, if we know each node's position
in preorder and postorder.)

21. If NODE(P) is a binary operator, pointers to its two operands are P1 = LLINK(P)
and P2 = RLINK(P1) = \$P. Algorithm D makes use of the fact that P2\$ = P, so
that RLINK(P1) may be changed to Q1, a pointer to the derivative of NODE(P1); then
RLINK(P1) is reset later in step D3. For ternary operations, we would have, say,
P1 = LLINK(P), P2 = RLINK(P1), P3 = RLINK(P2) = \$P, so it is difficult to generalize
the binary trick. After computing the derivative Q1, we could set RLINK(P1) ← Q1 temporarily, and then after computing the next derivative Q2 we could set RLINK(Q2) ← Q1
and RLINK(P2) ← Q2 and reset RLINK(P1) ← P2. But this is certainly inelegant, and it
becomes progressively more so as the degree of the operator becomes higher. Therefore
the device of temporarily changing RLINK(P1) in Algorithm D is definitely a *trick*,

not a *technique*. A more aesthetic way to control a differentiation process, because it generalizes to operators of higher degree and does not rely on isolated tricks, can be based on Algorithm 2.3.3F; see exercise 2.3.3–3.

22. From the definition it follows immediately that the relation is transitive; that is, if $T \subseteq T'$ and $T' \subseteq T''$ then $T \subseteq T''$. (In fact the relation is easily seen to be a partial ordering.) If we let f be the function taking nodes into themselves, clearly $l(T) \subseteq T$ and $r(T) \subseteq T$. Therefore if $T \subseteq l(T')$ or $T \subseteq r(T')$ we must have $T \subseteq T'$.

Suppose f_l and f_r are functions that respectively show $l(T) \subseteq l(T')$ and $r(T) \subseteq r(T')$. Let $f(u) = f_l(u)$ if u is in $l(T)$, $f(u) = \text{root}(T')$ if u is root(T), otherwise $f(u) = f_r(u)$. Now it follows easily that f shows $T \subseteq T'$; for example, if we let $r'(T)$ denote $r(T) \setminus \text{root}(T)$ we have preorder$(T) = \text{root}(T)$ preorder$(l(T))$ preorder$(r'(T))$; preorder$(T') = f(\text{root}(T))$ preorder$(l(T'))$ preorder$(r'(T'))$.

The converse does not hold: Consider the subtrees with roots b and b' in Fig. 25.

SECTION 2.3.3

1. Yes, we can reconstruct them just as (3) is deduced from (4), but interchanging LTAG and RTAG, LLINK and RLINK, and using a queue instead of a stack.

2. Make the following changes in Algorithm F: Step F1, change to "last node of the forest in preorder." Step F2, change "$f(x_d), \ldots, f(x_1)$" to "$f(x_1), \ldots, f(x_d)$" in two places. Step F4, "If P is the first node in preorder, terminate the algorithm. (Then the stack contains $f(\text{root}(T_1)), \ldots, f(\text{root}(T_m))$, from top to bottom, where $T_1, \ldots, T_m$ are the trees of the given forest, from left to right.) Otherwise set P to its predecessor in preorder (P ← P − c in the given representation), and return to F2."

3. In step D1, also set S ← Λ. (S is a link variable that links to the top of the stack.) Step D2 becomes, for example, "If NODE(P) denotes a unary operator, set Q ← S, S ← RLINK(Q), P1 ← LLINK(P); if it denotes a binary operator, set Q ← S, Q1 ← RLINK(Q), S ← RLINK(Q1), P1 ← LLINK(P), P2 ← RLINK(P1). Then perform DIFF[TYPE(P)]." Step D3 becomes "Set RLINK(Q) ← S, S ← Q." Step D4 becomes "Set P ← P$." The operation LLINK(DY) ← Q may be avoided in step D5 if we assume that S ≡ LLINK(DY). This technique clearly generalizes to ternary and higher-order operators.

4. A representation like (10) takes $n - m$ LLINKs and $n + (n - m)$ RLINKs. The difference in total number of links is $n - 2m$ between the two forms of representation. Arrangement (10) is superior when the LLINK and INFO fields require about the same amount of space in a node and when m is rather large, namely when the nonterminal nodes have rather large degrees.

5. It would certainly be silly to include threaded RLINKs, since an RLINK thread just points to PARENT anyway. Threaded LLINKs as in 2.3.2–(4) would be useful if it is necessary to move leftward in the tree, for example if we wanted to traverse a tree in reverse postorder, or in family order; but these operations are not significantly harder without threaded LLINKs unless the nodes tend to have very high degrees.

6. L1. Set P ← FIRST, FIRST ← Λ.

L2. If P = Λ, terminate. Otherwise set Q ← RLINK(P).

L3. If PARENT(P) = Λ, set RLINK(P) ← FIRST, FIRST ← P; otherwise set R ← PARENT(P), RLINK(P) ← LCHILD(R), LCHILD(R) ← P.

L4. Set P ← Q and return to L2. ∎

7. $\{1,5\}\{2,3,4,7\}\{6,8,9\}$.

8. Perform step E3 of Algorithm E, then test if $j = k$.

9. PARENT$[k]$:   5   0   2   2   0   8   2   2   8
    k :   1   2   3   4   5   6   7   8   9

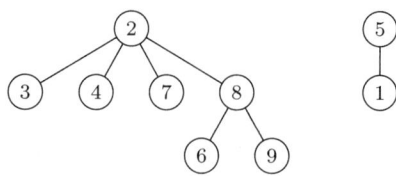

10. One idea is to set PARENT of each *root* node to the negative of the number of nodes in its tree (these values being easily kept up to date); then if $|\text{PARENT}[j]| > |\text{PARENT}[k]|$ in step E4, the roles of j and k are interchanged. This technique (due to M. D. McIlroy) ensures that each operation takes $O(\log n)$ steps.

For still more speed, we can use the following suggestion due to Alan Tritter: In step E4, set PARENT$[x] \leftarrow k$ for all values $x \neq k$ that were encountered in step E3. This makes an extra pass up the trees, but it collapses them so that future searches are faster. (See Section 7.4.1.)

11. It suffices to define the transformation that is done for each input $(\text{P}, j, \text{Q}, k)$:

> **T1.** If PARENT(P) $\neq \Lambda$, set $j \leftarrow j + \text{DELTA(P)}$, P $\leftarrow$ PARENT(P), and repeat this step.
>
> **T2.** If PARENT(Q) $\neq \Lambda$, set $k \leftarrow k + \text{DELTA(Q)}$, Q $\leftarrow$ PARENT(Q), and repeat this step.
>
> **T3.** If P $=$ Q, check that $j = k$ (otherwise the input erroneously contains contradictory equivalences). If P $\neq$ Q, set DELTA(Q) $\leftarrow j - k$, PARENT(Q) $\leftarrow$ P, LBD(P) $\leftarrow \min(\text{LBD(P)}, \text{LBD(Q)} + \text{DELTA(Q)})$, and UBD(P) $\leftarrow \max(\text{UBD(P)}, \text{UBD(Q)} + \text{DELTA(Q)})$. ∎

Note: It is possible to allow the ARRAY X$[l{:}u]$ declarations to occur intermixed with equivalences, or to allow assignment of certain addresses of variables before others are equivalenced to them, etc., under suitable conditions that are not difficult to understand. For further development of this algorithm, see *CACM* **7** (1964), 301–303, 506.

12. (a) Yes. (If this condition is not required, it would be possible to avoid the loops on S that appear in steps A2 and A9.) (b) Yes.

13. The crucial fact is that the UP chain leading upward from P always mentions the same variables and the same exponents for these variables as the UP chain leading upward from Q, except that the latter chain may include additional steps for variables with exponent zero. (This condition holds throughout most of the algorithm, except during the execution of steps A9 and A10.) Now we get to step A8 either from A3 or from A10, and in each case it was verified that EXP(Q) $\neq 0$. Therefore EXP(P) $\neq 0$, and in particular it follows that P $\neq \Lambda$, Q $\neq \Lambda$, UP(P) $\neq \Lambda$, UP(Q) $\neq \Lambda$; the result stated in the exercise now follows. Thus the proof depends on showing that the UP chain condition stated above is preserved by the actions of the algorithm.

16. We prove (by induction on the number of nodes in a *single tree T*) that if P is a pointer to T, and if the stack is initially empty, steps F2 through F4 will end with the single value $f(\text{root}(T))$ on the stack. This is true for $n = 1$. If $n > 1$, there are

$0 < d = \text{DEGREE}(\text{root}(T))$ subtrees $T_1, \ldots, T_d$; by induction and the nature of a stack, and since postorder consists of $T_1, \ldots, T_d$ followed by $\text{root}(T)$, the algorithm computes $f(T_1), \ldots, f(T_d)$, and then $f(\text{root}(T))$, as desired. The validity of Algorithm F for forests follows.

17. G1. Set the stack empty, and let P point to the root of the tree (the last node in postorder). Evaluate $f(\text{NODE(P)})$.

   G2. Push DEGREE(P) copies of $f(\text{NODE(P)})$ onto the stack.

   G3. If P is the first node in postorder, terminate the algorithm. Otherwise set P to its predecessor in postorder (this would be simply $P \leftarrow P - c$ in (9)).

   G4. Evaluate $f(\text{NODE(P)})$ using the value at the top of the stack, which is equal to $f(\text{NODE(PARENT(P))})$. Pop this value off the stack, and return to G2. ∎

Note: An algorithm analogous to this one can be based on preorder instead of postorder as in exercise 2. In fact, family order or level order could be used; in the latter case we would use a queue instead of a stack.

18. The INFO1 and RLINK tables, together with the suggestion for computing LTAG in the text, give us the equivalent of a binary tree represented in the usual manner. The idea is to traverse this tree in postorder, counting degrees as we go:

   P1. Let R, D, and I be stacks that are initially empty; then set $R \Leftarrow n + 1$, $D \Leftarrow 0$, $j \leftarrow 0$, $k \leftarrow 0$.

   P2. If $\text{top}(R) > j + 1$, go to P5. (If an LTAG field were present, we could have tested $\text{LTAG}[j] = 0$ instead of $\text{top}(R) > j + 1$.)

   P3. If I is empty, terminate the algorithm; otherwise set $i \Leftarrow I$, $k \leftarrow k + 1$, $\text{INFO2}[k] \leftarrow \text{INFO1}[i]$, $\text{DEGREE}[k] \Leftarrow D$.

   P4. If $\text{RLINK}[i] = 0$, go to P3; otherwise delete the top of R (which will equal $\text{RLINK}[i]$).

   P5. Set $\text{top}(D) \leftarrow \text{top}(D) + 1$, $j \leftarrow j + 1$, $I \Leftarrow j$, $D \Leftarrow 0$, and if $\text{RLINK}[j] \neq 0$ set $R \Leftarrow \text{RLINK}[j]$. Go to P2. ∎

19. (a) This property is equivalent to saying that SCOPE links do not cross each other. (b) The first tree of the forest contains $d_1 + 1$ elements, and we can proceed by induction. (c) The condition of (a) is preserved when we take minima.

   Notes: By exercise 2.3.2–20, it follows that $d_1 d_2 \ldots d_n$ can also be interpreted in terms of inversions: If the kth node in postorder is the p_kth node in preorder, then d_k is the number of elements $> k$ that appear to the left of k in $p_1 p_2 \ldots p_n$.

   A similar scheme, in which we list the number of descendants of each node in *postorder* of the forest, leads to sequences of numbers $c_1 c_2 \ldots c_n$ characterized by the properties (i) $0 \leq c_k < k$ and (ii) $k \geq j \geq k - c_k$ implies $j - c_j \geq k - c_k$. Algorithms based on such sequences have been investigated by J. M. Pallo, *Comp. J.* **29** (1986), 171–175. Notice that c_k is the size of the left subtree of the kth node in symmetric order of the corresponding binary tree. We can also interpret d_k as the size of the *right* subtree of the kth node in symmetric order of a suitable binary tree, namely the binary tree that corresponds to the given forest by the dual method of exercise 2.3.2–5.

   The relation $d_k \leq d'_k$ for $1 \leq k \leq n$ defines an interesting lattice ordering of forests and binary trees, first introduced in another way by D. Tamari [Thèse (Paris, 1951)]; see exercise 6.2.3–32.

SECTION 2.3.4.1

1. (B, A, C, D, B), (B, A, C, D, E, B), (B, D, C, A, B), (B, D, E, B), (B, E, D, B), (B, E, D, C, A, B).

2. Let $(V_0, V_1, \ldots, V_n)$ be a walk of smallest possible length from V to V'. If now $V_j = V_k$ for some $j < k$, then $(V_0, \ldots, V_j, V_{k+1}, \ldots, V_n)$ would be a shorter walk.

3. (The fundamental path traverses e_3 and e_4 once, but cycle C_2 traverses them -1 times, giving a net total of zero.) Traverse the following edges: e_1, e_2, e_6, e_7, e_9, e_{10}, e_{11}, e_{12}, e_{14}.

4. If not, let G'' be the subgraph of G' obtained by deleting each edge e_j for which $E_j = 0$. Then G'' is a finite graph that has no cycles and at least one edge, so by the proof of Theorem A there is at least one vertex, V, that is adjacent to exactly one other vertex, V'. Let e_j be the edge joining V to V'; then Kirchhoff's equation (1) at vertex V is $E_j = 0$, contradicting the definition of G''.

5. $A = 1 + E_8$, $B = 1 + E_8 - E_2$, $C = 1 + E_8$, $D = 1 + E_8 - E_5$, $E = 1 + E_{17} - E_{21}$, $F = 1 + E_{13}'' + E_{17} - E_{21}$, $G = 1 + E_{13}''$, $H = E_{17} - E_{21}$, $J = E_{17}$, $K = E_{19}'' + E_{20}$, $L = E_{17} + E_{19}'' + E_{20} - E_{21}$, $P = E_{17} + E_{20} - E_{21}$, $Q = E_{20}$, $R = E_{17} - E_{21}$, $S = E_{25}$. *Note:* In this case it is also possible to solve for $E_2, E_5, \ldots, E_{25}$ in terms of $A, B, \ldots, S$; hence there are nine independent solutions, explaining why we eliminated six variables in Eq. 1.3.3–(8).

6. (The following solution is based on the idea that we may print out each edge that does not make a cycle with the preceding edges.) Use Algorithm 2.3.3E, with each pair (a_i, b_i) representing $a_i \equiv b_i$ in the notation of that algorithm. The only change is to print (a_i, b_i) if $j \neq k$ in step E4.

To show that this algorithm is valid, we must prove that (a) the algorithm prints out no edges that form a cycle, and (b) if G contains at least one free subtree, the algorithm prints out $n - 1$ edges. Define $j \equiv k$ if there exists a path from V_j to V_k or if $j = k$. This is clearly an equivalence relation, and moreover $j \equiv k$ if and only if this relation can be deduced from the equivalences $a_1 \equiv b_1$, $\ldots$, $a_m \equiv b_m$. Now (a) holds because the algorithm prints out no edges that form a cycle with previously printed edges; (b) is true because PARENT$[k] = 0$ for precisely one k if all vertices are equivalent.

A more efficient algorithm can, however, be based on depth-first search; see Algorithm 2.3.5A and Section 7.4.1.

7. Fundamental cycles: $C_0 = e_0 + e_1 + e_4 + e_9$ (fundamental path is $e_1 + e_4 + e_9$); $C_5 = e_5 + e_3 + e_2$; $C_6 = e_6 - e_2 + e_4$; $C_7 = e_7 - e_4 - e_3$; $C_8 = e_8 - e_9 - e_4 - e_3$. Therefore we find $E_1 = 1$, $E_2 = E_5 - E_6$, $E_3 = E_5 - E_7 - E_8$, $E_4 = 1 + E_6 - E_7 - E_8$, $E_9 = 1 - E_8$.

8. Each step in the reduction process combines two arrows e_i and e_j that start at the same box, and it suffices to prove that such steps can be reversed. Thus we are given the value of $e_i + e_j$ after combination, and we must assign consistent values to e_i and e_j before the combination. There are three essentially different situations:

Case 1	Case 2	Case 3

Before

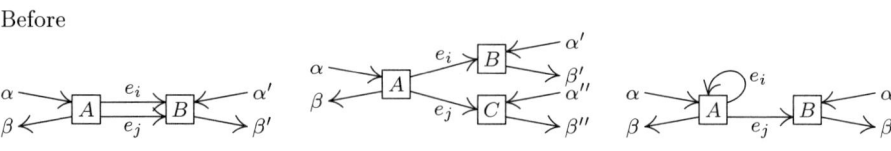

After

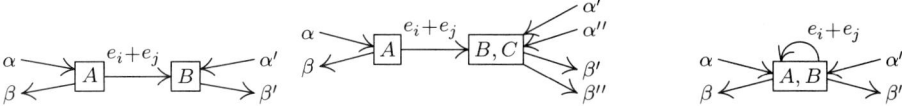

Here A, B, and C stand for vertices or supervertices, and the α's and β's stand for the other given flows besides $e_i + e_j$; these flows may each be distributed among several edges, although only one is shown. In Case 1 (e_i and e_j lead to the same box), we may choose e_i arbitrarily, then $e_j \leftarrow (e_i + e_j) - e_i$. In Case 2 ($e_i$ and e_j lead to different boxes), we must set $e_i \leftarrow \beta' - \alpha'$, $e_j \leftarrow \beta'' - \alpha''$. In Case 3 ($e_i$ is a loop but e_j is not), we must set $e_j \leftarrow \beta' - \alpha'$, $e_i \leftarrow (e_i + e_j) - e_j$. In each case we have reversed the combination step as desired.

The result of this exercise essentially proves that the number of fundamental cycles in the reduced flow chart is the minimum number of vertex flows that must be measured to determine all the others. In the given example, the reduced flow chart reveals that only three vertex flows (e.g., a, c, d) need to be measured, while the original chart of exercise 7 has four independent edge flows. We save one measurement every time Case 1 occurs during the reduction.

A similar reduction procedure could be based on combining the arrows flowing *into* a given box, instead of those flowing out. It can be shown that this would yield the same reduced flow chart, except that the supervertices would contain different names.

The construction in this exercise is based on ideas due to Armen Nahapetian and F. Stevenson. For further comments, see A. Nahapetian, *Acta Informatica* **3** (1973), 37–41; D. E. Knuth and F. Stevenson, *BIT* **13** (1973), 313–322.

9. Each edge from a vertex to itself becomes a "fundamental cycle" all by itself. If there are $k + 1$ edges $e, e', \ldots, e^{(k)}$ between vertices V and V', make k fundamental cycles $e' \pm e$, $\ldots$, $e^{(k)} \pm e$ (choosing $+$ or $-$ according as the edges go in the opposite or the same direction), and then proceed as if only edge e were present.

Actually this situation would be much simpler conceptually if we had defined a graph in such a way that multiple edges are allowed between vertices, and edges are allowed from a vertex to itself; paths and cycles would be defined in terms of edges instead of vertices. Such a definition is, in fact, made for directed graphs in Section 2.3.4.2.

10. If the terminals have all been connected together, the corresponding graph must be connected in the technical sense. A minimum number of wires will involve no cycles, so we must have a free tree. By Theorem A, a free tree contains $n - 1$ wires, and a graph with n vertices and $n - 1$ edges is a free tree if and only if it is connected.

11. It is sufficient to prove that when $n > 1$ and $c(n - 1, n)$ is the minimum of the $c(i, n)$, there exists at least one minimum cost tree in which T_{n-1} is wired to T_n. (For, any minimum cost tree with $n > 1$ terminals and with T_{n-1} wired to T_n must also be a minimum cost tree with $n - 1$ terminals if we regard T_{n-1} and T_n as "common," using the convention stated in the algorithm.)

To prove the statement above, suppose we have a minimum cost tree in which T_{n-1} is not wired to T_n. If we add the wire $T_{n-1} \longrightarrow T_n$ we obtain a cycle, and any of the other wires in that cycle may be removed; removing the other wire touching T_n gives us another tree, whose total cost is not greater than the original, and $T_{n-1} \longrightarrow T_n$ appears in that tree.

12. Keep two auxiliary tables, $a(i)$ and $b(i)$, for $1 \le i < n$, representing the fact that the cheapest connection from T_i to a chosen terminal is to $T_{b(i)}$, and its cost is $a(i)$; initially $a(i) = c(i, n)$ and $b(i) = n$. Then do the following operation $n - 1$ times: Find i such that $a(i) = \min_{1 \le j < n} a(j)$; connect T_i to $T_{b(i)}$; for $1 \le j < n$ if $c(i, j) < a(j)$ set $a(j) \leftarrow c(i, j)$ and $b(j) \leftarrow i$; and set $a(i) \leftarrow \infty$. Here $c(i, j)$ means $c(j, i)$ when $j < i$.

(It is somewhat more efficient to avoid the use of ∞, keeping instead a one-way linked list of those j that have not yet been chosen. With or without this straightforward improvement, the algorithm takes $O(n^2)$ operations.) See also E. W. Dijkstra, *Proc. Nederl. Akad. Wetensch.* **A63** (1960), 196–199; D. E. Knuth, *The Stanford GraphBase* (New York: ACM Press, 1994), 460–497. Significantly better algorithms to find a minimum-cost spanning tree are discussed in Section 7.5.4.

13. If there is no path from V_i to V_j, for some $i \ne j$, then no product of the transpositions will move i to j. So if all permutations are generated, the graph must be connected. Conversely if it is connected, remove edges if necessary until we have a free tree. Then renumber the vertices so that V_n is adjacent to only one other vertex, namely V_{n-1}. (See the proof of Theorem A.) Now the transpositions other than $(n-1 \ n)$ form a free tree with $n - 1$ vertices; so by induction if π is any permutation of $\{1, 2, \ldots, n\}$ that leaves n fixed, π can be written as a product of those transpositions. If π moves n to j then $\pi(j \ n-1)(n-1 \ n) = \rho$ fixes n; hence $\pi = \rho(n-1 \ n)(j \ n-1)$ can be written as a product of the given transpositions.

SECTION 2.3.4.2

1. Let $(e_1, \ldots, e_n)$ be an oriented walk of smallest possible length from V to V'. If now $\text{init}(e_j) = \text{init}(e_k)$ for $j < k$, $(e_1, \ldots, e_{j-1}, e_k, \ldots, e_n)$ would be a shorter walk; a similar argument applies if $\text{fin}(e_j) = \text{fin}(e_k)$ for $j < k$. Hence $(e_1, \ldots, e_n)$ is simple.

2. Those cycles in which all signs are the same: C_0, C_8, C_{13}'', C_{17}, C_{19}'', C_{20}.

3. For example, use three vertices A, B, C, with arcs from A to B and A to C.

4. If there are no oriented cycles, Algorithm 2.2.3T topologically sorts G. If there is an oriented cycle, topological sorting is clearly impossible. (Depending on how this exercise is interpreted, oriented cycles of length 1 could be excluded from consideration.)

5. Let k be the smallest integer such that $\text{fin}(e_k) = \text{init}(e_j)$ for some $j \le k$. Then $(e_j, \ldots, e_k)$ is an oriented cycle.

6. False (on a technicality), just because there may be several different arcs from one vertex to another.

7. True for finite directed graphs: If we start at any vertex V and follow the only possible oriented path, we never encounter any vertex twice, so we must eventually reach the vertex R (the only vertex with no successor). For infinite directed graphs the result is obviously false since we might have vertices $R, V_1, V_2, V_3, \ldots$ and arcs from V_j to V_{j+1} for $j \ge 1$.

9. All arcs point upward.

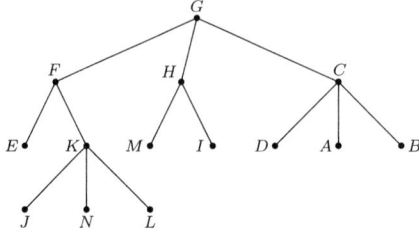

10. G1. Set $k \leftarrow P[j]$, $P[j] \leftarrow 0$.

    G2. If $k = 0$, stop; otherwise set $m \leftarrow P[k]$, $P[k] \leftarrow j$, $j \leftarrow k$, $k \leftarrow m$, and repeat step G2. ∎

11. This algorithm combines Algorithm 2.3.3E with the method of the preceding exercise, so that all oriented trees have arcs that correspond to actual arcs in the directed graph; $S[j]$ is an auxiliary table that tells whether an arc goes from j to $P[j]$ ($S[j] = +1$) or from $P[j]$ to j ($S[j] = -1$). Initially $P[1] = \cdots = P[n] = 0$. The following steps may be used to process each arc (a, b):

    C1. Set $j \leftarrow a$, $k \leftarrow P[j]$, $P[j] \leftarrow 0$, $s \leftarrow S[j]$.

    C2. If $k = 0$, go to C3; otherwise set $m \leftarrow P[k]$, $t \leftarrow S[k]$, $P[k] \leftarrow j$, $S[k] \leftarrow -s$, $s \leftarrow t$, $j \leftarrow k$, $k \leftarrow m$, and repeat step C2.

    C3. (Now a appears as the root of its tree.) Set $j \leftarrow b$, and then if $P[j] \neq 0$ repeatedly set $j \leftarrow P[j]$ until $P[j] = 0$.

    C4. If $j = a$, go to C5; otherwise set $P[a] \leftarrow b$, $S[a] \leftarrow +1$, print (a, b) as an arc belonging to the free subtree, and terminate.

    C5. Print "CYCLE" followed by "(a, b)".

    C6. If $P[b] = 0$ terminate. Otherwise if $S[b] = +1$, print "$+(b, P[b])$", else print "$-(P[b], b)$"; set $b \leftarrow P[b]$ and repeat step C6. ∎

Note: This algorithm will take at most $O(m \log n)$ steps if we incorporate the suggestion of McIlroy in answer 2.3.3–10. But there is a much better solution that needs only $O(m)$ steps: Use depth-first search to construct a "palm tree," with one fundamental cycle for each "frond" [R. E. Tarjan, *SICOMP* **1** (1972), 146–150].

12. It equals the in-degree; the out-degree of each vertex can be only 0 or 1.

13. Define a sequence of oriented subtrees of G as follows: G_0 is the vertex R alone. G_{k+1} is G_k, plus any vertex V of G that is not in G_k but for which there is an arc from V to V' where V' *is* in G_k, plus one such arc $e[V]$ for each such vertex. It is immediate by induction that G_k is an oriented tree for all $k \geq 0$, and that if there is an oriented path of length k from V to R in G then V is in G_k. Therefore G_∞, the set of all V and $e[V]$ in any of the G_k, is the desired oriented subtree of G.

14. $(e_{12}, e_{20}, e_{00}, e'_{01}, e_{10}, e_{01}, e'_{12}, e_{22}, e_{21})$, $(e_{12}, e_{20}, e_{00}, e'_{01}, e'_{12}, e_{22}, e_{21}, e_{10}, e_{01})$,
    $(e_{12}, e_{20}, e'_{01}, e_{10}, e_{00}, e_{01}, e'_{12}, e_{22}, e_{21})$, $(e_{12}, e_{20}, e'_{01}, e'_{12}, e_{22}, e_{21}, e_{10}, e_{00}, e_{01})$,
    $(e_{12}, e_{22}, e_{20}, e_{00}, e'_{01}, e_{10}, e_{01}, e'_{12}, e_{21})$, $(e_{12}, e_{22}, e_{20}, e_{00}, e'_{01}, e'_{12}, e_{21}, e_{10}, e_{01})$,
    $(e_{12}, e_{22}, e_{20}, e'_{01}, e_{10}, e_{00}, e_{01}, e'_{12}, e_{21})$, $(e_{12}, e_{22}, e_{20}, e'_{01}, e'_{12}, e_{21}, e_{10}, e_{00}, e_{01})$,

in lexicographic order; the eight possibilities come from the independent choices of which of e_{00} or e'_{01}, e_{10} or e'_{12}, e_{20} or e_{22}, should precede the other.

15. True for finite graphs: If it is connected and balanced and has more than one vertex, it has an Eulerian trail that touches all the vertices. (But false in general.)

16. Consider the directed graph G with vertices $V_1, \ldots, V_{13}$ and with an arc from V_j to V_k for each k in pile j; this graph is balanced. Winning the game is equivalent to tracing out an Eulerian trail in G, because the game ends when the fourth arc to V_{13} is encountered (namely, when the fourth king turns up). Now if the game is won, the stated digraph is an oriented subtree by Lemma E. Conversely if the stated digraph is an oriented tree, the game is won by Theorem D.

17. $\frac{1}{13}$. This answer can be obtained, as the author first obtained it, by laborious enumeration of oriented trees of special types and the application of generating functions, etc., based on the methods of Section 2.3.4.4. But such a simple answer deserves a simple, direct proof, and indeed there is one [see Tor B. Staver, *Norsk Matematisk Tidsskrift* **28** (1946), 88–89]. Define an order for turning up *all* cards of the deck, as follows: Obey the rules of the game until getting stuck, then "cheat" by turning up the first available card (find the first pile that is not empty, going clockwise from pile 1) and continue as before, until eventually all cards have been turned up. The cards *in the order of turning up* are in completely random order (since the value of a card need not be specified until after it is turned up). So the problem is just to calculate the probability that in a randomly shuffled deck the last card is a king. More generally the probability that k cards are still face down when the game is over is the probability that the last king in a random shuffle is followed by k cards, namely $4!\binom{51-k}{3}\frac{48!}{52!}$. Hence a person playing this game without cheating will turn up an average of exactly 42.4 cards per game. *Note:* Similarly, it can be shown that the probability that the player will have to "cheat" k times in the process described above is exactly given by the Stirling number $\left[\begin{smallmatrix}13\\k+1\end{smallmatrix}\right]/13!$. (See Eq. 1.2.10–(9) and exercise 1.2.10–7; the case of a more general card deck is considered in exercise 1.2.10–18.)

18. (a) If there is a cycle $(V_0, V_1, \ldots, V_k)$, where necessarily $3 \le k \le n$, the sum of the k rows of A corresponding to the k edges of this cycle, with appropriate signs, is a row of zeros; so if G is not a free tree the determinant of A_0 is zero.

But if G is a free tree we may regard it as an ordered tree with root V_0, and we can rearrange the rows and columns of A_0 so that columns are in preorder and so that the kth row corresponds to the edge from the kth vertex (column) to its parent. Then the matrix is triangular with ± 1's on the diagonal, so the determinant is ± 1.

(b) By the Binet–Cauchy formula (exercise 1.2.3–46) we have

$$\det A_0^T A_0 = \sum_{1 \le i_1 < \cdots < i_n \le m} (\det A_{i_1 \ldots i_n})^2$$

where $A_{i_1 \ldots i_n}$ represents a matrix consisting of rows $i_1, \ldots, i_n$ of A_0 (thus corresponding to a choice of n edges of G). The result now follows from (a).

[See S. Okada and R. Onodera, *Bull. Yamagata Univ.* **2** (1952), 89–117.]

19. (a) The conditions $a_{00} = 0$ and $a_{jj} = 1$ are just conditions (a), (b) of the definition of oriented tree. If G is not an oriented tree there is an oriented cycle (by exercise 7), and the rows of A_0 corresponding to the vertices in this oriented cycle will sum to a row of zeros; hence $\det A_0 = 0$. If G is an oriented tree, assign an arbitrary order to the children of each family and regard G as an ordered tree. Now permute rows and columns of A_0 until they correspond to preorder of the vertices. Since the same permutation has been applied to the rows as to the columns, the determinant is unchanged; and the resulting matrix is triangular with $+1$ in every diagonal position.

(b) We may assume that $a_{0j} = 0$ for all j, since no arc emanating from V_0 can participate in an oriented subtree. We may also assume that $a_{jj} > 0$ for all $j \ge 1$ since otherwise the whole jth row is zero and there obviously are no oriented subtrees. Now use induction on the number of arcs: If $a_{jj} > 1$ let e be some arc leading from V_j; let B_0 be a matrix like A_0 but with arc e deleted, and let C_0 be the matrix like A_0 but with all arcs *except* e that lead from V_j deleted. *Example:* If $A_0 = \left(\begin{smallmatrix} 3 & -2 \\ -1 & 2 \end{smallmatrix}\right)$, $j = 1$, and e is an arc from V_1 to V_0, then $B_0 = \left(\begin{smallmatrix} 2 & -2 \\ -1 & 2 \end{smallmatrix}\right)$, $C_0 = \left(\begin{smallmatrix} 1 & 0 \\ -1 & 2 \end{smallmatrix}\right)$. In general we have $\det A_0 = \det B_0 + \det C_0$, since the matrices agree in all rows except row j, and A_0 is the sum of B_0 and C_0 in that row. Moreover, the number of oriented subtrees of G is the number of subtrees that do *not* use e (namely, $\det B_0$, by induction) plus the number that *do* use e (namely, $\det C_0$).

Notes: The matrix A is often called the *Laplacian* of the graph, by analogy with a similar concept in the theory of partial differential equations. If we delete any set S of rows from the matrix A, and the same set of columns, the determinant of the resulting matrix is the number of oriented forests whose roots are the vertices $\{V_k \mid k \in S\}$ and whose arcs belong to the given digraph. The matrix tree theorem for oriented trees was stated without proof by J. J. Sylvester in 1857 (see exercise 28), then forgotten for many years until it was independently rediscovered by W. T. Tutte [*Proc. Cambridge Phil. Soc.* **44** (1948), 463–482, §3]. The first published proof in the special case of *undirected* graphs, when the matrix A is symmetric, was given by C. W. Borchardt [*Crelle* **57** (1860), 111–121]. Several authors have ascribed the theorem to Kirchhoff, but Kirchhoff proved a quite different (though related) result.

20. Using exercise 18 we find $B = A_0^T A_0$. Or, using exercise 19, B is the matrix A_0 for the directed graph G' with two arcs (one in each direction) in place of each edge of G; each free subtree of G corresponds uniquely to an oriented subtree of G' with root V_0, since the directions of the arcs are determined by the choice of root.

21. Construct the matrices A and A^* as in exercise 19. For the example graphs G and G^* in Figs. 36 and 37,

$$
A = \begin{pmatrix} 2 & -2 & 0 \\ -1 & 3 & -2 \\ -1 & -1 & 2 \end{pmatrix}, \quad
A^* = \begin{array}{c} \\ [00] \\ [10] \\ [20] \\ [01] \\ [01] \\ [21] \\ [12] \\ [12] \\ [22] \end{array}
\begin{array}{ccc|ccc|ccc}
[00] & [10] & [20] & [01] & [01] & [21] & [12] & [12] & [22] \\
\hline
2 & 0 & 0 & -1 & -1 & 0 & 0 & 0 & 0 \\
-1 & 3 & 0 & -1 & -1 & 0 & 0 & 0 & 0 \\
-1 & 0 & 3 & -1 & -1 & 0 & 0 & 0 & 0 \\
0 & -1 & 0 & 3 & 0 & 0 & -1 & -1 & 0 \\
0 & -1 & 0 & 0 & 3 & 0 & -1 & -1 & 0 \\
0 & -1 & 0 & 0 & 0 & 3 & -1 & -1 & 0 \\
0 & 0 & -1 & 0 & 0 & -1 & 3 & 0 & -1 \\
0 & 0 & -1 & 0 & 0 & -1 & 0 & 3 & -1 \\
0 & 0 & -1 & 0 & 0 & -1 & 0 & 0 & 2
\end{array}.
$$

Add the indeterminate λ to every diagonal element of A and A^*. If $t(G)$ and $t(G^*)$ are the numbers of oriented subtrees of G and G^*, we then have $\det A = \lambda t(G) + O(\lambda^2)$, $\det A^* = \lambda t(G^*) + O(\lambda^2)$. (The number of oriented subtrees of a balanced graph is the same for any given root, by exercise 22, but we do not need that fact.)

If we group vertices V_{jk} for equal k the matrix A^* can be partitioned as shown above. Let $B_{kk'}$ be the submatrix of A^* consisting of the rows for V_{jk} and the columns for $V_{j'k'}$, for all j and j' such that V_{jk} and $V_{j'k'}$ are in G^*. By adding the 2nd, ..., mth columns of each submatrix to the first column and then subtracting the first row of each submatrix from the 2nd, ..., mth rows, the matrix A^* is transformed so that

$$
B_{kk'} = \begin{pmatrix} a_{kk'} & * & \cdots & * \\ 0 & 0 & \cdots & 0 \\ \vdots & \vdots & \ddots & \vdots \\ 0 & 0 & \cdots & 0 \end{pmatrix} \quad \text{for } k \neq k', \qquad
B_{kk} = \begin{pmatrix} \lambda + a_{kk} & * & \cdots & * \\ 0 & \lambda + m & \cdots & 0 \\ \vdots & \vdots & \ddots & \vdots \\ 0 & 0 & \cdots & \lambda + m \end{pmatrix}.
$$

The asterisks in the top rows of the transformed submatrices turn out to be irrelevant, because the determinant of A^* is now seen to be $(\lambda + m)^{(m-1)n}$ times

$$
\det \begin{pmatrix} \lambda + a_{00} & a_{01} & \cdots & a_{0(n-1)} \\ a_{10} & \lambda + a_{11} & \cdots & a_{1(n-1)} \\ \vdots & \vdots & \ddots & \vdots \\ a_{(n-1)0} & a_{(n-1)1} & \cdots & \lambda + a_{(n-1)(n-1)} \end{pmatrix} = \lambda t(G) + O(\lambda^2).
$$

Notice that when $n = 1$ and there are m arcs from V_0 to itself, we find in particular that exactly m^{m-1} oriented trees are possible on m labeled nodes. This result will be obtained by quite different methods in Section 2.3.4.4.

This derivation can be generalized to determine the number of oriented subtrees of G^* when G is an *arbitrary* directed graph; see R. Dawson and I. J. Good, *Ann. Math. Stat.* **28** (1957), 946–956; D. E. Knuth, *Journal of Combinatorial Theory* **3** (1967), 309–314. An alternative, purely combinatorial proof has been given by J. B. Orlin, *Journal of Combinatorial Theory* **B25** (1978), 187–198.

22. The total number is $(\sigma_1 + \cdots + \sigma_n)$ times the number of Eulerian trails starting with a given edge e_1, where $\text{init}(e_1) = V_1$. Each such trail determines an oriented subtree with root V_1 by Lemma E, and for each of the T oriented subtrees there are $\prod_{j=1}^{n}(\sigma_j - 1)!$ walks satisfying the three conditions of Theorem D, corresponding to the different order in which the arcs $\{e \mid \text{init}(e) = V_j, e \neq e[V_j], e \neq e_1\}$ are entered into P. (Exercise 14 provides a simple example.)

23. Construct the directed graph G_k with m^{k-1} vertices as in the hint, and denote by $[x_1, \ldots, x_k]$ the arc mentioned there. For each function that has maximum period length, we can define a unique corresponding Eulerian trail, by letting $f(x_1, \ldots, x_k) = x_{k+1}$ if arc $[x_1, \ldots, x_k]$ is followed by $[x_2, \ldots, x_{k+1}]$. (We regard Eulerian trails as being the same if one is just a cyclic permutation of the other.) Now $G_k = G_{k-1}^*$ in the sense of exercise 21, so G_k has $m^{m^{k-1}-m^{k-2}}$ times as many oriented subtrees as G_{k-1}; by induction G_k has $m^{m^{k-1}-1}$ oriented subtrees, and $m^{m^{k-1}-k}$ with a given root. Therefore by exercise 22 the number of functions with maximum period, namely the number of Eulerian trails of G_k starting with a given arc, is $m^{-k}(m!)^{m^{k-1}}$. [For $m = 2$ this result is due to C. Flye Sainte-Marie, *L'Intermédiaire des Mathématiciens* **1** (1894), 107–110.]

24. Define a new directed graph having E_j copies of e_j, for $0 \leq j \leq m$. This graph is balanced, hence it contains an Eulerian trail $(e_0, \ldots)$ by Theorem G. The desired oriented walk comes by deleting the edge e_0 from this Eulerian trail.

25. Assign an arbitrary order to all arcs in the sets $I_j = \{e \mid \text{init}(e) = V_j\}$ and $F_j = \{e \mid \text{fin}(e) = V_j\}$. For each arc e in I_j, let $\text{ATAG}(e) = 0$ and $\text{ALINK}(e) = e'$ if e' follows e in the ordering of I_j; also let $\text{ATAG}(e) = 1$ and $\text{ALINK}(e) = e'$ if e is last in I_j and e' is first in F_j. Let $\text{ALINK}(e) = \Lambda$ in the latter case if F_j is empty. Define BLINK and BTAG by the same rules, reversing the roles of init and fin.

Examples (using alphabetic order in each set of arcs):

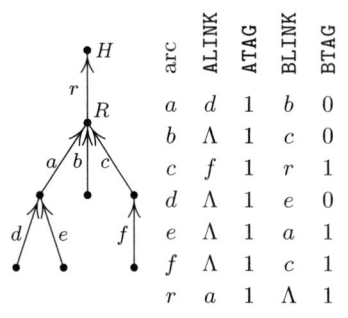

arc	ALINK	ATAG	BLINK	BTAG
a	d	1	b	0
b	Λ	1	c	0
c	f	1	r	1
d	Λ	1	e	0
e	Λ	1	a	1
f	Λ	1	c	1
r	a	1	Λ	1

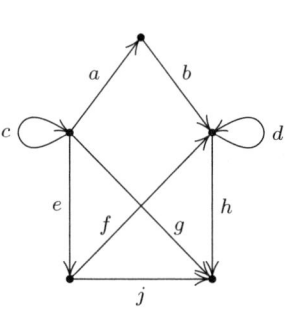

arc	ALINK	ATAG	BLINK	BTAG
a	c	0	b	1
b	a	1	d	0
c	e	0	a	1
d	h	0	f	0
e	g	0	f	1
f	j	0	d	1
g	c	1	h	0
h	b	1	j	0
j	e	1	Λ	1

Note: If in the oriented tree representation we add another arc from H to itself, we get an interesting situation: Either we get the standard conventions 2.3.1–(8) with LLINK, LTAG, RLINK, RTAG *interchanged* in the list head, or (if the new arc is placed last in the ordering) we get the standard conventions except RTAG $= 0$ in the node associated with the root of the tree.

This exercise is based on an idea communicated to the author by W. C. Lynch. Can tree traversal algorithms like Algorithm 2.3.1S be generalized to classes of digraphs that are not oriented trees, using such a representation?

27. Let a_{ij} be the sum of $p(e)$ over all arcs e from V_i to V_j. We are to prove that $t_j = \sum_i a_{ij} t_i$ for all j. Since $\sum_i a_{ji} = 1$, we must prove that $\sum_i a_{ji} t_j = \sum_i a_{ij} t_i$. But this is not difficult, because both sides of the equation represent the sum of all products $p(e_1) \dots p(e_n)$ taken over subgraphs $\{e_1, \dots, e_n\}$ of G such that $\mathrm{init}(e_i) = V_i$ and such that there is a unique oriented cycle contained in $\{e_1, \dots, e_n\}$, where this cycle includes V_j. Removing any arc of the cycle yields an oriented tree; the left-hand side of the equation is obtained by factoring out the arcs that leave V_j, while the right-hand side corresponds to those that enter V_j.

In a sense, this exercise is a combination of exercises 19 and 26.

28. Every term in the expansion is $a_{1p_1} \dots a_{mp_m} b_{1q_1} \dots b_{nq_n}$, where $0 \le p_i \le n$ for $1 \le i \le m$ and $0 \le q_j \le m$ for $1 \le j \le n$, times some integer coefficient. Represent this product as a directed graph on the vertices $\{0, u_1, \dots, u_m, v_1, \dots, v_n\}$, with arcs from u_i to v_{p_i} and from v_j to u_{q_j}, where $u_0 = v_0 = 0$.

If the digraph contains a cycle, the integer coefficient is zero. For each cycle corresponds to a factor of the form

$$a_{i_0 j_0} b_{j_0 i_1} a_{i_1 j_1} \dots a_{i_{k-1} j_{k-1}} b_{j_{k-1} i_0} \qquad (*)$$

where the indices $(i_0, i_1, \dots, i_{k-1})$ are distinct and so are the indices $(j_0, j_1, \dots, j_{k-1})$. The sum of all terms containing $(*)$ as a factor is $(*)$ times the determinant obtained by setting $a_{i_l j} \leftarrow [j = j_l]$ for $0 \le j \le n$ and $b_{j_l i} \leftarrow [i = i_{(l+1) \bmod k}]$ for $0 \le i \le m$, for $0 \le l < k$, leaving the variables in the other $m + n - 2k$ rows unchanged. This determinant is identically zero, because the sum of rows i_0, i_1, $\dots$, i_{k-1} in the top section equals the sum of rows j_0, j_1, $\dots$, j_{k-1} in the bottom section.

On the other hand, if the directed graph contains no cycles, the integer coefficient is $+1$. This follows because each factor a_{ip_i} and b_{jq_j} must have come from the diagonal of the determinant: If any off-diagonal element $a_{i_0 j_0}$ is chosen in row i_0 of the top section, we must choose some off-diagonal $b_{j_0 i_1}$ from row j_0 of the bottom section, hence we must choose some off-diagonal $a_{i_1 j_1}$ from row i_1 of the top section, etc., forcing a cycle.

Thus the coefficient is $+1$ if and only if the corresponding digraph is an oriented tree with root 0. The number of such terms (hence the number of such oriented trees) is obtained by setting each a_{ij} and b_{ji} to 1; for example,

$$\det \begin{pmatrix} 4 & 0 & 1 & 1 & 1 \\ 0 & 4 & 1 & 1 & 1 \\ 1 & 1 & 3 & 0 & 0 \\ 1 & 1 & 0 & 3 & 0 \\ 1 & 1 & 0 & 0 & 3 \end{pmatrix} = \det \begin{pmatrix} 4 & 0 & 1 & 1 & 1 \\ -4 & 4 & 0 & 0 & 0 \\ 1 & 1 & 3 & 0 & 0 \\ 0 & 0 & -3 & 3 & 0 \\ 0 & 0 & -3 & 0 & 3 \end{pmatrix} = \det \begin{pmatrix} 4 & 0 & 3 & 1 & 1 \\ 0 & 4 & 0 & 0 & 0 \\ 2 & 1 & 3 & 0 & 0 \\ 0 & 0 & 0 & 3 & 0 \\ 0 & 0 & 0 & 0 & 3 \end{pmatrix}$$

$$= \det \begin{pmatrix} 4 & 3 \\ 2 & 3 \end{pmatrix} \cdot 4 \cdot 3 \cdot 3.$$

In general we obtain $\det \binom{n+1 \quad n}{m \quad m+1} \cdot (n+1)^{m-1} \cdot (m+1)^{n-1}$.

Notes: J. J. Sylvester considered the special case $m = n$ and $a_{10} = a_{20} = \cdots = a_{m0} = 0$ in *Quarterly J. of Pure and Applied Math.* **1** (1857), 42–56, where he conjectured (correctly) that the total number of terms is then $n^n(n+1)^{n-1}$. He also stated without proof that the $(n+1)^{n-1}$ nonzero terms present when $a_{ij} = \delta_{ij}$ correspond to all connected cycle-free graphs on $\{0, 1, \ldots, n\}$. In that special case, he reduced the determinant to the form in the matrix tree theorem of exercise 19, e.g.,

$$\det \begin{pmatrix} b_{10} + b_{12} + b_{13} & -b_{12} & -b_{13} \\ -b_{21} & b_{20} + b_{21} + b_{23} & -b_{23} \\ -b_{31} & -b_{32} & b_{30} + b_{31} + b_{32} \end{pmatrix}.$$

Cayley quoted this result in *Crelle* **52** (1856), 279, ascribing it to Sylvester; thus it is ironic that the theorem about the number of such graphs is often attributed to Cayley.

By negating the first m rows of the given determinant, then negating the first m columns, we can reduce this exercise to the matrix tree theorem.

[Matrices having the general form considered in this exercise are important in iterative methods for the solution of partial differential equations, and they are said to have "Property $\mathcal{A}$." See, for example, Louis A. Hageman and David M. Young, *Applied Iterative Methods* (Academic Press, 1981), Chapter 9.]

SECTION 2.3.4.3

1. The root is the empty sequence; arcs go from $(x_1, \ldots, x_n)$ to $(x_1, \ldots, x_{n-1})$.

2. Take one tetrad type and rotate it $180°$ to get another tetrad type; these two types clearly tile the plane (without further rotations), by repeating a 2×2 pattern.

3. Consider the set of tetrad types for all positive integers j. The right half plane can be tiled in uncountably many ways; but whatever square is placed in the center of the plane puts a finite limit on the distance it can be continued to the left.

4. Systematically enumerate all possible ways to tile an $n \times n$ block, for $n = 1, 2, \ldots$, looking for toroidal solutions within these blocks. If there is no way to tile the plane, the infinity lemma tells us there is an n with no $n \times n$ solutions. If there *is* a way to tile the plane, the assumption tells us that there is an n with an $n \times n$ solution containing a rectangle that yields a toroidal solution. Hence in either case the algorithm will terminate.

[But the stated assumption is false, as shown in the next exercise; and in fact there is no algorithm that will determine in a finite number of steps whether or not there exists a way to tile the plane with a given set of types. On the other hand, if such a tiling does exist, there is always a tiling that is *quasitoroidal*, in the sense that each of its $n \times n$ blocks occurs at least once in every $f(n) \times f(n)$ block, for some function f. See B. Durand, *Theoretical Computer Science* **221** (1999), 61–75.]

5. Start by noticing that we need classes $\begin{smallmatrix} \alpha & \beta \\ \gamma & \delta \end{smallmatrix}$ replicated in 2×2 groups in any solution. Then, step 1: Considering just the α squares, show that the pattern $\begin{smallmatrix} a & b \\ c & d \end{smallmatrix}$ must be replicated in 2×2 groups of α squares. Step $n > 1$: Determine a pattern that must appear in a cross-shaped region of height and width $2^n - 1$. The middle of the crosses has the pattern $\begin{smallmatrix} Na & Nb \\ Nc & Nd \end{smallmatrix}$ replicated throughout the plane.

For example, after step 3 we will know the contents of 7×7 blocks throughout the plane, separated by unit length strips, every eight units. The 7×7 blocks that are of class Na in the center have the form

αa	βKQ	αb	βQP	αa	βBK	αb
γPJ	δNa	γRB	δQK	γLJ	δNb	γPB
αc	βDS	αd	βQTY	αc	βBS	αd
γPQ	δPJ	γPXB	δNa	γRQ	δRB	γRB
αa	βUK	αb	βDP	αa	βBK	αb
γTJ	δNc	γSB	δDS	γSJ	δNd	γTB
αc	βQS	αd	βDT	αc	βBS	αd

The middle column and the middle row is the "cross" just filled in during step 3; the other four 3 × 3 squares were filled in after step 2; the squares just to the right and below this 7 × 7 square are part of a 15 × 15 cross to be filled in at step 4.

For a similar construction that leads to a set of only 35 tetrad types having nothing but nontoroidal solutions, see R. M. Robinson, *Inventiones Math.* **12** (1971), 177–209. Robinson also exhibits a set of *six* squarish shapes that tile the plane only nontoroidally, even when rotations and reflections are allowed. In 1974, Roger Penrose discovered a set of only *two* polygons, based on the golden ratio instead of a square grid, that tile the plane only aperiodically; this led to a set of only 16 tetrad types with only nontoroidal solutions [see B. Grünbaum and G. C. Shephard, *Tilings and Patterns* (Freeman, 1987), Chapters 10–11; Martin Gardner, *Penrose Tiles to Trapdoor Ciphers* (Freeman, 1989), Chapters 1–2].

6. Let k and m be fixed. Consider an oriented tree whose vertices each represent, for some n, one of the partitions of $\{1, \ldots, n\}$ into k parts, containing no arithmetic progression of length m. A node that partitions $\{1, \ldots, n + 1\}$ is a child of one for $\{1, \ldots, n\}$ if the two partitions agree on $\{1, \ldots, n\}$. If there were an infinite path to the root we would have a way to divide *all* integers into k sets with no arithmetic progression of length m. Hence, by the infinity lemma and van der Waerden's theorem, this tree is finite. (If $k = 2$, $m = 3$, the tree can be rapidly calculated by hand, and the least value of N is 9. See *Studies in Pure Mathematics*, ed. by L. Mirsky (Academic Press, 1971), 251–260, for van der Waerden's interesting account of how the proof of his theorem was discovered.)

7. The positive integers can be partitioned into two sets S_0 and S_1 such that neither set contains any infinite *computable* sequence (see exercise 3.5–32). So in particular there is no infinite arithmetic progression. Theorem K does not apply because there is no way to put partial solutions into a tree with finite degrees at each vertex.

8. Let a "counterexample sequence" be an infinite sequence of trees that violates Kruskal's theorem, if such sequences exist. Assume that the theorem is false; then let T_1 be a tree with the smallest possible number of nodes such that T_1 can be the first tree in a counterexample sequence; if $T_1, \ldots, T_j$ have been chosen, let T_{j+1} be a tree with the smallest possible number of nodes such that $T_1, \ldots, T_j, T_{j+1}$ is the beginning of a counterexample sequence. This process defines a counterexample sequence $\langle T_n \rangle$. None of these T's is just a root. Now, we look at this sequence very carefully:

(a) Suppose there is a subsequence T_{n_1}, T_{n_2}, ... for which $l(T_{n_1})$, $l(T_{n_2})$, ... is a counterexample sequence. This is impossible; otherwise $T_1, \ldots, T_{n_1-1}, l(T_{n_1})$, $l(T_{n_2})$, ... would be a counterexample sequence, contradicting the definition of T_{n_1}.

(b) Because of (a), there are only finitely many j for which $l(T_j)$ cannot be embedded in $l(T_k)$ for any $k > j$. Therefore by taking n_1 larger than any such j we can find a subsequence for which $l(T_{n_1}) \subseteq l(T_{n_2}) \subseteq l(T_{n_3}) \subseteq \cdots$.

(c) Now by the result of exercise 2.3.2–22, $r(T_{n_j})$ cannot be embedded in $r(T_{n_k})$ for any $k > j$, else $T_{n_j} \subseteq T_{n_k}$. Therefore $T_1, \ldots, T_{n_1-1}, r(T_{n_1}), r(T_{n_2}), \ldots$ is a counterexample sequence. But this contradicts the definition of T_{n_1}.

Notes: Kruskal, in *Trans. Amer. Math. Soc.* **95** (1960), 210–225, actually proved a stronger result, using a weaker notion of embedding. His theorem does not follow directly from the infinity lemma, although the results are vaguely similar. Indeed, Kőnig himself proved a special case of Kruskal's theorem, showing that there is no infinite sequence of pairwise incomparable n-tuples of nonnegative integers, where comparability means that all components of one n-tuple are $\leq$ the corresponding components of the other [*Matematikai és Fizikai Lapok* **39** (1932), 27–29]. For further developments, see *J. Combinatorial Theory* **A13** (1972), 297–305. See also N. Dershowitz, *Inf. Proc. Letters* **9** (1979), 212–215, for applications to termination of algorithms.

SECTION 2.3.4.4

1. $\ln A(z) = \ln z + \sum_{k \geq 1} a_k \ln\left(\dfrac{1}{1 - z^k}\right) = \ln z + \sum_{k,t \geq 1} \dfrac{a_k z^{kt}}{t} = \ln z + \sum_{t \geq 1} \dfrac{A(z^t)}{t}.$

2. By differentiation, and equating the coefficients of z^n, we obtain the identity

$$n a_{n+1} = \sum_{k \geq 1} \sum_{d \backslash k} d a_d a_{n+1-k}.$$

Now interchange the order of summation.

4. (a) $A(z)$ certainly converges at least for $|z| < \frac{1}{4}$, since a_n is less than the number of *ordered* trees b_{n-1}. Since $A(1)$ is infinite and all coefficients are positive, there is a positive number $\alpha \leq 1$ such that $A(z)$ converges for $|z| < \alpha$, and there is a singularity at $z = \alpha$. Let $\psi(z) = A(z)/z$; since $\psi(z) > e^{z\psi(z)}$, we see that $\psi(z) = m$ implies $z < \ln m/m$, so $\psi(z)$ is bounded and $\lim_{z \to \alpha-} \psi(z)$ exists. Thus $\alpha < 1$, and by Abel's limit theorem $a = \alpha \cdot \exp(a + \frac{1}{2} A(\alpha^2) + \frac{1}{3} A(\alpha^3) + \cdots)$.

(b) $A(z^2), A(z^3), \ldots$ are analytic for $|z| < \sqrt{\alpha}$, and $\frac{1}{2} A(z^2) + \frac{1}{3} A(z^3) + \cdots$ converges uniformly in a slightly smaller disk.

(c) If $\partial F/\partial w = a - 1 \neq 0$, the implicit function theorem implies that there is an analytic function $f(z)$ in a neighborhood of $(\alpha, a/\alpha)$ such that $F(z, f(z)) = 0$. But this implies $f(z) = A(z)/z$, contradicting the fact that $A(z)$ is singular at α.

(d) Obvious.

(e) $\partial F/\partial w = A(z) - 1$ and $|A(z)| < A(\alpha) = 1$, since the coefficients of $A(z)$ are all positive. Hence, as in (c), $A(z)$ is regular at all such points.

(f) Near $(\alpha, 1/\alpha)$ we have the identity $0 = \beta(z - \alpha) + (\alpha/2)(w - 1/\alpha)^2 + $ higher order terms, where $w = A(z)/z$; so w is an analytic function of $\sqrt{z - \alpha}$ here by the implicit function theorem. Consequently there is a region $|z| < \alpha_1$ minus a cut $[\alpha, \alpha_1]$ in which $A(z)$ has the stated form. (The minus sign is chosen since a plus sign would make the coefficients ultimately negative.)

(g) Any function of the stated form has coefficient asymptotically $\dfrac{\sqrt{2\beta}}{\alpha^n}\binom{1/2}{n}$. Note that

$$\binom{3/2}{n} = O\left(\frac{1}{n}\binom{1/2}{n}\right).$$

For further details, and asymptotic values of the number of free trees, see R. Otter, *Ann. Math.* (2) **49** (1948), 583–599.

5.
$$c_n = \sum_{j_1 + 2j_2 + \cdots = n} \binom{c_1 + j_1 - 1}{j_1} \cdots \binom{c_n + j_n - 1}{j_n} - c_n, \quad n > 1.$$

Therefore

$$2C(z) + 1 - z = (1-z)^{-c_1}(1-z^2)^{-c_2}(1-z^3)^{-c_3}\cdots = \exp\big(C(z) + \tfrac{1}{2}C(z^2) + \cdots\big).$$

We find $C(z) = z + z^2 + 2z^3 + 5z^4 + 12z^5 + 33z^6 + 90z^7 + 261z^8 + 766z^9 + \cdots$. When $n > 1$, the number of series-parallel networks with n edges is $2c_n$ [see P. A. MacMahon, *Proc. London Math. Soc.* **22** (1891), 330–339].

6. $zG(z)^2 = 2G(z) - 2 - zG(z^2)$; $G(z) = 1 + z + z^2 + 2z^3 + 3z^4 + 6z^5 + 11z^6 + 23z^7 + 46z^8 + 98z^9 + \cdots$. The function $F(z) = 1 - zG(z)$ satisfies the simpler relation $F(z^2) = 2z + F(z)^2$. [J. H. M. Wedderburn, *Annals of Math.* (2) **24** (1922), 121–140.]

7. $g_n = ca^n n^{-3/2}(1 + O(1/n))$, where $c \approx 0.7916031835775$, $a \approx 2.483253536173$.

8.

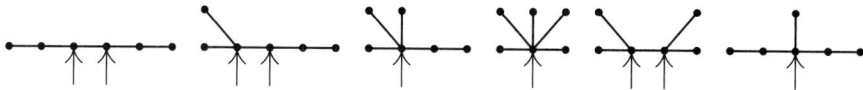

9. If there are two centroids, by considering a path from one to the other we find that there can't be intermediate points, so any two centroids are adjacent. A tree cannot contain three mutually adjacent vertices, so there are at most two.

10. If X and Y are adjacent, let $s(X,Y)$ be the number of vertices in the Y subtree of X. Then $s(X,Y) + s(Y,X) = n$. The argument in the text shows that if Y is a centroid, weight$(X) = s(X,Y)$. Therefore if both X and Y are centroids, weight$(X) =$ weight$(Y) = n/2$.

In terms of this notation, the argument in the text goes on to show that if $s(X,Y) \geq s(Y,X)$, there is a centroid in the Y subtree of X. So if two free trees with m vertices are joined by an edge between X and Y, we obtain a free tree in which $s(X,Y) = m = s(Y,X)$, and there must be two centroids (namely X and Y).

[It is a nice programming exercise to compute $s(X,Y)$ for all adjacent X and Y in $O(n)$ steps; from this information we can quickly find the centroid(s). An efficient algorithm for centroid location was first given by A. J. Goldman, *Transportation Sci.* **5** (1971), 212–221.]

11. $zT(z)^t = T(z) - 1$; thus $z + T(z)^{-t} = T(z)^{1-t}$. By Eq. 1.2.9–(21), $T(z) = \sum_n A_n(1, -t)z^n$, so the number of t-ary trees is

$$\binom{1 + tn}{n}\frac{1}{1 + tn} = \binom{tn}{n}\frac{1}{(t-1)n + 1}.$$

12. Consider the directed graph that has one arc from V_i to V_j for all $i \neq j$. The matrix A_0 of exercise 2.3.4.2–19 is a combinatorial $(n-1) \times (n-1)$ matrix with $n-1$ on the diagonal and -1 off the diagonal. So its determinant is

$$\big(n + (n-1)(-1)\big)n^{n-2} = n^{n-2},$$

the number of oriented trees with a given root. (Exercise 2.3.4.2–20 could also be used.)

13.

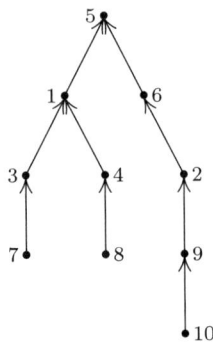

14. True, since the root will not become a leaf until all other branches have been removed.

15. In the canonical representation, $V_1, V_2, \ldots, V_{n-1}, f(V_{n-1})$ is a topological sort of the oriented tree considered as a directed graph, but this order would not in general be output by Algorithm 2.2.3T. Algorithm 2.2.3T can be changed so that it determines the values of $V_1, V_2, \ldots, V_{n-1}$ if the "insert into queue" operation of step T6 is replaced by a procedure that adjusts links so that the entries of the list appear in ascending order from front to rear; then the queue becomes a priority queue.

(However, a general priority queue isn't needed to find the canonical representation; we only need to sweep through the vertices from 1 to n, looking for leaves, while pruning off paths from new leaves less than the sweep pointer; see the following exercise.)

16. **D1.** Set $\text{C}[1] \leftarrow \cdots \leftarrow \text{C}[n] \leftarrow 0$, then set $\text{C}[f(V_j)] \leftarrow \text{C}[f(V_j)]+1$ for $1 \le j < n$. (Thus vertex k is a leaf if and only if $\text{C}[k] = 0$.) Set $k \leftarrow 0$ and $j \leftarrow 1$.

D2. Increase k one or more times until $\text{C}[k] = 0$, then set $l \leftarrow k$.

D3. Set $\text{PARENT}[l] \leftarrow f(V_j)$, $l \leftarrow f(V_j)$, $\text{C}[l] \leftarrow \text{C}[l] - 1$, and $j \leftarrow j+1$.

D4. If $j = n$, set $\text{PARENT}[l] \leftarrow 0$ and terminate the algorithm.

D5. If $\text{C}[l] = 0$ and $l < k$, go to D3; otherwise go back to D2. ∎

17. There must be exactly one cycle $x_1, x_2, \ldots, x_k$ where $f(x_j) = x_{j+1}$ and $f(x_k) = x_1$. We will enumerate all f having a cycle of length k such that the iterates of each x ultimately come into this cycle. Define the canonical representation $f(V_1)$, $f(V_2)$, $\ldots, f(V_{m-k})$ as in the text; now $f(V_{m-k})$ is in the cycle, so we continue to get a "canonical representation" by writing down the rest of the cycle $f(f(V_{m-k}))$, $f(f(f(V_{m-k})))$, etc. For example, the function with $m = 13$ whose graph is shown here leads to the representation 3, 1, 8, 8, 1, 12, 12, 2, 3, 4, 5, 1. We obtain a sequence of $m - 1$ numbers in which the last k are distinct. Conversely, from any such sequence we can reverse the construction (assuming that k is known); hence there are precisely $m^{\underline{k}} m^{m-k-1}$ such functions having a k-cycle. (For related results, see exercise 3.1–14. The formula $m^{m-1}Q(m)$ was first obtained by L. Katz, *Annals of Math. Statistics* **26** (1955), 512–517.)

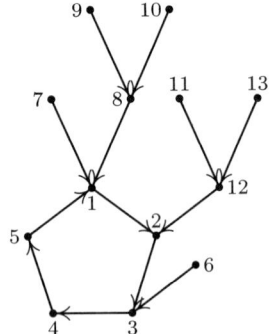

18. To reconstruct the tree from a sequence $s_1, s_2, \ldots, s_{n-1}$, begin with s_1 as the root and successively attach arcs to the tree that point to $s_1, s_2, \ldots$; if vertex s_k has appeared earlier, leave the initial vertex of the arc leading to s_{k-1} nameless, otherwise give this vertex the name s_k. After all $n-1$ arcs have been placed, give names to all vertices that remain nameless by using the numbers that have not yet appeared, assigning names in increasing order to nameless vertices in the order of their creation.

For example, from 3, 1, 4, 1, 5, 9, 2, 6, 5 we would construct the tree shown on the right. There is no simple connection between this method and the one in the text. Several more representations are possible; see the article by E. H. Neville, *Proc. Cambridge Phil. Soc.* **49** (1953), 381–385.

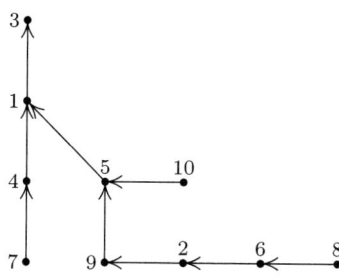

19. The canonical representation will have precisely $n - k$ different values, so we enumerate the sequences of $n-1$ numbers with this property. The answer is $n^{n-k} \left\{ {n-1 \atop n-k} \right\}$.

20. Consider the canonical representation of such trees. We are asking how many terms of $(x_1 + \cdots + x_n)^{n-1}$ have k_0 exponents zero, k_1 exponents one, etc. This is plainly the coefficient of such a term times the number of such terms, namely

$$\frac{(n-1)!}{(0!)^{k_0}(1!)^{k_1} \ldots (n!)^{k_n}} \times \frac{n!}{k_0!\, k_1! \ldots k_n!}.$$

21. There are none with $2m$ vertices; if there are $n = 2m + 1$ vertices, the answer is obtained from exercise 20 with $k_0 = m + 1$, $k_2 = m$, namely $\binom{2m+1}{m}(2m)!/2^m$.

22. Exactly n^{n-2}; for if X is a particular vertex, the free trees are in one-to-one correspondence with oriented trees having root X.

23. It is possible to put the labels on every unlabeled, ordered tree in $n!$ ways, and each of these labeled, ordered trees is distinct. So the total number is $n!\, b_{n-1} = (2n-2)!/(n-1)!$.

24. There are as many with one given root as with another, so the answer in general is $1/n$ times the answer in exercise 23; and in this particular case the answer is 30.

25. For $0 \le q < n$, $r(n,q) = (n-q)n^{q-1}$. (The special case $s = 1$ in Eq. (24).)

26. $(k = 7)$

27. Given a function g from $\{1, 2, \ldots, r\}$ to $\{1, 2, \ldots, q\}$ such that adding arcs from V_k to $U_{g(k)}$ introduces no oriented cycles, construct a sequence $a_1, \ldots, a_r$ as follows: Call vertex V_k "free" if there is no oriented path from V_j to V_k for any $j \neq k$. Since there are no oriented cycles, there must be at least one free vertex. Let b_1 be the smallest integer for which V_{b_1} is free; and assuming that $b_1, \ldots, b_t$ have been chosen, let b_{t+1} be the smallest integer different from $b_1, \ldots, b_t$ for which $V_{b_{t+1}}$ is free in the graph obtained by deleting the arcs from V_{b_k} to $U_{g(b_k)}$ for $1 \leq k \leq t$. This rule defines a permutation $b_1 b_2 \ldots b_r$ of the integers $\{1, 2, \ldots, r\}$. Let $a_k = g(b_k)$ for $1 \leq k \leq r$; this defines a sequence such that $1 \leq a_k \leq q$ for $1 \leq k < r$, and $1 \leq a_r \leq p$.

Conversely if such a sequence $a_1, \ldots, a_r$ is given, call a vertex V_k "free" if there is no j for which $a_j > p$ and $f(a_j) = k$. Since $a_r \leq p$ there are at most $r - 1$ non-free vertices. Let b_1 be the smallest integer for which V_{b_1} is free; and assuming that $b_1, \ldots, b_t$ have been chosen, let b_{t+1} be the smallest integer different from $b_1, \ldots, b_t$ for which $V_{b_{t+1}}$ is free with respect to the sequence $a_{t+1}, \ldots, a_r$. This rule defines a permutation $b_1 b_2 \ldots b_r$ of the integers $\{1, 2, \ldots, r\}$. Let $g(b_k) = a_k$ for $1 \leq k \leq r$; this defines a function such that adding arcs from V_k to $U_{g(k)}$ introduces no oriented cycles.

28. Let f be any of the n^{m-1} functions from $\{2, \ldots, m\}$ to $\{1, 2, \ldots, n\}$, and consider the directed graph with vertices $U_1, \ldots, U_m, V_1, \ldots, V_n$ and arcs from U_k to $V_{f(k)}$ for $1 < k \leq m$. Apply exercise 27 with $p = 1$, $q = m$, $r = n$, to show that there are m^{n-1} ways to add further arcs from the V's to the U's to obtain an oriented tree with root U_1. Since there is a one-to-one correspondence between the desired set of free trees and the set of oriented trees with root U_1, the answer is $n^{m-1} m^{n-1}$. [This construction can be extensively generalized; see D. E. Knuth, *Canadian J. Math.* **20** (1968), 1077–1086.]

29. If $y = x^t$, then $(tz)y = \ln y$, and we see that it is sufficient to prove the identity for $t = 1$. Now if $zx = \ln x$ we know by exercise 25 that $x^m = \sum_k E_k(m, 1) z^k$ for nonnegative integers m. Hence

$$x^r = e^{zxr} = \sum_k \frac{(zxr)^k}{k!} = \sum_{j,k} \frac{r^k z^{k+j} E_j(k, 1)}{k!} = \sum_k \frac{z^k}{k!} \sum_j \binom{k}{j} j! E_j(k-j, 1) r^{k-j}$$

$$= \sum_k \frac{z^k}{k!} \sum_j \binom{k-1}{j} k^j r^{k-j} = \sum_k z^k E_k(r, 1).$$

[Exercise 4.7–22 derives considerably more general results.]

30. Each graph described defines a set $C_x \subseteq \{1, \ldots, n\}$, where j is in C_x if and only if there is a path from t_j to r_i for some $i \leq x$. For a given C_x each graph described is composed of two independent parts: one of the $x(x + \epsilon_1 z_1 + \cdots + \epsilon_n z_n)^{\epsilon_1 + \cdots + \epsilon_n - 1}$ graphs on the vertices r_i, s_{jk}, t_j for $i \leq x$ and $j \in C_x$, where $\epsilon_j = [j \in C_x]$, plus one of the $y(y + (1 - \epsilon_1) z_1 + \cdots + (1 - \epsilon_n) z_n)^{(1-\epsilon_1) + \cdots + (1-\epsilon_n) - 1}$ graphs on the other vertices.

31. $G(z) = z + G(z)^2 + G(z)^3 + G(z)^4 + \cdots = z + G(z)^2/(1 - G(z))$. Hence $G(z) = \frac{1}{4}(1 + z - \sqrt{1 - 6z + z^2}) = z + z^2 + 3z^3 + 11z^4 + 45z^5 + \cdots$. [*Notes:* Another problem equivalent to this one was posed and solved by E. Schröder, *Zeitschrift für Mathematik und Physik* **15** (1870), 361–376, who determined the number of ways to insert nonoverlapping diagonals in a convex $(n + 1)$-gon. These numbers for $n > 1$ are just half the values obtained in exercise 2.2.1–11, since Pratt's grammar allows the root node of the associated parse tree to have degree one. The asymptotic value is calculated in exercise 2.2.1–12. Curiously, the value $[z^{10}] G(z) = 103049$ seems to have been calculated already by Hipparchus in the second century B.C., as the number of "affirmative compound propositions that can be made from only ten simple propositions"; see R. P. Stanley, *AMM* **104** (1997), 344–350; F. Acerbi, *Archive for History of Exact Sciences* **57** (2003), 465–502.]

32. Zero if $n_0 \neq 1 + n_2 + 2n_3 + 3n_4 + \cdots$ (see exercise 2.3–21), otherwise

$$(n_0 + n_1 + \cdots + n_m - 1)!/n_0! \, n_1! \ldots n_m!.$$

To prove this result we recall that an unlabeled tree with $n = n_0 + n_1 + \cdots + n_m$ nodes is characterized by the sequence $d_1 \, d_2 \ldots d_n$ of the degrees of the nodes in postorder (Section 2.3.3). Furthermore such a sequence of degrees corresponds to a tree if and only if $\sum_{j=1}^{k}(1 - d_j) > 0$ for $0 < k \leq n$. (This important property of Polish postfix notation is readily proved by induction; see Algorithm 2.3.3F with f a function that creates a tree, like the **TREE** function of Section 2.3.2.) In particular, d_1 must be 0. The answer to our problem is therefore the number of sequences $d_2 \ldots d_n$ with n_j occurrences of j for $j > 0$, namely the multinomial coefficient

$$\binom{n-1}{n_0 - 1, \, n_1, \ldots, n_m},$$

minus the number of such sequences $d_2 \ldots d_n$ for which $\sum_{j=2}^{k}(1 - d_j) < 0$ for some $k \geq 2$.

We may enumerate the latter sequences as follows: Let t be minimal such that $\sum_{j=2}^{t}(1 - d_j) < 0$; then $\sum_{j=2}^{t}(1 - d_j) = -s$ where $1 \leq s < d_t$, and we may form the subsequence $d_2' \ldots d_n' = d_{t-1} \ldots d_2 0 d_{t+1} \ldots d_n$, which has n_j occurrences of j for $j \neq d_t$, $n_j - 1$ occurrences of j for $j = d_t$. Now $\sum_{j=2}^{k}(1 - d_j')$ is equal to d_t when $k = n$, and equal to $d_t - s$ when $k = t$; when $k < t$, it is

$$\sum_{2 \leq j < t}(1 - d_j) - \sum_{2 \leq j \leq t-k}(1 - d_j) \leq \sum_{2 \leq j < t}(1 - d_j) = d_t - s - 1.$$

It follows that, given s and any sequence $d_2' \ldots d_n'$, the construction can be reversed; hence the number of sequences $d_2 \ldots d_n$ that have a given value of d_t and s is the multinomial coefficient

$$\binom{n-1}{n_0, \ldots, n_{d_t} - 1, \ldots, n_m}.$$

The number of sequences $d_2 \ldots d_n$ that correspond to trees is therefore obtained by summing over the possible values of d_t and s:

$$\sum_{j=0}^{m}(1 - j)\binom{n-1}{n_0, \ldots, n_j - 1, \ldots, n_m} = \frac{(n-1)!}{n_0! \, n_1! \ldots n_m!} \sum_{j=0}^{m}(1 - j)n_j$$

and the latter sum is 1.

An even simpler proof of this result has been given by G. N. Raney (*Transactions of the American Math. Society* **94** (1960), 441–451). If $d_1 \, d_2 \ldots d_n$ is any sequence with n_j appearances of j, there is precisely one cyclic rearrangement $d_k \ldots d_n d_1 \ldots d_{k-1}$ that corresponds to a tree, namely the rearrangement where k is maximal such that $\sum_{j=1}^{k-1}(1 - d_j)$ is minimal. [This argument in the case of binary trees was apparently first discovered by C. S. Peirce in an unpublished manuscript; see his *New Elements of Mathematics* **4** (The Hague: Mouton, 1976), 303–304. It was discovered in the case of t-ary trees by Dvoretzky and Motzkin, *Duke Math. J.* **14** (1947), 305–313.]

Still another proof, by G. Bergman, inductively replaces $d_k d_{k+1}$ by $(d_k + d_{k+1} - 1)$ if $d_k > 0$ [*Algebra Universalis* **8** (1978), 129–130].

The methods above can be generalized to show that the number of (ordered, unlabeled) forests having f trees and n_j nodes of degree j is $(n-1)!\,f/n_0!\,n_1!\ldots n_m!$, provided that the condition $n_0 = f + n_2 + 2n_3 + \cdots$ is satisfied.

33. Consider the number of trees with n_1 nodes labeled 1, n_2 nodes labeled 2, ..., and such that each node labeled j has degree e_j. Let this number be $c(n_1, n_2, \ldots)$, with the specified degrees $e_1, e_2, \ldots$ regarded as fixed. The generating function $G(z_1, z_2, \ldots) = \sum c(n_1, n_2, \ldots) z_1^{n_1} z_2^{n_2} \ldots$ satisfies the identity $G = z_1 G^{e_1} + \cdots + z_r G^{e_r}$, since $z_j G^{e_j}$ enumerates the trees whose root is labeled j. And by the result of the previous exercise,

$$
c(n_1, n_2, \ldots) = \begin{cases} \dfrac{(n_1 + n_2 + \cdots - 1)!}{n_1!\,n_2!\ldots}, & \text{if } (1 - e_1)n_1 + (1 - e_2)n_2 + \cdots = 1; \\ 0, & \text{otherwise.} \end{cases}
$$

More generally, since G^f enumerates the number of ordered forests having such labels, we have for integer $f > 0$

$$
w^f = \sum_{f = (1 - e_1)n_1 + (1 - e_2)n_2 + \cdots} \frac{(n_1 + n_2 + \cdots - 1)!\,f}{n_1!\,n_2!\ldots} z_1^{n_1} z_2^{n_2} \ldots.
$$

These formulas are meaningful when $r = \infty$, and they are essentially equivalent to Lagrange's inversion formula.

SECTION 2.3.4.5

1. There are $\binom{8}{5}$ in all, since the nodes numbered 8, 9, 10, 11, 12 may be attached in any of eight positions below 4, 5, 6, and 7.

2.

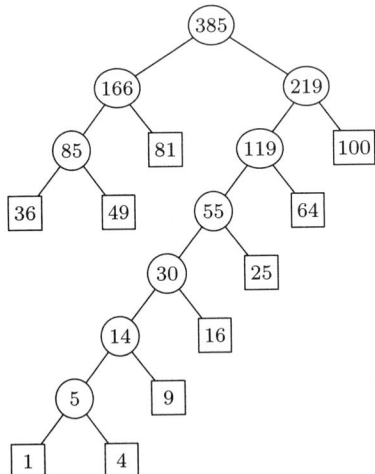

3. By induction on m, the condition is necessary. Conversely if $\sum_{j=1}^{m} 2^{-l_j} = 1$, we want to construct an extended binary tree with path lengths $l_1, \ldots, l_m$. When $m = 1$, we have $l_1 = 0$ and the construction is trivial. Otherwise we may assume that the l's are ordered so that $l_1 = l_2 = \cdots = l_q > l_{q+1} \geq l_{q+2} \geq \cdots \geq l_m > 0$ for some q with $1 \leq q \leq m$. Now $2^{l_1 - 1} = \sum_{j=1}^{m} 2^{l_1 - l_j - 1} = \frac{1}{2} q + \text{integer}$, hence q is even. By induction on m there is a tree with path lengths $l_1 - 1, l_3, l_4, \ldots, l_m$; take such a tree and replace one of the external nodes at level $l_1 - 1$ by an internal node whose children are at level $l_1 = l_2$.

4. First, find a tree by Huffman's method. If $w_j < w_{j+1}$, then $l_j \geq l_{j+1}$, since the tree is optimal. The construction in the answer to exercise 3 now gives us another tree with these same path lengths and with the weights in the proper sequence. For example, the tree (11) becomes

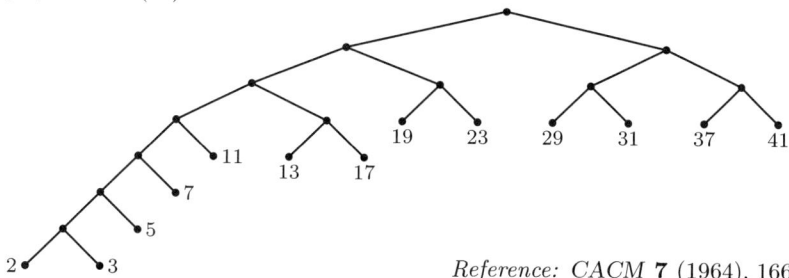

Reference: CACM **7** (1964), 166–169.

5. (a) $b_{np} = \sum_{\substack{k+l=n-1 \\ r+s+n-1=p}} b_{kr} b_{ls}$. Hence $zB(w, wz)^2 = B(w, z) - 1$.

(b) Take the partial derivative with respect to w:

$$2zB(w, wz)\big(B_w(w, wz) + zB_z(w, wz)\big) = B_w(w, z).$$

Therefore if $H(z) = B_w(1, z) = \sum_n h_n z^n$, we find $H(z) = 2zB(z)\big(H(z) + zB'(z)\big)$; and the known formula for $B(z)$ implies

$$H(z) = \frac{1}{1 - 4z} - \frac{1}{z}\left(\frac{1 - z}{\sqrt{1 - 4z}} - 1\right), \qquad \text{so} \qquad h_n = 4^n - \frac{3n + 1}{n + 1}\binom{2n}{n}.$$

The average value is h_n/b_n. (c) Asymptotically, this comes to $n\sqrt{\pi n} - 3n + O(\sqrt{n})$.

For the solution to similar problems, see John Riordan, *IBM J. Res. and Devel.* **4** (1960), 473–478; A. Rényi and G. Szekeres, *J. Australian Math. Soc.* **7** (1967), 497–507; John Riordan and N. J. A. Sloane, *J. Australian Math. Soc.* **10** (1969), 278–282; and exercise 2.3.1–11.

6. $n + s - 1 = tn$.

7. $E = (t - 1)I + tn$.

8. Summation by parts gives $\sum_{k=1}^{n} \lfloor \log_t((t-1)k) \rfloor = nq - \sum k$, where the sum on the right is over values of k such that $0 \leq k \leq n$ and $(t-1)k + 1 = t^j$ for some j. The latter sum may be rewritten $\sum_{j=1}^{q}(t^j - 1)/(t - 1)$.

9. Induction on the size of the tree.

10. By adding extra *zero* weights, if necessary, we may assume that $m \bmod (t - 1) = 1$. To obtain a t-ary tree with minimum weighted path length, combine the smallest t values at each step and replace them by their sum. The proof is essentially the same as the binary case. The desired ternary tree is shown.

F. K. Hwang has observed [*SIAM J. Appl. Math.* **37** (1979), 124–127] that a similar procedure is valid for minimum weighted path length trees having any prescribed multiset of degrees: Combine the smallest t weights at each step, where t is as small as possible.

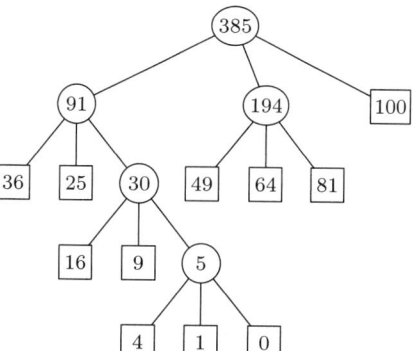

11. The "Dewey" notation is the binary representation of the node number.

12. By exercise 9, it is the internal path length divided by n, plus 1. (This result holds for general trees as well as binary trees.)

13. [See J. van Leeuwen, *Proc. 3rd International Colloq. Automata, Languages and Programming* (Edinburgh University Press, 1976), 382–410.]

> **H1.** [Initialize.] Set $A[m - 1 + i] \leftarrow w_i$ for $1 \leq i \leq m$. Then set $A[2m] \leftarrow \infty$, $x \leftarrow m$, $i \leftarrow m + 1$, $j \leftarrow m - 1$, $k \leftarrow m$. (During this algorithm $A[i] \leq \cdots \leq A[2m - 1]$ is the queue of unused external weights; $A[k] \geq \cdots \geq A[j]$ is the queue of unused internal weights, empty if $j < k$; the current left and right pointers are x and y.)
>
> **H2.** [Find right pointer.] If $j < k$ or $A[i] \leq A[j]$, set $y \leftarrow i$ and $i \leftarrow i + 1$; otherwise set $y \leftarrow j$ and $j \leftarrow j - 1$.
>
> **H3.** [Create internal node.] Set $k \leftarrow k - 1$, $L[k] \leftarrow x$, $R[k] \leftarrow y$, $A[k] \leftarrow A[x] + A[y]$.
>
> **H4.** [Done?] Terminate the algorithm if $k = 1$.
>
> **H5.** [Find left pointer.] (At this point $j \geq k$ and the queues contain a total of k unused weights. If $A[y] < 0$ we have $j = k$, $i = y + 1$, and $A[i] > A[j]$.) If $A[i] \leq A[j]$, set $x \leftarrow i$ and $i \leftarrow i + 1$; otherwise set $x \leftarrow j$ and $j \leftarrow j - 1$. Return to step H2. ∎

14. The proof for $k = m - 1$ applies with little change. [See *SIAM J. Appl. Math.* **21** (1971), 518.]

15. Use the combined-weight functions (a) $1 + \max(w_1, w_2)$ and (b) $xw_1 + xw_2$, respectively, instead of $w_1 + w_2$ in (9). [Part (a) is due to M. C. Golumbic, *IEEE Trans.* **C-25** (1976), 1164–1167; part (b) to T. C. Hu, D. Kleitman, and J. K. Tamaki, *SIAM J. Appl. Math.* **37** (1979), 246–256. Huffman's problem is the limiting case of (b) as $x \to 1$, since $\sum(1 + \epsilon)^{l_j} w_j = \sum w_j + \epsilon \sum w_j l_j + O(\epsilon^2)$.]

D. Stott Parker, Jr., has pointed out that a Huffman-like algorithm will also find the minimum of $w_1 x^{l_1} + \cdots + w_m x^{l_m}$ when $0 < x < 1$, if the two *maximum* weights are combined at each step as in part (b). In particular, the minimum of $w_1 2^{-l_1} + \cdots + w_m 2^{-l_m}$, when $w_1 \leq \cdots \leq w_m$, is $w_1/2 + \cdots + w_{m-1}/2^{m-1} + w_m/2^{m-1}$. See D. E. Knuth, *J. Comb. Theory* **A32** (1982), 216–224, for further generalizations.

16. Let $l_{m+1} = l'_{m+1} = 0$. Then

$$\sum_{j=1}^{m} w_j l_j \leq \sum_{j=1}^{m} w_j l'_j = \sum_{k=1}^{m} (l'_k - l'_{k+1}) \sum_{j=1}^{k} w_j \leq \sum_{k=1}^{m} (l'_k - l'_{k+1}) \sum_{j=1}^{k} w'_j = \sum_{j=1}^{m} w'_j l'_j,$$

since $l'_j \geq l'_{j+1}$ as in exercise 4. The same proof holds for many other kinds of optimum trees, including those of exercise 10.

17. (a) This is exercise 14. (b) We can extend $f(n)$ to a concave function $f(x)$, so the stated inequality holds. Now $F(m)$ is the minimum of $\sum_{j=1}^{m-1} f(s_j)$, where the s_j are internal node weights of an extended binary tree on the weights $1, 1, \ldots, 1$. Huffman's algorithm, which constructs the complete binary tree with $m - 1$ internal nodes in this case, yields the optimum tree. The choice $k = 2^{\lceil \lg(n/3) \rceil}$ defines a binary tree with the same internal weights, so it yields the minimum in the recurrence, for each n. [*SIAM J. Appl. Math.* **31** (1976), 368–378.] We can evaluate $F(n)$ in $O(\log n)$ steps; see exercises 5.2.3–20 and 5.2.3–21. If $f(n)$ is convex instead of concave, so that $\Delta^2 f(n) \geq 0$, the solution to the recurrence is obtained when $k = \lfloor n/2 \rfloor$.

SECTION 2.3.4.6

1. Choose one edge of the polygon and call it the base. Given a triangulation, let the triangle on the base correspond to the root of a binary tree, and let the other two sides of that triangle define bases of left and right subpolygons, which correspond to left and right subtrees in the same way. We proceed recursively until reaching "2-sided" polygons, which correspond to empty binary trees.

Stating this correspondence another way, we can label the non-base edges of a triangulated polygon with the integers $0, \ldots, n$; and when two adjacent sides of a triangle are labeled α and β in clockwise order, we can label the third side $(\alpha\beta)$. The label of the base then characterizes the binary tree and the triangulation. For example,

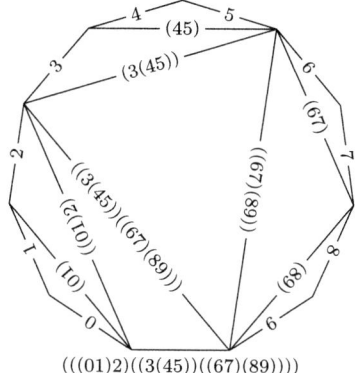

$$(((01)2)((3(45))((67)(89))))$$

corresponds to the binary tree shown in 2.3.1–(1). [See H. G. Forder, *Mathematical Gazette* **45** (1961), 199–201.]

2. (a) Take a base edge as in exercise 1, and give it d descendants if that edge is part of a $(d+1)$-gon in the dissected r-gon. The other d edges are then bases for subtrees. This defines a correspondence between Kirkman's problem and all ordered trees with $r-1$ leaves and $k+1$ nonleaves, having no nodes of degree 1. (When $k = r-3$ we have the situation of exercise 1.)

(b) There are $\binom{r+k}{k+1}\binom{r-3}{k}$ sequences $d_1 d_2 \ldots d_{r+k}$ of nonnegative integers such that $r-1$ of the d's are 0, none of them are 1, and the sum is $r+k-1$. Exactly one of the cyclic permutations $d_1 d_2 \ldots d_{r+k}$, $d_2 \ldots d_{r+k} d_1$, $\ldots$, $d_{r+k} d_1 \ldots d_{r+k-1}$ satisfies the additional property that $\sum_{j=1}^{q} (1-d_j) > 0$ for $1 \le q \le r+k$.

[Kirkman gave evidence for his conjecture in *Philos. Trans.* **147** (1857), 217–272, §22. Cayley proved it in *Proc. London Math. Soc.* **22** (1891), 237–262, without noticing the connection to trees.]

3. (a) Let the vertices be $\{1, 2, \ldots, n\}$. Draw an RLINK from i to j if i and j are consecutive elements of the same part and $i < j$; draw an LLINK from j to $j+1$ if $j+1$ is the smallest of its part. Then there are $k-1$ nonnull LLINKs, $n-k$ nonnull RLINKs, and we have a binary tree whose nodes are $12 \ldots n$ in preorder. Using the natural correspondence of Section 2.3.2, this rule defines a one-to-one correspondence between "partitions of an n-gon's vertices into k noncrossing parts" and "forests with n vertices and $n-k+1$ leaves." Interchanging LLINK with RLINK also gives "forests with n vertices and k leaves."

(b) A forest with n vertices and k leaves also corresponds to a sequence of nested parentheses, containing n left parentheses, n right parentheses, and k occurrences of "()". We can enumerate such sequences as follows:

Say that a string of 0s and 1s is an (m, n, k) string if there are m 0s, n 1s, and k occurrences of "01". Then 0010101001110 is a $(7, 6, 4)$ string. The number of (m, n, k) strings is $\binom{m}{k}\binom{n}{k}$, because we are free to choose which 0s and 1s will form the 01 pairs.

Let $S(\alpha)$ be the number of 0s in α minus the number of 1s. We say that a string σ is *good* if $S(\alpha) \geq 0$ whenever α is a prefix of σ (in other words, if $\sigma = \alpha\beta$ implies that $S(\alpha) \geq 0$); otherwise σ is *bad*. The following alternative to the "reflection principle" of exercise 2.2.1–4 establishes a one-to-one correspondence between bad (n, n, k) strings and arbitrary $(n-1, n+1, k)$ strings:

Any bad (n, n, k) string σ can be written uniquely in the form $\sigma = \alpha 0\beta$, where $\overline{\alpha}^R$ and β are good. (Here $\overline{\alpha}^R$ is the string obtained from α by reversing it and complementing all the bits.) Then $\sigma' = \alpha 1\beta$ is an $(n-1, n+1, k)$ string. Conversely, every $(n-1, n+1, k)$ string can be written uniquely in the form $\alpha 1\beta$ where $\overline{\alpha}^R$ and β are good, and $\alpha 0\beta$ is then a bad (n, n, k) string.

Thus the number of forests with n vertices and k leaves is $\binom{n}{k}\binom{n}{k} - \binom{n-1}{k}\binom{n+1}{k} = \binom{n-1}{k-1}\binom{n}{k} - \binom{n-1}{k}\binom{n}{k-1} = n!\,(n-1)!/(n-k+1)!\,(n-k)!\,k!\,(k-1)!$, a so-called *Narayana number* [T. V. Narayana, *Comptes Rendus Acad. Sci.* **240** (Paris, 1955), 1188–1189].

Notes: G. Kreweras, *Discrete Math.* **1** (1972), 333–350, enumerated noncrossing partitions in a different way. The partial ordering of partitions by refinement leads to an interesting partial ordering of forests, different from the one discussed in exercise 2.3.3–19; see Y. Poupard, *Cahiers du Bureau Univ. de Recherche Opér.* **16** (1971), Chapter 8; *Discrete Math.* **2** (1972), 279–288; P. Edelman, *Discrete Math.* **31** (1980), 171–180, **40** (1982), 171–179; N. Dershowitz and S. Zaks, *Discrete Math.* **64** (1986), 215–218.

A third way to define a natural lattice ordering of forests was introduced by R. Stanley in *Fibonacci Quarterly* **13** (1975), 215–232: Suppose we represent a forest by a string σ of 0s and 1s representing left and right parentheses as above; then $\sigma \leq \sigma'$ if and only if $S(\sigma_k) \leq S(\sigma'_k)$ for all k, where σ_k denotes the first k bits of σ. Stanley's lattice is *distributive*, unlike the other two.

4. Let $m = n + 2$; by exercise 1, we want a correspondence between triangulated m-gons and $(m-1)$-rowed friezes. First let's look more closely at the previous correspondence, by giving a "top-down" labeling to the edges of a triangulation instead of the "bottom-up" one considered earlier: Assign the empty label ϵ to the base, then recursively give the labels αL and αR to the opposite edges of a triangle whose base is labeled α. For example, the previous diagram becomes

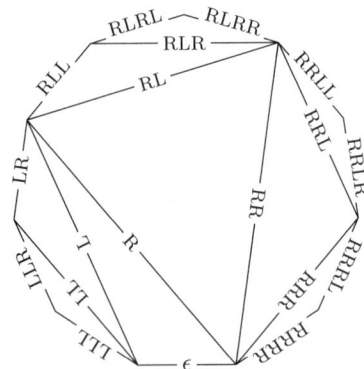

under these new conventions. If the base edge in this example is called 10, while the other edges are 0 to 9 as before, we can write $0 = 10LLL$, $1 = 10LLR$, $2 = 10LR$,

$3 = 10RLL$, etc. Any of the other edges can also be chosen as the base; thus, if 0 is chosen we have $1 = 0L$, $2 = 0RL$, $3 = 0RRLLL$, etc. It is not difficult to verify that if $u = v\alpha$ we have $v = u\alpha^T$, where α^T is obtained by reading α from right to left and interchanging L with R. For example, $10 = 0RRR = 1LRR = 2LR = 3RRL$, etc. If u, v, and w are edges of the polygon with $w = u\alpha L\gamma$ and $w = v\beta R\gamma$, then $u = v\beta L\alpha^T$ and $v = u\alpha R\beta^T$.

Given a triangulation of a polygon whose edges are numbered $0, 1, \ldots, m-1$, we define (u, v) for any pair of distinct edges u and v as follows: Let $u = v\alpha$, and interpret α as a 2×2 matrix by letting $L = \left(\begin{smallmatrix} 1 & 1 \\ 0 & 1 \end{smallmatrix}\right)$ and $R = \left(\begin{smallmatrix} 1 & 0 \\ 1 & 1 \end{smallmatrix}\right)$. Then (u, v) is defined to be the element in the upper left corner of α. Notice that α^T is the transpose of the matrix α, since $R = L^T$; hence we have $(v, u) = (u, v)$. Notice also that $(u, v) = 1$ if and only if u_- and v_- are joined by an edge of the triangulation, where u_- denotes the vertex between edges u and $u - 1$.

Let $(u, u) = 0$ for all polygon edges u. We can now prove that $v = u\alpha$ implies

$$\alpha = \begin{pmatrix} (u, v) & (u, v+1) \\ (u+1, v) & (u+1, v+1) \end{pmatrix} \qquad \text{for all } u \neq v, \qquad (*)$$

where $u+1$ and $v+1$ are the clockwise successors of u and v. The proof is by induction on m: Eq. $(*)$ is trivial when $m = 2$, since the two parallel edges u and v are then related by $u = v\epsilon$, and $\alpha = \epsilon$ is the identity matrix. If any triangulation is augmented by extending some edge v with a triangle $v\, v'\, v''$, then $v = u\alpha$ implies $v' = u\alpha L$ and $v'' = u\alpha R$; hence (u, v') and (u, v'') in the extended polygon are respectively equal to (u, v) and $(u, v) + (u, v+1)$ in the original one. It follows that

$$\alpha L = \begin{pmatrix} (u, v') & (u, v'') \\ (u+1, v') & (u+1, v'') \end{pmatrix} \quad \text{and} \quad \alpha R = \begin{pmatrix} (u, v'') & (u, v''+1) \\ (u+1, v'') & (u+1, v''+1) \end{pmatrix},$$

and $(*)$ remains true in the extended polygon.

The frieze pattern corresponding to the given triangulation is now defined to be the periodic sequence

$$\begin{array}{ccccccccc}
(0,1) & (1,2) & (2,3) & \cdots & (m{-}1,0) & (0,1) & (1,2) & \cdots \\
(0,2) & (1,3) & (2,4) & \cdots & (m{-}1,1) & (0,2) & (1,3) & \cdots \\
(m{-}1,2) & (0,3) & (1,4) & \cdots & (m{-}2,1) & (m{-}1,2) & (0,3) & \cdots \\
(m{-}1,3) & (0,4) & (1,5) & \cdots & (m{-}2,2) & (m{-}1,3) & (0,4) & \cdots
\end{array}$$

and so on until $m - 1$ rows have been defined; the final row begins with $(\lceil m/2 \rceil + 1, \lceil m/2 \rceil)$ when $m > 3$. Condition $(*)$ proves that this pattern is a frieze, namely that

$$(u, v)(u+1, v+1) - (u, v+1)(u+1, v) = 1, \qquad (**)$$

because $\det L = \det R = 1$ implies $\det \alpha = 1$. Our example triangulation yields

```
1  1  1  1  1  1  1  1  1  1  1  1  1  1  1  1  1  1  1  1   ...
 1  2  4  2  1  5  1  3  1  4  3  1  2  4  2  1  5  1  3  1  4  ...
2  1  7  7  1  4  4  2  2  3 11  2  1  7  7  1  4  4  2  2  3   ...
 1  3 12  3  3  3  7  1  5  8  7  1  3 12  3  3  3  7  1  5  8  ...
3  2  5  5  8  2  5  3  2 13  5  3  2  5  5  8  2  5  3  2 13   ...
 5  3  2 13  5  3  2  5  5  8  2  5  3  2 13  5  3  2  5  5  8  ...
3  7  1  5  8  7  1  3 12  3  3  3  7  1  5  8  7  1  3 12  3   ...
 4  2  2  3 11  2  1  7  7  1  4  4  2  2  3 11  2  1  7  7  1  ...
5  1  3  1  4  3  1  2  4  2  1  5  1  3  1  4  3  1  2  4  2   ...
 1  1  1  1  1  1  1  1  1  1  1  1  1  1  1  1  1  1  1  1  1  ...
```

The relation $(u, v) = 1$ defines the edges of the triangulation, hence different triangulations yield different friezes. To complete the proof of one-to-one correspondence, we must show that every $(m - 1)$-rowed frieze pattern of positive integers is obtained in this way from some triangulation.

Given any frieze of $m - 1$ rows, extend it by putting a new row 0 at the top and a new row m at the bottom, both consisting entirely of zeros. Now let the elements of row 0 be called $(0, 0)$, $(1, 1)$, $(2, 2)$, etc., and for all nonnegative integers $u < v \leq u + m$ let (u, v) be the element in the diagonal southeast of (u, u) and in the diagonal southwest of (v, v). By assumption, condition $(**)$ holds for all $u < v < u + m$. We can in fact extend $(**)$ to the considerably more general relation

$$(t, u)(v, w) + (t, w)(u, v) = (t, v)(u, w) \qquad \text{for } t \leq u \leq v \leq w \leq t + m. \qquad (***)$$

For if $(***)$ is false, let (t, u, v, w) be a counterexample with the smallest value of $(w - t)m + u - t + w - v$. Clearly $t \neq u$ and $v \neq w$. *Case 1:* $t + 1 < u$. Then $(***)$ holds for $(t, t + 1, v, w)$, $(t, t + 1, u, v)$, and $(t + 1, u, v, w)$, so we find $((t, u)(v, w) + (t, w)(u, v))(t + 1, v) = (t, v)(u, w)(t + 1, v)$; this implies $(t + 1, v) = 0$, a contradiction. *Case 2:* $v + 1 < w$. Then $(***)$ holds for $(t, u, w - 1, w)$, $(u, v, w - 1, w)$, and $(t, u, v, w - 1)$; we obtain a similar contradiction $(u, w - 1) = 0$. *Case 3:* $u = t + 1$ and $w = v + 1$. In this case $(***)$ reduces to $(**)$.

Now we set $u = t + 1$ and $w = t + m$ in $(***)$, obtaining $(t, v) = (v, t + m)$ for $t \leq v \leq t + m$, because $(t + 1, t + m) = 1$ and $(t, t + m) = 0$. We conclude that the entries of any $(m - 1)$-rowed frieze are periodic: $(u, v) = (v, u + m) = (u + m, v + m) = (v + m, u + 2m) = \cdots$.

Every frieze pattern of positive integers contains a 1 in row 2. For if we set $t = 0$, $v = u + 1$, and $w = u + 2$ in $(***)$ we get $(0, u + 1)(u, u + 2) = (0, u) + (0, u + 2)$, hence $(0, u + 2) - (0, u + 1) \geq (0, u + 1) - (0, u)$ if and only if $(u, u + 2) \geq 2$. This cannot hold for all u in the range $0 \leq u \leq m - 2$, because $(0, 1) - (0, 0) = 1$ and $(0, m) - (0, m - 1) = -1$.

Finally, if $m > 3$ we cannot have two consecutive 1s in row 2, because $(u, u + 2) = (u + 1, u + 3) = 1$ implies $(u, u + 3) = 0$. Therefore we can reduce the frieze to another one with m reduced by 1, as illustrated here for 7 rows reduced to 6:

1	1	1	1	1	1	1	1	$\cdots$	1	1	1	1	1	1	1 $\cdots$
a	b	c	$d{+}1$	1	$e{+}1$	y	z	$\cdots$	a	b	c	d	e	y	$z \cdots$
p	q	$c{+}r$	d	e	$u{+}y$	v	w	$\cdots$	p	q	r	s	u	v	$w \cdots$
u	$q{+}v$	r	s	u	$q{+}v$	r	s	$\cdots$	u	v	w	p	q	r	$s \cdots$
$u{+}y$	v	w	p	q	$c{+}r$	d	e	$\cdots$	y	z	a	b	c	d	$e \cdots$
y	z	a	b	c	$d{+}1$	1	$e{+}1$	$\cdots$	1	1	1	1	1	1	1 $\cdots$
1	1	1	1	1	1	1	1	$\cdots$							

The reduced frieze corresponds to a triangulation, by induction, and the unreduced frieze corresponds to attaching one more triangle. [*Math. Gazette* **57** (1974), 87–94, 175–183; Conway and Guy, *The Book of Numbers* (New York: Copernicus, 1996), 74–76, 96–97, 101–102.]

Notes: This proof demonstrates that the function (u, v), which we defined on any triangulation via 2×2 matrices, satisfies $(***)$ whenever (t, u, v, w) are edges of the polygon in clockwise order. We can express each (u, v) as a polynomial in the numbers $a_j = (j - 1, j + 1)$; these polynomials are essentially identical to the "continuants" discussed in Section 4.5.3, except for the signs of individual terms. In fact, $(j, k) = i^{1-k+j} K_{k-j-1}(ia_{j+1}, ia_{j+2}, \ldots, ia_{k-1})$. Thus $(***)$ is equivalent to Euler's identity for continuants in the answer to exercise 4.5.3–32. The matrices L and R have the interesting property that any 2×2 matrix of nonnegative integers with determinant 1 can be expressed uniquely as a product of L's and R's.

Many other interesting relationships are present; for example, the numbers in row 2 of an integer frieze count the number of triangles touching each vertex of the corresponding triangulated polygon. The total number of occurrences of $(u, v) = 1$ in the basic region $0 \leq u < v - 1 < m - 1$ and $(u, v) \neq (0, m - 1)$ is the number of diagonals (chords) of the triangulation, namely $m - 3 = n - 1$. The total number of 2s is also $n - 1$, because $(u, v) = 2$ if and only if u_- and v_- are opposing vertices of the two triangles adjacent to a chord.

Another interpretation of (u, v) was found by D. Broline, D. W. Crowe, and I. M. Isaacs [*Geometriæ Dedicata* **3** (1974), 171–176]: It is the number of ways to match the $v - u - 1$ vertices between edges u and $v - 1$ with distinct triangles adjacent to those vertices.

SECTION 2.3.5

1. A List structure is a directed graph in which the arcs leaving each vertex are ordered, and where some of the vertices that have out-degree 0 are designated "atoms." Furthermore there is a vertex S such that there is an oriented path from S to V for all vertices $V \neq S$. (With directions of arcs reversed, S would be a "root.")

2. Not in the same way, since thread links in the usual representation lead back to "PARENT," which is not unique for sub-Lists. The representation discussed in exercise 2.3.4.2–25, or some similar method, could perhaps be used (but this idea has not yet been exploited at the time of writing).

3. As mentioned in the text, we prove also that P = P0 upon termination. If only P0 is to be marked, the algorithm certainly operates correctly. If $n > 1$ nodes are to be marked, we must have ATOM(P0) = 0. Step E4 then sets ALINK(P0) ← Λ and executes the algorithm with P0 replaced by ALINK(P0) and T replaced by P0. By induction (note that since MARK(P0) is now 1, all links to P0 are equivalent to Λ by steps E4 and E5), we see that ultimately we will mark all nodes on paths that start with ALINK(P0) and do not pass through P0; and we will then get to step E6 with T = P0 and P = ALINK(P0). Now since ATOM(T) = 1, step E6 restores ALINK(P0) and ATOM(P0) and we reach step E5. Step E5 sets BLINK(P0) ← Λ, etc., and a similar argument shows that we will ultimately mark all nodes on paths that start with BLINK(P0) and do not pass through P0 or nodes reachable from ALINK(P0). Then we will get to E6 with T = P0, P = BLINK(P0), and finally we get to E6 with T = Λ, P = P0.

4. The program that follows incorporates the suggested improvements in the speed of processing atoms that appear in the text after the statement of Algorithm E.

In steps E4 and E5 of the algorithm, we want to test if MARK(Q) = 0. If NODE(Q) = +0, this is an unusual case that can be handled properly by setting it to −0 and treating it as if it were originally −0, since it has ALINK and BLINK both Λ. This simplification is not reflected in the timing calculations below.

rI1 ≡ P, rI2 ≡ T, rI3 ≡ Q, and rX ≡ −1 (for setting MARKs).

```
01  MARK  EQU   0:0
02  ATOM  EQU   1:1
03  ALINK EQU   2:3
04  BLINK EQU   4:5
```

05	E1	LD1 P0	1	*E1. Initialize.* P $\leftarrow$ P0.
06		ENT2 0	1	T $\leftarrow$ Λ.
07		ENTX -1	1	rX $\leftarrow$ -1.
08	E2	STX 0,1(MARK)	1	*E2. Mark.* MARK(P) $\leftarrow$ 1.
09	E3	LDA 0,1(ATOM)	1	*E3. Atom?*
10		JAZ E4	1	Jump if ATOM(P) = 0.
11	E6	J2Z DONE	n	*E6. Up.*
12		ENT3 0,2	$n-1$	Q $\leftarrow$ T.
13		LDA 0,3(ATOM)	$n-1$	
14		JANZ 1F	$n-1$	Jump if ATOM(T) = 1.
15		LD2 0,3(BLINK)	t_2	T $\leftarrow$ BLINK(Q).
16		ST1 0,3(BLINK)	t_2	BLINK(Q) $\leftarrow$ P.
17		ENT1 0,3	t_2	P $\leftarrow$ Q.
18		JMP E6	t_2	
19	1H	STZ 0,2(ATOM)	t_1	ATOM(T) $\leftarrow$ 0.
20		LD2 0,3(ALINK)	t_1	T $\leftarrow$ ALINK(Q).
21		ST1 0,3(ALINK)	t_1	ALINK(Q) $\leftarrow$ P.
22		ENT1 0,3	t_1	P $\leftarrow$ Q.
23	E5	LD3 0,1(BLINK)	n	*E5. Down BLINK.* Q $\leftarrow$ BLINK(P).
24		J3Z E6	n	Jump if Q = Λ.
25		LDA 0,3	$n-b_2$	
26		STX 0,3(MARK)	$n-b_2$	MARK(Q) $\leftarrow$ 1.
27		JANP E6	$n-b_2$	Jump if NODE(Q) was already marked.
28		LDA 0,3(ATOM)	t_2+a_2	
29		JANZ E6	t_2+a_2	Jump if ATOM(Q) = 1.
30		ST2 0,1(BLINK)	t_2	BLINK(P) $\leftarrow$ T.
31	E4A	ENT2 0,1	$n-1$	T $\leftarrow$ P.
32		ENT1 0,3	$n-1$	P $\leftarrow$ Q.
33	E4	LD3 0,1(ALINK)	n	*E4. Down ALINK.* Q $\leftarrow$ ALINK(P).
34		J3Z E5	n	Jump if Q = Λ.
35		LDA 0,3	$n-b_1$	
36		STX 0,3(MARK)	$n-b_1$	MARK(Q) $\leftarrow$ 1.
37		JANP E5	$n-b_1$	Jump if NODE(Q) was already marked.
38		LDA 0,3(ATOM)	t_1+a_1	
39		JANZ E5	t_1+a_1	Jump if ATOM(Q) = 1.
40		STX 0,1(ATOM)	t_1	ATOM(P) $\leftarrow$ 1.
41		ST2 0,1(ALINK)	t_1	ALINK(P) $\leftarrow$ T.
42		JMP E4A	t_1	T $\leftarrow$ P, P $\leftarrow$ Q, to E4. ∎

By Kirchhoff's law, $t_1 + t_2 + 1 = n$. The total time is $(34n + 4t_1 + 3a - 5b - 8)u$, where n is the number of nonatomic nodes marked, a is the number of atoms marked, b is the number of Λ links encountered in marked nonatomic nodes, and t_1 is the number of times we went down an ALINK ($0 \leq t_1 < n$).

5. (The following is the fastest known marking algorithm for a one-level memory.)

S1. Set MARK(P0) $\leftarrow$ 1. If ATOM(P0) = 1, the algorithm terminates; otherwise set S $\leftarrow$ 0, R $\leftarrow$ P0, T $\leftarrow$ Λ.

S2. Set P $\leftarrow$ BLINK(R). If P = Λ or MARK(P) = 1, go to S3. Otherwise set MARK(P) $\leftarrow$ 1. Now if ATOM(P) = 1, go to S3; otherwise if S < N set S $\leftarrow$ S + 1, STACK[S] $\leftarrow$ P, and go to S3; otherwise go to S5.

S3. Set P ← ALINK(R). If P = Λ or MARK(P) = 1, go to S4. Otherwise set MARK(P) ← 1. Now if ATOM(P) = 1, go to S4; otherwise set R ← P and return to S2.

S4. If S = 0, terminate the algorithm; otherwise set R ← STACK[S], S ← S − 1, and go to S2.

S5. Set Q ← ALINK(P). If Q = Λ or MARK(Q) = 1, go to S6. Otherwise set MARK(Q) ← 1. Now if ATOM(Q) = 1, go to S6; otherwise set ATOM(P) ← 1, ALINK(P) ← T, T ← P, P ← Q, go to S5.

S6. Set Q ← BLINK(P). If Q = Λ or MARK(Q) = 1, go to S7; otherwise set MARK(Q) ← 1. Now if ATOM(Q) = 1, go to S7; otherwise set BLINK(P) ← T, T ← P, P ← Q, go to S5.

S7. If T = Λ, go to S3. Otherwise set Q ← T. If ATOM(Q) = 1, set ATOM(Q) ← 0, T ← ALINK(Q), ALINK(Q) ← P, P ← Q, and return to S6. If ATOM(Q) = 0, set T ← BLINK(Q), BLINK(Q) ← P, P ← Q, and return to S7. ∎

Reference: CACM **10** (1967), 501–506.

6. From the second phase of garbage collection (or perhaps also the initial phase, if all mark bits are set to zero at that time).

7. Delete steps E2 and E3, and delete "ATOM(P) ← 1" in E4. Set MARK(P) ← 1 in step E5 and use "MARK(Q) = 0", "MARK(Q) = 1" in step E6 in place of the present "ATOM(Q) = 1", "ATOM(Q) = 0" respectively. The idea is to set the MARK bit only after the left subtree has been marked. This algorithm works even if the tree has overlapping (shared) subtrees, but it does not work for all recursive List structures such as those with NODE(ALINK(Q)) an ancestor of NODE(Q). (Note that ALINK of a marked node is never changed.)

8. *Solution 1:* Analogous to Algorithm E, but simpler.

F1. Set T ← Λ, P ← P0.

F2. Set MARK(P) ← 1, and set P ← P + SIZE(P).

F3. If MARK(P) = 1, go to F5.

F4. Set Q ← LINK(P). If Q ≠ Λ and MARK(Q) = 0, set LINK(P) ← T, T ← P, P ← Q and go to F2. Otherwise set P ← P − 1 and return to F3.

F5. If T = Λ, stop. Otherwise set Q ← T, T ← LINK(Q), LINK(Q) ← P, P ← Q − 1, and return to F3. ∎

A similar algorithm, which sometimes decreases the storage overhead and which avoids all pointers into the middle of nodes, has been suggested by Lars-Erik Thorelli, *BIT* **12** (1972), 555–568.

Solution 2: Analogous to Algorithm D. For this solution, we assume that the SIZE field is large enough to contain a link address. Such an assumption is probably not justified by the statement of the problem, but it lets us use a slightly faster method than the first solution when it is applicable.

G1. Set T ← Λ, MARK(P0) ← 1, P ← P0 + SIZE(P0).

G2. If MARK(P) = 1, go to G5.

G3. Set Q ← LINK(P), P ← P − 1.

G4. If Q ≠ Λ and MARK(Q) = 0, set MARK(Q) ← 1, S ← SIZE(Q), SIZE(Q) ← T, T ← Q + S. Go back to G2.

G5. If $T = \Lambda$, stop. Otherwise set $P \leftarrow T$ and find the first value of $Q = P, P - 1,$ $P - 2, \ldots$ for which $\mathtt{MARK(Q)} = 1$; set $T \leftarrow \mathtt{SIZE(Q)}$ and $\mathtt{SIZE(Q)} \leftarrow P - Q$. Go back to G2. ∎

9. H1. Set $L \leftarrow 0$, $K \leftarrow M + 1$, $\mathtt{MARK(0)} \leftarrow 1$, $\mathtt{MARK}(M + 1) \leftarrow 0$.

H2. Increase L by one, and if $\mathtt{MARK(L)} = 1$ repeat this step.

H3. Decrease K by one, and if $\mathtt{MARK(K)} = 0$ repeat this step.

H4. If $L > K$, go to step H5; otherwise set $\mathtt{NODE(L)} \leftarrow \mathtt{NODE(K)}$, $\mathtt{ALINK(K)} \leftarrow L$, $\mathtt{MARK(K)} \leftarrow 0$, and return to H2.

H5. For $L = 1, 2, \ldots, K$ do the following: Set $\mathtt{MARK(L)} \leftarrow 0$. If $\mathtt{ATOM(L)} = 0$ and $\mathtt{ALINK(L)} > K$, set $\mathtt{ALINK(L)} \leftarrow \mathtt{ALINK(ALINK(L))}$. If $\mathtt{ATOM(L)} = 0$ and $\mathtt{BLINK(L)} > K$, set $\mathtt{BLINK(L)} \leftarrow \mathtt{ALINK(BLINK(L))}$. ∎

See also exercise 2.5–33.

10. Z1. [Initialize.] Set $F \leftarrow \mathtt{P0}$, $R \Leftarrow \mathtt{AVAIL}$, $\mathtt{NODE(R)} \leftarrow \mathtt{NODE(F)}$, $\mathtt{REF(F)} \leftarrow R$. (Here F and R are pointers for a queue set up in the $\mathtt{REF}$ fields of all header nodes encountered.)

Z2. [Begin new List.] Set $P \leftarrow F$, $Q \leftarrow \mathtt{REF(P)}$.

Z3. [Advance to right.] Set $P \leftarrow \mathtt{RLINK(P)}$. If $P = \Lambda$, go to Z6.

Z4. [Copy one node.] Set $\mathtt{Q1} \Leftarrow \mathtt{AVAIL}$, $\mathtt{RLINK(Q)} \leftarrow \mathtt{Q1}$, $Q \leftarrow \mathtt{Q1}$, $\mathtt{NODE(Q)} \leftarrow \mathtt{NODE(P)}$.

Z5. [Translate sub-List link.] If $\mathtt{T(P)} = 1$, set $\mathtt{P1} \leftarrow \mathtt{REF(P)}$, and if $\mathtt{REF(P1)} = \Lambda$ set $\mathtt{REF(R)} \leftarrow \mathtt{P1}$, $R \Leftarrow \mathtt{AVAIL}$, $\mathtt{REF(P1)} \leftarrow R$, $\mathtt{NODE(R)} \leftarrow \mathtt{NODE(P1)}$, $\mathtt{REF(Q)} \leftarrow R$. If $\mathtt{T(P)} = 1$ and $\mathtt{REF(P1)} \neq \Lambda$, set $\mathtt{REF(Q)} \leftarrow \mathtt{REF(P1)}$. Go to Z3.

Z6. [Move to next List.] Set $\mathtt{RLINK(Q)} \leftarrow \Lambda$. If $\mathtt{REF(F)} \neq R$, set $F \leftarrow \mathtt{REF(REF(F))}$ and return to Z2. Otherwise set $\mathtt{REF(R)} \leftarrow \Lambda$, $P \leftarrow \mathtt{P0}$.

Z7. [Final cleanup.] Set $Q \leftarrow \mathtt{REF(P)}$. If $Q \neq \Lambda$, set $\mathtt{REF(P)} \leftarrow \Lambda$ and $P \leftarrow Q$ and repeat step Z7. ∎

Of course, this use of the $\mathtt{REF}$ fields makes it impossible to do garbage collection with Algorithm D; moreover, Algorithm D is ruled out by the fact that the Lists aren't well-formed during the copying.

Several elegant List-moving and List-copying algorithms that make substantially weaker assumptions about List representation have been devised. See D. W. Clark, *CACM* **19** (1976), 352–354; J. M. Robson, *CACM* **20** (1977), 431–433.

11. Here is a pencil-and-paper method that can be written out more formally to answer the problem: First attach a unique name (e.g., a capital letter) to each List in the given set; in the example we might have $A = (a\colon C, b, a\colon F)$, $F = (b\colon D)$, $B = (a\colon F, b, a\colon E)$, $C = (b\colon G)$, $G = (a\colon C)$, $D = (a\colon F)$, $E = (b\colon G)$. Now make a list of pairs of List names that must be proved equal. Successively add pairs to this list until either a contradiction is found because we have a pair that disagree on the first level (then the originally given Lists are unequal), or until the list of pairs does not imply any further pairs (then the originally given Lists are equal). In the example, this list of pairs would originally contain only the given pair, AB; then it gets the further pairs CF, EF (by matching A and B), DG (from CF); and then we have a self-consistent set.

To prove the validity of this method, observe that (i) if it returns the answer "unequal", the given Lists are unequal; (ii) if the given Lists are unequal, it returns the answer "unequal"; (iii) it always terminates.

12. When the `AVAIL` list contains N nodes, where N is a specified constant to be chosen as discussed below, initiate another coroutine that shares computer time with the main routine and does the following: (a) Marks all N nodes on the `AVAIL` list; (b) marks all other nodes that are accessible to the program; (c) links all unmarked nodes together to prepare a new `AVAIL` list for use when the current `AVAIL` list is empty, and (d) resets the mark bits in all nodes. One must choose N and the ratio of time sharing so that operations (a), (b), (c), and (d) are guaranteed to be complete before N nodes are taken from the `AVAIL` list, yet the main routine is running sufficiently fast. It is necessary to use some care in step (b) to make sure that all nodes "accessible to the program" are included, as the program continues to run; details are omitted here. If the list formed in (c) has fewer than N nodes, it may be necessary to stop eventually because memory space might become exhausted. [For further information, see Guy L. Steele Jr., *CACM* **18** (1975), 495–508; P. Wadler, *CACM* **19** (1976), 491–500; E. W. Dijkstra, L. Lamport, A. J. Martin, C. S. Scholten, and E. F. M. Steffens, *CACM* **21** (1978), 966–975; H. G. Baker, Jr., *CACM* **21** (1978), 280–294.]

SECTION 2.4

1. Preorder.

2. It is essentially proportional to the number of Data Table entries created.

3. Change step A5 to:

A5'. [Remove top level.] Remove the top stack entry; and if the new level number at the top of the stack is $\geq$ L, let (L1,P1) be the new entry at the top of the stack and repeat this step. Otherwise set SIB(P1) $\leftarrow$ Q and then let (L1,P1) be the new entry at the top of the stack.

4. (Solution by David S. Wise.) Rule (c) is violated if and only if there is a data item whose *complete qualification* A_0 OF ... OF A_n is also a COBOL reference to some other data item. Since the parent A_1 OF ... OF A_n must also satisfy rule (c), we may assume that this other data item is a descendant of the same parent. Therefore Algorithm A would be extended to check, as each new data item is added to the Data Table, whether its parent is an ancestor of any other item of the same name, or if the parent of any other item of the same name is in the stack. (When the parent is Λ, it is everybody's ancestor and always on the stack.)

On the other hand, if we leave Algorithm A as it stands, the COBOL programmer will get an error message from Algorithm B when trying to use an illegal item. Only `MOVE CORRESPONDING` can make use of such items without error.

5. Make these changes:

Step	replace	by
B1.	P $\leftarrow$ LINK(P_0)	P $\leftarrow$ LINK(INFO(T))
B2.	$k \leftarrow 0$	K $\leftarrow$ T
B3.	$k < n$	RLINK(K) $\neq \Lambda$
B4.	$k \leftarrow k + 1$	K $\leftarrow$ RLINK(K)
B6.	NAME(S) $= P_k$	NAME(S) $=$ INFO(K)

6. A simple modification of Algorithm B makes it search only for complete references (if $k = n$ and PARENT(S) $\neq \Lambda$ in step B3, or if NAME(S) $\neq P_k$ in step B6, set P $\leftarrow$ PREV(P) and go to B2). The idea is to run through this modified Algorithm B first; then, if Q is *still* Λ, to perform the unmodified algorithm.

7. MOVE MONTH OF DATE OF SALES TO MONTH OF DATE OF PURCHASES. MOVE DAY OF DATE OF SALES TO DAY OF DATE OF PURCHASES. MOVE YEAR OF DATE OF SALES TO YEAR OF

DATE OF PURCHASES. MOVE ITEM OF TRANSACTION OF SALES TO ITEM OF TRANSACTION OF PURCHASES. MOVE QUANTITY OF TRANSACTION OF SALES TO QUANTITY OF TRANSACTION OF PURCHASES. MOVE PRICE OF TRANSACTION OF SALES TO PRICE OF TRANSACTION OF PURCHASES. MOVE TAX OF TRANSACTION OF SALES TO TAX OF TRANSACTION OF PURCHASES.

8. If and only if α or β is an elementary item. (It may be of interest to note that the author failed to handle this case properly in his first draft of Algorithm C, and it actually made the algorithm more complicated.)

9. "MOVE CORRESPONDING α TO β", if neither α nor β is elementary, is equivalent to the set of statements "MOVE CORRESPONDING A OF α TO A OF β" taken over all names A common to groups α and β. (This is a more elegant way to state the definition than the more traditional and more cumbersome definition of "MOVE CORRESPONDING" given in the text.) We may verify that Algorithm C satisfies this definition, using an inductive proof that steps C2 through C5 will ultimately terminate with P = P0 and Q = Q0. Further details of the proof are filled in as we have done many times before in a "tree induction" (see, for example, the proof of Algorithm 2.3.1T).

10. (a) Set S1 ← LINK(P_k). Then repeatedly set S1 ← PREV(S1) zero or more times until either S1 = Λ (NAME(S) $\neq P_k$) or S1 = S (NAME(S) = P_k). (b) Set P1 ← P and then set P1 ← PREV(P1) zero or more times until PREV(P1) = Λ; do a similar operation with variables Q1 and Q; then test if P1 = Q1. Alternatively, if the Data Table entries are ordered so that PREV(P) < P for all P, a faster test can be made in an obvious way depending on whether P > Q or not, following the PREV links of the larger to see if the smaller is encountered.

11. A minuscule improvement in the speed of step C4 would be achieved by adding a new link field SIB1(P) $\equiv$ CHILD(PARENT(P)). More significantly, we could modify the CHILD and SIB links so that NAME(SIB(P)) > NAME(P); this would speed up the search in step C3 considerably because it would require only one pass over each family to find the matching members. This change would therefore remove the only "search" present in Algorithm C. Algorithms A and C are readily modified for this interpretation, and the reader may find it an interesting exercise. (However, if we consider the relative frequency of MOVE CORRESPONDING statements and the usual size of family groups, the resulting speedup will not be terribly significant in the translation of actual COBOL programs.)

12. Leave steps B1, B2, B3 unchanged; change the other steps thus:

> **B4′.** Set $k \leftarrow k + 1$, R ← LINK(P_k).

> **B5′.** If R = Λ, set P ← PREV(P) and go to B2′ (we haven't found a match). If R < S ≤ SCOPE(R), set S ← R and go to B3′. Otherwise set R ← PREV(R) and repeat step B5′. ∎

This algorithm does *not* adapt to the PL/I convention of exercise 6.

13. Use the same algorithm, minus the operations that set NAME, PARENT, CHILD, and SIB. Whenever removing the top stack entry in step A5, set SCOPE(P1) ← Q − 1. When the input is exhausted in step A2, simply set L ← 0 and continue, then terminate the algorithm if L = 0 in step A7.

14. The following algorithm, using an auxiliary stack, has steps numbered to show a direct correspondence with the text's algorithm.

> **C1′.** Set P ← P0, Q ← Q0, and set the stack contents empty.

C2. If SCOPE(P) = P or SCOPE(Q) = Q, output (P,Q) as one of the desired pairs and go to C5. Otherwise put (P,Q) on the stack and set P ← P + 1, Q ← Q + 1.

C3. Determine if P and Q point to entries with the same name (see exercise 10(b)). If so, go to C2. If not, let (P1,Q1) be the entry at the top of the stack; if SCOPE(Q) < SCOPE(Q1), set Q ← SCOPE(Q) + 1 and repeat step C3.

C4. Let (P1,Q1) be the entry at the top of the stack. If SCOPE(P) < SCOPE(P1), set P ← SCOPE(P) + 1, Q ← Q1 + 1, and go back to C3. If SCOPE(P) = SCOPE(P1), set P ← P1, Q ← Q1 and remove the top entry of the stack.

C5. If the stack is empty, the algorithm terminates. Otherwise go to C4. ∎

SECTION 2.5

1. In such fortuitous circumstances, a stack-like operation may be used as follows: Let the memory pool area be locations 0 through M − 1, and let AVAIL point to the lowest free location. To reserve N words, report failure if AVAIL + N ≥ M, otherwise set AVAIL ← AVAIL + N. To free these N words, just set AVAIL ← AVAIL − N.

Similarly, cyclic queue-like operation is appropriate for a first-in-first-out discipline.

2. The amount of storage space for an item of length l is $k\lceil l/(k-b)\rceil$, which has the average value $kL/(k-b) + (1-\alpha)k$, where α is assumed to be $1/2$, independent of k. This expression is a minimum (for real values of k) when $k = b + \sqrt{2bL}$. So choose k to be the integer just above or just below this value, whichever gives the lowest value of $kL/(k-b) + \frac{1}{2}k$. For example, if $b = 1$ and $L = 10$, we would choose $k \approx 1 + \sqrt{20} = 5$ or 6; both are equally good. For much greater detail about this problem, see *JACM* **12** (1965), 53–70.

4. rI1 ≡ Q, rI2 ≡ P.

A1	LDA	N	rA ← N.
	ENT2	AVAIL	P ← LOC(AVAIL).
A2A	ENT1	0,2	Q ← P.
A2	LD2	0,1(LINK)	P ← LINK(Q).
	J2N	OVERFLOW	If P = Λ, no room.
A3	CMPA	0,2(SIZE)	
	JG	A2A	Jump if N > SIZE(P).
A4	SUB	0,2(SIZE)	rA ← N − SIZE(P) ≡ K.
	JANZ	*+3	Jump if K ≠ 0.
	LDX	0,2(LINK)	
	STX	0,1(LINK)	LINK(Q) ← LINK(P).
	STA	0,2(SIZE)	SIZE(P) ← K.
	LD1	0,2(SIZE)	Optional ending,
	INC1	0,2	sets rI1 ← P + K. ∎

5. Probably not. The unavailable storage area just before location P will subsequently become available, and its length will be increased by the amount K; an increase of 99 would not be negligible.

6. The idea is to try to search in different parts of the AVAIL list each time. We can use a "roving pointer," called ROVER for example, which is treated as follows: In step A1, set Q ← ROVER. After step A4, set ROVER ← LINK(Q) if LINK(Q) ≠ Λ, otherwise set ROVER ← LOC(AVAIL). In step A2, when P = Λ the first time during a particular execution of Algorithm A, set Q ← LOC(AVAIL) and repeat step A2. When P = Λ the *second* time, the algorithm terminates unsuccessfully. In this way ROVER will tend to point to a random spot in the AVAIL list, and the sizes will be more balanced. At the beginning of the program, set ROVER ← LOC(AVAIL); it is *also* necessary to set ROVER to LOC(AVAIL) everywhere else in the program where the block whose address equals the current setting of ROVER is taken out of the AVAIL list. (Sometimes, however, it is useful to have small blocks at the beginning, as in the strict first-fit method; for example, we might want to keep a sequential stack at the high end of memory. In such cases we can reduce the search time by using trees as suggested in exercise 6.2.3–30.)

7. 2000, 1000 with requests of sizes 800, 1300. [An example where *worst-fit* succeeds, while best-fit fails, has been constructed by R. J. Weiland.]

8. In step A1″, also set M ← ∞, R ← Λ. In step A2″, if P = Λ go to A6″. In step A3″, go to A5″ instead of to A4″. Add new steps as follows:

> **A5″.** [Better fit?] If M > SIZE(P), set R ← Q and M ← SIZE(P). Then set Q ← P and return to A2″.
>
> **A6″.** [Any found?] If R = Λ, the algorithm terminates unsuccessfully. Otherwise set Q ← R, P ← LINK(Q), and go to A4″. ∎

9. Obviously if we are so lucky as to find SIZE(P) = N, we have a best fit and it is not necessary to search farther. (When there are only very few different block sizes, this occurs rather often.) If a "boundary tag" method like Algorithm C is being used, it is possible to maintain the AVAIL list in sorted order by size; so the length of search could be cut down to half the length of the list or less, on the average. But the best solution is to make the AVAIL list into a balanced tree structure as described in Section 6.2.3, if it is expected to be long.

10. Make the following changes:

Step B2, for "P > P0" read "P ≥ P0".

At the beginning of step B3, insert "If P0 + N > P and P ≠ Λ, set N ← max(N, P + SIZE(P) − P0), P ← LINK(P), and repeat step B3."

Step B4, for "Q + SIZE(Q) = P0", read "Q + SIZE(Q) ≥ P0"; and for "SIZE(Q) ← SIZE(Q) + N" read "SIZE(Q) ← max(SIZE(Q), P0 + N − Q)".

11. If P0 is greater than ROVER, we can set Q ← ROVER instead of Q ← LOC(AVAIL) in step B1. If there are n entries in the AVAIL list, the average number of iterations of step B2 is $(2n+3)(n+2)/(6n+6) = \frac{1}{3}n + \frac{5}{6} + O\left(\frac{1}{n}\right)$. For example if $n = 2$ we get 9 equally probable situations, where P1 and P2 point to the two existing available blocks:

	PO < P1	P1 < PO < P2	P2 < PO
ROVER = P1	1	1	2
ROVER = P2	1	2	1
ROVER = LOC(AVAIL)	1	2	3

This chart shows the number of iterations needed in each case. The average is

$$\frac{1}{9}\left(\binom{2}{2} + \binom{3}{2} + \binom{4}{2} + \binom{3}{2} + \binom{2}{2}\right) = \frac{1}{9}\left(\binom{5}{3} + \binom{4}{3}\right) = \frac{14}{9}.$$

12. **A1*.** Set P ← ROVER, F ← 0.

> **A2*.** If P = LOC(AVAIL) and F = 0, set P ← AVAIL, F ← 1, and repeat step A2*. If P = LOC(AVAIL) and F ≠ 0, the algorithm terminates unsuccessfully.
>
> **A3*.** If SIZE(P) ≥ N, go to A4*; otherwise set P ← LINK(P) and return to A2*.

A4*. Set ROVER ← LINK(P), K ← SIZE(P) − N. If K < c (where c is a constant ≥ 2), set LINK(LINK(P + 1)) ← ROVER, LINK(ROVER + 1) ← LINK(P + 1), L ← P; otherwise set L ← P + K, SIZE(P) ← SIZE(L − 1) ← K, TAG(L − 1) ← "−", SIZE(L) ← N. Finally set TAG(L) ← TAG(L + SIZE(L) − 1) ← "+". ∎

13. rI1 ≡ P, rX ≡ F, rI2 ≡ L.

```
LINK   EQU  4:5
SIZE   EQU  1:2
TSIZE  EQU  0:2
TAG    EQU  0:0
A1     LDA  N            rA ← N.
       SLA  3            Shift into SIZE field.
       ENTX 0            F ← 0.
       LD1  ROVER        P ← ROVER.
       JMP  A2
A3     CMPA 0,1(SIZE)
       JLE  A4           Jump if N ≤ SIZE(P).
       LD1  0,1(LINK)    P ← LINK(P).
A2     ENT2 -AVAIL,1     rI2 ← P − LOC(AVAIL).
       J2NZ A3
       JXNZ OVERFLOW     Is F ≠ 0?
       ENTX 1            Set F ← 1.
       LD1  AVAIL(LINK)  P ← AVAIL.
       JMP  A2
A4     LD2  0,1(LINK)
       ST2  ROVER        ROVER ← LINK(P).
       LDA  0,1(SIZE)    rA ≡ K ← SIZE(P) − N.
       SUB  N
       CMPA =c=
       JGE  1F           Jump if K ≥ c.
       LD3  1,1(LINK)    rI3 ← LINK(P + 1).
       ST2  0,3(LINK)    LINK(rI3) ← ROVER.
       ST3  1,2(LINK)    LINK(ROVER + 1) ← rI3.
       ENT2 0,1          L ← P.
       LD3  0,1(SIZE)    rI3 ← SIZE(P).
       JMP  2F
1H     STA  0,1(SIZE)    SIZE(P) ← K.
       LD2  0,1(SIZE)
       INC2 0,1          L ← P + K.
       LDAN 0,1(SIZE)    rA ← −K.
       STA  -1,2(TSIZE)  SIZE(L − 1) ← K, TAG(L − 1) ← "−".
       LD3  N            rI3 ← N.
2H     ST3  0,2(TSIZE)   TAG(L) ← "+", also set SIZE(L) ← rI3.
       INC3 0,2
       STZ  -1,3(TAG)    TAG(L + SIZE(L) − 1) ← "+". ∎
```

14. (a) This field is needed to locate the beginning of the block, in step C2. It could be replaced (perhaps to advantage) by a link to the first word of the block. See also exercise 19. (b) This field is needed because we sometimes need to reserve more than N words (for example if K = 1), and the amount reserved must be known when the block is subsequently freed.

15, 16. $rI1 \equiv P0$, $rI2 \equiv P1$, $rI3 \equiv F$, $rI4 \equiv B$, $rI6 \equiv -N$.

```
C1 LD1  P0                    C1.
   LD2  0,1(SIZE)
   ENN6 0,2                   N ← SIZE(P0).
   INC2 0,1                   P1 ← P0 + N.
   LD5  0,2(TSIZE)
   J5N  C4                    To C4 if TAG(P1) = "−".
C2 LD5  -1,1(TSIZE)           C2.
   J5N  C7                    To C7 if TAG(P0 − 1) = "−".
C3 LD3  AVAIL(LINK)           C3. Set F ← AVAIL.
   ENT4 AVAIL                 B ← LOC(AVAIL).
   JMP  C5                    To C5.
C4 INC6 0,5                   C4. N ← N + SIZE(P1).
   LD3  0,2(LINK)             F ← LINK(P1).
   LD4  1,2(LINK)             B ← LINK(P1 + 1).
   CMP2 ROVER                 (New code, because of the ROVER
   JNE  *+3                      feature of exercise 12:
   ENTX AVAIL                 If P1 = ROVER,
   STX  ROVER                     set ROVER ← LOC(AVAIL).)
   DEC2 0,5                   P1 ← P1 + SIZE(P1).
   LD5  -1,1(TSIZE)
   J5N  C6                    To C6 if TAG(P0 − 1) = "−".
C5 ST3  0,1(LINK)             C5. LINK(P0) ← F.
   ST4  1,1(LINK)             LINK(P0 + 1) ← B.
   ST1  1,3(LINK)             LINK(F + 1) ← P0.
   ST1  0,4(LINK)             LINK(B) ← P0.
   JMP  C8                    To C8.
C6 ST3  0,4(LINK)             C6. LINK(B) ← F.
   ST4  1,3(LINK)             LINK(F + 1) ← B.
C7 INC6 0,5                   C7. N ← N + SIZE(P0 − 1).
   INC1 0,5                   P0 ← P0 − SIZE(P0 − 1).
C8 ST6  0,1(TSIZE)            C8. SIZE(P0) ← N, TAG(P0) ← "−".
   ST6  -1,2(TSIZE)           SIZE(P1 − 1) ← N, TAG(P1 − 1) ← "−".  ▮
```

17. Both LINK fields equal to LOC(AVAIL).

18. Algorithm A reserves the upper end of a large block. When storage is completely available, the first-fit method actually begins by reserving the high-order locations, but once these become available again they are not re-reserved since a fit is usually found already in the lower locations; thus the initial large block at the lower end of memory quickly disappears with first-fit. A large block rarely is the best fit, however, so the best-fit method leaves a large block at the beginning of memory.

19. Use the algorithm of exercise 12, except delete the references to SIZE(L − 1), TAG(L − 1), and TAG(L + SIZE(L) − 1) from step A4*; also insert the following new step between steps A2* and A3*:

> **A2.5*.** Set P1 ← P + SIZE(P). If TAG(P1) = "+", proceed to step A3. Otherwise set P2 ← LINK(P1), LINK(P2 + 1) ← LINK(P1 + 1), LINK(LINK(P1 + 1)) ← P2, SIZE(P) ← SIZE(P) + SIZE(P1). If ROVER = P1, set ROVER ← P2. Repeat step A2.5*.

Clearly the situation of (2), (3), (4) can't occur here; the only real effect on storage allocation is that the search here will tend to be longer than in exercise 12, and sometimes K will be less than c although there is really another available block preceding this one that we do not know about.

(An alternative is to take the collapsing out of the inner loop A3*, and to do the collapsing only in step A4* before the final allocation or in the inner loop when the algorithm would otherwise have terminated unsuccessfully. This alternative requires a simulation study to see if it is an improvement or not.)

[This method, with a few refinements, has proved to be quite satisfactory in the implementations of TEX and METAFONT. See *TEX: The Program* (Addison–Wesley, 1986), §125.]

20. When a buddy is found to be available, during the collapsing loop, we want to remove that block from its AVAIL[k] list, but we do not know which links to update unless (i) we do a possibly long search, or (ii) the list is doubly linked.

21. If $n = 2^k \alpha$, where $1 \leq \alpha \leq 2$, a_n is $2^{2k+1}(\alpha - \frac{2}{3}) + \frac{1}{3}$, and b_n is $2^{2k-1}\alpha^2 + 2^{k-1}\alpha$. The ratio a_n/b_n for large n is essentially $4(\alpha - \frac{2}{3})/\alpha^2$, which takes its minimum value $\frac{4}{3}$ when $\alpha = 1$ and 2, and its maximum value $\frac{3}{2}$ when $\alpha = 1\frac{1}{3}$. So a_n/b_n approaches no limit; it oscillates between these two extremes. The averaging methods of Section 4.2.4 do, however, yield an average ratio of $4(\ln 2)^{-1} \int_1^2 (\alpha - \frac{2}{3})\, d\alpha/\alpha^3 = (\ln 2)^{-1} \approx 1.44$.

22. This idea requires a TAG field in several words of the 11-word block, not only in the first word. It is a workable idea, if those extra TAG bits can be spared, and it would appear to be especially suitable for use in computer hardware.

23. 011011110100; 011011100000.

24. This would introduce a bug in the program; we may get to step S1 when TAG(0) = 1, since S2 may return to S1. To make it work, add "TAG(L) ← 0" after "L ← P" in step S2. (It is easier to assume instead that TAG(2^m) = 0.)

25. The idea is absolutely correct. (Criticism need not be negative.) The list heads AVAIL[k] may be eliminated for $n < k \leq m$; the algorithms of the text may be used if "m" is changed to "n" in steps R1, S1. The initial conditions (13) and (14) should be changed to indicate 2^{m-n} blocks of size 2^n instead of one block of size 2^m.

26. Using the binary representation of M, we can easily modify the initial conditions (13), (14) so that all memory locations are divided into blocks whose size is a power of two, with blocks in decreasing order of size. In Algorithm S, TAG(P) should be regarded as 0 whenever $P \geq M - 2^k$.

27. rI1 $\equiv$ k, rI2 $\equiv$ j, rI3 $\equiv$ $j - k$, rI4 $\equiv$ L, LOC(AVAIL[j]) = AVAIL + j; assume that there is an auxiliary table TWO[j] = 2^j, stored in location TWO + j, for $0 \leq j \leq m$. Assume further that "+" and "−" represent tags of 0 and 1, and that TAG(LOC(AVAIL[j])) = "−"; but TAG(LOC(AVAIL[$m + 1$])) = "+" is a sentinel.

```
00  KVAL  EQU   5:5
01  TAG   EQU   0:0
02  LINKF EQU   1:2
03  LINKB EQU   3:4
04  TLNKF EQU   0:2
05  R1    LD1   K              1    R1. Find block.
06        ENT2  0,1            1    j ← k.
07        ENT3  0              1
08        LD4   AVAIL,2(LINKF) 1
```

09	1H	ENT5 AVAIL,2	$1+R$	
10		DEC5 0,4	$1+R$	
11		J5NZ R2	$1+R$	Jump if AVAILF[j] $\neq$ LOC(AVAIL[j]).
12		INC2 1	R	Increase j.
13		INC3 1	R	
14		LD4N AVAIL,2(TLNKF)	R	
15		J4NN 1B	R	Is $j \leq m$?
16		JMP OVERFLOW		
17	R2	LD5 0,4(LINKB)	1	*R2. Remove from list.*
18		ST5 AVAIL,2(LINKB)	1	AVAILB[j] $\leftarrow$ LINKB(L).
19		ENTA AVAIL,2	1	
20		STA 0,5(LINKF)	1	LINKF(L) $\leftarrow$ LOC(AVAIL[j]).
21		STZ 0,4(TAG)	1	TAG(L) $\leftarrow$ 0.
22	R3	J3Z DONE	1	*R3. Split required?*
23	R4	DEC3 1	R	*R4. Split.*
24		DEC2 1	R	Decrease j.
25		LD5 TWO,2	R	rI5 $\equiv$ P.
26		INC5 0,4	R	P $\leftarrow$ L + 2^j.
27		ENNA AVAIL,2	R	
28		STA 0,5(TLNKF)	R	TAG(P) $\leftarrow$ 1, LINKF(P) $\leftarrow$ LOC(AVAIL[j]).
29		STA 0,5(LINKB)	R	LINKB(P) $\leftarrow$ LOC(AVAIL[j]).
30		ST5 AVAIL,2(LINKF)	R	AVAILF[j] $\leftarrow$ P.
31		ST5 AVAIL,2(LINKB)	R	AVAILB[j] $\leftarrow$ P.
32		ST2 0,5(KVAL)	R	KVAL(P) $\leftarrow$ j.
33		J3P R4	R	Go to R3.
34	DONE	...		∎

28. rI1 $\equiv$ k, rI5 $\equiv$ P, rI4 $\equiv$ L; assume TAG(2^m) = "+".

01	S1	LD4 L	1	*S1. Is buddy available?*
02		LD1 K	1	
03	1H	ENTA 0,4	$1+S$	
04		XOR TWO,1	$1+S$	rA $\leftarrow$ buddy$_k$(L).
05		STA TEMP	$1+S$	
06		LD5 TEMP	$1+S$	P $\leftarrow$ rA.
07		LDA 0,5	$1+S$	
08		JANN S3	$1+S$	Jump if TAG(P) = 0.
09		CMP1 0,5(KVAL)	$B+S$	
10		JNE S3	$B+S$	Jump if KVAL(P) $\neq$ k.
11	S2	LD2 0,5(LINKB)	S	*S2. Combine with buddy.*
12		LD3 0,5(LINKF)	S	
13		ST3 0,2(LINKF)	S	LINKF(LINKB(P)) $\leftarrow$ LINKF(P).
14		ST2 0,3(LINKB)	S	LINKB(LINKF(P)) $\leftarrow$ LINKB(P).
15		INC1 1	S	Increase k.
16		CMP4 TEMP	S	
17		JL 1B	S	
18		ENT4 0,5	A	If L > P, set L $\leftarrow$ P.
19		JMP 1B	A	
20	S3	LD2 AVAIL,1(LINKF)	1	*S3. Put on list.*
21		ENNA AVAIL,1	1	
22		STA 0,4(0:4)	1	TAG(L) $\leftarrow$ 1, LINKB(L) $\leftarrow$ LOC(AVAIL[k]).

23	ST2	0,4(LINKF)	1	LINKF(L) ← AVAILF[k].
24	ST1	0,4(KVAL)	1	KVAL(L) ← k.
25	ST4	0,2(LINKB)	1	LINKB(AVAILF[k]) ← L.
26	ST4	AVAIL,1(LINKF)	1	AVAIL[k] ← L. ■

29. Yes, but only at the expense of some searching, or (better) an additional table of TAG bits packed somehow. (It is tempting to suggest that buddies not be joined together during Algorithm S, but only in Algorithm R if there is no block large enough to meet the request; but that would probably lead to a badly fragmented memory.)

31. See David L. Russell, *SICOMP* **6** (1977), 607–621.

32. Steven Crain points out that the method always frees all blocks and starts afresh before 16667 units of time have elapsed; hence the stated limit certainly exists. *Proof:* Let $u_n = n + t_n$, so that $g_n = \lfloor \frac{5}{4} \min(10000, f(u_{n-1} - n), f(u_{n-2} - n), \ldots, f(u_0 - n)) \rfloor$. Let $x_0 = 0$ and $x_1 = u_0$, and $x_{k+1} = \max(u_0, \ldots, u_{x_k-1})$ for $k \geq 1$. If $x_k > x_{k-1}$ then

$$u_n \leq n + \frac{5}{4} f(x_k - n) = \frac{5}{4} x_k - \frac{1}{4} n \leq \frac{5}{4} x_k - \frac{1}{4} x_{k-1} \qquad \text{for } x_{k-1} \leq n < x_k;$$

therefore $x_{k+1} - x_k \leq \frac{1}{4}(x_k - x_{k-1})$, and we must have $x_k = x_{k-1}$ before reaching time $12500 + \lfloor 12500/4 \rfloor + \lfloor 12500/4^2 \rfloor + \cdots$.

33. **G1.** [Clear LINKs.] Set P ← 1, and repeat the operation LINK(P) ← Λ, P ← P + SIZE(P) until P = AVAIL. (This merely sets the LINK field in the first word of each node to Λ; we may assume in most cases that this step is unnecessary, since LINK(P) is set to Λ in step G9 below and it can be set to Λ by the storage allocator.)

    G2. [Initialize marking phase.] Set TOP ← USE, LINK(TOP) ← AVAIL, LINK(AVAIL) ← Λ. (TOP points to the top of a stack as in Algorithm 2.3.5D.)

    G3. [Pop up stack.] Set P ← TOP, TOP ← LINK(TOP). If TOP = Λ, go to G5.

    G4. [Put new links on stack.] For $1 \leq k \leq$ T(P), do the following operations: Set Q ← LINK(P + k); then if Q ≠ Λ and LINK(Q) = Λ, set LINK(Q) ← TOP, TOP ← Q. Then go back to G3.

    G5. [Initialize next phase.] (Now P = AVAIL, and the marking phase has been completed so that the first word of each accessible node has a nonnull LINK. Our next goal is to combine adjacent inaccessible nodes, for speed in later steps, and to assign new addresses to the accessible nodes.) Set Q ← 1, LINK(AVAIL) ← Q, SIZE(AVAIL) ← 0, P ← 1. (Location AVAIL is being used as a sentinel to signify the end of a loop in subsequent phases.)

    G6. [Assign new addresses.] If LINK(P) = Λ, go to G7. Otherwise if SIZE(P) = 0, go to G8. Otherwise set LINK(P) ← Q, Q ← Q + SIZE(P), P ← P + SIZE(P), and repeat this step.

    G7. [Collapse available areas.] If LINK(P + SIZE(P)) = Λ, increase SIZE(P) by SIZE(P + SIZE(P)) and repeat this step. Otherwise set P ← P + SIZE(P) and return to G6.

    G8. [Translate all links.] (Now the LINK field in the first word of each accessible node contains the address to which the node will be moved.) Set USE ← LINK(USE), and AVAIL ← Q. Then set P ← 1, and repeat the following operation until SIZE(P) = 0: If LINK(P) ≠ Λ, set LINK(Q) ← LINK(LINK(Q)) for all Q such that P < Q ≤ P + T(P) and LINK(Q) ≠ Λ; then regardless of the value of LINK(P), set P ← P + SIZE(P).

G9. [Move.] Set P ← 1, and repeat the following operation until SIZE(P) = 0: Set Q ← LINK(P), and if Q ≠ Λ set LINK(P) ← Λ and NODE(Q) ← NODE(P); then whether Q = Λ or not, set P ← P + SIZE(P). (The operation NODE(Q) ← NODE(P) implies the movement of SIZE(P) words; we always have Q ≤ P, so it is safe to move the words in order from smallest location to largest.) ∎

[This method is called the "LISP 2 garbage collector." An interesting alternative, which does not require the LINK field at the beginning of a node, can be based on the idea of linking together all pointers that point to each node — see Lars-Erik Thorelli, *BIT* **16** (1976), 426–441; R. B. K. Dewar and A. P. McCann, *Software Practice & Exp.* **7** (1977), 95–113; F. Lockwood Morris, *CACM* **21** (1978), 662–665, **22** (1979), 571; H. B. M. Jonkers, *Inf. Proc. Letters* **9** (1979), 26–30; J. J. Martin, *CACM* **25** (1982), 571–581; F. Lockwood Morris, *Inf. Proc. Letters* **15** (1982), 139–142, **16** (1983), 215. Other methods have been published by B. K. Haddon and W. M. Waite, *Comp. J.* **10** (1967), 162–165; B. Wegbreit, *Comp. J.* **15** (1972), 204–208; D. A. Zave, *Inf. Proc. Letters* **3** (1975), 167–169. Cohen and Nicolau have analyzed four of these approaches in *ACM Trans. Prog. Languages and Systems* **5** (1983), 532–553.]

34. Let TOP ≡ rI1, Q ≡ rI2, P ≡ rI3, k ≡ rI4, SIZE(P) ≡ rI5. Assume further that Λ = 0, and LINK(0) ≠ 0 to simplify step G4. Step G1 is omitted.

```
01  LINK  EQU  4:5
02  INFO  EQU  0:3
03  SIZE  EQU  1:2
04  T     EQU  3:3
05  G2    LD1  USE          1          G2. Initialize marking phase. TOP ← USE.
06        LD2  AVAIL        1
07        ST2  0,1(LINK)    1          LINK(TOP) ← AVAIL.
08        STZ  0,2(LINK)    1          LINK(AVAIL) ← Λ.
09  G3    ENT3 0,1          a + 1      G3. Pop up stack. P ← TOP.
10        LD1  0,1(LINK)    a + 1      TOP ← LINK(TOP).
11        J1Z  G5           a + 1      To G5 if TOP = Λ.
12  G4    LD4  0,3(T)       a          G4. Put new links on stack. k ← T(P).
13  1H    J4Z  G3           a + b      k = 0?
14        INC3 1            b          P ← P + 1.
15        DEC4 1            b          k ← k − 1.
16        LD2  0,3(LINK)    b          Q ← LINK(P).
17        LDA  0,2(LINK)    b
18        JANZ 1B           b          Jump if LINK(Q) ≠ Λ.
19        ST1  0,2(LINK)    a − 1      Otherwise set LINK(Q) ← TOP,
20        ENT1 0,2          a − 1        TOP ← Q.
21        JMP  1B           a − 1
22  G5    ENT2 1            1          G5. Initialize next phase. Q ← 1.
23        ST2  0,3          1          LINK(AVAIL) ← 1, SIZE(AVAIL) ← 0.
24        ENT3 1            1          P ← 1.
25        JMP  G6           1
26  1H    ST2  0,3(LINK)    a          LINK(P) ← Q.
27        INC2 0,5          a          Q ← Q + SIZE(P).
28        INC3 0,5          a          P ← P + SIZE(P).
29  G6    LDA  0,3(LINK)    a + 1      G6. Assign new addresses.
30  G6A   LD5  0,3(SIZE)    a + c + 1
```

31		JAZ	G7	$a+c+1$	Jump if LINK(P) $= \Lambda$.
32		J5NZ	1B	$a+1$	Jump if SIZE(P) $\neq 0$.
33	G8	LD1	USE	1	*G8. Translate all links.*
34		LDA	0,1(LINK)	1	
35		STA	USE	1	USE $\leftarrow$ LINK(USE).
36		ST2	AVAIL	1	AVAIL $\leftarrow$ Q.
37		ENT3	1	1	P $\leftarrow$ 1.
38		JMP	G8P	1	
39	1H	LD6	0,6(SIZE)	d	
40		INC5	0,6	d	rI5 $\leftarrow$ rI5 + SIZE(P + SIZE(P)).
41	G7	ENT6	0,3	$c+d$	*G7. Collapse available areas.*
42		INC6	0,5	$c+d$	rI6 $\leftarrow$ P + SIZE(P).
43		LDA	0,6(LINK)	$c+d$	
44		JAZ	1B	$c+d$	Jump if LINK(rI6) $\equiv \Lambda$.
45		ST5	0,3(SIZE)	c	SIZE(P) $\leftarrow$ rI5.
46		INC3	0,5	c	P $\leftarrow$ P + SIZE(P).
47		JMP	G6A	c	
48	2H	DEC4	1	b	$k \leftarrow k - 1$.
49		INC2	1	b	Q $\leftarrow$ Q + 1.
50		LD6	0,2(LINK)	b	
51		LDA	0,6(LINK)	b	
52		STA	0,2(LINK)	b	LINK(Q) $\leftarrow$ LINK(LINK(Q)).
53	1H	J4NZ	2B	$a+b$	Jump if $k \neq 0$.
54	3H	INC3	0,5	$a+c$	P $\leftarrow$ P + SIZE(P).
55	G8P	LDA	0,3(LINK)	$1+a+c$	
56		LD5	0,3(SIZE)	$1+a+c$	
57		JAZ	3B	$1+a+c$	Is LINK(P) $= \Lambda$?
58		LD4	0,3(T)	$1+a$	$k \leftarrow$ T(P).
59		ENT2	0,3	$1+a$	Q $\leftarrow$ P.
60		J5NZ	1B	$1+a$	Jump unless SIZE(P) $= 0$.
61	G9	ENT3	1	1	*G9. Move.* P $\leftarrow$ 1.
62		ENT1	1	1	Set rI1 for MOVE instructions.
63		JMP	G9P	1	
64	1H	STZ	0,3(LINK)	a	LINK(P) $\leftarrow \Lambda$.
65		ST5	*+1(4:4)	a	
66		MOVE	0,3(*)	a	NODE(rI1) $\leftarrow$ NODE(P), rI1 $\leftarrow$ rI1 + SIZE(P).
67	3H	INC3	0,5	$a+c$	P $\leftarrow$ P + SIZE(P).
68	G9P	LDA	0,3(LINK)	$1+a+c$	
69		LD5	0,3(SIZE)	$1+a+c$	
70		JAZ	3B	$1+a+c$	Jump if LINK(P) $= \Lambda$.
71		J5NZ	1B	$1+a$	Jump unless SIZE(P) $= 0$. ▌

In line 66 we are assuming that the size of each node is sufficiently small that it can be moved with a single MOVE instruction; this seems a fair assumption for most cases when this kind of garbage collection is applicable.

The total running time for this program is $(44a + 17b + 2w + 25c + 8d + 47)u$, where a is the number of accessible nodes, b is the number of link fields therein, c is the number of inaccessible nodes that are *not* preceded by an inaccessible node, d is the number of inaccessible nodes that *are* preceded by an inaccessible node, and w is the total number of words in the accessible nodes. If the memory contains n nodes, with ρn of them inaccessible, then we may estimate $a = (1-\rho)n$, $c = (1-\rho)\rho n$, $d = \rho^2 n$. Example: five-word nodes (on the average), with two link fields per node (on the average), and a memory of 1000 nodes. Then when $\rho = \frac{1}{5}$, it takes $374u$ per available node recovered; when $\rho = \frac{1}{2}$, it takes $104u$; and when $\rho = \frac{4}{5}$, it takes only $33u$.

36. A single customer will be able to sit in one of the sixteen seats 1, 3, 4, 6, ..., 23. If a pair enters, there must be room for them; otherwise there are at least two people in seats $(1, 2, 3)$, at least two in $(4, 5, 6)$, ..., at least two in $(19, 20, 21)$, and at least one in 22 or 23, so at least fifteen people are already seated.

37. First sixteen single males enter, and she seats them. There are 17 gaps of empty seats between the occupied seats, counting one gap at each end, with a gap of length zero assumed between adjacent occupied seats. The total number of empty seats, namely the sum of all seventeen gaps, is 6. Suppose x of the gaps are of odd length; then $6 - x$ spaces are available to seat pairs. (Note that $6 - x$ is even and ≥ 0.) Now each of the customers 1, 3, 5, 7, 9, 11, 13, 15, from left to right, who has an even gap on both sides, finishes his lunch and walks out. Each odd gap prevents at most one of these eight diners from leaving, hence at least $8 - x$ people leave. There *still* are only $6 - x$ spaces available to seat pairs. But now $(8 - x)/2$ pairs enter.

38. The arguments generalize readily; $N(n, 2) = \lfloor(3n - 1)/2\rfloor$ for $n \geq 1$. [When the hostess uses a first-fit strategy instead of an optimal one, Robson has proved that the necessary and sufficient number of seats is $\lfloor(5n - 2)/3\rfloor$.]

39. Divide memory into three independent regions of sizes $N(n_1, m)$, $N(n_2, m)$, and $N(2m - 2, m)$. To process a request for space, put each block into the first region for which the stated capacity is not exceeded, using the relevant optimum strategy for that region. This cannot fail, for if we were unable to fill a request for x locations we must have at least $(n_1 - x + 1) + (n_2 - x + 1) + (2m - x - 1) > n_1 + n_2 - x$ locations already occupied.

Now if $f(n) = N(n, m) + N(2m - 2, m)$, we have the subadditive law $f(n_1 + n_2) \leq f(n_1) + f(n_2)$. Hence $\lim f(n)/n$ exists. (*Proof:* $f(a + bc) \leq f(a) + bf(c)$; hence $\limsup_{n\to\infty} f(n)/n = \max_{0 \leq a < c} \limsup_{b\to\infty} f(a+bc)/(a+bc) \leq f(c)/c$ for all c; hence $\limsup_{n\to\infty} f(n)/n \leq \liminf_{n\to\infty} f(n)/n$.) Therefore $\lim N(n, m)/n$ exists.

[From exercise 38 we know that $N(2) = \frac{3}{2}$. The value $N(m)$ is not known for any $m > 2$. It is not difficult to show that the multiplicative factor for just two block sizes, 1 and b, is $2 - 1/b$; hence $N(3) \geq 1\frac{2}{3}$. Robson's methods imply that $N(3) \leq 1\frac{11}{12}$, and $2 \leq N(4) \leq 2\frac{1}{6}$.]

40. Robson has proved that $N(2^r) \leq 1 + r$, by using the following strategy: Allocate to each block of size k, where $2^m \leq k < 2^{m+1}$, the first available block of k locations starting at a multiple of 2^m.

Let $N(\{b_1, b_2, \ldots, b_n\})$ denote the multiplicative factor when all block sizes are constrained to lie in the set $\{b_1, b_2, \ldots, b_n\}$, so that $N(n) = N(\{1, 2, \ldots, n\})$. Robson and S. Krogdahl have discovered that $N(\{b_1, b_2, \ldots, b_n\}) = n - (b_1/b_2 + \cdots + b_{n-1}/b_n)$ whenever b_i is a multiple of b_{i-1} for $1 < i \leq n$; indeed, Robson has established the *exact* formula $N(2^r m, \{1, 2, 4, \ldots, 2^r\}) = 2^r m(1 + \frac{1}{2}r) - 2^r + 1$. Thus in particular, $N(n) \geq 1 + \frac{1}{2}\lfloor\lg n\rfloor$. He also has derived the upper bound $N(n) \leq 1.1825 \ln n + O(1)$, and he conjectures tentatively that $N(n) = H_n$. This conjecture would follow if $N(\{b_1, b_2, \ldots, b_n\})$ were equal to $n - (b_1/b_2 + \cdots + b_{n-1}/b_n)$ in general, but this is unfortunately not the case since Robson has proved that $N(\{3, 4\}) \geq 1\frac{4}{15}$. (See *Inf. Proc. Letters* **2** (1973), 96–97; *JACM* **21** (1974), 491–499.)

41. Consider maintaining the blocks of size 2^k: The requests for sizes 1, 2, 4, ..., 2^{k-1} will periodically call for a new block of size 2^k to be split, or a block of that size will be returned. We can prove by induction on k that the total storage consumed by such split blocks never exceeds kn; for after every request to split a block of size 2^{k+1}, we are using at most kn locations in split 2^k-blocks and at most n locations in unsplit ones.

This argument can be strengthened to show that $a_r n$ cells suffice, where $a_0 = 1$ and $a_k = 1 + a_{k-1}(1 - 2^{-k})$; we have

$k =$	0	1	2	3	4	5
$a_k =$	1	$1\frac{1}{2}$	$2\frac{1}{8}$	$2\frac{55}{64}$	$3\frac{697}{1024}$	$4\frac{18535}{32768}$

Conversely for $r \leq 5$ it can be shown that a buddy system sometimes *requires* as many as $a_r n$ cells, if the mechanism of steps R1 and R2 is modified to choose the worst possible available 2^j-block to split instead of the first such block.

Robson's proof that $N(2^r) \leq 1 + r$ (see exercise 40) is easily modified to show that such a "leftmost" strategy will never need more than $(1 + \frac{1}{2}r)n$ cells to allocate space for blocks of sizes 1, 2, 4, ..., 2^r, since blocks of size 2^k will never be placed in locations $\geq (1 + \frac{1}{2}k)n$. Although his algorithm seems very much like the buddy system, it turns out that no buddy system will be this good, even if we modify steps R1 and R2 to choose the best possible available 2^j-block to split. For example, consider the following sequence of "snapshots" of the memory, for $n = 16$ and $r = 3$:

```
11111111   11111111   00000000   00000000
10101010   10101010   2-2-2-2-   00000000
11110000   11110000   2-110000   00000000
11111111   11110000   11110000   00000000
10101010   10102-2-   10102-2-   00000000
10001000   10002-00   10002-00   4---4---
10000000   10000000   10000000   4---0000
```

Here 0 denotes an available location and k denotes the beginning of a k-block. In a similar way there is a sequence of operations, whenever n is a multiple of 16, that forces $\frac{3}{16}n$ blocks of size 8 to be $\frac{1}{8}$ full, and another $\frac{1}{16}n$ to be $\frac{1}{2}$ full. If n is a multiple of 128, a subsequent request for $\frac{9}{128}n$ blocks of size 8 will require more than $2.5n$ memory cells. (The buddy system allows unwanted 1s to creep into $\frac{3}{16}n$ of the 8-blocks, since there are no other available 2s to be split at a crucial time; the "leftmost" algorithm keeps all 1s confined.)

42. We can assume that $m \geq 6$. The main idea is to establish the occupancy pattern $R_{m-2}(F_{m-3}R_1)^k$ at the beginning of the memory, for $k = 0, 1, \ldots$, where R_j and F_j denote reserved and free blocks of size j. The transition from k to $k + 1$ begins with

$$R_{m-2}(F_{m-3}R_1)^k \rightarrow R_{m-2}(F_{m-3}R_1)^k R_{m-2}R_{m-2}$$
$$\rightarrow R_{m-2}(F_{m-3}R_1)^{k-1} F_{2m-4}R_{m-2}$$
$$\rightarrow R_{m-2}(F_{m-3}R_1)^{k-1} R_m R_{m-5}R_1 R_{m-2}$$
$$\rightarrow R_{m-2}(F_{m-3}R_1)^{k-1} F_m R_{m-5}R_1 ;$$

then the commutation sequence $F_{m-3}R_1 F_m R_{m-5}R_1 \rightarrow F_{m-3}R_1 R_{m-2}R_2 R_{m-5}R_1 \rightarrow F_{2m-4}R_2 R_{m-5}R_1 \rightarrow R_m R_{m-5}R_1 R_2 R_{m-5}R_1 \rightarrow F_m R_{m-5}R_1 F_{m-3}R_1$ is used k times until we get $F_m R_{m-5}R_1(F_{m-3}R_1)^k \rightarrow F_{2m-5}R_1(F_{m-3}R_1)^k \rightarrow R_{m-2}(F_{m-3}R_1)^{k+1}$. Finally, when k gets large enough, there is an endgame that forces overflow unless the memory size is at least $(n - 4m + 11)(m - 2)$; details appear in *Comp. J.* **20** (1977),

242–244. [Notice that the worst conceivable worst case, which begins with the pattern $F_{m-1}R_1F_{m-1}R_1F_{m-1}R_1\ldots$, is only slightly worse than this; the next-fit strategy of exercise 6 can produce this pessimal pattern.]

43. We will show that if $D_1, D_2, \ldots$ is any sequence of numbers such that $D_1/m + D_2/(m+1) + \cdots + D_m/(2m-1) \geq 1$ for all $m \geq 1$, and if $C_m = D_1/1 + D_2/2 + \cdots + D_m/m$, then $N_{\mathrm{FF}}(n,m) \leq nC_m$. In particular, since

$$\frac{1}{m} + \frac{1}{m+1} + \cdots + \frac{1}{2m+1} = 1 - \frac{1}{2} + \cdots + \frac{1}{2m-3} - \frac{1}{2m-2} + \frac{1}{2m-1} > \ln 2,$$

the constant sequence $D_m = 1/\ln 2$ satisfies the necessary conditions. The proof is by induction on m. Let $N_j = nC_j$ for $j \geq 1$, and suppose that some request for a block of size m cannot be allocated in the leftmost N_m cells of memory. Then $m > 1$. For $0 \leq j < m$, we let N_j' denote the rightmost position allocated to blocks of sizes $\leq j$, or 0 if all reserved blocks are larger than j; by induction we have $N_j' \leq N_j$. Furthermore we let N_m' be the rightmost occupied position $\leq N_m$, so that $N_m' \geq N_m - m + 1$. Then the interval $(N_{j-1}' \mathinner{.\,.} N_j']$ contains at least $\lceil j(N_j' - N_{j-1}')/(m+j-1) \rceil$ occupied cells, since its free blocks are of size $< m$ and its reserved blocks are of size $\geq j$. It follows that $n - m \geq$ number of occupied cells $\geq \sum_{j=1}^{m} j(N_j' - N_{j-1}')/(m+j-1) = mN_m'/(2m-1) - (m-1)\sum_{j=1}^{m-1} N_j'/(m+j)(m+j-1) > mN_m/(2m-1) - m - (m-1)\sum_{j=1}^{m-1} N_j\big(1/(m+j-1) - 1/(m+j)\big) = \sum_{j=1}^{m} nD_j/(m+j-1) - m \geq n - m$, a contradiction.

[This proof establishes slightly more than was asked. If we define the D's by $D_1/m + \cdots + D_m/(2m-1) = 1$, then the sequence $C_1, C_2, \ldots$ is $1, \frac{7}{4}, \frac{161}{72}, \frac{7483}{2880}, \ldots$; and the result can be improved further, even in the case $m = 2$, as in exercise 38.]

44. $\lceil F^{-1}(1/N) \rceil, \lceil F^{-1}(2/N) \rceil, \ldots, \lceil F^{-1}(N/N) \rceil$.

APPENDIX A

TABLES OF NUMERICAL QUANTITIES

Table 1

QUANTITIES THAT ARE FREQUENTLY USED IN STANDARD SUBROUTINES
AND IN ANALYSIS OF COMPUTER PROGRAMS (40 DECIMAL PLACES)

$$\sqrt{2} = 1.41421\ 35623\ 73095\ 04880\ 16887\ 24209\ 69807\ 85697-$$
$$\sqrt{3} = 1.73205\ 08075\ 68877\ 29352\ 74463\ 41505\ 87236\ 69428+$$
$$\sqrt{5} = 2.23606\ 79774\ 99789\ 69640\ 91736\ 68731\ 27623\ 54406+$$
$$\sqrt{10} = 3.16227\ 76601\ 68379\ 33199\ 88935\ 44432\ 71853\ 37196-$$
$$\sqrt[3]{2} = 1.25992\ 10498\ 94873\ 16476\ 72106\ 07278\ 22835\ 05703-$$
$$\sqrt[3]{3} = 1.44224\ 95703\ 07408\ 38232\ 16383\ 10780\ 10958\ 83919-$$
$$\sqrt[4]{2} = 1.18920\ 71150\ 02721\ 06671\ 74999\ 70560\ 47591\ 52930-$$
$$\ln 2 = 0.69314\ 71805\ 59945\ 30941\ 72321\ 21458\ 17656\ 80755+$$
$$\ln 3 = 1.09861\ 22886\ 68109\ 69139\ 52452\ 36922\ 52570\ 46475-$$
$$\ln 10 = 2.30258\ 50929\ 94045\ 68401\ 79914\ 54684\ 36420\ 76011+$$
$$1/\ln 2 = 1.44269\ 50408\ 88963\ 40735\ 99246\ 81001\ 89213\ 74266+$$
$$1/\ln 10 = 0.43429\ 44819\ 03251\ 82765\ 11289\ 18916\ 60508\ 22944-$$
$$\pi = 3.14159\ 26535\ 89793\ 23846\ 26433\ 83279\ 50288\ 41972-$$
$$1° = \pi/180 = 0.01745\ 32925\ 19943\ 29576\ 92369\ 07684\ 88612\ 71344+$$
$$1/\pi = 0.31830\ 98861\ 83790\ 67153\ 77675\ 26745\ 02872\ 40689+$$
$$\pi^2 = 9.86960\ 44010\ 89358\ 61883\ 44909\ 99876\ 15113\ 53137-$$
$$\sqrt{\pi} = \Gamma(1/2) = 1.77245\ 38509\ 05516\ 02729\ 81674\ 83341\ 14518\ 27975+$$
$$\Gamma(1/3) = 2.67893\ 85347\ 07747\ 63365\ 56929\ 40974\ 67764\ 41287-$$
$$\Gamma(2/3) = 1.35411\ 79394\ 26400\ 41694\ 52880\ 28154\ 51378\ 55193+$$
$$e = 2.71828\ 18284\ 59045\ 23536\ 02874\ 71352\ 66249\ 77572+$$
$$1/e = 0.36787\ 94411\ 71442\ 32159\ 55237\ 70161\ 46086\ 74458+$$
$$e^2 = 7.38905\ 60989\ 30650\ 22723\ 04274\ 60575\ 00781\ 31803+$$
$$\gamma = 0.57721\ 56649\ 01532\ 86060\ 65120\ 90082\ 40243\ 10422-$$
$$\ln \pi = 1.14472\ 98858\ 49400\ 17414\ 34273\ 51353\ 05871\ 16473-$$
$$\phi = 1.61803\ 39887\ 49894\ 84820\ 45868\ 34365\ 63811\ 77203+$$
$$e^\gamma = 1.78107\ 24179\ 90197\ 98523\ 65041\ 03107\ 17954\ 91696+$$
$$e^{\pi/4} = 2.19328\ 00507\ 38015\ 45655\ 97696\ 59278\ 73822\ 34616+$$
$$\sin 1 = 0.84147\ 09848\ 07896\ 50665\ 25023\ 21630\ 29899\ 96226-$$
$$\cos 1 = 0.54030\ 23058\ 68139\ 71740\ 09366\ 07442\ 97660\ 37323+$$
$$-\zeta'(2) = 0.93754\ 82543\ 15843\ 75370\ 25740\ 94567\ 86497\ 78979-$$
$$\zeta(3) = 1.20205\ 69031\ 59594\ 28539\ 97381\ 61511\ 44999\ 07650-$$
$$\ln \phi = 0.48121\ 18250\ 59603\ 44749\ 77589\ 13424\ 36842\ 31352-$$
$$1/\ln \phi = 2.07808\ 69212\ 35027\ 53760\ 13226\ 06117\ 79576\ 77422-$$
$$-\ln \ln 2 = 0.36651\ 29205\ 81664\ 32701\ 24391\ 58232\ 66946\ 94543-$$

Table 2

QUANTITIES THAT ARE FREQUENTLY USED IN STANDARD SUBROUTINES
AND IN ANALYSIS OF COMPUTER PROGRAMS (45 OCTAL PLACES)

The names at the left of the "=" signs are given in decimal notation.

$0.1 =$	$0.06314\ 63146\ 31463\ 14631\ 46314\ 63146\ 31463\ 14631\ 46315-$
$0.01 =$	$0.00507\ 53412\ 17270\ 24365\ 60507\ 53412\ 17270\ 24365\ 60510-$
$0.001 =$	$0.00040\ 61115\ 64570\ 65176\ 76355\ 44264\ 16254\ 02030\ 44672+$
$0.0001 =$	$0.00003\ 21556\ 13530\ 70414\ 54512\ 75170\ 33021\ 15002\ 35223-$
$0.00001 =$	$0.00000\ 24761\ 32610\ 70664\ 36041\ 06077\ 17401\ 56063\ 34417-$
$0.000001 =$	$0.00000\ 02061\ 57364\ 05536\ 66151\ 55323\ 07746\ 44470\ 26033+$
$0.0000001 =$	$0.00000\ 00153\ 27745\ 15274\ 53644\ 12741\ 72312\ 20354\ 02151+$
$0.00000001 =$	$0.00000\ 00012\ 57143\ 56106\ 04303\ 47374\ 77341\ 01512\ 63327+$
$0.000000001 =$	$0.00000\ 00001\ 04560\ 27640\ 46655\ 12262\ 71426\ 40124\ 21742+$
$0.0000000001 =$	$0.00000\ 00000\ 06676\ 33766\ 35367\ 55653\ 37265\ 34642\ 01627-$
$\sqrt{2} =$	$1.32404\ 74631\ 77167\ 46220\ 42627\ 66115\ 46725\ 12575\ 17435+$
$\sqrt{3} =$	$1.56663\ 65641\ 30231\ 25163\ 54453\ 50265\ 60361\ 34073\ 42223-$
$\sqrt{5} =$	$2.17067\ 36334\ 57722\ 47602\ 57471\ 63003\ 00563\ 55620\ 32021-$
$\sqrt{10} =$	$3.12305\ 40726\ 64555\ 22444\ 02242\ 57101\ 41466\ 33775\ 22532+$
$\sqrt[3]{2} =$	$1.20505\ 05746\ 15345\ 05342\ 10756\ 65334\ 25574\ 22415\ 03024+$
$\sqrt[3]{3} =$	$1.34233\ 50444\ 22175\ 73134\ 67363\ 76133\ 05334\ 31147\ 60121-$
$\sqrt[4]{2} =$	$1.14067\ 74050\ 61556\ 12455\ 72152\ 64430\ 60271\ 02755\ 73136+$
$\ln 2 =$	$0.54271\ 02775\ 75071\ 73632\ 57117\ 07316\ 30007\ 71366\ 53640+$
$\ln 3 =$	$1.06237\ 24752\ 55006\ 05227\ 32440\ 63065\ 25012\ 35574\ 55337+$
$\ln 10 =$	$2.23273\ 06735\ 52524\ 25405\ 56512\ 66542\ 56026\ 46050\ 50705+$
$1/\ln 2 =$	$1.34252\ 16624\ 53405\ 77027\ 35750\ 37766\ 40644\ 35175\ 04353+$
$1/\ln 10 =$	$0.33626\ 75425\ 11562\ 41614\ 52325\ 33525\ 27655\ 14756\ 06220-$
$\pi =$	$3.11037\ 55242\ 10264\ 30215\ 14230\ 63050\ 56006\ 70163\ 21122+$
$1° = \pi/180 =$	$0.01073\ 72152\ 11224\ 72344\ 25603\ 54276\ 63351\ 22056\ 11544+$
$1/\pi =$	$0.24276\ 30155\ 62344\ 20251\ 23760\ 47257\ 50765\ 15156\ 70067-$
$\pi^2 =$	$11.67517\ 14467\ 62135\ 71322\ 25561\ 15466\ 30021\ 40654\ 34103-$
$\sqrt{\pi} = \Gamma(1/2) =$	$1.61337\ 61106\ 64736\ 65247\ 47035\ 40510\ 15273\ 34470\ 17762-$
$\Gamma(1/3) =$	$2.53347\ 35234\ 51013\ 61316\ 73106\ 47644\ 54653\ 00106\ 66046-$
$\Gamma(2/3) =$	$1.26523\ 57112\ 14154\ 74312\ 54572\ 37655\ 60126\ 23231\ 02452+$
$e =$	$2.55760\ 52130\ 50535\ 51246\ 52773\ 42542\ 00471\ 72363\ 61661+$
$1/e =$	$0.27426\ 53066\ 13167\ 46761\ 52726\ 75436\ 02440\ 52371\ 03355+$
$e^2 =$	$7.30714\ 45615\ 23355\ 33460\ 63507\ 35040\ 32664\ 25356\ 50217+$
$\gamma =$	$0.44742\ 14770\ 67666\ 06172\ 23215\ 74376\ 01002\ 51313\ 25521-$
$\ln \pi =$	$1.11206\ 40443\ 47503\ 36413\ 65374\ 52661\ 52410\ 37511\ 46057+$
$\phi =$	$1.47433\ 57156\ 27751\ 23701\ 27634\ 71401\ 40271\ 66710\ 15010+$
$e^\gamma =$	$1.61772\ 13452\ 61152\ 65761\ 22477\ 36553\ 53327\ 17554\ 21260+$
$e^{\pi/4} =$	$2.14275\ 31512\ 16162\ 52370\ 35530\ 11342\ 53525\ 44307\ 02171-$
$\sin 1 =$	$0.65665\ 24436\ 04414\ 73402\ 03067\ 23644\ 11612\ 07474\ 14505-$
$\cos 1 =$	$0.42450\ 50037\ 32406\ 42711\ 07022\ 14666\ 27320\ 70675\ 12321+$
$-\zeta'(2) =$	$0.74001\ 45144\ 53253\ 42362\ 42107\ 23350\ 50074\ 46100\ 27706+$
$\zeta(3) =$	$1.14735\ 00023\ 60014\ 20470\ 15613\ 42561\ 31715\ 10177\ 06614+$
$\ln \phi =$	$0.36630\ 26256\ 61213\ 01145\ 13700\ 41004\ 52264\ 30700\ 40646+$
$1/\ln \phi =$	$2.04776\ 60111\ 17144\ 41512\ 11436\ 16575\ 00355\ 43630\ 40651+$
$-\ln\ln 2 =$	$0.27351\ 71233\ 67265\ 63650\ 17401\ 56637\ 26334\ 31455\ 57005-$

Several of the 40-digit values in Table 1 were computed on a desk calculator by John W. Wrench, Jr., for the first edition of this book. When computer software for such calculations became available during the 1970s, all of his contributions proved to be correct. See the answer to exercise 1.3.3–23 for the 40-digit value of another fundamental constant.

Table 3

VALUES OF HARMONIC NUMBERS, BERNOULLI NUMBERS,
AND FIBONACCI NUMBERS, FOR SMALL VALUES OF n

n	H_n	B_n	F_n	n
0	0	1	0	0
1	1	$-1/2$	1	1
2	3/2	1/6	1	2
3	11/6	0	2	3
4	25/12	$-1/30$	3	4
5	137/60	0	5	5
6	49/20	1/42	8	6
7	363/140	0	13	7
8	761/280	$-1/30$	21	8
9	7129/2520	0	34	9
10	7381/2520	5/66	55	10
11	83711/27720	0	89	11
12	86021/27720	$-691/2730$	144	12
13	1145993/360360	0	233	13
14	1171733/360360	7/6	377	14
15	1195757/360360	0	610	15
16	2436559/720720	$-3617/510$	987	16
17	42142223/12252240	0	1597	17
18	14274301/4084080	43867/798	2584	18
19	275295799/77597520	0	4181	19
20	55835135/15519504	$-174611/330$	6765	20
21	18858053/5173168	0	10946	21
22	19093197/5173168	854513/138	17711	22
23	444316699/118982864	0	28657	23
24	1347822955/356948592	$-236364091/2730$	46368	24
25	34052522467/8923714800	0	75025	25
26	34395742267/8923714800	8553103/6	121393	26
27	312536252003/80313433200	0	196418	27
28	315404588903/80313433200	$-23749461029/870$	317811	28
29	9227046511387/2329089562800	0	514229	29
30	9304682830147/2329089562800	8615841276005/14322	832040	30

For any x, let $H_x = \sum_{n \geq 1} \left(\dfrac{1}{n} - \dfrac{1}{n+x} \right)$. Then

$$H_{1/2} = 2 - 2\ln 2,$$

$$H_{1/3} = 3 - \tfrac{1}{2}\pi/\sqrt{3} - \tfrac{3}{2}\ln 3,$$

$$H_{2/3} = \tfrac{3}{2} + \tfrac{1}{2}\pi/\sqrt{3} - \tfrac{3}{2}\ln 3,$$

$$H_{1/4} = 4 - \tfrac{1}{2}\pi - 3\ln 2,$$

$$H_{3/4} = \tfrac{4}{3} + \tfrac{1}{2}\pi - 3\ln 2,$$

$$H_{1/5} = 5 - \tfrac{1}{2}\pi\phi^{3/2}5^{-1/4} - \tfrac{5}{4}\ln 5 - \tfrac{1}{2}\sqrt{5}\ln\phi,$$

$$H_{2/5} = \tfrac{5}{2} - \tfrac{1}{2}\pi\phi^{-3/2}5^{-1/4} - \tfrac{5}{4}\ln 5 + \tfrac{1}{2}\sqrt{5}\ln\phi,$$

$$H_{3/5} = \tfrac{5}{3} + \tfrac{1}{2}\pi\phi^{-3/2}5^{-1/4} - \tfrac{5}{4}\ln 5 + \tfrac{1}{2}\sqrt{5}\ln\phi,$$

$$H_{4/5} = \tfrac{5}{4} + \tfrac{1}{2}\pi\phi^{3/2}5^{-1/4} - \tfrac{5}{4}\ln 5 - \tfrac{1}{2}\sqrt{5}\ln\phi,$$

$$H_{1/6} = 6 - \tfrac{1}{2}\pi\sqrt{3} - 2\ln 2 - \tfrac{3}{2}\ln 3,$$

$$H_{5/6} = \tfrac{6}{5} + \tfrac{1}{2}\pi\sqrt{3} - 2\ln 2 - \tfrac{3}{2}\ln 3,$$

and, in general, when $0 < p < q$ (see exercise 1.2.9–19),

$$H_{p/q} = \frac{q}{p} - \frac{\pi}{2}\cot\frac{p}{q}\pi - \ln 2q + 2 \sum_{1 \leq n < q/2} \cos\frac{2pn}{q}\pi \cdot \ln\sin\frac{n}{q}\pi.$$

INDEX TO NOTATIONS

In the following formulas, letters that are not further qualified have the following significance:

j, k	integer-valued arithmetic expression
m, n	nonnegative integer-valued arithmetic expression
x, y	real-valued arithmetic expression
f	real-valued or complex-valued function
P	pointer-valued expression (either Λ or a computer address)
S, T	set or multiset
α	string of symbols

Formal symbolism	Meaning	Where defined
$V \leftarrow E$	give variable V the value of expression E	1.1
$U \leftrightarrow V$	interchange the values of variables U and V	1.1
A_n or $A[n]$	the nth element of linear array A	1.1
A_{mn} or $A[m, n]$	the element in row m and column n of rectangular array A	1.1
NODE(P)	the node (group of variables that are individually distinguished by their field names) whose address is P, assuming that P $\neq \Lambda$	2.1
F(P)	the variable in NODE(P) whose field name is F	2.1
CONTENTS(P)	contents of computer word whose address is P	2.1
LOC(V)	address of variable V within a computer	2.1
P $\Leftarrow$ AVAIL	set the value of pointer variable P to the address of a new node	2.2.3
AVAIL $\Leftarrow$ P	return NODE(P) to free storage; all its fields lose their identity	2.2.3
$\text{top}(S)$	node at the top of a nonempty stack S	2.2.1
$X \Leftarrow S$	pop up S to X: set $X \leftarrow \text{top}(S)$; then delete $\text{top}(S)$ from nonempty stack S	2.2.1
$S \Leftarrow X$	push down X onto S: insert the value X as a new entry on top of stack S	2.2.1

Formal symbolism	Meaning	Where defined
$(B \Rightarrow E;\ E')$	conditional expression: denotes E if B is true, E' if B is false	
$[B]$	characteristic function of condition B: $(B \Rightarrow 1;\ 0)$	1.2.3
δ_{kj}	Kronecker delta: $[j = k]$	1.2.3
$[z^n]\,g(z)$	coefficient of z^n in power series $g(z)$	1.2.9
$\displaystyle\sum_{R(k)} f(k)$	sum of all $f(k)$ such that the variable k is an integer and relation $R(k)$ is true	1.2.3
$\displaystyle\prod_{R(k)} f(k)$	product of all $f(k)$ such that the variable k is an integer and relation $R(k)$ is true	1.2.3
$\displaystyle\min_{R(k)} f(k)$	minimum value of all $f(k)$ such that the variable k is an integer and relation $R(k)$ is true	1.2.3
$\displaystyle\max_{R(k)} f(k)$	maximum value of all $f(k)$ such that the variable k is an integer and relation $R(k)$ is true	1.2.3
$j\backslash k$	j divides k: $k \bmod j = 0$ and $j > 0$	1.2.4
$S \setminus T$	set difference: $\{a \mid a$ in S and a not in $T\}$	
$\gcd(j, k)$	greatest common divisor of j and k: $\left(j = k = 0 \Rightarrow 0;\ \max_{d\backslash j,\, d\backslash k} d\right)$	1.1
$j \perp k$	j is relatively prime to k: $\gcd(j, k) = 1$	1.2.4
A^T	transpose of rectangular array A: $A^T[j, k] = A[k, j]$	
α^R	left-right reversal of α	
x^y	x to the y power (when x is positive)	1.2.2
x^k	x to the kth power: $\left(k \geq 0 \Rightarrow \prod_{0 \leq j < k} x;\ 1/x^{-k}\right)$	1.2.2
$x^{\bar{k}}$	x to the k rising: $\Gamma(x + k)/\Gamma(x) =$ $\left(k \geq 0 \Rightarrow \prod_{0 \leq j < k} (x + j);\ 1/(x + k)^{\overline{-k}}\right)$	1.2.5
$x^{\underline{k}}$	x to the k falling: $x!/(x - k)! =$ $\left(k \geq 0 \Rightarrow \prod_{0 \leq j < k} (x - j);\ 1/(x - k)^{\underline{-k}}\right)$	1.2.5

Formal symbolism	Meaning	Where defined
$n!$	n factorial: $\Gamma(n+1) = n^{\underline{n}}$	1.2.5
$\binom{x}{k}$	binomial coefficient: $(k < 0 \Rightarrow 0;\ x^{\underline{k}}/k!)$	1.2.6
$\binom{n}{n_1, n_2, \ldots, n_m}$	multinomial coefficient (defined only when $n = n_1 + n_2 + \cdots + n_m$)	1.2.6
$\left[\begin{matrix} n \\ m \end{matrix}\right]$	Stirling number of the first kind: $$\sum_{0<k_1<k_2<\cdots<k_{n-m}<n} k_1 k_2 \ldots k_{n-m}$$	1.2.6
$\left\{\begin{matrix} n \\ m \end{matrix}\right\}$	Stirling number of the second kind: $$\sum_{1\leq k_1\leq k_2\leq\cdots\leq k_{n-m}\leq m} k_1 k_2 \ldots k_{n-m}$$	1.2.6
$\{a \mid R(a)\}$	set of all a such that the relation $R(a)$ is true	
$\{a_1, \ldots, a_n\}$	the set or multiset $\{a_k \mid 1 \leq k \leq n\}$	
$\{x\}$	fractional part (used in contexts where a real value, not a set, is implied): $x - \lfloor x \rfloor$	1.2.11.2
$a_1 + a_2 + \cdots + a_n$	n-fold sum: $\sum_{j=1}^{n} a_j$	1.2.3
$[a \mathinner{.\,.} b]$	closed interval: $\{x \mid a \leq x \leq b\}$	1.2.2
$(a \mathinner{.\,.} b)$	open interval: $\{x \mid a < x < b\}$	1.2.2
$[a \mathinner{.\,.} b)$	half-open interval: $\{x \mid a \leq x < b\}$	1.2.2
$(a \mathinner{.\,.} b]$	half-closed interval: $\{x \mid a < x \leq b\}$	1.2.2
$|S|$	cardinality: the number of elements in set S	
$|x|$	absolute value of x: $(x \geq 0 \Rightarrow x;\ -x)$	
$|\alpha|$	length of α	
$\lfloor x \rfloor$	floor of x, greatest integer function: $\max_{k \leq x} k$	1.2.4
$\lceil x \rceil$	ceiling of x, least integer function: $\min_{k \geq x} k$	1.2.4
$x \bmod y$	mod function: $\big(y = 0 \Rightarrow x;\ x - y\lfloor x/y \rfloor\big)$	1.2.4
$x \equiv x'$ (modulo y)	relation of congruence: $x \bmod y = x' \bmod y$	1.2.4
$O\big(f(n)\big)$	big-oh of $f(n)$, as the variable $n \to \infty$	1.2.11.1
$O\big(f(z)\big)$	big-oh of $f(z)$, as the variable $z \to 0$	1.2.11.1
$\Omega\big(f(n)\big)$	big-omega of $f(n)$, as the variable $n \to \infty$	1.2.11.1
$\Theta\big(f(n)\big)$	big-theta of $f(n)$, as the variable $n \to \infty$	1.2.11.1

Formal symbolism	Meaning	Where defined
$\log_b x$	logarithm, base b, of x (when $x > 0$, $b > 0$, and $b \neq 1$): the y such that $x = b^y$	1.2.2
$\ln x$	natural logarithm: $\log_e x$	1.2.2
$\lg x$	binary logarithm: $\log_2 x$	1.2.2
$\exp x$	exponential of x: e^x	1.2.9
$\langle X_n \rangle$	the infinite sequence X_0, X_1, X_2, ... (here the letter n is part of the symbolism)	1.2.9
$f'(x)$	derivative of f at x	1.2.9
$f''(x)$	second derivative of f at x	1.2.10
$f^{(n)}(x)$	nth derivative: $\big(n = 0 \Rightarrow f(x); \; g'(x) \big)$, where $g(x) = f^{(n-1)}(x)$	1.2.11.2
$H_n^{(x)}$	harmonic number of order x: $\displaystyle\sum_{1 \leq k \leq n} 1/k^x$	1.2.7
H_n	harmonic number: $H_n^{(1)}$	1.2.7
F_n	Fibonacci number: $(n \leq 1 \Rightarrow n; \; F_{n-1} + F_{n-2})$	1.2.8
B_n	Bernoulli number: $n! \, [z^n] \, z/(e^z - 1)$	1.2.11.2
$\det(A)$	determinant of square matrix A	1.2.3
$\text{sign}(x)$	sign of x: $[x > 0] - [x < 0]$	
$\zeta(x)$	zeta function: $\lim_{n \to \infty} H_n^{(x)}$ (when $x > 1$)	1.2.7
$\Gamma(x)$	gamma function: $(x - 1)! = \gamma(x, \infty)$	1.2.5
$\gamma(x, y)$	incomplete gamma function: $\int_0^y e^{-t} t^{x-1} \, dt$	1.2.11.3
γ	Euler's constant: $\lim_{n \to \infty}(H_n - \ln n)$	1.2.7
e	base of natural logarithms: $\sum_{n \geq 0} 1/n!$	1.2.2
π	circle ratio: $4 \sum_{n \geq 0} (-1)^n/(2n + 1)$	1.2.2
∞	infinity: larger than any number	
Λ	null link (pointer to no address)	2.1
ϵ	empty string (string of length zero)	
$\emptyset$	empty set (set with no elements)	
ϕ	golden ratio: $\frac{1}{2}\big(1 + \sqrt{5}\big)$	1.2.8
$\varphi(n)$	Euler's totient function: $\displaystyle\sum_{0 \leq k < n} [k \perp n]$	1.2.4
$x \approx y$	x is approximately equal to y	1.2.5, 4.2.2

Formal symbolism	Meaning	Where defined
$\Pr\bigl(S(X)\bigr)$	probability that statement $S(X)$ is true, for random values of X	1.2.10
$\mathrm{E}\,X$	expected value of X: $\sum_x x \Pr(X = x)$	1.2.10
$\mathrm{mean}(g)$	mean value of the probability distribution represented by generating function g: $g'(1)$	1.2.10
$\mathrm{var}(g)$	variance of the probability distribution represented by generating function g: $$g''(1) + g'(1) - g'(1)^2$$	1.2.10
$(\min x_1, \text{ave } x_2,$ $\max x_3, \text{dev } x_4)$	a random variable having minimum value x_1, average (expected) value x_2, maximum value x_3, standard deviation x_4	1.2.10
P*	address of preorder successor of NODE(P) in a binary tree or tree	2.3.1, 2.3.2
P$	address of inorder successor of NODE(P) in a binary tree, postorder successor in a tree	2.3.1, 2.3.2
P♯	address of postorder successor of NODE(P) in a binary tree	2.3.1
*P	address of preorder predecessor of NODE(P) in a binary tree or tree	2.3.1, 2.3.2
$P	address of inorder predecessor of NODE(P) in a binary tree, postorder predecessor in a tree	2.3.1, 2.3.2
♯P	address of postorder predecessor of NODE(P) in a binary tree	2.3.1
▌	end of algorithm, program, or proof	1.1
␣	one blank space	1.3.1
rA	register A (accumulator) of MIX	1.3.1
rX	register X (extension) of MIX	1.3.1
$rI1, \ldots, rI6$	(index) registers I1, ..., I6 of MIX	1.3.1
rJ	(jump) register J of MIX	1.3.1
(L:R)	partial field of MIX word, $0 \leq \text{L} \leq \text{R} \leq 5$	1.3.1
OP ADDRESS,I(F)	notation for MIX instruction	1.3.1, 1.3.2
u	unit of time in MIX	1.3.1
*	"self" in MIXAL	1.3.2
OF, 1F, 2F, ..., 9F	"forward" local symbol in MIXAL	1.3.2
OB, 1B, 2B, ..., 9B	"backward" local symbol in MIXAL	1.3.2
OH, 1H, 2H, ..., 9H	"here" local symbol in MIXAL	1.3.2

APPENDIX C

INDEX TO ALGORITHMS AND THEOREMS

Numerical experimentations are necessary
to fully understand the algorithms and theorems in this book.

— STÉPHANE MALLAT, *A Wavelet Tour of Signal Processing* (1998)

INDEX AND GLOSSARY

Some Men pretend to understand a Book
by scouting thro' the Index:
as if a Traveller should go about to describe a Palace
when he had seen nothing but the Privy.

— JONATHAN SWIFT, *Mechanical Operation of the Spirit* (1704)

When an index entry refers to a page containing a relevant exercise, see also the *answer* to that exercise for further information. An answer page is not indexed here unless it refers to a topic not included in the statement of the exercise.

(), 164, *see* Identity permutation.
0-2-trees, 317.
  oriented, 398.
0-origin indexing, 254, 282, 299–301,
  305–306.
2-d trees, 564.
γ (Euler's constant), 75, 107, 114, 619–620.
π (circle ratio), 21, 619–620.
  as "random" example, 397.
  Wallis's product for, 52, 116.
ϕ (golden ratio), 13, 18, 21, 80, 83–86,
  619–620.

A-register of MIX, 125.
Aardenne-Ehrenfest, Tatyana van, 375, 379.
Aarons, Roger Michael, 528.
Abel, Niels Henrik, 58, 498.
  binomial theorem, 58, 71–73, 398.
  limit theorem, 95, 588.
Absolute error, 116.
Absolute value, 21.
Absolutely convergent series, 29.
ACE computer, 193, 229.
  Pilot, 230.
Acerbi, Fabio, 593.
Adams, Charles William, 230.
ADD, 131–132, 208.
Add to list: *see* Insertion.
Addition of polynomials, 275–280, 357–359.
Address: A number used to identify a
  position in memory.
  field of MIXAL line, 145, 151–153.
  of node, 233.
  portion of MIX instruction, 127.
Address transfer operators of MIX,
  133–134, 210.
Adjacent vertices of a graph, 363.
Adobe Systems, 202.
Aebly, Jakob, 536.
Agenda, 288, 291, 296, *see* Priority queue.
Aho, Alfred Vaino, 560.
Ahrens, Wilhelm Ernst Martin Georg, 162.
Alhazen, *see* Ibn al-Haytham.
al-Khwārizmī, Abū 'Abd Allāh
  Muḥammad ibn Mūsā
  (أبو عبد الله محمد بن موسى الخوارزمي),
  1, 79.

ALF (alphabetic data), 151, 152, 155.
Algebraic formulas, 313.
  differentiation, 90, 338–347, 459.
  manipulation of, 459–462.
  representation as trees, 337, 459.
  simplification of, 339, 347.
ALGOL language, viii, 202, 229.
Algorithm, origin of word, 1–2.
Algorithms, 1–9.
  analysis of, vi, 7, 96–107, 170–172, 179,
    250, 253, 268, 278–280, 324–326, 331,
    380–382, 444–445, 451.
  communication of, 16.
  effective, 6, 8, 9.
  equivalence between, 467.
  form of in this book, 2–4.
  hardware-oriented, 26, 252, 611.
  how to read, 4, 16.
  proof of, 5–6, 13–17, 321, 361, 422, 434.
  properties of, 4–6, 9.
  random paths in, 380–381.
  set-theoretic definition, 7–9.
  theory of, 7, 9.
Allocation of tables, *see* Dynamic storage
  allocation, Linked allocation,
  Representation, Sequential allocation.
Alpern, Steven Robert, 526.
Alphameric character: A letter, digit, or
  special character symbol.
  codes for MIX, 136, 138, 140–141.
AMM: American Mathematical Monthly,
  published by the Mathematical
  Association of America since 1894.
Amortized running time, 254.
Analysis of algorithms, vi, 7, 96–107,
  170–172, 179, 250, 253, 268, 278–280,
  324–326, 331, 380–382, 444–445, 451.
Analytical Engine, 1, 229.
Ancestor, in a tree structure, 311, 348, 562.
Anticipated input, 216, *see* Buffering.
Antisymmetric relation, 261.
Apostol, Tom Mike, 28.
Arabic mathematics, 1, 162.
Araújo, Saulo, 565.
Arbogast, Louis François Antoine, 52, 105.
Arborescences, 363, *see* Oriented trees.
Arc digraph, 379.
Arc in a directed graph, 372.

d'Imperio, Mary Evelyn, 462.
Dahl, Ole-Johan, 229, 230, 461, 462.
Dahm, David Michael, 433, 434.
Data (originally the plural of "datum",
    but now used collectively as singular
    or plural, like "information"):
    Representation in a precise, formalized
    language of some facts or concepts,
    often numeric or alphabetic values,
    to facilitate manipulation by a
    computational method, 215.
  packed, 128, 158.
Data organization: A way to represent
    information in a data structure,
    together with algorithms that access
    and/or modify the structure.
Data structure: A table of data including
    structural relationships, 232–465.
  linear list structures, 238–298.
  List structures, 408–423.
  multilinked structures, 424–434.
  orthogonal lists, 298–307, 424–434.
  tree structures, 308–408.
Daughter, in a tree structure, 311.
David, Florence Nightingale, 66.
Davies, David Julian Meredith, 445.
Davis, Philip Jacob, 50.
Dawson, Reed, 584.
de Bruijn, Nicolaas Govert, 121, 122, 375,
    379, 380, 478, 504, 543, 565.
de Moivre, Abraham, 74, 83, 87, 106,
    182, 474, 536.
De Morgan, Augustus, 17.
Deallocation, see Liberation.
Debugging: Detecting and removing
    bugs (errors), 192–193, 201, 257,
    297, 413, 556.
DEC1 (decrease rI1), 134, 210.
DECA (decrease rA), 134, 210.
Decimal computer: A computer that
    manipulates numbers primarily in the
    decimal (radix ten) number system.
Decimal number system, 21, 619.
DECX (decrease rX), 134, 210.
Defined symbol, an assembly language, 153.
Definition, circular, see Circular definition.
Degree, of node in tree, 308, 317, 377.
  of vertex in directed graph, 372.
Deletion of a node: Removing it from a
    data structure and possibly returning
    it to available storage.
  from available space list, see Reservation.
  from deque, 251, 297.
  from doubly linked list, 281, 290–291, 297.
  from doubly linked ring structure, 358.
  from linear list, 239.
  from linked list, 236, 255, 276, 305.
  from queue, 242, 244–245, 254, 261,
    265, 273–274.
  from stack, 241, 242, 244–245, 247, 254,
    259, 269, 273–274, 278, 458.
  from tree, 358.
  from two-dimensional list, 305.

Demuth, Howard B., 120.
Depth-first search, 578, 581.
Deque: Double-ended queue, 239–243, 269.
  deletion from, 251, 297.
  input-restricted, 239–243, 416.
  insertion into, 251, 297.
  linked allocation, 280, 297.
  output-restricted, 239–243, 269, 274.
  sequential allocation, 251.
Derangements, 180, 183.
Derivative, 90, 338.
Dershowitz, Nachum (נחום דרשוביץ),
    518, 588, 598.
Descendant, in a tree structure, 311,
    348, 562.
Determinant of a square matrix, 37–39,
    81, 378–379, 382.
Deuel, Phillip DeVere, Jr., 556.
Deutsch, Laurence Peter, 418, 421, 422.
Dewar, Robert Berriedale Keith, 614.
Dewey, Melville (= Melvil) Louis Kossuth,
    notation for binary trees (due to
    Galton), 317, 331, 346, 405.
  notation for trees, 313, 317, 382–383, 460.
Diaconis, Persi Warren, 491.
Diagonals of polygons, 408.
Diagrams of structural information,
    234, 279.
  before-and-after, 260–261, 278, 281, 571.
  binary trees, 312, 318, 563.
  List structures, 315–317, 408–409.
  tree structures, 309–315, 337, 346,
    349, 460.
Dickman, Karl Daniel, 525.
Dickson, Leonard Eugene, 81, 484.
Dictionaries of English, 1–2, 215–216.
Differences of polynomials, 64.
Differentiation, 90, 338–347, 459.
  chain rule for, 52.
Digamma function $\psi(z)$, 44, 75, 493.
Digit: One of the symbols used in radix
    notation; usually a decimal digit, one
    of the symbols 0, 1, ..., or 9.
Digraphs, 372, see Directed graphs.
Dijkstra, Edsger Wybe, 17, 191, 230, 231,
    240, 459, 462, 545, 580, 605.
d'Imperio, Mary Evelyn, 462.
Directed graphs, 372–374, 422.
  as flow charts, 364–365, 377.
  balanced, 374–375.
  connected, 363.
  regular, 379.
  strongly connected, 372, 377.
Discrete system simulation, 203, 282–298.
  synchronous, 282, 298.
Disjoint sets: Sets with no common
    elements.
Disk files, 136–137, 435, 463.

Keller, Helen Adams, 123.

Kepler, Johannes, 80, 81.

Kilmer, Alfred Joyce, 232.

King, James Cornelius, 20.

Kinkelin, Hermann, 504.

Kirchhoff, Gustav Robert, 406, 583.
    law of conservation of flow, 97, 170–171,
        268, 278, 364–370, 380.

Kirkman, Thomas Penyngton, 408.

Kirschenhofer, Peter, 506.

Klarner, David Anthony, 86.

Kleitman, Daniel J (Isaiah Solomon),
        547, 596.

Knopp, Konrad Hermann Theodor, 48, 498.

Knotted lists, 459.

Knowlton, Kenneth Charles, 462.

Knuth, Donald Ervin (高德纳), ii, iv, xi, 11,
        33, 66, 120, 193, 201, 202, 296, 297, 395,
        457, 461, 471, 484, 499, 504, 523, 525,
        565, 579, 580, 584, 592, 596, 633, 652.

Knuth, Nancy Jill Carter (高精蘭), x, xx.

Kolmogorov, Andrei Nikolaevich
        (Колмогоров, Андрей Николаевич),
        104, 105, 464.

Kőnig, Dénes, 382, 406, 588.

Koster, Cornelis (= Kees) Hermanus
        Antonius, 461.

Kozelka, Robert Marvin, 544.

Kramp, Christian, 49, 486.

Krattenthaler, Christian, 39.

Kreweras, Germain, 598.

Krogdahl, Stein, 616.

Kronecker, Leopold, delta notation,
        33, 61, 624.

Kruskal, Joseph Bernard, Jr., 386, 588.

Kummer, Ernst Eduard, 70.

Kung, Hsiang Tsung (孔祥重), 563.

Labeled trees, enumeration of, 389, 407.

Labelle, Gilbert, 395.

Lagrange (= de la Grange), Joseph
        Louis, Comte,
    inversion formula, 392, 594.

Lamé, Gabriel, 407.

Lamport, Leslie B., 605.

Language: A set of strings of symbols,
        usually accompanied by conventions
        that assign a "meaning" to each string
        in the set, 5, 241, 460–461.
    machine, viii–x, 124.

Laplace (= de la Place), Pierre Simon,
        Marquis de, 87.
    transform, 94.

Laplacian matrix of a graph, 583.

Lapko, Olga Georgievna (Лапко, Ольга
        Георгиевна), 652.

Large programs, writing, 191–193.

Larus, James Richard, 369.

Last in, first out, 240, 452, 459, see Stack.
    almost, 446, 449, 455.

Latency, 228, 457.

Lattice: An algebraic system that
        generalizes operations like ∪ and ∩.
    defined on forests, 577, 598.
    free, 347.

Laurent, Paul Mathieu Hermann, series, 473.

Lawson, Harold Wilbur, Jr., 433, 461.

LCHILD field, 352–353, 359–360.

LD1 (load rI1), 129, 208.

LD1N (load rI1 negative), 129, 208.

LDA (load rA), 129, 208.

LDAN (load rA negative), 129, 208.

LDX (load rX), 129, 208.

LDXN (load rX negative), 129, 208.

Leaf of tree, 308, see Terminal node.

Least-recently-used replacement, 452.

Leeuwen, Jan van, 596.

Left-child/right-sibling links, 335, 348.

Left-sibling/right-child links, 346.

Left subtree in binary tree, 312, 318.

Left-to-right maximum or minimum,
        97–101, 104–106, 179.

Legendre (= Le Gendre), Adrien Marie,
        48, 49, 51.
    symbol, 45.

Léger, Émile, 80.

Lehmer, Derrick Henry, 465.

Leibniz, Gottfried Wilhelm, Freiherr
        von, 2, 51.

Leighton, Frank Thomson, 450–451.

Leiner, Alan Lewine, 231.

Lenormande, Claude, 527.

Lentin, André, 527.

Leonardo of Pisa, 79–80, 84.

Leroux, Pierre, 395.

Letter frequencies in English, 159.

Level of node in a tree, 308, 316, 317.

Level order, 351, 564, 577.
    sequential representation, 351, 359.

LeVeque, William Judson, 466.

Lévy, Paul, 105.

Levy, Silvio Vieira Ferreira, xi.

Lexicographic order, 20, 299–300, 306, 564.

Liberation of reserved storage, 256, 259,
        291, 413–414, 420–421, 438–442,
        443–444, 452–456.

LIFO, 240, 459, see Stack.

Lilius, Aloysius, 159.

Lindstrom, Gary Edward, 567–568.

Line printer, 136–137.

Lineal chart, 310–311.

Linear extensions, see Topological sorting.

Linear lists, 232, 238–307.

Linear ordering, 20, 262, 270.
    embedding a partial ordering into, 262,
        see Topological sorting.
    of binary trees, 333.
    of trees, 346.

Linear probing, 451.

Linear recurrences, 83, 88.

Martin, Johannes Jakob, 614.
Math. Comp.: Mathematics of Computation
    (1960–), a publication of the American
    Mathematical Society since 1965;
    founded by the National Research
    Council of the National Academy
    of Sciences under the original title
    *Mathematical Tables and Other Aids
    to Computation* (1943–1959).
Mathematical induction, 11–21, 32, 316, 475.
    generalized, 20.
Matiyasevich, Yuri Vladimirovich
    (Матиясевич, Юрий Владимирович),
    86.
Matrix: A two-dimensional array,
    298–299, 315.
    Cauchy, 37–38, 475.
    characteristic polynomial of, 499.
    combinatorial, 37–38, 589.
    determinant of, 37–39, 81, 378–379, 382.
    extendible, 307.
    Hilbert, 38.
    incidence, 270.
    inverse of, 37–38, 73, 307.
    multiplication, 306.
    permanent of, 51.
    representation of, 158–159, 298–307.
    singular, 307.
    sparse, 302–306.
    transpose of, 182.
    triangular, 300, 305.
    tridiagonal, 307.
    unimodular, 601.
    Vandermonde, 37–38, 475.
Matrix (Bush), Irving Joshua, 35, 36.
Matrix tree theorem, 378–379, 586.
Mauchly, John William, 230.
Maurolico, Francesco, 17.
Maximum, algorithm to find, 96–101,
    145, 186.
Maximum norm, 106.
McCall's, v.
McCann, Anthony Paul, 614.
McCarthy, John, 460–461.
McEliece, Robert James, 477.
McIlroy, Malcolm Douglas, 576, 581.
McKeeman, William Marshall, 230.
Mealy, George, 462.
Mean value, *see* Expected value.
Meek, Homer Vergil, 230.
Meggitt, John Edward, 471.
Melville, Robert Christian, 540.
Memory: Part of a computer system
    used to store data, 126.
    cell of, 127.
    hierarchy, 199, 421, 435, 463.
    map, 435–436.
    types of, 238.
Merner, Jack Newton Forsythe, 229.
Merrett, Timothy Howard, 560.

Merrington, Maxine, 66.
Meton of Athens (Μέτων ὁ Ἀθηναῖος),
    cycle, 160.
METAFONT, iv, xi, 611, 652.
METAPOST, xi, 652.
Military game, 273, 550.
Miller, Kenneth William, 123.
Ming, An-T'u (明安圖), 407.
Minimum path length, 399–406.
Minimum spanning tree, 371.
Minimum wire length, 371.
Minsky, Marvin Lee, 423.
Mirimanoff, Dmitri (Мириманов, Дмитрий
    Семёнович), 536.
Mirsky, Leon, 587.
Mitchell, William Charles, 525.
MIX computer, viii–x, 124–144.
    assembly language for, 144–157.
    extensions to, 143, 228, 251–252, 455.
    instructions, summary, 140–141.
    simulator of, 203–212.
Mix Barrington, David Arno, 526.
MIXAL: MIX Assembly Language, 144–157,
    235–236.
Mixed-radix number system, 300.
Mixture of probability distributions, 106.
MMIX computer, 124, 187, 215, 325.
Mock, Owen Russell, 231.
mod, 39–40.
modulo, 40.
Mohammed, John Llewelyn, 527.
Moivre, Abraham de, 74, 83, 87, 106,
    182, 474, 536.
Moments of probability distributions, 105.
Monitor routine, 212, *see* Trace routine.
Monte Carlo method: Experiments with
    random data, 254, 445–447.
Moon, John Wesley, 407.
Moore School of Electrical Engineering, 230.
Mordell, Louis Joel, 479.
Morris, Francis Lockwood, 18, 614.
Morris, Joseph Martin, 567.
Morrison, Emily Kramer, 229.
Morrison, Philip, 229.
Moser, Leo, 66.
Mother, in a tree structure, 311.
Motzkin, Theodor (= Theodore) Samuel
    (תיאודור שמואל מוצקין), 85, 593.
MOVE, 135, 142, 193, 211.
MOVE CORRESPONDING, 426, 430–431, 434.
MUG: MIX User's Group, 643.
MUL (multiply), 131–132, 208.
Multilinked structures, 232, 288–289,
    357, 424–434, 458.
Multilist representation, 301.
Multinomial coefficients, 65, 394.
Multinomial theorem, 65.
Multipass algorithms, 198–200, 201–202.
Multiple: x is a multiple of y if $x = ky$
    for some integer k.
Multiple entrances to subroutines, 189.

We must not ... think that computation,
that is ratiocination,
has place only in numbers.

— THOMAS HOBBES, *Elementary Philosophy* (1656)

THIS BOOK was composed on a Sun SPARCstation with Computer Modern typefaces, using the TEX and METAFONT software as described in the author's books *Computers & Typesetting* (Reading, Mass.: Addison–Wesley, 1986), Volumes A–E. The illustrations were produced with John Hobby's METAPOST system. Some names in the index were typeset with additional fonts developed by Yannis Haralambous (Greek, Hebrew, Arabic), Olga G. Lapko (Cyrillic), Frans J. Velthuis (Devanagari), Masatoshi Watanabe (Japanese), and Linbo Zhang (Chinese).

00	*1*	**01**	*2*	**02**	*2*	**03**	*10*
No operation		$rA \leftarrow rA + V$		$rA \leftarrow rA - V$		$rAX \leftarrow rA \times V$	
NOP(0)		ADD(0:5) FADD(6)		SUB(0:5) FSUB(6)		MUL(0:5) FMUL(6)	
08	*2*	**09**	*2*	**10**	*2*	**11**	*2*
$rA \leftarrow V$		$rI1 \leftarrow V$		$rI2 \leftarrow V$		$rI3 \leftarrow V$	
LDA(0:5)		LD1(0:5)		LD2(0:5)		LD3(0:5)	
16	*2*	**17**	*2*	**18**	*2*	**19**	*2*
$rA \leftarrow -V$		$rI1 \leftarrow -V$		$rI2 \leftarrow -V$		$rI3 \leftarrow -V$	
LDAN(0:5)		LD1N(0:5)		LD2N(0:5)		LD3N(0:5)	
24	*2*	**25**	*2*	**26**	*2*	**27**	*2*
$M(F) \leftarrow rA$		$M(F) \leftarrow rI1$		$M(F) \leftarrow rI2$		$M(F) \leftarrow rI3$	
STA(0:5)		ST1(0:5)		ST2(0:5)		ST3(0:5)	
32	*2*	**33**	*2*	**34**	*1*	**35**	*1+T*
$M(F) \leftarrow rJ$		$M(F) \leftarrow 0$		Unit F busy?		Control, unit F	
STJ(0:2)		STZ(0:5)		JBUS(0)		IOC(0)	
40	*1*	**41**	*1*	**42**	*1*	**43**	*1*
$rA : 0$, jump		$rI1 : 0$, jump		$rI2 : 0$, jump		$rI3 : 0$, jump	
JA[+]		J1[+]		J2[+]		J3[+]	
48	*1*	**49**	*1*	**50**	*1*	**51**	*1*
$rA \leftarrow [rA]? \pm M$		$rI1 \leftarrow [rI1]? \pm M$		$rI2 \leftarrow [rI2]? \pm M$		$rI3 \leftarrow [rI3]? \pm M$	
INCA(0) DECA(1) ENTA(2) ENNA(3)		INC1(0) DEC1(1) ENT1(2) ENN1(3)		INC2(0) DEC2(1) ENT2(2) ENN2(3)		INC3(0) DEC3(1) ENT3(2) ENN3(3)	
56	*2*	**57**	*2*	**58**	*2*	**59**	*2*
$CI \leftarrow rA(F) : V$		$CI \leftarrow rI1(F) : V$		$CI \leftarrow rI2(F) : V$		$CI \leftarrow rI3(F) : V$	
CMPA(0:5) FCMP(6)		CMP1(0:5)		CMP2(0:5)		CMP3(0:5)	

General form:

C	*t*
Description	
OP(F)	

C = operation code, $(5:5)$ field of instruction
F = op variant, $(4:4)$ field of instruction
M = address of instruction after indexing
$V = M(F)$ = contents of F field of location M
OP = symbolic name for operation
(F) = normal F setting
t = execution time; T = interlock time

THE ART OF
COMPUTER PROGRAMMING

THIRD EDITION

DONALD E. KNUTH *Stanford University*

▲
▼▼ **ADDISON–WESLEY**

Volume 2 / **Seminumerical Algorithms**

THE ART OF
COMPUTER PROGRAMMING

THIRD EDITION

Upper Saddle River, NJ · Boston · Indianapolis · San Francisco
New York · Toronto · Montréal · London · Munich · Paris · Madrid
Capetown · Sydney · Tokyo · Singapore · Mexico City

TEX is a trademark of the American Mathematical Society

METAFONT is a trademark of Addison–Wesley

The quotation on page 61 is reprinted by permission of Grove Press, Inc.

The publisher offers excellent discounts on this book when ordered in quantity for bulk purposes or special sales, which may include electronic versions and/or custom covers and content particular to your business, training goals, marketing focus, and branding interests. For more information, please contact:

> U.S. Corporate and Government Sales   (800) 382–3419
> corpsales@pearsontechgroup.com

For sales outside the U.S., please contact:

> International Sales   international@pearsoned.com

Visit us on the Web: informit.com/aw

Library of Congress Cataloging-in-Publication Data

```
Knuth, Donald Ervin, 1938-
  The art of computer programming / Donald Ervin Knuth.
  xiv,764 p.  24 cm.
  Includes bibliographical references and index.
  Contents: v. 1. Fundamental algorithms. -- v. 2. Seminumerical
algorithms. -- v. 3. Sorting and searching. -- v. 4a. Combinatorial
algorithms, part 1.
  Contents: v. 2. Seminumerical algorithms. -- 3rd ed.
  ISBN 978-0-201-89683-1 (v. 1, 3rd ed.)
  ISBN 978-0-201-89684-8 (v. 2, 3rd ed.)
  ISBN 978-0-201-89685-5 (v. 3, 2nd ed.)
  ISBN 978-0-201-03804-0 (v. 4a)
  1. Electronic digital computers--Programming.  2. Computer
algorithms.   I. Title.
QA76.6.K64  1997
005.1--DC21                                          97-2147
```

Internet page http://www-cs-faculty.stanford.edu/~knuth/taocp.html contains current information about this book and related books.

ISBN-13 978-0-201-89684-8
ISBN-10   0-201-89684-2

Text printed in the United States at Courier Westford in Westford, Massachusetts.
Twenty-eighth printing, January 2012

PREFACE

THE ALGORITHMS discussed in this book deal directly with numbers; yet I
believe they are properly called *seminumerical*, because they lie on the borderline
between numeric and symbolic calculation. Each algorithm not only computes
the desired answers to a numerical problem, it also is intended to blend well
with the internal operations of a digital computer. In many cases people are
not able to appreciate the full beauty of such an algorithm unless they also
have some knowledge of a computer's machine language; the efficiency of the
corresponding machine program is a vital factor that cannot be divorced from
the algorithm itself. The problem is to find the best ways to make computers
deal with numbers, and this involves tactical as well as numerical considerations.
Therefore the subject matter of this book is unmistakably a part of computer
science, as well as of numerical mathematics.

Some people working in "higher levels" of numerical analysis will regard the
topics treated here as the domain of system programmers. Other people working
in "higher levels" of system programming will regard the topics treated here as
the domain of numerical analysts. But I hope that there are a few people left who
will want to look carefully at these basic methods. Although the methods reside
perhaps on a low level, they underlie all of the more grandiose applications of
computers to numerical problems, so it is important to know them well. We are
concerned here with the interface between numerical mathematics and computer
programming, and it is the mating of both types of skills that makes the subject
so interesting.

There is a noticeably higher percentage of mathematical material in this
book than in other volumes of this series, because of the nature of the subjects
treated. In most cases the necessary mathematical topics are developed here
starting almost from scratch (or from results proved in Volume 1), but in several
easily recognizable sections a knowledge of calculus has been assumed.

This volume comprises Chapters 3 and 4 of the complete series. Chapter 3
is concerned with "random numbers": It is not only a study of various ways to
generate random sequences, it also investigates statistical tests for randomness,

v

as well as the transformation of uniform random numbers into other types of random quantities; the latter subject illustrates how random numbers are used in practice. I have also included a section about the nature of randomness itself. Chapter 4 is my attempt to tell the fascinating story of what people have discovered about the processes of arithmetic, after centuries of progress. It discusses various systems for representing numbers, and how to convert between them; and it treats arithmetic on floating point numbers, high-precision integers, rational fractions, polynomials, and power series, including the questions of factoring and finding greatest common divisors.

Each of Chapters 3 and 4 can be used as the basis of a one-semester college course at the junior to graduate level. Although courses on "Random Numbers" and on "Arithmetic" are not presently a part of many college curricula, I believe the reader will find that the subject matter of these chapters lends itself nicely to a unified treatment of material that has real educational value. My own experience has been that these courses are a good means of introducing elementary probability theory and number theory to college students. Nearly all of the topics usually treated in such introductory courses arise naturally in connection with applications, and the presence of these applications can be an important motivation that helps the student to learn and to appreciate the theory. Furthermore, each chapter gives a few hints of more advanced topics that will whet the appetite of many students for further mathematical study.

For the most part this book is self-contained, except for occasional discussions relating to the MIX computer explained in Volume 1. Appendix B contains a summary of the mathematical notations used, some of which are a little different from those found in traditional mathematics books.

Preface to the Third Edition

When the second edition of this book was completed in 1980, it represented the first major test case for prototype systems of electronic publishing called TEX and METAFONT. I am now pleased to celebrate the full development of those systems by returning to the book that inspired and shaped them. At last I am able to have all volumes of The Art of Computer Programming in a consistent format that will make them readily adaptable to future changes in printing and display technology. The new setup has allowed me to make many thousands of improvements that I have been wanting to incorporate for a long time.

In this new edition I have gone over every word of the text, trying to retain the youthful exuberance of my original sentences while perhaps adding some more mature judgment. Dozens of new exercises have been added; dozens of old exercises have been given new and improved answers. Changes appear everywhere, but most significantly in Sections 3.5 (about theoretical guarantees of randomness), 3.6 (about portable random-number generators), 4.5.2 (about the binary gcd algorithm), and 4.7 (about composition and iteration of power series).

The Art of Computer Programming is, however, still a work in progress. Research on seminumerical algorithms continues to grow at a phenomenal rate. Therefore some parts of this book are headed by an "under construction" icon, to apologize for the fact that the material is not up-to-date. My files are bursting with important material that I plan to include in the final, glorious, fourth edition of Volume 2, perhaps 16 years from now; but I must finish Volumes 4 and 5 first, and I do not want to delay their publication any more than absolutely necessary.

I am enormously grateful to the many hundreds of people who have helped me to gather and refine this material during the past 35 years. Most of the hard work of preparing the new edition was accomplished by Silvio Levy, who expertly edited the electronic text, and by Jeffrey Oldham, who converted nearly all of the original illustrations to METAPOST format. I have corrected every error that alert readers detected in the second edition (as well as some mistakes that, alas, nobody noticed); and I have tried to avoid introducing new errors in the new material. However, I suppose some defects still remain, and I want to fix them as soon as possible. Therefore I will cheerfully award $2.56 to the first finder of each technical, typographical, or historical error. The webpage cited on page iv contains a current listing of all corrections that have been reported to me.

Stanford, California   D. E. K.
July 1997

> When a book has been eight years in the making,
> there are too many colleagues, typists, students,
> teachers, and friends to thank.
> Besides, I have no intention of giving such people
> the usual exoneration from responsibility for errors which remain.
> They should have corrected me!
> And sometimes they are even responsible for ideas
> which may turn out in the long run to be wrong.
> Anyway, to such fellow explorers, my thanks.
> — EDWARD F. CAMPBELL, JR. (1975)

> *'Defendit numerus,'* [there is safety in numbers]
> is the maxim of the foolish;
> *'Deperdit numerus,'* [there is ruin in numbers]
> of the wise.
> — C. C. COLTON (1820)

NOTES ON THE EXERCISES

THE EXERCISES in this set of books have been designed for self-study as well as for classroom study. It is difficult, if not impossible, for anyone to learn a subject purely by reading about it, without applying the information to specific problems and thereby being encouraged to think about what has been read. Furthermore, we all learn best the things that we have discovered for ourselves. Therefore the exercises form a major part of this work; a definite attempt has been made to keep them as informative as possible and to select problems that are enjoyable as well as instructive.

In many books, easy exercises are found mixed randomly among extremely difficult ones. A motley mixture is, however, often unfortunate because readers like to know in advance how long a problem ought to take — otherwise they may just skip over all the problems. A classic example of such a situation is the book *Dynamic Programming* by Richard Bellman; this is an important, pioneering work in which a group of problems is collected together at the end of some chapters under the heading "Exercises and Research Problems," with extremely trivial questions appearing in the midst of deep, unsolved problems. It is rumored that someone once asked Dr. Bellman how to tell the exercises apart from the research problems, and he replied, "If you can solve it, it is an exercise; otherwise it's a research problem."

Good arguments can be made for including both research problems and very easy exercises in a book of this kind; therefore, to save the reader from the possible dilemma of determining which are which, *rating numbers* have been provided to indicate the level of difficulty. These numbers have the following general significance:

Rating   Interpretation

00   An extremely easy exercise that can be answered immediately if the material of the text has been understood; such an exercise can almost always be worked "in your head."

10   A simple problem that makes you think over the material just read, but is by no means difficult. You should be able to do this in one minute at most; pencil and paper may be useful in obtaining the solution.

20   An average problem that tests basic understanding of the text material, but you may need about fifteen or twenty minutes to answer it completely.

30 A problem of moderate difficulty and/or complexity; this one may involve more than two hours' work to solve satisfactorily, or even more if the TV is on.

40 Quite a difficult or lengthy problem that would be suitable for a term project in classroom situations. A student should be able to solve the problem in a reasonable amount of time, but the solution is not trivial.

50 A research problem that has not yet been solved satisfactorily, as far as the author knew at the time of writing, although many people have tried. If you have found an answer to such a problem, you ought to write it up for publication; furthermore, the author of this book would appreciate hearing about the solution as soon as possible (provided that it is correct).

By interpolation in this "logarithmic" scale, the significance of other rating numbers becomes clear. For example, a rating of *17* would indicate an exercise that is a bit simpler than average. Problems with a rating of *50* that are subsequently solved by some reader may appear with a *40* rating in later editions of the book, and in the errata posted on the Internet (see page iv).

The remainder of the rating number divided by 5 indicates the amount of detailed work required. Thus, an exercise rated *24* may take longer to solve than an exercise that is rated *25*, but the latter will require more creativity.

The author has tried earnestly to assign accurate rating numbers, but it is difficult for the person who makes up a problem to know just how formidable it will be for someone else to find a solution; and everyone has more aptitude for certain types of problems than for others. It is hoped that the rating numbers represent a good guess at the level of difficulty, but they should be taken as general guidelines, not as absolute indicators.

This book has been written for readers with varying degrees of mathematical training and sophistication; as a result, some of the exercises are intended only for the use of more mathematically inclined readers. The rating is preceded by an *M* if the exercise involves mathematical concepts or motivation to a greater extent than necessary for someone who is primarily interested only in programming the algorithms themselves. An exercise is marked with the letters "*HM*" if its solution necessarily involves a knowledge of calculus or other higher mathematics not developed in this book. An "*HM*" designation does *not* necessarily imply difficulty.

Some exercises are preceded by an arrowhead, "▶"; this designates problems that are especially instructive and especially recommended. Of course, no reader/student is expected to work *all* of the exercises, so those that seem to be the most valuable have been singled out. (This distinction is not meant to detract from the other exercises!) Each reader should at least make an attempt to solve all of the problems whose rating is *10* or less; and the arrows may help to indicate which of the problems with a higher rating should be given priority.

Solutions to most of the exercises appear in the answer section. Please use them wisely; do not turn to the answer until you have made a genuine effort to

solve the problem by yourself, or unless you absolutely do not have time to work this particular problem. *After* getting your own solution or giving the problem a decent try, you may find the answer instructive and helpful. The solution given will often be quite short, and it will sketch the details under the assumption that you have earnestly tried to solve it by your own means first. Sometimes the solution gives less information than was asked; often it gives more. It is quite possible that you may have a better answer than the one published here, or you may have found an error in the published solution; in such a case, the author will be pleased to know the details. Later printings of this book will give the improved solutions together with the solver's name where appropriate.

When working an exercise you may generally use the answers to previous exercises, unless specifically forbidden from doing so. The rating numbers have been assigned with this in mind; thus it is possible for exercise $n + 1$ to have a lower rating than exercise n, even though it includes the result of exercise n as a special case.

Summary of codes:		*00* Immediate
		10 Simple (one minute)
		20 Medium (quarter hour)
▶	Recommended	*30* Moderately hard
M	Mathematically oriented	*40* Term project
HM	Requiring "higher math"	*50* Research problem

EXERCISES

▶ **1.** [*00*] What does the rating "*M20*" mean?

2. [*10*] Of what value can the exercises in a textbook be to the reader?

3. [*34*] Leonhard Euler conjectured in 1772 that the equation $w^4 + x^4 + y^4 = z^4$ has no solution in positive integers, but Noam Elkies proved in 1987 that infinitely many solutions exist [see *Math. Comp.* **51** (1988), 825–835]. Find all integer solutions such that $0 \leq w \leq x \leq y < z < 10^6$.

4. [*M50*] Prove that when n is an integer, $n > 4$, the equation $w^n + x^n + y^n = z^n$ has no solution in positive integers w, x, y, z.

Exercise is the beste instrument in learnyng.
— ROBERT RECORDE, *The Whetstone of Witte* (1557)

CONTENTS

JMK
JSK

CHAPTER THREE

RANDOM NUMBERS

Any one who considers arithmetical
methods of producing random digits
is, of course, in a state of sin.
— JOHN VON NEUMANN (1951)

Lest men suspect your tale untrue,
Keep probability in view.
— JOHN GAY (1727)

There wanted not some beams of light
to guide men in the exercise of their Stocastick faculty.
— JOHN OWEN (1662)

3.1. INTRODUCTION

NUMBERS that are "chosen at random" are useful in many different kinds of applications. For example:

a) *Simulation.* When a computer is being used to simulate natural phenomena, random numbers are required to make things realistic. Simulation covers many fields, from the study of nuclear physics (where particles are subject to random collisions) to operations research (where people come into, say, an airport at random intervals).

b) *Sampling.* It is often impractical to examine all possible cases, but a random sample will provide insight into what constitutes "typical" behavior.

c) *Numerical analysis.* Ingenious techniques for solving complicated numerical problems have been devised using random numbers. Several books have been written on this subject.

d) *Computer programming.* Random values make a good source of data for testing the effectiveness of computer algorithms. More importantly, they are crucial to the operation of *randomized algorithms*, which are often far superior to their deterministic counterparts. This use of random numbers is the primary application of interest to us in this series of books; it accounts for the fact that random numbers are already being considered here in Chapter 3, before most of the other computer algorithms have appeared.

1

e) *Decision making.* There are reports that many executives make their decisions by flipping a coin or by throwing darts, etc. It is also rumored that some college professors prepare their grades on such a basis. Sometimes it is important to make a completely "unbiased" decision. Randomness is also an essential part of optimal strategies in the theory of matrix games.

f) *Cryptography.* A source of unbiased bits is crucial for many types of secure communications, when data needs to be concealed.

g) *Aesthetics.* A little bit of randomness makes computer-generated graphics and music seem more lively. For example, a pattern like

□□□□□□□□   tends to look   □□□□□□□□
□□□□□□□□   □□□□□□□□
□□□□□□□□ more appealing than □□□□□□□□

in certain contexts. [See D. E. Knuth, *Bull. Amer. Math. Soc.* **1** (1979), 369.]

h) *Recreation.* Rolling dice, shuffling decks of cards, spinning roulette wheels, etc., are fascinating pastimes for just about everybody. These traditional uses of random numbers have suggested the name "Monte Carlo method," a general term used to describe any algorithm that employs random numbers.

People who think about this topic almost invariably get into philosophical discussions about what the word "random" means. In a sense, there is no such thing as a random number; for example, is 2 a random number? Rather, we speak of a *sequence of independent random numbers* with a specified *distribution*, and this means loosely that each number was obtained merely by chance, having nothing to do with other numbers of the sequence, and that each number has a specified probability of falling in any given range of values.

A *uniform* distribution on a finite set of numbers is one in which each possible number is equally probable. A distribution is generally understood to be uniform unless some other distribution is specifically mentioned.

Each of the ten digits 0 through 9 will occur about $\frac{1}{10}$ of the time in a (uniform) sequence of random digits. Each pair of two successive digits should occur about $\frac{1}{100}$ of the time, and so on. Yet if we take a truly random sequence of a million digits, it will not always have exactly 100,000 zeros, 100,000 ones, etc. In fact, chances of this are quite slim; a *sequence* of such sequences will have this character on the average.

Any specified sequence of a million digits is as probable as any other. Thus, if we are choosing a million digits at random and if the first 999,999 of them happen to come out to be zero, the chance that the final digit is zero is still exactly $\frac{1}{10}$, in a truly random situation. These statements seem paradoxical to many people, yet no contradiction is really involved.

There are several ways to formulate decent abstract definitions of randomness, and we will return to this interesting subject in Section 3.5; but for the moment, let us content ourselves with an intuitive understanding of the concept.

Many years ago, people who needed random numbers in their scientific work would draw balls out of a "well-stirred urn," or they would roll dice or deal out cards. A table of over 40,000 random digits, "taken at random from census reports," was published in 1927 by L. H. C. Tippett. Since then, a number of devices have been built to generate random numbers mechanically. The first such machine was used in 1939 by M. G. Kendall and B. Babington-Smith to produce a table of 100,000 random digits. The Ferranti Mark I computer, first installed in 1951, had a built-in instruction that put 20 random bits into the accumulator using a resistance noise generator; this feature had been recommended by A. M. Turing. In 1955, the RAND Corporation published a widely used table of a million random digits obtained with the help of another special device. A famous random-number machine called ERNIE has been used for many years to pick the winning numbers in the British Premium Savings Bonds lottery. [F. N. David describes the early history in *Games, Gods, and Gambling* (1962). See also Kendall and Babington-Smith, *J. Royal Stat. Soc.* **A101** (1938), 147–166; **B6** (1939), 51–61; S. H. Lavington's discussion of the Mark I in *CACM* **21** (1978), 4–12; the review of the RAND table in *Math. Comp.* **10** (1956), 39–43; and the discussion of ERNIE by W. E. Thomson, *J. Royal Stat. Soc.* **A122** (1959), 301–333.]

Shortly after computers were introduced, people began to search for efficient ways to obtain random numbers within computer programs. A table could be used, but this method is of limited utility because of the memory space and input time requirement, because the table may be too short, and because it is a bit of a nuisance to prepare and maintain the table. A machine such as ERNIE might be attached to the computer, as in the Ferranti Mark I, but this has proved to be unsatisfactory since it is impossible to reproduce calculations exactly a second time when checking out a program; moreover, such machines have tended to suffer from malfunctions that are extremely difficult to detect. Advances in technology made tables useful again during the 1990s, because a billion well-tested random bytes could easily be made accessible. George Marsaglia helped resuscitate random tables in 1995 by preparing a demonstration disk that contained 650 random megabytes, generated by combining the output of a noise-diode circuit with deterministically scrambled rap music. (He called it "white and black noise.")

The inadequacy of mechanical methods in the early days led to an interest in the production of random numbers using a computer's ordinary arithmetic operations. John von Neumann first suggested this approach in about 1946; his idea was to take the square of the previous random number and to extract the middle digits. For example, if we are generating 10-digit numbers and the previous value was 5772156649, we square it to get

$$33317792380594909201;$$

the next number is therefore 7923805949.

There is a fairly obvious objection to this technique: How can a sequence generated in such a way be random, since each number is completely determined by its predecessor? (See von Neumann's comment at the beginning of this chapter.) The answer is that the sequence *isn't* random, but it *appears* to be. In typical applications the actual relationship between one number and its successor has no physical significance; hence the nonrandom character is not really undesirable. Intuitively, the middle square seems to be a fairly good scrambling of the previous number.

Sequences generated in a deterministic way such as this are often called *pseudorandom* or *quasirandom* sequences in the highbrow technical literature, but in most places of this book we shall simply call them random sequences, with the understanding that they only *appear* to be random. Being "apparently random" is perhaps all that can be said about any random sequence anyway. Random numbers generated deterministically on computers have worked quite well in nearly every application, provided that a suitable method has been carefully selected. Of course, deterministic sequences aren't always the answer; they certainly shouldn't replace ERNIE for the lotteries.

Von Neumann's original "middle-square method" has actually proved to be a comparatively poor source of random numbers. The danger is that the sequence tends to get into a rut, a short cycle of repeating elements. For example, if zero ever appears as a number of the sequence, it will continually perpetuate itself.

Several people experimented with the middle-square method in the early 1950s. Working with numbers that have four digits instead of ten, G. E. Forsythe tried 16 different starting values and found that 12 of them led to sequences ending with the cycle 6100, 2100, 4100, 8100, 6100, ..., while two of them degenerated to zero. More extensive tests were carried out by N. Metropolis, mostly in the binary number system. He showed that when 20-bit numbers are being used, there are 13 different cycles into which the middle-square sequence might degenerate, the longest of which has a period of length 142.

It is fairly easy to restart the middle-square method on a new value when zero has been detected, but long cycles are somewhat harder to avoid. Exercises 6 and 7 discuss some interesting ways to determine the cycles of periodic sequences, using very little memory space.

A theoretical disadvantage of the middle-square method is given in exercises 9 and 10. On the other hand, working with 38-bit numbers, Metropolis obtained a sequence of about 750,000 numbers before degeneracy occurred, and the resulting $750,000 \times 38$ bits satisfactorily passed statistical tests for randomness. [*Symp. on Monte Carlo Methods* (Wiley, 1956), 29–36.] This experience showed that the middle-square method *can* give usable results, but it is rather dangerous to put much faith in it until after elaborate computations have been performed.

Many random number generators in use when this chapter was first written were not very good. People have traditionally tended to avoid learning about such subroutines; old methods that were comparatively unsatisfactory have been passed down blindly from one programmer to another, until the users have no understanding of the original limitations. We shall see in this chapter that the most important facts about random number generators are not difficult to learn, although prudence is necessary to avoid common pitfalls.

It is not easy to invent a foolproof source of random numbers. This fact was convincingly impressed upon the author in 1959, when he attempted to create a fantastically good generator using the following peculiar approach:

Algorithm K (*"Super-random" number generator*). Given a 10-digit decimal number X, this algorithm may be used to change X to the number that should come next in a supposedly random sequence. Although the algorithm might be expected to yield quite a random sequence, reasons given below show that it is not, in fact, very good at all. (The reader need not study this algorithm in great detail except to observe how complicated it is; note, in particular, steps K1 and K2.)

K1. [Choose number of iterations.] Set $Y \leftarrow \lfloor X/10^9 \rfloor$, the most significant digit of X. (We will execute steps K2 through K13 exactly $Y + 1$ times; that is, we will apply randomizing transformations a *random* number of times.)

K2. [Choose random step.] Set $Z \leftarrow \lfloor X/10^8 \rfloor \bmod 10$, the second most significant digit of X. Go to step K$(3 + Z)$. (That is, we now jump to a *random* step in the program.)

K3. [Ensure $\geq 5 \times 10^9$.] If $X < 5000000000$, set $X \leftarrow X + 5000000000$.

K4. [Middle square.] Replace X by $\lfloor X^2/10^5 \rfloor \bmod 10^{10}$, that is, by the middle of the square of X.

K5. [Multiply.] Replace X by $(1001001001\, X) \bmod 10^{10}$.

K6. [Pseudo-complement.] If $X < 100000000$, then set $X \leftarrow X + 9814055677$; otherwise set $X \leftarrow 10^{10} - X$.

K7. [Interchange halves.] Interchange the low-order five digits of X with the high-order five digits; that is, set $X \leftarrow 10^5(X \bmod 10^5) + \lfloor X/10^5 \rfloor$, the middle 10 digits of $(10^{10} + 1)X$.

K8. [Multiply.] Same as step K5.

K9. [Decrease digits.] Decrease each nonzero digit of the decimal representation of X by one.

K10. [99999 modify.] If $X < 10^5$, set $X \leftarrow X^2 + 99999$; otherwise set $X \leftarrow X - 99999$.

K11. [Normalize.] (At this point X cannot be zero.) If $X < 10^9$, set $X \leftarrow 10X$ and repeat this step.

K12. [Modified middle square.] Replace X by $\lfloor X(X - 1)/10^5 \rfloor \bmod 10^{10}$, that is, by the middle 10 digits of $X(X - 1)$.

K13. [Repeat?] If $Y > 0$, decrease Y by 1 and return to step K2. If $Y = 0$, the algorithm terminates with X as the desired "random" value. ∎

(The machine-language program corresponding to this algorithm was intended to be so complicated that a person reading a listing of it without explanatory comments wouldn't know what the program was doing.)

Considering all the contortions of Algorithm K, doesn't it seem plausible that it should produce almost an infinite supply of unbelievably random numbers? No! In fact, when this algorithm was first put onto a computer, it almost immediately converged to the 10-digit value 6065038420, which — by extraordinary

Table 1

A COLOSSAL COINCIDENCE: THE NUMBER 6065038420
IS TRANSFORMED INTO ITSELF BY ALGORITHM K.

Step	X (after)		Step	X (after)	
K1	6065038420		K9	1107855700	
K3	6065038420		K10	1107755701	
K4	6910360760		K11	1107755701	
K5	8031120760		K12	1226919902	$Y = 3$
K6	1968879240		K5	0048821902	
K7	7924019688		K6	9862877579	
K8	9631707688		K7	7757998628	
K9	8520606577		K8	2384626628	
K10	8520506578		K9	1273515517	
K11	8520506578		K10	1273415518	
K12	0323372207	$Y = 6$	K11	1273415518	
K6	9676627793		K12	5870802097	$Y = 2$
K7	2779396766		K11	5870802097	
K8	4942162766		K12	3172562687	$Y = 1$
K9	3831051655		K4	1540029446	
K10	3830951656		K5	7015475446	
K11	3830951656		K6	2984524554	
K12	1905867781	$Y = 5$	K7	2455429845	
K12	3319967479	$Y = 4$	K8	2730274845	
K6	6680032521		K9	1620163734	
K7	3252166800		K10	1620063735	
K8	2218966800		K11	1620063735	
			K12	6065038420	$Y = 0$

coincidence — is transformed into itself by the algorithm (see Table 1). With another starting number, the sequence began to repeat after 7401 values, in a cyclic period of length 3178.

The moral of this story is that *random numbers should not be generated with a method chosen at random*. Some theory should be used.

In the following sections we shall consider random number generators that are superior to the middle-square method and to Algorithm K. The corresponding sequences are guaranteed to have certain desirable random properties, and no degeneracy will occur. We shall explore the reasons for this random-like behavior in some detail, and we shall also consider techniques for manipulating random numbers. For example, one of our investigations will be the shuffling of a simulated deck of cards within a computer program.

Section 3.6 summarizes this chapter and lists several bibliographic sources.

EXERCISES

▶ **1.** [*20*] Suppose that you wish to obtain a decimal digit at random, not using a computer. Which of the following methods would be suitable?

a) Open a telephone directory to a random place by sticking your finger in it some-where, and use the units digit of the first number found on the selected page.

b) Same as (a), but use the units digit of the *page* number.

c) Roll a die that is in the shape of a regular icosahedron, whose twenty faces have been labeled with the digits 0, 0, 1, 1, ..., 9, 9. Use the digit that appears on top, when the die comes to rest. (A felt-covered table with a hard surface is recommended for rolling dice.)

d) Expose a geiger counter to a source of radioactivity for one minute (shielding yourself) and use the units digit of the resulting count. Assume that the geiger counter displays the number of counts in decimal notation, and that the count is initially zero.

e) Glance at your wristwatch; and if the position of the second-hand is between $6n$ and $6(n+1)$ seconds, choose the digit n.

f) Ask a friend to think of a random digit, and use the digit he names.

g) Ask an enemy to think of a random digit, and use the digit he names.

h) Assume that 10 horses are entered in a race and that you know nothing whatever about their qualifications. Assign to these horses the digits 0 to 9, in arbitrary fashion, and after the race use the winner's digit.

2. [*M22*] In a random sequence of a million decimal digits, what is the probability that there are exactly 100,000 of each possible digit?

3. [*10*] What number follows 1010101010 in the middle-square method?

4. [*20*] (a) Why can't the value of X be zero when step K11 of Algorithm K is performed? What would be wrong with the algorithm if X could be zero? (b) Use Table 1 to deduce what happens when Algorithm K is applied repeatedly with the starting value $X = 3830951656$.

5. [*15*] Explain why, in any case, Algorithm K should not be expected to provide infinitely many random numbers, in the sense that (even if the coincidence given in Table 1 had not occurred) one knows in advance that any sequence generated by Algorithm K will eventually be periodic.

▶ **6.** [*M21*] Suppose that we want to generate a sequence of integers $X_0, X_1, X_2, \ldots$, in the range $0 \le X_n < m$. Let $f(x)$ be any function such that $0 \le x < m$ implies $0 \le f(x) < m$. Consider a sequence formed by the rule $X_{n+1} = f(X_n)$. (Examples are the middle-square method and Algorithm K.)

a) Show that the sequence is ultimately periodic, in the sense that there exist numbers λ and μ for which the values

$$X_0, X_1, \ldots, X_\mu, \ldots, X_{\mu+\lambda-1}$$

are distinct, but $X_{n+\lambda} = X_n$ when $n \ge \mu$. Find the maximum and minimum possible values of μ and λ.

b) (R. W. Floyd.) Show that there exists an $n > 0$ such that $X_n = X_{2n}$; and the smallest such value of n lies in the range $\mu \le n \le \mu + \lambda$. Furthermore the value of X_n is unique in the sense that if $X_n = X_{2n}$ and $X_r = X_{2r}$, then $X_r = X_n$.

c) Use the idea of part (b) to design an algorithm that calculates μ and λ for any given function f and any given X_0, using only $O(\mu+\lambda)$ steps and only a bounded number of memory locations.

▶ **7.** [*M21*] (R. P. Brent, 1977.) Let $\ell(n)$ be the greatest power of 2 that is less than or equal to n; thus, for example, $\ell(15) = 8$ and $\ell(\ell(n)) = \ell(n)$.

a) Show that, in terms of the notation in exercise 6, there exists an $n > 0$ such that $X_n = X_{\ell(n)-1}$. Find a formula that expresses the least such n in terms of the periodicity numbers μ and λ.

b) Apply this result to design an algorithm that can be used in conjunction with any random number generator of the type $X_{n+1} = f(X_n)$, to prevent it from cycling indefinitely. Your algorithm should calculate the period length λ, and it should use only a small amount of memory space — you must not simply store all of the computed sequence values!

8. [*23*] Make a complete examination of the middle-square method in the case of two-digit decimal numbers.

a) We might start the process out with any of the 100 possible values 00, 01, ..., 99. How many of these values lead ultimately to the repeating cycle 00, 00, ...? [*Example:* Starting with 43, we obtain the sequence 43, 84, 05, 02, 00, 00, 00, ...]

b) How many possible final cycles are there? How long is the longest cycle?

c) What starting value or values will give the largest number of distinct elements before the sequence repeats?

9. [*M14*] Prove that the middle-square method using $2n$-digit numbers to the base b has the following disadvantage: If the sequence includes any number whose most significant n digits are zero, the succeeding numbers will get smaller and smaller until zero occurs repeatedly.

10. [*M16*] Under the assumptions of the preceding exercise, what can you say about the sequence of numbers following X if the *least* significant n digits of X are zero? What if the least significant $n + 1$ digits are zero?

▶ **11.** [*M26*] Consider sequences of random number generators having the form described in exercise 6. If we choose $f(x)$ and X_0 at random — in other words, if we assume that each of the m^m possible functions $f(x)$ is equally probable and that each of the m possible values of X_0 is equally probable — what is the probability that the sequence will eventually degenerate into a cycle of length $\lambda = 1$? [*Note:* The assumptions of this problem give a natural way to think of a "random" random number generator of this type. A method such as Algorithm K may be expected to behave somewhat like the generator considered here; the answer to this problem gives a measure of how colossal the coincidence of Table 1 really is.]

▶ **12.** [*M31*] Under the assumptions of the preceding exercise, what is the average length of the final cycle? What is the average length of the sequence before it begins to cycle? (In the notation of exercise 6, we wish to examine the average values of λ and of $\mu + \lambda$.)

13. [*M42*] If $f(x)$ is chosen at random in the sense of exercise 11, what is the average length of the *longest* cycle obtainable by varying the starting value X_0? [*Note:* We have already considered the analogous problem in the case that $f(x)$ is a random permutation; see exercise 1.3.3–23.]

14. [*M38*] If $f(x)$ is chosen at random in the sense of exercise 11, what is the average number of distinct final cycles obtainable by varying the starting value? [See exercise 8(b).]

15. [*M15*] If $f(x)$ is chosen at random in the sense of exercise 11, what is the probability that none of the final cycles has length 1, regardless of the choice of X_0?

16. [*15*] A sequence generated as in exercise 6 must begin to repeat after at most m values have been generated. Suppose we generalize the method so that X_{n+1} depends on X_{n-1} as well as on X_n; formally, let $f(x, y)$ be a function such that $0 \le x, y < m$ implies $0 \le f(x, y) < m$. The sequence is constructed by selecting X_0 and X_1 arbitrarily, and then letting

$$X_{n+1} = f(X_n, X_{n-1}), \qquad \text{for } n > 0.$$

What is the maximum period conceivably attainable in this case?

17. [*10*] Generalize the situation in the previous exercise so that X_{n+1} depends on the preceding k values of the sequence.

18. [*M20*] Invent a method analogous to that of exercise 7 for finding cycles in the general form of random number generator discussed in exercise 17.

19. [*HM47*] Solve the problems of exercises 11 through 15 asymptotically for the more general case that X_{n+1} depends on the preceding k values of the sequence; each of the m^{m^k} functions $f(x_1, \ldots, x_k)$ is to be considered equally probable. [*Note:* The number of functions that yield the *maximum* period is analyzed in exercise 2.3.4.2–23.]

20. [*30*] Find all nonnegative $X < 10^{10}$ that lead ultimately via Algorithm K to the self-reproducing number in Table 1.

21. [*40*] Prove or disprove: The mapping $X \mapsto f(X)$ defined by Algorithm K has exactly five cycles, of lengths 3178, 1606, 1024, 943, and 1.

22. [*21*] (H. Rolletschek.) Would it be a good idea to generate random numbers by using the sequence $f(0), f(1), f(2), \ldots$, where f is a random function, instead of using $x_0, f(x_0), f(f(x_0))$, etc.?

▶ **23.** [*M26*] (D. Foata and A. Fuchs, 1970.) Show that each of the m^m functions $f(x)$ considered in exercise 6 can be represented as a sequence $(x_0, x_1, \ldots, x_{m-1})$ having the following properties:

i) $(x_0, x_1, \ldots, x_{m-1})$ is a permutation of $(f(0), f(1), \ldots, f(m-1))$.

ii) $(f(0), \ldots, f(m-1))$ can be uniquely reconstructed from $(x_0, x_1, \ldots, x_{m-1})$.

iii) The elements that appear in cycles of f are $\{x_0, x_1, \ldots, x_{k-1}\}$, where k is the largest subscript such that these k elements are distinct.

iv) $x_j \notin \{x_0, x_1, \ldots, x_{j-1}\}$ implies $x_{j-1} = f(x_j)$, unless x_j is the smallest element in a cycle of f.

v) $(f(0), f(1), \ldots, f(m-1))$ is a permutation of $(0, 1, \ldots, m-1)$ if and only if $(x_0, x_1, \ldots, x_{m-1})$ represents the *inverse* of that permutation by the "unusual correspondence" of Section 1.3.3.

vi) $x_0 = x_1$ if and only if $(x_1, \ldots, x_{m-1})$ represents an oriented tree by the construction of exercise 2.3.4.4–18, with $f(x)$ the parent of x.

3.2. GENERATING UNIFORM RANDOM NUMBERS

IN THIS SECTION we shall consider methods for generating a sequence of random fractions — random *real numbers U_n, uniformly distributed between zero and one.* Since a computer can represent a real number with only finite accuracy, we shall actually be generating integers X_n between zero and some number m; the fraction

$$U_n = X_n/m$$

will then lie between zero and one. Usually m is the word size of the computer, so X_n may be regarded (conservatively) as the integer contents of a computer word with the radix point assumed at the extreme right, and U_n may be regarded (liberally) as the contents of the same word with the radix point assumed at the extreme left.

3.2.1. The Linear Congruential Method

By far the most popular random number generators in use today are special cases of the following scheme, introduced by D. H. Lehmer in 1949. [See *Proc. 2nd Symp. on Large-Scale Digital Calculating Machinery* (Cambridge, Mass.: Harvard University Press, 1951), 141–146.] We choose four magic integers:

$$
\begin{array}{lll}
m, & \text{the modulus;} & 0 < m. \\
a, & \text{the multiplier;} & 0 \le a < m. \\
c, & \text{the increment;} & 0 \le c < m. \\
X_0, & \text{the starting value;} & 0 \le X_0 < m.
\end{array}
\tag{1}
$$

The desired sequence of random numbers $\langle X_n \rangle$ is then obtained by setting

$$X_{n+1} = (aX_n + c) \bmod m, \qquad n \ge 0. \tag{2}$$

This is called a *linear congruential sequence.* Taking the remainder mod m is somewhat like determining where a ball will land in a spinning roulette wheel.

For example, the sequence obtained when $m = 10$ and $X_0 = a = c = 7$ is

$$7, \ 6, \ 9, \ 0, \ 7, \ 6, \ 9, \ 0, \ \ldots. \tag{3}$$

As this example shows, the sequence is not always "random" for all choices of m, a, c, and X_0; the principles of choosing the magic numbers appropriately will be investigated carefully in later parts of this chapter.

Example (3) illustrates the fact that the congruential sequences always get into a loop: There is ultimately a cycle of numbers that is repeated endlessly. This property is common to all sequences having the general form $X_{n+1} = f(X_n)$, when f transforms a finite set into itself; see exercise 3.1–6. The repeating cycle is called the *period*; sequence (3) has a period of length 4. A useful sequence will of course have a relatively long period.

The special case $c = 0$ deserves explicit mention, since the number generation process is a little faster when $c = 0$ than it is when $c \ne 0$. We shall see later that the restriction $c = 0$ cuts down the length of the period of the sequence, but it is still possible to make the period reasonably long. Lehmer's original generation method had $c = 0$, although he mentioned $c \neq 0$ as a possibility; the fact that $c \neq 0$ can lead to longer periods is due to Thomson [*Comp. J.* **1** (1958), 83, 86] and, independently, to Rotenberg [*JACM* **7** (1960), 75–77]. The terms *multiplicative congruential method* and *mixed congruential method* are used by many authors to denote linear congruential sequences with $c = 0$ and $c \neq 0$, respectively.

The letters m, a, c, and X_0 will be used throughout this chapter in the sense described above. Furthermore, we will find it useful to define

$$b = a - 1, \qquad (4)$$

in order to simplify many of our formulas.

We can immediately reject the case $a = 1$, for this would mean that $X_n = (X_0 + nc) \bmod m$, and the sequence would certainly not behave as a random sequence. The case $a = 0$ is even worse. Hence for practical purposes we may assume that

$$a \geq 2, \qquad b \geq 1. \qquad (5)$$

Now we can prove a generalization of Eq. (2),

$$X_{n+k} = \left(a^k X_n + (a^k - 1)c/b\right) \bmod m, \qquad k \geq 0, \quad n \geq 0, \qquad (6)$$

which expresses the $(n+k)$th term directly in terms of the nth term. (The special case $n = 0$ in this equation is worthy of note.) It follows that the subsequence consisting of every kth term of $\langle X_n \rangle$ is another linear congruential sequence, having the multiplier $a^k \bmod m$ and the increment $\left((a^k - 1)c/b\right) \bmod m$.

An important corollary of (6) is that the general sequence defined by m, a, c, and X_0 can be expressed very simply in terms of the special case where $c = 1$ and $X_0 = 0$. Let

$$Y_0 = 0, \qquad Y_{n+1} = (aY_n + 1) \bmod m. \qquad (7)$$

According to Eq. (6) we will have $Y_k \equiv (a^k - 1)/b$ (modulo m), hence the general sequence defined in (2) satisfies

$$X_n = (AY_n + X_0) \bmod m, \qquad \text{where } A = (X_0 b + c) \bmod m. \qquad (8)$$

EXERCISES

1. [*10*] Example (3) shows a situation in which $X_4 = X_0$, so the sequence begins again from the beginning. Give an example of a linear congruential sequence with $m = 10$ for which X_0 never appears again in the sequence.

▶ **2.** [*M20*] Show that if a and m are relatively prime, the number X_0 will always appear in the period.

3. [*M10*] If a and m are not relatively prime, explain why the sequence will be somewhat handicapped and probably not very random; hence we will generally want the multiplier a to be relatively prime to the modulus m.

4. [*11*] Prove Eq. (6).

5. [*M20*] Equation (6) holds for $k \geq 0$. If possible, give a formula that expresses X_{n+k} in terms of X_n for *negative* values of k.

3.2.1.1. Choice of modulus. Our current goal is to find good values for the parameters that define a linear congruential sequence. Let us first consider the proper choice of the number m. We want m to be rather large, since the period cannot have more than m elements. (Even if we intend to generate only random zeros and ones, we should *not* take $m = 2$, for then the sequence would at best have the form $\ldots, 0, 1, 0, 1, 0, 1, \ldots$! Methods for getting random zeros and ones from linear congruential sequences are discussed in Section 3.4.)

Another factor that influences our choice of m is speed of generation: We want to pick a value so that the computation of $(aX_n + c) \bmod m$ is fast.

Consider MIX as an example. We can compute $y \bmod m$ by putting y in registers A and X and dividing by m; assuming that y and m are positive, we see that $y \bmod m$ will then appear in register X. But division is a comparatively slow operation, and it can be avoided if we take m to be a value that is especially convenient, such as the *word size* of our computer.

Let w be the computer's word size, namely 2^e on an e-bit binary computer or 10^e on an e-digit decimal machine. (In this book we shall often use the letter e to denote an arbitrary integer exponent, instead of the base of natural logarithms, hoping that the context will make our notation unambiguous. Physicists have a similar problem when they use e for the charge on an electron.) The result of an addition operation is usually given modulo w, except on ones'-complement machines; and multiplication mod w is also quite simple, since the desired result is the lower half of the product. Thus, the following program computes the quantity $(aX + c) \bmod w$ efficiently:

```
LDA   A       rA ← a.
MUL   X       rAX ← (rA) · X.
SLAX  5       rA ← rAX mod w.                          (1)
ADD   C       rA ← (rA + c) mod w.    ∎
```

The result appears in register A. The overflow toggle might be on at the conclusion of these instructions; if that is undesirable, the code should be followed by, say, "JOV *+1" to turn it off.

A clever technique that is less commonly known can be used to perform computations modulo $w + 1$. For reasons to be explained later, we will generally want $c = 0$ when $m = w + 1$, so we merely need to compute $(aX) \bmod (w + 1)$. The following program does this:

```
01  LDAN X       rA ← −X.
02  MUL  A       rAX ← (rA) · a.
03  STX  TEMP
04  SUB  TEMP    rA ← rA − rX.                         (2)
05  JANN *+3     Exit if rA ≥ 0.
06  INCA 2       rA ← rA + 2.
07  ADD  =w−1=   rA ← rA + w − 1.    ∎
```

Register A now contains the value $(aX) \bmod (w + 1)$. Of course, this value might lie anywhere between 0 and w, inclusive, so the reader may legitimately wonder how we can represent so many values in the A-register! (The register obviously cannot hold a number larger than $w-1$.) The answer is that the result equals w if and only if program (2) turns overflow on, assuming that overflow was initially off. We could represent w by 0, since (2) will not normally be used when $X = 0$; but it is most convenient simply to reject the value w if it appears in the congruential sequence modulo $w+1$. Then we can also avoid overflow, simply by changing lines 05 and 06 of (2) to "JANN *+4; INCA 2; JAP *-5".

To prove that code (2) actually does determine $(aX) \bmod (w+1)$, note that in line 04 we are subtracting the lower half of the product from the upper half. No overflow can occur at this step; and if $aX = qw + r$, with $0 \le r < w$, we will have the quantity $r - q$ in register A after line 04. Now

$$aX = q(w+1) + (r-q),$$

and we have $-w < r - q < w$ since $q < w$; hence $(aX) \bmod (w+1)$ equals either $r - q$ or $r - q + (w+1)$, depending on whether $r - q \ge 0$ or $r - q < 0$.

A similar technique can be used to get the product of two numbers modulo $(w-1)$; see exercise 8.

In later sections we shall require a knowledge of the prime factors of m in order to choose the multiplier a correctly. Table 1 lists the complete factorization of $w \pm 1$ into primes for nearly every known computer word size; the methods of Section 4.5.4 can be used to extend this table if desired.

The reader may well ask why we bother to consider using $m = w \pm 1$, when the choice $m = w$ is so manifestly convenient. The reason is that when $m = w$, the right-hand digits of X_n are much less random than the left-hand digits. If d is a divisor of m, and if

$$Y_n = X_n \bmod d, \tag{3}$$

we can easily show that

$$Y_{n+1} = (aY_n + c) \bmod d. \tag{4}$$

(For $X_{n+1} = aX_n + c - qm$ for some integer q, and taking both sides mod d causes the quantity qm to drop out when d is a factor of m.)

To illustrate the significance of Eq. (4), let us suppose, for example, that we have a binary computer. If $m = w = 2^e$, the low-order four bits of X_n are the numbers $Y_n = X_n \bmod 2^4$. The gist of Eq. (4) is that the low-order four bits of $\langle X_n \rangle$ form a congruential sequence that has a period of length 16 or less. Similarly, the low-order five bits are periodic with a period of at most 32; and the least significant bit of X_n is either constant or strictly alternating.

This situation does not occur when $m = w \pm 1$; in such a case, the low-order bits of X_n will behave just as randomly as the high-order bits do. If, for example, $w = 2^{35}$ and $m = 2^{35} - 1$, the numbers of the sequence will not be very random if we consider only their remainders mod 31, 71, 127, or 122921 (see Table 1); but the low-order bit, which represents the numbers of the sequence taken mod 2, should be satisfactorily random.

Another alternative is to let m be the largest prime number less than w. This prime may be found by using the techniques of Section 4.5.4, and a table of suitably large primes appears in that section.

Table 1

PRIME FACTORIZATIONS OF $w \pm 1$

$2^e - 1$	e	$2^e + 1$
$7 \cdot 31 \cdot 151$	15	$3^2 \cdot 11 \cdot 331$
$3 \cdot 5 \cdot 17 \cdot 257$	16	65537
131071	17	$3 \cdot 43691$
$3^3 \cdot 7 \cdot 19 \cdot 73$	18	$5 \cdot 13 \cdot 37 \cdot 109$
524287	19	$3 \cdot 174763$
$3 \cdot 5^2 \cdot 11 \cdot 31 \cdot 41$	20	$17 \cdot 61681$
$7^2 \cdot 127 \cdot 337$	21	$3^2 \cdot 43 \cdot 5419$
$3 \cdot 23 \cdot 89 \cdot 683$	22	$5 \cdot 397 \cdot 2113$
$47 \cdot 178481$	23	$3 \cdot 2796203$
$3^2 \cdot 5 \cdot 7 \cdot 13 \cdot 17 \cdot 241$	24	$97 \cdot 257 \cdot 673$
$31 \cdot 601 \cdot 1801$	25	$3 \cdot 11 \cdot 251 \cdot 4051$
$3 \cdot 2731 \cdot 8191$	26	$5 \cdot 53 \cdot 157 \cdot 1613$
$7 \cdot 73 \cdot 262657$	27	$3^4 \cdot 19 \cdot 87211$
$3 \cdot 5 \cdot 29 \cdot 43 \cdot 113 \cdot 127$	28	$17 \cdot 15790321$
$233 \cdot 1103 \cdot 2089$	29	$3 \cdot 59 \cdot 3033169$
$3^2 \cdot 7 \cdot 11 \cdot 31 \cdot 151 \cdot 331$	30	$5^2 \cdot 13 \cdot 41 \cdot 61 \cdot 1321$
2147483647	31	$3 \cdot 715827883$
$3 \cdot 5 \cdot 17 \cdot 257 \cdot 65537$	32	$641 \cdot 6700417$
$7 \cdot 23 \cdot 89 \cdot 599479$	33	$3^2 \cdot 67 \cdot 683 \cdot 20857$
$3 \cdot 43691 \cdot 131071$	34	$5 \cdot 137 \cdot 953 \cdot 26317$
$31 \cdot 71 \cdot 127 \cdot 122921$	35	$3 \cdot 11 \cdot 43 \cdot 281 \cdot 86171$
$3^3 \cdot 5 \cdot 7 \cdot 13 \cdot 19 \cdot 37 \cdot 73 \cdot 109$	36	$17 \cdot 241 \cdot 433 \cdot 38737$
$223 \cdot 616318177$	37	$3 \cdot 1777 \cdot 25781083$
$3 \cdot 174763 \cdot 524287$	38	$5 \cdot 229 \cdot 457 \cdot 525313$
$7 \cdot 79 \cdot 8191 \cdot 121369$	39	$3^2 \cdot 2731 \cdot 22366891$
$3 \cdot 5^2 \cdot 11 \cdot 17 \cdot 31 \cdot 41 \cdot 61681$	40	$257 \cdot 4278255361$
$13367 \cdot 164511353$	41	$3 \cdot 83 \cdot 8831418697$
$3^2 \cdot 7^2 \cdot 43 \cdot 127 \cdot 337 \cdot 5419$	42	$5 \cdot 13 \cdot 29 \cdot 113 \cdot 1429 \cdot 14449$
$431 \cdot 9719 \cdot 2099863$	43	$3 \cdot 2932031007403$
$3 \cdot 5 \cdot 23 \cdot 89 \cdot 397 \cdot 683 \cdot 2113$	44	$17 \cdot 353 \cdot 2931542417$
$7 \cdot 31 \cdot 73 \cdot 151 \cdot 631 \cdot 23311$	45	$3^3 \cdot 11 \cdot 19 \cdot 331 \cdot 18837001$
$3 \cdot 47 \cdot 178481 \cdot 2796203$	46	$5 \cdot 277 \cdot 1013 \cdot 1657 \cdot 30269$
$2351 \cdot 4513 \cdot 13264529$	47	$3 \cdot 283 \cdot 165768537521$
$3^2 \cdot 5 \cdot 7 \cdot 13 \cdot 17 \cdot 97 \cdot 241 \cdot 257 \cdot 673$	48	$193 \cdot 65537 \cdot 22253377$
$179951 \cdot 3203431780337$	59	$3 \cdot 2833 \cdot 37171 \cdot 1824726041$
$3^2 \cdot 5^2 \cdot 7 \cdot 11 \cdot 13 \cdot 31 \cdot 41 \cdot 61 \cdot 151 \cdot 331 \cdot 1321$	60	$17 \cdot 241 \cdot 61681 \cdot 4562284561$
$7^2 \cdot 73 \cdot 127 \cdot 337 \cdot 92737 \cdot 649657$	63	$3^3 \cdot 19 \cdot 43 \cdot 5419 \cdot 77158673929$
$3 \cdot 5 \cdot 17 \cdot 257 \cdot 641 \cdot 65537 \cdot 6700417$	64	$274177 \cdot 67280421310721$

$10^e - 1$	e	$10^e + 1$
$3^3 \cdot 7 \cdot 11 \cdot 13 \cdot 37$	6	$101 \cdot 9901$
$3^2 \cdot 239 \cdot 4649$	7	$11 \cdot 909091$
$3^2 \cdot 11 \cdot 73 \cdot 101 \cdot 137$	8	$17 \cdot 5882353$
$3^4 \cdot 37 \cdot 333667$	9	$7 \cdot 11 \cdot 13 \cdot 19 \cdot 52579$
$3^2 \cdot 11 \cdot 41 \cdot 271 \cdot 9091$	10	$101 \cdot 3541 \cdot 27961$
$3^2 \cdot 21649 \cdot 513239$	11	$11^2 \cdot 23 \cdot 4093 \cdot 8779$
$3^3 \cdot 7 \cdot 11 \cdot 13 \cdot 37 \cdot 101 \cdot 9901$	12	$73 \cdot 137 \cdot 99990001$
$3^2 \cdot 11 \cdot 17 \cdot 73 \cdot 101 \cdot 137 \cdot 5882353$	16	$353 \cdot 449 \cdot 641 \cdot 1409 \cdot 69857$

In most applications, the low-order bits are insignificant, and the choice $m = w$ is quite satisfactory — provided that the programmer using the random numbers does so wisely.

Our discussion so far has been based on a "signed magnitude" computer like MIX. Similar ideas apply to machines that use complement notations, although there are some instructive variations. For example, a DECsystem 20 computer has 36 bits with two's complement arithmetic; when it computes the product of two nonnegative integers, the lower half contains the least significant 35 bits with a plus sign. On this machine we should therefore take $w = 2^{35}$, not 2^{36}. The 32-bit two's complement arithmetic on IBM System/370 computers is different: The lower half of a product contains a full 32 bits. Some programmers have felt that this is a disadvantage, since the lower half can be negative when the operands are positive, and it is a nuisance to correct this; but actually it is a distinct *advantage* from the standpoint of random number generation, since we can take $m = 2^{32}$ instead of 2^{31} (see exercise 4).

EXERCISES

1. [*M12*] In exercise 3.2.1–3 we concluded that the best congruential generators will have the multiplier a relatively prime to m. Show that when $m = w$ in this case it is possible to compute $(aX + c) \bmod w$ in just *three* MIX instructions, rather than the four in (1), with the result appearing in register X.

2. [*16*] Write a MIX subroutine having the following characteristics:

> Calling sequence: JMP RANDM
>
> Entry conditions: Location XRAND contains an integer X.
>
> Exit conditions: $X \leftarrow \text{rA} \leftarrow (aX + c) \bmod w$, rX $\leftarrow 0$, overflow off.

(Thus a call on this subroutine will produce the next random number of a linear congruential sequence.)

▶ **3.** [*M25*] Many computers do not provide the ability to divide a two-word number by a one-word number; they provide only operations on single-word numbers, such as $\text{himult}(x, y) = \lfloor xy/w \rfloor$ and $\text{lomult}(x, y) = xy \bmod w$, when x and y are nonnegative integers less than the word size w. Explain how to evaluate $ax \bmod m$ in terms of himult and lomult, assuming that $0 \le a, x < m < w$ and that $m \perp w$. You may use precomputed constants that depend on a, m, and w.

▶ **4.** [*21*] Discuss the calculation of linear congruential sequences with $m = 2^{32}$ on two's-complement machines such as the System/370 series.

5. [*20*] Given that m is less than the word size, and that x and y are nonnegative integers less than m, show that the difference $(x - y) \bmod m$ may be computed in just four MIX instructions, without requiring any division. What is the best code for the sum $(x + y) \bmod m$?

▶ **6.** [*20*] The previous exercise suggests that subtraction mod m is easier to perform than addition mod m. Discuss sequences generated by the rule

$$X_{n+1} = (aX_n - c) \bmod m.$$

Are these sequences essentially different from linear congruential sequences as defined in the text? Are they more suited to efficient computer calculation?

7. [*M24*] What patterns can you spot in Table 1?

▶ **8.** [*20*] Write a MIX program analogous to (2) that computes $(aX) \bmod (w-1)$. The values 0 and $w - 1$ are to be treated as equivalent in the input and output of your program.

▶ **9.** [*M25*] Most high-level programming languages do not provide a good way to divide a two-word integer by a one-word integer, nor do they provide the himult operation of exercise 3. The purpose of this exercise is to find a reasonable way to cope with such limitations when we wish to evaluate $ax \bmod m$ for variable x and for constants $0 < a < m$.

a) Prove that if $q = \lfloor m/a \rfloor$, we have $a(x - (x \bmod q)) = \lfloor x/q \rfloor (m - (m \bmod a))$.

b) Use the identity of (a) to evaluate $ax \bmod m$ without computing any numbers that exceed m in absolute value, assuming that $a^2 \leq m$.

10. [*M26*] The solution to exercise 9(b) sometimes works also when $a^2 > m$. Exactly how many multipliers a are there for which the intermediate results in that method never exceed m, for all x between 0 and m?

11. [*M30*] Continuing exercise 9, show that it is possible to evaluate $ax \bmod m$ using only the following basic operations:

i) $u \times v$, where $u \geq 0$, $v \geq 0$, and $uv < m$;
ii) $\lfloor u/v \rfloor$, where $0 < v \leq u < m$;
iii) $(u - v) \bmod m$, where $0 \leq u, v < m$.

In fact, it is always possible to do this with at most 12 operations of types (i) and (ii), and with a bounded number of operations of type (iii), not counting the precomputation of constants that depend on a and m. For example, explain how to proceed when a is 62089911 and m is $2^{31} - 1$. (These constants appear in Table 3.3.4–1.)

▶ **12.** [*M28*] Consider computations by pencil and paper or an abacus.

a) What's a good way to multiply a given 10-digit number by 10, modulo 9999998999?

b) Same question, but multiply instead by 999999900 (modulo 9999998999).

c) Explain how to compute the powers $999999900^n \bmod 9999998999$, for $n = 1, 2, 3, \dots$.

d) Relate such computations to the decimal expansion of $1/9999998999$.

e) Show that these ideas make it possible to implement certain kinds of linear congruential generators that have extremely large moduli, using only a few operations per generated number.

13. [*M24*] Repeat the previous exercise, but with modulus 9999999001 and with multipliers 10 and 8999999101.

14. [*M25*] Generalize the ideas of the previous two exercises, obtaining a large family of linear congruential generators with extremely large moduli.

3.2.1.2. Choice of multiplier. In this section we shall consider how to choose the multiplier a so as to produce a *period of maximum length*. A long period is essential for any sequence that is to be used as a source of random numbers; indeed, we would hope that the period contains considerably more numbers than will ever be used in a single application. Therefore we shall concern ourselves in this section with the question of period length. The reader should keep in mind, however, that a long period is only one desirable criterion for the randomness of a linear congruential sequence. For example, when $a = c = 1$, the sequence is simply $X_{n+1} = (X_n + 1) \bmod m$, and this obviously has a period of length m, yet it is anything but random. Other considerations affecting the choice of a multiplier will be given later in this chapter.

Since only m different values are possible, the period surely cannot be longer than m. Can we achieve the maximum length, m? The example above shows that it is always possible, although the choice $a = c = 1$ does not yield a desirable sequence. Let us investigate *all* possible choices of a, c, and X_0 that give a period of length m. It turns out that all such values of the parameters can be characterized very simply; when m is the product of distinct primes, only $a = 1$ will produce the full period, but when m is divisible by a high power of some prime there is considerable latitude in the choice of a. The following theorem makes it easy to tell if the maximum period is achieved.

Theorem A. *The linear congruential sequence defined by m, a, c, and X_0 has period length m if and only if*

i) *c is relatively prime to m;*

ii) *$b = a - 1$ is a multiple of p, for every prime p dividing m;*

iii) *b is a multiple of 4, if m is a multiple of 4.*

The ideas used in the proof of this theorem go back at least a hundred years. But the first proof of the theorem in this particular form was given by M. Greenberger in the special case $m = 2^e$ [see *JACM* **8** (1961), 163–167], and the sufficiency of conditions (i), (ii), and (iii) in the general case was shown by Hull and Dobell [see *SIAM Review* **4** (1962), 230–254]. To prove the theorem we will first consider some auxiliary number-theoretic results that are of interest in themselves.

Lemma P. *Let p be a prime number, and let e be a positive integer, where $p^e > 2$. If*

$$x \equiv 1 \ (\text{modulo } p^e), \qquad x \not\equiv 1 \ (\text{modulo } p^{e+1}), \tag{1}$$

then

$$x^p \equiv 1 \ (\text{modulo } p^{e+1}), \qquad x^p \not\equiv 1 \ (\text{modulo } p^{e+2}). \tag{2}$$

Proof. We have $x = 1 + qp^e$ for some integer q that is not a multiple of p. By the binomial formula

$$x^p = 1 + \binom{p}{1} qp^e + \cdots + \binom{p}{p-1} q^{p-1} p^{(p-1)e} + q^p p^{pe}$$

$$= 1 + qp^{e+1} \left(1 + \frac{1}{p}\binom{p}{2} qp^e + \frac{1}{p}\binom{p}{3} q^2 p^{2e} + \cdots + \frac{1}{p}\binom{p}{p} q^{p-1} p^{(p-1)e} \right).$$

The quantity in parentheses is an integer, and, in fact, every term inside the parentheses is a multiple of p except the first term. For if $1 < k < p$, the binomial coefficient $\binom{p}{k}$ is divisible by p (see exercise 1.2.6–10); hence

$$\frac{1}{p}\binom{p}{k} q^{k-1} p^{(k-1)e}$$

is divisible by $p^{(k-1)e}$. And the last term is $q^{p-1}p^{(p-1)e-1}$, which is divisible by p since $(p-1)e > 1$ when $p^e > 2$. So $x^p \equiv 1 + qp^{e+1}$ (modulo p^{e+2}), and this completes the proof. (*Note:* A generalization of this result appears in exercise 3.2.2–11(a).) ∎

Lemma Q. *Let the decomposition of m into prime factors be*

$$m = p_1^{e_1} \ldots p_t^{e_t}. \tag{3}$$

The length λ of the period of the linear congruential sequence determined by (X_0, a, c, m) is the least common multiple of the lengths λ_j of the periods of the linear congruential sequences $(X_0 \bmod p_j^{e_j}, a \bmod p_j^{e_j}, c \bmod p_j^{e_j}, p_j^{e_j})$, $1 \leq j \leq t$.

Proof. By induction on t, it suffices to prove that if m_1 and m_2 are relatively prime, the length λ of the period of the linear congruential sequence determined by the parameters $(X_0, a, c, m_1 m_2)$ is the least common multiple of the lengths λ_1 and λ_2 of the periods of the sequences determined by $(X_0 \bmod m_1, a \bmod m_1, c \bmod m_1, m_1)$ and $(X_0 \bmod m_2, a \bmod m_2, c \bmod m_2, m_2)$. We observed in the previous section, Eq. (4), that if the elements of these three sequences are respectively denoted by X_n, Y_n, and Z_n, we will have

$$Y_n = X_n \bmod m_1 \qquad \text{and} \qquad Z_n = X_n \bmod m_2, \qquad \text{for all } n \geq 0.$$

Therefore, by Law D of Section 1.2.4, we find that

$$X_n = X_k \qquad \text{if and only if} \qquad Y_n = Y_k \quad \text{and} \quad Z_n = Z_k. \tag{4}$$

Let λ' be the least common multiple of λ_1 and λ_2; we wish to prove that $\lambda' = \lambda$. Since $X_n = X_{n+\lambda}$ for all suitably large n, we have $Y_n = Y_{n+\lambda}$ (hence λ is a multiple of λ_1) and $Z_n = Z_{n+\lambda}$ (hence λ is a multiple of λ_2), so we must have $\lambda \geq \lambda'$. Furthermore, we know that $Y_n = Y_{n+\lambda'}$ and $Z_n = Z_{n+\lambda'}$ for all suitably large n; therefore, by (4), $X_n = X_{n+\lambda'}$. This proves $\lambda \leq \lambda'$. ∎

Now we are ready to prove Theorem A. Lemma Q tells us that it suffices to prove the theorem when m is a power of a prime number, because

$$p_1^{e_1} \ldots p_t^{e_t} = \lambda = \operatorname{lcm}(\lambda_1, \ldots, \lambda_t) \leq \lambda_1 \ldots \lambda_t \leq p_1^{e_1} \ldots p_t^{e_t}$$

will be true if and only if $\lambda_j = p_j^{e_j}$ for $1 \leq j \leq t$.

Assume therefore that $m = p^e$, where p is prime and e is a positive integer. The theorem is obviously true when $a = 1$, so we may take $a > 1$. The period can be of length m if and only if each possible integer $0 \leq x < m$ occurs in the period, since no value occurs in the period more than once. Therefore the period is of length m if and only if the period of the sequence with $X_0 = 0$ is of length m, and we are justified in supposing that $X_0 = 0$. By formula 3.2.1–(6) we have

$$X_n = \left(\frac{a^n - 1}{a - 1} \right) c \bmod m. \tag{5}$$

If c is not relatively prime to m, this value X_n could never be equal to 1, so condition (i) of the theorem is necessary. The period has length m if and only if the smallest positive value of n for which $X_n = X_0 = 0$ is $n = m$. By (5) and condition (i), our theorem now reduces to proving the following fact:

Lemma R. *Assume that $1 < a < p^e$, where p is prime. If λ is the smallest positive integer for which $(a^\lambda - 1)/(a - 1) \equiv 0$ (modulo p^e), then*

$$\lambda = p^e \quad \text{if and only if} \quad \begin{cases} a \equiv 1 \ (\text{modulo } p) & \text{when} \quad p > 2, \\ a \equiv 1 \ (\text{modulo } 4) & \text{when} \quad p = 2. \end{cases}$$

Proof. Assume that $\lambda = p^e$. If $a \not\equiv 1$ (modulo p), then $(a^n - 1)/(a - 1) \equiv 0$ (modulo p^e) if and only if $a^n - 1 \equiv 0$ (modulo p^e). The condition $a^{p^e} - 1 \equiv 0$ (modulo p^e) then implies that $a^{p^e} \equiv 1$ (modulo p); but by Theorem 1.2.4F we have $a^{p^e} \equiv a$ (modulo p), hence $a \not\equiv 1$ (modulo p) leads to a contradiction. And if $p = 2$ and $a \equiv 3$ (modulo 4), we have

$$(a^{2^{e-1}} - 1)/(a - 1) \equiv 0 \ (\text{modulo } 2^e)$$

by exercise 8. These arguments show that it is necessary in general to have $a = 1 + qp^f$, where $p^f > 2$ and q is not a multiple of p, whenever $\lambda = p^e$.

It remains to be shown that this condition is *sufficient* to make $\lambda = p^e$. By repeated application of Lemma P, we find that

$$a^{p^g} \equiv 1 \ (\text{modulo } p^{f+g}), \qquad a^{p^g} \not\equiv 1 \ (\text{modulo } p^{f+g+1}),$$

for all $g \geq 0$, and therefore

$$\begin{aligned} (a^{p^g} - 1)/(a - 1) &\equiv 0 \ (\text{modulo } p^g), \\ (a^{p^g} - 1)/(a - 1) &\not\equiv 0 \ (\text{modulo } p^{g+1}). \end{aligned} \tag{6}$$

In particular, $(a^{p^e} - 1)/(a - 1) \equiv 0$ (modulo p^e). Now the congruential sequence $(0, a, 1, p^e)$ has $X_n = (a^n - 1)/(a - 1) \bmod p^e$; therefore it has a period of length λ, that is, $X_n = 0$ if and only if n is a multiple of λ. Hence p^e is a multiple of λ. This can happen only if $\lambda = p^g$ for some g, and the relations in (6) imply that $\lambda = p^e$, completing the proof. ∎

The proof of Theorem A is now complete. ∎

We will conclude this section by considering the special case of pure multiplicative generators, when $c = 0$. Although the random number generation process is slightly faster in this case, Theorem A shows us that the maximum period length cannot be achieved. In fact, this is quite obvious, since the sequence now satisfies the relation

$$X_{n+1} = aX_n \bmod m, \tag{7}$$

and the value $X_n = 0$ should never appear, lest the sequence degenerate to zero. In general, if d is any divisor of m and if X_n is a multiple of d, all succeeding elements $X_{n+1}, X_{n+2}, \ldots$ of the multiplicative sequence will be multiples of d. So when $c = 0$, we will want X_n to be relatively prime to m for all n, and this limits the length of the period to at most $\varphi(m)$, the number of integers between 0 and m that are relatively prime to m.

It may be possible to achieve an acceptably long period even if we stipulate that $c = 0$. Let us now try to find conditions on the multiplier so that the period is as long as possible in this special case.

According to Lemma Q, the period of the sequence depends entirely on the periods of the sequences when $m = p^e$, so let us consider that situation. We have $X_n = a^n X_0 \bmod p^e$, and it is clear that the period will be of length 1 if a is a multiple of p, so we take a to be relatively prime to p. Then the period is the smallest integer λ such that $X_0 = a^\lambda X_0 \bmod p^e$. If the greatest common divisor of X_0 and p^e is p^f, this condition is equivalent to

$$a^\lambda \equiv 1 \pmod{p^{e-f}}. \tag{8}$$

By Euler's theorem (exercise 1.2.4–28), $a^{\varphi(p^{e-f})} \equiv 1 \pmod{p^{e-f}}$; hence λ is a divisor of

$$\varphi(p^{e-f}) = p^{e-f-1}(p-1).$$

When a is relatively prime to m, the smallest integer λ for which $a^\lambda \equiv 1$ (modulo m) is conventionally called the *order* of a modulo m. Any such value of a that has the *maximum* possible order modulo m is called a *primitive element* modulo m.

Let $\lambda(m)$ denote the order of a primitive element, namely the maximum possible order, modulo m. The remarks above show that $\lambda(p^e)$ is a divisor of $p^{e-1}(p-1)$; with a little care (see exercises 11 through 16 below) we can give the precise value of $\lambda(m)$ in all cases as follows:

$$\lambda(2) = 1, \qquad \lambda(4) = 2, \qquad \lambda(2^e) = 2^{e-2} \quad \text{if} \quad e \geq 3;$$
$$\lambda(p^e) = p^{e-1}(p-1), \qquad \text{if} \quad p > 2; \tag{9}$$
$$\lambda(p_1^{e_1} \ldots p_t^{e_t}) = \operatorname{lcm}\bigl(\lambda(p_1^{e_1}), \ldots, \lambda(p_t^{e_t})\bigr).$$

Our remarks may be summarized in the following theorem:

Theorem B. [C. F. Gauss, *Disquisitiones Arithmeticæ* (1801), §90–92.] *The maximum period possible when $c = 0$ is $\lambda(m)$, where $\lambda(m)$ is defined in (9). This period is achieved if*

i) X_0 *is relatively prime to* m;

ii) a *is a primitive element modulo* m. ▌

Notice that we can obtain a period of length $m - 1$ if m is prime; this is just one less than the maximum length, so for all practical purposes such a period is as long as we want.

The question now is, how can we find primitive elements modulo m? The exercises at the close of this section tell us that there is a fairly simple answer when m is prime or a power of a prime, namely the results stated in our next theorem.

Theorem C. *The number a is a primitive element modulo p^e if and only if one of the following cases applies:*

i) $p = 2$, $e = 1$, *and a is odd;*

ii) $p = 2$, $e = 2$, and $a \bmod 4 = 3$;

iii) $p = 2$, $e = 3$, and $a \bmod 8 = 3$, 5, or 7;

iv) $p = 2$, $e \geq 4$, and $a \bmod 8 = 3$ or 5;

v) p is odd, $e = 1$, $a \not\equiv 0$ (modulo p), and $a^{(p-1)/q} \not\equiv 1$ (modulo p) for any prime divisor q of $p - 1$;

vi) p is odd, $e > 1$, a satisfies the conditions of (v), and $a^{p-1} \not\equiv 1$ (modulo p^2). ∎

Conditions (v) and (vi) of this theorem are readily tested on a computer for large values of p, by using the efficient methods for evaluating powers discussed in Section 4.6.3, if we know the factors of $p - 1$.

Theorem C applies to powers of primes only. But if we are given values a_j that are primitive modulo $p_j^{e_j}$, it is possible to find a single value a such that $a \equiv a_j$ (modulo $p_j^{e_j}$), for $1 \leq j \leq t$, using the Chinese remainder algorithm discussed in Section 4.3.2; this number a will be a primitive element modulo $p_1^{e_1} \dots p_t^{e_t}$. Hence there is a reasonably efficient way to construct multipliers satisfying the condition of Theorem B, for any modulus m of moderate size, although the calculations can be somewhat lengthy in the general case.

In the common case $m = 2^e$, with $e \geq 4$, the conditions above simplify to the single requirement that $a \equiv 3$ or 5 (modulo 8). In this case, one-fourth of all possible multipliers will make the period length equal to $m/4$, and $m/4$ is the maximum possible when $c = 0$.

The second most common case is when $m = 10^e$. Using Lemmas P and Q, it is not difficult to obtain necessary and sufficient conditions for the achievement of the maximum period in the case of a decimal computer (see exercise 18):

Theorem D. *If* $m = 10^e$, $e \geq 5$, $c = 0$, *and* X_0 *is not a multiple of 2 or 5, the period of the linear congruential sequence is* $5 \times 10^{e-2}$ *if and only if* $a \bmod 200$ *equals one of the following 32 values:*

$$3, 11, 13, 19, 21, 27, 29, 37, 53, 59, 61, 67, 69, 77, 83, 91, 109, 117,$$
$$123, 131, 133, 139, 141, 147, 163, 171, 173, 179, 181, 187, 189, 197. \quad (10)$$
∎

EXERCISES

1. [*10*] What is the length of the period of the linear congruential sequence with $X_0 = 5772156648$, $a = 3141592621$, $c = 2718281829$, and $m = 10000000000$?

2. [*10*] Are the following two conditions sufficient to guarantee the maximum length period, when m is a power of 2? "(i) c is odd; (ii) $a \bmod 4 = 1$."

3. [*13*] Suppose that $m = 10^e$, where $e \geq 2$, and suppose further that c is odd and not a multiple of 5. Show that the linear congruential sequence will have the maximum length period if and only if $a \bmod 20 = 1$.

4. [*M20*] Assume that $m = 2^e$ and $X_0 = 0$. If the numbers a and c satisfy the conditions of Theorem A, what is the value of $X_{2^{e-1}}$?

5. [*14*] Find all multipliers a that satisfy the conditions of Theorem A when $m = 2^{35} + 1$. (The prime factors of m may be found in Table 3.2.1.1–1.)

▶ **6.** [*20*] Find all multipliers a that satisfy the conditions of Theorem A when $m = 10^6 - 1$. (See Table 3.2.1.1–1.)

▶ **7.** [*M23*] The period of a congruential sequence need not start with X_0, but we can always find indices $\mu \geq 0$ and $\lambda > 0$ such that $X_{n+\lambda} = X_n$ whenever $n \geq \mu$, and for which μ and λ are the smallest possible values with this property. (See exercises 3.1–6 and 3.2.1–1.) If μ_j and λ_j are the indices corresponding to the sequences

$$(X_0 \bmod p_j^{e_j}, \ a \bmod p_j^{e_j}, \ c \bmod p_j^{e_j}, \ p_j^{e_j}),$$

and if μ and λ correspond to the composite sequence $(X_0, a, c, p_1^{e_1} \dots p_t^{e_t})$, Lemma Q states that λ is the least common multiple of $\lambda_1, \dots, \lambda_t$. What is the value of μ in terms of the values of $\mu_1, \dots, \mu_t$? What is the maximum possible value of μ obtainable by varying X_0, a, and c, when $m = p_1^{e_1} \dots p_t^{e_t}$ is fixed?

8. [*M20*] Show that if $a \bmod 4 = 3$, we have $(a^{2^{e-1}} - 1)/(a - 1) \equiv 0 \pmod{2^e}$ when $e > 1$. (Use Lemma P.)

▶ **9.** [*M22*] (W. E. Thomson.) When $c = 0$ and $m = 2^e \geq 16$, Theorems B and C say that the period has length 2^{e-2} if and only if the multiplier a satisfies $a \bmod 8 = 3$ or $a \bmod 8 = 5$. Show that every such sequence is essentially a linear congruential sequence with $m = 2^{e-2}$, having *full* period, in the following sense:

a) If $X_{n+1} = (4c + 1)X_n \bmod 2^e$, and $X_n = 4Y_n + 1$, then

$$Y_{n+1} = ((4c + 1)Y_n + c) \bmod 2^{e-2}.$$

b) If $X_{n+1} = (4c - 1)X_n \bmod 2^e$, and $X_n = ((-1)^n(4Y_n + 1)) \bmod 2^e$, then

$$Y_{n+1} = ((1 - 4c)Y_n - c) \bmod 2^{e-2}.$$

[*Note:* In these formulas, c is an odd integer. The literature contains several statements to the effect that sequences with $c = 0$ satisfying Theorem B are somehow more random than sequences satisfying Theorem A, in spite of the fact that the period is only one-fourth as long in the case of Theorem B. This exercise refutes such statements; in essence, we must give up two bits of the word length in order to save the addition of c, when m is a power of 2.]

10. [*M21*] For what values of m is $\lambda(m) = \varphi(m)$?

▶ **11.** [*M28*] Let x be an odd integer greater than 1. (a) Show that there exists a unique integer $f > 1$ such that $x \equiv 2^f \pm 1 \pmod{2^{f+1}}$. (b) Given that $1 < x < 2^e - 1$ and that f is the corresponding integer from part (a), show that the order of x modulo 2^e is 2^{e-f}. (c) In particular, this proves parts (i)–(iv) of Theorem C.

12. [*M26*] Let p be an odd prime. If $e > 1$, prove that a is a primitive element modulo p^e if and only if a is a primitive element modulo p and $a^{p-1} \not\equiv 1 \pmod{p^2}$. (For the purposes of this exercise, assume that $\lambda(p^e) = p^{e-1}(p-1)$. This fact is proved in exercises 14 and 16 below.)

13. [*M22*] Let p be prime. Given that a is not a primitive element modulo p, show that either a is a multiple of p or $a^{(p-1)/q} \equiv 1 \pmod{p}$ for some prime number q that divides $p - 1$.

14. [*M18*] If $e > 1$ and p is an odd prime, and if a is a primitive element modulo p, prove that either a or $a + p$ is a primitive element modulo p^e. [*Hint:* See exercise 12.]

15. [*M29*] (a) Let a_1 and a_2 be relatively prime to m, and let their orders modulo m be λ_1 and λ_2, respectively. If λ is the least common multiple of λ_1 and λ_2, prove that $a_1^{\kappa_1} a_2^{\kappa_2}$ has order λ modulo m, for suitable integers κ_1 and κ_2. [*Hint:* Consider first the case that λ_1 is relatively prime to λ_2.] (b) Let $\lambda(m)$ be the maximum order of any element modulo m. Prove that $\lambda(m)$ is a multiple of the order of each element modulo m; that is, prove that $a^{\lambda(m)} \equiv 1$ (modulo m) whenever a is relatively prime to m. (Do not use Theorem B.)

▶ **16.** [*M24*] (*Existence of primitive roots.*) Let p be a prime number.
  a) Consider the polynomial $f(x) = x^n + c_1 x^{n-1} + \cdots + c_n$, where the c's are integers. Given that a is an integer for which $f(a) \equiv 0$ (modulo p), show that there exists a polynomial
$$q(x) = x^{n-1} + q_1 x^{n-2} + \cdots + q_{n-1}$$
  with integer coefficients such that $f(x) \equiv (x-a)q(x)$ (modulo p) for all integers x.
  b) Let $f(x)$ be a polynomial as in (a). Show that $f(x)$ has at most n distinct "roots" modulo p; that is, there are at most n integers a, with $0 \le a < p$, such that $f(a) \equiv 0$ (modulo p).
  c) Because of exercise 15(b), the polynomial $f(x) = x^{\lambda(p)} - 1$ has $p-1$ distinct roots; hence there is an integer a with order $p-1$.

17. [*M26*] Not all of the values listed in Theorem D would be found by the text's construction; for example, 11 is not primitive modulo 5^e. How can this be possible, when 11 *is* primitive modulo 10^e, according to Theorem D? Which of the values listed in Theorem D are primitive elements modulo *both* 2^e and 5^e?

18. [*M25*] Prove Theorem D. (See the previous exercise.)

19. [*40*] Make a table of some suitable multipliers, a, for each of the values of m listed in Table 3.2.1.1–1, assuming that $c = 0$.

▶ **20.** [*M24*] (G. Marsaglia.) The purpose of this exercise is to study the period length of an *arbitrary* linear congruential sequence. Let $Y_n = 1 + a + \cdots + a^{n-1}$, so that $X_n = (AY_n + X_0) \bmod m$ for some constant A by Eq. 3.2.1–(8).
  a) Prove that the period length of $\langle X_n \rangle$ is the period length of $\langle Y_n \bmod m' \rangle$, where $m' = m/\gcd(A, m)$.
  b) Prove that the period length of $\langle Y_n \bmod p^e \rangle$ satisfies the following when p is prime: (i) If $a \bmod p = 0$, it is 1. (ii) If $a \bmod p = 1$, it is p^e, except when $p = 2$ and $e \ge 2$ and $a \bmod 4 = 3$. (iii) If $p = 2$, $e \ge 2$, and $a \bmod 4 = 3$, it is twice the order of a modulo p^e (see exercise 11), unless $a \equiv -1$ (modulo 2^e) when it is 2. (iv) If $a \bmod p > 1$, it is the order of a modulo p^e.

21. [*M25*] In a linear congruential sequence of maximum period, let $X_0 = 0$ and let s be the least positive integer such that $a^s \equiv 1$ (modulo m). Prove that $\gcd(X_s, m) = s$.

▶ **22.** [*M25*] Discuss the problem of finding moduli $m = b^k \pm b^l \pm 1$ so that the subtract-with-borrow and add-with-carry generators of exercise 3.2.1.1–14 will have very long periods.

3.2.1.3. Potency. In the preceding section, we showed that the maximum period can be obtained when $b = a - 1$ is a multiple of each prime dividing m; and b must also be a multiple of 4 if m is a multiple of 4. If z is the radix of the machine being used — so that $z = 2$ for a binary computer, and $z = 10$ for a decimal computer — and if m is the word size z^e, the multiplier

$$a = z^k + 1, \qquad 2 \le k < e \tag{1}$$

satisfies these conditions. Theorem 3.2.1.2A also says that we may take $c = 1$. The recurrence relation now has the form

$$X_{n+1} = \left((z^k + 1)X_n + 1\right) \bmod z^e, \tag{2}$$

and this equation suggests that we can avoid the multiplication; merely shifting and adding will suffice.

For example, suppose we choose $a = B^2 + 1$, where B is the byte size of MIX. The code

$$\texttt{LDA X; \quad SLA 2; \quad ADD X; \quad INCA 1} \tag{3}$$

can be used in place of the instructions given in Section 3.2.1.1, and the execution time decreases from $16u$ to $7u$.

For this reason, multipliers having form (1) have been widely discussed in the literature, and indeed they have been recommended by many authors. However, the early years of experimentation with this method showed conclusively that *multipliers having the simple form in* (1) *should be avoided*. The generated numbers just aren't random enough.

Later in this chapter we shall be discussing some rather sophisticated theory that accounts for the badness of all the linear congruential random number generators known to be bad. However, some generators $\bigl($such as (2)$\bigr)$ are sufficiently awful that a comparatively simple theory can be used to rule them out. This simple theory is related to the concept of "potency," which we shall now discuss.

The *potency* of a linear congruential sequence with maximum period is defined to be the least integer s such that

$$b^s \equiv 0 \pmod{m}. \tag{4}$$

(Such an integer s will always exist when the multiplier satisfies the conditions of Theorem 3.2.1.2A, since b is a multiple of every prime dividing m.)

We may analyze the randomness of the sequence by taking $X_0 = 0$, since 0 occurs somewhere in the period. With this assumption, Eq. 3.2.1–(6) reduces to

$$X_n = \left((a^n - 1)c/b\right) \bmod m;$$

and if we expand $a^n - 1 = (b + 1)^n - 1$ by the binomial theorem, we find that

$$X_n = c\left(n + \binom{n}{2}b + \cdots + \binom{n}{s}b^{s-1}\right) \bmod m. \tag{5}$$

All terms in b^s, b^{s+1}, etc., may be ignored, since they are multiples of m.

Equation (5) can be instructive, so we shall consider some special cases. If $a = 1$, the potency is 1; and $X_n \equiv cn \pmod{m}$, as we have already observed, so the sequence is surely not random. If the potency is 2, we have $X_n \equiv cn + cb\binom{n}{2}$, and again the sequence is not very random; indeed,

$$X_{n+1} - X_n \equiv c + cbn$$

in this case, so the differences between consecutively generated numbers change in a simple way from one value of n to the next. The point (X_n, X_{n+1}, X_{n+2}) always lies on one of the four planes

$$x - 2y + z = d + m, \qquad\qquad x - 2y + z = d - m,$$
$$x - 2y + z = d, \qquad\qquad x - 2y + z = d - 2m,$$

in three-dimensional space, where $d = cb \bmod m$.

If the potency is 3, the sequence begins to look somewhat more random, but there is a high degree of dependency between X_n, X_{n+1}, and X_{n+2}; tests show that sequences with potency 3 are still not sufficiently good. Reasonable results have been reported when the potency is 4 or more, but they have been disputed by other people. A potency of at least 5 would seem to be required for sufficiently random values.

Suppose, for example, that $m = 2^{35}$ and $a = 2^k + 1$. Then $b = 2^k$, so we find that the value $b^2 = 2^{2k}$ is a multiple of m when $k \geq 18$: The potency is 2. If $k = 17, 16, \ldots, 12$, the potency is 3, and a potency of 4 is achieved for $k = 11, 10, 9$. The only acceptable multipliers, from the standpoint of potency, therefore have $k \leq 8$. This means $a \leq 257$, and we shall see later that *small* multipliers are also to be avoided. We have now eliminated all multipliers of the form $2^k + 1$ when $m = 2^{35}$.

When m is equal to $w \pm 1$, where w is the word size, m is generally not divisible by high powers of primes, and a high potency is impossible (see exercise 6). So in this case, the maximum-period method should *not* be used; the pure-multiplication method with $c = 0$ should be applied instead.

It must be emphasized that high potency is necessary but not sufficient for randomness; we use the concept of potency only to reject impotent generators, not to accept the potent ones. Linear congruential sequences should pass the "spectral test" discussed in Section 3.3.4 before they are considered to be acceptably random.

EXERCISES

1. [*M10*] Show that, no matter what the byte size B of MIX happens to be, the code (3) yields a random number generator of maximum period.

2. [*10*] What is the potency of the generator represented by the MIX code (3)?

3. [*11*] When $m = 2^{35}$, what is the potency of the linear congruential sequence with $a = 3141592621$? What is the potency if the multiplier is $a = 2^{23} + 2^{13} + 2^2 + 1$?

4. [*15*] Show that if $m = 2^e \geq 8$, maximum potency is achieved when $a \bmod 8 = 5$.

5. [*M20*] Given that $m = p_1^{e_1} \ldots p_t^{e_t}$ and $a = 1 + kp_1^{f_1} \ldots p_t^{f_t}$, where a satisfies the conditions of Theorem 3.2.1.2A and k is relatively prime to m, show that the potency is $\max(\lceil e_1/f_1 \rceil, \ldots, \lceil e_t/f_t \rceil)$.

▶ **6.** [*20*] Which of the values of $m = w \pm 1$ in Table 3.2.1.1–1 can be used in a linear congruential sequence of maximum period whose potency is 4 or more? (Use the result of exercise 5.)

7. [*M20*] When a satisfies the conditions of Theorem 3.2.1.2A, it is relatively prime to m; hence there is a number a' such that $aa' \equiv 1$ (modulo m). Show that a' can be expressed simply in terms of b.

▶ **8.** [*M26*] A random number generator defined by $X_{n+1} = (2^{17} + 3)X_n \bmod 2^{35}$ and $X_0 = 1$ was subjected to the following test: Let $Y_n = \lfloor 20X_n/2^{35} \rfloor$; then Y_n should be a random integer between 0 and 19, and the triples $(Y_{3n}, Y_{3n+1}, Y_{3n+2})$ should take on each of the 8000 possible values from $(0, 0, 0)$ to $(19, 19, 19)$ with nearly equal frequency. But with 1,000,000 values of n tested, many triples never occurred, and others occurred much more often than they should have. Can you account for this failure?

3.2.2. Other Methods

Of course, linear congruential sequences are not the only sources of random numbers that have been proposed for computer use. In this section we shall review the most significant alternatives. Some of these methods are quite important, while others are interesting chiefly because they are not as good as a person might expect.

One of the common fallacies encountered in connection with random number generation is the idea that we can take a good generator and modify it a little, in order to get an "even more random" sequence. This is often false. For example, we know that

$$X_{n+1} = (aX_n + c) \bmod m \tag{1}$$

leads to reasonably good random numbers; wouldn't the sequence produced by

$$X_{n+1} = \big((aX_n) \bmod (m+1) + c\big) \bmod m \tag{2}$$

be even *more* random? The answer is, the new sequence is probably a great deal *less* random. For the whole theory breaks down, and in the absence of any theory about the behavior of the sequence (2), we come into the area of generators of the type $X_{n+1} = f(X_n)$ with the function f chosen at random; exercises 3.1–11 through 3.1–15 show that these sequences probably behave much more poorly than the sequences obtained from the more disciplined function (1).

Let us consider another approach, in an attempt to obtain a genuine improvement of sequence (1). The linear congruential method can be generalized to, say, a quadratic congruential method:

$$X_{n+1} = (dX_n^2 + aX_n + c) \bmod m. \tag{3}$$

Exercise 8 generalizes Theorem 3.2.1.2A to obtain necessary and sufficient conditions on a, c, and d such that the sequence defined by (3) has a period of the maximum length m; the restrictions are not much more severe than in the linear method.

An interesting quadratic method has been proposed by R. R. Coveyou when m is a power of two: Let

$$X_0 \bmod 4 = 2, \qquad X_{n+1} = X_n(X_n + 1) \bmod 2^e, \qquad n \geq 0. \tag{4}$$

This sequence can be computed with about the same efficiency as (1), without any worries of overflow. It has an interesting connection with von Neumann's original middle-square method: If we let Y_n be $2^e X_n$, so that Y_n is a double-precision number obtained by placing e zeros to the right of the binary representation of X_n, then Y_{n+1} consists of precisely the middle $2e$ digits of $Y_n^2 + 2^e Y_n$! In other words, Coveyou's method is almost identical to a somewhat degenerate double-precision middle-square method, yet it is guaranteed to have a long period; further evidence of its randomness is proved in Coveyou's paper cited in the answer to exercise 8.

Other generalizations of Eq. (1) also suggest themselves; for example, we might try to extend the period length of the sequence. The period of a linear congruential sequence is fairly long; when m is approximately the word size of the computer, we usually get periods on the order of 10^9 or more, and typical calculations will use only a very small portion of the sequence. On the other hand, when we discuss the idea of "accuracy" in Section 3.3.4 we will see that the period length influences the degree of randomness achievable in a sequence. Therefore it can be desirable to seek a longer period, and several methods are available for this purpose. One technique is to make X_{n+1} depend on both X_n and X_{n-1}, instead of just on X_n; then the period length can be as high as m^2, since the sequence will not begin to repeat until we have $(X_{n+\lambda}, X_{n+\lambda+1}) = (X_n, X_{n+1})$. John Mauchly, in an unpublished paper presented to a statistics conference in 1949, extended the middle square method by using the recurrence $X_n = \text{middle}(X_{n-1} \cdot X_{n-6})$.

The simplest sequence in which X_{n+1} depends on more than one of the preceding values is the Fibonacci sequence,

$$X_{n+1} = (X_n + X_{n-1}) \bmod m. \tag{5}$$

This generator was considered in the early 1950s, and it usually gives a period length greater than m. But tests have shown that the numbers produced by the Fibonacci recurrence are definitely *not* satisfactorily random, and so our main interest in (5) as a source of random numbers is that it makes a nice "bad example." We may also consider generators of the form

$$X_{n+1} = (X_n + X_{n-k}) \bmod m, \tag{6}$$

when k is a comparatively large value. This recurrence was introduced by Green, Smith, and Klem [*JACM* **6** (1959), 527–537], who reported that, when $k \leq 15$, the sequence fails to pass the "gap test" described in Section 3.3.2, although when $k = 16$ the test was satisfactory.

A much better type of additive generator was devised in 1958 by G. J. Mitchell and D. P. Moore [unpublished], who suggested the somewhat unusual sequence defined by

$$X_n = (X_{n-24} + X_{n-55}) \bmod m, \qquad n \geq 55, \tag{7}$$

where m is even, and where $X_0, \ldots, X_{54}$ are arbitrary integers not all even. The constants 24 and 55 in this definition were not chosen at random; they are special values that happen to define a sequence whose least significant bits, $\langle X_n \bmod 2 \rangle$, will have a period of length $2^{55} - 1$. Therefore the sequence $\langle X_n \rangle$ must have a period at least this long. Exercise 30 proves that (7) has a period of length exactly $2^{e-1}(2^{55} - 1)$ when $m = 2^e$.

At first glance Eq. (7) may not seem to be extremely well suited to machine implementation, but in fact there is a very efficient way to generate the sequence using a cyclic list:

Algorithm A (*Additive number generator*). Memory cells $Y[1], Y[2], \ldots, Y[55]$ are initially set to the values $X_{54}, X_{53}, \ldots, X_0$, respectively; j is initially equal to 24 and k is 55. Successive performances of this algorithm will produce the numbers $X_{55}, X_{56}, \ldots$ as output.

A1. [Add.] (If we are about to output X_n at this point, $Y[j]$ now equals X_{n-24} and $Y[k]$ equals X_{n-55}.) Set $Y[k] \leftarrow (Y[k] + Y[j]) \bmod 2^e$, and output $Y[k]$.

A2. [Advance.] Decrease j and k by 1. If now $j = 0$, set $j \leftarrow 55$; otherwise if $k = 0$, set $k \leftarrow 55$. (We cannot have both $j = 0$ and $k = 0$.) ∎

This algorithm in MIX is simply the following:

Program A (*Additive number generator*). Assuming that index registers 5 and 6, representing j and k, are not touched by the remainder of the program in which this routine is embedded, the following code performs Algorithm A and leaves the result in register A.

```
    LDA   Y,6    A1. Add.
    ADD   Y,5    Y_k + Y_j (overflow possible)
    STA   Y,6        → Y_k.
    DEC5  1      A2. Advance. j ← j − 1.
    DEC6  1      k ← k − 1.
    J5P   *+2
    ENT5  55     If j = 0, set j ← 55.
    J6P   *+2
    ENT6  55     If k = 0, set k ← 55.  ∎
```

This generator is usually faster than the other methods we have been discussing, since it does not require any multiplication. Besides its speed, it has the longest period we have seen yet, except in exercise 3.2.1.2–22. Furthermore, as Richard Brent has observed, it can be made to work correctly with floating point numbers, avoiding the need to convert between integers and fractions (see exercise 23). Therefore it may well prove to be the very *best* source of random numbers for practical purposes. The main reason why it is difficult to recommend sequences like (7) wholeheartedly is that there is still very little theory to prove that they do or do not have desirable randomness properties; essentially all we know for sure is that the period is very long, and this is not enough. John Reiser (Ph.D. thesis, Stanford University, 1977) has shown, however, that an additive sequence like (7) will be well distributed in high dimensions, provided that a certain plausible conjecture is true (see exercise 26).

The numbers 24 and 55 in (7) are commonly called *lags*, and the numbers X_n defined by (7) are said to form a *lagged Fibonacci sequence*. Lags like $(24, 55)$ work well because of theoretical results developed in some of the exercises

Table 1

LAGS THAT YIELD LONG PERIODS MOD 2

$(24, 55)$	$(37, 100)$	$(83, 258)$	$(273, 607)$	$(576, 3217)$	$(7083, 19937)$
$(38, 89)$	$(30, 127)$	$(107, 378)$	$(1029, 2281)$	$(4187, 9689)$	$(9739, 23209)$

For extensions of this table, see N. Zierler and J. Brillhart, *Information and Control* **13** (1968), 541–554, **14** (1969), 566–569, **15** (1969), 67–69; Y. Kurita and M. Matsumoto, *Math. Comp.* **56** (1991), 817–821; Heringa, Blöte, and Compagner, *Int. J. Mod. Phys.* **C3** (1992), 561–564.

below. It is of course better to use somewhat larger lags when an application happens to use, say, groups of 55 values at a time; the numbers generated by (7) will never have X_n lying strictly between X_{n-24} and X_{n-55} (see exercise 2). J.-M. Normand, H. J. Herrmann, and M. Hajjar detected slight biases in the numbers generated by (7) when they did extensive high-precision Monte Carlo studies requiring 10^{11} random numbers [*J. Statistical Physics* **52** (1988), 441–446]; but larger values of k decreased the bad effects. Table 1 lists several useful pairs (l, k) for which the sequence $X_n = (X_{n-l} + X_{n-k}) \bmod 2^e$ has period length $2^{e-1}(2^k - 1)$. The case $(l, k) = (30, 127)$ should be large enough for most applications, especially in combination with other randomness-enhancing techniques that we will discuss later.

George Marsaglia [*Comp. Sci. and Statistics: Symposium on the Interface* **16** (1984), 3–10] has suggested replacing (7) by

$$X_n = (X_{n-24} \cdot X_{n-55}) \bmod m, \qquad n \geq 55, \qquad (7')$$

where m is a multiple of 4 and where X_0 through X_{54} are odd, not all congruent to 1 (modulo 4). Then the second-least significant bits have a period of $2^{55} - 1$, while the most significant bits are more thoroughly mixed than before since they depend on all bits of X_{n-24} and X_{n-55} in an essential way. Exercise 31 shows that the period length of sequence $(7')$ is only slightly less than that of (7).

Lagged Fibonacci generators have been used successfully in many situations since 1958, so it came as a shock to discover in the 1990s that they actually fail an extremely simple, non-contrived test for randomness (see exercise 3.3.2–31). A workaround that avoids such problems by discarding appropriate elements of the sequence is described near the end of this section.

Instead of considering purely additive or purely multiplicative sequences, we can construct useful random number generators by taking general linear combinations of $X_{n-1}, \ldots, X_{n-k}$ for small k. In this case the best results occur when the modulus m is a large *prime*; for example, m can be chosen to be the largest prime number that fits in a single computer word (see Table 4.5.4–2). When $m = p$ is prime, the theory of finite fields tells us that it is possible to find multipliers $a_1, \ldots, a_k$ such that the sequence defined by

$$X_n = (a_1 X_{n-1} + \cdots + a_k X_{n-k}) \bmod p \qquad (8)$$

has period length $p^k - 1$; here $X_0, \ldots, X_{k-1}$ may be chosen arbitrarily but not all zero. (The special case $k = 1$ corresponds to a multiplicative congruential sequence with prime modulus, with which we are already familiar.) The constants

$a_1, \dots, a_k$ in (8) have the desired property if and only if the polynomial

$$f(x) = x^k - a_1 x^{k-1} - \cdots - a_k \tag{9}$$

is a "primitive polynomial modulo p," that is, if and only if this polynomial has a root that is a primitive element of the field with p^k elements (see exercise 4.6.2–16).

Of course, the mere fact that suitable constants $a_1, \dots, a_k$ *exist* giving a period of length $p^k - 1$ is not enough for practical purposes; we must be able to *find* them, and we can't simply try all p^k possibilities, since p is on the order of the computer's word size. Fortunately there are exactly $\varphi(p^k - 1)/k$ suitable choices of $(a_1, \dots, a_k)$, so there is a fairly good chance of hitting one after making a few random tries. But we also need a way to tell quickly whether or not (9) is a primitive polynomial modulo p; it is certainly unthinkable to generate up to $p^k - 1$ elements of the sequence and wait for a repetition! Methods of testing for primitivity modulo p are discussed by Alanen and Knuth in *Sankhyā* **A26** (1964), 305–328. The following criteria can be used: Let $r = (p^k - 1)/(p - 1)$.

i) $(-1)^{k-1} a_k$ must be a primitive root modulo p. (See Section 3.2.1.2.)

ii) The polynomial x^r must be congruent to $(-1)^{k-1} a_k$, modulo $f(x)$ and p.

iii) The degree of $x^{r/q} \bmod f(x)$, using polynomial arithmetic modulo p, must be positive, for each prime divisor q of r.

Efficient ways to compute the polynomial $x^n \bmod f(x)$, using polynomial arithmetic modulo a given prime p, are discussed in Section 4.6.2.

In order to carry out this test, we need to know the prime factorization of $r = (p^k - 1)/(p - 1)$, and this is the limiting factor in the calculation; r can be factored in a reasonable amount of time when $k = 2, 3$, and perhaps 4, but higher values of k are difficult to handle when p is large. Even $k = 2$ essentially doubles the number of "significant random digits" over what is achievable with $k = 1$, so larger values of k will rarely be necessary.

An adaptation of the spectral test (Section 3.3.4) can be used to rate the sequence of numbers generated by (8); see exercise 3.3.4–24. The considerations of that section show that we should *not* make the obvious choice of $a_1 = +1$ or -1 when a primitive polynomial of that form exists; it is better to pick large, essentially "random" values of $a_1, \dots, a_k$ that satisfy the conditions, and to verify the choice by applying the spectral test. A significant amount of computation is involved in finding $a_1, \dots, a_k$, but all known evidence indicates that the result will be a very satisfactory source of random numbers. We essentially achieve the randomness of a linear congruential generator with k-tuple precision, using only single precision operations.

The special case $p = 2$ is of independent interest. Sometimes a random number generator is desired that merely produces a random sequence of *bits* — zeros and ones — instead of fractions between zero and one. There is a simple way to generate a highly random bit sequence on a binary computer, manipulating k-bit words: Start with an arbitrary nonzero binary word X. To get the next random bit of the sequence, do the following operations, shown in MIX's language (see exercise 16):

```
LDA   X    (Assume that overflow is now "off.")
ADD   X    Shift left one bit.
JNOV  *+2  Jump if the high bit was originally zero.           (10)
XOR   A    Otherwise adjust the number with "exclusive or."
STA   X        ▮
```

The fourth instruction here is the "exclusive or" operation found on nearly all binary computers (see exercise 2.5–28 and Section 7.1); it changes each bit position of rA in which location A has a "1" bit. The value in location A is the binary constant $(a_1 \ldots a_k)_2$, where $x^k - a_1 x^{k-1} - \cdots - a_k$ is a primitive polynomial modulo 2 as above. After the code (10) has been executed, the next bit of the generated sequence may be taken as the least significant bit of word X. Alternatively, we could consistently use the most significant bit of X, if the most significant bit is more convenient.

```
1011
0101
1010
0111
1110
1111
1101
1001
0001
0010
0100
1000
0011
0110
1100
1011
```

Fig. 1. Successive contents of the computer word X in the binary method, assuming that $k = 4$ and CONTENTS(A) = $(0011)_2$.

For example, consider Fig. 1, which illustrates the sequence generated for $k = 4$ and CONTENTS(A) = $(0011)_2$. This is, of course, an unusually small value for k. The right-hand column shows the sequence of bits of the sequence, namely $1101011110001001\ldots$, repeating in a period of length $2^k - 1 = 15$. This sequence is quite random, considering that it was generated with only four bits of memory; to see this, consider the adjacent sets of four bits occurring in the period, namely 1101, 1010, 0101, 1011, 0111, 1111, 1110, 1100, 1000, 0001, 0010, 0100, 1001, 0011, 0110. In general, every possible adjacent set of k bits occurs exactly once in the period, except the set of all zeros, since the period length is $2^k - 1$; thus, adjacent sets of k bits are essentially independent. We shall see in Section 3.5 that this is a very strong criterion for randomness when k is, say, 30 or more. Theoretical results illustrating the randomness of this sequence are given in an article by R. C. Tausworthe, *Math. Comp.* **19** (1965), 201–209.

Primitive polynomials modulo 2 of degree $\leq$ 168 have been tabulated by W. Stahnke, *Math. Comp.* **27** (1973), 977–980. When $k = 35$, we may take

$$\text{CONTENTS(A)} = (00000000000000000000000000000000101)_2,$$

but the considerations of exercises 18 and 3.3.4–24 imply that it would be better to find "random" constants that define primitive polynomials modulo 2.

Caution: Several people have been trapped into believing that this random bit-generation technique can be used to generate random whole-word fractions $(.X_0X_1 \ldots X_{k-1})_2$, $(.X_kX_{k+1} \ldots X_{2k-1})_2$, $\ldots$; but it is actually a poor source of random fractions, even though the bits are individually quite random. Exercise 18 explains why.

Mitchell and Moore's additive generator (7) is essentially based on the concept of primitive polynomials: The polynomial $x^{55} + x^{24} + 1$ is primitive, and Table 1 is essentially a listing of certain primitive trinomials modulo 2. A generator almost identical to that of Mitchell and Moore was independently discovered in 1971 by T. G. Lewis and W. H. Payne [*JACM* **20** (1973), 456–468], but using "exclusive or" instead of addition; this makes the period length exactly $2^{55} - 1$. Each bit position in the sequence of Lewis and Payne runs through the same periodic sequence, but has its own starting point. Experience has shown that (7) gives better results.

We have now seen that sequences with $0 \le X_n < m$ and period $m^k - 1$ can be constructed without great difficulty, when X_n is a suitable function of $X_{n-1}, \ldots, X_{n-k}$ and when m is prime. The highest conceivable period for *any* sequence defined by a relation of the form

$$X_n = f(X_{n-1}, \ldots, X_{n-k}), \qquad 0 \le X_n < m, \tag{11}$$

is easily seen to be m^k. M. H. Martin [*Bull. Amer. Math. Soc.* **40** (1934), 859–864] was the first person to show that functions achieving this maximum period are possible for all m and k. His method is easy to state (exercise 17) and reasonably efficient to program (exercise 29), but it is unsuitable for random number generation because it changes the value of $X_{n-1} + \cdots + X_{n-k}$ very slowly: All k-tuples occur, but not in a very random order. A better class of functions f that yield the maximum period m^k is considered in exercise 21. The corresponding programs are, in general, not as efficient for random number generation as other methods we have described, but they do give demonstrable randomness when the period as a whole is considered.

Many other schemes have been proposed for random number generation. The most interesting of these alternative methods may well be the *inversive congruential sequences* suggested by Eichenauer and Lehn [*Statistische Hefte* **27** (1986), 315–326]:

$$X_{n+1} = (aX_n^{-1} + c) \bmod p. \tag{12}$$

Here p is prime, X_n ranges over the set $\{0, 1, \ldots, p-1, \infty\}$, and inverses are defined by $0^{-1} = \infty$, $\infty^{-1} = 0$, otherwise $X^{-1}X \equiv 1$ (modulo p). Since 0 is always followed by ∞ and then by c in this sequence, we could simply define $0^{-1} = 0$ for purposes of implementation; but the theory is cleaner and easier to develop when $0^{-1} = \infty$. Efficient algorithms suitable for hardware implementation are available for computing X^{-1} modulo p; see, for example, exercise 4.5.2–39. Unfortunately, however, this operation is not in the repertoire of most computers. Exercise 35 shows that many choices of a and c yield the maximum period length $p + 1$. Exercise 37 demonstrates the most important property: Inversive congruential sequences are completely free of the lattice structure that is characteristic of linear congruential sequences.

Another important class of techniques deals with the *combination* of random number generators. There will always be people who feel that the linear congruential methods, additive methods, etc., are all too simple to give sufficiently random sequences; and it may never be possible to *prove* that their skepticism is unjustified — indeed, they may be right — so it is pretty useless to argue the point. There are reasonably efficient ways to combine two sequences into a third one that should be haphazard enough to satisfy all but the most hardened skeptic.

Suppose we have two sequences $X_0, X_1, \ldots$ and $Y_0, Y_1, \ldots$ of random numbers between 0 and $m - 1$, preferably generated by two unrelated methods. Then we can, for example, use one random sequence to permute the elements of another, as suggested by M. D. MacLaren and G. Marsaglia [*JACM* **12** (1965), 83–89; see also Marsaglia and Bray, *CACM* **11** (1968), 757–759]:

Algorithm M (*Randomizing by shuffling*). Given methods for generating two sequences $\langle X_n \rangle$ and $\langle Y_n \rangle$, this algorithm will successively output the terms of a "considerably more random" sequence. We use an auxiliary table $V[0], V[1], \ldots, V[k - 1]$, where k is some number chosen for convenience, usually in the neighborhood of 100. Initially, the V-table is filled with the first k values of the X-sequence.

M1. [Generate X, Y.] Set X and Y equal to the next members of the sequences $\langle X_n \rangle$ and $\langle Y_n \rangle$, respectively.

M2. [Extract j.] Set $j \leftarrow \lfloor kY/m \rfloor$, where m is the modulus used in the sequence $\langle Y_n \rangle$; that is, j is a random value, $0 \le j < k$, determined by Y.

M3. [Exchange.] Output $V[j]$ and then set $V[j] \leftarrow X$. ∎

As an example, assume that Algorithm M is applied to the following two sequences, with $k = 64$:

$$X_0 = 5772156649, \qquad X_{n+1} = (3141592653X_n + 2718281829) \bmod 2^{35};$$
$$Y_0 = 1781072418, \qquad Y_{n+1} = (2718281829Y_n + 3141592653) \bmod 2^{35}. \tag{13}$$

On intuitive grounds it appears safe to predict that the sequence obtained by applying Algorithm M to (13) will satisfy virtually *anyone's* requirements for randomness in a computer-generated sequence, because the relationship between nearby terms of the output has been almost entirely obliterated. Furthermore, the time required to generate this sequence is only slightly more than twice as long as it takes to generate the sequence $\langle X_n \rangle$ alone.

Exercise 15 proves that the period length of Algorithm M's output will be the least common multiple of the period lengths of $\langle X_n \rangle$ and $\langle Y_n \rangle$, in most situations of practical interest. In particular, if we reject the value 0 when it occurs in the Y-sequence, so that $\langle Y_n \rangle$ has period length $2^{35} - 1$, the numbers generated by Algorithm M from (13) will have a period of length $2^{70} - 2^{35}$. [See J. Arthur Greenwood, *Computer Science and Statistics: Symposium on the Interface* **9** (1976), 222–227.]

However, there is an even better way to shuffle the elements of a sequence, discovered by Carter Bays and S. D. Durham [*ACM Trans. Math. Software* **2** (1976), 59–64]. Their approach, although it appears to be superficially similar to Algorithm M, can give surprisingly better performance even though it requires only one input sequence $\langle X_n \rangle$ instead of two:

Algorithm B (*Randomizing by shuffling*). Given a method for generating a sequence $\langle X_n \rangle$, this algorithm will successively output the terms of a "considerably more random" sequence, using an auxiliary table $V[0], V[1], \ldots, V[k-1]$ as in Algorithm M. Initially the V-table is filled with the first k values of the X-sequence, and an auxiliary variable Y is set equal to the $(k+1)$st value.

B1. [Extract j.] Set $j \leftarrow \lfloor kY/m \rfloor$, where m is the modulus used in the sequence $\langle X_n \rangle$; that is, j is a random value, $0 \le j < k$, determined by Y.

B2. [Exchange.] Set $Y \leftarrow V[j]$, output Y, and then set $V[j]$ to the next member of the sequence $\langle X_n \rangle$. ∎

The reader is urged to work exercises 3 and 5, in order to get a feeling for the difference between Algorithms M and B.

On MIX we may implement Algorithm B by taking k equal to the byte size, obtaining the following simple generation scheme once the initialization has been done:

```
LD6   Y(1:1)    j ← high-order byte of Y.
LDA   X         rA ← Xn.
INCA  1         (see exercise 3.2.1.1–1)
MUL   A         rX ← Xn+1.
STX   X         "n ← n + 1."
LDA   V,6
STA   Y         Y ← V[j].
STX   V,6       V[j] ← Xn.  ∎
```

$$(14)$$

The output appears in register A. Notice that Algorithm B requires only four instructions of overhead per generated number.

F. Gebhardt [*Math. Comp.* **21** (1967), 708–709] found that satisfactory random sequences were produced by Algorithm M even when it was applied to a sequence as nonrandom as the Fibonacci sequence, with $X_n = F_{2n} \bmod m$ and $Y_n = F_{2n+1} \bmod m$. However, it is also possible for Algorithm M to produce a sequence *less* random than the original sequences, if $\langle X_n \rangle$ and $\langle Y_n \rangle$ are strongly related, as shown in exercise 3. Such problems do not seem to arise with Algorithm B. Since Algorithm B won't make a sequence any less random, and since it enhances the randomness with very little extra cost, it can be recommended for use in combination with any other random number generator.

Shuffling methods have an inherent defect, however: They change only the order of the generated numbers, not the numbers themselves. For most purposes the order is the critical thing, but if a random number generator fails the "birthday spacings" test discussed in Section 3.3.2 or the random walk test of exercise 3.3.2–31 it will not fare much better after it has been shuffled. Shuffling also has the comparative disadvantage that it does not allow us to start at a given place in the period, or to skip quickly from X_n to X_{n+k} for large k.

Many people have therefore suggested combining two sequences $\langle X_n \rangle$ and $\langle Y_n \rangle$ in a much simpler way, which avoids both of the defects of shuffling: We can use a combination like

$$Z_n = (X_n - Y_n) \bmod m \qquad (15)$$

when $0 \le X_n < m$ and $0 \le Y_n < m' \le m$. Exercises 13 and 14 discuss the period length of such sequences; exercise 3.3.2–23 shows that (15) tends to enhance the randomness when the seeds X_0 and Y_0 are chosen independently.

An even simpler way to remove the structural biases of arithmetically generated numbers was proposed already in the early days of computing by J. Todd and O. Taussky Todd [*Symp. on Monte Carlo Methods* (Wiley, 1956), 15–28]: We can just throw away some numbers of the sequence. Their suggestion was of little use with linear congruential generators, but it has become quite appropriate nowadays in connection with generators like (7) that have extremely long periods, because we have plenty of numbers to discard.

The simplest way to improve the randomness of (7) is to use only every jth term, for some small j. But a better scheme, which may be even simpler, is to use (7) to produce, say, 500 random numbers in an array and to use only the first 55 of them. After those 55 have been consumed, we generate 500 more in the same way. This idea was proposed by Martin Lüscher [*Computer Physics Communications* **79** (1994), 100–110], motivated by the theory of chaos in dynamical systems: We can regard (7) as a process that maps 55 values $(X_{n-55}, \ldots, X_{n-1})$ into another vector of 55 values $(X_{n+t-55}, \ldots, X_{n+t-1})$. Suppose we generate $t \ge 55$ values and use the first 55 of them. Then if $t = 55$ the new vector of values is rather close to the old; but if $t \approx 500$ there is almost no correlation between old and new (see exercise 33). For the analogous case of add-with-carry or subtract-with-borrow generators (exercise 3.2.1.1–14), the vectors are in fact known to be the radix-b representation of numbers in a linear congruential generator, and the relevant multiplier when we generate t numbers at a time is b^{-t}. Lüscher's theory for this case can therefore be confirmed with the spectral test of Section 3.3.4. A portable random number generator, based on a lagged Fibonacci sequence enhanced with Lüscher's approach, appears in Section 3.6, together with further commentary.

Random number generators typically do only a few multiplications and/or additions to get from one element of the sequence to the next. When such generators are combined as suggested above, common sense tells us that the resulting sequences ought to be indistinguishable from truly random numbers. But intuitive hunches are no substitute for rigorous mathematical proof. If we are willing to do more work—say 1000 or 1000000 times as much—we can obtain sequences for which substantially better theoretical guarantees of randomness are available.

For example, consider the sequence of bits $B_1, B_2, \ldots$ generated by

$$X_{n+1} = X_n^2 \bmod M, \qquad B_n = X_n \bmod 2, \qquad (16)$$

[Blum, Blum, and Shub, *SICOMP* **15** (1986), 364–383], or the more elaborate sequence generated by

$$X_{n+1} = X_n^2 \bmod M, \qquad B_n = X_n \cdot Z \bmod 2, \tag{17}$$

where the dot product of r-bit binary numbers $(x_{r-1} \ldots x_0)_2$ and $(z_{r-1} \ldots z_0)_2$ is $x_{r-1}z_{r-1} + \cdots + x_0 z_0$; here Z is an r-bit "mask," and r is the number of bits in M. The modulus M should be the product of two large primes of the form $4k + 3$, and the starting value X_0 should be relatively prime to M. Rule (17), suggested by Leonid Levin, is a take-off on von Neumann's original middle-square method; we will call it the *muddle-square method*, because it jumbles the bits of the squares. Rule (16) is, of course, the special case $Z = 1$.

Section 3.5F contains a proof that, when X_0, Z, and M are chosen at random, the sequences generated by (16) and (17) pass all statistical tests for randomness that require no more work than factoring large numbers. In other words, the bits cannot be distinguished from truly random numbers by any computation lasting less than 100 years on today's fastest computers, when M is suitably large, unless it is possible to find the factors of a nontrivial fraction of such numbers much more rapidly than is presently known. Formula (16) is simpler than (17), but the modulus M in (16) has to be somewhat larger than it does in (17) if we want to achieve the same statistical guarantees.

EXERCISES

▶ **1.** [*12*] In practice, we form random numbers using $X_{n+1} = (aX_n + c) \bmod m$, where the X's are *integers*, afterwards treating them as the *fractions* $U_n = X_n/m$. The recurrence relation for U_n is actually

$$U_{n+1} = (aU_n + c/m) \bmod 1.$$

Discuss the generation of random sequences using this relation *directly*, by making use of floating point arithmetic on the computer.

▶ **2.** [*M20*] A good source of random numbers will have $X_{n-1} < X_{n+1} < X_n$ about one-sixth of the time, since each of the six possible relative orders of X_{n-1}, X_n, and X_{n+1} should be equally probable. However, show that the ordering above *never* occurs if the Fibonacci sequence (5) is used.

3. [*23*] (a) What sequence comes from Algorithm M if

$$X_0 = 0, \quad X_{n+1} = (5X_n + 3) \bmod 8, \qquad Y_0 = 0, \quad Y_{n+1} = (5Y_n + 1) \bmod 8,$$

and $k = 4$? (Note that the potency is two, so $\langle X_n \rangle$ and $\langle Y_n \rangle$ aren't extremely random to start with.) (b) What happens if Algorithm B is applied to this same sequence $\langle X_n \rangle$ with $k = 4$?

4. [*00*] Why is the most significant byte used in the first line of program (14), instead of some other byte?

▶ **5.** [*20*] Discuss using $X_n = Y_n$ in Algorithm M, in order to improve the speed of generation. Is the result analogous to Algorithm B?

6. [*10*] In the binary method (10), the text states that the low-order bit of X is random, if the code is performed repeatedly. Why isn't the entire *word* X random?

7. [*20*] Show that a complete sequence of length 2^e (that is, a sequence in which each of the 2^e possible sets of e adjacent bits occurs just once in the period) may be obtained if program (10) is changed to the following:

```
LDA   X           LDA   A           JNOV  *+3           XOR   A
JANZ  *+2         ADD   X           JAZ   *+2           STA   X  ▐
```

8. [*M39*] Prove that the quadratic congruential sequence (3) has period length m if and only if the following conditions are satisfied:

  i) c *is relatively prime to* m;
 ii) d *and* $a - 1$ *are both multiples of* p, *for all odd primes* p *dividing* m;
iii) d *is even, and* $d \equiv a - 1$ (modulo 4), *if* m *is a multiple of* 4;
     $d \equiv a - 1$ (modulo 2), *if* m *is a multiple of* 2;
 iv) $d \not\equiv 3c$ (modulo 9), *if* m *is a multiple of* 9.

[*Hint:* The sequence defined by $X_0 = 0$, $X_{n+1} = dX_n^2 + aX_n + c$ modulo m has a period of length m only if the same sequence modulo any divisor r of m has period length r.]

▶ **9.** [*M24*] (R. R. Coveyou.) Use the result of exercise 8 to prove that the modified middle-square method (4) has a period of length 2^{e-2}.

10. [*M29*] Show that if X_0 and X_1 are not both even and if $m = 2^e$, the period of the Fibonacci sequence (5) is $3 \cdot 2^{e-1}$.

11. [*M36*] The purpose of this exercise is to analyze certain properties of integer sequences satisfying the recurrence relation

$$X_n = a_1 X_{n-1} + \cdots + a_k X_{n-k}, \qquad n \geq k.$$

If we can calculate the period length of this sequence modulo $m = p^e$, when p is prime, the period length with respect to an arbitrary modulus m is the least common multiple of the period lengths for the prime power factors of m.

  a) If $f(z)$, $a(z)$, $b(z)$ are polynomials with integer coefficients, let us write $a(z) \equiv b(z)$ (modulo $f(z)$ and m) if $a(z) = b(z) + f(z)u(z) + mv(z)$ for some polynomials $u(z)$ and $v(z)$ with integer coefficients. Prove that the following statement holds when $f(0) = 1$ and $p^e > 2$: If $z^\lambda \equiv 1$ (modulo $f(z)$ and p^e) and $z^\lambda \not\equiv 1$ (modulo $f(z)$ and p^{e+1}), then $z^{p\lambda} \equiv 1$ (modulo $f(z)$ and p^{e+1}) and $z^{p\lambda} \not\equiv 1$ (modulo $f(z)$ and p^{e+2}).
  b) Let $f(z) = 1 - a_1 z - \cdots - a_k z^k$, and let

$$G(z) = 1/f(z) = A_0 + A_1 z + A_2 z^2 + \cdots.$$

  Let $\lambda(m)$ denote the period length of $\langle A_n \bmod m \rangle$. Prove that $\lambda(m)$ is the smallest positive integer λ such that $z^\lambda \equiv 1$ (modulo $f(z)$ and m).
  c) Given that p is prime, $p^e > 2$, and $\lambda(p^e) \neq \lambda(p^{e+1})$, prove that $\lambda(p^{e+r}) = p^r \lambda(p^e)$ for all $r \geq 0$. (Thus, to find the period length of the sequence $\langle A_n \bmod 2^e \rangle$, we can compute $\lambda(4)$, $\lambda(8)$, $\lambda(16)$, ... until we find the smallest $e \geq 3$ such that $\lambda(2^e) \neq \lambda(4)$; then the period length is determined mod 2^e for all e. Exercise 4.6.3–26 explains how to calculate X_n for large n in $O(\log n)$ operations.)
  d) Show that any sequence of integers satisfying the recurrence stated at the beginning of this exercise has the generating function $g(z)/f(z)$, for some polynomial $g(z)$ with integer coefficients.
  e) Given that the polynomials $f(z)$ and $g(z)$ in part (d) are relatively prime modulo p (see Section 4.6.1), prove that the sequence $\langle X_n \bmod p^e \rangle$ has exactly the same

period length as the special sequence $\langle A_n \bmod p^e \rangle$ in (b). (No longer period could be obtained by *any* choice of $X_0, \ldots, X_{k-1}$, since the general sequence is a linear combination of "shifts" of the special sequence.) [*Hint:* By exercise 4.6.2–22 (Hensel's lemma), there exist polynomials such that $a(z)f(z) + b(z)g(z) \equiv 1$ (modulo p^e).]

▶ **12.** [*M28*] Find integers X_0, X_1, a, b, and c such that the sequence

$$X_{n+1} = (aX_n + bX_{n-1} + c) \bmod 2^e, \qquad n \geq 1,$$

has the longest period length of all sequences of this type. [*Hint:* It follows that $X_{n+2} = \big((a+1)X_{n+1} + (b-a)X_n - bX_{n-1}\big) \bmod 2^e$; see exercise 11(c).]

13. [*M20*] Let $\langle X_n \rangle$ and $\langle Y_n \rangle$ be sequences of integers mod m with periods of lengths λ_1 and λ_2, and combine them by letting $Z_n = (X_n + Y_n) \bmod m$. Show that if λ_1 and λ_2 are relatively prime, the sequence $\langle Z_n \rangle$ has a period of length $\lambda_1 \lambda_2$.

14. [*M24*] Let X_n, Y_n, Z_n, λ_1, λ_2 be as in the previous exercise. Suppose that the prime factorization of λ_1 is $2^{e_2} 3^{e_3} 5^{e_5} \ldots$, and similarly suppose that $\lambda_2 = 2^{f_2} 3^{f_3} 5^{f_5} \ldots$. Let $g_p = \big(\max(e_p, f_p)$ if $e_p \neq f_p$, otherwise $0\big)$, and let $\lambda_0 = 2^{g_2} 3^{g_3} 5^{g_5} \ldots$. Show that the period length λ' of the sequence $\langle Z_n \rangle$ is a multiple of λ_0, and it is a divisor of $\lambda = \mathrm{lcm}(\lambda_1, \lambda_2)$. In particular, $\lambda' = \lambda$ if ($e_p \neq f_p$ or $e_p = f_p = 0$) for each prime p.

15. [*M27*] Let the sequence $\langle X_n \rangle$ in Algorithm M have period length λ_1, and assume that all elements of its period are distinct. Let $q_n = \min\{r \mid r > 0 \text{ and } \lfloor kY_{n-r}/m \rfloor = \lfloor kY_n/m \rfloor\}$. Assume that $q_n < \frac{1}{2}\lambda_1$ for all $n \geq n_0$, and that the sequence $\langle q_n \rangle$ has period length λ_2. Let λ be the least common multiple of λ_1 and λ_2. Prove that the output sequence $\langle Z_n \rangle$ produced by Algorithm M has a period of length λ.

▶ **16.** [*M28*] Let `CONTENTS(A)` in method (10) be $(a_1 a_2 \ldots a_k)_2$ in binary notation. Show that the generated sequence of low-order bits X_0, X_1, ... satisfies the relation

$$X_n = (a_1 X_{n-1} + a_2 X_{n-2} + \cdots + a_k X_{n-k}) \bmod 2.$$

[This may be regarded as another way to define the sequence, although the connection between this relation and the efficient code (10) is not apparent at first glance!]

17. [*M33*] (M. H. Martin, 1934.) Let m and k be positive integers, and let $X_1 = X_2 = \cdots = X_k = 0$. For all $n > 0$, set X_{n+k} equal to the largest nonnegative value $y < m$ such that the k-tuple $(X_{n+1}, \ldots, X_{n+k-1}, y)$ has not already occurred in the sequence; in other words, $(X_{n+1}, \ldots, X_{n+k-1}, y)$ must differ from $(X_{r+1}, \ldots, X_{r+k})$ for $0 \leq r < n$. In this way, each possible k-tuple will occur at most once in the sequence. Eventually the process will terminate, when we reach a value of n such that $(X_{n+1}, \ldots, X_{n+k-1}, y)$ has already occurred in the sequence for all nonnegative $y < m$. For example, if $m = k = 3$ the sequence is 00022212202112102012001110100, and the process terminates at this point. (a) Prove that when the sequence terminates, we have $X_{n+1} = \cdots = X_{n+k-1} = 0$. (b) Prove that *every* k-tuple $(a_1, a_2, \ldots, a_k)$ of elements with $0 \leq a_j < m$ occurs in the sequence; hence the sequence terminates when $n = m^k$. [*Hint:* Prove that the k-tuple $(a_1, \ldots, a_s, 0, \ldots, 0)$ appears, when $a_s \neq 0$, by induction on s.] Note that if we now define $f(X_n, \ldots, X_{n+k-1}) = X_{n+k}$ for $1 \leq n \leq m^k$, setting $X_{m^k + k} = 0$, we obtain a function of maximum possible period.

18. [*M22*] Let $\langle X_n \rangle$ be the sequence of bits generated by method (10), with $k = 35$ and `CONTENTS(A)` $= (00000000000000000000000000000000101)_2$. Let U_n be the binary fraction $(.X_{nk} X_{nk+1} \ldots X_{nk+k-1})_2$; show that this sequence $\langle U_n \rangle$ fails the serial test on pairs (Section 3.3.2B) when $d = 8$.

19. [*M41*] For each prime p specified in the first column of Table 2 in Section 4.5.4, find suitable constants a_1 and a_2 as suggested in the text, such that the period length of (8), when $k = 2$, is $p^2 - 1$. (See Eq. 3.3.4–(39) for an example.)

20. [*M40*] Calculate constants suitable for use as CONTENTS(A) in method (10), having approximately the same number of zeros as ones, for $2 \le k \le 64$.

21. [*M35*] (D. Rees.) The text explains how to find functions f such that the sequence (11) has period length $m^k - 1$, provided that m is prime and $X_0, \dots, X_{k-1}$ are not all zero. Show that such functions can be modified to obtain sequences of type (11) with period length m^k, for *all* integers m. [*Hints:* Consider the results of exercises 7 and 13, and sequences such as $\langle pX_{2n} + X_{2n+1} \rangle$.]

▶ **22.** [*M24*] The text restricts discussion of the extended linear sequences (8) to the case that m is prime. Prove that reasonably long periods can also be obtained when m is "squarefree," that is, the product of distinct primes. (Examination of Table 3.2.1.1–1 shows that $m = w \pm 1$ often satisfies this hypothesis; many of the results of the text can therefore be carried over to that case, which is somewhat more convenient for calculation.)

▶ **23.** [*20*] Discuss the sequence defined by $X_n = (X_{n-55} - X_{n-24}) \bmod m$ as an alternative to (7).

24. [*M20*] Let $0 < l < k$. Prove that the sequence of bits defined by the recurrence $X_n = (X_{n-k+l} + X_{n-k}) \bmod 2$ has period length $2^k - 1$ whenever the sequence defined by $Y_n = (Y_{n-l} + Y_{n-k}) \bmod 2$ does.

25. [*26*] Discuss the alternative to Program A that changes all 55 entries of the Y table every 55th time a random number is required.

26. [*M48*] (J. F. Reiser.) Let p be prime and let k be a positive integer. Given integers $a_1, \dots, a_k$ and $x_1, \dots, x_k$, let λ_α be the period of the sequence $\langle X_n \rangle$ generated by the recurrence

$$X_n = x_n \bmod p^\alpha, \quad 0 \le n < k; \qquad X_n = (a_1 X_{n-1} + \dots + a_k X_{n-k}) \bmod p^\alpha, \quad n \ge k;$$

and let N_α be the number of 0s that occur in the period (the number of indices j such that $\mu_\alpha \le j < \mu_\alpha + \lambda_\alpha$ and $X_j = 0$). Prove or disprove the following conjecture: There exists a constant c (depending possibly on p and k and $a_1, \dots, a_k$) such that $N_\alpha \le c p^{\alpha(k-2)/(k-1)}$ for all α and all $x_1, \dots, x_k$.

[*Notes:* Reiser has proved that if the recurrence has maximum period length mod p (that is, if $\lambda_1 = p^k - 1$), and if the conjecture holds, then the k-dimensional discrepancy of $\langle X_n \rangle$ will be $O(\alpha^k p^{-\alpha/(k-1)})$ as $\alpha \to \infty$; thus an additive generator like (7) would be well distributed in 55 dimensions, when $m = 2^e$ and the entire period is considered. (See Section 3.3.4 for the definition of discrepancy in k dimensions.) The conjecture is a very weak condition, for if $\langle X_n \rangle$ takes on each value about equally often and if $\lambda_\alpha = p^{\alpha-1}(p^k - 1)$, the quantity $N_\alpha \approx (p^k - 1)/p$ does not grow at all as α increases. Reiser has verified the conjecture for $k = 3$. On the other hand he has shown that it is possible to find unusually bad starting values $x_1, \dots, x_k$ (depending on α) so that $N_{2\alpha} \ge p^\alpha$, provided that $\lambda_\alpha = p^{\alpha-1}(p^k - 1)$ and $k \ge 3$ and α is sufficiently large.]

27. [*M30*] Suppose Algorithm B is being applied to a sequence $\langle X_n \rangle$ whose period length is λ, where $\lambda \gg k$. Show that for fixed k and all sufficiently large λ, the output of the sequence will eventually be periodic with the same period length λ, unless $\langle X_n \rangle$ isn't very random to start with. [*Hint:* Find a pattern of consecutive values of $\lfloor kX_n/m \rfloor$ that causes Algorithm B to "synchronize" its subsequent behavior.]

28. [*40*] (A. G. Waterman.) Experiment with linear congruential sequences with m the square or cube of the computer word size, while a and c are single-precision numbers.

▶ **29.** [*40*] Find a good way to compute the function $f(x_1, \ldots, x_k)$ defined by Martin's sequence in exercise 17, given only the k-tuple $(x_1, \ldots, x_k)$.

30. [*M37*] (R. P. Brent.) Let $f(x) = x^k - a_1 x^{k-1} - \cdots - a_k$ be a primitive polynomial modulo 2, and suppose that $X_0, \ldots, X_{k-1}$ are integers not all even.

    a) Prove that the period of the recurrence $X_n = (a_1 X_{n-1} + \cdots + a_k X_{n-k}) \bmod 2^e$ is $2^{e-1}(2^k - 1)$ for all $e \geq 1$ if and only if $f(x)^2 + f(-x)^2 \not\equiv 2f(x^2)$ and $f(x)^2 + f(-x)^2 \not\equiv 2(-1)^k f(-x^2)$ (modulo 8). [*Hint:* We have $x^{2^k} \equiv -x$ (modulo 4 and $f(x)$) if and only if $f(x)^2 + f(-x)^2 \equiv 2f(x^2)$ (modulo 8).]

    b) Prove that this condition always holds when the polynomial $f(x) = x^k \pm x^l \pm 1$ is primitive modulo 2 and $k > 2$.

31. [*M30*] (G. Marsaglia.) What is the period length of the sequence $(7')$ when $m = 2^e \geq 8$? Assume that $X_0, \ldots, X_{54}$ are not all $\equiv \pm 1$ (modulo 8).

32. [*M21*] What recurrences are satisfied by the elements of the subsequences $\langle X_{2n} \rangle$ and $\langle X_{3n} \rangle$, when $X_n = (X_{n-24} + X_{n-55}) \bmod m$?

▶ **33.** [*M23*] (a) Let $g_n(z) = X_{n+30} + X_{n+29}z + \cdots + X_n z^{30} + X_{n+54}z^{31} + \cdots + X_{n+31}z^{54}$, where the X's satisfy the lagged Fibonacci recurrence (7). Find a simple relation between $g_n(z)$ and $g_{n+t}(z)$. (b) Express X_{500} in terms of $X_0, \ldots, X_{54}$.

34. [*M25*] Prove that the inversive congruential sequence (12) has period $p+1$ if and only if the polynomial $f(x) = x^2 - cx - a$ has the following two properties: (i) $x^{p+1} \bmod f(x)$ is a nonzero constant, when computed with polynomial arithmetic modulo p; (ii) $x^{(p+1)/q} \bmod f(x)$ has degree 1 for every prime q that divides $p+1$. [*Hint:* Consider powers of the matrix $\left(\begin{smallmatrix} 0 & 1 \\ a & c \end{smallmatrix} \right)$.]

35. [*HM35*] How many pairs (a, c) satisfy the conditions of exercise 34?

36. [*M25*] Prove that the inversive congruential sequence $X_{n+1} = (aX_n^{-1} + c) \bmod 2^e$, $X_0 = 1$, $e \geq 3$, has period length 2^{e-1} whenever $a \bmod 4 = 1$ and $c \bmod 4 = 2$.

▶ **37.** [*HM32*] Let p be prime and assume that $X_{n+1} = (aX_n^{-1} + c) \bmod p$ defines an inversive congruential sequence of period $p + 1$. Also let $0 \leq b_1 < \cdots < b_d \leq p$, and consider the set

$$V = \{(X_{n+b_1}, X_{n+b_2}, \ldots, X_{n+b_d}) \mid 0 \leq n \leq p \text{ and } X_{n+b_j} \neq \infty \text{ for } 1 \leq j \leq d\}.$$

This set contains $p + 1 - d$ vectors, any d of which lie in some $(d-1)$-dimensional hyperplane $H = \{(v_1, \ldots, v_d) \mid r_1 v_1 + \cdots + r_d v_d \equiv r_0 \pmod{p}\}$, where $(r_1, \ldots, r_d) \not\equiv (0, \ldots, 0)$. Prove that no $d + 1$ vectors of V lie in the same hyperplane.

3.3. STATISTICAL TESTS

OUR MAIN PURPOSE is to obtain sequences that behave as if they are random. So
far we have seen how to make the period of a sequence so long that for practical
purposes it never will repeat; this is an important criterion, but it by no means
guarantees that the sequence will be useful in applications. How then are we to
decide whether a sequence is sufficiently random?

If we were to give some randomly chosen man a pencil and paper and ask him
to write down 100 random decimal digits, chances are very slim that he would
produce a satisfactory result. People tend to avoid things that seem nonrandom,
such as pairs of equal adjacent digits (although about one out of every 10 digits
should equal its predecessor). And if we would show that same man a table of
truly random digits, he would quite probably tell us they are not random at all;
his eye would spot certain apparent regularities.

According to Dr. I. J. Matrix and Donald C. Rehkopf (as quoted by Martin
Gardner in *Scientific American*, January, 1965), "Mathematicians consider the
decimal expansion of π a random series, but to a modern numerologist it is rich
with remarkable patterns." Dr. Matrix has pointed out, for example, that the
first repeated two-digit number in π's expansion is 26, and its second appearance
comes in the middle of a curious repetition pattern:

$$3.14159265358979323846264338327950 \tag{1}$$

After listing a dozen or so further properties of these digits, he observed that π,
when correctly interpreted, conveys the entire history of the human race!

We all notice patterns in our telephone numbers, license numbers, etc., as
aids to memory. The point of these remarks is that we cannot be trusted to judge
by ourselves whether a sequence of numbers is random or not. Some unbiased
mechanical tests must be applied.

The theory of statistics provides us with some quantitative measures for
randomness. There is literally no end to the number of tests that can be
conceived; we will discuss the tests that have proved to be most useful, most
instructive, and most readily adapted to computer calculation.

If a sequence behaves randomly with respect to tests T_1, T_2, ..., T_n, we
cannot be *sure* in general that it will not be a miserable failure when it is
subjected to a further test T_{n+1}. Yet each test gives us more and more confidence
in the randomness of the sequence. In practice, we apply about half a dozen
different kinds of statistical tests to a sequence, and if it passes them satisfactorily
we consider it to be random — it is then presumed innocent until proven guilty.

Every sequence that is to be used extensively should be tested carefully, so
the following sections explain how to administer the tests in an appropriate way.
Two kinds of tests are distinguished: *empirical tests*, for which the computer
manipulates groups of numbers of the sequence and evaluates certain statistics;
and *theoretical tests*, for which we establish characteristics of the sequence by

using number-theoretic methods based on the recurrence rule used to form the sequence.

If the evidence doesn't come out as desired, the reader may wish to try the techniques in *How to Lie With Statistics* by Darrell Huff (Norton, 1954).

3.3.1. General Test Procedures for Studying Random Data

A. "Chi-square" tests. The chi-square test (χ^2 test) is perhaps the best known of all statistical tests, and it is a basic method that is used in connection with many other tests. Before considering the idea in general, let us consider a particular example of the chi-square test as it might be applied to dice throwing. Using two "true" dice (each of which, independently, is assumed to yield the values 1, 2, 3, 4, 5, or 6 with equal probability), the following table gives the probability of obtaining a given total, s, on a single throw:

$$\begin{array}{lccccccccccc}
\text{value of } s = & 2 & 3 & 4 & 5 & 6 & 7 & 8 & 9 & 10 & 11 & 12 \\
\text{probability, } p_s = & \frac{1}{36} & \frac{1}{18} & \frac{1}{12} & \frac{1}{9} & \frac{5}{36} & \frac{1}{6} & \frac{5}{36} & \frac{1}{9} & \frac{1}{12} & \frac{1}{18} & \frac{1}{36}
\end{array} \quad (1)$$

For example, a value of 4 can be thrown in three ways: $1+3$, $2+2$, $3+1$; this constitutes $\frac{3}{36} = \frac{1}{12} = p_4$ of the 36 possible outcomes.

If we throw the dice n times, we should obtain the value s approximately np_s times on the average. For example, in 144 throws we should get the value 4 about 12 times. The following table shows what results were *actually* obtained in a particular sequence of 144 throws of the dice:

$$\begin{array}{lccccccccccc}
\text{value of } s = & 2 & 3 & 4 & 5 & 6 & 7 & 8 & 9 & 10 & 11 & 12 \\
\text{observed number, } Y_s = & 2 & 4 & 10 & 12 & 22 & 29 & 21 & 15 & 14 & 9 & 6 \\
\text{expected number, } np_s = & 4 & 8 & 12 & 16 & 20 & 24 & 20 & 16 & 12 & 8 & 4
\end{array} \quad (2)$$

Notice that the observed number was different from the expected number in all cases; in fact, random throws of the dice will hardly ever come out with *exactly* the right frequencies. There are 36^{144} possible sequences of 144 throws, all of which are equally likely. One of these sequences consists of all 2s ("snake eyes"), and anyone throwing 144 snake eyes in a row would be convinced that the dice were loaded. Yet the sequence of all 2s is just as probable as any other particular sequence if we specify the outcome of each throw of each die.

In view of this, how can we test whether or not a given pair of dice is loaded? The answer is that we can't make a definite yes-no statement, but we can give a *probabilistic* answer. We can say how probable or improbable certain types of events are.

A fairly natural way to proceed in the example above is to consider the squares of the differences between the observed numbers Y_s and the expected numbers np_s. We can add these together, obtaining

$$V = (Y_2 - np_2)^2 + (Y_3 - np_3)^2 + \cdots + (Y_{12} - np_{12})^2. \quad (3)$$

A bad set of dice should result in a relatively high value of V; and for any given value of V we can ask, "What is the probability that V is this high, using true dice?" If this probability is very small, say $\frac{1}{100}$, we would know that only about one time in 100 would true dice give results so far away from the expected numbers, and we would have definite grounds for suspicion. (Remember, however, that even *good* dice would give such a high value of V about one time in a hundred, so a cautious person would repeat the experiment to see if the high value of V is repeated.)

The statistic V in (3) gives equal weight to $(Y_7 - np_7)^2$ and $(Y_2 - np_2)^2$, although $(Y_7 - np_7)^2$ is likely to be a good deal higher than $(Y_2 - np_2)^2$ since 7s occur about six times as often as 2s. It turns out that the "right" statistic, at least one that has proved to be most important, will give $(Y_7 - np_7)^2$ only $\frac{1}{6}$ as much weight as $(Y_2 - np_2)^2$, and we should change (3) to the following formula:

$$V = \frac{(Y_2 - np_2)^2}{np_2} + \frac{(Y_3 - np_3)^2}{np_3} + \cdots + \frac{(Y_{12} - np_{12})^2}{np_{12}}. \tag{4}$$

This is called the "chi-square" statistic of the observed quantities $Y_2, \ldots, Y_{12}$ in the dice-throwing experiment. For the data in (2), we find that

$$V = \frac{(2-4)^2}{4} + \frac{(4-8)^2}{8} + \cdots + \frac{(9-8)^2}{8} + \frac{(6-4)^2}{4} = 7\frac{7}{48}. \tag{5}$$

The important question now is, of course, "Does $7\frac{7}{48}$ constitute an improbably high value for V to assume?" Before answering this question, let us consider the general application of the chi-square method.

In general, suppose that every observation can fall into one of k categories. We take n *independent observations*; this means that the outcome of one observation has absolutely no effect on the outcome of any of the others. Let p_s be the probability that each observation falls into category s, and let Y_s be the number of observations that actually *do* fall into category s. We form the statistic

$$V = \sum_{s=1}^{k} \frac{(Y_s - np_s)^2}{np_s}. \tag{6}$$

In our example above, there are eleven possible outcomes of each throw of the dice, so $k = 11$. $\big($Eq. (6) is a slight change of notation from Eq. (4), since we are numbering the possibilities from 1 to k instead of from 2 to 12.$\big)$

By expanding $(Y_s - np_s)^2 = Y_s^2 - 2np_sY_s + n^2p_s^2$ in (6), and using the facts that

$$\begin{aligned} Y_1 + Y_2 + \cdots + Y_k &= n, \\ p_1 + p_2 + \cdots + p_k &= 1, \end{aligned} \tag{7}$$

we arrive at the formula

$$V = \frac{1}{n} \sum_{s=1}^{k} \left(\frac{Y_s^2}{p_s}\right) - n, \tag{8}$$

which often makes the computation of V somewhat easier.

Table 1

SELECTED PERCENTAGE POINTS OF THE CHI-SQUARE DISTRIBUTION

	$p = 1\%$	$p = 5\%$	$p = 25\%$	$p = 50\%$	$p = 75\%$	$p = 95\%$	$p = 99\%$
$\nu = 1$	0.00016	0.00393	0.1015	0.4549	1.323	3.841	6.635
$\nu = 2$	0.02010	0.1026	0.5754	1.386	2.773	5.991	9.210
$\nu = 3$	0.1148	0.3518	1.213	2.366	4.108	7.815	11.34
$\nu = 4$	0.2971	0.7107	1.923	3.357	5.385	9.488	13.28
$\nu = 5$	0.5543	1.1455	2.675	4.351	6.626	11.07	15.09
$\nu = 6$	0.8721	1.635	3.455	5.348	7.841	12.59	16.81
$\nu = 7$	1.239	2.167	4.255	6.346	9.037	14.07	18.48
$\nu = 8$	1.646	2.733	5.071	7.344	10.22	15.51	20.09
$\nu = 9$	2.088	3.325	5.899	8.343	11.39	16.92	21.67
$\nu = 10$	2.558	3.940	6.737	9.342	12.55	18.31	23.21
$\nu = 11$	3.053	4.575	7.584	10.34	13.70	19.68	24.72
$\nu = 12$	3.571	5.226	8.438	11.34	14.85	21.03	26.22
$\nu = 15$	5.229	7.261	11.04	14.34	18.25	25.00	30.58
$\nu = 20$	8.260	10.85	15.45	19.34	23.83	31.41	37.57
$\nu = 30$	14.95	18.49	24.48	29.34	34.80	43.77	50.89
$\nu = 50$	29.71	34.76	42.94	49.33	56.33	67.50	76.15
$\nu > 30$	$\nu + \sqrt{2\nu}x_p + \frac{2}{3}x_p^2 - \frac{2}{3} + O\left(1/\sqrt{\nu}\right)$						
$x_p =$	-2.33	-1.64	$-.674$	0.00	0.674	1.64	2.33

(For further values, see *Handbook of Mathematical Functions*, edited by M. Abramowitz and
I. A. Stegun (Washington, D.C.: U.S. Government Printing Office, 1964), Table 26.8. See also
Eq. (22) and exercise 16.)

Now we turn to the important question, "What constitutes a reasonable
value of V?" This is found by referring to a table such as Table 1, which gives values of "the chi-square distribution with ν degrees of freedom" for various values
of ν. The line of the table with $\nu = k - 1$ is to be used; *the number of "degrees of
freedom" is $k-1$, one less than the number of categories.* (Intuitively, this means
that $Y_1, Y_2, \ldots, Y_k$ are not completely independent, since Eq. (7) shows that Y_k
can be computed if $Y_1, \ldots, Y_{k-1}$ are known; hence, $k - 1$ degrees of freedom are
present. This argument is not rigorous, but the theory below justifies it.)

If the table entry in row ν under column p is x, it means, "The quantity V
in Eq. (8) will be less than or equal to x with approximate probability p, if n
is large enough." For example, the 95 percent entry in row 10 is 18.31; we will
have $V > 18.31$ only about 5 percent of the time.

Let us assume that our dice-throwing experiment has been simulated on a computer using some sequence of supposedly random numbers, with the following results:

value of $s =$	2	3	4	5	6	7	8	9	10	11	12	
Experiment 1, $Y_s =$	4	10	10	13	20	18	18	11	13	14	13	(9)
Experiment 2, $Y_s =$	3	7	11	15	19	24	21	17	13	9	5	

We can compute the chi-square statistic in the first case, getting the value $V_1 = 29\frac{59}{120}$, and in the second case we get $V_2 = 1\frac{17}{120}$. Referring to the table entries for 10 degrees of freedom, we see that V_1 is *much too high*; V will be greater than 23.21 only about one percent of the time! (By using more extensive tables, we find in fact that V will be as high as V_1 only 0.1 percent of the time.) Therefore Experiment 1 represents a significant departure from random behavior.

On the other hand, V_2 is quite low, since the observed values Y_s in Experiment 2 are quite close to the expected values np_s in (2). The chi-square table tells us, in fact, that V_2 is *much too low*: The observed values are so close to the expected values, we cannot consider the result to be random! (Indeed, reference to other tables shows that such a low value of V occurs only 0.03 percent of the time when there are 10 degrees of freedom.) Finally, the value $V = 7\frac{7}{48}$ computed in (5) can also be checked with Table 1. It falls between the entries for 25 percent and 50 percent, so we cannot consider it to be significantly high or significantly low; thus the observations in (2) are satisfactorily random with respect to this test.

It is somewhat remarkable that the same table entries are used no matter what the value of n is, and no matter what the probabilities p_s are. Only the number $\nu = k - 1$ affects the results. In actual fact, however, the table entries are not exactly correct: *The chi-square distribution is an approximation that is valid only for large enough values of n.* How large should n be? A common rule of thumb is to take n large enough so that each of the expected values np_s is five or more; preferably, however, take n much larger than this, to get a more powerful test. In our examples above we took $n = 144$, so np_2 was only 4, violating the stated rule of thumb. This was done only because the author tired of throwing the dice; it makes the entries in Table 1 less accurate for our application. Experiments run on a computer, with $n = 1000$, or 10000, or even 100000, would be much better than this. We could also combine the data for $s = 2$ and $s = 12$; then the test would have only nine degrees of freedom but the chi-square approximation would be more accurate.

We can get an idea of how crude an approximation is involved by considering the case when there are only two categories, having probabilities p_1 and p_2. Suppose $p_1 = \frac{1}{4}$ and $p_2 = \frac{3}{4}$. According to the stated rule of thumb, we should have $n \geq 20$ to have a satisfactory approximation, so let's check that out. When $n = 20$, the possible values of V are $(Y_1 - 5)^2/5 + (5 - Y_1)^2/15 = \frac{4}{15}r^2$ for $-5 \leq r \leq 15$; we wish to know how well the row $\nu = 1$ of Table 1 describes the distribution of V. The chi-square distribution varies continuously, while the actual distribution of V has rather big jumps, so we need some convention for representing the exact distribution. If the distinct possible outcomes of the experiment lead to the values $V_0 \leq V_1 \leq \cdots \leq V_n$ with respective probabilities π_0, π_1, ..., π_n, suppose that a given percentage p falls in the range $\pi_0 + \cdots + \pi_{j-1} < p < \pi_0 + \cdots + \pi_{j-1} + \pi_j$. We would like to represent p by a "percentage point" x such that V is less than x with probability $\leq p$ and V is greater than x with probability $\leq 1-p$. It is not difficult to see that the only such number is $x = V_j$. In our example for $n = 20$ and $\nu = 1$, it turns out that the percentage points of the exact distribution, corresponding to the approximations in Table 1 for $p = 1\%$, 5%, 25%, 50%, 75%, 95%, and 99%, respectively, are

$$0, \quad 0, \quad .27, \quad .27, \quad 1.07, \quad 4.27, \quad 6.67$$

(to two decimal places). For example, the percentage point for $p = 95\%$ is 4.27, while Table 1 gives the estimate 3.841. The latter value is too low; it tells us (incorrectly) to reject the value $V = 4.27$ at the 95% level, while in fact the probability that $V \geq 4.27$ is more than 6.5%. When $n = 21$, the situation changes slightly because the expected values $np_1 = 5.25$ and $np_2 = 15.75$ can never be obtained exactly; the percentage points for $n = 21$ are

$$.02, \quad .02, \quad .14, \quad .40, \quad 1.29, \quad 3.57, \quad 5.73.$$

We would expect Table 1 to be a better approximation when $n = 50$, but the corresponding tableau actually turns out to be further from Table 1 in some respects than it was for $n = 20$:

$$.03, \quad .03, \quad .03, \quad .67, \quad 1.31, \quad 3.23, \quad 6.$$

Here are the values when $n = 300$:

$$0, \quad 0, \quad .07, \quad .44, \quad 1.44, \quad 4, \quad 6.42.$$

Even in this case, when np_s is ≥ 75 in each category, the entries in Table 1 are good to only about one significant digit.

The proper choice of n is somewhat obscure. If the dice are actually biased, the fact will be detected as n gets larger and larger. (See exercise 12.) But large values of n will tend to smooth out *locally* nonrandom behavior, when blocks of numbers with a strong bias are followed by blocks of numbers with the opposite bias. Locally nonrandom behavior is not an issue when actual dice are rolled, since the same dice are used throughout the test, but a sequence of numbers generated by computer might very well display such anomalies. Perhaps a chi-square test should be made for several different values of n. At any rate, n should always be rather large.

We can summarize the chi-square test as follows. A fairly large number, n, of independent observations is made. (It is important to avoid using the chi-square method unless the observations are independent. See, for example, exercise 10, which considers the case when half of the observations depend on the other half.) We count the number of observations falling into each of k categories and compute the quantity V given in Eqs. (6) and (8). Then V is compared with the numbers in Table 1, with $\nu = k - 1$. If V is less than the 1% entry or greater than the 99% entry, we reject the numbers as not sufficiently random. If V lies

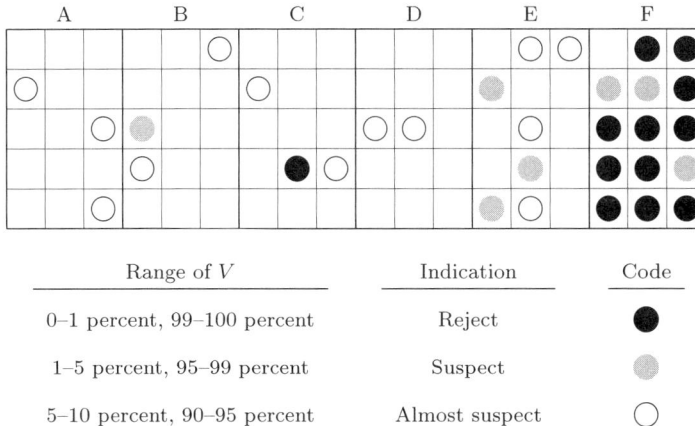

Fig. 2. Indications of "significant" deviations in 90 chi-square tests (see also Fig. 5).

between the 1% and 5% entries or between the 95% and 99% entries, the numbers are "suspect"; if (by interpolation in the table) V lies between the 5% and 10% entries, or the 90% and 95% entries, the numbers might be "almost suspect." The chi-square test is often done at least three times on different sets of data, and if at least two of the three results are suspect the numbers are regarded as not sufficiently random.

For example, see Fig. 2, which shows schematically the results of applying five different types of chi-square tests on each of six sequences of random numbers. Each test in this illustration was applied to three different blocks of numbers of the sequence. Generator A is the MacLaren–Marsaglia method (Algorithm 3.2.2M applied to the sequences in 3.2.2–(13)); Generator E is the Fibonacci method, 3.2.2–(5); and the other generators are linear congruential sequences with the following parameters:

Generator B: $X_0 = 0,$ $a = 3141592653,$ $c = 2718281829,$ $m = 2^{35}.$

Generator C: $X_0 = 0,$ $a = 2^7 + 1,$ $c = 1,$ $m = 2^{35}.$

Generator D: $X_0 = 47594118,$ $a = 23,$ $c = 0,$ $m = 10^8 + 1.$

Generator F: $X_0 = 314159265,$ $a = 2^{18} + 1,$ $c = 1,$ $m = 2^{35}.$

From Fig. 2 we conclude that (so far as these tests are concerned) Generators A, B, D are satisfactory, Generator C is on the borderline and should probably be rejected, Generators E and F are definitely unsatisfactory. Generator F has, of course, low potency; Generators C and D have been discussed in the literature, but their multipliers are too small. (Generator D is the original multiplicative generator proposed by Lehmer in 1948; Generator C is the original linear congruential generator with $c \neq 0$ proposed by Rotenberg in 1960.)

Instead of using the "suspect," "almost suspect," etc., criteria for judging the results of chi-square tests, one can employ a less *ad hoc* procedure discussed later in this section.

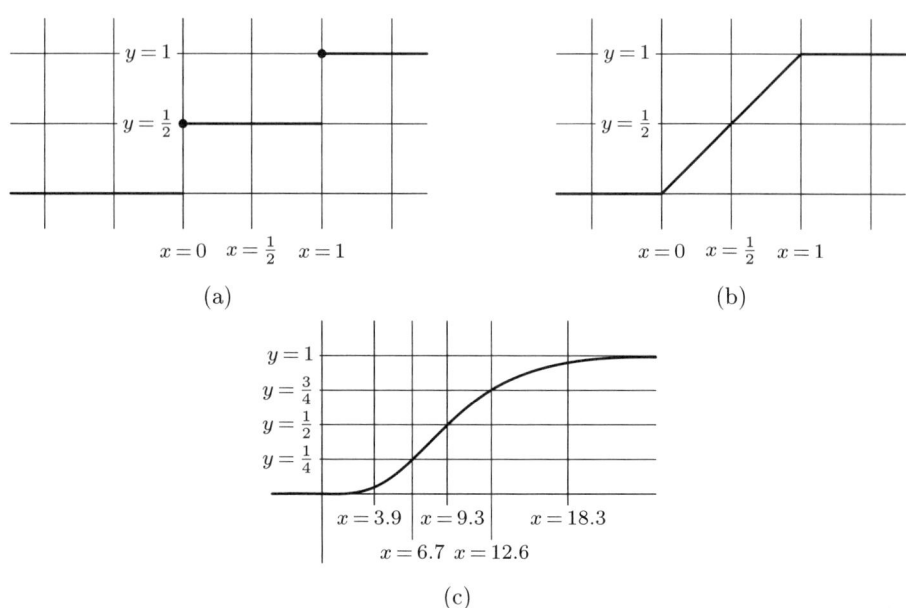

Fig. 3. Examples of distribution functions.

B. The Kolmogorov–Smirnov test. As we have seen, the chi-square test applies to the situation when observations can fall into a finite number of categories. It is not unusual, however, to consider random quantities that range over infinitely many values, such as a random fraction (a random real number between 0 and 1). Even though only finitely many real numbers can be represented in a computer, we want our random values to behave essentially as if all real numbers in $[0..1)$ were equally likely.

A general notation for specifying probability distributions, whether they are finite or infinite, is commonly used in the study of probability and statistics. Suppose we want to specify the distribution of the values of a random quantity, X; we do this in terms of the *distribution function* $F(x)$, where

$$F(x) = \Pr(X \le x) = \text{probability that } (X \le x).$$

Three examples are shown in Fig. 3. First we see the distribution function for a *random bit*, namely for the case when X takes on only the two values 0 and 1, each with probability $\frac{1}{2}$. Part (b) of the figure shows the distribution function for a *uniformly distributed random real number* between zero and one; here the probability that $X \le x$ is simply equal to x when $0 \le x \le 1$. For example, the probability that $X \le \frac{2}{3}$ is, naturally, $\frac{2}{3}$. And part (c) shows the limiting distribution of the value V in the chi-square test (shown here with 10 degrees of freedom); this is a distribution that we have already seen represented in another way in Table 1. Notice that $F(x)$ always increases from 0 to 1 as x increases from $-\infty$ to $+\infty$.

If we make n independent observations of the random quantity X, thereby obtaining the values X_1, X_2, ..., X_n, we can form the *empirical distribution function $F_n(x)$*, where

$$F_n(x) = \frac{\text{number of } X_1, X_2, \ldots, X_n \text{ that are} \leq x}{n}. \qquad (10)$$

Figure 4 illustrates three empirical distribution functions (shown as zigzag lines, although strictly speaking the vertical lines are not part of the graph of $F_n(x)$), superimposed on a graph of the assumed actual distribution function $F(x)$. As n gets large, $F_n(x)$ should be a better and better approximation to $F(x)$.

(a)
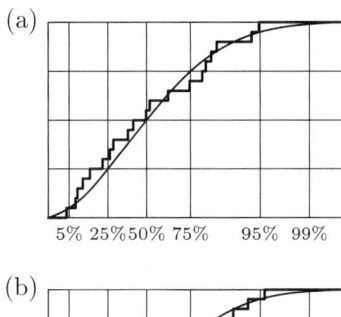
5% 25%50% 75%   95% 99%

(b)
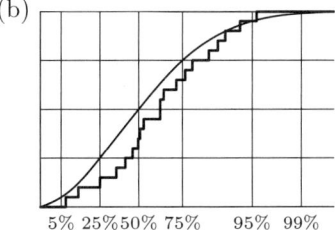
5% 25%50% 75%   95% 99%

(c)
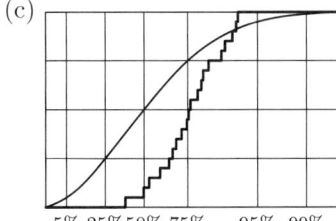
5% 25%50% 75%   95% 99%

Fig. 4. Examples of empirical distributions. The x value marked "5%" is the percentage point where $F(x) = 0.05$.

The Kolmogorov–Smirnov test (KS test) may be used when $F(x)$ has no jumps. It is based on the *difference between $F(x)$ and $F_n(x)$*. A bad source of random numbers will give empirical distribution functions that do not approximate $F(x)$ sufficiently well. Figure 4(b) shows an example in which the X_i are consistently too high, so the empirical distribution function is too low. Part (c) of the figure shows an even worse example; it is plain that such great deviations between $F_n(x)$ and $F(x)$ are extremely improbable, and the KS test is used to tell us how improbable they are.

To make the KS test, we form the following statistics:

$$K_n^+ = \sqrt{n} \sup_{-\infty < x < +\infty} \left(F_n(x) - F(x) \right);$$

$$K_n^- = \sqrt{n} \sup_{-\infty < x < +\infty} \left(F(x) - F_n(x) \right). \tag{11}$$

Here K_n^+ measures the greatest amount of deviation when F_n is greater than F, and K_n^- measures the maximum deviation when F_n is less than F. The statistics for the examples of Fig. 4 are

	Fig. 4(a)	Fig. 4(b)	Fig. 4(c)	
K_{20}^+	0.492	0.134	0.313	(12)
K_{20}^-	0.536	1.027	2.101	

(*Note:* The factor $\sqrt{n}$ that appears in Eqs. (11) may seem puzzling at first. Exercise 6 shows that, for fixed x, the standard deviation of $F_n(x)$ is proportional to $1/\sqrt{n}$; hence the factor $\sqrt{n}$ magnifies the statistics K_n^+ and K_n^- in such a way that this standard deviation is independent of n.)

As in the chi-square test, we may now look up the values K_n^+, K_n^- in a percentile table to determine if they are significantly high or low. Table 2 may be used for this purpose, both for K_n^+ and K_n^-. For example, the probability is 75 percent that K_{20}^- will be 0.7975 or less. Unlike the chi-square test, the table entries are *not* merely approximations that hold for large values of n; Table 2 gives exact values (except, of course, for roundoff error), and the KS test may be used reliably for any value of n.

As they stand, formulas (11) are not readily adapted to computer calculation, since we are asking for a least upper bound over infinitely many values of x. But from the fact that $F(x)$ is increasing and the fact that $F_n(x)$ increases only in finite steps, we can derive a simple procedure for evaluating the statistics K_n^+ and K_n^-:

Step 1. Obtain independent observations $X_1, X_2, \ldots, X_n$.

Step 2. Rearrange the observations so that they are sorted into ascending order, $X_1 \leq X_2 \leq \cdots \leq X_n$. (Efficient sorting algorithms are the subject of Chapter 5. But it is possible to avoid sorting in this case, as shown in exercise 23.)

Step 3. The desired statistics are now given by the formulas

$$K_n^+ = \sqrt{n} \max_{1 \leq j \leq n} \left(\frac{j}{n} - F(X_j) \right);$$

$$K_n^- = \sqrt{n} \max_{1 \leq j \leq n} \left(F(X_j) - \frac{j-1}{n} \right). \tag{13}$$

An appropriate choice of the number of observations, n, is slightly easier to make for this test than it is for the χ^2 test, although some of the considerations are similar. If the random variables X_j actually belong to the probability distribution $G(x)$, while they were assumed to belong to the distribution given by $F(x)$, we want n to be comparatively large, in order to reject the hypothesis that $G(x) = F(x)$; for we need n large enough that the empirical distributions

Table 2

SELECTED PERCENTAGE POINTS OF THE DISTRIBUTIONS K_n^+ AND K_n^-

	$p = 1\%$	$p = 5\%$	$p = 25\%$	$p = 50\%$	$p = 75\%$	$p = 95\%$	$p = 99\%$
$n = 1$	0.01000	0.05000	0.2500	0.5000	0.7500	0.9500	0.9900
$n = 2$	0.01400	0.06749	0.2929	0.5176	0.7071	1.0980	1.2728
$n = 3$	0.01699	0.07919	0.3112	0.5147	0.7539	1.1017	1.3589
$n = 4$	0.01943	0.08789	0.3202	0.5110	0.7642	1.1304	1.3777
$n = 5$	0.02152	0.09471	0.3249	0.5245	0.7674	1.1392	1.4024
$n = 6$	0.02336	0.1002	0.3272	0.5319	0.7703	1.1463	1.4144
$n = 7$	0.02501	0.1048	0.3280	0.5364	0.7755	1.1537	1.4246
$n = 8$	0.02650	0.1086	0.3280	0.5392	0.7797	1.1586	1.4327
$n = 9$	0.02786	0.1119	0.3274	0.5411	0.7825	1.1624	1.4388
$n = 10$	0.02912	0.1147	0.3297	0.5426	0.7845	1.1658	1.4440
$n = 11$	0.03028	0.1172	0.3330	0.5439	0.7863	1.1688	1.4484
$n = 12$	0.03137	0.1193	0.3357	0.5453	0.7880	1.1714	1.4521
$n = 15$	0.03424	0.1244	0.3412	0.5500	0.7926	1.1773	1.4606
$n = 20$	0.03807	0.1298	0.3461	0.5547	0.7975	1.1839	1.4698
$n = 30$	0.04354	0.1351	0.3509	0.5605	0.8036	1.1916	1.4801
$n > 30$	\multicolumn{7}{c}{$y_p - \frac{1}{6}n^{-1/2} + O(1/n)$, where $y_p^2 = \frac{1}{2}\ln(1/(1-p))$}
$y_p =$	0.07089	0.1601	0.3793	0.5887	0.8326	1.2239	1.5174

(To extend this table, see Eqs. (25) and (26), and the answer to exercise 20.)

$G_n(x)$ and $F_n(x)$ are expected to be observably different. On the other hand, large values of n will tend to average out locally nonrandom behavior, and such undesirable behavior is a significant danger in most computer applications of random numbers; this makes a case for *smaller* values of n. A good compromise would be to take n equal to, say, 1000, and to make a fairly large number of calculations of K_{1000}^+ on different parts of a random sequence, thereby obtaining values

$$K_{1000}^+(1), \qquad K_{1000}^+(2), \qquad \ldots, \qquad K_{1000}^+(r). \qquad (14)$$

We can also apply the KS test *again* to *these* results: Let $F(x)$ now be the distribution function for K_{1000}^+, and determine the empirical distribution $F_r(x)$ obtained from the observed values in (14). Fortunately, the function $F(x)$ in this case is very simple; for a large value of n like $n = 1000$, the distribution of K_n^+ is closely approximated by

$$F_\infty(x) = 1 - e^{-2x^2}, \qquad x \geq 0. \qquad (15)$$

The same remarks apply to K_n^-, since K_n^+ and K_n^- have the same expected behavior. *This method of using several tests for moderately large n, then combining the observations later in another KS test, will tend to detect both local and global nonrandom behavior.*

For example, the author conducted the following simple experiment while writing this chapter: The "maximum-of-5" test described in the next section was applied to a set of 1000 uniform random numbers, yielding 200 observations X_1, X_2, ..., X_{200} that were supposed to belong to the distribution $F(x) = x^5$ for $0 \le x \le 1$. The observations were divided into 20 groups of 10 each, and the statistic K_{10}^+ was computed for each group. The 20 values of K_{10}^+ thus obtained led to the empirical distributions shown in Fig. 4. The smooth curve shown in each of the diagrams in Fig. 4 is the actual distribution the statistic K_{10}^+ should have. Figure 4(a) shows the empirical distribution of K_{10}^+ obtained from the sequence

$$Y_{n+1} = (3141592653 Y_n + 2718281829) \bmod 2^{35}, \qquad U_n = Y_n/2^{35},$$

and it is satisfactorily random. Part (b) of the figure came from the Fibonacci method; this sequence has *globally* nonrandom behavior — that is, it can be shown that the observations X_n in the maximum-of-5 test do not have the correct distribution $F(x) = x^5$. Part (c) came from the notorious and impotent linear congruential sequence $Y_{n+1} = ((2^{18} + 1) Y_n + 1) \bmod 2^{35}$, $U_n = Y_n/2^{35}$.

The KS test applied to the data in Fig. 4 gives the results shown in (12). Referring to Table 2 for $n = 20$, we see that the values of K_{20}^+ and K_{20}^- for Fig. 4(b) are almost suspect (they lie at about the 5 percent and 88 percent levels), but they are not quite bad enough to be rejected outright. The value of K_{20}^- for Fig. 4(c) is, of course, completely out of line, so the maximum-of-5 test shows a definite failure of that random number generator.

We would expect the KS test in this experiment to have more difficulty locating global nonrandomness than local nonrandomness, since the basic observations in Fig. 4 were made on samples of only 10 numbers each. If we were to take 20 groups of 1000 numbers each, part (b) would show a much more significant deviation. To illustrate this point, a *single* KS test was applied to all 200 of the observations that led to Fig. 4, and the following results were obtained:

	Fig. 4(a)	Fig. 4(b)	Fig. 4(c)	
K_{200}^+	0.477	1.537	2.819	(16)
K_{200}^-	0.817	0.194	0.058	

The global nonrandomness of the Fibonacci generator has definitely been detected here.

We may summarize the Kolmogorov–Smirnov test as follows. We are given n *independent observations* X_1, ..., X_n taken from some distribution specified by a *continuous* function $F(x)$. That is, $F(x)$ must be like the functions shown in Fig. 3(b) and 3(c), having no jumps like those in Fig. 3(a). The procedure explained just before Eqs. (13) is carried out on these observations, and we obtain the statistics K_n^+ and K_n^-. These statistics should be distributed according to Table 2.

Some comparisons between the KS test and the χ^2 test can now be made. In the first place, we should observe that the KS test may be used in conjunction with the χ^2 test, to give a better procedure than the *ad hoc* method we mentioned when summarizing the χ^2 test. (That is, there is a better way to proceed than to make three tests and to consider how many of the results were "suspect.") Suppose we have made, say, 10 independent χ^2 tests on different parts of a random sequence, so that values $V_1, V_2, \ldots, V_{10}$ have been obtained. It is not a good policy simply to count how many of the V's are suspiciously large or small. This procedure will work in extreme cases, and very large or very small values may mean that the sequence has too much local nonrandomness; but a better general method would be to plot the empirical distribution of these 10 values and to compare it to the correct distribution, which may be obtained from Table 1. The empirical distribution gives a clearer picture of the results of the χ^2 tests, and in fact the statistics K_{10}^+ and K_{10}^- could be determined from the empirical χ^2 values as an indication of success or failure. With only 10 values or even as many as 100 this could all be done easily by hand, using graphical methods; with a larger number of V's, a computer subroutine for calculating the chi-square distribution would be necessary. Notice that *all 20 of the observations in Fig. 4(c) fall between the 5 and 95 percent levels*, so we would not have regarded *any* of them as suspicious, individually; yet collectively the empirical distribution shows that these observations are not at all right.

An important difference between the KS test and the chi-square test is that the KS test applies to distributions $F(x)$ having no jumps, while the chi-square test applies to distributions having nothing but jumps (since all observations are divided into k categories). The two tests are thus intended for different sorts of applications. Yet it is possible to apply the χ^2 test even when $F(x)$ is continuous, if we divide the domain of $F(x)$ into k parts and ignore all variations within each part. For example, if we want to test whether or not $U_1, U_2, \ldots, U_n$ can be considered to come from the uniform distribution between zero and one, we want to test if they have the distribution $F(x) = x$ for $0 \leq x \leq 1$. This is a natural application for the KS test. But we might also divide up the interval from 0 to 1 into $k = 100$ equal parts, count how many U's fall into each part, and apply the chi-square test with 99 degrees of freedom. There are not many theoretical results available at the present time to compare the effectiveness of the KS test versus the chi-square test. The author has found some examples in which the KS test pointed out nonrandomness more clearly than the χ^2 test, and others in which the χ^2 test gave a more significant result. If, for example, the 100 categories mentioned above are numbered $0, 1, \ldots, 99$, and if the deviations from the expected values are positive in compartments 0 to 49 but negative in compartments 50 to 99, then the empirical distribution function will be much further from $F(x)$ than the χ^2 value would indicate; but if the positive deviations occur in compartments $0, 2, \ldots, 98$ and the negative ones occur in $1, 3, \ldots, 99$, the empirical distribution function will tend to hug $F(x)$ much more closely. The

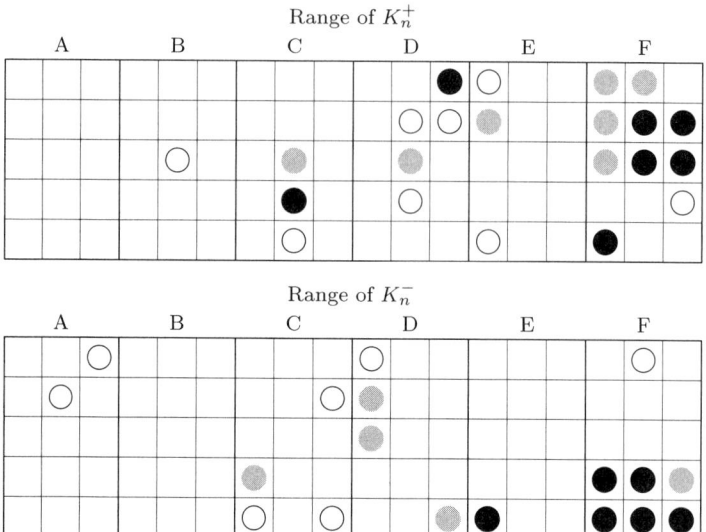

Fig. 5. The KS tests applied to the same data as Fig. 2.

kinds of deviations measured are therefore somewhat different. A χ^2 test was applied to the 200 observations that led to Fig. 4, with $k = 10$, and the respective values of V were 9.4, 17.7, and 39.3; so in this particular case the values were quite comparable to the KS values given in (16). Since the χ^2 test is intrinsically less accurate, and since it requires comparatively large values of n, the KS test has several advantages when a continuous distribution is to be tested.

A further example will also be of interest. The data that led to Fig. 2 were chi-square statistics based on $n = 200$ observations of the maximum-of-t criterion for $1 \le t \le 5$, with the range divided into 10 equally probable parts. KS statistics K_{200}^{+} and K_{200}^{-} can be computed from exactly the same sets of 200 observations, and the results can be tabulated in just the same way as we did in Fig. 2 (showing which KS values are beyond the 99-percent level, etc.); the results in this case are shown in Fig. 5. Notice that Generator D (Lehmer's original method) shows up very badly in Fig. 5, while chi-square tests *on the very same data* revealed no difficulty in Fig. 2; contrariwise, Generator E (the Fibonacci method) does not look so bad in Fig. 5. The good generators, A and B, passed all tests satisfactorily. The reasons for the discrepancies between Fig. 2 and Fig. 5 are primarily that (a) the number of observations, 200, is really not large enough for a powerful test, and (b) the "reject," "suspect," "almost suspect" ranking criterion is itself suspect.

(Incidentally, it is not fair to blame Lehmer for using a "bad" random number generator in the 1940s, since his actual use of Generator D was quite valid. The ENIAC computer was a highly parallel machine, programmed by means of a plugboard; Lehmer set it up so that one of its accumulators was repeatedly multiplying its own contents by 23 (modulo $10^8 + 1$), yielding a new value every few milliseconds. Since this multiplier 23 is too small, we know that each value obtained by such a process is too strongly related to the preceding value to be considered sufficiently random; but the durations of time between actual *uses* of the values in the special accumulator by the accompanying program were comparatively long and subject to some fluctuation. So the effective multiplier was 23^k for large, *varying* values of k.)

C. History, bibliography, and theory. The chi-square test was introduced by Karl Pearson in 1900 [*Philosophical Magazine*, Series 5, **50**, 157–175]. Pearson's important paper is regarded as one of the foundations of modern statistics, since before that time people would simply plot experimental results graphically and assert that they were correct. In his paper, Pearson gave several interesting examples of the previous misuse of statistics; and he also proved that certain runs at roulette (which he had experienced during two weeks at Monte Carlo in 1892) were so far from the expected frequencies that odds against the assumption of an honest wheel were some 10^{29} to one! A general discussion of the chi-square test and an extensive bibliography appear in the survey article by William G. Cochran, *Annals Math. Stat.* **23** (1952), 315–345.

Let us now consider a brief derivation of the theory behind the chi-square test. The exact probability that $Y_1 = y_1, \ldots, Y_k = y_k$ is easily seen to be

$$\frac{n!}{y_1! \ldots y_k!} p_1^{y_1} \ldots p_k^{y_k}. \tag{17}$$

If we assume that Y_s has the value y_s with the Poisson probability

$$\frac{e^{-np_s}(np_s)^{y_s}}{y_s!},$$

and that the Y's are independent, then $(Y_1, \ldots, Y_k)$ will equal $(y_1, \ldots, y_k)$ with probability

$$\prod_{s=1}^{k} \frac{e^{-np_s}(np_s)^{y_s}}{y_s!},$$

and $Y_1 + \cdots + Y_k$ will equal n with probability

$$\sum_{\substack{y_1+\cdots+y_k=n \\ y_1,\ldots,y_k \geq 0}} \prod_{s=1}^{k} \frac{e^{-np_s}(np_s)^{y_s}}{y_s!} = \frac{e^{-n}n^n}{n!}.$$

If we assume that they are independent *except* for the condition $Y_1 + \cdots + Y_k = n$, the probability that $(Y_1, \ldots, Y_k) = (y_1, \ldots, y_k)$ is the quotient

$$\left(\prod_{s=1}^{k} \frac{e^{-np_s}(np_s)^{y_s}}{y_s!} \right) \Big/ \left(\frac{e^{-n}n^n}{n!} \right),$$

which equals (17). *We may therefore regard the Y's as independently Poisson distributed, except for the fact that they have a fixed sum.*

It is convenient to make a change of variables,

$$Z_s = \frac{Y_s - np_s}{\sqrt{np_s}},\tag{18}$$

so that $V = Z_1^2 + \cdots + Z_k^2$. The condition $Y_1 + \cdots + Y_k = n$ is equivalent to requiring that

$$\sqrt{p_1}\,Z_1 + \cdots + \sqrt{p_k}\,Z_k = 0.\tag{19}$$

Let us consider the $(k-1)$-dimensional space S of all vectors $(Z_1, \ldots, Z_k)$ such that (19) holds. For large values of n, each Z_s has approximately the normal distribution (see exercise 1.2.10–15); therefore points in a differential volume $dz_2 \ldots dz_k$ of S occur with probability *approximately* proportional to $\exp\left(-(z_1^2 + \cdots + z_k^2)/2\right)$. (It is at this point in the derivation that the chi-square method becomes only an approximation for large n.) The probability that $V \leq v$ is now

$$\frac{\int_{(z_1,\ldots,z_k)\text{ in }S\text{ and }z_1^2+\cdots+z_k^2\leq v}\exp\left(-(z_1^2 + \cdots + z_k^2)/2\right)dz_2 \ldots dz_k}{\int_{(z_1,\ldots,z_k)\text{ in }S}\exp\left(-(z_1^2 + \cdots + z_k^2)/2\right)dz_2 \ldots dz_k}.\tag{20}$$

Since the hyperplane (19) passes through the origin of k-dimensional space, the numerator in (20) is an integration over the interior of a $(k-1)$-dimensional hypersphere centered at the origin. An appropriate transformation to generalized polar coordinates with radius χ and angles $\omega_1, \ldots, \omega_{k-2}$ transforms (20) into

$$\frac{\int_{\chi^2\leq v}e^{-\chi^2/2}\chi^{k-2}f(\omega_1,\ldots,\omega_{k-2})\,d\chi\,d\omega_1\ldots d\omega_{k-2}}{\int e^{-\chi^2/2}\chi^{k-2}f(\omega_1,\ldots,\omega_{k-2})\,d\chi\,d\omega_1\ldots d\omega_{k-2}}$$

for some function f (see exercise 15); then integration over the angles $\omega_1, \ldots, \omega_{k-2}$ gives a constant factor that cancels from numerator and denominator. We finally obtain the formula

$$\frac{\int_0^{\sqrt{v}}e^{-\chi^2/2}\chi^{k-2}\,d\chi}{\int_0^{\infty}e^{-\chi^2/2}\chi^{k-2}\,d\chi}\tag{21}$$

for the approximate probability that $V \leq v$.

Our derivation of (21) uses the symbol χ to stand for the radial length, just as Pearson did in his original paper; this is how the χ^2 test got its name. Substituting $t = \chi^2/2$, the integrals can be expressed in terms of the incomplete gamma function, which we discussed in Section 1.2.11.3:

$$\lim_{n\to\infty}\Pr(V\leq v) = \gamma\left(\frac{k-1}{2},\frac{v}{2}\right)\Big/\Gamma\left(\frac{k-1}{2}\right).\tag{22}$$

This is the definition of the chi-square distribution with $k-1$ degrees of freedom.

We now turn to the KS test. In 1933, A. N. Kolmogorov proposed a test based on the statistic

$$K_n = \sqrt{n}\max_{-\infty<x<+\infty}\left|F_n(x) - F(x)\right| = \max(K_n^+, K_n^-).\tag{23}$$

N. V. Smirnov discussed several modifications of this test in 1939, including the individual examination of K_n^+ and K_n^- as we have suggested above. There is a large family of similar tests, but the K_n^+ and K_n^- statistics seem to be most convenient for computer application. A comprehensive review of the literature concerning KS tests and their generalizations, including an extensive bibliography, appears in a monograph by J. Durbin, *Regional Conf. Series on Applied Math.* **9** (SIAM, 1973).

To study the distribution of K_n^+ and K_n^-, we begin with the following basic fact: *If X is a random variable with the continuous distribution $F(x)$, then $F(X)$ is a uniformly distributed real number between 0 and 1.* To prove this, we need only verify that if $0 \leq y \leq 1$ we have $F(X) \leq y$ with probability y. Since F is continuous, $F(x_0) = y$ for some x_0; thus the probability that $F(X) \leq y$ is the probability that $X \leq x_0$. By definition, the latter probability is $F(x_0)$, that is, it is y.

Let $Y_j = nF(X_j)$, for $1 \leq j \leq n$, where the X's have been sorted as in Step 2 preceding Eq. (13). Then the variables Y_j are essentially the same as independent, uniformly distributed random numbers between 0 and n that have been sorted into nondecreasing order, $Y_1 \leq Y_2 \leq \cdots \leq Y_n$; and the first equation of (13) may be transformed into

$$K_n^+ = \frac{1}{\sqrt{n}} \max(1 - Y_1, 2 - Y_2, \ldots, n - Y_n).$$

If $0 \leq t \leq n$, the probability that $K_n^+ \leq t/\sqrt{n}$ is therefore the probability that $Y_j \geq j - t$ for $1 \leq j \leq n$. This is not hard to express in terms of n-dimensional integrals,

$$\frac{\int_{\alpha_n}^n dy_n \int_{\alpha_{n-1}}^{y_n} dy_{n-1} \cdots \int_{\alpha_1}^{y_2} dy_1}{\int_0^n dy_n \int_0^{y_n} dy_{n-1} \cdots \int_0^{y_2} dy_1}, \qquad \text{where} \qquad \alpha_j = \max(j - t, 0). \qquad (24)$$

The denominator here is immediately evaluated: It is found to be $n^n/n!$, which makes sense since the hypercube of all vectors $(y_1, y_2, \ldots, y_n)$ with $0 \leq y_j < n$ has volume n^n, and it can be divided into $n!$ equal parts corresponding to each possible ordering of the y's. The integral in the numerator is a little more difficult, but it yields to the attack suggested in exercise 17, and we get the general formulas

$$\Pr\left(K_n^+ \leq \frac{t}{\sqrt{n}}\right) = \frac{t}{n^n} \sum_{0 \leq k \leq t} \binom{n}{k}(k - t)^k(t + n - k)^{n-k-1} \qquad (25)$$

$$= 1 - \frac{t}{n^n} \sum_{t < k \leq n} \binom{n}{k}(k - t)^k(t + n - k)^{n-k-1}. \qquad (26)$$

The distribution of K_n^- is exactly the same. Equation (26) was first obtained by N. V. Smirnov [*Uspekhi Mat. Nauk* **10** (1944), 176–206]; see also Z. W. Birnbaum and Fred H. Tingey, *Annals Math. Stat.* **22** (1951), 592–596. Smirnov derived the asymptotic formula

$$\Pr(K_n^+ \le s) = 1 - e^{-2s^2}\left(1 - \frac{2}{3}s/\sqrt{n} + O(1/n)\right) \tag{27}$$

for all fixed $s \ge 0$; this yields the approximations for large n that appear in Table 2.

Abel's binomial theorem, Eq. 1.2.6–(16), shows the equivalence of (25) and (26). We can extend Table 2 using either formula, but there is an interesting tradeoff: Although the sum in (25) has only about $s\sqrt{n}$ terms, when $s = t/\sqrt{n}$ is given, it must be evaluated with multiple-precision arithmetic, because the terms are large and their leading digits cancel out. No such problem arises in (26), since its terms are all positive; but (26) has $n - s\sqrt{n}$ terms.

EXERCISES

1. [00] What line of the chi-square table should be used to check whether or not the value $V = 7\frac{7}{48}$ of Eq. (5) is improbably high?

2. [20] If two dice are "loaded" so that, on one die, the value 1 will turn up exactly twice as often as any of the other values, and the other die is similarly biased towards 6, compute the probability p_s that a total of exactly s will appear on the two dice, for $2 \le s \le 12$.

▶ **3.** [23] Some dice that were loaded as described in the previous exercise were rolled 144 times, and the following values were observed:

value of $s =$	2	3	4	5	6	7	8	9	10	11	12
observed number, $Y_s =$	2	6	10	16	18	32	20	13	16	9	2

Apply the chi-square test to *these* values, using the probabilities in (1), pretending that the dice are not in fact known to be faulty. Does the chi-square test detect the bad dice? If not, explain why not.

▶ **4.** [23] The author actually obtained the data in experiment 1 of (9) by simulating dice in which one was normal, the other was loaded so that it always turned up 1 or 6. (The latter two possibilities were equally probable.) Compute the probabilities that replace (1) in this case, and by using a chi-square test decide if the results of that experiment are consistent with the dice being loaded in this way.

5. [22] Let $F(x)$ be the uniform distribution, Fig. 3(b). Find K_{20}^+ and K_{20}^- for the following 20 observations:

0.414, 0.732, 0.236, 0.162, 0.259, 0.442, 0.189, 0.693, 0.098, 0.302,
0.442, 0.434, 0.141, 0.017, 0.318, 0.869, 0.772, 0.678, 0.354, 0.718,

and state whether these observations are significantly different from the expected behavior with respect to either of these two tests.

6. [M20] Consider $F_n(x)$, as given in Eq. (10), for fixed x. What is the probability that $F_n(x) = s/n$, given an integer s? What is the mean value of $F_n(x)$? What is the standard deviation?

7. [M15] Show that K_n^+ and K_n^- can never be negative. What is the largest possible value K_n^+ can have?

8. [00] The text describes an experiment in which 20 values of the statistic K_{10}^+ were obtained in the study of a random sequence. These values were plotted, to obtain

Fig. 4, and a KS statistic was computed from the resulting graph. Why were the table entries for $n = 20$ used to study the resulting statistic, instead of the table entries for $n = 10$?

▶ **9.** [*20*] The experiment described in the text consisted of plotting 20 values of K_{10}^+, computed from the maximum-of-5 test applied to different parts of a random sequence. We could have computed also the corresponding 20 values of K_{10}^-; since K_{10}^- has the same distribution as K_{10}^+, we could lump together the 40 values thus obtained (that is, 20 of the K_{10}^+'s and 20 of the K_{10}^-'s), and a KS test could be applied so that we would get new values K_{40}^+, K_{40}^-. Discuss the merits of this idea.

▶ **10.** [*20*] Suppose a chi-square test is done by making n observations, and the value V is obtained. Now we repeat the test on these same n observations over again (getting, of course, the same results), and we put together the data from both tests, regarding it as a single chi-square test with $2n$ observations. (This procedure violates the text's stipulation that all of the observations must be independent of one another.) How is the second value of V related to the first one?

11. [*10*] Solve exercise 10 substituting the KS test for the chi-square test.

12. [*M28*] Suppose a chi-square test is made on a set of n observations, assuming that p_s is the probability that each observation falls into category s; but suppose that in actual fact the observations have probability $q_s \neq p_s$ of falling into category s. (See exercise 3.) We would, of course, like the chi-square test to detect the fact that the p_s assumption was incorrect. Show that this *will* happen, if n is large enough. Prove also the analogous result for the KS test.

13. [*M24*] Prove that Eqs. (13) are equivalent to Eqs. (11).

▶ **14.** [*HM26*] Let Z_s be given by Eq. (18). Show directly by using Stirling's approximation that the multinomial probability

$$n! p_1^{Y_1} \dots p_k^{Y_k}/Y_1! \dots Y_k! = e^{-V/2}/\sqrt{(2n\pi)^{k-1} p_1 \dots p_k} + O(n^{-k/2}),$$

if $Z_1, Z_2, \dots, Z_k$ are bounded as $n \to \infty$. (This idea leads to a proof of the chi-square test that is much closer to "first principles," and requires less handwaving, than the derivation in the text.)

15. [*HM24*] Polar coordinates in two dimensions are conventionally defined by the equations $x = r \cos\theta$ and $y = r \sin\theta$. For the purposes of integration, we have $dx\, dy = r\, dr\, d\theta$. More generally, in n-dimensional space we can let

$$x_k = r \sin\theta_1 \dots \sin\theta_{k-1} \cos\theta_k, \quad 1 \le k < n, \quad \text{and} \quad x_n = r \sin\theta_1 \dots \sin\theta_{n-1}.$$

Show that in this case

$$dx_1\, dx_2 \dots dx_n = |r^{n-1} \sin^{n-2}\theta_1 \dots \sin\theta_{n-2}\, dr\, d\theta_1 \dots d\theta_{n-1}|.$$

▶ **16.** [*HM35*] Generalize Theorem 1.2.11.3A to find the value of

$$\gamma(x + 1, x + z\sqrt{2x} + y)/\Gamma(x + 1),$$

for large x and fixed y, z. Disregard terms of the answer that are $O(1/x)$. Use this result to find the approximate solution, t, to the equation

$$\gamma\left(\frac{\nu}{2}, \frac{t}{2}\right) \bigg/ \Gamma\left(\frac{\nu}{2}\right) = p,$$

for large ν and fixed p, thereby accounting for the asymptotic formulas indicated in Table 1. [*Hint:* See exercise 1.2.11.3–8.]

17. [*HM26*] Let t be a fixed real number. For $0 \le k \le n$, let

$$P_{nk}(x) = \int_{n-t}^{x} dx_n \int_{n-1-t}^{x_n} dx_{n-1} \cdots \int_{k+1-t}^{x_{k+2}} dx_{k+1} \int_{0}^{x_{k+1}} dx_k \cdots \int_{0}^{x_2} dx_1;$$

by convention, let $P_{00}(x) = 1$. Prove the following relations:

a) $P_{nk}(x) = \displaystyle\int_{n}^{x+t} dx_n \int_{n-1}^{x_n} dx_{n-1} \cdots \int_{k+1}^{x_{k+2}} dx_{k+1} \int_{t}^{x_{k+1}} dx_k \cdots \int_{t}^{x_2} dx_1.$

b) $P_{n0}(x) = (x+t)^n/n! - (x+t)^{n-1}/(n-1)!.$

c) $P_{nk}(x) - P_{n(k-1)}(x) = \dfrac{(k-t)^k}{k!} P_{(n-k)0}(x-k)$, if $1 \le k \le n$.

d) Obtain a general formula for $P_{nk}(x)$, and apply it to the evaluation of Eq. (24).

18. [*M20*] Give a "simple" reason why K_n^- has the same probability distribution as K_n^+.

19. [*HM48*] Develop tests, analogous to the Kolmogorov–Smirnov test, for use with multivariate distributions $F(x_1, \ldots, x_r) = \Pr(X_1 \le x_1, \ldots, X_r \le x_r)$. (Such procedures could be used, for example, in place of the "serial test" in the next section.)

20. [*HM41*] Deduce further terms of the asymptotic behavior of the KS distribution, extending (27).

21. [*M40*] Although the text states that the KS test should be applied only when $F(x)$ is a continuous distribution function, it is, of course, possible to try to compute K_n^+ and K_n^- even when the distribution has jumps. Analyze the probable behavior of K_n^+ and K_n^- for various discontinuous distributions $F(x)$. Compare the effectiveness of the resulting statistical test with the chi-square test on several samples of random numbers.

22. [*HM46*] Investigate the "improved" KS test suggested in the answer to exercise 6.

23. [*M22*] (T. Gonzalez, S. Sahni, and W. R. Franta.) (a) Suppose that the maximum value in formula (13) for the KS statistic K_n^+ occurs at a given index j where $\lfloor nF(X_j) \rfloor = k$. Prove that $F(X_j) = \max_{1 \le i \le n}\{F(X_i) \mid \lfloor nF(X_i) \rfloor = k\}$. (b) Design an algorithm that calculates K_n^+ and K_n^- in $O(n)$ steps (without sorting).

▶ **24.** [*40*] Experiment with various probability distributions (p, q, r) on three categories, where $p + q + r = 1$, by computing the exact distribution of the chi-square statistic V for various n, thereby determining how accurate an approximation the chi-square distribution with two degrees of freedom really is.

25. [*HM26*] Suppose $Y_i = \sum_{j=1}^{n} a_{ij} X_j + \mu_i$ for $1 \le i \le m$, where $X_1, \ldots, X_n$ are independent random variables with mean zero and unit variance, and the matrix $A = (a_{ij})$ has rank n.

a) Express the covariance matrix $C = (c_{ij})$, where $c_{ij} = E(Y_i - \mu_i)(Y_j - \mu_j)$, in terms of the matrix A.

b) Prove that if $\bar{C} = (\bar{c}_{ij})$ is any matrix such that $C\bar{C}C = C$, the statistic

$$W = \sum_{i=1}^{m} \sum_{j=1}^{m} (Y_i - \mu_i)(Y_j - \mu_j)\bar{c}_{ij}$$

is equal to $X_1^2 + \cdots + X_n^2$. [Consequently, if the X_j have the normal distribution, W has the chi-square distribution with n degrees of freedom.]

*The equanimity of your average tosser of coins
depends upon a law ... which ensures that
he will not upset himself by losing too much
nor upset his opponent by winning too often.*

— TOM STOPPARD, *Rosencrantz & Guildenstern are Dead* (1966)

3.3.2. Empirical Tests

In this section we shall discuss eleven kinds of specific tests that have traditionally been applied to sequences in order to investigate their randomness. The discussion of each test has two parts: (a) a "plug-in" description of how to perform the test; and (b) a study of the theoretical basis for the test. (Readers who lack mathematical training may wish to skip over the theoretical discussions. Conversely, mathematically inclined readers may find the associated theory quite interesting, even if they never intend to test random number generators, since some instructive combinatorial questions are involved here. Indeed, this section introduces several topics that will be important to us later in quite different contexts.)

Each test is applied to a sequence

$$\langle U_n \rangle = U_0, U_1, U_2, \ldots \tag{1}$$

of real numbers, which purports to be independently and uniformly distributed between zero and one. Some of the tests are designed primarily for integer-valued sequences, instead of the real-valued sequence (1). In this case, the auxiliary sequence

$$\langle Y_n \rangle = Y_0, Y_1, Y_2, \ldots \tag{2}$$

defined by the rule

$$Y_n = \lfloor dU_n \rfloor \tag{3}$$

is used instead. This is a sequence of integers that purports to be independently and uniformly distributed between 0 and $d - 1$. The number d is chosen for convenience; for example, we might have $d = 64 = 2^6$ on a binary computer, so that Y_n represents the six most significant bits of the binary representation of U_n. The value of d should be large enough so that the test is meaningful, but not so large that the test becomes impracticably difficult to carry out.

The quantities U_n, Y_n, and d will have the significance stated above throughout this section, although the value of d will probably be different in different tests.

A. Equidistribution test (Frequency test). The first requirement that sequence (1) must meet is that its numbers are, in fact, uniformly distributed between zero and one. There are two ways to make this test: (a) Use the Kolmogorov–Smirnov test, with $F(x) = x$ for $0 \le x \le 1$. (b) Let d be a convenient number, such as 100 on a decimal computer, 64 or 128 on a binary computer, and use the sequence (2) instead of (1). For each integer r, $0 \le r < d$, count the number of times that $Y_j = r$ for $0 \le j < n$, and then apply the chi-square test using $k = d$ and probability $p_s = 1/d$ for each category.

The theory behind this test has been covered in Section 3.3.1.

B. Serial test. More generally, we want pairs of successive numbers to be uniformly distributed in an independent manner. The sun comes up just about as often as it goes down, in the long run, but that doesn't make its motion random.

To carry out the serial test, we simply count the number of times that the pair $(Y_{2j}, Y_{2j+1}) = (q, r)$ occurs, for $0 \leq j < n$; these counts are to be made for each pair of integers (q, r) with $0 \leq q, r < d$, and the chi-square test is applied to these $k = d^2$ categories with probability $1/d^2$ in each category. As with the equidistribution test, d may be any convenient number, but it will be somewhat smaller than the values suggested above since a valid chi-square test should have n large compared to k (say $n \geq 5d^2$ at least).

Clearly we can generalize this test to triples, quadruples, etc., instead of pairs (see exercise 2); however, the value of d must then be severely reduced in order to avoid having too many categories. When quadruples and larger numbers of adjacent elements are considered, we therefore make use of less exact tests such as the poker test or the maximum test described below.

Notice that $2n$ numbers of the sequence (2) are used in this test in order to make n observations. It would be a mistake to perform the serial test on the pairs (Y_0, Y_1), (Y_1, Y_2), ..., (Y_{n-1}, Y_n); can the reader see why? We might perform another serial test on the pairs (Y_{2j+1}, Y_{2j+2}), and expect the sequence to pass both tests, remembering that the tests aren't independent of each other. Alternatively, George Marsaglia has proved that, if the pairs (Y_0, Y_1), (Y_1, Y_2), ..., (Y_{n-1}, Y_n) are used, and if we use the usual chi-square method to compute both the statistics V_2 for the serial test and V_1 for the frequency test on $Y_0, \ldots, Y_{n-1}$ with the same value of d, then $V_2 - V_1$ should have the chi-square distribution with $d(d-1)$ degrees of freedom when n is large. (See exercise 24.)

C. Gap test. Another test is used to examine the length of "gaps" between occurrences of U_j in a certain range. If α and β are two real numbers with $0 \leq \alpha < \beta \leq 1$, we want to consider the lengths of consecutive subsequences U_j, U_{j+1}, ..., U_{j+r} in which U_{j+r} lies between α and β but the other U's do not. (This subsequence of $r + 1$ numbers represents a gap of length r.)

Algorithm G (*Data for gap test*). The following algorithm, applied to the sequence (1) for any given values of α and β, counts the number of gaps of lengths 0, 1, ..., $t - 1$ and the number of gaps of length $\geq t$, until n gaps have been tabulated.

G1. [Initialize.] Set $j \leftarrow -1$, $s \leftarrow 0$, and set COUNT$[r] \leftarrow 0$ for $0 \leq r \leq t$.

G2. [Set r zero.] Set $r \leftarrow 0$.

G3. [$\alpha \leq U_j < \beta$?] Increase j by 1. If $U_j \geq \alpha$ and $U_j < \beta$, go to step G5.

G4. [Increase r.] Increase r by one, and return to step G3.

G5. [Record the gap length.] (A gap of length r has now been found.) If $r \geq t$, increase COUNT$[t]$ by one, otherwise increase COUNT$[r]$ by one.

G6. [n gaps found?] Increase s by one. If $s < n$, return to step G2. ∎

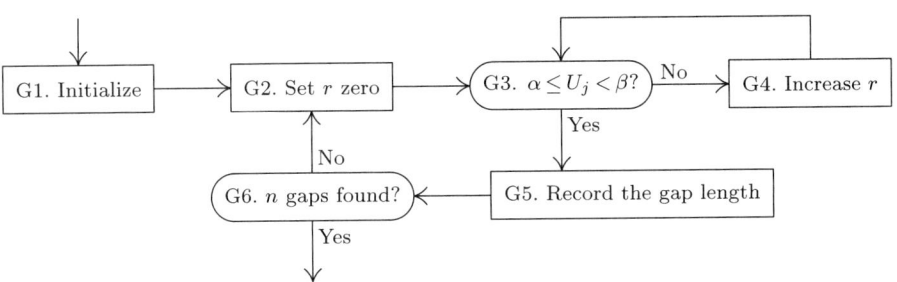

Fig. 6. Gathering data for the gap test. (Algorithms for the "coupon-collector's test" and the "run test" are similar.)

After Algorithm G has been performed, the chi-square test is applied to the $k = t + 1$ values of COUNT[0], COUNT[1], ..., COUNT[t], using the following probabilities:

$$p_r = p(1 - p)^r, \quad \text{for } 0 \le r \le t - 1; \qquad p_t = (1 - p)^t. \tag{4}$$

Here $p = \beta - \alpha$ is the probability that $\alpha \le U_j < \beta$. The values of n and t are to be chosen, as usual, so that each of the values of COUNT[r] is expected to be 5 or more, preferably more.

The gap test is often applied with $\alpha = 0$ or $\beta = 1$ in order to omit one of the comparisons in step G3. The special cases $(\alpha, \beta) = (0, \frac{1}{2})$ or $(\frac{1}{2}, 1)$ give rise to tests that are sometimes called "runs above the mean" and "runs below the mean," respectively.

The probabilities in Eq. (4) are easily deduced, so this derivation is left to the reader. Notice that the gap test as described above observes the lengths of n *gaps*; it does not observe the gap lengths among n *numbers*. If the sequence $\langle U_n \rangle$ is sufficiently nonrandom, Algorithm G might not terminate. Other gap tests that examine a fixed number of U's have also been proposed (see exercise 5).

D. Poker test (Partition test). The "classical" poker test considers n groups of five successive integers, $\{Y_{5j}, Y_{5j+1}, \ldots, Y_{5j+4}\}$ for $0 \le j < n$, and observes which of the following seven patterns is matched by each (orderless) quintuple:

$$
\begin{aligned}
\text{All different:} \quad & abcde \\
\text{One pair:} \quad & aabcd \\
\text{Two pairs:} \quad & aabbc \\
\text{Three of a kind:} \quad & aaabc \\
\text{Full house:} \quad & aaabb \\
\text{Four of a kind:} \quad & aaaab \\
\text{Five of a kind:} \quad & aaaaa
\end{aligned}
$$

A chi-square test is based on the number of quintuples in each category.

It is reasonable to ask for a somewhat simpler version of this test, to facilitate the programming involved. A good compromise would simply be to count the number of *distinct* values in the set of five. We would then have five categories:

$$5 \text{ values} = \text{all different};$$
$$4 \text{ values} = \text{one pair};$$
$$3 \text{ values} = \text{two pairs, or three of a kind};$$
$$2 \text{ values} = \text{full house, or four of a kind};$$
$$1 \text{ value} = \text{five of a kind}.$$

This breakdown is easier to determine systematically, and the test is nearly as good.

In general we can consider n groups of k successive numbers, and we can count the number of k-tuples with r different values. A chi-square test is then made, using the probability

$$p_r = \frac{d(d-1)\dots(d-r+1)}{d^k} \left\{ {k \atop r} \right\} \tag{5}$$

that there are r different. (The Stirling numbers $\left\{ {k \atop r} \right\}$ are defined in Section 1.2.6, and they can readily be computed using the formulas given there.) Since the probability p_r is very small when $r = 1$ or 2, we generally lump a few categories of low probability together before the chi-square test is applied.

To derive the proper formula for p_r, we must count how many of the d^k k-tuples of numbers between 0 and $d-1$ have exactly r different elements, and divide the total by d^k. Since $d(d-1)\dots(d-r+1)$ is the number of ordered choices of r things from a set of d objects, we need only show that $\left\{ {k \atop r} \right\}$ is the number of ways to partition a set of k elements into exactly r parts. Therefore exercise 1.2.6–64 completes the derivation of Eq. (5).

E. Coupon collector's test. The next test is related to the poker test somewhat as the gap test is related to the frequency test. We use the sequence Y_0, Y_1, ..., and we observe the lengths of segments Y_{j+1}, Y_{j+2}, ..., Y_{j+r} that are required to get a "complete set" of integers from 0 to $d-1$. Algorithm C describes this precisely:

Algorithm C (*Data for coupon collector's test*). Given a sequence of integers $Y_0, Y_1, \dots$, with $0 \le Y_j < d$, this algorithm counts the lengths of n consecutive "coupon collector" segments. At the conclusion of the algorithm, COUNT[r] is the number of segments with length r, for $d \le r < t$, and COUNT[t] is the number of segments with length $\ge t$.

C1. [Initialize.] Set $j \leftarrow -1$, $s \leftarrow 0$, and set COUNT[r] $\leftarrow 0$ for $d \le r \le t$.

C2. [Set q, r zero.] Set $q \leftarrow r \leftarrow 0$, and set OCCURS[$k$] $\leftarrow 0$ for $0 \le k < d$.

C3. [Next observation.] Increase r and j by 1. If OCCURS[Y_j] $\ne 0$, repeat this step.

C4. [Complete set?] Set OCCURS[Y_j] $\leftarrow 1$ and $q \leftarrow q + 1$. (The subsequence observed so far contains q distinct values; if $q = d$, we therefore have a complete set.) If $q < d$, return to step C3.

C5. [Record the length.] If $r \geq t$, increase COUNT$[t]$ by one, otherwise increase COUNT$[r]$ by one.

C6. [n found?] Increase s by one. If $s < n$, return to step C2. ∎

For an example of this algorithm, see exercise 7. We may think of a boy collecting d types of coupons, which are randomly distributed in his breakfast cereal boxes; he must keep eating more cereal until he has one coupon of each type.

A chi-square test is to be applied to COUNT$[d]$, COUNT$[d+1]$, ..., COUNT$[t]$, with $k = t - d + 1$, after Algorithm C has counted n lengths. The corresponding probabilities are

$$p_r = \frac{d!}{d^r} \begin{Bmatrix} r-1 \\ d-1 \end{Bmatrix}, \qquad d \leq r < t; \qquad p_t = 1 - \frac{d!}{d^{t-1}} \begin{Bmatrix} t-1 \\ d \end{Bmatrix}. \qquad (6)$$

To derive these probabilities, we simply note that if q_r denotes the probability that a subsequence of length r is *incomplete*, then

$$q_r = 1 - \frac{d!}{d^r} \begin{Bmatrix} r \\ d \end{Bmatrix}$$

by Eq. (5); for this means we have an r-tuple of elements that do not have all d different values. Then (6) follows from the relations $p_t = q_{t-1}$ and

$$p_r = q_{r-1} - q_r \qquad \text{for } d \leq r < t.$$

For formulas that arise in connection with *generalizations* of the coupon collector's test, see exercises 9 and 10 and also the papers by George Pólya, *Zeitschrift für angewandte Math. und Mech.* **10** (1930), 96–97; Hermann von Schelling, *AMM* **61** (1954), 306–311.

F. Permutation test. Divide the input sequence into n groups of t elements each, that is, $(U_{jt}, U_{jt+1}, \ldots, U_{jt+t-1})$ for $0 \leq j < n$. The elements in each group can have $t!$ possible relative orderings; the number of times each ordering appears is counted, and a chi-square test is applied with $k = t!$ and with probability $1/t!$ for each ordering.

For example, if $t = 3$ we would have six possible categories, according to whether $U_{3j} < U_{3j+1} < U_{3j+2}$ or $U_{3j} < U_{3j+2} < U_{3j+1}$ or $\cdots$ or $U_{3j+2} < U_{3j+1} < U_{3j}$. We assume in this test that equality between U's does not occur; such an assumption is justified, for the probability that two U's are equal is zero.

A convenient way to perform the permutation test on a computer makes use of the following algorithm, which is of interest in itself:

Algorithm P (*Analyze a permutation*). Given a sequence of distinct elements $(U_1, \ldots, U_t)$, we compute an integer $f(U_1, \ldots, U_t)$ such that

$$0 \leq f(U_1, \ldots, U_t) < t!,$$

and $f(U_1, \ldots, U_t) = f(V_1, \ldots, V_t)$ if and only if $(U_1, \ldots, U_t)$ and $(V_1, \ldots, V_t)$ have the same relative ordering.

P1. [Initialize.] Set $r \leftarrow t$, $f \leftarrow 0$. (During this algorithm we will have $0 \leq f < t!/r!$.)

P2. [Find maximum.] Find the maximum of $\{U_1, \ldots, U_r\}$, and suppose that U_s is the maximum. Set $f \leftarrow r \cdot f + s - 1$.

P3. [Exchange.] Exchange $U_r \leftrightarrow U_s$.

P4. [Decrease r.] Decrease r by one. If $r > 1$, return to step P2. ∎

The sequence $(U_1, \ldots, U_t)$ will have been sorted into ascending order when this algorithm stops. To prove that the result f uniquely characterizes the *initial* order of $(U_1, \ldots, U_t)$, we note that Algorithm P can be run backwards:

> For $r = 2, 3, \ldots, t$,
> set $s \leftarrow f \bmod r$, $f \leftarrow \lfloor f/r \rfloor$,
> and exchange $U_r \leftrightarrow U_{s+1}$.

It is easy to see that this will undo the effects of steps P2–P4; hence no two permutations can yield the same value of f, and Algorithm P performs as advertised.

The essential idea that underlies Algorithm P is a mixed-radix representation called the "factorial number system": Every integer in the range $0 \leq f < t!$ can be uniquely written in the form

$$f = \big(\ldots (c_{t-1} \times (t-1) + c_{t-2}) \times (t-2) + \cdots + c_2\big) \times 2 + c_1$$
$$= (t-1)!\, c_{t-1} + (t-2)!\, c_{t-2} + \cdots + 2!\, c_2 + 1!\, c_1 \qquad (7)$$

where the "digits" c_j are integers satisfying

$$0 \leq c_j \leq j, \qquad \text{for } 1 \leq j < t. \qquad (8)$$

In Algorithm P, $c_{r-1} = s - 1$ when step P2 is performed for a given value of r.

G. Run test. A sequence may also be tested for "runs up" and "runs down." This means that we examine the length of *monotone* portions of the original sequence (segments that are increasing or decreasing).

As an example of the precise definition of a run, consider the sequence of ten digits "1298536704". Putting a vertical line at the left and right and between X_j and X_{j+1} whenever $X_j > X_{j+1}$, we obtain

$$|1\ 2\ 9|8|5|3\ 6\ 7|0\ 4|, \qquad (9)$$

which displays the "runs up": There is a run of length 3, followed by two runs of length 1, followed by another run of length 3, followed by a run of length 2. The algorithm of exercise 12 shows how to tabulate the length of "runs up."

Unlike the gap test and the coupon collector's test (which are in many other respects similar to this test), we *should not apply a chi-square test to the run counts*, since adjacent runs are *not* independent. A long run will tend to be followed by a short run, and conversely. This lack of independence is enough to invalidate a straightforward chi-square test. Instead, the following statistic may be computed, when the run lengths have been determined as in exercise 12:

$$V = \frac{1}{n-6} \sum_{1 \le i,j \le 6} (\text{COUNT}[i] - nb_i)(\text{COUNT}[j] - nb_j) a_{ij}, \qquad (10)$$

where n is the length of the sequence, and the matrices of coefficients $A = (a_{ij})_{1 \le i,j \le 6}$ and $B = (b_i)_{1 \le i \le 6}$ are given by

$$A = \begin{pmatrix} 4529.4 & 9044.9 & 13568 & 18091 & 22615 & 27892 \\ 9044.9 & 18097 & 27139 & 36187 & 45234 & 55789 \\ 13568 & 27139 & 40721 & 54281 & 67852 & 83685 \\ 18091 & 36187 & 54281 & 72414 & 90470 & 111580 \\ 22615 & 45234 & 67852 & 90470 & 113262 & 139476 \\ 27892 & 55789 & 83685 & 111580 & 139476 & 172860 \end{pmatrix}, \quad B = \begin{pmatrix} \frac{1}{6} \\ \frac{5}{24} \\ \frac{11}{120} \\ \frac{19}{720} \\ \frac{29}{5040} \\ \frac{1}{840} \end{pmatrix}.$$

$$(11)$$

(The values of a_{ij} shown here are approximate only; exact values can be obtained from formulas derived below.) *The statistic V in* (10) *should have the chi-square distribution with six, not five, degrees of freedom*, when n is large. The value of n should be, say, 4000 or more. The same test can be applied to "runs down."

A vastly simpler and more practical run test appears in exercise 14, so a reader who is interested only in testing random number generators should skip the next few pages and go on to the "maximum-of-t test" after looking at exercise 14. On the other hand it is instructive from a mathematical standpoint to see how a complicated run test with interdependent runs can be treated, so we shall now digress for a moment.

Given any permutation of n elements, let $Z_{pi} = 1$ if position i is the beginning of an ascending run of length p or more, and let $Z_{pi} = 0$ otherwise. For example, consider the permutation (9) with $n = 10$; we have

$$Z_{11} = Z_{21} = Z_{31} = Z_{14} = Z_{15} = Z_{16} = Z_{26} = Z_{36} = Z_{19} = Z_{29} = 1,$$

and all other Z's are zero. With this notation,

$$R'_p = Z_{p1} + Z_{p2} + \cdots + Z_{pn} \qquad (12)$$

is the number of runs of length $\ge p$, and

$$R_p = R'_p - R'_{p+1} \qquad (13)$$

is the number of runs of length p exactly. Our goal is to compute the mean value of R_p, and also the *covariance*

$$\text{covar}(R_p, R_q) = \text{mean}\big((R_p - \text{mean}(R_p))(R_q - \text{mean}(R_q))\big),$$

which measures the interdependence of R_p and R_q. These mean values are to be computed as the average over the set of all $n!$ permutations.

Equations (12) and (13) show that the answers can be expressed in terms of the mean values of Z_{pi} and of $Z_{pi}Z_{qj}$, so as the first step of the derivation we obtain the following results (assuming that $i < j$):

$$\frac{1}{n!}\sum Z_{pi} = \begin{cases} \dfrac{p+\delta_{i1}}{(p+1)!}, & \text{if } i \le n-p+1; \\ 0, & \text{otherwise.} \end{cases}$$

$$\frac{1}{n!}\sum Z_{pi}Z_{qj} = \begin{cases} \dfrac{(p+\delta_{i1})q}{(p+1)!\,(q+1)!}, & \text{if } i+p < j \le n-q+1; \quad (14) \\ \dfrac{p+\delta_{i1}}{(p+1)!\,q!} - \dfrac{p+q+\delta_{i1}}{(p+q+1)!}, & \text{if } i+p = j \le n-q+1; \\ 0, & \text{otherwise.} \end{cases}$$

The $\sum$-signs stand for summation over all possible permutations. To illustrate the calculations involved here, we will work the most difficult case, when $i+p = j \le n-q+1$, and when $i > 1$. The quantity $Z_{pi}Z_{qj}$ is either zero or one, so the summation consists of counting all permutations $U_1 U_2 \ldots U_n$ for which $Z_{pi} = Z_{qj} = 1$, that is, all permutations such that

$$U_{i-1} > U_i < \cdots < U_{i+p-1} > U_{i+p} < \cdots < U_{i+p+q-1}. \quad (15)$$

The number of such permutations may be enumerated as follows: There are $\binom{n}{p+q+1}$ ways to choose the elements for the positions indicated in (15); there are

$$(p+q+1)\binom{p+q}{p} - \binom{p+q+1}{p+1} - \binom{p+q+1}{1} + 1 \quad (16)$$

ways to arrange them in the order (15), as shown in exercise 13; and there are $(n-p-q-1)!$ ways to arrange the remaining elements. Thus there are $\binom{n}{p+q+1}(n-p-q-1)!$ times (16) ways in all, and we divide by $n!$ to get the desired formula.

From relations (14) a rather lengthy calculation leads to

$$\operatorname{mean}(R'_p) = (n+1)p/(p+1)! - (p-1)/p!, \qquad 1 \le p \le n; \quad (17)$$

$$\begin{aligned} \operatorname{covar}(R'_p, R'_q) &= \operatorname{mean}(R'_p R'_q) - \operatorname{mean}(R'_p)\operatorname{mean}(R'_q) \\ &= \sum_{1 \le i,j \le n} \frac{1}{n!}\sum Z_{pi}Z_{qj} - \operatorname{mean}(R'_p)\operatorname{mean}(R'_q) \\ &= \begin{cases} \operatorname{mean}(R'_t) + f(p,q,n), & \text{if } p+q \le n, \\ \operatorname{mean}(R'_t) - \operatorname{mean}(R'_p)\operatorname{mean}(R'_q), & \text{if } p+q > n, \end{cases} \quad (18) \end{aligned}$$

where $t = \max(p,q)$, $s = p+q$, and

$$f(p,q,n) = (n+1)\left(\frac{s(1-pq)+pq}{(p+1)!\,(q+1)!} - \frac{2s}{(s+1)!}\right) + 2\binom{s-1}{s!} \\ + \frac{(s^2-s-2)pq - s^2 - p^2 q^2 + 1}{(p+1)!\,(q+1)!}. \quad (19)$$

This expression for the covariance is unfortunately quite complicated, but it is necessary for a successful run test as described above. From these formulas it is easy to compute

$$\text{mean}(R_p) = \text{mean}(R'_p) - \text{mean}(R'_{p+1}),$$

$$\text{covar}(R_p, R'_q) = \text{covar}(R'_p, R'_q) - \text{covar}(R'_{p+1}, R'_q), \qquad (20)$$

$$\text{covar}(R_p, R_q) = \text{covar}(R_p, R'_q) - \text{covar}(R_p, R'_{q+1}).$$

In *Annals Math. Stat.* **15** (1944), 163–165, J. Wolfowitz proved that the quantities $R_1, R_2, \ldots, R_{t-1}, R'_t$ become normally distributed as $n \to \infty$, subject to the mean and covariance expressed above; this implies that the following test for runs is valid: Given a sequence of n random numbers, compute the number of runs R_p of length p for $1 \le p < t$, and also the number of runs R'_t of length t or more. Let

$$Q_1 = R_1 - \text{mean}(R_1), \quad \ldots, \quad Q_{t-1} = R_{t-1} - \text{mean}(R_{t-1}),$$

$$Q_t = R'_t - \text{mean}(R'_t). \qquad (21)$$

Form the matrix C of the covariances of the R's; for example, $C_{13} = \text{covar}(R_1, R_3)$, while $C_{1t} = \text{covar}(R_1, R'_t)$. When $t = 6$, we have

$$C = nC_1 + C_2, \qquad (22)$$

where

$$C_1 = \begin{pmatrix}
\frac{23}{180} & \frac{-7}{360} & \frac{-5}{336} & \frac{-433}{60480} & \frac{-13}{5670} & \frac{-121}{181440} \\
\frac{-7}{360} & \frac{2843}{20160} & \frac{-989}{20160} & \frac{-7159}{362880} & \frac{-10019}{1814400} & \frac{-1303}{907200} \\
\frac{-5}{336} & \frac{-989}{20160} & \frac{54563}{907200} & \frac{-21311}{1814400} & \frac{-62369}{19958400} & \frac{-7783}{9979200} \\
\frac{-433}{60480} & \frac{-7159}{362880} & \frac{-21311}{1814400} & \frac{886657}{39916800} & \frac{-257699}{239500800} & \frac{-62611}{239500800} \\
\frac{-13}{5670} & \frac{-10019}{1814400} & \frac{-62369}{19958400} & \frac{-257699}{239500800} & \frac{29874811}{5448643200} & \frac{-1407179}{21794572800} \\
\frac{-121}{181440} & \frac{-1303}{907200} & \frac{-7783}{9979200} & \frac{-62611}{239500800} & \frac{-1407179}{21794572800} & \frac{2134697}{1816214400}
\end{pmatrix},$$

$$C_2 = \begin{pmatrix}
\frac{83}{180} & \frac{-29}{180} & \frac{-11}{210} & \frac{-41}{12096} & \frac{91}{25920} & \frac{41}{18144} \\
\frac{-29}{180} & \frac{-305}{4032} & \frac{319}{20160} & \frac{2557}{72576} & \frac{10177}{604800} & \frac{413}{64800} \\
\frac{-11}{210} & \frac{319}{20160} & \frac{-58747}{907200} & \frac{19703}{604800} & \frac{239471}{19958400} & \frac{39517}{9979200} \\
\frac{-41}{12096} & \frac{2557}{72576} & \frac{19703}{604800} & \frac{-220837}{4435200} & \frac{1196401}{239500800} & \frac{360989}{239500800} \\
\frac{91}{25920} & \frac{10177}{604800} & \frac{239471}{19958400} & \frac{1196401}{239500800} & \frac{-139126639}{7264857600} & \frac{4577641}{10897286400} \\
\frac{41}{18144} & \frac{413}{64800} & \frac{39517}{9979200} & \frac{360989}{239500800} & \frac{4577641}{10897286400} & \frac{-122953057}{21794572800}
\end{pmatrix}$$

if $n \ge 12$. Now form $A = (a_{ij})$, the inverse of the matrix C, and compute $\sum_{i,j=1}^{t} Q_i Q_j a_{ij}$. The result for large n should have approximately the chi-square distribution with t degrees of freedom.

The matrix A given earlier in (11) is the inverse of C_1 to five significant figures. The true inverse, A, is $n^{-1} C_1^{-1} - n^{-2} C_1^{-1} C_2 C_1^{-1} + n^{-3} C_1^{-1} C_2 C_1^{-1} C_2 C_1^{-1} - \cdots$, and it turns out that $C_1^{-1} C_2 C_1^{-1}$ is very nearly equal to $-6 C_1^{-1}$. Therefore by (10), $V \approx Q^T C_1^{-1} Q / (n - 6)$, where $Q = (Q_1 \ldots Q_t)^T$.

H. Maximum-of-t test. For $0 \le j < n$, let $V_j = \max(U_{tj}, U_{tj+1}, \ldots, U_{tj+t-1})$. Now apply the Kolmogorov–Smirnov test to the sequence V_0, V_1, ..., V_{n-1}, with the distribution function $F(x) = x^t$, $0 \le x \le 1$. Alternatively, apply the equidistribution test to the sequence V_0^t, V_1^t, ..., V_{n-1}^t.

To verify this test, we must show that the distribution function for the V_j is $F(x) = x^t$. The probability that $\max(U_1, U_2, \ldots, U_t) \le x$ is the probability that $U_1 \le x$ and $U_2 \le x$ and ... and $U_t \le x$, which is the product of the individual probabilities, namely $xx \ldots x = x^t$.

I. Collision test. Chi-square tests can be made only when a nontrivial number of items are expected in each category. But another kind of test can be used when the number of categories is much larger than the number of observations; this test is related to "hashing," an important method for information retrieval that we shall study in Section 6.4.

Suppose we have m urns and we throw n balls at random into those urns, where m is much greater than n. Most of the balls will land in urns that were previously empty, but if a ball falls into an urn that already contains at least one ball we say that a "collision" has occurred. The collision test counts the number of collisions, and a generator passes this test if it doesn't induce too many or too few collisions.

To fix the ideas, suppose $m = 2^{20}$ and $n = 2^{14}$. Then each urn will receive only one 64th of a ball, on the average. The probability that a given urn will contain exactly k balls is $p_k = \binom{n}{k} m^{-k} (1 - m^{-1})^{n-k}$, so the expected number of collisions per urn is

$$\sum_{k \ge 1} (k-1)p_k = \sum_{k \ge 0} k p_k - \sum_{k \ge 1} p_k = \frac{n}{m} - 1 + p_0.$$

Since $p_0 = (1 - m^{-1})^n = 1 - nm^{-1} + \binom{n}{2} m^{-2}$ − smaller terms, we find that the average total number of collisions taken over all m urns is slightly less than $n^2/(2m) = 128$. (The actual value is ≈ 127.33.)

We can use the collision test to rate a random number generator in a large number of dimensions. For example, when $m = 2^{20}$ and $n = 2^{14}$ we can test the 20-dimensional randomness of a number generator by letting $d = 2$ and forming 20-dimensional vectors $V_j = (Y_{20j}, Y_{20j+1}, \ldots, Y_{20j+19})$ for $0 \le j < n$. We keep a table of $m = 2^{20}$ bits to determine collisions, one bit for each possible value of the vector V_j; on a computer with 32 bits per word, this amounts to 2^{15} words. Initially all 2^{20} bits of this table are cleared to zero; then for each V_j, if the corresponding bit is already 1 we record a collision, otherwise we set the bit to 1. This test can also be used in 10 dimensions with $d = 4$, and so on.

To decide if the test is passed, we can use the following table of percentage points when $m = 2^{20}$ and $n = 2^{14}$:

collisions $\le$	101	108	119	126	134	145	153
with probability	.009	.043	.244	.476	.742	.946	.989

The theory underlying these probabilities is the same we used in the poker test, Eq. (5); the probability that c collisions occur is the probability that $n - c$ urns are occupied, namely

$$\frac{m(m-1)\dots(m-n+c+1)}{m^n}\left\{{n \atop n-c}\right\}.$$

Although m and n are very large, it is not difficult to compute these probabilities using the following method:

Algorithm S (*Percentage points for collision test*). Given m and n, this algorithm determines the distribution of the number of collisions that occur when n balls are scattered into m urns. An auxiliary array $A[0]$, $A[1]$, ..., $A[n]$ of floating point numbers is used for the computation; actually $A[j]$ will be nonzero only for $j_0 \le j \le j_1$, and $j_1 - j_0$ will be at most of order $\log n$, so it would be possible to get by with considerably less storage.

S1. [Initialize.] Set $A[j] \leftarrow 0$ for $0 \le j \le n$; then set $A[1] \leftarrow 1$ and $j_0 \leftarrow j_1 \leftarrow 1$. Then do step S2 exactly $n-1$ times and go on to step S3.

S2. [Update probabilities.] (Performing this step once corresponds to tossing a ball into an urn; $A[j]$ represents the probability that exactly j of the urns are occupied.) Set $j_1 \leftarrow j_1 + 1$. Then for $j \leftarrow j_1, j_1 - 1, \dots, j_0$ (in this order), set $A[j] \leftarrow (j/m)A[j] + \big((1+1/m) - (j/m)\big)A[j-1]$. If $A[j]$ has become very small as a result of this calculation, say $A[j] < 10^{-20}$, set $A[j] \leftarrow 0$; and in such a case, decrease j_1 by 1 if $j = j_1$, or increase j_0 by 1 if $j = j_0$.

S3. [Compute the answers.] In this step we make use of an auxiliary table $(T_1, T_2, \dots, T_{\text{tmax}}) = (.01, .05, .25, .50, .75, .95, .99, 1.00)$ containing the specified percentage points of interest. Set $p \leftarrow 0$, $t \leftarrow 1$, and $j \leftarrow j_0 - 1$. Do the following iteration until $t = \text{tmax}$: Increase j by 1, and set $p \leftarrow p + A[j]$; then if $p > T_t$, output $n - j - 1$ and $1 - p$ (meaning that with probability $1 - p$ there are at most $n - j - 1$ collisions) and repeatedly increase t by 1 until $p \le T_t$. ∎

J. Birthday spacings test. George Marsaglia introduced a new kind of test in 1984: We throw n balls into m urns, as in the collision test, but now we think of the urns as "days of a year" and the balls as "birthdays." Suppose the birthdays are $(Y_1, \dots, Y_n)$, where $0 \le Y_k < m$. Sort them into nondecreasing order $Y_{(1)} \le \cdots \le Y_{(n)}$; then define n "spacings" $S_1 = Y_{(2)} - Y_{(1)}, \dots, S_{n-1} = Y_{(n)} - Y_{(n-1)}$, $S_n = Y_{(1)} + m - Y_{(n)}$; finally sort the spacings into order, $S_{(1)} \le \cdots \le S_{(n)}$. Let R be the number of equal spacings, namely the number of indices j such that $1 < j \le n$ and $S_{(j)} = S_{(j-1)}$. When $m = 2^{25}$ and $n = 512$, we should have

$R =$	0	1	2	3 or more
with probability	.368801577	.369035243	.183471182	.078691997

(The average number of equal spacings for this choice of m and n should be approximately 1.) Repeat the test 1000 times, say, and do a chi-square test with 3 degrees of freedom to compare the empirical R's with the correct distribution; this will tell whether or not the generator produces reasonably random birthday spacings. Exercises 28–30 develop the theory behind this test and formulas for other values of m and n.

Such a test of birthday spacings is important primarily because of the remarkable fact that lagged Fibonacci generators consistently *fail* it, although they pass the other traditional tests quite nicely. [Dramatic examples of such failures were reported by Marsaglia, Zaman, and Tsang in *Stat. and Prob. Letters* **9** (1990), 35–39.] Consider, for example, the sequence

$$X_n = (X_{n-24} + X_{n-55}) \bmod m$$

of Eq. 3.2.2–(7). The numbers of this sequence satisfy

$$X_n + X_{n-86} \equiv X_{n-24} + X_{n-31} \quad (\text{modulo } m)$$

because both sides are congruent to $X_{n-24} + X_{n-55} + X_{n-86}$. Therefore two pairs of differences are equal:

$$X_n - X_{n-24} \equiv X_{n-31} - X_{n-86},$$

and

$$X_n - X_{n-31} \equiv X_{n-24} - X_{n-86}.$$

Whenever X_n is reasonably close to X_{n-24} or X_{n-31} (as it should be in a truly random sequence), the difference has a good chance of showing up in two of the spacings. So we get significantly more cases of equality — typically $R \approx 2$ on the average, not 1. But if we discount from R any equal spacings that arise from the stated congruence, the resulting statistic R' usually does pass the birthday test. (One way to avoid failure is to discard certain elements of the sequence, using for example only X_0, X_2, X_4, ... as random numbers; then we never get all four elements of the set $\{X_n, X_{n-24}, X_{n-31}, X_{n-86}\}$, and the birthday spacings are no problem. An even better way to avoid the problem is to discard consecutive batches of numbers, as suggested by Lüscher; see Section 3.2.2.) Similar remarks apply to the subtract-with-borrow and add-with-carry generators of exercise 3.2.1.1–14.

K. Serial correlation test. We may also compute the following statistic:

$$C = \frac{n(U_0 U_1 + U_1 U_2 + \cdots + U_{n-2} U_{n-1} + U_{n-1} U_0) - (U_0 + U_1 + \cdots + U_{n-1})^2}{n(U_0^2 + U_1^2 + \cdots + U_{n-1}^2) - (U_0 + U_1 + \cdots + U_{n-1})^2}. \quad (23)$$

This is the "serial correlation coefficient," a measure of the extent to which U_{j+1} depends on U_j.

Correlation coefficients appear frequently in statistical work. If we have n quantities U_0, U_1, ..., U_{n-1} and n others V_0, V_1, ..., V_{n-1}, the correlation coefficient between them is defined to be

$$C = \frac{n \sum (U_j V_j) - (\sum U_j)(\sum V_j)}{\sqrt{\left(n \sum U_j^2 - (\sum U_j)^2\right)\left(n \sum V_j^2 - (\sum V_j)^2\right)}}. \quad (24)$$

All summations in this formula are to be taken over the range $0 \le j < n$; Eq. (23) is the special case $V_j = U_{(j+1) \bmod n}$. The denominator of (24) is zero when $U_0 = U_1 = \cdots = U_{n-1}$ or $V_0 = V_1 = \cdots = V_{n-1}$; we exclude that case from discussion.

A correlation coefficient always lies between -1 and $+1$. When it is zero or very small, it indicates that the quantities U_j and V_j are (relatively speaking) independent of each other, whereas a value of ± 1 indicates total linear dependence. In fact, $V_j = \alpha \pm \beta U_j$ for all j in the latter case, for some constants α and β. (See exercise 17.)

Therefore it is desirable to have C in Eq. (23) close to zero. In actual fact, since $U_0 U_1$ is not completely independent of $U_1 U_2$, the serial correlation coefficient is not expected to be *exactly* zero. (See exercise 18.) A "good" value of C will be between $\mu_n - 2\sigma_n$ and $\mu_n + 2\sigma_n$, where

$$\mu_n = \frac{-1}{n-1}, \qquad \sigma_n^2 = \frac{n^2}{(n-1)^2(n-2)}, \qquad n > 2. \qquad (25)$$

We expect C to be between these limits about 95 percent of the time.

The formula for σ_n^2 in (25) is an upper bound, valid for serial correlations between independent random variables from an arbitrary distribution. When the U's are uniformly distributed, the true variance is obtained by subtracting $\frac{24}{5} n^{-2} + O(n^{-7/3} \log n)$. (See exercise 20.)

Instead of simply computing the correlation coefficient between the observations $(U_0, U_1, \ldots, U_{n-1})$ and their immediate successors $(U_1, \ldots, U_{n-1}, U_0)$, we can also compute it between $(U_0, U_1, \ldots, U_{n-1})$ and any cyclically shifted sequence $(U_q, \ldots, U_{n-1}, U_0, \ldots, U_{q-1})$; the cyclic correlations should be small for $0 < q < n$. A straightforward computation of Eq. (24) for all q would require about n^2 multiplications, but it is actually possible to compute all the correlations in only $O(n \log n)$ steps by using "fast Fourier transforms." (See Section 4.6.4; see also L. P. Schmid, *CACM* **8** (1965), 115.)

L. Tests on subsequences. External programs often call for random numbers in batches. For example, if a program works with three random variables X, Y, and Z, it may consistently invoke the generation of three random numbers at a time. In such applications it is important that the subsequences consisting of every *third* term of the original sequence be random. If the program requires q numbers at a time, the sequences

$$U_0, U_q, U_{2q}, \ldots; \quad U_1, U_{q+1}, U_{2q+1}, \ldots; \quad \ldots; \quad U_{q-1}, U_{2q-1}, U_{3q-1}, \ldots$$

can each be put through the tests described above for the original sequence U_0, U_1, U_2, $\ldots$.

Experience with linear congruential sequences has shown that these derived sequences rarely if ever behave less randomly than the original sequence, unless q has a large factor in common with the period length. On a binary computer with m equal to the word size, for example, a test of the subsequences for $q = 8$ will tend to give the poorest randomness for all $q < 16$; and on a decimal computer, $q = 10$ yields the subsequences most likely to be unsatisfactory. (This can be explained somewhat on the grounds of potency, since such values of q will tend to lower the potency. Exercise 3.2.1.2–20 provides a more detailed explanation.)

M. Historical remarks and further discussion. Statistical tests arose naturally in the course of scientists' efforts to "prove" or "disprove" hypotheses about various observed data. The best-known early papers dealing with the testing of artificially generated numbers for randomness are two articles by M. G. Kendall and B. Babington-Smith in the *Journal of the Royal Statistical Society* **101** (1938), 147–166, and in the supplement to that journal, **6** (1939), 51–61. Those papers were concerned with the testing of random digits between 0 and 9, rather than random real numbers; for this purpose, the authors discussed the frequency test, serial test, gap test, and poker test, although they misapplied the serial test. Kendall and Babington-Smith also used a variant of the coupon collector's test; the method described in this section was introduced by R. E. Greenwood in *Math. Comp.* **9** (1955), 1–5.

The run test has a rather interesting history. Originally, tests were made on runs up and down at once: A run up would be followed by a run down, then another run up, and so on. Note that the run test and the permutation test do not depend on the uniform distribution of the U's, but only on the fact that $U_i = U_j$ occurs with probability zero when $i \neq j$; therefore these tests can be applied to many types of random sequences. The run test in primitive form was originated by J. Bienaymé [*Comptes Rendus Acad. Sci.* **81** (Paris, 1875), 417–423]. Some sixty years later, W. O. Kermack and A. G. McKendrick published two extensive papers on the subject [*Proc. Royal Society Edinburgh* **57** (1937), 228–240, 332–376]; as an example they stated that Edinburgh rainfall between the years 1785 and 1930 was "entirely random in character" with respect to the run test (although they examined only the mean and standard deviation of the run lengths). Several other people began using the test, but it was not until 1944 that the use of the chi-square method in connection with this test was shown to be incorrect. A paper by H. Levene and J. Wolfowitz in *Annals Math. Stat.* **15** (1944), 58–69, introduced the correct run test (for runs up and down, alternately) and discussed the fallacies in earlier misuses of that test. Separate tests for runs up and runs down, as proposed in the text above, are more suited to computer application, so we have not given the more complex formulas for the alternate-up-and-down case. See the survey paper by D. E. Barton and C. L. Mallows, *Annals Math. Stat.* **36** (1965), 236–260.

Of all the tests we have discussed, the frequency test and the serial correlation test seem to be the weakest, in the sense that nearly all random number generators pass them. Theoretical grounds for the weakness of these tests are discussed briefly in Section 3.5 (see exercise 3.5–26). The run test, on the other hand, is rather strong: The results of exercises 3.3.3–23 and 24 suggest that linear congruential generators tend to have runs somewhat longer than normal if the multiplier is not large enough, so the run test of exercise 14 is definitely to be recommended.

The collision test is also highly recommended, since it has been specially designed to detect the deficiencies of many poor generators that have unfortunately become widespread. Based on ideas of H. Delgas Christiansen [Inst. Math. Stat. and Oper. Res., Tech. Univ. Denmark (October 1975), unpublished], this test was the first to be developed after the advent of computers; it is specifically intended for computer use, and unsuitable for hand calculation.

The reader probably wonders, *"Why are there so many tests?"* It has been said that more computer time is spent testing random numbers than using them in applications! This is untrue, although it is possible to go overboard in testing.

The need for making several tests has been amply documented. People have found, for example, that some numbers generated by a variant of the middle-square method have passed the frequency test, gap test, and poker test, yet flunked the serial test. Linear congruential sequences with small multipliers have been known to pass many tests, yet fail on the run test because there are too few runs of length one. The maximum-of-t test has also been used to ferret out some bad generators that otherwise seemed to perform respectably. A subtract-with-borrow generator fails the gap test when the maximum gap length exceeds the largest lag; see Vattulainen, Kankaala, Saarinen, and Ala-Nissila, *Computer Physics Communications* **86** (1995), 209–226, where a variety of other tests are also reported. Lagged Fibonacci generators, which are theoretically guaranteed to have equally distributed least-significant bits, still fail some simple variants of the 1-bit equidistribution test (see exercises 31 and 35, also 3.6–14).

Perhaps the main reason for doing extensive testing on random number generators is that people misusing Mr. X's random number generator will hardly ever admit that their programs are at fault: They will blame the generator, until Mr. X can *prove* to them that his numbers are sufficiently random. On the other hand, if the source of random numbers is only for Mr. X's personal use, he might decide not to bother to test them, since the techniques recommended in this chapter have a high probability of being satisfactory.

As computers become faster, more random numbers are consumed than ever before, and random number generators that once were satisfactory are no longer good enough for sophisticated applications in physics, combinatorics, stochastic geometry, etc. George Marsaglia has therefore introduced a number of *stringent tests*, which go well beyond classical methods like the gap and poker tests, in order to meet the new challenges. For example, he found that the sequence $X_{n+1} = (62605X_n + 113218009) \bmod 2^{29}$ had a noticeable bias in the following experiment: Generate 2^{21} random numbers X_n and extract their 10 leading bits $Y_n = \lfloor X_n/2^{19} \rfloor$. Count how many of the 2^{20} possible pairs (y, y') of 10-bit numbers do *not* occur among $(Y_1, Y_2), (Y_2, Y_3), \ldots, (Y_{2^{21}-1}, Y_{2^{21}})$. There ought to be about 141909.33 missing pairs, with standard deviation $\approx$ 290.46 (see exercise 34). But six consecutive trials, starting with $X_1 = 1234567$, produced counts that were all between 1.5 and 3.5 standard deviations too low. The distribution was a bit too "flat" to be random — probably because 2^{21} numbers is a significant fraction, $1/256$, of the entire period. A similar generator with multiplier 69069 and modulus 2^{30} proved to be better. Marsaglia and Zaman call this procedure a "monkey test," because it counts the number of two-character combinations that a monkey will miss after typing randomly on a keyboard with 1024 keys; see *Computers and Math.* **26**, 9 (November 1993), 1–10, for the analysis of several monkey tests.

EXERCISES

1. [10] Why should the serial test described in part B be applied to (Y_0, Y_1), (Y_2, Y_3), ..., (Y_{2n-2}, Y_{2n-1}) instead of to (Y_0, Y_1), (Y_1, Y_2), ..., (Y_{n-1}, Y_n)?

2. [10] State an appropriate way to generalize the serial test to triples, quadruples, etc., instead of pairs.

▶ **3.** [M20] How many U's need to be examined in the gap test (Algorithm G) before n gaps have been found, on the average, assuming that the sequence is random? What is the standard deviation of this quantity?

4. [M12] Prove that the probabilities in (4) are correct for the gap test.

5. [M23] The "classical" gap test used by Kendall and Babington-Smith considers the numbers U_0, U_1, ..., U_{N-1} to be a cyclic sequence with U_{N+j} identified with U_j. Here N is a fixed number of U's that are to be subjected to the test. If n of the numbers U_0, ..., U_{N-1} fall into the range $\alpha \le U_j < \beta$, there are n gaps in the cyclic sequence. Let Z_r be the number of gaps of length r, for $0 \le r < t$, and let Z_t be the number of gaps of length $\ge t$; show that the quantity $V = \sum_{0 \le r \le t} (Z_r - np_r)^2 / np_r$ should have the chi-square distribution with t degrees of freedom, in the limit as N goes to infinity, where p_r is given in Eq. (4).

6. [40] (H. Geiringer.) A frequency count of the first 2000 decimal digits in the representation of $e = 2.71828\ldots$ gave a χ^2 value of 1.06, indicating that the actual frequencies of the digits 0, 1, ..., 9 are much too close to their expected values to be considered randomly distributed. (In fact, $\chi^2 \ge 1.15$ with probability 99.9 percent.) The same test applied to the first 10,000 digits of e gives the reasonable value $\chi^2 = 8.61$; but the fact that the first 2000 digits are so evenly distributed is still surprising. Does the same phenomenon occur in the representation of e to other bases? [See *AMM* **72** (1965), 483–500.]

7. [08] Apply the coupon collector's test procedure (Algorithm C), with $d = 3$ and $n = 7$, to the sequence 1101221022120202001212201010201121. What lengths do the seven subsequences have?

▶ **8.** [M22] How many U's need to be examined in the coupon collector's test, on the average, before n complete sets have been found by Algorithm C, assuming that the sequence is random? What is the standard deviation? [*Hint:* See Eq. 1.2.9–(28).]

9. [M21] Generalize the coupon collector's test so that the search stops as soon as w distinct values have been found, where w is a fixed positive integer less than or equal to d. What probabilities should be used in place of (6)?

10. [M23] Solve exercise 8 for the more general coupon collector's test described in exercise 9.

11. [00] The "runs up" in a particular permutation are displayed in (9); what are the "runs down" in that permutation?

12. [20] Let U_0, U_1, ..., U_{n-1} be n distinct numbers. Write an algorithm that determines the lengths of all ascending runs in the sequence. When your algorithm terminates, COUNT[r] should be the number of runs of length r, for $1 \le r \le 5$, and COUNT[6] should be the number of runs of length 6 or more.

13. [M23] Show that (16) is the number of permutations of $p+q+1$ distinct elements having the pattern (15).

▶ **14.** [*M15*] If we "throw away" the element that immediately follows a run, so that when X_j is greater than X_{j+1} we start the next run with X_{j+2}, the run lengths are independent, and a simple chi-square test may be used (instead of the horribly complicated method derived in the text). What are the appropriate run-length probabilities for this simple run test?

15. [*M10*] In the maximum-of-t test, why are V_0^t, V_1^t, ..., V_{n-1}^t supposed to be uniformly distributed between zero and one?

▶ **16.** [*15*] Mr. J. H. Quick (a student) wanted to perform the maximum-of-t test for several different values of t.

a) Letting $Z_{jt} = \max(U_j, U_{j+1}, \dots, U_{j+t-1})$, he found a clever way to go from the sequence $Z_{0(t-1)}, Z_{1(t-1)}, \dots$, to the sequence $Z_{0t}, Z_{1t}, \dots$, using very little time and space. What was his bright idea?

b) He decided to modify the maximum-of-t method so that the jth observation would be $\max(U_j, \dots, U_{j+t-1})$; in other words, he took $V_j = Z_{jt}$ instead of $V_j = Z_{(tj)t}$ as the text says. He reasoned that *all* of the Z's should have the same distribution, so the test is even stronger if each Z_{jt}, $0 \le j < n$, is used instead of just every tth one. But when he tried a chi-square equidistribution test on the values of V_j^t, he got extremely high values of the statistic V, which got even higher as t increased. Why did this happen?

17. [*M25*] Given any numbers $U_0, \dots, U_{n-1}, V_0, \dots, V_{n-1}$, let their mean values be

$$\bar{u} = \frac{1}{n} \sum_{0 \le k < n} U_k, \qquad \bar{v} = \frac{1}{n} \sum_{0 \le k < n} V_k.$$

a) Let $U_k' = U_k - \bar{u}$, $V_k' = V_k - \bar{v}$. Show that the correlation coefficient C given in Eq. (24) is equal to

$$\sum_{0 \le k < n} U_k' V_k' \Big/ \sqrt{\sum_{0 \le k < n} U_k'^2} \sqrt{\sum_{0 \le k < n} V_k'^2}.$$

b) Let $C = N/D$, where N and D denote the numerator and denominator of the expression in part (a). Show that $N^2 \le D^2$, hence $-1 \le C \le 1$; and obtain a formula for the difference $D^2 - N^2$. [*Hint:* See exercise 1.2.3–30.]

c) If $C = \pm 1$, show that $\alpha U_k + \beta V_k = \tau$, $0 \le k < n$, for some constants α, β, and τ, not all zero.

18. [*M20*] (a) Show that if $n = 2$, the serial correlation coefficient (23) is always equal to -1 (unless the denominator is zero). (b) Similarly, show that when $n = 3$, the serial correlation coefficient always equals $-\frac{1}{2}$. (c) Show that the denominator in (23) is zero if and only if $U_0 = U_1 = \cdots = U_{n-1}$.

19. [*M30*] (J. P. Butler.) Let $U_0, \dots, U_{n-1}$ be independent random variables having the same distribution. Prove that the expected value of the serial correlation coefficient (23), averaged over all cases with nonzero denominator, is $-1/(n-1)$.

20. [*HM41*] Continuing the previous exercise, prove that the variance of (23) is equal to $n^2/(n-1)^2(n-2) - n^3 \operatorname{E}((U_0-U_1)^4/D^2)/2(n-2)$, where D is the denominator of (23) and E denotes the expected value over all cases with $D \ne 0$. What is the asymptotic value of $\operatorname{E}((U_0 - U_1)^4/D^2)$ when each U_j is uniformly distributed?

21. [*19*] What value of f is computed by Algorithm P if it is presented with the permutation $(1, 2, 9, 8, 5, 3, 6, 7, 0, 4)$?

22. [*18*] For what permutation of $\{0,1,2,3,4,5,6,7,8,9\}$ will Algorithm P produce the value $f = 1024$?

23. [*M22*] Let $\langle Y_n \rangle$ and $\langle Y_n' \rangle$ be integer sequences having period lengths λ and λ', respectively, with $0 \leq Y_n, Y_n' < d$; also let $Z_n = (Y_n + Y_{n+r}') \bmod d$, where r is chosen at random between 0 and $\lambda' - 1$. Show that $\langle Z_n \rangle$ passes the t-dimensional serial test at least as well as $\langle Y_n \rangle$ does, in the following sense: Let $P(x_1, \ldots, x_t)$ and $Q(x_1, \ldots, x_t)$ be the probabilities that the t-tuple $(x_1, \ldots, x_t)$ occurs in $\langle Y_n \rangle$ and $\langle Z_n \rangle$:

$$P(x_1, \ldots, x_t) = \frac{1}{\lambda} \sum_{n=0}^{\lambda-1} [(Y_n, \ldots, Y_{n+t-1}) = (x_1, \ldots, x_t)];$$

$$Q(x_1, \ldots, x_t) = \frac{1}{\lambda\lambda'} \sum_{n=0}^{\lambda-1} \sum_{r=0}^{\lambda'-1} [(Z_n, \ldots, Z_{n+t-1}) = (x_1, \ldots, x_t)].$$

Then $\displaystyle\sum_{(x_1, \ldots, x_t)} \left(Q(x_1, \ldots, x_t) - d^{-t}\right)^2 \leq \sum_{(x_1, \ldots, x_t)} \left(P(x_1, \ldots, x_t) - d^{-t}\right)^2$.

24. [*HM37*] (G. Marsaglia.) Show that the serial test on n overlapping t-tuples $(Y_1, Y_2, \ldots, Y_t)$, $(Y_2, Y_3, \ldots, Y_{t+1})$, $\ldots$, $(Y_n, Y_1, \ldots, Y_{t-1})$ can be carried out as follows: For each string $\alpha = a_1 \ldots a_m$ with $0 \leq a_i < d$, let $N(\alpha)$ be the number of times α occurs as a substring of $Y_1 Y_2 \ldots Y_n Y_1 \ldots Y_{m-1}$, and let $P(\alpha) = P(a_1) \ldots P(a_m)$ be the probability that α occurs at any given position; individual digits may occur with differing probabilities $P(0)$, $P(1)$, $\ldots$, $P(d-1)$. Compute the statistic

$$V = \frac{1}{n} \sum_{|\alpha|=t} \frac{N(\alpha)^2}{P(\alpha)} - \frac{1}{n} \sum_{|\alpha|=t-1} \frac{N(\alpha)^2}{P(\alpha)}.$$

Then V should have the chi-square distribution with $d^t - d^{t-1}$ degrees of freedom when n is large. [*Hint:* Use exercise 3.3.1–25.]

25. [*M46*] Why is $C_1^{-1} C_2 C_1^{-1} \approx -6C_1^{-1}$, when C_1 and C_2 are the matrices defined after (22)?

26. [*HM30*] Let U_1, U_2, $\ldots$, U_n be independent uniform deviates in $[0..1)$, and let $U_{(1)} \leq U_{(2)} \leq \cdots \leq U_{(n)}$ be their values after sorting; also define the spacings $S_1 = U_{(2)} - U_{(1)}$, $\ldots$, $S_{n-1} = U_{(n)} - U_{(n-1)}$, $S_n = U_{(1)} + 1 - U_{(n)}$ and sorted spacings $S_{(1)} \leq \cdots \leq S_{(n)}$ as in the birthday spacings test. It is convenient in the following calculations to use the notation x_+^n as an abbreviation for the expression $x^n[x \geq 0]$.

   a) Given any real numbers s_1, s_2, $\ldots$, s_n, prove that the simultaneous inequalities $S_1 \geq s_1$, $S_2 \geq s_2$, $\ldots$, $S_n \geq s_n$ occur with probability $(1 - s_1 - s_2 - \cdots - s_n)_+^{n-1}$.

   b) Consequently the smallest spacing $S_{(1)}$ is $\leq s$ with probability $1 - (1 - ns)_+^{n-1}$.

   c) What are the distribution functions $F_k(s) = \Pr(S_{(k)} \leq s)$, for $1 \leq k \leq n$?

   d) Calculate the mean and variance of each $S_{(k)}$.

▶ **27.** [*HM26*] (*Iterated spacings.*) In the notation of the previous exercise, show that the numbers $S_1' = nS_{(1)}$, $S_2' = (n-1)(S_{(2)} - S_{(1)})$, $\ldots$, $S_n' = 1(S_{(n)} - S_{(n-1)})$ have the same joint probability distribution as the original spacings S_1, $\ldots$, S_n of n uniform deviates. Therefore we can sort them into order, $S_{(1)}' \leq \cdots \leq S_{(n)}'$, and repeat this transformation to get yet another set of random spacings S_1'', $\ldots$, S_n'', etc. Each successive set of spacings $S_1^{(k)}$, $\ldots$, $S_n^{(k)}$ can be subjected to the Kolmogorov–Smirnov test, using

$$K_{n-1}^+ = \sqrt{n-1} \max_{1 \le j < n} \left(\frac{j}{n-1} - S_1^{(k)} - \cdots - S_j^{(k)} \right),$$

$$K_{n-1}^- = \sqrt{n-1} \max_{1 \le j < n} \left(S_1^{(k)} + \cdots + S_j^{(k)} - \frac{j-1}{n-1} \right).$$

Examine the transformation from $(S_1, \ldots, S_n)$ to $(S_1', \ldots, S_n')$ in detail in the cases $n = 2$ and $n = 3$; explain why continued repetition of this process will break down eventually when it is applied to computer-generated numbers with finite precision. (One way to compare random number generators is to see how long they can continue to survive such a torture test.)

28. [*M26*] Let $b_{nrs}(m)$ be the number of n-tuples $(y_1, \ldots, y_n)$ with $0 \le y_j < m$ that have exactly r equal spacings and s zero spacings. Thus, the probability that $R = r$ in the birthday spacings test is $\sum_{s=0}^{r+1} b_{nrs}(m)/m^n$. Also let $p_n(m)$ be the number of partitions of m into at most n parts (exercise 5.1.1–15). (a) Express $b_{n00}(m)$ in terms of partitions. [*Hint:* Consider cases with small m and n.] (b) Show that there is a simple relation between $b_{nrs}(m)$ and $b_{(n-s)(r+1-s)0}(m)$ when $s > 0$. (c) Deduce an explicit formula for the probability that no spacings are equal.

29. [*M35*] Continuing exercise 28, find simple expressions for the generating functions $b_{nr}(z) = \sum_{m \ge 0} b_{nr0}(m)z^m/m$, when $r = 0$, 1, and 2.

30. [*HM41*] Continuing the previous exercises, prove that if $m = n^3/\alpha$ we have

$$p_n(m) = \frac{m^{n-1}e^{\alpha/4}}{n!\,(n-1)!} \left(1 - \frac{13\alpha^2}{288n} + \frac{169\alpha^4 + 2016\alpha^3 - 1728\alpha^2 - 41472\alpha}{165888n^2} + O(n^{-3}) \right)$$

for fixed α as $n \to \infty$. Find a similar formula for $q_n(m)$, the number of partitions of m into n *distinct* positive parts. Deduce the asymptotic probabilities that the birthday spacings test finds R equal to 0, 1, and 2, to within $O(1/n)$.

▶ **31.** [*M21*] The recurrence $Y_n = (Y_{n-24} + Y_{n-55}) \bmod 2$, which describes the least significant bits of the lagged Fibonacci generator 3.2.2–(7) as well as the second-least significant bits of 3.2.2–(7'), is known to have period length $2^{55} - 1$; hence every possible nonzero pattern of bits $(Y_n, Y_{n+1}, \ldots, Y_{n+54})$ occurs equally often. Nevertheless, prove that if we generate 79 consecutive random bits $Y_n, \ldots, Y_{n+78}$ starting at a random point in the period, the probability is more than 51% that there are more 1s than 0s. If we use such bits to define a "random walk" that moves to the right when the bit is 1 and to the left when the bit is 0, we'll finish to the right of our starting point significantly more than half of the time. [*Hint:* Find the generating function $\sum_{k=0}^{79} \Pr(Y_n + \cdots + Y_{n+78} = k)\, z^k$.]

32. [*M20*] True or false: If X and Y are independent, identically distributed random variables with mean 0, and if they are more likely to be positive than negative, then $X + Y$ is more likely to be positive than negative.

33. [*HM32*] Find the asymptotic value of the probability that $k + l$ consecutive bits generated by the recurrence $Y_n = (Y_{n-l} + Y_{n-k}) \bmod 2$ have more 1s than 0s, when $k > 2l$ and the period length of this recurrence is $2^k - 1$, assuming that k is large.

34. [*HM29*] Explain how to estimate the mean and variance of the number of two-letter combinations that do not occur consecutively in a random string of length n on an m-letter alphabet. Assume that m is large and $n \approx 2m^2$.

▶ **35.** [*HM32*] (J. H. Lindholm, 1968.) Suppose we generate random bits $\langle Y_n \rangle$ using the recurrence

$$Y_n = (a_1 Y_{n-1} + a_2 Y_{n-2} + \cdots + a_k Y_{n-k}) \bmod 2,$$

for some choice of $a_1, \ldots, a_k$ such that the period length is $2^k - 1$; start with $Y_0 = 1$ and $Y_1 = \cdots = Y_{k-1} = 0$. Let $Z_n = (-1)^{Y_n+1} = 2Y_n - 1$ be a random sign, and consider the statistic $S_m = Z_n + Z_{n+1} + \cdots + Z_{n+m-1}$, where n is a random point in the period.

a) Prove that $\mathrm{E}\,S_m = m/N$, where $N = 2^k - 1$.

b) What is $\mathrm{E}\,S_m^2$? Assume that $m \leq N$. *Hint:* See exercise 3.2.2–16.

c) What would $\mathrm{E}\,S_m$ and $\mathrm{E}\,S_m^2$ be if the Z's were truly random?

d) Assuming that $m \leq N$, prove that $\mathrm{E}\,S_m^3 = m^3/N - 6B(N+1)/N$, where

$$B = \sum_{0 < i < j < m} \left[(Y_{i+1} Y_{i+2} \ldots Y_{i+k-1})_2 = (Y_{j+1} Y_{j+2} \ldots Y_{j+k-1})_2 \right] (m - j).$$

e) Evaluate B in the special case considered in exercise 31: $m = 79$ and $Y_n = (Y_{n-24} + Y_{n-55}) \bmod 2$.

*3.3.3. Theoretical Tests

Although it is always possible to test a random number generator using the methods in the previous section, it is far better to have *a priori* tests: theoretical results that tell us in advance how well those tests will come out. Such theoretical results give us much more understanding about the generation methods than empirical, trial-and-error results do. In this section we shall study the linear congruential sequences in more detail; if we know what the results of certain tests will be before we actually generate the numbers, we have a better chance of choosing a, m, and c properly.

The development of this kind of theory is quite difficult, although some progress has been made. The results obtained so far are generally for *statistical tests made over the entire period*. Not all statistical tests make sense when they are applied over a full period — for example, the equidistribution test will give results that are too perfect — but the serial test, gap test, permutation test, maximum test, etc., can be fruitfully analyzed in this way. Such studies will detect *global* nonrandomness of a sequence, that is, improper behavior in very large samples.

The theory we shall discuss is quite illuminating, but it does not eliminate the need for testing local nonrandomness by the methods of Section 3.3.2. Indeed, the task of proving anything useful about short subsequences appears to be very hard. Only a few theoretical results are known about the behavior of linear congruential sequences over less than a full period; they will be discussed at the end of Section 3.3.4. (See also exercise 18.)

Let us begin with a proof of a simple *a priori* law, for the least complicated case of the permutation test. The gist of our first theorem is that we have $X_{n+1} < X_n$ about half the time, provided that the sequence has high potency.

Theorem P. *Let a, c, and m generate a linear congruential sequence with maximum period; let $b = a - 1$ and let d be the greatest common divisor of m and b. The probability that $X_{n+1} < X_n$ is equal to $\frac{1}{2} + r$, where*

$$r = \big(2(c \bmod d) - d\big)/2m; \tag{1}$$

hence $|r| < d/2m$.

Proof. The proof of this theorem involves some techniques that are of interest in themselves. First we define

$$s(x) = (ax + c) \bmod m. \tag{2}$$

Thus, $X_{n+1} = s(X_n)$, and the theorem reduces to counting the number of integers x such that $0 \le x < m$ and $s(x) < x$, since every such integer occurs somewhere in the period. We want to show that this number is

$$\tfrac{1}{2}\big(m + 2(c \bmod d) - d\big). \tag{3}$$

The function $\lceil (x - s(x))/m \rceil$ is equal to 1 when $x > s(x)$, and it is 0 otherwise; hence the count we wish to obtain can be written simply as

$$\sum_{0 \le x < m} \left\lceil \frac{x - s(x)}{m} \right\rceil = \sum_{0 \le x < m} \left\lceil \frac{x}{m} - \left(\frac{ax + c}{m} - \left\lfloor \frac{ax + c}{m} \right\rfloor \right) \right\rceil$$

$$= \sum_{0 \le x < m} \left(\left\lfloor \frac{ax + c}{m} \right\rfloor - \left\lfloor \frac{bx + c}{m} \right\rfloor \right). \tag{4}$$

(Recall that $\lceil -y \rceil = -\lfloor y \rfloor$ and $b = a - 1$.) Such sums can be evaluated by the method of exercise 1.2.4–37, where we have proved that

$$\sum_{0 \le j < k} \left\lfloor \frac{hj + c}{k} \right\rfloor = \frac{(h-1)(k-1)}{2} + \frac{g-1}{2} + g\lfloor c/g \rfloor, \qquad g = \gcd(h, k), \tag{5}$$

whenever h and k are integers and $k > 0$. Since a is relatively prime to m, this formula yields

$$\sum_{0 \le x < m} \left\lfloor \frac{ax + c}{m} \right\rfloor = \frac{(a-1)(m-1)}{2} + c,$$

$$\sum_{0 \le x < m} \left\lfloor \frac{bx + c}{m} \right\rfloor = \frac{(b-1)(m-1)}{2} + \frac{d-1}{2} + c - (c \bmod d),$$

and (3) follows immediately. ∎

The proof of Theorem P indicates that *a priori* tests can indeed be carried out, provided that we are able to deal satisfactorily with sums involving the $\lfloor\ \rfloor$ and $\lceil\ \rceil$ functions. In many cases the most powerful technique for dealing with floor and ceiling functions is to replace them by two somewhat more symmetrical operations:

$$\delta(x) = \lfloor x \rfloor + 1 - \lceil x \rceil = [x \text{ is an integer}]; \tag{6}$$

$$((x)) = x - \lfloor x \rfloor - \tfrac{1}{2} + \tfrac{1}{2}\delta(x) = x - \lceil x \rceil + \tfrac{1}{2} - \tfrac{1}{2}\delta(x) = x - \tfrac{1}{2}\big(\lfloor x \rfloor + \lceil x \rceil\big). \tag{7}$$

The latter function is a "sawtooth" function familiar in the study of Fourier series; its graph is shown in Fig. 7. The reason for choosing to work with $((x))$ rather than $\lfloor x \rfloor$ or $\lceil x \rceil$ is that $((x))$ possesses several very useful properties:

$$((-x)) = -((x)); \tag{8}$$

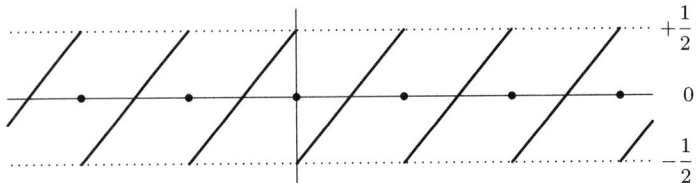

Fig. 7. The sawtooth function $((x))$.

$$((x+n)) = ((x)), \quad \text{integer } n; \tag{9}$$

$$((nx)) = ((x)) + \left(\left(x + \frac{1}{n}\right)\right) + \cdots + \left(\left(x + \frac{n-1}{n}\right)\right), \quad \text{integer } n \geq 1. \tag{10}$$

(See exercises 1.2.4–38 and 1.2.4–39(a,b,g).)

In order to get some practice working with these functions, let us prove Theorem P again, this time without relying on exercise 1.2.4–37. With the help of Eqs. (7), (8), (9), we can show that

$$\left\lceil \frac{x - s(x)}{m} \right\rceil = \frac{x - s(x)}{m} - \left(\left(\frac{x - s(x)}{m}\right)\right) + \frac{1}{2} - \frac{1}{2}\delta\left(\frac{x - s(x)}{m}\right)$$

$$= \frac{x - s(x)}{m} - \left(\left(\frac{x - (ax + c)}{m}\right)\right) + \frac{1}{2}$$

$$= \frac{x - s(x)}{m} + \left(\left(\frac{bx + c}{m}\right)\right) + \frac{1}{2} \tag{11}$$

since $\big(x - s(x)\big)/m$ is never an integer. Now

$$\sum_{0 \leq x < m} \frac{x - s(x)}{m} = 0$$

since both x and $s(x)$ take on each value of $\{0, 1, \ldots, m-1\}$ exactly once; hence (11) yields

$$\sum_{0 \leq x < m} \left\lceil \frac{x - s(x)}{m} \right\rceil = \sum_{0 \leq x < m} \left(\left(\frac{bx + c}{m}\right)\right) + \frac{m}{2}. \tag{12}$$

Let $b = b_0 d$, $m = m_0 d$, where b_0 and m_0 are relatively prime. We know that $(b_0 x) \bmod m_0$ takes on the values $\{0, 1, \ldots, m_0 - 1\}$ in some order as x varies from 0 to $m_0 - 1$. By (9) and (10) and the fact that

$$\left(\left(\frac{b(x + m_0) + c}{m}\right)\right) = \left(\left(\frac{bx + c}{m}\right)\right)$$

we have

$$\sum_{0 \leq x < m} \left(\left(\frac{bx + c}{m}\right)\right) = d \sum_{0 \leq x < m_0} \left(\left(\frac{bx + c}{m}\right)\right)$$

$$= d \sum_{0 \le x < m_0} \left(\left(\frac{c}{m} + \frac{b_0 x}{m_0} \right) \right) = d \left(\left(\frac{c}{d} \right) \right). \qquad (13)$$

Theorem P follows immediately from (12) and (13).

One consequence of Theorem P is that practically *any* choice of a and c will give a reasonable probability that $X_{n+1} < X_n$, at least over the entire period, except those that have large d. A large value of d corresponds to low potency, and we already know that generators of low potency are undesirable.

The next theorem gives us a more stringent condition for the choice of the parameters a and c; we will consider the *serial correlation test* applied over the entire period. The quantity C defined in Section 3.3.2, Eq. (23), is

$$C = \left(m \sum_{0 \le x < m} x s(x) - \left(\sum_{0 \le x < m} x \right)^2 \right) \Big/ \left(m \sum_{0 \le x < m} x^2 - \left(\sum_{0 \le x < m} x \right)^2 \right). \quad (14)$$

Let x' be the element such that $s(x') = 0$. We have

$$s(x) = m \left(\left(\frac{ax + c}{m} \right) \right) + \frac{m}{2} [x \ne x']. \qquad (15)$$

The formulas we are about to derive can be expressed most easily in terms of the sum

$$\sigma(h, k, c) = 12 \sum_{0 \le j < k} \left(\left(\frac{j}{k} \right) \right) \left(\left(\frac{hj + c}{k} \right) \right), \qquad (16)$$

an important function that arises in several mathematical problems. It is called a *generalized Dedekind sum*, since Richard Dedekind introduced the function $\sigma(h, k, 0)$ in 1876 when commenting on one of Riemann's incomplete manuscripts. [See B. Riemann's *Gesammelte math. Werke*, 2nd ed. (1892), 466–478.]

Using the well-known formulas

$$\sum_{0 \le x < m} x = \frac{m(m-1)}{2} \quad \text{and} \quad \sum_{0 \le x < m} x^2 = \frac{m(m - \frac{1}{2})(m-1)}{3},$$

it is a straightforward matter to transform Eq. (14) into

$$C = \frac{m\sigma(a, m, c) - 3 + 6(m - x' - c)}{m^2 - 1}. \qquad (17)$$

(See exercise 5.) Since m is usually very large, we may discard terms of order $1/m$, and we have the approximation

$$C \approx \sigma(a, m, c)/m, \qquad (18)$$

with an error of less than $6/m$ in absolute value.

The serial correlation test now reduces to determining the value of the Dedekind sum $\sigma(a, m, c)$. Evaluating $\sigma(a, m, c)$ directly from its definition (16) is hardly any easier than evaluating the correlation coefficient itself directly, but fortunately there are simple methods available for computing Dedekind sums quite rapidly.

Lemma B (*"Reciprocity law" for Dedekind sums*). *Let h, k, c be integers. If $0 \le c < k$, $0 < h \le k$, and if h is relatively prime to k, then*

$$\sigma(h,k,c) + \sigma(k,h,c) = \frac{h}{k} + \frac{k}{h} + \frac{1}{hk} + \frac{6c^2}{hk} - 6\left\lfloor \frac{c}{h} \right\rfloor - 3e(h,c), \qquad (19)$$

where

$$e(h,c) = [c=0] + [c \bmod h \ne 0]. \qquad (20)$$

Proof. We leave it to the reader to prove that, under these hypotheses,

$$\sigma(h,k,c) + \sigma(k,h,c) = \sigma(h,k,0) + \sigma(k,h,0) + \frac{6c^2}{hk} - 6\left\lfloor \frac{c}{h} \right\rfloor - 3e(h,c) + 3. \quad (21)$$

(See exercise 6.) The lemma now must be proved only in the case $c = 0$.

The proof we will give, based on complex roots of unity, is essentially due to L. Carlitz. There is actually a simpler proof that uses only elementary manipulations of sums (see exercise 7) — but the following method reveals more of the mathematical tools that are available for problems of this kind and it is therefore much more instructive.

Let $f(x)$ and $g(x)$ be polynomials defined as follows:

$$\begin{aligned} f(x) &= 1 + x + \cdots + x^{k-1} = (x^k - 1)/(x - 1) \\ g(x) &= x + 2x^2 + \cdots + (k-1)x^{k-1} \\ &= xf'(x) = kx^k/(x-1) - x(x^k-1)/(x-1)^2. \end{aligned} \qquad (22)$$

If ω is the complex kth root of unity $e^{2\pi i/k}$, we have by Eq. 1.2.9–(13)

$$\frac{1}{k} \sum_{0 \le j < k} \omega^{-jr} g(\omega^j x) = rx^r, \qquad \text{if } 0 \le r < k. \qquad (23)$$

Set $x = 1$; then $g(\omega^j x) = k/(\omega^j - 1)$ if $j \ne 0$, otherwise it equals $k(k-1)/2$. Therefore

$$r \bmod k = \sum_{0 < j < k} \frac{\omega^{-jr}}{\omega^j - 1} + \tfrac{1}{2}(k-1), \qquad \text{if } r \text{ is an integer.}$$

(Eq. (23) shows that the right-hand side equals r when $0 \le r < k$, and it is unchanged when multiples of k are added to r.) Hence

$$\left(\!\left(\frac{r}{k}\right)\!\right) = \frac{1}{k} \sum_{0 < j < k} \frac{\omega^{-jr}}{\omega^j - 1} - \frac{1}{2k} + \frac{1}{2}\delta\!\left(\frac{r}{k}\right). \qquad (24)$$

This important formula, which holds whenever r is an integer, allows us to reduce many calculations involving $((r/k))$ to sums involving kth roots of unity, and it brings a whole new range of techniques into the picture. In particular, we get the following formula when $h \perp k$:

$$\sigma(h,k,0) + \frac{3(k-1)}{k^2} = \frac{12}{k^2} \sum_{0 < r < k} \sum_{0 < i < k} \sum_{0 < j < k} \frac{\omega^{-ir}}{\omega^i - 1} \frac{\omega^{-jhr}}{\omega^j - 1}. \qquad (25)$$

The right-hand side of this formula may be simplified by carrying out the sum on r; we have $\sum_{0 \le r < k} \omega^{rs} = f(\omega^s) = 0$ if $s \bmod k \ne 0$. Equation (25) now reduces to

$$\sigma(h, k, 0) + \frac{3(k-1)}{k} = \frac{12}{k} \sum_{0 < j < k} \frac{1}{(\omega^{-jh} - 1)(\omega^j - 1)}. \tag{26}$$

A similar formula is obtained for $\sigma(k, h, 0)$, with $\zeta = e^{2\pi i/h}$ replacing ω.

It is not obvious what we can do with the sum in (26), but there is an elegant way to proceed, based on the fact that each term of the sum is a function of ω^j, where $0 < j < k$; hence the sum is essentially taken over the kth roots of unity other than 1. Whenever $x_1, x_2, \ldots, x_n$ are distinct complex numbers, we have the identity

$$\sum_{j=1}^{n} \frac{1}{(x_j - x_1) \ldots (x_j - x_{j-1})(x - x_j)(x_j - x_{j+1}) \ldots (x_j - x_n)}$$
$$= \frac{1}{(x - x_1) \ldots (x - x_n)}, \tag{27}$$

which follows from the usual method of expanding the right-hand side into partial fractions. Moreover, if $q(x) = (x - y_1)(x - y_2) \ldots (x - y_m)$, we have

$$q'(y_j) = (y_j - y_1) \ldots (y_j - y_{j-1})(y_j - y_{j+1}) \ldots (y_j - y_m); \tag{28}$$

this identity may often be used to simplify expressions like those in the left-hand side of (27). When h and k are relatively prime, the numbers $\omega, \omega^2, \ldots, \omega^{k-1}, \zeta, \zeta^2, \ldots, \zeta^{h-1}$ are all distinct; we can therefore consider formula (27) in the special case of the polynomial $(x - \omega) \ldots (x - \omega^{k-1})(x - \zeta) \ldots (x - \zeta^{h-1}) = (x^k - 1)(x^h - 1)/(x - 1)^2$, obtaining the following identity in x:

$$\frac{1}{h} \sum_{0 < j < h} \frac{\zeta^j(\zeta^j - 1)^2}{(\zeta^{jk} - 1)(x - \zeta^j)} + \frac{1}{k} \sum_{0 < j < k} \frac{\omega^j(\omega^j - 1)^2}{(\omega^{jh} - 1)(x - \omega^j)} = \frac{(x-1)^2}{(x^h - 1)(x^k - 1)}. \tag{29}$$

This identity has many interesting consequences, and it leads to numerous reciprocity formulas for sums of the type given in Eq. (26). For example, if we differentiate (29) twice with respect to x and let $x \to 1$, we find that

$$\frac{2}{h} \sum_{0 < j < h} \frac{\zeta^j(\zeta^j - 1)^2}{(\zeta^{jk} - 1)(1 - \zeta^j)^3} + \frac{2}{k} \sum_{0 < j < k} \frac{\omega^j(\omega^j - 1)^2}{(\omega^{jh} - 1)(1 - \omega^j)^3}$$
$$= \frac{1}{6}\left(\frac{h}{k} + \frac{k}{h} + \frac{1}{hk}\right) + \frac{1}{2} - \frac{1}{2h} - \frac{1}{2k}.$$

Replace j by $h - j$ and by $k - j$ in these sums and use (26) to get

$$\frac{1}{6}\left(\sigma(k, h, 0) + \frac{3(h-1)}{h}\right) + \frac{1}{6}\left(\sigma(h, k, 0) + \frac{3(k-1)}{k}\right)$$
$$= \frac{1}{6}\left(\frac{h}{k} + \frac{k}{h} + \frac{1}{hk}\right) + \frac{1}{2} - \frac{1}{2h} - \frac{1}{2k},$$

which is equivalent to the desired result. ∎

Lemma B gives us an explicit function $f(h, k, c)$ such that

$$\sigma(h, k, c) = f(h, k, c) - \sigma(k, h, c) \tag{30}$$

whenever $0 < h \le k$, $0 \le c < k$, and h is relatively prime to k. From the definition (16) it is clear that

$$\sigma(k, h, c) = \sigma(k \bmod h, h, c \bmod h). \tag{31}$$

Therefore we can use (30) iteratively to evaluate $\sigma(h, k, c)$, using a process that reduces the parameters as in Euclid's algorithm.

Further simplifications occur when we examine this iterative procedure more closely. Let us set $m_1 = k$, $m_2 = h$, $c_1 = c$, and form the following tableau:

$$
\begin{aligned}
m_1 &= a_1 m_2 + m_3 & c_1 &= b_1 m_2 + c_2 \\
m_2 &= a_2 m_3 + m_4 & c_2 &= b_2 m_3 + c_3 \\
m_3 &= a_3 m_4 + m_5 & c_3 &= b_3 m_4 + c_4 \\
m_4 &= a_4 m_5 & c_4 &= b_4 m_5 + c_5
\end{aligned}
\tag{32}
$$

Here

$$
\begin{aligned}
a_j &= \lfloor m_j / m_{j+1} \rfloor, & b_j &= \lfloor c_j / m_{j+1} \rfloor, \\
m_{j+2} &= m_j \bmod m_{j+1}, & c_{j+1} &= c_j \bmod m_{j+1},
\end{aligned}
\tag{33}
$$

and it follows that

$$0 \le m_{j+1} < m_j, \qquad 0 \le c_j < m_j. \tag{34}$$

We have assumed for convenience that Euclid's algorithm terminates in (32) after four iterations; this assumption will reveal the pattern that holds in the general case. Since h and k were relatively prime to start with, we must have $m_5 = 1$ and $c_5 = 0$ in (32).

Let us assume also that $c_3 \ne 0$ but $c_4 = 0$, in order to get a feeling for the effect this has on the recurrence. Equations (30) and (31) yield

$$
\begin{aligned}
\sigma(h, k, c) &= \sigma(m_2, m_1, c_1) \\
&= f(m_2, m_1, c_1) - \sigma(m_3, m_2, c_2) \\
&= \cdots \\
&= f(m_2, m_1, c_1) - f(m_3, m_2, c_2) + f(m_4, m_3, c_3) - f(m_5, m_4, c_4).
\end{aligned}
$$

The first part, $h/k + k/h$, of the formula for $f(h, k, c)$ in (19) contributes

$$\frac{m_2}{m_1} + \frac{m_1}{m_2} - \frac{m_3}{m_2} - \frac{m_2}{m_3} + \frac{m_4}{m_3} + \frac{m_3}{m_4} - \frac{m_5}{m_4} - \frac{m_4}{m_5}$$

to the total, and this simplifies to

$$\frac{h}{k} + \frac{m_1 - m_3}{m_2} - \frac{m_2 - m_4}{m_3} + \frac{m_3 - m_5}{m_4} - \frac{m_4}{m_5} = \frac{h}{k} + a_1 - a_2 + a_3 - a_4.$$

The next part of (19), $1/hk$, also leads to a simple contribution; according to Eq. 4.5.3–(9) and other formulas in Section 4.5.3, we have

$$\frac{1}{m_1 m_2} - \frac{1}{m_2 m_3} + \frac{1}{m_3 m_4} - \frac{1}{m_4 m_5} = \frac{h'}{k} - 1, \tag{35}$$

where h' is the unique integer satisfying

$$h'h \equiv 1 \pmod{k}, \quad 0 < h' \le k. \tag{36}$$

Adding up all the contributions, and remembering our assumption that $c_4 = 0$ (so that $e(m_4, c_3) = 0$, see (20)), we find that

$$\sigma(h, k, c) = \frac{h + h'}{k} + (a_1 - a_2 + a_3 - a_4) - 6(b_1 - b_2 + b_3 - b_4)$$

$$+ 6 \left(\frac{c_1^2}{m_1 m_2} - \frac{c_2^2}{m_2 m_3} + \frac{c_3^2}{m_3 m_4} - \frac{c_4^2}{m_4 m_5} \right) + 2,$$

in terms of the assumed tableau (32). Similar results hold in general:

Theorem D. *Let h, k, c be integers with $0 < h \le k$, $0 \le c < k$, and h relatively prime to k. Form the "Euclidean tableau" as defined in (33) above, and assume that the process stops after t steps with $m_{t+1} = 1$. Let s be the smallest subscript such that $c_s = 0$, and let h' be defined by (36). Then*

$$\sigma(h, k, c) = \frac{h + h'}{k} + \sum_{1 \le j \le t} (-1)^{j+1} \left(a_j - 6b_j + 6\frac{c_j^2}{m_j m_{j+1}} \right)$$

$$+ 3\big((-1)^s + \delta_{s1}\big) - 2 + (-1)^t. \quad \blacksquare$$

Euclid's algorithm is analyzed carefully in Section 4.5.3; the quantities a_1, $a_2, \ldots, a_t$ are called the *partial quotients* of h/k. Theorem 4.5.3F tells us that the number of iterations, t, will never exceed $\log_\phi k$; hence Dedekind sums can be evaluated rapidly. The terms $c_j^2/m_j m_{j+1}$ can be simplified further, and an efficient algorithm for evaluating $\sigma(h, k, c)$ appears in exercise 17.

Now that we have analyzed generalized Dedekind sums, let us apply our knowledge to the determination of serial correlation coefficients.

Example 1. *Find the serial correlation when $m = 2^{35}$, $a = 2^{34} + 1$, $c = 1$.*

Solution. We have

$$C = \big(2^{35}\sigma(2^{34} + 1, 2^{35}, 1) - 3 + 6(2^{35} - (2^{34} - 1) - 1)\big)/(2^{70} - 1),$$

by Eq. (17). To evaluate $\sigma(2^{34} + 1, 2^{35}, 1)$, we can form the tableau

$m_1 = 2^{35}$		$c_1 = 1$	
$m_2 = 2^{34} + 1$	$a_1 = 1$	$c_2 = 1$	$b_1 = 0$
$m_3 = 2^{34} - 1$	$a_2 = 1$	$c_3 = 1$	$b_2 = 0$
$m_4 = 2$	$a_3 = 2^{33} - 1$	$c_4 = 1$	$b_3 = 0$
$m_5 = 1$	$a_4 = 2$	$c_5 = 0$	$b_4 = 1$

Since $h' = 2^{34} + 1$, the value according to Theorem D comes to $2^{33} - 3 + 2^{-32}$. Thus

$$C = (2^{68} + 5)/(2^{70} - 1) = \tfrac{1}{4} + \epsilon, \quad |\epsilon| < 2^{-67}. \tag{37}$$

Such a correlation is much, much too high for randomness. Of course, this generator has very low potency, and we have already rejected it as nonrandom.

Example 2. *Find the approximate serial correlation when* $m = 10^{10}$, $a = 10001$, $c = 2113248653$.

Solution. We have $C \approx \sigma(a, m, c)/m$, and the computation proceeds as follows:

$m_1 = 10000000000$			$c_1 = 2113248653$		
$m_2 =$	10001	$a_1 = 999900$	$c_2 =$	7350	$b_1 = 211303$
$m_3 =$	100	$a_2 =$ 100	$c_3 =$	50	$b_2 =$ 73
$m_4 =$	1	$a_3 =$ 100	$c_4 =$	0	$b_3 =$ 50

$$\sigma(m_2, m_1, c_1) = -31.6926653544; \qquad C \approx -3 \cdot 10^{-9}. \tag{38}$$

This is a very respectable value of C indeed. But the generator has a potency of only 3, *so it is not really a very good source of random numbers in spite of the fact that it has low serial correlation.* It is necessary to have a low serial correlation, but not sufficient.

Example 3. *Estimate the serial correlation for general* a, m, *and* c.

Solution. If we consider just one application of (30), we have

$$\sigma(a, m, c) \approx \frac{m}{a} + 6\frac{c^2}{am} - 6\frac{c}{a} - \sigma(m, a, c).$$

Now $|\sigma(m, a, c)| < a$ by exercise 12, and therefore

$$C \approx \frac{\sigma(a, m, c)}{m} \approx \frac{1}{a}\left(1 - 6\frac{c}{m} + 6\left(\frac{c}{m}\right)^2\right). \tag{39}$$

The error in this approximation is less than $(a + 6)/m$ in absolute value.

The estimate in (39) was the first theoretical result known about the randomness of congruential generators. R. R. Coveyou [*JACM* **7** (1960), 72–74] obtained it by averaging over all *real* numbers x between 0 and m instead of considering only the integer values (see exercise 21); then Martin Greenberger [*Math. Comp.* **15** (1961), 383–389] gave a rigorous derivation including an estimate of the error term.

So began one of the saddest chapters in the history of computer science! Although the approximation above is quite correct, it has been grievously misapplied in practice; people abandoned the perfectly good generators they had been using and replaced them by terrible generators that looked good from the standpoint of (39). For more than a decade, the most common random number generators in daily use were seriously deficient, solely because of a theoretical advance.

> *A little Learning is a dang'rous Thing.*
> — ALEXANDER POPE, *An Essay on Criticism*, 215 (1711)

If we are to learn by past mistakes, we had better look carefully at how (39) has been misused. In the first place people assumed uncritically that a small serial correlation over the whole period would be a pretty good guarantee of randomness; but in fact it doesn't even ensure a small serial correlation for 1000 consecutive elements of the sequence (see exercise 14).

Secondly, (39) and its error term will ensure a relatively small value of C only when $a \approx \sqrt{m}$; therefore people suggested choosing multipliers near $\sqrt{m}$. In fact, we shall see that nearly all multipliers give a value of C that is substantially less than $1/\sqrt{m}$, hence (39) is not a very good approximation to the true behavior. Minimizing a crude upper bound for C does not minimize C.

In the third place, people observed that (39) yields its best estimate when

$$c/m \approx \tfrac{1}{2} \pm \tfrac{1}{6}\sqrt{3}, \tag{40}$$

since these values are the roots of $1 - 6x + 6x^2 = 0$. "In the absence of any other criterion for choosing c, we might as well use this one." The latter statement is not incorrect, but it is misleading at best, since experience has shown that the value of c has hardly any influence on the true value of the serial correlation when a is a good multiplier; the choice (40) reduces C substantially only in cases like Example 2 above. And we are fooling ourselves in such cases, since the bad multiplier will reveal its deficiencies in other ways.

Clearly we need a better estimate than (39); and such an estimate is now available thanks to Theorem D, which stems principally from the work of Ulrich Dieter [*Math. Comp.* **25** (1971), 855–883]. Theorem D implies that $\sigma(a, m, c)$ *will be small if the partial quotients of a/m are small.* Indeed, by analyzing generalized Dedekind sums still more closely, it is possible to obtain quite a sharp estimate:

Theorem K. *Under the assumptions of Theorem D, we always have*

$$-\frac{1}{2} \sum_{\substack{1 \le j \le t \\ j \text{ odd}}} a_j - \sum_{\substack{1 \le j \le t \\ j \text{ even}}} a_j \le \sigma(h, k, c) \le \sum_{\substack{1 \le j \le t \\ j \text{ odd}}} a_j + \frac{1}{2} \sum_{\substack{1 \le j \le t \\ j \text{ even}}} a_j - \frac{1}{2}. \tag{41}$$

Proof. See D. E. Knuth, *Acta Arithmetica* **33** (1977), 297–325, where it is shown further that these bounds are essentially the best possible when large partial quotients are present. ∎

Example 4. *Estimate the serial correlation for* $a = 3141592621$, $m = 2^{35}$, *c odd.*

Solution. The partial quotients of a/m are 10, 1, 14, 1, 7, 1, 1, 1, 3, 3, 3, 5, 2, 1, 8, 7, 1, 4, 1, 2, 4, 2; hence by Theorem K

$$-55 \le \sigma(a, m, c) \le 67.5,$$

and the serial correlation is guaranteed to be extremely low for all c.

Note that this bound is considerably better than we could obtain from (39), since the error in (39) is of order a/m; our "random" multiplier has turned out to be much better than one specifically chosen to look good on the basis of (39). In fact, it is possible to show that the *average* value of $\sum_{j=1}^{t} a_j$, taken over all multipliers a relatively prime to m, is

$$\frac{6}{\pi^2}(\ln m)^2 + O\big((\log m)(\log\log m)^4\big)$$

(see exercise 4.5.3–35). Therefore the probability that a random multiplier has large $\sum_{j=1}^{t} a_j$, say larger than $(\log m)^{2+\epsilon}$ for some fixed $\epsilon > 0$, approaches zero as $m \to \infty$. This substantiates the empirical evidence that almost all linear congruential sequences have extremely low serial correlation over the entire period.

The exercises below show that other *a priori* tests, such as the serial test over the entire period, can also be expressed in terms of a few generalized Dedekind sums. It follows from Theorem K that linear congruential sequences will pass those tests provided that certain specified fractions (depending on a and m but not on c) have small partial quotients. In particular, the result of exercise 19 implies that *the serial test on pairs will be passed satisfactorily if and only if a/m has no large partial quotients.*

The book *Dedekind Sums* by Hans Rademacher and Emil Grosswald (Math. Assoc. of America, Carus Monograph No. 16, 1972) discusses the history and properties of Dedekind sums and their generalizations. Further theoretical tests, including the serial test in higher dimensions, are discussed in Section 3.3.4.

EXERCISES — First Set

1. [*M10*] Express $x \bmod y$ in terms of the sawtooth and δ functions.

2. [*HM22*] What is the Fourier series expansion (in terms of sines and cosines) of the function $((x))$?

3. [*M23*] (N. J. Fine.) Prove that $|\sum_{k=0}^{n-1}((2^k x + \frac{1}{2}))| < 1$ for all real numbers x.

▶ **4.** [*M19*] If $m = 10^{10}$, what is the highest possible value of d (in the notation of Theorem P), given that the potency of the generator is 10?

5. [*M21*] Carry out the derivation of Eq. (17).

6. [*M27*] Assume that $hh' + kk' = 1$.

a) Show, without using Lemma B, that

$$\sigma(h,k,c) = \sigma(h,k,0) + 12\sum_{0<j<c}\left(\left(\frac{h'j}{k}\right)\right) + 6\left(\left(\frac{h'c}{k}\right)\right)$$

for all integers $c \geq 0$.

b) Show that $\left(\left(\frac{h'j}{k}\right)\right) + \left(\left(\frac{k'j}{h}\right)\right) = \frac{j}{hk} - \frac{1}{2}\delta\left(\frac{j}{h}\right)$ if $0 < j < k$.

c) Under the assumptions of Lemma B, prove Eq. (21).

▶ **7.** [*M24*] Give a proof of the reciprocity law (19), when $c = 0$, by using the general reciprocity law of exercise 1.2.4–45.

▶ **8.** [*M34*] (L. Carlitz.) Let

$$\rho(p,q,r) = 12\sum_{0\leq j<r}\left(\left(\frac{jp}{r}\right)\right)\left(\left(\frac{jq}{r}\right)\right).$$

By generalizing the method of proof used in Lemma B, prove the following beautiful identity due to H. Rademacher: If each of p, q, r is relatively prime to the other two,

$$\rho(p, q, r) + \rho(q, r, p) + \rho(r, p, q) = \frac{p}{qr} + \frac{q}{rp} + \frac{r}{pq} - 3.$$

(The reciprocity law for Dedekind sums, with $c = 0$, is the special case $r = 1$.)

9. [*M40*] Is there a simple proof of Rademacher's identity (exercise 8) along the lines of the proof in exercise 7 of a special case?

10. [*M20*] Show that when $0 < h < k$ it is possible to express $\sigma(k - h, k, c)$ and $\sigma(h, k, -c)$ easily in terms of $\sigma(h, k, c)$.

11. [*M30*] The formulas given in the text show us how to evaluate $\sigma(h, k, c)$ when h and k are relatively prime and c is an integer. For the general case, prove that

a) $\sigma(dh, dk, dc) = \sigma(h, k, c)$, for integer $d > 0$;

b) $\sigma(h, k, c + \theta) = \sigma(h, k, c) + 6((h'c/k))$, for integer c, real $0 < \theta < 1$, $h \perp k$, and $hh' \equiv 1$ (modulo k).

12. [*M24*] Show that if h is relatively prime to k and c is an integer, $|\sigma(h, k, c)| \le (k - 1)(k - 2)/k$.

13. [*M24*] Generalize Eq. (26) so that it gives an expression for $\sigma(h, k, c)$.

▶ **14.** [*M20*] The linear congruential generator that has $m = 2^{35}$, $a = 2^{18} + 1$, $c = 1$, was given the serial correlation test on three batches of 1000 consecutive numbers, and the result was a very high correlation, between 0.2 and 0.3, in each case. What is the serial correlation of this generator, taken over all 2^{35} numbers of the period?

15. [*M21*] Generalize Lemma B so that it applies to all *real* values of c, $0 \le c < k$.

16. [*M24*] Given the Euclidean tableau defined in (33), let $p_0 = 1$, $p_1 = a_1$, and $p_j = a_j p_{j-1} + p_{j-2}$ for $1 < j \le t$. Show that the complicated portion of the sum in Theorem D can be rewritten as follows, making it possible to avoid noninteger computations:

$$\sum_{1 \le j \le t} (-1)^{j+1} \frac{c_j^2}{m_j m_{j+1}} = \frac{1}{m_1} \sum_{1 \le j \le t} (-1)^{j+1} b_j (c_j + c_{j+1}) p_{j-1}.$$

[*Hint:* Prove that $\sum_{1 \le j \le r} (-1)^{j+1}/m_j m_{j+1} = (-1)^{r+1} p_{r-1}/m_1 m_{r+1}$ for $1 \le r \le t$.]

17. [*M22*] Design an algorithm that evaluates $\sigma(h, k, c)$ for integers h, k, c satisfying the hypotheses of Theorem D. Your algorithm should use only integer arithmetic (of unlimited precision), and it should produce the answer in the form $A + B/k$ where A and B are integers. (See exercise 16.) If possible, use only a finite number of variables for temporary storage, instead of maintaining arrays such as $a_1, a_2, \ldots, a_t$.

▶ **18.** [*M23*] (U. Dieter.) Given positive integers h, k, z, let

$$S(h, k, c, z) = \sum_{0 \le j < z} \left(\left(\frac{hj + c}{k} \right) \right).$$

Show that this sum can be evaluated in closed form, in terms of generalized Dedekind sums and the sawtooth function. [*Hint:* When $z \le k$, the quantity $\lfloor j/k \rfloor - \lfloor (j - z)/k \rfloor$ equals 1 for $0 \le j < z$, and it equals 0 for $z \le j < k$, so we can introduce this factor and sum over $0 \le j < k$.]

▶ **19.** [*M23*] Show that the *serial test* can be analyzed over the full period, in terms of generalized Dedekind sums, by finding a formula for the probability that $\alpha \leq X_n < \beta$ and $\alpha' \leq X_{n+1} < \beta'$ when α, β, α', β' are given integers with $0 \leq \alpha < \beta \leq m$ and $0 \leq \alpha' < \beta' \leq m$. [*Hint:* Consider the quantity $\lfloor (x-\alpha)/m \rfloor - \lfloor (x-\beta)/m \rfloor$.]

20. [*M29*] (U. Dieter.) Extend Theorem P by obtaining a formula for the probability that $X_n > X_{n+1} > X_{n+2}$, in terms of generalized Dedekind sums.

EXERCISES — Second Set

In many cases, exact computations with integers are quite difficult to carry out, but we can attempt to study the probabilities that arise when we take the average over all real values of x instead of restricting the calculation to integer values. Although these results are only approximate, they shed some light on the subject.

It is convenient to deal with numbers U_n between zero and one; for linear congruential sequences, $U_n = X_n/m$, and we have $U_{n+1} = \{aU_n + \theta\}$, where $\theta = c/m$ and $\{x\}$ denotes x mod 1. For example, the formula for serial correlation now becomes

$$ C = \left(\int_0^1 x\{ax + \theta\}\, dx - \left(\int_0^1 x\, dx \right)^2 \right) \Big/ \left(\int_0^1 x^2\, dx - \left(\int_0^1 x\, dx \right)^2 \right). $$

▶ **21.** [*HM23*] (R. R. Coveyou.) What is the value of C in the formula just given?

▶ **22.** [*M22*] Let a be an integer, and let $0 \leq \theta < 1$. If x is a random real number, uniformly distributed between 0 and 1, and if $s(x) = \{ax + \theta\}$, what is the probability that $s(x) < x$? (This is the "real number" analog of Theorem P.)

23. [*M28*] The previous exercise gives the probability that $U_{n+1} < U_n$. What is the probability that $U_{n+2} < U_{n+1} < U_n$, assuming that U_n is a random real number between zero and one?

24. [*M29*] Under the assumptions of the preceding problem, except with $\theta = 0$, show that $U_n > U_{n+1} > \cdots > U_{n+t-1}$ occurs with probability

$$ \frac{1}{t!} \left(1 + \frac{1}{a} \right) \cdots \left(1 + \frac{t-2}{a} \right). $$

What is the average length of a descending run starting at U_n, assuming that U_n is selected at random between zero and one?

▶ **25.** [*M25*] Let α, β, α', β' be real numbers with $0 \leq \alpha < \beta \leq 1$, $0 \leq \alpha' < \beta' \leq 1$. Under the assumptions of exercise 22, what is the probability that $\alpha \leq x < \beta$ and $\alpha' \leq s(x) < \beta'$? (This is the "real number" analog of exercise 19.)

26. [*M21*] Consider a "Fibonacci" generator, where $U_{n+1} = \{U_n + U_{n-1}\}$. Assuming that U_1 and U_2 are independently chosen at random between 0 and 1, find the probability that $U_1 < U_2 < U_3$, $U_1 < U_3 < U_2$, $U_2 < U_1 < U_3$, etc. [*Hint:* Divide the unit square $\{(x,y) \mid 0 \leq x, y < 1\}$ into six parts, depending on the relative order of x, y, and $\{x+y\}$, and determine the area of each part.]

27. [*M32*] In the Fibonacci generator of the preceding exercise, let U_0 and U_1 be chosen independently in the unit square except that $U_0 > U_1$. Determine the probability that U_1 is the beginning of an upward run of length k, so that $U_0 > U_1 < \cdots < U_k > U_{k+1}$. Compare this with the corresponding probabilities for a random sequence.

28. [*M35*] According to Eq. 3.2.1.3–(5), a linear congruential generator with potency 2 satisfies the condition $X_{n-1} - 2X_n + X_{n+1} \equiv (a-1)c \pmod{m}$. Consider a generator

that abstracts this situation: Let $U_{n+1} = \{\alpha + 2U_n - U_{n-1}\}$. As in exercise 26, divide
the unit square into parts that show the relative order of U_1, U_2, and U_3 for each pair
(U_1, U_2). Are there any values of α for which all six possible orders are achieved with
probability $\frac{1}{6}$, assuming that U_1 and U_2 are chosen at random in the unit square?

3.3.4. The Spectral Test

In this section we shall study an especially important way to check the quality of
linear congruential random number generators. Not only do all good generators
pass this test, all generators now known to be bad actually *fail* it. Thus it
is by far the most powerful test known, and it deserves particular attention.
Our discussion will also bring out some fundamental limitations on the degree
of randomness that we can expect from linear congruential sequences and their
generalizations.

The spectral test embodies aspects of both the empirical and theoretical
tests studied in previous sections: It is like the theoretical tests because it deals
with properties of the full period of the sequence, and it is like the empirical
tests because it requires a computer program to determine the results.

A. Ideas underlying the test. The most important randomness criteria seem
to rely on properties of the joint distribution of t consecutive elements of the
sequence, and the spectral test deals directly with this distribution. If we have
a sequence $\langle U_n \rangle$ of period m, the basic idea is to analyze the set of all m points

$$\{\,(U_n, U_{n+1}, \ldots, U_{n+t-1}) \mid 0 \le n < m\,\} \tag{1}$$

in t-dimensional space.

For simplicity we shall assume that we have a linear congruential sequence
(X_0, a, c, m) of maximum period length m (so that $c \ne 0$), or that m is prime
and $c = 0$ and the period length is $m - 1$. In the latter case we shall add the
point $(0, 0, \ldots, 0)$ to the set (1), so that there are always m points in all; this
extra point has a negligible effect when m is large, and it makes the theory much
simpler. Under these assumptions, (1) can be rewritten as

$$\left\{\frac{1}{m}\bigl(x, s(x), s(s(x)), \ldots, s^{[t-1]}(x)\bigr) \,\middle|\, 0 \le x < m\right\}, \tag{2}$$

where

$$s(x) = (ax + c) \bmod m \tag{3}$$

is the successor of x. We are considering only the set of all such points in t
dimensions, not the order in which those points are actually generated. But the
order of generation is reflected in the dependence between components of the
vectors; and the spectral test studies such dependence for various dimensions t
by dealing with the totality of all points (2).

For example, Fig. 8 shows a typical small case in 2 and 3 dimensions, for
the generator with

$$s(x) = (137x + 187) \bmod 256. \tag{4}$$

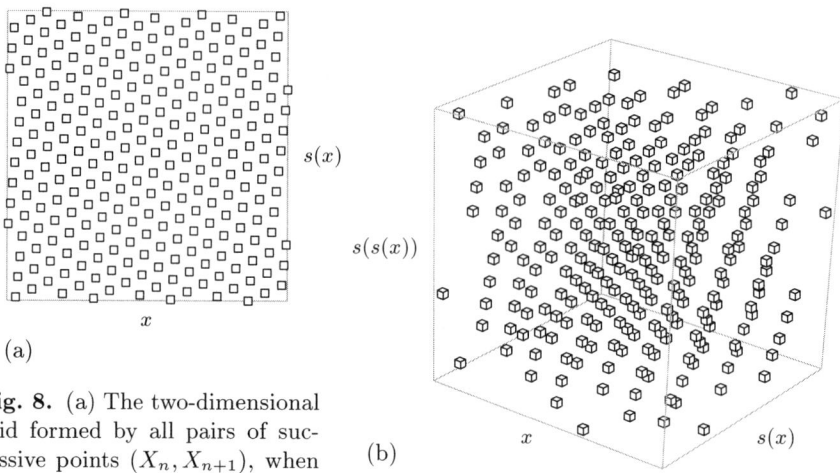

$s(x)$

$s(s(x))$

x

(a)

(b)

x $s(x)$

Fig. 8. (a) The two-dimensional grid formed by all pairs of successive points (X_n, X_{n+1}), when $X_{n+1} = (137X_n + 187) \bmod 256$. (b) The three-dimensional grid of triplets (X_n, X_{n+1}, X_{n+2}).

Of course a generator with period length 256 will hardly be random, but 256 is small enough that we can draw the diagram and gain some understanding before we turn to the larger m's that are of practical interest.

Perhaps the most striking thing about the pattern of boxes in Fig. 8(a) is that we can cover them all by a fairly small number of parallel lines; indeed, there are many different families of parallel lines that will hit all the points. For example, a set of 20 nearly vertical lines will do the job, as will a set of 21 lines that tilt upward at roughly a 30° angle. We commonly observe similar patterns when driving past farmlands that have been planted in a systematic manner.

If the same generator is considered in three dimensions, we obtain 256 points in a cube, obtained by appending a "height" component $s(s(x))$ to each of the 256 points $(x, s(x))$ in the plane of Fig. 8(a), as shown in Fig. 8(b). Let's imagine that this 3-D crystal structure has been made into a physical model, a cube that we can turn in our hands; as we rotate it, we will notice various families of parallel planes that encompass all of the points. In the words of Wallace Givens, the random numbers stay "mainly in the planes."

At first glance we might think that such systematic behavior is so nonrandom as to make congruential generators quite worthless; but more careful reflection, remembering that m is quite large in practice, provides a better insight. The regular structure in Fig. 8 is essentially the "grain" we see when examining our random numbers under a high-power microscope. If we take truly random numbers between 0 and 1, and round or truncate them to finite accuracy so that each is an integer multiple of $1/\nu$ for some given number ν, then the t-dimensional points (1) we obtain will have an extremely regular character when viewed through a microscope.

Let $1/\nu_2$ be the maximum distance between lines, taken over all families of parallel straight lines that cover the points $\{(x/m, s(x)/m)\}$ in two dimensions. We shall call ν_2 the two-dimensional *accuracy* of the random number generator, since the pairs of successive numbers have a fine structure that is essentially good to one part in ν_2. Similarly, let $1/\nu_3$ be the maximum distance between planes, taken over all families of parallel planes that cover all points $\{(x/m, s(x)/m, s(s(x))/m)\}$; we shall call ν_3 the accuracy in three dimensions. The t-dimensional accuracy ν_t is the reciprocal of the maximum distance between hyperplanes, taken over all families of parallel $(t-1)$-dimensional hyperplanes that cover all points $\{(x/m, s(x)/m, \ldots, s^{[t-1]}(x)/m)\}$.

The essential difference between periodic sequences and truly random sequences that have been truncated to multiples of $1/\nu$ is that the accuracy of truly random sequences is the same in all dimensions, while that of periodic sequences decreases as t increases. Indeed, since there are only m points in the t-dimensional cube when m is the period length, we can't achieve a t-dimensional accuracy of more than about $m^{1/t}$.

When the independence of t consecutive values is considered, computer-generated random numbers will behave essentially as if we took truly random numbers and truncated them to $\lg \nu_t$ bits, where ν_t decreases with increasing t. In practice, such varying accuracy is usually all we need. We don't insist that the 10-dimensional accuracy be 2^{32}, in the sense that all $(2^{32})^{10}$ possible 10-tuples $(U_n, U_{n+1}, \ldots, U_{n+9})$ should be equally likely on a 32-bit machine; for such large values of t we want only a few of the leading bits of $(U_n, U_{n+1}, \ldots, U_{n+t-1})$ to behave as if they were independently random.

On the other hand when an application demands high resolution of the random number sequence, simple linear congruential sequences will necessarily be inadequate. A generator with longer period should be used instead, even though only a small fraction of the period will actually be generated. Squaring the period length will essentially square the accuracy in higher dimensions; that is, it will double the effective number of bits of precision.

The spectral test is based on the values of ν_t for small t, say $2 \le t \le 6$. Dimensions 2, 3, and 4 seem to be adequate to detect important deficiencies in a sequence, but since we are considering the entire period it is wise to be somewhat cautious and go up into another dimension or two; on the other hand the values of ν_t for $t \ge 10$ seem to be of no practical significance whatever. (This is fortunate, because it appears to be rather difficult to calculate the accuracy ν_t precisely when $t \ge 10$.)

There is a vague relation between the spectral test and the serial test; for example, a special case of the serial test, taken over the entire period as in exercise 3.3.3–19, counts the number of boxes in each of 64 subsquares of Fig. 8(a). The main difference is that the spectral test rotates the dots so as to discover the least favorable orientation. We shall return to the serial test later in this section.

It may appear at first that we should apply the spectral test only for one suitably high value of t; if a generator passes the test in three dimensions, it seems plausible that it should also pass the 2-D test, hence we might as well omit the latter. The fallacy in this reasoning occurs because we apply more stringent conditions in lower dimensions. A similar situation occurs with the serial test:

Consider a generator that (quite properly) has almost the same number of points in each subcube of the unit cube, when the unit cube has been divided into 64 subcubes of size $\frac{1}{4} \times \frac{1}{4} \times \frac{1}{4}$; this same generator might yield completely *empty* subsquares of the unit square, when the unit square has been divided into 64 subsquares of size $\frac{1}{8} \times \frac{1}{8}$. Since we increase our expectations in lower dimensions, a separate test for each dimension is required.

It is not always true that $\nu_t \leq m^{1/t}$, although this upper bound is valid when the points form a rectangular grid. For example, it turns out that $\nu_2 = \sqrt{274} > \sqrt{256}$ in Fig. 8, because a nearly hexagonal structure brings the m points closer together than would be possible in a strictly rectangular arrangement.

In order to develop an algorithm that computes ν_t efficiently, we must look more deeply at the associated mathematical theory. Therefore a reader who is not mathematically inclined is advised to skip to part D of this section, where the spectral test is presented as a "plug-in" method accompanied by several examples. But the mathematics behind the spectral test requires only some elementary manipulations of vectors.

Some authors have suggested using the minimum number N_t of parallel covering lines or hyperplanes as the criterion, instead of the maximum distance $1/\nu_t$ between them. However, this number N_t does not appear to be as important as the concept of accuracy defined above, because it is biased by how nearly the slope of the lines or hyperplanes matches the coordinate axes of the cube. For example, the 20 nearly vertical lines that cover all the points of Fig. 8(a) are actually $1/\sqrt{328}$ units apart, according to Eq. (14) below with $(u_1, u_2) = (18, -2)$; this might falsely imply an accuracy of one part in $\sqrt{328}$, or perhaps even an accuracy of one part in 20. The true accuracy of only one part in $\sqrt{274}$ is realized only for the larger family of 21 lines with a slope of $7/15$; another family of 24 lines, with a slope of $-11/13$, also has a greater inter-line distance than the 20-line family, since $1/\sqrt{290} > 1/\sqrt{328}$. The precise way in which families of lines act at the boundaries of the unit hypercube does not seem to be an especially "clean" or significant criterion. However, for those people who prefer to count hyperplanes, it is possible to compute N_t using a method quite similar to the way in which we shall calculate ν_t (see exercise 16).

*B. Theory behind the test. In order to analyze the basic set (2), we start with the observation that

$$\frac{1}{m} s^{[j]}(x) = \left(\frac{a^j x + (1 + a + \cdots + a^{j-1})c}{m} \right) \bmod 1. \qquad (5)$$

We can get rid of the "mod 1" operation by extending the set periodically, making infinitely many copies of the original t-dimensional hypercube, proceeding in all directions. This gives us the set

$$L = \left\{ \left(\frac{x}{m} + k_1, \frac{s(x)}{m} + k_2, \ldots, \frac{s^{[t-1]}(x)}{m} + k_t \right) \middle| \text{ integer } x, k_1, k_2, \ldots, k_t \right\}$$

$$= \left\{ V_0 + \left(\frac{x}{m} + k_1, \frac{ax}{m} + k_2, \ldots, \frac{a^{t-1}x}{m} + k_t \right) \middle| \text{ integer } x, k_1, k_2, \ldots, k_t \right\},$$

where

$$V_0 = \frac{1}{m} \left(0,\ c,\ (1+a)c,\ \ldots,\ (1+a+\cdots+a^{t-2})c \right) \qquad (6)$$

is a constant vector. The variable k_1 is redundant in this representation of L, because we can change $(x, k_1, k_2, \ldots, k_t)$ to $(x+k_1 m,\ 0,\ k_2-ak_1,\ \ldots,\ k_t-a^{t-1}k_1)$, reducing k_1 to zero without loss of generality. Therefore we obtain the comparatively simple formula

$$L = \{ V_0 + y_1 V_1 + y_2 V_2 + \cdots + y_t V_t \mid \text{integer } y_1, y_2, \ldots, y_t \}, \qquad (7)$$

where

$$V_1 = \frac{1}{m}(1, a, a^2, \ldots, a^{t-1}); \qquad (8)$$

$$V_2 = (0, 1, 0, \ldots, 0), \quad V_3 = (0, 0, 1, \ldots, 0), \quad \ldots, \quad V_t = (0, 0, 0, \ldots, 1). \qquad (9)$$

The points $(x_1, x_2, \ldots, x_t)$ of L that satisfy $0 \le x_j < 1$ for all j are precisely the m points of our original set (2).

Notice that the increment c appears only in V_0, and the effect of V_0 is merely to shift all elements of L without changing their relative distances; hence c does not affect the spectral test in any way, and we might as well assume that $V_0 = (0, 0, \ldots, 0)$ when we are calculating ν_t. When V_0 is the zero vector we have a *lattice* of points

$$L_0 = \{ y_1 V_1 + y_2 V_2 + \cdots + y_t V_t \mid \text{integer } y_1, y_2, \ldots, y_t \}, \qquad (10)$$

and our goal is to study the distances between adjacent $(t-1)$-dimensional hyperplanes, in families of parallel hyperplanes that cover all the points of L_0.

A family of parallel $(t-1)$-dimensional hyperplanes can be defined by a nonzero vector $U = (u_1, \ldots, u_t)$ that is perpendicular to all of them; and the set of points on a particular hyperplane is then

$$\{ (x_1, \ldots, x_t) \mid x_1 u_1 + \cdots + x_t u_t = q \}, \qquad (11)$$

where q is a different constant for each hyperplane in the family. In other words, each hyperplane is the set of all vectors X for which the *dot product* $X \cdot U$ has a given value q. In our case the hyperplanes are all separated by a fixed distance, and one of them contains $(0, 0, \ldots, 0)$; hence we can adjust the magnitude of U so that the set of all *integer* values q gives all the hyperplanes in the family. Then the distance between neighboring hyperplanes is the minimum distance from $(0, 0, \ldots, 0)$ to the hyperplane for $q = 1$, namely

$$\min_{\text{real } x_1, \ldots, x_t} \left\{ \sqrt{x_1^2 + \cdots + x_t^2} \ \middle| \ x_1 u_1 + \cdots + x_t u_t = 1 \right\}. \qquad (12)$$

Cauchy's inequality (see exercise 1.2.3–30) tells us that

$$(x_1 u_1 + \cdots + x_t u_t)^2 \le (x_1^2 + \cdots + x_t^2)(u_1^2 + \cdots + u_t^2), \qquad (13)$$

hence the minimum in (12) occurs when each $x_j = u_j/(u_1^2+\cdots+u_t^2)$; the distance between neighboring hyperplanes is

$$1/\sqrt{u_1^2 + \cdots + u_t^2} = 1/\text{length}(U). \tag{14}$$

In other words, the quantity ν_t that we seek is precisely the length of the shortest vector U that defines a family of hyperplanes $\{X \cdot U = q \mid \text{integer } q\}$ containing all the elements of L_0.

Such a vector $U = (u_1, \ldots, u_t)$ must be nonzero, and it must satisfy $V \cdot U = $ integer for all V in L_0. In particular, since the points $(1, 0, \ldots, 0)$, $(0, 1, \ldots, 0)$, $\ldots$, $(0, 0, \ldots, 1)$ are all in L_0, all of the u_j must be integers. Furthermore since V_1 is in L_0, we must have $\frac{1}{m}(u_1 + au_2 + \cdots + a^{t-1}u_t) = $ integer, i.e.,

$$u_1 + au_2 + \cdots + a^{t-1}u_t \equiv 0 \pmod{m}. \tag{15}$$

Conversely, any nonzero integer vector $U = (u_1, \ldots, u_t)$ satisfying (15) defines a family of hyperplanes with the required properties, since all of L_0 will be covered: The dot product $(y_1 V_1 + \cdots + y_t V_t) \cdot U$ will be an integer for all integers $y_1, \ldots, y_t$. We have proved that

$$
\begin{aligned}
\nu_t^2 &= \min_{(u_1,\ldots,u_t)\neq(0,\ldots,0)} \left\{ u_1^2 + \cdots + u_t^2 \mid u_1 + au_2 + \cdots + a^{t-1}u_t \equiv 0 \pmod{m} \right\} \\
&= \min_{(x_1,\ldots,x_t)\neq(0,\ldots,0)} \left((mx_1 - ax_2 - a^2 x_3 - \cdots - a^{t-1}x_t)^2 + x_2^2 + x_3^2 + \cdots + x_t^2 \right).
\end{aligned} \tag{16}
$$

C. Deriving a computational method. We have now reduced the spectral test to the problem of finding the minimum value (16); but how on earth can we determine that minimum value in a reasonable amount of time? A brute-force search is out of the question, since m is very large in cases of practical interest.

It will be interesting and probably more useful if we develop a computational method for solving an even more general problem: *Find the minimum value of the quantity*

$$f(x_1, \ldots, x_t) = (u_{11}x_1 + \cdots + u_{t1}x_t)^2 + \cdots + (u_{1t}x_1 + \cdots + u_{tt}x_t)^2 \tag{17}$$

over all nonzero integer vectors $(x_1, \ldots, x_t)$, given any nonsingular matrix of coefficients $U = (u_{ij})$. The expression (17) is called a "positive definite quadratic form" in t variables. Since U is nonsingular, (17) cannot be zero unless the x_j are all zero.

Let us write $U_1, \ldots, U_t$ for the rows of U. Then (17) may be written

$$f(x_1, \ldots, x_t) = (x_1 U_1 + \cdots + x_t U_t) \cdot (x_1 U_1 + \cdots + x_t U_t), \tag{18}$$

the square of the length of the vector $x_1 U_1 + \cdots + x_t U_t$. The nonsingular matrix U has an inverse, which means that we can find uniquely determined vectors $V_1, \ldots, V_t$ such that

$$U_i \cdot V_j = \delta_{ij}, \qquad 1 \leq i, j \leq t. \tag{19}$$

For example, in the special form (16) that arises in the spectral test, we have

$$
\begin{aligned}
U_1 &= (\quad m, 0, 0, \ldots, 0), & V_1 &= \tfrac{1}{m}(1, a, a^2, \ldots, a^{t-1}), \\
U_2 &= (\quad -a, 1, 0, \ldots, 0), & V_2 &= \quad (0, 1, \ 0, \ldots, \quad 0), \\
U_3 &= (\quad -a^2, 0, 1, \ldots, 0), & V_3 &= \quad (0, 0, \ 1, \ldots, \quad 0), \quad (20)
\end{aligned}
$$

$$
\begin{aligned}
\cdots \quad \cdots \quad \cdots \quad \cdots \quad \cdots \\
U_t = (-a^{t-1}, 0, 0, \ldots, 1), \qquad V_t = \quad (0, 0, \ 0, \ldots, \quad 1).
\end{aligned}
$$

These V_j are precisely the vectors (8), (9) that we used to define our original lattice L_0. As the reader may well suspect, this is not a coincidence — indeed, if we had begun with an arbitrary lattice L_0, defined by any set of linearly independent vectors $V_1, \ldots, V_t$, the argument we have used above can be generalized to show that the maximum separation between hyperplanes in a covering family is equivalent to minimizing (17), where the coefficients u_{ij} are defined by (19). (See exercise 2.)

Our first step in minimizing (18) is to reduce it to a finite problem, namely to show that we won't need to test infinitely many vectors $(x_1, \ldots, x_t)$ when finding the minimum. This is where the vectors $V_1, \ldots, V_t$ come in handy; we have

$$
x_k = (x_1 U_1 + \cdots + x_t U_t) \cdot V_k,
$$

and Cauchy's inequality tells us that

$$
\big((x_1 U_1 + \cdots + x_t U_t) \cdot V_k\big)^2 \le f(x_1, \ldots, x_t)(V_k \cdot V_k).
$$

Hence we have derived a useful upper bound on each coordinate x_k:

Lemma A. *Let $(x_1, \ldots, x_t)$ be a nonzero vector that minimizes (18) and let $(y_1, \ldots, y_t)$ be any nonzero integer vector. Then*

$$
x_k^2 \le f(y_1, \ldots, y_t)(V_k \cdot V_k), \qquad \text{for } 1 \le k \le t. \tag{21}
$$

In particular, letting $y_i = \delta_{ij}$ for all i,

$$
x_k^2 \le (U_j \cdot U_j)(V_k \cdot V_k), \qquad \text{for } 1 \le j, k \le t. \quad \blacksquare \tag{22}
$$

Lemma A reduces the problem to a finite search, but the right-hand side of (21) is usually much too large to make an exhaustive search feasible; we need at least one more idea. On such occasions, an old maxim provides sound advice: "If you can't solve a problem as it is stated, change it into a simpler problem that has the same answer." For example, Euclid's algorithm has this form; if we don't know the gcd of the input numbers, we change them into smaller numbers having the same gcd. (In fact, a slightly more general approach probably underlies the discovery of nearly all algorithms: "If you can't solve a problem directly, change it into one or more simpler problems, from whose solution you can solve the original one.")

In our case, a simpler problem is one that requires less searching because the right-hand side of (22) is smaller. The key idea we shall use is that it is possible to change one quadratic form into another one that is equivalent for all practical purposes. Let j be any fixed subscript, $1 \leq j \leq t$; let $(q_1, \ldots, q_{j-1}, q_{j+1}, \ldots, q_t)$ be any sequence of $t-1$ integers; and consider the following transformation of the vectors:

$$V'_i = V_i - q_i V_j, \qquad x'_i = x_i - q_i x_j, \qquad U'_i = U_i, \qquad \text{for } i \neq j;$$
$$V'_j = V_j, \qquad\qquad x'_j = x_j, \qquad\qquad U'_j = U_j + \sum_{i \neq j} q_i U_i. \qquad (23)$$

It is easy to see that the new vectors $U'_1, \ldots, U'_t$ define a quadratic form f' for which $f'(x'_1, \ldots, x'_t) = f(x_1, \ldots, x_t)$; furthermore the basic orthogonality condition (19) remains valid, because it is easy to check that $U'_i \cdot V'_j = \delta_{ij}$. As $(x_1, \ldots, x_t)$ runs through all nonzero integer vectors, so does $(x'_1, \ldots, x'_t)$; hence the new form f' has the same minimum as f.

Our goal is to use transformation (23), replacing U_i by U'_i and V_i by V'_i for all i, in order to make the right-hand side of (22) small; and the right-hand side of (22) will be small when both $U_j \cdot U_j$ and $V_k \cdot V_k$ are small. Therefore it is natural to ask the following two questions about the transformation (23):

a) *What choice of q_i makes $V'_i \cdot V'_i$ as small as possible?*

b) *What choice of $q_1, \ldots, q_{j-1}, q_{j+1}, \ldots, q_t$ makes $U'_j \cdot U'_j$ as small as possible?*

It is easiest to solve these questions first for *real* values of the q_i. Question (a) is quite simple, since

$$(V_i - q_i V_j) \cdot (V_i - q_i V_j) = V_i \cdot V_i - 2q_i \, V_i \cdot V_j + q_i^2 \, V_j \cdot V_j$$
$$= (V_j \cdot V_j)\left(q_i - (V_i \cdot V_j / V_j \cdot V_j)\right)^2 + V_i \cdot V_i - (V_i \cdot V_j)^2 / V_j \cdot V_j,$$

and the minimum occurs when

$$q_i = V_i \cdot V_j \, / \, V_j \cdot V_j. \qquad (24)$$

Geometrically, we are asking what multiple of V_j should be subtracted from V_i so that the resulting vector V'_i has minimum length, and the answer is to choose q_i so that V'_i is perpendicular to V_j (that is, to make $V'_i \cdot V_j = 0$); the following diagram makes this plain.

$$(25)$$

Turning to question (b), we want to choose the q_i so that $U_j + \sum_{i \neq j} q_i U_i$ has minimum length; geometrically, we want to start with U_j and add some vector in the $(t-1)$-dimensional hyperplane whose points are the sums of multiples of $\{U_i \mid i \neq j\}$. Again the best solution is to choose things so that U'_j is perpendicular to the hyperplane, making $U'_j \cdot U_k = 0$ for all $k \neq j$:

$$U_j \cdot U_k + \sum_{i \neq j} q_i (U_i \cdot U_k) = 0, \qquad 1 \leq k \leq t, \qquad k \neq j. \qquad (26)$$

(See exercise 12 for a rigorous proof that a solution to question (b) must satisfy these $t - 1$ equations.)

Now that we have answered questions (a) and (b), we are in a bit of a quandary; should we choose the q_i according to (24), so that the $V_i' \cdot V_i'$ are minimized, or according to (26), so that $U_j' \cdot U_j'$ is minimized? Either of these alternatives makes an improvement in the right-hand side of (22), so it is not immediately clear which choice should get priority. Fortunately, there is a very simple answer to this dilemma: Conditions (24) and (26) are exactly the same! (See exercise 7.) Therefore questions (a) and (b) have the same answer; we have a happy state of affairs in which we can reduce the length of both the U's and the V's simultaneously. Indeed, we have just rediscovered the *Gram–Schmidt orthogonalization process* [see *Crelle* **94** (1883), 41–73].

Our joy must be tempered with the realization that we have dealt with questions (a) and (b) only for *real* values of the q_i. Our application restricts us to integer values, so we cannot make V_i' exactly perpendicular to V_j. The best we can do for question (a) is to let q_i be the *nearest integer* to $V_i \cdot V_j \,/\, V_j \cdot V_j$ (see (25)). It turns out that this is *not* always the best solution to question (b); in fact U_j' may at times be longer than U_j. However, the bound (21) is never increased, since we can remember the smallest value of $f(y_1, \ldots, y_t)$ found so far. Thus a choice of q_i based solely on question (a) is quite satisfactory.

If we apply transformation (23) repeatedly in such a way that none of the vectors V_i gets longer and at least one gets shorter, we can never get into a loop; that is, we will never be considering the same quadratic form again after a sequence of nontrivial transformations of this kind. But eventually we will get stuck, in the sense that none of the transformations (23) for $1 \le j \le t$ will be able to shorten any of the vectors V_1, ..., V_t. At that point we can revert to an exhaustive search, using the bounds of Lemma A, which will now be quite small in most cases. Occasionally these bounds (21) will be poor, and another type of transformation will usually get the algorithm unstuck again and reduce the bounds (see exercise 18). However, transformation (23) by itself has proved to be quite adequate for the spectral test; in fact, it has proved to be amazingly powerful when the computations are arranged as in the algorithm discussed below.

*D. How to perform the spectral test. Here now is an efficient computational procedure that follows from our considerations. R. W. Gosper and U. Dieter have observed that it is possible to use the results of lower dimensions to make the spectral test significantly faster in higher dimensions. This refinement has been incorporated into the following algorithm, together with Gauss's significant simplification of the two-dimensional case (exercise 5).

Algorithm S (*The spectral test*). This algorithm determines the value of

$$\nu_t = \min\left\{ \sqrt{x_1^2 + \cdots + x_t^2} \;\middle|\; x_1 + ax_2 + \cdots + a^{t-1}x_t \equiv 0 \pmod{m} \right\} \quad (27)$$

for $2 \le t \le T$, given a, m, and T, where $0 < a < m$ and a is relatively prime to m. (The minimum is taken over all nonzero integer vectors $(x_1, \ldots, x_t)$, and the number ν_t measures the t-dimensional accuracy of random number generators, as discussed in the text above.) All arithmetic within this algorithm is done on integers whose magnitudes rarely if ever exceed m^2, except in step S7; in fact, nearly all of the integer variables will be less than m in absolute value during the computation.

When ν_t is being calculated for $t \geq 3$, the algorithm works with two $t \times t$ matrices U and V, whose row vectors are denoted by $U_i = (u_{i1}, \ldots, u_{it})$ and $V_i = (v_{i1}, \ldots, v_{it})$ for $1 \leq i \leq t$. These vectors satisfy the conditions

$$u_{i1} + au_{i2} + \cdots + a^{t-1}u_{it} \equiv 0 \ (\text{modulo } m), \qquad 1 \leq i \leq t; \tag{28}$$

$$U_i \cdot V_j = m\delta_{ij}, \qquad 1 \leq i, j \leq t. \tag{29}$$

(Thus the V_j of our previous discussion have been multiplied by m, to ensure that their components are integers.) There are three other auxiliary vectors, $X = (x_1, \ldots, x_t)$, $Y = (y_1, \ldots, y_t)$, and $Z = (z_1, \ldots, z_t)$. During the entire algorithm, r will denote $a^{t-1} \bmod m$ and s will denote the smallest upper bound for ν_t^2 that has been discovered so far.

S1. [Initialize.] Set $t \leftarrow 2$, $h \leftarrow a$, $h' \leftarrow m$, $p \leftarrow 1$, $p' \leftarrow 0$, $r \leftarrow a$, $s \leftarrow 1 + a^2$. (The first steps of this algorithm handle the case $t = 2$ by a special method, very much like Euclid's algorithm; we will have

$$h - ap \equiv h' - ap' \equiv 0 \ (\text{modulo } m) \qquad \text{and} \qquad hp' - h'p = \pm m \tag{30}$$

during this phase of the calculation.)

S2. [Euclidean step.] Set $q \leftarrow \lfloor h'/h \rfloor$, $u \leftarrow h' - qh$, $v \leftarrow p' - qp$. If $u^2 + v^2 < s$, set $s \leftarrow u^2 + v^2$, $h' \leftarrow h$, $h \leftarrow u$, $p' \leftarrow p$, $p \leftarrow v$, and repeat step S2.

S3. [Compute ν_2.] Set $u \leftarrow u - h$, $v \leftarrow v - p$; and if $u^2 + v^2 < s$, set $s \leftarrow u^2 + v^2$, $h' \leftarrow u$, $p' \leftarrow v$. Then output $\sqrt{s} = \nu_2$. (The validity of this calculation for the two-dimensional case is proved in exercise 5. Now we will set up the U and V matrices satisfying (28) and (29), in preparation for calculations in higher dimensions.) Set

$$U \leftarrow \begin{pmatrix} -h & p \\ -h' & p' \end{pmatrix}, \qquad V \leftarrow \pm \begin{pmatrix} p' & h' \\ -p & -h \end{pmatrix},$$

where the $-$ sign is chosen for V if and only if $p' > 0$.

S4. [Advance t.] If $t = T$, the algorithm terminates. (Otherwise we want to increase t by 1. At this point U and V are $t \times t$ matrices satisfying (28) and (29), and we must enlarge them by adding an appropriate new row and column.) Set $t \leftarrow t + 1$ and $r \leftarrow (ar) \bmod m$. Set U_t to the new row $(-r, 0, 0, \ldots, 0, 1)$ of t elements, and set $u_{it} \leftarrow 0$ for $1 \leq i < t$. Set V_t to the new row $(0, 0, 0, \ldots, 0, m)$. Finally, for $1 \leq i < t$, set $q \leftarrow \text{round}(v_{i1}r/m)$, $v_{it} \leftarrow v_{i1}r - qm$, and $U_t \leftarrow U_t + qU_i$. (Here "round($x$)" denotes the nearest integer to x, e.g., $\lfloor x + 1/2 \rfloor$. We are essentially setting $v_{it} \leftarrow v_{i1}r$ and immediately applying transformation (23) with $j = t$, since the numbers $|v_{i1}r|$ are so large they ought to be reduced at once.) Finally set $s \leftarrow \min(s, U_t \cdot U_t)$, $k \leftarrow t$, and $j \leftarrow 1$. (In the following steps, j denotes the current row index for transformation (23), and k denotes the last such index where the transformation shortened at least one of the V_i.)

S5. [Transform.] For $1 \leq i \leq t$, do the following operations: If $i \neq j$ and $2|V_i \cdot V_j| > V_j \cdot V_j$, set $q \leftarrow \text{round}(V_i \cdot V_j / V_j \cdot V_j)$, $V_i \leftarrow V_i - qV_j$, $U_j \leftarrow U_j + qU_i$, $s \leftarrow \min(s, U_j \cdot U_j)$, and $k \leftarrow j$. (We omit the transformation when $2|V_i \cdot V_j|$ exactly equals $V_j \cdot V_j$; exercise 19 shows that this precaution keeps the algorithm from looping endlessly.)

S6. [Advance j.] If $j = t$, set $j \leftarrow 1$; otherwise set $j \leftarrow j + 1$. Now if $j \neq k$, return to step S5. (If $j = k$, we have gone through $t - 1$ consecutive cycles of no transformation, so the transformation process is stuck.)

S7. [Prepare for search.] (Now the absolute minimum will be determined, using an exhaustive search over all $(x_1, \ldots, x_t)$ satisfying condition (21) of Lemma A.) Set $X \leftarrow Y \leftarrow (0, \ldots, 0)$, set $k \leftarrow t$, and set

$$z_j \leftarrow \left\lfloor \sqrt{\lfloor (V_j \cdot V_j)s/m^2 \rfloor} \right\rfloor, \qquad \text{for } 1 \leq j \leq t. \tag{31}$$

(We will examine all $X = (x_1, \ldots, x_t)$ with $|x_j| \leq z_j$ for $1 \leq j \leq t$. Usually $|z_j| \leq 1$, but L. C. Killingbeck noticed in 1999 that larger values occur for about 0.00001 of all multipliers when $m = 2^{64}$. During the exhaustive search, the vector Y will always be equal to $x_1U_1 + \cdots + x_tU_t$, so that $f(x_1, \ldots, x_t) = Y \cdot Y$. Since $f(-x_1, \ldots, -x_t) = f(x_1, \ldots, x_t)$, we shall examine only vectors whose first nonzero component is positive. The method is essentially that of counting in steps of one, regarding $(x_1, \ldots, x_t)$ as the digits in a balanced number system with mixed radices $(2z_1+1, \ldots, 2z_t+1)$; see Section 4.1.)

S8. [Advance x_k.] If $x_k = z_k$, go to S10. Otherwise increase x_k by 1 and set $Y \leftarrow Y + U_k$.

S9. [Advance k.] Set $k \leftarrow k + 1$. Then if $k \leq t$, set $x_k \leftarrow -z_k$, $Y \leftarrow Y - 2z_kU_k$, and repeat step S9. But if $k > t$, set $s \leftarrow \min(s, Y \cdot Y)$.

S10. [Decrease k.] Set $k \leftarrow k - 1$. If $k \geq 1$, return to S8. Otherwise output $\nu_t = \sqrt{s}$ (the exhaustive search is completed) and return to S4. ∎

In practice Algorithm S is applied for $T = 5$ or 6, say; it usually works reasonably well when $T = 7$ or 8, but it can be terribly slow when $T \geq 9$ since the exhaustive search tends to make the running time grow as 3^T. (If the minimum value ν_t occurs at many different points, the exhaustive search will hit them all; hence we typically find that all $z_k = 1$ for large t. As remarked above, the values of ν_t are generally irrelevant for practical purposes when t is large.)

An example will help to make Algorithm S clear. Consider the linear congruential sequence defined by

$$m = 10^{10}, \qquad a = 3141592621, \qquad c = 1, \qquad X_0 = 0. \tag{32}$$

Six cycles of the Euclidean algorithm in steps S2 and S3 suffice to prove that the minimum nonzero value of $x_1^2 + x_2^2$ with

$$x_1 + 3141592621x_2 \equiv 0 \pmod{10^{10}}$$

occurs for $x_1 = 67654$, $x_2 = 226$; hence the two-dimensional accuracy of this generator is

$$\nu_2 = \sqrt{67654^2 + 226^2} \approx 67654.37748.$$

Passing to three dimensions, we seek the minimum nonzero value of $x_1^2 + x_2^2 + x_3^2$ such that

$$x_1 + 3141592621x_2 + 3141592621^2 x_3 \equiv 0 \pmod{10^{10}}. \tag{33}$$

Step S4 sets up the matrices

$$U = \begin{pmatrix} -67654 & -226 & 0 \\ -44190611 & 191 & 0 \\ 5793866 & 33 & 1 \end{pmatrix}, \quad V = \begin{pmatrix} -191 & -44190611 & 2564918569 \\ -226 & 67654 & 1307181134 \\ 0 & 0 & 10000000000 \end{pmatrix}.$$

The first iteration of step S5, with $q = 1$ for $i = 2$ and $q = 4$ for $i = 3$, changes them to

$$U = \begin{pmatrix} -21082801 & 97 & 4 \\ -44190611 & 191 & 0 \\ 5793866 & 33 & 1 \end{pmatrix}, \quad V = \begin{pmatrix} -191 & -44190611 & 2564918569 \\ -35 & 44258265 & -1257737435 \\ 764 & 176762444 & -259674276 \end{pmatrix}.$$

(The first row U_1 has actually gotten longer in this transformation, although eventually the rows of U should get shorter.)

The next fourteen iterations of step S5 have $(j, q_1, q_2, q_3) = (2, -2, *, 0)$, $(3, 0, 3, *)$, $(1, *, -10, -1)$, $(2, -1, *, -6)$, $(3, -1, 0, *)$, $(1, *, 0, 2)$, $(2, 0, *, -1)$, $(3, 3, 4, *)$, $(1, *, 0, 0)$, $(2, -5, *, 0)$, $(3, 1, 0, *)$, $(1, *, -3, -1)$, $(2, 0, *, 0)$, $(3, 0, 0, *)$. Now the transformation process is stuck, but the rows of the matrices have become significantly shorter:

$$U = \begin{pmatrix} -1479 & 616 & -2777 \\ -3022 & 104 & 918 \\ -227 & -983 & -130 \end{pmatrix}, \quad V = \begin{pmatrix} -888874 & 601246 & -2994234 \\ -2809871 & 438109 & 1593689 \\ -854296 & -9749816 & -1707736 \end{pmatrix}. \tag{34}$$

The search limits (z_1, z_2, z_3) in step S7 turn out to be $(0, 0, 1)$, so U_3 is the shortest solution to (33); we have

$$\nu_3 = \sqrt{227^2 + 983^2 + 130^2} \approx 1017.21089.$$

Only a few iterations were needed to find this value, although condition (33) looks quite formidable at first glance. Our computation has proved that all points (U_n, U_{n+1}, U_{n+2}) produced by the random number generator (32) lie on a family of parallel planes about 0.001 units apart, but not on any family of planes that differ by more than 0.001 units.

The exhaustive search in steps S8–S10 reduces the value of s only rarely. One such case, found in 1982 by R. Carling and K. Levine, occurs when $a = 464680339$, $m = 2^{29}$, and $t = 5$; another case arose when the author calculated ν_6^2 for line 21 of Table 1, later in this section.

E. Ratings for various generators. So far we haven't really given a criterion that tells us whether or not a particular random number generator passes or flunks the spectral test. In fact, spectral success depends on the application, since some applications demand higher resolution than others. It appears that

$\nu_t \geq 2^{30/t}$ for $2 \leq t \leq 6$ will be quite adequate for most purposes (although the author must admit choosing this criterion partly because 30 is conveniently divisible by 2, 3, 5, and 6).

For some purposes we would like a criterion that is relatively independent of m, so we can say that a particular multiplier is good or bad with respect to the set of all other multipliers for the given m, without examining any others. A reasonable figure of merit for rating the goodness of a particular multiplier seems to be the volume of the ellipsoid in t-space defined by the relation

$$(x_1 m - x_2 a - \cdots - x_t a^{t-1})^2 + x_2^2 + \cdots + x_t^2 \leq \nu_t^2,$$

since this volume tends to indicate how likely it is that nonzero *integer* points $(x_1, \ldots, x_t)$ — corresponding to solutions of (15) — are in the ellipsoid. We therefore propose to calculate this volume, namely

$$\mu_t = \frac{\pi^{t/2}\, \nu_t^t}{(t/2)!\, m}, \tag{35}$$

as an indication of the effectiveness of the multiplier a for the given m. In this formula,

$$\left(\frac{t}{2}\right)! = \left(\frac{t}{2}\right)\left(\frac{t}{2} - 1\right) \cdots \left(\frac{1}{2}\right)\sqrt{\pi}, \qquad \text{for } t \text{ odd.} \tag{36}$$

Thus, in six or fewer dimensions the merit is computed as follows:

$$\mu_2 = \pi\nu_2^2/m, \qquad \mu_3 = \tfrac{4}{3}\pi\nu_3^3/m, \qquad \mu_4 = \tfrac{1}{2}\pi^2\nu_4^4/m,$$
$$\mu_5 = \tfrac{8}{15}\pi^2\nu_5^5/m, \qquad \mu_6 = \tfrac{1}{6}\pi^3\nu_6^6/m.$$

We might say that the multiplier a passes the spectral test if μ_t is 0.1 or more for $2 \leq t \leq 6$, and it "passes with flying colors" if $\mu_t \geq 1$ for all these t. A low value of μ_t means that we have probably picked a very unfortunate multiplier, since very few lattices will have integer points so close to the origin. Conversely, a high value of μ_t means that we have found an unusually good multiplier for the given m; but it does not mean that the random numbers are necessarily very good, since m might be too small. Only the values ν_t truly indicate the degree of randomness.

Table 1 shows what sorts of values occur in typical sequences. Each line of the table considers a particular generator, and lists ν_t^2, μ_t, and the "number of bits of accuracy" $\lg \nu_t$. Lines 1 through 4 show the generators that were the subject of Figs. 2 and 5 in Section 3.3.1. The generators in lines 1 and 2 suffer from too small a multiplier; a diagram like Fig. 8 will have a nearly vertical "stripes" when a is small. The terrible generator in line 3 has a good μ_2 but very poor μ_3 and μ_4; like nearly all generators of potency 2, it has $\nu_3 = \sqrt{6}$ and $\nu_4 = 2$ (see exercise 3). Line 4 shows a "random" multiplier; this generator has satisfactorily passed numerous empirical tests for randomness, but it does not have especially high values of $\mu_2, \ldots, \mu_6$. In fact, the value of μ_5 flunks our criterion.

Line 5 shows the generator of Fig. 8. It passes the spectral test with very high-flying colors, when μ_2 through μ_6 are considered, but of course m is so small that the numbers can hardly be called random; the ν_t values are terribly low.

Table 1

SAMPLE RESULTS OF THE SPECTRAL TEST

Line	a	m	ν_2^2	ν_3^2	ν_4^2	ν_5^2	ν_6^2
1	23	10^8+1	530	530	530	530	447
2	2^7+1	2^{35}	16642	16642	16642	15602	252
3	$2^{18}+1$	2^{35}	34359738368	6	4	4	4
4	3141592653	2^{35}	2997222016	1026050	27822	1118	1118
5	137	256	274	30	14	6	4
6	3141592621	10^{10}	4577114792	1034718	62454	1776	542
7	3141592221	10^{10}	4293881050	276266	97450	3366	2382
8	4219755981	10^{10}	10721093248	2595578	49362	5868	820
9	4160984121	10^{10}	9183801602	4615650	16686	6840	1344
10	$2^{24}+2^{13}+5$	2^{35}	8364058	8364058	21476	16712	1496
11	5^{13}	2^{35}	33161885770	2925242	113374	13070	2256
12	$2^{16}+3$	2^{29}	536936458	118	116	116	116
13	1812433253	2^{32}	4326934538	1462856	15082	4866	906
14	1566083941	2^{32}	4659748970	2079590	44902	4652	662
15	69069	2^{32}	4243209856	2072544	52804	6990	242
16	2650845021	2^{32}	4938969760	2646962	68342	8778	1506
17	314159269	$2^{31}-1$	1432232969	899290	36985	3427	1144
18	62089911	$2^{31}-1$	1977289717	1662317	48191	6101	1462
19	16807	$2^{31}-1$	282475250	408197	21682	4439	895
20	48271	$2^{31}-1$	1990735345	1433881	47418	4404	1402
21	40692	$2^{31}-249$	1655838865	1403422	42475	6507	1438
22	44485709377909	2^{46}	5.6×10^{13}	1180915002	1882426	279928	26230
23	31167285	2^{48}	3.2×10^{14}	4111841446	17341510	306326	59278
24	see (38)		2.4×10^{18}	4.7×10^{11}	1.9×10^9	3194548	1611610
25	see (39)		$(2^{31}-1)^2$	1.4×10^{12}	643578623	12930027	837632
26	see the text	2^{64}	8.8×10^{18}	6.4×10^{12}	4.1×10^9	45662836	1846368
27	see the text	$\approx 2^{78}$	$2^{62}+1$	4281084902	2.2×10^9	1.8×10^9	1862407
28	$2^{-24\cdot389}$	$\approx 2^{576}$	1.8×10^{173}	3.5×10^{115}	4.4×10^{86}	2×10^{69}	5×10^{57}
29	$(2^{32}-5)^{-400}$	$\approx 2^{1376}$	1.6×10^{414}	8.6×10^{275}	1×10^{207}	2×10^{165}	8×10^{137}

Line 6 is the generator discussed in (32) above. Line 7 is a similar example, having an abnormally low value of μ_3. Line 8 shows a nonrandom multiplier for the same modulus m; all of its partial quotients are 1, 2, or 3. Such multipliers have been suggested by I. Borosh and H. Niederreiter because the Dedekind sums are likely to be especially small and because they produce best results in the two-dimensional serial test (see Section 3.3.3 and exercise 30). The particular example in line 8 has only one '3' as a partial quotient; there is no multiplier congruent to 1 modulo 20 whose partial quotients with respect to 10^{10} are only 1s and 2s. The generator in line 9 shows another multiplier chosen with malice aforethought, following a suggestion by A. G. Waterman that guarantees a reasonably high value of μ_2 (see exercise 11). Line 10 is interesting because it has high μ_3 in spite of very low μ_2 (see exercise 8).

Line 11 of Table 1 is a reminder of the good old days — it once was used extensively, following a suggestion of O. Taussky in the early 1950s. But computers for which 2^{35} was an appropriate modulus began to fade in importance during the late 60s, and they disappeared almost completely in the 80s, as machines

$$\left(\epsilon = \tfrac{1}{10}\right)$$

$\lg \nu_2$	$\lg \nu_3$	$\lg \nu_4$	$\lg \nu_5$	$\lg \nu_6$	μ_2	μ_3	μ_4	μ_5	μ_6	Line
4.5	4.5	4.5	4.5	4.4	$2\epsilon^5$	$5\epsilon^4$	0.01	0.34	4.62	1
7.0	7.0	7.0	7.0	4.0	$2\epsilon^6$	$3\epsilon^4$	0.04	4.66	$2\epsilon^3$	2
17.5	1.3	1.0	1.0	1.0	3.14	$2\epsilon^9$	$2\epsilon^9$	$5\epsilon^9$	ϵ^8	3
15.7	10.0	7.4	5.1	5.1	0.27	0.13	0.11	0.01	0.21	4
4.0	2.5	1.9	1.3	1.0	3.36	2.69	3.78	1.81	1.29	5
16.0	10.0	8.0	5.4	4.5	1.44	0.44	1.92	0.07	0.08	6
16.0	9.0	8.3	5.9	5.6	1.35	0.06	4.69	0.35	6.98	7
16.7	10.7	7.8	6.3	4.8	3.37	1.75	1.20	1.39	0.28	8
16.5	11.1	7.0	6.4	5.2	2.89	4.15	0.14	2.04	1.25	9
11.5	11.5	7.2	7.0	5.3	$8\epsilon^4$	2.95	0.07	5.53	0.50	10
17.5	10.7	8.4	6.8	5.6	3.03	0.61	1.85	2.99	1.73	11
14.5	3.4	3.4	3.4	3.4	3.14	ϵ^5	ϵ^4	ϵ^3	0.02	12
16.0	10.2	6.9	6.1	4.9	3.16	1.73	0.26	2.02	0.89	13
16.1	10.5	7.7	6.1	4.7	3.41	2.92	2.32	1.81	0.35	14
16.0	10.5	7.8	6.4	4.0	3.10	2.91	3.20	5.01	0.02	15
16.1	10.7	8.0	6.6	5.3	3.61	4.20	5.37	8.85	4.11	16
15.2	9.9	7.6	5.9	5.1	2.10	1.66	3.14	1.69	3.60	17
15.4	10.3	7.8	6.3	5.3	2.89	4.18	5.34	7.13	7.52	18
14.0	9.3	7.2	6.1	4.9	0.41	0.51	1.08	3.22	1.73	19
15.4	10.2	7.8	6.1	5.2	2.91	3.35	5.17	3.15	6.63	20
15.3	10.2	7.7	6.3	5.2	2.42	3.24	4.15	8.37	7.16	21
22.8	15.1	10.4	9.0	7.3	2.48	2.42	0.25	3.10	1.33	22
24.1	16.0	12.0	9.1	7.9	3.60	3.92	5.27	0.97	3.82	23
30.5	19.4	15.4	10.8	10.3	1.65	0.29	3.88	0.02	4.69	24
31.0	20.2	14.6	11.8	9.8	3.14	1.49	0.44	0.69	0.66	25
31.5	21.3	16.0	12.7	10.4	1.50	3.68	4.52	4.02	1.76	26
31.0	16.0	15.5	15.4	10.4	$5\epsilon^5$	$4\epsilon^9$	$8\epsilon^5$	2.56	ϵ^4	27
288.	192.	144.	115.	95.9	2.27	3.46	3.92	2.49	2.98	28
688.	458.	344.	275.	229.	3.10	2.04	2.85	1.15	1.33	29

upper bounds from (40):   3.63   5.92   9.87   14.89   23.87

with 32-bit arithmetic began to proliferate. This switch to a comparatively small word size called for comparatively greater care. Line 12 was, alas, the generator actually used on such machines in most of the world's scientific computing centers for more than a decade; its very name RANDU is enough to bring dismay into the eyes and stomachs of many computer scientists! The actual generator is defined by

$$X_0 \text{ odd}, \qquad X_{n+1} = (65539X_n) \bmod 2^{31}, \tag{37}$$

and exercise 20 indicates that 2^{29} is the appropriate modulus for the spectral test. Since $9X_n - 6X_{n+1} + X_{n+2} \equiv 0$ (modulo 2^{31}), the generator fails most three-dimensional criteria for randomness, and it should never have been used. Almost any multiplier $\equiv 5$ (modulo 8) would be better. (A curious fact about RANDU, noticed by R. W. Gosper, is that $\nu_4 = \nu_5 = \nu_6 = \nu_7 = \nu_8 = \nu_9 = \sqrt{116}$, hence μ_9 is a spectacular 11.98.) Lines 13 and 14 are the Borosh–Niederreiter and Waterman multipliers for modulus 2^{32}. Line 16 was found by L. C. Killingbeck, who carried out an exhaustive search of all multipliers $a \equiv 1 \bmod 4$ when $m = 2^{32}$. Line 23, similarly, was found by M. Lavaux and F. Janssens in a (nonexhaustive) computer search for spectrally good multipliers having a very high μ_2. Line 22 is for the multiplier used with $c = 0$ and $m = 2^{48}$ in the Cray X-MP library; line 26 (whose excellent multiplier 6364136223846793005 is too big to fit in the column) is due to C. E. Haynes. Line 15 was nominated by George Marsaglia as "a candidate for the best of all multipliers," after a computer search for nearly cubical lattices in dimensions 2 through 5, partly because it is easy to remember [*Applications of Number Theory to Numerical Analysis*, edited by S. K. Zaremba (New York: Academic Press, 1972), 275].

Line 17 uses a random primitive root, modulo the prime $2^{31} - 1$, as multiplier. Line 18 shows the spectrally best primitive root for $2^{31} - 1$, found in an exhaustive search by G. S. Fishman and L. R. Moore III [*SIAM J. Sci. Stat. Comput.* **7** (1986), 24–45]. The adequate but less outstanding multiplier $16807 = 7^5$ in line 19 is actually used most often for that modulus, after being proposed by Lewis, Goodman, and Miller in *IBM Systems J.* **8** (1969), 136–146; it has been one of the main generators in the popular IMSL subroutine library since 1971. The main reason for continued use of $a = 16807$ is that a^2 is less than the modulus m, hence $ax \bmod m$ can be implemented with reasonable efficiency in high-level languages using the technique of exercise 3.2.1.1–9. However, such small multipliers have known defects. S. K. Park and K. W. Miller noticed that the same implementation technique applies also to certain multipliers greater than $\sqrt{m}$, so they asked G. S. Fishman to find the best "efficiently portable" multiplier in this wider class; the result appears in line 20 [*CACM* **31** (1988), 1192–1201]. Line 21 shows another good multiplier, due to P. L'Ecuyer [*CACM* **31** (1988), 742–749, 774]; this one uses a slightly smaller prime modulus.

When the generators of lines 20 and 21 are combined by subtraction as suggested in Eq. 3.2.2–(15), so that the generated numbers $\langle Z_n \rangle$ satisfy

$$X_{n+1} = 48271 X_n \bmod (2^{31} - 1), \qquad Y_{n+1} = 40692 Y_n \bmod (2^{31} - 249),$$
$$Z_n = (X_n - Y_n) \bmod (2^{31} - 1), \tag{38}$$

exercise 32 shows that it is reasonable to rate $\langle Z_n \rangle$ with the spectral test for $m = (2^{31} - 1)(2^{31} - 249)$ and $a = 1431853894371298687$. (This value of a satisfies $a \bmod (2^{31} - 1) = 48271$ and $a \bmod (2^{31} - 249) = 40692$.) The results appear on line 24. We needn't worry too much about the low value of μ_5, since $\nu_5 > 1000$. Generator (38) has a period of length $(2^{31} - 2)(2^{31} - 250)/62 \approx 7 \times 10^{16}$.

Line 25 of the table represents the sequence

$$X_n = (271828183 X_{n-1} - 314159269 X_{n-2}) \bmod (2^{31} - 1), \tag{39}$$

which can be shown to have period length $(2^{31} - 1)^2 - 1$; it has been analyzed with the generalized spectral test of exercise 24.

The last three lines of Table 1 are based on add-with-carry and subtract-with-borrow methods, which simulate linear congruential sequences that have extremely large moduli (see exercise 3.2.1.1–14). Line 27 is for the generator

$$X_n = (X_{n-1} + 65430 X_{n-2} + C_n) \bmod 2^{31},$$
$$C_{n+1} = \lfloor (X_{n-1} + 65430 X_{n-2} + C_n)/2^{31} \rfloor,$$

which corresponds to $\mathcal{X}_{n+1} = (65430 \cdot 2^{31} + 1)\mathcal{X}_n \bmod (65430 \cdot 2^{62} + 2^{31} - 1)$; the numbers in the table refer to the "super-values"

$$\mathcal{X}_n = (65430 \cdot 2^{31} + 1)X_{n-1} + 65430X_{n-2} + C_n$$

rather than to the values X_n actually computed and used as random numbers. Line 28 represents a more typical subtract-with-borrow generator

$$X_n = (X_{n-10} - X_{n-24} - C_n) \bmod 2^{24}, \quad C_{n+1} = [X_{n-10} < X_{n-24} + C_n],$$

but modified by generating 389 elements of the sequence and then using only the first (or last) 24. This generator, called RANLUX, was recommended by Martin Lüscher after it passed many stringent tests that previous generators failed [*Computer Physics Communications* **79** (1994), 100–110]. A similar sequence,

$$X_n = (X_{n-22} - X_{n-43} - C_n) \bmod (2^{32} - 5), \quad C_{n+1} = [X_{n-22} < X_{n-43} + C_n],$$

with 43 elements used after 400 are generated, appears in line 29; this sequence is discussed in the answer to exercise 3.2.1.2–22. In both cases the table entries refer to the spectral test on multiprecision numbers $\mathcal{X}_n$ instead of to the individual "digits" X_n, but the high μ values indicate that the process of generating 389 or 400 numbers before selecting 24 or 43 is an excellent way to remove biases due to the extreme simplicity of the generation scheme.

Theoretical upper bounds on μ_t, which can never be transcended for any m, are shown just below Table 1; it is known that every lattice with m points per unit volume has

$$\nu_t \leq \gamma_t^{1/2} m^{1/t}, \tag{40}$$

where γ_t takes the respective values

$$(4/3)^{1/2}, \quad 2^{1/3}, \quad 2^{1/2}, \quad 2^{3/5}, \quad (64/3)^{1/6}, \quad 4^{3/7}, \quad 2 \tag{41}$$

for $t = 2, \ldots, 8$. [See exercise 9 and J. W. S. Cassels, *Introduction to the Geometry of Numbers* (Berlin: Springer, 1959), 332; J. H. Conway and N. J. A. Sloane, *Sphere Packings, Lattices and Groups* (New York: Springer, 1988), 20.] These bounds hold for lattices generated by vectors with arbitrary real coordinates. For example, the optimum lattice for $t = 2$ is hexagonal, and it is generated by vectors of length $2/\sqrt{3m}$ that form two sides of an equilateral triangle. In three dimensions the optimum lattice is generated by vectors V_1, V_2, V_3 that can be rotated into the form $(v, v, -v)$, $(v, -v, v)$, $(-v, v, v)$, where $v = 1/\sqrt[3]{4m}$.

*F. Relation to the serial test. In a series of important papers published during the 1970s, Harald Niederreiter showed how to analyze the distribution of the t-dimensional vectors (1) by means of exponential sums. One of the main consequences of his theory is that the serial test in several dimensions will be passed by any generator that passes the spectral test, even when we consider only a sufficiently large part of the period instead of the whole period. We shall now turn briefly to a study of his interesting methods, in the case of linear congruential sequences (X_0, a, c, m) of period length m.

The first idea we need is the notion of *discrepancy* in t dimensions, a quantity that we shall define as the difference between the expected number and the actual number of t-dimensional vectors $(x_n, x_{n+1}, \ldots, x_{n+t-1})$ falling into a hyper-rectangular region, maximized over all such regions. To be precise, let $\langle x_n \rangle$ be a sequence of integers in the range $0 \le x_n < m$. We define

$$D_N^{(t)} = \max_R \left| \frac{\text{number of } (x_n, \ldots, x_{n+t-1}) \text{ in } R \text{ for } 0 \le n < N}{N} - \frac{\text{volume of } R}{m^t} \right|$$

(42)

where R ranges over all sets of points of the form

$$R = \{(y_1, \ldots, y_t) \mid \alpha_1 \le y_1 < \beta_1, \ldots, \alpha_t \le y_t < \beta_t\};$$ (43)

here α_j and β_j are integers in the range $0 \le \alpha_j < \beta_j \le m$, for $1 \le j \le t$. The volume of R is clearly $(\beta_1 - \alpha_1) \ldots (\beta_t - \alpha_t)$. To get the discrepancy $D_N^{(t)}$, we imagine looking at all these sets R and finding the one with the greatest excess or deficiency of points $(x_n, \ldots, x_{n+t-1})$.

An upper bound for the discrepancy can be found by using exponential sums. Let $\omega = e^{2\pi i/m}$ be a primitive mth root of unity. If $(x_1, \ldots, x_t)$ and $(y_1, \ldots, y_t)$ are two vectors with all components in the range $0 \le x_j, y_j < m$, we have

$$\sum_{0 \le u_1, \ldots, u_t < m} \omega^{(x_1-y_1)u_1 + \cdots + (x_t-y_t)u_t} = \begin{cases} m^t & \text{if } (x_1, \ldots, x_t) = (y_1, \ldots, y_t), \\ 0 & \text{if } (x_1, \ldots, x_t) \ne (y_1, \ldots, y_t). \end{cases}$$

Therefore the number of vectors $(x_n, \ldots, x_{n+t-1})$ in R for $0 \le n < N$, when R is defined by (43), can be expressed as

$$\frac{1}{m^t} \sum_{0 \le n < N} \sum_{0 \le u_1, \ldots, u_t < m} \omega^{x_n u_1 + \cdots + x_{n+t-1} u_t} \sum_{\alpha_1 \le y_1 < \beta_1} \cdots \sum_{\alpha_t \le y_t < \beta_t} \omega^{-(y_1 u_1 + \cdots + y_t u_t)}.$$

When $u_1 = \cdots = u_t = 0$ in this sum, we get N/m^t times the volume of R; hence we can express $D_N^{(t)}$ as the maximum over R of

$$\left| \frac{1}{Nm^t} \sum_{0 \le n < N} \sum_{\substack{0 \le u_1, \ldots, u_t < m \\ (u_1, \ldots, u_t) \ne (0, \ldots, 0)}} \omega^{x_n u_1 + \cdots + x_{n+t-1} u_t} \sum_{\alpha_1 \le y_1 < \beta_1} \cdots \sum_{\alpha_t \le y_t < \beta_t} \omega^{-(y_1 u_1 + \cdots + y_t u_t)} \right|.$$

Since complex numbers satisfy $|w + z| \le |w| + |z|$ and $|wz| = |w||z|$, it follows that

$$D_N^{(t)} \le \max_R \frac{1}{m^t} \sum_{\substack{0 \le u_1, \ldots, u_t < m \\ (u_1, \ldots, u_t) \ne (0, \ldots, 0)}} \left| \sum_{\alpha_1 \le y_1 < \beta_1} \cdots \sum_{\alpha_t \le y_t < \beta_t} \omega^{-(y_1 u_1 + \cdots + y_t u_t)} \right| g(u_1, \ldots, u_t)$$

$$\le \frac{1}{m^t} \sum_{\substack{0 \le u_1, \ldots, u_t < m \\ (u_1, \ldots, u_t) \ne (0, \ldots, 0)}} \max_R \left| \sum_{\alpha_1 \le y_1 < \beta_1} \cdots \sum_{\alpha_t \le y_t < \beta_t} \omega^{-(y_1 u_1 + \cdots + y_t u_t)} \right| g(u_1, \ldots, u_t)$$

$$= \sum_{\substack{0 \le u_1,\dots,u_t < m \\ (u_1,\dots,u_t) \ne (0,\dots,0)}} f(u_1,\dots,u_t)\, g(u_1,\dots,u_t), \tag{44}$$

where

$$g(u_1,\dots,u_t) = \left| \frac{1}{N} \sum_{0 \le n < N} \omega^{x_n u_1 + \cdots + x_{n+t-1} u_t} \right|;$$

$$f(u_1,\dots,u_t) = \max_R \frac{1}{m^t} \left| \sum_{\alpha_1 \le y_1 < \beta_1} \cdots \sum_{\alpha_t \le y_t < \beta_t} \omega^{-(y_1 u_1 + \cdots + y_t u_t)} \right|$$

$$= \max_R \left| \frac{1}{m} \sum_{\alpha_1 \le y_1 < \beta_1} \omega^{-u_1 y_1} \right| \cdots \left| \frac{1}{m} \sum_{\alpha_t \le y_t < \beta_t} \omega^{-u_t y_t} \right|.$$

Both f and g can be simplified further in order to get a good upper bound on $D_N^{(t)}$. We have

$$\left| \frac{1}{m} \sum_{\alpha \le y < \beta} \omega^{-uy} \right| = \left| \frac{1}{m} \frac{\omega^{-\beta u} - \omega^{-\alpha u}}{\omega^{-u} - 1} \right| \le \frac{2}{m\,|\omega^u - 1|} = \frac{1}{m \sin(\pi u/m)}$$

when $u \ne 0$, and the sum is ≤ 1 when $u = 0$; hence

$$f(u_1,\dots,u_t) \le r(u_1,\dots,u_t), \tag{45}$$

where

$$r(u_1,\dots,u_t) = \prod_{\substack{1 \le k \le t \\ u_k \ne 0}} \frac{1}{m \sin(\pi u_k/m)}. \tag{46}$$

Furthermore, when $\langle x_n \rangle$ is generated modulo m by a linear congruential sequence, we have

$$x_n u_1 + \cdots + x_{n+t-1} u_t = x_n u_1 + (ax_n + c)u_2 + \cdots + \bigl(a^{t-1} x_n + c(a^{t-2} + \cdots + 1)\bigr)u_t$$

$$= (u_1 + au_2 + \cdots + a^{t-1} u_t)x_n + h(u_1,\dots,u_t)$$

where $h(u_1,\dots,u_t)$ is independent of n; hence

$$g(u_1,\dots,u_t) = \left| \frac{1}{N} \sum_{0 \le n < N} \omega^{q(u_1,\dots,u_t)x_n} \right|, \tag{47}$$

where

$$q(u_1,\dots,u_t) = u_1 + au_2 + \cdots + a^{t-1} u_t. \tag{48}$$

Now here is where the connection to the spectral test comes in: We will show that the sum $g(u_1,\dots,u_t)$ is rather small unless $q(u_1,\dots,u_t) \equiv 0$ (modulo m); in other words, the contributions to (44) arise mainly from the solutions to (15). Furthermore exercise 27 shows that $r(u_1,\dots,u_t)$ is rather small when $(u_1,\dots,u_t)$ is a "large" solution to (15). Hence the discrepancy $D_N^{(t)}$ will be rather small when (15) has only "large" solutions, namely when the spectral test is passed. Our remaining task is to quantify these qualitative statements by making careful calculations.

In the first place, let's consider the size of $g(u_1, \ldots, u_t)$. When $N = m$, so that the sum (47) is over an entire period, we have $g(u_1, \ldots, u_t) = 0$ except when $(u_1, \ldots, u_t)$ satisfies (15), so the discrepancy is bounded above in this case by the sum of $r(u_1, \ldots, u_t)$ taken over all the nonzero solutions of (15). But let's consider also what happens in a sum like (47) when N is less than m and $q(u_1, \ldots, u_t)$ is not a multiple of m. We have

$$\sum_{0 \le n < N} \omega^{x_n} = \sum_{0 \le n < N} \frac{1}{m} \sum_{0 \le k < m} \omega^{-nk} \sum_{0 \le j < m} \omega^{x_j + jk}$$

$$= \sum_{0 \le k < m} \left(\frac{1}{m} \sum_{0 \le n < N} \omega^{-nk} \right) S_{k0}, \tag{49}$$

where

$$S_{kl} = \sum_{0 \le j < m} \omega^{x_{j+l} + jk}. \tag{50}$$

Now $S_{kl} = \omega^{-lk} S_{k0}$, so $|S_{kl}| = |S_{k0}|$ for all l, and we can calculate this common value by further exponential-summery:

$$|S_{k0}|^2 = \frac{1}{m} \sum_{0 \le l < m} |S_{kl}|^2$$

$$= \frac{1}{m} \sum_{0 \le l < m} \sum_{0 \le j < m} \omega^{x_{j+l} + jk} \sum_{0 \le i < m} \omega^{-x_{i+l} - ik}$$

$$= \frac{1}{m} \sum_{0 \le i,j < m} \omega^{(j-i)k} \sum_{0 \le l < m} \omega^{x_{j+l} - x_{i+l}}$$

$$= \frac{1}{m} \sum_{0 \le i < m} \sum_{i \le j < m+i} \omega^{(j-i)k} \sum_{0 \le l < m} \omega^{(a^{j-i}-1)x_{i+l} + (a^{j-i}-1)c/(a-1)}.$$

Let s be minimum such that $a^s \equiv 1$ (modulo m), and let

$$s' = (a^s - 1)c/(a-1) \bmod m.$$

Then s is a divisor of m (see Lemma 3.2.1.2P), and $x_{n+js} \equiv x_n + js'$ (modulo m). The sum on l vanishes unless $j - i$ is a multiple of s, so we find that

$$|S_{k0}|^2 = m \sum_{0 \le j < m/s} \omega^{jsk + js'}.$$

We have $s' = q's$ where q' is relatively prime to m (see exercise 3.2.1.2–21), so it turns out that

$$|S_{k0}| = \begin{cases} 0 & \text{if } k + q' \not\equiv 0 \text{ (modulo } m/s), \\ m/\sqrt{s} & \text{if } k + q' \equiv 0 \text{ (modulo } m/s). \end{cases} \tag{51}$$

Putting this information back into (49), and recalling the derivation of (45), shows that

$$\left| \sum_{0 \le n < N} \omega^{x_n} \right| \le \frac{m}{\sqrt{s}} \sum_k r(k), \qquad (52)$$

where the sum is over $0 \le k < m$ such that $k + q' \equiv 0 \pmod{m/s}$. Exercise 25 can now be used to estimate the remaining sum, and we find that

$$\left| \sum_{0 \le n < N} \omega^{x_n} \right| \le \frac{2}{\pi} \sqrt{s} \ln s + O\left(\frac{m}{\sqrt{s}}\right). \qquad (53)$$

The same upper bound applies also to $|\sum_{0 \le n < N} \omega^{q x_n}|$ for any $q \not\equiv 0 \pmod{m}$, since the effect is to replace m in this derivation by a divisor of m. In fact, the upper bound gets even smaller when q has a factor in common with m, since s and $m/\sqrt{s}$ generally become smaller. (See exercise 26.)

We have now proved that the $g(u_1, \ldots, u_t)$ part of our upper bound (44) on the discrepancy is small, if N is large enough and if $(u_1, \ldots, u_t)$ does not satisfy the spectral test congruence (15). Exercise 27 proves that the $f(u_1, \ldots, u_t)$ part of our upper bound is small, when summed over all the nonzero vectors $(u_1, \ldots, u_t)$ satisfying (15), provided that all such vectors are far away from $(0, \ldots, 0)$. Putting these results together leads to the following theorem of Niederreiter:

Theorem N. *Let $\langle X_n \rangle$ be a linear congruential sequence (X_0, a, c, m) of period length $m > 1$, and let s be the least positive integer such that $a^s \equiv 1 \pmod{m}$. Then the t-dimensional discrepancy $D_N^{(t)}$ corresponding to the first N values of $\langle X_n \rangle$, as defined in (42), satisfies*

$$D_N^{(t)} = O\left(\frac{\sqrt{s} \log s (\log m)^t}{N}\right) + O\left(\frac{m(\log m)^t}{N\sqrt{s}}\right) + O\big((\log m)^t r_{\max}\big); \quad (54)$$

$$D_m^{(t)} = O\big((\log m)^t r_{\max}\big). \qquad (55)$$

Here $r_{\max}$ is the maximum value of the quantity $r(u_1, \ldots, u_t)$ defined in (46), taken over all nonzero integer vectors $(u_1, \ldots, u_t)$ satisfying (15).

Proof. The first two O-terms in (54) come from vectors $(u_1, \ldots, u_t)$ in (44) that do not satisfy (15), since exercise 25 proves that $f(u_1, \ldots, u_t)$ summed over all $(u_1, \ldots, u_t)$ is $O\big(((2/\pi) \ln m)^t\big)$ and exercise 26 bounds each $g(u_1, \ldots, u_t)$. (These terms are missing from (55) since $g(u_1, \ldots, u_t) = 0$ in that case.) The remaining O-term in (54) and (55) comes from nonzero vectors $(u_1, \ldots, u_t)$ that do satisfy (15), using the bound derived in exercise 27. (By examining this proof carefully, we could replace each O in these formulas by an explicit function of t.) ∎

Eq. (55) relates to the serial test in t dimensions over the entire period, while Eq. (54) gives us useful information about the distribution of the first N generated values when N is less than m, provided that N is not too small.

Notice that (54) will guarantee low discrepancy only when s is sufficiently large, otherwise the $m/\sqrt{s}$ term will dominate. If $m = p_1^{e_1} \ldots p_r^{e_r}$ and $\gcd(a-1, m) = p_1^{f_1} \ldots p_r^{f_r}$, then s equals $p_1^{e_1-f_1} \ldots p_r^{e_r-f_r}$ by Lemma 3.2.1.2P; thus, the largest values of s correspond to high potency. In the common case $m = 2^e$ and $a \equiv 5$ (modulo 8), we have $s = \frac{1}{4}m$, so $D_N^{(t)}$ is $O\big(\sqrt{m}\,(\log m)^{t+1}/N\big) + O\big((\log m)^t r_{\max}\big)$. It is not difficult to prove that

$$r_{\max} \leq \frac{1}{\sqrt{8}\,\nu_t} \tag{56}$$

(see exercise 29). Therefore Eq. (54) says in particular that the discrepancy will be low in t dimensions if the spectral test is passed and if N is somewhat larger than $\sqrt{m}\,(\log m)^{t+1}$.

In a sense Theorem N is almost too strong, for the result in exercise 30 shows that linear congruential sequences like those in lines 8 and 13 of Table 1 have a discrepancy of order $(\log m)^2/m$ in two dimensions. The discrepancy in this case is extremely small in spite of the fact that there are parallelogram-shaped regions of area $\approx 1/\sqrt{m}$ containing no points (U_n, U_{n+1}). The fact that discrepancy can change so drastically when the points are rotated warns us that the serial test may not be as meaningful a measure of randomness as the rotation-invariant spectral test.

G. Historical remarks. In 1959, while deriving upper bounds for the error in the evaluation of t-dimensional integrals by the Monte Carlo method, N. M. Korobov devised a way to rate the multiplier of a linear congruential sequence. His rather complicated formula is related to the spectral test, since it is strongly influenced by "small" solutions to (15); but it is not quite the same. Korobov's test has been the subject of an extensive literature, surveyed by Kuipers and Niederreiter in *Uniform Distribution of Sequences* (New York: Wiley, 1974), §2.5.

The spectral test was originally formulated by R. R. Coveyou and R. D. MacPherson [*JACM* **14** (1967), 100–119], who introduced it in an interesting indirect way. Instead of working with the grid structure of successive points, they considered random number generators as sources of t-dimensional "waves." The numbers $\sqrt{x_1^2 + \cdots + x_t^2}$ such that $x_1 + \cdots + a^{t-1}x_t \equiv 0$ (modulo m) in their original treatment were the wave "frequencies," or points in the "spectrum" defined by the random number generator, with low-frequency waves being the most damaging to randomness; hence the name *spectral test*. Coveyou and MacPherson introduced a procedure analogous to Algorithm S for performing their test, based on the principle of Lemma A. However, their original procedure (which used matrices UU^T and VV^T instead of U and V) dealt with extremely large numbers; the idea of working directly with U and V was independently suggested by F. Janssens and by U. Dieter. [See *Math. Comp.* **29** (1975), 827–833.]

Several other authors pointed out that the spectral test could be understood in far more concrete terms; by introducing the study of the grid and lattice structures corresponding to linear congruential sequences, the fundamental limitations on randomness became graphically clear. See G. Marsaglia, *Proc. Nat. Acad. Sci.*

61 (1968), 25–28; W. W. Wood, *J. Chem. Phys.* **48** (1968), 427; R. R. Coveyou, *Studies in Applied Math.* **3** (Philadelphia: SIAM, 1969), 70–111; W. A. Beyer, R. B. Roof, and D. Williamson, *Math. Comp.* **25** (1971), 345–360; G. Marsaglia and W. A. Beyer, *Applications of Number Theory to Numerical Analysis*, edited by S. K. Zaremba (New York: Academic Press, 1972), 249–285, 361–370.

R. G. Stoneham showed, by using estimates of exponential sums, that $p^{1/2+\epsilon}$ or more elements of the sequence $a^k X_0 \bmod p$ have asymptotically small discrepancy, when a is a primitive root modulo the prime p [*Acta Arithmetica* **22** (1973), 371–389]. This work was extended as explained above in a number of papers by Harald Niederreiter [*Math. Comp.* **28** (1974), 1117–1132; **30** (1976), 571–597; *Advances in Math.* **26** (1977), 99–181; *Bull. Amer. Math. Soc.* **84** (1978), 957–1041]. See also Niederreiter's book *Random Number Generation and Quasi-Monte Carlo Methods* (Philadelphia: SIAM, 1992).

EXERCISES

1. [*M10*] To what does the spectral test reduce in *one* dimension? (In other words, what happens when $t = 1$?)

2. [*HM20*] Let V_1, ..., V_t be linearly independent vectors in t-space, let L_0 be the lattice of points defined by (10), and let U_1, ..., U_t be defined by (19). Prove that the maximum distance between $(t-1)$-dimensional hyperplanes, over all families of parallel hyperplanes that cover L_0, is $1/\min\{f(x_1,\ldots,x_t)^{1/2} \mid (x_1,\ldots,x_t) \neq (0,\ldots,0)\}$, where f is defined in (17).

3. [*M24*] Determine ν_3 and ν_4 for all linear congruential generators of potency 2 and period length m.

▶ **4.** [*M23*] Let u_{11}, u_{12}, u_{21}, u_{22} be elements of a 2×2 integer matrix such that $u_{11} + au_{12} \equiv u_{21} + au_{22} \equiv 0$ (modulo m) and $u_{11}u_{22} - u_{21}u_{12} = m$.

  a) Prove that all integer solutions (y_1, y_2) to the congruence $y_1 + ay_2 \equiv 0$ (modulo m) have the form $(y_1, y_2) = (x_1u_{11}+x_2u_{21}, x_1u_{12}+x_2u_{22})$ for integer x_1, x_2.

  b) If, in addition, $2|u_{11}u_{21} + u_{12}u_{22}| \leq u_{21}^2 + u_{12}^2 \leq u_{21}^2 + u_{22}^2$, prove that $(y_1, y_2) = (u_{11}, u_{12})$ minimizes $y_1^2 + y_2^2$ over all nonzero solutions to the congruence.

5. [*M30*] Prove that steps S1 through S3 of Algorithm S correctly perform the spectral test in two dimensions. [*Hint:* See exercise 4, and prove that $(h'+h)^2+(p'+p)^2 \geq h^2+p^2$ at the beginning of step S2.]

6. [*M30*] Let $a_0, a_1, \ldots, a_{t-1}$ be the partial quotients of a/m as defined in Section 3.3.3, and let $A = \max_{0 \leq j < t} a_j$. Prove that $\mu_2 > 2\pi/(A+1+1/A)$.

7. [*HM22*] Prove that questions (a) and (b) following Eq. (23) have the same solution for real values of $q_1, \ldots, q_{j-1}, q_{j+1}, \ldots, q_t$ (see (24) and (26)).

8. [*M18*] Line 10 of Table 1 has a very low value of μ_2, yet μ_3 is quite satisfactory. What is the highest possible value of μ_3 when $\mu_2 = 10^{-6}$ and $m = 10^{10}$?

9. [*HM32*] (C. Hermite, 1846.) Let $f(x_1,\ldots,x_t)$ be a positive definite quadratic form, defined by the matrix U as in (17), and let θ be the minimum value of f at nonzero integer points. Prove that $\theta \leq (\frac{4}{3})^{(t-1)/2} |\det U|^{2/t}$. [*Hints:* If W is any integer matrix of determinant 1, the matrix WU defines a form equivalent to f; and if S is any orthogonal matrix (that is, if $S^{-1} = S^T$), the matrix US defines a form identically equal to f. Show that there is an equivalent form g whose minimum θ occurs at

$(1, 0, \ldots, 0)$. Then prove the general result by induction on t, writing $g(x_1, \ldots, x_t) = \theta(x_1 + \beta_2 x_2 + \cdots + \beta_t x_t)^2 + h(x_2, \ldots, x_t)$ where h is a positive definite quadratic form in $t - 1$ variables.]

10. [*M28*] Let y_1 and y_2 be relatively prime integers such that $y_1 + ay_2 \equiv 0$ (modulo m) and $y_1^2 + y_2^2 < \sqrt{4/3}\, m$. Show that there exist integers u_1 and u_2 such that $u_1 + au_2 \equiv 0$ (modulo m), $u_1 y_2 - u_2 y_1 = m$, $2\,|u_1 y_1 + u_2 y_2| \le \min(u_1^2 + u_2^2, y_1^2 + y_2^2)$, and $(u_1^2 + u_2^2) \times (y_1^2 + y_2^2) \ge m^2$. (Hence $\nu_2^2 = \min(u_1^2 + u_2^2, y_1^2 + y_2^2)$ by exercise 4.)

▶ **11.** [*HM30*] (Alan G. Waterman, 1974.) Invent a reasonably efficient procedure that computes multipliers $a \equiv 1$ (modulo 4) for which there exists a relatively prime solution to the congruence $y_1 + ay_2 \equiv 0$ (modulo m) with $y_1^2 + y_2^2 = \sqrt{4/3}\, m - \epsilon$, where $\epsilon > 0$ is as small as possible, given $m = 2^e$. (By exercise 10, this choice of a will guarantee that $\nu_2^2 \ge m^2/(y_1^2 + y_2^2) > \sqrt{3/4}\, m$, and there is a chance that ν_2^2 will be near its optimum value $\sqrt{4/3}\, m$. In practice we will compute several such multipliers having small ϵ, choosing the one with best spectral values $\nu_2, \nu_3, \ldots$.)

12. [*HM23*] Prove, without geometrical handwaving, that any solution to question (b) following Eq. (23) must also satisfy the set of equations (26).

13. [*HM22*] Lemma A uses the fact that U is nonsingular to prove that a positive definite quadratic form attains a definite, nonzero minimum value at nonzero integer points. Show that this hypothesis is necessary, by exhibiting a quadratic form (19) whose matrix of coefficients is singular, and for which the values of $f(x_1, \ldots, x_t)$ get arbitrarily near zero (but never reach it) at nonzero integer points $(x_1, \ldots, x_t)$.

14. [*24*] Perform Algorithm S by hand, for $m = 100$, $a = 41$, $T = 3$.

▶ **15.** [*M20*] Let U be an integer vector satisfying (15). How many of the $(t-1)$-dimensional hyperplanes defined by U intersect the unit hypercube $\{(x_1, \ldots, x_t) \mid 0 \le x_j < 1$ for $1 \le j \le t\}$? (This is approximately the number of hyperplanes in the family that will suffice to cover L_0.)

16. [*M30*] (U. Dieter.) Show how to modify Algorithm S in order to calculate the minimum number N_t of parallel hyperplanes intersecting the unit hypercube as in exercise 15, over all U satisfying (15). [*Hint:* What are appropriate analogs to positive definite quadratic forms and to Lemma A?]

17. [*20*] Modify Algorithm S so that, in addition to computing the quantities ν_t, it outputs all integer vectors $(u_1, \ldots, u_t)$ satisfying (15) such that $u_1^2 + \cdots + u_t^2 = \nu_t^2$, for $2 \le t \le T$.

18. [*M30*] This exercise is about the worst case of Algorithm S.
  a) By considering "combinatorial matrices," whose elements have the form $y + x\delta_{ij}$ (see exercise 1.2.3–39), find 3×3 matrices of integers U and V satisfying (29) such that the transformation of step S5 does nothing for any j, but the corresponding values of z_k in (31) are so huge that exhaustive search is out of the question. (The matrix U need not satisfy (28); we are interested here in *arbitrary* positive definite quadratic forms of determinant m.)
  b) Although transformation (23) is of no use for the matrices constructed in (a), find another transformation that does produce a substantial reduction.

▶ **19.** [*HM25*] Suppose step S5 were changed slightly, so that a transformation with $q = 1$ would be performed when $2V_i \cdot V_j = V_j \cdot V_j$. (Thus, $q = \lfloor (V_i \cdot V_j / V_j \cdot V_j) + \frac{1}{2} \rfloor$ whenever $i \ne j$.) Would it be possible for Algorithm S to get into an infinite loop?

20. [*M23*] Discuss how to carry out an appropriate spectral test for linear congruential sequences having $c = 0$, X_0 odd, $m = 2^e$, $a \bmod 8 = 3$ or 5. (See exercise 3.2.1.2–9.)

21. [*M20*] (R. W. Gosper.) A certain application uses random numbers in batches of four, but "throws away" the second of each set. How can we study the grid structure of $\left\{ \frac{1}{m}(X_{4n}, X_{4n+2}, X_{4n+3}) \right\}$, given a linear congruential generator of period $m = 2^e$?

22. [*M46*] What is the best upper bound on μ_3, given that μ_2 is very near its maximum value $\sqrt{4/3}\,\pi$? What is the best upper bound on μ_2, given that μ_3 is very near its maximum value $\frac{4}{3}\pi\sqrt{2}$?

23. [*M46*] Let U_i, V_j be vectors of real numbers with $U_i \cdot V_j = \delta_{ij}$ for $1 \le i, j \le t$, and such that $U_i \cdot U_i = 1$, $2|U_i \cdot U_j| \le 1$, $2|V_i \cdot V_j| \le V_j \cdot V_j$ for $i \ne j$. How large can $V_1 \cdot V_1$ be? (This question relates to the bounds in step S7, if both (23) and the transformation of exercise 18(b) fail to make any reductions. The maximum value known to be achievable is $(t+2)/3$, which occurs when $U_1 = I_1$, $U_j = \frac{1}{2}I_1 + \frac{1}{2}\sqrt{3}\,I_j$, $V_1 = I_1 - (I_2 + \cdots + I_t)/\sqrt{3}$, $V_j = 2I_j/\sqrt{3}$, for $2 \le j \le t$, where $(I_1, \ldots, I_t)$ is the identity matrix; this construction is due to B. V. Alexeev.)

▶ **24.** [*M28*] Generalize the spectral test to second-order sequences of the form $X_n = (aX_{n-1} + bX_{n-2}) \bmod p$, having period length $p^2 - 1$. (See Eq. 3.2.2–(8).) How should Algorithm S be modified?

25. [*HM24*] Let d be a divisor of m and let $0 \le q < d$. Prove that $\sum r(k)$, summed over all $0 \le k < m$ such that $k \bmod d = q$, is at most $(2/d\pi) \ln(m/d) + O(1)$. (Here $r(k)$ is defined in Eq. (46) when $t = 1$.)

26. [*M22*] Explain why the derivation of (53) leads to a similar bound on

$$\left| \sum_{0 \le n < N} \omega^{qx_n} \right|$$

for $0 < q < m$.

27. [*HM39*] (E. Hlawka, H. Niederreiter.) Let $r(u_1, \ldots, u_t)$ be the function defined in (46). Prove that $\sum r(u_1, \ldots, u_t)$, summed over all $0 \le u_1, \ldots, u_t < m$ such that $(u_1, \ldots, u_t) \ne (0, \ldots, 0)$ and (15) holds, is at most $2((\pi + 2\pi \lg m)^t r_{\max})$, where $r_{\max}$ is the maximum term $r(u_1, \ldots, u_t)$ in the sum.

▶ **28.** [*M28*] (H. Niederreiter.) Find an analog of Theorem N for the case $m =$ prime, $c = 0$, $a =$ primitive root modulo m, $X_0 \ne 0$ (modulo m). [*Hint:* Your exponential sums should involve $\zeta = e^{2\pi i/(m-1)}$ as well as ω.] Prove that in this case the "average" primitive root has discrepancy $D_{m-1}^{(t)} = O\left(t(\log m)^t/\varphi(m-1)\right)$, hence good primitive roots exist for all m.

29. [*HM22*] Prove that the quantity $r_{\max}$ of exercise 27 is never larger than $1/(\sqrt{8}\,\nu_t)$.

30. [*M33*] (S. K. Zaremba.) Prove that $r_{\max} = O\left(\max(a_1, \ldots, a_s)/m\right)$ in two dimensions, where a_1, $\ldots$, a_s are the partial quotients obtained when Euclid's algorithm is applied to m and a. [*Hint:* We have $a/m = //a_1, \ldots, a_s//$, in the notation of Section 4.5.3; apply exercise 4.5.3–42.]

31. [*HM47*] (I. Borosh.) Prove that for all sufficiently large m there exists a number a relatively prime to m such that all partial quotients of a/m are ≤ 3. Furthermore the set of all m satisfying this condition but with all partial quotients ≤ 2 has positive density.

▶ **32.** [*M21*] Let $m_1 = 2^{31} - 1$ and $m_2 = 2^{31} - 249$ be the moduli of generator (38).

a) Show that if $U_n = (X_n/m_1 - Y_n/m_2) \bmod 1$, we have $U_n \approx Z_n/m_1$.

b) Let $W_0 = (X_0 m_2 - Y_0 m_1) \bmod m$ and $W_{n+1} = aW_n \bmod m$, where a and m have the values stated in the text following (38). Prove that there is a simple relation between W_n and U_n.

In the next edition of this book, I plan to introduce a new Section 3.3.5, entitled "The L^3 Algorithm." It will be a digression from the general topic of Random Numbers, but it will continue the discussion of lattice basis reduction in Section 3.3.4. Its main topic will be the now-classic algorithm of A. K. Lenstra, H. W. Lenstra, Jr., and L. Lovász [Math. Annalen **261** (1982), 515–534] for finding a near-optimum set of basis vectors, and improvements to that algorithm made subsequently by other researchers. Examples of the latter can be found in the following papers and their bibliographies: M. Seysen, Combinatorica **13** (1993), 363–375; C. P. Schnorr and H. H. Hörner, Lecture Notes in Comp. Sci. **921** (1995), 1–12.

3.4. OTHER TYPES OF RANDOM QUANTITIES

WE HAVE NOW SEEN how to make a computer generate a sequence of numbers U_0, U_1, U_2, ... that behaves as if each number were independently selected at random between zero and one with the uniform distribution. Applications of random numbers often call for other kinds of distributions, however; for example, if we want to make a random choice from among k alternatives, we want a random *integer* between 1 and k. If some simulation process calls for a random waiting time between occurrences of independent events, a random number with the *exponential distribution* is desired. Sometimes we don't even want random *numbers* — we want a random *permutation* (a random arrangement of n objects) or a random *combination* (a random choice of k objects from a collection of n).

In principle, any of these other random quantities can be obtained from the uniform deviates U_0, U_1, U_2, ...; people have devised a number of important "random tricks" for the efficient transformation of uniform deviates. A study of these techniques also gives us insight into the proper use of random numbers in any Monte Carlo application.

It is conceivable that someday somebody will invent a random number generator that produces one of these other random quantities *directly*, instead of getting it indirectly via the uniform distribution. But no direct methods have as yet proved to be practical, except for the "random bit" generator described in Section 3.2.2. (See also exercise 3.4.1–31, where the uniform distribution is used primarily for initialization, after which the method is almost entirely direct.)

The discussion in the following section assumes the existence of a random sequence of uniformly distributed real numbers between zero and one. A new uniform deviate U is generated whenever we need it. These numbers are usually represented in a computer word with the radix point assumed at the left.

3.4.1. Numerical Distributions

This section summarizes the best techniques known for producing numbers from various important distributions. Many of the methods were originally suggested by John von Neumann in the early 1950s, and they have gradually been improved upon by other people, notably George Marsaglia, J. H. Ahrens, and U. Dieter.

A. Random choices from a finite set. The simplest and most common type of distribution required in practice is a random *integer*. An integer between 0 and 7 can be extracted from three bits of U on a binary computer; in such a case, these bits should be extracted from the *most significant* (left-hand) part of the computer word, since the least significant bits produced by many random number generators are not sufficiently random. (See the discussion in Section 3.2.1.1.)

In general, to get a random integer X between 0 and $k - 1$, we can *multiply* by k, and let $X = \lfloor kU \rfloor$. On MIX, we would write

$$\begin{array}{ll} \texttt{LDA} & \texttt{U} \\ \texttt{MUL} & \texttt{K} \end{array} \qquad (1)$$

and after these two instructions have been executed the desired integer will appear in register A. If a random integer between 1 and k is desired, we add one to this result. (The instruction "INCA 1" would follow (1).)

This method gives each integer with nearly equal probability. There is a slight error because the computer word size is finite (see exercise 2); but the error is quite negligible if k is small, for example if $k/m < 1/10000$.

In a more general situation we might want to give different weights to different integers. Suppose that the value $X = x_1$ is to be obtained with probability p_1, and $X = x_2$ with probability p_2, ..., $X = x_k$ with probability p_k. We can generate a uniform number U and let

$$X = \begin{cases} x_1, & \text{if } 0 \le U < p_1; \\ x_2, & \text{if } p_1 \le U < p_1 + p_2; \\ \vdots & \\ x_k, & \text{if } p_1 + p_2 + \cdots + p_{k-1} \le U < 1. \end{cases} \tag{2}$$

(Note that $p_1 + p_2 + \cdots + p_k = 1$.)

There is a "best possible" way to do the comparisons of U against various values of $p_1 + p_2 + \cdots + p_s$, as implied in (2); this situation is discussed in Section 2.3.4.5. Special cases can be handled by more efficient methods; for example, to obtain one of the eleven values 2, 3, ..., 12 with the respective "dice" probabilities $\frac{1}{36}, \frac{2}{36}, \ldots, \frac{6}{36}, \ldots, \frac{2}{36}, \frac{1}{36}$, we could compute two independent random integers between 1 and 6 and add them together.

However, there is actually a faster way to select $x_1, \ldots, x_k$ with arbitrarily given probabilities, based on an ingenious approach introduced by A. J. Walker [*Electronics Letters* **10**, 8 (1974), 127–128; *ACM Trans. Math. Software* **3** (1977), 253–256]. Suppose we form kU and consider the integer part $K = \lfloor kU \rfloor$ and fraction part $V = (kU) \bmod 1$ separately; for example, after the code (1) we will have K in register A and V in register X. Then we can always obtain the desired distribution by doing the operations

$$\text{if} \quad V < P_K \quad \text{then} \quad X \leftarrow x_{K+1} \quad \text{otherwise} \quad X \leftarrow Y_K, \tag{3}$$

for some appropriate tables $(P_0, \ldots, P_{k-1})$ and $(Y_0, \ldots, Y_{k-1})$. Exercise 7 shows how such tables can be computed in general. Walker's method is sometimes called the method of "aliases."

On a binary computer it is usually helpful to assume that k is a power of 2, so that multiplication can be replaced by shifting; this can be done without loss of generality by introducing additional x's that occur with probability zero. For example, let's consider dice again; suppose we want $X = j$ to occur with the following 16 probabilities:

$j =$	0	1	2	3	4	5	6	7	8	9	10	11	12	13	14	15
$p_j =$	0	0	$\frac{1}{36}$	$\frac{2}{36}$	$\frac{3}{36}$	$\frac{4}{36}$	$\frac{5}{36}$	$\frac{6}{36}$	$\frac{5}{36}$	$\frac{4}{36}$	$\frac{3}{36}$	$\frac{2}{36}$	$\frac{1}{36}$	0	0	0

We can do this using (3), if $k = 16$ and $x_{j+1} = j$ for $0 \le j < 16$, and if the P and Y tables are set up as follows:

$j =$	0	1	2	3	4	5	6	7	8	9	10	11	12	13	14	15
$P_j =$	0	0	$\frac{4}{9}$	$\frac{8}{9}$	1	$\frac{7}{9}$	1	1	1	$\frac{7}{9}$	$\frac{7}{9}$	$\frac{8}{9}$	$\frac{4}{9}$	0	0	0
$Y_j =$	5	9	7	4	$*$	6	$*$	$*$	$*$	8	4	7	10	6	7	8

(When $P_j = 1$, Y_j is not used.) For example, the value 7 occurs with probability $\frac{1}{16} \cdot \left((1 - P_2) + P_7 + (1 - P_{11}) + (1 - P_{14}) \right) = \frac{6}{36}$ as required. It is a peculiar way to throw dice, but the results are indistinguishable from the real thing.

The probabilities p_j can be represented implicitly by nonnegative weights $w_1, w_2, \ldots, w_k$; if we denote the sum of the weights by W, then $p_j = w_j/W$. In many applications the individual weights vary dynamically. Matias, Vitter, and Ni [*SODA* **4** (1993), 361–370] have shown how to update a weight and generate X in constant expected time.

B. General methods for continuous distributions. The most general real-valued distribution can be expressed in terms of its "distribution function" $F(x)$, which specifies the probability that a random quantity X will not exceed x:

$$F(x) = \Pr(X \le x). \tag{4}$$

This function always increases monotonically from zero to one; that is,

$$F(x_1) \le F(x_2), \quad \text{if } x_1 \le x_2; \qquad F(-\infty) = 0, \qquad F(+\infty) = 1. \tag{5}$$

Examples of distribution functions are given in Section 3.3.1, Fig. 3. If $F(x)$ is continuous and strictly increasing (so that $F(x_1) < F(x_2)$ when $x_1 < x_2$), it takes on all values between zero and one, and there is an *inverse function* $F^{[-1]}(y)$ such that, for $0 < y < 1$,

$$y = F(x) \qquad \text{if and only if} \qquad x = F^{[-1]}(y). \tag{6}$$

In general, when $F(x)$ is continuous and strictly increasing, we can compute a random quantity X with distribution $F(x)$ by setting

$$X = F^{[-1]}(U), \tag{7}$$

where U is uniform. This works because the probability that $X \le x$ is the probability that $F^{[-1]}(U) \le x$, namely the probability that $U \le F(x)$, namely $F(x)$.

The problem now reduces to one of numerical analysis, namely to find good methods for evaluating $F^{[-1]}(U)$ to the desired accuracy. Numerical analysis lies outside the scope of this seminumerical book; yet a number of important shortcuts are available to speed up the general approach of (7), and we will consider them here.

In the first place, if X_1 is a random variable having the distribution $F_1(x)$ and if X_2 is an independent random variable with the distribution $F_2(x)$, then

$$\begin{aligned} \max(X_1, X_2) \quad &\text{has the distribution} \quad F_1(x)F_2(x), \\ \min(X_1, X_2) \quad &\text{has the distribution} \quad F_1(x) + F_2(x) - F_1(x)F_2(x). \end{aligned} \tag{8}$$

(See exercise 4.) For example, a uniform deviate U has the distribution $F(x) = x$, for $0 \leq x \leq 1$; if $U_1, U_2, \ldots, U_t$ are independent uniform deviates, then $\max(U_1, U_2, \ldots, U_t)$ has the distribution function $F(x) = x^t$, for $0 \leq x \leq 1$. This formula is the basis of the "maximum-of-t test" given in Section 3.3.2; the inverse function is $F^{[-1]}(y) = \sqrt[t]{y}$. In the special case $t = 2$, we see therefore that the two formulas

$$X = \sqrt{U} \quad \text{and} \quad X = \max(U_1, U_2) \tag{9}$$

will give equivalent distributions to the random variable X, although this is not obvious at first glance. We need not take the square root of a uniform deviate.

The number of tricks like this is endless: *Any* algorithm that employs random numbers as input will give a random quantity with *some* distribution as output. The problem is to find general methods for constructing the algorithm, given the distribution function of the output. Instead of discussing such methods in purely abstract terms, we shall study how they can be applied in important cases.

C. The normal distribution. Perhaps the most important nonuniform, continuous distribution is the *normal distribution with mean zero and standard deviation one:*

$$F(x) = \frac{1}{\sqrt{2\pi}} \int_{-\infty}^{x} e^{-t^2/2} \, dt. \tag{10}$$

The significance of this distribution was indicated in Section 1.2.10. In this case the inverse function $F^{[-1]}$ is not especially easy to compute; but we shall see that several other techniques are available.

1) *The polar method*, due to G. E. P. Box, M. E. Muller, and G. Marsaglia. (See *Annals Math. Stat.* **29** (1958), 610–611; and Boeing Scientific Res. Lab. report D1-82-0203 (1962).)

Algorithm P (*Polar method for normal deviates*). This algorithm calculates two independent normally distributed variables, X_1 and X_2.

P1. [Get uniform variables.] Generate two independent random variables, U_1 and U_2, uniformly distributed between zero and one. Set $V_1 \leftarrow 2U_1 - 1$, $V_2 \leftarrow 2U_2 - 1$. (Now V_1 and V_2 are uniformly distributed between -1 and $+1$. On most computers it will be preferable to have V_1 and V_2 represented in floating point form.)

P2. [Compute S.] Set $S \leftarrow V_1^2 + V_2^2$.

P3. [Is $S \geq 1$?] If $S \geq 1$, return to step P1. (Steps P1 through P3 are executed 1.27 times on the average, with a standard deviation of 0.59; see exercise 6.)

P4. [Compute X_1, X_2.] If $S = 0$, set $X_1 \leftarrow X_2 \leftarrow 0$; otherwise set

$$X_1 \leftarrow V_1 \sqrt{\frac{-2\ln S}{S}}, \qquad X_2 \leftarrow V_2 \sqrt{\frac{-2\ln S}{S}}. \tag{11}$$

These are the normally distributed variables desired. ∎

To prove the validity of this method, we use elementary analytic geometry and calculus: If $S < 1$ in step P3, the point in the plane with Cartesian coordinates (V_1, V_2) is a *random point uniformly distributed inside the unit circle*. Transforming to polar coordinates $V_1 = R\cos\Theta$, $V_2 = R\sin\Theta$, we find

$$S = R^2, \quad X_1 = \sqrt{-2\ln S}\cos\Theta, \quad X_2 = \sqrt{-2\ln S}\sin\Theta.$$

Using also the polar coordinates $X_1 = R'\cos\Theta'$, $X_2 = R'\sin\Theta'$, we find that $\Theta' = \Theta$ and $R' = \sqrt{-2\ln S}$. It is clear that R' and Θ' are independent, since R and Θ are independent inside the unit circle. Also, Θ' is uniformly distributed between 0 and 2π; and the probability that $R' \leq r$ is the probability that $-2\ln S \leq r^2$, namely the probability that $S \geq e^{-r^2/2}$. This equals $1 - e^{-r^2/2}$, since $S = R^2$ is uniformly distributed between zero and one. The probability that R' lies between r and $r + dr$ is therefore the differential of $1 - e^{-r^2/2}$, namely $re^{-r^2/2}\,dr$. Similarly, the probability that Θ' lies between θ and $\theta + d\theta$ is $(1/2\pi)\,d\theta$. The joint probability that $X_1 \leq x_1$ and that $X_2 \leq x_2$ now can be computed; it is

$$\int_{\{(r,\theta)\,|\,r\cos\theta\leq x_1,\; r\sin\theta\leq x_2\}} \frac{1}{2\pi} e^{-r^2/2} r\, dr\, d\theta$$

$$= \frac{1}{2\pi} \int_{\{(x,y)\,|\,x\leq x_1,\; y\leq x_2\}} e^{-(x^2+y^2)/2}\, dx\, dy$$

$$= \left(\sqrt{\frac{1}{2\pi}} \int_{-\infty}^{x_1} e^{-x^2/2}\, dx\right)\left(\sqrt{\frac{1}{2\pi}} \int_{-\infty}^{x_2} e^{-y^2/2}\, dy\right).$$

This calculation proves that X_1 and X_2 are independent and normally distributed, as desired.

2) *The rectangle-wedge-tail method*, introduced by G. Marsaglia. Here we use the function

$$F(x) = \mathrm{erf}(x/\sqrt{2}) = \sqrt{\frac{2}{\pi}} \int_0^x e^{-t^2/2}\, dt, \qquad x \geq 0, \tag{12}$$

which gives the distribution of the *absolute value* of a normal deviate. After X has been computed according to distribution (12), we will attach a random sign to its value, and this will make it a true normal deviate.

The rectangle-wedge-tail approach is based on several important general techniques that we shall explore as we develop the algorithm. The first key idea is to regard $F(x)$ as a *mixture* of several other functions, namely to write

$$F(x) = p_1 F_1(x) + p_2 F_2(x) + \cdots + p_n F_n(x), \tag{13}$$

where F_1, F_2, ..., F_n are appropriate distributions and p_1, p_2, ..., p_n are nonnegative probabilities that sum to 1. If we generate a random variable X by choosing distribution F_j with probability p_j, it is easy to see that X will have distribution F overall. Some of the distributions $F_j(x)$ may be rather difficult to handle, even harder than F itself, but we can usually arrange things so that the

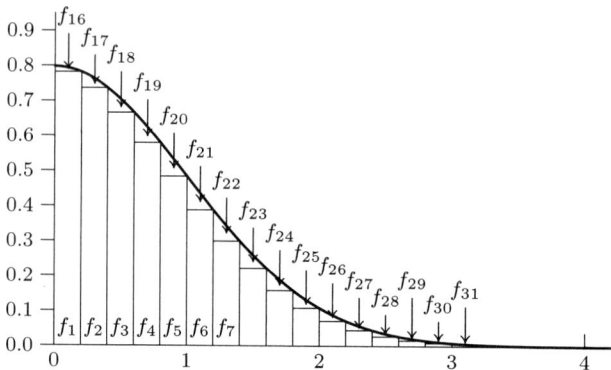

Fig. 9. The density function divided into 31 parts. The area of each part represents the average number of times a random number with that density is to be computed.

probability p_j is very small in that case. Most of the distributions $F_j(x)$ will be quite easy to accommodate, since they will be trivial modifications of the uniform distribution. The resulting method yields an extremely efficient program, since its *average* running time is very small.

It is easier to understand the method if we work with the *derivatives* of the distributions instead of the distributions themselves. Let

$$f(x) = F'(x), \qquad f_j(x) = F_j{}'(x)$$

be the *density functions* of the probability distributions. Equation (13) becomes

$$f(x) = p_1 f_1(x) + p_2 f_2(x) + \cdots + p_n f_n(x). \tag{14}$$

Each $f_j(x)$ is ≥ 0, and the total area under the graph of $f_j(x)$ is 1; so there is a convenient graphical way to display the relation (14): The area under $f(x)$ is divided into n parts, with the part corresponding to $f_j(x)$ having area p_j. See Fig. 9, which illustrates the situation in the case of interest to us here, with $f(x) = F'(x) = \sqrt{2/\pi}\, e^{-x^2/2}$; the area under this curve has been divided into $n = 31$ parts. There are 15 rectangles, which represent $p_1 f_1(x), \ldots, p_{15} f_{15}(x)$; there are 15 wedge-shaped pieces, which represent $p_{16} f_{16}(x), \ldots, p_{30} f_{30}(x)$; and the remaining part $p_{31} f_{31}(x)$ is the "tail," namely the entire graph of $f(x)$ for $x \geq 3$.

The rectangular parts $f_1(x), \ldots, f_{15}(x)$ represent *uniform distributions.* For example, $f_3(x)$ represents a random variable uniformly distributed between $\frac{2}{5}$ and $\frac{3}{5}$. The altitude of $p_j f_j(x)$ is $f(j/5)$, hence the area of the jth rectangle is

$$p_j = \frac{1}{5} f(j/5) = \sqrt{\frac{2}{25\pi}}\, e^{-j^2/50}, \qquad \text{for } 1 \leq j \leq 15. \tag{15}$$

In order to generate such rectangular portions of the distribution, we simply compute

$$X = \tfrac{1}{5} U + S, \tag{16}$$

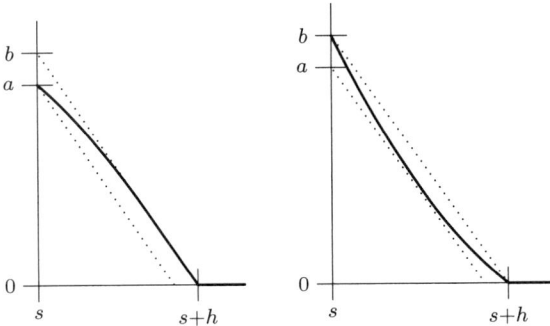

Fig. 10. Density functions for which Algorithm L may be used to generate random numbers.

where U is uniform and S takes the value $(j - 1)/5$ with probability p_j. Since $p_1 + \cdots + p_{15} = .9183$, we can use simple uniform deviates like this about 92 percent of the time.

In the remaining 8 percent, we will usually have to generate one of the wedge-shaped distributions $F_{16}, \ldots, F_{30}$. Typical examples of what we need to do are shown in Fig. 10. When $x < 1$, the curved part is concave, and when $x > 1$ it is convex, but in each case the curved part is reasonably close to a straight line, and it can be enclosed in two parallel lines as shown.

To handle these wedge-shaped distributions, we will rely on yet another general technique, von Neumann's *rejection method* for obtaining a complicated density from another one that "encloses" it. The polar method described above is a simple example of such an approach: Steps P1–P3 obtain a random point inside the unit circle by first generating a random point in a larger square, rejecting it and starting over again if the point was outside the circle.

The general rejection method is even more powerful than this. To generate a random variable X with density f, let g be another probability density function such that

$$f(t) \le cg(t) \tag{17}$$

for all t, where c is a constant. Now generate X according to density g, and also generate an independent uniform deviate U. If $U \ge f(X)/cg(X)$, reject X and start again with another X and U. When the condition $U < f(X)/cg(X)$ finally occurs, the resulting X will have density f as desired. [*Proof:* $X \le x$ will occur with probability $p(x) = \int_{-\infty}^{x} \left(g(t)\, dt \cdot f(t)/cg(t) \right) + qp(x)$, where the quantity $q = \int_{-\infty}^{\infty} \left(g(t)\, dt \cdot (1 - f(t)/cg(t)) \right) = 1 - 1/c$ is the probability of rejection; hence $p(x) = \int_{-\infty}^{x} f(t)\, dt.$]

The rejection technique is most efficient when c is small, since there will be c iterations on the average before a value is accepted. (See exercise 6.) In some cases $f(x)/cg(x)$ is always 0 or 1; then U need not be generated. In other cases if $f(x)/cg(x)$ is hard to compute, we may be able to "squeeze" it between two bounding functions

$$r(x) \le f(x)/cg(x) \le s(x) \tag{18}$$

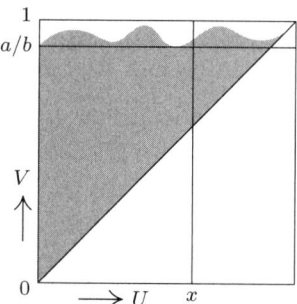

Fig. 11. Region of "acceptance" in Algorithm L.

that are much simpler, and the exact value of $f(x)/cg(x)$ need not be calculated unless $r(x) \le U < s(x)$. The following algorithm solves the wedge problem by developing the rejection method still further.

Algorithm L (*Nearly linear densities*). This algorithm may be used to generate a random variable X for any distribution whose density $f(x)$ satisfies the following conditions (see Fig. 10):

$$f(x) = 0, \qquad \text{for } x < s \text{ and for } x > s + h;$$
$$a - b(x - s)/h \le f(x) \le b - b(x - s)/h, \qquad \text{for } s \le x \le s + h. \tag{19}$$

L1. [Get $U \le V$.] Generate two independent random variables U and V, uniformly distributed between zero and one. If $U > V$, exchange $U \leftrightarrow V$.

L2. [Easy case?] If $V \le a/b$, go to L4.

L3. [Try again?] If $V > U + (1/b)f(s + hU)$, go back to step L1. (If a/b is close to 1, this step of the algorithm will not be necessary very often.)

L4. [Compute X.] Set $X \leftarrow s + hU$. ∎

When step L4 is reached, the point (U, V) is a random point in the area shaded in Fig. 11, namely, $0 \le U \le V \le U + (1/b)f(s + hU)$. Conditions (19) ensure that

$$\frac{a}{b} \le U + \frac{1}{b}f(s + hU) \le 1.$$

Now the probability that $X \le s + hx$, for $0 \le x \le 1$, is the area that lies to the left of the vertical line $U = x$ in Fig. 11, divided by the total area, namely

$$\int_0^x \frac{1}{b}f(s + hu)\, du \Big/ \int_0^1 \frac{1}{b}f(s + hu)\, du = \int_s^{s+hx} f(v)\, dv;$$

therefore X has the correct distribution.

With appropriate constants a_j, b_j, s_j, Algorithm L will take care of the wedge-shaped densities f_{j+15} of Fig. 9, for $1 \le j \le 15$. The final distribution, F_{31}, needs to be treated only about one time in 370; it is used whenever a result $X \ge 3$ is to be computed. Exercise 11 shows that a standard rejection scheme can be used for this "tail." We are ready to consider the procedure in its entirety:

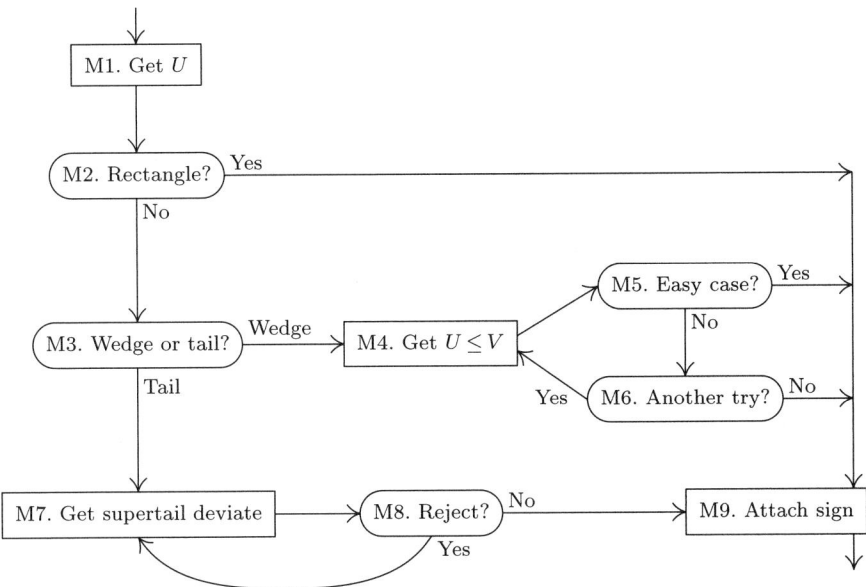

Fig. 12. The "rectangle-wedge-tail" algorithm for generating normal deviates.

Algorithm M (*Rectangle-wedge-tail method for normal deviates*). For this algorithm we use auxiliary tables $(P_0, \ldots, P_{31})$, $(Q_1, \ldots, Q_{15})$, $(Y_0, \ldots, Y_{31})$, $(Z_0, \ldots, Z_{31})$, $(S_1, \ldots, S_{16})$, $(D_{16}, \ldots, D_{30})$, $(E_{16}, \ldots, E_{30})$, constructed as explained in exercise 10; examples appear in Table 1. We assume that a binary computer is being used; a similar procedure could be worked out for decimal machines.

M1. [Get U.] Generate a uniform random number $U = (.b_0 b_1 b_2 \ldots b_t)_2$. (Here the b's are the bits in the binary representation of U. For reasonable accuracy, t should be at least 24.) Set $\psi \leftarrow b_0$. (Later, ψ will be used to determine the sign of the result.)

M2. [Rectangle?] Set $j \leftarrow (b_1 b_2 b_3 b_4 b_5)_2$, a binary number determined by the leading bits of U, and set $f \leftarrow (.b_6 b_7 \ldots b_t)_2$, the fraction determined by the remaining bits. If $f \geq P_j$, set $X \leftarrow Y_j + f Z_j$ and go to M9. Otherwise if $j \leq 15$ (that is, $b_1 = 0$), set $X \leftarrow S_j + f Q_j$ and go to M9. (This is an adaptation of Walker's alias method (3).)

M3. [Wedge or tail?] (Now $16 \leq j \leq 31$, and each particular value j occurs with probability p_j.) If $j = 31$, go to M7.

M4. [Get $U \leq V$.] Generate two new uniform deviates, U and V; if $U > V$, exchange $U \leftrightarrow V$. (We are now performing a special case of Algorithm L.) Set $X \leftarrow S_{j-15} + \frac{1}{5}U$.

M5. [Easy case?] If $V \leq D_j$, go to M9.

Table 1

EXAMPLE OF TABLES USED WITH ALGORITHM M*

j	P_j	P_{j+16}	Q_j	Y_j	Y_{j+16}	Z_j	Z_{j+16}	S_{j+1}	D_{j+15}	E_{j+15}
0	.000	.067		0.00	0.59	0.20	0.21	0.0		
1	.849	.161	.236	− 0.92	0.96	1.32	0.24	0.2	.505	25.00
2	.970	.236	.206	− 5.86	−0.06	6.66	0.26	0.4	.773	12.50
3	.855	.285	.234	− 0.58	0.12	1.38	0.28	0.6	.876	8.33
4	.994	.308	.201	−33.16	1.31	34.96	0.29	0.8	.939	6.25
5	.995	.304	.201	−39.51	0.31	41.31	0.29	1.0	.986	5.00
6	.933	.280	.214	− 2.57	1.12	2.97	0.28	1.2	.995	4.06
7	.923	.241	.217	− 1.61	0.54	2.61	0.26	1.4	.987	3.37
8	.727	.197	.275	0.67	0.75	0.73	0.25	1.6	.979	2.86
9	1.000	.152	.200		0.56		0.24	1.8	.972	2.47
10	.691	.112	.289	0.35	0.17	0.65	0.23	2.0	.966	2.16
11	.454	.079	.440	− 0.17	0.38	0.37	0.22	2.2	.960	1.92
12	.287	.052	.698	0.92	−0.01	0.28	0.21	2.4	.954	1.71
13	.174	.033	1.150	0.36	0.39	0.24	0.21	2.6	.948	1.54
14	.101	.020	1.974	− 0.02	0.20	0.22	0.20	2.8	.942	1.40
15	.057	.086	3.526	0.19	0.78	0.21	0.22	3.0	.936	1.27

*In practice, this data would be given with much greater precision; the table shows only enough figures so that interested readers will be able to test their own algorithms for computing the values more accurately. The values of Q_0, Y_9, Z_9, D_{15}, and E_{15} are not used.

M6. [Another try?] If $V > U + E_j(e^{(S_j^2 - 14 - X^2)/2} - 1)$, go back to step M4; otherwise go to M9. (This step is executed with low probability.)

M7. [Get supertail deviate.] Generate two new independent uniform deviates, U and V, and set $X \leftarrow \sqrt{9 - 2\ln V}$.

M8. [Reject?] If $UX \geq 3$, go back to step M7. (This will occur only about one-twelfth as often as we reach step M8.)

M9. [Attach sign.] If $\psi = 1$, set $X \leftarrow -X$. ∎

This algorithm is a very pretty example of mathematical theory intimately interwoven with programming ingenuity — a fine illustration of the art of computer programming! Only steps M1, M2, and M9 need to be performed most of the time, and the other steps aren't terribly slow either. The first publications of the rectangle-wedge-tail method were by G. Marsaglia, *Annals Math. Stat.* **32** (1961), 894–899; G. Marsaglia, M. D. MacLaren, and T. A. Bray, *CACM* **7** (1964), 4–10. Further refinements of Algorithm M have been developed by G. Marsaglia, K. Ananthanarayanan, and N. J. Paul, *Inf. Proc. Letters* **5** (1976), 27–30.

3) *The odd-even method*, due to G. E. Forsythe. An amazingly simple technique for generating random deviates with a density of the general exponential form

$$f(x) = Ce^{-h(x)} \, [a \leq x < b], \qquad (20)$$

when

$$0 \leq h(x) \leq 1 \qquad \text{for } a \leq x < b, \qquad (21)$$

was discovered by John von Neumann and G. E. Forsythe about 1950. The idea is based on the rejection method described earlier, letting $g(x)$ be the uniform distribution on $[a .. b]$: We set $X \leftarrow a + (b - a)U$, where U is a uniform deviate, and then we want to accept X with probability $e^{-h(X)}$. The latter operation could be done by comparing $e^{-h(X)}$ to V, or $h(X)$ to $-\ln V$, when V is another uniform deviate, but the job can be done without applying any transcendental functions in the following interesting way. Set $V_0 \leftarrow h(X)$, then generate uniform deviates $V_1, V_2, \ldots$ until finding some $K \geq 1$ with $V_{K-1} < V_K$. For fixed X and k, the probability that $h(X) \geq V_1 \geq \cdots \geq V_k$ is $1/k!$ times the probability that $\max(V_1, \ldots, V_k) \leq h(X)$, namely $h(X)^k/k!$; hence the probability that $K = k$ is $h(X)^{k-1}/(k-1)! - h(X)^k/k!$, and the probability that K is odd is

$$\sum_{k \text{ odd}, k \geq 1} \left(\frac{h(X)^{k-1}}{(k-1)!} - \frac{h(X)^k}{k!} \right) = e^{-h(X)}. \tag{22}$$

Therefore we reject X and try again if K is even; we accept X as a random variable with density (20) if K is odd. We usually won't have to generate many V's in order to determine K, since the average value of K (given X) is $\sum_{k \geq 0} \Pr(K > k) = \sum_{k \geq 0} h(X)^k/k! = e^{h(X)} \leq e$.

Forsythe realized some years later that this approach leads to an efficient method for calculating normal deviates, without the need for any auxiliary routines to calculate square roots or logarithms as in Algorithms P and M. His procedure, with an improved choice of intervals $[a \mathinner{.\,.} b]$ due to J. H. Ahrens and U. Dieter, can be summarized as follows.

Algorithm F (*Odd-even method for normal deviates*). This algorithm generates normal deviates on a binary computer, assuming approximately $t + 1$ bits of accuracy. It requires a table of values $d_j = a_j - a_{j-1}$, for $1 \leq j \leq t + 1$, where a_j is defined by the relation

$$\sqrt{\frac{2}{\pi}} \int_{a_j}^{\infty} e^{-x^2/2} \, dx = \frac{1}{2^j}. \tag{23}$$

F1. [Get U.] Generate a uniform random number $U = (.b_0 b_1 \ldots b_t)_2$, where b_0, $b_1, \ldots, b_t$ denote the bits in binary notation. Set $\psi \leftarrow b_0$, $j \leftarrow 1$, and $a \leftarrow 0$.

F2. [Find first zero b_j.] If $b_j = 1$, set $a \leftarrow a + d_j$, $j \leftarrow j + 1$, and repeat this step. (If $j = t + 1$, treat b_j as zero.)

F3. [Generate candidate.] (Now $a = a_{j-1}$, and the current value of j occurs with probability $\approx 2^{-j}$. We will generate X in the range $[a_{j-1} \mathinner{.\,.} a_j)$, using the rejection method above, with $h(x) = x^2/2 - a^2/2 = y^2/2 + ay$ where $y = x - a$. Exercise 12 proves that $h(x) \leq 1$ as required in (21).) Set $Y \leftarrow d_j$ times $(.b_{j+1} \ldots b_t)_2$ and $V \leftarrow (\frac{1}{2}Y + a)Y$. (Since the average value of j is 2, there will usually be enough significant bits in $(.b_{j+1} \ldots b_t)_2$ to provide decent accuracy. The calculations are readily done in fixed point arithmetic.)

F4. [Reject?] Generate a uniform deviate U. If $V < U$, go on to step F5. Otherwise set V to a new uniform deviate; and repeat step F4 if the new V is $\leq U$. Otherwise (that is, if K is even, in the discussion above), replace U by a new uniform deviate $(.b_0 b_1 \ldots b_t)_2$ and go back to F3.

F5. [Return X.] Set $X \leftarrow a + Y$. If $\psi = 1$, set $X \leftarrow -X$. ∎

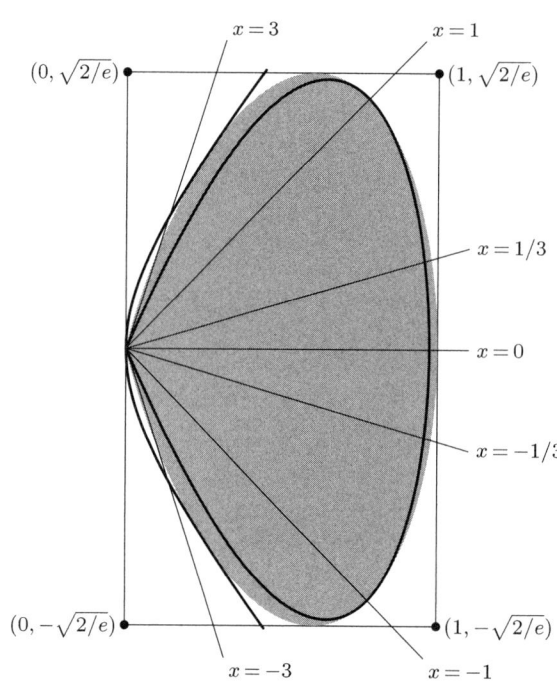

Fig. 13. Region of "acceptance" in the ratio-of-uniforms method for normal deviates. Lengths of lines with coordinate ratio x have the normal distribution.

Values of d_j for $1 \le j \le 47$ appear in a paper by Ahrens and Dieter, *Math. Comp.* **27** (1973), 927–937; their paper discusses refinements of the algorithm that improve its speed at the expense of more tables. Algorithm F is attractive since it is almost as fast as Algorithm M and it is easier to implement. The average number of uniform deviates per normal deviate is 2.53947; R. P. Brent [*CACM* **17** (1974), 704–705] has shown how to reduce this number to 1.37446 at the expense of two subtractions and one division per uniform deviate saved.

4) *Ratios of uniform deviates.* There is yet another good way to generate normal deviates, discovered by A. J. Kinderman and J. F. Monahan in 1976. Their idea is to generate a random point (U, V) in the region defined by

$$0 < u \le 1, \qquad -2u\sqrt{\ln(1/u)} \le v \le 2u\sqrt{\ln(1/u)}, \qquad (24)$$

and then to output the ratio $X \leftarrow V/U$. The shaded area of Fig. 13 is the magic region (24) that makes this all work. Before we study the associated theory, let us first state the algorithm so that its efficiency and simplicity are manifest:

Algorithm R (*Ratio method for normal deviates*). This algorithm generates normal deviates X.

R1. [Get U, V.] Generate two independent uniform deviates U and V, where U is nonzero, and set $X \leftarrow \sqrt{8/e}\,\left(V - \frac{1}{2}\right)/U$. (Now X is the ratio of the coordinates $\left(U, \sqrt{8/e}\,\left(V - \frac{1}{2}\right)\right)$ of a random point in the rectangle that encloses the shaded region in Fig. 13. We will accept X if the corresponding point actually lies "in the shade," otherwise we will try again.)

R2. [Optional upper bound test.] If $X^2 \leq 5 - 4e^{1/4}U$, output X and terminate the algorithm. (This step can be omitted if desired; it tests whether or not the selected point is in the interior region of Fig. 13, making it unnecessary to calculate a logarithm.)

R3. [Optional lower bound test.] If $X^2 \geq 4e^{-1.35}/U + 1.4$, go back to R1. (This step could also be omitted; it tests whether or not the selected point is outside the exterior region of Fig. 13, making it unnecessary to calculate a logarithm.)

R4. [Final test.] If $X^2 \leq -4\ln U$, output X and terminate the algorithm. Otherwise go back to R1. ∎

Exercises 20 and 21 work out the timing analysis; four different algorithms are analyzed, since steps R2 and R3 can be included or omitted depending on one's preference. The following table shows how many times each step will be performed, on the average, depending on which of the optional tests is applied:

Step	Neither	R2 only	R3 only	Both	
R1	1.369	1.369	1.369	1.369	
R2	0	1.369	0	1.369	(25)
R3	0	0	1.369	0.467	
R4	1.369	0.467	1.134	0.232	

Thus it pays to omit the optional tests if there is a very fast logarithm operation, but if the log routine is rather slow it pays to include them.

But why does it work? One reason is that we can calculate the probability that $X \leq x$, and it turns out to be the correct value (10). But such a calculation isn't very easy unless one happens to hit on the right trick, and anyway it is better to understand how the algorithm might have been discovered in the first place. Kinderman and Monahan derived it by working out the following theory that can be used with any well-behaved density function $f(x)$ [see *ACM Trans. Math. Software* **3** (1977), 257–260].

In general, suppose that a point (U, V) has been generated uniformly over the region of the (u, v)-plane defined by

$$u > 0, \qquad u^2 \leq g(v/u) \tag{26}$$

for some nonnegative integrable function g. If we set $X \leftarrow V/U$, the probability that $X \leq x$ can be calculated by integrating $du\,dv$ over the region defined by the two relations in (26) plus the auxiliary condition $v/u \leq x$, then dividing by the same integral without this extra condition. Letting $v = tu$, so that $dv = u\,dt$, the integral becomes

$$\int_{-\infty}^{x} dt \int_{0}^{\sqrt{g(t)}} u\,du = \frac{1}{2}\int_{-\infty}^{x} g(t)\,dt.$$

Hence the probability that $X \leq x$ is

$$\int_{-\infty}^{x} g(t)\,dt \bigg/ \int_{-\infty}^{+\infty} g(t)\,dt. \tag{27}$$

The normal distribution comes out when $g(t) = e^{-t^2/2}$; and the condition $u^2 \le g(v/u)$ simplifies in this case to $(v/u)^2 \le -4 \ln u$. It is easy to see that the set of all such pairs (u, v) is entirely contained in the rectangle of Fig. 13.

The bounds in steps R2 and R3 define interior and exterior regions with simpler boundary equations. The well-known inequality

$$e^x \ge 1 + x,$$

which holds for all real numbers x, can be used to show that

$$1 + \ln c - cu \ \le \ -\ln u \ \le \ 1/(cu) - 1 + \ln c \qquad (28)$$

for any constant $c > 0$. Exercise 21 proves that $c = e^{1/4}$ is the best possible constant to use in step R2. The situation is more complicated in step R3, and there doesn't seem to be a simple expression for the optimum c in that case, but computational experiments show that the best value for R3 is $\approx e^{1.35}$. The approximating curves (28) are tangent to the true boundary when $u = 1/c$.

With an improved approximation to the acceptance region [see J. L. Leva, *ACM Trans. Math. Software* **18** (1992), 449–455] we can, in fact, reduce the expected number of logarithm computations to only 0.012.

It is possible to obtain a faster method by partitioning the region into subregions, most of which can be handled more quickly. Of course, this means that auxiliary tables will be needed, as in Algorithms M and F. An interesting alternative that requires fewer auxiliary table entries has been suggested by Ahrens and Dieter in *CACM* **31** (1988), 1330–1337.

5) *Normal deviates from normal deviates.* Exercise 31 discusses an interesting approach that saves time by working directly with normal deviates instead of basing everything on uniform deviates. This method, introduced by C. S. Wallace in 1996, has comparatively little theoretical support at the present time, but it has successfully passed a number of empirical tests.

6) *Variations of the normal distribution.* So far we have considered the normal distribution with mean zero and standard deviation one. If X has this distribution, then

$$Y = \mu + \sigma X \qquad (29)$$

has the normal distribution with mean μ and standard deviation σ. Furthermore, if X_1 and X_2 are independent normal deviates with mean zero and standard deviation one, and if

$$Y_1 = \mu_1 + \sigma_1 X_1, \qquad Y_2 = \mu_2 + \sigma_2 \left(\rho X_1 + \sqrt{1 - \rho^2}\, X_2 \right), \qquad (30)$$

then Y_1 and Y_2 are *dependent* random variables, normally distributed with means μ_1, μ_2 and standard deviations σ_1, σ_2, and with correlation coefficient ρ. (For a generalization to n variables, see exercise 13.)

D. The exponential distribution. After uniform deviates and normal deviates, the next most important random quantity is an *exponential deviate*. Such numbers occur in "arrival time" situations; for example, if a radioactive substance emits alpha particles at a rate such that one particle is emitted every μ seconds on the average, then the time between two successive emissions has the exponential distribution with mean μ. This distribution is defined by the formula

$$F(x) = 1 - e^{-x/\mu}, \qquad x \geq 0. \tag{31}$$

1) *Logarithm method.* Clearly, if $y = F(x) = 1 - e^{-x/\mu}$, then $x = F^{[-1]}(y) = -\mu \ln(1-y)$. Therefore $-\mu \ln(1-U)$ has the exponential distribution by Eq. (7). Since $1 - U$ is uniformly distributed when U is, we conclude that

$$X = -\mu \ln U \tag{32}$$

is exponentially distributed with mean μ. (The case $U = 0$ must be treated specially; we can substitute any convenient value ϵ for 0, since the probability of this case is extremely small.)

2) *Random minimization method.* We saw in Algorithm F that there are simple and fast alternatives to calculating the logarithm of a uniform deviate. The following especially efficient approach has been developed by G. Marsaglia, M. Sibuya, and J. H. Ahrens [see *CACM* **15** (1972), 876–877]:

Algorithm S (*Exponential distribution with mean μ*). This algorithm produces exponential deviates on a binary computer, using uniform deviates with $(t+1)$-bit accuracy. The constants

$$Q[k] = \frac{\ln 2}{1!} + \frac{(\ln 2)^2}{2!} + \cdots + \frac{(\ln 2)^k}{k!}, \qquad k \geq 1, \tag{33}$$

should be precomputed, extending until $Q[k] > 1 - 2^{-t}$.

S1. [Get U and shift.] Generate a $(t+1)$-bit uniform random binary fraction $U = (.b_0 b_1 b_2 \ldots b_t)_2$; locate the first zero bit b_j, and shift off the leading $j+1$ bits, setting $U \leftarrow (.b_{j+1} \ldots b_t)_2$. (As in Algorithm F, the average number of discarded bits is 2.)

S2. [Immediate acceptance?] If $U < \ln 2$, set $X \leftarrow \mu(j \ln 2 + U)$ and terminate the algorithm. (Note that $Q[1] = \ln 2$.)

S3. [Minimize.] Find the least $k \geq 2$ such that $U < Q[k]$. Generate k new uniform deviates $U_1, \ldots, U_k$ and set $V \leftarrow \min(U_1, \ldots, U_k)$.

S4. [Deliver the answer.] Set $X \leftarrow \mu(j + V) \ln 2$. ∎

Alternative ways to generate exponential deviates (for example, a ratio of uniforms as in Algorithm R) might also be used.

E. Other continuous distributions. Let us now consider briefly how to handle some other distributions that arise reasonably often in practice.

1) *The gamma distribution* of order $a > 0$ is defined by

$$F(x) = \frac{1}{\Gamma(a)} \int_0^x t^{a-1} e^{-t} \, dt, \qquad x \geq 0. \tag{34}$$

When $a = 1$, this is the exponential distribution with mean 1; when $a = \frac{1}{2}$, it is the distribution of $\frac{1}{2}Z^2$, where Z has the normal distribution (mean 0, variance 1). If X and Y are independent gamma-distributed random variables, of order a and b, respectively, then $X + Y$ has the gamma distribution of order $a + b$. Thus, for example, the sum of k independent exponential deviates with mean 1 has the gamma distribution of order k. If the logarithm method (32) is being used to generate these exponential deviates, we need compute only one logarithm: $X \leftarrow -\ln(U_1 \ldots U_k)$, where $U_1, \ldots, U_k$ are nonzero uniform deviates. This technique handles all integer orders a; to complete the picture, a suitable method for $0 < a < 1$ appears in exercise 16.

The simple logarithm method is much too slow when a is large, since it requires $\lfloor a \rfloor$ uniform deviates. Moreover, there is a substantial risk that the product $U_1 \ldots U_{\lfloor a \rfloor}$ will cause floating point underflow. For large a, the following algorithm due to J. H. Ahrens is reasonably efficient, and it is easy to write in terms of standard subroutines. [See *Ann. Inst. Stat. Math.* **13** (1962), 231–237.]

Algorithm A (*Gamma distribution of order $a > 1$*).

A1. [Generate candidate.] Set $Y \leftarrow \tan(\pi U)$, where U is a uniform deviate, and set $X \leftarrow \sqrt{2a-1}\, Y + a - 1$. (In place of $\tan(\pi U)$ we could use a polar method, calculating a ratio V_2/V_1 as in step P4 of Algorithm P.)

A2. [Accept?] If $X \leq 0$, return to A1. Otherwise generate a uniform deviate V, and return to A1 if $V > (1 + Y^2)\exp\big((a-1)\ln(X/(a-1)) - \sqrt{2a-1}\,Y\big)$. Otherwise accept X. ∎

The average number of times step A1 is performed is < 1.902 when $a \geq 3$.

There is also an attractive approach for large a based on the remarkable fact that gamma deviates are approximately equal to aX^3, where X is normally distributed with mean $1 - 1/(9a)$ and standard deviation $1/\sqrt{9a}$; see E. B. Wilson and M. M. Hilferty, *Proc. Nat. Acad. Sci.* **17** (1931), 684–688; G. Marsaglia, *Computers and Math.* **3** (1977), 321–325.*

For a somewhat complicated but significantly faster algorithm, which generates a gamma deviate in about twice the time to generate a normal deviate, see J. H. Ahrens and U. Dieter, *CACM* **25** (1982), 47–54. This article contains an instructive discussion of the design principles used to construct the algorithm.

2) *The beta distribution* with positive parameters a and b is defined by

$$F(x) = \frac{\Gamma(a+b)}{\Gamma(a)\,\Gamma(b)} \int_0^x t^{a-1}(1-t)^{b-1}\, dt, \qquad 0 \leq x \leq 1. \tag{35}$$

Let X_1 and X_2 be independent gamma deviates of order a and b, respectively, and set $X \leftarrow X_1/(X_1 + X_2)$. Another method, useful for small a and b, is to set

$$Y_1 \leftarrow U_1^{1/a} \qquad \text{and} \qquad Y_2 \leftarrow U_2^{1/b}$$

repeatedly until $Y_1 + Y_2 \leq 1$; then $X \leftarrow Y_1/(Y_1 + Y_2)$. [See M. D. Jöhnk, *Metrika* **8** (1964), 5–15.] Still another approach, if a and b are integers and not

---

* Change "$+(3a-1)$" to "$-(3a-1)$" in Step 3 of the algorithm on page 323.

too large, is to set X to the bth largest of $a+b-1$ independent uniform deviates (see exercise 9 at the beginning of Chapter 5). See also the more direct method described by R. C. H. Cheng, *CACM* **21** (1978), 317–322.

3) *The chi-square distribution* with ν degrees of freedom (Eq. 3.3.1–(22)) is obtained by setting $X \leftarrow 2Y$, where Y is a random variable having the gamma distribution of order $\nu/2$.

4) *The F-distribution* (variance-ratio distribution) with ν_1 and ν_2 degrees of freedom is defined by

$$F(x) = \frac{\nu_1^{\nu_1/2}\,\nu_2^{\nu_2/2}\,\Gamma\big((\nu_1+\nu_2)/2\big)}{\Gamma(\nu_1/2)\,\Gamma(\nu_2/2)} \int_0^x t^{\nu_1/2-1}(\nu_2+\nu_1 t)^{-\nu_1/2-\nu_2/2}\,dt, \quad (36)$$

where $x \geq 0$. Let Y_1 and Y_2 be independent, having the chi-square distribution with ν_1 and ν_2 degrees of freedom, respectively; set $X \leftarrow Y_1\nu_2/Y_2\nu_1$. Or set $X \leftarrow \nu_2 Y/\nu_1(1-Y)$, where Y is a beta variate with parameters $\nu_1/2$ and $\nu_2/2$.

5) *The t-distribution* with ν degrees of freedom is defined by

$$F(x) = \frac{\Gamma\big((\nu+1)/2\big)}{\sqrt{\pi\nu}\,\Gamma(\nu/2)} \int_{-\infty}^x (1+t^2/\nu)^{-(\nu+1)/2}\,dt. \quad (37)$$

Let Y_1 be a normal deviate (mean 0, variance 1) and let Y_2 be independent of Y_1, having the chi-square distribution with ν degrees of freedom; set $X \leftarrow Y_1/\sqrt{Y_2/\nu}$. Alternatively, when $\nu > 2$, let Y_1 be a normal deviate and let Y_2 independently have the exponential distribution with mean $2/(\nu-2)$; set $Z \leftarrow Y_1^2/(\nu-2)$ and reject (Y_1, Y_2) if $e^{-Y_2-Z} \geq 1-Z$, otherwise set

$$X \leftarrow Y_1/\sqrt{(1-2/\nu)(1-Z)}.$$

The latter method is due to George Marsaglia, *Math. Comp.* **34** (1980), 235–236. [See also A. J. Kinderman, J. F. Monahan, and J. G. Ramage, *Math. Comp.* **31** (1977), 1009–1018.]

6) *Random point on an n-dimensional sphere with radius one.* Let X_1, X_2, ..., X_n be independent normal deviates (mean 0, variance 1); the desired point on the unit sphere is

$$(X_1/r, X_2/r, \ldots, X_n/r), \quad \text{where } r = \sqrt{X_1^2 + X_2^2 + \cdots + X_n^2}. \quad (38)$$

If the X's are calculated using the polar method, Algorithm P, we compute two independent X's each time, and we have $X_1^2 + X_2^2 = -2\ln S$ in the notation of that algorithm; this saves a little of the time needed to evaluate r. The validity of (38) comes from the fact that the distribution function for the point $(X_1,\ldots,X_n)$ has a density that depends only on its distance from the origin, so when it is projected onto the unit sphere it has the uniform distribution. This method was first suggested by G. W. Brown, in *Modern Mathematics for the Engineer*, First series, edited by E. F. Beckenbach (New York: McGraw–Hill,

1956), 302. To get a random point *inside* the n-sphere, R. P. Brent suggests taking a point on the surface and multiplying it by $U^{1/n}$.

In three dimensions a significantly simpler method can be used, since each individual coordinate is uniformly distributed between -1 and 1: Find V_1, V_2, and S by steps P1–P3 of Algorithm P; then the desired random point on the surface of a globe is $(\alpha V_1, \alpha V_2, 2S - 1)$, where $\alpha = 2\sqrt{1 - S}$. [Robert E. Knop, *CACM* **13** (1970), 326.]

F. Important integer-valued distributions. A probability distribution that consists only of integer values can essentially be handled by the techniques described at the beginning of this section; but some of these distributions are so important in practice, they deserve special mention here.

1) *The geometric distribution.* If some event occurs with probability p, the number N of independent trials needed between occurrences of the event (or until the event occurs for the first time) has the geometric distribution. We have $N = 1$ with probability p, $N = 2$ with probability $(1 - p)p$, ..., $N = n$ with probability $(1 - p)^{n-1}p$. This is essentially the situation we have already considered in the gap test of Section 3.3.2; it is also directly related to the number of times certain loops in the algorithms of this section are executed, like steps P1–P3 of the polar method.

A convenient way to generate a variable with this distribution is to set

$$N \leftarrow \lceil \ln U / \ln(1 - p) \rceil. \tag{39}$$

To check this formula, we observe that $\lceil \ln U / \ln(1 - p) \rceil = n$ if and only if $n - 1 < \ln U / \ln(1 - p) \le n$, that is, $(1 - p)^{n-1} > U \ge (1 - p)^n$, and this happens with probability $(1 - p)^{n-1}p$ as required. The quantity $\ln U$ can optionally be replaced by $-Y$, where Y has the exponential distribution with mean 1.

The special case $p = \frac{1}{2}$ is quite simple on a binary computer, since formula (39) reduces to setting $N \leftarrow \lceil -\lg U \rceil$; that is, N is one more than the number of leading zero bits in the binary representation of U.

2) *The binomial distribution* (t, p). If some event occurs with probability p, and if we carry out t independent trials, the total number N of occurrences equals n with probability $\binom{t}{n} p^n (1 - p)^{t-n}$. (See Section 1.2.10.) In other words if we generate U_1, ..., U_t, we want to count how many of these are $< p$. For small t we can obtain N in exactly this way.

For large t, we can generate a beta variate X with integer parameters a and b where $a + b - 1 = t$; this effectively gives us the bth largest of t elements, without bothering to generate the other elements. Now if $X \ge p$, we set $N \leftarrow N_1$ where N_1 has the binomial distribution $(a - 1, p/X)$, since this tells us how many of $a - 1$ random numbers in the range $[0 .. X)$ are $< p$; and if $X < p$, we set $N \leftarrow a + N_1$ where N_1 has the binomial distribution $\big(b - 1, (p - X)/(1 - X)\big)$, since N_1 tells us how many of $b - 1$ random numbers in the range $[X .. 1)$ are $< p$. By choosing $a = 1 + \lfloor t/2 \rfloor$, the parameter t will be reduced to a reasonable size after about $\lg t$ reductions of this kind. (This approach is due to J. H. Ahrens, who has also suggested an alternative for medium-sized t; see exercise 27.)

3) *The Poisson distribution* with mean μ. The Poisson distribution is related to the exponential distribution as the binomial distribution is related to the geometric: It represents the number of occurrences, per unit time, of an event that can occur at any instant of time. For example, the number of alpha particles emitted by a radioactive substance in a single second has a Poisson distribution.

According to this principle, we can produce a Poisson deviate N by generating independent exponential deviates X_1, X_2, ... with mean $1/\mu$, stopping as soon as $X_1 + \cdots + X_m \geq 1$; then $N \leftarrow m - 1$. The probability that $X_1 + \cdots + X_m \geq 1$ is the probability that a gamma deviate of order m is $\geq \mu$, and this comes to $\int_\mu^\infty t^{m-1} e^{-t}\, dt / (m-1)!$; hence the probability that $N = n$ is

$$\frac{1}{n!} \int_\mu^\infty t^n e^{-t}\, dt - \frac{1}{(n-1)!} \int_\mu^\infty t^{n-1} e^{-t}\, dt = e^{-\mu} \frac{\mu^n}{n!}, \qquad n \geq 0. \qquad (40)$$

If we generate exponential deviates by the logarithm method, the recipe above tells us to stop when $-(\ln U_1 + \cdots + \ln U_m)/\mu \geq 1$. Simplifying this expression, we see that the desired Poisson deviate can be obtained by calculating $e^{-\mu}$, converting it to a fixed point representation, then generating one or more uniform deviates U_1, U_2, ... until the product satisfies $U_1 \ldots U_m \leq e^{-\mu}$, finally setting $N \leftarrow m-1$. On the average this requires the generation of $\mu+1$ uniform deviates, so it is a very useful approach when μ is not too large.

When μ is large, we can obtain a method of order $\log \mu$ by using the fact that we know how to handle the gamma and binomial distributions for large orders: First generate X with the gamma distribution of order $m = \lfloor \alpha\mu \rfloor$, where α is a suitable constant. (Since X is equivalent to $-\ln(U_1 \ldots U_m)$, we are essentially bypassing m steps of the previous method.) If $X < \mu$, set $N \leftarrow m + N_1$, where N_1 is a Poisson deviate with mean $\mu - X$; and if $X \geq \mu$, set $N \leftarrow N_1$, where N_1 has the binomial distribution $(m - 1, \mu/X)$. This method is due to J. H. Ahrens and U. Dieter, whose experiments suggest that $\frac{7}{8}$ is a good choice for α.

The validity of the stated reduction when $X \geq \mu$ is a consequence of the following important principle: "Let X_1, ..., X_m be independent exponential deviates with the same mean; let $S_j = X_1 + \cdots + X_j$ and let $V_j = S_j/S_m$ for $1 \leq j \leq m$. Then the distribution of V_1, V_2, ..., V_{m-1} is the same as the distribution of $m - 1$ independent uniform deviates sorted into increasing order." To establish this principle formally, we compute the probability that $V_1 \leq v_1$, ..., $V_{m-1} \leq v_{m-1}$, given the value of $S_m = s$, for arbitrary values $0 \leq v_1 \leq \cdots \leq v_{m-1} \leq 1$: Let $f(v_1, v_2, \ldots, v_{m-1})$ be the $(m - 1)$-fold integral

$$\int_0^{v_1 s} \mu e^{-t_1/\mu}\, dt_1 \int_0^{v_2 s - t_1} \mu e^{-t_2/\mu}\, dt_2 \cdots$$

$$\times \int_0^{v_{m-1} s - t_1 - \cdots - t_{m-2}} \mu e^{-t_{m-1}/\mu}\, dt_{m-1} \cdot \mu e^{-(s - t_1 - \cdots - t_{m-1})/\mu};$$

then

$$\frac{f(v_1, v_2, \ldots, v_{m-1})}{f(1, 1, \ldots, 1)} = \frac{\int_0^{v_1} du_1 \int_{u_1}^{v_2} du_2 \ldots \int_{u_{m-2}}^{v_{m-1}} du_{m-1}}{\int_0^1 du_1 \int_{u_1}^1 du_2 \ldots \int_{u_{m-2}}^1 du_{m-1}},$$

by making the substitution $t_1 = su_1$, $t_1 + t_2 = su_2$, ..., $t_1 + \cdots + t_{m-1} = su_{m-1}$. The latter ratio is the corresponding probability that uniform deviates $U_1, \ldots, U_{m-1}$ satisfy $U_1 \le v_1, \ldots, U_{m-1} \le v_{m-1}$, given that they also satisfy $U_1 \le \cdots \le U_{m-1}$.

A more efficient but somewhat more complicated technique for binomial and Poisson deviates is sketched in exercise 22.

G. For further reading. A facsimile of a letter from von Neumann dated May 21, 1947, in which the rejection method first saw the light of day, appears in *Stanislaw Ulam 1909–1984*, a special issue of *Los Alamos Science* (Los Alamos National Lab., 1987), 135–136. The book *Non-Uniform Random Variate Generation* by L. Devroye (Springer, 1986) discusses many more algorithms for the generation of random variables with nonuniform distributions, together with a careful consideration of the efficiency of each technique on typical computers.

W. Hörmann and G. Derflinger [*ACM Trans. Math. Software* **19** (1993), 489–495] have pointed out that it can be dangerous to use the rejection method in connection with linear congruential generators that have small multipliers $a \approx \sqrt{m}$.

From a theoretical point of view it is interesting to consider *optimal* ways to generate random variables with a given distribution, in the sense that the method produces the desired result from the minimum possible number of random bits. For the beginnings of a theory dealing with such questions, see D. E. Knuth and A. C. Yao, *Algorithms and Complexity*, edited by J. F. Traub (New York: Academic Press, 1976), 357–428.

Exercise 16 is recommended as a review of many of the techniques in this section.

EXERCISES

1. [*10*] If α and β are real numbers with $\alpha < \beta$, how would you generate a random real number uniformly distributed between α and β?

2. [*M16*] Assuming that mU is a random integer between 0 and $m - 1$, what is the *exact* probability that $\lfloor kU \rfloor = r$, if $0 \le r < k$? Compare this with the desired probability $1/k$.

▶ **3.** [*14*] Discuss treating U as an integer and computing its *remainder* mod k to get a random integer between 0 and $k - 1$, instead of multiplying as suggested in the text. Thus (1) would be changed to

```
ENTA 0;   LDX U;   DIV K,
```

with the result appearing in register X. Is this a good method?

4. [*M20*] Prove the two relations in (8).

▶ **5.** [*21*] Suggest an efficient way to compute a random variable with the distribution $F(x) = px + qx^2 + rx^3$, where $p \ge 0$, $q \ge 0$, $r \ge 0$, and $p + q + r = 1$.

6. [*HM21*] A quantity X is computed by the following method:

Step 1. Generate two independent uniform deviates U and V.

Step 2. If $U^2 + V^2 \ge 1$, return to step 1; otherwise set $X \leftarrow U$.

What is the distribution function of X? How many times will step 1 be performed? (Give the mean and standard deviation.)

▶ **7.** [*20*] (A. J. Walker.) Suppose we have a bunch of cubes of k different colors, say n_j cubes of color C_j for $1 \leq j \leq k$, and we also have k boxes $\{B_1, \ldots, B_k\}$ each of which can hold exactly n cubes. Furthermore $n_1 + \cdots + n_k = kn$, so the cubes will just fit in the boxes. Prove (constructively) that there is always a way to put the cubes into the boxes so that each box contains at most two different colors of cubes; in fact, there is a way to do it so that, whenever box B_j contains two colors, one of those colors is C_j. Show how to use this principle to compute the P and Y tables required in (3), given a probability distribution $(p_1, \ldots, p_k)$.

8. [*M15*] Show that operation (3) could be changed to

$$\text{if} \quad U < P_K \quad \text{then} \quad X \leftarrow x_{K+1} \quad \text{otherwise} \quad X \leftarrow Y_K$$

(thus using the original value of U instead of V) if this were more convenient, by suitably modifying P_0, P_1, ..., P_{k-1}.

9. [*HM10*] Why is the curve $f(x)$ of Fig. 9 concave for $x < 1$, convex for $x > 1$?

▶ **10.** [*HM24*] Explain how to calculate auxiliary constants P_j, Q_j, Y_j, Z_j, S_j, D_j, E_j so that Algorithm M delivers answers with the correct distribution.

▶ **11.** [*HM27*] Prove that steps M7–M8 of Algorithm M generate a random variable with the appropriate tail of the normal distribution; in other words, the probability that $X \leq x$ should be exactly

$$\int_3^x e^{-t^2/2} \, dt \Big/ \int_3^\infty e^{-t^2/2} \, dt, \qquad x \geq 3.$$

[*Hint:* Show that it is a special case of the rejection method, with $g(t) = Cte^{-t^2/2}$ for some C.]

12. [*HM23*] (R. P. Brent.) Prove that the numbers a_j defined in (23) satisfy the relation

$$a_j^2 - a_{j-1}^2 < 2 \ln 2 \qquad \text{for all } j \geq 1.$$

[*Hint:* If $f(x) = e^{x^2/2} \int_x^\infty e^{-t^2/2} \, dt$, show that $f(x) > f(y)$ for $0 \leq x < y$.]

13. [*HM25*] Given a set of n independent normal deviates, $X_1, X_2, \ldots, X_n$, with mean 0 and variance 1, show how to find constants b_j and a_{ij}, $1 \leq j \leq i \leq n$, so that if

$$Y_1 = b_1 + a_{11}X_1, \quad Y_2 = b_2 + a_{21}X_1 + a_{22}X_2, \quad \ldots, \quad Y_n = b_n + a_{n1}X_1 + \cdots + a_{nn}X_n,$$

then Y_1, Y_2, ..., Y_n are dependent normally distributed variables, Y_j has mean μ_j, and the Y's have a given covariance matrix (c_{ij}). (The covariance, c_{ij}, of Y_i and Y_j is defined to be the average value of $(Y_i - \mu_i)(Y_j - \mu_j)$. In particular, c_{jj} is the variance of Y_j, the square of its standard deviation. Not all matrices (c_{ij}) can be covariance matrices, and your construction is, of course, only supposed to work whenever a solution to the given conditions is possible.)

14. [*M21*] If X is a random variable with the continuous distribution $F(x)$, and if c is a (possibly negative) constant, what is the distribution of cX?

15. [*HM21*] If X_1 and X_2 are independent random variables with the respective distributions $F_1(x)$ and $F_2(x)$, and with densities $f_1(x) = F_1'(x)$, $f_2(x) = F_2'(x)$, what are the distribution and density functions of the quantity $X_1 + X_2$?

▶ **16.** [*HM22*] (J. H. Ahrens.) Develop an algorithm for gamma deviates of order a when $0 < a \leq 1$, using the rejection method with $cg(t) = t^{a-1}/\Gamma(a)$ for $0 < t < 1$, and with $cg(t) = e^{-t}/\Gamma(a)$ for $t \geq 1$.

▶ **17.** [*M24*] What is the *distribution function* $F(x)$ for the geometric distribution with probability p? What is the *generating function* $G(z)$? What are the mean and standard deviation of this distribution?

18. [*M24*] Suggest a method to compute a random integer N for which N takes the value n with probability $np^2(1-p)^{n-1}$, $n \geq 0$. (The case of particular interest is when p is rather small.)

19. [*22*] The *negative binomial distribution* (t, p) has integer values $N = n$ with probability $\binom{t-1+n}{n}p^t(1-p)^n$. (Unlike the ordinary binomial distribution, t need not be an integer, since this quantity is nonnegative for all n whenever $t > 0$.) Generalizing exercise 18, explain how to generate integers N with this distribution when t is a small positive integer. What method would you suggest if $t = p = \frac{1}{2}$?

20. [*M20*] Let A be the area of the shaded region in Fig. 13, and let R be the area of the enclosing rectangle. Let I be the area of the interior region recognized by step R2, and let E be the area between the exterior region rejected in step R3 and the outer rectangle. Determine the number of times each step of Algorithm R is performed, for each of its four variants as in (25), in terms of A, R, I, and E.

21. [*HM29*] Derive formulas for the quantities A, R, I, and E defined in exercise 20. (For I and especially E you may wish to use an interactive computer algebra system.) Show that $c = e^{1/4}$ is the best possible constant in step R2 for tests of the form "$X^2 \leq 4(1 + \ln c) - 4cU$."

22. [*HM40*] Can the exact Poisson distribution for large μ be obtained by generating an appropriate normal deviate, converting it to an integer in some convenient way, and applying a (possibly complicated) correction a small percent of the time?

23. [*HM23*] (J. von Neumann.) Are the following two ways to generate a random quantity X equivalent (that is, does the quantity X have the same distribution)?

> **Method 1:** Set $X \leftarrow \sin((\pi/2)U)$, where U is uniform.

> **Method 2:** Generate two uniform deviates, U and V; if $U^2 + V^2 \geq 1$, repeat until $U^2 + V^2 < 1$. Then set $X \leftarrow |U^2 - V^2|/(U^2 + V^2)$.

24. [*HM40*] (S. Ulam, J. von Neumann.) Let V_0 be a randomly selected real number between 0 and 1, and define the sequence $\langle V_n \rangle$ by the rule $V_{n+1} = 4V_n(1 - V_n)$. If this computation is done with perfect accuracy, the result should be a sequence with the distribution $\sin^2 \pi U$, where U is uniform, that is, with distribution function $F(x) = \int_0^x dx/\sqrt{2\pi x(1-x)}$. For if we write $V_n = \sin^2 \pi U_n$, we find that $U_{n+1} = (2U_n) \bmod 1$; and by the fact that almost all real numbers have a random binary expansion (see Section 3.5), this sequence U_n is equidistributed. But if the computation of V_n is done with only finite accuracy, the argument breaks down because we soon are dealing with noise from the roundoff error. [See von Neumann's *Collected Works* **5**, 768–770.]

Analyze the sequence $\langle V_n \rangle$ defined in the preceding paragraph, when only finite accuracy is present, both empirically (for various different choices of V_0) and theoretically. Does the sequence have a distribution resembling the expected distribution?

25. [*M25*] Let X_1, X_2, ..., X_5 be binary words each of whose bits is independently 0 or 1 with probability $\frac{1}{2}$. What is the probability that a given bit position of $X_1 \mid (X_2 \,\&\, (X_3 \mid (X_4 \,\&\, X_5)))$ contains a 1? Generalize.

26. [*M18*] Let N_1 and N_2 be independent Poisson deviates with means μ_1 and μ_2, where $\mu_1 > \mu_2 \geq 0$. Prove or disprove: (a) $N_1 + N_2$ has the Poisson distribution with mean $\mu_1 + \mu_2$. (b) $N_1 - N_2$ has the Poisson distribution with mean $\mu_1 - \mu_2$.

27. [*22*] (J. H. Ahrens.) On most binary computers there is an efficient way to count the number of 1s in a binary word (see Section 7.1). Hence there is a nice way to obtain the binomial distribution (t, p) when $p = \frac{1}{2}$, simply by generating t random bits and counting the number of 1s.

Design an algorithm that produces the binomial distribution (t, p) for *arbitrary p*, using only a subroutine for the special case $p = \frac{1}{2}$ as a source of random data. [*Hint:* Simulate a process that first looks at the most significant bits of t uniform deviates, then at the second bit of those deviates whose leading bit is not sufficient to determine whether or not their value is $< p$, etc.]

28. [*HM35*] (R. P. Brent.) Develop a method to generate a random point on the surface of the ellipsoid defined by $\sum a_k x_k^2 = 1$, where $a_1 \geq \cdots \geq a_n > 0$.

29. [*M20*] (J. L. Bentley and J. B. Saxe.) Find a simple way to generate n numbers $X_1, \ldots, X_n$ that are uniform between 0 and 1 except for the fact that they are sorted: $X_1 \leq \cdots \leq X_n$. Your algorithm should take only $O(n)$ steps.

30. [*M30*] Explain how to generate a set of random points (X_j, Y_j) such that, if R is any rectangle of area α contained in the unit square, the number of (X_j, Y_j) lying in R has the Poisson distribution with mean $\alpha\mu$.

31. [*HM39*] (*Direct generation of normal deviates.*)
a) Prove that if $a_1^2 + \cdots + a_k^2 = 1$ and if $X_1, \ldots, X_k$ are independent normal deviates with mean 0 and variance 1, then $a_1 X_1 + \cdots + a_k X_k$ is a normal deviate with mean 0 and variance 1.
b) The result of (a) suggests that we can generate new normal deviates from old ones, just as we obtain new uniform deviates from old ones. For example, we might use the idea of 3.2.2–(7), but with a recurrence like
$$X_n = (X_{n-24} + X_{n-55})/\sqrt{2} \quad \text{or} \quad X_n = \tfrac{3}{5}X_{n-24} + \tfrac{4}{5}X_{n-55},$$
after a set of normal deviates $X_0, \ldots, X_{54}$ has been computed initially. Explain why this is *not* a good idea.
c) Show, however, that there *is* a suitable way to generate normal deviates quickly from other normal deviates, by using a refinement of the idea in (a) and (b). [*Hint:* If X and Y are independent normal deviates, so are $X' = X\cos\theta + Y\sin\theta$ and $Y' = -X\sin\theta + Y\cos\theta$, for any angle θ.]

32. [*HM30*] (C. S. Wallace.) Let X and Y be independent exponential deviates with mean 1. Show that X' and Y' are, likewise, independent exponential deviates with mean 1, if we obtain them from X and Y in any of the following ways:
a) Given $0 < \lambda < 1$,
$$X' = (1-\lambda)X - \lambda Y + (X+Y)[(1-\lambda)X < \lambda Y], \qquad Y' = X + Y - X'.$$
b) $(X', Y') = \begin{cases} (2X, Y-X), & \text{if } X \leq Y; \\ (2Y, X-Y), & \text{if } X > Y. \end{cases}$
c) If $X = (\ldots x_2 x_1 x_0 . x_{-1} x_{-2} x_{-3} \ldots)_2$ and $Y = (\ldots y_2 y_1 y_0 . y_{-1} y_{-2} y_{-3} \ldots)_2$ in binary notation, then X' and Y' have the "shuffled" values
$$X' = (\ldots x_2 y_1 x_0 . y_{-1} x_{-2} y_{-3} \ldots)_2, \qquad Y' = (\ldots y_2 x_1 y_0 . x_{-1} y_{-2} x_{-3} \ldots)_2.$$

33. [*20*] Algorithms P, M, F, and R generate normal deviates by consuming an unknown number of uniform random variables $U_1, U_2, \ldots$. How can they be modified so that the output is a function of just one U?

3.4.2. Random Sampling and Shuffling

Many data processing applications call for an unbiased choice of n records at random from a file containing N records. This problem arises, for example, in quality control or other statistical calculations where sampling is needed. Usually N is very large, so that it is impossible to contain all the data in memory at once; and the individual records themselves are often very large, so that we can't even hold n records in memory. Therefore we seek an efficient procedure for selecting n records by deciding either to accept or to reject each record as it comes along, writing the accepted records onto an output file.

Several methods have been devised for this problem. The most obvious approach is to select each record with probability n/N; this may sometimes be appropriate, but it gives only an *average* of n records in the sample. The standard deviation is $\sqrt{n(1 - n/N)}$, and the sample might turn out to be either too large for the desired application or too small to give the necessary results.

Fortunately, a simple modification of the "obvious" procedure gives us what we want: The $(t+1)$st record should be selected with probability $(n-m)/(N-t)$, if m items have already been selected. This is the appropriate probability, since of all the possible ways to choose n things from N such that m values occur in the first t, exactly

$$\binom{N-t-1}{n-m-1} \bigg/ \binom{N-t}{n-m} = \frac{n-m}{N-t} \tag{1}$$

of them select the $(t+1)$st element.

The idea developed in the preceding paragraph leads immediately to the following algorithm:

Algorithm S (*Selection sampling technique*). To select n records at random from a set of N, where $0 < n \leq N$.

S1. [Initialize.] Set $t \leftarrow 0$, $m \leftarrow 0$. (During this algorithm, m represents the number of records selected so far, and t is the total number of input records that we have dealt with.)

S2. [Generate U.] Generate a random number U, uniformly distributed between zero and one.

S3. [Test.] If $(N - t)U \geq n - m$, go to step S5.

S4. [Select.] Select the next record for the sample, and increase m and t by 1. If $m < n$, go to step S2; otherwise the sample is complete and the algorithm terminates.

S5. [Skip.] Skip the next record (do not include it in the sample), increase t by 1, and go back to step S2. ∎

This algorithm may appear to be unreliable at first glance and, in fact, to be incorrect; but a careful analysis (see the exercises below) shows that it is completely trustworthy. It is not difficult to verify that

a) At most N records are input (we never run off the end of the file before choosing n items).

b) The sample is completely unbiased. In particular, the probability that any given element is selected, such as the last element of the file, is n/N.

Statement (b) is true in spite of the fact that we are *not* selecting the $(t+1)$st item with probability n/N, but rather with the probability in Eq. (1)! This has caused some confusion in the published literature. Can the reader explain this seeming contradiction?

(*Note:* When using Algorithm S, one should be careful to use a different source of random numbers U each time the program is run, to avoid connections between the samples obtained on different days. This can be done, for example, by choosing a different value of X_0 for the linear congruential method each time. The seed value X_0 could be set to the current date, or to the last random number X that was generated on the previous run of the program.)

We will usually not have to pass over all N records. In fact, since (b) above says that the last record is selected with probability n/N, we will terminate the algorithm *before* considering the last record exactly $(1 - n/N)$ of the time. The average number of records considered when $n = 2$ is about $\frac{2}{3}N$, and the general formulas are given in exercises 5 and 6.

Algorithm S and a number of other sampling techniques are discussed in a paper by C. T. Fan, Mervin E. Muller, and Ivan Rezucha, *J. Amer. Stat. Assoc.* **57** (1962), 387–402. The method was independently discovered by T. G. Jones, *CACM* **5** (1962), 343.

A problem arises if we don't know the value of N in advance, since the precise value of N is crucial in Algorithm S. Suppose we want to select n items at random from a file, without knowing exactly how many are present in that file. We could first go through and count the records, then take a second pass to select them; but it is generally better to sample $m \geq n$ of the original items on the first pass, where m is much less than N, so that only m items must be considered on the second pass. The trick, of course, is to do this in such a way that the final result is a truly random sample of the original file.

Since we don't know when the input is going to end, we must keep track of a random sample of the input records seen so far, thus always being prepared for the end. As we read the input we will construct a "reservoir" that contains only the records that have appeared among the previous samples. The first n records always go into the reservoir. When the $(t+1)$st record is being input, for $t \geq n$, we will have in memory a table of n indices pointing to the records that we have chosen from among the first t. The problem is to maintain this situation with t increased by one, namely to find a new random sample from among the $t+1$ records now known to be present. It is not hard to see that we should include the new record in the new sample with probability $n/(t+1)$, and in such a case it should replace a random element of the previous sample.

Thus, the following procedure does the job:

Algorithm R (*Reservoir sampling*). To select n records at random from a file of unknown size $\geq n$, given $n > 0$. An auxiliary file called the "reservoir" contains all records that are candidates for the final sample. The algorithm uses a table of distinct indices $I[j]$ for $1 \leq j \leq n$, each of which points to one of the records in the reservoir.

R1. [Initialize.] Input the first n records and copy them to the reservoir. Set $I[j] \leftarrow j$ for $1 \leq j \leq n$, and set $t \leftarrow m \leftarrow n$. (If the file being sampled has fewer than n records, it will of course be necessary to abort the algorithm and report failure. During this algorithm, indices $I[1], \ldots, I[n]$ point to the records in the current sample; m is the size of the reservoir; and t is the number of input records dealt with so far.)

R2. [End of file?] If there are no more records to be input, go to step R6.

R3. [Generate and test.] Increase t by 1, then generate a random integer M between 1 and t (inclusive). If $M > n$, go to R5.

R4. [Add to reservoir.] Copy the next record of the input file to the reservoir, increase m by 1, and set $I[M] \leftarrow m$. (The record previously pointed to by $I[M]$ is being replaced in the sample by the new record.) Go back to R2.

R5. [Skip.] Skip over the next record of the input file (do not include it in the reservoir), and return to step R2.

R6. [Second pass.] Sort the I table entries so that $I[1] < \cdots < I[n]$; then go through the reservoir, copying the records with these indices into the output file that is to hold the final sample. ∎

Algorithm R is due to Alan G. Waterman. The reader may wish to work out the example of its operation that appears in exercise 9.

If the records are sufficiently short, it is of course unnecessary to have a reservoir at all; we can keep the n records of the current sample in memory at all times, and the algorithm becomes much simpler (see exercise 10).

The natural question to ask about Algorithm R is, "What is the expected size of the reservoir?" Exercise 11 shows that the average value of m is exactly $n(1 + H_N - H_n)$; this is approximately $n(1 + \ln(N/n))$. So if $N/n = 1000$, the reservoir will contain only about $1/125$ as many items as the original file.

Notice that Algorithms S and R can be used to obtain samples for several independent categories simultaneously. For example, if we have a large file of names and addresses of U.S. residents, we could pick random samples of exactly 10 people from each of the 50 states without making 50 passes through the file, and without first sorting the file by state.

Significant improvements to both Algorithms S and R are possible, when n/N is small, if we generate a single random variable to tell us how many records should be skipped instead of deciding whether or not to skip each record. (See exercise 8.)

The sampling problem can be regarded as the computation of a random *combination*, according to the conventional definition of combinations of N things taken n at a time (see Section 1.2.6). Now let us consider the problem of computing a random *permutation* of t objects; we will call this the *shuffling* problem, since shuffling a deck of cards is nothing more than subjecting the deck to a random permutation.

A moment's reflection is enough to convince any card player that traditional shuffling procedures are miserably inadequate. There is no hope of obtaining each of the $t!$ permutations with anywhere near equal probability by such methods. Expert bridge players reportedly make use of this fact when deciding whether or not to finesse. At least seven "riffle shuffles" of a 52-card deck are needed to reach a distribution within 10% of uniform, and 14 random riffles are guaranteed to do so [see Aldous and Diaconis, *AMM* **93** (1986), 333–348].

If t is small, we can obtain a random permutation very quickly by generating a random integer between 1 and $t!$. For example, when $t = 4$, a random number between 1 and 24 suffices to select a random permutation from a table of all possibilities. But for large t, it is necessary to be more careful if we want to claim that each permutation is equally likely, since $t!$ is much larger than the accuracy of individual random numbers.

A suitable shuffling procedure can be obtained by recalling Algorithm 3.3.2P, which gives a simple correspondence between each of the $t!$ possible permutations and a sequence of numbers $(c_1, c_2, \ldots, c_{t-1})$, with $0 \leq c_j \leq j$. It is easy to compute such a set of numbers at random, and we can use the correspondence to produce a random permutation.

Algorithm P (*Shuffling*). Let X_1, X_2, ..., X_t be a set of t numbers to be shuffled.

P1. [Initialize.] Set $j \leftarrow t$.

P2. [Generate U.] Generate a random number U, uniformly distributed between zero and one.

P3. [Exchange.] Set $k \leftarrow \lfloor jU \rfloor + 1$. (Now k is a random integer, between 1 and j. Exercise 3.4.1–3 explains that k should *not* be computed by taking a remainder modulo j.) Exchange $X_k \leftrightarrow X_j$.

P4. [Decrease j.] Decrease j by 1. If $j > 1$, return to step P2. ∎

This algorithm was first published by R. A. Fisher and F. Yates [*Statistical Tables* (London, 1938), Example 12], in ordinary language, and by R. Durstenfeld [*CACM* **7** (1964), 420] in computer language. If we merely wish to generate a random permutation of $\{1, \ldots, t\}$ instead of shuffling a given sequence $(X_1, \ldots, X_t)$, we can avoid the exchange operation $X_k \leftrightarrow X_j$ by letting j increase from 1 to t and setting $X_j \leftarrow X_k$, $X_k \leftarrow j$; see D. E. Knuth, *The Stanford GraphBase* (New York: ACM Press, 1994), 104.

R. Salfi [*COMPSTAT 1974* (Vienna: 1974), 28–35] has pointed out that Algorithm P cannot possibly generate more than m distinct permutations when we obtain the uniform U's with a linear congruential sequence of modulus m,

or indeed whenever we use a recurrence $U_{n+1} = f(U_n)$ for which U_n can take
only m different values, because the final permutation in such cases is entirely
determined by the value of the first U that is generated. Thus, for example,
if $m = 2^{32}$, certain permutations of 13 elements will never occur, since $13! \approx
1.45 \times 2^{32}$. In most applications we don't really *want* to see all 13! permutations;
yet it is disconcerting to know that the excluded ones are determined by a fairly
simple mathematical rule such as a lattice structure (see Section 3.3.4).

This problem does not arise when we use a lagged Fibonacci generator like
3.2.2–(7) with a sufficiently long period. But even with such methods we cannot
get all permutations uniformly unless we are able to specify at least $t!$ different
seed values to initialize the generator. In other words, we can't get $\lg t!$ truly
random bits out unless we put $\lg t!$ truly random bits in. Section 3.5 shows that
we need not despair about this.

Algorithm P can easily be modified to yield a random permutation of a
random combination (see exercise 15). For a discussion of random combinatorial
objects of other kinds (e.g., partitions), see Section 7.2 and/or the book *Combinatorial Algorithms* by Nijenhuis and Wilf (New York: Academic Press, 1975).

EXERCISES

1. [*M12*] Explain Eq. (1).

2. [*20*] Prove that Algorithm S never tries to read more than N records of its
input file.

▶ **3.** [*22*] The $(t+1)$st item in Algorithm S is selected with probability $(n-m)/(N-t)$,
not n/N, yet the text claims that the sample is unbiased; thus each item should be
selected with the *same* probability. How can both of these statements be true?

4. [*M23*] Let $p(m,t)$ be the probability that exactly m items are selected from among
the first t in the selection sampling technique. Show directly from Algorithm S that

$$p(m,t) = \binom{t}{m}\binom{N-t}{n-m}\bigg/\binom{N}{n}, \qquad \text{for } 0 \le t \le N.$$

5. [*M24*] What is the average value of t when Algorithm S terminates? (In other
words, how many of the N records have been passed, on the average, before the sample
is complete?)

6. [*M24*] What is the standard deviation of the value computed in exercise 5?

7. [*M25*] Prove that any *given* choice of n records from the set of N is obtained by
Algorithm S with probability $1/\binom{N}{n}$. Therefore the sample is completely unbiased.

▶ **8.** [*M39*] (J. S. Vitter.) Algorithm S computes one uniform deviate for each input
record it handles. The purpose of this exercise is to consider a more efficient approach
in which we calculate more quickly the proper number X of input records to skip before
the first selection is made.

a) What is the probability that $X \ge k$, given k?
b) Show that the result of (a) allows us to calculate X by generating only one
   uniform U and then doing $O(X)$ other calculations.
c) Show that we may also set $X \leftarrow \min(Y_N, Y_{N-1}, \ldots, Y_{N-n+1})$, where the Y's are
   independent and each Y_t is a random integer in the range $0 \le Y_t < t$.

d) For maximum speed, show that X can also be calculated in $O(1)$ steps, on the average, using a "squeeze method" like Eq. 3.4.1–(18).

9. [12] Let $n = 3$. If Algorithm R is applied to a file containing 20 records numbered 1 thru 20, and if the random numbers generated in step R3 are respectively

$$4, 1, 6, 7, 5, 3, 5, 11, 11, 3, 7, 9, 3, 11, 4, 5, 4,$$

which records go into the reservoir? Which are in the final sample?

10. [15] Modify Algorithm R so that the reservoir is eliminated, assuming that the n records of the current sample can be held in memory.

▶ **11.** [M25] Let p_m be the probability that exactly m elements are put into the reservoir during the first pass of Algorithm R. Determine the generating function $G(z) = \sum_m p_m z^m$, and find the mean and standard deviation. (Use the ideas of Section 1.2.10.)

12. [M26] The gist of Algorithm P is that any permutation π can be uniquely written as a product of transpositions in the form $\pi = (a_t t) \ldots (a_3 3)(a_2 2)$, where $1 \le a_j \le j$ for $t \ge j > 1$. Prove that there is also a unique representation of the form $\pi = (b_2 2)(b_3 3) \ldots (b_t t)$, where $1 \le b_j \le j$ for $1 < j \le t$, and design an algorithm that computes the b's from the a's in $O(t)$ steps.

13. [M23] (S. W. Golomb.) One of the most common ways to shuffle cards is to divide the deck into two parts as equal as possible, and to "riffle" them together. (According to the discussion of card-playing etiquette in Hoyle's rules of card games, "A shuffle of this sort should be made about three times to mix the cards thoroughly.") Consider a deck of $2n - 1$ cards $X_1, X_2, \ldots, X_{2n-1}$; a "perfect shuffle" s divides this deck into $X_1, X_2, \ldots, X_n$ and $X_{n+1}, \ldots, X_{2n-1}$, then perfectly interleaves them to obtain X_1, $X_{n+1}, X_2, X_{n+2}, \ldots, X_{2n-1}, X_n$. The "cut" operation c^j changes $X_1, X_2, \ldots, X_{2n-1}$ into $X_{j+1}, \ldots, X_{2n-1}, X_1, \ldots, X_j$. Show that by combining perfect shuffles and cuts, at most $(2n - 1)(2n - 2)$ different arrangements of the deck are possible, if $n > 1$.

14. [22] A cut-and-riffle permutation of $a_0 a_1 \ldots a_{n-1}$ changes it to a sequence that contains the subsequences

$$a_x \, a_{(x+1) \bmod n} \cdots a_{(y-1) \bmod n} \qquad \text{and} \qquad a_y \, a_{(y+1) \bmod n} \cdots a_{(x-1) \bmod n}$$

intermixed in some way, for some x and y. Thus, 3890145267 is a cut-and-riffle of 0123456789, with $x = 3$ and $y = 8$.

a) Beginning with 52 playing cards arranged in the standard order

2 3 4 5 6 7 8 9 10 J Q K A ♣   2 3 4 5 6 7 8 9 10 J Q K A ♦   2 3 4 5 6 7 8 9 10 J Q K A ♥   2 3 4 5 6 7 8 9 10 J Q K A ♠,

Mr. J. H. Quick (a student) did a random cut-and-riffle; then he removed the leftmost card and inserted it in a random place, obtaining the sequence

9 10 K J Q A K A 2 Q 3 2 3 4 5 6 7 4 8 9 5 10 6 J 7 Q 8 K 9 10 J Q A K 2 3 A 4 2 3 4 5 6 5 6 7 8 7 9 10 J 8.

Which card did he move from the leftmost position?

b) Starting again with the deck in its original order, Quick now did *three* cut-and-riffles before moving the leftmost card to a new place:

10 J Q 3 4 5 6 J J Q 4 6 K A 2 3 K 4 7 5 6 Q A 7 5 A 8 7 6 K K 9 A 7 8 9 10 8 10 8 2 5 J 2 3 Q 4 9 3 2 9 10.

Which card did he move this time?

▶ **15.** [*30*] (Ole-Johan Dahl.) If $X_k = k$ for $1 \le k \le t$ at the start of Algorithm P, and if we terminate the algorithm when j reaches the value $t - n$, the sequence X_{t-n+1}, $\ldots$, X_t is a random permutation of a random combination of n elements. Show how to simulate the effect of this procedure using only $O(n)$ cells of memory.

▶ **16.** [*M25*] Devise a way to compute a random sample of n records from N, given N and n, based on the idea of hashing (Section 6.4). Your method should use $O(n)$ storage locations and an average of $O(n)$ units of time, and it should present the sample as a sorted set of integers $1 \le X_1 < X_2 < \cdots < X_n \le N$.

17. [*M22*] (R. W. Floyd.) Prove that the following algorithm generates a random sample S of n integers from $\{1, \ldots, N\}$: Set $S \leftarrow \emptyset$; then for $j \leftarrow N - n + 1, N - n + 2$, $\ldots$, N (in this order), set $k \leftarrow \lfloor jU \rfloor + 1$ and

$$ S \leftarrow \begin{cases} S \cup \{k\}, & \text{if } k \notin S; \\ S \cup \{j\}, & \text{if } k \in S. \end{cases} $$

▶ **18.** [*M32*] People sometimes try to shuffle n items $(X_1, X_2, \ldots, X_n)$ by successively interchanging

$$ X_1 \leftrightarrow X_{k_1}, \ X_2 \leftrightarrow X_{k_2}, \ \ldots, \ X_n \leftrightarrow X_{k_n}, $$

where the indices k_j are independent and uniformly random between 1 and n.

Consider the directed graph with vertices $\{1, 2, \ldots, n\}$ and with arcs from j to k_j for $1 \le j \le n$. Describe the digraphs of this type for which, if we start with the elements $(X_1, X_2, \ldots, X_n) = (1, 2, \ldots, n)$, the stated interchanges produce the respective permutations (a) $(n, 1, 2, \ldots)$; (b) $(1, 2, \ldots, n)$; (c) $(2, \ldots, n, 1)$. Conclude that these three permutations are obtained with wildly different probabilities.

▶ **19.** [*M28*] (*Priority sampling.*) Consider a file of N items in which the kth item has a positive weight w_k. Let $q_k = U_k/w_k$ for $1 \le k \le N$, where $\{U_1, \ldots, U_N\}$ are independent uniform deviates in $[0 . . 1)$. If r is any real number, define

$$ \widehat{w}_k^{(r)} = \begin{cases} \max(w_k, 1/r), & \text{if } q_k < r; \\ 0, & \text{if } q_k \ge r; \end{cases} \qquad \widehat{w}_k^{(r+)} = \begin{cases} \max(w_k, 1/r), & \text{if } q_k \le r; \\ 0, & \text{if } q_k > r. \end{cases} $$

a) If r is the nth smallest element of $\{q_1, \ldots, q_N\}$, prove that the expected value $\mathrm{E}\, \widehat{w}_1^{(r)} \widehat{w}_2^{(r)} \ldots w_k^{(r)}$ is $w_1 w_2 \ldots w_k$, for $1 \le k < n \le N$. *Hint:* Show that, if s is the $(n-k)$th smallest element of $\{q_{k+1}, \ldots, q_N\}$, we have $\widehat{w}_1^{(r)} \ldots \widehat{w}_k^{(r)} = \widehat{w}_1^{(s+)} \ldots \widehat{w}_k^{(s+)}$. (Notice that the quantity s is independent of $\{U_1, \ldots, U_k\}$.)

b) Consequently $\mathrm{E}\, \widehat{w}_{j_1}^{(r)} \ldots \widehat{w}_{j_k}^{(r)} = w_{j_1} \ldots w_{j_k}$ when $j_1 < \cdots < j_k$.

c) Show that, if $n > 2$, the variance $\mathrm{Var}(\widehat{w}_{j_1}^{(r)} + \cdots + \widehat{w}_{j_k}^{(r)})$ is $\mathrm{Var}(\widehat{w}_{j_1}^{(r)}) + \cdots + \mathrm{Var}(\widehat{w}_{j_k}^{(r)})$.

d) Given n, explain how to modify the reservoir sampling method so that the value of r and the $n - 1$ items with subscripts $\{j \mid q_j < r\}$ can be obtained with one pass through a file of unknown size N. *Hint:* Use a priority queue of size n.

> *By means of the thread one understands the ball of yarn,*
> *so we'll be satisfied and assured by having this sample.*
> — MIGUEL DE CERVANTES, *El Ingenioso Hidalgo*
> *Don Quixote de la Mancha* (1605)

*3.5. WHAT IS A RANDOM SEQUENCE?

A. Introductory remarks. We have seen in this chapter how to generate sequences

$$\langle U_n \rangle = U_0, \ U_1, \ U_2, \ \ldots \tag{1}$$

of real numbers in the range $0 \leq U_n < 1$, and we have called them "random" sequences even though they are completely deterministic in character. To justify this terminology, we claimed that the numbers "behave as if they are truly random." Such a statement may be satisfactory for practical purposes (at the present time), but it sidesteps a very important philosophical and theoretical question: Precisely what do we mean by "random behavior"? A quantitative definition is needed. It is undesirable to talk about concepts that we do not really understand, especially since many apparently paradoxical statements can be made about random numbers.

The mathematical theory of probability and statistics scrupulously avoids the issue. It refrains from making absolute statements, and instead expresses everything in terms of how much *probability* is to be attached to statements involving random sequences of events. The axioms of probability theory are set up so that abstract probabilities can be computed readily, but nothing is said about what probability really signifies, or how this concept can be applied meaningfully to the actual world. In the book *Probability, Statistics, and Truth* (New York: Macmillan, 1957), R. von Mises discusses this situation in detail, and presents the view that a proper definition of probability depends on obtaining a proper definition of a random sequence.

Let us paraphrase here some statements made by two of the many authors who have commented on the subject.

> *D. H. Lehmer* (1951): "A random sequence is a vague notion embodying the idea of a sequence in which each term is unpredictable to the uninitiated and whose digits pass a certain number of tests, traditional with statisticians and depending somewhat on the uses to which the sequence is to be put."

> *J. N. Franklin* (1962): "The sequence (1) is random if it has every property that is shared by all infinite sequences of independent samples of random variables from the uniform distribution."

Franklin's statement essentially generalizes Lehmer's to say that the sequence must satisfy *all* statistical tests. His definition is not completely precise, and we will see later that a reasonable interpretation of his statement leads us to conclude that there is no such thing as a random sequence! So let us begin with Lehmer's less restrictive statement and attempt to make *it* precise. What we really want is a relatively short list of mathematical properties, each of which is satisfied by our intuitive notion of a random sequence; furthermore, the list is to be complete enough so that we are willing to agree that *any* sequence satisfying these properties is "random." In this section, we will develop what seems to be an adequate definition of randomness according to these criteria, although many interesting questions remain to be answered.

Let u and v be real numbers, $0 \le u < v \le 1$. If U is a random variable that is uniformly distributed between 0 and 1, the probability that $u \le U < v$ is equal to $v - u$. For example, the probability that $\frac{1}{5} \le U < \frac{3}{5}$ is $\frac{2}{5}$. How can we translate this property of the single number U into a property of the infinite sequence U_0, U_1, U_2, ...? The obvious answer is to count how many times U_n lies between u and v, and the average number of times should equal $v - u$. Our intuitive idea of probability is based in this way on the frequency of occurrence.

More precisely, let $\nu(n)$ be the number of values of j, $0 \le j < n$, such that $u \le U_j < v$; we want the ratio $\nu(n)/n$ to approach the value $v - u$ as n approaches infinity:

$$\lim_{n \to \infty} \frac{\nu(n)}{n} = v - u. \tag{2}$$

If this condition holds for all choices of u and v, the sequence is said to be *equidistributed*.

Let $S(n)$ be a statement about the integer n and the sequence U_0, U_1, ...; for example, $S(n)$ might be the statement considered above, "$u \le U_n < v$." We can generalize the idea used in the preceding paragraph to define the probability that $S(n)$ is true with respect to a particular infinite sequence.

Definition A. *Let $\nu(n)$ be the number of values of j, $0 \le j < n$, such that $S(j)$ is true. We say that $S(n)$ is true with probability λ if the limit as n tends to infinity of $\nu(n)/n$ equals λ. Symbolically:* $\Pr\bigl(S(n)\bigr) = \lambda$ *if* $\lim_{n \to \infty} \nu(n)/n = \lambda$. ∎

In terms of this notation, the sequence U_0, U_1, ... is equidistributed if and only if $\Pr(u \le U_n < v) = v - u$, for all real numbers u, v with $0 \le u < v \le 1$.

A sequence might be equidistributed without being random. For example, if U_0, U_1, ... and V_0, V_1, ... are equidistributed sequences, it is not hard to show that the sequence

$$W_0, W_1, W_2, W_3, \ldots = \tfrac{1}{2}U_0,\ \tfrac{1}{2}+\tfrac{1}{2}V_0,\ \tfrac{1}{2}U_1,\ \tfrac{1}{2}+\tfrac{1}{2}V_1,\ \ldots \tag{3}$$

is also equidistributed, since the subsequence $\frac{1}{2}U_0$, $\frac{1}{2}U_1$, ... is equidistributed between 0 and $\frac{1}{2}$, while the alternate terms $\frac{1}{2} + \frac{1}{2}V_0$, $\frac{1}{2} + \frac{1}{2}V_1$, ..., are equidistributed between $\frac{1}{2}$ and 1. But in the sequence of W's, a value less than $\frac{1}{2}$ is always followed by a value greater than or equal to $\frac{1}{2}$, and conversely; hence the sequence is not random by any reasonable definition. A stronger property than equidistribution is needed.

A natural generalization of the equidistribution property, which removes the objection stated in the preceding paragraph, is to consider adjacent pairs of numbers of our sequence. We can require the sequence to satisfy the condition

$$\Pr(u_1 \le U_n < v_1 \ \text{ and }\ u_2 \le U_{n+1} < v_2) = (v_1 - u_1)(v_2 - u_2) \tag{4}$$

for any four numbers u_1, v_1, u_2, v_2 with $0 \le u_1 < v_1 \le 1$, $0 \le u_2 < v_2 \le 1$. And in general, for any positive integer k we can require our sequence to be *k-distributed* in the following sense:

Definition B. *The sequence* (1) *is said to be k-distributed if*

$$\Pr(u_1 \le U_n < v_1, \ \ldots, \ u_k \le U_{n+k-1} < v_k) = (v_1 - u_1)\ldots(v_k - u_k) \quad (5)$$

for all choices of real numbers u_j, v_j, *with* $0 \le u_j < v_j \le 1$ *for* $1 \le j \le k$. ∎

An equidistributed sequence is a 1-distributed sequence. Notice that if $k > 1$, a k-distributed sequence is always $(k-1)$-distributed, since we may set $u_k = 0$ and $v_k = 1$ in Eq. (5). Thus, in particular, any sequence that is known to be 4-distributed must also be 3-distributed, 2-distributed, and equidistributed. We can investigate the largest k for which a given sequence is k-distributed; and this leads us to formulate a stronger property:

Definition C. *A sequence is said to be* ∞-*distributed if it is k-distributed for all positive integers k.* ∎

So far we have considered "$[0\mathbin{..}1)$ sequences," that is, sequences of real numbers lying between zero and one. The same ideas apply to integer-valued sequences; let us say that the sequence $\langle X_n \rangle = X_0, X_1, X_2, \ldots$ is a *b-ary sequence* if each X_n is one of the integers $0, 1, \ldots, b-1$. Thus, a 2-ary (binary) sequence is a sequence of zeros and ones.

We also define a *k-digit b-ary number* as a string of k integers $x_1 x_2 \ldots x_k$, where $0 \le x_j < b$ for $1 \le j \le k$.

Definition D. *A b-ary sequence is said to be k-distributed if*

$$\Pr(X_n X_{n+1} \ldots X_{n+k-1} = x_1 x_2 \ldots x_k) = 1/b^k \quad (6)$$

for all b-ary numbers $x_1 x_2 \ldots x_k$. ∎

It is clear from this definition that if $U_0, U_1, \ldots$ is a k-distributed $[0\mathbin{..}1)$ sequence, then the sequence $\lfloor bU_0 \rfloor, \lfloor bU_1 \rfloor, \ldots$ is a k-distributed b-ary sequence. (If we set $u_j = x_j/b$, $v_j = (x_j + 1)/b$, $X_n = \lfloor bU_n \rfloor$, Eq. (5) becomes Eq. (6).) Furthermore, every k-distributed b-ary sequence is also $(k-1)$-distributed, if $k > 1$: We add together the probabilities for the b-ary numbers $x_1 \ldots x_{k-1} 0$, $x_1 \ldots x_{k-1} 1$, $\ldots$, $x_1 \ldots x_{k-1} (b-1)$ to obtain

$$\Pr(X_n \ldots X_{n+k-2} = x_1 \ldots x_{k-1}) = 1/b^{k-1}.$$

(Probabilities for disjoint events are additive; see exercise 5.) It therefore is natural to speak of an ∞-distributed b-ary sequence, as in Definition C above.

The representation of a positive real number in the radix-b number system may be regarded as a b-ary sequence; for example, π corresponds to the 10-ary sequence 3, 1, 4, 1, 5, 9, 2, 6, 5, 3, 5, 8, 9, ... People have conjectured that this sequence is ∞-distributed, but nobody has yet been able to prove that it is even 1-distributed.

Let us analyze these concepts a little more closely in the case when k equals a million. A binary sequence that is 1000000-distributed is going to have runs of a million zeros in a row! Similarly, a $[0\mathbin{..}1)$ sequence that is 1000000-distributed is going to have runs of a million consecutive values each of which is less than $\frac{1}{2}$.

It is true that this will happen only $(\frac{1}{2})^{1000000}$ of the time, on the average, but the fact is that it *does* happen. Indeed, this phenomenon will occur in any truly random sequence, using our intuitive notion of "truly random." One can easily imagine that such a situation will have a drastic effect if this set of a million "truly random" numbers is being used in a computer-simulation experiment; there would be good reason to complain about the random number generator. However, if we have a sequence of numbers that never has runs of a million consecutive U's less than $\frac{1}{2}$, the sequence is not random, and it will not be a suitable source of numbers for other conceivable applications that use extremely long blocks of U's as input. In summary, *a truly random sequence will exhibit local nonrandomness*. Local nonrandomness is necessary in some applications, but it is disastrous in others. We are forced to conclude that no sequence of "random" numbers can be adequate for every application.

In a similar vein, one may argue that it is impossible to judge whether a *finite* sequence is random or not; any particular sequence is just as likely as any other one. These facts are definitely stumbling blocks if we are ever to have a useful definition of randomness, but they are not really cause for alarm. It is still possible to give a definition for the randomness of infinite sequences of real numbers in such a way that the corresponding theory (viewed properly) will give us a great deal of insight concerning the ordinary finite sequences of rational numbers that are actually generated on a computer. Furthermore, we shall see later in this section that there are several plausible definitions of randomness for finite sequences.

B. ∞-distributed sequences. Let us now make a brief study of the theory of sequences that are ∞-distributed. To describe the theory adequately, we will need to use a bit of higher mathematics, so we assume in the remainder of this subsection that the reader knows the material ordinarily taught in an "advanced calculus" course.

First it is convenient to generalize Definition A, since the limit appearing there does not exist for all sequences. We define

$$\overline{\Pr}\big(S(n)\big) = \limsup_{n\to\infty} \frac{\nu(n)}{n}, \qquad \underline{\Pr}\big(S(n)\big) = \liminf_{n\to\infty} \frac{\nu(n)}{n}. \tag{7}$$

Then $\Pr\big(S(n)\big)$, if it exists, is the common value of $\underline{\Pr}\big(S(n)\big)$ and $\overline{\Pr}\big(S(n)\big)$.

We have seen that a k-distributed $[0\mathinner{.\,.}1)$ sequence leads to a k-distributed b-ary sequence, if U is replaced by $\lfloor bU \rfloor$. Our first theorem shows that a converse result is also true.

Theorem A. *Let $\langle U_n \rangle = U_0, U_1, U_2, \ldots$ be a $[0\mathinner{.\,.}1)$ sequence. If the sequence*

$$\langle \lfloor b_j U_n \rfloor \rangle = \lfloor b_j U_0 \rfloor, \; \lfloor b_j U_1 \rfloor, \; \lfloor b_j U_2 \rfloor, \; \ldots$$

is a k-distributed b_j-ary sequence for all b_j in an infinite sequence of integers $1 < b_1 < b_2 < b_3 < \cdots$, then the original sequence $\langle U_n \rangle$ is k-distributed.

As an example of this theorem, suppose that $b_j = 2^j$. The sequence $\lfloor 2^j U_0 \rfloor$, $\lfloor 2^j U_1 \rfloor$, $\ldots$ is essentially the sequence of the first j bits of the binary representations of U_0, U_1, ... If all these integer sequences are k-distributed, in the sense of Definition D, then the real-valued sequence U_0, U_1, ... must also be k-distributed in the sense of Definition B.

Proof of Theorem A. If the sequence $\lfloor bU_0 \rfloor$, $\lfloor bU_1 \rfloor$, ... is k-distributed, it follows by the addition of probabilities that Eq. (5) holds whenever each u_j and v_j is a rational number with denominator b. Now let u_j, v_j be any real numbers, and let u'_j, v'_j be rational numbers with denominator b such that

$$u'_j \leq u_j < u'_j + 1/b, \qquad v'_j \leq v_j < v'_j + 1/b.$$

Let $S(n)$ be the statement that $u_1 \leq U_n < v_1, \ldots, u_k \leq U_{n+k-1} < v_k$. We have

$$\overline{\Pr}\bigl(S(n)\bigr) \leq \Pr\Bigl(u'_1 \leq U_n < v'_1 + \frac{1}{b}, \ldots, u'_k \leq U_{n+k-1} < v'_k + \frac{1}{b}\Bigr)$$

$$= \Bigl(v'_1 - u'_1 + \frac{1}{b}\Bigr) \ldots \Bigl(v'_k - u'_k + \frac{1}{b}\Bigr);$$

$$\underline{\Pr}\bigl(S(n)\bigr) \geq \Pr\Bigl(u'_1 + \frac{1}{b} \leq U_n < v'_1, \ldots, u'_k + \frac{1}{b} \leq U_{n+k-1} < v'_k\Bigr)$$

$$= \Bigl(v'_1 - u'_1 - \frac{1}{b}\Bigr) \ldots \Bigl(v'_k - u'_k - \frac{1}{b}\Bigr).$$

Now $\bigl|(v'_j - u'_j \pm 1/b) - (v_j - u_j)\bigr| \leq 2/b$. Since our inequalities hold for all $b = b_j$, and since $b_j \to \infty$ as $j \to \infty$, we have

$$(v_1 - u_1) \ldots (v_k - u_k) \leq \underline{\Pr}\bigl(S(n)\bigr) \leq \overline{\Pr}\bigl(S(n)\bigr) \leq (v_1 - u_1) \ldots (v_k - u_k). \quad \blacksquare$$

The next theorem is our main tool for proving things about k-distributed sequences.

Theorem B. *Suppose that $\langle U_n \rangle$ is a k-distributed $[0 .. 1)$ sequence, and let $f(x_1, x_2, \ldots, x_k)$ be a Riemann-integrable function of k variables; then*

$$\lim_{n \to \infty} \frac{1}{n} \sum_{0 \leq j < n} f(U_j, U_{j+1}, \ldots, U_{j+k-1}) = \int_0^1 \cdots \int_0^1 f(x_1, x_2, \ldots, x_k)\, dx_1 \ldots dx_k. \tag{8}$$

Proof. The definition of a k-distributed sequence states that this result is true in the special case that

$$f(x_1, \ldots, x_k) = [u_1 \leq x_1 < v_1, \ldots, u_k \leq x_k < v_k] \tag{9}$$

for some constants u_1, v_1, ..., u_k, v_k. Therefore Eq. (8) is true whenever $f = a_1 f_1 + a_2 f_2 + \cdots + a_m f_m$ and when each f_j is a function of type (9); in other words, Eq. (8) holds whenever f is a "step-function" obtained by partitioning the unit k-dimensional cube into subcells whose faces are parallel to the coordinate axes, and assigning a constant value to f on each subcell.

    Now let f be any Riemann-integrable function. If ϵ is any positive number, we know (by the definition of Riemann-integrability) that there exist step functions $\underline{f}$ and $\overline{f}$ such that $\underline{f}(x_1, \ldots, x_k) \leq f(x_1, \ldots, x_k) \leq \overline{f}(x_1, \ldots, x_k)$, and such that the difference of the integrals of $\underline{f}$ and $\overline{f}$ is less than ϵ. Since Eq. (8) holds for $\underline{f}$ and $\overline{f}$, and since

$$\frac{1}{n}\sum_{0\le j<n} \underline{f}(U_j,\ldots,U_{j+k-1}) \le \frac{1}{n}\sum_{0\le j<n} f(U_j,\ldots,U_{j+k-1})$$

$$\le \frac{1}{n}\sum_{0\le j<n} \overline{f}(U_j,\ldots,U_{j+k-1}),$$

we conclude that Eq. (8) is true also for f. ∎

Theorem B can be applied, for example, to the *permutation test* of Section 3.3.2. Let $(p_1,p_2,\ldots,p_k)$ be any permutation of the numbers $\{1,2,\ldots,k\}$; we want to show that

$$\Pr(U_{n+p_1-1} < U_{n+p_2-1} < \cdots < U_{n+p_k-1}) = 1/k!. \tag{10}$$

To prove this, assume that the sequence $\langle U_n\rangle$ is k-distributed, and let

$$f(x_1,\ldots,x_k) = [x_{p_1} < x_{p_2} < \cdots < x_{p_k}].$$

We have

$$\Pr(U_{n+p_1-1} < U_{n+p_2-1} < \cdots < U_{n+p_k-1})$$

$$= \int_0^1 \cdots \int_0^1 f(x_1,\ldots,x_k)\,dx_1\ldots dx_k$$

$$= \int_0^1 dx_{p_k} \int_0^{x_{p_k}} \cdots \int_0^{x_{p_3}} dx_{p_2} \int_0^{x_{p_2}} dx_{p_1} = \frac{1}{k!}.$$

Corollary P. *If a $[0..1)$ sequence is k-distributed, it satisfies the permutation test of order k, in the sense of Eq. (10).* ∎

We can also show that the *serial correlation test* is satisfied:

Corollary S. *If a $[0..1)$ sequence is $(k+1)$-distributed, the serial correlation coefficient between U_n and U_{n+k} tends to zero:*

$$\lim_{n\to\infty} \frac{\frac{1}{n}\sum U_j U_{j+k} - \left(\frac{1}{n}\sum U_j\right)\left(\frac{1}{n}\sum U_{j+k}\right)}{\sqrt{\left(\frac{1}{n}\sum U_j^2 - \left(\frac{1}{n}\sum U_j\right)^2\right)\left(\frac{1}{n}\sum U_{j+k}^2 - \left(\frac{1}{n}\sum U_{j+k}\right)^2\right)}} = 0.$$

(All summations here are for $0 \le j < n$.)

Proof. By Theorem B, the quantities

$$\frac{1}{n}\sum U_j U_{j+k}, \qquad \frac{1}{n}\sum U_j^2, \qquad \frac{1}{n}\sum U_{j+k}^2, \qquad \frac{1}{n}\sum U_j, \qquad \frac{1}{n}\sum U_{j+k}$$

tend to the respective limits $\frac{1}{4}, \frac{1}{3}, \frac{1}{3}, \frac{1}{2}, \frac{1}{2}$ as $n \to \infty$. ∎

Let us now consider some slightly more general distribution properties of sequences. We have defined the notion of k-distribution by considering all of the adjacent k-tuples; for example, a sequence is 2-distributed if and only if the points

$$(U_0, U_1), \ (U_1, U_2), \ (U_2, U_3), \ (U_3, U_4), \ (U_4, U_5), \ \ldots$$

are equidistributed in the unit square. It is quite possible, however, that this can happen while alternate pairs of points $(U_1, U_2), (U_3, U_4), (U_5, U_6), \ldots$ are *not* equidistributed; if the density of points (U_{2n-1}, U_{2n}) is deficient in some area, the other points (U_{2n}, U_{2n+1}) might compensate. For example, the periodic binary sequence

$$\langle X_n \rangle = 0,0,0,1, \ 0,0,0,1, \ 1,1,0,1, \ 1,1,0,1, \ 0,0,0,1, \ \ldots, \quad (11)$$

with a period of length 16, is seen to be 3-distributed; yet the sequence of even-numbered elements $\langle X_{2n} \rangle = 0, 0, 0, 0, 1, 0, 1, 0, \ldots$ has three times as many zeros as ones, while the subsequence of odd-numbered elements $\langle X_{2n+1} \rangle = 0, 1,$ 0, 1, 1, 1, 1, 1, $\ldots$ has three times as many ones as zeros.

Suppose the sequence $\langle U_n \rangle$ is ∞-distributed. Example (11) shows that the subsequence of alternate terms $\langle U_{2n} \rangle = U_0, U_2, U_4, U_6, \ldots$ is not obviously guaranteed to be ∞-distributed or even 1-distributed. But we shall see that $\langle U_{2n} \rangle$ is, in fact, ∞-distributed, and much more is true.

Definition E. *A $[0 \mathrel{.\,.} 1)$ sequence $\langle U_n \rangle$ is said to be (m, k)-distributed if*

$$\Pr(u_1 \leq U_{mn+j} < v_1, \ u_2 \leq U_{mn+j+1} < v_2, \ \ldots, \ u_k \leq U_{mn+j+k-1} < v_k)$$
$$= (v_1 - u_1) \ldots (v_k - u_k)$$

for all choices of real numbers u_r, v_r with $0 \leq u_r < v_r \leq 1$ for $1 \leq r \leq k$, and for all integers j with $0 \leq j < m$. ∎

Thus a k-distributed sequence is the special case $m = 1$ in Definition E; the case $m = 2$ means that the k-tuples starting in even positions must have the same density as the k-tuples starting in odd positions, etc.

The following properties of Definition E are obvious:

An (m, k)-distributed sequence is (m, κ)-distributed for $1 \leq \kappa \leq k$. (12)

An (m, k)-distributed sequence is (d, k)-distributed for all divisors d of m. (13)

(See exercise 8.) We can also define the concept of an (m, k)-distributed b-ary sequence, as in Definition D; and the proof of Theorem A remains valid for (m, k)-distributed sequences.

The next theorem, which is in many ways rather surprising, shows that the property of being ∞-distributed is very strong indeed, much stronger than we imagined it to be when we first considered the definition of the concept.

Theorem C (Ivan Niven and H. S. Zuckerman). *An ∞-distributed sequence is (m, k)-distributed for all positive integers m and k.*

Proof. It suffices to prove the theorem for b-ary sequences, by using the generalization of Theorem A just mentioned. Furthermore, we may assume that $m = k$, because (12) and (13) tell us that the sequence will be (m, k)-distributed if it is (mk, mk)-distributed.

So we will prove that *any ∞-distributed b-ary sequence $X_0, X_1, \ldots$ is (m, m)-distributed for all positive integers m.* Our proof is a simplified version of the original one given by Niven and Zuckerman in *Pacific J. Math.* **1** (1951), 103–109.

The key idea we shall use is an important technique that applies to many situations in mathematics: "If the sum of m quantities and the sum of their squares are both consistent with the hypothesis that the m quantities are equal, then that hypothesis is true." In a strong form, this principle may be stated as follows:

Lemma E. *Given m sequences of numbers $\langle y_{jn} \rangle = y_{j0}, y_{j1}, \ldots$ for $1 \leq j \leq m$, suppose that*

$$\lim_{n \to \infty} (y_{1n} + y_{2n} + \cdots + y_{mn}) = m\alpha,$$

$$\limsup_{n \to \infty} (y_{1n}^2 + y_{2n}^2 + \cdots + y_{mn}^2) \leq m\alpha^2. \tag{14}$$

Then for each j, $\lim_{n \to \infty} y_{jn}$ exists and equals α.

An incredibly simple proof of this lemma is given in exercise 9.   ∎

Resuming our proof of Theorem C, let $x = x_1 x_2 \ldots x_m$ be a b-ary number, and say that x *occurs* at position p if $X_{p-m+1} X_{p-m+2} \ldots X_p = x$. Let $\nu_j(n)$ be the number of occurrences of x at position p when $p < n$ and $p \bmod m = j$. Let $y_{jn} = \nu_j(n)/n$; we wish to prove that

$$\lim_{n \to \infty} y_{jn} = \frac{1}{mb^m}. \tag{15}$$

First we know that

$$\lim_{n \to \infty} (y_{0n} + y_{1n} + \cdots + y_{(m-1)n}) = \frac{1}{b^m}, \tag{16}$$

since the sequence is m-distributed. By Lemma E and Eq. (16), the theorem will be proved if we can show that

$$\limsup_{n \to \infty} (y_{0n}^2 + y_{1n}^2 + \cdots + y_{(m-1)n}^2) \leq \frac{1}{mb^{2m}}. \tag{17}$$

This inequality is not obvious yet; some rather delicate maneuvering is necessary before we can prove it. Let q be a multiple of m, and consider

$$C(n) = \sum_{0 \leq j < m} \binom{\nu_j(n) - \nu_j(n - q)}{2}. \tag{18}$$

This is the number of pairs of occurrences of x in positions p_1 and p_2 for which $n - q \leq p_1 < p_2 < n$ and $p_2 - p_1$ is a multiple of m. Consider now the sum

$$S_N = \sum_{n=1}^{N+q} C(n). \tag{19}$$

Each pair of occurrences of x in positions p_1 and p_2 with $p_1 < p_2 < p_1 + q$, where $p_2 - p_1$ is a multiple of m and $p_1 \leq N$, is counted exactly $p_1 + q - p_2$ times in the total S_N (namely, when $p_2 < n \leq p_1 + q$); and the pairs of such occurrences with $N < p_1 < p_2 < N + q$ are counted exactly $N + q - p_2$ times.

Let $d_t(n)$ be the number of pairs of occurrences of x in positions p_1 and p_2 with $p_1 + t = p_2 < n$. The analysis above shows that

$$\sum_{0 < t < q/m} (q - mt) d_{mt}(N + q) \geq S_N \geq \sum_{0 < t < q/m} (q - mt) d_{mt}(N). \qquad (20)$$

Since the original sequence is q-distributed,

$$\lim_{N \to \infty} \frac{1}{N} d_{mt}(N) = \frac{1}{b^{2m}} \qquad (21)$$

for all t, $0 < t < q/m$, and therefore by (20) we have

$$\lim_{N \to \infty} \frac{S_N}{N} = \sum_{0 < t < q/m} \frac{q - mt}{b^{2m}} = \frac{q(q - m)}{2mb^{2m}}. \qquad (22)$$

This fact will prove the theorem, after some manipulation.

By definition,

$$2S_N = \sum_{n=1}^{N+q} \sum_{0 \leq j < m} \left((\nu_j(n) - \nu_j(n - q))^2 - (\nu_j(n) - \nu_j(n - q)) \right),$$

and we can remove the unsquared terms by applying (16) to get

$$\lim_{N \to \infty} \frac{T_N}{N} = \frac{q(q - m)}{mb^{2m}} + \frac{q}{b^m}, \qquad (23)$$

where

$$T_N = \sum_{n=1}^{N+q} \sum_{0 \leq j < m} \left(\nu_j(n) - \nu_j(n - q) \right)^2.$$

Using the inequality

$$\frac{1}{r} \left(\sum_{j=1}^{r} a_j \right)^2 \leq \sum_{j=1}^{r} a_j^2$$

(see exercise 1.2.3–30), we find that

$$\limsup_{N \to \infty} \sum_{0 \leq j < m} \frac{1}{N(N+q)} \left(\sum_{n=1}^{N+q} (\nu_j(n) - \nu_j(n - q)) \right)^2 \leq \frac{q(q - m)}{mb^{2m}} + \frac{q}{b^m}. \qquad (24)$$

We also have

$$q\nu_j(N) \leq \sum_{N < n \leq N+q} \nu_j(n) = \sum_{n=1}^{N+q} (\nu_j(n) - \nu_j(n - q)) \leq q\nu_j(N + q),$$

and putting this into (24) gives

$$\limsup_{N \to \infty} \sum_{0 \le j < m} \left(\frac{\nu_j(N)}{N} \right)^2 \le \frac{q - m}{qmb^{2m}} + \frac{1}{qb^m}. \tag{25}$$

This formula has been established whenever q is a multiple of m; and if we let $q \to \infty$ we obtain (17), completing the proof.

For a possibly simpler proof, see J. W. S. Cassels, *Pacific J. Math.* **2** (1952), 555–557. ∎

Exercises 29 and 30 illustrate the nontriviality of this theorem, and they also demonstrate the fact that a q-distributed sequence will have probabilities deviating from the true (m, m)-distribution probabilities by essentially $1/\sqrt{q}$ at most. (See (25).) The full hypothesis of ∞-distribution is necessary for the proof of the theorem.

As a result of Theorem C, we can prove that an ∞-distributed sequence passes the serial test, the maximum-of-t test, the collision test, the birthday spacings test, and the tests on subsequences mentioned in Section 3.3.2. It is not hard to show that the gap test, the poker test, and the run test are also satisfied (see exercises 12 through 14). The coupon collector's test is considerably more difficult to deal with, but it too is passed (see exercises 15 and 16).

The existence of ∞-distributed sequences of a rather simple type is guaranteed by the next theorem.

Theorem F (J. N. Franklin). *The $[0 \,.\, .\, 1)$ sequence $U_0, U_1, U_2, \ldots$ with*

$$U_n = \theta^n \bmod 1 \tag{26}$$

is ∞-distributed for almost all real numbers $\theta > 1$. That is, the set

$$\{\theta \mid \theta > 1 \text{ and } (26) \text{ is not } \infty\text{-distributed}\}$$

is of measure zero.

The proofs of this theorem and some generalizations are given in *Math. Comp.* **17** (1963), 28–59. ∎

Franklin has shown that θ must be a transcendental number for (26) to be ∞-distributed. Early in the 1960s, the powers $\langle \pi^n \bmod 1 \rangle$ were laboriously computed for $n \le 10000$ using multiple-precision arithmetic; and the most significant 35 bits of each of these numbers, stored on a disk file, were used successfully as a source of uniform deviates. According to Theorem F, the probability that the powers $\langle \pi^n \bmod 1 \rangle$ are ∞-distributed is equal to 1; yet there are uncountably many real numbers, so the theorem gives us no information about whether the sequence for π is really ∞-distributed or not. It is a fairly safe bet that nobody in our lifetimes will ever *prove* that this particular sequence is *not* ∞-distributed; but it might not be. Because of these considerations, one may legitimately wonder if there is any *explicit* sequence that is ∞-distributed: *Is there an algorithm to compute real numbers U_n for all $n \ge 0$, such that* *the sequence* $\langle U_n \rangle$ *is* ∞-*distributed?* The answer is yes, as shown for example by D. E. Knuth in *BIT* **5** (1965), 246–250. The sequence constructed there consists entirely of rational numbers; in fact, each number U_n has a terminating representation in the binary number system. Another construction of an explicit ∞-distributed sequence, somewhat more complicated than the sequence just cited, follows from Theorem W below. See also N. M. Korobov, *Izv. Akad. Nauk SSSR* **20** (1956), 649–660.

C. Does ∞-**distributed** = **random?** In view of all the theoretical results about ∞-distributed sequences, we can be sure of one thing: The concept of an ∞-distributed sequence is an important one in mathematics. There is also a good deal of evidence that the following statement might be a valid formulation of the intuitive idea of randomness:

Definition R1. *A* $[0..1)$ *sequence is defined to be "random" if it is an* ∞-*distributed sequence.* ∎

We have seen that sequences meeting this definition will satisfy all the statistical tests of Section 3.3.2 and many more.

Let us attempt to criticize this definition objectively. First of all, is every "truly random" sequence ∞-distributed? There are uncountably many sequences $U_0, U_1, \ldots$ of real numbers between zero and one. If a truly random number generator is sampled to give values $U_0, U_1, \ldots$, any of the possible sequences may be considered equally likely, and some of the sequences (indeed, uncountably many of them) are not even equidistributed. On the other hand, using any reasonable definition of probability on this space of all possible sequences leads us to conclude that a random sequence is ∞-distributed *with probability one.* We are therefore led to formalize Franklin's definition of randomness (as given at the beginning of this section) in the following way:

Definition R2. *A* $[0..1)$ *sequence* $\langle U_n \rangle$ *is defined to be "random" if, whenever* P *is a property such that* $P(\langle V_n \rangle)$ *holds with probability one for a sequence* $\langle V_n \rangle$ *of independent samples of random variables from the uniform distribution, then* $P(\langle U_n \rangle)$ *is true.* ∎

Is it perhaps possible that Definition R1 is equivalent to Definition R2? Let us try out some possible objections to Definition R1, and see whether these criticisms are valid.

In the first place, Definition R1 deals only with limiting properties of the sequence as $n \to \infty$. There are ∞-distributed sequences in which the first million elements are all zero; should such a sequence be considered random?

This objection is not very substantial. If ϵ is any positive number, there is no reason why the first million elements of a sequence should not all be less than ϵ. With probability one, a truly random sequence contains infinitely many runs of a million consecutive elements less than ϵ, so why can't this happen at the beginning of the sequence?

On the other hand, consider Definition R2 and let P be the property that all elements of the sequence are distinct; P is true with probability one, so any sequence with a million zeros is not random by *this* criterion.

Now let P be the property that *no* element of the sequence is equal to zero; again, P is true with probability one, so by Definition R2 any sequence with a zero element is nonrandom. More generally, however, let x_0 be any fixed number between zero and one, and let P be the property that no element of the sequence is equal to x_0; Definition R2 now says that no random sequence may contain the element x_0! We can now prove that *no sequence satisfies the condition of Definition R2.* (For if U_0, U_1, ... is such a sequence, take $x_0 = U_0$.)

Therefore if R1 is too weak a definition, R2 is certainly too strong. The "right" definition must be less strict than R2. We have not really shown that R1 is too weak, however, so let us continue to attack it some more. As mentioned above, an ∞-distributed sequence of *rational* numbers has been constructed. (Indeed, this is not so surprising; see exercise 18.) Almost all real numbers are irrational; perhaps we should insist that

$$\Pr(U_n \text{ is rational}) = 0$$

for a random sequence.

The definition of equidistribution, Eq. (2), says that $\Pr(u \le U_n < v) = v - u$. There is an obvious way to generalize this definition, using measure theory: "If $S \subseteq [0 \mathbin{..} 1)$ is a set of measure μ, then

$$\Pr(U_n \in S) = \mu, \tag{27}$$

for all random sequences $\langle U_n \rangle$." In particular, if S is the set of rationals, it has measure zero, so no sequence of rational numbers is equidistributed in this generalized sense. It is reasonable to expect that Theorem B could be extended to Lebesgue integration instead of Riemann integration, if property (27) is stipulated. However, once again we find that definition (27) is too strict, for *no* sequence satisfies that property. If U_0, U_1, ... is any sequence, the set $S = \{U_0, U_1, \ldots\}$ is of measure zero, yet $\Pr(U_n \in S) = 1$. Thus, by the force of the same argument we used to exclude rationals from random sequences, we can exclude all random sequences.

So far Definition R1 has proved to be defensible. There are, however, some quite valid objections to it. For example, if we have a random sequence in the intuitive sense, the infinite subsequence

$$U_0, \ U_1, \ U_4, \ U_9, \ \ldots, \ U_{n^2}, \ \ldots \tag{28}$$

should also be a random sequence. This is not always true for an ∞-distributed sequence. In fact, if we take any ∞-distributed sequence and set $U_{n^2} \leftarrow 0$ for all n, the counts $\nu_k(n)$ that appear in the test of k-distributivity are changed by at most $\sqrt{n}$, so the limits of the ratios $\nu_k(n)/n$ remain unchanged. Definition R1 unfortunately fails to satisfy this randomness criterion.

Perhaps we should strengthen R1 as follows:

Definition R3. *A* $[0 .. 1)$ *sequence is said to be "random" if each of its infinite subsequences is* ∞-*distributed.* ∎

Once again, however, the definition turns out to be too strict; any equidistributed sequence $\langle U_n \rangle$ has a monotonic subsequence with $U_{s_0} < U_{s_1} < U_{s_2} < \cdots$.

The secret is to restrict the subsequences so that they could be defined by a person who does not look at U_n before deciding whether or not it is to be in the subsequence. The following definition now suggests itself:

Definition R4. *A* $[0 .. 1)$ *sequence* $\langle U_n \rangle$ *is said to be "random" if, for every effective algorithm that specifies an infinite sequence of distinct nonnegative integers* s_n *for* $n \geq 0$, *the subsequence* $U_{s_0}, U_{s_1}, U_{s_2}, \ldots$ *corresponding to this algorithm is* ∞-*distributed.* ∎

The algorithms referred to in Definition R4 are effective procedures that compute s_n, given n. (See the discussion in Section 1.1.) Thus, for example, the sequence $\langle \pi^n \bmod 1 \rangle$ will *not* satisfy R4, since it is either not equidistributed or there is an effective algorithm that determines an infinite subsequence s_n with $(\pi^{s_0} \bmod 1) < (\pi^{s_1} \bmod 1) < (\pi^{s_2} \bmod 1) < \cdots$. Similarly, *no explicitly defined sequence can satisfy Definition R4*; this is appropriate, if we agree that no explicitly defined sequence can really be random. The explicit-looking sequence $\langle \theta^n \bmod 1 \rangle$ actually does, however, satisfy Definition R4, for almost all real numbers $\theta > 1$; this is no contradiction, since almost all θ are uncomputable by algorithms. J. F. Koksma proved that $\langle \theta^{s_n} \bmod 1 \rangle$ is 1-distributed for almost all $\theta > 1$, if $\langle s_n \rangle$ is any sequence of distinct positive integers [*Compositio Math.* **2** (1935), 250–258]; H. Niederreiter and R. F. Tichy strengthened Koksma's theorem, replacing "1-distributed" by "∞-distributed" [*Mathematika* **32** (1985), 26–32]. Only countably many sequences $\langle s_n \rangle$ are effectively definable, so $\langle \theta^n \bmod 1 \rangle$ almost always satisfies R4.

Definition R4 is much stronger than Definition R1; but it is still reasonable to claim that Definition R4 is too weak. For example, let $\langle U_n \rangle$ be a truly random sequence, and define the subsequence $\langle U_{s_n} \rangle$ by the following rules: $s_0 = 0$; and if $n > 0$, s_n is the smallest integer $\geq n$ for which $U_{s_n - 1}, U_{s_n - 2}, \ldots, U_{s_n - n}$ are all less than $\frac{1}{2}$. Thus we are considering the subsequence of values following the first consecutive run of n values less than $\frac{1}{2}$. Suppose that "$U_n < \frac{1}{2}$" corresponds to the value "heads" in the flipping of a coin. Gamblers tend to feel that a long run of "heads" makes the opposite condition, "tails," more probable, assuming that a true coin is being used; and the subsequence $\langle U_{s_n} \rangle$ just defined corresponds to a gambling system for a man who places his nth bet on the coin toss following the first run of n consecutive "heads." The gambler may think that $\Pr(U_{s_n} \geq \frac{1}{2})$ is more than $\frac{1}{2}$, but of course in a truly random sequence $\langle U_{s_n} \rangle$ will be completely random. No gambling system will ever be able to beat the odds! Definition R4 says nothing about subsequences formed according to such a gambling system, so apparently we need something more.

Let us define a "subsequence rule" $\mathcal{R}$ as an infinite sequence of functions $\langle f_n(x_1, \ldots, x_n) \rangle$ where, for $n \geq 0$, f_n is a function of n variables, and the value of $f_n(x_1, \ldots, x_n)$ is either 0 or 1. Here $x_1, \ldots, x_n$ are elements of some set S. (Thus, in particular, f_0 is a constant function, either 0 or 1.) A subsequence rule $\mathcal{R}$ defines a subsequence of any infinite sequence $\langle X_n \rangle$ of elements of S as follows: *The* n*th term* X_n *is in the subsequence* $\langle X_n \rangle \mathcal{R}$ *if and only if* $f_n(X_0, X_1, \ldots, X_{n-1}) = 1$. Note that the subsequence $\langle X_n \rangle \mathcal{R}$ thus defined is not necessarily infinite, and it may in fact contain no elements at all.

For example, the gambler's subsequence just described corresponds to the following subsequence rule: "$f_0 = 1$; and for $n > 0$, $f_n(x_1, \ldots, x_n) = 1$ if and only if there is some k in the range $0 < k \le n$ such that the k consecutive parameters $x_m, x_{m-1}, \ldots, x_{m-k+1}$ are all $< \frac{1}{2}$ when $m = n$ but not when $k \le m < n$."

A subsequence rule $\mathcal{R}$ is said to be *computable* if there is an effective algorithm that determines the value of $f_n(x_1, \ldots, x_n)$, when n and $x_1, \ldots, x_n$ are given as input. We had better restrict ourselves to computable subsequence rules when trying to define randomness, lest we obtain an overly restrictive definition like R3 above. But effective algorithms cannot deal nicely with arbitrary real numbers as inputs; for example, if a real number x is specified by an infinite radix-10 expansion, there is no algorithm to determine if x is $< \frac{1}{3}$ or not, since all digits of the number $0.333\ldots$ have to be examined. Therefore computable subsequence rules do not apply to all $[0 \mathbin{.\,.} 1)$ sequences, and it is convenient to base our next definition on b-ary sequences.

Definition R5. *A* b*-ary sequence is said to be "random" if every infinite subsequence defined by a computable subsequence rule is 1-distributed.* ∎

A $[0 \mathbin{.\,.} 1)$ *sequence* $\langle U_n \rangle$ *is said to be "random" if the* b*-ary sequence* $\langle \lfloor bU_n \rfloor \rangle$ *is "random" for all integers* $b \ge 2$.

Note that Definition R5 says only "1-distributed," not "∞-distributed." It is interesting to verify that this may be done without loss of generality. For we may define an obviously computable subsequence rule $\mathcal{R}(a_1 \ldots a_k)$ as follows, given any b-ary number $a_1 \ldots a_k$: Let $f_n(x_1, \ldots, x_n) = 1$ if and only if $n \ge k - 1$ and $x_{n-k+1} = a_1, \ldots, x_{n-1} = a_{k-1}, x_n = a_k$. Now if $\langle X_n \rangle$ is a k-distributed b-ary sequence, this rule $\mathcal{R}(a_1 \ldots a_k)$ — which selects the subsequence consisting of those terms just following an occurrence of $a_1 \ldots a_k$ — defines an infinite subsequence; and if this subsequence is 1-distributed, each of the $(k + 1)$-tuples $a_1 \ldots a_k a_{k+1}$ for $0 \le a_{k+1} < b$ occurs with probability $1/b^{k+1}$ in $\langle X_n \rangle$. Thus we can prove that a sequence satisfying Definition R5 is k-distributed for all k, by induction on k. Similarly, by considering the "composition" of subsequence rules — if $\mathcal{R}_1$ defines an infinite subsequence $\langle X_n \rangle \mathcal{R}_1$, then we can define $\mathcal{R}_1 \mathcal{R}_2$ to be the subsequence rule for which $\langle X_n \rangle \mathcal{R}_1 \mathcal{R}_2 = (\langle X_n \rangle \mathcal{R}_1) \mathcal{R}_2$ — we find that all subsequences considered in Definition R5 are ∞-distributed. (See exercise 32.)

The fact that ∞-distribution comes out of Definition R5 as a very special case is encouraging, and it is a good indication that we may at last have found the definition of randomness we have been seeking. But alas, there still is a problem. It is not clear that sequences satisfying Definition R5 must satisfy Definition R4. The "computable subsequence rules" we have just specified always enumerate subsequences $\langle X_{s_n} \rangle$ for which $s_0 < s_1 < \cdots$, but $\langle s_n \rangle$ does not have to be monotone in R4; it must only satisfy the condition $s_n \neq s_m$ for $n \neq m$.

To meet this objection, we may combine Definitions R4 and R5 as follows:

Definition R6. *A b-ary sequence $\langle X_n \rangle$ is said to be "random" if, for every effective algorithm that specifies an infinite sequence of distinct nonnegative integers $\langle s_n \rangle$ as a function of n and the values of $X_{s_0}, \ldots, X_{s_{n-1}}$, the subsequence $\langle X_{s_n} \rangle$ corresponding to this algorithm is "random" in the sense of Definition R5.*

A $[0 \mathinner{.\,.} 1)$ sequence $\langle U_n \rangle$ is said to be "random" if the b-ary sequence $\langle \lfloor bU_n \rfloor \rangle$ is "random" for all integers $b \geq 2$. ∎

The author contends[*] that this definition surely meets all reasonable philosophical requirements for randomness, so it provides an answer to the principal question posed in this section.

D. Existence of random sequences. We have seen that Definition R3 is too strong, in the sense that no sequence can satisfy that definition; and the formulation of Definitions R4, R5, and R6 above was carried out in an attempt to recapture the essential characteristics of Definition R3. In order to show that Definition R6 is not overly restrictive, it is still necessary for us to prove that sequences satisfying all these conditions exist. Intuitively, we feel quite sure that there is no problem, because we believe that a truly random sequence exists and satisfies R6; but a proof is really necessary to show that the definition is consistent.

An interesting method for constructing sequences satisfying Definition R5 has been found by A. Wald, starting with a very simple 1-distributed sequence.

Lemma T. *Let the sequence of real numbers $\langle V_n \rangle$ be defined in terms of the binary system as follows:*

$$V_0 = 0, \qquad V_1 = .1, \qquad V_2 = .01, \qquad V_3 = .11, \qquad V_4 = .001, \qquad \ldots$$

$$V_n = .c_r \ldots c_1 1 \qquad \text{if } n = 2^r + c_1 2^{r-1} + \cdots + c_r. \tag{29}$$

Let $I_{b_1 \ldots b_r}$ denote the set of all real numbers in $[0 \mathinner{.\,.} 1)$ whose binary representation begins with $0.b_1 \ldots b_r$; thus

$$I_{b_1 \ldots b_r} = \big[(0.b_1 \ldots b_r)_2 \mathinner{.\,.} (0.b_1 \ldots b_r)_2 + 2^{-r} \big). \tag{30}$$

Then if $\nu(n)$ denotes the number of V_k in $I_{b_1 \ldots b_r}$ for $0 \leq k < n$, we have

$$\big| \nu(n)/n - 2^{-r} \big| \leq 1/n. \tag{31}$$

Proof. Since $\nu(n)$ is the number of k for which $k \bmod 2^r = (b_r \ldots b_1)_2$, we have $\nu(n) = t$ or $t+1$ when $\lfloor n/2^r \rfloor = t$. Hence $\big| \nu(n) - n/2^r \big| \leq 1$. ∎

It follows from (31) that the sequence $\langle \lfloor 2^r V_n \rfloor \rangle$ is an equidistributed 2^r-ary sequence; hence by Theorem A, $\langle V_n \rangle$ is an equidistributed $[0 \mathinner{.\,.} 1)$ sequence. Indeed, it is pretty clear that $\langle V_n \rangle$ is about as equidistributed as a $[0 \mathinner{.\,.} 1)$ sequence can be. (For further discussion of this and related sequences, see J. G. van der

---

[*] At least, he made such a contention when originally preparing this material in 1966.

Corput, *Proc. Koninklijke Nederl. Akad. Wetenschappen* **38** (1935), 813–821, 1058–1066; J. H. Halton, *Numerische Math.* **2** (1960), 84–90, 196; S. Haber, *J. Research National Bur. Standards* **B70** (1966), 127–136; R. Béjian and H. Faure, *Comptes Rendus Acad. Sci.* **A285** (Paris, 1977), 313–316; H. Faure, *J. Number Theory* **22** (1986), 4–20; S. Tezuka, *ACM Trans. Modeling and Comp. Simul.* **3** (1993), 99–107. L. H. Ramshaw has shown that the sequence $\langle \phi n \bmod 1 \rangle$ is slightly more equally distributed than $\langle V_n \rangle$; see *J. Number Theory* **13** (1981), 138–175.)

Now let $\mathcal{R}_1, \mathcal{R}_2, \ldots$ be infinitely many subsequence rules; we seek a sequence $\langle U_n \rangle$ for which all the infinite subsequences $\langle U_n \rangle \mathcal{R}_j$ are equidistributed.

Algorithm W (*Wald sequence*). Given an infinite sequence of subsequence rules $\mathcal{R}_1, \mathcal{R}_2, \ldots$ that define subsequences of $[0 .. 1)$ sequences of rational numbers, this procedure defines a $[0 .. 1)$ sequence $\langle U_n \rangle$. The computation involves infinitely many auxiliary variables $C[a_1, \ldots, a_r]$, where $r \geq 1$ and where $a_j = 0$ or 1 for $1 \leq j \leq r$. These variables are initially all zero.

W1. [Initialize n.] Set $n \leftarrow 0$.

W2. [Initialize r.] Set $r \leftarrow 1$.

W3. [Test $\mathcal{R}_r$.] If the element U_n is to be in the subsequence defined by $\mathcal{R}_r$, based on the values of U_k for $0 \leq k < n$, set $a_r \leftarrow 1$; otherwise set $a_r \leftarrow 0$.

W4. [Is case $[a_1, \ldots, a_r]$ unfinished?] If $C[a_1, \ldots, a_r] < 3 \cdot 4^{r-1}$, go to W6.

W5. [Increase r.] Set $r \leftarrow r + 1$ and return to W3.

W6. [Set U_n.] Increase the value of $C[a_1, \ldots, a_r]$ by 1 and let k be its new value. Set $U_n \leftarrow V_k$, where V_k is defined in Lemma T above.

W7. [Advance n.] Increase n by 1 and return to W2. ∎

Strictly speaking, this is not an algorithm, since it doesn't terminate; but we could of course easily modify the procedure to make it stop when n reaches a given value. In order to grasp the idea of the construction, the reader is advised to try it out manually, replacing the number $3 \cdot 4^{r-1}$ of step W4 by 2^r during this exercise.

Algorithm W is not meant to be a practical source of random numbers. It is intended to serve only a theoretical purpose:

Theorem W. *Let $\langle U_n \rangle$ be the sequence of rational numbers defined by Algorithm W, and let k be a positive integer. If the subsequence $\langle U_n \rangle \mathcal{R}_k$ is infinite, it is 1-distributed.*

Proof. Let $A[a_1, \ldots, a_r]$ denote the (possibly empty) subsequence of $\langle U_n \rangle$ containing precisely those elements U_n that, for all $j \leq r$, belong to subsequence $\langle U_n \rangle \mathcal{R}_j$ if $a_j = 1$ and do not belong to subsequence $\langle U_n \rangle \mathcal{R}_j$ if $a_j = 0$.

It suffices to prove, for all $r \geq 1$ and all pairs of binary numbers $a_1 \ldots a_r$ and $b_1 \ldots b_r$, that $\Pr(U_n \in I_{b_1 \ldots b_r}) = 2^{-r}$ with respect to the subsequence $A[a_1, \ldots, a_r]$, whenever the latter is infinite. (See Eq. (30).) For if $r \geq k$, the infinite sequence $\langle U_n \rangle \mathcal{R}_k$ is the finite union of the disjoint subsequences

$A[a_1, \ldots, a_r]$ for $a_k = 1$ and $a_j = 0$ or 1 for $1 \le j \le r$, $j \ne k$; and it follows that $\Pr(U_n \in I_{b_1 \ldots b_r}) = 2^{-r}$ with respect to $\langle U_n \rangle \mathcal{R}_k$. (See exercise 33.) This is enough to show that the sequence is 1-distributed, by Theorem A.

Let $B[a_1, \ldots, a_r]$ denote the subsequence of $\langle U_n \rangle$ that consists of the values for those n in which $C[a_1, \ldots, a_r]$ is increased by one in step W6 of the algorithm. By the algorithm, $B[a_1, \ldots, a_r]$ is a finite sequence with at most $3 \cdot 4^{r-1}$ elements. All but a finite number of the members of $A[a_1, \ldots, a_r]$ come from the subsequences $B[a_1, \ldots, a_r, \ldots, a_t]$, where $a_j = 0$ or 1 for $r < j \le t$.

Now assume that $A[a_1, \ldots, a_r]$ is infinite, and let $A[a_1, \ldots, a_r] = \langle U_{s_n} \rangle$, where $s_0 < s_1 < s_2 < \cdots$. If N is a large integer, with $4^r \le 4^q < N \le 4^{q+1}$, it follows that the number of values of $k < N$ for which U_{s_k} is in $I_{b_1 \ldots b_r}$ is (except for finitely many elements at the beginning of the subsequence)

$$\nu(N) = \nu(N_1) + \cdots + \nu(N_m).$$

Here m is the number of subsequences $B[a_1, \ldots, a_t]$ listed above in which U_{s_k} appears for some $k < N$; N_j is the number of values of k with U_{s_k} in the corresponding subsequence; and $\nu(N_j)$ is the number of such values that are also in $I_{b_1 \ldots b_r}$. Therefore by Lemma T,

$$\left| \nu(N) - 2^{-r} N \right| = \left| \nu(N_1) - 2^{-r} N_1 + \cdots + \nu(N_m) - 2^{-r} N_m \right|$$
$$\le \left| \nu(N_1) - 2^{-r} N_1 \right| + \cdots + \left| \nu(N_m) - 2^{-r} N_m \right|$$
$$\le m \le 1 + 2 + 4 + \cdots + 2^{q-r+1} < 2^{q+1}.$$

The inequality on m follows here from the fact that, by our choice of N, the element U_{s_N} is in $B[a_1, \ldots, a_t]$ for some $t \le q + 1$.

We have proved that $|\nu(N)/N - 2^{-r}| \le 2^{q+1}/N < 2/\sqrt{N}$. $\blacksquare$

To show finally that sequences satisfying Definition R5 exist, we note first that if $\langle U_n \rangle$ is a $[0 \mathbin{..} 1)$ sequence of rational numbers and if $\mathcal{R}$ is a computable subsequence rule for a b-ary sequence, we can make $\mathcal{R}$ into a computable subsequence rule $\mathcal{R}'$ for $\langle U_n \rangle$ by letting $f'_n(x_1, \ldots, x_n)$ in $\mathcal{R}'$ equal $f_n(\lfloor bx_1 \rfloor, \ldots, \lfloor bx_n \rfloor)$ in $\mathcal{R}$. If the $[0 \mathbin{..} 1)$ sequence $\langle U_n \rangle \mathcal{R}'$ is equidistributed, so is the b-ary sequence $\langle \lfloor bU_n \rfloor \rangle \mathcal{R}'$. Now the set of all computable subsequence rules for b-ary sequences, for all values of b, is countable (since only countably many effective algorithms are possible), so they may be listed in some sequence $\mathcal{R}_1, \mathcal{R}_2, \ldots$; therefore Algorithm W defines a $[0 \mathbin{..} 1)$ sequence that is random in the sense of Definition R5.

This brings us to a somewhat paradoxical situation. As we mentioned earlier, no effective algorithm can define a sequence that satisfies Definition R4, and for the same reason there is no effective algorithm that defines a sequence satisfying Definition R5. A proof of the existence of such random sequences is necessarily nonconstructive; how then can Algorithm W construct such a sequence?

There is no contradiction here; we have merely stumbled on the fact that the set of all effective algorithms cannot be enumerated by an effective algorithm. In other words, there is no effective algorithm to select the jth computable subsequence rule $\mathcal{R}_j$; this happens because there is no effective algorithm to determine if a computational method ever terminates. But important large classes of algorithms *can* be systematically enumerated; thus, for example, Algorithm W shows that it is possible to construct, with an effective algorithm, a sequence that satisfies Definition R5 if we restrict consideration to subsequence rules that are "primitive recursive."

By modifying step W6 of Algorithm W, so that it sets $U_n \leftarrow V_{k+t}$ instead of V_k, where t is any nonnegative integer depending on $a_1, \ldots, a_r$, we can show that there are *uncountably* many $[0 .. 1)$ sequences satisfying Definition R5.

The following theorem shows still another way to prove the existence of uncountably many random sequences, using a less direct argument based on measure theory, even if the strong definition R6 is used:

Theorem M. *Let the real number x, $0 \le x < 1$, correspond to the binary sequence $\langle X_n \rangle$ if the binary representation of x is $(0.X_0X_1\ldots)_2$. Under this correspondence, almost all x correspond to binary sequences that are random in the sense of Definition R6. (In other words, the set of all real x that correspond to a binary sequence that is nonrandom by Definition R6 has measure zero.)*

Proof. Let $\mathcal{S}$ be an effective algorithm that determines an infinite sequence of distinct nonnegative integers $\langle s_n \rangle$, where the choice of s_n depends only on n and X_{s_k} for $0 \le k < n$; and let $\mathcal{R}$ be a computable subsequence rule. Then any binary sequence $\langle X_n \rangle$ leads to a subsequence $\langle X_{s_n} \rangle \mathcal{R}$, and Definition R6 says this subsequence must either be finite or 1-distributed. It suffices to prove that for fixed $\mathcal{R}$ and $\mathcal{S}$ the set $N(\mathcal{R}, \mathcal{S})$ of all real x corresponding to $\langle X_n \rangle$, such that $\langle X_{s_n} \rangle \mathcal{R}$ is infinite and not 1-distributed, has measure zero. For x has a nonrandom binary representation if and only if x is in $\bigcup N(\mathcal{R}, \mathcal{S})$, taken over the countably many choices of $\mathcal{R}$ and $\mathcal{S}$.

Therefore let $\mathcal{R}$ and $\mathcal{S}$ be fixed. Consider the set $T(a_1 a_2 \ldots a_r)$ defined for all binary numbers $a_1 a_2 \ldots a_r$ as the set of all x corresponding to $\langle X_n \rangle$, such that $\langle X_{s_n} \rangle \mathcal{R}$ has $\ge r$ elements whose first r elements are respectively equal to $a_1, a_2, \ldots, a_r$. Our first result is that

$$T(a_1 a_2 \ldots a_r) \text{ has measure} \le 2^{-r}. \tag{32}$$

To prove this, we start by observing that $T(a_1 a_2 \ldots a_r)$ is a measurable set: Each element of $T(a_1 a_2 \ldots a_r)$ is a real number $x = (0.X_0 X_1 \ldots)_2$ for which there exists an integer m such that algorithm $\mathcal{S}$ determines distinct values $s_0, s_1, \ldots, s_m$, and rule $\mathcal{R}$ determines a subsequence of $X_{s_0}, X_{s_1}, \ldots, X_{s_m}$ such that X_{s_m} is the rth element of this subsequence. The set of all real $y = (0.Y_0 Y_1 \ldots)_2$ such that $Y_{s_k} = X_{s_k}$ for $0 \le k \le m$ also belongs to $T(a_1 a_2 \ldots a_r)$, and this is a measurable set consisting of the finite union of dyadic subintervals $I_{b_1 \ldots b_t}$. Since there are only countably many such dyadic intervals, we see that $T(a_1 a_2 \ldots a_r)$ is a countable union of dyadic intervals, and it is therefore measurable. Furthermore, this argument can be extended to show that the measure of $T(a_1 \ldots a_{r-1} 0)$ equals the measure of $T(a_1 \ldots a_{r-1} 1)$, since the latter is a union of dyadic intervals obtained from the former by requiring that $Y_{s_k} = X_{s_k}$ for $0 \le k < m$ and $Y_{s_m} \ne X_{s_m}$. Now since

$$T(a_1 \ldots a_{r-1}0) \cup T(a_1 \ldots a_{r-1}1) \subseteq T(a_1 \ldots a_{r-1}),$$

the measure of $T(a_1 a_2 \ldots a_r)$ is at most one-half the measure of $T(a_1 \ldots a_{r-1})$. The inequality (32) follows by induction on r.

Now that (32) has been established, the remainder of the proof is essentially to show that the binary representations of almost all real numbers are equidistributed. For $0 < \epsilon < 1$, let $B(r, \epsilon)$ be $\bigcup T(a_1 \ldots a_r)$, where the union is taken over all binary strings $a_1 \ldots a_r$ for which the number $\nu(r)$ of ones among $a_1 \ldots a_r$ satisfies

$$\left| \nu(r) - \tfrac{1}{2}r \right| \ge \epsilon r.$$

The number of such binary strings is $C(r, \epsilon) = \sum \binom{r}{k}$ summed over all values of k with $|k - \tfrac{1}{2}r| \ge \epsilon r$. Exercise 1.2.10–21 proves that $C(r, \epsilon) \le 2^{r+1}e^{-\epsilon^2 r}$; hence by (32),

$$B(r, \epsilon) \text{ has measure} \le 2^{-r}C(r, \epsilon) \le 2e^{-\epsilon^2 r}. \tag{33}$$

The next step is to define

$$B^*(r, \epsilon) = B(r, \epsilon) \cup B(r+1, \epsilon) \cup B(r+2, \epsilon) \cup \cdots.$$

The measure of $B^*(r, \epsilon)$ is at most $\sum_{k \ge r} 2e^{-\epsilon^2 k}$, and this is the remainder of a convergent series, so

$$\lim_{r \to \infty} \left(\text{measure of } B^*(r, \epsilon) \right) = 0. \tag{34}$$

Now if x is a real number whose binary expansion $(0.X_0 X_1 \ldots)_2$ leads to an infinite sequence $\langle X_{s_n} \rangle \mathcal{R}$ that is not 1-distributed, and if $\nu(r)$ denotes the number of ones in the first r elements of the latter sequence, then

$$\left| \nu(r)/r - \tfrac{1}{2} \right| \ge \epsilon,$$

for some $\epsilon > 0$ and infinitely many r. This means x is in $B^*(r, \epsilon)$ for all r. So finally we find that

$$N(\mathcal{R}, \mathcal{S}) = \bigcup_{t \ge 2} \bigcap_{r \ge 1} B^*(r, 1/t);$$

and, by (34), $\bigcap_{r \ge 1} B^*(r, 1/t)$ has measure zero for all t. Hence $N(\mathcal{R}, \mathcal{S})$ has measure zero. ∎

From the existence of *binary* sequences satisfying Definition R6, we can show the existence of $[0 .. 1)$ sequences that are random in this sense. For details, see exercise 36. The consistency of Definition R6 is thereby established.

E. Random finite sequences. An argument was given above to indicate that it is impossible to define the concept of randomness for finite sequences: Any given finite sequence is as likely as any other. Still, nearly everyone would agree that the sequence 011101001 is "more random" than 101010101, and even the latter sequence is "more random" than 000000000. Although it is true that truly random sequences will exhibit locally nonrandom behavior, we would expect such behavior only in a long finite sequence, not in a short one.

Several ways to define the randomness of a finite sequence have been proposed, and only a few of the ideas will be sketched here. For simplicity, we shall restrict our consideration to the case of b-ary sequences.

Given a b-ary sequence $X_0, X_1, \ldots, X_{N-1}$, we can say that

$$\Pr\big(S(n)\big) \approx p, \qquad \text{if } \big|\nu(N)/N - p\big| \leq 1/\sqrt{N}, \tag{35}$$

where $\nu(n)$ is the quantity appearing in Definition A at the beginning of this section. The sequence above can be called "k-distributed" if

$$\Pr(X_n X_{n+1}\ldots X_{n+k-1} = x_1 x_2 \ldots x_k) \approx 1/b^k \tag{36}$$

for all b-ary numbers $x_1 x_2 \ldots x_k$. (Compare with Definition D. Unfortunately a sequence might turn out to be k-distributed by this new definition when it is not $(k-1)$-distributed.)

A definition of randomness may now be given analogous to Definition R1, as follows:

Definition Q1. *A b-ary sequence of length N is "random" if it is k-distributed (in the sense above) for all positive integers $k \leq \log_b N$.* ∎

According to this definition, for example, there are 178 nonrandom binary sequences of length 11:

```
00000001111  10000000111  11000000011  11100000001  11110000000
00000001110  10000000110  11000000010  11100000000  11010000000
00000001101  10000000101  11000000001  10100000001  10110000000
00000001011  10000000011  01000000011  01100000001  01110000000
00000000111
```

plus 01010101010 and all sequences with nine or more zeros, plus all sequences obtained from the preceding sequences by interchanging ones and zeros.

Similarly, we can formulate a definition for finite sequences analogous to Definition R6. Let **A** be a set of algorithms, each of which is a selection-and-choice procedure that gives a subsequence $\langle X_{s_n} \rangle \mathcal{R}$ as in the proof of Theorem M.

Definition Q2. *The b-ary sequence $X_0, X_1, \ldots, X_{N-1}$ is (n, ϵ)-random with respect to a set of algorithms **A**, if for every subsequence $X_{t_1}, X_{t_2}, \ldots, X_{t_m}$ determined by an algorithm of **A** we have either $m < n$ or*

$$\left| \frac{1}{m}\nu_a(X_{t_1}, \ldots, X_{t_m}) - \frac{1}{b} \right| \leq \epsilon \qquad \text{for } 0 \leq a < b.$$

Here $\nu_a(x_1, \ldots, x_m)$ is the number of a's in the sequence $x_1, \ldots, x_m$. ∎

(In other words, every sufficiently long subsequence determined by an algorithm of **A** must be approximately equidistributed.) The basic idea in this case is to let **A** be a set of "simple" algorithms; the number (and the complexity) of the algorithms in **A** can grow as N grows.

As an example of Definition Q2, let us consider binary sequences, and let **A** be just the following four algorithms:

a) Take the whole sequence.
b) Take alternate terms of the sequence, starting with the first.
c) Take the terms of the sequence following a zero.
d) Take the terms of the sequence following a one.

Now a sequence $X_0, X_1, \ldots, X_7$ is $(4, \frac{1}{8})$-random with respect to **A** if:

by (a), $\left|\frac{1}{8}(X_0 + X_1 + \cdots + X_7) - \frac{1}{2}\right| \leq \frac{1}{8}$, that is, if there are 3, 4, or 5 ones;

by (b), $\left|\frac{1}{4}(X_0 + X_2 + X_4 + X_6) - \frac{1}{2}\right| \leq \frac{1}{8}$, that is, if there are exactly 2 ones in even-numbered positions;

by (c), there are three possibilities depending on how many zeros occupy positions $X_0, \ldots, X_6$: If there are 2 or 3 zeros here, there is no condition to test (since $n = 4$); if there are 4 zeros, they must respectively be followed by two zeros and two ones; and if there are 5 zeros, they must respectively be followed by two or three zeros;

by (d), we get conditions similar to those implied by (c).

It turns out that only the following binary sequences of length 8 are $(4, \frac{1}{8})$-random with respect to these rules:

00001011	00101001	01001110	01101000
00011010	00101100	01011011	01101100
00011011	00110010	01011110	01101101
00100011	00110011	01100010	01110010
00100110	00110110	01100011	01110110
00100111	00111001	01100110	

plus those obtained by interchanging 0 and 1 consistently.

It is clear that we could make the set of algorithms so large that no sequences satisfy the definition, when n and ϵ are reasonably small. A. N. Kolmogorov has proved that an (n, ϵ)-random binary sequence *will* always exist, for any given N, if the number of algorithms in **A** does not exceed

$$\frac{1}{2}e^{2n\epsilon^2(1-\epsilon)}. \qquad (37)$$

This result is not nearly strong enough to show that sequences satisfying Definition Q1 will exist, but the latter can be constructed efficiently using the procedure of Rees in exercise 3.2.2–21. A generalized spectral test, based on discrete Fourier transforms, can be used to test how well a sequence measures up to Definition Q1 [see A. Compagner, *Physical Rev.* **E52** (1995), 5634–5645].

Still another interesting approach to a definition of randomness has been taken by Per Martin-Löf [*Information and Control* **9** (1966), 602–619]. Given a finite b-ary sequence $X_1, \ldots, X_N$, let $l(X_1, \ldots, X_N)$ be the length of the shortest Turing machine program that generates this sequence. (Alternatively, we could use other classes of effective algorithms, such as those discussed in Section 1.1.) Then $l(X_1, \ldots, X_N)$ is a measure of the "patternlessness" of the sequence, and we may equate this idea with randomness. The sequences of length N that maximize $l(X_1, \ldots, X_N)$ may be called random. (From the standpoint of practical random number generation by computer, this is, of course, the worst definition of "randomness" that can be imagined!)

Essentially the same definition of randomness was given independently by G. Chaitin at about the same time; see *JACM* **16** (1969), 145–159. It is interesting to note that even though this definition makes no reference to equidistribution properties as our other definitions have, Martin-Löf and Chaitin have proved that random sequences of this type also have the expected equidistribution properties. In fact, Martin-Löf has demonstrated that such sequences satisfy *all* computable statistical tests for randomness, in an appropriate sense.

For further developments in the definition of random finite sequences, see A. K. Zvonkin and L. A. Levin, *Uspekhi Mat. Nauk* **25**, 6 (November 1970), 85–127 [English translation in *Russian Math. Surveys* **25**, 6 (November 1970), 83–124]; L. A. Levin, *Doklady Akad. Nauk SSSR* **212** (1973), 548–550; L. A. Levin, *Information and Control* **61** (1984), 15–37.

F. Pseudorandom numbers. It is comforting from a theoretical standpoint to know that random finite sequences of various flavors exist, but such theorems don't answer the questions faced by real-world programmers. More recent developments have led to a more relevant theory, based on the study of *sets* of finite sequences. More precisely, we consider *multisets* in which sequences may appear more than once.

Let S be a multiset containing bit strings (binary sequences) of length N; we call S an *N-source*. Let $\$_N$ denote the special N-source that contains all 2^N possible N-bit strings. Each element of S represents a sequence that we might use as a source of pseudorandom bits; choosing different "seed" values leads to different elements of S. For example, S might be

$$\{B_1 B_2 \ldots B_N \mid B_j \text{ is the most significant bit of } X_j\} \qquad (38)$$

in the linear congruential sequence defined by $X_{j+1} = (aX_j + c) \bmod 2^e$, where there is one string $B_1 B_2 \ldots B_N$ for each of the 2^e starting values X_0.

The basic idea of pseudorandom sequences, as we have seen throughout this chapter, is to get N bits that appear to be random, although we rely only on a few "truly random" bits when we choose the seed value. In the example just considered, we need e truly random bits to select X_0; in general, selecting a member of S amounts to using $\lg |S|$ truly random bits, after which we proceed deterministically. If $N = 10^6$ and $|S| = 2^{32}$, we are getting more than 30,000 "apparently random" bits for each truly random bit expended. With $\$_N$ instead of S, we get no such amplification, because $\lg |\$_N| = N$.

What does it mean to be "apparently random"? A. C. Yao proposed a good definition in 1982: Consider any algorithm A that looks at a bit string $B = B_1 \ldots B_N$ and outputs the value $A(B) = 0$ or 1. We may think of A as a test for randomness; for example, A might compute the distribution of runs of consecutive 0s and 1s, outputting 1 if the run lengths differ significantly from the expected distribution. Whatever A does, we can consider the probability $P(A, S)$ that $A(B) = 1$ when B is a randomly chosen element of S, and we can compare it to the probability $P(A, \$_N)$ that $A(B) = 1$ when B is a truly random bit string of length N. If $P(A, S)$ is extremely close to $P(A, \$_N)$ for all statistical tests A, we cannot tell the difference between the sequences of S and truly random binary sequences.

Definition P. *We say that an N-source S passes statistical test A with tolerance ϵ if $\left| P(A, S) - P(A, \$_N) \right| < \epsilon$. It fails the test if $\left| P(A, S) - P(A, \$_N) \right| \geq \epsilon$.* ∎

The algorithm A need not be designed by statisticians. *Any* algorithm can be considered a statistical test for randomness, according to Definition P. We allow A to flip coins (that is, to use truly random bits) as it performs its calculations. The only requirement is that A must output 0 or 1.

Well, actually there is another requirement: We insist that A must deliver its output in a reasonable time, at least on the average. We're not interested in algorithms that will take many years to run, because we will never notice any disparities between S and $\$_N$ if our computers cannot detect them during our lifetime. The sequences of S contain only $\lg |S|$ bits of information, so there surely are algorithms that will eventually detect the redundancy; but we don't care, as long as S is able to pass all the tests that really matter.

These qualitative ideas can be quantified, as we will now see. The theory is rather subtle, but it is sufficiently beautiful and important that readers who take the time to study the details carefully will be amply rewarded.

In the following discussion, the *running time $T(A)$* of an algorithm A on N-bit strings is defined to be the maximum of the expected number of steps needed to output $A(B)$, maximized over all $B \in \$_N$; the expected number is averaged over all coin flips made by the algorithm.

The first step in our quantitative analysis is to show that we may restrict the tests to be of a very special kind. Let A_k be an algorithm that depends only on the first k bits of the input string $B = B_1 \ldots B_N$, where $0 \leq k < N$, and let $A_k^P(B) = \left(A_k(B) + B_{k+1} + 1 \right) \bmod 2$. Thus A_k^P outputs 1 if and only if A_k has successfully predicted B_{k+1}; we call A_k^P a *prediction* test.

Lemma P1. *Let S be an N-source. If S fails test A with tolerance ϵ, there is an integer $k \in \{0, 1, \ldots, N-1\}$ and a prediction test A_k^P with $T(A_k^P) \leq T(A) + O(N)$ such that S fails A_k^P with tolerance ϵ/N.*

Proof. By complementing the output of A, if necessary, we may assume that $P(A, S) - P(A, \$_N) \geq \epsilon$. Consider the algorithms F_k that begin by flipping $N - k$ coins and replacing $B_{k+1} \ldots B_N$ by random bits $B'_{k+1} \ldots B'_N$ before executing A. Algorithm F_N is the same as A, while F_0 acts on S as if A were acting on $\$_N$. Let $p_k = P(F_k, S)$. Since $\sum_{k=0}^{N-1} (p_{k+1} - p_k) = p_N - p_0 = P(A, S) - P(A, \$_N) \geq \epsilon$, there is some k such that $p_{k+1} - p_k \geq \epsilon/N$.

Let A_k^P be the algorithm that performs the computations of F_k and predicts the value $\left(F_k(B) + B'_{k+1} + 1 \right) \bmod 2$; in other words, it outputs

$$A_k^P(B) = \left(F_k(B) + B_{k+1} + B'_{k+1} \right) \bmod 2. \tag{39}$$

A careful analysis of probabilities shows that $P(A_k^P, S) - P(A_k^P, \$_N) = p_{k+1} - p_k$. (See exercise 40.) ∎

Most N-sources S of practical interest are *shift-symmetric* in the sense that every substring $B_1 \ldots B_k$, $B_2 \ldots B_{k+1}$, $\ldots$, $B_{N-k+1} \ldots B_N$ of length k has the same probability distribution. This holds, for example, when S corresponds to a linear congruential sequence as in (38). In such cases we can improve on Lemma P1 by taking $k = N - 1$:

Lemma P2. *If S is a shift-symmetric N-source that fails test A with tolerance ϵ, there is an algorithm A' with $T(A') \leq T(A) + O(N)$ that predicts B_N from $B_1 \ldots B_{N-1}$ with probability at least $\frac{1}{2} + \epsilon/N$.*

Proof. If $P(A, S) > P(A, \$_N)$, let A' be the A_k^P in the proof of Lemma P1, but applied to $B_{N-k} \ldots B_{N-1} 0 \ldots 0$ instead of $B_1 \ldots B_N$. Then A' has the same average behavior, because of shift-symmetry. If $P(A, S) < P(A, \$_N)$, let A' be $1 - A_k^P$ in the same fashion. Clearly $P(A', \$_N) = \frac{1}{2}$. ∎

Now let's specialize S even more, by supposing that each of the sequences $B_1 B_2 \ldots B_N$ has the form $f\big(g(X_0)\big) f\big(g(g(X_0))\big) \ldots f\big(g^{[N]}(X_0)\big)$ as X_0 ranges over some set X, where g is a permutation of X and $f(x)$ is 0 or 1 for all $x \in X$. Our linear congruential example satisfies this restriction, with $X = \{0, 1, \ldots, 2^e - 1\}$, $g(x) = (ax + c) \bmod 2^e$, and $f(x) = $ most significant bit of x. Such N-sources will be called *iterative*.

Lemma P3. *If S is an iterative N-source that fails test A with tolerance ϵ, there is an algorithm A' with $T(A') \leq T(A) + O(N)$ that predicts B_1 from $B_2 \ldots B_N$ with probability at least $\frac{1}{2} + \epsilon/N$.*

Proof. An iterative N-source is shift-symmetric, and so is its reflection $S^R = \{B_N \ldots B_1 \mid B_1 \ldots B_N \in S\}$. Therefore Lemma P2 applies to S^R. ∎

The permutation $g(x) = (ax + c) \bmod 2^e$ is easy to invert, in the sense that we can determine x from $g(x)$ whenever a is odd. But many easily computed permutation functions are "one-way" — hard to invert — and we will see that this makes them provably good sources of pseudorandom numbers.

Lemma P4. *Let S be an iterative N-source corresponding to f, g, and X. If S fails test A with tolerance ϵ, there is an algorithm G that correctly guesses $f(x)$, given $g(x)$, with probability $\geq \frac{1}{2} + \epsilon/N$, when x is a random element of X. The running time $T(G)$ is at most $T(A) + O(N)\big(T(f) + T(g)\big)$.*

Proof. Given $y = g(x)$, the desired algorithm G computes $B_2 = f\big(g(x)\big)$, $B_3 = f\big(g(g(x))\big)$, $\ldots$, $B_N = f\big(g^{[N-1]}(x)\big)$ and applies the algorithm A' of Lemma P3. It guesses $f(x) = B_1$ with probability $\geq \frac{1}{2} + \epsilon/N$, because g is a permutation of X, and $B_1 \ldots B_N$ is the element of S corresponding to the seed value X_0 for which we have $g(X_0) = x$. ∎

In order to use Lemma P4, we need to amplify the ability to guess a single bit $f(x)$ to an ability to guess x itself, given only the value of $g(x)$. There is a nice general way to do this, using the properties of Boolean functions, if we extend S so that many different functions $f(x)$ need to be guessed. (However, the method is somewhat technical, so the first-time reader may want to skip down to Theorem G before looking closely at the details that follow.)

Suppose $G(z_1 \ldots z_R)$ is a binary-valued function on R-bit strings that is good at guessing a function of the form $f(z_1 \ldots z_R) = (x_1 z_1 + \cdots + x_R z_R) \bmod 2$ for some fixed $x = x_1 \ldots x_R$. It is convenient to measure the success of G by computing the expected value

$$s = \mathrm{E}\big((-1)^{G(z_1 \ldots z_R) + x_1 z_1 + \cdots + x_R z_R}\big), \tag{40}$$

averaged over all possibilities for $z_1 \ldots z_R$. This is the sum of correct guesses minus incorrect guesses, divided by 2^R; so if p is the probability that G is correct, we have $s = p - (1 - p)$, or $p = \frac{1}{2} + \frac{1}{2}s$.

For example, suppose $R = 4$ and $G(z_1 z_2 z_3 z_4) = [z_1 \neq z_2][z_3 + z_4 < 2]$. This function has success rate $s = \frac{3}{4}$ (and $p = \frac{7}{8}$) if $x = 1100$, because it equals $x \cdot z \bmod 2 = (z_1 + z_2) \bmod 2$ for all 4-bit strings z except 0111 or 1011. It also has success rate $\frac{1}{4}$ when $x = 0000$, 0011, 1101, or 1110; so there are five plausible possibilities for x. The other eleven x's make $s \leq 0$.

The following algorithm magically discovers x in most cases when G is a successful guesser in the sense just described. More precisely, the algorithm constructs a short list that has a good chance of containing x.

Algorithm L (*Amplification of linear guesses*). Given a binary-valued function $G(z_1 \ldots z_R)$ and a positive integer k, this algorithm outputs a list of 2^k binary sequences $x = x_1 \ldots x_R$ with the property that x is likely to be output when $G(z_1 \ldots z_R)$ is a good approximation to the function $(x_1 z_1 + \cdots + x_R z_R) \bmod 2$.

L1. [Construct a random matrix.] Generate random bits B_{ij} for $1 \leq i \leq k$ and $1 \leq j \leq R$.

L2. [Compute signs.] For $1 \leq i \leq R$, and for all bit strings $b = b_1 \ldots b_k$, compute

$$h_i(b) = \sum_{c \neq 0} (-1)^{b \cdot c + G(cB + e_i)} \tag{41}$$

where e_i is the R-bit string $0 \ldots 010 \ldots 0$ having 1 in position i, and where cB is the string $d_1 \ldots d_R$ with $d_j = (B_{1j} c_1 + \cdots + B_{kj} c_k) \bmod 2$. (In other words the binary vector $c_1 \ldots c_k$ is multiplied by the $k \times R$ binary matrix B.) The sum is taken over all $2^k - 1$ bit strings $c_1 \ldots c_k \neq 0 \ldots 0$. It can be evaluated for each i with $k \cdot 2^k$ additions and subtractions, using Yates's method for the Hadamard transform; see the remarks following Eq. 4.6.4–(38).

L3. [Output the guesses.] For all 2^k choices of $b = b_1 \ldots b_k$, output the string $x(b) = [h_1(b) < 0] \ldots [h_R(b) < 0]$. ∎

To prove that Algorithm L works properly, we must show that a given string x will probably be output whenever it deserves to be. Notice first that if we change G to G', where $G'(z) = (G(z) + z_j) \bmod 2$, the original $G(z)$ is a good approximation to $x \cdot z \bmod 2$ if and only if the new $G'(z)$ is a good approximation to $(x + e_j) \cdot z \bmod 2$, where e_j is the unit-vector string defined in step L2. Moreover, if we apply the algorithm to G' instead of G, we get

$$h'_i(b) = \sum_{c \neq 0} (-1)^{b \cdot c + G(cB + e_i) + (cB + e_i) \cdot e_j} = (-1)^{\delta_{ij}} h_i\big((b + B_j) \bmod 2\big),$$

where B_j is column j of B. Therefore step L3 outputs the vectors $x'(b) = x\big((b + B_j) \bmod 2\big) + e_j$, modulo 2. As b runs through all k-bit strings, so does $(b + B_j) \bmod 2$, and the effect is to complement bit j of every x in the output.

We need therefore prove only that the vector $x = 0 \ldots 0$ is likely to be output whenever $G(z)$ is a good approximation to the constant function 0. We will show, in fact, that $x(0 \ldots 0)$ equals $0 \ldots 0$ in step L3 with high probability, whenever $G(z)$ is a lot more likely to be 0 than 1 and k is sufficiently large. More precisely, the condition

$$\sum_{c \neq 0} (-1)^{G(cB + e_i)} > 0$$

holds for $1 \le i \le R$ with probability $> \frac{1}{2}$, if $s = \mathrm{E}\big((-1)^{G(z)}\big)$ is positive when averaged over all 2^R possibilities for z and if k is large enough.

The key observation is that, for each fixed $c = c_1 \ldots c_k \neq 0 \ldots 0$, the string $d = cB$ is uniformly distributed: Every value of d occurs with probability $1/2^R$, because the bits of B are random. Furthermore, when $c \neq c' = c'_1 \ldots c'_k$, the strings $d = cB$ and $d' = c'B$ are *independent*: Every value of the pair (d, d') occurs with probability $1/2^{2R}$. Therefore we can argue as in the proof of Chebyshev's inequality that, for any fixed i, the sum $\sum_{c \neq 0} (-1)^{G(cB + e_i)}$ is negative with probability at most $1/((2^k - 1)s^2)$. (Exercise 42 contains the details.) It follows that $R/((2^k - 1)s^2)$ is an upper bound on the probability that $x(0)$ is nonzero in step L3.

Theorem G. *If $s = \mathrm{E}\big((-1)^{G(z) + x \cdot z}\big) > 0$ and $2^k > \lceil 2R/s^2 \rceil$, Algorithm L outputs x with probability $\ge \frac{1}{2}$. The running time is $O(k2^k R)$ plus the time to make $2^k R$ evaluations of G.* ∎

Now we are ready to prove that the muddle-square sequence of Eq. 3.2.2–(17) is a good source of (pseudo)random numbers. Suppose $2^{R-1} < M = PQ < 2^R$, where P and Q are prime numbers of the form $4k + 3$ in the respective ranges $2^{(R-2)/2} < P < 2^{(R-1)/2}$, $2^{R/2} < Q < 2^{(R+1)/2}$. We will call M an R-bit *Blum integer*, because the importance of such numbers for cryptography was first pointed out by Manuel Blum [*COMPCON* **24** (Spring 1982), 133–137]. Blum originally suggested that P and Q both have $R/2$ bits, but Algorithm 4.5.4D shows that it is better to choose P and Q as stated here so that $Q - P > .29 \times 2^{R/2}$.

Choose X_0 at random in the range $0 < X_0 < M$, with $X_0 \perp M$; also let Z be a random R-bit mask. We can construct an iterative N-source S by letting X be the set of all (x, z, m) that are possibilities for (X_0, Z, M), with the further restriction that $x \equiv a^2 \pmod{m}$ for some a. The function $g(x, z, m) = (x^2 \bmod m, z, m)$ is easily shown to be a permutation of X (see, for example, exercise 4.5.4–35). The function $f(x, z, m)$ that extracts bits in this iterative source is $x \cdot z \bmod 2$. Our starting value (X_0, Z, M) isn't necessarily in X, but $g(X_0, Z, M)$ is uniformly distributed in X, because exactly four values of X_0 have a given square $X_0^2 \bmod M$.

Theorem P. *Let S be the N-source defined by the muddle-square method on R-bit moduli, and suppose S fails some statistical test A with tolerance $\epsilon \geq 1/2^N$. Then we can construct an algorithm F that finds factors of random R-bit Blum integers $M = PQ$ having the form described above, with success probability at least $\epsilon/(4N)$ and with running time $T(F) = O(N^2 R^2 \epsilon^{-2} T(A) + N^3 R^4 \epsilon^{-2})$.*

Proof. Multiplication mod M can be done in $O(R^2)$ steps; hence $T(f) + T(g) = O(R^2)$. Lemma P4 therefore asserts the existence of a guessing algorithm G with success rate ϵ/N and $T(G) \leq T(A) + O(NR^2)$. We can construct G from A using the method of exercise 41. This algorithm G has the property that $s = \mathrm{E}\big((-1)^{G(y,z,m)+z\cdot x}\big) \geq (\frac{1}{2} + \epsilon/N) - (\frac{1}{2} - \epsilon/N) = 2\epsilon/N$, where the expected value is taken over all $(x, z, m) \in X$, and where $(y, z, m) = g(x, z, m)$.

The desired algorithm F proceeds as follows. Given a random $M = PQ$ with unknown P and Q, it computes a random X_0 between 0 and M, and stops immediately with a known factorization if $\gcd(X_0, M) \neq 1$. Otherwise it applies Algorithm L with $G(z) = G(X_0^2 \bmod M, z, M)$ and $k = \lceil \lg(1 + 2N^2 R/\epsilon^2) \rceil$. If one of the 2^k values x output by that algorithm satisfies $x^2 \equiv X_0^2$ (modulo M), there is a 50:50 chance that $x \not\equiv \pm X_0$; then $\gcd(X_0 - x, M)$ and $\gcd(X_0 + x, M)$ are the prime factors of M. (See Rabin's "SQRT box" in Section 4.5.4.)

The running time of this algorithm is clearly $O(N^2 R^2 \epsilon^{-2} T(A) + N^3 R^4 \epsilon^{-2})$, since $\epsilon \geq 2^{-N}$. The probability that it succeeds in factoring M can be estimated as follows. Let $n = |X|/2^R$ be the number of choices of (x, m), and let $s_{xm} = 2^{-R} \sum (-1)^{G(y,z,m)+z\cdot x}$ summed over all R-bit numbers z; thus $s = \sum_{x,m} s_{xm}/n \geq 2\epsilon/N$. Let t be the number of (x, m) such that $s_{xm} \geq \epsilon/N$. The probability that our algorithm deals with such a pair (x, m) is

$$\frac{t}{n} \geq \sum_{x,m} [s_{xm} \geq \epsilon/N] \frac{s_{xm}}{n} = \sum_{x,m} (1 - [s_{xm} < \epsilon/N]) \frac{s_{xm}}{n}$$

$$\geq \frac{2\epsilon}{N} - \sum_{x,m} [s_{xm} < \epsilon/N] \frac{s_{xm}}{n} \geq \frac{\epsilon}{N}.$$

And in such a case it finds x with probability $\geq \frac{1}{2}$, by Theorem G, since we have $2^k > \lceil 2R/s_{xm}^2 \rceil$; so it finds a factor with probability $\geq \frac{1}{4}$. ∎

What does Theorem P imply, from a practical standpoint? Our proof shows that the constant implied by the O is small; let us assume that the running time for factoring is at most $10(N^2 R^2 \epsilon^{-2} T(A) + N^3 R^4 \epsilon^{-2})$. Many of the world's greatest mathematicians have worked on the problem of factoring large numbers, especially after factoring was shown to be highly relevant to cryptography in the late 1970s. Since they haven't found a good solution, we have excellent reason to believe that factoring is hard; hence Theorem P will show that $T(A)$ must be large on all algorithms that detect nonrandomness of muddle-square bits.

Long computations are conveniently measured in MIP-years, the number of instructions executed per Gregorian year by a machine that performs a million instructions per Gregorian second — namely 31,556,952,000,000 ≈ 3.16×10^{13}. In 1995, the time to factor a number of 120 decimal digits (400 bits), using the most highly tuned algorithms, was more than 250 MIP-years. The most optimistic researchers who have worked on factorization would be astonished if an algorithm were discovered that requires only $\exp\left(R^{1/4}(\ln R)^{3/4}\right)$ instructions as $R \to \infty$. But let us assume that such a breakthrough has been achieved, for at least a not-too-small fraction of the R-bit Blum integers M. Then we could factor many numbers of about 50000 bits (15000 digits) in 2×10^{25} MIP-years. If we generate $N = 1000$ random bits by muddle-square with $R = 50000$, and if we assume that all algorithms that are good enough to factor at least $\frac{1}{400000}$ of the 50000-bit Blum integers must run at least 2×10^{25} MIP-years, Theorem P tells us that every such set of 1000 bits will pass all statistical tests for randomness whose running time $T(A)$ is less than 70000 MIP-years: No such algorithm A will be able to distinguish such bits from a truly random sequence with probability $\geq \epsilon = \frac{1}{100}$.

Impressive? No. Such a result is hardly surprising, since we need to specify about 150000 truly random bits just to start up the muddle-square method with X_0, Z, and M when $R = 50000$. Of *course* we should be able to get 1000 random bits back from such an investment!

But in general, the formula becomes

$$T(A) \geq \frac{1}{100000} N^{-2} R^{-2} \exp\left(R^{1/4}(\ln R)^{3/4}\right) - NR^2,$$

under our conservative assumptions, when $\epsilon = \frac{1}{100}$; the NR^2 term is negligible when R is large. So let's set $R = 200000$ and $N = 10^{10}$. Then we get ten billion pseudorandom muddle-bits from $\approx 3R = 600000$ truly random bits, passing all statistical tests that require fewer than 7.486×10^{10} MIP-years = 74.86 gigaMIP-years. With $R = 333333$ and $N = 10^{13}$ the computation time needed to detect any statistical bias increases to 535 teraMIP-years.

The simple pseudorandom generator 3.2.2–(16), which avoids the random mask Z, can also be shown to pass all polynomial-time tests for randomness if factoring is intractable. (See exercise 4.5.4–43.) But the known performance guarantees for the simpler method are somewhat weaker than for muddle-square; currently they are $O\left(N^4 R \epsilon^{-4} \log(NR\epsilon^{-1})\right)$ versus the $O(N^2 R^2 \epsilon^{-2})$ of Theorem P.

Everyone believes that there is no factoring algorithm for R-bit numbers whose running time is polynomial in R. If that conjecture is true in a stronger form, so that we cannot even factor $1/R^k$ of the R-bit Blum integers in polynomial time for any fixed k, Theorem P proves that the muddle-square method generates pseudorandom numbers that pass all polynomial-time statistical tests for randomness.

Stating this another way: If you generate random bits with the muddle-square method for suitably chosen N and R, you either get numbers that pass all reasonable statistical tests, or you get fame and fortune for discovering a new factorization algorithm.

G. Summary, history, and bibliography. We have defined several degrees of randomness that a sequence might possess.

An infinite sequence that is ∞-distributed satisfies a great many useful properties that are expected of random sequences, and there is a rich theory concerning ∞-distributed sequences. (The exercises below develop several important properties of such sequences that have not been mentioned in the text.) Definition R1 is therefore an appropriate basis for theoretical studies of randomness.

The concept of an ∞-distributed b-ary sequence was introduced in 1909 by Emile Borel. He essentially defined the concept of an (m, k)-distributed sequence, and showed that the b-ary representations of almost all real numbers are (m, k)-distributed for all m and k. He called such numbers *entirely normal* to base b, and he stated Theorem C informally without apparently realizing that it required proof [*Rendiconti Circ. Mat. Palermo* **27** (1909), 247–271, §12.]

The notion of an ∞-distributed sequence of *real* numbers, also called a *completely equidistributed sequence*, first appeared in a note by N. M. Korobov in *Doklady Akad. Nauk SSSR* **62** (1948), 21–22. Korobov and several of his colleagues developed the theory of such sequences quite extensively in a series of papers during the 1950s. Completely equidistributed sequences were independently studied by Joel N. Franklin, *Math. Comp.* **17** (1963), 28–59, in a paper that is particularly noteworthy because it was inspired by the problem of random number generation. The book *Uniform Distribution of Sequences* by L. Kuipers and H. Niederreiter (New York: Wiley, 1974) is an extraordinarily complete source of information about the rich mathematical literature concerning k-distributed sequences of all kinds.

We have seen, however, that ∞-distributed sequences need not be sufficiently haphazard to qualify completely as "random." Three definitions, R4, R5, and R6, were formulated above to provide the additional conditions; and Definition R6, in particular, seems to be an appropriate way to define the concept of an infinite random sequence. It is a precise, quantitative statement that may well coincide with the intuitive idea of true randomness.

Historically, the development of these definitions was primarily influenced by the quest of R. von Mises for a good definition of "probability." In *Math. Zeitschrift* **5** (1919), 52–99, von Mises proposed a definition similar in spirit to Definition R5, although stated too strongly (like our Definition R3) so that no sequences satisfying the conditions could possibly exist. Many people noticed this discrepancy, and A. H. Copeland [*Amer. J. Math.* **50** (1928), 535–552] suggested weakening von Mises's definition by substituting what he called "admissible numbers" (or Bernoulli sequences). These are equivalent to ∞-distributed $[0..1)$ sequences in which all entries U_n have been replaced by 1 if $U_n < p$ or by 0 if $U_n \geq p$, for a given probability p. Thus Copeland was essentially suggesting a return to Definition R1. Then Abraham Wald showed that it is not necessary to weaken von Mises's definition so drastically, and he proposed substituting a countable set of subsequence rules. In an important paper [*Ergebnisse eines math. Kolloquiums* **8** (Vienna: 1937), 38–72], Wald essentially proved Theorem W, although he made the erroneous assertion that the sequence constructed by Algorithm W also satisfies the stronger condition that $\Pr(U_n \in A) =$ measure of A, for all Lebesgue measurable $A \subseteq [0 .. 1)$. We have observed that no sequence can satisfy this property.

The concept of "computability" was still very much in its infancy when Wald wrote his paper, and A. Church [*Bull. Amer. Math. Soc.* **46** (1940), 130–135] showed how the precise notion of "effective algorithm" could be added to Wald's theory to make his definitions completely rigorous. The extension to Definition R6 was due essentially to A. N. Kolmogorov [*Sankhyā* **A25** (1963), 369–376], who proposed Definition Q2 for finite sequences at the same time. Another definition of randomness for finite sequences, somewhere "between" Definitions Q1 and Q2, had been formulated many years earlier by A. S. Besicovitch [*Math. Zeitschrift* **39** (1934), 146–156].

The publications of Church and Kolmogorov considered only binary sequences for which $\Pr(X_n = 1) = p$ for a given probability p. Our discussion in this section has been slightly more general, since a $[0 .. 1)$ sequence essentially represents all p at once. The von Mises–Wald–Church definition has been refined in yet another interesting way by J. V. Howard, *Zeitschr. für math. Logik und Grundlagen der Math.* **21** (1975), 215–224.

Another important contribution was made by Donald W. Loveland [*Zeitschr. für math. Logik und Grundlagen der Math.* **12** (1966), 279–294], who discussed Definitions R4, R5, R6, and several intermediate concepts. Loveland proved that there are R5-random sequences that do not satisfy R4, thereby establishing the need for a stronger definition such as R6. In fact, he defined a rather simple permutation $\langle f(n) \rangle$ of the nonnegative integers, and an Algorithm W' analogous to Algorithm W, such that

$$\overline{\Pr}(U_{f(n)} \geq \tfrac{1}{2}) - \underline{\Pr}(U_{f(n)} \geq \tfrac{1}{2}) \geq \tfrac{1}{2}$$

for every R5-random sequence $\langle U_n \rangle$ produced by Algorithm W' when it is given an infinite set of subsequence rules $\mathcal{R}_k$.

Although Definition R6 is intuitively much stronger than R4, it is apparently not a simple matter to prove this rigorously, and for several years it was an open question whether or not R4 implies R6. Finally Thomas Herzog and James C. Owings, Jr., discovered how to construct a large family of sequences that satisfy R4 but not R6. [See *Zeitschr. für math. Logik und Grundlagen der Math.* **22** (1976), 385–389.]

Kolmogorov wrote another significant paper [*Problemy Peredači Informatsii* **1** (1965), 3–11] in which he considered the problem of defining the "information content" of a sequence, and this work led to Chaitin and Martin-Löf's interesting definition of finite random sequences via "patternlessness." [See *IEEE Trans.* **IT-14** (1968), 662–664.] The ideas can also be traced to R. J. Solomonoff, *Information and Control* **7** (1964), 1–22, 224–254; *IEEE Trans.* **IT-24** (1978), 422–432; *J. Computer and System Sciences* **55** (1997), 73–88.

For a philosophical discussion of random sequences, see K. R. Popper, *The Logic of Scientific Discovery* (London, 1959), especially the interesting construction on pages 162–163, which he first published in 1934.

Further connections between random sequences and recursive function theory have been explored by D. W. Loveland, *Trans. Amer. Math. Soc.* **125** (1966), 497–510. See also C.-P. Schnorr [*Zeitschr. Wahr. verw. Geb.* **14** (1969), 27–35], who found strong relations between random sequences and the "species of measure zero" defined by L. E. J. Brouwer in 1919. Schnorr's subsequent book *Zufälligkeit und Wahrscheinlichkeit* [*Lecture Notes in Math.* **218** (Berlin: Springer, 1971)] gives a detailed treatment of the entire subject of randomness and makes an excellent introduction to the ever-growing advanced literature on the topic. Important developments during the next two decades are surveyed in *An Introduction to Kolmogorov Complexity and Its Applications* (Springer, 1993), by Ming Li and Paul M. B. Vitányi.

The foundations of the theory of pseudorandom sequences and effective information were laid by Manuel Blum, Silvio Micali, and Andrew Yao [*FOCS* **23** (1982), 80–91, 112–117; *SICOMP* **13** (1984), 850–864], who constructed the first explicit sequences that pass all feasible statistical tests. Blum and Micali introduced the notion of a "hard-core bit," a Boolean function f such that $f(x)$ and $g(x)$ are easily computed although $f(g^{[-1]}(x))$ is not; their paper was the origin of Lemma P4. Leonid Levin developed the theory further [*Combinatorica* **7** (1987), 357–363], then he and Oded Goldreich [*STOC* **21** (1989), 25–32] analyzed algorithms such as the muddle-square method and showed that similar use of a mask yields hard-core bits in many further cases. Finally Charles Rackoff refined the methods of that paper by introducing and analyzing Algorithm L [see L. Levin, [*J. Symbolic Logic* **58** (1993), 1102–1103].

Many other authors have contributed to the theory — notably Impagliazzo, Levin, Luby, and Håstad, who showed [*SICOMP* **28** (1999), 1364–1396] that pseudorandom sequences can be constructed from any one-way function — but such results are beyond the scope of this book. The practical implications of theoretical work on pseudorandomness were first investigated empirically by P. L'Ecuyer and R. Proulx, *Proc. Winter Simulation Conf.* **22** (1989), 467–476.

> *If the numbers are not random,*
> *they are at least higgledy-piggledy.*
> — GEORGE MARSAGLIA (1984)

EXERCISES

1. [*10*] Can a periodic sequence be equidistributed?

2. [*10*] Consider the periodic binary sequence 0, 0, 1, 1, 0, 0, 1, 1, ... Is it 1-distributed? Is it 2-distributed? Is it 3-distributed?

3. [*M22*] Construct a periodic ternary sequence that is 3-distributed.

4. [*HM14*] Prove that $\Pr(S(n) \text{ and } T(n)) + \Pr(S(n) \text{ or } T(n)) = \Pr(S(n)) + \Pr(T(n))$, for any two statements $S(n)$ and $T(n)$, provided that at least three of the limits exist. For example, if a sequence is 2-distributed, we would find that

$$\Pr(u_1 \leq U_n < v_1 \text{ or } u_2 \leq U_{n+1} < v_2) = v_1 - u_1 + v_2 - u_2 - (v_1 - u_1)(v_2 - u_2).$$

▶ **5.** [*HM22*] Let $U_n = (2^{\lfloor \lg(n+1) \rfloor}/3) \bmod 1$. What is $\Pr(U_n < \frac{1}{2})$?

6. [*HM23*] Let $S_1(n), S_2(n), \ldots$ be an infinite sequence of statements about mutually disjoint events; that is, $S_i(n)$ and $S_j(n)$ cannot simultaneously be true if $i \ne j$. Assume that $\Pr(S_j(n))$ exists for each $j \ge 1$. Show that $\underline{\Pr}(S_j(n))$ is true for some $j \ge 1) \ge \sum_{j \ge 1} \Pr(S_j(n))$, and give an example to show that equality need not hold.

7. [*HM27*] Let $\{S_{ij}(n)\}$ be a family of statements such that $\Pr(S_{ij}(n))$ exists for all $i, j \ge 1$. Assume that for all $n > 0$, $S_{ij}(n)$ is true for exactly one pair of integers i, j. If $\sum_{i,j \ge 1} \Pr(S_{ij}(n)) = 1$, does it follow that "$\Pr(S_{ij}(n)$ is true for some $j \ge 1)$" exists for all $i \ge 1$, and that it equals $\sum_{j \ge 1} \Pr(S_{ij}(n))$?

8. [*M15*] Prove (13).

9. [*HM20*] Prove Lemma E. [*Hint:* Consider $\sum_{j=1}^{m} (y_{jn} - \alpha)^2$.]

▶ **10.** [*HM22*] Where was the fact that m divides q used in the proof of Theorem C?

11. [*M10*] Use Theorem C to prove that if a sequence $\langle U_n \rangle$ is ∞-distributed, so is the subsequence $\langle U_{2n} \rangle$.

12. [*HM20*] Show that a k-distributed sequence passes the "maximum-of-k test," in the following sense: $\Pr(u \le \max(U_n, U_{n+1}, \ldots, U_{n+k-1}) < v) = v^k - u^k$.

▶ **13.** [*HM27*] Show that an ∞-distributed $[0 \mathbin{.\,.} 1)$ sequence passes the "gap test" in the following sense: If $0 \le \alpha < \beta \le 1$ and $p = \beta - \alpha$, let $f(0) = 0$, and for $n \ge 1$ let $f(n)$ be the smallest integer $m > f(n-1)$ such that $\alpha \le U_m < \beta$; then

$$\Pr(f(n) - f(n-1) = k) = p(1-p)^{k-1}.$$

14. [*HM25*] Show that an ∞-distributed sequence passes the "run test" in the following sense: If $f(0) = 0$ and if, for $n \ge 1$, $f(n)$ is the smallest integer $m > f(n-1)$ such that $U_{m-1} > U_m$, then

$$\Pr(f(n) - f(n-1) = k) = 2k/(k+1)! - 2(k+1)/(k+2)!.$$

▶ **15.** [*HM30*] Show that an ∞-distributed sequence passes the "coupon-collector's test" when there are only two kinds of coupons, in the following sense: Let $X_1, X_2, \ldots$ be an ∞-distributed binary sequence. Let $f(0) = 0$, and for $n \ge 1$ let $f(n)$ be the smallest integer $m > f(n-1)$ such that $\{X_{f(n-1)+1}, \ldots, X_m\}$ is the set $\{0, 1\}$. Prove that $\Pr(f(n) - f(n-1) = k) = 2^{1-k}$, for $k \ge 2$. (See exercise 7.)

16. [*HM38*] Does the coupon-collector's test hold for ∞-distributed sequences when there are more than two kinds of coupons? (See the previous exercise.)

17. [*HM50*] If r is any given rational number, Franklin has proved that the sequence $\langle r^n \bmod 1 \rangle$ is not 2-distributed. But is there any rational number r for which this sequence is equidistributed? In particular, is the sequence equidistributed when $r = \frac{3}{2}$? [See K. Mahler, *Mathematika* **4** (1957), 122–124.]

▶ **18.** [*HM22*] Prove that if $U_0, U_1, \ldots$ is k-distributed, so is the sequence $V_0, V_1, \ldots$, where $V_n = \lfloor nU_n \rfloor / n$.

19. [*HM35*] Consider a modification of Definition R4 that requires the subsequences to be only 1-distributed instead of ∞-distributed. Is there a sequence that satisfies this weaker definition, but that is not ∞-distributed? (Is the weaker definition really weaker?)

▶ **20.** [*HM36*] (N. G. de Bruijn and P. Erdős.) The first n points of any $[0..1)$ sequence $\langle U_n \rangle$ with $U_0 = 0$ divide the interval $[0..1)$ into n subintervals; let those subintervals have lengths $l_n^{(1)} \geq l_n^{(2)} \geq \cdots \geq l_n^{(n)}$. Clearly $l_n^{(1)} \geq \frac{1}{n} \geq l_n^{(n)}$, because $l_n^{(1)} + \cdots + l_n^{(n)} = 1$. One way to measure the equitability of the distribution of $\langle U_n \rangle$ is to consider

$$\bar{L} = \limsup_{n \to \infty} n l_n^{(1)} \qquad \text{and} \qquad \underline{L} = \liminf_{n \to \infty} n l_n^{(n)}.$$

a) What are $\bar{L}$ and $\underline{L}$ for van der Corput's sequence (29)?
b) Show that $l_{n+k-1}^{(1)} \geq l_n^{(k)}$ for $1 \leq k \leq n$. Use this result to prove that $\bar{L} \geq 1/\ln 2$.
c) Prove that $\underline{L} \leq 1/\ln 4$. [*Hint:* For each n there are numbers $a_1, \ldots, a_{2n}$ such that $l_{2n}^{(k)} \geq l_{n+a_k}^{(n+a_k)}$ for $1 \leq k \leq 2n$. Moreover, each integer $2, \ldots, n$ occurs at most twice in $\{a_1, \ldots, a_{2n}\}$.]
d) Show that the sequence $\langle W_n \rangle$ defined by $W_n = \lg(2n+1) \bmod 1$ satisfies $1/\ln 2 > n l_n^{(1)} \geq n l_n^{(n)} > 1/\ln 4$ for all n; hence it achieves the optimum $\bar{L}$ and $\underline{L}$.

21. [*HM40*] (L. H. Ramshaw.)
a) Continuing the previous exercise, is the sequence $\langle W_n \rangle$ equidistributed?
b) Show that $\langle W_n \rangle$ is the only $[0..1)$ sequence for which we have $\sum_{j=1}^{k} l_n^{(j)} \leq \lg(1 + k/n)$ whenever $1 \leq k \leq n$.
c) Let $\langle f_n(l_1, \ldots, l_n) \rangle$ be any sequence of continuous functions on the sets of n-tuples $\{(l_1, \ldots, l_n) \mid l_1 \geq \cdots \geq l_n \text{ and } l_1 + \cdots + l_n = 1\}$, satisfying the following two properties:

$$f_{mn}(\tfrac{1}{m}l_1, \ldots, \tfrac{1}{m}l_1, \tfrac{1}{m}l_2, \ldots, \tfrac{1}{m}l_2, \ldots, \tfrac{1}{m}l_n, \ldots, \tfrac{1}{m}l_n) = f_n(l_1, \ldots, l_n);$$

if $\sum_{j=1}^{k} l_j \geq \sum_{j=1}^{k} l_j'$ for $1 \leq k \leq n$ then $f_n(l_1, \ldots, l_n) \geq f_n(l_1', \ldots, l_n')$.

[Examples are: $n l_n^{(1)}$; $-n l_n^{(n)}$; $l_n^{(1)}/l_n^{(n)}$; $n(l_n^{(1)2} + \cdots + l_n^{(n)2})$.] Let

$$\bar{F} = \limsup_{n \to \infty} f_n(l_n^{(1)}, \ldots, l_n^{(n)})$$

for the sequence $\langle W_n \rangle$. Show that $f_n(l_n^{(1)}, \ldots, l_n^{(n)}) \leq \bar{F}$ for all n, with respect to $\langle W_n \rangle$; also $\limsup_{n \to \infty} f_n(l_n^{(1)}, \ldots, l_n^{(n)}) \geq \bar{F}$ with respect to every other $[0..1)$ sequence.

▶ **22.** [*HM30*] (Hermann Weyl.) Show that the $[0..1)$ sequence $\langle U_n \rangle$ is k-distributed if and only if

$$\lim_{N \to \infty} \frac{1}{N} \sum_{0 \leq n < N} \exp(2\pi i(c_1 U_n + \cdots + c_k U_{n+k-1})) = 0$$

for every set of integers $c_1, c_2, \ldots, c_k$ not all zero.

23. [*M32*] (a) Show that a $[0..1)$ sequence $\langle U_n \rangle$ is k-distributed if and only if all of the sequences $\langle (c_1 U_n + c_2 U_{n+1} + \cdots + c_k U_{n+k-1}) \bmod 1 \rangle$ are 1-distributed, whenever $c_1, c_2, \ldots, c_k$ are integers not all zero. (b) Show that a b-ary sequence $\langle X_n \rangle$ is k-distributed if and only if all of the sequences $\langle (c_1 X_n + c_2 X_{n+1} + \cdots + c_k X_{n+k-1}) \bmod b \rangle$ are 1-distributed, whenever $c_1, c_2, \ldots, c_k$ are integers with $\gcd(c_1, \ldots, c_k) = 1$.

▶ **24.** [*M35*] (J. G. van der Corput.) (a) Prove that the $[0..1)$ sequence $\langle U_n \rangle$ is equidistributed whenever the sequences $\langle (U_{n+k} - U_n) \bmod 1 \rangle$ are equidistributed for all $k > 0$. (b) Consequently $\langle (\alpha_d n^d + \cdots + \alpha_1 n + \alpha_0) \bmod 1 \rangle$ is equidistributed, when $d > 0$ and α_d is irrational.

25. [*HM20*] A sequence is called a "white sequence" if all serial correlations are zero; that is, if the equation in Corollary S is true for *all* $k \geq 1$. (By Corollary S, an ∞-distributed sequence is white.) Show that if a $[0 \ldots 1)$ sequence is equidistributed, it is white if and only if

$$\lim_{n \to \infty} \frac{1}{n} \sum_{0 \leq j < n} (U_j - \tfrac{1}{2})(U_{j+k} - \tfrac{1}{2}) = 0, \qquad \text{for all } k \geq 1.$$

26. [*HM34*] (J. Franklin.) A white sequence, as defined in the previous exercise, can definitely fail to be random. Let $U_0, U_1, \ldots$ be an ∞-distributed sequence, and define the sequence $V_0, V_1, \ldots$ as follows:

$$\begin{aligned}
(V_{2n-1}, V_{2n}) &= (U_{2n-1}, U_{2n}) & \text{if } (U_{2n-1}, U_{2n}) \in G, \\
(V_{2n-1}, V_{2n}) &= (U_{2n}, U_{2n-1}) & \text{if } (U_{2n-1}, U_{2n}) \notin G,
\end{aligned}$$

where G is the set

$$\{(x, y) \mid x - \tfrac{1}{2} \leq y \leq x \text{ or } x + \tfrac{1}{2} \leq y\}.$$

Show that (a) $V_0, V_1, \ldots$ is equidistributed and white; (b) $\Pr(V_n > V_{n+1}) = \frac{5}{8}$. (This points out the weakness of the serial correlation test.)

27. [*HM48*] What is the highest possible value for $\Pr(V_n > V_{n+1})$ in an equidistributed, white sequence? (D. Coppersmith has constructed such a sequence achieving the value $\frac{7}{8}$.)

▶ **28.** [*HM21*] Use the sequence (11) to construct a $[0 \ldots 1)$ sequence that is 3-distributed, for which $\Pr(U_{2n} \geq \tfrac{1}{2}) = \frac{3}{4}$.

29. [*HM34*] Let $X_0, X_1, \ldots$ be a $(2k)$-distributed binary sequence. Show that

$$\overline{\Pr}(X_{2n} = 0) \leq \frac{1}{2} + \binom{2k-1}{k} \bigg/ 2^{2k}.$$

▶ **30.** [*M39*] Construct a binary sequence that is $(2k)$-distributed, and for which

$$\Pr(X_{2n} = 0) = \frac{1}{2} + \binom{2k-1}{k} \bigg/ 2^{2k}.$$

(Therefore the inequality in the previous exercise is the best possible.)

31. [*M30*] Show that $[0 \ldots 1)$ sequences exist that satisfy Definition R5, yet $\nu_n/n \geq \frac{1}{2}$ for all $n > 0$, where ν_n is the number of $j < n$ for which $U_j < \frac{1}{2}$. (This might be considered a nonrandom property of the sequence.)

32. [*M24*] Given that $\langle X_n \rangle$ is a "random" b-ary sequence according to Definition R5, and that $\mathcal{R}$ is a computable subsequence rule that specifies an infinite subsequence $\langle X_n \rangle \mathcal{R}$, show that the latter subsequence is not only 1-distributed, it is "random" by Definition R5.

33. [*HM22*] Let $\langle U_{r_n} \rangle$ and $\langle U_{s_n} \rangle$ be infinite disjoint subsequences of a sequence $\langle U_n \rangle$. (Thus, $r_0 < r_1 < r_2 < \cdots$ and $s_0 < s_1 < s_2 < \cdots$ are increasing sequences of integers and $r_m \neq s_n$ for any m, n.) Let $\langle U_{t_n} \rangle$ be the combined subsequence, so that $t_0 < t_1 < t_2 < \cdots$ and the set $\{t_n\} = \{r_n\} \cup \{s_n\}$. Show that if $\Pr(U_{r_n} \in A) = \Pr(U_{s_n} \in A) = p$, then $\Pr(U_{t_n} \in A) = p$.

▶ **34.** [*M25*] Define subsequence rules $\mathcal{R}_1, \mathcal{R}_2, \mathcal{R}_3, \ldots$ such that Algorithm W can be used with these rules to give an effective algorithm to construct a $[0 \ldots 1)$ sequence satisfying Definition R1.

▶ **35.** [*HM35*] (D. W. Loveland.) Show that if a binary sequence $\langle X_n \rangle$ is R5-random, and if $\langle s_n \rangle$ is any computable sequence as in Definition R4, then $\overline{\Pr}(X_{s_n} = 1) \geq \frac{1}{2}$ and $\underline{\Pr}(X_{s_n} = 1) \leq \frac{1}{2}$.

36. [*HM30*] Let $\langle X_n \rangle$ be a binary sequence that is "random" according to Definition R6. Show that the $[0 \mathinner{.\,.} 1)$ sequence $\langle U_n \rangle$ defined in binary notation by the scheme

$$U_0 = (0.X_0)_2, \quad U_1 = (0.X_1 X_2)_2, \quad U_2 = (0.X_3 X_4 X_5)_2, \quad U_3 = (0.X_6 X_7 X_8 X_9)_2, \quad \ldots$$

is random in the sense of Definition R6.

37. [*M37*] (D. Coppersmith.) Define a sequence that satisfies Definition R4 but not Definition R5. [*Hint:* Consider changing U_0, U_1, U_4, U_9, ... in a truly random sequence.]

38. [*M49*] (A. N. Kolmogorov.) Given N, n, and ϵ, what is the smallest number of algorithms in a set **A** such that no (n, ϵ)-random binary sequences of length N exist with respect to **A**? (If exact formulas cannot be given, can asymptotic formulas be found? The point of this problem is to discover how close the bound (37) comes to being "best possible.")

39. [*HM45*] (W. M. Schmidt.) Let U_n be a $[0 \mathinner{.\,.} 1)$ sequence, and let $\nu_n(u)$ be the number of nonnegative integers $j \leq n$ such that $0 \leq U_j < u$. Prove that there is a positive constant c such that, for any N and for any $[0 \mathinner{.\,.} 1)$ sequence $\langle U_n \rangle$, we have

$$|\nu_n(u) - un| > c \ln N$$

for some n and u with $0 \leq n < N$, $0 \leq u < 1$. (In other words, no $[0 \mathinner{.\,.} 1)$ sequence can be *too* equidistributed.)

40. [*M28*] Complete the proof of Lemma P1.

41. [*M21*] Lemma P2 shows the existence of a prediction test, but its proof relies on the existence of a suitable k without explaining how we could find k constructively from A. Show that any algorithm A can be converted into an algorithm A' with $T(A') \leq T(A) + O(N)$ that predicts B_N from $B_1 \ldots B_{N-1}$ with probability at least $\frac{1}{2} + (P(A, S) - P(A, \$_N))/N$ on any shift-symmetric N-source S.

▶ **42.** [*M28*] (*Pairwise independence.*)
  a) Let X_1, ..., X_n be random variables having mean value $\mu = \mathrm{E}\, X_j$ and variance $\sigma^2 = \mathrm{E}\, X_j^2 - (\mathrm{E}\, X_j)^2$ for $1 \leq j \leq n$. Prove Chebyshev's inequality

$$\Pr((X_1 + \cdots + X_n - n\mu)^2 \geq tn\sigma^2) \leq 1/t,$$

  under the additional assumption that $\mathrm{E}(X_i X_j) = (\mathrm{E}\, X_i)(\mathrm{E}\, X_j)$ whenever $i \neq j$.
  b) Let B be a random $k \times R$ binary matrix. Prove that if c and c' are fixed nonzero k-bit vectors, with $c \neq c'$, the vectors cB and $c'B$ are independent random R-bit vectors (modulo 2).
  c) Apply (a) and (b) to the analysis of Algorithm L.

43. [*20*] It seems just as difficult to find the factors of any *fixed* R-bit Blum integer M as to find the factors of a *random* R-bit integer. Why then is Theorem P stated for random M instead of fixed M?

▶ **44.** [*16*] (I. J. Good.) Can a valid table of random digits contain just one misprint?

3.6. SUMMARY

WE HAVE COVERED a fairly large number of topics in this chapter: How to generate random numbers, how to test them, how to modify them in applications, and how to derive theoretical facts about them. Perhaps the main question in many readers' minds will be, "What is the result of all this theory? What is a simple, virtuous generator that I can use in my programs in order to have a reliable source of random numbers?"

The detailed investigations in this chapter suggest that the following procedure gives the simplest random number generator for the machine language of most computers: At the beginning of the program, set an integer variable X to some value X_0. This variable X is to be used only for the purpose of random number generation. Whenever a new random number is required by the program, set

$$X \leftarrow (aX + c) \bmod m \qquad (1)$$

and use the new value of X as the random value. It is necessary to choose X_0, a, c, and m properly, and to use the random numbers wisely, according to the following principles:

i) The "seed" number X_0 may be chosen arbitrarily. If the program is run several times and a different source of random numbers is desired each time, set X_0 to the last value attained by X on the preceding run; or (if more convenient) set X_0 to the current date and time. If the program may need to be rerun later with the *same* random numbers (for example, when debugging), be sure to print out X_0 if it isn't otherwise known.

ii) The number m should be large, say at least 2^{30}. It may conveniently be taken as the computer's word size, since this makes the computation of $(aX + c) \bmod m$ quite efficient. Section 3.2.1.1 discusses the choice of m in more detail. The computation of $(aX + c) \bmod m$ must be done *exactly*, with no roundoff error.

iii) If m is a power of 2 (that is, if a binary computer is being used), pick a so that $a \bmod 8 = 5$. If m is a power of 10 (that is, if a decimal computer is being used), choose a so that $a \bmod 200 = 21$. This choice of a together with the choice of c given below ensures that the random number generator will produce all m different possible values of X before it starts to repeat (see Section 3.2.1.2) and ensures high "potency" (see Section 3.2.1.3).

iv) The multiplier a should preferably be chosen between $.01m$ and $.99m$, and its binary or decimal digits should *not* have a simple, regular pattern. By choosing some haphazard constant like $a = 3141592621$ (which satisfies both of the conditions in (iii)), one almost always obtains a reasonably good multiplier. Further testing should of course be done if the random number generator is to be used extensively; for example, there should be no large quotients when Euclid's algorithm is used to find the gcd of a and m (see Section 3.3.3). The multiplier should pass the spectral test (Section 3.3.4) and several tests of Section 3.3.2, before it is considered to have a truly clean bill of health.

v) The value of c is immaterial when a is a good multiplier, except that c must have no factor in common with m when m is the computer's word size. Thus we may choose $c = 1$ or $c = a$. Many people have used $c = 0$ together with $m = 2^e$, but they are sacrificing two bits of accuracy and half of the seed values just to save a few nanoseconds of running time (see exercise 3.2.1.2–9).

vi) The least significant (right-hand) digits of X are not very random, so decisions based on the number X should always be influenced primarily by the most significant digits. It is generally best to think of X as a random fraction X/m between 0 and 1, that is, to visualize X with a radix point at its left, rather than to regard X as a random integer between 0 and $m - 1$. To compute a random integer between 0 and $k - 1$, one should multiply by k and truncate the result. (Don't divide by k; see exercise 3.4.1–3.)

vii) An important limitation on the randomness of sequence (1) is discussed in Section 3.3.4, where it is shown that the "accuracy" in t dimensions will be only about one part in $\sqrt[t]{m}$. Monte Carlo applications requiring higher resolution can improve the randomness by employing techniques discussed in Section 3.2.2.

viii) At most about $m/1000$ numbers should be generated; otherwise the future will behave more and more like the past. If $m = 2^{32}$, this means that a new scheme (for example, a new multiplier a) should be adopted after every few million random numbers are consumed.

The comments above apply primarily to machine-language coding. Some of the ideas work fine also in higher-level languages for programming; for example, (1) becomes just 'X=a*X+c' in the C language, if X is of type **unsigned long** and if m is the modulus of **unsigned long** arithmetic (usually 2^{32} or 2^{64}). But C gives us no good way to regard X as a fraction, as required in (vi) above, unless we convert to double-precision floating point numbers.

Another variant of (1) is therefore often used in languages like C: We choose m to be a prime number near the largest easily computed integer, and we let a be a primitive root of m; the appropriate increment c for this case is zero. Then (1) can be implemented entirely with simple arithmetic on numbers that remain between $-m$ and $+m$, using the technique of exercise 3.2.1.1–9. For example, when $a = 48271$ and $m = 2^{31} - 1$ (see line 20 of Table 3.3.4–1), we can compute $X \leftarrow aX \bmod m$ with the C code

```
#define MM 2147483647              /* a Mersenne prime */
#define AA 48271   /* this does well in the spectral test */
#define QQ 44488   /* MM / AA */
#define RR 3399    /* MM % AA; it is important that RR<QQ */
X=AA*(X%QQ)-RR*(X/QQ);
if (X<0) X+=MM;
```

here X is type `long`, and X should be initialized to a nonzero seed value less than MM. Since MM is prime, the least-significant bits of X are just as random as the most-significant bits, so the precautions of (vi) no longer need to be taken.

If you need millions and millions of random numbers, you can combine that routine with another, as in Eq. 3.3.4–(38), by writing some additional code:

```
#define MMM 2147483399            /* a non-Mersenne prime */
#define AAA 40692      /* another spectral success story */
#define QQQ 52774      /* MMM / AAA */
#define RRR 3791       /* MMM % AAA; again less than QQQ */
Y=AAA*(Y%QQQ)-RRR*(Y/QQQ);
if (Y<0) Y+=MMM;
Z=X-Y; if (Z<=0) Z+=MM-1;
```

Like X, the variable Y needs to be initially nonzero. This code deviates slightly from 3.3.4–(38) so that the output, Z, always lies strictly between 0 and $2^{31} - 1$, as recommended by Liviu Lalescu. The period length of the Z sequence is about 74 quadrillion, and its numbers now have about twice as many bits of accuracy as the X numbers do.

This method is portable and fairly simple, but not very fast. An alternative scheme based on lagged Fibonacci sequences with subtraction (exercise 3.2.2–23) is even more attractive, because it not only allows easy portability between computers, it is considerably faster, and it delivers random numbers of better quality because the t-dimensional accuracy is probably good for $t \leq 100$. Here is a C subroutine $ran\_array(\textbf{long } aa[], \textbf{ int } n)$ that generates n new random numbers and places them into a given array aa, using the recurrence

$$X_j = (X_{j-100} - X_{j-37}) \bmod 2^{30}. \tag{2}$$

This recurrence is particularly well suited to modern computers. The value of n must be at least 100; larger values like 1000 are recommended.

```
#define KK 100                              /* the long lag */
#define LL  37                              /* the short lag */
#define MM (1L<<30)                         /* the modulus */
#define mod_diff(x,y) (((x)-(y))&(MM-1))    /* (x-y) mod MM */
long ran_x[KK];                        /* the generator state */
void ran_array(long aa[],int n) { /* put n new values in aa */
  register int i,j;
  for (j=0;j<KK;j++) aa[j]=ran_x[j];
  for (;j<n;j++) aa[j]=mod_diff(aa[j-KK],aa[j-LL]);
  for (i=0;i<LL;i++,j++) ran_x[i]=mod_diff(aa[j-KK],aa[j-LL]);
  for (;i<KK;i++,j++) ran_x[i]=mod_diff(aa[j-KK],ran_x[i-LL]);
}
```

All information about numbers that will be generated by future calls to ran_array appears in ran_x, so you can make a copy of that array in the midst of a computation if you want to restart at the same point later without going all the way back to the beginning of the sequence. The tricky thing about using a recurrence like (2) is, of course, to get everything started properly in the first place, by setting up suitable values of $X_0, \ldots, X_{99}$. The following subroutine *ran_start*(**long** *seed*) initializes the generator nicely when given any seed number between 0 and $2^{30} - 3 = 1{,}073{,}741{,}821$ inclusive:

```
#define TT  70      /* guaranteed separation between streams */
#define is_odd(x)   ((x)&1)               /* the units bit of x */
void ran_start(long seed) { /* use this to set up ran_array */
  register int t,j;
  long x[KK+KK-1];                      /* the preparation buffer */
  register long ss=(seed+2)&(MM-2);
  for (j=0;j<KK;j++) {
    x[j]=ss;                            /* bootstrap the buffer */
    ss<<=1; if (ss>=MM) ss-=MM-2;   /* cyclic shift 29 bits */
  }
  x[1]++;                         /* make x[1] (and only x[1]) odd */
  for (ss=seed&(MM-1),t=TT-1; t; ) {
    for (j=KK-1;j>0;j--)
      x[j+j]=x[j], x[j+j-1]=0;                        /* "square" */
    for (j=KK+KK-2;j>=KK;j--)
      x[j-(KK-LL)]=mod_diff(x[j-(KK-LL)],x[j]),
      x[j-KK]=mod_diff(x[j-KK],x[j]);
    if (is_odd(ss)) {                       /* "multiply by z" */
      for (j=KK;j>0;j--)  x[j]=x[j-1];
      x[0]=x[KK];               /* shift the buffer cyclically */
      x[LL]=mod_diff(x[LL],x[KK]);
    }
    if (ss) ss>>=1; else t--;
  }
  for (j=0;j<LL;j++) ran_x[j+KK-LL]=x[j];
  for (;j<KK;j++) ran_x[j-LL]=x[j];
  for (j=0;j<10;j++) ran_array(x,KK+KK-1);     /* warm it up */
}
```

(This program incorporates improvements to the author's original *ran_start* routine, recommended by Richard Brent and Pedro Gimeno in November 2001.)

The somewhat curious maneuverings of *ran_start* are explained in exercise 9, which proves that the sequences of numbers generated from different starting seeds are independent of each other: *Every block of 100 consecutive values* X_n, $X_{n+1}, \ldots, X_{n+99}$ *in the subsequent output of* ran_array *will be distinct from the blocks that occur with another seed*. (Strictly speaking, this is known to be true only when $n < 2^{70}$; but there are fewer than 2^{55} nanoseconds in a year.) Several processes can therefore start in parallel with different seeds and be sure that they are doing independent calculations; different groups of scientists working on a problem in different computer centers can be sure that they are not duplicating the work of others if they restrict themselves to disjoint sets of seeds. Thus, more than one billion essentially disjoint batches of random numbers are provided by the single routines *ran_array* and *ran_start*. And if that is not enough, you can replace the program parameters 100 and 37 by other values from Table 3.2.2–1.

These C routines use the bitwise-and operation '&' for efficiency, so they are not strictly portable unless the computer uses two's complement representation for integers. Almost all modern computers are based on two's complement arithmetic, but '&' is not really necessary for this algorithm. Exercise 10 shows how to get exactly the same sequences of numbers in FORTRAN, using no such tricks. Although the programs illustrated here are designed to generate 30-bit integers, they are easily modified to generate random 52-bit fractions between 0 and 1, on computers that have reliable floating point arithmetic; see exercise 11.

You may wish to include *ran_array* in a library of subroutines, or you may find that somebody else has already done so. One way to check whether an implementation of *ran_array* and *ran_start* conforms with the code above is to run the following rudimentary test program:

```
int main() { register int m; long a[2009];
  ran_start(310952);
  for (m=0;m<2009;m++) ran_array(a,1009);
  printf("%ld\n", ran_x[0]);
  ran_start(310952);
  for (m=0;m<1009;m++) ran_array(a,2009);
  printf("%ld\n", ran_x[0]); return 0;
}
```

The printed output should be **995235265** (twice).

Caution: The numbers generated by *ran_array* fail the birthday spacings test of Section 3.3.2J, and they have other deficiencies that sometimes show up in high-resolution simulations (see exercises 3.3.2–31 and 3.3.2–35). One way to avoid the birthday spacings problem is simply to use only half of the numbers (skipping the odd-numbered elements); but that doesn't cure the other problems. An even better procedure is to follow Martin Lüscher's suggestion, discussed in Section 3.2.2: Use *ran_array* to generate, say, 1009 numbers, but use only the first 100 of these. (See exercise 15.) *This method has modest theoretical support and no known defects.* Most users will not need such a precaution, but it is definitely less risky, and it allows a convenient tradeoff between randomness and speed.

A great deal is known about linear congruential sequences like (1), but comparatively little has yet been proved about the randomness properties of lagged Fibonacci sequences like (2). Both approaches seem to be reliable in practice, if they are used with the caveats already stated.

When this chapter was first written in the late 1960s, a truly horrible random number generator called RANDU was commonly used on most of the world's computers (see Section 3.3.4). The authors of many contributions to the science of random number generation have often been unaware that particular methods they were advocating would prove to be inadequate. A particularly noteworthy example was the experience of Alan M. Ferrenberg and his colleagues, reported in *Physical Review Letters* **69** (1992), 3382–3384: They tested their algorithms for a three-dimensional problem by considering first a related two-dimensional problem with a known answer, and discovered that supposedly super-quality modern random number generators gave wrong results in the fifth decimal place. By contrast, an old-fashioned run-of-the-mill linear congruential generator, $X \leftarrow 16807X \bmod (2^{31} - 1)$, worked fine. Perhaps further research will show that even the random number generators recommended here are unsatisfactory; we hope this is not the case, but the history of the subject warns us to be cautious. The most prudent policy for a person to follow is to run each Monte Carlo program at least twice using quite different sources of random numbers, before taking the answers of the program seriously; this will not only give an indication of the stability of the results, it also will guard against the danger of trusting in a generator with hidden deficiencies. (Every random number generator will fail in at least one application.)

Excellent bibliographies of the pre-1972 literature on random number generation have been compiled by Richard E. Nance and Claude Overstreet, Jr., *Computing Reviews* **13** (1972), 495–508, and by E. R. Sowey, *International Stat. Review* **40** (1972), 355–371. The period 1972–1984 is covered by Sowey in *International Stat. Review* **46** (1978), 89–102; *J. Royal Stat. Soc.* **A149** (1986), 83–107. Subsequent developments are discussed by Shu Tezuka, *Uniform Random Numbers* (Boston: Kluwer, 1995).

For a detailed study of the use of random numbers in numerical analysis, see J. M. Hammersley and D. C. Handscomb, *Monte Carlo Methods* (London: Methuen, 1964). This book shows that some numerical methods are enhanced by using numbers that are "quasirandom," designed specifically for a certain purpose (not necessarily satisfying the statistical tests we have discussed). The origins of Monte Carlo methods for computers are discussed by N. Metropolis and R. Eckhardt in *Stanislaw Ulam 1909–1984*, a special issue of *Los Alamos Science* **15** (1987), 125–137.

Every reader is urged to work exercise 6 in the following set of problems.

EXERCISES

1. [*21*] Write a `MIX` subroutine with the following characteristics, using method (1):

   Calling sequence:　`JMP RANDI`

   Entry conditions:　rA $= k$, a positive integer < 5000.

   Exit conditions:　rA $\leftarrow$ a random integer Y, $1 \leq Y \leq k$, with each integer about equally probable; rX $=$?; overflow off.

▶ 2. [*15*] Some people have been afraid that computers will someday take over the world; but they are reassured by the statement that a machine cannot do anything really new, since it is only obeying the commands of its master, the programmer. Lady Lovelace wrote in 1844, "The Analytical Engine has no pretensions to *originate* anything. It can do *whatever we know how to order it* to perform." Her statement has been elaborated further by many philosophers. Discuss this topic, with random number generators in mind.

3. [*32*] (*A dice game.*) Write a program that simulates a roll of two dice, each of which takes on the values 1, 2, ..., 6 with equal probability. If the total is 7 or 11 on the first roll, the game is won; a total of 2, 3, or 12 loses; and on any other total, call that total the "point" and continue rolling dice until either a 7 occurs (a loss) or the point occurs again (a win).

Play ten games. The result of each roll of the dice should be printed in the form $m\,n$, where m and n are the contents of the two dice, followed by some appropriate comment (like "snake eyes" or "little Joe" or "the hard way", etc.).

4. [*40*] (*Solitaire or patience.*) Some people spend a lot of valuable time playing card games of solitaire, and perhaps automation will make an important inroad in this area. Write a program that (i) shuffles a simulated deck of cards; (ii) plays some common game of solitaire based on the order of the cards in the deck; and (iii) displays the result of the game, showing how close the program came to winning. Cumulative statistics should be kept. The program might be set up to "cheat" upon request.

5. [*46*] (*Creative writing by computer.*) A television program entitled "The Thinking Machine," broadcast by the CBS television network on October 26, 1960, featured (among other things) two Western-style playlets that were written by a computer program. Here are the two scripts as they were printed out by the computer:

Saga #1. (The gun is in the right hand; the money is in the left hand; the glass is on the table; the bottle is on the table; the holster is on the robber; the sheriff's gun is in the sheriff's right hand; the sheriff's holster is on the sheriff.)

ROBBER: (The robber is at the window.) Go to door; open door; go thru door; close door; go to corner; put money down at corner; go to table; put gun on table; sit and fidget; sit at table; pick up glass with right hand (empty); put glass on table; pick up bottle with right hand; pour; put bottle on table; pick up glass with right hand; take a drink from glass; put glass on table; pick up bottle with right hand; sit at table; sit at table; go to corner; go to window; go to table; put bottle on table; sit and fidget; sit at table; sit and fidget; go to window; go to table; pick up glass with right hand.

SHERIFF: (The sheriff is at the window.) See robber; (robber sees sheriff); go to door.

ROBBER: Put glass on table; pick up gun with right hand; check gun.

SHERIFF: Wait; open door; see robber; (robber sees sheriff); go thru door.

ROBBER: Go to window; aim; fire; SHERIFF NICKED.

SHERIFF: Go to window; aim; fire; MISSED; go to door; go to window.

ROBBER: Go to door; aim; aim.

SHERIFF: Aim; fire; MISSED.

ROBBER: Fire; SHERIFF NICKED.

SHERIFF: Go to door; aim; fire; MISSED; go thru door; aim.

ROBBER: Aim; fire; MISSED; aim; fire; MISSED.

SHERIFF: Fire; MISSED; go to window; aim; fire; MISSED.

ROBBER: Aim; fire; MISSED; aim; fire; MISSED; aim; fire; SHERIFF NICKED.

SHERIFF: Aim; fire; ROBBER HIT.

ROBBER: Drop gun; robber dies.

SHERIFF: Put gun in holster; go to table; pick up glass with right hand (empty); take glass from right hand with left hand; pick up bottle with right hand; pour; put bottle on table; take glass from left hand with right hand; take a drink from glass; take glass from right hand with left hand; pick up bottle with right hand; pour; put bottle on table; take glass from left hand with right hand; take a drink from glass; put glass on table; go to corner; pick up money with right hand; go to door; go thru door; close door. CURTAIN.

Saga #2. (The gun is in the right hand; the money is in the left hand; the glass is on the table; the bottle is on the table; the holster is on the robber; the sheriff's gun is in the sheriff's right hand; the sheriff's holster is on the sheriff.)

ROBBER: (The robber is at the window.) Go to door; open door; go thru door; close door; go to corner; put money down at corner; go to window; put gun down at window; lean on window and look; lean on window and look; go to corner; count money; go to table; pick up glass with right hand (empty); take glass from right hand with left hand; pick up bottle with right hand; pour; put bottle on table; take glass from left hand with right hand; take a drink from glass; put glass on table; pick up bottle with right hand; pour; go to corner; put bottle down at corner; go to window; pick up gun with right hand; check gun; put gun in holster; go to table; pick up glass with right hand; take a drink from glass; go to window; put glass down at window.

SHERIFF: (The sheriff is at the window.) See robber; (robber sees sheriff); go to door.

ROBBER: Take gun from holster with right hand; check gun; go to door; check gun; put gun down at door.

SHERIFF: Open door; see robber; (robber sees sheriff); go thru door; go to window.

ROBBER: Pick up gun with right hand.

SHERIFF: Go to table.

ROBBER: Aim; fire; MISSED; aim; fire; SHERIFF HIT; blow out barrel; put gun in holster.

SHERIFF: Drop gun; sheriff dies.

ROBBER: Go to corner; pick up money with right hand; go to door; go thru door; close door. CURTAIN.

A careful reading of these scripts reveals the highly intense drama present here. The computer program was careful to keep track of the locations of each player, the contents of his hands, etc. Actions taken by the players were random, governed by certain probabilities; the probability of a foolish action was increased depending on how much that player had had to drink and on how often he had been nicked by a shot. The reader will be able to deduce further properties of the program by studying the sample scripts.

Of course, even the best scripts are rewritten before they are produced, and this is especially true when an inexperienced writer has prepared the original draft. Here are the scripts just as they were actually used in the show:

Saga #1.   Music up.
MS Robber peering thru window of shack.
CU Robber's face.
MS Robber entering shack.
CU Robber sees whiskey bottle on table.
CU Sheriff outside shack.
MS Robber sees sheriff.
LS Sheriff in doorway over shoulder of robber, both draw.
MS Sheriff drawing gun.
LS Shooting it out. Robber gets shot.
MS Sheriff picking up money bags.
MS Robber staggering.
MS Robber dying. Falls across table, after trying to take last shot at sheriff.
MS Sheriff walking thru doorway with money.
MS of robber's body, now still, lying across table top. Camera dollies back. (Laughter)

Saga #2.   Music up.
CU of window. Robber appears.
MS Robber entering shack with two sacks of money.
MS Robber puts money bags on barrel.
CU Robber — sees whiskey on table.
MS Robber pouring himself a drink at table. Goes to count money. Laughs.
MS Sheriff outside shack.
MS thru window.
MS Robber sees sheriff thru window.
LS Sheriff entering shack. Draw. Shoot it out.
CU Sheriff. Writhing from shot.
M/2 shot Sheriff staggering to table for a drink . . . falls dead.
MS Robber leaves shack with money bags.*

[*Note:* CU = "close up", MS = "medium shot", etc. The details above were kindly furnished to the author by Thomas H. Wolf, producer of the television show, who suggested the idea of a computer-written playlet in the first place, and also by Douglas T. Ross and Harrison R. Morse who produced the computer program.]

In the summer of 1952, Christopher Strachey had used the hardware random number generator of the Ferranti Mark I to compose the following letter:

Honey Dear
     My sympathetic affection beautifully attracts your affectionate enthusiasm. You are my loving adoration: my breathless adoration. My fellow feeling breathlessly hopes for your dear eagerness. My lovesick adoration cherishes your avid ardour.

                                          Yours wistfully,
                                          M. U. C.

[*Encounter* **3** (1954), 4, 25–31; another example appears in the article on Electronic Computers in the 64th edition of *Pears Cyclopedia* (London, 1955), 190–191.]

The reader will undoubtedly have many ideas about how to teach a computer to do creative writing; and that is the point of this exercise.

▶ **6.** [*40*] Look at the subroutine library of each computer installation in your organization, and replace the random number generators by good ones. Try to avoid being too shocked at what you find.

▶ **7.** [*M40*] A programmer decided to encipher his files by using a linear congruential sequence $\langle X_n \rangle$ of period 2^{32} generated by (1) with $m = 2^{32}$. He took the most significant bits $\lfloor X_n/2^{16} \rfloor$ and exclusive-or'ed them onto his data, but kept the parameters a, c, and X_0 secret.

Show that this isn't a very secure scheme, by devising a method that deduces the multiplier a and the first difference $X_1 - X_0$ in a reasonable amount of time, given only the values of $\lfloor X_n/2^{16} \rfloor$ for $0 \le n < 150$.

8. [*M15*] Suggest a good way to test whether an implementation of linear congruential generators is working properly.

9. [*HM32*] Let X_0, X_1, ... be the numbers produced by *ran_array* after *ran_start* has initialized the generation process with seed s, and consider the polynomials

$$P_n(z) = X_{n+62}z^{99} + X_{n+61}z^{98} + \cdots + X_n z^{37} + X_{n+99}z^{36} + \cdots + X_{n+64}z + X_{n+63}.$$

a) Prove that $P_n(z) \equiv z^{h(s)-n}$ (modulo 2 and $z^{100} + z^{37} + 1$), for some exponent $h(s)$.
b) Express $h(s)$ in terms of the binary representation of s.
c) Prove that if X_0', X_1', ... is the sequence of numbers produced by the same routines from the seed $s' \ne s$, we have $X_{n+k} \equiv X_{n'+k}'$ (modulo 2) for $0 \le k < 100$ only if $|n - n'| \ge 2^{70} - 1$.

10. [*22*] Convert the C code for *ran_array* and *ran_start* to FORTRAN 77 subroutines that generate exactly the same sequences of numbers.

▶ **11.** [*M25*] Assuming that floating point arithmetic on numbers of type **double** is properly rounded in the sense of Section 4.2.2 (hence exact when the values are suitably restricted), convert the C routines *ran_array* and *ran_start* to similar programs that deliver double-precision random fractions in the range $[0 . . 1)$, instead of 30-bit integers.

▶ **12.** [*M21*] What random number generator would be suitable for a minicomputer that does arithmetic only on integers in the range $[-32768 . . 32767]$?

13. [*M25*] Compare the subtract-with-borrow generators of exercise 3.2.1.1–12 to the lagged Fibonacci generators implemented in the programs of this section.

▶ **14.** [*M35*] (*The future versus the past.*) Let $X_n = (X_{n-37} + X_{n-100}) \bmod 2$ and consider the sequence

$$\langle Y_0, Y_1, \ldots \rangle = \langle X_0, X_1, \ldots, X_{99}, X_{200}, X_{201}, \ldots, X_{299}, X_{400}, X_{401}, \ldots, X_{499}, X_{600}, \ldots \rangle.$$

(This sequence corresponds to calling *ran_array*$(a, 200)$ repeatedly and looking only at the least significant bits, after discarding half of the elements.) The following experiment was repeated one million times using the sequence $\langle Y_n \rangle$: "Generate 100 random bits; then if 60 or more of them were 0, generate one more bit and print it." The result was to print 14527 0s and 13955 1s; but the probability that 28482 random bits contain at most 13955 1s is only about .000358.

Give a mathematical explanation why so many 0s were output.

▶ **15.** [*25*] Write C code that makes it convenient to generate the random integers obtained from *ran_array* by discarding all but the first 100 of every 1009 elements, as recommended in the text.

CHAPTER FOUR

ARITHMETIC

*Seeing there is nothing (right well beloued Students in the Mathematickes)
that is so troublesome to Mathematicall practise, nor that doth more molest
and hinder Calculators, then the Multiplications, Diuisions, square and
cubical Extractions of great numbers, which besides the tedious
expence of time, are for the most part subiect to many slippery errors.
I began therefore to consider in my minde, by what certaine and
ready Art I might remoue those hindrances.*

— JOHN NEPAIR [NAPIER] (1616)

I do hate sums. There is no greater mistake than to call arithmetic an exact
*science. There are . . . hidden laws of Number which it requires a mind
like mine to perceive. For instance, if you add a sum from the bottom up,
and then again from the top down, the result is always different.*

— M. P. LA TOUCHE (1878)

*I cannot conceive that anybody will require multiplications at the rate
of 40,000, or even 4,000 per hour; such a revolutionary change as the
octonary scale should not be imposed upon mankind in general
for the sake of a few individuals.*

— F. H. WALES (1936)

Most numerical analysts have no interest in arithmetic.

— B. PARLETT (1979)

THE CHIEF PURPOSE of this chapter is to make a careful study of the four
basic processes of arithmetic: addition, subtraction, multiplication, and division. Many people regard arithmetic as a trivial thing that children learn and
computers do, but we will see that arithmetic is a fascinating topic with many
interesting facets. It is important to make a thorough study of efficient methods for calculating with numbers, since arithmetic underlies so many computer
applications.

Arithmetic is, in fact, a lively subject that has played an important part in
the history of the world, and it still is undergoing rapid development. In this
chapter, we shall analyze algorithms for doing arithmetic operations on many
types of quantities, such as "floating point" numbers, extremely large numbers,
fractions (rational numbers), polynomials, and power series; and we will also
discuss related topics such as radix conversion, factoring of numbers, and the
evaluation of polynomials.

4.1. POSITIONAL NUMBER SYSTEMS

THE WAY WE DO ARITHMETIC is intimately related to the way we represent the numbers we deal with, so it is appropriate to begin our study of the subject with a discussion of the principal means for representing numbers.

Positional notation using base b (or *radix* b) is defined by the rule

$$(\ldots a_3 a_2 a_1 a_0 . a_{-1} a_{-2} \ldots)_b$$
$$= \cdots + a_3 b^3 + a_2 b^2 + a_1 b^1 + a_0 + a_{-1} b^{-1} + a_{-2} b^{-2} + \cdots; \qquad (1)$$

for example, $(520.3)_6 = 5 \cdot 6^2 + 2 \cdot 6^1 + 0 + 3 \cdot 6^{-1} = 192\frac{1}{2}$. Our conventional decimal number system is, of course, the special case when b is ten, and when the a's are chosen from the "decimal digits" 0, 1, 2, 3, 4, 5, 6, 7, 8, 9; in this case the subscript b in (1) may be omitted.

The simplest generalizations of the decimal number system are obtained when we take b to be an integer greater than 1 and when we require the a's to be integers in the range $0 \le a_k < b$. This gives us the standard binary ($b = 2$), ternary ($b = 3$), quaternary ($b = 4$), quinary ($b = 5$), ... number systems. In general, we could take b to be any nonzero number, and we could choose the a's from any specified set of numbers; this leads to some interesting situations, as we shall see.

The dot that appears between a_0 and a_{-1} in (1) is called the *radix point*. (When $b = 10$, it is also called the decimal point, and when $b = 2$, it is sometimes called the binary point, etc.) Continental Europeans often use a comma instead of a dot to denote the radix point; the English formerly used a raised dot.

The a's in (1) are called the *digits* of the representation. A digit a_k for large k is often said to be "more significant" than the digits a_k for small k; accordingly, the leftmost or "leading" digit is referred to as the *most significant digit* and the rightmost or "trailing" digit is referred to as the *least significant digit*. In the standard binary system the binary digits are often called *bits*; in the standard hexadecimal system (radix sixteen) the hexadecimal digits zero through fifteen are usually denoted by

> either   0, 1, 2, 3, 4, 5, 6, 7, 8, 9, a, b, c, d, e, f
> or   0, 1, 2, 3, 4, 5, 6, 7, 8, 9, A, B, C, D, E, F.

The historical development of number representations is a fascinating story, since it parallels the development of civilization itself. We would be going far afield if we were to examine this history in minute detail, but it will be instructive to look at its main features here.

The earliest forms of number representations, still found in primitive cultures, are generally based on groups of fingers, piles of stones, etc., usually with special conventions about replacing a larger pile or group of, say, five or ten objects by one object of a special kind or in a special place. Such systems lead naturally to the earliest ways of representing numbers in written form, as in the systems of Babylonian, Egyptian, Greek, Chinese, and Roman numerals; but such notations are comparatively inconvenient for performing arithmetic operations except in the simplest cases.

During the twentieth century, historians of mathematics have made extensive studies of early cuneiform tablets found by archæologists in the Middle East. These studies show that the Babylonian people actually had two distinct systems of number representation: The numbers used in everyday business transactions were written in a notation based on grouping by tens, hundreds, etc.; this notation was inherited from earlier Mesopotamian civilizations, and large numbers were seldom required. When more difficult mathematical problems were considered, however, Babylonian mathematicians made extensive use of a sexagesimal (radix sixty) positional notation that was highly developed at least as early as 1750 B.C. This notation was unique in that it was actually a *floating point* form of representation with exponents omitted; the proper scale factor or power of sixty was to be supplied by the context, so that, for example, the numbers 2, 120, 7200, and $\frac{1}{30}$ were all written in an identical manner. The notation was especially convenient for multiplication and division, using auxiliary tables, since radix-point alignment had no effect on the answer. As examples of this Babylonian notation, consider the following excerpts from early tables: The square of 30 is 15 (which may also be read, "The square of $\frac{1}{2}$ is $\frac{1}{4}$"); the reciprocal of $81 = (1\ 21)_{60}$ is $(44\ 26\ 40)_{60}$; and the square of the latter is $(32\ 55\ 18\ 31\ 6\ 40)_{60}$. The Babylonians had a symbol for zero, but because of their "floating point" philosophy, it was used only within numbers, not at the right end to denote a scale factor. For the interesting story of early Babylonian mathematics, see O. Neugebauer, *The Exact Sciences in Antiquity* (Princeton, N. J.: Princeton University Press, 1952), and B. L. van der Waerden, *Science Awakening*, translated by A. Dresden (Groningen: P. Noordhoff, 1954); see also D. E. Knuth, *CACM* **15** (1972), 671–677; **19** (1976), 108.

Fixed point positional notation was apparently first conceived by the Maya Indians in central America some 2000 years ago; their radix-20 system was highly developed, especially in connection with astronomical records and calendar dates. They began to use a written sign for zero about A.D. 200. But the Spanish conquerors destroyed nearly all of the Maya books on history and science, so we have comparatively little knowledge about the degree of sophistication that native Americans had reached in arithmetic. Special-purpose multiplication tables have been found, but no examples of division are known. [See J. Eric S. Thompson, *Contrib. to Amer. Anthropology and History* **7** (Carnegie Inst. of Washington, 1941), 37–67; J. Justeson, "Pratiche di calcolo nell'antica mesoamerica," *Storia della Scienza* **2** (Rome: Istituto della Enciclopedia Italiana, 2001), 976–990.]

Several centuries before Christ, the Greek people employed an early form of the abacus to do their arithmetical calculations, using sand and/or pebbles on a board that had rows or columns corresponding in a natural way to our decimal system. It is perhaps surprising to us that the same positional notation was never adapted to written forms of numbers, since we are so accustomed to decimal reckoning with pencil and paper; but the greater ease of calculating by abacus (since handwriting was not a common skill, and since abacus users need not memorize addition and multiplication tables) probably made the Greeks feel it would be silly even to suggest that computing could be done better on "scratch paper." At the same time Greek astronomers did make use of a sexagesimal positional notation for fractions, which they had learned from the Babylonians.

Our decimal notation, which differs from the more ancient forms primarily because of its fixed radix point, together with its symbol for zero to mark an empty position, was developed first in India within the Hindu culture. The exact date when this notation first appeared is quite uncertain; about A.D. 600 seems to be a good guess. Hindu science was highly developed at that time, particularly in astronomy. The earliest known Hindu manuscripts that show decimal notation have numbers written backwards (with the most significant digit at the right), but soon it became standard to put the most significant digit at the left.

The Hindu principles of decimal arithmetic were brought to Persia about A.D. 750, as several important works were translated into Arabic; a picturesque account of this development is given in a Hebrew document by Abraham Ibn Ezra, which has been translated into English in *AMM* **25** (1918), 99–108. Not long after this, al-Khwārizmī wrote his Arabic textbook on the subject. (As noted in Chapter 1, our word "algorithm" comes from al-Khwārizmī's name.) His work was translated into Latin and was a strong influence on Leonardo Pisano (Fibonacci), whose book on arithmetic (A.D. 1202) played a major role in the spreading of Hindu-Arabic numerals into Europe. It is interesting to note that the left-to-right order of writing numbers was unchanged during these two transitions, although Arabic is written from right to left while Hindu and Latin scholars generally wrote from left to right. A detailed account of the subsequent propagation of decimal numeration and arithmetic into all parts of Europe during the period 1200–1600 has been given by David Eugene Smith in his *History of Mathematics* **1** (Boston: Ginn and Co., 1923), Chapters 6 and 8.

Decimal notation was applied at first only to integer numbers, not to fractions. Arabic astronomers, who required fractions in their star charts and other tables, continued to use the notation of Ptolemy (the famous Greek astronomer), a notation based on sexagesimal fractions. This system still survives today in our trigonometric units of degrees, minutes, and seconds, and also in our units of time, as a remnant of the original Babylonian sexagesimal notation. Early European mathematicians also used sexagesimal fractions when dealing with noninteger numbers; for example, Fibonacci gave the value

$$1° \ 22' \ 7'' \ 42''' \ 33^{IV} \ 4^{V} \ 40^{VI}$$

as an approximation to the root of the equation $x^3 + 2x^2 + 10x = 20$. (The correct answer is $1° \ 22' \ 7'' \ 42''' \ 33^{IV} \ 4^{V} \ 38^{VI} \ 30^{VII} \ 50^{VIII} \ 15^{IX} \ 43^{X} \ \ldots$.)

The use of decimal notation also for tenths, hundredths, etc., in a similar way seems to be a comparatively minor change; but, of course, it is hard to break with tradition, and sexagesimal fractions have an advantage over decimal fractions because numbers such as $\frac{1}{3}$ can be expressed exactly, in a simple way.

Chinese mathematicians — who never used sexagesimals — were apparently the first people to work with the equivalent of decimal fractions, although their numeral system (lacking zero) was not originally a positional number system in the strict sense. Chinese units of weights and measures were decimal, so that

Tsu Ch'ung-Chih (who died in A.D. 500 or 501) was able to express an approximation to π in the following form:

3 chang, 1 ch'in, 4 ts'un, 1 fen, 5 li, 9 hao, 2 miao, 7 hu.

Here chang, ..., hu are units of length; 1 hu (the diameter of a silk thread) equals 1/10 miao, etc. The use of such decimal-like fractions was fairly widespread in China after about 1250.

An embryonic form of truly positional decimal fractions appeared in a 10th-century arithmetic text, written in Damascus by an obscure mathematician named al-Uqlīdisī ("the Euclidean"). He occasionally marked the place of a decimal point, for example in connection with a problem about compound interest, the computation of 135 times $(1.1)^n$ for $1 \le n \le 5$. [See A. S. Saidan, *The Arithmetic of al-Uqlīdisī* (Dordrecht: D. Reidel, 1975), 110, 114, 343, 355, 481–485.] But he did not develop the idea very fully, and his trick was soon forgotten. Al-Samaw'al of Baghdad and Baku, writing in 1172, understood that $\sqrt{10} = 3.162277\ldots$, but he had no convenient way to write such approximations down. Several centuries passed before decimal fractions were reinvented by a Persian mathematician, al-Kāshī, who died in 1429. Al-Kāshī was a highly skillful calculator, who gave the value of 2π as follows, correct to 16 decimal places:

integer		fractions														
0	6	2	8	3	1	8	5	3	0	7	1	7	9	5	8	6	5

This was by far the best approximation to π known until Ludolph van Ceulen laboriously calculated 35 decimal places during the period 1586–1610.

Decimal fractions began to appear sporadically in Europe; for example, a so-called "Turkish method" was used to compute $153.5 \times 16.25 = 2494.375$. Giovanni Bianchini developed them further, with applications to surveying, prior to 1450; but like al-Uqlīdisī, his work seems to have had little influence. Christof Rudolff and François Viète suggested the idea again in 1525 and 1579. Finally, an arithmetic text by Simon Stevin, who independently hit on the idea of decimal fractions in 1585, became popular. Stevin's work, and the discovery of logarithms soon afterwards, made decimal fractions commonplace in Europe during the 17th century. [For further remarks and references, see D. E. Smith, *History of Mathematics* **2** (1925), 228–247; V. J. Katz, *A History of Mathematics* (1993), 225–228, 345–348; and G. Rosińska, *Quart. J. Hist. Sci. Tech.* **40** (1995), 17–32.]

The binary system of notation has its own interesting history. Many primitive tribes in existence today are known to use a binary or "pair" system of counting (making groups of two instead of five or ten), but they do not count in a true radix-2 system, since they do not treat powers of 2 in a special manner. See *The Diffusion of Counting Practices* by Abraham Seidenberg, *Univ. of Calif. Publ. in Math.* **3** (1960), 215–300, for interesting details about primitive number systems. Another "primitive" example of an essentially binary system is the conventional musical notation for expressing rhythms and durations of time.

Nondecimal number systems were discussed in Europe during the seventeenth century. For many years astronomers had occasionally used sexagesimal arithmetic both for the integer and the fractional parts of numbers, primarily when performing multiplication [see John Wallis, *Treatise of Algebra* (Oxford: 1685), 18–22, 30]. The fact that *any* integer greater than 1 could serve as radix was apparently first stated in print by Blaise Pascal in *De Numeris Multiplicibus*, which was written about 1658 [see Pascal's *Œuvres Complètes* (Paris: Éditions du Seuil, 1963), 84–89]. Pascal wrote, "Denaria enim ex instituto hominum, non ex necessitate naturæ ut vulgus arbitratur, et sane satis inepte, posita est"; i.e., "The decimal system has been established, somewhat foolishly to be sure, according to man's custom, not from a natural necessity as most people think." He stated that the duodecimal (radix twelve) system would be a welcome change, and he gave a rule for testing a duodecimal number for divisibility by nine. Erhard Weigel tried to drum up enthusiasm for the quaternary (radix four) system in a series of publications beginning in 1673. A detailed discussion of radix-twelve arithmetic was given by Joshua Jordaine, *Duodecimal Arithmetick* (London: 1687).

Although decimal notation was almost exclusively used for arithmetic during that era, other systems of weights and measures were rarely if ever based on multiples of 10, and business transactions required a good deal of skill in adding quantities such as pounds, shillings, and pence. For centuries merchants had therefore learned to compute sums and differences of quantities expressed in peculiar units of currency, weights, and measures; thus they were doing arithmetic in nondecimal number systems. The common units of liquid measure in England, dating from the 13th century or earlier, are particularly noteworthy:

2 gills = 1 chopin
2 chopins = 1 pint
2 pints = 1 quart
2 quarts = 1 pottle
2 pottles = 1 gallon
2 gallons = 1 peck
2 pecks = 1 demibushel

2 demibushels = 1 bushel or firkin
2 firkins = 1 kilderkin
2 kilderkins = 1 barrel
2 barrels = 1 hogshead
2 hogsheads = 1 pipe
2 pipes = 1 tun

Quantities of liquid expressed in gallons, pottles, quarts, pints, etc. were essentially written in binary notation. Perhaps the true inventors of binary arithmetic were British wine merchants!

The first known appearance of pure binary notation was about 1605 in some unpublished manuscripts of Thomas Harriot (1560–1621). Harriot was a creative man who first became famous by coming to America as a representative of Sir Walter Raleigh. He invented (among other things) a notation like that now used for "less than" and "greater than" relations; but for some reason he chose not to publish many of his discoveries. Excerpts from his notes on binary arithmetic have been reproduced by John W. Shirley, *Amer. J. Physics* **19** (1951), 452–454; Harriot's discovery of binary notation was first cited by Frank Morley in *The Scientific Monthly* **14** (1922), 60–66.

The first published treatment of the binary system appeared in the work of a prominent Cistercian bishop, Juan Caramuel de Lobkowitz, *Mathesis Biceps* **1**

(Campaniæ: 1670), 45–48. Caramuel discussed the representation of numbers in radices 2, 3, 4, 5, 6, 7, 8, 9, 10, 12, and 60 at some length, but gave no examples of arithmetic operations in nondecimal systems except in the sexagesimal case.

Ultimately, an article by G. W. Leibniz [*Mémoires de l'Académie Royale des Sciences* (Paris, 1703), 110–116], which illustrated binary addition, subtraction, multiplication, and division, really brought binary notation into the limelight, and his article is usually referred to as the birth of radix-2 arithmetic. Leibniz later referred to the binary system quite frequently. He did not recommend it for practical calculations, but he stressed its importance in number-theoretical investigations, since patterns in number sequences are often more apparent in binary notation than they are in decimal; he also saw a mystical significance in the fact that everything is expressible in terms of zero and one. Leibniz's unpublished manuscripts show that he had been interested in binary notation as early as 1679, when he referred to it as a "bimal" system (analogous to "decimal").

A careful study of Leibniz's early work with binary numbers has been made by Hans J. Zacher, *Die Hauptschriften zur Dyadik von G. W. Leibniz* (Frankfurt am Main: Klostermann, 1973). Zacher points out that Leibniz was familiar with John Napier's so-called "local arithmetic," a way for calculating with stones that amounts to using a radix-2 abacus. [Napier had published the idea of local arithmetic as an appendix to his little book *Rhabdologia* in 1617; it may be called the world's first "binary computer," and it is surely the world's cheapest, although Napier felt that it was more amusing than practical. See Martin Gardner's discussion in *Knotted Doughnuts and Other Mathematical Entertainments* (New York: Freeman, 1986), Chapter 8.]

It is interesting to note that the important concept of negative powers to the right of the radix point was not yet well understood at that time. Leibniz asked James Bernoulli to calculate π in the binary system, and Bernoulli "solved" the problem by taking a 35-digit approximation to π, multiplying it by 10^{35}, and then expressing this integer in the binary system as his answer. On a smaller scale this would be like saying that $\pi \approx 3.14$, and $(314)_{10} = (100111010)_2$; hence π in binary is 100111010! [See Leibniz, *Math. Schriften*, edited by C. I. Gerhardt, **3** (Halle: 1855), 97; two of the 118 bits in the answer are incorrect, due to computational errors.] The motive for Bernoulli's calculation was apparently to see whether any simple pattern could be observed in this representation of π.

Charles XII of Sweden, whose talent for mathematics perhaps exceeded that of all other kings in the history of the world, hit on the idea of radix-8 arithmetic about 1717. This was probably his own invention, although he had met Leibniz briefly in 1707. Charles felt that radix 8 or 64 would be more convenient for calculation than the decimal system, and he considered introducing octal arithmetic into Sweden; but he died in battle before decreeing such a change. [See *The Works of Voltaire* **21** (Paris: E. R. DuMont, 1901), 49; E. Swedenborg, *Gentleman's Magazine* **24** (1754), 423–424.]

Octal notation was proposed also in colonial America before 1750, by the Rev. Hugh Jones, professor at the College of William and Mary [see *Gentleman's Magazine* **15** (1745), 377–379; H. R. Phalen, *AMM* **56** (1949), 461–465].

More than a century later, a prominent Swedish-American civil engineer named John W. Nystrom decided to carry Charles XII's plans a step further, by devising a complete system of numeration, weights, and measures based on radix-16 arithmetic. He wrote, "I am not afraid, or do not hesitate, to advocate a binary system of arithmetic and metrology. I know I have nature on my side; if I do not succeed to impress upon you its utility and great importance to mankind, it will reflect that much less credit upon our generation, upon our scientific men and philosophers." Nystrom devised special means for pronouncing hexadecimal numbers; for example, $(C0160)_{16}$ was to be read "vybong, bysanton." His entire system was called the Tonal System, and it is described in *J. Franklin Inst.* **46** (1863), 263–275, 337–348, 402–407. A similar system, but using radix 8, was worked out by Alfred B. Taylor [*Proc. Amer. Pharmaceutical Assoc.* **8** (1859), 115–216; *Proc. Amer. Philosophical Soc.* **24** (1887), 296–366]. Increased use of the French (metric) system of weights and measures prompted extensive debate about the merits of decimal arithmetic during that era; indeed, octal arithmetic was even being proposed in France [J. D. Collenne, *Le Système Octaval* (Paris: 1845); Aimé Mariage, *Numération par Huit* (Paris: Le Nonnant, 1857)].

The binary system was well known as a curiosity ever since Leibniz's time, and about 20 early references to it have been compiled by R. C. Archibald [*AMM* **25** (1918), 139–142]. It was applied chiefly to the calculation of powers, as explained in Section 4.6.3, and to the analysis of certain games and puzzles. Giuseppe Peano [*Atti della R. Accademia delle Scienze di Torino* **34** (1898), 47–55] used binary notation as the basis of a "logical" character set of 256 symbols. Joseph Bowden [*Special Topics in Theoretical Arithmetic* (Garden City: 1936), 49] gave his own system of nomenclature for hexadecimal numbers.

The book *History of Binary and Other Nondecimal Numeration* by Anton Glaser (Los Angeles: Tomash, 1981) contains an informative and nearly complete discussion of the development of binary notation, including English translations of many of the works cited above [see *Historia Math.* **10** (1983), 236–243].

Much of the recent history of number systems is connected with the development of calculating machines. Charles Babbage's notebooks for 1838 show that he considered using nondecimal numbers in his Analytical Engine [see M. V. Wilkes, *Historia Math.* **4** (1977), 421]. Increased interest in mechanical devices for arithmetic, especially for multiplication, led several people in the 1930s to consider the binary system for this purpose. A particularly delightful account of such activity appears in the article "Binary Calculation" by E. William Phillips [*Journal of the Institute of Actuaries* **67** (1936), 187–221] together with a record of the discussion that followed a lecture he gave on the subject. Phillips began by saying, "The ultimate aim [of this paper] is to persuade the whole civilized world to abandon decimal numeration and to use octonal [that is, radix 8] numeration in its place."

Modern readers of Phillips's article will perhaps be surprised to discover that a radix-8 number system was properly referred to as "octonary" or "octonal," according to all dictionaries of the English language at that time, just as the radix-10 number system is properly called either "denary" or "decimal"; the word "octal" did not appear in English language dictionaries until 1961, and it apparently originated as a term for the base of a certain class of vacuum tubes. The word "hexadecimal," which has crept into our language even more recently, is a mixture of Greek and Latin stems; more proper terms would be "senidenary" or "sedecimal" or even "sexadecimal," but the latter is perhaps too risqué for computer programmers.

The comment by Mr. Wales that is quoted at the beginning of this chapter has been taken from the discussion printed with Phillips's paper. Another man who attended the same lecture objected to the octal system for business purposes: "5% becomes $3.\dot{1}46\dot{3}$ per 64, which sounds rather horrible."

Phillips got the inspiration for his proposals from an electronic circuit that was capable of counting in binary [C. E. Wynn-Williams, *Proc. Roy. Soc. London* **A136** (1932), 312–324]. Electromechanical and electronic circuitry for general arithmetic operations was developed during the late 1930s, notably by John V. Atanasoff and George R. Stibitz in the U.S.A., L. Couffignal and R. Valtat in France, Helmut Schreyer and Konrad Zuse in Germany. All of these inventors used the binary system, although Stibitz later developed excess-3 binary-coded-decimal notation. A fascinating account of these early developments, including reprints and translations of important contemporary documents, appears in Brian Randell's book *The Origins of Digital Computers* (Berlin: Springer, 1973).

The first American high-speed computers, built in the early 1940s, used decimal arithmetic. But in 1946, an important memorandum by A. W. Burks, H. H. Goldstine, and J. von Neumann, in connection with the design of the first stored-program computers, gave detailed reasons for making a radical departure from tradition and using base-two notation [see John von Neumann, *Collected Works* **5**, 41–65]. Since then binary computers have multiplied. After a dozen years of experience with binary machines, a discussion of the relative advantages and disadvantages of radix-2 notation was given by W. Buchholz in his paper "Fingers or Fists?" [*CACM* **2**, 12 (December 1959), 3–11].

The MIX computer used in this book has been defined so that it can be either binary or decimal. It is interesting to note that nearly all MIX programs can be expressed without knowing whether binary or decimal notation is being used — even when we are doing calculations involving multiple-precision arithmetic. Thus we find that the choice of radix does not significantly influence computer programming. (Noteworthy exceptions to this statement, however, are the "Boolean" algorithms discussed in Section 7.1; see also Algorithm 4.5.2B.)

There are several different ways to represent *negative* numbers in a computer, and this sometimes influences the way arithmetic is done. In order to understand these notations, let us first consider MIX as if it were a decimal computer; then each word contains 10 digits and a sign, for example

$$-12345\ 67890. \tag{2}$$

This is called the *signed magnitude* representation. Such a representation agrees with common notational conventions, so it is preferred by many programmers. A potential disadvantage is that minus zero and plus zero can both be represented, while they usually should mean the same number; this possibility requires some care in practice, although it turns out to be useful at times.

Most mechanical calculators that do decimal arithmetic use another system called *ten's complement* notation. If we subtract 1 from 00000 00000, we get 99999 99999 in this notation; in other words, no explicit sign is attached to the number, and calculation is done modulo 10^{10}. The number $-12345\ 67890$ would appear as

$$87654\ 32110 \tag{3}$$

in ten's complement notation. It is conventional to regard any number whose leading digit is 5, 6, 7, 8, or 9 as a negative value in this notation, although with respect to addition and subtraction there is no harm in regarding (3) as the number $+87654\ 32110$ if it is convenient to do so. Notice that there is no problem of minus zero in such a system.

The major difference between signed magnitude and ten's complement notations in practice is that shifting right does not divide the magnitude by ten; for example, the number $-11 = \dots 99989$, shifted right one, gives $\dots 99998 = -2$ (assuming that a shift to the right inserts "9" as the leading digit when the number shifted is negative). In general, x shifted right one digit in ten's complement notation will give $\lfloor x/10 \rfloor$, whether x is positive or negative.

A possible disadvantage of the ten's complement system is the fact that it is not symmetric about zero; the p-digit negative number $500\dots 0$ is not the negative of any p-digit positive number. Thus it is possible that changing x to $-x$ will cause overflow. (See exercises 7 and 31 for a discussion of radix-complement notation with *infinite* precision.)

Another notation that has been used since the earliest days of high-speed computers is called *nines' complement* representation. In this case the number $-12345\ 67890$ would appear as

$$87654\ 32109. \tag{4}$$

Each digit of a negative number $(-x)$ is equal to 9 minus the corresponding digit of x. It is not difficult to see that the nines' complement notation for a negative number is always one less than the corresponding ten's complement notation. Addition and subtraction are done modulo $10^{10} - 1$, which means that a carry off the left end is to be added at the right end. (See the discussion of arithmetic modulo $w - 1$ in Section 3.2.1.1.) Again there is a potential problem with minus zero, since 99999 99999 and 00000 00000 denote the same value.

The ideas just explained for radix-10 arithmetic apply in a similar way to radix-2 arithmetic, where we have *signed magnitude*, *two's complement*, and *ones' complement* notations. Two's complement arithmetic on n-bit numbers is arithmetic modulo 2^n; ones' complement arithmetic is modulo $2^n - 1$. The MIX computer, as used in the examples of this chapter, deals only with signed magnitude arithmetic; however, alternative procedures for complement notations are discussed in the accompanying text when it is important to do so.

Detail-oriented readers and copy editors should notice the position of the apostrophe in terms like "two's complement" and "ones' complement": A two's complement number is complemented with respect to a single power of 2, while a ones' complement number is complemented with respect to a long sequence of 1s. Indeed, there is also a "twos' complement notation," which has radix 3 and complementation with respect to $(2 \ldots 22)_3$.

Descriptions of machine language often tell us that a computer's circuitry is set up with the radix point at a particular place within each numeric word. Such statements should usually be disregarded. It is better to learn the rules concerning where the radix point will appear in the result of an instruction if we assume that it lies in a certain place beforehand. For example, in the case of MIX we could regard our operands either as integers with the radix point at the extreme right, or as fractions with the radix point at the extreme left, or as some mixture of these two extremes; the rules for the appearance of the radix point after addition, subtraction, multiplication, or division are straightforward.

It is easy to see that there is a simple relation between radix b and radix b^k:

$$(\ldots a_3 a_2 a_1 a_0 . a_{-1} a_{-2} \ldots)_b = (\ldots A_3 A_2 A_1 A_0 . A_{-1} A_{-2} \ldots)_{b^k}, \qquad (5)$$

where

$$A_j = (a_{kj+k-1} \ldots a_{kj+1} a_{kj})_b;$$

see exercise 8. Thus we have simple techniques for converting at sight between, say, binary and hexadecimal notation.

Many interesting variations on positional number systems are possible in addition to the standard b-ary systems discussed so far. For example, we might have numbers in base (-10), so that

$$(\ldots a_3 a_2 a_1 a_0 . a_{-1} a_{-2} \ldots)_{-10}$$
$$= \cdots + a_3 (-10)^3 + a_2 (-10)^2 + a_1 (-10)^1 + a_0 + \cdots$$
$$= \cdots - 1000 a_3 + 100 a_2 - 10 a_1 + a_0 - \tfrac{1}{10} a_{-1} + \tfrac{1}{100} a_{-2} - \cdots .$$

Here the individual digits satisfy $0 \le a_k \le 9$ just as in the decimal system. The number 12345 67890 appears in the "negadecimal" system as

$$(1 \ 93755 \ 73910)_{-10}, \qquad (6)$$

since the latter represents $10305070900 - 9070503010$. It is interesting to note that the negative of this number, $-12345 \ 67890$, would be written

$$(28466 \ 48290)_{-10}, \qquad (7)$$

and, in fact, *every real number whether positive or negative can be represented without a sign* in the -10 system.

Negative-base systems were first considered by Vittorio Grünwald [*Giornale di Matematiche di Battaglini* **23** (1885), 203–221, 367], who explained how to perform the four arithmetic operations in such systems; Grünwald also discussed root extraction, divisibility tests, and radix conversion. However, his work seems to have had no effect on other research, since it was published in a rather obscure journal, and it was soon forgotten. The next publication about negative-base systems was apparently by A. J. Kempner [*AMM* **43** (1936), 610–617], who discussed the properties of noninteger radices and remarked in a footnote that negative radices would be feasible too. After twenty more years the idea was rediscovered again, this time by Z. Pawlak and A. Wakulicz [*Bulletin de l'Académie Polonaise des Sciences*, Classe III, **5** (1957), 233–236; Série des sciences techniques **7** (1959), 713–721], and also by L. Wadel [*IRE Transactions* **EC-6** (1957), 123]. Experimental computers called SKRZAT 1 and BINEG, which used -2 as the radix of arithmetic, were built in Poland in the late 1950s; see N. M. Blachman, *CACM* **4** (1961), 257; R. W. Marczyński, *Ann. Hist. Computing* **2** (1980), 37–48. For further references see *IEEE Transactions* **EC-12** (1963), 274–277; *Computer Design* **6** (May 1967), 52–63. There is evidence that the idea of negative bases occurred independently to quite a few people. For example, D. E. Knuth had discussed negative-radix systems in 1955, together with a further generalization to complex-valued bases, in a short paper submitted to a "science talent search" contest for high-school seniors.

The base $2i$ gives rise to a system called the "quater-imaginary" number system (by analogy with "quaternary"), which has the unusual feature that *every complex number can be represented with the digits* 0, 1, 2, *and* 3 *without a sign*. [See D. E. Knuth, *CACM* **3** (1960), 245–247; **4** (1961), 355.] For example,

$$(11210.31)_{2i} = 1 \cdot 16 + 1 \cdot (-8i) + 2 \cdot (-4) + 1 \cdot (2i) + 3 \cdot (-\tfrac{1}{2}i) + 1(-\tfrac{1}{4}) = 7\tfrac{3}{4} - 7\tfrac{1}{2}i.$$

Here the number $(a_{2n} \ldots a_1 a_0 . a_{-1} \ldots a_{-2k})_{2i}$ is equal to

$$(a_{2n} \ldots a_2 a_0 . a_{-2} \ldots a_{-2k})_{-4} + 2i(a_{2n-1} \ldots a_3 a_1 . a_{-1} \ldots a_{-2k+1})_{-4},$$

so conversion to and from quater-imaginary notation reduces to conversion to and from negative quaternary representation of the real and imaginary parts. The interesting property of this system is that it allows multiplication and division of complex numbers to be done in a fairly unified manner without treating real and imaginary parts separately. For example, we can multiply two numbers in this system much as we do with any base, merely using a different carry rule: Whenever a digit exceeds 3 we subtract 4 and carry -1 two columns to the left; when a digit is negative, we add 4 to it and carry $+1$ two columns to the left. The following example shows this peculiar carry rule at work:

```
              1 2 2 3 1      [9 − 10i]
          × 1 2 2 3 1        [9 − 10i]
            ─────────
              1 2 2 3 1
    1 0 3 2 0 2 1 3
        1 3 0 2 2
      1 3 0 2 2
    1 2 2 3 1
    ───────────────────
    0 2 1 3 3 3 1 2 1      [−19 − 180i]
```

A similar system that uses just the digits 0 and 1 may be based on $\sqrt{2}\,i$, but this requires an infinite nonrepeating expansion for the simple number "i" itself. Vittorio Grünwald proposed using the digits 0 and $1/\sqrt{2}$ in odd-numbered positions, to avoid such a problem; but that actually spoils the whole system [see *Commentari dell'Ateneo di Brescia* (1886), 43–54].

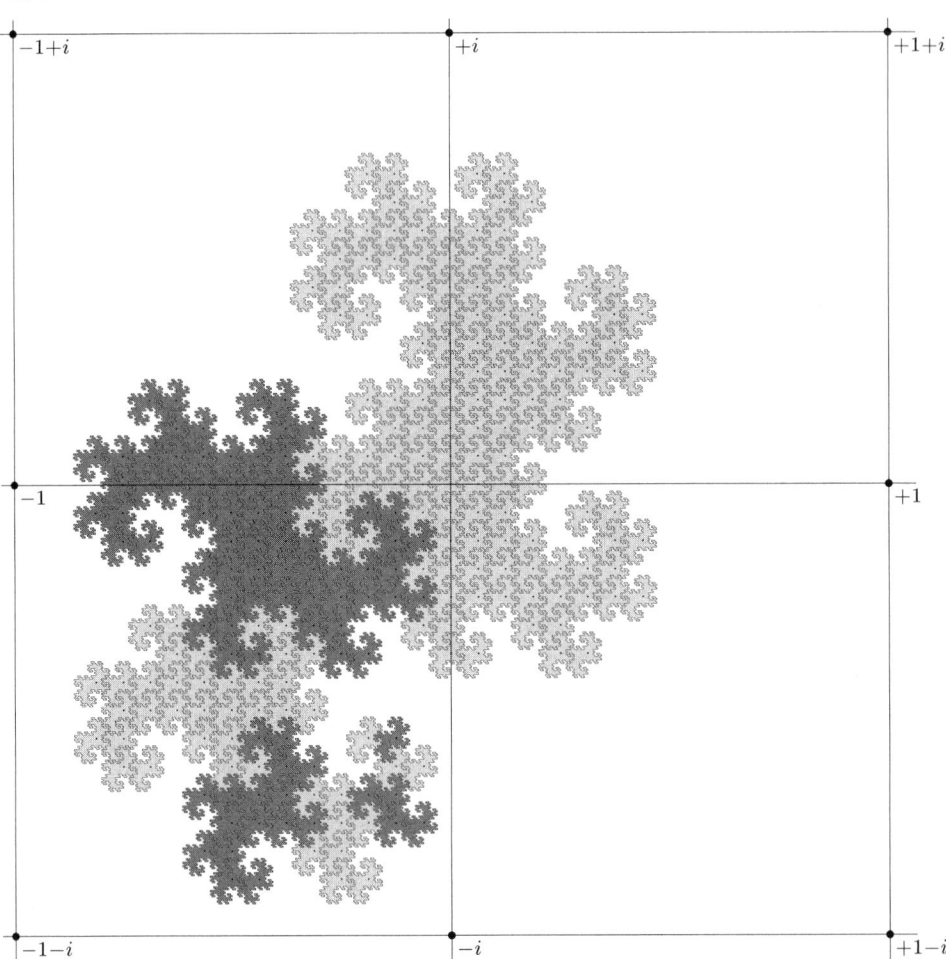

Fig. 1. The fractal set S called the "twindragon."

Another "binary" complex number system may be obtained by using the base $i - 1$, as suggested by W. Penney [*JACM* **12** (1965), 247–248]:

$$(\ldots a_4 a_3 a_2 a_1 a_0 . a_{-1} \ldots)_{i-1}$$
$$= \cdots - 4a_4 + (2i+2)a_3 - 2ia_2 + (i-1)a_1 + a_0 - \tfrac{1}{2}(i+1)a_{-1} + \cdots.$$

In this system, only the digits 0 and 1 are needed. One way to demonstrate that every complex number has such a representation is to consider the interesting set S shown in Fig. 1; this set is, by definition, all points that can be written as $\sum_{k \geq 1} a_k (i - 1)^{-k}$, for an infinite sequence a_1, a_2, a_3, ... of zeros and ones. It is also known as the "twindragon fractal" [see M. F. Barnsley, *Fractals Everywhere*, second edition (Academic Press, 1993), 306, 310]. Figure 1 shows that S can be decomposed into 256 pieces congruent to $\frac{1}{16}S$. Notice that if the diagram of S is rotated counterclockwise by 135°, we obtain two adjacent sets congruent to

$(1/\sqrt{2})\,S$, because $(i-1)S = S \cup (S+1)$. For details of a proof that S contains all complex numbers that are of sufficiently small magnitude, see exercise 18.

Perhaps the prettiest number system of all is the *balanced ternary* notation, which consists of radix-3 representation using -1, 0, and $+1$ as "trits" (ternary digits) instead of 0, 1, and 2. If we let the symbol $\bar{1}$ stand for -1, we have the following examples of balanced ternary numbers:

Balanced ternary	Decimal
$10\bar{1}$	8
$1\bar{1}0.\bar{1}\bar{1}$	$32\frac{5}{9}$
$\bar{1}\bar{1}0.11$	$-32\frac{5}{9}$
$\bar{1}\bar{1}10$	-33
$0.11111\ldots$	$\frac{1}{2}$

One way to find the representation of a number in the balanced ternary system is to start by representing it in ordinary ternary notation; for example,

$$208.3 = (21201.022002200220\ldots)_3.$$

(A very simple pencil-and-paper method for converting to ternary notation is given in exercise 4.4–12.) Now add the infinite number $\ldots 11111.11111\ldots$ in ternary notation; we obtain, in the example above, the infinite number

$$(\ldots 11111210012.210121012101\ldots)_3.$$

Finally, subtract $\ldots 11111.11111\ldots$ by decrementing each digit; we get

$$208.3 = (10\bar{1}\bar{1}01.10\bar{1}010\bar{1}010\bar{1}0\ldots)_3. \tag{8}$$

This process may clearly be made rigorous if we replace the artificial infinite number $\ldots 11111.11111\ldots$ by a number with suitably many ones.

The balanced ternary number system has many pleasant properties:

a) The negative of a number is obtained by interchanging 1 and $\bar{1}$.

b) The sign of a number is given by its most significant nonzero trit, and in general we can compare any two numbers by reading them from left to right and using lexicographic order, as in the decimal system.

c) The operation of rounding to the nearest integer is identical to truncation; in other words, we simply delete everything to the right of the radix point.

Addition in the balanced ternary system is quite simple, using the table

$\bar{1}$	$\bar{1}$	$\bar{1}$	$\bar{1}$	$\bar{1}$	$\bar{1}$	$\bar{1}$	$\bar{1}$	$\bar{1}$	0	0	0	0	0	0	0	0	0	1	1	1	1	1	1	1	1	1
$\bar{1}$	$\bar{1}$	$\bar{1}$	0	0	0	1	1	1	$\bar{1}$	$\bar{1}$	$\bar{1}$	0	0	0	1	1	1	$\bar{1}$	$\bar{1}$	$\bar{1}$	0	0	0	1	1	1
$\bar{1}$	0	1	$\bar{1}$	0	1	$\bar{1}$	0	1	$\bar{1}$	0	1	$\bar{1}$	0	1	$\bar{1}$	0	1	$\bar{1}$	0	1	$\bar{1}$	0	1	$\bar{1}$	0	1
$\bar{1}0$	$\bar{1}\bar{1}$	$\bar{1}$	$\bar{1}\bar{1}$	$\bar{1}$	0	$\bar{1}$	0	1	$\bar{1}\bar{1}$	$\bar{1}$	0	$\bar{1}$	0	1	0	1	$1\bar{1}$	$\bar{1}$	0	1	0	1	$1\bar{1}$	1	$1\bar{1}$	10

(The three inputs to the addition are the digits of the numbers to be added and the carry digit.) Subtraction is negation followed by addition. Multiplication also reduces to negation and addition, as in the following example:

$$
\begin{array}{r}
1\ \bar{1}\ 0\ \bar{1} \quad [17] \\
\times\ 1\ \bar{1}\ 0\ \bar{1} \quad [17] \\
\hline
\bar{1}\ 1\ 0\ 1 \\
\bar{1}\ 1\ 0\ 1 \\
1\ \bar{1}\ 0\ \bar{1} \\
\hline
0\ 1\ 1\ \bar{1}\ \bar{1}\ 0\ 1 \quad [289]
\end{array}
$$

Representation of numbers in the balanced ternary system is implicitly present in a famous mathematical puzzle, commonly called "Bachet's problem of weights" — although it was already stated by Fibonacci four centuries before Bachet wrote his book, and by Ṭabarī in Persia more than 100 years before Fibonacci. [See W. Ahrens, *Mathematische Unterhaltungen und Spiele* 1 (Leipzig: Teubner, 1910), Section 3.4; H. Hermelink, *Janus* 65 (1978), 105–117.] Positional number systems with negative digits were invented by J. Colson [*Philos. Trans.* 34 (1726), 161–173], then forgotten and rediscovered about 100 years later by Sir John Leslie [*The Philosophy of Arithmetic* (Edinburgh: 1817); see pages 33–34, 54, 64–65, 117, 150], and by A. Cauchy [*Comptes Rendus Acad. Sci.* 11 (Paris, 1840), 789–798]. Cauchy pointed out that negative digits make it unnecessary for a person to memorize the multiplication table past 5×5. A claim that such number systems were known in India long ago [J. Bharati, *Vedic Mathematics* (Delhi: Motilal Banarsidass, 1965)] has been refuted by K. S. Shukla [*Mathematical Education* 5,3 (1989), 129–133]. The first true appearance of "pure" balanced ternary notation was in an article by Léon Lalanne [*Comptes Rendus Acad. Sci.* 11 (Paris, 1840), 903–905], who was a designer of mechanical devices for arithmetic. Thomas Fowler independently invented and constructed a balanced ternary calculator at about the same time [see *Report British Assoc. Adv. Sci.* 10 (1840), 55; 11 (1841), 39–40]. The balanced ternary number system was mentioned only rarely for the next 100 years, until the development of the first electronic computers at the Moore School of Electrical Engineering in 1945–1946; at that time it was given serious consideration as a possible replacement for the decimal system. The complexity of arithmetic circuitry for balanced ternary arithmetic is not much greater than it is for the binary system, and a given number requires only $\ln 2/\ln 3 \approx 63\%$ as many digit positions for its representation. Discussions of the balanced ternary system appear in *AMM* 57 (1950), 90–93, and in *High-speed Computing Devices*, Engineering Research Associates (McGraw–Hill, 1950), 287–289. The experimental Russian computer SETUN was based on balanced ternary notation [see *CACM* 3 (1960), 149–150], and perhaps the symmetric properties and simple arithmetic of this number system will prove to be quite important someday — when the "flip-flop" is replaced by a "flip-flap-flop."

Positional notation generalizes in another important way to a *mixed-radix* system. Given a sequence of numbers $\langle b_n \rangle$ (where n may be negative), we define

$$
\begin{bmatrix} \ldots, a_3, a_2, a_1, a_0;\ a_{-1},\ a_{-2}, \ldots \\ \ldots, b_3, b_2, b_1, b_0;\ b_{-1},\ b_{-2}, \ldots \end{bmatrix}
$$
$$
= \cdots + a_3 b_2 b_1 b_0 + a_2 b_1 b_0 + a_1 b_0 + a_0 + a_{-1}/b_{-1} + a_{-2}/b_{-1} b_{-2} + \cdots. \quad (9)
$$

In the simplest mixed-radix systems, we work only with integers; we let b_0, b_1, b_2, ... be integers greater than one, and deal only with numbers that have no radix point, where a_n is required to lie in the range $0 \le a_n < b_n$.

One of the most important mixed-radix systems is the *factorial number system*, where $b_n = n + 2$. Using this system, which was known in 13th-century India, we can represent every positive integer uniquely in the form

$$c_n\, n! + c_{n-1}\, (n-1)! + \cdots + c_2\, 2! + c_1, \tag{10}$$

where $0 \le c_k \le k$ for $1 \le k \le n$, and $c_n \ne 0$. (See Algorithms 3.3.2P and 3.4.2P.)

Mixed-radix systems are familiar in everyday life, when we deal with units of measure. For example, the quantity "3 weeks, 2 days, 9 hours, 22 minutes, 57 seconds, and 492 milliseconds" is equal to

$$\begin{bmatrix} 3, & 2, & 9, & 22, & 57; & 492 \\ & 7, & 24, & 60, & 60; & 1000 \end{bmatrix} \text{ seconds.}$$

The quantity "10 pounds, 6 shillings, and thruppence ha'penny" was once equal to $\begin{bmatrix} 10, & 6, & 3; & 1 \\ & 20, & 12; & 2 \end{bmatrix}$ pence in British currency, before Great Britain changed to a purely decimal monetary system.

It is possible to add and subtract mixed-radix numbers by using a straightforward generalization of the usual addition and subtraction algorithms, provided of course that the same mixed-radix system is being used for both operands (see exercise 4.3.1–9). Similarly, we can easily multiply or divide a mixed-radix number by small integer constants, using simple extensions of the familiar pencil-and-paper methods.

Mixed-radix systems were first discussed in full generality by Georg Cantor [*Zeitschrift für Math. und Physik* **14** (1869), 121–128]. Exercises 26 and 29 give further information about them.

Several questions concerning *irrational* radices have been investigated by W. Parry, *Acta Math. Acad. Sci. Hung.* **11** (1960), 401–416.

Besides the systems described in this section, several other ways to represent numbers are mentioned elsewhere in this series of books: the combinatorial number system (exercise 1.2.6–56); the Fibonacci number system (exercises 1.2.8–34, 5.4.2–10); the phi number system (exercise 1.2.8–35); modular representations (Section 4.3.2); Gray code (Section 7.2.1); and Roman numerals (Section 9.1).

EXERCISES

1. [*15*] Express -10, -9, ..., 9, 10 in the number system whose radix is -2.

▶ **2.** [*24*] Consider the following four number systems: (a) binary (signed magnitude); (b) negabinary (radix -2); (c) balanced ternary; and (d) radix $b = \frac{1}{10}$. Use each of these four number systems to express each of the following three numbers: (i) -49; (ii) $-3\frac{1}{7}$ (show the repeating cycle); (iii) π (to a few significant figures).

3. [*20*] Express $-49 + i$ in the quater-imaginary system.

4. [*15*] Assume that we have a MIX program in which location A contains a number for which the radix point lies between bytes 3 and 4, while location B contains a number whose radix point lies between bytes 2 and 3. (The leftmost byte is number 1.) Where will the radix point be, in registers A and X, after the following instructions?

(a) `LDA A;    MUL B`   (b) `LDA A;    SRAX 5;    DIV B`

5. [*00*] Explain why a negative integer in nines' complement notation has a representation in ten's complement notation that is always one greater, if the representations are regarded as positive.

6. [*16*] What are the largest and smallest p-bit integers that can be represented in (a) signed magnitude binary notation (including one bit for the sign), (b) two's complement notation, (c) ones' complement notation?

7. [*M20*] The text defines ten's complement notation only for integers represented in a single computer word. Is there a way to define a ten's complement notation *for all real numbers*, having "infinite precision," analogous to the text's definition? Is there a similar way to define a nines' complement notation for all real numbers?

8. [*M10*] Prove Eq. (5).

▸ **9.** [*15*] Change the following *octal* numbers to *hexadecimal* notation, using the hexadecimal digits 0, 1, . . . , 9, A, B, C, D, E, F: *12*; *5655*; *2550276*; *76545336*; *3726755*.

10. [*M22*] Generalize Eq. (5) to mixed-radix notation as in (9).

11. [*22*] Design an algorithm that uses the -2 number system to compute the sum of $(a_n \ldots a_1 a_0)_{-2}$ and $(b_n \ldots b_1 b_0)_{-2}$, obtaining the answer $(c_{n+2} \ldots c_1 c_0)_{-2}$.

12. [*23*] Specify algorithms that convert (a) the binary signed magnitude number $\pm(a_n \ldots a_0)_2$ to its negabinary form $(b_{n+2} \ldots b_0)_{-2}$; and (b) the negabinary number $(b_{n+1} \ldots b_0)_{-2}$ to its signed magnitude form $\pm(a_{n+1} \ldots a_0)_2$.

▸ **13.** [*M21*] In the decimal system there are some numbers with two infinite decimal expansions; for example, $2.3599999\ldots = 2.3600000\ldots$. Does the *negadecimal* (base -10) system have unique expansions, or are there real numbers with two different infinite expansions in this base also?

14. [*14*] Multiply $(11321)_{2i}$ by itself in the quater-imaginary system using the method illustrated in the text.

15. [*M24*] What are the sets $S = \{\sum_{k \geq 1} a_k b^{-k} \mid a_k \text{ an allowable digit}\}$, analogous to Fig. 1, for the negative decimal and for the quater-imaginary number systems?

16. [*M24*] Design an algorithm to add 1 to $(a_n \ldots a_1 a_0)_{i-1}$ in the $i-1$ number system.

17. [*M30*] It may seem peculiar that $i - 1$ has been suggested as a number-system base, instead of the similar but intuitively simpler number $i + 1$. Can every complex number $a + bi$, where a and b are integers, be represented in a positional number system to base $i + 1$, using only the digits 0 and 1?

18. [*HM32*] Show that the twindragon of Fig. 1 is a closed set that contains a neighborhood of the origin. (Consequently, every complex number has a binary representation with radix $i - 1$.)

▸ **19.** [*23*] (David W. Matula.) Let D be a set of b integers, containing exactly one solution to the congruence $x \equiv j$ (modulo b) for $0 \leq j < b$. Prove that all integers m (positive, negative, or zero) can be represented in the form $m = (a_n \ldots a_0)_b$, where all the a_j are in D, if and only if all integers in the range $l \leq m \leq u$ can be so represented, where $l = -\max\{a \mid a \in D\}/(b-1)$ and $u = -\min\{a \mid a \in D\}/(b-1)$. For example, $D = \{-1, 0, \ldots, b-2\}$ satisfies the conditions for all $b \geq 3$. [*Hint:* Design an algorithm that constructs a suitable representation.]

20. [*HM28*] (David W. Matula.) Consider a decimal number system that uses the digits $D = \{-1, 0, 8, 17, 26, 35, 44, 53, 62, 71\}$ instead of $\{0, 1, \ldots, 9\}$. The result of exercise 19 implies (as in exercise 18) that all real numbers have an infinite decimal expansion using digits from D.

In the usual decimal system, exercise 13 points out that some numbers have two representations. (a) Find a real number that has *more* than two D-decimal representations. (b) Show that no real number has infinitely many D-decimal representations. (c) Show that uncountably many numbers have two or more D-decimal representations.

▶ **21.** [*M22*] (C. E. Shannon.) Can every real number (positive, negative, or zero) be expressed in a "balanced decimal" system, that is, in the form $\sum_{k \leq n} a_k 10^k$, for some integer n and some sequence a_n, a_{n-1}, a_{n-2}, ..., where each a_k is one of the ten numbers $\{-4\frac{1}{2}, -3\frac{1}{2}, -2\frac{1}{2}, -1\frac{1}{2}, -\frac{1}{2}, \frac{1}{2}, 1\frac{1}{2}, 2\frac{1}{2}, 3\frac{1}{2}, 4\frac{1}{2}\}$? (Although zero is not one of the allowed digits, we implicitly assume that a_{n+1}, a_{n+2}, ... are zero.) Find all representations of zero in this number system, and find all representations of unity.

22. [*HM25*] Let $\alpha = -\sum_{m \geq 1} 10^{-m^2}$. Given $\epsilon > 0$ and any real number x, prove that there is a "decimal" representation such that $0 < |x - \sum_{k=0}^{n} a_k 10^k| < \epsilon$, where each a_k is allowed to be only one of the three values 0, 1, or α. (No negative powers of 10 are used in this representation!)

23. [*HM30*] Let D be a set of b real numbers such that every positive real number has a representation $\sum_{k \leq n} a_k b^k$ with all $a_k \in D$. Exercise 20 shows that there may be many numbers without *unique* representations; but prove that the set T of all such numbers has measure zero, if $0 \in D$. Show that this conclusion need not be true if $0 \notin D$.

24. [*M35*] Find infinitely many different sets D of ten nonnegative integers satisfying the following three conditions: (i) $\gcd(D) = 1$; (ii) $0 \in D$; (iii) every positive real number can be represented in the form $\sum_{k \leq n} a_k 10^k$ with all $a_k \in D$.

25. [*M25*] (S. A. Cook.) Let b, u, and v be positive integers, where $b \geq 2$ and $0 < v < b^m$. Show that the radix-b representation of u/v does not contain a run of m consecutive digits equal to $b - 1$, anywhere to the right of the radix point. (By convention, no runs of infinitely many $(b-1)$'s are permitted in the standard radix-b representation.)

▶ **26.** [*HM30*] (N. S. Mendelsohn.) Let $\langle \beta_n \rangle$ be a sequence of real numbers defined for all integers n, $-\infty < n < \infty$, such that

$$\beta_n < \beta_{n+1}; \qquad \lim_{n \to \infty} \beta_n = \infty; \qquad \lim_{n \to -\infty} \beta_n = 0.$$

Let $\langle c_n \rangle$ be an arbitrary sequence of positive integers that is defined for all integers n, $-\infty < n < \infty$. Let us say that a number x has a "generalized representation" if there is an integer n and an infinite sequence of integers a_n, a_{n-1}, a_{n-2}, ... such that $x = \sum_{k \leq n} a_k \beta_k$, where $a_n \neq 0$, $0 \leq a_k \leq c_k$, and $a_k < c_k$ for infinitely many k.

Show that every positive real number x has exactly one generalized representation if and only if

$$\beta_{n+1} = \sum_{k \leq n} c_k \beta_k \qquad \text{for all } n.$$

(Consequently, the mixed-radix systems with integer bases all have this property; and mixed-radix systems with $\beta_1 = (c_0+1)\beta_0$, $\beta_2 = (c_1+1)(c_0+1)\beta_0$, ..., $\beta_{-1} = \beta_0/(c_{-1}+1)$, ... are the most general number systems of this type.)

27. [*M21*] Show that every nonzero integer has a unique "reversing binary representation"

$$2^{e_0} - 2^{e_1} + \cdots + (-1)^t 2^{e_t},$$

where $e_0 < e_1 < \cdots < e_t$.

▶ **28.** [*M24*] Show that every nonzero complex number of the form $a + bi$ where a and b are integers has a unique "revolving binary representation"

$$(1+i)^{e_0} + i(1+i)^{e_1} - (1+i)^{e_2} - i(1+i)^{e_3} + \cdots + i^t(1+i)^{e_t},$$

where $e_0 < e_1 < \cdots < e_t$. (Compare with exercise 27.)

29. [*M35*] (N. G. de Bruijn.) Let S_0, S_1, S_2, ... be sets of nonnegative integers; we will say that the collection $\{S_0, S_1, S_2, \ldots\}$ has Property B if every nonnegative integer n can be written in the form

$$n = s_0 + s_1 + s_2 + \cdots, \qquad s_j \in S_j,$$

in exactly one way. (Property B implies that $0 \in S_j$ for all j, since $n = 0$ can only be represented as $0 + 0 + 0 + \cdots$.) Any mixed-radix number system with radices b_0, b_1, b_2, ... provides an example of a collection of sets satisfying Property B, if we let $S_j = \{0, B_j, \ldots, (b_j - 1)B_j\}$, where $B_j = b_0 b_1 \ldots b_{j-1}$; here the representation of $n = s_0 + s_1 + s_2 + \cdots$ corresponds in an obvious manner to its mixed-radix representation (9). Furthermore, if the collection $\{S_0, S_1, S_2, \ldots\}$ has Property B, and if A_0, A_1, A_2, ... is any partition of the nonnegative integers (so that we have $A_0 \cup A_1 \cup A_2 \cup \cdots = \{0, 1, 2, \ldots\}$ and $A_i \cap A_j = \emptyset$ for $i \neq j$; some A_j's may be empty), then the "collapsed" collection $\{T_0, T_1, T_2, \ldots\}$ also has Property B, where T_j is the set of all sums $\sum_{i \in A_j} s_i$ taken over all possible choices of $s_i \in S_i$.

Prove that *any* collection $\{T_0, T_1, T_2, \ldots\}$ that satisfies Property B may be obtained by collapsing some collection $\{S_0, S_1, S_2, \ldots\}$ that corresponds to a mixed-radix number system.

30. [*M39*] (N. G. de Bruijn.) The negabinary number system shows us that every integer (positive, negative, or zero) has a unique representation of the form

$$(-2)^{e_1} + (-2)^{e_2} + \cdots + (-2)^{e_t}, \qquad e_1 > e_2 > \cdots > e_t \geq 0, \qquad t \geq 0.$$

The purpose of this exercise is to explore generalizations of this phenomenon.

a) Let b_0, b_1, b_2, ... be a sequence of integers such that every integer n has a unique representation of the form

$$n = b_{e_1} + b_{e_2} + \cdots + b_{e_t}, \qquad e_1 > e_2 > \cdots > e_t \geq 0, \qquad t \geq 0.$$

(Such a sequence $\langle b_n \rangle$ is called a "binary basis.") Show that there is an index j such that b_j is odd, but b_k is even for all $k \neq j$.

b) Prove that a binary basis $\langle b_n \rangle$ can always be rearranged into the form d_0, $2d_1$, $4d_2$, ... $= \langle 2^n d_n \rangle$, where each d_k is odd.

c) If each of d_0, d_1, d_2, ... in (b) is ± 1, prove that $\langle b_n \rangle$ is a binary basis if and only if there are infinitely many $+1$'s and infinitely many -1's.

d) Prove that 7, $-13 \cdot 2$, $7 \cdot 2^2$, $-13 \cdot 2^3$, ..., $7 \cdot 2^{2k}$, $-13 \cdot 2^{2k+1}$, ... is a binary basis, and find the representation of $n = 1$.

▶ **31.** [*M35*] A generalization of two's complement arithmetic, called "2-adic numbers," was introduced by K. Hensel in *Crelle* **127** (1904), 51–84. (In fact he treated *p-adic numbers*, for any prime p.) A 2-adic number may be regarded as a binary number

$$u = (\ldots u_3 u_2 u_1 u_0 . u_{-1} \ldots u_{-n})_2,$$

whose representation extends infinitely far to the left of the binary point, but only finitely many places to the right. Addition, subtraction, and multiplication of 2-adic numbers are done according to the ordinary procedures of arithmetic, which can in principle be extended indefinitely to the left. For example,

$$7 = (\ldots 000000000000111)_2 \qquad\qquad \tfrac{1}{7} = (\ldots 110110110110111)_2$$

$$-7 = (\ldots 111111111111001)_2 \qquad\qquad -\tfrac{1}{7} = (\ldots 001001001001001)_2$$

$$\tfrac{7}{4} = (\ldots 000000000000001.11)_2 \qquad\qquad \tfrac{1}{10} = (\ldots 110011001100110.1)_2$$

$$\sqrt{-7} = (\ldots 100000010110101)_2 \quad \text{or} \quad (\ldots 011111101001011)_2.$$

Here 7 appears as the ordinary binary integer seven, while -7 is its two's complement (extending infinitely to the left); it is easy to verify that the ordinary procedure for addition of binary numbers will give $-7 + 7 = (\ldots 00000)_2 = 0$, when the procedure is continued indefinitely. The values of $\tfrac{1}{7}$ and $-\tfrac{1}{7}$ are the unique 2-adic numbers that, when formally multiplied by 7, give 1 and -1, respectively. The values of $\tfrac{7}{4}$ and $\tfrac{1}{10}$ are examples of 2-adic numbers that are not 2-adic "integers," since they have nonzero bits to the right of the binary point. The two values of $\sqrt{-7}$, which are negatives of each other, are the only 2-adic numbers that, when formally squared, yield the value $(\ldots 111111111111001)_2$.

a) Prove that any 2-adic number u can be divided by any nonzero 2-adic number v to obtain a unique 2-adic number w satisfying $u = vw$. (Hence the set of 2-adic numbers forms a "field"; see Section 4.6.1.)

b) Prove that the 2-adic representation of the rational number $-1/(2n+1)$ may be obtained as follows, when n is a positive integer: First find the ordinary binary expansion of $+1/(2n+1)$, which has the periodic form $(0.\alpha\alpha\alpha\ldots)_2$ for some string α of 0s and 1s. Then $-1/(2n+1)$ is the 2-adic number $(\ldots \alpha\alpha\alpha)_2$.

c) Prove that the representation of a 2-adic number u is ultimately periodic (that is, $u_{N+\lambda} = u_N$ for all large N, for some $\lambda \geq 1$) if and only if u is rational (that is, $u = m/n$, for some integers m and n).

d) Prove that, when n is an integer, $\sqrt{n}$ is a 2-adic number if and only if it satisfies $n \bmod 2^{2k+3} = 2^{2k}$ for some nonnegative integer k. (Thus, the possibilities are either $n \bmod 8 = 1$, or $n \bmod 32 = 4$, etc.)

32. [*M40*] (I. Z. Ruzsa.) Construct infinitely many integers whose ternary representation uses only 0s and 1s and whose quinary representation uses only 0s, 1s, and 2s.

33. [*M40*] (D. A. Klarner.) Let D be any set of integers, let b be any positive integer, and let k_n be the number of distinct integers that can be written as n-digit numbers $(a_{n-1} \ldots a_1 a_0)_b$ to base b with digits a_i in D. Prove that the sequence $\langle k_n \rangle$ satisfies a linear recurrence relation, and explain how to compute the generating function $\sum_n k_n z^n$. Illustrate your algorithm by showing that k_n is a Fibonacci number in the case $b = 3$ and $D = \{-1, 0, 3\}$.

▶ **34.** [*22*] (G. W. Reitwiesner, 1960.) Explain how to represent a given integer n in the form $(\ldots a_2 a_1 a_0)_2$, where each a_j is -1, 0, or 1, using the fewest nonzero digits.

4.2. FLOATING POINT ARITHMETIC

IN THIS SECTION we shall study the basic principles of arithmetic operations on "floating point" numbers, by analyzing the internal mechanisms underlying such calculations. Perhaps many readers will have little interest in this subject, since their computers either have built-in floating point instructions or their operating systems include suitable subroutines. But, in fact, the material of this section should not merely be the concern of computer-design engineers or of a small clique of people who write library subroutines for new machines; *every* well-rounded programmer ought to have a knowledge of what goes on during the elementary steps of floating point arithmetic. This subject is not at all as trivial as most people think, and it involves a surprising amount of interesting information.

4.2.1. Single-Precision Calculations

A. Floating point notation. We have discussed "fixed point" notation for numbers in Section 4.1; in such a case the programmer knows where the radix point is assumed to lie in the numbers being manipulated. For many purposes, however, it is considerably more convenient to let the position of the radix point be dynamically variable or "floating" as a program is running, and to carry with each number an indication of its current radix point position. This idea has been used for many years in scientific calculations, especially for expressing very large numbers like Avogadro's number $N = 6.02214 \times 10^{23}$, or very small numbers like Planck's constant $h = 6.6261 \times 10^{-27}$ erg sec.

In this section we shall work with *base b, excess q, floating point numbers with p digits*: Such numbers will be represented by pairs of values (e, f), denoting

$$(e, f) = f \times b^{e-q}. \tag{1}$$

Here e is an integer having a specified range, and f is a signed fraction. We will adopt the convention that

$$|f| < 1;$$

in other words, the radix point appears at the left of the positional representation of f. More precisely, the stipulation that we have p-digit numbers means that $b^p f$ is an integer, and that

$$-b^p < b^p f < b^p. \tag{2}$$

The term "floating binary" implies that $b = 2$, "floating decimal" implies $b = 10$, etc. Using excess-50 floating decimal numbers with 8 digits, we can write, for example,

Avogadro's number $N = (74, +.60221400)$;

Planck's constant $h = (24, +.66261000)$. $\qquad$ (3)

The two components e and f of a floating point number are called the *exponent* and the *fraction* parts, respectively. (Other names are occasionally used for this purpose, notably "characteristic" and "mantissa"; but it is an abuse of terminology to call the fraction part a mantissa, since that term has quite a different meaning in connection with logarithms. Furthermore the English word mantissa means "a worthless addition.")

The MIX computer assumes that its floating point numbers have the form

$$\boxed{\pm} \;\boxed{e}\;\boxed{f}\;\boxed{f}\;\boxed{f}\;\boxed{f}\;. \tag{4}$$

Here we have base b, excess q, floating point notation with four bytes of precision, where b is the byte size (e.g., $b = 64$ or $b = 100$), and q is equal to $\lfloor \frac{1}{2}b \rfloor$. The fraction part is $\pm f f f f$, and e is the exponent, which lies in the range $0 \le e < b$. This internal representation is typical of the conventions in most existing computers, although b is a much larger base than usual.

B. Normalized calculations. A floating point number (e, f) is *normalized* if the most significant digit of the representation of f is nonzero, so that

$$1/b \le |f| < 1; \tag{5}$$

or if $f = 0$ and e has its smallest possible value. It is possible to tell which of two normalized floating point numbers has a greater magnitude by comparing the exponent parts first, and then testing the fraction parts only if the exponents are equal.

Most floating point routines now in use deal almost entirely with normalized numbers: Inputs to the routines are assumed to be normalized, and the outputs are always normalized. Under these conventions we lose the ability to represent a few numbers of very small magnitude — for example, the value $(0, .00000001)$ can't be normalized without producing a negative exponent — but we gain in speed, uniformity, and the ability to give relatively simple bounds on the relative error in our computations. (Unnormalized floating point arithmetic is discussed in Section 4.2.2.)

Let us now study the normalized floating point operations in detail. At the same time we can consider the construction of subroutines for these operations, assuming that we have a computer without built-in floating point hardware.

Machine-language subroutines for floating point arithmetic are usually written in a very machine-dependent manner, using many of the wildest idiosyncrasies of the computer at hand. Therefore floating point addition subroutines for two different machines usually bear little superficial resemblance to each other. Yet a careful study of numerous subroutines for both binary and decimal computers reveals that these programs actually have quite a lot in common, and it is possible to discuss the topics in a machine-independent way.

The first (and by far the most difficult!) algorithm we shall discuss in this section is a procedure for floating point addition,

$$(e_u, f_u) \oplus (e_v, f_v) = (e_w, f_w). \tag{6}$$

Since floating point arithmetic is inherently approximate, not exact, we will use "round" symbols

$$\oplus, \quad \ominus, \quad \otimes, \quad \oslash$$

to stand for floating point addition, subtraction, multiplication, and division, respectively, in order to distinguish approximate operations from the true ones.

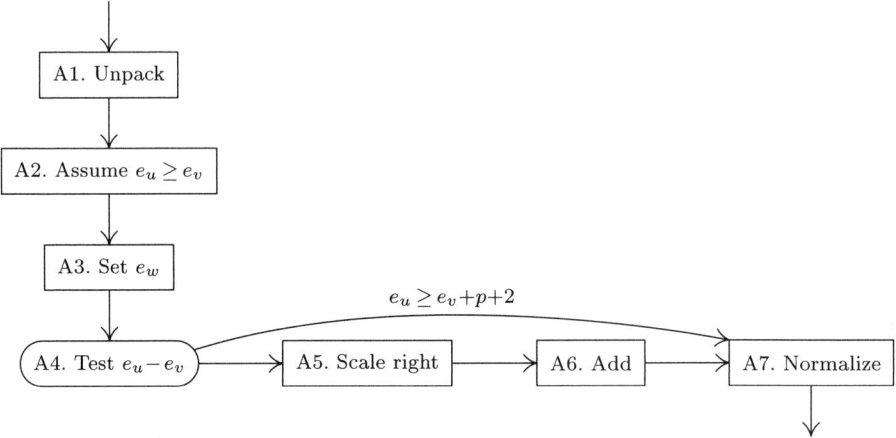

Fig. 2. Floating point addition.

The basic idea involved in floating point addition is fairly simple: Assuming that $e_u \geq e_v$, we take $e_w = e_u$, $f_w = f_u + f_v/b^{e_u - e_v}$ (thereby aligning the radix points for a meaningful addition), and normalize the result. But several situations can arise that make this process nontrivial, and the following algorithm explains the method more precisely.

Algorithm A (*Floating point addition*). Given base b, excess q, p-digit, normalized floating point numbers $u = (e_u, f_u)$ and $v = (e_v, f_v)$, this algorithm forms the sum $w = u \oplus v$. The same procedure may be used for floating point subtraction, if $-v$ is substituted for v.

A1. [Unpack.] Separate the exponent and fraction parts of the representations of u and v.

A2. [Assume $e_u \geq e_v$.] If $e_u < e_v$, interchange u and v. (In many cases, it is best to combine step A2 with step A1 or with some of the later steps.)

A3. [Set e_w.] Set $e_w \leftarrow e_u$.

A4. [Test $e_u - e_v$.] If $e_u - e_v \geq p+2$ (large difference in exponents), set $f_w \leftarrow f_u$ and go to step A7. (Actually, since we are assuming that u is normalized, we could terminate the algorithm; but it is occasionally useful to be able to normalize a possibly unnormalized number by adding zero to it.)

A5. [Scale right.] Shift f_v to the right $e_u - e_v$ places; that is, divide it by $b^{e_u - e_v}$. [*Note:* This will be a shift of up to $p + 1$ places, and the next step (which adds f_u to f_v) thereby requires an accumulator capable of holding $2p + 1$ base-b digits to the right of the radix point. If such a large accumulator is not available, it is possible to shorten the requirement to $p + 2$ or $p + 3$ places if proper precautions are taken; the details are given in exercise 5.]

A6. [Add.] Set $f_w \leftarrow f_u + f_v$.

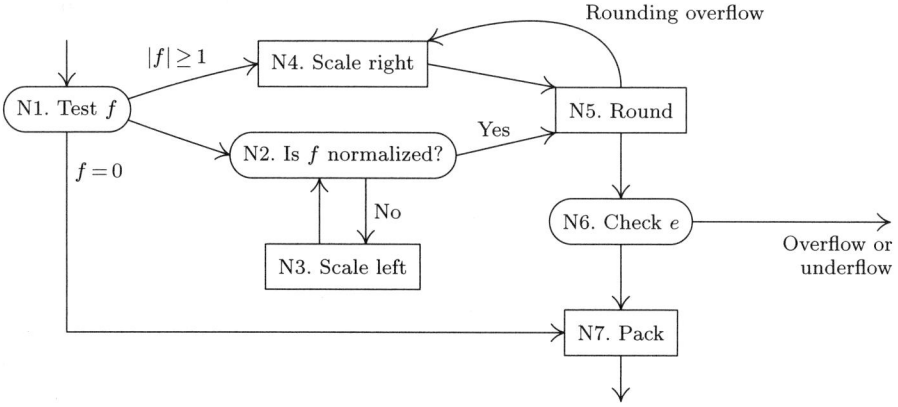

Fig. 3. Normalization of (e, f).

A7. [Normalize.] (At this point (e_w, f_w) represents the sum of u and v, but $|f_w|$ may have more than p digits, and it may be greater than unity or less than $1/b$.) Perform Algorithm N below, to normalize and round (e_w, f_w) into the final answer. ▮

Algorithm N (*Normalization*). A "raw exponent" e and a "raw fraction" f are converted to normalized form, rounding if necessary to p digits. This algorithm assumes that $|f| < b$.

N1. [Test f.] If $|f| \geq 1$ ("fraction overflow"), go to step N4. If $f = 0$, set e to its lowest possible value and go to step N7.

N2. [Is f normalized?] If $|f| \geq 1/b$, go to step N5.

N3. [Scale left.] Shift f to the left by one digit position (that is, multiply it by b), and decrease e by 1. Return to step N2.

N4. [Scale right.] Shift f to the right by one digit position (that is, divide it by b), and increase e by 1.

N5. [Round.] Round f to p places. (We take this to mean that f is changed to the nearest multiple of b^{-p}. It is possible that $(b^p f) \bmod 1 = \frac{1}{2}$ so that there are *two* nearest multiples; if b is even, we change f to the nearest multiple f' of b^{-p} such that $b^p f' + \frac{1}{2}b$ is odd. Further discussion of rounding appears in Section 4.2.2.) It is important to note that this rounding operation can make $|f| = 1$ ("rounding overflow"); in such a case, return to step N4.

N6. [Check e.] If e is too large, that is, greater than its allowed range, an *exponent overflow* condition is sensed. If e is too small, an *exponent underflow* condition is sensed. (See the discussion below; since the result cannot be expressed as a normalized floating point number in the required range, special action is necessary.)

N7. [Pack.] Put e and f together into the desired output representation. ▮

Some simple examples of floating point addition are given in exercise 4.

The following MIX subroutines, for addition and subtraction of numbers having the form (4), show how Algorithms A and N can be expressed as computer programs. The subroutines below are designed to take one input u from symbolic location ACC, and the other input v comes from register A upon entrance to the subroutine. The output w appears both in register A and location ACC. Thus, a fixed point coding sequence

$$\text{LDA A;   ADD B;   SUB C;   STA D} \qquad (7)$$

would correspond to the floating point coding sequence

$$\text{LDA A, STA ACC;   LDA B, JMP FADD;   LDA C, JMP FSUB;   STA D.} \qquad (8)$$

Program A (*Addition, subtraction, and normalization*). The following program is a subroutine for Algorithm A, and it is also designed so that the normalization portion can be used by other subroutines that appear later in this section. In this program and in many others throughout this chapter, OFLO stands for a subroutine that prints out a message to the effect that MIX's overflow toggle was unexpectedly found to be on. The byte size b is assumed to be a multiple of 4. The normalization routine NORM assumes that $rI2 = e$ and $rAX = f$, where $rA = 0$ implies $rX = 0$ and $rI2 < b$.

00	BYTE	EQU	1(4:4)	Byte size b
01	EXP	EQU	1:1	Definition of exponent field
02	FSUB	STA	TEMP	Floating point subtraction subroutine:
03		LDAN	TEMP	Change sign of operand.
04	FADD	STJ	EXITF	Floating point addition subroutine:
05		JOV	OFLO	Ensure that overflow is off.
06		STA	TEMP	TEMP $\leftarrow v$.
07		LDX	ACC	$rX \leftarrow u$.
08		CMPA	ACC(EXP)	Steps A1, A2, A3 are combined here:
09		JGE	1F	Jump if $e_v \geq e_u$.
10		STX	FU(0:4)	FU $\leftarrow \pm f f f f 0$.
11		LD2	ACC(EXP)	$rI2 \leftarrow e_w$.
12		STA	FV(0:4)	
13		LD1N	TEMP(EXP)	$rI1 \leftarrow -e_v$.
14		JMP	4F	
15	1H	STA	FU(0:4)	FU $\leftarrow \pm f f f f 0$ (u,v interchanged).
16		LD2	TEMP(EXP)	$rI2 \leftarrow e_w$.
17		STX	FV(0:4)	
18		LD1N	ACC(EXP)	$rI1 \leftarrow -e_v$.
19	4H	INC1	0,2	$rI1 \leftarrow e_u - e_v$. (Step A4 unnecessary.)
20	5H	LDA	FV	A5. Scale right.
21		ENTX	0	Clear rX.
22		SRAX	0,1	Shift right $e_u - e_v$ places.
23	6H	ADD	FU	A6. Add.
24		JOV	N4	A7. Normalize. Jump if fraction overflow.
25		JXZ	NORM	Easy case?
26		LD1	FV(0:1)	Check for opposite signs.
27		JAP	1F	

28		J1N	N2	If not, normalize.
29		JMP	2F	
30	1H	J1P	N2	
31	2H	SRC	5	$|rX| \leftrightarrow |rA|$.
32		DECX	1	(rX is positive.)
33		STA	TEMP	(The operands had opposite signs;
34		STA	HALF(0:0)	we must adjust the registers
35		LDAN	TEMP	before rounding and normalization.)
36		ADD	HALF	
37		ADD	HALF	Complement the least significant portion.
38		SRC	5	Jump into normalization routine.
39		JMP	N2	
40	HALF	CON	1//2	One half the word size (Sign varies)
41	FU	CON	0	Fraction part f_u
42	FV	CON	0	Fraction part f_v
43	NORM	JAZ	ZRO	*N1. Test f.*
44	N2	CMPA	=0=(1:1)	*N2. Is f normalized?*
45		JNE	N5	To N5 if leading byte nonzero.
46	N3	SLAX	1	*N3. Scale left.*
47		DEC2	1	Decrease e by 1.
48		JMP	N2	Return to N2.
49	N4	ENTX	1	*N4. Scale right.*
50		SRC	1	Shift right, insert "1" with proper sign.
51		INC2	1	Increase e by 1.
52	N5	CMPA	=BYTE/2=(5:5)	*N5. Round.*
53		JL	N6	Is $|tail| < \frac{1}{2}b$?
54		JG	5F	
55		JXNZ	5F	Is $|tail| > \frac{1}{2}b$?
56		STA	TEMP	$|tail| = \frac{1}{2}b$; round to odd.
57		LDX	TEMP(4:4)	
58		JXO	N6	To N6 if rX is odd.
59	5H	STA	*+1(0:0)	Store sign of rA.
60		INCA	BYTE	Add b^{-4} to $|f|$. (Sign varies)
61		JOV	N4	Check for rounding overflow.
62	N6	J2N	EXPUN	*N6. Check e.* Underflow if $e < 0$.
63	N7	ENTX	0,2	*N7. Pack.* rX $\leftarrow e$.
64		SRC	1	
65	ZRO	DEC2	BYTE	rI2 $\leftarrow e - b$.
66	8H	STA	ACC	
67	EXITF	J2N	*	Exit, unless $e \geq b$.
68	EXPOV	HLT	2	Exponent overflow detected
69	EXPUN	HLT	1	Exponent underflow detected
70	ACC	CON	0	Floating point accumulator ∎

The rather long section of code from lines 26 to 40 is needed because MIX has only a 5-byte accumulator for adding signed numbers while in general $2p+1 = 9$ places of accuracy are required by Algorithm A. The program could be shortened to about half its present length if we were willing to sacrifice a little bit of its accuracy, but we shall see in the next section that full accuracy is important. Line 58 uses a nonstandard MIX instruction defined in Section 4.5.2. The running time for floating point addition and subtraction depends on several factors that are analyzed in Section 4.2.4.

Now let us consider multiplication and division, which are simpler than addition, and somewhat similar to each other.

Algorithm M (*Floating point multiplication or division*). Given base b, excess q, p-digit, normalized floating point numbers $u = (e_u, f_u)$ and $v = (e_v, f_v)$, this algorithm forms the product $w = u \otimes v$ or the quotient $w = u \oslash v$.

M1. [Unpack.] Separate the exponent and fraction parts of the representations of u and v. (Sometimes it is convenient, but not necessary, to test the operands for zero during this step.)

M2. [Operate.] Set

$$
\begin{aligned}
e_w \leftarrow e_u + e_v - q, \qquad & f_w \leftarrow f_u f_v \qquad && \text{for multiplication;} \\
e_w \leftarrow e_u - e_v + q + 1, \quad & f_w \leftarrow (b^{-1} f_u)/f_v \quad && \text{for division.}
\end{aligned}
\tag{9}
$$

(Since the input numbers are assumed to be normalized, it follows that either $f_w = 0$, or $1/b^2 \le |f_w| < 1$, or a division-by-zero error has occurred.) If necessary, the representation of f_w may be reduced to $p+2$ or $p+3$ digits at this point, as in exercise 5.

M3. [Normalize.] Perform Algorithm N on (e_w, f_w) to normalize, round, and pack the result. (*Note:* Normalization is simpler in this case, since scaling left occurs at most once, and since rounding overflow cannot occur after division.) ∎

The following MIX subroutines, intended to be used in connection with Program A, illustrate the machine considerations that arise in Algorithm M.

Program M (*Floating point multiplication and division*).

```
01 Q      EQU  BYTE/2      q is half the byte size
02 FMUL   STJ  EXITF       Floating point multiplication subroutine:
03        JOV  OFLO        Ensure that overflow is off.
04        STA  TEMP        TEMP ← v.
05        LDX  ACC         rX ← u.
06        STX  FU(0:4)     FU ← ±f f f f 0.
07        LD1  TEMP(EXP)
08        LD2  ACC(EXP)
09        INC2 -Q,1        rI2 ← e_u + e_v - q.
10        SLA  1
11        MUL  FU          Multiply f_u times f_v.
12        JMP  NORM        Normalize, round, and exit.
13 FDIV   STJ  EXITF       Floating point division subroutine:
14        JOV  OFLO        Ensure that overflow is off.
15        STA  TEMP        TEMP ← v.
16        STA  FV(0:4)     FV ← ±f f f f 0.
17        LD1  TEMP(EXP)
18        LD2  ACC(EXP)
19        DEC2 -Q,1        rI2 ← e_u - e_v + q.
```

```
20        ENTX  0
21        LDA   ACC
22        SLA   1          rA ← f_u.
23        CMPA  FV(1:5)
24        JL    *+3        Jump if |f_u| < |f_v|.
25        SRA   1          Otherwise, scale f_u right
26        INC2  1              and increase rI2 by 1.
27        DIV   FV         Divide.
28        JNOV  NORM       Normalize, round, and exit.
29 DVZRO  HLT   3          Unnormalized or zero divisor  ▮
```

The most noteworthy feature of this program is the provision for division in lines 23–26, which is made in order to ensure enough accuracy to round the answer. If $|f_u| < |f_v|$, straightforward application of Algorithm M would leave a result of the form "$\pm 0\, f\, f\, f\, f$" in register A, and this would not allow a proper rounding without a careful analysis of the remainder (which appears in register X). So the program computes $f_w \leftarrow f_u/f_v$ in this case, ensuring that f_w is either zero or normalized in all cases; rounding can proceed with five significant bytes, possibly testing whether the remainder is zero.

We occasionally need to convert values between fixed and floating point representations. A "fix-to-float" routine is easily obtained with the help of the normalization algorithm above; for example, in MIX, the following subroutine converts an integer to floating point form:

```
01 FLOT  STJ   EXITF     Assume that rA = u, an integer.
02        JOV   OFLO      Ensure that overflow is off.
03        ENT2  Q+5       Set raw exponent.                    (10)
04        ENTX  0
05        JMP   NORM      Normalize, round, and exit.  ▮
```

A "float-to-fix" subroutine is the subject of exercise 14.

The debugging of floating point subroutines is usually a difficult job, since there are so many cases to consider. Here is a list of common pitfalls that often trap a programmer or machine designer who is preparing floating point routines:

1) *Losing the sign.* On many machines (not MIX), shift instructions between registers will affect the sign, and the shifting operations used in normalizing and scaling numbers must be carefully analyzed. The sign is also lost frequently when minus zero is present. (For example, Program A is careful to retain the sign of register A in lines 33–37. See also exercise 6.)

2) *Failure to treat exponent underflow or overflow properly.* The size of e_w should not be checked until *after* the rounding and normalization, because preliminary tests may give an erroneous indication. Exponent underflow and overflow can occur on floating point addition and subtraction, not only during multiplication and division; and even though this is a rather rare occurrence, it must be tested each time. Enough information should be retained so that meaningful corrective actions are possible after overflow or underflow has occurred.

It has unfortunately become customary in many instances to ignore exponent underflow and simply to set underflowed results to zero with no indication of error. This causes a serious loss of accuracy in most cases (indeed, it is the loss of *all* the significant digits), and the assumptions underlying floating point arithmetic have broken down; so the programmer really must be told when underflow has occurred. Setting the result to zero is appropriate only in certain cases when the result is later to be added to a significantly larger quantity. When exponent underflow is not detected, we find mysterious situations in which $(u \otimes v) \otimes w$ is zero, but $u \otimes (v \otimes w)$ is not, since $u \otimes v$ results in exponent underflow but $u \otimes (v \otimes w)$ can be calculated without any exponents falling out of range. Similarly, we can find positive numbers a, b, c, d, and y such that

$$(a \otimes y \oplus b) \oslash (c \otimes y \oplus d) \approx \tfrac{2}{3},$$
$$(a \oplus b \oslash y) \oslash (c \oplus d \oslash y) = 1 \tag{11}$$

if exponent underflow is not detected. (See exercise 9.) Even though floating point routines are not precisely accurate, such a disparity as (11) is certainly unexpected when a, b, c, d, and y are all *positive*! Exponent underflow is usually not anticipated by a programmer, so it needs to be reported.*

3) *Inserted garbage.* When scaling to the left it is important to keep from introducing anything but zeros at the right. For example, note the "ENTX 0" instruction in line 21 of Program A, and the all-too-easily-forgotten "ENTX 0" instruction in line 04 of the FLOT subroutine (10). (But it would be a mistake to clear register X after line 27 in the division subroutine.)

4) *Unforeseen rounding overflow.* When a number like .999999997 is rounded to 8 digits, a carry will occur to the left of the decimal point, and the result must be scaled to the right. Many people have mistakenly concluded that rounding overflow is impossible during multiplication, since they look at the maximum value of $|f_u f_v|$, which is $1 - 2b^{-p} + b^{-2p}$; and this cannot round up to 1. The fallacy in this reasoning is exhibited in exercise 11. Curiously, it turns out that the phenomenon of rounding overflow *is* impossible during floating point division (see exercise 12).

---

* On the other hand, we must admit that today's high-level programming languages give the programmer little or no satisfactory way to make use of the information that a floating point routine wants to provide; and the MIX programs in this section, which simply halt when errors are detected, are even worse. There are numerous important applications in which exponent underflow is relatively harmless, and it is desirable to find a way for programmers to cope with such situations easily and safely. The practice of silently replacing underflows by zero has been thoroughly discredited, but there is another alternative that has recently been gaining much favor, namely to modify the definition that we have given for floating point numbers, allowing an unnormalized fraction part when the exponent has its smallest possible value. This idea of "gradual underflow," which was first embodied in the hardware of the Electrologica X8 computer, adds only a small amount of complexity to the algorithms, and it makes exponent underflow impossible during addition or subtraction. The simple formulas for relative error in Section 4.2.2 no longer hold in the presence of gradual underflow, so the topic is beyond the scope of this book. However, by using formulas like round$(x) = x(1-\delta)+\epsilon$, where $|\delta| < b^{1-p}/2$ and $|\epsilon| < b^{-p-q}/2$, one can show that gradual underflow succeeds in many important cases. See W. M. Kahan and J. Palmer, *ACM SIGNUM Newsletter* (October 1979), 13–21.

There is a school of thought that says it is harmless to "round" a value like .999999997 to .99999999 instead of to 1.0000000, since this does not increase the worst-case bounds on relative error. The floating decimal number 1.0000000 may be said to represent all real values in the interval

$$[1.0000000 - 5 \times 10^{-8} \, .. \, 1.0000000 + 5 \times 10^{-8}],$$

while .99999999 represents all values in the much smaller interval

$$(.99999999 - 5 \times 10^{-9} \, .. \, .99999999 + 5 \times 10^{-9}).$$

Even though the latter interval does not contain the original value .999999997, each number of the second interval is contained in the first, so subsequent calculations with the second interval are no less accurate than with the first. This ingenious argument is, however, incompatible with the mathematical philosophy of floating point arithmetic expressed in Section 4.2.2.

5) *Rounding before normalizing.* Inaccuracies are caused by premature rounding in the wrong digit position. This error is obvious when rounding is being done to the left of the appropriate position; but it is also dangerous in the less obvious cases where rounding is first done too far to the right, followed by rounding in the true position. For this reason it is a mistake to round during the "scaling-right" operation in step A5, except as prescribed in exercise 5. (The special case of rounding in step N5, then rounding again after rounding overflow has occurred, is harmless, however, because rounding overflow always yields ± 1.0000000 and such values are unaffected by the subsequent rounding process.)

6) *Failure to retain enough precision in intermediate calculations.* Detailed analyses of the accuracy of floating point arithmetic, made in the next section, suggest strongly that normalizing floating point routines should always deliver a properly rounded result to the maximum possible accuracy. There should be no exceptions to this dictum, even in cases that occur with extremely low probability; the appropriate number of significant digits should be retained throughout the computations, as stated in Algorithms A and M.

C. Floating point hardware. Nearly every large computer intended for scientific calculations includes floating point arithmetic as part of its repertoire of built-in operations. Unfortunately, the design of such hardware usually includes some anomalies that result in dismally poor behavior in certain circumstances, and we hope that future computer designers will pay more attention to providing the proper behavior than they have in the past. It costs only a little more to build the machine right, and considerations in the following section show that substantial benefits will be gained. Yesterday's compromises are no longer appropriate for modern machines, based on what we know now.

The MIX computer, which is being used as an example of a "typical" machine in this series of books, has an optional "floating point attachment" (available at extra cost) that includes the following seven operations:

• FADD, FSUB, FMUL, FDIV, FLOT, FCMP (C = 1, 2, 3, 4, 5, 56, respectively; F = 6). The contents of rA after the operation "FADD V" are precisely the same as the contents of rA after the operations

$$\text{STA ACC; LDA V; JMP FADD}$$

where FADD is the subroutine that appears earlier in this section, except that both operands are automatically normalized before entry to the subroutine if they were not already in normalized form. (If exponent underflow occurs during this pre-normalization, but not during the normalization of the answer, no underflow is signalled.) Similar remarks apply to FSUB, FMUL, and FDIV. The contents of rA after the operation "FLOT" are the contents after "JMP FLOT" in the subroutine (10) above.

The contents of rA are unchanged by the operation "FCMP V". This instruction sets the comparison indicator to LESS, EQUAL, or GREATER, depending on whether the contents of rA are "definitely less than," "approximately equal to," or "definitely greater than" V, as discussed in the next section. The precise action is defined by the subroutine FCMP of exercise 4.2.2–17 with EPSILON in location 0.

No register other than rA is affected by any of the floating point operations. If exponent overflow or underflow occurs, the overflow toggle is turned on and the exponent of the answer is given modulo the byte size. Division by zero leaves undefined garbage in rA. Execution times: $4u$, $4u$, $9u$, $11u$, $3u$, $4u$, respectively.

• FIX ($C = 5$; $F = 7$). The contents of rA are replaced by the integer "round(rA)", rounding to the nearest integer as in step N5 of Algorithm N. However, if this answer is too large to fit in the register, the overflow toggle is set on and the result is undefined. Execution time: $3u$.

Sometimes it is helpful to use floating point operators in a nonstandard way. For example, if the operation FLOT had not been included as part of MIX's floating point attachment, we could easily achieve its effect on 4-byte numbers by writing

```
FLOT STJ  9F
     SLA  1
     ENTX Q+4
     SRC  1                                                    (12)
     FADD =0=
9H   JMP  *    ▮
```

This routine is not strictly equivalent to the FLOT operator, since it assumes that the 1:1 byte of rA is zero, and it destroys rX. The handling of more general situations is a little tricky, because rounding overflow can occur even during a FLOT operation.

Similarly, suppose MIX had a FADD operation but not FIX. If we wanted to round a number u from floating point form to the nearest fixed point integer, and if we knew that the number was nonnegative and would fit in at most three bytes, we could write

$$\text{FADD FUDGE}$$

where location FUDGE contains the constant

| + | Q+4 | 1 | 0 | 0 | 0 |

;

the result in rA would be

| + | Q+4 | 1 | round(u) |

.   (13)

D. History and bibliography. The origins of floating point notation can be traced back to Babylonian mathematicians (1800 B.C. or earlier), who made extensive use of radix-60 floating point arithmetic but did not have a notation for the exponents. The appropriate exponent was always somehow "understood" by whoever was doing the calculations. At least one case has been found in which the wrong answer was given because addition was performed with improper alignment of the operands, but such examples are very rare; see O. Neugebauer, *The Exact Sciences in Antiquity* (Princeton, N. J.: Princeton University Press, 1952), 26–27. Another early contribution to floating point notation is due to the Greek mathematician Apollonius (3rd century B.C.), who apparently was the first to explain how to simplify multiplication by collecting powers of 10 separately from their coefficients, at least in simple cases. [For a discussion of Apollonius's method, see Pappus, *Mathematical Collections* (4th century A.D.).] After the Babylonian civilization died out, the first significant uses of floating point notation for products and quotients did not emerge until much later, about the time logarithms were invented (1600) and shortly afterwards when Oughtred invented the slide rule (1630). The modern notation " x^n " for exponents was being introduced at about the same time; separate symbols for x squared, x cubed, etc., had been in use before this.

Floating point arithmetic was incorporated into the design of some of the earliest computers. It was independently proposed by Leonardo Torres y Quevedo in Madrid, 1914; by Konrad Zuse in Berlin, 1936; and by George Stibitz in New Jersey, 1939. Zuse's machines used a floating binary representation that he called "semi-logarithmic notation"; he also incorporated conventions for dealing with special quantities like "∞" and "undefined." The first American computers to operate with floating point arithmetic hardware were the Bell Laboratories' Model V and the Harvard Mark II, both of which were relay calculators designed in 1944. [See B. Randell, *The Origins of Digital Computers* (Berlin: Springer, 1973), 100, 155, 163–164, 259–260; *Proc. Symp. Large-Scale Digital Calculating Machinery* (Harvard, 1947), 41–68, 69–79; *Datamation* **13** (April 1967), 35–44 (May 1967), 45–49; *Zeit. für angew. Math. und Physik* **1** (1950), 345–346.]

The use of floating binary arithmetic was seriously considered in 1944–1946 by researchers at the Moore School in their plans for the first *electronic* digital computers, but they found that floating point circuitry was much harder to implement with tubes than with relays. The group realized that scaling was a problem in programming; but they knew that it was only a very small part of a total programming job in those days. Indeed, explicit fixed-point scaling seemed to be well worth the time and trouble it took, since it tended to keep programmers aware of the numerical accuracy they were getting. Furthermore, the machine designers argued that floating point representation would consume valuable memory space, since the exponents must be stored; and they noted that floating point hardware was not readily adapted to multiple-precision calculations. [See von Neumann's *Collected Works* **5** (New York: Macmillan, 1963), 43, 73–74.] At that time, of course, they were designing the first stored-program computer and the second electronic computer, and their choice had to be *either* fixed point *or* floating point arithmetic, not both. They anticipated the coding of floating binary subroutines, and in fact "shift left" and "shift right" instructions were put into their design primarily to make such routines more efficient. The first machine to have both kinds of arithmetic in its hardware was apparently a computer developed at General Electric Company [see *Proc. 2nd Symp. Large-Scale Digital Calculating Machinery* (Cambridge, Mass.: Harvard University Press, 1951), 65–69].

Floating point subroutines and interpretive systems for early machines were coded by D. J. Wheeler and others, and the first publication of such routines was in *The Preparation of Programs for an Electronic Digital Computer* by Wilkes, Wheeler, and Gill (Reading, Mass.: Addison–Wesley, 1951), subroutines A1–A11, pages 35–37 and 105–117. It is interesting to note that floating *decimal* subroutines are described here, although a binary computer was being used; in other words, the numbers were represented as $10^e f$, not $2^e f$, and therefore the scaling operations required multiplication or division by 10. On this particular machine such decimal scaling was almost as easy as shifting, and the decimal approach greatly simplified input/output conversions.

Most published references to the details of floating point arithmetic routines are scattered in technical memorandums distributed by various computer manufacturers, but there have been occasional appearances of these routines in the open literature. Besides the reference above, the following are of historical interest: R. H. Stark and D. B. MacMillan, *Math. Comp.* **5** (1951), 86–92, where a plugboard-wired program is described; D. McCracken, *Digital Computer Programming* (New York: Wiley, 1957), 121–131; J. W. Carr III, *CACM* **2**, 5 (May 1959), 10–15; W. G. Wadey, *JACM* **7** (1960), 129–139; D. E. Knuth, *JACM* **8** (1961), 119–128; O. Kesner, *CACM* **5** (1962), 269–271; F. P. Brooks and K. E. Iverson, *Automatic Data Processing* (New York: Wiley, 1963), 184–199. For a discussion of floating point arithmetic from a computer designer's standpoint, see "Floating point operation" by S. G. Campbell, in *Planning a Computer System*, edited by W. Buchholz (New York: McGraw–Hill, 1962), 92–121; A. Padegs, *IBM Systems J.* **7** (1968), 22–29. Additional references, which deal primarily with the accuracy of floating point methods, are given in Section 4.2.2.

A revolutionary change in floating point hardware took place when most manufacturers began to adopt ANSI/IEEE Standard 754 during the late 1980s. Relevant references are: *IEEE Micro* **4** (1984), 86–100; W. J. Cody, *Comp. Sci. and Statistics: Symp. on the Interface* **15** (1983), 133–139; W. M. Kahan, *Mini/Micro West-83 Conf. Record* (1983), Paper 16/1; D. Goldberg, *Computing Surveys* **23** (1991), 5–48, 413; W. J. Cody and J. T. Coonen, *ACM Trans. Math. Software* **19** (1993), 443–451.

The MMIX computer, which will replace MIX in the next edition of this book, will naturally conform to the new standard.

EXERCISES

1. [*10*] How would Avogadro's number and Planck's constant (3) be represented in base 100, excess 50, four-digit floating point notation? (This would be the representation used by MIX, as in (4), when the byte size is 100.)

2. [*12*] Assume that the exponent e is constrained to lie in the range $0 \le e \le E$; what are the largest and smallest positive values that can be written as base b, excess q, p-digit floating point numbers? What are the largest and smallest positive values that can be written as *normalized* floating point numbers with these specifications?

3. [*11*] (K. Zuse, 1936.) Show that if we are using normalized floating binary arithmetic, there is a way to increase the precision slightly without loss of memory space: A p-bit fraction part can be represented using only $p - 1$ bit positions of a computer word, if the range of exponent values is decreased very slightly.

▸ **4.** [*16*] Assume that $b = 10$, $p = 8$. What result does Algorithm A give for $(50, +.98765432) \oplus (49, +.33333333)$? For $(53, -.99987654) \oplus (54, +.10000000)$? For $(45, -.50000001) \oplus (54, +.10000000)$?

▸ **5.** [*24*] Let us say that $x \sim y$ (with respect to a given radix b) if x and y are real numbers satisfying the following conditions:

$$\lfloor x/b \rfloor = \lfloor y/b \rfloor;$$
$$x \bmod b = 0 \iff y \bmod b = 0;$$
$$0 < x \bmod b < \tfrac{1}{2}b \iff 0 < y \bmod b < \tfrac{1}{2}b;$$
$$x \bmod b = \tfrac{1}{2}b \iff y \bmod b = \tfrac{1}{2}b;$$
$$\tfrac{1}{2}b < x \bmod b < b \iff \tfrac{1}{2}b < y \bmod b < b.$$

Prove that if f_v is replaced by $b^{-p-2}F_v$ between steps A5 and A6 of Algorithm A, where $F_v \sim b^{p+2}f_v$, the result of that algorithm will be unchanged. (If F_v is an integer and b is even, this operation essentially truncates f_v to $p+2$ places while remembering whether any nonzero digits have been dropped, thereby minimizing the length of register that is needed for the addition in step A6.)

6. [*20*] If the result of a FADD instruction is zero, what will be the sign of rA, according to the definitions of MIX's floating point attachment given in this section?

7. [*27*] Discuss floating point arithmetic using balanced ternary notation.

8. [*20*] Give examples of normalized eight-digit floating decimal numbers u and v for which addition yields (a) exponent underflow, (b) exponent overflow, assuming that exponents must satisfy $0 \le e < 100$.

9. [*M24*] (W. M. Kahan.) Assume that the occurrence of exponent underflow causes the result to be replaced by zero, with no error indication given. Using excess zero, eight-digit floating decimal numbers with e in the range $-50 \le e < 50$, find positive values of a, b, c, d, and y such that (11) holds.

10. [*12*] Give an example of normalized eight-digit floating decimal numbers u and v for which rounding overflow occurs in addition.

▸ **11.** [*M20*] Give an example of normalized, excess 50, eight-digit floating decimal numbers u and v for which rounding overflow occurs in multiplication.

12. [*M25*] Prove that rounding overflow cannot occur during the normalization phase of floating point division.

13. [*30*] When doing "interval arithmetic" we don't want to round the results of a floating point computation; we want rather to implement operations such as $\triangledown$ and $\triangle$, which give the tightest possible representable bounds on the true sum:

$$u \triangledown v \le u + v \le u \triangle v.$$

How should the algorithms of this section be modified for such a purpose?

14. [*25*] Write a MIX subroutine that begins with an arbitrary floating point number in register A, not necessarily normalized, and converts it to the nearest fixed point integer (or determines that the number is too large in absolute value to make such a conversion possible).

▸ **15.** [*28*] Write a MIX subroutine, to be used in connection with the other subroutines of this section, that calculates $u \pmod 1$, namely $u - \lfloor u \rfloor$ rounded to the nearest floating point number, given a floating point number u. Notice that when u is a very small negative number, $u \pmod 1$ should be rounded so that the result is unity (even though $u \bmod 1$ has been defined to be always *less* than unity, as a real number).

16. [*HM21*] (Robert L. Smith.) Design an algorithm to compute the real and imaginary parts of the complex number $(a+bi)/(c+di)$, given real floating point values a, b, c, and d with $c+di \ne 0$. Avoid the computation of c^2+d^2, since it would cause floating point overflow even when $|c|$ or $|d|$ is approximately the square root of the maximum allowable floating point value.

17. [*40*] (John Cocke.) Explore the idea of extending the range of floating point numbers by defining a single-word representation in which the precision of the fraction decreases as the magnitude of the exponent increases.

18. [*25*] Consider a binary computer with 36-bit words, on which positive floating binary numbers are represented as $(0\,e_1 e_2 \ldots e_8 f_1 f_2 \ldots f_{27})_2$; here $(e_1 e_2 \ldots e_8)_2$ is an excess $(10000000)_2$ exponent and $(f_1 f_2 \ldots f_{27})_2$ is a 27-bit fraction. Negative floating point numbers are represented by the *two's complement* of the corresponding positive representation (see Section 4.1). Thus, 1.5 is $201|600000000$ in octal notation, while -1.5 is $576|200000000$; the octal representations of 1.0 and -1.0 are $201|400000000$ and $576|400000000$, respectively. (A vertical line is used here to show the boundary between exponent and fraction.) Note that bit f_1 of a normalized positive number is always 1, while it is almost always zero for negative numbers; the exceptional cases are representations of -2^k.

Suppose that the exact result of a floating point operation has the octal code $572|740000000|01$; this (negative) 33-bit fraction must be normalized and rounded to 27 bits. If we shift left until the leading fraction bit is zero, we get $576|000000000|20$, but this rounds to the illegal value $576|000000000$; we have over-normalized, since the correct answer is $575|400000000$. On the other hand if we start (in some other problem) with the value $572|740000000|05$ and stop before over-normalizing it, we get $575|400000000|50$, which rounds to the unnormalized number $575|400000001$; subsequent normalization yields $576|000000002$ while the correct answer is $576|000000001$.

Give a simple, correct rounding rule that resolves this dilemma on such a machine (without abandoning two's complement notation).

19. [*24*] What is the running time for the FADD subroutine in Program A, in terms of relevant characteristics of the data? What is the maximum running time, over all inputs that do not cause exponent overflow or underflow?

Round numbers are always false.
— SAMUEL JOHNSON (1750)

I shall speak in round numbers, not absolutely accurate,
yet not so wide from truth as to vary the result materially.
— THOMAS JEFFERSON (1824)

4.2.2. Accuracy of Floating Point Arithmetic

Floating point computation is by nature inexact, and programmers can easily misuse it so that the computed answers consist almost entirely of "noise." One of the principal problems of numerical analysis is to determine how accurate the results of certain numerical methods will be. There's a credibility gap: We don't know how much of the computer's answers to believe. Novice computer users solve this problem by implicitly trusting in the computer as an infallible authority; they tend to believe that all digits of a printed answer are significant. Disillusioned computer users have just the opposite approach; they are constantly afraid that their answers are almost meaningless. Many serious mathematicians have attempted to analyze a sequence of floating point operations rigorously, but have found the task so formidable that they have tried to be content with plausibility arguments instead.

A thorough examination of error analysis techniques is beyond the scope of this book, but in the present section we shall study some of the low-level characteristics of floating point arithmetic errors. Our goal is to discover how to perform floating point arithmetic in such a way that reasonable analyses of error propagation are facilitated as much as possible.

A rough (but reasonably useful) way to express the behavior of floating point arithmetic can be based on the concept of "significant figures" or *relative error*. If we are representing an exact real number x inside a computer by using the approximation $\hat{x} = x(1 + \epsilon)$, the quantity $\epsilon = (\hat{x} - x)/x$ is called the relative error of approximation. Roughly speaking, the operations of floating point multiplication and division do not magnify the relative error by very much; but floating point subtraction of nearly equal quantities (and floating point addition, $u \oplus v$, where u is nearly equal to $-v$) can very greatly increase the relative error. So we have a general rule of thumb, that a substantial loss of accuracy is expected from such additions and subtractions, but not from multiplications and divisions. On the other hand, the situation is somewhat paradoxical and needs to be understood properly, since the "bad" additions and subtractions are always performed with perfect accuracy! (See exercise 25.)

One of the consequences of the possible unreliability of floating point addition is that the associative law breaks down:

$$(u \oplus v) \oplus w \neq u \oplus (v \oplus w), \qquad \text{for many } u, v, w. \tag{1}$$

For example,

$(11111113. \oplus -11111111.) \oplus 7.5111111 = 2.0000000 \oplus 7.5111111 = 9.5111111;$

$11111113. \oplus (-11111111. \oplus 7.5111111) = 11111113. \oplus -11111103. = 10.000000.$

(All examples in this section are given in eight-digit floating decimal arithmetic, with exponents indicated by an explicit decimal point. Recall that, as in Section 4.2.1, the symbols $\oplus$, $\ominus$, $\otimes$, $\oslash$ are used to stand for floating point operations that correspond to the exact operations $+$, $-$, $\times$, $/$.)

In view of the failure of the associative law, the comment of Mrs. La Touche that appears at the beginning of this chapter makes a good deal of sense with respect to floating point arithmetic. Mathematical notations like "$a_1 + a_2 + a_3$" or "$\sum_{k=1}^{n} a_k$" are inherently based upon the assumption of associativity, so a programmer must be especially careful not to assume implicitly that the associative law is valid.

A. An axiomatic approach. Although the associative law is not valid, the commutative law

$$u \oplus v = v \oplus u \tag{2}$$

does hold, and this law can be a valuable conceptual asset in programming and in the analysis of programs. Equation (2) suggests that we should look for additional examples of important laws that *are* satisfied by $\oplus$, $\ominus$, $\otimes$, and $\oslash$; it is not unreasonable to say that *floating point routines should be designed to preserve as many of the ordinary mathematical laws as possible.* If more axioms are valid, it becomes easier to write good programs, and programs also become more portable from machine to machine.

Let us therefore consider some of the other basic laws that are valid for normalized floating point operations as described in the previous section. First we have

$$u \ominus v = u \oplus -v; \tag{3}$$
$$-(u \oplus v) = -u \oplus -v; \tag{4}$$
$$u \oplus v = 0 \quad \text{if and only if} \quad v = -u; \tag{5}$$
$$u \oplus 0 = u. \tag{6}$$

From these laws we can derive further identities; for example (exercise 1),

$$u \ominus v = -(v \ominus u). \tag{7}$$

Identities (2) to (6) are easily deduced from the algorithms in Section 4.2.1. The following rule is slightly less obvious:

$$\text{if} \quad u \le v \quad \text{then} \quad u \oplus w \le v \oplus w. \tag{8}$$

Instead of attempting to prove this rule by analyzing Algorithm 4.2.1A, let us go back to the basic principle by which that algorithm was designed. (Algorithmic proofs aren't always easier than mathematical ones.) Our idea was that the floating point operations should satisfy

$$u \oplus v = \text{round}(u + v), \qquad u \ominus v = \text{round}(u - v),$$
$$u \otimes v = \text{round}(u \times v), \qquad u \oslash v = \text{round}(u \,/\, v), \tag{9}$$

where round(x) denotes the best floating point approximation to x as defined in Algorithm 4.2.1N. We have

$$\text{round}(-x) = -\text{round}(x), \tag{10}$$

$$x \leq y \quad \text{implies} \quad \text{round}(x) \leq \text{round}(y), \tag{11}$$

and these fundamental relations yield properties (2) through (8) immediately. We can also write down several more identities:

$$u \otimes v = v \otimes u, \quad (-u) \otimes v = -(u \otimes v), \quad 1 \otimes v = v;$$
$$u \otimes v = 0 \quad \text{if and only if} \quad u = 0 \text{ or } v = 0;$$
$$(-u) \oslash v = u \oslash (-v) = -(u \oslash v);$$
$$0 \oslash v = 0, \quad u \oslash 1 = u, \quad u \oslash u = 1.$$

If $u \leq v$ and $w > 0$, then $u \otimes w \leq v \otimes w$ and $u \oslash w \leq v \oslash w$; also $w \oslash u \geq w \oslash v$ when $v \geq u > 0$. If $u \oplus v = u + v$, then $(u \oplus v) \ominus v = u$; and if $u \otimes v = u \times v \neq 0$, then $(u \otimes v) \oslash v = u$. We see that a good deal of regularity is present in spite of the inexactness of the floating point operations, when things have been defined properly.

Several familiar rules of algebra are still, of course, conspicuously absent from the collection of identities above. The associative law for floating point multiplication is not strictly true, as shown in exercise 3, and the distributive law between $\otimes$ and $\oplus$ can fail rather badly: Let $u = 20000.000$, $v = -6.0000000$, and $w = 6.0000003$; then

$$(u \otimes v) \oplus (u \otimes w) = -120000.00 \oplus 120000.01 = .010000000$$

$$u \otimes (v \oplus w) = 20000.000 \otimes .00000030000000 = .0060000000$$

so

$$u \otimes (v \oplus w) \neq (u \otimes v) \oplus (u \otimes w). \tag{12}$$

On the other hand we do have $b \otimes (v \oplus w) = (b \otimes v) \oplus (b \otimes w)$, when b is the floating point radix, since

$$\text{round}(bx) = b\,\text{round}(x). \tag{13}$$

(Strictly speaking, the identities and inequalities we are considering in this section implicitly assume that exponent underflow and overflow do not occur. The function round(x) is undefined when $|x|$ is too small or too large, and equations such as (13) hold only when both sides are defined.)

The failure of Cauchy's fundamental inequality

$$(x_1^2 + \cdots + x_n^2)(y_1^2 + \cdots + y_n^2) \geq (x_1 y_1 + \cdots + x_n y_n)^2$$

is another important example of the breakdown of traditional algebra in the presence of floating point arithmetic. Exercise 7 shows that Cauchy's inequality can fail even in the simple case $n = 2$, $x_1 = x_2 = 1$. Novice programmers who calculate the standard deviation of some observations by using the textbook formula

$$\sigma = \sqrt{\left(n \sum_{1 \le k \le n} x_k^2 - \left(\sum_{1 \le k \le n} x_k\right)^2\right) \Big/ n(n-1)} \tag{14}$$

often find themselves taking the square root of a negative number! A much better way to calculate means and standard deviations with floating point arithmetic is to use the recurrence formulas

$$M_1 = x_1, \qquad M_k = M_{k-1} \oplus (x_k \ominus M_{k-1}) \oslash k, \tag{15}$$
$$S_1 = 0, \qquad S_k = S_{k-1} \oplus (x_k \ominus M_{k-1}) \otimes (x_k \ominus M_k), \tag{16}$$

for $2 \le k \le n$, where $\sigma = \sqrt{S_n/(n-1)}$. [See B. P. Welford, *Technometrics* **4** (1962), 419–420.] With this method S_n can never be negative, and we avoid other serious problems encountered by the naïve method of accumulating sums, as shown in exercise 16. (See exercise 19 for a summation technique that provides an even better guarantee on the accuracy.)

Although algebraic laws do not always hold exactly, we can often show that they aren't too far off base. When $b^{e-1} \le |x| < b^e$ we have round$(x) = x + \rho(x)$, where $|\rho(x)| \le \frac{1}{2}b^{e-p}$; hence

$$\text{round}(x) = x(1 + \delta(x)), \tag{17}$$

where the relative error is bounded independently of x:

$$|\delta(x)| = \frac{|\rho(x)|}{|x|} \le \frac{|\rho(x)|}{b^{e-1} + |\rho(x)|} \le \frac{\frac{1}{2}b^{e-p}}{b^{e-1} + \frac{1}{2}b^{e-p}} < \frac{1}{2}b^{1-p}. \tag{18}$$

We can use this inequality to estimate the relative error of normalized floating point calculations in a simple way, since $u \oplus v = (u + v)(1 + \delta(u + v))$, etc.

As an example of typical error-estimation procedures, let us consider the associative law for multiplication. Exercise 3 shows that $(u \otimes v) \otimes w$ is not in general equal to $u \otimes (v \otimes w)$; but the situation in this case is much better than it was with respect to the associative law of addition (1) and the distributive law (12). In fact, we have

$$(u \otimes v) \otimes w = \big((uv)(1 + \delta_1)\big) \otimes w = uvw(1 + \delta_1)(1 + \delta_2),$$
$$u \otimes (v \otimes w) = u \otimes \big((vw)(1 + \delta_3)\big) = uvw(1 + \delta_3)(1 + \delta_4),$$

for some $\delta_1, \delta_2, \delta_3, \delta_4$, provided that no exponent underflow or overflow occurs, where $|\delta_j| < \frac{1}{2}b^{1-p}$ for each j. Hence

$$\frac{(u \otimes v) \otimes w}{u \otimes (v \otimes w)} = \frac{(1 + \delta_1)(1 + \delta_2)}{(1 + \delta_3)(1 + \delta_4)} = 1 + \delta,$$

where

$$|\delta| < 2b^{1-p}/\left(1 - \frac{1}{2}b^{1-p}\right)^2. \tag{19}$$

The number b^{1-p} occurs so often in such analyses, it has been given a special name, one *ulp*, meaning one unit in the last place of the fraction part. Floating point operations are correct to within half an ulp, and the calculation of uvw by two floating point multiplications will be correct within about one ulp (ignoring second-order terms). Hence the associative law for multiplication holds to within about two ulps of relative error.

We have shown that $(u \otimes v) \otimes w$ is approximately equal to $u \otimes (v \otimes w)$, except when exponent overflow or underflow is a problem. It is worthwhile to study this intuitive idea of approximate equality in more detail; can we make such a statement more precise in a reasonable way?

Programmers who use floating point arithmetic almost never want to test if two computed values are exactly equal to each other (or at least they hardly ever should try to do so), because this is an extremely improbable occurrence. For example, if a recurrence relation

$$x_{n+1} = f(x_n)$$

is being used, where the theory in some textbook says that x_n approaches a limit as $n \to \infty$, it is usually a mistake to wait until $x_{n+1} = x_n$ for some n, since the sequence x_n might be periodic with a longer period due to the rounding of intermediate results. The proper procedure is to wait until $|x_{n+1} - x_n| < \delta$, for some suitably chosen number δ; but since we don't necessarily know the order of magnitude of x_n in advance, it is even better to wait until

$$|x_{n+1} - x_n| \leq \epsilon |x_n|; \tag{20}$$

now ϵ is a number that is much easier to select. Relation (20) is another way of saying that x_{n+1} and x_n are approximately equal; and our discussion indicates that a relation of "approximately equal" would be more useful than the traditional relation of equality, when floating point computations are involved, if we could only define a suitable approximation relation.

In other words, the fact that strict equality of floating point values is of little importance implies that we ought to have a new operation, *floating point comparison*, which is intended to help assess the relative values of two floating point quantities. The following definitions seem to be appropriate for base b, excess q, floating point numbers $u = (e_u, f_u)$ and $v = (e_v, f_v)$:

$$u \prec v \quad (\epsilon) \qquad \text{if and only if} \qquad v - u > \epsilon \max(b^{e_u - q}, b^{e_v - q}); \tag{21}$$

$$u \sim v \quad (\epsilon) \qquad \text{if and only if} \qquad |v - u| \leq \epsilon \max(b^{e_u - q}, b^{e_v - q}); \tag{22}$$

$$u \succ v \quad (\epsilon) \qquad \text{if and only if} \qquad u - v > \epsilon \max(b^{e_u - q}, b^{e_v - q}); \tag{23}$$

$$u \approx v \quad (\epsilon) \qquad \text{if and only if} \qquad |v - u| \leq \epsilon \min(b^{e_u - q}, b^{e_v - q}). \tag{24}$$

These definitions apply to unnormalized values as well as to normalized ones. Notice that exactly one of the conditions $u \prec v$ (definitely less than), $u \sim v$ (approximately equal to), or $u \succ v$ (definitely greater than) must always hold for any given pair of values u and v. The relation $u \approx v$ is somewhat stronger than $u \sim v$, and it might be read "u is essentially equal to v." All of the relations are specified in terms of a positive real number ϵ that measures the degree of approximation being considered.

One way to view the definitions above is to associate a "neighborhood" set $N(u) = \{x \mid |x - u| \le \epsilon b^{e_u - q}\}$ with each floating point number u; thus, $N(u)$ represents a set of values near u based on the exponent of u's floating point representation. In these terms, we have $u \prec v$ if and only if $N(u) < v$ and $u < N(v)$; $u \sim v$ if and only if $u \in N(v)$ or $v \in N(u)$; $u \succ v$ if and only if $u > N(v)$ and $N(u) > v$; $u \approx v$ if and only if $u \in N(v)$ and $v \in N(u)$. (Here we are assuming that the parameter ϵ, which measures the degree of approximation, is a constant; a more complete notation would indicate the dependence of $N(u)$ upon ϵ.)

Here are some simple consequences of definitions (21)–(24):

$$\text{if} \quad u \prec v \quad (\epsilon) \quad \text{then} \quad v \succ u \quad (\epsilon); \tag{25}$$

$$\text{if} \quad u \approx v \quad (\epsilon) \quad \text{then} \quad u \sim v \quad (\epsilon); \tag{26}$$

$$u \approx u \quad (\epsilon); \tag{27}$$

$$\text{if} \quad u \prec v \quad (\epsilon) \quad \text{then} \quad u < v; \tag{28}$$

$$\text{if} \quad u \prec v \quad (\epsilon_1) \quad \text{and} \quad \epsilon_1 \ge \epsilon_2 \quad \text{then} \quad u \prec v \quad (\epsilon_2); \tag{29}$$

$$\text{if} \quad u \sim v \quad (\epsilon_1) \quad \text{and} \quad \epsilon_1 \le \epsilon_2 \quad \text{then} \quad u \sim v \quad (\epsilon_2); \tag{30}$$

$$\text{if} \quad u \approx v \quad (\epsilon_1) \quad \text{and} \quad \epsilon_1 \le \epsilon_2 \quad \text{then} \quad u \approx v \quad (\epsilon_2); \tag{31}$$

$$\text{if} \quad u \prec v \quad (\epsilon_1) \quad \text{and} \quad v \prec w \quad (\epsilon_2) \quad \text{then} \quad u \prec w \quad \bigl(\min(\epsilon_1, \epsilon_2)\bigr); \tag{32}$$

$$\text{if} \quad u \approx v \quad (\epsilon_1) \quad \text{and} \quad v \approx w \quad (\epsilon_2) \quad \text{then} \quad u \sim w \quad (\epsilon_1 + \epsilon_2). \tag{33}$$

Moreover, we can prove without difficulty that

$$|u - v| \le \epsilon|u| \quad \text{and} \quad |u - v| \le \epsilon|v| \quad \text{implies} \quad u \approx v \quad (\epsilon); \tag{34}$$

$$|u - v| \le \epsilon|u| \quad \text{or} \quad |u - v| \le \epsilon|v| \quad \text{implies} \quad u \sim v \quad (\epsilon); \tag{35}$$

and conversely, for *normalized* floating point numbers u and v, when $\epsilon < 1$,

$$u \approx v \quad (\epsilon) \quad \text{implies} \quad |u - v| \le b\epsilon|u| \quad \text{and} \quad |u - v| \le b\epsilon|v|; \tag{36}$$

$$u \sim v \quad (\epsilon) \quad \text{implies} \quad |u - v| \le b\epsilon|u| \quad \text{or} \quad |u - v| \le b\epsilon|v|. \tag{37}$$

Let $\epsilon_0 = b^{1-p}$ be one ulp. The derivation of (17) establishes the inequality $|x - \text{round}(x)| = |\rho(x)| < \frac{1}{2}\epsilon_0 \min\bigl(|x|, |\text{round}(x)|\bigr)$, hence

$$x \approx \text{round}(x) \quad (\tfrac{1}{2}\epsilon_0); \tag{38}$$

it follows that $u \oplus v \approx u + v$ $(\frac{1}{2}\epsilon_0)$, etc. The approximate associative law for multiplication derived above can be recast as follows: We have

$$\bigl|(u \otimes v) \otimes w - u \otimes (v \otimes w)\bigr| < \frac{2\epsilon_0}{(1 - \frac{1}{2}\epsilon_0)^2} |u \otimes (v \otimes w)|$$

by (19), and the same inequality is valid with $(u \otimes v) \otimes w$ and $u \otimes (v \otimes w)$ interchanged. Hence by (34),

$$(u \otimes v) \otimes w \approx u \otimes (v \otimes w) \quad (\epsilon) \tag{39}$$

whenever $\epsilon \ge 2\epsilon_0/(1 - \frac{1}{2}\epsilon_0)^2$. For example, if $b = 10$ and $p = 8$ we may take $\epsilon = 0.00000021$.

The relations $\prec, \sim, \succ$, and $\approx$ are useful within numerical algorithms, and it is therefore a good idea to provide routines for comparing floating point numbers as well as for doing arithmetic on them.

Let us now shift our attention back to the question of finding *exact* relations that are satisfied by the floating point operations. It is interesting to note that floating point addition and subtraction are not completely intractable from an axiomatic standpoint, since they do satisfy the nontrivial identities stated in the following theorems.

Theorem A. *Let u and v be normalized floating point numbers. Then*

$$\big((u \oplus v) \ominus u\big) + \big((u \oplus v) \ominus \big((u \oplus v) \ominus u\big)\big) = u \oplus v, \qquad (40)$$

provided that no exponent overflow or underflow occurs.

This rather cumbersome-looking identity can be rewritten in a simpler manner: Let

$$
\begin{aligned}
u' &= (u \oplus v) \ominus v, & v' &= (u \oplus v) \ominus u; \\
u'' &= (u \oplus v) \ominus v', & v'' &= (u \oplus v) \ominus u'.
\end{aligned}
\qquad (41)
$$

Intuitively, u' and u'' should be approximations to u, and v' and v'' should be approximations to v. Theorem A tells us that

$$u \oplus v = u' + v'' = u'' + v'. \qquad (42)$$

This is a stronger statement than the identity

$$u \oplus v = u' \oplus v'' = u'' \oplus v', \qquad (43)$$

which follows by rounding (42).

Proof. Let us say that t is a *tail* of x modulo b^e if

$$t \equiv x \pmod{b^e}, \qquad |t| \le \tfrac{1}{2} b^e; \qquad (44)$$

thus, $x - \text{round}(x)$ is always a tail of x. The proof of Theorem A rests largely on the following simple fact proved in exercise 11:

Lemma T. *If t is a tail of the floating point number x, then $x \ominus t = x - t$.* ∎

Let $w = u \oplus v$. Theorem A holds trivially when $w = 0$. By multiplying all variables by a suitable power of b, we may assume without loss of generality that $e_w = p$. Then $u + v = w + r$, where r is a tail of $u + v$ modulo 1. Furthermore $u' = \text{round}(w - v) = \text{round}(u - r) = u - r - t$, where t is a tail of $u - r$ modulo b^e and $e = e_{u'} - p$.

If $e \le 0$, then $t \equiv u - r \equiv -v \pmod{b^e}$, hence t is a tail of $-v$ and $v'' = \text{round}(w - u') = \text{round}(v + t) = v + t$; this proves (40). If $e > 0$, then $|u - r| \ge b^p - \tfrac{1}{2}$; and since $|r| \le \tfrac{1}{2}$, we have $|u| \ge b^p - 1$. It follows that u is an integer, so r is a tail of v modulo 1. If $u' = u$, then $t = -r$ is a tail of $-v$. Otherwise the relation $\text{round}(u - r) \ne u$ implies that $|u| = b^p - 1$, $|r| = \tfrac{1}{2}$, $|u'| = b^p$, $t = r$; again t is a tail of $-v$. ∎

Theorem A exhibits a regularity property of floating point addition, but it doesn't seem to be an especially useful result. The following identity is more significant:

Theorem B. *Under the hypotheses of Theorem A and* (41),

$$u + v = (u \oplus v) + \big((u \ominus u') \oplus (v \ominus v'')\big). \tag{45}$$

Proof. In fact, we can show that $u \ominus u' = u - u'$, $v \ominus v'' = v - v''$, and $(u - u') \oplus (v - v'') = (u - u') + (v - v'')$, hence (45) will follow from Theorem A. Using the notation of the preceding proof, these relations are respectively equivalent to

$$\text{round}(t + r) = t + r, \qquad \text{round}(t) = t, \qquad \text{round}(r) = r. \tag{46}$$

Exercise 12 establishes the theorem in the special case $|e_u - e_v| \geq p$. Otherwise $u + v$ has at most $2p$ significant digits and it is easy to see that $\text{round}(r) = r$. If now $e > 0$, the proof of Theorem A shows that $t = -r$ or $t = r = \pm\frac{1}{2}$. If $e \leq 0$ we have $t + r \equiv u$ and $t \equiv -v$ (modulo b^e); this is enough to prove that $t + r$ and t round to themselves, provided that $e_u \geq e$ and $e_v \geq e$. But either $e_u < 0$ or $e_v < 0$ would contradict our hypothesis that $|e_u - e_v| < p$, since $e_w = p$. ∎

Theorem B gives *an explicit formula for the difference* between $u + v$ and $u \oplus v$, in terms of quantities that can be calculated directly using five operations of floating point arithmetic. If the radix b is 2 or 3, we can improve on this result, obtaining the exact value of the correction term with only two floating point operations and one (fixed point) comparison of absolute values:

Theorem C. *If $b \leq 3$ and $|u| \geq |v|$, then*

$$u + v = (u \oplus v) + \big(u \ominus (u \oplus v)\big) \oplus v. \tag{47}$$

Proof. Following the conventions of preceding proofs again, we wish to show that $v \ominus v' = r$. It suffices to show that $v' = w - u$, because (46) will then yield $v \ominus v' = \text{round}(v - v') = \text{round}(u + v - w) = \text{round}(r) = r$.

We shall in fact prove (47) whenever $b \leq 3$ and $e_u \geq e_v$. If $e_u \geq p$, then r is a tail of v modulo 1, hence $v' = w \ominus u = v \ominus r = v - r = w - u$ as desired. If $e_u < p$, then we must have $e_u = p - 1$, and $w - u$ is a multiple of b^{-1}; it will therefore round to itself if its magnitude is less than $b^{p-1} + b^{-1}$. Since $b \leq 3$, we have indeed $|w - u| \leq |w - u - v| + |v| \leq \frac{1}{2} + (b^{p-1} - b^{-1}) < b^{p-1} + b^{-1}$. This completes the proof. ∎

The proofs of Theorems A, B, and C do not rely on the precise definitions of $\text{round}(x)$ in the ambiguous cases when x is exactly midway between consecutive floating point numbers; any way of resolving the ambiguity will suffice for the validity of everything we have proved so far.

No rounding rule can be best for every application. For example, we generally want a special rule when computing our income tax. But for most numerical calculations the best policy appears to be the rounding scheme specified in Algorithm 4.2.1N, which insists that the least significant digit should always be made even (or always odd) when an ambiguous value is rounded. This is not a trivial technicality, of interest only to nit-pickers; it is an important practical consideration, since the ambiguous case arises surprisingly often and a biased rounding rule produces significantly poor results. For example, consider decimal arithmetic and assume that remainders of 5 are always rounded upwards. Then if $u = 1.0000000$ and $v = 0.55555555$ we have $u \oplus v = 1.5555556$; and if we floating-subtract v from this result we get $u' = 1.0000001$. Adding and subtracting v from u' gives 1.0000002, and the next time we get 1.0000003, etc.; the result keeps growing although we are adding and subtracting the same value.

This phenomenon, called *drift*, will not occur when we use a stable rounding rule based on the parity of the least significant digit. More precisely:

Theorem D. $\big(((u \oplus v) \ominus v) \oplus v\big) \ominus v = (u \oplus v) \ominus v.$

For example, if $u = 1.2345679$ and $v = -0.23456785$, we find

$$u \oplus v = 1.0000000, \qquad\qquad (u \oplus v) \ominus v = 1.2345678,$$
$$((u \oplus v) \ominus v) \oplus v = 0.99999995, \qquad \big(((u \oplus v) \ominus v) \oplus v\big) \ominus v = 1.2345678.$$

The proof for general u and v seems to require a case analysis even more detailed than that in the theorems above; see the references below. ∎

Theorem D is valid both for "round to even" and "round to odd"; how should we choose between these possibilities? When the radix b is odd, ambiguous cases never arise except during floating point division, and the rounding in such cases is comparatively unimportant. For *even* radices, there is reason to prefer the following rule: "Round to even when $b/2$ is odd, round to odd when $b/2$ is even." The least significant digit of a floating point fraction occurs frequently as a remainder to be rounded off in subsequent calculations, and this rule avoids generating the digit $b/2$ in the least significant position whenever possible; its effect is to provide some memory of an ambiguous rounding so that subsequent rounding will tend to be unambiguous. For example, if we were to round to odd in the decimal system, repeated rounding of the number 2.44445 to one less place each time leads to the sequence 2.4445, 2.445, 2.45, 2.5, 3; if we round to even, such situations do not occur, although repeated rounding of a number like 2.5454 will lead to almost as much error. [See Roy A. Keir, *Inf. Proc. Letters* **3** (1975), 188–189.] Some people prefer rounding to even in all cases, so that the least significant digit will tend to be 0 more often. Exercise 23 demonstrates this advantage of round-to-even. Neither alternative conclusively dominates the other; fortunately the base is usually $b = 2$ or $b = 10$, when everyone agrees that round-to-even is best.

A reader who has checked some of the details of the proofs above will realize the immense simplification that has been afforded by the simple rule $u \oplus v = \text{round}(u + v)$. If our floating point addition routine would fail to give this result even in a few rare cases, the proofs would become enormously more complicated and perhaps they would even break down completely.

Theorem B fails if truncation arithmetic is used in place of rounding, that is, if we let $u \oplus v = \text{trunc}(u + v)$ and $u \ominus v = \text{trunc}(u - v)$, where $\text{trunc}(x)$ for a positive real x is the largest floating point number $\leq x$. An exception to Theorem B would then occur for cases such as $(20, +.10000001) \oplus (10, -.10000001) = (20, +.10000000)$, when the difference between $u+v$ and $u \oplus v$ cannot be expressed exactly as a floating point number; and also for cases such as $12345678 \oplus .012345678$, when it can be.

Many people feel that, since floating point arithmetic is inexact by nature, there is no harm in making it just a little bit less exact in certain rather rare cases, if it is convenient to do so. This policy saves a few cents in the design of computer hardware, or a small percentage of the average running time of a subroutine. But our discussion shows that such a policy is mistaken. We could save about five percent of the running time of the FADD subroutine, Program 4.2.1A, and about 25 percent of its space, if we took the liberty of rounding incorrectly in a few cases, but we are much better off leaving it as it is. The reason is not to glorify "bit chasing"; a more fundamental issue is at stake here: *Numerical subroutines should deliver results that satisfy simple, useful mathematical laws whenever possible.* The crucial formula $u \oplus v = \text{round}(u + v)$ is a regularity property that makes a great deal of difference between whether mathematical analysis of computational algorithms is worth doing or worth avoiding. Without any underlying symmetry properties, the job of proving interesting results becomes extremely unpleasant. *The enjoyment of one's tools is an essential ingredient of successful work.*

B. Unnormalized floating point arithmetic. The policy of normalizing all floating point numbers may be construed in two ways: We may look on it favorably by saying that it is an attempt to get the maximum possible accuracy obtainable with a given degree of precision, or we may consider it to be potentially dangerous since it tends to imply that the results are more accurate than they really are. When we normalize the result of $(1, +.31428571) \ominus (1, +.31415927)$ to $(-2, +.12644000)$, we are suppressing information about the possibly greater inaccuracy of the latter quantity. Such information would be retained if the answer were left as $(1, +.00012644)$.

The input data to a problem is frequently not known as precisely as the floating point representation allows. For example, the values of Avogadro's number and Planck's constant are not known to eight significant digits, and it might be more appropriate to denote them, respectively, by

$$(27, +.00060221) \qquad \text{and} \qquad (-23, +.00066261)$$

instead of by $(24, +.60221400)$ and $(-26, +.66261000)$. It would be nice if we could give our input data for each problem in an unnormalized form that expresses how much precision is assumed, and if the output would indicate just how much precision is known in the answer. Unfortunately, this is a terribly difficult problem, although the use of unnormalized arithmetic can help to give some indication. For example, we can say with a fair degree of certainty that the product of Avogadro's number by Planck's constant is $(1, +.00039903)$, and that their sum is $(27, +.00060221)$. (The purpose of this example is not to suggest that any important physical significance should be attached to the sum and product of these fundamental constants; the point is that it is possible to preserve a little of the information about precision in the result of calculations with imprecise quantities, when the original operands are independent of each other.)

The rules for unnormalized arithmetic are simply this: Let l_u be the number of leading zeros in the fraction part of $u = (e_u, f_u)$, so that l_u is the largest integer $\leq p$ with $|f_u| < b^{-l_u}$. Then addition and subtraction are performed just as in Algorithm 4.2.1A, except that all scaling to the left is suppressed. Multiplication and division are performed as in Algorithm 4.2.1M, except that the answer is scaled right or left so that precisely $\max(l_u, l_v)$ leading zeros appear. Essentially the same rules have been used in manual calculation for many years.

It follows that, for unnormalized computations,

$$e_{u \oplus v}, \; e_{u \ominus v} = \max(e_u, e_v) + (0 \text{ or } 1) \tag{48}$$

$$e_{u \otimes v} = e_u + e_v - q - \min(l_u, l_v) - (0 \text{ or } 1) \tag{49}$$

$$e_{u \oslash v} = e_u - e_v + q - l_u + l_v + \max(l_u, l_v) + (0 \text{ or } 1). \tag{50}$$

When the result of a calculation is zero, an unnormalized zero (often called an "order of magnitude zero") is given as the answer; this indicates that the answer may not truly be zero, we just don't know any of its significant digits.

Error analysis takes a somewhat different form with unnormalized floating point arithmetic. Let us define

$$\delta_u = \tfrac{1}{2} b^{e_u - q - p} \qquad \text{if } u = (e_u, f_u). \tag{51}$$

This quantity depends on the representation of u, not just on the value $b^{e_u - q} f_u$. Our rounding rule tells us that

$$|u \oplus v - (u + v)| \leq \delta_{u \oplus v}, \qquad |u \ominus v - (u - v)| \leq \delta_{u \ominus v},$$

$$|u \otimes v - (u \times v)| \leq \delta_{u \otimes v}, \qquad |u \oslash v - (u \, / \, v)| \leq \delta_{u \oslash v}.$$

These inequalities apply to normalized as well as unnormalized arithmetic; the main difference between the two types of error analysis is the definition of the exponent of the result of each operation $\big($Eqs. (48) to (50)$\big)$.

We have remarked that the relations $\prec$, $\sim$, $\succ$, and $\approx$ defined earlier in this section are valid and meaningful for unnormalized numbers as well as for normalized numbers. As an example of the use of these relations, let us prove an approximate associative law for unnormalized addition, analogous to (39):

$$(u \oplus v) \oplus w \approx u \oplus (v \oplus w) \quad (\epsilon), \tag{52}$$

for suitable ϵ. We have

$$|(u \oplus v) \oplus w - (u + v + w)| \leq |(u \oplus v) \oplus w - \big((u \oplus v) + w\big)| + |u \oplus v - (u + v)|$$

$$\leq \delta_{(u \oplus v) \oplus w} + \delta_{u \oplus v}$$

$$\leq 2\delta_{(u \oplus v) \oplus w}.$$

A similar formula holds for $|u \oplus (v \oplus w) - (u + v + w)|$. Now since $e_{(u \oplus v) \oplus w} = \max(e_u, e_v, e_w) + (0, 1, \text{ or } 2)$, we have $\delta_{(u \oplus v) \oplus w} \leq b^2 \delta_{u \oplus (v \oplus w)}$. Therefore we find that (52) is valid when $\epsilon \geq b^{2-p} + b^{-p}$; unnormalized addition is not as erratic as normalized addition with respect to the associative law.

It should be emphasized that unnormalized arithmetic is by no means a panacea. There are examples where it indicates greater accuracy than is present (for example, addition of a great many small quantities of about the same magnitude, or evaluation of x^n for large n); and there are many more examples when it indicates poor accuracy while normalized arithmetic actually does produce good results. There is an important reason why no straightforward one-operation-at-a-time method of error analysis can be completely satisfactory, namely the fact that operands are usually not independent of each other. This means that errors tend to cancel or reinforce each other in strange ways. For example, suppose that x is approximately $1/2$, and suppose that we have an approximation $y = x + \delta$ with absolute error δ. If we now wish to compute $x(1-x)$, we can form $y(1-y)$; if $x = \frac{1}{2} + \epsilon$ we find $y(1-y) = x(1-x) - 2\epsilon\delta - \delta^2$, so the absolute error has decreased substantially: It has been multiplied by a factor of $2\epsilon + \delta$. This is just one case where multiplication of imprecise quantities can lead to a quite accurate result when the operands are not independent of each other. A more obvious example is the computation of $x \ominus x$, which can be obtained with perfect accuracy regardless of how bad an approximation to x we begin with.

The extra information that unnormalized arithmetic gives us can often be more important than the information it destroys during an extended calculation, but (as usual) we must use it with care. Examples of the proper use of unnormalized arithmetic are discussed by R. L. Ashenhurst and N. Metropolis in *Computers and Computing, AMM,* Slaught Memorial Papers **10** (February 1965), 47–59; by N. Metropolis in *Numer. Math.* **7** (1965), 104–112; and by R. L. Ashenhurst in *Error in Digital Computation* **2**, edited by L. B. Rall (New York: Wiley, 1965), 3–37. Appropriate methods for computing standard mathematical functions with both input and output in unnormalized form are given by R. L. Ashenhurst in *JACM* **11** (1964), 168–187. An extension of unnormalized arithmetic, which remembers that certain values are known to be *exact*, has been discussed by N. Metropolis in *IEEE Trans.* **C-22** (1973), 573–576.

C. Interval arithmetic. Another approach to the problem of error determination is the so-called interval or range arithmetic, in which rigorous upper and lower bounds on each number are maintained during the calculations. Thus, for example, if we know that $u_0 \leq u \leq u_1$ and $v_0 \leq v \leq v_1$, we represent this by the interval notation $u = [u_0 .. u_1]$, $v = [v_0 .. v_1]$. The sum $u \oplus v$ is $[u_0 \bigtriangledown v_0 .. u_1 \bigtriangleup v_1]$, where $\bigtriangledown$ denotes "lower floating point addition," the greatest representable number less than or equal to the true sum, and $\bigtriangleup$ is defined similarly (see exercise 4.2.1–13). Furthermore $u \ominus v = [u_0 \bigtriangledown v_1 .. u_1 \bigtriangleup v_0]$; and if u_0 and v_0 are positive, we have $u \otimes v = [u_0 \bigtriangledown v_0 .. u_1 \bigtriangleup v_1]$, $u \oslash v = [u_0 \bigtriangledown v_1 .. u_1 \bigtriangleup v_0]$. For example, we might represent Avogadro's number and Planck's constant as

$$N = \big[(24, +.60221331) .. (24, +.60221403)\big],$$
$$h = \big[(-26, +.66260715) .. (-26, +.66260795)\big];$$

their sum and product would then turn out to be

$$N \oplus h = \big[(24, +.60221331) .. (24, +.60221404)\big],$$
$$N \otimes h = \big[(-2, +.39903084) .. (-2, +.39903181)\big].$$

If we try to divide by $[v_0 .. v_1]$ when $v_0 < 0 < v_1$, there is a possibility of division by zero. Since the philosophy underlying interval arithmetic is to provide rigorous error estimates, a divide-by-zero error should be signalled in this case. However, overflow and underflow need not be treated as fatal errors in interval arithmetic, if special conventions are introduced as discussed in exercise 24.

Interval arithmetic takes only about twice as long as ordinary arithmetic, and it provides truly reliable error estimates. Considering the difficulty of mathematical error analyses, this is indeed a small price to pay. Since the intermediate values in a calculation often depend on each other, as explained above, the final estimates obtained with interval arithmetic will tend to be pessimistic; and iterative numerical methods often have to be redesigned if we want to deal with intervals. However, the prospects for effective use of interval arithmetic look very good, so efforts should be made to increase its availability and to make it as user-friendly as possible.

D. History and bibliography. Jules Tannery's classic treatise on decimal calculations, *Leçons d'Arithmétique* (Paris: Colin, 1894), stated that positive numbers should be rounded upwards if the first discarded digit is 5 or more; since exactly half of the decimal digits are 5 or more, he felt that this rule would round upwards exactly half of the time, on the average, so it would produce compensating errors. The idea of "round to even" in the ambiguous cases seems to have been mentioned first by James B. Scarborough in the first edition of his pioneering book *Numerical Mathematical Analysis* (Baltimore: Johns Hopkins Press, 1930), 2; in the second (1950) edition he amplified his earlier remarks, stating that "It should be obvious to any thinking person that when a 5 is cut off, the preceding digit should be increased by 1 in only *half* the cases," and he recommended round-to-even in order to achieve this.

The first analysis of floating point arithmetic was given by F. L. Bauer and K. Samelson, *Zeitschrift für angewandte Math. und Physik* **4** (1953), 312–316. The next publication was not until over five years later: J. W. Carr III, *CACM* **2**, 5 (May 1959), 10–15. See also P. C. Fischer, *Proc. ACM Nat. Meeting* **13** (1958), Paper 39. The book *Rounding Errors in Algebraic Processes* (Englewood Cliffs: Prentice–Hall, 1963), by J. H. Wilkinson, shows how to apply error analysis of the individual arithmetic operations to the error analysis of large-scale problems; see also his treatise on *The Algebraic Eigenvalue Problem* (Oxford: Clarendon Press, 1965).

Additional early work on floating point accuracy is summarized in two important papers that can be especially recommended for further study: W. M. Kahan, *Proc. IFIP Congress* (1971), **2**, 1214–1239; R. P. Brent, *IEEE Trans.* **C-22** (1973), 601–607. Both papers include useful theory and demonstrate that it pays off in practice.

The relations $\prec$, $\sim$, $\succ$, $\approx$ introduced in this section are similar to ideas published by A. van Wijngaarden in *BIT* **6** (1966), 66–81. Theorems A and B above were inspired by some related work of Ole Møller, *BIT* **5** (1965), 37–50, 251–255; Theorem C is due to T. J. Dekker, *Numer. Math.* **18** (1971), 224–242. Extensions and refinements of all three theorems have been published by S. Linnainmaa, *BIT* **14** (1974), 167–202. W. M. Kahan introduced Theorem D in some unpublished notes; for a complete proof and further commentary, see J. F. Reiser and D. E. Knuth, *Inf. Proc. Letters* **3** (1975), 84–87, 164.

Unnormalized floating point arithmetic was recommended by F. L. Bauer and K. Samelson in the article cited above, and it was independently used by J. W. Carr III at the University of Michigan in 1953. Several years later, the MANIAC III computer was designed to include both kinds of arithmetic in its hardware; see R. L. Ashenhurst and N. Metropolis, *JACM* **6** (1959), 415–428, *IEEE Trans.* **EC-12** (1963), 896–901; R. L. Ashenhurst, *Proc. Spring Joint Computer Conf.* **21** (1962), 195–202. See also H. L. Gray and C. Harrison, Jr., *Proc. Eastern Joint Computer Conf.* **16** (1959), 244–248, and W. G. Wadey, *JACM* **7** (1960), 129–139, for further early discussions of unnormalized arithmetic.

For early developments in interval arithmetic, and some modifications, see A. Gibb, *CACM* **4** (1961), 319–320; B. A. Chartres, *JACM* **13** (1966), 386–403; and the book *Interval Analysis* by Ramon E. Moore (Prentice–Hall, 1966). The subsequent flourishing of this subject is described in Moore's later book, *Methods and Applications of Interval Analysis* (Philadelphia: SIAM, 1979).

An extension of the Pascal language that allows variables to be of type "interval" was developed at the University of Karlsruhe in the early 1980s. For a description of this language, which also includes numerous other features for scientific computing, see *Pascal-SC* by Bohlender, Ullrich, Wolff von Gudenberg, and Rall (New York: Academic Press, 1987).

The book *Grundlagen des numerischen Rechnens: Mathematische Begründung der Rechnerarithmetik* by Ulrich Kulisch (Mannheim: Bibl. Inst., 1976) is entirely devoted to the study of floating point arithmetic systems. See also Kulisch's article in *IEEE Trans.* **C-26** (1977), 610–621, and his more recent book written jointly with W. L. Miranker, entitled *Computer Arithmetic in Theory and Practice* (New York: Academic Press, 1981).

An excellent summary of more recent work on floating point error analysis appears in the book *Accuracy and Stability of Numerical Algorithms* by N. J. Higham (Philadelphia: SIAM, 1996).

EXERCISES

Note: Normalized floating point arithmetic is assumed unless the contrary is specified.

1. [*M18*] Prove that identity (7) is a consequence of (2) through (6).

2. [*M20*] Use identities (2) through (8) to prove that $(u \oplus x) \oplus (v \oplus y) \geq u \oplus v$ whenever $x \geq 0$ and $y \geq 0$.

3. [*M20*] Find eight-digit floating decimal numbers u, v, and w such that

$$u \otimes (v \otimes w) \neq (u \otimes v) \otimes w,$$

and such that no exponent overflow or underflow occurs during the computations.

4. [*10*] Is it possible to have floating point numbers u, v, and w for which exponent overflow occurs during the calculation of $u \otimes (v \otimes w)$ but not during the calculation of $(u \otimes v) \otimes w$?

5. [*M20*] Is $u \oslash v = u \otimes (1 \oslash v)$ an identity, for all floating point numbers u and $v \neq 0$ such that no exponent overflow or underflow occurs?

6. [*M22*] Are either of the following two identities valid for all floating point numbers u? (a) $0 \ominus (0 \ominus u) = u$; (b) $1 \oslash (1 \oslash u) = u$.

7. [*M21*] Let $u^{②}$ stand for $u \otimes u$. Find floating binary numbers u and v such that $(u \oplus v)^{②} > 2(u^{②} + v^{②})$.

▶ **8.** [*20*] Let $\epsilon = 0.0001$; which of the relations

$$u \prec v \quad (\epsilon), \qquad u \sim v \quad (\epsilon), \qquad u \succ v \quad (\epsilon), \qquad u \approx v \quad (\epsilon)$$

hold for the following pairs of base 10, excess 0, eight-digit floating point numbers?

a) $u = (1, +.31415927)$, $v = (1, +.31416000)$;
b) $u = (0, +.99997000)$, $v = (1, +.10000039)$;
c) $u = (24, +.60221400)$, $v = (27, +.00060221)$;
d) $u = (24, +.60221400)$, $v = (31, +.00000006)$;
e) $u = (24, +.60221400)$, $v = (28, +.00000000)$.

9. [*M22*] Prove (33), and explain why the conclusion cannot be strengthened to the relation $u \approx w \ (\epsilon_1 + \epsilon_2)$.

▶ **10.** [*M25*] (W. M. Kahan.) A certain computer performs floating point arithmetic without proper rounding, and, in fact, its floating point multiplication routine ignores all but the first p most significant digits of the $2p$-digit product $f_u f_v$. (Thus when $f_u f_v < 1/b$, the least-significant digit of $u \otimes v$ always comes out to be zero, due to subsequent normalization.) Show that this causes the monotonicity of multiplication to fail; in other words, exhibit positive normalized floating point numbers u, v, and w such that $u < v$ but $u \otimes w > v \otimes w$ on this machine.

11. [*M20*] Prove Lemma T.

12. [*M24*] Carry out the proof of Theorem B and (46) when $|e_u - e_v| \geq p$.

▶ **13.** [*M25*] Some programming languages (and even some computers) make use of floating point arithmetic only, with no provision for exact calculations with integers. If operations on integers are desired, we can, of course, represent an integer as a floating point number; and when the floating point operations satisfy the basic definitions in (9), we know that all floating point operations will be exact, provided that the operands and the answer can each be represented exactly with p significant digits. Therefore — so long as we know that the numbers aren't too large — we can add, subtract, or multiply integers with no inaccuracy due to rounding errors.

But suppose that a programmer wants to determine if m is an exact multiple of n, when m and $n \neq 0$ are integers. Suppose further that a subroutine is available to calculate the quantity $\text{round}(u \bmod 1) = u \ (\text{mod}) \ 1$ for any given floating point number u, as in exercise 4.2.1–15. One good way to determine whether or not m is a multiple of n might be to test whether or not $(m \oslash n) \ (\text{mod}) \ 1 = 0$, using the assumed subroutine; but perhaps rounding errors in the floating point calculations will invalidate this test in certain cases.

Find suitable conditions on the range of integer values $n \neq 0$ and m, such that m is a multiple of n if and only if $(m \oslash n) \ (\text{mod}) \ 1 = 0$. In other words, show that if m and n are not too large, this test is valid.

14. [*M27*] Find a suitable ϵ such that $(u \otimes v) \otimes w \approx u \otimes (v \otimes w)$ (ϵ), when *unnormalized* multiplication is being used. (This generalizes (39), since unnormalized multiplication is exactly the same as normalized multiplication when the input operands u, v, and w are normalized.)

▶ **15.** [*M24*] (H. Björk.) Does the computed midpoint of an interval always lie between the endpoints? (In other words, does $u \le v$ imply that $u \le (u \oplus v) \oslash 2 \le v$?)

16. [*M28*] (a) What is $\left(\cdots ((x_1 \oplus x_2) \oplus x_3) \oplus \cdots \oplus x_n \right)$ when $n = 10^6$ and $x_k = 1.1111111$ for all k, using eight-digit floating decimal arithmetic? (b) What happens when Eq. (14) is used to calculate the standard deviation of these particular values x_k? What happens when Eqs. (15) and (16) are used instead? (c) Prove that $S_k \ge 0$ in (16), for all choices of $x_1, \ldots, x_k$.

17. [*28*] Write a MIX subroutine, FCMP, that compares the floating point number u in location ACC with the floating point number v in register A, setting the comparison indicator to LESS, EQUAL, or GREATER according as $u \prec v$, $u \sim v$, or $u \succ v$ (ϵ); here ϵ is stored in location EPSILON as a nonnegative fixed point quantity with the radix point assumed at the left of the word. Assume normalized inputs.

18. [*M40*] In unnormalized arithmetic is there a suitable number ϵ such that

$$u \otimes (v \oplus w) \approx (u \otimes v) \oplus (u \otimes w) \quad (\epsilon) \,?$$

▶ **19.** [*M30*] (W. M. Kahan.) Consider the following procedure for floating point summation of $x_1, x_2, \ldots, x_n$:

$$s_0 = c_0 = 0;$$
$$y_k = x_k \ominus c_{k-1}, \quad s_k = s_{k-1} \oplus y_k, \quad c_k = (s_k \ominus s_{k-1}) \ominus y_k, \qquad \text{for } 1 \le k \le n.$$

Let the relative errors in these operations be defined by the equations

$$y_k = (x_k - c_{k-1})(1 + \eta_k), \qquad s_k = (s_{k-1} + y_k)(1 + \sigma_k),$$
$$c_k = ((s_k - s_{k-1})(1 + \gamma_k) - y_k)(1 + \delta_k),$$

where $|\eta_k|, |\sigma_k|, |\gamma_k|, |\delta_k| \le \epsilon$. Prove that $s_n - c_n = \sum_{k=1}^n (1 + \theta_k) x_k$, where $|\theta_k| \le 2\epsilon + O(n\epsilon^2)$. [Theorem C says that if $b = 2$ and $|s_{k-1}| \ge |y_k|$ we have $s_{k-1} + y_k = s_k - c_k$ exactly. But in this exercise we want to obtain an estimate that is valid *even when floating point operations are not carefully rounded*, assuming only that each operation has bounded relative error.]

20. [*25*] (S. Linnainmaa.) Find all u and v for which $|u| \ge |v|$ and (47) fails.

21. [*M35*] (T. J. Dekker.) Theorem C shows how to do exact addition of floating binary numbers. Explain how to do *exact multiplication*: Express the product uv in the form $w + w'$, where w and w' are computed from two given floating binary numbers u and v, using only the operations $\oplus$, $\ominus$, and $\otimes$.

22. [*M30*] Can drift occur in floating point multiplication/division? Consider the sequence $x_0 = u$, $x_{2n+1} = x_{2n} \otimes v$, $x_{2n+2} = x_{2n+1} \oslash v$, given u and $v \ne 0$; what is the largest subscript k such that $x_k \ne x_{k+2}$ is possible?

▶ **23.** [*M26*] Prove or disprove: $u \ominus (u \pmod{1}) = \lfloor u \rfloor$, for all floating point u.

24. [*M27*] Consider the set of all intervals $[u_l \mathbin{..} u_r]$, where u_l and u_r are either nonzero floating point numbers or the special symbols $+0$, -0, $+\infty$, $-\infty$; each interval must have $u_l \leq u_r$, and $u_l = u_r$ is allowed only when u_l is finite and nonzero. The interval $[u_l \mathbin{..} u_r]$ stands for all floating point x such that $u_l \leq x \leq u_r$, where we agree that

$$-\infty < -x < -0 < 0 < +0 < +x < +\infty$$

for all positive x. (Thus, $[1 \mathbin{..} 2]$ means $1 \leq x \leq 2$; $[+0 \mathbin{..} 1]$ means $0 < x \leq 1$; $[-0 \mathbin{..} 1]$ means $0 \leq x \leq 1$; $[-0 \mathbin{..} +0]$ denotes the single value 0; and $[-\infty \mathbin{..} +\infty]$ stands for everything.) Show how to define appropriate arithmetic operations on all such intervals, without resorting to overflow or underflow or other anomalous indications except when dividing by an interval that includes zero.

▶ **25.** [*15*] When people speak about inaccuracy in floating point arithmetic they often ascribe errors to "cancellation" that occurs during the subtraction of nearly equal quantities. But when u and v are approximately equal, the difference $u \ominus v$ is obtained exactly, with no error. What do these people really mean?

26. [*M21*] Given that u, u', v, and v' are positive floating point numbers with $u \sim u'$ (ϵ) and $v \sim v'$ (ϵ), prove that there's a small ϵ' such that $u \oplus v \sim u' \oplus v'$ (ϵ'), assuming normalized arithmetic.

27. [*M27*] (W. M. Kahan.) Prove that $1 \oslash (1 \oslash (1 \oslash u)) = 1 \oslash u$ for all $u \neq 0$.

28. [*HM30*] (H. G. Diamond.) Suppose $f(x)$ is a strictly increasing function on some interval $[x_0 \mathbin{..} x_1]$, and let $g(x)$ be the inverse function. (For example, f and g might be "exp" and "ln", or "tan" and "arctan".) If x is a floating point number such that $x_0 \leq x \leq x_1$, let $\hat{f}(x) = \text{round}(f(x))$, and if y is another such that $f(x_0) \leq y \leq f(x_1)$, let $\hat{g}(y) = \text{round}(g(y))$; furthermore, let $h(x) = \hat{g}(\hat{f}(x))$, whenever this is defined. Although $h(x)$ won't always be equal to x, due to rounding, we expect $h(x)$ to be fairly near x.

Prove that if the precision b^p is at least 3, and if f is strictly concave or strictly convex (that is, $f''(x)$ has the same sign for all x in $[x_0 \mathbin{..} x_1]$), then repeated application of h will be *stable* in the sense that

$$h(h(h(x))) = h(h(x)),$$

for all x such that both sides of this equation are defined. In other words, there will be no "drift" if the subroutines are properly implemented.

▶ **29.** [*M25*] Give an example to show that the condition $b^p \geq 3$ is necessary in the previous exercise.

▶ **30.** [*M30*] (W. M. Kahan.) Let $f(x) = 1 + x + \cdots + x^{106} = (1 - x^{107})/(1 - x)$ for $x < 1$, and let $g(y) = f((\frac{1}{3} - y^2)(3 + 3.45y^2))$ for $0 < y < 1$. Evaluate $g(y)$ on one or more pocket calculators, for $y = 10^{-3}$, 10^{-4}, 10^{-5}, 10^{-6}, and explain all inaccuracies in the results you obtain. (Since most present-day calculators do not round correctly, the results are often surprising. Note that $g(\epsilon) = 107 - 10491.35\epsilon^2 + 659749.9625\epsilon^4 - 30141386.26625\epsilon^6 + O(\epsilon^8)$.)

31. [*M25*] (U. Kulisch.) When the polynomial $2y^2 + 9x^4 - y^4$ is evaluated for $x = 408855776$ and $y = 708158977$ using standard 53-bit double-precision floating point arithmetic, the result is $\approx -3.7 \times 10^{19}$. Evaluating it in the alternative form $2y^2 + (3x^2 - y^2)(3x^2 + y^2)$ gives $\approx +1.0 \times 10^{18}$. The true answer, however, is 1.0 (exactly). Explain how to construct similar examples of numerical instability.

*4.2.3. Double-Precision Calculations

Up to now we have considered "single-precision" floating point arithmetic, which essentially means that the floating point values we have dealt with can be stored in a single machine word. When single-precision floating point arithmetic does not yield sufficient accuracy for a given application, the precision can be increased by suitable programming techniques that use two or more words of memory to represent each number.

Although we shall discuss the general question of high-precision calculations in Section 4.3, it is appropriate to give a separate discussion of double-precision here. Special techniques apply to double precision that are comparatively inappropriate for higher precisions; and double precision is a reasonably important topic in its own right, since it is the first step beyond single precision and it is applicable to many problems that do not require extremely high precision.

Well, that paragraph was true when the author wrote the first edition of this book in the 1960s. But computers have evolved in such a way that the old motivations for double-precision floating point have mostly disappeared; the present section is therefore primarily of historical interest. In the planned fourth edition of this book, Section 4.2.1 will be renamed "Normalized Calculations," and the present Section 4.2.3 will be replaced by a discussion of "Exceptional Numbers." The new material will focus on special aspects of ANSI/IEEE Standard 754: denormal numbers, infinities, and the so-called NaNs that represent undefined or otherwise unusual quantities. (See the references at the end of Section 4.2.1.) Meanwhile, let us take one last look at the older ideas, in order to see what lessons they can still teach us.

Double-precision calculations are almost always required for floating point rather than fixed point arithmetic, except perhaps in statistical work where fixed point double-precision is commonly used to calculate sums of squares and cross products; since fixed point versions of double-precision arithmetic are simpler than floating point versions, we shall confine our discussion here to the latter.

Double precision is quite frequently desired not only to extend the precision of the fraction parts of floating point numbers, but also to increase the range of the exponent part. Thus we shall deal in this section with the following two-word format for double-precision floating point numbers in the MIX computer:

$$\boxed{\pm}\ \boxed{e}\ \boxed{e}\ \boxed{f}\ \boxed{f}\ \boxed{f} \qquad \boxed{}\ \boxed{f}\ \boxed{f}\ \boxed{f}\ \boxed{f}\ \boxed{f}. \qquad (1)$$

Here two bytes are used for the exponent and eight bytes are used for the fraction. The exponent is "excess $b^2/2$," where b is the byte size. The sign will appear in the most significant word; it is convenient to ignore the sign of the other word completely.

Our discussion of double-precision arithmetic will be quite machine-oriented, because it is only by studying the problems involved in coding these routines that a person can properly appreciate the subject. A careful study of the MIX programs below is therefore essential to the understanding of the material.

In this section we shall depart from the idealistic goals of accuracy stated in the previous two sections; our double-precision routines will *not* round their results, and a little bit of error will sometimes be allowed to creep in. Users dare not trust these routines too much. There was ample reason to squeeze out every possible drop of accuracy in the single-precision case, but now we face a different situation: (a) The extra programming required to ensure true double-precision rounding in all cases is considerable; fully accurate routines would take, say, twice as much space and half again as much time. It was comparatively easy to make our single-precision routines perfect, but double precision brings us face to face with our machine's limitations. A similar situation occurs with respect to other floating point subroutines; we can't expect the cosine routine to compute round(cos x) exactly for all x, since that turns out to be virtually impossible. Instead, the cosine routine should provide the best relative error it can achieve with reasonable speed, for all reasonable values of x. Of course, the designer of the routine should try to make the computed function satisfy simple mathematical laws whenever possible — for example,

$$\boxed{\cos}\,(-x) = \boxed{\cos}\,x; \quad |\boxed{\cos}\,x| \leq 1; \quad \boxed{\cos}\,x \geq \boxed{\cos}\,y \text{ for } 0 \leq x \leq y < \pi.$$

(b) Single-precision arithmetic is a "staple food" that everybody who wants to employ floating point arithmetic must use, but double precision is usually for situations where such clean results aren't as important. The difference between seven- and eight-place accuracy can be noticeable, but we rarely care about the difference between 15- and 16-place accuracy. Double precision is most often used for intermediate steps during the calculation of single-precision results; its full potential isn't needed. (c) It will be instructive for us to analyze these procedures in order to see how inaccurate they can be, since they typify the types of short cuts generally taken in bad single-precision routines (see exercises 7 and 8).

Let us now consider addition and subtraction operations from this standpoint. Subtraction is, of course, converted to addition by changing the sign of the second operand. Addition is performed by separately adding together the least-significant halves and the most-significant halves, propagating "carries" appropriately.

A difficulty arises, however, since we are doing signed magnitude arithmetic: it is possible to add the least-significant halves and to get the wrong sign (namely, when the signs of the operands are opposite and the least-significant half of the smaller operand is bigger than the least-significant half of the larger operand). The simplest solution is to anticipate the correct sign; so in step A2 of Algorithm 4.2.1A we will now assume not only that $e_u \geq e_v$ but also that $|u| \geq |v|$. Then we can be sure that the final sign will be the sign of u. In other respects, double-precision addition is very much like its single-precision counterpart, except that everything needs to be done twice.

Program A (*Double-precision addition*). The subroutine DFADD adds a double-precision floating point number v, having the form (1), to a double-precision floating point number u, assuming that v is initially in rAX (registers A and X), and that u is initially stored in locations ACC and ACCX. The answer appears both in rAX and in (ACC, ACCX). The subroutine DFSUB subtracts v from u under the same conventions.

Both input operands are assumed to be normalized, and the answer is normalized. The last portion of this program is a double-precision normalization procedure that is used by other subroutines of this section. Exercise 5 shows how to improve the program significantly.

01	ABS	EQU	1:5	Field definition for absolute value
02	SIGN	EQU	0:0	Field definition for sign
03	EXPD	EQU	1:2	Double-precision exponent field
04	DFSUB	STA	TEMP	Double-precision subtraction:
05		LDAN	TEMP	Change sign of v.
06	DFADD	STJ	EXITDF	Double-precision addition:
07		CMPA	ACC(ABS)	Compare $|v|$ with $|u|$.
08		JG	1F	
09		JL	2F	
10		CMPX	ACCX(ABS)	
11		JLE	2F	
12	1H	STA	ARG	If $|v| > |u|$, interchange $u \leftrightarrow v$.
13		STX	ARGX	
14		LDA	ACC	
15		LDX	ACCX	
16		ENT1	ACC	(ACC and ACCX are in consecutive
17		MOVE	ARG(2)	locations.)
18	2H	STA	TEMP	
19		LD1N	TEMP(EXPD)	rI1 $\leftarrow -e_v$.
20		LD2	ACC(EXPD)	rI2 $\leftarrow e_u$.
21		INC1	0,2	rI1 $\leftarrow e_u - e_v$.
22		SLAX	2	Remove exponent.
23		SRAX	1,1	Scale right.
24		STA	ARG	0 v_1 v_2 v_3 v_4
25		STX	ARGX	v_5 v_6 v_7 v_8 v_9
26		STA	ARGX(SIGN)	Store true sign of v in both halves.
27		LDA	ACC	(We know that u has the sign of the answer.)
28		LDX	ACCX	rAX $\leftarrow u$.
29		SLAX	2	Remove exponent.
30		STA	ACC	u_1 u_2 u_3 u_4 u_5
31		SLAX	4	
32		ENTX	1	
33		STX	EXPO	EXPO $\leftarrow 1$ (see below).
34		SRC	1	1 u_5 u_6 u_7 u_8
35		STA	1F(SIGN)	A trick, see comments in text.
36		ADD	ARGX(0:4)	Add 0 v_5 v_6 v_7 v_8.
37		SRAX	4	
38	1H	DECA	1	Recover from inserted 1. (Sign varies)
39		ADD	ACC(0:4)	Add most significant halves.
40		ADD	ARG	(Overflow cannot occur)

41	DNORM	JANZ 1F	Normalization routine:
42		JXNZ 1F	f_w in rAX, $e_w = $ EXPO $+$ rI2.
43	DZERO	STA ACC	If $f_w = 0$, set $e_w \leftarrow 0$.
44		JMP 9F	
45	2H	SLAX 1	Normalize to the left.
46		DEC2 1	
47	1H	CMPA =0=(1:1)	Is the leading byte zero?
48		JE 2B	
49		SRAX 2	(Rounding omitted)
50		STA ACC	
51		LDA EXPO	Compute final exponent.
52		INCA 0,2	
53		JAN EXPUND	Is it negative?
54		STA ACC(EXPD)	
55		CMPA =1(3:3)=	Is it more than two bytes?
56		JL 8F	
57	EXPOVD	HLT 20	
58	EXPUND	HLT 10	
59	8H	LDA ACC	Bring answer into rA.
60	9H	STX ACCX	
61	EXITDF	JMP *	Exit from subroutine.
62	ARG	CON 0	
63	ARGX	CON 0	
64	ACC	CON 0	Floating point accumulator
65	ACCX	CON 0	
66	EXPO	CON 0	Part of "raw exponent" ▮

When the least-significant halves are added together in this program, an extra digit "1" is inserted at the left of the word that is known to have the correct sign. After the addition, this byte can be 0, 1, or 2, depending on the circumstances, and all three cases are handled simultaneously in this way. (Compare this with the rather cumbersome method of complementation that is used in Program 4.2.1A.)

It is worth noting that register A can be zero after the instruction on line 40 has been performed; and, because of the way MIX defines the sign of a zero result, the accumulator contains the correct sign that is to be attached to the result if register X is nonzero. If lines 39 and 40 were interchanged, the program would be incorrect, even though both instructions are "ADD"!

Now let us consider double-precision multiplication. The product has four components, shown schematically in Fig. 4. Since we need only the leftmost eight bytes, it is convenient to ignore the digits to the right of the vertical line in the diagram; in particular, we need not even compute the product of the two least-significant halves.

Program M (*Double-precision multiplication*). The input and output conventions for this subroutine are the same as for Program A.

01	BYTE	EQU 1(4:4)	Byte size
02	QQ	EQU BYTE*BYTE/2	Excess of double-precision exponent

$$
\begin{array}{llll}
u\ u\ u\ u\ u & u\ u\ u\ 0\ 0 & = u_m + \epsilon u_l \\
v\ v\ v\ v\ v & v\ v\ v\ 0\ 0 & = v_m + \epsilon v_l \\
\hline
x\ x\ x\ x\ x & x\ 0\ 0\ 0\ 0 & = \epsilon^2 u_l \times v_l \\
\end{array}
$$

$$
\begin{array}{l|ll}
x\ x\ x\ x & x & x\ x\ x\ 0\ 0 \qquad = \epsilon\, u_m \times v_l \\
x\ x\ x\ x & x & x\ x\ x\ 0\ 0 \qquad = \epsilon\, u_l \times v_m \\
\end{array}
$$

$$
x\ x\ x\ x\ x \quad x\ x\ x\ x \,|\, x \qquad\qquad = u_m \times v_m
$$

$$
w\ w\ w\ w\ w \quad w\ w\ w\ w\,|\,w \quad w\ w\ w\ w\ w \quad w\ 0\ 0\ 0\ 0
$$

Fig. 4. Double-precision multiplication of eight-byte fraction parts.

03	DFMUL	STJ	EXITDF	Double-precision multiplication:
04		STA	TEMP	
05		SLAX	2	Remove exponent.
06		STA	ARG	v_m
07		STX	ARGX	v_l
08		LDA	TEMP(EXPD)	
09		ADD	ACC(EXPD)	
10		STA	EXPO	EXPO $\leftarrow e_u + e_v$.
11		ENT2	-QQ	rI2 $\leftarrow$ -QQ.
12		LDA	ACC	
13		LDX	ACCX	
14		SLAX	2	Remove exponent.
15		STA	ACC	u_m
16		STX	ACCX	u_l
17		MUL	ARGX	$u_m \times v_l$
18		STA	TEMP	
19		LDA	ARG(ABS)	
20		MUL	ACCX(ABS)	$|v_m \times u_l|$
21		SRA	1	$0\ x\ x\ x\ x$
22		ADD	TEMP(1:4)	(Overflow cannot occur)
23		STA	TEMP	
24		LDA	ARG	
25		MUL	ACC	$v_m \times u_m$
26		STA	TEMP(SIGN)	Store true sign of result.
27		STA	ACC	Now prepare to add all the
28		STX	ACCX	partial products together.
29		LDA	ACCX(0:4)	$0\ x\ x\ x\ x$
30		ADD	TEMP	(Overflow cannot occur)
31		SRAX	4	
32		ADD	ACC	(Overflow cannot occur)
33		JMP	DNORM	Normalize and exit. $\blacksquare$

Notice the careful treatment of signs in this program, and note also the fact that the range of exponents makes it impossible to compute the final exponent using an index register. Program M is perhaps too slipshod in accuracy, since it uses only the information to the left of the vertical line in Fig. 4; this can make the least significant byte as much as 2 in error. A little more accuracy can be achieved as discussed in exercise 4.

Double-precision floating division is the most difficult routine, or at least the most frightening prospect we have encountered so far in this chapter. Actually, it is not terribly complicated, once we see how to do it; let us write the numbers to be divided in the form $(u_m + \epsilon u_l)/(v_m + \epsilon v_l)$, where ϵ is the reciprocal of the word size of the computer, and where v_m is assumed to be normalized. The fraction can now be expanded as follows:

$$\frac{u_m + \epsilon u_l}{v_m + \epsilon v_l} = \frac{u_m + \epsilon u_l}{v_m} \left(\frac{1}{1 + \epsilon(v_l/v_m)} \right)$$
$$= \frac{u_m + \epsilon u_l}{v_m} \left(1 - \epsilon\left(\frac{v_l}{v_m}\right) + \epsilon^2\left(\frac{v_l}{v_m}\right)^2 - \cdots \right). \qquad (2)$$

Since $0 \le |v_l| < 1$ and $1/b \le |v_m| < 1$, we have $|v_l/v_m| < b$, and the error from dropping terms involving ϵ^2 can be disregarded. Our method therefore is to compute $w_m + \epsilon w_l = (u_m + \epsilon u_l)/v_m$, and then to subtract ϵ times $w_m v_l/v_m$ from the result.

In the following program, lines 27–32 do the lower half of a double-precision addition, using another method for forcing the appropriate sign as an alternative to the trick of Program A.

Program D (*Double-precision division*). This program adheres to the same conventions as Programs A and M.

01	DFDIV	STJ	EXITDF	Double-precision division:
02		JOV	OFLO	Ensure that overflow is off.
03		STA	TEMP	
04		SLAX	2	Remove exponent.
05		STA	ARG	v_m
06		STX	ARGX	v_l
07		LDA	ACC(EXPD)	
08		SUB	TEMP(EXPD)	
09		STA	EXPO	EXPO $\leftarrow e_u - e_v$.
10		ENT2	QQ+1	rI2 $\leftarrow$ QQ $+ 1$.
11		LDA	ACC	
12		LDX	ACCX	
13		SLAX	2	Remove exponent.
14		SRAX	1	(See Algorithm 4.2.1M)
15		DIV	ARG	If overflow, it is detected below.
16		STA	ACC	w_m
17		SLAX	5	Use remainder in further division.
18		DIV	ARG	
19		STA	ACCX	$\pm w_l$
20		LDA	ARGX(1:4)	
21		ENTX	0	
22		DIV	ARG(ABS)	rA $\leftarrow \lfloor \lfloor b^4 v_l/v_m \rfloor \rfloor / b^5$.
23		JOV	DVZROD	Did division cause overflow?
24		MUL	ACC(ABS)	rAX $\leftarrow |w_m v_l/bv_m|$, approximately.
25		SRAX	4	Multiply by b, and save
26		SLC	5	the leading byte in rX.

27		SUB	ACCX(ABS)	Subtract $|w_l|$.
28		DECA	1	Force minus sign.
29		SUB	WM1	
30		JOV	*+2	If no overflow, carry one more
31		INCX	1	to upper half.
32		SLC	5	(Now rA $\leq$ 0)
33		ADD	ACC(ABS)	rA $\leftarrow |w_m| - |$rA$|$.
34		STA	ACC(ABS)	(Now rA $\geq$ 0)
35		LDA	ACC	rA $\leftarrow w_m$ with correct sign.
36		JMP	DNORM	Normalize and exit.
37	DVZROD	HLT	30	Unnormalized or zero divisor
38	1H	EQU	1(1:1)	
39	WM1	CON	1B-1,BYTE-1(1:1)	Word size minus one ▮

Here is a table of the approximate average computation times for these double-precision subroutines, compared to the single-precision subroutines that appear in Section 4.2.1:

	Single precision	Double precision
Addition	$45.5u$	$84u$
Subtraction	$49.5u$	$88u$
Multiplication	$48u$	$109u$
Division	$52u$	$126.5u$

For extension of the methods of this section to triple-precision floating point fraction parts, see Y. Ikebe, *CACM* **8** (1965), 175–177.

EXERCISES

1. [*16*] Try the double-precision division technique by hand, with $\epsilon = \frac{1}{1000}$, when dividing 180000 by 314159. (Thus, let $(u_m, u_l) = (.180, .000)$ and $(v_m, v_l) = (.314, .159)$, and find the quotient using the method suggested in the text following (2).)

2. [*20*] Would it be a good idea to insert the instruction "ENTX 0" between lines 30 and 31 of Program M, in order to keep unwanted information left over in register X from interfering with the accuracy of the results?

3. [*M20*] Explain why overflow cannot occur during Program M.

4. [*22*] How should Program M be changed so that extra accuracy is achieved, essentially by moving the vertical line in Fig. 4 over to the right one position? Specify all changes that are required, and determine the difference in execution time caused by these changes.

▶ **5.** [*24*] How should Program A be changed so that extra accuracy is achieved, essentially by working with a nine-byte accumulator instead of an eight-byte accumulator to the right of the radix point? Specify all changes that are required, and determine the difference in execution time caused by these changes.

6. [*23*] Assume that the double-precision subroutines of this section and the single-precision subroutines of Section 4.2.1 are being used in the same main program. Write a subroutine that converts a single-precision floating point number into double-precision form (1), and write another subroutine that converts a double-precision floating point number into single-precision form (reporting exponent overflow or underflow if the conversion is impossible).

▶ **7.** [*M30*] Estimate the accuracy of the double-precision subroutines in this section, by finding bounds δ_1, δ_2, and δ_3 on the relative errors

$$\left|((u \oplus v) - (u + v))/(u + v)\right|, \qquad \left|((u \otimes v) - (u \times v))/(u \times v)\right|,$$
$$\left|((u \oslash v) - (u/v))/(u/v)\right|.$$

8. [*M28*] Estimate the accuracy of the "improved" double-precision subroutines of exercises 4 and 5, in the sense of exercise 7.

9. [*M42*] T. J. Dekker [*Numer. Math.* **18** (1971), 224–242] has suggested an alternative approach to double precision, based entirely on single-precision floating binary calculations. For example, Theorem 4.2.2C states that $u + v = w + r$, where $w = u \oplus v$ and $r = (u \ominus w) \oplus v$, if $|u| \geq |v|$ and the radix is 2; here $|r| \leq |w|/2^p$, so the pair (w, r) may be considered a double-precision version of $u + v$. To add two such pairs $(u, u') \oplus (v, v')$, where $|u'| \leq |u|/2^p$ and $|v'| \leq |v|/2^p$ and $|u| \geq |v|$, Dekker suggests computing $u + v = w + r$ (exactly), then $s = (r \oplus v') \oplus u'$ (an approximate remainder), and finally returning the value $(w \oplus s, (w \ominus (w \oplus s)) \oplus s)$.

Study the accuracy and efficiency of this approach when it is used recursively to produce quadruple-precision calculations.

4.2.4. Distribution of Floating Point Numbers

In order to analyze the average behavior of floating point arithmetic algorithms (and in particular to determine their average running time), we need some statistical information that allows us to determine how often various cases arise. The purpose of this section is to discuss the empirical and theoretical properties of the distribution of floating point numbers.

A. Addition and subtraction routines. The execution time for a floating point addition or subtraction depends largely on the initial difference of exponents, and also on the number of normalization steps required (to the left or to the right). No way is known to give a good theoretical model that tells what characteristics to expect, but extensive empirical investigations have been made by D. W. Sweeney [*IBM Systems J.* **4** (1965), 31–42].

By means of a special tracing routine, Sweeney ran six "typical" large-scale numerical programs, selected from several different computing laboratories, and examined each floating addition or subtraction operation very carefully. Over 250,000 floating point addition-subtractions were involved in gathering this data. About one out of every ten instructions executed by the tested programs was either FADD or FSUB.

Subtraction is the same as addition preceded by negating the second operand, so we can give all the statistics as if we were merely doing addition. Sweeney's results can be summarized as follows:

One of the two operands to be added was found to be equal to zero about 9 percent of the time, and this was usually the accumulator (ACC). The other 91 percent of the cases split about equally between operands of the same or of

Table 1

EMPIRICAL DATA FOR OPERAND ALIGNMENTS BEFORE ADDITION

$|e_u - e_v|$	$b = 2$	$b = 10$	$b = 16$	$b = 64$
0	0.33	0.47	0.47	0.56
1	0.12	0.23	0.26	0.27
2	0.09	0.11	0.10	0.04
3	0.07	0.03	0.02	0.02
4	0.07	0.01	0.01	0.02
5	0.04	0.01	0.02	0.00
over 5	0.28	0.13	0.11	0.09
average	3.1	0.9	0.8	0.5

Table 2

EMPIRICAL DATA FOR NORMALIZATION AFTER ADDITION

	$b = 2$	$b = 10$	$b = 16$	$b = 64$
Shift right 1	0.20	0.07	0.06	0.03
No shift	0.59	0.80	0.82	0.87
Shift left 1	0.07	0.08	0.07	0.06
Shift left 2	0.03	0.02	0.01	0.01
Shift left 3	0.02	0.00	0.01	0.00
Shift left 4	0.02	0.01	0.00	0.01
Shift left > 4	0.06	0.02	0.02	0.02

opposite signs, and about equally between cases where $|u| \leq |v|$ or $|v| \leq |u|$. The computed answer was zero about 1.4 percent of the time.

The difference between exponents had a behavior approximately given by the probabilities shown in Table 1, for various radices b. (The "over 5" line of that table includes essentially all of the cases when one operand was zero, but the "average" line does not include these cases.)

When u and v have the same sign and are normalized, then $u + v$ either requires one shift to the *right* (for fraction overflow), or no normalization shifts whatever. When u and v have opposite signs, we have zero or more *left* shifts during the normalization. Table 2 gives the observed number of shifts required; the last line of that table includes all cases where the result was zero. The average number of left shifts per normalization was about 0.9 when $b = 2$; about 0.2 when $b = 10$ or 16; and about 0.1 when $b = 64$.

B. The fraction parts. Further analysis of floating point routines can be based on the *statistical distribution of the fraction parts* of randomly chosen normalized floating point numbers. The facts are quite surprising, and there is an interesting theory that accounts for the unusual phenomena that are observed.

For convenience let us assume temporarily that we are dealing with floating *decimal* arithmetic (radix 10); modifications of the following discussion to any other positive integer base b will be very straightforward. Suppose we are given a "random" positive normalized number $(e, f) = 10^e \cdot f$. Since f is normalized, we know that its leading digit is 1, 2, 3, 4, 5, 6, 7, 8, or 9, and we might naturally expect each of these nine possible leading digits to occur about one-ninth of the time. But, in fact, the behavior in practice is quite different. For example, the leading digit tends to be equal to 1 more than 30 percent of the time!

One way to test the assertion just made is to take a table of physical constants (like the speed of light or the acceleration of gravity) from some standard reference. If we look at the *Handbook of Mathematical Functions* (U.S. Dept of Commerce, 1964), for example, we find that 8 of the 28 different physical constants given in Table 2.3, roughly 29 percent, have leading digit equal to 1. The decimal values of $n!$ for $1 \leq n \leq 100$ include exactly 30 entries beginning with 1; so do the decimal values of 2^n and of F_n, for $1 \leq n \leq 100$. We might also try looking at census reports, or a Farmer's Almanack (but not a telephone directory).

In the days before pocket calculators, the pages in well-used tables of logarithms tended to get quite dirty in the front, while the last pages stayed relatively clean and neat. This phenomenon was apparently first mentioned in print by the astronomer Simon Newcomb [*Amer. J. Math.* **4** (1881), 39–40], who gave good grounds for believing that the leading digit d occurs with probability $\log_{10}(1 + 1/d)$. The same distribution was discovered empirically, many years later, by Frank Benford, who reported the results of 20,229 observations taken from different sources [*Proc. Amer. Philosophical Soc.* **78** (1938), 551–572].

In order to account for this leading-digit law, let's take a closer look at the way we write numbers in floating point notation. If we take any positive number u, its fraction part is determined by the formula $10f_u = 10^{(\log_{10} u) \bmod 1}$; hence its leading digit is less than d if and only if

$$(\log_{10} u) \bmod 1 < \log_{10} d. \tag{1}$$

Now if we have a "random" positive number U, chosen from some reasonable distribution that might occur in nature, we might expect that $(\log_{10} U) \bmod 1$ would be uniformly distributed between zero and one, at least to a very good approximation. (Similarly, we expect $U \bmod 1$, $U^2 \bmod 1$, $\sqrt{U + \pi} \bmod 1$, etc., to be uniformly distributed. We expect a roulette wheel to be unbiased, for essentially the same reason.) Therefore by (1) the leading digit will be 1 with probability $\log_{10} 2 \approx 30.103$ percent; it will be 2 with probability $\log_{10} 3 - \log_{10} 2 \approx 17.609$ percent; and, in general, if r is any real value between 1 and 10, we ought to have $10f_U \leq r$ approximately $\log_{10} r$ of the time.

The fact that leading digits tend to be small makes the most obvious techniques of "average error" estimation for floating point calculations invalid. The relative error due to rounding is usually a little more than expected.

Of course, it may justly be said that the heuristic argument above does not prove the stated law. It merely shows us a plausible reason why the leading digits behave the way they do. An interesting approach to the analysis of leading digits has been suggested by R. Hamming: Let $p(r)$ be the probability that $10f_U \leq r$, where $1 \leq r \leq 10$ and f_U is the normalized fraction part of a random normalized floating point number U. If we think of random quantities in the real world, we observe that they are measured in terms of arbitrary units; and if we were to change the definition of a meter or a gram, many of the fundamental physical constants would have different values. Suppose then that all of the numbers in the universe are suddenly multiplied by a constant factor c; our universe of random floating point quantities should be essentially unchanged by this transformation, so $p(r)$ should not be affected.

Multiplying everything by c has the effect of transforming $(\log_{10} U) \bmod 1$ into $(\log_{10} U + \log_{10} c) \bmod 1$. It is now time to set up formulas that describe the desired behavior; we may assume that $1 \le c \le 10$. By definition,

$$p(r) = \Pr\big((\log_{10} U) \bmod 1 \le \log_{10} r\big).$$

By our assumption, we should also have

$$p(r) = \Pr\big((\log_{10} U + \log_{10} c) \bmod 1 \le \log_{10} r\big)$$

$$= \begin{cases} \Pr\big((\log_{10} U \bmod 1) \le \log_{10} r - \log_{10} c \\ \qquad \text{or } (\log_{10} U \bmod 1) \ge 1 - \log_{10} c\big), & \text{if } c \le r; \\ \Pr\big((\log_{10} U \bmod 1) \le \log_{10} r + 1 - \log_{10} c \\ \qquad \text{and } (\log_{10} U \bmod 1) \ge 1 - \log_{10} c\big), & \text{if } c \ge r; \end{cases}$$

$$= \begin{cases} p(r/c) + 1 - p(10/c), & \text{if } c \le r; \\ p(10r/c) - p(10/c), & \text{if } c \ge r. \end{cases} \qquad (2)$$

Let us now extend the function $p(r)$ to values outside the range $1 \le r \le 10$, by defining $p(10^n r) = p(r) + n$; then if we replace $10/c$ by d, the last equation of (2) may be written

$$p(rd) = p(r) + p(d). \qquad (3)$$

If our assumption about invariance of the distribution under multiplication by a constant factor is valid, then Eq. (3) must hold for all $r > 0$ and $1 \le d \le 10$. The facts that $p(1) = 0$ and $p(10) = 1$ now imply that

$$1 = p(10) = p\big((\sqrt[n]{10})^n\big) = p(\sqrt[n]{10}) + p\big((\sqrt[n]{10})^{n-1}\big) = \cdots = np(\sqrt[n]{10});$$

hence we deduce that $p(10^{m/n}) = m/n$ for all positive integers m and n. If we now decide to require that p is continuous, we are forced to conclude that $p(r) = \log_{10} r$, and this is the desired law.

Although this argument may be more convincing than the first one, it doesn't really hold up under scrutiny if we stick to conventional notions of probability. The traditional way to make the argument above rigorous is to assume that there is some underlying distribution of numbers $F(u)$ such that a given positive number U is $\le u$ with probability $F(u)$; then the probability of concern to us is

$$p(r) = \sum_m \big(F(10^m r) - F(10^m)\big), \qquad (4)$$

summed over all values $-\infty < m < \infty$. Our assumptions about scale invariance and continuity have led us to conclude that

$$p(r) = \log_{10} r.$$

Using the same argument, we could "prove" that

$$\sum_m \left(F(b^m r) - F(b^m)\right) = \log_b r, \qquad (5)$$

for each integer $b \geq 2$, when $1 \leq r \leq b$. But there *is* no distribution function F that satisfies this equation for all such b and r! (See exercise 7.)

One way out of the difficulty is to regard the logarithm law $p(r) = \log_{10} r$ as only a very close *approximation* to the true distribution. The true distribution itself may perhaps be changing as the universe expands, becoming a better and better approximation as time goes on; and if we replace 10 by an arbitrary base b, the approximation might be less accurate (at any given time) as b gets larger. Another rather appealing way to resolve the dilemma, by abandoning the traditional idea of a distribution function, has been suggested by R. A. Raimi, *AMM* **76** (1969), 342–348.

The hedging in the last paragraph is probably a very unsatisfactory explanation, and so the following further calculation (which sticks to rigorous mathematics and avoids any intuitive, yet paradoxical, notions of probability) should be welcome. Let us consider the distribution of the leading digits of the *positive integers*, instead of the distribution for some imagined set of real numbers. The investigation of this topic is quite interesting, not only because it sheds some light on the probability distributions of floating point data, but also because it makes a particularly instructive example of how to combine the methods of discrete mathematics with the methods of infinitesimal calculus.

In the following discussion, let r be a fixed real number, $1 \leq r \leq 10$; we will attempt to make a reasonable definition of $p(r)$, the "probability" that the representation $10^{e_N} \cdot f_N$ of a "random" positive integer N has $10 f_N < r$, assuming infinite precision.

To start, let us try to find the probability using a limiting method like the definition of "Pr" in Section 3.5. One nice way to rephrase that definition is to define

$$P_0(n) = \left[n = 10^e \cdot f \text{ where } 10f < r\right] = \left[(\log_{10} n) \bmod 1 < \log_{10} r\right]. \quad (6)$$

Now $P_0(1)$, $P_0(2)$, $\ldots$ is an infinite sequence of zeros and ones, with ones to represent the cases that contribute to the probability we are seeking. We can try to "average out" this sequence, by defining

$$P_1(n) = \frac{1}{n} \sum_{k=1}^{n} P_0(k). \qquad (7)$$

Thus if we generate a random integer between 1 and n using the techniques of Chapter 3, and convert it to floating decimal form (e, f), the probability that $10f < r$ is exactly $P_1(n)$. It is natural to let $\lim_{n \to \infty} P_1(n)$ be the "probability" $p(r)$ we are after, and that is just what we did in Definition 3.5A.

But in this case the limit does not exist. For example, let us consider the subsequence

$$P_1(s), P_1(10s), P_1(100s), \ldots, P_1(10^n s), \ldots,$$

where s is a real number, $1 \le s \le 10$. If $s \le r$, we find that

$$P_1(10^n s) = \frac{1}{10^n s}\left(\lceil r \rceil - 1 + \lceil 10r \rceil - 10 + \cdots + \lceil 10^{n-1} r \rceil - 10^{n-1} + \lfloor 10^n s \rfloor + 1 - 10^n\right)$$

$$= \frac{1}{10^n s}\left(r(1 + 10 + \cdots + 10^{n-1}) + O(n) + \lfloor 10^n s \rfloor - 1 - 10 - \cdots - 10^n\right)$$

$$= \frac{1}{10^n s}\left(\tfrac{1}{9}(10^n r - 10^{n+1}) + \lfloor 10^n s \rfloor + O(n)\right). \tag{8}$$

As $n \to \infty$, $P_1(10^n s)$ therefore approaches the limiting value $1 + (r-10)/9s$. The same calculation is valid for the case $s > r$ if we replace $\lfloor 10^n s \rfloor + 1$ by $\lceil 10^n r \rceil$; thus we obtain the limiting value $10(r-1)/9s$ when $s \ge r$. [See J. Franel, *Naturforschende Gesellschaft, Vierteljahrsschrift* **62** (Zürich: 1917), 286–295.]

In other words, the sequence $\langle P_1(n) \rangle$ has subsequences $\langle P_1(10^n s) \rangle$ whose limit goes from $(r-1)/9$ up to $10(r-1)/9r$ and down again to $(r-1)/9$, as s goes from 1 to r to 10. We see that $P_1(n)$ has no limit as $n \to \infty$; and the values of $P_1(n)$ for large n are not particularly good approximations to our conjectured limit $\log_{10} r$ either!

Since $P_1(n)$ doesn't approach a limit, we can try to use the same idea as (7) once again, to "average out" the anomalous behavior. In general, let

$$P_{m+1}(n) = \frac{1}{n}\sum_{k=1}^{n} P_m(k). \tag{9}$$

Then $P_{m+1}(n)$ will tend to be a more well-behaved sequence than $P_m(n)$. Let us try to confirm this with quantitative calculations; our experience with the special case $m = 0$ indicates that it might be worthwhile to consider the subsequence $P_{m+1}(10^n s)$. The following results can, in fact, be derived:

Lemma Q. *For any integer $m \ge 1$ and any real number $\epsilon > 0$, there are functions $Q_m(s)$, $R_m(s)$ and an integer $N_m(\epsilon)$, such that whenever $n > N_m(\epsilon)$ and $1 \le s \le 10$, we have*

$$|P_m(10^n s) - Q_m(s) - R_m(s)[s > r]| < \epsilon. \tag{10}$$

Furthermore the functions $Q_m(s)$ and $R_m(s)$ satisfy the relations

$$Q_m(s) = \frac{1}{s}\left(\frac{1}{9}\int_1^{10} Q_{m-1}(t)\, dt + \int_1^s Q_{m-1}(t)\, dt + \frac{1}{9}\int_r^{10} R_{m-1}(t)\, dt\right);$$

$$R_m(s) = \frac{1}{s}\int_r^s R_{m-1}(t)\, dt; \tag{11}$$

$$Q_0(s) = 1, \qquad R_0(s) = -1.$$

Proof. Consider the functions $Q_m(s)$ and $R_m(s)$ defined by (11), and let

$$S_m(t) = Q_m(t) + R_m(t)[t > r]. \tag{12}$$

We will prove the lemma by induction on m.

First note that $Q_1(s) = \big(1 + (s-1) - (10-r)/9\big)/s = 1 + (r-10)/9s$, and $R_1(s) = (r-s)/s$. From (8) we find that $|P_1(10^n s) - S_1(s)| = O(n)/10^n$; this establishes the lemma when $m = 1$.

Now for $m > 1$, we have

$$P_m(10^n s) = \frac{1}{s}\left(\sum_{0 \le j < n} \frac{1}{10^{n-j}} \sum_{10^j \le k < 10^{j+1}} \frac{1}{10^j} P_{m-1}(k) + \sum_{10^n \le k \le 10^n s} \frac{1}{10^n} P_{m-1}(k)\right),$$

and we want to approximate this quantity. By induction, the difference

$$\left| \sum_{10^j \le k \le 10^j q} \frac{1}{10^j} P_{m-1}(k) - \sum_{10^j \le k \le 10^j q} \frac{1}{10^j} S_{m-1}\left(\frac{k}{10^j}\right) \right| \qquad (13)$$

is less than $q\epsilon$ when $1 \le q \le 10$ and $j > N_{m-1}(\epsilon)$. Since $S_{m-1}(t)$ is continuous, it is a Riemann-integrable function; and the difference

$$\left| \sum_{10^j \le k \le 10^j q} \frac{1}{10^j} S_{m-1}\left(\frac{k}{10^j}\right) - \int_1^q S_{m-1}(t)\, dt \right| \qquad (14)$$

is less than ϵ for all j greater than some number N, independent of q, by the definition of integration. We may choose N to be $> N_{m-1}(\epsilon)$. Therefore for $n > N$, the difference

$$\left| P_m(10^n s) - \frac{1}{s}\left(\sum_{0 \le j < n} \frac{1}{10^{n-j}} \int_1^{10} S_{m-1}(t)\, dt + \int_1^s S_{m-1}(t)\, dt\right) \right| \qquad (15)$$

is bounded by $\sum_{j=0}^{N}(M/10^{n-j}) + \sum_{N<j<n}(11\epsilon/10^{n-j}) + 11\epsilon$, if M is an upper bound for $(13) + (14)$ that is valid for all positive integers j. Finally, the sum $\sum_{0 \le j < n}(1/10^{n-j})$, which appears in (15), is equal to $(1 - 1/10^n)/9$; so

$$\left| P_m(10^n s) - \frac{1}{s}\left(\frac{1}{9}\int_1^{10} S_{m-1}(t)\, dt + \int_1^s S_{m-1}(t)\, dt\right) \right|$$

can be made smaller than, say, 20ϵ, if n is taken large enough. Comparing this with (10) and (11) completes the proof. ∎

The gist of Lemma Q is that we have the limiting relationship

$$\lim_{n \to \infty} P_m(10^n s) = S_m(s). \qquad (16)$$

Also, since $S_m(s)$ is not constant as s varies, the limit

$$\lim_{n \to \infty} P_m(n)$$

(which would be our desired "probability") does not exist for any m. The situation is shown in Fig. 5, which shows the values of $S_m(s)$ when m is small and $r = 2$.

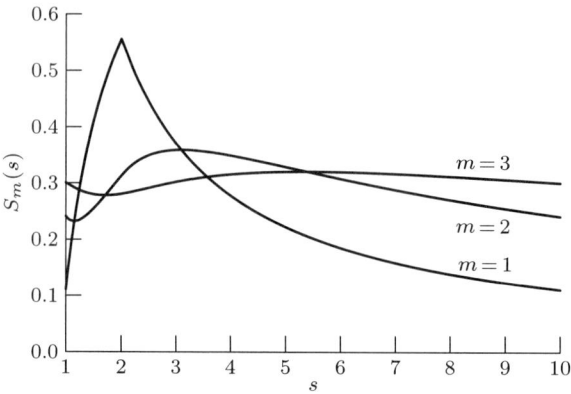

Fig. 5. The probability that the leading digit is 1.

Even though $S_m(s)$ is not a constant, so that we do not have a definite limit for $P_m(n)$, notice that already for $m = 3$ in Fig. 5 the value of $S_m(s)$ stays very close to $\log_{10} 2 \approx 0.30103$. Therefore we have good reason to suspect that $S_m(s)$ is very close to $\log_{10} r$ for all large m, and, in fact, that the sequence of functions $\langle S_m(s) \rangle$ converges uniformly to the constant function $\log_{10} r$.

It is interesting to prove this conjecture by explicitly calculating $Q_m(s)$ and $R_m(s)$ for all m, as in the proof of the following theorem:

Theorem F. *Let $S_m(s)$ be the limit defined in* (16). *For all $\epsilon > 0$, there exists a number $N(\epsilon)$ such that*

$$|S_m(s) - \log_{10} r| < \epsilon, \qquad \text{for } 1 \le s \le 10, \tag{17}$$

whenever $m > N(\epsilon)$.

Proof. In view of Lemma Q, we can prove this result if we can show that there is a number M depending on ϵ such that, for $1 \le s \le 10$ and for all $m > M$, we have

$$|Q_m(s) - \log_{10} r| < \epsilon \qquad \text{and} \qquad |R_m(s)| < \epsilon. \tag{18}$$

It is not difficult to solve the recurrence formula (11) for R_m: We have $R_0(s) = -1$, $R_1(s) = -1 + r/s$, $R_2(s) = -1 + (r/s)(1 + \ln(s/r))$, and in general

$$R_m(s) = -1 + \frac{r}{s}\left(1 + \frac{1}{1!}\ln\frac{s}{r} + \cdots + \frac{1}{(m-1)!}\left(\ln\frac{s}{r}\right)^{m-1}\right). \tag{19}$$

For the stated range of s, this converges uniformly to $-1 + (r/s)\exp(\ln(s/r)) = 0$.

The recurrence (11) for Q_m takes the form

$$Q_m(s) = \frac{1}{s}\left(c_m + 1 + \int_1^s Q_{m-1}(t)\,dt\right), \tag{20}$$

where

$$c_m = \frac{1}{9}\left(\int_1^{10} Q_{m-1}(t)\,dt + \int_r^{10} R_{m-1}(t)\,dt\right) - 1. \tag{21}$$

And the solution to recurrence (20) is easily found by trying out the first few cases and guessing at a formula that can be proved by induction; we find that

$$Q_m(s) = 1 + \frac{1}{s}\left(c_m + \frac{1}{1!}c_{m-1}\ln s + \cdots + \frac{1}{(m-1)!}c_1(\ln s)^{m-1}\right). \qquad (22)$$

It remains for us to calculate the coefficients c_m, which by (19), (21), and (22) satisfy the relations

$$c_1 = (r - 10)/9;$$

$$c_{m+1} = \frac{1}{9}\left(c_m \ln 10 + \frac{1}{2!}c_{m-1}(\ln 10)^2 + \cdots + \frac{1}{m!}c_1(\ln 10)^m\right.$$
$$\left. + r\left(1 + \frac{1}{1!}\ln\frac{10}{r} + \cdots + \frac{1}{m!}\left(\ln\frac{10}{r}\right)^m\right) - 10\right). \qquad (23)$$

This sequence appears at first to be very complicated, but actually we can analyze it without difficulty with the help of generating functions. Let

$$C(z) = c_1 z + c_2 z^2 + c_3 z^3 + \cdots;$$

then since $10^z = 1 + z \ln 10 + (1/2!)(z \ln 10)^2 + \cdots$, we deduce that

$$c_{m+1} = \frac{1}{10}c_{m+1} + \frac{9}{10}c_{m+1}$$
$$= \frac{1}{10}\left(c_{m+1} + c_m \ln 10 + \cdots + \frac{1}{m!}c_1(\ln 10)^m\right) + \frac{r}{10}\left(1 + \cdots + \frac{1}{m!}\left(\ln\frac{10}{r}\right)^m\right) - 1$$

is the coefficient of z^{m+1} in the function

$$\frac{1}{10}C(z)10^z + \frac{r}{10}\left(\frac{10}{r}\right)^z\left(\frac{z}{1-z}\right) - \frac{z}{1-z}. \qquad (24)$$

This condition holds for all values of m, so (24) must equal $C(z)$, and we obtain the explicit formula

$$C(z) = \frac{-z}{1-z}\left(\frac{(10/r)^{z-1} - 1}{10^{z-1} - 1}\right). \qquad (25)$$

We want to study asymptotic properties of the coefficients of $C(z)$, to complete our analysis. The large parenthesized factor in (25) approaches $\ln(10/r)/\ln 10 = 1 - \log_{10} r$ as $z \to 1$, so we see that

$$C(z) + \frac{1 - \log_{10} r}{1 - z} = R(z) \qquad (26)$$

is an analytic function of the complex variable z in the circle

$$|z| < \left|1 + \frac{2\pi i}{\ln 10}\right|.$$

In particular, $R(z)$ converges for $z = 1$, so its coefficients approach zero. This proves that the coefficients of $C(z)$ behave like those of $(\log_{10} r - 1)/(1 - z)$, that is,

$$\lim_{m \to \infty} c_m = \log_{10} r - 1.$$

Finally, we may combine this with (22), to show that $Q_m(s)$ approaches

$$1 + \frac{\log_{10} r - 1}{s}\left(1 + \ln s + \frac{1}{2!}(\ln s)^2 + \cdots\right) = \log_{10} r$$

uniformly for $1 \le s \le 10$. ∎

Therefore we have established the logarithmic law for integers by direct calculation, at the same time seeing that it is an extremely good approximation to the average behavior although it is never precisely achieved.

The proofs of Lemma Q and Theorem F given above are slight simplifications and amplifications of methods due to B. J. Flehinger, *AMM* **73** (1966), 1056–1061. Many authors have written about the distribution of initial digits, showing that the logarithmic law is a good approximation for many underlying distributions; see the surveys by Ralph A. Raimi, *AMM* **83** (1976), 521–538, and Peter Schatte, *J. Information Processing and Cybernetics* **24** (1988), 443–455, for a comprehensive review of the literature.

Exercise 17 discusses an approach to the definition of probability under which the logarithmic law holds exactly, over the integers. Furthermore, exercise 18 demonstrates that *any* reasonable definition of probability over the integers must lead to the logarithmic law, if it assigns a value to the probability of leading digits.

Floating point computations operate primarily on noninteger numbers, of course; we have studied integers because of their familiarity and their simplicity. When arbitrary real numbers are considered, theoretical results are more difficult to obtain, but evidence is accumulating that the same statistics apply, in the sense that repeated calculations with real numbers will nearly always tend to yield better and better approximations to a logarithmic distribution of fraction parts. For example, Peter Schatte [*Zeitschrift für angewandte Math. und Mechanik* **53** (1973), 553–565] showed that, under mild restrictions, the products of independent, identically distributed random real variables approach the logarithmic distribution. The sums of such variables do too, but only in the sense of repeated averaging. Similar results have been obtained by J. L. Barlow and E. H. Bareiss, *Computing* **34** (1985), 325–347.

EXERCISES

1. [*13*] Given that u and v are nonzero floating decimal numbers *with the same sign*, what is the approximate probability that fraction overflow occurs during the calculation of $u \oplus v$, according to Tables 1 and 2?

2. [*42*] Make further tests of floating point addition and subtraction, to confirm or improve on the accuracy of Tables 1 and 2.

3. [15] What is the probability that the two leading digits of a floating decimal number are "23", according to the logarithmic law?

4. [M18] The text points out that the front pages of a well-used table of logarithms get dirtier than the back pages do. What if we had an *antilogarithm* table instead, namely a table that tells us the value of x when $\log_{10} x$ is given; which pages of such a table would be the dirtiest?

▶ **5.** [M20] Let U be a random real number that is uniformly distributed in the interval $0 < U < 1$. What is the distribution of the leading digits of U?

6. [23] If we have binary computer words containing $n + 1$ bits, we might use p bits for the fraction part of floating binary numbers, one bit for the sign, and $n - p$ bits for the exponent. This means that the range of values representable, namely the ratio of the largest positive normalized value to the smallest, is essentially $2^{2^{n-p}}$. The same computer word could be used to represent floating *hexadecimal* numbers, that is, floating point numbers with radix 16, with $p + 2$ bits for the fraction part $((p + 2)/4$ hexadecimal digits) and $n - p - 2$ bits for the exponent; then the range of values would be $16^{2^{n-p-2}} = 2^{2^{n-p}}$, the same as before, and with more bits in the fraction part. This may sound as if we are getting something for nothing, but the normalization condition for base 16 is weaker in that there may be up to three leading zero bits in the fraction part; thus not all of the $p + 2$ bits are "significant."

On the basis of the logarithmic law, what are the probabilities that the fraction part of a positive normalized radix 16 floating point number has exactly 0, 1, 2, and 3 leading zero bits? Discuss the desirability of hexadecimal versus binary.

7. [HM28] Prove that there is no distribution function $F(u)$ that satisfies (5) for each integer $b \geq 2$, and for all real values r in the range $1 \leq r \leq b$.

8. [HM23] Does (10) hold when $m = 0$ for suitable $N_0(\epsilon)$?

9. [HM25] (P. Diaconis.) Let $P_1(n)$, $P_2(n)$, ... be any sequence of functions defined by repeatedly averaging a given function $P_0(n)$ according to Eq. (9). Prove that $\lim_{m \to \infty} P_m(n) = P_0(1)$ for all fixed n.

▶ **10.** [HM28] The text shows that $c_m = \log_{10} r - 1 + \epsilon_m$, where ϵ_m approaches zero as $m \to \infty$. Obtain the next term in the asymptotic expansion of c_m.

11. [M15] Given that U is a random variable distributed according to the logarithmic law, prove that $1/U$ is also.

12. [HM25] (R. W. Hamming.) The purpose of this exercise is to show that the result of floating point multiplication tends to obey the logarithmic law more perfectly than the operands do. Let U and V be random, normalized, positive floating point numbers, whose fraction parts are independently distributed with the respective density functions $f(x)$ and $g(x)$. Thus, $f_u \leq r$ and $f_v \leq s$ with probability $\int_{1/b}^{r} \int_{1/b}^{s} f(x)g(y)\,dy\,dx$, for $1/b \leq r, s \leq 1$. Let $h(x)$ be the density function of the fraction part of $U \times V$ (unrounded). Define the *abnormality* $A(f)$ of a density function f to be the maximum relative error,

$$A(f) = \max_{1/b \leq x \leq 1} \left| \frac{f(x) - l(x)}{l(x)} \right|,$$

where $l(x) = 1/(x \ln b)$ is the density of the logarithmic distribution.

Prove that $A(h) \leq \min(A(f), A(g))$. (In particular, if either factor has logarithmic distribution the product does also.)

▶ **13.** [*M20*] The floating point multiplication routine, Algorithm 4.2.1M, requires zero or one left shifts during normalization, depending on whether $f_u f_v \geq 1/b$ or not. Assuming that the input operands are independently distributed according to the logarithmic law, what is the probability that no left shift is needed for normalization of the result?

▶ **14.** [*HM30*] Let U and V be random, normalized, positive floating point numbers whose fraction parts are independently distributed according to the logarithmic law, and let p_k be the probability that the difference in their exponents is k. Assuming that the distribution of the exponents is independent of the fraction parts, give an equation for the probability that "fraction overflow" occurs during the floating point addition of $U \oplus V$, in terms of the base b and the quantities p_0, p_1, p_2, ... Compare this result with exercise 1. (Ignore rounding.)

15. [*HM28*] Let U, V, p_0, p_1, ... be as in exercise 14, and assume that radix 10 arithmetic is being used. Show that regardless of the values of p_0, p_1, p_2, ..., the sum $U \oplus V$ will *not* obey the logarithmic law exactly, and in fact the probability that $U \oplus V$ has leading digit 1 is always strictly *less* than $\log_{10} 2$.

16. [*HM28*] (P. Diaconis.) Let $P_0(n)$ be 0 or 1 for each n, and define "probabilities" $P_{m+1}(n)$ by repeated averaging, as in (9). Show that if $\lim_{n\to\infty} P_1(n)$ does not exist, neither does $\lim_{n\to\infty} P_m(n)$ for any m. [*Hint:* Prove that $a_n \to 0$ whenever we have $(a_1 + \cdots + a_n)/n \to 0$ and $a_{n+1} \leq a_n + M/n$, for some fixed constant $M > 0$.]

▶ **17.** [*HM25*] (M. Tsuji.) Another way to define the value of $\Pr(S(n))$ is to evaluate the quantity $\lim_{n\to\infty} \left(H_n^{-1} \sum_{k=1}^{n} [S(k)]/k\right)$; it can be shown that this *harmonic probability* exists and is equal to $\Pr(S(n))$, whenever the latter exists according to Definition 3.5A. Prove that the harmonic probability of the statement "$(\log_{10} n) \bmod 1 < r$" exists and equals r. (Thus, initial digits of integers satisfy the logarithmic law *exactly* in this sense.)

▶ **18.** [*HM30*] Let $P(S)$ be any real-valued function defined on sets S of positive integers, but not necessarily on all such sets, satisfying the following rather weak axioms:

  i) If $P(S)$ and $P(T)$ are defined and $S \cap T = \emptyset$, then $P(S \cup T) = P(S) + P(T)$.
  ii) If $P(S)$ is defined, then $P(S+1) = P(S)$, where $S + 1 = \{n + 1 \mid n \in S\}$.
  iii) If $P(S)$ is defined, then $P(2S) = \frac{1}{2}P(S)$, where $2S = \{2n \mid n \in S\}$.
  iv) If S is the set of *all* positive integers, then $P(S) = 1$.
  v) If $P(S)$ is defined, then $P(S) \geq 0$.

Assume furthermore that $P(L_a)$ is defined for all positive integers a, where L_a is the set of all integers whose decimal representation begins with a:

$$L_a = \{n \mid 10^m a \leq n < 10^m (a + 1) \text{ for some integer } m\} .$$

(In this definition, m may be negative; for example, 1 is an element of L_{10}, but not of L_{11}.) Prove that $P(L_a) = \log_{10}(1 + 1/a)$ for all integers $a \geq 1$.

19. [*HM25*] (R. L. Duncan.) Prove that the leading digits of Fibonacci numbers obey the logarithmic law of fraction parts: $\Pr(10 f_{F_n} < r) = \log_{10} r$.

20. [*HM40*] Sharpen (16) by finding the asymptotic behavior of $P_m(10^n s) - S_m(s)$ as $n \to \infty$.

4.3. MULTIPLE-PRECISION ARITHMETIC

LET US NOW consider operations on numbers that have arbitrarily high precision. For simplicity in exposition, we shall assume that we are working with integers, instead of with numbers that have an embedded radix point.

4.3.1. The Classical Algorithms

In this section we shall discuss algorithms for

a) addition or subtraction of n-place integers, giving an n-place answer and a carry;

b) multiplication of an m-place integer by an n-place integer, giving an $(m+n)$-place answer;

c) division of an $(m+n)$-place integer by an n-place integer, giving an $(m+1)$-place quotient and an n-place remainder.

These may be called *the classical algorithms*, since the word "algorithm" was used only in connection with these processes for several centuries. The term "n-place integer" means any nonnegative integer less than b^n, where b is the radix of ordinary positional notation in which the numbers are expressed; such numbers can be written using at most n "places" in this notation.

It is a straightforward matter to apply the classical algorithms for integers to numbers with embedded radix points or to extended-precision floating point numbers, in the same way that arithmetic operations defined for integers in MIX are applied to these more general problems.

In this section we shall study algorithms that do operations (a), (b), and (c) above for integers expressed in radix b notation, where b is any given integer that is 2 or more. Thus the algorithms are quite general definitions of arithmetic processes, and as such they are unrelated to any particular computer. But the discussion in this section will also be somewhat machine-oriented, since we are chiefly concerned with efficient methods for doing high-precision calculations by computer. Although our examples are based on the mythical MIX, essentially the same considerations apply to nearly every other machine.

The most important fact to understand about extended-precision numbers is that they may be regarded as numbers written in radix w notation, where w is the computer's word size. For example, an integer that fills 10 words on a computer whose word size is $w = 10^{10}$ has 100 decimal digits; but we will consider it to be a 10-place number to the base 10^{10}. This viewpoint is justified for the same reason that we may convert, say, from binary to hexadecimal notation, simply by grouping the bits together. (See Eq. 4.1–(5).)

In these terms, we are given the following primitive operations to work with:

a_0) addition or subtraction of one-place integers, giving a one-place answer and a carry;

b_0) multiplication of a one-place integer by another one-place integer, giving a two-place answer;

c_0) division of a two-place integer by a one-place integer, provided that the quotient is a one-place integer, and yielding also a one-place remainder.

By adjusting the word size, if necessary, nearly all computers will have these three operations available; so we will construct algorithms (a), (b), and (c) mentioned above in terms of the primitive operations (a$_0$), (b$_0$), and (c$_0$).

Since we are visualizing extended-precision integers as base b numbers, it is sometimes helpful to think of the situation when $b = 10$, and to imagine that we are doing the arithmetic by hand. Then operation (a$_0$) is analogous to memorizing the addition table; (b$_0$) is analogous to memorizing the multiplication table; and (c$_0$) is essentially memorizing the multiplication table in reverse. The more complicated operations (a), (b), (c) on high-precision numbers can now be done using the simple addition, subtraction, multiplication, and long-division procedures that children are taught in elementary school. In fact, most of the algorithms we shall discuss in this section are essentially nothing more than mechanizations of familiar pencil-and-paper operations. Of course, we must state the algorithms much more precisely than they have ever been stated in the fifth grade, and we should also attempt to minimize computer memory and running time requirements.

To avoid a tedious discussion and cumbersome notations, we shall assume first that all the numbers we deal with are *nonnegative*. The additional work of computing the signs, etc., is quite straightforward, although some care is necessary when dealing with complemented numbers on computers that do not use a signed magnitude representation. Such issues are discussed near the end of this section.

First comes addition, which of course is very simple, but it is worth careful study since the same ideas occur also in the other algorithms.

Algorithm A (*Addition of nonnegative integers*). Given nonnegative n-place integers $(u_{n-1} \ldots u_1 u_0)_b$ and $(v_{n-1} \ldots v_1 v_0)_b$, this algorithm forms their radix-b sum, $(w_n w_{n-1} \ldots w_1 w_0)_b$. Here w_n is the carry, and it will always be equal to 0 or 1.

A1. [Initialize.] Set $j \leftarrow 0$, $k \leftarrow 0$. (The variable j will run through the various digit positions, and the variable k will keep track of carries at each step.)

A2. [Add digits.] Set $w_j \leftarrow (u_j + v_j + k) \bmod b$, and $k \leftarrow \lfloor (u_j + v_j + k)/b \rfloor$. (By induction on the computation, we will always have

$$u_j + v_j + k \le (b-1) + (b-1) + 1 < 2b.$$

Thus k is being set to 1 or 0, depending on whether a carry occurs or not; equivalently, $k \leftarrow [u_j + v_j + k \ge b]$.)

A3. [Loop on j.] Increase j by one. Now if $j < n$, go back to step A2; otherwise set $w_n \leftarrow k$ and terminate the algorithm. ∎

For a formal proof that Algorithm A is valid, see exercise 4.

A MIX program for this addition process might take the following form:

Program A (*Addition of nonnegative integers*). Let $\mathrm{LOC}(u_j) \equiv \mathtt{U}+j$, $\mathrm{LOC}(v_j) \equiv \mathtt{V} + j$, $\mathrm{LOC}(w_j) \equiv \mathtt{W} + j$, $\mathrm{rI1} \equiv j - n$, $\mathrm{rA} \equiv k$, word size $\equiv b$, $\mathtt{N} \equiv n$.

```
01       ENN1 N         1          A1. Initialize. j ← 0.
02        JOV OFLO      1          Ensure that overflow is off.
03    1H ENTA 0         N + 1 − K  k ← 0.
04        J1Z  3F       N + 1 − K  Exit the loop if j = n.
05    2H ADD  U+N,1      N          A2. Add digits.
06        ADD  V+N,1     N
07        STA  W+N,1     N
08        INC1 1         N          A3. Loop on j. j ← j + 1.
09        JNOV 1B        N          If no overflow, set k ← 0.
10        ENTA 1         K          Otherwise, set k ← 1.
11        J1N  2B        K          To A2 if j < n.
12    3H STA  W+N        1          Store final carry in wₙ.  ∎
```

The running time for this program is $10N + 6$ cycles, independent of the number of carries, K. The quantity K is analyzed in detail at the close of this section.

Many modifications of Algorithm A are possible, and only a few of these are mentioned in the exercises below. A chapter on generalizations of this algorithm might be entitled "How to design addition circuits for a digital computer."

The problem of subtraction is similar to addition, but the differences are worth noting:

Algorithm S (*Subtraction of nonnegative integers*). Given nonnegative n-place integers $(u_{n-1} \ldots u_1 u_0)_b \geq (v_{n-1} \ldots v_1 v_0)_b$, this algorithm forms their nonnegative radix-b difference, $(w_{n-1} \ldots w_1 w_0)_b$.

S1. [Initialize.] Set $j \leftarrow 0$, $k \leftarrow 0$.

S2. [Subtract digits.] Set $w_j \leftarrow (u_j - v_j + k) \bmod b$, and $k \leftarrow \lfloor (u_j - v_j + k)/b \rfloor$. (In other words, k is set to -1 or 0, depending on whether a borrow occurs or not, namely whether $u_j - v_j + k < 0$ or not. In the calculation of w_j, we must have $-b = 0 - (b - 1) + (-1) \leq u_j - v_j + k \leq (b - 1) - 0 + 0 < b$; hence $0 \leq u_j - v_j + k + b < 2b$, and this suggests the method of computer implementation explained below.)

S3. [Loop on j.] Increase j by one. Now if $j < n$, go back to step S2; otherwise terminate the algorithm. (When the algorithm terminates, we should have $k = 0$; the condition $k = -1$ will occur if and only if $(v_{n-1} \ldots v_1 v_0)_b > (u_{n-1} \ldots u_1 u_0)_b$, contrary to the given assumptions. See exercise 12.) ∎

In a MIX program to implement subtraction, it is most convenient to retain the value $1 + k$ instead of k throughout the algorithm, so that we can calculate $u_j - v_j + (1 + k) + (b - 1)$ in step S2. (Recall that b is the word size.) This is illustrated in the following code.

Program S (*Subtraction of nonnegative integers*). This program is analogous to the code in Program A, but with rA $\equiv 1 + k$. Here, as in other programs of this section, location WM1 contains the constant $b - 1$, the largest possible value that can be stored in a MIX word; see Program 4.2.3D, lines 38–39.

```
01       ENN1 N         1          S1. Initialize. j ← 0.
02        JOV OFLO      1          Ensure that overflow is off.
```

```
03  1H  J1Z   DONE     K + 1    Terminate if j = n.
04      ENTA  1        K        Set k ← 0.
05  2H  ADD   U+N,1    N        S2. Subtract digits.
06      SUB   V+N,1    N        Compute u_j − v_j + k + b.
07      ADD   WM1      N
08      STA   W+N,1    N        (May be minus zero)
09      INC1  1        N        S3. Loop on j. j ← j + 1.
10      JOV   1B       N        If overflow, set k ← 0.
11      ENTA  0        N − K    Otherwise set k ← −1.
12      J1N   2B       N − K    Back to S2 if j < n.
13      HLT   5                 (Error, v > u)   ▮
```

The running time for this program is $12N + 3$ cycles, slightly longer than the corresponding amount for Program A.

The reader may wonder if it would not be worthwhile to have a combined addition-subtraction routine in place of the two algorithms A and S. But an examination of the code shows that it is generally better to use two different routines, so that the inner loops of the computations can be performed as rapidly as possible, since the programs are so short.

Our next problem is multiplication, and here we carry the ideas used in Algorithm A a little further:

Algorithm M (*Multiplication of nonnegative integers*). Given nonnegative integers $(u_{m-1} \ldots u_1 u_0)_b$ and $(v_{n-1} \ldots v_1 v_0)_b$, this algorithm forms their radix-b product $(w_{m+n-1} \ldots w_1 w_0)_b$. (The conventional pencil-and-paper method is based on forming the partial products $(u_{m-1} \ldots u_1 u_0) \times v_j$ first, for $0 \le j < n$, and then adding these products together with appropriate scale factors; but in a computer it is best to do the addition concurrently with the multiplication, as described in this algorithm.)

M1. [Initialize.] Set w_{m-1}, w_{m-2}, $\ldots$, w_0 all to zero. Set $j \leftarrow 0$. (If those positions were not cleared to zero in this step, one can show that the steps below would set

$$(w_{m+n-1} \ldots w_0)_b \leftarrow (u_{m-1} \ldots u_0)_b \times (v_{n-1} \ldots v_0)_b + (w_{m-1} \ldots w_0)_b.$$

This more general multiply-and-add operation is often useful.)

M2. [Zero multiplier?] If $v_j = 0$, set $w_{j+m} \leftarrow 0$ and go to step M6. (This test might save time if there is a reasonable chance that v_j is zero, but it may be omitted without affecting the validity of the algorithm.)

M3. [Initialize i.] Set $i \leftarrow 0$, $k \leftarrow 0$.

M4. [Multiply and add.] Set $t \leftarrow u_i \times v_j + w_{i+j} + k$; then set $w_{i+j} \leftarrow t \bmod b$ and $k \leftarrow \lfloor t/b \rfloor$. (Here the carry k will always be in the range $0 \le k < b$; see below.)

M5. [Loop on i.] Increase i by one. Now if $i < m$, go back to step M4; otherwise set $w_{j+m} \leftarrow k$.

M6. [Loop on j.] Increase j by one. Now if $j < n$, go back to step M2; otherwise the algorithm terminates.   ▮

Table 1

MULTIPLICATION OF 914 BY 84

Step	i	j	u_i	v_j	t	w_4	w_3	w_2	w_1	w_0
M5	0	0	4	4	16	.	.	0	0	6
M5	1	0	1	4	05	.	.	0	5	6
M5	2	0	9	4	36	.	.	6	5	6
M6	3	0	.	4	36	.	3	6	5	6
M5	0	1	4	8	37	.	3	6	7	6
M5	1	1	1	8	17	.	3	7	7	6
M5	2	1	9	8	76	.	6	7	7	6
M6	3	1	.	8	76	7	6	7	7	6

Algorithm M is illustrated in Table 1, assuming that $b = 10$, by showing the states of the computation at the beginning of steps M5 and M6. A proof of Algorithm M appears in the answer to exercise 14.

The two inequalities

$$0 \le t < b^2, \qquad 0 \le k < b \qquad\qquad (1)$$

are crucial for an efficient implementation of this algorithm, since they point out how large a register is needed for the computations. These inequalities may be proved by induction as the algorithm proceeds, for if we have $k < b$ at the start of step M4, we have

$$u_i \times v_j + w_{i+j} + k \le (b-1) \times (b-1) + (b-1) + (b-1) = b^2 - 1 < b^2.$$

The following MIX program shows the considerations that are necessary when Algorithm M is implemented on a computer. The coding for step M4 would be a little simpler if our computer had a "multiply-and-add" instruction, or if it had a double-length accumulator for addition.

Program M (*Multiplication of nonnegative integers*). This program is analogous to Program A. $rI1 \equiv i - m$, $rI2 \equiv j - n$, $rI3 \equiv i + j$, CONTENTS(CARRY) $\equiv k$.

01		ENT1	M-1	1	M1. Initialize.
02		JOV	OFLO	1	Ensure that overflow is off.
03		STZ	W,1	M	$w_{rI1} \leftarrow 0$.
04		DEC1	1	M	
05		J1NN	*-2	M	Repeat for $m > rI1 \ge 0$.
06		ENN2	N	1	$j \leftarrow 0$.
07	1H	LDX	V+N,2	N	M2. Zero multiplier?
08		JXZ	8F	N	If $v_j = 0$, set $w_{j+m} \leftarrow 0$ and go to M6.
09		ENN1	M	$N - Z$	M3. Initialize i. $i \leftarrow 0$.
10		ENT3	N,2	$N - Z$	$(i + j) \leftarrow j$.
11		ENTX	0	$N - Z$	$k \leftarrow 0$.
12	2H	STX	CARRY	$(N - Z)M$	M4. Multiply and add.
13		LDA	U+M,1	$(N - Z)M$	
14		MUL	V+N,2	$(N - Z)M$	$rAX \leftarrow u_i \times v_j$.
15		SLC	5	$(N - Z)M$	Interchange $rA \leftrightarrow rX$.
16		ADD	W,3	$(N - Z)M$	Add w_{i+j} to lower half.

17		JNOV	*+2	$(N-Z)M$	Did overflow occur?
18		INCX	1	K	If so, carry 1 into upper half.
19		ADD	CARRY	$(N-Z)M$	Add k to lower half.
20		JNOV	*+2	$(N-Z)M$	Did overflow occur?
21		INCX	1	K'	If so, carry 1 into upper half.
22		STA	W,3	$(N-Z)M$	$w_{i+j} \leftarrow t \bmod b$.
23		INC1	1	$(N-Z)M$	M5. Loop on i. $i \leftarrow i+1$.
24		INC3	1	$(N-Z)M$	$(i+j) \leftarrow (i+j)+1$.
25		J1N	2B	$(N-Z)M$	Back to M4 with rX = $\lfloor t/b \rfloor$ if $i < m$.
26	8H	STX	W+M+N,2	N	Set $w_{j+m} \leftarrow k$.
27		INC2	1	N	M6. Loop on j. $j \leftarrow j+1$.
28		J2N	1B	N	Repeat until $j = n$. ∎

The execution time of Program M depends on the number of places, M, in the multiplicand u; the number of places, N, in the multiplier v; the number of zeros, Z, in the multiplier; and the number of carries, K and K', that occur during the addition to the lower half of the product in the computation of t. If we approximate both K and K' by the reasonable (although somewhat pessimistic) values $\frac{1}{2}(N-Z)M$, we find that the total running time comes to $28MN + 4M + 10N + 3 - Z(28M+3)$ cycles. If step M2 were deleted, the running time would be $28MN + 4M + 7N + 3$ cycles, so that step is advantageous only if the density of zero positions within the multiplier is $Z/N > 3/(28M+3)$. If the multiplier is chosen completely at random, the ratio Z/N is expected to be only about $1/b$, which is extremely small. We conclude that step M2 is usually *not* worthwhile, unless b is small.

Algorithm M is not the fastest way to multiply when m and n are large, although it has the advantage of simplicity. Speedier but more complicated methods are discussed in Section 4.3.3; it is possible to multiply numbers faster than Algorithm M even when $m = n = 4$.

The final algorithm of concern to us in this section is long division, in which we want to divide $(m+n)$-place integers by n-place integers. Here the ordinary pencil-and-paper method involves a certain amount of guesswork and ingenuity on the part of the person doing the division; we must either eliminate this guesswork from the algorithm or develop some theory to explain it more carefully.

A moment's reflection about the ordinary process of long division shows that the general problem breaks down into simpler steps, each of which is the division of an $(n+1)$-place dividend u by the n-place divisor v, where $0 \le u/v < b$; the remainder r after each step is less than v, so we may use the quantity $rb + (\text{next place of dividend})$ as the new u in the succeeding step. For example, if we are asked to divide 3142 by 53, we first divide 314 by 53, getting 5 and a remainder of 49; then we divide 492 by 53, getting 9 and a remainder of 15; thus we have a quotient of 59 and a remainder of 15. It is clear that this same idea works in general, and so our search for an appropriate division algorithm reduces to the following problem (Fig. 6):

Let $u = (u_n u_{n-1} \ldots u_1 u_0)_b$ and $v = (v_{n-1} \ldots v_1 v_0)_b$ be nonnegative integers in radix-b notation, where $u/v < b$. Find an algorithm to determine $q = \lfloor u/v \rfloor$.

$$q$$
$$v_{n-1} \ldots v_1 v_0 \,\overline{)\, u_n u_{n-1} \ldots u_1 u_0}$$
$$\xleftarrow{\hspace{1em}} qv \xrightarrow{\hspace{1em}}$$
$$\xleftarrow{\hspace{1em}} r \xrightarrow{\hspace{1em}}$$

Fig. 6. Wanted: a way to determine q rapidly.

We may observe that the condition $u/v < b$ is equivalent to the condition that $u/b < v$, which is the same as $\lfloor u/b \rfloor < v$. This is simply the condition that $(u_n u_{n-1} \ldots u_1)_b < (v_{n-1} v_{n-2} \ldots v_0)_b$. Furthermore, if we write $r = u - qv$, then q is the unique integer such that $0 \le r < v$.

The most obvious approach to this problem is to make a guess about q, based on the most significant digits of u and v. It isn't obvious that such a method will be reliable enough, but it is worth investigating; let us therefore set

$$\hat{q} = \min\left(\left\lfloor \frac{u_n b + u_{n-1}}{v_{n-1}} \right\rfloor, \, b - 1 \right). \tag{2}$$

This formula says that $\hat{q}$ is obtained by dividing the two leading digits of u by the leading digit of v; and if the result is b or more we can replace it by $(b-1)$.

It is a remarkable fact, which we will now investigate, that this value $\hat{q}$ is always a very good approximation to the desired answer q, so long as v_{n-1} is reasonably large. In order to analyze how close $\hat{q}$ comes to q, we will first prove that $\hat{q}$ is never too small.

Theorem A. *In the notation above, $\hat{q} \ge q$.*

Proof. Since $q \le b - 1$, the theorem is certainly true if $\hat{q} = b - 1$. Otherwise we have $\hat{q} = \lfloor (u_n b + u_{n-1})/v_{n-1} \rfloor$, hence $\hat{q} v_{n-1} \ge u_n b + u_{n-1} - v_{n-1} + 1$. It follows that

$$u - \hat{q}v \le u - \hat{q} v_{n-1} b^{n-1}$$
$$\le u_n b^n + \cdots + u_0 - (u_n b^n + u_{n-1} b^{n-1} - v_{n-1} b^{n-1} + b^{n-1})$$
$$= u_{n-2} b^{n-2} + \cdots + u_0 - b^{n-1} + v_{n-1} b^{n-1} < v_{n-1} b^{n-1} \le v.$$

Since $u - \hat{q}v < v$, we must have $\hat{q} \ge q$. ∎

We will now prove that $\hat{q}$ cannot be much larger than q in practical situations. Assume that $\hat{q} \ge q + 3$. We have

$$\hat{q} \le \frac{u_n b + u_{n-1}}{v_{n-1}} = \frac{u_n b^n + u_{n-1} b^{n-1}}{v_{n-1} b^{n-1}} \le \frac{u}{v_{n-1} b^{n-1}} < \frac{u}{v - b^{n-1}}.$$

(The case $v = b^{n-1}$ is impossible, for if $v = (100 \ldots 0)_b$ then $q = \hat{q}$.) Furthermore, the relation $q > (u/v) - 1$ implies that

$$3 \le \hat{q} - q < \frac{u}{v - b^{n-1}} - \frac{u}{v} + 1 = \frac{u}{v}\left(\frac{b^{n-1}}{v - b^{n-1}} \right) + 1.$$

Therefore

$$\frac{u}{v} > 2\left(\frac{v - b^{n-1}}{b^{n-1}} \right) \ge 2(v_{n-1} - 1).$$

Finally, since $b - 4 \geq \hat{q} - 3 \geq q = \lfloor u/v \rfloor \geq 2(v_{n-1} - 1)$, we have $v_{n-1} < \lfloor b/2 \rfloor$. This proves the result we seek:

Theorem B. *If $v_{n-1} \geq \lfloor b/2 \rfloor$, then $\hat{q} - 2 \leq q \leq \hat{q}$.* ∎

The most important part of this theorem is that *the conclusion is independent of b*; no matter how large the radix is, the trial quotient $\hat{q}$ will never be more than 2 in error.

The condition that $v_{n-1} \geq \lfloor b/2 \rfloor$ is very much like a normalization requirement; in fact, it is exactly the condition of floating-binary normalization in a binary computer. One simple way to ensure that v_{n-1} is sufficiently large is to multiply both u and v by $\lfloor b/(v_{n-1} + 1) \rfloor$; this does not change the value of u/v, nor does it increase the number of places in v, and exercise 23 proves that it will always make the new value of v_{n-1} large enough. (Another way to normalize the divisor is discussed in exercise 28.)

Now that we have armed ourselves with all of these facts, we are in a position to write the desired long-division algorithm. This algorithm uses a slightly improved choice of $\hat{q}$ in step D3, which guarantees that $q = \hat{q}$ or $\hat{q} - 1$; in fact, the improved choice of $\hat{q}$ made here is almost always accurate.

Algorithm D (*Division of nonnegative integers*). Given nonnegative integers $u = (u_{m+n-1} \ldots u_1 u_0)_b$ and $v = (v_{n-1} \ldots v_1 v_0)_b$, where $v_{n-1} \neq 0$ and $n > 1$, we form the radix-b quotient $\lfloor u/v \rfloor = (q_m q_{m-1} \ldots q_0)_b$ and the remainder $u \bmod v = (r_{n-1} \ldots r_1 r_0)_b$. (When $n = 1$, the simpler algorithm of exercise 16 should be used.)

D1. [Normalize.] Set $d \leftarrow \lfloor b/(v_{n-1} + 1) \rfloor$. Then set $(u_{m+n} u_{m+n-1} \ldots u_1 u_0)_b$ equal to $(u_{m+n-1} \ldots u_1 u_0)_b$ times d; similarly, set $(v_{n-1} \ldots v_1 v_0)_b$ equal to $(v_{n-1} \ldots v_1 v_0)_b$ times d. (Notice the introduction of a new digit position u_{m+n} at the left of u_{m+n-1}; if $d = 1$, all we need to do in this step is to set $u_{m+n} \leftarrow 0$. On a binary computer it may be preferable to choose d to be a power of 2 instead of using the value suggested here; any value of d that results in $v_{n-1} \geq \lfloor b/2 \rfloor$ will suffice. See also exercise 37.)

D2. [Initialize j.] Set $j \leftarrow m$. (The loop on j, steps D2 through D7, will be essentially a division of $(u_{j+n} \ldots u_{j+1} u_j)_b$ by $(v_{n-1} \ldots v_1 v_0)_b$ to get a single quotient digit q_j; see Fig. 6.)

D3. [Calculate $\hat{q}$.] Set $\hat{q} \leftarrow \lfloor (u_{j+n} b + u_{j+n-1})/v_{n-1} \rfloor$ and let $\hat{r}$ be the remainder, $(u_{j+n} b + u_{j+n-1}) \bmod v_{n-1}$. Now test if $\hat{q} \geq b$ or $\hat{q} v_{n-2} > b\hat{r} + u_{j+n-2}$; if so, decrease $\hat{q}$ by 1, increase $\hat{r}$ by v_{n-1}, and repeat this test if $\hat{r} < b$. (The test on v_{n-2} determines at high speed most of the cases in which the trial value $\hat{q}$ is one too large, and it eliminates *all* cases where $\hat{q}$ is two too large; see exercises 19, 20, 21.)

D4. [Multiply and subtract.] Replace $(u_{j+n} u_{j+n-1} \ldots u_j)_b$ by

$$(u_{j+n} u_{j+n-1} \ldots u_j)_b - \hat{q}(0 v_{n-1} \ldots v_1 v_0)_b.$$

This computation (analogous to steps M3, M4, and M5 of Algorithm M) consists of a simple multiplication by a one-place number, combined with

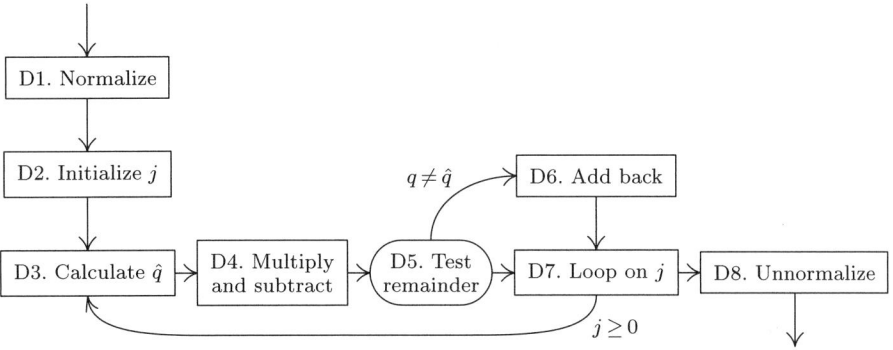

Fig. 7. Long division.

a subtraction. The digits $(u_{j+n}, u_{j+n-1}, \ldots, u_j)$ should be kept positive; if the result of this step is actually negative, $(u_{j+n}u_{j+n-1}\ldots u_j)_b$ should be left as the true value plus b^{n+1}, namely as the b's complement of the true value, and a "borrow" to the left should be remembered.

D5. [Test remainder.] Set $q_j \leftarrow \hat{q}$. If the result of step D4 was negative, go to step D6; otherwise go on to step D7.

D6. [Add back.] (The probability that this step is necessary is very small, on the order of only $2/b$, as shown in exercise 21; test data to activate this step should therefore be specifically contrived when debugging. See exercise 22.) Decrease q_j by 1, and add $(0v_{n-1}\ldots v_1 v_0)_b$ to $(u_{j+n}u_{j+n-1}\ldots u_{j+1}u_j)_b$. (A carry will occur to the left of u_{j+n}, and it should be ignored since it cancels with the borrow that occurred in D4.)

D7. [Loop on j.] Decrease j by one. Now if $j \geq 0$, go back to D3.

D8. [Unnormalize.] Now $(q_m \ldots q_1 q_0)_b$ is the desired quotient, and the desired remainder may be obtained by dividing $(u_{n-1} \ldots u_1 u_0)_b$ by d. ∎

The representation of Algorithm D as a MIX program has several points of interest:

Program D (*Division of nonnegative integers*). The conventions of this program are analogous to Program A; $\text{rI1} \equiv i - n$, $\text{rI2} \equiv j$, $\text{rI3} \equiv i + j$.

001	D1 JOV	OFLO	1	*D1. Normalize.*
$\cdots$				(See exercise 25)
039	D2 ENT2	M	1	*D2. Initialize j.* $j \leftarrow m$.
040	STZ	V+N	1	Set $v_n \leftarrow 0$, for convenience in D4.
041	D3 LDA	U+N,2(1:5)	$M+1$	*D3. Calculate $\hat{q}$.*
042	LDX	U+N-1,2	$M+1$	$\text{rAX} \leftarrow u_{j+n}b + u_{j+n-1}$.
043	DIV	V+N-1	$M+1$	$\text{rA} \leftarrow \lfloor \text{rAX}/v_{n-1} \rfloor$.
044	JOV	1F	$M+1$	Jump if quotient $\geq b$.
045	STA	QHAT	$M+1$	$\hat{q} \leftarrow \text{rA}$.
046	STX	RHAT	$M+1$	$\hat{r} \leftarrow u_{j+n}b + u_{j+n-1} - \hat{q}v_{n-1}$
047	JMP	2F	$M+1$	$= (u_{j+n}b + u_{j+n-1}) \bmod v_{n-1}$.

048	1H LDX	WM1		rX ← $b - 1$.
049	LDA	U+N-1,2		rA ← u_{j+n-1}. (Here $u_{j+n} = v_{n-1}$.)
050	JMP	4F		
051	3H LDX	QHAT	E	
052	DECX	1	E	Decrease $\hat{q}$ by one.
053	LDA	RHAT	E	Adjust $\hat{r}$ accordingly:
054	4H STX	QHAT	E	$\hat{q} \leftarrow$ rX.
055	ADD	V+N-1	E	rA ← $\hat{r} + v_{n-1}$.
056	JOV	D4	E	(If $\hat{r}$ will be $\geq b$, $\hat{q}v_{n-2}$ will be $< \hat{r}b$.)
057	STA	RHAT	E	$\hat{r} \leftarrow$ rA.
058	LDA	QHAT	E	
059	2H MUL	V+N-2	$M + E + 1$	
060	CMPA	RHAT	$M + E + 1$	Test if $\hat{q}v_{n-2} \leq \hat{r}b + u_{j+n-2}$.
061	JL	D4	$M + E + 1$	
062	JG	3B	E	
063	CMPX	U+N-2,2		
064	JG	3B		If not, $\hat{q}$ is too large.
065	D4 ENTX	1	$M + 1$	_D4. Multiply and subtract._
066	ENN1	N	$M + 1$	$i \leftarrow 0$.
067	ENT3	0,2	$M + 1$	$(i + j) \leftarrow j$.
068	2H STX	CARRY	$(M + 1)(N + 1)$	(Here $1 - b <$ rX $\leq +1$.)
069	LDAN	V+N,1	$(M + 1)(N + 1)$	
070	MUL	QHAT	$(M + 1)(N + 1)$	rAX ← $-\hat{q}v_i$.
071	SLC	5	$(M + 1)(N + 1)$	Interchange rA ↔ rX.
072	ADD	CARRY	$(M + 1)(N + 1)$	Add the contribution from the
073	JNOV	*+2	$(M + 1)(N + 1)$	digit to the right, plus 1.
074	DECX	1	K	If sum is $\leq -b$, carry -1.
075	ADD	U,3	$(M + 1)(N + 1)$	Add u_{i+j}.
076	ADD	WM1	$(M + 1)(N + 1)$	Add $b - 1$ to force $+$ sign.
077	JNOV	*+2	$(M + 1)(N + 1)$	If no overflow, carry -1.
078	INCX	1	K'	rX $\equiv$ carry $+ 1$.
079	STA	U,3	$(M + 1)(N + 1)$	$u_{i+j} \leftarrow$ rA (may be minus zero).
080	INC1	1	$(M + 1)(N + 1)$	
081	INC3	1	$(M + 1)(N + 1)$	
082	J1NP	2B	$(M + 1)(N + 1)$	Repeat for $0 \leq i \leq n$.
083	D5 LDA	QHAT	$M + 1$	_D5. Test remainder._
084	STA	Q,2	$M + 1$	Set $q_j \leftarrow \hat{q}$.
085	JXP	D7	$M + 1$	(Here rX $= 0$ or 1, since $v_n = 0$.)
086	D6 DECA	1		_D6. Add back._
087	STA	Q,2		Set $q_j \leftarrow \hat{q} - 1$.
088	ENN1	N		$i \leftarrow 0$.
089	ENT3	0,2		$(i + j) \leftarrow j$.
090	1H ENTA	0		(This is essentially Program A.)
091	2H ADD	U,3		
092	ADD	V+N,1		
093	STA	U,3		
094	INC1	1		
095	INC3	1		
096	JNOV	1B		

097	ENTA 1		
098	J1NP 2B		
099	D7 DEC2 1	$M+1$	*D7. Loop on j.*
100	J2NN D3	$M+1$	Repeat for $m \geq j \geq 0$.
101	D8 $\cdots$		(See exercise 26) ∎

Note how easily the rather complex-appearing calculations and decisions of step D3 can be handled inside the machine. Notice also that the program for step D4 is analogous to Program M, except that the ideas of Program S have also been incorporated.

The running time for Program D can be estimated by considering the quantities M, N, E, K, and K' shown in the program. (These quantities ignore several situations that occur only with very low probability; for example, we may assume that lines 048–050, 063–064, and step D6 are never executed.) Here $M+1$ is the number of words in the quotient; N is the number of words in the divisor; E is the number of times $\hat{q}$ is adjusted downwards in step D3; K and K' are the number of times certain carry adjustments are made during the multiply-subtract loop. If we assume that $K + K'$ is approximately $(N+1)(M+1)$, and that E is approximately $\frac{1}{2}M$, we get a total running time of approximately $30MN + 30N + 89M + 111$ cycles, plus $67N + 23.5M + 4$ more if $d > 1$. (The program segments of exercises 25 and 26 are included in these totals.) When M and N are large, this is only about seven percent longer than the time needed by Program M to multiply the quotient by the divisor.

When the radix b is comparatively small, so that b^2 is less than the computer's word size, multiprecision division can be speeded up by not reducing individual digits of intermediate results to the range $[0 .. b)$; see D. M. Smith, *Math. Comp.* **65** (1996), 157–163. Further commentary on Algorithm D appears in the exercises at the close of this section.

It is possible to debug programs for multiple-precision arithmetic by using the multiplication and addition routines to check the result of the division routine, etc. The following type of test data is occasionally useful:

$$(t^m - 1)(t^n - 1) = t^{m+n} - t^n - t^m + 1.$$

If $m < n$, this number has the radix-t expansion

$$\underbrace{(t-1) \quad \cdots \quad (t-1)}_{m-1 \text{ places}} \ (t-2) \ \underbrace{(t-1) \quad \cdots \quad (t-1)}_{n-m \text{ places}} \ \underbrace{0 \quad \cdots \quad 0}_{m-1 \text{ places}} \ 1;$$

for example, $(10^3 - 1)(10^8 - 1) = 99899999001$. In the case of Program D, it is also necessary to find some test cases that cause the rarely executed parts of the program to be exercised; some portions of that program would probably never get tested even if a million random test cases were tried. (See exercise 22.)

Now that we have seen how to operate with signed magnitude numbers, let us consider what approach should be taken to the same problems when a computer with complement notation is being used. For two's complement and ones' complement notations, it is usually best to let the radix b be *one half* of the word size; thus for a 32-bit computer word we would use $b = 2^{31}$ in the algorithms above. The sign bit of all but the most significant word of a multiple-precision number will be zero, so that no anomalous sign correction takes place during the computer's multiplication and division operations. In fact, the basic meaning of complement notation requires that we consider all but the most significant word to be nonnegative. For example, assuming an 8-bit word, the two's complement number

$$11011111 \quad 1111110 \quad 1101011$$

(where the sign bit is shown only in the most significant word) is properly thought of as

$$-2^{21} + (1011111)_2 \cdot 2^{14} + (1111110)_2 \cdot 2^7 + (1101011)_2.$$

On the other hand, some binary computers that work with two's complement notation also provide true unsigned arithmetic as well. For example, let x and y be 32-bit operands. A computer might regard them as two's complement numbers in the range $-2^{31} \leq x, y < 2^{31}$, or as unsigned numbers in the range $0 \leq x, y < 2^{32}$. If we ignore overflow, the 32-bit sum $(x + y) \bmod 2^{32}$ is the same under either interpretation; but overflow occurs in different circumstances when we change the assumed range. If the computer allows easy computation of the carry bit $\lfloor (x + y)/2^{32} \rfloor$ in the unsigned interpretation, and if it provides a full 64-bit product of unsigned 32-bit integers, we can use $b = 2^{32}$ instead of $b = 2^{31}$ in our high-precision algorithms.

Addition of signed numbers is slightly easier when complement notations are being used, since the routine for adding n-place nonnegative integers can be used for arbitrary n-place integers; the sign appears only in the first word, so the less significant words may be added together irrespective of the actual sign. (Special attention must be given to the leftmost carry when ones' complement notation is being used, however; it must be added into the least significant word, and possibly propagated further to the left.) Similarly, we find that subtraction of signed numbers is slightly simpler with complement notation. On the other hand, multiplication and division seem to be done most easily by working with nonnegative quantities and doing suitable complementation operations beforehand to make sure that both operands are nonnegative. It may be possible to avoid this complementation by devising some tricks for working directly with negative numbers in a complement notation, and it is not hard to see how this could be done in double-precision multiplication; but care should be taken not to slow down the inner loops of the subroutines when high precision is required.

Let us now turn to an analysis of the quantity K that arises in Program A, namely the number of carries that occur when two n-place numbers are being added together. Although K has no effect on the total running time of Program A, it does affect the running time of the Program A's counterparts that deal with complement notations, and its analysis is interesting in itself as a significant application of generating functions.

Suppose that u and v are independent random n-place integers, uniformly distributed in the range $0 \leq u, v < b^n$. Let p_{nk} be the probability that exactly k carries occur in the addition of u to v, *and* that one of these carries occurs in the most significant position (so that $u + v \geq b^n$). Similarly, let q_{nk} be the probability that exactly k carries occur, but that there is no carry in the most significant position. Then it is not hard to see that, for all k and n,

$$p_{0k} = 0, \qquad p_{(n+1)(k+1)} = \frac{b+1}{2b}p_{nk} + \frac{b-1}{2b}q_{nk},$$

$$q_{0k} = \delta_{0k}, \qquad q_{(n+1)k} = \frac{b-1}{2b}p_{nk} + \frac{b+1}{2b}q_{nk}; \qquad (3)$$

this happens because $(b-1)/2b$ is the probability that $u_{n-1} + v_{n-1} \geq b$ and $(b+1)/2b$ is the probability that $u_{n-1} + v_{n-1} + 1 \geq b$, when u_{n-1} and v_{n-1} are independently and uniformly distributed integers in the range $0 \leq u_{n-1}, v_{n-1} < b$.

To obtain further information about these quantities p_{nk} and q_{nk}, we set up the generating functions

$$P(z,t) = \sum_{k,n} p_{nk} z^k t^n, \qquad Q(z,t) = \sum_{k,n} q_{nk} z^k t^n. \qquad (4)$$

From (3) we have the basic relations

$$P(z,t) = zt\left(\frac{b+1}{2b}P(z,t) + \frac{b-1}{2b}Q(z,t)\right),$$

$$Q(z,t) = 1 + t\left(\frac{b-1}{2b}P(z,t) + \frac{b+1}{2b}Q(z,t)\right).$$

These two equations are readily solved for $P(z,t)$ and $Q(z,t)$; and if we let

$$G(z,t) = P(z,t) + Q(z,t) = \sum_n G_n(z)t^n,$$

where $G_n(z)$ is the generating function for the total number of carries when n-place numbers are added, we find that

$$G(z,t) = (b - zt)/p(z,t), \quad \text{where } p(z,t) = b - \tfrac{1}{2}(1+b)(1+z)t + zt^2. \qquad (5)$$

Note that $G(1,t) = 1/(1-t)$, and this checks with the fact that $G_n(1)$ must equal 1 (it is the sum of all the possible probabilities). Taking partial derivatives of (5) with respect to z, we find that

$$\frac{\partial G}{\partial z} = \sum_n G_n'(z)t^n = \frac{-t}{p(z,t)} + \frac{t(b-zt)(b+1-2t)}{2p(z,t)^2};$$

$$\frac{\partial^2 G}{\partial z^2} = \sum_n G_n''(z)t^n = \frac{-t^2(b+1-2t)}{p(z,t)^2} + \frac{t^2(b-zt)(b+1-2t)^2}{2p(z,t)^3}.$$

Now let us put $z = 1$ and expand in partial fractions:

$$\sum_n G_n'(1)t^n = \frac{t}{2}\left(\frac{1}{(1-t)^2} - \frac{1}{(b-1)(1-t)} + \frac{1}{(b-1)(b-t)}\right),$$

$$\sum_n G_n''(1)t^n = \frac{t^2}{2}\left(\frac{1}{(1-t)^3} - \frac{1}{(b-1)^2(1-t)} + \frac{1}{(b-1)^2(b-t)} + \frac{1}{(b-1)(b-t)^2}\right).$$

It follows that the average number of carries, the mean value of K, is

$$G'_n(1) = \frac{1}{2}\left(n - \frac{1}{b-1}\left(1 - \left(\frac{1}{b}\right)^n\right)\right);\qquad(6)$$

the variance is

$$\begin{aligned}&G''_n(1) + G'_n(1) - G'_n(1)^2\\ &= \frac{1}{4}\left(n + \frac{2n}{b-1} - \frac{2b+1}{(b-1)^2} + \frac{2b+2}{(b-1)^2}\left(\frac{1}{b}\right)^n - \frac{1}{(b-1)^2}\left(\frac{1}{b}\right)^{2n}\right).\qquad(7)\end{aligned}$$

So the number of carries is just slightly less than $\frac{1}{2}n$ under these assumptions.

History and bibliography.   The early history of the classical algorithms described in this section is left as an interesting project for the reader, and only the history of their implementation on computers will be traced here.

The use of 10^n as an assumed radix when multiplying large numbers on a desk calculator was discussed by D. N. Lehmer and J. P. Ballantine, *AMM* **30** (1923), 67–69.

Double-precision arithmetic on digital computers was first treated by J. von Neumann and H. H. Goldstine in their introductory notes on programming, originally published in 1947 [J. von Neumann, *Collected Works* **5**, 142–151]. Theorems A and B above are due to D. A. Pope and M. L. Stein [*CACM* **3** (1960), 652–654], whose paper also contains a bibliography of earlier work on double-precision routines. Other ways of choosing the trial quotient $\hat{q}$ have been discussed by A. G. Cox and H. A. Luther, *CACM* **4** (1961), 353 [divide by $v_{n-1}+1$ instead of v_{n-1}], and by M. L. Stein, *CACM* **7** (1964), 472–474 [divide by v_{n-1} or $v_{n-1} + 1$ according to the magnitude of v_{n-2}]; E. V. Krishnamurthy [*CACM* **8** (1965), 179–181] showed that examination of the single-precision remainder in the latter method leads to an improvement over Theorem B. Krishnamurthy and Nandi [*CACM* **10** (1967), 809–813] suggested a way to replace the normalization and unnormalization operations of Algorithm D by a calculation of $\hat{q}$ based on several leading digits of the operands. G. E. Collins and D. R. Musser have carried out an interesting analysis of the original Pope and Stein algorithm [*Information Processing Letters* **6** (1977), 151–155].

Several alternative approaches to division have also been suggested:

1) "Fourier division" [J. Fourier, *Analyse des Équations Déterminées* (Paris: 1831), §2.21]. This method, which was often used on desk calculators, essentially obtains each new quotient digit by increasing the precision of the divisor and the dividend at each step. Some rather extensive tests by the author have indicated that such a method is inferior to the divide-and-correct technique above, but there may be some applications in which Fourier division is practical. See D. H. Lehmer, *AMM* **33** (1926), 198–206; J. V. Uspensky, *Theory of Equations* (New York: McGraw–Hill, 1948), 159–164.

2) "Newton's method" for evaluating the reciprocal of a number was extensively used in early computers when there was no single-precision division instruction. The idea is to find some initial approximation x_0 to the number $1/v$, then to let

$x_{n+1} = 2x_n - vx_n^2$. This method converges rapidly to $1/v$, since $x_n = (1 - \epsilon)/v$ implies that $x_{n+1} = (1 - \epsilon^2)/v$. Convergence to third order, with ϵ replaced by $O(\epsilon^3)$ at each step, can be obtained using the formula

$$x_{n+1} = x_n + x_n(1 - vx_n) + x_n(1 - vx_n)^2$$
$$= x_n \left(1 + (1 - vx_n)(1 + (1 - vx_n)) \right),$$

and similar formulas hold for fourth-order convergence, etc.; see P. Rabinowitz, *CACM* **4** (1961), 98. For calculations on extremely large numbers, Newton's second-order method and subsequent multiplication by u can actually be considerably faster than Algorithm D, if we increase the precision of x_n at each step and if we also use the fast multiplication routines of Section 4.3.3. (See Algorithm 4.3.3R for details.) Some related iterative schemes have been discussed by E. V. Krishnamurthy, *IEEE Trans.* **C-19** (1970), 227–231.

3) Division methods have also been based on the evaluation of

$$\frac{u}{v + \epsilon} = \frac{u}{v} \left(1 - \left(\frac{\epsilon}{v}\right) + \left(\frac{\epsilon}{v}\right)^2 - \left(\frac{\epsilon}{v}\right)^3 + \cdots \right).$$

See H. H. Laughlin, *AMM* **37** (1930), 287–293. We have used this idea in the double-precision case $\big($Eq. 4.2.3–(2)$\big)$.

Besides the references just cited, the following early articles concerning multiple-precision arithmetic are also of interest: High-precision routines for floating point calculations using ones' complement arithmetic were described by A. H. Stroud and D. Secrest, *Comp. J.* **6** (1963), 62–66. Extended-precision subroutines for use in FORTRAN programs were described by B. I. Blum, *CACM* **8** (1965), 318–320, and for use in ALGOL by M. Tienari and V. Suokonautio, *BIT* **6** (1966), 332–338. Arithmetic on integers with *unlimited* precision, making use of linked memory allocation techniques, was elegantly introduced by G. E. Collins, *CACM* **9** (1966), 578–589. For a much larger repertoire of multiple-precision operations, including logarithms and trigonometric functions, see R. P. Brent, *ACM Trans. Math. Software* **4** (1978), 57–81; D. M. Smith, *ACM Trans. Math. Software* **17** (1991), 273–283, **24** (1998), 359–367.

Human progress in calculation has traditionally been measured by the number of decimal digits of π that were known at a given point in history. Section 4.1 mentions some of the early developments; by 1719, Thomas Fantet de Lagny had computed π to 127 decimal places [*Mémoires Acad. Sci.* (Paris, 1719), 135–145; a typographical error affected the 113th digit]. After better formulas were discovered, a famous mental calculator from Hamburg named Zacharias Dase needed less than two months to calculate 200 decimal digits correctly in 1844 [*Crelle* **27** (1844), 198]. Then William Shanks published 607 decimals of π in 1853, and continued to extend his calculations until he had obtained 707 digits in 1873. [See W. Shanks, *Contributions to Mathematics* (London: 1853); *Proc. Royal Soc. London* **21** (1873), 318–319; **22** (1873), 45–46; J. C. V. Hoffmann, *Zeit. für math. und naturwiss. Unterricht* **26** (1895), 261–264.] Shanks's 707-place value was widely quoted in mathematical reference books for many years, but D. F. Ferguson noticed in 1945 that it contained several mistakes beginning at the 528th decimal place [*Math. Gazette* **30** (1946), 89–90]. G. Reitwiesner and his colleagues used 70 hours of computing time on ENIAC during Labor Day weekend in 1949 to obtain 2037 correct decimals [*Math. Tables and Other Aids to Comp.* **4** (1950), 11–15]. F. Genuys reached 10,000 digits in 1958, after 100 minutes on an IBM 704 [*Chiffres* **1** (1958), 17–22]; shortly afterwards, the first 100,000 digits were published by D. Shanks [no relation to William] and J. W. Wrench, Jr. [*Math. Comp.* **16** (1962), 76–99], after about 8 hours on an IBM 7090 and another 4.5 hours for checking. Their check actually revealed a transient hardware error, which went away when the computation was repeated. One million digits of π were computed by Jean Guilloud and Martine Bouyer of the French Atomic Energy Commission in 1973, after nearly 24 hours of computer time on a CDC 7600 [see A. Shibata, *Surikagaku* **20** (1982), 65–73]. Amazingly, Dr. I. J. Matrix had correctly predicted seven years earlier that the millionth digit would turn out to be "5" [Martin Gardner, *New Mathematical Diversions* (Simon and Schuster, 1966), addendum to Chapter 8]. The billion-digit barrier was passed in 1989 by Gregory V. Chudnovsky and David V. Chudnovsky, and independently by Yasumasa Kanada and Yoshiaki Tamura; the Chudnovskys extended their calculation to two billion digits in 1991, after 250 hours of computation on a home-built parallel machine. [See Richard Preston, *The New Yorker* **68**, 2 (2 March 1992), 36–67. The novel formula used by the Chudnovskys is described in *Proc. Nat. Acad. Sci.* **86** (1989), 8178–8182.] Yasumasa Kanada and Daisuke Takahashi obtained more than 51.5 billion digits in July, 1997, using two independent methods that required respectively 29.0 and 37.1 hours on a HITACHI SR2201 computer with 1024 processing elements. Stay tuned for new records as we move into a new millennium.

We have restricted our discussion in this section to arithmetic techniques for use in computer programming. Many algorithms for *hardware* implementation of arithmetic operations are also quite interesting, but they appear to be inapplicable to high-precision software routines; see, for example, G. W. Reitwiesner, "Binary Arithmetic," *Advances in Computers* **1** (New York: Academic Press, 1960), 231–308; O. L. MacSorley, *Proc. IRE* **49** (1961), 67–91; G. Metze, *IRE Trans.* **EC-11** (1962), 761–764; H. L. Garner, "Number Systems and Arithmetic," *Advances in Computers* **6** (New York: Academic Press, 1965), 131–194. An infamous but very instructive bug in the division routine of the 1994 Pentium chip is discussed by A. Edelman in *SIAM Review* **39** (1997), 54–67. The minimum achievable execution time for hardware addition and multiplication operations has been investigated by S. Winograd, *JACM* **12** (1965), 277–285, **14** (1967), 793–802; by R. P. Brent, *IEEE Trans.* **C-19** (1970), 758–759; and by R. W. Floyd, *FOCS* **16** (1975), 3–5. See also Section 4.3.3E.

EXERCISES

1. [*42*] Study the early history of the classical algorithms for arithmetic by looking up the writings of, say, Sun Tsŭ, al-Khwārizmī, al-Uqlīdisī, Fibonacci, and Robert

Recorde, and by translating their methods as faithfully as possible into precise algorithmic notation.

2. [15] Generalize Algorithm A so that it does "column addition," obtaining the sum of m nonnegative n-place integers. (Assume that $m \leq b$.)

3. [21] Write a MIX program for the algorithm of exercise 2, and estimate its running time as a function of m and n.

4. [M21] Give a formal proof of the validity of Algorithm A, using the method of inductive assertions explained in Section 1.2.1.

5. [21] Algorithm A adds the two inputs by going from right to left, but sometimes the data is more readily accessible from left to right. Design an algorithm that produces the same answer as Algorithm A, but that generates the digits of the answer from left to right, going back to change previous values if a carry occurs to make a previous value incorrect. [*Note:* Early Hindu and Arabic manuscripts dealt with addition from left to right in this way, probably because it was customary to work from left to right on an abacus; the right-to-left addition algorithm was a refinement due to al-Uqlīdisī, perhaps because Arabic is written from right to left.]

▶ **6.** [22] Design an algorithm that adds from left to right (as in exercise 5), but never stores a digit of the answer until this digit cannot possibly be affected by future carries; there is to be no changing of any answer digit once it has been stored. [*Hint:* Keep track of the number of consecutive $(b-1)$'s that have not yet been stored in the answer.] This sort of algorithm would be appropriate, for example, in a situation where the input and output numbers are to be read and written from left to right on magnetic tapes, or if they appear in straight linear lists.

7. [M26] Determine the average number of times the algorithm of exercise 5 will find that a carry makes it necessary to go back and change k digits of the partial answer, for $k = 1, 2, \ldots, n$. (Assume that both inputs are independently and uniformly distributed between 0 and $b^n - 1$.)

8. [M26] Write a MIX program for the algorithm of exercise 5, and determine its average running time based on the expected number of carries as computed in the text.

▶ **9.** [21] Generalize Algorithm A to obtain an algorithm that adds two n-place numbers in a *mixed-radix* number system, with bases b_0, b_1, ... (from right to left). Thus the least significant digits lie between 0 and $b_0 - 1$, the next digits lie between 0 and $b_1 - 1$, etc.; see Eq. 4.1–(9).

10. [18] Would Program S work properly if the instructions on lines 06 and 07 were interchanged? If the instructions on lines 05 and 06 were interchanged?

11. [10] Design an algorithm that compares two nonnegative n-place integers $u = (u_{n-1} \ldots u_1 u_0)_b$ and $v = (v_{n-1} \ldots v_1 v_0)_b$, to determine whether $u < v$, $u = v$, or $u > v$.

12. [16] Algorithm S assumes that we know which of the two input operands is the larger; if this information is not known, we could go ahead and perform the subtraction anyway, and we would find that an extra borrow is still present at the end of the algorithm. Design another algorithm that could be used (if there is a borrow present at the end of Algorithm S) to complement $(w_{n-1} \ldots w_1 w_0)_b$ and therefore to obtain the absolute value of the difference of u and v.

13. [21] Write a MIX program that multiplies $(u_{n-1} \ldots u_1 u_0)_b$ by v, where v is a single-precision number (that is, $0 \leq v < b$), producing the answer $(w_n \ldots w_1 w_0)_b$. How much running time is required?

▶ **14.** [*M22*] Give a formal proof of the validity of Algorithm M, using the method of inductive assertions explained in Section 1.2.1. (See exercise 4.)

15. [*M20*] If we wish to form the product of two n-place fractions, $(.u_1u_2\ldots u_n)_b \times (.v_1v_2\ldots v_n)_b$, and to obtain only an n-place approximation $(.w_1w_2\ldots w_n)_b$ to the result, Algorithm M could be used to obtain a $2n$-place answer that is subsequently rounded to the desired approximation. But this involves about twice as much work as is necessary for reasonable accuracy, since the products u_iv_j for $i+j > n+2$ contribute very little to the answer.

Give an estimate of the maximum error that can occur, if these products u_iv_j for $i + j > n + 2$ are not computed during the multiplication, but are assumed to be zero.

▶ **16.** [*20*] (*Short division.*) Design an algorithm that divides a nonnegative n-place integer $(u_{n-1}\ldots u_1u_0)_b$ by v, where v is a single-precision number (that is, $0 < v < b$), producing the quotient $(w_{n-1}\ldots w_1w_0)_b$ and remainder r.

17. [*M20*] In the notation of Fig. 6, assume that $v_{n-1} \geq \lfloor b/2 \rfloor$; show that if $u_n = v_{n-1}$, we must have $q = b - 1$ or $b - 2$.

18. [*M20*] In the notation of Fig. 6, show that if $q' = \lfloor (u_nb+u_{n-1})/(v_{n-1}+1) \rfloor$, then $q' \leq q$.

▶ **19.** [*M21*] In the notation of Fig. 6, let $\hat{q}$ be an approximation to q, and let $\hat{r} = u_nb + u_{n-1} - \hat{q}v_{n-1}$. Assume that $v_{n-1} > 0$. Show that if $\hat{q}v_{n-2} > b\hat{r} + u_{n-2}$, then $q < \hat{q}$. [*Hint:* Strengthen the proof of Theorem A by examining the influence of v_{n-2}.]

20. [*M22*] Using the notation and assumptions of exercise 19, show that if $\hat{q}v_{n-2} \leq b\hat{r} + u_{n-2}$ and $\hat{q} < b$, then $\hat{q} = q$ or $q = \hat{q} - 1$.

▶ **21.** [*M23*] Show that if $v_{n-1} \geq \lfloor b/2 \rfloor$, and if $\hat{q}v_{n-2} \leq b\hat{r} + u_{n-2}$ but $\hat{q} \neq q$ in the notation of exercises 19 and 20, then $u \bmod v \geq (1 - 2/b)v$. (The latter event occurs with approximate probability $2/b$, so that when b is the word size of a computer we must have $q_j = \hat{q}$ in Algorithm D except in very rare circumstances.)

▶ **22.** [*24*] Find an example of a four-digit number divided by a three-digit number for which step D6 is necessary in Algorithm D, when the radix b is 10.

23. [*M23*] Given that v and b are integers, and that $1 \leq v < b$, prove that we always have $\lfloor b/2 \rfloor \leq v\lfloor b/(v+1) \rfloor < (v+1)\lfloor b/(v+1) \rfloor \leq b$.

24. [*M20*] Using the law of the distribution of leading digits explained in Section 4.2.4, give an approximate formula for the probability that $d = 1$ in Algorithm D. (When $d = 1$, we can omit most of the calculation in steps D1 and D8.)

25. [*26*] Write a MIX routine for step D1, which is needed to complete Program D.

26. [*21*] Write a MIX routine for step D8, which is needed to complete Program D.

27. [*M20*] Prove that at the beginning of step D8 in Algorithm D, the unnormalized remainder $(u_{n-1}\ldots u_1u_0)_b$ is always an exact multiple of d.

28. [*M30*] (A. Svoboda, *Stroje na Zpracování Informací* **9** (1963), 25–32.) Let $v = (v_{n-1}\ldots v_1v_0)_b$ be any radix b integer, where $v_{n-1} \neq 0$. Perform the following operations:

N1. If $v_{n-1} < b/2$, multiply v by $\lfloor (b+1)/(v_{n-1}+1) \rfloor$. Let the result of this step be $(v_nv_{n-1}\ldots v_1v_0)_b$.

N2. If $v_n = 0$, set $v \leftarrow v + (1/b)\lfloor b(b - v_{n-1})/(v_{n-1}+1) \rfloor v$; let the result of this step be $(v_nv_{n-1}\ldots v_0.v_{-1}\ldots)_b$. Repeat step N2 until $v_n \neq 0$. ∎

Prove that step N2 will be performed at most three times, and that we must always have $v_n = 1$, $v_{n-1} = 0$ at the end of the calculations.

[*Note:* If u and v are both multiplied by the constants above, we do not change the value of the quotient u/v, and the divisor has been converted into the form $(10v_{n-2} \ldots v_0.v_{-1}v_{-2}v_{-3})_b$. This form of the divisor is very convenient because, in the notation of Algorithm D, we may simply take $\hat{q} = u_{j+n}$ as a trial divisor at the beginning of step D3, or $\hat{q} = b - 1$ when $(u_{j+n+1}, u_{j+n}) = (1, 0)$.]

29. [*15*] Prove or disprove: At the beginning of step D7 of Algorithm D, we always have $u_{j+n} = 0$.

▶ **30.** [*22*] If memory space is limited, it may be desirable to use the same storage locations for both input and output during the performance of some of the algorithms in this section. Is it possible to have $w_0, w_1, \ldots, w_{n-1}$ stored in the same respective locations as $u_0, \ldots, u_{n-1}$ or $v_0, \ldots, v_{n-1}$ during Algorithm A or S? Is it possible to have the quotient $q_0, \ldots, q_m$ occupy the same locations as $u_n, \ldots, u_{m+n}$ in Algorithm D? Is there any permissible overlap of memory locations between input and output in Algorithm M?

31. [*28*] Assume that $b = 3$ and that $u = (u_{m+n-1} \ldots u_1 u_0)_3$, $v = (v_{n-1} \ldots v_1 v_0)_3$ are integers in *balanced ternary* notation (see Section 4.1), $v_{n-1} \neq 0$. Design a long-division algorithm that divides u by v, obtaining a remainder whose absolute value does not exceed $\frac{1}{2}|v|$. Try to find an algorithm that would be efficient if incorporated into the arithmetic circuitry of a balanced ternary computer.

32. [*M40*] Assume that $b = 2i$ and that u and v are complex numbers expressed in the quater-imaginary number system. Design algorithms that divide u by v, perhaps obtaining a suitable remainder of some sort, and compare their efficiency.

33. [*M40*] Design an algorithm for taking square roots, analogous to Algorithm D and to the traditional pencil-and-paper method for extracting square roots.

34. [*40*] Develop a set of computer subroutines for doing the four arithmetic operations on arbitrary integers, putting no constraint on the size of the integers except for the implicit assumption that the total memory capacity of the computer should not be exceeded. (Use linked memory allocation, so that no time is wasted in finding room to put the results.)

35. [*40*] Develop a set of computer subroutines for "decuple-precision floating point" arithmetic, using excess 0, base b, nine-place floating point number representation, where b is the computer word size, and allowing a full word for the exponent. (Thus each floating point number is represented in 10 words of memory, and all scaling is done by moving full words instead of by shifting within the words.)

36. [*M25*] Explain how to compute $\ln \phi$ to high precision, given a suitably precise approximation to ϕ, using only multiprecision addition, subtraction, and division by small numbers.

▶ **37.** [*20*] (E. Salamin.) Explain how to avoid the normalization and unnormalization steps of Algorithm D, when d is a power of 2 on a binary computer, without changing the sequence of trial quotient digits computed by that algorithm. (How can $\hat{q}$ be computed in step D3 if the normalization of step D1 hasn't been done?)

38. [*M35*] Suppose u and v are integers in the range $0 \le u, v < 2^n$. Devise a way to compute the geometric mean $\lfloor \sqrt{uv} + \frac{1}{2} \rfloor$ by doing $O(n)$ operations of addition, subtraction, and comparison of $(n+2)$-bit numbers. [*Hint:* Use a "pipeline" to combine the classical methods of multiplication and square rooting.]

39. [*25*] (D. Bailey, P. Borwein, and S. Plouffe, 1996.) Explain how to compute the nth bit of the binary representation of π without knowing the previous $n - 1$ bits, by using the identity

$$\pi = \sum_{k \geq 0} \frac{1}{16^k} \left(\frac{4}{8k + 1} - \frac{2}{8k + 4} - \frac{1}{8k + 5} - \frac{1}{8k + 6} \right)$$

and doing $O(n \log n)$ arithmetic operations on $O(\log n)$-bit integers. (Assume that the binary digits of π do not have surprisingly long stretches of consecutive 0s or 1s.)

40. [*M24*] Sometimes we want to divide u by v when we know that the remainder will be zero. Show that if u is a $2n$-place number and v is an n-place number with $u \bmod v = 0$, we can save about 75% of the work of Algorithm D if we compute half of the quotient from left to right and the other half from right to left.

▶ **41.** [*M26*] Many applications of high-precision arithmetic require repeated calculations modulo a fixed n-place number w, where w is relatively prime to the base b. We can speed up such calculations by using a trick due to Peter L. Montgomery [*Math. Comp.* **44** (1985), 519–521], which streamlines the remaindering process by essentially working from right to left instead of left to right.

a) Given $u = \pm(u_{m+n-1} \dots u_1 u_0)_b$, $w = (w_{n-1} \dots w_1 w_0)_b$, and a number w' such that $w_0 w' \bmod b = 1$, show how to compute $v = \pm(v_{n-1} \dots v_1 v_0)_b$ such that $b^m v \bmod w = u \bmod w$.

b) Given n-place signed integers u, v, w with $|u|, |v| < w$, and given w' as in (a), show how to calculate an n-place integer t such that $|t| < w$ and $b^n t \equiv uv$ (modulo w).

c) How do the algorithms of (a) and (b) facilitate arithmetic mod w?

42. [*HM35*] Given m and b, let P_{nk} be the probability that $\lfloor (u_1 + \dots + u_m)/b^n \rfloor = k$, when $u_1, \dots, u_m$ are random n-place integers in radix b. (This is the distribution of w_n in the column addition algorithm of exercise 2.) Show that $P_{nk} = \frac{1}{m!} \left\langle {m \atop k} \right\rangle + O(b^{-n})$, where $\left\langle {m \atop k} \right\rangle$ is an Eulerian number (see Section 5.1.3).

▶ **43.** [*22*] Shades of gray or components of color values in digitized images are usually represented as 8-bit numbers u in the range $[0 \mathinner{.\,.} 255]$, denoting the fraction $u/255$. Given two such fractions $u/255$ and $v/255$, graphical algorithms often need to compute their approximate product $w/255$, where w is the nearest integer to $uv/255$. Prove that w can be obtained from the efficient formula

$$t = uv + 128, \qquad w = \lfloor (\lfloor t/256 \rfloor + t)/256 \rfloor.$$

*4.3.2. Modular Arithmetic

Another interesting alternative is available for doing arithmetic on large integer numbers, based on some simple principles of number theory. The idea is to have several *moduli* $m_1, m_2, \dots, m_r$ that contain no common factors, and to work indirectly with *residues* $u \bmod m_1$, $u \bmod m_2$, $\dots$, $u \bmod m_r$ instead of directly with the number u.

For convenience in notation throughout this section, let

$$u_1 = u \bmod m_1, \qquad u_2 = u \bmod m_2, \qquad \dots, \qquad u_r = u \bmod m_r. \qquad (1)$$

It is easy to compute $(u_1, u_2, \dots, u_r)$ from an integer number u by means of division; and it is important to note that no information is lost in this process (if

u isn't too large), since we can recompute u from $(u_1, u_2, \ldots, u_r)$. For example, if $0 \leq u < v \leq 1000$, it is impossible to have $(u \bmod 7, u \bmod 11, u \bmod 13)$ equal to $(v \bmod 7, v \bmod 11, v \bmod 13)$. This is a consequence of the "Chinese remainder theorem" stated below.

We may therefore regard $(u_1, u_2, \ldots, u_r)$ as a new type of internal computer representation, a "modular representation," of the integer u.

The advantages of a modular representation are that addition, subtraction, and multiplication are very simple:

$$(u_1, \ldots, u_r) + (v_1, \ldots, v_r) = \big((u_1 + v_1) \bmod m_1, \ldots, (u_r + v_r) \bmod m_r\big), \quad (2)$$

$$(u_1, \ldots, u_r) - (v_1, \ldots, v_r) = \big((u_1 - v_1) \bmod m_1, \ldots, (u_r - v_r) \bmod m_r\big), \quad (3)$$

$$(u_1, \ldots, u_r) \times (v_1, \ldots, v_r) = \big((u_1 \times v_1) \bmod m_1, \ldots, (u_r \times v_r) \bmod m_r\big). \quad (4)$$

To derive (4), for example, we need to show that

$$uv \bmod m_j = (u \bmod m_j)(v \bmod m_j) \bmod m_j$$

for each modulus m_j. But this is a basic fact of elementary number theory: $x \bmod m_j = y \bmod m_j$ if and only if $x \equiv y$ (modulo m_j); furthermore if $x \equiv x'$ and $y \equiv y'$, then $xy \equiv x'y'$ (modulo m_j); hence $(u \bmod m_j)(v \bmod m_j) \equiv uv$ (modulo m_j).

The main disadvantage of a modular representation is that we cannot easily test whether $(u_1, \ldots, u_r)$ is greater than $(v_1, \ldots, v_r)$. It is also difficult to test whether or not overflow has occurred as the result of an addition, subtraction, or multiplication, and it is even more difficult to perform division. When such operations are required frequently in conjunction with addition, subtraction, and multiplication, the use of modular arithmetic can be justified only if fast means of conversion to and from the modular representation are available. Therefore conversion between modular and positional notation is one of the principal topics of interest to us in this section.

The processes of addition, subtraction, and multiplication using (2), (3), and (4) are called residue arithmetic or *modular arithmetic*. The range of numbers that can be handled by modular arithmetic is equal to $m = m_1 m_2 \ldots m_r$, the product of the moduli; and if each m_j is near our computer's word size we can deal with n-place numbers when $r \approx n$. Therefore we see that the amount of time required to add, subtract, or multiply n-place numbers using modular arithmetic is essentially proportional to n (not counting the time to convert in and out of modular representation). This is no advantage at all when addition and subtraction are considered, but it can be a considerable advantage with respect to multiplication since the conventional method of Section 4.3.1 requires an execution time proportional to n^2.

Moreover, on a computer that allows many operations to take place simultaneously, modular arithmetic can be a significant advantage even for addition and subtraction; the operations with respect to different moduli can all be done at the same time, so we obtain a substantial increase in speed. The same kind of decrease in execution time could not be achieved by the conventional techniques discussed in the previous section, since carry propagation must be considered. Perhaps highly parallel computers will someday make simultaneous operations commonplace, so that modular arithmetic will be of significant importance in "real-time" calculations when a quick answer to a single problem requiring high precision is needed. (With highly parallel computers, it is often preferable to run k *separate* programs simultaneously, instead of running a *single* program k times as fast, since the latter alternative is more complicated but does not utilize the machine any more efficiently. "Real-time" calculations are exceptions that make the inherent parallelism of modular arithmetic more significant.)

Now let us examine the basic fact that underlies the modular representation of numbers:

Theorem C (*Chinese Remainder Theorem*). *Let m_1, m_2, ..., m_r be positive integers that are relatively prime in pairs; that is,*

$$m_j \perp m_k \qquad \text{when } j \neq k. \tag{5}$$

Let $m = m_1 m_2 \ldots m_r$, and let a, u_1, u_2, ..., u_r be integers. Then there is exactly one integer u that satisfies the conditions

$$a \leq u < a + m, \qquad \text{and} \qquad u \equiv u_j \pmod{m_j} \quad \text{for } 1 \leq j \leq r. \tag{6}$$

Proof. If $u \equiv v \pmod{m_j}$ for $1 \leq j \leq r$, then $u - v$ is a multiple of m_j for all j, so (5) implies that $u - v$ is a multiple of $m = m_1 m_2 \ldots m_r$. This argument shows that there is *at most* one solution of (6). To complete the proof we must now show the existence of *at least* one solution, and this can be done in two simple ways:

Method 1 ("Nonconstructive" proof). As u runs through the m distinct values $a \leq u < a + m$, the r-tuples $(u \bmod m_1, \ldots, u \bmod m_r)$ must also run through m distinct values, since (6) has at most one solution. But there are exactly $m_1 m_2 \ldots m_r$ possible r-tuples $(v_1, \ldots, v_r)$ such that $0 \leq v_j < m_j$. Therefore each r-tuple must occur exactly once, and there must be some value of u for which $(u \bmod m_1, \ldots, u \bmod m_r) = (u_1, \ldots, u_r)$.

Method 2 ("Constructive" proof). We can find numbers M_j for $1 \leq j \leq r$ such that

$$M_j \equiv 1 \pmod{m_j} \qquad \text{and} \qquad M_j \equiv 0 \pmod{m_k} \quad \text{for } k \neq j. \tag{7}$$

This follows because (5) implies that m_j and m/m_j are relatively prime, so we may take

$$M_j = (m/m_j)^{\varphi(m_j)} \tag{8}$$

by Euler's theorem (exercise 1.2.4–28). Now the number

$$u = a + \big((u_1 M_1 + u_2 M_2 + \cdots + u_r M_r - a) \bmod m\big) \tag{9}$$

satisfies all the conditions of (6). ∎

A very special case of this theorem was stated by the Chinese mathematician Sun Tsŭ, who gave a rule called tái-yen ("great generalization"). The date of his writing is very uncertain; it is thought to be between A.D. 280 and 473. Mathematicians in mediæval India developed the techniques further, with their methods of *kuṭṭaka* (see Section 4.5.2), but Theorem C was first stated and proved in its proper generality by Ch'in Chiu-Shao in his *Shu Shu Chiu Chang* (1247); the latter work considers also the case where the moduli might have common factors as in exercise 3. [See J. Needham, *Science and Civilisation in China* **3** (Cambridge University Press, 1959), 33–34, 119–120; Y. Li and S. Du, *Chinese Mathematics* (Oxford: Clarendon, 1987), 92–94, 105, 161–166; K. Shen, *Archive for History of Exact Sciences* **38** (1988), 285–305.] Numerous early contributions to this theory have been summarized by L. E. Dickson in his *History of the Theory of Numbers* **2** (Carnegie Inst. of Washington, 1920), 57–64.

As a consequence of Theorem C, we may use modular representation for numbers in any consecutive interval of $m = m_1 m_2 \dots m_r$ integers. For example, we could take $a = 0$ in (6), and work only with nonnegative integers u less than m. On the other hand, when addition and subtraction are being done, as well as multiplication, it is usually most convenient to assume that all of the moduli $m_1, m_2, \dots, m_r$ are odd numbers, so that $m = m_1 m_2 \dots m_r$ is odd, and to work with integers in the range

$$-\frac{m}{2} < u < \frac{m}{2}, \tag{10}$$

which is completely symmetrical about zero.

In order to perform the basic operations listed in (2), (3), and (4), we need to compute $(u_j + v_j) \bmod m_j$, $(u_j - v_j) \bmod m_j$, and $u_j v_j \bmod m_j$, when $0 \le u_j, v_j < m_j$. If m_j is a single-precision number, it is most convenient to form $u_j v_j \bmod m_j$ by doing a multiplication and then a division operation. For addition and subtraction, the situation is a little simpler, since no division is necessary; the following formulas may conveniently be used:

$$(u_j + v_j) \bmod m_j = u_j + v_j - m_j [u_j + v_j \ge m_j]. \tag{11}$$

$$(u_j - v_j) \bmod m_j = u_j - v_j + m_j [u_j < v_j]. \tag{12}$$

(See Section 3.2.1.1.) Since we want m to be as large as possible, it is easiest to let m_1 be the largest odd number that fits in a computer word, to let m_2 be the largest odd number $< m_1$ that is relatively prime to m_1, to let m_3 be the largest odd number $< m_2$ that is relatively prime to both m_1 and m_2, and so on until enough m_j's have been found to give the desired range m. Efficient ways to determine whether or not two integers are relatively prime are discussed in Section 4.5.2.

As a simple example, suppose that we have a decimal computer whose words hold only two digits, so that the word size is 100. Then the procedure described in the previous paragraph would give

$$m_1 = 99, \quad m_2 = 97, \quad m_3 = 95, \quad m_4 = 91, \quad m_5 = 89, \quad m_6 = 83, \tag{13}$$

and so on.

On binary computers it is sometimes desirable to choose the m_j in a different way, by selecting

$$m_j = 2^{e_j} - 1. \tag{14}$$

In other words, each modulus is one less than a power of 2. Such a choice of m_j often makes the basic arithmetic operations simpler, because it is relatively easy to work modulo $2^{e_j} - 1$, as in ones' complement arithmetic. When the moduli are chosen according to this strategy, it is helpful to relax the condition $0 \leq u_j < m_j$ slightly, so that we require only

$$0 \leq u_j < 2^{e_j}, \qquad u_j \equiv u \pmod{2^{e_j} - 1}. \tag{15}$$

Thus, the value $u_j = m_j = 2^{e_j} - 1$ is allowed as an optional alternative to $u_j = 0$; this does not affect the validity of Theorem C, and it means we are allowing u_j to be any e_j-bit binary number. Under this assumption, the operations of addition and multiplication modulo m_j become the following:

$$u_j \oplus v_j = \big((u_j + v_j) \bmod 2^{e_j}\big) + [u_j + v_j \geq 2^{e_j}]. \tag{16}$$

$$u_j \otimes v_j = (u_j v_j \bmod 2^{e_j}) \;\oplus\; \lfloor u_j v_j / 2^{e_j} \rfloor. \tag{17}$$

(Here $\oplus$ and $\otimes$ refer to the operations done on the individual components of $(u_1, \ldots, u_r)$ and $(v_1, \ldots, v_r)$ when adding or multiplying, respectively, using the convention (15).) Equation (12) is still good for subtraction, or we can use

$$u_j \ominus v_j = \big((u_j - v_j) \bmod 2^{e_j}\big) - [u_j < v_j]. \tag{18}$$

These operations can be performed efficiently even when 2^{e_j} is larger than the computer's word size, since it is a simple matter to compute the remainder of a positive number modulo a power of 2, or to divide a number by a power of 2. In (17) we have the sum of the "upper half" and the "lower half" of the product, as discussed in exercise 3.2.1.1–8.

If moduli of the form $2^{e_j} - 1$ are to be used, we must know under what conditions the number $2^e - 1$ is relatively prime to the number $2^f - 1$. Fortunately, there is a very simple rule:

$$\gcd(2^e - 1, 2^f - 1) = 2^{\gcd(e,f)} - 1. \tag{19}$$

This formula states in particular that $2^e - 1$ and $2^f - 1$ are *relatively prime if and only if e and f are relatively prime.* Equation (19) follows from Euclid's algorithm and the identity

$$(2^e - 1) \bmod (2^f - 1) = 2^{e \bmod f} - 1. \tag{20}$$

(See exercise 6.) On a computer with word size 2^{32}, we could therefore choose $m_1 = 2^{32} - 1$, $m_2 = 2^{31} - 1$, $m_3 = 2^{29} - 1$, $m_4 = 2^{27} - 1$, $m_5 = 2^{25} - 1$; this would permit efficient addition, subtraction, and multiplication of integers in a range of size $m_1 m_2 m_3 m_4 m_5 > 2^{143}$.

As we have already observed, the operations of conversion to and from modular representation are very important. If we are given a number u, its modular representation $(u_1, \ldots, u_r)$ may be obtained by simply dividing u by

$m_1, \ldots, m_r$ and saving the remainders. A possibly more attractive procedure, if $u = (v_m v_{m-1} \ldots v_0)_b$, is to evaluate the polynomial

$$\left(\ldots (v_m b + v_{m-1}) b + \cdots \right) b + v_0$$

using modular arithmetic. When $b = 2$ and when the modulus m_j has the special form $2^{e_j} - 1$, both of these methods reduce to quite a simple procedure: Consider the binary representation of u with blocks of e_j bits grouped together,

$$u = a_t A^t + a_{t-1} A^{t-1} + \cdots + a_1 A + a_0, \qquad (21)$$

where $A = 2^{e_j}$ and $0 \le a_k < 2^{e_j}$ for $0 \le k \le t$. Then

$$u \equiv a_t + a_{t-1} + \cdots + a_1 + a_0 \pmod{2^{e_j} - 1}, \qquad (22)$$

since $A \equiv 1$, so we obtain u_j by adding the e_j-bit numbers $a_t \oplus \cdots \oplus a_1 \oplus a_0$, using (16). This process is similar to the familiar device of "casting out nines" that determines $u \bmod 9$ when u is expressed in the decimal system.

Conversion back from modular form to positional notation is somewhat more difficult. It is interesting in this regard to notice how the study of computation changes our viewpoint towards mathematical proofs: Theorem C tells us that the conversion from $(u_1, \ldots, u_r)$ to u is possible, and two proofs are given. The first proof we considered is a classical one that relies only on very simple concepts, namely the facts that

i) any number that is a multiple of m_1, of m_2, ..., and of m_r, must be a multiple of $m_1 m_2 \ldots m_r$ when the m_j's are pairwise relatively prime; and

ii) if m pigeons are put into m pigeonholes with no two pigeons in the same hole, then there must be one in each hole.

By traditional notions of mathematical aesthetics, this is no doubt the nicest proof of Theorem C; but from a computational standpoint it is completely worthless. It amounts to saying, "Try $u = a, a + 1, \ldots$ until you find a value for which $u \equiv u_1 \pmod{m_1}, \ldots, u \equiv u_r \pmod{m_r}$."

The second proof of Theorem C is more explicit; it shows how to compute r new constants $M_1, \ldots, M_r$, and to get the solution in terms of these constants by formula (9). This proof uses more complicated concepts (for example, Euler's theorem), but it is much more satisfactory from a computational standpoint, since the constants $M_1, \ldots, M_r$ need to be determined only once. On the other hand, the determination of M_j by Eq. (8) is certainly not trivial, since the evaluation of Euler's φ-function requires, in general, the factorization of m_j into prime powers. There are much better ways to compute M_j than to use (8); in this respect we can see again the distinction between mathematical elegance and computational efficiency. But even if we find M_j by the best possible method, we're stuck with the fact that M_j is a multiple of the huge number m/m_j. Thus, (9) forces us to do a lot of high-precision calculation, and such calculation is just what we wished to avoid by modular arithmetic in the first place.

So we need an even *better* proof of Theorem C if we are going to have a really usable method of conversion from $(u_1, \ldots, u_r)$ to u. Such a method was suggested by H. L. Garner in 1958; it can be carried out using $\binom{r}{2}$ constants c_{ij} for $1 \leq i < j \leq r$, where

$$c_{ij} \, m_i \equiv 1 \pmod{m_j}. \tag{23}$$

These constants c_{ij} are readily computed using Euclid's algorithm, since for any given i and j Algorithm 4.5.2X will determine a and b such that $am_i + bm_j = \gcd(m_i, m_j) = 1$, and we may take $c_{ij} = a$. When the moduli have the special form $2^{e_j} - 1$, a simple method of determining c_{ij} is given in exercise 6.

Once the c_{ij} have been determined satisfying (23), we can set

$$
\begin{aligned}
v_1 &\leftarrow u_1 \bmod m_1, \\
v_2 &\leftarrow (u_2 - v_1) \, c_{12} \bmod m_2, \\
v_3 &\leftarrow \big((u_3 - v_1) \, c_{13} - v_2\big) \, c_{23} \bmod m_3, \\
&\;\;\vdots \\
v_r &\leftarrow \big(\ldots((u_r - v_1) \, c_{1r} - v_2) \, c_{2r} - \cdots - v_{r-1}\big) \, c_{(r-1)r} \bmod m_r.
\end{aligned}
\tag{24}
$$

Then

$$u = v_r m_{r-1} \ldots m_2 m_1 + \cdots + v_3 m_2 m_1 + v_2 m_1 + v_1 \tag{25}$$

is a number satisfying the conditions

$$0 \leq u < m, \qquad u \equiv u_j \pmod{m_j} \quad \text{for } 1 \leq j \leq r. \tag{26}$$

(See exercise 8; another way of rewriting (24) that does not involve as many auxiliary constants is given in exercise 7.) Equation (25) is a *mixed-radix representation* of u, which can be converted to binary or decimal notation using the methods of Section 4.4. If $0 \leq u < m$ is not the desired range, an appropriate multiple of m can be added or subtracted after the conversion process.

The advantage of the computation shown in (24) is that the calculation of v_j can be done using only arithmetic mod m_j, which is already built into the modular arithmetic algorithms. Furthermore, (24) allows parallel computation: We can start with $(v_1, \ldots, v_r) \leftarrow (u_1 \bmod m_1, \ldots, u_r \bmod m_r)$, then at time j for $1 \leq j < r$ we simultaneously set $v_k \leftarrow (v_k - v_j) c_{jk} \bmod m_k$ for $j < k \leq r$. An alternative way to compute the mixed-radix representation, allowing similar possibilities for parallelism, has been discussed by A. S. Fraenkel, *Proc. ACM Nat. Conf.* **19** (Philadelphia: 1964), E1.4.

It is important to observe that the mixed-radix representation (25) is sufficient to compare the magnitudes of two modular numbers. For if we know that $0 \leq u < m$ and $0 \leq u' < m$, then we can tell if $u < u'$ by first doing the conversion to $(v_1, \ldots, v_r)$ and $(v_1', \ldots, v_r')$, then testing if $v_r < v_r'$, or if $v_r = v_r'$ and $v_{r-1} < v_{r-1}'$, etc., according to lexicographic order. It is not necessary to convert all the way to binary or decimal notation if we only want to know whether $(u_1, \ldots, u_r)$ is less than $(u_1', \ldots, u_r')$.

The operation of comparing two numbers, or of deciding if a modular number is negative, is intuitively very simple, so we would expect to have a much easier way to make this test than the conversion to mixed-radix form. But the following theorem shows that there is little hope of finding a substantially better method, since the range of a modular number depends essentially on all bits of all the residues $(u_1, \ldots, u_r)$:

Theorem S (Nicholas Szabó, 1961). *In terms of the notation above, assume that $m_1 < \sqrt{m}$, and let L be any value in the range*

$$m_1 \leq L \leq m - m_1. \tag{27}$$

Let g be any function such that the set $\{g(0), g(1), \ldots, g(m_1 - 1)\}$ contains fewer than m_1 values. Then there are numbers u and v such that

$$g(u \bmod m_1) = g(v \bmod m_1), \quad u \bmod m_j = v \bmod m_j \quad \text{for } 2 \leq j \leq r; \tag{28}$$
$$0 \leq u < L \leq v < m. \tag{29}$$

Proof. By hypothesis, there must exist numbers $u \neq v$ satisfying (28), since g must take on the same value for two different residues. Let (u, v) be a pair of values with $0 \leq u < v < m$ satisfying (28), for which u is a minimum. Since $u' = u - m_1$ and $v' = v - m_1$ also satisfy (28), we must have $u' < 0$ by the minimality of u. Hence $u < m_1 \leq L$; and if (29) does not hold, we must have $v < L$. But $v > u$, and $v - u$ is a multiple of $m_2 \ldots m_r = m/m_1$, so $v \geq v - u \geq m/m_1 > m_1$. Therefore, if (29) does not hold for (u, v), it will be satisfied for the pair $(u'', v'') = (v - m_1, u + m - m_1)$. $\blacksquare$

Of course, a similar result can be proved for any m_j in place of m_1; and we could also replace (29) by the condition "$a \leq u < a + L \leq v < a + m$" with only minor changes in the proof. Therefore Theorem S shows that many simple functions cannot be used to determine the range of a modular number.

Let us now reiterate the main points of the discussion in this section: Modular arithmetic can be a significant advantage for applications in which the predominant calculations involve exact multiplication (or raising to a power) of large integers, combined with addition and subtraction, but where there is very little need to divide or compare numbers, *or to test whether intermediate results "overflow" out of range.* (It is important not to forget the latter restriction; methods are available to test for overflow, as in exercise 12, but they are so complicated that they nullify the advantages of modular arithmetic.) Several applications of modular computations have been discussed by H. Takahasi and Y. Ishibashi, *Information Proc. in Japan* **1** (1961), 28–42.

An example of such an application is the exact solution of linear equations with rational coefficients. For various reasons it is desirable in this case to assume that the moduli $m_1, m_2, \ldots, m_r$ are all prime numbers; the linear equations can be solved independently modulo each m_j. A detailed discussion of this procedure has been given by I. Borosh and A. S. Fraenkel [*Math. Comp.* **20** (1966), 107–112], with further improvements by A. S. Fraenkel and D. Loewenthal [*J. Res. National Bureau of Standards* **75B** (1971), 67–75]. By means of their method, the nine independent solutions of a system of 111 linear equations in 120 unknowns were obtained exactly in less than 20 minutes on a CDC 1604 computer. The same procedure is worthwhile also for solving simultaneous linear equations with floating point coefficients, when the matrix of coefficients is ill-conditioned. The modular technique (treating the given floating point coefficients as exact rational numbers) gives a method for obtaining the *true* answers in less time than conventional methods can produce reliable *approximate* answers! [See M. T. McClellan, *JACM* **20** (1973), 563–588, for further developments of this approach; and see also E. H. Bareiss, *J. Inst. Math. and Appl.* **10** (1972), 68–104, for a discussion of its limitations.]

The published literature concerning modular arithmetic is mostly oriented towards hardware design, since the carry-free properties of modular arithmetic make it attractive from the standpoint of high-speed operation. The idea was first published by A. Svoboda and M. Valach in the Czechoslovakian journal *Stroje na Zpracování Informací (Information Processing Machines)* **3** (1955), 247–295; then independently by H. L. Garner [*IRE Trans.* **EC-8** (1959), 140–147]. The use of moduli of the form $2^{e_j} - 1$ was suggested by A. S. Fraenkel [*JACM* **8** (1961), 87–96], and several advantages of such moduli were demonstrated by A. Schönhage [*Computing* **1** (1966), 182–196]. See the book *Residue Arithmetic and Its Applications to Computer Technology* by N. S. Szabó and R. I. Tanaka (New York: McGraw–Hill, 1967), for additional information and a comprehensive bibliography of the subject. A Russian book published in 1968 by I. Y. Akushsky and D. I. Yuditsky includes a chapter about complex moduli [see *Rev. Roumaine de Math. Pures et Appl.* **15** (1970), 159–160].

Further discussion of modular arithmetic can be found in Section 4.3.3B.

> *The notice-board had said he was in Room 423,*
> *but the numbering system, nominally consecutive,*
> *seemed to have been applied on a plan that could only*
> *have been the work of a lunatic or a mathematician.*
> — ROBERT BARNARD, *The Case of the Missing Brontë* (1983)

EXERCISES

1. [*20*] Find all integers u that satisfy all of the following conditions: $u \bmod 7 = 1$, $u \bmod 11 = 6$, $u \bmod 13 = 5$, $0 \le u < 1000$.

2. [*M20*] Would Theorem C still be true if we allowed a, u_1, u_2, $\ldots$, u_r and u to be arbitrary real numbers (not just integers)?

▸ **3.** [*M26*] (*Generalized Chinese Remainder Theorem.*) Let m_1, m_2, $\ldots$, m_r be positive integers. Let m be the least common multiple of m_1, m_2, $\ldots$, m_r, and let a, u_1, u_2, $\ldots$, u_r be any integers. Prove that there is exactly one integer u that satisfies the conditions

$$a \le u < a + m, \qquad u \equiv u_j \text{ (modulo } m_j), \qquad 1 \le j \le r,$$

provided that

$$u_i \equiv u_j \text{ (modulo } \gcd(m_i, m_j)), \qquad 1 \le i < j \le r;$$

and there is no such integer u when the latter condition fails to hold.

4. [*20*] Continue the process shown in (13); what would m_7, m_8, m_9, $\ldots$ be?

▸ **5.** [*M23*] (a) Suppose that the method of (13) is continued until no more m_j can be chosen. Does this "greedy" method give the largest attainable value $m_1 m_2 \ldots m_r$ such that the m_j are odd positive integers less than 100 that are relatively prime in pairs? (b) What is the largest possible $m_1 m_2 \ldots m_r$ when each residue u_j must fit in eight bits of memory?

6. [*M22*] Let e, f, and g be nonnegative integers.
a) Show that $2^e \equiv 2^f$ (modulo $2^g - 1$) if and only if $e \equiv f$ (modulo g).
b) Given that $e \bmod f = d$ and $ce \bmod f = 1$, prove the identity

$$((1 + 2^d + \cdots + 2^{(c-1)d}) \cdot (2^e - 1)) \bmod (2^f - 1) = 1.$$

(Thus, we have a comparatively simple formula for the inverse of $2^e - 1$, modulo $2^f - 1$, as required in (23).)

▸ **7.** [*M21*] Show that (24) can be rewritten as follows:

$$v_1 \leftarrow u_1 \bmod m_1,$$
$$v_2 \leftarrow (u_2 - v_1)\, c_{12} \bmod m_2,$$
$$v_3 \leftarrow (u_3 - (v_1 + m_1 v_2))\, c_{13} c_{23} \bmod m_3,$$

$$\vdots$$

$$v_r \leftarrow (u_r - (v_1 + m_1(v_2 + m_2(v_3 + \cdots + m_{r-2} v_{r-1}) \ldots)))\, c_{1r} \ldots c_{(r-1)r} \bmod m_r.$$

If the formulas are rewritten in this way, we see that only $r - 1$ constants $C_j = c_{1j} \ldots c_{(j-1)j} \bmod m_j$ are needed instead of $r(r-1)/2$ constants c_{ij} as in (24). Discuss the relative merits of this version of the formula as compared to (24), from the standpoint of computer calculation.

8. [*M21*] Prove that the number u defined by (24) and (25) satisfies (26).

9. [*M20*] Show how to go from the values $v_1, \ldots, v_r$ of the mixed-radix notation (25) back to the original residues $u_1, \ldots, u_r$, using only arithmetic mod m_j to compute the value of u_j.

10. [*M25*] An integer u that lies in the symmetrical range (10) might be represented by finding the numbers $u_1, \ldots, u_r$ such that $u \equiv u_j$ (modulo m_j) and $-m_j/2 < u_j < m_j/2$, instead of insisting that $0 \le u_j < m_j$ as in the text. Discuss the modular arithmetic procedures that would be appropriate in connection with such a symmetrical representation (including the conversion process, (24)).

11. [*M23*] Assume that all the m_j are odd, and that $u = (u_1, \ldots, u_r)$ is known to be even, where $0 \le u < m$. Find a reasonably fast method to compute $u/2$ using modular arithmetic.

12. [*M10*] Prove that, if $0 \le u, v < m$, the modular addition of u and v causes overflow (lies outside the range allowed by the modular representation) if and only if the sum is less than u. (Thus the overflow detection problem is equivalent to the comparison problem.)

▸ **13.** [*M25*] (*Automorphic numbers.*) An n-digit decimal number $x > 1$ is called an "automorph" by recreational mathematicians if the last n digits of x^2 are equal to x. For example, 9376 is a 4-digit automorph, since $9376^2 = 87909376$. [See *Scientific American* **218** (January 1968), 125.]

a) Prove that an n-digit number $x > 1$ is an automorph if and only if $x \bmod 5^n = 0$ or 1 and $x \bmod 2^n = 1$ or 0, respectively. (Thus, if $m_1 = 2^n$ and $m_2 = 5^n$, the only two n-digit automorphs are the numbers M_1 and M_2 in (7).)

b) Prove that if x is an n-digit automorph, then $(3x^2 - 2x^3) \bmod 10^{2n}$ is a $2n$-digit automorph.

c) Given that $cx \equiv 1 \pmod{y}$, find a simple formula for a number c' depending on c and x but not on y, such that $c'x^2 \equiv 1 \pmod{y^2}$.

▶ **14.** [*M30*] (*Mersenne multiplication.*) The cyclic convolution of $(x_0, x_1, \ldots, x_{n-1})$ and $(y_0, y_1, \ldots, y_{n-1})$ is defined to be $(z_0, z_1, \ldots, z_{n-1})$, where

$$z_k = \sum_{i+j \equiv k \,(\text{modulo } n)} x_i y_j, \qquad \text{for } 0 \le k < n.$$

We will study efficient algorithms for cyclic convolution in Sections 4.3.3 and 4.6.4.

Consider q-bit integers u and v that are represented in the form

$$u = \sum_{k=0}^{n-1} u_k 2^{\lfloor kq/n \rfloor}, \qquad v = \sum_{k=0}^{n-1} v_k 2^{\lfloor kq/n \rfloor},$$

where $0 \le u_k, v_k < 2^{\lfloor (k+1)q/n \rfloor - \lfloor kq/n \rfloor}$. (This representation is a mixture of radices $2^{\lfloor q/n \rfloor}$ and $2^{\lceil q/n \rceil}$.) Suggest a good way to find the representation of

$$w = (uv) \bmod (2^q - 1),$$

using an appropriate cyclic convolution. [*Hint:* Do not be afraid of floating point arithmetic.]

*4.3.3. How Fast Can We Multiply?

The conventional procedure for multiplication in positional number systems, Algorithm 4.3.1M, requires approximately cmn operations to multiply an m-place number by an n-place number, where c is a constant. In this section, let us assume for convenience that $m = n$, and let us consider the following question: *Does every general computer algorithm for multiplying two n-place numbers require an execution time proportional to n^2, as n increases?*

(In this question, a "general" algorithm means one that accepts, as input, the number n and two arbitrary n-place numbers in positional notation; the algorithm is supposed to output their product in positional form. Certainly if we were allowed to choose a different algorithm for each value of n, the question would be of no interest, since multiplication could be done for any specific value of n by a "table-lookup" operation in some huge table. The term "computer algorithm" is meant to imply an algorithm that is suitable for implementation on a digital computer like MIX, and the execution time is to be the time it takes to perform the algorithm on such a computer.)

A. Digital methods. The answer to the question above is, rather surprisingly, "No," and, in fact, it is not very difficult to see why. For convenience, let us assume throughout this section that we are working with integers expressed in binary notation. If we have two $2n$-bit numbers $u = (u_{2n-1} \ldots u_1 u_0)_2$ and $v = (v_{2n-1} \ldots v_1 v_0)_2$, we can write

$$u = 2^n U_1 + U_0, \qquad v = 2^n V_1 + V_0, \tag{1}$$

where $U_1 = (u_{2n-1} \ldots u_n)_2$ is the "most significant half" of the number u and $U_0 = (u_{n-1} \ldots u_0)_2$ is the "least significant half"; similarly $V_1 = (v_{2n-1} \ldots v_n)_2$ and $V_0 = (v_{n-1} \ldots v_0)_2$. Now we have

$$uv = (2^{2n} + 2^n)U_1V_1 + 2^n(U_1 - U_0)(V_0 - V_1) + (2^n + 1)U_0V_0. \qquad (2)$$

This formula reduces the problem of multiplying $2n$-bit numbers to three multiplications of n-bit numbers, namely U_1V_1, $(U_1 - U_0)(V_0 - V_1)$, and U_0V_0, plus some simple shifting and adding operations.

Formula (2) can be used to multiply double-precision inputs when we want a quadruple-precision result, and it will be just a little faster than the traditional method on many machines. But the main advantage of (2) is that we can use it to define a recursive process for multiplication that is significantly faster than the familiar order-n^2 method when n is large: If $T(n)$ is the time required to perform multiplication of n-bit numbers, we have

$$T(2n) \le 3T(n) + cn \qquad (3)$$

for some constant c, since the right-hand side of (2) uses just three multiplications plus some additions and shifts. Relation (3) implies by induction that

$$T(2^k) \le c(3^k - 2^k), \qquad k \ge 1, \qquad (4)$$

if we choose c to be large enough so that this inequality is valid when $k = 1$; therefore we have

$$T(n) \le T\big(2^{\lceil \lg n \rceil}\big) \le c\big(3^{\lceil \lg n \rceil} - 2^{\lceil \lg n \rceil}\big) < 3c \cdot 3^{\lg n} = 3cn^{\lg 3}. \qquad (5)$$

Relation (5) shows that the running time for multiplication can be reduced from order n^2 to order $n^{\lg 3} \approx n^{1.585}$, so the recursive method is much faster than the traditional method when n is large. Exercise 18 discusses an implementation of this approach.

(A similar but slightly more complicated method for doing multiplication with running time of order $n^{\lg 3}$ was apparently first suggested by A. Karatsuba in *Doklady Akad. Nauk SSSR* **145** (1962), 293–294 [English translation in *Soviet Physics–Doklady* **7** (1963), 595–596]. Curiously, this idea does not seem to have been discovered before 1962; none of the "calculating prodigies" who have become famous for their ability to multiply large numbers mentally have been reported to use any such method, although formula (2) adapted to decimal notation would seem to lead to a reasonably easy way to multiply eight-digit numbers in one's head.)

The running time can be reduced still further, in the limit as n approaches infinity, if we observe that the method just used is essentially the special case $r = 1$ of a more general method that yields

$$T\big((r+1)n\big) \le (2r+1)T(n) + cn \qquad (6)$$

for any fixed r. This more general method can be obtained as follows: Let

$$u = (u_{(r+1)n-1} \ldots u_1 u_0)_2 \qquad \text{and} \qquad v = (v_{(r+1)n-1} \ldots v_1 v_0)_2$$

be broken into $r + 1$ pieces,

$$u = U_r 2^{rn} + \cdots + U_1 2^n + U_0, \qquad v = V_r 2^{rn} + \cdots + V_1 2^n + V_0, \qquad (7)$$

where each U_j and each V_j is an n-bit number. Consider the polynomials

$$U(x) = U_r x^r + \cdots + U_1 x + U_0, \qquad V(x) = V_r x^r + \cdots + V_1 x + V_0, \qquad (8)$$

and let

$$W(x) = U(x)V(x) = W_{2r} x^{2r} + \cdots + W_1 x + W_0. \qquad (9)$$

Since $u = U(2^n)$ and $v = V(2^n)$, we have $uv = W(2^n)$, so we can easily compute uv if we know the coefficients of $W(x)$. The problem is to find a good way to compute the coefficients of $W(x)$ by using only $2r + 1$ multiplications of n-bit numbers plus some further operations that involve only an execution time proportional to n. This can be done by computing

$$U(0)V(0) = W(0), \quad U(1)V(1) = W(1), \quad \ldots, \quad U(2r)V(2r) = W(2r). \qquad (10)$$

The coefficients of a polynomial of degree $2r$ can be written as a linear combination of the values of that polynomial at $2r + 1$ distinct points; computing such a linear combination requires an execution time at most proportional to n. (Actually, the products $U(j)V(j)$ are not strictly products of n-bit numbers, but they are products of at most $(n + t)$-bit numbers, where t is a fixed value depending on r. It is easy to design a multiplication routine for $(n + t)$-bit numbers that requires only $T(n) + c_1 n$ operations, where $T(n)$ is the number of operations needed for n-bit multiplications, since two products of t-bit by n-bit numbers can be done in $c_2 n$ operations when t is fixed.) Therefore we obtain a method of multiplication satisfying (6).

Relation (6) implies that $T(n) \leq c_3 n^{\log_{r+1}(2r+1)} < c_3 n^{1 + \log_{r+1} 2}$, if we argue as in the derivation of (5), so we have now proved the following result:

Theorem A. *Given $\epsilon > 0$, there exists a multiplication algorithm such that the number of elementary operations $T(n)$ needed to multiply two n-bit numbers satisfies*

$$T(n) < c(\epsilon) n^{1+\epsilon}, \qquad (11)$$

for some constant $c(\epsilon)$ independent of n. ∎

This theorem is still not the result we are after. It is unsatisfactory for practical purposes because the method becomes quite complicated as $\epsilon \to 0$ (and therefore as $r \to \infty$), causing $c(\epsilon)$ to grow so rapidly that extremely huge values of n are needed before we have any significant improvement over (5). And it is unsatisfactory for theoretical purposes because it does not make use of the full power of the polynomial method on which it is based. We can obtain a better result if we let r *vary* with n, choosing larger and larger values of r as n increases. This idea is due to A. L. Toom [*Doklady Akad. Nauk SSSR* **150** (1963), 496–498, English translation in *Soviet Mathematics* **4** (1963), 714–716], who used it to show that computer circuitry for the multiplication of n-bit numbers can be constructed with a fairly small number of components as n grows. S. A. Cook [*On the Minimum Computation Time of Functions* (Thesis, Harvard University, 1966), 51–77] showed later that Toom's method can be adapted to fast computer programs.

Before we discuss the Toom–Cook algorithm any further, let us study a small example of the transition from $U(x)$ and $V(x)$ to the coefficients of $W(x)$. This example will not demonstrate the efficiency of the method, since the numbers are too small, but it reveals some useful simplifications that we can make in the general case. Suppose that we want to multiply $u = 1234$ times $v = 2341$; in binary notation this is

$$u = (0100\ 1101\ 0010)_2 \text{ times } v = (1001\ 0010\ 0101)_2. \qquad (12)$$

Let $r = 2$; the polynomials $U(x)$ and $V(x)$ in (8) are

$$U(x) = 4x^2 + 13x + 2, \qquad V(x) = 9x^2 + 2x + 5.$$

Hence we find, for $W(x) = U(x)V(x)$,

$$
\begin{aligned}
U(0) &= 2, & U(1) &= 19, & U(2) &= 44, & U(3) &= 77, & U(4) &= 118; \\
V(0) &= 5, & V(1) &= 16, & V(2) &= 45, & V(3) &= 92, & V(4) &= 157; \\
W(0) &= 10, & W(1) &= 304, & W(2) &= 1980, & W(3) &= 7084, & W(4) &= 18526. & (13)
\end{aligned}
$$

Our job is to compute the five coefficients of $W(x)$ from the latter five values.

An attractive little algorithm can be used to compute the coefficients of a polynomial $W(x) = W_{m-1}x^{m-1} + \cdots + W_1 x + W_0$ when the values $W(0)$, $W(1)$, $\ldots$, $W(m-1)$ are given. Let us first write

$$W(x) = a_{m-1} x^{\underline{m-1}} + a_{m-2} x^{\underline{m-2}} + \cdots + a_1 x^{\underline{1}} + a_0, \qquad (14)$$

where $x^{\underline{k}} = x(x-1)\ldots(x-k+1)$, and where the coefficients a_j are unknown. The falling factorial powers have the important property that

$$W(x+1) - W(x) = (m-1)a_{m-1} x^{\underline{m-2}} + (m-2)a_{m-2} x^{\underline{m-3}} + \cdots + a_1;$$

hence by induction we find that, for all $k \geq 0$,

$$\frac{1}{k!}\left(W(x+k) - \binom{k}{1}W(x+k-1) + \binom{k}{2}W(x+k-2) - \cdots + (-1)^k W(x) \right)$$

$$= \binom{m-1}{k} a_{m-1} x^{\underline{m-1-k}} + \binom{m-2}{k} a_{m-2} x^{\underline{m-2-k}} + \cdots + \binom{k}{k} a_k. \qquad (15)$$

Denoting the left-hand side of (15) by $(1/k!)\,\Delta^k W(x)$, we see that

$$\frac{1}{k!}\Delta^k W(x) = \frac{1}{k}\left(\frac{1}{(k-1)!}\Delta^{k-1}W(x+1) - \frac{1}{(k-1)!}\Delta^{k-1}W(x) \right)$$

and $(1/k!)\,\Delta^k\,W(0) = a_k$. So the coefficients a_j can be evaluated using a very simple method, illustrated here for the polynomial $W(x)$ in (13):

$$
\begin{array}{lllll}
10 \\
 & 294 \\
304 & & 1382/2 =\ \ 691 \\
 & 1676 & & 1023/3 = 341 \\
1980 & & 3428/2 = 1714 & & 144/4 = 36 \qquad (16)\\
 & 5104 & & 1455/3 = 485 \\
7084 & & 6338/2 = 3169 \\
 & 11442 \\
18526
\end{array}
$$

The leftmost column of this tableau is a listing of the given values of $W(0)$, $W(1)$, ..., $W(4)$; the kth succeeding column is obtained by computing the difference between successive values of the preceding column and dividing by k. The coefficients a_j appear at the top of the columns, so that $a_0 = 10$, $a_1 = 294$, ..., $a_4 = 36$, and we have

$$W(x) = 36x^4 + 341x^3 + 691x^2 + 294x^1 + 10$$
$$= \big(((36(x-3) + 341)(x-2) + 691)(x-1) + 294\big)x + 10. \qquad (17)$$

In general, we can write

$$W(x) = \big(\ldots((a_{m-1}(x-m+2) + a_{m-2})(x-m+3) + a_{m-3})(x-m+4) + \cdots + a_1\big)x + a_0,$$

and this formula shows how the coefficients W_{m-1}, ..., W_1, W_0 can be obtained from the a's:

$$
\begin{array}{ccccc}
\boxed{\begin{array}{l}36\\ \ \end{array}} & 341 \\
 & -3\cdot 36 \\
\boxed{\begin{array}{l}36\\ \ \end{array}} & 233 & 691 \\
 & -2\cdot 36 & -2\cdot 233 & & \qquad (18)\\
\boxed{\begin{array}{l}36\\ \ \end{array}} & 161 & 225 & 294 \\
 & -1\cdot 36 & -1\cdot 161 & -1\cdot 225 \\
36 & 125 & 64 & 69 & \boxed{10}
\end{array}
$$

Here the numbers below the horizontal lines successively show the coefficients of the polynomials

$$a_{m-1},$$
$$a_{m-1}(x - m + 2) + a_{m-2},$$
$$\big(a_{m-1}(x - m + 2) + a_{m-2}\big)(x - m + 3) + a_{m-3}, \qquad \text{etc.}$$

From this tableau we have

$$W(x) = 36x^4 + 125x^3 + 64x^2 + 69x + 10, \qquad (19)$$

so the answer to our original problem is $1234 \cdot 2341 = W(16) = 2888794$, where $W(16)$ is obtained by adding and shifting. A generalization of this method for obtaining coefficients is discussed in Section 4.6.4.

The basic Stirling number identity of Eq. 1.2.6–(45),

$$x^n = \left\{{n \atop n}\right\} x^{\underline{n}} + \cdots + \left\{{n \atop 1}\right\} x^{\underline{1}} + \left\{{n \atop 0}\right\},$$

shows that if the coefficients of $W(x)$ are nonnegative, so are the numbers a_j, and in such a case *all of the intermediate results in the computation above are nonnegative*. This further simplifies the Toom–Cook multiplication algorithm, which we will now consider in detail. (Impatient readers should, however, skip to subsection C below.)

Algorithm T (*High-precision multiplication of binary numbers*). Given a positive integer n and two nonnegative n-bit integers u and v, this algorithm forms their $2n$-bit product, w. Four auxiliary stacks are used to hold the long numbers that are manipulated during the procedure:

Stacks U, V:	Temporary storage of $U(j)$ and $V(j)$ in step T4.
Stack C:	Numbers to be multiplied, and control codes.
Stack W:	Storage of $W(j)$.

These stacks may contain either binary numbers or special control symbols called code-1, code-2, and code-3. The algorithm also constructs an auxiliary table of numbers q_k, r_k; this table is maintained in such a manner that it may be stored as a linear list, where a single pointer that traverses the list (moving back and forth) can be used to access the current table entry of interest.

(Stacks C and W are used to control the recursive mechanism of this multiplication algorithm in a reasonably straightforward manner that is a special case of general procedures discussed in Chapter 8.)

T1. [Compute q, r tables.] Set stacks U, V, C, and W empty. Set

$$k \leftarrow 1, \qquad q_0 \leftarrow q_1 \leftarrow 16, \qquad r_0 \leftarrow r_1 \leftarrow 4, \qquad Q \leftarrow 4, \qquad R \leftarrow 2.$$

Now if $q_{k-1} + q_k < n$, set

$$k \leftarrow k+1, \qquad Q \leftarrow Q + R, \qquad R \leftarrow \lfloor \sqrt{Q} \rfloor, \qquad q_k \leftarrow 2^Q, \qquad r_k \leftarrow 2^R,$$

and repeat this operation until $q_{k-1} + q_k \geq n$. (*Note:* The calculation of $R \leftarrow \lfloor \sqrt{Q} \rfloor$ does not require a square root to be taken, since we may simply set $R \leftarrow R+1$ if $(R+1)^2 \leq Q$ and leave R unchanged if $(R+1)^2 > Q$; see exercise 2. In this step we build the sequences

k =	0	1	2	3	4	5	6	$\cdots$
q_k =	2^4	2^4	2^6	2^8	2^{10}	2^{13}	2^{16}	$\cdots$
r_k =	2^2	2^2	2^2	2^2	2^3	2^3	2^4	$\cdots$

The multiplication of 70000-bit numbers would cause this step to terminate with $k = 6$, since $70000 < 2^{13} + 2^{16}$.)

T2. [Put u, v on stack.] Put code-1 on stack C, then place u and v onto stack C as numbers of exactly $q_{k-1} + q_k$ bits each.

T3. [Check recursion level.] Decrease k by 1. If $k = 0$, the top of stack C now contains two 32-bit numbers, u and v; remove them, set $w \leftarrow uv$ using a built-in routine for multiplying 32-bit numbers, and go to step T10. If $k > 0$, set $r \leftarrow r_k$, $q \leftarrow q_k$, $p \leftarrow q_{k-1} + q_k$, and go on to step T4.

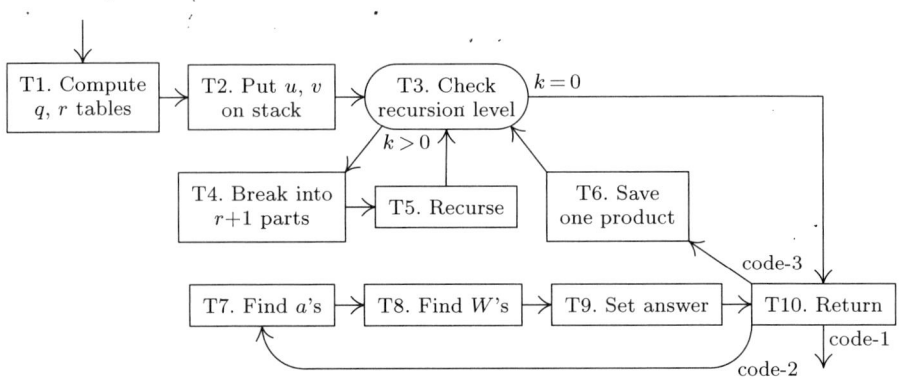

Fig. 8. The Toom–Cook algorithm for high-precision multiplication.

T4. [Break into $r + 1$ parts.] Let the number at the top of stack C be regarded as a list of $r + 1$ numbers with q bits each, $(U_r \ldots U_1 U_0)_{2^q}$. (The top of stack C now contains an $(r + 1)q = (q_k + q_{k+1})$-bit number.) For $j = 0, 1, \ldots, 2r$, compute the p-bit numbers

$$\big(\ldots (U_r j + U_{r-1})j + \cdots + U_1\big)j + U_0 = U(j)$$

and successively put these values onto stack U. (The bottom of stack U now contains $U(0)$, then comes $U(1)$, etc., with $U(2r)$ on top. We have

$$U(j) \le U(2r) < 2^q\big((2r)^r + (2r)^{r-1} + \cdots + 1\big) < 2^{q+1}(2r)^r \le 2^p,$$

by exercise 3.) Then remove $U_r \ldots U_1 U_0$ from stack C.

Now the top of stack C contains another list of $r + 1$ q-bit numbers, $V_r \ldots V_1 V_0$, and the p-bit numbers

$$\big(\ldots (V_r j + V_{r-1})j + \cdots + V_1\big)j + V_0 = V(j)$$

should be put onto stack V in the same way. After this has been done, remove $V_r \ldots V_1 V_0$ from stack C.

T5. [Recurse.] Successively put the following items onto stack C, at the same time emptying stacks U and V:

$$\text{code-2}, V(2r), U(2r), \text{code-3}, V(2r-1), U(2r-1), \ldots,$$
$$\text{code-3}, V(1), U(1), \text{code-3}, V(0), U(0).$$

Go back to step T3.

T6. [Save one product.] (At this point the multiplication algorithm has set w to one of the products $W(j) = U(j)V(j)$.) Put w onto stack W. (This number w contains $2(q_k + q_{k-1})$ bits.) Go back to step T3.

T7. [Find a's.] Set $r \leftarrow r_k$, $q \leftarrow q_k$, $p \leftarrow q_{k-1} + q_k$. (At this point stack W contains a sequence of numbers ending with $W(0), W(1), \ldots, W(2r)$ from bottom to top, where each $W(j)$ is a $2p$-bit number.)

Now for $j = 1, 2, 3, \ldots, 2r$, perform the following loop: For $t = 2r$, $2r - 1, 2r - 2, \ldots, j$, set $W(t) \leftarrow \big(W(t) - W(t-1)\big)/j$. (Here j must increase and t must decrease. The quantity $\big(W(t) - W(t-1)\big)/j$ will always be a nonnegative integer that fits in $2p$ bits; see (16).)

T8. [Find W's.] For $j = 2r - 1, 2r - 2, \ldots, 1$, perform the following loop: For $t = j, j+1, \ldots, 2r - 1$, set $W(t) \leftarrow W(t) - jW(t+1)$. (Here j must decrease and t must increase. The result of this operation will again be a nonnegative $2p$-bit integer; see (18).)

T9. [Set answer.] Set w to the $2(q_k + q_{k+1})$-bit integer

$$\big(\ldots \big(W(2r)2^q + W(2r - 1)\big)2^q + \cdots + W(1)\big)2^q + W(0).$$

Remove $W(2r), \ldots, W(0)$ from stack W.

T10. [Return.] Set $k \leftarrow k + 1$. Remove the top of stack C. If it is code-3, go to step T6. If it is code-2, put w onto stack W and go to step T7. And if it is code-1, terminate the algorithm (w is the answer). $\blacksquare$

Let us now estimate the running time, $T(n)$, for Algorithm T, in terms of some things we shall call "cycles," that is, elementary machine operations. Step T1 takes $O(q_k)$ cycles, even if we represent the number q_k internally as a long string of q_k bits followed by some delimiter, since $q_k + q_{k-1} + \cdots + q_0$ will be $O(q_k)$. Step T2 obviously takes $O(q_k)$ cycles.

Now let t_k denote the amount of computation required to get from step T3 to step T10 for a particular value of k (after k has been decreased at the beginning of step T3). Step T3 requires $O(q)$ cycles at most. Step T4 involves r multiplications of q-bit numbers by $(\lg 2r)$-bit numbers, and r additions of p-bit numbers, all repeated $4r + 2$ times. Thus we need a total of $O(r^2 q \log r)$ cycles. Step T5 requires moving $4r + 2$ p-bit numbers, so it involves $O(rq)$ cycles. Step T6 requires $O(q)$ cycles, and it is done $2r + 1$ times per iteration. The recursion involved when the algorithm essentially invokes itself (by returning to step T3) requires t_{k-1} cycles, $2r + 1$ times. Step T7 requires $O(r^2)$ subtractions of p-bit numbers and divisions of $2p$-bit by $(\lg 2r)$-bit numbers, so it requires $O(r^2 q \log r)$ cycles. Similarly, step T8 requires $O(r^2 q \log r)$ cycles. Step T9 involves $O(rq)$ cycles, and T10 takes hardly any time at all.

Summing up, we have $T(n) = O(q_k) + O(q_k) + t_{k-1}$, where (if $q = q_k$ and $r = r_k$) the main contribution to the running time satisfies

$$t_k = O(q) + O(r^2 q \log r) + O(rq) + (2r + 1)O(q) + O(r^2 q \log r)$$
$$+ O(r^2 q \log r) + O(rq) + O(q) + (2r + 1)t_{k-1}$$

$$= O(r^2 q \log r) + (2r + 1)t_{k-1}.$$

Thus there is a constant c such that

$$t_k \le c r_k^2 q_k \lg r_k + (2r_k + 1)t_{k-1}.$$

To complete the estimation of t_k we can prove by brute force that

$$t_k \le C q_{k+1} 2^{2.5\sqrt{\lg q_{k+1}}} \tag{20}$$

for some constant C. Let us choose $C > 20c$, and let us also take C large enough so that (20) is valid for $k \leq k_0$, where k_0 will be specified below. Then when $k > k_0$, let $Q_k = \lg q_k$, $R_k = \lg r_k$; we have by induction

$$t_k \leq c q_k r_k^2 \lg r_k + (2r_k + 1) C q_k 2^{2.5\sqrt{Q_k}} = C q_{k+1} 2^{2.5\sqrt{\lg q_{k+1}}} (\eta_1 + \eta_2),$$

where

$$\eta_1 = \frac{c}{C} R_k 2^{R_k - 2.5\sqrt{Q_{k+1}}} < \frac{1}{20} R_k 2^{-R_k} < 0.05,$$

$$\eta_2 = \left(2 + \frac{1}{r_k}\right) 2^{2.5(\sqrt{Q_k} - \sqrt{Q_{k+1}})} \to 2^{-1/4} < 0.85,$$

since

$$\sqrt{Q_{k+1}} - \sqrt{Q_k} = \sqrt{Q_k + \lfloor\sqrt{Q_k}\rfloor} - \sqrt{Q_k} \to \tfrac{1}{2}$$

as $k \to \infty$. It follows that we can find k_0 such that $\eta_2 < 0.95$ for all $k > k_0$, and this completes the proof of (20) by induction.

Finally, therefore, we are ready to estimate $T(n)$. Since $n > q_{k-1} + q_{k-2}$, we have $q_{k-1} < n$; hence

$$r_{k-1} = 2^{\lfloor\sqrt{\lg q_{k-1}}\rfloor} < 2^{\sqrt{\lg n}}, \qquad \text{and} \qquad q_k = r_{k-1} q_{k-1} < n 2^{\sqrt{\lg n}}.$$

Thus

$$t_{k-1} \leq C q_k 2^{2.5\sqrt{\lg q_k}} < C n 2^{\sqrt{\lg n} + 2.5(\sqrt{\lg n} + 1)},$$

and, since $T(n) = O(q_k) + t_{k-1}$, we have derived the following theorem:

Theorem B. *There is a constant c_0 such that the execution time of Algorithm T is less than $c_0 n 2^{3.5\sqrt{\lg n}}$ cycles.* ∎

Since $n 2^{3.5\sqrt{\lg n}} = n^{1 + 3.5/\sqrt{\lg n}}$, this result is noticeably stronger than Theorem A. By adding a few complications to the algorithm, pushing the ideas to their apparent limits (see exercise 5), we can improve the estimated execution time to

$$T(n) = O(n 2^{\sqrt{2\lg n}} \log n). \tag{21}$$

*B. A modular method. There is another way to multiply large numbers very rapidly, based on the ideas of modular arithmetic as presented in Section 4.3.2. It is very hard to believe at first that this method can be of advantage, since a multiplication algorithm based on modular arithmetic must include the choice of moduli and the conversion of numbers into and out of modular representation, besides the actual multiplication operation itself. In spite of these formidable difficulties, A. Schönhage discovered that all of these operations can be carried out quite rapidly.

In order to understand the essential mechanism of Schönhage's method, we shall look at a special case. Consider the sequence defined by the rules

$$q_0 = 1, \qquad q_{k+1} = 3q_k - 1, \tag{22}$$

so that $q_k = 3^k - 3^{k-1} - \cdots - 1 = \tfrac{1}{2}(3^k + 1)$. We will study a procedure that multiplies p_k-bit numbers, where $p_k = (18q_k + 8)$, in terms of a method for multiplying p_{k-1}-bit numbers. Thus, if we know how to multiply numbers having $p_0 = 26$ bits, the procedure to be described will show us how to multiply numbers of $p_1 = 44$ bits, then 98 bits, then 260 bits, etc., eventually increasing the number of bits by almost a factor of 3 at each step.

When multiplying p_k-bit numbers, the idea is to use the six moduli

$$m_1 = 2^{6q_k-1} - 1, \qquad m_2 = 2^{6q_k+1} - 1, \qquad m_3 = 2^{6q_k+2} - 1,$$
$$m_4 = 2^{6q_k+3} - 1, \qquad m_5 = 2^{6q_k+5} - 1, \qquad m_6 = 2^{6q_k+7} - 1. \qquad (23)$$

These moduli are relatively prime, by Eq. 4.3.2–(19), since the exponents

$$6q_k - 1, \quad 6q_k + 1, \quad 6q_k + 2, \quad 6q_k + 3, \quad 6q_k + 5, \quad 6q_k + 7 \qquad (24)$$

are always relatively prime (see exercise 6). The six moduli in (23) are capable of representing numbers up to $m = m_1 m_2 m_3 m_4 m_5 m_6 > 2^{36q_k+16} = 2^{2p_k}$, so there is no chance of overflow in the multiplication of p_k-bit numbers u and v. Thus we can use the following method, when $k > 0$:

a) Compute $u_1 = u \bmod m_1, \ldots, u_6 = u \bmod m_6$; and $v_1 = v \bmod m_1, \ldots, v_6 = v \bmod m_6$.

b) Multiply u_1 by v_1, u_2 by v_2, $\ldots$, u_6 by v_6. These are numbers of at most $6q_k + 7 = 18q_{k-1} + 1 < p_{k-1}$ bits, so the multiplications can be performed by using the assumed p_{k-1}-bit multiplication procedure.

c) Compute $w_1 = u_1 v_1 \bmod m_1$, $w_2 = u_2 v_2 \bmod m_2$, $\ldots$, $w_6 = u_6 v_6 \bmod m_6$.

d) Compute w such that $0 \le w < m$, $w \bmod m_1 = w_1, \ldots, w \bmod m_6 = w_6$.

Let t_k be the amount of time needed for this process. It is not hard to see that operation (a) takes $O(p_k)$ cycles, since the determination of $u \bmod (2^e - 1)$ is quite simple (like "casting out nines"), as shown in Section 4.3.2. Similarly, operation (c) takes $O(p_k)$ cycles. Operation (b) requires essentially $6t_{k-1}$ cycles. This leaves us with operation (d), which seems to be quite a difficult computation; but Schönhage has found an ingenious way to perform step (d) in $O(p_k \log p_k)$ cycles, and this is the crux of the method. As a consequence, we have

$$t_k = 6t_{k-1} + O(p_k \log p_k).$$

Since $p_k = 3^{k+2} + 17$, we can show that the time for n-bit multiplication is

$$T(n) = O(n^{\log_3 6}) = O(n^{1.631}). \qquad (25)$$

(See exercise 7.)

Although the modular method is more complicated than the $O(n^{\lg 3})$ procedure discussed at the beginning of this section, Eq. (25) shows that it does, in fact, lead to an execution time substantially better than $O(n^2)$ for the multiplication of n-bit numbers. Thus we have seen how to improve on the classical method by using either of two completely different approaches.

Let us now analyze operation (d) above. Assume that we are given a set of positive integers $e_1 < e_2 < \cdots < e_r$, relatively prime in pairs; let

$$m_1 = 2^{e_1} - 1, \qquad m_2 = 2^{e_2} - 1, \qquad \ldots, \qquad m_r = 2^{e_r} - 1. \qquad (26)$$

We are also given numbers w_1, ..., w_r such that $0 \le w_j \le m_j$. Our job is to determine the binary representation of the number w that satisfies the conditions

$$0 \le w < m_1 m_2 \ldots m_r,$$
$$w \equiv w_1 \ (\text{modulo } m_1), \qquad \ldots, \qquad w \equiv w_r \ (\text{modulo } m_r). \tag{27}$$

The method is based on (24) and (25) of Section 4.3.2. First we compute

$$w_j' = (\ldots((w_j - w_1')c_{1j} - w_2')c_{2j} - \cdots - w_{j-1}')c_{(j-1)j} \bmod m_j, \tag{28}$$

for $j = 2, \ldots, r$, where $w_1' = w_1 \bmod m_1$; then we compute

$$w = (\ldots(w_r' m_{r-1} + w_{r-1}')m_{r-2} + \cdots + w_2')m_1 + w_1'. \tag{29}$$

Here c_{ij} is a number such that $c_{ij}m_i \equiv 1 \ (\text{modulo } m_j)$; these numbers c_{ij} are not given, they must be determined from the e_j's.

The calculation of (28) for all j involves $\binom{r}{2}$ additions modulo m_j, each of which takes $O(e_r)$ cycles, plus $\binom{r}{2}$ multiplications by c_{ij}, modulo m_j. The calculation of w by formula (29) involves r additions and r multiplications by m_j; it is easy to multiply by m_j, since this is just adding, shifting, and subtracting, so it is clear that the evaluation of Eq. (29) takes $O(r^2 e_r)$ cycles. We will soon see that each of the multiplications by c_{ij}, modulo m_j, requires only $O(e_r \log e_r)$ cycles, and therefore *it is possible to complete the entire job of conversion in* $O(r^2 e_r \log e_r)$ *cycles.*

These observations leave us with the following problem to solve: Given relatively prime positive integers e and f with $e < f$, and a nonnegative integer $u < 2^f$, compute the value of $(cu) \bmod (2^f - 1)$, where c is the number such that $(2^e - 1)c \equiv 1 \ (\text{modulo } 2^f - 1)$; this entire computation must be done in $O(f \log f)$ cycles. The result of exercise 4.3.2–6 gives a formula for c that suggests a suitable procedure. First we find the least positive integer b such that

$$be \equiv 1 \ (\text{modulo } f). \tag{30}$$

Euclid's algorithm will discover b in $O((\log f)^3)$ cycles, since it requires $O(\log f)$ iterations when applied to e and f, and each iteration requires $O((\log f)^2)$ cycles. Alternatively, we could be very sloppy here without violating the total time constraint, by simply trying $b = 1, 2$, etc., until (30) is satisfied; such a process would take $O(f \log f)$ cycles in all. Once b has been found, exercise 4.3.2–6 tells us that

$$c = c[b] = \left(\sum_{0 \le j < b} 2^{je} \right) \bmod (2^f - 1). \tag{31}$$

A brute-force multiplication of $(cu) \bmod (2^f - 1)$ would not be good enough to solve the problem, since we do not know how to multiply general f-bit numbers in $O(f \log f)$ cycles. But the special form of c provides a clue: The binary representation of c is composed of bits in a regular pattern, and Eq. (31) shows that the number $c[2b]$ can be obtained in a simple way from $c[b]$. This suggests that we can rapidly multiply a number u by $c[b]$ if we build $c[b]u$ up in $\lg b$ steps in a suitably clever manner, such as the following: Suppose b is

$$b = (b_s \ldots b_2 b_1 b_0)_2$$

in binary notation; we can calculate four sequences a_k, d_k, u_k, v_k defined by

$$
\begin{aligned}
a_0 &= e, & a_k &= 2a_{k-1} \bmod f; \\
d_0 &= b_0 e, & d_k &= (d_{k-1} + b_k \, a_k) \bmod f; \\
u_0 &= u, & u_k &= (u_{k-1} + 2^{a_{k-1}} u_{k-1}) \bmod (2^f - 1); \\
v_0 &= b_0 u, & v_k &= (v_{k-1} + b_k \, 2^{d_{k-1}} u_k) \bmod (2^f - 1).
\end{aligned}
\tag{32}
$$

It is easy to prove by induction on k that

$$
\begin{aligned}
a_k &= (2^k e) \bmod f; & u_k &= (c[2^k]u) \bmod (2^f - 1); \\
d_k &= \big((b_k \ldots b_1 b_0)_2 \, e\big) \bmod f; & v_k &= \big(c[(b_k \ldots b_1 b_0)_2]u\big) \bmod (2^f - 1).
\end{aligned}
\tag{33}
$$

Hence the desired result, $(c[b]u) \bmod (2^f - 1)$, is v_s. The calculation of a_k, d_k, u_k, and v_k from a_{k-1}, d_{k-1}, u_{k-1}, v_{k-1} takes $O(\log f) + O(\log f) + O(f) + O(f) = O(f)$ cycles; consequently the entire calculation can be done in $s\,O(f) = O(f \log f)$ cycles as desired.

The reader will find it instructive to study the ingenious method represented by (32) and (33) very carefully. Similar techniques are discussed in Section 4.6.3.

Schönhage's paper [*Computing* **1** (1966), 182–196] shows that these ideas can be extended to the multiplication of n-bit numbers using $r \approx 2^{\sqrt{2 \lg n}}$ moduli, obtaining a method analogous to Algorithm T. We shall not dwell on the details here, since Algorithm T is always superior; in fact, an even better method is next on our agenda.

C. Discrete Fourier transforms. The critical problem in high-precision multiplication is the determination of "convolution products" such as

$$u_r v_0 + u_{r-1} v_1 + \cdots + u_0 v_r, \tag{34}$$

and there is an intimate relation between convolutions and an important mathematical concept called "Fourier transformation." If $\omega = \exp(2\pi i/K)$ is a Kth root of unity, the one-dimensional Fourier transform of the sequence of complex numbers $(u_0, u_1, \ldots, u_{K-1})$ is defined to be the sequence $(\hat{u}_0, \hat{u}_1, \ldots, \hat{u}_{K-1})$, where

$$\hat{u}_s = \sum_{0 \le t < K} \omega^{st} u_t, \qquad 0 \le s < K. \tag{35}$$

Letting $(\hat{v}_0, \hat{v}_1, \ldots, \hat{v}_{K-1})$ be defined in the same way, as the Fourier transform of $(v_0, v_1, \ldots, v_{K-1})$, it is not difficult to see that $(\hat{u}_0 \hat{v}_0, \hat{u}_1 \hat{v}_1, \ldots, \hat{u}_{K-1} \hat{v}_{K-1})$ is the transform of $(w_0, w_1, \ldots, w_{K-1})$, where

$$
\begin{aligned}
w_r &= u_r v_0 + u_{r-1} v_1 + \cdots + u_0 v_r + u_{K-1} v_{r+1} + \cdots + u_{r+1} v_{K-1} \\
&= \sum_{i+j \equiv r \pmod{K}} u_i v_j.
\end{aligned}
\tag{36}
$$

When $K \geq 2n - 1$ and $u_n = u_{n+1} = \cdots = u_{K-1} = v_n = v_{n+1} = \cdots = v_{K-1} = 0$, the w's are just what we need for multiplication, since the terms $u_{K-1}v_{r+1} + \cdots + u_{r+1}v_{K-1}$ vanish when $0 \leq r \leq 2n - 2$. In other words, *the transform of a convolution product is the ordinary product of the transforms.* This idea is actually a special case of Toom's use of polynomials (see (10)), with x replaced by roots of unity.

If K is a power of 2, the discrete Fourier transform (35) can be obtained quite rapidly when the computations are arranged in a certain way, and so can the inverse transform (determining the w's from the $\hat{w}$'s). This property of Fourier transforms was exploited by V. Strassen in 1968, who discovered how to multiply large numbers faster than was possible under all previously known schemes. He and A. Schönhage later refined the method and published improved procedures in *Computing* **7** (1971), 281–292. Similar ideas, but with all-integer methods, had been worked out independently by J. M. Pollard [*Math. Comp.* **25** (1971), 365–374]. In order to understand their approach to the problem, let us first take a look at the mechanism of fast Fourier transforms.

Given a sequence of $K = 2^k$ complex numbers $(u_0, \ldots, u_{K-1})$, and given the complex number

$$\omega = \exp(2\pi i/K), \tag{37}$$

the sequence $(\hat{u}_0, \ldots, \hat{u}_{K-1})$ defined in (35) can be calculated rapidly by carrying out the following scheme. (In these formulas the parameters s_j and t_j are either 0 or 1, so that each "pass" represents 2^k elementary computations.)

Pass 0. Let $A^{[0]}(t_{k-1}, \ldots, t_0) = u_t$, where $t = (t_{k-1} \ldots t_0)_2$.

Pass 1. Set $A^{[1]}(s_{k-1}, t_{k-2}, \ldots, t_0) \leftarrow$
$$A^{[0]}(0, t_{k-2}, \ldots, t_0) + \omega^{2^{k-1}s_{k-1}} A^{[0]}(1, t_{k-2}, \ldots, t_0).$$

Pass 2. Set $A^{[2]}(s_{k-1}, s_{k-2}, t_{k-3}, \ldots, t_0) \leftarrow$
$$A^{[1]}(s_{k-1}, 0, t_{k-3}, \ldots, t_0) + \omega^{2^{k-2}(s_{k-2}s_{k-1})_2} A^{[1]}(s_{k-1}, 1, t_{k-3}, \ldots, t_0).$$

$\cdots$

Pass k. Set $A^{[k]}(s_{k-1}, \ldots, s_1, s_0) \leftarrow$
$$A^{[k-1]}(s_{k-1}, \ldots, s_1, 0) + \omega^{(s_0 s_1 \ldots s_{k-1})_2} A^{[k-1]}(s_{k-1}, \ldots, s_1, 1).$$

It is fairly easy to prove by induction that we have

$$A^{[j]}(s_{k-1}, \ldots, s_{k-j}, t_{k-j-1}, \ldots, t_0) = \sum_{0 \leq t_{k-1}, \ldots, t_{k-j} \leq 1} \omega^{2^{k-j}(s_{k-j} \ldots s_{k-1})_2 (t_{k-1} \ldots t_{k-j})_2} u_t, \tag{38}$$

where $t = (t_{k-1} \ldots t_1 t_0)_2$, so that

$$A^{[k]}(s_{k-1}, \ldots, s_1, s_0) = \hat{u}_s, \qquad \text{where } s = (s_0 s_1 \ldots s_{k-1})_2. \tag{39}$$

(It is important to notice that the binary digits of s are reversed in the final result (39). Section 4.6.4 contains further discussion of transforms such as this.)

To get the inverse Fourier transform $(u_0, \ldots, u_{K-1})$ from the values of $(\hat{u}_0, \ldots, \hat{u}_{K-1})$, notice that the "double transform" is

$$\hat{\hat{u}}_r = \sum_{0 \leq s < K} \omega^{rs} \hat{u}_s = \sum_{0 \leq s,t < K} \omega^{rs} \omega^{st} u_t$$

$$= \sum_{0 \leq t < K} u_t \left(\sum_{0 \leq s < K} \omega^{s(t+r)} \right) = K u_{(-r) \bmod K}, \qquad (40)$$

since the geometric series $\sum_{0 \leq s < K} \omega^{sj}$ sums to zero unless j is a multiple of K. Therefore the inverse transform can be computed in the same way as the transform itself, except that the final results must be divided by K and shuffled slightly.

Returning to the problem of integer multiplication, suppose we wish to compute the product of two n-bit integers u and v. As in Algorithm T we shall work with groups of bits; let

$$2n \leq 2^k l < 4n, \qquad K = 2^k, \qquad L = 2^l, \qquad (41)$$

and write

$$u = (U_{K-1} \ldots U_1 U_0)_L, \qquad v = (V_{K-1} \ldots V_1 V_0)_L, \qquad (42)$$

regarding u and v as K-place numbers in radix L so that each digit U_j or V_j is an l-bit integer. Actually the leading digits U_j and V_j are zero for all $j \geq K/2$, because $2^{k-1} l \geq n$. We will select appropriate values for k and l later; at the moment our goal is to see what happens in general, so that we can choose k and l intelligently when all the facts are before us.

The next step of the multiplication procedure is to compute the Fourier transforms $(\hat{u}_0, \ldots, \hat{u}_{K-1})$ and $(\hat{v}_0, \ldots, \hat{v}_{K-1})$ of the sequences $(u_0, \ldots, u_{K-1})$ and $(v_0, \ldots, v_{K-1})$, where we define

$$u_t = U_t / 2^{k+l}, \qquad v_t = V_t / 2^{k+l}. \qquad (43)$$

This scaling is done for convenience so that each u_t and v_t is less than 2^{-k}, ensuring that the absolute values $|\hat{u}_s|$ and $|\hat{v}_s|$ will be less than 1 for all s.

An obvious problem arises here, since the complex number ω can't be represented exactly in binary notation. How are we going to compute a reliable Fourier transform? By a stroke of good luck, it turns out that everything will work properly if we do the calculations with only a modest amount of precision. For the moment let us bypass this question and assume that infinite-precision calculations are being performed; we shall analyze later how much accuracy is actually needed.

Once the $\hat{u}_s$ and $\hat{v}_s$ have been found, we let $\hat{w}_s = \hat{u}_s \hat{v}_s$ for $0 \leq s < K$ and determine the inverse Fourier transform $(w_0, \ldots, w_{K-1})$. As explained above, we now have

$$w_r = \sum_{i+j=r} u_i v_j = \sum_{i+j=r} U_i V_j / 2^{2k+2l},$$

Table 1

MULTIPLICATION VIA DISCRETE FOURIER TRANSFORMATION

s	$2^7\hat{u}_s$	$2^7\hat{v}_s$	$2^{14}\hat{w}_s$	$2^{14}\hat{\hat{w}}_s$	$2^{14}w_s = W_s$
0	19	16	304	80	10
1	$2 + 4i + 13\omega$	$5 + 9i + 2\omega$	$-26 + 64i + 69\omega - 125\bar{\omega}$	0	69
2	$-2 + 13i$	$-4 + 2i$	$-18 - 56i$	0	64
3	$2 - 4i - 13\bar{\omega}$	$5 - 9i - 2\bar{\omega}$	$-26 - 64i + 125\omega - 69\bar{\omega}$	0	125
4	-7	12	-84	288	36
5	$2 + 4i - 13\omega$	$5 + 9i - 2\omega$	$-26 + 64i - 69\omega + 125\bar{\omega}$	1000	0
6	$-2 - 13i$	$-4 - 2i$	$-18 + 56i$	512	0
7	$2 - 4i + 13\bar{\omega}$	$5 - 9i + 2\bar{\omega}$	$-26 - 64i - 125\omega + 69\bar{\omega}$	552	0

so the integers $W_r = 2^{2k+2l}w_r$ are the coefficients in the desired product

$$u \cdot v = W_{K-2} L^{K-2} + \cdots + W_1 L + W_0. \tag{44}$$

Since $0 \le W_r < (r+1)L^2 < KL^2$, each W_r has at most $k + 2l$ bits, so it will not be difficult to compute the binary representation when the W's are known unless k is large compared to l.

For example, suppose we want to multiply $u = 1234$ times $v = 2341$ when the parameters are $k = 3$ and $l = 4$. The computation of $(\hat{u}_0, \ldots, \hat{u}_7)$ from u proceeds as follows $\big($see $(12)\big)$:

$(r,s,t) =$	$(0,0,0)$	$(0,0,1)$	$(0,1,0)$	$(0,1,1)$	$(1,0,0)$	$(1,0,1)$	$(1,1,0)$	$(1,1,1)$
$2^7 A^{[0]}(r,s,t) =$	2	13	4	0	0	0	0	0
$2^7 A^{[1]}(r,s,t) =$	2	13	4	0	2	13	4	0
$2^7 A^{[2]}(r,s,t) =$	6	13	-2	13	$2 + 4i$	13	$2 - 4i$	13
$2^7 A^{[3]}(r,s,t) =$	19	-7	$-2 + 13i$	$-2 - 13i$	$\alpha + \beta$	$\alpha - \beta$	$\bar{\alpha} - \bar{\beta}$	$\bar{\alpha} + \bar{\beta}$

Here $\alpha = 2 + 4i$, $\beta = 13\omega$, and $\omega = (1+i)/\sqrt{2}$; this gives us the column headed $2^7\hat{u}_s$ in Table 1. The column for $\hat{v}_s$ is obtained from v in the same way; then we multiply $\hat{u}_s$ by $\hat{v}_s$ to get $\hat{w}_s$. Transforming again gives us w_s and W_s, using relation (40). Once again we obtain the convolution products in (19), this time using complex numbers instead of sticking to an all-integer method.

Let us try to estimate how much time this method takes on large numbers, if m-bit fixed point arithmetic is used in calculating the Fourier transforms. Exercise 10 shows that all of the quantities $A^{[j]}$ during all the passes of the transform calculations will be less than 1 in magnitude because of the scaling (43), hence it suffices to deal with m-bit fractions $(.a_{-1} \ldots a_{-m})_2$ for the real and imaginary parts of all the intermediate quantities. Simplifications are possible because the inputs u_t and v_t are real-valued; only K real values instead of $2K$ need to be carried in each step (see exercise 4.6.4–14). We will ignore such refinements in order to keep complications to a minimum.

The first job is to compute ω and its powers. For simplicity we shall make a table of the values $\omega^0, \ldots, \omega^{K-1}$. Let

$$\omega_r = \exp(2\pi i/2^r), \tag{45}$$

so that $\omega_1 = -1$, $\omega_2 = i$, $\omega_3 = (1 + i)/\sqrt{2}$, ..., $\omega_k = \omega$. If $\omega_r = x_r + iy_r$ and $r \geq 2$, we have $\omega_{r+1} = x_{r+1} + iy_{r+1}$ where

$$x_{r+1} = \sqrt{\frac{1 + x_r}{2}}, \qquad y_{r+1} = \frac{y_r}{2x_{r+1}}. \qquad (46)$$

[See S. R. Tate, *IEEE Transactions* **SP-43** (1995), 1709–1711.] The calculation of ω_1, ω_2, ..., ω_k takes negligible time compared with the other computations we need, so we can use any straightforward algorithm for square roots. Once the ω_r have been calculated we can compute all of the powers ω^j by noting that

$$\omega^j = \omega_1^{j_{k-1}} \ldots \omega_{k-1}^{j_1} \omega_k^{j_0} \qquad \text{if } j = (j_{k-1} \ldots j_1 j_0)_2. \qquad (47)$$

This method of calculation keeps errors from propagating, since each ω^j is a product of at most k of the ω_r's. The total time to calculate all the ω^j is $O(KM)$, where M is the time to do an m-bit complex multiplication, because only one multiplication is needed to obtain each ω^j from a previously computed value. The subsequent steps will require more than $O(KM)$ cycles, so the powers of ω have been computed at negligible cost.

Each of the three Fourier transformations comprises k passes, each of which involves K operations of the form $a \leftarrow b + \omega^j c$, so the total time to calculate the Fourier transforms is

$$O(kKM) = O(Mnk/l).$$

Finally, the work involved in computing the binary digits of $u \cdot v$ using (44) is $O(K(k+l)) = O(n + nk/l)$. Summing over all operations, we find that the total time to multiply n-bit numbers u and v will be $O(n) + O(Mnk/l)$.

Now let's see how large the intermediate precision m needs to be, so that we know how large M needs to be. For simplicity we shall be content with safe estimates of the accuracy, instead of finding the best possible bounds. It will be convenient to compute all the ω^j in such a way that our approximations $(\omega^j)'$ will satisfy $|(\omega^j)'| \leq 1$; this condition is easy to guarantee if we truncate towards zero instead of rounding, because $x_{r+1}^2 + y_{r+1}^2 = (1 + x_r^2 + y_r^2 + 2x_r)/(2 + 2x_r)$ in (46). The operations we need to perform with m-bit fixed point complex arithmetic are all obtained by replacing an exact computation of the form $a \leftarrow b + \omega^j c$ by the approximate computation

$$a' \leftarrow \text{truncate}\big(b' + (\omega^j)'c'\big), \qquad (48)$$

where b', $(\omega^j)'$, and c' are previously computed approximations; all of these complex numbers and their approximations are bounded by 1 in absolute value. If $|b' - b| \leq \delta_1$, $|(\omega^j)' - \omega^j| \leq \delta_2$, and $|c' - c| \leq \delta_3$, it is not difficult to see that we will have $|a' - a| < \delta + \delta_1 + \delta_2 + \delta_3$, where

$$\delta = |2^{-m} + 2^{-m} i| = 2^{1/2-m}, \qquad (49)$$

because we have $|(\omega^j)'c' - \omega^j c| = |((\omega^j)' - \omega^j)c' + \omega^j(c' - c)| \leq \delta_2 + \delta_3$, and δ exceeds the maximum truncation error. The approximations $(\omega^j)'$ are obtained by starting with approximations ω_r' to the numbers defined in (46), and we may assume that (46) is performed with sufficient precision to make $|\omega_r' - \omega_r| < \delta$. Then (47) implies that $\left|(\omega^j)' - \omega^j\right| < (2k-1)\delta$ for all j, because the error is due to at most k approximations and $k-1$ truncations.

If we have errors of at most ϵ before any pass of the fast Fourier transform, the operations of that pass therefore have the form (48) where $\delta_1 = \delta_3 = \epsilon$ and $\delta_2 = (2k-1)\delta$; the errors after the pass will then be at most $2\epsilon + 2k\delta$. There is no error in Pass 0, so we find by induction on j that the maximum error after Pass j is bounded by $(2^j - 1) \cdot 2k\delta$, and the computed values of $\hat{u}_s$ will satisfy $|(\hat{u}_s)' - \hat{u}_s| < (2^k - 1) \cdot 2k\delta$. A similar formula will hold for $(\hat{v}_s)'$; and we will have

$$|(\hat{w}_s)' - \hat{w}_s| < 2(2^k - 1) \cdot 2k\delta + \delta < (4k2^k - 2k)\delta.$$

During the inverse transformation there is an additional accumulation of errors, but the division by $K = 2^k$ ameliorates most of this; by the same argument we find that the computed values w_r' will satisfy

$$\left|(\hat{w}_r)' - \hat{w}_r\right| < 2^k(4k2^k - 2k)\delta + (2^k - 1)2k\delta; \quad |w_r' - w_r| < 4k2^k\delta. \tag{50}$$

We need enough precision to make $2^{2k+2l} w_r'$ round to the correct integer W_r, hence we need

$$2^{2k+2l+2+\lg k + k + 1/2 - m} \le \tfrac{1}{2}; \tag{51}$$

that is, $m \ge 3k + 2l + \lg k + 7/2$. This will hold if we simply require that

$$k \ge 7 \quad \text{and} \quad m \ge 4k + 2l. \tag{52}$$

Relations (41) and (52) can be used to determine parameters k, l, m so that multiplication takes $O(n) + O(Mnk/l)$ units of time, where M is the time to multiply m-bit fractions.

If we are using MIX, for example, suppose we want to multiply binary numbers having $n = 2^{13} = 8192$ bits each. We can choose $k = 11$, $l = 8$, $m = 60$, so that the necessary m-bit operations are nothing more than double-precision arithmetic. The running time M needed to do fixed point m-bit complex multiplication will therefore be comparatively small. With triple-precision operations we can go up for example to $k = l = 15$, $n \le 15 \cdot 2^{14}$, which takes us way beyond MIX's memory capacity. On a larger machine we could multiply a pair of gigabit numbers if we took $k = l = 27$ and $m = 144$.

Further study of the choice of k, l, and m leads in fact to a rather surprising conclusion: *For all practical purposes we can assume that M is constant, and the Schönhage–Strassen multiplication technique will have a running time linearly proportional to n.* The reason is that we can choose $k = l$ and $m = 6k$; this choice of k is always less than $\lg n$, so we will never need to use more than sextuple precision unless n is larger than the word size of our computer. (In particular, n would have to be larger than the capacity of an index register, so we probably couldn't fit the numbers u and v in main memory.)

The practical problem of fast multiplication is therefore solved, except for improvements in the constant factor. In fact, the all-integer convolution algorithm of exercise 4.6.4–59 is probably a better choice for practical high-precision multiplication. Our interest in multiplying large numbers is partly theoretical, however, because it is interesting to explore the ultimate limits of computational complexity. So let's forget practical considerations momentarily and suppose that n is extremely huge, perhaps much larger than the number of atoms in the universe. We can let m be approximately $6 \lg n$, and use the same algorithm recursively to do the m-bit multiplications. The running time will satisfy $T(n) = O\big(nT(\log n)\big)$; hence

$$T(n) \leq C\,n(C \lg n)(C \lg \lg n)(C \lg \lg \lg n)\ldots, \qquad (53)$$

where the product continues until reaching a factor with $\lg \ldots \lg n \leq 2$.

Schönhage and Strassen showed how to improve this theoretical upper bound to $O(n \log n \log \log n)$ in their paper, by using *integer* numbers ω to carry out fast Fourier transforms on integers, modulo numbers of the form $2^e + 1$. This upper bound applies to Turing machines, namely to computers with bounded memory and a finite number of arbitrarily long tapes.

If we allow ourselves a more powerful computer, with random access to any number of words of bounded size, Schönhage has pointed out that the upper bound drops to $O(n \log n)$. For we can choose $k = l$ and $m = 6k$, and we have time to build a complete multiplication table of all possible products xy for $0 \leq x, y < 2^{\lceil m/12 \rceil}$. (The number of such products is 2^k or 2^{k+1}, and we can compute each table entry by addition from one of its predecessors in $O(k)$ steps, hence $O(k2^k) = O(n)$ steps will suffice for the calculation.) In this case M is the time needed to do 12-place arithmetic in radix $2^{\lceil m/12 \rceil}$, and it follows that $M = O(k) = O(\log n)$ because 1-place multiplication can be done by table lookup. (The time to access a word of memory is assumed to be proportional to the number of bits in the address of that word.)

Moreover, Schönhage discovered in 1979 that a *pointer machine* can carry out n-bit multiplication in $O(n)$ steps; see exercise 12. Such devices (which are also called "storage modification machines" and "linking automata") seem to provide the best models of computation when $n \to \infty$, as discussed at the end of Section 2.6. So we can conclude that multiplication in $O(n)$ steps is possible for theoretical purposes as well as in practice.

An unusual general-purpose computer called Little Fermat, with a special ability to multiply large integers rapidly, was designed in 1986 by D. V. Chudnovsky, G. V. Chudnovsky, M. M. Denneau, and S. G. Younis. Its hardware featured fast arithmetic modulo $2^{256} + 1$ on 257-bit words; a convolution of 256-word arrays could then be done using 256 single-word multiplications, together with three discrete transforms that required only addition, subtraction, and shifting. This made it possible to multiply two 10^6-bit integers in less than 0.1 second, based on a pipelined cycle time of approximately 60 nanoseconds [*Proc. Third Int. Conf. on Supercomputing* **2** (International Supercomputing Institute, 1988), 498–499; *Contemporary Math.* **143** (1993), 136].

D. Division. Now that we have efficient routines for multiplication, let's consider the inverse problem. It turns out that division can be performed just as fast as multiplication, except for a constant factor.

To divide an n-bit number u by an n-bit number v, we can first find an n-bit approximation to $1/v$, then multiply by u to get an approximation $\hat{q}$ to u/v; finally, we can make the slight correction necessary to $\hat{q}$ to ensure that $0 \leq u - qv < v$ by using another multiplication. From this reasoning, we see that it suffices to have an efficient way to approximate the reciprocal of an n-bit number. The following algorithm does this, using "Newton's method" as explained at the end of Section 4.3.1.

Algorithm R (*High-precision reciprocal*). Let v have the binary representation $v = (0.v_1 v_2 v_3 \ldots)_2$, where $v_1 = 1$. This algorithm computes an approximation z to $1/v$, such that

$$|z - 1/v| \leq 2^{-n}. \tag{54}$$

R1. [Initial approximation.] Set $z \leftarrow \frac{1}{4} \lfloor 32/(4v_1 + 2v_2 + v_3) \rfloor$ and $k \leftarrow 0$.

R2. [Newtonian iteration.] (At this point we have a number z of the binary form $(xx.xx \ldots x)_2$ with $2^k + 1$ places after the radix point, and $z \leq 2$.) Calculate $z^2 = (xxx.xx \ldots x)_2$ exactly, using a high-speed multiplication routine. Then calculate $V_k z^2$ exactly, where $V_k = (0.v_1 v_2 \ldots v_{2^{k+1}+3})_2$. Then set $z \leftarrow 2z - V_k z^2 + r$, where $0 \leq r < 2^{-2^{k+1}-1}$ is added if necessary to round z up so that it is a multiple of $2^{-2^{k+1}-1}$. Finally, set $k \leftarrow k + 1$.

R3. [Test for end.] If $2^k < n$, go back to step R2; otherwise the algorithm terminates. ∎

This algorithm is based on a suggestion by S. A. Cook. A similar technique has been used in computer hardware [see Anderson, Earle, Goldschmidt, and Powers, *IBM J. Res. Dev.* **11** (1967), 48–52]. Of course, it is necessary to check the accuracy of Algorithm R quite carefully, because it comes very close to being inaccurate. We will prove by induction that

$$z \leq 2 \qquad \text{and} \qquad |z - 1/v| \leq 2^{-2^k} \tag{55}$$

at the beginning and end of step R2.

For this purpose, let $\delta_k = 1/v - z_k$, where z_k is the value of z after k iterations of step R2. To start the induction on k, we have

$$\delta_0 = 1/v - 8/v' + (32/v' - \lfloor 32/v' \rfloor)/4 = \eta_1 + \eta_2,$$

where $v' = (v_1 v_2 v_3)_2$ and $\eta_1 = (v' - 8v)/vv'$, so that we have $-\frac{1}{2} < \eta_1 \leq 0$ and $0 \leq \eta_2 < \frac{1}{4}$. Hence $|\delta_0| < \frac{1}{2}$. Now suppose that (55) has been verified for k; then

$$
\begin{aligned}
\delta_{k+1} = 1/v - z_{k+1} &= 1/v - z_k - z_k(1 - z_k V_k) - r \\
&= \delta_k - z_k(1 - z_k v) - z_k^2(v - V_k) - r \\
&= \delta_k - (1/v - \delta_k)v\delta_k - z_k^2(v - V_k) - r \\
&= v\delta_k^2 - z_k^2(v - V_k) - r.
\end{aligned}
$$

Now $0 \leq v\delta_k^2 < \delta_k^2 \leq (2^{-2^k})^2 = 2^{-2^{k+1}}$, and

$$0 \leq z^2(v - V_k) + r < 4(2^{-2^{k+1}-3}) + 2^{-2^{k+1}-1} = 2^{-2^{k+1}},$$

so $|\delta_{k+1}| \le 2^{-2^{k+1}}$. We must still verify the first inequality of (55); to show that $z_{k+1} \le 2$, there are three cases:

a) $V_k = \frac{1}{2}$; then $z_{k+1} = 2$.

b) $V_k \ne \frac{1}{2} = V_{k-1}$; then $z_k = 2$, so $2z_k - z_k^2 V_k \le 2 - 2^{-2^{k+1}-1}$.

c) $V_{k-1} \ne \frac{1}{2}$; then $z_{k+1} = 1/v - \delta_{k+1} < 2 - 2^{-2^{k+1}} \le 2$, since $k > 0$.

The running time of Algorithm R is bounded by

$$2T(4n) + 2T(2n) + 2T(n) + 2T(\tfrac{1}{2}n) + \cdots + O(n)$$

steps, where $T(n)$ is an upper bound on the time needed to do a multiplication of n-bit numbers. If $T(n)$ has the form $nf(n)$ for some monotonically nondecreasing function $f(n)$, we have

$$T(4n) + T(2n) + T(n) + \cdots < T(8n), \qquad (56)$$

so division can be done with a speed comparable to that of multiplication except for a constant factor.

R. P. Brent has shown that functions such as $\log x$, $\exp x$, and $\arctan x$ can be evaluated to n significant bits in $O\big(M(n)\log n\big)$ steps, if it takes $M(n)$ units of time to multiply n-bit numbers [*JACM* **23** (1976), 242–251].

E. Multiplication in real time. It is natural to wonder if multiplication of n-bit numbers can be accomplished in just n steps. We have come from order n^2 down to order n, so perhaps we can squeeze the time down to the absolute minimum. In fact, it is actually possible to output the answer as fast as we input the digits, if we leave the domain of conventional computer programming and allow ourselves to build a computer that has an unlimited number of components all acting at once.

A *linear iterative array* of automata is a set of devices M_1, M_2, M_3, ... that can each be in a finite set of "states" at each step of a computation. The machines M_2, M_3, ... all have *identical* circuitry, and their state at time $t + 1$ is a function of their own state at time t as well as the states of their left and right neighbors at time t. The first machine M_1 is slightly different: Its state at time $t + 1$ is a function of its own state and that of M_2, at time t, and also of the *input* at time t. The *output* of a linear iterative array is a function defined on the states of M_1.

Let $u = (u_{n-1} \ldots u_1 u_0)_2$, $v = (v_{n-1} \ldots v_1 v_0)_2$, and $q = (q_{n-1} \ldots q_1 q_0)_2$ be binary numbers, and let $uv + q = w = (w_{2n-1} \ldots w_1 w_0)_2$. It is a remarkable fact that a linear iterative array can be constructed, independent of n, that will output w_0, w_1, w_2, ... at times 1, 2, 3, ..., if it is given the inputs (u_0, v_0, q_0), (u_1, v_1, q_1), (u_2, v_2, q_2), ... at times 0, 1, 2, ...

We can state this phenomenon in the language of computer hardware by saying that it is possible to design a single integrated circuit module with the following property: If we wire together sufficiently many of these chips in a straight line, with each module communicating only with its left and right neighbors, the resulting circuitry will produce the $2n$-bit product of n-bit numbers in exactly $2n$ clock pulses.

Table 2

MULTIPLICATION IN A LINEAR ITERATIVE ARRAY

Time	u_j v_j	q_j	c	x_0 y_0	x_1 y_1	x y	z_2 z_1 z_0	c	x_0 y_0	x_1 y_1	x y	z_2 z_1 z_0	c	x_0 y_0	x_1 y_1	x y	z_2 z_1 z_0
				Module M_1					**Module M_2**					**Module M_3**			
0	1 / 1	1	0	0 / 0	0 / 0	0 / 0	0 0 0	0	0 / 0	0 / 0	0 / 0	0 0 0	0	0 / 0	0 / 0	0 / 0	0 0 0
1	1 / 1	1	1	1 / 1	0 / 0	0 / 0	0 1 0	0	0 / 0	0 / 0	0 / 0	0 0 0	0	0 / 0	0 / 0	0 / 0	0 0 0
2	1 / 1	0	2	1 / 1	1 / 1	0 / 0	1 0 0	0	0 / 0	0 / 0	0 / 0	0 0 0	0	0 / 0	0 / 0	0 / 0	0 0 0
3	0 / 0	1	3	1 / 1	1 / 1	1 / 1	0 1 1	0	0 / 0	0 / 0	0 / 0	0 0 1	0	0 / 0	0 / 0	0 / 0	0 0 0
4	1 / 1	0	3	1 / 1	1 / 1	0 / 0	1 0 1	1	1 / 1	0 / 0	0 / 0	0 0 1	0	0 / 0	0 / 0	0 / 0	0 0 0
5	0 / 0	0	3	1 / 1	1 / 1	1 / 1	0 1 1	2	1 / 1	0 / 0	0 / 0	0 0 1	0	0 / 0	0 / 0	0 / 0	0 0 0
6	0 / 0	0	3	1 / 1	1 / 1	0 / 0	1 0 0	3	1 / 1	0 / 0	1 / 1	0 1 0	0	0 / 0	0 / 0	0 / 0	0 0 0
7	0 / 0	0	3	1 / 1	1 / 1	0 / 0	0 0 0	3	1 / 1	0 / 0	0 / 0	0 1 0	1	1 / 1	0 / 0	0 / 0	0 0 1
8	0 / 0	0	3	1 / 1	1 / 1	0 / 0	0 0 0	3	1 / 1	0 / 0	0 / 0	0 1 0	2	1 / 1	0 / 0	0 / 0	0 0 0
9	0 / 0	0	3	1 / 1	1 / 1	0 / 0	0 0 0	3	1 / 1	0 / 0	0 / 0	0 0 1	3	1 / 1	0 / 0	0 / 0	0 0 0
10	0 / 0	0	3	1 / 1	1 / 1	0 / 0	0 0 1	3	1 / 1	0 / 0	0 / 0	0 0 0	3	1 / 1	0 / 0	0 / 0	0 0 0
11	0 / 0	0	3	1 / 1	1 / 1	0 / 0	0 0 0	3	1 / 1	0 / 0	0 / 0	0 0 0	3	1 / 1	0 / 0	0 / 0	0 0 0

The basic idea can be understood as follows. At time 0, machine M_1 senses (u_0, v_0, q_0) and it therefore is able to output $(u_0 v_0 + q_0) \bmod 2$ at time 1. Then it sees (u_1, v_1, q_1) and it can output $(u_0 v_1 + u_1 v_0 + q_1 + k_1) \bmod 2$, where k_1 is the "carry" left over from the previous step, at time 2. Next it sees (u_2, v_2, q_2) and outputs $(u_0 v_2 + u_1 v_1 + u_2 v_0 + q_2 + k_2) \bmod 2$; furthermore, its state holds the values of u_2 and v_2 so that machine M_2 will be able to sense these values at time 3, and M_2 will be able to compute $u_2 v_2$ for the benefit of M_1 at time 4. Machine M_1 essentially arranges to start M_2 multiplying the sequence (u_2, v_2), (u_3, v_3), $\ldots$, and M_2 will ultimately give M_3 the job of multiplying (u_4, v_4), (u_5, v_5), etc. Fortunately, things just work out so that no time is lost. The reader will find it interesting to deduce further details from the formal description that follows.

Each automaton has 2^{11} states $(c, x_0, y_0, x_1, y_1, x, y, z_2, z_1, z_0)$, where $0 \le c < 4$ and each of the x's, y's, and z's is either 0 or 1. Initially, all the devices are in state $(0,0,0,0,0,0,0,0,0,0)$. Suppose that a machine M_j, for $j > 1$, is in state $(c, x_0, y_0, x_1, y_1, x, y, z_2, z_1, z_0)$ at time t, and its left neighbor M_{j-1} is in state $(c^l, x_0^l, y_0^l, x_1^l, y_1^l, x^l, y^l, z_2^l, z_1^l, z_0^l)$ while its right neighbor M_{j+1} is in state $(c^r, x_0^r, y_0^r, x_1^r, y_1^r, x^r, y^r, z_2^r, z_1^r, z_0^r)$ at that time. Then machine M_j will go into state $(c', x_0', y_0', x_1', y_1', x', y', z_2', z_1', z_0')$ at time $t+1$, where

$$
\begin{aligned}
c' &= \min(c+1, 3) &&\text{if } c^l = 3, &&0 &&\text{otherwise;} \\
(x_0', y_0') &= (x^l, y^l) &&\text{if } c = 0, &&(x_0, y_0) &&\text{otherwise;} \\
(x_1', y_1') &= (x^l, y^l) &&\text{if } c = 1, &&(x_1, y_1) &&\text{otherwise;} \\
(x', y') &= (x^l, y^l) &&\text{if } c \ge 2, &&(x, y) &&\text{otherwise;}
\end{aligned}
\tag{57}
$$

and $(z_2' z_1' z_0')_2$ is the binary notation for

$$
z_0^r + z_1 + z_2^l + \begin{cases}
x^l y^l & \text{if } c = 0; \\
x_0 y^l + x^l y_0 & \text{if } c = 1; \\
x_0 y^l + x_1 y_1 + x^l y_0 & \text{if } c = 2; \\
x_0 y^l + x_1 y + x y_1 + x^l y_0 & \text{if } c = 3.
\end{cases}
\tag{58}
$$

The leftmost machine M_1 behaves in almost the same way as the others; it acts exactly as if there were a machine to its left in state $(3, 0, 0, 0, 0, u, v, q, 0, 0)$ when it is receiving the inputs (u, v, q). The output of the array is the z_0 component of M_1.

Table 2 shows an example of this array acting on the inputs

$$
u = v = (\ldots 00010111)_2, \qquad q = (\ldots 00001011)_2.
$$

The output sequence appears in the lower right portion of the states of M_1:

$$
0, 0, 1, 1, 1, 0, 0, 0, 0, 1, 0, \ldots,
$$

representing the number $(\ldots 01000011100)_2$ from right to left.

This construction is based on a similar one first published by A. J. Atrubin, *IEEE Trans.* **EC-14** (1965), 394–399.

Fast as it is, the iterative array is optimum only when the input bits arrive one at a time. If the input bits are all present simultaneously, we prefer parallel circuitry that will obtain the product of two n-bit numbers after $O(\log n)$ levels of delay. Efficient circuits of that kind have been described, for example, by C. S. Wallace, *IEEE Trans.* **EC-13** (1964), 14–17; D. E. Knuth, *The Stanford GraphBase* (New York: ACM Press, 1994), 270–279.

S. Winograd [*JACM* **14** (1967), 793–802] has investigated the minimum multiplication time achievable in a logical circuit when n is given and when the inputs are available all at once in arbitrarily coded form. For similar questions when multiplication and addition must both be supported simultaneously, see A. C. Yao, *STOC* **13** (1981), 308–311; Mansour, Nisan, and Tiwari, *STOC* **22** (1990), 235–243.

> *Multiplication is mie vexation,*
> *And Division is quite as bad:*
> *The Golden Rule is mie stumbling stule,*
> *And Practice drives me mad.*
>
> — Manuscript collected by J. O. HALLIWELL (c. 1570)

EXERCISES

1. [*22*] The idea expressed in (2) can be generalized to the decimal system, if the radix 2 is replaced by 10. Using this generalization, calculate 1234 times 2341 (reducing this product of four-digit numbers to three products of two-digit numbers, and reducing each of the latter to products of one-digit numbers).

2. [*M22*] Prove that, in step T1 of Algorithm T, the value of R either stays the same or increases by one when we set $R \leftarrow \lfloor \sqrt{Q} \rfloor$. (Therefore, as observed in that step, we need not calculate a square root.)

3. [*M22*] Prove that the sequences q_k and r_k defined in Algorithm T satisfy the inequality $2^{q_k+1}(2r_k)^{r_k} \leq 2^{q_{k-1}+q_k}$, when $k > 0$.

▶ **4.** [*28*] (K. Baker.) Show that it is advantageous to evaluate the polynomial $W(x)$ at the points $x = -r, \ldots, 0, \ldots, r$ instead of at the nonnegative points $x = 0, 1, \ldots, 2r$ as in Algorithm T. The polynomial $U(x)$ can be written

$$U(x) = U_e(x^2) + xU_o(x^2),$$

and similarly $V(x)$ and $W(x)$ can be expanded in this way; show how to exploit this idea, obtaining faster calculations in steps T7 and T8.

▶ **5.** [*35*] Show that if in step T1 of Algorithm T we set $R \leftarrow \lceil \sqrt{2Q} \rceil + 1$ instead of setting $R \leftarrow \lfloor \sqrt{Q} \rfloor$, with suitable initial values of q_0, q_1, r_0, and r_1, then (20) can be improved to $t_k \leq q_{k+1} 2^{\sqrt{2 \lg q_{k+1}}} (\lg q_{k+1})$.

6. [*M23*] Prove that the six numbers in (24) are relatively prime in pairs.

7. [*M23*] Prove (25).

8. [*M20*] True or false: We can ignore the bit reversal $(s_{k-1}, \ldots, s_0) \to (s_0, \ldots, s_{k-1})$ in (39), because the inverse Fourier transform will reverse the bits again anyway.

9. [*M15*] Suppose the Fourier transformation method of the text is applied with all occurrences of ω replaced by ω^q, where q is some fixed integer. Find a simple relation between the numbers $(\tilde{u}_0, \tilde{u}_1, \ldots, \tilde{u}_{K-1})$ obtained by this general procedure and the numbers $(\hat{u}_0, \hat{u}_1, \ldots, \hat{u}_{K-1})$ obtained when $q = 1$.

10. [*M26*] The scaling in (43) makes it clear that all the complex numbers $A^{[j]}$ computed by pass j of the transformation subroutine will be less than 2^{j-k} in absolute value, during the calculations of $\hat{u}_s$ and $\hat{v}_s$ in the Schönhage–Strassen multiplication algorithm. Show that all of the $A^{[j]}$ will be less than 1 in absolute value during the *third* Fourier transformation (the calculation of $\hat{w}_r$).

▶ **11.** [*M26*] If n is fixed, how many of the automata in the linear iterative array defined by (57) and (58) are needed to compute the product of n-bit numbers? (Notice that the automaton M_j is influenced only by the component z_0^r of the machine on its right, so we may remove all automata whose z_0 component is always zero whenever the inputs are n-bit numbers.)

▶ **12.** [*M41*] (A. Schönhage.) The purpose of this exercise is to prove that a simple form of pointer machine can multiply n-bit numbers in $O(n)$ steps. The machine has no built-in facilities for arithmetic; all it does is work with nodes and pointers. Each node has the same finite number of link fields, and there are finitely many link registers. The only operations this machine can do are:

i) read one bit of input and jump if that bit is 0;

ii) output 0 or 1;

iii) load a register with the contents of another register or with the contents of a link field in a node pointed to by a register;

iv) store the contents of a register into a link field in a node pointed to by a register;

v) jump if two registers are equal;

vi) create a new node and make a register point to it;

vii) halt.

Implement the Fourier-transform multiplication method efficiently on such a machine. [*Hints:* First show that if N is any positive integer, it is possible to create N nodes representing the integers $\{0, 1, \ldots, N-1\}$, where the node representing p has pointers to the nodes representing $p+1$, $\lfloor p/2 \rfloor$, and $2p$. These nodes can be created in $O(N)$ steps. Show that arithmetic with radix N can now be simulated without difficulty: For example, it takes $O(\log N)$ steps to find the node for $(p+q) \bmod N$ and to determine if $p+q \geq N$, given pointers to p and q; and multiplication can be simulated in $O(\log N)^2$ steps. Now consider the algorithm in the text, with $k = l$ and $m = 6k$ and $N = 2^{\lceil m/13 \rceil}$, so that all quantities in the fixed point arithmetic calculations are 13-place integers with radix N. Finally, show that each pass of the fast Fourier transformations can be done in $O(K + (N \log N)^2) = O(K)$ steps, using the following idea: Each of the K necessary assignments can be "compiled" into a bounded list of instructions for a simulated MIX-like computer whose word size is N, and instructions for K such machines acting in parallel can be simulated in $O(K + (N \log N)^2)$ steps if they are first sorted so that all identical instructions are performed together. (Two instructions are identical if they have the same operation code, the same register contents, and the same memory operand contents.) Note that $N^2 = O(n^{12/13})$, so $(N \log N)^2 = O(K)$.]

13. [*M25*] (A. Schönhage.) What is a good upper bound on the time needed to multiply an m-bit number by an n-bit number, when both m and n are very large but n is much larger than m, based on the results discussed in this section for the case $m = n$?

14. [*M42*] Write a program for Algorithm T, incorporating the improvements of exercise 4. Compare it with a program for Algorithm 4.3.1M and with a program based on (2), to see how large n must be before Algorithm T is an improvement.

15. [*M49*] (S. A. Cook.) A multiplication algorithm is said to be *online* if the $(k+1)$st input bits of the operands, from right to left, are not read until the kth output bit has been produced. What are the fastest possible online multiplication algorithms achievable on various species of automata?

▶ **16.** [*25*] Prove that it takes only $O(K \log K)$ arithmetic operations to evaluate the discrete Fourier transform (35), even when K is not a power of 2. [*Hint:* Rewrite (35) in the form

$$\hat{u}_s = \omega^{-s^2/2} \sum_{0 \le t < K} \omega^{(s+t)^2/2} \omega^{-t^2/2} u_t$$

and express this sum as a convolution product.]

17. [*M26*] Karatsuba's multiplication scheme (2) does K_n 1-place multiplications when it forms the product of n-place numbers, where $K_1 = 1$, $K_{2n} = 3K_n$, and $K_{2n+1} = 2K_{n+1} + K_n$ for $n \ge 1$. "Solve" this recurrence by finding an explicit formula for K_n when $n = 2^{e_1} + 2^{e_2} + \cdots + 2^{e_t}$, $e_1 > e_2 > \cdots > e_t \ge 0$.

▶ **18.** [*M30*] Devise a scheme to allocate memory for the intermediate results when multiplication is performed by a recursive algorithm based on (2): Given two N-place integers u and v, each in N consecutive places of memory, show how to arrange the computation so that the product uv appears in the least significant $2N$ places of a $(3N + O(\log N))$-place area of working storage.

▶ **19.** [*M23*] Show how to compute $uv \bmod m$ with a bounded number of operations that meet the ground rules of exercise 3.2.1.1–11, if you are also allowed to test whether one operand is less than another. Both u and v are variable, but m is constant. *Hint:* Consider the decomposition in (2).

4.4. RADIX CONVERSION

IF OUR ANCESTORS had invented arithmetic by counting with their two fists or
their eight fingers, instead of their ten "digits," we would never have to worry
about writing binary-decimal conversion routines. (And we would perhaps never
have learned as much about number systems.) In this section, we shall discuss
the conversion of numbers from positional notation with one radix into positional
notation with another radix; this process is, of course, most important on binary
computers when converting decimal input data into binary form, and converting
binary answers into decimal form.

A. The four basic methods. Binary-decimal conversion is one of the most
machine-dependent operations of all, since computer designers keep inventing
different ways to provide for it in the hardware. Therefore we shall discuss
only the general principles involved, from which programmers can select the
procedures that are best suited to their machines.

We shall assume that only nonnegative numbers enter into the conversion,
since the manipulation of signs is easily accounted for.

Let us assume that we are converting from radix b to radix B. (Mixed-
radix generalizations are considered in exercises 1 and 2.) Most radix-conversion
routines are based on multiplication and division, using one of the four methods
below. The first two methods apply to integers (radix point at the right), and the
others to fractions (radix point at the left). It is often impossible to express a terminating radix-b fraction $(0.u_{-1}u_{-2}\dots u_{-m})_b$ *exactly* as a terminating radix-B
fraction $(0.U_{-1}U_{-2}\dots U_{-M})_B$. For example, the fraction $\frac{1}{10}$ has the infinite
binary representation $(0.0001100110011\dots)_2$. Therefore methods of rounding
the result to M places are sometimes necessary.

Method 1a (Division by B using radix-b arithmetic). Given an integer u, we
can obtain its radix-B representation $(\dots U_2U_1U_0)_B$ as follows:

$$U_0 = u \bmod B, \quad U_1 = \lfloor u/B \rfloor \bmod B, \quad U_2 = \lfloor \lfloor u/B \rfloor / B \rfloor \bmod B, \quad \dots,$$

stopping when $\lfloor \dots \lfloor \lfloor u/B \rfloor / B \rfloor \dots / B \rfloor = 0$.

Method 1b (Multiplication by b using radix-B arithmetic). If u has the radix-b
representation $(u_m \dots u_1 u_0)_b$, we can use radix-B arithmetic to evaluate the
polynomial $u_m b^m + \dots + u_1 b + u_0 = u$ in the form

$$\big((\dots (u_m\, b + u_{m-1})\, b + \dots)\, b + u_1 \big)\, b + u_0.$$

Method 2a (Multiplication by B using radix-b arithmetic). Given a fractional
number u, we can obtain the digits of its radix-B representation $(.U_{-1}U_{-2}\dots)_B$
as follows:

$$U_{-1} = \lfloor uB \rfloor, \quad U_{-2} = \lfloor \{uB\}B \rfloor, \quad U_{-3} = \lfloor \{\{uB\}B\}B \rfloor, \quad \dots,$$

where $\{x\}$ denotes $x \bmod 1 = x - \lfloor x \rfloor$. If it is desired to round the result
to M places, the computation can be stopped after U_{-M} has been calculated,

and U_{-M} should be increased by unity if $\{\dots\{\{uB\}B\}\dots B\}$ is greater than $\frac{1}{2}$. (Note, however, that this may cause carries to propagate, and these carries must be incorporated into the answer using radix-B arithmetic. It would be simpler to add the constant $\frac{1}{2}B^{-M}$ to the original number u before the calculation begins, but this may lead to an incorrect answer when $\frac{1}{2}B^{-M}$ cannot be represented exactly as a radix-b number inside the computer. Note further that it is possible for the answer to round up to $(1.00\dots0)_B$, if $b^m \geq 2B^M$.)

Exercise 3 shows how to extend this method so that M is *variable*, just large enough to represent the original number to a specified accuracy. In this case the problem of carries does not occur.

Method 2b (Division by b using radix-B arithmetic). If u has the radix-b representation $(0.u_{-1}u_{-2}\dots u_{-m})_b$, we can use radix-$B$ arithmetic to evaluate $u_{-1}b^{-1} + u_{-2}b^{-2} + \cdots + u_{-m}b^{-m}$ in the form

$$\big((\dots(u_{-m}/b + u_{1-m})/b + \cdots + u_{-2})/b + u_{-1}\big)/b.$$

Care should be taken to control errors that might occur due to truncation or rounding in the division by b; these are often negligible, but not always.

To summarize, Methods 1a, 1b, 2a, and 2b give us two ways to convert integers and two ways to convert fractions; and it is certainly possible to convert between integers and fractions by multiplying or dividing by an appropriate power of b or B. Therefore there are at least four methods to choose from when trying to do radix conversion.

B. Single-precision conversion. To illustrate these four methods, let us assume that MIX is a binary computer, and suppose that we want to convert a nonnegative binary integer u to a decimal integer. Thus $b = 2$ and $B = 10$. Method 1a could be programmed as follows:

```
      ENT1 0          Set j ← 0.
      LDX  U
      ENTA 0          Set rAX ← u.
 1H   DIV  =10=       (rA,rX) ← (⌊rAX/10⌋, rAX mod 10).        (1)
      STX  ANSWER,1   U_j ← rX.
      INC1 1          j ← j + 1.
      SRAX 5          rAX ← rA.
      JXP  1B         Repeat until result is zero.  ∎
```

This requires $18M + 4$ cycles to obtain M digits.

Method 1a uses division by 10; Method 2a uses *multiplication* by 10, so it might be a little faster. But in order to use Method 2a, we must deal with fractions, and this leads to an interesting situation. Let w be the word size of the computer, and assume that $u < 10^n < w$. With a single division we can find q and r, where

$$wu = 10^n q + r, \qquad 0 \leq r < 10^n. \tag{2}$$

Now if we apply Method 2a to the fraction $(q+1)/w$, we will obtain the digits of u from left to right, in n steps, since

$$\left\lfloor 10^n \frac{q+1}{w} \right\rfloor = \left\lfloor u + \frac{10^n - r}{w} \right\rfloor = u. \tag{3}$$

(This idea is due to P. A. Samet, *Software Practice & Experience* **1** (1971), 93–96.)

Here is the corresponding MIX program:

```
      JOV   OFLO        Ensure that overflow is off.
      LDA   U
      LDX   =10ⁿ=       rAX ← wu + 10ⁿ.
      DIV   =10ⁿ=       rA ← q + 1, rX ← r.
      JOV   ERROR       Jump if u ≥ 10ⁿ.
      ENT1  n-1         Set j ← n − 1.                           (4)
2H    MUL   =10=        Now imagine the radix point at the left, rA = x.
      STA   ANSWER,1    Set Uⱼ ← ⌊10x⌋.
      SLAX  5           x ← {10x}.
      DEC1  1           j ← j − 1.
      J1NN  2B          Repeat for n > j ≥ 0.  ∎
```

This slightly longer routine requires $16n + 19$ cycles, so it is a little faster than program (1) if $n = M \geq 8$; when leading zeros are present, (1) will be faster.

Program (4) as it stands cannot be used to convert integers $u \geq 10^m$ when $10^m < w < 10^{m+1}$, since we would need to take $n = m + 1$. In this case we can obtain the leading digit of u by computing $\lfloor u/10^m \rfloor$; then $u \bmod 10^m$ can be converted as above with $n = m$.

The fact that the answer digits are obtained from left to right may be an advantage in some applications (for example, when typing out an answer one digit at a time). Thus we see that a fractional method can be used for conversion of integers, although the use of inexact division makes a little bit of numerical analysis necessary.

We can avoid the division by 10 in Method 1a if we do two multiplications instead. This alternative can be important, because radix conversion is often done by "satellite" computers that have no built-in division capability. If we let x be an approximation to $\frac{1}{10}$, so that

$$\frac{1}{10} < x < \frac{1}{10} + \frac{1}{w},$$

it is easy to prove (see exercise 7) that $\lfloor ux \rfloor = \lfloor u/10 \rfloor$ or $\lfloor u/10 \rfloor + 1$, so long as $0 \leq u < w$. Therefore, if we compute $u - 10\lfloor ux \rfloor$, we will be able to determine the value of $\lfloor u/10 \rfloor$:

$$\lfloor u/10 \rfloor = \lfloor ux \rfloor - \big[u < 10\lfloor ux \rfloor \big]. \tag{5}$$

At the same time we will have determined $u \bmod 10$. A MIX program for conversion using (5) appears in exercise 8; it requires about 33 cycles per digit.

If the computer has neither division nor multiplication in its repertoire of built-in instructions, we can still use Method 1a for conversion by judiciously shifting and adding, as explained in exercise 9.

Another way to convert from binary to decimal is to use Method 1b, but to do this we need to simulate doubling in a *decimal* number system. This approach is generally most suitable for incorporation into computer hardware; however, it is possible to program the doubling process for decimal numbers, using binary addition, binary shifting, and binary extraction or masking (bitwise AND) as shown in Table 1, which was suggested by Peter L. Montgomery.

Table 1
DOUBLING A BINARY-CODED DECIMAL NUMBER

Operation	General form	Example
1. Given number	$u_{11}\,u_{10}\,u_9\,u_8\ \ u_7\,u_6\,u_5\,u_4\ \ u_3\,u_2\,u_1\,u_0$	$0011\,0110\,1001 = 3\,6\,9$
2. Add 3 to each digit	$v_{11}\,v_{10}\,v_9\,v_8\ \ v_7\,v_6\,v_5\,v_4\ \ v_3\,v_2\,v_1\,v_0$	$0110\,1001\,1100$
3. Extract each high bit	$v_{11}\ \ 0\ \ 0\ \ 0\ \ v_7\,0\ \ 0\ \ 0\ \ v_3\,0\ \ 0\ \ 0$	$0000\,1000\,1000$
4. Shift right 2 and subtract	$0\ \ v_{11}\,v_{11}0\ \ 0\ \ v_7\,v_7\,0\ \ 0\ \ v_3\,v_3\,0$	$0000\,0110\,0110$
5. Add original number	$w_{11}w_{10}w_9w_8\ \ w_7w_6w_5w_4\ \ w_3w_2w_1w_0$	$0011\,1100\,1111$
6. Add original number	$x_{12}\,x_{11}\,x_{10}\,x_9\,x_8\ \ x_7\,x_6\,x_5\,x_4\ \ x_3\,x_2\,x_1\,x_0$	$0\,0111\,0011\,1000 = 7\,3\,8$

This method changes each individual digit d into $2d$ when $0 \le d \le 4$, and into $6 + 2d = (2d - 10) + 2^4$ when $5 \le d \le 9$; and that is just what is needed to double decimal numbers encoded with 4 bits per digit.

Another related idea is to keep a table of the powers of two in decimal form, and to add the appropriate powers together by simulating decimal addition. A survey of bit-manipulation techniques appears in Section 7.1.

Finally, even Method 2b can be used for the conversion of binary integers to decimal integers. We can find q as in (2), and then we can simulate the decimal division of $q + 1$ by w, using a "halving" process (exercise 10) that is similar to the doubling process just described, retaining only the first n digits to the right of the radix point in the answer. In this situation, Method 2b does not seem to offer advantages over the other three methods already discussed, but we have confirmed the remark made earlier that at least four distinct methods are available for converting integers from one radix to another.

Now let us consider decimal-to-binary conversion (so that $b = 10$, $B = 2$). Method 1a simulates a decimal division by 2; this is feasible (see exercise 10), but it is primarily suitable for incorporation in hardware instead of programs.

Method 1b is the most practical method for decimal-to-binary conversion in the great majority of cases. The following MIX code assumes that there are at least two digits in the number $(u_m \ldots u_1 u_0)_{10}$ being converted, and that $10^{m+1} < w$ so that overflow is not an issue:

```
    ENT1 M-1        Set j ← m − 1.
    LDA  INPUT+M    Set U ← u_m.
1H  MUL  =10=
    SLAX 5                                          (6)
    ADD  INPUT,1    U ← 10U + u_j.
    DEC1 1
    J1NN 1B         Repeat for m > j ≥ 0.   ▌
```

The multiplication by 10 could be replaced by shifting and adding.

A trickier but perhaps faster method, which uses about $\lg m$ multiplications, extractions, and additions instead of $m − 1$ multiplications and additions, is described in exercise 19.

For the conversion of decimal fractions $(0.u_{-1} u_{-2} \ldots u_{-m})_{10}$ to binary form, we can use Method 2b; or, more commonly, we can first convert the integer $(u_{-1} u_{-2} \ldots u_{-m})_{10}$ by Method 1b and then divide by 10^m.

C. Hand calculation. It is occasionally necessary for computer programmers to convert numbers by hand, and since this is a subject not yet taught in elementary schools, it may be worthwhile to examine it briefly here. There are simple pencil-and-paper methods for converting between decimal and octal notations, and these methods are easily learned, so they should be more widely known.

Converting octal integers to decimal. The simplest conversion is from octal to decimal; this technique was apparently first published by Walter Soden, *Math. Comp.* **7** (1953), 273–274. To do the conversion, write down the given octal number; then at the kth step, double the k leading digits using decimal arithmetic, and subtract this from the $k + 1$ leading digits using decimal arithmetic. The process terminates in m steps if the given number has $m + 1$ digits. It is a good idea to insert a radix point to show which digits are being doubled, as shown in the following example, in order to prevent embarrassing mistakes.

Example 1. Convert $(5325121)_8$ to decimal.

$$
\begin{array}{r}
5.3\ 2\ 5\ 1\ 2\ 1 \\
-\ 1\ 0 \\
\hline
4\ 3.2\ 5\ 1\ 2\ 1 \\
-\ \ \ 8\ 6 \\
\hline
3\ 4\ 6.5\ 1\ 2\ 1 \\
-\ \ \ 6\ 9\ 2 \\
\hline
2\ 7\ 7\ 3.1\ 2\ 1 \\
-\ \ \ 5\ 5\ 4\ 6 \\
\hline
2\ 2\ 1\ 8\ 5.2\ 1 \\
-\ \ \ 4\ 4\ 3\ 7\ 0 \\
\hline
1\ 7\ 7\ 4\ 8\ 2.1 \\
-\ \ \ 3\ 5\ 4\ 9\ 6\ 4 \\
\hline
1\ 4\ 1\ 9\ 8\ 5\ 7 \qquad \textit{Answer: } (1419857)_{10}.
\end{array}
$$

A reasonably good check on the computations may be had by "casting out nines": The sum of the digits of the decimal number must be congruent modulo 9 to the alternating sum and difference of the digits of the octal number, with the rightmost digit of the latter given a plus sign. In the example above, we have $1 + 4 + 1 + 9 + 8 + 5 + 7 = 35$, and $1 - 2 + 1 - 5 + 2 - 3 + 5 = -1$; the difference is 36 (a multiple of 9). If this test fails, it can be applied to the $k + 1$ leading digits after the kth step, and the error can be located using a "binary search" procedure; in other words, we can locate the error by first checking the middle result, then using the same procedure on the first or second half of the calculation, depending on whether the middle result is incorrect or correct.

The "casting-out-nines" process is only about 89 percent reliable, because there is one chance in nine that two *random* integers will differ by a multiple of nine. An even better check is to convert the answer back to octal by using an inverse method, which we shall now consider.

Converting decimal integers to octal. A similar procedure can be used for the opposite conversion: Write down the given decimal number; then at the kth step, double the k leading digits using *octal* arithmetic, and *add* these to the $k + 1$ leading digits using *octal* arithmetic. The process terminates in m steps if the given number has $m + 1$ digits.

Example 2. Convert $(1419857)_{10}$ to octal.

$$
\begin{array}{r}
1\;.4\;\;1\;\;9\;\;8\;\;5\;\;7 \\
+\quad 2 \qquad\qquad\qquad\quad \\
\hline
1\;\;6\;.1\;\;9\;\;8\;\;5\;\;7 \\
+\quad 3\;\;4 \qquad\qquad\qquad \\
\hline
2\;\;1\;\;5\;.9\;\;8\;\;5\;\;7 \\
+\quad 4\;\;3\;\;2 \qquad\qquad \\
\hline
2\;\;6\;\;1\;\;3\;.8\;\;5\;\;7 \\
+\quad 5\;\;4\;\;2\;\;6 \qquad\quad \\
\hline
3\;\;3\;\;5\;\;6\;\;6\;.5\;\;7 \\
+\quad 6\;\;7\;\;3\;\;5\;\;4 \quad\; \\
\hline
4\;\;2\;\;5\;\;2\;\;4\;\;1\;.7 \\
+\;1\;\;0\;\;5\;\;2\;\;5\;\;0\;\;2 \\
\hline
5\;\;3\;\;2\;\;5\;\;1\;\;2\;\;1 \\
\end{array}
\qquad \textit{Answer: } (5325121)_8.
$$

(Notice that the nonoctal digits 8 and 9 enter into this octal computation.) The answer can be checked as discussed above. This method was published by Charles P. Rozier, *IEEE Trans.* **EC-11** (1962), 708–709.

The two procedures just given are essentially Method 1b of the general radix-conversion procedures. Doubling and subtracting in decimal notation is like multiplying by $10 - 2 = 8$; doubling and adding in octal notation is like multiplying by $8 + 2 = 10$. There is a similar method for hexadecimal/decimal conversions, but it is a little more difficult since it involves multiplication by 6 instead of by 2.

To keep these two methods straight in our minds, it is not hard to remember that we must subtract to go from octal to decimal, since the decimal representation of a number is smaller; similarly we must add to go from decimal to octal. The computations are performed using the radix of the *answer*, not the radix of the given number, otherwise we couldn't get the desired answer.

Converting fractions. No equally fast method of converting fractions manually is known. The best way seems to be Method 2a, with doubling and adding or subtracting to simplify the multiplications by 10 or by 8. In this case, we reverse the addition-subtraction criterion, adding when we convert to decimal and subtracting when we convert to octal; we also use the radix of the given input number, *not* the radix of the answer, in this computation (see Examples 3 and 4). The process is about twice as hard as the method that we used for integers.

Example 3. Convert $(.14159)_{10}$ to octal.

```
      .1 4 1 5 9
       2 8 3 1 8 −
     ―――――――――――――
    1 .1 3 2 7 2
         2 6 5 4 4 −
       ―――――――――――――
    1 .0 6 1 7 6
           1 2 3 5 2 −
         ―――――――――――――
    0 .4 9 4 0 8
             9 8 8 1 6 −
           ―――――――――――――
    3 .9 5 2 6 4
             1 9 0 5 2 8 −
           ―――――――――――――――
    7 .6 2 1 1 2
               1 2 4 2 2 4 −
             ―――――――――――――――
    4 .9 6 8 9 6        Answer: $(.110374\ldots)_8$.
```

Example 4. Convert $(.110374)_8$ to decimal.

```
      .1 1 0 3 7 4
       2 2 0 7 7 0 +
     ―――――――――――――――
    1 .3 2 4 7 3 0
         6 5 1 6 6 0 +
       ―――――――――――――――
    4 .1 2 1 1 6 0
           2 4 2 3 4 0 +
         ―――――――――――――――
    1 .4 5 4 1 4 0
             1 1 3 0 3 0 0 +
           ―――――――――――――――――
    5 .6 7 1 7 0 0
               1 5 6 3 6 0 0 +
             ―――――――――――――――――
    8 .5 0 2 6 0 0
                 1 2 0 5 4 0 0 +
               ―――――――――――――――――
    6 .2 3 3 4 0 0     Answer: $(.141586\ldots)_{10}$.
```

D. Floating point conversion. When floating point values are to be converted, it is necessary to deal with both the exponent and the fraction parts simultaneously, since conversion of the exponent will affect the fraction part. Given the number $f \cdot 2^e$ to be converted to decimal, we may express 2^e in the form $F \cdot 10^E$ (usually by means of auxiliary tables), and then convert Ff to decimal. Alternatively, we can multiply e by $\log_{10} 2$ and round this to the nearest integer E; then divide $f \cdot 2^e$ by 10^E and convert the result. Conversely, given the number $F \cdot 10^E$ to be converted to binary, we may convert F and then multiply it by the floating point number 10^E (again by using auxiliary tables). Obvious techniques can be used to reduce the maximum size of the auxiliary tables by using several multiplications and/or divisions, although this can cause rounding errors to propagate. Exercise 17 considers the minimization of error.

E. Multiple-precision conversion. When converting extremely long numbers, it is most convenient to start by converting blocks of digits, which can be handled by single-precision techniques, and then to combine these blocks by using simple multiple-precision techniques. For example, suppose that 10^n is the highest power of 10 less than the computer word size. Then:

a) To convert a multiple-precision *integer* from binary to decimal, divide it repeatedly by 10^n (thus converting from binary to radix 10^n by Method 1a). Single-precision operations will give the n decimal digits for each place of the radix-10^n representation.

b) To convert a multiple-precision *fraction* from binary to decimal, proceed similarly, multiplying by 10^n (that is, using Method 2a with $B = 10^n$).

c) To convert a multiple-precision integer from decimal to binary, convert blocks of n digits first; then use Method 1b to convert from radix 10^n to binary.

d) To convert a multiple-precision fraction from decimal to binary, convert first to radix 10^n as in (c), then use Method 2b.

F. History and Bibliography. Radix-conversion techniques implicitly originated in ancient problems dealing with weights, measures, and currencies, where mixed-radix systems were generally involved. Auxiliary tables were usually prepared to help people make the conversions. During the seventeenth century, when sexagesimal fractions were being supplanted by decimal fractions, it was necessary to convert between the two systems in order to use existing books of astronomical tables; a systematic method to transform fractions from radix 60 to radix 10 and vice versa was given in the 1667 edition of William Oughtred's *Clavis Mathematicæ*, Chapter 6, Section 18. (This material was not present in the original 1631 edition of Oughtred's book.) Conversion rules had already been given by al-Kāshī of Samarkand in his *Key to Arithmetic* (1427), where Methods 1a, 1b, and 2a are clearly explained [*Istoriko-Mat. Issled.* **7** (1954), 126–135], but his work was unknown in Europe. The 18th century American mathematician Hugh Jones used the words "octavation" and "decimation" to describe octal/decimal conversions, but his methods were not as clever as his terminology. A. M. Legendre [*Théorie des Nombres* (Paris: 1798), 229] noted that positive integers may be conveniently converted to binary form if they are repeatedly divided by 64.

In 1946, H. H. Goldstine and J. von Neumann gave prominent consideration to radix conversion in their classic memoir, *Planning and Coding Problems for an Electronic Computing Instrument*, because it was necessary to justify the use of binary arithmetic; see John von Neumann, *Collected Works* **5** (New York: Macmillan, 1963), 127–142. Another early discussion of radix conversion on binary computers was published by F. Koons and S. Lubkin, *Math. Comp.* **3** (1949), 427–431, who suggested a rather unusual method. The first discussion of floating point conversion was given somewhat later by F. L. Bauer and K. Samelson [*Zeit. für angewandte Math. und Physik* **4** (1953), 312–316].

The following articles are, similarly, of historic interest: A note by G. T. Lake [*CACM* **5** (1962), 468–469] mentioned some hardware techniques for conversion and gave clear examples. A. H. Stroud and D. Secrest [*Comp. J.* **6** (1963), 62–66] discussed conversion of multiple-precision floating point numbers. The conversion of *unnormalized* floating point numbers, preserving the amount of "significance" implied by the representation, was discussed by H. Kanner [*JACM* **12** (1965), 242–246] and by N. Metropolis and R. L. Ashenhurst [*Math. Comp.* **19** (1965), 435–441]. See also K. Sikdar, *Sankhyā* **B30** (1968), 315–334, and the references cited in his paper.

Detailed subroutines for formatted input and output of integers and floating point numbers in the C programming language have been given by P. J. Plauger in *The Standard C Library* (Prentice–Hall, 1992), 301–331.

EXERCISES

▶ **1.** [*25*] Generalize Method 1b so that it works with arbitrary mixed-radix notations, converting

$$a_m b_{m-1} \ldots b_1 b_0 + \cdots + a_1 b_0 + a_0 \quad \text{into} \quad A_M B_{M-1} \ldots B_1 B_0 + \cdots + A_1 B_0 + A_0,$$

where $0 \le a_j < b_j$ and $0 \le A_J < B_J$ for $0 \le j < m$ and $0 \le J < M$.

Give an example of your generalization by manually converting "3 days, 9 hours, 12 minutes, and 37 seconds" into long tons, hundredweights, stones, pounds, and ounces. (Let one second equal one ounce. The British system of weights has 1 stone = 14 pounds, 1 hundredweight = 8 stone, 1 long ton = 20 hundredweight.) In other words, let $b_0 = 60$, $b_1 = 60$, $b_2 = 24$, $m = 3$, $B_0 = 16$, $B_1 = 14$, $B_2 = 8$, $B_3 = 20$, $M = 4$; the problem is to find $A_4, \ldots, A_0$ in the proper ranges such that $3b_2 b_1 b_0 + 9 b_1 b_0 + 12 b_0 + 37 = A_4 B_3 B_2 B_1 B_0 + A_3 B_2 B_1 B_0 + A_2 B_1 B_0 + A_1 B_0 + A_0$, using a systematic method that generalizes Method 1b. (All arithmetic is to be done in a mixed-radix system.)

2. [*25*] Generalize Method 1a so that it works with mixed-radix notations, as in exercise 1, and give an example of your generalization by manually solving the same conversion problem stated in exercise 1.

▶ **3.** [*25*] (D. Taranto.) When fractions are being converted, there is no obvious way to decide how many digits to give in the answer. Design a simple generalization of Method 2a that, given two positive radix-b fractions u and ϵ between 0 and 1, converts u to a rounded radix-B equivalent U that has just enough places M to the right of the radix point to ensure that $|U - u| < \epsilon$. (In particular if u is a multiple of b^{-m} and $\epsilon = b^{-m}/2$, the value of U will have just enough digits so that u can be recomputed exactly, given U and m. Note that M might be zero; for example, if $\epsilon \leq \frac{1}{2}$ and $u > 1 - \epsilon$, the proper answer is $U = 1$.)

4. [*M21*] (a) Prove that every real number with a terminating *binary* representation also has a terminating *decimal* representation. (b) Find a simple condition on the positive integers b and B that is satisfied if and only if every real number that has a terminating radix-b representation also has a terminating radix-B representation.

5. [*M20*] Show that program (4) would still work if the instruction "LDX =10^n=" were replaced by "LDX =c=" for certain other constants c.

6. [*30*] Discuss using Methods 1a, 1b, 2a, and 2b when b or B is -2.

7. [*M18*] Given that $0 < \alpha \leq x \leq \alpha + 1/w$ and $0 \leq u \leq w$, where u is an integer, prove that $\lfloor ux \rfloor$ is equal to either $\lfloor \alpha u \rfloor$ or $\lfloor \alpha u \rfloor + 1$. Furthermore $\lfloor ux \rfloor = \lfloor \alpha u \rfloor$ exactly, if $u < \alpha w$ and α^{-1} is an integer.

8. [*24*] Write a MIX program analogous to (1) that uses (5) and includes no division instructions.

▸ **9.** [*M29*] The purpose of this exercise is to compute $\lfloor u/10 \rfloor$ with binary shifting and addition operations only, when u is a nonnegative integer. Let $v_0(u) = 3\lfloor u/2 \rfloor + 3$ and

$$v_{k+1}(u) = v_k(u) + \lfloor v_k(u)/2^{2^{k+2}} \rfloor \qquad \text{for } k \geq 0.$$

Given k, what is the smallest nonnegative integer u such that $\lfloor v_k[u]/16 \rfloor \neq \lfloor u/10 \rfloor$?

10. [*22*] Table 1 shows how a binary-coded decimal number can be doubled by using various shifting, extracting, and addition operations on a binary computer. Give an analogous method that computes *half* of a binary-coded decimal number (throwing away the remainder if the number is odd).

11. [*16*] Convert $(57721)_8$ to decimal.

▸ **12.** [*22*] Invent a rapid pencil-and-paper method for converting integers from ternary notation to decimal, and illustrate your method by converting $(1212011210210)_3$ into decimal. How would you go from decimal to ternary?

▸ **13.** [*25*] Assume that locations $U + 1$, $U + 2$, ..., $U + m$ contain a multiple-precision fraction $(.u_{-1}u_{-2} \ldots u_{-m})_b$, where b is the word size of MIX. Write a MIX routine that converts this fraction to decimal notation, truncating it to 180 decimal digits. The answer should be printed on two lines, with the digits grouped into 20 blocks of nine each separated by blanks. (Use the CHAR instruction.)

▸ **14.** [*M27*] (A. Schönhage.) The text's method of converting multiple-precision integers requires an execution time of order n^2 to convert an n-place integer, when n is large. Show that it is possible to convert n-digit decimal integers into binary notation in $O(M(n) \log n)$ steps, where $M(n)$ is an upper bound on the number of steps needed to multiply n-bit binary numbers that satisfies the "smoothness condition" $M(2n) \geq 2M(n)$.

15. [*M47*] Can the upper bound on the time to convert large integers given in the preceding exercise be substantially lowered? (See exercise 4.3.3–12.)

16. [*41*] Construct a fast linear iterative array for radix conversion from decimal to binary (see Section 4.3.3E).

17. [*M40*] Design "ideal" floating point conversion subroutines, taking p-digit decimal numbers into P-digit binary numbers and vice versa, in both cases producing a true rounded result in the sense of Section 4.2.2.

18. [*HM34*] (David W. Matula.) Let $\text{round}_b(u,p)$ be the function of b, u, and p that represents the best p-digit base b floating point approximation to u, in the sense of Section 4.2.2. Under the assumption that $\log_B b$ is irrational and that the range of exponents is unlimited, prove that

$$u = \text{round}_b(\text{round}_B(u, P), p)$$

holds for all p-digit base b floating point numbers u if and only if $B^{P-1} \geq b^p$. (In other words, an "ideal" input conversion of u into an independent base B, followed by an "ideal" output conversion of this result, will always yield u again if and only if the intermediate precision P is suitably large, as specified by the formula above.)

19. [*M23*] Let the decimal number $u = (u_7 \ldots u_1 u_0)_{10}$ be represented as the binary-coded decimal number $U = (u_7 \ldots u_1 u_0)_{16}$. Find appropriate constants c_i and masks m_i so that the operation $U \leftarrow U - c_i(U \mathbin{\&} m_i)$, repeated for $i = 1, 2, 3$, will convert U to the binary representation of u, where "$\&$" denotes extraction (bitwise AND).

4.5. RATIONAL ARITHMETIC

IT IS OFTEN IMPORTANT to know that the answer to some numerical problem is exactly $1/3$, not a floating point number that gets printed as "0.333333574". If arithmetic is done on fractions instead of on approximations to fractions, many computations can be done entirely *without any accumulated rounding errors*. This results in a comfortable feeling of security that is often lacking when floating point calculations have been made, and it means that the accuracy of the calculation cannot be improved upon.

> *Irrationality is the square root of all evil.*
> — DOUGLAS HOFSTADTER, *Metamagical Themas* (1983)

4.5.1. Fractions

When fractional arithmetic is desired, the numbers can be represented as pairs of integers, (u/u'), where u and u' are relatively prime to each other and $u' > 0$. The number zero is represented as $(0/1)$. In this form, $(u/u') = (v/v')$ if and only if $u = v$ and $u' = v'$.

Multiplication of fractions is, of course, easy; to form $(u/u') \times (v/v') = (w/w')$, we can simply compute uv and $u'v'$. The two products uv and $u'v'$ might not be relatively prime, but if $d = \gcd(uv, u'v')$, the desired answer is $w = uv/d$, $w' = u'v'/d$. (See exercise 2.) Efficient algorithms to compute the greatest common divisor are discussed in Section 4.5.2.

Another way to perform the multiplication is to find $d_1 = \gcd(u, v')$ and $d_2 = \gcd(u', v)$; then the answer is $w = (u/d_1)(v/d_2)$, $w' = (u'/d_2)(v'/d_1)$. (See exercise 3.) This method requires two gcd calculations, but it is not really slower than the former method; the gcd process involves a number of iterations that is essentially proportional to the logarithm of its inputs, so the total number of iterations needed to evaluate both d_1 and d_2 is essentially the same as the number of iterations during the single calculation of d. Furthermore, each iteration in the evaluation of d_1 and d_2 is potentially faster, because comparatively small numbers are being examined. If u, u', v, and v' are single-precision quantities, this method has the advantage that no double-precision numbers appear in the calculation unless it is impossible to represent both of the answers w and w' in single-precision form.

Division may be done in a similar manner; see exercise 4.

Addition and subtraction are slightly more complicated. The obvious procedure is to set $(u/u') \pm (v/v') = ((uv' \pm u'v)/u'v')$ and then to reduce this fraction to lowest terms by calculating $d = \gcd(uv' \pm u'v, u'v')$, as in the first multiplication method. But again it is possible to avoid working with such large numbers, if we start by calculating $d_1 = \gcd(u', v')$. If $d_1 = 1$, then the desired numerator and denominator are $w = uv' \pm u'v$ and $w' = u'v'$. (According to Theorem 4.5.2D, d_1 will be 1 about 61 percent of the time, if the denominators u' and v' are randomly distributed, so it is wise to single out this case.) If $d_1 > 1$, then let $t = u(v'/d_1) \pm v(u'/d_1)$ and calculate $d_2 = \gcd(t, d_1)$; finally the answer is $w = t/d_2$, $w' = (u'/d_1)(v'/d_2)$. (Exercise 6 proves that these values of w and w' are relatively prime to each other.) If single-precision numbers are being used, this method requires only single-precision operations, except that t may be a double-precision number or slightly larger (see exercise 7); since $\gcd(t, d_1) = \gcd(t \bmod d_1, d_1)$, the calculation of d_2 does not require double precision.

For example, to compute $(7/66) + (17/12)$, we form $d_1 = \gcd(66, 12) = 6$; then $t = 7 \cdot 2 + 17 \cdot 11 = 201$, and $d_2 = \gcd(201, 6) = 3$, so the answer is

$$\frac{201}{3} \Big/ \left(\frac{66}{6} \cdot \frac{12}{3} \right) = 67/44.$$

To help check out subroutines for rational arithmetic, inversion of matrices with known inverses (like Cauchy matrices, exercise 1.2.3–41) is suggested.

Experience with fractional calculations shows that in many cases the numbers grow to be quite large. So if u and u' are intended to be single-precision numbers for each fraction (u/u'), it is important to include tests for overflow in each of the addition, subtraction, multiplication, and division subroutines. For numerical problems in which perfect accuracy is important, a set of subroutines for fractional arithmetic with *arbitrary* precision allowed in numerator and denominator is very useful.

The methods of this section extend also to other number fields besides the rational numbers; for example, we could do arithmetic on quantities of the form $(u + u'\sqrt{5})/u''$, where u, u', u'' are integers, $\gcd(u, u', u'') = 1$, and $u'' > 0$; or on quantities of the form $(u + u'\sqrt[3]{2} + u''\sqrt[3]{4})/u'''$, etc.

Instead of insisting on exact calculations with fractions, it is interesting to consider also "fixed slash" and "floating slash" numbers, which are analogous to floating point numbers but based on rational fractions instead of radix-oriented fractions. In a binary fixed-slash scheme, the numerator and denominator of a representable fraction each consist of at most p bits, for some given p. In a floating-slash scheme, the *sum* of numerator bits plus denominator bits must be a total of at most q, for some given q, and another field of the representation is used to indicate how many of these q bits belong to the numerator. Infinity can be represented as $(1/0)$. To do arithmetic on such numbers, we define $x \oplus y = \mathrm{round}(x+y)$, $x \ominus y = \mathrm{round}(x-y)$, etc., where $\mathrm{round}(x) = x$ if x is representable, otherwise it is one of the two representable numbers that surround x.

It may seem at first that the best definition of $\mathrm{round}(x)$ would be to choose the representable number that is closest to x, by analogy with the way we round in floating point arithmetic. But experience has shown that it is best to bias our rounding towards "simple" numbers, since numbers with small numerator and denominator occur much more often than complicated fractions do. We want more numbers to round to $\frac{1}{2}$ than to $\frac{127}{255}$. The rounding rule that turns out to be most successful in practice is called "median rounding": If (u/u') and (v/v') are adjacent representable numbers, so that whenever $u/u' \le x \le v/v'$ we must have $\mathrm{round}(x)$ equal to (u/u') or (v/v'), the median rounding rule says that

$$\mathrm{round}(x) = \frac{u}{u'} \text{ for } x < \frac{u+v}{u'+v'}, \quad \mathrm{round}(x) = \frac{v}{v'} \text{ for } x > \frac{u+v}{u'+v'}. \tag{1}$$

If $x = (u+v)/(u'+v')$ exactly, we let round(x) be the neighboring fraction with the smallest denominator (or, if $u' = v'$, with the smallest numerator). Exercise 4.5.3–43 shows that it is not difficult to implement mediant rounding efficiently.

For example, suppose we are doing fixed slash arithmetic with $p = 8$, so that the representable numbers (u/u') have $-128 < u < 128$ and $0 \le u' < 256$ and $u \perp u'$. This isn't much precision, but it is enough to give us a feel for slash arithmetic. The numbers adjacent to $0 = (0/1)$ are $(-1/255)$ and $(1/255)$; according to the mediant rounding rule, we will therefore have round$(x) = 0$ if and only if $|x| \le 1/256$. Suppose we have a calculation that would take the overall form $\frac{22}{7} = \frac{314}{159} + \frac{1300}{1113}$ if we were working in exact rational arithmetic, but the intermediate quantities have had to be rounded to representable numbers. In this case $\frac{314}{159}$ would round to $(79/40)$ and $\frac{1300}{1113}$ would round to $(7/6)$. The rounded terms sum to $\frac{79}{40} + \frac{7}{6} = \frac{377}{120}$, which rounds to $(22/7)$; so we have obtained the correct answer even though three roundings were required. This example was not specially contrived. When the answer to a problem is a simple fraction, slash arithmetic tends to make the intermediate rounding errors cancel out.

Exact representation of fractions within a computer was first discussed in the literature by P. Henrici, *JACM* **3** (1956), 6–9. Fixed and floating slash arithmetic were proposed by David W. Matula, in *Applications of Number Theory to Numerical Analysis*, edited by S. K. Zaremba (New York: Academic Press, 1972), 486–489. Further developments of the idea are discussed by Matula and Kornerup in *Proc. IEEE Symp. Computer Arith.* **4** (1978), 29–38, 39–47; *Lecture Notes in Comp. Sci.* **72** (1979), 383–397; *Computing*, Suppl. **2** (1980), 85–111; *IEEE Trans.* **C-32** (1983), 378–388; *IEEE Trans.* **C-34** (1985), 3–18; *IEEE Trans.* **C-39** (1990), 1106–1115.

EXERCISES

1. [*15*] Suggest a reasonable computational method for comparing two fractions, to test whether or not $(u/u') < (v/v')$.

2. [*M15*] Prove that if $d = \gcd(u, v)$ then u/d and v/d are relatively prime.

3. [*M20*] Prove that $u \perp u'$ and $v \perp v'$ implies $\gcd(uv, u'v') = \gcd(u, v')\gcd(u', v)$.

4. [*11*] Design a division algorithm for fractions, analogous to the second multiplication method of the text. (Note that the sign of v must be considered.)

5. [*10*] Compute $(17/120) + (-27/70)$ by the method recommended in the text.

▶ **6.** [*M23*] Show that $u \perp u'$ and $v \perp v'$ implies $\gcd(uv' + vu', u'v') = d_1 d_2$, where $d_1 = \gcd(u', v')$ and $d_2 = \gcd(d_1, u(v'/d_1) + v(u'/d_1))$. (Hence if $d_1 = 1$ we have $(uv' + vu') \perp u'v'$.)

7. [*M22*] How large can the absolute value of the quantity t become, in the addition-subtraction method recommended in the text, if the numerators and denominators of the inputs are less than N in absolute value?

▶ **8.** [*22*] Discuss using $(1/0)$ and $(-1/0)$ as representations for ∞ and $-\infty$, and/or as representations of overflow.

9. [*M23*] If $1 \le u'$, $v' < 2^n$, show that $\lfloor 2^{2n}u/u'\rfloor = \lfloor 2^{2n}v/v'\rfloor$ implies $u/u' = v/v'$.

10. [*41*] Extend the subroutines suggested in exercise 4.3.1–34 so that they deal with "arbitrary" rational numbers.

11. [*M23*] Consider fractions of the form $(u + u'\sqrt{5})/u''$, where u, u', u'' are integers, $\gcd(u, u', u'') = 1$, and $u'' > 0$. Explain how to divide two such fractions and to obtain a quotient having the same form.

12. [*M16*] What is the largest finite floating slash number, given a bound q on the numerator length plus the denominator length? Which numbers round to $(0/1)$?

13. [*20*] (Matula and Kornerup.) Discuss the representation of floating slash numbers in a 32-bit word.

14. [*M23*] Explain how to compute the exact number of pairs of integers (u, u') such that $M_1 < u \le M_2$ and $N_1 < u' \le N_2$ and $u \perp u'$. (This can be used to determine how many numbers are representable in slash arithmetic. According to Theorem 4.5.2D, the number will be approximately $(6/\pi^2)(M_2 - M_1)(N_2 - N_1)$.)

15. [*42*] Modify one of the compilers at your installation so that it will replace all floating point calculations by floating slash calculations. Experiment with the use of slash arithmetic by running existing programs that were written by programmers who actually had floating point arithmetic in mind. (When special subroutines like square root or logarithm are called, your system should automatically convert slash numbers to floating point form before the subroutine is invoked, then back to slash form again afterwards. There should be a new option to print slash numbers in a fractional format; however, you should also print slash numbers in decimal notation as usual, if no changes are made to a user's source program.) Are the results better or worse, when floating slash numbers are substituted?

16. [*40*] Experiment with interval arithmetic on slash numbers.

4.5.2. The Greatest Common Divisor

If u and v are integers, not both zero, we say that their *greatest common divisor*, $\gcd(u, v)$, is the largest integer that evenly divides both u and v. This definition makes sense, because if $u \ne 0$ then no integer greater than $|u|$ can evenly divide u, but the integer 1 does divide both u and v; hence there must be a largest integer that divides them both. When u and v are both zero, every integer evenly divides zero, so the definition above does not apply; it is convenient to set

$$\gcd(0, 0) = 0. \tag{1}$$

The definitions just given obviously imply that

$$\gcd(u, v) = \gcd(v, u), \tag{2}$$
$$\gcd(u, v) = \gcd(-u, v), \tag{3}$$
$$\gcd(u, 0) = |u|. \tag{4}$$

In the previous section, we reduced the problem of expressing a rational number in lowest terms to the problem of finding the greatest common divisor of its numerator and denominator. Other applications of the greatest common divisor have been mentioned for example in Sections 3.2.1.2, 3.3.3, 4.3.2, 4.3.3. So the concept of $\gcd(u, v)$ is important and worthy of serious study.

The *least common multiple* of two integers u and v, written $\operatorname{lcm}(u, v)$, is a related idea that is also important. It is defined to be the smallest positive integer that is an integer multiple of both u and v; and $\operatorname{lcm}(u, 0) = \operatorname{lcm}(0, v) = 0$. The classical method for teaching children how to add fractions $u/u' + v/v'$ is to train them to find the "least common denominator," which is $\operatorname{lcm}(u', v')$.

According to the "fundamental theorem of arithmetic" (proved in exercise 1.2.4–21), each positive integer u can be expressed in the form

$$u = 2^{u_2} 3^{u_3} 5^{u_5} 7^{u_7} 11^{u_{11}} \ldots = \prod_{p \text{ prime}} p^{u_p}, \tag{5}$$

where the exponents u_2, u_3, ... are uniquely determined nonnegative integers, and where all but a finite number of the exponents are zero. From this canonical factorization of a positive integer, we immediately obtain one way to compute the greatest common divisor of u and v: By (2), (3), and (4), we may assume that u and v are positive integers, and if both of them have been canonically factored into primes we have

$$\gcd(u, v) = \prod_{p \text{ prime}} p^{\min(u_p, v_p)}, \tag{6}$$

$$\operatorname{lcm}(u, v) = \prod_{p \text{ prime}} p^{\max(u_p, v_p)}. \tag{7}$$

Thus, for example, the greatest common divisor of $u = 7000 = 2^3 \cdot 5^3 \cdot 7$ and $v = 4400 = 2^4 \cdot 5^2 \cdot 11$ is $2^{\min(3,4)} 5^{\min(3,2)} 7^{\min(1,0)} 11^{\min(0,1)} = 2^3 \cdot 5^2 = 200$. The least common multiple of the same two numbers is $2^4 \cdot 5^3 \cdot 7 \cdot 11 = 154000$.

From formulas (6) and (7) we can easily prove a number of basic identities concerning the gcd and the lcm:

$$\gcd(u, v)w = \gcd(uw, vw), \qquad \text{if } w \geq 0; \tag{8}$$

$$\operatorname{lcm}(u, v)w = \operatorname{lcm}(uw, vw), \qquad \text{if } w \geq 0; \tag{9}$$

$$u \cdot v = \gcd(u, v) \cdot \operatorname{lcm}(u, v), \qquad \text{if } u, v \geq 0; \tag{10}$$

$$\gcd\big(\operatorname{lcm}(u, v), \operatorname{lcm}(u, w)\big) = \operatorname{lcm}\big(u, \gcd(v, w)\big); \tag{11}$$

$$\operatorname{lcm}\big(\gcd(u, v), \gcd(u, w)\big) = \gcd\big(u, \operatorname{lcm}(v, w)\big). \tag{12}$$

The latter two formulas are "distributive laws" analogous to the familiar identity $uv + uw = u(v + w)$. Equation (10) reduces the calculation of $\gcd(u, v)$ to the calculation of $\operatorname{lcm}(u, v)$, and conversely.

Euclid's algorithm. Although Eq. (6) is useful for theoretical purposes, it is generally no help for calculating a greatest common divisor in practice, because it requires that we first determine the canonical factorization of u and v. There is no known way to find the prime factors of an integer very rapidly (see Section 4.5.4). But fortunately the greatest common divisor of two integers can be found efficiently without factoring, and in fact such a method was discovered more than 2250 years ago; it is *Euclid's algorithm*, which we have already examined in Sections 1.1 and 1.2.1.

Euclid's algorithm is found in Book 7, Propositions 1 and 2 of his *Elements* (c. 300 B.C.), but it probably wasn't his own invention. Some scholars believe that the method was known up to 200 years earlier, at least in its subtractive form, and it was almost certainly known to Eudoxus (c. 375 B.C.); see K. von Fritz, *Ann. Math.* (2) **46** (1945), 242–264. Aristotle (c. 330 B.C.) hinted at it in his *Topics*, 158b, 29–35. However, very little hard evidence about such early history has survived [see W. R. Knorr, *The Evolution of the Euclidean Elements* (Dordrecht: 1975)].

We might call Euclid's method the granddaddy of all algorithms, because it is the oldest nontrivial algorithm that has survived to the present day. (The chief rival for this honor is perhaps the ancient Egyptian method for multiplication, which was based on doubling and adding, and which forms the basis for efficient calculation of nth powers as explained in Section 4.6.3. But the Egyptian manuscripts merely give examples that are not completely systematic, and the examples were certainly not stated systematically; the Egyptian method is therefore not quite deserving of the name "algorithm." Several ancient Babylonian methods, for doing such things as solving special sets of quadratic equations in two variables, are also known. Genuine algorithms are involved in this case, not just special solutions to the equations for certain input parameters; even though the Babylonians invariably presented each method in conjunction with an example worked with particular input data, they regularly explained the general procedure in the accompanying text. [See D. E. Knuth, *CACM* **15** (1972), 671–677; **19** (1976), 108.] Many of these Babylonian algorithms predate Euclid by 1500 years, and they are the earliest known instances of written procedures for mathematics. But they do not have the stature of Euclid's algorithm, since they do not involve iteration and since they have been superseded by modern algebraic methods.)

In view of the importance of Euclid's algorithm, for historical as well as practical reasons, let us now consider how Euclid himself treated it. Paraphrased into modern terminology, this is essentially what he wrote:

Proposition. *Given two positive integers, find their greatest common divisor.*

Let A and C be the two given positive integers; it is required to find their greatest common divisor. If C divides A, then C is a common divisor of C and A, since it also divides itself. And it clearly is in fact the greatest, since no greater number than C will divide C.

But if C does not divide A, then continually subtract the lesser of the numbers A, C from the greater, until some number is left that divides the previous one. This will eventually happen, for if unity is left, it will divide the previous number.

Now let E be the positive remainder of A divided by C; let F be the positive remainder of C divided by E; and suppose that F is a divisor of E. Since F divides E and E divides $C - F$, F also divides $C - F$; but it also divides itself, so it divides C. And C divides $A - E$; therefore F also divides $A - E$. But it also divides E; therefore it divides A. Hence it is a common divisor of A and C.

I now claim that it is also the greatest. For if F is not the greatest common divisor of A and C, some larger number will divide them both. Let such a number be G.

Now since G divides C while C divides $A - E$, G divides $A - E$. G also divides the whole of A, so it divides the remainder E. But E divides $C - F$; therefore G also divides $C - F$. And G also divides the whole of C, so it divides the remainder F; that is, a greater number divides a smaller one. This is impossible.

Therefore no number greater than F will divide A and C, so F is their greatest common divisor.

Corollary. This argument makes it evident that any number dividing two numbers divides their greatest common divisor. *Q.E.D.*

Euclid's statements have been simplified here in one nontrivial respect: Greek mathematicians did not regard unity as a "divisor" of another positive integer. Two positive integers were either both equal to unity, or they were relatively prime, or they had a greatest common divisor. In fact, unity was not even considered to be a "number," and zero was of course nonexistent. These rather awkward conventions made it necessary for Euclid to duplicate much of his discussion, and he gave two separate propositions that are each essentially like the one appearing here.

In his discussion, Euclid first suggests subtracting the smaller of the two current numbers from the larger, repeatedly, until we get two numbers where one is a multiple of the other. But in the proof he really relies on taking the remainder of one number divided by another; and since he has no simple concept of zero, he cannot speak of the remainder when one number divides the other. It is reasonable to say that he imagines each *division* (not the individual subtractions) as a single step of the algorithm, and hence an "authentic" rendition of his algorithm can be phrased as follows:

Algorithm E (*Original Euclidean algorithm*). Given two integers A and C greater than unity, this algorithm finds their greatest common divisor.

E1. [Is A divisible by C?] If C divides A, the algorithm terminates with C as the answer.

E2. [Replace A by remainder.] If $A \bmod C$ is equal to unity, the given numbers were relatively prime, so the algorithm terminates. Otherwise replace the pair of values (A, C) by $(C, A \bmod C)$ and return to step E1. ▮

Euclid's "proof" quoted above is especially interesting because it is not really a proof at all! He verifies the result of the algorithm only if step E1 is performed once or thrice. Surely he must have realized that step E1 could take place more than three times, although he made no mention of such a possibility. Not having the notion of a proof by mathematical induction, he could only give a proof for a finite number of cases. (In fact, he often proved only the case $n = 3$ of a theorem that he wanted to establish for general n.) Although Euclid is justly famous for the great advances he made in the art of logical deduction, techniques for giving valid proofs by induction were not discovered until many centuries later, and the crucial ideas for proving the validity of *algorithms* are only now becoming really clear. (See Section 1.2.1 for a complete proof of Euclid's algorithm, together with a short discussion of general proof procedures for algorithms.)

It is worth noting that this algorithm for finding the greatest common divisor was chosen by Euclid to be the very first step in his development of the theory of numbers. The same order of presentation is still in use today in modern textbooks. Euclid also gave a method (Proposition 34) to find the least common multiple of two integers u and v, namely to divide u by $\gcd(u, v)$ and to multiply the result by v; this is equivalent to Eq. (10).

If we avoid Euclid's bias against the numbers 0 and 1, we can reformulate Algorithm E in the following way.

Algorithm A (*Modern Euclidean algorithm*). Given nonnegative integers u and v, this algorithm finds their greatest common divisor. (*Note:* The greatest common divisor of *arbitrary* integers u and v may be obtained by applying this algorithm to $|u|$ and $|v|$, because of Eqs. (2) and (3).)

A1. [$v = 0$?] If $v = 0$, the algorithm terminates with u as the answer.

A2. [Take $u \bmod v$.] Set $r \leftarrow u \bmod v$, $u \leftarrow v$, $v \leftarrow r$, and return to A1. (The operations of this step decrease the value of v, but they leave $\gcd(u, v)$ unchanged.) ∎

For example, we may calculate $\gcd(40902, 24140)$ as follows:

$$\gcd(40902, 24140) = \gcd(24140, 16762) = \gcd(16762, 7378)$$
$$= \gcd(7378, 2006) = \gcd(2006, 1360) = \gcd(1360, 646)$$
$$= \gcd(646, 68) = \gcd(68, 34) = \gcd(34, 0) = 34.$$

The validity of Algorithm A follows readily from Eq. (4) and the fact that

$$\gcd(u, v) = \gcd(v, u - qv), \qquad (13)$$

if q is any integer. Equation (13) holds because any common divisor of u and v is a divisor of both v and $u - qv$, and, conversely, any common divisor of v and $u - qv$ must divide both u and v.

The following MIX program illustrates the fact that Algorithm A can easily be implemented on a computer:

Program A (*Euclid's algorithm*). Assume that u and v are single-precision, nonnegative integers, stored respectively in locations U and V; this program puts $\gcd(u, v)$ into rA.

```
        LDX   U      1      rX ← u.
        JMP   2F     1
1H STX  V      T      v ← rX.
        SRAX  5      T      rAX ← rA.
        DIV   V      T      rX ← rAX mod v.
2H LDA  V      1+T    rA ← v.
        JXNZ  1B     1+T    Done if rX = 0. ∎
```

The running time for this program is $19T + 6$ cycles, where T is the number of divisions performed. The discussion in Section 4.5.3 shows that we may take $T = 0.842766 \ln N + 0.06$ as an approximate average value, when u and v are independently and uniformly distributed in the range $1 \le u, v \le N$.

A binary method. Since Euclid's patriarchal algorithm has been used for so many centuries, it is rather surprising that it might not be the best way to find the greatest common divisor after all. A quite different gcd algorithm, primarily suited to binary arithmetic, was devised by Josef Stein in 1961 [see *J. Comp. Phys.* **1** (1967), 397–405]. This new algorithm requires no division instruction; it relies solely on the operations of subtraction, parity testing, and halving of even numbers (which corresponds to a right shift in binary notation).

The binary gcd algorithm is based on four simple facts about positive integers u and v:

a) If u and v are both even, then $\gcd(u, v) = 2\gcd(u/2, v/2)$. [See Eq. (8).]
b) If u is even and v is odd, then $\gcd(u, v) = \gcd(u/2, v)$. [See Eq. (6).]
c) As in Euclid's algorithm, $\gcd(u, v) = \gcd(u - v, v)$. [See Eqs. (13), (2).]
d) If u and v are both odd, then $u - v$ is even, and $|u - v| < \max(u, v)$.

Algorithm B (*Binary gcd algorithm*). Given positive integers u and v, this algorithm finds their greatest common divisor.

B1. [Find power of 2.] Set $k \leftarrow 0$, and then repeatedly set $k \leftarrow k + 1$, $u \leftarrow u/2$, $v \leftarrow v/2$, zero or more times until u and v are not both even.

B2. [Initialize.] (Now the original values of u and v have been divided by 2^k, and at least one of their present values is odd.) If u is odd, set $t \leftarrow -v$ and go to B4. Otherwise set $t \leftarrow u$.

B3. [Halve t.] (At this point, t is even, and nonzero.) Set $t \leftarrow t/2$.

B4. [Is t even?] If t is even, go back to B3.

B5. [Reset $\max(u, v)$.] If $t > 0$, set $u \leftarrow t$; otherwise set $v \leftarrow -t$. (The larger of u and v has been replaced by $|t|$, except perhaps during the first time this step is performed.)

B6. [Subtract.] Set $t \leftarrow u - v$. If $t \neq 0$, go back to B3. Otherwise the algorithm terminates with $u \cdot 2^k$ as the output. ∎

As an example of Algorithm B, let us consider $u = 40902$, $v = 24140$, the same numbers we used when trying out Euclid's algorithm. Step B1 sets $k \leftarrow 1$, $u \leftarrow 20451$, $v \leftarrow 12070$. Then t is set to -12070, and replaced by -6035; then v is replaced by 6035, and the computation proceeds as follows:

u	v	t
20451	6035	$+14416, +7208, +3604, +1802, +901$;
901	6035	$-5134, -2567$;
901	2567	$-1666, -833$;
901	833	$+68, +34, +17$;
17	833	$-816, -408, -204, -102, -51$;
17	51	$-34, -17$;
17	17	0.

The answer is $17 \cdot 2^1 = 34$. A few more iterations were necessary here than we needed with Algorithm A, but each iteration was somewhat simpler since no division steps were used.

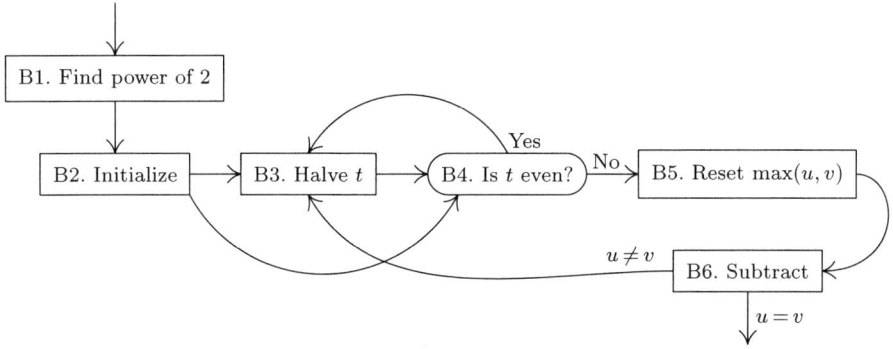

Fig. 9. Binary algorithm for the greatest common divisor.

A MIX program for Algorithm B requires just a little more code than for Algorithm A. In order to make such a program fairly typical of a binary computer's representation of Algorithm B, let us assume that MIX is extended to include the following operators:

• SLB (shift left AX binary). C = 6; F = 6.
The contents of registers A and X are "shifted left" M binary places; that is, $|rAX| \leftarrow |2^M rAX| \bmod B^{10}$, where B is the byte size. (As with all MIX shift commands, the signs of rA and rX are not affected.)

• SRB (shift right AX binary). C = 6; F = 7.
The contents of registers A and X are "shifted right" M binary places; that is, $|rAX| \leftarrow \lfloor |rAX|/2^M \rfloor$.

• JAE, JAO (jump A even, jump A odd). C = 40; F = 6, 7, respectively.
A JMP occurs if rA is even or odd, respectively.

• JXE, JXO (jump X even, jump X odd). C = 47; F = 6, 7, respectively.
Analogous to JAE, JAO.

Program B (*Binary gcd algorithm*). Assume that u and v are single-precision positive integers, stored respectively in locations U and V; this program uses Algorithm B to put $\gcd(u, v)$ into rA. Register assignments: $rA \equiv t$, $rI1 \equiv k$.

01	ABS	EQU	1:5	
02	B1	ENT1	0	1	*B1. Find power of 2.*
03		LDX	U	1	rX ← u.
04		LDAN	V	1	rA ← −v.
05		JMP	1F	1	
06	2H	SRB	1	A	Halve rA, rX.
07		INC1	1	A	k ← k + 1.
08		STX	U	A	u ← u/2.
09		STA	V(ABS)	A	v ← v/2.
10	1H	JXO	B4	1 + A	To B4 with t ← −v if u is odd.
11	B2	JAE	2B	B + A	*B2. Initialize.*

12		LDA	U	B	$t \leftarrow u$.
13	B3	SRB	1	D	B3. Halve t.
14	B4	JAE	B3	$1 - B + D$	B4. Is t even?
15	B5	JAN	1F	C	B5. Reset $\max(u, v)$.
16		STA	U	E	If $t > 0$, set $u \leftarrow t$.
17		SUB	V	E	$t \leftarrow u - v$.
18		JMP	2F	E	
19	1H	STA	V(ABS)	$C - E$	If $t < 0$, set $v \leftarrow -t$.
20	B6	ADD	U	$C - E$	B6. Subtract.
21	2H	JANZ	B3	C	To B3 if $t \neq 0$.
22		LDA	U	1	$rA \leftarrow u$.
23		ENTX	0	1	$rX \leftarrow 0$.
24		SLB	0,1	1	$rA \leftarrow 2^k \cdot rA$. ∎

The running time of this program is

$$9A + 2B + 6C + 3D + E + 13$$

units, where $A = k$, $B = 1$ if $t \leftarrow u$ in step B2 (otherwise $B = 0$), C is the number of subtraction steps, D is the number of halvings in step B3, and E is the number of times $t > 0$ in step B5. Calculations discussed later in this section imply that we may take $A = \frac{1}{3}$, $B = \frac{1}{3}$, $C = 0.71N - 0.5$, $D = 1.41N - 2.7$, and $E = 0.35N - 0.4$ as average values for these quantities, assuming random inputs u and v in the range $1 \leq u, v < 2^N$. The total running time is therefore about $8.8N + 5.2$ cycles, compared to about $11.1N + 7.1$ for Program A under the same assumptions. The worst possible running time for u and v in this range occurs when $A = 0$, $B = 1$, $C = N$, $D = 2N - 2$, $E = N - 1$; this amounts to $13N + 8$ cycles. (The corresponding value for Program A is $26.8N + 19$.)

Thus the greater speed of the iterations in Program B, due to the simplicity of the operations, compensates for the greater number of iterations required. We have found that the binary algorithm is about 20 percent faster than Euclid's algorithm on the MIX computer. Of course, the situation may be different on other computers, and in any event both programs are quite efficient; but it appears that not even a procedure as venerable as Euclid's algorithm can withstand progress.

The binary gcd algorithm itself might have a distinguished pedigree, since it may well have been known in ancient China. Chapter 1, Section 6 of a classic text called *Chiu Chang Suan Shu*, the "Nine Chapters on Arithmetic" (c. 1st century A.D.), gives the following method for reducing a fraction to lowest terms:

> If halving is possible, take half.
>
> Otherwise write down the denominator and the numerator, and subtract the smaller from the greater.
>
> Repeat until both numbers are equal.
>
> Simplify with this common value.

If the repeat instruction means to go back to the halving step instead of to repeat the subtraction step — this point isn't clear — the method is essentially Algorithm B. [See Y. Mikami, *The Development of Mathematics in China* and Japan (Leipzig: 1913), 11; K. Vogel, *Neun Bücher arithmetischer Technik* (Braunschweig: Vieweg, 1968), 8.]

V. C. Harris [*Fibonacci Quarterly* **8** (1970), 102–103; see also V. A. Lebesgue, *J. Math. Pures Appl.* **12** (1847), 497–520] has suggested an interesting cross between Euclid's algorithm and the binary algorithm. If u and v are odd, with $u \geq v > 0$, we can always write

$$u = qv \pm r$$

where $0 \leq r < v$ and r is even; if $r \neq 0$ we set $r \leftarrow r/2$ until r is odd, then set $u \leftarrow v$, $v \leftarrow r$ and repeat the process. In subsequent iterations, $q \geq 3$.

Extensions. We can extend the methods used to calculate $\gcd(u, v)$ in order to solve some slightly more difficult problems. For example, assume that we want to compute the greatest common divisor of n integers $u_1, u_2, \ldots, u_n$.

One way to calculate $\gcd(u_1, u_2, \ldots, u_n)$, assuming that the u's are all nonnegative, is to extend Euclid's algorithm in the following way: If all u_j are zero, the greatest common divisor is taken to be zero; otherwise if only one u_j is nonzero, it is the greatest common divisor; otherwise replace u_k by $u_k \bmod u_j$ for all $k \neq j$, where u_j is the minimum of the nonzero u's, and repeat the process.

The algorithm sketched in the preceding paragraph is a natural generalization of Euclid's method, and it can be justified in a similar manner. But there is a simpler method available, based on the easily verified identity

$$\gcd(u_1, u_2, \ldots, u_n) = \gcd\big(u_1, \gcd(u_2, \ldots, u_n)\big). \tag{14}$$

To calculate $\gcd(u_1, u_2, \ldots, u_n)$, we may therefore proceed as follows:

Algorithm C (*Greatest common divisor of n integers*). Given integers u_1, u_2, $\ldots$, u_n, where $n \geq 1$, this algorithm computes their greatest common divisor, using an algorithm for the case $n = 2$ as a subroutine.

C1. Set $d \leftarrow u_n$, $k \leftarrow n - 1$.

C2. If $d \neq 1$ and $k > 0$, set $d \leftarrow \gcd(u_k, d)$ and $k \leftarrow k - 1$ and repeat this step. Otherwise $d = \gcd(u_1, \ldots, u_n)$. ∎

This method reduces the calculation of $\gcd(u_1, \ldots, u_n)$ to repeated calculations of the greatest common divisor of two numbers at a time. It makes use of the fact that $\gcd(u_1, \ldots, u_k, 1) = 1$; and this will be helpful, since we will already have $\gcd(u_{n-1}, u_n) = 1$ more than 60 percent of the time, if u_{n-1} and u_n are chosen at random. In most cases the value of d will decrease rapidly during the first few stages of the calculation, and this will make the remainder of the computation quite fast. Here Euclid's algorithm has an advantage over Algorithm B, because its running time is primarily governed by the value of $\min(u, v)$, while the running time for Algorithm B is primarily governed by $\max(u, v)$; it would be reasonable to perform one iteration of Euclid's algorithm, replacing u by $u \bmod v$ if u is much larger than v, and then to continue with Algorithm B.

The assertion that $\gcd(u_{n-1}, u_n)$ will be equal to unity more than 60 percent of the time for random inputs is a consequence of the following well-known result of number theory:

Theorem D. [G. Lejeune Dirichlet, *Abhandlungen Königlich Preuß. Akad. Wiss.* (1849), 69–83.] *If u and v are integers chosen at random, the probability that $\gcd(u, v) = 1$ is $6/\pi^2 \approx .60793$.*

A precise formulation of this theorem, which defines carefully what is meant by being "chosen at random," appears in exercise 10 with a rigorous proof. Let us content ourselves here with a heuristic argument that shows why the theorem is plausible.

If we assume, without proof, the existence of a well-defined probability p that $u \perp v$, then we can determine the probability that $\gcd(u, v) = d$ for any positive integer d, because $\gcd(u, v) = d$ if and only if u is a multiple of d and v is a multiple of d and $u/d \perp v/d$. Thus the probability that $\gcd(u, v) = d$ is equal to $1/d$ times $1/d$ times p, namely p/d^2. Now let us sum these probabilities over all possible values of d; we should get

$$1 = \sum_{d \geq 1} p/d^2 = p\left(1 + \tfrac{1}{4} + \tfrac{1}{9} + \tfrac{1}{16} + \cdots\right).$$

Since the sum $1 + \tfrac{1}{4} + \tfrac{1}{9} + \cdots = H_\infty^{(2)}$ is equal to $\pi^2/6$ by Eq. 1.2.7–(7), we need $p = 6/\pi^2$ in order to make this equation come out right. ∎

Euclid's algorithm can be extended in another important way: We can calculate integers u' and v' such that

$$uu' + vv' = \gcd(u, v) \tag{15}$$

at the same time $\gcd(u, v)$ is being calculated. This extension of Euclid's algorithm can be described conveniently in vector notation:

Algorithm X (*Extended Euclid's algorithm*). Given nonnegative integers u and v, this algorithm determines a vector (u_1, u_2, u_3) such that $uu_1 + vu_2 = u_3 = \gcd(u, v)$. The computation makes use of auxiliary vectors (v_1, v_2, v_3), (t_1, t_2, t_3); all vectors are manipulated in such a way that the relations

$$ut_1 + vt_2 = t_3, \qquad uu_1 + vu_2 = u_3, \qquad uv_1 + vv_2 = v_3 \tag{16}$$

hold throughout the calculation.

X1. [Initialize.] Set $(u_1, u_2, u_3) \leftarrow (1, 0, u)$, $(v_1, v_2, v_3) \leftarrow (0, 1, v)$.

X2. [Is $v_3 = 0$?] If $v_3 = 0$, the algorithm terminates.

X3. [Divide, subtract.] Set $q \leftarrow \lfloor u_3/v_3 \rfloor$, and then set

$$(t_1, t_2, t_3) \leftarrow (u_1, u_2, u_3) - (v_1, v_2, v_3)q,$$
$$(u_1, u_2, u_3) \leftarrow (v_1, v_2, v_3), \qquad (v_1, v_2, v_3) \leftarrow (t_1, t_2, t_3).$$

Return to step X2. ∎

For example, let $u = 40902$, $v = 24140$. At step X2 we have

q	u_1	u_2	u_3	v_1	v_2	v_3
—	1	0	40902	0	1	24140
1	0	1	24140	1	−1	16762
1	1	−1	16762	−1	2	7378
2	−1	2	7378	3	−5	2006
3	3	−5	2006	−10	17	1360
1	−10	17	1360	13	−22	646
2	13	−22	646	−36	61	68
9	−36	61	68	337	−571	34
2	337	−571	34	−710	1203	0

The solution is therefore $337 \cdot 40902 - 571 \cdot 24140 = 34 = \gcd(40902, 24140)$.

Algorithm X can be traced to the *Āryabhatīya* (A.D. 499) by Āryabhaṭa of northern India. His description was rather cryptic, but later commentators such as Bhāskara I in the seventh century clarified the rule, which was called *kuṭṭaka* ("the pulverizer"). [See B. Datta and A. N. Singh, *History of Hindu Mathematics* **2** (Lahore: Motilal Banarsi Das, 1938), 89–116.] Its validity follows from (16) and the fact that the algorithm is identical to Algorithm A with respect to its manipulation of u_3 and v_3; a detailed proof of Algorithm X is discussed in Section 1.2.1. Gordon H. Bradley has observed that we can avoid a good deal of the calculation in Algorithm X by suppressing u_2, v_2, and t_2; then u_2 can be determined afterwards using the relation $uu_1 + vu_2 = u_3$.

Exercise 15 shows that the values of $|u_1|$, $|u_2|$, $|v_1|$, and $|v_2|$ remain bounded by the size of the inputs u and v. Algorithm B, which computes the greatest common divisor using properties of binary notation, can be extended in a similar way; see exercise 39. For some instructive extensions to Algorithm X, see exercises 18 and 19 in Section 4.6.1.

The ideas underlying Euclid's algorithm can also be applied to find a *general solution in integers* of any set of linear equations with integer coefficients. For example, suppose that we want to find all integers w, x, y, z that satisfy the two equations

$$10w + 3x + 3y + 8z = 1, \tag{17}$$
$$6w - 7x \qquad - 5z = 2. \tag{18}$$

We can introduce a new variable

$$\lfloor 10/3 \rfloor w + \lfloor 3/3 \rfloor x + \lfloor 3/3 \rfloor y + \lfloor 8/3 \rfloor z = 3w + x + y + 2z = t_1,$$

and use it to eliminate y; Eq. (17) becomes

$$(10 \bmod 3)w + (3 \bmod 3)x + 3t_1 + (8 \bmod 3)z = w + 3t_1 + 2z = 1, \tag{19}$$

and Eq. (18) remains unchanged. The new equation (19) may be used to eliminate w, and (18) becomes

$$6(1 - 3t_1 - 2z) - 7x - 5z = 2;$$

that is,

$$7x + 18t_1 + 17z = 4. \tag{20}$$

Now as before we introduce a new variable

$$x + 2t_1 + 2z = t_2$$

and eliminate x from (20):

$$7t_2 + 4t_1 + 3z = 4. \tag{21}$$

Another new variable can be introduced in the same fashion, in order to eliminate the variable z, which has the smallest coefficient:

$$2t_2 + t_1 + z = t_3.$$

Eliminating z from (21) yields

$$t_2 + t_1 + 3t_3 = 4, \tag{22}$$

and this equation, finally, can be used to eliminate t_2. We are left with two independent variables, t_1 and t_3; substituting back for the original variables, we obtain the general solution

$$\begin{aligned}
w &= 17 - 5t_1 - 14t_3, \\
x &= 20 - 5t_1 - 17t_3, \\
y &= -55 + 19t_1 + 45t_3, \\
z &= -8 + t_1 + 7t_3.
\end{aligned} \tag{23}$$

In other words, all integer solutions (w, x, y, z) to the original equations (17) and (18) are obtained from (23) by letting t_1 and t_3 independently run through all integers.

The general method that has just been illustrated is based on the following procedure: Find a nonzero coefficient c of smallest absolute value in the system of equations. Suppose that this coefficient appears in an equation having the form

$$cx_0 + c_1x_1 + \cdots + c_kx_k = d; \tag{24}$$

and assume for simplicity that $c > 0$. If $c = 1$, use this equation to eliminate the variable x_0 from the other equations remaining in the system; then repeat the procedure on the remaining equations. (If no more equations remain, the computation stops, and a general solution in terms of the variables not yet eliminated has essentially been obtained.) If $c > 1$, then if $c_1 \bmod c = \cdots = c_k \bmod c = 0$ check that $d \bmod c = 0$, otherwise there is no integer solution; then divide both sides of (24) by c and eliminate x_0 as in the case $c = 1$. Finally, if $c > 1$ and not all of $c_1 \bmod c$, ..., $c_k \bmod c$ are zero, then introduce a new variable

$$\lfloor c/c \rfloor x_0 + \lfloor c_1/c \rfloor x_1 + \cdots + \lfloor c_k/c \rfloor x_k = t; \tag{25}$$

eliminate the variable x_0 from the other equations, in favor of t, and replace the
original equation (24) by

$$ct + (c_1 \bmod c)x_1 + \cdots + (c_k \bmod c)x_k = d. \qquad (26)$$

(See (19) and (21) in the example above.)

This process must terminate, since each step reduces either the number of
equations or the size of the smallest nonzero coefficient in the system. When this
procedure is applied to the equation $ux + vy = 1$, for specific integers u and v,
it runs through essentially the steps of Algorithm X.

The transformation-of-variables procedure just explained is a simple and
straightforward way to solve linear equations when the variables are allowed
to take on integer values only, but it isn't the best method available for this
problem. Substantial refinements are possible, but beyond the scope of this
book. [See Henri Cohen, *A Course in Computational Algebraic Number Theory*
(New York: Springer, 1993), Chapter 2.]

Variants of Euclid's algorithm can be used also with Gaussian integers $u+iu'$
and in certain other quadratic number fields. See, for example, A. Hurwitz, *Acta
Math.* **11** (1887), 187–200; E. Kaltofen and H. Rolletschek, *Math. Comp.* **53**
(1989), 697–720; A. Knopfmacher and J. Knopfmacher, *BIT* **31** (1991), 286–
292.

High-precision calculation. If u and v are very large integers, requiring a
multiple-precision representation, the binary method (Algorithm B) is a simple
and fairly efficient means of calculating their greatest common divisor, since it
involves only subtractions and shifting.

By contrast, Euclid's algorithm seems much less attractive, since step A2
requires a multiple-precision division of u by v. But this difficulty is not really
as bad as it seems, since we will prove in Section 4.5.3 that the quotient $\lfloor u/v \rfloor$ is
almost always very small. For example, assuming random inputs, the quotient
$\lfloor u/v \rfloor$ will be less than 1000 approximately 99.856 percent of the time. Therefore
it is almost always possible to find $\lfloor u/v \rfloor$ and $(u \bmod v)$ using single-precision
calculations, together with the comparatively simple operation of calculating
$u - qv$ where q is a single-precision number. Furthermore, if it does turn out
that u is much larger than v (for instance, the initial input data might have this
form), we don't really mind having a large quotient q, since Euclid's algorithm
makes a great deal of progress when it replaces u by $u \bmod v$ in such a case.

A significant improvement in the speed of Euclid's algorithm when high-
precision numbers are involved can be achieved by using a method due to D. H.
Lehmer [*AMM* **45** (1938), 227–233]. Working only with the leading digits of
large numbers, it is possible to do most of the calculations with single-precision
arithmetic, and to make a substantial reduction in the number of multiple-
precision operations involved. The idea is to save time by doing a "virtual"
calculation instead of the actual one.

For example, let us consider the pair of eight-digit numbers $u = 27182818$,
$v = 10000000$, assuming that we are using a machine with only four-digit words.

Let $u' = 2718$, $v' = 1001$, $u'' = 2719$, $v'' = 1000$; then u'/v' and u''/v'' are approximations to u/v, with

$$u'/v' < u/v < u''/v''. \qquad (27)$$

The ratio u/v determines the sequence of quotients obtained in Euclid's algorithm. If we perform Euclid's algorithm simultaneously on the single-precision values (u', v') and (u'', v'') until we get a different quotient, it is not difficult to see that the same sequence of quotients would have appeared to this point if we had worked with the multiple-precision numbers (u, v). Thus, consider what happens when Euclid's algorithm is applied to (u', v') and to (u'', v''):

u'	v'	q'		u''	v''	q''
2718	1001	2		2719	1000	2
1001	716	1		1000	719	1
716	285	2		719	281	2
285	146	1		281	157	1
146	139	1		157	124	1
139	7	19		124	33	3

The first five quotients are the same in both cases, so they must be the true ones. But on the sixth step we find that $q' \neq q''$, so the single-precision calculations are suspended. We have gained the knowledge that the calculation would have proceeded as follows if we had been working with the original multiple-precision numbers:

u	v	q
u_0	v_0	2
v_0	$u_0 - 2v_0$	1
$u_0 - 2v_0$	$-u_0 + 3v_0$	2
$-u_0 + 3v_0$	$3u_0 - 8v_0$	1
$3u_0 - 8v_0$	$-4u_0 + 11v_0$	1
$-4u_0 + 11v_0$	$7u_0 - 19v_0$	?

$$(28)$$

(The next quotient lies somewhere between 3 and 19.) No matter how many digits are in u and v, the first five steps of Euclid's algorithm would be the same as (28), so long as (27) holds. We can therefore avoid the multiple-precision operations of the first five steps, and replace them all by a multiple-precision calculation of $-4u_0 + 11v_0$ and $7u_0 - 19v_0$. In this case we obtain $u = 1268728$, $v = 279726$; the calculation can now continue in a similar manner with $u' = 1268$, $v' = 280$, $u'' = 1269$, $v'' = 279$, etc. If we had a larger accumulator, more steps could be done by single-precision calculations. Our example showed that only five cycles of Euclid's algorithm were combined into one multiple step, but with (say) a word size of 10 digits we could do about twelve cycles at a time. Results proved in Section 4.5.3 imply that the number of multiple-precision cycles that can be replaced at each iteration is essentially proportional to the number of digits used in the single-precision calculations.

Lehmer's method can be formulated as follows:

Algorithm L (*Euclid's algorithm for large numbers*). Let u and v be nonnegative integers, with $u \geq v$, represented in multiple precision. This algorithm computes the greatest common divisor of u and v, making use of auxiliary single-precision p-digit variables $\hat{u}$, $\hat{v}$, A, B, C, D, T, q, and auxiliary multiple-precision variables t and w.

L1. [Initialize.] If v is small enough to be represented as a single-precision value, calculate $\gcd(u,v)$ by Algorithm A and terminate the computation. Otherwise, let $\hat{u}$ be the p leading digits of u, and let $\hat{v}$ be the corresponding digits of v; in other words, if radix-b notation is being used, $\hat{u} \leftarrow \lfloor u/b^k \rfloor$ and $\hat{v} \leftarrow \lfloor v/b^k \rfloor$, where k is as small as possible consistent with the condition $\hat{u} < b^p$.

Set $A \leftarrow 1$, $B \leftarrow 0$, $C \leftarrow 0$, $D \leftarrow 1$. (These variables represent the coefficients in (28), where

$$u = Au_0 + Bv_0, \quad \text{and} \quad v = Cu_0 + Dv_0, \tag{29}$$

in the equivalent actions of Algorithm A on multiple-precision numbers. We also have

$$u' = \hat{u} + B, \qquad v' = \hat{v} + D, \qquad u'' = \hat{u} + A, \qquad v'' = \hat{v} + C \tag{30}$$

in terms of the notation in the example worked above.)

L2. [Test quotient.] Set $q \leftarrow \lfloor (\hat{u} + A)/(\hat{v} + C) \rfloor$. If $q \neq \lfloor (\hat{u} + B)/(\hat{v} + D) \rfloor$, go to step L4. (This step tests if $q' \neq q''$, in the notation of the example above. Single-precision overflow can occur in special circumstances during the computation in this step, but only when $\hat{u} = b^p - 1$ and $A = 1$ or when $\hat{v} = b^p - 1$ and $D = 1$; the conditions

$$0 \leq \hat{u} + A \leq b^p, \qquad 0 \leq \hat{v} + C < b^p,$$
$$0 \leq \hat{u} + B < b^p, \qquad 0 \leq \hat{v} + D \leq b^p \tag{31}$$

will always hold, because of (30). It is possible to have $\hat{v}+C = 0$ or $\hat{v}+D = 0$, but not both simultaneously; therefore division by zero in this step is taken to mean "Go directly to L4.")

L3. [Emulate Euclid.] Set $T \leftarrow A - qC$, $A \leftarrow C$, $C \leftarrow T$, $T \leftarrow B - qD$, $B \leftarrow D$, $D \leftarrow T$, $T \leftarrow \hat{u} - q\hat{v}$, $\hat{u} \leftarrow \hat{v}$, $\hat{v} \leftarrow T$, and go back to step L2. (These single-precision calculations are the equivalent of multiple-precision operations, as in (28), under the conventions of (29).)

L4. [Multiprecision step.] If $B = 0$, set $t \leftarrow u \bmod v$, $u \leftarrow v$, $v \leftarrow t$, using multiple-precision division. (This happens only if the single-precision operations cannot simulate any of the multiple-precision ones. It implies that Euclid's algorithm requires a very large quotient, and this is an extremely rare occurrence.) Otherwise, set $t \leftarrow Au$, $t \leftarrow t+Bv$, $w \leftarrow Cu$, $w \leftarrow w+Dv$, $u \leftarrow t$, $v \leftarrow w$ (using straightforward multiple-precision operations). Go back to step L1. ∎

The values of A, B, C, D remain as single-precision numbers throughout this calculation, because of (31).

Algorithm L requires a somewhat more complicated program than Algorithm B, but with large numbers it will be faster on many computers. The binary technique of Algorithm B can, however, be speeded up in a similar way (see exercise 38), to the point where it continues to win. Algorithm L has the advantage that it determines the sequence of quotients obtained in Euclid's algorithm, and this has numerous applications (see, for example, exercises 43, 47, 49, and 51 in Section 4.5.3). See also exercise 4.5.3–46.

*Analysis of the binary algorithm. Let us conclude this section by studying the running time of Algorithm B, in order to justify the formulas stated earlier.

An exact determination of Algorithm B's behavior appears to be exceedingly difficult to derive, but we can begin to study it by means of an approximate model. Suppose that u and v are odd numbers, with $u > v$ and

$$\lfloor \lg u \rfloor = m, \qquad \lfloor \lg v \rfloor = n. \tag{32}$$

(Thus, u is an $(m + 1)$-bit number, and v is an $(n + 1)$-bit number.) Consider a subtract-and-shift cycle of Algorithm B, namely an operation that starts at step B6 and then stops after step B5 is finished. Every subtract-and-shift cycle with $u > v$ forms $u - v$ and shifts this quantity right until obtaining an odd number u' that replaces u. Under random conditions, we would expect to have $u' = (u - v)/2$ about one-half of the time, $u' = (u - v)/4$ about one-fourth of the time, $u' = (u - v)/8$ about one-eighth of the time, and so on. We have

$$\lfloor \lg u' \rfloor = m - k - r, \tag{33}$$

where k is the number of places that $u - v$ is shifted right, and where r is $\lfloor \lg u \rfloor - \lfloor \lg(u - v) \rfloor$, the number of bits lost at the left during the subtraction of v from u. Notice that $r \leq 1$ when $m \geq n + 2$, and $r \geq 1$ when $m = n$.

The interaction between k and r is quite messy (see exercise 20), but Richard Brent discovered a nice way to analyze the approximate behavior by assuming that u and v are large enough that a continuous distribution describes the ratio v/u, while k varies discretely. [See *Algorithms and Complexity*, edited by J. F. Traub (New York: Academic Press, 1976), 321–355.] Let us assume that u and v are large integers that are essentially random, except that they are odd and their ratio has a certain probability distribution. Then the least significant bits of the quantity $t = u - v$ in step B6 will be essentially random, except that t will be even. Hence t will be an odd multiple of 2^k with probability 2^{-k}; this is the approximate probability that k right shifts will be needed in the subtract-and-shift cycle. In other words, we obtain a reasonable approximation to the behavior of Algorithm B if we assume that step B4 always branches to B3 with probability $1/2$.

Let $G_n(x)$ be the probability that $\min(u, v)/\max(u, v)$ is $\geq x$ after n subtract-and-shift cycles have been performed under this assumption. If $u \geq v$ and if exactly k right shifts are performed, the ratio $X = v/u$ is changed to $X' =$

$\min\left(2^k v/(u-v), (u-v)/2^k v\right) = \min\left(2^k X/(1-X), (1-X)/2^k X\right)$. Thus we will have $X' \geq x$ if and only if $2^k X/(1-X) \geq x$ and $(1-X)/2^k X \geq x$; and this is the same as

$$\frac{1}{1 + 2^k/x} \leq X \leq \frac{1}{1 + 2^k x}. \tag{34}$$

Therefore $G_n(x)$ satisfies the interesting recurrence

$$G_{n+1}(x) = \sum_{k \geq 1} 2^{-k}\left(G_n\left(\frac{1}{1 + 2^k/x}\right) - G_n\left(\frac{1}{1 + 2^k x}\right)\right), \tag{35}$$

where $G_0(x) = 1 - x$ for $0 \leq x \leq 1$. Computational experiments indicate that $G_n(x)$ converges rapidly to a limiting distribution $G_\infty(x) = G(x)$, although a formal proof of convergence seems to be difficult. We shall assume that $G(x)$ exists; hence it satisfies

$$G(x) = \sum_{k \geq 1} 2^{-k}\left(G\left(\frac{1}{1 + 2^k/x}\right) - G\left(\frac{1}{1 + 2^k x}\right)\right), \quad \text{for } 0 < x \leq 1; \tag{36}$$

$$G(0) = 1; \qquad\qquad\qquad G(1) = 0. \tag{37}$$

Let

$$S(x) = \frac{1}{2}G\left(\frac{1}{1 + 2x}\right) + \frac{1}{4}G\left(\frac{1}{1 + 4x}\right) + \frac{1}{8}G\left(\frac{1}{1 + 8x}\right) + \cdots$$

$$= \sum_{k \geq 1} 2^{-k}G\left(\frac{1}{1 + 2^k x}\right); \tag{38}$$

then we have

$$G(x) = S(1/x) - S(x). \tag{39}$$

It is convenient to define

$$G(1/x) = -G(x), \tag{40}$$

so that (39) holds for all $x > 0$. As x runs from 0 to ∞, $S(x)$ increases from 0 to 1, hence $G(x)$ decreases from $+1$ to -1. Of course $G(x)$ is no longer a probability when $x > 1$; but it is meaningful nevertheless (see exercise 23).

We will assume that there are power series $\alpha(x)$, $\beta(x)$, $\gamma_m(x)$, $\delta_m(x)$, $\lambda(x)$, $\mu(x)$, $\sigma_m(x)$, $\tau_m(x)$, and $\rho(x)$ such that

$$G(x) = \alpha(x) \lg x + \beta(x) + \sum_{m=1}^{\infty} \left(\gamma_m(x) \cos 2\pi m \lg x + \delta_m(x) \sin 2\pi m \lg x\right), \tag{41}$$

$$S(x) = \lambda(x) \lg x + \mu(x) + \sum_{m=1}^{\infty} \left(\sigma_m(x) \cos 2\pi m \lg x + \tau_m(x) \sin 2\pi m \lg x\right), \tag{42}$$

$$\rho(x) = G(1 + x) = \rho_1 x + \rho_2 x^2 + \rho_3 x^3 + \rho_4 x^4 + \rho_5 x^5 + \rho_6 x^6 + \cdots, \tag{43}$$

because it can be shown that the solutions $G_n(x)$ to (35) have this property for $n \geq 1$. (See, for example, exercise 30.) The power series converge for $|x| < 1$.

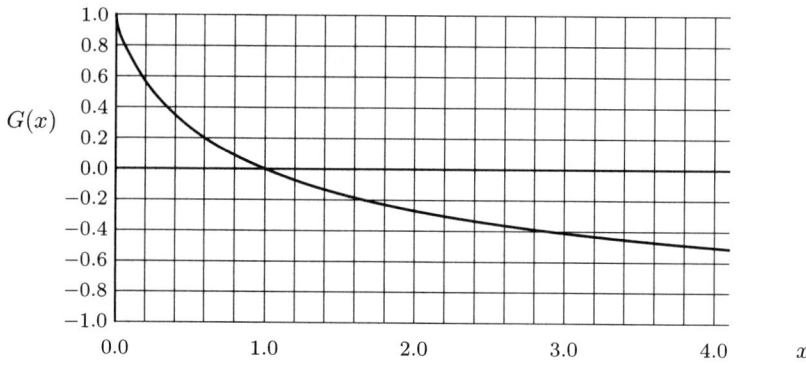

Fig. 10. The limiting distribution of ratios in the binary gcd algorithm.

What can we deduce about $\alpha(x)$, $\ldots$, $\rho(x)$ from equations (36)–(43)? In the first place we have

$$2S(x) = G\big(1/(1+2x)\big) + S(2x) = S(2x) - \rho(2x) \tag{44}$$

from (38), (40), and (43). Consequently Eq. (42) holds if and only if

$$2\lambda(x) = \lambda(2x); \tag{45}$$

$$2\mu(x) = \mu(2x) + \lambda(2x) - \rho(2x); \tag{46}$$

$$2\sigma_m(x) = \sigma_m(2x), \qquad 2\tau_m(x) = \tau_m(2x), \qquad \text{for } m \geq 1. \tag{47}$$

Relation (45) tells us that $\lambda(x)$ is simply a constant multiple of x; we will write

$$\lambda(x) = -\lambda x \tag{48}$$

because the constant is negative. (The relevant coefficient turns out to be

$$\lambda = 0.39792\,26811\,88316\,64407\,67071\,61142\,65498\,23098+, \tag{49}$$

but no easy way to compute it is known.) Relation (46) tells us that $\rho_1 = -\lambda$, and that $2\mu_k = 2^k \mu_k - 2^k \rho_k$ when $k > 1$; in other words,

$$\mu_k = \rho_k/(1 - 2^{1-k}), \qquad \text{for } k \geq 2. \tag{50}$$

We also know from (47) that the two families of power series

$$\sigma_m(x) = \sigma_m x, \qquad \tau_m(x) = \tau_m x \tag{51}$$

are simply linear functions. (This is not true for $\gamma_m(x)$ and $\delta_m(x)$.)

Replacing x by $1/2x$ in (44) yields

$$2S(1/2x) = S(1/x) + G(x/(1+x)), \tag{52}$$

and (39) converts this equation to a relation between G and S when x is near 0:

$$2G(2x) + 2S(2x) = G(x) + S(x) + G(x/(1+x)). \tag{53}$$

The coefficients of $\lg x$ must agree when both sides of this equation are expanded in power series, hence

$$2\alpha(2x) - 4\lambda x = \alpha(x) - \lambda x + \alpha(x/(1+x)). \tag{54}$$

Equation (54) is a recurrence that defines $\alpha(x)$. In fact, let us consider the function $\psi(z)$ that satisfies

$$\psi(z) = \frac{1}{2}\left(z + \psi\left(\frac{z}{2}\right) + \psi\left(\frac{z}{2+z}\right)\right), \qquad \psi(0) = 0, \quad \psi'(0) = 1. \tag{55}$$

Then (54) says that

$$\alpha(x) = \frac{3}{2}\lambda\psi(x). \tag{56}$$

Moreover, iteration of (55) yields

$$
\begin{aligned}
\psi(z) &= \frac{z}{2}\left(\frac{1}{1} + \frac{1}{2}\left(\frac{1}{2} + \frac{1}{2+z}\right) + \frac{1}{4}\left(\frac{1}{4} + \frac{1}{4+z} + \frac{1}{4+2z} + \frac{1}{4+3z}\right) + \cdots\right) \\
&= \frac{z}{2}\sum_{k\geq 0}\frac{1}{2^k}\sum_{0\leq j < 2^k}\frac{1}{2^k + jz}.
\end{aligned}
\tag{57}
$$

It follows that the power series expansion of $\psi(z)$ is

$$\psi(z) = \sum_{n\geq 1}(-1)^{n-1}\psi_n z^n, \qquad \psi_n = \frac{1}{2n}\sum_{k=0}^{n-1}\frac{B_k}{2^{k+1} - 1}\binom{n}{k} + \frac{\delta_{n1}}{2}; \tag{58}$$

see exercise 27. This formula for ψ_n is surprisingly similar to an expression that arises in connection with digital search tree algorithms, Eq. 6.3–(18). Exercise 28 proves that $\psi_n = \Theta(n^{-2})$.

We now know $\alpha(x)$, except for the constant $\lambda = -\rho_1$, and (50) relates $\mu(x)$ to $\rho(x)$ except for the coefficient μ_1. The answer to exercise 25 shows that the coefficients of $\rho(x)$ can all be expressed in terms of ρ_1, ρ_3, ρ_5, $\ldots$; moreover, the constants σ_m and τ_m can be computed by the method used to solve exercise 29, and complicated relations also hold between the coefficients of the functions $\gamma_m(x)$ and $\delta_m(x)$. However, there seems to be no way to compute all the coefficients of the various functions that enter into $G(x)$ except to iterate the recurrence (36) by elaborate numerical methods.

Once we have computed a good approximation to $G(x)$, we can estimate the asymptotic average running time of Algorithm B as follows: If $u \geq v$ and if k right shifts are performed, the quantity $Y = uv$ is changed to $Y' = (u - v)v/2^k$; hence the ratio Y/Y' is $2^k/(1-X)$, where $X = v/u$ is $\geq x$ with probability $G(x)$. Therefore the number of bits in uv decreases on the average by the constant

$$b = \operatorname{E}\lg(Y/Y') = \sum_{k\geq 1}2^{-k}\left(f_k(0) + \int_0^1 G(x)f_k'(x)\,dx\right),$$

where $f_k(x) = \lg\big(2^k/(1-x)\big)$; we have

$$b = \sum_{k \geq 1} 2^{-k} \left(k + \int_0^1 \frac{G(x)\,dx}{(1-x)\ln 2} \right) = 2 + \int_0^1 \frac{G(x)\,dx}{(1-x)\ln 2}. \qquad (59)$$

When eventually $u = v$, the expected value of $\lg uv$ will be approximately 0.9779 (see exercise 14); therefore the total number of subtract-and-shift cycles of Algorithm B will be approximately $1/b$ times the initial value of $\lg uv$. By symmetry, this is about $2/b$ times the initial value of $\lg u$. Numerical computations carried out by Richard Brent in 1997 give the value

$$2/b = 0.70597\ 12461\ 01916\ 39152\ 93141\ 35852\ 88176\ 66677+ \qquad (60)$$

for this fundamental constant.

A deeper study of these functions by Brigitte Vallée led her to suspect that the constants λ and b might be related by the remarkable formula

$$\frac{\lambda}{b} = \frac{2\ln 2}{\pi^2}. \qquad (61)$$

Sure enough, the values computed by Brent agree perfectly with this tantalizing conjecture. Vallée has successfully analyzed Algorithm B using rigorous "dynamical" methods of great interest [see *Algorithmica* **22** (1998), 660–685].

Let us return to our assumption in (32) that u and v are odd and in the ranges $2^m \leq u < 2^{m+1}$ and $2^n \leq v < 2^{n+1}$. Empirical tests of Algorithm B with several million random inputs and with various values of m and n in the range $29 \leq m, n \leq 37$ indicate that the actual average behavior of the algorithm is given by

$$\begin{aligned} C &\approx \tfrac{1}{2}m + 0.203n + 1.9 - 0.4(0.6)^{m-n}, \\ D &\approx m + 0.41n\ - 0.5 - 0.7(0.6)^{m-n}, \end{aligned} \qquad m \geq n, \qquad (62)$$

with a rather small standard deviation from these observed average values. The coefficients $\tfrac{1}{2}$ and 1 of m in (62) can be verified rigorously (see exercise 21).

If we assume instead that u and v are to be *any* integers, independently and uniformly distributed over the ranges

$$1 \leq u < 2^N, \qquad 1 \leq v < 2^N, \qquad (63)$$

then we can calculate the average values of C and D from the data already given:

$$C \approx 0.70N + O(1), \qquad D \approx 1.41N + O(1). \qquad (64)$$

(See exercise 22.) This agrees perfectly with the results of further empirical tests, made on several million random inputs for $N \leq 30$; the latter tests show that we may take

$$C = 0.70N - 0.5, \qquad D = 1.41N - 2.7 \qquad (65)$$

as decent estimates of the values, given this distribution of the inputs u and v.

The theoretical analysis in Brent's continuous model of Algorithm B predicts that C and D will be asymptotically equal to $2N/b$ and $4N/b$ under assumption (63), where $2/b \approx 0.70597$ is the constant in (60). The agreement with experiment is so good that Brent's constant $2/b$ must be the true value of the number "0.70" in (65), and we should replace 0.203 by 0.206 in (62).

This completes our study of the average values of C and D. The other three quantities that appear in the running time of Algorithm B are quite easy to analyze; see exercises 6, 7, and 8.

Now that we know approximately how Algorithm B behaves on the average, let's consider a "worst case" scenario: What values of u and v are in some sense the hardest to handle? If we assume as before that

$$\lfloor \lg u \rfloor = m \qquad \text{and} \qquad \lfloor \lg v \rfloor = n,$$

we want to find u and v that make the algorithm run most slowly. The subtractions take somewhat longer than the shifts, when the auxiliary bookkeeping is considered, so this question may be rephrased by asking for the inputs u and v that require the most subtractions. The answer is somewhat surprising; the maximum value of C is exactly

$$\max(m, n) + 1, \tag{66}$$

although a naïve analysis would predict that substantially higher values of C are possible (see exercise 35). The derivation of the worst case (66) is quite interesting, so it has been left as an amusing problem for readers to work out for themselves (see exercises 36 and 37).

EXERCISES

1. [*M21*] How can (8), (9), (10), (11), and (12) be derived easily from (6) and (7)?

2. [*M22*] Given that u divides $v_1 v_2 \dots v_n$, prove that u divides

$$\gcd(u, v_1) \gcd(u, v_2) \dots \gcd(u, v_n).$$

3. [*M23*] Show that the number of ordered pairs of positive integers (u, v) such that $\text{lcm}(u, v) = n$ is the number of divisors of n^2.

4. [*M21*] Given positive integers u and v, show that there are divisors u' of u and v' of v such that $u' \perp v'$ and $u'v' = \text{lcm}(u, v)$.

▶ **5.** [*M26*] Invent an algorithm (analogous to Algorithm B) for calculating the greatest common divisor of two integers based on their *balanced ternary* representation. Demonstrate your algorithm by applying it to the calculation of $\gcd(40902, 24140)$.

6. [*M22*] Given that u and v are random positive integers, find the mean and the standard deviation of the quantity A that enters into the timing of Program B. (This is the number of right shifts applied to both u and v during the preparatory phase.)

7. [*M20*] Analyze the quantity B that enters into the timing of Program B.

▶ **8.** [*M25*] Show that in Program B, the average value of E is approximately equal to $\frac{1}{2}C_{\text{ave}}$, where C_{ave} is the average value of C.

9. [*18*] Using Algorithm B and hand calculation, find $\gcd(31408, 2718)$. Also find integers m and n such that $31408m + 2718n = \gcd(31408, 2718)$, using Algorithm X.

▶ **10.** [*HM24*] Let q_n be the number of ordered pairs of integers (u, v) lying in the range $1 \le u, v \le n$ such that $u \perp v$. The object of this exercise is to prove that we have $\lim_{n\to\infty} q_n/n^2 = 6/\pi^2$, thereby establishing Theorem D.

a) Use the principle of inclusion and exclusion (Section 1.3.3) to show that

$$q_n = n^2 - \sum_{p_1} \lfloor n/p_1 \rfloor^2 + \sum_{p_1 < p_2} \lfloor n/p_1 p_2 \rfloor^2 - \cdots,$$

where the sums are taken over all *prime* numbers p_i.

b) The *Möbius function* $\mu(n)$ is defined by the rules $\mu(1) = 1$, $\mu(p_1 p_2 \ldots p_r) = (-1)^r$ if $p_1, p_2, \ldots, p_r$ are distinct primes, and $\mu(n) = 0$ if n is divisible by the square of a prime. Show that $q_n = \sum_{k\ge 1} \mu(k) \lfloor n/k \rfloor^2$.

c) As a consequence of (b), prove that $\lim_{n\to\infty} q_n/n^2 = \sum_{k\ge 1} \mu(k)/k^2$.

d) Prove that $(\sum_{k\ge 1} \mu(k)/k^2)(\sum_{m\ge 1} 1/m^2) = 1$. *Hint:* When the series are absolutely convergent we have

$$\left(\sum_{k\ge 1} a_k/k^z \right) \left(\sum_{m\ge 1} b_m/m^z \right) = \sum_{n\ge 1} \left(\sum_{d\backslash n} a_d b_{n/d} \right) \Big/ n^z.$$

11. [*M22*] What is the probability that $\gcd(u, v) \le 3$? (See Theorem D.) What is the *average* value of $\gcd(u, v)$?

12. [*M24*] (E. Cesàro.) If u and v are random positive integers, what is the average number of (positive) divisors they have in common? [*Hint:* See the identity in exercise 10(d), with $a_k = b_m = 1$.]

13. [*HM23*] Given that u and v are random *odd* positive integers, show that they are relatively prime with probability $8/\pi^2$.

▶ **14.** [*HM25*] What is the expected value of $\ln \gcd(u, v)$ when u and v are (a) random positive integers? (b) random positive odd integers?

15. [*M21*] What are the values of v_1 and v_2 when Algorithm X terminates?

▶ **16.** [*M22*] Design an algorithm to *divide u by v modulo m*, given positive integers u, v, and m, with v relatively prime to m. In other words, your algorithm should find w, in the range $0 \le w < m$, such that $u \equiv vw$ (modulo m).

▶ **17.** [*M20*] Given two integers u and v such that $uv \equiv 1$ (modulo 2^e), explain how to compute an integer u' such that $u'v \equiv 1$ (modulo 2^{2e}). [This leads to a fast algorithm for computing the reciprocal of an odd number modulo a power of 2, since we can start with a table of all such reciprocals for $e = 8$ or $e = 16$.]

▶ **18.** [*M24*] Show how Algorithm L can be extended (as Algorithm A was extended to Algorithm X) to obtain solutions of (15) when u and v are large.

19. [*21*] Use the text's method to find a general solution in integers to the following sets of equations:

a)	$3x + 7y + 11z = 1$	b)	$3x + 7y + 11z = 1$
	$5x + 7y - 5z = 3$		$5x + 7y - 5z = -3$

20. [*M37*] Let u and v be odd integers, independently and uniformly distributed in the ranges $2^m \le u < 2^{m+1}$, $2^n \le v < 2^{n+1}$. What is the *exact* probability that a single subtract-and-shift cycle in Algorithm B reduces u and v to the ranges $2^{m'} \le u < 2^{m'+1}$, $2^{n'} \le v < 2^{n'+1}$, as a function of m, n, m', and n'?

21. [*HM26*] Let C_{mn} and D_{mn} be the average number of subtraction steps and shift steps, respectively, in Algorithm B, when u and v are odd, $\lfloor \lg u \rfloor = m$, $\lfloor \lg v \rfloor = n$. Show that for fixed n, $C_{mn} = \frac{1}{2}m + O(1)$ and $D_{mn} = m + O(1)$ as $m \to \infty$.

22. [*M28*] Continuing the previous exercise, show that if $C_{mn} = \alpha m + \beta n + \gamma$ for some constants α, β, and γ, then

$$\sum_{1 \le n < m \le N} (N-m)(N-n)2^{m+n-2}C_{mn} = 2^{2N}\left(\tfrac{11}{27}(\alpha+\beta)N + O(1)\right),$$

$$\sum_{1 \le n \le N} (N-n)^2 2^{2n-2} C_{nn} = 2^{2N}\left(\tfrac{5}{27}(\alpha+\beta)N + O(1)\right).$$

▶ **23.** [*M20*] What is the probability that $v/u \le x$ after n subtract-and-shift cycles of Algorithm B, when the algorithm begins with large random integers? (Here x is any real number ≥ 0; we do not assume that $u \ge v$.)

24. [*M20*] Suppose $u > v$ in step B6, and assume that the ratio v/u has Brent's limiting distribution G. What is the probability that $u < v$ the next time step B6 is encountered?

25. [*M21*] Equation (46) implies that $\rho_1 = -\lambda$; prove that $\rho_2 = \lambda/2$.

26. [*M22*] Prove that when $G(x)$ satisfies (36)–(40) we have

$$2G(x) - 5G(2x) + 2G(4x) = G(1+2x) - 2G(1+4x) + 2G(1+1/x) - G(1+1/2x).$$

27. [*M22*] Prove (58), which expresses ψ_n in terms of Bernoulli numbers.

28. [*HM36*] Study the asymptotic behavior of ψ_n. *Hint:* See exercise 6.3–34.

▶ **29.** [*HM26*] (R. P. Brent.) Find $G_1(x)$, the distribution of $\min(u,v)/\max(u,v)$ after the first subtract-and-shift cycle of Algorithm B as defined in (35). *Hint:* Let $S_{n+1}(x) = \sum_{k=1}^{\infty} 2^{-k} G_n\bigl(1/(1+2^k x)\bigr)$, and use the method of Mellin transforms for harmonic sums [see P. Flajolet, X. Gourdon, and P. Dumas, *Theor. Comp. Sci.* **144** (1995), 3–58].

30. [*HM39*] Continuing the previous exercise, determine $G_2(x)$.

31. [*HM46*] Prove or disprove Vallée's conjecture (61).

32. [*HM42*] Is there a unique continuous function $G(x)$ that satisfies (36) and (37)?

33. [*M46*] Analyze Harris's "binary Euclidean algorithm," stated after Program B.

34. [*HM49*] Find a rigorous proof that Brent's model describes the asymptotic behavior of Algorithm B.

35. [*M23*] Consider a directed graph with vertices (m,n) for all nonnegative integers $m, n \ge 0$, having arcs from (m,n) to (m',n') whenever it is possible for a subtract-and-shift cycle of Algorithm B to transform integers u and v with $\lfloor \lg u \rfloor = m$ and $\lfloor \lg v \rfloor = n$ into integers u' and v' with $\lfloor \lg u' \rfloor = m'$ and $\lfloor \lg v' \rfloor = n'$; there also is a special "Stop" vertex, with arcs from (n,n) to Stop for all $n \ge 0$. What is the length of the longest path from (m,n) to Stop? (This gives an upper bound on the maximum running time of Algorithm B.)

▶ **36.** [*M28*] Given $m \ge n \ge 1$, find values of u and v with $\lfloor \lg u \rfloor = m$ and $\lfloor \lg v \rfloor = n$ such that Algorithm B requires $m+1$ subtraction steps.

37. [*M32*] Prove that the subtraction step B6 of Algorithm B is never executed more than $1 + \lfloor \lg \max(u,v) \rfloor$ times.

▶ **38.** [*M32*] (R. W. Gosper.) Demonstrate how to modify Algorithm B for large numbers, using ideas analogous to those in Algorithm L.

▶ **39.** [*M28*] (V. R. Pratt.) Extend Algorithm B to an Algorithm Y that is analogous to Algorithm X.

▶ **40.** [*M25*] (R. P. Brent and H. T. Kung.) The following variant of the binary gcd algorithm is better than Algorithm B from the standpoint of hardware implementation, because it does not require testing the sign of $u - v$. Assume that u is odd; u and v can be either positive or negative.

K1. [Initialize.] Set $c \leftarrow 0$. (This counter estimates the difference between $\lg |u|$ and $\lg |v|$.)

K2. [Done?] If $v = 0$, terminate with $|u|$ as the answer.

K3. [Make v odd.] Set $v \leftarrow v/2$ and $c \leftarrow c + 1$ zero or more times, until v is odd.

K4. [Make $c \leq 0$.] If $c > 0$, interchange $u \leftrightarrow v$ and set $c \leftarrow -c$.

K5. [Reduce.] Set $w \leftarrow (u+v)/2$. If w is even, set $v \leftarrow w$; otherwise set $v \leftarrow w - v$. Return to step K2. ∎

Prove that step K2 is performed at most $2 + 2\lg\max(|u|, |v|)$ times.

41. [*M22*] Use Euclid's algorithm to find a simple formula for $\gcd(10^m - 1, 10^n - 1)$ when m and n are nonnegative integers.

42. [*M30*] Evaluate the determinant

$$\begin{vmatrix} \gcd(1,1) & \gcd(1,2) & \ldots & \gcd(1,n) \\ \gcd(2,1) & \gcd(2,2) & \ldots & \gcd(2,n) \\ \vdots & \vdots & & \vdots \\ \gcd(n,1) & \gcd(n,2) & \ldots & \gcd(n,n) \end{vmatrix}.$$

*4.5.3. Analysis of Euclid's Algorithm

The execution time of Euclid's algorithm depends on T, the number of times the division step A2 is performed. (See Algorithm 4.5.2A and Program 4.5.2A.) The quantity T is also an important factor in the running time of other algorithms, such as the evaluation of functions satisfying a reciprocity formula (see Section 3.3.3). We shall see in this section that the mathematical analysis of this quantity T is interesting and instructive.

Relation to continued fractions. Euclid's algorithm is intimately connected with *continued fractions*, which are expressions of the form

$$\cfrac{b_1}{a_1 + \cfrac{b_2}{a_2 + \cfrac{b_3}{\cdots \cfrac{}{a_{n-1}+\cfrac{b_n}{a_n}}}}} = b_1 / \big(a_1 + b_2/(a_2 + b_3/(\cdots/(a_{n-1} + b_n/a_n)\ldots))\big).$$

$$(1)$$

Continued fractions have a beautiful theory that is the subject of several classic books, such as O. Perron, *Die Lehre von den Kettenbrüchen*, 3rd edition (Stuttgart: Teubner, 1954), 2 volumes; A. Khinchin, *Continued Fractions*, translated by Peter Wynn (Groningen: P. Noordhoff, 1963); and H. S. Wall, *Analytic Theory of Continued Fractions* (New York: Van Nostrand, 1948). See also Claude Brezinski, *History of Continued Fractions and Padé Approximants* (Springer, 1991), for the early history of the subject. It is necessary to limit ourselves to a comparatively brief treatment of the theory here, studying only those aspects that give us more insight into the behavior of Euclid's algorithm.

The continued fractions of primary interest to us are those in which all of the b's in (1) are equal to unity. For convenience in notation, let us define

$$//x_1, x_2, \ldots, x_n// = 1/(x_1 + 1/(x_2 + 1/(\cdots/(x_{n-1} + 1/x_n)\ldots))). \qquad (2)$$

Thus, for example,

$$//x_1// = \frac{1}{x_1}, \qquad //x_1, x_2// = \frac{1}{x_1 + 1/x_2} = \frac{x_2}{x_1 x_2 + 1}. \qquad (3)$$

If $n = 0$, the symbol $//x_1, \ldots, x_n//$ is taken to mean 0. Let us also define the so-called *continuant polynomials* $K_n(x_1, x_2, \ldots, x_n)$ of n variables, for $n \geq 0$, by the rule

$$K_n(x_1, x_2, \ldots, x_n) = \begin{cases} 1, & \text{if } n = 0; \\ x_1, & \text{if } n = 1; \\ x_1 K_{n-1}(x_2, \ldots, x_n) + K_{n-2}(x_3, \ldots, x_n), & \text{if } n > 1. \end{cases} \qquad (4)$$

Thus $K_2(x_1, x_2) = x_1 x_2 + 1$, $K_3(x_1, x_2, x_3) = x_1 x_2 x_3 + x_1 + x_3$, etc. In general, as noted by L. Euler in the eighteenth century, $K_n(x_1, x_2, \ldots, x_n)$ is the sum of all terms obtainable by starting with $x_1 x_2 \ldots x_n$ and deleting zero or more nonoverlapping pairs of consecutive variables $x_j x_{j+1}$; there are F_{n+1} such terms.

The basic property of continuants is the explicit formula

$$//x_1, x_2, \ldots, x_n// = K_{n-1}(x_2, \ldots, x_n)/K_n(x_1, x_2, \ldots, x_n), \qquad n \geq 1. \qquad (5)$$

This can be proved by induction, since it implies that

$$x_0 + //x_1, \ldots, x_n// = K_{n+1}(x_0, x_1, \ldots, x_n)/K_n(x_1, \ldots, x_n);$$

hence $//x_0, x_1, \ldots, x_n//$ is the reciprocal of the latter quantity.

The K-polynomials are symmetrical in the sense that

$$K_n(x_1, x_2, \ldots, x_n) = K_n(x_n, \ldots, x_2, x_1). \qquad (6)$$

This follows from Euler's observation above, and as a consequence we have

$$K_n(x_1, \ldots, x_n) = x_n K_{n-1}(x_1, \ldots, x_{n-1}) + K_{n-2}(x_1, \ldots, x_{n-2}) \qquad (7)$$

for $n > 1$. The K-polynomials also satisfy the important identity

$$K_n(x_1, \ldots, x_n) K_n(x_2, \ldots, x_{n+1}) - K_{n+1}(x_1, \ldots, x_{n+1}) K_{n-1}(x_2, \ldots, x_n)$$
$$= (-1)^n, \qquad n \geq 1. \qquad (8)$$

(See exercise 4.) The latter equation in connection with (5) implies that

$$//x_1, \ldots, x_n// = \frac{1}{q_0 q_1} - \frac{1}{q_1 q_2} + \frac{1}{q_2 q_3} - \cdots + \frac{(-1)^{n-1}}{q_{n-1} q_n},$$
$$\text{where } q_k = K_k(x_1, \ldots, x_k). \qquad (9)$$

Thus the K-polynomials are intimately related to continued fractions.

Every real number X in the range $0 \le X < 1$ has a *regular continued fraction* defined as follows: Let $X_0 = X$, and for all $n \ge 0$ such that $X_n \ne 0$ let

$$A_{n+1} = \lfloor 1/X_n \rfloor, \qquad X_{n+1} = 1/X_n - A_{n+1}. \tag{10}$$

If $X_n = 0$, the quantities A_{n+1} and X_{n+1} are not defined, and the regular continued fraction for X is $/\!/A_1, \ldots, A_n/\!/$. If $X_n \ne 0$, this definition guarantees that $0 \le X_{n+1} < 1$, so each of the A's is a positive integer. Definition (10) also implies that

$$X = X_0 = \frac{1}{A_1 + X_1} = \frac{1}{A_1 + 1/(A_2 + X_2)} = \cdots;$$

hence

$$X = /\!/A_1, \ldots, A_{n-1}, A_n + X_n/\!/ \tag{11}$$

for all $n \ge 1$, whenever X_n is defined. In particular, we have $X = /\!/A_1, \ldots, A_n/\!/$ when $X_n = 0$. If $X_n \ne 0$, the number X always lies *between* $/\!/A_1, \ldots, A_n/\!/$ and $/\!/A_1, \ldots, A_n + 1/\!/$, since by (7) the quantity $q_n = K_n(A_1, \ldots, A_n + X_n)$ increases monotonically from $K_n(A_1, \ldots, A_n)$ up to $K_n(A_1, \ldots, A_n + 1)$ as X_n increases from 0 to 1, and by (9) the continued fraction increases or decreases when q_n increases, according as n is even or odd. In fact,

$$
\begin{aligned}
|X - /\!/A_1, \ldots, A_n/\!/| &= |/\!/A_1, \ldots, A_n + X_n/\!/ - /\!/A_1, \ldots, A_n/\!/| \\
&= |/\!/A_1, \ldots, A_n, 1/X_n/\!/ - /\!/A_1, \ldots, A_n/\!/| \\
&= \left| \frac{K_n(A_2, \ldots, A_n, 1/X_n)}{K_{n+1}(A_1, \ldots, A_n, 1/X_n)} - \frac{K_{n-1}(A_2, \ldots, A_n)}{K_n(A_1, \ldots, A_n)} \right| \\
&= 1 / \big(K_n(A_1, \ldots, A_n) K_{n+1}(A_1, \ldots, A_n, 1/X_n) \big) \\
&\le 1 / \big(K_n(A_1, \ldots, A_n) K_{n+1}(A_1, \ldots, A_n, A_{n+1}) \big) \tag{12}
\end{aligned}
$$

by (5), (7), (8), and (10). Therefore $/\!/A_1, \ldots, A_n/\!/$ is an extremely close approximation to X, unless n is small. If X_n is nonzero for all n, we obtain an *infinite continued fraction* $/\!/A_1, A_2, A_3, \ldots /\!/$, whose value is defined to be

$$\lim_{n \to \infty} /\!/A_1, A_2, \ldots, A_n/\!/;$$

from inequality (12) it is clear that this limit equals X.

The regular continued fraction expansion of real numbers has several properties analogous to the representation of numbers in the decimal system. If we use the formulas above to compute the regular continued fraction expansions of some familiar real numbers, we find, for example, that

$$\tfrac{8}{29} = /\!/3, 1, 1, 1, 2/\!/;$$

$$\sqrt{\tfrac{8}{29}} = /\!/1, 1, 9, 2, 2, 3, 2, 2, 9, 1, 2, 1, 9, 2, 2, 3, 2, 2, 9, 1, 2, 1, 9, 2, 2, 3, 2, 2, 9, 1, \ldots /\!/;$$

$$\sqrt[3]{2} = 1 + /\!/3, 1, 5, 1, 1, 4, 1, 1, 8, 1, 14, 1, 10, 2, 1, 4, 12, 2, 3, 2, 1, 3, 4, 1, 1, 2, 14, 3, \ldots /\!/;$$

$$\pi = 3 + /\!/7, 15, 1, 292, 1, 1, 1, 2, 1, 3, 1, 14, 2, 1, 1, 2, 2, 2, 2, 1, 84, 2, 1, 1, 15, 3, 13, \ldots /\!/;$$

$$e = 2 + /\!/1, 2, 1, 1, 4, 1, 1, 6, 1, 1, 8, 1, 1, 10, 1, 1, 12, 1, 1, 14, 1, 1, 16, 1, 1, 18, 1, \ldots /\!/;$$

$$\gamma = /\!/1, 1, 2, 1, 2, 1, 4, 3, 13, 5, 1, 1, 8, 1, 2, 4, 1, 1, 40, 1, 11, 3, 7, 1, 7, 1, 1, 5, 1, 49, \ldots /\!/;$$

$$\phi = 1 + /\!/1, 1, 1, 1, 1, 1, 1, 1, 1, 1, 1, 1, 1, 1, 1, 1, 1, 1, 1, 1, 1, 1, 1, 1, 1, 1, 1, 1, \ldots /\!/. \quad (13)$$

The numbers A_1, A_2, ... are called the *partial quotients* of X. Notice the regular pattern that appears in the partial quotients for $\sqrt{8/29}$, ϕ, and e; the reasons for this behavior are discussed in exercises 12 and 16. There is no apparent pattern in the partial quotients for $\sqrt[3]{2}$, π, or γ.

It is interesting to note that the ancient Greeks' first definition of real numbers, once they had discovered the existence of irrationals, was essentially stated in terms of infinite continued fractions. (Later they adopted the suggestion of Eudoxus that $x = y$ should be defined instead as "$x < r$ if and only if $y < r$, for all rational r.") See O. Becker, *Quellen und Studien zur Geschichte Math., Astron., Physik* **B2** (1933), 311–333.

When X is a rational number, the regular continued fraction corresponds in a natural way to Euclid's algorithm. Let us assume that $X = v/u$, where $u > v \geq 0$. The regular continued fraction process starts with $X_0 = X$; let us define $U_0 = u$, $V_0 = v$. Assuming that $X_n = V_n/U_n \neq 0$, (10) becomes

$$A_{n+1} = \lfloor U_n/V_n \rfloor, \qquad X_{n+1} = U_n/V_n - A_{n+1} = (U_n \bmod V_n)/V_n. \quad (14)$$

Therefore, if we define

$$U_{n+1} = V_n, \qquad V_{n+1} = U_n \bmod V_n, \quad (15)$$

the condition $X_n = V_n/U_n$ holds throughout the process. Furthermore, (15) is precisely the transformation made on the variables u and v in Euclid's algorithm (see Algorithm 4.5.2A, step A2). For example, since $\frac{8}{29} = /\!/3, 1, 1, 1, 2/\!/$, we know that Euclid's algorithm applied to $u = 29$ and $v = 8$ will require exactly five division steps, and the quotients $\lfloor u/v \rfloor$ in step A2 will be successively 3, 1, 1, 1, and 2. The last partial quotient A_n must always be 2 or more when $X_n = 0$ and $n \geq 1$, since X_{n-1} is less than unity.

From this correspondence with Euclid's algorithm we can see that the regular continued fraction for X terminates at some step with $X_n = 0$ if and only if X is rational; for it is obvious that X_n cannot be zero if X is irrational, and, conversely, we know that Euclid's algorithm always terminates. If the partial quotients obtained during Euclid's algorithm are A_1, A_2, ..., A_n, then we have, by (5),

$$\frac{v}{u} = \frac{K_{n-1}(A_2, \ldots, A_n)}{K_n(A_1, A_2, \ldots, A_n)}. \quad (16)$$

This formula holds also if Euclid's algorithm is applied for $u < v$, when $A_1 = 0$. Furthermore, because of relation (8), the continuants $K_{n-1}(A_2, \ldots, A_n)$ and $K_n(A_1, A_2, \ldots, A_n)$ are relatively prime, and the fraction on the right-hand side of (16) is in lowest terms; therefore

$$u = K_n(A_1, A_2, \ldots, A_n)d, \qquad v = K_{n-1}(A_2, \ldots, A_n)d, \quad (17)$$

where $d = \gcd(u, v)$.

The worst case. We can now apply these observations to determine the behavior of Euclid's algorithm in the worst case, or in other words to give an upper bound on the number of division steps. The worst case occurs when the inputs are consecutive Fibonacci numbers:

Theorem F. *For $n \geq 1$, let u and v be integers with $u > v > 0$ such that Euclid's algorithm applied to u and v requires exactly n division steps, and such that u is as small as possible satisfying these conditions. Then $u = F_{n+2}$ and $v = F_{n+1}$.*

Proof. By (17), we must have $u = K_n(A_1, A_2, \ldots, A_n)d$, where A_1, A_2, $\ldots$, A_n, and d are positive integers and $A_n \geq 2$. Since K_n is a polynomial with nonnegative coefficients, involving all of the variables, the minimum value is achieved only when $A_1 = 1$, $\ldots$, $A_{n-1} = 1$, $A_n = 2$, $d = 1$. Putting these values in (17) yields the desired result. ∎

This theorem has the historical claim of being the first practical application of the Fibonacci sequence; since then many other applications of Fibonacci numbers to algorithms and to the study of algorithms have been discovered. The result is essentially due to T. F. de Lagny [*Mém. Acad. Sci.* **11** (Paris, 1733), 363–364], who tabulated the first several continuants and observed that Fibonacci numbers give the smallest numerator and denominator for continued fractions of a given length. He did not explicitly mention gcd calculation, however; the connection between Fibonacci numbers and Euclid's algorithm was first pointed out by É. Léger [*Correspondance Math. et Physique* **9** (1837), 483–485.]

Shortly afterwards, P. J. É. Finck [*Traité Élémentaire d'Arithmétique* (Strasbourg: 1841), 44] proved by another method that $\gcd(u, v)$ takes at most $2 \lg v + 1$ steps, when $u > v > 0$; and G. Lamé [*Comptes Rendus Acad. Sci.* **19** (Paris, 1844), 867–870] improved this to $5\lceil \log_{10}(v + 1)\rceil$. Full details about these pioneering studies in the analysis of algorithms appear in an interesting review by J. O. Shallit, *Historia Mathematica* **21** (1994), 401–419. A more precise estimate of the worst case is, however, a direct consequence of Theorem F:

Corollary L. *If $0 \leq v < N$, the number of division steps required when Algorithm 4.5.2A is applied to u and v is at most $\lfloor \log_\phi (3 - \phi)N \rfloor$.*

Proof. After step A1 we have $v > u \bmod v$. Therefore by Theorem F, the maximum number of steps, n, occurs when $v = F_{n+1}$ and $u \bmod v = F_n$. Since $F_{n+1} < N$, we have $\phi^{n+1}/\sqrt{5} < N$ $\left(\text{see Eq. 1.2.8–(15)}\right)$; thus $\phi^n < (\sqrt{5}/\phi)N = (3 - \phi)N$. ∎

The quantity $\log_\phi (3 - \phi)N$ is approximately equal to $2.078 \ln N + .6723 \approx 4.785 \log_{10} N + .6723$. See exercises 31, 36, and 38 for extensions of Theorem F.

An approximate model. Now that we know the maximum number of division steps that can occur, let us attempt to find the *average* number. Let $T(m, n)$ be the number of division steps that occur when $u = m$ and $v = n$ are input to Euclid's algorithm. Thus

$$T(m, 0) = 0; \qquad T(m, n) = 1 + T(n, m \bmod n) \qquad \text{if } n \geq 1. \qquad (18)$$

Let T_n be the average number of division steps when $v = n$ and when u is chosen at random; since only the value of $u \bmod v$ affects the algorithm after the first division step, we have

$$T_n = \frac{1}{n} \sum_{0 \le k < n} T(k, n). \tag{19}$$

For example, $T(0, 5) = 1$, $T(1, 5) = 2$, $T(2, 5) = 3$, $T(3, 5) = 4$, $T(4, 5) = 3$, so

$$T_5 = \tfrac{1}{5}(1 + 2 + 3 + 4 + 3) = 2\tfrac{3}{5}.$$

Our goal is to estimate T_n for large n. One idea is to try an approximation suggested by R. W. Floyd: We might assume that, for $0 \le k < n$, the value of n is essentially "random" modulo k, so that we can set

$$T_n \approx 1 + \frac{1}{n}(T_0 + T_1 + \cdots + T_{n-1}).$$

Then $T_n \approx S_n$, where the sequence $\langle S_n \rangle$ is the solution to the recurrence relation

$$S_0 = 0, \qquad S_n = 1 + \frac{1}{n}(S_0 + S_1 + \cdots + S_{n-1}), \qquad n \ge 1. \tag{20}$$

This recurrence is easy to solve by noting that

$$S_{n+1} = 1 + \frac{1}{n+1}(S_0 + S_1 + \cdots + S_{n-1} + S_n)$$

$$= 1 + \frac{1}{n+1}\big(n(S_n - 1) + S_n\big) = S_n + \frac{1}{n+1};$$

hence S_n is $1 + \frac{1}{2} + \cdots + \frac{1}{n} = H_n$, a harmonic number. The approximation $T_n \approx S_n$ now suggests that we might have $T_n \approx \ln n + O(1)$.

Comparison of this approximation with tables of the true value of T_n show, however, that $\ln n$ is too large; T_n does not grow this fast. Our tentative assumption that n is random modulo k must therefore be too pessimistic. And indeed, a closer look shows that the average value of $n \bmod k$ is less than the average value of $\frac{1}{2}k$, in the range $1 \le k \le n$:

$$\frac{1}{n} \sum_{1 \le k \le n} (n \bmod k) = \frac{1}{n} \sum_{1 \le k, q \le n} (n - qk)\,\big[\lfloor n/(q+1)\rfloor < k \le \lfloor n/q \rfloor\big]$$

$$= n - \frac{1}{n} \sum_{1 \le q \le n} q \left(\binom{\lfloor n/q \rfloor + 1}{2} - \binom{\lfloor n/(q+1)\rfloor + 1}{2}\right)$$

$$= n - \frac{1}{n} \sum_{1 \le q \le n} \binom{\lfloor n/q \rfloor + 1}{2}$$

$$= \left(1 - \frac{\pi^2}{12}\right) n + O(\log n) \tag{21}$$

$\big($see exercise 4.5.2–10(c)$\big)$. This is only about $.1775n$, not $.25n$; so the value of $n \bmod k$ tends to be smaller than Floyd's model predicts, and Euclid's algorithm works faster than we might expect.

A continuous model. The behavior of Euclid's algorithm with $v = N$ is essentially determined by the behavior of the regular continued fraction process when $X = 0/N, 1/N, \ldots, (N-1)/N$. When N is very large, we therefore want to study the behavior of regular continued fractions when X is essentially a random real number, uniformly distributed in $[0 \ldots 1)$. Consider the distribution function

$$F_n(x) = \Pr(X_n \leq x), \qquad \text{for } 0 \leq x \leq 1, \tag{22}$$

given a uniform distribution of $X = X_0$. By the definition of regular continued fractions, we have $F_0(x) = x$, and

$$F_{n+1}(x) = \sum_{k \geq 1} \Pr(k \leq 1/X_n \leq k + x)$$

$$= \sum_{k \geq 1} \Pr\big(1/(k+x) \leq X_n \leq 1/k\big)$$

$$= \sum_{k \geq 1} \big(F_n(1/k) - F_n\big(1/(k+x)\big)\big). \tag{23}$$

If the distributions $F_0(x)$, $F_1(x)$, ... defined by these formulas approach a limiting distribution $F_\infty(x) = F(x)$, we will have

$$F(x) = \sum_{k \geq 1} \big(F(1/k) - F\big(1/(k+x)\big)\big). \tag{24}$$

(An analogous relation, 4.5.2–(36), arose in our study of the binary gcd algorithm.) One function that satisfies (24) is $F(x) = \log_b(1+x)$, for any base $b > 1$; see exercise 19. The further condition $F(1) = 1$ implies that we should take $b = 2$. Thus it is reasonable to make a guess that $F(x) = \lg(1+x)$, and that $F_n(x)$ approaches this behavior.

We might conjecture, for example, that $F(\frac{1}{2}) = \lg(\frac{3}{2}) \approx 0.58496$; let us see how close $F_n(\frac{1}{2})$ comes to this value for small n. We have $F_0(\frac{1}{2}) = 0.50000$, and

$$F_1(x) = \sum_{k \geq 1} \left(\frac{1}{k} - \frac{1}{k+x}\right) = H_x;$$

$$F_1(\tfrac{1}{2}) = H_{1/2} = 2 - 2\ln 2 \approx 0.61371;$$

$$F_2(\tfrac{1}{2}) = H_{2/2} - H_{2/3} + H_{2/4} - H_{2/5} + H_{2/6} - H_{2/7} + \cdots .$$

(See Table 3 of Appendix A.) The power series expansion

$$H_x = \zeta(2)x - \zeta(3)x^2 + \zeta(4)x^3 - \zeta(5)x^4 + \cdots \tag{25}$$

makes it feasible to compute the numerical value

$$F_2(\tfrac{1}{2}) = 0.57655\,93276\,99914\,08418\,82618\,72122\,27055\,92452\,- . \tag{26}$$

We're getting closer to 0.58496; but it is not immediately clear how to get a good estimate of $F_n(\frac{1}{2})$ for $n = 3$, much less for really large values of n.

The distributions $F_n(x)$ were first studied by C. F. Gauss, who first thought of the problem on February 5, 1799. His notebook for 1800 lists various recurrence relations and gives a brief table of values, including the (inaccurate) approximation $F_2(\frac{1}{2}) \approx 0.5748$. After performing these calculations, Gauss wrote, "Tam complicatæ evadunt, ut nulla spes superesse videatur"; i.e., "They come out so complicated that no hope appears to be left." Twelve years later, he wrote a letter to Laplace in which he posed the problem as one he could not resolve to his satisfaction. He said, "I found by very simple reasoning that, for n infinite, $F_n(x) = \log(1 + x)/\log 2$. But the efforts that I made since then in my inquiries to assign $F_n(x) - \log(1 + x)/\log 2$ for very large but not infinite values of n were fruitless." He never published his "very simple reasoning," and it is not completely clear that he had found a rigorous proof. [See Gauss's *Werke*, vol. 10^1, 552–556.] More than 100 years went by before a proof was finally published, by R. O. Kuz'min [*Atti del Congresso Internazionale dei Matematici* **6** (Bologna, 1928), 83–89], who showed that

$$F_n(x) = \lg(1 + x) + O(e^{-A\sqrt{n}})$$

for some positive constant A. The error term was improved to $O(e^{-An})$ by Paul Lévy shortly afterwards [*Bull. Soc. Math. de France* **57** (1929), 178–194]*; but Gauss's problem, namely to find the asymptotic behavior of $F_n(x) - \lg(1 + x)$, was not really resolved until 1974, when Eduard Wirsing published a beautiful analysis of the situation [*Acta Arithmetica* **24** (1974), 507–528]. We shall study the simplest aspects of Wirsing's approach here, since his method is an instructive use of linear operators.

If G is any function of x defined for $0 \le x \le 1$, let SG be the function defined by

$$SG(x) = \sum_{k \ge 1} \left(G\left(\frac{1}{k}\right) - G\left(\frac{1}{k + x}\right) \right). \tag{27}$$

Thus, S is an operator that changes one function into another. In particular, by (23) we have $F_{n+1}(x) = SF_n(x)$, hence

$$F_n = S^n F_0. \tag{28}$$

(In this discussion F_n stands for a distribution function, *not* for a Fibonacci number.) Notice that S is a "linear operator"; that is, $S(cG) = c(SG)$ for all constants c, and $S(G_1 + G_2) = SG_1 + SG_2$.

Now if G has a bounded first derivative, we can differentiate (27) term by term to show that

$$(SG)'(x) = \sum_{k \ge 1} \frac{1}{(k + x)^2} G'\left(\frac{1}{k + x}\right); \tag{29}$$

hence SG also has a bounded first derivative. (Term-by-term differentiation of a convergent series is justified when the series of derivatives is uniformly

---

* An exposition of Lévy's interesting proof appeared in the first edition of this book.

convergent; see, for example, K. Knopp, *Theory and Application of Infinite Series* (Glasgow: Blackie, 1951), §47.)

Let $H = SG$, and let $g(x) = (1+x)G'(x)$, $h(x) = (1+x)H'(x)$. It follows that

$$h(x) = \sum_{k \geq 1} \frac{1+x}{(k+x)^2} \left(1 + \frac{1}{k+x}\right)^{-1} g\left(\frac{1}{k+x}\right)$$

$$= \sum_{k \geq 1} \left(\frac{k}{k+1+x} - \frac{k-1}{k+x}\right) g\left(\frac{1}{k+x}\right).$$

In other words, $h = Tg$, where T is the linear operator defined by

$$Tg(x) = \sum_{k \geq 1} \left(\frac{k}{k+1+x} - \frac{k-1}{k+x}\right) g\left(\frac{1}{k+x}\right). \tag{30}$$

Continuing, we see that if g has a bounded first derivative, we can differentiate term by term to show that Tg does also:

$$(Tg)'(x) = -\sum_{k \geq 1} \left(\left(\frac{k}{(k+1+x)^2} - \frac{k-1}{(k+x)^2}\right) g\left(\frac{1}{k+x}\right)\right.$$

$$\left. + \left(\frac{k}{k+1+x} - \frac{k-1}{k+x}\right) \frac{1}{(k+x)^2} g'\left(\frac{1}{k+x}\right)\right)$$

$$= -\sum_{k \geq 1} \left(\frac{k}{(k+1+x)^2} \left(g\left(\frac{1}{k+x}\right) - g\left(\frac{1}{k+1+x}\right)\right)\right.$$

$$\left. + \frac{1+x}{(k+x)^3(k+1+x)} g'\left(\frac{1}{k+x}\right)\right).$$

There is consequently a third linear operator, U, such that $(Tg)' = -U(g')$, namely

$$U\varphi(x) = \sum_{k \geq 1} \left(\frac{k}{(k+1+x)^2} \int_{1/(k+1+x)}^{1/(k+x)} \varphi(t)\, dt + \frac{1+x}{(k+x)^3(k+1+x)} \varphi\left(\frac{1}{k+x}\right)\right). \tag{31}$$

What is the relevance of all this to our problem? Well, if we set

$$F_n(x) = \lg(1+x) + R_n\big(\lg(1+x)\big), \tag{32}$$

$$f_n(x) = (1+x) F_n'(x) = \frac{1}{\ln 2}\big(1 + R_n'\big(\lg(1+x)\big)\big), \tag{33}$$

we have

$$f_n'(x) = R_n''\big(\lg(1+x)\big)\big/\big((\ln 2)^2(1+x)\big); \tag{34}$$

the effect of the $\lg(1+x)$ term disappears, after these transformations. Furthermore, since $F_n = S^n F_0$, we have $f_n = T^n f_0$ and $f_n' = (-1)^n U^n f_0'$. Both F_n and f_n have bounded derivatives, by induction on n. Thus (34) becomes

$$(-1)^n R_n''\big(\lg(1+x)\big) = (1+x)(\ln 2)^2\, U^n f_0'(x). \tag{35}$$

Now $F_0(x) = x$, $f_0(x) = 1 + x$, and $f_0'(x)$ is the constant function 1. We are going to show that the operator U^n takes the constant function into a function with very small values, hence $|R_n''(x)|$ must be very small for $0 \leq x \leq 1$. Finally we can clinch the argument by showing that $R_n(x)$ itself is small: Since we have $R_n(0) = R_n(1) = 0$, it follows from a well-known interpolation formula (see exercise 4.6.4–15 with $x_0 = 0$, $x_1 = x$, $x_2 = 1$) that

$$R_n(x) = -\frac{x(1-x)}{2} R_n''(\xi_n(x)) \tag{36}$$

for some function $\xi_n(x)$, where $0 \leq \xi_n(x) \leq 1$ when $0 \leq x \leq 1$.

Thus everything hinges on our being able to prove that U^n produces small function values, where U is the linear operator defined in (31). Notice that U is a *positive* operator, in the sense that $U\varphi(x) \geq 0$ for all x if $\varphi(x) \geq 0$ for all x. It follows that U is order-preserving: If $\varphi_1(x) \leq \varphi_2(x)$ for all x then we have $U\varphi_1(x) \leq U\varphi_2(x)$ for all x.

One way to exploit this property is to find a function φ for which we can calculate $U\varphi$ exactly, and to use constant multiples of this function to bound the ones that we are really interested in. First let us look for a function g such that Tg is easy to compute. If we consider functions defined for all $x \geq 0$, instead of only on $[0 \, . \, . \, 1]$, it is easy to remove the summation from (27) by observing that

$$SG(x + 1) - SG(x) = G\left(\frac{1}{1+x}\right) - \lim_{k \to \infty} G\left(\frac{1}{k+x}\right) = G\left(\frac{1}{1+x}\right) - G(0) \tag{37}$$

when G is continuous. Since $T\big((1 + x)G'\big) = (1 + x)(SG)'$, it follows (see exercise 20) that

$$\frac{Tg(x)}{1+x} - \frac{Tg(1+x)}{2+x} = \left(\frac{1}{1+x} - \frac{1}{2+x}\right) g\left(\frac{1}{1+x}\right). \tag{38}$$

If we set $Tg(x) = 1/(1 + x)$, we find that the corresponding value of $g(x)$ is $1 + x - 1/(1+x)$. Let $\varphi(x) = g'(x) = 1 + 1/(1+x)^2$, so that $U\varphi(x) = -(Tg)'(x) = 1/(1 + x)^2$; this is the function φ we have been looking for.

For this choice of φ we have $2 \leq \varphi(x)/U\varphi(x) = (1+x)^2 + 1 \leq 5$ for $0 \leq x \leq 1$, hence

$$\tfrac{1}{5}\varphi \leq U\varphi \leq \tfrac{1}{2}\varphi.$$

By the positivity of U and φ we can apply U to this inequality again, obtaining $\tfrac{1}{25}\varphi \leq \tfrac{1}{5}U\varphi \leq U^2\varphi \leq \tfrac{1}{2}U\varphi \leq \tfrac{1}{4}\varphi$; and after $n - 1$ applications we have

$$5^{-n}\varphi \leq U^n\varphi \leq 2^{-n}\varphi \tag{39}$$

for this particular φ. Let $\chi(x) = f_0'(x) = 1$ be the constant function; then for $0 \leq x \leq 1$ we have $\tfrac{5}{4}\chi \leq \varphi \leq 2\chi$, hence

$$\tfrac{5}{8}5^{-n}\chi \leq \tfrac{1}{2}5^{-n}\varphi \leq \tfrac{1}{2}U^n\varphi \leq U^n\chi \leq \tfrac{4}{5}U^n\varphi \leq \tfrac{4}{5}2^{-n}\varphi \leq \tfrac{8}{5}2^{-n}\chi.$$

It follows by (35) that

$$\tfrac{5}{8}(\ln 2)^2 5^{-n} \leq (-1)^n R_n''(x) \leq \tfrac{16}{5}(\ln 2)^2 2^{-n}, \qquad \text{for } 0 \leq x \leq 1;$$

hence by (32) and (36) we have proved the following result:

Theorem W.   *The distribution $F_n(x)$ equals $\lg(1+x) + O(2^{-n})$ as $n \to \infty$.*
In fact, $F_n(x) - \lg(1+x)$ lies between $\frac{5}{16}(-1)^{n+1}5^{-n}\big(\ln(1+x)\big)\big(\ln 2/(1+x)\big)$
and $\frac{8}{5}(-1)^{n+1}2^{-n}\big(\ln(1+x)\big)\big(\ln 2/(1+x)\big)$, for $0 \le x \le 1$. ∎

With a slightly different choice of φ, we can obtain tighter bounds (see exercise 21). In fact, Wirsing went much further in his paper, proving that

$$F_n(x) = \lg(1+x) + (-\lambda)^n \Psi(x) + O\big(x(1-x)(\lambda - 0.031)^n\big), \qquad (40)$$

where

$$\begin{aligned}
\lambda &= 0.30366\,30028\,98732\,65859\,74481\,21901\,55623\,31109- \\
&= /\!/3, 3, 2, 2, 3, 13, 1, 174, 1, 1, 1, 2, 2, 2, 1, 1, 1, 2, 2, 1, \ldots /\!/
\end{aligned} \qquad (41)$$

is a fundamental constant (apparently unrelated to more familiar constants), and where Ψ is an interesting function that is analytic in the entire complex plane except for the negative real axis from -1 to $-\infty$. Wirsing's function satisfies $\Psi(0) = \Psi(1) = 0$, $\Psi'(0) < 0$, and $S\Psi = -\lambda\Psi$; thus by (37) it satisfies the identity

$$\Psi(z) - \Psi(z+1) = \frac{1}{\lambda}\Psi\left(\frac{1}{1+z}\right). \qquad (42)$$

Furthermore, Wirsing demonstrated that

$$\Psi\left(-\frac{u}{v} + \frac{i}{N}\right) = c\lambda^{-n}\log N + O(1) \qquad \text{as } N \to \infty, \qquad (43)$$

where c is a constant and $n = T(u, v)$ is the number of iterations when Euclid's algorithm is applied to the integers $u > v > 0$.

A complete solution to Gauss's problem was found a few years later by K. I. Babenko [*Doklady Akad. Nauk SSSR* **238** (1978), 1021–1024], who used powerful techniques of functional analysis to prove that

$$F_n(x) = \lg(1+x) + \sum_{j \ge 2} \lambda_j^n \, \Psi_j(x) \qquad (44)$$

for all $0 \le x \le 1$, $n \ge 1$. Here $|\lambda_2| > |\lambda_3| \ge |\lambda_4| \ge \cdots$, and each $\Psi_j(z)$ is an analytic function in the complex plane except for a cut at $[-\infty\,..\,-1]$. The function Ψ_2 is Wirsing's Ψ, and $\lambda_2 = -\lambda$, while $\lambda_3 \approx 0.10088$, $\lambda_4 \approx -0.03550$, $\lambda_5 \approx 0.01284$, $\lambda_6 \approx -0.00472$, $\lambda_7 \approx 0.00175$. Babenko also established further properties of the eigenvalues λ_j, proving in particular that they are exponentially small as $j \to \infty$, and that the sum for $j \ge k$ in (44) is bounded by $(\pi^2/6)|\lambda_k|^{n-1}\min(x, 1-x)$. [Further information appears in papers by Babenko and Yuriev, *Doklady Akad. Nauk SSSR* **240** (1978), 1273–1276; Mayer and Roepstorff, *J. Statistical Physics* **47** (1987), 149–171; **50** (1988), 331–344; D. Hensley, *J. Number Theory* **49** (1994), 142–182; Daudé, Flajolet, and Vallée, *Combinatorics, Probability and Computing* **6** (1997), 397–433; Flajolet and Vallée, *Theoretical Comp. Sci.* **194** (1998), 1–34.] The 40-place value of λ in (41) was computed by John Hershberger.

From continuous to discrete. We have now derived results about the probability distributions for continued fractions when X is a real number uniformly distributed in the interval $[0 \mathinner{.\,.} 1)$. But a real number is rational with probability zero — almost all numbers are irrational — so these results do not apply directly to Euclid's algorithm. Before we can apply Theorem W to our problem, some technicalities must be overcome. Consider the following observation based on elementary measure theory:

Lemma M. *Let* $I_1, I_2, \ldots, J_1, J_2, \ldots$ *be pairwise disjoint intervals contained in the interval* $[0 \mathinner{.\,.} 1)$, *and let*

$$\mathcal{I} = \bigcup_{k \geq 1} I_k, \qquad \mathcal{J} = \bigcup_{k \geq 1} J_k, \qquad \mathcal{K} = [0 \mathinner{.\,.} 1] \setminus (\mathcal{I} \cup \mathcal{J}).$$

Assume that $\mathcal{K}$ *has measure zero. Let* P_n *be the set* $\{0/n, 1/n, \ldots, (n-1)/n\}$. *Then*

$$\lim_{n \to \infty} \frac{|\mathcal{I} \cap P_n|}{n} = \mu(\mathcal{I}). \tag{45}$$

Here $\mu(\mathcal{I})$ *is the Lebesgue measure of* $\mathcal{I}$, *namely,* $\sum_{k \geq 1} \text{length}(I_k)$; *and* $|\mathcal{I} \cap P_n|$ *denotes the number of elements in the set* $\mathcal{I} \cap P_n$.

Proof. Let $\mathcal{I}_N = \bigcup_{1 \leq k \leq N} I_k$ and $\mathcal{J}_N = \bigcup_{1 \leq k \leq N} J_k$. Given $\epsilon > 0$, find N large enough so that $\mu(\mathcal{I}_N) + \mu(\mathcal{J}_N) \geq 1 - \epsilon$, and let

$$\mathcal{K}_N = \mathcal{K} \cup \bigcup_{k > N} I_k \cup \bigcup_{k > N} J_k.$$

If I is an interval, having any of the forms $(a \mathinner{.\,.} b)$ or $[a \mathinner{.\,.} b)$ or $(a \mathinner{.\,.} b]$ or $[a \mathinner{.\,.} b]$, it is clear that $\mu(I) = b - a$ and

$$n\mu(I) - 1 \leq |I \cap P_n| \leq n\mu(I) + 1.$$

Now let $r_n = |\mathcal{I}_N \cap P_n|$, $s_n = |\mathcal{J}_N \cap P_n|$, $t_n = |\mathcal{K}_N \cap P_n|$; we have

$$r_n + s_n + t_n = n;$$
$$n\mu(\mathcal{I}_N) - N \leq r_n \leq n\mu(\mathcal{I}_N) + N;$$
$$n\mu(\mathcal{J}_N) - N \leq s_n \leq n\mu(\mathcal{J}_N) + N.$$

Furthermore $r_n \leq |\mathcal{I} \cap P_n| \leq r_n + t_n$, because $\mathcal{I}_N \subseteq \mathcal{I} \subseteq \mathcal{I}_N \cup \mathcal{K}$. Consequently

$$\mu(\mathcal{I}) - \frac{N}{n} - \epsilon \leq \mu(\mathcal{I}_N) - \frac{N}{n} \leq \frac{r_n}{n} \leq \frac{r_n + t_n}{n}$$

$$= 1 - \frac{s_n}{n} \leq 1 - \mu(\mathcal{J}_N) + \frac{N}{n} \leq \mu(\mathcal{I}) + \frac{N}{n} + \epsilon.$$

Given ϵ, this holds for all n; so $\lim_{n \to \infty} r_n/n = \lim_{n \to \infty} (r_n + t_n)/n = \mu(\mathcal{I})$.   ∎

Exercise 25 shows that Lemma M is not trivial, in the sense that some rather restrictive hypotheses are needed to prove (45).

Distribution of partial quotients. Now we put Theorem W and Lemma M together to derive some solid facts about Euclid's algorithm.

Theorem E. *Let $p_k(a, n)$ be the probability that the $(k + 1)$st quotient A_{k+1} in Euclid's algorithm is equal to a, when $u = n$ and when v is equally likely to be any of the numbers $\{0, 1, \ldots, n - 1\}$. Then*

$$\lim_{n \to \infty} p_k(a, n) = F_k\left(\frac{1}{a}\right) - F_k\left(\frac{1}{a+1}\right),$$

where $F_k(x)$ is the distribution function (22).

Proof. The set $\mathcal{I}$ of all X in $[0 \mathinner{.\,.} 1)$ for which $A_{k+1} = a$ is a union of disjoint intervals, and so is the set $\mathcal{J}$ of all X for which $A_{k+1} \neq a$. Lemma M therefore applies, with $\mathcal{K}$ the set of all X for which A_{k+1} is undefined. Furthermore, $F_k(1/a) - F_k\left(1/(a+1)\right)$ is the probability that $1/(a + 1) < X_k \leq 1/a$, which is $\mu(\mathcal{I})$, the probability that $A_{k+1} = a$. ∎

As a consequence of Theorems E and W, we can say that a quotient equal to a occurs with the approximate probability

$$\lg(1 + 1/a) - \lg\left(1 + 1/(a + 1)\right) = \lg\left((a + 1)^2/((a + 1)^2 - 1)\right).$$

Thus

a quotient of 1 occurs about $\lg(\frac{4}{3}) \approx 41.504$ percent of the time;

a quotient of 2 occurs about $\lg(\frac{9}{8}) \approx 16.993$ percent of the time;

a quotient of 3 occurs about $\lg(\frac{16}{15}) \approx 9.311$ percent of the time;

a quotient of 4 occurs about $\lg(\frac{25}{24}) \approx 5.889$ percent of the time.

Actually, if Euclid's algorithm produces the quotients A_1, A_2, $\ldots$, A_t, the nature of the proofs above will guarantee this behavior only for A_k when k is comparatively small with respect to t; the values A_{t-1}, A_{t-2}, $\ldots$ are not covered by this proof. But we can in fact show that the distribution of the last quotients A_{t-1}, A_{t-2}, $\ldots$ is essentially the same as the first.

For example, consider the regular continued fraction expansions for the set of all proper fractions whose denominator is 29:

$\frac{1}{29} = /\!/29/\!/$	$\frac{8}{29} = /\!/3, 1, 1, 1, 2/\!/$	$\frac{15}{29} = /\!/1, 1, 14/\!/$	$\frac{22}{29} = /\!/1, 3, 7/\!/$
$\frac{2}{29} = /\!/14, 2/\!/$	$\frac{9}{29} = /\!/3, 4, 2/\!/$	$\frac{16}{29} = /\!/1, 1, 4, 3/\!/$	$\frac{23}{29} = /\!/1, 3, 1, 5/\!/$
$\frac{3}{29} = /\!/9, 1, 2/\!/$	$\frac{10}{29} = /\!/2, 1, 9/\!/$	$\frac{17}{29} = /\!/1, 1, 2, 2, 2/\!/$	$\frac{24}{29} = /\!/1, 4, 1, 4/\!/$
$\frac{4}{29} = /\!/7, 4/\!/$	$\frac{11}{29} = /\!/2, 1, 1, 1, 3/\!/$	$\frac{18}{29} = /\!/1, 1, 1, 1, 3/\!/$	$\frac{25}{29} = /\!/1, 6, 4/\!/$
$\frac{5}{29} = /\!/5, 1, 4/\!/$	$\frac{12}{29} = /\!/2, 2, 2, 2/\!/$	$\frac{19}{29} = /\!/1, 1, 1, 9/\!/$	$\frac{26}{29} = /\!/1, 8, 1, 2/\!/$
$\frac{6}{29} = /\!/4, 1, 5/\!/$	$\frac{13}{29} = /\!/2, 4, 3/\!/$	$\frac{20}{29} = /\!/1, 2, 4, 2/\!/$	$\frac{27}{29} = /\!/1, 13, 2/\!/$
$\frac{7}{29} = /\!/4, 7/\!/$	$\frac{14}{29} = /\!/2, 14/\!/$	$\frac{21}{29} = /\!/1, 2, 1, 1, 1, 2/\!/$	$\frac{28}{29} = /\!/1, 28/\!/$

Several things can be observed in this table.

a) As mentioned earlier, the last quotient is always 2 or more. Furthermore, we have the obvious identity

$$/\!/x_1, \ldots, x_{n-1}, x_n + 1/\!/ = /\!/x_1, \ldots, x_{n-1}, x_n, 1/\!/, \tag{46}$$

which shows how continued fractions whose last quotient is unity are related to regular continued fractions.

b) The values in the right-hand columns have a simple relationship to the values in the left-hand columns; can the reader see the correspondence before reading any further? The relevant identity is

$$1 - /\!/x_1, x_2, \ldots, x_n/\!/ = /\!/1, x_1 - 1, x_2, \ldots, x_n/\!/; \qquad (47)$$

see exercise 9.

c) There is symmetry between left and right in the first two columns: If $/\!/A_1, A_2, \ldots, A_t/\!/$ occurs, so does $/\!/A_t, \ldots, A_2, A_1/\!/$. This will always be the case (see exercise 26).

d) If we examine all of the quotients in the table, we find that there are 96 in all, of which $\frac{39}{96} \approx 40.6$ percent are equal to 1, $\frac{21}{96} \approx 21.9$ percent are equal to 2, $\frac{8}{96} \approx 8.3$ percent are equal to 3; this agrees reasonably well with the probabilities listed above.

The number of division steps. Let us now return to our original problem and investigate T_n, the average number of division steps when $v = n$. $\big($See Eq. (19).$\big)$ Here are some sample values of T_n:

$n =$	95	96	97	98	99	100	101	102	103	104	105
$T_n =$	5.0	4.4	5.3	4.8	4.7	4.6	5.3	4.6	5.3	4.7	4.6

$n =$	996	997	998	999	1000	1001	$\cdots$	9999	10000	10001
$T_n =$	6.5	7.3	7.0	6.8	6.4	6.7	$\cdots$	8.6	8.3	9.1

$n =$	49998	49999	50000	50001	$\cdots$	99999	100000	100001
$T_n =$	9.8	10.6	9.7	10.0	$\cdots$	10.7	10.3	11.0

Notice the somewhat erratic behavior; T_n tends to be larger than its neighbors when n is prime, and it is correspondingly lower when n has many divisors. (In this list, 97, 101, 103, 997, and 49999 are primes; $10001 = 73 \cdot 137$; $49998 = 2 \cdot 3 \cdot 13 \cdot 641$; $50001 = 3 \cdot 7 \cdot 2381$; $99999 = 3 \cdot 3 \cdot 41 \cdot 271$; and $100001 = 11 \cdot 9091$.) It is not difficult to understand why this happens: If $\gcd(u, v) = d$, Euclid's algorithm applied to u and v behaves essentially the same as if it were applied to u/d and v/d. Therefore, when $v = n$ has several divisors, there are many choices of u for which n behaves as if it were smaller.

Accordingly let us consider *another* quantity, τ_n, which is the average number of division steps when $v = n$ and when u is *relatively prime* to n. Thus

$$\tau_n = \frac{1}{\varphi(n)} \sum_{\substack{0 \le m < n \\ m \perp n}} T(m, n). \qquad (48)$$

It follows that

$$T_n = \frac{1}{n} \sum_{d \backslash n} \varphi(d) \tau_d. \qquad (49)$$

Here is a table of τ_n for the same values of n considered above:

$n =$	95	96	97	98	99	100	101	102	103	104	105
$\tau_n =$	5.4	5.3	5.3	5.6	5.2	5.2	5.4	5.3	5.4	5.3	5.6

$n =$	996	997	998	999	1000	1001	$\cdots$	9999	10000	10001
$\tau_n =$	7.2	7.3	7.3	7.3	7.3	7.4	$\cdots$	9.21	9.21	9.22

$n =$	49998	49999	50000	50001	$\cdots$	99999	100000	100001
$\tau_n =$	10.59	10.58	10.57	10.59	$\cdots$	11.170	11.172	11.172

Clearly τ_n is much more well-behaved than T_n, and it should be more susceptible to analysis. Inspection of a table of τ_n for small n reveals some curious anomalies; for example, $\tau_{50} = \tau_{100}$ and $\tau_{60} = \tau_{120}$. But as n grows, the values of τ_n behave quite regularly indeed, as the table indicates, and they show no significant relation to the factorization properties of n. If these values τ_n are plotted as functions of $\ln n$ on graph paper, for the values of τ_n given above, they lie very nearly on the straight line

$$\tau_n \approx 0.843 \ln n + 1.47. \tag{50}$$

We can account for this behavior if we study the regular continued fraction process a little further. In Euclid's algorithm as expressed in (15) we have

$$\frac{V_0}{U_0} \frac{V_1}{U_1} \cdots \frac{V_{t-1}}{U_{t-1}} = \frac{V_{t-1}}{U_0},$$

since $U_{k+1} = V_k$; therefore if $U = U_0$ and $V = V_0$ are relatively prime, and if there are t division steps, we have

$$X_0 X_1 \ldots X_{t-1} = 1/U.$$

Setting $U = N$ and $V = m < N$, we find that

$$\ln X_0 + \ln X_1 + \cdots + \ln X_{t-1} = -\ln N. \tag{51}$$

We know the approximate distribution of X_0, X_1, X_2, $\ldots$, so we can use this equation to estimate

$$t = T(N, m) = T(m, N) - 1.$$

Returning to the formulas preceding Theorem W, we find that the average value of $\ln X_n$, when X_0 is a real number uniformly distributed in $[0 \mathinner{.\,.} 1)$, is

$$\int_0^1 \ln x \, F_n'(x) \, dx = \int_0^1 \ln x \, f_n(x) \, dx / (1 + x), \tag{52}$$

where $f_n(x)$ is defined in (33). Now

$$f_n(x) = \frac{1}{\ln 2} + O(2^{-n}), \tag{53}$$

using the facts we have derived earlier (see exercise 23); hence the average value of $\ln X_n$ is very well approximated by

$$
\frac{1}{\ln 2}\int_0^1 \frac{\ln x}{1+x}\,dx = -\frac{1}{\ln 2}\int_0^\infty \frac{ue^{-u}}{1+e^{-u}}\,du
$$

$$
= -\frac{1}{\ln 2}\sum_{k\geq 1}(-1)^{k+1}\int_0^\infty ue^{-ku}\,du
$$

$$
= -\frac{1}{\ln 2}\left(1 - \frac{1}{4} + \frac{1}{9} - \frac{1}{16} + \frac{1}{25} - \cdots\right)
$$

$$
= -\frac{1}{\ln 2}\left(1 + \frac{1}{4} + \frac{1}{9} + \cdots - 2\left(\frac{1}{4} + \frac{1}{16} + \frac{1}{36} + \cdots\right)\right)
$$

$$
= -\frac{1}{2\ln 2}\left(1 + \frac{1}{4} + \frac{1}{9} + \cdots\right)
$$

$$
= -\pi^2/(12\ln 2).
$$

By (51) we therefore expect to have the approximate formula

$$
-t\pi^2/(12\ln 2) \approx -\ln N;
$$

that is, t should be approximately equal to $\big((12\ln 2)/\pi^2\big)\ln N$. This constant $(12\ln 2)/\pi^2 = 0.842765913\ldots$ agrees perfectly with the empirical formula (50) obtained earlier, so we have good reason to believe that the formula

$$
\tau_n \approx \frac{12\ln 2}{\pi^2}\ln n + 1.47 \tag{54}
$$

indicates the true asymptotic behavior of τ_n as $n \to \infty$.

If we assume that (54) is valid, we obtain the formula

$$
T_n \approx \frac{12\ln 2}{\pi^2}\left(\ln n - \sum_{d\backslash n}\frac{\Lambda(d)}{d}\right) + 1.47, \tag{55}
$$

where $\Lambda(d)$ is *von Mangoldt's function* defined by the rules

$$
\Lambda(n) = \begin{cases} \ln p, & \text{if } n = p^r \text{ for } p \text{ prime and } r \geq 1; \\ 0, & \text{otherwise.} \end{cases} \tag{56}
$$

(See exercise 27.) For example,

$$
T_{100} \approx \frac{12\ln 2}{\pi^2}\left(\ln 100 - \frac{\ln 2}{2} - \frac{\ln 2}{4} - \frac{\ln 5}{5} - \frac{\ln 5}{25}\right) + 1.47
$$

$$
\approx (0.843)(4.605 - 0.347 - 0.173 - 0.322 - 0.064) + 1.47
$$

$$
\approx 4.59;
$$

the exact value of T_{100} is 4.56.

We can also estimate the average number of division steps when u and v are both uniformly distributed between 1 and N, by calculating

$$\frac{1}{N^2} \sum_{m=1}^{N} \sum_{n=1}^{N} T(m,n) = \frac{2}{N^2} \sum_{n=1}^{N} n T_n - \frac{1}{2} - \frac{1}{2N}. \tag{57}$$

Assuming formula (55), exercise 29 shows that this sum has the form

$$\frac{12 \ln 2}{\pi^2} \ln N + O(1), \tag{58}$$

and empirical calculations with the same numbers used to derive Eq. 4.5.2–(65) show good agreement with the formula

$$\frac{12 \ln 2}{\pi^2} \ln N + 0.06. \tag{59}$$

Of course we have not yet *proved* anything about T_n and τ_n in general; so far we have only been considering plausible reasons why certain formulas ought to hold. Fortunately it is now possible to supply rigorous proofs, based on a careful analysis by several mathematicians.

The leading coefficient $12\pi^{-2} \ln 2$ in the formulas above was established first, in independent studies by Gustav Lochs, John D. Dixon, and Hans A. Heilbronn. Lochs [*Monatshefte für Math.* **65** (1961), 27–52] derived a formula equivalent to the fact that (57) equals $(12\pi^{-2} \ln 2) \ln N + a + O(N^{-1/2})$, where $a \approx 0.065$. Unfortunately his paper remained essentially unknown for many years, perhaps because it computed only an average value from which we cannot derive definite information about T_n for any particular n. Dixon [*J. Number Theory* **2** (1970), 414–422] developed the theory of the $F_n(x)$ distributions to show that individual partial quotients are essentially independent of each other in an appropriate sense, and proved that for all positive ϵ we have $|T(m,n) - (12\pi^{-2} \ln 2) \ln n| < (\ln n)^{(1/2)+\epsilon}$ except for $\exp(-c(\epsilon)(\log N)^{\epsilon/2}) N^2$ values of m and n in the range $1 \le m < n \le N$, where $c(\epsilon) > 0$. Heilbronn's approach was completely different, working entirely with integers instead of continuous variables. His idea, which is presented in slightly modified form in exercises 33 and 34, is based on the fact that τ_n can be related to the number of ways to represent n in a certain manner. Furthermore, his paper [*Number Theory and Analysis*, edited by Paul Turán (New York: Plenum, 1969), 87–96] shows that the distribution of individual partial quotients 1, 2, ... that we have discussed above actually applies to the entire collection of partial quotients belonging to the fractions having a given denominator; this is a sharper form of Theorem E. A still sharper result was obtained several years later by J. W. Porter [*Mathematika* **22** (1975), 20–28], who established that

$$\tau_n = \frac{12 \ln 2}{\pi^2} \ln n + C + O(n^{-1/6+\epsilon}), \tag{60}$$

where $C \approx 1.46707\,80794$ is the constant

$$\frac{6 \ln 2}{\pi^2} \left(3 \ln 2 + 4\gamma - \frac{24}{\pi^2} \zeta'(2) - 2 \right) - \frac{1}{2}; \tag{61}$$

see D. E. Knuth, *Computers and Math. with Applic.* **2** (1976), 137–139. Thus the conjecture (50) is fully proved. Using (60), Graham H. Norton [*J. Symbolic Computation* **10** (1990), 53–58] extended the calculations of exercise 29 to confirm Lochs's work, proving that the empirical constant 0.06 in (59) is actually

$$\frac{6\ln 2}{\pi^2}\left(3\ln 2 + 4\gamma - \frac{12}{\pi^2}\zeta'(2) - 3\right) - 1 = 0.06535\,14259\dots\,. \tag{62}$$

D. Hensley proved in *J. Number Theory* **49** (1994), 142–182, that the variance of τ_n is proportional to $\log n$.

The average running time for Euclid's algorithm on multiple-precision integers, using classical algorithms for arithmetic, was shown to be of order

$$\bigl(1 + \log\bigl(\max(u,v)/\gcd(u,v)\bigr)\bigr)\log\min(u,v) \tag{63}$$

by G. E. Collins, in *SICOMP* **3** (1974), 1–10.

Summary. We have found that the worst case of Euclid's algorithm occurs when its inputs u and v are consecutive Fibonacci numbers (Theorem F); the number of division steps when $0 \le v < N$ will never exceed $\lceil 4.8\log_{10} N - 0.32 \rceil$. We have determined the frequency of the values of various partial quotients, showing, for example, that the division step finds $\lfloor u/v \rfloor = 1$ about 41 percent of the time (Theorem E). And, finally, the theorems of Heilbronn and Porter prove that the average number T_n of division steps when $v = n$ is approximately

$$\bigl((12\ln 2)/\pi^2\bigr)\ln n \approx 1.9405\log_{10} n,$$

minus a correction term based on the divisors of n as shown in Eq. (55).

EXERCISES

▶ **1.** [*20*] Since the quotient $\lfloor u/v \rfloor$ is equal to unity more than 40 percent of the time in Algorithm 4.5.2A, it may be advantageous on some computers to make a test for this case and to avoid the division when the quotient is unity. Is the following MIX program for Euclid's algorithm more efficient than Program 4.5.2A?

```
        LDX   U     rX ← u.                SRAX  5     rAX ← rA.
        JMP   2F                           JL    2F    Is u − v < v?
1H STX  V     v ← rX.                      DIV   V     rX ← rAX mod v.
        SUB   V     rA ← u − v.       2H LDA V     rA ← v.
        CMPA  V                            JXNZ  1B    Done if rX = 0.  ■
```

2. [*M21*] Evaluate the matrix product $\begin{pmatrix} x_1 & 1 \\ 1 & 0 \end{pmatrix}\begin{pmatrix} x_2 & 1 \\ 1 & 0 \end{pmatrix}\cdots\begin{pmatrix} x_n & 1 \\ 1 & 0 \end{pmatrix}.$

3. [*M21*] What is the value of $\det\begin{pmatrix} x_1 & 1 & 0 & \cdots & 0 \\ -1 & x_2 & 1 & & 0 \\ 0 & -1 & x_3 & 1 & \vdots \\ \vdots & & -1 & \ddots & 1 \\ 0 & 0 & \cdots & -1 & x_n \end{pmatrix}?$

4. [*M20*] Prove Eq. (8).

5. [*HM25*] Let x_1, x_2, ... be a sequence of real numbers that are each greater than some positive real number ϵ. Prove that the infinite continued fraction $/\!/x_1, x_2, \ldots /\!/ = \lim_{n\to\infty} /\!/x_1, \ldots, x_n/\!/$ exists. Show also that $/\!/x_1, x_2, \ldots /\!/$ need not exist if we assume only that $x_j > 0$ for all j.

6. [*M23*] Prove that the regular continued fraction expansion of a number is *unique* in the following sense: If B_1, B_2, ... are positive integers, then the infinite continued fraction $/\!/B_1, B_2, \ldots /\!/$ is an irrational number X between 0 and 1 whose regular continued fraction has $A_n = B_n$ for all $n \geq 1$; and if B_1, ..., B_m are positive integers with $B_m > 1$, then the regular continued fraction for $X = /\!/B_1, \ldots, B_m/\!/$ has $A_n = B_n$ for $1 \leq n \leq m$.

7. [*M26*] Find all permutations $p(1)p(2)\ldots p(n)$ of the integers $\{1, 2, \ldots, n\}$ such that $K_n(x_1, x_2, \ldots, x_n) = K_n(x_{p(1)}, x_{p(2)}, \ldots, x_{p(n)})$ is an identity for all x_1, x_2, ..., x_n.

8. [*M20*] Show that $-1/X_n = /\!/A_n, \ldots, A_1, -X/\!/$, whenever X_n is defined, in the regular continued fraction process.

9. [*M21*] Show that continued fractions satisfy the following identities:

a) $/\!/x_1, \ldots, x_n/\!/ = /\!/x_1, \ldots, x_k + /\!/x_{k+1}, \ldots, x_n/\!/ /\!/$, $1 \leq k \leq n$;

b) $/\!/0, x_1, x_2, \ldots, x_n/\!/ = x_1 + /\!/x_2, \ldots, x_n/\!/$, $n \geq 1$;

c) $/\!/x_1, \ldots, x_{k-1}, x_k, 0, x_{k+1}, x_{k+2}, \ldots, x_n/\!/ = /\!/x_1, \ldots, x_{k-1}, x_k + x_{k+1}, x_{k+2}, \ldots, x_n/\!/$,
   $1 \leq k < n$;

d) $1 - /\!/x_1, x_2, \ldots, x_n/\!/ = /\!/1, x_1 - 1, x_2, \ldots, x_n/\!/$, $n \geq 1$.

10. [*M28*] By the result of exercise 6, every irrational real number X has a unique regular continued fraction representation of the form

$$X = A_0 + /\!/A_1, A_2, A_3, \ldots /\!/,$$

where A_0 is an integer and A_1, A_2, A_3, ... are positive integers. Show that if X has this representation then the regular continued fraction for $1/X$ is

$$1/X = B_0 + /\!/B_1, \ldots, B_m, A_5, A_6, \ldots /\!/$$

for suitable integers B_0, B_1, ..., B_m. (The case $A_0 < 0$ is, of course, the most interesting.) Explain how to determine the B's in terms of A_0, A_1, A_2, A_3, and A_4.

11. [*M30*] (J.-A. Serret, 1850.) Let $X = A_0 + /\!/A_1, A_2, A_3, A_4, \ldots /\!/$ and $Y = B_0 + /\!/B_1, B_2, B_3, B_4, \ldots /\!/$ be the regular continued fraction representations of two real numbers X and Y, in the sense of exercise 10. Show that these representations "eventually agree," in the sense that $A_{m\,|\,k} = B_{n\,|\,k}$ for some m and n and for all $k \geq 0$, if and only if we have $X = (qY + r)/(sY + t)$ for some integers q, r, s, t with $|qt - rs| = 1$. (This theorem is the analog, for continued fraction representations, of the simple result that the representations of X and Y in the decimal system eventually agree if and only if $X = (10^q Y + r)/10^s$ for some integers q, r, and s.)

▶ **12.** [*M30*] A *quadratic irrationality* is a number of the form $(\sqrt{D} - U)/V$, where D, U, and V are integers, $D > 0$, $V \neq 0$, and D is not a perfect square. We may assume without loss of generality that V is a divisor of $D - U^2$, for otherwise the number may be rewritten as $(\sqrt{DV^2} - U|V|)/(V|V|)$.

a) Prove that the regular continued fraction expansion (in the sense of exercise 10) of a quadratic irrationality $X = (\sqrt{D} - U)/V$ is obtained by the following formulas:

$$V_0 = V, \qquad\qquad A_0 = \lfloor X \rfloor, \qquad\qquad U_0 = U + A_0 V;$$
$$V_{n+1} = (D - U_n^2)/V_n, \quad A_{n+1} = \lfloor (\sqrt{D} + U_n)/V_{n+1} \rfloor, \quad U_{n+1} = A_{n+1} V_{n+1} - U_n.$$

b) Prove that $0 < U_n < \sqrt{D}$, $0 < V_n < 2\sqrt{D}$, for all $n > N$, where N is some integer depending on X; hence the regular continued fraction representation of every quadratic irrationality is eventually periodic. [*Hint:* Show that

$$(-\sqrt{D} - U)/V = A_0 + //A_1, \ldots, A_n, -V_n/(\sqrt{D} + U_n)//,$$

and use Eq. (5) to prove that $(\sqrt{D} + U_n)/V_n$ is positive when n is large.]

c) Letting $p_n = K_{n+1}(A_0, A_1, \ldots, A_n)$ and $q_n = K_n(A_1, \ldots, A_n)$, prove the identity $V p_n^2 + 2U p_n q_n + ((U^2 - D)/V) q_n^2 = (-1)^{n+1} V_{n+1}$.

d) Prove that the regular continued fraction representation of an irrational number X is eventually periodic if and only if X is a quadratic irrationality. (This is the continued fraction analog of the fact that the decimal expansion of a real number X is eventually periodic if and only if X is rational.)

13. [*M40*] (J. Lagrange, 1767.) Let $f(x) = a_n x^n + \cdots + a_0$, $a_n > 0$, be a polynomial having exactly one real root $\xi > 1$, where ξ is irrational and $f'(\xi) \neq 0$. Experiment with a computer program to find the first thousand or so partial quotients of ξ, using the following algorithm (which essentially involves only addition):

L1. Set $A \leftarrow 1$.

L2. For $k = 0, 1, \ldots, n-1$ (in this order) and for $j = n-1, \ldots, k$ (in this order), set $a_j \leftarrow a_{j+1} + a_j$. (This step replaces $f(x)$ by $g(x) = f(x+1)$, a polynomial whose roots are one less than those of f.)

L3. If $a_n + a_{n-1} + \cdots + a_0 < 0$, set $A \leftarrow A + 1$ and return to L2.

L4. Output A (which is the value of the next partial quotient). Replace the coefficients $(a_n, a_{n-1}, \ldots, a_0)$ by $(-a_0, -a_1, \ldots, -a_n)$ and return to L1. (This step replaces $f(x)$ by a polynomial whose roots are reciprocals of those of f.) ∎

For example, starting with $f(x) = x^3 - 2$, the algorithm will output "1" (changing $f(x)$ to $x^3 - 3x^2 - 3x - 1$); then "3" (changing $f(x)$ to $10x^3 - 6x^2 - 6x - 1$); etc.

14. [*M22*] (A. Hurwitz, 1891.) Show that the following rules make it possible to find the regular continued fraction expansion of $2X$, given the partial quotients of X:

$$2// 2a, b, c, \ldots // = // a, 2b + 2//c, \ldots ////;$$
$$2// 2a + 1, b, c, \ldots // = // a, 1, 1 + 2//b - 1, c, \ldots ////.$$

Use this idea to find the regular continued fraction expansion of $\frac{1}{2}e$, given the expansion of e in (13).

▶ **15.** [*M31*] (R. W. Gosper.) Generalizing exercise 14, design an algorithm that computes the continued fraction $X_0 + //X_1, X_2, \ldots //$ for $(ax + b)/(cx + d)$, given the continued fraction $x_0 + //x_1, x_2, \ldots //$ for x, and given integers a, b, c, d with $ad \neq bc$. Make your algorithm an "online coroutine" that outputs as many X_k as possible before inputting each x_j. Demonstrate how your algorithm computes $(97x + 39)/(-62x - 25)$ when $x = -1 + //5, 1, 1, 1, 2, 1, 2//$.

16. [*HM30*] (L. Euler, 1731.) Let $f_0(z) = (e^z - e^{-z})/(e^z + e^{-z}) = \tanh z$, and let $f_{n+1}(z) = 1/f_n(z) - (2n+1)/z$. Prove that, for all n, $f_n(z)$ is an analytic function of the complex variable z in a neighborhood of the origin, and it satisfies the differential equation $f_n'(z) = 1 - f_n(z)^2 - 2n f_n(z)/z$. Use this fact to prove that

$$\tanh z = //z^{-1}, 3z^{-1}, 5z^{-1}, 7z^{-1}, \ldots //;$$

then apply Hurwitz's rule (exercise 14) to prove that

$$e^{-1/n} = /\!/\, \overline{1, (2m+1)n - 1, 1}\,/\!/, \qquad m \geq 0.$$

(This notation denotes the infinite continued fraction $/\!/\, 1,\, n - 1,\, 1,\, 1,\, 3n - 1,\, 1,\, 1,$ $5n - 1,\, 1,\, \ldots /\!/$.) Also find the regular continued fraction expansion of $e^{-2/n}$ when $n > 0$ is odd.

▶ **17.** [*M23*] (a) Prove that $/\!/ x_1, -x_2 /\!/ = /\!/ x_1 - 1, 1, x_2 - 1 /\!/$. (b) Generalize this identity, obtaining a formula for $/\!/ x_1, -x_2, x_3, -x_4, x_5, -x_6, \ldots, x_{2n-1}, -x_{2n} /\!/$ in which all partial quotients are positive integers when the x's are large positive integers. (c) The result of exercise 16 implies that $\tan 1 = /\!/ 1, -3, 5, -7, \ldots /\!/$. Find the regular continued fraction expansion of $\tan 1$.

18. [*M25*] Show that $/\!/ a_1, a_2, \ldots, a_m, x_1, a_1, a_2, \ldots, a_m, x_2, a_1, a_2, \ldots, a_m, x_3, \ldots /\!/\, -$ $/\!/ a_m, \ldots, a_2, a_1, x_1, a_m, \ldots, a_2, a_1, x_2, a_m, \ldots, a_2, a_1, x_3, \ldots /\!/$ does not depend on x_1, $x_2, x_3, \ldots$. *Hint:* Multiply both continued fractions by $K_m(a_1, a_2, \ldots, a_m)$.

19. [*M20*] Prove that $F(x) = \log_b(1 + x)$ satisfies Eq. (24).

20. [*HM20*] Derive (38) from (37).

21. [*HM29*] (E. Wirsing.) The bounds (39) were obtained for a function φ corresponding to g with $Tg(x) = 1/(x + 1)$. Show that the function corresponding to $Tg(x) = 1/(x + c)$ yields better bounds, when $c > 0$ is an appropriate constant.

22. [*HM46*] (K. I. Babenko.) Develop efficient means to calculate accurate approximations to the quantities λ_j and $\Psi_j(x)$ in (44), for small $j \geq 3$ and for $0 \leq x \leq 1$.

23. [*HM23*] Prove (53), using results from the proof of Theorem W.

24. [*M22*] What is the average value of a partial quotient A_n in the regular continued fraction expansion of a random real number?

25. [*HM25*] Find an example of a set $\mathcal{I} = I_1 \cup I_2 \cup I_3 \cup \cdots \subseteq [0 \,..\, 1]$, where the I's are disjoint intervals, for which (45) does not hold.

26. [*M23*] Show that if the numbers $\{1/n, 2/n, \ldots, \lfloor n/2 \rfloor/n\}$ are expressed as regular continued fractions, the result is symmetric between left and right, in the sense that $/\!/ A_t, \ldots, A_2, A_1 /\!/$ appears whenever $/\!/ A_1, A_2, \ldots, A_t /\!/$ does.

27. [*M21*] Derive (55) from (49) and (54).

28. [*M23*] Prove the following identities involving the three number-theoretic functions $\varphi(n)$, $\mu(n)$, $\Lambda(n)$:

a) $\displaystyle\sum_{d \backslash n} \mu(d) = \delta_{n1}.$
b) $\displaystyle\ln n = \sum_{d \backslash n} \Lambda(d), \qquad n = \sum_{d \backslash n} \varphi(d).$

c) $\displaystyle\Lambda(n) = \sum_{d \backslash n} \mu\!\left(\frac{n}{d}\right) \ln d, \qquad \varphi(n) = \sum_{d \backslash n} \mu\!\left(\frac{n}{d}\right) d.$

29. [*M23*] Assuming that T_n is given by (55), show that (57) equals (58).

▶ **30.** [*HM32*] The following "greedy" variant of Euclid's algorithm is often suggested: Instead of replacing v by $u \bmod v$ during the division step, replace it by $|(u \bmod v) - v|$ if $u \bmod v > \frac{1}{2}v$. Thus, for example, if $u = 26$ and $v = 7$, we have $\gcd(26, 7) = \gcd(-2, 7) = \gcd(7, 2)$; -2 is the *remainder of smallest magnitude* when multiples of 7 are subtracted from 26. Compare this procedure with Euclid's algorithm; estimate the number of division steps this method saves, on the average.

▶ **31.** [*M35*] Find the worst case of the modification of Euclid's algorithm suggested in exercise 30: What are the smallest inputs $u > v > 0$ that require n division steps?

32. [*20*] (a) A Morse code sequence of length n is a string of r dots and s dashes, where $r + 2s = n$. For example, the Morse code sequences of length 4 are

$$\bullet\bullet\bullet\bullet, \quad \bullet\bullet-, \quad \bullet-\bullet, \quad -\bullet\bullet, \quad --.$$

Noting that the continuant $K_4(x_1, x_2, x_3, x_4)$ is $x_1 x_2 x_3 x_4 + x_1 x_2 + x_1 x_4 + x_3 x_4 + 1$, find and prove a simple relation between $K_n(x_1, \ldots, x_n)$ and Morse code sequences of length n. (b) (L. Euler, *Novi Comm. Acad. Sci. Pet.* **9** (1762), 53–69.) Prove that

$$K_{m+n}(x_1, \ldots, x_{m+n}) = K_m(x_1, \ldots, x_m) K_n(x_{m+1}, \ldots, x_{m+n})$$
$$+ K_{m-1}(x_1, \ldots, x_{m-1}) K_{n-1}(x_{m+2}, \ldots, x_{m+n}).$$

33. [*M32*] Let $h(n)$ be the number of representations of n in the form

$$n = xx' + yy', \qquad x > y > 0, \qquad x' > y' > 0, \qquad x \perp y, \qquad \text{integer } x, x', y, y'.$$

a) Show that if the conditions are relaxed to allow $x' = y'$, the number of representations is $h(n) + \lfloor (n-1)/2 \rfloor$.

b) Show that for fixed $y > 0$ and $0 < t \le y$, where $t \perp y$, and for each fixed x' in the range $0 < x' < n/(y+t)$ such that $x't \equiv n$ (modulo y), there is exactly one representation of n satisfying the restrictions of (a) and the condition $x \equiv t$ (modulo y).

c) Consequently, $h(n) = \sum \lceil (n/(y+t) - t')/y \rceil - \lfloor (n-1)/2 \rfloor$, where the sum is over all positive integers y, t, t' such that $t \perp y$, $t \le y$, $t' \le y$, $tt' \equiv n$ (modulo y).

d) Show that each of the $h(n)$ representations can be expressed uniquely in the form

$$x = K_m(x_1, \ldots, x_m), \qquad\qquad y = K_{m-1}(x_1, \ldots, x_{m-1}),$$
$$x' = K_k(x_{m+1}, \ldots, x_{m+k}) d, \qquad y' = K_{k-1}(x_{m+2}, \ldots, x_{m+k}) d,$$

where m, k, d, and the x_j are positive integers with $x_1 \ge 2$, $x_{m+k} \ge 2$, and d is a divisor of n. The identity of exercise 32 now implies that $n/d = K_{m+k}(x_1, \ldots, x_{m+k})$. Conversely, any given sequence of positive integers $x_1, \ldots, x_{m+k}$ such that $x_1 \ge 2$, $x_{m+k} \ge 2$, and $K_{m+k}(x_1, \ldots, x_{m+k})$ divides n, corresponds in this way to $m+k-1$ representations of n.

e) Therefore $nT_n = \lfloor (5n-3)/2 \rfloor + 2h(n)$.

34. [*HM40*] (H. Heilbronn.) Let $h_d(n)$ be the number of representations of n as in exercise 33 such that $xd < x'$, plus half the number of representations with $xd = x'$.

a) Let $g(n)$ be the number of representations without the requirement that $x \perp y$. Prove that

$$h(n) = \sum_{d\backslash n} \mu(d) g\left(\frac{n}{d}\right), \qquad g(n) = 2 \sum_{d\backslash n} h_d\left(\frac{n}{d}\right).$$

b) Generalizing exercise 33(b), show that for $d \ge 1$, $h_d(n) = \sum(n/(y(y+t))) + O(n)$, where the sum is over all integers y and t such that $t \perp y$ and $0 < t \le y < \sqrt{n/d}$.

c) Show that $\sum (y/(y+t)) = \varphi(y) \ln 2 + O(\sigma_{-1}(y))$, where the sum is over the range $0 < t \le y$, $t \perp y$, and where $\sigma_{-1}(y) = \sum_{d\backslash y}(1/d)$.

d) Show that $\sum_{y=1}^{n} \varphi(y)/y^2 = \sum_{d=1}^{n} \mu(d) H_{\lfloor n/d \rfloor}/d^2$.

e) Hence we have the asymptotic formula

$$T_n = ((12 \ln 2)/\pi^2)\left(\ln n - \sum_{d\backslash n} \Lambda(d)/d\right) + O(\sigma_{-1}(n)^2).$$

35. [*HM41*] (A. C. Yao and D. E. Knuth.) Prove that the sum of all partial quotients for the fractions m/n, for $1 \le m < n$, is equal to $2(\sum \lfloor x/y \rfloor + \lfloor n/2 \rfloor)$, where the sum is over all representations $n = xx' + yy'$ satisfying the conditions of exercise 33(a). Show that $\sum \lfloor x/y \rfloor = 3\pi^{-2} n(\ln n)^2 + O(n \log n \,(\log \log n)^2)$, and apply this to the "ancient" form of Euclid's algorithm that uses only subtraction instead of division.

36. [*M25*] (G. H. Bradley.) What is the smallest value of u_n such that the calculation of $\gcd(u_1, \ldots, u_n)$ by Algorithm 4.5.2C requires N divisions, if Euclid's algorithm is used throughout? Assume that $N \ge n \ge 3$.

37. [*M38*] (T. S. Motzkin and E. G. Straus.) Let $a_1, \ldots, a_n$ be positive integers. Show that $\max K_n(a_{p(1)}, \ldots, a_{p(n)})$, over all permutations $p(1) \ldots p(n)$ of $\{1, 2, \ldots, n\}$, occurs when $a_{p(1)} \ge a_{p(n)} \ge a_{p(2)} \ge a_{p(n-1)} \ge \cdots$; and the minimum occurs when $a_{p(1)} \le a_{p(3)} \le a_{p(5)} \le \cdots \le a_{p(6)} \le a_{p(4)} \le a_{p(2)}$.

38. [*M25*] (J. Mikusiński.) Let $L(n) = \max_{m \ge 0} T(m, n)$. Theorem F shows that $L(n) \le \log_\phi(\sqrt{5}\, n + 1) - 2$; prove that $2L(n) \ge \log_\phi(\sqrt{5}\, n + 1) - 2$.

▶ **39.** [*M25*] (R. W. Gosper.) If a baseball player's batting average is .334, what is the smallest possible number of times he has been at bat? [Note for non-baseball-fans: Batting average = (number of hits)/(times at bat), rounded to three decimal places.]

▶ **40.** [*M28*] (*The Stern–Brocot tree.*) Consider an infinite binary tree in which each node is labeled with the fraction $(p_l + p_r)/(q_l + q_r)$, where p_l/q_l is the label of the node's nearest left ancestor and p_r/q_r is the label of the node's nearest right ancestor. (A left ancestor is one that precedes a node in symmetric order, while a right ancestor follows the node. See Section 2.3.1 for the definition of symmetric order.) If the node has no left ancestors, $p_l/q_l = 0/1$; if it has no right ancestors, $p_r/q_r = 1/0$. Thus the label of the root is $1/1$; the labels of its two children are $1/2$ and $2/1$; the labels of the four nodes on level 2 are $1/3$, $2/3$, $3/2$, and $3/1$, from left to right; the labels of the eight nodes on level 3 are $1/4$, $2/5$, $3/5$, $3/4$, $4/3$, $5/3$, $5/2$, $4/1$; and so on.

   Prove that p is relatively prime to q in each label p/q; furthermore, the node labeled p/q precedes the node labeled p'/q' in symmetric order if and only if the labels satisfy $p/q < p'/q'$. Find a connection between the continued fraction for the label of a node and the path to that node, thereby showing that each positive rational number appears as the label of exactly one node in the tree.

41. [*M40*] (J. Shallit, 1979.) Show that the regular continued fraction expansion of

$$\frac{1}{2^1} + \frac{1}{2^3} + \frac{1}{2^7} + \cdots = \sum_{n \ge 1} \frac{1}{2^{2^n - 1}}$$

contains only 1s and 2s and has a fairly simple pattern. Prove that the partial quotients of Liouville's numbers $\sum_{n \ge 1} l^{-n!}$ also have a regular pattern, when l is any integer ≥ 2. [The latter numbers, introduced by J. Liouville in *J. de Math. Pures et Appl.* **16** (1851), 133–142, were the first explicitly defined numbers to be proved *transcendental*. The former number and similar constants were first proved transcendental by A. J. Kempner, *Trans. Amer. Math. Soc.* **17** (1916), 476–482.]

42. [*M30*] (J. Lagrange, 1798.) Let X have the regular continued fraction expansion $/\!/A_1, A_2, \ldots /\!/$, and let $q_n = K_n(A_1, \ldots, A_n)$. Let $\|x\|$ denote the distance from x to the nearest integer, namely $\min_p |x - p|$. Show that $\|qX\| \ge \|q_{n-1}X\|$ for $1 \le q < q_n$. (Thus the denominators q_n of the so-called convergents $p_n/q_n = /\!/A_1, \ldots, A_n /\!/$ are the "record-breaking" integers that make $\|qX\|$ achieve new lows.)

43. [*M30*] (D. W. Matula.) Show that the "mediant rounding" rule for fixed slash or floating slash numbers, Eq. 4.5.1–(1), can be implemented simply as follows, when the number $x > 0$ is not representable: Let the regular continued fraction expansion of x be $a_0 + //a_1, a_2, \ldots //$, and let $p_n = K_{n+1}(a_0, \ldots, a_n)$, $q_n = K_n(a_1, \ldots, a_n)$. Then round$(x) = (p_i/q_i)$, where (p_i/q_i) is representable but (p_{i+1}/q_{i+1}) is not. [*Hint:* See exercise 40.]

44. [*M25*] Suppose we are doing fixed slash arithmetic with mediant rounding, where the fraction (u/u') is representable if and only if $|u| < M$ and $0 \le u' < N$ and $u \perp u'$. Prove or disprove the identity $((u/u') \oplus (v/v')) \ominus (v/v') = (u/u')$ for all representable (u/u') and (v/v'), provided that $u' < \sqrt{N}$ and no overflow occurs.

45. [*M25*] Show that Euclid's algorithm (Algorithm 4.5.2A) applied to two n-bit binary numbers requires $O(n^2)$ units of time, as $n \to \infty$. (The same upper bound obviously holds for Algorithm 4.5.2B.)

46. [*M43*] Can the upper bound $O(n^2)$ in exercise 45 be decreased, if another algorithm for calculating the greatest common divisor is used?

47. [*M40*] Develop a computer program to find as many partial quotients of x as possible, when x is a real number given with high precision. Use your program to calculate the first several thousand partial quotients of Euler's constant γ, which can be calculated as explained by D. W. Sweeney in *Math. Comp.* **17** (1963), 170–178. (If γ is a rational number, you might discover its numerator and denominator, thereby resolving a famous problem in mathematics. According to the theory in the text, we expect to get about 0.97 partial quotients per decimal digit, when the given number is random. Multiprecision division is not necessary; see Algorithm 4.5.2L and the article by J. W. Wrench, Jr. and D. Shanks, *Math. Comp.* **20** (1966), 444–447.)

48. [*M21*] Let $T_0 = (1, 0, u)$, $T_1 = (0, 1, v)$, $\ldots$, $T_{n+1} = ((-1)^{n+1}v/d, (-1)^n u/d, 0)$ be the sequence of vectors computed by Algorithm 4.5.2X (the extended Euclidean algorithm), and let $//a_1, \ldots, a_n//$ be the regular continued fraction for v/u. Express T_j in terms of continuants involving $a_1, \ldots, a_n$, for $1 < j \le n$.

49. [*M33*] By adjusting the final iteration of Algorithm 4.5.2X so that a_n is optionally replaced by two partial quotients $(a_n - 1, 1)$, we can assume that the number of iterations, n, has a given parity. Continuing the previous exercise, let λ and μ be arbitrary positive real numbers and let $\theta = \sqrt{\lambda\mu v/d}$, where $d = \gcd(u, v)$. Prove that if n is even, and if $T_j = (x_j, y_j, z_j)$, we have $\min_{j=1}^{n+1} |\lambda x_j + \mu z_j - [j \text{ even}]\theta| \le \theta$.

▶ **50.** [*M25*] Given an irrational number $\alpha \in (0..1)$ and real numbers β and γ with $0 \le \beta < \gamma < 1$, let $f(\alpha, \beta, \gamma)$ be the smallest nonnegative integer n such that $\beta \le \alpha n \bmod 1 < \gamma$. (Such an integer exists because of Weyl's theorem, exercise 3.5–22.) Design an algorithm to compute $f(\alpha, \beta, \gamma)$.

▶ **51.** [*M30*] (*Rational reconstruction.*) The number 28481 turns out to be equal to $41/316$ (modulo 199999), in the sense that $316 \cdot 28481 \equiv 41$. How could a person discover this? Given integers a and m with $m > a > 1$, explain how to find integers x and y such that $ax \equiv y$ (modulo m), $x \perp y$, $0 < x \le \sqrt{m/2}$, and $|y| \le \sqrt{m/2}$, or to determine that no such x and y exist. Can there be more than one solution?

4.5.4. Factoring into Primes

Several of the computational methods we have encountered in this book rest on the fact that every positive integer n can be expressed in a unique way in the form

$$n = p_1 p_2 \ldots p_t, \qquad p_1 \leq p_2 \leq \cdots \leq p_t, \qquad (1)$$

where each p_k is prime. (When $n = 1$, this equation holds for $t = 0$.) It is unfortunately not a simple matter to find this prime factorization of n, or to determine whether or not n is prime. So far as anyone knows, it is a great deal harder to factor a large number n than to compute the greatest common divisor of two large numbers m and n; therefore we should avoid factoring large numbers whenever possible. But several ingenious ways to speed up the factoring process have been discovered, and we will now investigate some of them. [A comprehensive history of factoring before 1950 has been compiled by H. C. Williams and J. O. Shallit, *Proc. Symp. Applied Math.* **48** (1993), 481–531.]

Divide and factor. First let us consider the most obvious algorithm for factorization: If $n > 1$, we can divide n by successive primes $p = 2, 3, 5, \ldots$ until discovering the smallest p for which $n \bmod p = 0$. Then p is the smallest prime factor of n, and the same process may be applied to $n \leftarrow n/p$ in an attempt to divide this new value of n by p and by higher primes. If at any stage we find that $n \bmod p \neq 0$ but $\lfloor n/p \rfloor \leq p$, we can conclude that n is prime; for if n is not prime, then by (1) we must have $n \geq p_1^2$, but $p_1 > p$ implies that $p_1^2 \geq (p+1)^2 > p(p+1) > p^2 + (n \bmod p) \geq \lfloor n/p \rfloor p + (n \bmod p) = n$. This leads us to the following procedure:

Algorithm A (*Factoring by division*). Given a positive integer N, this algorithm finds the prime factors $p_1 \leq p_2 \leq \cdots \leq p_t$ of N as in Eq. (1). The method makes use of an auxiliary sequence of trial divisors

$$2 = d_0 < d_1 < d_2 < d_3 < \cdots, \qquad (2)$$

which includes all prime numbers $\leq \sqrt{N}$ (and possibly values that are *not* prime, if convenient). The sequence of d's must also include at least one value such that $d_k \geq \sqrt{N}$.

A1. [Initialize.] Set $t \leftarrow 0$, $k \leftarrow 0$, $n \leftarrow N$. (During this algorithm the variables t, k, n are related by the following condition: "$n = N/p_1 \ldots p_t$, and n has no prime factors less than d_k.")

A2. [$n = 1$?] If $n = 1$, the algorithm terminates.

A3. [Divide.] Set $q \leftarrow \lfloor n/d_k \rfloor$, $r \leftarrow n \bmod d_k$. (Here q and r are the quotient and remainder obtained when n is divided by d_k.)

A4. [Zero remainder?] If $r \neq 0$, go to step A6.

A5. [Factor found.] Increase t by 1, and set $p_t \leftarrow d_k$, $n \leftarrow q$. Return to step A2.

A6. [Low quotient?] If $q > d_k$, increase k by 1 and return to step A3.

A7. [n is prime.] Increase t by 1, set $p_t \leftarrow n$, and terminate the algorithm. ∎

As an example of Algorithm A, consider the factorization of the number $N = 25852$. We find immediately that $N = 2 \cdot 12926$; hence $p_1 = 2$. Furthermore, $12926 = 2 \cdot 6463$, so $p_2 = 2$. But now $n = 6463$ is not divisible by $2, 3, 5, \ldots, 19$;

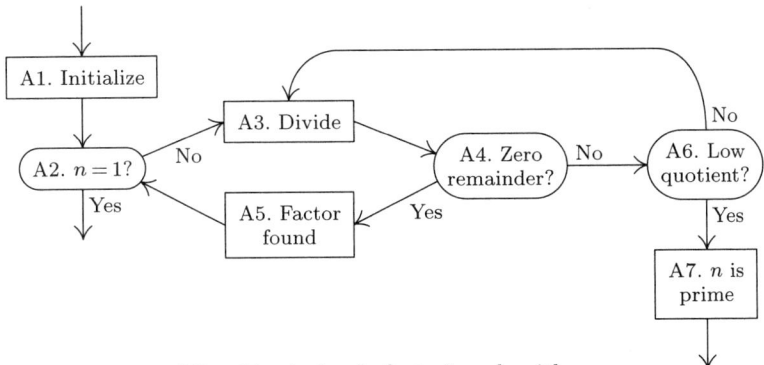

Fig. 11. A simple factoring algorithm.

we find that $n = 23 \cdot 281$, hence $p_3 = 23$. Finally $281 = 12 \cdot 23 + 5$ and $12 \le 23$; hence $p_4 = 281$. The determination of 25852's factors has therefore involved a total of 12 division operations; on the other hand, if we had tried to factor the slightly smaller number 25849 (which is prime), at least 38 division operations would have been performed. This illustrates the fact that Algorithm A requires a running time roughly proportional to $\max(p_{t-1}, \sqrt{p_t})$. (If $t = 1$, this formula is valid if we adopt the convention $p_0 = 1$.)

The sequence d_0, d_1, d_2, ... of trial divisors used in Algorithm A can be taken to be simply 2, 3, 5, 7, 11, 13, 17, 19, 23, 25, 29, 31, 35, ..., where we alternately add 2 and 4 after the first three terms. This sequence contains all numbers that are not multiples of 2 or 3; it also includes numbers such as 25, 35, 49, etc., which are not prime, but the algorithm will still give the correct answer. A further savings of 20 percent in computation time can be made by removing the numbers $30m \pm 5$ from the list for $m \ge 1$, thereby eliminating all of the spurious multiples of 5. The exclusion of multiples of 7 shortens the list by 14 percent more, etc. A compact bit table can be used to govern the choice of trial divisors.

If N is known to be small, it is reasonable to have a table of all the necessary primes as part of the program. For example, if N is less than a million, we need only include the 168 primes less than a thousand (followed by the value $d_{168} = 1000$, to terminate the list in case N is a prime larger than 997^2). Such a table can be set up by means of a short auxiliary program; see, for example, Algorithm 1.3.2P or exercise 8.

How many trial divisions are necessary in Algorithm A? Let $\pi(x)$ be the number of primes $\le x$, so that $\pi(2) = 1$, $\pi(10) = 4$; the asymptotic behavior of this function has been studied extensively by many of the world's greatest mathematicians, beginning with Legendre in 1798. Numerous advances made during the nineteenth century culminated in 1899, when Charles de La Vallée Poussin proved that, for some $A > 0$,

$$\pi(x) = \int_2^x \frac{dt}{\ln t} + O\left(xe^{-A\sqrt{\log x}}\right). \tag{3}$$

[*Mém. Couronnés Acad. Roy. Belgique* **59** (1899), 1–74; see also J. Hadamard, *Bull. Soc. Math. de France* **24** (1896), 199–220.] Integrating by parts yields

$$\pi(x) = \frac{x}{\ln x} + \frac{x}{(\ln x)^2} + \frac{2!\,x}{(\ln x)^3} + \cdots + \frac{r!\,x}{(\ln x)^{r+1}} + O\left(\frac{x}{(\log x)^{r+2}}\right) \quad (4)$$

for all fixed $r \geq 0$. The error term in (3) has subsequently been improved; for example, it can be replaced by $O\big(x\exp(-A(\log x)^{3/5}/(\log\log x)^{1/5})\big)$. [See A. Walfisz, *Weyl'sche Exponentialsummen in der neueren Zahlentheorie* (Berlin: 1963), Chapter 5.] Bernhard Riemann conjectured in 1859 that

$$\pi(x) \approx \sum_{k=1}^{\lg x} \frac{\mu(k)}{k} L\big(\sqrt[k]{x}\big) \;=\; L(x) - \frac{1}{2}L\big(\sqrt{x}\big) - \frac{1}{3}L\big(\sqrt[3]{x}\big) + \cdots \quad (5)$$

where $L(x) = \int_2^x dt/\ln t$, and his formula agrees well with actual counts when x is of reasonable size:

x	$\pi(x)$	$L(x)$	Riemann's formula
10^3	168	176.6	168.3
10^6	78498	78626.5	78527.4
10^9	50847534	50849233.9	50847455.4
10^{12}	37607912018	37607950279.8	37607910542.2
10^{15}	29844570422669	29844571475286.5	29844570495886.9
10^{18}	24739954287740860	24739954309690414.0	24739954284239494.4

(See exercise 41.) However, the distribution of large primes is not that simple, and Riemann's conjecture (5) was disproved by J. E. Littlewood in 1914; see Hardy and Littlewood, *Acta Math.* **41** (1918), 119–196, where it is shown that there is a positive constant C such that

$$\pi(x) > L(x) + C\sqrt{x}\,\log\log\log x/\log x$$

for infinitely many x. Littlewood's result shows that prime numbers are inherently somewhat mysterious, and it will be necessary to develop deep properties of mathematics before their distribution is really understood. Riemann made another much more plausible conjecture, the famous "Riemann hypothesis," which states that the complex function $\zeta(z)$ is zero only when the real part of z is equal to $1/2$, except in the trivial cases where z is a negative even integer. This hypothesis, if true, would imply that $\pi(x) = L(x) + O\big(\sqrt{x}\log x\big)$; see exercise 25. Richard Brent has used a method of D. H. Lehmer to verify Riemann's hypothesis computationally for all "small" values of z, by showing that $\zeta(z)$ has exactly 75,000,000 zeros whose imaginary part is in the range $0 < \Im z < 32585736.4$; all of these zeros have $\Re z = \frac{1}{2}$ and $\zeta'(z) \neq 0$. [*Math. Comp.* **33** (1979), 1361–1372.]

In order to analyze the average behavior of Algorithm A, we would like to know how large the largest prime factor p_t will tend to be. This question was first investigated by Karl Dickman [*Arkiv för Mat., Astron. och Fys.* **22A**, 10 (1930), 1–14], who studied the probability that a random integer between 1 and x will have its largest prime factor $\leq x^\alpha$. Dickman gave a heuristic argument to show that this probability approaches the limiting value $F(\alpha)$ as $x \to \infty$, where F can be calculated from the functional equation

$$F(\alpha) = \int_0^\alpha F\left(\frac{t}{1-t}\right) \frac{dt}{t}, \quad \text{for } 0 \le \alpha \le 1; \qquad F(\alpha) = 1, \quad \text{for } \alpha \ge 1. \quad (6)$$

His argument was essentially this: Given $0 < t < 1$, the number of integers less than x whose largest prime factor is between x^t and x^{t+dt} is $xF'(t)\,dt$. The number of primes p in that range is $\pi(x^{t+dt}) - \pi(x^t) = \pi(x^t + (\ln x)x^t\, dt) - \pi(x^t) = x^t\, dt/t$. For every such p, the number of integers n such that "$np \le x$ and the largest prime factor of n is $\le p$" is the number of $n \le x^{1-t}$ whose largest prime factor is $\le (x^{1-t})^{t/(1-t)}$, namely $x^{1-t}\,F(t/(1-t))$. Hence $xF'(t)\,dt = (x^t\, dt/t)(x^{1-t}F(t/(1-t)))$, and (6) follows by integration. This heuristic argument can be made rigorous; V. Ramaswami [*Bull. Amer. Math. Soc.* **55** (1949), 1122–1127] showed that the probability in question for fixed α is asymptotically $F(\alpha) + O(1/\log x)$, as $x \to \infty$, and many other authors have extended the analysis [see the survey by Karl K. Norton, *Memoirs Amer. Math. Soc.* **106** (1971), 9–27].

If $\frac{1}{2} \le \alpha \le 1$, formula (6) simplifies to

$$F(\alpha) = 1 - \int_\alpha^1 F\left(\frac{t}{1-t}\right) \frac{dt}{t} = 1 - \int_\alpha^1 \frac{dt}{t} = 1 + \ln \alpha.$$

Thus, for example, the probability that a random positive integer $\le x$ has a prime factor $> \sqrt{x}$ is $1 - F(\frac{1}{2}) = \ln 2$, about 69 percent. In all such cases, Algorithm A must work hard.

The net result of this discussion is that Algorithm A will give the answer rather quickly if we want to factor a six-digit number; but for large N the amount of computer time for factorization by trial division will rapidly exceed practical limits, unless we are unusually lucky.

Later in this section we will see that there are fairly good ways to determine whether or not a reasonably large number n is prime, without trying all divisors up to $\sqrt{n}$. Therefore Algorithm A would often run faster if we inserted a primality test between steps A2 and A3; the running time for this improved algorithm would then be roughly proportional to p_{t-1}, the *second-largest* prime factor of N, instead of to $\max(p_{t-1}, \sqrt{p_t})$. By an argument analogous to Dickman's (see exercise 18), we can show that the second-largest prime factor of a random integer $\le x$ will be $\le x^\beta$ with approximate probability $G(\beta)$, where

$$G(\beta) = \int_0^\beta \left(G\left(\frac{t}{1-t}\right) - F\left(\frac{t}{1-t}\right)\right) \frac{dt}{t}, \quad \text{for } 0 \le \beta \le \frac{1}{2}. \quad (7)$$

Clearly $G(\beta) = 1$ for $\beta \ge \frac{1}{2}$. (See Fig. 12.) Numerical evaluation of (6) and (7) yields the following "percentage points":

$F(\alpha), G(\beta) =$	.01	.05	.10	.20	.35	.50	.65	.80	.90	.95	.99
$\alpha \approx$	.2697	.3348	.3785	.4430	.5220	.6065	.7047	.8187	.9048	.9512	.9900
$\beta \approx$	.0056	.0273	.0531	.1003	.1611	.2117	.2582	.3104	.3590	.3967	.4517

Thus, the second-largest prime factor will be $\le x^{.2117}$ about half the time, etc.

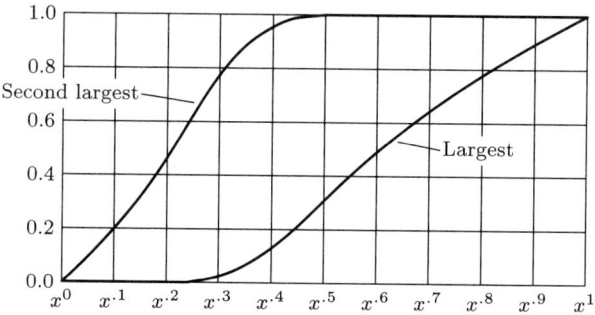

Fig. 12. Probability distribution functions for the
two largest prime factors of a random integer $\leq x$.

The *total number of prime factors*, t, has also been intensively analyzed.
Obviously $1 \leq t \leq \lg N$, but these lower and upper bounds are seldom achieved.
It is possible to prove that if N is chosen at random between 1 and x, the
probability that $t \leq \ln\ln x + c\sqrt{\ln\ln x}$ approaches

$$\frac{1}{\sqrt{2\pi}} \int_{-\infty}^{c} e^{-u^2/2}\, du \qquad (8)$$

as $x \to \infty$, for any fixed c. In other words, the distribution of t is essentially
normal, with mean and variance $\ln\ln x$; about 99.73 percent of all the large
integers $\leq x$ have $|t - \ln\ln x| \leq 3\sqrt{\ln\ln x}$. Furthermore the average value of
$t - \ln\ln x$ for $1 \leq N \leq x$ is known to approach

$$\gamma + \sum_{p \text{ prime}} \left(\ln(1 - 1/p) + 1/(p-1) \right) = \gamma + \sum_{n \geq 2} \frac{\varphi(n)\ln\zeta(n)}{n}$$

$$= 1.03465\,38818\,97437\,91161\,97942\,98464\,63825\,46703+. \qquad (9)$$

[See G. H. Hardy and E. M. Wright, *An Introduction to the Theory of Numbers*,
5th edition (Oxford, 1979), §22.11; see also P. Erdös and M. Kac, *Amer. J. Math.*
62 (1940), 738–742.]

The size of prime factors has a remarkable connection with permutations:
The average number of bits in the kth largest prime factor of a random n-bit
integer is asymptotically the same as the average length of the kth largest cycle
of a random n-element permutation, as $n \to \infty$. [See D. E. Knuth, *Selected
Papers on Analysis of Algorithms* (2000), 329–330, 336–337, for references to
the relevant literature.] It follows that Algorithm A usually finds a few small
factors and then begins a long-drawn-out search for the big ones that are left.

An excellent exposition of the probability distribution of the prime factors
of a random integer has been given by Patrick Billingsley, *AMM* **80** (1973),
1099–1115; see also his paper in *Annals of Probability* **2** (1974), 749–791.

Factoring by pseudorandom cycles. Near the beginning of Chapter 3, we
observed that "a random number generator chosen at random isn't very random."
This principle, which worked against us in that chapter, has the redeeming virtue

that it leads to a surprisingly efficient method of factorization, discovered by
J. M. Pollard [*BIT* **15** (1975), 331–334]. The number of computational steps
in Pollard's method is on the order of $\sqrt{p_{t-1}}$, so it is significantly faster than
Algorithm A when N is large. According to (7) and Fig. 12, the running time
will usually be well under $N^{1/4}$.

Let $f(x)$ be any polynomial with integer coefficients, and consider the two
sequences defined by

$$x_0 = y_0 = A; \qquad x_{m+1} = f(x_m) \bmod N, \qquad y_{m+1} = f(y_m) \bmod p, \qquad (10)$$

where p is any prime factor of N. It follows that

$$y_m = x_m \bmod p, \qquad \text{for } m \geq 1. \qquad (11)$$

Now exercise 3.1–7 shows that we will have $y_m = y_{\ell(m)-1}$ for some $m \geq 1$,
where $\ell(m)$ is the greatest power of 2 that is $\leq m$. Thus $x_m - x_{\ell(m)-1}$ will
be a multiple of p. Furthermore if $f(y) \bmod p$ behaves as a random mapping
from the set $\{0, 1, \ldots, p-1\}$ into itself, exercise 3.1–12 shows that the average
value of the least such m will be of order $\sqrt{p}$. In fact, exercise 4 below shows
that this average value for random mappings is less than $1.625\,Q(p)$, where the
function $Q(p) \approx \sqrt{\pi p / 2}$ was defined in Section 1.2.11.3. If the different prime
divisors of N correspond to different values of m (as they almost surely will, when
N is large), we will be able to find them by calculating $\gcd(x_m - x_{\ell(m)-1}, N)$
for $m = 1, 2, 3, \ldots$, until the unfactored residue is prime. Pollard called his
technique the "rho method," because an eventually periodic sequence such as
$y_0, y_1, \ldots$ is reminiscent of the Greek letter ρ.

From the theory in Chapter 3, we know that a linear polynomial $f(x) = ax + c$ will not be sufficiently random for our purposes. The next-simplest
case is quadratic, say $f(x) = x^2 + 1$. We don't *know* that this function is
sufficiently random, but our lack of knowledge tends to support the hypothesis
of randomness, and empirical tests show that this f does work essentially as
predicted. In fact, f is probably slightly *better* than random, since $x^2 + 1$ takes
on only $\frac{1}{2}(p+1)$ distinct values mod p; see Arney and Bender, *Pacific J. Math.*
103 (1982), 269–294. Therefore the following procedure is reasonable:

Algorithm B (*Factoring by the rho method*). This algorithm outputs the prime
factors of a given integer $N \geq 2$, with high probability, although there is a chance
that it will fail.

B1. [Initialize.] Set $x \leftarrow 5$, $x' \leftarrow 2$, $k \leftarrow 1$, $l \leftarrow 1$, $n \leftarrow N$. (During this
algorithm, n is the unfactored part of N, and the variables x and x' represent
the quantities $x_m \bmod n$ and $x_{\ell(m)-1} \bmod n$ in (10), where $f(x) = x^2 + 1$,
$A = 2$, $l = \ell(m)$, and $k = 2l - m$.)

B2. [Test primality.] If n is prime (see the discussion below), output n; the
algorithm terminates.

B3. [Factor found?] Set $g \leftarrow \gcd(x' - x, n)$. If $g = 1$, go on to step B4; otherwise
output g. Now if $g = n$, the algorithm terminates (and it has failed, because

we know that n isn't prime). Otherwise set $n \leftarrow n/g$, $x \leftarrow x \bmod n$, $x' \leftarrow x' \bmod n$, and return to step B2. (Note that g may not be prime; this should be tested. In the rare event that g isn't prime, its prime factors won't be determinable with this algorithm.)

B4. [Advance.] Set $k \leftarrow k - 1$. If $k = 0$, set $x' \leftarrow x$, $l \leftarrow 2l$, $k \leftarrow l$. Set $x \leftarrow (x^2 + 1) \bmod n$ and return to B3. ∎

As an example of Algorithm B, let's try to factor $N = 25852$ again. The third execution of step B3 will output $g = 4$ (which isn't prime). After six more iterations the algorithm finds the factor $g = 23$. Algorithm B has not distinguished itself in this example, but of course it was designed to factor *big* numbers. Algorithm A takes much longer to find large prime factors, but it can't be beat when it comes to removing the small ones. In practice, we should run Algorithm A awhile before switching over to Algorithm B.

We can get a better idea of Algorithm B's prowess by considering the ten largest six-digit primes. The number of iterations, $m(p)$, that Algorithm B needs to find the factor p is given in the following table:

$p =$	999863	999883	999907	999917	999931	999953	999959	999961	999979	999983
$m(p) =$	276	409	2106	1561	1593	1091	474	1819	395	814

Experiments by Tomás Oliveira e Silva indicate that $m(p)$ has an average value of about $2\sqrt{p}$, and it never exceeds $16\sqrt{p}$ when $p < 1000000000$. The maximum $m(p)$ for $p < 10^9$ is $m(850112303) = 416784$; and the maximum of $m(p)/\sqrt{p}$ occurs when $p = 695361131$, $m(p) = 406244$. According to these experimental results, almost all 18-digit numbers can be factored in fewer than 64,000 iterations of Algorithm B (compared to roughly 50,000,000 divisions in Algorithm A).

The time-consuming operations in each iteration of Algorithm B are the multiple-precision multiplication and division in step B4, and the gcd in step B3. The technique of "Montgomery multiplication" (exercise 4.3.1–41) will speed this up. Moreover, if the gcd operation is slow, Pollard suggests gaining speed by accumulating the product mod n of, say, ten consecutive $(x' - x)$ values before taking each gcd; this replaces 90 percent of the gcd operations by a single multiplication mod N while only slightly increasing the chance of failure. He also suggests starting with $m = q$ instead of $m = 1$ in step B1, where q is, say, one tenth of the number of iterations you are planning to use.

In those rare cases where failure occurs for large N, we could try using $f(x) = x^2 + c$ for some $c \neq 0$ or 1. The value $c = -2$ should also be avoided, since the recurrence $x_{m+1} = x_m^2 - 2$ has solutions of the form $x_m = r^{2^m} + r^{-2^m}$. Other values of c do not seem to lead to simple relationships mod p, and they should all be satisfactory when used with suitable starting values.

Richard Brent used a modification of Algorithm B to discover the prime factor 1238926361552897 of $2^{256} + 1$. [See *Math. Comp.* **36** (1981), 627–630; **38** (1982), 253–255.]

Fermat's method. Another approach to the factoring problem, which was used by Pierre de Fermat in 1643, is more suited to finding large factors than small ones. [Fermat's original description of his method, translated into English, can be found in L. E. Dickson's monumental *History of the Theory of Numbers* **1** (Carnegie Inst. of Washington, 1919), 357. An equivalent idea had in fact been used already by Nārāyaṇa Paṇḍita in his remarkable book *Gaṇita Kaumudī* (1356); see Parmanand Singh, *Gaṇita Bhāratī* **22** (2000), 72–74.]

Assume that $N = uv$, where $u \leq v$. For practical purposes we may assume that N is odd; this means that u and v are odd, and we can let

$$x = (u + v)/2, \qquad y = (v - u)/2, \qquad (12)$$
$$N = x^2 - y^2, \qquad 0 \leq y < x \leq N. \qquad (13)$$

Fermat's method consists of searching systematically for values of x and y that satisfy Eq. (13). The following algorithm shows how factoring can therefore be done *without using any multiplication or division:*

Algorithm C (*Factoring by addition and subtraction*). Given an odd number N, this algorithm determines the largest factor of N less than or equal to $\sqrt{N}$.

C1. [Initialize.] Set $a \leftarrow 2\lfloor\sqrt{N}\rfloor + 1$, $b \leftarrow 1$, $r \leftarrow \lfloor\sqrt{N}\rfloor^2 - N$. (During this algorithm a, b, and r correspond respectively to $2x+1$, $2y+1$, and x^2-y^2-N as we search for a solution to (13); we will have $|r| < a$ and $b < a$.)

C2. [Done?] If $r = 0$, the algorithm terminates; we have

$$N = \big((a - b)/2\big)\big((a + b - 2)/2\big),$$

and $(a - b)/2$ is the largest factor of N less than or equal to $\sqrt{N}$.

C3. [Increase a.] Set $r \leftarrow r + a$ and $a \leftarrow a + 2$.

C4. [Increase b.] Set $r \leftarrow r - b$ and $b \leftarrow b + 2$.

C5. [Test r.] Return to step C4 if $r > 0$, otherwise go back to C2. ∎

The reader may find it amusing to find the factors of 377 by hand, using this algorithm. The number of steps needed to find the factors u and v of $N = uv$ is essentially proportional to $(a+b-2)/2 - \lfloor\sqrt{N}\rfloor = v - \lfloor\sqrt{N}\rfloor$; this can, of course, be a very large number, although each step can be done very rapidly on most computers. An improvement that requires only $O(N^{1/3})$ operations in the worst case has been developed by R. S. Lehman [*Math. Comp.* **28** (1974), 637–646].

It is not quite correct to call Algorithm C "Fermat's method," since Fermat used a somewhat more streamlined approach. Algorithm C's main loop is quite fast on computers, but it is not very suitable for hand calculation. Fermat didn't actually maintain the running value of y; he would look at $x^2 - N$ and guess whether or not this quantity was a perfect square by looking at its least significant digits. (The last two digits of a perfect square must be 00, $e1$, $e4$, 25, $o6$, or $e9$, where e is an even digit and o is an odd digit.) Therefore he avoided the operations of steps C4 and C5, replacing them by an occasional determination that a certain number is not a perfect square.

Fermat's method of looking at the rightmost digits can, of course, be generalized by using other moduli. Suppose for clarity that $N = 8616460799$, a number whose historic significance is explained below, and consider the following table:

m	if $x \bmod m$ is	then $x^2 \bmod m$ is	and $(x^2 - N) \bmod m$ is
3	$0, 1, 2$	$0, 1, 1$	$1, 2, 2$
5	$0, 1, 2, 3, 4$	$0, 1, 4, 4, 1$	$1, 2, 0, 0, 2$
7	$0, 1, 2, 3, 4, 5, 6$	$0, 1, 4, 2, 2, 4, 1$	$5, 6, 2, 0, 0, 2, 6$
8	$0, 1, 2, 3, 4, 5, 6, 7$	$0, 1, 4, 1, 0, 1, 4, 1$	$1, 2, 5, 2, 1, 2, 5, 2$
11	$0, 1, 2, 3, 4, 5, 6, 7, 8, 9, 10$	$0, 1, 4, 9, 5, 3, 3, 5, 9, 4, 1$	$10, 0, 3, 8, 4, 2, 2, 4, 8, 3, 0$

If $x^2 - N$ is to be a perfect square y^2, it must have a residue mod m consistent with this fact, for all m. For example, if $N = 8616460799$ and $x \bmod 3 \neq 0$, then $(x^2 - N) \bmod 3 = 2$, so $x^2 - N$ cannot be a perfect square; therefore x must be a multiple of 3 whenever $N = x^2 - y^2$. The table tells us, in fact, that

$$
\begin{aligned}
x \bmod 3 &= 0; \\
x \bmod 5 &= 0,\ 2,\ \text{or } 3; \\
x \bmod 7 &= 2,\ 3,\ 4,\ \text{or } 5; \\
x \bmod 8 &= 0 \text{ or } 4 \ (\text{hence } x \bmod 4 = 0); \\
x \bmod 11 &= 1,\ 2,\ 4,\ 7,\ 9,\ \text{or } 10.
\end{aligned}
\tag{14}
$$

This narrows down the search for x considerably. For example, x must be a multiple of 12. We must have $x \geq \lceil \sqrt{N} \rceil = 92825$, and the least such multiple of 12 is 92832. This value has residues $(2, 5, 3)$ modulo $(5, 7, 11)$ respectively, so it fails (14) with respect to modulus 11. Increasing x by 12 changes the residue mod 5 by 2, mod 7 by 5, and mod 11 by 1; so it is easy to see that the first value of $x \geq 92825$ that satisfies all of the conditions in (14) is $x = 92880$. Now $92880^2 - N = 10233601$, and the pencil-and-paper method for square root tells us that $10233601 = 3199^2$ is indeed a perfect square. Therefore we have found the desired solution $x = 92880$, $y = 3199$, and the factorization is

$$8616460799 = (x - y)(x + y) = 89681 \cdot 96079.$$

This value of N is interesting because the English economist and logician W. S. Jevons introduced it as follows in a well-known book: "Given any two numbers, we may by a simple and infallible process obtain their product, but it is quite another matter when a large number is given to determine its factors. Can the reader say what two numbers multiplied together will produce the number 8,616,460,799? I think it unlikely that anyone but myself will ever know." [*The Principles of Science* (1874), Chapter 7.] We have just seen, however, that Fermat could have factored N in less than 10 minutes, on the back of an envelope! Jevons's point about the difficulty of factoring versus multiplying is well taken, but only if we form the product of numbers that aren't so close to each other.

In place of the moduli considered in (14), we can use any powers of distinct primes. For example, if we had used 25 in place of 5, we would find that the only permissible values of $x \bmod 25$ are 0, 5, 7, 10, 15, 18, and 20. This gives more information than (14). In general, we will get more information modulo p^2 than we do modulo p, for odd primes p, whenever $x^2 - N \equiv 0$ (modulo p) has a solution x. Individual primes p and q are, however, preferable to moduli like p^2 unless p is quite small, because we tend to get even more information $\bmod pq$.

The modular method just used is called a *sieve procedure*, since we can imagine passing all integers through a "sieve" for which only those values with $x \bmod 3 = 0$ come out, then sifting these numbers through another sieve that allows only numbers with $x \bmod 5 = 0$, 2, or 3 to pass, etc. Each sieve by itself will remove about half of the remaining values (see exercise 6); and when we sieve with respect to moduli that are relatively prime in pairs, each sieve is independent of the others because of the Chinese remainder theorem (Theorem 4.3.2C). So if we sieve with respect to, say, 30 different primes, only about one value in every 2^{30} will need to be examined to see if $x^2 - N$ is a perfect square y^2.

Algorithm D (*Factoring with sieves*). Given an odd number N, this algorithm determines the largest factor of N less than or equal to $\sqrt{N}$. The procedure uses moduli m_1, m_2, ..., m_r that are relatively prime to each other in pairs and relatively prime to N. We assume that we have access to r *sieve tables* $S[i,j]$ for $0 \le j < m_i$, $1 \le i \le r$, where

$$S[i,j] = \big[j^2 - N \equiv y^2 \text{ (modulo } m_i \text{) has a solution } y \big].$$

D1. [Initialize.] Set $x \leftarrow \lceil \sqrt{N} \rceil$, and set $k_i \leftarrow (-x) \bmod m_i$ for $1 \le i \le r$. (Throughout this algorithm the index variables k_1, k_2, ..., k_r will be set so that $k_i = (-x) \bmod m_i$.)

D2. [Sieve.] If $S[i, k_i] = 1$ for $1 \le i \le r$, go to step D4.

D3. [Step x.] Set $x \leftarrow x + 1$, and set $k_i \leftarrow (k_i - 1) \bmod m_i$ for $1 \le i \le r$. Return to step D2.

D4. [Test $x^2 - N$.] Set $y \leftarrow \lfloor \sqrt{x^2 - N} \rfloor$ or to $\lceil \sqrt{x^2 - N} \rceil$. If $y^2 = x^2 - N$, then $(x - y)$ is the desired factor, and the algorithm terminates. Otherwise return to step D3. ∎

There are several ways to make this procedure run fast. For example, we have seen that if $N \bmod 3 = 2$, then x must be a multiple of 3; we can set $x = 3x'$, and use a different sieve corresponding to x', increasing the speed threefold. If $N \bmod 9 = 1$, 4, or 7, then x must be congruent respectively to ± 1, ± 2, or ± 4 (modulo 9); so we run two sieves (one for x' and one for x'', where $x = 9x' + a$ and $x = 9x'' - a$) to increase the speed by a factor of $4\frac{1}{2}$. If $N \bmod 4 = 3$, then $x \bmod 4$ is known and the speed is increased by an additional factor of 4; in the other case, when $N \bmod 4 = 1$, x must be odd so the speed may be doubled. Another way to double the speed of the algorithm (at the expense of storage space) is to combine pairs of moduli, using $m_{r-k} m_k$ in place of m_k for $1 \le k < \frac{1}{2}r$.

An even more important method of speeding up Algorithm D is to use the Boolean operations found on most binary computers. Let us assume, for example, that MIX is a binary computer with 30 bits per word. The tables $S[i, k_i]$ can be kept in memory with one bit per entry; thus 30 values can be stored in a single word. The operation AND, which replaces the kth bit of the accumulator by zero if the kth bit of a specified word in memory is zero, for $1 \le k \le 30$, can be used to process 30 values of x at once! For convenience, we can make several copies of the tables $S[i,j]$ so that the table entries for m_i involve $\operatorname{lcm}(m_i, 30)$ bits; then the sieve tables for each modulus fill an integral number of words. Under these assumptions, 30 executions of the main loop in Algorithm D are equivalent to code of the following form:

```
D2 LD1   K1      rI1 ← k'₁.
   LDA   S1,1    rA ← S'[1,rI1].
   DEC1  1       rI1 ← rI1 − 1.
   J1NN  *+2
   INC1  M1      If rI1 < 0, set rI1 ← rI1 + lcm(m₁,30).
   ST1   K1      k'₁ ← rI1.
   LD1   K2      rI1 ← k'₂.
   AND   S2,1    rA ← rA & S'[2,rI1].
   DEC1  1       rI1 ← rI1 − 1.
   J1NN  *+2
   INC1  M2      If rI1 < 0, set rI1 ← rI1 + lcm(m₂,30).
   ST1   K2      k'₂ ← rI1.
   LD1   K3      rI1 ← k'₃.
   ...           (m₃ through m_r are like m₂)
   ST1   Kr      k'_r ← rI1.
   INCX  30      x ← x + 30.
   JAZ   D2      Repeat if all sieved out.  ∎
```

The number of cycles for 30 iterations is essentially $2 + 8r$; if $r = 11$, this means three cycles are being used on each iteration, just as in Algorithm C, and Algorithm C involves $y = \frac{1}{2}(v - u)$ more iterations.

If the table entries for m_i do not come out to be an integral number of words, further shifting of the table entries would be necessary on each iteration in order to align the bits properly. This would add quite a lot of coding to the main loop and it would probably make the program too slow to compete with Algorithm C unless $v/u \leq 100$ (see exercise 7).

Sieve procedures can be applied to a variety of other problems, not necessarily having much to do with arithmetic. A survey of these techniques has been prepared by Marvin C. Wunderlich, *JACM* **14** (1967), 10–19.

F. W. Lawrence proposed the construction of special sieve machines for factorization in the 19th century [*Quart. J. of Pure and Applied Math.* **28** (1896), 285–311], and E. O. Carissan completed such a device with 14 moduli in 1919. [See Shallit, Williams, and Morain, *Math. Intelligencer* **17**,3 (1995), 41–47, for the interesting story of how Carissan's long-lost sieve was rediscovered and preserved for posterity.] D. H. Lehmer and his associates constructed and used many different sieve devices during the period 1926–1989, beginning with bicycle chains and later using photoelectric cells and other kinds of technology; see, for example, *AMM* **40** (1933), 401–406. Lehmer's electronic delay-line sieve, which began operating in 1965, processed one million numbers per second. By 1995 it was possible to construct a machine that sieved 6144 million numbers per second, performing 256 iterations of steps D2 and D3 in about 5.2 nanoseconds [see Lukes, Patterson, and Williams, *Nieuw Archief voor Wiskunde* (4) **13** (1995),

113–139]. Another way to factor with sieves was described by D. H. and Emma Lehmer in *Math. Comp.* **28** (1974), 625–635.

Primality testing. None of the algorithms we have discussed so far is an efficient way to determine that a large number n is prime. Fortunately, there are other methods available for settling this question; efficient techniques have been devised by É. Lucas and others, notably D. H. Lehmer [see *Bull. Amer. Math. Soc.* **33** (1927), 327–340].

According to Fermat's theorem (Theorem 1.2.4F), we have

$$x^{p-1} \bmod p = 1$$

whenever p is prime and x is not a multiple of p. Furthermore, there are efficient ways to calculate $x^{n-1} \bmod n$, requiring only $O(\log n)$ operations of multiplication mod n. (We shall study them in Section 4.6.3 below.) Therefore we can often determine that n is *not* prime when this relationship fails.

For example, Fermat once verified that the numbers $2^1 + 1$, $2^2 + 1$, $2^4 + 1$, $2^8 + 1$, and $2^{16} + 1$ are prime. In a letter to Mersenne written in 1640, Fermat conjectured that $2^{2^n} + 1$ is always prime, but said he was unable to determine definitely whether the number $4294967297 = 2^{32} + 1$ is prime or not. Neither Fermat nor Mersenne ever resolved this problem, although they could have done it as follows: The number $3^{2^{32}} \bmod (2^{32} + 1)$ can be computed by doing 32 operations of squaring modulo $2^{32} + 1$, and the answer is 3029026160; therefore (by Fermat's own theorem, which he discovered in the same year 1640!) the number $2^{32} + 1$ is *not* prime. This argument gives us absolutely no idea what the factors are, but it answers Fermat's question.

Fermat's theorem is a powerful test for showing nonprimality of a given number. When n is not prime, it is always possible to find a value of $x < n$ such that $x^{n-1} \bmod n \neq 1$; experience shows that, in fact, such a value can almost always be found very quickly. There are some rare values of n for which $x^{n-1} \bmod n$ is frequently equal to unity, but then n has a factor less than $\sqrt[3]{n}$; see exercise 9.

The same method can be extended to prove that a large prime number n really *is* prime, by using the following idea: *If there is a number x for which the order of x modulo n is equal to $n - 1$, then n is prime.* (The order of x modulo n is the smallest positive integer k such that $x^k \bmod n = 1$; see Section 3.2.1.2.) For this condition implies that the numbers $x^1 \bmod n$, ..., $x^{n-1} \bmod n$ are distinct and relatively prime to n, so they must be the numbers 1, 2, ..., $n-1$ in some order; thus n has no proper divisors. If n is prime, such a number x (called a *primitive root* of n) will always exist; see exercise 3.2.1.2–16. In fact, primitive roots are rather numerous. There are $\varphi(n - 1)$ of them, and this is quite a substantial number, since $n/\varphi(n - 1) = O(\log \log n)$.

It is unnecessary to calculate $x^k \bmod n$ for all $k \leq n - 1$ to determine if the order of x is $n - 1$ or not. The order of x will be $n - 1$ if and only if

  i) $x^{n-1} \bmod n = 1$;

 ii) $x^{(n-1)/p} \bmod n \neq 1$ for all primes p that divide $n - 1$.

For x^s mod $n = 1$ if and only if s is a multiple of the order of x modulo n. If the two conditions hold, and if k is the order of x modulo n, we therefore know that k is a divisor of $n - 1$, but not a divisor of $(n - 1)/p$ for any prime factor p of $n - 1$; the only remaining possibility is $k = n - 1$. This completes the proof that conditions (i) and (ii) suffice to establish the primality of n.

Exercise 10 shows that we can in fact use different values of x for each of the primes p, and n will still be prime. We may restrict consideration to prime values of x, since the order of uv modulo n divides the least common multiple of the orders of u and v by exercise 3.2.1.2–15. Conditions (i) and (ii) can be tested efficiently by using the rapid methods for evaluating powers of numbers discussed in Section 4.6.3. But it is necessary to know the prime factors of $n-1$, so we have an interesting situation in which the factorization of n depends on that of $n - 1$.

An example. The study of a reasonably typical large factorization will help to fix the ideas we have discussed so far. Let us try to find the prime factors of $2^{214} + 1$, a 65-digit number. The factorization can be initiated with a bit of clairvoyance if we notice that

$$2^{214} + 1 = (2^{107} - 2^{54} + 1)(2^{107} + 2^{54} + 1); \qquad (15)$$

this is a special case of the factorization $4x^4 + 1 = (2x^2 + 2x + 1)(2x^2 - 2x + 1)$, which Euler communicated to Goldbach in 1742 [P. H. Fuss, *Correspondance Math. et Physique* **1** (1843), 145]. The problem now boils down to examining each of the 33-digit factors in (15).

A computer program readily discovers that $2^{107} - 2^{54} + 1 = 5 \cdot 857 \cdot n_0$, where

$$n_0 = 3786680906166005726421925 3397 \qquad (16)$$

is a 29-digit number having no prime factors less than 1000. A multiple-precision calculation using Algorithm 4.6.3A shows that

$$3^{n_0 - 1} \bmod n_0 = 1,$$

so we suspect that n_0 is prime. It is certainly out of the question to prove that n_0 is prime by trying the 10 million million or so potential divisors, but the method discussed above gives a feasible test for primality: Our next goal is to factor $n_0 - 1$. With little difficulty, our computer will tell us that

$$n_0 - 1 = 2 \cdot 2 \cdot 19 \cdot 107 \cdot 353 \cdot n_1, \qquad n_1 = 13191270754108226049301.$$

Here $3^{n_1 - 1} \bmod n_1 \neq 1$, so n_1 is not prime; by continuing Algorithm A or Algorithm B we obtain another factor,

$$n_1 = 91813 \cdot n_2, \qquad n_2 = 143675413657196977.$$

This time $3^{n_2 - 1} \bmod n_2 = 1$, so we will try to prove that n_2 is prime. Casting out factors < 1000 yields $n_2 - 1 = 2 \cdot 2 \cdot 2 \cdot 2 \cdot 3 \cdot 3 \cdot 547 \cdot n_3$, where $n_3 = 1824032775457$. Since $3^{n_3 - 1} \bmod n_3 \neq 1$, we know that n_3 cannot be prime, and Algorithm A finds that $n_3 = 1103 \cdot n_4$, where $n_4 = 1653701519$. The number n_4 behaves like a prime (that is, $3^{n_4 - 1} \bmod n_4 = 1$), so we calculate

$$n_4 - 1 = 2 \cdot 7 \cdot 19 \cdot 23 \cdot 137 \cdot 1973.$$

Good; this is our first complete factorization. We are now ready to backtrack to the previous subproblem, proving that n_4 is prime. Using the procedure suggested by exercise 10, we compute the following values:

x	p	$x^{(n_4-1)/p} \bmod n_4$	$x^{n_4-1} \bmod n_4$	
2	2	1	(1)	
2	7	766408626	(1)	
2	19	332952683	(1)	
2	23	1154237810	(1)	
2	137	373782186	(1)	(17)
2	1973	490790919	(1)	
3	2	1	(1)	
5	2	1	(1)	
7	2	1653701518	1	

(Here "(1)" means a result of 1 that needn't be computed since it can be deduced from previous calculations.) Thus n_4 is prime, and $n_2 - 1$ has been completely factored. A similar calculation shows that n_2 is prime, and this complete factorization of $n_0 - 1$ finally shows, after still another calculation like (17), that n_0 is prime.

The last three lines of (17) represent a search for an integer x that satisfies $x^{(n_4-1)/2} \not\equiv x^{n_4-1} \equiv 1$ (modulo n_4). If n_4 is prime, we have only a 50-50 chance of success, so the case $p = 2$ is typically the hardest one to verify. We could streamline this part of the calculation by using the law of quadratic reciprocity (see exercise 23), which tells us for example that $5^{(q-1)/2} \equiv 1$ (modulo q) whenever q is a prime congruent to ± 1 (modulo 5). Merely calculating $n_4 \bmod 5$ would have told us right away that $x = 5$ could not possibly help in showing that n_4 is prime. In fact, however, the result of exercise 26 implies that the case $p = 2$ doesn't really need to be considered at all when testing n for primality, unless $n - 1$ is divisible by a high power of 2, so we could have dispensed with the last three lines of (17) entirely.

The next quantity to be factored is the other half of (15), namely

$$n_5 = 2^{107} + 2^{54} + 1.$$

Since $3^{n_5-1} \bmod n_5 \neq 1$, we know that n_5 is not prime, and Algorithm B shows that $n_5 = 843589 \cdot n_6$, where $n_6 = 192343993140277293096491917$. Unfortunately, $3^{n_6-1} \bmod n_6 \neq 1$, so we are left with a 27-digit nonprime. Continuing Algorithm B might well exhaust our patience (not our budget — we're using idle time on a weekend rather than "prime time"). But the sieve method of Algorithm D will be able to crack n_6 into its two factors,

$$n_6 = 8174912477117 \cdot 23528569104401.$$

(It turns out that Algorithm B would also have succeeded, after 6,432,966 iterations.) The factors of n_6 could not have been discovered by Algorithm A in a reasonable length of time.

Now the computation is complete: $2^{214} + 1$ has the prime factorization

$$5 \cdot 857 \cdot 843589 \cdot 8174912477117 \cdot 23528569104401 \cdot n_0,$$

where n_0 is the 29-digit prime in (16). A certain amount of good fortune entered into these calculations, for if we had not started with the known factorization (15) it is quite probable that we would first have cast out the small factors, reducing n to $n_6 n_0$. This 55-digit number would have been much more difficult to factor — Algorithm D would be useless and Algorithm B would have to work overtime because of the high precision necessary.

Dozens of further numerical examples can be found in an article by John Brillhart and J. L. Selfridge, *Math. Comp.* **21** (1967), 87–96.

Improved primality tests. The procedure just illustrated requires the complete factorization of $n-1$ before we can prove that n is prime, so it will bog down for large n. Another technique, which uses the factorization of $n+1$ instead, is described in exercise 15; if $n-1$ turns out to be too hard, $n+1$ might be easier.

Significant improvements are available for dealing with large n. For example, it is not difficult to prove a stronger converse of Fermat's theorem that requires only a partial factorization of $n-1$. Exercise 26 shows that we could have avoided most of the calculations in (17); the three conditions $2^{n_4-1} \bmod n_4 = \gcd(2^{(n_4-1)/23} - 1, n_4) = \gcd(2^{(n_4-1)/1973} - 1, n_4) = 1$ are sufficient by themselves to prove that n_4 is prime. Brillhart, Lehmer, and Selfridge have in fact developed a method that works when the numbers $n-1$ and $n+1$ have been only partially factored [*Math. Comp.* **29** (1975), 620–647, Corollary 11]: Suppose $n - 1 = f^- r^-$ and $n + 1 = f^+ r^+$, where we know the complete factorizations of f^- and f^+, and we also know that all factors of r^- and r^+ are $\geq b$. If the product $\left(b^3 f^- f^+ \max(f^-, f^+)\right)$ is greater than $2n$, a small amount of additional computation, described in their paper, will determine whether or not n is prime. Therefore numbers of up to 35 digits can usually be tested for primality in a fraction of a second, simply by casting out all prime factors < 30030 from $n \pm 1$ [see J. L. Selfridge and M. C. Wunderlich, *Congressus Numerantium* **12** (1974), 109–120]. The partial factorization of other quantities like $n^2 \pm n + 1$ and $n^2 + 1$ can be used to improve this method still further [see H. C. Williams and J. S. Judd, *Math. Comp.* **30** (1976), 157–172, 867–886].

In practice, when n has no small prime factors and $3^{n-1} \bmod n = 1$, further calculations almost always show that n is prime. (One of the rare exceptions in the author's experience is $n = \frac{1}{7}(2^{28} - 9) = 2341 \cdot 16381$.) On the other hand, some nonprime values of n are definitely bad news for the primality test we have discussed, because it might happen that $x^{n-1} \bmod n = 1$ for all x relatively prime to n (see exercise 9). The smallest such number is $n = 3 \cdot 11 \cdot 17 = 561$; here $\lambda(n) = \mathrm{lcm}(2, 10, 16) = 80$ in the notation of Eq. 3.2.1.2–(9), so $x^{80} \bmod 561 = 1 = x^{560} \bmod 561$ whenever x is relatively prime to 561. Our procedure would repeatedly fail to show that such an n is nonprime, until we had stumbled across one of its divisors. To improve the method, we need a quick way to determine the nonprimality of nonprime n, even in such pathological cases.

The following surprisingly simple procedure is guaranteed to do the job with high probability:

Algorithm P (*Probabilistic primality test*). Given an odd integer n, this algorithm attempts to decide whether or not n is prime. By repeating the algorithm several times, as explained in the remarks below, it is possible to be extremely confident about the primality of n, in a precise sense, yet the primality will not be rigorously proved. Let $n = 1 + 2^k q$, where q is odd.

P1. [Generate x.] Let x be a random integer in the range $1 < x < n$.

P2. [Exponentiate.] Set $j \leftarrow 0$ and $y \leftarrow x^q \bmod n$. (As in our previous primality test, $x^q \bmod n$ should be calculated in $O(\log q)$ steps; see Section 4.6.3.)

P3. [Done?] (Now $y = x^{2^j q} \bmod n$.) If $y = n - 1$, or if $y = 1$ and $j = 0$, terminate the algorithm and say "n is probably prime." If $y = 1$ and $j > 0$, go to P5.

P4. [Increase j.] Increase j by 1. If $j < k$, set $y \leftarrow y^2 \bmod n$ and return to P3.

P5. [Not prime.] Terminate and say "n is definitely not prime." ▮

The idea underlying Algorithm P is that if $x^q \bmod n \neq 1$ and $n = 1 + 2^k q$ is prime, the sequence of values

$$x^q \bmod n, \quad x^{2q} \bmod n, \quad x^{4q} \bmod n, \quad \ldots, \quad x^{2^k q} \bmod n$$

will end with 1, and the value just preceding the first appearance of 1 will be $n - 1$. (The only solutions to $y^2 \equiv 1$ (modulo p) are $y \equiv \pm 1$, when p is prime, since $(y - 1)(y + 1)$ must be a multiple of p.)

Exercise 22 proves the basic fact that Algorithm P will be wrong at most $1/4$ of the time, for all n. Actually it will rarely fail at all, for most n; but the crucial point is that the probability of failure is bounded *regardless* of the value of n.

Suppose we invoke Algorithm P repeatedly, choosing x independently and at random whenever we get to step P1. If the algorithm ever reports that n is nonprime, we can be sure this is so. But if the algorithm reports 25 times in a row that n is "probably prime," we can say that n is "almost surely prime." For the probability is less than $(1/4)^{25}$ that such a 25-times-in-a-row procedure gives the wrong information about its input. This is less than one chance in a quadrillion; even if we tested a billion different numbers with such a procedure, the expected number of mistakes would be less than $\frac{1}{1000000}$. It's much more likely that our computer has dropped a bit in its calculations, due to hardware malfunctions or cosmic radiations, than that Algorithm P has repeatedly guessed wrong!

Probabilistic algorithms like this lead us to question our traditional standards of reliability. Do we really *need* to have a rigorous proof of primality? For people unwilling to abandon traditional notions of proof, Gary L. Miller has demonstrated (in slightly weaker form) that if a certain well-known conjecture in number theory called the Extended Riemann Hypothesis can be proved, then either n is prime or there is an $x < 2(\ln n)^2$ such that Algorithm P will discover the nonprimality of n. [See *J. Comp. System Sci.* **13** (1976), 300–317. The constant 2 in this upper bound is due to Eric Bach, *Math. Comp.* **55** (1990), 355–380. See Chapter 8 of *Algorithmic Number Theory* **1** by E. Bach and J. O.

Shallit (MIT Press, 1996), for an exposition of various generalizations of the Riemann hypothesis.] Thus, we would have a rigorous way to test primality in $O(\log n)^5$ elementary operations, as opposed to a probabilistic method whose running time is $O(\log n)^3$, if the Extended Riemann Hypothesis were proved. But one might well ask whether any purported proof of that hypothesis will ever be as reliable as repeated application of Algorithm P on random x's.

A probabilistic test for primality was proposed in 1974 by R. Solovay and V. Strassen, who devised the interesting but more complicated test described in exercise 23(b). [See *SICOMP* **6** (1977), 84–85; **7** (1978), 118.] Algorithm P is a simplified version of a procedure due to M. O. Rabin, based in part on ideas of Gary L. Miller [see *Algorithms and Complexity* (1976), 35–36], and independently discovered by J. L. Selfridge. B. Arazi [*Comp. J.* **37** (1994), 219–222] has observed that Algorithm P can be speeded up significantly for large n by using Montgomery's fast method for remainders (exercise 4.3.1–41).

A completely rigorous and deterministic way to test for primality in polynomial time was finally discovered in 2002 by Manindra Agrawal, Neeraj Kayal, and Nitin Saxena, who proved the following result:

Theorem A. *Let r be an integer such that $n \perp r$ and the order of n modulo r exceeds $(\lg n)^2$. Then n is prime if and only if the polynomial congruence*

$$(z + a)^n \equiv z^n + a \qquad (\text{modulo } z^r - 1 \text{ and } n)$$

holds for $0 \leq z \leq \sqrt{r}\, \lg n$. (See exercise 3.2.2–11(a).) ∎

An excellent exposition of this theorem has been prepared by Andrew Granville [*Bull. Amer. Math. Soc.* **42** (2005), 3–38], who presents an elementary proof that it yields a primality test with running time $\Omega(\log n)^6$ and $O(\log n)^{11}$. He also explains a subsequent improvement due to H. Lenstra and C. Pomerance, who showed that the running time can be reduced to $O(\log n)^{6+\epsilon}$ if the polynomial $z^r - 1$ is replaced by a more general family of polynomials. And he discusses refinements by P. Berrizbeitia, Q. Cheng, P. Mihăilescu, R. Avanzi, and D. Bernstein, leading to a probabilistic algorithm by which a proof of primality can almost surely be found in $O(\log n)^{4+\epsilon}$ steps whenever n is prime.

Factoring via continued fractions. The factorization procedures we have discussed so far will often balk at numbers of 30 digits or more, and another idea is needed if we are to go much further. Fortunately there is such an idea; in fact, there were two ideas, due respectively to A. M. Legendre and M. Kraitchik, which led D. H. Lehmer and R. E. Powers to devise a new technique many years ago [*Bull. Amer. Math. Soc.* **37** (1931), 770–776]. However, the method was not used at the time because it was comparatively unsuitable for desk calculators. This negative judgment prevailed until the late 1960s, when John Brillhart found that the Lehmer–Powers approach deserved to be resurrected, since it was quite well suited to computer programming. In fact, he and Michael A. Morrison later developed it into the champion of all multiprecision factorization methods that were known in the 1970s. Their program would handle typical 25-digit numbers in about 30 seconds, and 40-digit numbers in about 50 minutes, on an IBM

360/91 computer [see *Math. Comp.* **29** (1975), 183–205]. The method had its
first triumphant success in 1970, discovering that $2^{128}+1 = 59649589127497217 \cdot$
5704689200685129054721.

The basic idea is to search for numbers x and y such that

$$x^2 \equiv y^2 \text{ (modulo } N), \qquad 0 < x, y < N, \qquad x \neq y, \qquad x + y \neq N. \qquad (18)$$

Fermat's method imposes the stronger requirement $x^2 - y^2 = N$, but actually
the congruence (18) is enough to split N into factors: It implies that N is a
divisor of $x^2 - y^2 = (x-y)(x+y)$, yet N divides neither $x-y$ nor $x+y$; hence
$\gcd(N, x-y)$ and $\gcd(N, x+y)$ are proper factors of N that can be found by
the efficient methods of Section 4.5.2.

One way to discover solutions of (18) is to look for values of x such that
$x^2 \equiv a \text{ (modulo } N)$, for small values of $|a|$. As we will see, it is often a simple
matter to piece together solutions of this congruence to obtain solutions of (18).
Now if $x^2 = a + kNd^2$ for some k and d, with small $|a|$, the fraction x/d is a good
approximation to $\sqrt{kN}$; conversely, if x/d is an especially good approximation
to $\sqrt{kN}$, the difference $|x^2 - kNd^2|$ will be small. This observation suggests
looking at the continued fraction expansion of $\sqrt{kN}$, since we have seen in
Eq. 4.5.3–(12) and exercise 4.5.3–42 that continued fractions yield good rational
approximations.

Continued fractions for quadratic irrationalities have many pleasant properties, which are proved in exercise 4.5.3–12. The algorithm below makes use of
these properties to derive solutions to the congruence

$$x^2 \equiv (-1)^{e_0} p_1^{e_1} p_2^{e_2} \dots p_m^{e_m} \text{ (modulo } N). \qquad (19)$$

Here we use a fixed set of small primes $p_1 = 2$, $p_2 = 3$, $\dots$, up to p_m; only
primes p such that either $p = 2$ or $(kN)^{(p-1)/2} \bmod p \leq 1$ should appear in this
list, since other primes will never be factors of the numbers generated by the
algorithm (see exercise 14). If $(x_1, e_{01}, e_{11}, \dots, e_{m1})$, $\dots$, $(x_r, e_{0r}, e_{1r}, \dots, e_{mr})$
are solutions of (19) such that the vector sum

$$(e_{01}, e_{11}, \dots, e_{m1}) + \dots + (e_{0r}, e_{1r}, \dots, e_{mr}) = (2e'_0, 2e'_1, \dots, 2e'_m) \qquad (20)$$

is *even* in each component, then

$$x = (x_1 \dots x_r) \bmod N, \qquad y = \left((-1)^{e'_0} p_1^{e'_1} \dots p_m^{e'_m}\right) \bmod N \qquad (21)$$

yields a solution to (18), except for the possibility that $x \equiv \pm y$. Condition (20)
essentially says that the vectors are linearly dependent modulo 2, so we must
have a solution to (20) if we have found at least $m + 2$ solutions to (19).

Algorithm E (*Factoring via continued fractions*). Given a positive integer N
and a positive integer k such that kN is not a perfect square, this algorithm
attempts to discover solutions to the congruence (19) for a given sequence of
primes p_1, $\dots$, p_m, by analyzing the convergents of the continued fraction for
$\sqrt{kN}$. (Another algorithm, which uses the outputs to discover factors of N, is
the subject of exercise 12.)

Table 1

AN ILLUSTRATION OF ALGORITHM E

$N = 197209$, $k = 1$, $m = 3$, $p_1 = 2$, $p_2 = 3$, $p_3 = 5$

	U	V	A	P	S	T	Output
After E1:	876	73	12	5329	1	—	
After E4:	882	145	6	5329	0	29	
After E4:	857	37	23	32418	1	37	
After E4:	751	720	1	159316	0	1	$159316^2 \equiv +2^4 \cdot 3^2 \cdot 5^1$
After E4:	852	143	5	191734	1	143	
After E4:	681	215	3	131941	0	43	
After E4:	863	656	1	193139	1	41	
After E4:	883	33	26	127871	0	11	
After E4:	821	136	6	165232	1	17	
After E4:	877	405	2	133218	0	1	$133218^2 \equiv +2^0 \cdot 3^4 \cdot 5^1$
After E4:	875	24	36	37250	1	1	$37250^2 \equiv -2^3 \cdot 3^1 \cdot 5^0$
After E4:	490	477	1	93755	0	53	

E1. [Initialize.] Set $D \leftarrow kN$, $R \leftarrow \lfloor\sqrt{D}\rfloor$, $R' \leftarrow 2R$, $U' \leftarrow R'$, $V \leftarrow D - R^2$, $V' \leftarrow 1$, $A \leftarrow \lfloor R'/V \rfloor$, $U \leftarrow R' - (R' \bmod V)$, $P' \leftarrow R$, $P \leftarrow (AR+1) \bmod N$, $S \leftarrow 1$. (This algorithm follows the general procedure of exercise 4.5.3–12, finding the continued fraction expansion of $\sqrt{kN}$. The variables U, U', V, V', P, P', A, and S represent, respectively, what that exercise calls $\lfloor\sqrt{D}\rfloor + U_n$, $\lfloor\sqrt{D}\rfloor + U_{n-1}$, V_n, V_{n-1}, $p_n \bmod N$, $p_{n-1} \bmod N$, A_n, and $n \bmod 2$, where n is initially 1. We will always have $0 < V \le U \le R'$, so the highest precision is needed only for P and P'.)

E2. [Advance U, V, S.] Set $T \leftarrow V$, $V \leftarrow A(U' - U) + V'$, $V' \leftarrow T$, $A \leftarrow \lfloor U/V \rfloor$, $U' \leftarrow U$, $U \leftarrow R' - (U \bmod V)$, $S \leftarrow 1 - S$.

E3. [Factor V.] (Now we have $P^2 - kNQ^2 = (-1)^S V$, for some Q relatively prime to P, by exercise 4.5.3–12(c).) Set $(e_0, e_1, \ldots, e_m) \leftarrow (S, 0, \ldots, 0)$, $T \leftarrow V$. Now do the following, for $1 \le j \le m$: If $T \bmod p_j = 0$, set $T \leftarrow T/p_j$ and $e_j \leftarrow e_j + 1$, and repeat this process until $T \bmod p_j \ne 0$.

E4. [Solution?] If $T = 1$, output the values $(P, e_0, e_1, \ldots, e_m)$, which comprise a solution to (19). (If enough solutions have been generated, we may terminate the algorithm now.)

E5. [Advance P, P'.] If $V \ne 1$, set $T \leftarrow P$, $P \leftarrow (AP + P') \bmod N$, $P' \leftarrow T$, and return to step E2. Otherwise the continued fraction process has started to repeat its cycle, except perhaps for S, so the algorithm terminates. (The cycle will usually be so long that this doesn't happen.) ∎

We can illustrate the application of Algorithm E to relatively small numbers by considering the case $N = 197209$, $k = 1$, $m = 3$, $p_1 = 2$, $p_2 = 3$, $p_3 = 5$. The computation begins as shown in Table 1.

Continuing the computation gives 25 outputs in the first 100 iterations; in other words, the algorithm is finding solutions quite rapidly. But some of the solutions are trivial. For example, if the computation above were continued 14 more times, we would obtain the output $197197^2 \equiv 2^4 \cdot 3^2 \cdot 5^0$, which is of no interest since $197197 \equiv -12$. The first two solutions above are already enough to complete the factorization: We have found that

$$(159316 \cdot 133218)^2 \equiv (2^2 \cdot 3^3 \cdot 5^1)^2 \pmod{197209};$$

thus (18) holds with $x = (159316 \cdot 133218) \bmod 197209 = 126308$, $y = 540$. By Euclid's algorithm, $\gcd(126308 - 540, 197209) = 199$; hence we obtain the pretty factorization

$$197209 = 199 \cdot 991.$$

We can get some understanding of why Algorithm E factors large numbers so successfully by considering a heuristic analysis of its running time, following unpublished ideas that R. Schroeppel communicated to the author in 1975. Let us assume for convenience that $k = 1$. The number of outputs needed to produce a factorization of N will be roughly proportional to the number m of small primes being cast out. Each execution of step E3 takes about order $m \log N$ units of time, so the total running time will be roughly proportional to $m^2 \log N/P$, where P is the probability of a successful output per iteration. If we make the conservative assumption that V is randomly distributed between 0 and $2\sqrt{N}$, the probability P is $(2\sqrt{N})^{-1}$ times the number of integers $< 2\sqrt{N}$ whose prime factors are all in the set $\{p_1, \ldots, p_m\}$. Exercise 29 gives a lower bound for P, from which we conclude that the running time is at most of order

$$\frac{2\sqrt{N}\, m^2 \log N}{m^r/r!}, \qquad \text{where } r = \left\lfloor \frac{\log 2\sqrt{N}}{\log p_m} \right\rfloor. \tag{22}$$

If we let $\ln m$ be approximately $\frac{1}{2}\sqrt{\ln N \ln \ln N}$, we have $r \approx \sqrt{\ln N/\ln \ln N} - 1$, assuming that $p_m = O(m \log m)$, so formula (22) reduces to

$$\exp\left(2\sqrt{(\ln N)(\ln \ln N)}\ + \ O\left((\log N)^{1/2}(\log \log N)^{-1/2}(\log \log \log N)\right)\right).$$

Stating this another way, the running time of Algorithm E is expected to be at most $N^{\epsilon(N)}$ under reasonably plausible assumptions, where the exponent $\epsilon(N) \approx 2\sqrt{\ln \ln N/\ln N}$ goes to 0 as $N \to \infty$.

When N is in a practical range, we should of course be careful not to take such asymptotic estimates too seriously. For example, if $N = 10^{50}$ we have $N^{1/\alpha} = (\lg N)^\alpha$ when $\alpha \approx 4.75$, and the same relation holds for $\alpha \approx 8.42$ when $N = 10^{200}$. The function $N^{\epsilon(N)}$ has an order of growth that is sort of a cross between $N^{1/\alpha}$ and $(\lg N)^\alpha$; but all three of these forms are about the same, unless N is intolerably large. Extensive computational experiments by M. C. Wunderlich have shown that a well-tuned version of Algorithm E performs much better than our estimate would indicate [see *Lecture Notes in Math.* **751** (1979), 328–342]; although $2\sqrt{\ln \ln N/\ln N} \approx .41$ when $N = 10^{50}$, he obtained running times of about $N^{0.15}$ while factoring thousands of numbers in the range $10^{13} \le N \le 10^{42}$.

Algorithm E begins its attempt to factorize N by essentially replacing N by kN, and this is a rather curious way to proceed (if not downright stupid).

"Excuse me, do you mind if I multiply your number by 3 before I try to factor it?" Nevertheless, it turns out to be a good idea, since certain values of k will make the V numbers potentially divisible by more small primes, hence they will be more likely to factor completely in step E3. On the other hand, a large value of k will make the V numbers larger, hence they will be less likely to factor completely; we want to balance these tendencies by choosing k wisely. Consider, for example, the divisibility of V by powers of 5. We have $P^2 - kNQ^2 = (-1)^S V$ in step E3, so if 5 divides V we have $P^2 \equiv kNQ^2$ (modulo 5). In this congruence Q cannot be a multiple of 5, since it is relatively prime to P, so we may write $(P/Q)^2 \equiv kN$ (modulo 5). If we assume that P and Q are random relatively prime integers, so that the 24 possible pairs $(P \bmod 5, Q \bmod 5) \neq (0,0)$ are equally likely, the probability that 5 divides V is therefore $\frac{4}{24}$, $\frac{8}{24}$, 0, 0, or $\frac{8}{24}$ according as $kN \bmod 5$ is 0, 1, 2, 3, or 4. Similarly the probability that 25 divides V is 0, $\frac{40}{600}$, 0, 0, $\frac{40}{600}$ respectively, unless kN is a multiple of 25. In general, given an odd prime p with $(kN)^{(p-1)/2} \bmod p = 1$, we find that V is a multiple of p^e with probability $2/(p^{e-1}(p+1))$; and the average number of times p divides V comes to $2p/(p^2 - 1)$. This analysis, suggested by R. Schroeppel, suggests that the best choice of k is the value that maximizes

$$\sum_{j=1}^{m} f(p_j, kN) \log p_j - \frac{1}{2} \log k, \tag{23}$$

where f is the function defined in exercise 28, since this is essentially the expected value of $\ln(\sqrt{N}/T)$ when we reach step E4.

Best results will be obtained with Algorithm E when both k and m are well chosen. The proper choice of m can only be made by experimental testing, since the asymptotic analysis we have made is too crude to give sufficiently precise information, and since a variety of refinements to the algorithm tend to have unpredictable effects. For example, we can make an important improvement by comparing step E3 with Algorithm A: The factoring of V can stop whenever we find $T \bmod p_j \neq 0$ and $\lfloor T/p_j \rfloor \leq p_j$, since T will then be either 1 or prime. If T is a prime greater than p_m (it will be at most $p_m^2 + p_m - 1$ in such a case), we can still output $(P, e_0, \ldots, e_m, T)$, since a complete factorization has been obtained. The second phase of the algorithm will use only those outputs whose prime T's have occurred at least twice. This modification gives the effect of a much longer list of primes, without increasing the factorization time. Wunderlich's experiments indicate that $m \approx 150$ works well in the presence of this refinement, when N is in the neighborhood of 10^{40}.

Since step E3 is by far the most time-consuming part of the algorithm, Morrison, Brillhart, and Schroeppel have suggested several ways to abort this step when success becomes improbable: (a) Whenever T changes to a single-precision value, continue only if $\lfloor T/p_j \rfloor > p_j$ and $3^{T-1} \bmod T \neq 1$. (b) Give up if T is still $> p_m^2$ after casting out factors $< \frac{1}{10}p_m$. (c) Cast out factors only up to p_5, say, for batches of 100 or so consecutive V's; continue the factorization later, but only on the V from each batch that has produced the smallest residual T. (Before casting out the factors up to p_5, it is wise to calculate $V \bmod p_1^{f_1} p_2^{f_2} p_3^{f_3} p_4^{f_4} p_5^{f_5}$, where the f's are small enough to make $p_1^{f_1} p_2^{f_2} p_3^{f_3} p_4^{f_4} p_5^{f_5}$ fit in single precision, but large enough to make $V \bmod p_i^{f_i+1} = 0$ unlikely. One single-precision remainder will therefore characterize the value of V modulo five small primes.)

For estimates of the cycle length in the output of Algorithm E, see H. C. Williams, *Math. Comp.* **36** (1981), 593–601.

*A theoretical upper bound. From the standpoint of computational complexity, we would like to know if there is any method of factorization whose expected running time can be proved to be $O(N^{\epsilon(N)})$, where $\epsilon(N) \to 0$ as $N \to \infty$. We have seen that Algorithm E probably has such behavior, but it seems hopeless to find a rigorous proof, because continued fractions are not sufficiently well disciplined. The first proof that a good factorization algorithm exists in this sense was discovered by John Dixon in 1978; Dixon showed, in fact, that it suffices to consider a simplified version of Algorithm E, in which the continued fraction apparatus is removed but the basic idea of (18) remains.

Dixon's method [*Math. Comp.* **36** (1981), 255–260] is simply this, assuming that N is known to have at least two distinct prime factors, and that N is not divisible by the first m primes $p_1, p_2, \ldots, p_m$: Choose a random integer X in the range $0 < X < N$, and let $V = X^2 \bmod N$. If $V = 0$, the number $\gcd(X, N)$ is a proper factor of N. Otherwise cast out all of the small prime factors of V as in step E3; in other words, express V in the form

$$V = p_1^{e_1} \ldots p_m^{e_m} T, \tag{24}$$

where T is not divisible by any of the first m primes. If $T = 1$, the algorithm proceeds as in step E4 to output $(X, e_1, \ldots, e_m)$, which represents a solution to (19) with $e_0 = 0$. This process continues with new random values of X until there are sufficiently many outputs to discover a factor of N by the method of exercise 12.

In order to analyze this algorithm, we want to find bounds on (a) the probability that a random X will yield an output, and (b) the probability that a large number of outputs will be required before a factor is found. Let $P(m, N)$ be the probability (a), namely the probability that $T = 1$ when X is chosen at random. After M values of X have been tried, we will obtain $MP(m, N)$ outputs, on the average; and the number of outputs has a binomial distribution, so the standard deviation is less than the square root of the mean. The probability (b) is fairly easy to deal with, since exercise 13 proves that the algorithm needs more than $m + k$ outputs with probability $\leq 2^{-k}$.

Exercise 30 proves that $P(m, N) \geq m^r/(r! N)$ when $r = 2\lfloor \log N/(2 \log p_m) \rfloor$, so we can estimate the running time almost as we did in (22) but with the quantity $2\sqrt{N}$ replaced by N. This time we choose

$$r = \sqrt{2 \ln N / \ln \ln N} + \theta,$$

where $|\theta| \leq 1$ and r is even, and we choose m so that

$$r = \ln N / \ln p_m + O(1/\log \log N);$$

this means

$$\ln p_m = \sqrt{\frac{\ln N \ln\ln N}{2}} - \frac{\theta}{2}\ln\ln N + O(1),$$

$$\ln m = \ln \pi(p_m) = \ln p_m - \ln\ln p_m + O(1/\log p_m)$$

$$= \sqrt{\frac{\ln N \ln\ln N}{2}} - \frac{\theta+1}{2}\ln\ln N + O(\log\log\log N),$$

$$\frac{m^r}{r!\,N} = \exp\bigl(-\sqrt{2\ln N \ln\ln N} + O(r\log\log\log N)\bigr).$$

We will choose M so that $Mm^r/(r!\,N) \geq 4m$; thus the expected number of outputs $MP(m, N)$ will be at least $4m$. The running time of the algorithm is of order $Mm\log N$, plus $O(m^3)$ steps for exercise 12; it turns out that $O(m^3)$ is less than $Mm\log N$, which is

$$\exp\bigl(\sqrt{8(\ln N)(\ln\ln N)} + O\bigl((\log N)^{1/2}(\log\log N)^{-1/2}(\log\log\log N)\bigr)\bigr).$$

The probability that this method fails to find a factor is negligibly small, since the probability is at most $e^{-m/2}$ that fewer than $2m$ outputs are obtained (see exercise 31), while the probability is at most 2^{-m} that no factors are found from the first $2m$ outputs, and $m \gg \ln N$. We have proved the following slight strengthening of Dixon's original theorem:

Theorem D. *There is an algorithm whose running time is $O(N^{\epsilon(N)})$, where $\epsilon(N) = c\sqrt{\ln\ln N/\ln N}$ and c is any constant greater than $\sqrt{8}$, that finds a nontrivial factor of N with probability $1 - O(1/N)$, whenever N has at least two distinct prime divisors.* ∎

Other approaches. Another factorization technique was suggested by John M. Pollard [*Proc. Cambridge Phil. Soc.* **76** (1974), 521–528], who gave a practical way to discover prime factors p of N when $p - 1$ has no large prime factors. The latter algorithm (see exercise 19) is probably the first thing to try after Algorithms A and B have run too long on a large N.

A survey paper by R. K. Guy, written in collaboration with J. H. Conway, *Congressus Numerantium* **16** (1976), 49–89, gave a unique perspective on the developments up till that time. Guy stated, "I shall be surprised if anyone regularly factors numbers of size 10^{80} without special form during the present century"; and he was indeed destined to be surprised many times during the next 20 years.

Tremendous advances in factorization techniques for large numbers were made during the 1980s, beginning with Carl Pomerance's *quadratic sieve method* of 1981 [see *Lecture Notes in Comp. Sci.* **209** (1985), 169–182]. Then Hendrik Lenstra devised the *elliptic curve method* [*Annals of Math.* (2) **126** (1987), 649–673], which heuristically is expected to take about $\exp\bigl(\sqrt{(2+\epsilon)(\ln p)(\ln\ln p)}\bigr)$ multiplications to find a prime factor p. This is asymptotically the square root of the running time in our estimate for Algorithm E when $p \approx \sqrt{N}$, and it becomes even better when N has relatively small prime factors. An excellent exposition of this method has been given by Joseph H. Silverman and John Tate in *Rational Points on Elliptic Curves* (New York: Springer, 1992), Chapter 4.

John Pollard came back in 1988 with another new technique, which has become known as the *number field sieve*; see *Lecture Notes in Math.* **1554** (1993) for a series of papers about this method, which is the current champion for factoring extremely large integers. Its running time is predicted to be of order

$$\exp\big((64/9 + \epsilon)^{1/3}(\ln N)^{1/3}(\ln\ln N)^{2/3}\big) \tag{25}$$

as $N \to \infty$. The crossover point at which a well-tuned version of the number field sieve begins to beat a well-tuned version of the quadratic sieve appears to be at $N \approx 10^{112}$, according to A. K. Lenstra.

Details of the new methods are beyond the scope of this book, but we can get an idea of their effectiveness by noting some of the early success stories in which unfactored Fermat numbers of the form $2^{2^k}+1$ were cracked. For example, the factorization

$$2^{512} + 1 = 2424833 \cdot$$
$$7455602825647884420833739573620045491878366342657 \cdot p_{99}$$

was found by the number field sieve, after four months of computation that occupied otherwise idle time on about 700 workstations [Lenstra, Lenstra, Manasse, and Pollard, *Math. Comp.* **61** (1993), 319–349; **64** (1995), 1357]; here p_{99} denotes a 99-digit prime number. The next Fermat number has twice as many digits, but it yielded to the elliptic curve method on October 20, 1995:

$$2^{1024} + 1 = 45592577 \cdot 6487031809 \cdot$$
$$4659775785220018543264560743076778192897 \cdot p_{252}.$$

[Richard Brent, *Math. Comp.* **68** (1999), 429–451.] In fact, Brent had already used the elliptic curve method to resolve the next case as early as 1988:

$$2^{2048} + 1 = 319489 \cdot 974849 \cdot$$
$$167988556341760475137 \cdot 3560841906445833920513 \cdot p_{564};$$

by a stroke of good luck, all but one of the prime factors was $< 10^{22}$, so the elliptic curve method was a winner.

What about $2^{4096} + 1$? At present, that number seems completely out of reach. It has five factors $< 10^{16}$, but the unfactored residual has 1187 decimal digits. The next case, $2^{8192} + 1$, has four known factors $< 10^{27}$ [Crandall and Fagin, *Math. Comp.* **62** (1994), 321; Brent, Crandall, Dilcher, and van Halewyn, *Math. Comp.* **69** (2000), 1297–1304] and a huge unfactored residual.

Secret factors. Worldwide interest in the problem of factorization increased dramatically in 1977, when R. L. Rivest, A. Shamir, and L. Adleman discovered a way to encode messages that can apparently be decoded only by knowing the factors of a large number N, even though the method of encoding is known to everyone. Since a significant number of the world's greatest mathematicians have been unable to find efficient methods of factoring, this scheme [*CACM* **21** (1978), 120–126] almost certainly provides a secure way to protect confidential data and communications in computer networks.

Let us imagine a small electronic device called an *RSA box* that has two large prime numbers p and q stored in its memory. We will assume that $p-1$ and $q-1$ are not divisible by 3. The RSA box is connected somehow to a computer, and it has told the computer the product $N = pq$; however, no human being will be able to discover the values of p and q except by factoring N, since the RSA box is cleverly designed to self-destruct if anybody tries to tamper with it. In other words, it will erase its memory if it is jostled or if it is subjected to any radiation that could change or read out the data stored inside. Furthermore, the RSA box is sufficiently reliable that it never needs to be maintained; we simply would discard it and buy another, if an emergency arose or if it wore out. The prime factors p and q were generated by the RSA box itself, using some scheme based on truly random phenomena in nature like cosmic rays. The important point is that *nobody* knows p or q, not even a person or organization that owns or has access to this RSA box; there is no point in bribing or blackmailing anyone or holding anybody hostage in order to discover N's factors.

To send a secret message to the owner of an RSA box whose product number is N, you break the message up into a sequence of numbers $(x_1, \ldots, x_k)$, where each x_i lies in the range $0 \le x_i < N$; then you transmit the numbers

$$(x_1^3 \bmod N, \ \ldots, \ x_k^3 \bmod N).$$

The RSA box, knowing p and q, can decode the message, because it has pre-computed a number $d < N$ such that $3d \equiv 1 \ \big(\text{modulo } (p-1)(q-1)\big)$; it can now compute each secret component $(x_i^3 \bmod N)^d \bmod N = x_i$ in a reasonable amount of time, using the method of Section 4.6.3. Naturally the RSA box keeps this magic number d to itself; in fact, the RSA box might choose to remember only d instead of p and q, because its only duties after having computed N are to protect its secrets and to take cube roots mod N.

Such an encoding scheme is ineffective if $x < \sqrt[3]{N}$, since $x^3 \bmod N = x^3$ and the cube root will easily be found. The logarithmic law of leading digits in Section 4.2.4 implies that the leading place x_1 of a k-place message $(x_1, \ldots, x_k)$ will be less than $\sqrt[3]{N}$ about $\frac{1}{3}$ of the time, so this is a problem that needs to be resolved. Exercise 32 presents one way to avoid the difficulty.

The security of the RSA encoding scheme relies on the fact that nobody has been able to discover how to take cube roots quickly mod N without knowing N's factors. It seems likely that no such method will be found, but we cannot be absolutely sure. So far all that can be said for certain is that all of the ordinary ways to discover cube roots will fail. For example, there is essentially no point in trying to compute the number d as a function of N; the reason is that if d is known, or in fact if any number m of reasonable size is known such that $x^m \bmod N = 1$ holds for a significant number of x's, then we can find the factors of N in a few more steps (see exercise 34). Thus, any method of attack based explicitly or implicitly on finding such an m can be no better than factoring.

Some precautions are necessary, however. If the same message is sent to three different people on a computer network, a person who knows x^3 modulo N_1, N_2, and N_3 could reconstruct $x^3 \bmod N_1 N_2 N_3 = x^3$ by the Chinese remainder theorem, so x would no longer be a secret. In fact, even if a "time-stamped" message $(2^{\lceil \lg t_i \rceil} x + t_i)^3 \bmod N_i$ is sent to seven different people, with known or guessable t_i, the value of x can be deduced (see exercise 44). Therefore some cryptographers have recommended encoding with the exponent $2^{16} + 1 = 65537$ instead of 3; this exponent is prime, and the computation of $x^{65537} \bmod N$ takes only about 8.5 times as long as the computation of $x^3 \bmod N$. [*CCITT Recommendations Blue Book* (Geneva: International Telecommunication Union, 1989), Fascicle VIII.8, Recommendation X.509, Annex C, pages 74–76.] The original proposal of Rivest, Shamir, and Adleman was to encode x by $x^a \bmod N$ where a is any exponent prime to $\varphi(N)$, not just $a = 3$; in practice, however, we prefer an exponent for which encoding is faster than decoding.

The numbers p and q shouldn't merely be "random" primes in order to make the RSA scheme effective. We have mentioned that $p-1$ and $q-1$ should not be divisible by 3, since we want to ensure that unique cube roots exist modulo N. Another condition is that $p-1$ should have at least one very large prime factor, and so should $q-1$; otherwise N can be factored using the algorithm of exercise 19. In fact, that algorithm essentially relies on finding a fairly small number m with the property that $x^m \bmod N$ is frequently equal to 1, and we have just seen that such an m is dangerous. When $p-1$ and $q-1$ have large prime factors p_1 and q_1, the theory in exercise 34 implies that m is either a multiple of $p_1 q_1$ (hence m will be hard to discover) or the probability that $x^m \equiv 1$ will be less than $1/p_1 q_1$ (hence $x^m \bmod N$ will almost never be 1). Besides this condition, we don't want p and q to be close to each other, lest Algorithm D succeed in discovering them; in fact, we don't want the ratio p/q to be near a simple fraction, otherwise Lehman's generalization of Algorithm C could find them.

The following procedure for generating p and q is almost surely unbreakable: Start with a truly random number p_0 between, say, 10^{80} and 10^{81}. Search for the first prime number p_1 greater than p_0; this will require testing about $\frac{1}{2} \ln p_0 \approx 90$ odd numbers, and it will be sufficient to have p_1 a "probable prime" with probability $> 1 - 2^{-100}$ after 50 trials of Algorithm P. Then choose another truly random number p_2 between, say, 10^{39} and 10^{40}. Search for the first prime number p of the form $kp_1 + 1$ where $k \geq p_2$, k is even, and $k \equiv p_1 \pmod 3$. This will require testing about $\frac{1}{3} \ln p_1 p_2 \approx 90$ numbers before a prime p is found. The prime p will be about 120 digits long; a similar construction can be used to find a prime q about 130 digits long. For extra security, it is probably advisable to check that neither $p+1$ nor $q+1$ consists entirely of rather small prime factors (see exercise 20). The product $N = pq$, whose order of magnitude will be about 10^{250}, now meets all of our requirements, and it is inconceivable at this time that such an N could be factored.

For example, suppose we knew a method that could factor a 250-digit number N in $N^{0.1}$ microseconds. This amounts to 10^{25} microseconds, and there are only 31,556,952,000,000 μs per year, so we would need more than 3×10^{11} years of CPU time to complete the factorization. Even if a government agency purchased 10 billion computers and set them all to working on this problem, it would take more than 31 years before one of them would crack N into factors;

meanwhile the fact that the government had purchased so many specialized machines would leak out, and people would start using 300-digit N's.

Since the encoding method $x \mapsto x^3 \bmod N$ is known to everyone, there are additional advantages besides the fact that the code can be cracked only by the RSA box. Such "public key" systems were first published by W. Diffie and M. E. Hellman in *IEEE Trans.* **IT-22** (1976), 644–654. As an example of what can be done when the encoding method is public knowledge, suppose Alice wants to communicate with Bob securely via electronic mail, *signing* her letter so that Bob can be sure nobody else has forged it. Let $E_A(M)$ be the encoding function for messages M sent to Alice, let $D_A(M)$ be the decoding done by Alice's RSA box, and let $E_B(M)$, $D_B(M)$ be the corresponding encoding and decoding functions for Bob's RSA box. Then Alice can send a signed message by affixing her name and the date to some confidential message, then transmitting $E_B\big(D_A(M)\big)$ to Bob, using her machine to compute $D_A(M)$. When Bob gets this message, his RSA box converts it to $D_A(M)$, and he knows E_A so he can compute $M = E_A\big(D_A(M)\big)$. This should convince him that the message did indeed come from Alice; nobody else could have sent the message $D_A(M)$. (Well, Bob himself now knows $D_A(M)$, so he could impersonate Alice by passing $E_X\big(D_A(M)\big)$ to Xavier. To defeat any such attempted forgery, the content of M should clearly indicate that it is for Bob's eyes only.)

We might ask, how do Alice and Bob know each other's encoding functions E_A and E_B? It wouldn't do simply to have them stored in a public file, since some Charlie could tamper with that file, substituting an N that he has computed by himself; Charlie could then surreptitiously intercept and decode a private message before Alice or Bob would discover that something is amiss. The solution is to keep the product numbers N_A and N_B in a special public directory that has its own RSA box and its own widely publicized product number N_D. When Alice wants to know how to communicate with Bob, she asks the directory for Bob's product number; the directory computer sends her a *signed* message giving the value of N_B. Nobody can forge such a message, so it must be legitimate.

An interesting alternative to the RSA scheme has been proposed by Michael Rabin [MIT Lab. for Comp. Sci., report TR-212 (1979)], who suggests encoding by the function $x^2 \bmod N$ instead of $x^3 \bmod N$. In this case the decoding mechanism, which we can call a SQRT box, returns four different messages; the reason is that four different numbers have the same square modulo N, namely x, $-x$, $fx \bmod N$, and $(-fx) \bmod N$, where

$$f = (p^{q-1} - q^{p-1}) \bmod N.$$

If we agree in advance that x is even, or that $x < \frac{1}{2}N$, then the ambiguity drops to two messages, presumably only one of which makes any sense. The ambiguity can in fact be eliminated entirely, as shown in exercise 35. Rabin's scheme has the important property that it is provably as difficult to find square roots mod N as to find the factorization $N = pq$; for by taking the square root of $x^2 \bmod N$ when x is chosen at random, we have a 50-50 chance of finding a value y such that $x^2 \equiv y^2$ and $x \not\equiv \pm y$, after which $\gcd(x - y, N) = p$ or q. However, the system has a fatal flaw that does not seem to be present in the RSA scheme (see exercise 33): Anyone with access to a SQRT box can easily determine the factors of its N. This not only permits cheating by dishonest employees, or threats of extortion, it also allows people to reveal their p and q, after which they might claim that their "signature" on some transmitted document was a forgery. Thus it is clear that the goal of secure communication leads to subtle problems quite different from those we usually face in the design and analysis of algorithms.

Historical note: It was revealed in 1997 that Clifford Cocks had considered the encoding of messages by the transformation $x^{pq} \bmod pq$ already in 1973, but his work was kept secret.

The largest known primes. We have discussed several computational methods elsewhere in this book that require the use of large prime numbers, and the techniques just described can be used to discover primes of up to, say, 25 digits or fewer, with relative ease. Table 2 shows the ten largest primes that are less than the word size of typical computers. (Some other useful primes appear in the answers to exercises 3.2.1.2–22 and 4.6.4–57.)

Actually much larger primes of special forms are known, and it is occasionally important to find primes that are as large as possible. Let us therefore conclude this section by investigating the interesting manner in which the largest explicitly known primes have been discovered. Such primes are of the form $2^n - 1$, for various special values of n, and so they are especially suited to certain applications of binary computers.

A number of the form $2^n - 1$ cannot be prime unless n is prime, since $2^{uv} - 1$ is divisible by $2^u - 1$. In 1644, Marin Mersenne astonished his contemporaries by stating, in essence, that the numbers $2^p - 1$ are prime for $p = 2, 3, 5, 7, 13, 17, 19, 31, 67, 127, 257$, and for no other p less than 257. (This statement appeared in connection with a discussion of perfect numbers in the preface to his *Cogitata Physico-Mathematica*. Curiously, he also made the following remark: "To tell if a given number of 15 or 20 digits is prime or not, all time would not suffice for the test, whatever use is made of what is already known.") Mersenne, who had corresponded frequently with Fermat, Descartes, and others about similar topics in previous years, gave no proof of his assertions, and for over 200 years nobody knew whether he was correct. Euler showed that $2^{31} - 1$ is prime in 1772, after having tried unsuccessfully to prove this in previous years. About 100 years later, É. Lucas discovered that $2^{127} - 1$ is prime, but $2^{67} - 1$ was questionable; therefore Mersenne might not be completely accurate. Then I. M. Pervushin proved in 1883 that $2^{61} - 1$ is prime [see *Istoriko-Mat. Issledovaniĭa* **6** (1953), 559], and this touched off speculation that Mersenne had only made a copying error, writing 67 for 61. Eventually other errors in Mersenne's statement were discovered; R. E. Powers [*AMM* **18** (1911), 195] showed that $2^{89} - 1$ is prime, as had been conjectured by some earlier writers, and three years later he proved that $2^{107} - 1$ also is prime. M. Kraitchik found in 1922 that $2^{257} - 1$ is *not* prime [see his *Recherches sur la Théorie des Nombres* (Paris: 1924), 21]; computational errors may have crept in to his calculations, but his conclusion has turned out to be correct.

Table 2

USEFUL PRIME NUMBERS

N	a_1	a_2	a_3	a_4	a_5	a_6	a_7	a_8	a_9	a_{10}
2^{15}	19	49	51	55	61	75	81	115	121	135
2^{16}	15	17	39	57	87	89	99	113	117	123
2^{17}	1	9	13	31	49	61	63	85	91	99
2^{18}	5	11	17	23	33	35	41	65	75	93
2^{19}	1	19	27	31	45	57	67	69	85	87
2^{20}	3	5	17	27	59	69	129	143	153	185
2^{21}	9	19	21	55	61	69	105	111	121	129
2^{22}	3	17	27	33	57	87	105	113	117	123
2^{23}	15	21	27	37	61	69	135	147	157	159
2^{24}	3	17	33	63	75	77	89	95	117	167
2^{25}	39	49	61	85	91	115	141	159	165	183
2^{26}	5	27	45	87	101	107	111	117	125	135
2^{27}	39	79	111	115	135	187	199	219	231	235
2^{28}	57	89	95	119	125	143	165	183	213	273
2^{29}	3	33	43	63	73	75	93	99	121	133
2^{30}	35	41	83	101	105	107	135	153	161	173
2^{31}	1	19	61	69	85	99	105	151	159	171
2^{32}	5	17	65	99	107	135	153	185	209	267
2^{33}	9	25	49	79	105	285	301	303	321	355
2^{34}	41	77	113	131	143	165	185	207	227	281
2^{35}	31	49	61	69	79	121	141	247	309	325
2^{36}	5	17	23	65	117	137	159	173	189	233
2^{37}	25	31	45	69	123	141	199	201	351	375
2^{38}	45	87	107	131	153	185	191	227	231	257
2^{39}	7	19	67	91	135	165	219	231	241	301
2^{40}	87	167	195	203	213	285	293	299	389	437
2^{41}	21	31	55	63	73	75	91	111	133	139
2^{42}	11	17	33	53	65	143	161	165	215	227
2^{43}	57	67	117	175	255	267	291	309	319	369
2^{44}	17	117	119	129	143	149	287	327	359	377
2^{45}	55	69	81	93	121	133	139	159	193	229
2^{46}	21	57	63	77	167	197	237	287	305	311
2^{47}	115	127	147	279	297	339	435	541	619	649
2^{48}	59	65	89	93	147	165	189	233	243	257
2^{59}	55	99	225	427	517	607	649	687	861	871
2^{60}	93	107	173	179	257	279	369	395	399	453
2^{63}	25	165	259	301	375	387	391	409	457	471
2^{64}	59	83	95	179	189	257	279	323	353	363
10^6	17	21	39	41	47	69	83	93	117	137
10^7	9	27	29	57	63	69	71	93	99	111
10^8	11	29	41	59	69	153	161	173	179	213
10^9	63	71	107	117	203	239	243	249	261	267
10^{10}	33	57	71	119	149	167	183	213	219	231
10^{11}	23	53	57	93	129	149	167	171	179	231
10^{12}	11	39	41	63	101	123	137	143	153	233
10^{16}	63	83	113	149	183	191	329	357	359	369

The ten largest primes less than N are $N - a_1, \ldots, N - a_{10}$.

Numbers of the form $2^p - 1$ are now called *Mersenne numbers*, and it is known that Mersenne primes are obtained for p equal to

2, 3, 5, 7, 13, 17, 19, 31, 61, 89, 107, 127, 521, 607, 1279, 2203, 2281,
3217, 4253, 4423, 9689, 9941, 11213, 19937, 21701, 23209, 44497, 86243,
110503, 132049, 216091, 756839, 859433, 1257787, 1398269,
2976221, 3021377, 6972593, 13466917, 20996011, 24036583,
25964951, 30402457, 32582657, 37156667, 42643801, 43112609, ... (26)

The first entries above 100000 were found by David Slowinski and associates while testing new supercomputers [see *J. Recreational Math.* **11** (1979), 258–261]; he found 756839, 859433, and 1257787 in collaboration with Paul Gage during the 1990s. But the remaining exponents, beginning with 1398269, were found respectively by Joël Armengaud, Gordon Spence, Roland Clarkson, Nayan Hajratwala, Michael Cameron, Michael Shafer, Josh Findley, Martin Nowak, Curtis Cooper/Steven Boone, Hans-Michael Elvenich, Odd Magnar Strindmo, and Edson Smith using off-the-shelf personal computers, most recently in 2009. They used a program by George Woltman, who launched the Great Internet Mersenne Prime Search project (GIMPS) in 1996, with Internet administrative software contributed subsequently by Scott Kurowski.

Notice that the prime $8191 = 2^{13} - 1$ does not occur in (26); Mersenne had stated that $2^{8191} - 1$ is prime, and others had conjectured that any Mersenne prime could perhaps be used in the exponent.

The search for large primes has not been systematic, because people have generally tried to set a hard-to-beat world record instead of spending time with smaller exponents. For example, $2^{132049} - 1$ was proved prime in 1983, and $2^{216091} - 1$ in 1984, but the case $2^{110503} - 1$ was not discovered until 1988. Therefore one or more unknown Mersenne primes less than $2^{43112609} - 1$ might still exist. According to Woltman, all exponents $< 25{,}000{,}000$ were checked as of March 1, 2008; his volunteers are systematically filling the remaining gaps.

Since $2^{43112609} - 1$ has nearly 13 million decimal digits, it is clear that some special techniques have been used to prove that such numbers are prime. An efficient way to test the primality of a given Mersenne number $2^p - 1$ was first devised by É. Lucas [*Amer. J. Math.* **1** (1878), 184–239, 289–321, especially page 316] and improved by D. H. Lehmer [*Annals of Math.* (2) **31** (1930), 419–448, especially page 443]. The Lucas–Lehmer test, which is a special case of the method now used for testing the primality of n when the factors of $n + 1$ are known, is the following:

Theorem L. *Let q be an odd prime, and define the sequence $\langle L_n \rangle$ by the rule*

$$L_0 = 4, \qquad L_{n+1} = (L_n^2 - 2) \bmod (2^q - 1). \qquad (27)$$

Then $2^q - 1$ is prime if and only if $L_{q-2} = 0$.

For example, $2^3 - 1$ is prime since $L_1 = (4^2 - 2) \bmod 7 = 0$. This test is particularly well suited to binary computers, since calculation mod $(2^q - 1)$ is so convenient; see Section 4.3.2. Exercise 4.3.2–14 explains how to save time when q is extremely large.

Proof. We will prove Theorem L using only very simple principles of number theory, by investigating several features of recurring sequences that are of independent interest. Consider the sequences $\langle U_n \rangle$ and $\langle V_n \rangle$ defined by

$$U_0 = 0, \qquad U_1 = 1, \qquad U_{n+1} = 4U_n - U_{n-1};$$
$$V_0 = 2, \qquad V_1 = 4, \qquad V_{n+1} = 4V_n - V_{n-1}. \tag{28}$$

The following equations are readily proved by induction:

$$V_n = U_{n+1} - U_{n-1}; \tag{29}$$
$$U_n = \left((2 + \sqrt{3})^n - (2 - \sqrt{3})^n\right)/\sqrt{12}; \tag{30}$$
$$V_n = (2 + \sqrt{3})^n + (2 - \sqrt{3})^n; \tag{31}$$
$$U_{m+n} = U_m U_{n+1} - U_{m-1} U_n. \tag{32}$$

Let us now prove an auxiliary result, when p is prime and $e \geq 1$:

$$\text{if} \qquad U_n \equiv 0 \ (\text{modulo } p^e) \qquad \text{then} \qquad U_{np} \equiv 0 \ (\text{modulo } p^{e+1}). \tag{33}$$

This follows from the more general considerations of exercise 3.2.2–11, but a direct proof can be given for sequence (28). Assume that $U_n = bp^e$, $U_{n+1} = a$. By (32) and (28), $U_{2n} = bp^e(2a - 4bp^e) \equiv 2aU_n$ (modulo p^{e+1}), while we have $U_{2n+1} = U_{n+1}^2 - U_n^2 \equiv a^2$. Similarly, $U_{3n} = U_{2n+1}U_n - U_{2n}U_{n-1} \equiv 3a^2 U_n$ and $U_{3n+1} = U_{2n+1}U_{n+1} - U_{2n}U_n \equiv a^3$. In general,

$$U_{kn} \equiv ka^{k-1}U_n \qquad \text{and} \qquad U_{kn+1} \equiv a^k \ (\text{modulo } p^{e+1}),$$

so (33) follows if we take $k = p$.

From formulas (30) and (31) we can obtain other expressions for U_n and V_n, expanding $(2 \pm \sqrt{3})^n$ by the binomial theorem:

$$U_n = \sum_k \binom{n}{2k+1} 2^{n-2k-1} 3^k, \qquad V_n = \sum_k \binom{n}{2k} 2^{n-2k+1} 3^k. \tag{34}$$

Now if we set $n = p$, where p is an odd prime, and if we use the fact that $\binom{p}{k}$ is a multiple of p except when $k = 0$ or $k = p$, we find that

$$U_p \equiv 3^{(p-1)/2}, \qquad V_p \equiv 4 \qquad (\text{modulo } p). \tag{35}$$

If $p \neq 3$, Fermat's theorem tells us that $3^{p-1} \equiv 1$; hence $(3^{(p-1)/2} - 1) \times (3^{(p-1)/2} + 1) \equiv 0$, and $3^{(p-1)/2} \equiv \pm 1$. When $U_p \equiv -1$, we have $U_{p+1} = 4U_p - U_{p-1} = 4U_p + V_p - U_{p+1} \equiv -U_{p+1}$; hence $U_{p+1} \bmod p = 0$. When $U_p \equiv +1$, we have $U_{p-1} = 4U_p - U_{p+1} = 4U_p - V_p - U_{p-1} \equiv -U_{p-1}$; hence $U_{p-1} \bmod p = 0$. We have proved that, for all primes p, there is an integer $\epsilon(p)$ such that

$$U_{p+\epsilon(p)} \bmod p = 0, \qquad |\epsilon(p)| \leq 1. \tag{36}$$

Now if N is any positive integer, and if $m = m(N)$ is the smallest positive integer such that $U_{m(N)} \bmod N = 0$, we have

$$U_n \bmod N = 0 \qquad \text{if and only if} \qquad n \text{ is a multiple of } m(N). \tag{37}$$

(This number $m(N)$ is called the *rank of apparition* of N in the sequence.) To prove (37), observe that the sequence $U_m, U_{m+1}, U_{m+2}, \ldots$ is congruent (modulo N) to aU_0, aU_1, aU_2, $\ldots$, where $a = U_{m+1} \bmod N$ is relatively prime to N because $\gcd(U_n, U_{n+1}) = 1$.

With these preliminaries out of the way, we are ready to prove Theorem L. By (27) and induction,

$$L_n = V_{2^n} \bmod (2^q - 1). \qquad (38)$$

Furthermore, the identity $2U_{n+1} = 4U_n + V_n$ implies that $\gcd(U_n, V_n) \le 2$, since any common factor of U_n and V_n must divide U_n and $2U_{n+1}$, while $U_n \perp U_{n+1}$. So U_n and V_n have no odd factor in common, and if $L_{q-2} = 0$ we must have

$$U_{2^{q-1}} = U_{2^{q-2}} V_{2^{q-2}} \equiv 0 \text{ (modulo } 2^q - 1),$$
$$U_{2^{q-2}} \not\equiv 0 \text{ (modulo } 2^q - 1).$$

Now if $m = m(2^q - 1)$ is the rank of apparition of $2^q - 1$, it must be a divisor of 2^{q-1} but not of 2^{q-2}; thus $m = 2^{q-1}$. We will prove that $n = 2^q - 1$ must therefore be prime: Let the factorization of n be $p_1^{e_1} \ldots p_r^{e_r}$. All primes p_j are greater than 3, since n is odd and congruent to $(-1)^q - 1 = -2$ (modulo 3). From (33), (36), and (37) we know that $U_t \equiv 0$ (modulo $2^q - 1$), where

$$t = \operatorname{lcm}\big(p_1^{e_1-1}(p_1 + \epsilon_1), \ldots, p_r^{e_r-1}(p_r + \epsilon_r)\big),$$

and each ϵ_j is ± 1. It follows that t is a multiple of $m = 2^{q-1}$. Let $n_0 = \prod_{j=1}^r p_j^{e_j-1}(p_j + \epsilon_j)$; we have $n_0 \le \prod_{j=1}^r p_j^{e_j-1}(p_j + \frac{1}{5}p_j) = (\frac{6}{5})^r n$. Also, because $p_j + \epsilon_j$ is even, $t \le n_0/2^{r-1}$, since a factor of two is lost each time the least common multiple of two even numbers is taken. Combining these results, we have $m \le t \le 2(\frac{3}{5})^r n < 4(\frac{3}{5})^r m < 3m$; hence $r \le 2$ and $t = m$ or $t = 2m$, a power of 2. Therefore $e_1 = 1$, $e_r = 1$, and if n is not prime we must have $n = 2^q - 1 = (2^k + 1)(2^l - 1)$ where $2^k + 1$ and $2^l - 1$ are prime. The latter factorization is obviously impossible when q is odd, so n is prime.

Conversely, suppose that $n = 2^q - 1$ is prime; we must show that $V_{2^{q-2}} \equiv 0$ (modulo n). For this purpose it suffices to prove that $V_{2^{q-1}} \equiv -2$ (modulo n), since $V_{2^{q-1}} = (V_{2^{q-2}})^2 - 2$. Now

$$V_{2^{q-1}} = \big((\sqrt{2} + \sqrt{6})/2\big)^{n+1} + \big((\sqrt{2} - \sqrt{6})/2\big)^{n+1}$$

$$= 2^{-n} \sum_k \binom{n+1}{2k} \sqrt{2}^{n+1-2k} \sqrt{6}^{2k} = 2^{(1-n)/2} \sum_k \binom{n+1}{2k} 3^k.$$

Since n is an odd prime, the binomial coefficient

$$\binom{n+1}{2k} = \binom{n}{2k} + \binom{n}{2k-1}$$

is divisible by n except when $2k = 0$ and $2k = n + 1$; hence

$$2^{(n-1)/2} V_{2^{q-1}} \equiv 1 + 3^{(n+1)/2} \text{ (modulo } n).$$

Here $2 \equiv (2^{(q+1)/2})^2$, so $2^{(n-1)/2} \equiv (2^{(q+1)/2})^{(n-1)} \equiv 1$ by Fermat's theorem. Finally, by a simple case of the law of quadratic reciprocity (see exercise 23), $3^{(n-1)/2} \equiv -1$, since $n \bmod 3 = 1$ and $n \bmod 4 = 3$. This means $V_{2^{q-1}} \equiv -2$, so we must have $V_{2^{q-2}} \equiv 0$ as desired. ∎

An anonymous author whose works are now preserved in Italian libraries had discovered by 1460 that $2^{17} - 1$ and $2^{19} - 1$ are prime. Ever since then, the world's largest explicitly known prime numbers have almost always been Mersenne primes. But the situation might change, since Mersenne primes are getting harder to find, and since exercise 27 presents an efficient test for primes of other forms. [See E. Picutti, *Historia Math.* **16** (1989), 123–136; Hugh C. Williams, *Édouard Lucas and Primality Testing* (1998), Chapter 2.]

EXERCISES

1. [*10*] If the sequence d_0, d_1, d_2, ... of trial divisors in Algorithm A contains a number that is not prime, why will it never appear in the output?

2. [*15*] If it is known that the input N to Algorithm A is equal to 3 or more, could step A2 be eliminated?

3. [*M20*] Show that there is a number P with the following property: If $1000 \le n \le 1000000$, then n is prime if and only if $\gcd(n, P) = 1$.

4. [*M29*] In the notation of exercise 3.1–7 and Section 1.2.11.3, prove that the average value of the least n such that $X_n = X_{\ell(n)-1}$ lies between $1.5Q(m) - 0.5$ and $1.625Q(m) - 0.5$.

5. [*21*] Use Fermat's method (Algorithm D) to find the factors of 11111 by hand, when the moduli are 3, 5, 7, 8, and 11.

6. [*M24*] If p is an odd prime and if N is not a multiple of p, prove that the number of integers x such that $0 \le x < p$ and $x^2 - N \equiv y^2$ (modulo p) has a solution y is equal to $(p \pm 1)/2$.

7. [*25*] Discuss the problems of programming the sieve of Algorithm D on a binary computer when the table entries for modulus m_i do not exactly fill an integral number of memory words.

▶ **8.** [*23*] (*The sieve of Eratosthenes*, 3rd century B.C.) The following procedure evidently discovers all odd prime numbers less than a given integer N, since it removes all the nonprime numbers: Start with all the odd numbers between 1 and N; then successively strike out the multiples p_k^2, $p_k(p_k + 2)$, $p_k(p_k + 4)$, ..., of the kth prime p_k, for $k = 2, 3, 4, \ldots$, until reaching a prime p_k with $p_k^2 > N$.

Show how to adapt the procedure just described into an algorithm that is directly suited to efficient computer calculation, using no multiplication.

9. [*M25*] Let n be an odd number, $n \ge 3$. Show that if the number $\lambda(n)$ of Theorem 3.2.1.2B is a divisor of $n-1$ but not equal to $n-1$, then n must have the form $p_1 p_2 \ldots p_t$ where the p's are distinct primes and $t \ge 3$.

▶ **10.** [*M26*] (John Selfridge.) Prove that if, for each prime divisor p of $n - 1$, there is a number x_p such that $x_p^{(n-1)/p} \bmod n \ne 1$ but $x_p^{n-1} \bmod n = 1$, then n is prime.

11. [*M20*] What outputs does Algorithm E give when $N = 197209$, $k = 5$, $m = 1$? [*Hint:* $\sqrt{5 \cdot 197209} = 992 + //\overline{1,495,2,495,1,1984}//$.]

▶ **12.** [*M28*] Design an algorithm that uses the outputs of Algorithm E to find a proper factor of N, if Algorithm E has produced enough outputs to deduce a solution of (18).

13. [*HM25*] (J. D. Dixon.) Prove that whenever the algorithm of exercise 12 is presented with a solution $(x, e_0, \ldots, e_m)$ whose exponents are linearly dependent modulo 2 on the exponents of previous solutions, the probability is 2^{1-d} that a factorization will not be found, when N has d distinct prime factors and x is chosen at random.

14. [*M20*] Prove that the number T in step E3 of Algorithm E will never be a multiple of an odd prime p for which $(kN)^{(p-1)/2} \bmod p > 1$.

▶ **15.** [*M34*] (Lucas and Lehmer.) Let P and Q be relatively prime integers, and let $U_0 = 0$, $U_1 = 1$, $U_{n+1} = PU_n - QU_{n-1}$ for $n \geq 1$. Prove that if N is a positive integer relatively prime to $2P^2 - 8Q$, and if $U_{N+1} \bmod N = 0$, while $U_{(N+1)/p} \bmod N \neq 0$ for each prime p dividing $N + 1$, then N is prime. (This gives a test for primality when the factors of $N + 1$ are known instead of the factors of $N - 1$. We can evaluate U_m in $O(\log m)$ steps as in exercise 4.6.3–26.) [*Hint:* See the proof of Theorem L.]

16. [*M50*] Are there infinitely many Mersenne primes?

17. [*M25*] (V. R. Pratt.) A complete proof of primality by the converse of Fermat's theorem takes the form of a tree whose nodes have the form (q, x), where q and x are positive integers satisfying the following arithmetic conditions: (i) If (q_1, x_1), ..., (q_t, x_t) are the children of (q, x) then $q = q_1 \ldots q_t + 1$. [In particular, if (q, x) is childless, then $q = 2$.] (ii) If (r, y) is a child of (q, x), then $x^{(q-1)/r} \bmod q \neq 1$. (iii) For each node (q, x), we have $x^{q-1} \bmod q = 1$. From these conditions it follows that q is prime and x is a primitive root modulo q, for all nodes (q, x). [For example, the tree

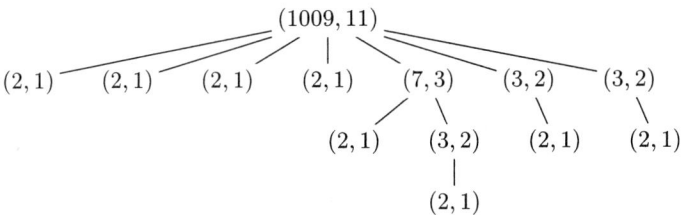

demonstrates that 1009 is prime.] Prove that such a tree with root (q, x) has at most $f(q)$ nodes, where f is a rather slowly growing function.

▶ **18.** [*HM23*] Give a heuristic proof of (7), analogous to the text's derivation of (6). What is the approximate probability that $p_{t-1} \leq \sqrt{p_t}$?

▶ **19.** [*M25*] (J. M. Pollard.) Show how to compute a number M that is divisible by all odd primes p such that $p - 1$ is a divisor of some given number D. [*Hint:* Consider numbers of the form $a^n - 1$.] Such an M is useful in factorization, for by computing $\gcd(M, N)$ we may discover a factor of N. Extend this idea to an efficient method that has high probability of discovering prime factors p of a given large number N, when all prime power factors of $p - 1$ are less than 10^3 except for at most one prime factor less than 10^5. [For example, the second-largest prime dividing (15) would be detected by this method, since it is $1 + 2^4 \cdot 5^2 \cdot 67 \cdot 107 \cdot 199 \cdot 41231$.]

20. [*M40*] Consider exercise 19 with $p + 1$ replacing $p - 1$.

21. [*M49*] (R. K. Guy.) Let $m(p)$ be the number of iterations required by Algorithm B to cast out the prime factor p. Is $m(p) = O(\sqrt{p} \log p)$ as $p \to \infty$?

▶ **22.** [*M30*] (M. O. Rabin.) Let p_n be the probability that Algorithm P guesses wrong, when n is an odd integer ≥ 3. Show that $p_n < \frac{1}{4}$ for all n.

23. [*M35*] The *Jacobi symbol* $\left(\frac{p}{q}\right)$ is defined to be -1, 0, or $+1$ for all integers $p \geq 0$ and all odd integers $q > 1$ by the rules $\left(\frac{p}{q}\right) \equiv p^{(q-1)/2}$ (modulo q) when q is prime;

$\left(\frac{p}{q}\right) = \left(\frac{p}{q_1}\right) \ldots \left(\frac{p}{q_t}\right)$ when q is the product $q_1 \ldots q_t$ of t primes (not necessarily distinct). Thus it generalizes the Legendre symbol of exercise 1.2.4–47.

a) Prove that $\left(\frac{p}{q}\right)$ satisfies the following relationships, hence it can be computed efficiently: $\left(\frac{0}{q}\right) = 0$; $\left(\frac{1}{q}\right) = 1$; $\left(\frac{p}{q}\right) = \left(\frac{p \bmod q}{q}\right)$; $\left(\frac{2}{q}\right) = (-1)^{(q^2-1)/8}$; $\left(\frac{pp'}{q}\right) = \left(\frac{p}{q}\right)\left(\frac{p'}{q}\right)$; $\left(\frac{p}{q}\right) = (-1)^{(p-1)(q-1)/4}\left(\frac{q}{p}\right)$ if both p and q are odd. [The latter law, which is a reciprocity relation reducing the evaluation of $\left(\frac{p}{q}\right)$ to the evaluation of $\left(\frac{q}{p}\right)$, has been proved in exercise 1.2.4–47(d) when both p and q are prime, so you may assume its validity in that special case.]

b) (Solovay and Strassen.) Prove that if n is odd but not prime, the number of integers x such that $1 \le x < n$ and $0 \ne \left(\frac{x}{n}\right) \equiv x^{(n-1)/2}$ (modulo n) is at most $\frac{1}{2}\varphi(n)$. (Thus, the following testing procedure correctly determines whether or not a given n is prime, with probability at least $1/2$ for all fixed n: "Generate x at random with $1 \le x < n$. If $0 \ne \left(\frac{x}{n}\right) \equiv x^{(n-1)/2}$ (modulo n), say that n is probably prime, otherwise say that n is definitely not prime.")

c) (L. Monier.) Prove that if n and x are numbers for which Algorithm P concludes that "n is probably prime", then $0 \ne \left(\frac{x}{n}\right) \equiv x^{(n-1)/2}$ (modulo n). [Hence Algorithm P is always superior to the test in (b).]

▶ **24.** [*M25*] (L. Adleman.) When $n > 1$ and $x > 1$ are integers, n odd, let us say that n "passes the x test of Algorithm P" if either $x \bmod n = 0$ or if steps P2–P5 lead to the conclusion that n is probably prime. Prove that, for any N, there exists a set of positive integers $x_1, \ldots, x_m \le N$ with $m \le \lfloor \lg N \rfloor$ such that a positive odd integer in the range $1 < n \le N$ is prime if and only if it passes the x test of Algorithm P for $x = x_1 \bmod n$, $\ldots$, $x = x_m \bmod n$. Thus, the probabilistic test for primality can in principle be converted into an efficient test that leaves nothing to chance. (You need not show how to compute the x_j efficiently; just prove that they exist.)

25. [*HM41*] (B. Riemann.) Prove that

$$\pi(x) + \frac{\pi(x^{1/2})}{2} + \frac{\pi(x^{1/3})}{3} + \cdots = \int_2^x \frac{dt}{\ln t} - 2\sum \int_{-\infty}^{\sigma} \frac{e^{(t+i\tau)\ln x} \, dt}{t + i\tau} + O(1),$$

where the sum is over all complex $\sigma + i\tau$ such that $\tau > 0$ and $\zeta(\sigma + i\tau) = 0$.

▶ **26.** [*M25*] (H. C. Pocklington, 1914.) Let $N = fr + 1$, where $0 < r \le f + 1$. Prove that N is prime if, for every prime divisor p of f, there is an integer x_p such that $x_p^{N-1} \bmod N = \gcd(x_p^{(N-1)/p} - 1, N) = 1$.

▶ **27.** [*M30*] Show that there is a way to test numbers of the form $N = 5 \cdot 2^n + 1$ for primality, using approximately the same number of squarings mod N as the Lucas–Lehmer test for Mersenne primes in Theorem L. [*Hint:* See the previous exercise.]

28. [*M27*] Given a prime p and a positive integer d, what is the value of $f(p, d)$, the average number of times that p divides $A^2 - dB^2$ (counting multiplicity), when A and B are random integers that are independent except for the condition $A \perp B$?

29. [*M25*] Prove that the number of positive integers $\le n$ whose prime factors are all contained in a given set of primes $\{p_1, \ldots, p_m\}$ is at least $m^r/r!$, when $r = \lfloor \log n / \log p_m \rfloor$ and $p_1 < \cdots < p_m$.

30. [*HM35*] (J. D. Dixon and Claus-Peter Schnorr.) Let $p_1 < \cdots < p_m$ be primes that do not divide the odd number N, and let r be an even integer $\le \log N / \log p_m$. Prove that the number of integers X in the range $0 \le X < N$ such that $X^2 \bmod N =$

$p_1^{e_1} \ldots p_m^{e_m}$ is at least $m^r/r!$. *Hint:* Let the prime factorization of N be $q_1^{f_1} \ldots q_d^{f_d}$. Show that a sequence of exponents $(e_1, \ldots, e_m)$ leads to 2^d solutions X whenever we have $e_1 + \cdots + e_m \leq r$ and $p_1^{e_1} \ldots p_m^{e_m}$ is a quadratic residue modulo q_i for $1 \leq i \leq d$. Such exponent sequences can be obtained as ordered pairs $(e_1', \ldots, e_m'; e_1'', \ldots, e_m'')$ where $e_1' + \cdots + e_m' \leq \frac{1}{2}r$ and $e_1'' + \cdots + e_m'' \leq \frac{1}{2}r$ and

$$(p_1^{e_1'} \ldots p_m^{e_m'})^{(q_i-1)/2} \equiv (p_1^{e_1''} \ldots p_m^{e_m''})^{(q_i-1)/2} \pmod{q_i} \qquad \text{for } 1 \leq i \leq d.$$

31. [*M20*] Use exercise 1.2.10–21 to estimate the probability that Dixon's factorization algorithm (as described preceding Theorem D) obtains fewer than $2m$ outputs.

▶ **32.** [*M21*] Show how to modify the RSA encoding scheme so that there is no problem with messages $< \sqrt[3]{N}$, in such a way that the length of messages is not substantially increased.

33. [*M50*] Prove or disprove: If a reasonably efficient algorithm exists that has a nonnegligible probability of being able to find $x \bmod N$, given a number $N = pq$ whose prime factors satisfy $p \equiv q \equiv 2 \pmod 3$ and given the value of $x^3 \bmod N$, then there is a reasonably efficient algorithm that has a nonnegligible probability of being able to find the factors of N. [If this could be proved, it would not only show that the cube root problem is as difficult as factoring, it would also show that the RSA scheme has the same fatal flaw as the SQRT scheme.]

34. [*M30*] (Peter Weinberger.) Suppose $N = pq$ in the RSA scheme, and suppose you know a number m such that $x^m \bmod N = 1$ for at least 10^{-12} of all positive integers x. Explain how you could go about factoring N without great difficulty, if m is not too large (say $m < N^{10}$).

▶ **35.** [*M25*] (H. C. Williams, 1979.) Let N be the product of two primes p and q, where $p \bmod 8 = 3$ and $q \bmod 8 = 7$. Prove that the Jacobi symbol satisfies $(\frac{-x}{N}) = (\frac{x}{N}) = -(\frac{2x}{N})$, and use this property to design an encoding/decoding scheme analogous to Rabin's SQRT box but with no ambiguity of messages.

36. [*HM24*] The asymptotic analysis following (22) is too coarse to give meaningful values unless N is extremely large, since $\ln \ln N$ is always rather small when N is in a practical range. Carry out a more precise analysis that gives insight into the behavior of (22) for reasonable values of N; also explain how to choose a value of $\ln m$ that minimizes (22) except for a factor of size at most $\exp(O(\log \log N))$.

37. [*M27*] Prove that the square root of every positive integer D has a periodic continued fraction of the form

$$\sqrt{D} = R + /\!/a_1, \ldots, a_n, 2R, a_1, \ldots, a_n, 2R, a_1, \ldots, a_n, 2R, \ldots /\!/,$$

unless D is a perfect square, where $R = \lfloor \sqrt{D} \rfloor$ and $(a_1, \ldots, a_n)$ is a *palindrome* (that is, $a_i = a_{n+1-i}$ for $1 \leq i \leq n$).

38. [*25*] (*Useless primes.*) For $0 \leq d \leq 9$, find P_d, the largest 50-digit prime number that has the maximum possible number of decimal digits equal to d. (First maximize the number of d's, then find the largest such prime.)

39. [*40*] Many primes p have the property that $2p + 1$ is also prime; for example, $5 \to 11 \to 23 \to 47$. More generally, say that q is a *successor* of p if p and q are both prime and $q = 2^k p + 1$ for some $k \geq 0$. For example, $2 \to 3 \to 7 \to 29 \to 59 \to 1889 \to 3779 \to 7559 \to 4058207223809 \to 32465657790473 \to 4462046030502692971872857 \to 95\langle30 \text{ omitted digits}\rangle37 \to \cdots$; the smallest successor of $95 \ldots 37$ has 103 digits. Find the longest chain of successive primes that you can.

▶ **40.** [*M36*] (A. Shamir.) Consider an abstract computer that can perform the operations $x + y$, $x - y$, $x \cdot y$, and $\lfloor x/y \rfloor$ on integers x and y of arbitrary length, in just one unit of time, no matter how large those integers are. The machine stores integers in a random-access memory and it can select different program steps depending on whether or not $x = y$, given x and y. The purpose of this exercise is to demonstrate that there is an amazingly fast way to factorize numbers on such a computer. (Therefore it will probably be quite difficult to show that factorization is inherently complicated on *real* machines, although we suspect that it is.)

a) Find a way to compute $n!$ in $O(\log n)$ steps on such a computer, given an integer value $n \geq 2$. [*Hint:* If A is a sufficiently large integer, the binomial coefficients $\binom{m}{k} = m!/(m-k)!\,k!$ can be computed readily from the value of $(A+1)^m$.]

b) Show how to compute a number $f(n)$ in $O(\log n)$ steps on such a computer, given an integer value $n \geq 2$, having the following properties: $f(n) = n$ if n is prime, otherwise $f(n)$ is a proper (but not necessarily prime) divisor of n. [*Hint:* If $n \neq 4$, one such function $f(n)$ is $\gcd(m(n), n)$, where $m(n) = \min\{m \mid m! \bmod n = 0\}$.]

(As a consequence of (b), we can completely factor a given number n by doing only $O(\log n)^2$ arithmetic operations on arbitrarily large integers: Given a partial factorization $n = n_1 \ldots n_r$, each nonprime n_i can be replaced by $f(n_i) \cdot (n_i/f(n_i))$ in $\sum O(\log n_i) = O(\log n)$ steps, and this refinement can be repeated until all n_i are prime.)

▶ **41.** [*M28*] (Lagarias, Miller, and Odlyzko.) The purpose of this exercise is to show that the number of primes less than N^3 can be calculated by looking only at the primes less than N^2, and thus to evaluate $\pi(N^3)$ in $O(N^{2+\epsilon})$ steps.

Say that an "m-survivor" is a positive integer whose prime factors all exceed m; thus, an m-survivor remains in the sieve of Eratosthenes (exercise 8) after all multiples of primes $\leq m$ have been sieved out. Let $f(x, m)$ be the number of m-survivors that are $\leq x$, and let $f_k(x, m)$ be the number of such survivors that have exactly k prime factors (counting multiplicity).

a) Prove that $\pi(N^3) = \pi(N) + f(N^3, N) - 1 - f_2(N^3, N)$.

b) Explain how to compute $f_2(N^3, N)$ from the values of $\pi(x)$ for $x \leq N^2$. Use your method to evaluate $f_2(1000, 10)$ by hand.

c) Same question as (b), but evaluate $f(N^3, N)$ instead of $f_2(N^3, N)$. [*Hint:* Use the identity $f(x, p_j) = f(x, p_{j-1}) - f(x/p_j, p_{j-1})$, where p_j is the jth prime and $p_0 = 1$.]

d) Discuss data structures for the efficient evaluation of the quantities in (b) and (c).

42. [*M35*] (H. W. Lenstra, Jr.) Given $0 < r < s < N$ with $r \perp s$ and $N \perp s$, show that it is possible to find all divisors of N that are $\equiv r$ (modulo s) by performing $O(\lceil N/s^3 \rceil^{1/2} \log s)$ well-chosen arithmetic operations on $(\lg N)$-bit numbers. [*Hint:* Apply exercise 4.5.3–49.]

▶ **43.** [*M43*] Let $m = pq$ be an r-bit Blum integer as in Theorem 3.5P, and let $Q_m = \{y \mid y = x^2 \bmod m$ for some $x\}$. Then Q_m has $(p+1)(q+1)/4$ elements, and every element $y \in Q_m$ has a unique square root $x = \sqrt{y}$ such that $x \in Q_m$. Suppose $G(y)$ is an algorithm that correctly guesses $\sqrt{y} \bmod 2$ with probability $\geq \frac{1}{2} + \epsilon$, when y is a random element of Q_m. The goal of this exercise is to prove that the problem solved by G is almost as hard as the problem of factoring m.

a) Construct an algorithm $A(G, m, \epsilon, y, \delta)$ that uses random numbers and algorithm G to guess whether a given integer y is in Q_m, without necessarily computing $\sqrt{y}$. Your algorithm should guess correctly with probability $\geq 1 - \delta$, and its running time $T(A)$ should be at most $O(\epsilon^{-2}(\log \delta^{-1})T(G))$, assuming that $T(G) \geq r^2$. (If $T(G) < r^2$, replace $T(G)$ by $(T(G) + r^2)$ in this formula.)

b) Construct an algorithm $F(G, m, \epsilon)$ that finds the factors of m with expected running time $T(F) = O(r^2(\epsilon^{-6} + \epsilon^{-4}(\log \epsilon^{-1})T(G)))$.

Hints: For fixed $y \in Q_m$, and for $0 \leq v < m$, let $\tau v = v\sqrt{y} \bmod m$ and $\lambda v = \tau v \bmod 2$. Notice that $\lambda(-v) + \lambda v = 1$ and $\lambda(v_1 + \cdots + v_n) = (\lambda v_1 + \cdots + \lambda v_n + \lfloor(\tau v_1 + \cdots + \tau v_m)/m\rfloor) \bmod 2$. Furthermore we have $\tau(\frac{1}{2}v) = \frac{1}{2}(\tau v + m\lambda v)$; here $\frac{1}{2}v$ stands for $(\frac{m+1}{2}v) \bmod m$. If $\pm v \in Q_m$ we have $\tau(\pm v) = \sqrt{v^2 y}$; therefore algorithm G gives us a way to guess λv for about half of all v.

44. [*M35*] (J. Håstad.) Show that it is not difficult to find x when $a_{i0} + a_{i1}x + a_{i2}x^2 + a_{i3}x^3 \equiv 0$ (modulo m_i), $0 < x < m_i$, $\gcd(a_{i0}, a_{i1}, a_{i2}, a_{i3}, m_i) = 1$, and $m_i > 10^{27}$ for $1 \leq i \leq 7$, if $m_i \perp m_j$ for $1 \leq i < j \leq 7$. (All variables are integers; all but x are known.) *Hint:* When L is any nonsingular matrix of real numbers, the algorithm of Lenstra, Lenstra, and Lovász [*Mathematische Annalen* **261** (1982), 515–534] efficiently finds a nonzero integer vector $v = (v_1, \ldots, v_n)$ such that length$(vL) \leq \sqrt{n2^n} |\det L|^{1/n}$.

▶ **45.** [*M41*] (J. M. Pollard and Claus-Peter Schnorr.) Show that there is an efficient way to solve the congruence

$$x^2 - ay^2 \equiv b \quad \text{(modulo } n)$$

for integers x and y, given integers a, b, and n with $ab \perp n$ and n odd, even if the factorization of n is unknown. [*Hint:* Use the identity $(x_1^2 - ay_1^2)(x_2^2 - ay_2^2) = x^2 - ay^2$, where $x = x_1x_2 - ay_1y_2$ and $y = x_1y_2 + x_2y_1$.]

46. [*HM30*] (L. Adleman.) Let p be a rather large prime number and let a be a primitive root modulo p; thus, all integers b in the range $1 \leq b < p$ can be written $b = a^n \bmod p$, for some unique n with $1 \leq n < p$.

Design an algorithm that almost always finds n, given b, in $O(p^\epsilon)$ steps for all $\epsilon > 0$, using ideas similar to those of Dixon's factoring algorithm. [*Hint:* Start by building a repertoire of numbers n_i such that $a^{n_i} \bmod p$ has only small prime factors.]

47. [*M50*] A certain literary quotation $x = x_1x_2$, represented in ASCII code, has the enciphered value $(x_1^3 \bmod N, x_2^3 \bmod N) =$

(14E97EF5C531D92591B89CDBAB48444A04612C01AA29C2A8FA10FA804EF7AC3CE03D7D3667C4D3E132A24A68
E6797FE28650DC3ADF327474B86B0CBD5387A49872CE012269A59B3E4B3BD83B74681A78AD7B6D1772A7451B,
15B025E2AEE095A9542590184CF62F72B2E8E8DD794AEF8511F2591E6BC2C8B8A8E48AF1FE04FF2FD933E730
9205A3418DBB9BB8C6A7665DA309531735FE86C741D1261B34CB2668FA34D0C0C28575A2454E3DB00E408AC7)

in hexadecimal notation, where N is

17B2353B9595ECA69FEF80940160C4084286D1255FFE49D114F2E633F82C88D5224FC4AA6F9104CED2BCA810
BEA76157FFDC78F9656A0ED9B3F6CCAB99001B8B2571F4EBD095925F07F9BEE5111E8375DFD71593628AD8D1.

What is x?

The problem of distinguishing prime numbers from composites,
and of resolving composite numbers into their prime factors,
is one of the most important and useful in all of arithmetic.
... The dignity of science seems to demand that every aid to the solution
of such an elegant and celebrated problem be zealously cultivated.

— C. F. GAUSS, *Disquisitiones Arithmeticæ*, Article 329 (1801)

4.6. POLYNOMIAL ARITHMETIC

THE TECHNIQUES we have been studying apply in a natural way to many types of mathematical quantities, not simply to numbers. In this section we shall deal with polynomials, which are the next step up from numbers. Formally speaking, a *polynomial over* S is an expression of the form

$$u(x) = u_n x^n + \cdots + u_1 x + u_0, \tag{1}$$

where the *coefficients* u_n, ..., u_1, u_0 are elements of some algebraic system S, and the *variable* x may be regarded as a formal symbol with an indeterminate meaning. We will assume that the algebraic system S is a *commutative ring with identity*; this means that S admits the operations of addition, subtraction, and multiplication, satisfying the customary properties: Addition and multiplication are binary operations defined on S; they are associative and commutative, and multiplication distributes over addition. There is an additive identity element 0 and a multiplicative identity element 1, such that $a + 0 = a$ and $a \cdot 1 = a$ for all a in S. Subtraction is the inverse of addition, but we assume nothing about the possibility of division as an inverse to multiplication. The polynomial $0x^{n+m} + \cdots + 0x^{n+1} + u_n x^n + \cdots + u_1 x + u_0$ is regarded as the same polynomial as (1), although its expression is formally different.

We say that (1) is a polynomial of *degree* n and *leading coefficient* u_n if $u_n \neq 0$; and in this case we write

$$\deg(u) = n, \qquad \ell(u) = u_n. \tag{2}$$

By convention, we also set

$$\deg(0) = -\infty, \qquad \ell(0) = 0, \tag{3}$$

where "0" denotes the zero polynomial whose coefficients are all zero. We say that $u(x)$ is a *monic polynomial* if its leading coefficient $\ell(u)$ is 1.

Arithmetic on polynomials consists primarily of addition, subtraction, and multiplication; in some cases, further operations such as division, exponentiation, factoring, and taking the greatest common divisor are important. Addition, subtraction, and multiplication are defined in a natural way, as though the variable x were an element of S: We add or subtract polynomials by adding or subtracting the coefficients of like powers of x. Multiplication is done by the rule

$$(u_r x^r + \cdots + u_0)(v_s x^s + \cdots + v_0) = w_{r+s} x^{r+s} + \cdots + w_0, $$

where

$$w_k = u_0 v_k + u_1 v_{k-1} + \cdots + u_{k-1} v_1 + u_k v_0. \tag{4}$$

In the latter formula u_i or v_j are treated as zero if $i > r$ or $j > s$.

The algebraic system S is usually the set of integers, or the rational numbers; or it may itself be a set of polynomials (in variables other than x), in which case (1) is a *multivariate* polynomial, a polynomial in several variables. Another important case occurs when the algebraic system S consists of the integers 0, 1, ..., $m - 1$, with addition, subtraction, and multiplication performed mod m

$\big($see Eq. 4.3.2–$(11)\big)$; this is called *polynomial arithmetic modulo m*. Polynomial arithmetic modulo 2, when each of the coefficients is 0 or 1, is especially
important.

The reader should note the similarity between polynomial arithmetic and
multiple-precision arithmetic (Section 4.3.1), where the radix b is substituted
for x. The chief difference is that the coefficient u_k of x^k in polynomial arithmetic
bears no essential relation to its neighboring coefficients $u_{k\pm1}$, so the idea of
"carrying" from one place to the next is absent. In fact, polynomial arithmetic
modulo b is essentially identical to multiple-precision arithmetic with radix b,
except that all carries are suppressed. For example, compare the multiplication
of $(1101)_2$ by $(1011)_2$ in the binary number system with the analogous multiplication of $x^3 + x^2 + 1$ by $x^3 + x + 1$ modulo 2:

Binary system	Polynomials modulo 2
1101	1101
× 1011	× 1011
1101	1101
1101	1101
1101	1101
10001111	1111111

The product of these polynomials modulo 2 is obtained by suppressing all carries,
and it is $x^6 + x^5 + x^4 + x^3 + x^2 + x + 1$. If we had multiplied the same polynomials
over the integers, without taking residues modulo 2, the result would have been
$x^6 + x^5 + x^4 + 3x^3 + x^2 + x + 1$; again carries are suppressed, but in this case
the coefficients can get arbitrarily large.

In view of this strong analogy with multiple-precision arithmetic, it is unnecessary to discuss polynomial addition, subtraction, and multiplication much further in this section. However, we should point out some aspects that often make
polynomial arithmetic somewhat different from multiple-precision arithmetic in
practice: There is often a tendency to have a large number of zero coefficients,
and polynomials of huge degrees, so special forms of representation are desirable;
see Section 2.2.4. Furthermore, arithmetic on polynomials in several variables
leads to routines that are best understood in a recursive framework; this situation
is discussed in Chapter 8.

Although the techniques of polynomial addition, subtraction, and multiplication are comparatively straightforward, several other important aspects of
polynomial arithmetic deserve special examination. The following subsections
therefore discuss *division* of polynomials, with associated techniques such as
finding greatest common divisors and factoring. We shall also discuss the problem of efficient *evaluation* of polynomials, namely the task of finding the value
of $u(x)$ when x is a given element of S, using as few operations as possible. The
special case of evaluating x^n rapidly when n is large is quite important by itself,
so it is discussed in detail in Section 4.6.3.

The first major set of computer subroutines for doing polynomial arithmetic
was the ALPAK system [W. S. Brown, J. P. Hyde, and B. A. Tague, *Bell System*

Tech. J. **42** (1963), 2081–2119; **43** (1964), 785–804, 1547–1562]. Another early landmark in this field was the PM system of George Collins [*CACM* **9** (1966), 578–589]; see also C. L. Hamblin, *Comp. J.* **10** (1967), 168–171.

EXERCISES

1. [*10*] If we are doing polynomial arithmetic modulo 10, what is $7x+2$ minus x^2+5? What is $6x^2 + x + 3$ times $5x^2 + 2$?

2. [*17*] True or false: (a) The product of monic polynomials is monic. (b) The product of polynomials of degrees m and n has degree $m+n$. (c) The sum of polynomials of degrees m and n has degree $\max(m, n)$.

3. [*M20*] If each of the coefficients $u_r, \ldots, u_0, v_s, \ldots, v_0$ in (4) is an integer satisfying the conditions $|u_i| \leq m_1$, $|v_j| \leq m_2$, what is the maximum absolute value of the product coefficients w_k?

▶ **4.** [*21*] Can the multiplication of polynomials modulo 2 be facilitated by using the ordinary arithmetic operations on a binary computer, if coefficients are packed into computer words?

▶ **5.** [*M21*] Show how to multiply two polynomials of degree $\leq n$, modulo 2, with an execution time proportional to $O(n^{\lg 3})$ when n is large, by adapting Karatsuba's method (see Section 4.3.3).

4.6.1. Division of Polynomials

It is possible to divide one polynomial by another in essentially the same way that we divide one multiple-precision integer by another, when arithmetic is being done on polynomials over a *field*. A field S is a commutative ring with identity, in which exact division is possible as well as the operations of addition, subtraction, and multiplication; this means as usual that whenever u and v are elements of S, and $v \neq 0$, there is an element w in S such that $u = vw$. The most important fields of coefficients that arise in applications are

a) the rational numbers (represented as fractions, see Section 4.5.1);

b) the real or complex numbers (represented within a computer by means of floating point approximations; see Section 4.2);

c) the integers modulo p where p is prime (where division can be implemented as suggested in exercise 4.5.2–16);

d) *rational functions* over a field, that is, quotients of two polynomials whose coefficients are in that field, the denominator being monic.

Of special importance is the field of integers modulo 2, whose only elements are 0 and 1. Polynomials over this field (namely polynomials modulo 2) have many analogies to integers expressed in binary notation; and rational functions over this field have striking analogies to rational numbers whose numerator and denominator are represented in binary notation.

Given two polynomials $u(x)$ and $v(x)$ over a field, with $v(x) \neq 0$, we can divide $u(x)$ by $v(x)$ to obtain a quotient polynomial $q(x)$ and a remainder polynomial $r(x)$ satisfying the conditions

$$u(x) = q(x) \cdot v(x) + r(x), \qquad \deg(r) < \deg(v). \tag{1}$$

It is easy to see that there is at most one pair of polynomials $\big(q(x), r(x)\big)$ satisfying these relations; for if $\big(q_1(x), r_1(x)\big)$ and $\big(q_2(x), r_2(x)\big)$ both satisfy (1) with respect to the same polynomials $u(x)$ and $v(x)$, then $q_1(x)v(x) + r_1(x) = q_2(x)v(x) + r_2(x)$, so $\big(q_1(x) - q_2(x)\big)v(x) = r_2(x) - r_1(x)$. Now if $q_1(x) - q_2(x)$ is nonzero, we have $\deg\big((q_1 - q_2) \cdot v\big) = \deg(q_1 - q_2) + \deg(v) \geq \deg(v) > \deg(r_2 - r_1)$, a contradiction; hence $q_1(x) - q_2(x) = 0$ and $r_1(x) = r_2(x)$.

The following algorithm, which is essentially the same as Algorithm 4.3.1D for multiple-precision division but without any concerns of carries, may be used to determine $q(x)$ and $r(x)$:

Algorithm D (*Division of polynomials over a field*). Given polynomials

$$u(x) = u_m x^m + \cdots + u_1 x + u_0, \qquad v(x) = v_n x^n + \cdots + v_1 x + v_0$$

over a field S, where $v_n \neq 0$ and $m \geq n \geq 0$, this algorithm finds the polynomials

$$q(x) = q_{m-n} x^{m-n} + \cdots + q_0, \qquad r(x) = r_{n-1} x^{n-1} + \cdots + r_0$$

over S that satisfy (1).

D1. [Iterate on k.] Do step D2 for $k = m - n, \ m - n - 1, \ \ldots, \ 0$; then terminate the algorithm with $(r_{n-1}, \ldots, r_0) = (u_{n-1}, \ldots, u_0)$.

D2. [Division loop.] Set $q_k \leftarrow u_{n+k}/v_n$, and then set $u_j \leftarrow u_j - q_k v_{j-k}$ for $j = n+k-1, \ n+k-2, \ \ldots, \ k$. (The latter operation amounts to replacing $u(x)$ by $u(x) - q_k x^k v(x)$, a polynomial of degree $< n + k$.) ▌

An example of Algorithm D appears below in (5). The number of arithmetic operations is essentially proportional to $n(m - n + 1)$. Note that explicit division of coefficients is done only at the beginning of step D2, and the divisor is always v_n; thus if $v(x)$ is a monic polynomial (with $v_n = 1$), there is no actual division at all. If multiplication is easier to perform than division it will be preferable to compute $1/v_n$ at the beginning of the algorithm and to multiply by this quantity in step D2.

We shall often write $u(x) \bmod v(x)$ for the remainder $r(x)$ in (1).

Unique factorization domains. If we restrict consideration to polynomials over a field, we are not coming to grips with many important cases, such as polynomials over the integers or polynomials in several variables. Let us therefore now consider the more general situation that the algebraic system S of coefficients is a *unique factorization domain*, not necessarily a field. This means that S is a commutative ring with identity, and that

i) $uv \neq 0$, whenever u and v are nonzero elements of S;
ii) every nonzero element u of S is either a *unit* or has a "unique" representation as a product of *primes* $p_1, \ldots, p_t$:

$$u = p_1 \ldots p_t, \qquad t \geq 1. \tag{2}$$

A *unit* is an element that has a reciprocal, namely an element u such that $uv = 1$ for some v in S; and a *prime* is a nonunit element p such that the equation $p = qr$

can be true only if either q or r is a unit. The representation (2) is to be unique in the sense that if $p_1 \ldots p_t = q_1 \ldots q_s$, where all the p's and q's are primes, then $s = t$ and there is a permutation $\pi_1 \ldots \pi_t$ of $\{1, \ldots, t\}$ such that $p_1 = a_1 q_{\pi_1}, \ldots,$ $p_t = a_t q_{\pi_t}$ for some units $a_1, \ldots, a_t$. In other words, factorization into primes is unique, except for unit multiples and except for the order of the factors.

Any field is a unique factorization domain, in which each nonzero element is a unit and there are no primes. The integers form a unique factorization domain in which the units are $+1$ and -1, and the primes are ± 2, ± 3, ± 5, ± 7, ± 11, etc. The case that S is the set of all integers is of principal importance, because it is often preferable to work with integer coefficients instead of arbitrary rational coefficients.

One of the key facts about polynomials (see exercise 10) is that *the polynomials over a unique factorization domain form a unique factorization domain.* A polynomial that is prime in this domain is usually called an *irreducible polynomial.* By using the unique factorization theorem repeatedly, we can prove that multivariate polynomials over the integers, or over any field, in any number of variables, can be uniquely factored into irreducible polynomials. For example, the multivariate polynomial $90x^3 - 120x^2y + 18x^2yz - 24xy^2z$ over the integers is the product of five irreducible polynomials $2 \cdot 3 \cdot x \cdot (3x - 4y) \cdot (5x + yz)$. The same polynomial, as a polynomial over the rationals, is the product of three irreducible polynomials $(6x) \cdot (3x - 4y) \cdot (5x + yz)$; this factorization can also be written $x \cdot (90x - 120y) \cdot (x + \frac{1}{5}yz)$ and in infinitely many other ways, although the factorization is essentially unique.

As usual, we say that $u(x)$ is a *multiple* of $v(x)$, and that $v(x)$ is a *divisor* of $u(x)$, if $u(x) = v(x)q(x)$ for some polynomial $q(x)$. If we have an algorithm to tell whether or not u is a multiple of v for arbitrary nonzero elements u and v of a unique factorization domain S, and to determine w if $u = v \cdot w$, then Algorithm D gives us a method to tell whether or not $u(x)$ is a multiple of $v(x)$ for arbitrary nonzero polynomials $u(x)$ and $v(x)$ over S. For if $u(x)$ is a multiple of $v(x)$, it is easy to see that u_{n+k} must be a multiple of v_n each time we get to step D2, hence the quotient $u(x)/v(x)$ will be found. Applying this observation recursively, we obtain an algorithm that decides if a given polynomial over S, in any number of variables, is a multiple of another given polynomial over S, and the algorithm will find the quotient when it exists.

A set of elements of a unique factorization domain is said to be *relatively prime* if no prime of that unique factorization domain divides all of them. A polynomial over a unique factorization domain is called *primitive* if its coefficients are relatively prime. (This concept should not be confused with the quite different idea of "primitive polynomials modulo p" discussed in Section 3.2.2.) The following fact, introduced for the case of polynomials over the integers by C. F. Gauss in article 42 of his celebrated book *Disquisitiones Arithmeticæ* (Leipzig: 1801), is of prime importance:

Lemma G (Gauss's Lemma). *The product of primitive polynomials over a unique factorization domain is primitive.*

Proof. Let $u(x) = u_m x^m + \cdots + u_0$ and $v(x) = v_n x^n + \cdots + v_0$ be primitive polynomials. If p is any prime of the domain, we must show that p does not divide all the coefficients of $u(x)v(x)$. By assumption, there is an index j such that u_j is not divisible by p, and an index k such that v_k is not divisible by p. Let j and k be as small as possible; then the coefficient of x^{j+k} in $u(x)v(x)$ is

$$u_j v_k + u_{j+1} v_{k-1} + \cdots + u_{j+k} v_0 + u_{j-1} v_{k+1} + \cdots + u_0 v_{k+j},$$

and it is easy to see that this is not a multiple of p (since its first term isn't, but all of its other terms are). ∎

If a nonzero polynomial $u(x)$ over a unique factorization domain S is not primitive, we can write $u(x) = p_1 \cdot u_1(x)$, where p_1 is a prime of S dividing all the coefficients of $u(x)$, and where $u_1(x)$ is another nonzero polynomial over S. All of the coefficients of $u_1(x)$ have one less prime factor than the corresponding coefficients of $u(x)$. Now if $u_1(x)$ is not primitive, we can write $u_1(x) = p_2 \cdot u_2(x)$, etc.; this process must ultimately terminate in a representation $u(x) = c \cdot u_k(x)$, where c is an element of S and $u_k(x)$ is primitive. In fact, we have the following companion to Lemma G:

Lemma H. *Any nonzero polynomial $u(x)$ over a unique factorization domain S can be factored in the form $u(x) = c \cdot v(x)$, where c is in S and $v(x)$ is primitive. Furthermore, this representation is unique, in the sense that if $u = c_1 \cdot v_1(x) = c_2 \cdot v_2(x)$, then $c_1 = ac_2$ and $v_2(x) = av_1(x)$ where a is a unit of S.*

Proof. We have shown that such a representation exists, so only the uniqueness needs to be proved. Assume that $c_1 \cdot v_1(x) = c_2 \cdot v_2(x)$, where $v_1(x)$ and $v_2(x)$ are primitive. Let p be any prime of S. If p^k divides c_1, then p^k also divides c_2; otherwise p^k would divide all the coefficients of $c_2 \cdot v_2(x)$, so p would divide all the coefficients of $v_2(x)$, a contradiction. Similarly, p^k divides c_2 only if p^k divides c_1. Hence, by unique factorization, $c_1 = ac_2$ where a is a unit; and $0 = ac_2 \cdot v_1(x) - c_2 \cdot v_2(x) = c_2 \cdot \big(av_1(x) - v_2(x)\big)$, so $av_1(x) - v_2(x) = 0$. ∎

Therefore we may write any nonzero polynomial $u(x)$ as

$$u(x) = \operatorname{cont}(u) \cdot \operatorname{pp}\big(u(x)\big), \tag{3}$$

where $\operatorname{cont}(u)$, the *content* of u, is an element of S, and $\operatorname{pp}\big(u(x)\big)$, the *primitive part* of $u(x)$, is a primitive polynomial over S. When $u(x) = 0$, it is convenient to define $\operatorname{cont}(u) = \operatorname{pp}\big(u(x)\big) = 0$. Combining Lemmas G and H gives us the relations

$$\operatorname{cont}(u \cdot v) = a \operatorname{cont}(u) \operatorname{cont}(v),$$
$$\operatorname{pp}\big(u(x) \cdot v(x)\big) = b \operatorname{pp}\big(u(x)\big) \operatorname{pp}\big(v(x)\big), \tag{4}$$

where a and b are units, depending on the way contents are calculated, with $ab = 1$. When we are working with polynomials over the integers, the only units are $+1$ and -1, and it is conventional to define $\operatorname{pp}\big(u(x)\big)$ so that its leading coefficient is positive; then (4) is true with $a = b = 1$. When working with polynomials over a field we may take $\operatorname{cont}(u) = \ell(u)$, so that $\operatorname{pp}\big(u(x)\big)$ is monic; in this case again (4) holds with $a = b = 1$, for all $u(x)$ and $v(x)$.

For example, if we are dealing with polynomials over the integers, let $u(x) = -26x^2 + 39$ and $v(x) = 21x + 14$. Then

$$\text{cont}(u) = -13, \qquad \text{pp}\big(u(x)\big) = 2x^2 - 3,$$
$$\text{cont}(v) = +7, \qquad \text{pp}\big(v(x)\big) = 3x + 2,$$
$$\text{cont}(u \cdot v) = -91, \qquad \text{pp}\big(u(x) \cdot v(x)\big) = 6x^3 + 4x^2 - 9x - 6.$$

Greatest common divisors. When there is unique factorization, it makes sense to speak of a *greatest common divisor* of two elements; this is a common divisor that is divisible by as many primes as possible. $\big($See Eq. 4.5.2–(6).$\big)$ Since a unique factorization domain may have many units, however, there is ambiguity in this definition of greatest common divisor; if w is a greatest common divisor of u and v, so is $a \cdot w$, when a is any unit. Conversely, the assumption of unique factorization implies that if w_1 and w_2 are both greatest common divisors of u and v, then $w_1 = a \cdot w_2$ for some unit a. In other words it does not make sense, in general, to speak of "the" greatest common divisor of u and v; there is a set of greatest common divisors, each one being a unit multiple of the others.

Let us now consider the problem of finding a greatest common divisor of two given polynomials over an algebraic system S, a question originally raised by Pedro Nuñez in his *Libro de Algebra* (Antwerp: 1567). If S is a field, the problem is relatively simple; our division algorithm, Algorithm D, can be extended to an algorithm that computes greatest common divisors, just as Euclid's algorithm (Algorithm 4.5.2A) yields the greatest common divisor of two given integers based on a division algorithm for integers:

If $v(x) = 0$, then $\gcd\big(u(x), v(x)\big) = u(x)$;
otherwise $\gcd\big(u(x), v(x)\big) = \gcd\big(v(x), r(x)\big)$,

where $r(x)$ is given by (1). This procedure is called Euclid's algorithm for polynomials over a field. It was first used by Simon Stevin in *L'Arithmetique* (Leiden: 1585); see A. Girard, *Les Œuvres Mathématiques de Simon Stevin* **1** (Leiden: 1634), 56.

For example, let us determine the gcd of $x^8 + x^6 + 10x^4 + 10x^3 + 8x^2 + 2x + 8$ and $3x^6 + 5x^4 + 9x^2 + 4x + 8$, mod 13, by using Euclid's algorithm for polynomials over the integers modulo 13. First, writing only the coefficients to show the steps of Algorithm D, we have

```
                                      9  0  7
           3 0 5 0 9 4 8 ) 1 0 1 0 10 10  8  2  8
                           1 0 6 0  3 10  7
                           ─────────────────────
                             0 8 0  7  0  1  2  8
                                8 0  9  0 11  2  4
                                ──────────────────
                                  0 11  0  3  0  4
```
$$(5)$$

so that $x^8 + x^6 + 10x^4 + 10x^3 + 8x^2 + 2x + 8$ equals

$$(9x^2 + 7)(3x^6 + 5x^4 + 9x^2 + 4x + 8) + (11x^4 + 3x^2 + 4).$$

Similarly,

$$3x^6 + 5x^4 + 9x^2 + 4x + 8 = (5x^2 + 5)(11x^4 + 3x^2 + 4) \; + \; (4x + 1);$$
$$11x^4 + 3x^2 + 4 = (6x^3 + 5x^2 + 6x + 5)(4x + 1) \; + \; 12;$$
$$4x + 1 = (9x + 12) \cdot 12 \; + \; 0. \tag{6}$$

(The equality sign here means congruence modulo 13, since all arithmetic on the coefficients has been done mod 13.) This computation shows that 12 is a greatest common divisor of the two original polynomials. Now any nonzero element of a field is a unit of the domain of polynomials over that field, so it is conventional in the case of fields to divide the result of the algorithm by its leading coefficient, producing a *monic* polynomial that is called *the* greatest common divisor of the two given polynomials. The gcd computed in (6) is accordingly taken to be 1, not 12. The last step in (6) could have been omitted, for if $\deg(v) = 0$, then $\gcd(u(x), v(x)) = 1$, no matter what polynomial is chosen for $u(x)$. Exercise 4 determines the average running time for Euclid's algorithm on random polynomials modulo p.

Let us now turn to the more general situation in which our polynomials are given over a unique factorization domain that is not a field. From Eqs. (4) we can deduce the important relations

$$\mathrm{cont}\big(\gcd(u, v)\big) = a \cdot \gcd\big(\mathrm{cont}(u), \mathrm{cont}(v)\big),$$
$$\mathrm{pp}\big(\gcd(u(x), v(x))\big) = b \cdot \gcd\big(\mathrm{pp}(u(x)), \mathrm{pp}(v(x))\big), \tag{7}$$

where a and b are units. Here $\gcd\big(u(x), v(x)\big)$ denotes any particular polynomial in x that is a greatest common divisor of $u(x)$ and $v(x)$. Equations (7) reduce the problem of finding greatest common divisors of arbitrary polynomials to the problem of finding greatest common divisors of *primitive* polynomials.

Algorithm D for division of polynomials over a field can be generalized to a *pseudo-division* of polynomials over any algebraic system that is a commutative ring with identity. We can observe that Algorithm D requires explicit division only by $\ell(v)$, the leading coefficient of $v(x)$, and that step D2 is carried out exactly $m - n + 1$ times; thus if $u(x)$ and $v(x)$ start with integer coefficients, and if we are working over the rational numbers, then the only denominators that appear in the coefficients of $q(x)$ and $r(x)$ are divisors of $\ell(v)^{m-n+1}$. This suggests that we can always find polynomials $q(x)$ and $r(x)$ such that

$$\ell(v)^{m-n+1} u(x) = q(x)v(x) + r(x), \qquad \deg(r) < n, \tag{8}$$

where $m = \deg(u)$ and $n = \deg(v)$, for any polynomials $u(x)$ and $v(x) \neq 0$, provided that $m \geq n$.

Algorithm R (*Pseudo-division of polynomials*). Given polynomials

$$u(x) = u_m x^m + \cdots + u_1 x + u_0, \qquad v(x) = v_n x^n + \cdots + v_1 x + v_0,$$

where $v_n \neq 0$ and $m \geq n \geq 0$, this algorithm finds polynomials $q(x) = q_{m-n}x^{m-n} + \cdots + q_0$ and $r(x) = r_{n-1}x^{n-1} + \cdots + r_0$ satisfying (8).

R1. [Iterate on k.] Do step R2 for $k = m - n$, $m - n - 1$, $\ldots$, 0; then terminate the algorithm with $(r_{n-1}, \ldots, r_0) = (u_{n-1}, \ldots, u_0)$.

R2. [Multiplication loop.] Set $q_k \leftarrow u_{n+k} v_n^k$, and set $u_j \leftarrow v_n u_j - u_{n+k} v_{j-k}$ for $j = n + k - 1$, $n + k - 2$, $\ldots$, 0. (When $j < k$ this means that $u_j \leftarrow v_n u_j$, since we treat v_{-1}, v_{-2}, $\ldots$ as zero. These multiplications could have been avoided if we had started the algorithm by replacing u_t by $v_n^{m-n-t} u_t$, for $0 \le t < m - n$.) ∎

An example calculation appears below in (10). It is easy to prove the validity of Algorithm R by induction on $m - n$, since each execution of step R2 essentially replaces $u(x)$ by $\ell(v) u(x) - \ell(u) x^k v(x)$, where $k = \deg(u) - \deg(v)$. Notice that no division whatever is used in this algorithm; the coefficients of $q(x)$ and $r(x)$ are themselves certain polynomial functions of the coefficients of $u(x)$ and $v(x)$. If $v_n = 1$, the algorithm is identical to Algorithm D. If $u(x)$ and $v(x)$ are polynomials over a unique factorization domain, we can prove as before that the polynomials $q(x)$ and $r(x)$ are unique; therefore another way to do the pseudo-division over a unique factorization domain is to multiply $u(x)$ by v_n^{m-n+1} and apply Algorithm D, knowing that all the quotients in step D2 will exist.

Algorithm R can be extended to a "generalized Euclidean algorithm" for primitive polynomials over a unique factorization domain, in the following way: Let $u(x)$ and $v(x)$ be primitive polynomials with $\deg(u) \ge \deg(v)$, and determine the polynomial $r(x)$ satisfying (8) by means of Algorithm R. Now we can prove that $\gcd\big(u(x), v(x)\big) = \gcd\big(v(x), r(x)\big)$: Any common divisor of $u(x)$ and $v(x)$ divides $v(x)$ and $r(x)$; conversely, any common divisor of $v(x)$ and $r(x)$ divides $\ell(v)^{m-n+1} u(x)$, and it must be primitive $\big($since $v(x)$ is primitive$\big)$ so it divides $u(x)$. If $r(x) = 0$, we therefore have $\gcd\big(u(x), v(x)\big) = v(x)$; on the other hand if $r(x) \ne 0$, we have $\gcd\big(v(x), r(x)\big) = \gcd\big(v(x), \mathrm{pp}(r(x))\big)$ since $v(x)$ is primitive, so the process can be iterated.

Algorithm E (*Generalized Euclidean algorithm*). Given nonzero polynomials $u(x)$ and $v(x)$ over a unique factorization domain S, this algorithm calculates a greatest common divisor of $u(x)$ and $v(x)$. We assume that auxiliary algorithms exist to calculate greatest common divisors of elements of S, and to divide a by b in S when $b \ne 0$ and a is a multiple of b.

E1. [Reduce to primitive.] Set $d \leftarrow \gcd\big(\mathrm{cont}(u), \mathrm{cont}(v)\big)$, using the assumed algorithm for calculating greatest common divisors in S. $\big($By definition, $\mathrm{cont}(u)$ is a greatest common divisor of the coefficients of $u(x)$.$\big)$ Replace $u(x)$ by the polynomial $u(x)/\mathrm{cont}(u) = \mathrm{pp}\big(u(x)\big)$; similarly, replace $v(x)$ by $\mathrm{pp}\big(v(x)\big)$.

E2. [Pseudo-division.] Calculate $r(x)$ using Algorithm R. $\big($It is unnecessary to calculate the quotient polynomial $q(x)$.$\big)$ If $r(x) = 0$, go to E4. If $\deg(r) = 0$, replace $v(x)$ by the constant polynomial "1" and go to E4.

E3. [Make remainder primitive.] Replace $u(x)$ by $v(x)$ and replace $v(x)$ by $\mathrm{pp}\big(r(x)\big)$. Go back to step E2. (This is the "Euclidean step," analogous to the other instances of Euclid's algorithm that we have seen.)

E4. [Attach the content.] The algorithm terminates, with $d \cdot v(x)$ as the desired answer. ∎

As an example of Algorithm E, let us calculate the gcd of the polynomials

$$u(x) = x^8 + x^6 - 3x^4 - 3x^3 + 8x^2 + 2x - 5,$$
$$v(x) = 3x^6 + 5x^4 - 4x^2 - 9x + 21, \tag{9}$$

over the integers. These polynomials are primitive, so step E1 sets $d \leftarrow 1$. In step E2 we have the pseudo-division

$$
\begin{array}{r}
1\quad 0\quad -6 \\[2pt]
3\ 0\ 5\ 0\ -4\ -9\ 21\ )\ \overline{\ 1\ 0\quad 1\ 0\ -3\ -3\ \ 8\ \ 2\ \ -5\ } \\
3\ 0\qquad 3\ 0\ -9\ -9\ 24\ \ 6\ -15 \\
3\ 0\qquad 5\ 0\ -4\ -9\ 21 \\
\hline
0\ -2\ 0\ \ -5\quad 0\ \ 3\ \ 6\ -15 \\
0\ -6\ 0\ -15\quad 0\ \ 9\ 18\ -45 \\
0\quad 0\ 0\quad 0\quad 0\ \ 0\ \ 0\quad 0 \\
\hline
-6\ 0\ -15\quad 0\ \ 9\ 18\ -45 \\
-18\ 0\ -45\quad 0\ 27\ 54\ -135 \\
-18\ 0\ -30\quad 0\ 24\ 54\ -126 \\
\hline
-15\quad 0\ \ 3\quad 0\quad -9
\end{array}
\tag{10}
$$

Here the quotient $q(x)$ is $1 \cdot 3^2 x^2 + 0 \cdot 3^1 x + -6 \cdot 3^0$; we have

$$27u(x) = v(x)(9x^2 - 6) + (-15x^4 + 3x^2 - 9). \tag{11}$$

Now step E3 replaces $u(x)$ by $v(x)$ and $v(x)$ by $\mathrm{pp}(r(x)) = 5x^4 - x^2 + 3$. The subsequent calculation is summarized in the following table, where only the coefficients are shown:

$u(x)$	$v(x)$	$r(x)$
$1, 0, 1, 0, -3, -3, 8, 2, -5$	$3, 0, 5, 0, -4, -9, 21$	$-15, 0, 3, 0, -9$
$3, 0, 5, 0, -4, -9, 21$	$5, 0, -1, 0, 3$	$-585, -1125, 2205$
$5, 0, -1, 0, 3$	$13, 25, -49$	$-233150, 307500$
$13, 25, -49$	$4663, -6150$	143193869

(12)

It is instructive to compare this calculation with the computation of the same greatest common divisor over the *rational* numbers, instead of over the integers, by using Euclid's algorithm for polynomials over a field as described earlier in this section. The following surprisingly complicated sequence appears:

$u(x)$	$v(x)$
$1, 0, 1, 0, -3, -3, 8, 2, -5$	$3, 0, 5, 0, -4, -9, 21$
$3, 0, 5, 0, -4, -9, 21$	$-\frac{5}{9}, 0, \frac{1}{9}, 0, -\frac{1}{3}$
$-\frac{5}{9}, 0, \frac{1}{9}, 0, -\frac{1}{3}$	$-\frac{117}{25}, -9, \frac{441}{25}$
$-\frac{117}{25}, -9, \frac{441}{25}$	$\frac{233150}{19773}, -\frac{102500}{6591}$
$\frac{233150}{19773}, -\frac{102500}{6591}$	$-\frac{1288744821}{543589225}$

(13)

To improve that algorithm, we can reduce $u(x)$ and $v(x)$ to monic polynomials at each step, since this removes unit factors that make the coefficients more complicated than necessary; this is actually Algorithm E over the rationals:

$$
\begin{array}{cc}
u(x) & v(x) \\[4pt]
1, 0, 1, 0, -3, -3, 8, 2, -5 & 1, 0, \tfrac{5}{3}, 0, -\tfrac{4}{3}, -3, 7 \\[4pt]
1, 0, \tfrac{5}{3}, 0, -\tfrac{4}{3}, -3, 7 & 1, 0, -\tfrac{1}{5}, 0, \tfrac{3}{5} \\[4pt]
1, 0, -\tfrac{1}{5}, 0, \tfrac{3}{5} & 1, \tfrac{25}{13}, -\tfrac{49}{13} \\[4pt]
1, \tfrac{25}{13}, -\tfrac{49}{13} & 1, -\tfrac{6150}{4663} \\[4pt]
1, -\tfrac{6150}{4663} & 1
\end{array}
\qquad (14)
$$

In both (13) and (14) the sequence of polynomials is essentially the same as (12), which was obtained by Algorithm E over the integers; the only difference is that the polynomials have been multiplied by certain rational numbers. Whether we have $5x^4 - x^2 + 3$ or $-\tfrac{5}{9}x^4 + \tfrac{1}{9}x^2 - \tfrac{1}{3}$ or $x^4 - \tfrac{1}{5}x^2 + \tfrac{3}{5}$, the computations are essentially the same. But either algorithm using rational arithmetic tends to run slower than the all-integer Algorithm E, since rational arithmetic usually requires more evaluations of integer gcds within each step when the polynomials have large degree.

It is instructive to compare (12), (13), and (14) with (6) above, where we determined the gcd of the same polynomials $u(x)$ and $v(x)$ modulo 13 with considerably less labor. Since $\ell(u)$ and $\ell(v)$ are not multiples of 13, the fact that $\gcd\bigl(u(x), v(x)\bigr) = 1$ modulo 13 is sufficient to prove that $u(x)$ and $v(x)$ are relatively prime over the integers (and therefore over the rational numbers). We will return to this time-saving observation at the close of Section 4.6.2.

The subresultant algorithm. An ingenious algorithm that is generally superior to Algorithm E, and that gives us further information about Algorithm E's behavior, was discovered by George E. Collins [*JACM* **14** (1967), 128–142] and subsequently improved by W. S. Brown and J. F. Traub [*JACM* **18** (1971), 505–514; see also W. S. Brown, *ACM Trans. Math. Software* **4** (1978), 237–249]. This algorithm avoids the calculation of primitive parts in step E3, dividing instead by an element of S that is known to be a factor of $r(x)$:

Algorithm C (*Greatest common divisor over a unique factorization domain*). This algorithm has the same input and output assumptions as Algorithm E, and has the advantage that fewer calculations of greatest common divisors of coefficients are needed.

C1. [Reduce to primitive.] As in step E1 of Algorithm E, set $d \leftarrow \gcd\bigl(\mathrm{cont}(u),$ $\mathrm{cont}(v)\bigr)$, and replace $\bigl(u(x), v(x)\bigr)$ by $\bigl(\mathrm{pp}\bigl(u(x)\bigr), \mathrm{pp}\bigl(v(x)\bigr)\bigr)$. Set $g \leftarrow h \leftarrow 1$.

C2. [Pseudo-division.] Set $\delta \leftarrow \deg(u) - \deg(v)$. Calculate $r(x)$ using Algorithm R. If $r(x) = 0$, go to C4. If $\deg(r) = 0$, replace $v(x)$ by the constant polynomial "1" and go to C4.

C3. [Adjust remainder.] Replace the polynomial $u(x)$ by $v(x)$, and replace $v(x)$ by $r(x)/gh^\delta$. (At this point all coefficients of $r(x)$ are multiples of gh^δ.)

Then set $g \leftarrow \ell(u)$, $h \leftarrow h^{1-\delta}g^{\delta}$ and return to C2. (The new value of h will be in the domain S, even if $\delta > 1$.)

C4. [Attach the content.] Return $d \cdot \mathrm{pp}\big(v(x)\big)$ as the answer. ∎

If we apply this algorithm to the polynomials (9) considered earlier, the following sequence of results is obtained at the beginning of step C2:

$u(x)$	$v(x)$	g	h	
$1, 0, 1, 0, -3, -3, 8, 2, -5$	$3, 0, 5, 0, -4, -9, 21$	1	1	
$3, 0, 5, 0, -4, -9, 21$	$-15, 0, 3, 0, -9$	3	9	
$-15, 0, 3, 0, -9$	$65, 125, -245$	-15	25	
$65, 125, -245$	$-9326, 12300$	65	169	(15)

At the conclusion of the algorithm, $r(x)/gh^{\delta} = 260708$.

The sequence of polynomials consists of integral multiples of the polynomials in the sequence produced by Algorithm E. In spite of the fact that the polynomials are not reduced to primitive form, the coefficients are kept to a reasonable size because of the reduction factor in step C3.

In order to analyze Algorithm C and to prove that it is valid, let us call the sequence of polynomials it produces $u_1(x)$, $u_2(x)$, $u_3(x)$, $\ldots$, where $u_1(x) = u(x)$ and $u_2(x) = v(x)$. Let $\delta_j = n_j - n_{j+1}$ for $j \geq 1$, where $n_j = \deg(u_j)$; and let $g_1 = h_1 = 1$, $g_j = \ell(u_j)$, $h_j = h_{j-1}^{1-\delta_{j-1}}g_j^{\delta_{j-1}}$ for $j \geq 2$. Then we have

$$g_2^{\delta_1+1}u_1(x) = u_2(x)q_1(x) + g_1 h_1^{\delta_1}u_3(x), \qquad n_3 < n_2;$$
$$g_3^{\delta_2+1}u_2(x) = u_3(x)q_2(x) + g_2 h_2^{\delta_2}u_4(x), \qquad n_4 < n_3; \qquad (16)$$
$$g_4^{\delta_3+1}u_3(x) = u_4(x)q_3(x) + g_3 h_3^{\delta_3}u_5(x), \qquad n_5 < n_4;$$

and so on. The process terminates when $n_{k+1} = \deg(u_{k+1}) \leq 0$. We must show that $u_3(x)$, $u_4(x)$, $\ldots$, have coefficients in S, namely that the factors $g_j h_j^{\delta_j}$ exactly divide all coefficients of the remainders, and we must also show that the h_j values all belong to S. The proof is rather involved, and it can be most easily understood by considering an example.

Suppose, as in (15), that $n_1 = 8$, $n_2 = 6$, $n_3 = 4$, $n_4 = 2$, $n_5 = 1$, $n_6 = 0$, so that $\delta_1 = \delta_2 = \delta_3 = 2$, $\delta_4 = \delta_5 = 1$. Let us write $u_1(x) = a_8x^8 + a_7x^7 + \cdots + a_0$, $u_2(x) = b_6x^6 + b_5x^5 + \cdots + b_0$, $\ldots$, $u_5(x) = e_1x + e_0$, $u_6(x) = f_0$, so that $h_1 = 1$, $h_2 = b_6^2$, $h_3 = c_4^2/b_6^2$, $h_4 = d_2^2b_6^2/c_4^2$. In these terms it is helpful to consider the array shown in Table 1. For concreteness, let us assume that the coefficients of the polynomials are integers. We have $b_6^3u_1(x) = u_2(x)q_1(x) + u_3(x)$; so if we multiply row A_5 by b_6^3 and subtract appropriate multiples of rows B_7, B_6, and B_5 (corresponding to the coefficients of $q_1(x)$) we will get row C_5. If we also multiply row A_4 by b_6^3 and subtract multiples of rows B_6, B_5, and B_4, we get row C_4. In a similar way, we have $c_4^3u_2(x) = u_3(x)q_2(x) + b_6^5u_4(x)$; so we can multiply row B_3 by c_4^3, subtract integer multiples of rows C_5, C_4, and C_3, then divide by b_6^5 to obtain row D_3.

In order to prove that $u_4(x)$ has integer coefficients, let us consider the matrix

$$
\begin{matrix}
A_2 \\ A_1 \\ A_0 \\ B_4 \\ B_3 \\ B_2 \\ B_1 \\ B_0
\end{matrix}
\begin{pmatrix}
a_8 & a_7 & a_6 & a_5 & a_4 & a_3 & a_2 & a_1 & a_0 & 0 & 0 \\
0 & a_8 & a_7 & a_6 & a_5 & a_4 & a_3 & a_2 & a_1 & a_0 & 0 \\
0 & 0 & a_8 & a_7 & a_6 & a_5 & a_4 & a_3 & a_2 & a_1 & a_0 \\
b_6 & b_5 & b_4 & b_3 & b_2 & b_1 & b_0 & 0 & 0 & 0 & 0 \\
0 & b_6 & b_5 & b_4 & b_3 & b_2 & b_1 & b_0 & 0 & 0 & 0 \\
0 & 0 & b_6 & b_5 & b_4 & b_3 & b_2 & b_1 & b_0 & 0 & 0 \\
0 & 0 & 0 & b_6 & b_5 & b_4 & b_3 & b_2 & b_1 & b_0 & 0 \\
0 & 0 & 0 & 0 & b_6 & b_5 & b_4 & b_3 & b_2 & b_1 & b_0
\end{pmatrix} = M. \qquad (17)
$$

The indicated row operations and a permutation of rows will transform M into

$$
\begin{matrix}
B_4 \\ B_3 \\ B_2 \\ B_1 \\ C_2 \\ C_1 \\ C_0 \\ D_0
\end{matrix}
\begin{pmatrix}
b_6 & b_5 & b_4 & b_3 & b_2 & b_1 & b_0 & 0 & 0 & 0 & 0 \\
0 & b_6 & b_5 & b_4 & b_3 & b_2 & b_1 & b_0 & 0 & 0 & 0 \\
0 & 0 & b_6 & b_5 & b_4 & b_3 & b_2 & b_1 & b_0 & 0 & 0 \\
0 & 0 & 0 & b_6 & b_5 & b_4 & b_3 & b_2 & b_1 & b_0 & 0 \\
0 & 0 & 0 & 0 & c_4 & c_3 & c_2 & c_1 & c_0 & 0 & 0 \\
0 & 0 & 0 & 0 & 0 & c_4 & c_3 & c_2 & c_1 & c_0 & 0 \\
0 & 0 & 0 & 0 & 0 & 0 & c_4 & c_3 & c_2 & c_1 & c_0 \\
0 & 0 & 0 & 0 & 0 & 0 & 0 & 0 & d_2 & d_1 & d_0
\end{pmatrix} = M'. \qquad (18)
$$

Because of the way M' has been derived from M, we must have

$$ b_6^3 \cdot b_6^3 \cdot b_6^3 \cdot (c_4^3/b_6^5) \cdot \det M_0 = \pm \det M_0', $$

if M_0 and M_0' represent any square matrices obtained by selecting eight corresponding columns from M and M'. For example, let us select the first seven columns and the column containing d_1; then

$$
b_6^3 \cdot b_6^3 \cdot b_6^3 \cdot (c_4^3/b_6^5) \cdot \det
\begin{pmatrix}
a_8 & a_7 & a_6 & a_5 & a_4 & a_3 & a_2 & 0 \\
0 & a_8 & a_7 & a_6 & a_5 & a_4 & a_3 & a_0 \\
0 & 0 & a_8 & a_7 & a_6 & a_5 & a_4 & a_1 \\
b_6 & b_5 & b_4 & b_3 & b_2 & b_1 & b_0 & 0 \\
0 & b_6 & b_5 & b_4 & b_3 & b_2 & b_1 & 0 \\
0 & 0 & b_6 & b_5 & b_4 & b_3 & b_2 & 0 \\
0 & 0 & 0 & b_6 & b_5 & b_4 & b_3 & b_0 \\
0 & 0 & 0 & 0 & b_6 & b_5 & b_4 & b_1
\end{pmatrix}
= \pm b_6^4 \cdot c_4^3 \cdot d_1.
$$

Since $b_6 c_4 \neq 0$, this proves that d_1 is an integer. Similarly, d_2 and d_0 are integers.

In general, we can show that $u_{j+1}(x)$ has integer coefficients in a similar manner. If we start with the matrix M consisting of rows $A_{n_2-n_j}$ through A_0 and $B_{n_1-n_j}$ through B_0, and if we perform the row operations indicated in Table 1, we will obtain a matrix M' consisting in some order of rows $B_{n_1-n_j}$ through $B_{n_3-n_j+1}$, then $C_{n_2-n_j}$ through $C_{n_4-n_j+1}$, $\ldots$, $P_{n_{j-2}-n_j}$ through P_1, then $Q_{n_{j-1}-n_j}$ through Q_0, and finally R_0 (a row containing the coefficients of $u_{j+1}(x)$). Extracting appropriate columns shows that

$$
(g_2^{\delta_1+1}/g_1 h_1^{\delta_1})^{n_2-n_j+1}(g_3^{\delta_2+1}/g_2 h_2^{\delta_2})^{n_3-n_j+1} \ldots (g_j^{\delta_{j-1}+1}/g_{j-1} h_{j-1}^{\delta_{j-1}})^{n_j-n_j+1}
$$
$$
\times \det M_0 = \pm g_2^{n_1-n_3} g_3^{n_2-n_4} \ldots g_{j-1}^{n_{j-2}-n_j} g_j^{n_{j-1}-n_j+1} r_t, \qquad (19)
$$

Table 1

COEFFICIENTS THAT ARISE IN ALGORITHM C

Row name	Row														Multiply by	Replace by row
A_5	a_8	a_7	a_6	a_5	a_4	a_3	a_2	a_1	a_0	0	0	0	0	0	b_6^3	C_5
A_4	0	a_8	a_7	a_6	a_5	a_4	a_3	a_2	a_1	a_0	0	0	0	0	b_6^3	C_4
A_3	0	0	a_8	a_7	a_6	a_5	a_4	a_3	a_2	a_1	a_0	0	0	0	b_6^3	C_3
A_2	0	0	0	a_8	a_7	a_6	a_5	a_4	a_3	a_2	a_1	a_0	0	0	b_6^3	C_2
A_1	0	0	0	0	a_8	a_7	a_6	a_5	a_4	a_3	a_2	a_1	a_0	0	b_6^3	C_1
A_0	0	0	0	0	0	a_8	a_7	a_6	a_5	a_4	a_3	a_2	a_1	a_0	b_6^3	C_0
B_7	b_6	b_5	b_4	b_3	b_2	b_1	b_0	0	0	0	0	0	0	0		
B_6	0	b_6	b_5	b_4	b_3	b_2	b_1	b_0	0	0	0	0	0	0		
B_5	0	0	b_6	b_5	b_4	b_3	b_2	b_1	b_0	0	0	0	0	0		
B_4	0	0	0	b_6	b_5	b_4	b_3	b_2	b_1	b_0	0	0	0	0		
B_3	0	0	0	0	b_6	b_5	b_4	b_3	b_2	b_1	b_0	0	0	0	c_4^3/b_6^5	D_3
B_2	0	0	0	0	0	b_6	b_5	b_4	b_3	b_2	b_1	b_0	0	0	c_4^3/b_6^5	D_2
B_1	0	0	0	0	0	0	b_6	b_5	b_4	b_3	b_2	b_1	b_0	0	c_4^3/b_6^5	D_1
B_0	0	0	0	0	0	0	0	b_6	b_5	b_4	b_3	b_2	b_1	b_0	c_4^3/b_6^5	D_0
C_5	0	0	0	0	c_4	c_3	c_2	c_1	c_0	0	0	0	0	0		
C_4	0	0	0	0	0	c_4	c_3	c_2	c_1	c_0	0	0	0	0		
C_3	0	0	0	0	0	0	c_4	c_3	c_2	c_1	c_0	0	0	0		
C_2	0	0	0	0	0	0	0	c_4	c_3	c_2	c_1	c_0	0	0		
C_1	0	0	0	0	0	0	0	0	c_4	c_3	c_2	c_1	c_0	0	$d_2^2 b_6^4/c_4^5$	E_1
C_0	0	0	0	0	0	0	0	0	0	c_4	c_3	c_2	c_1	c_0	$d_2^2 b_6^4/c_4^5$	E_0
D_3	0	0	0	0	0	0	0	0	d_2	d_1	d_0	0	0	0		
D_2	0	0	0	0	0	0	0	0	0	d_2	d_1	d_0	0	0		
D_1	0	0	0	0	0	0	0	0	0	0	d_2	d_1	d_0	0		
D_0	0	0	0	0	0	0	0	0	0	0	0	d_2	d_1	d_0	$e_2^2 c_4^2/d_2^3 b_6^2$	F_0
E_1	0	0	0	0	0	0	0	0	0	0	0	e_1	e_0	0		
E_0	0	0	0	0	0	0	0	0	0	0	0	0	e_1	e_0		
F_0	0	0	0	0	0	0	0	0	0	0	0	0	0	f_0		

where r_t is a given coefficient of $u_{j+1}(x)$ and M_0 is a submatrix of M. The h's have been chosen very cleverly so that this equation simplifies to

$$\det M_0 = \pm r_t \qquad (20)$$

(see exercise 24). Therefore *every coefficient of $u_{j+1}(x)$ can be expressed as the determinant of an $(n_1 + n_2 - 2n_j + 2) \times (n_1 + n_2 - 2n_j + 2)$ matrix whose elements are coefficients of $u(x)$ and $v(x)$.*

It remains to be shown that the cleverly chosen h's also are integers. A similar technique applies: Let's look, for example, at the matrix

$$
\begin{array}{c}
A_1 \\ A_0 \\ B_3 \\ B_2 \\ B_1 \\ B_0
\end{array}
\left(
\begin{array}{cccccccccc}
a_8 & a_7 & a_6 & a_5 & a_4 & a_3 & a_2 & a_1 & a_0 & 0 \\
0 & a_8 & a_7 & a_6 & a_5 & a_4 & a_3 & a_2 & a_1 & a_0 \\
b_6 & b_5 & b_4 & b_3 & b_2 & b_1 & b_0 & 0 & 0 & 0 \\
0 & b_6 & b_5 & b_4 & b_3 & b_2 & b_1 & b_0 & 0 & 0 \\
0 & 0 & b_6 & b_5 & b_4 & b_3 & b_2 & b_1 & b_0 & 0 \\
0 & 0 & 0 & b_6 & b_5 & b_4 & b_3 & b_2 & b_1 & b_0
\end{array}
\right) = M. \qquad (21)
$$

Row operations as specified in Table 1, and permutation of rows, leads to

$$
\begin{matrix}
B_3 \\
B_2 \\
B_1 \\
B_0 \\
C_1 \\
C_0
\end{matrix}
\begin{pmatrix}
b_6 & b_5 & b_4 & b_3 & b_2 & b_1 & b_0 & 0 & 0 & 0 \\
0 & b_6 & b_5 & b_4 & b_3 & b_2 & b_1 & b_0 & 0 & 0 \\
0 & 0 & b_6 & b_5 & b_4 & b_3 & b_2 & b_1 & b_0 & 0 \\
0 & 0 & 0 & b_6 & b_5 & b_4 & b_3 & b_2 & b_1 & b_0 \\
0 & 0 & 0 & 0 & c_4 & c_3 & c_2 & c_1 & c_0 & 0 \\
0 & 0 & 0 & 0 & 0 & c_4 & c_3 & c_2 & c_1 & c_0
\end{pmatrix} = M'; \qquad (22)
$$

hence if we consider any submatrices M_0 and M_0' obtained by selecting six corresponding columns of M and M' we have $b_6^3 \cdot b_6^3 \cdot \det M_0 = \pm \det M_0'$. When M_0 is chosen to be the first six columns of M, we find that $\det M_0 = \pm c_4^2 / b_6^2 = \pm h_3$, so h_3 is an integer.

In general, to show that h_j is an integer for $j \geq 3$, we start with the matrix M consisting of rows $A_{n_2 - n_j - 1}$ through A_0 and $B_{n_1 - n_j - 1}$ through B_0; then we perform appropriate row operations until obtaining a matrix M' consisting of rows $B_{n_1 - n_j - 1}$ through $B_{n_3 - n_j}$, then $C_{n_2 + n_j - 1}$ through $C_{n_4 - n_j}, \ldots, P_{n_{j-2} - n_j - 1}$ through P_0, then $Q_{n_{j-1} - n_j - 1}$ through Q_0. Letting M_0 be the first $n_1 + n_2 - 2n_j$ columns of M, we obtain

$$
(g_2^{\delta_1 + 1} / g_1 h_1^{\delta_1})^{n_2 - n_j} (g_3^{\delta_2 + 1} / g_2 h_2^{\delta_2})^{n_3 - n_j} \ldots (g_j^{\delta_{j-1} + 1} / g_{j-1} h_{j-1}^{\delta_{j-1}})^{n_j - n_j} \det M_0
$$
$$
= \pm g_2^{n_1 - n_3} g_3^{n_2 - n_4} \ldots g_{j-1}^{n_{j-2} - n_j} g_j^{n_{j-1} - n_j}, \quad (23)
$$

an equation that neatly simplifies to

$$
\det M_0 = \pm h_j. \qquad (24)
$$

(This proof, although stated for the domain of integers, obviously applies to any unique factorization domain.)

In the process of verifying Algorithm C, we have also learned that every element of S dealt with by the algorithm can be expressed as a determinant whose entries are the coefficients of the primitive parts of the original polynomials. A well-known theorem of Hadamard (see exercise 15) states that

$$
|\det(a_{ij})| \leq \prod_{1 \leq i \leq n} \left(\sum_{1 \leq j \leq n} a_{ij}^2 \right)^{1/2}; \qquad (25)
$$

therefore every coefficient appearing in the polynomials computed by Algorithm C is at most

$$
N^{m+n} (m+1)^{n/2} (n+1)^{m/2}, \qquad (26)
$$

if all coefficients of the given polynomials $u(x)$ and $v(x)$ are bounded by N in absolute value. This same upper bound applies to the coefficients of all polynomials $u(x)$ and $v(x)$ computed during the execution of Algorithm E, since the polynomials obtained in Algorithm E are always divisors of the polynomials obtained in Algorithm C.

This upper bound on the coefficients is extremely gratifying, because it is much better than we would ordinarily have a right to expect. For example, consider what happens if we avoid the corrections in steps E3 and C3, merely replacing $v(x)$ by $r(x)$. This is the simplest gcd algorithm, and it is the one that traditionally appears in textbooks on algebra (for theoretical purposes, not intended for practical calculations). If we suppose that $\delta_1 = \delta_2 = \cdots = 1$, we find that the coefficients of $u_3(x)$ are bounded by N^3, the coefficients of $u_4(x)$ are bounded by N^7, those of $u_5(x)$ by N^{17}, ...; the coefficients of $u_k(x)$ are bounded by N^{a_k}, where $a_k = 2a_{k-1} + a_{k-2}$. Thus the upper bound, in place of (26) for $m = n + 1$, would be approximately

$$N^{0.5(2.414)^n}, \tag{27}$$

and experiments show that the simple algorithm does in fact have this behavior; the number of digits in the coefficients grows exponentially at each step! In Algorithm E, by contrast, the growth in the number of digits is only slightly more than linear at most.

Another byproduct of our proof of Algorithm C is the fact that the degrees of the polynomials will almost always decrease by 1 at each step, so that the number of iterations of step C2 (or E2) will usually be $\deg(v)$ if the given polynomials are "random." In order to see why this happens, notice for example that we could have chosen the first eight columns of M and M' in (17) and (18); then we would have found that $u_4(x)$ has degree less than 3 if and only if $d_3 = 0$, that is, if and only if

$$\det \begin{pmatrix} a_8 & a_7 & a_6 & a_5 & a_4 & a_3 & a_2 & a_1 \\ 0 & a_8 & a_7 & a_6 & a_5 & a_4 & a_3 & a_2 \\ 0 & 0 & a_8 & a_7 & a_6 & a_5 & a_4 & a_3 \\ b_6 & b_5 & b_4 & b_3 & b_2 & b_1 & b_0 & 0 \\ 0 & b_6 & b_5 & b_4 & b_3 & b_2 & b_1 & b_0 \\ 0 & 0 & b_6 & b_5 & b_4 & b_3 & b_2 & b_1 \\ 0 & 0 & 0 & b_6 & b_5 & b_4 & b_3 & b_2 \\ 0 & 0 & 0 & 0 & b_6 & b_5 & b_4 & b_3 \end{pmatrix} = 0.$$

In general, δ_j will be greater than 1 for $j > 1$ if and only if a similar determinant in the coefficients of $u(x)$ and $v(x)$ is zero. Since such a determinant is a nonzero multivariate polynomial in the coefficients, it will be nonzero "almost always," or "with probability 1." (See exercise 16 for a more precise formulation of this statement, and see exercise 4 for a related proof.) The example polynomials in (15) have both δ_2 and δ_3 equal to 2, so they are exceptional indeed.

The considerations above can be used to derive the well-known fact that two polynomials are relatively prime if and only if their *resultant* is nonzero; the resultant is a determinant having the form of rows A_5 through A_0 and B_7 through B_0 in Table 1. (This is "Sylvester's determinant"; see exercise 12. Further properties of resultants are discussed in B. L. van der Waerden, *Modern Algebra*, translated by Fred Blum (New York: Ungar, 1949), Sections 27–28.) From the standpoint discussed above, we could say that the gcd is "almost always" of degree zero, since Sylvester's determinant is almost never zero. But many calculations of practical interest would never be undertaken if there weren't some reasonable chance that the gcd would be a polynomial of positive degree.

We can see exactly what happens during Algorithms E and C when the gcd is not 1 by considering $u(x) = w(x)u_1(x)$ and $v(x) = w(x)u_2(x)$, where $u_1(x)$ and $u_2(x)$ are relatively prime and $w(x)$ is primitive. Then if the polynomials $u_1(x)$, $u_2(x)$, $u_3(x)$, ... are obtained when Algorithm E works on $u(x) = u_1(x)$ and $v(x) = u_2(x)$, it is easy to see that the sequence obtained for $u(x) = w(x)u_1(x)$ and $v(x) = w(x)u_2(x)$ is simply $w(x)u_1(x)$, $w(x)u_2(x)$, $w(x)u_3(x)$, $w(x)u_4(x)$, etc. With Algorithm C the behavior is different: If the polynomials $u_1(x)$, $u_2(x)$, $u_3(x)$, ... are obtained when Algorithm C is applied to $u(x) = u_1(x)$ and $v(x) = u_2(x)$, and if we assume that $\deg(u_{j+1}) = \deg(u_j) - 1$ (which is almost always true when $j > 1$), then the sequence

$$w(x)u_1(x), \ w(x)u_2(x), \ \ell^2 w(x)u_3(x), \ \ell^4 w(x)u_4(x), \ \ell^6 w(x)u_5(x), \ \ldots \quad (28)$$

is obtained when Algorithm C is applied to $u(x) = w(x)u_1(x)$ and $v(x) = w(x)u_2(x)$, where $\ell = \ell(w)$. (See exercise 13.) Even though these additional ℓ-factors are present, Algorithm C will be superior to Algorithm E, because it is easier to deal with slightly larger polynomials than to calculate primitive parts repeatedly.

Polynomial remainder sequences such as those in Algorithms C and E are not useful merely for finding greatest common divisors and resultants. Another important application is to the enumeration of real roots, for a given polynomial in a given interval, according to the famous theorem of J. Sturm [*Mém. Présentés par Divers Savants* **6** (Paris, 1835), 271–318]. Let $u(x)$ be a polynomial over the real numbers, having distinct complex roots. We shall see in the next section that the roots are distinct if and only if $\gcd\big(u(x), u'(x)\big) = 1$, where $u'(x)$ is the derivative of $u(x)$; accordingly, there is a polynomial remainder sequence proving that $u(x)$ is relatively prime to $u'(x)$. We set $u_0(x) = u(x)$, $u_1(x) = u'(x)$, and (following Sturm) we negate the sign of all remainders, obtaining

$$\begin{aligned}
c_1 u_0(x) &= u_1(x)q_1(x) - d_1 u_2(x), \\
c_2 u_1(x) &= u_2(x)q_2(x) - d_2 u_3(x), \\
&\vdots \\
c_k u_{k-1}(x) &= u_k(x)q_k(x) - d_k u_{k+1}(x),
\end{aligned} \quad (29)$$

for some positive constants c_j and d_j, where $\deg(u_{k+1}) = 0$. We say that the *variation* $V(u, a)$ of $u(x)$ at a is the number of changes of sign in the sequence $u_0(a)$, $u_1(a)$, ..., $u_{k+1}(a)$, not counting zeros. For example, if the sequence of signs is 0, +, −, −, 0, +, +, −, we have $V(u, a) = 3$. Sturm's theorem asserts that *the number of roots of $u(x)$ in the interval $a < x \le b$ is $V(u, a) - V(u, b)$*; and the proof is surprisingly short (see exercise 22).

Although Algorithms C and E are interesting, they aren't the whole story. Important alternative ways to calculate polynomial gcds over the integers are discussed at the end of Section 4.6.2. There is also a general determinant-evaluation algorithm that may be said to include Algorithm C as a special case; see E. H. Bareiss, *Math. Comp.* **22** (1968), 565–578.

⟨R⟩ *In the fourth edition of this book I plan to redo the exposition of the
present section, taking into proper account the 19th-century research on
determinants, as well as the work of W. Habicht, Comm. Math. Helvetici* **21**
*(1948), 99–116. An excellent discussion of the latter has been given by R. Loos in
Computing, Supplement 4 (1982), 115–137. An interesting method for evaluating
determinants, derived by C. L. Dodgson (aka Lewis Carroll) from a theorem of
Jacobi, is also highly relevant to these methods. See D. E. Knuth, Electronic J.
Combinatorics* **3**, 2 *(1996), paper #R5, §3, for a summary of the early history of
identities between determinants of submatrices.*

EXERCISES

1. [*10*] Compute the pseudo-quotient $q(x)$ and pseudo-remainder $r(x)$, namely the
polynomials satisfying (8), when $u(x) = x^6 + x^5 - x^4 + 2x^3 + 3x^2 - x + 2$ and $v(x) = 2x^3 + 2x^2 - x + 3$, over the integers.

2. [*15*] What is the greatest common divisor of $3x^6 + x^5 + 4x^4 + 4x^3 + 3x^2 + 4x + 2$
and its "reverse" $2x^6 + 4x^5 + 3x^4 + 4x^3 + 4x^2 + x + 3$, modulo 7?

▶ **3.** [*M25*] Show that Euclid's algorithm for polynomials over a field S can be extended
to find polynomials $U(x)$ and $V(x)$ over S such that

$$u(x)V(x) + U(x)v(x) = \gcd(u(x), v(x)).$$

(See Algorithm 4.5.2X.) What are the degrees of the polynomials $U(x)$ and $V(x)$ that
are computed by this extended algorithm? Prove that if S is the field of rational
numbers, and if $u(x) = x^m - 1$ and $v(x) = x^n - 1$, then the extended algorithm yields
polynomials $U(x)$ and $V(x)$ having *integer* coefficients. Find $U(x)$ and $V(x)$ when
$u(x) = x^{21} - 1$ and $v(x) = x^{13} - 1$.

▶ **4.** [*M30*] Let p be prime, and suppose that Euclid's algorithm applied to the polynomials $u(x)$ and $v(x)$ modulo p yields a sequence of polynomials having respective
degrees m, n, n_1, ..., n_t, $-\infty$, where $m = \deg(u)$, $n = \deg(v)$, and $n_t \geq 0$. Assume
that $m \geq n$. If $u(x)$ and $v(x)$ are monic polynomials, independently and uniformly
distributed over all the p^{m+n} pairs of monic polynomials having respective degrees
m and n, what are the average values of the three quantities t, $n_1 + \cdots + n_t$, and
$(n - n_1)n_1 + \cdots + (n_{t-1} - n_t)n_t$, as functions of m, n, and p? (These three quantities
are the fundamental factors in the running time of Euclid's algorithm applied to
polynomials modulo p, assuming that division is done by Algorithm D.) [*Hint:* Show
that $u(x) \bmod v(x)$ is uniformly distributed and independent of $v(x)$.]

5. [*M22*] What is the probability that $u(x)$ and $v(x)$ are relatively prime modulo p,
if $u(x)$ and $v(x)$ are independently and uniformly distributed monic polynomials of
degree n?

6. [*M23*] We have seen that Euclid's Algorithm 4.5.2A for integers can be directly
adapted to an algorithm for the greatest common divisor of polynomials. Can the
binary gcd algorithm, Algorithm 4.5.2B, be adapted in an analogous way to an algorithm that applies to polynomials?

7. [*M10*] What are the units in the domain of all polynomials over a unique factorization domain S?

▶ **8.** [*M22*] Show that if a polynomial with integer coefficients is irreducible over the
domain of integers, it is irreducible when considered as a polynomial over the field of
rational numbers.

9. [*M25*] Let $u(x)$ and $v(x)$ be primitive polynomials over a unique factorization domain S. Prove that $u(x)$ and $v(x)$ are relatively prime if and only if there are polynomials $U(x)$ and $V(x)$ over S such that $u(x)V(x) + U(x)v(x)$ is a polynomial of degree zero. [*Hint:* Extend Algorithm E, as Algorithm 4.5.2A is extended in exercise 3.]

10. [*M28*] Prove that the polynomials over a unique factorization domain form a unique factorization domain. [*Hint:* Use the result of exercise 9 to help show that there is at most one kind of factorization possible.]

11. [*M22*] What row names would have appeared in Table 1 if the sequence of degrees had been 9, 6, 5, 2, $-\infty$ instead of 8, 6, 4, 2, 1, 0?

▶ **12.** [*M24*] Let $u_1(x)$, $u_2(x)$, $u_3(x)$, ... be a sequence of polynomials obtained during a run of Algorithm C. "Sylvester's matrix" is the square matrix formed from rows A_{n_2-1} through A_0 and B_{n_1-1} through B_0 (in a notation analogous to that of Table 1). Show that if $u_1(x)$ and $u_2(x)$ have a common factor of positive degree, then the determinant of Sylvester's matrix is zero; conversely, given that $\deg(u_k) = 0$ for some k, show that the determinant of Sylvester's matrix is nonzero by deriving a formula for its absolute value in terms of $\ell(u_j)$ and $\deg(u_j)$, $1 \le j \le k$.

13. [*M22*] Show that the leading coefficient ℓ of the primitive part of $\gcd\bigl(u(x), v(x)\bigr)$ enters into Algorithm C's polynomial sequence as shown in (28), when $\delta_1 = \delta_2 = \cdots = \delta_{k-1} = 1$. What is the behavior for general δ_j?

14. [*M29*] Let $r(x)$ be the pseudo-remainder when $u(x)$ is pseudo-divided by $v(x)$. If $\deg(u) \ge \deg(v) + 2$ and $\deg(v) \ge \deg(r) + 2$, show that $r(x)$ is a multiple of $\ell(v)$.

15. [*M26*] Prove Hadamard's inequality (25). [*Hint:* Consider the matrix AA^T.]

▶ **16.** [*M22*] Let $f(x_1, \ldots, x_n)$ be a multivariate polynomial that is not identically zero, and let $r(S_1, \ldots, S_n)$ be the set of roots $(x_1, \ldots, x_n)$ of $f(x_1, \ldots, x_n) = 0$ such that $x_1 \in S_1$, ..., $x_n \in S_n$. If the degree of f is at most $d_j \le |S_j|$ in the variable x_j, prove that

$$|r(S_1, \ldots, S_n)| \le |S_1| \ldots |S_n| - (|S_1| - d_1) \ldots (|S_n| - d_n).$$

Therefore the probability of finding a root at random, $|r(S_1, \ldots, S_n)|/|S_1| \ldots |S_n|$, approaches zero as the sets S_j get bigger. [This inequality has many applications in the design of randomized algorithms, because it provides a good way to test whether a complicated sum of products of sums is identically zero without expanding out all the terms.]

17. [*M32*] (*P. M. Cohn's algorithm for division of string polynomials.*) Let A be an *alphabet*, that is, a set of symbols. A *string* α on A is a sequence of $n \ge 0$ symbols, $\alpha = a_1 \ldots a_n$, where each a_j is in A. The *length* of α, denoted by $|\alpha|$, is the number n of symbols. A *string polynomial* on A is a finite sum $U = \sum_k r_k \alpha_k$, where each r_k is a nonzero rational number and each α_k is a string on A; we assume that $\alpha_j \ne \alpha_k$ when $j \ne k$. The *degree* of U, $\deg(U)$, is defined to be $-\infty$ if $U = 0$ (that is, if the sum is empty), otherwise $\deg(U) = \max |\alpha_k|$. The sum and product of string polynomials are defined in an obvious manner; thus, $(\sum_j r_j \alpha_j)(\sum_k s_k \beta_k) = \sum_{j,k} r_j s_k \alpha_j \beta_k$, where the product of two strings is obtained by simply juxtaposing them, after which we collect like terms. For example, if $A = \{a, b\}$, $U = ab + ba - 2a - 2b$, and $V = a + b - 1$, then $\deg(U) = 2$, $\deg(V) = 1$, $V^2 = aa + ab + ba + bb - 2a - 2b + 1$, and $V^2 - U = aa + bb + 1$. Clearly $\deg(UV) = \deg(U) + \deg(V)$, and $\deg(U + V) \le \max(\deg(U), \deg(V))$, with equality in the latter formula if $\deg(U) \ne \deg(V)$. (String polynomials may be regarded as ordinary multivariate polynomials over the field of rational numbers, except that the variables are *not commutative* under multiplication. In the conventional language of pure mathematics, the set of string polynomials with the operations defined here is the "free associative algebra" generated by A over the rationals.)

a) Let Q_1, Q_2, U, and V be string polynomials with $\deg(U) \geq \deg(V)$ and such that $\deg(Q_1 U - Q_2 V) < \deg(Q_1 U)$. Give an algorithm to find a string polynomial Q such that $\deg(U - QV) < \deg(U)$. (Thus if we are given U and V such that $Q_1 U = Q_2 V + R$ and $\deg(R) < \deg(Q_1 U)$, for some Q_1 and Q_2, then there is a solution to these conditions with $Q_1 = 1$.)

b) Given that U and V are string polynomials with $\deg(V) > \deg(Q_1 U - Q_2 V)$ for some Q_1 and Q_2, show that the result of (a) can be improved to find a quotient Q such that $U = QV + R$, $\deg(R) < \deg(V)$. (This is the analog of (1) for string polynomials; part (a) showed that we can make $\deg(R) < \deg(U)$, under weaker hypotheses.)

c) A *homogeneous polynomial* is one whose terms all have the same degree (length). If U_1, U_2, V_1, V_2 are homogeneous string polynomials with $U_1 V_1 = U_2 V_2$ and $\deg(V_1) \geq \deg(V_2)$, show that there is a homogeneous string polynomial U such that $U_2 = U_1 U$ and $V_1 = U V_2$.

d) Given that U and V are homogeneous string polynomials with $UV = VU$, prove that there is a homogeneous string polynomial W such that $U = rW^m$, $V = sW^n$ for some integers m, n and rational numbers r, s. Give an algorithm to compute such a W having the largest possible degree. (This algorithm is of interest, for example, when $U = \alpha$ and $V = \beta$ are strings satisfying $\alpha\beta = \beta\alpha$; then W is simply a string γ. When $U = x^m$ and $V = x^n$, the solution of largest degree is the string $W = x^{\gcd(m,n)}$, so this algorithm includes a gcd algorithm for integers as a special case.)

▶ **18.** [*M24*] (*Euclidean algorithm for string polynomials.*) Let V_1 and V_2 be string polynomials, not both zero, having a *common left multiple*. (This means that there exist string polynomials U_1 and U_2, not both zero, such that $U_1 V_1 = U_2 V_2$.) The purpose of this exercise is to find an algorithm to compute their *greatest common right divisor* $\gcd(V_1, V_2)$ and their *least common left multiple* $\mathrm{lclm}(V_1, V_2)$. The latter quantities are defined as follows: $\gcd(V_1, V_2)$ is a common right divisor of V_1 and V_2 (that is, $V_1 = W_1 \gcd(V_1, V_2)$ and $V_2 = W_2 \gcd(V_1, V_2)$ for some W_1 and W_2), and any common right divisor of V_1 and V_2 is a right divisor of $\gcd(V_1, V_2)$; $\mathrm{lclm}(V_1, V_2) = Z_1 V_1 = Z_2 V_2$ for some Z_1 and Z_2, and any common left multiple of V_1 and V_2 is a left multiple of $\mathrm{lclm}(V_1, V_2)$.

For example, let $U_1 = abbbab + abbab - bbab + ab - 1$, $V_1 = babab + abab + ab - b$; $U_2 = abb + ab - b$, $V_2 = babbabab + bababab + babab + abab - babb - 1$. Then we have $U_1 V_1 = U_2 V_2 = abbbabbabab + abbabbabab + abbbababab + abbababab - bbabbabab + abbbabab - bbababab + 2abbabab - abbbabb + ababab - abbabb - bbabab - babab + bbabb - abb - ab + b$. For these string polynomials it can be shown that $\gcd(V_1, V_2) = ab + 1$, and $\mathrm{lclm}(V_1, V_2) = U_1 V_1$.

The division algorithm of exercise 17 may be restated thus: If V_1 and V_2 are string polynomials, with $V_2 \neq 0$, and if $U_1 \neq 0$ and U_2 satisfy the equation $U_1 V_1 = U_2 V_2$, then there exist string polynomials Q and R such that

$$V_1 = QV_2 + R, \qquad \text{where } \deg(R) < \deg(V_2).$$

It follows readily that Q and R are uniquely determined; they do not depend on the given U_1 and U_2. Furthermore the result is right-left symmetric, in the sense that

$$U_2 = U_1 Q + R', \qquad \text{where } \deg(R') = \deg(U_1) - \deg(V_2) + \deg(R) < \deg(U_1).$$

Show that this division algorithm can be extended to an algorithm that computes $\text{lclm}(V_1, V_2)$ and $\text{gcrd}(V_1, V_2)$; in fact, the extended algorithm finds string polynomials Z_1 and Z_2 such that $Z_1 V_1 + Z_2 V_2 = \text{gcrd}(V_1, V_2)$. [*Hint:* Use auxiliary variables u_1, u_2, v_1, v_2, w_1, w_2, w_1', w_2', z_1, z_2, z_1', z_2', whose values are string polynomials; start by setting $u_1 \leftarrow U_1$, $u_2 \leftarrow U_2$, $v_1 \leftarrow V_1$, $v_2 \leftarrow V_2$, and throughout the algorithm maintain the conditions

$$
\begin{aligned}
U_1 w_1 + U_2 w_2 &= u_1, & z_1 V_1 + z_2 V_2 &= v_1, \\
U_1 w_1' + U_2 w_2' &= u_2, & z_1' V_1 + z_2' V_2 &= v_2, \\
u_1 z_1 - u_2 z_1' &= (-1)^n U_1, & w_1 v_1 - w_1' v_2 &= (-1)^n V_1, \\
-u_1 z_2 + u_2 z_2' &= (-1)^n U_2, & -w_2 v_1 + w_2' v_2 &= (-1)^n V_2
\end{aligned}
$$

at the nth iteration. This might be regarded as the "ultimate" extension of Euclid's algorithm.]

19. [*M39*] (*Common divisors of square matrices.*) Exercise 18 shows that the concept of greatest common right divisor can be meaningful when multiplication is not commutative. Prove that any two $n \times n$ matrices A and B of integers have a greatest common right matrix divisor D. [*Suggestion:* Design an algorithm whose inputs are A and B, and whose outputs are integer matrices D, P, Q, X, Y, where $A = PD$, $B = QD$, and $D = XA + YB$.] Find a greatest common right divisor of the matrices $\left(\begin{smallmatrix} 1 & 2 \\ 3 & 4 \end{smallmatrix}\right)$ and $\left(\begin{smallmatrix} 4 & 3 \\ 2 & 1 \end{smallmatrix}\right)$.

20. [*M40*] Investigate *approximate* polynomial gcds and the accuracy of Euclid's algorithm: What can be said about calculation of the greatest common divisor of polynomials whose coefficients are floating point numbers?

21. [*M25*] Prove that the computation time required by Algorithm C to compute the gcd of two nth degree polynomials over the integers is $O(n^4 (\log Nn)^2)$, if the coefficients of the given polynomials are bounded by N in absolute value.

22. [*M23*] Prove Sturm's theorem. [*Hint:* Some sign sequences are impossible.]

23. [*M22*] Prove that if $u(x)$ in (29) has $\deg(u)$ real roots, then we have $\deg(u_{j+1}) = \deg(u_j) - 1$ for $0 \le j \le k$.

24. [*M21*] Show that (19) simplifies to (20) and (23) simplifies to (24).

25. [*M24*] (W. S. Brown.) Prove that all the polynomials $u_j(x)$ in (16) for $j \ge 3$ are multiples of $\gcd(\ell(u), \ell(v))$, and explain how to improve Algorithm C accordingly.

▶ **26.** [*M26*] The purpose of this exercise is to give an analog for polynomials of the fact that continued fractions with positive integer entries give the best approximations to real numbers (exercise 4.5.3–42).

Let $u(x)$ and $v(x)$ be polynomials over a field, with $\deg(u) > \deg(v)$, and let $a_1(x)$, $a_2(x)$, ... be the quotient polynomials when Euclid's algorithm is applied to $u(x)$ and $v(x)$. For example, the sequence of quotients in (5) and (6) is $9x^2 + 7$, $5x^2 + 5$, $6x^3 + 5x^2 + 6x + 5$, $9x + 12$. We wish to show that the convergents $p_n(x)/q_n(x)$ of the continued fraction $// a_1(x), a_2(x), \ldots //$ are the "best approximations" of low degree to the rational function $v(x)/u(x)$, where we have $p_n(x) = K_{n-1}(a_2(x), \ldots, a_n(x))$ and $q_n(x) = K_n(a_1(x), \ldots, a_n(x))$ in terms of the continuant polynomials of Eq. 4.5.3–(4). By convention, we let $p_0(x) = q_{-1}(x) = 0$, $p_{-1}(x) = q_0(x) = 1$.

Prove that if $p(x)$ and $q(x)$ are polynomials such that $\deg(q) < \deg(q_n)$ and $\deg(pu - qv) \le \deg(p_{n-1}u - q_{n-1}v)$, for some $n \ge 1$, then $p(x) = cp_{n-1}(x)$ and $q(x) = cq_{n-1}(x)$ for some constant c. In particular, each $q_n(x)$ is a "record-breaking" polynomial in the sense that no nonzero polynomial $q(x)$ of smaller degree can make the quantity $p(x)u(x) - q(x)v(x)$, for any polynomial $p(x)$, achieve a degree as small as $p_n(x)u(x) - q_n(x)v(x)$.

27. [*M23*] Suggest a way to speed up the division of $u(x)$ by $v(x)$ when we know in advance that the remainder will be zero.

*4.6.2. Factorization of Polynomials

Let us now consider the problem of *factoring* polynomials, not merely finding the greatest common divisor of two or more of them.

Factoring modulo p. As in the case of integer numbers (Sections 4.5.2, 4.5.4), the problem of factoring seems to be more difficult than finding the greatest common divisor. But factorization of polynomials modulo a prime integer p is not as hard to do as we might expect. It is much easier to find the factors of an arbitrary polynomial of degree n, modulo 2, than to use any known method to find the factors of an arbitrary n-bit binary number. This surprising situation is a consequence of an instructive factorization algorithm discovered in 1967 by Elwyn R. Berlekamp [*Bell System Technical J.* **46** (1967), 1853–1859].

Let p be a prime number; all arithmetic on polynomials in the following discussion will be done modulo p. Suppose that someone has given us a polynomial $u(x)$, whose coefficients are chosen from the set $\{0, 1, \ldots, p - 1\}$; we may assume that $u(x)$ is monic. Our goal is to express $u(x)$ in the form

$$u(x) = p_1(x)^{e_1} \ldots p_r(x)^{e_r}, \tag{1}$$

where $p_1(x)$, $\ldots$, $p_r(x)$ are distinct, monic, irreducible polynomials.

As a first step, we can use a standard technique to determine whether any of the exponents $e_1, \ldots, e_r$ are greater than unity. If

$$u(x) = u_n x^n + \cdots + u_0 = v(x)^2 w(x), \tag{2}$$

then the derivative (formed in the usual way, but modulo p) is

$$u'(x) = n u_n x^{n-1} + \cdots + u_1 = 2v(x)v'(x)w(x) + v(x)^2 w'(x), \tag{3}$$

and this is a multiple of the squared factor $v(x)$. Therefore our first step in factoring $u(x)$ is to form

$$\gcd\big(u(x), u'(x)\big) = d(x). \tag{4}$$

If $d(x)$ is equal to 1, we know that $u(x)$ is *squarefree*, the product of distinct primes $p_1(x) \ldots p_r(x)$. If $d(x)$ is not equal to 1 and $d(x) \neq u(x)$, then $d(x)$ is a proper factor of $u(x)$; the relation between the factors of $d(x)$ and the factors of $u(x)/d(x)$ speeds up the factorization process nicely in this case (see exercises 34 and 36). Finally, if $d(x) = u(x)$, we must have $u'(x) = 0$; hence the coefficient u_k of x^k is nonzero only when k is a multiple of p. This means that $u(x)$ can be written as a polynomial of the form $v(x^p)$, and in such a case we have

$$u(x) = v(x^p) = \big(v(x)\big)^p; \tag{5}$$

the factorization process can be completed by finding the irreducible factors of $v(x)$ and raising them to the pth power.

Identity (5) may appear somewhat strange to the reader; it is an important fact that is basic to Berlekamp's algorithm and to several other methods we shall discuss. We can prove it as follows: If $v_1(x)$ and $v_2(x)$ are any polynomials modulo p, then

$$\big(v_1(x)+v_2(x)\big)^p = v_1(x)^p + \binom{p}{1}v_1(x)^{p-1}v_2(x) + \cdots + \binom{p}{p-1}v_1(x)v_2(x)^{p-1} + v_2(x)^p$$
$$= v_1(x)^p + v_2(x)^p,$$

since the binomial coefficients $\binom{p}{1}, \ldots, \binom{p}{p-1}$ are all multiples of p. Furthermore if a is any integer, we have $a^p \equiv a$ (modulo p) by Fermat's theorem. Therefore when $v(x) = v_m x^m + v_{m-1}x^{m-1} + \cdots + v_0$, we find that

$$v(x)^p = (v_m x^m)^p + (v_{m-1}x^{m-1})^p + \cdots + (v_0)^p$$
$$= v_m x^{mp} + v_{m-1}x^{(m-1)p} + \cdots + v_0 = v(x^p).$$

The remarks above show that the problem of factoring a polynomial reduces to the problem of factoring a squarefree polynomial. Let us therefore assume that

$$u(x) = p_1(x)p_2(x)\ldots p_r(x) \qquad (6)$$

is the product of distinct primes. How can we be clever enough to discover the $p_j(x)$'s when only $u(x)$ is given? Berlekamp's idea is to make use of the Chinese remainder theorem, which is valid for polynomials just as it is valid for integers (see exercise 3). If $(s_1, s_2, \ldots, s_r)$ is any r-tuple of integers mod p, the Chinese remainder theorem implies that *there is a unique polynomial $v(x)$ such that*

$$v(x) \equiv s_1 \;\big(\text{modulo } p_1(x)\big), \quad \ldots, \quad v(x) \equiv s_r \;\big(\text{modulo } p_r(x)\big),$$
$$\deg(v) < \deg(p_1) + \deg(p_2) + \cdots + \deg(p_r) = \deg(u). \qquad (7)$$

The notation "$g(x) \equiv h(x) \;\big(\text{modulo } f(x)\big)$" that appears here has the same meaning as "$g(x) \equiv h(x) \;\big(\text{modulo } f(x) \text{ and } p\big)$" in exercise 3.2.2–11, since we are considering polynomial arithmetic modulo p. The polynomial $v(x)$ in (7) gives us a way to get at the factors of $u(x)$, for if $r \geq 2$ and $s_1 \neq s_2$, we will have $\gcd\big(u(x), v(x) - s_1\big)$ divisible by $p_1(x)$ but not by $p_2(x)$.

Since this observation shows that we can get information about the factors of $u(x)$ from appropriate solutions $v(x)$ of (7), let us analyze (7) more closely. In the first place we can observe that the polynomial $v(x)$ satisfies the condition $v(x)^p \equiv s_j^p = s_j \equiv v(x) \;\big(\text{modulo } p_j(x)\big)$ for $1 \leq j \leq r$; therefore

$$v(x)^p \equiv v(x) \;\big(\text{modulo } u(x)\big), \qquad \deg(v) < \deg(u). \qquad (8)$$

In the second place we have the basic polynomial identity

$$x^p - x \equiv (x - 0)(x - 1)\ldots\big(x - (p-1)\big) \;(\text{modulo } p) \qquad (9)$$

(see exercise 6); hence

$$v(x)^p - v(x) = \big(v(x) - 0\big)\big(v(x) - 1\big)\ldots\big(v(x) - (p-1)\big) \qquad (10)$$

is an identity for any polynomial $v(x)$, when we are working modulo p. If $v(x)$ satisfies (8), it follows that $u(x)$ divides the left-hand side of (10), so every irreducible factor of $u(x)$ must divide one of the p relatively prime factors of the right-hand side of (10). In other words, *all* solutions of (8) must have the form of (7), for some $s_1, s_2, \ldots, s_r$; there are exactly p^r solutions of (8).

The solutions $v(x)$ to congruence (8) therefore provide a key to the factorization of $u(x)$. It may seem harder to find all solutions to (8) than to factor $u(x)$ in the first place, but in fact this is not true, since the set of solutions to (8) is closed under addition. Let $\deg(u) = n$; we can construct the $n \times n$ matrix

$$Q = \begin{pmatrix} q_{0,0} & q_{0,1} & \cdots & q_{0,n-1} \\ \vdots & \vdots & & \vdots \\ q_{n-1,0} & q_{n-1,1} & \cdots & q_{n-1,n-1} \end{pmatrix} \qquad (11)$$

where

$$x^{pk} \equiv q_{k,n-1}x^{n-1} + \cdots + q_{k,1}x + q_{k,0} \pmod{u(x)}. \qquad (12)$$

Then $v(x) = v_{n-1}x^{n-1} + \cdots + v_1 x + v_0$ is a solution to (8) if and only if

$$(v_0, v_1, \ldots, v_{n-1})Q = (v_0, v_1, \ldots, v_{n-1}); \qquad (13)$$

for the latter equation holds if and only if

$$v(x) = \sum_j v_j x^j = \sum_j \sum_k v_k q_{k,j} x^j \equiv \sum_k v_k x^{pk} = v(x^p) \equiv v(x)^p \pmod{u(x)}.$$

Berlekamp's factoring algorithm therefore proceeds as follows:

B1. [Remove duplicate factors.] Ensure that $u(x)$ is squarefree; in other words, if $\gcd(u(x), u'(x)) \neq 1$, reduce the problem of factoring $u(x)$, as stated earlier in this section.

B2. [Get Q.] Form the matrix Q defined by (11) and (12). This can be done in different ways, depending on the size of p, as explained below.

B3. [Find null space.] "Triangularize" the matrix $Q - I$, where $I = (\delta_{ij})$ is the $n \times n$ identity matrix, finding its rank $n - r$ and finding linearly independent vectors $v^{[1]}, \ldots, v^{[r]}$ such that $v^{[j]}(Q - I) = (0, 0, \ldots, 0)$ for $1 \leq j \leq r$. (The first vector $v^{[1]}$ may always be taken as $(1, 0, \ldots, 0)$, representing the trivial solution $v^{[1]}(x) = 1$ to (8). The computation can be done using appropriate column operations, as explained in Algorithm N below.) *At this point, r is the number of irreducible factors of $u(x)$, because the solutions to (8) are the p^r polynomials corresponding to the vectors $t_1 v^{[1]} + \cdots + t_r v^{[r]}$ for all choices of integers $0 \leq t_1, \ldots, t_r < p$. Therefore if $r = 1$ we know that $u(x)$ is irreducible, and the procedure terminates.*

B4. [Split.] Calculate $\gcd(u(x), v^{[2]}(x) - s)$ for $0 \leq s < p$, where $v^{[2]}(x)$ is the polynomial represented by vector $v^{[2]}$. The result will be a nontrivial factorization of $u(x)$, because $v^{[2]}(x) - s$ is nonzero and has degree less than $\deg(u)$, and by exercise 7 we have

$$u(x) = \prod_{0 \leq s < p} \gcd(v(x) - s, u(x)) \qquad (14)$$

whenever $v(x)$ satisfies (8).

If the use of $v^{[2]}(x)$ does not succeed in splitting $u(x)$ into r factors, further factors can be obtained by calculating $\gcd\big(v^{[k]}(x) - s, w(x)\big)$ for $0 \leq s < p$ and all factors $w(x)$ found so far, for $k = 3, 4, \ldots$, until r factors are obtained. (If we choose $s_i \neq s_j$ in (7), we obtain a solution $v(x)$ to (8) that distinguishes $p_i(x)$ from $p_j(x)$; some $v^{[k]}(x) - s$ will be divisible by $p_i(x)$ and not by $p_j(x)$, so this procedure will eventually find all of the factors.)

If p is 2 or 3, the calculations of this step are quite efficient; but if p is more than 25, say, there is a much better way to proceed, as we shall see later. ∎

Historical notes: M. C. R. Butler [*Quart. J. Math.* **5** (1954), 102–107] observed that the matrix $Q - I$ corresponding to a squarefree polynomial with r irreducible factors will have rank $n - r$, modulo p. Indeed, this fact was implicit in a more general result of K. Petr [*Časopis pro Pěstování Matematiky a Fysiky* **66** (1937), 85–94], who determined the characteristic polynomial of Q. See also Š. Schwarz, *Quart. J. Math.* **7** (1956), 110–124.

As an example of Algorithm B, let us now determine the factorization of

$$u(x) = x^8 + x^6 + 10x^4 + 10x^3 + 8x^2 + 2x + 8 \tag{15}$$

modulo 13. (This polynomial appears in several of the examples in Section 4.6.1.) A quick calculation using Algorithm 4.6.1E shows that $\gcd\big(u(x), u'(x)\big) = 1$; therefore $u(x)$ is squarefree, and we turn to step B2. Step B2 involves calculating the Q matrix, which in this case is an 8×8 array. The first row of Q is always $(1, 0, 0, \ldots, 0)$, representing the polynomial $x^0 \bmod u(x) = 1$. The second row represents $x^{13} \bmod u(x)$, and, in general, $x^k \bmod u(x)$ may readily be determined as follows (for relatively small values of k): If

$$u(x) = x^n + u_{n-1}x^{n-1} + \cdots + u_1 x + u_0$$

and if

$$x^k \equiv a_{k,n-1}x^{n-1} + \cdots + a_{k,1}x + a_{k,0} \big(\text{modulo } u(x)\big),$$

then

$$x^{k+1} \equiv a_{k,n-1}x^n + \cdots + a_{k,1}x^2 + a_{k,0}x$$
$$\equiv a_{k,n-1}\big(-u_{n-1}x^{n-1} - \cdots - u_1 x - u_0\big) + a_{k,n-2}x^{n-1} + \cdots + a_{k,0}x$$
$$= a_{k+1,n-1}x^{n-1} + \cdots + a_{k+1,1}x + a_{k+1,0},$$

where

$$a_{k+1,j} = a_{k,j-1} - a_{k,n-1}u_j. \tag{16}$$

In this formula $a_{k,-1}$ is treated as zero, so that $a_{k+1,0} = -a_{k,n-1}u_0$. The simple "shift register" recurrence (16) makes it easy to calculate $x^k \bmod u(x)$ for $k = 1$, $2, 3, \ldots, (n-1)p$. Inside a computer, this calculation is of course generally done by maintaining a one-dimensional array $(a_{n-1}, \ldots, a_1, a_0)$ and repeatedly setting

$$t \leftarrow a_{n-1}, \ a_{n-1} \leftarrow (a_{n-2} - tu_{n-1}) \bmod p, \ \ldots, \ a_1 \leftarrow (a_0 - tu_1) \bmod p,$$

and $a_0 \leftarrow (-tu_0) \bmod p$. (We have seen similar procedures in connection with random number generation, 3.2.2–(10).) For the example polynomial $u(x)$ in (15), we obtain the following sequence of coefficients of $x^k \bmod u(x)$, using arithmetic modulo 13:

k	$a_{k,7}$	$a_{k,6}$	$a_{k,5}$	$a_{k,4}$	$a_{k,3}$	$a_{k,2}$	$a_{k,1}$	$a_{k,0}$
0	0	0	0	0	0	0	0	1
1	0	0	0	0	0	0	1	0
2	0	0	0	0	0	1	0	0
3	0	0	0	0	1	0	0	0
4	0	0	0	1	0	0	0	0
5	0	0	1	0	0	0	0	0
6	0	1	0	0	0	0	0	0
7	1	0	0	0	0	0	0	0
8	0	12	0	3	3	5	11	5
9	12	0	3	3	5	11	5	0
10	0	4	3	2	8	0	2	8
11	4	3	2	8	0	2	8	0
12	3	11	8	12	1	2	5	7
13	11	5	12	10	11	7	1	2

Therefore the second row of Q is $(2, 1, 7, 11, 10, 12, 5, 11)$. Similarly we may determine $x^{26} \bmod u(x), \ldots, x^{91} \bmod u(x)$, and we find that

$$Q = \begin{pmatrix} 1 & 0 & 0 & 0 & 0 & 0 & 0 & 0 \\ 2 & 1 & 7 & 11 & 10 & 12 & 5 & 11 \\ 3 & 6 & 4 & 3 & 0 & 4 & 7 & 2 \\ 4 & 3 & 6 & 5 & 1 & 6 & 2 & 3 \\ 2 & 11 & 8 & 8 & 3 & 1 & 3 & 11 \\ 6 & 11 & 8 & 6 & 2 & 7 & 10 & 9 \\ 5 & 11 & 7 & 10 & 0 & 11 & 7 & 12 \\ 3 & 3 & 12 & 5 & 0 & 11 & 9 & 12 \end{pmatrix},$$

$$Q - I = \begin{pmatrix} 0 & 0 & 0 & 0 & 0 & 0 & 0 & 0 \\ 2 & 0 & 7 & 11 & 10 & 12 & 5 & 11 \\ 3 & 6 & 3 & 3 & 0 & 4 & 7 & 2 \\ 4 & 3 & 6 & 4 & 1 & 6 & 2 & 3 \\ 2 & 11 & 8 & 8 & 2 & 1 & 3 & 11 \\ 6 & 11 & 8 & 6 & 2 & 6 & 10 & 9 \\ 5 & 11 & 7 & 10 & 0 & 11 & 6 & 12 \\ 3 & 3 & 12 & 5 & 0 & 11 & 9 & 11 \end{pmatrix}.$$

$$(17)$$

That finishes step B2; the next step of Berlekamp's procedure requires finding the "null space" of $Q - I$. In general, suppose that A is an $n \times n$ matrix over a field, whose rank $n - r$ is to be determined; suppose further that we wish to determine linearly independent vectors $v^{[1]}, v^{[2]}, \ldots, v^{[r]}$ such that $v^{[1]}A = v^{[2]}A = \cdots = v^{[r]}A = (0, \ldots, 0)$. An algorithm for this calculation can be based on the observation that any column of A may be multiplied by a nonzero quantity, and any multiple of one of its columns may be added to a different column, without changing the rank or the vectors $v^{[1]}, \ldots, v^{[r]}$. (These transformations amount to replacing A by AB, where B is a nonsingular matrix.) The following well-known "triangularization" procedure may therefore be used.

Algorithm N (*Null space algorithm*). Let A be an $n \times n$ matrix, whose elements a_{ij} belong to a field and have subscripts in the range $0 \leq i, j < n$. This algorithm outputs r vectors $v^{[1]}, \ldots, v^{[r]}$, which are linearly independent over the field and satisfy $v^{[j]}A = (0, \ldots, 0)$, where $n - r$ is the rank of A.

N1. [Initialize.] Set $c_0 \leftarrow c_1 \leftarrow \cdots \leftarrow c_{n-1} \leftarrow -1$, $r \leftarrow 0$. (During the calculation we will have $c_j \geq 0$ only if $a_{c_j j} = -1$ and all other entries of row c_j are zero.)

N2. [Loop on k.] Do step N3 for $k = 0, 1, \ldots, n - 1$, then terminate the algorithm.

N3. [Scan row for dependence.] If there is some j in the range $0 \leq j < n$ such that $a_{kj} \neq 0$ and $c_j < 0$, then do the following: Multiply column j of A by $-1/a_{kj}$ (so that a_{kj} becomes equal to -1); then add a_{ki} times column j to column i for all $i \neq j$; finally set $c_j \leftarrow k$. (Since it is not difficult to show that $a_{sj} = 0$ for all $s < k$, these operations have no effect on rows $0, 1, \ldots, k - 1$ of A.)

   On the other hand, if there is no j in the range $0 \leq j < n$ such that $a_{kj} \neq 0$ and $c_j < 0$, then set $r \leftarrow r + 1$ and output the vector

$$v^{[r]} = (v_0, v_1, \ldots, v_{n-1})$$

defined by the rule

$$v_j = \begin{cases} a_{ks}, & \text{if } c_s = j \geq 0; \\ 1, & \text{if } j = k; \\ 0, & \text{otherwise.} \end{cases} \tag{18}$$

   An example will reveal the mechanism of this algorithm. Let A be the matrix $Q - I$ of (17) over the field of integers modulo 13. When $k = 0$, we output the vector $v^{[1]} = (1, 0, 0, 0, 0, 0, 0, 0)$. When $k = 1$, we may take j in step N3 to be either 0, 2, 3, 4, 5, 6, or 7; the choice here is completely arbitrary, although it affects the particular vectors that are chosen to be output by the algorithm. For hand calculation, it is most convenient to pick $j = 5$, since $a_{15} = 12 = -1$ already; the column operations of step N3 then change A to the matrix

$$\begin{pmatrix} 0 & 0 & 0 & 0 & 0 & 0 & 0 & 0 \\ 0 & 0 & 0 & 0 & 0 & \text{⑫} & 0 & 0 \\ 11 & 6 & 5 & 8 & 1 & 4 & 1 & 7 \\ 3 & 3 & 9 & 5 & 9 & 6 & 6 & 4 \\ 4 & 11 & 2 & 6 & 12 & 1 & 8 & 9 \\ 5 & 11 & 11 & 7 & 10 & 6 & 1 & 10 \\ 1 & 11 & 6 & 1 & 6 & 11 & 9 & 3 \\ 12 & 3 & 11 & 9 & 6 & 11 & 12 & 2 \end{pmatrix}.$$

(The circled element in column "5", row "1", is used here to indicate that $c_5 = 1$. Remember that Algorithm N numbers the rows and columns of the matrix starting with 0, not 1.) When $k = 2$, we may choose $j = 4$ and proceed in a similar way, obtaining the following matrices, which all have the same null space as $Q - I$:

$$k = 2$$

$$\begin{pmatrix} 0 & 0 & 0 & 0 & 0 & 0 & 0 & 0 \\ 0 & 0 & 0 & 0 & 0 & \boxed{12} & 0 & 0 \\ 0 & 0 & 0 & 0 & \boxed{12} & 0 & 0 & 0 \\ 8 & 1 & 3 & 11 & 4 & 9 & 10 & 6 \\ 2 & 4 & 7 & 1 & 1 & 5 & 9 & 3 \\ 12 & 3 & 0 & 5 & 3 & 5 & 4 & 5 \\ 0 & 1 & 2 & 5 & 7 & 0 & 3 & 0 \\ 11 & 6 & 7 & 0 & 7 & 0 & 6 & 12 \end{pmatrix}$$

$$k = 3$$

$$\begin{pmatrix} 0 & 0 & 0 & 0 & 0 & 0 & 0 & 0 \\ 0 & 0 & 0 & 0 & 0 & \boxed{12} & 0 & 0 \\ 0 & 0 & 0 & 0 & \boxed{12} & 0 & 0 & 0 \\ 0 & \boxed{12} & 0 & 0 & 0 & 0 & 0 & 0 \\ 9 & 9 & 8 & 9 & 11 & 8 & 8 & 5 \\ 1 & 10 & 4 & 11 & 4 & 4 & 0 & 0 \\ 5 & 12 & 12 & 7 & 3 & 4 & 6 & 7 \\ 2 & 7 & 2 & 12 & 9 & 11 & 11 & 2 \end{pmatrix}$$

$$k = 4$$

$$\begin{pmatrix} 0 & 0 & 0 & 0 & 0 & 0 & 0 & 0 \\ 0 & 0 & 0 & 0 & 0 & \boxed{12} & 0 & 0 \\ 0 & 0 & 0 & 0 & \boxed{12} & 0 & 0 & 0 \\ 0 & \boxed{12} & 0 & 0 & 0 & 0 & 0 & 0 \\ 0 & 0 & 0 & 0 & 0 & 0 & 0 & \boxed{12} \\ 1 & 10 & 4 & 11 & 4 & 4 & 0 & 0 \\ 8 & 2 & 6 & 10 & 11 & 11 & 0 & 9 \\ 1 & 6 & 4 & 11 & 2 & 0 & 0 & 10 \end{pmatrix}$$

$$k = 5$$

$$\begin{pmatrix} 0 & 0 & 0 & 0 & 0 & 0 & 0 & 0 \\ 0 & 0 & 0 & 0 & 0 & \boxed{12} & 0 & 0 \\ 0 & 0 & 0 & 0 & \boxed{12} & 0 & 0 & 0 \\ 0 & \boxed{12} & 0 & 0 & 0 & 0 & 0 & 0 \\ 0 & 0 & 0 & 0 & 0 & 0 & 0 & \boxed{12} \\ \boxed{12} & 0 & 0 & 0 & 0 & 0 & 0 & 0 \\ 5 & 0 & 0 & 0 & 5 & 5 & 0 & 9 \\ 12 & 9 & 0 & 0 & 11 & 9 & 0 & 10 \end{pmatrix}$$

Now every column that has no circled entry is completely zero; so when $k = 6$ and $k = 7$ the algorithm outputs two more vectors, namely

$$v^{[2]} = (0, 5, 5, 0, 9, 5, 1, 0), \qquad v^{[3]} = (0, 9, 11, 9, 10, 12, 0, 1).$$

From the form of matrix A after $k = 5$, it is evident that these vectors satisfy the equation $vA = (0, \ldots, 0)$. Since the computation has produced three linearly independent vectors, $u(x)$ must have exactly three irreducible factors.

Finally we can go to step B4 of the factoring procedure. The calculation of $\gcd\bigl(u(x),\, v^{[2]}(x) - s\bigr)$ for $0 \le s < 13$, where $v^{[2]}(x) = x^6 + 5x^5 + 9x^4 + 5x^2 + 5x$, gives $x^5 + 5x^4 + 9x^3 + 5x + 5$ as the answer when $s = 0$, and $x^3 + 8x^2 + 4x + 12$ when $s = 2$; the gcd is unity for other values of s. Therefore $v^{[2]}(x)$ gives us only two of the three factors. Turning to $\gcd\bigl(v^{[3]}(x) - s,\, x^5 + 5x^4 + 9x^3 + 5x + 5\bigr)$, where $v^{[3]}(x) = x^7 + 12x^5 + 10x^4 + 9x^3 + 11x^2 + 9x$, we obtain the factor $x^4 + 2x^3 + 3x^2 + 4x + 6$ when $s = 6$, $x + 3$ when $s = 8$, and unity otherwise. Thus the complete factorization is

$$u(x) = (x^4 + 2x^3 + 3x^2 + 4x + 6)(x^3 + 8x^2 + 4x + 12)(x + 3). \qquad (19)$$

Let us now estimate the running time of Berlekamp's method when an nth degree polynomial is factored modulo p. First assume that p is relatively small, so that the four arithmetic operations can be done modulo p in essentially a fixed length of time. (Division modulo p can be converted to multiplication, by storing a table of reciprocals as suggested in exercise 9; for example, when working modulo 13, we have $\frac{1}{2} = 7$, $\frac{1}{3} = 9$, etc.) The computation in step B1 takes $O(n^2)$ units of time; step B2 takes $O(pn^2)$. For step B3 we use Algorithm N, which requires $O(n^3)$ units of time at most. Finally, in step B4 we can observe that the calculation of $\gcd\big(f(x), g(x)\big)$ by Euclid's algorithm takes $O\big(\deg(f)\deg(g)\big)$ units of time; hence the calculation of $\gcd\big(v^{[j]}(x) - s, w(x)\big)$ for fixed j and s and for all factors $w(x)$ of $u(x)$ found so far takes $O(n^2)$ units. Step B4 therefore requires $O(prn^2)$ units of time at most. *Berlekamp's procedure factors an arbitrary polynomial of degree n, modulo p, in $O(n^3 + prn^2)$ steps,* when p is a small prime; and exercise 5 shows that the average number of factors, r, is approximately $\ln n$. Thus the algorithm is much faster than any known methods of factoring n-digit numbers in the p-ary number system.

Of course, when n and p are small, a trial-and-error factorization procedure analogous to Algorithm 4.5.4A will be even faster than Berlekamp's method. Exercise 1 implies that it is a good idea to cast out factors of small degree first when p is small, before going to any more complicated procedure, even when n is large.

When p is large, a different implementation of Berlekamp's procedure would be used for the calculations. Division modulo p would not be done with an auxiliary table of reciprocals; instead the method of exercise 4.5.2–16, which takes $O\big((\log p)^2\big)$ steps, would probably be used. Then step B1 would take $O\big(n^2(\log p)^2\big)$ units of time; similarly, step B3 would take $O\big(n^3(\log p)^2\big)$. In step B2, we can form $x^p \bmod u(x)$ in a more efficient way than (16) when p is large: Section 4.6.3 shows that this value can be obtained by essentially using $O(\log p)$ operations of squaring $\bmod\, u(x)$, going from $x^k \bmod u(x)$ to $x^{2k} \bmod u(x)$, together with the operation of multiplying by x. The squaring operation is relatively easy to perform if we first make an auxiliary table of $x^m \bmod u(x)$ for $m = n,\, n+1,\, \ldots,\, 2n-2$; if $x^k \bmod u(x) = c_{n-1}x^{n-1} + \cdots + c_1 x + c_0$, then

$$x^{2k} \bmod u(x) = \big(c_{n-1}^2 x^{2n-2} + \cdots + (c_1 c_0 + c_1 c_0)x + c_0^2\big) \bmod u(x),$$

where $x^{2n-2},\, \ldots,\, x^n$ can be replaced by polynomials in the auxiliary table. The total time to compute $x^p \bmod u(x)$ comes to $O\big(n^2(\log p)^3\big)$ units, and we obtain the second row of Q. To get further rows of Q, we can compute $x^{2p} \bmod u(x)$, $x^{3p} \bmod u(x),\, \ldots$, simply by multiplying repeatedly by $x^p \bmod u(x)$, in a fashion analogous to squaring $\bmod\, u(x)$; step B2 is completed in $O\big(n^3(\log p)^2\big)$ additional units of time. Thus steps B1, B2, and B3 take a total of $O\big(n^2(\log p)^3 + n^3(\log p)^2\big)$ time units; these three steps tell us the number of factors of $u(x)$.

But when p is large and we get to step B4, we are asked to calculate a greatest common divisor for p different values of s, and that is out of the question if p is even moderately large. This hurdle was first surmounted by Hans Zassenhaus [*J. Number Theory* **1** (1969), 291–311], who showed how to determine all of the "useful" values of s (see exercise 14); but an even better way to proceed was found by Zassenhaus and Cantor in 1980. If $v(x)$ is any solution to (8), we know that $u(x)$ divides $v(x)^p - v(x) = v(x) \cdot \big(v(x)^{(p-1)/2} + 1\big) \cdot \big(v(x)^{(p-1)/2} - 1\big)$. This suggests that we calculate

$$\gcd\big(u(x),\, v(x)^{(p-1)/2} - 1\big); \tag{20}$$

with a little bit of luck, (20) will be a nontrivial factor of $u(x)$. In fact, we can determine exactly how much luck is involved, by considering (7). Let $v(x) \equiv s_j$ (modulo $p_j(x)$) for $1 \le j \le r$; then $p_j(x)$ divides $v(x)^{(p-1)/2} - 1$ if and only if $s_j^{(p-1)/2} \equiv 1$ (modulo p). We know that exactly $(p-1)/2$ of the integers s in the range $0 \le s < p$ satisfy $s^{(p-1)/2} \equiv 1$ (modulo p), hence about half of the $p_j(x)$ will appear in the gcd (20). More precisely, if $v(x)$ is a random solution of (8), where all p^r solutions are equally likely, the probability that the gcd (20) equals $u(x)$ is exactly

$$\big((p-1)/2p\big)^r,$$

and the probability that it equals 1 is $\big((p+1)/2p\big)^r$. The probability that a nontrivial factor will be obtained is therefore

$$1 - \left(\frac{p-1}{2p}\right)^r - \left(\frac{p+1}{2p}\right)^r = 1 - \frac{1}{2^{r-1}}\left(1 + \binom{r}{2}p^{-2} + \binom{r}{4}p^{-4} + \cdots\right) \ge \frac{4}{9},$$

for all $r \ge 2$ and $p \ge 3$.

It is therefore a good idea to replace step B4 by the following procedure, unless p is quite small: Set $v(x) \leftarrow a_1 v^{[1]}(x) + a_2 v^{[2]}(x) + \cdots + a_r v^{[r]}(x)$, where the coefficients a_j are randomly chosen in the range $0 \le a_j < p$. Let the current partial factorization of $u(x)$ be $u_1(x) \ldots u_t(x)$ where t is initially 1. Compute

$$g_i(x) = \gcd\big(u_i(x), v(x)^{(p-1)/2} - 1\big)$$

for all i such that $\deg(u_i) > 1$; replace $u_i(x)$ by $g_i(x) \cdot \big(u_i(x)/g_i(x)\big)$ and increase the value of t, whenever a nontrivial gcd is found. Repeat this process for different choices of $v(x)$ until $t = r$.

If we assume (as we may) that only $O(\log r)$ random solutions $v(x)$ to (8) will be needed, we can give an upper bound on the time required to perform this alternative to step B4. It takes $O\big(rn(\log p)^2\big)$ steps to compute $v(x)$; and if $\deg(u_i) = d$, it takes $O\big(d^2(\log p)^3\big)$ steps to compute $v(x)^{(p-1)/2} \bmod u_i(x)$ and $O\big(d^2(\log p)^2\big)$ further steps to compute $\gcd\big(u_i(x), v(x)^{(p-1)/2} - 1\big)$. Thus the total time is $O(n^2(\log p)^3 \log r)$.

Distinct-degree factorization. We shall now turn to a somewhat simpler way to find factors modulo p. The ideas we have studied so far in this section involve many instructive insights into computational algebra, so the author does not apologize to the reader for presenting them; but it turns out that the problem of factorization modulo p can actually be solved without relying on so many concepts.

In the first place we can make use of the fact that an irreducible polynomial $q(x)$ of degree d is a divisor of $x^{p^d} - x$, and it is not a divisor of $x^{p^c} - x$ for $1 \le c < d$; see exercise 16. We can therefore cast out the irreducible factors of each degree separately, by adopting the following strategy.

D1. [Go squarefree.] Rule out squared factors, as in Berlekamp's method. Also set $v(x) \leftarrow u(x)$, $w(x) \leftarrow$ "x", and $d \leftarrow 0$. (Here $v(x)$ and $w(x)$ are variables that have polynomials as values.)

D2. [If not done, take pth power.] (At this point $w(x) = x^{p^d} \bmod v(x)$; all of the irreducible factors of $v(x)$ are distinct and have degree $> d$.) If $d + 1 > \frac{1}{2}\deg(v)$, the procedure terminates since we either have $v(x) = 1$ or $v(x)$ is irreducible. Otherwise increase d by 1 and replace $w(x)$ by $w(x)^p \bmod v(x)$.

D3. [Extract factors.] Find $g_d(x) = \gcd(w(x) - x, v(x))$. (This is the product of all the irreducible factors of $u(x)$ whose degree is d.) If $g_d(x) \neq 1$, replace $v(x)$ by $v(x)/g_d(x)$ and $w(x)$ by $w(x) \bmod v(x)$; and if the degree of $g_d(x)$ is greater than d, use the algorithm below to find its factors. Return to step D2. ∎

This procedure determines the product of all irreducible factors of each degree d, and therefore it tells us how many factors there are of each degree. Since the three factors of our example polynomial (19) have different degrees, they would all be discovered without any need to factorize the polynomials $g_d(x)$.

To complete the method, we need a way to split the polynomial $g_d(x)$ into its irreducible factors when $\deg(g_d) > d$. Michael Rabin pointed out in 1976 that this can be done by doing arithmetic in the field of p^d elements. David G. Cantor and Hans Zassenhaus discovered in 1979 that there is an even simpler way to proceed, based on the following identity: If p is any odd prime, we have

$$g_d(x) = \gcd(g_d(x), t(x)) \; \gcd(g_d(x), t(x)^{(p^d-1)/2} + 1) \; \gcd(g_d(x), t(x)^{(p^d-1)/2} - 1) \tag{21}$$

for all polynomials $t(x)$, since $t(x)^{p^d} - t(x)$ is a multiple of all irreducible polynomials of degree d. (We may regard $t(x)$ as an element of the field of size p^d, when that field consists of all polynomials modulo an irreducible $f(x)$ as in exercise 16.) Now exercise 29 shows that $\gcd(g_d(x), t(x)^{(p^d-1)/2} - 1)$ will be a nontrivial factor of $g_d(x)$ about 50 percent of the time, when $t(x)$ is a random polynomial of degree $\leq 2d - 1$; hence we will not need many random trials to discover all of the factors. We may assume without loss of generality that $t(x)$ is monic, since integer multiples of $t(x)$ make no difference except possibly to change $t(x)^{(p^d-1)/2}$ into its negative. Thus in the case $d = 1$, we can take $t(x) = x + s$, where s is chosen at random.

Sometimes this procedure will in fact succeed for $d > 1$ when only linear polynomials $t(x)$ are used. For example, there are eight irreducible polynomials $f(x)$ of degree 3, modulo 3, and they will all be distinguished by calculating $\gcd(f(x), (x + s)^{13} - 1)$ for $0 \leq s < 3$:

$f(x)$	$s = 0$	$s = 1$	$s = 2$
$x^3 + 2x + 1$	1	1	1
$x^3 + 2x + 2$	$f(x)$	$f(x)$	$f(x)$
$x^3 + x^2 + 2$	$f(x)$	$f(x)$	1
$x^3 + x^2 + x + 2$	$f(x)$	1	$f(x)$
$x^3 + x^2 + 2x + 1$	1	$f(x)$	$f(x)$
$x^3 + 2x^2 + 1$	1	$f(x)$	1
$x^3 + 2x^2 + x + 1$	1	1	$f(x)$
$x^3 + 2x^2 + 2x + 2$	$f(x)$	1	1

Exercise 31 contains a partial explanation of why linear polynomials can be effective. But when there are more than 2^p irreducible polynomials of degree d, some irreducibles must exist that cannot be distinguished by linear choices of $t(x)$.

An alternative to (21) that works when $p = 2$ is discussed in exercise 30. Faster algorithms for distinct-degree factorization when p is very large have been found by J. von zur Gathen, V. Shoup, and E. Kaltofen; the running time is $O(n^{2+\epsilon} + n^{1+\epsilon} \log p)$ arithmetic operations modulo p for numbers of practical size, and $O(n^{(5+\omega+\epsilon)/4} \log p)$ such operations as $n \to \infty$, when ω is the exponent of "fast" matrix multiplication in exercise 4.6.4–66. [See *Computational Complexity* **2** (1992), 187–224; *J. Symbolic Comp.* **20** (1995), 363–397; *Math. Comp.* **67** (1998), 1179–1197.]

Historical notes: The idea of finding all the linear factors of a squarefree polynomial $f(x)$ modulo p by first calculating $g(x) = \gcd\big(x^{p-1} - 1, f(x)\big)$ and then calculating $\gcd\big(g(x), (x + s)^{(p-1)/2} \pm 1\big)$ for arbitrary s is due to A. M. Legendre, *Mémoires Acad. Sci.* (Paris, 1785), 484–490; his motive was to find all of the integer solutions to Diophantine equations of the form $f(x) = py$, that is, $f(x) \equiv 0$ (modulo p). The more general degree-separation technique embodied in Algorithm D was discovered by C. F. Gauss before 1800, but not published [see his *Werke* **2** (1876), 237], and then by Évariste Galois in the now-classic paper that launched the theory of finite fields [*Bulletin des Sciences Mathématiques, Physiques et Chimiques* **13** (1830), 428–435; reprinted in *J. de Math. Pures et Appliquées* **11** (1846), 398–407]. However, this work of Gauss and Galois was ahead of its time, and not well understood until J. A. Serret gave a detailed exposition somewhat later [*Mémoires Acad. Sci.*, series 2, **35** (Paris, 1866), 617–688; Algorithm D is in §7]. Special procedures for splitting $g_d(x)$ into irreducible factors were devised subsequently by various authors, but methods of full generality that would work efficiently for large p were apparently not discovered until the advent of computers made them desirable. The first such randomized algorithm with a rigorously analyzed running time was published by E. Berlekamp [*Math. Comp.* **24** (1970), 713–735]; it was refined and simplified by Robert T. Moenck [*Math. Comp.* **31** (1977), 235–250], M. O. Rabin [*SICOMP* **9** (1980), 273–280], D. G. Cantor and H. J. Zassenhaus [*Math. Comp.* **36** (1981), 587–592]. Paul Camion independently found a generalization to special classes of multivariate polynomials [*Comptes Rendus Acad. Sci.* **A291** (Paris, 1980), 479–482; *IEEE Trans.* **IT-29** (1983), 378–385].

The average number of operations needed to factor a random polynomial mod p has been analyzed by P. Flajolet, X. Gourdon, and D. Panario, *Lecture Notes in Comp. Sci.* **1099** (1996), 232–243.

Factoring over the integers. It is somewhat more difficult to find the complete factorization of polynomials with integer coefficients when we are *not* working modulo p, but some reasonably efficient methods are available for this purpose.

Isaac Newton gave a method for finding linear and quadratic factors of polynomials with integer coefficients in his *Arithmetica Universalis* (1707). His method was extended by N. Bernoulli in 1708 and, more explicitly, by an astronomer named Friedrich von Schubert in 1793, who showed how to find all factors of degree n in a finite number of steps; see M. Mignotte and D. Ştefănescu, *Revue d'Hist. Math.* **7** (2001), 67–89. L. Kronecker rediscovered their approach independently, about 90 years later; but unfortunately the method is very inefficient when n is five or more. Much better results can be obtained with the help of the "mod p" factorization methods presented above.

Suppose that we want to find the irreducible factors of a given polynomial

$$u(x) = u_n x^n + u_{n-1} x^{n-1} + \cdots + u_0, \qquad u_n \neq 0,$$

over the integers. As a first step, we can divide by the greatest common divisor of the coefficients; this leaves us with a *primitive* polynomial. We may also assume that $u(x)$ is squarefree, by dividing out $\gcd\bigl(u(x), u'(x)\bigr)$ as in exercise 34.

Now if $u(x) = v(x)w(x)$, where each of these polynomials has integer coefficients, we obviously have $u(x) \equiv v(x)w(x)$ (modulo p) for all primes p, so there is a nontrivial factorization modulo p unless p divides $\ell(u)$. An efficient algorithm for factoring $u(x)$ modulo p can therefore be used in an attempt to reconstruct possible factorizations of $u(x)$ over the integers.

For example, let

$$u(x) = x^8 + x^6 - 3x^4 - 3x^3 + 8x^2 + 2x - 5. \tag{22}$$

We have seen above in (19) that

$$u(x) \equiv (x^4 + 2x^3 + 3x^2 + 4x + 6)(x^3 + 8x^2 + 4x + 12)(x + 3) \pmod{13}; \tag{23}$$

and the complete factorization of $u(x)$ modulo 2 shows one factor of degree 6 and another of degree 2 (see exercise 10). From (23) we can see that $u(x)$ has no factor of degree 2, so it must be irreducible over the integers.

This particular example was perhaps too simple; experience shows that most irreducible polynomials can be recognized as such by examining their factors modulo a few primes, but it is *not* always so easy to establish irreducibility. For example, there are polynomials that can be properly factored modulo p for all primes p, with consistent degrees of the factors, yet they are irreducible over the integers (see exercise 12).

A large family of irreducible polynomials is exhibited in exercise 38, and exercise 27 proves that almost all polynomials are irreducible over the integers. But we usually aren't trying to factor a random polynomial; there is probably some reason to expect a nontrivial factor or else the calculation would not have been attempted in the first place. We need a method that identifies factors when they are there.

In general if we try to find the factors of $u(x)$ by considering its behavior modulo different primes, the results will not be easy to combine. For example, if $u(x)$ is actually the product of four quadratic polynomials, we will have trouble matching up their images with respect to different prime moduli. Therefore it is desirable to stick to a single prime and to see how much mileage we can get out of it, once we feel that the factors modulo this prime have the right degrees.

One idea is to work modulo a very *large* prime p, big enough so that the coefficients in any true factorization $u(x) = v(x)w(x)$ over the integers must actually lie between $-p/2$ and $p/2$. Then all possible integer factors can be read off from the factors that we know how to compute mod p.

Exercise 20 shows how to obtain fairly good bounds on the coefficients of polynomial factors. For example, if (22) were reducible it would have a factor $v(x)$ of degree ≤ 4, and the coefficients of v would be at most 34 in magnitude by the results of that exercise. So all potential factors of $u(x)$ will be fairly evident if we work modulo any prime $p > 68$. Indeed, the complete factorization modulo 71 is

$$(x + 12)(x + 25)(x^2 - 13x - 7)(x^4 - 24x^3 - 16x^2 + 31x - 12),$$

and we see immediately that none of these polynomials could be a factor of (22) over the integers since the constant terms do not divide 5; furthermore there is no way to obtain a divisor of (22) by grouping two of these factors, since none of the conceivable constant terms 12×25, $12 \times (-7)$, $12 \times (-12)$ is congruent to ± 1 or ± 5 (modulo 71).

Incidentally, it is not trivial to obtain good bounds on the coefficients of polynomial factors, since a lot of cancellation can occur when polynomials are multiplied. For example, the innocuous-looking polynomial $x^n - 1$ has irreducible factors whose coefficients exceed $\exp(n^{1/\lg\lg n})$ for infinitely many n. [See R. C. Vaughan, *Michigan Math. J.* **21** (1974), 289–295.] The factorization of $x^n - 1$ is discussed in exercise 32.

Instead of using a large prime p, which might need to be truly enormous if $u(x)$ has large degree or large coefficients, we can also make use of small p, provided that $u(x)$ is squarefree mod p. For in this case, an important construction known as Hensel's Lemma can be used to extend a factorization modulo p in a unique way to a factorization modulo p^e for arbitrarily high exponents e (see exercise 22). If we apply Hensel's Lemma to (23) with $p = 13$ and $e = 2$, we obtain the unique factorization

$$u(x) \equiv (x - 36)(x^3 - 18x^2 + 82x - 66)(x^4 + 54x^3 - 10x^2 + 69x + 84)$$

(modulo 169). Calling these factors $v_1(x)v_3(x)v_4(x)$, we see that $v_1(x)$ and $v_3(x)$ are not factors of $u(x)$ over the integers, nor is their product $v_1(x)v_3(x)$ when the coefficients have been reduced modulo 169 to the range $(-\frac{169}{2} \mathinner{.\,.} \frac{169}{2})$. Thus we have exhausted all possibilities, proving once again that $u(x)$ is irreducible over the integers — this time using only its factorization modulo 13.

The example we have been considering is atypical in one important respect: We have been factoring the *monic* polynomial $u(x)$ in (22), so we could assume that all its factors were monic. What should we do if $u_n > 1$? In such a case, the leading coefficients of all but one of the polynomial factors can be varied almost arbitrarily modulo p^e; we certainly don't want to try all possibilities. Perhaps the reader has already noticed this problem. Fortunately there is a simple way out: The factorization $u(x) = v(x)w(x)$ implies a factorization $u_n u(x) = v_1(x)w_1(x)$ where $\ell(v_1) = \ell(w_1) = u_n = \ell(u)$. ("Excuse me, do you mind if I multiply your polynomial by its leading coefficient before I factor it?") We can proceed essentially as above, but using $p^e > 2B$ where B now bounds the maximum coefficient for factors of $u_n u(x)$ instead of $u(x)$. Another way to solve the leading coefficient problem is discussed in exercise 40.

Putting these observations all together results in the following procedure:

F1. [Factor modulo a prime power.] Find the unique squarefree factorization

$$u(x) \equiv \ell(u)v_1(x)\dots v_r(x) \pmod{p^e},$$

where p^e is sufficiently large as explained above, and where the $v_j(x)$ are monic. (This will be possible for all but a few primes p; see exercise 23.) Also set $d \leftarrow 1$.

F2. [Try the d-element subfactors.] For every combination of factors $v(x) = v_{i_1}(x)\dots v_{i_d}(x)$, with $i_1 = 1$ if $d = \frac{1}{2}r$, form the unique polynomial $\bar{v}(x) \equiv \ell(u)v(x) \pmod{p^e}$ whose coefficients all lie in the interval $[-\frac{1}{2}p^e \mathinner{.\,.} \frac{1}{2}p^e)$. If $\bar{v}(x)$ divides $\ell(u)u(x)$, output the factor $\mathrm{pp}(\bar{v}(x))$, divide $u(x)$ by this factor, and remove the corresponding $v_i(x)$ from the list of factors modulo p^e; decrease r by the number of factors removed, and terminate if $d > \frac{1}{2}r$.

F3. [Loop on d.] Increase d by 1, and return to F2 if $d \le \frac{1}{2}r$. ∎

At the conclusion of this process, the current value of $u(x)$ will be the final irreducible factor of the originally given polynomial. Notice that if $|u_0| < |u_n|$, it is preferable to do all of the work with the reverse polynomial $u_0 x^n + \cdots + u_n$, whose factors are the reverses of the factors of $u(x)$.

The procedure as stated requires $p^e > 2B$, where B is a bound on the coefficients of *any* divisor of $u_n u(x)$, but we can use a much smaller value of B if we only guarantee it to be valid for divisors of degree $\le \frac{1}{2}\deg(u)$. In this case the divisibility test in step F2 should be applied to $w(x) = v_1(x)\dots v_r(x)/v(x)$ instead of $v(x)$, whenever $\deg(v) > \frac{1}{2}\deg(u)$.

We can decrease B still more if we decide to guarantee only that B should bound the coefficients of *at least one* proper divisor of $u(x)$. (For example, when we're factoring a nonprime integer N instead of a polynomial, some of the divisors might be very large, but at least one will be $\le \sqrt{N}$.) This idea, due to B. Beauzamy, V. Trevisan, and P. S. Wang [*J. Symbolic Comp.* **15** (1993), 393–413], is discussed in exercise 21. The divisibility test in step F2 must then be applied to both $v(x)$ and $w(x)$, but the computations are faster because p^e is often much smaller.

The algorithm above contains an obvious bottleneck: We may have to test as many as $2^{r-1} - 1$ potential factors $v(x)$. The average value of 2^r in a random situation is about n, or perhaps $n^{1.5}$ (see exercise 5), but in nonrandom situations we will want to speed up this part of the routine as much as we can. One way to rule out spurious factors quickly is to compute the trailing coefficient $\bar{v}(0)$ first, continuing only if this divides $\ell(u)u(0)$; the complications explained in the preceding paragraphs do not have to be considered unless this divisibility condition is satisfied, since such a test is valid even when $\deg(v) > \frac{1}{2}\deg(u)$.

Another important way to speed up the procedure is to reduce r so that it tends to reflect the true number of factors. The distinct degree factorization algorithm above can be applied for various small primes p_j, thus obtaining for each prime a set D_j of possible degrees of factors modulo p_j; see exercise 26. We can represent D_j as a string of n binary bits. Now we compute the intersection $\bigcap D_j$, namely the bitwise "and" of these strings, and we perform step F2 only for

$$\deg(i_1) + \cdots + \deg(i_d) \in \bigcap D_j.$$

Furthermore p is chosen to be that p_j having the smallest value of r. This technique is due to David R. Musser, whose experience suggests trying about five primes p_j [see *JACM* **25** (1978), 271–282]. Of course we would stop immediately if the current $\bigcap D_j$ shows that $u(x)$ is irreducible.

Musser has given a complete discussion of a factorization method similar to the steps above, in *JACM* **22** (1975), 291–308. Steps F1–F3 incorporate an improvement suggested in 1978 by G. E. Collins, namely to look for trial divisors by taking combinations of d factors at a time rather than combinations of total degree d. This improvement is important because of the statistical behavior of the modulo-p factors of polynomials that are irreducible over the rationals (see exercise 37).

A. K. Lenstra, H. W. Lenstra, Jr., and L. Lovász introduced their famous "LLL algorithm" in order to obtain rigorous worst-case bounds on the amount of computation needed to factor a polynomial over the integers [*Math. Annalen* **261** (1982), 515–534]. Their method requires no random numbers, and its running time for $u(x)$ of degree n is $O\big(n^{12} + n^9 (\log \|u\|)^3\big)$ bit operations, where $\|u\|$ is defined in exercise 20. This estimate includes the time to search for a suitable prime number p and to find all factors modulo p with Algorithm B. Of course, heuristic methods that use randomization run noticeably faster in practice.

Greatest common divisors. Similar techniques can be used to calculate greatest common divisors of polynomials: If $\gcd\big(u(x), v(x)\big) = d(x)$ over the integers, and if $\gcd\big(u(x), v(x)\big) = q(x)$ (modulo p) where $q(x)$ is monic, then $d(x)$ is a common divisor of $u(x)$ and $v(x)$ modulo p; hence

$$d(x) \text{ divides } q(x) \text{ (modulo } p). \tag{24}$$

If p does not divide the leading coefficients of both u and v, it does not divide the leading coefficient of d; in such a case $\deg(d) \le \deg(q)$. When $q(x) = 1$ for such a prime p, we must therefore have $\deg(d) = 0$, and $d(x) = \gcd\big(\text{cont}(u), \text{cont}(v)\big)$. This justifies the remark made in Section 4.6.1 that the simple computation of $\gcd\big(u(x), v(x)\big)$ modulo 13 in 4.6.1–(6) is enough to prove that $u(x)$ and $v(x)$ are relatively prime over the integers; the comparatively laborious calculations of Algorithm 4.6.1E or Algorithm 4.6.1C are unnecessary. Since two random primitive polynomials are almost always relatively prime over the integers, and since they are relatively prime modulo p with probability $1 - 1/p$ by exercise 4.6.1–5, it is usually a good idea to do the computations modulo p.

As remarked before, we need good methods also for the nonrandom polynomials that arise in practice. Therefore we wish to sharpen our techniques and discover how to find $\gcd\big(u(x), v(x)\big)$ in general, over the integers, based entirely on information that we obtain working modulo primes p. We may assume that $u(x)$ and $v(x)$ are primitive.

Instead of calculating $\gcd\big(u(x), v(x)\big)$ directly, it will be convenient to search instead for the polynomial

$$\bar{d}(x) = c \cdot \gcd\big(u(x), v(x)\big), \tag{25}$$

where the constant c is chosen so that

$$\ell(\bar{d}) = \gcd\big(\ell(u), \ell(v)\big). \tag{26}$$

This condition will always hold for suitable c, since the leading coefficient of any common divisor of $u(x)$ and $v(x)$ must be a divisor of $\gcd\big(\ell(u), \ell(v)\big)$. Once $\bar{d}(x)$ has been found satisfying these conditions, we can readily compute $\mathrm{pp}\big(\bar{d}(x)\big)$, which is the true greatest common divisor of $u(x)$ and $v(x)$. Condition (26) is convenient since it avoids the uncertainty of unit multiples of the gcd; we have used essentially the same idea to control the leading coefficients in our factorization routine.

If p is a sufficiently large prime, based on the bounds for coefficients in exercise 20 applied either to $\ell(\bar{d})u(x)$ or $\ell(\bar{d})v(x)$, let us compute the unique polynomial $\bar{q}(x) \equiv \ell(\bar{d})q(x)$ (modulo p) having all coefficients in $[-\frac{1}{2}p .. \frac{1}{2}p)$. When $\mathrm{pp}\big(\bar{q}(x)\big)$ divides both $u(x)$ and $v(x)$, it must equal $\gcd\big(u(x), v(x)\big)$ because of (24). On the other hand if it does not divide both $u(x)$ and $v(x)$ we must have $\deg(q) > \deg(d)$. A study of Algorithm 4.6.1E reveals that this will be the case only if p divides the leading coefficient of one of the nonzero remainders computed by that algorithm with exact integer arithmetic; otherwise Euclid's algorithm modulo p deals with precisely the same sequence of polynomials as Algorithm 4.6.1E except for nonzero constant multiples (modulo p). So only a small number of "unlucky" primes can cause us to miss the gcd, and we will soon find a lucky prime if we keep trying.

If the bound on coefficients is so large that single-precision primes p are insufficient, we can compute $\bar{d}(x)$ modulo several primes p until it has been determined via the Chinese remainder algorithm of Section 4.3.2. This approach, which is due to W. S. Brown and G. E. Collins, has been described in detail by Brown in *JACM* **18** (1971), 478–504. Alternatively, as suggested by J. Moses and D. Y. Y. Yun [*Proc. ACM Conf.* **28** (1973), 159–166], we can use Hensel's method to determine $\bar{d}(x)$ modulo p^e for sufficiently large e. Hensel's construction appears to be computationally superior to the Chinese remainder approach; but it is valid directly only when

$$d(x) \perp u(x)/d(x) \qquad \text{or} \qquad d(x) \perp v(x)/d(x), \tag{27}$$

since the idea is to apply the techniques of exercise 22 to one of the factorizations $\ell(\bar{d})u(x) \equiv \bar{q}(x)u_1(x)$ or $\ell(\bar{d})v(x) \equiv \bar{q}(x)v_1(x)$ (modulo p). Exercises 34 and 35 show that it is possible to arrange things so that (27) holds whenever necessary. (The notation

$$u(x) \perp v(x) \tag{28}$$

used in (27) means that $u(x)$ and $v(x)$ are relatively prime, by analogy with the notation used for relatively prime integers.)

The gcd algorithms sketched here are significantly faster than those of Section 4.6.1 except when the polynomial remainder sequence is very short. Perhaps the best general procedure would be to start with the computation of $\gcd\big(u(x), v(x)\big)$ modulo a fairly small prime p, not a divisor of both $\ell(u)$ and $\ell(v)$. If the result $q(x)$ is 1, we're done; if it has high degree, we use Algorithm 4.6.1C; otherwise we use one of the methods above, first computing a bound for the coefficients of $\bar{d}(x)$ based on the coefficients of $u(x)$ and $v(x)$, and on the (small) degree of $q(x)$. As in the factorization problem, we should apply this procedure to the reverses of $u(x), v(x)$ and reverse the result, if the trailing coefficients are simpler than the leading ones.

Multivariate polynomials. Similar techniques lead to useful algorithms for factorization or gcd calculations on multivariate polynomials with integer coefficients. It is convenient to deal with the polynomial $u(x_1, \ldots, x_t)$ by working modulo the irreducible polynomials $x_2 - a_2$, $\ldots$, $x_t - a_t$, which play the role of p in the discussion above. Since $v(x) \bmod (x - a) = v(a)$, the value of

$$u(x_1, \ldots, x_t) \bmod \{x_2 - a_2, \ldots, x_t - a_t\}$$

is the univariate polynomial $u(x_1, a_2, \ldots, a_t)$. When the integers a_2, $\ldots$, a_t are chosen so that $u(x_1, a_2, \ldots, a_t)$ has the same degree in x_1 as the original polynomial $u(x_1, x_2, \ldots, x_t)$, an appropriate generalization of Hensel's construction will "lift" squarefree factorizations of this univariate polynomial to factorizations modulo $\{(x_2 - a_2)^{n_2}, \ldots, (x_t - a_t)^{n_t}\}$, where n_j is the degree of x_j in u; at the same time we can also work modulo an appropriate integer prime p. As many as possible of the a_j should be zero, so that sparseness of the intermediate results is retained. For details, see P. S. Wang, *Math. Comp.* **32** (1978), 1215–1231, in addition to the papers by Musser and by Moses and Yun cited earlier.

Significant computational experience has been accumulating since the days when the pioneering papers cited above were written. See R. E. Zippel, *Effective Polynomial Computation* (Boston: Kluwer, 1993) for a more recent survey. Moreover, it is now possible to factor polynomials that are given implicitly by a "black box" computational procedure, even when both input and output polynomials would fill the universe if they were written out explicitly [see E. Kaltofen and B. M. Trager, *J. Symbolic Comp.* **9** (1990), 301–320; Y. N. Lakshman and B. David Saunders, *SICOMP* **24** (1995), 387–397].

> *The asymptotically best algorithms frequently turn out*
> *to be worst on all problems for which they are used.*
> — D. G. CANTOR and H. ZASSENHAUS (1981)

EXERCISES

▶ **1.** [*M24*] Let p be prime, and let $u(x)$ be a random polynomial of degree n, assuming that each of the p^n monic polynomials is equally likely. Show that if $n \geq 2$, the probability that $u(x)$ has a linear factor mod p lies between $(1 + p^{-1})/2$ and $(2 + p^{-2})/3$, inclusive. Give a closed form for this probability when $n \geq p$. What is the average number of linear factors?

▶ **2.** [*M25*] (a) Show that any monic polynomial $u(x)$, over a unique factorization domain, may be expressed uniquely in the form

$$u(x) = v(x)^2 w(x),$$

where $w(x)$ is squarefree (has no factor of positive degree of the form $d(x)^2$) and both $v(x)$ and $w(x)$ are monic. (b) (E. R. Berlekamp.) How many monic polynomials of degree n are squarefree modulo p, when p is prime?

3. [*M25*] (*The Chinese remainder theorem for polynomials.*) Let $u_1(x), \ldots, u_r(x)$ be polynomials over a field S, with $u_j(x) \perp u_k(x)$ for all $j \neq k$. For any given polynomials $w_1(x), \ldots, w_r(x)$ over S, prove that there is a unique polynomial $v(x)$ over S such that $\deg(v) < \deg(u_1) + \cdots + \deg(u_r)$ and $v(x) \equiv w_j(x)$ (modulo $u_j(x)$) for $1 \leq j \leq r$. Does this result hold also when S is the set of all integers?

4. [*HM28*] Let a_{np} be the number of monic irreducible polynomials of degree n, modulo a prime p. Find a formula for the generating function $G_p(z) = \sum_n a_{np} z^n$. [*Hint:* Prove the following identity connecting power series: $f(z) = \sum_{j \geq 1} g(z^j)/j^t$ if and only if $g(z) = \sum_{n \geq 1} \mu(n) f(z^n)/n^t$.] What is $\lim_{p \to \infty} a_{np}/p^n$?

5. [*HM30*] Let A_{np} be the average number of irreducible factors of a randomly selected polynomial of degree n, modulo a prime p. Show that $\lim_{p \to \infty} A_{np} = H_n$. What is the limiting average value of 2^r, when r is the number of irreducible factors?

6. [*M21*] (J. L. Lagrange, 1771.) Prove the congruence (9). [*Hint:* Factor $x^p - x$ in the field of p elements.]

7. [*M22*] Prove Eq. (14).

8. [*HM20*] How can we be sure that the vectors output by Algorithm N are linearly independent?

9. [*20*] Explain how to construct a table of reciprocals mod 101 in a simple way, given that 2 is a primitive root of 101.

▶ **10.** [*21*] Find the complete factorization of the polynomial $u(x)$ in (22), modulo 2, using Berlekamp's procedure.

11. [*22*] Find the complete factorization of the polynomial $u(x)$ in (22), modulo 5.

▶ **12.** [*M22*] Use Berlekamp's algorithm to determine the number of factors of $u(x) = x^4 + 1$, modulo p, for all primes p. [*Hint:* Consider the cases $p = 2$, $p = 8k + 1$, $p = 8k + 3$, $p = 8k + 5$, $p = 8k + 7$ separately; what is the matrix Q? You need not discover the factors; just determine how many there are.]

13. [*M25*] Continuing the previous exercise, give an explicit formula for the factors of $x^4 + 1$, modulo p, for all odd primes p, in terms of the quantities $\sqrt{-1}$, $\sqrt{2}$, $\sqrt{-2}$ when such square roots exist modulo p.

14. [*M25*] (H. Zassenhaus.) Let $v(x)$ be a solution to (8), and let $w(x) = \prod(x - s)$ where the product is over all $0 \leq s < p$ such that $\gcd(u(x), v(x) - s) \neq 1$. Explain how to compute $w(x)$, given $u(x)$ and $v(x)$. [*Hint:* Eq. (14) implies that $w(x)$ is the polynomial of least degree such that $u(x)$ divides $w(v(x))$.]

▶ **15.** [*M27*] (*Square roots modulo a prime.*) Design an algorithm to calculate the square root of a given integer u modulo a given prime p, that is, to find an integer v such that $v^2 \equiv u$ (modulo p) whenever such a v exists. Your algorithm should be efficient even for very large primes p. (For $p \neq 2$, a solution to this problem leads to a procedure for solving any given quadratic equation modulo p, using the quadratic formula in the usual way.) *Hint:* Consider what happens when the factorization methods of this section are applied to the polynomial $x^2 - u$.

16. [*M30*] (*Finite fields.*) The purpose of this exercise is to prove basic properties of the fields introduced by É. Galois in 1830.

a) Given that $f(x)$ is an irreducible polynomial modulo a prime p, of degree n, prove that the p^n polynomials of degree less than n form a field under arithmetic modulo $f(x)$ and p. [*Note:* The existence of irreducible polynomials of each degree is proved in exercise 4; therefore fields with p^n elements exist for all primes p and all $n \geq 1$.]

b) Show that any field with p^n elements has a "primitive root" element ξ such that the elements of the field are $\{0, 1, \xi, \xi^2, \dots, \xi^{p^n - 2}\}$. [*Hint:* Exercise 3.2.1.2–16 provides a proof in the special case $n = 1$.]

c) If $f(x)$ is an irreducible polynomial modulo p, of degree n, prove that $x^{p^m} - x$ is divisible by $f(x)$ if and only if m is a multiple of n. (It follows that we can test irreducibility rather quickly: A given nth degree polynomial $f(x)$ is irreducible modulo p if and only if $x^{p^n} - x$ is divisible by $f(x)$ and $x^{p^{n/q}} - x \perp f(x)$ for all primes q that divide n.)

17. [*M23*] Let F be a field with 13^2 elements. How many elements of F have order f, for each integer f with $1 \leq f < 13^2$? (The *order* of an element a is the least positive integer m such that $a^m = 1$.)

▶ **18.** [*M25*] Let $u(x) = u_n x^n + \dots + u_0, u_n \neq 0$, be a primitive polynomial with integer coefficients, and let $v(x)$ be the monic polynomial defined by

$$v(x) = u_n^{n-1} \cdot u(x/u_n) = x^n + u_{n-1} x^{n-1} + u_{n-2} u_n x^{n-2} + \dots + u_0 u_n^{n-1}.$$

(a) Given that $v(x)$ has the complete factorization $p_1(x) \dots p_r(x)$ over the integers, where each $p_j(x)$ is monic, what is the complete factorization of $u(x)$ over the integers?
(b) If $w(x) = x^m + w_{m-1} x^{m-1} + \dots + w_0$ is a factor of $v(x)$, prove that w_k is a multiple of u_n^{m-1-k} for $0 \leq k < m$.

19. [*M20*] (*Eisenstein's criterion.*) Perhaps the best-known class of irreducible polynomials over the integers was introduced by T. Schönemann in *Crelle* **32** (1846), 100, then popularized by G. Eisenstein in *Crelle* **39** (1850), 166–169: Let p be prime and let $u(x) = u_n x^n + \dots + u_0$ have the following properties: (i) u_n is not divisible by p; (ii) $u_{n-1}, \dots, u_0$ are divisible by p; (iii) u_0 is not divisible by p^2. Show that $u(x)$ is irreducible over the integers.

20. [*HM33*] If $u(x) = u_n x^n + \dots + u_0$ is any polynomial over the complex numbers, let $\|u\| = (|u_n|^2 + \dots + |u_0|^2)^{1/2}$.

a) Let $u(x) = (x - \alpha) w(x)$ and $v(x) = (\bar\alpha x - 1) w(x)$, where α is any complex number and $\bar\alpha$ is its complex conjugate. Prove that $\|u\| = \|v\|$.

b) Let $u_n (x - \alpha_1) \dots (x - \alpha_n)$ be the complete factorization of $u(x)$ over the complex numbers, and write $M(u) = |u_n| \prod_{j=1}^n \max(1, |\alpha_j|)$. Prove that $M(u) \leq \|u\|$.

c) Show that $|u_j| \leq \binom{n-1}{j} M(u) + \binom{n-1}{j-1} |u_n|$, for $0 \leq j \leq n$.

d) Combine these results to prove that if $u(x) = v(x) w(x)$ and $v(x) = v_m x^m + \dots + v_0$, where u, v, w all have integer coefficients, then the coefficients of v are bounded by

$$|v_j| \leq \binom{m-1}{j} \|u\| + \binom{m-1}{j-1} |u_n|.$$

21. [*HM32*] Continuing exercise 20, we can also derive useful bounds on the coefficients of *multivariate* polynomial factors over the integers. For convenience we will let boldface letters stand for sequences of t integers; thus, instead of writing

$$u(x_1, \ldots, x_t) = \sum_{j_1, \ldots, j_t} u_{j_1 \ldots j_t} x_1^{j_1} \ldots x_t^{j_t}$$

we will write simply $u(\mathbf{x}) = \sum_{\mathbf{j}} u_{\mathbf{j}} \mathbf{x}^{\mathbf{j}}$. Notice the convention for $\mathbf{x}^{\mathbf{j}}$; we also write $\mathbf{j}! = j_1! \ldots j_t!$ and $\Sigma \mathbf{j} = j_1 + \cdots + j_t$.

a) Prove the identity

$$\sum_{\mathbf{j},\mathbf{k}} \frac{1}{\mathbf{j}!\,\mathbf{k}!} \sum_{\mathbf{p},\mathbf{q} \geq 0} [\mathbf{p} - \mathbf{j} = \mathbf{q} - \mathbf{k}] a_{\mathbf{p}} b_{\mathbf{q}} \frac{\mathbf{p}!\,\mathbf{q}!}{(\mathbf{p} - \mathbf{j})!} \sum_{\mathbf{r},\mathbf{s} \geq 0} [\mathbf{r} - \mathbf{j} = \mathbf{s} - \mathbf{k}] c_{\mathbf{r}} d_{\mathbf{s}} \frac{\mathbf{r}!\,\mathbf{s}!}{(\mathbf{r} - \mathbf{j})!}$$

$$= \sum_{\mathbf{i} \geq 0} \mathbf{i}! \sum_{\mathbf{p},\mathbf{s} \geq 0} [\mathbf{p} + \mathbf{s} = \mathbf{i}] a_{\mathbf{p}} d_{\mathbf{s}} \sum_{\mathbf{q},\mathbf{r} \geq 0} [\mathbf{q} + \mathbf{r} = \mathbf{i}] b_{\mathbf{q}} c_{\mathbf{r}} .$$

b) The polynomial $u(\mathbf{x}) = \sum_{\mathbf{j}} u_{\mathbf{j}} \mathbf{x}^{\mathbf{j}}$ is called *homogeneous* of degree n if each term has total degree n; thus we have $\Sigma \mathbf{j} = n$ whenever $u_{\mathbf{j}} \neq 0$. Consider the weighted sum of coefficients $B(u) = \sum_{\mathbf{j}} \mathbf{j}! |u_{\mathbf{j}}|^2$. Use part (a) to show that $B(u) \geq B(v)B(w)$ whenever $u(\mathbf{x}) = v(\mathbf{x})w(\mathbf{x})$ is homogeneous.

c) The *Bombieri norm* $[u]$ of a polynomial $u(\mathbf{x})$ is defined to be $\sqrt{B(u)/n!}$ when u is homogeneous of degree n. It is also defined for nonhomogeneous polynomials, by adding a new variable x_{t+1} and multiplying each term by a power of x_{t+1} so that u becomes homogeneous without increasing its maximum degree. For example, let $u(x) = 4x^3 + x - 2$; the corresponding homogeneous polynomial is $4x^3 + xy^2 - 2y^3$, and we have $[u]^2 = (3!\,0!\,4^2 + 1!\,2!\,1^2 + 0!\,3!\,2^2)/3! = 16 + \frac{1}{3} + 4$. If $u(x, y, z) = 3xy^3 - z^2$ we have, similarly, $[u]^2 = (1!\,3!\,0!\,0!\,3^2 + 0!\,0!\,2!\,2!\,1^2)/4! = \frac{9}{4} + \frac{1}{6}$. What does part (b) tell us about the relation between $[u]$, $[v]$, and $[w]$, when $u(\mathbf{x}) = v(\mathbf{x})w(\mathbf{x})$?

d) Prove that if $u(x)$ is a reducible polynomial of degree n in one variable, it has a factor whose coefficients are at most $n!^{1/4}[u]^{1/2}/(n/4)!$ in absolute value. What is the corresponding result for homogeneous polynomials in t variables?

e) Calculate $[u]$ both explicitly and asymptotically when $u(x) = (x^2 - 1)^n$.

f) Prove that $[u][v] \geq [uv]$.

g) Show that $2^{-n/2}M(u) \leq [u] \leq 2^{n/2}M(u)$, when $u(x)$ is a polynomial of degree n and $M(u)$ is the quantity defined in exercise 20. (Therefore the bound in part (d) is roughly the square root of the bound we obtained in that exercise.)

▶ **22.** [*M24*] (*Hensel's Lemma.*) Let $u(x)$, $v_e(x)$, $w_e(x)$, $a(x)$, $b(x)$ be polynomials with integer coefficients, satisfying the relations

$$u(x) \equiv v_e(x)w_e(x) \pmod{p^e}, \qquad a(x)v_e(x) + b(x)w_e(x) \equiv 1 \pmod{p},$$

where p is prime, $e \geq 1$, $v_e(x)$ is monic, $\deg(a) < \deg(w_e)$, $\deg(b) < \deg(v_e)$, and $\deg(u) = \deg(v_e) + \deg(w_e)$. Show how to compute polynomials $v_{e+1}(x) \equiv v_e(x)$ and $w_{e+1}(x) \equiv w_e(x) \pmod{p^e}$, satisfying the same conditions with e increased by 1. Furthermore, prove that $v_{e+1}(x)$ and $w_{e+1}(x)$ are unique, modulo p^{e+1}.

Use your method for $p = 2$ to prove that (22) is irreducible over the integers, starting with its factorization modulo 2 found in exercise 10. (Note that Euclid's extended algorithm, exercise 4.6.1–3, will get the process started for $e = 1$.)

23. [*HM23*] Let $u(x)$ be a squarefree polynomial with integer coefficients. Prove that there are only finitely many primes p such that $u(x)$ is not squarefree modulo p.

24. [*M20*] The text speaks only of factorization over the integers, not over the field of rational numbers. Explain how to find the complete factorization of a polynomial with rational coefficients, over the field of rational numbers.

25. [*M25*] What is the complete factorization of $x^5 + x^4 + x^2 + x + 2$ over the field of rational numbers?

26. [*20*] Let d_1, ..., d_r be the degrees of the irreducible factors of $u(x)$ modulo p, with proper multiplicity, so that $d_1 + \cdots + d_r = n = \deg(u)$. Explain how to compute the set $\{\deg(v) \mid u(x) \equiv v(x)w(x) \text{ (modulo } p) \text{ for some } v(x), w(x)\}$ by performing $O(r)$ operations on binary bit strings of length n.

27. [*HM30*] Prove that a random primitive polynomial over the integers is "almost always" irreducible, in some appropriate sense.

28. [*M25*] The distinct-degree factorization procedure is "lucky" when there is at most one irreducible polynomial of each degree d; then $g_d(x)$ never needs to be broken into factors. What is the probability of such a lucky circumstance, when factoring a random polynomial of degree n, modulo p, for fixed n as $p \to \infty$?

29. [*M22*] Let $g(x)$ be a product of two or more distinct irreducible polynomials of degree d, modulo an odd prime p. Prove that $\gcd\big(g(x), t(x)^{(p^d-1)/2} - 1\big)$ will be a proper factor of $g(x)$ with probability $\geq 1/2 - 1/(2p^{2d})$, for any fixed $g(x)$, when $t(x)$ is selected at random from among the p^{2d} polynomials of degree $< 2d$ modulo p.

30. [*M25*] Prove that if $q(x)$ is an irreducible polynomial of degree d, modulo p, and if $t(x)$ is any polynomial, then the value of $\big(t(x)+t(x)^p+t(x)^{p^2}+\cdots+t(x)^{p^{d-1}}\big) \bmod q(x)$ is an integer (that is, a polynomial of degree ≤ 0). Use this fact to design a randomized algorithm for factoring a product $g_d(x)$ of degree-d irreducibles, analogous to (21), for the case $p = 2$.

31. [*HM30*] Let p be an odd prime and let $d \geq 1$. Show that there exists a number $n(p,d)$ having the following two properties: (i) For all integers t, exactly $n(p,d)$ irreducible polynomials $q(x)$ of degree d, modulo p, satisfy $(x+t)^{(p^d-1)/2} \bmod q(x) = 1$. (ii) For all integers $0 \leq t_1 < t_2 < p$, exactly $n(p,d)$ irreducible polynomials $q(x)$ of degree d, modulo p, satisfy $(x + t_1)^{(p^d-1)/2} \bmod q(x) = (x + t_2)^{(p^d-1)/2} \bmod q(x)$.

▶ **32.** [*M30*] (*Cyclotomic polynomials.*) Let $\Psi_n(x) = \prod_{1\leq k\leq n,\, k\perp n}(x - \omega^k)$, where $\omega = e^{2\pi i/n}$; thus, the roots of $\Psi_n(x)$ are the complex nth roots of unity that aren't mth roots for $m < n$.

a) Prove that $\Psi_n(x)$ is a polynomial with integer coefficients, and that

$$x^n - 1 = \prod_{d\backslash n} \Psi_d(x); \qquad \Psi_n(x) = \prod_{d\backslash n}(x^d - 1)^{\mu(n/d)}.$$

  (See exercises 4.5.2–10(b) and 4.5.3–28(c).)

b) Prove that $\Psi_n(x)$ is irreducible over the integers, hence the formula above is the complete factorization of $x^n - 1$ over the integers. [*Hint:* If $f(x)$ is an irreducible factor of $\Psi_n(x)$ over the integers, and if ζ is a complex number with $f(\zeta) = 0$, prove that $f(\zeta^p) = 0$ for all primes p not dividing n. It may help to use the fact that $x^n - 1$ is squarefree modulo p for all such primes.]

c) Discuss the calculation of $\Psi_n(x)$, and tabulate the values for $n \leq 15$.

33. [*M18*] True or false: If $u(x) \neq 0$ and the complete factorization of $u(x)$ modulo p is $p_1(x)^{e_1} \ldots p_r(x)^{e_r}$, then $u(x)/\gcd(u(x), u'(x)) = p_1(x) \ldots p_r(x)$.

▶ **34.** [*M25*] (*Squarefree factorization.*) It is clear that any primitive polynomial of a unique factorization domain can be expressed in the form $u(x) = u_1(x) u_2(x)^2 u_3(x)^3 \ldots$, where the polynomials $u_i(x)$ are squarefree and relatively prime to each other. This representation, in which $u_j(x)$ is the product of all the irreducible polynomials that divide $u(x)$ exactly j times, is unique except for unit multiples; and it is a useful way to represent polynomials that participate in multiplication, division, and gcd operations.

Let $\mathrm{GCD}(u(x), v(x))$ be a procedure that returns three answers:

$$\mathrm{GCD}(u(x), v(x)) = \big(d(x), u(x)/d(x), v(x)/d(x)\big), \quad \text{where } d(x) = \gcd(u(x), v(x)).$$

The modular method described in the text following Eq. (25) always ends with a trial division of $u(x)/d(x)$ and $v(x)/d(x)$, to make sure that no "unlucky prime" has been used, so the quantities $u(x)/d(x)$ and $v(x)/d(x)$ are byproducts of the gcd computation; thus we can compute $\mathrm{GCD}(u(x), v(x))$ essentially as fast as $\gcd(u(x), v(x))$ when we are using a modular method.

Devise a procedure that obtains the squarefree representation $\big(u_1(x), u_2(x), \ldots\big)$ of a given primitive polynomial $u(x)$ over the integers. Your algorithm should perform exactly e computations of a GCD, where e is the largest subscript with $u_e(x) \neq 1$; furthermore, each GCD calculation should satisfy (27), so that Hensel's construction can be used.

35. [*M22*] (D. Y. Y. Yun.) Design an algorithm that computes the squarefree representation $\big(w_1(x), w_2(x), \ldots\big)$ of $w(x) = \gcd(u(x), v(x))$ over the integers, given the squarefree representations $\big(u_1(x), u_2(x), \ldots\big)$ and $\big(v_1(x), v_2(x), \ldots\big)$ of $u(x)$ and $v(x)$.

36. [*M27*] Extend the procedure of exercise 34 so that it will obtain the squarefree representation $\big(u_1(x), u_2(x), \ldots\big)$ of a given polynomial $u(x)$ when the coefficient arithmetic is performed modulo p.

37. [*HM24*] (George E. Collins.) Let $d_1, \ldots, d_r$ be positive integers whose sum is n, and let p be prime. What is the probability that the irreducible factors of a random nth-degree integer polynomial $u(x)$ have degrees $d_1, \ldots, d_r$, when it is completely factored modulo p? Show that this probability is asymptotically the same as the probability that a random permutation on n elements has cycles of lengths $d_1, \ldots, d_r$.

38. [*HM27*] (*Perron's criterion.*) Let $u(x) = x^n + u_{n-1} x^{n-1} + \cdots + u_0$ be a polynomial with integer coefficients such that $u_0 \neq 0$ and either $|u_{n-1}| > 1 + |u_{n-2}| + \cdots + |u_0|$ or $(u_{n-1} = 0$ and $u_{n-2} > 1 + |u_{n-3}| + \cdots + |u_0|)$. Show that $u(x)$ is irreducible over the integers. [*Hint:* Prove that almost all of u's roots are less than 1 in absolute value.]

39. [*HM42*] (David G. Cantor.) Show that if the polynomial $u(x)$ is irreducible over the integers, it has a "succinct" proof of irreducibility, in the sense that the number of bits in the proof is at most a polynomial in $\deg(u)$ and the length of the coefficients. (Only a bound on the *length* of proof is requested here, as in exercise 4.5.4–17, not a bound on the time needed to find such a proof.) *Hint:* If $v(x)$ is irreducible and t is any polynomial over the integers, all factors of $v(t(x))$ have degree $\geq \deg(v)$. Perron's criterion gives a large supply of irreducible polynomials $v(x)$.

▶ **40.** [*M20*] (P. S. Wang.) If u_n is the leading coefficient of $u(x)$ and B is a bound on coefficients of some factor of u, the text's factorization algorithm requires us to find a factorization modulo p^e where $p^e > 2|u_n|B$. But $|u_n|$ might be larger than B, when B is chosen by the method of exercise 21. Show that if $u(x)$ is reducible, there is a way to recover one of its true factors from a factorization modulo p^e whenever $p^e \geq 2B^2$, by using the algorithm of exercise 4.5.3–51.

41. [*M47*] (Beauzamy, Trevisan, and Wang.) Prove or disprove: There is a constant c such that, if $f(x)$ is any integer polynomial with all coefficients $\leq B$ in absolute value, then one of its irreducible factors has coefficients bounded by cB.

4.6.3. Evaluation of Powers

In this section we shall study the interesting problem of computing x^n efficiently, given x and n, where n is a positive integer. Suppose, for example, that we need to compute x^{16}; we could simply start with x and multiply by x fifteen times. But it is possible to obtain the same answer with only four multiplications, if we repeatedly take the square of each partial result, successively forming x^2, x^4, x^8, x^{16}.

The same idea applies, in general, to any value of n, in the following way: Write n in the binary number system (suppressing zeros at the left). Then replace each "1" by the pair of letters SX, replace each "0" by S, and cross off the "SX" that now appears at the left. The result is a rule for computing x^n, if "S" is interpreted as the operation of *squaring*, and if "X" is interpreted as the operation of *multiplying by x*. For example, if $n = 23$, its binary representation is 10111; so we form the sequence SX S SX SX SX and remove the leading SX to obtain the rule SSXSXSX. This rule states that we should "square, square, multiply by x, square, multiply by x, square, and multiply by x"; in other words, we should successively compute x^2, x^4, x^5, x^{10}, x^{11}, x^{22}, x^{23}.

This binary method is easily justified by a consideration of the sequence of exponents in the calculation: If we reinterpret "S" as the operation of multiplying by 2 and "X" as the operation of adding 1, and if we start with 1 instead of x, the rule will lead to a computation of n because of the properties of the binary number system. The method is quite ancient; it appeared before A.D. 400 in Piṅgala's Hindu classic *Chandaḥśāstra* [see B. Datta and A. N. Singh, *History of Hindu Mathematics* **2** (Lahore: Motilal Banarsi Das, 1935), 76]. There seem to be no other references to this method outside of India during the next several centuries, but a clear discussion of how to compute 2^n efficiently for arbitrary n was given by al-Uqlīdisī of Damascus in A.D. 952; see *The Arithmetic of al-Uqlīdisī* by A. S. Saidan (Dordrecht: D. Reidel, 1975), 341–342, where the general ideas are illustrated for $n = 51$. See also al-Bīrūnī's *Chronology of Ancient Nations*, edited and translated by E. Sachau (London: 1879), 132–136; this eleventh-century Arabic work had great influence.

The S-and-X binary method for obtaining x^n requires no temporary storage except for x and the current partial result, so it is well suited for incorporation in the hardware of a binary computer. The method can also be readily programmed; but it requires that the binary representation of n be scanned from left to right. Computer programs generally prefer to go the other way, because the available operations of division by 2 and remainder mod 2 will deduce the binary representation from right to left. Therefore the following algorithm, based on a right-to-left scan of the number, is often more convenient:

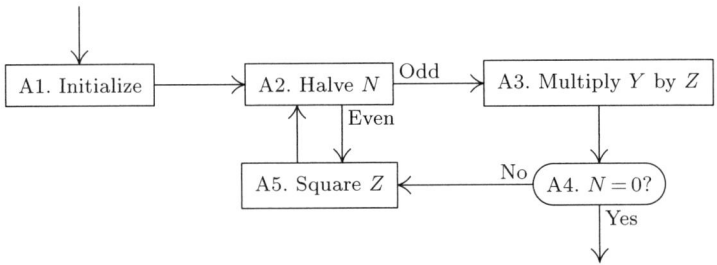

Fig. 13. Evaluation of x^n, based on a right-to-left scan of the binary notation for n.

Algorithm A (*Right-to-left binary method for exponentiation*). This algorithm evaluates x^n, where n is a positive integer. (Here x belongs to any algebraic system in which an associative multiplication, with identity element 1, has been defined.)

A1. [Initialize.] Set $N \leftarrow n$, $Y \leftarrow 1$, $Z \leftarrow x$.

A2. [Halve N.] (At this point, $x^n = Y Z^N$.) Set $t \leftarrow N \bmod 2$ and $N \leftarrow \lfloor N/2 \rfloor$. If $t = 0$, skip to step A5.

A3. [Multiply Y by Z.] Set $Y \leftarrow Z$ times Y.

A4. [$N = 0$?] If $N = 0$, the algorithm terminates, with Y as the answer.

A5. [Square Z.] Set $Z \leftarrow Z$ times Z, and return to step A2. ∎

As an example of Algorithm A, consider the steps in the evaluation of x^{23}:

	N	Y	Z
After step A1	23	1	x
After step A5	11	x	x^2
After step A5	5	x^3	x^4
After step A5	2	x^7	x^8
After step A5	1	x^7	x^{16}
After step A4	0	x^{23}	x^{16}

A MIX program corresponding to Algorithm A appears in exercise 2.

The great calculator al-Kāshī stated Algorithm A in A.D. 1427 [*Istoriko-Mat. Issledovaniia* **7** (1954), 256–257]. The method is closely related to a procedure for multiplication that was actually used by Egyptian mathematicians as early as 2000 B.C.; for if we change step A3 to "$Y \leftarrow Y + Z$" and step A5 to "$Z \leftarrow Z + Z$", and if we set Y to zero instead of unity in step A1, the algorithm terminates with $Y = nx$. [See A. B. Chace, *The Rhind Mathematical Papyrus* (1927); W. W. Struve, *Quellen und Studien zur Geschichte der Mathematik* **A1** (1930).] This is a practical method for multiplication by hand, since it involves only the simple operations of doubling, halving, and adding. It is often called the "Russian peasant method" of multiplication, since Western visitors to Russia in the nineteenth century found the method in wide use there.

The number of multiplications required by Algorithm A is

$$\lfloor \lg n \rfloor + \nu(n),$$

where $\nu(n)$ is the number of ones in the binary representation of n. This is one more multiplication than the left-to-right binary method mentioned at the beginning of this section would require, due to the fact that the first execution of step A3 is simply a multiplication by unity.

Because of the bookkeeping time required by this algorithm, the binary method is usually not of importance for small values of n, say $n \leq 10$, unless the time for a multiplication is comparatively large. If the value of n is known in advance, the left-to-right binary method is preferable. In some situations, such as the calculation of $x^n \bmod u(x)$ discussed in Section 4.6.2, it is much easier to multiply by x than to perform a general multiplication or to square a value, so binary methods for exponentiation are primarily suited for quite large n in such cases. If we wish to calculate the exact multiple-precision value of x^n, when x is an integer greater than the computer word size, binary methods are not much help unless n is so huge that the high-speed multiplication routines of Section 4.3.3 are involved; and such applications are rare. Similarly, binary methods are usually inappropriate for raising a polynomial to a power; see R. J. Fateman, *SICOMP* **3** (1974), 196–213, for a discussion of the extensive literature on polynomial exponentiation.

The point of these remarks is that binary methods are nice, but not a panacea. They are most applicable when the time to multiply $x^j \cdot x^k$ is essentially independent of j and k (for example, when we are doing floating point multiplication, or multiplication mod m); in such cases the running time is reduced from order n to order $\log n$.

Fewer multiplications. Several authors have published statements (without proof) that the binary method actually gives the *minimum* possible number of multiplications. But that is not true. The smallest counterexample is $n = 15$, when the binary method needs six multiplications, yet we can calculate $y = x^3$ in two multiplications and $x^{15} = y^5$ in three more, achieving the desired result with only five multiplications. Let us now discuss some other procedures for evaluating x^n, assuming that n is known in advance. Such procedures are of interest, for example, when an optimizing compiler is generating machine code.

The *factor method* is based on a factorization of n. If $n = pq$, where p is the smallest prime factor of n and $q > 1$, we may calculate x^n by first calculating x^p and then raising this quantity to the qth power. If n is prime, we may calculate x^{n-1} and multiply by x. And, of course, if $n = 1$, we have x^n with no calculation at all. Repeated application of these rules gives a procedure for evaluating x^n, given any value of n. For example, if we want to calculate x^{55}, we first evaluate $y = x^5 = x^4 x = (x^2)^2 x$; then we form $y^{11} = y^{10} y = (y^2)^5 y$. The whole process takes eight multiplications, while the binary method would have required nine. The factor method is better than the binary method on the average, but there are cases ($n = 33$ is the smallest example) where the binary method excels.

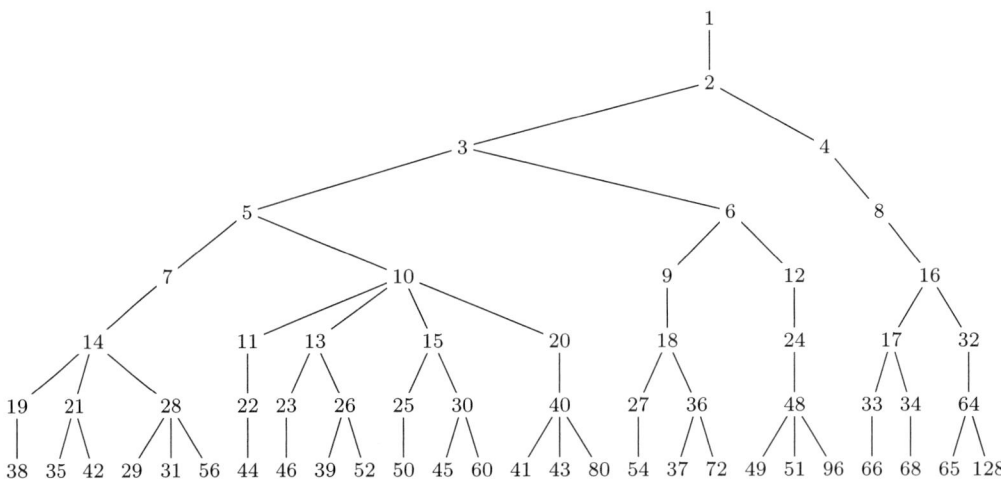

Fig. 14. The "power tree."

The binary method can be generalized to an *m-ary method* as follows: Let $n = d_0 m^t + d_1 m^{t-1} + \cdots + d_t$, where $0 \le d_j < m$ for $0 \le j \le t$. The computation begins by forming x, x^2, x^3, ..., x^{m-1}. (Actually, only those powers x^{d_j} such that d_j appears in the representation of n are needed, and this observation often saves some of the work.) Then raise x^{d_0} to the mth power and multiply by x^{d_1}; we have computed $y_1 = x^{d_0 m + d_1}$. Next, raise y_1 to the mth power and multiply by x^{d_2}, obtaining $y_2 = x^{d_0 m^2 + d_1 m + d_2}$. The process continues in this way until $y_t = x^n$ has been computed. Whenever $d_j = 0$, it is of course unnecessary to multiply by x^{d_j}. Notice that this method reduces to the left-to-right binary method discussed earlier, when $m = 2$; there is also a less obvious right-to-left m-ary method that takes more memory but only a few more steps (see exercise 9). If m is a small prime, the m-ary method will be particularly efficient for calculating powers of one polynomial modulo another, when the coefficients are treated modulo m, because of Eq. 4.6.2–(5).

A systematic method that gives the minimum number of multiplications for all of the relatively small values of n (in particular, for most n that occur in practical applications) is indicated in Fig. 14. To calculate x^n, find n in this tree; then the path from the root to n indicates a sequence of exponents that occur in an efficient evaluation of x^n. The rule for generating this "power tree" appears in exercise 5. Computer tests have shown that the power tree gives optimum results for all of the n listed in the figure. But for large enough values of n the power tree method is not always optimum; the smallest examples are $n = 77$, 154, 233. The first case for which the power tree is superior to both the binary method and the factor method is $n = 23$. The first case for which the factor method beats the power tree method is $n = 19879 = 103 \cdot 193$; such cases are quite rare. (For $n \le 100{,}000$ the power tree method is better than the factor method 88,803 times; it ties 11,191 times; and it loses only 6 times.)

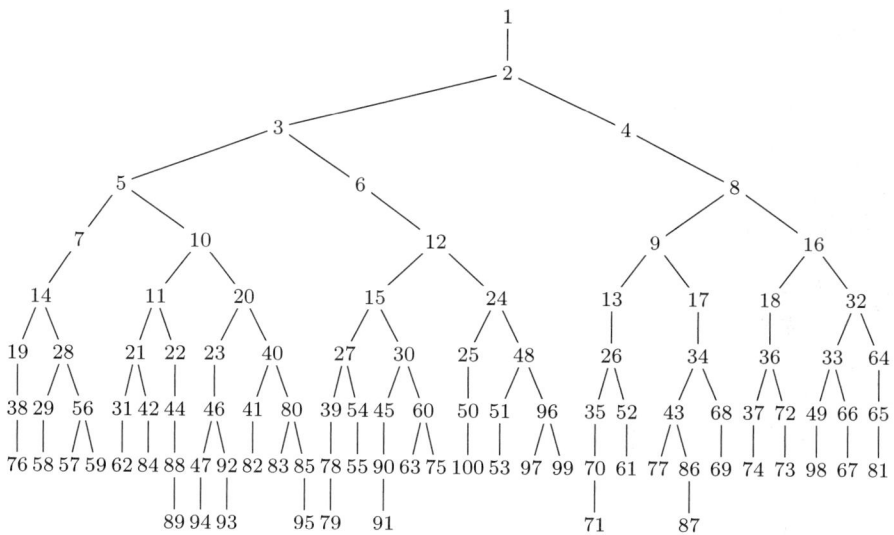

Fig. 15. A tree that minimizes the number of multiplications, for $n \leq 100$.

Addition chains. The most economical way to compute x^n by multiplication is a mathematical problem with an interesting history. We shall now examine it in detail, not only because it is classical and interesting in its own right, but because it is an excellent example of the theoretical questions that arise in the study of optimum methods of computation.

Although we are concerned with multiplication of powers of x, the problem can easily be reduced to addition, since the exponents are additive. This leads us to the following abstract formulation: An *addition chain for* n is a sequence of integers

$$1 = a_0, \quad a_1, \quad a_2, \quad \ldots, \quad a_r = n \tag{1}$$

with the property that

$$a_i = a_j + a_k, \qquad \text{for some } k \leq j < i, \tag{2}$$

for all $i = 1, 2, \ldots, r$. One way of looking at this definition is to consider a simple computer that has an accumulator and is capable of the three operations LDA, STA, and ADD; the machine begins with the number 1 in its accumulator, and it proceeds to compute the number n by adding together previous results. Notice that a_1 must equal 2, and a_2 is either 2, 3, or 4.

The shortest length, r, for which there exists an addition chain for n is denoted by $l(n)$. Thus $l(1) = 0$, $l(2) = 1$, $l(3) = l(4) = 2$, etc. Our goal in the remainder of this section is to discover as much as we can about this function $l(n)$. The values of $l(n)$ for small n are displayed in tree form in Fig. 15, which shows how to calculate x^n with the fewest possible multiplications for all $n \leq 100$.

The problem of determining $l(n)$ was apparently first raised by H. Dellac in 1894, and a partial solution by E. de Jonquières mentioned the factor method [see L'*Intermédiaire des Mathématiciens* **1** (1894), 20, 162–164]. In his solution, de Jonquières listed what he felt were the values of $l(p)$ for all prime numbers $p < 200$, but his table entries for $p = 107, 149, 163, 179, 199$ were one too high.

The factor method tells us immediately that

$$l(mn) \le l(m) + l(n), \qquad (3)$$

since we can take the chains $1, a_1, \ldots, a_r = m$ and $1, b_1, \ldots, b_s = n$ and form the chain $1, a_1, \ldots, a_r, a_r b_1, \ldots, a_r b_s = mn$.

We can also recast the m-ary method into addition-chain terminology. Consider the case $m = 2^k$, and write $n = d_0 m^t + d_1 m^{t-1} + \cdots + d_t$ in the m-ary number system; the corresponding addition chain takes the form

$$1, 2, 3, \ldots, m - 2, m - 1,$$
$$2d_0, 4d_0, \ldots, md_0, md_0 + d_1,$$
$$2(md_0 + d_1), 4(md_0 + d_1), \ldots, m(md_0 + d_1), m^2 d_0 + md_1 + d_2,$$
$$\ldots, \qquad m^t d_0 + m^{t-1} d_1 + \cdots + d_t. \qquad (4)$$

The length of this chain is $m - 2 + (k+1)t$; and it can often be reduced by deleting certain elements of the first row that do not occur among the coefficients d_j, plus elements among $2d_0, 4d_0, \ldots$ that already appear in the first row. Whenever digit d_j is zero, the step at the right end of the corresponding line may, of course, be dropped. Furthermore, we can omit all the even numbers (except 2) in the first row, if we bring values of the form $d_j/2^e$ into the computation e steps earlier. [See E. Wattel and G. A. Jensen, *Math. Centrum Report* ZW1968-001 (1968), 18 pp.; E. G. Thurber, *Duke Math. J.* **40** (1973), 907–913.]

The simplest case of the m-ary method is the binary method ($m = 2$), when the general scheme (4) simplifies to the "S" and "X" rule mentioned at the beginning of this section: The binary addition chain for $2n$ is the binary chain for n followed by $2n$; for $2n + 1$ it is the binary chain for $2n$ followed by $2n + 1$. From the binary method we conclude that

$$l(2^{e_0} + 2^{e_1} + \cdots + 2^{e_t}) \le e_0 + t, \qquad \text{if } e_0 > e_1 > \cdots > e_t \ge 0. \qquad (5)$$

Let us now define two auxiliary functions for convenience in our subsequent discussion:

$$\lambda(n) = \lfloor \lg n \rfloor; \qquad (6)$$

$$\nu(n) = \text{number of 1s in the binary representation of } n. \qquad (7)$$

Thus $\lambda(17) = 4$, $\nu(17) = 2$; these functions may be defined by the recurrence relations

$$\lambda(1) = 0, \qquad \lambda(2n) = \lambda(2n + 1) = \lambda(n) + 1; \qquad (8)$$

$$\nu(1) = 1, \qquad \nu(2n) = \nu(n), \qquad \nu(2n + 1) = \nu(n) + 1. \qquad (9)$$

In terms of these functions, the binary addition chain for n requires exactly $\lambda(n) + \nu(n) - 1$ steps, and (5) becomes

$$l(n) \le \lambda(n) + \nu(n) - 1. \qquad (10)$$

Special classes of chains. We may assume without any loss of generality that an addition chain is *ascending*,

$$1 = a_0 < a_1 < a_2 < \cdots < a_r = n. \tag{11}$$

For if any two a's are equal, one of them may be dropped; and we can also rearrange the sequence (1) into ascending order and remove terms $> n$ without destroying the addition chain property (2). *From now on we shall consider only ascending chains,* without explicitly mentioning this assumption.

It is convenient at this point to define a few special terms relating to addition chains. By definition we have, for $1 \leq i \leq r$,

$$a_i = a_j + a_k \tag{12}$$

for some j and k, $0 \leq k \leq j < i$. If this relation holds for more than one pair (j, k), we let j be as large as possible. Let us say that step i of (11) is a *doubling*, if $j = k = i - 1$; then a_i has the maximum possible value $2a_{i-1}$ that can follow the ascending chain $1, a_1, \ldots, a_{i-1}$. If j (but not necessarily k) equals $i - 1$, let us say that step i is a *star step*. The importance of star steps is explained below. Finally let us say that step i is a *small step* if $\lambda(a_i) = \lambda(a_{i-1})$. Since $a_{i-1} < a_i \leq 2a_{i-1}$, the quantity $\lambda(a_i)$ is always equal to either $\lambda(a_{i-1})$ or $\lambda(a_{i-1}) + 1$; it follows that, in any chain (11), *the length r is equal to $\lambda(n)$ plus the number of small steps.*

Several elementary relations hold between these types of steps: Step 1 is always a doubling. A doubling obviously is a star step, but never a small step. A doubling must be followed by a star step. Furthermore if step i is *not* a small step, then step $i + 1$ is either a small step or a star step, or both; putting this another way, if step $i + 1$ is neither small nor star, step i must have been small.

A *star chain* is an addition chain that involves only star steps. This means that each term a_i is the sum of a_{i-1} and a previous a_k; the simple "computer" discussed above after Eq. (2) makes use only of the two operations STA and ADD (not LDA) in a star chain, since each new term of the sequence utilizes the preceding result in the accumulator. Most of the addition chains we have discussed so far are star chains. The minimum length of a star chain for n is denoted by $l^*(n)$; clearly

$$l(n) \leq l^*(n). \tag{13}$$

We are now ready to derive some nontrivial facts about addition chains. First we can show that there must be fairly many doublings if r is not far from $\lambda(n)$.

Theorem A. *If the addition chain (11) includes d doublings and $f = r - d$ nondoublings, then*

$$n \leq 2^{d-1} F_{f+3}. \tag{14}$$

Proof. By induction on $r = d + f$, we see that (14) is certainly true when $r = 1$. When $r > 1$, there are three cases: If step r is a doubling, then $\frac{1}{2}n = a_{r-1} \leq 2^{d-2}F_{f+3}$; hence (14) follows. If steps r and $r - 1$ are both nondoublings, then $a_{r-1} \leq 2^{d-1}F_{f+2}$ and $a_{r-2} \leq 2^{d-1}F_{f+1}$; hence $n = a_r \leq$

$a_{r-1} + a_{r-2} \le 2^{d-1}(F_{f+2} + F_{f+1}) = 2^{d-1}F_{f+3}$ by the definition of the Fibonacci sequence. Finally, if step r is a nondoubling but step $r-1$ is a doubling, then $a_{r-2} \le 2^{d-2}F_{f+2}$ and $n = a_r \le a_{r-1} + a_{r-2} = 3a_{r-2}$. Now $2F_{f+3} - 3F_{f+2} = F_{f+1} - F_f \ge 0$; hence $n \le 2^{d-1}F_{f+3}$ in all cases. ∎

The method of proof we have used shows that inequality (14) is "best possible" under the stated assumptions; the addition chain

$$1, 2, \ldots, 2^{d-1}, 2^{d-1}F_3, 2^{d-1}F_4, \ldots, 2^{d-1}F_{f+3} \qquad (15)$$

has d doublings and f nondoublings.

Corollary A. *If the addition chain* (11) *includes f nondoublings and s small steps, then*

$$s \le f \le 3.271s. \qquad (16)$$

Proof. Obviously $s \le f$. We have $2^{\lambda(n)} \le n \le 2^{d-1}F_{f+3} \le 2^d\phi^f = 2^{\lambda(n)+s}(\phi/2)^f$, since $d + f = \lambda(n) + s$, and since $F_{f+3} \le 2\phi^f$ when $f \ge 0$. Hence $0 \le s\ln 2 + f\ln(\phi/2)$, and (16) follows from the fact that $\ln 2/\ln(2/\phi) \approx 3.2706$. ∎

Values of $l(n)$ for special n. It is easy to show by induction that $a_i \le 2^i$, and therefore $\lg n \le r$ in any addition chain (11). Hence

$$l(n) \ge \lceil \lg n \rceil. \qquad (17)$$

This lower bound, together with the upper bound (10) given by the binary method, gives us the values

$$l(2^A) = A; \qquad (18)$$

$$l(2^A + 2^B) = A + 1, \qquad \text{if } A > B. \qquad (19)$$

In other words, the binary method is optimum when $\nu(n) \le 2$. With some further calculation we can extend these formulas to the case $\nu(n) = 3$:

Theorem B. $\qquad l(2^A + 2^B + 2^C) = A + 2, \qquad \text{if } A > B > C. \qquad (20)$

Proof. We can, in fact, prove a stronger result that will be of use to us later in this section: *All addition chains with exactly one small step have one of the following six types* (where all steps indicated by "..." represent doublings):

Type 1. $1, \ldots, 2^A, 2^A + 2^B, \ldots, 2^{A+C} + 2^{B+C}$; $A > B \ge 0, C \ge 0$.

Type 2. $1, \ldots, 2^A, 2^A + 2^B, 2^{A+1} + 2^B, \ldots, 2^{A+C+1} + 2^{B+C}$; $A > B \ge 0$, $C \ge 0$.

Type 3. $1, \ldots, 2^A, 2^A + 2^{A-1}, 2^{A+1} + 2^{A-1}, 2^{A+2}, \ldots, 2^{A+C}$; $A > 0, C \ge 2$.

Type 4. $1, \ldots, 2^A, 2^A + 2^{A-1}, 2^{A+1} + 2^A, 2^{A+2}, \ldots, 2^{A+C}$; $A > 0, C \ge 2$.

Type 5. $1, \ldots, 2^A, 2^A + 2^{A-1}, \ldots, 2^{A+C} + 2^{A+C-1}, 2^{A+C+1} + 2^{A+C-2}, \ldots,$ $2^{A+C+D+1} + 2^{A+C+D-2}$; $A > 0, C > 0, D \ge 0$.

Type 6. $1, \ldots, 2^A, 2^A + 2^B, 2^{A+1}, \ldots, 2^{A+C}$; $A > B \ge 0, C \ge 1$.

A straightforward hand calculation shows that these six types exhaust all possibilities. By Corollary A, there are at most three nondoublings when there is one small step; this maximum occurs only in sequences of Type 3. All of the above are star chains, except Type 6 when $B < A - 1$.

The theorem now follows from the observation that

$$l(2^A + 2^B + 2^C) \leq A + 2;$$

and $l(2^A + 2^B + 2^C)$ must be greater than $A + 1$, since none of the six possible types have $\nu(n) > 2$. ∎

(E. de Jonquières stated without proof in 1894 that $l(n) \geq \lambda(n) + 2$ when $\nu(n) > 2$. The first published demonstration of Theorem B was by A. A. Gioia, M. V. Subbarao, and M. Sugunamma in *Duke Math. J.* **29** (1962), 481–487.)

The calculation of $l(2^A + 2^B + 2^C + 2^D)$, when $A > B > C > D$, is more involved. By the binary method it is at most $A+3$, and by the proof of Theorem B it is at least $A + 2$. The value $A + 2$ is possible, since we know that the binary method is not optimal when $n = 15$ or $n = 23$. The complete behavior when $\nu(n) = 4$ can be determined, as we shall now see.

Theorem C. *If $\nu(n) \geq 4$ then $l(n) \geq \lambda(n) + 3$, except in the following circumstances when $A > B > C > D$ and $l(2^A + 2^B + 2^C + 2^D)$ equals $A + 2$:*

Case 1. $A - B = C - D$. (Example: $n = 15$.)

Case 2. $A - B = C - D + 1$. (Example: $n = 23$.)

Case 3. $A - B = 3$, $C - D = 1$. (Example: $n = 39$.)

Case 4. $A - B = 5$, $B - C = C - D = 1$. (Example: $n = 135$.)

Proof. When $l(n) = \lambda(n) + 2$, there is an addition chain for n having just two small steps; such an addition chain starts out as one of the six types in the proof of Theorem B, followed by a small step, followed by a sequence of nonsmall steps. Let us say that n is "special" if $n = 2^A + 2^B + 2^C + 2^D$ for one of the four cases listed in the theorem. We can obtain addition chains of the required form for each special n, as shown in exercise 13; therefore it remains for us to prove that no chain with exactly two small steps contains any elements with $\nu(a_i) \geq 4$ except when a_i is special.

Let a "counterexample chain" be an addition chain with two small steps such that $\nu(a_r) \geq 4$, but a_r is not special. If counterexample chains exist, let $1 = a_0 < a_1 < \cdots < a_r = n$ be a counterexample chain of shortest possible length. Then step r is not a small step, since none of the six types in the proof of Theorem B can be followed by a small step with $\nu(n) \geq 4$ except when n is special. Furthermore, step r is not a doubling, otherwise $a_0, \ldots, a_{r-1}$ would be a shorter counterexample chain; and step r is a star step, otherwise $a_0, \ldots, a_{r-2}, a_r$ would be a shorter counterexample chain. Thus

$$a_r = a_{r-1} + a_{r-k}, \qquad k \geq 2; \qquad \text{and } \lambda(a_r) = \lambda(a_{r-1}) + 1. \tag{21}$$

Let c be the number of carries that occur when a_{r-1} is added to a_{r-k} in the binary number system by Algorithm 4.3.1A. Using the fundamental relation

$$\nu(a_r) = \nu(a_{r-1}) + \nu(a_{r-k}) - c, \tag{22}$$

we can prove that *step $r - 1$ is not a small step* (see exercise 14).

Let $m = \lambda(a_{r-1})$. Since neither r nor $r - 1$ is a small step, $c \geq 2$; and $c = 2$ can hold only when $a_{r-1} \geq 2^m + 2^{m-1}$.

Now let us suppose that $r - 1$ is not a star step. Then $r - 2$ is a small step, and $a_0, \ldots, a_{r-3}, a_{r-1}$ is a chain with only one small step; hence $\nu(a_{r-1}) \leq 2$ and $\nu(a_{r-2}) \leq 4$. The relation (22) can now hold only if $\nu(a_r) = 4$, $\nu(a_{r-1}) = 2$, $k = 2$, $c = 2$, $\nu(a_{r-2}) = 4$. From $c = 2$ we conclude that $a_{r-1} = 2^m + 2^{m-1}$; hence $a_0, a_1, \ldots, a_{r-3} = 2^{m-1} + 2^{m-2}$ is an addition chain with only one small step, and it must be of Type 1, so a_r belongs to Case 3. Thus $r - 1$ *is a star step*.

Now assume that $a_{r-1} = 2^t a_{r-k}$ for some t. If $\nu(a_{r-1}) \leq 3$, then by (22), $c = 2$, $k = 2$, and we see that a_r must belong to Case 3. On the other hand, if $\nu(a_{r-1}) = 4$ then a_{r-1} is special, and it is easy to see by considering each case that a_r also belongs to one of the four cases. (Case 4 arises, for example, when $a_{r-1} = 90$, $a_{r-k} = 45$; or $a_{r-1} = 120$, $a_{r-k} = 15$.) Therefore we may conclude that $a_{r-1} \neq 2^t a_{r-k}$ for any t.

We have proved that $a_{r-1} = a_{r-2} + a_{r-q}$ for some $q \geq 2$. If $k = 2$, then $q > 2$, and $a_0, a_1, \ldots, a_{r-2}, 2a_{r-2}, 2a_{r-2} + a_{r-q} = a_r$ is a counterexample sequence in which $k > 2$; therefore we may assume that $k > 2$.

Let us now suppose that $\lambda(a_{r-k}) = m - 1$; the case $\lambda(a_{r-k}) < m - 1$ may be ruled out by similar arguments, as shown in exercise 14. If $k = 4$, both $r - 2$ and $r - 3$ are small steps; hence $a_{r-4} = 2^{m-1}$, and (22) is impossible. Therefore $k = 3$; step $r - 2$ is small, $\nu(a_{r-3}) = 2$, $c = 2$, $a_{r-1} \geq 2^m + 2^{m-1}$, and $\nu(a_{r-1}) = 4$. There must be at least two carries when a_{r-2} is added to $a_{r-1} - a_{r-2}$; hence $\nu(a_{r-2}) = 4$, and a_{r-2} (being special and $\geq \frac{1}{2}a_{r-1}$) has the form $2^{m-1}+2^{m-2}+2^{d+1}+2^d$ for some d. Now a_{r-1} is either $2^m+2^{m-1}+2^{d+1}+2^d$ or $2^m + 2^{m-1} + 2^{d+2} + 2^{d+1}$, and in both cases a_{r-3} must be $2^{m-1} + 2^{m-2}$, so a_r belongs to Case 3. ∎

E. G. Thurber [*Pacific J. Math.* **49** (1973), 229–242] has extended Theorem C to show that $l(n) \geq \lambda(n) + 4$ when $\nu(n) > 8$. It seems reasonable to conjecture that $l(n) \geq \lambda(n) + \lg \nu(n)$ in general, since A. Schönhage has come very close to proving this (see exercise 28).

*Asymptotic values. Theorem C indicates that it is probably quite difficult to get exact values of $l(n)$ for large n, when $\nu(n) > 4$; however, we can determine the approximate behavior in the limit as $n \to \infty$.

Theorem D. [A. Brauer, *Bull. Amer. Math. Soc.* **45** (1939), 736–739.]

$$\lim_{n \to \infty} l^*(n)/\lambda(n) = \lim_{n \to \infty} l(n)/\lambda(n) = 1. \tag{23}$$

Proof. The addition chain (4) for the 2^k-ary method is a star chain if we delete the second occurrence of any element that appears twice in the chain; for if a_i

is the first element among $2d_0$, $4d_0$, ... of the second line that is not present in the first line, we have $a_i \leq 2(m-1)$; hence $a_i = (m-1) + a_j$ for some a_j in the first line. By totaling up the length of the chain, we have

$$\lambda(n) \leq l(n) \leq l^*(n) < (1+1/k) \lg n + 2^k \qquad (24)$$

for all $k \geq 1$. The theorem follows if we choose, say, $k = \lfloor \frac{1}{2} \lg \lambda(n) \rfloor$. ∎

If we let $k = \lambda\lambda(n) - 2\lambda\lambda\lambda(n)$ in (24) for large n, where $\lambda\lambda(n)$ denotes $\lambda(\lambda(n))$, we obtain the stronger asymptotic bound

$$l(n) \leq l^*(n) \leq \lambda(n) + \lambda(n)/\lambda\lambda(n) + O\big(\lambda(n)\lambda\lambda\lambda(n)/\lambda\lambda(n)^2\big). \qquad (25)$$

The second term $\lambda(n)/\lambda\lambda(n)$ is essentially the best that can be obtained from (24). A much deeper analysis of lower bounds can be carried out, to show that this term $\lambda(n)/\lambda\lambda(n)$ is, in fact, essential in (25). In order to see why this is so, let us consider the following fact:

Theorem E. [Paul Erdős, *Acta Arithmetica* **6** (1960), 77–81.] *Let ϵ be a positive real number. The number of addition chains* (11) *such that*

$$\lambda(n) = m, \qquad r \leq m + (1-\epsilon)m/\lambda(m) \qquad (26)$$

is less than α^m, for some $\alpha < 2$, for all suitably large m. (In other words, the number of addition chains so short that (26) is satisfied is substantially less than the number of values of n such that $\lambda(n) = m$, when m is large.)

Proof. We want to estimate the number of possible addition chains, and for this purpose our first goal is to get an improvement of Theorem A that enables us to deal more satisfactorily with nondoublings.

Lemma P. *Let $\delta < \sqrt{2} - 1$ be a fixed positive real number. Call step i of an addition chain a "ministep" if it is not a doubling and if $a_i < a_j(1+\delta)^{i-j}$ for some j, where $0 \leq j < i$. If the addition chain contains s small steps and t ministeps, then*

$$t \leq s/(1-\theta), \qquad \text{where } (1+\delta)^2 = 2^\theta. \qquad (27)$$

Proof. For each ministep i_k, $1 \leq k \leq t$, we have $a_{i_k} < a_{j_k}(1+\delta)^{i_k-j_k}$ for some $j_k < i_k$. Let I_1, ..., I_t be the intervals $(j_1 .. i_1]$, ..., $(j_t .. i_t]$, where the notation $(j .. i]$ stands for the set of all integers k such that $j < k \leq i$. It is possible (see exercise 17) to find nonoverlapping intervals J_1, ..., $J_h = (j'_1 .. i'_1]$, ..., $(j'_h .. i'_h]$ such that

$$I_1 \cup \cdots \cup I_t = J_1 \cup \cdots \cup J_h,$$
$$a_{i'_k} < a_{j'_k}(1+\delta)^{2(i'_k - j'_k)}, \qquad \text{for } 1 \leq k \leq h. \qquad (28)$$

Now for all steps i outside of the intervals J_1, ..., J_h we have $a_i \leq 2a_{i-1}$; hence if we let

$$q = (i'_1 - j'_1) + \cdots + (i'_h - j'_h),$$

we have $2^{\lambda(n)} \leq n \leq 2^{r-q}(1+\delta)^{2q} = 2^{\lambda(n)+s-(1-\theta)q} \leq 2^{\lambda(n)+s-(1-\theta)t}$. ∎

Returning to the proof of Theorem E, let us choose $\delta = 2^{\epsilon/4} - 1$, and let us divide the r steps of each addition chain into three classes:

$$t \text{ ministeps}, \qquad u \text{ doublings}, \qquad v \text{ other steps}, \qquad t + u + v = r. \qquad (29)$$

Counting another way, we have s small steps, where $s + m = r$. By the hypotheses, Theorem A, and Lemma P, we obtain the relations

$$s \leq (1 - \epsilon)m/\lambda(m), \qquad t + v \leq 3.271s, \qquad t \leq s/(1 - \epsilon/2). \qquad (30)$$

Given s, t, u, v satisfying these conditions, there are

$$\binom{r}{t, u, v} = \binom{r}{t + v}\binom{t + v}{v} \qquad (31)$$

ways to assign the steps to the specified classes. Given such a distribution of the steps, let us consider how the non-ministeps can be selected: If step i is one of the "other" steps in (29), $a_i \geq (1 + \delta)a_{i-1}$, so $a_i = a_j + a_k$, where $\delta a_{i-1} \leq a_k \leq a_j \leq a_{i-1}$. Also $a_j \leq a_i/(1 + \delta)^{i-j} \leq 2a_{i-1}/(1 + \delta)^{i-j}$, so $\delta \leq 2/(1 + \delta)^{i-j}$. This gives at most β choices for j, where β is a constant that depends only on δ. There are also at most β choices for k, so the number of ways to assign j and k for each of the non-ministeps is at most

$$\beta^{2v}. \qquad (32)$$

Finally, once the "j" and "k" have been selected for each of the non-ministeps, there are fewer than

$$\binom{r^2}{t} \qquad (33)$$

ways to choose the j and the k for the ministeps: We select t distinct pairs $(j_1, k_1), \ldots, (j_t, k_t)$ of indices in the range $0 \leq k_h \leq j_h < r$, in fewer than (33) ways. Then for each ministep i, in turn, we use a pair of indices (j_h, k_h) such that

a) $j_h < i$;
b) $a_{j_h} + a_{k_h}$ is as small as possible among the pairs not already used for smaller ministeps i;
c) $a_i = a_{j_h} + a_{k_h}$ satisfies the definition of ministep.

If no such pair (j_h, k_h) exists, we get no addition chain; on the other hand, any addition chain with ministeps in the designated places must be selected in one of these ways, so (33) is an upper bound on the possibilities.

Thus the total number of possible addition chains satisfying (26) is bounded by (31) times (32) times (33), summed over all relevant s, t, u, and v. The proof of Theorem E can now be completed by means of a rather standard estimation of these functions (exercise 18). ∎

Corollary E. The value of $l(n)$ is asymptotically $\lambda(n) + \lambda(n)/\lambda\lambda(n)$, for almost all n. More precisely, there is a function $f(n)$ such that $f(n) \to 0$ as $n \to \infty$, and

$$\Pr\big(\big|l(n) - \lambda(n) - \lambda(n)/\lambda\lambda(n)\big| \geq f(n)\lambda(n)/\lambda\lambda(n)\big) = 0. \qquad (34)$$

(See Section 3.5 for the definition of this probability "Pr".)

Proof. The upper bound (25) shows that (34) holds without the absolute value signs. The lower bound comes from Theorem E, if we let $f(n)$ decrease to zero slowly enough so that, when $f(n) \le \epsilon$, the value N is so large that at most ϵN values $n \le N$ have $l(n) \le \lambda(n) + (1 - \epsilon)\lambda(n)/\lambda\lambda(n)$. ▮

*Star chains. Optimistic people find it reasonable to suppose that $l(n) = l^*(n)$; given an addition chain of minimal length $l(n)$, it appears hard to believe that we cannot find one of the same length that satisfies the (apparently mild) star condition. But in 1958 Walter Hansen proved the remarkable theorem that, for certain large values of n, the value of $l(n)$ is definitely less than $l^*(n)$, and he also proved several related theorems that we shall now investigate.

Hansen's theorems begin with an investigation of the detailed structure of a star chain. Let $n = 2^{e_0} + 2^{e_1} + \cdots + 2^{e_t}$, where $e_0 > e_1 > \cdots > e_t \ge 0$, and let $1 = a_0 < a_1 < \cdots < a_r = n$ be a star chain for n. If there are d doublings in this chain, we define the auxiliary sequence

$$0 = d_0 \le d_1 \le d_2 \le \cdots \le d_r = d, \tag{35}$$

where d_i is the number of doublings among steps $1, 2, \ldots, i$. We also define a sequence of "multisets" $S_0, S_1, \ldots, S_r$, which keep track of the powers of 2 present in the chain. (A *multiset* is a mathematical entity that is like a set, but it is allowed to contain repeated elements; an object may be an element of a multiset several times, and its multiplicity of occurrences is relevant. See exercise 19 for familiar examples of multisets.) The multisets S_i are defined by the rules

a) $S_0 = \{0\}$;

b) If $a_{i+1} = 2a_i$, then $S_{i+1} = S_i + 1 = \{x + 1 \mid x \in S_i\}$;

c) If $a_{i+1} = a_i + a_k$, $k < i$, then $S_{i+1} = S_i \uplus S_k$.

(The symbol $\uplus$ means that the multisets are combined, adding the multiplicities.) From this definition it follows that

$$a_i = \sum_{x \in S_i} 2^x, \tag{36}$$

where the terms in this sum are not necessarily distinct. In particular,

$$n = 2^{e_0} + 2^{e_1} + \cdots + 2^{e_t} = \sum_{x \in S_r} 2^x. \tag{37}$$

The number of elements in the latter sum is at most 2^f, where $f = r - d$ is the number of nondoublings.

Since n has two different binary representations in (37), we can partition the multiset S_r into multisets $M_0, M_1, \ldots, M_t$ such that

$$2^{e_j} = \sum_{x \in M_j} 2^x, \qquad 0 \le j \le t. \tag{38}$$

This can be done by arranging the elements of S_r into nondecreasing order $x_1 \le x_2 \le \cdots$ and taking $M_t = \{x_1, x_2, \ldots, x_k\}$, where $2^{x_1} + \cdots + 2^{x_k} = 2^{e_t}$.

This must be possible, since e_t is the smallest of the e's. Similarly, $M_{t-1} = \{x_{k+1}, x_{k+2}, \ldots, x_{k'}\}$, and so on; the process is easily visualized in binary notation. An example appears below.

Let M_j contain m_j elements (counting multiplicities); then $m_j \leq 2^f - t$, since S_r has at most 2^f elements and it has been partitioned into $t+1$ nonempty multisets. By Eq. (38), we can see that

$$e_j \geq x > e_j - m_j, \qquad \text{for all } x \in M_j. \tag{39}$$

Our examination of the star chain's structure is completed by forming the multisets M_{ij} that record the ancestral history of M_j. The multiset S_i is partitioned into $t+1$ multisets as follows:

a) $M_{rj} = M_j$;

b) If $a_{i+1} = 2a_i$, then $M_{ij} = M_{(i+1)j} - 1 = \{x - 1 \mid x \in M_{(i+1)j}\}$;

c) If $a_{i+1} = a_i + a_k$, $k < i$, then (since $S_{i+1} = S_i \uplus S_k$) we let $M_{ij} = M_{(i+1)j}$ minus S_k, that is, we remove the elements of S_k from $M_{(i+1)j}$. If some element of S_k appears in two or more different multisets $M_{(i+1)j}$, we remove it from the set with the largest possible value of j; this rule uniquely defines M_{ij} for each j, when i is fixed.

From this definition it follows that

$$e_j + d_i - d \geq x > e_j + d_i - d - m_j, \qquad \text{for all } x \in M_{ij}. \tag{40}$$

As an example of this detailed construction, let us consider the star chain 1, 2, 3, 5, 10, 20, 23, for which $t = 3$, $r = 6$, $d = 3$, $f = 3$. We obtain the following array of multisets:

$(d_0, d_1, \ldots, d_6)$:	0	1	1	1	2	3	3		
$(a_0, a_1, \ldots, a_6)$:	1	2	3	5	10	20	23		
$(M_{03}, M_{13}, \ldots, M_{63})$:							0	M_3	$e_3 = 0,\ m_3 = 1$
$(M_{02}, M_{12}, \ldots, M_{62})$:							1	M_2	$e_2 = 1,\ m_2 = 1$
$(M_{01}, M_{11}, \ldots, M_{61})$:			0	0	1	2	2	M_1	$e_1 = 2,\ m_1 = 1$
$(M_{00}, M_{10}, \ldots, M_{60})$:	0	1	1	1	2	3	3	M_0	$e_0 = 4,\ m_0 = 2$
				1	2	3	3		
	S_0	S_1	S_2	S_3	S_4	S_5	S_6		

Thus $M_{40} = \{2, 2\}$, etc. From the construction we can see that d_i is the largest element of S_i; hence

$$d_i \in M_{i0}. \tag{41}$$

The most important part of this structure comes from Eq. (40); one of its immediate consequences is

Lemma K. *If M_{ij} and M_{uv} both contain a common integer x, then*

$$-m_v < (e_j - e_v) - (d_u - d_i) < m_j. \quad \blacksquare \tag{42}$$

Although Lemma K may not look extremely powerful, it says (when m_j and m_v are reasonably small and when M_{ij} contains an element in common with M_{uv}) that the number of doublings between steps u and i is approximately equal to the difference between the exponents e_v and e_j. This imposes a certain amount of regularity on the addition chain; and it suggests that we might be able to prove a result analogous to Theorem B above, that $l^*(n) = e_0 + t$, if the exponents e_j are far enough apart. The next theorem shows how this can in fact be done.

Theorem H. [W. Hansen, *Crelle* **202** (1959), 129–136.] *Let* $n = 2^{e_0} + 2^{e_1} + \cdots + 2^{e_t}$, *where* $e_0 > e_1 > \cdots > e_t \geq 0$. *If*

$$e_0 > 2e_1 + 2.271(t - 1) \qquad \text{and} \qquad e_{i-1} \geq e_i + 2m \quad \text{for } 1 \leq i \leq t, \tag{43}$$

where $m = 2^{\lfloor 3.271(t-1) \rfloor} - t$, *then* $l^*(n) = e_0 + t$.

Proof. We may assume that $t > 2$, since the result of the theorem is true without restriction on the e's when $t \leq 2$. Suppose that we have a star chain $1 = a_0 < a_1 < \cdots < a_r = n$ for n with $r \leq e_0 + t - 1$. Let the integers d, f, $d_0, \ldots, d_r$, and the multisets M_j, S_i, M_{ij} reflect the structure of this chain, as defined above. By Corollary A, we know that $f \leq \lfloor 3.271(t - 1) \rfloor$; therefore the value of m is a bona fide upper bound for the number m_j of elements in each multiset M_j.

In the summation

$$a_i = \left(\sum_{x \in M_{i0}} 2^x \right) + \left(\sum_{x \in M_{i1}} 2^x \right) + \cdots + \left(\sum_{x \in M_{it}} 2^x \right),$$

no carries propagate from the term corresponding to M_{ij} to the term corresponding to $M_{i(j-1)}$, if we think of this sum as being carried out in the binary number system, since the e's are so far apart. (See (40).) In particular, the sum of all the terms for $j \neq 0$ will not carry up to affect the terms for $j = 0$, so we must have

$$a_i \geq \sum_{x \in M_{i0}} 2^x \geq 2^{\lambda(a_i)}, \qquad 0 \leq i \leq r. \tag{44}$$

In order to prove Theorem H, we would like to show that in some sense the t extra powers of n must be put in "one at a time," so we want to find a way to tell at which step each of these terms essentially enters the addition chain.

Let j be a number between 1 and t. Since M_{0j} is empty and $M_{rj} = M_j$ is nonempty, we can find the *first* step i for which M_{ij} is not empty.

From the way in which the M_{ij} are defined, we know that step i is a non-doubling: $a_i = a_{i-1} + a_u$ for some $u < i - 1$. We also know that all the elements of M_{ij} are elements of S_u. We will prove that a_u must be relatively small compared to a_i.

Let x_j be an element of M_{ij}. Then since $x_j \in S_u$, there is some v for which $x_j \in M_{uv}$. It follows that

$$d_i - d_u > m, \tag{45}$$

that is, at least $m + 1$ doublings occur between steps u and i. For if $d_i - d_u \leq m$, Lemma K tells us that $|e_j - e_v| < 2m$; hence $v = j$. But this is impossible, because M_{uj} is empty by our choice of step i.

All elements of S_u are less than or equal to $e_1 + d_i - d$. For if $x \in S_u \subseteq S_i$ and $x > e_1 + d_i - d$, then $x \in M_{u0}$ and $x \in M_{i0}$ by (40); so Lemma K implies that $|d_i - d_u| < m$, contradicting (45). In fact, this argument proves that M_{i0} has no elements in common with S_u, so $M_{(i-1)0} = M_{i0}$. From (44) we have $a_{i-1} \geq 2^{\lambda(a_i)}$, and therefore *step i is a small step.*

We can now deduce what is probably the key fact in this entire proof: *All elements of S_u are in M_{u0}.* For if not, let x be an element of S_u with $x \notin M_{u0}$. Since $x \geq 0$, (40) implies that $e_1 \geq d - d_u$, hence

$$e_0 = f + d - s \leq 2.271s + d \leq 2.271(t - 1) + e_1 + d_u.$$

By hypothesis (43), this implies $d_u > e_1$. But $d_u \in S_u$ by (41), and it cannot be in M_{i0}, hence $d_u \leq e_1 + d_i - d \leq e_1$, a contradiction.

Going back to our element x_j in M_{ij}, we have $x_j \in M_{uv}$; and we have proved that $v = 0$. Therefore, by equation (40) again,

$$e_0 + d_u - d \geq x_j > e_0 + d_u - d - m_0. \tag{46}$$

For all $j = 1, 2, \ldots, t$ we have determined a number x_j satisfying (46), and a small step i at which the term 2^{e_j} may be said to have entered into the addition chain. If $j \neq j'$, the step i at which this occurs cannot be the same for both j and j'; for (46) would tell us that $|x_j - x_{j'}| < m$, while elements of M_{ij} and $M_{ij'}$ must differ by more than m, since e_j and $e_{j'}$ are so far apart. We are forced to conclude that the chain contains at least t small steps; but this is a contradiction. ∎

Theorem F (W. Hansen).

$$l(2^A + xy) \leq A + \nu(x) + \nu(y) - 1, \qquad \text{if } \lambda(x) + \lambda(y) \leq A. \tag{47}$$

Proof. An addition chain (which is *not* a star chain in general) may be constructed by combining the binary and factor methods. Let $x = 2^{x_1} + \cdots + 2^{x_u}$ and $y = 2^{y_1} + \cdots + 2^{y_v}$, where $x_1 > \cdots > x_u \geq 0$ and $y_1 > \cdots > y_v \geq 0$.

The first steps of the chain form successive powers of 2, until 2^{A-y_1} is reached; in between these steps, the additional values $2^{x_{u-1}} + 2^{x_u}$, $2^{x_{u-2}} + 2^{x_{u-1}} + 2^{x_u}$, $\ldots$, and x are inserted in the appropriate places. After a chain up to $2^{A-y_i} + x(2^{y_1-y_i} + \cdots + 2^{y_{i-1}-y_i})$ has been formed, we continue by adding x and doubling the resulting sum $y_i - y_{i+1}$ times; this yields

$$2^{A-y_{i+1}} + x(2^{y_1-y_{i+1}} + \cdots + 2^{y_i-y_{i+1}}).$$

If this construction is done for $i = 1, 2, \ldots, v$, assuming for convenience that $y_{v+1} = 0$, we have an addition chain for $2^A + xy$ as desired. ∎

Theorem F enables us to find values of n for which $l(n) < l^*(n)$, since Theorem H gives an explicit value of $l^*(n)$ in certain cases. For example, let $x = 2^{1016} + 1$, $y = 2^{2032} + 1$, and let

$$n = 2^{6103} + xy = 2^{6103} + 2^{3048} + 2^{2032} + 2^{1016} + 1.$$

According to Theorem F, we have $l(n) \leq 6106$. But Theorem H also applies, with $m = 508$, and this proves that $l^*(n) = 6107$.

Extensive computer calculations have shown that $n = 12509$ is the smallest value with $l(n) < l^*(n)$. No star chain for this value of n is as short as the sequence 1, 2, 4, 8, 16, 17, 32, 64, 128, 256, 512, 1024, 1041, 2082, 4164, 8328, 8345, 12509. The smallest n with $\nu(n) = 5$ and $l(n) \neq l^*(n)$ is $16537 = 2^{14} + 9 \cdot 17$ (see exercise 15).

Jan van Leeuwen has generalized Theorem H to show that

$$l^*(k2^{e_0}) + t \leq l^*(kn) \leq l^*(k2^{e_t}) + e_0 - e_t + t$$

for all fixed $k \geq 1$, if the exponents $e_0 > \cdots > e_t$ are far enough apart [*Crelle* **295** (1977), 202–207].

Some conjectures. Although it was reasonable to guess at first glance that $l(n) = l^*(n)$, we have now seen that this is false. Another plausible conjecture [first made by A. Goulard, and supposedly "proved" by E. de Jonquières in *L'Interméd. des Math.* **2** (1895), 125–126] is that $l(2n) = l(n) + 1$; a doubling step is so efficient, it seems unlikely that there could be any shorter chain for $2n$ than to add a doubling step to the shortest chain for n. But computer calculations show that this conjecture also fails, since $l(191) = l(382) = 11$. (A star chain of length 11 for 382 is not hard to find; for example, 1, 2, 4, 5, 9, 14, 23, 46, 92, 184, 198, 382. The number 191 is minimal such that $l(n) = 11$, and it seems to be nontrivial to prove by hand that $l(191) > 10$. The author's computer-generated proof of this fact, using a backtrack method that will be sketched in Section 7.2.2, involved a detailed examination of 102 cases.) The smallest four values of n such that $l(2n) = l(n)$ are $n = 191, 701, 743, 1111$; E. G. Thurber proved in *Pacific J. Math.* **49** (1973), 229–242, that the third of these is a member of an infinite family of such n, namely $23 \cdot 2^k + 7$ for all $k \geq 5$. Neill Clift found in 2007 that $l(n) = l(2n) = l(4n) = 31$ when $n = 30958077$; and in 2008, astonishingly, he discovered that $l(n) > l(2n) = 34$ when $n = 375494703$. Kevin R. Hebb has shown that $l(n) - l(mn)$ can get arbitrarily large, for all fixed integers m not a power of 2 [*Notices Amer. Math. Soc.* **21** (1974), A–294]. The smallest case in which $l(n) > l(mn)$ is $l((2^{13} + 1)/3) = 15$.

Let $c(r)$ be the smallest value of n such that $l(n) = r$. The computation of $l(n)$ seems to be hardest for this sequence of n's, which begins as follows:

r	$c(r)$	r	$c(r)$	r	$c(r)$
1	2	14	1087	27	2211837
2	3	15	1903	28	4169527
3	5	16	3583	29	7624319
4	7	17	6271	30	14143037
5	11	18	11231	31	25450463
6	19	19	18287	32	46444543
7	29	20	34303	33	89209343
8	47	21	65131	34	155691199
9	71	22	110591	35	298695487
10	127	23	196591	36	550040063
11	191	24	357887	37	994660991
12	379	25	685951	38	1886023151
13	607	26	1176431	39	3502562143

For $r \leq 11$, the value of $c(r)$ is approximately equal to $c(r-1) + c(r-2)$, and this fact led to speculation by several people that $c(r)$ grows like the function ϕ^r; but the result of Theorem D $\bigl($with $n = c(r)\bigr)$ implies that $r/\lg c(r) \to 1$ as $r \to \infty$. The values listed here for $r > 18$ have been computed by Achim Flammenkamp, except that $c(24)$ was first computed by Daniel Bleichenbacher, and $c(29)$ through $c(39)$ by Neill Clift. Flammenkamp notes that $c(r)$ is fairly well approximated by the formula $2^r \exp(-\theta r/\lg r)$ for $10 \leq r \leq 39$, where θ is near $\ln 2$; this agrees nicely with the upper bound (25). Several people had conjectured at one time that $c(r)$ would always be a prime number, in view of the factor method; but $c(15)$, $c(18)$, and $c(21)$ are all divisible by 11. Perhaps no conjecture about addition chains is safe!

Tabulated values of $l(n)$ show that this function is surprisingly smooth; for example, $l(n) = 13$ for all n in the range $1125 \leq n \leq 1148$. The computer calculations show that a table of $l(n)$ may be prepared for $2 \leq n \leq 1000$ by using the formula

$$l(n) = \min(l(n-1) + 1, l_n) - \delta_n, \tag{48}$$

where $l_n = \infty$ if n is prime, otherwise $l_n = l(p) + l(n/p)$ if p is the smallest prime dividing n; and $\delta_n = 1$ for n in Table 1, $\delta_n = 0$ otherwise.

Let $d(r)$ be the number of solutions n to the equation $l(n) = r$. The following table lists the first few values of $d(r)$, according to Flammenkamp and Clift:

r	$d(r)$	r	$d(r)$	r	$d(r)$	r	$d(r)$	r	$d(r)$	r	$d(r)$
1	1	6	15	11	246	16	4490	21	90371	26	1896704
2	2	7	26	12	432	17	8170	22	165432	27	3501029
3	3	8	44	13	772	18	14866	23	303475	28	6465774
4	5	9	78	14	1382	19	27128	24	558275	29	11947258
5	9	10	136	15	2481	20	49544	25	1028508	30	22087489

Surely $d(r)$ must be an increasing function of r, but there is no evident way to prove this seemingly simple assertion, much less to determine the asymptotic growth of $d(r)$ for large r.

The most famous problem about addition chains that is still outstanding is the *Scholz–Brauer conjecture*, which states that

$$l(2^n - 1) \leq n - 1 + l(n). \tag{49}$$

Notice that $2^n - 1$ is the worst case for the binary method, because $\nu(2^n - 1) = n$. E. G. Thurber [*Discrete Math.* **16** (1976), 279–289] has shown that several of these values, including the case $n = 32$, can actually be calculated by hand. Computer calculations by Neill Clift [*Computing* **91** (2011), 265–284] show that $l(2^n - 1)$ is in fact exactly equal to $n - 1 + l(n)$ for $1 \leq n \leq 64$. Arnold Scholz coined the name "addition chain" (in German) and posed (49) as a problem in 1937 [*Jahresbericht der Deutschen Mathematiker-Vereinigung*, Abteilung II, **47** (1937), 41–42]; Alfred Brauer proved in 1939 that

$$l^*(2^n - 1) \leq n - 1 + l^*(n). \tag{50}$$

Table 1

VALUES OF n FOR SPECIAL ADDITION CHAINS

23	163	229	319	371	413	453	553	599	645	707	741	813	849	903
43	165	233	323	373	419	455	557	611	659	709	749	825	863	905
59	179	281	347	377	421	457	561	619	667	711	759	835	869	923
77	203	283	349	381	423	479	569	623	669	713	779	837	887	941
83	211	293	355	382	429	503	571	631	677	715	787	839	893	947
107	213	311	359	395	437	509	573	637	683	717	803	841	899	955
149	227	317	367	403	451	551	581	643	691	739	809	845	901	983

Hansen's theorems show that $l(n)$ can be less than $l^*(n)$, so more work is definitely necessary in order to prove or disprove (49). As a step in this direction, Hansen has defined the concept of an l^0-*chain*, which lies "between" l-chains and l^*-chains. In an l^0-chain, some of the elements are underlined; the condition is that $a_i = a_j + a_k$, where a_j is the largest underlined element less than a_i.

As an example of an l^0-chain (certainly not a minimum one), consider

$$1, \underline{2}, \underline{4}, 5, \underline{8}, 10, 12, \underline{18}; \qquad (51)$$

it is easy to verify that the difference between each element and the previous underlined element is in the chain. We let $l^0(n)$ denote the minimum length of an l^0-chain for n. Clearly $l(n) \le l^0(n) \le l^*(n)$.

Hansen pointed out that the chain constructed in Theorem F is an l^0-chain (see exercise 22); and he also established the following improvement of Eq. (50):

Theorem G. $l^0(2^n - 1) \le n - 1 + l^0(n)$.

Proof. Let $1 = a_0, a_1, \ldots, a_r = n$ be an l^0-chain of minimum length for n, and let $1 = b_0, b_1, \ldots, b_t = n$ be the subsequence of underlined elements. (We may assume that n is underlined.) Then we can get an l^0-chain for $2^n - 1$ as follows:

a) Include the $l^0(n) + 1$ numbers $2^{a_i} - 1$, for $0 \le i \le r$, underlined if and only if a_i is underlined.

b) Include the numbers $2^i(2^{b_j} - 1)$, for $0 \le j < t$ and for $0 < i \le b_{j+1} - b_j$, all underlined. (This is a total of $b_1 - b_0 + \cdots + b_t - b_{t-1} = n - 1$ numbers.)

c) Sort the numbers from (a) and (b) into ascending order.

We may easily verify that this gives an l^0-chain: The numbers of (b) are all equal to twice some other element of (a) or (b); furthermore, this element is the preceding underlined element. If $a_i = b_j + a_k$, where b_j is the largest underlined element less than a_i, then $a_k = a_i - b_j \le b_{j+1} - b_j$, so $2^{a_k}(2^{b_j} - 1) = 2^{a_i} - 2^{a_k}$ appears underlined in the chain, just preceding $2^{a_i} - 1$. Since $2^{a_i} - 1$ is equal to $(2^{a_i} - 2^{a_k}) + (2^{a_k} - 1)$, where both of these values appear in the chain, we have an addition chain with the l^0 property. ∎

The chain corresponding to (51), constructed in the proof of Theorem G, is

$\underline{1}, \underline{2}, 3, \underline{6}, \underline{12}, 15, \underline{30}, 31, \underline{60}, \underline{120}, \underline{240}, 255, \underline{510}, \underline{1020}, 1023, \underline{2040},$
$\qquad\qquad 4080, 4095, \underline{8160}, \underline{16320}, \underline{32640}, \underline{65280}, \underline{130560}, \underline{261120}, 262143.$

Computations by Neill Clift have shown that $l(n) < l^0(n)$ when $n = 5784689$ (see exercise 42). This is the smallest case where Eq. (49) remains in doubt.

Graphical representation. An addition chain (1) corresponds in a natural way to a directed graph, where the vertices are labeled a_i for $0 \le i \le r$, and where we draw arcs from a_j to a_i and from a_k to a_i as a representation of each step $a_i = a_j + a_k$ in (2). For example, the addition chain 1, 2, 3, 6, 12, 15, 27, 39, 78, 79 that appears in Fig. 15 corresponds to the directed graph

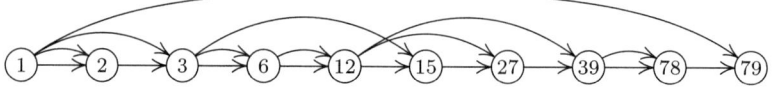

If $a_i = a_j + a_k$ for more than one pair of indices (j, k), we choose a definite j and k for purposes of this construction.

In general, all but the first vertex of such a directed graph will be at the head of exactly two arcs; however, this is not really an important property of the graph, because it conceals the fact that many different addition chains can be essentially equivalent. If a vertex has out-degree 1, it is used in only one later step, hence the later step is essentially a sum of three inputs $a_j + a_k + a_m$ that might be computed either as $(a_j+a_k)+a_m$ or as $a_j+(a_k+a_m)$ or as $a_k+(a_j+a_m)$. These three choices are immaterial, but the addition-chain conventions force us to distinguish between them. We can avoid such redundancy by deleting any vertex whose out-degree is 1 and attaching the arcs from its predecessors to its successor. For example, the graph above would become

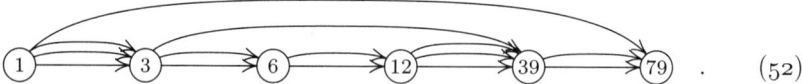   (52)

We can also delete any vertex whose out-degree is 0, except of course the final vertex a_r, since such a vertex corresponds to a useless step in the addition chain.

In this way every addition chain leads to a reduced directed graph that contains one "source" vertex (labeled 1) and one "sink" vertex (labeled n); every vertex but the source has in-degree ≥ 2 and every vertex but the sink has out-degree ≥ 2. Conversely, any such directed graph without oriented cycles corresponds to at least one addition chain, since we can topologically sort the vertices and write down $d - 1$ addition steps for each vertex of in-degree $d > 0$. The length of the addition chain, exclusive of useless steps, can be reconstructed by looking at the reduced graph; it is

$$(\text{number of arcs}) - (\text{number of vertices}) + 1, \qquad (53)$$

since deletion of a vertex of out-degree 1 also deletes one arc.

We say that two addition chains are *equivalent* if they have the same reduced directed graph. For example, the addition chain 1, 2, 3, 6, 12, 15, 24, 39, 40, 79 is equivalent to the chain we began with, since it also leads to (52). This example shows that a non-star chain can be equivalent to a star chain. An addition chain is equivalent to a star chain if and only if its reduced directed graph can be topologically sorted in only one way.

An important property of this graph representation has been pointed out by N. Pippenger: The label of each vertex is exactly equal to the number of oriented paths from the source to that vertex. Thus, the problem of finding an optimal addition chain for n is equivalent to minimizing the quantity (53) over all directed graphs that have one source vertex and one sink vertex and exactly n oriented paths from the source to the sink.

This characterization has a surprising corollary, because of the symmetry of the directed graph. If we reverse the directions of all the arcs, the source and the sink exchange roles, and we obtain another directed graph corresponding to a set of addition chains for the same n; these addition chains have the same length (53) as the chain we started with. For example, if we make the arrows in (52) run from right to left, and if we relabel the vertices according to the number of paths from the right-hand vertex, we get

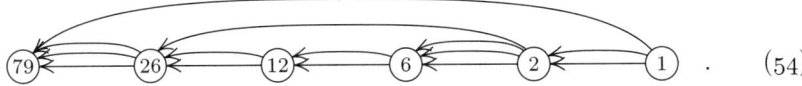

$$(54)$$

One of the star chains corresponding to this reduced directed graph is

$$1, 2, 4, 6, 12, 24, 26, 52, 78, 79;$$

we may call this a *dual* of the original addition chain.

Exercises 39 and 40 discuss important consequences of this graphical representation and the duality principle.

EXERCISES

1. [*15*] What is the value of Z when Algorithm A terminates?

2. [*24*] Write a MIX program for Algorithm A, to calculate $x^n \bmod w$ given integers n and x, where w is the word size. Assume that MIX has the binary operations SRB, JAE, etc., that are described in Section 4.5.2. Write another program that computes $x^n \bmod w$ in a serial manner (multiplying repeatedly by x), and compare the running times of these programs.

▶ **3.** [*22*] How is x^{975} calculated by (a) the binary method? (b) the ternary method? (c) the quaternary method? (d) the factor method?

4. [*M20*] Find a number n for which the octal (2^3-ary) method gives ten fewer multiplications than the binary method.

▶ **5.** [*24*] Figure 14 shows the first eight levels of the "power tree." The $(k+1)$st level of this tree is defined as follows, assuming that the first k levels have been constructed: Take each node n of the kth level, from left to right in turn, and attach below it the nodes

$$n + 1, \ n + a_1, \ n + a_2, \ \ldots, \ n + a_{k-1} = 2n$$

(in this order), where $1, a_1, a_2, \ldots, a_{k-1}$ is the path from the root of the tree to n; but discard any node that duplicates a number that has already appeared in the tree.

Design an efficient algorithm that constructs the first $r+1$ levels of the power tree. [*Hint:* Make use of two sets of variables LINKU[j], LINKR[j] for $0 \le j \le 2^r$; these point upwards and to the right, respectively, if j is a number in the tree.]

6. [*M26*] If a slight change is made to the definition of the power tree that is given in exercise 5, so that the nodes below n are attached in *decreasing* order

$$n + a_{k-1}, \ldots, n + a_2, n + a_1, n + 1$$

instead of increasing order, we get a tree whose first five levels are

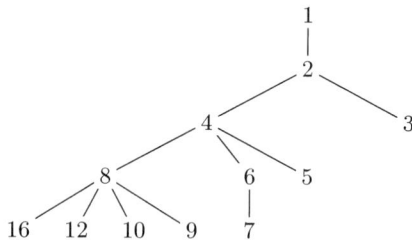

Show that this tree gives a method of computing x^n that requires exactly as many multiplications as the binary method; therefore it is not as good as the power tree, although it has been constructed in almost the same way.

7. [*M21*] Prove that there are infinitely many values of n

a) for which the factor method is better than the binary method;
b) for which the binary method is better than the factor method;
c) for which the power tree method is better than both the binary and factor methods.

(Here the "better" method is the one that computes x^n using fewer multiplications.)

8. [*M21*] Prove that the power tree (exercise 5) never gives more multiplications for the computation of x^n than the binary method.

▶ **9.** [*25*] Design an exponentiation procedure that is analogous to Algorithm A, but based on radix $m = 2^e$. Your method should perform approximately $\lg n + \nu + m$ multiplications, where ν is the number of nonzero digits in the m-ary representation of n.

10. [*10*] Figure 15 shows a tree that indicates one way to compute x^n with the fewest possible multiplications, for all $n \le 100$. How can this tree be conveniently represented within a computer, in just 100 memory locations?

▶ **11.** [*M26*] The tree of Fig. 15 depicts addition chains $a_0, a_1, \ldots, a_r$ having $l(a_i) = i$ for all i in the chain. Find all addition chains for n that have this property, when $n = 43$ and when $n = 77$. Show that any tree such as Fig. 15 must include either the path 1, 2, 4, 8, 9, 17, 34, 43, 77 or the path 1, 2, 4, 8, 9, 17, 34, 68, 77.

12. [*M10*] Is it possible to extend the tree shown in Fig. 15 to an infinite tree that yields a minimum-multiplication rule for computing x^n, for all positive integers n?

13. [*M21*] Find a star chain of length $A + 2$ for each of the four cases listed in Theorem C. (Consequently Theorem C holds also with l replaced by l^*.)

14. [*M29*] Complete the proof of Theorem C, by demonstrating that (a) step $r - 1$ is not a small step; and (b) $\lambda(a_{r-k})$ cannot be less than $m - 1$, where $m = \lambda(a_{r-1})$.

15. [*M43*] Write a computer program to extend Theorem C, characterizing all n such that $l(n) = \lambda(n) + 3$ and characterizing all n such that $l^*(n) = \lambda(n) + 3$.

16. [*HM15*] Show that Theorem D is not trivially true just because of the binary method; if $l^B(n)$ denotes the length of the addition chain for n produced by the binary S-and-X method, the ratio $l^B(n)/\lambda(n)$ does not approach a limit as $n \to \infty$.

17. [*M25*] Explain how to find the intervals $J_1, \ldots, J_h$ that are required in the proof of Lemma P.

18. [*HM24*] Let β be a positive constant. Show that there is a constant $\alpha < 2$ such that

$$\sum \binom{m+s}{t+v}\binom{t+v}{v}\beta^{2v}\binom{(m+s)^2}{t} < \alpha^m$$

for all large m, where the sum is over all s, t, v satisfying (30).

19. [*M23*] A "multiset" is like a set, but it may contain identical elements repeated a finite number of times. If A and B are multisets, we define new multisets $A \uplus B$, $A \cup B$, and $A \cap B$ in the following way: An element occurring exactly a times in A and b times in B occurs exactly $a + b$ times in $A \uplus B$, exactly $\max(a,b)$ times in $A \cup B$, and exactly $\min(a,b)$ times in $A \cap B$. (A "set" is a multiset that contains no elements more than once; if A and B are sets, so are $A \cup B$ and $A \cap B$, and the definitions given in this exercise agree with the customary definitions of set union and intersection.)

  a) The prime factorization of a positive integer n is a multiset N whose elements are primes, where $\prod_{p \in N} p = n$. The fact that every positive integer can be uniquely factored into primes gives us a one-to-one correspondence between the positive integers and the finite multisets of prime numbers; for example, if $n = 2^2 \cdot 3^3 \cdot 17$, the corresponding multiset is $N = \{2, 2, 3, 3, 3, 17\}$. If M and N are the multisets corresponding respectively to m and n, what multisets correspond to $\gcd(m, n)$, $\operatorname{lcm}(m, n)$, and mn?

  b) Every monic polynomial $f(z)$ over the complex numbers corresponds in a natural way to the multiset F of its "roots"; we have $f(z) = \prod_{\zeta \in F}(z - \zeta)$. If $f(z)$ and $g(z)$ are the polynomials corresponding to the finite multisets F and G of complex numbers, what polynomials correspond to $F \uplus G$, $F \cup G$, and $F \cap G$?

  c) Find as many interesting identities as you can that hold between multisets, with respect to the three operations $\uplus$, $\cup$, $\cap$.

20. [*M20*] What are the sequences S_i and M_{ij} ($0 \leq i \leq r$, $0 \leq j \leq t$) arising in Hansen's structural decomposition of star chains (a) of Type 3? (b) of Type 5? (The six "types" are defined in the proof of Theorem B.)

▶ **21.** [*M26*] (W. Hansen.) Let q be any positive integer. Find a value of n such that $l(n) \leq l^*(n) - q$.

22. [*M20*] Prove that the addition chain constructed in the proof of Theorem F is an l^0-chain.

23. [*M20*] Prove Brauer's inequality (50).

▶ **24.** [*M22*] Generalize the proof of Theorem G to show that $l^0((B^n - 1)/(B - 1)) \leq (n - 1)\,l^0(B) + l^0(n)$, for any integer $B > 1$; and prove that $l(2^{mn} - 1) \leq l(2^m - 1) + mn - m + l^0(n)$.

25. [*20*] Let y be a fraction, $0 < y < 1$, expressed in the binary number system as $y = (.d_1 \ldots d_k)_2$. Design an algorithm to compute x^y using the operations of multiplication and square-root extraction.

▶ **26.** [*M25*] Design an efficient algorithm that computes the nth Fibonacci number F_n, modulo m, given large integers n and m.

27. [*M23*] (A. Flammenkamp.) What is the smallest n for which every addition chain contains at least eight small steps?

28. [*HM33*] (A. Schönhage.) The object of this exercise is to give a fairly short proof that $l(n) \geq \lambda(n) + \lg \nu(n) - O(\log \log(\nu(n) + 1))$.

a) When $x = (x_k \ldots x_0.x_{-1} \ldots)_2$ and $y = (y_k \ldots y_0.y_{-1} \ldots)_2$ are real numbers written in binary notation, let us write $x \subseteq y$ if $x_j \leq y_j$ for all j. Give a simple rule for constructing the smallest number z with the property that $x' \subseteq x$ and $y' \subseteq y$ implies $x' + y' \subseteq z$. Denoting this number by $x \nabla y$, prove that $\nu(x \nabla y) \leq \nu(x) + \nu(y)$.

b) Given any addition chain (11) with $r = l(n)$, let the sequence $d_0, d_1, \ldots, d_r$ be defined as in (35), and define the sequence $A_0, A_1, \ldots, A_r$ by the following rules: $A_0 = 1$; if $a_i = 2a_{i-1}$ then $A_i = 2A_{i-1}$; otherwise if $a_i = a_j + a_k$ for some $0 \leq k \leq j < i$, then $A_i = A_{i-1} \nabla (A_{i-1}/2^{d_j - d_k})$. Prove that this sequence "covers" the given chain, in the sense that $a_i \subseteq A_i$ for $0 \leq i \leq r$.

c) Let δ be a positive integer (to be selected later). Call the nondoubling step $a_i = a_j + a_k$ a "baby step" if $d_j - d_k \geq \delta$, otherwise call it a "close step." Let $B_0 = 1$; $B_i = 2B_{i-1}$ if $a_i = 2a_{i-1}$; $B_i = B_{i-1} \nabla (B_{i-1}/2^{d_j - d_k})$ if $a_i = a_j + a_k$ is a baby step; and $B_i = \rho(2B_{i-1})$ otherwise, where $\rho(x)$ is the least number y such that $x/2^e \subseteq y$ for $0 \leq e \leq \delta$. Show that $A_i \subseteq B_i$ and $\nu(B_i) \leq (1 + \delta c_i) 2^{b_i}$ for $0 \leq i \leq r$, where b_i and c_i respectively denote the number of baby steps and close steps $\leq i$. [*Hint:* Show that the 1s in B_i appear in consecutive blocks of size $\geq 1 + \delta c_i$.]

d) We now have $l(n) = r = b_r + c_r + d_r$ and $\nu(n) \leq \nu(B_r) \leq (1 + \delta c_r) 2^{b_r}$. Explain how to choose δ in order to obtain the inequality stated at the beginning of this exercise. [*Hint:* See (16), and note that $n \leq 2^r \alpha^{b_r}$ for some $\alpha < 1$ depending on δ.]

29. [*M49*] Is $\nu(n) \leq 2^{l(n) - \lambda(n)}$ for all positive integers n? (If so, we have the lower bound $l(2^n - 1) \geq n - 1 + \lceil \lg n \rceil$; see (17) and (49).)

30. [*20*] An *addition-subtraction chain* has the rule $a_i = a_j \pm a_k$ in place of (2); the imaginary computer described in the text has a new operation code, SUB. (This corresponds in practice to evaluating x^n using both multiplications and divisions.) Find an addition-subtraction chain, for some n, that has fewer than $l(n)$ steps.

31. [*M46*] (D. H. Lehmer.) Explore the problem of minimizing $\epsilon q + (r - q)$ in an addition chain (1), where q is the number of "simple" steps in which $a_i = a_{i-1} + 1$, given a small positive "weight" ϵ. (This problem comes closer to reality for many calculations of x^n, if multiplication by x is simpler than a general multiplication; see the applications in Section 4.6.2.)

32. [*M30*] (A. C. Yao, F. F. Yao, R. L. Graham.) Associate the "cost" $a_j a_k$ with each step $a_i = a_j + a_k$ of an addition chain (1). Show that the left-to-right binary method yields a chain of minimum total cost, for all positive integers n.

33. [*15*] How many addition chains of length 9 have (52) as their reduced directed graph?

34. [*M23*] The binary addition chain for $n = 2^{e_0} + \cdots + 2^{e_t}$, when $e_0 > \cdots > e_t \geq 0$, is $1, 2, \ldots, 2^{e_0 - e_1}, 2^{e_0 - e_1} + 1, \ldots, 2^{e_0 - e_2} + 2^{e_1 - e_2}, 2^{e_0 - e_2} + 2^{e_1 - e_2} + 1, \ldots, n$. This corresponds to the S-and-X method described at the beginning of this section, while Algorithm A corresponds to the addition chain obtained by sorting the two sequences $(1, 2, 4, \ldots, 2^{e_0})$ and $(2^{e_{t-1}} + 2^{e_t}, 2^{e_{t-2}} + 2^{e_{t-1}} + 2^{e_t}, \ldots, n)$ into increasing order. Prove or disprove: Each of these addition chains is a dual of the other.

35. [*M27*] How many addition chains without useless steps are equivalent to each of the addition chains discussed in exercise 34, when $e_0 > e_1 + 1$?

▶ **36.** [*25*] (E. G. Straus.) Find a way to compute a general *monomial* $x_1^{n_1} x_2^{n_2} \ldots x_m^{n_m}$ in at most $2\lambda(\max(n_1, n_2, \ldots, n_m)) + 2^m - m - 1$ multiplications.

37. [*HM30*] (A. C. Yao.) Let $l(n_1, \ldots, n_m)$ be the length of the shortest addition chain that contains m given numbers $n_1 < \cdots < n_m$. Prove that $l(n_1, \ldots, n_m) \leq \lambda(n_m) + m\lambda(n_m)/\lambda\lambda(n_m) + O(\lambda(n_m)\lambda\lambda\lambda(n_m)/\lambda\lambda(n_m)^2)$, thereby generalizing (25).

38. [*M47*] What is the asymptotic value of $l(1, 4, 9, \ldots, m^2) - m$, as $m \to \infty$, in the notation of exercise 37?

▶ **39.** [*M25*] (J. Olivos, 1979.) Let $l([n_1, n_2, \ldots, n_m])$ be the minimum number of multiplications needed to evaluate the monomial $x_1^{n_1} x_2^{n_2} \ldots x_m^{n_m}$ in the sense of exercise 36, where each n_i is a positive integer. Prove that this problem is equivalent to the problem of exercise 37, by showing that $l([n_1, n_2, \ldots, n_m]) = l(n_1, n_2, \ldots, n_m) + m - 1$. [*Hint:* Consider directed graphs like (52) that have more than one source vertex.]

▶ **40.** [*M21*] (J. Olivos.) Generalizing the factor method and Theorem F, prove that

$$l(m_1 n_1 + \cdots + m_t n_t) \leq l(m_1, \ldots, m_t) + l(n_1, \ldots, n_t) + t - 1,$$

where $l(n_1, \ldots, n_t)$ is defined in exercise 37.

41. [*M40*] (P. Downey, B. Leong, R. Sethi.) Let G be a connected graph with n vertices $\{1, \ldots, n\}$ and m edges, where the edges join u_j to v_j for $1 \leq j \leq m$. Prove that $l(1, 2, \ldots, 2^{An}, 2^{Au_1} + 2^{Av_1} + 1, \ldots, 2^{Au_m} + 2^{Av_m} + 1) = An + m + k$ for all sufficiently large A, where k is the minimum number of vertices in a vertex cover for G (namely a set that contains either u_j or v_j for $1 \leq j \leq m$).

42. [*22*] (Neill Clift, 2005.) Show that neither 1, 2, 4, 8, 16, 32, 64, 65, 97, 128, 256, 353, 706, 1412, 2824, 5648, 11296, 22592, 45184, 90368, 180736, 361472, 361537, 723074, 1446148, 2892296, 5784592, 5784689 nor its dual is an l^0-chain.

43. [*M50*] Is $l(2^n - 1) \leq n - 1 + l(n)$ for all integers $n > 0$? Does equality always hold?

4.6.4. Evaluation of Polynomials

Now that we know efficient ways to evaluate the special polynomial x^n, let us consider the general problem of computing an nth degree polynomial

$$u(x) = u_n x^n + u_{n-1} x^{n-1} + \cdots + u_1 x + u_0, \qquad u_n \neq 0, \tag{1}$$

for given values of x. This problem arises frequently in practice.

In the following discussion we shall concentrate on minimizing the number of operations required to evaluate polynomials by computer, blithely assuming that all arithmetic operations are exact. Polynomials are most commonly evaluated using floating point arithmetic, which is not exact, and different schemes for the evaluation will, in general, give different answers. A numerical analysis of the accuracy achieved depends on the coefficients of the particular polynomial being considered, and is beyond the scope of this book; the reader should be careful to investigate the accuracy of any calculations undertaken with floating point arithmetic. In most cases the methods we shall describe turn out to be reasonably satisfactory from a numerical standpoint, but many bad examples can also be given. [See Webb Miller, *SICOMP* **4** (1975), 97–107, for a survey of the literature on stability of fast polynomial evaluation, and for a demonstration that certain kinds of numerical stability cannot be guaranteed for some families of high-speed algorithms.]

Throughout this section we will act as if the variable x were a single number. But it is important to keep in mind that most of the methods we will discuss are valid also when the variables are large objects like multiprecision numbers, polynomials, or matrices. In such cases efficient formulas lead to even bigger payoffs, especially when we can reduce the number of multiplications.

A beginning programmer will often evaluate the polynomial (1) in a manner that corresponds directly to its conventional textbook form: First $u_n x^n$ is calculated, then $u_{n-1} x^{n-1}$, ..., $u_1 x$, and finally all of the terms of (1) are added together. But even if the efficient methods of Section 4.6.3 are used to evaluate the powers of x in this approach, the resulting calculation is needlessly slow unless nearly all of the coefficients u_k are zero. If the coefficients are all nonzero, an obvious alternative would be to evaluate (1) from right to left, computing the values of x^k and $u_k x^k + \cdots + u_0$ for $k = 1, \ldots, n$. Such a process involves $2n - 1$ multiplications and n additions, and it might also require further instructions to store and retrieve intermediate results from memory.

Horner's rule. One of the first things a novice programmer is usually taught is an elegant way to rearrange this computation, by evaluating $u(x)$ as follows:

$$u(x) = \bigl(\ldots (u_n x + u_{n-1}) x + \cdots \bigr) x + u_0. \tag{2}$$

Start with u_n, multiply by x, add u_{n-1}, multiply by x, ..., multiply by x, add u_0. This form of the computation is usually called "Horner's rule"; we have already seen it used in connection with radix conversion in Section 4.4. The entire process requires n multiplications and n additions, minus one addition for each coefficient that is zero. Furthermore, there is no need to store partial results, since each quantity arising during the calculation is used immediately after it has been computed.

W. G. Horner gave this rule early in the nineteenth century [*Philosophical Transactions*, Royal Society of London **109** (1819), 308–335] in connection with a procedure for calculating polynomial roots. The fame of the latter method [see J. L. Coolidge, *Mathematics of Great Amateurs* (Oxford, 1949), Chapter 15] accounts for the fact that Horner's name has been attached to (2); but actually Isaac Newton had made use of the same idea more than 150 years earlier. For example, in a well-known work entitled *De Analysi per Æquationes Infinitas*, originally written in 1669, Newton wrote

$$\overline{\overline{y - 4 \times y : + 5}} \times y : - 12 \times y : + 17$$

for the polynomial $y^4 - 4y^3 + 5y^2 - 12y + 17$, while illustrating what later came to be known as Newton's method for rootfinding. This clearly shows the idea of (2), since he often denoted grouping by using horizontal lines and colons instead of parentheses. Newton had been using the idea for several years in unpublished notes. [See *The Mathematical Papers of Isaac Newton*, edited by D. T. Whiteside, **1** (1967), 490, 531; **2** (1968), 222.] Independently, a method equivalent to Horner's had in fact been used in 13th-century China by Ch'in Chiu-Shao [see Y. Mikami, *The Development of Mathematics in China and Japan* (1913), 73–77].

Several generalizations of Horner's rule have been suggested. Let us first consider evaluating $u(z)$ when z is a complex number, while the coefficients u_k are real. In particular, when $z = e^{i\theta} = \cos\theta + i\sin\theta$, the polynomial $u(z)$ is essentially two Fourier series,

$$(u_0 + u_1\cos\theta + \cdots + u_n\cos n\theta) + i(u_1\sin\theta + \cdots + u_n\sin n\theta).$$

Complex addition and multiplication can obviously be reduced to a sequence of ordinary operations on real numbers:

real + complex	requires	1 addition
complex + complex	requires	2 additions
real × complex	requires	2 multiplications
complex × complex	requires	4 multiplications, 2 additions
	or	3 multiplications, 5 additions

(See exercise 41. Subtraction is considered here as if it were equivalent to addition.) Therefore Horner's rule (2) uses either $4n - 2$ multiplications and $3n - 2$ additions or $3n - 1$ multiplications and $6n - 5$ additions to evaluate $u(z)$ when $z = x + iy$ is complex. Actually $2n - 4$ of these additions can be saved, since we are multiplying by the same number z each time. An alternative procedure for evaluating $u(x + iy)$ is to let

$$a_1 = u_n, \qquad b_1 = u_{n-1}, \qquad r = x + x, \quad s = x^2 + y^2;$$
$$a_j = b_{j-1} + ra_{j-1}, \quad b_j = u_{n-j} - sa_{j-1}, \qquad 1 < j \le n. \tag{3}$$

Then it is easy to prove by induction that $u(z) = za_n + b_n$. This scheme [*BIT* **5** (1965), 142; see also G. Goertzel, *AMM* **65** (1958), 34–35] requires only $2n + 2$ multiplications and $2n + 1$ additions, so it is an improvement over Horner's rule when $n \ge 3$. In the case of Fourier series, when $z = e^{i\theta}$, we have $s = 1$, so the number of multiplications drops to $n + 1$. The moral of this story is that a good programmer does not make indiscriminate use of the built-in complex-arithmetic features of high-level programming languages.

Consider the process of dividing the polynomial $u(x)$ by $x - x_0$, using Algorithm 4.6.1D to obtain $u(x) = (x - x_0)q(x) + r(x)$; here $\deg(r) < 1$, so $r(x)$ is a constant independent of x, and $u(x_0) = 0 \cdot q(x_0) + r = r$. An examination of this division process reveals that the computation is essentially the same as Horner's rule for evaluating $u(x_0)$. Similarly, if we divide $u(z)$ by the polynomial $(z - z_0)(z - \bar{z}_0) = z^2 - 2x_0z + x_0^2 + y_0^2$, the resulting computation turns out to be equivalent to (3); we obtain $u(z) = (z - z_0)(z - \bar{z}_0)q(z) + a_nz + b_n$, hence $u(z_0) = a_nz_0 + b_n$.

In general, if we divide $u(x)$ by $f(x)$ to obtain $u(x) = f(x)q(x) + r(x)$, and if $f(x_0) = 0$, we have $u(x_0) = r(x_0)$; this observation leads to further generalizations of Horner's rule. For example, we may let $f(x) = x^2 - x_0^2$; this yields the "second-order" Horner's rule

$$u(x) = \left(\ldots (u_{2\lfloor n/2\rfloor}x^2 + u_{2\lfloor n/2\rfloor-2})x^2 + \cdots\right)x^2 + u_0$$
$$+ \left((\ldots (u_{2\lceil n/2\rceil-1}x^2 + u_{2\lceil n/2\rceil-3})x^2 + \cdots)x^2 + u_1\right)x. \tag{4}$$

The second-order rule uses $n+1$ multiplications and n additions (see exercise 5); so it is no improvement over Horner's rule from this standpoint. But there are at least two circumstances in which (4) is useful: If we want to evaluate both $u(x)$ and $u(-x)$, this approach yields $u(-x)$ with just one more addition operation; two values can be obtained almost as cheaply as one. Moreover, if we have a computer that allows parallel computations, the two lines of (4) may be evaluated independently, so we save about half the running time.

When our computer allows parallel computation on k arithmetic units at once, a "kth-order" Horner's rule $\left(\text{obtained in a similar manner from } f(x) = x^k - x_0^k\right)$ may be used. Another attractive method for parallel computation has been suggested by G. Estrin [*Proc. Western Joint Computing Conf.* **17** (1960), 33–40]; for $n = 7$, Estrin's method is:

Processor 1	Processor 2	Processor 3	Processor 4	Processor 5
$a_1 = u_7 x + u_6$	$b_1 = u_5 x + u_4$	$c_1 = u_3 x + u_2$	$d_1 = u_1 x + u_0$	x^2
$a_2 = a_1 x^2 + b_1$		$c_2 = c_1 x^2 + d_1$		x^4
$a_3 = a_2 x^4 + c_2$				

Here $a_3 = u(x)$. However, an interesting analysis by W. S. Dorn [*IBM J. Res. and Devel.* **6** (1962), 239–245] shows that these methods might not actually be an improvement over the second-order rule, if each arithmetic unit must access a memory that communicates with only one processor at a time.

Tabulating polynomial values. If we wish to evaluate an nth degree polynomial at many points in an arithmetic progression $\big($that is, if we want to calculate $u(x_0)$, $u(x_0 + h)$, $u(x_0 + 2h)$, $\ldots\big)$, the process can be reduced to addition only, after the first few steps. For if we start with any sequence of numbers $(\alpha_0, \alpha_1, \ldots, \alpha_n)$ and apply the transformation

$$\alpha_0 \leftarrow \alpha_0 + \alpha_1, \quad \alpha_1 \leftarrow \alpha_1 + \alpha_2, \quad \ldots, \quad \alpha_{n-1} \leftarrow \alpha_{n-1} + \alpha_n, \qquad (5)$$

we find that k applications of (5) yields

$$\alpha_j^{(k)} = \binom{k}{0}\beta_j + \binom{k}{1}\beta_{j+1} + \binom{k}{2}\beta_{j+2} + \cdots, \qquad 0 \le j \le n,$$

where β_j denotes the initial value of α_j and $\beta_j = 0$ for $j > n$. In particular,

$$\alpha_0^{(k)} = \binom{k}{0}\beta_0 + \binom{k}{1}\beta_1 + \cdots + \binom{k}{n}\beta_n \qquad (6)$$

is a polynomial of degree n in k. By properly choosing the β's, as shown in exercise 7, we can set things up so that this quantity $\alpha_0^{(k)}$ is the desired value $u(x_0 + kh)$, for all k. In other words, each execution of the n additions in (5) will produce the next value of the given polynomial.

Caution: Rounding errors can accumulate after many repetitions of (5), and an error in α_j produces a corresponding error in the coefficients of x^0, $\ldots$, x^j in the polynomial being computed. Therefore the values of the α's should be "refreshed" after a large number of iterations.

Derivatives and changes of variable. Sometimes we want to find the coefficients of $u(x+x_0)$, given a constant x_0 and the coefficients of $u(x)$. For example, if $u(x) = 3x^2 + 2x - 1$, then $u(x-2) = 3x^2 - 10x + 7$. This is analogous to a radix conversion problem, converting from base x to base $x + 2$. By Taylor's theorem, the new coefficients are given by the derivatives of $u(x)$ at $x = x_0$, namely

$$u(x + x_0) = u(x_0) + u'(x_0)x + \left(u''(x_0)/2!\right)x^2 + \cdots + \left(u^{(n)}(x_0)/n!\right)x^n, \qquad (7)$$

so the problem is equivalent to evaluating $u(x)$ and all its derivatives.

If we write $u(x) = q(x)(x - x_0) + r$, then $u(x + x_0) = q(x + x_0)x + r$; so r is the constant coefficient of $u(x + x_0)$, and the problem reduces to finding the coefficients of $q(x + x_0)$, where $q(x)$ is a known polynomial of degree $n - 1$. Thus the following algorithm is indicated:

H1. Set $v_j \leftarrow u_j$ for $0 \le j \le n$.

H2. For $k = 0, 1, \ldots, n - 1$ (in this order), set $v_j \leftarrow v_j + x_0 v_{j+1}$ for $j = n - 1$, $\ldots, k + 1, k$ (in this order). ∎

At the conclusion of step H2 we have $u(x + x_0) = v_n x^n + \cdots + v_1 x + v_0$. This procedure was a principal part of Horner's root-finding method, and when $k = 0$ it is exactly rule (2) for evaluating $u(x_0)$.

Horner's method requires $(n^2 + n)/2$ multiplications and $(n^2 + n)/2$ additions; but notice that if $x_0 = 1$ we avoid all of the multiplications. Fortunately we can reduce the general problem to the case $x_0 = 1$ by introducing comparatively few multiplications and divisions:

S1. Compute and store the values $x_0^2, \ldots, x_0^n$.

S2. Set $v_j \leftarrow u_j x_0^j$ for $0 \le j \le n$. $\left(\text{Now } v(x) = u(x_0 x).\right)$

S3. Perform step H2 but with $x_0 = 1$. $\left(\text{Now } v(x) = u\left(x_0(x+1)\right) = u(x_0 x + x_0).\right)$

S4. Set $v_j \leftarrow v_j / x_0^j$ for $0 < j \le n$. $\left(\text{Now } v(x) = u(x + x_0) \text{ as desired.}\right)$ ∎

This idea, due to M. Shaw and J. F. Traub [*JACM* **21** (1974), 161–167], has the same number of additions and the same numerical stability as Horner's method; but it needs only $2n - 1$ multiplications and $n - 1$ divisions, since $v_n = u_n$. About $\frac{1}{2}n$ of these multiplications can, in turn, be avoided (see exercise 6).

If we want only the first few or the last few derivatives, Shaw and Traub have observed that there are further ways to save time. For example, if we just want to evaluate $u(x)$ and $u'(x)$, we can do the job with $2n - 1$ additions and about $n + \sqrt{2n}$ multiplications/divisions as follows:

D1. Compute and store the values $x^2, x^3, \ldots, x^t, x^{2t}$, where $t = \left\lceil \sqrt{n/2} \right\rceil$.

D2. Set $v_j \leftarrow u_j x^{f(j)}$ for $0 \le j \le n$, where $f(j) = t - 1 - \left((n - 1 - j) \bmod 2t\right)$ for $0 \le j < n$, and $f(n) = t$.

D3. Set $v_j \leftarrow v_j + v_{j+1} x^{g(j)}$ for $j = n-1, \ldots, 1, 0$; here $g(j) = 2t$ when $n - 1 - j$ is a positive multiple of $2t$, otherwise $g(j) = 0$ and the multiplication by $x^{g(j)}$ need not be done.

D4. Set $v_j \leftarrow v_j + v_{j+1} x^{g(j)}$ for $j = n - 1, \ldots, 2, 1$. Now $v_0 / x^{f(0)} = u(x)$ and $v_1 / x^{f(1)} = u'(x)$. ∎

Adaptation of coefficients. Let us now return to our original problem of evaluating a given polynomial $u(x)$ as rapidly as possible, for "random" values of x. The importance of this problem is due partly to the fact that standard functions such as $\sin x$, $\cos x$, e^x, etc., are usually computed by subroutines that rely on the evaluation of certain polynomials; such polynomials are evaluated so often, it is desirable to find the fastest possible way to do the computation.

Arbitrary polynomials of degree five and higher can be evaluated with fewer operations than Horner's rule requires, if we first "adapt" or "precondition" the coefficients u_0, u_1, $\ldots$, u_n. This adaptation process might involve a lot of work, as explained below; but the preliminary calculation is not wasted, since it must be done only once while the polynomial will be evaluated many times. For examples of "adapted" polynomials for standard functions, see V. Y. Pan, *USSR Computational Math. and Math. Physics* **2** (1963), 137–146.

The simplest case for which adaptation of coefficients is helpful occurs for a fourth degree polynomial:

$$u(x) = u_4 x^4 + u_3 x^3 + u_2 x^2 + u_1 x + u_0, \qquad u_4 \neq 0. \tag{8}$$

This equation can be rewritten in a form originally suggested by T. S. Motzkin,

$$y = (x + \alpha_0)x + \alpha_1, \qquad u(x) = \big((y + x + \alpha_2)y + \alpha_3\big)\alpha_4, \tag{9}$$

for suitably "adapted" coefficients α_0, α_1, α_2, α_3, α_4. The computation in this scheme involves three multiplications, five additions, and (on a one-accumulator machine like MIX) one instruction to store the partial result y into temporary storage. By comparison with Horner's rule, we have traded a multiplication for an addition and a possible storage command. Even this comparatively small savings is worthwhile if the polynomial is to be evaluated often. (Of course, if the time for multiplication is comparable to the time for addition, (9) gives no improvement; we will see that a general fourth-degree polynomial always requires at least eight arithmetic operations for its evaluation.)

By equating coefficients in (8) and (9), we obtain formulas for computing the α_j's in terms of the u_k's:

$$\alpha_0 = \tfrac{1}{2}(u_3/u_4 - 1), \qquad \beta = u_2/u_4 - \alpha_0(\alpha_0 + 1), \qquad \alpha_1 = u_1/u_4 - \alpha_0\beta,$$
$$\alpha_2 = \beta - 2\alpha_1, \qquad \alpha_3 = u_0/u_4 - \alpha_1(\alpha_1 + \alpha_2), \qquad \alpha_4 = u_4. \tag{10}$$

A similar scheme, which evaluates a fourth-degree polynomial in the same number of steps as (9), appears in exercise 18; this alternative method will give greater numerical accuracy than (9) in certain cases, although it yields poorer accuracy in others.

Polynomials that arise in practice often have a rather small leading coefficient, so that the division by u_4 in (10) leads to instability. In such a case it is usually preferable to replace x by $|u_4|^{1/4}x$ as the first step, reducing (8) to a polynomial whose leading coefficient is ± 1. A similar transformation applies to polynomials of higher degrees. This idea is due to C. T. Fike [*CACM* **10** (1967), 175–178], who has presented several interesting examples.

Any polynomial of the fifth degree may be evaluated using four multiplications, six additions, and one storing, by using the rule $u(x) = U(x)x + u_0$, where $U(x) = u_5 x^4 + u_4 x^3 + u_3 x^2 + u_2 x + u_1$ is evaluated as in (9). Alternatively, we can do the evaluation with four multiplications, five additions, and three storings, if the calculations take the form

$$y = (x + \alpha_0)^2, \qquad u(x) = \big(((y + \alpha_1)y + \alpha_2)(x + \alpha_3) + \alpha_4\big)\alpha_5. \qquad (11)$$

The determination of the α's this time requires the solution of a cubic equation (see exercise 19).

On many computers the number of "storing" operations required by (11) is less than 3; for example, we may be able to compute $(x + \alpha_0)^2$ without storing $x + \alpha_0$. In fact, most computers nowadays have more than one arithmetic register for floating point calculations, so we can avoid storing altogether. Because of the wide variety of features available for arithmetic on different computers, we shall henceforth in this section count only the arithmetic operations, not the operations of storing and loading an accumulator. The computation schemes can usually be adapted to any particular computer in a straightforward manner, so that very few of these auxiliary operations are necessary; on the other hand, it must be remembered that overhead costs might well overshadow the fact that we are saving a multiplication or two, especially if the machine code is being produced by a compiler that does not optimize.

A polynomial $u(x) = u_6 x^6 + \cdots + u_1 x + u_0$ of degree six can always be evaluated using four multiplications and seven additions, with the scheme

$$z = (x + \alpha_0)x + \alpha_1, \qquad w = (x + \alpha_2)z + \alpha_3,$$
$$u(x) = \big((w + z + \alpha_4)w + \alpha_5\big)\alpha_6. \qquad (12)$$

[See D. E. Knuth, *CACM* **5** (1962), 595–599.] This saves two of the six multiplications required by Horner's rule. Here again we must solve a cubic equation: Since $\alpha_6 = u_6$, we may assume that $u_6 = 1$. Under this assumption, let

$$\beta_1 = (u_5 - 1)/2, \qquad \beta_2 = u_4 - \beta_1(\beta_1 + 1),$$
$$\beta_3 = u_3 - \beta_1\beta_2, \qquad \beta_4 = \beta_1 - \beta_2, \qquad \beta_5 = u_2 - \beta_1\beta_3.$$

Let β_6 be a real root of the cubic equation

$$2y^3 + (2\beta_4 - \beta_2 + 1)y^2 + (2\beta_5 - \beta_2\beta_4 - \beta_3)y + (u_1 - \beta_2\beta_5) = 0. \qquad (13)$$

(This equation always has a real root, since the polynomial on the left approaches $+\infty$ for large positive y, and it approaches $-\infty$ for large negative y; it must assume the value zero somewhere in between.) Now if we define

$$\beta_7 = \beta_6^2 + \beta_4\beta_6 + \beta_5, \qquad \beta_8 = \beta_3 - \beta_6 - \beta_7,$$

we have finally

$$\alpha_0 = \beta_2 - 2\beta_6, \qquad \alpha_2 = \beta_1 - \alpha_0, \qquad \alpha_1 = \beta_6 - \alpha_0\alpha_2,$$
$$\alpha_3 = \beta_7 - \alpha_1\alpha_2, \qquad \alpha_4 = \beta_8 - \beta_7 - \alpha_1, \qquad \alpha_5 = u_0 - \beta_7\beta_8. \qquad (14)$$

We can illustrate this procedure with a contrived example: Suppose that we want to evaluate $x^6 + 13x^5 + 49x^4 + 33x^3 - 61x^2 - 37x + 3$. We obtain $\alpha_6 = 1$, $\beta_1 = 6$, $\beta_2 = 7$, $\beta_3 = -9$, $\beta_4 = -1$, $\beta_5 = -7$, and so we meet with the cubic equation

$$2y^3 - 8y^2 + 2y + 12 = 0. \tag{15}$$

This equation has $\beta_6 = 2$ as a root, and we continue to find

$$\beta_7 = -5, \qquad \beta_8 = -6,$$
$$\alpha_0 = 3, \quad \alpha_2 = 3, \quad \alpha_1 = -7, \quad \alpha_3 = 16, \quad \alpha_4 = 6, \quad \alpha_5 = -27.$$

The resulting scheme is therefore

$$z = (x+3)x - 7, \qquad w = (x+3)z + 16, \qquad u(x) = (w+z+6)w - 27.$$

By sheer coincidence the quantity $x + 3$ appears twice here, so we have found a method that uses three multiplications and six additions.

Another method for handling sixth-degree equations has been suggested by V. Y. Pan [*Problemy Kibernetiki* **5** (1961), 17–29]. His method requires one more addition operation, but it involves only rational operations in the preliminary steps; no cubic equation needs to be solved. We may proceed as follows:

$$z = (x + \alpha_0)x + \alpha_1, \qquad w = z + x + \alpha_2,$$
$$u(x) = \big(((z - x + \alpha_3)w + \alpha_4)z + \alpha_5\big)\alpha_6. \tag{16}$$

To determine the α's, we divide the polynomial once again by $u_6 = \alpha_6$ so that $u(x)$ becomes monic. It can then be verified that $\alpha_0 = u_5/3$ and that

$$\alpha_1 = (u_1 - \alpha_0 u_2 + \alpha_0^2 u_3 - \alpha_0^3 u_4 + 2\alpha_0^5)/(u_3 - 2\alpha_0 u_4 + 5\alpha_0^3). \tag{17}$$

Note that Pan's method requires that the denominator in (17) does not vanish. In other words, (16) can be used only when

$$27u_3 u_6^2 - 18u_6 u_5 u_4 + 5u_5^3 \neq 0; \tag{18}$$

in fact, this quantity should not be so small that α_1 becomes too large. Once α_1 has been determined, the remaining α's may be determined from the equations

$$\beta_1 = 2\alpha_0, \qquad\qquad\qquad \beta_2 = u_4 - \alpha_0\beta_1 - \alpha_1,$$
$$\beta_3 = u_3 - \alpha_0\beta_2 - \alpha_1\beta_1, \qquad \beta_4 = u_2 - \alpha_0\beta_3 - \alpha_1\beta_2,$$
$$\alpha_3 = \tfrac{1}{2}\big(\beta_3 - (\alpha_0 - 1)\beta_2 + (\alpha_0 - 1)(\alpha_0^2 - 1)\big) - \alpha_1,$$
$$\alpha_2 = \beta_2 - (\alpha_0^2 - 1) - \alpha_3 - 2\alpha_1, \qquad \alpha_4 = \beta_4 - (\alpha_2 + \alpha_1)(\alpha_3 + \alpha_1),$$
$$\alpha_5 = u_0 - \alpha_1\beta_4. \tag{19}$$

We have discussed the cases of degree $n = 4$, 5, 6 in detail because the smaller values of n arise most frequently in applications. Let us now consider a general evaluation scheme for nth degree polynomials, a method that involves at most $\lfloor n/2 \rfloor + 2$ multiplications and n additions.

Theorem E. *Every nth degree polynomial* (1) *with real coefficients, $n \geq 3$, can be evaluated by the scheme*

$$y = x + c, \qquad w = y^2; \qquad z = \begin{cases} (u_n y + \alpha_0)y + \beta_0, & n \text{ even,} \\ u_n y + \beta_0, & n \text{ odd,} \end{cases}$$

$$u(x) = \big(\ldots((z(w - \alpha_1) + \beta_1)(w - \alpha_2) + \beta_2)\ldots\big)(w - \alpha_m) + \beta_m, \qquad (20)$$

for suitable real parameters c, α_k and β_k, where $m = \lceil n/2 \rceil - 1$. In fact, it is possible to select these parameters so that $\beta_m = 0$.

Proof. Let us first examine the circumstances under which the α's and β's can be chosen in (20), if c is fixed. Let

$$p(x) = u(x - c) = a_n x^n + a_{n-1} x^{n-1} + \cdots + a_1 x + a_0. \qquad (21)$$

We want to show that $p(x)$ has the form $p_1(x)(x^2 - \alpha_m) + \beta_m$ for some polynomial $p_1(x)$ and some constants α_m, β_m. If we divide $p(x)$ by $x^2 - \alpha_m$, we can see that the remainder β_m is a constant only if the auxiliary polynomial

$$q(x) = a_{2m+1} x^m + a_{2m-1} x^{m-1} + \cdots + a_1, \qquad (22)$$

formed from every odd-numbered coefficient of $p(x)$, is a multiple of $x - \alpha_m$. Conversely, if $q(x)$ has $x - \alpha_m$ as a factor, then $p(x) = p_1(x)(x^2 - \alpha_m) + \beta_m$, for some constant β_m that may be determined by division.

Similarly, we want $p_1(x)$ to have the form $p_2(x)(x^2 - \alpha_{m-1}) + \beta_{m-1}$, and this is the same as saying that $q(x)/(x - \alpha_m)$ is a multiple of $x - \alpha_{m-1}$; for if $q_1(x)$ is the polynomial corresponding to $p_1(x)$ as $q(x)$ corresponds to $p(x)$, we have $q_1(x) = q(x)/(x - \alpha_m)$. Continuing in the same way, we find that the parameters $\alpha_1, \beta_1, \ldots, \alpha_m, \beta_m$ will exist if and only if

$$q(x) = a_{2m+1}(x - \alpha_1)\ldots(x - \alpha_m). \qquad (23)$$

In other words, either $q(x)$ is identically zero (and this can happen only when n is even), or else $q(x)$ is an mth degree polynomial having all real roots.

Now we have a surprising fact discovered by J. Eve [*Numer. Math.* **6** (1964), 17–21]: *If $p(x)$ has at least $n - 1$ complex roots whose real parts are all nonnegative, or all nonpositive, then the corresponding polynomial $q(x)$ is identically zero or has all real roots.* (See exercise 23.) Since $u(x) = 0$ if and only if $p(x + c) = 0$, we need merely choose the parameter c large enough that at least $n-1$ of the roots of $u(x) = 0$ have a real part $\geq -c$, and (20) will apply whenever $a_{n-1} = u_{n-1} - ncu_n \neq 0$.

We can also determine c so that these conditions are fulfilled and also that $\beta_m = 0$. First the n roots of $u(x) = 0$ are determined. If $a + bi$ is a root having the largest or the smallest real part, and if $b \neq 0$, let $c = -a$ and $\alpha_m = -b^2$; then $x^2 - \alpha_m$ is a factor of $u(x - c)$. If the root with smallest or largest real part is real, but the root with *second* smallest (or second largest) real part is nonreal, the same transformation applies. If the two roots with smallest (or largest) real parts are both real, they can be expressed in the form $a-b$ and $a+b$, respectively; let $c = -a$ and $\alpha_m = b^2$. Again $x^2 - \alpha_m$ is a factor of $u(x - c)$. (Still other values of c are often possible; see exercise 24.) The coefficient a_{n-1} will be nonzero for at least one of these alternatives, unless $q(x)$ is identically zero. ∎

Note that this method of proof usually gives at least two values of c, and we also have the chance to permute $\alpha_1, \ldots, \alpha_{m-1}$ in $(m-1)!$ ways. Some of these alternatives may give more desirable numerical accuracy than others.

Questions of numerical accuracy do not arise, of course, when we are working with integers modulo m instead of with real numbers. Scheme (9) works for $n = 4$ when m is relatively prime to $2u_4$, and (16) works for $n = 6$ when m is relatively prime to $6u_6$ and to the denominator of (17). Exercise 44 shows that $n/2 + O(\log n)$ multiplications and $O(n)$ additions suffice for any monic nth degree polynomial modulo any m.

*Polynomial chains. Now let us consider questions of optimality. What are the *best possible* schemes for evaluating polynomials of various degrees, in terms of the minimum possible number of arithmetic operations? This question was first analyzed by A. M. Ostrowski in the case that no preliminary adaptation of coefficients is allowed [*Studies in Mathematics and Mechanics Presented to R. von Mises* (New York: Academic Press, 1954), 40–48], and by T. S. Motzkin in the case of adapted coefficients [see *Bull. Amer. Math. Soc.* **61** (1955), 163].

In order to investigate this question, we can extend Section 4.6.3's concept of addition chains to the notion of *polynomial chains*. A polynomial chain is a sequence of the form

$$x = \lambda_0, \quad \lambda_1, \quad \ldots, \quad \lambda_r = u(x), \tag{24}$$

where $u(x)$ is some polynomial in x, and for $1 \le i \le r$

$$\begin{aligned} \text{either } \lambda_i &= (\pm\lambda_j) \circ \lambda_k, & 0 \le j, k < i, \\ \text{or } \lambda_i &= \alpha_j \circ \lambda_k, & 0 \le k < i. \end{aligned} \tag{25}$$

Here "$\circ$" denotes any of the three operations "+", "−", or "×", and α_j denotes a so-called parameter. Steps of the first kind are called *chain steps*, and steps of the second kind are called *parameter steps*. We shall assume that a different parameter α_j is used in each parameter step; if there are s parameter steps, they should involve $\alpha_1, \alpha_2, \ldots, \alpha_s$ in this order.

It follows that the polynomial $u(x)$ at the end of the chain has the form

$$u(x) = q_n x^n + \cdots + q_1 x + q_0, \tag{26}$$

where $q_n, \ldots, q_1, q_0$ are polynomials in $\alpha_1, \alpha_2, \ldots, \alpha_s$ with integer coefficients. We shall interpret the parameters $\alpha_1, \alpha_2, \ldots, \alpha_s$ as real numbers, and we shall therefore restrict ourselves to considering the evaluation of polynomials with real coefficients. The *result set* R of a polynomial chain is defined to be the set of all vectors $(q_n, \ldots, q_1, q_0)$ of real numbers that occur as $\alpha_1, \alpha_2, \ldots, \alpha_s$ independently assume all possible real values.

If for every choice of $t+1$ distinct integers $j_0, \ldots, j_t \in \{0, 1, \ldots, n\}$ there is a nonzero multivariate polynomial $f_{j_0 \ldots j_t}$ with integer coefficients such that $f_{j_0 \ldots j_t}(q_{j_0}, \ldots, q_{j_t}) = 0$ for all $(q_n, \ldots, q_1, q_0)$ in R, let us say that the result set R has at most t *degrees of freedom*, and that the chain (24) has at most t degrees of freedom. We also say that the chain (24) *computes* a given polynomial $u(x) = u_n x^n + \cdots + u_1 x + u_0$ if $(u_n, \ldots, u_1, u_0)$ is in R. It follows that a polynomial chain with at most n degrees of freedom cannot compute all nth degree polynomials (see exercise 27).

As an example of a polynomial chain, consider the following chain corresponding to Theorem E, when n is odd:

$$
\begin{aligned}
\lambda_0 &= x \\
\lambda_1 &= \alpha_1 + \lambda_0 \\
\lambda_2 &= \lambda_1 \times \lambda_1 \\
\lambda_3 &= \alpha_2 \times \lambda_1 \\
\left.
\begin{aligned}
\lambda_{1+3i} &= \alpha_{1+2i} + \lambda_{3i} \\
\lambda_{2+3i} &= \alpha_{2+2i} + \lambda_2 \\
\lambda_{3+3i} &= \lambda_{1+3i} \times \lambda_{2+3i}
\end{aligned}
\right\} &\quad 1 \le i < n/2.
\end{aligned}
\tag{27}
$$

There are $\lfloor n/2 \rfloor + 2$ multiplications and n additions; $\lfloor n/2 \rfloor + 1$ chain steps and $n + 1$ parameter steps. By Theorem E, the result set R includes the set of all $(u_n, \ldots, u_1, u_0)$ with $u_n \neq 0$, so (27) computes all polynomials of degree n. We cannot prove that R has at most n degrees of freedom, since the result set has $n + 1$ independent components.

A polynomial chain with s parameter steps has at most s degrees of freedom. In a sense, this is obvious: We can't compute a function with t degrees of freedom using fewer than t arbitrary parameters. But this intuitive fact is not easy to prove formally; for example, there are continuous functions ("space-filling curves") that map the real line onto a plane, and such functions map a single parameter into two independent parameters. For our purposes, we need to verify that no polynomial functions with integer coefficients can have such a property; a proof appears in exercise 28.

Given this fact, we can proceed to prove the results we seek:

Theorem M (T. S. Motzkin, 1954). *A polynomial chain with $m > 0$ multiplications has at most $2m$ degrees of freedom.*

Proof. Let μ_1, μ_2, $\ldots$, μ_m be the λ_i's of the chain that are multiplication operations. Then

$$
\mu_i = S_{2i-1} \times S_{2i} \quad \text{for } 1 \le i \le m \qquad \text{and} \qquad u(x) = S_{2m+1}, \tag{28}
$$

where each S_j is a certain sum of μ's, x's, and α's. Write $S_j = T_j + \beta_j$, where T_j is a sum of μ's and x's while β_j is a sum of α's.

Now $u(x)$ is expressible as a polynomial in x, β_1, $\ldots$, β_{2m+1} with integer coefficients. Since the β's are expressible as linear functions of α_1, $\ldots$, α_s, the set of values represented by all real values of β_1, $\ldots$, β_{2m+1} contains the result set of the chain. Therefore there are at most $2m + 1$ degrees of freedom; this can be improved to $2m$ when $m > 0$, as shown in exercise 30. ∎

An example of the construction in the proof of Theorem M appears in exercise 25. A similar result can be proved for additions:

Theorem A (É. G. Belaga, 1958). *A polynomial chain containing q additions and subtractions has at most $q + 1$ degrees of freedom.*

Proof. [*Problemy Kibernetiki* **5** (1961), 7–15.] Let $\kappa_1, \ldots, \kappa_q$ be the λ_i's of the chain that correspond to addition or subtraction operations. Then

$$\kappa_i = \pm T_{2i-1} \pm T_{2i} \quad \text{for } 1 \leq i \leq q \qquad \text{and} \qquad u(x) = T_{2q+1}, \qquad (29)$$

where each T_j is a product of κ's, x's, and α's. We may write $T_j = A_j B_j$, where A_j is a product of α's and B_j is a product of κ's and x's. The following transformation may now be made to the chain, successively for $i = 1, 2, \ldots, q$: Let $\beta_i = A_{2i}/A_{2i-1}$, so that $\kappa_i = A_{2i-1}(\pm B_{2i-1} \pm \beta_i B_{2i})$. Then change κ_i to $\pm B_{2i-1} \pm \beta_i B_{2i}$, and replace each occurrence of κ_i in future formulas T_{2i+1}, $T_{2i+2}, \ldots, T_{2q+1}$ by $A_{2i-1}\kappa_i$. (This replacement may change the values of A_{2i+1}, $A_{2i+2}, \ldots, A_{2q+1}$.)

After the transformation has been done for all i, let $\beta_{q+1} = A_{2q+1}$; then $u(x)$ can be expressed as a polynomial in $\beta_1, \ldots, \beta_{q+1}$, and x, with integer coefficients. We are almost ready to complete the proof, but we must be careful because the polynomials obtained as $\beta_1, \ldots, \beta_{q+1}$ range over all real values may not include all polynomials representable by the original chain (see exercise 26); it is possible to have $A_{2i-1} = 0$, for some values of the α's, and this makes β_i undefined.

To complete the proof, let us observe that the result set R of the original chain can be written $R = R_1 \cup R_2 \cup \cdots \cup R_q \cup R'$, where R_i is the set of result vectors possible when $A_{2i-1} = 0$, and where R' is the set of result vectors possible when all α's are nonzero. The discussion above proves that R' has at most $q+1$ degrees of freedom. If $A_{2i-1} = 0$, then $T_{2i-1} = 0$, so addition step κ_i may be dropped to obtain another chain computing the result set R_i; by induction we see that each R_i has at most q degrees of freedom. Hence by exercise 29, R has at most $q + 1$ degrees of freedom. ∎

Theorem C. *If a polynomial chain (24) computes all nth degree polynomials $u(x) = u_n x^n + \cdots + u_0$, for some $n \geq 2$, then it includes at least $\lfloor n/2 \rfloor + 1$ multiplications and at least n addition-subtractions.*

Proof. Let there be m multiplication steps. By Theorem M, the chain has at most $2m$ degrees of freedom, so $2m \geq n + 1$. Similarly, by Theorem A there are $\geq n$ addition-subtractions. ∎

This theorem states that no *single* method having fewer than $\lfloor n/2 \rfloor + 1$ multiplications or fewer than n additions can evaluate all possible nth degree polynomials. The result of exercise 29 allows us to strengthen this and say that no finite collection of such polynomial chains will suffice for all polynomials of a given degree. Some special polynomials can, of course, be evaluated more efficiently; all we have really proved is that polynomials whose coefficients are *algebraically independent*, in the sense that they satisfy no nontrivial polynomial equation, require $\lfloor n/2 \rfloor + 1$ multiplications and n additions. Unfortunately the coefficients we deal with in computers are always rational numbers, so the theorems above don't really apply; in fact, exercise 42 shows that we can always get by with $O(\sqrt{n})$ multiplications (and a possibly huge number of additions). From a practical standpoint, the bounds of Theorem C apply to "almost all" coefficients, and they seem to apply to all reasonable schemes for evaluation. Furthermore it is possible to obtain lower bounds corresponding to those of Theorem C even in the rational case: By strengthening the proofs above, V. Strassen has shown, for example, that the polynomial

$$u(x) = \sum_{k=0}^{n} 2^{2^{kn^3}} x^k \qquad (30)$$

cannot be evaluated by any polynomial chain of length $< n^2/\lg n$ unless the chain has at least $\frac{1}{2}n - 2$ multiplications and $n - 4$ additions [*SICOMP* **3** (1974), 128–149]. The coefficients of (30) are very large; but it is also possible to find polynomials whose coefficients are just 0s and 1s, such that every polynomial chain computing them involves at least $\sqrt{n}/(4 \lg n)$ chain multiplications, for all sufficiently large n, even when the parameters α_j are allowed to be arbitrary complex numbers. [See R. J. Lipton, *SICOMP* **7** (1978), 61–69; C.-P. Schnorr, *Lecture Notes in Comp. Sci.* **53** (1977), 135–147.] Jean-Paul van de Wiele has shown that the evaluation of certain 0–1 polynomials requires a total of at least $cn/\log n$ arithmetic operations, for some $c > 0$ [*FOCS* **19** (1978), 159–165].

A gap still remains between the lower bounds of Theorem C and the actual operation counts known to be achievable, except in the trivial case $n = 2$. Theorem E gives $\lfloor n/2 \rfloor + 2$ multiplications, not $\lfloor n/2 \rfloor + 1$, although it does achieve the minimum number of additions. Our special methods for $n = 4$ and $n = 6$ have the minimum number of multiplications, but one extra addition. When n is odd, it is not difficult to prove that the lower bounds of Theorem C cannot be achieved simultaneously for both multiplications and additions; see exercise 33. For $n = 3$, 5, and 7, it is possible to show that at least $\lfloor n/2 \rfloor + 2$ multiplications are necessary. Exercises 35 and 36 show that the lower bounds of Theorem C cannot both be achieved when $n = 4$ or $n = 6$; thus the methods we have discussed are best possible, for $n < 8$. When n is even, Motzkin proved that $\lfloor n/2 \rfloor + 1$ multiplications are sufficient, but his construction involves an indeterminate number of additions (see exercise 39). An optimal scheme for $n = 8$ was found by V. Y. Pan, who showed that $n + 1$ additions are necessary and sufficient for this case when there are $\lfloor n/2 \rfloor + 1$ multiplications; he also showed that $\lfloor n/2 \rfloor + 1$ multiplications and $n + 2$ additions will suffice for all even $n \geq 10$. Pan's paper [*STOC* **10** (1978), 162–172] also establishes the exact minimum number of multiplications and additions needed when calculations are done entirely with complex numbers instead of reals, for all degrees n. Exercise 40 discusses the interesting situation that arises for odd values of $n \geq 9$.

It is clear that the results we have obtained about chains for polynomials in a single variable can be extended without difficulty to multivariate polynomials.

For example, if we want to find an optimum scheme for polynomial evaluation *without* adaptation of coefficients, we can regard $u(x)$ as a polynomial in the $n + 2$ variables x, u_n, ..., u_1, u_0; exercise 38 shows that n multiplications and n additions are necessary in this case. Indeed, A. Borodin [*Theory of Machines and Computations*, edited by Z. Kohavi and A. Paz (New York: Academic Press, 1971), 45–58] has proved that Horner's rule (2) is essentially the *only* way to compute $u(x)$ in $2n$ operations without preconditioning.

With minor variations, the methods above can be extended to chains involving division, that is, to rational functions as well as polynomials. Curiously, the continued-fraction analog of Horner's rule now turns out to be optimal from an operation-count standpoint, if multiplication and division speeds are equal, even when preconditioning is allowed (see exercise 37).

Sometimes division is helpful during the evaluation of polynomials, even though polynomials are defined only in terms of multiplication and addition; we have seen examples of this in the Shaw–Traub algorithms for polynomial derivatives. Another example is the polynomial

$$x^n + \cdots + x + 1;$$

since this polynomial can be written $(x^{n+1} - 1)/(x - 1)$, we can evaluate it with $l(n + 1)$ multiplications (see Section 4.6.3), two subtractions, and one division, while techniques that avoid division seem to require about three times as many operations (see exercise 43).

Special multivariate polynomials. The *determinant* of an $n \times n$ matrix may be considered to be a polynomial in n^2 variables x_{ij}, $1 \leq i, j \leq n$. If $x_{11} \neq 0$, we have

$$\det \begin{pmatrix} x_{11} & x_{12} & \cdots & x_{1n} \\ x_{21} & x_{22} & \cdots & x_{2n} \\ x_{31} & x_{32} & \cdots & x_{3n} \\ \vdots & \vdots & & \vdots \\ x_{n1} & x_{n2} & \cdots & x_{nn} \end{pmatrix} = x_{11} \det \begin{pmatrix} x_{22} - (x_{21}/x_{11})x_{12} & \cdots & x_{2n} - (x_{21}/x_{11})x_{1n} \\ x_{32} - (x_{31}/x_{11})x_{12} & \cdots & x_{3n} - (x_{31}/x_{11})x_{1n} \\ \vdots & & \vdots \\ x_{n2} - (x_{n1}/x_{11})x_{12} & \cdots & x_{nn} - (x_{n1}/x_{11})x_{1n} \end{pmatrix}. \tag{31}$$

The determinant of an $n \times n$ matrix may therefore be evaluated by evaluating the determinant of an $(n - 1) \times (n - 1)$ matrix and performing an additional $(n - 1)^2 + 1$ multiplications, $(n - 1)^2$ additions, and $n - 1$ divisions. Since a 2×2 determinant can be evaluated with two multiplications and one addition, we see that the determinant of almost all matrices (namely those for which no division by zero is needed) can be computed with at most $(2n^3 - 3n^2 + 7n - 6)/6$ multiplications, $(2n^3 - 3n^2 + n)/6$ additions, and $(n^2 - n - 2)/2$ divisions.

When zero occurs, the determinant is even easier to compute. For example, if $x_{11} = 0$ but $x_{21} \neq 0$, we have

$$\det \begin{pmatrix} 0 & x_{12} & \cdots & x_{1n} \\ x_{21} & x_{22} & \cdots & x_{2n} \\ x_{31} & x_{32} & \cdots & x_{3n} \\ \vdots & \vdots & & \vdots \\ x_{n1} & x_{n2} & \cdots & x_{nn} \end{pmatrix} = -x_{21} \det \begin{pmatrix} x_{12} & \cdots & x_{1n} \\ x_{32} - (x_{31}/x_{21})x_{22} & \cdots & x_{3n} - (x_{31}/x_{21})x_{2n} \\ \vdots & & \vdots \\ x_{n2} - (x_{n1}/x_{21})x_{22} & \cdots & x_{nn} - (x_{n1}/x_{21})x_{2n} \end{pmatrix}. \tag{32}$$

Here the reduction to an $(n-1) \times (n-1)$ determinant saves $n-1$ of the multiplications and $n-1$ of the additions used in (31), in compensation for the additional bookkeeping required to recognize this case. Thus any determinant can be evaluated with roughly $\frac{2}{3}n^3$ arithmetic operations (including division); this is remarkable, since it is a polynomial with $n!$ terms and n variables in each term.

If we want to evaluate the determinant of a matrix with *integer* elements, the procedure of (31) and (32) appears to be unattractive since it requires rational arithmetic. However, we can use the method to evaluate the determinant mod p, for any prime p, since division mod p is possible (exercise 4.5.2–16). If this is done for sufficiently many primes, the exact value of the determinant can be found as explained in Section 4.3.2, since Hadamard's inequality 4.6.1–(25) gives an upper bound on the magnitude.

The coefficients of the *characteristic polynomial* $\det(xI - X)$ of an $n \times n$ matrix X can also be computed in $O(n^3)$ steps; see J. H. Wilkinson, *The Algebraic Eigenvalue Problem* (Oxford: Clarendon Press, 1965), 353–355, 410–411. Exercise 70 discusses an interesting division-free method that involves $O(n^4)$ steps.

The *permanent* of a matrix is a polynomial that is very similar to the determinant; the only difference is that all of its nonzero coefficients are $+1$. Thus we have

$$\text{per} \begin{pmatrix} x_{11} & \cdots & x_{1n} \\ \vdots & & \vdots \\ x_{n1} & \cdots & x_{nn} \end{pmatrix} = \sum x_{1j_1} x_{2j_2} \ldots x_{nj_n}, \tag{33}$$

summed over all permutations $j_1 j_2 \ldots j_n$ of $\{1, 2, \ldots, n\}$. It would seem that this function should be even easier to compute than its more complicated-looking cousin, but no way to evaluate the permanent as efficiently as the determinant is known. Exercises 9 and 10 show that substantially fewer than $n!$ operations will suffice, for large n, but the execution time of all known methods still grows exponentially with the size of the matrix. In fact, Leslie G. Valiant has shown that it is as difficult to compute the permanent of a given 0–1 matrix as it is to count the number of accepting computations of a nondeterministic polynomial-time Turing machine, if we ignore polynomial factors in the running time of the calculation. Therefore a polynomial-time evaluation algorithm for permanents would imply that scores of other well known problems that have resisted efficient solution would be solvable in polynomial time. On the other hand, Valiant proved that the permanent of an $n \times n$ integer matrix can be evaluated modulo 2^k in $O(n^{4k-3})$ steps for all $k \geq 2$. [See *Theoretical Comp. Sci.* **8** (1979), 189–201.]

Another fundamental operation involving matrices is, of course, *matrix multiplication:* If $X = (x_{ij})$ is an $m \times n$ matrix, $Y = (y_{jk})$ is an $n \times s$ matrix, and $Z = (z_{ik})$ is an $m \times s$ matrix, then the formula $Z = XY$ means that

$$z_{ik} = \sum_{j=1}^{n} x_{ij} y_{jk}, \qquad 1 \leq i \leq m, \qquad 1 \leq k \leq s. \tag{34}$$

This equation may be regarded as the computation of ms simultaneous polynomials in $mn + ns$ variables; each polynomial is the "inner product" of two n-place vectors. A straightforward calculation would involve mns multiplications and $ms(n-1)$ additions; but S. Winograd discovered in 1967 that there is a way to trade about half of the multiplications for additions:

$$z_{ik} = \sum_{1 \le j \le n/2} (x_{i,2j} + y_{2j-1,k})(x_{i,2j-1} + y_{2j,k}) - a_i - b_k + x_{in}y_{nk}[n \text{ odd}];$$

$$a_i = \sum_{1 \le j \le n/2} x_{i,2j}\,x_{i,2j-1}; \qquad b_k = \sum_{1 \le j \le n/2} y_{2j-1,k}\,y_{2j,k}. \qquad (35)$$

This scheme uses $\lceil n/2 \rceil ms + \lfloor n/2 \rfloor (m+s)$ multiplications and $(n+2)ms + (\lfloor n/2 \rfloor - 1)(ms + m + s)$ additions or subtractions; the total number of operations has increased slightly, but the number of multiplications has roughly been halved. [See *IEEE Trans.* **C-17** (1968), 693–694.] Winograd's surprising construction led many people to look more closely at the problem of matrix multiplication, and it touched off widespread speculation that $n^3/2$ multiplications might be necessary to multiply $n \times n$ matrices, because of the somewhat similar lower bound that was known to hold for polynomials in one variable.

An even better scheme for large n was discovered by Volker Strassen in 1968; he found a way to compute the product of 2×2 matrices with only seven multiplications, without relying on the commutativity of multiplication as in (35). Since $2n \times 2n$ matrices can be partitioned into four $n \times n$ matrices, his idea can be used recursively to obtain the product of $2^k \times 2^k$ matrices with only 7^k multiplications instead of $(2^k)^3 = 8^k$. The number of additions also grows as order 7^k. Strassen's original 2×2 identity [*Numer. Math.* **13** (1969), 354–356] used 7 multiplications and 18 additions; S. Winograd later discovered the following more economical formula:

$$\begin{pmatrix} a & b \\ c & d \end{pmatrix}\begin{pmatrix} A & C \\ B & D \end{pmatrix} = \begin{pmatrix} aA+bB & w+v+(a+b-c-d)D \\ w+u+d(B+C-A-D) & w+u+v \end{pmatrix}, \qquad (36)$$

where $u = (c-a)(C-D)$, $v = (c+d)(C-A)$, $w = aA + (c+d-a)(A+D-C)$. If intermediate results are appropriately saved, this involves 7 multiplications and only 15 additions; by induction on k, we can multiply $2^k \times 2^k$ matrices with 7^k multiplications and $5(7^k - 4^k)$ additions. The total number of operations needed to multiply $n \times n$ matrices has therefore been reduced from order n^3 to $O(n^{\lg 7}) = O(n^{2.8074})$. A similar reduction applies also to the evaluation of determinants and matrix inverses; see J. R. Bunch and J. E. Hopcroft, *Math. Comp.* **28** (1974), 231–236.

Strassen's exponent $\lg 7$ resisted numerous attempts at improvement until 1978, when Viktor Pan discovered that it could be lowered to $\log_{70} 143640 \approx 2.795$ (see exercise 60). This new breakthrough led to further intensive analysis of the problem, and the combined efforts of D. Bini, M. Capovani, D. Coppersmith, G. Lotti, F. Romani, A. Schönhage, V. Pan, and S. Winograd, produced a dramatic reduction in the asymptotic running time. Exercises 60–67 discuss some of the interesting techniques by which such upper bounds have been established; in particular, exercise 66 contains a reasonably simple proof that $O(n^{2.55})$

operations suffice. The best upper bound known as of 1997 is $O(n^{2.376})$, due to Coppersmith and Winograd [*J. Symbolic Comp.* **9** (1990), 251–280]. By contrast, the best current lower bound is $2n^2 - 1$ (see exercise 12).

These theoretical results are quite striking, but from a practical standpoint they are of little use because n must be very large before we overcome the effect of additional bookkeeping costs. Richard Brent [Stanford Computer Science report CS157 (March 1970), see also *Numer. Math.* **16** (1970), 145–156] found that a careful implementation of Winograd's scheme (35), with appropriate scaling for numerical stability, became better than the conventional method only when $n \geq 40$, and it saved only about 7 percent of the running time when $n = 100$. For complex arithmetic the situation was somewhat different; scheme (35) became advantageous for $n > 20$, and saved 18 percent when $n = 100$. He estimated that Strassen's scheme (36) would not begin to excel over (35) until $n \approx 250$; and such enormous matrices rarely occur in practice unless they are very sparse, when other techniques apply. Furthermore, the known methods of order n^ω where $\omega < 2.7$ have such large constants of proportionality that they require more than 10^{23} multiplications before they start to beat (36).

By contrast, the methods we shall discuss next are eminently practical and have found wide use. The *discrete Fourier transform* f of a complex-valued function F of n variables, over respective domains of $m_1, \ldots, m_n$ elements, is defined by the equation

$$f(s_1,\ldots,s_n) = \sum_{\substack{0 \leq t_1 < m_1 \\ \cdots \\ 0 \leq t_n < m_n}} \exp\left(2\pi i\left(\frac{s_1 t_1}{m_1} + \cdots + \frac{s_n t_n}{m_n}\right)\right) F(t_1,\ldots,t_n) \quad (37)$$

for $0 \leq s_1 < m_1, \ldots, 0 \leq s_n < m_n$; the name "transform" is justified because we can recover the values $F(t_1,\ldots,t_n)$ from the values $f(s_1,\ldots,s_n)$, as shown in exercise 13. In the important special case that all $m_j = 2$, we have

$$f(s_1,\ldots,s_n) = \sum_{0 \leq t_1,\ldots,t_n \leq 1} (-1)^{s_1 t_1 + \cdots + s_n t_n} F(t_1,\ldots,t_n) \quad (38)$$

for $0 \leq s_1,\ldots,s_n \leq 1$, and this may be regarded as a simultaneous evaluation of 2^n linear polynomials in 2^n variables $F(t_1,\ldots,t_n)$. A well-known technique due to F. Yates [*The Design and Analysis of Factorial Experiments* (Harpenden: Imperial Bureau of Soil Sciences, 1937)] can be used to reduce the number of additions implied in (38) from $2^n(2^n - 1)$ to $n2^n$. Yates's method can be understood by considering the case $n = 3$: Let $X_{t_1 t_2 t_3} = F(t_1, t_2, t_3)$.

Given	First step	Second step	Third step
X_{000}	$X_{000}+X_{001}$	$X_{000}+X_{001}+X_{010}+X_{011}$	$X_{000}+X_{001}+X_{010}+X_{011}+X_{100}+X_{101}+X_{110}+X_{111}$
X_{001}	$X_{010}+X_{011}$	$X_{100}+X_{101}+X_{110}+X_{111}$	$X_{000}-X_{001}+X_{010}-X_{011}+X_{100}-X_{101}+X_{110}-X_{111}$
X_{010}	$X_{100}+X_{101}$	$X_{000}-X_{001}+X_{010}-X_{011}$	$X_{000}+X_{001}-X_{010}-X_{011}+X_{100}+X_{101}-X_{110}-X_{111}$
X_{011}	$X_{110}+X_{111}$	$X_{100}-X_{101}+X_{110}-X_{111}$	$X_{000}-X_{001}-X_{010}+X_{011}+X_{100}-X_{101}-X_{110}+X_{111}$
X_{100}	$X_{000}-X_{001}$	$X_{000}+X_{001}-X_{010}-X_{011}$	$X_{000}+X_{001}+X_{010}+X_{011}-X_{100}-X_{101}-X_{110}-X_{111}$
X_{101}	$X_{010}-X_{011}$	$X_{100}+X_{101}-X_{110}-X_{111}$	$X_{000}-X_{001}+X_{010}-X_{011}-X_{100}+X_{101}-X_{110}+X_{111}$
X_{110}	$X_{100}-X_{101}$	$X_{000}-X_{001}-X_{010}+X_{011}$	$X_{000}+X_{001}-X_{010}-X_{011}-X_{100}-X_{101}+X_{110}+X_{111}$
X_{111}	$X_{110}-X_{111}$	$X_{100}-X_{101}-X_{110}+X_{111}$	$X_{000}-X_{001}-X_{010}+X_{011}-X_{100}+X_{101}+X_{110}-X_{111}$

To get from the "Given" to the "First step" requires four additions and four subtractions; and the interesting feature of Yates's method is that exactly the same transformation that takes us from "Given" to "First step" will take us from "First step" to "Second step" and from "Second step" to "Third step." In each case we do four additions, then four subtractions; and after three steps we magically have the desired Fourier transform $f(s_1, s_2, s_3)$ in the place originally occupied by $F(s_1, s_2, s_3)$.

This special case is often called the *Hadamard transform* or the *Walsh transform* of 2^n data elements, since the corresponding pattern of signs was studied by J. Hadamard [*Bull. Sci. Math.* (2) **17** (1893), 240–246] and by J. L. Walsh [*Amer. J. Math.* **45** (1923), 5–24]. Notice that the number of sign changes from left to right in the "Third step" assumes the respective values

$$0,\ 7,\ 3,\ 4,\ 1,\ 6,\ 2,\ 5;$$

this is a permutation of the numbers $\{0, 1, 2, 3, 4, 5, 6, 7\}$. Walsh observed that there will be exactly $0, 1, \ldots, 2^n - 1$ sign changes in the general case, if we permute the transformed elements appropriately, so the coefficients provide discrete approximations to sine waves with various frequencies. (See Section 7.2.1.1 for further discussion of the Hadamard–Walsh coefficients.)

Yates's method can be generalized to the evaluation of any discrete Fourier transform, and, in fact, to the evaluation of any set of sums that can be written in the general form

$$f(s_1, s_2, \ldots, s_n) =$$

$$\sum_{\substack{0 \le t_1 < m_1 \\ \cdots \\ 0 \le t_n < m_n}} g_1(s_1, s_2, \ldots, s_n, t_1) g_2(s_2, \ldots, s_n, t_2) \ldots g_n(s_n, t_n) F(t_1, t_2, \ldots, t_n) \quad (39)$$

for $0 \le s_j < m_j$, given the functions $g_j(s_j, \ldots, s_n, t_j)$. We proceed as follows.

$$f_0(t_1, t_2, t_3, \ldots, t_n) = F(t_1, t_2, t_3, \ldots, t_n);$$

$$f_1(s_n, t_1, t_2, \ldots, t_{n-1}) = \sum_{0 \le t_n < m_n} g_n(s_n, t_n) f_0(t_1, t_2, \ldots, t_n);$$

$$f_2(s_{n-1}, s_n, t_1, \ldots, t_{n-2}) = \sum_{0 \le t_{n-1} < m_{n-1}} g_{n-1}(s_{n-1}, s_n, t_{n-1}) f_1(s_n, t_1, \ldots, t_{n-1});$$

$$\vdots$$

$$f_n(s_1, s_2, s_3, \ldots, s_n) = \sum_{0 \le t_1 < m_1} g_1(s_1, \ldots, s_n, t_1) f_{n-1}(s_2, s_3, \ldots, s_n, t_1);$$

$$f(s_1, s_2, s_3, \ldots, s_n) = f_n(s_1, s_2, s_3, \ldots, s_n). \quad (40)$$

For Yates's method as shown above, $g_j(s_j, \ldots, s_n, t_j) = (-1)^{s_j t_j}$; $f_0(t_1, t_2, t_3)$ represents the "Given"; $f_1(s_3, t_1, t_2)$ represents the "First step"; and so on. Whenever a desired set of sums can be put into the form of (39), for reasonably simple functions $g_j(s_j, \ldots, s_n, t_j)$, the scheme (40) will reduce the amount of computation from order N^2 to order $N \log N$ or thereabouts, where $N = m_1 \ldots m_n$ is the number of data points. Furthermore this scheme is ideally suited to parallel computation. The important special case of one-dimensional Fourier transforms is discussed in exercises 14 and 53; we have considered the one-dimensional case also in Section 4.3.3C.

Let us consider one more special case of polynomial evaluation. *Lagrange's interpolation polynomial* of order n, which we shall write as

$$u_{[n]}(x) = y_0 \frac{(x-x_1)(x-x_2)\ldots(x-x_n)}{(x_0-x_1)(x_0-x_2)\ldots(x_0-x_n)} + y_1 \frac{(x-x_0)(x-x_2)\ldots(x-x_n)}{(x_1-x_0)(x_1-x_2)\ldots(x_1-x_n)}$$
$$+ \cdots + y_n \frac{(x-x_0)(x-x_1)\ldots(x-x_{n-1})}{(x_n-x_0)(x_n-x_1)\ldots(x_n-x_{n-1})}, \quad (41)$$

is the only polynomial of degree $\leq n$ in x that takes on the respective values $y_0, y_1, \ldots, y_n$ at the $n+1$ distinct points $x = x_0, x_1, \ldots, x_n$. (For it is evident from (41) that $u_{[n]}(x_k) = y_k$ for $0 \leq k \leq n$. If $f(x)$ is any such polynomial of degree $\leq n$, then $g(x) = f(x) - u_{[n]}(x)$ is of degree $\leq n$, and $g(x)$ is zero for $x = x_0, x_1, \ldots, x_n$; therefore $g(x)$ must be a multiple of the polynomial $(x - x_0)(x - x_1)\ldots(x - x_n)$. The degree of the latter polynomial is greater than n, so $g(x) = 0$.) If we assume that the values of a function in some table are well approximated by a polynomial, formula (41) may therefore be used to "interpolate" for values of the function at points x not appearing in the table. Lagrange presented (41) to his class at the Paris École Normale in 1795 [see his *Œuvres* **7** (Paris: 1877), 286]; but Edward Waring of Cambridge University actually deserves the credit, because he had already presented the same formula quite clearly and explicitly in *Philosophical Transactions* **69** (1779), 59–67.

There seem to be quite a few additions, subtractions, multiplications, and divisions in Waring and Lagrange's formula; in fact, there are exactly n additions, $2n^2 + 2n$ subtractions, $2n^2 + n - 1$ multiplications, and $n + 1$ divisions. But fortunately (as we might be conditioned to suspect by now), improvement is possible.

The basic idea for simplifying (41) is to exploit the fact that

$$u_{[n]}(x) - u_{[n-1]}(x) = 0 \qquad \text{for } x = x_0, \ldots, x_{n-1};$$

thus $u_{[n]}(x) - u_{[n-1]}(x)$ is a polynomial of degree n or less, and a multiple of $(x - x_0)\ldots(x - x_{n-1})$. We conclude that $u_{[n]}(x) = \alpha_n(x - x_0)\ldots(x - x_{n-1}) + u_{[n-1]}(x)$, where α_n is a constant. This leads us to *Newton's interpolation formula*

$$u_{[n]}(x) = \alpha_n(x - x_0)(x - x_1)\ldots(x - x_{n-1}) + \cdots$$
$$+ \alpha_2(x - x_0)(x - x_1) + \alpha_1(x - x_0) + \alpha_0, \quad (42)$$

where the α's are some coefficients that we want to determine from the given numbers $x_0, x_1, \ldots, x_n, y_0, y_1, \ldots, y_n$. Notice that this formula holds for all n; the coefficient α_k does not depend on $x_{k+1}, \ldots, x_n$, or on $y_{k+1}, \ldots, y_n$. Once the α's are known, Newton's interpolation formula is convenient for calculation, since we may generalize Horner's rule once again and write

$$u_{[n]}(x) = ((\dots(\alpha_n(x-x_{n-1}) + \alpha_{n-1})(x-x_{n-2}) + \dots)(x-x_0) + \alpha_0). \quad (43)$$

This requires n multiplications and $2n$ additions. Alternatively, we may evaluate each of the individual terms of (42) from right to left; with $2n-1$ multiplications and $2n$ additions we thereby calculate all of the values $u_{[0]}(x)$, $u_{[1]}(x)$, $\dots$, $u_{[n]}(x)$, and this indicates whether or not an interpolation process is converging.

The coefficients α_k in Newton's formula may be found by computing the *divided differences* in the following tableau (shown for $n = 3$):

y_0
$\quad (y_1 - y_0)/(x_1 - x_0) = y_1'$
$y_1 \qquad\qquad\qquad\qquad\qquad (y_2' - y_1')/(x_2 - x_0) = y_2''$
$\quad (y_2 - y_1)/(x_2 - x_1) = y_2' \qquad\qquad\qquad\qquad\qquad (y_3'' - y_2'')/(x_3 - x_0) = y_3'''$
$y_2 \qquad\qquad\qquad\qquad\qquad (y_3' - y_2')/(x_3 - x_1) = y_3''$
$\quad (y_3 - y_2)/(x_3 - x_2) = y_3'$
y_3
$\hfill (44)$

It is possible to prove that $\alpha_0 = y_0$, $\alpha_1 = y_1'$, $\alpha_2 = y_2''$, etc., and to show that the divided differences have important relations to the derivatives of the function being interpolated; see exercise 15. Therefore the following calculation (corresponding to (44)) may be used to obtain the α's:

Start with $(\alpha_0, \alpha_1, \dots, \alpha_n) \leftarrow (y_0, y_1, \dots, y_n)$;
then, for $k = 1, 2, \dots, n$ (in this order),
set $\alpha_j \leftarrow (\alpha_j - \alpha_{j-1})/(x_j - x_{j-k})$ for $j = n, n-1, \dots, k$ (in this order).

This process requires $\frac{1}{2}(n^2 + n)$ divisions and $n^2 + n$ subtractions, so about three-fourths of the work implied in (41) has been saved.

For example, suppose that we want to estimate 1.5! from the values of 0!, 1!, 2!, and 3!, using a cubic polynomial. The divided differences are

x	y	y'	y''	y'''
0	1			
		0		
1	1		$\frac{1}{2}$	
		1		$\frac{1}{3}$
2	2		$\frac{3}{2}$	
		4		
3	6			

so $u_{[0]}(x) = u_{[1]}(x) = 1$, $u_{[2]}(x) = \frac{1}{2}x(x - 1) + 1$, $u_{[3]}(x) = \frac{1}{3}x(x - 1)(x - 2) + \frac{1}{2}x(x-1)+1$. Setting $x = 1.5$ in $u_{[3]}(x)$ gives $-.125+.375+1 = 1.25$; presumably the "correct" value is $\Gamma(2.5) = \frac{3}{4}\sqrt{\pi} \approx 1.33$. (But there are of course many other sequences that begin with the numbers 1, 1, 2, and 6.)

If we want to interpolate several polynomials that have the same interpolation points x_0, x_1, $\dots$, x_n but varying values y_0, y_1, $\dots$, y_n, it is desirable to rewrite (41) in a form suggested by W. J. Taylor [*J. Research Nat. Bur. Standards* **35** (1945), 151–155]:

$$u_{[n]}(x) = \left(\frac{y_0 w_0}{x - x_0} + \dots + \frac{y_n w_n}{x - x_n}\right) \bigg/ \left(\frac{w_0}{x - x_0} + \dots + \frac{w_n}{x - x_n}\right), \quad (45)$$

when $x \notin \{x_0, x_1, \ldots, x_n\}$, where

$$w_k = 1/(x_k - x_0) \ldots (x_k - x_{k-1})(x_k - x_{k+1}) \ldots (x_k - x_n). \qquad (46)$$

This form is also recommended for its numerical stability [see P. Henrici, *Essentials of Numerical Analysis* (New York: Wiley, 1982), 237–243]. The denominator of (45) is the partial fraction expansion of $1/(x - x_0)(x - x_1) \ldots (x - x_n)$.

An important and somewhat surprising application of polynomial interpolation was discovered by Adi Shamir [*CACM* **22** (1979), 612–613], who observed that polynomials mod p can be used to "share a secret." This means that we can design a system of secret keys or passwords such that the knowledge of any $n+1$ of the keys enables efficient calculation of a magic number N that unlocks a door (say), but the knowledge of any n of the keys gives no information whatsoever about N. Shamir's amazingly simple solution to this problem is to choose a random polynomial $u(x) = u_n x^n + \cdots + u_1 x + u_0$, where $0 \le u_i < p$ and p is a large prime number. Each part of the secret is an integer x in the range $0 < x < p$, together with the value of $u(x) \bmod p$; and the supersecret number N is the constant term u_0. Given $n + 1$ values $u(x_i)$, we can deduce N by interpolation. But if only n values of $u(x_i)$ are given, there is a unique polynomial $u(x)$ having a given constant term but the same values at x_1, $\ldots$, x_n; thus the n values do not make one particular N more likely than any other.

It is instructive to note that evaluation of the interpolation polynomial is just a special case of the Chinese remainder algorithm of Section 4.3.2 and exercise 4.6.2–3, since we know the values of $u_{[n]}(x)$ modulo the relatively prime polynomials $x - x_0$, $\ldots$, $x - x_n$. (As we have seen in Section 4.6.2 and in the discussion following (3), $f(x) \bmod (x - x_0) = f(x_0)$.) Under this interpretation, Newton's formula (42) is precisely the "mixed-radix representation" of Eq. 4.3.2–(25); and 4.3.2–(24) yields another way to compute α_0, $\ldots$, α_n using the same number of operations as (44).

By applying fast Fourier transforms, it is possible to reduce the running time for interpolation to $O\big(n (\log n)^2\big)$, and a similar reduction can also be made for related algorithms such as the solution to the Chinese remainder problem and the evaluation of an nth degree polynomial at n different points. [See E. Horowitz, *Inf. Proc. Letters* **1** (1972), 157–163; A. Borodin and R. Moenck, *J. Comp. Syst. Sci.* **8** (1974), 336–385; A. Borodin, *Complexity of Sequential and Parallel Numerical Algorithms*, edited by J. F. Traub (New York: Academic Press, 1973), 149–180; D. Bini and V. Pan, *Polynomial and Matrix Computations* **1** (Boston: Birkhäuser, 1994), Chapter 1.] However, these observations are primarily of theoretical interest, since the known algorithms have a rather large overhead factor that makes them unattractive unless n is quite large.

A remarkable extension of the method of divided differences, which applies to quotients of polynomials as well as to polynomials, was introduced by T. N. Thiele in 1909. Thiele's method of "reciprocal differences" is discussed in L. M. Milne-Thompson's *Calculus of Finite Differences* (London: MacMillan, 1933), Chapter 5; see also R. W. Floyd, *CACM* **3** (1960), 508.

Bilinear forms. Several of the problems we have considered in this section are special cases of the general problem of evaluating a set of *bilinear forms*

$$z_k = \sum_{i=1}^{m}\sum_{j=1}^{n} t_{ijk}x_iy_j, \qquad \text{for } 1 \le k \le s, \tag{47}$$

where the t_{ijk} are specific coefficients belonging to some given field. The three-dimensional array (t_{ijk}) is called an $m \times n \times s$ *tensor*, and we can display it by writing down s matrices of size $m \times n$, one for each value of k. For example, the problem of multiplying complex numbers, namely the problem of evaluating

$$z_1 + iz_2 = (x_1 + ix_2)(y_1 + iy_2) = (x_1y_1 - x_2y_2) + i(x_1y_2 + x_2y_1), \tag{48}$$

is the problem of computing the bilinear form specified by the $2 \times 2 \times 2$ tensor

$$\begin{pmatrix} 1 & 0 \\ 0 & -1 \end{pmatrix} \begin{pmatrix} 0 & 1 \\ 1 & 0 \end{pmatrix}.$$

Matrix multiplication as defined in (34) is the problem of evaluating a set of bilinear forms corresponding to a particular $mn \times ns \times ms$ tensor. Fourier transforms (37) can also be cast in this mold, although they are linear instead of bilinear, if we let the x's be constant rather than variable.

The evaluation of bilinear forms is most easily studied if we restrict ourselves to what might be called *normal* evaluation schemes, in which all chain multiplications take place between a linear combination of the x's and a linear combination of the y's. Thus, we form r products

$$w_l = (a_{1l}x_1 + \cdots + a_{ml}x_m)(b_{1l}y_1 + \cdots + b_{nl}y_n), \qquad \text{for } 1 \le l \le r, \tag{49}$$

and obtain the z's as linear combinations of these products,

$$z_k = c_{k1}w_1 + \cdots + c_{kr}w_r, \qquad \text{for } 1 \le k \le s. \tag{50}$$

Here all the a's, b's, and c's belong to a given field of coefficients. By comparing (50) to (47), we see that a normal evaluation scheme is correct for the tensor (t_{ijk}) if and only if

$$t_{ijk} = a_{i1}b_{j1}c_{k1} + \cdots + a_{ir}b_{jr}c_{kr} \tag{51}$$

for $1 \le i \le m$, $1 \le j \le n$, and $1 \le k \le s$.

A nonzero tensor (t_{ijk}) is said to be of rank one if there are three vectors $(a_1, \ldots, a_m)$, $(b_1, \ldots, b_n)$, $(c_1, \ldots, c_s)$ such that $t_{ijk} = a_ib_jc_k$ for all i, j, k. We can extend this definition to all tensors by saying that *the rank of (t_{ijk}) is the minimum number r such that (t_{ijk}) is expressible as the sum of r rank-one tensors* in the given field. Comparing this definition with Eq. (51) shows that the rank of a tensor is the minimum number of chain multiplications in a normal evaluation of the corresponding bilinear forms. Incidentally, when $s = 1$ the tensor (t_{ijk}) is just an ordinary matrix, and the rank of (t_{ij1}) as a tensor is the same as its rank as a matrix (see exercise 49). The concept of tensor rank was introduced by F. L. Hitchcock in *J. Math. and Physics* **6** (1927), 164–189; its application to the complexity of polynomial evaluation was pointed out in an important paper by V. Strassen, *Crelle* **264** (1973), 184–202.

Winograd's scheme (35) for matrix multiplication is "abnormal" because it mixes x's and y's before multiplying them. The Strassen–Winograd scheme (36), on the other hand, does not rely on the commutativity of multiplication, so it is normal. In fact, (36) corresponds to the following way to represent the $4 \times 4 \times 4$ tensor for 2×2 matrix multiplication as a sum of seven rank-one tensors:

$$
\begin{pmatrix}1&0&0&0\\0&1&0&0\\0&0&0&0\\0&0&0&0\end{pmatrix}
\begin{pmatrix}0&0&0&0\\0&0&0&0\\1&0&0&0\\0&1&0&0\end{pmatrix}
\begin{pmatrix}0&0&1&0\\0&0&0&1\\0&0&0&0\\0&0&0&0\end{pmatrix}
\begin{pmatrix}0&0&0&0\\0&0&0&0\\0&0&1&0\\0&0&0&1\end{pmatrix}
=
\begin{pmatrix}1&0&0&0\\0&0&0&0\\0&0&0&0\\0&0&0&0\end{pmatrix}
\begin{pmatrix}1&0&0&0\\0&0&0&0\\0&0&0&0\\0&0&0&0\end{pmatrix}
\begin{pmatrix}1&0&0&0\\0&0&0&0\\0&0&0&0\\0&0&0&0\end{pmatrix}
\begin{pmatrix}1&0&0&0\\0&0&0&0\\0&0&0&0\\0&0&0&0\end{pmatrix}
$$

$$
+
\begin{pmatrix}0&0&0&0\\0&1&0&0\\0&0&0&0\\0&0&0&0\end{pmatrix}
\begin{pmatrix}0&0&0&0\\0&0&0&0\\0&0&0&0\\0&0&0&0\end{pmatrix}
\begin{pmatrix}0&0&0&0\\0&0&0&0\\0&0&0&0\\0&0&0&0\end{pmatrix}
\begin{pmatrix}0&0&0&0\\0&0&0&0\\0&0&0&0\\0&0&0&0\end{pmatrix}
+
\begin{pmatrix}0&0&0&0\\0&0&0&0\\0&0&0&0\\0&0&0&0\end{pmatrix}
\begin{pmatrix}0&0&\bar1&1\\0&0&0&0\\0&0&1&\bar1\\0&0&0&0\end{pmatrix}
\begin{pmatrix}0&0&0&0\\0&0&0&0\\0&0&0&0\\0&0&0&0\end{pmatrix}
\begin{pmatrix}0&0&\bar1&1\\0&0&0&0\\0&0&1&\bar1\\0&0&0&0\end{pmatrix}
$$

$$
+
\begin{pmatrix}0&0&0&0\\0&0&0&0\\0&0&0&0\\0&0&0&0\end{pmatrix}
\begin{pmatrix}0&0&0&0\\0&0&0&0\\0&0&0&0\\\bar1&1&1&\bar1\end{pmatrix}
\begin{pmatrix}0&0&0&0\\0&0&0&0\\0&0&0&0\\0&0&0&0\end{pmatrix}
\begin{pmatrix}0&0&0&0\\0&0&0&0\\0&0&0&0\\0&0&0&0\end{pmatrix}
+
\begin{pmatrix}0&0&0&0\\0&0&0&0\\0&0&0&0\\0&0&0&0\end{pmatrix}
\begin{pmatrix}0&0&0&0\\0&0&0&0\\0&0&0&0\\0&0&0&0\end{pmatrix}
\begin{pmatrix}0&0&0&0\\0&0&0&0\\\bar1&0&1&0\\\bar1&0&1&0\end{pmatrix}
\begin{pmatrix}0&0&0&0\\0&0&0&0\\\bar1&0&1&0\\\bar1&0&1&0\end{pmatrix}
$$

$$
+
\begin{pmatrix}0&0&0&0\\0&0&0&0\\0&0&0&0\\0&0&0&0\end{pmatrix}
\begin{pmatrix}0&0&0&0\\0&0&0&0\\0&0&0&0\\0&0&0&0\end{pmatrix}
\begin{pmatrix}0&0&0&1\\0&0&0&1\\0&0&0&\bar1\\0&0&0&\bar1\end{pmatrix}
\begin{pmatrix}0&0&0&0\\0&0&0&0\\0&0&0&0\\0&0&0&0\end{pmatrix}
+
\begin{pmatrix}0&0&0&0\\0&0&0&0\\0&0&0&0\\0&0&0&0\end{pmatrix}
\begin{pmatrix}\bar1&0&1&\bar1\\0&0&0&0\\1&0&\bar1&1\\1&0&\bar1&1\end{pmatrix}
\begin{pmatrix}\bar1&0&1&\bar1\\0&0&0&0\\1&0&\bar1&1\\1&0&\bar1&1\end{pmatrix}
\begin{pmatrix}\bar1&0&1&\bar1\\0&0&0&0\\1&0&\bar1&1\\1&0&\bar1&1\end{pmatrix}.
$$

$$(52)$$

(Here $\bar1$ stands for -1.)

The fact that (51) is symmetric in i, j, k and invariant under a variety of transformations makes the study of tensor rank mathematically tractable, and it also leads to some surprising consequences about bilinear forms. We can permute the indices i, j, k to obtain "transposed" bilinear forms, and the transposed tensor clearly has the same rank; but the corresponding bilinear forms are conceptually quite different. For example, a normal scheme for evaluating an $(m \times n)$ times $(n \times s)$ matrix product implies the existence of a normal scheme to evaluate an $(n \times s)$ times $(s \times m)$ matrix product, using the same number of chain multiplications. In matrix terms these two problems hardly seem to be related at all — they involve different numbers of dot products, on vectors of different sizes — but in tensor terms they are equivalent. [See V. Y. Pan, *Uspekhi Mat. Nauk* **27**, 5 (September–October 1972), 249–250; J. E. Hopcroft and J. Musinski, *SICOMP* **2** (1973), 159–173.]

When the tensor (t_{ijk}) can be represented as a sum (51) of r rank-one tensors, let A, B, C be the matrices (a_{il}), (b_{jl}), (c_{kl}) of respective sizes $m \times r$, $n \times r$, $s \times r$; we shall say that (A, B, C) is a *realization* of the tensor (t_{ijk}). For example, the realization of 2×2 matrix multiplication in (52) can be specified by the matrices

$$
A = \begin{pmatrix}1&0&\bar1&0&0&1&\bar1\\0&1&0&0&0&1&0\\0&0&1&0&1&\bar1&1\\0&0&0&1&1&\bar1&1\end{pmatrix}, \quad
B = \begin{pmatrix}1&0&0&\bar1&\bar1&0&1\\0&1&0&1&0&0&0\\0&0&1&1&1&0&\bar1\\0&0&\bar1&\bar1&0&1&1\end{pmatrix}, \quad
C = \begin{pmatrix}1&1&0&0&0&0&0\\1&0&1&1&0&0&1\\1&0&0&0&1&1&1\\1&0&1&0&1&0&1\end{pmatrix}. \quad (53)
$$

An $m \times n \times s$ tensor (t_{ijk}) can also be represented as a matrix by grouping its subscripts together. We shall write $(t_{(ij)k})$ for the $mn \times s$ matrix whose rows are indexed by the pair of subscripts $\langle i, j \rangle$ and whose columns are indexed by k. Similarly, $(t_{k(ij)})$ stands for the $s \times mn$ matrix that contains t_{ijk} in row k and column $\langle i, j \rangle$; $(t_{(ik)j})$ is an $ms \times n$ matrix, and so on. The indices of an array need not be integers, and we are using ordered pairs as indices here. We can use this notation to derive the following simple but useful lower bound on the rank of a tensor.

Lemma T. *Let* (A, B, C) *be a realization of an* $m \times n \times s$ *tensor* (t_{ijk}). *Then* $\text{rank}(A) \geq \text{rank}(t_{i(jk)})$, $\text{rank}(B) \geq \text{rank}(t_{j(ik)})$, *and* $\text{rank}(C) \geq \text{rank}(t_{k(ij)})$; *consequently*

$$\text{rank}(t_{ijk}) \geq \max\big(\text{rank}(t_{i(jk)}), \text{rank}(t_{j(ik)}), \text{rank}(t_{k(ij)})\big).$$

Proof. It suffices by symmetry to show that $r \geq \text{rank}(A) \geq \text{rank}(t_{i(jk)})$. Since A is an $m \times r$ matrix, it is obvious that A cannot have rank greater than r. Furthermore, according to (51), the matrix $(t_{i(jk)})$ is equal to AQ, where Q is the $r \times ns$ matrix defined by $Q_{l\langle j,k\rangle} = b_{jl}c_{kl}$. If x is any row vector such that $xA = 0$ then $xAQ = 0$, hence all linear dependencies in A occur also in AQ. It follows that $\text{rank}(AQ) \leq \text{rank}(A)$. ∎

As an example of the use of Lemma T, let us consider the problem of polynomial multiplication. Suppose we want to multiply a general polynomial of degree 2 by a general polynomial of degree 3, obtaining the coefficients of the product:

$$(x_0 + x_1 u + x_2 u^2)(y_0 + y_1 u + y_2 u^2 + y_3 u^3)$$
$$= z_0 + z_1 u + z_2 u^2 + z_3 u^3 + z_4 u^4 + z_5 u^5. \quad (54)$$

This is the problem of evaluating six bilinear forms corresponding to the $3 \times 4 \times 6$ tensor

$$\begin{pmatrix} 1\,0\,0\,0 \\ 0\,0\,0\,0 \\ 0\,0\,0\,0 \end{pmatrix} \begin{pmatrix} 0\,1\,0\,0 \\ 1\,0\,0\,0 \\ 0\,0\,0\,0 \end{pmatrix} \begin{pmatrix} 0\,0\,1\,0 \\ 0\,1\,0\,0 \\ 1\,0\,0\,0 \end{pmatrix} \begin{pmatrix} 0\,0\,0\,1 \\ 0\,0\,1\,0 \\ 0\,1\,0\,0 \end{pmatrix} \begin{pmatrix} 0\,0\,0\,0 \\ 0\,0\,0\,1 \\ 0\,0\,1\,0 \end{pmatrix} \begin{pmatrix} 0\,0\,0\,0 \\ 0\,0\,0\,0 \\ 0\,0\,0\,1 \end{pmatrix}. \quad (55)$$

For brevity, we may write (54) as $x(u)y(u) = z(u)$, letting $x(u)$ denote the polynomial $x_0 + x_1 u + x_2 u^2$, etc. (We have come full circle from the way we began this section, since Eq. (1) refers to $u(x)$, not $x(u)$; the notation has changed because the *coefficients* of the polynomials are now the variables of interest to us.)

If each of the six matrices in (55) is regarded as a vector of length 12 indexed by $\langle i, j \rangle$, it is clear that the vectors are linearly independent, since they are nonzero in different positions; hence the rank of (55) is at least 6 by Lemma T. Conversely, it is possible to obtain the coefficients $z_0, z_1, \ldots, z_5$ by making only six chain multiplications, for example by computing

$$x(0)y(0), \ x(1)y(1), \ \ldots, \ x(5)y(5); \quad (56)$$

this gives the values of $z(0), z(1), \ldots, z(5)$, and the formulas developed above for interpolation will yield the coefficients of $z(u)$. The evaluation of $x(j)$

and $y(j)$ can be carried out entirely in terms of additions and/or parameter multiplications, and the interpolation formula merely takes linear combinations of these values. Thus, all of the chain multiplications are shown in (56), and the rank of (55) is 6. (We used essentially this same technique when multiplying high-precision numbers in Algorithm 4.3.3T.)

The realization (A, B, C) of (55) sketched in the paragraph above turns out to be

$$\begin{pmatrix} 1 & 1 & 1 & 1 & 1 & 1 \\ 0 & 1 & 2 & 3 & 4 & 5 \\ 0 & 1 & 4 & 9 & 16 & 25 \end{pmatrix}, \begin{pmatrix} 1 & 1 & 1 & 1 & 1 & 1 \\ 0 & 1 & 2 & 3 & 4 & 5 \\ 0 & 1 & 4 & 9 & 16 & 25 \\ 0 & 1 & 8 & 27 & 64 & 125 \end{pmatrix}, \begin{pmatrix} 120 & 0 & 0 & 0 & 0 & 0 \\ -274 & 600 & -600 & 400 & -150 & 24 \\ 225 & -770 & 1070 & -780 & 305 & -50 \\ -85 & 355 & -590 & 490 & -205 & 35 \\ 15 & -70 & 130 & -120 & 55 & -10 \\ -1 & 5 & -10 & 10 & -5 & 1 \end{pmatrix} \times \frac{1}{120}. \quad (57)$$

Thus, the scheme does indeed achieve the minimum number of chain multiplications, but it is completely impractical because it involves so many additions and parameter multiplications. We shall now study a practical approach to the generation of more efficient schemes, introduced by S. Winograd.

In the first place, to evaluate the coefficients of $x(u)y(u)$ when $\deg(x) = m$ and $\deg(y) = n$, we can use the identity

$$x(u)y(u) = \big(x(u)y(u) \bmod p(u)\big) + x_m y_n p(u), \quad (58)$$

when $p(u)$ is any monic polynomial of degree $m+n$. The polynomial $p(u)$ should be chosen so that the coefficients of $x(u)y(u) \bmod p(u)$ are easy to evaluate.

In the second place, to evaluate the coefficients of $x(u)y(u) \bmod p(u)$, when the polynomial $p(u)$ can be factored into $q(u)r(u)$ where $\gcd\big(q(u), r(u)\big) = 1$, we can use the identity

$$x(u)y(u) \bmod q(u)r(u) = \big(a(u)r(u)(x(u)y(u) \bmod q(u))$$
$$+ b(u)q(u)(x(u)y(u) \bmod r(u))\big) \bmod q(u)r(u) \quad (59)$$

where $a(u)r(u) + b(u)q(u) = 1$; this is essentially the Chinese remainder theorem applied to polynomials.

In the third place, we can always evaluate the coefficients of the polynomial $x(u)y(u) \bmod p(u)$ by using the trivial identity

$$x(u)y(u) \bmod p(u) = \big(x(u) \bmod p(u)\big)\big(y(u) \bmod p(u)\big) \bmod p(u). \quad (60)$$

Repeated application of (58), (59), and (60) tends to produce efficient schemes, as we shall see.

For our example problem (54), let us choose $p(u) = u^5 - u$ and apply (58); the reason for this choice of $p(u)$ will appear as we proceed. Writing $p(u) = u(u^4 - 1)$, rule (59) reduces to

$$x(u)y(u) \bmod u(u^4 - 1) = \big(-(u^4 - 1)x_0 y_0 + u^4(x(u)y(u) \bmod (u^4 - 1))\big)$$
$$\bmod (u^5 - u). \quad (61)$$

Here we have used the fact that $x(u)y(u) \bmod u = x_0 y_0$; in general it is a good idea to choose $p(u)$ in such a way that $p(0) = 0$, so that this simplification can be

used. If we could now determine the coefficients w_0, w_1, w_2, w_3 of the polynomial
$x(u)y(u) \bmod (u^4 - 1) = w_0 + w_1 u + w_2 u^2 + w_3 u^3$, our problem would be solved,
since

$$u^4\big(x(u)y(u) \bmod (u^4 - 1)\big) \bmod (u^5 - u) = w_0 u^4 + w_1 u + w_2 u^2 + w_3 u^3,$$

and the combination of (58) and (61) would reduce to

$$x(u)y(u) = x_0 y_0 + (w_1 - x_2 y_3)u + w_2 u^2 + w_3 u^3 + (w_0 - x_0 y_0)u^4 + x_2 y_3 u^5. \quad (62)$$

(This formula can, of course, be verified directly.)

The problem remaining to be solved is to compute $x(u)y(u) \bmod (u^4 - 1)$;
and this subproblem is interesting in itself. Let us momentarily allow $x(u)$ to be
of degree 3 instead of degree 2. Then the coefficients of $x(u)y(u) \bmod (u^4 - 1)$
are respectively

$$x_0 y_0 + x_1 y_3 + x_2 y_2 + x_3 y_1, \quad x_0 y_1 + x_1 y_0 + x_2 y_3 + x_3 y_2,$$

$$x_0 y_2 + x_1 y_1 + x_2 y_0 + x_3 y_3, \quad x_0 y_3 + x_1 y_2 + x_2 y_1 + x_3 y_0,$$

and the corresponding tensor is

$$\begin{pmatrix} 1\,0\,0\,0 \\ 0\,0\,0\,1 \\ 0\,0\,1\,0 \\ 0\,1\,0\,0 \end{pmatrix} \begin{pmatrix} 0\,1\,0\,0 \\ 1\,0\,0\,0 \\ 0\,0\,0\,1 \\ 0\,0\,1\,0 \end{pmatrix} \begin{pmatrix} 0\,0\,1\,0 \\ 0\,1\,0\,0 \\ 1\,0\,0\,0 \\ 0\,0\,0\,1 \end{pmatrix} \begin{pmatrix} 0\,0\,0\,1 \\ 0\,0\,1\,0 \\ 0\,1\,0\,0 \\ 1\,0\,0\,0 \end{pmatrix}. \quad (63)$$

In general when $\deg(x) = \deg(y) = n-1$, the coefficients of $x(u)y(u) \bmod (u^n - 1)$
are called the *cyclic convolution* of $(x_0, x_1, \ldots, x_{n-1})$ and $(y_0, y_1, \ldots, y_{n-1})$. The
kth coefficient w_k is the bilinear form $\sum x_i y_j$ summed over all i and j with
$i + j \equiv k$ (modulo n).

The cyclic convolution of degree 4 can be obtained by applying rule (59).
The first step is to find the factors of $u^4 - 1$, namely $(u - 1)(u + 1)(u^2 + 1)$. We
could write this as $(u^2 - 1)(u^2 + 1)$, then apply rule (59), then use (59) again on
the part modulo $(u^2 - 1) = (u-1)(u+1)$; but it is easier to generalize the Chinese
remainder rule (59) directly to the case of several relatively prime factors. For
example, we have

$$x(u)y(u) \bmod q_1(u)q_2(u)q_3(u)$$
$$= \big(a_1(u)q_2(u)q_3(u)\big(x(u)y(u) \bmod q_1(u)\big) + a_2(u)q_1(u)q_3(u)\big(x(u)y(u) \bmod q_2(u)\big)$$
$$+ a_3(u)q_1(u)q_2(u)\big(x(u)y(u) \bmod q_3(u)\big)\big) \bmod q_1(u)q_2(u)q_3(u), \quad (64)$$

where $a_1(u)q_2(u)q_3(u) + a_2(u)q_1(u)q_3(u) + a_3(u)q_1(u)q_2(u) = 1$. (This equation
can also be understood in another way, by noting that the partial fraction expansion of $1/q_1(u)q_2(u)q_3(u)$ is $a_1(u)/q_1(u) + a_2(u)/q_2(u) + a_3(u)/q_3(u)$.) From (64)
we obtain

$$x(u)y(u) \bmod (u^4 - 1) = \big(\tfrac{1}{4}(u^3 + u^2 + u + 1)x(1)y(1) - \tfrac{1}{4}(u^3 - u^2 + u - 1)x(-1)y(-1)$$
$$- \tfrac{1}{2}(u^2 - 1)\big(x(u)y(u) \bmod (u^2 + 1)\big)\big) \bmod (u^4 - 1). \quad (65)$$

The remaining problem is to evaluate $x(u)y(u) \bmod (u^2 + 1)$, and it is time
to invoke rule (60). First we reduce $x(u)$ and $y(u) \bmod (u^2 + 1)$, obtaining

$X(u) = (x_0 - x_2) + (x_1 - x_3)u$, $Y(u) = (y_0 - y_2) + (y_1 - y_3)u$. Then (60) tells us to evaluate $X(u)Y(u) = Z_0 + Z_1 u + Z_2 u^2$, and to reduce this in turn modulo $(u^2 + 1)$, obtaining $(Z_0 - Z_2) + Z_1 u$. The job of computing $X(u)Y(u)$ is simple; we can use rule (58) with $p(u) = u(u + 1)$ and we get

$$Z_0 = X_0 Y_0, \quad Z_1 = X_0 Y_0 - (X_0 - X_1)(Y_0 - Y_1) + X_1 Y_1, \quad Z_2 = X_1 Y_1.$$

(We have thereby rediscovered the trick of Eq. 4.3.3–(2) in a more systematic way.) Putting everything together yields the following realization (A, B, C) of degree-4 cyclic convolution:

$$\begin{pmatrix} 1 & 1 & 1 & 0 & 1 \\ 1 & \bar{1} & 0 & 1 & \bar{1} \\ 1 & 1 & \bar{1} & 0 & \bar{1} \\ 1 & \bar{1} & 0 & \bar{1} & 1 \end{pmatrix}, \quad \begin{pmatrix} 1 & 1 & 1 & 0 & 1 \\ 1 & \bar{1} & 0 & 1 & \bar{1} \\ 1 & 1 & \bar{1} & 0 & \bar{1} \\ 1 & \bar{1} & 0 & \bar{1} & 1 \end{pmatrix}, \quad \begin{pmatrix} 1 & 1 & 2 & \bar{2} & 0 \\ 1 & \bar{1} & 2 & 2 & \bar{2} \\ 1 & 1 & \bar{2} & 2 & 0 \\ 1 & \bar{1} & 2 & \bar{2} & 2 \end{pmatrix} \times \frac{1}{4}. \qquad (66)$$

Here $\bar{1}$ stands for -1 and $\bar{2}$ stands for -2.

The tensor for cyclic convolution of degree n satisfies

$$t_{i,j,k} = t_{k,-j,i}, \qquad (67)$$

treating the subscripts modulo n, since $t_{ijk} = 1$ if and only if $i + j \equiv k$ (modulo n). Thus if (a_{il}), (b_{jl}), (c_{kl}) is a realization of the cyclic convolution, so is (c_{kl}), $(b_{-j,l})$, (a_{il}); in particular, we can realize (63) by transforming (66) into

$$\begin{pmatrix} 1 & 1 & 2 & \bar{2} & 0 \\ 1 & \bar{1} & 2 & 2 & \bar{2} \\ 1 & 1 & \bar{2} & 2 & 0 \\ 1 & \bar{1} & 2 & \bar{2} & 2 \end{pmatrix} \times \frac{1}{4}, \quad \begin{pmatrix} 1 & 1 & 1 & 0 & 1 \\ 1 & \bar{1} & 0 & \bar{1} & 1 \\ 1 & 1 & \bar{1} & 0 & \bar{1} \\ 1 & \bar{1} & 0 & 1 & \bar{1} \end{pmatrix}, \quad \begin{pmatrix} 1 & 1 & 1 & 0 & 1 \\ 1 & \bar{1} & 0 & 1 & \bar{1} \\ 1 & 1 & \bar{1} & 0 & \bar{1} \\ 1 & \bar{1} & 0 & \bar{1} & 1 \end{pmatrix}. \qquad (68)$$

Now all of the complicated scalars appear in the A matrix. This is important in practice, since we often want to compute the convolution for many values of y_0, y_1, y_2, y_3 but for a fixed choice of x_0, x_1, x_2, x_3. In such a situation, the arithmetic on x's can be done once and for all, and we need not count it. Thus (68) leads to the following scheme for evaluating the cyclic convolution w_0, w_1, w_2, w_3 when x_0, x_1, x_2, x_3 are known in advance:

$$s_1 = y_0 + y_2, \quad s_2 = y_1 + y_3, \quad s_3 = s_1 + s_2, \quad s_4 = s_1 - s_2,$$
$$s_5 = y_0 - y_2, \quad s_6 = y_3 - y_1, \quad s_7 = s_5 - s_6;$$
$$m_1 = \tfrac{1}{4}(x_0 + x_1 + x_2 + x_3) \cdot s_3, \quad m_2 = \tfrac{1}{4}(x_0 - x_1 + x_2 - x_3) \cdot s_4,$$
$$m_3 = \tfrac{1}{2}(x_0 + x_1 - x_2 - x_3) \cdot s_5, \quad m_4 = \tfrac{1}{2}(-x_0 + x_1 + x_2 - x_3) \cdot s_6, \quad m_5 = \tfrac{1}{2}(x_3 - x_1) \cdot s_7;$$
$$t_1 = m_1 + m_2, \quad t_2 = m_3 + m_5, \quad t_3 = m_1 - m_2, \quad t_4 = m_4 - m_5;$$
$$w_0 = t_1 + t_2, \quad w_1 = t_3 + t_4, \quad w_2 = t_1 - t_2, \quad w_3 = t_3 - t_4. \qquad (69)$$

There are 5 multiplications and 15 additions, while the definition of cyclic convolution involves 16 multiplications and 12 additions. We will prove later that 5 multiplications are necessary.

Going back to our original multiplication problem (54), using (62), we have derived the realization

$$
\begin{pmatrix} 4 & 0 & 1 & 1 & 2 & \bar 2 & 0 \\ 0 & 0 & 1 & \bar 1 & 2 & 2 & \bar 2 \\ 0 & 4 & 1 & 1 & \bar 2 & 2 & 0 \end{pmatrix} \times \frac{1}{4},
\begin{pmatrix} 1 & 0 & 1 & 1 & 1 & 0 & 1 \\ 0 & 0 & 1 & \bar 1 & 0 & \bar 1 & 1 \\ 0 & 0 & 1 & 1 & \bar 1 & 0 & \bar 1 \\ 0 & 1 & 1 & \bar 1 & 0 & 1 & \bar 1 \end{pmatrix},
\begin{pmatrix} 1 & 0 & 0 & 0 & 0 & 0 & 0 \\ 0 & \bar 1 & 1 & \bar 1 & 0 & 1 & \bar 1 \\ 0 & 0 & 1 & 1 & \bar 1 & 0 & \bar 1 \\ 0 & 0 & 1 & \bar 1 & 0 & \bar 1 & 1 \\ \bar 1 & 0 & 1 & 1 & 1 & 0 & 1 \\ 0 & 1 & 0 & 0 & 0 & 0 & 0 \end{pmatrix}. \quad (70)
$$

This scheme uses one more than the minimum number of chain multiplications, but it requires far fewer parameter multiplications than (57). Of course, it must be admitted that the scheme is still rather complicated: If our goal is simply to compute the coefficients z_0, z_1, ..., z_5 of the product of two given polynomials $(x_0 + x_1 u + x_2 u^2)(y_0 + y_1 u + y_2 u^2 + y_3 u^3)$, as a one-shot problem, our best bet may well be to use the obvious method that does 12 multiplications and 6 additions — unless (say) the x's and y's are matrices. Another reasonably attractive scheme, which requires 8 multiplications and 18 additions, appears in exercise 58(b). Notice that if the x's are fixed as the y's vary, (70) does the evaluation with 7 multiplications and 17 additions. Even though this scheme isn't especially useful as it stands, our derivation has illustrated important techniques that are useful in a variety of other situations. For example, Winograd has used this approach to compute Fourier transforms using significantly fewer multiplications than the fast Fourier transform algorithm needs (see exercise 53).

Let us conclude this section by determining the exact rank of the $n \times n \times n$ tensor that corresponds to the multiplication of two polynomials modulo a third,

$$
z_0 + z_1 u + \cdots + z_{n-1} u^{n-1}
$$
$$
= (x_0 + x_1 u + \cdots + x_{n-1} u^{n-1})(y_0 + y_1 u + \cdots + y_{n-1} u^{n-1}) \bmod p(u). \quad (71)
$$

Here $p(u)$ stands for any given monic polynomial of degree n; in particular, $p(u)$ might be $u^n - 1$, so one of the results of our investigation will be to deduce the rank of the tensor corresponding to cyclic convolution of degree n. It will be convenient to write $p(u)$ in the form

$$
p(u) = u^n - p_{n-1} u^{n-1} - \cdots - p_1 u - p_0, \quad (72)
$$

so that $u^n \equiv p_0 + p_1 u + \cdots + p_{n-1} u^{n-1} \pmod{p(u)}$.

The tensor element t_{ijk} is the coefficient of u^k in $u^{i+j} \bmod p(u)$; and this is the element in row i, column k of the matrix P^j, where

$$
P = \begin{pmatrix} 0 & 1 & 0 & \cdots & 0 \\ 0 & 0 & 1 & \cdots & 0 \\ \vdots & \vdots & \vdots & & \vdots \\ 0 & 0 & 0 & \cdots & 1 \\ p_0 & p_1 & p_2 & \cdots & p_{n-1} \end{pmatrix} \quad (73)
$$

is called the *companion matrix* of $p(u)$. (The indices i, j, k in our discussion will run from 0 to $n - 1$ instead of from 1 to n.) It is convenient to transpose the tensor, for if $T_{ijk} = t_{ikj}$ the individual layers of (T_{ijk}) for $k = 0, 1, 2, \ldots, n-1$ are simply given by the matrices

$$I \quad P \quad P^2 \quad \ldots \quad P^{n-1}. \tag{74}$$

The first rows of the matrices in (74) are respectively the unit vectors $(1, 0, 0, \ldots, 0)$, $(0, 1, 0, \ldots, 0)$, $(0, 0, 1, \ldots, 0)$, $\ldots$, $(0, 0, 0, \ldots, 1)$, hence a linear combination $\sum_{k=0}^{n-1} v_k P^k$ will be the zero matrix if and only if the coefficients v_k are all zero. Furthermore, most of these linear combinations are actually nonsingular matrices, for we have

$$(w_0, w_1, \ldots, w_{n-1}) \sum_{k=0}^{n-1} v_k P^k = (0, 0, \ldots, 0)$$

$$\text{if and only if} \quad v(u)w(u) \equiv 0 \pmod{p(u)},$$

where $v(u) = v_0 + v_1 u + \cdots + v_{n-1} u^{n-1}$ and $w(u) = w_0 + w_1 u + \cdots + w_{n-1} u^{n-1}$. Thus, $\sum_{k=0}^{n-1} v_k P^k$ is a singular matrix if and only if the polynomial $v(u)$ is a multiple of some factor of $p(u)$. We are now ready to prove the desired result.

Theorem W (S. Winograd, 1975). *Let $p(u)$ be a monic polynomial of degree n whose complete factorization over a given infinite field is*

$$p(u) = p_1(u)^{e_1} \ldots p_q(u)^{e_q}. \tag{75}$$

Then the rank of the tensor (74) corresponding to the bilinear forms (71) is $2n - q$ over this field.

Proof. The bilinear forms can be evaluated with only $2n - q$ chain multiplications by using rules (58), (59), (60) in an appropriate fashion, so we must prove only that the rank r is $\geq 2n - q$. The discussion above establishes the fact that $\operatorname{rank}(T_{(ij)k}) = n$; hence by Lemma T, any $n \times r$ realization (A, B, C) of (T_{ijk}) has $\operatorname{rank}(C) = n$. Our strategy will be to use Lemma T again, by finding a vector $(v_0, v_1, \ldots, v_{n-1})$ that has the following two properties:

i) The vector $(v_0, v_1, \ldots, v_{n-1})C$ has at most $q + r - n$ nonzero coefficients.
ii) The matrix $v(P) = \sum_{k=0}^{n-1} v_k P^k$ is nonsingular.

This and Lemma T will prove that $q + r - n \geq n$, since the identity

$$\sum_{l=1}^{r} a_{il} b_{jl} \left(\sum_{k=0}^{n-1} v_k c_{kl} \right) = v(P)_{ij}$$

shows how to realize the $n \times n \times 1$ tensor $v(P)$ of rank n with $q + r - n$ chain multiplications.

We may assume for convenience that the first n columns of C are linearly independent. Let D be the $n \times n$ matrix such that the first n columns of DC are equal to the identity matrix. Our goal will be achieved if there is a linear combination $(v_0, v_1, \ldots, v_{n-1})$ of at most q rows of D, such that $v(P)$ is nonsingular; such a vector will satisfy conditions (i) and (ii).

Since the rows of D are linearly independent, no irreducible factor $p_\lambda(u)$ can divide the polynomials corresponding to every row. Given a vector

$$w = (w_0, w_1, \ldots, w_{n-1}),$$

let covered(w) be the set of all λ such that $w(u)$ is not a multiple of $p_\lambda(u)$. From two vectors v and w we can find a linear combination $v + \alpha w$ such that

$$\text{covered}(v + \alpha w) = \text{covered}(v) \cup \text{covered}(w), \qquad (76)$$

for some α in the field. The reason is that if λ is covered by v or w but not both, then λ is covered by $v + \alpha w$ for all nonzero α; if λ is covered by both v and w but λ is not covered by $v + \alpha w$, then λ is covered by $v + \beta w$ for all $\beta \neq \alpha$. By trying $q+1$ different values of α, at least one must yield (76). In this way we can systematically construct a linear combination of at most q rows of D, covering all λ for $1 \leq \lambda \leq q$. ∎

One of the most important corollaries of Theorem W is that the rank of a tensor can depend on the field from which we draw the elements of the realization (A, B, C). For example, consider the tensor corresponding to cyclic convolution of degree 5; this is equivalent to multiplication of polynomials mod $p(u) = u^5 - 1$. Over the field of rational numbers, the complete factorization of $p(u)$ is $(u - 1) \times (u^4 + u^3 + u^2 + u + 1)$ by exercise 4.6.2–32, so the tensor rank is $10 - 2 = 8$. On the other hand, the complete factorization over the real numbers, in terms of the number $\phi = \frac{1}{2}(1 + \sqrt{5})$, is $(u - 1)(u^2 + \phi u + 1)(u^2 - \phi^{-1}u + 1)$; thus, the rank is only 7, if we allow arbitrary real numbers to appear in A, B, C. Over the complex numbers the rank is 5. This phenomenon does not occur in two-dimensional tensors (matrices), where the rank can be determined by evaluating determinants of submatrices and testing for 0. The rank of a matrix does not change when the field containing its elements is embedded in a larger field, but the rank of a tensor *can* decrease when the field gets larger.

In the paper that introduced Theorem W [*Math. Systems Theory* **10** (1977), 169–180], Winograd went on to show that *all* realizations of (71) in $2n - q$ chain multiplications correspond to the use of (59), when q is greater than 1. Furthermore he has shown that the only way to evaluate the coefficients of $x(u)y(u)$ in $\deg(x) + \deg(y) + 1$ chain multiplications is to use interpolation or to use (58) with a polynomial that splits into distinct linear factors in the field. Finally he has proved that the only way to evaluate $x(u)y(u) \bmod p(u)$ in $2n - 1$ chain multiplications when $q = 1$ is essentially to use (60). These results hold for *all* polynomial chains, not only "normal" ones. He has extended the results to multivariate polynomials in *SICOMP* **9** (1980), 225–229.

The tensor rank of an arbitrary $m \times n \times 2$ tensor in a suitably large field has been determined by Joseph Ja'Ja', *SICOMP* **8** (1979), 443–462; *JACM* **27** (1980), 822–830. See also his interesting discussion of commutative bilinear forms in *SICOMP* **9** (1980), 713–728. However, the problem of computing the tensor rank of an arbitrary $n \times n \times n$ tensor over any finite field is NP-complete [J. Håstad, *Journal of Algorithms* **11** (1990), 644–654].

For further reading. In this section we have barely scratched the surface of a very large subject in which many beautiful theories are emerging. Considerably more comprehensive treatments can be found in the books *Computational Complexity of Algebraic and Numeric Problems* by A. Borodin and I. Munro (New York: American Elsevier, 1975); *Polynomial and Matrix Computations* **1** by D. Bini and V. Pan (Boston: Birkhäuser, 1994); *Algebraic Complexity Theory* by P. Bürgisser, M. Clausen, and M. Amin Shokrollahi (Heidelberg: Springer, 1997).

EXERCISES

1. [*15*] What is a good way to evaluate an "odd" polynomial

$$u(x) = u_{2n+1}x^{2n+1} + u_{2n-1}x^{2n-1} + \cdots + u_1x?$$

▶ **2.** [*M20*] Instead of computing $u(x + x_0)$ by steps H1 and H2 as in the text, discuss the application of Horner's rule (2) when *polynomial* multiplication and addition are used instead of arithmetic in the domain of coefficients.

3. [*20*] Give a method analogous to Horner's rule, for evaluating a polynomial in two variables $\sum_{i+j\leq n} u_{ij}x^iy^j$. (This polynomial has $(n + 1)(n + 2)/2$ coefficients, and its "total degree" is n.) Count the number of additions and multiplications you use.

4. [*M20*] The text shows that scheme (3) is superior to Horner's rule when we are evaluating a polynomial with real coefficients at a complex point z. Compare (3) to Horner's rule when *both* the coefficients and the variable z are complex numbers; how many (real) multiplications and addition-subtractions are required by each method?

5. [*M15*] Count the number of multiplications and additions required by the second-order rule (4).

6. [*22*] (L. de Jong and J. van Leeuwen.) Show how to improve on steps S1, ..., S4 of the Shaw–Traub algorithm by computing only about $\frac{1}{2}n$ powers of x_0.

7. [*M25*] How can β_0, ..., β_n be calculated so that (6) has the value $u(x_0 + kh)$ for all integers k?

8. [*M20*] The factorial power $x^{\underline{k}}$ is defined to be $k!\binom{x}{k} = x(x - 1)\ldots(x - k + 1)$. Explain how to evaluate $u_nx^{\underline{n}} + \cdots + u_1x^{\underline{1}} + u_0$ with at most n multiplications and $2n - 1$ additions, starting with x and the $n + 3$ constants u_n, ..., u_0, 1, $n - 1$.

9. [*M25*] (H. J. Ryser.) Show that if $X = (x_{ij})$ is an $n \times n$ matrix, then

$$\operatorname{per}(X) = \sum(-1)^{n-\epsilon_1-\cdots-\epsilon_n} \prod_{1\leq i\leq n} \sum_{1\leq j\leq n} \epsilon_j x_{ij}$$

summed over all 2^n choices of ϵ_1, ..., ϵ_n equal to 0 or 1 independently. Count the number of addition and multiplication operations required to evaluate $\operatorname{per}(X)$ by this formula.

10. [*M21*] The permanent of an $n \times n$ matrix $X = (x_{ij})$ may be calculated as follows: Start with the n quantities x_{11}, x_{12}, ..., x_{1n}. For $1 \leq k < n$, assume that the $\binom{n}{k}$ quantities A_{kS} have been computed, for all k-element subsets S of $\{1, 2, \ldots, n\}$, where $A_{kS} = \sum x_{1j_1} \ldots x_{kj_k}$ summed over all $k!$ permutations $j_1 \ldots j_k$ of the elements of S; then form all of the sums

$$A_{(k+1)S} = \sum_{j\in S} A_{k(S\setminus\{j\})} x_{(k+1)j}.$$

We have $\operatorname{per}(X) = A_{n\{1,\ldots,n\}}$. How many additions and multiplications does this method require? How much temporary storage is needed?

11. [*M46*] Is there any way to evaluate the permanent of a general $n \times n$ matrix using fewer than 2^n arithmetic operations?

12. [*M50*] What is the minimum number of multiplications required to form the product of two $n \times n$ matrices? What is the smallest exponent ω such that $O(n^{\omega+\epsilon})$ multiplications are sufficient for all $\epsilon > 0$? (Find good upper and lower bounds for small n as well as large n.)

13. [*M23*] Find the inverse of the general discrete Fourier transform (37), by expressing $F(t_1, \ldots, t_n)$ in terms of the values of $f(s_1, \ldots, s_n)$. [*Hint:* See Eq. 1.2.9–(13).]

▶ **14.** [*HM28*] (*Fast Fourier transforms.*) Show that the scheme (40) can be used to evaluate the one-dimensional discrete Fourier transform

$$f(s) = \sum_{0 \le t < 2^n} F(t)\,\omega^{st}, \qquad \omega = e^{2\pi i/2^n}, \qquad 0 \le s < 2^n,$$

using arithmetic on complex numbers. Estimate the number of arithmetic operations performed.

▶ **15.** [*HM28*] The nth *divided difference* $f(x_0, x_1, \ldots, x_n)$ of a function $f(x)$ at $n+1$ distinct points x_0, x_1, $\ldots$, x_n is defined by the formula

$$f(x_0, x_1, \ldots, x_n) = \big(f(x_0, x_1, \ldots, x_{n-1}) - f(x_1, \ldots, x_{n-1}, x_n)\big)/(x_0 - x_n),$$

for $n > 0$. Thus $f(x_0, x_1, \ldots, x_n) = \sum_{k=0}^n f(x_k)/\prod_{0 \le j \le n,\, j \ne k}(x_k - x_j)$ is a symmetric function of its $n+1$ arguments. (a) Prove that $f(x_0, \ldots, x_n) = f^{(n)}(\theta)/n!$, for some θ between $\min(x_0, \ldots, x_n)$ and $\max(x_0, \ldots, x_n)$, if the nth derivative $f^{(n)}(x)$ exists and is continuous. [*Hint:* Prove the identity

$$f(x_0, x_1, \ldots, x_n) = \int_0^1 dt_1 \int_0^{t_1} dt_2 \ldots \int_0^{t_{n-1}} dt_n f^{(n)}\big(x_0(1 - t_1) + x_1(t_1 - t_2) + \cdots$$
$$+ \, x_{n-1}(t_{n-1} - t_n) + x_n(t_n - 0)\big).$$

This formula also defines $f(x_0, x_1, \ldots, x_n)$ in a useful manner when the x_j are not distinct.] (b) If $y_j = f(x_j)$, show that $\alpha_j = f(x_0, \ldots, x_j)$ in Newton's interpolation polynomial (42).

16. [*M22*] How can we readily compute the coefficients of $u_{[n]}(x) = u_n x^n + \cdots + u_0$, if we are given the values of x_0, x_1, $\ldots$, x_{n-1}, α_0, α_1, $\ldots$, α_n in Newton's interpolation polynomial (42)?

17. [*M20*] Show that the interpolation formula (45) reduces to a very simple expression involving binomial coefficients when $x_k = x_0 + kh$ for $0 \le k \le n$. [*Hint:* See exercise 1.2.6–48.]

18. [*M20*] If the fourth-degree scheme (9) were changed to

$$y = (x + \alpha_0)x + \alpha_1, \qquad u(x) = ((y - x + \alpha_2)y + \alpha_3)\alpha_4,$$

what formulas for computing the α_j's in terms of the u_k's would take the place of (10)?

▶ **19.** [*M24*] Explain how to determine the adapted coefficients α_0, α_1, $\ldots$, α_5 in (11) from the coefficients u_5, $\ldots$, u_1, u_0 of $u(x)$, and find the α's for the particular polynomial $u(x) = x^5 + 5x^4 - 10x^3 - 50x^2 + 13x + 60$.

▶ **20.** [*21*] Write a MIX program that evaluates a fifth-degree polynomial according to scheme (11); try to make the program as efficient as possible, by making slight modifications to (11). Use MIX's floating point arithmetic operators FADD and FMUL, which are described in Section 4.2.1.

21. [*20*] Find two additional ways to evaluate the polynomial $x^6 + 13x^5 + 49x^4 + 33x^3 - 61x^2 - 37x + 3$ by scheme (12), using the two roots of (15) that were not considered in the text.

22. [*18*] What is the scheme for evaluating $x^6 - 3x^5 + x^4 - 2x^3 + x^2 - 3x - 1$, using Pan's method (16)?

23. [*HM30*] (J. Eve.) Let $f(z) = a_n z^n + a_{n-1} z^{n-1} + \cdots + a_0$ be a polynomial of degree n with real coefficients, having at least $n - 1$ roots with a nonnegative real part. Let

$$g(z) = a_n z^n + a_{n-2} z^{n-2} + \cdots + a_{n \bmod 2} z^{n \bmod 2},$$

$$h(z) = a_{n-1} z^{n-1} + a_{n-3} z^{n-3} + \cdots + a_{(n-1) \bmod 2} z^{(n-1) \bmod 2}.$$

Assume that $h(z)$ is not identically zero.

a) Show that $g(z)$ has at least $n - 2$ imaginary roots (that is, roots whose real part is zero), and $h(z)$ has at least $n - 3$ imaginary roots. [*Hint:* Consider the number of times the path $f(z)$ circles the origin as z goes around the path shown in Fig. 16, for a sufficiently large radius R.]

b) Prove that the squares of the roots of $g(z) = 0$ and $h(z) = 0$ are all real.

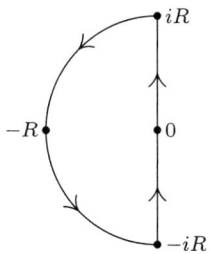

Fig. 16. Proof of Eve's theorem.

▶ **24.** [*M24*] Find values of c and α_k, β_k satisfying the conditions of Theorem E, for the polynomial $u(x) = (x + 7)(x^2 + 6x + 10)(x^2 + 4x + 5)(x + 1)$. Choose these values so that $\beta_2 = 0$. Give two different solutions.

25. [*M20*] When the construction in the proof of Theorem M is applied to the (inefficient) polynomial chain

$$\lambda_1 = \alpha_1 + \lambda_0, \qquad \lambda_2 = -\lambda_0 - \lambda_0, \qquad \lambda_3 = \lambda_1 + \lambda_1, \qquad \lambda_4 = \alpha_2 \times \lambda_3,$$

$$\lambda_5 = \lambda_0 - \lambda_0, \qquad \lambda_6 = \alpha_6 - \lambda_5, \qquad \lambda_7 = \alpha_7 \times \lambda_6, \qquad \lambda_8 = \lambda_7 \times \lambda_7,$$

$$\lambda_9 = \lambda_1 \times \lambda_4, \qquad \lambda_{10} = \alpha_8 - \lambda_9, \qquad \lambda_{11} = \lambda_3 - \lambda_{10},$$

how can $\beta_1, \beta_2, \ldots, \beta_9$ be expressed in terms of $\alpha_1, \ldots, \alpha_8$?

▶ **26.** [*M21*] (a) Give the polynomial chain corresponding to Horner's rule for evaluating polynomials of degree $n = 3$. (b) Using the construction that appears in the text's proof of Theorem A, express κ_1, κ_2, κ_3, and the result polynomial $u(x)$ in terms of β_1, β_2, β_3, β_4, and x. (c) Show that the result set obtained in (b), as β_1, β_2, β_3, and β_4 independently assume all real values, omits certain vectors in the result set of (a).

27. [*M22*] Let R be a set that includes all $(n+1)$-tuples $(q_n, \ldots, q_1, q_0)$ of real numbers such that $q_n \neq 0$; prove that R does not have at most n degrees of freedom.

28. [*HM20*] Show that if $f_0(\alpha_1, \ldots, \alpha_s)$, $\ldots$, $f_s(\alpha_1, \ldots, \alpha_s)$ are multivariate polynomials with integer coefficients, then there is a nonzero polynomial $g(x_0, \ldots, x_s)$ with integer coefficients such that $g\big(f_0(\alpha_1, \ldots, \alpha_s), \ldots, f_s(\alpha_1, \ldots, \alpha_s)\big) = 0$ for all real α_1, $\ldots$, α_s. (Hence any polynomial chain with s parameters has at most s degrees of freedom.) [*Hint:* Use the theorems about "algebraic dependence" that are found, for example, in B. L. van der Waerden's *Modern Algebra*, translated by Fred Blum (New York: Ungar, 1949), Section 64.]

▶ **29.** [*M20*] Let R_1, R_2, $\ldots$, R_m all be sets of $(n + 1)$-tuples of real numbers having at most t degrees of freedom. Show that the union $R_1 \cup R_2 \cup \cdots \cup R_m$ also has at most t degrees of freedom.

▶ **30.** [*M28*] Prove that a polynomial chain with m_c chain multiplications and m_p parameter multiplications has at most $2m_c + m_p + \delta_{0m_c}$ degrees of freedom. [*Hint:* Generalize Theorem M, showing that the first chain multiplication and each parameter multiplication can essentially introduce only one new parameter into the result set.]

31. [*M23*] Prove that a polynomial chain capable of computing all *monic* polynomials of degree n has at least $\lfloor n/2 \rfloor$ multiplications and at least n addition-subtractions.

32. [*M24*] Find a polynomial chain of minimum possible length that can compute all polynomials of the form $u_4 x^4 + u_2 x^2 + u_0$; and prove that its length is minimal.

▶ **33.** [*M25*] Let $n \geq 3$ be odd. Prove that a polynomial chain with $\lfloor n/2 \rfloor + 1$ multiplication steps cannot compute all polynomials of degree n unless it has at least $n + 2$ addition-subtraction steps. [*Hint:* See exercise 30.]

34. [*M26*] Let λ_0, λ_1, $\ldots$, λ_r be a polynomial chain in which all of the addition and subtraction steps are parameter steps, and in which there is at least one parameter multiplication. Assume that this scheme has m multiplications and $k = r - m$ addition-subtractions, and that the polynomial computed by the chain has maximum degree n. Prove that all polynomials computable by this chain, for which the coefficient of x^n is not zero, can be computed by another chain that has at most m multiplications and at most k additions, and no subtractions; furthermore the last step of the new chain should be the only parameter multiplication.

▶ **35.** [*M25*] Show that any polynomial chain that computes a general fourth-degree polynomial using three multiplications must have at least five addition-subtractions. [*Hint:* Assume that there are only four addition-subtractions, and show that exercise 34 applies; therefore the scheme must have a particular form that is incapable of representing all fourth-degree polynomials.]

36. [*M27*] Continuing the previous exercise, show that any polynomial chain that computes a general sixth-degree polynomial using only four multiplications must have at least seven addition-subtractions.

37. [*M21*] (T. S. Motzkin.) Show that "almost all" rational functions of the form

$$(u_n x^n + u_{n-1} x^{n-1} + \cdots + u_1 x + u_0)/(x^n + v_{n-1} x^{n-1} + \cdots + v_1 x + v_0),$$

with coefficients in a field S, can be evaluated using the scheme

$$\alpha_1 + \beta_1/(x + \alpha_2 + \beta_2/(x + \cdots + \beta_n/(x + \alpha_{n+1}) \ldots)),$$

for suitable α_j, β_j in S. (This continued fraction scheme has n divisions and $2n$ additions; by "almost all" rational functions we mean all except those whose coefficients satisfy some nontrivial polynomial equation.) Determine the α's and β's for the rational function $(x^2 + 10x + 29)/(x^2 + 8x + 19)$.

▶ **38.** [*HM32*] (V. Y. Pan, 1962.) The purpose of this exercise is to prove that Horner's rule is really optimal if no preliminary adaptation of coefficients is made; we need n multiplications and n additions to compute $u_n x^n + \cdots + u_1 x + u_0$, if the variables u_n, ..., u_1, u_0, x, and arbitrary constants are given. Consider chains that are as before except that u_n, ..., u_1, u_0, x are each considered to be variables; we may say, for example, that $\lambda_{-j-1} = u_j$, $\lambda_0 = x$. In order to show that Horner's rule is best, it is convenient to prove a somewhat more general theorem: Let $A = (a_{ij})$, $0 \le i \le m$, $0 \le j \le n$, be an $(m+1) \times (n+1)$ matrix of real numbers, of rank $n+1$; and let $B = (b_0, \ldots, b_m)$ be a vector of real numbers. Prove that *any polynomial chain that computes*

$$P(x; u_0, \ldots, u_n) = \sum_{i=0}^{m} (a_{i0} u_0 + \cdots + a_{in} u_n + b_i) x^i$$

involves at least n chain multiplications. (Note that this does not mean only that we are considering some fixed chain in which the parameters α_j are assigned values depending on A and B; it means that both the chain *and* the values of the α's may depend on the given matrix A and vector B. No matter how A, B, and the values of α_j are chosen, it is impossible to compute $P(x; u_0, \ldots, u_n)$ without doing n "chain-step" multiplications.) The assumption that A has rank $n+1$ implies that $m \ge n$. [*Hint:* Show that from any such scheme we can derive another that has fewer chain multiplications and that has n decreased by one.]

39. [*M29*] (T. S. Motzkin, 1954.) Show that schemes of the form

$$w_1 = x(x + \alpha_1) + \beta_1, \qquad w_k = w_{k-1}(w_1 + \gamma_k x + \alpha_k) + \delta_k x + \beta_k \quad \text{for } 1 < k \le m,$$

where the α_k, β_k are real and the γ_k, δ_k are integers, can be used to evaluate all monic polynomials of degree $2m$ over the real numbers. (We may have to choose α_k, β_k, γ_k, and δ_k differently for different polynomials.) Try to let $\delta_k = 0$ whenever possible.

40. [*M41*] Can the lower bound in the number of multiplications in Theorem C be raised from $\lfloor n/2 \rfloor + 1$ to $\lceil n/2 \rceil + 1$? (See exercise 33.)

41. [*22*] Show that the real and imaginary parts of $(a + bi)(c + di)$ can be obtained by doing 3 multiplications and 5 additions of real numbers, where two of the additions involve a and b only.

42. [*36*] (M. Paterson and L. Stockmeyer.) (a) Prove that a polynomial chain with $m \ge 2$ chain multiplications has at most $m^2 + 1$ degrees of freedom. (b) Show that for all $n \ge 2$ there exist polynomials of degree n, all of whose coefficients are 0 or 1, that cannot be evaluated by any polynomial chain with fewer than $\lfloor \sqrt{n} \rfloor$ multiplications, if we require all parameters α_j to be integers. (c) Show that any polynomial of degree n with integer coefficients can be evaluated by an all-integer algorithm that performs at most $2\lfloor \sqrt{n} \rfloor$ multiplications, if we don't care how many additions we do.

43. [*22*] Explain how to evaluate $x^n + \cdots + x + 1$ with $2l(n+1) - 2$ multiplications and $l(n+1)$ additions (no divisions or subtractions), where $l(n)$ is the function studied in Section 4.6.3.

▶ **44.** [*M25*] Show that any monic polynomial $u(x) = x^n + u_{n-1} x^{n-1} + \cdots + u_0$ can be evaluated with $\frac{1}{2} n + O(\log n)$ multiplications and $\le \frac{5}{4} n$ additions, using parameters α_1, α_2, ... that are polynomials in u_{n-1}, u_{n-2}, ... with integer coefficients. [*Hint:* Consider first the case $n = 2^l$.]

▶ **45.** [*HM22*] Let (t_{ijk}) be an $m \times n \times s$ tensor, and let F, G, H be nonsingular matrices of respective sizes $m \times m$, $n \times n$, $s \times s$. If

$$T_{ijk} = \sum_{i'=1}^{m} \sum_{j'=1}^{n} \sum_{k'=1}^{s} F_{ii'} G_{jj'} H_{kk'} t_{i'j'k'}$$

for all i, j, k, prove that the tensor (T_{ijk}) has the same rank as (t_{ijk}). [*Hint:* Consider what happens when F^{-1}, G^{-1}, H^{-1} are applied in the same way to (T_{ijk}).]

46. [*M28*] Prove that all pairs (z_1, z_2) of bilinear forms in (x_1, x_2) and (y_1, y_2) can be evaluated with at most three chain multiplications. In other words, show that every $2 \times 2 \times 2$ tensor has rank ≤ 3.

47. [*M25*] Prove that for all m, n, and s there exists an $m \times n \times s$ tensor whose rank is at least $\lceil mns/(m+n+s) \rceil$. Conversely, show that every $m \times n \times s$ tensor has rank at most $mns/\max(m,n,s)$.

48. [*M21*] If (t_{ijk}) and (t'_{ijk}) are tensors of sizes $m \times n \times s$ and $m' \times n' \times s'$, respectively, their *direct sum* $(t_{ijk}) \oplus (t'_{ijk}) = (t''_{ijk})$ is the $(m+m') \times (n+n') \times (s+s')$ tensor defined by $t''_{ijk} = t_{ijk}$ if $i \leq m$, $j \leq n$, $k \leq s$; $t''_{ijk} = t'_{i-m,j-n,k-s}$ if $i > m$, $j > n$, $k > s$; and $t''_{ijk} = 0$ otherwise. Their direct product $(t_{ijk}) \otimes (t'_{ijk}) = (t'''_{ijk})$ is the $mm' \times nn' \times ss'$ tensor defined by $t_{\langle ii' \rangle \langle jj' \rangle \langle kk' \rangle} = t_{ijk} t'_{i'j'k'}$. Derive the upper bounds $\operatorname{rank}(t''_{ijk}) \leq \operatorname{rank}(t_{ijk}) + \operatorname{rank}(t'_{ijk})$ and $\operatorname{rank}(t'''_{ijk}) \leq \operatorname{rank}(t_{ijk}) \cdot \operatorname{rank}(t'_{ijk})$.

▶ **49.** [*HM25*] Show that the rank of an $m \times n \times 1$ tensor (t_{ijk}) is the same as its rank as an $m \times n$ matrix (t_{ij1}), according to the traditional definition of matrix rank as the maximum number of linearly independent rows.

50. [*HM20*] (S. Winograd.) Let (t_{ijk}) be the $mn \times n \times m$ tensor corresponding to multiplication of an $m \times n$ matrix by an $n \times 1$ column vector. Prove that the rank of (t_{ijk}) is mn.

▶ **51.** [*M24*] (S. Winograd.) Devise an algorithm for cyclic convolution of degree 2 that uses 2 multiplications and 4 additions, not counting operations on the x_i. Similarly, devise an algorithm for degree 3, using 4 multiplications and 11 additions. (See (69), which solves the analogous problem for degree 4.)

52. [*M25*] (S. Winograd.) Let $n = n'n''$ where $n' \perp n''$. Given normal schemes for cyclic convolutions of degrees n' and n'', using respectively (m', m'') chain multiplications, (p', p'') parameter multiplications, and (a', a'') additions, show how to construct a normal scheme for cyclic convolution of degree n using $m'm''$ chain multiplications, $p'n'' + m'p''$ parameter multiplications, and $a'n'' + m'a''$ additions.

53. [*HM40*] (S. Winograd.) Let ω be a complex mth root of unity, and consider the one-dimensional discrete Fourier transform

$$f(s) = \sum_{t=1}^{m} F(t) \omega^{st}, \qquad \text{for } 1 \leq s \leq m.$$

a) When $m = p^e$ is a power of an odd prime, show that efficient normal schemes for computing cyclic convolutions of degrees $(p-1)p^k$, for $0 \leq k < e$, will lead to efficient algorithms for computing the Fourier transform on m complex numbers. Give a similar construction for the case $p = 2$.

b) When $m = m'm''$ and $m' \perp m''$, show that Fourier transformation algorithms for m' and m'' can be combined to yield a Fourier transformation algorithm for m elements.

54. [*M23*] Theorem W refers to an infinite field. How many elements must a finite field have in order for the proof of Theorem W to be valid?

55. [*HM22*] Determine the rank of tensor (74) when P is an *arbitrary* $n \times n$ matrix.

56. [*M32*] (V. Strassen.) Show that any polynomial chain that evaluates a set of *quadratic forms* $\sum_{i=1}^{n} \sum_{j=1}^{n} \tau_{ijk} x_i x_j$ for $1 \le k \le s$ must use at least $\frac{1}{2}\operatorname{rank}(\tau_{ijk} + \tau_{jik})$ chain multiplications altogether. [*Hint:* Show that the minimum number of chain multiplications is the minimum rank of (t_{ijk}) taken over all tensors (t_{ijk}) such that $t_{ijk} + t_{jik} = \tau_{ijk} + \tau_{jik}$ for all i, j, k.] Conclude that if a polynomial chain evaluates a set of bilinear forms (47) corresponding to a tensor (t_{ijk}), whether normal or abnormal, it must use at least $\frac{1}{2}\operatorname{rank}(t_{ijk})$ chain multiplications.

57. [*M20*] Show that fast Fourier transforms can be used to compute the coefficients of the product $x(u)y(u)$ of two given polynomials of degree n, using $O(n \log n)$ operations of (exact) addition and multiplication of complex numbers. [*Hint:* Consider the product of Fourier transforms of the coefficients.]

58. [*HM28*] (a) Show that any realization (A, B, C) of the polynomial multiplication tensor (55) must have the following property: Any nonzero linear combination of the three rows of A must be a vector with at least four nonzero elements; and any nonzero linear combination of the four rows of B must have at least three nonzero elements. (b) Find a realization (A, B, C) of (55) that uses only 0, +1, and −1 as elements, where $r = 8$. Try to use as many 0s as possible.

▶ **59.** [*M40*] (H. J. Nussbaumer, 1980.) The text defines the cyclic convolution of two sequences $(x_0, x_1, \ldots, x_{n-1})$ and $(y_0, y_1, \ldots, y_{n-1})$ to be the sequence $(z_0, z_1, \ldots, z_{n-1})$ where $z_k = x_0 y_k + \cdots + x_k y_0 + x_{k+1} y_{n-1} + \cdots + x_{n-1} y_{k+1}$. Let us define the *negacyclic convolution* similarly, but with

$$z_k = x_0 y_k + \cdots + x_k y_0 - (x_{k+1} y_{n-1} + \cdots + x_{n-1} y_{k+1}).$$

Construct efficient algorithms for cyclic and negacyclic convolution over the integers when n is a power of 2. Your algorithms should deal entirely with integers, and they should perform at most $O(n \log n)$ multiplications and at most $O(n \log n \log \log n)$ additions or subtractions or divisions of even numbers by 2. [*Hint:* A cyclic convolution of order $2n$ can be reduced to cyclic and negacyclic convolutions of order n, using (59).]

60. [*M27*] (V. Y. Pan.) The problem of $(m \times n)$ times $(n \times s)$ matrix multiplication corresponds to an $mn \times ns \times sm$ tensor $(t_{\langle i,j' \rangle \langle j,k' \rangle \langle k,i' \rangle})$ where $t_{\langle i,j' \rangle \langle j,k' \rangle \langle k,i' \rangle} = 1$ if and only if $i' = i$ and $j' = j$ and $k' = k$. The rank of this tensor $T(m, n, s)$ is the smallest number r such that numbers $a_{ij'l}$, $b_{jk'l}$, $c_{ki'l}$ exist satisfying

$$\sum_{\substack{1 \le i \le m \\ 1 \le j \le n \\ 1 \le k \le s}} x_{ij} y_{jk} z_{ki} = \sum_{1 \le l \le r} \left(\sum_{\substack{1 \le i \le m \\ 1 \le j' \le n}} a_{ij'l} x_{ij'} \right) \left(\sum_{\substack{1 \le j \le n \\ 1 \le k' \le s}} b_{jk'l} y_{jk'} \right) \left(\sum_{\substack{1 \le k \le s \\ 1 \le i' \le m}} c_{ki'l} z_{ki'} \right).$$

Let $M(n)$ be the rank of $T(n, n, n)$. The purpose of this exercise is to exploit the symmetry of such a trilinear representation, obtaining efficient realizations of matrix multiplication over the integers when $m = n = s = 2\nu$. For convenience we divide the indices $\{1, \ldots, n\}$ into two subsets $O = \{1, 3, \ldots, n-1\}$ and $E = \{2, 4, \ldots, n\}$ of ν elements each, and we set up a one-to-one correspondence between O and E by the rule $\tilde{i} = i + 1$ if $i \in O$; $\tilde{i} = i - 1$ if $i \in E$. Thus we have $\tilde{\tilde{i}} = i$ for all indices i.

a) The identity

$$abc + ABC = (a + A)(b + B)(c + C) - (a + A)bC - A(b + B)c - aB(c + C)$$

implies that

$$\sum_{1 \le i,j,k \le n} x_{ij} y_{jk} z_{ki} = \sum_{(i,j,k) \in S} (x_{ij} + x_{\bar{k}\bar{\imath}})(y_{jk} + y_{\bar{\imath}\bar{\jmath}})(z_{ki} + z_{\bar{\jmath}\bar{k}}) - \Sigma_1 - \Sigma_2 - \Sigma_3,$$

where $S = E \times E \times E \cup E \times E \times O \cup E \times O \times E \cup O \times E \times E$ is the set of all triples of indices containing at most one odd index; Σ_1 is the sum of all terms of the form $(x_{ij} + x_{\bar{k}\bar{\imath}}) y_{jk} z_{\bar{\jmath}\bar{k}}$ for $(i,j,k) \in S$; and Σ_2, Σ_3 similarly are sums of the terms $x_{\bar{k}\bar{\imath}}(y_{jk} + y_{\bar{\imath}\bar{\jmath}}) z_{ki}$, $x_{ij} y_{\bar{\imath}\bar{\jmath}}(z_{ki} + z_{\bar{\jmath}\bar{k}})$. Clearly S has $4\nu^3 = \frac{1}{2}n^3$ terms. Show that each of $\Sigma_1, \Sigma_2, \Sigma_3$ can be realized as the sum of $3\nu^2$ trilinear terms; furthermore, if the 3ν triples of the forms $(i,i,\bar{\imath})$ and $(i,\bar{\imath},i)$ and $(\bar{\imath},i,i)$ are removed from S, we can modify Σ_1, Σ_2, and Σ_3 in such a way that the identity is still valid, without adding any new trilinear terms. Thus $M(n) \le \frac{1}{2}n^3 + \frac{9}{4}n^2 - \frac{3}{2}n$ when n is even.

b) Apply the method of (a) to show that two *independent* matrix multiplication problems of the respective sizes $m \times n \times s$ and $s \times m \times n$ can be performed with $mns + mn + ns + sm$ noncommutative multiplications.

61. [*M26*] Let (t_{ijk}) be a tensor over an arbitrary field. We define $\text{rank}_d(t_{ijk})$ as the minimum value of r such that there is a realization of the form

$$\sum_{l=1}^{r} a_{il}(u) b_{jl}(u) c_{kl}(u) = t_{ijk} u^d + O(u^{d+1}),$$

where $a_{il}(u)$, $b_{jl}(u)$, $c_{kl}(u)$ are polynomials in u over the field. Thus rank_0 is the ordinary rank of a tensor. Prove that

a) $\text{rank}_{d+1}(t_{ijk}) \le \text{rank}_d(t_{ijk})$;

b) $\text{rank}(t_{ijk}) \le \binom{d+2}{2} \text{rank}_d(t_{ijk})$;

c) $\text{rank}_d((t_{ijk}) \oplus (t'_{ijk})) \le \text{rank}_d(t_{ijk}) + \text{rank}_d(t'_{ijk})$, in the sense of exercise 48;

d) $\text{rank}_{d+d'}((t_{ijk}) \otimes (t'_{ijk})) \le \text{rank}_d(t_{ijk}) \cdot \text{rank}_{d'}(t'_{ijk})$;

e) $\text{rank}_{d+d'}((t_{ijk}) \otimes (t'_{ijk})) \le \text{rank}_{d'}(r(t'_{ijk}))$, where $r = \text{rank}_d(t_{ijk})$ and rT denotes the direct sum $T \oplus \cdots \oplus T$ of r copies of T.

62. [*M24*] The *border rank* of (t_{ijk}), denoted by $\underline{\text{rank}}(t_{ijk})$, is $\min_{d \ge 0} \text{rank}_d(t_{ijk})$, where rank_d is defined in exercise 61. Prove that the tensor $\begin{pmatrix} 1 & 0 \\ 0 & 1 \end{pmatrix} \begin{pmatrix} 0 & 1 \\ 0 & 0 \end{pmatrix}$ has rank 3 but border rank 2, over every field.

63. [*HM30*] Let $T(m,n,s)$ be the tensor for matrix multiplication as in exercise 60, and let $M(N)$ be the rank of $T(N,N,N)$.

a) Show that $T(m,n,s) \otimes T(M,N,S) = T(mM, nN, sS)$.

b) Show that $\text{rank}_d(T(mN, nN, sN)) \le \text{rank}_d(M(N)T(m,n,s))$ (see exercise 61(e)).

c) If $T(m,n,s)$ has rank $\le r$, show that $M(N) = O(N^{\omega(m,n,s,r)})$ as $N \to \infty$, where $\omega(m,n,s,r) = 3 \log r / \log mns$.

d) If $T(m,n,s)$ has border rank $\le r$, show that $M(N) = O(N^{\omega(m,n,s,r)} (\log N)^2)$.

64. [*M30*] (A. Schönhage.) Show that $\text{rank}_2(T(3,3,3)) \le 21$, so $M(N) = O(N^{2.78})$.

▶ **65.** [*M27*] (A. Schönhage.) Show that $\text{rank}_2(T(m,1,n) \oplus T(1,(m-1)(n-1),1)) = mn + 1$. *Hint:* Consider the trilinear form

$$\sum_{i=1}^{m} \sum_{j=1}^{n} (x_i + u X_{ij})(y_j + u Y_{ij})(Z + u^2 z_{ij}) - (x_1 + \cdots + x_m)(y_1 + \cdots + y_n) Z$$

when $\sum_{i=1}^{m} X_{ij} = \sum_{j=1}^{n} Y_{ij} = 0$.

66. [*HM33*] We can now use the result of exercise 65 to sharpen the asymptotic bounds of exercise 63.

a) Prove that the limit $\omega = \lim_{n\to\infty} \log M(n)/\log n$ exists.

b) Prove that $(mns)^{\omega/3} \le \underline{\mathrm{rank}}(T(m,n,s))$.

c) Let t be the tensor $T(m,n,s) \oplus T(M,N,S)$. Prove that $(mns)^{\omega/3} + (MNS)^{\omega/3} \le \underline{\mathrm{rank}}(t)$. *Hint:* Consider direct products of t with itself.

d) Therefore $16^{\omega/3} + 9^{\omega/3} \le 17$, and we have $\omega < 2.55$.

67. [*HM40*] (D. Coppersmith and S. Winograd.) By generalizing exercises 65 and 66 we can obtain even better upper bounds on ω.

a) Say that the tensor (t_{ijk}) is *nondegenerate* if $\mathrm{rank}(t_{i(jk)}) = m$, $\mathrm{rank}(t_{j(ki)}) = n$, and $\mathrm{rank}(t_{k(ij)}) = s$, in the notation of Lemma T. Prove that the tensor $T(m,n,s)$ for $mn \times ns$ matrix multiplication is nondegenerate.

b) Show that the direct sum of nondegenerate tensors is nondegenerate.

c) An $m \times n \times s$ tensor t with realization (A,B,C) of length r is called *improvable* if it is nondegenerate and there are nonzero elements $d_1, \ldots, d_r$ such that $\sum_{l=1}^{r} a_{il}b_{jl}d_l = 0$ for $1 \le i \le m$ and $1 \le j \le n$. Prove that in such a case $t \oplus T(1,q,1)$ has border rank $\le r$, where $q = r - m - n$. *Hint:* There are $q \times r$ matrices V and W such that $\sum_{l=1}^{r} v_{il}b_{jl}d_l = \sum_{l=1}^{r} a_{il}w_{jl}d_l = 0$ and $\sum_{l=1}^{r} v_{il}w_{jl}d_l = \delta_{ij}$ for all relevant i and j.

d) Explain why the result of exercise 65 is a special of (c).

e) Prove that $\mathrm{rank}(T(m,n,s)) \le r$ implies
$$\mathrm{rank}_2\bigl(T(m,n,s) \oplus T(1, r - n(m+s-1), 1)\bigr) \le r + n.$$

f) Therefore ω is strictly less than $\log M(n)/\log n$ for all $n > 1$.

g) Generalize (c) to the case where (A,B,C) realizes t only in the weaker sense of exercise 61.

h) From (d) we have $\underline{\mathrm{rank}}(T(3,1,3) \oplus T(1,4,1)) \le 10$; thus by exercise 61(d) we also have $\underline{\mathrm{rank}}(T(9,1,9) \oplus 2T(3,4,3) \oplus T(1,16,1)) \le 100$. Prove that if we simply delete the rows of A and B that correspond to the $16 + 16$ variables of $T(1,16,1)$, we obtain a realization of $T(9,1,9) \oplus 2T(3,4,3)$ that is improvable. Therefore we have in fact $\underline{\mathrm{rank}}(T(9,1,9) \oplus 2T(3,4,3) \oplus T(1,34,1)) \le 100$.

i) Generalizing exercise 66(c), show that
$$\sum_{p=1}^{t} (m_p n_p s_p)^{\omega/3} \le \underline{\mathrm{rank}}\left(\bigoplus_{p=1}^{t} T(m_p, n_p, s_p)\right).$$

j) Therefore $\omega < 2.5$.

68. [*M45*] Is there a way to evaluate the polynomial
$$\sum_{1 \le i < j \le n} x_i x_j = x_1 x_2 + \cdots + x_{n-1} x_n$$

with fewer than $n - 1$ multiplications and $2n - 4$ additions? (There are $\binom{n}{2}$ terms.)

▶ **69.** [*HM27*] (V. Strassen, 1973.) Show that the determinant (31) of an $n \times n$ matrix can be evaluated by doing $O(n^5)$ multiplications and $O(n^5)$ additions or subtractions, and no divisions. [*Hint:* Consider $\det(I + Y)$ where $Y = X - I$.]

▶ **70.** [*HM25*] The *characteristic polynomial* $f_X(\lambda)$ of a matrix X is defined to be $\det(\lambda I - X)$. Prove that if $X = \begin{pmatrix} x & u \\ v & Y \end{pmatrix}$, where X, u, v, and Y are respectively of sizes $n \times n$, $1 \times (n-1)$, $(n-1) \times 1$, and $(n-1) \times (n-1)$, we have

$$f_X(\lambda) = f_Y(\lambda) \left(\lambda - x - \frac{uv}{\lambda} - \frac{uYv}{\lambda^2} - \frac{uY^2v}{\lambda^3} - \cdots \right).$$

Show that this relation allows us to compute the coefficients of f_X with about $\frac{1}{4}n^4$ multiplications, $\frac{1}{4}n^4$ addition-subtractions, and no divisions. *Hint:* Use the identity

$$\begin{pmatrix} A & B \\ C & D \end{pmatrix} = \begin{pmatrix} I & 0 \\ 0 & D \end{pmatrix} \begin{pmatrix} A - BD^{-1}C & B \\ 0 & I \end{pmatrix} \begin{pmatrix} I & 0 \\ D^{-1}C & I \end{pmatrix},$$

which holds for any matrices A, B, C, and D of respective sizes $l \times l$, $l \times m$, $m \times l$, and $m \times m$ when D is nonsingular.

▶ **71.** [*HM30*] A *quolynomial chain* is like a polynomial chain except that it allows division as well as addition, subtraction, and multiplication. Prove that if $f(x_1, \ldots, x_n)$ can be computed by a quolynomial chain that has m chain multiplications and d divisions, then $f(x_1, \ldots, x_n)$ and all n of its partial derivatives $\partial f(x_1, \ldots, x_n)/\partial x_k$ for $1 \le k \le n$ can be computed by a single quolynomial chain that has at most $3m+d$ chain multiplications and $2d$ divisions. (Consequently, for example, any efficient method for calculating the determinant of a matrix leads to an efficient method for calculating all of its cofactors, hence an efficient method for computing the inverse matrix.)

72. [*M48*] Is it possible to determine the rank of any given tensor (t_{ijk}) over, say, the field of rational numbers, in a finite number of steps?

73. [*HM25*] (J. Morgenstern, 1973.) Prove that any polynomial chain for the discrete Fourier transform (37) has at least $\frac{1}{2}m_1 \ldots m_n \lg m_1 \ldots m_n$ addition-subtractions, if there are no chain multiplications and if every parameter multiplication is by a complex-valued constant with $|\alpha_j| \le 1$. *Hint:* Consider the matrices of the linear transformations computed by the first k steps. How big can their determinants be?

74. [*HM35*] (A. Nozaki, 1978.) Most of the theory of polynomial evaluation is concerned with bounds on chain multiplications, but multiplication by noninteger constants can also be essential. The purpose of this exercise is to develop an appropriate theory of constants. Let us say that vectors $v_1, \ldots, v_s$ of real numbers are *Z-dependent* if there are integers $(k_1, \ldots, k_s)$ such that $\gcd(k_1, \ldots, k_s) = 1$ and $k_1 v_1 + \cdots + k_s v_s$ is an all-integer vector. If no such $(k_1, \ldots, k_s)$ exist, the vectors $v_1, \ldots, v_s$ are *Z-independent*.

a) Prove that if the columns of an $r \times s$ matrix V are Z-independent, so are the columns of VU, when U is any $s \times s$ unimodular matrix (a matrix of integers whose determinant is ± 1).

b) Let V be an $r \times s$ matrix with Z-independent columns. Prove that a polynomial chain to evaluate the elements of Vx from inputs $x_1, \ldots, x_s$, where $x = (x_1, \ldots, x_s)^T$, needs at least s multiplications.

c) Let V be an $r \times t$ matrix having s columns that are Z-independent. Prove that a polynomial chain to evaluate the elements of Vx from inputs $x_1, \ldots, x_t$, where $x = (x_1, \ldots, x_t)^T$, needs at least s multiplications.

d) Show how to compute the pair of values $\{x/2 + y, x + y/3\}$ from x and y using only one multiplication, although two multiplications are needed to compute the pair $\{x/2 + y, x + y/2\}$.

*4.7. MANIPULATION OF POWER SERIES

IF WE ARE GIVEN two power series

$$U(z) = U_0 + U_1 z + U_2 z^2 + \cdots, \qquad V(z) = V_0 + V_1 z + V_2 z^2 + \cdots, \qquad (1)$$

whose coefficients belong to a field, we can form their sum, their product, and sometimes their quotient, to obtain new power series. A polynomial is obviously a special case of a power series, in which there are only finitely many terms.

Of course, only a finite number of terms can be represented and stored within a computer, so it makes sense to ask whether power series arithmetic is even possible on computers; and if it is possible, what makes it different from polynomial arithmetic? The answer is that we work with only the first N coefficients of the power series, where N is a parameter that may in principle be arbitrarily large; instead of ordinary polynomial arithmetic, we are essentially doing polynomial arithmetic modulo z^N, and this often leads to a somewhat different point of view. Furthermore, special operations like "reversion" can be performed on power series but not on polynomials, since polynomials are not closed under those operations.

Manipulation of power series has many applications to numerical analysis, but perhaps its greatest use is the determination of asymptotic expansions (as we have seen in Section 1.2.11.3), or the calculation of quantities defined by certain generating functions. The latter applications make it desirable to calculate the coefficients exactly, instead of with floating point arithmetic. All of the algorithms in this section, with obvious exceptions, can be done using rational operations only, so the techniques of Section 4.5.1 can be used to obtain exact results when desired.

The calculation of $W(z) = U(z) \pm V(z)$ is, of course, trivial, since we have $W_n = [z^n] W(z) = U_n \pm V_n$ for $n = 0, 1, 2, \ldots$. It is also easy to calculate the coefficients of $W(z) = U(z)V(z)$, using the familiar convolution rule

$$W_n = \sum_{k=0}^{n} U_k V_{n-k} = U_0 V_n + U_1 V_{n-1} + \cdots + U_n V_0. \qquad (2)$$

The quotient $W(z) = U(z)/V(z)$, when $V_0 \neq 0$, can be obtained by interchanging U and W in (2); we obtain the rule

$$W_n = \left(U_n - \sum_{k=0}^{n-1} W_k V_{n-k} \right) \Big/ V_0$$

$$= (U_n - W_0 V_n - W_1 V_{n-1} - \cdots - W_{n-1} V_1)/V_0. \qquad (3)$$

This recurrence relation for the W's makes it easy to determine $W_0, W_1, W_2, \ldots$ successively, without inputting U_n and V_n until after W_{n-1} has been computed. A power series manipulation algorithm with that property is traditionally called *online*; with an online algorithm, we can determine N coefficients $W_0, W_1, \ldots,$ W_{N-1} of the result without knowing N in advance, so we could in principle run the algorithm indefinitely and compute the entire power series. We can also run an online algorithm until any desired condition is met. (The opposite of "online" is "offline.")

If the coefficients U_k and V_k are integers but the W_k are not, the recurrence relation (3) involves computation with fractions. This can be avoided by the all-integer approach described in exercise 2.

Let us now consider the operation of computing $W(z) = V(z)^\alpha$, where α is an "arbitrary" power. For example, we could calculate the square root of $V(z)$ by taking $\alpha = \frac{1}{2}$, or we could find $V(z)^{-10}$ or even $V(z)^\pi$. If V_m is the first nonzero coefficient of $V(z)$, we have

$$V(z) = V_m z^m \left(1 + (V_{m+1}/V_m)z + (V_{m+2}/V_m)z^2 + \cdots\right),$$
$$V(z)^\alpha = V_m^\alpha z^{\alpha m} \left(1 + (V_{m+1}/V_m)z + (V_{m+2}/V_m)z^2 + \cdots\right)^\alpha. \tag{4}$$

This will be a power series if and only if αm is a nonnegative integer. If α itself is not an integer, there's more than one possibility for $V_m^\alpha z^{\alpha m}$ here.

From (4) we can see that the problem of computing general powers can be reduced to the case that $V_0 = 1$; then the problem is to compute the coefficients of

$$W(z) = (1 + V_1 z + V_2 z^2 + V_3 z^3 + \cdots)^\alpha. \tag{5}$$

Clearly $W_0 = 1^\alpha = 1$.

The obvious way to find the coefficients of (5) is to use the binomial theorem, Eq. 1.2.9–(19), or (if α is a positive integer) to try repeated squaring as in Section 4.6.3. But Leonhard Euler discovered a much simpler and more efficient way to obtain power series powers [*Introductio in Analysin Infinitorum* **1** (1748), §76]: If $W(z) = V(z)^\alpha$, we have by differentiation

$$W_1 + 2W_2 z + 3W_3 z^2 + \cdots = W'(z) = \alpha V(z)^{\alpha-1} V'(z); \tag{6}$$

therefore

$$W'(z)V(z) = \alpha W(z)V'(z). \tag{7}$$

If we now equate the coefficients of z^{n-1} in (7), we find that

$$\sum_{k=0}^{n} k W_k V_{n-k} = \alpha \sum_{k=0}^{n} (n-k) W_k V_{n-k}, \tag{8}$$

and this gives us a useful computational rule valid for all $n \geq 1$:

$$W_n = \sum_{k=1}^{n} \left(\left(\frac{\alpha+1}{n}\right)k - 1\right) V_k W_{n-k}$$
$$= \left((\alpha+1-n)V_1 W_{n-1} + (2\alpha+2-n)V_2 W_{n-2} + \cdots + n\alpha V_n W_0\right)/n. \tag{9}$$

Equation (9) leads to a simple online algorithm by which we can successively determine $W_1, W_2, \ldots$, using approximately $2n$ multiplications to compute the nth coefficient. Notice the special case $\alpha = -1$, in which (9) becomes the special case $U(z) = V_0 = 1$ of (3).

A similar technique can be used to form $f(V(z))$ when f is any function that satisfies a simple differential equation. (For example, see exercise 4.) A comparatively straightforward "power series method" is often used to obtain

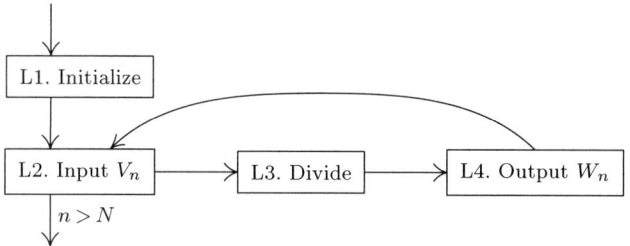

Fig. 17. Power series reversion by Algorithm L.

the solution of differential equations; this technique is explained in nearly all textbooks about differential equations.

Reversion of series. The transformation of power series that is perhaps of greatest interest is called "reversion of series." This problem is to solve the equation

$$z = t + V_2 t^2 + V_3 t^3 + V_4 t^4 + \cdots \tag{10}$$

for t, obtaining the coefficients of the power series

$$t = z + W_2 z^2 + W_3 z^3 + W_4 z^4 + \cdots. \tag{11}$$

Several interesting ways to achieve such a reversion are known. We might say that the "classical" method is one based on Lagrange's remarkable inversion formula [*Mémoires Acad. Royale des Sciences et Belles-Lettres de Berlin* **24** (1768), 251–326], which states that

$$W_n = \frac{1}{n} \left[t^{n-1} \right] (1 + V_2 t + V_3 t^2 + \cdots)^{-n}. \tag{12}$$

For example, we have $(1-t)^{-5} = \binom{4}{4} + \binom{5}{4} t + \binom{6}{4} t^2 + \cdots$; hence the fifth coefficient, W_5, in the reversion of $z = t - t^2$ is equal to $\binom{8}{4}/5 = 14$. This checks with the formulas for enumerating binary trees in Section 2.3.4.4.

Relation (12), which has a simple algorithmic proof (see exercise 16), shows that we can revert the series (10) if we successively compute the negative powers $(1 + V_2 t + V_3 t^2 + \cdots)^{-n}$ for $n = 1, 2, 3, \ldots$. A straightforward application of this idea would lead to an online reversion algorithm that uses approximately $N^3/2$ multiplications to find N coefficients, but Eq. (9) makes it possible to work with only the first n coefficients of $(1 + V_2 t + V_3 t^2 + \cdots)^{-n}$, obtaining an online algorithm that requires only about $N^3/6$ multiplications.

Algorithm L (*Lagrangian power series reversion*). This online algorithm inputs the value of V_n in (10) and outputs the value of W_n in (11), for $n = 2, 3, 4, \ldots, N$. (The number N need not be specified in advance; any desired termination criterion may be substituted.)

L1. [Initialize.] Set $n \leftarrow 1$, $U_0 \leftarrow 1$. (The relation

$$(1 + V_2 t + V_3 t^2 + \cdots)^{-n} = U_0 + U_1 t + \cdots + U_{n-1} t^{n-1} + O(t^n) \tag{13}$$

will be maintained throughout this algorithm.)

L2. [Input V_n.] Increase n by 1. If $n > N$, the algorithm terminates; otherwise input the next coefficient, V_n.

L3. [Divide.] Set $U_k \leftarrow U_k - U_{k-1}V_2 - \cdots - U_1 V_k - U_0 V_{k+1}$, for $k = 1, 2, \ldots,$ $n - 2$ (in this order); then set

$$U_{n-1} \leftarrow -2U_{n-2}V_2 - 3U_{n-3}V_3 - \cdots - (n-1)U_1 V_{n-1} - n U_0 V_n.$$

$\big($We have thereby divided $U(z)$ by $V(z)/z$; see (3) and (9).$\big)$

L4. [Output W_n.] Output U_{n-1}/n (which is W_n) and return to L2. ∎

When applied to the example $z = t - t^2$, Algorithm L computes

n	V_n	U_0	U_1	U_2	U_3	U_4	W_n
1	1	1					1
2	−1	1	2				1
3	0	1	3	6			2
4	0	1	4	10	20		5
5	0	1	5	15	35	70	14

Exercise 8 shows that a slight modification of Algorithm L will solve a considerably more general problem with only a little more effort.

Let us now consider solving the equation

$$U_1 z + U_2 z^2 + U_3 z^3 + \cdots = t + V_2 t^2 + V_3 t^3 + \cdots \qquad (14)$$

for t, obtaining the coefficients of the power series

$$t = W_1 z + W_2 z^2 + W_3 z^3 + W_4 z^4 + \cdots. \qquad (15)$$

Eq. (10) is the special case $U_1 = 1$, $U_2 = U_3 = \cdots = 0$. If $U_1 \neq 0$, we may assume that $U_1 = 1$, if we replace z by $(U_1 z)$; but we shall consider the general equation (14), since U_1 might equal zero.

Algorithm T (*General power series reversion*). This online algorithm inputs the values of U_n and V_n in (14) and outputs the value of W_n in (15), for $n = 1, 2, 3, \ldots, N$. An auxiliary matrix T_{mn}, $1 \le m \le n \le N$, is used in the calculations.

T1. [Initialize.] Set $n \leftarrow 1$. Let the first two inputs (namely, U_1 and V_1) be stored in T_{11} and V_1, respectively. (We must have $V_1 = 1$.)

T2. [Output W_n.] Output the value of T_{1n} (which is W_n).

T3. [Input U_n, V_n.] Increase n by 1. If $n > N$, the algorithm terminates; otherwise store the next two inputs (namely, U_n and V_n) in T_{1n} and V_n.

T4. [Multiply.] Set

$$T_{mn} \leftarrow T_{11}T_{m-1,n-1} + T_{12}T_{m-1,n-2} + \cdots + T_{1,n-m+1}T_{m-1,m-1}$$

and $T_{1n} \leftarrow T_{1n} - V_m T_{mn}$, for $2 \le m \le n$. $\big($After this step we have

$$t^m = T_{mm}z^m + T_{m,m+1}z^{m+1} + \cdots + T_{mn}z^n + O(z^{n+1}), \qquad (16)$$

for $1 \le m \le n$. It is easy to verify (16) by induction for $m \ge 2$, and when $m = 1$, we have $U_n = T_{1n} + V_2 T_{2n} + \cdots + V_n T_{nn}$ by (14) and (16).$\big)$ Return to step T2. ∎

Equation (16) explains the mechanism of this algorithm, which is due to Henry C. Thacher, Jr. [*CACM* **9** (1966), 10–11]. The running time is essentially the same as Algorithm L, but considerably more storage space is required. An example of this algorithm is worked out in exercise 9.

Still another approach to power series reversion has been proposed by R. P. Brent and H. T. Kung [*JACM* **25** (1978), 581–595], based on the fact that standard iterative procedures used to find roots of equations over the real numbers can also be applied to equations over power series. In particular, we can consider Newton's method for computing approximations to a real number t such that $f(t) = 0$, given a function f that is well-behaved near t: If x is a good approximation to t, then $\phi(x) = x - f(x)/f'(x)$ will be even better, for if we write $x = t + \epsilon$ we have $f(x) = f(t) + \epsilon f'(t) + O(\epsilon^2)$, $f'(x) = f'(t) + O(\epsilon)$; consequently $\phi(x) = t + \epsilon - \bigl(0 + \epsilon f'(t) + O(\epsilon^2)\bigr)/\bigl(f'(t) + O(\epsilon)\bigr) = t + O(\epsilon^2)$. Applying this idea to power series, let $f(x) = V(x) - U(z)$, where U and V are the power series in Eq. (14). We wish to find the power series t in z such that $f(t) = 0$. Let $x = W_1 z + \cdots + W_{n-1} z^{n-1} = t + O(z^n)$ be an "approximation" to t of order n; then $\phi(x) = x - f(x)/f'(x)$ will be an approximation of order $2n$, since the assumptions of Newton's method hold for this f and t.

In other words, we can use the following procedure:

Algorithm N (*General power series reversion by Newton's method*). This "semi-online" algorithm inputs the values of U_n and V_n in (14) for $2^k \le n < 2^{k+1}$ and then outputs the values of W_n in (15) for $2^k \le n < 2^{k+1}$, thereby producing its answers in batches of 2^k at a time, for $k = 0, 1, 2, \ldots, K$.

N1. [Initialize.] Set $N \leftarrow 1$. (We will have $N = 2^k$.) Input the first coefficients U_1 and V_1 (where $V_1 = 1$), and set $W_1 \leftarrow U_1$.

N2. [Output.] Output W_n for $N \le n < 2N$.

N3. [Input.] Set $N \leftarrow 2N$. If $N > 2^K$, the algorithm terminates; otherwise input the values U_n and V_n for $N \le n < 2N$.

N4. [Newtonian step.] Use an algorithm for power series composition (see exercise 11) to evaluate the coefficients Q_j and R_j ($0 \le j < N$) in the power series

$$U_1 z + \cdots + U_{2N-1} z^{2N-1} - V(W_1 z + \cdots + W_{N-1} z^{N-1})$$
$$= R_0 z^N + R_1 z^{N+1} + \cdots + R_{N-1} z^{2N-1} + O(z^{2N}),$$
$$V'(W_1 z + \cdots + W_{N-1} z^{N-1}) = Q_0 + Q_1 z + \cdots + Q_{N-1} z^{N-1} + O(z^N),$$

where $V(x) = x + V_2 x^2 + \cdots$ and $V'(x) = 1 + 2V_2 x + \cdots$. Then set $W_N, \ldots,$ W_{2N-1} to the coefficients in the power series

$$\frac{R_0 + R_1 z + \cdots + R_{N-1} z^{N-1}}{Q_0 + Q_1 z + \cdots + Q_{N-1} z^{N-1}} = W_N + \cdots + W_{2N-1} z^{N-1} + O(z^N)$$

and return to step N2. ∎

The running time for this algorithm to obtain the coefficients up to $N = 2^K$ is $T(N)$, where

$$T(2N) = T(N) + \text{(time to do step N4)} + O(N). \tag{17}$$

Straightforward algorithms for composition and division in step N4 will take order N^3 steps, so Algorithm N will run slower than Algorithm T. However, Brent and Kung have found a way to do the required composition of power series with $O(N \log N)^{3/2}$ arithmetic operations, and exercise 6 gives an even faster algorithm for division; hence (17) shows that power series reversion can be achieved by doing only $O(N \log N)^{3/2}$ operations as $N \to \infty$. (On the other hand the constant of proportionality is such that N must be really large before Algorithms L and T lose out to this "high-speed" method.)

Historical note: J. N. Bramhall and M. A. Chapple published the first $O(N^3)$ method for power series reversion in *CACM* **4** (1961), 317–318, 503. It was an offline algorithm essentially equivalent to the method of exercise 16, with running time approximately the same as that of Algorithms L and T.

Iteration of series. If we want to study the behavior of an iterative process $x_n \leftarrow f(x_{n-1})$, we are interested in studying the n-fold composition of a given function f with itself, namely $x_n = f(f(\ldots f(x_0)\ldots))$. Let us define $f^{[0]}(x) = x$ and $f^{[n]}(x) = f(f^{[n-1]}(x))$, so that

$$f^{[m+n]}(x) = f^{[m]}(f^{[n]}(x)) \tag{18}$$

for all integers m, $n \geq 0$. In many cases the notation $f^{[n]}(x)$ makes sense also when n is a negative integer, namely if $f^{[n]}$ and $f^{[-n]}$ are inverse functions such that $x = f^{[n]}(f^{[-n]}(x))$; if inverse functions are unique, (18) holds for *all* integers m and n. Reversion of series is essentially the operation of finding the inverse power series $f^{[-1]}(x)$; for example, Eqs. (10) and (11) essentially state that $z = V(W(z))$ and that $t = W(V(t))$, so $W = V^{[-1]}$.

Suppose we are given two power series $V(z) = z + V_2 z^2 + \cdots$ and $W(z) = z + W_2 z^2 + \cdots$ such that $W = V^{[-1]}$. Let u be any nonzero constant, and consider the function

$$U(z) = W(uV(z)). \tag{19}$$

It is easy to see that $U(U(z)) = W(u^2 V(z))$, and in general that

$$U^{[n]}(z) = W(u^n V(z)) \tag{20}$$

for all integers n. Therefore we have a simple expression for the nth iterate $U^{[n]}$, which can be calculated with roughly the same amount of work for all n. Furthermore, we can even use (20) to define $U^{[n]}$ for noninteger values of n; the "half iterate" $U^{[1/2]}$, for example, is a function such that $U^{[1/2]}(U^{[1/2]}(z)) = U(z)$. (There are two such functions $U^{[1/2]}$, obtained by using $\sqrt{u}$ and $-\sqrt{u}$ as the value of $u^{1/2}$ in (20).)

We obtained the simple state of affairs in (20) by starting with V and u, then defining U. But in practice we generally want to go the other way: Starting with some given function U, we want to find V and u such that (19) holds, namely such that

$$V\big(U(z)\big) = u\,V(z). \tag{21}$$

Such a function V is called the *Schröder function* of U, because it was introduced by Ernst Schröder in *Math. Annalen* **3** (1871), 296–322. Let us now look at the problem of finding the Schröder function $V(z) = z + V_2 z^2 + \cdots$ of a given power series $U(z) = U_1 z + U_2 z^2 + \cdots$. Clearly $u = U_1$ if (21) is to hold.

Expanding (21) with $u = U_1$ and equating coefficients of z leads to a sequence of equations that begins

$$U_1^2 V_2 + U_2 = U_1 V_2,$$
$$U_1^3 V_3 + 2U_1 U_2 V_2 + U_3 = U_1 V_3,$$
$$U_1^4 V_4 + 3U_1^2 U_2 V_3 + 2U_1 U_3 V_2 + U_2^2 V_2 + U_4 = U_1 V_4,$$

and so on. Clearly there is no solution when $U_1 = 0$ (unless trivially $U_2 = U_3 = \cdots = 0$); otherwise there is a unique solution unless U_1 is a root of unity. We might have expected that something funny would happen when $U_1^n = 1$, since Eq. (20) tells us that $U^{[n]}(z) = z$ if the Schröder function exists in that case. For the moment let us assume that U_1 is nonzero and not a root of unity; then the Schröder function does exist, and the next question is how to compute it without doing too much work.

The following procedure has been suggested by R. P. Brent and J. F. Traub. Equation (21) leads to subproblems of a similar but more complicated form, so we set ourselves a more general task whose subtasks have the same form: Let us try to find $V(z) = V_0 + V_1 z + \cdots + V_{n-1} z^{n-1}$ such that

$$V\big(U(z)\big) = W(z)V(z) + S(z) + O(z^n), \tag{22}$$

given $U(z)$, $W(z)$, $S(z)$, and n, where n is a power of 2 and $U(0) = 0$. If $n = 1$ we simply let $V_0 = S(0)/\big(1 - W(0)\big)$, with $V_0 = 1$ if $S(0) = 0$ and $W(0) = 1$. Furthermore it is possible to go from n to $2n$: First we find $R(z)$ such that

$$V\big(U(z)\big) = W(z)V(z) + S(z) - z^n R(z) + O(z^{2n}). \tag{23}$$

Then we compute

$$\hat{W}(z) = W(z)\big(z/U(z)\big)^n + O(z^n), \qquad \hat{S}(z) = R(z)\big(z/U(z)\big)^n + O(z^n), \tag{24}$$

and find $\hat{V}(z) = V_n + V_{n+1} z + \cdots + V_{2n-1} z^{n-1}$ such that

$$\hat{V}\big(U(z)\big) = \hat{W}(z)\hat{V}(z) + \hat{S}(z) + O(z^n). \tag{25}$$

It follows that the function $V^*(z) = V(z) + z^n \hat{V}(z)$ satisfies

$$V^*\big(U(z)\big) = W(z)V^*(z) + S(z) + O(z^{2n}),$$

as desired.

The running time $T(n)$ of this procedure satisfies

$$T(2n) = 2T(n) + C(n), \tag{26}$$

where $C(n)$ is the time to compute $R(z)$, $\hat{W}(z)$, and $\hat{S}(z)$. The function $C(n)$ is dominated by the time to compute $V(U(z))$ modulo z^{2n}, and $C(n)$ presumably grows faster than order $n^{1+\epsilon}$; therefore the solution $T(n)$ to (26) will be of order $C(n)$. For example, if $C(n) = cn^3$ we have $T(n) \approx \frac{4}{3}cn^3$; or if $C(n)$ is $O(n \log n)^{3/2}$ using "fast" composition, we have $T(n) = O(n \log n)^{3/2}$.

The procedure breaks down when $W(0) = 1$ and $S(0) \neq 0$, so we need to investigate when this can happen. It is easy to prove by induction on n that the solution of (22) by the Brent–Traub method entails consideration of exactly n subproblems, in which the coefficient of $V(z)$ on the right-hand side takes the respective values $W(z)(z/U(z))^j + O(z^n)$ for $0 \le j < n$ in some order. If $W(0) = U_1$ and if U_1 is not a root of unity, we therefore have $W(0) = 1$ only when $j = 1$; the procedure will fail in this case only if (22) has no solution for $n = 2$.

Consequently the Schröder function for U can be found by solving (22) for $n = 2, 4, 8, 16, \ldots$, with $W(z) = U_1$ and $S(z) = 0$, whenever U_1 is nonzero and not a root of unity.

If $U_1 = 1$, there is no Schröder function unless $U(z) = z$. But Brent and Traub have found a fast way to compute $U^{[n]}(z)$ even when $U_1 = 1$, by making use of a function $V(z)$ such that

$$V(U(z)) = U'(z)V(z). \tag{27}$$

If two functions $U(z)$ and $\hat{U}(z)$ both satisfy (27), for the same V, it is easy to check that their composition $U(\hat{U}(z))$ does too; therefore all iterates of $U(z)$ are solutions of (27). Suppose we have $U(z) = z + U_k z^k + U_{k+1} z^{k+1} + \cdots$ where $k \ge 2$ and $U_k \neq 0$. Then it can be shown that there is a unique power series of the form $V(z) = z^k + V_{k+1} z^{k+1} + V_{k+2} z^{k+2} + \cdots$ satisfying (27). Conversely if such a function $V(z)$ is given, and if $k \ge 2$ and U_k are given, then there is a unique power series of the form $U(z) = z + U_k z^k + U_{k+1} z^{k+1} + \cdots$ satisfying (27). The desired iterate $U^{[n]}(z)$ is the unique power series $P(z)$ satisfying

$$V(P(z)) = P'(z)V(z) \tag{28}$$

such that $P(z) = z + nU_k z^k + \cdots$. Both $V(z)$ and $P(z)$ can be found by appropriate algorithms (see exercise 14).

If U_1 is a kth root of unity, but not equal to 1, the same method can be applied to the function $U^{[k]}(z) = z + \cdots$, and $U^{[k]}(z)$ can be found from $U(z)$ by doing $l(k)$ composition operations (see Section 4.6.3). We can also handle the case $U_1 = 0$: If $U(z) = U_k z^k + U_{k+1} z^{k+1} + \cdots$ where $k \ge 2$ and $U_k \neq 0$, the idea is to find a solution to the equation $V(U(z)) = U_k V(z)^k$; then

$$U^{[n]}(z) = V^{[-1]}\left(U_k^{[(k^n-1)/(k-1)]} V(z)^{k^n}\right). \tag{29}$$

Finally, if $U(z) = U_0 + U_1 z + \cdots$ where $U_0 \neq 0$, let α be a "fixed point" such that $U(\alpha) = \alpha$, and let

$$\hat{U}(z) = U(\alpha + z) - \alpha = zU'(\alpha) + z^2 U''(\alpha)/2! + \cdots; \tag{30}$$

then $U^{[n]}(z) = \hat{U}^{[n]}(z-\alpha)+\alpha$. Further details can be found in Brent and Traub's paper [*SICOMP* **9** (1980), 54–66]. The V function of (27) had previously been considered by M. Kuczma, *Functional Equations in a Single Variable* (Warsaw: PWN–Polish Scientific, 1968), Lemma 9.4, and implicitly by E. Jabotinsky a few years earlier (see exercise 23).

Algebraic functions. The coefficients of each power series $W(z)$ that satisfies a general equation of the form

$$A_n(z)W(z)^n + \cdots + A_1(z)W(z) + A_0(z) = 0, \qquad (31)$$

where each $A_i(z)$ is a polynomial, can be computed efficiently by using methods due to H. T. Kung and J. F. Traub; see *JACM* **25** (1978), 245–260. See also D. V. Chudnovsky and G. V. Chudnovsky, *J. Complexity* **2** (1986), 271–294; **3** (1987), 1–25.

EXERCISES

1. [*M10*] The text explains how to divide $U(z)$ by $V(z)$ when $V_0 \neq 0$; how should the division be done when $V_0 = 0$?

2. [*20*] If the coefficients of $U(z)$ and $V(z)$ are integers and $V_0 \neq 0$, find a recurrence relation for the integers $V_0^{n+1}W_n$, where W_n is defined by (3). How could you use this for power series division?

3. [*M15*] Does formula (9) give the right results when $\alpha = 0$? When $\alpha = 1$?

▶ **4.** [*HM23*] Show that simple modifications of (9) can be used to calculate $e^{V(z)}$ when $V_0 = 0$, and $\ln V(z)$ when $V_0 = 1$.

5. [*M00*] What happens when a power series is reverted twice — that is, if the output of Algorithm L or T is reverted again?

▶ **6.** [*M21*] (H. T. Kung.) Apply Newton's method to the computation of $W(z) = 1/V(z)$, when $V(0) \neq 0$, by finding the power series root of the equation $f(x) = 0$, where $f(x) = x^{-1} - V(z)$.

7. [*M23*] Use Lagrange's inversion formula (12) to find a simple expression for the coefficient W_n in the reversion of $z = t - t^m$.

▶ **8.** [*M25*] If $W(z) = W_1 z + W_2 z^2 + W_3 z^3 + \cdots = G_1 t + G_2 t^2 + G_3 t^3 + \cdots = G(t)$, where $z = V_1 t + V_2 t^2 + V_3 t^3 + \cdots$ and $V_1 \neq 0$, Lagrange proved that

$$W_n = \frac{1}{n}[t^{n-1}]\, G'(t)/(V_1 + V_2 t + V_3 t^2 + \cdots)^n\,.$$

(Equation (12) is the special case $G_1 = V_1 = 1$, $G_2 = G_3 = \cdots = 0$.) Extend Algorithm L so that it obtains the coefficients $W_1, W_2, \ldots$ in this more general situation, without substantially increasing its running time.

9. [*11*] Find the values of T_{mn} computed by Algorithm T as it determines the first five coefficients in the reversion of $z = t - t^2$.

10. [*M20*] Given that $y = x^\alpha + a_1 x^{\alpha+1} + a_2 x^{\alpha+2} + \cdots$, $\alpha \neq 0$, show how to compute the coefficients in the expansion $x = y^{1/\alpha} + b_2 y^{2/\alpha} + b_3 y^{3/\alpha} + \cdots$.

▶ **11.** [*M25*] (*Composition of power series.*) Let

$$U(z) = U_0 + U_1 z + U_2 z^2 + \cdots \quad \text{and} \quad V(z) = V_1 z + V_2 z^2 + V_3 z^3 + \cdots.$$

Design an algorithm that computes the first N coefficients of $U(V(z))$.

12. [*M20*] Find a connection between polynomial division and power series division: Given polynomials $u(x)$ and $v(x)$ of respective degrees m and n over a field, show how to find the polynomials $q(x)$ and $r(x)$ such that $u(x) = q(x)v(x) + r(x)$ and $\deg(r) < n$, using only operations on power series.

13. [*M27*] (*Rational function approximation.*) It is occasionally desirable to find polynomials whose quotient has the same initial terms as a given power series. For example, if $W(z) = 1 + z + 3z^2 + 7z^3 + \cdots$, there are essentially four different ways to express $W(z)$ as $w_1(z)/w_2(z) + O(z^4)$ where $w_1(z)$ and $w_2(z)$ are polynomials with $\deg(w_1) + \deg(w_2) < 4$:

$$(1 + z + 3z^2 + 7z^3) / 1 = 1 + z + 3z^2 + 7z^3 + 0z^4 + \cdots,$$

$$(3 - 4z + 2z^2) / (3 - 7z) = 1 + z + 3z^2 + 7z^3 + \tfrac{49}{3} z^4 + \cdots,$$

$$(1 - z) / (1 - 2z - z^2) = 1 + z + 3z^2 + 7z^3 + 17z^4 + \cdots,$$

$$1 / (1 - z - 2z^2 - 2z^3) = 1 + z + 3z^2 + 7z^3 + 15z^4 + \cdots.$$

Rational functions of this kind are commonly called *Padé approximations*, since they were studied extensively by H. E. Padé [*Annales Scient. de l'École Normale Supérieure* (3) **9** (1892), S1–S93; (3) **16** (1899), 395–426].

Show that all Padé approximations $W(z) = w_1(z)/w_2(z) + O(z^N)$ with $\deg(w_1) + \deg(w_2) < N$ can be obtained by applying an extended Euclidean algorithm to the polynomials z^N and $W_0 + W_1 z + \cdots + W_{N-1} z^{N-1}$; and design an all-integer algorithm for the case that each W_i is an integer. [*Hint:* See exercise 4.6.1–26.]

▶ **14.** [*HM30*] Fill in the details of Brent and Traub's method for calculating $U^{[n]}(z)$ when $U(z) = z + U_k z^k + \cdots$, using (27) and (28).

15. [*HM20*] For what functions $U(z)$ does $V(z)$ have the simple form z^k in (27)? What do you deduce about the iterates of $U(z)$?

16. [*HM21*] Let $W(z) = G(t)$ as in exercise 8. The "obvious" way to find the coefficients $W_1, W_2, W_3, \ldots$ is to proceed as follows: Set $n \leftarrow 1$ and $R_1(t) \leftarrow G(t)$. Then preserve the relation $W_n V(t) + W_{n+1} V(t)^2 + \cdots = R_n(t)$ by repeatedly setting $W_n \leftarrow [t] R_n(t)/V_1$, $R_{n+1}(t) \leftarrow R_n(t)/V(t) - W_n$, $n \leftarrow n + 1$.

Prove Lagrange's formula of exercise 8 by showing that

$$\frac{1}{n}[t^{n-1}] R'_{k+1}(t) t^n / V(t)^n = \frac{1}{n+1}[t^n] R'_k(t) t^{n+1} / V(t)^{n+1}, \quad \text{for all } n \geq 1 \text{ and } k \geq 1.$$

▶ **17.** [*M20*] Given the power series $V(z) = V_1 z + V_2 z^2 + V_3 z^3 + \cdots$, we define the *power matrix* of V as the infinite array of coefficients $v_{nk} = \frac{n!}{k!}[z^n] V(z)^k$; the nth *poweroid* of V is then defined to be $V_n(x) = v_{n0} + v_{n1} x + \cdots + v_{nn} x^n$. Prove that poweroids satisfy the general convolution law

$$V_n(x + y) = \sum_k \binom{n}{k} V_k(x) V_{n-k}(y).$$

(For example, when $V(z) = z$ we have $V_n(x) = x^n$, and this is the binomial theorem. When $V(z) = \ln(1/(1-z))$ we have $v_{nk} = \begin{bmatrix} n \\ k \end{bmatrix}$ by Eq. 1.2.9–(26); hence the poweroid $V_n(x)$ is $x^{\overline{n}}$, and the identity is the result proved in exercise 1.2.6–33. When $V(z) = e^z - 1$ we have $V_n(x) = \sum_k \left\{ {n \atop k} \right\} x^k$ and the formula is equivalent to

$$\binom{l+m}{m} \left\{ {n \atop l+m} \right\} = \sum_k \binom{n}{k} \left\{ {k \atop l} \right\} \left\{ {n-k \atop m} \right\},$$

an identity we haven't seen before. Several other triangular arrays of coefficients that
arise in combinatorial mathematics and the analysis of algorithms also turn out to be
the power matrices of power series.)

18. [*HM22*] Continuing exercise 17, prove that poweroids also satisfy

$$xV_n(x+y) = (x+y)\sum_k \binom{n-1}{k-1} V_k(x) V_{n-k}(y).$$

[*Hint:* Consider the derivative of $e^{xV(z)}$.]

19. [*M25*] Continuing exercise 17, express all the numbers v_{nk} in terms of the numbers
$v_n = v_{n1} = n!\, V_n$ of the first column, and find a simple recurrence by which all columns
can be computed from the sequence $v_1, v_2, \ldots$. Show in particular that if all the v_n
are integers, then all the v_{nk} are integers.

20. [*HM20*] Continuing exercise 17, suppose we have $W(z) = U(V(z))$ and $U_0 = 0$.
Prove that the power matrix of W is the product of the power matrices of V and U:
$w_{nk} = \sum_j v_{nj} u_{jk}$.

▶ **21.** [*HM27*] Continuing the previous exercises, suppose $V_1 \neq 0$ and let $W(z) = -V^{[-1]}(-z)$. The purpose of this exercise is to show that the power matrices of V
and W are "dual" to each other; for example, when $V(z) = \ln(1/(1-z))$ we have
$V^{[-1]}(z) = 1 - e^{-z}$, $W(z) = e^z - 1$, and the corresponding power matrices are the
well-known Stirling triangles $v_{nk} = \begin{bmatrix} n \\ k \end{bmatrix}$, $w_{nk} = \begin{Bmatrix} n \\ k \end{Bmatrix}$.

a) Prove that the inversion formulas 1.2.6–(47) for Stirling numbers hold in general:

$$\sum_k v_{nk} w_{km} (-1)^{n-k} = \sum_k w_{nk} v_{km} (-1)^{n-k} = \delta_{mn}.$$

b) The relation $v_{n(n-k)} = n^{\underline{k}} [z^k] (V(z)/z)^{n-k}$ shows that, for fixed k, the quantity
$v_{n(n-k)}/V_1^n$ is a polynomial in n of degree $\leq 2k$. We can therefore define

$$v_{\alpha(\alpha-k)} = \alpha^{\underline{k}} [z^k] (V(z)/z)^{\alpha-k}$$

for arbitrary α when k is a nonnegative integer, as we did for Stirling numbers in
Section 1.2.6. Prove that $v_{(-k)(-n)} = w_{nk}$. (This generalizes Eq. 1.2.6–(58).)

▶ **22.** [*HM27*] Given $U(z) = U_0 + U_1 z + U_2 z^2 + \cdots$ with $U_0 \neq 0$, the αth *induced function*
$U^{\{\alpha\}}(z)$ is the power series $V(z)$ defined implicitly by the equation

$$V(z) = U(zV(z)^\alpha).$$

a) Prove that $U^{\{0\}}(z) = U(z)$ and $U^{\{\alpha\}\{\beta\}}(z) = U^{\{\alpha+\beta\}}(z)$.

b) Let $B(z)$ be the simple binomial series $1 + z$. Where have we seen $B^{\{2\}}(z)$ before?

c) Prove that $[z^n] U^{\{\alpha\}}(z)^x = \frac{x}{x+n\alpha} [z^n] U(z)^{x+n\alpha}$. *Hint:* If $W(z) = z/U(z)^\alpha$, we
have $U^{\{\alpha\}}(z) = (W^{[-1]}(z)/z)^{1/\alpha}$.

d) Consequently any poweroid $V_n(x)$ satisfies not only the identities of exercises 17
and 18, but also

$$\frac{(x+y)V_n(x+y+n\alpha)}{x+y+n\alpha} = \sum_k \binom{n}{k} \frac{xV_k(x+k\alpha)}{x+k\alpha} \frac{yV_{n-k}(y+(n-k)\alpha)}{y+(n-k)\alpha};$$

$$\frac{V_n(x+y)}{y-n\alpha} = (x+y)\sum_k \binom{n-1}{k-1} \frac{V_k(x+k\alpha)}{x+k\alpha} \frac{V_{n-k}(y-k\alpha)}{y-k\alpha}.$$

[Special cases include Abel's binomial theorem, Eq. 1.2.6–(16); Rothe's identities
1.2.6–(26) and 1.2.6–(30); Torelli's sum, exercise 1.2.6–34.]

23. [*HM35*] (E. Jabotinsky.) Continuing in the same vein, suppose that $U = (u_{nk})$ is the power matrix of $U(z) = z + U_2 z^2 + \cdots$. Let $u_n = u_{n1} = n! \, U_n$.

a) Explain how to compute a matrix $\ln U$ so that the power matrix of $U^{[\alpha]}(z)$ is
$\exp(\alpha \ln U) = I + \alpha \ln U + (\alpha \ln U)^2/2! + \cdots$.

b) Let l_{nk} be the entry in row n and column k of $\ln U$, and let

$$l_n = l_{n1}, \qquad L(z) = l_2 \frac{z^2}{2!} + l_3 \frac{z^3}{3!} + l_4 \frac{z^4}{4!} + \cdots.$$

Prove that $l_{nk} = \binom{n}{k-1} l_{n+1-k}$ for $1 \le k \le n$. [*Hint:* $U^{[\epsilon]}(z) = z + \epsilon L(z) + O(\epsilon^2)$.]

c) Considering $U^{[\alpha]}(z)$ as a function of both α and z, prove that

$$\frac{\partial}{\partial \alpha} U^{[\alpha]}(z) = L(z) \frac{\partial}{\partial z} U^{[\alpha]}(z) = L\big(U^{[\alpha]}(z)\big).$$

(Consequently $L(z) = (l_k/k!)V(z)$, where $V(z)$ is the function in (27) and (28).)

d) Show that if $u_2 \ne 0$, the numbers l_n can be computed from the recurrence

$$l_2 = u_2, \qquad \sum_{k=2}^{n} \binom{n}{k} l_k u_{n+1-k} = \sum_{k=2}^{n} l_k u_{nk}.$$

How would you use this recurrence when $u_2 = 0$?

e) Prove the identity

$$u_n = \sum_{m=0}^{n-1} \frac{n!}{m!} \sum_{\substack{k_1 + \cdots + k_m = n+m-1 \\ k_1, \ldots, k_m \ge 2}} \frac{n_0}{k_1!} \frac{n_1}{k_2!} \cdots \frac{n_{m-1}}{k_m!} l_{k_1} l_{k_2} \ldots l_{k_m},$$

where $n_j = 1 + k_1 + \cdots + k_j - j$.

24. [*HM25*] Given the power series $U(z) = U_1 z + U_2 z^2 + \cdots$, where U_1 is not a root of unity, let $U = (u_{nk})$ be the power matrix of $U(z)$.

a) Explain how to compute a matrix $\ln U$ so that the power matrix of $U^{[\alpha]}(z)$ is
$\exp(\alpha \ln U) = I + \alpha \ln U + (\alpha \ln U)^2/2! + \cdots$.

b) Show that if $W(z)$ is not identically zero and if $U(W(z)) = W(U(z))$, then $W(z) = U^{[\alpha]}(z)$ for some complex number α.

25. [*M24*] If $U(z) = z + U_k z^k + U_{k+1} z^{k+1} + \cdots$ and $V(z) = z + V_l z^l + V_{l+1} z^{l+1} + \cdots$, where $k \ge 2$, $l \ge 2$, $U_k \ne 0$, $V_l \ne 0$, and $U(V(z)) = V(U(z))$, prove that we must have $k = l$ and $V(z) = U^{[\alpha]}(z)$ for $\alpha = V_k/U_k$.

26. [*M22*] Show that if $U(z) = U_0 + U_1 z + U_2 z^2 + \cdots$ and $V(z) = V_1 z + V_2 z^2 + \cdots$ are power series with all coefficients 0 or 1, we can obtain the first N coefficients of $U(V(z)) \bmod 2$ in $O(N^{1+\epsilon})$ steps, for any $\epsilon > 0$.

27. [*M22*] (D. Zeilberger.) Find a recurrence analogous to (9) for computing the coefficients of $W(z) = V(z)V(qz)\ldots V(q^{m-1}z)$, given q, m, and the coefficients of $V(z) = 1 + V_1 z + V_2 z^2 + \cdots$. Assume that q is not a root of unity.

▶ **28.** [*HM26*] A *Dirichlet series* is a sum of the form $V(z) = V_1/1^z + V_2/2^z + V_3/3^z + \cdots$; the product $U(z)V(z)$ of two such series is the Dirichlet series $W(z)$ where

$$W_n = \sum_{d \backslash n} U_d V_{n/d}.$$

Ordinary power series are special cases of Dirichlet series, since we have $V_0 + V_1 z +$ $V_2 z^2 + V_3 z^3 + \cdots = V_0/1^s + V_1/2^s + V_2/4^s + V_3/8^s + \cdots$ when $z = 2^{-s}$. In fact, Dirichlet series are essentially equivalent to power series $V(z_1, z_2, \dots)$ in arbitrarily many variables, where $z_k = p_k^{-s}$ and p_k is the kth prime number.

Find recurrence relations that generalize (9) and the formulas of exercise 4, assuming that a Dirichlet series $V(z)$ is given and that we want to calculate (a) $W(z) = V(z)^\alpha$ when $V_1 = 1$; (b) $W(z) = \exp V(z)$ when $V_1 = 0$; (c) $W(z) = \ln V(z)$ when $V_1 = 1$. [*Hint:* Let $t(n)$ be the total number of prime factors of n, including multiplicity, and let $\delta \sum_n V_n/n^z = \sum_n t(n) V_n/n^z$. Show that δ is analogous to a derivative; for example, $\delta e^{V(z)} = e^{V(z)} \delta V(z)$.]

It seems impossible *that any thing*
should really alter the *series of things,*
without the same power which first produced them.
— EDWARD STILLINGFLEET, *Origines Sacræ*, 2:3:2 (1662)

ANSWERS TO EXERCISES

This branch of mathematics is the only one, I believe,
in which good writers frequently get results entirely erroneous.
... It may be doubted if there is a single
extensive treatise on probabilities in existence
which does not contain solutions absolutely indefensible.

— C. S. PEIRCE, in *Popular Science Monthly* (1878)

NOTES ON THE EXERCISES

1. An average problem for a mathematically inclined reader.

3. (Solution by Roger Frye, after about 110 hours of computation on a Connection Machine in 1987.) $95800^4 + 217519^4 + 414560^4 = 422481^4$.

4. (One of the readers of the preliminary manuscript for this book reported that he had found a truly remarkable proof. But unfortunately the margin of his copy was too small to contain it.)

SECTION 3.1

1. (a) This will usually fail, since "round" telephone numbers are often selected by the telephone user when possible. In some communities, telephone numbers are perhaps assigned randomly. But it would be a mistake in any case to try to get several successive random numbers from the same page, since the same telephone number is often listed several times in a row.

(b) But do you use the left-hand page or the right-hand page? Say, use the left-hand page number, divide by 2, and take the units digit. The total number of pages should be a multiple of 20; but even so, this method will have some bias.

(c) The markings on the faces will slightly bias the die, but for practical purposes this method is quite satisfactory (and it has been used by the author in the preparation of several examples in this set of books). See *Math. Comp.* **15** (1961), 94–95, for further discussion of icosahedral dice.

(d) (This is a hard question thrown in purposely as a surprise.) The number is not quite uniformly random. If the average number of emissions per minute is m, the probability that the counter registers k is $e^{-m}m^k/k!$ (the Poisson distribution); so the digit 0 is selected with probability $e^{-m}\sum_{k\geq 0} m^{10k}/(10k)!$, etc. In particular, the units digit will be even with probability $e^{-m}\cosh m = \frac{1}{2} + \frac{1}{2}e^{-2m}$, and this is never equal to $\frac{1}{2}$ (although the error is negligibly small when m is large).

ANSWERS TO EXERCISES   539

It is almost legitimate to take ten readings $(m_0, \ldots, m_9)$ and then to output j if m_j is strictly less than m_i for all $i \neq j$; try again if the minimum value appears more than once. (See (h).) However, the parameter m isn't really constant in the real world.

(e) Okay, provided that the time since the previous digit selected in this way is random. However, there is possible bias in borderline cases.

(f, g) No. People usually think of certain digits (like 7) with higher probability.

(h) Okay; your assignment of numbers to the horses had probability $\frac{1}{10}$ of assigning a given digit to the winning horse (unless you know, say, the jockey).

2. The number of such sequences is the multinomial coefficient $1000000!/(100000!)^{10}$; the probability is this number divided by $10^{1000000}$, the total number of sequences of a million digits. By Stirling's approximation we find that the probability is close to $1/(16\pi^4 10^{22}\sqrt{2\pi}) \approx 2.56 \times 10^{-26}$, roughly one chance in 4×10^{25}.

3. 3040504030.

4. (a) Step K11 can be entered only from step K10 or step K2, and in either case we find it impossible for X to be zero by a simple argument. If X could be zero at that point, the algorithm would not terminate.

(b) If X is initially 3830951656, the computation is like many of the steps that appear in Table 1 except that we reach step K11 with $Y = 3$ instead of $Y = 5$; hence $3830951656 \to 5870802097$. Similarly, $5870802097 \to 1226919902 \to 3172562687 \to 3319967479 \to 6065038420 \to 6065038420 \to \cdots$.

5. Since only 10^{10} ten-digit numbers are possible, some value of X must be repeated during the first $10^{10}+1$ steps; and as soon as a value is repeated, the sequence continues to repeat its past behavior.

6. (a) Arguing as in the previous exercise, the sequence must eventually repeat a value; let this repetition occur for the first time at step $\mu + \lambda$, where $X_{\mu+\lambda} = X_\mu$. (This condition defines μ and λ.) We have $0 \leq \mu < m$, $0 < \lambda \leq m$, $\mu + \lambda \leq m$. The values $\mu = 0$, $\lambda = m$ are attained if and only if f is a cyclic permutation; and $\mu = m-1$, $\lambda = 1$ occurs, e.g., if $X_0 = 0$, $f(x) = x+1$ for $x < m-1$, and $f(m-1) = m-1$.

(b) We have, for $r > n$, $X_r = X_n$ if and only if $r - n$ is a multiple of λ and $n \geq \mu$. Hence $X_{2n} = X_n$ if and only if n is a multiple of λ and $n \geq \mu$. The desired results now follow immediately. [*Note:* Equivalently, the powers of an element in a finite semigroup include a unique idempotent element: Take $X_1 = a$, $f(x) = ax$. See G. Frobenius, *Sitzungsberichte preußische Akademie der Wissenschaften* (1895), 82–83.]

(c) Once n has been found, generate X_i and X_{n+i} for $i \geq 0$ until first finding $X_i = X_{n+i}$; then $\mu = i$. If none of the values of X_{n+i} for $0 < i < \mu$ is equal to X_n, it follows that $\lambda = n$, otherwise λ is the smallest such i.

7. (a) The least $n > 0$ such that $n - (\ell(n) - 1)$ is a multiple of λ and $\ell(n) - 1 \geq \mu$ is $n = 2^{\lceil \lg \max(\mu+1, \lambda) \rceil} - 1 + \lambda$. [This may be compared with the least $n > 0$ such that $X_{2n} = X_n$, namely $\lambda(\lceil \mu/\lambda \rceil + \delta_{\mu 0})$.]

(b) Start with $X = Y = X_0$, $k = m = 1$. (At key places in this algorithm we will have $X = X_{2m-k-1}$, $Y = X_{m-1}$, and $m = \ell(2m - k)$.) To generate the next random number, do the following steps: Set $X \leftarrow f(X)$ and $k \leftarrow k - 1$. If $X = Y$, stop (the period length λ is equal to $m - k$). Otherwise if $k = 0$, set $Y \leftarrow X$, $m \leftarrow 2m$, $k \leftarrow m$. Output X.

Notes: Brent has also considered a more general method in which the successive values of $Y = X_{n_i}$ satisfy $n_1 = 0$, $n_{i+1} = 1 + \lfloor pn_i \rfloor$ where p is any number greater than 1. He showed that the best choice of p, approximately 2.4771, saves about 3 percent of the iterations by comparison with $p = 2$. (See exercise 4.5.4–4.)

The method in part (b) has a serious deficiency, however, since it might generate a lot of nonrandom numbers before shutting off. For example, we might have a particularly bad case such as $\lambda = 1$, $\mu = 2^k$. A method based on Floyd's idea in exercise 6(b), namely one that maintains $Y = X_{2n}$ and $X = X_n$ for $n = 0, 1, 2, \ldots$, will require a few more function evaluations than Brent's method, but it will stop before any number has been output twice.

On the other hand, if f is unknown (for example, if we are receiving the values X_0, X_1, $\ldots$ online from an outside source) or if f is difficult to apply, the following cycle detection algorithm due to R. W. Gosper will be preferable: Maintain an auxiliary table T_0, T_1, $\ldots$, T_m, where $m = \lfloor \lg n \rfloor$ when receiving X_n. Initially $T_0 \leftarrow X_0$. For $n = 1, 2, \ldots$, compare X_n with each of T_0, $\ldots$, $T_{\lfloor \lg n \rfloor}$; if no match is found, set $T_{e(n)} \leftarrow X_n$, where $e(n) = \rho(n+1) = \max\{e \mid 2^e \text{ divides } n + 1\}$. But if a match $X_n = T_k$ is found, then $\lambda = n - \max\{l \mid l < n \text{ and } e(l) = k\}$. After X_n has been stored in $T_{e(n)}$, it is subsequently compared with X_{n+1}, X_{n+2}, $\ldots$, $X_{n+2^{e(n)+1}}$. Therefore the procedure stops immediately after generating $X_{\mu+\lambda+j}$, where $j \geq 0$ is minimum with $e(\mu+j) \geq \lceil \lg \lambda \rceil - 1$. With this method, no X value is generated more than twice, and at most $\max(1, 2^{\lceil \lg \lambda \rceil - 1})$ values are generated more than once. [MIT AI Laboratory Memo 239 (29 February 1972), Hack 132.]

R. Sedgewick, T. G. Szymanski, and A. C. Yao have analyzed a more complex algorithm based on parameters $m \geq 2$ and $g \geq 1$: An auxiliary table of size m contains X_0, X_b, $\ldots$, X_{qb} at the moment that X_n is computed, where $b = 2^{\lceil \lg n/m \rceil}$ and $q = \lceil n/b \rceil - 1$. If $n \bmod gb < b$, X_n is compared to the entries in the table; eventually equality occurs, and we can reconstruct μ and λ after doing at most $(g+1)2^{\lceil \lg(\mu+\lambda)\rceil + 1}$ further evaluations of f. If the evaluation of f costs τ units of time, and if testing X_n for membership in the table costs σ units, then g can be chosen so that the total running time is $(\mu + \lambda)(\tau + O(\frac{\sigma \tau}{m})^{1/2})$; this is optimum if $\sigma/\tau = O(m)$. Moreover, X_n is not computed unless $\mu + \lambda > mn/(m+4g+2)$, so we can use this method "online" to output elements that are guaranteed to be distinct, making only $2 + O(m^{-1/2})$ function evaluations per output. [$SICOMP$ **11** (1982), 376–390.]

8. (a, b) $00, 00, \ldots$ [62 starting values]; $10, 10, \ldots$ [19]; $60, 60, \ldots$ [15]; $50, 50, \ldots$ [1]; $24, 57, 24, 57, \ldots$ [3]. (c) 42 or 69; these both lead to a set of fifteen distinct values, namely (42 or 69), 76, 77, 92, 46, 11, 12, 14, 19, 36, 29, 84, 05, 02, 00.

9. Since $X < b^n$, we have $X^2 < b^{2n}$, and the middle square is $\lfloor X^2/b^n \rfloor \leq X^2/b^n$. If $X > 0$, then $X^2/b^n < Xb^n/b^n = X$.

10. If $X = ab^n$, the next number of the sequence has the same form; it is equal to $(a^2 \bmod b^n)b^n$. If a is a multiple of all the prime factors of b, the sequence will soon degenerate to zero; if not, the sequence will degenerate into a cycle of numbers having the same general form as X.

Further facts about the middle-square method have been found by B. Jansson, *Random Number Generators* (Stockholm: Almqvist & Wiksell, 1966), Section 3A. Numerologists will be interested to learn that the number 3792 is self-reproducing in the four-digit middle-square method, since $3792^2 = 14379264$; furthermore (as Jansson observed), it is "self-reproducing" in another sense, too, since its prime factorization is $3 \cdot 79 \cdot 2^4$!

11. The probability that $\mu = 0$ and $\lambda = 1$ is the probability that $X_1 = X_0$, namely $1/m$. The probability that $(\mu, \lambda) = (1, 1)$ or that $(\mu, \lambda) = (0, 2)$ is the probability that $X_1 \neq X_0$ and that X_2 has a certain value, so it is $(1 - 1/m)(1/m)$. Similarly, the probability that the sequence has any given μ and λ is a function only of $\mu + \lambda$, namely

$$P(\mu, \lambda) = \frac{1}{m} \prod_{1 \le k < \mu + \lambda} \left(1 - \frac{k}{m}\right).$$

For the probability that $\lambda = 1$, we have

$$\sum_{\mu \ge 0} \frac{1}{m} \prod_{k=1}^{\mu} \left(1 - \frac{k}{m}\right) = \frac{1}{m} Q(m),$$

where $Q(m)$ is defined in Section 1.2.11.3, Eq. (2). By Eq. (25) in that section, the probability is approximately $\sqrt{\pi/2m} \approx 1.25/\sqrt{m}$. The chance of Algorithm K converging as it did is only about one in 80000; the author was decidedly unlucky. But see exercise 15 for further comments on the "colossalness."

12. $\displaystyle\sum_{\substack{1 \le \lambda \le m \\ 0 \le \mu < m}} \lambda P(\mu, \lambda) = \frac{1}{m} \left(1 + 3\left(1 - \frac{1}{m}\right) + 6\left(1 - \frac{1}{m}\right)\left(1 - \frac{2}{m}\right) + \cdots\right) = \frac{1 + Q(m)}{2}.$

(See the previous answer. In general if $f(a_0, a_1, \dots) = \sum_{n \ge 0} a_n \prod_{k=1}^{n}(1 - k/m)$ then $f(a_0, a_1, \dots) = a_0 + f(a_1, a_2, \dots) - f(a_1, 2a_2, \dots))/m$; apply this identity with $a_n = (n + 1)/2$.) Therefore the average value of λ (and, by symmetry of $P(\mu, \lambda)$, also of $\mu + 1$) is approximately $\sqrt{\pi m/8} + \frac{1}{3}$. The average value of $\mu + \lambda$ is exactly $Q(m)$, approximately $\sqrt{\pi m/2} - \frac{1}{3}$. [For alternative derivations and further results, including asymptotic values for the moments, see A. Rapoport, *Bull. Math. Biophysics* **10** (1948), 145–157, and B. Harris, *Annals Math. Stat.* **31** (1960), 1045–1062; see also I. M. Sobol, *Theory of Probability and Its Applications* **9** (1964), 333–338. Sobol discusses the asymptotic period length for the more general sequence $X_{n+1} = f(X_n)$ if $n \not\equiv 0$ (modulo m), $X_{n+1} = g(X_n)$ if $n \equiv 0$ (modulo m), with both f and g random.]

13. [Paul Purdom and John Williams, *Trans. Amer. Math. Soc.* **133** (1968), 547–551.] Let T_{mn} be the number of functions that have n one-cycles and no cycles of length greater than one. Then

$$T_{mn} = \binom{m-1}{n-1} m^{m-n}.$$

(This is $\binom{m}{n} r(m, m-n)$ in exercise 2.3.4.4–25.) *Any* function is such a function followed by a permutation of the n elements that were the one-cycles. Hence $\sum_{n \ge 1} T_{mn} n! = m^m$.

Let P_{nk} be the number of permutations of n elements in which the longest cycle is of length k. Then the number of functions with a maximum cycle of length k is $\sum_{n \ge 1} T_{mn} P_{nk}$. To get the average value of k, we compute $\sum_{k \ge 1} \sum_{n \ge 1} k T_{mn} P_{nk}$, which by the result of exercise 1.3.3–23 is $\sum_{n \ge 1} T_{mn} n!(cn + \frac{1}{2}c + O(n^{-1}))$ where $c \approx .62433$. Summing, we get the average value $cQ(m) + \frac{1}{2}c + O(m^{1/2})$. (This is not substantially larger than the average value when X_0 is selected at random. The average value of $\max \mu$ is asymptotic to $Q(m) \ln 4$, and the average value of $\max(\mu + \lambda)$ is asymptotic to $1.9268 Q(m)$; see Flajolet and Odlyzko, *Lecture Notes in Comp. Sci.* **434** (1990), 329–354.)

14. Let $c_r(m)$ be the number of functions with exactly r different final cycles. From the recurrence $c_1(m) = (m - 1)! - \sum_{k>0} \binom{m}{k}(-1)^k (m - k)^k c_1(m - k)$, which comes by counting the number of functions whose image contains at most $m - k$ elements, we find the solution $c_1(m) = m^{m-1} Q(m)$. (See exercise 1.2.11.3–16.) Another way to obtain the value of $c_1(m)$, which is perhaps more elegant and revealing, is given in exercise 2.3.4.4–17. The value of $c_r(m)$ may be determined as in exercise 13:

$$c_r(m) = \sum_{n \geq 1} T_{mn} \begin{bmatrix} n \\ r \end{bmatrix} = m^{m-1} \left(\frac{1}{0!} \begin{bmatrix} 1 \\ r \end{bmatrix} + \frac{1}{1!} \begin{bmatrix} 2 \\ r \end{bmatrix} \frac{m-1}{m} + \frac{1}{2!} \begin{bmatrix} 3 \\ r \end{bmatrix} \frac{m-1}{m} \frac{m-2}{m} + \cdots \right).$$

The desired average value can now be computed; it is (see exercise 12)

$$E_m = \frac{1}{m} \left(H_1 + 2H_2 \frac{m-1}{m} + 3H_3 \frac{m-1}{m} \frac{m-2}{m} + \cdots \right)$$

$$= 1 + \frac{1}{2} \frac{m-1}{m} + \frac{1}{3} \frac{m-1}{m} \frac{m-2}{m} + \cdots.$$

This latter formula was obtained by quite different means by Martin D. Kruskal, *AMM* **61** (1954), 392–397. Using the integral representation

$$E_m = \int_0^\infty \left(\left(1 + \frac{x}{m} \right)^m - 1 \right) e^{-x} \frac{dx}{x},$$

he proved the asymptotic relation $\lim_{m \to \infty}(E_m - \frac{1}{2} \ln m) = \frac{1}{2}(\gamma + \ln 2)$. For further results and references, see John Riordan, *Annals Math. Stat.* **33** (1962), 178–185.

15. The probability that $f(x) \neq x$ for all x is $(m-1)^m/m^m$, which is approximately $1/e$. The existence of a self-repeating value in an algorithm like Algorithm K is therefore not "colossal" at all — it occurs with probability $1 - 1/e \approx .63212$. The only "colossal" thing was that the author happened to hit such a value when X_0 was chosen at random (see exercise 11).

16. The sequence will repeat when a pair of successive elements occurs for the second time. The maximum period is m^2. (See the next exercise.)

17. After selecting $X_0, \ldots, X_{k-1}$ arbitrarily, let $X_{n+1} = f(X_n, \ldots, X_{n-k+1})$, where $0 \leq x_1, \ldots, x_k < m$ implies that $0 \leq f(x_1, \ldots, x_k) < m$. The maximum period is m^k. This is an obvious upper bound, but it is not obvious that it can be attained; for constructive proofs that it can always be attained for suitable f, see exercises 3.2.2–17 and 3.2.2–21, and for the number of ways to attain it see exercise 2.3.4.2–23.

18. Same as exercise 7, but use the k-tuple of elements $(X_n, \ldots, X_{n-k+1})$ in place of the single element X_n.

19. Clearly $\Pr(\text{no final cycle has length } 1) = (m-1)^m/m^m$. R. Pemantle [*J. Algorithms* **54** (2005)72–84] has shown that $\Pr(\lambda = 1) = \Theta(m^{k/2})$, and that $\Pr((\mu + \lambda)^2 > 2m^k x$ and $\lambda/(\mu + \lambda) \leq y)$ rapidly approaches ye^{-x}, when $x > 0$, $0 < y < 1$, and $m \to \infty$. The k-dimensional analogs of exercises 13 and 14 remain unsolved.

20. It suffices to consider the simpler mapping $g(X)$ defined by steps K2–K13. Working backward from 6065038420, we obtain a total of 597 solutions; the smallest is 0009612809 and the largest is 9995371004.

21. We may work with $g(X)$ as in the previous exercise, but now we want to run the function forward instead of backward. There is an interesting tradeoff between time and space. Notice that the mechanism of step K1 tends to make the period length small. So does the existence of X's with large in-degree; for example, 512 choices of $X = *6********$ in step K2 will go to K10 with $X \leftarrow 0500000000$.

Scott Fluhrer has discovered *another* fixed point of Algorithm K, namely the value 5008502835(!). He also found the 3-cycle $0225923640 \to 2811514413 \to 0590051662 \to$

0225923640, making a total of seven cycles in all. Only 128 starting numbers lead to the repeating value 5008502835. Algorithm K is a *terrible* random number generator.

22. If f were truly random, this would be ideal; but how do we construct such f? The function defined by Algorithm K would work much better under this scheme, although it does have decidedly nonrandom properties (see the previous answer).

23. The function f permutes its cyclic elements; let $(x_0, \ldots, x_{k-1})$ be the "unusual" representation of the inverse of that permutation. Then proceed to define $x_k, \ldots, x_{m-1}$ as in exercise 2.3.4.4–18. [See *J. Combinatorial Theory* **8** (1970), 361–375.]

For example, if $m = 10$ and $\big(f(0), \ldots, f(9)\big) = (3, 1, 4, 1, 5, 9, 2, 6, 5, 4)$, we have $(x_0, \ldots, x_9) = (4, 9, 5, 1, 1, 3, 4, 2, 6, 5)$; if $(x_0, \ldots, x_9) = (3, 1, 4, 1, 5, 9, 2, 6, 5, 4)$, we have $\big(f(0), \ldots, f(9)\big) = (6, 4, 9, 3, 1, 1, 2, 5, 4, 5)$.

SECTION 3.2.1

1. Take X_0 even, a even, c odd. Then X_n is odd for $n > 0$.

2. Let X_r be the first repeated value in the sequence. If X_r were equal to X_k for some k where $0 < k < r$, we could prove that $X_{r-1} = X_{k-1}$, since X_n uniquely determines X_{n-1} when a is prime to m. Hence $k = 0$.

3. If d is the greatest common divisor of a and m, the quantity aX_n can take on at most m/d values. The situation can be even worse; for example, if $m = 2^e$ and if a is even, Eq. (6) shows that the sequence is eventually constant.

4. Induction on k.

5. If a is relatively prime to m, there is a number a' for which $aa' \equiv 1 \pmod{m}$. Then $X_{n-1} = (a'X_n - a'c) \bmod m$; and in general, if $b = a - 1$,

$$X_{n-k} = \big((a')^k X_n - c(a' + \cdots + (a')^k)\big) \bmod m$$
$$= \Big((a')^k X_n + ((a')^k - 1)c/b\Big) \bmod m$$

when $k \geq 0$, $n - k \geq 0$. If a is not relatively prime to m, it is not possible to determine X_{n-1} when X_n is given; multiples of $m/\gcd(a, m)$ may be added to X_{n-1} without changing the value of X_n. (See also exercise 3.2.1.3–7.)

SECTION 3.2.1.1

1. Let c' be a solution to the congruence $ac' \equiv c \pmod{m}$. (Thus, $c' = a'c \bmod m$, if a' is the number in the answer to exercise 3.2.1–5.) Then we have

```
        LDA X;   ADD CPRIME;   MUL A.
```

Overflow is possible on this addition operation. (From results derived later in the chapter, it is probably best to save a unit of time, taking $c = a$ and replacing the ADD instruction by "INCA 1". Then if $X_0 = 0$, overflow will not occur until the end of the period, so it won't occur in practice.)

```
2. RANDM STJ   1F                          1H     JNOV  *
         LDA   XRAND                               JMP   *-1
         MUL   2F                          XRAND CON   X0
         SLAX  5                           2H     CON   a
         ADD   3F    (or, INCA c, if c is small)   3H     CON   c
         STA   XRAND
```

3. Let $a' = aw \bmod m$, and let m' be such that $mm' \equiv 1$ (modulo w). Set $y \leftarrow$ lomult(a', x), $z \leftarrow$ himult(a', x), $t \leftarrow$ lomult(m', y), $u \leftarrow$ himult(m, t). Then we have $mt \equiv a'x$ (modulo w), hence $a'x - mt = (z - u)w$, hence $ax \equiv z - u$ (modulo m); it follows that $ax \bmod m = z - u + [z < u]m$.

4. Define the operation $x \underline{\bmod} 2^e = y$ if and only if $x \equiv y$ (modulo 2^e) and $-2^{e-1} \leq y < 2^{e-1}$. The congruential sequence $\langle Y_n \rangle$ defined by

$$Y_0 = X_0 \underline{\bmod} 2^{32}, \qquad Y_{n+1} = (aY_n + c) \underline{\bmod} 2^{32}$$

is easy to compute on 370-style machines, since the lower half of the product of y and z is $(yz) \underline{\bmod} 2^{32}$ for all two's complement numbers y and z, and since addition ignoring overflow also delivers its result $\underline{\bmod} 2^{32}$. This sequence has all the randomness properties of the standard linear congruential sequence $\langle X_n \rangle$, since $Y_n \equiv X_n$ (modulo 2^{32}). Indeed, the two's complement representation of Y_n is *identical* to the binary representation of X_n, for all n. [G. Marsaglia and T. A. Bray first pointed this out in *CACM* **11** (1968), 757–759.]

5. (a) Subtraction: LDA X; SUB Y; JANN *+2; ADD M. (b) Addition: LDA X; SUB M; ADD Y; JANN *+2; ADD M. (Note that if m is more than half the word size, the instruction "SUB M" must precede the instruction "ADD Y".)

6. The sequences are not essentially different, since adding the constant $(m - c)$ has the same effect as subtracting the constant c. The operation must be combined with multiplication, so a subtractive process has little merit over the additive one (at least in MIX's case), except when it is necessary to avoid affecting the overflow toggle.

7. The prime factors of $z^k - 1$ appear in the factorization of $z^{kr} - 1$. If r is odd, the prime factors of $z^k + 1$ appear in the factorization of $z^{kr} + 1$. And $z^{2k} - 1$ equals $(z^k - 1)(z^k + 1)$.

8.

```
   JOV  *+1    (Ensure that overflow is off.)
   LDA  X
   MUL  A
   STX  TEMP
   ADD  TEMP   Add lower half to upper half.
   JNOV *+2    If ≥ w, subtract w − 1.
   INCA 1      (Overflow is impossible in this step.)
```

Note: Since addition on an e-bit ones'-complement computer is mod $(2^e - 1)$, it is possible to combine the techniques of exercises 4 and 8, producing $(yz) \bmod (2^e - 1)$ by adding together the two e-bit halves of the product yz, for all ones' complement numbers y and z regardless of sign.

9. (a) Both sides equal $aq\lfloor x/q \rfloor$.

(b) Set $t \leftarrow a(x \bmod q) - r\lfloor x/q \rfloor$, where $r = m \bmod a$; the constants q and r can be precomputed. Then $ax \bmod m = t + [t < 0]m$, because we can prove that $t > -m$: Clearly $a(x \bmod q) \leq a(q - 1) < m$. Also $r\lfloor x/q \rfloor \leq r\lfloor(m - 1)/q \rfloor = r\lfloor a + (r - 1)/q \rfloor = ra \leq qa < m$ if $0 < r \leq q$; and $a^2 \leq m$ implies $r < a \leq q$. [This technique is implicit in a program published by B. A. Wichmann and I. D. Hill, *Applied Stat.* **31** (1982), 190.]

10. If $r > q$ and $x = m-1$ we have $r\lfloor x/q \rfloor \geq (q+1)(a+1) > m$. So the condition $r \leq q$ is necessary and sufficient for method 9(b) to be valid; this means $\frac{m}{q} - 1 \leq a \leq \frac{m}{q}$. Let $t = \lfloor \sqrt{m} \rfloor$. The intervals $[\frac{m}{q} - 1 \mathinner{.\,.} \frac{m}{q}]$ are disjoint for $1 \leq q \leq t$, and they include exactly 1 or 2 integers, depending on whether q is a divisor of m. These intervals account for all solutions with $a > \sqrt{m}$; they also include the case $a = t$, if $(\sqrt{m} \bmod 1) < \frac{1}{2}$, and the case $a = t - 1$ if $m = t^2$. Thus the total number of "lucky" multipliers is exactly $2\lfloor\sqrt{m}\rfloor + \lfloor d(m)/2\rfloor - [(\sqrt{m} \bmod 1) < \frac{1}{2}] - 1$, where $d(m)$ is the number of divisors of m.

11. We can assume that $a \le \frac{1}{2}m$; otherwise we can obtain $ax \bmod m$ from $(m-a)x \bmod m$. Then we can represent $a = a'a'' - a'''$, where a', a'', and a''' are all less than $\sqrt{m}$; for example, we can take $a' \approx \sqrt{m} - 1$ and $a'' = \lceil a/a' \rceil$. It follows that $ax \bmod m$ is $(a'(a''x \bmod m) \bmod m - (a'''x \bmod m)) \bmod m$, and the inner three operations can all be handled by exercise 9.

When $m = 2^{31} - 1$ we can take advantage of the fact that $m - 1$ has 192 divisors to find cases in which $m = q'a' + 1$, simplifying the general method because $r' = 1$. It turns out that 86 of these divisors lead to lucky a'' and a''', when $a = 62089911$; the best such case is probably $a' = 3641$, $a'' = 17053$, $a''' = 62$, because 3641 and 62 both divide $m - 1$. This decomposition yields the scheme

$$t \leftarrow 17053(x \bmod 125929) - 16410\lfloor x/125929\rfloor\,,$$
$$t \leftarrow 3641(t \bmod 589806) - \lfloor t/589806\rfloor\,,$$
$$t \leftarrow t - (62(x \bmod 34636833) - \lfloor x/34636833\rfloor)\,,$$

where "$-$" denotes subtraction mod m. The mod operations count as one multiplication and one subtraction, because $x \bmod q = x - q\lfloor x/q\rfloor$ and the operation $\lfloor x/q\rfloor$ has already been done; thus, we have performed seven multiplications, three divisions, and seven subtractions. But it's even better to notice that 62089911 itself has 24 divisors; they lead to five suitable factorizations with $a''' = 0$. For example, when $a' = 883$ and $a'' = 70317$ we need only six multiplications, two divisions, four subtractions:

$$t \leftarrow 883(x \bmod 2432031) - 274\lfloor x/2432031\rfloor\,,$$
$$t \leftarrow 70317(t \bmod 30540) - 2467\lfloor t/30540\rfloor\,.$$

[Can the worst-case number of multiplications plus divisions be reduced to at most 11, for all a and m, or is 12 the best upper bound? Another way to achieve 12 appears in exercise 4.3.3–19.]

12. (a) Let $m = 9999998999 = 10^{10} - 10^3 - 1$. To multiply $(x_9x_8 \ldots x_0)_{10}$ by 10 modulo m, use the fact that $10^{10}x_9 \equiv 10^3x_9 + x_9$: Add $(x_9000)_{10}$ to $(x_8x_7 \ldots x_0x_9)_{10}$. And to avoid circular shifting, imagine that the digits are arranged on a wheel: Just add the high-order digit x_9 to the digit x_2 three positions left, and point to x_8 as the new high-order digit. If $x_9 + x_2 \ge 10$, a carry propagates to the left. And if this carry ripples all the way to the left of x_8, it propagates not only to x_9 but also to the x_2 position; it may continue to propagate from both x_9 and x_2 before finally settling down. (The numbers might also become slightly larger than m. For example, 0999999900 goes to 9999999000 $= m + 1$, which goes to 9999999009 $= m + 10$. But a redundant representation isn't necessarily harmful.)

(b) This is the operation of *dividing* by 10, so we do the opposite of (a): Move the high-order digit pointer cyclically *left*, and *subtract* the new high-order digit from the digit three to its left. If the result of subtraction is negative, "borrow" in the usual fashion (Algorithm 4.3.1S); that is, decrease the preceding digit by 1. Borrowing may propagate as in (a), but never past the high-order digit position. This operation keeps the numbers nonnegative and less than m. (Thus, division by 10 turns out to be easier than multiplication by 10.)

(c) We can *remember* the borrow-bit instead of propagating it, because it can be incorporated into the subtraction on the next step. Thus, if we define digits x_n and borrow-bits b_n by the recurrence

$$x_n = (x_{n-10} - x_{n-3} - b_n) \bmod 10 = x_{n-10} - x_{n-3} - b_n + 10b_{n+1},$$

we have $999999900^n \bmod 9999998999 = X_n$ by induction on n, where

$$X_n = (x_{n-1}x_{n-2}x_{n-3}x_{n-4}x_{n-5}x_{n-6}x_{n-7}x_{n+2}x_{n+1}x_n)_{10} - 1000b_{n+3}$$
$$= (x_{n-1}x_{n-2}\ldots x_{n-10})_{10} - (x_{n-1}x_{n-2}x_{n-3})_{10} - b_n,$$

provided that the initial conditions are set up to make $X_0 = 1$. Notice that $10X_{n+1} = (x_n x_{n-1} x_{n-2} x_{n-3} x_{n-4} x_{n-5} x_{n-6} x_{n+3} x_{n+2} x_{n+1} 0)_{10} - 10000b_{n+4} = mx_n + X_n$; it follows that $0 \le X_n < m$ for all $n \ge 0$.

(d) If $0 \le U < m$, the first digit of the decimal representation of U/m is $\lfloor 10U/m \rfloor$, and the subsequent digits are the decimal representation of $(10U \bmod m)/m$; see, for example, Method 2a in Section 4.4. Thus $U/m = (.u_1u_2\ldots)_{10}$ if we set $U_0 = U$ and $U_n = 10U_{n-1} \bmod m = 10U_{n-1} - mu_n$. Informally, the digits of $1/m$ are the leading digits of $10^n \bmod m$ for $n = 1, 2, \ldots$, a sequence that is eventually periodic; these are the leading digits of $10^{-n} \bmod m$ in reverse order, so we have calculated them in (c).

A rigorous proof is, of course, preferable to handwaving. Let λ be the least positive integer with $10^\lambda \equiv 1$ (modulo m), and define $x_n = x_{n \bmod \lambda}$, $b_n = b_{n \bmod \lambda}$, $X_n = X_{n \bmod \lambda}$ for all $n < 0$. Then the recurrences for x_n, b_n, and X_n in (c) are valid for all integers n. If $U_0 = 1$ it follows that $U_n = X_{-n}$ and $u_n = x_{-n}$; hence

$$\frac{999999900^n \bmod 9999998999}{9999998999} = (.x_{n-1}x_{n-2}x_{n-3}\ldots)_{10}.$$

(e) Let w be the computer's word size, and use the recurrence

$$x_n = (x_{n-k} - x_{n-l} - b_n) \bmod w = x_{n-k} - x_{n-l} - b_n + wb_{n+1},$$

where $0 < l < k$ and k is large. Then $(.x_{n-1}x_{n-2}x_{n-3}\ldots)_w = X_n/m$, where $m = w^k - w^l - 1$ and $X_{n+1} = (w^{k-1} - w^{l-1})X_n \bmod m$. The relation

$$X_n = (x_{n-1}\ldots x_{n-k})_w - (x_{n-1}\ldots x_{n-l})_w - b_n$$

holds for $n \ge 0$; the values of $x_{-1}, \ldots, x_{-k}$, and b_0 should be such that $0 \le X_0 < m$.

Such random number generators, and the similar ones in the following exercise, were introduced by G. Marsaglia and A. Zaman [*Annals of Applied Probability* **1** (1991), 462–480], who called the method *subtract-with-borrow*. Their starting point was the radix-w representation of fractions with denominator m. The relation to linear congruential sequences was noticed by Shu Tezuka, and analyzed in detail by Tezuka, L'Ecuyer, and Couture [*ACM Trans. Modeling and Computer Simulation* **3** (1993), 315–331]. The period length is discussed in exercise 3.2.1.2–22.

13. Multiplication by 10 now requires *negating* the digit that is added. For this purpose it is convenient to represent a number with its last three digits negated; for example, $9876543210 = (9876544\bar{7}\bar{9}\bar{0})_{10}$. Then 10 times $(x_9\ldots x_3\bar{x}_2\bar{x}_1\bar{x}_0)_{10}$ is $(x_8\ldots x_3 x' \bar{x}_1 \bar{x}_0 \bar{x}_9)_{10}$ where $x' = x_9 - x_2$. Similarly, $(x_9\ldots x_3\bar{x}_2\bar{x}_1\bar{x}_0)_{10}$ divided by 10 is $(x_0 x_9 \ldots x_4 \bar{x}'' \bar{x}_2 \bar{x}_1)_{10}$ where $x'' = x_0 - x_3$. The recurrence

$$x_n = (x_{n-3} - x_{n-10} - b_n) \bmod 10 = x_{n-3} - x_{n-10} - b_n + 10b_{n+1}$$

yields $8999999101^n \bmod 9999999001 = X_n$ where

$$X_n = (x_{n-1}x_{n-2}x_{n-3}x_{n-4}x_{n-5}x_{n-6}x_{n-7}\bar{x}_{n+2}\bar{x}_{n+1}\bar{x}_n)_{10} + 1000b_{n+3}$$
$$= (x_{n-1}x_{n-2}\ldots x_{n-10})_{10} - (x_{n-1}x_{n-2}x_{n-3})_{10} + b_n.$$

When the radix is generalized from 10 to w, we find that the inverse powers of w modulo $w^k - w^l + 1$ are generated by

$$x_n = (x_{n-l} - x_{n-k} - b_n) \bmod w = x_{n-l} - x_{n-k} - b_n + w b_{n+1}$$

(the same as in exercise 12 but with k and l interchanged).

14. Mild generalization: We can effectively divide by b modulo $b^k - b^l \pm 1$ for any b less than or equal to the word size w, since the recurrence for x_n is almost as efficient when $b < w$ as it is when $b = w$.

Strong generalization: The recurrence

$$x_n = (a_1 x_{n-1} + \cdots + a_k x_{n-k} + c_n) \bmod b, \quad c_{n+1} = \left\lfloor \frac{a_1 x_{n-1} + \cdots + a_k x_{n-k} + c_n}{b} \right\rfloor$$

is equivalent to $X_n = b^{-1} X_{n-1} \bmod |m|$ in the sense that $X_n/|m| = (.x_{n-1} x_{n-2} \ldots)_b$, if we define

$$m = a_k b^k + \cdots + a_1 b - 1 \quad \text{and} \quad X_n = \left(\sum_{j=1}^{k} a_j (x_{n-1} \ldots x_{n-j})_b + c_n \right) (\operatorname{sign} m).$$

The initial values $x_{-1} \ldots x_{-k}$ and c_0 should be selected so that $0 \le X_0 < |m|$; we will then have $x_n = (b X_{n+1} - X_n)/|m|$ for $n \ge 0$. The values of x_j for $j < 0$ that appear in the formula $X_n/|m| = (.x_{n-1} x_{n-2} \ldots)_b$ are properly regarded as $x_{j \bmod \lambda}$, where $b^\lambda \equiv 1$ (modulo m); these values may differ from the numbers $x_{-1}, \ldots, x_{-k}$ that were initially supplied. The carry digits c_n will satisfy

$$\sum_{j=1}^{k} \min(0, a_j) \le c_n < \sum_{j=1}^{k} \max(0, a_j)$$

if the initial carry c_0 is in this range.

The special case $m = b^k + b^l - 1$, for which $a_j = \delta_{jl} + \delta_{jk}$, is of particular interest because it can be computed so easily; Marsaglia and Zaman called this the *add-with-carry* generator:

$$x_n = (x_{n-l} + x_{n-k} + c_n) \bmod b = x_{n-l} + x_{n-k} + c_n - b c_{n+1}.$$

Another potentially attractive possibility is to use $k = 2$ in a generator with, say, $b = 2^{31}$ and $m = 65430 b^2 + b - 1$. This modulus m is prime, and the period length turns out to be $(m-1)/2$. The spectral test of Section 3.3.4 indicates that the spacing between planes is good (large ν values), although of course the multiplier b^{-1} is poor in comparison with other multipliers for this particular modulus m.

Exercise 3.2.1.2–22 contains additional information about subtract-with-borrow and add-with-carry moduli that lead to extremely long periods.

SECTION 3.2.1.2

1. Period length m, by Theorem A. (See exercise 3.)

2. Yes, these conditions imply the conditions in Theorem A, since the only prime divisor of 2^e is 2, and any odd number is relatively prime to 2^e. (In fact, the conditions of the exercise are *necessary* and sufficient.)

3. By Theorem A, we need $a \equiv 1$ (modulo 4) and $a \equiv 1$ (modulo 5). By Law D of Section 1.2.4, this is equivalent to $a \equiv 1$ (modulo 20).

4. We know $X_{2^{e-1}} \equiv 0$ (modulo 2^{e-1}) by using Theorem A in the case $m = 2^{e-1}$. Also using Theorem A for $m = 2^e$, we know that $X_{2^{e-1}} \not\equiv 0$ (modulo 2^e). It follows that $X_{2^{e-1}} = 2^{e-1}$. More generally, we can use Eq. 3.2.1–(6) to prove that the second half of the period is essentially like the first half, since $X_{n+2^{e-1}} = (X_n + 2^{e-1})$ mod 2^e. (The quarters are similar too, see exercise 21.)

5. We need $a \equiv 1$ (modulo p) for $p = 3, 11, 43, 281, 86171$. By Law D of Section 1.2.4, this is equivalent to $a \equiv 1$ (modulo $3 \cdot 11 \cdot 43 \cdot 281 \cdot 86171$), so the *only* solution is the terrible multiplier $a = 1$.

6. (See the previous exercise.) The congruence $a \equiv 1$ (modulo $3 \cdot 7 \cdot 11 \cdot 13 \cdot 37$) implies that the solutions are $a = 1 + 111111k$, for $0 \le k \le 8$.

7. Using the notation of the proof of Lemma Q, μ is the smallest value such that $X_{\mu+\lambda} = X_\mu$; so it is the smallest value such that $Y_{\mu+\lambda} = Y_\mu$ and $Z_{\mu+\lambda} = Z_\mu$. This shows that $\mu = \max(\mu_1, \ldots, \mu_t)$. The highest achievable μ is $\max(e_1, \ldots, e_t)$, but nobody really wants to achieve it.

8. We have $a^2 \equiv 1$ (modulo 8); so $a^4 \equiv 1$ (modulo 16), $a^8 \equiv 1$ (modulo 32), etc. If a mod $4 = 3$, then $a - 1$ is twice an odd number; so $(a^{2^{e-1}} - 1)/(a - 1) \equiv 0$ (modulo 2^e) if and only if $(a^{2^{e-1}} - 1)/2 \equiv 0$ (modulo $2^{e+1}/2$), which is true.

9. Substitute for X_n in terms of Y_n and simplify. If X_0 mod $4 = 3$, the formulas of the exercise do not apply; but they do apply to the sequence $Z_n = (-X_n)$ mod 2^e, which has essentially the same behavior.

10. Only when $m = 1, 2, 4, p^e$, and $2p^e$, for odd primes p. In all other cases, the result of Theorem B is an improvement over Euler's theorem (exercise 1.2.4–28).

11. (a) Either $x+1$ or $x-1$ (not both) will be a multiple of 4, so $x \mp 1 = q2^f$, where q is odd and f is greater than 1. (b) In the given circumstances, $f < e$ and so $e \ge 3$. We have $\pm x \equiv 1$ (modulo 2^f) and $\pm x \not\equiv 1$ (modulo 2^{f+1}) and $f > 1$. Hence, by applying Lemma P, we find that $(\pm x)^{2^{e-f-1}} \not\equiv 1$ (modulo 2^e), while $x^{2^{e-f}} = (\pm x)^{2^{e-f}} \equiv 1$ (modulo 2^e). So the order is a divisor of 2^{e-f}, but not a divisor of 2^{e-f-1}. (c) 1 has order 1; $2^e - 1$ has order 2; the maximum period when $e \ge 3$ is therefore 2^{e-2}, and for $e \ge 4$ it is necessary to have $f = 2$, that is, $x \equiv 4 \pm 1$ (modulo 8).

12. If k is a proper divisor of $p - 1$ and if $a^k \equiv 1$ (modulo p), then by Lemma P we have $a^{kp^{e-1}} \equiv 1$ (modulo p^e). Similarly, if $a^{p-1} \equiv 1$ (modulo p^2), we find that $a^{(p-1)p^{e-2}} \equiv 1$ (modulo p^e). So in these cases a is *not* primitive. Conversely, if $a^{p-1} \not\equiv 1$ (modulo p^2), Theorem 1.2.4F and Lemma P tell us that $a^{(p-1)p^{e-2}} \not\equiv 1$ (modulo p^e), but $a^{(p-1)p^{e-1}} \equiv 1$ (modulo p^e). So the order is a divisor of $(p-1)p^{e-1}$ but not of $(p-1)p^{e-2}$; it therefore has the form kp^{e-1}, where k divides $p-1$. But if a is primitive modulo p, the congruence $a^{kp^{e-1}} \equiv a^k \equiv 1$ (modulo p) implies that $k = p - 1$.

13. Suppose a mod $p \ne 0$, and let λ be the order of a modulo p. By Theorem 1.2.4F, λ is a divisor of $p - 1$. If $\lambda < p - 1$, then $(p-1)/\lambda$ has a prime factor, q.

14. Let $0 < k < p$. If $a^{p-1} \equiv 1$ (modulo p^2), then $(a + kp)^{p-1} \equiv a^{p-1} + (p-1)a^{p-2}kp$ (modulo p^2); and this is $\not\equiv 1$, since $(p-1)a^{p-2}k$ is not a multiple of p. By exercise 12, $a + kp$ is primitive modulo p^e.

15. (a) If $\lambda_1 = p_1^{e_1} \ldots p_t^{e_t}$ and $\lambda_2 = p_1^{f_1} \ldots p_t^{f_t}$, let $\kappa_1 = p_1^{g_1} \ldots p_t^{g_t}$ and $\kappa_2 = p_1^{h_1} \ldots p_t^{h_t}$, where

$$g_j = e_j \quad \text{and} \quad h_j = 0, \qquad \text{if} \quad e_j < f_j,$$
$$g_j = 0 \quad \text{and} \quad h_j = f_j, \qquad \text{if} \quad e_j \ge f_j.$$

Now $a_1^{\kappa_1}$ and $a_2^{\kappa_2}$ have periods λ_1/κ_1 and λ_2/κ_2, and the latter are relatively prime. Furthermore $(\lambda_1/\kappa_1)(\lambda_2/\kappa_2) = \lambda$, so it suffices to consider the case when λ_1 is relatively prime to λ_2, that is, when $\lambda = \lambda_1\lambda_2$. Now let λ' be the order of a_1a_2. Since $(a_1a_2)^{\lambda'} \equiv 1$, we have $1 \equiv (a_1a_2)^{\lambda'\lambda_1} \equiv a_2^{\lambda'\lambda_1}$; hence $\lambda'\lambda_1$ is a multiple of λ_2. This implies that λ' is a multiple of λ_2, since λ_1 is relatively prime to λ_2. Similarly, λ' is a multiple of λ_1; hence λ' is a multiple of $\lambda_1\lambda_2$. But obviously $(a_1a_2)^{\lambda_1\lambda_2} \equiv 1$, so $\lambda' = \lambda_1\lambda_2$.

(b) If a_1 has order $\lambda(m)$ and if a_2 has order λ, by part (a) $\lambda(m)$ must be a multiple of λ, otherwise we could find an element of higher order, namely of order $\mathrm{lcm}(\lambda, \lambda(m))$.

16. (a) $f(x) = (x - a)(x^{n-1} + (a + c_1)x^{n-2} + \cdots + (a^{n-1} + \cdots + c_{n-1})) + f(a)$.
(b) The statement is clear when $n = 0$. If a is one root, $f(x) \equiv (x - a)q(x)$; therefore, if a' is any other root,

$$0 \equiv f(a') \equiv (a' - a)q(a'),$$

and since $a' - a$ is not a multiple of p, a' must be a root of $q(x)$. So if $f(x)$ has more than n distinct roots, $q(x)$ has more than $n - 1$ distinct roots. [J. L. Lagrange, *Mém. Acad. Roy. Sci. Berlin* **24** (1768), 181–250, §10.] (c) $\lambda(p) \geq p-1$, since $f(x)$ must have degree $\geq p-1$ in order to possess so many roots. But $\lambda(p) \leq p-1$ by Theorem 1.2.4F.

17. By Lemma P, $11^5 \equiv 1$ (modulo 25), $11^5 \not\equiv 1$ (modulo 125), etc.; so the order of 11 is 5^{e-1} (modulo 5^e), not the maximum value $\lambda(5^e) = 4 \cdot 5^{e-1}$. But by Lemma Q the total period length is the least common multiple of the period modulo 2^e (namely 2^{e-2}) and the period modulo 5^e (namely 5^{e-1}), and this is $2^{e-2}5^{e-1} = \lambda(10^e)$. The period modulo 5^e may be 5^{e-1} or $2 \cdot 5^{e-1}$ or $4 \cdot 5^{e-1}$, without affecting the length of period modulo 10^e, since the least common multiple is taken. The values that are primitive modulo 5^e are those congruent to 2, 3, 8, 12, 13, 17, 22, 23 modulo 25 (see exercise 12), namely 3, 13, 27, 37, 53, 67, 77, 83, 117, 123, 133, 147, 163, 173, 187, 197.

18. According to Theorem C, $a \bmod 8$ must be 3 or 5. Knowing the period of a modulo 5 and modulo 25 allows us to apply Lemma P to determine admissible values of $a \bmod 25$. Period $= 4 \cdot 5^{e-1}$: 2, 3, 8, 12, 13, 17, 22, 23; period $= 2 \cdot 5^{e-1}$: 4, 9, 14, 19; period $= 5^{e-1}$: 6, 11, 16, 21. Each of these 16 values yields one value of a, $0 \leq a < 200$, with $a \bmod 8 = 3$, and another value of a with $a \bmod 8 = 5$.

19. Several examples appear in lines 17–20 of Table 3.3.4–1.

20. (a) We have $AY_n + X_0 \equiv AY_{n+k} + X_0$ (modulo m) if and only if $Y_n \equiv Y_{n+k}$ (modulo m'). (b)(i) Obvious. (ii) Theorem A. (iii) $(a^n - 1)/(a - 1) \equiv 0$ (modulo 2^e) if and only if $a^n \equiv 1$ (modulo 2^{e+1}); if $a \not\equiv -1$, the order of a modulo 2^{e+1} is twice its order modulo 2^e. (iv) $(a^n - 1)/(a - 1) \equiv 0$ (modulo p^e) if and only if $a^n \equiv 1$.

21. $X_{n+s} \equiv X_n + X_s$ by Eq. 3.2.1–(6); and s is a divisor of m, since s is a power of p when m is a power of p. Hence a given integer q is a multiple of m/s if and only if $X_{qs} \equiv 0$, if and only if q is a multiple of $m/\gcd(X_s, m)$.

22. Algorithm 4.5.4P is able to test numbers of the form $m = b^k \pm b^l \pm 1$ for primality in a reasonable time when, say, $b \approx 2^{32}$ and $l < k \approx 100$; the calculations should be done in radix b so that the special form of m speeds up the operation of squaring mod m. (Consider, for example, squaring mod 9999998999 in decimal notation.) Algorithm 4.5.4P should, of course, be used only when m is known to have no small divisors.

Marsaglia and Zaman [*Annals of Applied Probability* **1** (1991), 474–475] showed that $m = b^{43} - b^{22} + 1$ is prime with primitive root b when b is the prime number $2^{32} - 5$. This required factoring $m-1 = b^{22}(b-1)(b^6+b^5+b^4+b^3+b^2+b+1)(b^{14}+b^7+1)$ in order to establish the primitivity of b; one of the 17 prime factors of $m - 1$ has 99 decimal digits. As a result, we can be sure that the sequence $x_n = (x_{n-22} - x_{n-43} - c_n) \bmod b =$

$x_{n-22} - x_{n-43} - c_n + bc_{n+1}$ has period length $m - 1 \approx 10^{414}$ for every nonzero choice of seed values $0 \le x_{-1}, \ldots, x_{-43} < b$ when $c_0 = 0$.

However, 43 is still a rather small value for k from the standpoint of the birthday spacings test (see Section 3.3.2J), and 22 is rather near $43/2$. Considerations of "mixing" indicate that we prefer values of k and l for which the first few partial quotients in the continued fraction of l/k are small. To avoid potential problems with this generator, it's a good idea to discard some of the numbers, as recommended by Lüscher (see Section 3.2.2).

Here are some prime numbers of the form $b^k \pm b^l \pm 1$ that satisfy the mixing constraint when $b = 2^{32}$ and $50 < k \le 100$: For subtract-with-borrow, $b^{57} - b^{17} - 1$, $b^{73} - b^{17} - 1$, $b^{86} - b^{62} - 1$, $b^{88} - b^{52} - 1$, $b^{95} - b^{61} - 1$; $b^{58} - b^{33} + 1$, $b^{62} - b^{17} + 1$, $b^{69} - b^{24} + 1$, $b^{70} - b^{57} + 1$, $b^{87} - b^{24} + 1$. For add-with-carry, $b^{56} + b^{22} - 1$, $b^{61} + b^{44} - 1$, $b^{74} + b^{27} - 1$, $b^{90} + b^{65} - 1$. (Less desirable from a mixing standpoint are the primes $b^{56} - b^5 - 1$, $b^{56} - b^{32} - 1$, $b^{66} - b^{57} - 1$, $b^{76} - b^{15} - 1$, $b^{84} - b^{26} - 1$, $b^{90} - b^{42} - 1$, $b^{93} - b^{18} - 1$; $b^{52} - b^8 + 1$, $b^{60} - b^{12} + 1$, $b^{67} - b^8 + 1$, $b^{67} - b^{63} + 1$, $b^{83} - b^{14} + 1$; $b^{65} + b^2 - 1$, $b^{76} + b^{11} - 1$, $b^{88} + b^{30} - 1$, $b^{92} + b^{48} - 1$.)

To calculate the period of the resulting sequences, we need to know the factors of $m - 1$; but this isn't feasible for such large numbers unless we are extremely lucky. Suppose we do succeed in finding the prime factors $q_1, \ldots, q_t$; then the probability that $b^{(m-1)/q} \bmod m = 1$ is extremely small, only $1/q$, except for the very small primes q. Therefore we can be quite confident that the period of $b^n \bmod m$ is extremely long even though we cannot factor $m - 1$.

Indeed, the period is almost certainly very long even if m is not prime. Consider, for example, the case $k = 10$, $l = 3$, $b = 10$ (which is much too small for random number generation but small enough that we can easily compute the exact results). In this case $\langle 10^n \bmod m \rangle$ has period length $\operatorname{lcm}(219, 11389520) = 2494304880$ when $m = 9999998999 = 439 \cdot 22779041$; 4999999500 when $m = 9999999001$; 5000000499 when $m = 10000000999$; and $\operatorname{lcm}(1, 16, 2686, 12162) = 130668528$ when $m = 10000001001 = 3 \cdot 17 \cdot 2687 \cdot 72973$. Rare choices of the seed values may shorten the period when m is not prime. But we can hardly go wrong if we choose, say, $k = 1000$, $l = 619$, and $b = 2^{16}$.

SECTION 3.2.1.3

1. $c = 1$ is always relatively prime to B^5; and every prime dividing $m = B^5$ is a divisor of B, so it divides $b = B^2$ to at least the second power.

2. Only 3, so the generator is not recommended in spite of its long period.

3. The potency is 18 in both cases (see the next exercise).

4. Since $a \bmod 4 = 1$, we must have $a \bmod 8 = 1$ or 5, so $b \bmod 8 = 0$ or 4. If b is an odd multiple of 4, and if b_1 is a multiple of 8, clearly $b^s \equiv 0$ (modulo 2^e) implies that $b_1^s \equiv 0$ (modulo 2^e), so b_1 cannot have higher potency than b.

5. The potency is the smallest value of s such that $f_j s \ge e_j$ for all j.

6. The modulus must be divisible by 2^7 or by p^4 (for odd prime p) in order to have a potency as high as 4. The only values are $m = 2^{27} + 1$ and $10^9 - 1$.

7. $a' = (1 - b + b^2 - \cdots) \bmod m$, where the terms in b^s, b^{s+1}, etc., are dropped (if s is the potency).

8. Since X_n is always odd,

$$X_{n+2} = (2^{34} + 3 \cdot 2^{18} + 9)X_n \bmod 2^{35} = (2^{34} + 6X_{n+1} - 9X_n) \bmod 2^{35}.$$

Given Y_n and Y_{n+1}, the possibilities for

$$Y_{n+2} \approx (10 + 6(Y_{n+1} + \epsilon_1) - 9(Y_n + \epsilon_2)) \bmod 20,$$

with $0 \le \epsilon_1 < 1$, $0 \le \epsilon_2 < 1$, are limited and nonrandom.

Note: If the multiplier suggested in exercise 3 were, say, $2^{33} + 2^{18} + 2^2 + 1$, instead of $2^{23} + 2^{13} + 2^2 + 1$, we would similarly find $X_{n+2} - 10X_{n+1} + 25X_n \equiv$ constant (modulo 2^{35}). In general, we do not want $a \pm \delta$ to be divisible by high powers of 2 when δ is small, else we get "second-order impotency." See Section 3.3.4 for a more detailed discussion.

The generator that appears in this exercise is discussed in an article by MacLaren and Marsaglia, *JACM* **12** (1965), 83–89. The deficiencies of such generators were first demonstrated by M. Greenberger, *CACM* **8** (1965), 177–179. Yet generators like this were still in widespread use more than ten years later (see the discussion of RANDU in Section 3.3.4).

SECTION 3.2.2

1. The method is useful only with great caution. In the first place, aU_n is likely to be so large that the addition of c/m that follows will lose almost all significance, and the "mod 1" operation will nearly destroy any vestiges of significance that might remain. We conclude that double-precision floating point arithmetic is necessary. Even with double precision, one must be sure that no rounding, etc., occurs to affect the numbers of the sequence in any way, since that would destroy the theoretical grounds for the good behavior of the sequence. (But see exercise 23.)

2. X_{n+1} equals either $X_{n-1} + X_n$ or $X_{n-1} + X_n - m$. If $X_{n+1} < X_n$ we must have $X_{n+1} = X_{n-1} + X_n - m$; hence $X_{n+1} < X_{n-1}$.

3. (a) The underlined numbers are $V[j]$ after step M3.

Output: initial	0 4 5 6 2 0 3(2 7 4 1 6 3 0 5) and repeats.
$V[0]$: 0	4 7 7 7 7 7 7 7 4 7 7 7 7 7 7 7 4 7 ...
$V[1]$: 3	3 3 3 3 3 3 2 5 5 5 5 5 5 5 2 5 5 5 ...
$V[2]$: 2	2 2 2 2 0 3 3 3 3 3 3 3 0 3 3 3 3 3 ...
$V[3]$: 5	5 5 6 1 1 1 1 1 1 1 6 1 1 1 1 1 1 1 ...
X:	4 7 6 1 0 3 2 5 4 7 6 1 0 3 2 5 4 7 ...
Y:	0 1 6 7 4 5 2 3 0 1 6 7 4 5 2 3 0 1 ...

So the potency has been reduced to 1! (See further comments in the answer to exercise 15.)

(b) The underlined numbers are $V[j]$ after step B2.

Output: initial	2 3 6 5 7 0 0 5 3 ... 4 6(3 0 ... 4 7)...
$V[0]$: 0	0 0 0 0 0 0 5 4 4 ... 1 1 1 1 ... 1 1 ...
$V[1]$: 3	3 6 1 1 1 1 1 1 1 ... 0 0 0 4 ... 0 0 ...
$V[2]$: 2	7 7 7 7 3 3 3 3 7 ... 6 2 2 2 ... 7 2 ...
$V[3]$: 5	5 5 5 0 0 2 2 2 2 ... 3 3 5 5 ... 3 3 ...
X: 4	7 6 1 0 3 2 5 4 7 ... 3 2 5 4 ... 3 2 ...

In this case the output is considerably better than the input; it enters a repeating cycle of length 40 after 46 steps: 236570 05314 72632 40110 37564 76025 12541 73625 03746 (30175 24061 52317 46203 74531 60425 16753 02647). The cycle can be found easily by applying the method of exercise 3.1–7 to the array above until a column is repeated.

4. The low-order byte of many random sequences (e.g., linear congruential sequences with m = word size) is much less random than the high-order byte. See Section 3.2.1.1.

5. The randomizing effect would be quite minimized, because $V[j]$ would always contain a number in a certain range, essentially $j/k \leq V[j]/m < (j+1)/k$. However, some similar approaches could be used: We could take $Y_n = X_{n-1}$, or we could choose j from X_n by extracting some digits from the middle instead of at the extreme left. None of these suggestions would produce a lengthening of the period analogous to the behavior of Algorithm B. (Exercise 27 shows, however, that Algorithm B doesn't necessarily increase the period length.)

6. For example, if $X_n/m < \frac{1}{2}$, then $X_{n+1} = 2X_n$.

7. [W. Mantel, *Nieuw Archief voor Wiskunde* (2) **1** (1897), 172–184.]

The subsequence of X values:	00...01 00...10 . . . 10...00 CONTENTS(A)	becomes:	00...01 00...10 . . . 10...00 00...00 CONTENTS(A)

8. We may assume that $X_0 = 0$ and $m = p^e$, as in the proof of Theorem 3.2.1.2A. First suppose that the sequence has period length p^e; it follows that the period of the sequence mod p^f has length p^f, for $1 \leq f \leq e$, otherwise some residues mod p^f would never occur. Clearly, c is not a multiple of p, for otherwise each X_n would be a multiple of p. If $p \leq 3$, it is easy to establish the necessity of conditions (iii) and (iv) by trial and error, so we may assume that $p \geq 5$. If $d \not\equiv 0$ (modulo p) then $dx^2 + ax + c \equiv d(x + a_1)^2 + c_1$ (modulo p^e) for some integers a_1 and c_1 and for all integers x; this quadratic takes the same value at the points x and $-x - 2a_1$, so it cannot assume all values modulo p^e. Hence $d \equiv 0$ (modulo p); and if $a \not\equiv 1$, we would have $dx^2 + ax + c \equiv x$ (modulo p) for some x, contradicting the fact that the sequence mod p has period length p.

To show the sufficiency of the conditions, we may assume by Theorem 3.2.1.2A and consideration of some trivial cases that $m = p^e$ where $e \geq 2$. If $p = 2$, we have $X_{n+2} \equiv X_n + 2$ (modulo 4), by trial; and if $p = 3$, we have $X_{n+3} \equiv X_n - d + 3c$ (modulo 9), using (i) and (ii). For $p \geq 5$, we can prove that $X_{n+p} \equiv X_n + pc$ (modulo p^2): Let $d = pr$, $a = 1 + ps$. Then if $X_n \equiv cn + pY_n$ (modulo p^2), we must have $Y_{n+1} \equiv n^2 c^2 r + ncs + Y_n$ (modulo p); hence $Y_n \equiv \binom{n}{3} 2c^2 r + \binom{n}{2}(c^2 r + cs)$ (modulo p). Thus Y_p mod $p = 0$, and the desired relation has been proved.

Now we can prove that the sequence $\langle X_n \rangle$ of integers defined in the "hint" satisfies the relation

$$X_{n+p^f} \equiv X_n + tp^f \pmod{p^{f+1}}, \qquad n \geq 0,$$

for some t with $t \bmod p \neq 0$, and for all $f \geq 1$. This suffices to prove that the sequence $\langle X_n \bmod p^e \rangle$ has period length p^e, for the length of the period is a divisor of p^e but not a divisor of p^{e-1}. The relation above has already been established for $f = 1$, and for $f > 1$ it can be proved by induction in the following manner: Let

$$X_{n+p^f} \equiv X_n + tp^f + Z_n p^{f+1} \pmod{p^{f+2}};$$

then the quadratic law for generating the sequence, with $d = pr$, $a = 1 + ps$, yields $Z_{n+1} \equiv 2rtnc + st + Z_n$ (modulo p). It follows that $Z_{n+p} \equiv Z_n$ (modulo p); hence

$$X_{n+kp^f} \equiv X_n + k(tp^f + Z_n p^{f+1}) \pmod{p^{f+2}}$$

for $k = 1, 2, 3, \ldots$; setting $k = p$ completes the proof.

   Notes: If $f(x)$ is a polynomial of degree higher than 2 and $X_{n+1} = f(X_n)$, the analysis is more complicated, although we can use the fact that $f(m + p^k) = f(m) + p^k f'(m) + p^{2k} f''(m)/2! + \cdots$ to prove that many polynomial recurrences give the maximum period. For example, Coveyou has proved that the period is $m = 2^e$ if $f(0)$ is odd, $f'(j) \equiv 1$, $f''(j) \equiv 0$, and $f(j+1) \equiv f(j) + 1$ (modulo 4) for $j = 0, 1, 2, 3$. [*Studies in Applied Math.* **3** (Philadelphia: SIAM, 1969), 70–111.]

   9. Let $X_n = 4Y_n + 2$; then the sequence Y_n satisfies the quadratic recurrence $Y_{n+1} = (4Y_n^2 + 5Y_n + 1) \bmod 2^{e-2}$.

   10. *Case 1:* $X_0 = 0$, $X_1 = 1$; hence $X_n \equiv F_n$. We seek the smallest n for which $F_n \equiv 0$ and $F_{n+1} \equiv 1$ (modulo 2^e). Since $F_{2n} = F_n(F_{n-1} + F_{n+1})$, $F_{2n+1} = F_n^2 + F_{n+1}^2$, we find by induction on e that, for $e > 1$, $F_{3 \cdot 2^{e-1}} \equiv 0$ and $F_{3 \cdot 2^{e-1}+1} \equiv 2^e + 1$ (modulo 2^{e+1}). This implies that the period is a divisor of $3 \cdot 2^{e-1}$ but not a divisor of $3 \cdot 2^{e-2}$, so it is either $3 \cdot 2^{e-1}$ or 2^{e-1}. But F_{2^e-1} is always odd (since only F_{3n} is even).

   Case 2: $X_0 = a$, $X_1 = b$. Then $X_n \equiv aF_{n-1} + bF_n$; we need to find the smallest positive n with $a(F_{n+1} - F_n) + bF_n \equiv a$ and $aF_n + bF_{n+1} \equiv b$. This implies that $(b^2 - ab - a^2)F_n \equiv 0$, $(b^2 - ab - a^2)(F_{n+1} - 1) \equiv 0$. And $b^2 - ab - a^2$ is odd (that is, prime to m); so the condition is equivalent to $F_n \equiv 0$, $F_{n+1} \equiv 1$.

   Methods to determine the period of $\langle F_n \rangle$ for any modulus appear in an article by D. D. Wall, *AMM* **67** (1960), 525–532. Further facts about the Fibonacci sequence mod 2^e have been derived by B. Jansson [*Random Number Generators* (Stockholm: Almqvist & Wiksell, 1966), Section 3C1].

   11. (a) We have $z^\lambda = 1 + f(z)u(z) + p^e v(z)$ for some $u(z)$ and $v(z)$, where $v(z) \not\equiv 0$ (modulo $f(z)$ and p). By the binomial theorem,

$$z^{\lambda p} = 1 + p^{e+1} v(z) + p^{2e+1} v(z)^2 (p-1)/2$$

plus further terms congruent to zero (modulo $f(z)$ and p^{e+2}). Since $p^e > 2$, we have $z^{\lambda p} \equiv 1 + p^{e+1} v(z)$ (modulo $f(z)$ and p^{e+2}). If $p^{e+1} v(z) \equiv 0$ (modulo $f(z)$ and p^{e+2}), there must exist polynomials $a(z)$ and $b(z)$ such that $p^{e+1}(v(z) + pa(z)) = f(z)b(z)$. Since $f(0) = 1$, this implies that $b(z)$ is a multiple of p^{e+1} (by Gauss's Lemma 4.6.1G); hence $v(z) \equiv 0$ (modulo $f(z)$ and p), a contradiction.

   (b) If $z^\lambda - 1 = f(z)u(z) + p^e v(z)$, then

$$G(z) = u(z)/(z^\lambda - 1) + p^e v(z)/f(z)(z^\lambda - 1);$$

hence $A_{n+\lambda} \equiv A_n$ (modulo p^e) for large n. Conversely, if $\langle A_n \rangle$ has the latter property then $G(z) = u(z) + v(z)/(1 - z^\lambda) + p^e H(z)$, for some polynomials $u(z)$ and $v(z)$, and some power series $H(z)$, all with integer coefficients. This implies the identity $1 - z^\lambda = u(z)f(z)(1 - z^\lambda) + v(z)f(z) + p^e H(z)f(z)(1 - z^\lambda)$; and $H(z)f(z)(1 - z^\lambda)$ is a polynomial since the other terms of the equation are polynomials.

   (c) It suffices to prove that $\lambda(p^e) \neq \lambda(p^{e+1})$ implies that $\lambda(p^{e+1}) = p\lambda(p^e) \neq \lambda(p^{e+2})$. Applying (a) and (b), we know that $\lambda(p^{e+2}) \neq p\lambda(p^e)$, and that $\lambda(p^{e+1})$ is a divisor of $p\lambda(p^e)$ but not of $\lambda(p^e)$. Hence if $\lambda(p^e) = p^f q$, where $q \bmod p \neq 0$, then $\lambda(p^{e+1})$ must be $p^{f+1}d$, where d is a divisor of q. But now $X_{n+p^{f+1}d} \equiv X_n$ (modulo p^e); hence $p^{f+1}d$ is a multiple of $p^f q$, hence $d = q$. [*Note:* The hypothesis $p^e > 2$ is necessary; for example, let $a_1 = 4$, $a_2 = -1$, $k = 2$; then $\langle A_n \rangle = 1, 4, 15, 56, 209, 780,$ $\ldots$; $\lambda(2) = 2$, $\lambda(4) = 4$, $\lambda(8) = 4$.]

(d) $g(z) = X_0 + (X_1 - a_1 X_0)z + \cdots + (X_{k-1} - a_1 X_{k-2} - a_2 X_{k-3} - \cdots - a_{k-1} X_0)z^{k-1}$.

(e) The derivation in (b) can be generalized to the case $G(z) = g(z)/f(z)$; then the assumption of period length λ implies that $g(z)(1 - z^\lambda) \equiv 0$ (modulo $f(z)$ and p^e); we treated only the special case $g(z) = 1$ above. But both sides of this congruence can be multiplied by Hensel's $b(z)$, and we obtain $1 - z^\lambda \equiv 0$ (modulo $f(z)$ and p^e).

Note: A more "elementary" proof of the result in (c) can be given without using generating functions, using methods analogous to those in the answer to exercise 8: If $A_{\lambda+n} = A_n + p^e B_n$, for $n = r, r+1, \ldots, r+k-1$ and some integers B_n, then this same relation holds for *all* $n \geq r$ if we define $B_{r+k}, B_{r+k+1}, \ldots$ by the given recurrence relation. Since the resulting sequence of B's is some linear combination of shifts of the sequence of A's, we will have $B_{\lambda+n} \equiv B_n$ (modulo p^e) for all large enough values of n. Now $\lambda(p^{e+1})$ must be some multiple of $\lambda = \lambda(p^e)$; for all large enough n we have $A_{n+j\lambda} = A_n + p^e(B_n + B_{n+\lambda} + B_{n+2\lambda} + \cdots + B_{n+(j-1)\lambda}) \equiv A_n + jp^e B_n$ (modulo p^{2e}) for $j = 1, 2, 3, \ldots$. No k consecutive B's are multiples of p; hence $\lambda(p^{e+1}) = p\lambda(p^e) \neq \lambda(p^{e+2})$ follows immediately when $e \geq 2$. We still must prove that $\lambda(p^{e+2}) \neq p\lambda(p^e)$ when p is odd and $e = 1$; here we let $B_{\lambda+n} = B_n + pC_n$, and observe that $C_{n+\lambda} \equiv C_n$ (modulo p) when n is large enough. Then $A_{n+p} \equiv A_n + p^2 \left(B_n + \binom{p}{2} C_n \right)$ (modulo p^3), and the proof is readily completed.

For the history of this problem, see Morgan Ward, *Trans. Amer. Math. Soc.* **35** (1933), 600–628; see also D. W. Robinson, *AMM* **73** (1966), 619–621.

12. The period length mod 2 can be at most 4; and the period length mod 2^{e+1} is at most twice the maximum length mod 2^e, by the considerations of the previous exercise. So the maximum conceivable period length is 2^{e+1}; this is achievable, for example, in the trivial case $a = 0$, $b = c = 1$.

13, 14. Clearly $Z_{n+\lambda} = Z_n$, so λ' is certainly a divisor of λ. Let the least common multiple of λ' and λ_1 be λ_1', and define λ_2' similarly. We have $X_n + Y_n \equiv Z_n \equiv Z_{n+\lambda_1'} \equiv X_n + Y_{n+\lambda_1'}$, so λ_1' is a multiple of λ_2. Similarly, λ_2' is a multiple of λ_1. This yields the desired result. (The result is "best possible" in the sense that sequences for which $\lambda' = \lambda_0$ can be constructed, as well as sequences for which $\lambda' = \lambda$.)

15. Algorithm M generates (X_{n+k}, Y_n) in step M1 and outputs $Z_n = X_{n+k-q_n}$ in step M3, for all sufficiently large n. Thus $\langle Z_n \rangle$ has a period of length λ', where λ' is the least positive integer such that $X_{n+k-q_n} = X_{n+\lambda'+k-q_{n+\lambda'}}$ for all large n. Since λ is a multiple of λ_1 and λ_2, it follows that λ' is a divisor of λ. (These observations are due to Alan G. Waterman.)

We also have $n + k - q_n \equiv n + \lambda' + k - q_{n+\lambda'}$ (modulo λ_1) for all large n, by the distinctness of the X's. The bound on $\langle q_n \rangle$ implies that $q_{n+\lambda'} = q_n + c$ for all large n, where $c \equiv \lambda'$ (modulo λ_1) and $|c| < \frac{1}{2}\lambda_1$. But c must be 0 since $\langle q_n \rangle$ is bounded. Hence $\lambda' \equiv 0$ (modulo λ_1), and $q_{n+\lambda'} = q_n$ for all large n; it follows that λ' is a multiple of λ_2 and λ_1, so $\lambda' = \lambda$.

Note: The answer to exercise 3.2.1.2–4 implies that when $\langle Y_n \rangle$ is a linear congruential sequence of maximum period modulo $m = 2^e$, the period length λ_2 will be at most 2^{e-2} when k is a power of 2.

16. There are several methods of proof.

(1) Using the theory of finite fields. In the field with 2^k elements let ξ satisfy $\xi^k = a_1 \xi^{k-1} + \cdots + a_k$. Let $f(b_1 \xi^{k-1} + \cdots + b_k) = b_k$, where each b_j is either zero

or one; this is a linear function. If word X in the generation algorithm is $(b_1 b_2 \ldots b_k)_2$ before (10) is executed, and if $b_1 \xi^{k-1} + \cdots + b_k \xi^0 = \xi^n$, then word X represents ξ^{n+1} after (10) is executed. Hence the sequence is $f(\xi^n)$, $f(\xi^{n+1})$, $f(\xi^{n+2})$, $\ldots$; and $f(\xi^{n+k}) = f(\xi^n \xi^k) = f(a_1 \xi^{n+k-1} + \cdots + a_k \xi^n) = a_1 f(\xi^{n+k-1}) + \cdots + a_k f(\xi^n)$.

(2) Using brute force, or elementary ingenuity. We are given a sequence X_{nj}, $n \geq 0$, $1 \leq j \leq k$, satisfying

$$X_{(n+1)j} \equiv X_{n(j+1)} + a_j X_{n1}, \quad 1 \leq j < k; \qquad X_{(n+1)k} \equiv a_k X_{n1} \pmod{2}.$$

We must show that this implies $X_{nk} \equiv a_1 X_{(n-1)k} + \cdots + a_k X_{(n-k)k}$, for $n \geq k$. Indeed, it implies $X_{nj} \equiv a_1 X_{(n-1)j} + \cdots + a_k X_{(n-k)j}$ when $1 \leq j \leq k \leq n$. This is clear for $j = 1$, since $X_{n1} \equiv a_1 X_{(n-1)1} + X_{(n-1)2} \equiv a_1 X_{(n-1)1} + a_2 X_{(n-2)1} + X_{(n-2)3}$, etc. For $j > 1$, we have by induction

$$\begin{aligned}
X_{nj} &\equiv X_{(n+1)(j-1)} - a_{j-1} X_{n1} \\
&\equiv \sum_{1 \leq i \leq k} a_i X_{(n+1-i)(j-1)} - a_{j-1} \sum_{1 \leq i \leq k} a_i X_{(n-i)1} \\
&\equiv \sum_{1 \leq i \leq k} a_i \left(X_{(n+1-i)(j-1)} - a_{j-1} X_{(n-i)1} \right) \\
&\equiv a_1 X_{(n-1)j} + \cdots + a_k X_{(n-k)j}.
\end{aligned}$$

This proof does *not* depend on the fact that operations were done modulo 2, or modulo any prime number.

17. (a) When the sequence terminates, the $(k-1)$-tuple $(X_{n+1}, \ldots, X_{n+k-1})$ occurs for the $(m+1)$st time. A given $(k-1)$-tuple $(X_{r+1}, \ldots, X_{r+k-1})$ can have only m distinct predecessors X_r, so one of these occurrences must be for $r = 0$. (b) Since the $(k-1)$-tuple $(0, \ldots, 0)$ occurs $(m+1)$ times, each possible predecessor appears, so the k-tuple $(a_1, 0, \ldots, 0)$ appears for all a_1, $0 \leq a_1 < m$. Let $1 \leq s < k$ and suppose we have proved that all k-tuples $(a_1, \ldots, a_s, 0, \ldots, 0)$ appear in the sequence when $a_s \neq 0$. By the construction, this k-tuple would not be in the sequence unless $(a_1, \ldots, a_s, 0, \ldots, 0, y)$ had appeared earlier for $1 \leq y < m$. Hence the $(k-1)$-tuple $(a_1, \ldots, a_s, 0, \ldots, 0)$ has appeared m times, and all m possible predecessors appear; this means that $(a, a_1, \ldots, a_s, 0, \ldots, 0)$ appears for $0 \leq a < m$. The proof is now complete by induction.

The result also follows from Theorem 2.3.4.2D, using the directed graph of exercise 2.3.4.2–23; the set of arcs from $(x_1, \ldots, x_j, 0, \ldots, 0)$ to $(x_2, \ldots, x_j, 0, 0, \ldots, 0)$, where $x_j \neq 0$ and $1 \leq j \leq k$, forms an oriented subtree related neatly to Dewey decimal notation.

18. By exercise 16, the most significant bit of U_{n+1} is completely determined by the first and third bits of U_n, so only 32 of the 64 possible pairs $(\lfloor 8U_n \rfloor, \lfloor 8U_{n+1} \rfloor)$ occur. [*Notes:* If we had used, say, 11-bit numbers $U_n = (.X_{11n} X_{11n+1} \ldots X_{11n+10})_2$, the sequence *would* be satisfactory for many applications. If another constant appears in A having more 1 bits, the generalized spectral test might give some indication of its suitability. See exercise 3.3.4–24; we could examine ν_t in dimensions $t = 36, 37, 38, \ldots$.]

21. [*J. London Math. Soc.* **21** (1946), 169–172.] Any sequence of period length $m^k - 1$ with no k consecutive zeros leads to a sequence of period length m^k by inserting a zero in the appropriate place, as in exercise 7; conversely, we can start with a sequence of period length m^k and delete an appropriate zero from the period, to form a sequence of the other type. Let us call these "(m, k) sequences" of types A and B. The hypothesis assures us of the existence of (p, k) sequences of type A, for all primes p and all $k \geq 1$; hence we have (p, k) sequences of type B for all such p and k.

To get a (p^e, k) sequence of type B, let $e = qr$, where q is a power of p and r is not a multiple of p. Start with a (p, qrk) sequence of type A, namely $X_0, X_1, X_2, \ldots$; then (using the p-ary number system) the grouped digits $(X_0 \ldots X_{q-1})_p, (X_q \ldots X_{2q-1})_p, \ldots$ form a (p^q, rk) sequence of type A, since q is relatively prime to $p^{qrk} - 1$ and the sequence therefore has a period length of $p^{qrk} - 1$. This leads to a (p^q, rk) sequence $\langle Y_n \rangle$ of type B; and $(Y_0 Y_1 \ldots Y_{r-1})_{p^q}, (Y_r Y_{r+1} \ldots Y_{2r-1})_{p^q}, \ldots$ is a (p^{qr}, k) sequence of type B by a similar argument, since r is relatively prime to p^{qk}.

To get an (m, k) sequence of type B for arbitrary m, we can combine (p^e, k) sequences for each of the prime power factors of m using the Chinese remainder theorem; but a simpler method is available. Let $\langle X_n \rangle$ be an (r, k) sequence of type B, and let $\langle Y_n \rangle$ be an (s, k) sequence of type B, where r and s are relatively prime; then $\langle (X_n + Y_n) \bmod rs \rangle$ is an (rs, k) sequence of type B, by exercise 13.

A simple, uniform construction that yields $(2, k)$ sequences for arbitrary k has been discovered by A. Lempel [*IEEE Trans.* **C-19** (1970), 1204–1209].

22. By the Chinese remainder theorem, we can find constants $a_1, \ldots, a_k$ having desired residues modulo each prime divisor of m. If $m = p_1 p_2 \ldots p_t$, the period length will be $\mathrm{lcm}(p_1^k - 1, \ldots, p_t^k - 1)$. In fact, we can achieve reasonably long periods for arbitrary m (not necessarily squarefree), as shown in exercise 11.

23. Subtraction may be faster than addition, see exercise 3.2.1.1–5; the period length is still $2^{e-1}(2^{55} - 1)$, by exercise 30. R. Brent has pointed out that the calculations can be done exactly on floating point numbers in $[0 .. 1)$; see exercise 3.6–11.

24. Run the sequence backwards. In other words, if $Z_n = Y_{-n}$ we have $Z_n = (Z_{n-k+l} - Z_{n-k}) \bmod 2 = (Z_{n-k+l} + Z_{n-k}) \bmod 2$.

25. This idea can save most of the overhead of subroutine calls. For example, suppose Program A is invoked by calling `JMP RANDM`, where we have

```
      RANDM STJ   1F
            LDA   Y,6
              ⋮                } Program A
            ENT6  55
      1H    JMP   *          ▮
```

The cost per random number is then $14 + \frac{2}{55}$ units of time. But suppose we generate random numbers by saying 'DEC6 1; J6Z RNGEN; LDA Y,6' instead, with the subroutine

```
      RNGEN STJ   1F              ENT6 31
            ENT6  24              LDA  Y,6
            LDA   Y+31,6          ADD  Y+24,6
            ADD   Y,6             STA  Y,6
            STA   Y+31,6          DEC6 1
            DEC6  1               J6P  *-4
            J6P   *-4             ENT6 55
                           1H     JMP  *      ▮
```

The cost is now only $(12 + \frac{6}{55})u$. [A similar implementation, expressed in the C language, is used in *The Stanford GraphBase* (New York: ACM Press, 1994), GB_FLIP.] Indeed, many applications find it preferable to generate an array of random numbers all at once. Moreover, the latter approach is essentially mandatory when we enhance the randomness with Lüscher's method; see the C and FORTRAN routines in Section 3.6.

27. Let $J_n = \lfloor kX_n/m \rfloor$. **Lemma.** *After the* $(k^2 + 7k - 2)/2$ *consecutive values*

$$0^{k+2}\ 1\ 0^{k+1}\ 2\ 0^k\ \ldots\ (k-1)\ 0^3$$

occur in the $\langle J_n \rangle$ *sequence, Algorithm B will have* $V[j] < m/k$ *for* $0 \le j < k$, *and also* $Y < m/k$. *Proof.* Let S_n be the set of positions j such that $V[j] < m/k$ just before X_n is generated, and let j_n be the index such that $V[j_n] \leftarrow X_n$. If $j_n \notin S_n$ and $J_n = 0$, then $S_{n+1} = S_n \cup \{j_n\}$ and $j_{n+1} > 0$; if $j_n \in S_n$ and $J_n = 0$, then $S_{n+1} = S_n$ and $j_{n+1} = 0$. After $k+2$ successive 0s, we must therefore have $0 \in S_n$ and $j_{n+1} = 0$. Then after "1 0^{k+1}" we must have $\{0,1\} \subseteq S_n$ and $j_{n+1} = 0$; after "2 0^k" we must have $\{0,1,2\} \subseteq S_n$ and $j_{n+1} = 0$; and so on.

Corollary. Let $l = (k^2 + 7k - 2)/2$. *If* $\lambda \geq lk^l$, *either Algorithm B yields a period of length* λ *or the sequence* $\langle X_n \rangle$ *is poorly distributed. Proof.* The probability that any given length-l pattern of J's does not occur in a random sequence of length λ is less than $(1 - k^{-l})^{\lambda/l} < \exp(-k^{-l}\lambda/l) \le e^{-1}$; hence the stated pattern should appear. After it does, the subsequent behavior of Algorithm B will be the same each time it reaches this part of the period. (When $k > 4$, we are requiring $\lambda > 10^{21}$, so this result is purely academic. But smaller bounds may be possible.)

29. The following algorithm performs about k^2 operations in the worst case, but its average running time is much faster, perhaps $O(\log k)$ or even $O(1)$:

X1. Set $(a_0, a_1, \ldots, a_k) \leftarrow (x_1, \ldots, x_k, m-1)$.

X2. Let i be minimum with $a_i > 0$ and $i > 0$. Do subroutine Y for $j = i+1$, $\ldots$, k, while $a_k > 0$.

X3. If $a_0 > a_k$, $f(x_1, \ldots, x_k) = a_0$; otherwise if $a_0 > 0$, $f(x_1, \ldots, x_k) = a_0 - 1$; otherwise $f(x_1, \ldots, x_k) = a_k$. ∎

Y1. Set $l \leftarrow 0$. (The subroutine in steps Y1–Y3 essentially tests the lexicographic relation $(a_i, \ldots, a_{i+k-1}) \geq (a_j, \ldots, a_{j+k-1})$, decreasing a_k if necessary to make this inequality true. We assume that $a_{k+1} = a_1$, $a_{k+2} = a_2$, etc.)

Y2. If $a_{i+l} > a_{j+l}$, exit the subroutine. Otherwise if $j + l = k$, set $a_k \leftarrow a_{i+l}$. Otherwise if $a_{i+l} = a_{j+l}$, go on to step Y3. Otherwise if $j + l > k$, decrease a_k by 1 and exit. Otherwise set $a_k \leftarrow 0$ and exit.

Y3. Increase l by 1, and return to step Y2 if $l < k$. ∎

This problem was first solved by H. Fredricksen when $m = 2$ [*J. Combinatorial Theory* **9** (1970), 1–5; **A12** (1972), 153–154]; in that special case the algorithm is simpler and it can be done with k-bit registers. See also H. Fredricksen and J. Maiorana, *Discrete Math.* **23** (1978), 207–210, who essentially discovered Algorithm 7.2.1.1F.

30. (a) By exercise 11, it suffices to show that the period length mod 8 is $4(2^k - 1)$; this will be true if and only if $x^{2(2^k-1)} \not\equiv 1$ (modulo 8 and $f(x)$), if and only if $x^{2^k-1} \not\equiv 1$ (modulo 4 and $f(x)$). Write $f(x) = f_e(x^2) + xf_o(x^2)$, where $f_e(x^2) = \frac{1}{2}(f(x) + f(-x))$. Then $f(x)^2 + f(-x)^2 \equiv 2f(x^2)$ (modulo 8) if and only if $f_e(x)^2 + xf_o(x)^2 \equiv f(x)$ (modulo 4); and the latter condition holds if and only if $f_e(x)^2 \equiv -xf_o(x)^2$ (modulo 4 and $f(x)$), because $f_e(x)^2 + xf_o(x)^2 = f(x) + O(x^{k-1})$. Furthermore, working modulo 2 and $f(x)$, we have $f_e(x)^2 \equiv f_e(x^2) \equiv xf_o(x^2) \equiv x^{2^k}f_o(x)^2$, hence $f_e(x) \equiv x^{2^{k-1}}f_o(x)$. Therefore $f_e(x)^2 \equiv x^{2^k}f_o(x)^2$ (modulo 4 and $f(x)$), and the hint follows. A similar argument proves that $x^{2^k} \equiv x$ (modulo 4 and $f(x)$) if and only if $f(x)^2 + f(-x)^2 \equiv 2(-1)^k f(-x^2)$ (modulo 8).

(b) The condition can hold only when l is odd and $k = 2l$. But then $f(x)$ is primitive modulo 2 only when $k = 2$. [*Math. Comp.* **63** (1994), 389–401.]

31. We have $X_n \equiv (-1)^{Y_n} 3^{Z_n} \bmod 2^e$ for some Y_n and Z_n, by Theorem 3.2.1.2C; hence $Y_n = (Y_{n-24} + Y_{n-55}) \bmod 2$ and $Z_n = (Z_{n-24} + Z_{n-55}) \bmod 2^{e-2}$. Since Z_k is odd if and only if $X_k \bmod 8 = 3$ or 5, the period length is $2^{e-3}(2^{55} - 1)$ by the previous exercise.

32. We can ignore the 'mod m' and put it back afterwards. The generating function $g(z) = \sum_n X_n z^n$ is a polynomial multiple of $1/(1 - z^{24} - z^{55})$; hence $\sum_n X_{2n} z^{2n} = \frac{1}{2}(g(z) + g(-z))$ is a polynomial divided by $(1 - z^{24} - z^{55})(1 - z^{24} + z^{55}) = 1 - 2z^{24} + z^{48} - z^{110}$. The first desired recurrence is therefore $X_{2n} = (2X_{2(n-12)} - X_{2(n-24)} + X_{2(n-55)}) \bmod m$. Similarly, $\sum_n X_{3n} z^{3n} = \frac{1}{3}(g(z) + g(\omega z) + g(\omega^2 z))$ where $\omega = e^{2\pi i/3}$, and we find $X_{3n} = (3X_{3(n-8)} - 3X_{3(n-16)} + X_{3(n-24)} + X_{3(n-55)}) \bmod m$.

33. (a) $g_{n+t}(z) \equiv z^t g_n(z)$ (modulo m and $1 + z^{31} - z^{55}$), by induction on t. (b) Since $z^{500} \bmod (1 + z^{31} - z^{55}) = 792z^2 + z^5 + 17z^6 + 715z^9 + 36z^{12} + z^{13} + 364z^{16} + 210z^{19} + 105z^{23} + 462z^{26} + 16z^{30} + 1287z^{33} + 9z^{36} + 18z^{37} + 1001z^{40} + 120z^{43} + z^{44} + 455z^{47} + 462z^{50} + 120z^{54}$ (see Algorithm 4.6.1D), we have $X_{500} = (792X_2 + X_5 + \cdots + 120X_{54}) \bmod m$.

[It is interesting to compare the similar formula $X_{165} = (X_0 + 3X_7 + X_{14} + 3X_{31} + 4X_{38} + X_{45}) \bmod m$ to the sparser recurrence for $\langle X_{3n} \rangle$ in the previous exercise. Lüscher's method of generating 165 numbers and using only the first 55 is clearly superior to the idea of generating 165 and using only $X_3, X_6, \ldots, X_{165}$.]

34. Let $q_0 = 0$, $q_1 = 1$, $q_{n+1} = cq_n + aq_{n-1}$. Then we have $\begin{pmatrix} 0 & 1 \\ a & c \end{pmatrix}^n = \begin{pmatrix} aq_{n-1} & q_n \\ aq_n & q_{n+1} \end{pmatrix}$, $X_n = (q_{n+1}X_0 + aq_n)/(q_n X_0 + aq_{n-1})$, and $x^n \bmod f(x) \equiv q_n x + aq_{n-1}$, for $n \geq 1$. Thus if $X_0 = 0$ we have $X_n = 0$ if and only if $x^n \bmod f(x)$ is a nonzero constant.

35. Conditions (i) and (ii) imply that $f(x)$ is irreducible. For if $f(x) = (x - r_1)(x - r_2)$ and $r_1 r_2 \neq 0$ we have $x^{p-1} \equiv 1$ if $r_1 \neq r_2$ and $x^p \equiv r_1$ if $r_1 = r_2$.

Let ξ be a primitive root of a field with p^2 elements, and suppose $\xi^{2k} = c_k \xi^k + a_k$. The quadratic polynomials we seek are precisely the polynomials $f_k(x) = x^2 - c_k x - a_k$ where $1 \leq k < p^2 - 1$ and $k \perp p + 1$. (See exercise 4.6.2–16.) Each polynomial occurs for two values of k; hence the number of solutions is $\frac{1}{2}(p^2 - 1) \prod_{q \backslash p+1, \, q \text{ prime}} (1 - 1/q)$.

36. In this case X_n is always odd, so X_n^{-1} exists mod 2^e. The sequence $\langle q_n \rangle$ defined in answer 34 is 0, 1, 2, 1, 0, 1, 2, 1, ... modulo 4. We also have $q_{2n} = q_n(q_{n+1} + aq_{n-1})$ and $q_{2n-1} = aq_{n-1}^2 + q_n^2$; hence $q_{2n+1} - aq_{2n-1} = (q_{n+1} - aq_{n-1})(q_{n+1} + aq_{n+1})$. Since $q_{n+1} + aq_{n+1} \equiv 2$ (modulo 4) when n is even, we deduce that q_{2^e} is an odd multiple of 2^e and $q_{2^e+1} - aq_{2^e-1}$ is an odd multiple of 2^{e+1}, for all $e \geq 0$. Therefore

$$q_{2^e} + aq_{2^e-1} \equiv q_{2^e+1} + aq_{2^e} + 2^{e+1} \quad (\text{modulo } 2^{e+2}).$$

And $X_{2^{e}-2} \equiv (q_{2^{e-2}+1} + aq_{2^{e-2}})/(q_{2^{e-2}} + aq_{2^{e-2}-1}) \not\equiv 1$ (modulo 2^e), while $X_{2^{e}-1} \equiv 1$. Conversely, we need $a \bmod 4 = 1$ and $c \bmod 4 = 2$; otherwise $X_{2n} \equiv 1$ (modulo 8). [Eichenauer, Lehn, and Topuzoğlu, *Math. Comp.* **51** (1988), 757–759.] The low-order bits of this sequence have a short period, so inversive generators with prime modulus are preferable.

37. We can assume that $b_1 = 0$. By exercise 34, a typical vector in V is

$$(x, (s_2' x + as_2)/(s_2 x + as_2''), \ldots, (s_d' x + as_d)/(s_d x + as_d'')),$$

where $s_j = q_{b_j}$, $s_j' = q_{b_j+1}$, $s_j'' = q_{b_j-1}$. This vector belongs to the hyperplane H if and only if

$$r_1 x + \frac{r_2 t_2}{x + u_2} + \cdots + \frac{r_d t_d}{x + u_d} \equiv r_0 - r_2 s_2' s_2^{-1} - \cdots - r_d s_d' s_d^{-1} \quad (\text{modulo } p),$$

where $t_j = a - a s'_j s''_j s_j^{-2} = -(-a)^{b_j} s_j^{-2}$ and $u_j = a s''_j s_j^{-1}$. But this relation is equivalent to a polynomial congruence of degree $\leq d$; so it cannot hold for $d+1$ values of x unless it holds for all x, including the distinct points $x = u_2, \ldots, x = u_d$. Hence $r_2 = \cdots = r_d \equiv 0$, and $r_1 \equiv 0$. [See J. Eichenauer-Herrmann, *Math. Comp.* **56** (1991), 297–301.]

Notes: If we consider the $(p+1-d) \times (d+1)$ matrix M with rows $\{(1, v_1, \ldots, v_d) \mid (v_1, \ldots, v_d) \in V\}$, this exercise is equivalent to the assertion that any $d+1$ rows of M are linearly independent modulo p. It is interesting to plot the points (X_n, X_{n+1}) for $p \approx 1000$ and $0 \leq n \leq p$; traces of circles, rather than straight lines, meet the eye.

SECTION 3.3.1

1. There are $k = 11$ categories, so the line $\nu = 10$ should be used.

2. $\frac{2}{49}, \frac{3}{49}, \frac{4}{49}, \frac{5}{49}, \frac{6}{49}, \frac{9}{49}, \frac{6}{49}, \frac{5}{49}, \frac{4}{49}, \frac{3}{49}, \frac{2}{49}$.

3. $V = 7\frac{173}{240}$, only very slightly higher than that obtained from the good dice! There are two reasons why we do not detect the weighting: (a) The new probabilities (see exercise 2) are not really very far from the old ones in Eq. (1). The sum of the two dice tends to smooth out the probabilities; if we counted instead each of the 36 possible pairs of values, we would probably detect the difference quite rapidly (assuming that the two dice are distinguishable). (b) A far more important reason is that n is too small for a significant difference to be detected. If the same experiment is done for large enough n, the faulty dice will be discovered (see exercise 12).

4. $p_s = \frac{1}{12}$ for $2 \leq s \leq 12$ and $s \neq 7$; $p_7 = \frac{1}{6}$. The value of V is $16\frac{1}{2}$, which falls between the 75% and 95% entries in Table 1; so it is reasonable, in spite of the fact that not too many sevens actually turned up.

5. $K_{20}^+ = 1.15$; $K_{20}^- = 0.215$; these values do not differ significantly from random behavior (being at about the 94% and 86% levels), but they are mighty close. (The data values in this exercise come from Appendix A, Table 1.)

6. The probability that $X_j \leq x$ is $F(x)$, so we have the binomial distribution discussed in Section 1.2.10: $F_n(x) = s/n$ with probability $\binom{n}{s} F(x)^s (1 - F(x))^{n-s}$; the mean is $F(x)$; the standard deviation is $\sqrt{F(x)(1 - F(x))/n}$. [See Eq. 1.2.10–(19). This suggests that a slightly better statistic would be to define

$$K_n^+ = \sqrt{n} \max_{-\infty < x < \infty} \big(F_n(x) - F(x)\big) / \sqrt{F(x)(1 - F(x))};$$

see exercise 22. We can calculate the mean and standard deviation of $F_n(y) - F_n(x)$, for $x < y$, and obtain the covariance of $F_n(x)$ and $F_n(y)$. Using these facts, it can be shown that for large values of n the function $F_n(x)$ behaves as a "Brownian motion," and techniques from this branch of probability theory may be used to study it. The situation is exploited in articles by J. L. Doob and M. D. Donsker, *Annals Math. Stat.* **20** (1949), 393–403 and **23** (1952), 277–281; their approach is generally regarded as the most enlightening way to study the KS tests.]

7. Set $j = n$ in Eq. (13) to see that K_n^+ is never negative, and that it can get as high as $\sqrt{n}$. Similarly, set $j = 1$ to make the same observations about K_n^-.

8. The new KS statistic was computed for 20 observations. The distribution of K_{10}^+ was used as $F(x)$ when the KS statistic was computed.

9. The idea is erroneous, because all of the observations must be *independent*. There is a relation between the statistics K_n^+ and K_n^- on the same data, so each test should be judged separately. (A high value of one tends to give a low value of the other.) Similarly, the entries in Figs. 2 and 5, which show 15 tests for each generator, do not show 15 independent observations, because the maximum-of-5 test is not independent of the maximum-of-4 test. The three tests of each horizontal row are independent (because they were done on different parts of the sequence), but the five tests in a column are somewhat correlated. The net effect of this is that the 95-percent probability levels, etc., which apply to one test, cannot legitimately be applied to a whole group of tests on the same data. Moral: When testing a random number generator, we may expect it to "pass" each of several tests, like the frequency test, maximum test, and run test; but an array of data from several different tests should not be considered as a unit since the tests themselves may not be independent. The K_n^+ and K_n^- statistics should be considered as two separate tests; a good source of random numbers will pass both.

10. Each Y_s is doubled, and np_s is doubled, so the numerators of (6) are quadrupled while the denominators only double. Hence the new value of V is twice as high as the old one.

11. The empirical distribution function stays the same; the values of K_n^+ and K_n^- are multiplied by $\sqrt{2}$.

12. Let $Z_s = (Y_s - nq_s)/\sqrt{nq_s}$. The value of V is n times

$$\sum_{s=1}^{k} (q_s - p_s + \sqrt{q_s/n} Z_s)^2 / p_s,$$

and the latter quantity stays bounded away from zero as n increases (since $Z_s n^{-1/4}$ is bounded with probability 1). Hence the value of V will increase to a value that is extremely improbable under the p_s assumption.

For the KS test, let $F(x)$ be the assumed distribution, $G(x)$ the actual distribution, and let $h = \max|G(x) - F(x)|$. Take n large enough so that $|F_n(x) - G(x)| > h/2$ occurs with very small probability; then $|F_n(x) - F(x)|$ will be improbably high under the assumed distribution $F(x)$.

13. (The "max" notation should really be replaced by "sup" since a least upper bound is meant; however, "max" was used in the text to avoid confusing too many readers by the less familiar "sup" notation.) For convenience, let $X_0 = -\infty$, $X_{n+1} = +\infty$. When $X_j \le x < X_{j+1}$, we have $F_n(x) = j/n$; therefore $\max(F_n(x) - F(x)) = j/n - F(X_j)$ and $\max(F(x) - F_n(x)) = F(X_{j+1}) - j/n$ in this interval. As j varies from 0 to n, all real values of x are considered; this proves that

$$K_n^+ = \sqrt{n} \max_{0 \le j \le n} \left(\frac{j}{n} - F(X_j) \right);$$

$$K_n^- = \sqrt{n} \max_{1 \le j \le n+1} \left(F(X_j) - \frac{j-1}{n} \right).$$

These equalities are equivalent to (13), since the extra term under the maximum signs is nonpositive and it must be redundant by exercise 7.

14. The logarithm of the left-hand side simplifies to

$$-\sum_{s=1}^{k} Y_s \ln\left(1 + \frac{Z_s}{\sqrt{np_s}} \right) + \frac{1-k}{2} \ln(2\pi n) - \frac{1}{2} \sum_{s=1}^{k} \ln p_s - \frac{1}{2} \sum_{s=1}^{k} \ln\left(1 + \frac{Z_s}{\sqrt{np_s}} \right) + O\left(\frac{1}{n} \right),$$

and this quantity simplifies further (upon expanding $\ln(1 + Z_s/\sqrt{np_s})$ and realizing that $\sum_{s=1}^{k} Z_s \sqrt{np_s} = 0$) to

$$-\frac{1}{2}\sum_{s=1}^{k} Z_s^2 + \frac{1-k}{2}\ln(2\pi n) - \frac{1}{2}\ln(p_1 \ldots p_k) + O\left(\frac{1}{\sqrt{n}}\right).$$

15. The corresponding Jacobian determinant is easily evaluated by (i) removing the factor r^{n-1} from the determinant, (ii) expanding the resulting determinant by the cofactors of the row containing "$\cos\theta_1 \ -\sin\theta_1 \ 0 \ldots 0$" (each of the cofactor determinants may be evaluated by induction), and (iii) recalling that $\sin^2\theta_1 + \cos^2\theta_1 = 1$.

16. $\displaystyle\int_0^{z\sqrt{2x}+y} \exp\left(-\frac{u^2}{2x} + \cdots\right) du = ye^{-z^2} + O\left(\frac{1}{\sqrt{x}}\right) + \int_0^{z\sqrt{2x}} \exp\left(-\frac{u^2}{2x} + \cdots\right) du.$

The latter integral is

$$\int_0^{z\sqrt{2x}} e^{-u^2/2x}\, du + \frac{1}{3x^2}\int_0^{z\sqrt{2x}} e^{-u^2/2x} u^3 \, du + O\left(\frac{1}{\sqrt{x}}\right).$$

When all is put together, the final result is

$$\frac{\gamma(x+1,\, x+z\sqrt{2x}+y)}{\Gamma(x+1)} = \frac{1}{\sqrt{2\pi}}\int_{-\infty}^{z\sqrt{2}} e^{-u^2/2}\, du + \frac{e^{-z^2}}{\sqrt{2\pi x}}(y - \tfrac{2}{3} - \tfrac{2}{3}z^2) + O\left(\frac{1}{x}\right).$$

If we set $z\sqrt{2} = x_p$ and write

$$\frac{1}{\sqrt{2\pi}}\int_{-\infty}^{z\sqrt{2}} e^{-u^2/2}\, du = p, \qquad x + 1 = \frac{\nu}{2}, \qquad \gamma\left(\frac{\nu}{2},\frac{t}{2}\right)\Big/\Gamma\left(\frac{\nu}{2}\right) = p,$$

where $t/2 = x + z\sqrt{2x} + y$, we can solve for y to obtain $y = \frac{2}{3}(1 + z^2) + O(1/\sqrt{x})$, which is consistent with the analysis above. The solution is therefore $t = \nu + 2\sqrt{\nu}z + \frac{4}{3}z^2 - \frac{2}{3} + O(1/\sqrt{\nu})$.

17. (a) Change of variable, $x_j \leftarrow x_j + t$.
    (b) Induction on n; by definition, $P_{n0}(x-t) = \displaystyle\int_n^x P_{(n-1)0}(x_n - t)\, dx_n$.
    (c) The left-hand side is

$$\int_n^{x+t} dx_n \cdots \int_{k+1}^{x_{k+2}} dx_{k+1} \quad \text{times} \quad \int_t^k dx_k \int_t^{x_k} dx_{k-1} \cdots \int_t^{x_2} dx_1.$$

    (d) From (b) and (c) we have $P_{nk}(x) = \displaystyle\sum_{r=0}^{k} \frac{(r-t)^r}{r!}\frac{(x+t-r)^{n-r-1}}{(n-r)!}(x+t-n).$
The numerator in (24) is $P_{n\lfloor t\rfloor}(n)$.

18. We may assume that $F(x) = x$ for $0 \le x \le 1$, as remarked in the text's derivation of (24). If $0 \le X_1 \le \cdots \le X_n \le 1$, let $Z_j = 1 - X_{n+1-j}$. We have $0 \le Z_1 \le \cdots \le Z_n \le 1$; and K_n^+ evaluated for $X_1, \ldots, X_n$ equals K_n^- evaluated for $Z_1, \ldots, Z_n$. This symmetrical relation gives a one-to-one correspondence between sets of equal volume for which K_n^+ and K_n^- fall in a given range.

20. For example, the term $O(1/n)$ is $-(\frac{4}{9}s^4 - \frac{2}{3}s^2)/n + O(n^{-3/2})$. A complete expansion has been obtained by H. A. Lauwerier, *Zeitschrift für Wahrscheinlichkeitstheorie und verwandte Gebiete* **2** (1963), 61–68.

23. Let m be any number $\geq n$. (a) If $\lfloor mF(X_i)\rfloor = \lfloor mF(X_j)\rfloor$ and $i > j$, then $i/n - F(X_i) > j/n - F(X_j)$. (b) Start with $a_k = 1.0$, $b_k = 0.0$, and $c_k = 0$ for $0 \leq k < m$. Then do the following for each observation X_j: Set $Y \leftarrow F(X_j)$, $k \leftarrow \lfloor mY\rfloor$, $a_k \leftarrow \min(a_k, Y)$, $b_k \leftarrow \max(b_k, Y)$, $c_k \leftarrow c_k + 1$. (Assume that $F(X_j) < 1$ so that $k < m$.) Then set $j \leftarrow 0$, $r^+ \leftarrow r^- \leftarrow 0$, and for $k = 0, 1, \ldots, m - 1$ (in this order) do the following whenever $c_k > 0$: Set $r^- \leftarrow \max(r^-, a_k - j/n)$, $j \leftarrow j + c_k$, $r^+ \leftarrow \max(r^+, j/n - b_k)$. Finally set $K_n^+ \leftarrow \sqrt{n}\,r^+$, $K_n^- \leftarrow \sqrt{n}\,r^-$. The time required is $O(m+n)$, and the precise value of n need not be known in advance. (If the estimate $(k + \frac12)/m$ is used for a_k and b_k, so that only the values c_k are actually computed for each k, we obtain estimates of K_n^+ and K_n^- good to within $\frac12\sqrt{n}/m$, even when $m < n$.) [*ACM Trans. Math. Software* **3** (1977), 60–64.]

25. (a) Since $c_{ij} = \mathrm{E}(\sum_{k=1}^{n} a_{ik}X_k \sum_{l=1}^{n} a_{jl}X_l) = \sum_{k=1}^{n} a_{ik}a_{jk}$, we have $C = AA^T$.

(b) Consider the singular value decomposition $A = UDV^T$, where U and V are orthogonal of sizes $m \times m$ and $n \times n$, and D is $m \times n$ with entries $d_{ij} = [i=j]\sigma_j$; the singular values σ_j are all positive. [See, for example, Golub and Van Loan, *Matrix Computations* (1996), §2.5.3.] If $C\bar{C}C = C$ we have $SBS = S$, where $S = DD^T$ and $B = U^T\bar{C}U$. Thus $s_{ij} = [i=j]\sigma_j^2$, where we let $\sigma_{n+1} = \cdots = \sigma_m = 0$, and $s_{ij} = \sum_{k,l} s_{ik}b_{kl}s_{lj} = \sigma_i^2\sigma_j^2 b_{ij}$. Consequently $b_{ij} = [i=j]/\sigma_j^2$ if $i, j \leq n$, and we deduce that D^TBD is the $n \times n$ identity matrix. Let $Y = (Y_1 - \mu_1, \ldots, Y_m - \mu_m)^T$ and $X = (X_1, \ldots, X_n)^T$; it follows that $W = Y^T\bar{C}Y = X^TA^T\bar{C}AX = X^TVD^TBDV^TX = X^TX$.

SECTION 3.3.2

1. The observations for a chi-square test must be independent. In the second sequence, successive observations are manifestly dependent, since the second component of one equals the first component of the next.

2. Form t-tuples $(Y_{jt}, \ldots, Y_{jt+t-1})$, for $0 \leq j < n$, and count how many of them are equal to each possible value. Apply the chi-square test with $k = d^t$ and with probability $1/d^t$ in each category. The number of observations, n, should be at least $5d^t$.

3. The probability that exactly j values are examined, namely the probability that U_{j-1} is the nth element that lies in the range $\alpha \leq U_{j-1} < \beta$, is easily seen to be

$$\binom{j-1}{n-1} p^n (1-p)^{j-n},$$

by enumeration of the possible places in which the other $n - 1$ occurrences can appear and by evaluation of the probability of such a pattern. The generating function is $G(z) = \big(pz/(1 - (1 - p)z)\big)^n$, which makes sense since the given distribution is the n-fold convolution of the same thing for $n = 1$. Hence the mean and variance are proportional to n; the number of U's to be examined is now easily found to have the characteristics $\big(\min n, \text{ave } n/p, \max \infty, \text{dev } \sqrt{n(1-p)}/p\big)$. A more detailed discussion of this probability distribution when $n = 1$ may be found in the answer to exercise 3.4.1–17; see also the considerably more general results of exercise 2.3.4.2–26.

4. The probability of a gap of length $\geq r$ is the probability that r consecutive U's lie outside the given range, namely $(1 - p)^r$. The probability of a gap of length exactly r is the probability for length $\geq r$ minus the probability for length $\geq (r + 1)$.

5. As N goes to infinity, so does n (with probability 1), hence this test is just the same as the gap test described in the text except for the length of the very last gap.

And the text's gap test certainly is asymptotic to the chi-square distribution stated, since the length of each gap is independent of the length of the others. [*Notes:* A quite complicated proof of this result by E. Bofinger and V. J. Bofinger appears in *Annals Math. Stat.* **32** (1961), 524–534. Their paper is noteworthy because it discusses several interesting variations of the gap test; they show, for example, that the quantity

$$\sum_{0 \le r \le t} \frac{(Y_r - (Np)p_r)^2}{(Np)p_r}$$

does *not* approach a chi-square distribution, although others had suggested this statistic as a "stronger" test because Np is the expected value of n.]

7. 5, 3, 5, 6, 5, 5, 4.

8. See exercise 10, with $w = d$.

9. (Change d to w in steps C1 and C4.) We have

$$p_r = \frac{d(d-1)\dots(d-w+1)}{d^r} \left\{ {r-1 \atop w-1} \right\}, \qquad \text{for } w \le r < t;$$

$$p_t = 1 - \frac{d!}{d^{t-1}} \left(\frac{1}{0!} \left\{ {t-1 \atop d} \right\} + \dots + \frac{1}{(d-w)!} \left\{ {t-1 \atop w} \right\} \right).$$

10. As in exercise 3, we really need consider only the case $n = 1$. The generating function for the probability that a coupon set has length r is

$$G(z) = \frac{d!}{(d-w)!} \sum_{r>0} \left\{ {r-1 \atop w-1} \right\} \left(\frac{z}{d} \right)^r = z^w \left(\frac{d-1}{d-z} \right) \dots \left(\frac{d-w+1}{d-(w-1)z} \right)$$

by the previous exercise and Eq. 1.2.9–(28). The mean and variance are readily computed using Theorem 1.2.10A and exercise 3.4.1–17. We find that

$$\text{mean}(G) = w + \left(\frac{d}{d-1} - 1 \right) + \dots + \left(\frac{d}{d-w+1} - 1 \right) = d(H_d - H_{d-w}) = \mu;$$

$$\text{var}(G) = d^2 (H_d^{(2)} - H_{d-w}^{(2)}) - d(H_d - H_{d-w}) = \sigma^2.$$

The number of U's examined, as the search for a coupon set is repeated n times, therefore has the characteristics $(\min wn, \text{ ave } \mu n, \max \infty, \text{ dev } \sigma\sqrt{n})$.

11. $\left| 1 \left| 2 \right| 9 \ \ 8 \ \ 5 \ \ 3 \left| 6 \right| 7 \ \ 0 \left| 4 \right| \right.$.

12. Algorithm R (*Data for run test*).

R1. [Initialize.] Set $j \leftarrow -1$, and set COUNT[1] $\leftarrow$ COUNT[2] $\leftarrow \dots \leftarrow$ COUNT[6] $\leftarrow 0$. Also set $U_n \leftarrow U_{n-1}$, for convenience in terminating the algorithm.

R2. [Set r zero.] Set $r \leftarrow 0$.

R3. [Is $U_j < U_{j+1}$?] Increase r and j by 1. If $U_j < U_{j+1}$, repeat this step.

R4. [Record the length.] If $r \ge 6$, increase COUNT[6] by one, otherwise increase COUNT[r] by one.

R5. [Done?] If $j < n - 1$, return to step R2. ∎

13. There are $(p+q+1)\binom{p+q}{p}$ ways to have $U_{i-1} \gtreqless U_i < \dots < U_{i+p-1} \gtreqless U_{i+p} < \dots < U_{i+p+q-1}$; subtract $\binom{p+q+1}{p+1}$ for those ways in which $U_{i-1} < U_i$, and subtract $\binom{p+q+1}{1}$ for those in which $U_{i+p-1} < U_{i+p}$; then add in 1 for the case that both $U_{i-1} < U_i$ and $U_{i+p-1} < U_{i+p}$, since this case has been subtracted out twice. (This is a special case of the inclusion-exclusion principle, which is explained further in Section 1.3.3.)

14. A run of length r occurs with probability $1/r! - 1/(r+1)!$, assuming distinct U's. Therefore we use $p_r = 1/r! - 1/(r+1)!$ for $r < t$ and $p_t = 1/t!$ for runs of length $\geq t$.

15. This is always true of $F(X)$ when F is continuous and X has distribution F; see the remarks following Eq. 3.3.1–(23).

16. (a) $Z_{jt} = \max(Z_{j(t-1)}, Z_{(j+1)(t-1)})$. If the $Z_{j(t-1)}$ are stored in memory, it is therefore a simple matter to transform this array into the set of Z_{jt} with no auxiliary storage required. (b) With his "improvement," each of the V's should indeed have the stated distribution, but the observations are no longer independent. In fact, when U_j is a relatively large value, all of $Z_{jt}, Z_{(j-1)t}, \ldots, Z_{(j-t+1)t}$ will be equal to U_j; so we almost have the effect of repeating the same data t times (and that would multiply V by t, as in exercise 3.3.1–10).

17. (b) By Binet's identity, the difference is $\sum_{0 \leq k < j < n}(U_k'V_j' - U_j'V_k')^2$, and this is certainly nonnegative. (c) Therefore if $D^2 = N^2$, we must have $U_k'V_j' - U_j'V_k' = 0$, for all pairs j, k. This means that the matrix

$$\begin{pmatrix} U_0' & U_1' & \cdots & U_{n-1}' \\ V_0' & V_1' & \cdots & V_{n-1}' \end{pmatrix}$$

has rank < 2, so its rows are linearly dependent. (A more elementary proof can be given, using the fact that $U_0'V_j' - U_j'V_0' = 0$ for $1 \leq j < n$ implies the existence of constants α, β such that $\alpha U_j' + \beta V_j' = 0$ for all j, provided that U_0' and V_0' are not both zero; the latter case can be avoided by a suitable renumbering.)

18. (a) The numerator is $-(U_0 - U_1)^2$, the denominator is $(U_0 - U_1)^2$. (b) The numerator in this case is $-(U_0^2 + U_1^2 + U_2^2 - U_0U_1 - U_1U_2 - U_2U_0)$; the denominator is $2(U_0^2 + \cdots - U_2U_0)$. (c) The denominator always equals $\sum_{0 \leq j < k < n}(U_j - U_k)^2$, by exercise 1.2.3–30 or 1.2.3–31.

19. The stated result holds, in fact, whenever the joint distribution of $U_0, \ldots, U_{n-1}$ is symmetrical (unchanged under permutations). Let $S_1 = U_0 + \cdots + U_{n-1}$, $S_2 = U_0^2 + \cdots + U_{n-1}^2$, $X = U_0U_1 + \cdots + U_{n-2}U_{n-1} + U_{n-1}U_0$, and $D = nS_2 - S_1^2$. Also let $\mathrm{E}\, f(U_0, \ldots, U_{n-1})$ denote the expected value of $f(U_0, \ldots, U_{n-1})$ subject to the condition $D \neq 0$. Since D is a symmetric function, we have $\mathrm{E}\, f(U_0, \ldots, U_{n-1}) = \mathrm{E}\, f(U_{p(0)}, \ldots, U_{p(n-1)})$ for all permutations p of $\{0, \ldots, n-1\}$. Therefore $\mathrm{E}\, S_2/D = n\,\mathrm{E}\, U_0^2/D$, $\mathrm{E}\, S_1^2/D = n(n-1)\,\mathrm{E}(U_0U_1/D) + n\,\mathrm{E}\, U_0^2/D$, and $\mathrm{E}\, X/D = n\,\mathrm{E}(U_0U_1/D)$. It follows that $1 = \mathrm{E}\,(nS_2 - S_1^2)/D = -(n-1)\,\mathrm{E}\,(nX - S_1^2)/D$. (Strictly speaking, $\mathrm{E}\, S_2/D$ and $\mathrm{E}\, S_1^2/D$ might be infinite, so we should be careful to work only with linear combinations of expected values that are known to exist.)

20. Let $E_{1111}, E_{211}, E_{22}, E_{31}$, and E_4 denote the respective values $\mathrm{E}(U_0U_1U_2U_3/D^2)$, $\mathrm{E}(U_0^2U_1U_2/D^2)$, $\mathrm{E}(U_0^2U_1^2/D^2)$, $\mathrm{E}(U_0^3U_1/D^2)$, $\mathrm{E}(U_0^4/D^2)$. Then we have $\mathrm{E}\, S_2^2/D^2 = n(n-1)E_{22} + nE_4$, $\mathrm{E}(S_2S_1^2/D^2) = n(n-1)(n-2)E_{211} + n(n-1)E_{22} + 2n(n-1)E_{31} + nE_4$, $\mathrm{E}\, S_1^4/D^2 = n(n-1)(n-2)(n-3)E_{1111} + 6n(n-1)(n-2)E_{211} + 3n(n-1)E_{22} + 4n(n-1)E_{31} + nE_4$, $\mathrm{E}\, X^2/D^2 = n(n-3)E_{1111} + 2nE_{211} + nE_{22}$, $\mathrm{E}(XS_1^2/D^2) = n(n-2)(n-3)E_{1111} + 5n(n-2)E_{211} + 2nE_{22} + 2nE_{31}$, $\mathrm{E}((U_0 - U_1)^4/D^2) = 6E_{22} - 8E_{31} + 2E_4$, and the first result follows.

Let $\delta = \alpha((\ln n)/n)^{1/3}$, $M = \alpha^3/2 + 1/3$, and $m = \lceil 1/\delta \rceil$. If we divide the range of the distribution into m equiprobable parts, we can show that each part will contain between $n\delta(1 - \delta)$ and $n\delta(1 + \delta)$ points, with probability $\geq 1 - O(n^{-M})$, using the tail inequalities 1.2.10–(24) and (25). Hence, if the distribution is uniform, $D = \frac{1}{12}n^2(1 + O(\delta))$ with at least this probability. If D is not in that range, we have

$0 \leq (U_0 - U_1)^4/D^2 \leq 1$. Since $\mathrm{E}((U_0 - U_1)^4) = \int_0^1 \int_0^1 (x - y)^4 \, dx \, dy = \frac{1}{15}$, we may conclude that $\mathrm{E}((U_0 - U_1)^4/D^2) = \frac{48}{5} n^{-4}(1 + O(\delta)) + O(n^{-M})$.

Note: Let N be the numerator of (23). When the variables all have the normal distribution, W. J. Dixon proved that the expected value of $e^{(wN+zD)/n}$ is

$$(1 - 2z - 2w)^{1/2}(1 - 2z + \sqrt{(1-2z)^2 - 4w^2}\,)^{-n/2} + O(w^n).$$

Differentiating with respect to w and integrating with respect to z, he found the moments $\mathrm{E}(N/D)^{2k-1} = (-\frac{1}{2})^{\overline{k}}/(n - \frac{1}{2})^{\overline{k}}$, $\mathrm{E}(N/D)^{2k} = (+\frac{1}{2})^{\overline{k}}/(n + \frac{1}{2})^{\overline{k}}$, when $n > 2k$. In particular, the variance in this case is exactly $1/(n + 1) - 1/(n - 1)^2$. [*Annals of Math. Stat.* **15** (1944), 119–144.]

21. The successive values of $c_{r-1} = s - 1$ in step P2 are 2, 3, 7, 6, 4, 2, 2, 1, 0; hence $f = 886862$.

22. $1024 = 6! + 2 \cdot 5! + 2 \cdot 4! + 2 \cdot 3! + 2 \cdot 2! + 0 \cdot 1!$, so we want the successive values of $s - 1$ in step P2 to be 0, 0, 0, 1, 2, 2, 2, 2, 0; working backwards, the permutation is $(9, 6, 5, 2, 3, 4, 0, 1, 7, 8)$.

23. Let $P'(x_1, \ldots, x_t) = \frac{1}{\lambda'} \sum_{n=0}^{\lambda'-1} [(Y'_n, \ldots, Y'_{n+t-1}) = (x_1, \ldots, x_t)]$. Then we have

$$Q(x_1, \ldots, x_t) = \sum_{(y_1, \ldots, y_t)} P'(y_1, \ldots, y_t) P((x_1 - y_1) \bmod d, \ldots, (x_t - y_t) \bmod d);$$

more compactly, $Q(x) = \sum_y P'(y) P(x - y)$. Hence, using the general inequality $(\mathrm{E}\,X)^2 \leq \mathrm{E}\,X^2$, we have $\sum_x (Q(x) - d^{-t})^2 = \sum_x (\sum_y P'(y)(P(x - y) - d^{-t}))^2 \leq \sum_x \sum_y P'(y)(P(x - y) - d^{-t})^2 = \sum_y P'(y) \sum_x (P(x) - d^{-t})^2 = \sum_x (P(x) - d^{-t})^2$. [See G. Marsaglia, *Comp. Sci. and Statistics: Symp. on the Interface* **16** (1984), 5–6. The result is of interest only when $d^t \leq 2\lambda$, since each $P(x)$ is a multiple of $1/\lambda$.]

24. Write $k : \alpha$ and $\alpha : k$ for the first k and last k elements of string α. Let $K(\alpha, \beta) = [\alpha = \beta]/P(\alpha)$, and let $\bar{C}$ be the $d^t \times d^t$ matrix with entries $\bar{c}_{\alpha\beta} = K(\alpha, \beta) - K(t-1 : \alpha, t - 1 : \beta)$. Let C be the covariance matrix of the random variables $N(\alpha)$ for $|\alpha| = t$, divided by n. These variables are subject to the constraint $\sum_{a=0}^{d-1} N(\alpha a) = \sum_{a=0}^{d-1} N(a\alpha)$ for each of d^{t-1} strings α, and we also have $\sum_{|\alpha|=t} N(\alpha) = n$; but all other linear constraints are derivable from these (see Theorem 2.3.4.2G). Therefore C has rank $d^t - d^{t-1}$, and by exercise 3.3.1–25 we need only show that $C\bar{C}C = C$.

It is not difficult to verify that $c_{\alpha\beta} = P(\alpha\beta) \sum_{|k| < t} T_k(\alpha, \beta)$, where $T_k(\alpha, \beta)$ is a term corresponding to the overlap that might occur when we superimpose β on α and slide it k positions to the right:

$$T_k(\alpha, \beta) = \begin{cases} K(t + k : \alpha, \ \beta : t + k) - 1, & \text{if } k \leq 0; \\ K(\alpha : t - k, \ t - k : \beta) - 1, & \text{if } k \geq 0. \end{cases}$$

For example, if $d = 2$, $t = 5$, $\alpha = 01101$, and $\beta = 10101$, we have $c_{\alpha\beta} = P(0)^4 P(1)^6 \times (P(01)^{-1} + P(101)^{-1} + P(1)^{-1} - 9)$. Entry $\alpha\beta$ of $C\bar{C}C$ is therefore $P(\alpha\beta)$ times

$$\sum_{|\gamma|=t-1} \sum_{a,b=0}^{d-1} P(\gamma ab) \sum_{|k| < t} \sum_{|l| < t} T_k(\alpha, \gamma a)(K(a, b) - 1) T_l(\gamma b, \beta).$$

Given k and l, the product $T_k(\alpha, \gamma a)(K(a, b) - 1) T_l(\gamma b, \beta)$ expands to eight terms, each of which usually sums to ± 1 when multiplied by $P(\gamma ab)$ and summed over all γab. For example, the sum of $P(\gamma ab) K(2 : \alpha, \ \gamma a : 2) K(a, b) K(3 : \gamma b, \ \beta : 3)$, when $\alpha = a_1 \ldots a_t$,

$\beta = b_1 \dots b_t$, $\gamma = c_1 \dots c_{t-1}$, and $t \geq 5$, is the sum of $P(c_4 \dots c_{t-2})$, which is 1. If $t = 4$, the same sum would be $K(a_1, b_4)$, but it would cancel with the sum of $P(\gamma ab)K(2 : \alpha, \gamma a : 2)(-1)K(3 : \gamma b, \beta : 3)$. The net result is therefore 0 unless $k \leq 0 \leq l$; otherwise it turns out to be $K(i : (\alpha : i - k), i : (\beta : i + l)) - K(i - 1 : (\alpha : i - k), i - 1 : (\beta : i + l))$, where $i = \min(t + k, t - l)$. The sum over k and l telescopes to $c_{\alpha\beta}$.

25. Empirical tests show, in fact, that when (22) is generalized to arbitrary t the ratios of corresponding elements of C_1^{-1} and $C_1^{-1}C_2C_1^{-1}$ are very nearly $-t$, when $t \geq 5$. For example, when $t = 6$ they all lie between -6.039 and -6.111; when $t = 20$ they all lie between -20.039 and -20.045. This phenomenon demands an explanation.

26. (a) The vectors $(S_1, \dots, S_n)$ are uniformly distributed points in the $(n - 1)$-dimensional polyhedron defined by the inequalities $S_1 \geq 0$, $\dots$, $S_n \geq 0$ in the hyperplane $S_1 + \dots + S_n = 1$. An easy induction proves that

$$\int_{s_1}^{\infty} dt_1 \int_{s_2}^{\infty} dt_2 \cdots \int_{s_{n-1}}^{\infty} dt_{n-1} \left[1 - t_1 - \cdots - t_{n-1} \geq s_n \right] = \frac{(1 - s_1 - s_2 - \cdots - s_n)_+^{n-1}}{(n-1)!}.$$

To get the probability, divide this integral by its value in the special case $s_1 = \cdots = s_n = 0$. [Bruno de Finetti, *Giornale Istituto Italiano degli Attuari* **27** (1964), 151–173.]

(b) The probability that $S_{(1)} \geq s$ is the probability that $S_1 \geq s$, $\dots$, $S_n \geq s$.

(c) The probability that $S_{(k)} \geq s$ is the probability that at most $k - 1$ of the S_j are $< s$; hence $1 - F_k(s) = G_1(s) + \cdots + G_{k-1}(s)$, where $G_j(s)$ is the probability that exactly j spacings are $< s$. By symmetry, $G_j(s)$ is $\binom{n}{j}$ times the probability that $S_1 < s$, $\dots$, $S_j < s$, $S_{j+1} \geq s$, $\dots$, $S_n \geq s$; and the latter is $\Pr(S_1 < s, \dots, S_{j-1} < s, S_j \geq 0, S_{j+1} \geq s, \dots, S_n \geq s) - \Pr(S_1 < s, \dots, S_{j-1} < s, S_j \geq s, \dots, S_n \geq s)$. Repeated application of (a) shows that $G_j(s) = \binom{n}{j} \sum_l \binom{j}{l}(-1)^{j-l}(1 - (n - l)s)_+^{n-1}$; hence

$$1 - F_k(s) = \sum_l \binom{n}{l}\binom{n-l-1}{k-l-1}(-1)^{k-l-1}(1 - (n-l)s)_+^{n-1}.$$

In particular, the largest spacing $S_{(n)}$ has distribution

$$F_n(s) = 1 - \sum_l \binom{n}{l}\binom{n-l-1}{n-l-1}(-1)^{n-l-1}(1 - (n-l)s)_+^{n-1} = \sum_l \binom{n}{l}(-1)^l(1 - ls)_+^{n-1}.$$

[Incidentally, the similar quantity $x^{n-1}(n - 1)!^{-1}F_n(x^{-1})$ turns out to be the *density* function for the *sum* $U_1 + \cdots + U_n$ of uniform deviates.]

(d) From the formulas $E\, s^r = r \int_0^1 (1 - F(s))s^{r-1}\, ds$ and $\int_0^1 s^r(1 - ks)_+^{n-1}\, ds = k^{-r-1}n^{-1}\binom{n+r}{r}^{-1}$, we find $E\, S_{(k)} = n^{-1}(H_n - H_{n-k})$ and, with a bit of algebra, $E\, S_{(k)}^2 = n^{-1}(n + 1)^{-1}(H_n^{(2)} - H_{n-k}^{(2)} + (H_n - H_{n-k})^2)$. Thus the variance of $S_{(k)}$ is equal to $n^{-1}(n + 1)^{-1}(H_n^{(2)} - H_{n-k}^{(2)} - (H_n - H_{n-k})^2/n)$.

[The distributions $F_k(s)$ were first found by W. A. Whitworth, in problem 667 of *DCC Exercises in Choice and Chance* (Cambridge, 1897). Whitworth also discovered an elegant way to compute the expected value of any polynomial in the functions $G_k(s) = F_k(s) - F_{k+1}(s)$; this was published in a booklet entitled *The Expectation of Parts* (Cambridge, 1898), and incorporated into the fifth edition of *Choice and Chance* (1901). Simplified expressions for the mean and variance and for a variety of more general spacing statistics were found by Barton and David, *J. Royal Stat. Soc.* **B18** (1956), 79–94. See R. Pyke, *J. Royal Stat. Soc.* **B27** (1965), 395–449, for a survey of the ways in which statisticians have traditionally analyzed spacings as clues to potential biases in data.]

27. Consider the polyhedron in the hyperplane $S_1 + \cdots + S_n = 1$ defined by the inequalities $S_1 \geq 0, \ldots, S_n \geq 0$. This polyhedron consists of $n!$ congruent subpolyhedra defined by the ordering of the S's (assuming that the S's are distinct), and the operation of sorting is an $n!$-to-1 folding of the large polyhedron to the subpolyhedron in which $S_1 \leq \cdots \leq S_n$. The transformation that takes $(S_{(1)}, \ldots, S_{(n)})$ to $(S_1', \ldots, S_n')$ is a 1-to-1 mapping that expands differential volumes by the factor $n!$. It takes the vertices $(\frac{1}{n}, \ldots, \frac{1}{n})$, $(0, \frac{1}{n-1}, \ldots, \frac{1}{n-1})$, $\ldots$, $(0, \ldots, 0, 1)$ of the subpolyhedron into the respective vertices $(1, 0, \ldots, 0)$, $(0, 1, 0, \ldots, 0)$, $\ldots$, $(0, \ldots, 0, 1)$, linearly stretching and distorting the overall shape in the process. (The Euclidean distance between vertices $(0, \ldots, 0, \frac{1}{j}, \ldots, \frac{1}{j})$ and $(0, \ldots, 0, \frac{1}{k}, \ldots, \frac{1}{k})$ in the subpolyhedron is $|j^{-1} - k^{-1}|^{1/2}$; the transformation produces a regular simplex in which all n vertices are $\sqrt{2}$ apart.)

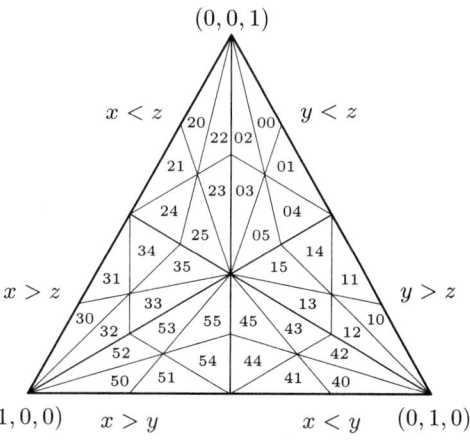

The behavior of iterated spacings is easiest to understand if we examine the details graphically when $n = 3$. In this case the polyhedron is simply an equilateral triangle, whose points are represented with barycentric coordinates (x, y, z), $x + y + z = 1$. The accompanying diagram illustrates the first two levels of a recursive decomposition of this triangle. Each of the 6^2 subtriangles has been labeled with a two-digit code pq, where p represents the applicable permutation when $(x, y, z) = (S_1, S_2, S_3)$ is sorted into $(S_{(1)}, S_{(2)}, S_{(3)})$, and q represents the permutation in the next stage when S_1', S_2', and S_3' are sorted, according to the following code:

$$0: x < y < z, \quad 1: x < z < y, \quad 2: y < x < z, \quad 3: y < z < x, \quad 4: z < x < y, \quad 5: z < y < x.$$

For example, the points of subtriangle 34 have $S_2 < S_3 < S_1$ and $S_3' < S_1' < S_2'$. We can continue this process to infinitely many levels; all points of the triangle with irrational barycentric coordinates thereby acquire a unique representation as an infinite radix-6 expansion. A tetrahedron can be subdivided similarly into 24, 24^2, 24^3, $\ldots$ subtetrahedra, and in general this procedure constructs a radix-$n!$ expansion for the points of any $(n-1)$-dimensional simplex.

When $n = 2$ the process is especially simple: If $x \notin \{0, \frac{1}{2}, 1\}$, the transformation takes spacings $(x, 1 - x) = (x, y)$ into either $(2x \bmod 1, 2y \bmod 1)$ or $(2y \bmod 1, 2x \bmod 1)$, depending on whether $x < y$ or $x > y$. Repeated tests therefore essentially shift the binary representation left one bit, possibly complementing the result. After at most $e+1$ iterations on e-bit numbers the process must converge to the fixed point $(0, 1)$. Permutation coding in the case $n = 2$ corresponds simply to folding and stretching a line; the first four levels of subdivision have the following four-bit codes:

$(0,1)$ |———+———+———+———+———+———+———+———+———| $(1,0)$

0000 0001 0011 0010 0110 0111 0101 0100 1100 1101 1111 1110 1010 1011 1001 1000

This sequence is exactly the Gray binary code studied in Section 7.2.1. In general, the radix-$n!$ permutation code for an n-simplex has the property that adjacent regions have identical codes except in one digit position. Each iteration of the spacing transformation shifts off the leftmost digit of the representation of each point. Note that equal birthday spacings are points near the boundary of the first-level decomposition.

This fundamental transformation from $(S_1, \ldots, S_n)$ to $(S_1', \ldots, S_n')$ is implicit in Whitworth's proof of Proposition LVI in the fifth edition of *Choice and Chance* (see the reference in answer 26). It was first studied explicitly by J. Durbin [*Biometrika* **48** (1961), 41–55], who was inspired by a similar construction of P. V. Sukhatme [*Annals of Eugenics* **8** (1937), 52–56]. The permutation coding for iterated spacings was introduced by H. E. Daniels [*Biometrika* **49** (1962), 139–149].

28. (a) The number of partitions of m into n distinct positive parts is $p_n\big(m - \binom{n+1}{2}\big)$, by exercise 5.1.1–16. These partitions can be permuted in $n!$ ways to yield n-tuples $(y_1, \ldots, y_n)$ with $0 = y_1 < y_2 < \cdots < y_n < m$; and each of these n-tuples leads to $(n-1)!$ n-tuples that have $y_1 = 0$ and $0 < y_2, \ldots, y_n < m$. Now add a constant mod m to each y_j; this preserves the spacings. Hence $b_{n00}(m) = mn!\,(n-1)!\,p_n\big(m - \binom{n+1}{2}\big)$.

(b) Zero spacings correspond to balls in the same urn, and they contribute $s-1$ to the count of equal spacings. Therefore $b_{nrs}(m) = \left\{ {n \atop n-s} \right\} b_{(n-s)(r+1-s)0}(m)$.

(c) Since $\left\{ {n \atop n-1} \right\} = \binom{n}{2}$, the probability is

$$n!\,(n-1)!\,m^{1-n}\left(p_n\left(m - \binom{n+1}{2}\right) - \frac{1}{2}p_{n-1}\left(m - \binom{n}{2}\right)\right).$$

29. By the previous answer and exercise 5.1.1–15 we have $b_{n0}(z) = n!\,(n-1)!\,z^{\binom{n+1}{2}}/(1-z)\ldots(1-z^n)$. When $r = 1$, the $n!$ in our previous derivation becomes $n!/2$, and the number of solutions to $0 < s_1 < \cdots < s_k \le s_{k+1} < \cdots < s_n$ with $s_1 + \cdots + s_n = m$ is the number of solutions to $0 \le s_1 - 1 \le \cdots \le s_k - k \le s_{k+1} - k \le \cdots \le s_n - n + 1$ with $(s_1 - 1) + \cdots + (s_k - k) + (s_{k+1} - k) + \cdots + (s_n - n + 1) = m - \binom{n}{2} - k$. Hence $b_{n1}(z) = \frac{1}{2}n!\,(n-1)!\sum_{k=1}^n (z^k - z^n)\,z^{\binom{n}{2}}/(1-z)\ldots(1-z^n)$. A similar argument shows that

$$\frac{b_{n2}(z)}{n!\,(n-1)!} = \left(\frac{1}{2!\,2!}\sum_{1 \le j < k < n}(z^j - z^n)(z^k - z^{n-1}) + \frac{1}{3!}\sum_{1 \le k < n}(z^k - z^n)(z^k - z^{n-1})\right)$$
$$\times \frac{z^{\binom{n-1}{2}}}{(1-z)\ldots(1-z^n)}.$$

We can obtain $b_{nr}(z)$ for general r from the formula

$$\frac{\sum_r b_{nr}(z)w^r}{n!\,(n-1)!\,z^n} = \sum_{0 \le b_1,\ldots,b_{n-1} \le 1}\frac{(z - b_1 z^n)\ldots(z^{n-1} - b_{n-1}z^n)}{c_1\ldots c_{n-1}(1-z)\ldots(1-z^n)}\left(\frac{w}{z^{n-1}}\right)^{b_1}\ldots\left(\frac{w}{z^1}\right)^{b_{n-1}}$$

where $c_k = 1 + b_k + b_k b_{k-1} + \cdots + b_k \ldots b_2 b_1 = 1 + b_k c_{k-1}$. (The special case $w = 1$ is interesting because the left side sums to $(1-z)^{-n}/n!$ in that case.)

30. This is a good problem for the saddle point method [N. G. de Bruijn, *Asymptotic Methods in Analysis* (North-Holland, 1961), Chapter 5]. We have $p_n(m) = \frac{1}{2\pi i}\oint e^{f(z)}\frac{dz}{z}$, where $f(z) = -m\ln z - \sum_{k=1}^n \ln(1 - z^k)$. Let $\rho = n/m$ and $\delta = \sqrt{n}/m$; integrating on the path $z = e^{-\rho + it\delta}$ gives $p_n(m) = \frac{\delta}{2\pi}\int_{-\pi/\delta}^{\pi/\delta}\exp\big(f(e^{-\rho + it\delta})\big)\,dt$. It is convenient to use the identity

$$g(se^t) = \sum_{j=0}^{n} \frac{t^j}{j!} \vartheta^j g(s) + \int_0^t \frac{u^n}{n!} \vartheta^{n+1} g(se^{t-u})\, du\,,$$

where $g = g(z)$ is any analytic function and ϑ is the operator $z\frac{d}{dz}$. When the function $\vartheta^j g$ is evaluated at e^z the result is the same as when $g(e^z)$ is differentiated j times with respect to z. This principle leads to the formula

$$\vartheta^j f(e^{-\rho}) = -m[j=1] + \frac{j!\,n}{\rho^j} + (-1)^j \sum_{k=1}^{n} \sum_{l \ge j} \frac{l^{\underline{j}}\,B_l}{l \cdot l!} k^l \rho^{l-j}\,,$$

because of another handy identity,

$$\ln\left(\frac{1 - e^{-z}}{z}\right) = \sum_{n \ge 1} \frac{B_n z^n}{n \cdot n!}\,.$$

Therefore we obtain an asymptotic expansion of the integrand,

$$\exp f(e^{-\rho + it\delta}) = \exp\left(\sum_{j \ge 0} \frac{i^j \delta^j t^j}{j!} \vartheta^j f(e^{-\rho})\right) = e^{-t^2/2 + f(e^{-\rho})} \exp(ic_1 t - c_2 t^2 - ic_3 t^3 + \cdots),$$

where $c_1 = \left(\frac{n(n+1)}{2} B_1 + \frac{n(n+1/2)(n+1)}{6} B_2 \rho\right)\delta + O(n^{-3})$, etc.; and it turns out that $c_j = O(n^{-3})$ for $j \ge 3$. Factoring out the constant term

$$\frac{\delta}{2\pi} e^{f(e^{-\rho})} = \frac{\delta}{2\pi\, n!\, \rho^n e^{-m\rho}} \exp\left(-\sum_{k=1}^{n} \sum_{l \ge 1} \frac{B_l}{l \cdot l!} k^l \rho^l\right)$$

$$= \frac{\sqrt{n}\, m^{n-1} e^{n + \alpha/4}}{2\pi\, n!\, n^n} \left(1 + \frac{18\alpha - \alpha^2}{72n} + \frac{108\alpha^2 - 36\alpha^3 + \alpha^4}{10368 n^2} + O(n^{-3})\right)$$

leaves us with an integral whose integrand is exponentially small when $|t| \ge n^\epsilon$. We can ignore larger values of t, because partial fraction expansion shows that the integrand is $O((m/n)^{n/2})$; none of the other roots of unity occurs more than $n/2$ times as a pole of the denominator. Hence we are allowed to "trade tails" [CMath, §9.4] and integrate over all t. The formulas $\int_{-\infty}^{\infty} e^{-t^2/2} t^j\, dt = (j-1)(j-3)\ldots(1)\sqrt{2\pi}$ [j even] and $n! = (n/e)^n \sqrt{2\pi n} \exp(\frac{1}{12} n^{-1} + O(n^{-3}))$ suffice to complete the evaluation.

With $q_n(m) = p_n\left(m - \binom{n+1}{2}\right)$ in place of $p_n(m)$ the calculation proceeds in the same way but with c_1 increased by $\frac{1}{2}\alpha(n^{1/2} - n^{-1/2})$ and with the additional factor $\exp\left(-\rho\binom{n+1}{2}\right)$. We get

$$q_n(m) = \frac{m^{n-1} e^{-\alpha/4}}{n!\,(n-1)!}\left(1 - \frac{13\alpha^2}{288n} + \frac{169\alpha^4 - 2016\alpha^3 - 1728\alpha^2 + 41472\alpha}{165888 n^2} + O(n^{-3})\right);$$

this matches the formula for $p_n(m)$ except that α has been changed to $-\alpha$. (In fact, if we define $p_n(m) = r_n\left(2m + \binom{n+1}{2}\right)$ and $q_n(m) = r_n\left(2m - \binom{n+1}{2}\right)$, the generating function $R_n(z) = \sum_m r_n(z^m) = \prod_{k=1}^{n} (z^{-k} - z^k)^{-1}$ satisfies $R_n(1/z) = (-1)^n R_n(z)$. This implies a duality formula $r_n(-m) = (-1)^{n-1} r_n(m)$, in the sense that this equation is identically true when we express $r_n(m)$ as a polynomial in m and roots of unity. Therefore we may say that $q_n(m) = p_n(-m)$. A general treatment of such duality can be found in G. Pólya, Math. Zeitschrift **29** (1928), 549–640, §44.) For further information see G. Szekeres, *Quarterly J. Math. Oxford* **2** (1951), 85–108; **4** (1953), 96–111.

The exact value of $q_n(m)$ when $m = 2^{25}$ and $n = 512$ is $7.08069\,34695\,90264\,094\ldots \times 10^{1514}$; our approximation gives the estimate $7.080693501 \times 10^{1514}$.

The probability that the birthday test finds $R = 0$ spacings is $b_{n00}(m)/m^n = n!\,(n-1)!\,m^{1-n}q_n(m) = e^{-\alpha/4} + O(n^{-1})$, by exercise 28, because the contribution from $b_{n01}(m)$ is $\approx \frac{\alpha}{2n}e^{-\alpha/4} = O(n^{-1})$. Inserting the factor $g_n(z) = \sum_{k=1}^{n-1}(z^{-k}-1)$ into the integrand for $q_n(m)$ has the effect of multiplying the result by $\frac{\alpha}{2} + O(n^{-1})$, because $g_n(e^{-\rho+it\delta}) = \binom{n}{2}\rho + O(n^3\rho^2) + itO(n^2\delta) - \frac{1}{2}t^2O(n^3\delta^2) + \cdots$. Similarly, the extra factor $\sum_{1\le j<k<n}(z^{-j}-1)(z^{-k}-1)$ essentially multiplies by $\frac{1}{8}n^4\rho^2 = \frac{1}{8}\alpha^2$, plus $O(n^{-1})$; other contributions to the probability that $R = 2$ are $O(n^{-1})$. In this way we find that the probability of r equal spacings is $e^{-\alpha/4}(\alpha/4)^r/r! + O(n^{-1})$, a Poisson distribution; more complicated terms arise if we carry the expansion out to $O(n^{-2})$.

31. The 79 bits consist of 24 sets of three, $\{Y_n, Y_{n+31}, Y_{n+55}\}$, $\{Y_{n+1}, Y_{n+32}, Y_{n+56}\}$, ..., $\{Y_{n+23}, Y_{n+54}, Y_{n+78}\}$, plus 7 additional bits $Y_{n+24}, \ldots, Y_{n+30}$. The latter bits are equally likely to be 0 or 1, but in each group of three the probability is $\frac{1}{4}$ that the bits will be $\{0,0,0\}$ and $\frac{3}{4}$ that they will be $\{0,1,1\}$. Therefore the probability generating function for the sum of bits is $f(z) = \left(\frac{1+z}{2}\right)^7\left(\frac{1+3z^2}{4}\right)^{24}$, a polynomial of degree 55. (Well, not quite; strictly speaking, it is $(2^{55}f(z) - 1)/(2^{55} - 1)$, because the all-0 case is excluded.) The coefficients of $2^{55}f(z)$ are easily computed by machine, and we find that the probability of more 1s than 0s is $18509401282464000/(2^{55} - 1) \approx 0.51374$.

Notes: This exercise is based on the discovery by Vattulainen, Ala-Nissila, and Kankaala [*Physical Review Letters* **73** (1994), 2513–2516] that a lagged Fibonacci generator fails a more complicated two-dimensional random walk test. Notice that the sequence $Y_{2n}, Y_{2n+2}, \ldots$ will fail the test too, because it satisfies the same recurrence. The bias toward 1s also carries over into the subsequence consisting of the even-valued elements generated by $X_n = (X_{n-55} \pm X_{n-24}) \bmod 2^e$; we tend to have more occurrences of $(\ldots 10)_2$ than $(\ldots 00)_2$ in binary notation.

There's nothing magic about the number 79 in this test; experiments show that a significant bias towards a majority of 1s is present also in random walks of length 101 or 1001 or 10001. But a formal proof seems to be difficult. After 86 steps the generating function is $\left(\frac{1+3z^2}{4}\right)^{17}\left(\frac{1+2z^2+4z^3+z^4}{8}\right)^7$; then we get the factors $(1 + 2z^2 + 5z^3 + 5z^4 + 10z^5 + 8z^6 + z^7)/32$; then $(1+2z^2+7z^3+7z^4+15z^5+25z^6+29z^7+28z^8+13z^9+z^{10})/128$, etc. The analysis becomes more and more complicated as the walks get longer.

Intuitively, the preponderance of 1s that arise in the first 79 steps ought to persist as long as the subsequent numbers are reasonably balanced between 0 and 1. The accompanying diagram shows the results of a much smaller case, the generator $Y_n = (Y_{n-2}+Y_{n-11}) \bmod 2$, which is easy to analyze exhaustively. In this case random walks of length 445 have a 64% chance of finishing to the right of the starting point; this bias disappears only when the length of the walk increases to half the period length (after which, of course, 0s are more likely, although the full period does lack one 0).

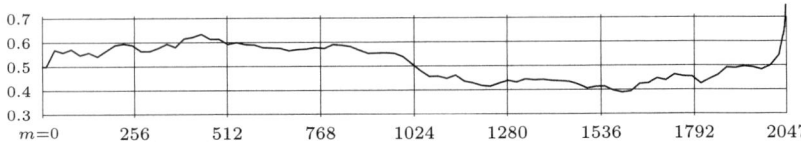

The probability that 1s outnumber 0s in random m-tuples when $Y_n = Y_{n-2} \oplus Y_{n-11}$.

Lüscher's discarding technique can be used to avoid the bias toward 1s (see the end of Section 3.2.2). For example, with lags 55 and 24, no deviation for randomness is observed for random walks of length 1001 when the numbers are generated in batches of 165, if only the first 55 numbers of each batch are used.

32. Not if, say, X and Y each take the values $(-n, m)$ with the respective probabilities $(m/(m+n), n/(m+n))$, where $m < n < (1 + \sqrt{2})m$. [Suppose two competitors differ by X after playing one round of golf. Then they are of equal strength based on their mean scores, but one might be more likely to win a one-round tournament while the other will more often win in two rounds. See T. M. Cover, *Amer. Statistician* **43** (1989), 277–278, for a discussion of similar phenomena.]

33. We essentially want $[z^{(k+l-1)/2}]\left(\frac{1+z}{2}\right)^{k-2l}\left(\frac{1+3z^2}{4}\right)^l/(1-z)$. Let $m = k - 2l$ and $n = l$; the desired coefficient is $\frac{1}{2\pi i}\oint e^{g(z)}\frac{dz}{z(1-z)}$, where $g(z) = m\ln\left(\frac{1+z}{2}\right) + n\ln\left(\frac{1+3z^2}{4}\right) - \left(\frac{m+3n-1}{2}\right)\ln z$. It is convenient (and saddle-wise) to integrate along the path $z = e^{\epsilon u}$ where $\epsilon^2 = 4/(m + 3n)$ and $u = -1 + it$ for $-\infty < t < \infty$. We have $g(e^{\epsilon u}) = -\epsilon u/2 + u^2/2 + c_3\epsilon u^3 + c_4\epsilon^2 u^4 + \cdots$, where $c_k = \epsilon^2\vartheta^k g(1)/k! = O(1)$. Also $1/(1 - e^{\epsilon u}) = \frac{-1}{\epsilon u} + \frac{1}{2} - B_2\epsilon u/2! - \cdots$. Multiplying out the integrand and using the facts that $\frac{1}{2\pi i}\int_{1-i\infty}^{1+i\infty} e^{u^2/2}\frac{du}{u} = \frac{1}{2}$ and $\frac{1}{2\pi i}\int_{a-i\infty}^{a+i\infty} e^{u^2/2}u^{2k}\,du = (-1)^k(2k-1)(2k-3)\ldots(1)\sqrt{2\pi}$ yields the asymptotic formula $\frac{1}{2} + (2\pi)^{-1/2}n(m + 3n)^{-3/2} + O((m + 3n)^{-3/2})$. If $m + 3n$ is even, the same asymptotic formula holds, provided that we give half of the coefficient of $z^{(m+3n)/2}$ to the 1s and half to the 0s. (This coefficient is $\left(\frac{2}{\pi(m+3n)}\right)^{1/2} + O((m-3n)^{-3/2})$.)

34. The number of strings of length n that exclude a given two-letter substring or pair of substrings is the coefficient of z^n in an appropriate generating function, and it can be written $ce^{n\tau}m^n + O(1)$ where c and τ have series expansions in powers of $\epsilon = 1/m$:

Case	Excluded	Generating function	c	τ
1	aa	$(1+z)/p(z)$	$1 + \epsilon^2 - 2\epsilon^3 + \cdots$	$-\epsilon^2 + \epsilon^3 - \frac{5}{2}\epsilon^4 + \cdots$
2	ab	$1/(1-mz+z^2)$	$1 + \epsilon^2 + 3\epsilon^4 + \cdots$	$-\epsilon^2 - \frac{3}{2}\epsilon^4 + \cdots$
3	aa, bb	$(1+z)/(p(z)+z^2)$	$1 + 2\epsilon^2 - 4\epsilon^3 + \cdots$	$-2\epsilon^2 + 2\epsilon^3 - 8\epsilon^4 + \cdots$
4	aa, bc	$(1+z)/(p(z)+z^2+z^3)$	$1 + 2\epsilon^2 - 2\epsilon^3 + \cdots$	$-2\epsilon^2 + \epsilon^3 - 7\epsilon^4 + \cdots$
5	ab, bc	$(1+z)/(1-mz+2z^2-z^3)$	$1 + 2\epsilon^2 - 2\epsilon^3 + \cdots$	$-2\epsilon^2 + \epsilon^3 - 6\epsilon^4 + \cdots$
6	ab, cd	$1/(1-mz+2z^2)$	$1 + 2\epsilon^2 + 12\epsilon^4 + \cdots$	$-2\epsilon^2 - 6\epsilon^4 + \cdots$

(Here a, b, c, d denote distinct letters and $p(z) = 1 - (m - 1)(z + z^2)$. It turns out that the effect of excluding $\{ab, ba\}$ or $\{aa, ab\}$ is equivalent to excluding $\{aa, bb\}$; excluding $\{ab, ac\}$ is equivalent to excluding $\{ab, cd\}$.) Let $S_n^{(j)}$ be the coefficient of z^n in Case j and let X be the total number of two-letter combinations that do not appear. Then $\mathrm{E}\,X = (mS_n^{(1)} + m^2 S_n^{(2)})/m^n$ and

$$\mathrm{E}\,X^2 = (mS_n^{(1)} + m^2(S_n^{(2)} + 6S_n^{(3)}) + 2m^3(S_n^{(4)} + S_n^{(5)} + S_n^{(6)}) + m^4 S_n^{(6)})/m^n.$$

35. (a) $\mathrm{E}\,S_m = N^{-1}\sum_{n=0}^{N-1}\sum_{j=0}^{m-1} Z_{n+j} = N^{-1}\sum_{j=0}^{m-1}\sum_{n=0}^{N-1} Z_{n+j} = m/N$, because $\sum_{n=0}^{N-1} Z_{n+j} = 2^{k-1} - (2^{k-1} - 1) = 1$.

(b) Let $\xi^k = a_1\xi^{k-1} + \cdots + a_k$, and define the linear function f as in the first solution to exercise 3.2.2–16. Then $Y_n = f(\xi^n)$, and it follows that $Y_{n+i} + Y_{n+j} = f(\xi^{n+i}) + f(\xi^{n+j}) \equiv f(\xi^{n+i} + \xi^{n+j}) = f(\xi^n\alpha)$ (modulo 2), where α is nonzero when $i \not\equiv j$ (modulo N). Hence $\mathrm{E}\,S_m^2 = N^{-1}\sum_{i=0}^{m-1}\sum_{j=0}^{m-1}\sum_{n=0}^{N-1} Z_{n+i}Z_{n+j} = N^{-1}(\sum_{i=0}^{m-1}\sum_{n=0}^{N-1} Z_{n+i}^2 - 2\sum_{0\leq i<j<m}\sum_{n=0}^{N-1} Z_n) = m - m(m - 1)/N$.

(c) $\mathrm{E}\sum_{j=0}^{m-1} Z_{n+j} = \sum_{j=0}^{m-1} \mathrm{E}\, Z_{n+j} = 0$ and $\mathrm{E}(\sum_{j=0}^{m-1} Z_{n+j})^2 = \sum_{j=0}^{m-1} \mathrm{E}\, Z_{n+j}^2 + \sum_{0 \le i < j < m}(\mathrm{E}\, Z_{n+i})(\mathrm{E}\, Z_{n+j}) = m$ when each Z_n is truly random. Thus the mean and variance of S_m are very close to the correct values when $m \ll N$.

(d) $\mathrm{E}\, S_m^3 = N^{-1}\sum_{h=0}^{m-1}\sum_{i=0}^{m-1}\sum_{j=0}^{m-1}\sum_{n=0}^{N-1} Z_{n+h} Z_{n+i} Z_{n+j}$. If any of h, i, or j are equal, the sum on n is 1; hence

$$\mathrm{E}\, S_m^3 = \frac{1}{N}\left(m^3 - m^{\underline{3}} + 6 \sum_{0 \le h < i < j < m}\ \sum_{n=0}^{N-1} Z_{n+h} Z_{n+i} Z_{n+j}\right).$$

Arguing as in (b), we find that the sum on n will be 1 if $\xi^h + \xi^i + \xi^j \ne 0$; otherwise it will be $-N$. Thus $\mathrm{E}\, S_m^3 = m^3 - 6B(N+1)/N$, where $B = \sum_{0 \le h < i < j < m}[\xi^h + \xi^i + \xi^j = 0] = \sum_{0 < i < j < m}[1 + \xi^i + \xi^j = 0]\,(m - j)$. Finally observe that $1 + \xi^i = \xi^j$ in the field if and only if $f(\xi^{i+l}) = f(\xi^{j+l})$ for $0 < l < k$, assuming that $0 < i < j < N$.

(e) The only nonzero term occurs for $i = 31$ and $j = 55$; hence $B = 79 - 55 = 24$. (The next nonzero term occurs when $i = 62$ and $j = 110$.) In a truly random situation, $\mathrm{E}\, S_m^3$ should be zero, so this value $\mathrm{E}\, S_{79}^3 \approx -144$ is distinctly nonrandom. Curiously it is negative, although exercise 31 showed that S_{79} is usually *positive*. The value of S_{79} tends to be more seriously negative when it does dip below zero.

Reference: IEEE Trans. **IT-14** (1968), 569–576. Experiments by M. Matsumoto and Y. Kurita [*ACM Trans. Modeling and Comp. Simul.* **2** (1992), 179–194; **4** (1994), 254–266] confirm that trinomial-based generators fail such distribution tests even when the lags are quite large. See also *ACM Trans. Modeling and Comp. Simul.* **6** (1996), 99–106, where they exhibit exponentially long subsequences of low density.

SECTION 3.3.3

1. $y((x/y)) + \frac{1}{2}y - \frac{1}{2}y\delta(x/y)$.

2. $((x)) = -\sum_{n \ge 1}\frac{1}{n\pi}\sin 2\pi nx$, which converges for all x. (The representation in Eq. (24) may be considered a "finite" Fourier series, for the case when x is rational.)

3. The sum is $((2^n x)) - ((x))$. [See *Trans. Amer. Math. Soc.* **65** (1949), 401.]

4. $d_{\max} = 2^{10} \cdot 5$. Note that we have $X_{n+1} < X_n$ with probability $\frac{1}{2} + \epsilon$, where

$$|\epsilon| < d/(2 \cdot 10^{10}) \le 1/(2 \cdot 5^9);$$

hence *every* potency-10 generator is respectable from the standpoint of Theorem P.

5. An intermediate result:

$$\sum_{0 \le x < m}\frac{x}{m}\frac{s(x)}{m} = \frac{1}{12}\sigma(a, m, c) + \frac{m}{4} - \frac{c}{2m} - \frac{x'}{2m}.$$

6. (a) Use induction and the formula

$$\left(\left(\frac{hj + c}{k}\right)\right) - \left(\left(\frac{hj + c - 1}{k}\right)\right) = \frac{1}{k} - \frac{1}{2}\delta\left(\frac{hj + c}{k}\right) - \frac{1}{2}\delta\left(\frac{hj + c - 1}{k}\right).$$

(b) Use the fact that $-\left(\left(\frac{h'j}{k}\right)\right) = -\left(\left(\frac{j}{hk} - \frac{k'j}{h}\right)\right) = \left(\left(\frac{k'j}{h}\right)\right) - \frac{j}{hk} + \frac{1}{2}\delta\left(\frac{k'j}{h}\right)$.

7. Take $m = h$, $n = k$, $k = 2$ in the second formula of exercise 1.2.4–45:

$$\sum_{0 \le j < k}\left(\frac{hj}{k} - \left(\left(\frac{hj}{k}\right)\right) + \frac{1}{2}\right)\left(\frac{hj}{k} - \left(\left(\frac{hj}{k}\right)\right) - \frac{1}{2}\right) + 2\sum_{0 < j < h}\left(\frac{kj}{h} - \left(\left(\frac{kj}{h}\right)\right) + \frac{1}{2}\right)j = kh(h-1).$$

The sums on the left simplify, and by standard manipulations we get

$$h^2 k - hk - \frac{h}{2} + \frac{h^2}{6k} + \frac{k}{12} + \frac{1}{4} - \frac{h}{6}\sigma(h, k, 0) - \frac{h}{6}\sigma(k, h, 0) + \frac{1}{12}\sigma(1, k, 0) = h^2 k - hk.$$

Since $\sigma(1, k, 0) = (k - 1)(k - 2)/k$, this reduces to the reciprocity law.

8. See *Duke Math. J.* **21** (1954), 391–397.

9. Begin with the interesting identity $\sum_{k=0}^{r-1}\lfloor kp/r\rfloor\lfloor kq/r\rfloor + \sum_{k=0}^{p-1}\lfloor kq/p\rfloor\lfloor kr/p\rfloor + \sum_{k=0}^{q-1}\lfloor kr/q\rfloor\lfloor kp/q\rfloor = (p - 1)(q - 1)(r - 1)$, for which a simple geometric proof is possible, assuming that $p \perp q$, $q \perp r$, and $r \perp p$. [U. Dieter, *Abh. Math. Sem. Univ. Hamburg* **21** (1957), 109–125.]

10. Obviously $\sigma(k - h, k, c) = -\sigma(h, k, -c)$, by (8). Replace j by $k - j$ in definition (16), to deduce that $\sigma(h, k, c) = \sigma(h, k, -c)$.

11. (a) $\displaystyle\sum_{0 \leq j < dk}\left(\left(\frac{j}{dk}\right)\right)\left(\left(\frac{hj+c}{k}\right)\right) = \sum_{\substack{0 \leq i < d \\ 0 \leq j < k}}\left(\left(\frac{ik+j}{dk}\right)\right)\left(\left(\frac{hj+c}{k}\right)\right)$; use (10) to sum on i.

(b) $\displaystyle\left(\left(\frac{hj + c + \theta}{k}\right)\right) = \left(\left(\frac{hj + c}{k}\right)\right) + \frac{\theta}{k} - \frac{1}{2}\delta\left(\frac{hj + c}{k}\right)$; now sum.

12. Since $\left(\left(\frac{hj+c}{k}\right)\right)$ runs through the same values as $\left(\left(\frac{j}{k}\right)\right)$ in some order, Cauchy's inequality implies that $\sigma(h, k, c)^2 \leq \sigma(h, k, 0)^2$; and $\sigma(1, k, 0)$ may be summed directly, see exercise 7.

13. $\displaystyle\sigma(h, k, c) + \frac{3(k - 1)}{k} = \frac{12}{k}\sum_{0 < j < k}\frac{\omega^{-cj}}{(\omega^{-hj} - 1)(\omega^j - 1)} + \frac{6}{k}(c \bmod k) - 6\left(\left(\frac{h'c}{k}\right)\right),$

if $hh' \equiv 1$ (modulo k).

14. $(2^{38} - 3 \cdot 2^{20} + 5)/(2^{70} - 1) \approx 2^{-32}$. An extremely satisfactory global value, in spite of the local nonrandomness!

15. Replace c^2 where it appears in (19) by $\lfloor c\rfloor\lceil c\rceil$.

16. The hinted identity is equivalent to $m_1 = p_r m_{r+1} + p_{r-1}m_{r+2}$ for $1 \leq r \leq t$; this follows by induction. (See also exercise 4.5.3–32.) Now replace c_j by $\sum_{j \leq r \leq t} b_r m_{r+1}$ and compare coefficients of $b_i b_j$ on both sides of the identity to be proved.

Note: For all exponents $e \geq 1$, a similar argument gives

$$\sum_{1 \leq j \leq t}(-1)^{j+1}\frac{c_j^e}{m_j m_{j+1}} = \frac{1}{m_1}\sum_{1 \leq j \leq t}(-1)^{j+1}b_j\frac{c_j^e - c_{j+1}^e}{c_j - c_{j+1}}p_{j-1}.$$

17. During this algorithm we will have $k = m_j$, $h = m_{j+1}$, $c = c_j$, $p = p_{j-1}$, $p' = p_{j-2}$, $s = (-1)^{j+1}$ for $j = 1, 2, \ldots, t + 1$.

D1. [Initialize.] Set $A \leftarrow 0$, $B \leftarrow h$, $p \leftarrow 1$, $p' \leftarrow 0$, $s \leftarrow 1$.

D2. [Divide.] Set $a \leftarrow \lfloor k/h\rfloor$, $b \leftarrow \lfloor c/h\rfloor$, $r \leftarrow c \bmod h$. (Now $a = a_j$, $b = b_j$, and $r = c_{j+1}$.)

D3. [Accumulate.] Set $A \leftarrow A + (a - 6b)s$, $B \leftarrow B + 6bp(c + r)s$. If $r \neq 0$ or $c = 0$, set $A \leftarrow A - 3s$. If $h = 1$, set $B \leftarrow B + ps$. (This subtracts $3e(m_{j+1}, c_j)$ and also takes care of the $\sum(-1)^{j+1}/m_j m_{j+1}$ terms.)

D4. [Prepare for next iteration.] Set $c \leftarrow r$, $s \leftarrow -s$; set $r \leftarrow k - ah$, $k \leftarrow h$, $h \leftarrow r$; set $r \leftarrow ap + p'$, $p' \leftarrow p$, $p \leftarrow r$. If $h > 0$, return to D2. ∎

At the conclusion of this algorithm, p will be equal to the original value k_0 of k, so the desired answer will be $A + B/p$. The final value of p' will be h' if $s < 0$, otherwise p' will be $k_0 - h'$. It would be possible to maintain B in the range $0 \le B < k_0$, by making appropriate adjustments to A, thereby requiring only single-precision operations (with double-precision products and dividends) if k_0 is a single-precision number.

18. A moment's thought shows that the formula

$$S(h, k, c, z) = \sum_{0 \le j < k} (\lfloor j/k \rfloor - \lfloor (j - z)/k \rfloor) (((hj + c)/k))$$

is in fact valid for all $z \ge 0$, not only when $k \ge z$. Writing $\lfloor j/k \rfloor - \lfloor (j - z)/k \rfloor = \frac{z}{k} + ((\frac{j-z}{k})) - ((\frac{j}{k})) + \frac{1}{2} \delta_{j0} - \frac{1}{2} \delta(\frac{j-z}{k})$ and carrying out the sums yields

$$S(h, k, c, z) = \frac{zd}{k} \left(\left(\frac{c}{d}\right)\right) + \frac{1}{12} \sigma(h, k, hz + c) - \frac{1}{12} \sigma(h, k, c) + \frac{1}{2} \left(\left(\frac{c}{k}\right)\right) - \frac{1}{2} \left(\left(\frac{hz + c}{k}\right)\right),$$

where $d = \gcd(h, k)$. [This formula allows us to express the probability that $X_{n+1} < X_n < \alpha$ in terms of generalized Dedekind sums, given α.]

19. The desired probability is

$$m^{-1} \sum_{x=0}^{m-1} \left(\left\lfloor \frac{x - \alpha}{m} \right\rfloor - \left\lfloor \frac{x - \beta}{m} \right\rfloor\right) \left(\left\lfloor \frac{s(x) - \alpha'}{m} \right\rfloor - \left\lfloor \frac{s(x) - \beta'}{m} \right\rfloor\right)$$

$$= m^{-1} \sum_{x=0}^{m-1} \left(\frac{\beta - \alpha}{m} + \left(\left(\frac{x - \beta}{m}\right)\right) - \left(\left(\frac{x - \alpha}{m}\right)\right) + \frac{1}{2} \delta\left(\frac{x - \alpha}{m}\right) - \frac{1}{2} \delta\left(\frac{x - \beta}{m}\right)\right)$$

$$\times \left(\frac{\beta' - \alpha'}{m} + \left(\left(\frac{s(x) - \beta'}{m}\right)\right) - \left(\left(\frac{s(x) - \alpha'}{m}\right)\right) + \frac{1}{2} \delta\left(\frac{s(x) - \alpha'}{m}\right) - \frac{1}{2} \delta\left(\frac{s(x) - \beta'}{m}\right)\right)$$

$$= \frac{\beta - \alpha}{m} \frac{\beta' - \alpha'}{m} + \frac{1}{12m} \Big(\sigma(a, m, c + a\alpha - \alpha') - \sigma(a, m, c + a\alpha - \beta')$$

$$+ \sigma(a, m, c + a\beta - \beta') - \sigma(a, m, c + a\beta - \alpha')\Big) + \epsilon,$$

where $|\epsilon| \le 2.5/m$.

[This approach is due to U. Dieter. The discrepancy between the true probability and the ideal value $\frac{\beta - \alpha}{m} \frac{\beta' - \alpha'}{m}$ is bounded by $\sum_{j=1}^{t} a_j/4m$, according to Theorem K; conversely, by choosing α, β, α', β' appropriately we will obtain a discrepancy of at least half this bound when there are large partial quotients, using the fact that Theorem K is "best possible." Note that when $a \approx \sqrt{m}$ the discrepancy cannot exceed $O(1/\sqrt{m})$, so even the locally nonrandom generator of exercise 14 will look good on the serial test over the full period; it appears that we should insist on an *extremely* small discrepancy.]

20. $\sum_{0 \le x < m} \lceil (x - s(x))/m \rceil \lceil (s(x) - s(s(x)))/m \rceil/m = \sum_{0 \le x < m} ((x - s(x))/m + (((bx + c)/m)) + \frac{1}{2}) ((s(x) - s(s(x)))/m + ((a(bx + c)/m)) + \frac{1}{2})/m$; and $x/m = ((x/m)) + \frac{1}{2} - \frac{1}{2} \delta(x/m)$, $s(x)/m = (((ax + c)/m)) + \frac{1}{2} - \frac{1}{2} \delta((ax + c)/m)$, $s(s(x))/m = (((a^2x + ac + c)/m)) + \frac{1}{2} - \frac{1}{2} \delta((a^2x + ac + c)/m)$. Let $s(x') = s(s(x'')) = 0$ and $d = \gcd(b, m)$. The sum now reduces to

$$\frac{1}{4} + \frac{1}{12m}(S_1 - S_2 + S_3 - S_4 + S_5 - S_6 + S_7 - S_8 + S_9) + \frac{d}{m}\left(\left(\frac{c}{d}\right)\right)$$

$$+ \frac{1}{2m} \left(\left(\left(\frac{x' - x''}{m}\right)\right) - \left(\left(\frac{x'}{m}\right)\right) + \left(\left(\frac{x''}{m}\right)\right) + \left(\left(\frac{ac + c}{m}\right)\right) - \left(\left(\frac{ac}{m}\right)\right) - \left(\left(\frac{c}{m}\right)\right) - \frac{1}{2}\right),$$

where $S_1 = \sigma(a, m, c)$, $S_2 = \sigma(a^2, m, ac + c)$, $S_3 = \sigma(ab, m, ac)$, $S_4 = \sigma(1, m, 0) = (m - 1)(m - 2)/m$, $S_5 = \sigma(a, m, c)$, $S_6 = \sigma(b, m, c)$, $S_7 = -\sigma(a' - 1, m, a'c)$, and $S_8 = -\sigma(a'(a' - 1), m, (a')^2 c)$, if $a'a \equiv 1$ (modulo m); and finally

$$S_9 = 12 \sum_{0 \le x < m} \left(\!\left(\frac{bx + c}{m}\right)\!\right)\left(\!\left(\frac{a(bx + c)}{m}\right)\!\right)$$

$$= 12d \sum_{0 \le x < m/d} \left(\!\left(\frac{x + c_0/d}{m/d}\right)\!\right)\left(\!\left(\frac{a(x + c_0/d)}{m/d}\right)\!\right)$$

$$= 12d \sum_{0 \le x < m/d} \left(\left(\!\left(\frac{x}{m/d}\right)\!\right) + \frac{c_0}{m} - \frac{1}{2}\delta_{x0}\right)\left(\!\left(\frac{a(x + c_0/d)}{m/d}\right)\!\right)$$

$$= d\left(\sigma(ad, m, ac_0) + 12\frac{c_0}{m}\left(\!\left(\frac{ac_0}{d}\right)\!\right) - 6\left(\!\left(\frac{ac_0}{m}\right)\!\right)\right)$$

where $c_0 = c \bmod d$. The grand total will be near $\frac{1}{6}$ when d is small and when the fractions a/m, $(a^2 \bmod m)/m$, $(ab \bmod m)/m$, b/m, $(a' - 1)/m$, $(a'(a' - 1) \bmod m)/m$, $((ad) \bmod m)/m$ all have small partial quotients. (Note that $a' - 1 \equiv -b + b^2 - \cdots$, as in exercise 3.2.1.3–7.)

21. Notice first that the main integral decomposes nicely:

$$s_n = \int_{x_n}^{x_{n+1}} x\{ax + \theta\}\,dx = \frac{1}{a^2}\left(\frac{1}{3} - \frac{\theta}{2} + \frac{n}{2}\right), \qquad \text{if } x_n = \frac{n - \theta}{a};$$

$$s = \int_0^1 x\{ax + \theta\}\,dx = s_0 + s_1 + \cdots + s_{a-1} + \int_{-\theta/a}^0 (ax + \theta)\,dx = \frac{1}{3a} - \frac{\theta}{2a} + \frac{a - 1}{4a} + \frac{\theta^2}{2a}.$$

Therefore $C = (s - (\frac{1}{2})^2)/(\frac{1}{3} - (\frac{1}{2})^2) = (1 - 6\theta + 6\theta^2)/a$.

22. We have $s(x) < x$ in the disjoint intervals $[\frac{1-\theta}{a} \mathinner{.\,.} \frac{1-\theta}{a-1})$, $[\frac{2-\theta}{a} \mathinner{.\,.} \frac{2-\theta}{a-1})$, $\ldots$, $[\frac{a-\theta}{a} \mathinner{.\,.} 1)$, which have total length

$$1 + \sum_{0 < j \le a-1} \left(\frac{j - \theta}{a - 1}\right) - \sum_{0 < j \le a} \left(\frac{j - \theta}{a}\right) = 1 + \frac{a}{2} - \theta - \frac{a + 1}{2} + \theta = \frac{1}{2}.$$

23. We have $s(s(x)) < s(x) < x$ when x is in $[\frac{k-\theta}{a} \mathinner{.\,.} \frac{k-\theta}{a-1})$ and $ax + \theta - k$ is in $[\frac{j-\theta}{a} \mathinner{.\,.} \frac{j-\theta}{a-1})$, for $0 < j \le k < a$; or when x is in $[\frac{a-\theta}{a} \mathinner{.\,.} 1)$ and $ax + \theta - a$ is either in $[\frac{j-\theta}{a} \mathinner{.\,.} \frac{j-\theta}{a-1})$ for $0 < j \le \lfloor a\theta \rfloor$ or in $[\frac{\lfloor a\theta \rfloor + 1 - \theta}{a} \mathinner{.\,.} \theta)$. The desired probability is

$$\sum_{0 < j \le k < a} \frac{j - \theta}{a^2(a - 1)} + \sum_{0 < j \le \lfloor a\theta \rfloor} \frac{j - \theta}{a^2(a - 1)} + \frac{1}{a^2}\max(0, \{a\theta\} + \theta - 1)$$

$$= \frac{1}{6} + \frac{1}{6a} - \frac{\theta}{2a} + \frac{1}{a^2}\left(\frac{\lfloor a\theta \rfloor(\lfloor a\theta \rfloor + 1 - 2\theta)}{2(a - 1)} + \max(0, \{a\theta\} + \theta - 1)\right),$$

which is $\frac{1}{6} + (1 - 3\theta + 3\theta^2)/6a + O(1/a^2)$ for large a. Note that $1 - 3\theta + 3\theta^2 \ge \frac{1}{4}$, so θ can't be chosen to make this probability come out right.

24. Proceed as in the previous exercise; the sum of the interval lengths is

$$\sum_{0 < j_1 \le \cdots \le j_{t-1} < a} \frac{j_1}{a^{t-1}(a - 1)} = \frac{1}{a^{t-1}(a - 1)}\binom{a + t - 2}{t}.$$

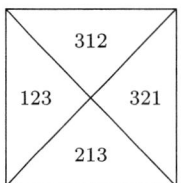

Fig. A–1. Permutation regions
for the Fibonacci generator.

Fig. A–2. Run-length regions
for the Fibonacci generator.

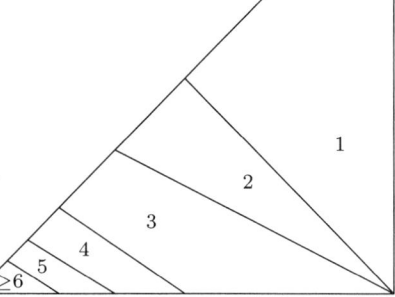

To compute the average length, let p_k be the probability of a run of length $\geq k$; the average is

$$\sum_{k\geq 1} p_k = \sum_{k\geq 1} \binom{a+k-2}{k} \frac{1}{a^{k-1}(a-1)} = \left(\frac{a}{a-1}\right)^a - \frac{a}{a-1}.$$

The value for a truly random sequence would be $e-1$; and our value is $e-1+(e/2-1)/a+O(1/a^2)$. [*Note:* The same result holds for an ascending run, since we have $U_n > U_{n+1}$ if and only if $1-U_n < 1-U_{n+1}$. This would lead us to suspect that runs in linear congruential sequences might be slightly longer than normal, so the run test should be applied to such generators.]

25. x must be in the interval $[(k+\alpha'-\theta)/a \mathrel{..} (k+\beta'-\theta)/a)$ for some k, and also in the interval $[\alpha \mathrel{..} \beta)$. Let $k_0 = \lceil a\alpha+\theta-\beta' \rceil$, $k_1 = \lceil a\beta+\theta-\beta' \rceil$. With due regard to boundary conditions, we get the probability

$$(k_1-k_0)(\beta'-\alpha')/a + \max(0, \beta-(k_1+\alpha'-\theta)/a) - \max(0, \alpha-(k_0+\alpha'-\theta)/a).$$

This is $(\beta-\alpha)(\beta'-\alpha')+\epsilon$, where $|\epsilon| < 2(\beta'-\alpha')/a$.

26. See Fig. A–1. The orderings $U_1 < U_3 < U_2$ and $U_2 < U_3 < U_1$ are impossible; the other four each have probability $\frac{1}{4}$.

27. $U_n = \{F_{n-1}U_0 + F_nU_1\}$. We need to have both $F_{k-1}U_0 + F_kU_1 < 1$ and $F_kU_0 + F_{k+1}U_1 > 1$. The half-unit-square in which $U_0 > U_1$ is broken up as shown in Fig. A–2, with various values of k indicated. The probability for a run of length k is $\frac{1}{2}$, if $k=1$; it is $1/F_{k-1}F_{k+1} - 1/F_kF_{k+2}$, if $k > 1$. The corresponding probabilities for a random sequence are $2k/(k+1)! - 2(k+1)/(k+2)!$; the following table compares the first few values.

k:	1	2	3	4	5
Probability in Fibonacci case:	$\frac{1}{2}$	$\frac{1}{3}$	$\frac{1}{10}$	$\frac{1}{24}$	$\frac{1}{65}$
Probability in random case:	$\frac{1}{3}$	$\frac{5}{12}$	$\frac{11}{60}$	$\frac{19}{360}$	$\frac{29}{2520}$

28. Fig. A–3 shows the various regions in the general case. The "213" region means $U_2 < U_1 < U_3$, if U_1 and U_2 are chosen at random; the "321" region means that $U_3 < U_2 < U_1$, etc. The probabilities for 123 and 321 are $\frac{1}{4} - \alpha/2 + \alpha^2/2$; the probabilities for all other cases are $\frac{1}{8} + \alpha/4 - \alpha^2/4$. To have all equal to $\frac{1}{6}$, we must have

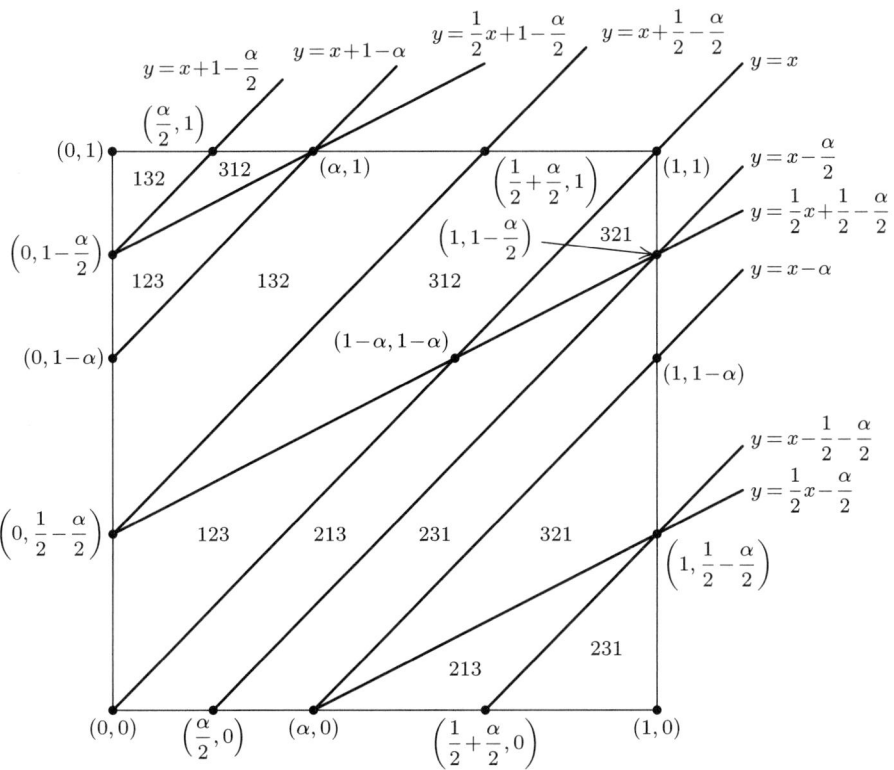

Fig. A–3. Permutation regions for a generator with potency 2; $\alpha = (a-1)c/m$.

$1 - 6\alpha + 6\alpha^2 = 0$. [This exercise establishes a theorem due to J. N. Franklin, *Math. Comp.* **17** (1963), 28–59, Theorem 13; other results of Franklin's paper are related to exercises 22 and 23.]

SECTION 3.3.4

1. For generators of maximum period, the 1-D accuracy ν_1 is always m, and $\mu_1 = 2$.

2. Let V be the matrix whose rows are $V_1, \ldots, V_t$. To minimize $Y \cdot Y$, subject to the condition that $Y \neq (0, \ldots, 0)$ and VY is an integer column vector X, is equivalent to minimizing $(V^{-1}X) \cdot (V^{-1}X)$, subject to the condition that X is a nonzero integer column vector. The columns of V^{-1} are $U_1, \ldots, U_t$.

3. $a^2 \equiv 2a - 1$ and $a^3 \equiv 3a - 2$ (modulo m). By considering all short solutions of (15), we find that $\nu_3^2 = 6$ and $\nu_4^2 = 4$, for the respective vectors $(1, -2, 1)$ and $(1, -1, -1, 1)$, except in the following cases:

$$m = 9, \quad a = 4 \text{ or } 7, \quad \nu_2^2 = \nu_3^2 = 5;$$
$$m = 9q, \quad a = 3q + 1 \text{ or } 6q + 1, \quad \nu_4^2 = 2.$$

4. (a) The unique choice for (x_1, x_2) is $\frac{1}{m}(y_1 u_{22} - y_2 u_{21}, -y_1 u_{12} + y_2 u_{11})$, and this is $\equiv \frac{1}{m}(y_1 u_{22} + y_2 a u_{22}, -y_1 u_{12} - y_2 a u_{12}) \equiv (0,0)$ (modulo 1); that is, x_1 and x_2 are integers. (b) When $(x_1, x_2) \neq (0,0)$, we have $(x_1 u_{11} + x_2 u_{21})^2 + (x_1 u_{12} + x_2 u_{22})^2 = x_1^2(u_{11}^2 + u_{12}^2) + x_2^2(u_{21}^2 + u_{22}^2) + 2x_1 x_2(u_{11} u_{21} + u_{12} u_{22})$, and by hypothesis this is $\geq (x_1^2 + x_2^2 - |x_1 x_2|)(u_{11}^2 + u_{12}^2) \geq u_{11}^2 + u_{12}^2$.

[Note that this is a stronger result than Lemma A, which tells us only that $x_1^2 \leq (u_{11}^2 + u_{12}^2)(u_{21}^2 + u_{22}^2)/m^2$ and that $x_2^2 \leq (u_{11}^2 + u_{12}^2)^2/m^2$, where the latter can be ≥ 1. The idea is essentially Gauss's notion of a reduced binary quadratic form, *Disquisitiones Arithmeticæ* (Leipzig: 1801), §171.]

5. Conditions (30) remain invariant; hence h cannot be zero in step S2, when a is relatively prime to m. Since h always decreases in that step, S2 eventually terminates with $u^2 + v^2 \geq s$. Notice that $pp' \leq 0$ throughout the calculation.

The hinted inequality surely holds the first time step S2 is encountered. The integer q' that minimizes $(h' - q'h)^2 + (p' - q'p)^2$ is $q' = \text{round}((h'h + p'p)/(h^2 + p^2))$, by Eq. (24). If $(h' - q'h)^2 + (p' - q'p)^2 < h^2 + p^2$ we must have $q' \neq 0$, $q' \neq -1$, hence $(p' - q'p)^2 \geq p^2$, hence $(h' - q'h)^2 < h^2$, i.e., $|h' - q'h| < h$, i.e., q' is q or $q+1$. We have $hu + pv \geq h(h' - q'h) + p(p' - q'p) \geq -\frac{1}{2}(h^2 + p^2)$, so if $u^2 + v^2 < s$ the next iteration of step S2 will preserve the assumption in the hint. If $u^2 + v^2 \geq s > (u-h)^2 + (v-p)^2$, we have $2|h(u-h) + p(v-p)| = 2(h(h-u) + p(p-v)) = (u-h)^2 + (v-p)^2 + h^2 + p^2 - (u^2 + v^2) \leq (u-h)^2 + (v-p)^2 \leq h^2 + p^2$, hence $(u-h)^2 + (v-p)^2$ is minimal by exercise 4. Finally if both $u^2 + v^2$ and $(u-h)^2 + (v-p)^2$ are $\geq s$, let $u' = h' - q'h$, $v' = p' - q'p$; then $2|hu' + pv'| \leq h^2 + p^2 \leq u'^2 + v'^2$, and $h^2 + p^2$ is minimal by exercise 4.

[Generalizations to finding the shortest 2-D vector with respect to other metrics are discussed by Kaib and Schnorr, *J. Algorithms* **21** (1996), 565–578.]

6. If $u^2 + v^2 \geq s > (u-h)^2 + (v-p)^2$ in the previous answer, we have $(v-p)^2 > v^2$, hence $(u-h)^2 < u^2$; and if $q = a_j$, so that $h' = a_j h + u$, we must have $a_{j+1} = 1$. It follows that $\nu_2^2 = \min_{0 \leq j < t}(m_j^2 + p_{j-1}^2)$, in the notation of exercise 3.3.3–16.

Now we have $m_0 = m_j p_j + m_{j+1} p_{j-1} = a_j m_j p_{j-1} + m_j p_{j-2} + m_{j+1} p_{j-1} < (a_j + 1 + 1/a_j) m_j p_{j-1} \leq (A + 1 + 1/A) m_j p_{j-1}$, and $m_j^2 + p_{j-1}^2 \geq 2 m_j p_{j-1}$, hence the result.

7. We shall prove, using condition (19), that $U_j \cdot U_k = 0$ for all $k \neq j$ if and only if $V_j \cdot V_k = 0$ for all $k \neq j$. Assume that $U_j \cdot U_k = 0$ for all $k \neq j$, and let $U_j = \alpha_1 V_1 + \cdots + \alpha_t V_t$. Then $U_j \cdot U_k = \alpha_k$ for all k, hence $U_j = \alpha_j V_j$, and $V_j \cdot V_k = \alpha_j^{-1}(U_j \cdot V_k) = 0$ for all $k \neq j$. A symmetric argument proves the converse.

8. Clearly $\nu_{t+1} \leq \nu_t$ (a fact used implicitly in Algorithm S, since s is not changed when t increases). For $t = 2$ this is equivalent to $(m\mu_2/\pi)^{1/2} \geq (\frac{3}{4} m\mu_3/\pi)^{1/3}$, i.e., $\mu_3 \leq \frac{4}{3}\sqrt{m/\pi}\,\mu_2^{3/2}$. This bound reduces to $\frac{4}{3} 10^{-4}/\sqrt{\pi}$ with the given parameters, but for large m and fixed μ_2 the bound (40) is better.

9. Let $f(y_1, \ldots, y_t) = \theta$; then $\gcd(y_1, \ldots, y_t) = 1$, so there is an integer matrix W of determinant 1 having $(y_1, \ldots, y_t)$ as its first row. (Prove the latter fact by induction on the magnitude of the smallest nonzero entry in the row.) Now if $X = (x_1, \ldots, x_t)$ is a row vector, we have $XW = X'$ if and only if $X = X'W^{-1}$, and W^{-1} is an integer matrix of determinant 1, hence the form g defined by WU satisfies $g(x_1, \ldots, x_t) = f(x_1', \ldots, x_t')$; furthermore $g(1, 0, \ldots, 0) = \theta$.

Without loss of generality, assume that $f = g$. If now S is any orthogonal matrix, the matrix US defines the same form as U, since $(XUS)(XUS)^T = (XU)(XU)^T$. Choosing S so that its first column is a multiple of U_1^T and its other columns are any suitable vectors, we have

$$US = \begin{pmatrix} \alpha_1 & 0 & \cdots & 0 \\ \alpha_2 & & & \\ \vdots & & U' & \\ \alpha_t & & & \end{pmatrix}$$

for some $\alpha_1, \alpha_2, \ldots, \alpha_t$ and some $(t-1) \times (t-1)$ matrix U'. Hence $f(x_1, \ldots, x_t) = (\alpha_1 x_1 + \cdots + \alpha_t x_t)^2 + h(x_2, \ldots, x_t)$. It follows that $\alpha_1 = \sqrt{\theta}$ [in fact, $\alpha_j = (U_1 \cdot U_j)/\sqrt{\theta}$ for $1 \leq j \leq t$] and that h is a positive definite quadratic form defined by U', where $\det U' = (\det U)/\sqrt{\theta}$. By induction on t, there are integers $(x_2, \ldots, x_t)$ with

$$h(x_2, \ldots, x_t) \leq \left(\tfrac{4}{3}\right)^{(t-2)/2} |\det U|^{2/(t-1)}/\theta^{1/(t-1)},$$

and for these integer values we can choose x_1 so that $|x_1 + (\alpha_2 x_2 + \cdots + \alpha_t x_t)/\alpha_1| \leq \tfrac{1}{2}$; equivalently, $(\alpha_1 x_1 + \cdots + \alpha_t x_t)^2 \leq \tfrac{1}{4}\theta$. Hence

$$\theta \leq f(x_1, \ldots, x_t) \leq \tfrac{1}{4}\theta + \left(\tfrac{4}{3}\right)^{(t-2)/2} |\det U|^{2/(t-1)}/\theta^{1/(t-1)}$$

and the desired inequality follows immediately.

[*Note:* For $t = 2$ the result is best possible. For general t, Hermite's theorem implies that $\mu_t \leq \pi^{t/2}(4/3)^{t(t-1)/4}/(t/2)!$. A fundamental theorem due to Minkowski ("Every t-dimensional convex set symmetric about the origin with volume $\geq 2^t$ contains a nonzero integer point") gives $\mu_t \leq 2^t$; this is stronger than Hermite's theorem for $t \geq 9$. Even stronger results are known, see (41).]

10. Since y_1 and y_2 are relatively prime, we can solve $u_1 y_2 - u_2 y_1 = m$; furthermore $(u_1 + qy_1)y_2 - (u_2 + qy_2)y_1 = m$ for all q, so we can ensure that $2|u_1 y_1 + u_2 y_2| \leq y_1^2 + y_2^2$ by choosing an appropriate integer q. Now $y_2(u_1 + au_2) \equiv y_2 u_1 - y_1 u_2 \equiv 0 \pmod{m}$, and y_2 must be relatively prime to m, hence $u_1 + au_2 \equiv 0$. Finally let $|u_1 y_1 + u_2 y_2| = \alpha m$, $u_1^2 + u_2^2 = \beta m$, $y_1^2 + y_2^2 = \gamma m$; we have $0 \leq \alpha \leq \tfrac{1}{2}\gamma$, and it remains to be shown that $\alpha \leq \tfrac{1}{2}\beta$ and $\beta\gamma \geq 1$. The identity $(u_1 y_2 - u_2 y_1)^2 + (u_1 y_1 + u_2 y_2)^2 = (u_1^2 + u_2^2)(y_1^2 + y_2^2)$ implies that $1 + \alpha^2 = \beta\gamma$. If $\alpha > \tfrac{1}{2}\beta$, we have $2\alpha\gamma > 1 + \alpha^2$, that is, $\gamma - \sqrt{\gamma^2 - 1} < \alpha \leq \tfrac{1}{2}\gamma$. But $\tfrac{1}{2}\gamma < \sqrt{\gamma^2 - 1}$ implies that $\gamma^2 > \tfrac{4}{3}$, a contradiction.

11. Since a is odd, $y_1 + y_2$ must be even. To avoid solutions with y_1 and y_2 both even, let $y_1 = x_1 + x_2$, $y_2 = x_1 - x_2$, and solve $x_1^2 + x_2^2 = m/\sqrt{3} - \epsilon$, with $x_1 \perp x_2$ and x_1 even; the corresponding multiplier a will be the solution to $(x_2 - x_1)a \equiv x_2 + x_1 \pmod{2^e}$. It is not difficult to prove that $a \equiv 1 \pmod{2^{k+1}}$ if and only if $x_1 \equiv 0 \pmod{2^k}$, so we get the best potency when $x_1 \bmod 4 = 2$. The problem reduces to finding relatively prime solutions to $x_1^2 + x_2^2 = N$ where N is a large integer of the form $4k + 1$. By factoring N over the Gaussian integers, we can see that solutions exist if and only if each prime factor of N (over the usual integers) has the form $4k + 1$.

According to a famous theorem of Fermat, every prime p of the form $4k + 1$ can be written $p = u^2 + v^2 = (u + iv)(u - iv)$, v even, in a unique way except for the signs of u and v. The numbers u and v can be calculated efficiently by solving $x^2 \equiv -1 \pmod{p}$, then calculating $u + iv = \gcd(x + i, p)$ by Euclid's algorithm over the Gaussian integers. [We can take $x = n^{(p-1)/4} \bmod p$ for almost half of all integers n. This application of a Euclidean algorithm is essentially the same as finding the least nonzero $u^2 + v^2$ such that $u \pm xv \equiv 0 \pmod{p}$. The values of u and v also appear when Euclid's algorithm for integers is applied in the ordinary way to p and x; see J. A. Serret and C. Hermite, *J. de Math. Pures et Appl.* **5** (1848), 12–15.] If the prime factorization of N is $p_1^{e_1} \ldots p_r^{e_r} = (u_1 + iv_1)^{e_1}(u_1 - iv_1)^{e_1} \ldots (u_r + iv_r)^{e_r}(u_r - iv_r)^{e_r}$, we get 2^{r-1} distinct solutions to $x_1^2 + x_2^2 = N$, $x_1 \perp x_2$, x_1 even, by letting $|x_2| + i|x_1| = (u_1 + iv_1)^{e_1}(u_2 \pm iv_2)^{e_2} \ldots (u_r \pm iv_r)^{e_r}$; and all such solutions are obtained in this way.

Note: When $m = 10^e$, a similar procedure can be used, but it is five times as much work since we must keep trying until finding a solution with $x_1 \equiv 0$ (modulo 10). For example, when $m = 10^{10}$ we have $\lfloor m/\sqrt{3} \rfloor = 5773502691$, and $5773502689 = 53 \cdot 108934013 = (7 + 2i)(7 - 2i)(2203 + 10202i)(2203 - 10202i)$. Of the two solutions $|x_2| + i|x_1| = (7 + 2i)(2203 + 10202i)$ or $(7 + 2i)(2203 - 10202i)$, the former gives $|x_1| = 67008$ (no good) and the latter gives $|x_1| = 75820$, $|x_2| = 4983$ (which is usable). Line 9 of Table 1 was obtained by taking $x_1 = 75820$, $x_2 = -4983$.

Line 14 of the table was obtained as follows: $\lfloor 2^{32}/\sqrt{3} \rfloor = 2479700524$; we drop down to $N = 2479700521$, which equals $37 \cdot 797 \cdot 84089$ and has four solutions $N = 4364^2 + 49605^2 = 26364^2 + 42245^2 = 38640^2 + 31411^2 = 11960^2 + 48339^2$. The corresponding multipliers are 2974037721, 2254986297, 4246248609, and 956772177. We try also $N - 4$, but it is ineligible because it is divisible by 3. On the other hand the prime number $N - 8 = 45088^2 + 21137^2$ leads to the multiplier 3825140801. Similarly, we get additional multipliers from $N - 20$, $N - 44$, $N - 48$, etc. The multiplier on line 14 is the best of the first sixteen multipliers found by this procedure; it's one of the four obtained from $N - 68$.

12. $U_j' \cdot U_j' = U_j \cdot U_j + 2\sum_{i \neq j} q_i(U_i \cdot U_j) + \sum_{i \neq j}\sum_{k \neq j} q_i q_k(U_i \cdot U_k)$. The partial derivative with respect to q_k is twice the left-hand side of (26). If the minimum can be achieved, these partial derivatives must all vanish.

13. $u_{11} = 1$, $u_{21} = $ irrational, $u_{12} = u_{22} = 0$.

14. After three Euclidean steps we find $\nu_2^2 = 5^2 + 5^2$, then S4 produces

$$U = \begin{pmatrix} -5 & 5 & 0 \\ -18 & -2 & 0 \\ 1 & -2 & 1 \end{pmatrix}, \qquad V = \begin{pmatrix} -2 & 18 & 38 \\ -5 & -5 & -5 \\ 0 & 0 & 100 \end{pmatrix}.$$

Transformations $(j, q_1, q_2, q_3) = (1, *, 0, 2)$, $(2, -4, *, 1)$, $(3, 0, 0, *)$, $(1, *, 0, 0)$ result in

$$U = \begin{pmatrix} -3 & 1 & 2 \\ -5 & -8 & -7 \\ 1 & -2 & 1 \end{pmatrix}, \qquad V = \begin{pmatrix} -22 & -2 & 18 \\ -5 & -5 & -5 \\ 9 & -31 & 29 \end{pmatrix}, \qquad Z = (0 \quad 0 \quad 1).$$

Thus $\nu_3 = \sqrt{6}$, as we already knew from exercise 3.

15. The largest achievable q in (11), minus the smallest achievable, plus 1, is $|u_1| + \cdots + |u_t| - \delta$, where $\delta = 1$ if $u_i u_j < 0$ for some i and j, otherwise $\delta = 0$. For example if $t = 5$, $u_1 > 0$, $u_2 > 0$, $u_3 > 0$, $u_4 = 0$, and $u_5 < 0$, the largest achievable value is $q = u_1 + u_2 + u_3 - 1$ and the smallest is $q = u_5 + 1 = -|u_5| + 1$.

[Note that the number of hyperplanes is unchanged when c varies, hence the same answer applies to the problem of covering L instead of L_0. However, the stated formula is *not* always exact for covering L_0, since the hyperplanes that intersect the unit hypercube may not all contain points of L_0. In the example above, we can never achieve the value $q = u_1 + u_2 + u_3 - 1$ in L_0 if $u_1 + u_2 + u_3 > m$; it is achievable if and only if there is a solution to $m - u_1 - u_2 - u_3 = x_1 u_1 + x_2 u_2 + x_3 u_3 + x_4|u_5|$ in nonnegative integers (x_1, x_2, x_3, x_4). It may be true that the stated limits are always achievable when $|u_1| + \cdots + |u_t|$ is minimal, but this does not appear to be obvious.]

16. It suffices to determine all solutions to (15) having minimum $|u_1| + \cdots + |u_t|$, subtracting 1 if any one of these solutions has components of opposite sign.

Instead of positive definite quadratic forms, we work with the somewhat similar function $f(x_1, \ldots, x_t) = |x_1 U_1 + \cdots + x_t U_t|$, defining $|Y| = |y_1| + \cdots + |y_t|$. Inequality (21) can be replaced by $|x_k| \le f(y_1, \ldots, y_t)\left(\max_{1 \le j \le t} |v_{kj}|\right)$.

Thus a workable algorithm can be obtained as follows. Replace steps S1 through S3 by: "Set $U \leftarrow (m)$, $V \leftarrow (1)$, $r \leftarrow 1$, $s \leftarrow m$, $t \leftarrow 1$." (Here U and V are 1×1 matrices; thus the two-dimensional case will be handled by the general method. A special procedure for $t = 2$ could, of course, be used; see the reference following the answer to exercise 5.) In steps S4 and S7, set $s \leftarrow \min(s, |U_k|)$. In step S7, set $z_k \leftarrow \lfloor \max_{1 \le j \le t} |v_{kj}| s/m \rfloor$. In step S9, set $s \leftarrow \min(s, |Y| - \delta)$; and in step S10, output $s = N_t$. Otherwise leave the algorithm as it stands, since it already produces suitably short vectors. [*Math. Comp.* **29** (1975), 827–833.]

17. When $k > t$ in S9, and if $Y \cdot Y \le s$, output Y and $-Y$; furthermore if $Y \cdot Y < s$, take back the previous output of vectors for this t. [In the author's experience preparing Table 1, there was exactly one vector (and its negative) output for each ν_t, except when $y_1 = 0$ or $y_t = 0$.]

18. (a) Let $x = m$, $y = (1 - m)/3$, $v_{ij} = y + x\delta_{ij}$, $u_{ij} = -y + \delta_{ij}$. Then $V_j \cdot V_k = \frac{1}{3}(m^2 - 1)$ for $j \ne k$, $V_k \cdot V_k = \frac{2}{3}(m^2 + \frac{1}{2})$, $U_j \cdot U_j = \frac{1}{3}(m^2 + 2)$, $z_k \approx \sqrt{\frac{2}{9}}\, m$. (This example satisfies (28) with $a = 1$ and works for all $m \equiv 1$ (modulo 3).)

(b) Interchange the roles of U and V in step S5. Also set $s \leftarrow \min(s, U_i \cdot U_i)$ for all U_i that change. For example, when $m = 64$ this transformation with $j = 1$, applied to the matrices of (a), reduces

$$V = \begin{pmatrix} 43 & -21 & -21 \\ -21 & 43 & -21 \\ -21 & -21 & 43 \end{pmatrix}, \quad U = \begin{pmatrix} 22 & 21 & 21 \\ 21 & 22 & 21 \\ 21 & 21 & 22 \end{pmatrix}$$

to

$$V = \begin{pmatrix} 1 & 1 & 1 \\ -21 & 43 & -21 \\ -21 & -21 & 43 \end{pmatrix}, \quad U = \begin{pmatrix} 22 & 21 & 21 \\ -1 & 1 & 0 \\ -1 & 0 & 1 \end{pmatrix}.$$

[Since the transformation can increase the length of V_j, an algorithm that incorporates both transformations must be careful to avoid infinite looping. See also exercise 23.]

19. No, since a product of non-identity matrices with all off-diagonal elements non-negative and all diagonal elements 1 cannot be the identity.

[However, looping would be possible if a subsequent transformation with $q = -1$ were performed when $-2V_i \cdot V_j = V_j \cdot V_j$; the rounding rule must be asymmetric with respect to sign if non-shortening transformations are allowed.]

20. When $a \bmod 8 = 5$, the points $2^{-e}(x, s(x), \ldots, s^{[t-1]}(x))$ for x in the period are the same as the points $2^{2-e}(y, \sigma(y), \ldots, \sigma^{t-1}(y))$ for $0 \le y < 2^{e-2}$, plus $2^{-e}(t, \ldots, t)$, where $\sigma(y) = (ay + \lfloor a/4 \rfloor t) \bmod 2^{e-2}$ and $t = X_0 \bmod 4$. So in this case we should use Algorithm S with $m = 2^{e-2}$.

When $a \bmod 8 = 3$, the maximum distance between parallel hyperplanes that cover the points $2^{-e}(x, s(x), \ldots, s^{[t-1]}(x))$ modulo 1 is the same as the maximum distance covering the points $2^{-e}(x, -s(x), \ldots, (-1)^{t-1} s^{[t-1]}(x))$, because the negation of coordinates doesn't change distance. The latter points are $2^{2-e}(y, \sigma(y), \ldots, \sigma^{t-1}(y))$ where $\sigma(y) = (-ay - \lceil a/4 \rceil t) \bmod 2^{e-2}$, plus a constant offset. Again we apply Algorithm S with $m = 2^{e-2}$; changing a to $m - a$ has no effect on the result.

21. $X_{4n+4} \equiv X_{4n}$ (modulo 4), so it is now appropriate to let $V_1 = (4, 4a^2, 4a^3)/m$, $V_2 = (0, 1, 0)$, $V_3 = (0, 0, 1)$ define the corresponding lattice L_0.

24. Let $m = p$; an analysis paralleling the text can be given. For example, when $t = 4$ we have $X_{n+3} = ((a^2 + b)X_{n+1} + abX_n) \bmod m$, and we want to minimize $u_1^2 + u_2^2 + u_3^2 + u_4^2 \neq 0$ such that $u_1 + bu_3 + abu_4 \equiv u_2 + au_3 + (a^2 + b)u_4 \equiv 0$ (modulo m).

Replace steps S1 through S3 by the operations of setting

$$U \leftarrow \begin{pmatrix} m & 0 \\ 0 & m \end{pmatrix}, \qquad V \leftarrow \begin{pmatrix} 1 & 0 \\ 0 & 1 \end{pmatrix}, \qquad R \leftarrow \begin{pmatrix} 1 & 0 \\ 0 & 1 \end{pmatrix}, \qquad s \leftarrow m^2, \qquad t \leftarrow 2,$$

and outputting $\nu_2 = m$. Replace step S4 by

> **S4'.** [Advance t.] If $t = T$, the algorithm terminates. Otherwise set $t \leftarrow t + 1$ and $R \leftarrow R\begin{pmatrix} 0 & b \\ 1 & a \end{pmatrix} \bmod m$. Set U_t to the new row $(-r_{12}, -r_{22}, 0, \dots, 0, 1)$ of t elements, and set $u_{it} \leftarrow 0$ for $1 \leq i < t$. Set V_t to the new row $(0, \dots, 0, m)$. For $1 \leq i < t$, set $q \leftarrow \text{round}((v_{i1}r_{12} + v_{i2}r_{22})/m)$, $v_{it} \leftarrow v_{i1}r_{12} + v_{i2}r_{22} - qm$, and $U_t \leftarrow U_t + qU_i$. Finally set $s \leftarrow \min(s, U_t \cdot U_t)$, $k \leftarrow t$, $j \leftarrow 1$.

[A similar generalization applies to all sequences of length $p^k - 1$ that satisfy the linear recurrence 3.2.2–(8). Additional numerical examples have been given by A. Grube, *Zeitschrift für angewandte Math. und Mechanik* **53** (1973), T223–T225; L'Ecuyer, Blouin, and Couture, *ACM Trans. Modeling and Comp. Simul.* **3** (1993), 87–98.]

25. The given sum is at most twice the quantity $\sum_{0 \leq k \leq m/(2d)} r(dk) = 1 + \frac{1}{d}f(m/d)$, where

$$f(m) = \frac{1}{m} \sum_{1 \leq k \leq m/2} \csc(\pi k/m)$$

$$= \frac{1}{m} \int_1^{m/2} \csc(\pi x/m) \, dx + O\left(\frac{1}{m}\right) = \frac{1}{\pi} \ln \tan\left(\frac{\pi}{2m}x\right) \Big|_1^{m/2} + O\left(\frac{1}{m}\right).$$

[When $d = 1$, we have $\sum_{0 \leq k < m} r(k) = (2/\pi)\ln m + 1 + (2/\pi)\ln(2e/\pi) + O(1/m)$.]

26. If $\gcd(q, m) = d$, the same derivation goes through with m replaced by m/d. Suppose we have $m = p_1^{e_1} \dots p_r^{e_r}$ and $\gcd(a - 1, m) = p_1^{f_1} \dots p_r^{f_r}$ and $d = p_1^{d_1} \dots p_r^{d_r}$. If m is replaced by m/d, then s is replaced by $p_1^{\max(0, e_1 - f_1 - d_1)} \dots p_r^{\max(0, e_r - f_r - d_r)}$. Since $m/d > 1$, we can also replace N by $N \bmod (m/d)$.

27. It is convenient to use the following functions: $\rho(x) = 1$ if $x = 0$, $\rho(x) = x$ if $0 < x \leq m/2$, $\rho(x) = m - x$ if $m/2 < x < m$; $\text{trunc}(x) = \lfloor x/2 \rfloor$ if $0 \leq x \leq m/2$, $\text{trunc}(x) = m - \lfloor (m - x)/2 \rfloor$ if $m/2 < x < m$; $L(x) = 0$ if $x = 0$, $L(x) = \lfloor \lg x \rfloor + 1$ if $0 < x \leq m/2$, $L(x) = -(\lfloor \lg(m - x) \rfloor + 1)$ if $m/2 < x < m$; and $l(x) = \max(1, 2^{|x|-1})$. Note that $l(L(x)) \leq \rho(x) < 2l(L(x))$ and $2\rho(x) \leq 1/r(x) = m\sin(\pi x/m) < \pi\rho(x)$, for $0 < x < m$.

Say that a vector $(u_1, \dots, u_t)$ is *bad* if it is nonzero and satisfies (15); and let $\rho_{\min}$ be the minimum value of $\rho(u_1) \dots \rho(u_t)$ over all bad $(u_1, \dots, u_t)$. The vector $(u_1, \dots, u_t)$ is said to be in class $(L(u_1), \dots, L(u_t))$. Thus there are at most $(2\lg m + 1)^t$ classes, and class $(L_1, \dots, L_t)$ contains at most $l(L_1) \dots l(L_t)$ vectors. Our proof is based on showing that the bad vectors in each fixed class contribute at most $2/\rho_{\min}$ to $\sum r(u_1, \dots, u_t)$; this establishes the desired bound, since $1/\rho_{\min} < \pi^t r_{\max}$.

Let $\mu = \lfloor \lg \rho_{\min} \rfloor$. The *$\mu$-fold truncation operator* on a vector is defined to be the following operation repeated μ times: "Let j be minimal such that $\rho(u_j) > 1$, and replace u_j by $\text{trunc}(u_j)$; but do nothing if $\rho(u_j) = 1$ for all j." (This operation essentially throws away one bit of information about $(u_1, \dots, u_t)$.) If $(u_1', \dots, u_t')$ and $(u_1'', \dots, u_t'')$ are two vectors of the same class having the same μ-fold truncation, we say they are *similar*; in this case it follows that $\rho(u'_1 - u''_1) \ldots \rho(u'_t - u''_t) < 2^\mu \leq \rho_{\min}$. For example, any two vectors of the form $((1x_2x_1)_2, 0, m-(1x_3)_2, (101x_5x_4)_2, (1101)_2)$ are similar when m is large and $\mu = 5$; the μ-fold truncation operator successively removes x_1, x_2, x_3, x_4, x_5. Since the difference of two bad vectors satisfies (15), it is impossible for two unequal bad vectors to be similar. Therefore class $(L_1, \ldots, L_t)$ can contain at most $\max(1, l(L_1) \ldots l(L_t)/2^\mu)$ bad vectors. If class $(L_1, \ldots, L_t)$ contains exactly one bad vector $(u_1, \ldots, u_t)$, we have $r(u_1, \ldots, u_t) \leq r_{\max} \leq 1/\rho_{\min}$; if it contains $\leq l(L_1) \ldots l(L_t)/2^\mu$ bad vectors, each of them has $r(u_1, \ldots, u_t) \leq 1/\rho(u_1) \ldots \rho(u_t) \leq 1/l(L_1) \ldots l(L_t)$, and we have $1/2^\mu < 2/\rho_{\min}$.

28. Let $\zeta = e^{2\pi i/(m-1)}$ and let $S_{kl} = \sum_{0 \leq j < m-1} \omega^{x_j + l} \zeta^{jk}$. The analog of (51) is $|S_{k0}| = \sqrt{m}$, hence the analog of (53) is

$$\left| N^{-1} \sum_{0 \leq n < N} \omega^{x_n} \right| = O((\sqrt{m} \log m)/N).$$

The analogous theorem now states that

$$D_N^{(t)} = O\left(\frac{\sqrt{m}\,(\log m)^{t+1}}{N} \right) + O\left((\log m)^t r_{\max}\right), \qquad D_{m-1}^{(t)} = O((\log m)^t r_{\max}).$$

In fact, $D_{m-1}^{(t)} \leq \frac{m-2}{m-1} \sum r(u_1, \ldots, u_t)$ [summed over nonzero solutions of (15)] $+ \frac{1}{m-1} \sum r(u_1, \ldots, u_t)$ [summed over all nonzero $(u_1, \ldots, u_t)$]. The latter sum is $O(\log m)^t$ by exercise 25 with $d = 1$, and the former sum is treated as in exercise 27.

Let us now consider the quantity $R(a) = \sum r(u_1, \ldots, u_t)$ summed over nonzero solutions of (15). Since m is prime, each $(u_1, \ldots, u_t)$ can be a solution to (15) for at most $t - 1$ values of a, hence $\sum_{0 < a < m} R(a) \leq (t-1) \sum r(u_1, \ldots, u_t) = O(t(\log m)^t)$. It follows that the average value of $R(a)$ taken over all $\varphi(m - 1)$ primitive roots is $O(t(\log m)^t/\varphi(m - 1))$.

Note: In general $1/\varphi(n) = O(\log \log n/n)$; we have therefore proved that *for all prime m and for all T there exists a primitive root a modulo m such that the linear congruential sequence $(1, a, 0, m)$ has discrepancy $D_{m-1}^{(t)} = O(m^{-1}T(\log m)^T \log \log m)$ for $1 \leq t \leq T$.* This method of proof does *not* extend to a similar result for linear congruential generators of period 2^e modulo 2^e, since for example the vector $(1, -3, 3, -1)$ solves (15) for about $2^{2e/3}$ values of a.

29. To get an upper bound, allow the nonzero components of $u = (u_1, \ldots, u_t)$ to be any real values $1 \leq |u_j| \leq \frac{1}{2}m$. If k components are nonzero, we have $r(u) \leq 1/(2^k \rho(u))$ in the notation of the answer to exercise 27. And if $u_1^2 + \cdots + u_t^2$ has a given value ν^2, we minimize $\rho(u)$ by taking $u_1 = \cdots = u_{k-1} = 1$ and $u_k^2 = \nu^2 - k + 1$. Thus $r(u) \leq 1/(2^k\sqrt{\nu^2 - k + 1})$. But $2^k\sqrt{\nu^2 - k + 1} \geq \sqrt{8}\nu$, since $\nu \geq k \geq 2$.

30. Let's first minimize $q|aq - mp|$ for $1 \leq q < m$ and $0 \leq p < a$. In the notation of exercise 4.5.3–42, we have $aq_n - mp_n = (-1)^n K_{s-n-1}(a_{n+2}, \ldots, a_s)$ for $0 \leq n \leq s$. In the range $q_{n-1} \leq q < q_n$ we have $|aq - mp| \geq |aq_{n-1} - mp_{n-1}|$; consequently $q|aq - mp| \geq q_{n-1}|aq_{n-1} - mp_{n-1}|$, and the minimum is $\min_{0 \leq n < s} q_n|aq_n - mp_n| = \min_{0 \leq n < s} K_n(a_1, \ldots, a_n) K_{s-n-1}(a_{n+2}, \ldots, a_s)$. By exercise 4.5.3–32 we have $m = K_n(a_1, \ldots, a_n) a_{n+1} K_{s-n-1}(a_{n+2}, \ldots, a_s) + K_n(a_1, \ldots, a_n) K_{s-n-2}(a_{n+3}, \ldots, a_s) + K_{n-1}(a_1, \ldots, a_{n-1}) K_{s-n-1}(a_{n+2}, \ldots, a_s)$; and our problem is essentially that of maximizing the quantity $m/K_n(a_1, \ldots, a_n) K_{s-n-1}(a_{n+2}, \ldots, a_s)$, which lies between a_{n+1} and $a_{n+1} + 2$.

Now let $A = \max(a_1, \ldots, a_s)$. Since $r(m - u) = r(u)$, we can assume that $r_{\max} = r(u)r(au \bmod m)$ for some u with $1 \leq u \leq \frac{1}{2}m$. Setting $u' = \min(au \bmod m, (-au) \bmod m)$, we have $r_{\max} = r(u)r(u')$. We know from the previous paragraph that $uu' \geq qq'$, where $A/m \leq 1/qq' \leq (A + 2)/m$. Furthermore $2u \leq r(u)^{-1} \leq \pi u$ for $0 < u \leq \frac{1}{2}m$, so $r_{\max} \leq 1/(4uu')$. Hence we have $r_{\max} \leq (A + 2)/(4m)$. (There is a similar lower bound, namely $r_{\max} > A/(\pi^2 m)$.)

31. Equivalently, the conjecture is that all large m can be written $m = K_n(a_1, \ldots, a_n)$ for some n and some $a_i \in \{1, 2, 3\}$. For fixed n the 3^n numbers $K_n(a_1, \ldots, a_n)$ have an average value of order $(1 + \sqrt{2})^n$, and their standard deviation is of order $(2.51527)^n$; so the conjecture is almost surely true. S. K. Zaremba conjectured in 1972 that all m can be represented with $a_i \leq 5$; T. W. Cusick made some progress on this problem in *Mathematika* **24** (1977), 166–172. It appears that only the cases $m = 54$ and $m = 150$ require $a_i = 5$, and the largest m's that require 4s are 2052, 2370, 5052, and 6234; at least, the author has found representations with $a_i \leq 3$ for all other integers less than 2000000. When we require $a_i \leq 2$, the average of $K_n(a_1, \ldots, a_n)$ is $\frac{4}{5}2^n + \frac{1}{5}(-2)^{-n}$, while the standard deviation grows as $(2.04033)^n$. The density of such numbers in the author's experiments (which considered 2^6 blocks of 2^{14} numbers each, for $m \leq 2^{20}$) appears to vary between .50 and .65.

[See I. Borosh and H. Niederreiter, *BIT* **25** (1980), 193–208, for a computational method that finds multipliers with small partial quotients. They have found 2-bounded solutions with $m = 2^e$ for $25 \leq e \leq 35$.]

32. (a) $U_n - Z_n/m_1 \equiv (m_2 - m_1)Y_n/m_1 m_2$ (modulo 1), and $(m_1 - m_2)/m_1 m_2 \approx 2^{-54}$. (Therefore we can analyze the high-order bits of Z_n by analyzing U_n. The low-order bits are probably random too, but this argument does not apply to them.) (b) We have $U_n = W_n/m$ for all n. The Chinese remainder theorem tells us that we need only verify the congruences $W_n \equiv X_n m_2$ (modulo m_1) and $W_n \equiv -Y_n m_1$ (modulo m_2), because $m_1 \perp m_2$. [Pierre L'Ecuyer and Shu Tezuka, *Math. Comp.* **57** (1991), 735–746.]

SECTION 3.4.1

1. $\alpha + (\beta - \alpha)U$.

2. Let $U = X/m$; then $\lfloor kU \rfloor = r \iff r \leq kX/m < r + 1 \iff mr/k \leq X < m(r + 1)/k \iff \lceil mr/k \rceil \leq X < \lceil m(r + 1)/k \rceil$. The exact probability is given by the formula $(1/m)(\lceil m(r + 1)/k \rceil - \lceil mr/k \rceil) = 1/k + \epsilon$, where $|\epsilon| < 1/m$.

3. If full-word random numbers are given, the result will deviate from the correct distribution by at most $1/m$, as in exercise 2; but all of the excess is given to the smallest results. Thus if $k \approx m/3$, the result will be less than $k/2$ about $\frac{2}{3}$ of the time. It is much better to obtain a perfectly uniform distribution by rejecting U if $U \geq k\lfloor m/k \rfloor$; see D. E. Knuth, *The Stanford GraphBase* (New York: ACM Press, 1994), 221.

On the other hand, if a linear congruential sequence is used, k must be relatively prime to the modulus m, lest the numbers have a very short period, by the results of Section 3.2.1.1. For example, if $k = 2$ and m is even, the numbers will at best be alternately 0 and 1. The method is slower than (1) in nearly every case, so it is not recommended.

Unfortunately, however, the "himult" operation in (1) is not supported in many high-level languages; see exercise 3.2.1.1–3. Division by m/k may be best when himult is unavailable.

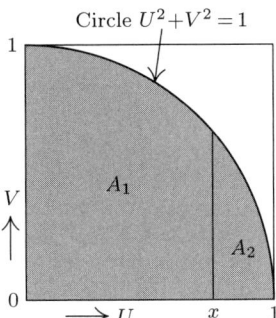

Fig. A–4. Region of "acceptance" for
the algorithm of exercise 6.

4. $\max(X_1, X_2) \leq x$ if and only if $X_1 \leq x$ and $X_2 \leq x$; $\min(X_1, X_2) \geq x$ if and only if $X_1 \geq x$ and $X_2 \geq x$. The probability that two independent events both happen is the product of the individual probabilities.

5. Obtain independent uniform deviates U_1 and U_2. Set $X \leftarrow U_2$. If $U_1 \geq p$, set $X \leftarrow \max(X, U_3)$, where U_3 is a third uniform deviate. If $U_1 \geq p + q$, also set $X \leftarrow \max(X, U_4)$, where U_4 is a fourth uniform deviate. This method can obviously be generalized to any polynomial, and indeed even to infinite power series (as shown for example in Algorithm S, which uses minimization instead of maximization).

We could also proceed as follows (suggested by M. D. MacLaren): If $U_1 < p$, set $X \leftarrow U_1/p$; otherwise if $U_1 < p + q$, set $X \leftarrow \max((U_1 - p)/q, U_2)$; otherwise set $X \leftarrow \max((U_1 - p - q)/r, U_2, U_3)$. This method requires less time than the other to obtain the uniform deviates, although it involves further arithmetical operations and it is slightly less stable numerically.

6. $F(x) = A_1/(A_1 + A_2)$, where A_1 and A_2 are the areas in Fig. A–4; so

$$F(x) = \frac{\int_0^x \sqrt{1 - y^2}\, dy}{\int_0^1 \sqrt{1 - y^2}\, dy} = \frac{2}{\pi} \arcsin x + \frac{2}{\pi} x \sqrt{1 - x^2}.$$

The probability of termination at step 2 is $p = \pi/4$, each time step 2 is encountered, so the number of executions of step 2 has the geometric distribution. The characteristics of this number are (min 1, ave $4/\pi$, max ∞, dev $(4/\pi)\sqrt{1 - \pi/4}$), by exercise 17.

7. If $k = 1$, then $n_1 = n$ and the problem is trivial. Otherwise it is always possible to find $i \neq j$ such that $n_i \leq n \leq n_j$. Fill B_i with n_i cubes of color C_i and $n - n_i$ of color C_j, then decrease n_j by $n - n_i$ and eliminate color C_i. We are left with the same sort of problem but with k reduced by 1; by induction, it's possible.

The following algorithm can be used to compute the P and Y tables: Form a list of pairs $(p_1, 1) \dots (p_k, k)$ and sort it by first components, obtaining a list $(q_1, a_1) \dots (q_k, a_k)$ where $q_1 \leq \dots \leq q_k$. Set $n \leftarrow k$; then repeat the following operations until $n = 0$: Set $P[a_1 - 1] \leftarrow kq_1$ and $Y[a_1 - 1] \leftarrow x_{a_n}$. Delete (q_1, a_1) and (q_n, a_n), then insert the new entry $(q_n - (1/k - q_1), a_n)$ into its proper place in the list and decrease n by 1.

(If $p_j < 1/k$ the algorithm will never put x_j in the Y table; this fact is used implicitly in Algorithm M. The algorithm attempts to maximize the probability that $V < P_K$ in (3), by always robbing from the richest remaining element and giving it to the poorest. However, it is very difficult to determine the absolute maximum of this probability, since such a task is at least as difficult as the "bin-packing problem"; see Section 7.9.)

8. Replace P_j by $(j + P_j)/k$ for $0 \le j < k$.

9. Consider the sign of $f''(x) = \sqrt{2/\pi}\,(x^2 - 1)e^{-x^2/2}$.

10. Let $S_j = (j-1)/5$ for $1 \le j \le 16$ and $p_{j+15} = F(S_{j+1}) - F(S_j) - p_j$ for $1 \le j \le 15$; also let $p_{31} = 1 - F(3)$ and $p_{32} = 0$. (Eq. (15) defines $p_1, \ldots, p_{15}$.) The algorithm of exercise 7 can now be used with $k = 32$ to compute P_j and Y_j, after which we will have $1 \le Y_j \le 15$ for $1 \le j \le 32$. Set $P_0 \leftarrow P_{32}$ (which is 0) and $Y_0 \leftarrow Y_{32}$. Then set $Z_j \leftarrow 1/(5 - 5P_j)$ and $Y_j \leftarrow \frac{1}{5}Y_j - Z_j$ for $0 \le j < 32$; $Q_j \leftarrow 1/(5P_j)$ for $1 \le j \le 15$.

Let $h = \frac{1}{5}$ and $f_{j+15}(x) = \sqrt{2/\pi}(e^{-x^2/2} - e^{-j^2/50})/p_{j+15}$ for $S_j \le x \le S_j + h$. Then let $a_j = f_{j+15}(S_j)$ for $1 \le j \le 5$, $b_j = f_{j+15}(S_j)$ for $6 \le j \le 15$; also $b_j = -hf'_{j+15}(S_j + h)$ for $1 \le j \le 5$, and $a_j = f_{j+15}(x_j) + (x_j - S_j)b_j/h$ for $6 \le j \le 15$, where x_j is the root of the equation $f'_{j+15}(x_j) = -b_j/h$. Finally set $D_{j+15} \leftarrow a_j/b_j$ for $1 \le j \le 15$ and $E_{j+15} \leftarrow 25/j$ for $1 \le j \le 5$, $E_{j+15} \leftarrow 1/(e^{(2j-1)/50} - 1)$ for $6 \le j \le 15$.

Table 1 was computed while making use of the following intermediate values: $(p_1, \ldots, p_{31}) = (.156, .147, .133, .116, .097, .078, .060, .044, .032, .022, .014, .009, .005,$ $.003, .002, .002, .005, .007, .009, .010, .009, .009, .008, .006, .005, .004, .002, .002, .001, .001,$ $.003)$; $(x_6, \ldots, x_{15}) = (1.115, 1.304, 1.502, 1.700, 1.899, 2.099, 2.298, 2.497, 2.697, 2.896)$; $(a_1, \ldots, a_{15}) = (7.5, 9.1, 9.5, 9.8, 9.9, 10.0, 10.0, 10.1, 10.1, 10.1, 10.1, 10.2, 10.2, 10.2, 10.2)$; $(b_1, \ldots, b_{15}) = (14.9, 11.7, 10.9, 10.4, 10.1, 10.1, 10.2, 10.3, 10.4, 10.5, 10.6, 10.7, 10.7, 10.8, 10.9)$.

11. Let $g(t) = e^{9/2}te^{-t^2/2}$ for $t \ge 3$. Since $G(x) = \int_3^x g(t)\,dt = 1 - e^{-(x^2-9)/2}$, a random variable X with density g can be computed by setting $X \leftarrow G^{[-1]}(1-V) = \sqrt{9 - 2\ln V}$. Now $e^{-t^2/2} \le (t/3)e^{-t^2/2}$ for $t \ge 3$, so we obtain a valid rejection method if we accept X with probability $f(X)/cg(X) = 3/X$.

12. We have $f'(x) = xf(x) - 1 < 0$ for $x \ge 0$, since $f(x) = x^{-1} - e^{x^2/2}\int_x^\infty e^{-t^2/2}\,dt/t^2$ for $x > 0$. Let $x = a_{j-1}$ and $y^2 = x^2 + 2\ln 2$; then

$$\sqrt{2/\pi}\int_y^\infty e^{-t^2/2}\,dt = \tfrac{1}{2}\sqrt{2/\pi}\,e^{-x^2/2}f(y) < \tfrac{1}{2}\sqrt{2/\pi}\,e^{-x^2/2}f(x) = 2^{-j},$$

hence $y > a_j$.

13. Take $b_j = \mu_j$; consider now the problem with $\mu_j = 0$ for each j. In matrix notation, if $Y = AX$, where $A = (a_{ij})$, we need $AA^T = C = (c_{ij})$. (In other notation, if $Y_j = \sum a_{jk}X_k$, then the average value of Y_iY_j is $\sum a_{ik}a_{jk}$.) If this matrix equation can be solved for A, it can be solved when A is triangular, since $A = BU$ for some orthogonal matrix U and some triangular B, and $BB^T = C$. The desired triangular solution can be obtained by solving the equations $a_{11}^2 = c_{11}$, $a_{11}a_{21} = c_{12}$, $a_{21}^2 + a_{22}^2 = c_{22}$, $a_{11}a_{31} = c_{13}$, $a_{21}a_{31} + a_{22}a_{32} = c_{23}$, $\ldots$, successively for a_{11}, a_{21}, a_{22}, a_{31}, a_{32}, etc. [*Note:* The covariance matrix must be positive semidefinite, since the average value of $\left(\sum y_jY_j\right)^2$ is $\sum c_{ij}y_iy_j$, which must be nonnegative. And there is always a solution when C is positive semidefinite, since $C = U^{-1}\text{diag}(\lambda_1, \ldots, \lambda_n)U$, where the eigenvalues λ_j are nonnegative, and $U^{-1}\text{diag}(\sqrt{\lambda_1}, \ldots, \sqrt{\lambda_n})U$ is a solution.]

14. $F(x/c)$ if $c > 0$; the step function $[x \ge 0]$ if $c = 0$; or $1 - F(x/c)$ if $c < 0$.

15. Distribution $\int_{-\infty}^\infty F_1(x - t)\,dF_2(t)$. Density $\int_{-\infty}^\infty f_1(x - t)f_2(t)\,dt$. This is called the *convolution* of the given distributions.

16. It is clear that $f(t) \le cg(t)$ for all t as required. Since $\int_0^\infty g(t)\,dt = 1$ we have $g(t) = Ct^{a-1}$ for $0 \le t < 1$, Ce^{-t} for $t \ge 1$, where $C = ae/(a + e)$. A random variable with density g is easy to obtain as a mixture of two distributions, $G_1(x) = x^a$ for $0 \le x < 1$, and $G_2(x) = 1 - e^{1-x}$ for $x \ge 1$:

G1. [Initialize.] Set $p \leftarrow e/(a+e)$. (This is the probability that G_1 should be used.)

G2. [Generate G deviate.] Generate independent uniform deviates U and V, where $V \neq 0$. If $U < p$, set $X \leftarrow V^{1/a}$ and $q \leftarrow e^{-X}$; otherwise set $X \leftarrow 1 - \ln V$ and $q \leftarrow X^{a-1}$. (Now X has density g, and $q = f(X)/cg(X)$.)

G3. [Reject?] Generate a new uniform deviate U. If $U \geq q$, return to G2. ∎

The average number of iterations is $c = (a+e)/(e\Gamma(a+1)) < 1.4$.

It is possible to streamline this procedure in several ways. First, we can replace V by an exponential deviate Y of mean 1, generated by Algorithm S, say, and then we set $X \leftarrow e^{-Y/a}$ or $X \leftarrow 1 + Y$ in the two cases. Moreover, if we set $q \leftarrow pe^{-X}$ in the first case and $q \leftarrow p + (1-p)X^{a-1}$ in the second, we can use the original U instead of a newly generated one in step G3. Finally if $U < p/e$ we can accept $V^{1/a}$ immediately, avoiding the calculation of q about 30 percent of the time.

17. (a) $F(x) = 1 - (1-p)^{\lfloor x \rfloor}$, for $x \geq 0$. (b) $G(z) = pz/(1-(1-p)z)$. (c) Mean $1/p$, standard deviation $\sqrt{1-p}/p$. To do the latter calculation, observe that if $H(z) = q + (1-q)z$, then $H'(1) = 1 - q$ and $H''(1) + H'(1) - (H'(1))^2 = q(1-q)$, so the mean and variance of $1/H(z)$ are $q-1$ and $q(q-1)$, respectively. (See Section 1.2.10.) In this case, $q = 1/p$; the extra factor z in the numerator of $G(z)$ adds 1 to the mean.

18. Set $N \leftarrow N_1 + N_2 - 1$, where N_1 and N_2 independently have the geometric distribution for probability p. (Consider the generating function.)

19. Set $N \leftarrow N_1 + \cdots + N_t - t$, where the N_j have the geometric distribution for p. (This is the number of failures before the tth success, when a sequence of independent trials are made each of which succeeds with probability p.)

For $t = p = \frac{1}{2}$, and in general when the mean value (namely $t(1-p)/p$) of the distribution is small, we can simply evaluate the probabilities $p_n = \binom{t-1+n}{n}p^t(1-p)^n$ consecutively for $n = 0, 1, 2, \ldots$ as in the following algorithm:

N1. [Initialize.] Set $N \leftarrow 0$, $q \leftarrow p^t$, $r \leftarrow q$, and generate a random uniform deviate U. (We will have $q = p_N$ and $r = p_0 + \cdots + p_N$ during this algorithm, which stops as soon as $U < r$.)

N2. [Iterate.] If $U \geq r$, set $N \leftarrow N + 1$, $q \leftarrow q(1-p)(t-1+N)/N$, $r \leftarrow r + q$, and repeat this step. Otherwise return N and terminate. ∎

[An interesting technique for the negative binomial distribution, for arbitrarily large real values of t, has been suggested by R. Léger: First generate a random gamma deviate X of order t, then let N be a random Poisson deviate of mean $X(1-p)/p$.]

20. $R1 = 1 + (1 - A/R) \cdot R1$. When R2 is performed, the algorithm terminates with probability I/R; when R3 is performed, it goes to R1 with probability E/R. We have

R1	R/A	R/A	R/A	R/A
R2	0	R/A	0	R/A
R3	0	0	R/A	$R/A - I/A$
R4	R/A	$R/A - I/A$	$R/A - E/A$	$R/A - I/A - E/A$

21. $R = \sqrt{8/e} \approx 1.71553$; $A = \sqrt{2}\Gamma(3/2) = \sqrt{\pi/2} \approx 1.25331$. Since

$$\int u\sqrt{a - bu}\, du = (a - bu)^{3/2}\left(\tfrac{2}{5}(a - bu) - \tfrac{2}{3}a\right)/b^2,$$

we have $I = 2 \int_0^{a/b} u\sqrt{a - bu}\, du = \frac{8}{15} a^{5/2}/b^2$ where $a = 4(1 + \ln c)$ and $b = 4c$; when $c = e^{1/4}$, I has its maximum value $\frac{5}{6}\sqrt{5/e} \approx 1.13020$. Finally the following integration formulas are needed for E:

$$\int \sqrt{bu - au^2}\, du = \tfrac{1}{8} b^2 a^{-3/2} \arcsin(2ua/b - 1) + \tfrac{1}{4} ba^{-1}\sqrt{bu - au^2}\,(2ua/b - 1),$$

$$\int \sqrt{bu + au^2}\, du = -\tfrac{1}{8} b^2 a^{-3/2} \ln(\sqrt{bu + au^2} + u\sqrt{a} + b/2\sqrt{a}) + \tfrac{1}{4} ba^{-1}\sqrt{bu + au^2}\,(2ua/b + 1),$$

where $a, b > 0$. Let the test in step R3 be "$X^2 \geq 4e^{x-1}/U - 4x$"; then the exterior region hits the top of the rectangle when $u = r(x) = (e^x - \sqrt{e^{2x} - 2ex})/2ex$. (Incidentally, $r(x)$ reaches its maximum value at $x = 1/2$, a point where it is *not* differentiable!) We have $E = 2 \int_0^{r(x)} (\sqrt{2/e} - \sqrt{bu - au^2})\, du$ where $b = 4e^{x-1}$ and $a = 4x$. The maximum value of E occurs near $x = -.35$, where we have $E \approx .29410$.

22. (Solution by G. Marsaglia.) Consider the "continuous Poisson distribution" defined by $G(x) = \int_\mu^\infty e^{-t} t^{x-1}\, dt / \Gamma(x)$, for $x > 0$; if X has this distribution then $\lfloor X \rfloor$ is Poisson distributed, since $G(x + 1) - G(x) = e^{-\mu}\mu^x/x!$. If μ is large, G is approximately normal, hence $G^{[-1]}(F_\mu(x))$ is approximately linear, where $F_\mu(x)$ is the distribution function for a normal deviate with mean and variance μ; that is, $F_\mu(x) = F((x - \mu)/\sqrt{\mu})$, where $F(x)$ is the normal distribution function (10). Let $g(x)$ be an efficiently computable function such that $|G^{[-1]}(F_\mu(x)) - g(x)| < \epsilon$ for $-\infty < x < \infty$; we can now generate Poisson deviates efficiently as follows: Generate a normal deviate X, and set $Y \leftarrow g(\mu + \sqrt{\mu}\, X)$, $N \leftarrow \lfloor Y \rfloor$, $M \leftarrow \lfloor Y + \tfrac{1}{2} \rfloor$. Then if $|Y - M| > \epsilon$, output N; otherwise output $M - [G^{[-1]}(F(X)) < M]$.

This approach applies also to the binomial distribution, with

$$G(x) = \int_p^1 u^{x-1}(1 - u)^{n-x}\, du \, \frac{\Gamma(t + 1)}{\Gamma(x)\,\Gamma(t + 1 - x)},$$

since $\lfloor G^{[-1]}(U) \rfloor$ is binomial with parameters (t, p) and G is approximately normal. [See also the alternative method proposed by Ahrens and Dieter in *Computing* **25** (1980), 193–208.]

23. Yes. The second method calculates $|\cos 2\theta|$, where θ is uniformly distributed between 0 and $\pi/2$. (Let $U = r \cos\theta$, $V = r \sin\theta$.)

25. $\frac{21}{32} = (.10101)_2$. In general, the binary representation is formed by using 1 for | and 0 for &, from left to right, then suffixing 1. This technique [see K. D. Tocher, *J. Roy. Stat. Soc.* **B16** (1954), 49] can lead to efficient generation of independent bits having a given probability p, and it can also be applied to the geometric and binomial distributions.

26. (a) True: $\sum_k \Pr(N_1 = k)\Pr(N_2 = n - k) = e^{-\mu_1 - \mu_2}(\mu_1 + \mu_2)^n/n!$. (b) False, unless $\mu_2 = 0$; otherwise $N_1 - N_2$ might be negative.

27. Let the binary representation of p be $(.b_1 b_2 b_3 \ldots)_2$, and proceed according to the following rules:

B1. [Initialize.] Set $m \leftarrow t$, $N \leftarrow 0$, $j \leftarrow 1$. (During this algorithm, m represents the number of simulated uniform deviates whose relation to p is still unknown, since they match p in their leading $j - 1$ bits; and N is the number of simulated deviates known to be less than p.)

B2. [Look at next column of bits.] Generate a random integer M with the binomial distribution $(m, \tfrac{1}{2})$. (Now M represents the number of unknown deviates that fail to match b_j.) Set $m \leftarrow m - M$, and if $b_j = 1$ set $N \leftarrow N + M$.

B3. [Done?] If $m = 0$, or if the remaining bits $(.b_{j+1}b_{j+2} \ldots)_2$ of p are all zero, the algorithm terminates. Otherwise, set $j \leftarrow j+1$ and return to step B2. ∎

[When $b_j = 1$ for infinitely many j, the average number of iterations A_t satisfies

$$A_0 = 0; \qquad A_n = 1 + \frac{1}{2^n} \sum_k \binom{n}{k} A_k, \quad \text{for } n \geq 1.$$

Letting $A(z) = \sum A_n z^n/n!$, we have $A(z) = e^z - 1 + A(\frac{1}{2}z)e^{z/2}$. Therefore $A(z)e^{-z} = 1 - e^{-z} + A(\frac{1}{2}z)e^{-z/2} = \sum_{k \geq 0}(1 - e^{-z/2^k}) = 1 - e^{-z} - \sum_{n \geq 1}(-z)^n/(n!(2^n - 1))$, and

$$A_m = 1 + \sum_{k \geq 1}\binom{n}{k}\frac{(-1)^{k+1}}{2^k - 1} = 1 + \frac{V_{n+1}}{n+1} = \lg n + \frac{\gamma}{\ln 2} + \frac{1}{2} + f_0(n) + O(n^{-1})$$

in the notation of exercise 5.2.2–48.]

28. Generate a random point $(y_1, \ldots, y_n)$ on the unit sphere, and let $\rho = \sqrt{\sum a_k y_k^2}$. Generate an independent uniform deviate U, and if $\rho^{n+1}U < K\sqrt{\sum a_k^2 y_k^2}$, output the point $(y_1/\rho, \ldots, y_n/\rho)$; otherwise start over. Here $K^2 = \min\{(\sum a_k y_k^2)^{n+1}/(\sum a_k^2 y_k^2) \mid \sum y_k^2 = 1\} = a_n^{n-1}$ if $na_n \geq a_1$, $((n+1)/(a_1 + a_n))^{n+1}(a_1 a_n/n)^n$ otherwise.

29. Let $X_{n+1} = 1$, then set $X_k \leftarrow X_{k+1}U_k^{1/k}$ or $X_k \leftarrow X_{k+1}e^{-Y_k/k}$ for $k = n, n-1$, ..., 1, where U_k is uniform or Y_k is exponential. [*ACM Trans. Math. Software* **6** (1980), 359–364. This technique was introduced in the 1960s by David Seneschal; see *Amer. Statistician* **26**, 4 (October 1972), 56–57. The alternative of generating n uniform numbers and sorting them is probably faster, with an appropriate sorting method, but the method suggested here is particularly valuable if only a few of the largest or smallest X's are desired. Notice that $(F^{[-1]}(X_1), \ldots, F^{[-1]}(X_n))$ will be sorted deviates having distribution F.]

30. Generate random numbers $Z_1 = -\mu^{-1}\ln U_1$, $Z_2 = Z_1 - \mu^{-1}\ln U_2$, ..., until $Z_{m+1} \geq 1$. Output $(X_j, Y_j) = f(Z_j)$ for $1 \leq j \leq m$, where $f((.b_1 b_2 \ldots b_{2r})_2) = ((.b_1 b_2 \ldots b_r)_2, (.b_{r+1}b_{r+2} \ldots b_{2r})_2)$. If the less significant bits are significantly less random than the more significant bits, it's safer (but slower) to let $f((.b_1 b_2 \ldots b_{2r})_2) = ((.b_1 b_3 \ldots b_{2r-1})_2, (.b_2 b_4 \ldots b_{2r})_2)$.

31. (a) It suffices to consider the case $k = 2$, since $a_1 X_1 + \cdots + a_k X_k = X\cos\theta + Y\sin\theta$ when $X = X_1$, $\cos\theta = a_1$, and $Y = (a_2 X_2 + \cdots + a_k X_k)/\sin\theta$. And

$$\Pr(X\cos\theta + Y\sin\theta \leq x) = \frac{1}{2\pi}\int_{s,t} e^{-s^2/2 - t^2/2}\,ds\,dt\,[s\cos\theta + t\sin\theta \leq x]$$

$$= \frac{1}{2\pi}\int_{u,v} e^{-u^2/2 - v^2/2}\,du\,dv\,[u \leq x] = (10),$$

from the substitution $u = s\cos\theta + t\sin\theta$, $v = -s\sin\theta + t\cos\theta$.

(b) There are numbers $\alpha > 1$ and $\beta > 1$ such that $(\alpha^{-24} + \alpha^{-55})/\sqrt{2} = 1$ and $\frac{3}{5}\beta^{-24} + \frac{4}{5}\beta^{-55} = 1$; so the numbers X_n will grow exponentially with n, by the properties of linear recurrences.

If we break out of the linear recurrence mold by, say, using the recurrence $X_n = X_{n-24}\cos\theta_n + X_{n-55}\sin\theta_n$, where θ_n is chosen uniformly in $[0 \mathinner{\ldotp\ldotp} 2\pi)$, we probably will obtain decent results; but this alternative would involve much more computation.

(c) Start with, say, 2048 normal deviates $X_0, \ldots, X_{1023}, Y_0, \ldots, Y_{1023}$. After having used about 1/3 of them, generate 2048 more as follows: Choose integers a, b, c, and d uniformly in $[0\mathinner{\ldotp\ldotp}1024)$, with a and c odd; then set

$$X_j' \leftarrow X_{(aj+b) \bmod 1024} \cos\theta + Y_{(cj+d) \bmod 1024} \sin\theta,$$
$$Y_j' \leftarrow -X_{(aj+b) \bmod 1024} \sin\theta + Y_{(cj+d) \bmod 1024} \cos\theta,$$

for $0 \le j < 1024$, where $\cos\theta$ and $\sin\theta$ are random ratios $(U^2 - V^2)/(U^2 + V^2)$ and $2UV/(U^2 + V^2)$, chosen as in exercise 23. We can reject U and V unless $|\cos\theta| \ge \frac{1}{2}$ and $|\sin\theta| \ge \frac{1}{2}$. The 2048 new deviates now replace the old ones. Notice that only a few operations were needed per new deviate.

This method does not diverge like the sequences considered in (b), because the sum of squares $\sum(X_j^2 + Y_j^2) = \sum((X_j')^2 + (Y_j')^2)$ remains at the constant value $S \approx 2048$, except for a slight roundoff error. On the other hand, the constancy of S is actually a defect of the method, because the sum of squares should really have the χ^2 distribution with 2048 degrees of freedom. To overcome this problem, the normal deviates actually delivered to the user should be not X_j but αX_j, where $\alpha^2 = \frac{1}{2}(Y_{1023} + \sqrt{4095})^2/S$ is a precomputed scale factor. (The quantity $\frac{1}{2}(Y_{1023} + \sqrt{4095})^2$ will be a reasonable approximation to the χ^2 deviate desired.)

References: C. S. Wallace [*ACM Trans. on Math. Software* **22** (1996), 119–127]; R. P. Brent [*Lecture Notes in Comp. Sci.* **1470** (1998), 1–20].

32. (a) This mapping $(X', Y') = f(X, Y)$ is a one-to-one correspondence from the set $\{x, y \ge 0\}$ to itself such that $x' + y' = x + y$ and $dx'\,dy' = dx\,dy$. We have

$$\frac{X'}{X'+Y'} = \left(\frac{X}{X+Y} - \lambda\right) \bmod 1, \qquad \frac{Y'}{X'+Y'} = \left(\frac{Y}{X+Y} + \lambda\right) \bmod 1.$$

(b) This mapping is a two-to-one correspondence such that $x' + y' = x + y$ and $dx'\,dy' = 2\,dx\,dy$.

(c) It suffices to consider the "j-flip" transformation

$$X' = (\ldots x_{j+2}x_{j+1}x_j y_{j-1} y_{j-2} y_{j-3} \ldots)_2,$$
$$Y' = (\ldots y_{j+2}y_{j+1}y_j x_{j-1} x_{j-2} x_{j-3} \ldots)_2,$$

for a fixed integer j, and then to compose j-flips for $j = 0, 1, -1, 2, -2, \ldots$, noticing that the joint probability distribution of X' and Y' converges as $|j| \to \infty$. Each j-flip is one-to-one, with $x' + y' = x + y$ and $dx'\,dy' = dx\,dy$.

33. Use U_1 as the seed for *another* random number generator (perhaps a linear congruential generator with a different multiplier); take U_2, U_3, $\ldots$ from that one.

SECTION 3.4.2

1. There are $\binom{N-t}{n-m}$ ways to pick $n - m$ records from the last $N - t$, and $\binom{N-t-1}{n-m-1}$ ways to pick $n - m - 1$ from $N - t - 1$ after selecting the $(t+1)$st item.

2. Step S3 will never go to step S5 when the number of records left to be examined is equal to $n - m$.

3. We should not confuse conditional and unconditional probabilities. The quantity m depends randomly on the selections that took place among the first t elements; if we take the average over all possible choices that could have occurred among these elements, we will find that $(n - m)/(N - t)$ is exactly n/N on the average. For example, consider the second element; if the first element was selected in the sample (this happens with probability n/N), the second element is selected with probability $(n - 1)/(N - 1)$; if the first element was not selected, the second is selected with

probability $n/(N-1)$.   The overall probability of selecting the second element is
$(n/N)((n-1)/(N-1)) + (1-n/N)(n/(N-1)) = n/N$.

4. From the algorithm,

$$p(m, t+1) = \left(1 - \frac{n-m}{N-t}\right)p(m,t) + \frac{n-(m-1)}{N-t}p(m-1,t).$$

The desired formula can be proved by induction on t. In particular, $p(n, N) = 1$.

5. In the notation of exercise 4, the probability that $t = k$ at termination is $q_k = p(n,k) - p(n, k-1) = \binom{k-1}{n-1}/\binom{N}{n}$. The average is $\sum_{k=0}^{N} kq_k = (N+1)n/(n+1)$.

6. Similarly, $\sum_{k=0}^{N} k(k+1)q_k = (N+2)(N+1)n/(n+2)$; the variance is therefore $(N+1)(N-n)n/(n+2)(n+1)^2$.

7. Suppose the choice is $1 \le x_1 < x_2 < \cdots < x_n \le N$. Let $x_0 = 0$, $x_{n+1} = N+1$. The choice is obtained with probability $p = \prod_{1 \le t \le N} p_t$, where

$$p_t = \begin{cases} (N-(t-1)-n+m)/(N-(t-1)), & \text{for } x_m < t < x_{m+1}; \\ (n-m)/(N-(t-1)), & \text{for } t = x_{m+1}. \end{cases}$$

The denominator of the product p is $N!$; the numerator contains the terms $N - n$, $N - n - 1$, $\ldots$, 1 for those t's that are not x's, and the terms n, $n-1$, $\ldots$, 1 for those t's that *are* x's. Hence $p = (N-n)!\,n!/N!$.

Example: $n = 3$, $N = 8$, $(x_1, x_2, x_3) = (2, 3, 7)$; $p = \frac{5}{8}\frac{3}{7}\frac{2}{6}\frac{4}{5}\frac{3}{4}\frac{2}{3}\frac{1}{2}\frac{1}{1}$.

8. (a) $p(0, k) = \binom{N-k}{n}/\binom{N}{n} = \binom{N-n}{k}/\binom{N}{k}$ of the $\binom{N}{n}$ samples omit the first k records.

(b) Set $X \leftarrow k-1$, where k is minimum with $U \ge \Pr(X \ge k)$. Thus, start with $X \leftarrow 0$, $p \leftarrow N-n$, $q \leftarrow N$, $R \leftarrow p/q$, and while $U < R$ set $X \leftarrow X+1$, $p \leftarrow p-1$, $q \leftarrow q-1$, $R \leftarrow Rp/q$. (This method is good when n/N is, say, $\ge 1/5$. We can assume that $n/N \le 1/2$; otherwise it's better to select $N-n$ *unsampled* items.)

(c) $\Pr(\min(Y_N, \ldots, Y_{N-n+1}) \ge k) = \prod_{j=0}^{n-1} \Pr(Y_{N-j} \ge k) = \prod_{j=0}^{n-1}((N-j-k)/(N-j))$. (This method is good if, say, $n \le 5$.)

(d) (See exercise 3.4.1–29.) The value $X \leftarrow \lfloor N(1 - U^{1/n})\rfloor$ needs to be rejected with probability only $O(n/N)$. Precise details are worked out carefully in *CACM* **27** (1984), 703–718, and a practical implementation appears in *ACM Trans. Math. Software* **13** (1987), 58–67. (This method is good when, say, $5 < n < \frac{1}{5}N$.)

After skipping X records and selecting the next, we set $n \leftarrow n-1$, $N \leftarrow N-X-1$, and repeat the process until $n = 0$. A similar approach speeds up the reservoir method; see *ACM Trans. Math. Software* **11** (1985), 37–57.

9. The reservoir gets seven records: 1, 2, 3, 5, 9, 13, 16. The final sample consists of records 2, 5, 16.

10. Delete step R6 and the variable m. Replace the I table by a table of records, initialized to the first n records in step R1, and with the new record replacing the Mth table entry in step R4.

11. Arguing as in Section 1.2.10, which considers the special case $n = 1$, we see that the generating function is

$$G(z) = z^n\left(\frac{1}{n+1} + \frac{n}{n+1}z\right)\left(\frac{2}{n+2} + \frac{n}{n+2}z\right)\cdots\left(\frac{N-n}{N} + \frac{n}{N}z\right).$$

The mean is $n + \sum_{n < t \le N}(n/t) = n(1 + H_N - H_n)$; and the variance turns out to be $n(H_N - H_n) - n^2(H_N^{(2)} - H_n^{(2)})$.

12. (Note that $\pi^{-1} = (b_t t) \ldots (b_3 3)(b_2 2)$, so we seek an algorithm that goes from the representation of π to that for π^{-1}.) Set $b_j \leftarrow j$ for $1 \le j \le t$. Then for $j = 2, 3, \ldots, t$ (in this order), interchange $b_j \leftrightarrow b_{a_j}$. Finally for $j = t, \ldots, 3, 2$ (in this order), set $b_{a_j} \leftarrow b_j$. (The algorithm is based on the fact that $(a_t t)\pi_1 = \pi_1(b_t t)$.)

13. Renumbering the deck $0, 1, \ldots, 2n-2$, we find that s takes card number x into card number $(2x)$ mod $(2n-1)$, while c takes card x into $(x-1)$ mod $(2n-1)$. We have (c followed by s) $= cs = sc^2$. Therefore any product of c's and s's can be transformed into the form $s^i c^k$. Also $2^{\varphi(2n-1)} \equiv 1$ modulo $(2n-1)$; since $s^{\varphi(2n-1)}$ and c^{2n-1} are the identity permutation, at most $(2n-1)\varphi(2n-1)$ arrangements are possible. (The *exact* number of different arrangements is $(2n-1)k$, where k is the order of 2 modulo $(2n-1)$. For if $s^k = c^j$, then c^j fixes the card 0, so $s^k = c^j = $ identity.) For further details, see *SIAM Review* **3** (1961), 293–297.

14. (a) ♀. We could have deduced this regardless of where he had moved it, unless he had put it into one of the first three or last two positions. (b) ♦. Three cut-and-riffles will produce an intermixture of at most eight cyclically increasing subsequences $a_{x_j} a_{(x_j+1) \bmod n} \cdots a_{(x_{j+1}-1) \bmod n}$; hence the subsequence 6♦ 5♦ 4♦ is a dead giveaway. [Several magic tricks are based on the fact that three cut-and-riffles are highly nonrandom; see Martin Gardner, *Mathematical Magic Show* (Knopf, 1977), Chapter 7.]

15. Set $Y_j \leftarrow j$ for $t - n < j \le t$. Then for $j = t, t-1, \ldots, t-n+1$ do the following operations: Set $k \leftarrow \lfloor jU \rfloor + 1$. If $k > t - n$ then set $X_j \leftarrow Y_k$ and $Y_k \leftarrow Y_j$; otherwise if $k = X_i$ for some $i > j$ (a symbol table algorithm could be used), then set $X_j \leftarrow Y_i$ and $Y_i \leftarrow Y_j$; otherwise set $X_j \leftarrow k$. (The idea is to let $Y_{t-n+1}, \ldots, Y_j$ represent $X_{t-n+1}, \ldots, X_j$, and if $i > j$ and $X_i \le t - n$ also to let Y_i represent X_{X_i}, in the execution of Algorithm P. It is interesting to prove the correctness of Dahl's algorithm. One basic observation is that, in step P2, $X_k \ne k$ implies $X_k > j$, for $1 \le k \le j$.)

16. We may assume that $n \le \frac{1}{2}N$, otherwise it suffices to find the $N - n$ elements *not* in the sample. Using a hash table of size $2n$, the idea is to generate random numbers between 1 and N, storing them in the table and discarding duplicates, until n distinct numbers have been generated. The average number of random numbers generated is $N/N + N/(N-1) + \cdots + N/(N-n+1) < 2n$, by exercise 3.3.2–10, and the average time to process each number is $O(1)$. We want to output the results in increasing order, and this can be done as follows: Using an ordered hash table (exercise 6.4–66) with linear probing, the hash table will appear as if the values had been inserted in increasing order and the average total number of probes will be less than $\frac{5}{2}n$. Thus if we use a monotonic hash address such as $\lfloor 2n(k-1)/N \rfloor$ for the key k, it will be a simple matter to output the keys in sorted order by making at most two passes over the table. [See *CACM* **29** (1986), 366–367.]

17. Show inductively that before step j, the set S is a random sample of $j - N - 1 + n$ integers from $\{1, \ldots, j-1\}$. [*CACM* **30** (1987), 754–757. Floyd's method can be used to speed up the solution to exercise 16. It is essentially dual to Dahl's algorithm in exercise 15, which operates for *decreasing* values of j; see exercise 12.]

18. (a) Oriented trees that essentially merge $(1, 2, \ldots)$ with $(n, n-1, \ldots)$, such as

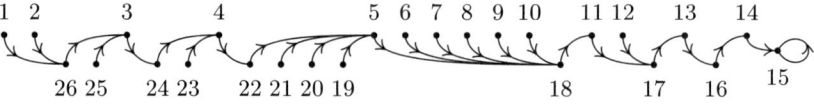

(b) Collections of 1-cycles and 2-cycles. (c) Binary search trees on the keys $(1, 2, \ldots, n)$, with k_j the parent of j (or j, at the root); see Section 6.2.2. The number of $(k_1, \ldots, k_n)$ in each case is (a) 2^{n-1}; (b) $t_n \geq \sqrt{n!}$, see 5.1.4–(40); (c) $\binom{2n}{n} \frac{1}{n+1}$. [Case (a) represents the least common permutation; case (b) represents the most common, when $n \geq 18$. See D. P. Robbins and E. D. Bolker, Æquationes Mathematicæ **22** (1981), 268–292; D. Goldstein and D. Moews, Æquationes Mathematicæ **65** (2003), 3–30.]

19. See N. Duffield, C. Lund, and M. Thorup, *JACM* **54** (2007), 32:1–32:37.

SECTION 3.5

1. A b-ary sequence, yes (see exercise 2); a $[0 \, . \, . \, 1)$ sequence, no (since only finitely many values are assumed by the elements).

2. It is 1-distributed and 2-distributed, but not 3-distributed (the binary number 111 never appears).

3. Repeat the sequence in exercise 3.2.2–17, with a period of length 27.

4. If $\nu_1(n)$, $\nu_2(n)$, $\nu_3(n)$, $\nu_4(n)$ are the counts for the four probabilities, we have $\nu_1(n) + \nu_2(n) = \nu_3(n) + \nu_4(n)$ for all n. So the desired result follows by addition of limits.

5. The sequence begins $\frac{1}{3}$, $\frac{2}{3}$, $\frac{2}{3}$, $\frac{1}{3}$, $\frac{1}{3}$, $\frac{1}{3}$, $\frac{1}{3}$, $\frac{2}{3}$, $\frac{2}{3}$, $\frac{2}{3}$, $\frac{2}{3}$, $\frac{2}{3}$, $\frac{2}{3}$, $\frac{2}{3}$, etc. When $n = 1, 3$, 7, 15, $\ldots$ we have $\nu(n) = 1, 1, 5, 5, \ldots$ so that $\nu(2^{2k-1} - 1) = \nu(2^{2k} - 1) = (2^{2k} - 1)/3$; hence $\nu(n)/n$ oscillates between $\frac{1}{3}$ and approximately $\frac{2}{3}$, and no limit exists. The probability is undefined. [The methods of Section 4.2.4 show, however, that a numerical value *can* meaningfully be assigned to $\Pr(U_n < \frac{1}{2}) = \Pr(\text{leading digit of the radix-4}$ representation of $n + 1$ is 1), namely $\log_4 2 = \frac{1}{2}$.]

6. By exercise 4 and induction, $\Pr(S_j(n)$ for some j, $1 \leq j \leq k) = \sum_{j=1}^{k} \Pr(S_j(n))$. As $k \to \infty$, the latter is a monotone sequence bounded by 1, so it converges; and $\underline{\Pr}(S_j(n)$ for some $j \geq 1) \geq \sum_{j=1}^{k} \Pr(S_j(n))$ for all k. For a counterexample to equality, it is not hard to arrange things so that $S_j(n)$ is always true for *some* j, yet $\Pr(S_j(n)) = 0$ for *all* j.

7. Let $p_i = \sum_{j \geq 1} \Pr(S_{ij}(n))$. The result of the preceding exercise can be generalized to $\underline{\Pr}(S_j(n)$ for some $j \geq 1) \geq \sum_{j \geq 1} \underline{\Pr}(S_j(n))$, for *any* disjoint statements $S_j(n)$. So we have $1 = \Pr(S_{ij}(n)$ for some $i, j \geq 1) \geq \sum_{i \geq 1} \underline{\Pr}(S_{ij}(n)$ for some $j \geq 1) \geq \sum_{i \geq 1} p_i = 1$, and hence $\underline{\Pr}(S_{ij}(n)$ for some $j \geq 1) = p_i$. Given $\epsilon > 0$, let I be large enough so that $\sum_{i=1}^{I} p_i \geq 1 - \epsilon$. Let

$$\phi_i(N) = (\text{number of } n < N \text{ with } S_{ij}(n) \text{ true for some } j \geq 1)/N.$$

Clearly $\sum_{i=1}^{I} \phi_i(N) \leq 1$, and for all large enough N we have $\sum_{i=2}^{I} \phi_i(N) \geq \sum_{i=2}^{I} p_i - \epsilon$; hence $\phi_1(N) \leq 1 - \phi_2(N) - \cdots - \phi_I(N) \leq 1 - p_2 - \cdots - p_I + \epsilon \leq 1 - (1 - \epsilon - p_1) + \epsilon = p_1 + 2\epsilon$. This proves that $\overline{\Pr}(S_{1j}(n)$ for some $j \geq 1) \leq p_1 + 2\epsilon$; hence $\Pr(S_{1j}(n)$ for some $j \geq 1) = p_1$, and the desired result holds for $i = 1$. By symmetry of the hypotheses, it holds for any value of i.

8. Add together the probabilities for j, $j + d$, $j + 2d$, $\ldots$, $m + j - d$ in Definition E.

9. $\limsup_{n \to \infty} (a_n + b_n) \leq \limsup_{n \to \infty} a_n + \limsup_{n \to \infty} b_n$; hence we find that

$$\limsup_{n \to \infty} \left((y_{1n} - \alpha)^2 + \cdots + (y_{mn} - \alpha)^2 \right) \leq m\alpha^2 - 2m\alpha^2 + m\alpha^2 = 0,$$

and this can happen only if each $(y_{jn} - \alpha)$ tends to zero.

10. In the evaluation of the sum in Eq. (22).

11. $\langle U_{2n} \rangle$ is k-distributed if $\langle U_n \rangle$ is $(2, 2k-1)$-distributed.

12. Apply Theorem B with $f(x_1, \ldots, x_k) = [u \le \max(x_1, \ldots, x_k) < v]$.

13. Let

$$p_k = \Pr(U_n \text{ begins a gap of length } k-1)$$
$$= \Pr(U_{n-1} \in [\alpha \mathinner{..} \beta),\ U_n \notin [\alpha \mathinner{..} \beta),\ \ldots,\ U_{n+k-2} \notin [\alpha \mathinner{..} \beta),\ U_{n+k-1} \in [\alpha \mathinner{..} \beta))$$
$$= p^2(1-p)^{k-1}.$$

It remains to translate this into the probability that $f(n) - f(n-1) = k$. Let $\nu_k(n) =$ (number of $j \le n$ with $f(j) - f(j-1) = k$); let $\mu_k(n) =$ (number of $j \le n$ with U_j the beginning of a gap of length $k-1$); and let $\mu(n)$ similarly count the number of $1 \le j \le n$ with $U_j \in [\alpha \mathinner{..} \beta)$. We have $\mu_k(f(n)) = \nu_k(n)$, $\mu(f(n)) = n$. As $n \to \infty$, we must have $f(n) \to \infty$, hence

$$\nu_k(n)/n = \big(\mu_k(f(n))/f(n)\big) \cdot \big(f(n)/\mu(f(n))\big) \to p_k/p = p(1-p)^{k-1}.$$

[We have only made use of the fact that the sequence is $(k+1)$-distributed.]

14. Let $p_k = \Pr(U_n \text{ begins a run of length } k)$

$$= \Pr(U_{n-1} > U_n < \cdots < U_{n+k-1} > U_{n+k})$$
$$= \frac{1}{(k+2)!}\left(\binom{k+2}{1}\binom{k+1}{1} - \binom{k+2}{1} - \binom{k+2}{1} + 1\right) = \frac{k}{(k+1)!} - \frac{k+1}{(k+2)!}$$

(see exercise 3.3.2–13). Now proceed as in the previous exercise to transfer this to $\Pr(f(n) - f(n-1) = k)$. [We have assumed only that the sequence is $(k+2)$-distributed.]

15. For $s, t \ge 0$ let

$$p_{st} = \Pr(X_{n-2t-3} = X_{n-2t-2} \ne X_{n-2t-1} \ne \cdots \ne X_{n-1} \text{ and } X_n = \cdots = X_{n+s} \ne X_{n+s+1})$$
$$= 2^{-s-2t-3};$$

for $t \ge 0$ let $q_t = \Pr(X_{n-2t-2} = X_{n-2t-1} \ne \cdots \ne X_{n-1}) = 2^{-2t-1}$. By exercise 7,

$$\Pr(X_n \text{ is not the beginning of a coupon set}) = \sum_{t \ge 0} q_t = \tfrac{2}{3};$$
$$\Pr(X_n \text{ is the beginning of coupon set of length } s+2) = \sum_{t \ge 0} p_{st} = \tfrac{1}{3} \cdot 2^{-s-1}.$$

Now proceed as in exercise 13.

16. (Solution by R. P. Stanley.) Whenever the subsequence $S = (b-1), (b-2), \ldots,$ $1, 0, 0, 1, \ldots, (b-2), (b-1)$ appears, a coupon set must end at the right of S, since some coupon set is completed in the first half of S. We now proceed to calculate the probability that a coupon set begins at position n by manipulating the probabilities that the last prior appearance of S ends at position $n-1$, $n-2$, etc., as in exercise 15.

18. Proceed as in the proof of Theorem A to calculate $\underline{\Pr}$ and $\overline{\Pr}$.

19. (Solution by T. Herzog.) Yes. For example, apply exercise 33 to the sequence $\langle U_{\lfloor n/2 \rfloor} \rangle$, when $\langle U_n \rangle$ satisfies R4 (or even its weaker version).

20. (a) 2 and $\tfrac{1}{2}$. (When n increases, we break $l_n^{(1)}$ in half.)

(b) Each new point breaks a single interval into two parts. Let ρ be equal to $\max_{k=0}^{n-1}\big((n+k)l_{n+k}^{(1)}\big)$. Then $1 = \sum_{k=1}^{n} l_n^{(k)} \le \sum_{k=0}^{n-1} l_{n+k}^{(1)} \le \sum_{k=0}^{n-1} \rho/(n+k) = \rho \ln 2 + O(1/n)$. So infinitely many m have $m l_m^{(1)} \ge 1/\ln 2 + O(1/m)$.

(c) To verify the hint, let $l_{2n}^{(k)}$ come from the interval with endpoints U_m and $U_{m'}$, and set $a_k = \max(m-n, m'-n, 1)$. Then $\rho = \min_{m=n+1}^{2n} m l_m^{(m)}$ implies $1 = \sum_{k=1}^{2n} l_{2n}^{(k)} \ge \sum_{k=1}^{2n} \rho/(n+a_k) \ge 2\rho \sum_{k=1}^{n} 1/(n+k)$; hence $2\rho \le 1/(H_{2n} - H_n) = 1/\ln 2 + O(1/n)$.

(d) We have $(l_n^{(1)}, \ldots, l_n^{(n)}) = (\lg \frac{n+1}{n}, \lg \frac{n+2}{n+1}, \ldots, \lg \frac{2n}{2n-1})$, because the $(n+1)$st point always breaks the largest interval into intervals of length $\lg \frac{2n+1}{2n}$ and $\lg \frac{2n+2}{2n+1}$. [*Indagationes Math.* **11** (1949), 14–17.]

21. (a) No! We have $\overline{\Pr}(W_n < \frac{1}{2}) \geq \limsup_{n\to\infty} \nu(\lceil 2^{n-1/2}\rceil)/\lceil 2^{n-1/2}\rceil = 2 - \sqrt{2}$, and $\underline{\Pr}(W_n < \frac{1}{2}) \leq \liminf_{n\to\infty} \nu(2^n)/2^n = \sqrt{2} - 1$, because $\nu(\lceil 2^{n-1/2}\rceil) = \nu(2^n) = \frac{1}{2}\sum_{k=0}^n (2^{k+1/2} - 2^k) + O(n)$.

(b, c) See *Indagationes Math.* **40** (1978), 527–541.

22. If the sequence is k-distributed, the limit is zero by integration and Theorem B. Conversely, note that if $f(x_1, \ldots, x_k)$ has an absolutely convergent Fourier series

$$f(x_1, \ldots, x_k) = \sum_{-\infty < c_1, \ldots, c_k < \infty} a(c_1, \ldots, c_k) \exp\bigl(2\pi i(c_1 x_1 + \cdots + c_k x_k)\bigr),$$

we have $\lim_{N\to\infty} \frac{1}{N} \sum_{0 \leq n < N} f(U_n, \ldots, U_{n+k-1}) = a(0, \ldots, 0) + \epsilon_r$, where

$$|\epsilon_r| \leq \sum_{\max\{|c_1|, \ldots, |c_k|\} > r} |a(c_1, \ldots, c_k)|,$$

so ϵ_r can be made arbitrarily small. Hence this limit is equal to

$$a(0, \ldots, 0) = \int_0^1 \cdots \int_0^1 f(x_1, \ldots, x_k)\, dx_1 \ldots dx_k,$$

and Eq. (8) holds for all sufficiently smooth functions f. The remainder of the proof shows that the function in (9) can be approximated by smooth functions to any desired accuracy.

23. (a) This follows immediately from exercise 22. (b) Use a discrete Fourier transform in an analogous way; see D. E. Knuth, *AMM* **75** (1968), 260–264.

24. (a) Let c be any nonzero integer; we must show, by exercise 22, that

$$\frac{1}{N} \sum_{n=0}^{N-1} e^{2\pi i c U_n} \to 0 \qquad \text{as} \quad N \to \infty.$$

This follows because, if K is any positive integer, we have $\sum_{k=0}^{K-1} \sum_{n=0}^{N-1} e^{2\pi i c U_{n+k}} = K \sum_{n=0}^{N-1} e^{2\pi i c U_n} + O(K^2)$. Hence, by Cauchy's inequality,

$$\frac{1}{N^2} \left| \sum_{n=0}^{N-1} e^{2\pi i c U_n} \right|^2 = \frac{1}{K^2 N^2} \left| \sum_{n=0}^{N-1} \sum_{k=0}^{K-1} e^{2\pi i c U_{n+k}} \right|^2 + O\left(\frac{K}{N}\right)$$

$$\leq \frac{1}{K^2 N} \sum_{n=0}^{N-1} \left| \sum_{k=0}^{K-1} e^{2\pi i c U_{n+k}} \right|^2 + O\left(\frac{K}{N}\right)$$

$$= \frac{1}{K} + \frac{2}{K^2 N} \Re\left(\sum_{0 \leq j < k < K} \sum_{n=0}^{N-1} e^{2\pi i c(U_{n+k} - U_{n+j})} \right) + O\left(\frac{K}{N}\right) \to \frac{1}{K}.$$

(b) When $d = 1$, exercise 22 tells us that $\langle (\alpha_1 n + \alpha_0) \bmod 1 \rangle$ is equidistributed if and only if α_1 is irrational. When $d > 1$, we can use (a) and induction on d. [*Acta Math.* **56** (1931), 373–456. The result in (b) had previously been obtained in a more complicated way by H. Weyl, *Nachr. Gesellschaft der Wiss. Göttingen, Math.-Phys. Kl.* (1914), 234–244. A similar argument proves that the polynomial sequence is equidistributed if at least one of the coefficients $\alpha_d, \ldots, \alpha_1$ is irrational.]

25. If the sequence is equidistributed, the denominator in Corollary S approaches $\frac{1}{12}$, and the numerator approaches the quantity in this exercise.

26. See *Math. Comp.* **17** (1963), 50–54. [Consider also the following example by A. G. Waterman: Let $\langle U_n \rangle$ be an equidistributed $[0 \mathinner{.\,.} 1)$ sequence and $\langle X_n \rangle$ an ∞-distributed binary sequence. Let $V_n = U_{\lfloor \sqrt{n} \rfloor}$ or $1 - U_{\lceil \sqrt{n} \rceil}$ according as X_n is 0 or 1. Then $\langle V_n \rangle$ is equidistributed and white, but $\Pr(V_n = V_{n+1}) = \frac{1}{2}$. Let $W_n = (V_n - \epsilon_n) \bmod 1$ where $\langle \epsilon_n \rangle$ is any sequence that decreases monotonically to 0; then $\langle W_n \rangle$ is equidistributed and white, yet $\Pr(W_n < W_{n+1}) = \frac{3}{4}$.]

28. Let $\langle U_n \rangle$ be ∞-distributed, and consider the sequence $\langle \frac{1}{2}(X_n + U_n) \rangle$. This is 3-distributed, using the fact that $\langle U_n \rangle$ is $(16, 3)$-distributed.

29. If $x = x_1 x_2 \ldots x_t$ is any binary number, we can consider the number $\nu_x^E(n)$ of times $X_p \ldots X_{p+t-1} = x$, where $1 \le p \le n$ and p is even. Similarly, let $\nu_x^O(n)$ count the number of times when p is odd. Let $\nu_x^E(n) + \nu_x^O(n) = \nu_x(n)$. Now

$$\nu_0^E(n) = \sum \nu_{0**\ldots*}^E(n) \approx \sum \nu_{*0*\ldots*}^O(n) \approx \sum \nu_{**0\ldots*}^E(n) \approx \cdots \approx \sum \nu_{***\ldots0}^O(n)$$

where the ν's in these summations have $2k$ subscripts, $2k-1$ of which are asterisks (meaning that they are being summed over — each sum is taken over 2^{2k-1} combinations of zeros and ones), and where "$\approx$" denotes approximate equality (except for an error of at most $2k$ due to end conditions). Therefore we find that

$$\tfrac{1}{n} 2k \nu_0^E(n) = \tfrac{1}{n}\left(\sum \nu_{*0*\ldots*}^E(n) + \cdots + \sum \nu_{***\ldots0}(n)\right) \tfrac{1}{n}\sum_x (r(x) - s(x))\nu_x^E(n) + O\left(\tfrac{1}{n}\right),$$

where $x = x_1 \ldots x_{2k}$ contains $r(x)$ zeros in odd positions and $s(x)$ zeros in even positions. By $(2k)$-distribution, the parenthesized quantity tends to $k(2^{2k-1})/2^{2k} = k/2$. The remaining sum is clearly a maximum if $\nu_x^E(n) = \nu_x(n)$ when $r(x) > s(x)$, and $\nu_x^E(n) = 0$ when $r(x) < s(x)$. So the maximum of the right-hand side becomes

$$\frac{k}{2} + \sum_{0 \le s < r \le k} (r - s) \binom{k}{r}\binom{k}{s}\Big/2^{2k} = \frac{k}{2} + k\binom{2k-1}{k}\Big/2^{2k}.$$

Now $\overline{\Pr}(X_{2n} = 0) \le \limsup_{n \to \infty} \nu_0^E(2n)/n$, so the proof is complete. Note that we have

$$\sum_{r,s}\binom{n}{r}\binom{n}{s}\max(r, s) = 2n2^{2n-2} + n\binom{2n-1}{n};$$

$$\sum_{r,s}\binom{n}{r}\binom{n}{s}\min(r, s) = 2n2^{2n-2} - n\binom{2n-1}{n}.$$

30. Construct a digraph with 2^{2k} nodes labeled $(Ex_1 \ldots x_{2k-1})$ and $(Ox_1 \ldots x_{2k-1})$, where each x_j is either 0 or 1. Let there be $1 + f(x_1, x_2, \ldots, x_{2k})$ directed arcs from $(Ex_1 \ldots x_{2k-1})$ to $(Ox_2 \ldots x_{2k})$, and $1 - f(x_1, x_2, \ldots, x_{2k})$ directed arcs leading from $(Ox_1 \ldots x_{2k-1})$ to $(Ex_2 \ldots x_{2k})$, where $f(x_1, x_2, \ldots, x_{2k}) = \operatorname{sign}(x_1 - x_2 + x_3 - x_4 + \cdots - x_{2k})$. We find that each node has the same number of arcs leading into it as there are leading out; for example, $(Ex_1 \ldots x_{2k-1})$ has $1 - f(0, x_1, \ldots, x_{2k-1}) + 1 - f(1, x_1, \ldots, x_{2k-1})$ leading in and $1 + f(x_1, \ldots, x_{2k-1}, 0) + 1 + f(x_1, \ldots, x_{2k-1}, 1)$ leading out, and $f(x, x_1, \ldots, x_{2k-1}) = -f(x_1, \ldots, x_{2k-1}, x)$. Drop all nodes that have no paths leading either in or out, namely $(Ex_1 \ldots x_{2k-1})$ if $f(0, x_1, \ldots, x_{2k-1}) = +1$,

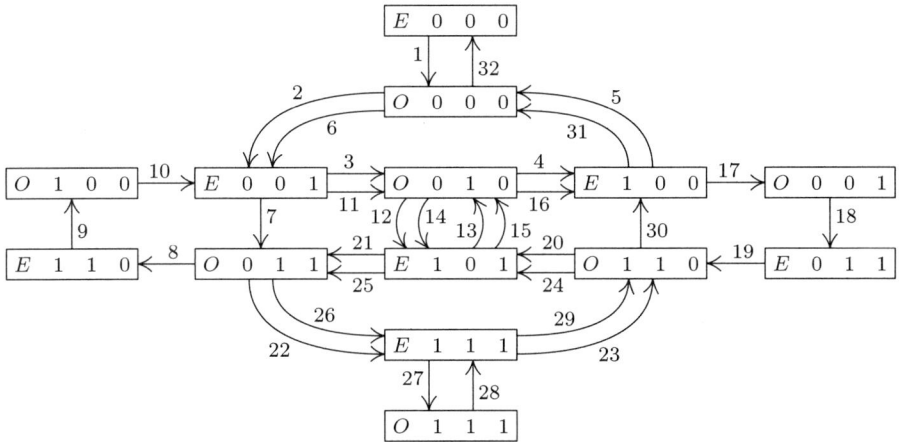

Fig. A–5. Directed graph for the construction in exercise 30.

or $(Ox_1 \ldots x_{2k-1})$ if $f(1, x_1, \ldots, x_{2k-1}) = -1$. The resulting directed graph is seen to be connected, since we can get from any node to $(E1010 \ldots 1)$ and from this to any desired node. By Theorem 2.3.4.2G, there is a cyclic path traversing each arc; this path has length 2^{2k+1}, and we may assume that it starts at node $(E00 \ldots 0)$. Construct a cyclic sequence with $X_1 = \cdots = X_{2k-1} = 0$, and $X_{n+2k-1} = x_{2k}$ if the nth arc of the path is from $(Ex_1 \ldots x_{2k-1})$ to $(Ox_2 \ldots x_{2k})$ or from $(Ox_1 \ldots x_{2k-1})$ to $(Ex_2 \ldots x_{2k})$. For example, the graph for $k = 2$ is shown in Fig. A–5; the arcs of the cyclic path are numbered from 1 to 32, and the cyclic sequence is

$$(00001000110010101001101110111110)(00001\ldots).$$

Notice that $\Pr(X_{2n} = 0) = \frac{11}{16}$ in this sequence. The sequence is clearly $(2k)$-distributed, since each $(2k)$-tuple $x_1 x_2 \ldots x_{2k}$ occurs

$$1 + f(x_1, \ldots, x_{2k}) + 1 - f(x_1, \ldots, x_{2k}) = 2$$

times in the cycle. The fact that $\Pr(X_{2n} = 0)$ has the desired value comes from the fact that the maximum value on the right-hand side in the proof of the preceding exercise has been achieved by this construction.

31. Use Algorithm W with rule $\mathcal{R}_1$ selecting the entire sequence. [For a generalization of this type of nonrandom behavior in R5-sequences, see Jean Ville, *Étude Critique de la Notion de Collectif* (Paris: 1939), 55–62. Perhaps R6 is also too weak, from this standpoint, but no such counterexample is presently known.]

32. If $\mathcal{R}, \mathcal{R}'$ are computable subsequence rules, so is $\mathcal{R}'' = \mathcal{R}\mathcal{R}'$ defined by the following functions: $f_n''(x_0, \ldots, x_{n-1}) = 1$ if and only if $\mathcal{R}$ defines the subsequence $x_{r_1}, \ldots, x_{r_k}$ of $x_0, \ldots, x_{n-1}$, where $k \geq 0$ and $0 \leq r_1 < \cdots < r_k < n$ and $f_k'(x_{r_1}, \ldots, x_{r_k}) = 1$.

Now $\langle X_n \rangle \mathcal{R}\mathcal{R}'$ is $(\langle X_n \rangle \mathcal{R})\mathcal{R}'$. The result follows immediately.

33. Given $\epsilon > 0$, find N_0 such that $N > N_0$ implies that both $|\nu_r(N)/N - p| < \epsilon$ and $|\nu_s(N)/N - p| < \epsilon$. Then find N_1 such that $N > N_1$ implies that t_N is r_M or s_M for some $M > N_0$. Now $N > N_1$ implies that

$$\left|\frac{\nu_t(N)}{N} - p\right| = \left|\frac{\nu_r(N_r) + \nu_s(N_s)}{N} - p\right| = \left|\frac{\nu_r(N_r) - pN_r + \nu_s(N_s) - pN_s}{N_r + N_s}\right| < \epsilon.$$

34. For example, if the binary representation of t is $(1\,0^{b-2}\,1\,0^{a_1}\,1\,1\,0^{a_2}\,1\,\ldots\,1\,0^{a_k})_2$, where "$0^a$" stands for a sequence of a consecutive zeros, let the rule $\mathcal{R}_t$ accept U_n if and only if $\lfloor bU_{n-k}\rfloor = a_1, \ldots, \lfloor bU_{n-1}\rfloor = a_k$.

35. Let $a_0 = s_0$ and $a_{m+1} = \max\{s_k \mid 0 \le k < 2^{a_m}\}$. Construct a subsequence rule that selects element X_n if and only if $n = s_k$ for some $k < 2^{a_m}$, when n is in the range $a_m \le n < a_{m+1}$. Then $\lim_{m\to\infty} \nu(a_m)/a_m = \frac{1}{2}$.

36. Let b and k be arbitrary but fixed integers greater than 1. Let $Y_n = \lfloor bU_n\rfloor$. An arbitrary infinite subsequence $\langle Z_n\rangle = \langle Y_{s_n}\rangle\mathcal{R}$ determined by algorithms $\mathcal{S}$ and $\mathcal{R}$ (as in the proof of Theorem M) corresponds in a straightforward but notationally hopeless manner to algorithms $\mathcal{S}'$ and $\mathcal{R}'$ that inspect $X_t, X_{t+1}, \ldots, X_{t+s}$ and/or select X_t, $X_{t+1}, \ldots, X_{t+\min(k-1,s)}$ of $\langle X_n\rangle$ if and only if $\mathcal{S}$ and $\mathcal{R}$ inspect and/or select Y_s, where $U_s = (0.X_tX_{t+1}\ldots X_{t+s})_2$. Algorithms $\mathcal{S}'$ and $\mathcal{R}'$ determine an infinite 1-distributed subsequence of $\langle X_n\rangle$ and in fact (as in exercise 32) this subsequence is ∞-distributed so it is $(k,1)$-distributed. Hence we find that $\underline{\Pr}(Z_n = a)$ and $\overline{\Pr}(Z_n = a)$ differ from $1/b$ by less than $1/2^k$.

[The result of this exercise is true if "R6" is replaced consistently by "R4" or "R5"; but it is false if "R1" is used, since $X_{\binom{n}{2}}$ might be identically zero.]

37. For $n \ge 2$ replace U_{n^2} by $\frac{1}{2}(U_{n^2} + \delta_n)$, where $\delta_n = 0$ or 1 according as the set $\{U_{(n-1)^2+1}, \ldots, U_{n^2-1}\}$ contains an even or odd number of elements less than $\frac{1}{2}$. [*Advances in Math.* **14** (1974), 333–334; see also the Ph.D. thesis of Thomas N. Herzog, Univ. of Maryland (1975).]

39. See *Acta Arithmetica* **21** (1972), 45–50. The best possible value of c is unknown.

40. Since F_k depends only on $B_1\ldots B_k$, we have $P(A_k^P, \$_N) = \frac{1}{2}$. Let $q(B_1\ldots B_k) = \Pr(B_{k+1} = 1 \mid B_1\ldots B_k)$, where the probability is taken over all elements of S having $B_1\ldots B_k$ as the first k bits. Similarly, let $q_b(B_1\ldots B_k) = \Pr(F_k = 1$ and $B'_{k+1} = b \mid B_1\ldots B_k)$. Then we have $\Pr(A_k^P = 1 \mid B_1\ldots B_k) = \Pr((F_k + B_{k+1} + B'_{k+1}) \bmod 2 = 1 \mid B_1\ldots B_k) = q\cdot(\frac{1}{2} - q_0 + q_1) + (1-q)\cdot(q_0 + \frac{1}{2} - q_1) = \frac{1}{2} - (q_0 + q_1) + 2(qq_1 + (1-q)q_0) = \frac{1}{2} - \Pr(F_k = 1 \mid B_1\ldots B_k) + 2\Pr(F_k = 1$ and $B'_{k+1} = B_{k+1} \mid B_1\ldots B_k)$. Hence $\Pr(A_k^P = 1) = \sum_{B_1\ldots B_k}\Pr(B_1\ldots B_k)\Pr(A_k^P = 1 \mid B_1\ldots B_k) = \frac{1}{2} - \Pr(F_k = 1) + \Pr(F_{k+1} = 1)$. [See Theorem 4 of Goldreich, Goldwasser, and Micali in *JACM* **33** (1986), 792–807.]

41. Choose k uniformly from $\{0, \ldots, N-1\}$ and use the construction in the proof of Lemma P1. Then the proof of P1 shows that A' will be equal to 1 with probability $\sum_{k=0}^{N-1}(\frac{1}{2} - p_k + p_{k+1})/N$.

42. (a) Let $X = X_1 + \cdots + X_n$. Clearly $\mathrm{E}(X) = n\mu$; and we have $\mathrm{E}((X - n\mu)^2) = \mathrm{E}\,X^2 - n^2\mu^2 = n\,\mathrm{E}\,X_j^2 + 2\sum_{1\le i<j\le n}(\mathrm{E}\,X_i)(\mathrm{E}\,X_j) - n^2\mu^2 = n\,\mathrm{E}\,X_j^2 - n\mu^2 = n\sigma^2$. Also $\mathrm{E}((X - n\mu)^2) = \sum_{x\ge 0} x\Pr((X - n\mu)^2 = x) \ge \sum_{x\ge tn\sigma^2} x\Pr((X - n\mu)^2 = x) \ge \sum_{x\ge tn\sigma^2} tn\sigma^2\Pr((X - n\mu)^2 = x) = tn\sigma^2\Pr((X - n\mu)^2 \ge tn\sigma^2)$.

(b) There is a position i where $c_i \ne c'_i$, say $c_i = 0$ and $c'_i = 1$. Then there's a position j where $c_j = 1$. For any fixed setting of B in the $k-2$ rows other than i or j, we have $(cB, c'B) = (d, d')$ if and only if rows i and j have particular values; this occurs with probability $1/2^{2R}$.

(c) In the notation of Algorithm L, take $n = 2^k - 1$ and $X_c = (-1)^{G(cB+e_i)}$; then $\mu = s$ and $\sigma^2 = 1 - s^2$. The probability that $X = \sum_{c \neq 0} X_c$ is negative is at most the probability that $(X - n\mu)^2 \geq n^2\mu^2$. By (a) this is at most $\sigma^2/(n\mu^2)$.

43. The conclusion for fixed M would be of no interest, since there obviously exists an algorithm to factor any fixed M (namely, an algorithm that knows the factors). The theory applies to *all* algorithms that have short running time, not only to algorithms that are effectively discoverable.

44. If every one-digit change to a random table yields a random table, all tables are random (or none are). If we don't allow degrees of randomness, the answer must therefore be, "Not always."

SECTION 3.6

1.

	RANDI STJ	9F	Store exit location.
	STA	8F	Store value of k.
	LDA	XRAND	rA $\leftarrow X$.
	MUL	7F	rAX $\leftarrow aX$.
	INCX	1009	rX $\leftarrow (aX + c) \bmod m$.
	JOV	*+1	Ensure that overflow is off.
	SLAX	5	rA $\leftarrow (aX + c) \bmod m$.
	STA	XRAND	Store X.
	MUL	8F	rA $\leftarrow \lfloor kX/m \rfloor$.
	INCA	1	Add 1, so that $1 \leq Y \leq k$.
9H	JMP	*	Return.
XRAND	CON	1	Value of X; $X_0 = 1$.
8H	CON	0	Temp storage of k.
7H	CON	3141592621	The multiplier a. ∎

2. Putting a random number generator into a program makes the results essentially unpredictable to the programmer. If the behavior of the machine on each problem were known in advance, few programs would ever be written. As Turing has said, the actions of a computer quite often *do* surprise its programmer, especially when a program is being debugged.

So the world had better watch out.

7. In fact, you only need the 2-bit values $\lfloor X_n/2^{16} \rfloor \bmod 4$; see D. E. Knuth, *IEEE Trans.* **IT-31** (1985), 49–52. J. Reeds, *Cryptologia* **1** (1977), 20–26, **3** (1979), 83–95, initiated the study of related problems; see also J. Boyar, *J. Cryptology* **1** (1989), 177–184. In *SICOMP* **17** (1988), 262–280, Frieze, Håstad, Kannan, Lagarias, and Shamir discuss general techniques that are useful in problems like this.

8. We can, say, generate $X_{1000000}$ by making one million successive calls, and compare it to the correct value $(a^{1000000}X_0 + (a^{1000000} - 1)c/(a - 1)) \bmod m$, which can also be expressed as $((a^{1000000}(X_0(a - 1) + c) - c) \bmod (a - 1)m)/(a - 1)$. The latter can be evaluated quickly by an independent method (see Algorithm 4.6.3A). For example, $48271^{1000000} \bmod 2147483647 = 1263606197$. Most errors will be detected, because recurrence (1) is not self-correcting.

9. (a) The values of $X_0, X_1, \ldots, X_{99}$ are not all even. The polynomial $z^{100} + z^{37} + 1$ is primitive (see Section 3.2.2); hence there is a number $h(s)$ such that $P_0(z) \equiv z^{h(s)}$

(modulo 2 and $z^{100} + z^{37} + 1$). Now $zP_{n+1}(z) = P_n(z) - X_n z^{37} - X_{n+63} + X_{n+63} z^{100} + X_{n+100} z^{37} \equiv P_n(z) + X_{n+63}(z^{100} + z^{37} + 1)$ (modulo 2), so the result holds by induction.

(b) The operations "square" and "multiply by z" in *ran_start* change $p(z) = x_{99} z^{99} + \cdots + x_1 z + x_0$ to $p(z)^2$ and $zp(z)$, respectively, modulo 2 and $z^{100} + z^{37} + 1$, because $p(z)^2 \equiv p(z^2)$. (We consider here only the low-order bits. The other bits are manipulated in an ad hoc way that tends to preserve and/or enhance whatever disorder they already have.) Therefore if $s = (1s_j \ldots s_1 s_0)_2$ we have $h(s) = (1s_0 s_1 \ldots s_j 1)_2 \cdot 2^{69}$.

(c) $z^{h(s)-n} \equiv z^{h(s')-n'}$ (modulo 2 and $z^{100} + z^{37} + 1$) implies that $h(s) - n \equiv h(s') - n'$ (modulo $2^{100} - 1$). Since $2^{69} \le h(s) < 2^{100} - 2^{69}$, we have $|n - n'| \ge |h(s) - h(s')| \ge 2^{70}$.

[This method of initialization was inspired by comments of R. P. Brent, *Proc. Australian Supercomputer Conf.* **5** (1992), 95–104, although Brent's algorithm was completely different. In general if the lags are $k > l$, if $0 \le s < 2^e$, and if the separation parameter t satisfies $t + e \le k$, this method of proof shows that $|n - n'| \ge 2^t - 1$, with $2^t - 1$ occurring only if $\{s, s'\} = \{0, 2^e - 1\}$.]

10. The following code belongs to the simplified language Subset FORTRAN, as defined by the American National Standards Institute, except for its use of PARAMETER statements for readability.

```
      SUBROUTINE RNARRY(AA,N)
      IMPLICIT INTEGER (A-Z)
      DIMENSION AA(*)
      PARAMETER (KK=100)
      PARAMETER (LL=37)
      PARAMETER (MM=2**30)
      COMMON /RSTATE/ RANX(KK)
      SAVE /RSTATE/
      DO 1 J=1,KK
1        AA(J)=RANX(J)
      DO 2 J=KK+1,N
         AA(J)=AA(J-KK)-AA(J-LL)
         IF (AA(J) .LT. 0) AA(J)=AA(J)+MM
2     CONTINUE
      DO 3 J=1,LL
         RANX(J)=AA(N+J-KK)-AA(N+J-LL)
         IF (RANX(J) .LT. 0) RANX(J)=RANX(J)+MM
3     CONTINUE
      DO 4 J=LL+1,KK
         RANX(J)=AA(N+J-KK)-RANX(J-LL)
         IF (RANX(J) .LT. 0) RANX(J)=RANX(J)+MM
4     CONTINUE
      END

      SUBROUTINE RNSTRT(SEED)
      IMPLICIT INTEGER (A-Z)
      PARAMETER (KK=100)
      PARAMETER (LL=37)
      PARAMETER (MM=2**30)
      PARAMETER (TT=70)
```

```
      PARAMETER (KKK=KK+KK-1)
      DIMENSION X(KKK)
      COMMON /RSTATE/ RANX(KK)
      SAVE /RSTATE/

      IF (SEED .LT. 0) THEN
         SSEED=MM-1-MOD(-1-SEED,MM)
      ELSE
         SSEED=MOD(SEED,MM)
      END IF

      SS=SSEED-MOD(SSEED,2)+2
      DO 1 J=1,KK
         X(J)=SS
         SS=SS+SS
         IF (SS .GE. MM) SS=SS-MM+2
1     CONTINUE
      X(2)=X(2)+1

      SS=SSEED
      T=TT-1
10    DO 12 J=KK,2,-1
         X(J+J-1)=X(J)
12       X(J+J-2)=0
      DO 14 J=KKK,KK+1,-1
         X(J-(KK-LL))=X(J-(KK-LL))-X(J)
         IF (X(J-(KK-LL)) .LT. 0) X(J-(KK-LL))=X(J-(KK-LL))+MM
         X(J-KK)=X(J-KK)-X(J)
         IF (X(J-KK) .LT. 0) X(J-KK)=X(J-KK)+MM
14    CONTINUE

      IF (MOD(SS,2) .EQ. 1) THEN
         DO 16 J=KK,1,-1
16          X(J+1)=X(J)
         X(1)=X(KK+1)
         X(LL+1)=X(LL+1)-X(KK+1)
         IF (X(LL+1) .LT. 0) X(LL+1)=X(LL+1)+MM
      END IF

      IF (SS .NE. 0) THEN
         SS=SS/2
      ELSE
         T=T-1
      END IF
      IF (T .GT. 0) GO TO 10

      DO 20 J=1,LL
20       RANX(J+KK-LL)=X(J)
      DO 21 J=LL+1,KK
21       RANX(J-LL)=X(J)
      DO 22 J=1,10
22       CALL RNARRY(X,KKK)
      END
```

11. Floating point arithmetic on 64-bit operands conforming to ANSI/IEEE Standard 754 allows us to compute $U_n = (U_{n-100} - U_{n-37}) \bmod 1$ with perfect accuracy for fractions U_n that are integer multiples of 2^{-53}. However, the following program uses the *additive* recurrence $U_n = (U_{n-100} + U_{n-37}) \bmod 1$ on integer multiples of 2^{-52} instead, because pipelined computers can subtract an integer part more quickly than they can branch conditionally on the sign of an intermediate result. The theory of exercise 9 applies equally well to this sequence.

A FORTRAN translation similar to the code in exercise 10 will generate exactly the same numbers as this C routine.

```
#define KK 100                                      /* the long lag */
#define LL   37                                      /* the short lag */
#define mod_sum(x,y) (((x)+(y))-(int)((x)+(y)))    /* (x+y) mod 1.0 */

double ran_u[KK];                                   /* the generator state */

void ranf_array(double aa[],int n) { /* aa gets n random fractions */
  register int i,j;
  for (j=0;j<KK;j++) aa[j]=ran_u[j];
  for (;j<n;j++) aa[j]=mod_sum(aa[j-KK],aa[j-LL]);
  for (i=0;i<LL;i++,j++) ran_u[i]=mod_sum(aa[j-KK],aa[j-LL]);
  for (;i<KK;i++,j++) ran_u[i]=mod_sum(aa[j-KK],ran_u[i-LL]);
}

#define TT  70              /* guaranteed separation between streams */
#define is_odd(s) ((s)&1)

void ranf_start(long seed) {      /* do this before using ranf_array */
  register int t,s,j;
  double u[KK+KK-1];
  double ulp=(1.0/(1L<<30))/(1L<<22);              /* 2 to the -52 */
  double ss=2.0*ulp*((seed&0x3fffffff)+2);

  for (j=0;j<KK;j++) {
    u[j]=ss;                                  /* bootstrap the buffer */
    ss+=ss;
    if (ss>=1.0) ss-=1.0-2*ulp;              /* cyclic shift of 51 bits */
  }
  u[1]+=ulp;                        /* make u[1] (and only u[1]) "odd" */
  for (s=seed&0x3fffffff,t=TT-1; t; ) {
    for (j=KK-1;j>0;j--)
      u[j+j]=u[j],u[j+j-1]=0.0;                      /* "square" */
    for (j=KK+KK-2;j>=KK;j--) {
      u[j-(KK-LL)]=mod_sum(u[j-(KK-LL)],u[j]);
      u[j-KK]=mod_sum(u[j-KK],u[j]);
    }
    if (is_odd(s)) {                           /* "multiply by z" */
      for (j=KK;j>0;j--) u[j]=u[j-1];
      u[0]=u[KK];                        /* shift the buffer cyclically */
      u[LL]=mod_sum(u[LL],u[KK]);
    }
    if (s) s>>=1; else t--;
  }
}
```

```
    for (j=0;j<LL;j++) ran_u[j+KK-LL]=u[j];
    for (;j<KK;j++) ran_u[j-LL]=u[j];
    for (j=0;j<10;j++) ranf_array(u,KK+KK-1);    /* warm everything up */
}
int main() {                                      /* a rudimentary test */
    register int m;
    double a[2009];
    ranf_start(310952);
    for (m=0;m<2009;m++)
        ranf_array(a,1009);
    printf("%.20f\n", ran_u[0]);        /* 0.36410514377569680455 */
    ranf_start(310952);
    for (m=0;m<1009;m++)
        ranf_array(a,2009);
    printf("%.20f\n", ran_u[0]);        /* 0.36410514377569680455 */
    return 0;
}
```

12. A simple linear congruential generator like (1) would fail, because m would be much too small. Good results are possible by combining three (not two) such generators, with multipliers and moduli $(157, 32363)$, $(146, 31727)$, $(142, 31657)$, as suggested by P. L'Ecuyer in *CACM* **31** (1988), 747–748. However, the best method is probably to use the C programs *ran_array* and *ran_start*, with the following changes to keep all numbers in range: 'long' becomes 'int'; 'MM' is defined to be '(1U<<15)'; and the type of variable ss should be **unsigned int**. This generates 15-bit integers, all of whose bits are usable. The seed is now restricted to the range $[0..32765]$. The "rudimentary test routine" will print $X_{1009 \times 2009} = 24130$, given the seed 12509.

13. A program for subtract-with-borrow would be very similar to *ran_array*, but slower because of the carry maintenance. As in exercise 11, floating point arithmetic could be used with perfect accuracy. It is possible to guarantee disjointness of the sequences produced from different seeds s by initializing the generator with the $(-n)$th element of the sequence, where $n = 2^{70s}$; this requires computing $b^n \bmod (b^k - b^l \pm 1)$. Squaring a radix-$b$ number mod $b^k - b^l \pm 1$ is, however, considerably more complicated than the analogous operation in program *ran_start*, and for k in a practical range it takes about $k^{1.6}$ operations instead of $O(k)$.

Both methods probably generate sequences of the same quality in practice, when they have roughly the same value of k. The only significant difference between them is a better theoretical guarantee and a provably immense period for the subtract-with-borrow method; the analysis of lagged Fibonacci generators is less complete. Experience shows that we should not reduce the value of k in subtract-with-borrow just because of these theoretical advantages. When all is said and done, lagged Fibonacci generators seem preferable from a practical standpoint; the subtract-with-borrow method is then valuable chiefly because of the insight it gives us into the excellent behavior of the simpler approach.

14. We have $X_{n+200} \equiv (X_n + X_{n+126})$ (modulo 2); see exercise 3.2.2–32. Hence $Y_{n+100} \equiv Y_n + Y_{n+26}$ when $n \bmod 100 > 73$. Similarly $X_{n+200} \equiv X_n + X_{n+26} + X_{n+89}$; hence $Y_{n+100} \equiv Y_n + Y_{n+26} + Y_{n+89}$ when $n \bmod 100 < 11$. Thus Y_{n+100} is a sum of only two or three elements of $\{Y_n, \ldots, Y_{n+99}\}$, in $26\% + 11\%$ of all cases; a preponderance of 0s will then tend to make $Y_{n+100} = 0$.

More precisely, consider the sequence $\langle u_1, u_2, \ldots \rangle = \langle 126, 89, 152, 115, 78, \ldots, 100,$ $63, 126, \ldots \rangle$ where $u_{n+1} = u_n - 37 + 100[u_n < 100]$. Then we have

$$X_{n+200} = (X_n + X_{n+v_1} + \cdots + X_{n+v_{k-2}} + X_{u_{k-1}}) \bmod 2,$$

where $v_j = u_j + (-1)^{[u_j \geq 100]} 100$; for example, $X_{n+200} \equiv X_n + X_{n+26} + X_{n+189} + X_{n+152} \equiv X_n + X_{n+26} + X_{n+189} + X_{n+52} + X_{n+115}$. If the subscripts are all $< n + t$ and $\geq n + 100 + t$, we obtain a k-term expression for Y_{n+100} when $n \bmod 100 = 100 - t$, for $1 \leq t \leq 100$. The case $t = 63$ is an exception, because $X_n + X_{n+1} + \cdots + X_{n+62} + X_{n+163} + X_{n+164} + \cdots + X_{n+199} \equiv 0$; in this case Y_{n+100} is independent of $\{Y_n, \ldots, Y_{n+99}\}$. The case $t = 64$ is interesting because it gives the 99-term relation $Y_{n+100} \equiv Y_{n+1} + Y_{n+2} + \cdots + Y_{n+99}$; this tends to be 0 in spite of the large number of terms, because most of the 100-tuples that have 40 or fewer 1s have even parity.

When there is a k-term relation, the probability that $Y_{n+100} = 1$ is

$$p_k = \sum_{l=0}^{40} \sum_{j=1}^{k} \binom{100-k}{l-j} \binom{k}{j} [j \text{ odd}] \Bigg/ \sum_{l=0}^{40} \binom{100}{l}.$$

The quantity t takes the values 100, 99, ..., 1, 100, 99, ..., 1, ... as bits are printed; so we find that the expected number of 1s printed is $10^6 (26p_2 + 11p_3 + 26p_4 + 11p_6 + 11p_9 + 4p_{12} + 4p_{20} + 3p_{28} + p_{47} + p_{74} + p_{99} + 1/2)/100 \approx 14043$. The expected number of digits printed is $10^6 \sum_{l=0}^{40} \binom{100}{l} / 2^{100} \approx 28444$, so the expected number of 0s is ≈ 14401.

The detectable bias goes away if more elements are discarded. For example, if we use only 100 elements of $ran\_array(a, 300)$, the probability can be shown to be $(26p_5 + 22p_6 + 19p_{10} + \cdots)/100$; with $ran\_array(a, 400)$ it is worse, $(15p_3 + 37p_6 + 15p_9 + \cdots)/100$, because $X_{n+400} \equiv X_n + X_{n+252}$. With $ran\_array(a, 1009)$ as recommended in the text we have $(17p_7 + 10p_{11} + 2p_{12} + \cdots)/100$, which can only be detected by such experiments if the threshold for printing is raised from 60 to, say, 75; but then the expected number of outputs is only about 0.28 per million trials.

[This exercise is based on ideas of Y. Kurita, H. Leeb, and M. Matsumoto, communicated to the author in 1997.]

15. The following program makes it possible to obtain a new random integer quickly with the expression $ran\_arr\_next()$, once ran_start has been called to get things started:

```
#define QUALITY 1009    /* recommended quality level for high-res use */
#define KK 100                                          /* the long lag */
long ran_arr_buf[QUALITY];
long ran_arr_sentinel=-1;
long *ran_arr_ptr=&ran_arr_sentinel; /* the next random number, or -1 */
#define ran_arr_next() (*ran_arr_ptr>=0? *ran_arr_ptr++: ran_arr_cycle())
long ran_arr_cycle()
{
  ran_array(ran_arr_buf,QUALITY);
  ran_arr_buf[KK]=-1; ran_arr_ptr=ran_arr_buf+1;
  return ran_arr_buf[0];
}
```

Reset $ran\_arr\_ptr = \&ran\_arr\_sentinel$ if ran_start is used again.

SECTION 4.1

1. $(1010)_{-2}$, $(1011)_{-2}$, $(1000)_{-2}$, ..., $(11000)_{-2}$, $(11001)_{-2}$, $(11110)_{-2}$.

2. (a) $-(110001)_2$, $-(11.001001001001\ldots)_2$, $(11.00100100001111110110101\ldots)_2$.

(b) $(11010011)_{-2}$, $(1101.001011001011\ldots)_{-2}$, $(111.0110010001000000101\ldots)_{-2}$.

(c) $(\bar{1}11\bar{1}\bar{1})_3$, $(\bar{1}0.0\bar{1}\bar{1}0110\bar{1}\bar{1}011\ldots)_3$, $(10.011\bar{1}\bar{1}111\bar{1}000\bar{1}011\bar{1}1101\bar{1}1111110\ldots)_3$.

(d) $-(9.4)_{1/10}$, $-(\ldots 7582417582413)_{1/10}$, $(\ldots 3462648323979853562951413)_{1/10}$.

3. $(1010113.2)_{2i}$.

4. (a) Between rA and rX. (b) The remainder in rX has radix point between bytes 3 and 4; the quotient in rA has radix point one byte to the right of the least significant portion of the register.

5. It has been subtracted from $999\ldots9 = 10^p - 1$, instead of from $1000\ldots0 = 10^p$.

6. (a, c) $2^{p-1} - 1$, $-(2^{p-1} - 1)$; (b) $2^{p-1} - 1$, -2^{p-1}.

7. A ten's complement representation for a negative number x can be obtained by considering $10^n + x$ (where n is large enough for this to be positive) and extending it on the left with infinitely many nines. The nines' complement representation can be obtained in the usual manner. (These two representations are equal for nonterminating decimals, otherwise the nines' complement representation has the form $\ldots(a)99999\ldots$ while the ten's complement representation has the form $\ldots(a+1)0000\ldots.$) The representations may be considered sensible if we regard the value of the infinite sum $N = 9 + 90 + 900 + 9000 + \cdots$ as -1, since $N - 10N = 9$.

See also exercise 31, which considers p-adic number systems. The latter agree with the p's complement notations considered here, for numbers whose radix-p representation is terminating, but there is no simple relation between the field of p-adic numbers and the field of real numbers.

8. $\sum_j a_j b^j = \sum_j (a_{kj+k-1} b^{k-1} + \cdots + a_{kj}) b^{kj}$.

9. A BAD ADOBE FACADE FADED. [*Note:* Other possible "number sentences" would be DO A DEED A DECADE; A CAD FED A BABE BEEF, COCOA, COFFEE; BOB FACED A DEAD DODO.]

10.
$$\begin{bmatrix} \ldots, a_3, a_2, a_1, a_0; \ a_{-1}, a_{-2}, \ldots \\ \ldots, b_3, b_2, b_1, b_0; \ b_{-1}, b_{-2}, \ldots \end{bmatrix} = \begin{bmatrix} \ldots, A_3, A_2, A_1, A_0; \ A_{-1}, A_{-2}, \ldots \\ \ldots, B_3, B_2, B_1, B_0; \ B_{-1}, B_{-2}, \ldots \end{bmatrix}, \quad \text{if}$$

$$A_j = \begin{bmatrix} a_{k_{j+1}-1}, a_{k_{j+1}-2}, \ldots, a_{k_j} \\ b_{k_{j+1}-2}, \ldots, b_{k_j} \end{bmatrix}, \qquad B_j = b_{k_{j+1}-1} \ldots b_{k_j},$$

where $\langle k_n \rangle$ is any doubly infinite sequence of integers with $k_{j+1} > k_j$ and $k_0 = 0$.

11. (The following algorithm works both for addition or subtraction, depending on whether the plus or minus sign is chosen.)

Start by setting $k \leftarrow a_{n+1} \leftarrow a_{n+2} \leftarrow b_{n+1} \leftarrow b_{n+2} \leftarrow 0$; then for $m = 0, 1,$ $\ldots, n+2$ do the following: Set $c_m \leftarrow a_m \pm b_m + k$; then if $c_m \geq 2$, set $k \leftarrow -1$ and $c_m \leftarrow c_m - 2$; otherwise if $c_m < 0$, set $k \leftarrow 1$ and $c_m \leftarrow c_m + 2$; otherwise (namely if $0 \leq c_m \leq 1$), set $k \leftarrow 0$.

12. (a) Subtract $\pm(\ldots a_3 0 a_1 0)_{-2}$ from $\pm(\ldots a_4 0 a_2 0 a_0)_{-2}$ in the negabinary system. (See also exercise 7.1.3–7 for a trickier solution that uses full-word bitwise operations.) (b) Subtract $(\ldots b_3 0 b_1 0)_2$ from $(\ldots b_4 0 b_2 0 b_0)_2$ in the binary system.

13. $(1.909090\ldots)_{-10} = (0.090909\ldots)_{-10} = \frac{1}{11}$.

14.

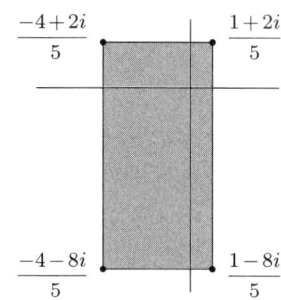

Fig. A–6. Fundamental region for quater-imaginary numbers.

$$
\begin{array}{ccccccc}
1 & 1 & 3 & 2 & 1 \\
1 & 1 & 3 & 2 & 1 \\
1 & 1 & 3 & 2 & 1 \\
1 & 1 & 2 & 0 & 2 \\
1 & 2 & 1 & 2 & 3 \\
1 & 1 & 3 & 2 & 1 \\
1 & 1 & 3 & 2 & 1 \\
\end{array}
$$

with the products labeled $[5-4i]$, $[5-4i]$, and the final sum $0\ 1\ 0\ 3\ 1\ 1\ 2\ 0\ 1$ labeled $[9-40i]$.

15. $\left[-\frac{10}{11}\mathinner{..}\frac{1}{11}\right]$, and the rectangle on the right.

16. It is tempting to try to do this in a very simple way, by using the rule $2 = (1100)_{i-1}$ to take care of carries; but that leads to a nonterminating method if, for example, we try to add 1 to $(11101)_{i-1} = -1$.

The following solution does the job by providing four related algorithms (namely for adding or subtracting 1 or i). If α is a string of zeros and ones, let α^P be a string of zeros and ones such that $(\alpha^P)_{i-1} = (\alpha)_{i-1} + 1$; and let α^{-P}, α^Q, α^{-Q} be defined similarly, with -1, $+i$, and $-i$ respectively in place of $+1$. Then

$$(\alpha 0)^P = \alpha 1; \qquad (\alpha x 1)^P = \alpha^Q x 0. \qquad\qquad (\alpha 0)^Q = \alpha^P 1; \qquad (\alpha 1)^Q = \alpha^{-Q} 0.$$
$$(\alpha x 0)^{-P} = \alpha^{-Q} x 1; \qquad (\alpha 1)^{-P} = \alpha 0. \qquad\qquad (\alpha 0)^{-Q} = \alpha^Q 1; \qquad (\alpha 1)^{-Q} = \alpha^{-P} 0.$$

Here x stands for either 0 or 1, and the strings are extended on the left with zeros if necessary. The processes will clearly always terminate. Hence every number of the form $a + bi$ with a and b integers is representable in the $i - 1$ system.

17. No (in spite of exercise 28); the number -1 cannot be so represented. This can be proved by constructing a set S as in Fig. 1. We do have the representations $-i = (0.1111\ldots)_{1+i}$, $i = (100.1111\ldots)_{1+i}$.

18. Let S_0 be the set of points $(a_7 a_6 a_5 a_4 a_3 a_2 a_1 a_0)_{i-1}$, where each a_k is 0 or 1. (Thus, S_0 is given by the 256 interior dots shown in Fig. 1, if that picture is multiplied by 16.) We first show that S is closed: If $\{y_1, y_2, \ldots\}$ is an infinite subset of S, we have $y_n = \sum_{k=1}^{\infty} a_{nk} 16^{-k}$, where each a_{nk} is in S_0. Construct a tree whose nodes are $(a_{n1}, \ldots, a_{nr})$, for $1 \le r \le n$, and let a node of this tree be an ancestor of another node if it is an initial subsequence of that node. By the infinity lemma (Theorem 2.3.4.3K) this tree has an infinite path $(a_1, a_2, a_3, \ldots)$; consequently $\sum_{k \ge 1} a_k 16^{-k}$ is a limit point of $\{y_1, y_2, \ldots\}$ in S.

By the answer to exercise 16, all numbers of the form $(a+bi)/16^k$ are representable, when a and b are integers. Therefore if x and y are arbitrary reals and $k \ge 1$, the number $z_k = (\lfloor 16^k x \rfloor + \lfloor 16^k y \rfloor i)/16^k$ is in $S + m + ni$ for some integers m and n. It can be shown that $S + m + ni$ is bounded away from the origin when $(m, n) \ne (0, 0)$. Consequently if $|x|$ and $|y|$ are sufficiently small and k is sufficiently large, we have $z_k \in S$, and $\lim_{k \to \infty} z_k = x + yi$ is in S.

[B. Mandelbrot named S the "twindragon" because he noticed that it is essentially obtained by joining two "dragon curves" belly-to-belly; see his book *Fractals: Form, Chance, and Dimension* (San Francisco: Freeman, 1977), 313–314, where he also stated that the dimension of the boundary is $2 \lg x \approx 1.523627$, where $x = 1 + 2x^{-2} \approx 1.69562$. Other properties of the dragon curve are described in C. Davis and D. E. Knuth, *J. Recr.*

Math. **3** (1970), 66–81, 133–149. The sets S for digits $\{0, 1\}$ and other complex bases are illustrated and analyzed by D. Goffinet in *AMM* **98** (1991), 249–255.]

    I. Kátai and J. Szabó have shown that the radix $-d+i$ yields a number system with digits $\{0, 1, \ldots, d^2\}$; see *Acta Scient. Math.* **37** (1975), 255–260. Further properties of such systems have been investigated by W. J. Gilbert, *Canadian J. Math.* **34** (1982), 1335–1348; *Math. Magazine* **57** (1984), 77–81. Another interesting case, with digits $\{0, 1, i, -1, -i\}$ and radix $2 + i$, has been suggested by V. Norton [*Math. Magazine* **57** (1984), 250–251]. For studies of number systems based on more general algebraic integers, see I. Kátai and B. Kovács, *Acta Math. Acad. Sci. Hung.* **37** (1981), 159–164, 405–407; B. Kovács, *Acta Math. Hung.* **58** (1991), 113–120; B. Kovács and A. Pethő, *Studia Scient. Math. Hung.* **27** (1992), 169–172.

19. If $m > u$ or $m < l$, find $a \in D$ such that $m \equiv a$ (modulo b); the desired representation will be a representation of $m' = (m - a)/b$ followed by a. Note that $m > u$ implies $l < m' < m$; $m < l$ implies $m < m' < u$; so the algorithm terminates.

    [There are no solutions when $b = 2$. The representation will be unique if and only if $0 \in D$; nonunique representation occurs for example when $D = \{-3, -1, 7\}$, $b = 3$, since $(\alpha)_3 = (\overline{3}77\overline{3}\alpha)_3$. When $b \geq 3$ it is not difficult to show that there are exactly 2^{b-3} solution sets D in which $|a| < b$ for all $a \in D$. Furthermore the set $D = \{0, 1, 2 - \epsilon_2 b^n, 3 - \epsilon_3 b^n, \ldots, b - 2 - \epsilon_{b-2} b^n, b - 1 - b^n\}$ gives unique representations, for all $b \geq 3$ and $n \geq 1$, when each ϵ_j is 0 or 1. *References: Proc. IEEE Symp. Comp. Arith.* **4** (1978), 1–9; *JACM* **29** (1982), 1131–1143.]

20. (a) $0.\overline{1}\overline{1}\overline{1} \ldots = \overline{1}.888 \ldots = \overline{1}8.\frac{111}{777} \ldots = \overline{1}8\frac{1}{7} \cdot \frac{222}{666} \ldots = \cdots = \overline{1}8\frac{123456}{765432} \cdot \frac{777}{111} \cdots$
has nine representations. (b) A "D-fraction" $.a_1 a_2 \ldots$ always lies between $-1/9$ and $+71/9$. Suppose x has ten or more D-decimal representations. Then for sufficiently large k, $10^k x$ has ten representations that differ to the left of the decimal point: $10^k x = n_1 + f_1 = \cdots = n_{10} + f_{10}$ where each f_j is a D-fraction. By uniqueness of integer representations, the n_j are distinct, say $n_1 < \cdots < n_{10}$, hence $n_{10} - n_1 \geq 9$; but this implies $f_1 - f_{10} \geq 9 > 71/9 - (-1/9)$, a contradiction. (c) Any number of the form $0.a_1 a_2 \ldots$, where each a_j is -1 or 8, equals $\overline{1}.a_1' a_2' \ldots$ where $a_j' = a_j + 9$ (and it even has six *more* representations $\overline{1}8.a_1'' a_2'' \ldots$, etc.).

21. We can convert to such a representation by using a method like that suggested in the text for converting to balanced ternary.

    In contrast to the system of exercise 20, zero can be represented in infinitely many ways, all obtained from $\frac{1}{2} + \sum_{k \geq 1} (-4\frac{1}{2}) \cdot 10^{-k}$ (or from the negative of this representation) by multiplying it by a power of ten. The representations of unity are $1\frac{1}{2} - \frac{1}{2}^*$, $\frac{1}{2} + \frac{1}{2}^*$, $5 - 3\frac{1}{2} - \frac{1}{2}^*$, $5 - 4\frac{1}{2} + \frac{1}{2}^*$, $50 - 45 - 3\frac{1}{2} - \frac{1}{2}^*$, $50 - 45 - 4\frac{1}{2} + \frac{1}{2}^*$, etc., where $\pm\frac{1}{2}^* = (\pm 4\frac{1}{2})(10^{-1} + 10^{-2} + \cdots)$. [*AMM* **57** (1950), 90–93.]

22. Given some approximation $b_n \ldots b_1 b_0$ with error $\sum_{k=0}^n b_k 10^k - x > 10^{-t}$ for $t > 0$, we will show how to reduce the error by approximately 10^{-t}. (The process can be started by finding a suitable $\sum_{k=0}^n b_k 10^k > x$; then a finite number of reductions of this type will make the error less than ϵ.) Simply choose $m > n$ so large that the decimal representation of $-10^m \alpha$ has a one in position 10^{-t} and no ones in positions 10^{-t+1}, 10^{-t+2}, $\ldots$, 10^n. Then $10^m \alpha + $ (a suitable sum of powers of 10 between 10^m and 10^n) $+ \sum_{k=0}^n b_k 10^k \approx \sum_{k=0}^n b_k 10^k - 10^{-t}$.

23. The set $S = \{\sum_{k \geq 1} a_k b^{-k} \mid a_k \in D\}$ is closed as in exercise 18, hence it is measurable, and in fact it has positive measure. Since $bS = \bigcup_{a \in D} (a + S)$, we have $b\mu(S) = \mu(bS) \leq \sum_{a \in D} \mu(a + S) = \sum_{a \in D} \mu(S) = b\mu(S)$, and we must therefore have

$\mu((a + S) \cap (a' + S)) = 0$ when $a \neq a' \in D$. Now T has measure zero if $0 \in D$, since T is a union of countably many sets of the form $b^k(n + ((a + S) \cap (a' + S)))$, $a \neq a'$, each of measure zero. On the other hand, as pointed out by K. A. Brakke, every real number has infinitely many representations in the number system of exercise 21.

[The set T cannot be empty, since the real numbers cannot be written as a countable union of disjoint, closed, bounded sets; see *AMM* **84** (1977), 827–828, and the more detailed analysis by Petkovšek in *AMM* **97** (1990), 408–411. If D has fewer than b elements, the set of numbers representable with radix b and digits from D has measure zero. If D has more than b elements and represents all reals, T has infinite measure.]

24. $\{2a \cdot 10^k + a' \mid 0 \leq a < 5, 0 \leq a' < 2\}$ or $\{5a' \cdot 10^k + a \mid 0 \leq a < 5, 0 \leq a' < 2\}$, for $k \geq 0$. [R. L. Graham has shown that there are no more sets of integer digits with these properties. And Andrew Odlyzko has shown that the restriction to integers is superfluous, in the sense that if the smallest two elements of D are 0 and 1, all the digits must be integers. *Proof.* Let $S = \{\sum_{k<0} a_k b^k \mid a_k \in D\}$ be the set of "fractions," and let $X = \{(a_n \ldots a_0)_b \mid a_k \in D\}$ be the set of "whole numbers"; then $[0 . . \infty) = \bigcup_{x \in X}(x + S)$, and $(x + S) \cap (x' + S)$ has measure zero for $x \neq x' \in X$. We have $(0 . . 1) \subseteq S$, and by induction on m we will prove that $(m . . m + 1) \subseteq x_m + S$ for some $x_m \in X$. Let $x_m \in X$ be such that $(m . . m + \epsilon) \cap (x_m + S)$ has positive measure for all $\epsilon > 0$. Then $x_m \leq m$, and x_m must be an integer lest $x_{\lfloor x_m \rfloor} + S$ overlap $x_m + S$ too much. If $x_m > 0$, the fact that $(m - x_m . . m - x_m + 1) \cap S$ has positive measure implies by induction that this measure is 1, and $(m . . m+1) \subseteq x_m + S$ since S is closed. If $x_m = 0$ and $(m . . m + 1) \not\subseteq S$, we must have $m < x'_m < m + 1$ for some $x'_m \in X$, where $(m . . x'_m) \subseteq S$; but then $1 + S$ overlaps $x'_m + S$. See *Proc. London Math. Soc.* (3) **18** (1978), 581–595.]

Note: If we drop the restriction $0 \in D$, there *are* many other cases, some of which are quite interesting, especially $\{1, 2, 3, 4, 5, 6, 7, 8, 9, 10\}$, $\{1, 2, 3, 4, 5, 51, 52, 53, 54, 55\}$, and $\{2, 3, 4, 5, 6, 52, 53, 54, 55, 56\}$. Alternatively if we allow negative digits we obtain many other solutions by the method of exercise 19, plus further sets of unusual digits like $\{-1, 0, 1, 2, 3, 4, 5, 6, 7, 18\}$ that don't meet the conditions stated there. It appears hopeless to find a nice characterization of all solutions with negative digits.

25. A positive number whose radix-b representation has m consecutive $(b-1)$'s to the right of the radix point must have the form $c/b^n + (b^m - \theta)/b^{n+m}$, where c and n are nonnegative integers and $0 < \theta \leq 1$. So if u/v has this form, we find that $b^{m+n}u = b^m cv + b^m v - \theta v$. Therefore θv is an integer that is a multiple of b^m. But $0 < \theta v \leq v < b^m$. [There can be arbitrarily long runs of other digits a, if $0 \leq a < b - 1$, for example in the representation of $a/(b - 1)$.]

26. The proof of "sufficiency" is a straightforward generalization of the usual proof for base b, by successively constructing the desired representation. The proof of "necessity" breaks into two parts: If β_{n+1} is greater than $\sum_{k \leq n} c_k \beta_k$ for some n, then $\beta_{n+1} - \epsilon$ has no representation for small ϵ. If $\beta_{n+1} \leq \sum_{k \leq n} c_k \beta_k$ for all n, but equality does not always hold, we can show that there are two representations for certain x. [See *Transactions of the Royal Society of Canada*, series III, **46** (1952), 45–55.]

27. Proof by induction on $|n|$: If n is even we must take $e_0 > 0$, and the result follows by induction, since $n/2$ has a unique such representation. If n is odd, we must take $e_0 = 0$, and the problem reduces to representing $-(n-1)/2$; if the latter quantity is either zero or one, there is obviously only one way to proceed, otherwise it has a unique reversing representation by induction. [A. D. Booth, in *Quarterly J. Mechanics and Applied Math.* **4** (1951), 236–240, applied this principle to two's complement multiplication.]

[It follows that every positive integer has exactly *two* such representations with *decreasing* exponents $e_0 > e_1 > \cdots > e_t$: one with t even and the other with t odd.]

28. A proof like that of exercise 27 may be given. Note that $a + bi$ is a multiple of $1 + i$ by a complex integer if and only if $a + b$ is even. This representation is intimately related to the dragon curve discussed in the answer to exercise 18.

29. It suffices to prove that any collection $\{T_0, T_1, T_2, \ldots\}$ satisfying Property B may be obtained by collapsing some collection $\{S_0, S_1, S_2, \ldots\}$, where $S_0 = \{0, 1, \ldots, b-1\}$ and all elements of S_1, S_2, ... are multiples of b.

To prove the latter statement, we may assume that $1 \in T_0$ and that there is a least element $b > 1$ such that $b \notin T_0$. We will prove, by induction on n, that if $nb \notin T_0$, then $nb + 1$, $nb + 2$, ..., $nb + b - 1$ are not in any of the T_j's; but if $nb \in T_0$, then so are $nb + 1$, ..., $nb + b - 1$. The result then follows with $S_1 = \{nb \mid nb \in T_0\}$, $S_2 = T_1$, $S_3 = T_2$, etc.

If $nb \notin T_0$, then $nb = t_0 + t_1 + \cdots$, where t_1, t_2, ... are multiples of b; hence $t_0 < nb$ is a multiple of b. By induction, $(t_0 + k) + t_1 + t_2 + \cdots$ is the representation of $nb + k$, for $0 < k < b$; hence $nb + k \notin T_j$ for any j.

If $nb \in T_0$ and $0 < k < b$, let the representation of $nb + k$ be $t_0 + t_1 + \cdots$. We cannot have $t_j = nb + k$ for $j \geq 1$, lest $nb + b$ have two representations $(b - k) + \cdots + (nb + k) + \cdots = (nb) + \cdots + b + \cdots$. By induction, $t_0 \bmod b = k$; and the representation $nb = (t_0 - k) + t_1 + \cdots$ implies that $t_0 = nb + k$.

[Reference: *Nieuw Archief voor Wiskunde* (3) **4** (1956), 15–17. A finite analog of this result was derived by P. A. MacMahon, *Combinatory Analysis* **1** (1915), 217–223.]

30. (a) Let A_j be the set of numbers n whose representation does not involve b_j; then by the uniqueness property, $n \in A_j$ if and only if $n + b_j \notin A_j$. Consequently we have $n \in A_j$ if and only if $n + 2b_j \in A_j$. It follows that, for $j \neq k$, $n \in A_j \cap A_k$ if and only if $n + 2b_j b_k \in A_j \cap A_k$. Let m be the number of integers $n \in A_j \cap A_k$ such that $0 \leq n < 2b_j b_k$. Then this interval contains exactly m integers that are in A_j but not A_k, exactly m in A_k but not A_j, and exactly m in neither A_j nor A_k; hence $4m = 2b_j b_k$. Therefore b_j and b_k cannot both be odd. But at least one b_j is odd, of course, since odd numbers can be represented.

(b) According to (a) we can renumber the b's so that b_0 is odd and b_1, b_2, ... are even; then $\frac{1}{2}b_1$, $\frac{1}{2}b_2$, ... must also be a binary basis, and the process can be iterated.

(c) If it is a binary basis, we must have positive and negative d_k's for arbitrarily large k, in order to represent $\pm 2^n$ when n is large. Conversely, the following algorithm may be used:

S1. [Initialize.] Set $k \leftarrow 0$.

S2. [Done?] If $n = 0$, terminate.

S3. [Choose.] If n is even, set $n \leftarrow n/2$. Otherwise include $2^k d_k$ in the representation, and set $n \leftarrow (n - d_k)/2$.

S4. [Advance k.] Increase k by 1 and return to S2. ∎

At each step the choice is forced; furthermore step S3 always decreases $|n|$ unless $n = -d_k$, hence the algorithm must terminate.

(d) Two iterations of steps S2–S4 in the preceding algorithm will change $4m \to m$, $4m + 1 \to m + 5$, $4m + 2 \to m + 7$, $4m + 3 \to m - 1$. Arguing as in exercise 19, we need only show that the algorithm terminates for $-2 \leq n \leq 8$; all other values of n are moved toward this interval. In this range $3 \to -1 \to -2 \to 6 \to 8 \to 2 \to 7 \to 0$ and $4 \to 1 \to 5 \to 6$. Thus $1 = 7 \cdot 2^0 - 13 \cdot 2^1 + 7 \cdot 2^2 - 13 \cdot 2^3 - 13 \cdot 2^5 - 13 \cdot 2^9 + 7 \cdot 2^{10}$.

Note: The choice $d_0, d_1, d_2, \ldots = 5, -3, 3, 5, -3, 3, \ldots$ also yields a binary basis. For further details see *Math. Comp.* **18** (1964), 537–546; A. D. Sands, *Acta Math. Acad. Sci. Hung.* **8** (1957), 65–86.

31. (See also the related exercises 3.2.2–11, 4.3.2–13, 4.6.2–22.)

(a) By multiplying numerator and denominator by suitable powers of 2, we may assume that $u = (\ldots u_2 u_1 u_0)_2$ and $v = (\ldots v_2 v_1 v_0)_2$ are 2-adic integers, where $v_0 = 1$. The following computational method now determines w, using the notation $u^{(n)}$ to stand for the integer $(u_{n-1} \ldots u_0)_2 = u \bmod 2^n$ when $n > 0$:

Let $w_0 = u_0$ and $w^{(1)} = w_0$. For $n = 1, 2, \ldots$, assume that we have found an integer $w^{(n)} = (w_{n-1} \ldots w_0)_2$ such that $u^{(n)} \equiv v^{(n)} w^{(n)}$ (modulo 2^n). Then we have $u^{(n+1)} \equiv v^{(n+1)} w^{(n)}$ (modulo 2^n), hence $w_n = 0$ or 1 according as the quantity $(u^{(n+1)} - v^{(n+1)} w^{(n)}) \bmod 2^{n+1}$ is 0 or 2^n.

(b) Find the smallest integer k such that $2^k \equiv 1$ (modulo $2n + 1$). Then we have $1/(2n+1) = m/(2^k - 1)$ for some integer m, $1 \le m < 2^{k-1}$. Let α be the k-bit binary representation of m; then $(0.\alpha\alpha\alpha \ldots)_2$ times $2n + 1$ is $(0.111 \ldots)_2 = 1$ in the binary system, and $(\ldots \alpha\alpha\alpha)_2$ times $2n + 1$ is $(\ldots 111)_2 = -1$ in the 2-adic system.

(c) If u is rational, say $u = m/(2^e n)$ where n is odd and positive, the 2-adic representation of u is periodic, because the set of numbers with periodic expansions includes $-1/n$ and is closed under the operations of negation, division by 2, and addition. Conversely, if $u_{N+\lambda} = u_N$ for all sufficiently large N, the 2-adic number $(2^\lambda - 1)2^r u$ is an integer for all sufficiently large r.

(d) The square of any number of the form $(\ldots u_2 u_1 1)_2$ has the form $(\ldots 001)_2$, hence the condition is necessary. To show the sufficiency, we can use the following procedure to compute $v = \sqrt{n}$ when $n \bmod 8 = 1$:

H1. [Initialize.] Set $m \leftarrow (n-1)/8$, $k \leftarrow 2$, $v_0 \leftarrow 1$, $v_1 \leftarrow 0$, $v \leftarrow 1$. (During this algorithm we will have $v = (v_{k-1} \ldots v_1 v_0)_2$ and $v^2 = n - 2^{k+1} m$.)

H2. [Transform.] If m is even, set $v_k \leftarrow 0$, $m \leftarrow m/2$. Otherwise set $v_k \leftarrow 1$, $m \leftarrow (m - v - 2^{k-1})/2$, $v \leftarrow v + 2^k$.

H3. [Advance k.] Increase k by 1 and return to H2. ∎

32. A more general result appears in *Math. Comp.* **29** (1975), 84–86.

33. Let K_n be the set of all such n-digit numbers, so that $k_n = |K_n|$. If S and T are any finite sets of integers, we shall say $S \sim T$ if $S = T + x$ for some integer x, and we shall write $k_n(S) = |\mathcal{K}_n(S)|$, where $\mathcal{K}_n(S)$ is the family of all subsets of K_n that are $\sim S$. When $n = 0$, we have $k_n(S) = 0$ unless $|S| \le 1$, since zero is the only "0-digit" number. When $n \ge 1$ and $S = \{s_1, \ldots, s_r\}$, we have

$$\mathcal{K}_n(S) = \bigcup_{0 \le j < b} \bigcup_{(a_1, \ldots, a_r)} \{\{t_1 b + a_1, \ldots, t_r b + a_r\} \mid$$

$$\{t_1, \ldots, t_r\} \in K_{n-1}(\{(s_i + j - a_i)/b \mid 1 \le i \le r\})\},$$

where the inner union is over all sequences of digits $(a_1, \ldots, a_r)$ satisfying the condition $a_i \equiv s_i + j$ (modulo b) for $1 \le i \le r$. In this formula we require $t_i - t_{i'} = (s_i - a_i)/b - (s_{i'} - a_{i'})/b$ for $1 \le i < i' \le r$, so that the naming of subscripts is uniquely determined. By the principle of inclusion and exclusion, therefore, we have $k_n(S) = \sum_{0 \le j < b} \sum_{m \ge 1} (-1)^{m-1} f(S, m, j)$, where $f(S, m, j)$ is the number of sets of integers that can be expressed as $\{t_1 b + a_1, \ldots, t_r b + a_r\}$ in the manner above for m different sequences $(a_1, \ldots, a_r)$, summed over all choices of m different sequences $(a_1, \ldots, a_r)$. Given m different sequences $(a_1^{(l)}, \ldots, a_r^{(l)})$ for $1 \le l \le m$, the number of such sets is $k_{n-1}(\{(s_i + j - a_i^{(l)})/b \mid 1 \le i \le r, 1 \le l \le m\})$. Thus there is a collection of sets $\mathcal{T}(S)$ such that

$$k_n(S) = \sum_{T \in \mathcal{T}(S)} c_T\, k_{n-1}(T),$$

where each c_T is an integer. Furthermore if $T \in \mathcal{T}(S)$, its elements are near those of S; we have $\min T \ge (\min S - \max D)/b$ and $\max T \le (\max S + b - 1 - \min D)/b$. Thus we obtain simultaneous recurrence relations for the sequences $\langle k_n(S) \rangle$, where S runs through the nonempty integer subsets of $[l \mathrel{..} u+1]$, in the notation of exercise 19. Since $k_n = k_n(S)$ for any one-element set S, the sequence $\langle k_n \rangle$ appears among these recurrences. The coefficients c_T can be computed from the first few values of $k_n(S)$, so we can obtain a system of equations defining the generating functions $k_S(z) = \sum k_n(S)z^n = [|S| \le 1] + z\sum_{T \in \mathcal{T}(S)} c_T k_T(z)$. [See J. Algorithms **2** (1981), 31–43.]

For example, when $D = \{-1, 0, 3\}$ and $b = 3$ we have $l = -\frac{3}{2}$ and $u = \frac{1}{2}$, so the relevant sets S are $\{0\}$, $\{0, 1\}$, $\{-1, 1\}$, and $\{-1, 0, 1\}$. The corresponding sequences for $n \le 3$ are $\langle 1, 3, 8, 21 \rangle$, $\langle 0, 1, 3, 8 \rangle$, $\langle 0, 0, 1, 4 \rangle$, and $\langle 0, 0, 0, 0 \rangle$; so we obtain

$$k_0(z) = 1 + z(3k_0(z) - k_{01}(z)), \qquad k_{02}(z) = z(k_{01}(z) + k_{02}(z)),$$
$$k_{01}(z) = zk_0(z), \qquad\qquad\qquad k_{012}(z) = 0,$$

and $k(z) = 1/(1 - 3z + z^2)$. In this case $k_n = F_{2n+2}$ and $k_n(\{0, 2\}) = F_{2n-1} - 1$.

34. There is exactly one string α_n on the symbols $\{\bar{1}, 0, 1\}$ such that $n = (\alpha_n)_2$ and α_n has no leading zeros or consecutive nonzeros: α_0 is empty, otherwise $\alpha_{2n} = \alpha_n 0$, $\alpha_{4n+1} = \alpha_n 01$, $\alpha_{4n-1} = \alpha_n 0\bar{1}$. Any string that represents n can be converted to this "canonical signed bit representation" by using the reductions $1\bar{1} \to 01$, $\bar{1}1 \to 0\bar{1}$, $01\ldots 11 \to 10\ldots 0\bar{1}$, $0\bar{1}\ldots \bar{1}\bar{1} \to \bar{1}0\ldots 01$, and inserting or deleting leading zeros. Since these reductions do not increase the number of nonzero digits, α_n has the fewest. [Advances in Computers **1** (1960), 244–260.] The number of nonzero digits in α_n, denoted by $\bar{\nu}(n)$, is the number of 1s in the ordinary representation that are immediately preceded by 0 or by the substring $00(10)^k 1$ for some $k \ge 0$. (See exercise 7.1.3–35.)

A generalization to radix $b > 2$ has been given by J. von zur Gathen, Computational Complexity **1** (1991), 360–394.

SECTION 4.2.1

1. $N = (62, +.60\ 22\ 14\ 00)$; $h = (37, +.66\ 26\ 10\ 00)$. Note that the quantity $10h$ would be $(38, +.06\ 62\ 61\ 00)$.

2. $b^{E-q}(1 - b^{-p})$, b^{-q-p}; $b^{E-q}(1 - b^{-p})$, b^{-q-1}.

3. When e does not have its smallest value, the most significant "one" bit (which appears in all such normalized numbers) need not appear in the computer word.

4. $(51, +.10209877)$; $(50, +.12346000)$; $(53, +.99999999)$. The third answer would be $(54, +.10000000)$ if the first operand had been $(45, -.50000000)$, since $b/2$ is odd.

5. If $x \sim y$ and m is an integer then $mb + x \sim mb + y$. Furthermore $x \sim y$ implies $x/b \sim y/b$, by considering all possible cases. Another crucial property is that x and y will round to the same integer, whenever $bx \sim by$.

Now if $b^{-p-2}F_v \ne f_v$ we must have $(b^{p+2}f_v) \bmod b \ne 0$; hence the transformation leaves f_v unchanged unless $e_u - e_v \ge 2$. Since u was normalized, it is nonzero and $|f_u + f_v| > b^{-1} - b^{-2} \ge b^{-2}$: The leading nonzero digit of $f_u + f_v$ must be at most two places to the right of the radix point, and the rounding operation will convert

$b^{p+j}(f_u + f_v)$ to an integer, where $j \leq 1$. The proof will be complete if we can show
that $b^{p+j+1}(f_u + f_v) \sim b^{p+j+1}(f_u + b^{-p-2}F_v)$. By the previous paragraph, we have
$b^{p+2}(f_u + f_v) \sim b^{p+2}f_u + F_v = b^{p+2}(f_u + b^{-p-2}F_v)$, which implies the desired result
for all $j \leq 1$. Similar remarks apply to step M2 of Algorithm M.

Note that, when $b > 2$ is even, such an integer F_v always exists; but when $b = 2$
we require $p+3$ bits (let $2F_v$ be an integer). When b is odd, an integer F_v always exists
except in the case of division by Algorithm M, when a remainder of $\frac{1}{2}b$ is possible.

6. (Consider the case $e_u = e_v$, $f_u = -f_v$ in Program A.) Register A retains its
previous sign, as in ADD.

7. Say that a number is normalized if and only if it is zero or its fraction part lies in the
range $\frac{1}{6} < |f| < \frac{1}{2}$. A $(p+1)$-place accumulator suffices for addition and subtraction;
rounding (except during division) is equivalent to truncation. A very pleasant system
indeed! We might represent numbers with excess-zero exponent, inserted between the
first and subsequent digits of the fraction, and complemented if the fraction is negative,
so that the order of fixed point numbers is preserved.

8. (a) $(06, +.12345679) \oplus (06, -.12345678)$, $(01, +.10345678) \oplus (00, -.94000000)$;
(b) $(99, +.87654321) \oplus$ itself, $(99, +.99999999) \oplus (91, +.50000000)$.

9. $a = c = (-50, +.10000000)$, $b = (-41, +.20000000)$, $d = (-41, +.80000000)$, $y = (11, +.10000000)$.

10. $(50, +.99999000) \oplus (55, +.99999000)$.

11. $(50, +.10000001) \otimes (50, +.99999990)$.

12. If $0 < |f_u| < |f_v|$, then $|f_u| \leq |f_v| - b^{-p}$; hence $1/b < |f_u/f_v| \leq 1 - b^{-p}/|f_v| < 1 - b^{-p}$. If $0 < |f_v| \leq |f_u|$, we have $1/b \leq |f_u/f_v|/b \leq ((1 - b^{-p})/(1/b))/b = 1 - b^{-p}$.

13. See J. Michael Yohe, *IEEE Trans.* **C-22** (1973), 577–586; see also exercise 4.2.2–24.

14.
```
     FIX STJ   9F            Float-to-fix subroutine:
         STA   TEMP
         LD1   TEMP(EXP)     rI1 ← e.
         SLA   1             rA ← ±f f f f 0.
         JAZ   9F            Is input zero?
         DEC1  1
         CMPA  =0=(1:1)      If leading byte is zero,
         JE    *-4             shift left again.
         ENN1  -Q-4,1
         J1N   FIXOVFLO      Is magnitude too large?
         ENTX  0
         SRAX  0,1
         CMPX  =1//2=
         JL    9F
         JG    *+2
         JAO   9F            The ambiguous case becomes odd, since b/2 is even.
         STA   *+1(0:0)      Round, if necessary.
         INCA  1             Add ±1 (overflow is impossible).
     9H  JMP   *             Exit from subroutine.  ▮
```

15.
```
     FP  STJ   EXITF         Fractional part subroutine:
         JOV   OFLO          Ensure that overflow is off.
         STA   TEMP          TEMP ← u.
```

```
       ENTX 0
       SLA  1              rA ← f_u.
       LD2  TEMP(EXP)      rI2 ← e_u.
       DEC2 Q
       J2NP *+3
       SLA  0,2            Remove integer part of u.
       ENT2 0
       JANN 1F
       ENN2 0,2            Fraction is negative: Find
       SRAX 0,2               its complement.
       ENT2 0
       JXNZ *+3
       JAZ  *+2
       INCA 1
       ADD  WM1            Add word size minus one.
  1H   INC2 Q              Prepare to normalize the answer.
       JMP  NORM           Normalize, round, and exit.
  8H   EQU  1(1:1)
  WM1  CON  8B-1,8B-1(1:4) Word size minus one ∎
```

16. If $|c| \geq |d|$, then set $r \leftarrow d \oslash c$, $s \leftarrow c \oplus (r \otimes d)$; $x \leftarrow \big(a \oplus (b \otimes r)\big) \oslash s$, $y \leftarrow \big(b \ominus (a \otimes r)\big) \oslash s$. Otherwise set $r \leftarrow c \oslash d$, $s \leftarrow d \oplus (r \otimes c)$; $x \leftarrow \big((a \otimes r) \oplus b\big) \oslash s$, $y \leftarrow \big((b \otimes r) \ominus a\big) \oslash s$. Then $x + iy$ is the desired approximation to $(a + bi)/(c + di)$. Computing $s' \leftarrow 1 \oslash s$ and multiplying twice by s' may be better than dividing twice by s. As with (11), gradual underflow is recommended for the calculation of r unless special precautions are taken. [*CACM* **5** (1962), 435. Other algorithms for complex arithmetic and function evaluation are given by P. Wynn, *BIT* **2** (1962), 232–255. For $|a + bi|$, see Paul Friedland, *CACM* **10** (1967), 665.]

17. See Robert Morris, *IEEE Trans.* **C-20** (1971), 1578–1579. Error analysis is more difficult with such systems, so interval arithmetic is correspondingly more desirable.

18. For positive numbers: Shift fraction left until $f_1 = 1$, then round, then if the fraction is zero (rounding overflow) shift it right again. For negative numbers: Shift fraction left until $f_1 = 0$, then round, then if the fraction is zero (rounding underflow) shift it right again.

19. $\big(73 - (5 - [\text{rounding digits are } \frac{b}{2} 0 \ldots 0])(6 - [\text{magnitude is rounded up}]) + [e_v < e_u] + [\text{first rounding digit is } \frac{b}{2}] - [\text{fraction overflow}] - 10[\text{result zero}] + 7[\text{rounding overflow}] + 7N + (3 + (16 + [\text{result negative}])[\text{opposite signs}])X\big)u$, where N is the number of left shifts during normalization, and X is the condition that rX receives nonzero digits and there is no fraction overflow. The maximum time of $84u$ occurs for example when

$$u = -50\ 01\ 00\ 00\ 00, \quad v = +45\ 49\ 99\ 99\ 99, \quad b = 100.$$

[The average time, considering the data in Section 4.2.4, will be less than $47u$.]

SECTION 4.2.2

1. $u \ominus v = u \oplus -v = -v \oplus u = -(v \oplus -u) = -(v \ominus u)$.

2. $u \oplus x \geq u \oplus 0 = u$, by (8), (2), (6); hence by (8) again, $(u \oplus x) \oplus v \geq u \oplus v$. Similarly, (8) and (6) together with (2) imply that $(u \oplus x) \oplus (v \oplus y) \geq (u \oplus x) \oplus v$.

3. $u = 8.0000001$, $v = 1.2500008$, $w = 8.0000008$; $(u \otimes v) \otimes w = 80.000064$, yet $u \otimes (v \otimes w) = 80.000057$.

4. Yes; let $1/u \approx v = w$, where v is large.

5. Not always; in decimal arithmetic take $u = v = 9$.

6. (a) Yes. (b) Only for $b + p \leq 4$ (try $u = 1 - b^{-p}$). But see exercise 27.

7. If u and v are consecutive floating binary numbers, $u \oplus v = 2u$ or $2v$. When it is $2v$ we often have $u^{\textcircled{2}} \oplus v^{\textcircled{2}} < 2v^{\textcircled{2}}$. For example, $u = (.10\ldots001)_2$, $v = (.10\ldots010)_2$, $u \oplus v = 2v$, and $u^{\textcircled{2}} + v^{\textcircled{2}} = (.10\ldots011)_2$.

8. (a) $\sim$, $\approx$; (b) $\sim$, $\approx$; (c) $\sim$, $\approx$; (d) $\sim$; (e) $\sim$.

9. $|u-w| \leq |u-v| + |v-w| \leq \epsilon_1 \min(b^{e_u-q}, b^{e_v-q}) + \epsilon_2 \min(b^{e_v-q}, b^{e_w-q}) \leq \epsilon_1 b^{e_u-q} + \epsilon_2 b^{e_w-q} \leq (\epsilon_1 + \epsilon_2) \max(b^{e_u-q}, b^{e_w-q})$. The result cannot be strengthened in general, since for example we might have e_u very small compared to both e_v and e_w, and this means that $u - w$ might be fairly large under the hypotheses.

10. We have $(.a_1 \ldots a_{p-1}a_p)_b \otimes (.9 \ldots 99)_b = (.a_1 \ldots a_{p-1}(a_p-1))_b$ if $a_p \geq 1$ and $a_1 \geq \frac{b}{2}$; here "9" stands for $b-1$. Furthermore, $(.a_1 \ldots a_{p-1}a_p)_b \otimes (1.0 \ldots 0)_b = (.a_1 \ldots a_{p-1}0)_b$, so the multiplication is not monotone if $b > 2$ and $a_p \geq 1 + [a_1 \geq \frac{b}{2}]$. But when $b = 2$, this argument can be extended to show that multiplication *is* monotone; obviously the "certain computer" had $b > 2$.

11. Without loss of generality, let x be an integer, $0 \leq x < b^p$. If $e \leq 0$, then $t = 0$. If $0 < e \leq p$, then $x - t$ has at most $p+1$ digits, the least significant being zero. If $e > p$, then $x - t = 0$. [The result holds also under the weaker hypothesis $|t| < b^e$; in that case we might have $x - t = b^e$ when $e > p$.]

12. Assume that $e_u = p$, $e_v \leq 0$, $u > 0$. Case 1, $u > b^{p-1}$. Case (1a), $w = u + 1$, $v \geq \frac{1}{2}$, $e_v = 0$. Then $u' = u$ or $u + 1$, $v' = 1$, $u'' = u$, $v'' = 1$ or 0. Case (1b), $w = u$, $|v| \leq \frac{1}{2}$. Then $u' = u$, $v' = 0$, $u'' = u$, $v'' = 0$. If $|v| = \frac{1}{2}$ and more general rounding is permitted we might also have $u' = u \pm 1$, $v'' = \mp 1$. Case (1c), $w = u - 1$, $v \leq -\frac{1}{2}$, $e_v = 0$. Then $u' = u$ or $u - 1$, $v' = -1$, $u'' = u$, $v'' = -1$ or 0. Case 2, $u = b^{p-1}$. Case (2a), $w = u + 1$, $v \geq \frac{1}{2}$, $e_v = 0$. Like (1a). Case (2b), $w = u$, $|v| \leq \frac{1}{2}$, $u' \geq u$. Like (1b). Case (2c), $w = u$, $|v| \leq \frac{1}{2}$, $u' < u$. Then $u' = u - j/b$ where $v = j/b + v_1$ and $|v_1| \leq \frac{1}{2}b^{-1}$ for some positive integer $j \leq \frac{1}{2}b$; we have $v' = 0$, $u'' = u$, $v'' = j/b$. Case (2d), $w < u$. Then $w = u - j/b$ where $v = -j/b + v_1$ and $|v_1| \leq \frac{1}{2}b^{-1}$ for some positive integer $j \leq b$; we have $(v', u'') = (-j/b, u)$, and $(u', v'') = (u, -j/b)$ or $(u - 1/b, (1-j)/b)$, the latter case only when $v_1 = \frac{1}{2}b^{-1}$. In all cases $u \ominus u' = u - u'$, $v \ominus v' = v - v'$, $u \ominus u'' = u - u''$, $v \ominus v'' = v - v''$, $\mathrm{round}(w - u - v) = w - u - v$.

13. Since $\mathrm{round}(x) = 0$ if and only if $x = 0$, we want to find a large set of integer pairs (m, n) with the property that $m \oslash n$ is an integer if and only if m/n is. Assume that $|m|, |n| < b^p$. If m/n is an integer, then $m \oslash n = m/n$ is also. Conversely if m/n is not an integer, but $m \oslash n$ is, we have $1/|n| \leq |m \oslash n - m/n| < \frac{1}{2}|m/n|b^{1-p}$, hence $|m| > 2b^{p-1}$. Our answer is therefore to require $|m| \leq 2b^{p-1}$ and $0 < |n| < b^p$. (Slightly weaker hypotheses are also possible.)

14. $|(u \otimes v) \otimes w - uvw| \leq |(u \otimes v) \otimes w - (u \otimes v)w| + |w| \, |u \otimes v - uv| \leq \delta_{(u \otimes v) \otimes w} + b^{e_w-q-l_w}\delta_{u \otimes v} \leq (1 + b)\delta_{(u \otimes v) \otimes w}$. Now $|e_{(u \otimes v) \otimes w} - e_{u \otimes (v \otimes w)}| \leq 2$, so we may take $\epsilon = \frac{1}{2}(1 + b)(1 + b^2)b^{-p}$.

15. $u \leq v$ implies that $(u \oplus u) \oslash 2 \leq (u \oplus v) \oslash 2 \leq (v \oplus v) \oslash 2$, so the condition holds for all u and v if and only if it holds whenever $u = v$. For base $b = 2$, the condition is therefore always satisfied (barring overflow); but for $b > 2$ there are numbers $v \neq w$ such that $v \oplus v = w \oplus w$, hence the condition fails. [On the other hand, the formula $u \oplus ((v \ominus u) \oslash 2)$ does give a midpoint in the correct range. *Proof.* It suffices to show that $u + (v \ominus u) \oslash 2 \le v$, i.e., $(v \ominus u) \oslash 2 \le v - u$; and it is easy to verify that round$(\frac{1}{2}$round$(x)) \le x$ for all $x \ge 0$.]

16. (a) Exponent changes occur at $\sum_{10} = 11.111111$, $\sum_{91} = 101.11110$, $\sum_{901} = 1001.1102$, $\sum_{9001} = 10001.020$, $\sum_{90009} = 100000.91$, $\sum_{900819} = 1000000.0$; therefore $\sum_{1000000} = 1109099.1$.

(b) After calculating $\sum_{k=1}^{n} 1.2345679 = 1224782.1$, (14) tries to take the square root of $-.0053187053$. But (15) and (16) are exact in this case. [If, however, $x_k = 1 + \lfloor (k-1)/2 \rfloor 10^{-7}$, (15) and (16) have errors of order n. See Chan and Lewis, *CACM* **22** (1979), 526–531, for further results on the accuracy of standard deviation calculations.]

(c) We need to show that $u \oplus ((v \ominus u) \oslash k)$ lies between u and v; see exercise 15.

17.
```
   FCMP STJ   9F              Floating point comparison subroutine:
        JOV   OFLO            Ensure that overflow is off.
        STA   TEMP
        LDAN  TEMP            v ← −v.
        (Copy here lines 07–20 of Program 4.2.1A.)
        LDX   FV(0:0)         Set rX to zero with the sign of f_v.
        DEC1  5
        J1N   *+2
        ENT1  0               Replace large difference in exponents
        SRAX  5,1                 by a smaller one.
        ADD   FU              rA ← difference of operands.
        JOV   7F              Fraction overflow: not ∼.
        CMPA  EPSILON(1:5)
        JG    8F              Jump if not ∼.
        JL    6F              Jump if ∼.
        JXZ   9F              Jump if ∼.
        JXP   1F              If |rA| = ε, check sign of rA × rX.
        JAP   9F              Jump if ∼. (rA ≠ 0)
        JMP   8F
7H      ENTX  1
        SRC   1               Make rA nonzero with same sign.
        JMP   8F
1H      JAP   8F              Jump if not ∼. (rA ≠ 0)
6H      ENTA  0
8H      CMPA  =0=             Set comparison indicator.
9H      JMP   *               Exit from subroutine.  ▮
```

19. Let $\gamma_k = \delta_k = \eta_k = \sigma_k = 0$ for $k > n$. It suffices to find the coefficient of x_1, since the coefficient of x_k will be just the same except with all subscripts increased by $k - 1$. Let (f_k, g_k) denote the coefficient of x_1 in $(s_k - c_k, c_k)$ respectively. Then $f_1 = (1+\eta_1)(1-\gamma_1-\gamma_1\delta_1-\gamma_1\sigma_1-\delta_1\sigma_1-\gamma_1\delta_1\sigma_1)$, $g_1 = (1+\delta_1)(1+\eta_1)(\gamma_1+\sigma_1+\gamma_1\sigma_1)$, and $f_k = (1-\gamma_k\sigma_k-\delta_k\sigma_k-\gamma_k\delta_k\sigma_k)f_{k-1} + (\gamma_k-\eta_k+\gamma_k\delta_k+\gamma_k\eta_k+\gamma_k\delta_k\eta_k+\gamma_k\eta_k\sigma_k+\delta_k\eta_k\sigma_k+\gamma_k\delta_k\eta_k\sigma_k)g_{k-1}$, $g_k = \sigma_k(1+\gamma_k)(1+\delta_k)f_{k-1} - (1+\delta_k)(\gamma_k+\gamma_k\eta_k+\eta_k\sigma_k+\gamma_k\eta_k\sigma_k)g_{k-1}$, for $1 < k \le n$. Thus $f_n = 1 + \eta_1 - \gamma_1 + (4n$ terms of 2nd order$) + ($higher order terms$) = 1 + \eta_1 - \gamma_1 + O(n\epsilon^2)$ is sufficiently small. [The Kahan summation formula was first published in *CACM* **8** (1965), 40; see also *Proc. IFIP Congress* (1971), **2**, 1232, and further developments by K. Ozawa, *J. Information Proc.* **6** (1983), 226–230. Kahan observed that $s_n \ominus c_n = \sum_{k=1}^{n}(1+\phi_k)x_k$ where $|\phi_k| \le 2\epsilon + O((n+1-k)\epsilon^2)$. For another approach to accurate summation, see R. J. Hanson, *CACM* **18** (1975), 57–58.

When some x's are negative and others are positive, we may be able to match them advantageously, as explained by T. O. Espelid, *SIAM Review* **37** (1995), 603–607. See also G. Bohlender, *IEEE Trans.* **C-26** (1977), 621–632, for algorithms that compute $\text{round}(x_1 + \cdots + x_n)$ and $\text{round}(x_1 \ldots x_n)$ *exactly*, given $\{x_1, \ldots, x_n\}$.]

20. By the proof of Theorem C, (47) fails for $e_w = p$ only if $|v| + \frac{1}{2} \geq |w - u| \geq b^{p-1} + b^{-1}$; hence $|f_u| \geq |f_v| \geq 1 - (\frac{1}{2}b - 1)b^{-p}$. We now find that a necessary and sufficient condition for failure is that $|f_w|$ is essentially rounded to 2 during the normalization process (actually to $2/b$ after scaling right for fraction overflow) — a very rare case indeed!

21. (Solution by G. W. Veltkamp.) Let $c = 2^{\lceil p/2 \rceil} + 1$; we may assume that $p \geq 2$, so c is representable. First compute $u' = u \otimes c$, $u_1 = (u \ominus u') \oplus u'$, $u_2 = u \ominus u_1$; similarly, $v' = v \otimes c$, $v_1 = (v \ominus v') \oplus v'$, $v_2 = v \ominus v_1$. Then set $w \leftarrow u \otimes v$, $w' \leftarrow (((u_1 \otimes v_1 \ominus w) \oplus (u_1 \otimes v_2)) \oplus (u_2 \otimes v_1)) \oplus (u_2 \otimes v_2)$.

It suffices to prove this when $u, v > 0$ and $e_u = e_v = p$, so that u and v are integers $\in [2^{p-1} .. 2^p]$. Then $u = u_1 + u_2$ where $2^{p-1} \leq u_1 \leq 2^p$, $u_1 \bmod 2^{\lceil p/2 \rceil} = 0$, and $|u_2| \leq 2^{\lceil p/2 \rceil - 1}$; similarly $v = v_1 + v_2$. The operations during the calculation of w' are exact, because $w - u_1 v_1$ is a multiple of 2^{p-1} such that $|w - u_1 v_1| \leq |w - uv| + |u_2 v_1 + u_1 v_2 + u_2 v_2| \leq 2^{p-1} + 2^{p + \lceil p/2 \rceil} + 2^{p-1}$; and similarly $|w - u_1 v_1 - u_1 v_2| \leq |w - uv| + |u_2 v| < 2^{p-1} + 2^{\lceil p/2 \rceil - 1 + p}$, where $w - u_1 v_1 - u_1 v_2$ is a multiple of $2^{\lceil p/2 \rceil}$.

22. We may assume that $b^{p-1} \leq u, v < b^p$. If $uv \leq b^{2p-1}$, then $x_1 = uv - r$ where $|r| \leq \frac{1}{2}b^{p-1}$, hence $x_2 = \text{round}(u - r/v) = x_0$ (since $|r/v| \leq \frac{1}{2}b^{p-1}/b^{p-1} \leq \frac{1}{2}$, and equality implies $v = b^{p-1}$ hence $r = 0$). If $uv > b^{2p-1}$, then $x_1 = uv - r$ where $|r| \leq \frac{1}{2}b^p$, hence $x_1/v = u - r/v < b^p + \frac{1}{2}b$ and $x_2 \leq b^p$. If $x_2 = b^p$, then $x_3 = x_1$ (since the condition $(b^p - \frac{1}{2})v \leq x_1$ implies that x_1 is a multiple of b^p, and we have $x_1 < b^p(v + \frac{1}{2})$). If $x_2 < b^p$ and $x_1 > b^{2p-1}$, then let $x_2 = x_1/v + q$ where $|q| \leq \frac{1}{2}$; we have $x_3 = \text{round}(x_1 + qv) = x_1$. Finally if $x_2 < b^p$, $x_1 = b^{2p-1}$, and $x_3 < b^{2p-1}$, then $x_4 = x_2$ by the first case above. This situation arises, for example, when $b = 10$, $p = 2$, $u = 19$, $v = 55$, $x_1 = 1000$, $x_2 = 18$, $x_3 = 990$.

23. If $u \geq 0$ or $u \leq -1$ we have $u \bmod\!\!\!\bmod 1 = u \bmod 1$, so the identity holds. If $-1 < u < 0$, then $u \bmod\!\!\!\bmod 1 = u \oplus 1 = u + 1 + r$ where $|r| \leq \frac{1}{2}b^{-p}$; the identity holds if and only if $\text{round}(1 + r) = 1$, so it always holds if we round to even. With the text's rounding rule the identity fails if and only if b is a multiple of 4 and $-1 < u < 0$ and $u \bmod 2b^{-p} = \frac{3}{2}b^{-p}$ (for example, $p = 3$, $b = 8$, $u = -(.0124)_8$).

24. Let $u = [u_l .. u_r]$, $v = [v_l .. v_r]$. Then $u \oplus v = [u_l \triangledown v_l .. u_r \triangle v_r]$, where $x \triangle y = y \triangle x$, $x \triangle +0 = x$ for all x, $x \triangle -0 = x$ for all $x \neq +0$, $x \triangle +\infty = +\infty$ for all $x \neq -\infty$, and $x \triangle -\infty$ needn't be defined; $x \triangledown y = -((-x) \triangle (-y))$. If $x \oplus y$ would overflow in normal floating point arithmetic because $x + y$ is too large, then $x \triangle y$ is $+\infty$ and $x \triangledown y$ is the largest representable number.

For subtraction, let $u \ominus v = u \oplus (-v)$, where $-v = [-v_r .. -v_l]$.

Multiplication is somewhat more complicated. The correct procedure is to let $u \otimes v = [\min(u_l \triangledown v_l, u_l \triangledown v_r, u_r \triangledown v_l, u_r \triangledown v_r) .. \max(u_l \triangle v_l, u_l \triangle v_r, u_r \triangle v_l, u_r \triangle v_r)]$, where $x \triangle y = y \triangle x$, $x \triangle (-y) = -(x \triangledown y) = (-x) \triangle y$; $x \triangle +0 = (+0$ for $x > 0$, -0 for $x < 0$); $x \triangle -0 = -(x \triangle +0)$; $x \triangle +\infty = (+\infty$ for $x > +0$, $-\infty$ for $x < -0)$. (It is possible to determine the min and max simply by looking at the signs of u_l, u_r, v_l, and v_r, thereby computing only two of the eight products, except when $u_l < 0 < u_r$ and $v_l < 0 < v_r$; in the latter case we compute four products, and the answer is $[\min(u_l \triangledown v_r, u_r \triangledown v_l) .. \max(u_l \triangle v_l, u_r \triangle v_r)]$.)

Finally, $u \oslash v$ is undefined if $v_l < 0 < v_r$; otherwise we use the formulas for multiplication with v_l and v_r replaced respectively by v_r^{-1} and v_l^{-1}, where $x \vartriangle y^{-1} = x \vartriangle y$, $x \triangledown y^{-1} = x \triangledown y$, $(\pm 0)^{-1} = \pm \infty$, $(\pm \infty)^{-1} = \pm 0$.

[See E. R. Hansen, *Math. Comp.* **22** (1968), 374–384. An alternative scheme, in which division by 0 gives no error messages and intervals may be neighborhoods of ∞, has been proposed by W. M. Kahan. In Kahan's scheme, for example, the reciprocal of $[-1 \mathinner{\ldotp\ldotp} +1]$ is $[+1 \mathinner{\ldotp\ldotp} -1]$, and an attempt to multiply an interval containing 0 by an interval containing ∞ yields $[-\infty \mathinner{\ldotp\ldotp} +\infty]$, the set of all numbers. See *Numerical Analysis*, Univ. Michigan Engineering Summer Conf. Notes No. 6818 (1968).]

25. Cancellation reveals *previous* errors in the computation of u and v. For example, if ϵ is small, we often get poor accuracy when computing $f(x + \epsilon) \ominus f(x)$, because the rounded calculation of $f(x + \epsilon)$ destroys much of the information about ϵ. It is desirable to rewrite such formulas as $\epsilon \otimes g(x, \epsilon)$, where $g(x, \epsilon) = (f(x + \epsilon) - f(x))/\epsilon$ is first computed symbolically. Thus, if $f(x) = x^2$ then $g(x, \epsilon) = 2x + \epsilon$; if $f(x) = \sqrt{x}$ then $g(x, \epsilon) = 1/(\sqrt{x + \epsilon} + \sqrt{x})$.

26. Let $e = \max(e_u, e_{u'})$, $e' = \max(e_v, e_{v'})$, $e'' = \max(e_{u \oplus v}, e_{u' \oplus v'})$, and assume that $q = 0$. Then $(u \oplus v) - (u' \oplus v') \le u + v + \frac{1}{2}b^{e'' - p} - u' - v' + \frac{1}{2}b^{e'' - p} \le \epsilon b^e + \epsilon b^{e'} + b^{e'' - p}$, and $e'' \ge \max(e, e')$. Hence $u \oplus v \sim u' \oplus v' \; (2\epsilon + b^{-p})$.

If $b = 2$ this estimate can be improved to $1.5\epsilon + b^{-p}$. For $\epsilon + b^{-p}$ is an upper bound if $u - u'$ and $v - v'$ have opposite signs, and in the other case we cannot have $e = e' = e''$.

27. The stated identity is a consequence of the fact that $1 \oslash (1 \oslash u) = u$ whenever $b^{-1} \le f_u \le b^{-1/2}$. If the latter were false, there would be integers x and y such that $b^{p-1} < x < b^{p-1/2}$ and either $y - \frac{1}{2} \le b^{2p-1}/x < b^{2p-1}/(x - \frac{1}{2}) \le y$ or $y \le b^{2p-1}/(x + \frac{1}{2}) < b^{2p-1}/x \le y + \frac{1}{2}$. But that is clearly impossible unless we have $x(x + \frac{1}{2}) > b^{2p-1}$, yet the latter condition implies $y = \lfloor b^{p-1/2} \rfloor = x$.

28. See *Math. Comp.* **32** (1978), 227–232.

29. When $b = 2$ and $p = 1$ and $x > 0$, we have $\operatorname{round}(x) = 2^{e(x)}$ where $e(x) = \lfloor \lg \frac{4}{3} x \rfloor$. Let $f(x) = x^\alpha$ and let $t(n) = \lfloor \lfloor \alpha n + \lg \frac{4}{3} \rfloor / \alpha + \lg \frac{4}{3} \rfloor$. Then $\hat{h}(2^e) = 2^{t(e)}$. When $\alpha = .99$ we find $\hat{h}(2^e) = 2^{e-1}$ for $41 < e \le 58$.

31. According to the theory in Section 4.5.3, the convergents to the continued fraction $\sqrt{3} = 1 + /\!/1, 2, 1, 2, \ldots /\!/$ are $p_n/q_n = K_{n+1}(1, 1, 2, 1, 2, \ldots)/K_n(1, 2, 1, 2, \ldots)$. These convergents are excellent approximations to $\sqrt{3}$, hence $3q_n^2 \approx p_n^2$; in fact, $3q_n^2 - p_n^2 = 2 - 3(n \bmod 2)$. The example given is $2p_{31}^2 + (3q_{31}^2 - p_{31}^2)(3q_{31}^2 + p_{31}^2) = 2p_{31}^2 - (p_{31}^2 - 1 + p_{31}^2) = 1$. Floating point subtraction of p_{31}^2 from $3q_{31}^2$ yields zero, unless we can represent $3q_{31}^2$ almost perfectly; subtracting p_{31}^4 from $9q_{31}^4$ generally gives rounding errors much larger than $2p_{31}^2$. Similar examples can be based on continued fraction approximations to any algebraic number.

SECTION 4.2.3

1. First, $(w_m, w_l) = (.573, .248)$; then $w_m v_l / v_m = .290$; so the answer is $(.572, .958)$. This in fact is the correct result to six decimals.

2. The answer is not affected, since the normalization routine truncates to eight places and can never look at this particular byte position. (Scaling to the left occurs at most once during normalization, since the inputs are normalized.)

3. Overflow obviously cannot occur at line 09, since we are adding two-byte quantities, or at line 22, since we are adding four-byte quantities. In line 30 we are computing the sum of three four-byte quantities, so this cannot overflow. Finally, in line 32, overflow is impossible because the product $f_u f_v$ must be less than unity.

4. Insert "JOV OFLO; ENT1 0" between lines 03 and 04. Replace lines 21–22 by "ADD TEMP(ABS); JNOV *+2; INC1 1", and change lines 28–31 to "SLAX 5; ADD TEMP; JNOV *+2; INC1 1; ENTX 0,1; SRC 5". This adds five lines of code and only 1, 2, or 3 units of execution time.

5. Insert "JOV OFLO" after line 06. Change lines 22, 31, 39 respectively to "SRAX 0,1", "SLAX 5", "ADD ACC". Between lines 40 and 41, insert "DEC2 1; JNOV DNORM; INC2 1; INCX 1; SRC 1". (It's tempting to remove the "DEC2 1" in favor of "STZ EXPO", but then "INC2 1" might overflow rI2!) This adds six lines of code; the running time *decreases* by $3u$, unless there is fraction overflow, when it increases by $7u$.

6.

DOUBLE	STJ	EXITDF	Convert to double precision:
	ENTX	0	Clear rX.
	STA	TEMP	
	LD2	TEMP(EXP)	rI2 ← e.
	INC2	QQ-Q	Correct for difference in excess.
	STZ	EXPO	EXPO ← 0.
	SLAX	1	Remove exponent.
	JMP	DNORM	Normalize and exit.
SINGLE	STJ	EXITF	Convert to single precision:
	JOV	OFLO	Ensure that overflow is off.
	STA	TEMP	
	LD2	TEMP(EXPD)	rI2 ← e.
	DEC2	QQ-Q	Correct for difference in excess.
	SLAX	2	Remove exponent.
	JMP	NORM	Normalize, round, and exit. ∎

7. All three routines give zero as the answer if and only if the exact result would be zero, so we need not worry about zero denominators in the expressions for relative error. The worst case of the addition routine is pretty bad: Visualized in decimal notation, if the inputs are 1.0000000 and .99999999, the answer is b^{-7} instead of b^{-8}; thus the maximum relative error δ_1 is $b - 1$, where b is the byte size.

For multiplication and division, we may assume that both operands are positive and have the same exponent QQ. The maximum error in multiplication is readily bounded by considering Fig. 4: When $uv \geq 1/b$, we have $0 \leq uv - u \otimes v < 3b^{-9} + (b - 1)b^{-9}$, so the relative error is bounded by $(b + 2)b^{-8}$. When $1/b^2 \leq uv < 1/b$, we have $0 \leq uv - u \otimes v < 3b^{-9}$, so the relative error in this case is bounded by $3b^{-9}/uv \leq 3b^{-7}$. We take δ_2 to be the larger of the two estimates, namely $3b^{-7}$.

Division requires a more careful analysis of Program D. The quantity actually computed by the subroutine is $\alpha - \delta - b\epsilon((\alpha - \delta'')(\beta - \delta') - \delta''') - \delta_n$ where $\alpha = (u_m + \epsilon u_l)/bv_m$, $\beta = v_l/bv_m$, and the nonnegative truncation errors ($\delta, \delta', \delta'', \delta'''$) are respectively less than ($b^{-10}, b^{-5}, b^{-5}, b^{-6}$); finally δ_n (the truncation during normalization) is nonnegative and less than either b^{-9} or b^{-8}, depending on whether scaling occurs or not. The actual value of the quotient is $\alpha/(1 + b\epsilon\beta) = \alpha - b\epsilon\alpha\beta + b^2\alpha\beta^2\delta''''$, where δ'''' is the nonnegative error due to truncation of the infinite series (2); here $\delta'''' < \epsilon^2 = b^{-10}$, since it is an alternating series. The relative error is therefore the absolute value of $(b\epsilon\delta' + b\epsilon\delta''\beta/\alpha + b\epsilon\delta'''/\alpha) - (\delta/\alpha + b\epsilon\delta'\delta''/\alpha + b^2\beta^2\delta'''' + \delta_n/\alpha)$, times

$(1 + b\epsilon\beta)$. The positive terms in this expression are bounded by $b^{-9} + b^{-8} + b^{-8}$, and the negative terms are bounded by $b^{-8} + b^{-12} + b^{-8}$ plus the contribution by the normalizing phase, which can be about b^{-7} in magnitude. It is therefore clear that the potentially greatest part of the relative error comes during the normalization phase, and that $\delta_3 = (b+2)b^{-8}$ is a safe upper bound for the relative error.

8. Addition: If $e_u \leq e_v + 1$, the entire relative error occurs during the normalization phase, so it is bounded above by b^{-7}. If $e_u \geq e_v + 2$, and if the signs are the same, again the entire error may be ascribed to normalization; if the signs are opposite, the error due to shifting digits out of the register is in the opposite direction from the subsequent error introduced during normalization. Both of these errors are bounded by b^{-7}, hence $\delta_1 = b^{-7}$. (This is substantially better then the result in exercise 7.)

Multiplication: An analysis as in exercise 7 gives $\delta_2 = (b+2)b^{-8}$.

SECTION 4.2.4

1. Since fraction overflow can occur only when the operands have the same sign, this is the probability that fraction overflow occurs divided by the probability that the operands have the same sign, namely, $7\%/(\frac{1}{2}(91\%)) \approx 15\%$.

3. $\log_{10} 2.4 - \log_{10} 2.3 \approx 1.84834\%$.

4. The pages would be uniformly gray.

5. The probability that $10 f_U \leq r$ is $(r-1)/10 + (r-1)/100 + \cdots = (r-1)/9$. So in this case the leading digits are *uniformly* distributed; for example, the leading digit is 1 with probability $\frac{1}{9}$.

6. The probability that there are three leading zero bits is $\log_{16} 2 = \frac{1}{4}$; the probability that there are two leading zero bits is $\log_{16} 4 - \log_{16} 2 = \frac{1}{4}$; and similarly for the other two cases. The "average" number of leading zero bits is $1\frac{1}{2}$, so the "average" number of "significant bits" is $p + \frac{1}{2}$. The worst case, $p - 1$ bits, occurs however with rather high probability. In practice, it is usually necessary to base error estimates on the worst case, since a chain of calculations is only as strong as its weakest link. In the error analysis of Section 4.2.2, the upper bound on relative rounding error for floating hex is 2^{1-p}. In the binary case we can have $p + 1$ significant bits in all normalized numbers (see exercise 4.2.1–3), with relative rounding errors bounded by 2^{-1-p}. Extensive computational experience confirms that floating binary produces significantly more accurate results than the equivalent floating hex, even when the binary numbers have a precision of p bits instead of $p + 1$.

Tables 1 and 2 show that hexadecimal arithmetic can be done a little faster, since fewer cycles are needed when scaling to the right or normalizing to the left. But this fact is insignificant compared to the substantial advantages of $b = 2$ over other radices (see also Theorem 4.2.2C and exercises 4.2.2–13, 15, 21), especially since floating binary can be made as fast as floating hex with only a tiny increase in total processor cost.

7. For example, suppose that $\sum_m \left(F(10^{km} \cdot 5^k) - F(10^{km}) \right) = \log 5^k / \log 10^k$ and also that $\sum_m \left(F(10^{km} \cdot 4^k) - F(10^{km}) \right) = \log 4^k / \log 10^k$; then

$$\sum_m \left(F(10^{km} \cdot 5^k) - F(10^{km} \cdot 4^k) \right) = \log_{10} \frac{5}{4}$$

for all k. But now let ϵ be a small positive number, and choose $\delta > 0$ so that $F(x) < \epsilon$ for $0 < x < \delta$, and choose $M > 0$ so that $F(x) > 1 - \epsilon$ for $x > M$. We can take k so large that $10^{-k} \cdot 5^k < \delta$ and $4^k > M$; hence by the monotonicity of F,

$$\sum_m \left(F(10^{km} \cdot 5^k) - F(10^{km} \cdot 4^k) \right)$$

$$\leq \sum_{m<0} \left(F(10^{km} \cdot 5^k) - F(10^{k(m-1)} \cdot 5^k) \right) + \sum_{m \geq 0} \left(F(10^{k(m+1)} \cdot 4^k) - F(10^{km} \cdot 4^k) \right)$$

$$= F(10^{-k} \cdot 5^k) + 1 - F(4^k) < 2\epsilon.$$

8. When $s > r$, $P_0(10^n s)$ is 1 for small n, and 0 when $\lfloor 10^n s \rfloor > \lfloor 10^n r \rfloor$. The least n for which this happens may be arbitrarily large, so no uniform bound can be given for $N_0(\epsilon)$ independent of s. (In general, calculus textbooks prove that such a uniform bound would imply that the limit function $S_0(s)$ would be continuous, and it isn't.)

9. Let $q_1, q_2, \ldots$ be such that $P_0(n) = q_1 \binom{n-1}{0} + q_2 \binom{n-1}{1} + \cdots$ for all n. It follows that $P_m(n) = 1^{-m} q_1 \binom{n-1}{0} + 2^{-m} q_2 \binom{n-1}{1} + \cdots$ for all m and n.

10. When $1 < r < 10$ the generating function $C(z)$ has simple poles at the points $1 + w_n$, where $w_n = 2\pi n i / \ln 10$, hence

$$C(z) = \frac{\log_{10} r - 1}{1 - z} + \sum_{n \neq 0} \frac{1 + w_n}{w_n} \frac{e^{-w_n \ln r} - 1}{(\ln 10)(z - 1 - w_n)} + E(z)$$

where $E(z)$ is analytic in the entire plane. Thus if $\theta = \arctan(2\pi / \ln 10)$,

$$c_m = \log_{10} r - 1 - \frac{2}{\ln 10} \sum_{n > 0} \Re\left(\frac{e^{-w_n \ln r} - 1}{w_n (1 + w_n)^m} \right) + e_m$$

$$= \log_{10} r - 1 + \frac{\sin(m\theta + 2\pi \log_{10} r) - \sin(m\theta)}{\pi (1 + 4\pi^2/(\ln 10)^2)^{m/2}} + O\left(\frac{1}{(1 + 16\pi^2/(\ln 10)^2)^{m/2}} \right).$$

11. When $(\log_b U) \bmod 1$ is uniformly distributed in $[0..1)$, so is $(\log_b 1/U) \bmod 1 = (1 - \log_b U) \bmod 1$.

12. We have

$$h(z) = \int_{1/b}^{z} f(x) \, dx \, g(z/bx)/bx + \int_{z}^{1} f(x) \, dx \, g(z/x)/x;$$

consequently

$$\frac{h(z) - l(z)}{l(z)} = \int_{1/b}^{z} f(x) \, dx \, \frac{g(z/bx) - l(z/bx)}{l(z/bx)} + \int_{z}^{1} f(x) \, dx \, \frac{g(z/x) - l(z/x)}{l(z/x)}.$$

Since $f(x) \geq 0$, $|(h(z) - l(z))/l(z)| \leq \int_{1/b}^{z} f(x) \, dx \, A(g) + \int_{z}^{1} f(x) \, dx \, A(g)$ for all z, hence $A(h) \leq A(g)$. By symmetry, $A(h) \leq A(f)$. [Bell System Tech. J. **49** (1970), 1609–1625.]

13. Let $X = (\log_b U) \bmod 1$ and $Y = (\log_b V) \bmod 1$, so that X and Y are independently and uniformly distributed in $[0..1)$. No left shift is needed if and only if $X + Y \geq 1$, and that occurs with probability $1/2$.

(Similarly, the probability is $1/2$ that floating point division by Algorithm 4.2.1M needs no normalization shifts; this analysis needs only the weaker assumption that both of the operands independently have the *same* distribution.)

14. For convenience, the calculations are shown here for $b = 10$. If $k = 0$, the probability of a carry is

$$\left(\frac{1}{\ln 10}\right)^2 \int_{\substack{1 \le x, y \le 10 \\ x+y \ge 10}} \frac{dx}{x}\frac{dy}{y}.$$

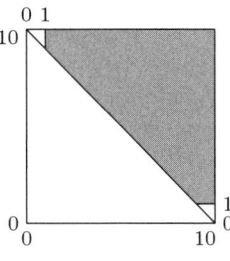

Fig. A–7.

(See Fig. A–7.) The value of the integral is

$$\int_0^{10} \frac{dy}{y} \int_{10-y}^{10} \frac{dx}{x} - 2\int_0^1 \frac{dy}{y} \int_{10-y}^{10} \frac{dx}{x},$$

and

$$\int_0^t \frac{dy}{y} \ln\left(\frac{1}{1-y/10}\right) = \int_0^t \left(\frac{1}{10} + \frac{y}{200} + \frac{y^2}{3000} + \cdots\right) dy = \frac{t}{10} + \frac{t^2}{400} + \frac{t^3}{9000} + \cdots.$$

(The latter integral is essentially a "dilogarithm.") Hence the probability of a carry when $k = 0$ is $(1/\ln 10)^2(\pi^2/6 - 2\sum_{n \ge 1} 1/n^2 10^n) \approx .27154$. [*Note:* When $b = 2$ and $k = 0$, fraction overflow *always* occurs, so this derivation proves that $\sum_{n \ge 1} 1/n^2 2^n = \pi^2/12 - (\ln 2)^2/2$.]

When $k > 0$, the probability is

$$\left(\frac{1}{\ln 10}\right)^2 \int_{10^{-k}}^{10^{1-k}} \frac{dy}{y} \int_{10-y}^{10} \frac{dx}{x} = \left(\frac{1}{\ln 10}\right)^2 \left(\sum_{n \ge 1} \frac{1}{n^2 10^{nk}} - \sum_{n \ge 1} \frac{1}{n^2 10^{n(k+1)}}\right).$$

Thus when $b = 10$, fraction overflow should occur with approximate probability $.272p_0 + .017p_1 + .002p_2 + \cdots$. When $b = 2$ the corresponding figures are $p_0 + .655p_1 + .288p_2 + .137p_3 + .067p_4 + .033p_5 + .016p_6 + .008p_7 + .004p_8 + .002p_9 + .001p_{10} + \cdots$.

Now if we use the probabilities from Table 1, dividing by .91 to eliminate zero operands and assuming that the probabilities are independent of the operand signs, we predict a probability of about 14 percent when $b = 10$, instead of the 15 percent in exercise 1. For $b = 2$, we predict about 48 percent, while the table yields 44 percent. These results are certainly in agreement within the limits of experimental error.

15. When $k = 0$, the leading digit is 1 if and only if there is a carry. (It is possible for fraction overflow and subsequent rounding to yield a leading digit of 2, when $b \ge 4$, but we are ignoring rounding in this exercise.) The probability of fraction overflow is approximately .272, as shown in the previous exercise, and $.272 < \log_{10} 2$.

When $k > 0$, the leading digit is 1 with probability

$$\left(\frac{1}{\ln 10}\right)^2 \left(\int_{10^{-k}}^{10^{1-k}} \frac{dy}{y} \int_{\substack{1 \le x < 2-y \\ \text{or } 10-y \le x < 10}} \frac{dx}{x}\right) < \left(\frac{1}{\ln 10}\right)^2 \left(\int_{10^{-k}}^{10^{1-k}} \frac{dy}{y} \int_{1 \le x \le 2} \frac{dx}{x}\right) = \log_{10} 2.$$

16. To prove the hint [which is due to Landau, *Prace Matematyczno-Fizyczne* **21** (1910), 103–113], assume first that $\limsup a_n = \lambda > 0$. Let $\epsilon = \lambda/(\lambda + 4M)$ and choose N so that $|a_1 + \cdots + a_n| < \frac{1}{10}\epsilon\lambda n$ for all $n > N$. Let $n > N/(1 - \epsilon)$, $n > 5/\epsilon$ be such that $a_n > \frac{1}{2}\lambda$. Then, by induction, $a_{n-k} \ge a_n - kM/(n - \epsilon n) > \frac{1}{4}\lambda$ for $0 \le k < \epsilon n$, and $\sum_{n-\epsilon n < k \le n} a_k \ge \frac{1}{4}\lambda(\epsilon n - 1) > \frac{1}{5}\lambda\epsilon n$. But

$$\left|\sum_{n-\epsilon n < k \le n} a_k\right| = \left|\sum_{1 \le k \le n} a_k - \sum_{1 \le k \le n-\epsilon n} a_k\right| \le \frac{1}{5}\epsilon\lambda n$$

since $n - \epsilon n > N$. A similar contradiction applies if $\liminf a_n < 0$.

Assuming that $P_{m+1}(n) \to \lambda$ as $n \to \infty$, let $a_k = P_m(k) - \lambda$. If $m > 0$, the a_k satisfy the hypotheses of the hint (see Eq. 4.2.2–(15)), since $0 \leq P_m(k) \leq 1$; hence $P_m(n) \to \lambda$.

17. See *J. Math. Soc. Japan* **4** (1952), 313–322. (The fact that harmonic probability extends ordinary probability follows from a theorem of Cesàro, [*Atti della Reale Accademia dei Lincei, Rendiconti* (4) **4** (1888), 452–457]. Persi Diaconis [Ph.D. thesis, Harvard University, 1974] has shown among other things that the definition of probability by repeated averaging is weaker than harmonic probability, in the following precise sense: If $\lim_{m\to\infty} \liminf_{n\to\infty} P_m(n) = \lim_{m\to\infty} \limsup_{n\to\infty} P_m(n) = \lambda$ then the harmonic probability is λ. On the other hand the statement "$10^{k^2} \leq n < 10^{k^2+k}$ for some integer $k > 0$" has harmonic probability $\frac{1}{2}$, while repeated averaging never settles down to give it any particular probability.)

18. Let $p(a) = P(L_a)$ and $p(a, b) = \sum_{a \leq k < b} p(k)$ for $1 \leq a < b$. Since $L_a = L_{10a} \cup L_{10a+1} \cup \cdots \cup L_{10a+9}$ for all a, we have $p(a) = p(10a, 10(a+1))$ by (i). Furthermore since $P(S) = P(2S) + P(2S + 1)$ by (i), (ii), (iii), we have $p(a) = p(2a, 2(a+1))$. It follows that $p(a, b) = p(2^m 10^n a, 2^m 10^n b)$ for all $m, n \geq 0$.

If $1 < b/a < b'/a'$, then $p(a, b) \leq p(a', b')$. The reason is that there exist integers m, n, m', n' such that $2^{m'} 10^{n'} a' \leq 2^m 10^n a < 2^m 10^n b \leq 2^{m'} 10^{n'} b'$ as a consequence of the fact that $\log 2/\log 10$ is irrational, hence we can apply (v). (See exercise 3.5–22 with $k = 1$ and $U_n = n \log 2/\log 10$.) In particular, $p(a) \geq p(a+1)$, and it follows that $p(a, b)/p(a, b+1) \geq (b - a)/(b + 1 - a)$. (See Eq. 4.2.2–(15).)

Now we can prove that $p(a, b) = p(a', b')$ whenever $b/a = b'/a'$; for $p(a, b) = p(10^n a, 10^n b) \leq c_n p(10^n a, 10^n b - 1) \leq c_n p(a', b')$, for arbitrarily large values of n, where $c_n = 10^n(b - a)/(10^n(b - a) - 1) = 1 + O(10^{-n})$.

For any positive integer n we have $p(a^n, b^n) = p(a^n, ba^{n-1}) + p(ba^{n-1}, b^2 a^{n-2}) + \cdots + p(b^{n-1}a, b^n) = np(a, b)$. If $10^m \leq a^n \leq 10^{m+1}$ and $10^{m'} \leq b^n \leq 10^{m'+1}$, then $p(10^{m+1}, 10^{m'}) \leq p(a^n, b^n) \leq p(10^m, 10^{m'+1})$ by (v). But $p(1, 10) = 1$ by (iv), hence $p(10^m, 10^{m'}) = m' - m$ for all $m' \geq m$. We conclude that $\lfloor \log_{10} b^n \rfloor - \lfloor \log_{10} a^n \rfloor - 1 \leq np(a, b) \leq \lfloor \log_{10} b^n \rfloor + \lfloor \log_{10} a^n \rfloor + 1$ for all n, and $p(a, b) = \log_{10}(b/a)$.

[This exercise was inspired by D. I. A. Cohen, who proved a slightly weaker result in *J. Combinatorial Theory* **A20** (1976), 367–370.]

19. Equivalently, $\langle (\log_{10} F_n) \bmod 1 \rangle$ is equidistributed in the sense of Definition 3.5B. Since $\log_{10} F_n = n \log_{10} \phi - \log_{10} \sqrt{5} + O(\phi^{-2n})$ by 1.2.8–(14), this is equivalent to equidistribution of $\langle n \log_{10} \phi \rangle$, which follows from ex. 3.5–22. [*Fibonacci Quarterly* **5** (1967), 137–140.] The same proof shows that the sequences $\langle b^n \rangle$ obey the logarithmic law for all integers $b > 1$ that aren't powers of 10 [Yaglom and Yaglom, *Challenging Problems with Elementary Solutions* (Moscow: 1954; English translation, 1964), Problem 91b].

Notes: Many other sequences of integers have this property. For example, Persi Diaconis [*Annals of Probability* **5** (1977), 72–81] showed that $\langle n! \rangle$ is one such sequence, and that binomial coefficients obey the logarithmic law too, in the sense that

$$\lim_{n\to\infty} \frac{1}{n+1} \sum_{k=0}^{n} [10 f_{\binom{n}{k}} < r] = \log_{10} r.$$

P. Schatte [*Math. Nachrichten* **148** (1990), 137–144] proved that the denominators of continued fraction approximations have logarithmic fraction parts, whenever the partial quotients have a repeating pattern with polynomial variation as in exercise

4.5.3–16. One interesting open question is whether the sequence $\langle 2!, (2!)!, ((2!)!)!, \ldots \rangle$ has logarithmic fraction parts; see J. H. Conway and M. J. T. Guy, *Eureka* **25** (1962), 18–19.

SECTION 4.3.1

2. If the ith number to be added is $u_i = (u_{i(n-1)} \ldots u_{i1} u_{i0})_b$, use Algorithm A with step A2 changed to the following:

A2′. [Add digits.] Set

$$w_j \leftarrow (u_{1j} + \cdots + u_{mj} + k) \bmod b, \quad \text{and} \quad k \leftarrow \lfloor (u_{1j} + \cdots + u_{mj} + k)/b \rfloor.$$

(The maximum value of k is $m - 1$, so step A3 would have to be altered if $m > b$.)

3.

	ENN1 N	1	
	JOV OFLO	1	Ensure that overflow is off.
	ENTX 0	1	$k \leftarrow 0$.
2H	SLAX 5	N	($\text{rX} \equiv$ next value of k)
	ENT3 M*N,1	N	($\text{LOC}(u_{ij}) \equiv \text{U} + n(i-1) + j$)
3H	ADD U,3	MN	$\text{rA} \leftarrow \text{rA} + u_{ij}$.
	JNOV *+2	MN	
	INCX 1	K	Carry one.
	DEC3 N	MN	Repeat for $m \geq i \geq 1$.
	J3NN 3B	MN	($\text{rI3} \equiv n(i-1) + j$)
	STA W+N,1	N	$w_j \leftarrow \text{rA}$.
	INC1 1	N	
	J1N 2B	N	Repeat for $0 \leq j < n$.
	STX W+N	1	Store final carry in w_n. ∎

Running time, assuming that $K = \frac{1}{2}MN$, is $5.5MN + 7N + 4$ cycles.

4. We may make the following assertion before A1: "$n \geq 1$; and $0 \leq u_i, v_i < b$ for $0 \leq i < n$." Before A2, we assert: "$0 \leq j < n$; $0 \leq u_i, v_i < b$ for $0 \leq i < n$; $0 \leq w_i < b$ for $0 \leq i < j$; $0 \leq k \leq 1$; and $(u_{j-1} \ldots u_0)_b + (v_{j-1} \ldots v_0)_b = (kw_{j-1} \ldots w_0)_b$." The latter statement means more precisely that

$$\sum_{0 \leq l < j} u_l b^l + \sum_{0 \leq l < j} v_l b^l = kb^j + \sum_{0 \leq l < j} w_l b^l.$$

Before A3, we assert: "$0 \leq j < n$; $0 \leq u_i, v_i < b$ for $0 \leq i < n$; $0 \leq w_i < b$ for $0 \leq i \leq j$; $0 \leq k \leq 1$; and $(u_j \ldots u_0)_b + (v_j \ldots v_0)_b = (kw_j \ldots w_0)_b$." After A3, we assert that $0 \leq w_i < b$ for $0 \leq i < n$; $0 \leq w_n \leq 1$; and $(u_{n-1} \ldots u_0)_b + (v_{n-1} \ldots v_0)_b = (w_n \ldots w_0)_b$.

It is a simple matter to complete the proof by verifying the necessary implications between the assertions and by showing that the algorithm always terminates.

5. B1. Set $j \leftarrow n - 1$, $w_n \leftarrow 0$.

B2. Set $t \leftarrow u_j + v_j$, $w_j \leftarrow t \bmod b$, $i \leftarrow j$.

B3. If $t \geq b$, set $i \leftarrow i + 1$, $t \leftarrow w_i + 1$, $w_i \leftarrow t \bmod b$, and repeat this step until $t < b$.

B4. Decrease j by one, and if $j \geq 0$ go back to B2. ∎

6. C1. Set $j \leftarrow n - 1$, $i \leftarrow n$, $r \leftarrow 0$.

C2. Set $t \leftarrow u_j + v_j$. If $t \geq b$, set $w_i \leftarrow r + 1$ and $w_k \leftarrow 0$ for $i > k > j$; then set $i \leftarrow j$ and $r \leftarrow t \bmod b$. Otherwise if $t < b - 1$, set $w_i \leftarrow r$ and $w_k \leftarrow b - 1$ for $i > k > j$; then set $i \leftarrow j$ and $r \leftarrow t$.

C3. Decrease j by one. If $j \geq 0$, go back to C2; otherwise set $w_i \leftarrow r$, and $w_k \leftarrow b - 1$ for $i > k \geq 0$. ∎

7. When $j = n - 3$, for example, we have $k = 0$ with probability $(b + 1)/2b$; $k = 1$ with probability $((b - 1)/2b)(1 - 1/b)$, namely the probability that a carry occurs and that the preceding digit wasn't $b - 1$; $k = 2$ with probability $((b - 1)/2b)(1/b)(1 - 1/b)$; and $k = 3$ with probability $((b - 1)/2b)(1/b)(1/b)(1)$. For fixed k we may add the probabilities as j varies from $n - 1$ to 0; this gives the mean number of times the carry propagates back k places,

$$m_k = \frac{b - 1}{2b^k}\left((n + 1 - k)\left(1 - \frac{1}{b}\right) + \frac{1}{b}\right).$$

As a check, we find that the average number of carries is

$$m_1 + 2m_2 + \cdots + nm_n = \frac{1}{2}\left(n - \frac{1}{b - 1}\left(1 - \left(\frac{1}{b}\right)^n\right)\right),$$

in agreement with (6).

```
8.     ENT1 N-1   1        3H LDA  W,2  K
       JOV  OFLO  1           INCA 1    K
       STZ  W+N   1           STA  W,2  K
    2H LDA  U,1   N           INC2 1    K
       ADD  V,1   N           JOV  3B   K
       STA  W,1   N        4H DEC1 1    N
       JNOV 4F    N           J1NN 2B   N  ∎
       ENT2 1,1   L
```

The running time depends on L, the number of positions in which $u_j + v_j \geq b$; and on K, the total number of carries. It is not difficult to see that K is the same quantity that appears in Program A. The analysis in the text shows that L has the average value $N((b - 1)/2b)$, and K has the average value $\frac{1}{2}(N - b^{-1} - b^{-2} - \cdots - b^{-n})$. So if we ignore terms of order $1/b$, the running time is $9N + L + 7K + 3 \approx 13N + 3$ cycles.

9. Replace "b" by "b_j" everywhere in step A2.

10. If lines 06 and 07 were interchanged, we would almost always have overflow, but register A might have a negative value at line 08, so this would not work. If the instructions on lines 05 and 06 were interchanged, the sequence of overflows occurring in the program would be slightly different in some cases, but the program would still be right.

11. This is equivalent to lexicographic comparison of strings: (i) Set $j \leftarrow n - 1$; (ii) if $u_j < v_j$, terminate $[u < v]$; if $u_j = v_j$ and $j = 0$, terminate $[u = v]$; if $u_j = v_j$ and $j > 0$, set $j \leftarrow j - 1$ and repeat (ii); if $u_j > v_j$, terminate $[u > v]$. This algorithm tends to be quite fast, since there is usually low probability that j will have to decrease very much before we encounter a case with $u_j \neq v_j$.

12. Use Algorithm S with $u_j = 0$ and $v_j = w_j$. Another borrow will occur at the end of the algorithm; this time it should be ignored.

13.

	ENN1	N	1	MUL	V	N	STA	W+N,1	N

```
13.   ENN1  N      1        MUL   V     N        STA   W+N,1  N
      JOV   OFLO   1        SLC   5     N        INC1  1      N
      ENTX  0      1        ADD   CARRY N        J1N   2B     N
2H    STX   CARRY  N        JNOV  *+2   N        STX   W+N    1   ▮
      LDA   U+N,1  N        INCX  1     K
```

The running time is $23N + K + 5$ cycles, and K is roughly $\frac{1}{2}N$.

14. The key inductive assertion is the one that should be valid at the beginning of step M4; all others are readily filled in from this one, which is as follows: $0 \le i < m$; $0 \le j < n$; $0 \le u_l < b$ for $0 \le l < m$; $0 \le v_l < b$ for $0 \le l < n$; $0 \le w_l < b$ for $0 \le l < j + m$; $0 \le k < b$; and, in the notation of the answer to exercise 4,

$$(w_{j+m-1} \ldots w_0)_b + kb^{i+j} = u \times (v_{j-1} \ldots v_0)_b + (u_{i-1} \ldots u_0)_b \times v_j b^j.$$

15. The error is nonnegative and less than $(n-2)b^{-n-1}$. [Similarly, if we ignore the products with $i + j > n + 3$, the error is bounded by $(n-3)b^{-n-2}$, etc.; but, in some cases, we must compute all of the products if we want to get the true rounded result. Further analysis shows that correctly rounded results of multiprecision floating point fractions can almost always be obtained by doing only about half the work needed to compute the full double-length product; moreover, a simple test will identify the rare cases for which full precision is needed. See W. Krandick and J. R. Johnson, *Proc. IEEE Symp. Computer Arithmetic* **11** (1993), 228–233.]

16. Q1. Set $r \leftarrow 0$, $j \leftarrow n - 1$.

Q2. Set $w_j \leftarrow \lfloor (rb + u_j)/v \rfloor$, $r \leftarrow (rb + u_j) \bmod v$.

Q3. Decrease j by 1, and return to Q2 if $j \ge 0$. ▮

17. $u/v > u_n b^n /(v_{n-1}+1)b^{n-1} = b\big(1 - 1/(v_{n-1}+1)\big) > b\big(1 - 1/(b/2)\big) = b - 2$.

18. $(u_n b + u_{n-1})/(v_{n-1}+1) \le u/(v_{n-1}+1)b^{n-1} < u/v$.

19. $u - \hat{q}v \le u - \hat{q}v_{n-1}b^{n-1} - \hat{q}v_{n-2}b^{n-2} = u_{n-2}b^{n-2} + \cdots + u_0 + \hat{r}b^{n-1} - \hat{q}v_{n-2}b^{n-2} < b^{n-2}(u_{n-2}+1+\hat{r}b - \hat{q}v_{n-2}) \le 0$. Since $u - \hat{q}v < 0$, $q < \hat{q}$.

20. If $q \le \hat{q} - 2$, then $u < (\hat{q}-1)v < \hat{q}(v_{n-1}b^{n-1} + (v_{n-2}+1)b^{n-2}) - v < \hat{q}v_{n-1}b^{n-1} + \hat{q}v_{n-2}b^{n-2} + b^{n-1} - v \le \hat{q}v_{n-1}b^{n-1} + (b\hat{r}+u_{n-2})b^{n-2} + b^{n-1} - v = u_n b^n + u_{n-1}b^{n-1} + u_{n-2}b^{n-2} + b^{n-1} - v \le u_n b^n + u_{n-1}b^{n-1} + u_{n-2}b^{n-2} \le u$. In other words, $u < u$, and this is a contradiction.

21. (Solution by G. K. Goyal.) The inequality $\hat{q}v_{n-2} \le b\hat{r} + u_{n-2}$ implies that we have $\hat{q} \le (u_n b^2 + u_{n-1}b + u_{n-2})/(v_{n-1}b + v_{n-2}) \le u/((v_{n-1}b + v_{n-2})b^{n-2})$. Now $u \bmod v = u - qv = v(1 - \alpha)$ where $0 < \alpha = 1 + q - u/v \le \hat{q} - u/v \le u\big(1/((v_{n-1}b + v_{n-2})b^{n-2}) - 1/v\big) = u(v_{n-3}b^{n-3} + \cdots)/((v_{n-1}b + v_{n-2})b^{n-2}v) < u/(v_{n-1}bv) \le \hat{q}/(v_{n-1}b) \le (b-1)/(v_{n-1}b)$, and this is at most $2/b$ since $v_{n-1} \ge \frac{1}{2}(b-1)$.

22. Let $u = 4100$, $v = 588$. We first try $\hat{q} = \lfloor \frac{41}{5} \rfloor = 8$, but $8 \cdot 8 > 10(41-40)+0$. Then we set $\hat{q} = 7$, and now we find $7 \cdot 8 < 10(41-35)+0$. But 7 times 588 equals 4116, so the true quotient is $q = 6$. (Incidentally, this example shows that Theorem B cannot be improved under the given hypotheses, when $b = 10$. Similarly, when $b = 2^{16}$ we can let $u = (\text{7fff800100000000})_{16}$, $v = (\text{800080020005})_{16}$.)

23. Obviously $v\lfloor b/(v+1) \rfloor < (v+1)\lfloor b/(v+1) \rfloor \le b$; and the lower bound certainly holds if $v \ge b/2$. Otherwise $v\lfloor b/(v+1) \rfloor \ge v(b-v)/(v+1) \ge (b-1)/2 > \lfloor b/2 \rfloor - 1$.

24. The approximate probability is only $\log_b 2$, not $\frac{1}{2}$. (For example, if $b = 2^{32}$, the probability that $v_{n-1} \ge 2^{31}$ is approximately $\frac{1}{32}$; this is still high enough to warrant the special test for $d = 1$ in steps D1 and D8.)

25.

002		ENTA 1	1	
003		ADD V+N-1	1	
004		STA TEMP	1	
005		ENTA 1	1	
006		JOV 1F	1	Jump if $v_{n-1} = b - 1$.
007		ENTX 0	1	
008		DIV TEMP	1	Otherwise compute $\lfloor b/(v_{n-1}+1)\rfloor$.
009		JOV DIVBYZERO	1	Jump if $v_{n-1} = 0$.
010	1H	STA D	1	
011		DECA 1	1	
012		JANZ *+3	1	Jump if $d \neq 1$.
013		STZ U+M+N	$1 - A$	Set $u_{m+n} \leftarrow 0$.
014		JMP D2	$1 - A$	
015		ENN1 N	A	Multiply v by d.
016		ENTX 0	A	
017	2H	STX CARRY	AN	
018		LDA V+N,1	AN	
019		MUL D	AN	
$\cdots$				(as in exercise 13)
026		J1N 2B	AN	
027		ENN1 M+N	A	(Now rX = 0.)
028	2H	STX CARRY	$A(M+N)$	Multiply u by d.
029		LDA U+M+N,1	$A(M+N)$	
$\cdots$				(as in exercise 13)
037		J1N 2B	$A(M+N)$	
038		STX U+M+N	A	∎

26. (See the algorithm of exercise 16.)

101	D8	LDA D	1	(Remainder will be left in
102		DECA 1	1	locations U through U+N-1)
103		JAZ DONE	1	Terminate if $d = 1$.
104		ENT1 N-1	A	rI1 $\equiv j$; $j \leftarrow n - 1$.
105		ENTA 0	A	$r \leftarrow 0$.
106	1H	LDX U,1	AN	rAX $\leftarrow rb + u_j$.
107		DIV D	AN	
108		STA U,1	AN	
109		SLAX 5	AN	$(u_j, r) \leftarrow (\lfloor \text{rAX}/d\rfloor, \text{rAX} \bmod d)$.
110		DEC1 1	AN	$j \leftarrow j - 1$.
111		J1NN 1B	AN	Repeat for $n > j \geq 0$. ∎

At this point, the division routine is complete; and by the next exercise, rAX = 0.

27. It is $du \bmod dv = d(u \bmod v)$.

28. For convenience, let us assume that v has a decimal point at the left, i.e., $v = (v_n.v_{n-1}v_{n-2}\ldots)_b$. After step N1 we have $\frac{1}{2} \leq v < 1 + 1/b$: For

$$v\left\lfloor \frac{b+1}{v_{n-1}+1}\right\rfloor \leq \frac{v(b+1)}{v_{n-1}+1} = \frac{v(1+1/b)}{(1/b)(v_{n-1}+1)} < 1 + \frac{1}{b},$$

and

$$v\left\lfloor \frac{b+1}{v_{n-1}+1}\right\rfloor \geq \frac{v(b+1-v_{n-1})}{v_{n-1}+1} \geq \frac{1}{b}\frac{v_{n-1}(b+1-v_{n-1})}{v_{n-1}+1}.$$

The latter quantity takes its smallest value when $v_{n-1} = 1$, since it is a concave function and the other extreme value is greater.

The formula in step N2 may be written $v \leftarrow \left\lfloor \dfrac{b(b+1)}{v_{n-1}+1} \right\rfloor \dfrac{v}{b}$, so we see as above that v will never become $\geq 1 + 1/b$.

The minimum value of v after one iteration of step N2 is $\geq$

$$\left(\frac{b(b+1) - v_{n-1}}{v_{n-1}+1}\right)\frac{v}{b} \geq \left(\frac{b(b+1) - v_{n-1}}{v_{n-1}+1}\right)\frac{v_{n-1}}{b^2} = \left(\frac{b(b+1)+1-t}{t}\right)\left(\frac{t-1}{b^2}\right)$$

$$= 1 + \frac{1}{b} + \frac{2}{b^2} - \frac{1}{b^2}\left(t + \frac{b(b+1)+1}{t}\right),$$

if $t = v_{n-1} + 1$. The minimum of this quantity occurs for $t = b/2 + 1$; a lower bound is $1 - 3/2b$. Hence $v_{n-1} \geq b - 2$, after one iteration of step N2. Finally, we have $(1 - 3/2b)(1 + 1/b)^2 > 1$, when $b \geq 5$, so at most two more iterations are needed. The assertion is easily verified when $b < 5$.

29. True, since $(u_{j+n} \ldots u_j)_b < v$.

30. In Algorithms A and S, such overlap is possible if the algorithms are rewritten slightly; for example, in Algorithm A we could rewrite step A2 thus: "Set $t \leftarrow u_j + v_j + k$, $w_j \leftarrow t \bmod b$, $k \leftarrow \lfloor t/b \rfloor$."

In Algorithm M, v_j may be in the same location as w_{j+n}. In Algorithm D, it is most convenient (as in Program D, exercise 26) to let $r_{n-1} \ldots r_0$ be the same as $u_{n-1} \ldots u_0$; and we can also let $q_m \ldots q_0$ be the same as $u_{m+n} \ldots u_n$, provided that no alteration of u_{j+n} is made in step D6. (Line 098 of Program D can safely be changed to "J1N 2B", since u_{j+n} isn't used in the subsequent calculation.)

31. Consider the situation of Fig. 6 with $u = (u_{j+n} \ldots u_{j+1} u_j)_3$ as in Algorithm D. If the leading nonzero digits of u and v have the same sign, set $r \leftarrow u - v$, $q \leftarrow 1$; otherwise set $r \leftarrow u + v$, $q \leftarrow -1$. Now if $|r| > |u|$, or if $|r| = |u|$ and the first nonzero digit of $u_{j-1} \ldots u_0$ has the same sign as the first nonzero digit of r, set $q \leftarrow 0$; otherwise set $u_{j+n} \ldots u_j$ equal to the digits of r.

32. See M. Nadler, *CACM* **4** (1961), 192–193; Z. Pawlak and A. Wakulicz, *Bull. de l'Acad. Polonaise des Sciences*, Classe III, **5** (1957), 233–236 (see also pages 803–804); and exercise 4.1–15.

34. See, for example, R. E. Maeder, *The Mathematica Journal* **6**, 2 (Spring 1996), 32–40; **6**, 3 (Summer 1996), 37–43.

36. Given ϕ with an accuracy of $\pm 2^{-2n}$, we can successively compute ϕ^{-1}, ϕ^{-2}, ... by subtraction until $\phi^{-k} < 2^{-n}$; the accumulated error will not exceed 2^{1-n}. Then we can use the series $\ln \phi = \ln((1 + \phi^{-3})/(1 - \phi^{-3})) = 2(\phi^{-3} + \frac{1}{3}\phi^{-9} + \frac{1}{5}\phi^{-15} + \cdots)$. [See William Schooling's article in *Napier Tercentenary Memorial*, edited by C. G. Knott (London: Longmans, 1915), 337–344.] An even better procedure, suggested in 1965 by J. W. Wrench, Jr., is to evaluate

$$\ln \phi = \frac{1}{2}\ln((1 + 5^{-1/2})/(1 - 5^{-1/2})) = (2\phi - 1)(5^{-1} + \frac{1}{3}5^{-2} + \frac{1}{5}5^{-3} + \cdots).$$

37. Let $d = 2^e$ so that $b > dv_{n-1} \geq b/2$. Instead of normalizing u and v in step D1, simply compute the two leading digits $v'v''$ of $2^e(v_{n-1}v_{n-2}v_{n-3})_b$ by shifting left e bits. In step D3, use (v', v'') instead of (v_{n-1}, v_{n-2}) and (u', u'', u''') instead of $(u_{j+n}, u_{j+n-1}, u_{j+n-2})$, where the digits $u'u''u'''$ are obtained from $(u_{j+n} \ldots u_{j+n-3})_b$ by shifting left e bits. Omit division by d in step D8. (In essence, u and v are being "virtually" shifted. This method saves computation when m is small compared to n.)

38. Set $k \leftarrow n$, $r \leftarrow 0$, $s \leftarrow 1$, $t \leftarrow 0$, $w \leftarrow u$; we will preserve the invariant relation $uv = 2^{2k}(r + s^2 - s) + 2^{2k-n}t + 2^{2k-2n}vw$ with $0 \leq t, w < 2^n$, and with $0 < r \leq 2s$ unless $(r, s) = (0, 1)$. While $k > 0$, let $4w = 2^n w' + w''$ and $4t + w'v = 2^n t' + t''$, where $0 \leq w'', t'' < 2^n$ and $0 \leq t' \leq 6$; then set $t \leftarrow t''$, $w \leftarrow w''$, $s \leftarrow 2s$, $r \leftarrow 4r + t' - s$, $k \leftarrow k - 1$. If $r \leq 0$, set $s \leftarrow s - 1$ and $r \leftarrow r + 2s$; otherwise, if $r > 2s$, set $r \leftarrow r - 2s$ and $s \leftarrow s + 1$ (this correction might need to be done twice). Repeat until $k = 0$. Then $uv = r + s^2 - s$, since w is always a multiple of 2^{2n-2k}. Consequently $r = 0$ if and only if $uv = 0$; otherwise the answer is s, because $uv - s \leq s^2 < uv + s$.

39. Let $S_j = \sum_{k \geq 0} 16^{-k}/(8k+j)$. We want to know whether or not $2^{n-1}\pi \bmod 1 < \frac{1}{2}$. Since $\pi = 4S_1 - 2S_4 - S_5 - S_6$, it suffices to have good estimates of $2^{n-1}S_j \bmod 1$. Now $2^{n-1}S_j$ is congruent (modulo 1) to $\sum_{0 \leq k < n/4} a_{njk}/(8k+j) + \sum_{k \geq n/4} 2^{n-1-4k}/(8k+j)$, where $a_{njk} = 2^{n-1-4k} \bmod (8k+j)$. Each term in the first sum can be approximated within 2^{-m} by computing a_{njk} in $O(\log n)$ operations (Section 4.6.3) and then finding the scaled quotient $\lfloor 2^m a_{njk}/(8k+j) \rfloor$. The second sum can be approximated within 2^{-m} by computing 2^m times its first $m/4$ terms. If $m \approx 2 \lg n$, the range of uncertainty will be $\approx 1/n$, and this will almost always be accurate enough. [*Math. Comp.* **66** (1997), 903–913.]

Notes: Let $\zeta = e^{\pi i/4} = (1 + i)/\sqrt{2}$ be an 8th root of unity, and consider the values $l_j = \ln(1 - \zeta^j/\sqrt{2})$. Then $l_0 = \ln(1 - 1/\sqrt{2})$, $l_1 = \bar{l}_7 = \frac{1}{2}\ln\frac{1}{2} - i\arctan 1$, $l_2 = \bar{l}_6 = \frac{1}{2}\ln\frac{3}{2} - i\arctan(1/\sqrt{2})$, $l_3 = \bar{l}_5 = \frac{1}{2}\ln\frac{5}{2} - i\arctan(1/3)$, $l_4 = \ln(1 + 1/\sqrt{2})$. Also $-S_j/2^{j/2} = \frac{1}{8}(l_0 + \zeta^{-j}l_1 + \cdots + \zeta^{-7j}l_7)$ for $1 \leq j \leq 8$ by 1.2.9–(13). Therefore $4S_1 - 2S_4 - S_5 - S_6 = 2l_0 - (2 - 2i)2l_1 + 2l_4 + (2 + 2i)l_7 = \pi$. Other identities of interest are:

$$\ln 2 = S_2 + \tfrac{1}{2}S_4 + \tfrac{1}{4}S_6 + \tfrac{1}{8}S_8;$$

$$\ln 3 = 2S_2 + \tfrac{1}{2}S_6;$$

$$\ln 5 = 2S_2 + 2S_4 + \tfrac{1}{2}S_6;$$

$$\sqrt{2}\,\ln(\sqrt{2} + 1) = S_1 + \tfrac{1}{2}S_3 + \tfrac{1}{4}S_5 + \tfrac{1}{8}S_7;$$

$$\sqrt{2}\,\arctan(1/\sqrt{2}) = S_1 - \tfrac{1}{2}S_3 + \tfrac{1}{4}S_5 - \tfrac{1}{8}S_7;$$

$$\arctan(1/3) = S_1 - S_2 - \tfrac{1}{2}S_4 - \tfrac{1}{4}S_5;$$

$$0 = 8S_1 - 8S_2 - 4S_3 - 8S_4 - 2S_5 - 2S_6 + S_7.$$

In general we have

$$\sum_{k \geq 0} \frac{z^{8k+1}}{8k+1} = A + B + C + D, \qquad \sum_{k \geq 0} \frac{z^{8k+5}}{8k+5} = A - B + C - D,$$

$$\sum_{k \geq 0} \frac{z^{8k+3}}{8k+3} = A - B - C + D, \qquad \sum_{k \geq 0} \frac{z^{8k+7}}{8k+7} = A + B - C - D,$$

where

$$A = \frac{1}{8}\ln\frac{1+z}{1-z}, \qquad B = \frac{1}{2^{7/2}}\ln\frac{1 + \sqrt{2}z + z^2}{1 - \sqrt{2}z + z^2},$$

$$C = \frac{1}{4}\arctan z, \qquad D = \frac{1}{2^{5/2}}\arctan\frac{\sqrt{2}z}{1 - z^2};$$

and

$$\sum_{k\geq 0}\frac{z^{mk+a}}{mk+a}=-\frac{1}{m}\Big(\ln(1-z)+(-1)^a[m\text{ even}]\ln(1+z)+f_{am}(z)\Big),$$

$$f_{am}(z)=\sum_{k=1}^{\lfloor(m-1)/2\rfloor}\Big(\cos\frac{2\pi ka}{m}\ln\Big(1-2z\cos\frac{2\pi k}{m}+z^2\Big)$$

$$-2\sin\frac{2\pi ka}{m}\arctan\frac{z\sin(2\pi k/m)}{1-z\cos(2\pi k/m)}\Big).$$

40. To get the most significant $n/2$ places, we need about $\sum_{k=1}^{n/2}\approx\frac18 n^2$ basic operations (see exercise 15). And we can get the least significant $n/2$ places by using a b-adic method when b is a power of 2 (see exercise 4.1–31): The problem is easily reduced to the case where v is odd. Let $u=(\ldots u_2 u_1 u_0)_b$, $v=(\ldots v_2 v_1 v_0)_b$, and $w=(\ldots w_2 w_1 w_0)_b$, where we want to solve $u=vw$ (modulo $b^{n/2}$). Compute v' such that $v'v\bmod b=1$ (see exercise 4.5.2–17). Then $w_0=v'u_0\bmod b$, and we can compute $u'=u-w_0v$, $w_1=v'u_0'\bmod b$, etc. The rightmost $n/2$ places are found after about $\frac18 n^2$ basic operations. So the total is $\frac14 n^2+O(n)$, while Algorithm D needs about $n^2+O(n)$. A pure right-to-left method for all n digits would require $\frac12 n^2+O(n)$. [See A. Schönhage and E. Vetter, *Lecture Notes in Comp. Sci.* **855** (1994), 448–459; W. Krandick and T. Jebelean, *J. Symbolic Computation* **21** (1996), 441–455.]

41. (a) If $m=0$, let $v=u$. Otherwise subtract xw from $(u_{m+n-1}\ldots u_1 u_0)_b$, where $x=u_0 w'\bmod b$; this zeroes out the units digit, so we have effectively reduced m by 1. (This operation is closely related to the computation of u/w in b-adic arithmetic, since $u/w=q+b^m v/w$ for some integer q; see exercise 4.1–31. It wins over ordinary division because we never have to correct a trial divisor. To compute w' when b is a power of 2, notice that if $w_0 w'\equiv 1$ (modulo 2^e) then $w_0 w''\equiv 1$ (modulo 2^{2e}) when $w''=(2-w_0 w')w'$, by the 2-adic analog of "Newton's method.")

(b) Apply (a) to the product uv. Memory space is conserved if we interlace multiplication and modulation as follows: Set $k\leftarrow 0$, $t\leftarrow 0$. Then while $k<n$, preserve the invariant relation $b^k t\equiv(u_{k-1}\ldots u_0)v$ (modulo w) by setting $t\leftarrow t+u_k v$, $t\leftarrow(t-xw)/b$, $k\leftarrow k+1$, where $x=t_0 w'\bmod b$ is chosen to make $t-xw$ a multiple of b. This solution assumes that t, u, and v have a signed magnitude representation; we can work also with nonnegative numbers $<2w$ or with complement notations, as discussed by Shand and Vuillemin and by Kornerup, [*IEEE Symp. Computer Arithmetic* **11** (1993), 252–259, 277–283]. If n is large, the techniques of Section 4.3.3 speed up the multiplication.

(c) Represent all numbers congruent to u (modulo w) by an internal value $r(u)$ where $r(u)\equiv b^n u$. Then addition and subtraction are handled as usual, while multiplication is $r(uv)=\text{bmult}(r(u),r(v))$, where bmult is the operation of (b). At the beginning of the computation, replace each operand u by $r(u)=\text{bmult}(u,a)$, using the precomputed constant $a=b^{2n}\bmod w$. At the end, replace each $r(u)$ by $u=\text{bmult}(r(u),1)$. [In the application to RSA encryption, Section 4.5.4, we could redefine the coding scheme so that precomputation and postcomputation are unnecessary.]

42. An interesting analysis by J. M. Holte in *AMM* **104** (1997), 138–149, establishes the exact formula

$$P_{nk}=\frac{1}{m!}\sum_j\genfrac{[}{]}{0pt}{}{m}{m-j}b^{-jn}\sum_{r=0}^{k}\binom{m+1}{r}(k+1-r)^{m-j}.$$

The inner sum is $\sum_{r=0}^{k}(-1)^r\binom{m+1}{r}(k+1-r)^m = \left\langle\begin{smallmatrix}m\\k\end{smallmatrix}\right\rangle$ when $j = 0$. (Exercise 5.1.3–25 explains why Eulerian numbers arise in this connection.)

43. By exercise 1.2.4–35 we have $w = \lfloor W/2^{16}\rfloor$, where $W = (2^8+1)t = (2^8+1)(uv+2^7)$. Therefore if $uv/255 > c+\frac{1}{2}$, we have $c < 2^8$, hence $w \geq \lfloor(2^{16}(c+1)+2^8-c)/2^{16}\rfloor \geq c+1$; if $uv/255 < c+\frac{1}{2}$, we have $w \leq \lfloor(2^{16}(c+1)-c-1)/2^{16}\rfloor = c$. [See J. F. Blinn, *IEEE Computer Graphics and Applic.* **14**, 6 (November 1994), 78–82.]

SECTION 4.3.2

1. The solution is unique since $7\cdot11\cdot13 = 1001$. The constructive proof of Theorem C tells us that the answer is $\big((11\cdot13)^6+6\cdot(7\cdot13)^{10}+5\cdot(7\cdot11)^{12}\big)$ mod 1001. But this answer is perhaps not explicit enough! By (24) we have $v_1 = 1$, $v_2 = (6-1)\cdot 8$ mod $11 = 7$, $v_3 = \big((5-1)\cdot 2 - 7\big)\cdot 6$ mod $13 = 6$, so $u = 6\cdot7\cdot11 + 7\cdot7 + 1 = 512$.

2. No. There is at most one such u; the additional condition $u_1 \equiv \cdots \equiv u_r$ (modulo 1) is necessary and sufficient, and it follows that such a generalization is not very interesting.

3. $u \equiv u_i$ (modulo m_i) implies that $u \equiv u_i$ (modulo $\gcd(m_i, m_j)$), so the condition $u_i \equiv u_j$ (modulo $\gcd(m_i, m_j)$) must surely hold if there is a solution. Furthermore if $u \equiv v$ (modulo m_j) for all j, then $u - v$ is a multiple of $\text{lcm}(m_1,\ldots,m_r) = m$; hence there is at most one solution.

The proof can now be completed in a nonconstructive manner by counting the number of different r-tuples $(u_1,\ldots,u_r)$ satisfying the conditions $0 \leq u_j < m_j$ and $u_i \equiv u_j$ (modulo $\gcd(m_i, m_j)$). If this number is m, there must be a solution since $(u \bmod m_1,\ldots,u \bmod m_r)$ takes on m distinct values as u goes from a to $a + m - 1$. Assume that $u_1, \ldots, u_{r-1}$ have been chosen satisfying the given conditions; we must now pick $u_r \equiv u_j$ (modulo $\gcd(m_j, m_r)$) for $1 \leq j < r$, and by the generalized Chinese remainder theorem for $r - 1$ elements there are

$$m_r/\text{lcm}\big(\gcd(m_1, m_r),\ldots,\gcd(m_{r-1}, m_r)\big) = m_r/\gcd\big(\text{lcm}(m_1,\ldots,m_{r-1}),m_r\big)$$
$$= \text{lcm}(m_1,\ldots,m_r)/\text{lcm}(m_1,\ldots,m_{r-1})$$

ways to do this. [This proof is based on identities (10), (11), (12), and (14) of Section 4.5.2.]

A constructive proof [A. S. Fraenkel, *Proc. Amer. Math. Soc.* **14** (1963), 790–791] generalizing (25) can be given as follows. Let $M_j = \text{lcm}(m_1,\ldots,m_j)$; we wish to find $u = v_r M_{r-1} + \cdots + v_2 M_1 + v_1$, where $0 \leq v_j < M_j/M_{j-1}$. Assume that $v_1, \ldots, v_{j-1}$ have already been determined; then we must solve the congruence

$$v_j M_{j-1} + v_{j-1}M_{j-2} + \cdots + v_1 \equiv u_j \quad (\text{modulo } m_j).$$

Here $v_{j-1}M_{j-2} + \cdots + v_1 \equiv u_i \equiv u_j$ (modulo $\gcd(m_i, m_j)$) for $i < j$ by hypothesis, so $c = u_j - (v_{j-1}M_{j-2} + \cdots + v_1)$ is a multiple of

$$\text{lcm}\big(\gcd(m_1, m_j),\ldots,\gcd(m_{j-1}, m_j)\big) = \gcd(M_{j-1}, m_j) = d_j.$$

We therefore must solve $v_j M_{j-1} \equiv c$ (modulo m_j). By Euclid's algorithm there is a number c_j such that $c_j M_{j-1} \equiv d_j$ (modulo m_j); hence we may take

$$v_j = (c_j\, c)/d_j \bmod (m_j/d_j).$$

Notice that, as in the nonconstructive proof, we have $m_j/d_j = M_j/M_{j-1}$.

4. (After $m_4 = 91 = 7 \cdot 13$, we have used up all products of two or more odd primes that can be less than 100, so m_5, ... must all be prime.) We find

$$
\begin{array}{lllll}
m_7 = 79, & m_8 = 73, & m_9 = 71, & m_{10} = 67, & m_{11} = 61, \\
m_{12} = 59, & m_{13} = 53, & m_{14} = 47, & m_{15} = 43, & m_{16} = 41, \\
m_{17} = 37, & m_{18} = 31, & m_{19} = 29, & m_{20} = 23, & m_{21} = 17,
\end{array}
$$

and then we are stuck ($m_{22} = 1$ does no good).

5. (a) No. The obvious upper bound,

$$
3^4 5^2 7^2 11^1 \ldots = \prod_{\substack{p \text{ odd} \\ p \text{ prime}}} p^{\lfloor \log_p 100 \rfloor},
$$

is attained if we choose $m_1 = 3^4$, $m_2 = 5^2$, etc. (It is more difficult, however, to maximize $m_1 \ldots m_r$ when r is fixed, or to maximize $e_1 + \cdots + e_r$ with relatively prime e_j as we would attempt to do when using moduli $2^{e_j} - 1$.) (b) Replacing 100 by 256 and allowing even moduli gives $2^8 3^5 5^3 \ldots 251^1 \approx 1.67 \cdot 10^{109}$.

6. (a) If $e = f + kg$, then $2^e = 2^f (2^g)^k \equiv 2^f \cdot 1^k$ (modulo $2^g - 1$). So if $2^e \equiv 2^f$ (modulo $2^g - 1$), we have $2^{e \bmod g} \equiv 2^{f \bmod g}$ (modulo $2^g - 1$); and since the latter quantities lie between zero and $2^g - 1$ we must have $e \bmod g = f \bmod g$. (b) By part (a), $(1 + 2^d + \cdots + 2^{(c-1)d}) \cdot (2^e - 1) \equiv (1 + 2^d + \cdots + 2^{(c-1)d}) \cdot (2^d - 1) = 2^{cd} - 1 \equiv 2^{ce} - 1 \equiv 2^1 - 1 = 1$ (modulo $2^f - 1$).

7. We have $v_j m_{j-1} \ldots m_1 \equiv u_j - (v_{j-1} m_{j-2} \ldots m_1 + \cdots + v_1)$ and $C_j m_{j-1} \ldots m_1 \equiv 1$ (modulo m_j) by (23), (25), and (26); see P. A. Pritchard, *CACM* **27** (1984), 57.

This method of rewriting the formulas uses the same number of arithmetic operations and fewer constants; but the number of constants is fewer only if we order the moduli so that $m_1 < m_2 < \cdots < m_r$, otherwise we would need a table of $m_i \bmod m_j$. This ordering of the moduli might seem to require more computation than if we made m_1 the largest, m_2 the next largest, etc., since there are many more operations to be done modulo m_r than modulo m_1; but since v_j can be as large as $m_j - 1$, we are better off with $m_1 < m_2 < \cdots < m_r$ in (24) also. So this idea appears to be preferable to the formulas in the text, although Section 4.3.3B shows that the formulas in the text are advantageous when the moduli have the form (14).

8. Modulo m_j: $m_{j-1} \ldots m_1 v_j \equiv m_{j-1} \ldots m_1 (\ldots ((u_j - v_1)c_{1j} - v_2)c_{2j} - \cdots - v_{j-1}) \times c_{(j-1)j} \equiv m_{j-2} \ldots m_1 (\ldots (u_j - v_1)c_{1j} - \cdots - v_{j-2})c_{(j-2)j} - v_{j-1} m_{j-2} \ldots m_1 \equiv \cdots \equiv u_j - v_1 - v_2 m_1 - \cdots - v_{j-1} m_{j-2} \ldots m_1$.

9. $u_r \leftarrow ((\ldots (v_r m_{r-1} + v_{r-1}) m_{r-2} + \cdots) m_1 + v_1) \bmod m_r$, ...,

$$
u_2 \leftarrow (v_2 m_1 + v_1) \bmod m_2, \quad u_1 \leftarrow v_1 \bmod m_1.
$$

(The computation should be done in this order, if we want to let u_j and v_j share the same memory locations, as they can in (24).)

10. If we redefine the "mod" operator so that it produces residues in the symmetrical range, the basic formulas (2), (3), (4) for arithmetic and (24), (25) for conversion remain the same, and the number u in (25) lies in the desired range (10). (Here (25) is a *balanced mixed-radix* notation, generalizing balanced ternary notation.) The comparison of two numbers may still be done from left to right, in the simple manner described in the text. Furthermore, it is possible to retain the value u_j in a single computer word, if we have signed magnitude representation within the computer, even if m_j is almost twice the word size. But the arithmetic operations analogous to (11) and (12) are more difficult, so it appears that this idea would result in slightly slower operation on most computers.

11. Multiply by $\frac{1}{2}(m+1) = \left(\frac{1}{2}(m_1+1), \ldots, \frac{1}{2}(m_r+1)\right)$. Note that $2t \cdot \frac{m+1}{2} \equiv t$ (modulo m). In general if v is relatively prime to m, then we can find (by Euclid's algorithm) a number $v' = (v'_1, \ldots, v'_r)$ such that $vv' \equiv 1$ (modulo m); and then if u is known to be a multiple of v we have $u/v = uv'$, where the latter is computed with modular multiplication. When v is not relatively prime to m, division is much harder.

12. Replace m_j by m in (11). [Another way to test for overflow, if m is odd, is to maintain extra bits $u_0 = u \bmod 2$ and $v_0 = v \bmod 2$. Then overflow has occurred if and only if $u_0 + v_0 \not\equiv w_1 + \cdots + w_r$ (modulo 2), where $(w_1, \ldots, w_r)$ are the mixed-radix digits corresponding to $u + v$.]

13. (a) $x^2 - x = (x-1)x \equiv 0$ (modulo 10^n) is equivalent to $(x-1)x \equiv 0$ (modulo p^n) for $p = 2$ and 5. Either x or $x-1$ must be a multiple of p, and then the other is relatively prime to p^n; so either x or $x-1$ must be a multiple of p^n. If $x \bmod 2^n = x \bmod 5^n = 0$ or 1, we must have $x \bmod 10^n = 0$ or 1; hence automorphs have $x \bmod 2^n \neq x \bmod 5^n$. (b) If $x = qp^n + r$, where $r = 0$ or 1, then $r \equiv r^2 \equiv r^3$, so $3x^2 - 2x^3 \equiv (6qp^nr + 3r) - (6qp^nr + 2r) \equiv r$ (modulo p^{2n}). (c) Let c' be $(3(cx)^2 - 2(cx)^3)/x^2 = 3c^2 - 2c^3x$.

Note: Since the last k digits of an n-digit automorph form a k-digit automorph, it makes sense to speak of the two ∞-digit automorphs, x and $1 - x$, which are 10-adic numbers (see exercise 4.1–31). The set of 10-adic numbers is equivalent under modular arithmetic to the set of ordered pairs (u_1, u_2), where u_1 is a 2-adic number and u_2 is a 5-adic number.

14. Find the cyclic convolution $(z_0, z_1, \ldots, z_{n-1})$ of floating point approximations to $(a_0u_0, a_1u_1, \ldots, a_{n-1}u_{n-1})$ and $(a_0v_0, a_1v_1, \ldots, a_{n-1}v_{n-1})$, where the constants $a_k = 2^{-(kq \bmod n)/n}$ have been precomputed. The identities $u = \sum_{k=0}^{n-1} u_k a_k 2^{kq/n}$ and $v = \sum_{k=0}^{n-1} v_k a_k 2^{kq/n}$ now imply that $w = \sum_{k=0}^{n-1} t_k a_k 2^{kq/n}$ where $t_k \approx z_k/a_k$. If sufficient accuracy has been maintained, each t_k will be very close to an integer. The representation of w can readily be found from those integers. [R. Crandall and B. Fagin, *Math. Comp.* **62** (1994), 305–324. For improved error bounds, and extensions to moduli of the form $k \cdot 2^n \pm 1$, see Colin Percival, *Math. Comp.* **72** (2002), 387–395.]

SECTION 4.3.3

1.

12×23 :	34×41 :	22×18 :	1234×2341 :
02	12	02	0276
02	12	02	0276
-01	$+03$	$+00$	-0396
06	04	16	1394
06	04	16	1394
0276	1394	0396	2888794

2. $\sqrt{Q + \lfloor\sqrt{Q}\rfloor} \le \sqrt{Q + \sqrt{Q}} < \sqrt{Q + 2\sqrt{Q} + 1} = \sqrt{Q} + 1$, so $\lfloor\sqrt{Q+R}\rfloor \le \lfloor\sqrt{Q}\rfloor + 1$.

3. The result is true when $k \le 2$, so assume that $k > 2$. Let $q_k = 2^{Q_k}$, $r_k = 2^{R_k}$, so that $R_k = \lfloor\sqrt{Q_k}\rfloor$ and $Q_k = Q_{k-1} + R_{k-1}$. We must show that $1 + (R_k+1)2^{R_k} \le 2^{Q_{k-1}}$; this inequality isn't close at all. One way is to observe that $1 + (R_k+1)2^{R_k} \le 1 + 2^{2R_k}$ and $2R_k < Q_{k-1}$ when $k > 2$. (The fact that $2R_k < Q_{k-1}$ is readily proved by induction since $R_{k+1} - R_k \le 1$ and $Q_k - Q_{k-1} \ge 2$.)

4. For $j = 1, \ldots, r$, calculate $U_e(j^2)$, $jU_o(j^2)$, $V_e(j^2)$, $jV_o(j^2)$; and by recursively calling the multiplication algorithm, calculate

$$W(j) = (U_e(j^2) + jU_o(j^2))(V_e(j^2) + jV_o(j^2)),$$
$$W(-j) = (U_e(j^2) - jU_o(j^2))(V_e(j^2) - jV_o(j^2)).$$

Then we have $W_e(j^2) = \frac{1}{2}(W(j) + W(-j))$, $W_o(j^2) = \frac{1}{2}(W(j) - W(-j))$. Also calculate $W_e(0) = U(0)V(0)$. Now construct difference tables for W_e and W_o, which are polynomials whose respective degrees are r and $r - 1$.

This method reduces the size of the numbers being handled, and reduces the number of additions and multiplications. Its only disadvantage is a longer program (since the control is somewhat more complex, and some of the calculations must be done with signed numbers).

Another possibility would perhaps be to evaluate W_e and W_o at 1^2, 2^2, 4^2, $\ldots$, $(2^r)^2$; although the numbers involved are larger, the calculations are faster, since all multiplications are replaced by shifting and all divisions are by binary numbers of the form $2^j(2^k - 1)$. (Simple procedures are available for dividing by such numbers.)

5. Start the q and r sequences out with q_0 and q_1 large enough so that the inequality in exercise 3 is valid. Then we will find in the formulas like those preceding Theorem B that we have $\eta_1 \to 0$ and $\eta_2 = (1 + 1/(2r_k))2^{1+\sqrt{2Q_k}-\sqrt{2Q_{k+1}}}(Q_k/Q_{k+1})$. The factor $Q_k/Q_{k+1} \to 1$ as $k \to \infty$, so we can ignore it if we want to show that $\eta_2 < 1 - \epsilon$ for all large k. Now $\sqrt{2Q_{k+1}} = \sqrt{2Q_k + 2\lceil\sqrt{2Q_k}\rceil + 2} \geq \sqrt{(2Q_k + 2\sqrt{2Q_k} + 1) + 1} \geq \sqrt{2Q_k} + 1 + 1/(3R_k)$. Hence $\eta_2 \leq (1 + 1/(2r_k))2^{-1/(3R_k)}$, and $\lg \eta_2 < 0$ for large enough k.

Note: Algorithm T can also be modified to define a sequence $q_0, q_1, \ldots$ of a similar type that is based on n, so that $n \approx q_k + q_{k+1}$ after step T1. This modification leads to the estimate (21).

6. Any common divisor of $6q+d_1$ and $6q+d_2$ must also divide their difference $d_2 - d_1$. The $\binom{6}{2}$ differences are 2, 3, 4, 6, 8, 1, 2, 4, 6, 1, 3, 5, 2, 4, 2, so we must only show that at most one of the given numbers is divisible by each of the primes 2, 3, 5. Clearly only $6q + 2$ is even, and only $6q + 3$ is a multiple of 3; and there is at most one multiple of 5, since $q_k \not\equiv 3 \pmod 5$.

7. Let $p_{k-1} < n \leq p_k$. We have $t_k \leq 6t_{k-1} + ck3^k$ for some constant c; so $t_k/6^k \leq t_{k-1}/6^{k-1} + ck/2^k \leq t_0 + c\sum_{j\geq 1} j/2^j = M$. Thus $t_k \leq M \cdot 6^k = O(p_k^{\log_3 6})$.

8. False. To see the fallacy, try it with $k = 2$.

9. $\tilde{u}_s = \hat{u}_{(qs) \bmod K}$. In particular, if $q = -1$ we get $\hat{u}_{(-r) \bmod K}$, which avoids data-flipping when computing inverse transforms.

10. $A^{[j]}(s_{k-1}, \ldots, s_{k-j}, t_{k-j-1}, \ldots, t_0)$ can be written

$$\sum_{0 \leq t_{k-1}, \ldots, t_{k-j} \leq 1} \omega^{2^{k-j}(s_{k-j}\ldots s_{k-1})_2 \cdot (t_{k-1}\ldots t_{k-j})_2} \left(\sum_{0 \leq p < K} \omega^{tp} u_p\right)\left(\sum_{0 \leq q < K} \omega^{tq} v_q\right),$$

and this is $\sum_{p,q} u_p v_q S(p, q)$, where $|S(p, q)| = 0$ or 2^j. We have $|S(p, q)| = 2^j$ for exactly $2^{2k}/2^j$ values of p and q.

11. An automaton cannot have $z_2 = 1$ until it has $c \geq 2$, and this occurs first for M_j at time $3j - 1$. It follows that M_j cannot have $z_2 z_1 z_0 \neq 000$ until time $3(j - 1)$. Furthermore, if M_j has $z_0 \neq 0$ at time t, we cannot change this to $z_0 = 0$ without affecting the output; but the output cannot be affected by this value of z_0 until at least time $t + j - 1$, so we must have $t + j - 1 \leq 2n$. Since the first argument we gave proves that $3(j - 1) \leq t$, we must have $4(j - 1) \leq 2n$, that is, $j - 1 \leq n/2$, i.e., $j \leq \lfloor n/2 \rfloor + 1$. This is the best possible bound, since the inputs $u = v = 2^n - 1$ require the use of M_j for all $j \leq \lfloor n/2 \rfloor + 1$. (For example, Table 2 shows that M_2 is needed to multiply two-bit numbers, at time 3.)

12. We can "sweep through" K lists of MIX-like instructions, executing the first instruction on each list, in $O(K + (N \log N)^2)$ steps as follows: (i) A radix list sort (Section 5.2.5) will group together all identical instructions, in time $O(K + N)$. (ii) Each set of j identical instructions can be performed in $O(\log N)^2 + O(j)$ steps, and there are $O(N^2)$ sets. A bounded number of sweeps will finish all the lists. The remaining details are straightforward; for example, arithmetic operations can be simulated by converting p and q to binary. [*SICOMP* **9** (1980), 490–508.]

13. If it takes $T(n)$ steps to multiply n-bit numbers, we can accomplish m-bit times n-bit multiplication by breaking the n-bit number into $\lceil n/m \rceil$ m-bit groups, using $\lceil n/m \rceil T(m) + O(n + m)$ operations. The results cited in the text therefore give an estimated running time of $O(n \log m \log \log m)$ on Turing machines, or $O(n \log m)$ on machines with random access to words of bounded size, or $O(n)$ on pointer machines.

15. The best upper bound known is $O(n(\log n)^2 \log \log n)$, due to M. J. Fischer and L. J. Stockmeyer [*J. Comp. and Syst. Sci.* **9** (1974), 317–331]; their construction works on multitape Turing machines, and is $O(n \log n)$ on pointer machines. The best lower bound known is of order $n \log n / \log \log n$, due to M. S. Paterson, M. J. Fischer, and A. R. Meyer [*SIAM/AMS Proceedings* **7** (1974), 97–111]; this applies to multitape Turing machines but not to pointer machines.

16. Let 2^k be the smallest power of 2 that exceeds $2K$. Set $a_t \leftarrow \omega^{-t^2/2} u_t$ and $b_t \leftarrow \omega^{(2K-2-t)^2/2}$, where $u_t = 0$ for $t \geq K$. We want to evaluate the convolutions $c_r = \sum_{j=0}^{r} a_j b_{r-j}$ for $r = 2K - 2 - s$, when $0 \leq s < K$. The convolutions can be found by using three fast Fourier transformations of order 2^k, as in the text's multiplication procedure. [Note that this technique, sometimes called the "chirp transform," works for any complex number ω, not necessarily a root of unity. See L. I. Bluestein, *Northeast Electronics Res. and Eng. Meeting Record* **10** (1968), 218–219; D. H. Bailey and P. N. Swarztrauber, *SIAM Review* **33** (1991), 389–404.]

17. The quantity $D_n = K_{n+1} - K_n$ satisfies $D_1 = 2$, $D_{2n} = 2D_n$, and $D_{2n+1} = D_n$; hence $D_n = 2^{e_1 - t + 2}$ when n has the stated form. It follows that $K_n = 3^{e_1} + \sum_{l=2}^{t} 3^{e_l} 2^{e_1 - e_l - l + 3}$, by induction on n.

Incidentally, K_n is odd, and we can multiply an n-place integer by an $(n + 1)$-place integer with $(K_n + K_{n+1})/2$ 1-place multiplications. The generating function $K(z) = \sum_{n \geq 1} K_n z^n$ satisfies $zK(z) + z^2 = K(z^2)(z + 1)(z + 2)$; hence $K(-1) = 1$ and $K(1) = \frac{1}{5}$.

18. The following scheme uses $3N + S_N$ places of working storage, where $S_1 = 0$, $S_{2n} = S_n$, and $S_{2n-1} = S_n + 1$, hence $S_n = e_1 - e_t - t + 2 - [t = 1]$ in the notation of the previous exercise. Let $N = 2n - \epsilon$, where ϵ is 0 or 1, and assume that $N > 1$. Given N-place numbers $u = 2^n U_1 + U_0$ and $v = 2^n V_1 + V_0$, we first form $|U_0 - U_1|$ and $|V_0 - V_1|$ in two n-place areas starting at positions 0 and n of the $(3N + S_N)$-place working area. Then we place their product into the working area starting at position $3n + S_n$. The next step is to form the $2(n - \epsilon)$-place product $U_1 V_1$, starting in position 0; using that product, we change the $3n - 2\epsilon$ places starting at position $3n + S_n$ to the value of

$U_1V_1 - (U_0 - U_1)(V_0 - V_1) + 2^nU_1V_1$. (Notice that $3n - 2\epsilon + 3n + S_n = 3N + S_N$.) Finally, we form the $2n$-place product U_0V_0 starting at position 0, and add it to the partial result starting at positions $2n + S_n$ and $3n + S_n$. We must also move the $2N$-place answer to its final position by shifting it down $2n + S_n$ positions.

The final move could be avoided by a trickier variation that cyclically rotates its output by a given amount within a designated working area. If the $2N$-place product is not allowed to be adjacent to the auxiliary working space, we need about N more places of memory (that is, a total of about $6N$ instead of $5N$ places, for the input, output, and temporary storage); see R. Maeder, *Lecture Notes in Comp. Sci.* **722** (1993), 59–65.

19. Let $m = s^2 + r$ where $-s < r \le s$. We can use (2) with $U_1 = \lfloor u/s \rfloor$, $U_0 = u \bmod s$, $V_1 = \lfloor v/s \rfloor$, $V_0 = v \bmod s$, and with s playing the role of 2^n. If we know the signs of $U_1 - U_0$ and $V_1 - V_0$ we know how to compute the product $|U_1 - U_0||V_1 - V_0|$, which is $< m$, and whether to add or subtract it. It remains to multiply by s and by $s^2 \equiv -r$. Each of these can be done with four multiplication/divisions, using exercise 3.2.1.1–9, but only seven are needed because one of the multiplications needed to compute $sx \bmod m$ is by r or $r+s$. Thus 14 multiplication/divisions are sufficient (or 12, in case $u = v$ or u is constant). Without the ability to compare operands, we can still do the job with one more multiplication, by computing U_0V_1 and U_1V_0 separately.

SECTION 4.4

1. We compute $(\ldots (a_mb_{m-1} + a_{m-1})b_{m-2} + \cdots + a_1)b_0 + a_0$ by adding and multiplying in the B_J system.

	T.	$= 20$(cwt.	$= 8$(st.	$= 14$(lb.	$= 16$ oz.)))
Start with zero	0	0	0	0	0
Add 3	0	0	0	0	3
Multiply by 24	0	0	0	4	8
Add 9	0	0	0	5	1
Multiply by 60	0	2	5	9	12
Add 12	0	2	5	10	8
Multiply by 60	8	3	1	0	0
Add 37	8	3	1	2	5

(Addition and multiplication by a constant in a mixed-radix system are readily done using a simple generalization of the usual carry rule; see exercise 4.3.1–9.)

2. We compute $\lfloor u/B_0 \rfloor$, $\lfloor \lfloor u/B_0 \rfloor / B_1 \rfloor$, etc., and the remainders are A_0, A_1, etc. The division is done in the b_j system.

	d.	$= 24$(h.	$= 60$(m.	$= 60$ s.))	
Start with u	3	9	12	37	
Divide by 16	0	5	4	32	Remainder $= 5$
Divide by 14	0	0	21	45	Remainder $= 2$
Divide by 8	0	0	2	43	Remainder $= 1$
Divide by 20	0	0	0	8	Remainder $= 3$
Divide by ∞	0	0	0	0	Remainder $= 8$

Answer: 8 T. 3 cwt. 1 st. 2 lb. 5 oz.

3. The following procedure due to G. L. Steele Jr. and Jon L White generalizes Taranto's algorithm for $B = 2$ originally published in *CACM* **2**, 7 (July 1959), 27.

A1. [Initialize.] Set $M \leftarrow 0$, $U_0 \leftarrow 0$.

A2. [Done?] If $u < \epsilon$ or $u > 1 - \epsilon$, go to step A4. (Otherwise no M-place fraction will satisfy the given conditions.)

A3. [Transform.] Set $M \leftarrow M + 1$, $U_{-M} \leftarrow \lfloor Bu \rfloor$, $u \leftarrow Bu \bmod 1$, $\epsilon \leftarrow B\epsilon$, and return to A2. (This transformation returns us to essentially the same state we were in before; the remaining problem is to convert u to U with fewest radix-B places so that $|U - u| < \epsilon$. Note, however, that ϵ may now be ≥ 1; in this case we could go immediately to step A4 instead of storing the new value of ϵ.)

A4. [Round.] If $u \geq \frac{1}{2}$, increase U_{-M} by 1. (If $u = \frac{1}{2}$ exactly, another rounding rule such as "increase U_{-M} by 1 only when it is odd" might be preferred; see Section 4.2.2.) ∎

Step A4 will never increase U_{-M} from $B - 1$ to B; for if $U_{-M} = B - 1$ we must have $M > 0$, but no $(M - 1)$-place fraction was sufficiently accurate. Steele and White go on to consider floating point conversions in their paper [*SIGPLAN Notices* **25**, 6 (June 1990), 112–126]. See also D. E. Knuth in *Beauty is Our Business*, edited by W. H. J. Feijen et al. (New York: Springer, 1990), 233–242.

4. (a) $1/2^k = 5^k/10^k$. (b) Every prime divisor of b divides B.

5. If and only if $10^n - 1 \leq c < w$; see (3).

7. $\alpha u \leq ux \leq \alpha u + u/w \leq \alpha u + 1$, hence $\lfloor \alpha u \rfloor \leq \lfloor ux \rfloor \leq \lfloor \alpha u + 1 \rfloor$. Furthermore, in the special case cited we have $ux < \alpha u + \alpha$ and $\lfloor \alpha u \rfloor = \lfloor \alpha u + \alpha - \epsilon \rfloor$ for $0 < \epsilon \leq \alpha$.

8.

```
      ENT1 0              LDA  TEMP      (Can occur only on
      LDA  U              DECA 1             the first iteration,
 1H   MUL  =1//10=        JMP  3B            by exercise 7.)
 3H   STA  TEMP      2H   STA  ANSWER,1 (May be minus zero.)
      MUL  =-10=          LDA  TEMP
      SLAX 5              INC1 1
      ADD  U              JAP  1B              ∎
      JANN 2F
```

9. Let $p_k = 2^{2^{k+2}}$. By induction on k we have $v_k(u) \leq \frac{16}{5}(1 - 1/p_k)(\lfloor u/2 \rfloor + 1)$; hence $\lfloor v_k(u)/16 \rfloor \leq \lfloor \lfloor u/2 \rfloor/5 \rfloor = \lfloor u/10 \rfloor$ for all integers $u \geq 0$. Furthermore, since $v_k(u+1) \geq v_k(u)$, the smallest counterexample to $\lfloor v_k(u)/16 \rfloor = \lfloor u/10 \rfloor$ must occur when u is a multiple of 10.

Now let $u = 10m$ be fixed, and suppose $v_k(u) \bmod p_k = r_k$ so that $v_{k+1}(u) = v_k(u) + (v_k(u) - r_k)/p_k$. The fact that $p_k^2 = p_{k+1}$ implies that there exist integers m_0, m_1, m_2, ... such that $m_0 = m$, $v_k(u) = (p_k - 1)m_k + x_k$, and $m_k = m_{k+1}p_k + x_k - r_k$, where $x_{k+1} = (p_k + 1)x_k - p_k r_k$. Unwinding this recurrence yields

$$v_k(u) = (p_k - 1)m_k + c_k - \sum_{j=0}^{k-1} p_j r_j \prod_{i=j+1}^{k-1} (p_i + 1), \qquad c_k = 3\frac{p_k - 1}{p_0 - 1}.$$

Furthermore $v_k(u) + m_k = v_{k+1}(u) + m_{k+1}$ is independent of k, and it follows that $v_k(u)/16 = m + (3 - m_k)/16$. So the minimal counterexample $u = 10y_k$ is obtained for $0 \leq k \leq 4$ by setting $m_k = 4$ and $r_j = p_j - 1$ in the formula $y_k = \frac{1}{16}(v_k + m_k - c_0)$. In hexadecimal notation, y_k turns out to be the final 2^k digits of 434243414342434.

Since $v_4(10y_4)$ is less than 2^{64}, the same counterexample is also minimal for all $k > 4$. One way to work with larger operands is to modify the method by starting with

$v_0(u) = 6\lfloor u/2 \rfloor + 6$ and letting $c_k = 6(p_k - 1)/(p_0 - 1)$, $m_0 = 2m$. (In effect, we are truncating one bit further to the right than before.) Then $\lfloor v_k(u)/32 \rfloor = \lfloor u/10 \rfloor$ when u is less than $10z_k$, for $1 \le k \le 7$, where $z_k = \frac{1}{32}(v_k + m_k - 6)$ when $m_k = 7$, $r_0 = 14$, and $r_j = p_j - 1$ for $j > 0$. For example, $z_4 = $ `1c342c3424342c34`. [This exercise is based on ideas of R. A. Vowels, *Australian Comp. J.* **24** (1992), 81–85.]

10. (i) Shift right one; (ii) Extract the left bit of each group; (iii) Shift the result of (ii) right two; (iv) Shift the result of (iii) right one, and add it to the result of (iii); (v) Subtract the result of (iv) from the result of (i).

11.
```
      5.7 7 2 1
    - 1 0
    ----------
    4 7.7 2 1
    -   9 4
    ----------
    3 8 3.2 1
    -   7 6 6
    ----------
    3 0 6 6.1
    -   6 1 3 2
    ----------
    2 4 5 2 9     Answer: (24529)₁₀.
```

12. First convert the ternary number to nonary (radix 9) notation, then proceed as in octal-to-decimal conversion but without doubling. Decimal to nonary is similar. In the given example, we have

```
  1.7 6 4 7 2 3
-   1
----------------
1 6.6 4 7 2 3
-   1 6
----------------
1 5 0.4 7 2 3
-   1 5 0
----------------
1 3 5 4.7 2 3
-   1 3 5 4
----------------
1 2 1 9 3.2 3
-   1 2 1 9 3
----------------
1 0 9 7 3 9.3
-   1 0 9 7 3 9
----------------
  9 8 7 6 5 4     Answer: (987654)₁₀.
```

```
      9.8 7 6 5 4
+       9
------------------
1 1 8.7 6 5 4
+     1 1 8
------------------
1 3 1 6.6 5 4
+     1 3 1 6
------------------
1 4 4 8 3.5 4
+     1 4 4 8 3
------------------
1 6 0 4 2 8.4
+     1 6 0 4 2 8
------------------
1 7 6 4 7 2 3     Answer: (1764723)₉.
```

13.
```
BUF     ALF   .⊔⊔⊔⊔          (Radix point on first line)
        ORIG  *+39
START   JOV   OFLO           Ensure that overflow is off.
        ENT2  -40            Set buffer pointer.
8H      ENT3  10             Set loop counter.
1H      ENT1  m              Begin multiplication routine.
        ENTX  0
2H      STX   CARRY
        ...                  (See exercise 4.3.1–13, with
        J1P   2B                 v = 10⁹ and W = U.)
        SLAX  5              rA ← next nine digits.
        CHAR
        STA   BUF+40,2(2:5)  Store next nine digits.
```

```
STX   BUF+41,2
INC2  2                      Increase buffer pointer.
DEC3  1
J3P   1B                     Repeat ten times.
OUT   BUF+20,2(PRINTER)
J2N   8B                     Repeat until both lines are printed.  ▮
```

14. Let $K(n)$ be the number of steps required to convert an n-digit decimal number to binary and at the same time to compute the binary representation of 10^n. Then we have $K(2n) \leq 2K(n) + O(M(n))$. *Proof.* Given the number $U = (u_{2n-1} \ldots u_0)_{10}$, compute $U_1 = (u_{2n-1} \ldots u_n)_{10}$ and $U_0 = (u_{n-1} \ldots u_0)_{10}$ and 10^n, in $2K(n)$ steps, then compute $U = 10^n U_1 + U_0$ and $10^{2n} = 10^n \cdot 10^n$ in $O(M(n))$ steps. It follows that $K(2^n) = O(M(2^n) + 2M(2^{n-1}) + 4M(2^{n-2}) + \cdots) = O(nM(2^n))$.

[Similarly, Schönhage has observed that we can convert a $(2^n \lg 10)$-bit number U from binary to decimal, in $O(nM(2^n))$ steps. First form $V = 10^{2^{n-1}}$ in $O(M(2^{n-1}) + M(2^{n-2}) + \cdots) = O(M(2^n))$ steps, then compute $U_0 = (U \bmod V)$ and $U_1 = \lfloor U/V \rfloor$ in $O(M(2^n))$ further steps, then convert U_0 and U_1.]

17. See W. D. Clinger, *SIGPLAN Notices* **25**, 6 (June 1990), 92–101, and the paper by Steele and White cited in the answer to exercise 3.

18. Let $U = \mathrm{round}_B(u, P)$ and $v = \mathrm{round}_b(U, p)$. We may assume that $u > 0$, so that $U > 0$ and $v > 0$. *Case 1: $v < u$.* Determine e and E such that $b^{e-1} < u \leq b^e$, $B^{E-1} \leq U < B^E$. Then $u \leq U + \frac{1}{2}B^{E-P}$ and $U \leq u - \frac{1}{2}b^{e-p}$; hence $B^{P-1} \leq B^{P-E}U < B^{P-E}u \leq b^{p-e}u \leq b^p$. *Case 2: $v > u$.* Determine e and E such that $b^{e-1} \leq u < b^e$, $B^{E-1} < U \leq B^E$. Then $u \geq U - \frac{1}{2}B^{E-P}$ and $U \geq u + \frac{1}{2}b^{e-p}$; hence $B^{P-1} \leq B^{P-E}(U - B^{E-P}) < B^{P-E}u \leq b^{p-e}u < b^p$. Thus we have proved that $B^{P-1} < b^p$ whenever $v \neq u$.

Conversely, if $B^{P-1} < b^p$, the proof above suggests that the most likely example for which $u \neq v$ will occur when u is a power of b and at the same time it is close to a power of B. We have $B^{P-1}b^p < B^{P-1}b^p + \frac{1}{2}b^p - \frac{1}{2}B^{P-1} - \frac{1}{4} = (B^{P-1} + \frac{1}{2})(b^p - \frac{1}{2})$; hence $1 < \alpha = 1/(1 - \frac{1}{2}b^{-p}) < 1 + \frac{1}{2}B^{1-P} = \beta$. There are integers e and E such that $\log_B \alpha < e \log_B b - E < \log_B \beta$, by exercise 4.5.3–50. Hence $\alpha < b^e/B^E < \beta$, for some e and E. Now we have $\mathrm{round}_B(b^e, P) = B^E$, and $\mathrm{round}_b(B^E, p) < b^e$. [*CACM* **11** (1968), 47–50; *Proc. Amer. Math. Soc.* **19** (1968), 716–723.]

For example, if $b^p = 2^{10}$ and $B^P = 10^4$, the number $u = 2^{6408} \approx .100049 \cdot 10^{1930}$ rounds down to $U = .1 \cdot 10^{1930} \approx (.11111111101111111111)_2 \cdot 2^{6408}$, which rounds down to $2^{6408} - 2^{6398}$. (The *smallest* example is actually $\mathrm{round}((.1111111001)_2 \cdot 2^{784}) = .1011 \cdot 10^{236}$, $\mathrm{round}(.1011 \cdot 10^{235}) = (.11111110010)_2 \cdot 2^{784}$, found by Fred J. Tydeman.)

19. $m_1 = (\mathtt{F0F0F0F0})_{16}$, $c_1 = 1 - 10/16$ makes $U = ((u_7 u_6)_{10} \ldots (u_1 u_0)_{10})_{256}$; then $m_2 = (\mathtt{FF00FF00})_{16}$, $c_2 = 1 - 10^2/16^2$ makes $U = ((u_7 u_6 u_5 u_4)_{10}(u_3 u_2 u_1 u_0)_{10})_{65536}$; and $m_3 = (\mathtt{FFFF0000})_{16}$, $c_3 = 1 - 10^4/16^4$ finishes the job. [Compare with Schönhage's algorithm in exercise 14. This technique is due to Roy A. Keir, circa 1958.]

SECTION 4.5.1

1. Test whether or not $uv' < u'v$, since the denominators are positive. (See also the answer to exercise 4.5.3–39.)

2. If $c > 1$ divides both u/d and v/d, then cd divides both u and v.

3. Let p be prime. If p^e is a divisor of uv and $u'v'$ for $e \geq 1$, then either $p^e \backslash u$ and $p^e \backslash v'$ or $p^e \backslash u'$ and $p^e \backslash v$; hence $p^e \backslash \gcd(u, v') \gcd(u', v)$. The converse follows by reversing the argument.

4. Let $d_1 = \gcd(u, v)$, $d_2 = \gcd(u', v')$; the answer is $w = (u/d_1)(v'/d_2)\text{sign}(v)$, $w' = |(u'/d_2)(v/d_1)|$, with a "divide by zero" error message if $v = 0$.

5. $d_1 = 10$, $t = 17 \cdot 7 - 27 \cdot 12 = -205$, $d_2 = 5$, $w = -41$, $w' = 168$.

6. Let $u'' = u'/d_1$, $v'' = v'/d_1$; our goal is to show that $\gcd(uv'' + u''v, d_1) = \gcd(uv'' + u''v, d_1 u''v'')$. If p is a prime that divides u'', then p does not divide u or v'', so p does not divide $uv'' + u''v$. A similar argument holds for prime divisors of v'', so no prime divisors of $u''v''$ affect the given gcd.

7. $(N-1)^2 + (N-2)^2 = 2N^2 - (6N - 5)$. If the inputs are n-bit binary numbers, $2n + 1$ bits may be necessary to represent t.

8. For multiplication and division these quantities obey the rules $x/0 = \text{sign}(x)\infty$, $(\pm\infty) \times x = x \times (\pm\infty) = (\pm\infty)/x = \pm\text{sign}(x)\infty$, $x/(\pm\infty) = 0$, provided that x is finite and nonzero, without change to the algorithms described. Furthermore, the algorithms can readily be modified so that $0/0 = 0 \times (\pm\infty) = (\pm\infty) \times 0 = \text{"}(0/0)\text{"}$, where the latter is a representation of "undefined." If either operand is undefined the result should be undefined also.

Since the multiplication and division subroutines can yield these fairly natural rules of extended arithmetic, it is sometimes worthwhile to modify the addition and subtraction operations so that they satisfy the rules $x \pm \infty = \pm\infty$, $x \pm (-\infty) = \mp\infty$, for x finite; $(\pm\infty) + (\pm\infty) = \pm\infty - (\mp\infty) = \pm\infty$; furthermore $(\pm\infty) + (\mp\infty) = (\pm\infty) - (\pm\infty) = (0/0)$; and if either or both operands are $(0/0)$, the result should also be $(0/0)$. Equality tests and comparisons may be treated in a similar manner.

The remarks above are independent of "overflow" indications. If ∞ is being used to suggest overflow, it is incorrect to let $1/\infty$ be equal to zero, lest inaccurate results be regarded as true answers. It is far better to represent overflow by $(0/0)$, and to adhere to the convention that the result of any operation is undefined if at least one of the inputs is undefined. This type of overflow indication has the advantage that final results of an extended calculation reveal exactly which answers are defined and which are not.

9. If $u/u' \neq v/v'$, then $1 \leq |uv' - u'v| = u'v'|u/u' - v/v'| < |2^{2n}u/u' - 2^{2n}v/v'|$; two quantities differing by more than unity cannot have the same "floor." (In other words, the first $2n$ bits to the right of the binary point are enough to characterize the value of a binary fraction, when there are n-bit denominators. We cannot improve this to $2n - 1$ bits, for if $n = 4$ we have $\frac{1}{13} = (.00010011\ldots)_2$, $\frac{1}{14} = (.00010010\ldots)_2$.)

11. To divide by $(v + v'\sqrt{5})/v''$, when v and v' are not both zero, multiply by the reciprocal, $(v - v'\sqrt{5})v''/(v^2 - 5v'^2)$, and reduce to lowest terms.

12. $((2^{q-1} - 1)/1)$; $\text{round}(x) = (0/1)$ if and only if $|x| \leq 2^{1-q}$. Similarly, $\text{round}(x) = (1/0)$ if and only if $x \geq 2^{q-1}$.

13. One idea is to limit numerator and denominator to a total of 27 bits, where we need only store 26 of these bits (since the leading bit of the denominator is 1 unless the denominator has length 0). This leaves room for a sign and five bits to indicate the denominator size. Another idea is to use 28 bits for numerator and denominator, which are to have a total of at most seven hexadecimal digits, together with a sign and a 3-bit field to indicate the number of hexadecimal digits in the denominator.

[Using the formulas in the next exercise, the first alternative leads to exactly 2140040119 finite representable numbers, while the second leads to 1830986459. The first alternative is preferable because it represents more values, and because it is cleaner and makes smoother transitions between ranges. With 64-bit words we would, similarly, limit numerator and denominator to a total of at most $64 - 6 = 58$ bits.]

14. The number of multiples of n in the interval $(a \mathinner{..} b]$ is $\lfloor b/n \rfloor - \lfloor a/n \rfloor$. Hence, by inclusion and exclusion, the answer to this problem is $S_0 - S_1 + S_2 - \cdots$, where S_k is $\sum (\lfloor M_2/P \rfloor - \lfloor M_1/P \rfloor)(\lfloor N_2/P \rfloor - \lfloor N_1/P \rfloor)$, summed over all products P of k distinct primes. We can also express the answer as

$$\sum_{n=1}^{\min(M_2, N_2)} \mu(n) \left(\lfloor M_2/n \rfloor - \lfloor M_1/n \rfloor \right) \left(\lfloor N_2/n \rfloor - \lfloor N_1/n \rfloor \right).$$

SECTION 4.5.2

1. Substitute min, max, $+$ consistently for gcd, lcm, $\times$, respectively (after making sure that the identities are correct when any variable is zero).

2. For prime p, let $u_p, v_{1p}, \ldots, v_{np}$ be the exponents of p in the canonical factorizations of $u, v_1, \ldots, v_n$. By hypothesis, $u_p \leq v_{1p} + \cdots + v_{np}$. We must show that $u_p \leq \min(u_p, v_{1p}) + \cdots + \min(u_p, v_{np})$, and this is certainly true if u_p is greater than or equal to each v_{jp}, or if u_p is less than some v_{jp}.

3. *Solution 1:* If $n = p_1^{e_1} \ldots p_r^{e_r}$, the number in each case is $(2e_1 + 1) \ldots (2e_r + 1)$. *Solution 2:* A one-to-one correspondence is obtained if we set $u = \gcd(d, n)$ and $v = n^2/\operatorname{lcm}(d, n)$ for each divisor d of n^2. [E. Cesàro, *Annali di Matematica Pura ed Applicata* (2) **13** (1885), 235–250, §12.]

4. See exercise 3.2.1.2–15(a).

5. Shift u and v right until neither is a multiple of 3, remembering the proper power of 3 that will appear in the gcd. Each subsequent iteration sets $t \leftarrow u + v$ or $t \leftarrow u - v$ (whichever is a multiple of 3), shifts t right until it is not a multiple of 3, then replaces $\max(u, v)$ by the result.

u	v	t
13634	24140	10506, 3502;
13634	3502	17136, 5712, 1904;
1904	3502	5406, 1802;
1904	1802	102, 34;
34	1802	1836, 612, 204, 68;
34	68	102, 34;
34	34	0.

The evidence that $\gcd(40902, 24140) = 34$ is now overwhelming.

6. The probability that both u and v are even is $\frac{1}{4}$; the probability that both are multiples of four is $\frac{1}{16}$; etc. Thus A has the distribution given by the generating function

$$\frac{3}{4} + \frac{3}{16}z + \frac{3}{64}z^2 + \cdots = \frac{3/4}{1 - z/4}.$$

The mean is $\frac{1}{3}$, and the standard deviation is $\sqrt{\frac{2}{9} + \frac{1}{3} - \frac{1}{9}} = \frac{2}{3}$. If u and v are independently and uniformly distributed with $1 \leq u, v < 2^N$, some small correction terms are needed; the mean is then actually

$$(2^N - 1)^{-2} \sum_{k=1}^{N} (2^{N-k} - 1)^2 = \frac{1}{3} - \frac{4}{3}(2^N - 1)^{-1} + N(2^N - 1)^{-2}.$$

7. When u and v are not both even, each of the cases (even, odd), (odd, even), (odd, odd) is equally probable, and $B = 1, 0, 0$ in these cases. Hence $B = \frac{1}{3}$ on the average. Actually, as in exercise 6, a small correction should be given to be strictly accurate when $1 \le u, v < 2^N$; the probability that $B = 1$ is actually

$$(2^N - 1)^{-2} \sum_{k=1}^{N} (2^{N-k} - 1)2^{N-k} = \frac{1}{3} - \frac{1}{3}(2^N - 1)^{-1}.$$

8. Let F be the number of subtraction steps in which $u > v$; then $E = F + B$. If we change the inputs from (u, v) to (v, u), the value of C stays unchanged, while F becomes $C - 1 - F$. Hence $E_{\text{ave}} = \frac{1}{2}(C_{\text{ave}} - 1) + B_{\text{ave}}$.

9. The binary algorithm first gets to B6 with $u = 1963$, $v = 1359$; then $t \leftarrow 604$, 302, 151, etc. The gcd is 302. Using Algorithm X we find that $2 \cdot 31408 - 23 \cdot 2718 = 302$.

10. (a) Two integers are relatively prime if and only if they are not both divisible by any prime number. (b) Rearrange the sum in (a), with denominators $k = p_1 \dots p_r$. (Each of the sums in (a) and (b) is actually finite.) (c) Since $(n/k)^2 - \lfloor n/k \rfloor^2 = O(n/k)$, we have $q_n - \sum_{k=1}^{n} \mu(k)(n/k)^2 = \sum_{k=1}^{n} O(n/k) = O(nH_n)$. Furthermore $\sum_{k>n}(n/k)^2 = O(n)$. (d) $\sum_{d\backslash n} \mu(d) = \delta_{1n}$. [In fact, we have the more general result

$$\sum_{d\backslash n} \mu(d) \left(\frac{n}{d}\right)^s = n^s - \sum \left(\frac{n}{p}\right)^s + \sum \left(\frac{n}{pq}\right)^s - \cdots,$$

as in part (b), where the sums on the right are over the prime divisors of n, and this is equal to $n^s(1 - 1/p_1^s) \dots (1 - 1/p_r^s)$ if $n = p_1^{e_1} \dots p_r^{e_r}$.]

   Notes: Similarly, we find that a set of k integers is relatively prime with probability $1/\zeta(k) = 1/(\sum_{n \ge 1} 1/n^k)$. This proof of Theorem D is due to F. Mertens, *Crelle* **77** (1874), 289–291. The technique actually gives a much stronger result, namely that $6\pi^{-2}mn + O(n \log m)$ pairs of integers $u \in [f(m) .. f(m) + m]$, $v \in [g(n) .. g(n) + n]$ are relatively prime, when $m \le n$, $f(m) = O(m)$, and $g(n) = O(n)$.

11. (a) $6/\pi^2$ times $1 + \frac{1}{4} + \frac{1}{9}$, namely $49/(6\pi^2) \approx .82746$. (b) $6/\pi^2$ times $1/1 + 2/4 + 3/9 + \cdots$, namely ∞. (This is true in spite of the results of exercises 12 and 14.)

12. [*Annali di Mat.* (2) **13** (1885), 235–250, §3.] Let $\sigma(n)$ be the number of positive divisors of n. The answer is

$$\sum_{k \ge 1} \sigma(k) \cdot \frac{6}{\pi^2 k^2} = \frac{6}{\pi^2} \left(\sum_{k \ge 1} \frac{1}{k^2}\right)^2 = \frac{\pi^2}{6}.$$

[Thus, the average is *less* than 2, although there are always at least two common divisors when u and v are not relatively prime.]

13. $1 + \frac{1}{9} + \frac{1}{25} + \cdots = 1 + \frac{1}{4} + \frac{1}{9} + \cdots - \frac{1}{4}(1 + \frac{1}{4} + \frac{1}{9} + \cdots)$.

14. (a) $L = (6/\pi^2) \sum_{d \ge 1} d^{-2} \ln d = -\zeta'(2)/\zeta(2) = \sum_{p \text{ prime}} (\ln p)/(p^2 - 1) \approx 0.56996$. (b) $(8/\pi^2) \sum_{d \ge 1} [d \text{ odd}] d^{-2} \ln d = L - \frac{1}{3} \ln 2 \approx 0.33891$.

15. $v_1 = \pm v/u_3$, $v_2 = \mp u/u_3$ (the sign depends on whether the number of iterations is even or odd). This follows from the fact that v_1 and v_2 are relatively prime to each other (throughout the algorithm), and that $v_1 u = -v_2 v$. [Hence $v_1 u = \text{lcm}(u, v)$ at the close of the algorithm, but this is not an especially efficient way to compute the least common multiple. For a generalization, see exercise 4.6.1–18.]

   Further details can be found in exercise 4.5.3–48.

16. Apply Algorithm X to v and m, thus obtaining a value x such that $xv \equiv 1$ (modulo m). (This can be done by simplifying Algorithm X so that u_2, v_2, and t_2 are not computed, since they are never used in the answer.) Then set $w \leftarrow ux \bmod m$. [It follows, as in exercise 4.5.3–45, that this process requires $O(n^2)$ units of time, when it is applied to large n-bit numbers. See exercises 17 and 39 for alternatives to Algorithm X.]

17. We can let $u' = (2u - vu^2) \bmod 2^{2e}$, as in Newton's method (see the end of Section 4.3.1). Equivalently, if $uv \equiv 1 + 2^e w$ (modulo 2^{2e}), let $u' = u + 2^e((-uw) \bmod 2^e)$.

18. Let u_1, u_2, u_3, v_1, v_2, v_3 be multiprecision variables, in addition to u and v. The extended algorithm will act the same on u_3 and v_3 as Algorithm L does on u and v. New multiprecision operations are to set $t \leftarrow Au_j$, $t \leftarrow t + Bv_j$, $w \leftarrow Cu_j$, $w \leftarrow w + Dv_j$, $u_j \leftarrow t$, $v_j \leftarrow w$ for all j, in step L4; also if $B = 0$ in that step to set $t \leftarrow u_j - qv_j$, $u_j \leftarrow v_j$, $v_j \leftarrow t$ for all j and for $q = \lfloor u_3/v_3 \rfloor$. A similar modification is made to step L1 if v_3 is small. The inner loop (steps L2 and L3) is unchanged.

19. (a) Set $t_1 = x + 2y + 3z$; then $3t_1 + y + 2z = 1$, $5t_1 - 3y - 20z = 3$. Eliminate y, then $14t_1 - 14z = 6$: No solution. (b) This time $14t_1 - 14z = 0$. Divide by 14, eliminate t_1; the general solution is $x = 8z - 2$, $y = 1 - 5z$, z arbitrary.

20. We can assume that $m \geq n$. If $m > n = 0$ we get to $(m - t, 0)$ with probability 2^{-t} for $1 \leq t < m$, to $(0, 0)$ with probability 2^{1-m}. *Valida vi*, the following values can be obtained for $n > 0$:

Case 1, $m = n$. From (n, n) we go to $(n - t, n)$ with probability $t/2^t - 5/2^{t+1} + 3/2^{2t}$, for $2 \leq t < n$. (These values are $\frac{1}{16}$, $\frac{7}{64}$, $\frac{27}{256}$, ...) To $(0, n)$ the probability is $n/2^{n-1} - 1/2^{n-2} + 1/2^{2n-2}$. To (n, k) the probability is the same as to (k, n). The algorithm terminates with probability $1/2^{n-1}$.

Case 2, $m = n + 1$. From $(n + 1, n)$ we get to (n, n) with probability $\frac{1}{8}$ when $n > 1$, or 0 when $n = 1$; to $(n - t, n)$ with probability $11/2^{t+3} - 3/2^{2t+1}$, for $1 \leq t < n - 1$. (These values are $\frac{5}{16}$, $\frac{1}{4}$, $\frac{19}{128}$, ...) We get to $(1, n)$ with probability $5/2^{n+1} - 3/2^{2n-1}$, for $n > 1$; to $(0, n)$ with probability $3/2^n - 1/2^{2n-1}$.

Case 3, $m \geq n + 2$. The probabilities are given by the following table:

$$(m - 1, n): \qquad 1/2 - 3/2^{m-n+2} - \delta_{n1}/2^{m+1};$$
$$(m - t, n): \qquad 1/2^t + 3/2^{m-n+t+1}, \qquad 1 < t < n;$$
$$(m - n, n): \qquad 1/2^n + 1/2^m, \qquad n > 1;$$
$$(m - n - t, n): \qquad 1/2^{n+t} + \delta_{t1}/2^{m-1}, \qquad 1 \leq t < m - n;$$
$$(0, n): \qquad 1/2^{m-1}.$$

The only thing interesting about these results is that they are so messy; but that makes them uninteresting.

21. Show that for fixed v and for $2^m < u < 2^{m+1}$, when m is large, each subtract-and-shift cycle of the algorithm reduces $\lfloor \lg u \rfloor$ by two, on the average.

22. Exactly $(N - m)2^{m-1+\delta_{m0}}$ integers u in the range $1 \leq u < 2^N$ have $\lfloor \lg u \rfloor = m$, after u has been shifted right until it is odd. Thus

$$(2^N - 1)^2 C = N^2 C_{00} + 2N \sum_{1 \leq n \leq N} (N - n)2^{n-1} C_{n0}$$

$$+ 2 \sum_{1 \leq n < m \leq N} (N - m)(N - n)2^{m+n-2} C_{mn} + \sum_{1 \leq n \leq N} (N - n)^2 2^{2n-2} C_{nn}.$$

(The same formula holds for D in terms of D_{mn}.)

The middle sum is $2^{2N-2} \sum_{0 \le m < n < N} mn 2^{-m-n} ((\alpha+\beta)N + \gamma - \alpha m - \beta n)$. Since

$$\sum_{0 \le m < n} m 2^{-m} = 2 - (n+1) 2^{1-n} \quad \text{and} \quad \sum_{0 \le m < n} m(m-1) 2^{-m} = 4 - (n^2 + n + 2) 2^{1-n},$$

the sum on m is

$$2^{2N-2} \sum_{0 \le n < N} n 2^{-n} \Big((\gamma - \alpha - \beta n + (\alpha+\beta)N)(2 - (n+1) 2^{1-n}) - \alpha(4 - (n^2 + n + 2) 2^{1-n}) \Big)$$

$$= 2^{2N-2} \Big((\alpha+\beta) N \sum_{n \ge 0} n 2^{-n} (2 - (n+1) 2^{1-n}) + O(1) \Big).$$

Thus the coefficient of $(\alpha + \beta)N$ in the answer is found to be $2^{-2}(4 - (\frac{4}{3})^3) = \frac{11}{27}$. A similar argument applies to the other sums.

Note: The *exact* value of the sums may be obtained after some tedious calculation by means of the general summation-by-parts formula

$$\sum_{0 \le k < n} k^{\underline{m}} z^k = \frac{m! \, z^m}{(1-z)^{m+1}} - \sum_{k=0}^{m} \frac{m^{\underline{k}} \, n^{\underline{m-k}} \, z^{n+k}}{(1-z)^{k+1}}.$$

23. If $x \le 1$ it is $\Pr(u \ge v \text{ and } v/u \le x) = \frac{1}{2}(1 - G_n(x))$. And if $x \ge 1$ it is $\frac{1}{2} + \Pr(u \le v$ and $v/u \ge 1/x) = \frac{1}{2} + \frac{1}{2} G_n(1/x)$; this also equals $\frac{1}{2}(1 - G_n(x))$ by (40).

24. $\sum_{k \ge 1} 2^{-k} G(1/(2^k + 1)) = S(1)$. This value, which has no obvious connection to classical constants, is approximately 0.5432582959.

25. Richard Brent has noted that $G(e^{-y})$ is an odd function that is analytic for all real values of y. If we let $G(e^{-y}) = \lambda_1 y + \lambda_3 y^3 + \lambda_5 y^5 + \cdots = \rho(e^{-y} - 1)$, we have $-\rho_1 = \lambda_1 = \lambda$, $\rho_2 = \frac{1}{2}\lambda$, $-\rho_3 = \frac{1}{3}\lambda + \lambda_3$, $\rho_4 = \frac{1}{4}\lambda + \frac{3}{2}\lambda_3$, $-\rho_5 = \frac{1}{5}\lambda + \frac{7}{4}\lambda_3 + \lambda_5$;

$$(-1)^n \rho_n = \sum_k \begin{bmatrix} n \\ k \end{bmatrix} \frac{k!}{n!} \lambda_k; \qquad \lambda_n = -\sum_k \begin{Bmatrix} n \\ k \end{Bmatrix} \frac{k!}{n!} \rho_k.$$

The first few values are $\lambda_1 \approx .3979226812$, $\lambda_3 \approx -.0210096400$, $\lambda_5 \approx .0013749841$, $\lambda_7 \approx -.0000960351$. *Wild conjecture:* $\lim_{k \to \infty} (-\lambda_{2k+1}/\lambda_{2k-1}) = 1/\pi^2$.

26. The left side is $2S(1/x) - 5S(1/2x) + 2S(1/4x) - 2S(x) + 5S(2x) - 2S(4x)$ by (39); the right side is $S(2x) - S(4x) + 2S(1/x) - S(1/2x) - 2S(x) + 4S(2x) - 4S(1/2x) + 2S(1/4x)$ by (44). The cases $x = 1$, $x = 1/\sqrt{2}$, and $x = \phi$ are perhaps the most interesting; for example, $x = \phi$ gives $2G(4\phi) - 5G(2\phi) + G(\phi^2/2) - G(\phi^3) = 2G(2\phi^2)$.

27. $2\psi_n = [z^n] z \sum_{k \ge 0} 2^{-2k} \sum_{j=0}^{2^k - 1} \sum_{l \ge 0} (jz/2^k)^l = \sum_{k \ge 1} 2^{-k(n+1)} \sum_{j=0}^{2^k - 1} j^{n-1} = \sum_{k \ge 1} 2^{-k(n+1)} \sum_{l=0}^{n-1} \binom{n}{l} B_l 2^{k(n-l)}/n$ by exercise 1.2.11.2–4, when $n > 1$; and of course $\sum_{k \ge 1} 2^{-k(l+1)} = 1/(2^{l+1} - 1)$.

28. Letting $S_n(m) = \sum_{k=1}^{m-1} (1 - k/m)^n$ and $T_n(m) = 1/(e^{n/m} - 1)$ as in exercise 6.3–34(b), we find $S_n(m) = T_n(m) + O(e^{-n/m} n/m^2)$ and $2\psi_{n+1} = \sum_{j \ge 1} 2^{-2j} S_n(2^j) = \tau_n + O(n^{-3})$, where $\tau_n = \sum_{j \ge 1} 2^{-2j} T_n(2^j)$. Since $\tau_{n+1} < \tau_n$ and $4\tau_{2n} - \tau_n = 1/(e^n - 1)$ is positive but exponentially small, it follows that $\tau_n = \Theta(n^{-2})$. More detailed information can be obtained by writing

$$\sum_{j \ge 1} \frac{1}{2^{2j}} \frac{1}{e^{n/2^j} - 1} = \frac{1}{2\pi i} \sum_{j \ge 1} \int_{3/2 - i\infty}^{3/2 + i\infty} \frac{\zeta(z) \Gamma(z) n^{-z}}{2^j (2-z)} \, dz = \frac{1}{2\pi i} \int_{3/2 - i\infty}^{3/2 + i\infty} \frac{\zeta(z) \Gamma(z) n^{-z}}{2^{2-z} - 1} \, dz.$$

The integral is the sum of the residues at the poles $2 + 2\pi ik/\ln 2$, namely n^{-2} times $\pi^2/(6\ln 2) + f(n)$, where

$$f(n) = 2\sum_{k\geq 1} \Re(\zeta(2 + 2\pi ik/\ln 2)\Gamma(2 + 2\pi ik/\ln 2)\exp(-2\pi ik\lg n)/\ln 2$$

is a periodic function of $\lg n$ whose "average" value is zero.

29. (Solution by P. Flajolet and B. Vallée.) If $f(x) = \sum_{k\geq 1} 2^{-k}g(2^kx)$ and $g^*(s) = \int_0^\infty g(x)x^{s-1}\,dx$, then $f^*(s) = \sum_{k\geq 1} 2^{-k(s+1)}g^*(s) = g^*(s)/(2^{s+1} - 1)$, and $f(x) = \frac{1}{2\pi i}\int_{c-i\infty}^{c+i\infty} f^*(s)x^{-s}\,ds$ under appropriate conditions. Letting $g(x) = 1/(1+x)$, we find that the transform in this case is $g^*(s) = \pi/\sin\pi s$ when $0 < \Re s < 1$; hence

$$f(x) = \sum_{k=1}^\infty \frac{1}{2^k}\frac{1}{1 + 2^kx} = \frac{1}{2\pi i}\int_{1/2-i\infty}^{1/2+i\infty} \frac{\pi x^{-s}\,ds}{(2^{s+1} - 1)\sin\pi s}.$$

It follows that $f(x)$ is the sum of the residues of $\frac{\pi}{\sin\pi s}x^{-s}/(2^{s+1}-1)$ for $\Re s \leq 0$, namely $1 + x\lg x + \frac{1}{2}x + xP(\lg x) - \frac{2}{i}x^2 + \frac{4}{3}x^3 - \frac{8}{7}x^4 + \cdots$, where

$$P(t) = \frac{2\pi}{\ln 2}\sum_{m=1}^\infty \frac{\sin 2\pi mt}{\sinh(2m\pi^2/\ln 2)}$$

is a periodic function whose absolute value never exceeds 8×10^{-12}. (The fact that $P(t)$ is so small caused Brent to overlook it in his original paper.)

The Mellin transform of $f(1/x)$ is $f^*(-s) = \pi/((1 - 2^{1-s})\sin\pi s)$ for $-1 < \Re s < 0$; thus $f(1/x) = \frac{1}{2\pi i}\int_{-1/2-i\infty}^{-1/2+i\infty} \frac{\pi}{\sin\pi s}x^{-s}\,ds/(1 - 2^{1-s})$, and we now want the residues of the integrand with $\Re s \leq -1$: $f(1/x) = \frac{1}{3}x - \frac{1}{7}x^2 + \cdots$. [This formula could also have been obtained directly.] We have $S_1(x) = 1 - f(x)$, and it follows that

$$G_1(x) = f(x) - f(1/x) = x\lg x + \frac{1}{2}x + xP(\lg x) - \frac{x^2}{1+x} + (1 - x^2)\phi(x),$$

where $\phi(x) = \sum_{k=0}^\infty (-1)^k x^k/(2^{k+1} - 1)$.

30. We have $G_2(x) = \Sigma_1(x) - \Sigma_1(1/x) + \Sigma_2(x) - \Sigma_2(1/x)$, where

$$\Sigma_1(x) = \sum_{k,l\geq 1} \frac{1}{2^{k+l}}\frac{1}{1 + 2^l(1 + 2^kx)}, \qquad \Sigma_2(x) = \sum_{k,l\geq 1} \frac{1}{2^k}\frac{1}{1 + 2^l + 2^kx}.$$

The Mellin transforms are $\Sigma_1^*(s) = \frac{\pi}{\sin\pi s}a(s)/(2^{s+1} - 1)$, $\Sigma_2^*(s) = \frac{\pi}{\sin\pi s}b(s)/(2^{s+1} - 1)$, where

$$a(s) = \sum_{l\geq 1}\frac{(1 + 2^{-l})^{s-1}}{2^{2l}} = \sum_{k\geq 0}\binom{s-1}{k}\frac{1}{2^{k+2} - 1},$$

$$b(s) = \sum_{l\geq 1}(2^l + 1)^{s-1} = \sum_{k\geq 0}\binom{s-1}{k}\frac{1}{2^{k+1-s} - 1}.$$

Therefore we obtain the following expansions for $0 \leq x \leq 1$:

$$\Sigma_1(x) = a(0) + a(-1)x(\lg x + \tfrac{1}{2}) - a'(1)x/\ln 2 + xA(\lg x) - \sum_{k\geq 2}\frac{2^{k-1}}{2^{k-1}-1}a(-k)(-x)^k,$$

$$\Sigma_2(x) = b(0) + b(-1)x(\lg x + \tfrac{1}{2}) - b'(1)x/\ln 2 + xB(\lg x) - \sum_{k\geq 2}\frac{2^{k-1}}{2^{k-1}-1}b(-k)(-x)^k,$$

$$\Sigma_1(1/x) = \sum_{k \geq 1} \frac{-a(k)(-x)^k}{2^{k+1} - 1},$$

$$\Sigma_2(1/x) = \sum_{k \geq 1} \frac{(-x)^k}{2^{k+1} - 1} \left(\lg x - \hat{b}(k) - \frac{1}{2} - \frac{1}{2^{k+1} - 1} + \frac{H_{k-1}}{\ln 2} + P_k(\lg x) \right),$$

$$\hat{b}(s) = \sum_{k=0}^{s-2} \binom{s-1}{k} \frac{1}{2^{k+1-s} - 1};$$

$$A(t) = \frac{1}{\ln 2} \sum_{m \geq 1} \Re \left(\frac{2\pi i}{\sinh(2m\pi^2/\ln 2)} a(-1 + 2m\pi i/\ln 2) e^{-2m\pi i t} \right),$$

$$B(t) = \frac{1}{\ln 2} \sum_{m \geq 1} \Re \left(\frac{2\pi i}{\sinh(2m\pi^2/\ln 2)} b(-1 + 2m\pi i/\ln 2) e^{-2m\pi i t} \right),$$

$$P_k(t) = \frac{1}{\ln 2} \sum_{m \geq 1} \Re \left(\frac{2\pi i}{\sinh(2m\pi^2/\ln 2)} \binom{k - 1 - 2m\pi i/\ln 2}{k - 1} e^{-2m\pi i t} \right).$$

32. Yes: See G. Maze, *J. Discrete Algorithms* **5** (2007), 176–186.

34. Brigitte Vallée [*Algorithmica* **22** (1998), 660–685] has found an elegant and rigorous analysis of Algorithm B, using an approach quite different from that of Brent. Indeed, her methods are sufficiently different that they are not yet known to predict the same behavior as Brent's heuristic model. Thus the problem of analyzing the binary gcd algorithm, now solved rigorously for the first time, continues to lead to ever more tantalizing questions of higher mathematics.

35. By induction, the length is $m + \lfloor n/2 \rfloor + 1 - [m = n = 1]$ when $m \geq n$. But exercise 37 shows that the algorithm cannot go as slowly as this.

36. Let $a_n = (2^n - (-1)^n)/3$; then $a_0, a_1, a_2, \ldots = 0, 1, 1, 3, 5, 11, 21, \ldots$. (This sequence of numbers has an interesting pattern of zeros and ones in its binary representation. Notice that $a_n = a_{n-1} + 2a_{n-2}$, and $a_n + a_{n+1} = 2^n$.) For $m > n$, let $u = 2^{m+1} - a_{n+2}$, $v = a_{n+2}$. For $m = n > 0$, let $u = a_{n+2}$ and $v = u + (-1)^n$. Another example for the case $m = n > 0$ is $u = 2^{n+1} - 2$, $v = 2^{n+1} - 1$; this choice takes more shifts, and gives $B = 1$, $C = n + 1$, $D = 2n$, $E = n$, the worst case for Program B.

37. (Solution by J. O. Shallit.) This is a problem where it appears to be necessary to prove *more* than was asked just to prove what was asked. Let $S(u, v)$ be the number of subtraction steps taken by Algorithm B on inputs u and v. We will prove that $S(u, v) \leq \lg(u + v)$. This will imply that $S(u, v) \leq \lfloor \lg(u + v) \rfloor \leq \lfloor \lg 2 \max(u, v) \rfloor = 1 + \lfloor \lg \max(u, v) \rfloor$ as desired.

Notice that $S(u, v) = S(v, u)$. If u is even, $S(u, v) = S(u/2, v)$; hence we may assume that u and v are odd. We may also assume that $u > v$, since $S(u, u) = 1$. Then $S(u, v) = 1 + S((u - v)/2, v) \leq 1 + \lg((u - v)/2 + v) = \lg(u + v)$ by induction.

It follows, incidentally, that the smallest case requiring n subtraction steps is $u = 2^{n-1} + 1$, $v = 2^{n-1} - 1$.

38. Keep track of the most significant and least significant words of the operands (the most significant is used to guess the sign of t and the least significant is to determine the amount of right shift), while building a 2×2 matrix A of single-precision integers such that $A\binom{u}{v} = \binom{u'w}{v'w}$, where w is the computer word size and where u' and v' are smaller than u and v. (Instead of dividing the simulated odd operand by 2, multiply the other one by 2, until obtaining multiples of w after exactly $\lg w$ shifts.) Experiments show this algorithm running four times as fast as Algorithm L, on at least one computer. With the similar algorithm of exercise 40 we don't need the most significant words.

A possibly faster binary algorithm has been described by J. Sorenson, *J. Algorithms* **16** (1994), 110–144; Shallit and Sorenson, *Lecture Notes in Comp. Sci.* **877** (1994), 169–183.

39. (Solution by Michael Penk.)

> **Y1.** [Find power of 2.] Same as step B1.
>
> **Y2.** [Initialize.] Set $(u_1, u_2, u_3) \leftarrow (1, 0, u)$ and $(v_1, v_2, v_3) \leftarrow (v, 1 - u, v)$. If u is odd, set $(t_1, t_2, t_3) \leftarrow (0, -1, -v)$ and go to Y4. Otherwise set $(t_1, t_2, t_3) \leftarrow (1, 0, u)$.
>
> **Y3.** [Halve t_3.] If t_1 and t_2 are both even, set $(t_1, t_2, t_3) \leftarrow (t_1, t_2, t_3)/2$; otherwise set $(t_1, t_2, t_3) \leftarrow (t_1 + v, t_2 - u, t_3)/2$. (In the latter case, $t_1 + v$ and $t_2 - u$ will both be even.)
>
> **Y4.** [Is t_3 even?] If t_3 is even, go back to Y3.
>
> **Y5.** [Reset $\max(u_3, v_3)$.] If t_3 is positive, set $(u_1, u_2, u_3) \leftarrow (t_1, t_2, t_3)$; otherwise set $(v_1, v_2, v_3) \leftarrow (v - t_1, -u - t_2, -t_3)$.
>
> **Y6.** [Subtract.] Set $(t_1, t_2, t_3) \leftarrow (u_1, u_2, u_3) - (v_1, v_2, v_3)$. Then if $t_1 \leq 0$, set $(t_1, t_2) \leftarrow (t_1 + v, t_2 - u)$. If $t_3 \neq 0$, go back to Y3. Otherwise the algorithm terminates with $(u_1, u_2, u_3 \cdot 2^k)$ as the output. ∎

It is clear that the relations in (16) are preserved, and that $0 \leq u_1, v_1, t_1 \leq v$, $0 \geq u_2, v_2, t_2 \geq -u$, $0 < u_3 \leq u$, $0 < v_3 \leq v$ after each of steps Y2–Y6. If u is odd after step Y1, then step Y3 can be simplified, since t_1 and t_2 are both even if and only if t_2 is even; similarly, if v is odd, then t_1 and t_2 are both even if and only if t_1 is even. Thus, as in Algorithm X, it is possible to suppress all calculations involving u_2, v_2, and t_2, provided that v is odd after step Y1. This condition is often known in advance (for example, it holds when v is prime and we are trying to compute u^{-1} modulo v).

See also A. W. Bojanczyk and R. P. Brent, *Computers and Math.* **14** (1987), 233, for a similar extension of the algorithm in exercise 40.

40. Let $m = \lg \max(|u|, |v|)$. We can show inductively that $|u| \leq 2^{m-(s-c)/2}$, $|v| \leq 2^{m-(s+c)/2}$ after we have performed the operation $c \leftarrow c + 1$ in step K3 s times. Therefore $s \leq 2m$. If K2 is executed t times, we have $t \leq s + 2$, because s increases every time except the first and last. [See *VLSI '83* (North-Holland, 1983), 145–154.]

Notes: When $u = 1$ and $v = 3 \cdot 2^k - 1$ and $k \geq 2$, we have $m = k + 2$, $s = 2k$, $t = k + 4$. When $u = u_j$ and $v = 2u_{j-1}$ in the sequence defined by $u_0 = 3$, $u_1 = 1$, $u_{j+1} = \min(|3u_j - 16u_{j-1}|, |5u_j - 16u_{j-1}|)$, we have $s = 2j + 2$, $t = 2j + 3$, and (empirically) $m \approx \phi j$. Can t be asymptotically larger than $2m/\phi$?

41. In general, since $(a^u - 1) \bmod (a^v - 1) = a^{u \bmod v} - 1$ (see Eq. 4.3.2–(20)), we find that $\gcd(a^m - 1, a^n - 1) = a^{\gcd(m,n)} - 1$ for all positive integers a.

42. Subtract the kth column from the $2k$th, $3k$th, $4k$th, etc., for $k = 1, 2, 3, \ldots$. The result is a triangular matrix with x_k on the diagonal in column k, where $m = \sum_{d \backslash m} x_d$. It follows that $x_m = \varphi(m)$, so the determinant is $\varphi(1)\varphi(2)\ldots\varphi(n)$.

[In general, "Smith's determinant," in which the (i, j) element is $f(\gcd(i, j))$ for an arbitrary function f, is equal to $\prod_{m=1}^{n} \sum_{d \backslash m} \mu(m/d) f(d)$, by the same argument. See L. E. Dickson, *History of the Theory of Numbers* **1** (Carnegie Inst. of Washington, 1919), 122–123.]

SECTION 4.5.3

1. The running time is about $19.02T + 6$, just a trifle slower than Program 4.5.2A.

2. $\begin{pmatrix} K_n(x_1, x_2, \ldots, x_{n-1}, x_n) & K_{n-1}(x_1, x_2, \ldots, x_{n-1}) \\ K_{n-1}(x_2, \ldots, x_{n-1}, x_n) & K_{n-2}(x_2, \ldots, x_{n-1}) \end{pmatrix}.$

3. $K_n(x_1, \ldots, x_n)$.

4. By induction, or by taking the determinant of the matrix product in exercise 2.

5. When the x's are positive, the q's of (9) are positive, and $q_{n+1} > q_{n-1}$; hence (9) is an alternating series of decreasing terms, and it converges if and only if $q_n q_{n+1} \to \infty$. By induction, if the x's are greater than ϵ, we have $q_n \geq (1 + \epsilon/2)^n c$, where c is chosen small enough to make this inequality valid for $n = 1$ and 2. But if $x_n = 1/2^n$, we have $q_n \leq 2 - 1/2^n$.

6. It suffices to prove that $A_1 = B_1$; and from the fact that $0 \leq /\!/x_1, \ldots, x_n/\!/ < 1$ whenever $x_1, \ldots, x_n$ are positive integers, we have $B_1 = \lfloor 1/X \rfloor = A_1$.

7. Only $1\,2\ldots n$ and $n\ldots 2\,1$. (The variable x_k appears in exactly $F_k\,F_{n+1-k}$ terms; hence x_1 and x_n can only be permuted into x_1 and x_n. If x_1 and x_n are fixed by the permutation, it follows by induction that $x_2, \ldots, x_{n-1}$ are also fixed.)

8. This is equivalent to

$$\frac{K_{n-2}(A_{n-1}, \ldots, A_2) - X K_{n-1}(A_{n-1}, \ldots, A_1)}{K_{n-1}(A_n, \ldots, A_2) - X K_n(A_n, \ldots, A_1)} = -\frac{1}{X_n},$$

and by (6) it is equivalent to

$$X = \frac{K_{n-1}(A_2, \ldots, A_n) + X_n K_{n-2}(A_2, \ldots, A_{n-1})}{K_n(A_1, \ldots, A_n) + X_n K_{n-1}(A_1, \ldots, A_{n-1})}.$$

9. (a) By definition. (b, d) Prove this when $n = 1$, then apply (a) to get the result for general n. (c) Prove it when $n = k + 1$, then apply (a).

10. If $A_0 > 0$, then $B_0 = 0$, $B_1 = A_0$, $B_2 = A_1$, $B_3 = A_2$, $B_4 = A_3$, $B_5 = A_4$, $m = 5$. If $A_0 = 0$, then $B_0 = A_1$, $B_1 = A_2$, $B_2 = A_3$, $B_3 = A_4$, $m = 3$. If $A_0 = -1$ and $A_1 = 1$, then $B_0 = -(A_2 + 2)$, $B_1 = 1$, $B_2 = A_3 - 1$, $B_3 = A_4$, $m = 3$. If $A_0 = -1$ and $A_1 > 1$, then $B_0 = -2$, $B_1 = 1$, $B_2 = A_1 - 2$, $B_3 = A_2$, $B_4 = A_3$, $B_5 = A_4$, $m = 5$. If $A_0 < -1$, then $B_0 = -1$, $B_1 = 1$, $B_2 = -A_0 - 2$, $B_3 = 1$, $B_4 = A_1 - 1$, $B_5 = A_2$, $B_6 = A_3$, $B_7 = A_4$, $m = 7$. [Actually, the last three cases involve eight subcases; if any of the B's is set to zero, the values should be "collapsed together" by using the rule of exercise 9(c). For example, if $A_0 = -1$ and $A_1 = A_3 = 1$, we actually have $B_0 = -(A_2 + 2)$, $B_1 = A_4 + 1$, $m = 1$. Double collapsing occurs when $A_0 = -2$ and $A_1 = 1$.]

11. Let $q_n = K_n(A_1, \ldots, A_n)$, $q'_n = K_n(B_1, \ldots, B_n)$, $p_n = K_{n+1}(A_0, \ldots, A_n)$, $p'_n = K_{n+1}(B_0, \ldots, B_n)$. By (5) and (11) we have $X = (p_m + p_{m-1}X_m)/(q_m + q_{m-1}X_m)$, $Y = (p'_n + p'_{n-1}Y_n)/(q'_n + q'_{n-1}Y_n)$; therefore if $X_m = Y_n$, the stated relation between X and Y holds by (8). Conversely, if $X = (qY + r)/(sY + t)$ and $|qt - rs| = 1$, we may assume that $s \geq 0$, and we can show that the partial quotients of X and Y eventually agree, by induction on s. The result is clear when $s = 0$, by exercise 9(d). If $s > 0$, let $q = as + s'$, where $0 \leq s' < s$. Then $X = a + 1/((sY + t)/(s'Y + r - at))$; since $s(r - at) - ts' = sr - tq$, and $s' < s$, we know by induction and exercise 10 that the partial quotients of X and Y eventually agree. [*J. de Math. Pures et Appl.* **15** (1850), 153–155. The fact that m is always odd in exercise 10 shows, by a close inspection of this proof, that $X_m = Y_n$ if and only if $X = (qY + r)/(sY + t)$, where $qt - rs = (-1)^{m-n}$.]

12. (a) Since $V_n V_{n+1} = D - U_n^2$, we know that $D - U_{n+1}^2$ is a multiple of V_{n+1}; hence by induction $X_n = (\sqrt{D} - U_n)/V_n$, where U_n and V_n are integers. [*Notes:* An algorithm based on this process has many applications to the solution of quadratic equations in integers; see, for example, H. Davenport, *The Higher Arithmetic* (London: Hutchinson, 1952); W. J. LeVeque, *Topics in Number Theory* (Reading, Mass.: Addison–Wesley, 1956); and see also Section 4.5.4. By exercise 1.2.4–35, we have

$$A_{n+1} = \begin{cases} \lfloor (\lfloor \sqrt{D} \rfloor + U_n)/V_{n+1} \rfloor, & \text{if } V_{n+1} > 0, \\ \lfloor (\lfloor \sqrt{D} \rfloor + 1 + U_n)/V_{n+1} \rfloor, & \text{if } V_{n+1} < 0; \end{cases}$$

hence such an algorithm need only work with the positive integer $\lfloor \sqrt{D} \rfloor$. Moreover, the identity $V_{n+1} = A_n(U_{n-1} - U_n) + V_{n-1}$ makes it unnecessary to divide when V_{n+1} is being determined.]

(b) Let $Y = (-\sqrt{D} - U)/V$, $Y_n = (-\sqrt{D} - U_n)/V_n$. The stated identity obviously holds by replacing $\sqrt{D}$ by $-\sqrt{D}$ in the proof of (a). We have

$$Y = (p_n/Y_n + p_{n-1})/(q_n/Y_n + q_{n-1}),$$

where p_n and q_n are defined in part (c) of this exercise; hence

$$Y_n = (-q_n/q_{n-1})(Y - p_n/q_n)/(Y - p_{n-1}/q_{n-1}).$$

But by (12), p_{n-1}/q_{n-1} and p_n/q_n are extremely close to X; since $X \neq Y$, $Y - p_n/q_n$ and $Y - p_{n-1}/q_{n-1}$ will have the same sign as $Y - X$ for all large n. This proves that $Y_n < 0$ for all large n; hence $0 < X_n < X_n - Y_n = 2\sqrt{D}/V_n$; V_n must be positive. Also $U_n < \sqrt{D}$, since $X_n > 0$. Hence $V_n < 2\sqrt{D}$, since $V_n \leq A_n V_n < \sqrt{D} + U_{n-1}$.

Finally, we want to show that $U_n > 0$. Since $X_n < 1$, we have $U_n > \sqrt{D} - V_n$, so we need only consider the case $V_n > \sqrt{D}$. Then $U_n = A_n V_n - U_{n-1} \geq V_n - U_{n-1} > \sqrt{D} - U_{n-1}$, and this is positive as we have already observed.

Notes: In the repeating cycle, $\sqrt{D} + U_n = A_n V_n + (\sqrt{D} - U_{n-1}) > V_n$; hence $\lfloor (\sqrt{D} + U_{n+1})/V_{n+1} \rfloor = \lfloor A_{n+1} + V_n/(\sqrt{D} + U_n) \rfloor = A_{n+1} = \lfloor (\sqrt{D} + U_n)/V_{n+1} \rfloor$. In other words A_{n+1} is determined by U_{n+1} and V_{n+1}; we can determine (U_n, V_n) from its successor (U_{n+1}, V_{n+1}) in the period. In fact, when $0 < V_n < \sqrt{D} + U_n$ and $0 < U_n < \sqrt{D}$, the arguments above prove that $0 < V_{n+1} < \sqrt{D} + U_{n+1}$ and $0 < U_{n+1} < \sqrt{D}$; moreover, if the pair (U_{n+1}, V_{n+1}) follows (U', V') with $0 < V' < \sqrt{D} + U'$ and $0 < U' < \sqrt{D}$, then $U' = U_n$ and $V' = V_n$. Hence (U_n, V_n) is part of the cycle if and only if $0 < V_n < \sqrt{D} + U_n$ and $0 < U_n < \sqrt{D}$.

(c) $\dfrac{-V_{n+1}}{V_n} = X_n Y_n = \dfrac{(q_n X - p_n)(q_n Y - p_n)}{(q_{n-1} X - p_{n-1})(q_{n-1} Y - p_{n-1})}.$

There is also a companion identity, namely

$$V p_n p_{n-1} + U(p_n q_{n-1} + p_{n-1} q_n) + ((U^2 - D)/V) q_n q_{n-1} = (-1)^n U_n.$$

(d) If $X_n = X_m$ for some $n \neq m$, then X is an irrational number that satisfies the quadratic equation $(q_n X - p_n)/(q_{n-1} X - p_{n-1}) = (q_m X - p_m)/(q_{m-1} X - p_{m-1})$.

The ideas underlying this exercise go back at least to Jayadeva in India, prior to A.D. 1073; see K. S. Shukla, *Gaṇita* **5** (1954), 1–20; C.-O. Selenius, *Historia Math.* **2** (1975), 167–184. Some of its aspects had also been discovered in Japan before 1750; see Y. Mikami, *The Development of Mathematics in China and Japan* (1913), 223–229. But the main principles of the theory of continued fractions for quadratics are largely due to Euler [*Novi Comment. Acad. Sci. Petrop.* **11** (1765), 28–66] and Lagrange [*Hist. Acad. Sci.* **24** (Berlin: 1768), 111–180].

14. As in exercise 9, we need only verify the stated identities when c is the last partial quotient, and this verification is trivial. Now Hurwitz's rule gives $2/e = //1, 2, 1, 2, 0, 1, 1, 1, 1, 1, 0, 2, 3, 2, 0, 1, 1, 3, 1, 1, 0, 2, 5, \ldots //$. Taking the reciprocal, collapsing out the zeros as in exercise 9, and taking note of the pattern that appears, we find (see exercise 16) that $e/2 = 1 + // \, 2, \overline{2m+1, \, 3, \, 1, \, 2m+1, \, 1, \, 3}//, \ m \geq 0$. [*Schriften der phys.-ökon. Gesellschaft zu Königsberg* **32** (1891), 59–62. Hurwitz also explained how to multiply by an arbitrary positive integer, in *Vierteljahrsschrift der Naturforschenden Gesellschaft in Zürich* **41** (1896), Jubelband II, 34–64, §2.]

15. (This procedure maintains four integers (A, B, C, D) with the invariant meaning that "our remaining job is to output the continued fraction for $(Ay+B)/(Cy+D)$, where y is the input yet to come.") Initially set $j \leftarrow k \leftarrow 0$, $(A, B, C, D) \leftarrow (a, b, c, d)$; then input x_j and set $(A, B, C, D) \leftarrow (Ax_j+B, A, Cx_j+D, C)$, $j \leftarrow j+1$, one or more times until $C + D$ has the same sign as C. (When $j \geq 1$ and the input has not terminated, we know that $1 < y < \infty$; and when $C + D$ has the same sign as C we know therefore that $(Ay + B)/(Cy + D)$ lies between $(A + B)/(C + D)$ and A/C.) Now comes the general step: If no integer lies strictly between $(A+B)/(C+D)$ and A/C, output $X_k \leftarrow \min(\lfloor A/C \rfloor, \lfloor (A+B)/(C+D) \rfloor)$, and set $(A, B, C, D) \leftarrow (C, D, A - X_kC, B - X_kD)$, $k \leftarrow k + 1$; otherwise input x_j and set $(A, B, C, D) \leftarrow (Ax_j + B, A, Cx_j + D, C)$, $j \leftarrow j + 1$. The general step is repeated ad infinitum. However, if at any time the *final* x_j is input, the algorithm immediately switches gears: It outputs the continued fraction for $(Ax_j + B)/(Cx_j + D)$, using Euclid's algorithm, and terminates.

The following tableau solves the requested example, where the matrix $\begin{pmatrix} B & A \\ D & C \end{pmatrix}$ begins at the upper left corner, then shifts right one on input, down one on output:

x_j	−1	5	1	1	1	2	1	2	∞
X_k	39	97	−58	−193					
−2	−25	−62	37	123					
2			16	53					
3			5	17	22				
7			1	2	3	5			
1				3	1	4	5	14	
1					2	1	3	7	
1						2	7	9	25
12						1	0	1	2
2									1
∞									0

M. Mendès France has shown that the number of quotients output per quotient input is asymptotically bounded between $1/r$ and r, where $r = 2\lfloor L(|ad - bc|)/2 \rfloor + 1$ and L is the function defined in exercise 38; this bound is best possible. [*Topics in Number Theory*, edited by P. Turán, *Colloquia Math. Soc. János Bolyai* **13** (1976), 183–194.]

Gosper has also shown that the algorithm above can be generalized to compute the continued fraction for $(axy + bx + cy + d)/(Axy + Bx + Cy + D)$ from those of x and y (in particular, to compute sums and products). [MIT AI Laboratory Memo 239 (29 February 1972), Hack 101.] For further developments, see J. Vuillemin, *ACM Conf. LISP and Functional Programming* **5** (1988), 14–27.

16. It is not difficult to prove by induction that $f_n(z) = z/(2n+1) + O(z^3)$ is an odd function with a convergent power series in a neighborhood of the origin, and that it satisfies the given differential equation. Hence

$$f_0(z) = //z^{-1} + f_1(z)// = \cdots = //z^{-1}, 3z^{-1}, \ldots, (2n+1)z^{-1} + f_{n+1}(z)//.$$

It remains to prove that $\lim_{n \to \infty} //z^{-1}, 3z^{-1}, \ldots, (2n+1)z^{-1}// = f_0(z)$. [Actually Euler, age 24, obtained continued fraction expansions for the considerably more general differential equation $f_n'(z) = az^m + bf_n(z)z^{m-1} + cf_n(z)^2$; but he did not bother to prove convergence, since formal manipulation and intuition were good enough in the eighteenth century.]

There are several ways to prove the desired limiting equation. First, letting $f_n(z) = \sum_k a_{nk} z^k$, we can argue from the equation

$$(2n+1)a_{n1} + (2n+3)a_{n3}z^2 + (2n+5)a_{n5}z^4 + \cdots = 1 - (a_{n1}z + a_{n3}z^3 + a_{n5}z^5 + \cdots)^2$$

that $(-1)^k a_{n(2k+1)}$ is a sum of terms of the form $c_k/(2n+1)^{k+1}(2n+b_{k1})\ldots(2n+b_{kk})$, where the c_k and b_{km} are positive integers independent of n. For example, we have $-a_{n7} = 4/(2n+1)^4(2n+3)(2n+5)(2n+7) + 1/(2n+1)^4(2n+3)^2(2n+7)$. Thus $|a_{(n+1)k}| \le |a_{nk}|$, and $|f_n(z)| \le \tan|z|$ for $|z| < \pi/2$. This uniform bound on $f_n(z)$ makes the convergence proof very simple. Careful study of this argument reveals that the power series for $f_n(z)$ actually converges for $|z| < \pi\sqrt{2n+1}/2$; therefore the singularities of $f_n(z)$ get farther and farther away from the origin as n grows, and the continued fraction actually represents $\tanh z$ *throughout* the complex plane.

Another proof gives further information of a different kind: If we let

$$A_n(z) = n! \sum_{k=0}^{n} \binom{2n-k}{n} \frac{z^k}{k!} = \sum_{k \ge 0} \frac{(n+k)! \, z^{n-k}}{k! \, (n-k)!} = z^n \, {}_2F_0(n+1, -n; ; -1/z),$$

then

$$A_{n+1}(z) = \sum_{k \ge 0} \frac{(n+k-1)! \, ((4n+2)k + (n+1-k)(n-k))}{k! \, (n+1-k)!} z^{n+1-k}$$

$$= (4n+2)A_n(z) + z^2 A_{n-1}(z).$$

It follows, by induction, that

$$K_n\left(\frac{1}{z}, \frac{3}{z}, \ldots, \frac{2n-1}{z}\right) = \frac{A_n(2z) + A_n(-2z)}{2^{n+1} z^n},$$

$$K_{n-1}\left(\frac{3}{z}, \ldots, \frac{2n-1}{z}\right) = \frac{A_n(2z) - A_n(-2z)}{2^{n+1} z^n}.$$

Hence

$$//z^{-1}, 3z^{-1}, \ldots, (2n-1)z^{-1}// = \frac{A_n(2z) - A_n(-2z)}{A_n(2z) + A_n(-2z)},$$

and we want to show that this ratio approaches $\tanh z$. By Equations 1.2.9–(11) and 1.2.6–(24),

$$e^z A_n(-z) = n! \sum_{m \ge 0} \frac{z^m}{m!} \left(\sum_{k=0}^{n} \binom{m}{k} \binom{2n-k}{n} (-1)^k \right) = \sum_{m \ge 0} \binom{2n-m}{n} z^m \frac{n!}{m!}.$$

Hence

$$e^z A_n(-z) - A_n(z) = R_n(z) = (-1)^n z^{2n+1} \sum_{k \ge 0} \frac{(n+k)! \, z^k}{(2n+k+1)! \, k!}.$$

We now have $(e^{2z} - 1)(A_n(2z) + A_n(-2z)) - (e^{2z} + 1)(A_n(2z) - A_n(-2z)) = 2R_n(2z)$; hence

$$\tanh z - /\!/ z^{-1}, 3z^{-1}, \dots, (2n-1)z^{-1} /\!/ = \frac{2R_n(2z)}{(A_n(2z) + A_n(-2z))(e^{2z} + 1)},$$

and we have an exact formula for the difference. When $|2z| \leq 1$, the factor $e^{2z} + 1$ is bounded away from zero, $|R_n(2z)| \leq e\, n!/(2n+1)!$, and

$$\frac{1}{2}|A_n(2z) + A_n(-2z)| \geq n! \left(\binom{2n}{n} - \binom{2n-2}{n} - \binom{2n-4}{n} - \binom{2n-6}{n} - \cdots \right)$$

$$\geq \frac{(2n)!}{n!} \left(1 - \frac{1}{4} - \frac{1}{16} - \frac{1}{64} - \cdots \right) = \frac{2}{3} \frac{(2n)!}{n!}.$$

Thus convergence is very rapid, even for complex values of z.

To go from this continued fraction to the continued fraction for e^z, we have $\tanh z = 1 - 2/(e^{2z} + 1)$; hence we get the continued-fraction representation for $(e^{2z} + 1)/2$ by simple manipulations. Hurwitz's rule gives the expansion of $e^{2z} + 1$, from which we may subtract unity. For n odd,

$$e^{-2/n} = /\!/ \overline{1, 3mn + \lfloor n/2 \rfloor, (12m+6)n, (3m+2)n + \lfloor n/2 \rfloor, 1} /\!/, \qquad m \geq 0.$$

Another derivation has been given by C. S. Davis, *J. London Math. Soc.* **20** (1945), 194–198. The continued fraction for e was first found empirically by Roger Cotes, *Philosophical Transactions* **29** (1714), 5–45, Proposition 1, Scholium 3. Euler communicated his results in a letter to Goldbach on November 25, 1731 [*Correspondance Mathématique et Physique*, edited by P. H. Fuss, **1** (St. Petersburg: 1843), 56–60], and he eventually published fuller descriptions in *Commentarii Acad. Sci. Petropolitanæ* **9** (1737), 98–137; **11** (1739), 32–81.

17. (b) $/\!/ x_1 - 1, 1, x_2 - 2, 1, x_3 - 2, 1, \dots, 1, x_{2n-1} - 2, 1, x_{2n} - 1 /\!/$. [*Note:* One can remove negative parameters from continuants by using the identity

$$K_{m+n+1}(x_1, \dots, x_m, -x, y_n, \dots, y_1)$$
$$= (-1)^{n-1} K_{m+n+2}(x_1, \dots, x_{m-1}, x_m - 1, 1, x - 1, -y_n, \dots, -y_1),$$

from which we obtain

$$K_{m+n+1}(x_1, \dots, x_m, -x, y_n, \dots, y_1)$$
$$= -K_{m+n+3}(x_1, \dots, x_{m-1}, x_m - 1, 1, x - 2, 1, y_n - 1, y_{n-1}, \dots, y_1)$$

after a second application. A similar identity appears in exercise 41.]

(c) $1 + /\!/ 1, 1, 3, 1, 5, 1, \dots /\!/ = 1 + /\!/ \overline{2m+1, 1} /\!/, \; m \geq 0$.

18. Since we have $K_m(a_1, a_2, \dots, a_m) /\!/ a_1, a_2, \dots, a_m, x /\!/ = K_{m-1}(a_2, \dots, a_m) + (-1)^m/(K_{m-1}(a_1, \dots, a_{m-1}) + K_m(a_1, a_2, \dots, a_m)x)$ by Eqs. (5) and (8), we also have $K_m(a_1, a_2, \dots, a_m) /\!/ a_1, a_2, \dots, a_m, x_1, a_1, a_2, \dots, a_m, x_2, a_1, a_2, \dots, a_m, x_3, a_1, \dots /\!/ = K_{m-1}(a_2, \dots, a_m) + /\!/ (-1)^m(C + Ax_1), C + Ax_2, (-1)^m(C + Ax_3), \dots /\!/$, where $A = K_m(a_1, a_2, \dots, a_m)$ and $C = K_{m-1}(a_2, \dots, a_m) + K_{m-1}(a_1, \dots, a_{m-1})$. Consequently the stated difference is $(K_{m-1}(a_2, \dots, a_m) - K_{m-1}(a_1, \dots, a_{m-1}))/K_m(a_1, a_2, \dots, a_m)$, by (6). [The case $m = 2$ was discussed by Euler in *Commentarii Acad. Sci. Petropolitanæ* **9** (1737), 98–137, §24–26.]

19. The sum for $1 \leq k \leq N$ is $\log_b((1+x)(N+1)/(N+1+x))$.

20. Let $H = SG$, $g(x) = (1+x)G'(x)$, $h(x) = (1+x)H'(x)$. Then (37) implies that $h(x+1)/(x+2) - h(x)/(x+1) = -(1+x)^{-2}g(1/(1+x))/(1+1/(1+x))$.

21. $\varphi(x) = c/(cx+1)^2 + (2-c)/((c-1)x+1)^2$, $U\varphi(x) = 1/(x+c)^2$. When $c \le 1$, the minimum of $\varphi(x)/U\varphi(x)$ occurs at $x = 0$ and is $2c^2 \le 2$. When $c \ge \phi$, the minimum occurs at $x = 1$ and is $\le \phi^2$. When $c \approx 1.31266$ the values at $x = 0$ and $x = 1$ are nearly equal and the minimum is > 3.2; the bounds $(0.29)^n\varphi \le U^n\varphi \le (0.31)^n\varphi$ are obtained. Still better bounds come from well-chosen linear combinations of the form $Tg(x) = \sum a_j/(x+c_j)$.

23. By the interpolation formula of exercise 4.6.4–15 with $x_0 = 0$, $x_1 = x$, $x_2 = x + \epsilon$, letting $\epsilon \to 0$, we have the general identity $R_n'(x) = (R_n(x) - R_n(0))/x + \frac{1}{2}xR_n''(\theta_n(x))$ for some $\theta_n(x)$ between 0 and x, whenever R_n is a function with continuous second derivative. Hence in this case $R_n'(x) = O(2^{-n})$.

24. ∞. [A. Khinchin, in *Compos. Math.* **1** (1935), 361–382, proved that the sum $A_1 + \cdots + A_n$ of the first n partial quotients of a real number X will be asymptotically $n \lg n$, for almost all X. Exercise 35 shows that the behavior is different for rational X.]

25. Any union of intervals can be written as a union of disjoint intervals, since we have $\bigcup_{k \ge 1} I_k = \bigcup_{k \ge 1}(I_k \setminus \bigcup_{1 \le j < k} I_j)$, and this is a disjoint union in which $I_k \setminus \bigcup_{1 \le j < k} I_j$ can be expressed as a finite union of disjoint intervals. Therefore we may take $\mathcal{I} = \bigcup I_k$, where I_k is an interval of length $\epsilon/2^k$ containing the kth rational number in $[0 .. 1]$, using some enumeration of the rationals. In this case $\mu(\mathcal{I}) \le \epsilon$, but $|\mathcal{I} \cap P_n| = n$ for all n.

26. The continued fractions $/\!/A_1, \ldots, A_t/\!/$ that appear are precisely those for which $A_1 > 1$, $A_t > 1$, and $K_t(A_1, A_2, \ldots, A_t)$ is a divisor of n. Therefore (6) completes the proof. [*Note:* If $m_1/n = /\!/A_1, \ldots, A_t/\!/$ and $m_2/n = /\!/A_t, \ldots, A_1/\!/$, where m_1 and m_2 are relatively prime to n, then $m_1 m_2 \equiv \pm 1$ (modulo n); this rule defines the correspondence. When $A_1 = 1$ an analogous symmetry is valid, according to (46).]

27. First prove the result for $n = p^e$, then for $n = rs$, where r and s are relatively prime. Alternatively, use the formulas in the next exercise.

28. (a) The left-hand side is multiplicative (see exercise 1.2.4–31), and it is easily evaluated when n is a power of a prime. (c) From (a), we have *Möbius's inversion formula*: If $f(n) = \sum_{d\backslash n} g(d)$, then $g(n) = \sum_{d\backslash n} \mu(n/d)f(d)$.

29. We have $\sum_{n=1}^{N} n \ln n = \frac{1}{2}N^2 \ln N + O(N^2)$ by Euler's summation formula (see exercise 1.2.11.2– 7). Also $\sum_{n=1}^{N} n \sum_{d\backslash n} \Lambda(d)/d = \sum_{d=1}^{N} \Lambda(d) \sum_{1 \le k \le N/d} k$, and this is $O(\sum_{d=1}^{N} \Lambda(d)N^2/d^2) = O(N^2)$. Indeed, $\sum_{d \ge 1} \Lambda(d)/d^2 = -\zeta'(2)/\zeta(2)$.

30. The modified algorithm affects the calculation if and only if the following division step in the unmodified algorithm would have the quotient 1, and in this case it avoids the following division step. The probability that a given division step is avoided is the probability that $A_k = 1$ and that this quotient is preceded by an even number of quotients equal to 1. By the symmetry condition, this is the probability that $A_k = 1$ and is *followed* by an even number of quotients equal to 1. The latter happens if and only if $X_{k-1} > \phi - 1 = 0.618\ldots$, where ϕ is the golden ratio: For $A_k = 1$ and $A_{k+1} > 1$ if and only if $\frac{2}{3} \le X_{k-1} < 1$; $A_k = A_{k+1} = A_{k+2} = 1$ and $A_{k+3} > 1$ if and only if $\frac{5}{8} \le X_{k-1} < \frac{2}{3}$; etc. Thus we save approximately $F_{k-1}(1) - F_{k-1}(\phi - 1) \approx 1 - \lg\phi \approx 0.306$ of the division steps. The average number of steps is approximately $((12\ln\phi)/\pi^2)\ln n$, when $v = n$ and u is relatively prime to n.

K. Vahlen [*Crelle* **115** (1895), 221–233] considered all algorithms that replace (u, v) by $(v, (\pm u) \bmod v)$ at each iteration when $u \bmod v \neq 0$. If $u \perp v$ there are exactly v such algorithms, and they can be represented as a binary tree with v leaves. The shallowest leaves, which correspond to the shortest possible number of iterations over all such gcd algorithms, occur when the least remainder is taken at each step; the deepest leaves occur when the greatest remainder is always chosen. [Similar ideas had been considered by Lagrange in *Hist. Acad. Sci.* **23** (Berlin: 1768), 111–180, §58.] For further results see N. G. de Bruijn and W. M. Zaring, *Nieuw Archief voor Wiskunde* (3) **1** (1953), 105–112; G. J. Rieger, *Math. Nachr.* **82** (1978), 157–180.

On many computers, the modified algorithm makes each division step longer; the idea of exercise 1, which saves *all* division steps when the quotient is unity, would be preferable in such cases.

31. Let $a_0 = 0$, $a_1 = 1$, $a_{n+1} = 2a_n + a_{n-1}$; then $a_n = ((1 + \sqrt{2})^n - (1 - \sqrt{2})^n)/2\sqrt{2}$, and the worst case (in the sense of Theorem F) occurs when $u = a_n + a_{n-1}$, $v = a_n$, $n \geq 2$. This result is due to A. Dupré [*J. de Math.* **11** (1846), 41–64], who also investigated more general "look-ahead" procedures suggested by J. Binet.

32. (b) $K_{m-1}(x_1, \ldots, x_{m-1}) K_{n-1}(x_{m+2}, \ldots, x_{m+n})$ corresponds to those Morse code sequences of length $m + n$ in which a dash occupies positions m and $m + 1$; the other term corresponds to the opposite case. (Alternatively, use exercise 2. The more general identity

$$K_{m+n}(x_1, \ldots, x_{m+n}) K_k(x_{m+1}, \ldots, x_{m+k}) =$$
$$K_{m+k}(x_1, \ldots, x_{m+k}) K_n(x_{m+1}, \ldots, x_{m+n})$$
$$+ (-1)^k K_{m-1}(x_1, \ldots, x_{m-1}) K_{n-k-1}(x_{m+k+2}, \ldots, x_{m+n})$$

also appeared in Euler's paper. Incidentally, "Morse code" was really invented by F. C. Gerke in 1848; Morse's prototypes were quite different.)

33. (a) The new representations are $x = m/d$, $y = (n - m)/d$, $x' = y' = d = \gcd(m, n - m)$, for $\frac{1}{2}n < m < n$. (b) The relation $(n/x') - y \leq x < n/x'$ defines x. (c) Count the x' satisfying (b). (d) A pair of integers $x > y > 0$ with $x \perp y$ can be uniquely written in the form $x = K_m(x_1, \ldots, x_m)$, $y = K_{m-1}(x_1, \ldots, x_{m-1})$, where $x_1 \geq 2$ and $m \geq 1$; here $y/x = //x_m, \ldots, x_1//$. (e) It suffices to show that $\sum_{1 \leq k \leq n/2} T(k, n) = 2\lfloor n/2 \rfloor + h(n)$; this follows from exercise 26.

34. (a) Dividing x and y by $\gcd(x, y)$ yields $g(n) = \sum_{d \backslash n} h(n/d)$; apply exercise 28(c), and use the symmetry between primed and unprimed variables. (b) For fixed y and t, the representations with $xd \geq x'$ have $x' < \sqrt{nd}$; hence there are $O(\sqrt{nd}/y)$ such representations. Now sum for $0 < t \leq y < \sqrt{n/d}$. (c) If $s(y)$ is the given sum, then $\sum_{d \backslash y} s(d) = y(H_{2y} - H_y) = k(y)$, say; hence $s(y) = \sum_{d \backslash y} \mu(d) k(y/d)$. Now $k(y) = y \ln 2 - 1/4 + O(1/y)$. (d) $\sum_{y=1}^{n} \varphi(y)/y^2 = \sum_{y=1}^{n} \sum_{d \backslash y} \mu(d)/yd = \sum_{cd \leq n} \mu(d)/cd^2$. (Similarly, $\sum_{y=1}^{n} \sigma_{-1}(y)/y^2 = O(1)$.) (e) $\sum_{k=1}^{n} \mu(k)/k^2 = 6/\pi^2 + O(1/n)$ (see exercise 4.5.2–10(d)); and $\sum_{k=1}^{n} \mu(k) \log k/k^2 = O(1)$. Hence $h_d(n) = n((3 \ln 2)/\pi^2) \ln(n/d) + O(n)$ for $d \geq 1$. Finally $h(n) = 2 \sum_{cd \backslash n} \mu(d) h_c(n/cd) = ((6 \ln 2)/\pi^2) n(\ln \ln n - \sum - \sum') + O(n\sigma_{-1}(n)^2)$, where the remaining sums are $\sum = \sum_{cd \backslash n} \mu(d) \ln(cd)/cd = 0$ and $\sum' = \sum_{cd \backslash n} \mu(d) \ln c/cd = \sum_{d \backslash n} \Lambda(d)/d$. [It is well known that $\sigma_{-1}(n) = O(\log \log n)$; see Hardy and Wright, *An Introduction to the Theory of Numbers*, §22.9.]

35. See *Proc. Nat. Acad. Sci.* **72** (1975), 4720–4722. M. L. V. Pitteway and C. M. A. Castle [*Bull. Inst. Math. and Its Applications* **24** (1988), 17–20] have found strong and tantalizing empirical evidence that the sum of all partial quotients is actually

$$\frac{\pi^2}{24(\ln 2)^2}\left(T_n + \frac{1}{2} - \frac{18(\ln 2)^2}{\pi^2}\right)^2 + \frac{6}{\pi^2}\sum_{\substack{p \text{ prime} \\ p^r \backslash n}}\left(\frac{4r}{p^r} - \frac{p+1}{p^{2r}}\frac{p^r - 1}{p-1}\right)(\ln p)^2$$

$$- 2.542875 + O(n^{-1/2}).$$

36. Working the algorithm backwards, assuming that $t_k - 1$ divisions occur in step C2 for a given value of k, we obtain minimum u_n when $\gcd(u_{k+1}, \ldots, u_n) = F_{t_1}\ldots F_{t_k}$ and $u_k \equiv F_{t_1}\ldots F_{t_{k-1}}F_{t_k-1}$ (modulo $\gcd(u_{k+1}, \ldots, u_n)$); here the t's are ≥ 2, $t_1 \geq 3$, and $t_1 + \cdots + t_{n-1} = N + n - 1$. One way to minimize $u_n = F_{t_1}\ldots F_{t_{n-1}}$ under these conditions is to take $t_1 = 3$, $t_2 = \cdots = t_{n-2} = 2$, $u_n = 2F_{N-n+2}$. If we stipulate also that $u_1 \geq u_2 \geq \cdots \geq u_n$, the solution $u_1 = 2F_{N-n+3}+1$, $u_2 = \cdots = u_{n-1} = 2F_{N-n+3}$, $u_n = 2F_{N-n+2}$ has minimum u_1. [See *CACM* **13** (1970), 433–436, 447–448.]

37. See *Proc. Amer. Math. Soc.* **7** (1956), 1014–1021; see also exercise 6.1–18.

38. Let $m = \lceil n/\phi \rceil$, so that $m/n = \phi^{-1} + \epsilon = //a_1, a_2, \ldots //$ where $0 < \epsilon < 1/n$. Let k be minimal such that $a_k \geq 2$; then $(\phi^{1-k} + (-1)^k F_{k-1}\epsilon)/(\phi^{-k} - (-1)^k F_k \epsilon) \geq 2$, hence k is even and $\phi^{-2} = 2 - \phi \leq \phi^k F_{k+2}\epsilon = (\phi^{2k+2} - \phi^{-2})\epsilon/\sqrt{5}$. [*Ann. Polon. Math.* **1** (1954), 203–206.]

39. At least 287 at bats; $//2, 1, 95// = 96/287 \approx .33449477$, and no fraction with denominator < 287 lies in the interval

$$[.3335\ldots.3345] = [//2, 1, 666// \ldots //2, 1, 94, 1, 1, 3//].$$

To solve the general question of the fraction in $[a\mathbin{..}b]$ with smallest denominator, where $0 < a < b < 1$, note that in terms of regular continued-fraction representations we have $//x_1, x_2, \ldots // < //y_1, y_2, \ldots //$ if and only if $(-1)^j x_j < (-1)^j y_j$ for the smallest j with $x_j \neq y_j$, where we place "∞" after the last partial quotient of a rational number. Thus if $a = //x_1, x_2, \ldots //$ and $b = //y_1, y_2, \ldots //$, and if j is minimal with $x_j \neq y_j$, the fractions in $[a\mathbin{..}b]$ have the form $c = //x_1, \ldots, x_{j-1}, z_j, \ldots, z_m//$ where $//z_j, \ldots, z_m//$ lies between $//x_j, x_{j+1}, \ldots //$ and $//y_j, y_{j+1}, \ldots //$ inclusive. Let $K_{-1} = 0$. The denominator

$$K_{j-1}(x_1, \ldots, x_{j-1})K_{m-j+1}(z_j, \ldots, z_m) + K_{j-2}(x_1, \ldots, x_{j-2})K_{m-j}(z_{j+1}, \ldots, z_m)$$

of c is minimized when $m = j$ and $z_j = (j \text{ odd} \Rightarrow y_j + [y_{j+1} \neq \infty]; x_j + [x_{j+1} \neq \infty])$. [Another way to derive this method comes from the theory in the following exercise.]

40. One can prove by induction that $p_r q_l - p_l q_r = 1$ at each node, hence p_l and q_l are relatively prime. Since $p/q < p'/q'$ implies that $p/q < (p + p')/(q + q') < p'/q'$, it is also clear that the labels on all left descendants of p/q are less than p/q, while the labels on all its right descendants are greater. Therefore each rational number occurs at most once as a label.

It remains to show that each rational does appear. If $p/q = //a_1, \ldots, a_r, 1//$, where each a_i is a positive integer, one can show by induction that the node labeled p/q is found by going left a_1 times, then right a_2 times, then left a_3 times, etc.

[The sequence of labels on successive levels of this tree was first studied by M. A. Stern, *Crelle* **55** (1858), 193–220, although the relation to binary trees is not explicit in his paper. The notion of obtaining all possible fractions by successively interpolating $(p + p')/(q + q')$ between adjacent elements p/q and p'/q' goes back much further: The essential ideas were published by Daniel Schwenter [*Deliciæ Physico-Mathematicæ*

(Nürnberg: 1636), Part 1, Problem 87; *Geometria Practica*, 3rd edition (1641), 68; see M. Cantor, *Geschichte der Math.* **2** (1900), 763–765], and by John Wallis in his *Treatise of Algebra* (1685), Chapters 10–11. C. Huygens put such ideas to good use when designing the gear-wheels of his planetarium [see *Descriptio Automati Planetarii* (1703), published after his death]. Lagrange gave a full description in *Hist. Acad. Sci.* **23** (Berlin: 1767), 311–352, §24, and in his additions to the French translation of Euler's algebra (1774), §18–§20. See also exercise 1.3.2–19; A. Brocot, *Revue Chronométrique* **3** (1861), 186–194; D. H. Lehmer, *AMM* **36** (1929), 59–67.]

41. In fact, the regular continued fractions for numbers of the general form

$$\frac{1}{l_1} + \frac{(-1)^{e_1}}{l_1^2 l_2} + \frac{(-1)^{e_2}}{l_1^4 l_2^2 l_3} + \cdots$$

have an interesting pattern, based on the continuant identity

$$K_{m+n+1}(x_1, \ldots, x_{m-1}, x_m - 1, 1, y_n - 1, y_{n-1}, \ldots, y_1) =$$
$$x_m K_{m-1}(x_1, \ldots, x_{m-1}) K_n(y_n, \ldots, y_1)$$
$$+ (-1)^n K_{m+n}(x_1, \ldots, x_{m-1}, 0, -y_n, -y_{n-1}, \ldots, -y_1).$$

This identity is most interesting when $y_n = x_{m-1}$, $y_{n-1} = x_{m-2}$, etc., since

$$K_{n+1}(z_1, \ldots, z_k, 0, z_{k+1}, \ldots, z_n) = K_{n-1}(z_1, \ldots, z_{k-1}, z_k + z_{k+1}, z_{k+2}, \ldots, z_n).$$

In particular we find that if $p_n/q_n = K_{n-1}(x_2, \ldots, x_n)/K_n(x_1, \ldots, x_n) = /\!/x_1, \ldots, x_n/\!/$, then $p_n/q_n + (-1)^n/q_n^2 r = /\!/x_1, \ldots, x_n, r - 1, 1, x_n - 1, x_{n-1}, \ldots, x_1/\!/$. By changing $/\!/x_1, \ldots, x_n/\!/$ to $/\!/x_1, \ldots, x_{n-1}, x_n - 1, 1/\!/$, we can control the sign $(-1)^n$ as desired.

For example, the partial sums of the first series have the following continued fractions of even length: $/\!/1, 1/\!/$; $/\!/1, 1, 1, 1, 0, 1/\!/ = /\!/1, 1, 1, 2/\!/$; $/\!/1, 1, 1, 2, 1, 1, 1, 1, 1, 1/\!/$; $/\!/1, 1, 1, 2, 1, 1, 1, 1, 1, 1, 1, 1, 0, 1, 1, 1, 1, 1, 2, 1, 1, 1/\!/ = /\!/1, 1, 1, 2, 1, 1, 1, 1, 1, 1, 1, 2, 1, 1, 1, 1, 2, 1, 1, 1/\!/$; and from this point on the sequence settles down and obeys a simple reflecting pattern. We find that the nth partial quotient a_n can be computed rapidly as follows, if $n - 1 = 20q + r$ where $0 \le r < 20$:

$$a_n = \begin{cases} 1, & \text{if } r = 0, 2, 4, 5, 6, 7, 9, 10, 12, 13, 14, 15, 17, \text{ or } 19; \\ 2, & \text{if } r = 3 \text{ or } 16; \\ 1 + (q + r) \bmod 2, & \text{if } r = 8 \text{ or } 11; \\ 2 - d_q, & \text{if } r = 1; \\ 1 + d_{q+1}, & \text{if } r = 18. \end{cases}$$

Here d_n is the "dragon sequence" defined by the rules $d_0 = 1$, $d_{2n} = d_n$, $d_{4n+1} = 0$, $d_{4n+3} = 1$; the Jacobi symbol $\left(\frac{-1}{n}\right)$ is $1 - 2d_n$. The dragon curve discussed in exercise 4.1–18 turns right at its nth step if and only if $d_n = 1$.

Liouville's numbers with $l \ge 3$ are equal to $/\!/l - 1, l + 1, l^2 - 1, 1, l, l - 1, l^{12} - 1, 1, l - 2, l, 1, l^2 - 1, l + 1, l - 1, l^{72} - 1, \ldots /\!/$. The nth partial quotient a_n depends on the dragon sequence on $n \bmod 4$ as follows: If $n \bmod 4 = 1$ it is $l - 2 + d_{n-1} + (\lfloor n/2 \rfloor \bmod 4)$ and if $n \bmod 4 = 2$ it is $l + 2 - d_{n+2} - (\lfloor n/2 \rfloor \bmod 4)$; if $n \bmod 4 = 0$ it is 1 or $l^{k!(k-1)} - 1$, depending on whether or not $d_n = 0$ or 1, where k is the largest power of 2 dividing n; and if $n \bmod 4 = 3$ it is $l^{k!(k-1)} - 1$ or 1, depending on whether $d_{n+1} = 0$ or 1, where k is the largest power of 2 dividing $n + 1$. When $l = 2$ the same rules apply, except that 0s must be removed, so there is a more complicated pattern depending on $n \bmod 24$.

[*References:* J. O. Shallit, *J. Number Theory* **11** (1979), 209–217; Allouche, Lubiw, Mendès France, van der Poorten, and Shallit, *Acta Arithmetica* **77** (1996), 77–96.]

42. Suppose that $\|qX\| = |qX - p|$. We can always find integers u and v such that $q = uq_{n-1} + vq_n$ and $p = up_{n-1} + vp_n$, where $p_n = K_{n-1}(A_2, \ldots, A_n)$, since $q_n p_{n-1} - q_{n-1} p_n = \pm 1$. The result is clear if $v = 0$. Otherwise we must have $uv < 0$, hence $u(q_{n-1}X - p_{n-1})$ has the same sign as $v(q_n X - p_n)$, and $|qX - p|$ is equal to $|u| |q_{n-1}X - p_{n-1}| + |v| |q_n X - p_n|$. This completes the proof, since $u \neq 0$. See Theorem 6.4S for a generalization.

43. If x is representable, so is the parent of x in the Stern–Brocot tree of exercise 40; thus the representable numbers form a subtree of that binary tree. Let (u/u') and (v/v') be adjacent representable numbers. Then one is an ancestor of the other; say (u/u') is an ancestor of (v/v'), since the other case is similar. Then (u/u') is the nearest left ancestor of (v/v'), so all numbers between u/u' and v/v' are left descendants of (v/v') and the mediant $((u+v)/(u'+v'))$ is its left child. According to the relation between regular continued fractions and the binary tree, the mediant and all of its left descendants will have (u/u') as their last representable p_i/q_i, while all of the mediant's right descendants will have (v/v') as one of the p_i/q_i. (The numbers p_i/q_i label the *parents* of the "turning-point" nodes on the path to x.)

44. A counterexample for $M = N = 100$ is $(u/u') = \frac{1}{3}$, $(v/v') = \frac{67}{99}$. However, the identity is almost always true, because of (12); it fails only when $u/u' + v/v'$ is very nearly equal to a fraction that is simpler than (u/u').

45. To determine A and r such that $u = Av + r$, $0 \leq r < v$, using ordinary long division, takes $O((1 + \log A)(\log u))$ units of time. If the quotients during the algorithm are A_1, A_2, $\ldots$, A_m, then $A_1 A_2 \ldots A_m \leq u$, so $\log A_1 + \cdots + \log A_m \leq \log u$. Also $m = O(\log u)$ by Corollary L.

46. Yes, to $O(n(\log n)^2 (\log \log n))$, even if we also need to compute the sequence of partial quotients that would be computed by Euclid's algorithm; see A. Schönhage, *Acta Informatica* **1** (1971), 139–144. Moreover, Schönhage's algorithm is asymptotically optimal for computing a continued fraction expansion, with respect to the multiplications and divisions it performs [V. Strassen, *SICOMP* **12** (1983), 1–27]. Algorithm 4.5.2L is better in practice unless n is quite large, but an efficient implementation for numbers exceeding about 1800 bits is sketched in the book *Fast Algorithms* by A. Schönhage, A. F. W. Grotefeld, and E. Vetter (Heidelberg: Spektrum Akademischer Verlag, 1994), §7.2.

48. $T_j = (K_{j-2}(-a_2, \ldots, -a_{j-1}), K_{j-1}(-a_1, \ldots, -a_{j-1}), K_{n-j}(a_{j+1}, \ldots, a_n)d) = ((-1)^j K_{j-2}(a_2, \ldots, a_{j-1}), (-1)^{j-1} K_{j-1}(a_1, \ldots, a_{j-1}), K_{n-j}(a_{j+1}, \ldots, a_n)d)$.

49. Since $\lambda x_1 + \mu z_1 = \mu v$ and $\lambda x_{n+1} + \mu z_{n+1} = -\lambda v/d$, there is an odd value of j such that $\lambda x_j + \mu z_j \geq 0$ and $\lambda x_{j+2} + \mu z_{j+2} \leq 0$. If $\lambda x_j + \mu z_j > \theta$ and $\lambda x_{j+2} + \mu z_{j+2} < -\theta$ we have $\mu > \theta/z_j$ and $\lambda > -\theta/x_{j+2}$. It follows that $0 < \lambda x_{j+1} + \mu z_{j+1} < \lambda \mu x_{j+1} z_j/\theta - \lambda \mu z_{j+1} x_{j+2}/\theta \leq 2\lambda \mu v/\theta = 2\theta$, because we have $|x_{k+1} z_k| = K_{k-1}(a_2, \ldots, a_k) K_{n-k}(a_{k+1}, \ldots, a_n) \leq K_{n-1}(a_2, \ldots, a_n) = v/d$ for all k. [H. W. Lenstra, Jr., *Math. Comp.* **42** (1984), 331–340.]

50. Let $k = \lceil \beta/\alpha \rceil$. If $k\alpha < \gamma$, the answer is k; otherwise it is

$$k - 1 + \left\lceil \frac{f((1/\alpha) \bmod 1, k - \gamma/\alpha, k - \beta/\alpha)}{\alpha} \right\rceil.$$

51. If $ax - mz = y$ and $x \perp y$ we have $x \perp mz$. Consider the Stern–Brocot tree of exercise 40, with an additional node labeled $0/1$. Attach the tag value $y = ax - mz$

together with each node label z/x. We want to find all nodes z/x whose tag y is at most $\theta = \sqrt{m/2}$ in absolute value and whose denominator x is also $\leq \theta$. The only possible path to such nodes keeps a positive tag to the left and a negative tag to the right. This rule defines a unique path, which moves to the right when the tag is positive and to the left when the tag is negative, stopping when the tag becomes zero. The same path is followed implicitly when Algorithm 4.5.2X is performed with $u = m$ and $v = a$, except that the algorithm skips ahead — it visits only nodes of the path just before the tag changes sign (the parents of the "turning point" nodes as in exercise 43).

Let z/x be the first node of the path whose tag y satisfies $|y| \leq \theta$. If $x > \theta$, there is no solution, since subsequent values on the path have even larger denominators. Otherwise $(\pm x, \mp y)$ is a solution, provided that $x \perp y$.

It is easy to see that there is no solution if $y = 0$, and that if $y \neq 0$ the tag on the next node of the path will not have the same sign as y. Therefore node z/x will be visited by Algorithm 4.5.2X, and we will have $x = x_j = K_{j-1}(a_1, \ldots, a_{j-1})$, $y = y_j = (-1)^{(j-1)}K_{n-j}(a_{j+1}, \ldots, a_n)d$, $z = z_j = K_{j-2}(a_2, \ldots, a_{j-1})$ for some j (see exercise 48). The next possibility for a solution will be the node labeled $z'/x' = (z_{j-1} + kz_j)/(x_{j-1} + kx_j)$ with tag $y' = y_{j-1} + ky_j$, where k is as small as possible such that $|y'| \leq \theta$; we have $y'y < 0$. However, x' must now exceed θ; otherwise we would have $m = K_n(a_1, \ldots, a_n)d = x'|y| + x|y'| \leq \theta^2 + \theta^2 = m$, and equality cannot hold.

This discussion proves that the problem can be solved efficiently by applying Algorithm 4.5.2X with $u = m$ and $v = a$, but with the following replacement for step X2: "If $v_3 \leq \sqrt{m/2}$, the algorithm terminates. The pair $(x, y) = (|v_2|, v_3 \operatorname{sign}(v_2))$ is then the unique solution, provided that $x \perp y$ and $x \leq \sqrt{m/2}$; otherwise there is no solution." [P. S. Wang, *Lecture Notes in Comp. Sci.* **162** (1983), 225–235; P. Kornerup and R. T. Gregory, *BIT* **23** (1983), 9–20.]

A similar method works if we require $0 < x \leq \theta_1$ and $|y| \leq \theta_2$, whenever $2\theta_1\theta_2 \leq m$.

SECTION 4.5.4

1. If d_k isn't prime, its prime factors are cast out before d_k is tried.

2. No; the algorithm would fail if $p_{t-1} = p_t$, giving "1" as a spurious prime factor.

3. Let P be the product of the first 168 primes. [*Note:* Although $P = 19590 \ldots 5910$ is a 416-digit number, such a gcd can be computed in much less time than it would take to do 168 divisions, if we just want to test whether or not n is prime.]

4. In the notation of exercise 3.1–11,

$$\sum_{\mu, \lambda} 2^{\lceil \lg \max(\mu+1, \lambda) \rceil} P(\mu, \lambda) = \frac{1}{m} \sum_{l \geq 1} f(l) \prod_{k=1}^{l-1} \left(1 - \frac{k}{m}\right),$$

where $f(l) = \sum_{1 \leq \lambda \leq l} 2^{\lceil \lg \max(l+1-\lambda, \lambda) \rceil}$. If $l = 2^{k+\theta}$, where $0 < \theta \leq 1$, we have

$$f(l) = l^2(3 \cdot 2^{-\theta} - 2 \cdot 2^{-2\theta}),$$

where the function $3 \cdot 2^{-\theta} - 2 \cdot 2^{-2\theta}$ reaches a maximum of $\frac{9}{8}$ at $\theta = \lg(4/3)$ and has a minimum of 1 at $\theta = 0$ and 1. Therefore the average value of $2^{\lceil \lg \max(\mu+1, \lambda) \rceil}$ lies between 1.0 and 1.125 times the average value of $\mu + \lambda$, and the result follows.

Notes: Richard Brent has observed that, as $m \to \infty$, the density $\prod_{k=1}^{l-1}(1 - k/m) = \exp(-l(l-1)/2m + O(l^3/m^2))$ approaches a normal distribution, and we may assume that θ is uniformly distributed. Then $3 \cdot 2^{-\theta} - 2 \cdot 2^{-2\theta}$ takes the average value $3/(4\ln 2)$, and the average number of iterations needed by Algorithm B comes to approximately $(3/(4\ln 2) + \frac{1}{2})\sqrt{\pi m/2} = 1.98277\sqrt{m}$. A similar analysis of the more general method in the answer to exercise 3.1–7 gives $\sim 1.92600\sqrt{m}$, when $p \approx 2.4771366$ is chosen "optimally" as the root of $(p^2 - 1)\ln p = p^2 - p + 1$. See *BIT* **20** (1980), 176–184.

Algorithm B is a refinement of Pollard's original algorithm, which was based on exercise 3.1–6(b) instead of the yet undiscovered result in exercise 3.1–7. He showed that the least n such that $X_{2n} = X_n$ has average value $\sim (\pi^2/12)Q(m) \approx 1.0308\sqrt{m}$; this constant $\pi^2/12$ is explained by Eq. 4.5.3–(21). Hence the average amount of work needed by his original algorithm is about $1.03081\sqrt{m}$ gcds (or multiplications mod m) and $3.09243\sqrt{m}$ squarings. This will actually be *better* than Algorithm B when the cost of gcd is more than about 1.17 times the cost of squaring — as it usually is with large numbers.

Brent noticed, however, that Algorithm B can be improved by not checking the gcd when $k > l/2$; if step B4 is repeated until $k \le l/2$, we will still detect the cycle, after $\lambda \lfloor \ell(\mu)/\lambda \rfloor = \ell(\mu) - (\ell(\mu) \bmod \lambda)$ further iterations. The average cost now becomes approximately $(3/(4\ln 2))\sqrt{\pi m/2} \approx 1.35611\sqrt{m}$ iterations when we square without taking the gcd, plus $((\ln \pi - \gamma)/(4\ln 2) + \frac{1}{2})\sqrt{\pi m/2} \approx .88319\sqrt{m}$ iterations when we do both. [See the analysis by Henri Cohen in *A Course in Computational Algebraic Number Theory* (Berlin: Springer, 1993), §8.5.]

5. Remarkably, $11111 \equiv 8616460799$ (modulo $3 \cdot 7 \cdot 8 \cdot 11$), so (14) is correct also for $N = 11111$ except with respect to the modulus 5. Since the residues $(x^2 - N) \bmod 5$ are 4, 0, 3, 3, 0, we must have $x \bmod 5 = 0$, 1, or 4. The first $x \ge \lceil \sqrt{N} \rceil = 106$ that satisfies all the conditions is $x = 144$; but the square root of $144^2 - 11111 = 9625$ is not an integer. The next case, however, gives $156^2 - 11111 = 13225 = 115^2$, and $11111 = (156 - 115) \cdot (156 + 115) = 41 \cdot 271$.

6. Let us count the number of solutions (x, y) of the congruence $N \equiv (x - y)(x + y)$ (modulo p), where $0 \le x, y < p$. Since $N \not\equiv 0$ and p is prime, $x + y \not\equiv 0$. For each $v \not\equiv 0$ there is a unique u (modulo p) such that $N \equiv uv$. The congruences $x - y \equiv u$, $x + y \equiv v$ now uniquely determine $x \bmod p$ and $y \bmod p$, since p is odd. Thus the stated congruence has exactly $p - 1$ solutions (x, y). If (x, y) is a solution, so is $(x, p - y)$ if $y \ne 0$, since $(p - y)^2 \equiv y^2$; and if (x, y_1) and (x, y_2) are solutions with $y_1 \ne y_2$, we have $y_1^2 \equiv y_2^2$; hence $y_1 = p - y_2$. Thus the number of different x values among the solutions (x, y) is $(p - 1)/2$ if $N \equiv x^2$ has no solutions, or $(p + 1)/2$ if $N \equiv x^2$ has solutions.

7. One procedure is to keep two indices for each modulus, one for the current word position and one for the current bit position; loading two words of the table and doing an indexed shift command will bring the table entries into proper alignment. (Many computers have special facilities for such bit manipulation.)

8. (We may assume that $N = 2M$ is even.) The following algorithm uses an auxiliary table $X[1]$, $X[2]$, ..., $X[M - 1]$, where $X[k]$ represents the primality of $2k + 1$.

S1. Set $X[k] \leftarrow 1$ for $1 \le k < M$. Also set $j \leftarrow 1$, $k \leftarrow 1$, $p \leftarrow 3$, $q \leftarrow 4$. (During this algorithm $p = 2j + 1$ and $q = 2j + 2j^2$.)

S2. If $X[j] = 0$, go to S4. Otherwise output p, which is prime, and set $k \leftarrow q$.

S3. If $k < M$, then set $X[k] \leftarrow 0$, $k \leftarrow k + p$, and repeat this step.

S4. Set $j \leftarrow j + 1$, $p \leftarrow p + 2$, $q \leftarrow q + 2p - 2$. If $j < M$, return to S2. ∎

A major part of this calculation could be made noticeably faster if q (instead of j) were tested against M in step S4, and if a new loop were appended that outputs $2j + 1$ for all remaining $X[j]$ that equal 1, suppressing the manipulation of p and q.

Notes: The original sieve of Eratosthenes was described in Book 1, Chapter 13 of Nicomachus's *Introduction to Arithmetic*. It is well known that $\sum_{p\,\mathrm{prime}}[p \le N]/p = \ln\ln N + M + O((\log N)^{-10000})$, where $M = \gamma + \sum_{k>2}\mu(k)\ln\zeta(k)/k$ is Mertens's constant $0.26149\,72128\,47642\,78375\,54268\,38608\,69585\,90516-$; see F. Mertens, *Crelle* **76** (1874), 46–62; Greene and Knuth, *Mathematics for the Analysis of Algorithms* (Boston: Birkhäuser, 1981), §4.2.3. In particular, the number of operations in the original algorithm described by Nicomachus is $N\ln\ln N + O(N)$. Improvements in the efficiency of sieve methods for generating primes are discussed in exercise 5.2.3–15 and in Section 7.1.3.

9. If p^2 is a divisor of n for some prime p, then p is a divisor of $\lambda(n)$, but not of $n-1$. If $n = p_1 p_2$, where $p_1 < p_2$ are primes, then $p_2 - 1$ is a divisor of $\lambda(n)$ and therefore $p_1 p_2 - 1 \equiv 0$ (modulo $p_2 - 1$). Since $p_2 \equiv 1$, this means $p_1 - 1$ is a multiple of $p_2 - 1$, contradicting the assumption $p_1 < p_2$. [Values of n for which $\lambda(n)$ properly divides $n-1$ are called *Carmichael numbers*. For example, here are some small Carmichael numbers with up to six prime factors: $3\cdot11\cdot17$, $5\cdot13\cdot17$, $7\cdot11\cdot13\cdot41$, $5\cdot7\cdot17\cdot19\cdot73$, $5\cdot7\cdot17\cdot73\cdot89\cdot107$. There are 8241 Carmichael numbers less than 10^{12}, and there are at least $\Omega(N^{2/7})$ Carmichael numbers less than N; see W. R. Alford, A. Granville, and C. Pomerance, *Annals of Math.* (2) **139** (1994), 703–722.]

10. Let k_p be the order of x_p modulo n, and let λ be the least common multiple of all the k_p's. Then λ is a divisor of $n-1$ but not of any $(n-1)/p$, so $\lambda = n-1$. Since $x_p^{\varphi(n)} \bmod n = 1$, $\varphi(n)$ is a multiple of k_p for all p, so $\varphi(n) \ge \lambda$. But $\varphi(n) < n-1$ when n is not prime. (Another way to carry out the proof is to construct an element x of order $n-1$ from the x_p's, by the method of exercise 3.2.1.2–15.)

11.

U	V	A	P	S	T	Output
1984	1	0	992	0	—	
1981	1981	1	992	1	1981	
1983	4	495	993	0	1	$993^2 \equiv +2^2$
1983	991	2	98109	1	991	
1981	4	495	2	0	1	$2^2 \equiv +2^2$
1984	1981	1	99099	1	1981	
1984	1	1984	99101	0	1	$99101^2 \equiv +2^0$

The factorization $199\cdot991$ is evident from the first or last outputs. The shortness of the cycle, and the appearance of the notorious number 1984, are probably just coincidences.

12. The following algorithm makes use of an auxiliary $(m+1) \times (m+1)$ matrix of integers E_{jk}, $0 \le j, k \le m$; a single-precision vector $(b_0, b_1, \ldots, b_m)$; and a multiple-precision vector $(x_0, x_1, \ldots, x_m)$ with entries in the range $0 \le x_k < N$.

F1. [Initialize.] Set $b_i \leftarrow -1$ for $0 \le i \le m$; then set $j \leftarrow 0$.

F2. [Next solution.] Get the next output $(x, e_0, e_1, \ldots, e_m)$ from Algorithm E. (It is convenient to regard Algorithms E and F as coroutines.) Set $k \leftarrow m$.

F3. [Search for odd.] If $k < 0$ go to step F5. Otherwise if e_k is even, set $k \leftarrow k-1$ and repeat this step.

F4. [Linear dependence?] If $b_k \ge 0$, then set $i \leftarrow b_k$, $x \leftarrow (x_i x) \bmod N$, $e_r \leftarrow e_r + E_{ir}$ for $0 \le r \le m$; set $k \leftarrow k-1$ and return to F3. Otherwise set $b_k \leftarrow j$, $x_j \leftarrow x$, $E_{jr} \leftarrow e_r$ for $0 \le r \le m$; set $j \leftarrow j+1$ and return to F2. (In the latter case we have a new linearly independent solution, modulo 2, whose first odd component is e_k. The values E_{jr} are not guaranteed to remain single-precision, but they tend to remain small when k decreases from m to 0 as recommended by Morrison and Brillhart.)

F5. [Try to factor.] (Now $e_0, e_1, \ldots, e_m$ are even.) Set

$$y \leftarrow \left((-1)^{e_0/2} p_1^{e_1/2} \ldots p_m^{e_m/2}\right) \bmod N.$$

If $x = y$ or if $x + y = N$, return to F2. Otherwise compute $\gcd(x - y, N)$, which is a proper factor of N, and terminate the algorithm. ∎

This algorithm finds a factor whenever it is possible to deduce one from the given outputs of Algorithm E. [*Proof.* Let the outputs of Algorithm E be $(X_i, E_{i0}, \ldots, E_{im})$ for $1 \le i \le t$, and suppose that we could find a factorization $N = N_1 N_2$ when $x \equiv X_1^{a_1} \ldots X_t^{a_t}$ and $y \equiv (-1)^{e_0/2} p_1^{e_1/2} \ldots p_m^{e_m/2}$ (modulo N), where $e_j = a_1 E_{1j} + \cdots + a_t E_{tj}$ is even for all j. Then $x \equiv \pm y$ (modulo N_1) and $x \equiv \mp y$ (modulo N_2). It is not difficult to see that this solution can be transformed into a pair (x, y) that appears in step F5, by a series of steps that systematically replace (x, y) by (xx', yy') where $x' \equiv \pm y'$ (modulo N).]

13. There are 2^d values of x having the same exponents $(e_0, \ldots, e_m)$, since we can choose the sign of x modulo $q_i^{f_i}$ arbitrarily when $N = q_1^{f_1} \ldots q_d^{f_d}$. Exactly two of these 2^d values will fail to yield a factor.

14. Since $P^2 \equiv kNQ^2$ (modulo p) for any prime divisor p of V, we get $1 \equiv P^{2(p-1)/2} \equiv (kNQ^2)^{(p-1)/2} \equiv (kN)^{(p-1)/2}$ (modulo p), if $P \not\equiv 0$.

15. $U_n = (a^n - b^n)/\sqrt{D}$, where $a = \frac{1}{2}(P + \sqrt{D})$, $b = \frac{1}{2}(P - \sqrt{D})$, $D = P^2 - 4Q$. Then $2^{n-1} U_n = \sum_k \binom{n}{2k+1} P^{n-2k-1} D^k$; so $U_p \equiv D^{(p-1)/2}$ (modulo p) if p is an odd prime. Similarly, if $V_n = a^n + b^n = U_{n+1} - QU_{n-1}$, then $2^{n-1} V_n = \sum_k \binom{n}{2k} P^{n-2k} D^k$, and $V_p \equiv P^p \equiv P$. Thus if $U_p \equiv -1$, we find that $U_{p+1} \bmod p = 0$. If $U_p \equiv 1$, we find that $(QU_{p-1}) \bmod p = 0$; here if Q is a multiple of p, $U_n \equiv P^{n-1}$ (modulo p) for $n > 0$, so U_n is never a multiple of p; if Q is not a multiple of p, $U_{p-1} \bmod p = 0$. Therefore as in Theorem L, $U_t \bmod N = 0$ if $N = p_1^{e_1} \ldots p_r^{e_r}$, $N \perp Q$, and $t = \text{lcm}_{1 \le j \le r} (p_j^{e_j-1}(p_j + \epsilon_j))$. Under the assumptions of this exercise, the rank of apparition of N is $N + 1$; hence N is prime to Q and t is a multiple of $N + 1$. Also, the assumptions of this exercise imply that each p_j is odd and each ϵ_j is ± 1, so $t \le 2^{1-r} \prod p_j^{e_j-1}(p_j + \frac{1}{3}p_j) = 2(\frac{2}{3})^r N$; hence $r = 1$ and $t = p_1^{e_1} + \epsilon_1 p_1^{e_1-1}$. Finally, therefore, $e_1 = 1$ and $\epsilon_1 = 1$.

Note: If this test for primality is to be any good, we must choose P and Q in such a way that the test will probably work. Lehmer suggests taking $P = 1$ so that $D = 1 - 4Q$, and choosing Q so that $N \perp QD$. (If the latter condition fails, we know already that N is not prime, unless $|QD| \ge N$.) Furthermore, the derivation above shows that we will want $\epsilon_1 = 1$, that is, $D^{(N-1)/2} \equiv -1$ (modulo N). This is another condition that determines the choice of Q. Furthermore, if D satisfies this condition, and if $U_{N+1} \bmod N \ne 0$, we know that N is *not* prime.

Example: If $P = 1$ and $Q = -1$, we have the Fibonacci sequence, with $D = 5$. Since $5^{11} \equiv -1$ (modulo 23), we might attempt to prove that 23 is prime by using the Fibonacci sequence:

$$\langle F_n \bmod 23 \rangle = 0, 1, 1, 2, 3, 5, 8, 13, 21, 11, 9, 20, 6, 3, 9, 12, 21, 10, 8, 18, 3, 21, 1, 22, 0, \ldots,$$

so 24 is the rank of apparition of 23 and the test works. However, the Fibonacci sequence cannot be used in this way to prove the primality of 13 or 17, since $F_7 \bmod$

$13 = 0$ and $F_9 \bmod 17 = 0$. When $p \equiv \pm 1$ (modulo 10), we have $5^{(p-1)/2} \bmod p = 1$, so F_{p-1} (not F_{p+1}) is divisible by p.

17. Let $f(q) = 2 \lg q - 1$. When $q = 2$ or 3, the tree has at most $f(q)$ nodes. When $q > 3$ is prime, let $q = 1 + q_1 \ldots q_t$ where $t \geq 2$ and $q_1, \ldots, q_t$ are prime. The size of the tree is $\leq 1 + \sum f(q_k) = 2 + f(q-1) - t < f(q)$. [*SICOMP* **4** (1975), 214–220.]

18. $x(G(\alpha) - F(\alpha))$ is the number of $n \leq x$ whose second-largest prime factor is $\leq x^\alpha$ and whose largest prime factor is $> x^\alpha$. Hence

$$xG'(t)\,dt = \left(\pi(x^{t+dt}) - \pi(x^t)\right) \cdot x^{1-t}\left(G(t/(1-t)) - F(t/(1-t))\right).$$

The probability that $p_{t-1} \leq \sqrt{p_t}$ is $\int_0^1 F(t/2(1-t))t^{-1}\,dt$. [Curiously, it can be shown that this also equals $\int_0^1 F(t/(1-t))\,dt$, the average value of $\log p_t / \log x$, and it also equals the Dickman–Golomb constant .62433 of exercises 1.3.3–23 and 3.1–13. The derivative $G'(0)$ can be shown to equal

$$\int_0^1 F(t/(1-t))t^{-2}\,dt = F(1) + 2F(\tfrac{1}{2}) + 3F(\tfrac{1}{3}) + \cdots = e^\gamma.$$

The third-largest prime factor has $H(\alpha) = \int_0^\alpha \left(H(t/(1-t)) - G(t/(1-t))\right)t^{-1}\,dt$ and $H'(0) = \infty$. See P. Billingsley, *Period. Math. Hungar.* **2** (1972), 283–289; J. Galambos, *Acta Arith.* **31** (1976), 213–218; D. E. Knuth and L. Trabb Pardo, *Theoretical Comp. Sci.* **3** (1976), 321–348; J. L. Hafner and K. S. McCurley, *J. Algorithms* **10** (1989), 531–556.]

19. $M = 2^D - 1$ is a multiple of all p for which the order of 2 modulo p divides D. To extend this idea, let $a_1 = 2$ and $a_{j+1} = a_j^{q_j} \bmod N$, where $q_j = p_j^{e_j}$, p_j is the jth prime, and $e_j = \lfloor \log 1000/\log p_j \rfloor$; let $A = a_{169}$. Now compute $b_q = \gcd(A^q - 1, N)$ for all primes q between 10^3 and 10^5. One way to do this is to start with $A^{1009} \bmod N$ and then to multiply alternately by $A^4 \bmod N$ and $A^2 \bmod N$. (A similar method was used in the 1920s by D. N. Lehmer, but he didn't publish it.) As with Algorithm B we can avoid most of the gcds by batching; for example, since $b_{30r-k} = \gcd(A^{30r} - A^k, N)$, we might try batches of 8, computing $c_r = (A^{30r} - A^{29})(A^{30r} - A^{23})\ldots(A^{30r} - A) \bmod N$, then $\gcd(c_r, N)$ for $33 < r \leq 3334$.

20. See H. C. Williams, *Math. Comp.* **39** (1982), 225–234.

21. Some interesting theory relevant to this conjecture has been introduced by Eric Bach, *Information and Computation* **90** (1991), 139–155.

22. Algorithm P fails only when the random number x does not reveal the fact that n is nonprime. Say x is *bad* if $x^q \bmod n = 1$ or if one of the numbers $x^{2^j q}$ is $\equiv -1$ (modulo n) for $0 \leq j < k$. Since 1 is bad, we have $p_n = [n \text{ nonprime}](b_n - 1)/(n-2) < [n \text{ nonprime}]b_n/(n-1)$, where b_n is the number of bad x such that $1 \leq x < n$.

Every bad x satisfies $x^{n-1} \equiv 1$ (modulo n). When p is prime, the number of solutions to the congruence $x^q \equiv 1$ (modulo p^e) for $1 \leq x < p^e$ is the same as the number of solutions of $qy \equiv 0$ (modulo $p^{e-1}(p-1)$) for $0 \leq y < p^{e-1}(p-1)$, namely $\gcd(q, p^{e-1}(p-1))$, since we may replace x by a^y where a is a primitive root.

Let $n = n_1^{e_1} \ldots n_r^{e_r}$, where the n_i are distinct primes. According to the Chinese remainder theorem, the number of solutions to the congruence $x^{n-1} \equiv 1$ (modulo n) is $\prod_{i=1}^r \gcd(n-1, n_i^{e_i-1}(n_i-1))$, and this is at most $\prod_{i=1}^r (n_i - 1)$ since n_i is relatively prime to $n - 1$. If some $e_i > 1$, we have $n_i - 1 \leq \frac{2}{9}n_i^{e_i}$, hence the number of solutions is at most $\frac{2}{9}n$; in this case $b_n \leq \frac{2}{9}n \leq \frac{1}{4}(n-1)$, since $n \geq 9$.

Therefore we may assume that n is the product $n_1 \ldots n_r$ of distinct primes. Let $n_i = 1 + 2^{k_i}q_i$, where $k_1 \leq \cdots \leq k_r$. Then $\gcd(n-1, n_i-1) = 2^{k_i'}q_i'$, where $k_i' =$

$\min(k, k_i)$ and $q_i' = \gcd(q, q_i)$. Modulo n_i, the number of x such that $x^q \equiv 1$ is q_i'; and the number of x such that $x^{2^j q} \equiv -1$ is $2^j q_i'$ for $0 \le j < k_i'$, otherwise 0. Since $k \ge k_1$, we have $b_n = q_1' \ldots q_r' \left(1 + \sum_{0 \le j < k_1} 2^{jr}\right)$.

To complete the proof, it suffices to show that $b_n \le \frac{1}{4} q_1 \ldots q_r 2^{k_1 + \cdots + k_r} = \frac{1}{4} \varphi(n)$, since $\varphi(n) < n - 1$. We have

$$\left(1 + \sum_{0 \le j < k_1} 2^{jr}\right)/2^{k_1 + \cdots + k_r} \le \left(1 + \sum_{0 \le j < k_1} 2^{jr}\right)/2^{k_1 r}$$
$$= 1/(2^r - 1) + (2^r - 2)/(2^{k_1 r}(2^r - 1)) \le 1/2^{r-1},$$

so the result follows unless $r = 2$ and $k_1 = k_2$. If $r = 2$, exercise 9 shows that $n - 1$ is not a multiple of both $n_1 - 1$ and $n_2 - 1$. Thus if $k_1 = k_2$ we cannot have both $q_1' = q_1$ and $q_2' = q_2$; it follows that $q_1' q_2' \le \frac{1}{3} q_1 q_2$ and $b_n \le \frac{1}{6} \varphi(n)$ in this case.

[*Reference: J. Number Theory* **12** (1980), 128–138.] This proof shows that p_n is near $\frac{1}{4}$ in only two cases, when n is $(1 + 2q_1)(1 + 4q_1)$ or a Carmichael number of the special form $(1 + 2q_1)(1 + 2q_2)(1 + 2q_3)$. For example, when $n = 49939 \cdot 99877$ we have $b_n = \frac{1}{4}(49938 \cdot 99876)$ and $p_n \approx .24999$; when $n = 1667 \cdot 2143 \cdot 4523$, we have $b_n = \frac{1}{4}(1666 \cdot 2142 \cdot 4522)$, $p_n \approx .24968$. See the next answer for further remarks.]

23. (a) The proofs are simple except perhaps for the reciprocity law. Let $p = p_1 \ldots p_s$ and $q = q_1 \ldots q_r$, where the p_i and q_j are prime. Then

$$\left(\frac{p}{q}\right) = \prod_{i,j}\left(\frac{p_i}{q_j}\right) = \prod_{i,j}(-1)^{(p_i - 1)(q_j - 1)/4}\left(\frac{q_j}{p_i}\right) = (-1)^{\sum_{i,j}(p_i - 1)(q_j - 1)/4}\left(\frac{q}{p}\right),$$

so we need only verify that $\sum_{i,j}(p_i - 1)(q_j - 1)/4 \equiv (p-1)(q-1)/4$ (modulo 2). But $\sum_{i,j}(p_i - 1)(q_j - 1)/4 = (\sum_i(p_i - 1)/2)(\sum_j(q_j - 1)/2)$ is odd if and only if an odd number of the p_i and an odd number of the q_j are $\equiv 3$ (modulo 4), and this holds if and only if $(p-1)(q-1)/4$ is odd. [C. G. J. Jacobi, *Bericht Königl. Preuß. Akad. Wiss. Berlin* **2** (1837), 127–136; V. A. Lebesgue, *J. Math. Pures Appl.* **12** (1847), 497–520, discussed the efficiency.]

(b) As in exercise 22, we may assume that $n = n_1 \ldots n_r$ where the $n_i = 1 + 2^{k_i} q_i$ are distinct primes, and $k_1 \le \cdots \le k_r$; we let $\gcd(n - 1, n_i - 1) = 2^{k_i'} q_i'$ and we call x *bad* if it falsely makes n look prime. Let $\Pi_n = \prod_{i=1}^r q_i' \, 2^{\min(k_i, k-1)}$ be the number of solutions of $x^{(n-1)/2} \equiv 1$. The number of bad x with $\left(\frac{x}{n}\right) = 1$ is Π_n, times an extra factor of $\frac{1}{2}$ if $k_1 < k$. (This factor $\frac{1}{2}$ is needed to ensure that $\left(\frac{x}{n_i}\right) = -1$ for an even number of the n_i with $k_i < k$.) The number of bad x with $\left(\frac{x}{n}\right) = -1$ is Π_n if $k_1 = k$, otherwise 0. [If $x^{(n-1)/2} \equiv -1$ (modulo n_i), we have $\left(\frac{x}{n_i}\right) = -1$ if $k_i = k$, $\left(\frac{x}{n_i}\right) = +1$ if $k_i > k$, and a contradiction if $k_i < k$. If $k_1 = k$, there are an odd number of k_i equal to k.]

Notes: The probability of a bad guess is $> \frac{1}{4}$ only if n is a Carmichael number with $k_r < k$; for example, $n = 7 \cdot 13 \cdot 19 = 1729$, a number made famous by Ramanujan in another context. Louis Monier has extended the analyses above to obtain the following closed formulas for the number of bad x in general:

$$b_n = \left(1 + \frac{2^{rk_1} - 1}{2^r - 1}\right)\prod_{i=1}^r q_i'; \qquad b_n' = \delta_n \prod_{i=1}^r \gcd\left(\frac{n-1}{2}, n_i - 1\right).$$

Here b_n' is the number of bad x in this exercise, and δ_n is either 2 (if $k_1 = k$), or $\frac{1}{2}$ (if $k_i < k$ and e_i is odd for some i), or 1 (otherwise).

(c) If $x^q \mod n = 1$, then $1 = \left(\frac{x^q}{n}\right) = \left(\frac{x}{n}\right)^q = \left(\frac{x}{n}\right)$. If $x^{2^j q} \equiv -1$ (modulo n), then the order of x modulo n_i must be an odd multiple of 2^{j+1} for all prime divisors n_i

of n. Let $n = n_1^{e_1} \dots n_r^{e_r}$ and $n_i = 1 + 2^{j+1} q_i''$; then $\left(\frac{x}{n_i}\right) = (-1)^{q_i''}$, so $\left(\frac{x}{n}\right) = +1$ or -1 according as $\sum e_i q_i''$ is even or odd. Since $n \equiv \left(1 + 2^{j+1} \sum e_i q_i''\right)$ (modulo 2^{j+2}), the sum $\sum e_i q_i''$ is odd if and only if $j + 1 = k$. [*Theoretical Comp. Sci.* **12** (1980), 97–108.]

24. Let M_1 be a matrix having one row for each nonprime odd number n in the range $1 \le n \le N$ and having $N-1$ columns numbered from 2 to N; the entry in row n column x is 1 if n fails the x test of Algorithm P, otherwise it is zero. When $N = qn + r$ and $0 \le r < n$, we know that row n contains at most $-1 + q(b_n + 1) + \min(b_n + 1, r) < q(\frac{1}{4}(n-1) + 1) + \min(b_n + 1, r) \le \frac{1}{3}qn + \min(\frac{1}{4}n, r) = \frac{1}{3}N + \min(\frac{1}{4}n - \frac{1}{3}r, \frac{2}{3}r) \le \frac{1}{3}N + \frac{1}{6}n \le \frac{1}{2}N$ entries equal to 0, so at least half of the entries in the matrix are 1. Thus, some column x_1 of M_1 has at least half of its entries equal to 1. Removing column x_1 and all rows in which this column contains 1 leaves a matrix M_2 having similar properties; a repetition of this construction produces matrix M_r with $N - r$ columns and fewer than $N/2^r$ rows, and with at least $\frac{1}{2}(N-1)$ entries per row equal to 1. [See *FOCS* **19** (1978), 78.]

[A similar proof implies the existence of a *single* infinite sequence $x_1 < x_2 < \cdots$ such that the number $n > 1$ is prime if and only if it passes the x test of Algorithm P for $x = x_1, \dots, x = x_m$, where $m = \frac{1}{2}\lfloor \lg n \rfloor (\lfloor \lg n \rfloor - 1)$. Does there exist a sequence $x_1 < x_2 < \cdots$ having this property but with $m = O(\log n)$?]

25. This theorem was first proved rigorously by von Mangoldt [*Crelle* **114** (1895), 255–305], who showed in fact that the $O(1)$ term is $C + \int_x^\infty dt/((t^2-1)t \ln t)$, minus $1/2k$ if x is the kth power of a prime. The constant C is $\operatorname{li} 2 - \ln 2 = \gamma + \ln\ln 2 + \sum_{n \ge 2} (\ln 2)^n / nn! = 0.35201\ 65995\ 57547\ 47542\ 73567\ 67736\ 43656\ 84471+$.

[For a summary of developments during the 100 years following von Mangoldt's paper, see A. A. Karatsuba, *Complex Analysis in Number Theory* (CRC Press, 1995). See also Eric Bach and Jeffrey Shallit, *Algorithmic Number Theory* **1** (MIT Press, 1996), Chapter 8, for an excellent introduction to the connection between Riemann's hypothesis and concrete problems about integers.]

26. If N is not prime, it has a prime factor $q \le \sqrt{N}$. By hypothesis, every prime divisor p of f has an integer x_p such that the order of x_p modulo q is a divisor of $N-1$ but not of $(N-1)/p$. Therefore if p^k divides f, the order of x_p modulo q is a multiple of p^k. Exercise 3.2.1.2–15 now tells us that there is an element x of order f modulo q. But this is impossible, since it implies that $q^2 \ge (f+1)^2 \ge (f+1)r \ge N$, and equality cannot hold. [*Proc. Camb. Phil. Soc.* **18** (1914), 29–30.]

27. If k is not divisible by 3 and if $k \le 2^n + 1$, the number $k \cdot 2^n + 1$ is prime if and only if $3^{2^{n-1}k} \equiv -1$ (modulo $k \cdot 2^n + 1$). For if this condition holds, $k \cdot 2^n + 1$ is prime by exercise 26; and if $k \cdot 2^n + 1$ is prime, the number 3 is a quadratic nonresidue mod $k \cdot 2^n + 1$ by the law of quadratic reciprocity, since $(k \cdot 2^n + 1) \bmod 12 = 5$. [This test was stated without proof by Proth in *Comptes Rendus Acad. Sci.* **87** (Paris, 1878), 926.]

To implement Proth's test with the necessary efficiency, we need to be able to compute $x^2 \bmod (k \cdot 2^n + 1)$ with about the same speed as we can compute the quantity $x^2 \bmod (2^n - 1)$. Let $x^2 = A \cdot 2^n + B$; then $x^2 \equiv B - \lfloor A/k \rfloor + 2^n (A \bmod k)$, so the remainder is easily obtained when k is small. (See also exercise 4.3.2–14.)

[To test numbers of the form $3 \cdot 2^n + 1$ for primality, the job is only slightly more difficult; we first try random single-precision numbers until finding one that is a quadratic nonresidue mod $3 \cdot 2^n + 1$ by the law of quadratic reciprocity, then use this number in place of "3" in the test above. If $n \bmod 4 \ne 0$, the number 5 can be used. It turns out that $3 \cdot 2^n + 1$ is prime when $n = 1, 2, 5, 6, 8, 12, 18, 30, 36, 41, 66, 189, 201, 209, 276, 353, 408, 438, 534, 2208, 2816, 3168, 3189, 3912, 20909, 34350, 42294,$

42665, 44685, 48150, 55182, 59973, 80190, 157169, 213321, and no other $n \leq 300000$; and $5 \cdot 2^n + 1$ is prime when $n = 1, 3, 7, 13, 15, 25, 39, 55, 75, 85, 127, 1947, 3313, 4687, 5947, 13165, 23473, 26607, 125413, 209787, 240937$, and no other $n \leq 300000$. See R. M. Robinson, *Proc. Amer. Math. Soc.* **9** (1958), 673–681; G. V. Cormack and H. C. Williams, *Math. Comp.* **35** (1980), 1419–1421; H. Dubner and W. Keller, *Math. Comp.* **64** (1995), 397–405; J. S. Young, *Math. Comp.* **67** (1998), 1735–1738.]

28. $f(p, p^2 d) = 2/(p+1) + f(p, d)/p$, since $1/(p+1)$ is the probability that A is a multiple of p. $f(p, pd) = 1/(p+1)$ when $d \bmod p \neq 0$. $f(2, 4k+3) = \frac{1}{3}$ since $A^2 - (4k+3)B^2$ cannot be a multiple of 4; $f(2, 8k+5) = \frac{2}{3}$ since $A^2 - (8k+5)B^2$ cannot be a multiple of 8; $f(2, 8k+1) = \frac{1}{3} + \frac{1}{3} + \frac{1}{3} + \frac{1}{6} + \frac{1}{12} + \cdots = \frac{4}{3}$. $f(p, d) = (2p/(p^2 - 1), 0)$ if $d^{(p-1)/2} \bmod p = (1, p-1)$, respectively, for odd p.

29. The number of solutions to the inequality $x_1 + \cdots + x_m \leq r$ in nonnegative integers x_i is $\binom{m+r}{r} \geq m^r/r!$, and each of these corresponds to a unique integer $p_1^{x_1} \ldots p_m^{x_m} \leq n$. [For sharper estimates, in the special case that p_j is the jth prime for all j, see N. G. de Bruijn, *Indag. Math.* **28** (1966), 240–247; H. Halberstam, *Proc. London Math. Soc.* (3) **21** (1970), 102–107.]

30. If $p_1^{e_1} \ldots p_m^{e_m} \equiv x_i^2$ (modulo q_i), we can find y_i such that $p_1^{e_1} \ldots p_m^{e_m} \equiv (\pm y_i)^2$ (modulo $q_i^{d_i}$), hence by the Chinese remainder theorem we obtain 2^d values of X such that $X^2 \equiv p_1^{e_1} \ldots p_m^{e_m}$ (modulo N). Such $(e_1, \ldots, e_m)$ correspond to at most $\binom{r}{r/2}$ pairs $(e_1', \ldots, e_m'; e_1'', \ldots, e_m'')$ having the hinted properties. Now for each of the 2^d binary numbers $a = (a_1 \ldots a_d)_2$, let n_a be the number of exponents $(e_1', \ldots, e_m')$ such that $(p_1^{e_1'} \ldots p_m^{e_m'})^{(q_i-1)/2} \equiv (-1)^{a_i}$ (modulo q_i); we have proved that the required number of integers X is $\geq 2^d (\sum_a n_a^2)/\binom{r}{r/2}$. Since $\sum_a n_a$ is the number of ways to choose at most $r/2$ objects from a set of m objects with repetitions permitted, namely $\binom{m+r/2}{r/2}$, we have $\sum_a n_a^2 \geq \binom{m+r/2}{r/2}^2/2^d \geq m^r/(2^d (r/2)!^2)$. [See *J. Algorithms* **3** (1982), 101–127, where Schnorr presents many further refinements of Theorem D.]

31. Set $n = M$, $pM = 4m$, and $\epsilon M = 2m$ to show that $\Pr(X \leq 2m) \leq e^{-m/2}$.

32. Let $M = \lfloor \sqrt[3]{N} \rfloor$, and let the places x_i of each message be restricted to the range $0 \leq x < M^3 - M^2$. If $x \geq M$, encode it as $x^3 \bmod N$ as before, but if $x < M$ change the encoding to $(x + yM)^3 \bmod N$, where y is a random number in the range $M^2 - M \leq y < M^2$. To decode, first take the cube root; and if the result is $M^3 - M^2$ or more, take the remainder mod M.

34. Let P be the probability that $x^m \bmod p = 1$ and let Q be the probability that $x^m \bmod q = 1$. The probability that $\gcd(x^m - 1, N) = p$ or q is $P(1 - Q) + Q(1 - P) = P + Q - 2PQ$. If $P \leq \frac{1}{2}$ or $Q \leq \frac{1}{2}$, this probability is $\geq 2(10^{-6} - 10^{-12})$, so we have a good chance of finding a factor after about $10^6 \log m$ arithmetic operations modulo N. On the other hand if $P > \frac{1}{2}$ and $Q > \frac{1}{2}$ then $P \approx Q \approx 1$, since we have the general formula $P = \gcd(m, p-1)/p$; thus m is a multiple of $\operatorname{lcm}(p-1, q-1)$ in this case. Let $m = 2^k r$ where r is odd, and form the sequence $x^r \bmod N$, $x^{2r} \bmod N$, ..., $x^{2^k r} \bmod N$; we find as in Algorithm P that the first appearance of 1 is preceded by a value y other than $N - 1$ with probability $\geq \frac{1}{2}$, hence $\gcd(y - 1, N) = p$ or q.

35. Let $f = (p^{q-1} - q^{p-1}) \bmod N$. Since $p \bmod 4 = q \bmod 4 = 3$, we have $\left(\frac{-1}{p}\right) = \left(\frac{-1}{q}\right) = \left(\frac{f}{p}\right) = -\left(\frac{f}{q}\right) = -1$, and we also have $\left(\frac{2}{p}\right) = -\left(\frac{2}{q}\right) = -1$. Given a message x in the range $0 \leq x \leq \frac{1}{8}(N-5)$, let $\bar{x} = 4x + 2$ or $8x + 4$, whichever satisfies $\left(\frac{\bar{x}}{N}\right) \geq 0$; then transmit the message $\bar{x}^2 \bmod N$.

To decode this message, we first use a SQRT box to find the unique number y such that $y^2 \equiv \bar{x}^2 \bmod N$ and $\left(\frac{y}{N}\right) \geq 0$ and y is even. Then $y = \bar{x}$, since the other square roots of $\bar{x}^2$ are $N - \bar{x}$ and $(\pm f\bar{x}) \bmod N$; the first of these is odd, and the other two either have negative Jacobi symbols or are simply $\bar{x}$ and $N - \bar{x}$. The decoding is now completed by setting $x \leftarrow \lfloor y/4 \rfloor$ if $y \bmod 4 = 2$, otherwise $x \leftarrow \lfloor y/8 \rfloor$.

Anybody who can decode such encodings can also find the factors of N, because the decoding of a false message $\bar{x}^2 \bmod N$ when $\left(\frac{\bar{x}}{N}\right) = -1$ reveals $(\pm f) \bmod N$, and $((\pm f) \bmod N) - 1$ has a nontrivial gcd with N. [*Reference: IEEE Transactions* **IT-26** (1980), 726–729.]

36. The mth prime equals $m \ln m + m \ln \ln m - m + m \ln \ln m / \ln m - 2m / \ln m + O(m(\log \log m)^2 (\log m)^{-2})$, by (4), although for this problem we need only the weaker estimate $p_m = m \ln m + O(m \log \log m)$. (We will assume that p_m is the mth prime, since this corresponds to the assumption that V is uniformly distributed.) If we choose $\ln m = \frac{1}{2} c \sqrt{\ln N \ln \ln N}$, where $c = O(1)$, we find that $r = c^{-1} \sqrt{\ln N / \ln \ln N} - c^{-2} - c^{-2}(\ln \ln \ln N / \ln \ln N) - 2c^{-2}(\ln \frac{1}{2}c)/\ln \ln N + O(\sqrt{\ln \ln N / \ln N})$. The estimated running time (22) now simplifies somewhat surprisingly to $\exp(f(c, N) \sqrt{\ln N \ln \ln N} + O(\log \log N))$, where we have $f(c, N) = c + (1 - (1 + \ln 2)/\ln \ln N)c^{-1}$. The value of c that minimizes $f(c, N)$ is $\sqrt{1 - (1 + \ln 2)/\ln \ln N}$, so we obtain the estimate

$$\exp(2\sqrt{\ln N \ln \ln N} \sqrt{1 - (1 + \ln 2)/\ln \ln N} + O(\log \log N)).$$

When $N = 10^{50}$ this gives $\epsilon(N) \approx .33$, which is still much larger than the observed behavior.

Note: The partial quotients of $\sqrt{D}$ seem to behave according to the distribution obtained for random real numbers in Section 4.5.3. For example, the first million partial quotients of the square root of the number $10^{18} + 314159$ include exactly (415236, 169719, 93180, 58606) cases where A_n is respectively (1, 2, 3, 4). Moreover, we have $V_{n+1} = |p_n^2 - D q_n^2| = 2\sqrt{D} q_n |p_n - \sqrt{D} q_n| + O(q_n^{-2})$ by exercise 4.5.3–12(c) and Eq. 4.5.3–(12). Therefore we can expect $V_n / 2\sqrt{D}$ to behave essentially like the quantity $\theta_n(x) = q_n |p_n - x q_n|$, where x is a random real number. The random variable θ_n is known to have the approximate density $\min(1, \theta^{-1} - 1)/\ln 2$ for $0 \leq \theta \leq 1$ [see Bosma, Jager, and Wiedijk, *Indag. Math.* **45** (1983), 281–299], which is uniform when $\theta \leq 1/2$. So something besides the size of V_n must account for the unreasonable effectiveness of Algorithm E.

37. Apply exercise 4.5.3–12 to the number $\sqrt{D} + R$, to see that the periodic part begins immediately, and run the period backwards to verify the palindromic property. [It follows that the second half of the period gives the same V's as the first, and Algorithm E could be shut down earlier by terminating it when $U = U'$ or $V = V'$ in step E5. However, the period is generally so long, we never even get close to halfway through it, so there is no point in making the algorithm more complicated.]

38. Let $r = (10^{50} - 1)/9$. Then $P_0 = 10^{49} + 9$; $P_1 = r + 3 \cdot 10^{46}$; $P_2 = 2r + 3 \cdot 10^{47} + 7$; $P_3 = 3r + 2 \cdot 10^{49}$; $P_4 = 4r + 2 \cdot 10^{49} - 3$; $P_5 = 5r + 3 \cdot 10^{49} + 4$; $P_6 = 6r + 2 \cdot 10^{48} + 3$; $P_7 = 7r + 2 \cdot 10^{25}$ (very pretty); $P_8 = 8r + 10^{38} - 7$; $P_9 = 9r - 8000$.

39. Notice that it's easy to prove the primality of q when $q - 1$ has just 2 and p as prime factors. The only successors of 2 are Fermat primes, and the existence or nonexistence of a sixth Fermat prime is one of the most famous unsolved problems of number theory. Thus we probably will never know how to determine whether or not an arbitrary integer has any successors. In some cases, however, this is possible; for example, John Selfridge proved in 1962 that 78557 and 271129 have none [see *AMM* **70**

(1963), 101–102], after W. Sierpiński had proved the existence of infinitely many odd numbers without a successor [*Elemente der Math.* **15** (1960), 73–74]. Perhaps 78557 is the smallest of these, although 69 other contenders for that honor still existed in 1983, according to G. Jaeschke and W. Keller [*Math. Comp.* **40** (1983), 381–384, 661–673; **45** (1985), 637].

For information on the more traditional "Cunningham" form of prime chain, in which the transitions are $p \to 2p \pm 1$, see Günter Löh, *Math. Comp.* **53** (1989), 751–759. In particular, Löh found that $554688278430 \cdot 2^k - 1$ is prime for $0 \le k < 12$.

40. [*Inf. Proc. Letters* **8** (1979), 28–31.] Notice that $x \bmod y = x - y \lfloor x/y \rfloor$ can be computed easily on such a machine, and we can get simple constants like $0 = x - x$, $1 = \lfloor x/x \rfloor$, $2 = 1 + 1$; we can test $x > 0$ by testing whether $x = 1$ or $\lfloor x/(x-1) \rfloor \ne 0$.

(a) First compute $l = \lfloor \lg n \rfloor$ in $O(\log n)$ steps, by repeatedly dividing by 2; at the same time compute $k = 2^l$ and $A = 2^{2^{l+1}}$ in $O(\log n)$ steps by repeatedly setting $k \leftarrow 2k$, $A \leftarrow A^2$. For the main computation, suppose we know that $t = A^m$, $u = (A+1)^m$, and $v = m!$; then we can increase the value of m by 1 by setting $m \leftarrow m+1$, $t \leftarrow At$, $u \leftarrow (A+1)u$, $v \leftarrow vm$; and we can *double* the value of m by setting $m \leftarrow 2m$, $u \leftarrow u^2$, $v \leftarrow (\lfloor u/t \rfloor \bmod A)v^2$, $t \leftarrow t^2$, provided that A is sufficiently large. (Consider the number u in radix-A notation; A must be greater than $\binom{2m}{m}$.) Now if $n = (a_l \ldots a_0)_2$, let $n_j = (a_l \ldots a_j)_2$; if $m = n_j$ and $k = 2^j$ and $j > 0$ we can decrease j by 1 by setting $k \leftarrow \lfloor k/2 \rfloor$, $m \leftarrow 2m + (\lfloor n/k \rfloor \bmod 2)$. Hence we can compute $n_j!$ for $j = l$, $l-1$, ..., 0 in $O(\log n)$ steps. [Another solution, due to Julia Robinson, is to compute $n! = \lfloor B^n / \binom{B}{n} \rfloor$ when $B > (2n)^{n+1}$; see *AMM* **80** (1973), 250–251, 266.]

(b) First compute $A = 2^{2^{l+2}}$ as in (a), then find the least $k \ge 0$ such that $2^{k+1}! \bmod n = 0$. If $\gcd(n, 2^k!) \ne 1$, let $f(n)$ be this value; note that this gcd can be computed in $O(\log n)$ steps by Euclid's algorithm. Otherwise we will find the least integer m such that $\binom{m}{\lfloor m/2 \rfloor} \bmod n = 0$, and let $f(n) = \gcd(m, n)$. (Note that in this case $2^k < m \le 2^{k+1}$, hence $\lceil m/2 \rceil \le 2^k$ and $\lceil m/2 \rceil!$ is relatively prime to n; therefore $\binom{m}{\lfloor m/2 \rfloor} \bmod n = 0$ if and only if $m! \bmod n = 0$. Furthermore $n \ne 4$.)

To compute m with a bounded number of registers, we can use Fibonacci numbers (see Algorithm 6.2.1F). Suppose we know that $s = F_j$, $s' = F_{j+1}$, $t = A^{F_j}$, $t' = A^{F_{j+1}}$, $u = (A+1)^{2F_j}$, $u' = (A+1)^{2F_{j+1}}$, $v = A^m$, $w = (A+1)^{2m}$, $\binom{2m}{m} \bmod n \ne 0$, and $\binom{2(m+s)}{m+s} \bmod n = 0$. It is easy to reach this state of affairs with $m = F_{j+1}$, for suitably large j, in $O(\log n)$ steps; furthermore A will be larger than $2^{2(m+s)}$. If $s = 1$, we set $f(n) = \gcd(2m+1, n)$ or $\gcd(2m+2, n)$, whichever is $\ne 1$, and terminate the algorithm. Otherwise we reduce j by 1 as follows: Set $r \leftarrow s$, $s \leftarrow s' - s$, $s' \leftarrow r$, $r \leftarrow t$, $t \leftarrow \lfloor t'/t \rfloor$, $t' \leftarrow r$, $r \leftarrow u$, $u \leftarrow \lfloor u'/u \rfloor$, $u' \leftarrow r$; then if $(\lfloor wu/vt \rfloor \bmod A) \bmod n \ne 0$, set $m \leftarrow m+s$, $w \leftarrow wu$, $v \leftarrow vt$.

[Can this problem be solved with fewer than $O(\log n)$ operations? Can the smallest, or the largest, prime factor of n be computed in $O(\log n)$ operations?]

41. (a) Clearly $\pi(x) = \pi(m) + f_1(x, m) = \pi(m) + f(x, m) - f_0(x, m) - f_2(x, m) - f_3(x, m) - \cdots$ when $1 \le m \le x$. Set $x = N^3$, $m = N$, and note that $f_k(N^3, N) = 0$ for $k > 2$.

(b) We have $f_2(N^3, N) = \sum_{N < p \le q} [pq \le N^3] = \sum_{N < p \le N^{3/2}} (\pi(N^3/p) - \pi(p) + 1) = \sum_{N < p \le N^{3/2}} \pi(N^3/p) - \binom{\pi(N^{3/2})}{2} + \binom{\pi(N)}{2}$, where p and q range over primes. Hence $f_2(1000, 10) = \pi(\frac{1000}{11}) + \pi(\frac{1000}{13}) + \pi(\frac{1000}{17}) + \pi(\frac{1000}{19}) + \pi(\frac{1000}{23}) + \pi(\frac{1000}{29}) + \pi(\frac{1000}{31}) - \binom{\pi(31)}{2} + \binom{\pi(10)}{2} = 24 + 21 + 16 + 15 + 14 + 11 + 11 - 55 + 6 = 63$.

(c) The hinted identity says simply that a p_j-survivor is a p_{j-1}-survivor that isn't a multiple of p_j. Clearly $f(N^3, N) = f(N^3, p_{\pi(N)})$. Apply the identity until reaching terms $f(x, p_j)$ where either $j = 0$ or $x \le N^2$; the result is

$$f(N^3, N) = \sum_{k=1}^{N-1} \mu(k) f\left(\frac{N^3}{k}, 1\right) - \sum_{j=1}^{\pi(N)} \sum_{N/p_j \le k < N} \mu(k) f\left(\frac{N^3}{kp_j}, p_{j-1}\right)[k \text{ is a } p_j\text{-survivor}].$$

Now $f(x, 1) = \lfloor x \rfloor$, so the first sum is $1000 - 500 - 333 - 200 + 166 - 142 = -9$ when $N = 10$. The second sum is $-f(\frac{1000}{10}, 1) - f(\frac{1000}{14}, 1) - f(\frac{1000}{15}, 2) - f(\frac{1000}{21}, 2) - f(\frac{1000}{35}, 3) = -100 - 71 - 33 - 24 - 9 = -237$. Hence $f(1000, 10) = -9 + 237 = 228$, and $\pi(1000) = 4 + 228 - 1 - 63 = 168$.

(d) If $N^2 \le 2^m$ we can construct an array in which $a_{2^m-1+n} = [n + 1$ is a p_j-survivor$]$ for $1 \le n \le N^2$ represents a sieve after j passes, and $a_n = a_{2n} + a_{2n+1}$ for $1 \le n < 2^m$. Then it is easy to compute $f(x, p_j)$ in $O(m)$ steps when $x \le N^2$, and to remove multiples of p from the sieve in $O(N^2 m/p)$ steps. The total running time to compute $f(N^3, N)$ will come to $O(N^2 \log N \log \log N)$, because $\sum_{j=1}^{\pi(N)} 1/p_j = O(\log \log N)$.

The storage requirement can be reduced from $2N^2 m$ to $2Nm$ if we break the sieve into N parts of size N and work on each part separately. Auxiliary tables of p_j for $1 \le j \le \pi(N)$, and of $\mu(k)$ and the least prime factor of k for $1 \le k \le N$, are helpful and easily constructed before the main computation begins.

[See *Math. Comp.* **44** (1985), 537–560. A similar procedure was first introduced by D. F. E. Meissel, *Math. Annalen* **2** (1870), 636–642; **3** (1871), 523–525; **21** (1883), 304; **25** (1885), 251–257. D. H. Lehmer made several refinements in *Illinois J. Math.* **3** (1959), 381–388. Neither Meissel nor Lehmer had a stopping rule for the recurrence that was as efficient as the method described above. Further refinements due to Marc Deléglise, Joël Rivat, Xavier Gourdon, and Tomás Oliveira e Silva have made it possible to deduce that $\pi(10^{23}) = 1925320391606803968923$; see *Revista do DETUA* **4** (2006), 759–768. Lagarias and Odlyzko also developed a completely different approach whereby $\pi(N)$ can be evaluated in $O(N^{1/2+\epsilon})$ steps, using principles of analytic number theory; see *J. Algorithms* **8** (1987), 173–191. But the constant in that O is impractically large.

42. L1. [Initialize.] Find $\bar{r}$ such that $r\bar{r} \equiv 1$ (modulo s); then set $r' \leftarrow n\bar{r} \bmod s$, $u \leftarrow r'\bar{r} \bmod s$, $v \leftarrow s$, $w \leftarrow (n - rr')\bar{r}/s \bmod s$, $\theta \leftarrow \lfloor \sqrt{N/s} \rfloor$, $(u_1, u_3) \leftarrow (1, u)$, $(v_1, v_3) \leftarrow (0, v)$. (We want to find all pairs of integers (λ, μ) such that $(\lambda s + r)(\mu s + r') = N$; this implies $\lambda u + \mu \equiv w$ (modulo s) and $\sqrt{\lambda \mu v} \le \theta$. We will perform Algorithm 4.5.2X with t_2, u_2, v_2 suppressed; the relations

$$\lambda t_3 + \mu t_1 \equiv w t_1, \quad \lambda u_3 + \mu u_1 \equiv w u_1, \quad \lambda v_3 + \mu v_1 \equiv w v_1 \quad \text{(modulo } s\text{)}$$

will remain invariant.)

L2. [Try for divisors.] If $v_1 = 0$, output $\lambda s + r$ whenever $\lambda s + r$ divides N and $0 \le \lambda \le \theta/s$. If $v_3 = 0$, output $N/(\mu s + r')$ whenever $\mu s + r'$ divides N and $0 \le \mu \le \theta/s$. Otherwise, for all k such that $|wv_1 + ks| \le \theta$ if $v_1 < 0$, or $0 < wv_1 + ks \le 2\theta$ if $v_1 > 0$, and for $\sigma = +1$ and -1, output $\lambda s + r$ if $d = (wv_1 s + ks^2 + v_3 r + v_1 r')^2 - 4v_1 v_3 N$ is a perfect square and if the numbers

$$\lambda = \frac{wv_1 s + ks^2 - v_3 r + v_1 r' + \sigma\sqrt{d}}{2v_3 s}, \quad \mu = \frac{wv_1 s + ks^2 + v_3 r - v_1 r' - \sigma\sqrt{d}}{2v_3 s}$$

are positive integers. (These are the solutions to $\lambda v_3 + \mu v_1 = wv_1 + ks$, $(\lambda s + r)(\mu s + r') = N$.)

L3. [Done?] If $v_3 = 0$, the algorithm terminates.

L4. [Divide and subtract.] Set $q \leftarrow \lfloor u_3/v_3 \rfloor$. If $u_3 = qv_3$ and $v_1 < 0$, decrease q by 1. Then set

$$(t_1, t_3) \leftarrow (u_1, u_3) - (v_1, v_3)q, \quad (u_1, u_3) \leftarrow (v_1, v_3), \quad (v_1, v_3) \leftarrow (t_1, t_3)$$

and return to step L2. $\blacksquare$

[See *Math. Comp.* **42** (1984), 331–340. The bounds in step L2 can be sharpened, for example to ensure that $d \geq 0$. Some factors may be output more than once.]

43. (a) First make sure that the Jacobi symbol $\left(\frac{y}{m}\right)$ is $+1$. (If it's 0, the task is easy; if it's -1, then $y \notin Q_m$.) Then choose random integers $x_1, \ldots, x_n$ in $[0 \ldots m)$ and let $X_j = [G(y^2 x_j^4 \bmod m) = (yx_j^2 \bmod m) \bmod 2]$. If $y \in Q_m$ we have $E\,X_j \geq \frac{1}{2} + \epsilon$; otherwise $m - y \in Q_m$ and $E\,X_j \leq \frac{1}{2} - \epsilon$. Report that $y \in Q_m$ if $X_1 + \cdots + X_n \geq \frac{1}{2}n$. The probability of failure is at most $e^{-2\epsilon^2 n}$, by exercise 1.2.10–21. Therefore we choose $n = \lceil \frac{1}{2}\epsilon^{-2} \ln \delta^{-1} \rceil$.

(b) Find an x with Jacobi symbol $\left(\frac{x}{m}\right) = -1$, and set $y \leftarrow x^2 \bmod m$. Then the prime factors of m are $\gcd(x + \sqrt{y}, m)$ and $\gcd(x - \sqrt{y}, m)$, so our task is to find $\pm\sqrt{y}$ when $y \in Q_m$ is given. If we can find τv for any nonzero v, we are done, since $\sqrt{y} = (v^{-1}\tau v) \bmod m$ unless $\gcd(v, m)$ is a factor of m.

Assume that $\epsilon = 2^{-e}$ for some $e \geq 1$. Choose random integers a and b in $[0 \ldots m)$, and assume that we know the binary fractions α_0 and β_0 such that

$$\left| \frac{\tau a}{m} - \alpha_0 \right| < \frac{\epsilon}{64}, \qquad \left| \frac{\tau b}{m} - \beta_0 \right| < \frac{\epsilon^3}{64};$$

here α_0 is an odd multiple of $\epsilon/64$, while β_0 is an odd multiple of $\epsilon^3/64$. Assume also that we know λa and λb. Of course we don't really know α_0, β_0, λa, or λb, but we will try all $32\epsilon^{-1} \times 32\epsilon^{-3} \times 2 \times 2$ possibilities. Spurious branches of the program, which operate under incorrect assumptions, will cause no harm.

Define the numbers $u_{tj} = 2^{-t}(a + (j + \frac{1}{2})b) \bmod m$ and $v_{tj} = 2^{-t-1}(a + jb) \bmod m$. Both u_{tj} and v_{tj} are uniformly distributed in $[0 \ldots m)$, because a and b were chosen at random. Furthermore, for fixed t, the numbers u_{tj} for $j_0 \leq j < j_0 + l$ are *pairwise independent*, and so are the numbers v_{tj} for $j_0 \leq j < j_0 + l$, as long as l does not exceed the smallest prime factor of m. We will make use of u_{tj} and v_{tj} only for $-2r\epsilon^{-2} \leq j < 2r\epsilon^{-2}$; if any of these values has a nonzero factor in common with m, we're done.

For all $v \perp m$ we define $\chi v = +1$ if $v \in Q_m$, $\chi v = -1$ if $-v \in Q_m$, and $\chi v = 0$ if $\left(\frac{v}{m}\right) = -1$. Notice that $\chi u_{(t+2)j} = \chi u_{tj}$, since $u_{tj} = (2^2 u_{(t+2)j}) \bmod m$. Therefore we can determine χu_{tj} and χv_{tj} for all t and j by applying algorithm A to u_{tj} and v_{tj} for $0 \leq t \leq 1$ and $-2r\epsilon^{-2} \leq j < 2r\epsilon^{-2}$. Setting $\delta = \frac{1}{1440}\epsilon^2 r^{-1}$ in that algorithm will ensure that all χ values are correct with probability $\geq 1 - \frac{1}{90}$.

The algorithm works in at most r stages. At the beginning of stage t, for $0 \leq t < r$, we assume that we know $\lambda 2^{-t}a$, $\lambda 2^{-t}b$, and fractions α_t, β_t such that

$$\left| \frac{\tau 2^{-t}a}{m} - \alpha_t \right| < \frac{\epsilon}{2^{t+6}}, \qquad \left| \frac{\tau 2^{-t}b}{m} - \beta_t \right| < \frac{\epsilon^3}{2^{t+6}}.$$

Define $\alpha_{t+1} = \frac{1}{2}(\alpha_t + \lambda 2^{-t}a)$ and $\beta_{t+1} = \frac{1}{2}(\beta_t + \lambda 2^{-t}b)$; this preserves the inequalities. The next step is to find $\lambda 2^{-t-1}b$, which satisfies

$$\lambda u_{tj} + \lambda 2^{-t}a + j\lambda 2^{-t}b + \lambda 2^{-t-1}b + \left\lfloor \frac{\tau 2^{-t}a + j\tau 2^{-t}b + \tau 2^{-t-1}b}{m} \right\rfloor \equiv 0 \quad (\text{modulo } 2).$$

Let $n = 4\min(r, 2^t)\epsilon^{-2}$; then when $|j| \le \frac{n}{2}$ we have

$$\left| \frac{\tau 2^{-t}a}{m} + j\frac{\tau 2^{-t}b}{m} + \frac{\tau 2^{-t-1}b}{m} - (\alpha_t + j\beta_t + \beta_{t+1}) \right| < \frac{\epsilon}{16}.$$

Therefore if $\chi u_{tj} = 1$ it is likely that $\lambda 2^{-t-1}b = G_j$, where $G_j = (G(u_{tj}^2 y \bmod m) + \lambda 2^{-t}a + j\lambda 2^{-t}b + \lfloor \alpha_t j\beta_t + \beta_{t+1} \rfloor) \bmod 2$. More precisely, we will have

$$\lfloor (\tau 2^{-t}a + j\tau 2^{-t}b + \tau 2^{-t-1}b)/m \rfloor = \lfloor \alpha_t + j\beta_t + \beta_{t+1} \rfloor$$

unless $\tau u_{tj} < \frac{\epsilon}{16}m$ or $\tau u_{tj} > \left(1 - \frac{\epsilon}{16}\right)m$. Let $Y_j = (2G_j - 1)\chi u_{tj}$. If $Y_j = +1$, it is a vote for $\lambda 2^{-t-1}b = 1$; if $Y_j = -1$, it is a vote for $\lambda 2^{-t-1}b = 0$; if $Y_j = 0$, it is an abstention. We will be democratic and set $\lambda 2^{-t-1}b = [\sum_{j=-n/2}^{n/2-1} Y_j \ge 0]$.

What is the probability that $\lambda 2^{-t-1}b$ is correct? Let $Z_j = -1$ if $\chi u_{tj} \ne 0$ and $(\tau u_{tj} < \frac{\epsilon}{16}m$ or $\tau u_{tj} > (1 - \frac{\epsilon}{16})m$ or $G(u_{tj}^2 y \bmod m) \ne \lambda u_{tj})$; otherwise let $Z_j = |\chi u_{tj}|$. Since Z_j is a function of u_{tj}, the random variables Z_j are pairwise independent and have the same distribution. Let $Z = \sum_{j=-n/2}^{n/2-1} Z_j$; if $Z > 0$, the value of $\lambda 2^{-t-1}b$ will be correct. The probability that $Z_j = 0$ is $\frac{1}{2}$, and the probability that $Z_j = +1$ is $\ge \frac{1}{4} + \frac{\epsilon}{2} - \frac{\epsilon}{8}$; therefore $\mathrm{E}\,Z_j \ge \frac{3}{4}\epsilon$. Clearly $\mathrm{var}(Z_j) \le \frac{1}{2}$. So the chance of error, in the branch of the program that has the correct assumptions, is at most $\Pr(Z \le 0) \le \Pr((Z - n\,\mathrm{E}\,Z_j)^2 \ge \frac{9}{16}n^2\epsilon^2) \le \frac{8}{9}n^{-1}\epsilon^2 = \frac{2}{9}\min(r, 2^t)^{-1}$, by Chebyshev's inequality (exercise 3.5–42).

A similar method, with v_{tj} in place of u_{tj}, can be used to determine $\lambda 2^{-t-1}a$ with error $\le \frac{2}{9}\min(r, 2^t)^{-1}$. Eventually we will have $\epsilon^3/2^{t+6} < 1/(2m)$, so $\tau 2^{-t}b$ will be the nearest integer to $m\beta_t$. Then we can compute $\sqrt{y} = (2^t b^{-1}\tau 2^{-t}b) \bmod m$; squaring this quantity will tell us if we are correct.

The total chance of making a mistake is bounded by $\frac{4}{9}\sum_{t\ge 1} 2^{-t} = \frac{4}{9}$ in stages $t < \lg n$, and by $\frac{4}{9}\sum_{t\le r} r^{-1} = \frac{4}{9}$ in subsequent stages. So the total chance of error, including the possibility that the χ values were not all correct, is at most $\frac{4}{9} + \frac{4}{9} + \frac{1}{90} = \frac{9}{10}$. At least $\frac{1}{10}$ of all runs of the program will succeed in finding $\sqrt{y}$; hence the factors of m will be found after repeating the process at most 10 times, on the average.

The total running time is dominated by $O(r\epsilon^{-4}\log(r\epsilon^{-2})T(G))$ for the χ computation, plus $O(r^2\epsilon^{-2}T(G))$ for subsequent guessing, plus $O(r^2\epsilon^{-6})$ for the calculations of α_t, β_t, $\lambda 2^{-t}a$, and $\lambda 2^{-t}b$ in all branches.

This procedure, which nicely illustrates many of the basic paradigms of randomized algorithms, is due to R. Fischlin and C. P. Schnorr [*J. Cryptology* **13** (2000), 221–244], who derived it from earlier approaches by Alexi, Chor, Goldreich, and Schnorr [*SICOMP* **17** (1988), 194–209] and by Ben-Or, Chor, and Shamir [*STOC* **15** (1983), 421–430]. When we combine it with Lemma 3.5P4, we get a theorem analogous to Theorem 3.5P, but with the sequence 3.2.2–(16) instead of 3.2.2–(17). Fischlin and Schnorr showed how to streamline the calculations so that their factoring algorithm takes $O(r\epsilon^{-4}\log(r\epsilon^{-1})T(G))$ steps; the resulting time bound for "cracking" 3.2.2–(16) is $T(F) = O(RN^4\epsilon^{-4}\log(RN\epsilon^{-1})(T(G) + R^2))$. The constant factor implied by this O is rather large, but not enormous. A similar method finds x from the RSA function $y = x^a \bmod m$ when $a \perp \varphi(m)$, if we can guess $y^{1/a} \bmod 2$ with probability $\ge \frac{1}{2} + \epsilon$.

44. Suppose $\sum_{j=0}^{d-1} a_{ij}x^j \equiv 0$ (modulo m_i), $\gcd(a_{i0}, a_{i1}, \ldots, a_{i(d-1)}, m_i) = 1$, and $|x| < m_i$ for $1 \le i \le k = d(d-1)/2 + 1$, where $m_i \perp m_j$ for $1 \le i < j \le k$. Also assume that $m = \min\{m_1, \ldots, m_k\} > n^{n/2}2^{n^2/2}d^d$, where $n = d + k$. First find

$u_1, \ldots, u_k$ such that $u_j \bmod m_i = \delta_{ij}$. Then set up the $n \times n$ matrix

$$L = \begin{pmatrix} M & & & & & & & \\ 0 & mM & & & & & & \\ \vdots & \vdots & \ddots & & & & & \\ 0 & 0 & \cdots & m^{d-1}M & & & & \\ a_{10}u_1 & ma_{11}u_1 & \cdots & m^{d-1}a_{1(d-1)}u_1 & M/m_1 d & & & \\ a_{20}u_2 & ma_{21}u_2 & \cdots & m^{d-1}a_{2(d-1)}u_2 & 0 & M/m_2 d & & \\ \vdots & \vdots & & \vdots & \vdots & \vdots & \ddots & \\ a_{k0}u_k & ma_{k1}u_k & \cdots & m^{d-1}a_{k(d-1)}u_k & 0 & 0 & \cdots & M/m_k d \end{pmatrix}$$

where $M = m_1 m_2 \ldots m_k$; all entries above the diagonal are zero, hence $\det L = M^{n-1}m^{k-1}d^{-k}$. Now let $v = (t_0, \ldots, t_{d-1}, v_1, \ldots, v_k)$ be a nonzero integer vector with $\mathrm{length}(vL) \leq \sqrt{n2^n}M^{(n-1)/n}m^{(k-1)/n}d^{-k/n}$. Since $M^{(n-1)/n} < M/m^{k/n}$, we have $\mathrm{length}(vL) < M/d$. Let $c_j = t_j M + \sum_{i=1}^{k} a_{ij}u_i v_i$ and $P(x) = c_0 + c_1 x + \cdots + c_{d-1}x^{d-1}$. Then $P(x) \equiv v_i(a_{i0} + a_{i1}x + \cdots + a_{i(d-1)}x^{d-1}) \equiv 0$ (modulo m_i), for $1 \leq i \leq k$; hence $P(x) \equiv 0$ (modulo M). Also $|m^j c_j| < M/d$; it follows that $P(x) = 0$. But $P(x)$ is not identically zero, because the conditions $v_i a_{ij} \equiv 0$ (modulo m_i) and $\gcd(a_{i0}, \ldots, a_{i(d-1)}, m_i) = 1$ imply $v_i \equiv 0$ (modulo m_i), while $|v_i M/m_i d| < M/d$ implies $|v_i| < m_i$; we cannot have $v_1 = \cdots = v_k = 0$. Thus we can find x (more precisely, at most $d - 1$ possibilities for x), and the total running time is polynomial in $\lg M$. [*Lecture Notes in Comp. Sci.* **218** (1985), 403–408.]

45. Fact 1. A solution always exists. Suppose first that n is prime. If $\left(\frac{b}{n}\right) = 1$, there is a solution with $y = 0$. If $\left(\frac{b}{n}\right) = -1$, let $j > 0$ be minimum such that we have $\left(\frac{-ja}{n}\right) = -1$; then $x_0^2 - a \equiv -ja$ and $b \equiv -ja(y_0)^2$ for some x_0 and y_0 (modulo n), hence $(x_0 y_0)^2 - ay_0^2 \equiv b$. Suppose next that we have found a solution $x^2 - ay^2 \equiv b$ (modulo n) and we want to extend this to a solution modulo n^2. We can always find c and d such that $(x+cn)^2 - a(y+dn)^2 \equiv b$ (modulo n^2), because $(x+cn)^2 - a(y+dn)^2 \equiv x^2 - ay^2 + (2cx - 2ayd)n$ and $\gcd(2x, 2ay) \perp n$. Thus a solution always exists when n is a power of an odd prime. (We need to assume that n is odd because, for example, there is no solution to $x^2 \pm y^2 \equiv 3$ (modulo 8).) Finally, a solution exists for all odd n, by the Chinese remainder theorem.

    Fact 2. The number of solutions, given a and n with $a \perp n$, is the same for all $b \perp n$. This follows from the hinted identity and Fact 1, for if $x_1^2 - ay_1^2 \equiv b$ then $(x_1 x_2 - ay_1 y_2, x_1 y_2 + x_2 y_1)$ runs through all solutions of $x^2 - ay^2 \equiv b$ as (x_2, y_2) runs through all solutions of $x^2 - ay^2 \equiv 1$. In other words, (x_2, y_2) is uniquely determined by (x_1, y_1) and (x, y), when $x_1^2 - ay_1^2 \perp n$.

    Fact 3. Given integers (a, s, z) such that $z^2 \equiv a$ (modulo s), we can find integers (x, y, m, t) with $x^2 - ay^2 = m^2 st$, where $(x, y) \neq (0, 0)$ and $t^2 \leq \frac{4}{3}|a|$. For if $z^2 = a + ms$, let (u, v) be a nonzero pair of integers that minimizes $(zu + mv)^2 + |a|u^2$. We can find (u, v) efficiently using the methods of Section 3.3.4, and $(zu+mv)^2 + |a|u^2 \leq (\frac{4}{3}|a|)^{1/2}$ by exercise 3.3.4–9. Therefore $(zu + mv)^2 - au^2 = mt$ where $t^2 \leq \frac{4}{3}|a|$. The hinted identity now solves $x^2 - ay^2 = (ms)(mt)$.

    Fact 4. It is easy to solve $x^2 - y^2 \equiv b$ (modulo n), because we can let $x = (b+1)/2$, $y = (b-1)/2$.

    Fact 5. It is not difficult to solve $x^2 + y^2 \equiv b$ (modulo n), because the method in exercise 3.3.4–11 solves $x^2 + y^2 = p$ when p is prime and $p \bmod 4 = 1$; one of the numbers $b, b + n, b + 2n, \ldots$ will be such a prime.

Now to solve the stated problem when $|a| > 1$ we can proceed as follows. Choose u and v at random between 1 and $n - 1$, then compute $w = (u^2 - av^2) \bmod n$ and $d = \gcd(w, n)$. If $1 < d < n$ or if $\gcd(v, n) > 1$ we can reduce n; the methods used to prove Fact 1 will lift solutions for factors of n to solutions for n itself. If $d = n$ and $v \perp n$, we have $(u/v)^2 \equiv a$ (modulo n), hence we can reduce a to 1. Otherwise $d = 1$; let $s = bw \bmod n$. This number s is uniformly distributed among the numbers prime to n, by Fact 2. If $\left(\frac{a}{s}\right) = 1$, try to solve $z^2 \equiv a$ (modulo s), assuming that s is prime (exercise 4.6.2–15). If unsuccessful, start over with another random choice of u and v. If successful, let $z^2 = a + ms$ and compute $d = \gcd(ms, n)$. If $d > 1$, reduce the problem as before. Otherwise use Fact 3 to find $x^2 - ay^2 = m^2 st$ with $t^2 \leq \frac{4}{3}|a|$; this makes $(x/m)^2 - a(y/m)^2 \equiv st$ (modulo n). If $t = 0$, reduce a to 1. Otherwise apply the algorithm recursively to solve $X^2 - tY^2 \equiv a$ (modulo n). (Since t is much smaller than a, only $O(\log \log n)$ levels of recursion will be necessary.) If $\gcd(Y, n) > 1$ we can reduce n or a; otherwise $(X/Y)^2 - a(1/Y)^2 \equiv t$ (modulo n). Finally the hinted identity yields a solution to $x'^2 - ay'^2 \equiv s$ (see Fact 2), which leads in turn to the desired solution because $u^2 - av^2 \equiv s/b$.

In practice only $O(\log n)$ random trials are needed before the assumptions about prime numbers made in this algorithm turn out to be true. But a formal proof would require us to assume the Extended Riemann Hypothesis [*IEEE Trans.* **IT-33** (1987), 702–709]. Adleman, Estes, and McCurley [*Math. Comp.* **48** (1987), 17–28] have developed a slower and more complicated algorithm that does not rely on any unproved hypotheses.

46. [*FOCS* **20** (1979), 55–60.] After finding $a^{n_i} \bmod p = \prod_{j=1}^{m} p_j^{e_{ij}}$ for enough n_i, we can solve $\sum_i x_{ijk} e_{ij} + (p - 1) t_{jk} = \delta_{jk}$ in integers x_{ijk}, t_{jk} for $1 \leq j, k \leq m$ (for example, as in 4.5.2–(23)), thereby knowing the solutions $N_j = \left(\sum_i x_{ijk} e_{jk}\right) \bmod (p-1)$ to $a^{N_j} \bmod p = p_j$. Then if $ba^{n'} \bmod p = \prod_{j=1}^{m} p_j^{e'_j}$, we have $n + n' \equiv \sum_{j=1}^{m} e'_j N_j$ (modulo $p - 1$). [Improved algorithms are known; see, for example, Coppersmith, Odlyzko, and Schroeppel, *Algorithmica* **1** (1986), 1–15.]

SECTION 4.6

1. $9x^2 + 7x + 7$; $5x^3 + 7x^2 + 2x + 6$.

2. (a) True. (b) False if the algebraic system S contains *zero divisors*, that is, nonzero numbers whose product is zero, as in exercise 1; otherwise true. (c) True when $m \neq n$, but false in general when $m = n$, since the leading coefficients might cancel.

3. Assume that $r \leq s$. For $0 \leq k \leq r$ the maximum is $m_1 m_2(k + 1)$; for $r \leq k \leq s$ it is $m_1 m_2(r + 1)$; for $s \leq k \leq r + s$ it is $m_1 m_2(r + s + 1 - k)$. The least upper bound valid for all k is $m_1 m_2(r + 1)$. (The solver of this exercise will know how to factor the polynomial $x^7 + 2x^6 + 3x^5 + 3x^4 + 3x^3 + 3x^2 + 2x + 1$.)

4. If one of the polynomials has fewer than 2^t nonzero coefficients, the product can be formed by putting exactly $t - 1$ zeros between each of the coefficients, then multiplying in the binary number system, and finally using a bitwise AND instruction (present on most binary computers, see Algorithm 4.5.4D) to zero out the extra bits. For example, if $t = 3$, the multiplication in the text would become $(1001000001)_2 \times (1000001001)_2 = (1001001011001001001)_2$; the desired answer is obtained if we AND this result with the constant $(1001001 \ldots 1001)_2$. A similar technique can be used to multiply polynomials with nonnegative coefficients that are not too large.

5. Polynomials of degree $\leq 2n$ can be written $U_1(x)x^n + U_0(x)$ where $\deg(U_1) \leq n$ and $\deg(U_0) \leq n$; and $\big(U_1(x)x^n + U_0(x)\big)\big(V_1(x)x^n + V_0(x)\big) = U_1(x)V_1(x)(x^{2n} + x^n) +$

$(U_1(x) + U_0(x))(V_1(x) + V_0(x))x^n + U_0(x)V_0(x)(x^n + 1)$. (This equation assumes that arithmetic is being done modulo 2.) Thus Eqs. 4.3.3–(3) and 4.3.3–(5) hold.

Notes: S. A. Cook has shown that Algorithm 4.3.3T can be extended in a similar way; and A. Schönhage [*Acta Informatica* **7** (1977), 395–398] has explained how to multiply polynomials mod 2 with only $O(n \log n \log \log n)$ bit operations. In fact, polynomials over any ring S can be multiplied with only $O(n \log n \log \log n)$ algebraic operations, even when S is an algebraic system in which multiplication need not be commutative or associative [D. G. Cantor and E. Kaltofen, *Acta Informatica* **28** (1991), 693–701]. See also exercises 4.6.4–57 and 4.6.4–58. But these ideas are not useful for sparse polynomials (having mostly zero coefficients).

SECTION 4.6.1

1. $q(x) = 1 \cdot 2^3 x^3 + 0 \cdot 2^2 x^2 - 2 \cdot 2x + 8 = 8x^3 - 4x + 8$; $r(x) = 28x^2 + 4x + 8$.

2. The monic sequence of polynomials produced during Euclid's algorithm has the coefficients $(1, 5, 6, 6, 1, 6, 3)$, $(1, 2, 5, 2, 2, 4, 5)$, $(1, 5, 6, 2, 3, 4)$, $(1, 3, 4, 6)$, 0. Hence the greatest common divisor is $x^3 + 3x^2 + 4x + 6$. (The greatest common divisor of a polynomial and its reverse is always symmetric, in the sense that it is a unit multiple of its own reverse.)

3. The procedure of Algorithm 4.5.2X is valid, with polynomials over S substituted for integers. When the algorithm terminates, we have $U(x) = u_2(x)$, $V(x) = u_1(x)$. Let $m = \deg(u)$, $n = \deg(v)$. It is easy to prove by induction that $\deg(u_3) + \deg(v_1) = n$, $\deg(u_3) + \deg(v_2) = m$, after step X3, throughout the execution of the algorithm, provided that $m \geq n$. Hence if m and n are greater than $d = \deg(\gcd(u, v))$ we have $\deg(U) < m - d$, $\deg(V) < n - d$; the exact degrees are $m - d_1$ and $n - d_1$, where d_1 is the degree of the next-to-last nonzero remainder. If $d = \min(m, n)$, say $d = n$, we have $U(x) = 0$ and $V(x) = 1$.

When $u(x) = x^m - 1$ and $v(x) = x^n - 1$, the identity $(x^m - 1) \bmod (x^n - 1) = x^{m \bmod n} - 1$ shows that all polynomials occurring during the calculation are monic, with integer coefficients. When $u(x) = x^{21} - 1$ and $v(x) = x^{13} - 1$, we have $V(x) = x^{11} + x^8 + x^6 + x^3 + 1$ and $U(x) = -(x^{19} + x^{16} + x^{14} + x^{11} + x^8 + x^6 + x^3 + x)$. [See also Eq. 3.3.3–(29), which gives an alternative formula for $U(x)$ and $V(x)$. See also exercise 4.3.2–6, with 2 replaced by x.]

4. Since the quotient $q(x)$ depends only on $v(x)$ and the first $m-n$ coefficients of $u(x)$, the remainder $r(x) = u(x) - q(x)v(x)$ is uniformly distributed and independent of $v(x)$. Hence each step of the algorithm may be regarded as independent of the others; this algorithm is much more well-behaved than Euclid's algorithm over the integers.

The probability that $n_1 = n - k$ is $p^{1-k}(1 - 1/p)$, and $t = 0$ with probability p^{-n}. Each succeeding step has essentially the same behavior; hence we can see that any given sequence of degrees $n, n_1, \ldots, n_t, -\infty$ occurs with probability $(p - 1)^t/p^n$. To find the average value of $f(n_1, \ldots, n_t)$, let S_t be the sum of $f(n_1, \ldots, n_t)$ over all sequences $n > n_1 > \cdots > n_t \geq 0$ having a given value of t; then the average is $\sum_t S_t(p - 1)^t/p^n$.

Let $f(n_1, \ldots, n_t) = t$; then $S_t = \binom{n}{t}t$, so the average is $n(1 - 1/p)$. Similarly, if $f(n_1, \ldots, n_t) = n_1 + \cdots + n_t$, then $S_t = \binom{n}{2}\binom{n-1}{t-1}$, and the average is $\binom{n}{2}(1 - 1/p)$. Finally, if $f(n_1, \ldots, n_t) = (n - n_1)n_1 + \cdots + (n_{t-1} - n_t)n_t$, then

$$S_t = \binom{n+2}{t+2} - (n+1)\binom{n+1}{t+1} + \binom{n+1}{2}\binom{n}{t},$$

and the average is $\binom{n+1}{2} - (n+1)p/(p-1) + (p/(p-1))^2(1 - 1/p^{n+1})$.

(The probability that $n_{j+1} = n_j - 1$ for $1 \le j \le t = n$ is $(1 - 1/p)^n$, obtained by setting $S_t = [t = n]$; so this probability approaches 1 as $p \to \infty$. As a consequence we have further evidence for the text's claim that Algorithm C almost always finds $\delta_2 = \delta_3 = \cdots = 1$, because any polynomials that fail the latter condition will fail the former condition modulo p for all p.)

5. Using the formulas developed in exercise 4, with $f(n_1, \ldots, n_t) = [n_t = 0]$, we find that the probability is $1 - 1/p$ if $n > 0$, 1 if $n = 0$.

6. Assuming that the constant terms $u(0)$ and $v(0)$ are nonzero, imagine a "right-to-left" division algorithm, $u(x) = v(x)q(x) + x^{m-n}r(x)$, where $\deg(r) < \deg(v)$. We obtain a gcd algorithm analogous to Algorithm 4.5.2B, which is essentially Euclid's algorithm applied to the "reverse" of the original inputs (see exercise 2), afterwards reversing the answer and multiplying by an appropriate power of x.

There is a similar algorithm analogous to the method of exercise 4.5.2–40. The average number of iterations for both algorithms has been found by G. H. Norton, *SICOMP* **18** (1989), 608–624; K. Ma and J. von zur Gathen, *J. Symbolic Comp.* **9** (1990), 429–455.

7. The units of S (as polynomials of degree zero).

8. If $u(x) = v(x)w(x)$, where $u(x)$ has integer coefficients while $v(x)$ and $w(x)$ have rational coefficients, there are nonzero integers m and n such that $m \cdot v(x)$ and $n \cdot w(x)$ have integer coefficients. Now $u(x)$ is primitive, so Eq. (4) implies that

$$u(x) = \mathrm{pp}((m \cdot v(x))(n \cdot w(x))) = \pm \mathrm{pp}(m \cdot v(x)) \mathrm{pp}(n \cdot w(x)).$$

9. We can extend Algorithm E as follows: Let $\big(u_1(x), u_2(x), u_3, u_4(x)\big)$ and $\big(v_1(x), v_2(x), v_3, v_4(x)\big)$ be quadruples that satisfy the relations $u_1(x)u(x) + u_2(x)v(x) = u_3u_4(x)$ and $v_1(x)u(x) + v_2(x)v(x) = v_3v_4(x)$. The extended algorithm starts with the quadruples $\big(1, 0, \mathrm{cont}(u), \mathrm{pp}(u(x))\big)$ and $\big(0, 1, \mathrm{cont}(v), \mathrm{pp}(v(x))\big)$ and manipulates them in such a way as to preserve the conditions above, where $u_4(x)$ and $v_4(x)$ run through the same sequence as $u(x)$ and $v(x)$ do in Algorithm E. If $au_4(x) = q(x)v_4(x) + br(x)$, we have $av_3\big(u_1(x), u_2(x)\big) - q(x)u_3\big(v_1(x), v_2(x)\big) = \big(r_1(x), r_2(x)\big)$, where $r_1(x)u(x) + r_2(x)v(x) = bu_3v_3r(x)$, so the extended algorithm can preserve the desired relations. If $u(x)$ and $v(x)$ are relatively prime, the extended algorithm eventually finds $r(x)$ of degree zero, and we obtain $U(x) = r_2(x)$, $V(x) = r_1(x)$ as desired. (In practice we would divide $r_1(x)$, $r_2(x)$, and bu_3v_3 by $\gcd(\mathrm{cont}(r_1), \mathrm{cont}(r_2))$.) Conversely, if such $U(x)$ and $V(x)$ exist, then $u(x)$ and $v(x)$ have no common prime divisors, since they are primitive and have no common divisors of positive degree.

10. By successively factoring reducible polynomials into polynomials of smaller degree, we must obtain a finite factorization of any polynomial into irreducibles. The factorization of the *content* is unique. To show that there is at most one factorization of the primitive part, the key result is to prove that if $u(x)$ is an irreducible factor of $v(x)w(x)$, but not a unit multiple of the irreducible polynomial $v(x)$, then $u(x)$ is a factor of $w(x)$. This can be proved by observing that $u(x)$ is a factor of $v(x)w(x)U(x) = rw(x) - w(x)u(x)V(x)$ by the result of exercise 9, where r is a nonzero constant.

11. The only row names needed would be A_1, A_0, B_4, B_3, B_2, B_1, B_0, C_1, C_0, D_0. In general, let $u_{j+2}(x) = 0$; then the rows needed for the proof are $A_{n_2 - n_j}$ through A_0, $B_{n_1 - n_j}$ through B_0, $C_{n_2 - n_j}$ through C_0, $D_{n_3 - n_j}$ through D_0, etc.

12. If $n_k = 0$, the text's proof of (24) shows that the value of the determinant is $\pm h_k$, and this equals $\pm \ell_k^{n_{k-1}} / \prod_{1 < j < k} \ell_j^{\delta_{j-1}(\delta_j - 1)}$. If the polynomials have a factor of positive degree, we can artificially assume that the polynomial zero has degree zero and use the same formula with $\ell_k = 0$.

Notes: The value $R(u, v)$ of Sylvester's determinant is called the *resultant* of u and v, and the quantity $(-1)^{\deg(u)(\deg(u)-1)/2} \ell(u)^{-1} R(u, u')$ is called the *discriminant* of u, where u' is the derivative of u. If $u(x)$ has the factored form $a(x - \alpha_1) \ldots (x - \alpha_m)$, and if $v(x) = b(x - \beta_1) \ldots (x - \beta_n)$, the resultant $R(u, v)$ is $a^n v(\alpha_1) \ldots v(\alpha_m) = (-1)^{mn} b^m u(\beta_1) \ldots u(\beta_n) = a^n b^m \prod_{i=1}^{m} \prod_{j=1}^{n} (\alpha_i - \beta_j)$. It follows that the polynomials of degree mn in y defined as the respective resultants with $v(x)$ of $u(y - x)$, $u(y + x)$, $x^m u(y/x)$, and $u(yx)$ have as respective roots the sums $\alpha_i + \beta_j$, differences $\alpha_i - \beta_j$, products $\alpha_i \beta_j$, and quotients α_i / β_j (when $v(0) \neq 0$). This idea has been used by R. G. K. Loos to construct algorithms for arithmetic on algebraic numbers [*Computing, Supplement* **4** (1982), 173–187].

If we replace each row A_i in Sylvester's matrix by

$$(b_0 A_i + b_1 A_{i+1} + \cdots + b_{n_2-1-i} A_{n_2-1}) - (a_0 B_i + a_1 B_{i+1} + \cdots + a_{n_2-1-i} B_{n_2-1}),$$

and then delete rows B_{n_2-1} through B_0 and the last n_2 columns, we obtain an $n_1 \times n_1$ determinant for the resultant instead of the original $(n_1 + n_2) \times (n_1 + n_2)$ determinant. In some cases the resultant can be evaluated efficiently by means of this determinant; see *CACM* **12** (1969), 23–30, 302–303.

J. T. Schwartz has shown that it is possible to evaluate resultants and Sturm sequences for polynomials of degree n with a total of $O(n(\log n)^2)$ arithmetic operations as $n \to \infty$. [See *JACM* **27** (1980), 701–717.]

13. One can show by induction on j that the values of $(u_{j+1}(x), g_{j+1}, h_j)$ are replaced respectively by $(\ell^{1+p_j} w(x) u_j(x), \ell^{2+p_j} g_j, \ell^{p_j} h_j)$ for $j \geq 2$, where $p_j = n_1 + n_2 - 2n_j$. [In spite of this growth, the bound (26) remains valid.]

14. Let p be a prime of the domain, and let j, k be maximum such that $p^k \backslash v_n = \ell(v)$, $p^j \backslash v_{n-1}$. Let $P = p^k$. By Algorithm R we may write $q(x) = a_0 + P a_1 x + \cdots + P^s a_s x^s$, where $s = m - n \geq 2$. Let us look at the coefficients of x^{n+1}, x^n, and x^{n-1} in $v(x)q(x)$, namely $P a_1 v_n + P^2 a_2 v_{n-1} + \cdots$, $a_0 v_n + P a_1 v_{n-1} + \cdots$, and $a_0 v_{n-1} + P a_1 v_{n-2} + \cdots$, each of which is a multiple of P^3. We conclude from the first that $p^j \backslash a_1$, from the second that $p^{\min(k, 2j)} \backslash a_0$, then from the third that $P \backslash a_0$. Hence $P \backslash r(x)$. [If m were only $n + 1$, the best we could prove would be that $p^{\lceil k/2 \rceil}$ divides $r(x)$; for example, consider $u(x) = x^3 + 1$, $v(x) = 4x^2 + 2x + 1$, $r(x) = 18$. On the other hand, an argument based on determinants of matrices like (21) and (22) can be used to show that $\ell(r)^{\deg(v)-\deg(r)-1} r(x)$ is always a multiple of $\ell(v)^{(\deg(u)-\deg(v))(\deg(v)-\deg(r)-1)}$.]

15. Let $c_{ij} = a_{i1} a_{j1} + \cdots + a_{in} a_{jn}$; we may assume that $c_{ii} > 0$ for all i. If $c_{ij} \neq 0$ for some $i \neq j$, we can replace row i and column i by $(c_{i1} - t c_{j1}, \ldots, c_{in} - t c_{jn})$, where $t = c_{ij}/c_{jj}$; this does not change the value of $\det C$, and it decreases the value of the upper bound we wish to prove, since c_{ii} is replaced by $c_{ii} - c_{ij}^2/c_{jj}$. Such replacements can be done in a systematic way for increasing i and for $j < i$, until $c_{ij} = 0$ for all $i \neq j$. [The latter algorithm is called the *Gram–Schmidt orthogonalization process*: See *Crelle* **94** (1883), 41–73; *Math. Annalen* **63** (1907), 442.] Then $\det(A)^2 = \det(AA^T) = c_{11} \ldots c_{nn}$.

16. A univariate polynomial of degree d over any unique factorization domain has at most d roots (see exercise 3.2.1.2–16(b)); so if $n = 1$ it is clear that $|r(S_1)| \leq d_1$. If $n > 1$ we have $f(x_1, \ldots, x_n) = g_0(x_2, \ldots, x_n) + x_1 g_1(x_2, \ldots, x_n) + \cdots + x_1^{d_1} g_{d_1}(x_2, \ldots, x_n)$ where g_k is nonzero for at least one k. Given $(x_2, \ldots, x_n)$, it follows that $f(x_1, \ldots, x_n)$ is zero for at most d_1 choices of x_1, unless $g_k(x_2, \ldots, x_n) = 0$; hence $|r(S_1, \ldots, S_n)| \leq$

$d_1(|S_2|-d_2)\dots(|S_n|-d_n)+|S_1|(|S_2|\dots|S_n|-(|S_2|-d_2)\dots(|S_n|-d_n))$. [R. A. DeMillo and R. J. Lipton, *Inf. Proc. Letters* **7** (1978), 193–195.]

Notes: The stated upper bound is best possible, because equality occurs for the polynomial $f(x_1,\dots,x_n) = \prod\{x_j - s_k \mid s_k \in S_j,\ 1 \le k \le d_j,\ 1 \le j \le n\}$. But there is another sense in which the upper bound can be significantly improved: Let $f_1(x_1,\dots,x_n) = f(x_1,\dots,x_n)$, and let $f_{j+1}(x_{j+1},\dots,x_n)$ be any nonzero coefficient of a power of x_j in $f_j(x_j,\dots,x_n)$. Then we can let d_j be the degree of x_j in f_j instead of the (often much larger) degree of x_j in f. For example, we could let $d_1 = 3$ and $d_2 = 1$ in the polynomial $x_1^3 x_2^9 - 3x_1^2 x_2 + x_2^{100} + 5$. This observation ensures that $d_1 + \cdots + d_n \le d$ when each term of f has total degree $\le d$; hence the probability in such cases is

$$\frac{|r(S,\dots,S)|}{|S|} \le 1 - \left(1 - \frac{d_1}{|S|}\right) \cdots \left(1 - \frac{d_n}{|S|}\right) \le \frac{d_1 + \cdots + d_n}{|S|} \le \frac{d}{|S|}$$

when all sets S_j are equal. If this probability is $\le \frac{1}{2}$, and if $f(x_1,\dots,x_n)$ turns out to be zero for 50 randomly selected vectors $(x_1,\dots,x_n)$, then $f(x_1,\dots,x_n)$ is identically zero with probability at least $1 - 2^{-50}$.

Moreover, if $f_j(x_j,\dots,x_n)$ has the special form $x_j^{e_j} f_{j+1}(x_{j+1},\dots,x_n)$ with $e_j > 0$ we can take $d_j = 1$, because x_j must then be 0 when $f_{j+1}(x_{j+1},\dots,x_n) \ne 0$. A sparse polynomial with only m nonzero terms will therefore have $d_j \le 1$ for at least $n - \lg m$ values of j.

Applications of this inequality to gcd calculation and other operations on sparse multivariate polynomials were introduced by R. Zippel, *Lecture Notes in Comp. Sci.* **72** (1979), 216–226. J. T. Schwartz [*JACM* **27** (1980), 701–717] gave further extensions, including a way to avoid large numbers by means of modular arithmetic: If the coefficients of f are integers, if P is a set of prime numbers all $\ge q$, and if $|f(x_1,\dots,x_n)| \le L$ whenever each $x_j \in S_j$, then the number of solutions to $f(x_1,\dots,x_n) \equiv 0$ (modulo p) for $p \in P$ is at most

$$|S_1|\dots|S_n||P| - (|S_1| - d_1)\dots(|S_n| - d_n)(|P| - \log_q L).$$

17. (a) For convenience, let us describe the algorithm only for $A = \{a,b\}$. The hypotheses imply that $\deg(Q_1 U) = \deg(Q_2 V) \ge 0$, $\deg(Q_1) \le \deg(Q_2)$. If $\deg(Q_1) = 0$, then Q_1 is just a nonzero rational number, so we set $Q = Q_2/Q_1$. Otherwise we let $Q_1 = aQ_{11} + bQ_{12} + r_1$, $Q_2 = aQ_{21} + bQ_{22} + r_2$, where r_1 and r_2 are rational numbers; it follows that

$$Q_1 U - Q_2 V = a(Q_{11}U - Q_{21}V) + b(Q_{12}U - Q_{22}V) + r_1 U - r_2 V.$$

We must have either $\deg(Q_{11}) = \deg(Q_1) - 1$ or $\deg(Q_{12}) = \deg(Q_1) - 1$. In the former case, $\deg(Q_{11}U - Q_{21}V) < \deg(Q_{11}U)$, by considering the terms of highest degree that start with a; so we may replace Q_1 by Q_{11}, Q_2 by Q_{21}, and repeat the process. Similarly in the latter case, we may replace (Q_1, Q_2) by (Q_{12}, Q_{22}) and repeat the process.

(b) We may assume that $\deg(U) \ge \deg(V)$. If $\deg(R) \ge \deg(V)$, note that $Q_1 U - Q_2 V = Q_1 R - (Q_2 - Q_1 Q)V$ has degree less than $\deg(V) \le \deg(Q_1 R)$, so we can repeat the process with U replaced by R; we obtain $R = Q'V + R'$, $U = (Q + Q')V + R'$, where $\deg(R') < \deg(R)$, so eventually a solution will be obtained.

(c) The algorithm of (b) gives $V_1 = UV_2 + R$, $\deg(R) < \deg(V_2)$; by homogeneity, $R = 0$ and U is homogeneous.

(d) We may assume that $\deg(V) \le \deg(U)$. If $\deg(V) = 0$, set $W \leftarrow U$; otherwise use (c) to find $U = QV$, so that $QVV = VQV$, $(QV - VQ)V = 0$. This implies that $QV = VQ$, so we can set $U \leftarrow V$, $V \leftarrow Q$ and repeat the process.

For further details about the subject of this exercise, see P. M. Cohn, *Proc. Cambridge Phil. Soc.* **57** (1961), 18–30. The considerably more difficult problem of characterizing *all* string polynomials such that $UV = VU$ has been solved by G. M. Bergman [Ph.D. thesis, Harvard University, 1967].

18. [P. M. Cohn, *Transactions of the Amer. Math. Soc.* **109** (1963), 332–356.]

S1. Set $u_1 \leftarrow U_1$, $u_2 \leftarrow U_2$, $v_1 \leftarrow V_1$, $v_2 \leftarrow V_2$, $z_1 \leftarrow z_2' \leftarrow w_1 \leftarrow w_2' \leftarrow 1$, $z_1' \leftarrow z_2 \leftarrow w_1' \leftarrow w_2 \leftarrow 0$, $n \leftarrow 0$.

S2. (At this point the identities given in the exercise hold, and $u_1 v_1 = u_2 v_2$; $v_2 = 0$ if and only if $u_1 = 0$.) If $v_2 = 0$, the algorithm terminates with $\gcd(V_1, V_2) = v_1$, $\mathrm{lclm}(V_1, V_2) = z_1' V_1 = -z_2' V_2$. (Also, by symmetry, we have $\gcd(U_1, U_2) = u_2$ and $\mathrm{lcrm}(U_1, U_2) = U_1 w_1 = -U_2 w_2$.)

S3. Find Q and R such that $v_1 = Qv_2 + R$, where $\deg(R) < \deg(v_2)$. (We have $u_1(Qv_2 + R) = u_2 v_2$, so $u_1 R = (u_2 - u_1 Q)v_2 = R'v_2$.)

S4. Set $(w_1, w_2, w_1', w_2', z_1, z_2, z_1', z_2', u_1, u_2, v_1, v_2) \leftarrow (w_1' - w_1 Q, w_2' - w_2 Q, w_1, w_2, z_1', z_2', z_1 - Qz_1', z_2 - Qz_2', u_2 - u_1 Q, u_1, v_2, v_1 - Qv_2)$ and $n \leftarrow n+1$. Go back to S2. ∎

This extension of Euclid's algorithm includes most of the features we have seen in previous extensions, all at the same time, so it provides new insight into the special cases already considered. To prove that it is valid, note first that $\deg(v_2)$ decreases in step S4, so the algorithm certainly terminates. At the conclusion of the algorithm, v_1 is a common right divisor of V_1 and V_2, since $w_1 v_1 = (-1)^n V_1$ and $-w_2 v_1 = (-1)^n V_2$; also if d is any common right divisor of V_1 and V_2, it is a right divisor of $z_1 V_1 + z_2 V_2 = v_1$. Hence $v_1 = \gcd(V_1, V_2)$. Also if m is any common left multiple of V_1 and V_2, we may assume without loss of generality that $m = U_1 V_1 = U_2 V_2$, since the sequence of values of Q does not depend on U_1 and U_2. Hence $m = (-1)^n(-u_2 z_1')V_1 = (-1)^n(u_2 z_2')V_2$ is a multiple of $z_1' V_1$.

In practice, if we just want to calculate $\gcd(V_1, V_2)$, we may suppress the computation of n, w_1, w_2, w_1', w_2', z_1, z_2, z_1', z_2'. These additional quantities were added to the algorithm primarily to make its validity more readily established.

Note: Nontrivial factorizations of string polynomials, such as the example given with this exercise, can be found from matrix identities such as

$$\begin{pmatrix} a & 1 \\ 1 & 0 \end{pmatrix}\begin{pmatrix} b & 1 \\ 1 & 0 \end{pmatrix}\begin{pmatrix} c & 1 \\ 1 & 0 \end{pmatrix}\begin{pmatrix} 0 & 1 \\ 1 & -c \end{pmatrix}\begin{pmatrix} 0 & 1 \\ 1 & -b \end{pmatrix}\begin{pmatrix} 0 & 1 \\ 1 & -a \end{pmatrix} = \begin{pmatrix} 1 & 0 \\ 0 & 1 \end{pmatrix},$$

since these identities hold even when multiplication is not commutative. For example,

$$(abc + a + c)(1 + ba) = (ab + 1)(cba + a + c).$$

(Compare this with the continuant polynomials of Section 4.5.3.)

19. [See Eugène Cahen, *Théorie des Nombres* **1** (Paris: 1914), 336–338.] If such an algorithm exists, D is a gcrd by the argument in exercise 18. Let us regard A and B as a single $2n \times n$ matrix C whose first n rows are those of A, and whose second n rows are those of B. Similarly, P and Q can be combined into a $2n \times n$ matrix R; X and Y can be combined into an $n \times 2n$ matrix Z. The desired conditions now reduce to two equations $C = RD$, $D = ZC$. If we can find a $2n \times 2n$ integer matrix U

with determinant ± 1 such that the last n rows of $U^{-1}C$ are all zero, then $R = $ (first n columns of U), $D = $ (first n rows of $U^{-1}C$), $Z = $ (first n rows of U^{-1}) solves the desired conditions. Hence, for example, the following algorithm may be used (with $m = 2n$):

Algorithm T (*Triangularization*). Let C be an $m \times n$ matrix of integers. This algorithm finds $m \times m$ integer matrices U and V such that $UV = I$ and VC is *upper triangular*. (This means that the entry in row i and column j of VC is zero if $i > j$.)

> **T1.** [Initialize.] Set $U \leftarrow V \leftarrow I$, the $m \times m$ identity matrix; and set $T \leftarrow C$. (Throughout the algorithm we will have $T = VC$ and $UV = I$.)

> **T2.** [Iterate on j.] Do step T3 for $j = 1, 2, \ldots, \min(m, n)$, then terminate the algorithm.

> **T3.** [Zero out column j.] Perform the following actions zero or more times until T_{ij} is zero for all $i > j$: Let T_{kj} be a nonzero element of $\{T_{ij}, T_{(i+1)j}, \ldots, T_{mj}\}$ having the smallest absolute value. Interchange rows k and j of T and of V; interchange columns k and j of U. Then subtract $\lfloor T_{ij}/T_{jj} \rfloor$ times row j from row i, in matrices T and V, and add the same multiple of column i to column j in matrix U, for $j < i \le m$. ∎

For the stated example, the algorithm yields $\begin{pmatrix} 1 & 2 \\ 3 & 4 \end{pmatrix} = \begin{pmatrix} 1 & 0 \\ 3 & 2 \end{pmatrix}\begin{pmatrix} 1 & 2 \\ 0 & -1 \end{pmatrix}$, $\begin{pmatrix} 4 & 3 \\ 2 & 1 \end{pmatrix} = \begin{pmatrix} 4 & 5 \\ 2 & 3 \end{pmatrix}\begin{pmatrix} 1 & 2 \\ 0 & -1 \end{pmatrix}$, $\begin{pmatrix} 1 & 2 \\ 0 & -1 \end{pmatrix} = \begin{pmatrix} 1 & 0 \\ 2 & -2 \end{pmatrix}\begin{pmatrix} 1 & 2 \\ 3 & 4 \end{pmatrix} + \begin{pmatrix} 0 & 0 \\ 1 & 0 \end{pmatrix}\begin{pmatrix} 4 & 3 \\ 2 & 1 \end{pmatrix}$. (Actually *any* matrix with determinant ± 1 would be a gcrd in this particular case.)

20. See V. Y. Pan, *Information and Computation* **167** (2001), 71–85.

21. To get an upper bound, we may assume that Algorithm R is used only when $m - n \le 1$; furthermore, the coefficients are bounded by (26) with $m = n$. [The stated formula is, in fact, the execution time observed in practice, not merely an upper bound. For more detailed information see G. E. Collins, *Proc. 1968 Summer Inst. on Symbolic Mathematical Computation*, edited by Robert G. Tobey (IBM Federal Systems Center: June 1969), 195–231.]

22. A sequence of signs cannot contain two consecutive zeros, since $u_{k+1}(x)$ is a nonzero constant in (29). Moreover we cannot have "+, 0, +" or "−, 0, −" as subsequences. The formula $V(u, a) - V(u, b)$ is clearly valid when $b = a$, so we must only verify it as b increases. The polynomials $u_j(x)$ have finitely many roots, and $V(u, b)$ changes only when b encounters or passes such roots. Let x be a root of some (possibly several) u_j. When b increases from $x - \epsilon$ to x, the sign sequence near j goes from "+, ±, −" to "+, 0, −" or from "−, ±, +" to "−, 0, +" if $j > 0$; and from "+, −" to "0, −" or from "−, +" to "0, +" if $j = 0$. (Since $u'(x)$ is the derivative, $u'(x)$ is negative when $u(x)$ is decreasing.) Thus the net change in V is $-\delta_{j0}$. When b increases from x to $x + \epsilon$, a similar argument shows that V remains unchanged.

　　[L. E. Heindel, *JACM* **18** (1971), 533–548, has applied these ideas to construct algorithms for isolating the real zeros of a given polynomial $u(x)$, in time bounded by a polynomial in $\deg(u)$ and $\log N$, where all coefficients y_j are integers with $|u_j| \le N$, and all operations are guaranteed to be exact.]

23. If v has $n-1$ real roots occurring between the n real roots of u, then (by considering sign changes) $u(x) \bmod v(x)$ has $n - 2$ real roots lying between the $n - 1$ roots of v.

24. First show that $h_j = g_j^{\delta_j - 1} g_{j-1}^{\delta_j - 2(1 - \delta_j - 1)} \cdots g_2^{\delta_1(1 - \delta_2) \cdots (1 - \delta_j - 1)}$. Then show that the exponent of g_2 on the left-hand side of (18) has the form $\delta_2 + \delta_1 x$, where $x = $

$\delta_2 + \cdots + \delta_{j-1} + 1 - \delta_2(\delta_3 + \cdots + \delta_{j-1} + 1) - \delta_3(1 - \delta_2)(\delta_4 + \cdots + \delta_{j-1} + 1) - \cdots -$
$\delta_{j-1}(1 - \delta_2) \ldots (1 - \delta_{j-2})(1)$. But $x = 1$, since it is seen to be independent of δ_{j-1}
and we can set $\delta_{j-1} = 0$, etc. A similar derivation works for $g_3, g_4, \ldots$, and a simpler
derivation works for (23).

25. Each coefficient of $u_j(x)$ can be expressed as a determinant in which one column
contains only $\ell(u)$, $\ell(v)$, and zeros. To use this fact, modify Algorithm C as follows:
In step C1, set $g \leftarrow \gcd(\ell(u), \ell(v))$ and $h \leftarrow 0$. In step C3, if $h = 0$, set $u(x) \leftarrow v(x)$,
$v(x) \leftarrow r(x)/g$, $h \leftarrow \ell(u)^\delta/g$, $g \leftarrow \ell(u)$, and return to C2; otherwise proceed as in the
unmodified algorithm. The effect of this new initialization is simply to replace $u_j(x)$
by $u_j(x)/\gcd(\ell(u), \ell(v))$ for all $j \geq 3$; thus, ℓ^{2j-4} will become ℓ^{2j-5} in (28).

26. In fact, even more is true. Note that the algorithm in exercise 3 computes $\pm p_n(x)$
and $\mp q_n(x)$ for $n \geq -1$. Let $e_n = \deg(q_n)$ and $d_n = \deg(p_n u - q_n v)$; we observed in exercise 3 that $d_{n-1} + e_n = \deg(u)$ for $n \geq 0$. We shall prove that the conditions $\deg(q) < e_n$
and $\deg(pu - qv) < d_{n-2}$ imply that $p(x) = c(x)p_{n-1}(x)$ and $q(x) = c(x)q_{n-1}(x)$: Given
such p and q, we can find $c(x)$ and $d(x)$ such that $p(x) = c(x)p_{n-1}(x) + d(x)p_n(x)$ and
$q(x) = c(x)q_{n-1}(x) + d(x)q_n(x)$, since $p_{n-1}(x)q_n(x) - p_n(x)q_{n-1}(x) = \pm 1$. Hence
$pu - qv = c(p_{n-1}u - q_{n-1}v) + d(p_n u - q_n v)$. If $d(x) \neq 0$, we must have $\deg(c) + e_{n-1} =$
$\deg(d) + e_n$, since $\deg(q) < \deg(q_n)$; it follows that $\deg(c) + d_{n-1} > \deg(d) + d_n$, since
this is surely true if $d_n = -\infty$ and otherwise we have $d_{n-1} + e_n = d_n + e_{n+1} > d_n + e_{n-1}$.
Therefore $\deg(pu - qv) = \deg(c) + d_{n-1}$. But we have assumed that $\deg(pu - qv) <$
$d_{n-2} = d_{n-1} + e_n - e_{n-1}$; so $\deg(c) < e_n - e_{n-1}$ and $\deg(d) < 0$, a contradiction.
   [This result is essentially due to L. Kronecker, *Monatsberichte Königl. preuß. Akad.
Wiss.* (Berlin: 1881), 535–600. It implies the following theorem: "Let $u(x)$ and $v(x)$
be relatively prime polynomials over a field and let $d \leq \deg(v) < \deg(u)$. If $q(x)$
is a polynomial of least degree such that there exist polynomials $p(x)$ and $r(x)$ with
$p(x)u(x) - q(x)v(x) = r(x)$ and $\deg(r) = d$, then $p(x)/q(x) = p_n(x)/q_n(x)$ for some n."
For if $d_{n-2} > d \geq d_{n-1}$, there are solutions $q(x)$ with $\deg(q) = e_{n-1} + d - d_{n-1} < e_n$,
and we have proved that all solutions of such low degree have the stated property.]

27. The ideas of answer 4.3.1–40 apply, but in simpler fashion because polynomial
arithmetic is carry-free; right-to-left division uses 4.7–(3). Alternatively, with large
values of n, we could divide Fourier transforms of the coefficients, using exercise 4.6.4–
57 in reverse.

SECTION 4.6.2

1. For any choice of $k \leq n$ distinct roots, there are p^{n-k} monic polynomials having
those roots at least once. Therefore by the principle of inclusion and exclusion (Section
1.3.3), the number of polynomials without linear factors is $\sum_{k \leq n} \binom{p}{k}p^{n-k}(-1)^k$, and it
is alternately $\leq$ and $\geq$ the partial sums of this series. The stated bounds correspond
to $k \leq 2$ and $k \leq 3$. When $n \geq p$ the probability of at least one linear factor is
$1 - (1 - 1/p)^p$. The average number of linear factors is p times the average number of
times x divides $u(x)$, so it is $1 + p^{-1} + \cdots + p^{1-n} = \frac{p}{p-1}(1 - p^{-n})$.
   [In a similar way, we find that there is an irreducible factor of degree 2 with
probability $\sum_{k \leq n/2} \binom{p(p-1)/2}{k}(-1)^k p^{-2k}$; this probability lies between $\frac{3}{8} - \frac{1}{4}p^{-1}$ and
$\frac{1}{2} - \frac{1}{2}p^{-1}$ when $n \geq 2$ and it approaches $1 - e^{-1/2}(1 + \frac{1}{2}p^{-1}) + O(p^{-2})$ as $n \to \infty$. The
average number of such factors is $\frac{1}{2} - \frac{1}{2}p^{-2\lfloor n/2 \rfloor}$.]
   Note: Let $u(x)$ be a fixed polynomial with integer coefficients. Peter Weinberger
has observed that, if $u(x)$ is irreducible over the integers, the average number of linear

factors of $u(x)$ modulo p approaches 1 as $p \to \infty$, because the Galois group of $u(x)$ is transitive and the average number of 1-cycles in a randomly chosen element of any transitive permutation group is 1. Thus, *the average number of linear factors of $u(x)$ modulo p is the number of irreducible factors of $u(x)$ over the integers, as $p \to \infty$.* [See the remarks in the answer to exercise 37, and *Proc. Symp. Pure Math.* **24** (Amer. Math. Soc., 1972), 321–332.]

2. (a) We know that $u(x)$ has a representation as a product of irreducible polynomials; and the leading coefficients of these polynomials must be units, since they divide the leading coefficient of $u(x)$. Therefore we may assume that $u(x)$ has a representation as a product of monic irreducible polynomials $p_1(x)^{e_1} \ldots p_r(x)^{e_r}$, where $p_1(x), \ldots, p_r(x)$ are distinct. This representation is unique, except for the order of the factors, so the conditions on $u(x)$, $v(x)$, $w(x)$ are satisfied if and only if

$$v(x) = p_1(x)^{\lfloor e_1/2 \rfloor} \ldots p_r(x)^{\lfloor e_r/2 \rfloor}, \qquad w(x) = p_1(x)^{e_1 \bmod 2} \ldots p_r(x)^{e_r \bmod 2}.$$

(b) The generating function for the number of monic polynomials of degree n is $1+pz+p^2z^2+\cdots = 1/(1-pz)$. The generating function for the number of polynomials of degree n having the form $v(x)^2$, where $v(x)$ is monic, is $1+pz^2+p^2z^4+\cdots = 1/(1-pz^2)$. If the generating function for the number of monic squarefree polynomials of degree n is $g(z)$, then we must have $1/(1-pz) = g(z)/(1-pz^2)$ by part (a). Hence $g(z) = (1-pz^2)/(1-pz) = 1+pz+(p^2-p)z^2+(p^3-p^2)z^3+\cdots$. The answer is $p^n - p^{n-1}$ for $n \geq 2$. [Curiously, this proves that $u(x) \perp u'(x)$ with probability $1-1/p$; it is the same as the probability that $u(x) \perp v(x)$ when $u(x)$ and $v(x)$ are *independent*, by exercise 4.6.1–5.]

Note: By a similar argument, every $u(x)$ has a unique representation $v(x)w(x)^r$, where $v(x)$ is not divisible by the rth power of any irreducible; the number of such monic polynomials $v(x)$ is $p^n - p^{n-r+1}$ for $n \geq r$.

3. Let $u(x) = u_1(x) \ldots u_r(x)$. There is *at most* one such $v(x)$, by the argument of Theorem 4.3.2C. There is *at least* one if, for each j, we can solve the system with $w_j(x) = 1$ and $w_k(x) = 0$ for $k \neq j$. A solution to the latter is $v_1(x) \prod_{k \neq j} u_k(x)$, where $v_1(x)$ and $v_2(x)$ can be found satisfying

$$v_1(x) \prod_{k \neq j} u_k(x) + v_2(x)u_j(x) = 1, \qquad \deg(v_1) < \deg(u_j),$$

by the extension of Euclid's algorithm (exercise 4.6.1–3).

Over the integers we cannot make $v(x) \equiv 1$ (modulo x) and $v(x) \equiv 0$ (modulo $x-2$) when $\deg(v) < 2$.

4. By unique factorization, we have $(1-pz)^{-1} = \prod_{n \geq 1}(1-z^n)^{-a_{np}}$; after taking logarithms, this can be rewritten

$$\ln(1/(1-pz)) = \sum_{k,j \geq 1} a_{kp} z^{kj}/j = \sum_{j \geq 1} G_p(z^j)/j.$$

The stated identity now yields the answer $G_p(z) = \sum_{m \geq 1} \mu(m)m^{-1}\ln(1/(1-pz^m))$, from which we obtain $a_{np} = \sum_{d \backslash n} \mu(n/d)p^d/n$; thus $\lim_{p \to \infty} a_{np}/p^n = 1/n$.

To prove the stated identity, note that

$$\sum_{n,j \geq 1} \mu(n)g(z^{nj})n^{-t}j^{-t} = \sum_{m \geq 1} g(z^m)m^{-t}\sum_{n \backslash m}\mu(n) = g(z).$$

[The numbers a_{np} were first found by Gauss; see his *Werke* **2**, 219–222.]

5. Let a_{npr} be the number of monic polynomials of degree n modulo p having exactly r irreducible factors. Then $\mathcal{G}_p(z, w) = \sum_{n,r \geq 0} a_{npr} z^n w^r = \exp(\sum_{k \geq 1} G_p(z^k) w^k / k) = \exp(\sum_{m \geq 1} a_{mw} \ln(1/(1 - pz^{-m})))$; see Eq. 1.2.9–(38). We have

$$\sum_{n \geq 0} A_{np} z^n = d\mathcal{G}_p(z/p, w)/dw \,|_{w=1} = (\textstyle\sum_{k \geq 1} G_p(z^k/p^k)) \, \mathcal{G}_p(z/p, 1)$$
$$= (\textstyle\sum_{n \geq 1} \ln(1/(1 - p^{1-n} z^n))) \varphi(n)/n)/(1 - z),$$

hence $A_{np} = H_n + 1/2p + O(p^{-2})$ for $n \geq 2$. The average value of 2^r is $[z^n] \mathcal{G}_p(z/p, 2) = n + 1 + (n-1)/p + O(np^{-2})$. (The variance is of order n^3, however: Set $w = 4$.)

6. For $0 \leq s < p$, $x - s$ is a factor of $x^p - x$ (modulo p) by Fermat's theorem. So $x^p - x$ is a multiple of $\text{lcm}(x - 0, x - 1, \ldots, x - (p-1)) = x^{\underline{p}}$. [*Note:* Therefore the Stirling numbers $\begin{bmatrix} p \\ k \end{bmatrix}$ are multiples of p except when $k = 1$ or $k = p$. Equation 1.2.6–(45) shows that the same statement is valid for Stirling numbers $\begin{Bmatrix} p \\ k \end{Bmatrix}$ of the other kind.]

7. The factors on the right are relatively prime, and each is a divisor of $u(x)$, so their product divides $u(x)$. On the other hand, $u(x)$ divides

$$v(x)^p - v(x) = \textstyle\prod_{0 \leq s < p}(v(x) - s),$$

so it divides the right-hand side by exercise 4.5.2–2.

8. The vector (18) is the only output whose kth component is nonzero.

9. For example, start with $x \leftarrow 1$ and $y \leftarrow 1$; then repeatedly set $R[x] \leftarrow y$, $x \leftarrow 2x \bmod 101$, $y \leftarrow 51y \bmod 101$, one hundred times.

10. The matrix $Q - I$ below has a null space generated by the two vectors $v^{[1]} = (1, 0, 0, 0, 0, 0, 0, 0)$, $v^{[2]} = (0, 1, 1, 0, 0, 1, 1, 1)$. The factorization is

$$(x^6 + x^5 + x^4 + x + 1)(x^2 + x + 1).$$

$p = 2$

$$\begin{pmatrix} 0 & 0 & 0 & 0 & 0 & 0 & 0 & 0 \\ 0 & 1 & 1 & 0 & 0 & 0 & 0 & 0 \\ 0 & 0 & 1 & 0 & 1 & 0 & 0 & 0 \\ 0 & 0 & 0 & 1 & 0 & 0 & 1 & 0 \\ 1 & 0 & 0 & 1 & 0 & 0 & 1 & 0 \\ 1 & 0 & 1 & 1 & 1 & 0 & 0 & 0 \\ 0 & 0 & 1 & 0 & 1 & 1 & 0 & 1 \\ 1 & 1 & 0 & 1 & 1 & 1 & 0 & 1 \end{pmatrix}$$

$p = 5$

$$\begin{pmatrix} 0 & 0 & 0 & 0 & 0 & 0 & 0 \\ 0 & 4 & 0 & 0 & 0 & 1 & 0 \\ 0 & 2 & 2 & 0 & 4 & 3 & 4 \\ 0 & 1 & 4 & 4 & 4 & 2 & 1 \\ 2 & 2 & 2 & 3 & 4 & 3 & 2 \\ 0 & 0 & 4 & 0 & 1 & 3 & 2 \\ 3 & 0 & 2 & 1 & 4 & 2 & 1 \end{pmatrix}$$

11. Removing the trivial factor x, the matrix $Q - I$ above has a null space generated by $(1, 0, 0, 0, 0, 0, 0)$ and $(0, 3, 1, 4, 1, 2, 1)$. The factorization is

$$x(x^2 + 3x + 4)(x^5 + 2x^4 + x^3 + 4x^2 + x + 3).$$

12. If $p = 2$, $(x + 1)^4 = x^4 + 1$. If $p = 8k + 1$, $Q - I$ is the zero matrix, so there are four factors. For other values of p we have

$$
\begin{array}{ccc}
p = 8k + 3 & p = 8k + 5 & p = 8k + 7
\end{array}
$$

$$Q - I = \begin{pmatrix} 0 & 0 & 0 & 0 \\ 0 & -1 & 0 & 1 \\ 0 & 0 & -2 & 0 \\ 0 & 1 & 0 & -1 \end{pmatrix} \quad \begin{pmatrix} 0 & 0 & 0 & 0 \\ 0 & -2 & 0 & 0 \\ 0 & 0 & 0 & 0 \\ 0 & 0 & 0 & -2 \end{pmatrix} \quad \begin{pmatrix} 0 & 0 & 0 & 0 \\ 0 & -1 & 0 & -1 \\ 0 & 0 & -2 & 0 \\ 0 & -1 & 0 & -1 \end{pmatrix}.$$

Here $Q - I$ has rank 2, so there are $4 - 2 = 2$ factors. [But it is easy to prove that $x^4 + 1$ is irreducible over the integers, since it has no linear factors and the coefficient of x in any factor of degree two must be less than or equal to 2 in absolute value by exercise 20. (See also exercise 32, since $x^4 + 1 = \Psi_8(x)$.) For all $k \geq 2$, H. P. F. Swinnerton-Dyer has exhibited polynomials of degree 2^k that are irreducible over the integers, but they split completely into linear and quadratic factors modulo every prime. For degree 8, his example is $x^8 - 16x^6 + 88x^4 + 192x^2 + 144$, having roots $\pm\sqrt{2}\pm\sqrt{3}\pm i$ [see *Math. Comp.* **24** (1970), 733–734]. According to the theorem of Frobenius cited in exercise 37, any irreducible polynomial of degree n whose Galois group contains no n-cycles will have factors modulo almost all primes.]

13. Case $p = 8k+1$: $\left(x + (1 + \sqrt{-1})/\sqrt{2}\right)\left(x + (1 - \sqrt{-1})/\sqrt{2}\right)\left(x - (1 + \sqrt{-1})/\sqrt{2}\right) \times$ $\left(x - (1 - \sqrt{-1})/\sqrt{2}\right)$. Case $p = 8k + 3$: $\left(x^2 + \sqrt{-2}x - 1\right)\left(x^2 - \sqrt{-2}x - 1\right)$. Case $p = 8k+5$: $\left(x^2 + \sqrt{-1}\right)\left(x^2 - \sqrt{-1}\right)$. Case $p = 8k+7$: $\left(x^2 + \sqrt{2}x + 1\right)\left(x^2 - \sqrt{2}x + 1\right)$. The factorization for $p = 8k + 7$ also holds over the field of real numbers.

14. Algorithm N can be adapted to find the coefficients of w: Let A be the $(r+1) \times n$ matrix whose kth row contains the coefficients of $v(x)^k \bmod u(x)$, for $0 \leq k \leq r$. Apply the method of Algorithm N until the first dependence is found in step N3; then the algorithm terminates with $w(x) = v_0 + v_1x + \cdots + v_kx^k$, where v_j is defined in (18). At this point $2 \leq k \leq r$; it is not necessary to know r in advance, since we can check for dependency after generating each row of A.

15. We may assume that $u \neq 0$ and that p is odd. Berlekamp's method applied to the polynomial $x^2 - u$ tells us that a square root exists if and only if $Q - I = O$ if and only if $u^{(p-1)/2} \bmod p = 1$; but we already knew that. The method of Cantor and Zassenhaus suggests that $\gcd\left(x^2 - u, (sx + t)^{(p-1)/2} - 1\right)$ will often be a nontrivial factor; and indeed one can show that $(p-1)/2 + (0, 1, \text{ or } 2)$ values of s will succeed. In practice, sequential choices seem to work just as well as random choices, so we obtain the following algorithm: "Evaluate $\gcd\left(x^2 - u, x^{(p-1)/2} - 1\right)$, $\gcd\left(x^2 - u, (x+1)^{(p-1)/2} - 1\right)$, $\gcd\left(x^2 - u, (x + 2)^{(p-1)/2} - 1\right)$, $\ldots$, until finding the first case where the gcd has the form $x + v$. Then $\sqrt{u} = \pm v$." The expected running time (with random s) will be $O(\log p)^3$ for large p.

A closer look shows that the first step of this algorithm succeeds if and only if $p \bmod 4 = 3$. For if $p = 2q + 1$ where q is odd, we have $x^q \bmod (x^2 - u) = u^{(q-1)/2}x$, and $\gcd(x^2 - u, x^q - 1) \equiv x - u^{(q+1)/2}$ since $u^q \equiv 1$ (modulo p). In fact, we see that the formula $\sqrt{u} = \pm u^{(p+1)/4} \bmod p$ gives the square root directly whenever $p \bmod 4 = 3$.

But when $p \bmod 4 = 1$, we will have $x^{(p-1)/2} \bmod (x^2 - u) = u^{(p-1)/4}$, and the gcd will be 1. The algorithm above should therefore be used only when $p \bmod 4 = 1$, and the first gcd should then be omitted.

A direct method that works nicely when $p \bmod 8 = 5$ was discovered in the 1990s by A. O. L. Atkin, based on the fact that $2^{(p-1)/2} \equiv -1$ in that case: Set $v \leftarrow (2u)^{(p-5)/8} \bmod p$ and $i \leftarrow (2uv^2) \bmod p$; then $\sqrt{u} = \pm(uv(i - 1)) \bmod p$, and we also have $\sqrt{-1} = \pm i$. [*Computational Perspectives on Number Theory* (Cambridge, Mass.: International Press, 1998), 1–11; see also H. C. Pocklington, *Proc. Camb. Phil. Soc.* **19** (1917), 57–59.]

When $p \bmod 8 = 1$, a trial-and-error method seems to be necessary. The following procedure due to Daniel Shanks often outperforms all other known algorithms in such cases: Suppose $p = 2^e q + 1$ where $e \geq 3$.

S1. Choose x at random in the range $1 < x < p$, and set $z = x^q \bmod p$. If $z^{2^{e-1}} \bmod p = 1$, repeat this step. (The average number of repetitions will be less than 2. Random numbers will not be needed in steps S2 and S3. In practice we can save time by trying small odd prime numbers x, and stopping with $z = x^q \bmod p$ when $p^{(x-1)/2} \bmod x = x - 1$; see exercise 1.2.4–47.)

S2. Set $y \leftarrow z$, $r \leftarrow e$, $x \leftarrow u^{(q-1)/2} \bmod p$, $v \leftarrow ux \bmod p$, $w \leftarrow ux^2 \bmod p$.

S3. If $w = 1$, stop; v is the answer. Otherwise find the smallest k such that $w^{2^k} \bmod p$ is equal to 1. If $k = r$, stop (there is no answer); otherwise set $(y, r, v, w) \leftarrow (y^{2^{r-k}}, k, vy^{2^{r-k-1}}, wy^{2^{r-k}})$ and repeat step S3. ∎

The validity of this algorithm follows from the invariant congruences $uw \equiv v^2$, $y^{2^{r-1}} \equiv -1$, $w^{2^{r-1}} \equiv 1$ (modulo p). When $w \neq 1$, step S3 performs $r+2$ multiplications mod p; hence the maximum number of multiplications in that step is less than $\binom{e+3}{2}$, and the average number is less than $\frac{1}{2}\binom{e+4}{2}$. Thus the running time is $O(\log p)^3$ for steps S1 and S2 plus order $e^2 (\log p)^2$ for step S3, compared to just $O(\log p)^3$ for the randomized method based on (21). But the constant factors in Shanks's method are small. [*Congressus Numerantium* **7**(1972), 58–62. A related but less efficient method was published by A. Tonelli, *Göttinger Nachrichten* (1891), 344–346. The first person to discover a square root algorithm with expected running time $O(\log p)^3$ was M. Cipolla, *Rendiconti Accad. Sci. Fis. Mat. Napoli* **9** (1903), 154–163.]

16. (a) Substitute polynomials modulo p for integers, in the proof for $n = 1$. (b) The proof for $n = 1$ carries over to any finite field. (c) Since $x = \xi^k$ for some k, $x^{p^n} = x$ in the field defined by $f(x)$. Furthermore, the elements y that satisfy the equation $y^{p^m} = y$ in the field are closed under addition, and closed under multiplication; so if $x^{p^m} = x$, then ξ (being a polynomial in x with integer coefficients) satisfies $\xi^{p^m} = \xi$.

17. If ξ is a primitive root, each nonzero element is some power of ξ. Hence the order must be a divisor of $13^2 - 1 = 2^3 \cdot 3 \cdot 7$, and $\varphi(f)$ elements have order f.

f	$\varphi(f)$	f	$\varphi(f)$	f	$\varphi(f)$	f	$\varphi(f)$
1	1	3	2	7	6	21	12
2	1	6	2	14	6	42	12
4	2	12	4	28	12	84	24
8	4	24	8	56	24	168	48

18. (a) $pp(p_1(u_n x)) \ldots pp(p_r(u_n x))$, by Gauss's lemma. For example, let

$$u(x) = 6x^3 - 3x^2 + 2x - 1, \qquad v(x) = x^3 - 3x^2 + 12x - 36 = (x^2 + 12)(x - 3);$$

then $pp(36x^2 + 12) = 3x^2 + 1$, $pp(6x - 3) = 2x - 1$. (This is a modern version of a fourteenth-century trick used for many years to help solve algebraic equations.)

(b) Let $pp(w(u_n x)) = \bar{w}_m x^m + \cdots + \bar{w}_0 = w(u_n x)/c$, where c is the content of $w(u_n x)$ as a polynomial in x. Then $w(x) = (c\bar{w}/u_n^m)x^m + \cdots + c\bar{w}_0$, hence $c\bar{w}_m = u_n^m$; since $\bar{w}_m$ is a divisor of u_n, c is a multiple of u_n^{m-1}.

19. If $u(x) = v(x)w(x)$ with $\deg(v)\deg(w) \geq 1$, then $u_n x^n \equiv v(x)w(x)$ (modulo p). By unique factorization modulo p, all but the leading coefficients of v and w are multiples of p, and p^2 divides $v_0 w_0 = u_0$.

20. (a) $\sum(\alpha u_j - u_{j-1})(\bar{\alpha}\bar{u}_j - \bar{u}_{j-1}) = \sum(u_j - \bar{\alpha}u_{j-1})(\bar{u}_j - \alpha\bar{u}_{j-1})$. (b) We may assume that $u_0 \neq 0$. Let $m(u) = \prod_{j=1}^n \min(1, |\alpha_j|) = |u_0|/M(u)$. Whenever $|\alpha_j| < 1$, change the factor $x - \alpha_j$ to $\bar{\alpha}_j x - 1$ in $u(x)$; this doesn't affect $\|u\|$, but it changes $|u_0|$ to $M(u)$. (c) $u_j = \pm u_n \sum \alpha_{i_1} \ldots \alpha_{i_{n-j}}$, an elementary symmetric function, hence $|u_j| \leq |u_n| \sum \beta_{i_1} \ldots \beta_{i_{n-j}}$ where $\beta_i = \max(1, |\alpha_i|)$. We complete the proof by showing that when $x_1 \geq 1, \ldots, x_n \geq 1$, and $x_1 \ldots x_n = M$, the elementary symmetric function

$\sigma_{nk} = \sum x_{i_1} \ldots x_{i_k}$ is $\leq \binom{n-1}{k-1} M + \binom{n-1}{k}$, the value assumed when $x_1 = \cdots = x_{n-1} = 1$ and $x_n = M$. (For if $x_1 \leq \cdots \leq x_n < M$, the transformation $x_n \leftarrow x_{n-1} x_n$, $x_{n-1} \leftarrow 1$ increases σ_{nk} by $\sigma_{(n-2)(k-1)}(x_n - 1)(x_{n-1} - 1)$, which is positive.) (d) $|v_j| \leq \binom{m-1}{j} M(v) + \binom{m-1}{j-1} |v_m| \leq \binom{m-1}{j} M(u) + \binom{m-1}{j-1} |u_n|$ since $M(v) \leq M(u)$ and $|v_m| \leq |u_n|$. [M. Mignotte, *Math. Comp.* **28** (1974), 1153–1157.]

Notes: This solution shows that $\binom{m-1}{j} M(u) + \binom{m-1}{j-1} |u_n|$ is an upper bound, so we would like to have a better estimate of $M(u)$. Several methods are known [W. Specht, *Math. Zeit.* **53** (1950), 357–363; Cerlienco, Mignotte, and Piras, *J. Symbolic Comp.* **4** (1987), 21–33]. The simplest and most rapidly convergent is perhaps the following procedure [see C. H. Graeffe, *Auflösung der höheren numerischen Gleichungen* (Zürich: 1837)]: Assuming that $u(x) = u_n(x - \alpha_1) \ldots (x - \alpha_n)$, let $\hat{u}(x) = u(\sqrt{x}) u(-\sqrt{x}) = (-1)^n u_n^2 (x - \alpha_1^2) \ldots (x - \alpha_n^2)$. Then $M(u)^2 = M(\hat{u}) \leq \|\hat{u}\|$. Hence we may set $c \leftarrow \|u\|$, $v \leftarrow u/c$, $t \leftarrow 0$, and then repeatedly set $t \leftarrow t + 1$, $c \leftarrow \|\hat{v}\|^{1/2^t} c$, $v \leftarrow \hat{v}/\|\hat{v}\|$. The invariant relations $M(u) = c M(v)^{1/2^t}$ and $\|v\| = 1$ guarantee that $M(u) \leq c$ at each step of the iteration. Notice that when $v(x) = v_0(x^2) + x v_1(x^2)$, we have $\hat{v}(x) = v_0(x)^2 - x v_1(x)^2$. It can be shown that if each $|\alpha_j|$ is $\leq \rho$ or $\geq 1/\rho$, then $M(u) = \|u\|(1 + O(\rho))$; hence c will be $M(u)(1 + O(\rho^{2^t}))$ after t steps.

For example, if $u(x)$ is the polynomial of (22), the successive values of c for $t = 0$, 1, 2, ... turn out to be 10.63, 12.42, 6.85, 6.64, 6.65, 6.6228, 6.62246, 6.62246, ... In this example $\rho \approx .90982$. Notice that convergence is not monotonic. Eventually $v(x)$ will converge to the monomial x^m, where m is the number of roots with $|\alpha_j| < 1$, assuming that $|\alpha_j| \neq 1$ for all j; in general, if there are k roots with $|\alpha_j| = 1$, the coefficients of x^m and x^{m+k} will not approach zero, while the coefficients of higher and lower powers of x will.

A famous formula due to Jensen [*Acta Math.* **22** (1899), 359–364] proves that $M(u)$ is the geometric mean of $|u(x)|$ on the unit circle, namely $\exp\left(\frac{1}{2\pi} \int_0^{2\pi} \ln|f(e^{i\theta})| \, d\theta\right)$. Exercise 21(a) will show, similarly, that $\|u\|$ is the root-mean-square of $|u(x)|$ on the unit circle. The inequality $M(u) \leq \|u\|$, which goes back to E. Landau [*Bull. Soc. Math. de France* **33** (1905), 251–261], can therefore be understood as a relation between mean values. The number $M(u)$ is often called the *Mahler measure* of a polynomial, because Kurt Mahler used it in *Mathematika* **7** (1960), 98–100. Incidentally, Jensen also proved that $\frac{1}{2\pi} \int_0^{2\pi} e^{im\theta} \ln|f(e^{i\theta})| \, d\theta = -\sum_{j=1}^{n} \alpha_j^m / (2m \max(|\alpha_j|, 1)^{2m})$ when $m > 0$.

21. (a) The coefficient of $a_p b_q c_r d_s$ is zero on both sides unless $\mathbf{p} + \mathbf{s} = \mathbf{q} + \mathbf{r}$. And when this condition holds, the coefficient on the right is $(\mathbf{p} + \mathbf{s})!$; on the left it is

$$\sum_j \binom{\mathbf{p}}{\mathbf{j}} \binom{\mathbf{s}}{\mathbf{r} - \mathbf{j}} \mathbf{q}! \, \mathbf{r}! = \binom{\mathbf{p} + \mathbf{s}}{\mathbf{r}} \mathbf{q}! \, \mathbf{r}! = (\mathbf{q} + \mathbf{r})! \, .$$

[B. Beauzamy and J. Dégot, *Trans. Amer. Math. Soc.* **345** (1995), 2607–2619; D. Zeilberger, *AMM* **101** (1994), 894–896.]

(b) Let $a_{\mathbf{p}} = v_{\mathbf{p}}$, $b_{\mathbf{q}} = w_{\mathbf{q}}$, $c_{\mathbf{r}} = \overline{v}_{\mathbf{r}}$, $d_{\mathbf{s}} = \overline{w}_{\mathbf{s}}$. Then the right side of (a) is $B(u)$, and the left side is a sum of nonnegative terms for each $\mathbf{j}$ and $\mathbf{k}$. If we consider only the terms where $\Sigma \mathbf{j}$ is the degree of v, the terms $v_{\mathbf{p}}/(\mathbf{p} - \mathbf{j})!$ vanish except when $\mathbf{p} = \mathbf{j}$. Those terms therefore reduce to

$$\sum_{\mathbf{j}, \mathbf{k}} \frac{1}{\mathbf{j}! \, \mathbf{k}!} \left| v_{\mathbf{j}} w_{\mathbf{k}} \mathbf{j}! \, \mathbf{k}! \right|^2 = B(v) B(w) \, .$$

[B. Beauzamy, E. Bombieri, P. Enflo, and H. Montgomery, *J. Number Theory* **36** (1990), 219–245.]

(c) Adding a new variable, if needed to make everything homogeneous, does not change the relation $u = vw$. Thus if v and w have total degrees m and n, respectively, we have $(m+n)!\,[u]^2 \geq m!\,[v]^2\,n!\,[w]^2$; in other words, $[v][w] \leq \binom{m+n}{m}^{1/2}[u]$.

Incidentally, one nice way to think of the Bombieri norm is to imagine that the variables are noncommutative. For example, instead of $3xy^3 - z^2w^2$ we could write $\frac{3}{4}xyyy + \frac{3}{4}yxyy + \frac{3}{4}yyxy + \frac{3}{4}yyyx - \frac{1}{6}zzww - \frac{1}{6}zwzw - \frac{1}{6}zwwz - \frac{1}{6}wzzw - \frac{1}{6}wzwz - \frac{1}{6}wwzz$. Then the Bombieri norm is the $\|\ \|$ norm on the new coefficients. Another interesting formula, when u is homogeneous of degree n, is

$$[u]^2 = \frac{1}{n!\,\pi^n}\int_{\mathbf{x}}\int_{\mathbf{y}} e^{-x_1^2 - \cdots - x_t^2 - y_1^2 - \cdots - y_t^2}\,|u(\mathbf{x} + i\mathbf{y})|^2\,d\mathbf{x}\,d\mathbf{y}\,.$$

(d) The one-variable case corresponds to $t = 2$. Suppose $u = vw$ where v is homogeneous of degree m in t variables. Then $|v_{\mathbf{k}}|^2\,\mathbf{k}!/m! \leq [v]^2$ for all $\mathbf{k}$, and $\mathbf{k}! \geq (m/t)!^t$ since $\log\Gamma(x)$ is convex for $x > 0$; therefore $|v_{\mathbf{k}}|^2 \leq m!\,[v]^2/(m/t)!^t$. We can assume that $m!\,[v]^2/(m/t)!^t \leq m'!\,[w]^2/(m'/t)!^t$, where $m' = n - m$ is the degree of w. Then

$$|v_{\mathbf{k}}|^2 \leq m!\,[v]^2/(m/t)!^t \leq m!^{1/2}m'!^{1/2}\,[v][w]/(m/t)!^{t/2}(m'/t)!^{t/2} \leq n!^{1/2}\,[u]/(n/2t)!^t\,.$$

(A better bound is obtained if we maximize the next-to-last expression over all degrees m for which a factor has not been ruled out.) The quantity $n!^{1/4}/(n/2t)!^{t/2}$ is $c_t(2t)^{n/4}n^{-(2t-1)/8}\bigl(1 + O(\frac{1}{n})\bigr)$, where $c_t = 2^{1/8}\pi^{-(2t-1)/8}t^{t/4}$ is ≈ 1.004 when $t = 2$.

Notice that we have not demonstrated the existence of an *irreducible* factor with such small coefficients; further splitting may be needed. See exercise 41.

(e) $[u]^2 = \sum_k \binom{n}{k}^2/\binom{2n}{2k} = \sum_k \binom{2k}{k}\binom{2n-2k}{n-k}/\binom{2n}{n} = 4^n/\binom{2n}{n} = \sqrt{\pi n} + O(n^{-1/2})$. If $v(x) = (x-1)^n$ and $w(x) = (x+1)^n$, we have $[v]^2 = [w]^2 = 2^n$; hence the inequality of (c) is an equality in this case.

(f) Let u and v be homogeneous of degree m and n. Then

$$[uv]^2 \leq \sum_k \frac{(\sum_j |u_j v_{\mathbf{k}-j}|)^2}{\binom{m+n}{k}} \leq \sum_k \left(\sum_j \frac{|u_j|^2}{\binom{m}{j}}\frac{|v_{\mathbf{k}-j}|^2}{\binom{n}{k-j}}\right)\left(\sum_j \frac{\binom{m}{j}\binom{n}{k-j}}{\binom{m+n}{k}}\right) = [u]^2[v]^2$$

by Cauchy's inequality. [B. Beauzamy, *J. Symbolic Comp.* **13** (1992), 465–472, Proposition 5.]

(g) By exercise 20, $\binom{n}{\lfloor n/2\rfloor}^{-1}M(u)^2 \leq \binom{n}{\lfloor n/2\rfloor}^{-1}\|u\|^2 = \binom{n}{\lfloor n/2\rfloor}^{-1}\sum_j |u_j|^2 \leq [u]^2 = \sum_j \binom{n}{j}^{-1}|u_j|^2 \leq \sum_j \binom{n}{j}M(u)^2 = 2^n M(u)^2$. The upper inequality also follows from (f), for if $u(x) = u_n\prod_{j=1}^n (x - \alpha_j)$ we have $[u]^2 \leq |u_n|^2\prod_{j=1}^n [x - \alpha_j]^2 = |u_n|^2\prod_{j=1}^n (1 + |\alpha_j|^2) \leq |u_n|^2\prod_{j=1}^n (2\max(1, |\alpha_j|)^2) = 2^n M(u)^2$.

22. More generally, assume that $u(x) \equiv v(x)w(x)$ (modulo q), $a(x)v(x) + b(x)w(x) \equiv 1$ (modulo p), $c \cdot \ell(v) \equiv 1$ (modulo r), $\deg(a) < \deg(w)$, $\deg(b) < \deg(v)$, and $\deg(u) = \deg(v) + \deg(w)$, where $r = \gcd(p, q)$ and p, q needn't be prime. We shall construct polynomials $V(x) \equiv v(x)$ and $W(x) \equiv w(x)$ (modulo q) such that $u(x) \equiv V(x)W(x)$ (modulo qr), $\ell(V) = \ell(v)$, $\deg(V) = \deg(v)$, $\deg(W) = \deg(w)$; furthermore, if r is prime, the results will be unique modulo qr.

The problem asks us to find $\bar{v}(x)$ and $\bar{w}(x)$ with $V(x) = v(x) + q\bar{v}(x)$, $W(x) = w(x) + q\bar{w}(x)$, $\deg(\bar{v}) < \deg(v)$, $\deg(\bar{w}) \leq \deg(w)$; and the other condition

$$\bigl(v(x) + q\bar{v}(x)\bigr)\bigl(w(x) + q\bar{w}(x)\bigr) \equiv u(x) \quad (\text{modulo } qr)$$

is equivalent to $\bar{w}(x)v(x) + \bar{v}(x)w(x) \equiv f(x)$ (modulo r), where $f(x)$ satisfies $u(x) \equiv v(x)w(x) + qf(x)$ (modulo qr). We have

$$(a(x)f(x) + t(x)w(x))v(x) + (b(x)f(x) - t(x)v(x))w(x) \equiv f(x) \quad \text{(modulo } r)$$

for all $t(x)$. Since $\ell(v)$ has an inverse modulo r, we can find a quotient $t(x)$ by Algorithm 4.6.1D such that $\deg(bf - tv) < \deg(v)$; for this $t(x)$, $\deg(af + tw) \leq \deg(w)$, since we have $\deg(f) \leq \deg(u) = \deg(v) + \deg(w)$. Thus the desired solution is $\bar{v}(x) = b(x)f(x) - t(x)v(x) = b(x)f(x) \bmod v(x)$, $\bar{w}(x) = a(x)f(x) + t(x)w(x)$. If $(\bar{\bar{v}}(x), \bar{\bar{w}}(x))$ is another solution, we have $(\bar{w}(x) - \bar{\bar{w}}(x))v(x) \equiv (\bar{\bar{v}}(x) - \bar{v}(x))w(x)$ (modulo r). Thus if r is prime, $v(x)$ must divide $\bar{\bar{v}}(x) - \bar{v}(x)$; but $\deg(\bar{\bar{v}} - \bar{v}) < \deg(v)$, so $\bar{\bar{v}}(x) = \bar{v}(x)$ and $\bar{\bar{w}}(x) = \bar{w}(x)$.

If p divides q, so that $r = p$, our choices of $V(x)$ and $W(x)$ also satisfy $a(x)V(x) + b(x)W(x) \equiv 1$ (modulo p), as required by Hensel's Lemma.

For $p = 2$, the factorization proceeds as follows (writing only the coefficients, and using bars for negative digits): Exercise 10 says that $v_1(x) = (\bar{1}\,1\,\bar{1})$, $w_1(x) = (\bar{1}\,\bar{1}\,\bar{1}\,0\,0\,\bar{1}\,\bar{1})$ in one-bit two's complement notation. Euclid's extended algorithm yields $a(x) = (1\,0\,0\,0\,0\,1)$, $b(x) = (1\,0)$. The factor $v(x) = x^2 + c_1 x + c_0$ must have $|c_1| \leq \lfloor 1 + \sqrt{113} \rfloor = 11$, $|c_0| \leq 10$, by exercise 20. Three applications of Hensel's lemma yield $v_4(x) = (1\,3\,\bar{1})$, $w_4(x) = (1\,\bar{3}\,\bar{5}\,\bar{4}\,4\,\bar{3}\,5)$. Thus $c_1 \equiv 3$ and $c_0 \equiv -1$ (modulo 16); the only possible quadratic factor of $u(x)$ is $x^2 + 3x - 1$. Division fails, so $u(x)$ is irreducible. (Since we have now proved the irreducibility of this beloved polynomial by four separate methods, it is unlikely that it has any factors.)

Hans Zassenhaus has observed that we can often speed up such calculations by increasing p as well as q: When $r = p$ in the notation above, we can find $A(x)$, $B(x)$ such that $A(x)V(x) + B(x)W(x) \equiv 1$ (modulo p^2), namely by taking $A(x) = a(x) + p\bar{a}(x)$, $B(x) = b(x) + p\bar{b}(x)$, where $\bar{a}(x)V(x) + \bar{b}(x)W(x) \equiv g(x)$ (modulo p), $a(x)V(x) + b(x)W(x) \equiv 1 - pg(x)$ (modulo p^2). We can also find C with $\ell(V)C \equiv 1$ (modulo p^2). In this way we can lift a squarefree factorization $u(x) \equiv v(x)w(x)$ (modulo p) to its unique extensions modulo p^2, p^4, p^8, p^{16}, etc. However, this "accelerated" procedure reaches a point of diminishing returns in practice, as soon as we get to double-precision moduli, since the time for multiplying multiprecision numbers in practical ranges outweighs the advantage of squaring the modulus directly. From a computational standpoint it seems best to work with the successive moduli p, p^2, p^4, p^8, $\ldots$, p^E, p^{E+e}, p^{E+2e}, p^{E+3e}, $\ldots$, where E is the smallest power of 2 with p^E greater than single precision and e is the largest integer such that p^e has single precision.

"Hensel's Lemma" was actually invented by C. F. Gauss about 1799, in the draft of an unfinished book called *Analysis Residuorum*, §373–374. Gauss incorporated most of the material from that manuscript into his *Disquisitiones Arithmeticæ* (1801), but his ideas about polynomial factorization were not published until after his death [see his *Werke* **2** (Göttingen, 1863), 238]. Meanwhile T. Schönemann had independently discovered the lemma and proved uniqueness [*Crelle* **32** (1846), 93–105, §59]. Hensel's name was attached to the method because it is basic to the theory of p-adic numbers (see exercise 4.1–31). The lemma can be generalized in several ways. First, if there are more factors, say $u(x) \equiv v_1(x)v_2(x)v_3(x)$ (modulo p), we can find $a_1(x)$, $a_2(x)$, $a_3(x)$ such that $a_1(x)v_2(x)v_3(x) + a_2(x)v_1(x)v_3(x) + a_3(x)v_1(x)v_2(x) \equiv 1$ (modulo p) and $\deg(a_i) < \deg(v_i)$. (In essence, $1/u(x)$ is expanded in partial fractions as $\sum a_i(x)/v_i(x)$.) An exactly analogous construction now allows us to lift the factorization without changing the leading coefficients of v_1 and v_2; we take $\bar{v}_1(x) = a_1(x)f(x) \bmod v_1(x)$, $\bar{v}_2(x) = a_2(x)f(x) \bmod v_2(x)$, etc. Another important generalization is to several simultaneous moduli, of the respective forms p^e, $(x_2 - a_2)^{n_2}$, ..., $(x_t - a_t)^{n_t}$, when performing multivariate gcds and factorizations. See D. Y. Y. Yun, Ph.D. Thesis (M.I.T., 1974).

23. The discriminant of $\mathrm{pp}(u(x))$ is a nonzero integer (see exercise 4.6.1–12), and there are multiple factors modulo p if and only if p divides the discriminant. [The factorization of (22) modulo 3 is $(x + 1)(x^2 - x - 1)^2(x^3 + x^2 - x + 1)$; squared factors for this polynomial occur only for $p = 3$, 23, 233, and 121702457. It is not difficult to prove that the smallest prime that is not unlucky is at most $O(n \log Nn)$, if $n = \deg(u)$ and if N bounds the coefficients of $u(x)$.]

24. Multiply a monic polynomial with rational coefficients by a suitable nonzero integer, to get a primitive polynomial over the integers. Factor this polynomial over the integers, and then convert the factors back to monic. (No factorizations are lost in this way; see exercise 4.6.1–8.)

25. Consideration of the constant term shows there are no factors of degree 1, so if the polynomial is reducible, it must have one factor of degree 2 and one of degree 3. Modulo 2 the factors are $x(x + 1)^2(x^2 + x + 1)$; this is not much help. Modulo 3 the factors are $(x + 2)^2(x^3 + 2x + 2)$. Modulo 5 they are $(x^2 + x + 1)(x^3 + 4x + 2)$. So we see that the answer is $(x^2 + x + 1)(x^3 - x + 2)$.

26. Begin with $D \leftarrow (0 \ldots 01)$, representing the set $\{0\}$. Then for $1 \le j \le r$, set $D \leftarrow D \mid (D \ll d_j)$, where $\mid$ denotes bitwise "or" and $D \ll d$ denotes D shifted left d bit positions. (Actually we need only work with a bit vector of length $\lceil (n + 1)/2 \rceil$, since $n - m$ is in the set if and only if m is.)

27. Exercise 4 says that a random polynomial of degree n is irreducible modulo p with rather low probability, about $1/n$. But the Chinese remainder theorem implies that a random monic polynomial of degree n over the integers will be reducible with respect to each of k distinct primes with probability about $(1 - 1/n)^k$, and this approaches zero as $k \to \infty$. Hence almost all polynomials over the integers are irreducible with respect to infinitely many primes; and almost all primitive polynomials over the integers are irreducible. [Another proof has been given by W. S. Brown, *AMM* **70** (1963), 965–969.]

28. See exercise 4; the probability is $[z^n](1 + a_{1p}z/p)(1 + a_{2p}z^2/p^2)(1 + a_{3p}z^3/p^3)\ldots$, which has the limiting value $g(z) = (1 + z)(1 + \frac{1}{2}z^2)(1 + \frac{1}{3}z^3)\ldots$. For $1 \le n \le 10$ the answers are 1, $\frac{1}{2}$, $\frac{5}{6}$, $\frac{7}{12}$, $\frac{37}{60}$, $\frac{79}{120}$, $\frac{173}{280}$, $\frac{101}{168}$, $\frac{127}{210}$, $\frac{1033}{1680}$. [Let $f(y) = \ln(1 + y) - y = O(y^2)$. We have

$$g(z) = \exp\left(\sum_{n \ge 1} z^n/n + \sum_{n \ge 1} f(z^n/n)\right) = h(z)/(1 - z),$$

and it can be shown that the limiting probability is $h(1) = \exp(\sum_{n \ge 1} f(1/n)) = e^{-\gamma} \approx .56146$ as $n \to \infty$. Indeed, N. G. de Bruijn has established the asymptotic formula $\lim_{p \to \infty} a_{np} = e^{-\gamma} + e^{-\gamma}/n + O(n^{-2} \log n)$. [See D. H. Lehmer, *Acta Arith.* **21** (1972), 379–388; D. H. Greene and D. E. Knuth, *Math. for the Analysis of Algorithms* (Boston: Birkhäuser, 1981), §4.1.6.] On the other hand the answers for $1 \le n \le 10$ when $p = 2$ are smaller: 1, $\frac{1}{4}$, $\frac{1}{2}$, $\frac{7}{16}$, $\frac{7}{16}$, $\frac{7}{16}$, $\frac{27}{64}$, $\frac{111}{256}$, $\frac{109}{256}$, $\frac{109}{256}$. A. Knopfmacher and R. Warlimont [*Trans. Amer. Math. Soc.* **347** (1995), 2235–2243] have shown that for fixed p the probability is $c_p + O(1/n)$, where $c_p = \prod_{m \ge 1} e^{-1/m}(1 + a_{mp}/p^m)$, $c_2 \approx .397$.]

29. Let $q_1(x)$ and $q_2(x)$ be any two of the irreducible divisors of $g(x)$. By the Chinese remainder theorem (exercise 3), choosing a random polynomial $t(x)$ of degree $< 2d$ is equivalent to choosing two random polynomials $t_1(x)$ and $t_2(x)$ of degrees $< d$, where $t_i(x) = t(x) \bmod q_i(x)$. The gcd will be a proper factor if $t_1(x)^{(p^d - 1)/2} \bmod q_1(x) = 1$

and $t_2(x)^{(p^d-1)/2} \bmod q_1(x) \neq 1$, or vice versa, and this condition holds for exactly $2((p^d - 1)/2)((p^d + 1)/2) = (p^{2d} - 1)/2$ choices of $t_1(x)$ and $t_2(x)$.

Notes: We are considering here only the behavior with respect to two irreducible factors, but the true behavior is probably much better. Suppose that each irreducible factor $q_i(x)$ has probability $\frac{1}{2}$ of dividing $t(x)^{(p^d-1)/2} - 1$ for each $t(x)$, independent of the behavior for other $q_j(x)$ and $t(x)$; and assume that $g(x)$ has r irreducible factors in all. Then if we encode each $q_i(x)$ by a sequence of 0s and 1s according as $q_i(x)$ does or doesn't divide $t(x)^{(p^d-1)/2} - 1$ for the successive t's tried, we obtain a random binary trie with r lieves (see Section 6.3). The cost associated with an internal node of this trie, having m lieves as descendants, is $O(m^2(\log p))$; and the solution to the recurrence $A_n = \binom{n}{2} + 2^{1-n} \sum \binom{n}{k} A_k$ is $A_n = 2\binom{n}{2}$, by exercise 5.2.2–36. Hence the sum of costs in the given random trie—representing the expected time to factor $g(x)$ completely—is $O(r^2(\log p)^3)$ under this plausible assumption. The plausible assumption becomes rigorously true if we choose $t(x)$ at random of degree $< rd$ instead of restricting it to degree $< 2d$.

30. Let $T(x) = x + x^p + \cdots + x^{p^{d-1}}$ be the *trace* of x and let $v(x) = T(t(x)) \bmod q(x)$. Since $t(x)^{p^d} = t(x)$ in the field of polynomial remainders modulo $q(x)$, we have $v(x)^p = v(x)$ in that field; in other words, $v(x)$ is one of the p roots of the equation $y^p - y = 0$. Hence $v(x)$ is an integer.

It follows that $\prod_{s=0}^{p-1} \gcd(g_d(x), T(t(x)) - s) = g_d(x)$. In particular, when $p = 2$ we can argue as in exercise 29 that $\gcd(g_d(x), T(t(x)))$ will be a proper factor of $g_d(x)$ with probability $\geq \frac{1}{2}$ when $g_d(x)$ has at least two irreducible factors and $t(x)$ is a random binary polynomial of degree $< 2d$.

[Note that $T(t(x)) \bmod g(x)$ can be computed by starting with $u(x) \leftarrow t(x)$ and setting $u(x) \leftarrow (t(x) + u(x)^p) \bmod g(x)$ repeatedly, $d - 1$ times. The method of this exercise is based on the polynomial factorization $x^{p^d} - x = \prod_{s=0}^{p-1}(T(x) - s)$, which holds for any p, while formula (21) is based on the polynomial factorization $x^{p^d} - x = x(x^{(p^d-1)/2} + 1)(x^{(p^d-1)/2} - 1)$ for odd p.]

The trace was introduced by Richard Dedekind, *Abhandlungen der Königl. Gesellschaft der Wissenschaften zu Göttingen* **29** (1882), 1–56. The technique of calculating $\gcd(f(x), T(x) - s)$ to find factors of $f(x)$ can be traced to A. Arwin, *Arkiv för Mat., Astr. och Fys.* **14**, 7 (1918), 1–46; but his method was incomplete because he did not consider $T(t(x))$ for $t(x) \neq x$. A complete factorization algorithm using traces was devised later by R. J. McEliece, *Math. Comp.* **23** (1969), 861–867; see also von zur Gathen and Shoup, *Computational Complexity* **2** (1992), 187–224, Algorithm 3.6, for asymptotically fast results.

Henri Cohen has observed that for $p = 2$ it suffices to test at most d special cases $t(x) = x, x^3, \ldots, x^{2d-1}$ when applying this method. One of these choices of $t(x)$ is guaranteed to split $g_d(x)$ whenever g_d is reducible, because we can obtain the effects of all polynomials $t(x)$ of degree $< 2d$ from these special cases using the facts that $T(t(x)^p) \equiv T(t(x))$ and $T(u(x)+t(x)) \equiv T(u(x))+T(t(x))$ (modulo $g_d(x)$). [*A Course in Computational Algebraic Number Theory* (Springer, 1993), Algorithm 3.4.8.]

31. If α is an element of the field of p^d elements, let $d(\alpha)$ be the *degree* of α, namely the smallest exponent e such that $\alpha^{p^e} = \alpha$. Then consider the polynomial

$$P_\alpha(x) = (x - \alpha)(x - \alpha^p) \ldots (x - \alpha^{p^{d-1}}) = q_\alpha(x)^{d/d(\alpha)},$$

where $q_\alpha(x)$ is an irreducible polynomial of degree $d(\alpha)$. As α runs through all elements of the field, the corresponding $q_\alpha(x)$ runs through every irreducible polynomial of degree e dividing d, where every such irreducible occurs exactly e times. We have $(x + t)^{(p^d-1)/2} \bmod q_\alpha(x) = 1$ if and only if $(\alpha + t)^{(p^d-1)/2} = 1$ in the field. If t is an integer, we have $d(\alpha + t) = d(\alpha)$, hence $n(p, d)$ is d^{-1} times the number of elements α of degree d such that $\alpha^{(p^d-1)/2} = 1$. Similarly, if $t_1 \neq t_2$ we want to count the number of elements of degree d such that $(\alpha + t_1)^{(p^d-1)/2} = (\alpha + t_2)^{(p^d-1)/2}$, or equivalently $((\alpha+t_1)/(\alpha+t_2))^{(p^d-1)/2} = 1$. As α runs through all the elements of degree d, so does the quantity $(\alpha + t_1)/(\alpha + t_2) = 1 + (t_1 - t_2)/(\alpha + t_2)$.

[We have $n(p, d) = \frac14 d^{-1} \sum_{c\backslash d}(3 + (-1)^c)\mu(c)(p^{d/c} - 1)$, which is about half the total number of irreducibles—exactly half, in fact, when d is odd. This proves that $\gcd(g_d(x), (x + t)^{(p^d-1)/2} - 1)$ has a good chance of finding factors of $g_d(x)$ when t is fixed and $g_d(x)$ is chosen at random; but a randomized algorithm is supposed to work with guaranteed probability for *fixed* $g_d(x)$ and *random* t, as in exercise 29.]

32. (a) Clearly $x^n - 1 = \prod_{d\backslash n}\Psi_d(x)$, since every complex nth root of unity is a primitive dth root for some unique $d\backslash n$. The second identity follows from the first; and $\Psi_n(x)$ has integer coefficients since it is expressed in terms of products and quotients of monic polynomials with integer coefficients.

(b) The condition in the hint suffices to prove that $f(x) = \Psi_n(x)$, so we shall take the hint. When p does not divide n, we have $x^n - 1 \perp nx^{n-1}$ modulo p, hence $x^n - 1$ is squarefree modulo p. Given $f(x)$ and ζ as in the hint, let $g(x)$ be the irreducible factor of $\Psi_n(x)$ such that $g(\zeta^p) = 0$. If $g(x) \neq f(x)$ then $f(x)$ and $g(x)$ are distinct factors of $\Psi_n(x)$, hence they are distinct factors of $x^n - 1$, hence they have no irreducible factors in common modulo p. However, ζ is a root of $g(x^p)$, so $\gcd(f(x), g(x^p)) \neq 1$ over the integers, hence $f(x)$ is a divisor of $g(x^p)$. By (5), $f(x)$ is a divisor of $g(x)^p$, modulo p, contradicting the assumption that $f(x)$ and $g(x)$ have no irreducible factors in common. Therefore $f(x) = g(x)$. [The irreducibility of $\Psi_n(x)$ was first proved for prime n by C. F. Gauss in *Disquisitiones Arithmeticæ* (Leipzig: 1801), Art. 341, and for general n by L. Kronecker, *J. de Math. Pures et Appliquées* **19** (1854), 177–192.]

(c) $\Psi_1(x) = x - 1$; and when p is prime, $\Psi_p(x) = 1 + x + \cdots + x^{p-1}$. If $n > 1$ is odd, it is not difficult to prove that $\Psi_{2n}(x) = \Psi_n(-x)$. If p divides n, the second identity in (a) shows that $\Psi_{pn}(x) = \Psi_n(x^p)$. If p does not divide n, we have $\Psi_{pn}(x) = \Psi_n(x^p)/\Psi_n(x)$. For nonprime $n \leq 15$ we have $\Psi_4(x) = x^2 + 1$, $\Psi_6(x) = x^2 - x + 1$, $\Psi_8(x) = x^4 + 1$, $\Psi_9(x) = x^6 + x^3 + 1$, $\Psi_{10}(x) = x^4 - x^3 + x^2 - x + 1$, $\Psi_{12}(x) = x^4 - x^2 + 1$, $\Psi_{14}(x) = x^6 - x^5 + x^4 - x^3 + x^2 - x + 1$, $\Psi_{15}(x) = x^8 - x^7 + x^5 - x^4 + x^3 - x + 1$. [The formula $\Psi_{pq}(x) = (1 + x^p + \cdots + x^{(q-1)p})(x - 1)/(x^q - 1)$ can be used to show that $\Psi_{pq}(x)$ has all coefficients ±1 or 0 when p and q are prime; but the coefficients of $\Psi_{pqr}(x)$ can be arbitrarily large.]

33. False; we lose all p_j with e_j divisible by p. True if $p > \deg(u)$. [See exercise 36.]

34. [D. Y. Y. Yun, *Proc. ACM Symp. Symbolic and Algebraic Comp.* (1976), 26–35.] Set $(t(x), v_1(x), w_1(x)) \leftarrow \text{GCD}(u(x), u'(x))$. If $t(x) = 1$, set $e \leftarrow 1$; otherwise set $(u_i(x), v_{i+1}(x), w_{i+1}(x)) \leftarrow \text{GCD}(v_i(x), w_i(x) - v_i'(x))$ for $i = 1, 2, \ldots, e - 1$, until finding $w_e(x) - v_e'(x) = 0$. Finally set $u_e(x) \leftarrow v_e(x)$.

To prove the validity of this algorithm, we observe that it computes the polynomials $t(x) = u_2(x)u_3(x)^2u_4(x)^3 \ldots$, $v_i(x) = u_i(x)u_{i+1}(x)u_{i+2}(x)\ldots$, and

$$w_i(x) = u_i'(x)u_{i+1}(x)u_{i+2}(x)\ldots + 2u_i(x)u_{i+1}'(x)u_{i+2}(x)\ldots + 3u_i(x)u_{i+1}(x)u_{i+2}'(x)\ldots + \cdots.$$

We have $t(x) \perp w_1(x)$, since an irreducible factor of $u_i(x)$ divides all but the ith term of $w_1(x)$, and it is relatively prime to that term. Furthermore we clearly have $u_i(x) \perp v_{i+1}(x)$.

[Although exercise 2(b) proves that most polynomials are squarefree, nonsquarefree polynomials actually occur often in practice; hence this method turns out to be quite important. See Paul S. Wang and Barry M. Trager, *SICOMP* **8** (1979), 300–305, for suggestions on how to improve the efficiency. Squarefree factorization modulo p is discussed by Bach and Shallit, *Algorithmic Number Theory* **1** (MIT Press, 1996), answer to exercise 7.27.]

35. We have $w_j(x) = \gcd\big(u_j(x), v_j^*(x)\big) \cdot \gcd\big(u_{j+1}^*(x), v_j(x)\big)$, where

$$u_j^*(x) = u_j(x)u_{j+1}(x)\dots \qquad \text{and} \qquad v_j^*(x) = v_j(x)v_{j+1}(x)\dots \,.$$

[Yun notes that the running time for squarefree factorization by the method of exercise 34 is at most about twice the running time to calculate $\gcd\big(u(x), u'(x)\big)$. Furthermore if we are given an arbitrary method for discovering squarefree factorization, the method of this exercise leads to a gcd procedure. (When $u(x)$ and $v(x)$ are squarefree, their gcd is simply $w_2(x)$ where $w(x) = u(x)v(x) = w_1(x)w_2(x)^2$; the polynomials $u_j(x)$, $v_j(x)$, $u_j^*(x)$, and $v_j^*(x)$ are all squarefree.) Hence the problem of converting a primitive polynomial of degree n to its squarefree representation is computationally *equivalent* to the problem of calculating the gcd of two nth degree polynomials, in the sense of asymptotic worst-case running time.]

36. Let $U_j(x)$ be the value computed for "$u_j(x)$" by the procedure of exercise 34. If $\deg(U_1) + 2\deg(U_2) + \dots = \deg(u)$, then $u_j(x) = U_j(x)$ for all j. But in general we will have $e < p$ and $U_j(x) = \prod_{k \geq 0} u_{j+pk}(x)$ for $1 \leq j < p$. To separate these factors further, we can calculate $t(x)/\big(U_2(x)U_3(x)^2 \dots U_{p-1}(x)^{p-2}\big) = \prod_{j \geq p} u_j(x)^{p\lfloor j/p \rfloor} = z(x^p)$. After recursively finding the squarefree representation of $z(x) = (z_1(x), z_2(x), \dots)$, we will have $z_k(x) = \prod_{0 \leq j < p} u_{j+pk}(x)$, so we can calculate the individual $u_i(x)$ by the formula $\gcd\big(U_j(x), z_k(x)\big) = u_{j+pk}(x)$ for $1 \leq j < p$. The polynomial $u_{pk}(x)$ will be left when the other factors of $z_k(x)$ have been removed.

Note: This procedure is fairly simple but the program is lengthy. If one's goal is to have a short program for complete factorization modulo p, rather than an extremely efficient one, it is probably easiest to modify the distinct-degree factorization routine so that it casts out $\gcd\big(x^{p^d} - x, u(x)\big)$ several times for the same value of d until the gcd is 1. In this case you needn't begin by calculating $\gcd\big(u(x), u'(x)\big)$ and removing multiple factors as suggested in the text, since the polynomial $x^{p^d} - x$ is squarefree.

37. The exact probability is $\prod_{j \geq 1}(a_{jp}/p^j)^{k_j}/k_j!$, where k_j is the number of d_i that are equal to j. Since $a_{jp}/p^j \approx 1/j$ by exercise 4, we get the formula of exercise 1.3.3–21.

Notes: This exercise says that if we fix the prime p and let the polynomial $u(x)$ be random, it will have a certain probability of splitting in a given way modulo p. A much harder problem is to fix the polynomial $u(x)$ and to let p be "random"; it turns out that the same asymptotic result holds for almost all $u(x)$. G. Frobenius proved in 1880 that the integer polynomial $u(x)$ splits modulo p into factors of degrees $d_1, \dots, d_r$, when p is a large prime chosen at random, with probability equal to the number of permutations in the Galois group G of $u(x)$ having cycle lengths $\{d_1, \dots, d_r\}$ divided by the total number of permutations in G. [If $u(x)$ has rational coefficients and distinct roots $\xi_1, \dots, \xi_n$ over the complex numbers, its Galois group is the (unique) group G of permutations such that the polynomial $\prod_{p(1)\dots p(n) \in G}(z + \xi_{p(1)}y_1 + \dots + \xi_{p(n)}y_n) = U(z, y_1, \dots, y_n)$ has rational coefficients and is irreducible over the rationals; see G. Frobenius, *Sitzungsberichte Königl. preuß. Akad. Wiss.* (Berlin: 1896), 689–703. The linear mapping $x \mapsto x^p$ is traditionally called the Frobenius automorphism because of this famous paper.] Furthermore B. L. van der Waerden proved in 1934 that almost all polynomials of degree n have the set of all $n!$ permutations as their Galois group [*Math. Annalen* **109** (1934), 13–16]. Therefore almost all fixed irreducible polynomials $u(x)$ will factor as we might expect them to, with respect to randomly chosen large primes p. See also N. Chebotarev, *Math. Annalen* **95** (1926), for a generalization of Frobenius's theorem to conjugacy classes of the Galois group.

38. The conditions imply that when $|z| = 1$ we have either $|u_{n-2}z^{n-2} + \cdots + u_0| < |u_{n-1}| - 1 \le |z^n + u_{n-1}z^{n-1}|$ or $|u_{n-3}z^{n-3} + \cdots + u_0| < u_{n-2} - 1 \le |z^n + u_{n-2}z^{n-2}|$. Therefore by Rouché's theorem [*J. École Polytechnique* **21**, 37 (1858), 1–34], $u(z)$ has at least $n - 1$ or $n - 2$ roots inside the circle $|z| = 1$. If $u(z)$ is reducible, it can be written $v(z)w(z)$ where v and w are monic integer polynomials. The products of the roots of v and of w are nonzero integers, so each factor has a root of absolute value ≥ 1. Hence the only possibility is that v and w both have exactly one such root and that $u_{n-1} = 0$. These roots must be real, since the complex conjugates are roots; hence $u(z)$ has a real root z_0 with $|z_0| \ge 1$. But this cannot be, for if $r = 1/z_0$ we have $0 = |1 + u_{n-2}r^2 + \cdots + u_0 r^n| \ge 1 + u_{n-2}r^2 - |u_{n-3}|r^3 - \cdots - |u_0|r^n > 1$. [O. Perron, *Crelle* **132** (1907), 288–307; for generalizations, see A. Brauer, *Amer. J. Math.* **70** (1948), 423–432, **73** (1951), 717–720.]

39. First we prove the hint: Let $u(x) = a(x - \alpha_1)\ldots(x - \alpha_n)$ have integer coefficients. The resultant of $u(x)$ with the polynomial $y - t(x)$ is a determinant, so it is a polynomial $r_t(y) = a^{\deg(t)}(y - t(\alpha_1))\ldots(y - t(\alpha_n))$ with integer coefficients (see exercise 4.6.1–12). If $u(x)$ divides $v(t(x))$ then $v(t(\alpha_1)) = 0$, hence $r_t(y)$ has a factor in common with $v(y)$. So if v is irreducible, we have $\deg(u) = \deg(r_t) \ge \deg(v)$.

Given an irreducible polynomial $u(x)$ for which a short proof of irreducibility is desired, we may assume that $u(x)$ is monic, by exercise 18, and that $\deg(u) \ge 3$. The idea is to show the existence of a polynomial $t(x)$ such that $v(y) = r_t(y)$ is irreducible by the criterion of exercise 38. Then all factors of $u(x)$ divide the polynomial $v(t(x))$, and this will prove that $u(x)$ is irreducible. The proof will be succinct if the coefficients of $t(x)$ are suitably small.

The polynomial $v(y) = (y - \beta_1)\ldots(y - \beta_n)$ can be shown to satisfy the criterion of exercise 38 if $n \ge 3$ and $\beta_1 \ldots \beta_n \ne 0$, and if the following "smallness condition" holds: $|\beta_j| \le 1/(4n)$ except when $j = n$ or when $\beta_j = \overline{\beta}_n$ and $|\Re\beta_j| \le 1/(4n)$. The calculations are straightforward, using the fact that $|v_0| + \cdots + |v_n| \le (1 + |\beta_1|)\ldots(1 + |\beta_n|)$.

Let $\alpha_1, \ldots, \alpha_r$ be real and $\alpha_{r+1}, \ldots, \alpha_{r+s}$ be complex, where $n = r + 2s$ and $\alpha_{r+s+j} = \overline{\alpha}_{r+j}$ for $1 \le j \le s$. Consider the linear expressions $S_j(a_0, \ldots, a_{n-1})$ defined to be $\Re(\sum_{i=0}^{n-1} a_i \alpha_j^i)$ for $1 \le j \le r + s$ and $\Im(\sum_{i=0}^{n-1} a_i \alpha_j^i)$ for $r + s < j \le n$. If $0 \le a_i < b$ and $B = \lceil \max_{j=1}^{n-1} \sum_{i=0}^{n-1} |\alpha_i|^j \rceil$, we have $|S_j(a_1, \ldots, a_{n-1})| < bB$. Thus if we choose $b > (16nB)^{n-1}$, there must be distinct vectors $(a_0, \ldots, a_{n-1})$ and $(a'_0, \ldots, a'_{n-1})$ such that $\lfloor 8nS_j(a_0, \ldots, a_{n-1}) \rfloor = \lfloor 8nS_j(a'_0, \ldots, a'_{n-1}) \rfloor$ for $1 \le j < n$, since there are b^n vectors but at most $(16nbB)^{n-1} < b^n$ possible $(n - 1)$-tuples of values. Let $t(x) = (a_0 - a'_0) + \cdots + (a_{n-1} - a'_{n-1})x^{n-1}$ and $\beta_j = t(\alpha_j)$. Then the smallness condition is satisfied. Furthermore $\beta_j \ne 0$; otherwise $t(x)$ would divide $u(x)$. [*J. Algorithms* **2** (1981), 385–392.]

40. Given a candidate factor $v(x) = x^d + a_{d-1}x^{d-1} + \cdots + a_0$, change each a_j to a rational fraction (modulo p^e), with numerators and denominators $\le B$. Then multiply by the least common denominator, and see if the resulting polynomial divides $u(x)$ over the integers. If not, no factor of $u(x)$ with coefficients bounded by B is congruent modulo p^e to a multiple of $v(x)$.

41. David Boyd notes that $4x^8 + 4x^6 + x^4 + 4x^2 + 4 = (2x^4 + 4x^3 + 5x^2 + 4x + 2) \times (2x^4 - 4x^3 + 5x^2 - 4x + 2)$, and he has found examples of higher degree to prove that c must be > 2 if it exists.

SECTION 4.6.3

1. x^m, where $m = 2^{\lfloor \lg n \rfloor}$ is the highest power of 2 less than or equal to n.

2. Assume that x is input in register A, and n in location NN; the output is in register X.

01	A1	ENTX	1	1	_A1. Initialize._	
02		STX	Y	1	$Y \leftarrow 1$.	
03		STA	Z	1	$Z \leftarrow x$.	
04		LDA	NN	1	$N \leftarrow n$.	
05		JAP	2F	1	To A2.	
06		JMP	DONE	0	Otherwise the answer is 1.	
07	5H	SRB	1	$L+1-K$		
08		STA	N	$L+1-K$	$N \leftarrow \lfloor N/2 \rfloor$.	
09	A5	LDA	Z	L	_A5. Square Z._	
10		MUL	Z	L		
11		STX	Z	L	$Z \leftarrow Z \times Z \bmod w$.	
12	A2	LDA	N	L	_A2. Halve N._	
13	2H	JAE	5B	$L+1$	To A5 if N is even.	
14		SRB	1	K		
15	A4	JAZ	4F	K	Jump if $N = 1$.	
16		STA	N	$K-1$	$N \leftarrow \lfloor N/2 \rfloor$.	
17	A3	LDA	Z	$K-1$	_A3. Multiply Y by Z._	
18		MUL	Y	$K-1$		
19		STX	Y	$K-1$	$Y \leftarrow Z \times Y \bmod w$.	
20		JMP	A5	$K-1$	To A5.	
21	4H	LDA	Z	1		
22		MUL	Y	1	Do the final multiplication. ∎	

The running time is $21L + 16K + 8$, where $L = \lambda(n)$ is one less than the number of bits in the binary representation of n, and $K = \nu(n)$ is the number of 1-bits in that representation.

For the serial program, we may assume that n is small enough to fit in an index register; otherwise serial exponentiation is out of the question. The following program leaves the output in register A:

01	S1	LD1	NN	1	rI1 $\leftarrow n$.
02		STA	X	1	$X \leftarrow x$.
03		JMP	2F	1	
04	1H	MUL	X	$N-1$	rA $\times$ X mod w
05		SLAX	5	$N-1$	$\rightarrow$ rA.
06	2H	DEC1	1	N	rI1 $\leftarrow$ rI1 $- 1$.
07		J1P	1B	N	Multiply again if rI1 > 0. ∎

The running time for this program is $14N - 7$; it is faster than the previous program when $n \le 7$, slower when $n \ge 8$.

3. The sequences of exponents are: (a) 1, 2, 3, 6, 7, 14, 15, 30, 60, 120, 121, 242, 243, 486, 487, 974, 975 [16 multiplications]; (b) 1, 2, 3, 4, 8, 12, 24, 36, 72, 108, 216, 324, 325, 650, 975 [14 multiplications]; (c) 1, 2, 3, 6, 12, 15, 30, 60, 120, 240, 243, 486, 972, 975 [13 multiplications]; (d) 1, 2, 3, 6, 12, 15, 30, 60, 75, 150, 300, 600, 900, 975 [13 multiplications]. [The smallest possible number of multiplications is 12; this is obtainable by combining the factor method with the binary method, since $975 = 15 \cdot (2^6 + 1)$.]

4. $(777777)_8 = 2^{18} - 1$.

5. **T1.** [Initialize.] Set $\mathtt{LINKU}[j] \leftarrow 0$ for $0 \le j \le 2^r$, and set $k \leftarrow 0$, $\mathtt{LINKR}[0] \leftarrow 1$, $\mathtt{LINKR}[1] \leftarrow 0$.

T2. [Change level.] (Now level k of the tree has been linked together from left to right, starting at $\mathtt{LINKR}[0]$.) If $k = r$, the algorithm terminates. Otherwise set $n \leftarrow \mathtt{LINKR}[0]$, $m \leftarrow 0$.

T3. [Prepare for n.] (Now n is a node on level k, and m points to the rightmost node currently on level $k + 1$.) Set $q \leftarrow 0$, $s \leftarrow n$.

T4. [Already in tree?] (Now s is a node in the path from the root to n.) If $\mathtt{LINKU}[n + s] \ne 0$, go to T6 (the value $n + s$ is already in the tree).

T5. [Insert below n.] If $q = 0$, set $m' \leftarrow n + s$. Then set $\mathtt{LINKR}[n + s] \leftarrow q$, $\mathtt{LINKU}[n + s] \leftarrow n$, $q \leftarrow n + s$.

T6. [Move up.] Set $s \leftarrow \mathtt{LINKU}[s]$. If $s \ne 0$, return to T4.

T7. [Attach group.] If $q \ne 0$, set $\mathtt{LINKR}[m] \leftarrow q$, $m \leftarrow m'$.

T8. [Move n.] Set $n \leftarrow \mathtt{LINKR}[n]$. If $n \ne 0$, return to T3.

T9. [End of level.] Set $\mathtt{LINKR}[m] \leftarrow 0$, $k \leftarrow k + 1$, and return to T2. ▮

6. Prove by induction that the path to the number $2^{e_0} + 2^{e_1} + \cdots + 2^{e_t}$, if $e_0 > e_1 > \cdots > e_t \ge 0$, is 1, 2, 2^2, ..., 2^{e_0}, $2^{e_0} + 2^{e_1}$, ..., $2^{e_0} + 2^{e_1} + \cdots + 2^{e_t}$; furthermore, the sequences of exponents on each level are in decreasing lexicographic order.

7. The binary and factor methods require one more step to compute x^{2n} than x^n; the power tree method requires at most one more step. Hence (a) $15 \cdot 2^k$; (b) $33 \cdot 2^k$; (c) $23 \cdot 2^k$; $k = 0, 1, 2, 3, \ldots$.

8. The power tree always includes the node $2m$ at one level below m, unless it occurs at the same level or an earlier level; and it always includes the node $2m + 1$ at one level below $2m$, unless it occurs at the same level or an earlier level. [It is not true that $2m$ is a child of m in the power tree for all m; the smallest example where this fails is $m = 2138$, which appears on level 15, while 4276 appears elsewhere on level 16. In fact, $2m$ sometimes occurs on the same level as m; the smallest example is $m = 6029$.]

9. Start with $N \leftarrow n$, $Z \leftarrow x$, and $Y_q \leftarrow 1$ for $1 \le q < m$, q odd; in general we will have $x^n = Y_1 Y_3^3 Y_5^5 \ldots Y_{m-1}^{m-1} Z^N$ as the algorithm proceeds. Assuming that $N > 0$, set $k \leftarrow N \bmod m$, $N \leftarrow \lfloor N/m \rfloor$. Then if $k = 0$, set $Z \leftarrow Z^m$ and repeat; otherwise if $k = 2^p q$ where q is odd, set $Z \leftarrow Z^{2^p}$, $Y_q \leftarrow Y_q \cdot Z$, and if $N > 0$ set $Z \leftarrow Z^{2^{e-p}}$ and repeat. Finally set $Y_k \leftarrow Y_k \cdot Y_{k+2}$ for $k = m - 3, m - 5, \ldots, 1$; the answer is $Y_1 (Y_3 Y_5 \ldots Y_{m-1})^2$. (About $m/2$ of the multiplications are by 1.)

10. By using the "PARENT" representation discussed in Section 2.3.3: Make use of a table $p[j]$, $1 \le j \le 100$, such that $p[1] = 0$ and $p[j]$ is the number of the node just above j for $j \ge 2$. (The fact that each node of this tree has degree at most two has no effect on the efficiency of this representation; it just makes the tree look prettier as an illustration.)

11. 1, 2, 3, 5, 10, 20, (23 or 40), 43; 1, 2, 4, 8, 9, 17, (26 or 34), 43; 1, 2, 4, 8, 9, 17, 34, (43 or 68), 77; 1, 2, 4, 5, 9, 18, 36, (41 or 72), 77. If either of the last two paths were in the tree we would have no possibility for $n = 43$, since the tree must contain either 1, 2, 3, 5 or 1, 2, 4, 8, 9.

12. No such infinite tree can exist, since $l(n) \neq l^*(n)$ for some n.

13. For Case 1, use a Type-1 chain followed by $2^{A+C} + 2^{B+C} + 2^A + 2^B$; or use the factor method. For Case 2, use a Type-2 chain followed by $2^{A+C+1} + 2^{B+C} + 2^A + 2^B$. For Case 3, use a Type-5 chain followed by addition of $2^A + 2^{A-1}$, or use the factor method. For Case 4, $n = 135 \cdot 2^D$, so we may use the factor method.

14. (a) It is easy to verify that steps $r - 1$ and $r - 2$ are not both small, so let us assume that step $r - 1$ is small and step $r - 2$ is not. If $c = 1$, then $\lambda(a_{r-1}) = \lambda(a_{r-k})$, so $k = 2$; and since $4 \leq \nu(a_r) = \nu(a_{r-1}) + \nu(a_{r-k}) - 1 \leq \nu(a_{r-1}) + 1$, we have $\nu(a_{r-1}) \geq 3$, making $r - 1$ a star step (lest $a_0, a_1, \ldots, a_{r-3}, a_{r-1}$ include only one small step). Then $a_{r-1} = a_{r-2} + a_{r-q}$ for some q, and if we replace a_{r-2}, a_{r-1}, a_r by $a_{r-2}, 2a_{r-2}, 2a_{r-2} + a_{r-q} = a_r$, we obtain another counterexample chain in which step r is small; but this is impossible. On the other hand, if $c \geq 2$, then $4 \leq \nu(a_r) \leq \nu(a_{r-1}) + \nu(a_{r-k}) - 2 \leq \nu(a_{r-1})$; hence $\nu(a_{r-1}) = 4$, $\nu(a_{r-k}) = 2$, and $c = 2$. This leads readily to an impossible situation by a consideration of the six types in the proof of Theorem B.

(b) If $\lambda(a_{r-k}) < m - 1$, we have $c \geq 3$, so $\nu(a_{r-k}) + \nu(a_{r-1}) \geq 7$ by (22); therefore both $\nu(a_{r-k})$ and $\nu(a_{r-1})$ are ≥ 3. All small steps must be $\leq r - k$, and $\lambda(a_{r-k}) = m - k + 1$. If $k \geq 4$, we must have $c = 4$, $k = 4$, $\nu(a_{r-1}) = \nu(a_{r-4}) = 4$; thus $a_{r-1} \geq 2^m + 2^{m-1} + 2^{m-2}$, and a_{r-1} must equal $2^m + 2^{m-1} + 2^{m-2} + 2^{m-3}$; but $a_{r-4} \geq \frac{1}{8}a_{r-1}$ now implies that $a_{r-1} = 8a_{r-4}$. Thus $k = 3$ and $a_{r-1} > 2^m + 2^{m-1}$. Since $a_{r-2} < 2^m$ and $a_{r-3} < 2^{m-1}$, step $r - 1$ must be a doubling; but step $r - 2$ is a nondoubling, since $a_{r-1} \neq 4a_{r-3}$. Furthermore, since $\nu(a_{r-3}) \geq 3$, $r - 3$ is a star step; and $a_{r-2} = a_{r-3} + a_{r-5}$ would imply that $a_{r-5} = 2^{m-2}$, hence we must have $a_{r-2} = a_{r-3} + a_{r-4}$. As in a similar case treated in the text, the only possibility is now seen to be $a_{r-4} = 2^{m-2} + 2^{m-3}$, $a_{r-3} = 2^{m-2} + 2^{m-3} + 2^{d+1} + 2^d$, $a_{r-1} = 2^m + 2^{m-1} + 2^{d+2} + 2^{d+1}$, and even this possibility is impossible.

15. Achim Flammenkamp [Diplomarbeit in Mathematics (Bielefeld University, 1991), Part 1] has shown that the numbers n with $\lambda(n) + 3 = l(n) < l^*(n)$ all have the form $2^A + 2^B + 2^C + 2^D + 2^E$ where $A > B > C > D > E$ and $B + E = C + D$; moreover, they are described precisely by not matching any of the following eight patterns where $|\epsilon| \leq 1$: $2^A + 2^{A-3} + 2^C + 2^{C-1} + 2^{2C+2-A}$, $2^A + 2^{A-1} + 2^C + 2^D + 2^{C+D+1-A}$, $2^A + 2^B + 2^{2B-A+3} + 2^{2B+2-A} + 2^{3B+5-2A}$, $2^A + 2^B + 2^{2B-A+\epsilon} + 2^D + 2^{B+D+\epsilon-A}$, $2^A + 2^B + 2^{B-1} + 2^D + 2^{D-1}$, $2^A + 2^B + 2^{B-2} + 2^D + 2^{D-2}$ $(A > B + 1)$, $2^A + 2^B + 2^C + 2^{2B+\epsilon-A} + 2^{B+C+\epsilon-A}$, $2^A + 2^B + 2^C + 2^{B+C+\epsilon-A} + 2^{2C+\epsilon-A}$.

16. $l^B(n) = \lambda(n) + \nu(n) - 1$; so if $n = 2^k$, $l^B(n)/\lambda(n) = 1$, but if $n = 2^{k+1} - 1$, $l^B(n)/\lambda(n) = 2$.

17. Let $i_1 < \cdots < i_t$. Delete any intervals I_k that can be removed without affecting the union $I_1 \cup \cdots \cup I_t$. (The interval $(j_k .. i_k]$ may be dropped out if either $j_{k+1} \leq j_k$ or $j_1 < j_2 < \cdots$ and $j_{k+1} \leq i_{k-1}$.) Now combine overlapping intervals $(j_1 .. i_1], \ldots, (j_d .. i_d]$ into an interval $(j' .. i'] = (j_1 .. i_d]$ and note that

$$a_{i'} < a_{j'}(1 + \delta)^{i_1 - j_1 + \cdots + i_d - j_d} \leq a_{j'}(1 + \delta)^{2(i' - j')},$$

since each point of $(j' .. i']$ is covered at most twice in $(j_1 .. i_1] \cup \cdots \cup (j_d .. i_d]$.

18. Call $f(m)$ a "nice" function if $(\log f(m))/m \to 0$ as $m \to \infty$. A polynomial in m is nice. The product of nice functions is nice. If $g(m) \to 0$ and c is a positive constant, then $c^{mg(m)}$ is nice; also $\binom{2m}{mg(m)}$ is nice, for by Stirling's approximation this is equivalent to saying that $g(m) \log(1/g(m)) \to 0$.

Now replace each term of the summation by the maximum term that is attained for any s, t, v. The total number of terms is nice, and so are $\binom{m+s}{t+v}$, $\binom{t+v}{v} \le 2^{t+v}$, and β^{2v}, because $(t+v)/m \to 0$. Finally, $\binom{(m+s)^2}{t} \le (2m)^{2t}/t! < (4em^2/t)^t$, where $(4e)^t$ is nice. Replacing t by its upper bound $(1-\epsilon/2)m/\lambda(m)$ shows that $(m^2/t)^t \le 2^{m(1-\epsilon/2)}f(m)$, where $f(m)$ is nice. Hence the entire sum is less than α^m for large m if $\alpha = 2^{1-\eta}$, where $0 < \eta < \frac{1}{2}\epsilon$.

19. (a) $M \cap N$, $M \cup N$, $M \uplus N$, respectively; see Eqs. 4.5.2–(6), 4.5.2–(7).

(b) $f(z)g(z)$, $\operatorname{lcm}(f(z), g(z))$, $\gcd(f(z), g(z))$. (For the same reasons as (a), because the monic irreducible polynomials over the complex numbers are precisely the polynomials $z - \zeta$.)

(c) Commutative laws $A \uplus B = B \uplus A$, $A \cup B = B \cup A$, $A \cap B = B \cap A$. Associative laws $A \uplus (B \uplus C) = (A \uplus B) \uplus C$, $A \cup (B \cup C) = (A \cup B) \cup C$, $A \cap (B \cap C) = (A \cap B) \cap C$. Distributive laws $A \cup (B \cap C) = (A \cup B) \cap (A \cup C)$, $A \cap (B \cup C) = (A \cap B) \cup (A \cap C)$, $A \uplus (B \cup C) = (A \uplus B) \cup (A \uplus C)$, $A \uplus (B \cap C) = (A \uplus B) \cap (A \uplus C)$. Idempotent laws $A \cup A = A$, $A \cap A = A$. Absorption laws $A \cup (A \cap B) = A$, $A \cap (A \cup B) = A$, $A \cap (A \uplus B) = A$, $A \cup (A \uplus B) = A \uplus B$. Identity and zero laws $\emptyset \uplus A = A$, $\emptyset \cup A = A$, $\emptyset \cap A = \emptyset$, where $\emptyset$ is the empty multiset. Counting law $A \uplus B = (A \cup B) \uplus (A \cap B)$. Further properties analogous to those of sets come from the partial ordering defined by the rule $A \subseteq B$ if and only if $A \cap B = A$ (if and only if $A \cup B = B$).

Notes: Other common applications of multisets are zeros and poles of meromorphic functions, invariants of matrices in canonical form, invariants of finite Abelian groups, etc.; multisets can be useful in combinatorial counting arguments and in the development of measure theory. The terminal strings of a noncircular context-free grammar form a multiset that is a set if and only if the grammar is unambiguous. The author's paper in *Theoretical Studies in Computer Science*, edited by J. D. Ullman (Academic Press, 1992), 1–13, discusses further applications to context-free grammars, and introduces the operation $A \cap B$, where each element that occurs a times in A and b times in B occurs ab times in $A \cap B$.

Although multisets appear frequently in mathematics, they often must be treated rather clumsily because there is currently no standard way to treat sets with repeated elements. Several mathematicians have voiced their belief that the lack of adequate terminology and notation for this common concept has been a definite handicap to the development of mathematics. (A multiset is, of course, formally equivalent to a mapping from a set into the nonnegative integers, but this formal equivalence is of little or no practical value for creative mathematical reasoning.) The author discussed this matter with many people during the 1960s in an attempt to find a good remedy. Some of the names suggested for the concept were list, bunch, bag, heap, sample, weighted set, collection, suite; but these words either conflicted with present terminology, had an improper connotation, or were too much of a mouthful to say and to write conveniently. Finally it became clear that such an important concept deserves a name of its own, and the word "multiset" was coined by N. G. de Bruijn. His suggestion was widely adopted during the 1970s, and it is now standard terminology.

The notation "$A \uplus B$" has been selected by the author to avoid conflict with existing notations and to stress the analogy with set union. It would not be as desirable to use

"$A+B$" for this purpose, since algebraists have found that $A+B$ is a good notation for the multiset $\{\alpha + \beta \mid \alpha \in A \text{ and } \beta \in B\}$. If A is a multiset of nonnegative integers, let $G(z) = \sum_{n \in A} z^n$ be a generating function corresponding to A. (Generating functions with nonnegative integer coefficients obviously correspond one-to-one with multisets of nonnegative integers.) If $G(z)$ corresponds to A and $H(z)$ to B, then $G(z) + H(z)$ corresponds to $A \uplus B$ and $G(z)H(z)$ corresponds to $A + B$. If we form "Dirichlet" generating functions $g(z) = \sum_{n \in A} 1/n^z$, $h(z) = \sum_{n \in B} 1/n^z$, then the product $g(z)h(z)$ corresponds to the multiset product AB.

20. Type 3: $(S_0, \ldots, S_r) = (M_{00}, \ldots, M_{r0}) = (\{0\}, \ldots, \{A\}, \{A-1, A\}, \{A-1, A, A\}, \{A-1, A-1, A, A, A\}, \ldots, \{A+C-3, A+C-3, A+C-2, A+C-2, A+C-2\})$.
Type 5: $(M_{00}, \ldots, M_{r0}) = (\{0\}, \ldots, \{A\}, \{A-1, A\}, \ldots, \{A+C-1, A+C\}, \{A+C-1, A+C-1, A+C\}, \ldots, \{A+C+D-1, A+C+D-1, A+C+D\})$; $(M_{01}, \ldots, M_{r1}) = (\emptyset, \ldots, \emptyset, \emptyset, \ldots, \emptyset, \{A+C-2\}, \ldots, \{A+C+D-2\})$, $S_i = M_{i0} \uplus M_{i1}$.

21. For example, let $u = 2^{8q+5}$, $x = (2^{(q+1)u} - 1)/(2^u - 1) = 2^{qu} + \cdots + 2^u + 1$, $y = 2^{(q+1)u} + 1$. Then $xy = (2^{2(q+1)u} - 1)/(2^u - 1)$. If $n = 2^{4(q+1)u} + xy$, we have $l(n) \leq 4(q+1)u + q + 2$ by Theorem F, but $l^*(n) = 4(q+1)u + 2q + 2$ by Theorem H.

22. Underline everything except the $u - 1$ insertions used in the calculation of x.

23. Theorem G (everything underlined).

24. Use the numbers $(B^{a_i} - 1)/(B - 1)$, $0 \leq i \leq r$, underlined when a_i is underlined; and $c_k B^{i-1}(B^{b_j} - 1)/(B - 1)$ for $0 \leq j < t$, $0 < i \leq b_{j+1} - b_j$, $1 \leq k \leq l^0(B)$, underlined when c_k is underlined, where $c_0, c_1, \ldots$ is a minimum length l^0-chain for B. To prove the second inequality, let $B = 2^m$ and use (3). (The second inequality is rarely, if ever, an improvement on Theorem G.)

25. We may assume that $d_k = 1$. Use the rule R $A_{k-1} \ldots A_1$, where $A_j = $ "XR" if $d_j = 1$, $A_j = $ "R" otherwise, and where "R" means take the square root, "X" means multiply by x. For example, if $y = (.1101101)_2$, the rule is R R XR XR R XR XR. (There exist binary square-root extraction algorithms suitable for computer hardware, requiring an execution time comparable to that of division; computers with such hardware could therefore calculate more general fractional powers using the technique in this exercise.)

26. If we know the pair (F_k, F_{k-1}), then we have $(F_{k+1}, F_k) = (F_k + F_{k-1}, F_k)$ and $(F_{2k}, F_{2k-1}) = (F_k^2 + 2F_k F_{k-1}, F_k^2 + F_{k-1}^2)$; so a binary method can be used to calculate (F_n, F_{n-1}), using $O(\log n)$ arithmetic operations. Perhaps better is to use the pair of values (F_k, L_k), where $L_k = F_{k-1} + F_{k+1}$ (see exercise 4.5.4–15); then we have $(F_{k+1}, L_{k+1}) = (\frac{1}{2}(F_k + L_k), \frac{1}{2}(5F_k + L_k))$, $(F_{2k}, L_{2k}) = (F_k L_k, L_k^2 - 2(-1)^k)$.

For the general linear recurrence $x_n = a_1 x_{n-1} + \cdots + a_d x_{n-d}$, we can compute x_n in $O(d^3 \log n)$ arithmetic operations by computing the nth power of an appropriate $d \times d$ matrix. [This observation is due to J. C. P. Miller and D. J. Spencer Brown, *Comp. J.* **9** (1966), 188–190.] In fact, as Richard Brent has observed, the number of operations can be reduced to $O(d^2 \log n)$, or even to $O(d \log d \log n)$ using exercise 4.7–6, if we first compute $x^n \bmod (x^d - a_1 x^{d-1} - \cdots - a_d)$ and then replace x^j by x_j.

27. The smallest n requiring s small steps must be $c(r)$ for some r. For if $c(r) < n < c(r+1)$ we have $l(n) - \lambda(n) \leq r - \lambda(c(r)) = l(c(r)) - \lambda(c(r))$. The answers for $1 \leq s \leq 8$ are therefore 3, 7, 29, 127, 1903, 65131, 4169527, 994660991.

28. (a) $x \nabla y = x \mid y \mid (x + y)$, where "$\mid$" is bitwise "or", see exercise 4.6.2–26; clearly $\nu(x \nabla y) \leq \nu(x \mid y) + \nu(x \& y) = \nu(x) + \nu(y)$. (b) Note first that $A_{i-1}/2^{d_{i-1}} \subseteq A_i/2^{d_i}$ for $1 \leq i \leq r$. Secondly, note that $d_j = d_{i-1}$ in a nondoubling; for otherwise $a_{i-1} \geq 2a_j \geq$

$a_j + a_k = a_i$. Hence $A_j \subseteq A_{i-1}$ and $A_k \subseteq A_{i-1}/2^{d_j - d_k}$. (c) An easy induction on i, except that close steps need closer attention. Let us say that m has property $P(\alpha)$ if the 1s in its binary representation all appear in consecutive blocks of $\geq \alpha$ in a row. If m and m' have $P(\alpha)$, so does $m \nabla m'$; if m has $P(\alpha)$ then $\rho(m)$ has $P(\alpha + \delta)$. Hence B_i has $P(1 + \delta c_i)$. Finally if m has $P(\alpha)$ then $\nu(\rho(m)) \leq (\alpha + \delta)\nu(m)/\alpha$; for $\nu(m) = \nu_1 + \cdots + \nu_q$, where each block size ν_j is $\geq \alpha$, hence $\nu(\rho(m)) \leq (\nu_1 + \delta) + \cdots + (\nu_q + \delta) \leq (1 + \delta/\alpha)\nu_1 + \cdots + (1 + \delta/\alpha)\nu_q$. (d) Let $f = b_r + c_r$ be the number of nondoublings and s the number of small steps. If $f \geq 3.271 \lg \nu(n)$ we have $s \geq \lg \nu(n)$ as desired, by (16). Otherwise we have $a_i \leq (1 + 2^{-\delta})^{b_i} 2^{c_i + d_i}$ for $0 \leq i \leq r$, hence $n \leq ((1 + 2^{-\delta})/2)^{b_r} 2^r$, and $r \geq \lg n + b_r - b_r \lg(1 + 2^{-\delta}) \geq \lg n + \lg \nu(n) - \lg(1 + \delta c_r) - b_r \lg(1 + 2^{-\delta})$. Let $\delta = \lceil \lg(f + 1) \rceil$; then $\ln(1 + 2^{-\delta}) \leq \ln(1 + 1/(f+1)) \leq 1/(f+1) \leq \delta/(1 + \delta f)$, and it follows that $\lg(1 + \delta x) + (f - x)\lg(1 + 2^{-\delta}) \leq \lg(1 + \delta f)$ for $0 \leq x \leq f$. Hence finally $l(n) \geq \lg n + \lg \nu(n) - \lg(1 + (3.271 \lg \nu(n))\lceil \lg(1 + 3.271 \lg \nu(n)) \rceil)$. [*Theoretical Comp. Sci.* **1** (1975), 1–12.]

29. In the paper just cited, Schönhage refined the method of exercise 28 to prove that $l(n) \geq \lg n + \lg \nu(n) - 2.13$ for all n. Can the remaining gap be closed?

30. $n = 31$ is the smallest example; $l(31) = 7$, but 1, 2, 4, 8, 16, 32, 31 is an addition-subtraction chain of length 6. [After proving Theorem E, Erdős stated that the same result holds also for addition-subtraction chains. Schönhage has extended the lower bound of exercise 28 to addition-subtraction chains, with $\nu(n)$ replaced by $\bar{\nu}(n)$ as defined in exercise 4.1–34. A generalized right-to-left binary method for exponentiation, which uses $\lambda(n) + \bar{\nu}(n) - 1$ multiplications when both x and x^{-1} are given, can be based on the representation α_n of that exercise.]

32. See *Discrete Math.* **23** (1978), 115–119. [This cost model corresponds to multiplication of large numbers by a classical method like Algorithm 4.3.1M. Empirical results with a more general model in which the cost is $(a_j a_k)^{\beta/2}$ have been obtained by D. P. McCarthy, *Math. Comp.* **46** (1986), 603–608; this model comes closer to the "fast multiplication" methods of Section 4.3.3, when two n-bit numbers are multiplied in $O(n^\beta)$ steps, but the cost function $a_j a_k^{\beta-1}$ would actually be more appropriate (see exercise 4.3.3–13). H. Zantema has analyzed the analogous problem when the cost of step i is $a_j + a_k$ instead of $a_j a_k$; see *J. Algorithms* **12** (1991), 281–307. In this case the optimum chains have total cost $\frac{5}{2}n + O(n^{1/2})$. Furthermore the optimum additive cost when n is odd is at least $\frac{5}{2}(n-1)$, with equality if and only if n can be written as a product of numbers of the form $2^k + 1$.]

33. Eight; there are four ways to compute $39 = 12 + 12 + 12 + 3$ and two ways to compute $79 = 39 + 39 + 1$.

34. The statement is true. The labels in the reduced graph of the binary chain are $\lfloor n/2^k \rfloor$ for $k = e_0, \ldots, 0$; they are $1, 2, \ldots, 2^{e_0}, n$ in the dual graph. [Similarly, the right-to-left m-ary method of exercise 9 is the dual of the left-to-right method.]

35. 2^t are equivalent to the binary chain; it would be 2^{t-1} if $e_0 = e_1 + 1$. The number of chains equivalent to the scheme of Algorithm A is the number of ways to compute the sum of $t + 2$ numbers of which two are identical. This is $\frac{1}{2}f_{t+1} + \frac{1}{2}f_t$, where f_m is the number of ways to compute the sum of $m + 1$ distinct numbers. When we take commutativity into account, we see that f_m is 2^{-m} times $(m + 1)!$ times the number of binary trees on m nodes, so $f_m = (2m - 1)(2m - 3) \ldots 1$.

36. First form the $2^m - m - 1$ products $x_1^{e_1} \ldots x_m^{e_m}$, for all sequences of exponents such that $0 \leq e_k \leq 1$ and $e_1 + \cdots + e_m \geq 2$. Let $n_k = (d_{k\lambda} \ldots d_{k1} d_{k0})_2$; to complete the calculation, take $x_1^{d_1\lambda} \ldots x_m^{d_m\lambda}$, then square and multiply by $x_1^{d_{1i}} \ldots x_m^{d_{mi}}$, for $i = \lambda - 1$, ..., 1, 0. [Straus showed in *AMM* **71** (1964), 807–808, that $2\lambda(n)$ may be replaced by $(1+\epsilon)\lambda(n)$ for any $\epsilon > 0$, by generalizing this binary method to 2^k-ary as in Theorem D.]

37. (Solution by D. J. Bernstein.) Let $n = n_m$. First compute 2^e for $1 \le e \le \lambda(n)$, then compute each n_j in $\lambda(n)/\lambda\lambda(n) + O(\lambda(n)\lambda\lambda\lambda(n)/\lambda\lambda(n)^2)$ further steps by the following variant of the 2^k-ary method, where $k = \lfloor \lg \lg n - 2 \lg \lg \lg n \rfloor$: For all odd $q < 2^k$, compute $y_q = \sum \{2^{kt+e} \mid d_t = 2^e q\}$ where $n_j = (\ldots d_1 d_0)_{2^k}$, in at most $\lfloor \frac{1}{k} \lg n \rfloor$ steps; then use the method in the final stages of answer 9 to compute $n_j = \sum q y_q$ with at most $2^k - 1$ further additions.

[A generalization of Theorem E gives the corresponding lower bound. Reference: *SICOMP* **5** (1976), 100–103.]

38. The following construction due to D. J. Newman provides the best upper bound currently known: Let $k = p_1 \ldots p_r$ be the product of the first r primes. Compute k and all quadratic residues mod k in $O(2^{-r}k \log k)$ steps (because there are approximately $2^{-r}k$ quadratic residues). Also compute all multiples of k that are $\le m^2$, in about m^2/k further steps. Now m additions suffice to compute $1^2, 2^2, \ldots, m^2$. We have $k = \exp(p_r + O(p_r/(\log p_r)^{1000}))$ where p_r is given by the formula in the answer to exercise 4.5.4–36; see, for example, Greene and Knuth, *Math. for the Analysis of Algorithms* (Boston: Birkhäuser, 1981), §4.1.6. So by choosing

$$r = \lfloor (1 + \tfrac{1}{2} \ln 2 / \lg \lg m) \ln m / \ln \ln m \rfloor$$

it follows that $l(1^2, \ldots, m^2) = m + O(m \cdot \exp(-(\tfrac{1}{2} \ln 2 - \epsilon) \ln m / \ln \ln m))$.

On the other hand, D. Dobkin and R. Lipton have shown that, for any $\epsilon > 0$, $l(1^2, \ldots, m^2) > m + m^{2/3-\epsilon}$ when m is sufficiently large [*SICOMP* **9** (1980), 121–125].

39. The quantity $l([n_1, n_2, \ldots, n_m])$ is the minimum of arcs $-$ vertices $+ m$ taken over all directed graphs having m vertices s_j whose in-degree is zero and one vertex t whose out-degree is zero, where there are exactly n_j oriented paths from s_j to t for $1 \le j \le m$. The quantity $l(n_1, n_2, \ldots, n_m)$ is the minimum of arcs $-$ vertices $+ 1$ taken over all directed graphs having one vertex s whose in-degree is zero and m vertices t_j whose out-degree is zero, where there are exactly n_j oriented paths from s to t_j for $1 \le j \le m$. These problems are dual to each other, if we change the direction of all the arcs. [See *J. Algorithms* **2** (1981), 13–21.]

Note: C. H. Papadimitriou has observed that this is a special case of a much more general theorem. Let $N = (n_{ij})$ be an $m \times p$ matrix of nonnegative integers having no row or column entirely zero. We can define $l(N)$ to be the minimum number of multiplications needed to compute the set of monomials $\{x_1^{n_{1j}} \ldots x_m^{n_{mj}} \mid 1 \le j \le p\}$. Now $l(N)$ is also the minimum of arcs $-$ vertices $+ m$ taken over all directed graphs having m vertices s_i whose in-degree is zero and p vertices t_j whose out-degree is zero, where there are exactly n_{ij} oriented paths from s_i to t_j for each i and j. By duality we have $l(N) = l(N^T) + m - p$. [*Bulletin of the EATCS* **13** (February 1981), 2–3.]

N. Pippenger has considerably extended the results of exercises 36 and 37. For example, if $L(m, p, n)$ is the maximum of $l(N)$ taken over all $m \times p$ matrices N of nonnegative integers $n_{ij} \le n$, he showed that $L(m, p, n) = \min(m, p) \lg n + H/\lg H + O(m + p + H(\log \log H)^{1/2}(\log H)^{-3/2})$, where $H = mp \lg(n + 1)$. [See *SICOMP* **9** (1980), 230–250.]

40. By exercise 39, it suffices to show that $l(m_1 n_1 + \cdots + m_t n_t) \le l(m_1, \ldots, m_t) + l([n_1, \ldots, n_t])$. But this is clear, since we can first form $\{x^{m_1}, \ldots, x^{m_t}\}$ and then compute the monomial $(x^{m_1})^{n_1} \ldots (x^{m_t})^{n_t}$.

Note: One strong way to state Olivos's theorem is that if $a_0, \ldots, a_r$ and $b_0, \ldots, b_s$ are any addition chains, then $l(\sum c_{ij} a_i b_j) \leq r + s + \sum c_{ij} - 1$ for any $(r+1) \times (s+1)$ matrix of nonnegative integers c_{ij}.

41. [*SICOMP* **10** (1981), 638–646.] The stated formula can be proved whenever $A \geq 9m^2$. Since this is a polynomial in m, and since the problem of finding a minimum vertex cover is NP-hard (see Section 7.9), the problem of computing $l(n_1, \ldots, n_m)$ is NP-complete. [It is unknown whether or not the problem of computing $l(n)$ is NP-complete. But it seems plausible that an optimum chain for, say, $\sum_{k=0}^{m-1} n_{k+1} 2^{Ak^2}$ would entail an optimum chain for $\{n_1, \ldots, n_m\}$, when A is sufficiently large.]

42. The condition fails at 128 (and in the dual 1, 2, ..., 16384, 16385, 16401, 32768, ... at 32768). Only two reduced digraphs of cost 27 exist; hence $l^0(5784689) = 28$. Furthermore, Clift's programs proved that $l^0(n) = l(n)$ for all smaller values of n.

SECTION 4.6.4

1. Set $y \leftarrow x^2$, then compute $((\ldots (u_{2n+1} y + u_{2n-1}) y + \cdots) y + u_1) x$.

2. Replacing x in (2) by the polynomial $x + x_0$ leads to the following procedure:

G1. Do step G2 for $k = n$, $n - 1$, ..., 0 (in this order), and stop.

G2. Set $v_k \leftarrow u_k$, and then set $v_j \leftarrow v_j + x_0 v_{j+1}$ for $j = k$, $k + 1$, ..., $n - 1$. (When $k = n$, this step simply sets $v_n \leftarrow u_n$.) ∎

The computations turn out to be identical to those in H1 and H2, but performed in a different order. (This process was Newton's original motivation for using scheme (2).)

3. The coefficient of x^k is a polynomial in y that may be evaluated by Horner's rule: $(\ldots (u_{n,0} x + (u_{n-1,1} y + u_{n-1,0})) x + \cdots) x + ((\ldots (u_{0,n} y + u_{0,n-1}) y + \cdots) y + u_{0,0})$. [For a "homogeneous" polynomial, such as $u_n x^n + u_{n-1} x^{n-1} y + \cdots + u_1 x y^{n-1} + u_0 y^n$, another scheme is more efficient: If $0 < |x| \leq |y|$, first divide x by y, evaluate a polynomial in x/y, then multiply by y^n.]

4. Rule (2) involves $4n$ or $3n$ real multiplications and $4n$ or $7n$ real additions; (3) is worse, it takes $4n + 2$ or $4n + 1$ multiplications, $4n + 2$ or $4n + 5$ additions.

5. One multiplication to compute x^2; $\lfloor n/2 \rfloor$ multiplications and $\lfloor n/2 \rfloor$ additions to evaluate the first line; $\lceil n/2 \rceil$ multiplications and $\lceil n/2 \rceil - 1$ additions to evaluate the second line; and one addition to add the two lines together. Total: $n + 1$ multiplications and n additions.

6. **J1.** Compute and store the values x_0^2, x_0^3, ..., $x_0^{\lceil n/2 \rceil}$.

J2. Set $v_j \leftarrow u_j x_0^{j - \lfloor n/2 \rfloor}$ for $0 \leq j \leq n$.

J3. For $k = 0, 1, \ldots, n - 1$, set $v_j \leftarrow v_j + v_{j+1}$ for $j = n - 1, \ldots, k + 1, k$.

J4. Set $v_j \leftarrow v_j x_0^{\lfloor n/2 \rfloor - j}$ for $0 \leq j \leq n$. ∎

There are $(n^2 + n)/2$ additions, $n + \lceil n/2 \rceil - 1$ multiplications, n divisions. Another multiplication and division can be saved by treating v_n and v_0 as special cases. *Reference: SIGACT News* **7**, 3 (Summer 1975), 32–34.

7. Let $x_j = x_0 + jh$, and consider (42) and (44). Set $y_j \leftarrow u(x_j)$ for $0 \leq j \leq n$. For $k = 1, 2, \ldots, n$ (in this order), set $y_j \leftarrow y_j - y_{j-1}$ for $j = n$, $n - 1$, ..., k (in this order). Now set $\beta_j \leftarrow y_j$ for all j.

However, rounding errors will accumulate as explained in the text, even if the operations of (5) are done with perfect accuracy. A better way to do the initialization, when (5) is performed with fixed point arithmetic, is to choose $\beta_0, \ldots, \beta_n$ so that

$$
\begin{pmatrix}
\binom{0}{0} & \binom{0}{1} & \cdots & \binom{0}{n} \\
\binom{d}{0} & \binom{d}{1} & \cdots & \binom{d}{n} \\
\vdots & \vdots & & \vdots \\
\binom{nd}{0} & \binom{nd}{1} & \cdots & \binom{nd}{n}
\end{pmatrix}
\begin{pmatrix}
\beta_0 \\ \beta_1 \\ \vdots \\ \beta_n
\end{pmatrix}
=
\begin{pmatrix}
u(x_0) \\ u(x_d) \\ \vdots \\ u(x_{nd})
\end{pmatrix}
+
\begin{pmatrix}
\epsilon_0 \\ \epsilon_1 \\ \vdots \\ \epsilon_n
\end{pmatrix},
$$

where $|\epsilon_0|, |\epsilon_1|, \ldots, |\epsilon_n|$ are as small as possible. [H. Hassler, *Proc. 12th Spring Conf. Computer Graphics* (Bratislava: Comenius University, 1996), 55–66.]

8. See (43).

9. [*Combinatorial Mathematics* (Buffalo: Math. Assoc. of America, 1963), 26–28.] This formula can be regarded as an application of the principle of inclusion and exclusion (Section 1.3.3), since the sum of the terms for $n - \epsilon_1 - \cdots - \epsilon_n = k$ is the sum of all $x_{1j_1} x_{2j_2} \ldots x_{nj_n}$ for which k values of the j_i do not appear. A direct proof can be given by observing that the coefficient of $x_{1j_1} \ldots x_{nj_n}$ is

$$
\sum (-1)^{n - \epsilon_1 - \cdots - \epsilon_n} \epsilon_{j_1} \ldots \epsilon_{j_n};
$$

if the j's are distinct, this equals unity, but if $j_1, \ldots, j_n \neq k$ then it is zero, since the terms for $\epsilon_k = 0$ cancel the terms for $\epsilon_k = 1$.

To evaluate the sum efficiently, we can start with $\epsilon_1 = 1$, $\epsilon_2 = \cdots = \epsilon_n = 0$, and we can then proceed through all combinations of the ϵ's in such a way that only one ϵ changes from one term to the next. (See "Gray binary code" in Section 7.2.1.1.) The first term costs $n - 1$ multiplications; the subsequent $2^n - 2$ terms each involve n additions, then $n - 1$ multiplications, then one more addition. Total: $(2^n - 1)(n - 1)$ multiplications, and $(2^n - 2)(n + 1)$ additions. Only $n + 1$ temporary storage locations are needed, one for the main partial sum and one for each factor of the current product.

10. $\sum_{1 \leq k < n} (k + 1)\binom{n}{k+1} = n(2^{n-1} - 1)$ multiplications and $\sum_{1 \leq k < n} k\binom{n}{k+1} = n2^{n-1} - 2^n + 1$ additions. This is approximately half as many arithmetic operations as the method of exercise 9, although it requires a more complicated program to control the sequence. Approximately $\binom{n}{\lceil n/2 \rceil} + \binom{n}{\lceil n/2 \rceil - 1}$ temporary storage locations must be used, and this grows exponentially large (on the order of $2^n/\sqrt{n}$).

The method in this exercise is equivalent to the unusual matrix factorization of the permanent function given by Jurkat and Ryser in *J. Algebra* **3** (1966), 1–27. It may also be regarded as an application of (39) and (40), in an appropriate sense.

11. Efficient methods are known for computing an approximate value, if the matrix is sufficiently dense; see A. Sinclair, *Algorithms for Random Generation and Counting* (Boston: Birkhäuser, 1993). But this problem asks for the exact value. There may be a way to evaluate the permanent with $O(c^n)$ operations for some $c < 2$.

12. Here is a brief summary of progress on this famous research problem: J. Hopcroft and L. R. Kerr proved, among other things, that seven multiplications are necessary in 2×2 matrix multiplication modulo 2 [*SIAM J. Appl. Math.* **20** (1971), 30–36]. R. L. Probert showed that all 7-multiplication schemes, in which each multiplication takes a linear combination of elements from one matrix and multiplies by a linear combination of elements from the other, must have at least 15 additions [*SICOMP* **5** (1976), 187–203]. The tensor rank of 2×2 matrix multiplication is 7 over every field [V. Y. Pan, *J. Algorithms* **2** (1981), 301–310]; the rank of $T(2, 3, 2)$, the tensor for the product of a 2×3 matrix by a 3×2 matrix, is 11 [V. B. Alekseyev, *J. Algorithms* **6** (1985),

71–85]. For $n \times n$ matrix multiplication, the best upper bound known when $n = 3$ is due to J. D. Laderman [*Bull. Amer. Math. Soc.* **82** (1976), 126–128], who showed that 23 noncommutative multiplications suffice. His construction has been generalized by Ondrej Sýkora, who exhibited a method requiring $n^3 - (n-1)^2$ noncommutative multiplications and $n^3 - n^2 + 11(n-1)^2$ additions; this result also reduces to (36) when $n = 2$ [*Lecture Notes in Comp. Sci.* **53** (1977), 504–512]. For $n = 5$, the current record is 100 noncommutative multiplications [O. M. Makarov, *USSR Comp. Math. and Math. Phys.* **27**, 1 (1987), 205–207]. The best lower bound known so far is due to Markus Bläser, who showed that $2n^2 + n - 3$ nonscalar multiplications are necessary for $n \geq 2$, and $mn + ns + m - n + s - 3$ in the $m \times n \times s$ case for $n \geq 2$ and $s \geq 2$ [*Computational Complexity* **8** (1999), 203–226]. If all calculations must be done without division, slightly better lower bounds were obtained by N. H. Bshouty [*SICOMP* **18** (1989), 759–765], who proved that $m \times n$ by $n \times s$ matrix multiplication mod 2 requires at least $\sum_{k=0}^{j-1} \lfloor ms/2^k \rfloor + \frac{1}{2}(n + (n \bmod j))(n - (n \bmod j) - j) + n \bmod j$ multiplications when $n \geq s \geq j \geq 1$; setting $m = n = s$ and $j \approx \lg n$ gives $2.5n^2 - \frac{1}{2}n \lg n + O(n)$.

The best upper bounds known for large n are discussed in the text, following (36).

13. By summing geometric series, we find that $F(t_1, \ldots, t_n)$ equals

$$\sum_{0 \leq s_1 < m_1, \ldots, 0 \leq s_n < m_n} \exp(-2\pi i(s_1 t_1/m_1 + \cdots + s_n t_n/m_n)) f(s_1, \ldots, s_n))/m_1 \ldots m_n.$$

The inverse transform times $m_1 \ldots m_n$ can be found by doing a regular transform and interchanging t_j with $m_j - t_j$ when $t_j \neq 0$; see exercise 4.3.3–9.

[If we regard $F(t_1, \ldots, t_n)$ as the coefficient of $x_1^{t_1} \ldots x_n^{t_n}$ in a multivariate polynomial, the discrete Fourier transform amounts to evaluation of this polynomial at roots of unity, and the inverse transform amounts to finding the interpolating polynomial.]

14. Let $m_1 = \cdots = m_n = 2$, $F(t_1, t_2, \ldots, t_n) = F(2^{n-1} t_n + \cdots + 2t_2 + t_1)$, and $f(s_1, s_2, \ldots, s_n) = f(2^{n-1} s_1 + 2^{n-2} s_2 + \cdots + s_n)$; note the reversal between t's and s's. Also let $g_k(s_k, \ldots, s_n, t_k)$ be ω raised to the $2^{k-1} t_k(s_n + 2s_{n-1} + \cdots + 2^{n-k} s_k)$ power. Replace $f_k(s_{n-k+1}, \ldots, s_n, t_1, \ldots, t_{n-k})$ by $f_k(t_1, \ldots, t_{n-k}, s_{n-k+1}, \ldots, s_n)$ in (40) if you prefer to work *in situ*.

At each iteration we essentially take 2^{n-1} pairs of complex numbers (α, β) and replace them by $(\alpha + \zeta\beta, \alpha - \zeta\beta)$, where ζ is a suitable power of ω, hence $\zeta = \cos\theta + i\sin\theta$ for some θ. If we take advantage of simplifications when $\zeta = \pm 1$ or $\pm i$, the total work comes to $((n-3) \cdot 2^{n-1} + 2)$ complex multiplications and $n \cdot 2^n$ complex additions; the techniques of exercise 41 can be used to reduce the real multiplications and additions used to implement these complex operations.

The number of complex multiplications can be reduced about 25 percent without changing the number of additions by combining passes k and $k + 1$ for $k = 1, 3, \ldots$; this means that 2^{n-2} quadruples $(\alpha, \beta, \gamma, \delta)$ are being replaced by

$$(\alpha + \zeta\beta + \zeta^2\gamma + \zeta^3\delta, \ \alpha + i\zeta\beta - \zeta^2\gamma - i\zeta^3\delta, \ \alpha - \zeta\beta + \zeta^2\gamma - \zeta^3\delta, \ \alpha - i\zeta\beta - \zeta^2\gamma + i\zeta^3\delta).$$

The total number of complex multiplications when n is even is thereby reduced to $(3n - 2)2^{n-3} - 5\lfloor 2^{n-1}/3 \rfloor$.

These calculations assume that the given numbers $F(t)$ are complex. If the $F(t)$ are real, then $f(s)$ is the complex conjugate of $f(2^n - s)$, so we can avoid the redundancy by computing only the 2^n independent real numbers $f(0), \Re f(1), \ldots, \Re f(2^{n-1} - 1), f(2^{n-1}), \Im f(1), \ldots, \Im f(2^{n-1} - 1)$. The entire calculation in this case can be done by working with 2^n real values, using the fact that $f_k(s_{n-k+1}, \ldots, s_n, t_1, \ldots, t_{n-k})$ will be the complex conjugate of $f_k(s'_{n-k+1}, \ldots, s'_n, t_1, \ldots, t_{n-k})$ when $(s_1 \ldots s_n)_2 +$

$(s'_1 \ldots s'_n)_2 \equiv 0$ (modulo 2^n). About half as many multiplications and additions are needed as in the complex case.

[The fast Fourier transform algorithm was discovered by C. F. Gauss in 1805 and independently rediscovered many times since, most notably by J. W. Cooley and J. W. Tukey, *Math. Comp.* **19** (1965), 297–301. Its interesting history has been traced by J. W. Cooley, P. A. W. Lewis, and P. D. Welch, *Proc. IEEE* **55** (1967), 1675–1677; M. T. Heideman, D. H. Johnson, and C. S. Burrus, *IEEE ASSP Magazine* **1**, 4 (October 1984), 14–21. Details concerning its use have been discussed by hundreds of authors, admirably summarized by Charles Van Loan, *Computational Frameworks for the Fast Fourier Transform* (Philadelphia: SIAM, 1992). For a survey of fast Fourier transforms on finite groups, see M. Clausen and U. Baum, *Fast Fourier Transforms* (Mannheim: Bibliographisches Institut Wissenschaftsverlag, 1993).]

15. (a) The hint follows by integration and induction. Let $f^{(n)}(\theta)$ take on all values between A and B inclusive, as θ varies from $\min(x_0, \ldots, x_n)$ to $\max(x_0, \ldots, x_n)$. Replacing $f^{(n)}$ by each of these bounds, in the stated integral, yields $A/n! \le f(x_0, \ldots, x_n) \le B/n!$. (b) It suffices to prove this for $j = n$. Let f be Newton's interpolation polynomial, then $f^{(n)}$ is the constant $n!\,\alpha_n$. [See *The Mathematical Papers of Isaac Newton*, edited by D. T. Whiteside, **4** (1971), 36–51, 70–73.]

16. Carry out the multiplications and additions of (43) as operations on polynomials. (The special case $x_0 = x_1 = \cdots = x_n$ is considered in exercise 2. We have used this method in step T8 of Algorithm 4.3.3T.)

17. For example, when $n = 5$ we have

$$u_{[5]}(x) = \frac{\dfrac{y_0}{x-x_0} - \dfrac{5y_1}{x-x_1} + \dfrac{10y_2}{x-x_2} - \dfrac{10y_3}{x-x_3} + \dfrac{5y_4}{x-x_4} - \dfrac{y_5}{x-x_5}}{\dfrac{1}{x-x_0} - \dfrac{5}{x-x_1} + \dfrac{10}{x-x_2} - \dfrac{10}{x-x_3} + \dfrac{5}{x-x_4} - \dfrac{1}{x-x_5}},$$

independent of the value of h.

18. $\alpha_0 = \frac{1}{2}(u_3/u_4 + 1)$, $\beta = u_2/u_4 - \alpha_0(\alpha_0 - 1)$, $\alpha_1 = \alpha_0\beta - u_1/u_4$, $\alpha_2 = \beta - 2\alpha_1$, $\alpha_3 = u_0/u_4 - \alpha_1(\alpha_1 + \alpha_2)$, $\alpha_4 = u_4$.

19. Since α_5 is the leading coefficient, we may assume without loss of generality that $u(x)$ is monic (namely that $u_5 = 1$). Then α_0 is a root of the equation $40z^3 - 24u_4z^2 + (4u_4^2 + 2u_3)z + (u_2 - u_3u_4) = 0$; this equation always has at least one real root, and it may have three. Once α_0 is determined, we have $\alpha_3 = u_4 - 4\alpha_0$, $\alpha_1 = u_3 - 4\alpha_0\alpha_3 - 6\alpha_0^2$, $\alpha_2 = u_1 - \alpha_0(\alpha_0\alpha_1 + 4\alpha_0^2\alpha_3 + 2\alpha_1\alpha_3 + \alpha_0^3)$, $\alpha_4 = u_0 - \alpha_3(\alpha_0^4 + \alpha_1\alpha_0^2 + \alpha_2)$.

For the given polynomial we are to solve the cubic equation $40z^3 - 120z^2 + 80z = 0$; this leads to three solutions $(\alpha_0, \alpha_1, \alpha_2, \alpha_3, \alpha_4, \alpha_5) = (0, -10, 13, 5, -5, 1)$, $(1, -20, 68, 1, 11, 1)$, $(2, -10, 13, -3, 27, 1)$.

20.

LDA	X	STA	TEMP2	FADD	$=\alpha_1=$	FMUL	TEMP1
FADD	$=\alpha_3=$	FMUL	TEMP2	FMUL	TEMP2	FADD	$=\alpha_4=$
STA	TEMP1	STA	TEMP2	FADD	$=\alpha_2=$	FMUL	$=\alpha_5=$ ∎
FADD	$=\alpha_0-\alpha_3=$						

21. $z = (x+1)x - 2$, $w = (x+5)z + 9$, $u(x) = (w+z-8)w - 8$; or $z = (x+9)x + 26$, $w = (x-3)z + 73$, $u(x) = (w+z-24)w - 12$.

22. $\alpha_6 = 1$, $\alpha_0 = -1$, $\alpha_1 = 1$, $\beta_1 = -2$, $\beta_2 = -2$, $\beta_3 = -2$, $\beta_4 = 1$, $\alpha_3 = -4$, $\alpha_2 = 0$, $\alpha_4 = 4$, $\alpha_5 = -2$. We form $z = (x-1)x+1$, $w = z+x$, and $u(x) = ((z-x-4)w+4)z-2$. Here one of the seven additions can be saved if we compute $w = x^2 + 1$, $z = w - x$.

23. (a) We may use induction on n; the result is trivial if $n < 2$. If $f(0) = 0$, then the result is true for the polynomial $f(z)/z$, so it holds for $f(z)$. If $f(iy) = 0$ for some real $y \neq 0$, then $g(\pm iy) = h(\pm iy) = 0$; since the result is true for $f(z)/(z^2 + y^2)$, it holds also for $f(z)$. Therefore we may assume that $f(z)$ has no roots whose real part is zero. Now the net number of times the given path circles the origin is the number of roots of $f(z)$ inside the region, which is at most 1. When R is large, the path $f(Re^{it})$ for $\pi/2 \leq t \leq 3\pi/2$ will circle the origin clockwise approximately $n/2$ times; so the path $f(it)$ for $-R \leq t \leq R$ must go counterclockwise around the origin at least $n/2 - 1$ times. For n even, this implies that $f(it)$ crosses the imaginary axis at least $n-2$ times, and the real axis at least $n - 3$ times; for n odd, $f(it)$ crosses the real axis at least $n - 2$ times and the imaginary axis at least $n - 3$ times. These are roots respectively of $g(it) = 0$, $h(it) = 0$.

(b) If not, g or h would have a root of the form $a + bi$ with $a \neq 0$ and $b \neq 0$. But this would imply the existence of at least three other such roots, namely $a - bi$ and $-a \pm bi$, while $g(z)$ and $h(z)$ have at most n roots.

24. The roots of u are -7, $-3 \pm i$, $-2 \pm i$, and -1; permissible values of c are 2 and 4 (but *not* 3, since $c = 3$ makes the sum of the roots equal to zero). *Case 1: $c = 2$.* Then $p(x) = (x + 5)(x^2 + 2x + 2)(x^2 + 1)(x - 1) = x^6 + 6x^5 + 6x^4 + 4x^3 - 5x^2 - 2x - 10$; $q(x) = 6x^2 + 4x - 2 = 6(x + 1)(x - \frac{1}{3})$. Let $\alpha_2 = -1$, $\alpha_1 = \frac{1}{3}$; $p_1(x) = x^4 + 6x^3 + 5x^2 - 2x - 10 = (x^2 + 6x + \frac{16}{3})(x^2 - \frac{1}{3}) - \frac{74}{9}$; $\alpha_0 = 6$, $\beta_0 = \frac{16}{3}$, $\beta_1 = -\frac{74}{9}$. *Case 2: $c = 4$.* A similar analysis gives $\alpha_2 = 9$, $\alpha_1 = -3$, $\alpha_0 = -6$, $\beta_0 = 12$, $\beta_1 = -26$.

25. $\beta_1 = \alpha_2$, $\beta_2 = 2\alpha_1$, $\beta_3 = \alpha_7$, $\beta_4 = \alpha_6$, $\beta_5 = \beta_6 = 0$, $\beta_7 = \alpha_1$, $\beta_8 = 0$, $\beta_9 = 2\alpha_1 - \alpha_8$.

26. (a) $\lambda_1 = \alpha_1 \times \lambda_0$, $\lambda_2 = \alpha_2 + \lambda_1$, $\lambda_3 = \lambda_2 \times \lambda_0$, $\lambda_4 = \alpha_3 + \lambda_3$, $\lambda_5 = \lambda_4 \times \lambda_0$, $\lambda_6 = \alpha_4 + \lambda_5$. (b) $\kappa_1 = 1 + \beta_1 x$, $\kappa_2 = 1 + \beta_2 \kappa_1 x$, $\kappa_3 = 1 + \beta_3 \kappa_2 x$, $u(x) = \beta_4 \kappa_3 = \beta_1 \beta_2 \beta_3 \beta_4 x^3 + \beta_2 \beta_3 \beta_4 x^2 + \beta_3 \beta_4 x + \beta_4$. (c) If any coefficient is zero, the coefficient of x^3 must also be zero in (b), while (a) yields an arbitrary polynomial $\alpha_1 x^3 + \alpha_2 x^2 + \alpha_3 x + \alpha_4$ of degree ≤ 3.

27. Otherwise there would be a nonzero polynomial $f(q_n, \ldots, q_1, q_0)$ with integer coefficients such that $q_n \cdot f(q_n, \ldots, q_1, q_0) = 0$ for all sets $(q_n, \ldots, q_0)$ of real numbers. This cannot happen, since it is easy to prove by induction on n that a nonzero polynomial always takes on some nonzero value. (See exercise 4.6.1–16. However, this result is false for *finite* fields in place of the real numbers.)

28. The indeterminate quantities $\alpha_1, \ldots, \alpha_s$ form an algebraic basis for the polynomial domain $Q[\alpha_1, \ldots, \alpha_s]$, where Q is the field of rational numbers. Since $s + 1$ is greater than the number of elements in a basis, the polynomials $f_j(\alpha_1, \ldots, \alpha_s)$ are algebraically dependent; this means that there is a nonzero polynomial g with rational coefficients such that $g\big(f_0(\alpha_1, \ldots, \alpha_s), \ldots, f_s(\alpha_1, \ldots, \alpha_s)\big)$ is identically zero.

29. Given $j_0, \ldots, j_t \in \{0, 1, \ldots, n\}$, there are nonzero polynomials with integer coefficients such that $g_j(q_{j_0}, \ldots, q_{j_t}) = 0$ for all $(q_n, \ldots, q_0)$ in R_j, $1 \leq j \leq m$. The product $g_1 g_2 \ldots g_m$ is therefore zero for all $(q_n, \ldots, q_0)$ in $R_1 \cup \cdots \cup R_m$.

30. Starting with the construction in Theorem M, we will prove that $m_p + (1 - \delta_{0m_c})$ of the β's may effectively be eliminated: If μ_i corresponds to a parameter multiplication, we have $\mu_i = \beta_{2i-1} \times (T_{2i} + \beta_{2i})$; add $c\beta_{2i-1}\beta_{2i}$ to each β_j for which $c\mu_i$ occurs in T_j, and replace β_{2i} by zero. This removes one parameter for each parameter multiplication. If μ_i is the first chain multiplication, then $\mu_i = (\gamma_1 x + \theta_1 + \beta_{2i-1}) \times (\gamma_2 x + \theta_2 + \beta_{2i})$, where γ_1, γ_2, θ_1, θ_2 are polynomials in $\beta_1, \ldots, \beta_{2i-2}$ with integer coefficients. Here θ_1 and θ_2 can be "absorbed" into β_{2i-1} and β_{2i}, respectively, so we may assume that

$\theta_1 = \theta_2 = 0$. Now add $c\beta_{2i-1}\beta_{2i}$ to each β_j for which $c\mu_i$ occurs in T_j; add $\beta_{2i-1}\gamma_2/\gamma_1$ to β_{2i}; and set β_{2i-1} to zero. The result set is unchanged by this elimination of β_{2i-1}, except for the values of $\alpha_1, \ldots, \alpha_s$ such that γ_1 is zero. [This proof is essentially due to V. Y. Pan, *Uspekhi Mat. Nauk* **21**, 1 (January–February 1966), 103–134.] The latter case can be handled as in the proof of Theorem A, since the polynomials with $\gamma_1 = 0$ can be evaluated by eliminating β_{2i} (as in the first construction, where μ_i corresponds to a parameter multiplication).

31. Otherwise we could add one parameter multiplication as a final step, and violate Theorem C. (The exercise is an improvement over Theorem A, in this special case, since there are only n degrees of freedom in the coefficients of a monic polynomial of degree n.)

32. $\lambda_1 = \lambda_0 \times \lambda_0$, $\lambda_2 = \alpha_1 \times \lambda_1$, $\lambda_3 = \alpha_2 + \lambda_2$, $\lambda_4 = \lambda_3 \times \lambda_1$, $\lambda_5 = \alpha_3 + \lambda_4$. We need at least three multiplications to compute $u_4 x^4$ (see Section 4.6.3), and at least two additions by Theorem A.

33. We must have $n + 1 \leq 2m_c + m_p + \delta_{0m_c}$, and $m_c + m_p = (n+1)/2$; so there are no parameter multiplications. Now the first λ_i whose leading coefficient (as a polynomial in x) is not an integer must be obtained by a chain addition; and there must be at least $n + 1$ parameters, so there are at least $n + 1$ parameter additions.

34. Transform the given chain step by step, and also define the "content" c_i of λ_i, as follows: (Intuitively, c_i is the leading coefficient of λ_i.) Define $c_0 = 1$. (a) If the step has the form $\lambda_i = \lambda_j + \lambda_k$, replace it by $\lambda_i = \beta_j + \lambda_k$, where $\beta_j = \alpha_j/c_k$; and define $c_i = c_k$. (b) If the step has the form $\lambda_i = \alpha_j - \lambda_k$, replace it by $\lambda_i = \beta_j + \lambda_k$, where $\beta_j = -\alpha_j/c_k$; and define $c_i = -c_k$. (c) If the step has the form $\lambda_i = \alpha_j \times \lambda_k$, replace it by $\lambda_i = \lambda_k$ (the step will be deleted later); and define $c_i = \alpha_j c_k$. (d) If the step has the form $\lambda_i = \lambda_j \times \lambda_k$, leave it unchanged; and define $c_i = c_j c_k$.

After this process is finished, delete all steps of the form $\lambda_i = \lambda_k$, replacing λ_i by λ_k in each future step that uses λ_i. Then add a final step $\lambda_{r+1} = \beta \times \lambda_r$, where $\beta = c_r$. This is the desired scheme, since it is easy to verify that the new λ_i are just the old ones divided by the factor c_i. The β's are given functions of the α's; division by zero is no problem, because if any $c_k = 0$ we must have $c_r = 0$ (hence the coefficient of x^n is zero), or else λ_k never contributes to the final result.

35. Since there are at least five parameter steps, the result is trivial unless there is at least one parameter multiplication; considering the ways in which three multiplications can form $u_4 x^4$, we see that there must be one parameter multiplication and two chain multiplications. Therefore the four addition-subtractions must each be parameter steps, and exercise 34 applies. We can now assume that only additions are used, and that we have a chain to compute a general *monic* fourth-degree polynomial with *two* chain multiplications and four parameter additions. The only possible scheme of this type that calculates a fourth-degree polynomial has the form

$$\lambda_1 = \alpha_1 + \lambda_0$$
$$\lambda_2 = \alpha_2 + \lambda_0$$
$$\lambda_3 = \lambda_1 \times \lambda_2$$
$$\lambda_4 = \alpha_3 + \lambda_3$$
$$\lambda_5 = \alpha_4 + \lambda_3$$
$$\lambda_6 = \lambda_4 \times \lambda_5$$
$$\lambda_7 = \alpha_5 + \lambda_6.$$

Actually this chain has one addition too many, but any correct scheme can be put into this form if we restrict some of the α's to be functions of the others. Now λ_7 has the form $(x^2 + Ax + B)(x^2 + Ax + C) + D = x^4 + 2Ax^3 + (E + A^2)x^2 + EAx + F$, where $A = \alpha_1 + \alpha_2$, $B = \alpha_1\alpha_2 + \alpha_3$, $C = \alpha_1\alpha_2 + \alpha_4$, $D = \alpha_6$, $E = B + C$, $F = BC + D$; and since this involves only three independent parameters it cannot represent a general monic fourth-degree polynomial.

36. As in the solution to exercise 35, we may assume that the chain computes a general monic polynomial of degree six, using only three chain multiplications and six parameter additions. The computation must take one of two general forms

<table>
<tr><td>

$\lambda_1 = \alpha_1 + \lambda_0$
$\lambda_2 = \alpha_2 + \lambda_0$
$\lambda_3 = \lambda_1 \times \lambda_2$
$\lambda_4 = \alpha_3 + \lambda_0$
$\lambda_5 = \alpha_4 + \lambda_3$
$\lambda_6 = \lambda_4 \times \lambda_5$
$\lambda_7 = \alpha_5 + \lambda_6$
$\lambda_8 = \alpha_6 + \lambda_6$
$\lambda_9 = \lambda_7 \times \lambda_8$
$\lambda_{10} = \alpha_7 + \lambda_9$

</td><td>

$\lambda_1 = \alpha_1 + \lambda_0$
$\lambda_2 = \alpha_2 + \lambda_0$
$\lambda_3 = \lambda_1 \times \lambda_2$
$\lambda_4 = \alpha_3 + \lambda_3$
$\lambda_5 = \alpha_4 + \lambda_3$
$\lambda_6 = \lambda_4 \times \lambda_5$
$\lambda_7 = \alpha_5 + \lambda_3$
$\lambda_8 = \alpha_6 + \lambda_6$
$\lambda_9 = \lambda_7 \times \lambda_8$
$\lambda_{10} = \alpha_7 + \lambda_9$

</td></tr>
</table>

where, as in exercise 35, an extra addition has been inserted to cover a more general case. Neither of these schemes can calculate a general sixth-degree monic polynomial, since the first case is a polynomial of the form

$$(x^3 + Ax^2 + Bx + C)(x^3 + Ax^2 + Bx + D) + E,$$

and the second case is a polynomial of the form

$$(x^4 + 2Ax^3 + (E + A^2)x^2 + EAx + F)(x^2 + Ax + G) + H;$$

both of these involve only five independent parameters.

37. Let $p_0(x) = u_n x^n + u_{n-1} x^{n-1} + \cdots + u_0$ and $q_0(x) = x^n + v_{n-1} x^{n-1} + \cdots + v_0$. For $1 \le j \le n$, divide $p_{j-1}(x)$ by the monic polynomial $q_{j-1}(x)$, obtaining $p_{j-1}(x) = \alpha_j q_{j-1}(x) + \beta_j q_j(x)$. Assume that a monic polynomial $q_j(x)$ of degree $n - j$ exists satisfying this relation; this will be true for almost all rational functions. Let $p_j(x) = q_{j-1}(x) - xvq_j(x)$. These definitions imply that $\deg(p_n) < 1$, so we may let $\alpha_{n+1} = p_n(x)$.

For the given rational function we have

j	α_j	β_j	$q_j(x)$	$p_j(x)$
0			$x^2 + 8x + 19$	$x^2 + 10x + 29$
1	1	2	$x + 5$	$3x + 19$
2	3	4	1	5

so $u(x)/v(x) = p_0(x)/q_0(x) = 1 + 2/(x + 3 + 4/(x + 5))$.

Notes: A general rational function of the stated form has $2n + 1$ "degrees of freedom," in the sense that it can be shown to have $2n + 1$ essentially independent parameters. If we generalize polynomial chains to quolynomial chains, which allow division operations as well as addition, subtraction, and multiplication (see exercise 71), we can obtain the following results with slight modifications to the proofs of Theorems A and M: *A quolynomial chain with q addition-subtraction steps has at most $q + 1$*

degrees of freedom. A quolynomial chain with m multiplication-division steps has at most $2m + 1$ degrees of freedom. Therefore a quolynomial chain that computes almost all rational functions of the stated form must have at least $2n$ addition-subtractions, and n multiplication-divisions; the method in this exercise is optimal.

38. The theorem is certainly true if $n = 0$. Assume that n is positive, and that a polynomial chain computing $P(x; u_0, \ldots, u_n)$ is given, where each of the parameters α_j has been replaced by a real number. Let $\lambda_i = \lambda_j \times \lambda_k$ be the first chain multiplication step that involves one of $u_0, \ldots, u_n$; such a step must exist because of the rank of A. Without loss of generality, we may assume that λ_j involves u_n; thus, λ_j has the form $h_0 u_0 + \cdots + h_n u_n + f(x)$, where $h_0, \ldots, h_n$ are real, $h_n \neq 0$, and $f(x)$ is a polynomial with real coefficients. (The h's and the coefficients of $f(x)$ are derived from the values assigned to the α's.)

Now change step i to $\lambda_i = \alpha \times \lambda_k$, where α is an arbitrary real number. (We could take $\alpha = 0$; general α is used here merely to show that there is a certain amount of flexibility available in the proof.) Add further steps to calculate

$$\lambda = (\alpha - f(x) - h_0 u_0 - \cdots - h_{n-1} u_{n-1})/h_n;$$

these new steps involve only additions and parameter multiplications (by suitable new parameters). Finally, replace $\lambda_{-n-1} = u_n$ everywhere in the chain by this new element λ. The result is a chain that calculates

$$Q(x; u_0, \ldots, u_{n-1}) = P(x; u_0, \ldots, u_{n-1}, (\alpha - f(x) - h_0 u_0 - \cdots - h_{n-1} u_{n-1})/h_n);$$

and this chain has one less chain multiplication. The proof will be complete if we can show that Q satisfies the hypotheses. The quantity $(\alpha - f(x))/h_n$ leads to a possibly increased value of m, and a new vector B'. If the columns of A are $A_0, A_1, \ldots, A_n$ (these vectors being linearly independent over the reals), the new matrix A' corresponding to Q has the column vectors

$$A_0 - (h_0/h_n)A_n, \qquad \ldots, \qquad A_{n-1} - (h_{n-1}/h_n)A_n,$$

plus perhaps a few rows of zeros to account for an increased value of m, and these columns are clearly also linearly independent. By induction, the chain that computes Q has at least $n - 1$ chain multiplications, so the original chain has at least n.

[Pan showed also that the use of division would give no improvement; see *Problemy Kibernetiki* **7** (1962), 21–30. Generalizations to the computation of several polynomials in several variables, with and without various kinds of preconditioning, have been given by S. Winograd, *Comm. Pure and Applied Math.* **23** (1970), 165–179.]

39. By induction on m. Let $w_m(x) = x^{2m} + u_{2m-1}x^{2m-1} + \cdots + u_0$, $w_{m-1}(x) = x^{2m-2} + v_{2m-3}x^{2m-3} + \cdots + v_0$, $a = \alpha_1 + \gamma_m$, $b = \alpha_m$, and let

$$f(r) = \sum_{i,j \geq 0} (-1)^{i+j} \binom{i+j}{j} u_{r+i+2j} a^i b^j.$$

It follows that $v_r = f(r + 2)$ for $r \geq 0$, and $\delta_m = f(1)$. If $\delta_m = 0$ and a is given, we have a polynomial of degree $m - 1$ in b, with leading coefficient $\pm(u_{2m-1} - ma) = \pm(\gamma_2 + \cdots + \gamma_m - m\gamma_m)$.

In Motzkin's unpublished notes he arranged to make $\delta_k = 0$ almost always, by choosing γ's so that this leading coefficient is $\neq 0$ when m is even and $= 0$ when m is odd; then we can almost always let b be a (real) root of an odd-degree polynomial.

40. No; S. Winograd found a way to compute all polynomials of degree 13 with only 7 (possibly complex) multiplications [*Comm. Pure and Applied Math.* **25** (1972), 455–457]. L. Revah found schemes that evaluate almost all polynomials of degree $n \geq 9$ with $\lfloor n/2 \rfloor + 1$ (possibly complex) multiplications [*SICOMP* **4** (1975), 381–392]; she also showed that when $n = 9$ it is possible to achieve $\lfloor n/2 \rfloor + 1$ multiplications only with at least $n + 3$ additions. By appending sufficiently many additions (see exercise 39), the "almost all" and "possibly complex" provisos disappear. V. Y. Pan [*STOC* **10** (1978), 162–172; IBM Research Report RC7754 (1979)] found schemes with $\lfloor n/2 \rfloor + 1$ (complex) multiplications and the minimum number $n + 2 + \delta_{n9}$ of (complex) additions, for all odd $n \geq 9$; his method for $n = 9$ is

$$v(x) = ((x + \alpha)^2 + \beta)(x + \gamma), \qquad w(x) = v(x) + x,$$
$$t_1(x) = (v(x) + \delta_1)(w(x) + \epsilon_1), \qquad t_2(x) = (v(x) + \delta_2)(w(x) + \epsilon_2),$$
$$u(x) = (t_1(x) + \zeta)(t_2(x) - t_1(x) + \eta) + \kappa.$$

The minimum number of *real* additions necessary, when the minimum number of (real) multiplications is achieved, remains unknown for $n \geq 9$.

41. $a(c + d) - (a + b)d + i(a(c + d) + (b - a)c)$. [Beware of numerical instability. Three multiplications are necessary, since complex multiplication is a special case of (71) with $p(u) = u^2 + 1$. Without the restriction on additions there are other possibilities. For example, the symmetric formula $ac - bd + i((a + b)(c + d) - ac - bd)$ was suggested by Peter Ungar in 1963; Eq. 4.3.3–(2) is similar, with 2^n in the role of i. See I. Munro, *STOC* **3** (1971), 40–44; S. Winograd, *Linear Algebra and Its Applications* **4** (1971), 381–388.]

Alternatively, if $a^2 + b^2 = 1$ and $t = (1 - a)/b = b/(1 + a)$, the algorithm "$w = c - td$, $v = d + bw$, $u = w - tv$" for calculating the product $(a + bi)(c + di) = u + iv$ has been suggested by Oscar Buneman [*J. Comp. Phys.* **12** (1973), 127–128]. In this method if $a = \cos \theta$ and $b = \sin \theta$, we have $t = \tan(\theta/2)$.

Helmut Alt and Jan van Leeuwen [*Computing* **27** (1981), 205–215] have shown that four real multiplications or divisions are necessary for computing $1/(a + bi)$, and four are sufficient for computing

$$\frac{a}{b + ci} = \frac{a}{b + c(c/b)} - i\frac{(c/b)a}{b + c(c/b)}.$$

Six multiplication-division operations and three addition-subtractions are necessary and sufficient to compute $(a + bi)/(c + di)$. [T. Lickteig, *SICOMP* **16** (1987), 278–311].

In spite of these lower bounds, one should remember that complex arithmetic need not be implemented in terms of real arithmetic. For example, the time needed to multiply two n-place complex numbers is asymptotically only about twice the time to multiply two n-place real numbers, using fast Fourier transforms.

42. (a) Let $\pi_1, \ldots, \pi_m$ be the λ_i's that correspond to chain multiplications; then $\pi_i = P_{2i-1} \times P_{2i}$ and $u(x) = P_{2m+1}$, where each P_j has the form $\beta_j + \beta_{j0}x + \beta_{j1}\pi_1 + \cdots + \beta_{jr(j)}\pi_{r(j)}$, where $r(j) \leq \lceil j/2 \rceil - 1$ and each of the β_j and β_{jk} is a polynomial in the α's with integer coefficients. We can systematically modify the chain (see exercise 30) so that $\beta_j = 0$ and $\beta_{jr(j)} = 1$, for $1 \leq j \leq 2m$; furthermore we can assume that $\beta_{30} = 0$. The result set now has at most $m + 1 + \sum_{j=1}^{2m}(\lceil j/2 \rceil - 1) = m^2 + 1$ degrees of freedom.

(b) Any such polynomial chain with at most m chain multiplications can be simulated by one with the form considered in (a), except that now we let $r(j) = \lceil j/2 \rceil - 1$ for $1 \leq j \leq 2m + 1$, and we do not assume that $\beta_{30} = 0$ or that $\beta_{jr(j)} = 1$ for $j \geq 3$.

This single canonical form involves $m^2 + 2m$ parameters. As the α's run through all integers and as we run through all chains, the β's run through at most 2^{m^2+2m} sets of values mod 2, hence the result set does also. In order to obtain all 2^n polynomials of degree n with 0–1 coefficients, we need $m^2 + 2m \geq n$.

(c) Set $m \leftarrow \lfloor \sqrt{n} \rfloor$ and compute x^2, x^3, ..., x^m. Let $u(x) = u_{m+1}(x)x^{(m+1)m} + \cdots + u_1(x)x^m + u_0(x)$, where each $u_j(x)$ is a polynomial of degree $\leq m$ with integer coefficients (hence it can be evaluated without any more multiplications). Now evaluate $u(x)$ by rule (2) as a polynomial in x^m with known coefficients. (The number of additions used is approximately the sum of the absolute values of the coefficients, so this algorithm is efficient on 0–1 polynomials. Paterson and Stockmeyer also gave another algorithm that uses about $\sqrt{2n}$ multiplications.)

References: SICOMP **2** (1973), 60–66; see also J. E. Savage, *SICOMP* **3** (1974), 150–158; J. Ganz, *SICOMP* **24** (1995), 473–483. For analogous results about additions, see Borodin and Cook, *SICOMP* **5** (1976), 146–157; Rivest and Van de Wiele, *Inf. Proc. Letters* **8** (1979), 178–180.

43. When $a_i = a_j + a_k$ is a step in some optimal addition chain for $n + 1$, compute $x^i = x^j x^k$ and $p_i = p_k x^j + p_j$, where $p_i = x^{i-1} + \cdots + x + 1$; omit the final calculation of x^{n+1}. We save one multiplication whenever $a_k = 1$, in particular when $i = 1$. (See exercise 4.6.3–31 with $\epsilon = \frac{1}{2}$.)

44. Let $l = \lfloor \lg n \rfloor$, and suppose x, x^2, x^4, ..., x^{2^l} have been precomputed. If $u(x)$ is monic of degree $n = 2m + 1$, we can write $u(x) = (x^{m+1} + \alpha)v(x) + w(x)$, where $v(x)$ and $w(x)$ are monic of degree m. This yields a method for $n = 2^{l+1} - 1 \geq 3$ that requires $2^l - 1$ further multiplications and $2^{l+1} + 2^{l-1} - 2$ additions. If $n = 2^l$ we can apply Horner's rule to reduce n by 1. And if $m = 2^l < n < 2^{l+1} - 1$, we can write $u(x) = x^m v(x) + w(x)$ where v and w are monic of degrees $n - m$ and m, respectively; by induction on l, this requires at most $\frac{1}{2}n + l - 1$ multiplications and $\frac{5}{4}n$ additions, after the precomputation. [See S. Winograd, *IBM Tech. Disclosure Bull.* **13** (1970), 1133–1135.]

Note: It is also possible to evaluate $u(x)$ with $\frac{1}{2}n + O(\sqrt{n})$ multiplications and $n + O(\sqrt{n})$ additions, under the same ground rules, if our goal is to minimize multiplications + additions. The generic polynomial

$$p_{jkm}(x) = \Big(\big(\dots (((x^m + \alpha_0)(x^{j+1} + \beta_1) + \alpha_1)(x^{j+2} + \beta_2)$$
$$+ \alpha_2) \cdots \big)(x^k + \beta_{k-j}) + \alpha_{k-j} \big)(x^j + \beta_0) \Big)$$

"covers" the coefficients of exponents $\{j, j + k, j + k + (k - 1), \dots, j + k + (k - 1) + \cdots + (j + 1), m' - k, m' - k + 1, \dots, m' - j\}$, where

$$m' = m + j + (j + 1) + \cdots + k = m + \binom{k+1}{2} - \binom{j}{2}.$$

By adding together such polynomials $p_{1km_1}(x)$, $p_{2km_2}(x)$, ..., $p_{kkm_k}(x)$ for $m_j = \binom{j+1}{2} + \binom{k-j+2}{2}$, we obtain an arbitrary monic polynomial of degree $k^2 + k + 1$. [Rabin and Winograd, *Comm. on Pure and Applied Math.* **25** (1972), 433–458, §2; this paper also proves that constructions with $\frac{1}{2}n + O(\log n)$ multiplications and $\leq (1 + \epsilon)n$ additions are possible for all $\epsilon > 0$, if n is large enough.]

45. It suffices to show that (T_{ijk})'s rank is *at most* that of (t_{ijk}), since we can obtain (t_{ijk}) back from (T_{ijk}) by transforming it in the same way with F^{-1}, G^{-1}, H^{-1}. If

$t_{ijk} = \sum_{l=1}^{r} a_{il} b_{jl} c_{kl}$ then it follows immediately that

$$T_{ijk} = \sum_{1 \le l \le r} \left(\sum_{i'=1}^{m} F_{ii'} a_{i'l}\right)\left(\sum_{j'=1}^{n} G_{jj'} b_{j'l}\right)\left(\sum_{k'=1}^{s} H_{kk'} c_{k'l}\right).$$

[H. F. de Groote has proved that all normal schemes that yield 2×2 matrix products with seven chain multiplications are equivalent, in the sense that they can be obtained from each other by nonsingular matrix multiplication as in this exercise. In this sense Strassen's algorithm is unique. See *Theor. Comp. Sci.* **7** (1978), 127–148.]

46. By exercise 45 we can add any multiple of a row, column, or plane to another one without changing the rank; we can also multiply a row, column, or plane by a nonzero constant, or transpose the tensor. A sequence of such operations can always be found to reduce a given $2 \times 2 \times 2$ tensor to one of the forms $\left(\begin{smallmatrix} 0 & 0 \\ 0 & 0 \end{smallmatrix}\right)\left(\begin{smallmatrix} 0 & 0 \\ 0 & 0 \end{smallmatrix}\right)$, $\left(\begin{smallmatrix} 1 & 0 \\ 0 & 0 \end{smallmatrix}\right)\left(\begin{smallmatrix} 0 & 0 \\ 0 & 0 \end{smallmatrix}\right)$, $\left(\begin{smallmatrix} 1 & 0 \\ 0 & 1 \end{smallmatrix}\right)\left(\begin{smallmatrix} 0 & 0 \\ 0 & 0 \end{smallmatrix}\right)$, $\left(\begin{smallmatrix} 1 & 0 \\ 0 & 0 \end{smallmatrix}\right)\left(\begin{smallmatrix} 0 & 0 \\ 0 & 1 \end{smallmatrix}\right)$, $\left(\begin{smallmatrix} 1 & 0 \\ 0 & 1 \end{smallmatrix}\right)\left(\begin{smallmatrix} 0 & 1 \\ q & r \end{smallmatrix}\right)$. The last tensor has rank 3 or 2 according as the polynomial $u^2 - ru - q$ has one or two irreducible factors in the field of interest, by Theorem W (see (74)).

47. A general $m \times n \times s$ tensor has mns degrees of freedom. By exercise 28 it is impossible to express all $m \times n \times s$ tensors in terms of the $(m + n + s)r$ elements of a realization (A, B, C) unless $(m + n + s)r \ge mns$. On the other hand, assume that $m \ge n \ge s$. The rank of an $m \times n$ matrix is at most n, so we can realize any tensor in ns chain multiplications by realizing each matrix plane separately. [Exercise 46 shows that this lower bound on the maximum tensor rank is not best possible, nor is the upper bound. Thomas D. Howell (Ph.D. thesis, Cornell Univ., 1976) has shown that there are tensors of rank $\ge \lceil mns/(m + n + s - 2) \rceil$ over the complex numbers.]

48. If (A, B, C) and (A', B', C') are realizations of (t_{ijk}) and (t'_{ijk}) of respective lengths r and r', then $A'' = A \oplus A'$, $B'' = B \oplus B'$, $C'' = C \oplus C'$, and $A''' = A \otimes A'$, $B''' = B \otimes B'$, $C''' = C \otimes C'$, are realizations of (t''_{ijk}) and (t'''_{ijk}) of respective lengths $r + r'$ and $r \cdot r'$.

Note: Many people have made the natural conjecture that $\mathrm{rank}((t_{ijk}) \oplus (t'_{ijk})) = \mathrm{rank}(t_{ijk}) + \mathrm{rank}(t'_{ijk})$, but the constructions in exercise 60(b) and exercise 65 make this seem much less plausible than it once was.

49. By Lemma T, $\mathrm{rank}(t_{ijk}) \ge \mathrm{rank}(t_{i(jk)})$. Conversely if M is a matrix of rank r we can transform it by row and column operations, finding nonsingular matrices F and G such that FMG has all entries 0 except for r diagonal elements that are 1; see Algorithm 4.6.2N. The tensor rank of FMG is therefore $\le r$; and it is the same as the tensor rank of M, by exercise 45.

50. Let $i = \langle i', i'' \rangle$ where $1 \le i' \le m$ and $1 \le i'' \le n$; then $t_{\langle i', i'' \rangle jk} = \delta_{i''j} \delta_{i'k}$, and it is clear that $\mathrm{rank}(t_{i(jk)}) = mn$ since $(t_{i(jk)})$ is a permutation matrix. By Lemma L, $\mathrm{rank}(t_{ijk}) \ge mn$. Conversely, since (t_{ijk}) has only mn nonzero entries, its rank is clearly $\le mn$. (There is consequently no normal scheme requiring fewer than the mn obvious multiplications. There is no such abnormal scheme either [*Comm. Pure and Appl. Math.* **3** (1970), 165–179]. But some savings can be achieved if the same matrix is used with $s > 1$ different column vectors, since this is equivalent to $(m \times n)$ times $(n \times s)$ matrix multiplication.)

51. (a) $s_1 = y_0 + y_1$, $s_2 = y_0 - y_1$; $m_1 = \frac{1}{2}(x_0 + x_1)s_1$, $m_2 = \frac{1}{2}(x_0 - x_1)s_2$; $w_0 = m_1 + m_2$, $w_1 = m_1 - m_2$. (b) Here are some intermediate steps, using the methodology in the text: $((x_0 - x_2) + (x_1 - x_2)u)((y_0 - y_2) + (y_1 - y_2)u) \bmod (u^2 + u + 1) = ((x_0 - x_2)(y_0 - y_2) - (x_1 - x_2)(y_1 - y_2)) + ((x_0 - x_2)(y_0 - y_2) - (x_1 - x_0)(y_1 - y_0))u$. The first realization is

$$\begin{pmatrix} 1 & 1 & \bar{1} & 0 \\ 1 & 0 & 1 & 1 \\ 1 & \bar{1} & 0 & \bar{1} \end{pmatrix}, \qquad \begin{pmatrix} 1 & 1 & \bar{1} & 0 \\ 1 & 0 & 1 & 1 \\ 1 & \bar{1} & 0 & \bar{1} \end{pmatrix}, \qquad \begin{pmatrix} 1 & 1 & 1 & \bar{2} \\ 1 & 1 & \bar{2} & 1 \\ 1 & \bar{2} & 1 & 1 \end{pmatrix} \times \frac{1}{3}.$$

The second realization is

$$\begin{pmatrix} 1 & 1 & 1 & \bar{2} \\ 1 & 1 & \bar{2} & 1 \\ 1 & \bar{2} & 1 & 1 \end{pmatrix} \times \frac{1}{3}, \qquad \begin{pmatrix} 1 & 1 & \bar{1} & 0 \\ 1 & \bar{1} & 0 & \bar{1} \\ 1 & 0 & 1 & 1 \end{pmatrix}, \qquad \begin{pmatrix} 1 & 1 & \bar{1} & 0 \\ 1 & 0 & 1 & 1 \\ 1 & \bar{1} & 0 & \bar{1} \end{pmatrix}.$$

The resulting algorithm computes $s_1 = y_0 + y_1$, $s_2 = y_0 - y_1$, $s_3 = y_2 - y_0$, $s_4 = y_2 - y_1$, $s_5 = s_1 + y_2$; $m_1 = \frac{1}{3}(x_0 + x_1 + x_2)s_5$, $m_2 = \frac{1}{3}(x_0 + x_1 - 2x_2)s_2$, $m_3 = \frac{1}{3}(x_0 - 2x_1 + x_2)s_3$, $m_4 = \frac{1}{3}(-2x_0 + x_1 + x_2)s_4$; $t_1 = m_1 + m_2$, $t_2 = m_1 - m_2$, $t_3 = m_1 + m_3$, $w_0 = t_1 - m_3$, $w_1 = t_3 + m_4$, $w_2 = t_2 - m_4$.

52. Let $k = \langle k', k'' \rangle$ when $k \bmod n' = k'$ and $k \bmod n'' = k''$. Then we wish to compute $w_{\langle k', k'' \rangle} = \sum x_{\langle i', i'' \rangle} y_{\langle j', j'' \rangle}$ summed for $i' + j' \equiv k'$ (modulo n') and $i'' + j'' \equiv k''$ (modulo n''). This can be done by applying the n' algorithm to the $2n'$ vectors $X_{i'}$ and $Y_{j'}$ of length n'', obtaining the n' vectors $W_{k'}$. Each vector addition becomes n'' additions, each parameter multiplication becomes n'' parameter multiplications, and each chain multiplication of vectors is replaced by a cyclic convolution of degree n''. [If the subalgorithms use the minimum number of chain multiplications over the rationals, this algorithm uses $2(n' - d(n'))(n'' - d(n''))$ more than the minimum, where $d(n)$ is the number of divisors of n, because of exercise 4.6.2–32 and Theorem W.]

53. (a) Let $n(k) = (p-1)p^{e-k-1} = \varphi(p^{e-k})$ for $0 \le k < e$, and $n(k) = 1$ for $k \ge e$. Represent the numbers $\{1, \ldots, m\}$ in the form $a^i p^k$ (modulo m), where $0 \le k \le e$ and $0 \le i < n(k)$, and a is a fixed primitive element modulo p^e. For example, when $m = 9$ we can let $a = 2$; the values are $\{2^0 3^0, 2^1 3^0, 2^0 3^1, 2^2 3^0, 2^5 3^0, 2^1 3^1, 2^4 3^0, 2^3 3^0, 2^0 3^2\}$. Then $f(a^i p^k) = \sum_{0 \le l \le e} \sum_{0 \le j < n(l)} \omega^{g(i,j,k,l)} F(a^j p^l)$ where $g(i, j, k, l) = a^{i+j} p^{k+l}$.

We shall compute $f_{ikl} = \sum_{0 \le j < n(l)} \omega^{g(i,j,k,l)} F(a^j p^l)$ for $0 \le i < n(k)$ and for each k and l. This is a cyclic convolution of degree $n(k+l)$ on the values $x_i = \omega^{a^i p^{k+l}}$ and $y_s = \sum_{0 \le j < n(l)}[s + j \equiv 0 \pmod{n(k+l)}] F(a^j p^l)$, since f_{ikl} is $\sum x_r y_s$ summed over $r + s \equiv i \pmod{n(k+l)}$. The Fourier transform is obtained by summing appropriate f_{ikl}'s. [*Note:* When linear combinations of the x_i are formed, for example as in (69), the result will be purely real or purely imaginary, when the cyclic convolution algorithm has been constructed by using rule (59) with $u^{n(k)} - 1 = (u^{n(k)/2} - 1)(u^{n(k)/2} + 1)$. The reason is that reduction mod $(u^{n(k)/2} - 1)$ produces a polynomial with real coefficients $\omega^j + \omega^{-j}$ while reduction mod $(u^{n(k)/2} + 1)$ produces a polynomial with imaginary coefficients $\omega^j - \omega^{-j}$.]

When $p = 2$ an analogous construction applies, using the representation $(-1)^i a^j 2^k$ (modulo m), where $0 \le k \le e$ and $0 \le i \le \min(e-k, 1)$ and $0 \le j < 2^{e-k-2}$. In this case we use the construction of exercise 52 with $n' = 2$ and $n'' = 2^{e-k-2}$; although these numbers are not relatively prime, the construction does yield the desired direct product of cyclic convolutions.

(b) Let $a'm' + a''m'' = 1$; and let $\omega' = \omega^{a''m''}$, $\omega'' = \omega^{a'm'}$. Define $s' = s \bmod m'$, $s'' = s \bmod m''$, $t' = t \bmod m'$, $t'' = t \bmod m''$, so that $\omega^{st} = (\omega')^{s't'}(\omega'')^{s''t''}$. It follows that $f(s', s'') = \sum_{t'=0}^{m'-1} \sum_{t''=0}^{m''-1} (\omega')^{s't'}(\omega'')^{s''t''} F(t', t'')$; in other words, the one-dimensional Fourier transform on m elements is actually a two-dimensional Fourier transform on $m' \times m''$ elements, in slight disguise.

We shall deal with "normal" algorithms consisting of (i) a number of sums s_i of the F's and s's; followed by (ii) a number of products m_j, each of which is obtained by multiplying one of the F's or S's by a real or imaginary number α_j; followed by (iii) a number of further sums t_k, each of which is formed from m's or t's (not F's or s's). The final values must be m's or t's. For example, the "normal" Fourier transform

scheme for $m = 5$ constructed from (69) and the method of part (a) is as follows:
$s_1 = F(1) + F(4)$, $s_2 = F(3) + F(2)$, $s_3 = s_1 + s_2$, $s_4 = s_1 - s_2$, $s_5 = F(1) - F(4)$,
$s_6 = F(2) - F(3)$, $s_7 = s_5 - s_6$; $m_1 = \frac{1}{4}(\omega + \omega^2 + \omega^4 + \omega^3)s_3$, $m_2 = \frac{1}{4}(\omega - \omega^2 + \omega^4 - \omega^3)s_4$,
$m_3 = \frac{1}{2}(\omega + \omega^2 - \omega^4 - \omega^3)s_5$, $m_4 = \frac{1}{2}(-\omega + \omega^2 + \omega^4 - \omega^3)s_6$, $m_5 = \frac{1}{2}(\omega^3 - \omega^2)s_7$,
$m_6 = 1 \cdot F(5)$, $m_7 = 1 \cdot s_3$; $t_0 = m_1 + m_6$, $t_1 = t_0 + m_2$, $t_2 = m_3 + m_5$, $t_3 = t_0 - m_2$,
$t_4 = m_4 - m_5$, $t_5 = t_1 + t_2$, $t_6 = t_3 + t_4$, $t_7 = t_1 - t_2$, $t_8 = t_3 - t_4$, $t_9 = m_6 + m_7$.
Note the multiplication by 1 shown in m_6 and m_7; this is required by our conventions,
and it is important to include such cases for use in recursive constructions (although
the multiplications need not really be done). Here $m_6 = f_{001}$, $m_7 = f_{010}$, $t_5 = f_{000} + f_{001} = f(2^0)$, $t_6 = f_{100} + f_{101} = f(2^1)$, etc. We can improve the scheme by
introducing $s_8 = s_3 + F(5)$, replacing m_1 by $(\frac{1}{4}(\omega + \omega^2 + \omega^4 + \omega^3) - 1)s_3$ [this is $-\frac{5}{4}s_3$],
replacing m_6 by $1 \cdot s_8$, and deleting m_7 and t_9; this saves one of the trivial multiplications
by 1, and it will be advantageous when the scheme is used to build larger ones. In the
improved scheme, $f(5) = m_6$, $f(1) = t_5$, $f(2) = t_6$, $f(3) = t_8$, $f(4) = t_7$.

Now suppose we have normal one-dimensional schemes for m' and m'', using
respectively (a', a'') complex additions, (t', t'') trivial multiplications by ± 1 or $\pm i$, and
a total of (c', c'') complex multiplications including the trivial ones. (The nontrivial
complex multiplications are all "simple" since they involve only two real multiplications
and no real additions.) We can construct a normal scheme for the two-dimensional
$m' \times m''$ case by applying the m' scheme to vectors $F(t', *)$ of length m''. Each s_i
step becomes m'' additions; each m_j becomes a Fourier transform on m'' elements,
but with all of the α's in this algorithm multiplied by α_j; and each t_k becomes m''
additions. Thus the new algorithm has $(a'm'' + c'a'')$ complex additions, $t't''$ trivial
multiplications, and a total of $c'c''$ complex multiplications.

Using these techniques, Winograd has found normal one-dimensional schemes for
the following small values of m with the following costs (a, t, c):

$m = 2$ $(2, 2, 2)$	$m = 7$ $(36, 1, 9)$
$m = 3$ $(6, 1, 3)$	$m = 8$ $(26, 6, 8)$
$m = 4$ $(8, 4, 4)$	$m = 9$ $(46, 1, 12)$
$m = 5$ $(17, 1, 6)$	$m = 16$ $(74, 8, 18)$

By combining these schemes as described above, we obtain methods that use fewer
arithmetic operations than the "fast Fourier transform" (FFT) discussed in exercise 14.
For example, when $m = 1008 = 7 \cdot 9 \cdot 16$, the costs come to $(17946, 8, 1944)$, so we can do
a Fourier transform on 1008 complex numbers with 3872 real multiplications and 35892
real additions. It is possible to improve on Winograd's method for combining relatively
prime moduli by using multidimensional convolutions, as shown by Nussbaumer and
Quandalle in *IBM J. Res. and Devel.* **22** (1978), 134–144; their ingenious approach
reduces the amount of computation needed for 1008-point complex Fourier transforms
to 3084 real multiplications and 34668 real additions. By contrast, the FFT on 1024
complex numbers involves 14344 real multiplications and 27652 real additions. If the
two-passes-at-once improvement in the answer to exercise 14 is used, however, the FFT
on 1024 complex numbers needs only 10936 real multiplications and 25948 additions,
and it is not difficult to implement. Therefore the subtler methods are faster only on
machines that take significantly longer to multiply than to add.

[*References: Proc. Nat. Acad. Sci. USA* **73** (1976), 1005–1006; *Math. Comp.* **32**
(1978), 175–199; *Advances in Math.* **32** (1979), 83–117; *IEEE Trans.* **ASSP-27** (1979),
169–181.]

54. $\max(2e_1\deg(p_1) - 1, \ldots, 2e_q\deg(p_q) - 1, q + 1)$.

55. $2n' - q'$, where n' is the degree of the minimum polynomial of P (the monic polynomial μ of least degree such that $\mu(P)$ is the zero matrix) and q' is the number of distinct irreducible factors it has. (Reduce P by similarity transformations.)

56. Let $t_{ijk} + t_{jik} = \tau_{ijk} + \tau_{jik}$, for all i, j, k. If (A, B, C) is a realization of (t_{ijk}) of rank r, then $\sum_{l=1}^{r} c_{kl}\left(\sum_i a_{il}x_i\right)\left(\sum_j b_{jl}x_j\right) = \sum_{i,j} t_{ijk}x_ix_j = \sum_{i,j} \tau_{ijk}x_ix_j$ for all k. Conversely, let the lth chain multiplication of a polynomial chain, for $1 \le l \le r$, be the product $\left(\alpha_l + \sum_i \alpha_{il}x_i\right)\left(\beta_l + \sum_j \beta_{jl}x_j\right)$, where α_l and β_l denote possible constant terms and/or nonlinear terms. All terms of degree 2 appearing at any step of the chain can be expressed as a linear combination $\sum_{l=1}^{r} c_l\left(\sum_i a_{il}x_i\right)\left(\sum_j b_{jl}x_j\right)$; hence the chain defines a tensor (t_{ijk}) of rank $\le r$ such that $t_{ijk} + t_{jik} = \tau_{ijk} + \tau_{jik}$. This establishes the hint. Now $\mathrm{rank}(\tau_{ijk} + \tau_{jik}) = \mathrm{rank}(t_{ijk} + t_{jik}) \le \mathrm{rank}(t_{ijk}) + \mathrm{rank}(t_{jik}) = 2\,\mathrm{rank}(t_{ijk})$.

A bilinear form in $x_1, \ldots, x_m, y_1, \ldots, y_n$ is a quadratic form in $m + n$ variables, where $\tau_{ijk} = t_{i,j-m,k}$ for $i \le m$ and $j > m$, otherwise $\tau_{ijk} = 0$. Now $\mathrm{rank}(\tau_{ijk}) + \mathrm{rank}(\tau_{jik}) \ge \mathrm{rank}(t_{ijk})$, since we obtain a realization of (t_{ijk}) by suppressing the last n rows of A and the first m rows of B in a realization (A, B, C) of $(\tau_{ijk} + \tau_{jik})$.

57. Let N be the smallest power of 2 that exceeds $2n$, and let $u_{n+1} = \cdots = u_{N-1} = v_{n+1} = \cdots = v_{N-1} = 0$. If $U_s = \sum_{t=0}^{N-1} \omega^{st}u_t$ and $V_s = \sum_{t=0}^{N-1} \omega^{st}v_t$ for $0 \le s < N$, where $\omega = e^{2\pi i/N}$, then $\sum_{s=0}^{N-1} \omega^{-st}U_sV_s = N\sum u_{t_1}v_{t_2}$, where the latter sum is taken over all t_1 and t_2 with $0 \le t_1, t_2 < N$, $t_1 + t_2 \equiv t$ (modulo N). The terms vanish unless $t_1 \le n$ and $t_2 \le n$, so $t_1 + t_2 < N$; thus the sum is the coefficient of z^t in the product $u(z)v(z)$. If we use the method of exercise 14 to compute the Fourier transforms and the inverse transforms, the number of complex operations is $O(N\log N) + O(N\log N) + O(N) + O(N\log N)$; and $N \le 4n$. [See Section 4.3.3C and the paper by J. M. Pollard, *Math. Comp.* **25** (1971), 365–374.]

When multiplying integer polynomials, it is possible to use an *integer* number ω that is of order 2^t modulo a prime p, and to determine the results modulo sufficiently many primes. Useful primes in this regard, together with their least primitive roots r (from which we take $\omega = r^{(p-1)/2^t} \bmod p$ when $p \bmod 2^t = 1$), can be found as described in Section 4.5.4. For $t = 9$, the ten largest cases $< 2^{35}$ are $p = 2^{35} - 512a + 1$, where $(a, r) = (28, 7), (31, 10), (34, 13), (56, 3), (58, 10), (76, 5), (80, 3), (85, 11), (91, 5), (101, 3)$; the ten largest cases $< 2^{31}$ are $p = 2^{31} - 512a + 1$, where $(a, r) = (1, 10), (11, 3), (19, 11), (20, 3), (29, 3), (35, 3), (55, 19), (65, 6), (95, 3), (121, 10)$. For larger t, all primes p of the form $2^tq + 1$ where $q < 32$ is odd and $2^{24} < p < 2^{36}$ are given by $(p - 1, r) = (11 \cdot 2^{21}, 3), (25 \cdot 2^{20}, 3), (27 \cdot 2^{20}, 5), (25 \cdot 2^{22}, 3), (27 \cdot 2^{22}, 7), (5 \cdot 2^{25}, 3), (7 \cdot 2^{26}, 3), (27 \cdot 2^{26}, 13), (15 \cdot 2^{27}, 31), (17 \cdot 2^{27}, 3), (3 \cdot 2^{30}, 5), (13 \cdot 2^{28}, 3), (29 \cdot 2^{27}, 3), (23 \cdot 2^{29}, 5)$. Some of the latter primes can be used with $\omega = 2^e$ for appropriate small e. For a discussion of such primes, see R. M. Robinson, *Proc. Amer. Math. Soc.* **9** (1958), 673–681; S. W. Golomb, *Math. Comp.* **30** (1976), 657–663. Additional all-integer methods are cited in the answer to exercise 4.6–5.

However, the method of exercise 59 will almost always be preferable in practice.

58. (a) In general if (A, B, C) realizes (t_{ijk}), then $((x_1, \ldots, x_m)A, B, C)$ is a realization of the $1 \times n \times s$ matrix whose entry in row j, column k is $\sum x_i t_{ijk}$. So there must be at least as many nonzero elements in $(x_1, \ldots, x_m)A$ as the rank of this matrix. In the case of the $m \times n \times (m+n-1)$ tensor corresponding to polynomial multiplication of degree $m - 1$ by degree $n - 1$, the corresponding matrix has rank n whenever $(x_1, \ldots, x_m) \ne (0, \ldots, 0)$. A similar statement holds with $A \leftrightarrow B$ and $m \leftrightarrow n$.

Notes: In particular, if we work over the field of 2 elements, this says that the rows of A modulo 2 form a "linear code" of m vectors having distance at least n, whenever (A, B, C) is a realization consisting entirely of integers. This observation, due to R. W. Brockett and D. Dobkin [*Linear Algebra and Its Applications* **19** (1978), 207–235, Theorem 14; see also Lempel and Winograd, *IEEE Trans.* **IT-23** (1977), 503–508; Lempel, Seroussi, and Winograd, *Theoretical Comp. Sci.* **22** (1983), 285–296], can be used to obtain nontrivial lower bounds on the rank over the integers. For example, M. R. Brown and D. Dobkin [*IEEE Trans.* **C-29** (1980), 337–340] have used it to show that realizations of $n \times n$ polynomial multiplication over the integers must have rank $\geq \alpha n$ for all sufficiently large n, when α is any real number less than

$$\alpha_{\min} = 3.52762\,68026\,32407\,48061\,54754\,08128\,07512\,70182+;$$

here $\alpha_{\min} = 1/H(\sin^2 \theta, \cos^2 \theta)$, where $H(p, q) = p \lg(1/p) + q \lg(1/q)$ is the binary entropy function and $\theta \approx 1.34686$ is the root of $\sin^2(\theta - \pi/4) = H(\sin^2 \theta, \cos^2 \theta)$. An all-integer realization of rank $O(n \log n)$, based on cyclotomic polynomials, has been constructed by M. Kaminski [*J. Algorithms* **9** (1988), 137–147].

$$\text{(b)} \begin{pmatrix} 1\,0\,0\,0\,0\,1\,1\,1 \\ 0\,1\,0\,0\,1\,1\,0\,1 \\ 0\,0\,1\,1\,0\,0\,1\,1 \end{pmatrix}, \begin{pmatrix} 1\,0\,0\,0\,0\,1\,1\,1 \\ 0\,1\,0\,0\,0\,1\,0\,1 \\ 0\,0\,1\,0\,0\,0\,1\,1 \\ 0\,0\,0\,1\,1\,0\,0\,1 \end{pmatrix}, \begin{pmatrix} 1\,0\,0\,0\,0\,0\,0\,0 \\ \bar{1}\,\bar{1}\,0\,0\,0\,1\,0\,0 \\ \bar{1}\,1\,\bar{1}\,0\,0\,0\,1\,0 \\ 1\,0\,0\,\bar{1}\,\bar{1}\,\bar{1}\,\bar{1}\,1 \\ 0\,0\,1\,0\,1\,0\,0\,0 \\ 0\,0\,0\,1\,0\,0\,0\,0 \end{pmatrix}.$$

The following economical ways to realize the multiplication of general polynomials of degrees 2, 3, and 4 have been presented by H. Cohen and A. K. Lenstra [see *Math. Comp.* **48** (1987), S1–S2]:

$$\begin{pmatrix} 1\,0\,0\,1\,1\,0 \\ 0\,1\,0\,1\,0\,1 \\ 0\,0\,1\,0\,1\,1 \end{pmatrix}, \text{same,} \begin{pmatrix} 1\,0\,0\,0\,0\,0 \\ \bar{1}\,\bar{1}\,0\,1\,0\,0 \\ \bar{1}\,1\,\bar{1}\,0\,1\,0 \\ 0\,\bar{1}\,\bar{1}\,0\,0\,1 \\ 0\,0\,1\,0\,0\,0 \end{pmatrix};$$

$$\begin{pmatrix} 1\,0\,0\,0\,1\,1\,0\,0\,1 \\ 0\,1\,0\,0\,1\,0\,0\,1\,1 \\ 0\,0\,1\,0\,0\,1\,1\,0\,1 \\ 0\,0\,0\,1\,0\,0\,1\,1\,1 \end{pmatrix}, \text{same,} \begin{pmatrix} 1\,0\,0\,0\,0\,0\,0\,0\,0 \\ \bar{1}\,\bar{1}\,0\,0\,1\,0\,0\,0\,0 \\ \bar{1}\,1\,\bar{1}\,0\,0\,1\,0\,0\,0 \\ 1\,1\,1\,1\,\bar{1}\,\bar{1}\,\bar{1}\,\bar{1}\,1 \\ 0\,\bar{1}\,1\,\bar{1}\,0\,0\,0\,1\,0 \\ 0\,0\,\bar{1}\,\bar{1}\,0\,0\,1\,0\,0 \\ 0\,0\,0\,1\,0\,0\,0\,0\,0 \end{pmatrix};$$

$$\begin{pmatrix} 1\,0\,0\,1\,1\,0\,1\,0\,1\,1\,0\,0\,0\,0 \\ 0\,1\,0\,1\,0\,1\,0\,1\,1\,0\,1\,0\,0\,0 \\ 0\,0\,1\,0\,1\,1\,0\,0\,0\,1\,1\,0\,0\,0 \\ 0\,0\,0\,0\,0\,0\,1\,0\,1\,1\,0\,1\,0\,1 \\ 0\,0\,0\,0\,0\,0\,1\,1\,0\,1\,0\,1\,1 \end{pmatrix}, \text{same,} \begin{pmatrix} 1\,0\,0\,0\,0\,0\,0\,0\,0\,0\,0\,0\,0\,0 \\ \bar{1}\,\bar{1}\,0\,1\,0\,0\,0\,0\,0\,0\,0\,0\,0\,0 \\ \bar{1}\,1\,\bar{1}\,0\,1\,0\,0\,0\,0\,0\,0\,0\,0\,0 \\ \bar{1}\,\bar{1}\,\bar{1}\,0\,0\,1\,1\,0\,0\,0\,0\,\bar{1}\,0\,0 \\ 1\,1\,1\,\bar{1}\,0\,0\,\bar{1}\,\bar{1}\,1\,0\,0\,1\,1\,\bar{1} \\ 1\,\bar{1}\,0\,0\,\bar{1}\,0\,\bar{1}\,1\,0\,1\,0\,0\,\bar{1}\,0 \\ 0\,1\,0\,0\,0\,\bar{1}\,0\,\bar{1}\,0\,0\,1\,1\,0\,0 \\ 0\,0\,0\,0\,0\,0\,0\,0\,0\,0\,\bar{1}\,\bar{1}\,1 \\ 0\,0\,0\,0\,0\,0\,0\,0\,0\,0\,0\,0\,1\,0 \end{pmatrix}.$$

In each case the A and B matrices are identical.

59. [*IEEE Trans.* **ASSP-28** (1980), 205–215.] Note that cyclic convolution is polynomial multiplication mod $u^n - 1$, and negacyclic convolution is polynomial multiplication mod $u^n + 1$. Let us now change notation, replacing n by 2^n; we shall consider recursive algorithms for cyclic and negacyclic convolution $(z_0, \ldots, z_{2^n-1})$ of $(x_0, \ldots, x_{2^n-1})$ with $(y_0, \ldots, y_{2^n-1})$. The algorithms are presented in unoptimized form, for brevity and ease in exposition; readers who implement them will notice that many things can be streamlined. For example, the final value of $Z_{2m-1}(w)$ in step N5 will always be zero.

C1. [Test for simple case.] If $n = 1$, set

$$z_0 \leftarrow x_0 y_0 + x_1 y_1, \qquad z_1 \leftarrow (x_0 + x_1)(y_0 + y_1) - z_0,$$

and terminate. Otherwise set $m \leftarrow 2^{n-1}$.

C2. [Remainderize.] For $0 \le k < m$, set $(x_k, x_{m+k}) \leftarrow (x_k + x_{m+k}, x_k - x_{m+k})$ and $(y_k, y_{m+k}) \leftarrow (y_k + y_{m+k}, y_k - y_{m+k})$. (Now we have $x(u) \bmod (u^m - 1) = x_0 + \cdots + x_{m-1} u^{m-1}$ and $x(u) \bmod (u^m + 1) = x_m + \cdots + x_{2m-1} u^{m-1}$; we will compute $x(u)y(u) \bmod (u^m - 1)$ and $x(u)y(u) \bmod (u^m + 1)$, then we will combine the results by (59).)

C3. [Recurse.] Set $(z_0, \ldots, z_{m-1})$ to the cyclic convolution of $(x_0, \ldots, x_{m-1})$ with $(y_0, \ldots, y_{m-1})$. Also set $(z_m, \ldots, z_{2m-1})$ to the negacyclic convolution of $(x_m, \ldots, x_{2m-1})$ with $(y_m, \ldots, y_{2m-1})$.

C4. [Unremainderize.] For $0 \le k < m$, set $(z_k, z_{m+k}) \leftarrow \frac{1}{2}(z_k + z_{m+k}, z_k - z_{m+k})$. Now $(z_0, \ldots, z_{2m-1})$ is the desired answer. ∎

N1. [Test for simple case.] If $n = 1$, set $t \leftarrow x_0(y_0 + y_1)$, $z_0 \leftarrow t - (x_0 + x_1)y_1$, $z_1 \leftarrow t + (x_1 - x_0)y_0$, and terminate. Otherwise set $m \leftarrow 2^{\lfloor n/2 \rfloor}$ and $r \leftarrow 2^{\lceil n/2 \rceil}$. (The following steps use 2^{n+1} auxiliary variables X_{ij} for $0 \le i < 2m$ and $0 \le j < r$, to represent $2m$ polynomials $X_i(w) = X_{i0} + X_{i1}w + \cdots + X_{i(r-1)}w^{r-1}$; similarly, there are 2^{n+1} auxiliary variables Y_{ij}.)

N2. [Initialize auxiliary polynomials.] Set $X_{ij} \leftarrow X_{(i+m)j} \leftarrow x_{mj+i}$, $Y_{ij} \leftarrow Y_{(i+m)j} \leftarrow y_{mj+i}$, for $0 \le i < m$ and $0 \le j < r$. (At this point we have $x(u) = X_0(u^m) + uX_1(u^m) + \cdots + u^{m-1}X_{m-1}(u^m)$, and a similar formula holds for $y(u)$. Our strategy will be to multiply these polynomials modulo $(u^{mr} + 1) = (u^{2^n} + 1)$, by operating modulo $(w^r + 1)$ on the polynomials $X(w)$ and $Y(w)$, finding their cyclic convolution of length $2m$ and thereby obtaining $x(u)y(u) \equiv Z_0(u^m) + uZ_1(u^m) + \cdots + u^{2m-1}Z_{2m-1}(u^m)$.)

N3. [Transform.] (Now we will essentially do a fast Fourier transform on the polynomials $(X_0, \ldots, X_{m-1}, 0, \ldots, 0)$ and $(Y_0, \ldots, Y_{m-1}, 0, \ldots, 0)$, using $w^{r/m}$ as a $(2m)$th root of unity. This is efficient, because multiplication by a power of w is not really a multiplication at all.) For $j = \lfloor n/2 \rfloor - 1, \ldots, 1, 0$ (in this order), do the following for all m binary numbers $s + t = (s_{\lfloor n/2 \rfloor} \ldots s_{j+1} 0 \ldots 0)_2 + (0 \ldots 0 t_{j-1} \ldots t_0)_2$: Replace $(X_{s+t}(w), X_{s+t+2^j}(w))$ by the pair of polynomials $(X_{s+t}(w) + w^{(r/m)s'}X_{s+t+2^j}(w), X_{s+t}(w) - w^{(r/m)s'}X_{s+t+2^j}(w))$, where $s' = 2^j(s_{j+1} \ldots s_{\lfloor n/2 \rfloor})_2$. (We are evaluating 4.3.3–(39), with $K = 2m$ and $\omega = w^{r/m}$; notice the bit-reversal in s'. The polynomial operation $X_i(w) \leftarrow X_i(w) + w^k X_l(w)$ means, more precisely, that we set $X_{ij} \leftarrow X_{ij} + X_{l(j-k)}$ for $k \le j < r$, and $X_{ij} \leftarrow X_{ij} - X_{l(j-k+r)}$ for $0 \le j < k$. A copy of $X_l(w)$ can be made without wasting much space.) Do the same transformation on the Y's.

N4. [Recurse.] For $0 \le i < 2m$, set $(Z_{i0}, \ldots, Z_{i(r-1)})$ to the negacyclic convolution of $(X_{i0}, \ldots, X_{i(r-1)})$ and $(Y_{i0}, \ldots, Y_{i(r-1)})$.

N5. [Untransform.] For $j = 0, 1, \ldots, \lfloor n/2 \rfloor$ (in this order), and for all m choices of s and t as in steps N3, set $(Z_{s+t}(w), Z_{s+t+2^j}(w))$ to

$$\tfrac{1}{2}\big(Z_{s+t}(w) + Z_{s+t+2^j}(w), \, w^{-(r/m)s'}(Z_{s+t}(w) - Z_{s+t+2^j}(w))\big).$$

N6. [Repack.] (Now we have accomplished the goal stated at the end of step N2, since it is easy to show that the transform of the Z's is the product of the transforms of the X's and the Y's.) Set $z_i \leftarrow Z_{i0} - Z_{(m+i)(r-1)}$ and $z_{mj+i} \leftarrow Z_{ij} + Z_{(m+i)(j-1)}$ for $0 < j < r$, for $0 \le i < m$. ∎

It is easy to verify that at most n extra bits of precision are needed for the intermediate variables in this calculation; for example, if $|x_i| \le M$ for $0 \le i < 2^n$ at the beginning of the algorithm, then all of the x and X variables will be bounded by $2^n M$ throughout. All of the z and Z variables will be bounded by $(2^n M)^2$, which is n more bits than required to hold the final convolution.

Algorithm N performs A_n addition-subtractions, D_n halvings, and M_n multiplications, where $A_1 = 5$, $D_1 = 0$, $M_1 = 3$; for $n > 1$ we have $A_n = \lfloor n/2 \rfloor 2^{n+2} + 2^{\lfloor n/2 \rfloor + 1} A_{\lceil n/2 \rceil} + (\lfloor n/2 \rfloor + 1) 2^{n+1} + 2^n$, $D_n = 2^{\lfloor n/2 \rfloor + 1} D_{\lceil n/2 \rceil} + (\lfloor n/2 \rfloor + 1) 2^{n+1}$, and $M_n = 2^{\lfloor n/2 \rfloor + 1} M_{\lceil n/2 \rceil}$. The solutions are $A_n = 11 \cdot 2^{n-1+\lceil \lg n \rceil} - 3 \cdot 2^n + 6 \cdot 2^n S_n$, $D_n = 4 \cdot 2^{n-1+\lceil \lg n \rceil} - 2 \cdot 2^n + 2 \cdot 2^n S_n$, $M_n = 3 \cdot 2^{n-1+\lceil \lg n \rceil}$; here S_n satisfies the recurrence $S_1 = 0$, $S_n = 2S_{\lceil n/2 \rceil} + \lfloor n/2 \rfloor$, and it is not difficult to prove the inequalities $\tfrac{1}{2} n \lceil \lg n \rceil \le S_n \le S_{n+1} \le \tfrac{1}{2} n \lg n + n$ for all $n \ge 1$. Algorithm C does approximately the same amount of work as Algorithm N.

60. (a) In Σ_1, for example, we can group all terms having a common value of j and k into a single trilinear term; this gives ν^2 trilinear terms when $(j,k) \in E \times E$, plus ν^2 when $(j,k) \in E \times O$ and ν^2 when $(j,k) \in O \times E$. When $\tilde{j} = k$ we can also include $-x_{j\tilde{j}} y_{j\tilde{j}} z_{\tilde{j}j}$ in Σ_1, free of charge. [In the case $n = 10$, the method multiplies 10×10 matrices with 710 noncommutative multiplications; this is almost as good as seven 5×5 multiplications by the method of Makarov cited in the answer to exercise 12, although Winograd's scheme (35) uses only 600 when commutativity is allowed. With a similar scheme, Pan showed for the first time that $M(n) < n^{2.8}$ for all large n, and this awakened great interest in the problem. See *SICOMP* **9** (1980), 321–342.]

(b) Here we simply let S be all the indices (i,j,k) of one problem, $\tilde{S}$ the indices $[k,i,j]$ of the other, and work with an $(mn+sm) \times (ns+mn) \times (sm+ns)$ tensor. [When $m = n = s = 10$, the result is quite surprising: We can multiply two separate 10×10 matrices with 1300 noncommutative multiplications, while no scheme is known that would multiply each of them with 650.]

61. (a) Replace $a_{il}(u)$ by $u a_{il}(u)$. (b) Let $a_{il}(u) = \sum_{\mu} a_{il\mu} u^{\mu}$, etc., in a polynomial realization of length $r = \operatorname{rank}_d(t_{ijk})$. Then $t_{ijk} = \sum_{\mu+\nu+\sigma=d} \sum_{l=1}^{r} a_{il\mu} b_{jl\nu} c_{kl\sigma}$. [This result can be improved to $\operatorname{rank}(t_{ijk}) \le (2d+1)\operatorname{rank}_d(t_{ijk})$ in an infinite field, because the trilinear form $\sum_{\mu+\nu+\sigma=d} a_\mu b_\nu c_\sigma$ corresponds to multiplication of polynomials modulo u^{d+1}, as pointed out by Bini and Pan. See *Calcolo* **17** (1980), 87–97.] (c, d) This is clear from the realizations in exercise 48.

(e) Suppose we have realizations of t and rt' such that $\sum_{l=1}^{r} a_{il} b_{jl} c_{kl} = t_{ijk} u^d + O(u^{d+1})$ and $\sum_{L=1}^{R} A_{\langle ii' \rangle L} B_{\langle jj' \rangle L} C_{\langle kk' \rangle L} = [i = j = k] t'_{i'j'k'} u^{d'} + O(u^{d'+1})$. Then

$$\sum_{L=1}^{R} \sum_{l=1}^{r} a_{il} A_{\langle li' \rangle L} \sum_{m=1}^{r} b_{jm} B_{\langle mj' \rangle L} \sum_{n=1}^{r} c_{kn} C_{\langle nk' \rangle L} = t_{ijk} t'_{i'j'k'} u^{d+d'} + O(u^{d+d'+1}).$$

62. The rank is 3, by the method of proof in Theorem W with $P = \left(\begin{smallmatrix} 0 & 1 \\ 0 & 0 \end{smallmatrix}\right)$. The border rank cannot be 1, since we cannot have $a_1(u)b_1(u)c_1(u) \equiv a_1(u)b_2(u)c_2(u) \equiv u^d$ and $a_1(u)b_2(u)c_1(u) \equiv a_1(u)b_1(u)c_2(u) \equiv 0$ (modulo u^{d+1}). The border rank is 2 because of the realization $\left(\begin{smallmatrix} 1 & 1 \\ u & 0 \end{smallmatrix}\right)$, $\left(\begin{smallmatrix} u & 0 \\ 1 & 1 \end{smallmatrix}\right)$, $\left(\begin{smallmatrix} 1 & -1 \\ 0 & u \end{smallmatrix}\right)$.

The notion of border rank was introduced by Bini, Capovani, Lotti, and Romani in *Information Processing Letters* **8** (1979), 234–235.

63. (a) Let the elements of $T(m,n,s)$ and $T(M,N,S)$ be denoted by $t_{\langle i,j'\rangle \langle j,k'\rangle \langle k,i'\rangle}$ and $T_{\langle I,J'\rangle \langle J,K'\rangle \langle K,I'\rangle}$, respectively. Each element $\mathcal{T}_{\langle \mathcal{I},J'\rangle \langle \mathcal{J},K'\rangle \langle \mathcal{K},\mathcal{I}'\rangle}$ of the direct product, where $\mathcal{I} = \langle i,I\rangle$, $\mathcal{J} = \langle j,J\rangle$, and $\mathcal{K} = \langle k,K\rangle$, is equal to $t_{\langle i,j'\rangle \langle j,k'\rangle \langle k,i'\rangle} \times T_{\langle I,J'\rangle \langle J,K'\rangle \langle K,I'\rangle}$ by definition, so it is $[\mathcal{I}' = \mathcal{I}$ and $\mathcal{J}' = \mathcal{J}$ and $\mathcal{K}' = \mathcal{K}]$.

(b) Apply exercise 61(e) with $M(N) = \underline{\mathrm{rank}}_0(T(N,N,N))$.

(c) We have $M(mns) \leq r^3$, since $T(mns, mns, mns) = T(m,n,s) \otimes T(n,s,m) \otimes T(s,m,n)$. If $M(n) \leq R$ we have $M(n^h) \leq R^h$ for all h, and it follows that $M(N) \leq M(n^{\lceil \log_n N\rceil}) \leq R^{\lceil \log_n N\rceil} \leq RN^{\log R/\log n}$. [This result appears in Pan's paper of 1972.]

(d) We have $M_d(mns) \leq r^3$ for some d, where $M_d(n) = \mathrm{rank}_d(T(n,n,n))$. If $M_d(n) \leq R$ we have $M_{hd}(n^h) \leq R^h$ for all h, and the stated formula follows since $M(n^h) \leq \binom{hd+2}{2}R^h$ by exercise 61(b). In an infinite field we save a factor of $\log N$. [This result is due to Bini and Schönhage, 1979.]

64. We have $\sum_k (f_k(u) + \sum_{j\neq k} g_{j,k}(u)) = u^2 \sum_{1\leq i,j,k\leq 3} x_{ij}y_{jk}z_{ki} + O(u^3)$, when $f_k(u) = (x_{k1} + u^2 x_{k2})(y_{2k} + u^2 y_{1k})z_{kk} + (x_{k1} + u^2 x_{k3})y_{3k}((1+u)z_{kk} - u(z_{k1} + z_{k2} + z_{k3})) - x_{k1}(y_{2k} + y_{3k})(z_{k1} + z_{k2} + z_{k3})$ and $g_{jk}(u) = (x_{k1} + u^2 x_{j2})(y_{2k} - uy_{1j})(z_{kj} - uz_{jk}) + (x_{k1} + u^2 x_{j3})(y_{2k} + uy_{1j})z_{kj}$. [The best upper bound known for rank($T(3,3,3)$) is 23; see the answer to exercise 12. The border rank of $T(2,2,2)$ remains unknown.]

65. The polynomial in the hint is $u^2 \sum_{i=1}^{m} \sum_{j=1}^{n} (x_i y_j z_{ij} + X_{ij}Y_{ij}Z) + O(u^3)$. Let X_{ij} and Y_{ij} be indeterminates for $1 \leq i < m$ and $1 \leq j < n$; also set $X_{in} = Y_{mj} = 0$, $X_{mj} = -\sum_{i=1}^{m-1} X_{ij}$, $Y_{in} = -\sum_{j=1}^{n-1} Y_{ij}$. Thus with $mn + 1$ multiplications of polynomials in the indeterminates we can compute $x_i y_j$ for each i and j and also $\sum_{i=1}^{m} \sum_{j=1}^{n} X_{ij}Y_{ij} = \sum_{i=1}^{m-1} \sum_{j=1}^{n-1} X_{ij}Y_{ij}$. [*SICOMP* **10** (1981), 434–455. In this classic paper Schönhage also derived, among other things, the results of exercises 64, 66, and 67(i).]

66. (a) Let $\omega = \liminf_{n\to\infty} \log M(n)/\log n$; we have $\omega \geq 2$ by Lemma T. For all $\epsilon > 0$, there is an N with $M(N) < N^{\omega + \epsilon}$. The argument of exercise 63(c) now shows that $\log M(n)/\log n < \omega + 2\epsilon$ for all sufficiently large n.

(b) This is an immediate consequence of exercise 63(d).

(c) Let $r = \underline{\mathrm{rank}}(t)$, $q = (mns)^{\omega/3}$, $Q = (MNS)^{\omega/3}$. Given $\epsilon > 0$, there is an integer constant c_ϵ such that $M(p) \leq c_\epsilon p^{\omega + \epsilon}$ for all positive integers p. For every integer $h > 0$ we have $t^h = \bigoplus_k \binom{h}{k} T(m^k M^{h-k}, n^k N^{h-k}, s^k S^{h-k})$, and $\underline{\mathrm{rank}}(t^h) \leq r^h$. Given h and k, let $p = \lfloor \binom{h}{k}^{1/(\omega + \epsilon)} \rfloor$. Then

$$\underline{\mathrm{rank}}(T(pm^k M^{h-k}, pn^k N^{h-k}, ps^k S^{h-k})) \leq \underline{\mathrm{rank}}(M(p)T(m^k M^{h-k}, n^k N^{h-k}, s^k S^{h-k}))$$
$$\leq \underline{\mathrm{rank}}(c_\epsilon \binom{h}{k} T(m^k M^{h-k}, n^k N^{h-k}, s^k S^{h-k}))$$
$$\leq c_\epsilon r^h$$

by exercise 63(b), and it follows from part (b) that

$$p^\omega q^k Q^{h-k} = (pm^k M^{h-k} pn^k N^{h-k} ps^k S^{h-k})^{\omega/3} \leq c_\epsilon r^h.$$

Since $p \geq \binom{h}{k}^{1/(\omega+\epsilon)}/2$ we have

$$\binom{h}{k} q^k Q^{h-k} \leq \binom{h}{k}^{\epsilon/(\omega+\epsilon)} (2p)^\omega q^k Q^{h-k} \leq 2^{\epsilon h/(\omega+\epsilon)} 2^\omega c_\epsilon r^h.$$

Therefore $(q+Q)^h \leq (h+1) 2^{\epsilon h/(\omega+\epsilon)} 2^\omega c_\epsilon r^h$ for all h. And it follows that we must have $q + Q \leq 2^{\epsilon/(\omega+\epsilon)} r$ for all $\epsilon > 0$.

(d) Set $m = n = 4$ in exercise 65, and note that $16^{0.85} + 9^{0.85} > 17$.

67. (a) The $mn \times mns^2$ matrix $(t_{\langle ij'\rangle(\langle jk'\rangle\langle ki'\rangle)})$ has rank mn because it is a permutation matrix when restricted to the mn rows for which $k = k' = 1$.

(b) $((t \oplus t')_{i(jk)})$ is essentially $(t_{i(jk)}) \oplus (t'_{i(jk)})$, plus $n's + sn'$ additional columns of zeros. [Similarly we have $((t \otimes t')_{i(jk)}) = (t_{i(jk)}) \otimes (t'_{i(jk)})$ for the direct product.]

(c) Let D be the diagonal matrix $\mathrm{diag}(d_1, \ldots, d_r)$, so that $ADB^T = O$. We know by Lemma T that $\mathrm{rank}(A) = m$ and $\mathrm{rank}(B) = n$; hence $\mathrm{rank}(AD) = m$ and $\mathrm{rank}(DB^T) = n$. We can assume without loss of generality that the first m columns of A are linearly independent. Since the columns of B^T are in the null space of AD, we may also assume that the last n columns of B are linearly independent. Write A in the partitioned form $(A_1 \, A_2 \, A_3)$ where A_1 is $m \times m$ (and nonsingular), A_2 is $m \times q$, and A_3 is $m \times n$. Also partition D so that $AD = (A_1 D_1 \, A_2 D_2 \, A_3 D_3)$. Then there is a $q \times r$ matrix $W = (W_1 \, I \, O)$ such that $ADW^T = O$, namely $W_1 = -D_2 A_2^T A_1^{-T} D_1^{-1}$. Similarly, we may write $B = (B_1 \, B_2 \, B_3)$, and we find $VDB^T = O$ when $V = (O \, I \, V_3)$ is the $q \times r$ matrix with $V_3 = -D_2 B_2^T B_3^{-T} D_3^{-1}$. Notice that $UDV^T = D_2$, so the hint is established (more or less — after all, it was just a hint).

Now we let $A_{il}(u) = a_{il}$ for $1 \leq i \leq m$, $A_{(m+i)l}(u) = uv_{il}/d_{m+i}$; $B_{jl}(u) = b_{jl}$ for $1 \leq j \leq n$, $B_{(n+j)l}(u) = w_{jl}u$; $C_{kl}(u) = u^2 c_{kl}$ for $1 \leq k \leq s$, $C_{(s+1)l}(u) = d_l$. It follows that $\sum_{l=1}^r A_{il}(u) B_{jl}(u) C_{kl}(u) = u^2 t_{ijk} + O(u^3)$ if $k \leq s$, $u^2 [i > m][j > n]$ if $k = s+1$. [In this proof we did not need to assume that t is nondegenerate with respect to C.]

(d) Consider the following realization of $T(m, 1, n)$ with $r = mn+1$: $a_{il} = [\lfloor l/n \rfloor = i-1]$, $b_{jl} = [l \bmod n = j]$, $b_{\langle ij\rangle l} = [l = (i-1)n + j]$, if $l \leq mn$; $a_{ir} = 1$, $b_{jr} = -1$, $c_{\langle ij\rangle r} = 0$. This is improvable with $d_l = 1$ for $1 \leq l \leq r$.

(e) The idea is to find an improvable realization of $T(m, n, s)$. Suppose (A, B, C) is a realization of length r. Given arbitrary integers $\alpha_1, \ldots, \alpha_m, \beta_1, \ldots, \beta_s$, extend A, B, and C by defining

$$A_{\langle ij'\rangle(r+p)} = \alpha_i[j'=p], \quad B_{\langle jk'\rangle(r+p)} = \beta_{k'}[j=p], \quad C_{\langle ki'\rangle(r+p)} = 0, \text{ for } 1 \leq p \leq n.$$

If $d_l = \sum_{i'=1}^m \sum_{k=1}^s \alpha_{i'} \beta_k c_{\langle ki'\rangle l}$ for $l \leq r$ and $d_l = -1$ otherwise, we have

$$\sum_{l=1}^{r+n} A_{\langle ij'\rangle l} B_{\langle jk'\rangle l} d_l = \sum_{i'=1}^m \sum_{k=1}^s \alpha_{i'} \beta_k \sum_{l=1}^r A_{\langle ij'\rangle l} B_{\langle jk'\rangle l} C_{\langle ki'\rangle l} - \sum_{p=1}^n \alpha_i[j'=p] \beta_{k'}[j=p]$$

$$= [j=j'] \alpha_i \beta_{k'} - [j=j'] \alpha_i \beta_{k'} = 0;$$

so this is improvable if $d_1 \ldots d_r \neq 0$. But $d_1 \ldots d_r$ is a polynomial in $(\alpha_1, \ldots, \alpha_m, \beta_1, \ldots, \beta_s)$, not identically zero, since we can assume without loss of generality that C has no all-zero columns. Therefore some choice of α's and β's will work.

(f) If $M(n) = n^\omega$ we have $M(n^h) = n^{h\omega}$, hence

$$\underline{\mathrm{rank}}(T(n^h, n^h, n^h) \oplus T(1, n^{h\omega} - n^h(2n^h - 1), 1)) \leq n^{h\omega} + n^h.$$

Exercise 66(c) now implies that $n^{h\omega} + (n^{h\omega} - 2n^{2h} + n^h)^{\omega/3} \leq n^{h\omega} + n^h$ for all h. Therefore $\omega = 2$; but this contradicts the lower bound $2n^2 - 1$ (see the answer to exercise 12).

(g) Let $f(u)$ and $g(u)$ be polynomials such that the elements of $Vf(u)$ and $Wg(u)$ are polynomials. Then we redefine

$$A_{(i+m)l} = u^{d+1}v_{il}f(u)/d_{i+m}, \ B_{(j+n)l} = u^{d+1}w_{jl}g(u)/p, \ C_{kl} = u^{d+e+2}c_{kl},$$

where $f(u)g(u) = pu^e + O(u^{e+1})$. It follows that $\sum_{l=1}^{r} A_{il}(u)B_{jl}(u)C_{kl}(u)$ is equal to $u^{d+e+2}t_{ijk} + O(u^{d+e+3})$ if $k \le s$, $u^{d+e+2}[i > m][j > n]$ if $k = s+1$. [*Note:* The result of (e) therefore holds over any field, if rank$_2$ is replaced by rank, since we can choose the α's and β's to be polynomials of the form $1 + O(u)$.]

(h) Let row p of C refer to the component $T(1, 16, 1)$. The key point is that $\sum_{l=1}^{r} a_{il}(u)b_{jl}(u)c_{pl}(u)$ is zero (not simply $O(u^{d+1})$) for all i and j that remain after deletion; moreover, $c_{pl}(u) \neq 0$ for all l. These properties are true in the constructions of parts (c) and (g), and they remain true when we take direct products.

(i) The proof generalizes from binomials to multinomials in a straightforward way.

(j) After part (h) we have $81^{\omega/3} + 2(36^{\omega/3}) + 34^{\omega/3} \le 100$, so $\omega < 2.52$. Squaring once again gives rank$(T(81, 1, 81) \oplus 4T(27, 4, 27) \oplus 2T(9, 34, 9) \oplus 4T(9, 16, 9) \oplus 4T(3, 136, 3) \oplus T(1, 3334, 1)) \le 10000$; this yields $\omega < 2.4999$. Success! Continued squaring leads to better and better bounds that converge rapidly to $2.497723729083\ldots$. If we had started with $T(4, 1, 4) \oplus T(1, 9, 1)$ instead of $T(3, 1, 3) \oplus T(1, 4, 1)$, the limiting bound would have been $2.51096309\ldots$.

[Similar tricks yield $\omega < 2.496$; see *SICOMP* **11** (1982), 472–492.]

68. T. M. Vari has shown that $n - 1$ multiplications are necessary, by proving that n multiplications are necessary to compute $x_1^2 + \cdots + x_n^2$ [Cornell Computer Science Report 120 (1972)]. C. Pandu Rangan showed that if we compute the polynomial as $L_1R_1 + \cdots + L_{n-1}R_{n-1}$, where the L's and R's are linear combinations of the x's, at least $n - 2$ additions are needed to form the L's and R's [*J. Algorithms* **4** (1983), 282–285]. But his lower bound does not obviously apply to all polynomial chains.

69. Let $y_{ij} = x_{ij} - [i = j]$, and apply the recursive construction (31) to the matrix $I + Y$, using arithmetic on power series in the n^2 variables y_{ij} but ignoring all terms of total degree $> n$. Each entry h of the array is represented as a sum $h_0 + h_1 + \cdots + h_n$, where h_k is the value of a homogeneous polynomial of degree k. Then every addition step becomes $n + 1$ additions, and every multiplication step becomes $\approx \frac{1}{2}n^2$ multiplications and $\approx \frac{1}{2}n^2$ additions. Furthermore, every division is by a quantity of the form $1 + h_1 + \cdots + h_n$, since all divisions in the recursive construction are by 1 when the y_{ij} are entirely zero; therefore division is slightly easier than multiplication (see Eq. 4.7–(3) when $V_0 = 1$). Since we stop when reaching a 2×2 determinant, we need not subtract 1 from y_{jj} when $j > n - 2$. It turns out that when redundant computations are suppressed, this method requires $20\binom{n}{5} + 8\binom{n}{4} + 12\binom{n}{3} - 4\binom{n}{2} + 5n - 4$ multiplications and $20\binom{n}{5} + 8\binom{n}{4} + 4\binom{n}{3} + 24\binom{n}{2} - n$ additions, thus $\frac{1}{6}n^5 - O(n^4)$ of each. A similar method can be used to eliminate division in many other cases; see *Crelle* **264** (1973), 184–202. (But the next exercise constructs an even faster divisionless scheme for determinants.)

70. Set $A = \lambda - x$, $B = -u$, $C = -v$, and $D = \lambda I - Y$ in the hinted identity, then take the determinant of both sides, using the fact that $I/\lambda + Y/\lambda^2 + Y^2/\lambda^3 + \cdots$ is the inverse of D as a formal power series in $1/\lambda$. We need to compute $uY^k v$ only for $0 \le k \le n - 2$, because we know that $f_X(\lambda)$ is a polynomial of degree n; thus, only $n^3 + O(n^2)$ multiplications and $n^3 + O(n^2)$ additions are needed to advance from degree $n - 1$ to degree n. Proceeding recursively, we obtain the coefficients of f_X from the elements of X after doing $6\binom{n}{4} + 7\binom{n}{3} + 2\binom{n}{2}$ multiplications and $6\binom{n}{4} + 5\binom{n}{3} + 2\binom{n}{2}$ addition-subtractions.

If we only want to compute $\det X = (-1)^n f_X(0)$, we save $3\binom{n}{2} - n + 1$ multiplications and $\binom{n}{2}$ additions. This division-free method for determinant evaluation is in fact quite economical when n has a moderate size; it beats the obvious cofactor expansion scheme when $n > 4$.

If ω is the exponent of matrix multiplication in exercise 66, the same approach leads to a division-free computation in $O(n^{\omega+1+\epsilon})$ steps, because the vectors uY^k for $0 \le k < n$ can be evaluated in $O(M(n)\log n)$ steps: Take a matrix whose first 2^l rows are uY^k for $0 \le k < 2^l$ and multiply it by Y^{2^l}; then the first 2^l rows of the product are uY^k for $2^l \le k < 2^{l+1}$. [See S. J. Berkowitz, *Inf. Processing Letters* **18** (1984), 147–150.] Of course such asymptotically "fast" matrix multiplication is strictly of theoretical interest. E. Kaltofen has shown how to evaluate determinants with only $O(n^{2+\epsilon}\sqrt{M(n)})$ additions, subtractions, and multiplications [*Proc. Int. Symp. Symb. Alg. Comp.* **17** (1992), 342–349]; his method is interesting even with $M(n) = n^3$.

71. Suppose $g_1 = u_1 \circ v_1, \ldots, g_r = u_r \circ v_r$, and $f = \alpha_1 g_1 + \cdots + \alpha_r g_r + p_0$, where $u_k = \beta_{k1}g_1 + \cdots + \beta_{k(k-1)}g_{k-1} + p_k$, $v_k = \gamma_{k1}g_1 + \cdots + \gamma_{k(k-1)}g_{k-1} + q_k$, each $\circ$ is "$\times$" or "$/$", and each p_j or q_j is a polynomial of degree ≤ 1 in $x_1, \ldots, x_n$. Compute auxiliary quantities w_k, y_k, z_k for $k = r, r-1, \ldots, 1$ as follows: $w_k = \alpha_k + \beta_{(k+1)k}y_{k+1} + \gamma_{(k+1)k}z_{k+1} + \cdots + \beta_{rk}y_r + \gamma_{rk}z_r$, and

$$\begin{aligned} y_k = w_k \times v_k, \quad & z_k = w_k \times u_k, \qquad && \text{if } g_k = u_k \times v_k; \\ y_k = w_k/v_k, \quad & z_k = -y_k \times g_k, \qquad && \text{if } g_k = u_k/v_k. \end{aligned}$$

Then $f' = p_0' + p_1'y_1 + q_1'z_1 + \cdots + p_r'y_r + q_r'z_r$, where $'$ denotes the derivative with respect to any of $x_1, \ldots, x_n$. [W. Baur and V. Strassen, *Theoretical Comp. Sci.* **22** (1983), 317–330. A related method had been published by S. Linnainmaa, *BIT* **16** (1976), 146–160, who applied it to analysis of rounding errors.] We save two chain multiplications if $g_r = u_r \times v_r$, since $w_r = \alpha_r$. Repeating the construction gives all second partial derivatives with at most $9m + 3d$ chain multiplications and $4d$ divisions.

72. There is an algorithm to compute the tensor rank over algebraically closed fields like the complex numbers, since this is a special case of the results of Alfred Tarski, *A Decision Method for Elementary Algebra and Geometry*, 2nd edition (Berkeley, California: Univ. of California Press, 1951); but the known methods do not make this computation really feasible except for very small tensors. Over the field of rational numbers, the problem isn't even known to be solvable in finite time.

73. In such a polynomial chain on N variables, the determinant of any $N \times N$ matrix for N of the linear forms known after l addition-subtraction steps is at most 2^l. And in the discrete Fourier transform, the matrix of the final $N = m_1 \ldots m_n$ linear forms has determinant $N^{N/2}$, since its square is N times a permutation matrix by exercise 13. [*JACM* **20** (1973), 305–306.]

74. (a) If $k = (k_1, \ldots, k_s)^T$ is a vector of relatively prime integers, so is Uk, since any common divisor of the elements of Uk divides all elements of $k = U^{-1}Uk$. Therefore VUk cannot have all integer components.

(b) Suppose there is a polynomial chain for Vx with t multiplications. If $t = 0$, the entries of V must all be integers, so $s = 0$. Otherwise let $\lambda_i = \alpha \times \lambda_k$ or $\lambda_i = \lambda_j \times \lambda_k$ be the first multiplication step. We can assume that $\lambda_k = n_1x_1 + \cdots + n_sx_s + \beta$ where $n_1, \ldots, n_s$ are integers, not all zero, and β is constant. Find a unimodular matrix U such that $(n_1, \ldots, n_s)U = (0, \ldots, 0, d)$, where $d = \gcd(n_1, \ldots, n_s)$. (The algorithm discussed before Eq. 4.5.2–(14) implicitly defines such a U.) Construct a new polynomial chain with inputs $y_1, \ldots, y_{s-1}$ as follows: First calculate $x = (x_1, \ldots, x_s)^T = U(y_1, \ldots, y_{s-1}, -\beta/d)^T$, then continue with the assumed polynomial chain for Vx. When step i of that chain is reached, we will have $\lambda_k = (n_1, \ldots, n_s)x + \beta = 0$, so we can simply set $\lambda_i = 0$ instead of multiplying. After Vx has been evaluated, add the constant vector $w\beta/d$ to the result, where w is the rightmost column of VU, and let W be the other $s - 1$ columns of VU. The new polynomial chain has computed $Vx + w\beta/d = VU(y_1, \ldots, y_{s-1}, -\beta/d)^T + w\beta/d = W(y_1, \ldots, y_{s-1})^T$, with $t - 1$ multiplications. But the columns of W are Z-independent, by part (a); hence $t - 1 \geq s - 1$, by induction on s, and we have $t \geq s$.

(c) Let $x_j = 0$ for the $t - s$ values of j that aren't in the set of Z-independent columns. Any chain for Vx then evaluates $V'x'$ for a matrix V' to which part (b) applies.

(d) $\lambda_1 = x - y$, $\lambda_2 = \lambda_1 + \lambda_1$, $\lambda_3 = \lambda_2 + x$, $\lambda_4 = (1/6) \times \lambda_3$, $\lambda_5 = \lambda_4 + \lambda_4$, $\lambda_6 = \lambda_5 + y \; (= x + y/3)$, $\lambda_7 = \lambda_6 - \lambda_1$, $\lambda_8 = \lambda_7 + \lambda_4 \; (= x/2 + y)$. But $\{x/2 + y, x + y/2\}$ needs two multiplications, since the columns of $\left(\begin{smallmatrix} 1/2 & 1 \\ 1 & 1/2 \end{smallmatrix}\right)$ are Z-independent. [*Journal of Information Processing* **1** (1978), 125–129.]

SECTION 4.7

1. Find the first nonzero coefficient V_m, as in (4), and divide both $U(z)$ and $V(z)$ by z^m (shifting the coefficients m places to the left). The quotient will be a power series if and only if $U_0 = \cdots = U_{m-1} = 0$.

2. We have $V_0^{n+1}W_n = V_0^n U_n - (V_0^1 W_0)(V_0^{n-1}V_n) - (V_0^2 W_1)(V_0^{n-2}V_{n-1}) - \cdots - (V_0^n W_{n-1})(V_0^0 V_1)$. Thus, we can start by replacing (U_j, V_j) by $(V_0^j U_j, V_0^{j-1}V_j)$ for $j \geq 1$, then set $W_n \leftarrow U_n - \sum_{k=0}^{n-1} W_k V_{n-k}$ for $n \geq 0$, finally replace W_j by W_j/V_0^{j+1} for $j \geq 0$. Similar techniques are possible in connection with other algorithms in this section.

3. Yes. When $\alpha = 0$, it is easy to prove by induction that $W_1 = W_2 = \cdots = 0$. When $\alpha = 1$, we find $W_n = V_n$, by the cute identity

$$\sum_{k=1}^{n} \left(\frac{k - (n - k)}{n} \right) V_k V_{n-k} = V_n V_0.$$

4. If $W(z) = e^{V(z)}$, then $W'(z) = V'(z)W(z)$; we find $W_0 = e^{V_0}$, and

$$W_n = \sum_{k=1}^{n} \frac{k}{n} V_k W_{n-k}, \qquad \text{for } n \geq 1.$$

If $W(z) = \ln V(z)$, the roles of V and W are reversed; hence when $V_0 = 1$ the rule is $W_0 = 0$ and $W_n = V_n + \sum_{k=1}^{n-1}(k/n - 1)V_k W_{n-k}$ for $n \geq 1$.

[By exercise 6, the logarithm can be obtained to order n in $O(n \log n)$ operations. R. P. Brent observes that $\exp(V(z))$ can also be calculated with this asymptotic speed by applying Newton's method to $f(x) = \ln x - V(z)$; therefore general exponentiation $(1+V(z))^\alpha = \exp(\alpha \ln(1+V(z)))$ is $O(n \log n)$ too. *Reference: Analytic Computational Complexity*, edited by J. F. Traub (New York: Academic Press, 1975), 172–176.]

5. We get the original series back. This can be used to test a reversion algorithm.

6. $\phi(x) = x + x(1 - xV(z))$; see Algorithm 4.3.3R. Thus after $W_0, \ldots, W_{N-1}$ are known, the idea is to input $V_N, \ldots, V_{2N-1}$, compute $(W_0 + \cdots + W_{N-1}z^{N-1}) \times (V_0 + \cdots + V_{2N-1}z^{2N-1}) = 1 + R_0 z^N + \cdots + R_{N-1}z^{2N-1} + O(z^{2N})$, and let $W_N + \cdots + W_{2N-1}z^{N-1} = -(W_0 + \cdots + W_{N-1}z^{N-1})(R_0 + \cdots + R_{N-1}z^{N-1}) + O(z^N)$.

[*Numer. Math.* **22** (1974), 341–348; this algorithm was, in essence, first published by M. Sieveking, *Computing* **10** (1972), 153–156.] Note that the total time for N coefficients is $O(N \log N)$ arithmetic operations if we use "fast" polynomial multiplication (exercise 4.6.4–57).

7. $W_n = \binom{mk}{k}/n$ when $n = (m-1)k + 1$, otherwise 0. (See exercise 2.3.4.4–11.)

8. G1. Input G_1 and V_1; set $n \leftarrow 1$, $U_0 \leftarrow 1/V_1$; output $W_1 = G_1 U_0$.

  G2. Increase n by 1. Terminate the algorithm if $n > N$; otherwise input V_n and G_n.

  G3. Set $U_k \leftarrow (U_k - \sum_{j=1}^{k} U_{k-j}V_{j+1})/V_1$ for $k = 0, 1, \ldots, n-2$ (in this order); then set $U_{n-1} \leftarrow -\sum_{k=2}^{n} kU_{n-k}V_k/V_1$.

  G4. Output $W_n = \sum_{k=1}^{n} kU_{n-k}G_k/n$ and return to G2. ∎

(The running time of the order N^3 algorithm is hereby increased by only order N^2.)

  Note: Algorithms T and N determine $V^{[-1]}(U(z))$; the algorithm in this exercise determines $G(V^{[-1]}(z))$, which is somewhat different. Of course, the results can all be obtained by a sequence of operations of reversion and composition (exercise 11), but it is helpful to have more direct algorithms for each case.

9.

	$n=1$	$n=2$	$n=3$	$n=4$	$n=5$
T_{1n}	1	1	2	5	14
T_{2n}		1	2	5	14
T_{3n}			1	3	9
T_{4n}				1	4
T_{5n}					1

10. Form $y^{1/\alpha} = x(1 + a_1 x + a_2 x^2 + \cdots)^{1/\alpha} = x(1 + c_1 x + c_2 x^2 + \cdots)$ by means of Eq. (9); then revert the latter series. (See the remarks following Eq. 1.2.11.3–(11).)

11. Set $W_0 \leftarrow U_0$, and set $(T_k, W_k) \leftarrow (V_k, 0)$ for $1 \le k \le N$. Then for $n = 1$, 2, $\ldots$, N, do the following: Set $W_j \leftarrow W_j + U_n T_j$ for $n \le j \le N$; and then set $T_j \leftarrow T_{j-1}V_1 + \cdots + T_n V_{j-n}$ for $j = N, N-1, \ldots, n+1$.

  Here $T(z)$ represents $V(z)^N$. An *online* power series algorithm for this problem, analogous to Algorithm T, could be constructed, but it would require about $N^2/2$ storage locations. There is also an online algorithm that solves this exercise and needs only $O(N)$ storage locations: We may assume that $V_1 = 1$, if U_k is replaced by $U_k V_1^k$ and V_k is replaced by V_k/V_1 for all k. Then we may revert $V(z)$ by Algorithm L, and use its output as input to the algorithm of exercise 8 with $G_1 = U_1$, $G_2 = U_2$, etc., thus computing $U(V^{[-1][-1]}(z)) - U_0$. See also exercise 20.

  Brent and Kung have constructed several algorithms that are asymptotically faster. For example, we can evaluate $U(x)$ for $x = V(z)$ by a slight variant of exercise 4.6.4–42(c), doing about $2\sqrt{N}$ chain multiplications of cost $M(N)$ and about N parameter multiplications of cost N, where $M(N)$ is the number of operations needed to multiply power series to order N; the total time is therefore $O(\sqrt{N}M(N) + N^2) = O(N^2)$. A still faster method can be based on the identity $U(V_0(z) + z^m V_1(z)) = U(V_0(z)) + z^m U'(V_0(z))V_1(z) + z^{2m} U''(V_0(z))V_1(z)^2/2! + \cdots$, extending to about N/m terms, where we choose $m \approx \sqrt{N/\log N}$; the first term $U(V_0(z))$ is evaluated in $O(mN(\log N)^2)$ operations using a method somewhat like that in exercise 4.6.4–43. Since we can go from $U^{(k)}(V_0(z))$ to $U^{(k+1)}(V_0(z))$ in $O(N \log N)$ operations by differentiating and dividing by $V_0'(z)$, the entire procedure takes $O(mN(\log N)^2 + (N/m) N \log N) = O(N \log N)^{3/2}$ operations. [*JACM* **25** (1978), 581–595.]

When the polynomials have m-bit integer coefficients, this algorithm involves roughly $N^{3/2+\epsilon}$ multiplications of $(N \lg m)$-bit numbers, so the total running time will be more than $N^{5/2}$. An alternative approach with asymptotic running time $O(N^{2+\epsilon})$ has been developed by P. Ritzmann [*Theoretical Comp. Sci.* **44** (1986), 1–16]. Composition can be done much faster modulo a small prime p (see exercise 26).

12. Polynomial division is trivial unless $m \geq n \geq 1$. Assuming the latter, the equation $u(x) = q(x)v(x) + r(x)$ is equivalent to $U(z) = Q(z)V(z) + z^{m-n+1}R(z)$ where $U(x) = x^m u(x^{-1})$, $V(x) = x^n v(x^{-1})$, $Q(x) = x^{m-n}q(x^{-1})$, and $R(x) = x^{n-1}r(x^{-1})$ are the "reverse" polynomials of u, v, q, and r.

To find $q(x)$ and $r(x)$, compute the first $m - n + 1$ coefficients of the power series $U(z)/V(z) = W(z) + O(z^{m-n+1})$; then compute the power series $U(z) - V(z)W(z)$, which has the form $z^{m-n+1}T(z)$ where $T(z) = T_0 + T_1 z + \cdots$. Note that $T_j = 0$ for all $j \geq n$; hence $Q(z) = W(z)$ and $R(z) = T(z)$ satisfy the requirements.

13. Apply exercise 4.6.1–3 with $u(z) = z^N$ and $v(z) = W_0 + \cdots + W_{N-1}z^{N-1}$; the desired approximations are the values of $v_3(z)/v_2(z)$ obtained during the course of the algorithm. Exercise 4.6.1–26 tells us that there are no further possibilities with relatively prime numerator and denominator. If each W_i is an integer, an all-integer extension of Algorithm 4.6.1C will have the desired properties.

Notes: See the book *History of Continued Fractions and Padé Approximants* by Claude Brezinski (Berlin: Springer, 1991) for further information. The case $N = 2n+1$ and $\deg(w_1) = \deg(w_2) = n$ is of particular interest, since it is equivalent to a so-called Toeplitz system; asymptotically fast methods for Toeplitz systems are surveyed in Bini and Pan, *Polynomial and Matrix Computations* **1** (Boston: Birkhäuser, 1994), §2.5. The method of this exercise can be generalized to arbitrary rational interpolation of the form $W(z) \equiv p(z)/q(z)$ (modulo $(z - z_1)\ldots(z - z_N)$), where the z_i's need not be distinct; thus, we can specify the value of $W(z)$ and some of its derivatives at several points. See Richard P. Brent, Fred G. Gustavson, and David Y. Y. Yun, *J. Algorithms* **1** (1980), 259–295.

14. If $U(z) = z + U_k z^k + \cdots$ and $V(z) = z^k + V_{k+1}z^{k+1} + \cdots$, we find that the difference $V(U(z)) - U'(z)V(z)$ is $\sum_{j\geq 1} z^{2k+j-1}j(U_k V_{k+j} - U_{k+j} + \text{(polynomial involving only}$ $U_k, \ldots, U_{k+j-1}, V_{k+1}, \ldots, V_{k+j-1}))$; hence $V(z)$ is unique if $U(z)$ is given and $U(z)$ is unique if $V(z)$ and U_k are given.

The solution depends on two auxiliary algorithms, the first of which solves the equation $V(z+z^kU(z)) = (1+z^{k-1}W(z))V(z)+z^{k-1}S(z)+O(z^{k-1+n})$ for $V(z) = V_0 + V_1 z + \cdots + V_{n-1}z^{n-1}$, given $U(z)$, $W(z)$, $S(z)$, and n. If $n = 1$, let $V_0 = -S(0)/W(0)$; or let V_0 be arbitrary when $S(0) = W(0) = 0$. To go from n to $2n$, let

$$V(z + z^kU(z)) = (1 + z^{k-1}W(z))V(z) + z^{k-1}S(z) - z^{k-1+n}R(z) + O(z^{k-1+2n}),$$
$$1 + z^{k-1}\hat{W}(z) = (z/(z + z^kU(z)))^n (1 + z^{k-1}W(z)) + O(z^{k-1+n}),$$
$$\hat{S}(z) = (z/(z + z^kU(z)))^n R(z) + O(z^n),$$

and let $\hat{V}(z) = V_n + V_{n+1}z + \cdots + V_{2n-1}z^{n-1}$ satisfy

$$\hat{V}(z + z^kU(z)) = (1 + z^{k-1}\hat{W}(z))\hat{V}(z) + z^{k-1}\hat{S}(z) + O(z^{k-1+n}).$$

The second algorithm solves $W(z)U(z) + zU'(z) = V(z) + O(z^n)$ for $U(z) = U_0 + U_1 z + \cdots + U_{n-1}z^{n-1}$, given $V(z)$, $W(z)$, and n. If $n = 1$, let $U_0 = V(0)/W(0)$, or let U_0 be arbitrary in case $V(0) = W(0) = 0$. To go from n to $2n$, let $W(z)U(z) + zU'(z) =$

$V(z) - z^n R(z) + O(z^{2n})$, and let $\hat{U}(z) = U_n + \cdots + U_{2n-1}z^{n-1}$ be a solution to the equation $(n + W(z))\hat{U}(z) + z\hat{U}'(z) = R(z) + O(z^n)$.

Resuming the notation of (27), the first algorithm can be used to solve $\hat{V}(U(z)) = U'(z)(z/U(z))^k\hat{V}(z)$ to any desired accuracy, and we set $V(z) = z^k\hat{V}(z)$. To find $P(z)$, suppose we have $V(P(z)) = P'(z)V(z) + O(z^{2k-1+n})$, an equation that holds for $n = 1$ when $P(z) = z + \alpha z^k$ and α is arbitrary. We can go from n to $2n$ by letting $V(P(z)) = P'(z)V(z) + z^{2k-1+n}R(z) + O(z^{2k-1+2n})$ and replacing $P(z)$ by $P(z) + z^{k+n}\hat{P}(z)$, where the second algorithm is used to find the polynomial $\hat{P}(z)$ such that $(k + n - zV'(P(z))/V(z))\hat{P}(z) + z\hat{P}'(z) = (z^k/V(z))R(z) + O(z^n)$.

15. The differential equation $U'(z)/U(z)^k = 1/z^k$ implies that $U(z)^{1-k} = z^{1-k} + c$ for some constant c. So we find $U^{[n]}(z) = z/(1 + cnz^{1-k})^{1/(k-1)}$.

A similar argument solves (27) for arbitrary $V(z)$: If $W'(z) = 1/V(z)$, we have $W(U^{[n]}(z)) = W(z) + nc$ for some c.

16. We want to show that $[t^n]\, t^{n+1}((n+1)R'_{k+1}(t)/V(t)^n - nR'_k(t)/V(t)^{n+1}) = 0$. This follows since $(n + 1)R'_{k+1}(t)/V(t)^n - nR'_k(t)/V(t)^{n+1} = \frac{d}{dt}(R_k(t)/V(t)^{n+1})$. Consequently we have $n^{-1}[t^{n-1}]\,R'_1(t)\,t^n/V(t)^n = (n-1)^{-1}[t^{n-2}]\,R'_2(t)\,t^{n-1}/V(t)^{n-1} = \cdots = 1^{-1}[t^0]\,R'_n(t)\,t/V(t) = [t]\,R_n(t)/V_1 = W_n$.

17. Equating coefficients of $x^l y^m$, the convolution formula states that $\binom{l+m}{m}v_{n(l+m)} = \sum_k \binom{n}{k}v_{kl}v_{(n-k)m}$, which is the same as $[z^n]\,V(z)^{l+m} = \sum_k ([z^k]V(z)^l)([z^{n-k}]\,V(z)^m)$, which is a special case of (2).

Notes: The name "poweroid" was introduced by J. F. Steffensen, who was the first of many authors to study the striking properties of these polynomials in general [*Acta Mathematica* **73** (1941), 333–366]. For a review of the literature, and for further discussion of the topics in the next several exercises, see D. E. Knuth, *The Mathematica Journal* **2** (1992), 67–78. One of the results proved in that paper is the asymptotic formula $V_n(x) = e^{xV(s)}(\frac{n}{es})^n(1 - V_2 y + O(y^2) + O(x^{-1}))$, if $V_1 = 1$ and $sV'(s) = y$ and $y = n/x$ is bounded as $x \to \infty$ and $n \to \infty$.

18. We have $V_n(x) = \sum_k x^k n!\,[z^n]\,V(z)^k/k! = n!\,[z^n]\,e^{xV(z)}$. Consequently $V_n(x)/x = (n-1)!\,[z^{n-1}]\,V'(z)\,e^{xV(z)}$ when $n > 0$. We get the stated identity by equating the coefficients of z^{n-1} in $V'(z)\,e^{(x+y)V(z)} = V'(z)\,e^{xV(z)}e^{yV(z)}$.

19. We have

$$v_{nm} = \frac{n!}{m!}\,[z^n]\left(\frac{v_1}{1!}z + \frac{v_2}{2!}z^2 + \frac{v_3}{3!}z^3 + \cdots\right)^m$$

$$= \sum_{\substack{k_1+k_2+\cdots+k_n=m \\ k_1+2k_2+\cdots+nk_n=n \\ k_1,k_2,\ldots,k_n \geq 0}} \frac{n!}{k_1!\,k_2!\ldots k_n!}\left(\frac{v_1}{1!}\right)^{k_1}\left(\frac{v_2}{2!}\right)^{k_2}\cdots\left(\frac{v_n}{n!}\right)^{k_n}$$

by the multinomial theorem 1.2.6–(42). These coefficients, called partial Bell polynomials [see *Annals of Math.* (2) **35** (1934), 258–277], arise also in Arbogast's formula, exercise 1.2.5–21, and we can associate the terms with set partitions as explained in the answer to that exercise. The recurrence

$$v_{nk} = \sum_j \binom{n-1}{j-1}v_j v_{(n-j)(k-1)}$$

shows how to calculate column k from columns 1 and $k-1$; it is readily interpreted with respect to partitions of $\{1,\ldots,n\}$, since there are $\binom{n-1}{j-1}$ ways to include the element n

in a subset of size j. The first few rows of the matrix are

$$v_1$$
$$v_2 \qquad v_1^2$$
$$v_3 \qquad 3v_1 v_2 \qquad\qquad v_1^3$$
$$v_4 \qquad 4v_1 v_3 + 3v_2^2 \qquad 6v_1^2 v_2 \qquad\qquad v_1^4$$
$$v_5 \qquad 5v_1 v_4 + 10 v_2 v_3 \qquad 15 v_1 v_2^2 + 10 v_1^2 v_3 \qquad 10 v_1^3 v_2 \qquad v_1^5$$

20. $[z^n] W(z)^k = \sum_j ([z^j] U(z)^k)([z^n] V(z)^j)$; hence $w_{nk} = (n!/k!) \sum_j ((k!/j!) u_{jk}) \times ((j!/n!)v_{nj})$. [E. Jabotinsky, *Comptes Rendus Acad. Sci.* **224** (Paris, 1947), 323–324.]

21. (a) If $U(z) = \alpha W(\beta z)$ we have $u_{nk} = \frac{n!}{k!} [z^n] (\alpha W(\beta(z))^k = \alpha^k \beta^n w_{nk}$; in particular, if $U(z) = V^{[-1]}(z) = -W(-z)$ we have $u_{nk} = (-1)^{n-k} w_{nk}$. So $\sum_k u_{nk} v_{km}$ and $\sum_k v_{nk} u_{km}$ correspond to the identity function z, by exercise 20.

(b) [Solution by Ira Gessel.] This identity is, in fact, equivalent to Lagrange's inversion formula: We have $w_{nk} = (-1)^{n-k} u_{nk} = (-1)^{n-k} \frac{n!}{k!} [z^n] V^{[-1]}(z)^k$, and the coefficient of z^n in $V^{[-1]}(z)^k$ is $n^{-1}[t^{n-1}] kt^{n+k-1}/V(t)^n$ by exercise 16. On the other hand we have defined $v_{(-k)(-n)}$ to be $(-k)^{\underline{n-k}} [z^{n-k}] (V(z)/z))^{-n}$, which equals $(-1)^{n-k}(n-1)\dots(k+1)k [z^{n-1}] z^{n+k-1}/V(z)^n$.

22. (a) If $V(z) = U^{\{\alpha\}}(z)$ and $W(z) = V^{\{\beta\}}(z)$, we have $W(z) = V(zW(z)^\beta) = U(zW(z)^\beta V(zW(z)^\beta)^\alpha) = U(zW(z)^{\alpha+\beta})$. (Notice the contrast between this law and the similar formulas $U^{[1]}(z) = U(z)$, $U^{[\alpha][\beta]}(z) = U^{[\alpha\beta]}(z)$ that apply to iteration.)

(b) $B^{\{2\}}(z)$ is the generating function for binary trees, 2.3.4.4–(12), which is $W(z)/z$ in the example $z = t - t^2$ following Algorithm L. Moreover, $B^{\{t\}}(z)$ is the generating function for t-ary trees, exercise 2.3.4.4–11.

(c) The hint is equivalent to $zU^{\{\alpha\}}(z)^\alpha = W^{[-1]}(z)$, which is equivalent to the formula $zU^{\{\alpha\}}(z)^\alpha / U(zU^{\{\alpha\}}(z)^\alpha)^\alpha = z$. Now Lagrange's inversion theorem (exercise 8) says that $[z^n] W^{[-1]}(z)^x = \frac{x}{n}[z^{-x}] W(z)^{-n}$ when x is a positive integer. (Here $W(z)^{-n}$ is a Laurent series — a power series divided by a power of z; we can use the notation $[z^m] V(z)$ for Laurent series as well as for power series.) Therefore $[z^n] U^{\{\alpha\}}(z)^x = [z^n] (W^{[-1]}(z)/z)^{x/\alpha} = [z^{n+x/\alpha}] W^{[-1]}(z)^{x/\alpha}$ is equal to $\frac{x/\alpha}{n+x/\alpha} [z^{-x/\alpha}] W(z)^{-n-x/\alpha} = \frac{x}{x+n\alpha} [z^{-x/\alpha}] z^{-n-x/\alpha} U(z)^{x+n\alpha}$ when x/α is a positive integer. We have verified the result for infinitely many α; that is sufficient, since the coefficients of $U^{\{\alpha\}}(z)^x$ are polynomials in α.

We've seen special cases of this result in exercises 1.2.6–25 and 2.3.4.4–29. One memorable consequence of the hint is the case $\alpha = -1$:

$$W(z) = zU(z) \qquad \text{if and only if} \qquad W^{[-1]}(z) = z/U^{\{-1\}}(z).$$

(d) If $U_0 = 1$ and $V_n(x)$ is the poweroid for $V(z) = \ln U(z)$, we've just proved that $xV_n(x + n\alpha)/(x + n\alpha)$ is the poweroid for $\ln U^{\{\alpha\}}(z)$. So we can plug this poweroid into the former identities, changing y to $y - \alpha n$ in the second formula.

23. (a) We have $U = I + T$ where T^n is zero in rows $\le n$. Hence $\ln U = T - \frac{1}{2}T^2 + \frac{1}{3}T^3 - \cdots$ will have the property that $\exp(\alpha \ln U) = I + \binom{\alpha}{1}T + \binom{\alpha}{2}T^2 + \cdots = U^\alpha$. Each entry of U^α is a polynomial in α, and the relations of exercise 19 hold whenever α is a positive integer; therefore U^α is a power matrix for all α, and its first column defines $U^{[\alpha]}(z)$. (In particular, U^{-1} is a power matrix; this is another way to revert $U(z)$.)

(b) Since $U^\epsilon = I + \epsilon \ln U + O(\epsilon^2)$, we have

$$l_{nk} = [\epsilon] u_{nk}^{[\epsilon]} = \frac{n!}{k!} [z^n][\epsilon] (z + \epsilon L(z) + O(\epsilon^2))^k = \frac{n!}{k!} [z^n] kz^{k-1} L(z).$$

(c) $\frac{\partial}{\partial \alpha} U^{[\alpha]}(z) = [\epsilon] U^{[\alpha+\epsilon]}(z)$, and we have

$$U^{[\alpha+\epsilon]}(z) = U^{[\alpha]}(U^{[\epsilon]}(z)) = U^{[\alpha]}(z + \epsilon L(z) + O(\epsilon^2)).$$

Also $U^{[\alpha+\epsilon]}(z) = U^{[\epsilon]}(U^{[\alpha]}(z)) = U^{[\alpha]}(z) + \epsilon L(U^{[\alpha]}(z)) + O(\epsilon^2)$.

(d) The identity follows from the fact that U commutes with $\ln U$. It determines l_{n-1} when $n \geq 4$, because the coefficient of l_{n-1} on the left is nu_2, while the coefficient on the right is $u_{n(n-1)} = \binom{n}{2}u_2$. Similarly, if $u_2 = \cdots = u_{k-1} = 0$ and $u_k \neq 0$, we have $l_k = u_k$ and the recurrence for $n \geq 2k$ determines $l_{k+1}, l_{k+2}, \ldots$: The left side has the form $l_n + \binom{n}{k-1}l_{n+1-k}u_k + \cdots$ and the right side has the form $l_n + \binom{n}{k}l_{n+1-k}u_k + \cdots$. In general, $l_2 = u_2$, $l_3 = u_3 - \frac{3}{2}u_2^2$, $l_4 = u_4 - 5u_2u_3 + \frac{9}{2}u_2^3$, $l_5 = u_5 - \frac{15}{2}u_2u_4 - 5u_3^2 + \frac{185}{6}u_2^2u_3 - 20u_2^4$.

(e) We have $U = \sum_m (\ln U)^m/m!$, and for fixed m the contribution to $u_n = u_{n1}$ from the mth term is $\sum l_{n_m n_{m-1}} \ldots l_{n_2 n_1} l_{n_1 n_0}$ summed over $n = n_m > \cdots > n_1 > n_0 = 1$. Now apply the result of part (b). [See *Trans. Amer. Math. Soc.* **108** (1963), 457–477.]

24. (a) By (21) and exercise 20, we have $U = VDV^{-1}$ where V is the power matrix of the Schröder function and D is the diagonal matrix $\text{diag}(u, u^2, u^3, \ldots)$. So we may take $\ln U = V \text{diag}(\ln u, 2\ln u, 3\ln u, \ldots)V^{-1}$. (b) The equation $WVDV^{-1} = VDV^{-1}W$ implies $(V^{-1}WV)D = D(V^{-1}WV)$. The diagonal entries of D are distinct, so $V^{-1}WV$ must be a diagonal matrix D'. Thus $W = VD'V^{-1}$, and W has the same Schröder function as U. It follows that $W_1 \neq 0$ and $W = VD^\alpha V^{-1}$, where $\alpha = (\ln W_1)/(\ln U_1)$.

25. We must have $k = l$ because $[z^{k+l-1}]U(V(z)) = U_{k+l-1} + V_{k+l-1} + kU_kV_l$. To complete the proof it suffices to show that $U_k = V_k$ and $U(V(z)) = V(U(z))$ implies $U(z) = V(z)$. Suppose l is minimal with $U_l \neq V_l$, and let $n = k + l - 1$. Then we have $u_{nk} - v_{nk} = \binom{n}{l}(u_l - v_l)$; $u_{nj} = v_{nj}$ for all $j > k$; $u_{nl} = \binom{n}{l}u_k$; and $u_{nj} = 0$ for $l < j < n$. Now the sum $\sum_j u_{nj}v_j = u_n + u_{nk}v_k + \cdots + u_{nl}v_l + v_n$ must be equal to $\sum_j v_{nj}u_j$; so we find $\binom{n}{l}(u_l - v_l)v_k = \binom{n}{k}v_k(u_l - v_l)$. But we have $\binom{k+l-1}{k} = \binom{k+l-1}{l}$ if and only if $k = l$.

[From this exercise and the previous one, we might suspect that $U(V(z)) = V(U(z))$ only when one of U and V is an iterate of the other. But this is not necessarily true when U_1 and V_1 are roots of unity. For example, if $V_1 = -1$ and $U(z) = V^{[2]}(z)$, V is not an iterate of $U^{[1/2]}$, nor is $U^{[1/2]}$ an iterate of V.]

26. Writing $U(z) = U_{[0]}(z^2) + zU_{[1]}(z^2)$, we have $U(V(z)) \equiv U_{[0]}(V_1z^2 + V_2z^4 + \cdots) + V(z)U_{[1]}(V_1z^2 + V_2z^4 + \cdots)$ (modulo 2). The running time satisfies $T(N) = 2T(N/2) + C(N)$, where $C(N)$ is essentially the time for polynomial multiplication mod z^N. We can make $C(N) = O(N^{1+\epsilon})$ by the method of, say, exercise 4.6.4–59; see also the answer to exercise 4.6–5.

A similar method works mod p in time $O(pN^{1+\epsilon})$. [D. J. Bernstein, *J. Symbolic Computation* **26** (1998), 339–341.]

27. From $(W(qz) - W(z))V(z) = W(z)(V(q^m z) - V(z))$ we obtain the recurrence $W_n = \sum_{k=1}^{n} V_k W_{n-k}(q^{km} - q^{n-k})/(q^n - 1)$. [*J. Difference Eqs. and Applics.* **1** (1995), 57–60.]

28. Note first that $\delta(U(z)V(z)) = (\delta U(z))V(z) + U(z)(\delta V(z))$, because $t(mn) = t(m) + t(n)$. Therefore $\delta(V(z)^n) = nV(z)^{n-1}\delta V(z)$ for all $n \geq 0$, by induction on n; and this is the identity we need to show that $\delta e^{V(z)} = \sum_{n \geq 0} \delta(V(z)^n/n!) = e^{V(z)}\delta V(z)$. Replacing $V(z)$ by $\ln V(z)$ in this equation gives $V(z)\delta \ln V(z) = \delta V(z)$;

hence $\delta\big(V(z)^\alpha\big) = \delta e^{\alpha \ln V(z)} = e^{\alpha \ln V(z)}\delta(\alpha \ln V(z)) = \alpha V(z)^{\alpha-1}$ for all complex numbers α.

It follows that the desired recurrences are

(a) $W_1 = 1$, $W_n = \sum_{d\backslash n,\, d>1}\big((\alpha+1)t(d)/t(n) - 1\big)V_d W_{n/d}$;

(b) $W_1 = 1$, $W_n = \sum_{d\backslash n,\, d>1}\big(t(d)/t(n)\big)V_d W_{n/d}$;

(c) $W_1 = 0$, $W_n = V_n + \sum_{d\backslash n,\, d>1}\big(t(d)/t(n) - 1\big)V_d W_{n/d}$.

[See H. W. Gould, *AMM* **81** (1974), 3–14. These formulas hold when t is any function such that $t(m) + t(n) = t(mn)$ and $t(n) = 0$ if and only if $n = 1$, but the suggested t is simplest. The method discussed here works also for power series in arbitrarily many variables; then t is the total degree of a term.]

> *"It is certainly an idea you have there," said Poirot, with some interest.*
> *"Yes, yes, I play the part of the computer.*
> *One feeds in the information —"*
> *"And supposing you come up with all the wrong answers?" said Mrs. Oliver.*
> *"That would be impossible," said Hercule Poirot.*
> *"Computers do not do that sort of a thing."*
> *"They're not supposed to," said Mrs. Oliver,*
> *"but you'd be surprised at the things that happen sometimes."*
> — AGATHA CHRISTIE, *Hallowe'en Party* (1969)

APPENDIX A

TABLES OF NUMERICAL QUANTITIES

Table 1

QUANTITIES THAT ARE FREQUENTLY USED IN STANDARD SUBROUTINES
AND IN ANALYSIS OF COMPUTER PROGRAMS (40 DECIMAL PLACES)

$$\sqrt{2} = 1.41421\ 35623\ 73095\ 04880\ 16887\ 24209\ 69807\ 85697-$$
$$\sqrt{3} = 1.73205\ 08075\ 68877\ 29352\ 74463\ 41505\ 87236\ 69428+$$
$$\sqrt{5} = 2.23606\ 79774\ 99789\ 69640\ 91736\ 68731\ 27623\ 54406+$$
$$\sqrt{10} = 3.16227\ 76601\ 68379\ 33199\ 88935\ 44432\ 71853\ 37196-$$
$$\sqrt[3]{2} = 1.25992\ 10498\ 94873\ 16476\ 72106\ 07278\ 22835\ 05703-$$
$$\sqrt[3]{3} = 1.44224\ 95703\ 07408\ 38232\ 16383\ 10780\ 10958\ 83919-$$
$$\sqrt[4]{2} = 1.18920\ 71150\ 02721\ 06671\ 74999\ 70560\ 47591\ 52930-$$
$$\ln 2 = 0.69314\ 71805\ 59945\ 30941\ 72321\ 21458\ 17656\ 80755+$$
$$\ln 3 = 1.09861\ 22886\ 68109\ 69139\ 52452\ 36922\ 52570\ 46475-$$
$$\ln 10 = 2.30258\ 50929\ 94045\ 68401\ 79914\ 54684\ 36420\ 76011+$$
$$1/\ln 2 = 1.44269\ 50408\ 88963\ 40735\ 99246\ 81001\ 89213\ 74266+$$
$$1/\ln 10 = 0.43429\ 44819\ 03251\ 82765\ 11289\ 18916\ 60508\ 22944-$$
$$\pi = 3.14159\ 26535\ 89793\ 23846\ 26433\ 83279\ 50288\ 41972-$$
$$1° = \pi/180 = 0.01745\ 32925\ 19943\ 29576\ 92369\ 07684\ 88612\ 71344+$$
$$1/\pi = 0.31830\ 98861\ 83790\ 67153\ 77675\ 26745\ 02872\ 40689+$$
$$\pi^2 = 9.86960\ 44010\ 89358\ 61883\ 44909\ 99876\ 15113\ 53137-$$
$$\sqrt{\pi} = \Gamma(1/2) = 1.77245\ 38509\ 05516\ 02729\ 81674\ 83341\ 14518\ 27975+$$
$$\Gamma(1/3) = 2.67893\ 85347\ 07747\ 63365\ 56929\ 40974\ 67764\ 41287-$$
$$\Gamma(2/3) = 1.35411\ 79394\ 26400\ 41694\ 52880\ 28154\ 51378\ 55193+$$
$$e = 2.71828\ 18284\ 59045\ 23536\ 02874\ 71352\ 66249\ 77572+$$
$$1/e = 0.36787\ 94411\ 71442\ 32159\ 55237\ 70161\ 46086\ 74458+$$
$$e^2 = 7.38905\ 60989\ 30650\ 22723\ 04274\ 60575\ 00781\ 31803+$$
$$\gamma = 0.57721\ 56649\ 01532\ 86060\ 65120\ 90082\ 40243\ 10422-$$
$$\ln \pi = 1.14472\ 98858\ 49400\ 17414\ 34273\ 51353\ 05871\ 16473-$$
$$\phi = 1.61803\ 39887\ 49894\ 84820\ 45868\ 34365\ 63811\ 77203+$$
$$e^{\gamma} = 1.78107\ 24179\ 90197\ 98523\ 65041\ 03107\ 17954\ 91696+$$
$$e^{\pi/4} = 2.19328\ 00507\ 38015\ 45655\ 97696\ 59278\ 73822\ 34616+$$
$$\sin 1 = 0.84147\ 09848\ 07896\ 50665\ 25023\ 21630\ 29899\ 96226-$$
$$\cos 1 = 0.54030\ 23058\ 68139\ 71740\ 09366\ 07442\ 97660\ 37323+$$
$$-\zeta'(2) = 0.93754\ 82543\ 15843\ 75370\ 25740\ 94567\ 86497\ 78979-$$
$$\zeta(3) = 1.20205\ 69031\ 59594\ 28539\ 97381\ 61511\ 44999\ 07650-$$
$$\ln \phi = 0.48121\ 18250\ 59603\ 44749\ 77589\ 13424\ 36842\ 31352-$$
$$1/\ln \phi = 2.07808\ 69212\ 35027\ 53760\ 13226\ 06117\ 79576\ 77422-$$
$$-\ln \ln 2 = 0.36651\ 29205\ 81664\ 32701\ 24391\ 58232\ 66946\ 94543-$$

Table 2

QUANTITIES THAT ARE FREQUENTLY USED IN STANDARD SUBROUTINES
AND IN ANALYSIS OF COMPUTER PROGRAMS (45 OCTAL PLACES)

The names at the left of the "=" signs are given in decimal notation.

$0.1 =$	*0.06314 63146 31463 14631 46314 63146 31463 14631 46315−*
$0.01 =$	*0.00507 53412 17270 24365 60507 53412 17270 24365 60510−*
$0.001 =$	*0.00040 61115 64570 65176 76355 44264 16254 02030 44672+*
$0.0001 =$	*0.00003 21556 13530 70414 54512 75170 33021 15002 35223−*
$0.00001 =$	*0.00000 24761 32610 70664 36041 06077 17401 56063 34417−*
$0.000001 =$	*0.00000 02061 57364 05536 66151 55323 07746 44470 26033+*
$0.0000001 =$	*0.00000 00153 27745 15274 53644 12741 72312 20354 02151+*
$0.00000001 =$	*0.00000 00012 57143 56106 04303 47374 77341 01512 63327+*
$0.000000001 =$	*0.00000 00001 04560 27640 46655 12262 71426 40124 21742+*
$0.0000000001 =$	*0.00000 00000 06676 33766 35367 55653 37265 34642 01627−*
$\sqrt{2} =$	*1.32404 74631 77167 46220 42627 66115 46725 12575 17435+*
$\sqrt{3} =$	*1.56663 65641 30231 25163 54453 50265 60361 34073 42223−*
$\sqrt{5} =$	*2.17067 36334 57722 47602 57471 63003 00563 55620 32021−*
$\sqrt{10} =$	*3.12305 40726 64555 22444 02242 57101 41466 33775 22532+*
$\sqrt[3]{2} =$	*1.20505 05746 15345 05342 10756 65334 25574 22415 03024+*
$\sqrt[3]{3} =$	*1.34233 50444 22175 73134 67363 76133 05334 31147 60121−*
$\sqrt[4]{2} =$	*1.14067 74050 61556 12455 72152 64430 60271 02755 73136+*
$\ln 2 =$	*0.54271 02775 75071 73632 57117 07316 30007 71366 53640+*
$\ln 3 =$	*1.06237 24752 55006 05227 32440 63065 25012 35574 55337+*
$\ln 10 =$	*2.23273 06735 52524 25405 56512 66542 56026 46050 50705+*
$1/\ln 2 =$	*1.34252 16624 53405 77027 35750 37766 40644 35175 04353+*
$1/\ln 10 =$	*0.33626 75425 11562 41614 52325 33525 27655 14756 06220−*
$\pi =$	*3.11037 55242 10264 30215 14230 63050 56006 70163 21122+*
$1° = \pi/180 =$	*0.01073 72152 11224 72344 25603 54276 63351 22056 11544+*
$1/\pi =$	*0.24276 30155 62344 20251 23760 47257 50765 15156 70067−*
$\pi^2 =$	*11.67517 14467 62135 71322 25561 15466 30021 40654 34103−*
$\sqrt{\pi} = \Gamma(1/2) =$	*1.61337 61106 64736 65247 47035 40510 15273 34470 17762−*
$\Gamma(1/3) =$	*2.53347 35234 51013 61316 73106 47644 54653 00106 66046−*
$\Gamma(2/3) =$	*1.26523 57112 14154 74312 54572 37655 60126 23231 02452+*
$e =$	*2.55760 52130 50535 51246 52773 42542 00471 72363 61661+*
$1/e =$	*0.27426 53066 13167 46761 52726 75436 02440 52371 03355+*
$e^2 =$	*7.30714 45615 23355 33460 63507 35040 32664 25356 50217+*
$\gamma =$	*0.44742 14770 67666 06172 23215 74376 01002 51313 25521−*
$\ln \pi =$	*1.11206 40443 47503 36413 65374 52661 52410 37511 46057+*
$\phi =$	*1.47433 57156 27751 23701 27634 71401 40271 66710 15010+*
$e^{\gamma} =$	*1.61772 13452 61152 65761 22477 36553 53327 17554 21260+*
$e^{\pi/4} =$	*2.14275 31512 16162 52370 35530 11342 53525 44307 02171−*
$\sin 1 =$	*0.65665 24436 04414 73402 03067 23644 11612 07474 14505−*
$\cos 1 =$	*0.42450 50037 32406 42711 07022 14666 27320 70675 12321+*
$-\zeta'(2) =$	*0.74001 45144 53253 42362 42107 23350 50074 46100 27706+*
$\zeta(3) =$	*1.14735 00023 60014 20470 15613 42561 31715 10177 06614+*
$\ln \phi =$	*0.36630 26256 61213 01145 13700 41004 52264 30700 40646+*
$1/\ln \phi =$	*2.04776 60111 17144 41512 11436 16575 00355 43630 40651+*
$-\ln \ln 2 =$	*0.27351 71233 67265 63650 17401 56637 26334 31455 57005−*

Several of the 40-digit values in Table 1 were computed on a desk calculator by John W. Wrench, Jr., for the first edition of this book. When computer software for such calculations became available during the 1970s, all of his contributions proved to be correct. The 40-digit values of other fundamental constants can be found in Eqs. 4.5.2–(60), 4.5.3–(26), 4.5.3–(41), 4.5.4–(9), and the answers to exercises 4.5.4–8, 4.5.4–25, 4.6.4–58.

Table 3

VALUES OF HARMONIC NUMBERS, BERNOULLI NUMBERS,
AND FIBONACCI NUMBERS, FOR SMALL VALUES OF n

n	H_n	B_n	F_n	n
0	0	1	0	0
1	1	$-1/2$	1	1
2	3/2	1/6	1	2
3	11/6	0	2	3
4	25/12	$-1/30$	3	4
5	137/60	0	5	5
6	49/20	1/42	8	6
7	363/140	0	13	7
8	761/280	$-1/30$	21	8
9	7129/2520	0	34	9
10	7381/2520	5/66	55	10
11	83711/27720	0	89	11
12	86021/27720	$-691/2730$	144	12
13	1145993/360360	0	233	13
14	1171733/360360	7/6	377	14
15	1195757/360360	0	610	15
16	2436559/720720	$-3617/510$	987	16
17	42142223/12252240	0	1597	17
18	14274301/4084080	43867/798	2584	18
19	275295799/77597520	0	4181	19
20	55835135/15519504	$-174611/330$	6765	20
21	18858053/5173168	0	10946	21
22	19093197/5173168	854513/138	17711	22
23	444316699/118982864	0	28657	23
24	1347822955/356948592	$-236364091/2730$	46368	24
25	34052522467/8923714800	0	75025	25
26	34395742267/8923714800	8553103/6	121393	26
27	312536252003/80313433200	0	196418	27
28	315404588903/80313433200	$-23749461029/870$	317811	28
29	9227046511387/2329089562800	0	514229	29
30	9304682830147/2329089562800	8615841276005/14322	832040	30

For any x, let $H_x = \sum_{n \geq 1} \left(\dfrac{1}{n} - \dfrac{1}{n+x} \right)$. Then

$$H_{1/2} = 2 - 2\ln 2,$$

$$H_{1/3} = 3 - \tfrac{1}{2}\pi/\sqrt{3} - \tfrac{3}{2}\ln 3,$$

$$H_{2/3} = \tfrac{3}{2} + \tfrac{1}{2}\pi/\sqrt{3} - \tfrac{3}{2}\ln 3,$$

$$H_{1/4} = 4 - \tfrac{1}{2}\pi - 3\ln 2,$$

$$H_{3/4} = \tfrac{4}{3} + \tfrac{1}{2}\pi - 3\ln 2,$$

$$H_{1/5} = 5 - \tfrac{1}{2}\pi\phi^{3/2}5^{-1/4} - \tfrac{5}{4}\ln 5 - \tfrac{1}{2}\sqrt{5}\ln\phi,$$

$$H_{2/5} = \tfrac{5}{2} - \tfrac{1}{2}\pi\phi^{-3/2}5^{-1/4} - \tfrac{5}{4}\ln 5 + \tfrac{1}{2}\sqrt{5}\ln\phi,$$

$$H_{3/5} = \tfrac{5}{3} + \tfrac{1}{2}\pi\phi^{-3/2}5^{-1/4} - \tfrac{5}{4}\ln 5 + \tfrac{1}{2}\sqrt{5}\ln\phi,$$

$$H_{4/5} = \tfrac{5}{4} + \tfrac{1}{2}\pi\phi^{3/2}5^{-1/4} - \tfrac{5}{4}\ln 5 - \tfrac{1}{2}\sqrt{5}\ln\phi,$$

$$H_{1/6} = 6 - \tfrac{1}{2}\pi\sqrt{3} - 2\ln 2 - \tfrac{3}{2}\ln 3,$$

$$H_{5/6} = \tfrac{6}{5} + \tfrac{1}{2}\pi\sqrt{3} - 2\ln 2 - \tfrac{3}{2}\ln 3,$$

and, in general, when $0 < p < q$ (see exercise 1.2.9–19),

$$H_{p/q} = \frac{q}{p} - \frac{\pi}{2}\cot\frac{p}{q}\pi - \ln 2q + 2\sum_{1 \leq n < q/2} \cos\frac{2pn}{q}\pi \cdot \ln\sin\frac{n}{q}\pi.$$

INDEX TO NOTATIONS

In the following formulas, letters that are not further qualified have the following significance:

j, k integer-valued arithmetic expression

m, n nonnegative integer-valued arithmetic expression

x, y real-valued arithmetic expression

z complex-valued arithmetic expression

f real-valued or complex-valued function

S, T set or multiset

Formal symbolism	Meaning	Where defined
∎	end of algorithm, program, or proof	1.1
A_n or $A[n]$	the nth element of linear array A	1.1
A_{mn} or $A[m, n]$	the element in row m and column n of rectangular array A	1.1
$V \leftarrow E$	give variable V the value of expression E	1.1
$U \leftrightarrow V$	interchange the values of variables U and V	1.1
$(B \Rightarrow E;\ E')$	conditional expression: denotes E if B is true, E' if B is false	
$[B]$	characteristic function of condition B: $(B \Rightarrow 1;\ 0)$	1.2.3
δ_{kj}	Kronecker delta: $[j = k]$	1.2.3
$[z^n]\, g(z)$	coefficient of z^n in power series $g(z)$	1.2.9
$\displaystyle\sum_{R(k)} f(k)$	sum of all $f(k)$ such that the variable k is an integer and relation $R(k)$ is true	1.2.3
$\displaystyle\prod_{R(k)} f(k)$	product of all $f(k)$ such that the variable k is an integer and relation $R(k)$ is true	1.2.3
$\displaystyle\min_{R(k)} f(k)$	minimum value of all $f(k)$ such that the variable k is an integer and relation $R(k)$ is true	1.2.3
$\displaystyle\max_{R(k)} f(k)$	maximum value of all $f(k)$ such that the variable k is an integer and relation $R(k)$ is true	1.2.3

Formal symbolism	Meaning	Where defined
$\Re z$	real part of z	1.2.2
$\Im z$	imaginary part of z	1.2.2
$\overline{z}$	complex conjugate: $\Re z - i\,\Im z$	1.2.2
A^T	transpose of rectangular array A: $$A^T[j,k] = A[k,j]$$	
x^y	x to the y power (when x is positive)	1.2.2
x^k	x to the kth power: $$\left(k \geq 0 \Rightarrow \prod_{0 \leq j < k} x; \quad 1/x^{-k}\right)$$	1.2.2
$x^{\overline{k}}$	x to the k rising: $\Gamma(x+k)/\Gamma(x) =$ $$\left(k \geq 0 \Rightarrow \prod_{0 \leq j < k} (x+j); \quad 1/(x+k)^{\overline{-k}}\right)$$	1.2.5
$x^{\underline{k}}$	x to the k falling: $x!/(x-k)! =$ $$\left(k \geq 0 \Rightarrow \prod_{0 \leq j < k} (x-j); \quad 1/(x-k)^{\underline{-k}}\right)$$	1.2.5
$n!$	n factorial: $\Gamma(n+1) = n^{\underline{n}}$	1.2.5
$f'(x)$	derivative of f at x	1.2.9
$f''(x)$	second derivative of f at x	1.2.10
$f^{(n)}(x)$	nth derivative: $\bigl(n = 0 \Rightarrow f(x); \ g'(x)\bigr)$, where $g(x) = f^{(n-1)}(x)$	1.2.11.2
$f^{[n]}(x)$	nth iterate: $\bigl(n = 0 \Rightarrow x; f(f^{[n-1]}(x))\bigr)$	4.7
$f^{\{n\}}(x)$	nth induced function: $$f^{\{n\}}(x) = f\bigl(xf^{\{n\}}(x)^n\bigr)$$	4.7
$H_n^{(x)}$	harmonic number of order x: $\displaystyle\sum_{1 \leq k \leq n} 1/k^x$	1.2.7
H_n	harmonic number: $H_n^{(1)}$	1.2.7
F_n	Fibonacci number: $(n \leq 1 \Rightarrow n; \ F_{n-1} + F_{n-2})$	1.2.8
B_n	Bernoulli number: $n!\,[z^n]\,z/(e^z - 1)$	1.2.11.2
$X \cdot Y$	dot product of vectors $X = (x_1, \ldots, x_n)$ and $Y = (y_1, \ldots, y_n)$: $x_1 y_1 + \cdots + x_n y_n$	3.3.4
$j \backslash k$	j divides k: $k \bmod j = 0$ and $j > 0$	1.2.4
$S \setminus T$	set difference: $\{a \mid a$ in S and a not in $T\}$	
$\oplus \ominus \otimes \oslash$	rounded or special operations	4.2.1

Formal symbolism	Meaning	Where defined
$(\dots a_1 a_0 . a_{-1} \dots)_b$	radix-b positional notation: $\sum_k a_k b^k$	4.1
$/\!/x_1, x_2, \dots, x_n/\!/$	continued fraction: $$1/\bigl(x_1 + 1/(x_2 + 1/(\cdots + 1/(x_n)\dots)))$$	4.5.3
$\dbinom{x}{k}$	binomial coefficient: $(k < 0 \Rightarrow 0;\ x^{\underline{k}}/k!)$	1.2.6
$\dbinom{n}{n_1, n_2, \dots, n_m}$	multinomial coefficient (defined only when $n = n_1 + n_2 + \cdots + n_m$)	1.2.6
$\left[\begin{smallmatrix} n \\ m \end{smallmatrix}\right]$	Stirling number of the first kind: $$\sum_{0 < k_1 < k_2 < \cdots < k_{n-m} < n} k_1 k_2 \dots k_{n-m}$$	1.2.6
$\left\{\begin{smallmatrix} n \\ m \end{smallmatrix}\right\}$	Stirling number of the second kind: $$\sum_{1 \le k_1 \le k_2 \le \cdots \le k_{n-m} \le m} k_1 k_2 \dots k_{n-m}$$	1.2.6
$\{a \mid R(a)\}$	set of all a such that the relation $R(a)$ is true	
$\{a_1, \dots, a_n\}$	the set or multiset $\{a_k \mid 1 \le k \le n\}$	
$\{x\}$	fractional part (used in contexts where a real value, not a set, is implied): $x - \lfloor x \rfloor$	1.2.11.2
$[a \mathinner{\ldotp\ldotp} b]$	closed interval: $\{x \mid a \le x \le b\}$	1.2.2
$(a \mathinner{\ldotp\ldotp} b)$	open interval: $\{x \mid a < x < b\}$	1.2.2
$[a \mathinner{\ldotp\ldotp} b)$	half-open interval: $\{x \mid a \le x < b\}$	1.2.2
$(a \mathinner{\ldotp\ldotp} b]$	half-closed interval: $\{x \mid a < x \le b\}$	1.2.2
$|S|$	cardinality: the number of elements in set S	
$|x|$	absolute value of x: $(x \ge 0 \Rightarrow x;\ -x)$	
$|z|$	absolute value of z: $\sqrt{z\bar{z}}$	1.2.2
$\lfloor x \rfloor$	floor of x, greatest integer function: $\max_{k \le x} k$	1.2.4
$\lceil x \rceil$	ceiling of x, least integer function: $\min_{k \ge x} k$	1.2.4
$((x))$	sawtooth function	3.3.3
$\langle X_n \rangle$	the infinite sequence $X_0, X_1, X_2, \dots$ (here the letter n is part of the symbolism)	1.2.9

Formal symbolism	Meaning	Where defined
γ	Euler's constant: $\lim_{n\to\infty}(H_n - \ln n)$	1.2.7
$\gamma(x, y)$	incomplete gamma function: $\int_0^y e^{-t}t^{x-1}\,dt$	1.2.11.3
$\Gamma(x)$	gamma function: $(x - 1)! = \gamma(x, \infty)$	1.2.5
$\delta(x)$	characteristic function of the integers	3.3.3
e	base of natural logarithms: $\sum_{n\geq 0} 1/n!$	1.2.2
$\zeta(x)$	zeta function: $\lim_{n\to\infty} H_n^{(x)}$ (when $x > 1$)	1.2.7
$K_n(x_1, \ldots, x_n)$	continuant polynomial	4.5.3
$\ell(u)$	leading coefficient of polynomial u	4.6
$l(n)$	length of shortest addition chain for n	4.6.3
$\Lambda(n)$	von Mangoldt's function	4.5.3
$\mu(n)$	Möbius function	4.5.2
$\nu(n)$	sideways sum	4.6.3
$O\big(f(n)\big)$	big-oh of $f(n)$, as the variable $n \to \infty$	1.2.11.1
$O\big(f(z)\big)$	big-oh of $f(z)$, as the variable $z \to 0$	1.2.11.1
$\Omega\big(f(n)\big)$	big-omega of $f(n)$, as the variable $n \to \infty$	1.2.11.1
$\Theta\big(f(n)\big)$	big-theta of $f(n)$, as the variable $n \to \infty$	1.2.11.1
$\pi(x)$	prime count: $\sum_{n\leq x}[n \text{ is prime}]$	4.5.4
π	circle ratio: $4\sum_{n\geq 0}(-1)^n/(2n + 1)$	4.3.1
ϕ	golden ratio: $\frac{1}{2}\big(1 + \sqrt{5}\,\big)$	1.2.8
$\emptyset$	empty set: $\{x \mid 0 = 1\}$	
$\varphi(n)$	Euler's totient function: $\sum_{0\leq k<n}[k \perp n]$	1.2.4
∞	infinity: larger than any number	4.2.2
$\det(A)$	determinant of square matrix A	1.2.3
$\operatorname{sign}(x)$	sign of x: $\big(x = 0 \Rightarrow 0;\ x/|x|\big)$	
$\deg(u)$	degree of polynomial u	4.6
$\operatorname{cont}(u)$	content of polynomial u	4.6.1
$\operatorname{pp}\big(u(x)\big)$	primitive part of polynomial u	4.6.1
$\log_b x$	logarithm, base b, of x (when $x > 0$, $b > 0$, and $b \neq 1$): the y such that $x = b^y$	1.2.2
$\ln x$	natural logarithm: $\log_e x$	1.2.2
$\lg x$	binary logarithm: $\log_2 x$	1.2.2
$\exp x$	exponential of x: e^x	1.2.9
$j \perp k$	j is relatively prime to k: $\gcd(j, k) = 1$	1.2.4

Formal symbolism	Meaning	Where defined
$\gcd(j, k)$	greatest common divisor of j and k: $$\left(j = k = 0 \Rightarrow 0; \; \max_{d \backslash j, \, d \backslash k} d\right)$$	4.5.2
$\text{lcm}(j, k)$	least common multiple of j and k: $$\left(jk = 0 \Rightarrow 0; \; \min_{d > 0, \, j \backslash d, \, k \backslash d} d\right)$$	4.5.2
$x \bmod y$	mod function: $\left(y = 0 \Rightarrow x; \; x - y \lfloor x/y \rfloor\right)$	1.2.4
$u(x) \bmod v(x)$	remainder of polynomial u after division by polynomial v	4.6.1
$x \equiv x' \pmod{y}$	relation of congruence: $x \bmod y = x' \bmod y$	1.2.4
$x \approx y$	x is approximately equal to y	3.5, 4.2.2
$\Pr\bigl(S(n)\bigr)$	probability that statement $S(n)$ is true, for random positive integers n	3.5
$\Pr\bigl(S(X)\bigr)$	probability that statement $S(X)$ is true, for random values of X	1.2.10
$\mathrm{E}\, X$	expected value of X: $\sum_x x \Pr(X = x)$	1.2.10
$\text{mean}(g)$	mean value of the probability distribution represented by generating function g: $g'(1)$	1.2.10
$\text{var}(g)$	variance of the probability distribution represented by generating function g: $$g''(1) + g'(1) - g'(1)^2$$	1.2.10
$(\min x_1, \text{ave } x_2, \max x_3, \text{dev } x_4)$	a random variable having minimum value x_1, average (expected) value x_2, maximum value x_3, standard deviation x_4	1.2.10
␣	one blank space	1.3.1
rA	register A (accumulator) of MIX	1.3.1
rX	register X (extension) of MIX	1.3.1
rI1, ..., rI6	(index) registers I1, ..., I6 of MIX	1.3.1
rJ	(jump) register J of MIX	1.3.1
(L:R)	partial field of MIX word, $0 \le \text{L} \le \text{R} \le 5$	1.3.1
OP ADDRESS,I(F)	notation for MIX instruction	1.3.1, 1.3.2
u	unit of time in MIX	1.3.1
*	"self" in MIXAL	1.3.2
OF, 1F, 2F, ..., 9F	"forward" local symbol in MIXAL	1.3.2
OB, 1B, 2B, ..., 9B	"backward" local symbol in MIXAL	1.3.2
OH, 1H, 2H, ..., 9H	"here" local symbol in MIXAL	1.3.2

APPENDIX C

INDEX TO ALGORITHMS AND THEOREMS

*At any step, arbitrary combinations of algorithms and theorems
can be applied to solve a given problem.*
— KARSTEN HOMANN and JACQUES CALMET (1995)

INDEX AND GLOSSARY

Seek and ye shall find.
— Matthew 7:7

When an index entry refers to a page containing a relevant exercise, see also the *answer* to that exercise for further information. An answer page is not indexed here unless it refers to a topic not included in the statement of the exercise.

THIS BOOK was composed on a Sun SPARCstation with Computer Modern typefaces, using the TEX and METAFONT software as described in the author's books *Computers & Typesetting* (Reading, Mass.: Addison–Wesley, 1986), Volumes A–E. The illustrations were produced with John Hobby's METAPOST system. Some names in the index were typeset with additional fonts developed by Yannis Haralambous (Greek, Hebrew, Arabic), Olga G. Lapko (Cyrillic), Frans J. Velthuis (Devanagari), Masatoshi Watanabe (Japanese), and Linbo Zhang (Chinese).

Character code:

00	01	02	03	04	05	06	07	08	09	10	11	12	13	14	15	16	17	18	19	20	21	22	23	24
␣	A	B	C	D	E	F	G	H	I	Δ	J	K	L	M	N	O	P	Q	R	Σ	Π	S	T	U

00	*1*	**01**	*2*	**02**	*2*	**03**	*10*
No operation		rA ← rA + V		rA ← rA − V		rAX ← rA × V	
NOP(0)		ADD(0:5) FADD(6)		SUB(0:5) FSUB(6)		MUL(0:5) FMUL(6)	
08	*2*	**09**	*2*	**10**	*2*	**11**	*2*
rA ← V		rI1 ← V		rI2 ← V		rI3 ← V	
LDA(0:5)		LD1(0:5)		LD2(0:5)		LD3(0:5)	
16	*2*	**17**	*2*	**18**	*2*	**19**	*2*
rA ← −V		rI1 ← −V		rI2 ← −V		rI3 ← −V	
LDAN(0:5)		LD1N(0:5)		LD2N(0:5)		LD3N(0:5)	
24	*2*	**25**	*2*	**26**	*2*	**27**	*2*
M(F) ← rA		M(F) ← rI1		M(F) ← rI2		M(F) ← rI3	
STA(0:5)		ST1(0:5)		ST2(0:5)		ST3(0:5)	
32	*2*	**33**	*2*	**34**	*1*	**35**	*1 + T*
M(F) ← rJ		M(F) ← 0		Unit F busy?		Control, unit F	
STJ(0:2)		STZ(0:5)		JBUS(0)		IOC(0)	
40	*1*	**41**	*1*	**42**	*1*	**43**	*1*
rA : 0, jump		rI1 : 0, jump		rI2 : 0, jump		rI3 : 0, jump	
JA[+]		J1[+]		J2[+]		J3[+]	
48	*1*	**49**	*1*	**50**	*1*	**51**	*1*
rA ← [rA]? ± M		rI1 ← [rI1]? ± M		rI2 ← [rI2]? ± M		rI3 ← [rI3]? ± M	
INCA(0) DECA(1) ENTA(2) ENNA(3)		INC1(0) DEC1(1) ENT1(2) ENN1(3)		INC2(0) DEC2(1) ENT2(2) ENN2(3)		INC3(0) DEC3(1) ENT3(2) ENN3(3)	
56	*2*	**57**	*2*	**58**	*2*	**59**	*2*
CI ← rA(F) : V		CI ← rI1(F) : V		CI ← rI2(F) : V		CI ← rI3(F) : V	
CMPA(0:5) FCMP(6)		CMP1(0:5)		CMP2(0:5)		CMP3(0:5)	

General form:

C	*t*
Description	
OP(F)	

C = operation code, (5 : 5) field of instruction
F = op variant, (4 : 4) field of instruction
M = address of instruction after indexing
V = M(F) = contents of F field of location M
OP = symbolic name for operation
(F) = normal F setting
t = execution time; T = interlock time

THE ART OF
COMPUTER PROGRAMMING

SECOND EDITION

DONALD E. KNUTH *Stanford University*

 ADDISON–WESLEY

Volume 3 / **Sorting and Searching**

THE ART OF
COMPUTER PROGRAMMING

SECOND EDITION

Upper Saddle River, NJ · Boston · Indianapolis · San Francisco
New York · Toronto · Montréal · London · Munich · Paris · Madrid
Capetown · Sydney · Tokyo · Singapore · Mexico City

TEX is a trademark of the American Mathematical Society

METAFONT is a trademark of Addison–Wesley

The author and publisher have taken care in the preparation of this book, but make no expressed or implied warranty of any kind and assume no responsibility for errors or omissions. No liability is assumed for incidental or consequential damages in connection with or arising out of the use of the information or programs contained herein.

The publisher offers excellent discounts on this book when ordered in quantity for bulk purposes or special sales, which may include electronic versions and/or custom covers and content particular to your business, training goals, marketing focus, and branding interests. For more information, please contact:

    U.S. Corporate and Government Sales   (800) 382–3419
    corpsales@pearsontechgroup.com

For sales outside the U.S., please contact:

    International Sales   international@pearsoned.com

Visit us on the Web: informit.com/aw

Library of Congress Cataloging-in-Publication Data

Knuth, Donald Ervin, 1938-
  The art of computer programming / Donald Ervin Knuth.
  xiv,782 p. 24 cm.
  Includes bibliographical references and index.
  Contents: v. 1. Fundamental algorithms. -- v. 2. Seminumerical
algorithms. -- v. 3. Sorting and searching. -- v. 4a. Combinatorial
algorithms, part 1.
  Contents: v. 3. Sorting and searching. -- 2nd ed.
  ISBN 978-0-201-89683-1 (v. 1, 3rd ed.)
  ISBN 978-0-201-89684-8 (v. 2, 3rd ed.)
  ISBN 978-0-201-89685-5 (v. 3, 2nd ed.)
  ISBN 978-0-201-03804-0 (v. 4a)
  1. Electronic digital computers--Programming. 2. Computer
algorithms. I. Title.
QA76.6.K64 1997
005.1--DC21   97-2147

Internet page http://www-cs-faculty.stanford.edu/~knuth/taocp.html contains current information about this book and related books.

ISBN-13 978-0-201-89685-5
ISBN-10   0-201-89685-0

Text printed in the United States at Courier Westford in Westford, Massachusetts.
Twenty-ninth printing, January 2012

PREFACE

Cookery is become an art,
a noble science;
cooks are gentlemen.
— TITUS LIVIUS, *Ab Urbe Condita* XXXIX.vi
(Robert Burton, *Anatomy of Melancholy* 1.2.2.2)

THIS BOOK forms a natural sequel to the material on information structures in Chapter 2 of Volume 1, because it adds the concept of linearly ordered data to the other basic structural ideas.

The title "Sorting and Searching" may sound as if this book is only for those systems programmers who are concerned with the preparation of general-purpose sorting routines or applications to information retrieval. But in fact the area of sorting and searching provides an ideal framework for discussing a wide variety of important general issues:

- How are good algorithms discovered?
- How can given algorithms and programs be improved?
- How can the efficiency of algorithms be analyzed mathematically?
- How can a person choose rationally between different algorithms for the same task?
- In what senses can algorithms be proved "best possible"?
- How does the theory of computing interact with practical considerations?
- How can external memories like tapes, drums, or disks be used efficiently with large databases?

Indeed, I believe that virtually *every* important aspect of programming arises somewhere in the context of sorting or searching!

This volume comprises Chapters 5 and 6 of the complete series. Chapter 5 is concerned with sorting into order; this is a large subject that has been divided chiefly into two parts, internal sorting and external sorting. There also are supplementary sections, which develop auxiliary theories about permutations (Section 5.1) and about optimum techniques for sorting (Section 5.3). Chapter 6 deals with the problem of searching for specified items in tables or files; this is subdivided into methods that search sequentially, or by comparison of keys, or by digital properties, or by hashing, and then the more difficult problem of secondary key retrieval is considered. There is a surprising amount of interplay between both chapters, with strong analogies tying the topics together. Two important varieties of information structures are also discussed, in addition to those considered in Chapter 2, namely priority queues (Section 5.2.3) and linear lists represented as balanced trees (Section 6.2.3).

Like Volumes 1 and 2, this book includes a lot of material that does not appear in other publications. Many people have kindly written to me about their ideas, or spoken to me about them, and I hope that I have not distorted the material too badly when I have presented it in my own words.

I have not had time to search the patent literature systematically; indeed, I decry the current tendency to seek patents on algorithms (see Section 5.4.5). If somebody sends me a copy of a relevant patent not presently cited in this book, I will dutifully refer to it in future editions. However, I want to encourage people to continue the centuries-old mathematical tradition of putting newly discovered algorithms into the public domain. There are better ways to earn a living than to prevent other people from making use of one's contributions to computer science.

Before I retired from teaching, I used this book as a text for a student's second course in data structures, at the junior-to-graduate level, omitting most of the mathematical material. I also used the mathematical portions of this book as the basis for graduate-level courses in the analysis of algorithms, emphasizing especially Sections 5.1, 5.2.2, 6.3, and 6.4. A graduate-level course on concrete computational complexity could also be based on Sections 5.3, and 5.4.4, together with Sections 4.3.3, 4.6.3, and 4.6.4 of Volume 2.

For the most part this book is self-contained, except for occasional discussions relating to the MIX computer explained in Volume 1. Appendix B contains a summary of the mathematical notations used, some of which are a little different from those found in traditional mathematics books.

Preface to the Second Edition

This new edition matches the third editions of Volumes 1 and 2, in which I have been able to celebrate the completion of TeX and METAFONT by applying those systems to the publications they were designed for.

The conversion to electronic format has given me the opportunity to go over every word of the text and every punctuation mark. I've tried to retain the youthful exuberance of my original sentences while perhaps adding some more mature judgment. Dozens of new exercises have been added; dozens of old exercises have been given new and improved answers. Changes appear everywhere, but most significantly in Sections 5.1.4 (about permutations and tableaux), 5.3 (about optimum sorting), 5.4.9 (about disk sorting), 6.2.2 (about entropy), 6.4 (about universal hashing), and 6.5 (about multidimensional trees and tries).

The Art of Computer Programming is, however, still a work in progress. Research on sorting and searching continues to grow at a phenomenal rate. Therefore some parts of this book are headed by an "under construction" icon, to apologize for the fact that the material is not up-to-date. For example, if I were teaching an undergraduate class on data structures today, I would surely discuss randomized structures such as treaps at some length; but at present, I am only able to cite the principal papers on the subject, and to announce plans for a future Section 6.2.5 (see page 478). My files are bursting with important material that I plan to include in the final, glorious, third edition of Volume 3, perhaps 17 years from now. But I must finish Volumes 4 and 5 first, and I do not want to delay their publication any more than absolutely necessary.

I am enormously grateful to the many hundreds of people who have helped me to gather and refine this material during the past 35 years. Most of the hard work of preparing the new edition was accomplished by Phyllis Winkler (who put the text of the first edition into TEX form), by Silvio Levy (who edited it extensively and helped to prepare several dozen illustrations), and by Jeffrey Oldham (who converted more than 250 of the original illustrations to METAPOST format). The production staff at Addison–Wesley has also been extremely helpful, as usual.

I have corrected every error that alert readers detected in the first edition — as well as some mistakes that, alas, nobody noticed — and I have tried to avoid introducing new errors in the new material. However, I suppose some defects still remain, and I want to fix them as soon as possible. Therefore I will cheerfully award $2.56 to the first finder of each technical, typographical, or historical error. The webpage cited on page iv contains a current listing of all corrections that have been reported to me.

Stanford, California   D. E. K.
February 1998

> *There are certain common Privileges of a Writer,*
> *the Benefit whereof, I hope, there will be no Reason to doubt;*
> *Particularly, that where I am not understood, it shall be concluded,*
> *that something very useful and profound is coucht underneath.*
> — JONATHAN SWIFT, *Tale of a Tub*, Preface (1704)

NOTES ON THE EXERCISES

THE EXERCISES in this set of books have been designed for self-study as well as for classroom study. It is difficult, if not impossible, for anyone to learn a subject purely by reading about it, without applying the information to specific problems and thereby being encouraged to think about what has been read. Furthermore, we all learn best the things that we have discovered for ourselves. Therefore the exercises form a major part of this work; a definite attempt has been made to keep them as informative as possible and to select problems that are enjoyable as well as instructive.

In many books, easy exercises are found mixed randomly among extremely difficult ones. A motley mixture is, however, often unfortunate because readers like to know in advance how long a problem ought to take — otherwise they may just skip over all the problems. A classic example of such a situation is the book *Dynamic Programming* by Richard Bellman; this is an important, pioneering work in which a group of problems is collected together at the end of some chapters under the heading "Exercises and Research Problems," with extremely trivial questions appearing in the midst of deep, unsolved problems. It is rumored that someone once asked Dr. Bellman how to tell the exercises apart from the research problems, and he replied, "If you can solve it, it is an exercise; otherwise it's a research problem."

Good arguments can be made for including both research problems and very easy exercises in a book of this kind; therefore, to save the reader from the possible dilemma of determining which are which, *rating numbers* have been provided to indicate the level of difficulty. These numbers have the following general significance:

Rating   Interpretation

00 An extremely easy exercise that can be answered immediately if the material of the text has been understood; such an exercise can almost always be worked "in your head."

10 A simple problem that makes you think over the material just read, but is by no means difficult. You should be able to do this in one minute at most; pencil and paper may be useful in obtaining the solution.

20 An average problem that tests basic understanding of the text material, but you may need about fifteen or twenty minutes to answer it completely.

30 A problem of moderate difficulty and/or complexity; this one may involve more than two hours' work to solve satisfactorily, or even more if the TV is on.

40 Quite a difficult or lengthy problem that would be suitable for a term project in classroom situations. A student should be able to solve the problem in a reasonable amount of time, but the solution is not trivial.

50 A research problem that has not yet been solved satisfactorily, as far as the author knew at the time of writing, although many people have tried. If you have found an answer to such a problem, you ought to write it up for publication; furthermore, the author of this book would appreciate hearing about the solution as soon as possible (provided that it is correct).

By interpolation in this "logarithmic" scale, the significance of other rating numbers becomes clear. For example, a rating of *17* would indicate an exercise that is a bit simpler than average. Problems with a rating of *50* that are subsequently solved by some reader may appear with a *40* rating in later editions of the book, and in the errata posted on the Internet (see page iv).

The remainder of the rating number divided by 5 indicates the amount of detailed work required. Thus, an exercise rated *24* may take longer to solve than an exercise that is rated *25*, but the latter will require more creativity.

The author has tried earnestly to assign accurate rating numbers, but it is difficult for the person who makes up a problem to know just how formidable it will be for someone else to find a solution; and everyone has more aptitude for certain types of problems than for others. It is hoped that the rating numbers represent a good guess at the level of difficulty, but they should be taken as general guidelines, not as absolute indicators.

This book has been written for readers with varying degrees of mathematical training and sophistication; as a result, some of the exercises are intended only for the use of more mathematically inclined readers. The rating is preceded by an *M* if the exercise involves mathematical concepts or motivation to a greater extent than necessary for someone who is primarily interested only in programming the algorithms themselves. An exercise is marked with the letters "*HM*" if its solution necessarily involves a knowledge of calculus or other higher mathematics not developed in this book. An "*HM*" designation does *not* necessarily imply difficulty.

Some exercises are preceded by an arrowhead, "▶"; this designates problems that are especially instructive and especially recommended. Of course, no reader/student is expected to work *all* of the exercises, so those that seem to be the most valuable have been singled out. (This distinction is not meant to detract from the other exercises!) Each reader should at least make an attempt to solve all of the problems whose rating is *10* or less; and the arrows may help to indicate which of the problems with a higher rating should be given priority.

Solutions to most of the exercises appear in the answer section. Please use them wisely; do not turn to the answer until you have made a genuine effort to

solve the problem by yourself, or unless you absolutely do not have time to work this particular problem. *After* getting your own solution or giving the problem a decent try, you may find the answer instructive and helpful. The solution given will often be quite short, and it will sketch the details under the assumption that you have earnestly tried to solve it by your own means first. Sometimes the solution gives less information than was asked; often it gives more. It is quite possible that you may have a better answer than the one published here, or you may have found an error in the published solution; in such a case, the author will be pleased to know the details. Later printings of this book will give the improved solutions together with the solver's name where appropriate.

When working an exercise you may generally use the answers to previous exercises, unless specifically forbidden from doing so. The rating numbers have been assigned with this in mind; thus it is possible for exercise $n + 1$ to have a lower rating than exercise n, even though it includes the result of exercise n as a special case.

Summary of codes:	*00* Immediate
	10 Simple (one minute)
	20 Medium (quarter hour)
▶ Recommended	*30* Moderately hard
M Mathematically oriented	*40* Term project
HM Requiring "higher math"	*50* Research problem

EXERCISES

▶ **1.** [*00*] What does the rating "*M20*" mean?

2. [*10*] Of what value can the exercises in a textbook be to the reader?

3. [*HM45*] Prove that when n is an integer, $n > 2$, the equation $x^n + y^n = z^n$ has no solution in positive integers x, y, z.

Two hours' daily exercise ... will be enough
to keep a hack fit for his work.
— M. H. MAHON, *The Handy Horse Book* (1865)

CONTENTS

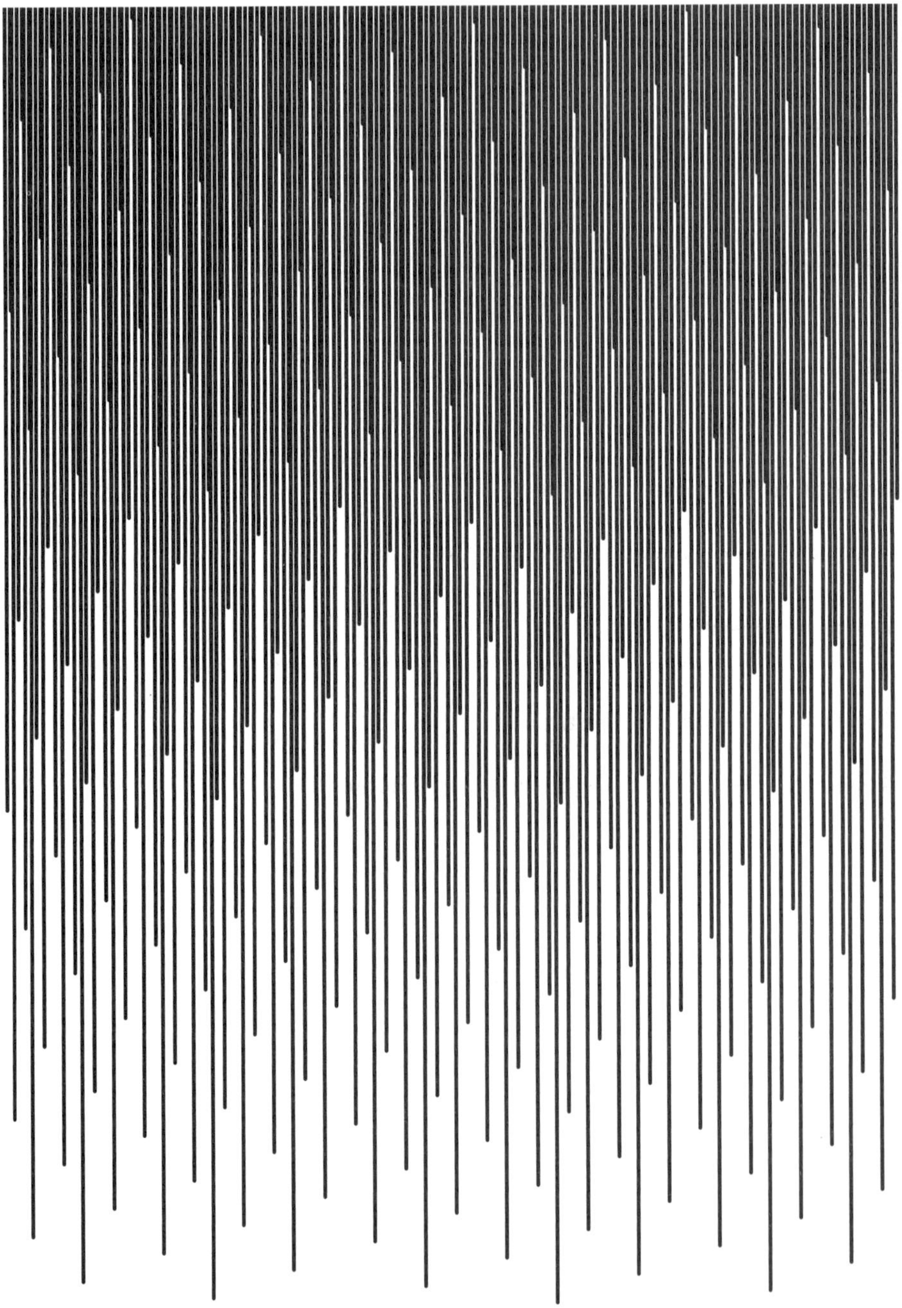

CHAPTER FIVE

SORTING

There is nothing more difficult to take in hand,
more perilous to conduct, or more uncertain in its success,
than to take the lead in the introduction of
a new order of things.
— NICCOLÒ MACHIAVELLI, *The Prince* (1513)

"But you can't look up all those license
numbers in time," Drake objected.
"We don't have to, Paul. We merely arrange a list
and look for duplications."
— PERRY MASON, in *The Case of the Angry Mourner* (1951)

"Treesort" Computer — With this new 'computer-approach'
to nature study you can quickly identify over 260
different trees of U.S., Alaska, and Canada,
even palms, desert trees, and other exotics.
To sort, you simply insert the needle.
— EDMUND SCIENTIFIC COMPANY, *Catalog* (1964)

IN THIS CHAPTER we shall study a topic that arises frequently in programming: the rearrangement of items into ascending or descending order. Imagine how hard it would be to use a dictionary if its words were not alphabetized! We will see that, in a similar way, the order in which items are stored in computer memory often has a profound influence on the speed and simplicity of algorithms that manipulate those items.

Although dictionaries of the English language define "sorting" as the process of separating or arranging things according to class or kind, computer programmers traditionally use the word in the much more special sense of marshaling things into ascending or descending order. The process should perhaps be called *ordering*, not sorting; but anyone who tries to call it "ordering" is soon led into confusion because of the many different meanings attached to that word. Consider the following sentence, for example: "Since only two of our tape drives were in working order, I was ordered to order more tape units in short order, in order to order the data several orders of magnitude faster." Mathematical terminology abounds with still more senses of order (the order of a group, the order of a permutation, the order of a branch point, relations of order, etc., etc.). Thus we find that the word "order" can lead to chaos.

Some people have suggested that "sequencing" would be the best name for the process of sorting into order; but this word often seems to lack the right connotation, especially when equal elements are present, and it occasionally conflicts with other terminology. It is quite true that "sorting" is itself an overused word ("I was sort of out of sorts after sorting that sort of data"), but it has become firmly established in computing parlance. Therefore we shall use the word "sorting" chiefly in the strict sense of sorting into order, without further apologies.

Some of the most important applications of sorting are:

a) *Solving the "togetherness" problem*, in which all items with the same identification are brought together. Suppose that we have 10000 items in arbitrary order, many of which have equal values; and suppose that we want to rearrange the data so that all items with equal values appear in consecutive positions. This is essentially the problem of sorting in the older sense of the word; and it can be solved easily by sorting the file in the new sense of the word, so that the values are in ascending order, $v_1 \leq v_2 \leq \cdots \leq v_{10000}$. The efficiency achievable in this procedure explains why the original meaning of "sorting" has changed.

b) *Matching items in two or more files.* If several files have been sorted into the same order, it is possible to find all of the matching entries in one sequential pass through them, without backing up. This is the principle that Perry Mason used to help solve a murder case (see the quotation at the beginning of this chapter). We can usually process a list of information most quickly by traversing it in sequence from beginning to end, instead of skipping around at random in the list, unless the entire list is small enough to fit in a high-speed random-access memory. Sorting makes it possible to use sequential accessing on large files, as a feasible substitute for direct addressing.

c) *Searching for information by key values.* Sorting is also an aid to searching, as we shall see in Chapter 6, hence it helps us make computer output more suitable for human consumption. In fact, a listing that has been sorted into alphabetic order often looks quite authoritative even when the associated numerical information has been incorrectly computed.

Although sorting has traditionally been used mostly for business data processing, it is actually a basic tool that every programmer should keep in mind for use in a wide variety of situations. We have discussed its use for simplifying algebraic formulas, in exercise 2.3.2–17. The exercises below illustrate the diversity of typical applications.

One of the first large-scale software systems to demonstrate the versatility of sorting was the LARC Scientific Compiler developed by J. Erdwinn, D. E. Ferguson, and their associates at Computer Sciences Corporation in 1960. This optimizing compiler for an extended FORTRAN language made heavy use of sorting so that the various compilation algorithms were presented with relevant parts of the source program in a convenient sequence. The first pass was a lexical scan that divided the FORTRAN source code into individual tokens, each representing an identifier or a constant or an operator, etc. Each token was assigned several sequence numbers; when sorted on the name and an appropriate sequence number, all the uses of a given identifier were brought together. The "defining entries" by which a user would specify whether an identifier stood for a function name, a parameter, or a dimensioned variable were given low sequence numbers, so that they would appear first among the tokens having a given identifier; this made it easy to check for conflicting usage and to allocate storage with respect to EQUIVALENCE declarations. The information thus gathered about each identifier was now attached to each token; in this way no "symbol table" of identifiers needed to be maintained in the high-speed memory. The updated tokens were then sorted on another sequence number, which essentially brought the source program back into its original order except that the numbering scheme was cleverly designed to put arithmetic expressions into a more convenient "Polish prefix" form. Sorting was also used in later phases of compilation, to facilitate loop optimization, to merge error messages into the listing, etc. In short, the compiler was designed so that virtually all the processing could be done sequentially from files that were stored in an auxiliary drum memory, since appropriate sequence numbers were attached to the data in such a way that it could be sorted into various convenient arrangements.

Computer manufacturers of the 1960s estimated that more than 25 percent of the running time on their computers was spent on sorting, when all their customers were taken into account. In fact, there were many installations in which the task of sorting was responsible for more than half of the computing time. From these statistics we may conclude that either (i) there are many important applications of sorting, or (ii) many people sort when they shouldn't, or (iii) inefficient sorting algorithms have been in common use. The real truth probably involves all three of these possibilities, but in any event we can see that sorting is worthy of serious study, as a practical matter.

Even if sorting were almost useless, there would be plenty of rewarding reasons for studying it anyway! The ingenious algorithms that have been discovered show that sorting is an extremely interesting topic to explore in its own right. Many fascinating unsolved problems remain in this area, as well as quite a few solved ones.

From a broader perspective we will find also that sorting algorithms make a valuable *case study* of how to attack computer programming problems in general. Many important principles of data structure manipulation will be illustrated in this chapter. We will be examining the evolution of various sorting techniques in an attempt to indicate how the ideas were discovered in the first place. By extrapolating this case study we can learn a good deal about strategies that help us design good algorithms for other computer problems.

Sorting techniques also provide excellent illustrations of the general ideas involved in the *analysis of algorithms* — the ideas used to determine performance characteristics of algorithms so that an intelligent choice can be made between competing methods. Readers who are mathematically inclined will find quite a few instructive techniques in this chapter for estimating the speed of computer algorithms and for solving complicated recurrence relations. On the other hand, the material has been arranged so that readers without a mathematical bent can safely skip over these calculations.

Before going on, we ought to define our problem a little more clearly, and introduce some terminology. We are given N items

$$R_1, R_2, \ldots, R_N$$

to be sorted; we shall call them *records*, and the entire collection of N records will be called a *file*. Each record R_j has a *key*, K_j, which governs the sorting process. Additional data, besides the key, is usually also present; this extra "satellite information" has no effect on sorting except that it must be carried along as part of each record.

An ordering relation "$<$" is specified on the keys so that the following conditions are satisfied for any key values a, b, c:

i) Exactly one of the possibilities $a < b$, $a = b$, $b < a$ is true. (This is called the law of trichotomy.)

ii) If $a < b$ and $b < c$, then $a < c$. (This is the familiar law of transitivity.)

Properties (i) and (ii) characterize the mathematical concept of *linear ordering*, also called *total ordering*. Any relationship "$<$" satisfying these two properties can be sorted by most of the methods to be mentioned in this chapter, although some sorting techniques are designed to work only with numerical or alphabetic keys that have the usual ordering.

The goal of sorting is to determine a permutation $p(1)\,p(2)\ldots p(N)$ of the indices $\{1, 2, \ldots, N\}$ that will put the keys into nondecreasing order:

$$K_{p(1)} \leq K_{p(2)} \leq \cdots \leq K_{p(N)}. \tag{1}$$

The sorting is called *stable* if we make the further requirement that records with equal keys should retain their original relative order. In other words, stable sorting has the additional property that

$$p(i) < p(j) \qquad \text{whenever} \quad K_{p(i)} = K_{p(j)} \quad \text{and} \quad i < j. \tag{2}$$

In some cases we will want the records to be physically rearranged in storage so that their keys are in order. But in other cases it will be sufficient merely to have an auxiliary table that specifies the permutation in some way, so that the records can be accessed in order of their keys.

A few of the sorting methods in this chapter assume the existence of either or both of the values "∞" and "$-\infty$", which are defined to be greater than or less than all keys, respectively:

$$-\infty < K_j < \infty, \qquad \text{for } 1 \leq j \leq N. \tag{3}$$

Such extreme values are occasionally used as artificial keys or as sentinel indicators. The case of equality is excluded in (3); if equality can occur, the algorithms can be modified so that they will still work, but usually at the expense of some elegance and efficiency.

Sorting can be classified generally into *internal sorting*, in which the records are kept entirely in the computer's high-speed random-access memory, and *external sorting*, when more records are present than can be held comfortably in memory at once. Internal sorting allows more flexibility in the structuring and accessing of the data, while external sorting shows us how to live with rather stringent accessing constraints.

The time required to sort N records, using a decent general-purpose sorting algorithm, is roughly proportional to $N \log N$; we make about $\log N$ "passes" over the data. This is the minimum possible time, as we shall see in Section 5.3.1, if the records are in random order and if sorting is done by pairwise comparisons of keys. Thus if we double the number of records, it will take a little more than twice as long to sort them, all other things being equal. (Actually, as N approaches infinity, a better indication of the time needed to sort is $N(\log N)^2$, if the keys are distinct, since the size of the keys must grow at least as fast as $\log N$; but for practical purposes, N never really approaches infinity.)

On the other hand, if the keys are known to be randomly distributed with respect to some continuous numerical distribution, we will see that sorting can be accomplished in $O(N)$ steps on the average.

EXERCISES — First Set

1. [*M20*] Prove, from the laws of trichotomy and transitivity, that the permutation $p(1)\,p(2)\ldots p(N)$ is *uniquely* determined when the sorting is assumed to be stable.

2. [*21*] Assume that each record R_j in a certain file contains *two* keys, a "major key" K_j and a "minor key" k_j, with a linear ordering $<$ defined on each of the sets of keys. Then we can define *lexicographic order* between pairs of keys (K, k) in the usual way:

$$(K_i, k_i) < (K_j, k_j) \quad \text{if} \quad K_i < K_j \quad \text{or if} \quad K_i = K_j \quad \text{and} \quad k_i < k_j.$$

Alice took this file and sorted it first on the major keys, obtaining n groups of records with equal major keys in each group,

$$K_{p(1)} = \cdots = K_{p(i_1)} < K_{p(i_1+1)} = \cdots = K_{p(i_2)} < \cdots < K_{p(i_{n-1}+1)} = \cdots = K_{p(i_n)},$$

where $i_n = N$. Then she sorted each of the n groups $R_{p(i_{j-1}+1)}, \ldots, R_{p(i_j)}$ on their minor keys.

Bill took the same original file and sorted it first on the minor keys; then he took the resulting file, and sorted it on the major keys.

Chris took the same original file and did a single sorting operation on it, using lexicographic order on the major and minor keys (K_j, k_j).

Did everyone obtain the same result?

3. [*M25*] Let $<$ be a relation on $K_1, \ldots, K_N$ that satisfies the law of trichotomy but *not* the transitive law. Prove that even without the transitive law it is possible to sort the records in a stable manner, meeting conditions (1) and (2); in fact, there are at least three arrangements that satisfy the conditions!

▶ **4.** [*21*] Lexicographers don't actually use strict lexicographic order in dictionaries, because uppercase and lowercase letters must be interfiled. Thus they want an ordering such as this:

$$\text{a} < \text{A} < \text{aa} < \text{AA} < \text{AAA} < \text{Aachen} < \text{aah} < \cdots < \text{zzz} < \text{ZZZ}.$$

Explain how to implement dictionary order.

▶ **5.** [*M28*] Design a binary code for all nonnegative integers so that if n is encoded as the string $\rho(n)$ we have $m < n$ if and only if $\rho(m)$ is lexicographically less than $\rho(n)$. Moreover, $\rho(m)$ should not be a prefix of $\rho(n)$ for any $m \neq n$. If possible, the length of $\rho(n)$ should be at most $\lg n + O(\log \log n)$ for all large n. (Such a code is useful if we want to sort texts that mix words and numbers, or if we want to map arbitrarily large alphabets into binary strings.)

6. [*15*] Mr. B. C. Dull (a MIX programmer) wanted to know if the number stored in location A is greater than, less than, or equal to the number stored in location B. So he wrote "LDA A; SUB B" and tested whether register A was positive, negative, or zero. What serious mistake did he make, and what should he have done instead?

7. [*17*] Write a MIX subroutine for multiprecision comparison of keys, having the following specifications:

Calling sequence: JMP COMPARE

Entry conditions: rI1 $= n$; CONTENTS$(A + k) = a_k$ and CONTENTS$(B + k) = b_k$, for $1 \leq k \leq n$; assume that $n \geq 1$.

Exit conditions: CI = GREATER, if $(a_n, \ldots, a_1) > (b_n, \ldots, b_1)$;
 CI = EQUAL,   if $(a_n, \ldots, a_1) = (b_n, \ldots, b_1)$;
 CI = LESS,   if $(a_n, \ldots, a_1) < (b_n, \ldots, b_1)$;
 rX and rI1 are possibly affected.

Here the relation $(a_n, \ldots, a_1) < (b_n, \ldots, b_1)$ denotes lexicographic ordering from left to right; that is, there is an index j such that $a_k = b_k$ for $n \geq k > j$, but $a_j < b_j$.

▶ **8.** [*30*] Locations A and B contain two numbers a and b, respectively. Show that it is possible to write a MIX program that computes and stores $\min(a, b)$ in location C, *without using any jump operators*. (Caution: Since you will not be able to test whether or not arithmetic overflow has occurred, it is wise to guarantee that overflow is impossible regardless of the values of a and b.)

9. [*M27*] After N independent, uniformly distributed random variables between 0 and 1 have been sorted into nondecreasing order, what is the probability that the rth smallest of these numbers is $\leq x$?

EXERCISES — Second Set

Each of the following exercises states a problem that a computer programmer might have had to solve in the old days when computers didn't have much random-access memory. Suggest a "good" way to solve the problem, *assuming that only a few thousand words of internal memory are available*, supplemented by about half a dozen tape units (enough tape units for sorting). Algorithms that work well under such limitations also prove to be efficient on modern machines.

10. [*15*] You are given a tape containing one million words of data. How do you determine how many distinct words are present on the tape?

11. [*18*] You are the U. S. Internal Revenue Service; you receive millions of "information" forms from organizations telling how much income they have paid to people, and millions of "tax" forms from people telling how much income they have been paid. How do you catch people who don't report all of their income?

12. [*M25*] (*Transposing a matrix.*) You are given a magnetic tape containing one million words, representing the elements of a 1000×1000 matrix stored in order by rows: $a_{1,1}\, a_{1,2} \ldots a_{1,1000}\, a_{2,1} \ldots a_{2,1000} \ldots a_{1000,1000}$. How do you create a tape in which the elements are stored by columns $a_{1,1}\,a_{2,1}\ldots a_{1000,1}\,a_{1,2}\ldots a_{1000,2}\ldots a_{1000,1000}$ instead? (Try to make less than a dozen passes over the data.)

13. [*M26*] How could you "shuffle" a large file of N words into a random rearrangement?

14. [*20*] You are working with two computer systems that have different conventions for the "collating sequence" that defines the ordering of alphameric characters. How do you make one computer sort alphameric files in the order used by the other computer?

15. [*18*] You are given a list of the names of a fairly large number of people born in the U.S.A., together with the name of the state where they were born. How do you count the number of people born in each state? (Assume that nobody appears in the list more than once.)

16. [*20*] In order to make it easier to make changes to large FORTRAN programs, you want to design a "cross-reference" routine; such a routine takes FORTRAN programs as input and prints them together with an index that shows each use of each identifier (that is, each name) in the program. How should such a routine be designed?

▶ **17.** [*33*] (*Library card sorting.*) Before the days of computerized databases, every library maintained a catalog of cards so that users could find the books they wanted. But the task of putting catalog cards into an order convenient for human use turned out to be quite complicated as library collections grew. The following "alphabetical" listing indicates many of the procedures recommended in the *American Library Association Rules for Filing Catalog Cards* (Chicago: 1942):

Text of card	Remarks
R. Accademia nazionale dei Lincei, Rome	Ignore foreign royalty (except British)
1812; ein historischer Roman.	Achtzehnhundertzwölf
Bibliothèque d'histoire révolutionnaire.	Treat apostrophe as space in French
Bibliothèque des curiosités.	Ignore accents on letters
Brown, Mrs. J. Crosby	Ignore designation of rank
Brown, John	Names with dates follow those without
Brown, John, mathematician	. . . and the latter are subarranged
Brown, John, of Boston	by descriptive words
Brown, John, 1715–1766	Arrange identical names by birthdate
BROWN, JOHN, 1715–1766	Works "about" follow works "by"
Brown, John, d. 1811	Sometimes birthdate must be estimated
Brown, Dr. John, 1810–1882	Ignore designation of rank
Brown-Williams, Reginald Makepeace	Treat hyphen as space
Brown America.	Book titles follow compound names
Brown & Dallison's Nevada directory.	& in English becomes "and"
Brownjohn, Alan	
Den', Vladimir Éduardovich, 1867–	Ignore apostrophe in names
The den.	Ignore an initial article
Den lieben langen Tag.	. . . provided it's in nominative case
Dix, Morgan, 1827–1908	Names precede words
1812 ouverture.	Dix-huit cent douze
Le XIXe siècle français.	Dix-neuvième
The 1847 issue of U. S. stamps.	Eighteen forty-seven
1812 overture.	Eighteen twelve
I am a mathematician.	(a book by Norbert Wiener)

Text of card	Remarks
IBM journal of research and development.	Initials are like one-letter words
ha-I ha-ehad.	Ignore initial article
Ia; a love story.	Ignore punctuation in titles
International Business Machines Corporation	
al-Khuwārizmī, Muḥammad ibn Mūsā,	
fl. 813–846	Ignore initial "al-" in Arabic names
Labour. A magazine for all workers.	Respell it "Labor"
Labor research association	
Labour, see Labor	Cross-reference card
McCall's cookbook	Ignore apostrophe in English
McCarthy, John, 1927–	Mc = Mac
Machine-independent computer	
programming.	Treat hyphen as space
MacMahon, Maj. Percy Alexander,	
1854–1929	Ignore designation of rank
Mrs. Dalloway.	"Mrs." = "Mistress"
Mistress of mistresses.	
Royal society of London	Don't ignore British royalty
St. Petersburger Zeitung.	"St." = "Saint", even in German
Saint-Saëns, Camille, 1835–1921	Treat hyphen as space
Ste-Marie, Gaston P	Sainte
Seminumerical algorithms.	(a book by Donald Ervin Knuth)
Uncle Tom's cabin.	(a book by Harriet Beecher Stowe)
U. S. bureau of the census.	"U. S." = "United States"
Vandermonde, Alexandre Théophile,	
1735–1796	
Van Valkenburg, Mac Elwyn, 1921–	Ignore space after prefix in surnames
Von Neumann, John, 1903–1957	
The whole art of legerdemain.	Ignore initial article
Who's afraid of Virginia Woolf?	Ignore apostrophe in English
Wijngaarden, Adriaan van, 1916–	Surname begins with uppercase letter

(Most of these rules are subject to certain exceptions, and there are many other rules not illustrated here.)

If you were given the job of sorting large quantities of catalog cards by computer, and eventually maintaining a very large file of such cards, and if you had no chance to change these long-standing policies of card filing, how would you arrange the data in such a way that the sorting and merging operations are facilitated?

18. [*M25*] (E. T. Parker.) Leonhard Euler once conjectured [*Nova Acta Acad. Sci. Petropolitanæ* **13** (1795), 45–63, §3; written in 1778] that there are no solutions to the equation

$$u^6 + v^6 + w^6 + x^6 + y^6 = z^6$$

in positive integers u, v, w, x, y, z. At the same time he conjectured that

$$x_1^n + \cdots + x_{n-1}^n = x_n^n$$

would have no positive integer solutions, for all $n \geq 3$, but this more general conjecture was disproved by the computer-discovered identity $27^5 + 84^5 + 110^5 + 133^5 = 144^5$; see L. J. Lander, T. R. Parkin, and J. L. Selfridge, *Math. Comp.* **21** (1967), 446–459.

Infinitely many counterexamples when $n = 4$ were subsequently found by Noam Elkies [*Math. Comp.* **51** (1988), 825–835]. Can you think of a way in which sorting would help in the search for counterexamples to Euler's conjecture when $n = 6$?

▸ **19.** [*24*] Given a file containing a million or so distinct 30-bit binary words $x_1, \ldots, x_N$, what is a good way to find all *complementary* pairs $\{x_i, x_j\}$ that are present? (Two words are complementary when one has 0 wherever the other has 1, and conversely; thus they are complementary if and only if their sum is $(11 \ldots 1)_2$, when they are treated as binary numbers.)

▸ **20.** [*25*] Given a file containing 1000 30-bit words $x_1, \ldots, x_{1000}$, how would you prepare a list of all pairs (x_i, x_j) such that $x_i = x_j$ except in at most two bit positions?

21. [*22*] How would you go about looking for five-letter anagrams such as CARET, CARTE, CATER, CRATE, REACT, RECTA, TRACE; CRUEL, LUCRE, ULCER; DOWRY, ROWDY, WORDY? [One might wish to know whether there are any sets of ten or more five-letter English anagrams besides the remarkable set

APERS, ASPER, PARES, PARSE, PEARS, PRASE, PRESA, RAPES, REAPS, SPAER, SPARE, SPEAR,

to which we might add the French word APRÈS.]

22. [*M28*] Given the specifications of a fairly large number of directed graphs, what approach will be useful for grouping the *isomorphic* ones together? (Directed graphs are isomorphic if there is a one-to-one correspondence between their vertices and a one-to-one correspondence between their arcs, where the correspondences preserve incidence between vertices and arcs.)

23. [*30*] In a certain group of 4096 people, everyone has about 100 acquaintances. A file has been prepared listing all pairs of people who are acquaintances. (The relation is symmetric: If x is acquainted with y, then y is acquainted with x. Therefore the file contains roughly 200,000 entries.) How would you design an algorithm to list all the k-person *cliques* in this group of people, given k? (A clique is an instance of mutual acquaintances: Everyone in the clique is acquainted with everyone else.) Assume that there are no cliques of size 25, so the total number of cliques cannot be enormous.

▸ **24.** [*30*] Three million men with distinct names were laid end-to-end, reaching from New York to California. Each participant was given a slip of paper on which he wrote down his own name and the name of the person immediately west of him in the line. The man at the extreme western end didn't understand what to do, so he threw his paper away; the remaining 2,999,999 slips of paper were put into a huge basket and taken to the National Archives in Washington, D.C. Here the contents of the basket were shuffled completely and transferred to magnetic tapes.

At this point an information scientist observed that there was enough information on the tapes to reconstruct the list of people in their original order. And a computer scientist discovered a way to do the reconstruction with fewer than 1000 passes through the data tapes, using only sequential accessing of tape files and a small amount of random-access memory. How was that possible?

[In other words, given the pairs (x_i, x_{i+1}), for $1 \le i < N$, in random order, where the x_i are distinct, how can the sequence $x_1 x_2 \ldots x_N$ be obtained, restricting all operations to serial techniques suitable for use with magnetic tapes? This is the problem of sorting into order when there is no easy way to tell which of two given keys precedes the other; we have already raised this question as part of exercise 2.2.3–25.]

25. [*M21*] (*Discrete logarithms.*) You know that p is a (rather large) prime number, and that a is a primitive root modulo p. Therefore, for all b in the range $1 \leq b < p$, there is a unique n such that $a^n \bmod p = b$, $1 \leq n < p$. (This n is called the index of b modulo p, with respect to a.) Explain how to find n, given b, without needing $\Omega(n)$ steps. [*Hint:* Let $m = \lceil \sqrt{p} \rceil$ and try to solve $a^{mn_1} \equiv ba^{-n_2}$ (modulo p) for $0 \leq n_1, n_2 < m$.]

*5.1. COMBINATORIAL PROPERTIES OF PERMUTATIONS

A PERMUTATION of a finite set is an arrangement of its elements into a row. Permutations are of special importance in the study of sorting algorithms, since they represent the unsorted input data. In order to study the efficiency of different sorting methods, we will want to be able to count the number of permutations that cause a certain step of a sorting procedure to be executed a certain number of times.

We have, of course, met permutations frequently in previous chapters. For example, in Section 1.2.5 we discussed two basic theoretical methods of constructing the $n!$ permutations of n objects; in Section 1.3.3 we analyzed some algorithms dealing with the cycle structure and multiplicative properties of permutations; in Section 3.3.2 we studied their "runs up" and "runs down." The purpose of the present section is to study several other properties of permutations, and to consider the general case where equal elements are allowed to appear. In the course of this study we will learn a good deal about combinatorial mathematics.

The properties of permutations are sufficiently pleasing to be interesting in their own right, and it is convenient to develop them systematically in one place instead of scattering the material throughout this chapter. But readers who are not mathematically inclined and readers who are anxious to dive right into sorting techniques are advised to go on to Section 5.2 immediately, since the present section actually has little *direct* connection to sorting.

*5.1.1. Inversions

Let $a_1 a_2 \ldots a_n$ be a permutation of the set $\{1, 2, \ldots, n\}$. If $i < j$ and $a_i > a_j$, the pair (a_i, a_j) is called an *inversion* of the permutation; for example, the permutation 3 1 4 2 has three inversions: $(3, 1)$, $(3, 2)$, and $(4, 2)$. Each inversion is a pair of elements that is out of sort, so the only permutation with no inversions is the sorted permutation $1\,2\ldots n$. This connection with sorting is the chief reason why we will be so interested in inversions, although we have already used the concept to analyze a dynamic storage allocation algorithm (see exercise 2.2.2–9).

The concept of inversions was introduced by G. Cramer in 1750 [*Intr. à l'Analyse des Lignes Courbes Algébriques* (Geneva: 1750), 657–659; see Thomas Muir, *Theory of Determinants* **1** (1906), 11–14], in connection with his famous rule for solving linear equations. In essence, Cramer defined the determinant of an $n \times n$ matrix in the following way:

$$\det \begin{pmatrix} x_{11} & x_{12} & \cdots & x_{1n} \\ \vdots & \vdots & & \vdots \\ x_{n1} & x_{n2} & \cdots & x_{nn} \end{pmatrix} = \sum (-1)^{\text{inv}(a_1 a_2 \ldots a_n)} x_{1a_1} x_{2a_2} \ldots x_{na_n},$$

summed over all permutations $a_1 a_2 \ldots a_n$ of $\{1, 2, \ldots, n\}$, where $\text{inv}(a_1 a_2 \ldots a_n)$ is the number of inversions of the permutation.

The *inversion table* $b_1 b_2 \ldots b_n$ of the permutation $a_1 a_2 \ldots a_n$ is obtained by letting b_j be the number of elements to the left of j that are greater than j.

In other words, b_j is the number of inversions whose second component is j. It follows, for example, that the permutation

$$5\ 9\ 1\ 8\ 2\ 6\ 4\ 7\ 3 \tag{1}$$

has the inversion table

$$2\ 3\ 6\ 4\ 0\ 2\ 2\ 1\ 0, \tag{2}$$

since 5 and 9 are to the left of 1; 5, 9, 8 are to the left of 2; etc. This permutation has 20 inversions in all. By definition the numbers b_j will always satisfy

$$0 \le b_1 \le n-1, \quad 0 \le b_2 \le n-2, \quad \ldots, \quad 0 \le b_{n-1} \le 1, \quad b_n = 0. \tag{3}$$

Perhaps the most important fact about inversions is the simple observation that *an inversion table uniquely determines the corresponding permutation.* We can go back from any inversion table $b_1 b_2 \ldots b_n$ satisfying (3) to the unique permutation that produces it, by successively determining the relative placement of the elements $n, n-1, \ldots, 1$ (in this order). For example, we can construct the permutation corresponding to (2) as follows: Write down the number 9; then place 8 after 9, since $b_8 = 1$. Similarly, put 7 after both 8 and 9, since $b_7 = 2$. Then 6 must follow two of the numbers already written down, because $b_6 = 2$; the partial result so far is therefore

$$9\ 8\ 6\ 7.$$

Continue by placing 5 at the left, since $b_5 = 0$; put 4 after four of the numbers; and put 3 after six numbers (namely at the extreme right), giving

$$5\ 9\ 8\ 6\ 4\ 7\ 3.$$

The insertion of 2 and 1 in an analogous way yields (1).

This correspondence is important because we can often translate a problem stated in terms of permutations into an equivalent problem stated in terms of inversion tables, and the latter problem may be easier to solve. For example, consider the simplest question of all: How many permutations of $\{1, 2, \ldots, n\}$ are possible? The answer must be the number of possible inversion tables, and they are easily enumerated since there are n choices for b_1, independently $n-1$ choices for b_2, ..., 1 choice for b_n, making $n(n-1) \ldots 1 = n!$ choices in all. Inversions are easy to count, because the b's are completely independent of each other, while the a's must be mutually distinct.

In Section 1.2.10 we analyzed the number of local maxima that occur when a permutation is read from right to left; in other words, we counted how many elements are larger than any of their successors. (The right-to-left maxima in (1), for example, are 3, 7, 8, and 9.) This is the number of j such that b_j has its maximum value, $n - j$. Since b_1 will equal $n - 1$ with probability $1/n$, and (independently) b_2 will be equal to $n - 2$ with probability $1/(n - 1)$, etc., it is clear by consideration of the inversions that the average number of right-to-left

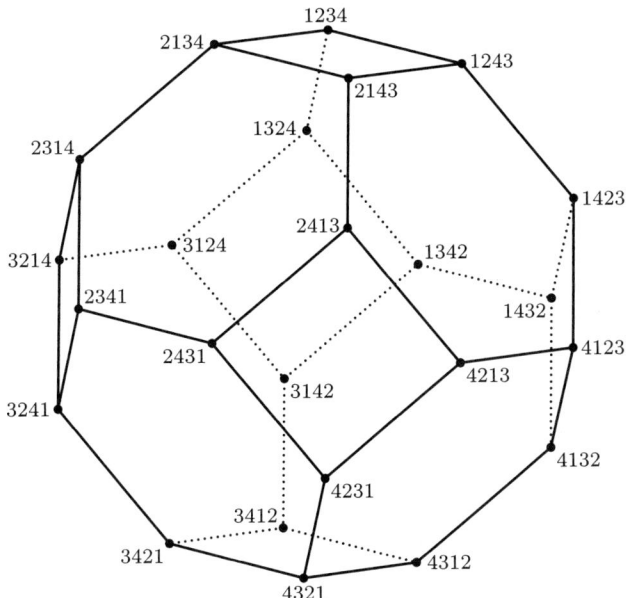

Fig. 1. The truncated octahedron, which shows the change in inversions when adjacent elements of a permutation are interchanged.

maxima is

$$\frac{1}{n} + \frac{1}{n-1} + \cdots + \frac{1}{1} = H_n.$$

The corresponding generating function is also easily derived in a similar way.

If we interchange two *adjacent* elements of a permutation, it is easy to see that the total number of inversions will increase or decrease by unity. Figure 1 shows the 24 permutations of $\{1, 2, 3, 4\}$, with lines joining permutations that differ by an interchange of adjacent elements; following any line downward inverts exactly one new pair. Hence the number of inversions of a permutation π is the length of a downward path from 1234 to π in Fig. 1; all such paths must have the same length.

Incidentally, the diagram in Fig. 1 may be viewed as a three-dimensional solid, the "truncated octahedron," which has 8 hexagonal faces and 6 square faces. This is one of the classical uniform polyhedra attributed to Archimedes (see exercise 10).

The reader should not confuse inversions of a permutation with the *inverse* of a permutation. Recall that we can write a permutation in two-line form

$$\begin{pmatrix} 1 & 2 & 3 & \ldots & n \\ a_1 & a_2 & a_3 & \ldots & a_n \end{pmatrix};$$
(4)

the inverse $a_1' \, a_2' \, a_3' \ldots a_n'$ of this permutation is the permutation obtained by interchanging the two rows and then sorting the columns into increasing order of the new top row:

$$\begin{pmatrix} a_1 & a_2 & a_3 & \ldots & a_n \\ 1 & 2 & 3 & \ldots & n \end{pmatrix} = \begin{pmatrix} 1 & 2 & 3 & \ldots & n \\ a'_1 & a'_2 & a'_3 & \ldots & a'_n \end{pmatrix}. \qquad (5)$$

For example, the inverse of $5\,9\,1\,8\,2\,6\,4\,7\,3$ is $3\,5\,9\,7\,1\,6\,8\,4\,2$, since

$$\begin{pmatrix} 5\ 9\ 1\ 8\ 2\ 6\ 4\ 7\ 3 \\ 1\ 2\ 3\ 4\ 5\ 6\ 7\ 8\ 9 \end{pmatrix} = \begin{pmatrix} 1\ 2\ 3\ 4\ 5\ 6\ 7\ 8\ 9 \\ 3\ 5\ 9\ 7\ 1\ 6\ 8\ 4\ 2 \end{pmatrix}.$$

Another way to define the inverse is to say that $a'_j = k$ if and only if $a_k = j$.

The inverse of a permutation was first defined by H. A. Rothe [in *Sammlung combinatorisch-analytischer Abhandlungen*, edited by C. F. Hindenburg, **2** (Leipzig: 1800), 263–305], who noticed an interesting connection between inverses and inversions: *The inverse of a permutation has exactly as many inversions as the permutation itself.* Rothe's proof of this fact was not the simplest possible one, but it is instructive and quite pretty nevertheless. We construct an $n \times n$ chessboard having a dot in column j of row i whenever $a_i = j$. Then we put ×'s in all squares that have dots lying both below (in the same column) and to their right (in the same row). For example, the diagram for $5\,9\,1\,8\,2\,6\,4\,7\,3$ is

×	×	×	×	●				
×	×	×	×		×	×	×	●
●								
	×	×	×		×	×	●	
	●							
		×	×		●			
		×	●					
		×				●		
		●						

The number of ×'s is the number of inversions, since it is easy to see that b_j is the number of ×'s in column j. Now if we transpose the diagram — interchanging rows and columns — we get the diagram corresponding to the inverse of the original permutation. Hence the number of ×'s (the number of inversions) is the same in both cases. Rothe used this fact to prove that the determinant of a matrix is unchanged when the matrix is transposed.

The analysis of several sorting algorithms involves the knowledge of how many permutations of n elements have exactly k inversions. Let us denote that number by $I_n(k)$; Table 1 lists the first few values of this function.

By considering the inversion table $b_1\, b_2 \ldots b_n$, it is obvious that $I_n(0) = 1$, $I_n(1) = n - 1$, and there is a symmetry property

$$I_n\left(\binom{n}{2} - k\right) = I_n(k). \qquad (6)$$

Table 1

PERMUTATIONS WITH k INVERSIONS

n	$I_n(0)$	$I_n(1)$	$I_n(2)$	$I_n(3)$	$I_n(4)$	$I_n(5)$	$I_n(6)$	$I_n(7)$	$I_n(8)$	$I_n(9)$	$I_n(10)$	$I_n(11)$
1	1	0	0	0	0	0	0	0	0	0	0	0
2	1	1	0	0	0	0	0	0	0	0	0	0
3	1	2	2	1	0	0	0	0	0	0	0	0
4	1	3	5	6	5	3	1	0	0	0	0	0
5	1	4	9	15	20	22	20	15	9	4	1	0
6	1	5	14	29	49	71	90	101	101	90	71	49

Furthermore, since each of the b's can be chosen independently of the others, it is not difficult to see that the generating function

$$G_n(z) = I_n(0) + I_n(1)z + I_n(2)z^2 + \cdots \qquad (7)$$

satisfies $G_n(z) = (1 + z + \cdots + z^{n-1})G_{n-1}(z)$; hence it has the comparatively simple form noticed by O. Rodrigues [*J. de Math.* **4** (1839), 236–240]:

$$(1 + z + \cdots + z^{n-1})\ldots(1 + z)(1) = (1 - z^n)\ldots(1 - z^2)(1 - z)/(1 - z)^n. \quad (8)$$

From this generating function, we can easily extend Table 1, and we can verify that the numbers below the zigzag line in that table satisfy

$$I_n(k) = I_n(k - 1) + I_{n-1}(k), \quad \text{for} \quad k < n. \qquad (9)$$

(This relation does *not* hold *above* the zigzag line.) A more complicated argument (see exercise 14) shows that, in fact, we have the formulas

$$I_n(2) = \binom{n}{2} - 1, \qquad\qquad n \geq 2;$$

$$I_n(3) = \binom{n+1}{3} - \binom{n}{1}, \qquad\qquad n \geq 3;$$

$$I_n(4) = \binom{n+2}{4} - \binom{n+1}{2}, \qquad\qquad n \geq 4;$$

$$I_n(5) = \binom{n+3}{5} - \binom{n+2}{3} + 1, \qquad n \geq 5;$$

in general, the formula for $I_n(k)$ contains about $1.6\sqrt{k}$ terms:

$$I_n(k) = \binom{n+k-2}{k} - \binom{n+k-3}{k-2} + \binom{n+k-6}{k-5} + \binom{n+k-8}{k-7} - \cdots$$

$$+ (-1)^j\left(\binom{n+k-u_j-1}{k-u_j} + \binom{n+k-u_j-j-1}{k-u_j-j}\right) + \cdots, \quad n \geq k, \quad (10)$$

where $u_j = (3j^2 - j)/2$ is a so-called "pentagonal number."

If we divide $G_n(z)$ by $n!$ we get the generating function $g_n(z)$ for the probability distribution of the number of inversions in a random permutation of n elements. This is the product

$$g_n(z) = h_1(z)h_2(z)\ldots h_n(z), \tag{11}$$

where $h_k(z) = (1 + z + \cdots + z^{k-1})/k$ is the generating function for the uniform distribution of a random nonnegative integer less than k. It follows that

$$\text{mean}(g_n) = \text{mean}(h_1) + \text{mean}(h_2) + \cdots + \text{mean}(h_n)$$

$$= \quad 0 \quad + \quad \frac{1}{2} \quad + \cdots + \quad \frac{n-1}{2} \quad = \frac{n(n-1)}{4}; \tag{12}$$

$$\text{var}(g_n) = \quad \text{var}(h_1) \quad + \quad \text{var}(h_2) \quad + \cdots + \quad \text{var}(h_n)$$

$$= \quad 0 \quad + \quad \frac{1}{4} \quad + \cdots + \quad \frac{n^2-1}{12} \quad = \frac{n(2n+5)(n-1)}{72}. \tag{13}$$

So the average number of inversions is rather large, about $\frac{1}{4}n^2$; the standard deviation is also rather large, about $\frac{1}{6}n^{3/2}$.

A remarkable discovery about the distribution of inversions was made by P. A. MacMahon [*Amer. J. Math.* **35** (1913), 281–322]. Let us define the *index* of the permutation $a_1 a_2 \ldots a_n$ as the sum of all subscripts j such that $a_j > a_{j+1}$, $1 \le j < n$. For example, the index of $5\,9\,1\,8\,2\,6\,4\,7\,3$ is $2 + 4 + 6 + 8 = 20$. By coincidence the index is the same as the number of inversions in this case. If we list the 24 permutations of $\{1, 2, 3, 4\}$, namely

Permutation	Index	Inversions	Permutation	Index	Inversions
1 2 3 4	0	0	3|1 2 4	1	2
1 2 4|3	3	1	3|1 4|2	4	3
1 3|2 4	2	1	3|2|1 4	3	3
1 3 4|2	3	2	3|2 4|1	4	4
1 4|2 3	2	2	3 4|1 2	2	4
1 4|3|2	5	3	3 4|2|1	5	5
2|1 3 4	1	1	4|1 2 3	1	3
2|1 4|3	4	2	4|1 3|2	4	4
2 3|1 4	2	2	4|2|1 3	3	4
2 3 4|1	3	3	4|2 3|1	4	5
2 4|1 3	2	3	4|3|1 2	3	5
2 4|3|1	5	4	4|3|2|1	6	6

we see that *the number of permutations having a given index, k, is the same as the number having k inversions.*

At first this fact might appear to be almost obvious, but further scrutiny makes it very mysterious. MacMahon gave an ingenious indirect proof, as follows: Let $\text{ind}(a_1 a_2 \ldots a_n)$ be the index of the permutation $a_1 a_2 \ldots a_n$, and let

$$H_n(z) = \sum z^{\text{ind}(a_1 a_2 \ldots a_n)} \tag{14}$$

be the corresponding generating function; the sum in (14) is over all permutations of $\{1, 2, \ldots, n\}$. We wish to show that $H_n(z) = G_n(z)$. For this purpose we will define a one-to-one correspondence between arbitrary n-tuples $(q_1, q_2, \ldots, q_n)$ of nonnegative integers, on the one hand, and ordered pairs of n-tuples

$$\big((a_1, a_2, \ldots, a_n),\ (p_1, p_2, \ldots, p_n)\big)$$

on the other hand, where $a_1 a_2 \ldots a_n$ is a permutation of the indices $\{1, 2, \ldots, n\}$ and $p_1 \geq p_2 \geq \cdots \geq p_n \geq 0$. This correspondence will satisfy the condition

$$q_1 + q_2 + \cdots + q_n = \operatorname{ind}(a_1 a_2 \ldots a_n) + (p_1 + p_2 + \cdots + p_n). \tag{15}$$

The generating function $\sum z^{q_1 + q_2 + \cdots + q_n}$, summed over all n-tuples of nonnegative integers $(q_1, q_2, \ldots, q_n)$, is $Q_n(z) = 1/(1-z)^n$; and the generating function $\sum z^{p_1 + p_2 + \cdots + p_n}$, summed over all n-tuples of integers $(p_1, p_2, \ldots, p_n)$ such that $p_1 \geq p_2 \geq \cdots \geq p_n \geq 0$, is

$$P_n(z) = 1/(1-z)(1-z^2)\ldots(1-z^n), \tag{16}$$

as shown in exercise 15. In view of (15), the one-to-one correspondence we are about to establish will prove that $Q_n(z) = H_n(z)P_n(z)$, that is,

$$H_n(z) = Q_n(z)/P_n(z). \tag{17}$$

But $Q_n(z)/P_n(z)$ is $G_n(z)$, by (8).

The desired correspondence is defined by a simple sorting procedure: Any n-tuple $(q_1, q_2, \ldots, q_n)$ can be rearranged into nonincreasing order $q_{a_1} \geq q_{a_2} \geq \cdots \geq q_{a_n}$ in a stable manner, where $a_1 a_2 \ldots a_n$ is a permutation such that $q_{a_j} = q_{a_{j+1}}$ implies $a_j < a_{j+1}$. We set $(p_1, p_2, \ldots, p_n) = (q_{a_1}, q_{a_2}, \ldots, q_{a_n})$ and then, for $1 \leq j < n$, subtract 1 from each of $p_1, \ldots, p_j$ for each j such that $a_j > a_{j+1}$. We still have $p_1 \geq p_2 \geq \cdots \geq p_n$, because p_j was strictly greater than p_{j+1} whenever $a_j > a_{j+1}$. The resulting pair $\big((a_1, a_2, \ldots, a_n), (p_1, p_2, \ldots, p_n)\big)$ satisfies (15), because the total reduction of the p's is $\operatorname{ind}(a_1 a_2 \ldots a_n)$. For example, if $n = 9$ and $(q_1, \ldots, q_9) = (3, 1, 4, 1, 5, 9, 2, 6, 5)$, we find $a_1 \ldots a_9 = 6\,8\,5\,9\,3\,1\,7\,2\,4$ and $(p_1, \ldots, p_9) = (5, 2, 2, 2, 2, 2, 1, 1, 1)$.

Conversely, we can easily go back to $(q_1, q_2, \ldots, q_n)$ when $a_1 a_2 \ldots a_n$ and $(p_1, p_2, \ldots, p_n)$ are given. (See exercise 17.) So the desired correspondence has been established, and MacMahon's index theorem has been proved.

D. Foata and M. P. Schützenberger discovered a surprising extension of MacMahon's theorem, about 65 years after MacMahon's original publication: *The number of permutations of n elements that have k inversions and index l is the same as the number that have l inversions and index k.* In fact, Foata and Schützenberger found a simple one-to-one correspondence between permutations of the first kind and permutations of the second (see exercise 25).

EXERCISES

1. [*10*] What is the inversion table for the permutation $2\,7\,1\,8\,4\,5\,9\,3\,6$? What permutation has the inversion table $5\,0\,1\,2\,1\,2\,0\,0$?

2. [*M20*] In the classical problem of Josephus (exercise 1.3.2–22), n men are initially arranged in a circle; the mth man is executed, the circle closes, and every mth man is repeatedly eliminated until all are dead. The resulting execution order is a permutation of $\{1, 2, \ldots, n\}$. For example, when $n = 8$ and $m = 4$ the order is $5\,4\,6\,1\,3\,8\,7\,2$ (man 1 is 5th out, etc.); the inversion table corresponding to this permutation is $3\,6\,3\,1\,0\,0\,1\,0$.

Give a simple recurrence relation for the elements $b_1\, b_2 \ldots b_n$ of the inversion table in the general Josephus problem for n men, when every mth man is executed.

3. [*18*] If the permutation $a_1\, a_2 \ldots a_n$ corresponds to the inversion table $b_1\, b_2 \ldots b_n$, what is the permutation $\bar{a}_1\, \bar{a}_2 \ldots \bar{a}_n$ that corresponds to the inversion table

$$(n - 1 - b_1)(n - 2 - b_2) \ldots (0 - b_n)\,?$$

▶ **4.** [*20*] Design an algorithm suitable for computer implementation that constructs the permutation $a_1\, a_2 \ldots a_n$ corresponding to a given inversion table $b_1\, b_2 \ldots b_n$ satisfying (3). [*Hint:* Consider a linked-memory technique.]

5. [*35*] The algorithm of exercise 4 requires an execution time roughly proportional to $n + b_1 + \cdots + b_n$ on typical computers, and this is $\Theta(n^2)$ on the average. Is there an algorithm whose worst-case running time is substantially better than order n^2?

▶ **6.** [*26*] Design an algorithm that computes the inversion table $b_1\, b_2 \ldots b_n$ corresponding to a given permutation $a_1\, a_2 \ldots a_n$ of $\{1, 2, \ldots, n\}$, where the running time is essentially proportional to $n \log n$ on typical computers.

7. [*20*] Several other kinds of inversion tables can be defined, corresponding to a given permutation $a_1\, a_2 \ldots a_n$ of $\{1, 2, \ldots, n\}$, besides the particular table $b_1\, b_2 \ldots b_n$ defined in the text; in this exercise we will consider three other types of inversion tables that arise in applications.

Let c_j be the number of inversions whose *first* component is j, that is, the number of elements to the *right* of j that are less than j. [Corresponding to (1) we have the table $0\,0\,0\,1\,4\,2\,1\,5\,7$; clearly $0 \le c_j < j$.] Let $B_j = b_{a_j}$ and $C_j = c_{a_j}$.

Show that $0 \le B_j < j$ and $0 \le C_j \le n - j$, for $1 \le j \le n$; furthermore show that the permutation $a_1\, a_2 \ldots a_n$ can be determined uniquely when either $c_1\, c_2 \ldots c_n$ or $B_1\, B_2 \ldots B_n$ or $C_1\, C_2 \ldots C_n$ is given.

8. [*M24*] Continuing the notation of exercise 7, let $a'_1\, a'_2 \ldots a'_n$ be the inverse of the permutation $a_1\, a_2 \ldots a_n$, and let the corresponding inversion tables be $b'_1\, b'_2 \ldots b'_n$, $c'_1\, c'_2 \ldots c'_n$, $B'_1\, B'_2 \ldots B'_n$, and $C'_1\, C'_2 \ldots C'_n$. Find as many interesting relations as you can between the numbers $a_j, b_j, c_j, B_j, C_j, a'_j, b'_j, c'_j, B'_j, C'_j$.

▶ **9.** [*M21*] Prove that, in the notation of exercise 7, the permutation $a_1\, a_2 \ldots a_n$ is an involution (that is, its own inverse) if and only if $b_j = C_j$ for $1 \le j \le n$.

10. [*HM20*] Consider Fig. 1 as a polyhedron in three dimensions. What is the diameter of the truncated octahedron (the distance between vertex 1234 and vertex 4321), if all of its edges have unit length?

11. [*M25*] If $\pi = a_1\, a_2 \ldots a_n$ is a permutation of $\{1, 2, \ldots, n\}$, let

$$E(\pi) = \{(a_i, a_j) \mid i < j,\, a_i > a_j\}$$

be the set of its inversions, and let

$$\bar{E}(\pi) = \{(a_i, a_j) \mid i > j,\, a_i > a_j\}$$

be the non-inversions.

a) Prove that $E(\pi)$ and $\bar{E}(\pi)$ are transitive. (A set S of ordered pairs is called *transitive* if (a, c) is in S whenever both (a, b) and (b, c) are in S.)

b) Conversely, let E be any transitive subset of $T = \{(x,y) \mid 1 \leq y < x \leq n\}$ whose complement $\bar{E} = T \setminus E$ is also transitive. Prove that there exists a permutation π such that $E(\pi) = E$.

12. [*M28*] Continuing the notation of the previous exercise, prove that if π_1 and π_2 are permutations and if E is the smallest transitive set containing $E(\pi_1) \cup E(\pi_2)$, then $\bar{E}$ is transitive. [Hence, if we say π_1 is "above" π_2 whenever $E(\pi_1) \subseteq E(\pi_2)$, a *lattice* of permutations is defined; there is a unique "lowest" permutation "above" two given permutations. Figure 1 is the lattice diagram when $n = 4$.]

13. [*M23*] It is well known that half of the terms in the expansion of a determinant have a plus sign, and half have a minus sign. In other words, there are just as many permutations with an *even* number of inversions as with an *odd* number, when $n \geq 2$. Show that, in general, the number of permutations having a number of inversions congruent to t modulo m is $n!/m$, regardless of the integer t, whenever $n \geq m$.

14. [*M24*] (F. Franklin.) A partition of n into k distinct parts is a representation $n = p_1 + p_2 + \cdots + p_k$, where $p_1 > p_2 > \cdots > p_k > 0$. For example, the partitions of 7 into distinct parts are 7, $6 + 1$, $5 + 2$, $4 + 3$, $4 + 2 + 1$. Let $f_k(n)$ be the number of partitions of n into k distinct parts; prove that $\sum_k (-1)^k f_k(n) = 0$, unless n has the form $(3j^2 \pm j)/2$, for some nonnegative integer j; in the latter case the sum is $(-1)^j$. For example, when $n = 7$ the sum is $-1 + 3 - 1 = 1$, and $7 = (3 \cdot 2^2 + 2)/2$. [*Hint:* Represent a partition as an array of dots, putting p_i dots in the ith row, for $1 \leq i \leq k$. Find the smallest j such that $p_{j+1} < p_j - 1$, and encircle the rightmost dots in the first j rows. If $j < p_k$, these j dots can usually be removed, tilted $45°$, and placed as a new $(k+1)$st row. On the other hand if $j \geq p_k$, the kth row of dots can usually be removed, tilted $45°$, and placed to the right of the circled dots. (See Fig. 2.) This process pairs off partitions having an odd number of rows with partitions having an even number of rows, in most cases, so only unpaired partitions must be considered in the sum.]

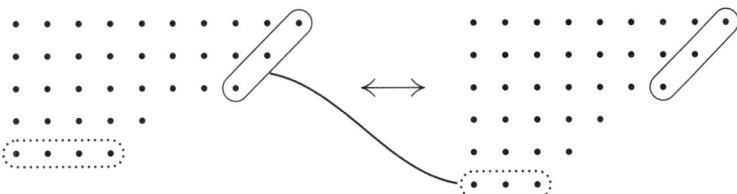

Fig. 2. Franklin's correspondence between partitions with distinct parts.

Note: As a consequence, we obtain Euler's formula

$$(1 - z)(1 - z^2)(1 - z^3)\ldots = 1 - z - z^2 + z^5 + z^7 - z^{12} - z^{15} + \cdots$$

$$= \sum_{-\infty < j < \infty} (-1)^j z^{(3j^2 + j)/2}.$$

The generating function for ordinary partitions (whose parts are not necessarily distinct) is $\sum p(n)z^n = 1/(1 - z)(1 - z^2)(1 - z^3)\ldots$; hence we obtain a nonobvious recurrence relation for the partition numbers,

$$p(n) = p(n-1) + p(n-2) - p(n-5) - p(n-7) + p(n-12) + p(n-15) - \cdots.$$

15. [*M23*] Prove that (16) is the generating function for partitions into at most n parts; that is, prove that the coefficient of z^m in $1/(1-z)(1-z^2)\dots(1-z^n)$ is the number of ways to write $m = p_1 + p_2 + \dots + p_n$ with $p_1 \geq p_2 \geq \dots \geq p_n \geq 0$. [*Hint:* Drawing dots as in exercise 14, show that there is a one-to-one correspondence between n-tuples $(p_1, p_2, \dots, p_n)$ such that $p_1 \geq p_2 \geq \dots \geq p_n \geq 0$ and sequences $(P_1, P_2, P_3, \dots)$ such that $n \geq P_1 \geq P_2 \geq P_3 \geq \dots \geq 0$, with the property that $p_1 + p_2 + \dots + p_n = P_1 + P_2 + P_3 + \dots$. In other words, partitions into at most n parts correspond to partitions into parts not exceeding n.]

16. [*M25*] (L. Euler.) Prove the following identities by interpreting both sides of the equations in terms of partitions:

$$\prod_{k \geq 0} \frac{1}{(1-q^k z)} = \frac{1}{(1-z)(1-qz)(1-q^2 z)\dots}$$

$$= 1 + \frac{z}{1-q} + \frac{z^2}{(1-q)(1-q^2)} + \dots = \sum_{n \geq 0} z^n \Big/ \prod_{k=1}^{n}(1-q^k).$$

$$\prod_{k \geq 0} (1+q^k z) = (1+z)(1+qz)(1+q^2 z)\dots$$

$$= 1 + \frac{z}{1-q} + \frac{z^2 q}{(1-q)(1-q^2)} + \dots = \sum_{n \geq 0} z^n q^{n(n-1)/2} \Big/ \prod_{k=1}^{n}(1-q^k).$$

17. [*20*] In MacMahon's correspondence defined at the end of this section, what are the 24 quadruples (q_1, q_2, q_3, q_4) for which $(p_1, p_2, p_3, p_4) = (0, 0, 0, 0)$?

18. [*M30*] (T. Hibbard, *CACM* **6** (1963), 210.) Let $n > 0$, and assume that a sequence of 2^n n-bit integers $X_0, \dots, X_{2^n-1}$ has been generated at random, where each bit of each number is independently equal to 1 with probability p. Consider the sequence $X_0 \oplus 0$, $X_1 \oplus 1$, $\dots$, $X_{2^n-1} \oplus (2^n - 1)$, where $\oplus$ denotes the "exclusive or" operation on the binary representations. Thus if $p = 0$, the sequence is $0, 1, \dots, 2^n - 1$, and if $p = 1$ it is $2^n - 1, \dots, 1, 0$; and when $p = \frac{1}{2}$, each element of the sequence is a random integer between 0 and $2^n - 1$. For general p this is a useful way to generate a sequence of random integers with a biased number of inversions, although the distribution of the elements of the sequence taken as a whole is uniform in the sense that each n-bit integer has the same distribution. What is the average number of inversions in such a sequence, as a function of the probability p?

19. [*M28*] (C. Meyer.) When m is relatively prime to n, we know that the sequence $(m \bmod n)(2m \bmod n)\dots((n-1)m \bmod n)$ is a permutation of $\{1, 2, \dots, n-1\}$. Show that the number of inversions of this permutation can be expressed in terms of Dedekind sums (see Section 3.3.3).

20. [*M43*] The following famous identity due to Jacobi [*Fundamenta Nova Theoriæ Functionum Ellipticarum* (1829), §64] is the basis of many remarkable relationships involving elliptic functions:

$$\prod_{k \geq 1} (1 - u^k v^{k-1})(1 - u^{k-1}v^k)(1 - u^k v^k)$$

$$= (1-u)(1-v)(1-uv)(1-u^2 v)(1-uv^2)(1-u^2 v^2)\dots$$

$$= 1 - (u+v) + (u^3 v + uv^3) - (u^6 v^3 + u^3 v^6) + \dots$$

$$= \sum_{-\infty < j < +\infty} (-1)^j u^{\binom{j}{2}} v^{\binom{j+1}{2}}.$$

For example, if we set $u = z$, $v = z^2$, we obtain Euler's formula of exercise 14. If we set $z = \sqrt{u/v}$, $q = \sqrt{uv}$, we obtain

$$\prod_{k \geq 1}(1 - q^{2k-1}z)(1 - q^{2k-1}z^{-1})(1 - q^{2k}) = \sum_{-\infty < n < \infty} (-1)^n z^n q^{n^2}.$$

Is there a combinatorial proof of Jacobi's identity, analogous to Franklin's proof of the special case in exercise 14? (Thus we want to consider "complex partitions"

$$m + ni = (p_1 + q_1 i) + (p_2 + q_2 i) + \cdots + (p_k + q_k i)$$

where the $p_j + q_j i$ are distinct nonzero complex numbers, p_j and q_j being nonnegative integers with $|p_j - q_j| \leq 1$. Jacobi's identity says that the number of such representations with k even is the same as the number with k odd, except when m and n are consecutive triangular numbers.) What other remarkable properties do complex partitions have?

▶ **21.** [*M25*] (G. D. Knott.) Show that the permutation $a_1 \ldots a_n$ is obtainable with a stack, in the sense of exercise 2.2.1–5 or 2.3.1–6, if and only if $C_j \leq C_{j+1} + 1$ for $1 \leq j < n$ in the notation of exercise 7.

22. [*M26*] Given a permutation $a_1 a_2 \ldots a_n$ of $\{1, 2, \ldots, n\}$, let h_j be the number of indices $i < j$ such that $a_i \in \{a_j + 1, a_j + 2, \ldots, a_j + 1\}$. (If $a_{j+1} < a_j$, the elements of this set "wrap around" from n to 1. When $j = n$ we use the set $\{a_n + 1, a_n + 2, \ldots, n\}$.) For example, the permutation $5\,9\,1\,8\,2\,6\,4\,7\,3$ leads to $h_1 \ldots h_9 = 0\,0\,1\,2\,1\,4\,2\,4\,6$.

   a) Prove that $a_1 a_2 \ldots a_n$ can be reconstructed from the numbers $h_1 h_2 \ldots h_n$.

   b) Prove that $h_1 + h_2 + \cdots + h_n$ is the index of $a_1 a_2 \ldots a_n$.

▶ **23.** [*M27*] (*Russian roulette.*) A group of n condemned men who prefer probability theory to number theory might choose to commit suicide by sitting in a circle and modifying Josephus's method (exercise 2) as follows: The first prisoner holds a gun and aims it at his head; with probability p he dies and leaves the circle. Then the second man takes the gun and proceeds in the same way. Play continues cyclically, with constant probability $p > 0$, until everyone is dead.

   Let $a_j = k$ if man k is the jth to die. Prove that the death order $a_1 a_2 \ldots a_n$ occurs with a probability that is a function only of n, p, and the index of the dual permutation $(n + 1 - a_n) \ldots (n + 1 - a_2)(n + 1 - a_1)$. What death order is least likely?

24. [*M26*] Given integers $t(1)\,t(2)\ldots t(n)$ with $t(j) \geq j$, the *generalized index* of a permutation $a_1 a_2 \ldots a_n$ is the sum of all subscripts j such that $a_j > t(a_{j+1})$, plus the total number of inversions such that $i < j$ and $t(a_j) \geq a_i > a_j$. Thus when $t(j) = j$ for all j, the generalized index is the same as the index; but when $t(j) \geq n$ for all j it is the number of inversions. Prove that the number of permutations whose generalized index equals k is the same as the number of permutations having k inversions. [*Hint:* Show that, if we take any permutation $a_1 \ldots a_{n-1}$ of $\{1, \ldots, n-1\}$ and insert the number n in all possible places, we increase the generalized index by the numbers $\{0, 1, \ldots, n-1\}$ in some order.]

▶ **25.** [*M30*] (Foata and Schützenberger.) If $\alpha = a_1 \ldots a_n$ is a permutation, let $\text{ind}(\alpha)$ be its index, and let $\text{inv}(\alpha)$ count its inversions.

   a) Define a one-to-one correspondence that takes each permutation α of $\{1, \ldots, n\}$ to a permutation $f(\alpha)$ that has the following two properties: (i) $\text{ind}(f(\alpha)) = \text{inv}(\alpha)$; (ii) for $1 \leq j < n$, the number j appears to the left of $j + 1$ in $f(\alpha)$ if and only if it appears to the left of $j + 1$ in α. What permutation does your construction assign to $f(\alpha)$ when $\alpha = 1\,9\,8\,2\,6\,3\,7\,4\,5$? For what permutation α is $f(\alpha) = 1\,9\,8\,2\,6\,3\,7\,4\,5$? [*Hint:* If $n > 1$, write $\alpha = x_1\alpha_1 x_2\alpha_2 \ldots x_k\alpha_k a_n$, where $x_1, \ldots, x_k$ are all the elements $< a_n$ if $a_1 < a_n$, otherwise $x_1, \ldots, x_k$ are all the elements $> a_n$; the other elements appear in (possibly empty) strings $\alpha_1, \ldots, \alpha_k$. Compare the number of inversions of $h(\alpha) = \alpha_1 x_1\alpha_2 x_2 \ldots \alpha_k x_k$ to $\mathrm{inv}(\alpha)$; in this construction the number a_n does not appear in $h(\alpha)$.]

b) Use f to define another one-to-one correspondence g having the following two properties: (i) $\mathrm{ind}(g(\alpha)) = \mathrm{inv}(\alpha)$; (ii) $\mathrm{inv}(g(\alpha)) = \mathrm{ind}(\alpha)$. [*Hint:* Consider inverse permutations.]

26. [*M25*] What is the statistical correlation coefficient between the number of inversions and the index of a random permutation? (See Eq. 3.3.2–(24).)

27. [*M37*] Prove that, in addition to (15), there is a simple relationship between $\mathrm{inv}(a_1\, a_2 \ldots a_n)$ and the n-tuple $(q_1, q_2, \ldots, q_n)$. Use this fact to generalize the derivation of (17), obtaining an algebraic characterization of the bivariate generating function

$$H_n(w, z) = \sum w^{\mathrm{inv}(a_1\, a_2 \ldots a_n)}\, z^{\mathrm{ind}(a_1\, a_2 \ldots a_n)},$$

where the sum is over all $n!$ permutations $a_1\, a_2 \ldots a_n$.

▶ **28.** [*25*] If $a_1\, a_2 \ldots a_n$ is a permutation of $\{1, 2, \ldots, n\}$, its *total displacement* is defined to be $\sum_{j=1}^{n} |a_j - j|$. Find upper and lower bounds for total displacement in terms of the number of inversions.

29. [*28*] If $\pi = a_1\, a_2 \ldots a_n$ and $\pi' = a'_1\, a'_2 \ldots a'_n$ are permutations of $\{1, 2, \ldots, n\}$, their product $\pi\pi'$ is $a'_{a_1}\, a'_{a_2} \ldots a'_{a_n}$. Let $\mathrm{inv}(\pi)$ denote the number of inversions, as in exercise 25. Show that $\mathrm{inv}(\pi\pi') \le \mathrm{inv}(\pi) + \mathrm{inv}(\pi')$, and that equality holds if and only if $\pi\pi'$ is "below" π' in the sense of exercise 12.

*5.1.2. Permutations of a Multiset

So far we have been discussing permutations of a *set* of elements; this is just a special case of the concept of permutations of a *multiset*. (A multiset is like a set except that it can have repetitions of identical elements. Some basic properties of multisets have been discussed in exercise 4.6.3–19.)

For example, consider the multiset

$$M = \{a, a, a, b, b, c, d, d, d, d\}, \tag{1}$$

which contains 3 a's, 2 b's, 1 c, and 4 d's. We may also indicate the multiplicities of elements in another way, namely

$$M = \{3 \cdot a, 2 \cdot b, c, 4 \cdot d\}. \tag{2}$$

A permutation* of M is an arrangement of its elements into a row; for example,

$$c\ a\ b\ d\ d\ a\ b\ d\ a\ d.$$

From another point of view we would call this a string of letters, containing 3 a's, 2 b's, 1 c, and 4 d's.

How many permutations of M are possible? If we regarded the elements of M as distinct, by subscripting them a_1, a_2, a_3, b_1, b_2, c_1, d_1, d_2, d_3, d_4,

---

* Sometimes called a "permatution."

we would have $10! = 3{,}628{,}800$ permutations; but many of those permutations would actually be the same when we removed the subscripts. In fact, each permutation of M would occur exactly $3!\,2!\,1!\,4! = 288$ times, since we can start with any permutation of M and put subscripts on the a's in 3! ways, on the b's (independently) in 2! ways, on the c in 1 way, and on the d's in 4! ways. Therefore the true number of permutations of M is

$$\frac{10!}{3!\,2!\,1!\,4!} = 12{,}600.$$

In general, we can see by this same argument that the number of permutations of any multiset is the multinomial coefficient

$$\binom{n}{n_1, n_2, \ldots} = \frac{n!}{n_1!\,n_2!\ldots}, \tag{3}$$

where n_1 is the number of elements of one kind, n_2 is the number of another kind, etc., and $n = n_1 + n_2 + \cdots$ is the total number of elements.

The number of permutations of a set has been known for more than 1500 years. The Hebrew *Book of Creation* (c. A.D. 400), which was the earliest literary product of Jewish philosophical mysticism, gives the correct values of the first seven factorials, after which it says "Go on and compute what the mouth cannot express and the ear cannot hear." [*Sefer Yetzirah*, end of Chapter 4. See Solomon Gandz, *Studies in Hebrew Astronomy and Mathematics* (New York: Ktav, 1970), 494–496; Aryeh Kaplan, *Sefer Yetzirah* (York Beach, Maine: Samuel Weiser, 1993).] This is one of the first two known enumerations of permutations in history. The other occurs in the Indian classic *Anuyogadvārasūtra* (c. 500), rule 97, which gives the formula

$$6 \times 5 \times 4 \times 3 \times 2 \times 1 - 2$$

for the number of permutations of six elements that are neither in ascending nor descending order. [See G. Chakravarti, *Bull. Calcutta Math. Soc.* **24** (1932), 79–88. The *Anuyogadvārasūtra* is one of the books in the canon of Jainism, a religious sect that flourishes in India.]

The corresponding formula for permutations of multisets seems to have appeared first in the *Līlāvatī* of Bhāskara (c. 1150), sections 270–271. Bhāskara stated the rule rather tersely, and illustrated it only with two simple examples $\{2, 2, 1, 1\}$ and $\{4, 8, 5, 5, 5\}$. Consequently the English translations of his work do not all state the rule correctly, although there is little doubt that Bhāskara knew what he was talking about. He went on to give the interesting formula

$$\frac{(4 + 8 + 5 + 5 + 5) \times 120 \times 11111}{5 \times 6}$$

for the sum of the 20 numbers $48555 + 45855 + \cdots$.

The correct rule for counting permutations when elements are repeated was apparently unknown in Europe until Marin Mersenne stated it without proof as Proposition 10 in his elaborate treatise on melodic principles [*Harmonie Universelle* **2**, also entitled *Traitez de la Voix et des Chants* (1636), 129–130].

Mersenne was interested in the number of tunes that could be made from a given collection of notes; he observed, for example, that a theme by Boesset,

can be rearranged in exactly $15!/(4!\,3!\,3!\,2!) = 756{,}756{,}000$ ways.

The general rule (3) also appeared in Jean Prestet's *Élémens des Mathématiques* (Paris: 1675), 351–352, one of the very first expositions of combinatorial mathematics to be written in the Western world. Prestet stated the rule correctly for a general multiset, but illustrated it only in the simple case $\{a, a, b, b, c, c\}$. A few years later, John Wallis's *Discourse of Combinations* (Oxford: 1685), Chapter 2 (published with his *Treatise of Algebra*) gave a clearer and somewhat more detailed discussion of the rule.

In 1965, Dominique Foata introduced an ingenious idea called the "intercalation product," which makes it possible to extend many of the known results about ordinary permutations to the general case of multiset permutations. [See *Publ. Inst. Statistique*, Univ. Paris, **14** (1965), 81–241; also *Lecture Notes in Math.* **85** (Springer, 1969).] Assuming that the elements of a multiset have been linearly ordered in some way, we may consider a *two-line notation* such as

$$\begin{pmatrix} a & a & a & b & b & c & d & d & d & d \\ c & a & b & d & d & a & b & d & a & d \end{pmatrix}, \tag{4}$$

where the top line contains the elements of M sorted into nondecreasing order and the bottom line is the permutation itself. The *intercalation product* $\alpha \mathbin{\mathsf{T}} \beta$ of two multiset permutations α and β is obtained by (a) expressing α and β in the two-line notation, (b) juxtaposing these two-line representations, and (c) sorting the columns into nondecreasing order of the top line. The sorting is supposed to be stable, in the sense that left-to-right order of elements in the bottom line is preserved when the corresponding top line elements are equal. For example, $c\,a\,d\,a\,b \mathbin{\mathsf{T}} b\,d\,d\,a\,d = c\,a\,b\,d\,d\,a\,b\,d\,a\,d$, since

$$\begin{pmatrix} a & a & b & c & d \\ c & a & d & a & b \end{pmatrix} \mathbin{\mathsf{T}} \begin{pmatrix} a & b & d & d & d \\ b & d & d & a & d \end{pmatrix} = \begin{pmatrix} a & a & a & b & b & c & d & d & d & d \\ c & a & b & d & d & a & b & d & a & d \end{pmatrix}. \tag{5}$$

It is easy to see that the intercalation product is associative:

$$(\alpha \mathbin{\mathsf{T}} \beta) \mathbin{\mathsf{T}} \gamma = \alpha \mathbin{\mathsf{T}} (\beta \mathbin{\mathsf{T}} \gamma); \tag{6}$$

it also satisfies two cancellation laws:

$$\begin{aligned} \pi \mathbin{\mathsf{T}} \alpha = \pi \mathbin{\mathsf{T}} \beta \quad &\text{implies} \quad \alpha = \beta, \\ \alpha \mathbin{\mathsf{T}} \pi = \beta \mathbin{\mathsf{T}} \pi \quad &\text{implies} \quad \alpha = \beta. \end{aligned} \tag{7}$$

There is an identity element,

$$\alpha \mathbin{\mathsf{T}} \epsilon = \epsilon \mathbin{\mathsf{T}} \alpha = \alpha, \tag{8}$$

where ϵ is the null permutation, the "arrangement" of the empty set. Although the commutative law is not valid in general (see exercise 2), we do have

$$\alpha \top \beta = \beta \top \alpha \qquad \text{if } \alpha \text{ and } \beta \text{ have no letters in common.} \tag{9}$$

In an analogous fashion we can extend the concept of *cycles* in permutations to cases where elements are repeated; we let

$$(x_1 \quad x_2 \quad \ldots \quad x_n) \tag{10}$$

stand for the permutation obtained in two-line form by sorting the columns of

$$\begin{pmatrix} x_1 & x_2 & \ldots & x_n \\ x_2 & x_3 & \ldots & x_1 \end{pmatrix} \tag{11}$$

by their top elements in a stable manner. For example, we have

$$(d\ b\ d\ d\ a\ c\ a\ a\ b\ d) = \begin{pmatrix} d & b & d & d & a & c & a & a & b & d \\ b & d & d & a & c & a & a & b & d & d \end{pmatrix} = \begin{pmatrix} a & a & a & b & b & c & d & d & d & d \\ c & a & b & d & d & a & b & d & a & d \end{pmatrix},$$

so the permutation (4) is actually a cycle. We might render this cycle in words by saying something like "d goes to b goes to d goes to d goes ... goes to d goes back." Note that these general cycles do not share all of the properties of ordinary cycles; $(x_1\ x_2 \ldots x_n)$ is not always the same as $(x_2 \ldots x_n\ x_1)$.

We observed in Section 1.3.3 that every permutation of a set has a unique representation (up to order) as a product of disjoint cycles, where the "product" of permutations is defined by a law of composition. It is easy to see that *the product of disjoint cycles is exactly the same as their intercalation*; this suggests that we might be able to generalize the previous results, obtaining a unique representation (in some sense) for any permutation of a multiset, as the intercalation of cycles. In fact there are at least two natural ways to do this, each of which has important applications.

Equation (5) shows one way to factor $c\ a\ b\ d\ d\ a\ b\ d\ a\ d$ as the intercalation of shorter permutations; let us consider the general problem of finding all factorizations $\pi = \alpha \top \beta$ of a given permutation π. It will be helpful to consider a particular permutation, such as

$$\pi = \begin{pmatrix} a & a & b & b & b & b & c & c & c & d & d & d & d & d \\ d & b & c & b & c & a & c & d & a & d & d & b & b & b & d \end{pmatrix}, \tag{12}$$

as we investigate the factorization problem.

If we can write this permutation π in the form $\alpha \top \beta$, where α contains the letter a at least once, then the leftmost a in the top line of the two-line notation for α must appear over the letter d, so α must also contain at least one occurrence of the letter d. If we now look at the leftmost d in the top line of α, we see in the same way that it must appear over the letter d, so α must contain at least *two* d's. Looking at the second d, we see that α also contains at least one b. We have deduced the partial result

$$\alpha = \begin{pmatrix} a & & b & & d & d & \\ d & \cdots & & \cdots & d & b & \cdots \end{pmatrix} \tag{13}$$

on the sole assumption that α is a left factor of π containing the letter a. Proceeding in the same manner, we find that the b in the top line of (13) must appear over the letter c, etc. Eventually this process will reach the letter a again, and we can identify this a with the first a if we choose to do so. The argument we have just made essentially proves that any left factor α of (12) that contains the letter a has the form $(d\ d\ b\ c\ d\ b\ b\ c\ a)\top\alpha'$, for some permutation α'. (It is convenient to write the a last in the cycle, instead of first; this arrangement is permissible since there is only one a.) Similarly, if we had assumed that α contains the letter b, we would have deduced that $\alpha = (c\ d\ d\ b)\top\alpha''$ for some α''.

In general, this argument shows that, *if we have any factorization $\alpha\top\beta = \pi$, where α contains a given letter y, exactly one cycle of the form*

$$(x_1\ \ldots\ x_n\ y), \qquad n \geq 0, \qquad x_1, \ldots, x_n \neq y, \tag{14}$$

is a left factor of α. This cycle is easily determined when π and y are given; it is the shortest left factor of π that contains the letter y. One of the consequences of this observation is the following theorem:

Theorem A. *Let the elements of the multiset M be linearly ordered by the relation "$<$". Every permutation π of M has a unique representation as the intercalation*

$$\pi = (x_{11}\ldots x_{1n_1}y_1)\top(x_{21}\ldots x_{2n_2}y_2)\top\cdots\top(x_{t1}\ldots x_{tn_t}y_t), \quad t \geq 0, \tag{15}$$

where the following two conditions are satisfied:

$$y_1 \leq y_2 \leq \cdots \leq y_t \qquad \text{and} \qquad y_i < x_{ij} \text{ for } 1 \leq j \leq n_i,\ 1 \leq i \leq t. \tag{16}$$

(In other words, the last element in each cycle is smaller than every other element, and the sequence of last elements is in nondecreasing order.)

Proof. If $\pi = \epsilon$, we obtain such a factorization by letting $t = 0$. Otherwise we let y_1 be the smallest element permuted; and we determine $(x_{11}\ldots x_{1n_1}y_1)$, the shortest left factor of π containing y_1, as in the example above. Now $\pi = (x_{11}\ \ldots\ x_{1n_1}\ y_1)\top\rho$ for some permutation ρ; by induction on the length, we can write

$$\rho = (x_{21}\ \ldots\ x_{2n_2}\ y_2)\top\cdots\top(x_{t1}\ \ldots\ x_{tn_t}\ y_t), \quad t \geq 1,$$

where (16) is satisfied. This proves the existence of such a factorization.

Conversely, to prove that the representation (15) satisfying (16) is unique, clearly $t = 0$ if and only if π is the null permutation ϵ. When $t > 0$, (16) implies that y_1 is the smallest element permuted, and that $(x_{11}\ \ldots\ x_{1n_1}\ y_1)$ is the shortest left factor containing y_1. Therefore $(x_{11}\ \ldots\ x_{1n_1}\ y_1)$ is uniquely determined; by the cancellation law (7) and induction, the representation is unique. ∎

For example, the "canonical" factorization of (12), satisfying the given conditions, is

$$(d\ d\ b\ c\ d\ b\ b\ c\ a)\top(b\ a)\top(c\ d\ b)\top(d), \tag{17}$$

if $a < b < c < d$.

It is important to note that we can actually drop the parentheses and the $_T$'s in this representation, without ambiguity! Each cycle ends just after the first appearance of the smallest remaining element. So this construction associates the permutation

$$\pi' = d\,d\,b\,c\,d\,b\,b\,c\,a\,b\,a\,c\,d\,b\,d$$

with the original permutation

$$\pi = d\,b\,c\,b\,c\,a\,c\,d\,a\,d\,d\,b\,b\,b\,d.$$

Whenever the two-line representation of π had a column of the form $\frac{y}{x}$, where $x < y$, the associated permutation π' has a corresponding pair of adjacent elements $\ldots y\,x\ldots$. Thus our example permutation π has three columns of the form $\frac{d}{b}$, and π' has three occurrences of the pair $d\,b$. In general this construction establishes the following remarkable theorem:

Theorem B. *Let M be a multiset. There is a one-to-one correspondence between the permutations of M such that, if π corresponds to π', the following conditions hold:*

a) *The leftmost element of π' equals the leftmost element of π.*

b) *For all pairs of permuted elements (x, y) with $x < y$, the number of occurrences of the column $\frac{y}{x}$ in the two-line notation of π is equal to the number of times x is immediately preceded by y in π'.* ∎

When M is a set, this is essentially the same as the "unusual correspondence" we discussed near the end of Section 1.3.3, with unimportant changes. The more general result in Theorem B is quite useful for enumerating special kinds of permutations, since we can often solve a problem based on a two-line constraint more easily than the equivalent problem based on an adjacent-pair constraint.

P. A. MacMahon considered problems of this type in his extraordinary book *Combinatory Analysis* **1** (Cambridge Univ. Press, 1915), 168–186. He gave a constructive proof of Theorem B in the special case that M contains only two different kinds of elements, say a and b; his construction for this case is essentially the same as that given here, although he expressed it quite differently. For the case of three different elements a, b, c, MacMahon gave a complicated nonconstructive proof of Theorem B; the general case was first proved constructively by Foata [*Comptes Rendus Acad. Sci.* **258** (Paris, 1964), 1672–1675].

As a nontrivial example of Theorem B, let us find the number of strings of letters a, b, c containing exactly

A	occurrences of the letter a;	
B	occurrences of the letter b;	
C	occurrences of the letter c;	
k	occurrences of the adjacent pair of letters ca;	
l	occurrences of the adjacent pair of letters cb;	
m	occurrences of the adjacent pair of letters ba.	(18)

The theorem tells us that this is the same as the number of two-line arrays of the form

$$
\begin{pmatrix}
\overbrace{a \quad \cdots \quad a}^{A} & \overbrace{b \quad \cdots \quad b}^{B} & \overbrace{c \quad \cdots \quad c}^{C} \\
\underbrace{\sqcup \cdots \sqcup}_{A-k-m \text{ a's}} & \underbrace{\sqcup \cdots \sqcup}_{m \text{ a's}} \quad \underbrace{\sqcup \cdots \sqcup}_{k \text{ a's}}
\end{pmatrix} .
$$

$$\underbrace{\qquad\qquad}_{B-l \text{ b's}} \quad \underbrace{\qquad}_{l \text{ b's}}$$

$$\underbrace{\qquad\qquad\qquad}_{C \text{ c's}}$$

(19)

The a's can be placed in the second line in

$$
\binom{A}{A-k-m}\binom{B}{m}\binom{C}{k} \qquad \text{ways;}
$$

then the b's can be placed in the remaining positions in

$$
\binom{B+k}{B-l}\binom{C-k}{l} \qquad \text{ways.}
$$

The positions that are still vacant must be filled by c's; hence the desired number is

$$
\binom{A}{A-k-m}\binom{B}{m}\binom{C}{k}\binom{B+k}{B-l}\binom{C-k}{l}.
$$

(20)

Let us return to the question of finding all factorizations of a given permutation. Is there such a thing as a "prime" permutation, one that has no intercalation factors except itself and ϵ? The discussion preceding Theorem A leads us quickly to conclude that *a permutation is prime if and only if it is a cycle with no repeated elements.* For if it is such a cycle, our argument proves that there are no left factors except ϵ and the cycle itself. And if a permutation contains a repeated element y, it has a nontrivial cyclic left factor in which y appears only once.

A nonprime permutation can be factored into smaller and smaller pieces until it has been expressed as a product of primes. Furthermore we can show that the factorization is unique, if we neglect the order of factors that commute:

Theorem C. *Every permutation of a multiset can be written as a product*

$$
\sigma_1 \top \sigma_2 \top \cdots \top \sigma_t, \qquad t \geq 0,
$$

(21)

where each σ_j is a cycle having no repeated elements. This representation is unique, in the sense that any two such representations of the same permutation may be transformed into each other by successively interchanging pairs of adjacent disjoint cycles.

The term "disjoint cycles" means cycles having no elements in common. As an example of this theorem, we can verify that the permutation

$$\begin{pmatrix} a & a & b & b & c & c & d \\ b & a & a & c & d & b & c \end{pmatrix}$$

has exactly five factorizations into primes, namely

$$(a\ b)\top(a)\top(c\ d)\top(b\ c) = (a\ b)\top(c\ d)\top(a)\top(b\ c)$$
$$= (a\ b)\top(c\ d)\top(b\ c)\top(a)$$
$$= (c\ d)\top(a\ b)\top(b\ c)\top(a)$$
$$= (c\ d)\top(a\ b)\top(a)\top(b\ c). \qquad (22)$$

Proof. We must show that the stated uniqueness property holds. By induction on the length of the permutation, it suffices to prove that if ρ and σ are unequal cycles having no repeated elements, and if

$$\rho\top\alpha = \sigma\top\beta,$$

then ρ and σ are disjoint, and

$$\alpha = \sigma\top\theta, \qquad \beta = \rho\top\theta,$$

for some permutation θ.

If y is any element of the cycle ρ, then any left factor of $\sigma\top\beta$ containing the element y must have ρ as a left factor. So if ρ and σ have an element in common, σ is a multiple of ρ; hence $\sigma = \rho$ (since they are primes), contradicting our assumption. Therefore the cycle containing y, having no elements in common with σ, must be a left factor of β. The proof is completed by using the cancellation law (7). ∎

As an example of Theorem C, let us consider permutations of the multiset $M = \{A \cdot a, B \cdot b, C \cdot c\}$ consisting of A a's, B b's, and C c's. Let $N(A, B, C, m)$ be the number of permutations of M whose two-line representation contains *no* columns of the forms $\frac{a}{a}$, $\frac{b}{b}$, $\frac{c}{c}$, and exactly m columns of the form $\frac{a}{b}$. It follows that there are exactly $A - m$ columns of the form $\frac{a}{c}$, $B - m$ of the form $\frac{c}{b}$, $C - B + m$ of the form $\frac{c}{a}$, $C - A + m$ of the form $\frac{b}{c}$, and $A + B - C - m$ of the form $\frac{b}{a}$. Hence

$$N(A, B, C, m) = \binom{A}{m}\binom{B}{C - A + m}\binom{C}{B - m}. \qquad (23)$$

Theorem C tells us that we can count these permutations in another way: Since columns of the form $\frac{a}{a}$, $\frac{b}{b}$, $\frac{c}{c}$ are excluded, the only possible prime factors of the permutation are

$$(a\ b), \qquad (a\ c), \qquad (b\ c), \qquad (a\ b\ c), \qquad (a\ c\ b). \qquad (24)$$

Each pair of these cycles has at least one letter in common, so the factorization into primes is completely unique. If the cycle $(a\ b\ c)$ occurs k times in the factorization, our previous assumptions imply that $(a\ b)$ occurs $m - k$ times,

$(b\ c)$ occurs $C - A + m - k$ times, $(a\ c)$ occurs $C - B + m - k$ times, and $(a\ c\ b)$ occurs $A + B - C - 2m + k$ times. Hence $N(A, B, C, m)$ is the number of permutations of these cycles (a multinomial coefficient), summed over k:

$$N(A, B, C, m)$$

$$= \sum_k \frac{(C+m-k)!}{(m-k)!\,(C-A+m-k)!\,(C-B+m-k)!\,k!\,(A+B-C-2m+k)!}$$

$$= \sum_k \binom{m}{k}\binom{A}{m}\binom{A-m}{C-B+m-k}\binom{C+m-k}{A}. \tag{25}$$

Comparing this with (23), we find that the following identity must be valid:

$$\sum_k \binom{m}{k}\binom{A-m}{C-B+m-k}\binom{C+m-k}{A} = \binom{B}{C-A+m}\binom{C}{B-m}. \tag{26}$$

This turns out to be the identity we met in exercise 1.2.6–31, namely

$$\sum_j \binom{M-R+S}{j}\binom{N+R-S}{N-j}\binom{R+j}{M+N} = \binom{R}{M}\binom{S}{N}, \tag{27}$$

with $M = A+B-C-m$, $N = C-B+m$, $R = B$, $S = C$, and $j = C-B+m-k$.

Similarly we can count the number of permutations of $\{A{\cdot}a,\ B{\cdot}b,\ C{\cdot}c,\ D{\cdot}d\}$ such that the number of columns of various types is specified as follows:

Column type:	$\begin{matrix}a\\d\end{matrix}$	$\begin{matrix}a\\b\end{matrix}$	$\begin{matrix}b\\a\end{matrix}$	$\begin{matrix}b\\c\end{matrix}$	$\begin{matrix}c\\b\end{matrix}$	$\begin{matrix}c\\d\end{matrix}$	$\begin{matrix}d\\a\end{matrix}$	$\begin{matrix}d\\c\end{matrix}$	
Frequency:	r	$A-r$	q	$B-q$	$B-A+r$	$D-r$	$A-q$	$D-A+q$	(28)

(Here $A + C = B + D$.) The possible cycles occurring in a prime factorization of such permutations are then

Cycle:	$(a\ b)$	$(b\ c)$	$(c\ d)$	$(d\ a)$	$(a\ b\ c\ d)$	$(d\ c\ b\ a)$	
Frequency:	$A-r-s$	$B-q-s$	$D-r-s$	$A-q-s$	s	$q-A+r+s$	(29)

for some s (see exercise 12). In this case the cycles $(a\ b)$ and $(c\ d)$ commute with each other, and so do $(b\ c)$ and $(d\ a)$, so we must count the number of distinct prime factorizations. It turns out (see exercise 10) that there is always a unique factorization such that no $(c\ d)$ is immediately followed by $(a\ b)$, and no $(d\ a)$ is immediately followed by $(b\ c)$. Hence by the result of exercise 13, we have

$$\sum_{s,t} \binom{B}{t}\binom{A-q-s}{A-r-s-t}\binom{B+D-r-s-t}{B-q-s}$$

$$\times \frac{D!}{(D-r-s)!\,(A-q-s)!\,s!\,(q-A+r+s)!}$$

$$= \binom{A}{r}\binom{B+D-A}{D-r}\binom{B}{q}\binom{D}{A-q}.$$

Taking out the factor $\binom{D}{A-q}$ from both sides and simplifying the factorials slightly leaves us with the complicated-looking five-parameter identity

$$\sum_{s,t} \binom{B}{t}\binom{A-r-t}{s}\binom{B+D-r-s-t}{D+q-r-t}\binom{D-A+q}{D-r-s}\binom{A-q}{r+t-q}$$

$$= \binom{A}{r}\binom{B+D-A}{D-r}\binom{B}{q}. \quad (30)$$

The sum on s can be performed using (27), and the resulting sum on t is easily evaluated; so, after all this work, we were not fortunate enough to discover any identities that we didn't already know how to derive. But at least we have learned how to count certain kinds of permutations, in two different ways, and these counting techniques are good training for the problems that lie ahead.

EXERCISES

1. [M05] *True or false:* Let M_1 and M_2 be multisets. If α is a permutation of M_1 and β is a permutation of M_2, then $\alpha \top \beta$ is a permutation of $M_1 \cup M_2$.

2. [10] The intercalation of $c\ a\ d\ a\ b$ and $b\ d\ d\ a\ d$ is computed in (5); find the intercalation $b\ d\ d\ a\ d \top c\ a\ d\ a\ b$ that is obtained when the factors are interchanged.

3. [M13] Is the converse of (9) valid? In other words, if α and β commute under intercalation, must they have no letters in common?

4. [M11] The canonical factorization of (12), in the sense of Theorem A, is given in (17) when $a < b < c < d$. Find the corresponding canonical factorization when $d < c < b < a$.

5. [M23] Condition (b) of Theorem B requires $x < y$; what would happen if we weakened the relation to $x \le y$?

6. [M15] How many strings are there that contain exactly m a's, n b's, and no other letters, with exactly k of the a's preceded immediately by a b?

7. [M21] How many strings on the letters a, b, c satisfying conditions (18) begin with the letter a? with the letter b? with c?

▶ **8.** [20] Find all factorizations of (12) into two factors $\alpha \top \beta$.

9. [33] Write computer programs that perform the factorizations of a given multiset permutation into the forms mentioned in Theorems A and C.

▶ **10.** [M30] *True or false:* Although the factorization into primes isn't quite unique, according to Theorem C, we can ensure uniqueness in the following way: "There is a linear ordering $\prec$ of the set of primes such that every permutation of a multiset has a unique factorization $\sigma_1 \top \sigma_2 \top \cdots \top \sigma_n$ into primes subject to the condition that $\sigma_i \preceq \sigma_{i+1}$ whenever σ_i commutes with σ_{i+1}, for $1 \le i < n$."

▶ **11.** [M26] Let $\sigma_1, \sigma_2, \ldots, \sigma_t$ be cycles without repeated elements. Define a partial ordering $\prec$ on the t objects $\{x_1, \ldots, x_t\}$ by saying that $x_i \prec x_j$ if $i < j$ and σ_i has at least one letter in common with σ_j. Prove the following connection between Theorem C and the notion of "topological sorting" (Section 2.2.3): *The number of distinct prime factorizations of $\sigma_1 \top \sigma_2 \top \cdots \top \sigma_t$ is the number of ways to sort the given partial ordering topologically.* (For example, corresponding to (22) we find that there are five ways to sort the ordering $x_1 \prec x_2$, $x_3 \prec x_4$, $x_1 \prec x_4$ topologically.) Conversely, given any partial ordering on t elements, there is a set of cycles $\{\sigma_1, \sigma_2, \ldots, \sigma_t\}$ that defines it in the stated way.

12. [*M16*] Show that (29) is a consequence of the assumptions of (28).

13. [*M21*] Prove that the number of permutations of the multiset

$$\{A \cdot a, \ B \cdot b, \ C \cdot c, \ D \cdot d, \ E \cdot e, \ F \cdot f\}$$

containing no occurrences of the adjacent pairs of letters ca and db is

$$\sum_t \binom{D}{A-t} \binom{A+B+E+F}{t} \binom{A+B+C+E+F-t}{B} \binom{C+D+E+F}{C,D,E,F}.$$

14. [*M30*] One way to define the inverse π^- of a general permutation π, suggested by other definitions in this section, is to interchange the lines of the two-line representation of π and then to do a stable sort of the columns in order to bring the top row into nondecreasing order. For example, if $a < b < c < d$, this definition implies that the inverse of $\ c\ a\ b\ d\ d\ a\ b\ d\ a\ d\ $ is $\ a\ c\ d\ a\ d\ a\ b\ b\ d\ d.$

Explore properties of this inversion operation; for example, does it have any simple relation with intercalation products? Can we count the number of permutations such that $\pi = \pi^-$?

▶ **15.** [*M25*] Prove that the permutation $a_1 \ldots a_n$ of the multiset

$$\{n_1 \cdot x_1, \ n_2 \cdot x_2, \ldots, n_m \cdot x_m\},$$

where $x_1 < x_2 < \cdots < x_m$ and $n_1 + n_2 + \cdots + n_m = n$, is a cycle if and only if the directed graph with vertices $\{x_1, x_2, \ldots, x_m\}$ and arcs from x_j to $a_{n_1 + \cdots + n_j}$ contains precisely one oriented cycle. In the latter case, the number of ways to represent the permutation in cycle form is the length of the oriented cycle. For example, the directed graph corresponding to

$$\begin{pmatrix} a & a & a & b & b & c & c & c & d & d \\ d & c & b & a & c & a & a & b & d & c \end{pmatrix} \qquad \text{is} \qquad$$

and the two ways to represent the permutation as a cycle are $(b\ a\ d\ d\ c\ a\ c\ a\ b\ c)$ and $(c\ a\ d\ d\ c\ a\ c\ b\ a\ b)$.

16. [*M35*] We found the generating function for *inversions* of permutations in the previous section, Eq. 5.1.1–(8), in the special case that a set was being permuted. Show that, in general, if a *multiset* is permuted, the generating function for inversions of $\{n_1 \cdot x_1, n_2 \cdot x_2, \ldots\}$ is the "z-multinomial coefficient"

$$\binom{n}{n_1, n_2, \ldots}_z = \frac{n!_z}{n_1!_z\ n_2!_z \cdots}, \qquad \text{where} \quad m!_z = \prod_{k=1}^m (1 + z + \cdots + z^{k-1}).$$

[Compare with (3) and with the definition of z-nomial coefficients in Eq. 1.2.6–(40).]

17. [*M24*] Find the average and standard deviation of the number of inversions in a random permutation of a given multiset, using the generating function found in exercise 16.

18. [*M30*] (P. A. MacMahon.) The *index* of a permutation $a_1\,a_2 \ldots a_n$ was defined in the previous section; and we proved that the number of permutations of a given set that have a given index k is the same as the number of permutations that have k inversions. Does the same result hold for permutations of a given multiset?

19. [*HM28*] Define the *Möbius function* $\mu(\pi)$ of a permutation π to be 0 if π contains repeated elements, otherwise $(-1)^k$ if π is the product of k primes. (Compare with the definition of the ordinary Möbius function, exercise 4.5.2–10.)

a) Prove that if $\pi \neq \epsilon$, we have

$$\sum \mu(\lambda) = 0,$$

summed over all permutations λ that are left factors of π (namely all λ such that $\pi = \lambda \top \rho$ for some ρ).

b) Given that $x_1 < x_2 < \cdots < x_m$ and $\pi = x_{i_1} x_{i_2} \ldots x_{i_n}$, where $1 \leq i_k \leq m$ for $1 \leq k \leq n$, prove that

$$\mu(\pi) = (-1)^n \epsilon(i_1 i_2 \ldots i_n), \quad \text{where} \quad \epsilon(i_1 i_2 \ldots i_n) = \text{sign} \prod_{1 \leq j < k \leq n} (i_k - i_j).$$

▶ **20.** [*HM33*] (D. Foata.) Let (a_{ij}) be any matrix of real numbers. In the notation of exercise 19(b), define $\nu(\pi) = a_{i_1 j_1} \ldots a_{i_n j_n}$, where the two-line notation for π is

$$\begin{pmatrix} x_{i_1} & x_{i_2} & \cdots & x_{i_n} \\ x_{j_1} & x_{j_2} & \cdots & x_{j_n} \end{pmatrix}.$$

This function is useful in the computation of generating functions for permutations of a multiset, because $\sum \nu(\pi)$, summed over all permutations π of the multiset

$$\{n_1 \cdot x_1, \ldots, n_m \cdot x_m\},$$

will be the generating function for the number of permutations satisfying certain restrictions. For example, if we take $a_{ij} = z$ for $i = j$, and $a_{ij} = 1$ for $i \neq j$, then $\sum \nu(\pi)$ is the generating function for the number of "fixed points" (columns in which the top and bottom entries are equal). In order to study $\sum \nu(\pi)$ for all multisets simultaneously, we consider the function

$$G = \sum \pi \nu(\pi)$$

summed over all π in the set $\{x_1, \ldots, x_m\}^*$ of all permutations of multisets involving the elements $x_1, \ldots, x_m$, and we look at the coefficient of $x_1^{n_1} \ldots x_m^{n_m}$ in G.

In this formula for G we are treating π as the product of the x's. For example, when $m = 2$ we have

$$G = 1 + x_1\nu(x_1) + x_2\nu(x_2) + x_1 x_1\nu(x_1 x_1) + x_1 x_2\nu(x_1 x_2) + x_2 x_1\nu(x_2 x_1) + x_2 x_2\nu(x_2 x_2) + \cdots$$

$$= 1 + x_1 a_{11} + x_2 a_{22} + x_1^2 a_{11}^2 + x_1 x_2 a_{11} a_{22} + x_1 x_2 a_{21} a_{12} + x_2^2 a_{22}^2 + \cdots.$$

Thus the coefficient of $x_1^{n_1} \ldots x_m^{n_m}$ in G is $\sum \nu(\pi)$ summed over all permutations π of $\{n_1 \cdot x_1, \ldots, n_m \cdot x_m\}$. It is not hard to see that this coefficient is also the coefficient of $x_1^{n_1} \ldots x_m^{n_m}$ in the expression

$$(a_{11}x_1 + \cdots + a_{1m}x_m)^{n_1} (a_{21}x_1 + \cdots + a_{2m}x_m)^{n_2} \ldots (a_{m1}x_1 + \cdots + a_{mm}x_m)^{n_m}.$$

The purpose of this exercise is to prove what P. A. MacMahon called a "Master Theorem" in his *Combinatory Analysis* **1** (1915), Section 3, namely the formula

$$G = 1/D, \quad \text{where} \quad D = \det \begin{pmatrix} 1 - a_{11}x_1 & -a_{12}x_2 & \cdots & -a_{1m}x_m \\ -a_{21}x_1 & 1 - a_{22}x_2 & & -a_{2m}x_m \\ \vdots & & & \vdots \\ -a_{m1}x_1 & -a_{m2}x_2 & \cdots & 1 - a_{mm}x_m \end{pmatrix}.$$

For example, if $a_{ij} = 1$ for all i and j, this formula gives

$$G = 1/(1 - (x_1 + x_2 + \cdots + x_m)),$$

and the coefficient of $x_1^{n_1} \ldots x_m^{n_m}$ turns out to be $(n_1 + \cdots + n_m)!/n_1! \ldots n_m!$, as it should. To prove the Master Theorem, show that

a) $\nu(\pi \top \rho) = \nu(\pi)\nu(\rho)$;

b) $D = \sum \pi\mu(\pi)\nu(\pi)$, in the notation of exercise 19, summed over all permutations π in $\{x_1, \ldots, x_m\}^*$;

c) therefore $D \cdot G = 1$.

21. [M21] Given $n_1, \ldots, n_m$, and $d \geq 0$, how many permutations $a_1 a_2 \ldots a_n$ of the multiset $\{n_1 \cdot 1, \ldots, n_m \cdot m\}$ satisfy $a_{j+1} \geq a_j - d$ for $1 \leq j < n = n_1 + \cdots + n_m$?

22. [M30] Let $P(x_1^{n_1} \ldots x_m^{n_m})$ denote the set of all possible permutations of the multiset $\{n_1 \cdot x_1, \ldots, n_m \cdot x_m\}$, and let $P_0(x_0^{n_0} x_1^{n_1} \ldots x_m^{n_m})$ be the subset of $P(x_0^{n_0} x_1^{n_1} \ldots x_m^{n_m})$ in which the first n_0 elements are $\neq x_0$.

a) Given a number t with $1 \leq t < m$, find a one-to-one correspondence between $P(1^{n_1} \ldots m^{n_m})$ and the set of all ordered pairs of permutations that belong respectively to $P_0(0^k 1^{n_1} \ldots t^{n_t})$ and $P_0(0^k (t+1)^{n_{t+1}} \ldots m^{n_m})$, for some $k \geq 0$. [Hint: For each $\pi = a_1 \ldots a_n \in P(1^{n_1} \ldots m^{n_m})$, let $l(\pi)$ be the permutation obtained by replacing $t+1, \ldots, m$ by 0 and erasing all 0s in the last $n_{t+1} + \cdots + n_m$ positions; similarly, let $r(\pi)$ be the permutation obtained by replacing $1, \ldots, t$ by 0 and erasing all 0s in the first $n_1 + \cdots + n_t$ positions.]

b) Prove that the number of permutations of $P_0(0^{n_0} 1^{n_1} \ldots m^{n_m})$ whose two-line form has p_j columns $\frac{0}{j}$ and q_j columns $\frac{j}{0}$ is

$$\frac{|P(x_1^{p_1} \ldots x_m^{p_m} y_1^{n_1 - p_1} \ldots y_m^{n_m - p_m})| \, |P(x_1^{q_1} \ldots x_m^{q_m} y_1^{n_1 - q_1} \ldots y_m^{n_m - q_m})|}{|P_0(0^{n_0} 1^{n_1} \ldots m^{n_m})|}.$$

c) Let $w_1, \ldots, w_m, z_1, \ldots, z_m$ be complex numbers on the unit circle. Define the weight $w(\pi)$ of a permutation $\pi \in P(1^{n_1} \ldots m^{n_m})$ as the product of the weights of its columns in two-line form, where the weight of $\frac{j}{k}$ is w_j/w_k if j and k are both $\leq t$ or both $> t$, otherwise it is z_j/z_k. Prove that the sum of $w(\pi)$ over all $\pi \in P(1^{n_1} \ldots m^{n_m})$ is

$$\sum_{k \geq 0} \frac{k!^2 (n_{\leq t} - k)! \, (n_{>t} - k)!}{n_1! \ldots n_m!} \left| \sum \binom{n_1}{p_1} \cdots \binom{n_m}{p_m} \left(\frac{w_1}{z_1}\right)^{p_1} \cdots \left(\frac{w_m}{z_m}\right)^{p_m} \right|^2,$$

where $n_{\leq t}$ is $n_1 + \cdots + n_t$, $n_{>t}$ is $n_{t+1} + \cdots + n_m$, and the inner sum is over all $(p_1, \ldots, p_m)$ such that $p_{\leq t} = p_{>t} = k$.

23. [M23] A strand of DNA can be thought of as a word on a four-letter alphabet. Suppose we copy a strand of DNA and break it completely into one-letter bases, then recombine those bases at random. If the resulting strand is placed next to the original, prove that the number of places in which they differ is more likely to be even than odd. [Hint: Apply the previous exercise.]

24. [27] Consider any relation R that might hold between two unordered pairs of letters; if $\{w, x\} R \{y, z\}$ we say $\{w, x\}$ *preserves* $\{y, z\}$, otherwise $\{w, x\}$ *moves* $\{y, z\}$.

The operation of *transposing* $\frac{w}{y}\frac{x}{z}$ with respect to R replaces $\frac{w}{y}\frac{x}{z}$ by $\frac{x}{y}\frac{w}{z}$ or $\frac{x}{z}\frac{w}{y}$, according as the pair $\{w, x\}$ preserves or moves the pair $\{y, z\}$, assuming that $w \neq x$ and $y \neq z$; if $w = x$ or $y = z$ the transposition always produces $\frac{x}{z}\frac{w}{y}$.

The operation of *sorting* a two-line array $\left(\begin{smallmatrix} x_1 & \cdots & x_n \\ y_1 & \cdots & y_n \end{smallmatrix}\right)$ with respect to R repeatedly finds the largest x_j such that $x_j > x_{j+1}$ and transposes columns j and $j+1$, until eventually $x_1 \leq \cdots \leq x_n$. (We do not require $y_1 \ldots y_n$ to be a permutation of $x_1 \ldots x_n$.)

a) Given $\left(\begin{smallmatrix} x_1 & \cdots & x_n \\ y_1 & \cdots & y_n \end{smallmatrix}\right)$, prove that for every $x \in \{x_1, \ldots, x_n\}$ there is a unique $y \in \{y_1, \ldots, y_n\}$ such that $\text{sort}\left(\begin{smallmatrix} x_1 & \cdots & x_n \\ y_1 & \cdots & y_n \end{smallmatrix}\right) = \text{sort}\left(\begin{smallmatrix} x & x_2' & \cdots & x_n' \\ y & y_2' & \cdots & y_n' \end{smallmatrix}\right)$ for some $x_2', y_2', \ldots, x_n', y_n'$.

b) Let $\left(\begin{smallmatrix} w_1 & \cdots & w_k \\ y_1 & \cdots & y_k \end{smallmatrix}\right) \circledR \left(\begin{smallmatrix} x_1 & \cdots & x_l \\ z_1 & \cdots & z_l \end{smallmatrix}\right)$ denote the result of sorting $\left(\begin{smallmatrix} w_1 & \cdots & w_k & x_1 & \cdots & x_l \\ y_1 & \cdots & y_k & z_1 & \cdots & z_l \end{smallmatrix}\right)$ with respect to R. For example, if R is always true, $\circledR$ sorts $\{w_1, \ldots, w_k, x_1, \ldots, x_l\}$, but it simply juxtaposes $y_1 \ldots y_k$ with $z_1 \ldots z_l$; if R is always false, $\circledR$ is the intercalation product $\top$. Generalize Theorem A by proving that every permutation π of a multiset M has a unique representation of the form

$$\pi = (x_{11} \ldots x_{1n_1} y_1) \circledR \left((x_{21} \ldots x_{2n_2} y_2) \circledR (\cdots \circledR (x_{t1} \ldots x_{tn_t} y_t) \cdots)\right)$$

satisfying (16), if we redefine cycle notation by letting the two-line array (11) correspond to the cycle $(x_2 \ldots x_n x_1)$ instead of to $(x_1 x_2 \ldots x_n)$. For example, suppose $\{w, x\} R \{y, z\}$ means that w, x, y, and z are distinct; then it turns out that the factorization of (12) analogous to (17) is

$$(d\,d\,b\,c\,a) \circledR \left((c\,b\,b\,a) \circledR \left((c\,d\,b) \circledR \left((d\,b) \circledR (d)\right)\right)\right).$$

(The operation $\circledR$ does not always obey the associative law; parentheses in the generalized factorization should be nested from right to left.)

*5.1.3. Runs

In Chapter 3 we analyzed the lengths of upward runs in permutations, as a way to test the randomness of a sequence. If we place a vertical line at both ends of a permutation $a_1 a_2 \ldots a_n$ and also between a_j and a_{j+1} whenever $a_j > a_{j+1}$, the *runs* are the segments between pairs of lines. For example, the permutation

$$|\,3\ 5\ 7\,|\,1\ 6\ 8\ 9\,|\,4\,|\,2\,|$$

has four runs. The theory developed in Section 3.3.2G determines the average number of runs of length k in a random permutation of $\{1, 2, \ldots, n\}$, as well as the covariance of the numbers of runs of lengths j and k. Runs are important in the study of sorting algorithms, because they represent sorted segments of the data, so we will now take up the subject of runs once again.

Let us use the notation

$$\left\langle {n \atop k} \right\rangle \tag{1}$$

to stand for the number of permutations of $\{1, 2, \ldots, n\}$ that have exactly k "descents" $a_j > a_{j+1}$, thus exactly $k+1$ ascending runs. These numbers $\left\langle {n \atop k} \right\rangle$ arise in several contexts, and they are usually called *Eulerian numbers* since Euler discussed them in his famous book *Institutiones Calculi Differentialis* (St. Petersburg: 1755), 485–487, after having introduced them several years earlier in a technical paper [*Comment. Acad. Sci. Imp. Petrop.* **8** (1736), 147–158, §13]; they should not be confused with the *Euler numbers* E_n discussed in exercise 5.1.4–23. The angle brackets in $\left\langle {n \atop k} \right\rangle$ remind us of the ">" sign in the definition of a descent. Of course $\left\langle {n \atop k} \right\rangle$ is also the number of permutations that have k "ascents" $a_j < a_{j+1}$.

We can use any given permutation of $\{1, \ldots, n-1\}$ to form n new permutations, by inserting the element n in all possible places. If the original permutation has k descents, exactly $k+1$ of these new permutations will have k descents; the remaining $n-1-k$ will have $k+1$, since we increase the number of descents unless we place the element n at the end of an existing run. For example, the six permutations formed from $3\,1\,2\,4\,5$ are

$$
\begin{array}{ccc}
6\,3\,1\,2\,4\,5, & 3\,6\,1\,2\,4\,5, & 3\,1\,6\,2\,4\,5, \\
3\,1\,2\,6\,4\,5, & 3\,1\,2\,4\,6\,5, & 3\,1\,2\,4\,5\,6;
\end{array}
$$

all but the second and last of these have two descents instead of one. Therefore we have the recurrence relation

$$\left\langle {n \atop k} \right\rangle = (k+1)\left\langle {n-1 \atop k} \right\rangle + (n-k)\left\langle {n-1 \atop k-1} \right\rangle, \quad \text{integer } n > 0, \text{ integer } k. \quad (2)$$

By convention we set

$$\left\langle {0 \atop k} \right\rangle = \delta_{k0}, \quad (3)$$

saying that the null permutation has no descents. The reader may find it interesting to compare (2) with the recurrence relations for Stirling numbers in Eqs. 1.2.6–(46). Table 1 lists the Eulerian numbers for small n.

Several patterns can be observed in Table 1. By definition, we have

$$\left\langle {n \atop 0} \right\rangle + \left\langle {n \atop 1} \right\rangle + \cdots + \left\langle {n \atop n} \right\rangle = n!; \quad (4)$$

$$\left\langle {n \atop 0} \right\rangle = 1; \quad (5)$$

$$\left\langle {n \atop n-1} \right\rangle = 1, \quad \left\langle {n \atop n} \right\rangle = 0, \quad \text{for } n \geq 1. \quad (6)$$

Eq. (6) follows from (5) because of a general rule of symmetry,

$$\left\langle {n \atop k} \right\rangle = \left\langle {n \atop n-1-k} \right\rangle, \quad \text{for } n \geq 1, \quad (7)$$

which comes from the fact that each nonnull permutation $a_1\,a_2\,\ldots\,a_n$ having k descents has $n-1-k$ ascents.

Another important property of the Eulerian numbers is the formula

$$\sum_k \left\langle {n \atop k} \right\rangle \binom{m+k}{n} = m^n, \quad n \geq 0, \quad (8)$$

which was discovered by the Chinese mathematician Li Shan-Lan and published in 1867. [See J.-C. Martzloff, *A History of Chinese Mathematics* (Berlin: Springer, 1997), 346–348; special cases for $n \leq 5$ had already been known to Yoshisuke Matsunaga in Japan, who died in 1744.] Li Shan-Lan's identity follows from the properties of sorting: Consider the m^n sequences $a_1\,a_2\,\ldots\,a_n$ such that $1 \leq a_i \leq m$. We can sort any such sequence into nondecreasing order in a stable manner, obtaining

$$a_{i_1} \leq a_{i_2} \leq \cdots \leq a_{i_n} \quad (9)$$

Table 1

EULERIAN NUMBERS

n	$\left\langle{n\atop0}\right\rangle$	$\left\langle{n\atop1}\right\rangle$	$\left\langle{n\atop2}\right\rangle$	$\left\langle{n\atop3}\right\rangle$	$\left\langle{n\atop4}\right\rangle$	$\left\langle{n\atop5}\right\rangle$	$\left\langle{n\atop6}\right\rangle$	$\left\langle{n\atop7}\right\rangle$	$\left\langle{n\atop8}\right\rangle$
0	1	0	0	0	0	0	0	0	0
1	1	0	0	0	0	0	0	0	0
2	1	1	0	0	0	0	0	0	0
3	1	4	1	0	0	0	0	0	0
4	1	11	11	1	0	0	0	0	0
5	1	26	66	26	1	0	0	0	0
6	1	57	302	302	57	1	0	0	0
7	1	120	1191	2416	1191	120	1	0	0
8	1	247	4293	15619	15619	4293	247	1	0
9	1	502	14608	88234	156190	88234	14608	502	1

where $i_1 i_2 \ldots i_n$ is a uniquely determined permutation of $\{1, 2, \ldots, n\}$ such that $a_{i_j} = a_{i_{j+1}}$ implies $i_j < i_{j+1}$; in other words, $i_j > i_{j+1}$ implies that $a_{i_j} < a_{i_{j+1}}$. If the permutation $i_1 i_2 \ldots i_n$ has k runs, we will show that the number of corresponding sequences $a_1 a_2 \ldots a_n$ is $\binom{m+n-k}{n}$. This will prove (8) if we replace k by $n - k$ and use (7), because $\left\langle{n\atop k}\right\rangle$ permutations have $n - k$ runs.

For example, if $n = 9$ and $i_1 i_2 \ldots i_n = 3\,5\,7\,1\,6\,8\,9\,4\,2$, we want to count the number of sequences $a_1 a_2 \ldots a_n$ such that

$$1 \le a_3 \le a_5 \le a_7 < a_1 \le a_6 \le a_8 \le a_9 < a_4 < a_2 \le m; \qquad (10)$$

this is the number of sequences $b_1 b_2 \ldots b_9$ such that

$$1 \le b_1 < b_2 < b_3 < b_4 < b_5 < b_6 < b_7 < b_8 < b_9 \le m + 5,$$

since we can let $b_1 = a_3$, $b_2 = a_5 + 1$, $b_3 = a_7 + 2$, $b_4 = a_1 + 2$, $b_5 = a_6 + 3$, etc. The number of choices of the b's is simply the number of ways of choosing 9 things out of $m + 5$, namely $\binom{m+5}{9}$; a similar proof works for general n and k, and for any permutation $i_1 i_2 \ldots i_n$ with k runs.

Since both sides of (8) are polynomials in m, we may replace m by any real number x, and we obtain an interesting representation of powers in terms of consecutive binomial coefficients:

$$x^n = \left\langle{n\atop0}\right\rangle\binom{x}{n} + \left\langle{n\atop1}\right\rangle\binom{x+1}{n} + \cdots + \left\langle{n\atop n-1}\right\rangle\binom{x+n-1}{n}, \quad n \ge 1. \quad (11)$$

For example,

$$x^3 = \binom{x}{3} + 4\binom{x+1}{3} + \binom{x+2}{3}.$$

This is the key property of Eulerian numbers that makes them useful in the study of discrete mathematics.

Setting $x = 1$ in (11) proves again that $\left\langle{n\atop n-1}\right\rangle = 1$, since the binomial coefficients vanish in all but the last term. Setting $x = 2$ yields

$$\left\langle{n\atop n-2}\right\rangle = \left\langle{n\atop1}\right\rangle = 2^n - n - 1, \quad n \ge 1. \qquad (12)$$

Setting $x = 3, 4, \ldots$ shows that relation (11) completely defines the numbers $\left\langle {n \atop k} \right\rangle$, and leads to a formula originally given by Euler:

$$\left\langle {n \atop k} \right\rangle = (k+1)^n - k^n \binom{n+1}{1} + (k-1)^n \binom{n+1}{2} - \cdots + (-1)^k 1^n \binom{n+1}{k}$$

$$= \sum_{j=0}^{k} (-1)^j \binom{n+1}{j} (k+1-j)^n, \qquad n \geq 0,\ k \geq 0. \tag{13}$$

Now let us study the generating function for runs. If we set

$$g_n(z) = \sum_k \left\langle {n \atop k-1} \right\rangle \frac{z^k}{n!}, \tag{14}$$

the coefficient of z^k is the probability that a random permutation of $\{1, 2, \ldots, n\}$ has exactly k runs. Since k runs are just as likely as $n+1-k$, the average number of runs must be $\frac{1}{2}(n+1)$, hence $g_n'(1) = \frac{1}{2}(n+1)$. Exercise 2(b) shows that there is a simple formula for *all* the derivatives of $g_n(z)$ at the point $z = 1$:

$$g_n^{(m)}(1) = \left\{ {n+1 \atop n+1-m} \right\} \Big/ \binom{n}{m}, \qquad n \geq m. \tag{15}$$

Thus in particular the variance $g_n''(1) + g_n'(1) - g_n'(1)^2$ comes to $(n+1)/12$, for $n \geq 2$, indicating a rather stable distribution about the mean. (We found this same quantity in Eq. 3.3.2–(18), where it was called $\operatorname{covar}(R_1', R_1')$.) Since $g_n(z)$ is a polynomial, we can use formula (15) to deduce the Taylor series expansions

$$g_n(z) = \frac{1}{n!} \sum_{k=0}^{n} (z-1)^{n-k} k! \left\{ {n+1 \atop k+1} \right\} = \frac{1}{n!} \sum_{k=0}^{n} z^{k+1} (1-z)^{n-k} k! \left\{ {n+1 \atop k+1} \right\}. \tag{16}$$

The second of these equations follows from the first, since

$$g_n(z) = z^{n+1} g_n(1/z), \qquad n \geq 1, \tag{17}$$

by the symmetry condition (7). The Stirling number recurrence

$$\left\{ {n+1 \atop k+1} \right\} = (k+1) \left\{ {n \atop k+1} \right\} + \left\{ {n \atop k} \right\}$$

gives two slightly simpler representations,

$$g_n(z) = \frac{1}{n!} \sum_{k=0}^{n} z(z-1)^{n-k} k! \left\{ {n \atop k} \right\} = \frac{1}{n!} \sum_{k=0}^{n} z^k (1-z)^{n-k} k! \left\{ {n \atop k} \right\}, \tag{18}$$

when $n \geq 1$. The super generating function

$$g(z, x) = \sum_{n \geq 0} \frac{g_n(z) x^n}{z} = \sum_{k, n \geq 0} \left\langle {n \atop k} \right\rangle \frac{z^k x^n}{n!} \tag{19}$$

is therefore equal to

$$\sum_{k,n\geq 0} \frac{((z-1)x)^n}{(z-1)^k} \left\{ {n \atop k} \right\} \frac{k!}{n!} = \sum_{k\geq 0} \left(\frac{e^{(z-1)x} - 1}{z-1} \right)^k = \frac{(1-z)}{e^{(z-1)x} - z}; \qquad (20)$$

this is another relation discussed by Euler.

Further properties of the Eulerian numbers may be found in a survey paper by L. Carlitz [*Math. Magazine* **32** (1959), 247–260]. See also J. Riordan, *Introduction to Combinatorial Analysis* (New York: Wiley, 1958), 38–39, 214–219, 234–237; D. Foata and M. P. Schützenberger, *Lecture Notes in Math.* **138** (Berlin: Springer, 1970).

Let us now consider the length of runs; how long will a run be, on the average? We have already studied the expected number of runs having a given length, in Section 3.3.2; the average run length is approximately 2, in agreement with the fact that about $\frac{1}{2}(n+1)$ runs appear in a random permutation of length n. For applications to sorting algorithms, a slightly different viewpoint is useful; we will consider the length of the kth run of the permutation from left to right, for $k = 1, 2, \ldots$.

For example, how long is the first (leftmost) run of a random permutation $a_1 a_2 \ldots a_n$? Its length is always ≥ 1, and its length is ≥ 2 exactly one-half the time (namely when $a_1 < a_2$). Its length is ≥ 3 exactly one-sixth of the time (when $a_1 < a_2 < a_3$), and, in general, its length is $\geq m$ with probability $q_m = 1/m!$, for $1 \leq m \leq n$. The probability that its length is exactly equal to m is therefore

$$p_m = q_m - q_{m+1} = 1/m! - 1/(m+1)!, \qquad \text{for } 1 \leq m < n;$$
$$p_n = 1/n!. \qquad (21)$$

The average length of the first run therefore equals

$$p_1 + 2p_2 + \cdots + np_n = (q_1 - q_2) + 2(q_2 - q_3) + \cdots + (n-1)(q_{n-1} - q_n) + nq_n$$

$$= q_1 + q_2 + \cdots + q_n = \frac{1}{1!} + \frac{1}{2!} + \cdots + \frac{1}{n!}. \qquad (22)$$

If we let $n \to \infty$, the limit is $e - 1 = 1.71828\ldots$, and for finite n the value is $e - 1 - \delta_n$ where δ_n is quite small;

$$\delta_n = \frac{1}{(n+1)!} \left(1 + \frac{1}{n+2} + \frac{1}{(n+2)(n+3)} + \cdots \right) \leq \frac{e-1}{(n+1)!}.$$

For practical purposes it is therefore convenient to study runs in a random *infinite* sequence of distinct numbers

$$a_1, a_2, a_3, \ldots;$$

by "random" we mean in this case that each of the $n!$ possible relative orderings of the first n elements in the sequence is equally likely. The average length of the first run in a random infinite sequence is exactly $e - 1$.

By slightly sharpening our analysis of the first run, we can ascertain the average length of the kth run in a random sequence. Let q_{km} be the probability that the first k runs have total length $\geq m$; then q_{km} is $1/m!$ times the number of permutations of $\{1, 2, \ldots, m\}$ that have $\leq k$ runs,

$$q_{km} = \left(\left\langle {m \atop 0} \right\rangle + \cdots + \left\langle {m \atop k-1} \right\rangle \right) \Big/ m! . \tag{23}$$

The probability that the first k runs have total length m is $q_{km} - q_{k(m+1)}$. Therefore if L_k denotes the average length of the kth run, we find that

$$L_1 + \cdots + L_k = \text{average total length of first } k \text{ runs}$$
$$= (q_{k1} - q_{k2}) + 2(q_{k2} - q_{k3}) + 3(q_{k3} - q_{k4}) + \cdots$$
$$= q_{k1} + q_{k2} + q_{k3} + \cdots .$$

Subtracting $L_1 + \cdots + L_{k-1}$ and using the value of q_{km} in (23) yields the desired formula

$$L_k = \frac{1}{1!} \left\langle {1 \atop k-1} \right\rangle + \frac{1}{2!} \left\langle {2 \atop k-1} \right\rangle + \frac{1}{3!} \left\langle {3 \atop k-1} \right\rangle + \cdots = \sum_{m \geq 1} \left\langle {m \atop k-1} \right\rangle \frac{1}{m!} . \tag{24}$$

Since $\left\langle {0 \atop k-1} \right\rangle = 0$ except when $k = 1$, L_k turns out to be the coefficient of z^{k-1} in the generating function $g(z, 1) - 1$ (see Eq. (19)), so we have

$$L(z) = \sum_{k \geq 0} L_k z^k = \frac{z(1-z)}{e^{z-1} - z} - z . \tag{25}$$

From Euler's formula (13) we obtain a representation of L_k as a polynomial in e:

$$L_k = \sum_{m \geq 0} \sum_{j=0}^{k} (-1)^{k-j} \binom{m+1}{k-j} \frac{j^m}{m!}$$

$$= \sum_{j=0}^{k} (-1)^{k-j} \sum_{m \geq 0} \binom{m}{k-j} \frac{j^m}{m!} + \sum_{j=0}^{k-1} (-1)^{k-j} \sum_{m \geq 0} \binom{m}{k-j-1} \frac{j^m}{m!}$$

$$= \sum_{j=0}^{k} \frac{(-1)^{k-j} j^{k-j}}{(k-j)!} \sum_{n \geq 0} \frac{j^n}{n!} + \sum_{j=0}^{k-1} \frac{(-1)^{k-j} j^{k-j-1}}{(k-j-1)!} \sum_{n \geq 0} \frac{j^n}{n!}$$

$$= k \sum_{j=0}^{k} \frac{(-1)^{k-j} j^{k-j-1}}{(k-j)!} e^j . \tag{26}$$

This formula for L_k was first obtained by B. J. Gassner [see *CACM* **10** (1967), 89–93]. In particular, we have

$$L_1 = e - 1 \qquad\qquad \approx 1.71828 \ldots ;$$
$$L_2 = e^2 - 2e \qquad\quad \approx 1.95249 \ldots ;$$
$$L_3 = e^3 - 3e^2 + \tfrac{3}{2}e \approx 1.99579 \ldots .$$

The second run is expected to be longer than the first, and the third run will be longer yet, on the average. This may seem surprising at first glance, but a moment's reflection shows that the first element of the second run tends to be

Table 2

AVERAGE LENGTH OF THE kTH RUN

k	L_k	k	L_k
1	1.71828 18284 59045+	10	2.00000 00012 05997+
2	1.95249 24420 12560−	11	2.00000 00001 93672+
3	1.99579 13690 84285−	12	1.99999 99999 99909+
4	2.00003 88504 76806−	13	1.99999 99999 97022−
5	2.00005 75785 89716+	14	1.99999 99999 99719+
6	2.00000 50727 55710−	15	2.00000 00000 00019+
7	1.99999 96401 44022+	16	2.00000 00000 00006+
8	1.99999 98889 04744+	17	2.00000 00000 00000+
9	1.99999 99948 43434−	18	2.00000 00000 00000−

small (it caused the first run to terminate); hence there is a better chance for the second run to go on longer. The first element of the third run will tend to be even smaller than that of the second.

The numbers L_k are important in the theory of replacement-selection sorting (Section 5.4.1), so it is interesting to study their values in detail. Table 2 shows the first 18 values of L_k to 15 decimal places. Our discussion in the preceding paragraph might lead us to suspect at first that $L_{k+1} > L_k$, but in fact the values oscillate back and forth. Notice that L_k rapidly approaches the limiting value 2; it is quite remarkable to see these monic polynomials in the transcendental number e converging to the rational number 2 so quickly! The polynomials (26) are also somewhat interesting from the standpoint of numerical analysis, since they provide an excellent example of the loss of significant figures when nearly equal numbers are subtracted; using 19-digit floating point arithmetic, Gassner concluded incorrectly that $L_{12} > 2$, and John W. Wrench, Jr., has remarked that 42-digit floating point arithmetic gives L_{28} correct to only 29 significant digits.

The asymptotic behavior of L_k can be determined by using simple principles of complex variable theory. The denominator of (25) is zero only when $e^{z-1} = z$, namely when

$$e^{x-1} \cos y = x \qquad \text{and} \qquad e^{x-1} \sin y = y, \tag{27}$$

if we write $z = x + iy$. Figure 3 shows the superimposed graphs of these two equations, and we note that they intersect at the points $z = z_0, z_1, \bar{z}_1, z_2, \bar{z}_2, \ldots$, where $z_0 = 1$,

$$z_1 = (3.08884\ 30156\ 13044-) + (7.46148\ 92856\ 54255-)\,i, \tag{28}$$

and the imaginary part $\Im(z_{k+1})$ is roughly equal to $\Im(z_k) + 2\pi$ for large k. Since

$$\lim_{z \to z_k} \left(\frac{1-z}{e^{z-1} - z} \right)(z - z_k) = -1, \qquad \text{for } k > 0,$$

and since the limit is -2 for $k = 0$, the function

$$R_m(z) = L(z) + \frac{2z}{z - z_0} + \frac{z}{z - z_1} + \frac{z}{z - \bar{z}_1} + \frac{z}{z - z_2} + \frac{z}{z - \bar{z}_2} + \cdots + \frac{z}{z - z_m} + \frac{z}{z - \bar{z}_m}$$

has no singularities in the complex plane for $|z| < |z_{m+1}|$. Hence $R_m(z)$ has a power series expansion $\sum_k \rho_k z^k$ that converges absolutely when $|z| < |z_{m+1}|$; it follows that $\rho_k M^k \to 0$ as $k \to \infty$, where $M = |z_{m+1}| - \epsilon$. The coefficients of $L(z)$ are the coefficients of

$$\frac{2z}{1-z} + \frac{z/z_1}{1 - z/z_1} + \frac{z/\bar{z}_1}{1 - z/\bar{z}_1} + \cdots + \frac{z/z_m}{1 - z/z_m} + \frac{z/\bar{z}_m}{1 - z/\bar{z}_m} + R_m(z),$$

namely,

$$L_n = 2 + 2r_1^{-n} \cos n\theta_1 + 2r_2^{-n} \cos n\theta_2 + \cdots + 2r_m^{-n} \cos n\theta_m + O(r_{m+1}^{-n}), \quad (29)$$

if we let

$$z_k = r_k e^{i\theta_k}. \quad (30)$$

This shows the asymptotic behavior of L_n. We have

$$
\begin{aligned}
r_1 &= \ \ 8.07556\ 64528\ 89526-, & \theta_1 &= 1.17830\ 39784\ 74668+; \\
r_2 &= 14.35456\ 68997\ 62106-, & \theta_2 &= 1.31268\ 53883\ 87636+; \\
r_3 &= 20.62073\ 15381\ 80628-, & \theta_3 &= 1.37427\ 90757\ 91688-; \\
r_4 &= 26.88795\ 29424\ 54546-, & \theta_4 &= 1.41049\ 72786\ 51865-; & (31)
\end{aligned}
$$

so the main contribution to $L_n - 2$ is due to r_1 and θ_1, and convergence of (29) is quite rapid. Further analysis [W. W. Hooker, *CACM* **12** (1969), 411–413] shows that $R_m(z) \to cz$ for some constant c as $m \to \infty$; hence the series $2\sum_{k \geq 0} r_k^{-n} \cos n\theta_k$ actually *converges* to L_n when $n > 1$. (See also exercise 28.)

A more careful examination of probabilities can be carried out to determine the complete probability distribution for the length of the kth run and for the total length of the first k runs (see exercises 9, 10, 11). The sum $L_1 + \cdots + L_k$ turns out to be asymptotically $2k - \frac{1}{3} + O(8^{-k})$.

Let us conclude this section by considering the properties of runs when equal elements are allowed to appear in the permutations. The famous nineteenth-century American astronomer Simon Newcomb amused himself by playing a game of solitaire related to this question. He would deal a deck of cards into a pile, so long as the face values were in nondecreasing order; but whenever the next card to be dealt had a face value lower than its predecessor, he would start a new pile. He wanted to know the probability that a given number of piles would be formed after the entire deck had been dealt out in this manner.

Simon Newcomb's problem therefore consists of finding the probability distribution of runs in a random permutation of a multiset. The general answer is rather complicated (see exercise 12), although we have already seen how to solve the special case when all cards have a distinct face value. We will content ourselves here with a derivation of the *average* number of piles that appear in the game.

Suppose first that there are m different types of cards, each occurring exactly p times. An ordinary bridge deck, for example, has $m = 13$ and $p = 4$ if suits are disregarded. A remarkable symmetry applying to this case was discovered

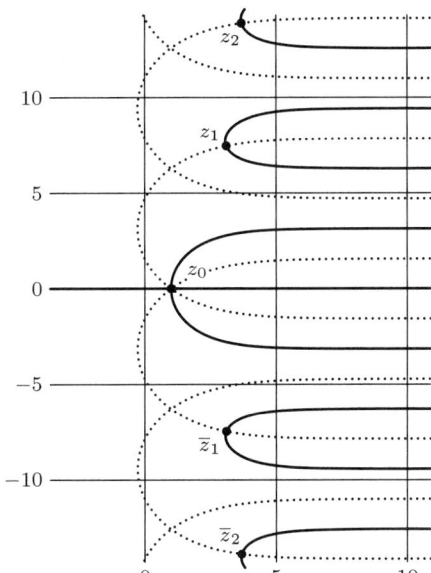

$$e^{x-1}\sin y = y \quad \text{————}$$
$$e^{x-1}\cos y = x \quad \cdots\cdots\cdots$$

Fig. 3. Roots of $e^{z-1} = z$.

by P. A. MacMahon [*Combinatory Analysis* **1** (Cambridge, 1915), 212–213]: The number of permutations with $k+1$ runs is the same as the number with $mp - p - k + 1$ runs. When $p = 1$, this relation is Eq. (7), but for $p > 1$ it is quite surprising.

We can prove the symmetry by setting up a one-to-one correspondence between the permutations in such a way that each permutation with $k+1$ runs corresponds to another having $mp - p - k + 1$ runs. The reader is urged to try discovering such a correspondence before reading further.

No very simple correspondence is evident; MacMahon's proof was based on generating functions instead of a combinatorial construction. But Foata's correspondence (Theorem 5.1.2B) provides a useful simplification, because it tells us that there is a one-to-one correspondence between multiset permutations with $k+1$ runs and permutations whose two-line notation contains exactly k columns $\frac{y}{x}$ with $x < y$.

Suppose the given multiset is $\{p \cdot 1, p \cdot 2, \ldots, p \cdot m\}$, and consider the permutation whose two-line notation is

$$\begin{pmatrix} 1 & \cdots & 1 & 2 & \cdots & 2 & \cdots & m & \cdots & m \\ x_{11} & \cdots & x_{1p} & x_{21} & \cdots & x_{2p} & \cdots & x_{m1} & \cdots & x_{mp} \end{pmatrix}. \tag{32}$$

We can associate this permutation with another one,

$$\begin{pmatrix} 1 & \cdots & 1 & 2 & \cdots & 2 & \cdots & m & \cdots & m \\ x'_{11} & \cdots & x'_{1p} & x'_{m1} & \cdots & x'_{mp} & \cdots & x'_{21} & \cdots & x'_{2p} \end{pmatrix}, \tag{33}$$

where $x' = m+1-x$. If (32) contains k columns of the form $\frac{y}{x}$ with $x < y$, then (33) contains $(m-1)p - k$ such columns; for we need only consider the case $y > 1$, and $x < y$ is equivalent to $x' \geq m+2-y$. Now (32) corresponds to a permutation with $k+1$ runs, and (33) corresponds to a permutation with $mp-p-k+1$ runs, and the transformation that takes (32) into (33) is reversible — it takes (33) back into (32). Therefore MacMahon's symmetry condition has been established. See exercise 14 for an example of this construction.

Because of the symmetry property, the average number of runs in a random permutation must be $\frac{1}{2}\big((k+1) + (mp-p-k+1)\big) = 1 + \frac{1}{2}p(m-1)$. For example, the average number of piles resulting from Simon Newcomb's solitaire game using a standard deck will be 25 (so it doesn't appear to be a very exciting way to play solitaire).

We can actually determine the average number of runs in general, using a fairly simple argument, given *any* multiset $\{n_1 \cdot x_1, n_2 \cdot x_2, \ldots, n_m \cdot x_m\}$ where the x's are distinct. Let $n = n_1 + n_2 + \cdots + n_m$, and imagine that all of the permutations $a_1 a_2 \ldots a_n$ of this multiset have been written down; we will count how often a_i is greater than a_{i+1}, for each fixed value of i, $1 \le i < n$. The number of times $a_i > a_{i+1}$ is just half of the number of times $a_i \ne a_{i+1}$; and it is not difficult to see that $a_i = a_{i+1} = x_j$ exactly $Nn_j(n_j-1)/n(n-1)$ times, where N is the total number of permutations. Hence $a_i = a_{i+1}$ exactly

$$\frac{N}{n(n-1)}\big(n_1(n_1-1) + \cdots + n_m(n_m-1)\big) = \frac{N}{n(n-1)}(n_1^2 + \cdots + n_m^2 - n)$$

times, and $a_i > a_{i+1}$ exactly

$$\frac{N}{2n(n-1)}\big(n^2 - (n_1^2 + \cdots + n_m^2)\big)$$

times. Summing over i and adding N, since a run ends at a_n in each permutation, we obtain the total number of runs among all N permutations:

$$N\left(\frac{n}{2} - \frac{1}{2n}(n_1^2 + \cdots + n_m^2) + 1\right). \tag{34}$$

Dividing by N gives the desired average number of runs.

Since runs are important in the study of "order statistics," there is a fairly large literature dealing with them, including several other types of runs not considered here. For additional information, see the book *Combinatorial Chance* by F. N. David and D. E. Barton (London: Griffin, 1962), Chapter 10; and the survey paper by D. E. Barton and C. L. Mallows, *Annals of Math. Statistics* **36** (1965), 236–260.

EXERCISES

1. [*M26*] Derive Euler's formula (13).

▶ 2. [*M22*] (a) Extend the idea used in the text to prove (8), considering those sequences $a_1 a_2 \ldots a_n$ that contain exactly q distinct elements, in order to prove the formula

$$\sum_k \left\langle {n \atop k} \right\rangle \binom{k}{n-q} = \left\{ {n \atop q} \right\} q!, \qquad \text{integer } q \ge 0.$$

(b) Use this identity to prove that

$$\sum_k \left\langle {n \atop k} \right\rangle \binom{k+1}{m} = \left\{ {n+1 \atop n+1-m} \right\} (n-m)!, \qquad \text{for } n \geq m.$$

3. [*HM25*] Evaluate the sum $\sum_k \left\langle {n \atop k} \right\rangle (-1)^k$.

4. [*M21*] What is the value of $\sum_k (-1)^k \left\{ {n \atop k} \right\} k! \binom{n-k}{m}$?

5. [*M20*] Deduce the value of $\left\langle {p \atop k} \right\rangle \bmod p$ when p is prime.

▶ **6.** [*M21*] Mr. B. C. Dull noticed that, by Eqs. (4) and (13),

$$n! = \sum_{k \geq 0} \left\langle {n \atop k} \right\rangle = \sum_{k \geq 0} \sum_{j \geq 0} (-1)^{k-j} \binom{n+1}{k-j} (j+1)^n.$$

Carrying out the sum on k first, he found that $\sum_{k \geq 0} (-1)^{k-j} \binom{n+1}{k-j} = 0$ for all $j \geq 0$; hence $n! = 0$ for all $n \geq 0$. Did he make a mistake?

7. [*HM40*] Is the probability distribution of runs, given by (14), asymptotically normal? (See exercise 1.2.10–13.)

8. [*M24*] (P. A. MacMahon.) Show that the probability that the first run of a sufficiently long permutation has length l_1, the second has length l_2, ..., and the kth has length $\geq l_k$, is

$$\det \begin{pmatrix} 1/l_1! & 1/(l_1+l_2)! & 1/(l_1+l_2+l_3)! & \cdots & 1/(l_1+l_2+l_3+\cdots+l_k)! \\ 1 & 1/l_2! & 1/(l_2+l_3)! & \cdots & 1/(l_2+l_3+\cdots+l_k)! \\ 0 & 1 & 1/l_3! & \cdots & 1/(l_3+\cdots+l_k)! \\ \vdots & & & & \vdots \\ 0 & 0 & \cdots & 1 & 1/l_k! \end{pmatrix}.$$

9. [*M30*] Let $h_k(z) = \sum p_{km} z^m$, where p_{km} is the probability that m is the total length of the first k runs in a random (infinite) sequence. Find "simple" expressions for $h_1(z)$, $h_2(z)$, and the super generating function $h(z, x) = \sum_k h_k(z) x^k$.

10. [*HM30*] Find the asymptotic behavior of the mean and variance of the distributions $h_k(z)$ in the preceding exercise, for large k.

11. [*M40*] Let $H_k(z) = \sum P_{km} z^m$, where P_{km} is the probability that m is the length of the kth run in a random (infinite) sequence. Express $H_1(z)$, $H_2(z)$, and the super generating function $H(z, x) = \sum_k H_k(z) x^k$ in terms of familiar functions.

12. [*M33*] (P. A. MacMahon.) Generalize Eq. (13) to permutations of a multiset, by proving that the number of permutations of $\{n_1 \cdot 1, n_2 \cdot 2, \ldots, n_m \cdot m\}$ having exactly k runs is

$$\sum_{j=0}^k (-1)^j \binom{n+1}{j} \binom{n_1 - 1 + k - j}{n_1} \binom{n_2 - 1 + k - j}{n_2} \cdots \binom{n_m - 1 + k - j}{n_m},$$

where $n = n_1 + n_2 + \cdots + n_m$.

13. [*05*] If Simon Newcomb's solitaire game is played with a standard bridge deck, ignoring face value but treating clubs < diamonds < hearts < spades, what is the average number of piles?

14. [*M18*] The permutation 3 1 1 1 2 3 1 4 2 3 3 4 2 2 4 4 has 5 runs; find the corresponding permutation with 9 runs, according to the text's construction for MacMahon's symmetry condition.

▶ **15.** [*M21*] (*Alternating runs.*) The classical nineteenth-century literature of combinatorial analysis did not treat the topic of runs in permutations, as we have considered
them, but several authors studied "runs" that are alternately ascending and descending.
Thus $5\,3\,2\,4\,7\,6\,1\,8$ was considered to have 4 runs: $5\,3\,2$, $2\,4\,7$, $7\,6\,1$, and $1\,8$. (The first
run would be ascending or descending, according as $a_1 < a_2$ or $a_1 > a_2$; thus $a_1\,a_2\dots a_n$
and $a_n \dots a_2\,a_1$ and $(n+1-a_1)(n+1-a_2)\dots(n+1-a_n)$ all have the same number
of alternating runs.) When n elements are being permuted, the maximum number of
runs of this kind is $n-1$.

Find the average number of alternating runs in a random permutation of the set
$\{1,2,\dots,n\}$. [*Hint:* Consider the proof of (34).]

16. [*M30*] Continuing the previous exercise, let $\left\langle\!\!\left\langle {n \atop k} \right\rangle\!\!\right\rangle$ be the number of permutations
of $\{1,2,\dots,n\}$ that have exactly k alternating runs. Find a recurrence relation, by
means of which a table of $\left\langle\!\!\left\langle {n \atop k} \right\rangle\!\!\right\rangle$ can be computed; and find the corresponding recurrence
relation for the generating function $G_n(z) = \sum_k \left\langle\!\!\left\langle {n \atop k} \right\rangle\!\!\right\rangle z^k/n!$. Use the latter recurrence
to discover a simple formula for the *variance* of the number of alternating runs in a
random permutation of $\{1,2,\dots,n\}$.

17. [*M25*] Among all 2^n sequences $a_1\,a_2\dots a_n$, where each a_j is either 0 or 1, how
many have exactly k runs (that is, $k-1$ occurrences of $a_j > a_{j+1}$)?

18. [*M28*] Among all $n!$ sequences $b_1\,b_2\dots b_n$ such that each b_j is an integer in the
range $0 \le b_j \le n - j$, how many have (a) exactly k descents (that is, k occurrences of
$b_j > b_{j+1}$)? (b) exactly k distinct elements?

 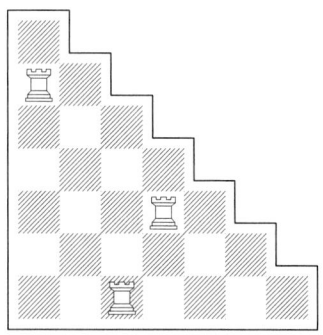

Fig. 4. Nonattacking rooks on a chessboard, with $k = 3$ rooks below the main diagonal.

▶ **19.** [*M26*] (I. Kaplansky and J. Riordan, 1946.) (a) In how many ways can n nonattacking rooks — no two in the same row or column — be placed on an $n \times n$ chessboard,
so that exactly k lie below the main diagonal? (b) In how many ways can k nonattacking
rooks be placed below the main diagonal of an $n \times n$ chessboard?

For example, Fig. 4 shows one of the 15619 ways to put eight nonattacking rooks
on a standard chessboard with exactly three rooks in the unshaded portion below the
main diagonal, together with one of the 1050 ways to put three nonattacking rooks on
a triangular board.

▶ **20.** [*M21*] A permutation is said to require k *readings* if we must scan it k times from
left to right in order to read off its elements in nondecreasing order. For example, the

permutation $4\,9\,1\,8\,2\,5\,3\,6\,7$ requires four readings: On the first we obtain 1, 2, 3; on the second we get 4, 5, 6, 7; then 8; then 9. Find a connection between runs and readings.

21. [*M22*] If the permutation $a_1\,a_2\ldots a_n$ of $\{1,2,\ldots,n\}$ has k runs and requires j readings, in the sense of exercise 20, what can be said about $a_n \ldots a_2\,a_1$?

22. [*M26*] (L. Carlitz, D. P. Roselle, and R. A. Scoville.) Show that there is no permutation of $\{1,2,\ldots,n\}$ with $n+1-r$ runs, and requiring s readings, if $rs < n$; but such permutations do exist if $n \geq n+1-r \geq s \geq 1$ and $rs \geq n$.

23. [*HM42*] (Walter Weissblum.) The "long runs" of a permutation $a_1\,a_2\ldots a_n$ are obtained by placing vertical lines just before a segment fails to be monotonic; long runs are either increasing or decreasing, depending on the order of their first two elements, so the length of each long run (except possibly the last) is ≥ 2. For example, $7\,5\mid 6\,2\mid 3\,8\,9\mid 1\,4$ has four long runs. Find the average length of the first two long runs of an infinite permutation, and prove that the limiting long-run length is

$$(1 + \cot \tfrac{1}{2})/(3 - \cot \tfrac{1}{2}) \approx 2.4202.$$

24. [*M30*] What is the average number of runs in sequences generated as in exercise 5.1.1–18, as a function of p?

25. [*M25*] Let $U_1,\ldots,U_n$ be independent uniform random numbers in $[0\,.\,.\,1)$. What is the probability that $\lfloor U_1 + \cdots + U_n \rfloor = k$?

26. [*M20*] Let ϑ be the operation $z\frac{d}{dz}$, which multiplies the coefficient of z^n in a generating function by n. Show that the result of applying ϑ to $1/(1-z)$ repeatedly, m times, can be expressed in terms of Eulerian numbers.

▶ **27.** [*M21*] An *increasing forest* is an oriented forest in which the nodes are labeled $\{1,2,\ldots,n\}$ in such a way that parents have smaller numbers than their children. Show that $\left\langle {n \atop k} \right\rangle$ is the number of n-node increasing forests with $k+1$ leaves.

28. [*HM35*] Find the asymptotic value of the numbers z_m in Fig. 3 as $m \to \infty$, and prove that $\sum_{m=1}^{\infty}(z_m^{-1} + \bar{z}_m^{-1}) = e - 5/2$.

▶ **29.** [*M30*] The permutation $a_1 \ldots a_n$ has a "peak" at a_j if $1 < j < n$ and $a_{j-1} < a_j > a_{j+1}$. Let s_{nk} be the number of permutations with exactly k peaks, and let t_{nk} be the number with k peaks *and* k descents. Prove that (a) $s_{nk} = \frac{1}{2}\left\langle {n \atop 2k} \right\rangle + \left\langle {n \atop 2k+1} \right\rangle + \frac{1}{2}\left\langle {n \atop 2k+2} \right\rangle$ (see exercise 16); (b) $s_{nk} = 2^{n-1-2k} t_{nk}$; (c) $\sum_k \left\langle {n \atop k} \right\rangle x^k = \sum_k t_{nk} x^k (1+x)^{n-1-2k}$.

*5.1.4. Tableaux and Involutions

To complete our survey of the combinatorial properties of permutations, we will discuss some remarkable relations that connect permutations with arrays of integers called tableaux. A *Young tableau of shape* $(n_1, n_2, \ldots, n_m)$, where $n_1 \geq n_2 \geq \cdots \geq n_m > 0$, is an arrangement of $n_1 + n_2 + \cdots + n_m$ distinct integers in an array of left-justified rows, with n_i elements in row i, such that the entries of each row are in increasing order from left to right, and the entries of each column are increasing from top to bottom. For example,

$$
\begin{array}{|c|c|c|c|c|c|}
\hline
1 & 2 & 5 & 9 & 10 & 15 \\
\hline
\end{array}
$$

(1)

is a Young tableau of shape $(6, 4, 4, 1)$. Such arrangements were introduced by Alfred Young as an aid to the study of matrix representations of permutations [see *Proc. London Math. Soc.* (2) **28** (1928), 255–292; Bruce E. Sagan, *The Symmetric Group* (Pacific Grove, Calif.: Wadsworth & Brooks/Cole, 1991)]. For simplicity, we will simply say "tableau" instead of "Young tableau."

An *involution* is a permutation that is its own inverse. For example, there are ten involutions of $\{1, 2, 3, 4\}$:

$$\begin{pmatrix} 1\ 2\ 3\ 4 \\ 1\ 2\ 3\ 4 \end{pmatrix} \quad \begin{pmatrix} 1\ 2\ 3\ 4 \\ 2\ 1\ 3\ 4 \end{pmatrix} \quad \begin{pmatrix} 1\ 2\ 3\ 4 \\ 3\ 2\ 1\ 4 \end{pmatrix} \quad \begin{pmatrix} 1\ 2\ 3\ 4 \\ 4\ 2\ 3\ 1 \end{pmatrix} \quad \begin{pmatrix} 1\ 2\ 3\ 4 \\ 1\ 3\ 2\ 4 \end{pmatrix}$$

$$\begin{pmatrix} 1\ 2\ 3\ 4 \\ 1\ 4\ 3\ 2 \end{pmatrix} \quad \begin{pmatrix} 1\ 2\ 3\ 4 \\ 1\ 2\ 4\ 3 \end{pmatrix} \quad \begin{pmatrix} 1\ 2\ 3\ 4 \\ 2\ 1\ 4\ 3 \end{pmatrix} \quad \begin{pmatrix} 1\ 2\ 3\ 4 \\ 3\ 4\ 1\ 2 \end{pmatrix} \quad \begin{pmatrix} 1\ 2\ 3\ 4 \\ 4\ 3\ 2\ 1 \end{pmatrix} \qquad (2)$$

The term "involution" originated in classical geometry problems; involutions in the general sense considered here were first studied by H. A. Rothe when he introduced the concept of inverses (see Section 5.1.1).

It may appear strange that we should be discussing both tableaux and involutions at the same time, but there is an extraordinary connection between these two apparently unrelated concepts: *The number of involutions of* $\{1, 2, \dots, n\}$ *is the same as the number of tableaux that can be formed from the elements* $\{1, 2, \dots, n\}$. For example, exactly ten tableaux can be formed from $\{1, 2, 3, 4\}$, namely,

corresponding respectively to the ten involutions (2).

This connection between involutions and tableaux is by no means obvious, and there is probably no very simple way to prove it. The proof we will discuss involves an interesting tableau-construction algorithm that has several other surprising properties. It is based on a special procedure that inserts new elements into a tableau.

For example, suppose that we want to insert the element 8 into the tableau

The method we will use starts by placing the 8 into row 1, in the spot previously occupied by 9, since 9 is the least element greater than 8 in that row. Element 9 is "bumped down" into row 2, where it displaces the 10. The 10 then "bumps" the 13 from row 3 to row 4; and since row 4 contains no element greater than 13, the process terminates by inserting 13 at the right end of row 4. Thus, tableau (4) has been transformed into

$$
\begin{array}{|c|c|c|c|c|c|}
\hline
1 & 3 & 5 & 8 & 12 & 16 \\
\hline
2 & 6 & 9 & 15 & \multicolumn{2}{c}{} \\
\cline{1-4}
4 & 10 & 14 & \multicolumn{3}{c}{} \\
\cline{1-3}
11 & 13 & \multicolumn{4}{c}{} \\
\cline{1-2}
17 & \multicolumn{5}{c}{} \\
\cline{1-1}
\end{array}
\qquad (5)
$$

     A precise description of this process, together with a proof that it always preserves the tableau properties, appears in Algorithm I.

Algorithm I (*Insertion into a tableau*). Let $P = (P_{ij})$ be a tableau of positive integers, and let x be a positive integer not in P. This algorithm transforms P into another tableau that contains x in addition to its original elements. The new tableau has the same shape as the old, except for the addition of a new position in row s, column t, where s and t are quantities determined by the algorithm.

     (Parenthesized remarks in this algorithm serve to prove its validity, since it is easy to verify inductively that the remarks are valid and that the array P remains a tableau throughout the process. For convenience we will assume that the tableau has been bordered by zeros at the top and left and with ∞'s to the right and below, so that P_{ij} is defined for all $i, j \geq 0$. If we define the relation

$$
a \lesssim b \qquad \text{if and only if} \qquad a < b \quad \text{or} \quad a = b = 0 \quad \text{or} \quad a = b = \infty, \qquad (6)
$$

the tableau inequalities can be expressed in the convenient form

$$
\begin{aligned}
P_{ij} = 0 \qquad &\text{if and only if} \qquad i = 0 \quad \text{or} \quad j = 0; \\
P_{ij} \lesssim P_{i(j+1)} \quad \text{and} \quad P_{ij} &\lesssim P_{(i+1)j}, \qquad \text{for all } i, j \geq 0.
\end{aligned} \qquad (7)
$$

The statement "$x \notin P$" means that either $x = \infty$ or $x \neq P_{ij}$ for all $i, j \geq 0$.)

I1. [Input x.] Set $i \leftarrow 1$, set $x_1 \leftarrow x$, and set j to the smallest value such that $P_{1j} = \infty$.

I2. [Find x_{i+1}.] (At this point $P_{(i-1)j} < x_i < P_{ij}$ and $x_i \notin P$.) If $x_i < P_{i(j-1)}$, decrease j by 1 and repeat this step. Otherwise set $x_{i+1} \leftarrow P_{ij}$ and set $r_i \leftarrow j$.

I3. [Replace by x_i.] (Now $P_{i(j-1)} < x_i < x_{i+1} = P_{ij} \lesssim P_{i(j+1)}$, $P_{(i-1)j} < x_i < x_{i+1} = P_{ij} \lesssim P_{(i+1)j}$, and $r_i = j$.) Set $P_{ij} \leftarrow x_i$.

I4. [Is $x_{i+1} = \infty$?] (Now $P_{i(j-1)} < P_{ij} = x_i < x_{i+1} \lesssim P_{i(j+1)}$, $P_{(i-1)j} < P_{ij} = x_i < x_{i+1} \lesssim P_{(i+1)j}$, $r_i = j$, and $x_{i+1} \notin P$.) If $x_{i+1} \neq \infty$, increase i by 1 and return to step I2.

I5. [Determine s, t.] Set $s \leftarrow i$, $t \leftarrow j$, and terminate the algorithm. (At this point the conditions

$$P_{st} \neq \infty \quad \text{and} \quad P_{(s+1)t} = P_{s(t+1)} = \infty \qquad (8)$$

are satisfied.) ∎

Algorithm I defines a "bumping sequence"

$$x = x_1 < x_2 < \cdots < x_s < x_{s+1} = \infty, \qquad (9)$$

as well as an auxiliary sequence of column indices

$$r_1 \geq r_2 \geq \cdots \geq r_s = t; \qquad (10)$$

element P_{ir_i} has been changed from x_{i+1} to x_i, for $1 \leq i \leq s$. For example, when we inserted 8 into (4), the bumping sequence was 8, 9, 10, 13, ∞, and the auxiliary sequence was 4, 3, 2, 2. We could have reformulated the algorithm so that it used much less temporary storage; only the current values of j, x_i, and x_{i+1} need to be remembered. But sequences (9) and (10) have been introduced so that we can prove interesting things about the algorithm.

The key fact we will use about Algorithm I is that it can be run backwards: Given the values of s and t determined in step I5, we can transform P back into its original form again, determining and removing the element x that was inserted. For example, consider (5) and suppose we are told that element 13 is in the position that used to be blank. Then 13 must have been bumped down from row 3 by the 10, since 10 is the greatest element less than 13 in that row; similarly the 10 must have been bumped from row 2 by the 9, and the 9 must have been bumped from row 1 by the 8. Thus we can go from (5) back to (4). The following algorithm specifies this process in detail:

Algorithm D (*Deletion from a tableau*). Given a tableau P and positive integers s, t satisfying (8), this algorithm transforms P into another tableau, having almost the same shape, but with ∞ in column t of row s. An element x, determined by the algorithm, is deleted from P.

(As in Algorithm I, parenthesized assertions are included here to facilitate a proof that P remains a tableau throughout the process.)

D1. [Input s, t.] Set $j \leftarrow t$, $i \leftarrow s$, $x_{s+1} \leftarrow \infty$.

D2. [Find x_i.] (At this point $P_{ij} < x_{i+1} \lesssim P_{(i+1)j}$ and $x_{i+1} \notin P$.) If $P_{i(j+1)} < x_{i+1}$, increase j by 1 and repeat this step. Otherwise set $x_i \leftarrow P_{ij}$ and $r_i \leftarrow j$.

D3. [Replace by x_{i+1}.] (Now $P_{i(j-1)} < P_{ij} = x_i < x_{i+1} \lesssim P_{i(j+1)}$, $P_{(i-1)j} < P_{ij} = x_i < x_{i+1} \lesssim P_{(i+1)j}$, and $r_i = j$.) Set $P_{ij} \leftarrow x_{i+1}$.

D4. [Is $i = 1$?] (Now $P_{i(j-1)} < x_i < x_{i+1} = P_{ij} \lesssim P_{i(j+1)}$, $P_{(i-1)j} < x_i < x_{i+1} = P_{ij} \lesssim P_{(i+1)j}$, and $r_i = j$.) If $i > 1$, decrease i by 1 and return to step D2.

D5. [Determine x.] Set $x \leftarrow x_1$; the algorithm terminates. (Now $0 < x < \infty$.) ∎

The parenthesized assertions appearing in Algorithms I and D are not only a useful way to prove that the algorithms preserve the tableau structure; they also serve to verify that *Algorithms I and D are perfect inverses of each other*. If we perform Algorithm I first, given some tableau P and some positive integer $x \notin P$, it will insert x and determine positive integers s, t satisfying (8); Algorithm D applied to the result will recompute x and will restore P. Conversely, if we perform Algorithm D first, given some tableau P and some positive integers s, t satisfying (8), it will modify P, deleting some positive integer x; Algorithm I applied to the result will recompute s, t and will restore P. The reason is that the parenthesized assertions of steps I3 and D4 are identical, as are the assertions of steps I4 and D3, and these assertions characterize the value of j uniquely. Hence the auxiliary sequences (9), (10) are the same in each case.

Now we are ready to prove a basic property of tableaux:

Theorem A. *There is a one-to-one correspondence between the set of all permutations of $\{1, 2, \ldots, n\}$ and the set of ordered pairs (P, Q) of tableaux formed from $\{1, 2, \ldots, n\}$, where P and Q have the same shape.*

(An example of this theorem appears within the proof that follows.)

Proof. It is convenient to prove a slightly more general result. Given any two-line array

$$\begin{pmatrix} q_1 & q_2 & \cdots & q_n \\ p_1 & p_2 & \cdots & p_n \end{pmatrix}, \qquad \begin{array}{l} q_1 < q_2 < \cdots < q_n, \\ p_1, p_2, \ldots, p_n \text{ distinct}, \end{array} \tag{11}$$

we will construct two corresponding tableaux P and Q, where the elements of P are $\{p_1, \ldots, p_n\}$ and the elements of Q are $\{q_1, \ldots, q_n\}$ and the shape of P is the shape of Q.

Let P and Q be empty initially. Then, for $i = 1, 2, \ldots, n$ (in this order), do the following operation: Insert p_i into tableau P using Algorithm I; then set $Q_{st} \leftarrow q_i$, where s and t specify the newly filled position of P.

For example, if the given permutation is $\left(\begin{smallmatrix} 1 & 3 & 5 & 6 & 8 \\ 7 & 2 & 9 & 5 & 3 \end{smallmatrix} \right)$, we obtain

	P	Q
Insert 7:	7	1
Insert 2:	2 / 7	1 / 3
Insert 9:	2 9 / 7	1 5 / 3
Insert 5:	2 5 / 7 9	1 5 / 3 6
Insert 3:	2 3 / 5 9 / 7	1 5 / 3 6 / 8

$$(12)$$

so the tableaux (P, Q) corresponding to $\left(\begin{smallmatrix} 1 & 3 & 5 & 6 & 8 \\ 7 & 2 & 9 & 5 & 3 \end{smallmatrix}\right)$ are

$$
P = \begin{array}{|c|c|} \hline 2 & 3 \\ \hline 5 & 9 \\ \hline 7 \\ \cline{1-1} \end{array} \; , \qquad
Q = \begin{array}{|c|c|} \hline 1 & 5 \\ \hline 3 & 6 \\ \hline 8 \\ \cline{1-1} \end{array} \; . \tag{13}
$$

It is clear from this construction that P and Q always have the same shape; furthermore, since we always add elements on the periphery of Q, in increasing order, Q is a tableau.

Conversely, given two equal-shape tableaux P and Q, we can find the corresponding two-line array (11) as follows. Let the elements of Q be

$$
q_1 < q_2 < \cdots < q_n.
$$

For $i = n, \ldots, 2, 1$ (in this order), let p_i be the element x that is removed when Algorithm D is applied to P, using the values s and t such that $Q_{st} = q_i$.

For example, this construction will start with (13) and will successively undo the calculation (12) until P is empty, and $\left(\begin{smallmatrix} 1 & 3 & 5 & 6 & 8 \\ 7 & 2 & 9 & 5 & 3 \end{smallmatrix}\right)$ is obtained.

Since Algorithms I and D are inverses of each other, the two constructions we have described are inverses of each other, and the one-to-one correspondence has been established. ∎

The correspondence defined in the proof of Theorem A has many startling properties, and we will now proceed to derive some of them. The reader is urged to work out the example in exercise 1, in order to become familiar with the construction, before proceeding further.

Once an element has been bumped from row 1 to row 2, it doesn't affect row 1 any longer; furthermore rows 2, 3, ... are built up from the sequence of bumped elements in exactly the same way as rows 1, 2, ... are built up from the original permutation. These facts suggest that we can look at the construction of Theorem A in another way, concentrating only on the first rows of P and Q. For example, the permutation $\left(\begin{smallmatrix} 1 & 3 & 5 & 6 & 8 \\ 7 & 2 & 9 & 5 & 3 \end{smallmatrix}\right)$ causes the following action in row 1, according to (12):

1:	Insert 7, set $Q_{11} \leftarrow 1$.
3:	Insert 2, bump 7.
5:	Insert 9, set $Q_{12} \leftarrow 5$.
6:	Insert 5, bump 9.
8:	Insert 3, bump 5.

$$\tag{14}$$

Thus the first row of P is 2 3, and the first row of Q is 1 5. Furthermore, the remaining rows of P and Q are the tableaux corresponding to the "bumped" two-line array

$$
\begin{pmatrix} 3 & 6 & 8 \\ 7 & 9 & 5 \end{pmatrix}. \tag{15}
$$

In order to study the behavior of the construction on row 1, we can consider the elements that go into a given column of this row. Let us say that (q_i, p_i) is in *class* t with respect to the two-line array

$$\begin{pmatrix} q_1 & q_2 & \cdots & q_n \\ p_1 & p_2 & \cdots & p_n \end{pmatrix}, \qquad \begin{matrix} q_1 < q_2 < \cdots < q_n, \\ p_1, p_2, \ldots, p_n \text{ distinct,} \end{matrix} \qquad (16)$$

if $p_i = P_{1t}$ after Algorithm I has been applied successively to $p_1, p_2, \ldots, p_i$, starting with an empty tableau P. (Remember that Algorithm I always inserts the given element into row 1.)

It is easy to see that (q_i, p_i) is in class 1 if and only if p_i has $i - 1$ inversions, that is, if and only if $p_i = \min\{p_1, p_2, \ldots, p_i\}$ is a "left-to-right minimum." If we cross out the columns of class 1 in (16), we obtain another two-line array

$$\begin{pmatrix} q_1' & q_2' & \cdots & q_m' \\ p_1' & p_2' & \cdots & p_m' \end{pmatrix} \qquad (17)$$

such that (q, p) is in class t with respect to (17) if and only if it is in class $t+1$ with respect to (16). The operation of going from (16) to (17) represents removing the leftmost position of row 1. This gives us a systematic way to determine the classes. For example in $\begin{pmatrix} 1 & 3 & 5 & 6 & 8 \\ 7 & 2 & 9 & 5 & 3 \end{pmatrix}$ the elements that are left-to-right minima are 7 and 2, so class 1 is $\{(1, 7), (3, 2)\}$; in the remaining array $\begin{pmatrix} 5 & 6 & 8 \\ 9 & 5 & 3 \end{pmatrix}$ all elements are minima, so class 2 is $\{(5, 9), (6, 5), (8, 3)\}$. In the "bumped" array (15), class 1 is $\{(3, 7), (8, 5)\}$ and class 2 is $\{(6, 9)\}$.

For any fixed value of t, the elements of class t can be labeled

$$(q_{i_1}, p_{i_1}), \ldots, (q_{i_k}, p_{i_k})$$

in such a way that

$$\begin{matrix} q_{i_1} < q_{i_2} < \cdots < q_{i_k}, \\ p_{i_1} > p_{i_2} > \cdots > p_{i_k}, \end{matrix} \qquad (18)$$

since the tableau position P_{1t} takes on the decreasing sequence of values $p_{i_1}, \ldots, p_{i_k}$ as the insertion algorithm proceeds. At the end of the construction we have

$$P_{1t} = p_{i_k}, \qquad Q_{1t} = q_{i_1}; \qquad (19)$$

and the "bumped" two-line array that defines rows 2, 3, ... of P and Q contains the columns

$$\begin{pmatrix} q_{i_2} & q_{i_3} & \cdots & q_{i_k} \\ p_{i_1} & p_{i_2} & \cdots & p_{i_{k-1}} \end{pmatrix} \qquad (20)$$

plus other columns formed in a similar way from the other classes.

These observations lead to a simple method for calculating P and Q by hand (see exercise 3), and they also provide us with the means to prove a rather unexpected result:

Theorem B. *If the permutation*

$$\begin{pmatrix} 1 & 2 & \cdots & n \\ a_1 & a_2 & \cdots & a_n \end{pmatrix}$$

corresponds to tableaux (P, Q) *in the construction of Theorem A, then the inverse permutation corresponds to* (Q, P).

This fact is quite startling, since P and Q are formed by such completely different methods in Theorem A, and since the inverse of a permutation is obtained by juggling the columns of the two-line array rather capriciously.

Proof. Suppose that we have a two-line array (16); its columns are essentially independent and can be rearranged. Interchanging the lines and sorting the columns so that the new top line is in increasing order gives the "inverse" array

$$\begin{pmatrix} q_1 & q_2 & \cdots & q_n \\ p_1 & p_2 & \cdots & p_n \end{pmatrix}^- = \begin{pmatrix} p_1 & p_2 & \cdots & p_n \\ q_1 & q_2 & \cdots & q_n \end{pmatrix}$$

$$= \begin{pmatrix} p'_1 & p'_2 & \cdots & p'_n \\ q'_1 & q'_2 & \cdots & q'_n \end{pmatrix}, \quad \begin{array}{l} p'_1 < p'_2 < \cdots < p'_n; \\ q'_1, q'_2, \ldots, q'_n \text{ distinct.} \end{array} \quad (21)$$

We will show that this operation corresponds to interchanging P and Q in the construction of Theorem A.

Exercise 2 reformulates our remarks about class determination so that the class of (q_i, p_i) doesn't depend on the fact that $q_1, q_2, \ldots, q_n$ are in ascending order. Since the resulting condition is symmetrical in the q's and the p's, the operation (21) does not destroy the class structure; if (q, p) is in class t with respect to (16), then (p, q) is in class t with respect to (21). If we therefore arrange the elements of the latter class t as

$$p_{i_k} < \cdots < p_{i_2} < p_{i_1},$$
$$q_{i_k} > \cdots > q_{i_2} > q_{i_1}, \quad (22)$$

by analogy with (18), we have

$$P_{1t} = q_{i_1}, \qquad Q_{1t} = p_{i_k} \quad (23)$$

as in (19), and the columns

$$\begin{pmatrix} p_{i_{k-1}} & \cdots & p_{i_2} & p_{i_1} \\ q_{i_k} & \cdots & q_{i_3} & q_{i_2} \end{pmatrix} \quad (24)$$

go into the "bumped" array as in (20). Hence the first rows of P and Q are interchanged. Furthermore the "bumped" two-line array for (21) is the inverse of the "bumped" two-line array for (16), so the proof is completed by induction on the number of rows in the tableaux. ∎

Corollary B. *The number of tableaux that can be formed from $\{1, 2, \ldots, n\}$ is the number of involutions on $\{1, 2, \ldots, n\}$.*

Proof. If π is an involution corresponding to (P, Q), then $\pi = \pi^-$ corresponds to (Q, P); hence $P = Q$. Conversely, if π is any permutation corresponding to (P, P), then π^- also corresponds to (P, P); hence $\pi = \pi^-$. So there is a one-to-one correspondence between involutions π and tableaux P. ∎

It is clear that the upper-left corner element of a tableau is always the smallest. This suggests a possible way to sort a set of numbers: First we can put the numbers into a tableau, by using Algorithm I repeatedly; this brings the smallest element to the corner. Then we delete the smallest element, rearranging

the remaining elements so that they form another tableau; then we delete the
new smallest element; and so on.

Let us therefore consider what happens when we delete the corner element
from the tableau

$$
\begin{array}{|c|c|c|c|c|c|}
\hline
1 & 3 & 5 & 7 & 11 & 15 \\ \cline{1-6}
2 & 6 & 8 & 14 \\ \cline{1-4}
4 & 9 & 13 \\ \cline{1-3}
10 & 12 \\ \cline{1-2}
16 \\ \cline{1-1}
\end{array}
\qquad (25)
$$

If the 1 is removed, the 2 must come to take its place. Then we can move the
4 up to where the 2 was, but we can't move the 10 to the position of the 4; the
9 can be moved instead, then the 12 in place of the 9. In general, we are led to
the following procedure.

Algorithm S (*Delete corner element*). Given a tableau P, this algorithm deletes
the upper left corner element of P and moves other elements so that the tableau
properties are preserved. The notational conventions of Algorithms I and D are
used.

S1. [Initialize.] Set $r \leftarrow 1$, $s \leftarrow 1$.

S2. [Done?] If $P_{rs} = \infty$, the process is complete.

S3. [Compare.] If $P_{(r+1)s} \lesssim P_{r(s+1)}$, go to step S5. (We examine the elements
just below and to the right of the vacant cell, and we will move the smaller
of the two.)

S4. [Shift left.] Set $P_{rs} \leftarrow P_{r(s+1)}$, $s \leftarrow s + 1$, and return to S3.

S5. [Shift up.] Set $P_{rs} \leftarrow P_{(r+1)s}$, $r \leftarrow r + 1$, and return to S2. ∎

It is easy to prove that P is still a tableau after Algorithm S has deleted its
corner element (see exercise 10). So if we repeat Algorithm S until P is empty,
we can read out its elements in increasing order. Unfortunately this doesn't
turn out to be as efficient a sorting algorithm as other methods we will see; its
minimum running time is proportional to $n^{1.5}$, but similar algorithms that use
trees instead of tableau structures have an execution time on the order of $n \log n$.

In spite of the fact that Algorithm S doesn't lead to a superbly efficient
sorting algorithm, it has some very interesting properties.

Theorem C (M. P. Schützenberger). *If P is the tableau formed by the construction of Theorem A from the permutation $a_1 a_2 \ldots a_n$, and if*

$$
a_i = \min\{a_1, a_2, \ldots, a_n\},
$$

then Algorithm S changes P to the tableau corresponding to $a_1 \ldots a_{i-1} a_{i+1} \ldots a_n$.

Proof. See exercise 13. ∎

After we apply Algorithm S to a tableau, let us put the deleted element into the newly vacated place P_{rs}, but in *italic type* to indicate that it isn't really part of the tableau. For example, after applying this procedure to the tableau (25) we would have

2	3	5	7	11	15
4	6	8	14		
9	12	13			
10	*1*				
16					

,

and two more applications yield

4	5	7	11	15	*2*
6	8	13	14		
9	12	*3*			
10	*1*				
16					

.

Continuing until all elements are removed gives

16	*14*	*13*	*12*	*10*	*2*
15	*9*	*6*	*4*		
11	*5*	*3*			
8	*1*				
7					

,   (26)

which has the same shape as the original tableau (25). This configuration may be called a *dual tableau*, since it is like a tableau except that the "dual order" has been used (reversing the roles of $<$ and $>$). Let us denote the dual tableau formed from P in this way by the symbol P^S.

From P^S we can determine P uniquely; in fact, we can obtain the original tableau P from P^S, by applying exactly the same algorithm — but reversing the order and the roles of italic and regular type, since P^S is a dual tableau. For example, two steps of the algorithm applied to (26) give

14	*13*	*12*	*10*	*2*	15
11	*9*	*6*	*4*		
8	*5*	*3*			
7	*1*				
16					

,

and eventually (25) will be reproduced again! This remarkable fact is one of the consequences of our next theorem.

Theorem D (C. Schensted, M. P. Schützenberger). *Let*

$$\begin{pmatrix} q_1 & q_2 & \cdots & q_n \\ p_1 & p_2 & \cdots & p_n \end{pmatrix} \tag{27}$$

be the two-line array corresponding to the tableaux (P, Q).

a) *Using dual (reverse) order on the q's, but not on the p's, the two-line array*

$$\begin{pmatrix} q_n & \cdots & q_2 & q_1 \\ p_n & \cdots & p_2 & p_1 \end{pmatrix} \tag{28}$$

  corresponds to $\bigl(P^T, (Q^S)^T\bigr)$.

As usual, "T" denotes the operation of transposing rows and columns; P^T is a tableau, while $(Q^S)^T$ is a dual tableau, since the order of the q's is reversed.

b) *Using dual order on the p's, but not on the q's, the two-line array* (27) *corresponds to* $\bigl((P^S)^T, Q^T\bigr)$.

c) *Using dual order on both the p's and the q's, the two-line array* (28) *corresponds to* (P^S, Q^S).

Proof. No simple proof of this theorem is known. The fact that case (a) corresponds to (P^T, X) for some dual tableau X is proved in exercise 5; hence by Theorem B, case (b) corresponds to (Y, Q^T) for some dual tableau Y, and Y must have the shape of P^T.

Let $p_i = \min\{p_1, \ldots, p_n\}$; since p_i is the "largest" element in the dual order, it appears on the periphery of Y, and it doesn't bump any elements in the construction of Theorem A. Thus, if we successively insert $p_1, \ldots, p_{i-1}, p_{i+1}, \ldots, p_n$ using the dual order, we get $Y - \{p_i\}$, that is, Y with p_i removed. By Theorem C if we successively insert $p_1, \ldots, p_{i-1}, p_{i+1}, \ldots, p_n$ using the normal order, we get the tableau $d(P)$ obtained by applying Algorithm S to P. By induction on n, $Y - \{p_i\} = \bigl(d(P)^S\bigr)^T$. But since

$$(P^S)^T - \{p_i\} = \bigl(d(P)^S\bigr)^T, \tag{29}$$

by definition of the operation S, and since Y has the same shape as $(P^S)^T$, we must have $Y = (P^S)^T$.

This proves part (b), and part (a) follows by an application of Theorem B. Applying parts (a) and (b) successively then shows that case (c) corresponds to $\bigl(((P^T)^S)^T, ((Q^S)^T)^T\bigr)$; and this is (P^S, Q^S) since $(P^S)^T = (P^T)^S$ by the row-column symmetry of operation S. ∎

In particular, this theorem establishes two surprising facts about the tableau insertion algorithm: If successive insertion of distinct elements $p_1, \ldots, p_n$ into an empty tableau yields tableau P, insertion in the opposite order $p_n, \ldots, p_1$ yields the *transposed* tableau P^T. And if we not only insert the p's in this order $p_n, \ldots, p_1$ but also interchange the roles of $<$ and $>$, as well as 0 and ∞, in the insertion process, we obtain the dual tableau P^S. The reader is urged to try out these processes on some simple examples. The unusual nature of these coincidences might lead us to suspect that some sort of witchcraft is operating behind the scenes! No simple explanation for these phenomena is yet known; there seems to be no obvious way to prove even that case (c) corresponds to tableaux having the same *shape* as P and Q, although the characterization of classes in exercise 2 does provide a significant clue.

The correspondence of Theorem A was given by G. de B. Robinson [*American J. Math.* **60** (1938), 745–760, §5], in a somewhat vague and different form, as part of his solution to a rather difficult problem in group theory. Robinson stated Theorem B without proof. Many years later, C. Schensted independently rediscovered the correspondence, which he described in terms of "bumping" as we have done in Algorithm I; Schensted also proved the "P" part of Theorem D(a) [see *Canadian J. Math.* **13** (1961), 179–191]. M. P. Schützenberger [*Math. Scand.* **12** (1963), 117–128] proved Theorem C and the "Q" part of Theorem D(a), from which (b) and (c) follow. It is possible to extend the correspondence to permutations of *multisets;* the case that $p_1, \ldots, p_n$ need not be distinct was considered by Schensted, and the "ultimate" generalization to the case that both the p's and the q's may contain repeated elements was investigated by Knuth [*Pacific J. Math.* **34** (1970), 709–727].

Let us now turn to a related question: *How many tableaux formed from* $\{1, 2, \ldots, n\}$ *have a given shape* $(n_1, n_2, \ldots, n_m)$, *where* $n_1 + n_2 + \cdots + n_m = n$? If we denote this number by $f(n_1, n_2, \ldots, n_m)$, and if we allow the parameters n_j to be arbitrary integers, the function f must satisfy the relations

$$f(n_1, n_2, \ldots, n_m) = 0 \qquad \text{unless} \qquad n_1 \geq n_2 \geq \cdots \geq n_m \geq 0; \tag{30}$$

$$f(n_1, n_2, \ldots, n_m, 0) = f(n_1, n_2, \ldots, n_m); \tag{31}$$

$$f(n_1, n_2, \ldots, n_m) = f(n_1-1, n_2, \ldots, n_m) + f(n_1, n_2-1, \ldots, n_m)$$
$$+ \cdots + f(n_1, n_2, \ldots, n_m-1),$$
$$\text{if} \quad n_1 \geq n_2 \geq \cdots \geq n_m \geq 1. \tag{32}$$

Recurrence (32) comes from the fact that a tableau with its largest element removed is always another tableau; for example, the number of tableaux of shape $(6, 4, 4, 1)$ is $f(5, 4, 4, 1) + f(6, 3, 4, 1) + f(6, 4, 3, 1) + f(6, 4, 4, 0) = f(5, 4, 4, 1) + f(6, 4, 3, 1) + f(6, 4, 4)$, since every tableau of shape $(6, 4, 4, 1)$ on $\{1, 2, \ldots, 15\}$ is formed by inserting the element 15 into the appropriate place in a tableau of shape $(5, 4, 4, 1)$, $(6, 4, 3, 1)$, or $(6, 4, 4)$. Schematically:

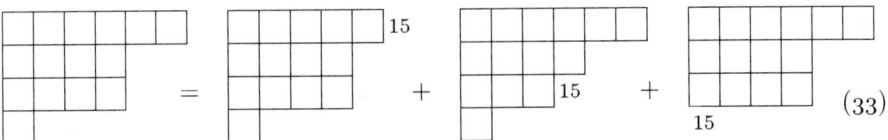

$$\tag{33}$$

The function $f(n_1, n_2, \ldots, n_m)$ that satisfies these relations has a fairly simple form,

$$f(n_1, n_2, \ldots, n_m) = \frac{\Delta(n_1 + m - 1, \, n_2 + m - 2, \, \ldots, \, n_m) \, n!}{(n_1 + m - 1)! \, (n_2 + m - 2)! \, \ldots \, n_m!}, \tag{34}$$

provided that the relatively mild conditions

$$n_1 + m - 1 \geq n_2 + m - 2 \geq \cdots \geq n_m$$

are satisfied; here Δ denotes the "square root of the discriminant" function

$$\Delta(x_1, x_2, \ldots, x_m) = \det \begin{pmatrix} x_1^{m-1} & x_2^{m-1} & \cdots & x_m^{m-1} \\ \vdots & \vdots & & \vdots \\ x_1^2 & x_2^2 & & x_m^2 \\ x_1 & x_2 & & x_m \\ 1 & 1 & \cdots & 1 \end{pmatrix} = \prod_{1 \leq i < j \leq m} (x_i - x_j). \qquad (35)$$

Formula (34) was derived by G. Frobenius [*Sitzungsberichte preuß. Akad. der Wissenschaften* (1900), 516–534, §3], in connection with an equivalent problem in group theory, using a rather deep group-theoretical argument; a combinatorial proof was given independently by MacMahon [*Philosophical Trans.* **A209** (1909), 153–175]. The formula can be established by induction, since relations (30) and (31) are readily proved and (32) follows by setting $y = -1$ in the identity of exercise 17.

Theorem A gives a remarkable identity in connection with this formula for the number of tableaux. If we sum over all shapes, we have

$$n! = \sum_{\substack{k_1 \geq k_2 \geq \cdots \geq k_n \geq 0 \\ k_1 + k_2 + \cdots + k_n = n}} f(k_1, k_2 \ldots, k_n)^2$$

$$= n!^2 \sum_{\substack{k_1 \geq k_2 \geq \cdots \geq k_n \geq 0 \\ k_1 + k_2 + \cdots + k_n = n}} \frac{\Delta(k_1 + n - 1, k_2 + n - 2, \ldots, k_n)^2}{(k_1 + n - 1)!^2 (k_2 + n - 2)!^2 \ldots k_n!^2}$$

$$= n!^2 \sum_{\substack{q_1 > q_2 > \cdots > q_n \geq 0 \\ q_1 + q_2 + \cdots + q_n = (n+1)n/2}} \frac{\Delta(q_1, q_2, \ldots, q_n)^2}{q_1!^2 \, q_2!^2 \, \ldots q_n!^2};$$

hence

$$\sum_{\substack{q_1 + q_2 + \cdots + q_n = (n+1)n/2 \\ q_1, q_2, \ldots, q_n \geq 0}} \frac{\Delta(q_1, q_2, \ldots, q_n)^2}{q_1!^2 \, q_2!^2 \, \ldots q_n!^2} = 1. \qquad (36)$$

The inequalities $q_1 > q_2 > \cdots > q_n$ have been removed in the latter sum, since the summand is a symmetric function of the q's that vanishes when $q_i = q_j$. A similar identity appears in exercise 24.

The formula for the number of tableaux can also be expressed in a much more interesting way, based on the idea of "hooks." The *hook* corresponding to a cell in a tableau is defined to be the cell itself plus the cells lying below and to its right. For example, the shaded area in Fig. 5 is the hook corresponding to cell $(2, 3)$ in row 2, column 3; it contains six cells. Each cell of Fig. 5 has been filled in with the length of its hook.

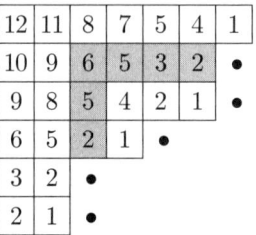

Fig. 5. Hooks and hook lengths.

If the shape of the tableau is $(n_1, n_2, \ldots, n_m)$, the longest hook has length $n_1 + m - 1$. Further examination of the hook lengths shows that row 1 contains all the lengths $n_1 + m - 1$, $n_1 + m - 2$, $\ldots$, 1 *except* for $(n_1 + m - 1) - (n_m)$, $(n_1 + m - 1) - (n_{m-1} + 1)$, $\ldots$, $(n_1 + m - 1) - (n_2 + m - 2)$. In Fig. 5, for example, the hook lengths in row 1 are 12, 11, 10, $\ldots$, 1 except for 10, 9, 6, 3, 2; the exceptions correspond to five nonexistent hooks, from nonexistent cells $(6, 3)$, $(5, 3)$, $(4, 5)$, $(3, 7)$, $(2, 7)$ leading up to cell $(1, 7)$. Similarly, row j contains all lengths $n_j + m - j$, $\ldots$, 1, except for $(n_j + m - j) - (n_m)$, $\ldots$, $(n_j + m - j) - (n_{j+1} + m - j - 1)$. It follows that the product of all the hook lengths is equal to

$$\frac{(n_1 + m - 1)! \, (n_2 + m - 2)! \ldots n_m!}{\Delta(n_1 + m - 1, n_2 + m - 2, \ldots, n_m)}.$$

This is just what happens in Eq. (34), so we have derived the following celebrated result due to J. S. Frame, G. de B. Robinson, and R. M. Thrall [*Canadian J. Math.* **6** (1954), 316–318]:

Theorem H. *The number of tableaux on* $\{1, 2, \ldots, n\}$ *having a specified shape is* $n!$ *divided by the product of the hook lengths.* ∎

Since this is such a simple rule, it deserves a simple proof; a heuristic argument runs as follows: Each element of the tableau is the smallest in its hook. If we fill the tableau shape at random, the probability that cell (i, j) will contain the minimum element of the corresponding hook is the reciprocal of the hook length; multiplying these probabilities over all i and j gives Theorem H. But unfortunately this argument is fallacious, since the probabilities are far from independent! No direct proof of Theorem H, based on combinatorial properties of hooks used correctly, was known until 1992 (see exercise 39), although researchers did discover several instructive indirect proofs (exercises 35, 36, and 38).

Theorem H has an interesting connection with the enumeration of trees, which we considered in Chapter 2. We observed that binary trees with n nodes correspond to permutations that can be obtained with a stack, and that such permutations correspond to sequences $a_1 a_2 \ldots a_{2n}$ of n S's and n X's, where the number of S's is never less than the number of X's as we read from left to right. (See exercises 2.2.1–3 and 2.3.1–6.) The latter sequences correspond in a natural way to tableaux of shape (n, n); we place in row 1 the indices i such that $a_i = $ S, and in row 2 we put those indices with $a_i = $ X. For example, the sequence

$$\text{S S S X X S S X X S X X}$$

corresponds to the tableau

1	2	3	6	7	10
4	5	8	9	11	12

$$(37)$$

The column constraint is satisfied in this tableau if and only if the number of X's never exceeds the number of S's from left to right. By Theorem H, the number of tableaux of shape (n, n) is

$$\frac{(2n)!}{(n + 1)!\,n!};$$

so this is the number of binary trees, in agreement with Eq. 2.3.4.4–(14). Furthermore, this argument solves the more general "ballot problem" considered in the answer to exercise 2.2.1–4, if we use tableaux of shape (n, m) for $n \geq m$. So Theorem H includes some rather complex enumeration problems as simple special cases.

Any tableau A of shape (n, n) on the elements $\{1, 2, \ldots, 2n\}$ corresponds to two tableaux (P, Q) of the same shape, in the following way suggested by MacMahon [*Combinatory Analysis* **1** (1915), 130–131]: Let P consist of the elements $\{1, \ldots, n\}$ as they appear in A; then Q is formed by taking the remaining elements, rotating the configuration by 180°, and replacing $n + 1, n + 2, \ldots, 2n$ by $n, n - 1, \ldots, 1$, respectively. For example, (37) splits into

1	2	3	6
4	5		

and

		7	10
8	9	11	12

;

rotation and renaming of the latter yields

$$P = \begin{array}{|c|c|c|c|} \hline 1 & 2 & 3 & 6 \\ \hline 4 & 5 \\ \cline{1-2} \end{array}, \qquad Q = \begin{array}{|c|c|c|c|} \hline 1 & 2 & 4 & 5 \\ \hline 3 & 6 \\ \cline{1-2} \end{array}. \qquad (38)$$

Conversely, any pair of equal-shape tableaux of at most two rows, each containing n cells, corresponds in this way to a tableau of shape (n, n). Hence by exercise 7 *the number of permutations $a_1 a_2 \ldots a_n$ of $\{1, 2, \ldots, n\}$ containing no decreasing subsequence $a_i > a_j > a_k$ for $i < j < k$ is the number of binary trees with n nodes.* An interesting one-to-one correspondence between such permutations and binary trees, more direct than the roundabout method via Algorithm I that we have used here, has been found by D. Rotem [*Inf. Proc. Letters* **4** (1975), 58–61]; similarly there is a rather direct correspondence between binary trees and permutations having no instances of $a_i > a_k > a_j$ for $i < j < k$ (see exercise 2.2.1–5).

The number of ways to fill a tableau of shape $(6, 4, 4, 1)$ is obviously the number of ways to put the labels $\{1, 2, \ldots, 15\}$ onto the vertices of the directed graph

$$(39)$$

in such a way that the label of vertex u is less than the label of vertex v whenever $u \rightarrow v$. In other words, it is the number of ways to sort the partial ordering (39) topologically, in the sense of Section 2.2.3.

In general, we can ask the same question for any directed graph that contains no oriented cycles. It would be nice if there were some simple formula generalizing Theorem H to the case of an arbitrary directed graph; but not all graphs have such pleasant properties as the graphs corresponding to tableaux. Some other classes of directed graphs for which the labeling problem has a simple solution are discussed in the exercises at the close of this section. Other exercises show that some directed graphs have *no* simple formula corresponding to Theorem H. For example, the number of ways to do the labeling is not always a divisor of $n!$.

To complete our investigations, let us count the total number of tableaux that can be formed from n distinct elements; we will denote this number by t_n. By Corollary B, t_n is the number of involutions of $\{1, 2, \ldots, n\}$. A permutation is its own inverse if and only if its cycle form consists solely of one-cycles (fixed points) and two-cycles (transpositions). Since t_{n-1} of the t_n involutions have (n) as a one-cycle, and since t_{n-2} of them have $(j\ n)$ as a two-cycle, for fixed $j < n$, we obtain the formula

$$t_n = t_{n-1} + (n-1)t_{n-2}, \tag{40}$$

which Rothe devised in 1800 to tabulate t_n for small n. The values for $n \geq 0$ are 1, 1, 2, 4, 10, 26, 76, 232, 764, 2620, 9496, ...

Counting another way, let us suppose that there are k two-cycles and $(n-2k)$ one-cycles. There are $\binom{n}{2k}$ ways to choose the fixed points, and the multinomial coefficient $(2k)!/(2!)^k$ is the number of ways to arrange the other elements into k distinguishable transpositions; dividing by $k!$ to make the transpositions indistinguishable we therefore obtain

$$t_n = \sum_{k=0}^{\lfloor n/2 \rfloor} t_n(k), \qquad t_n(k) = \frac{n!}{(n-2k)!\, 2^k k!}. \tag{41}$$

Unfortunately, this sum has no simple closed form (unless we choose to regard the Hermite polynomial $i^n 2^{-n/2} H_n(-i/\sqrt{2})$ as simple), so we resort to two indirect approaches in order to understand t_n better:

a) We can find the generating function

$$\sum_n t_n z^n/n! = e^{z+z^2/2}; \tag{42}$$

see exercise 25.

b) We can determine the asymptotic behavior of t_n. This is an instructive problem, because it involves some general techniques that will be useful to us in other connections, so we will conclude this section with an analysis of the asymptotic behavior of t_n.

The first step in analyzing the asymptotic behavior of (41) is to locate the main contribution to the sum. Since

$$\frac{t_n(k+1)}{t_n(k)} = \frac{(n-2k)(n-2k-1)}{2(k+1)}, \tag{43}$$

we can see that the terms gradually increase from $k = 0$ until $t_n(k+1) \approx t_n(k)$ when k is approximately $\frac{1}{2}(n - \sqrt{n}\,)$; then they decrease to zero when k exceeds $\frac{1}{2}n$. The main contribution clearly comes from the vicinity of $k = \frac{1}{2}(n - \sqrt{n}\,)$. It is usually preferable to have the main contribution at the value 0, so we write

$$k = \tfrac{1}{2}(n - \sqrt{n}\,) + x, \tag{44}$$

and we will investigate the size of $t_n(k)$ as a function of x.

One useful way to get rid of the factorials in $t_n(k)$ is to use Stirling's approximation, Eq. 1.2.11.2–(18). For this purpose it is convenient (as we shall see in a moment) to restrict x to the range

$$-n^{\epsilon+1/4} \le x \le n^{\epsilon+1/4}, \tag{45}$$

where $\epsilon = 0.001$, say, so that an error term can be included. A somewhat laborious calculation, which the author did by hand in the 60s but which is now easily done with the help of computer algebra, yields the formula

$$t_n(k) = \exp\bigl(\tfrac{1}{2}n\ln n - \tfrac{1}{2}n + \sqrt{n} - \tfrac{1}{4}\ln n - 2x^2/\sqrt{n} - \tfrac{1}{4} - \tfrac{1}{2}\ln\pi$$
$$- \tfrac{4}{3}x^3/n + 2x/\sqrt{n} + \tfrac{1}{3}/\sqrt{n} - \tfrac{4}{3}x^4/n\sqrt{n} + O(n^{5\epsilon-3/4})\bigr). \tag{46}$$

The restriction on x in (45) can be justified by the fact that we may set $x = \pm n^{\epsilon+1/4}$ to get an upper bound for all of the discarded terms, namely

$$e^{-2n^{2\epsilon}}\exp\bigl(\tfrac{1}{2}n\ln n - \tfrac{1}{2}n + \sqrt{n} - \tfrac{1}{4}\ln n - \tfrac{1}{4} - \tfrac{1}{2}\ln\pi + O(n^{3\epsilon-1/4})\bigr), \tag{47}$$

and if we multiply this by n we get an upper bound for the sum of the excluded terms. The upper bound is of lesser order than the terms we will compute for x in the restricted range (45), because of the factor $\exp(-2n^{2\epsilon})$, which is much smaller than any polynomial in n.

We can evidently remove the factor

$$\exp\bigl(\tfrac{1}{2}n\ln n - \tfrac{1}{2}n + \sqrt{n} - \tfrac{1}{4}\ln n - \tfrac{1}{4} - \tfrac{1}{2}\ln\pi + \tfrac{1}{3}/\sqrt{n}\,\bigr) \tag{48}$$

from the sum, and this leaves us with the task of summing

$$\exp\bigl(-2x^2/\sqrt{n} - \tfrac{4}{3}x^3/n + 2x/\sqrt{n} - \tfrac{4}{3}x^4/n\sqrt{n} + O(n^{5\epsilon-3/4})\bigr)$$

$$= \exp\left(\frac{-2x^2}{\sqrt{n}}\right)\left(1 - \frac{4}{3}\frac{x^3}{n} + \frac{8}{9}\frac{x^6}{n^2}\right)\left(1 + 2\frac{x}{\sqrt{n}} + 2\frac{x^2}{n}\right)$$

$$\times \left(1 - \frac{4}{3}\frac{x^4}{n\sqrt{n}}\right)\bigl(1 + O(n^{9\epsilon-3/4})\bigr) \tag{49}$$

over the range $x = \alpha, \alpha+1, \ldots, \beta-2, \beta-1$, where $-\alpha$ and β are approximately equal to $n^{\epsilon+1/4}$ (and not necessarily integers). Euler's summation formula, Eq. 1.2.11.2–(10), can be written

$$\sum_{\alpha \le x < \beta} f(x) = \int_\alpha^\beta f(x)\, dx - \frac{1}{2} f(x)\Big|_\alpha^\beta$$

$$+ \frac{1}{2} B_2 \frac{f'(x)}{1!}\Big|_\alpha^\beta + \cdots + \frac{1}{m+1} B_{m+1} \frac{f^{(m)}(x)}{m!}\Big|_\alpha^\beta + R_{m+1}, \quad (50)$$

by translation of the summation interval. Here $|R_m| \le (4/(2\pi)^m) \int_\alpha^\beta |f^{(m)}(x)|\, dx$. If we let $f(x) = x^t \exp(-2x^2/\sqrt{n}\,)$, where t is a fixed nonnegative integer, Euler's summation formula will give an asymptotic series for $\sum f(x)$ as $n \to \infty$, since

$$f^{(m)}(x) = n^{(t-m)/4} g^{(m)}(n^{-1/4}x), \qquad g(y) = y^t e^{-2y^2}, \quad (51)$$

and $g(y)$ is a well-behaved function independent of n. The derivative $g^{(m)}(y)$ is e^{-2y^2} times a polynomial in y, hence $R_m = O(n^{(t+1-m)/4}) \int_{-\infty}^{+\infty} |g^{(m)}(y)|\, dy = O(n^{(t+1-m)/4})$. Furthermore if we replace α and β by $-\infty$ and $+\infty$ in the right-hand side of (50), we make an error of at most $O(\exp(-2n^{2\epsilon}))$ in each term. Thus

$$\sum_{\alpha \le x < \beta} f(x) = \int_{-\infty}^\infty f(x)\, dx + O(n^{-m}), \qquad \text{for all } m \ge 0; \quad (52)$$

only the integral is really significant, given this particular choice of $f(x)$! The integral is not difficult to evaluate (see exercise 26), so we can multiply out and sum formula (49), giving $\sqrt{\pi/2}\,(n^{1/4} - \frac{1}{24}n^{-1/4} + O(n^{-1/2}))$. Thus

$$t_n = \frac{1}{\sqrt{2}} n^{n/2} e^{-n/2+\sqrt{n}-1/4} \big(1 + \tfrac{7}{24} n^{-1/2} + O(n^{-3/4})\big). \quad (53)$$

Actually the O-terms here should have an extra 9ϵ in the exponent, but our manipulations make it clear that this 9ϵ would disappear if we had carried further accuracy in the intermediate calculations. In principle, the method we have used could be extended to obtain $O(n^{-k})$ for any k, instead of $O(n^{-3/4})$. This asymptotic series for t_n was first determined (using a different method) by Moser and Wyman, *Canadian J. Math.* **7** (1955), 159–168.

The method we have used to derive (53) is an extremely useful technique for asymptotic analysis that was introduced by P. S. Laplace [*Mémoires Acad. Sci.* (Paris, 1782), 1–88]; it is discussed under the name "trading tails" in *CMath*, §9.4. For further examples and extensions of tail-trading, see the conclusion of Section 5.2.2.

EXERCISES

1. [*16*] What tableaux (P, Q) correspond to the two-line array

$$\begin{pmatrix} 1 & 2 & 3 & 4 & 5 & 6 & 7 & 8 & 9 \\ 6 & 4 & 9 & 5 & 7 & 1 & 2 & 8 & 3 \end{pmatrix},$$

in the construction of Theorem A? What two-line array corresponds to the tableaux

$$P = \begin{array}{|c|c|c|} \hline 1 & 4 & 7 \\ \hline 2 & 8 \\ \cline{1-2} 5 & 9 \\ \cline{1-2} \end{array}, \quad Q = \begin{array}{|c|c|c|} \hline 1 & 3 & 7 \\ \hline 4 & 5 \\ \cline{1-2} 8 & 9 \\ \cline{1-2} \end{array} \quad ?$$

2. [*M21*] Prove that (q, p) belongs to class t with respect to (16) if and only if t is the largest number of indices $i_1, \ldots, i_t$ such that

$$p_{i_1} < p_{i_2} < \cdots < p_{i_t} = p, \qquad q_{i_1} < q_{i_2} < \cdots < q_{i_t} = q.$$

▶ **3.** [*M24*] Show that the correspondence defined in the proof of Theorem A can also be carried out by constructing a table such as this:

Line 0	1	3	5	6	8
Line 1	7	2	9	5	3
Line 2	∞	7	∞	9	5
Line 3		∞		∞	7
Line 4				∞	

Here lines 0 and 1 constitute the given two-line array. For $k \geq 1$, line $k + 1$ is formed from line k by the following procedure:

a) Set $p \leftarrow \infty$.
b) Let column j be the leftmost column in which line k contains an integer $< p$, but line $k + 1$ is blank. If no such columns exist, and if $p = \infty$, line $k + 1$ is complete; if no such columns exist and $p < \infty$, return to (a).
c) Insert p into column j in line $k + 1$, then set p equal to the entry in column j of line k and return to (b).

Once the table has been constructed in this way, row k of P consists of those integers in line k that are not in line $(k + 1)$; row k of Q consists of those integers in line 0 that appear in a column containing ∞ in line $k + 1$.

▶ **4.** [*M30*] Let $a_1 \ldots a_{j-1} a_j \ldots a_n$ be a permutation of distinct elements, and assume that $1 < j \leq n$. The permutation $a_1 \ldots a_{j-2} a_j a_{j-1} a_{j+1} \ldots a_n$, obtained by interchanging a_{j-1} with a_j, is called "admissible" if either

i) $j \geq 3$ and a_{j-2} lies between a_{j-1} and a_j; or
ii) $j < n$ and a_{j+1} lies between a_{j-1} and a_j.

For example, exactly three admissible interchanges can be performed on the permutation $1\,5\,4\,6\,8\,3\,7$; we can interchange the 1 and the 5 since $1 < 4 < 5$; we can interchange the 8 and the 3 since $3 < 6 < 8$ (or since $3 < 7 < 8$); but we cannot interchange the 5 and the 4, or the 3 and the 7.

a) Prove that an admissible interchange does not change the tableau P formed from the permutation by successive insertion of the elements $a_1, a_2, \ldots, a_n$ into an initially empty tableau.
b) Conversely, prove that any two permutations that have the same P tableau can be transformed into each other by a sequence of one or more admissible interchanges. [*Hint:* Given that the shape of P is $(n_1, n_2, \ldots, n_m)$, show that any permutation that corresponds to P can be transformed into the "canonical permutation" $P_{m1} \ldots P_{mn_m} \ldots P_{21} \ldots P_{2n_2} P_{11} \ldots P_{1n_1}$ by a sequence of admissible interchanges.]

▶ **5.** [*M22*] Let P be the tableau corresponding to the permutation $a_1 a_2 \ldots a_n$; use exercise 4 to prove that P^T is the tableau corresponding to $a_n \ldots a_2 a_1$.

6. [*M26*] (M. P. Schützenberger.) Let π be an involution with k fixed points. Prove that the tableau corresponding to π, in the proof of Corollary B, has exactly k columns of odd length.

7. [*M20*] (C. Schensted.) Let P be the tableau corresponding to the permutation $a_1 a_2 \ldots a_n$. Prove that the number of *columns* in P is the longest length c of an increasing subsequence $a_{i_1} < a_{i_2} < \cdots < a_{i_c}$, where $i_1 < i_2 < \cdots < i_c$; the number of *rows* in P is the longest length r of a decreasing subsequence $a_{j_1} > a_{j_2} > \cdots > a_{j_r}$, where $j_1 < j_2 < \cdots < j_r$.

8. [*M18*] (P. Erdős, G. Szekeres.) Prove that any permutation containing more than n^2 elements has a monotonic subsequence of length greater than n; but there are permutations of n^2 elements with no monotonic subsequences of length greater than n. [*Hint:* See the previous exercise.]

9. [*M24*] Continuing exercise 8, find a "simple" formula for the exact number of permutations of $\{1, 2, \ldots, n^2\}$ that have no monotonic subsequences of length greater than n.

10. [*M20*] Prove that P is a tableau when Algorithm S terminates, if it was a tableau initially.

11. [*20*] Given only the values of r and s after Algorithm S terminates, is it possible to restore P to its original condition?

12. [*M24*] How many times is step S3 performed, if Algorithm S is used repeatedly to delete all elements of a tableau P whose shape is $(n_1, n_2, \ldots, n_m)$? What is the minimum of this quantity, taken over all shapes with $n_1 + n_2 + \cdots + n_m = n$?

13. [*M28*] Prove Theorem C.

14. [*M43*] Find a more direct proof of Theorem D, part (c).

15. [*M20*] How many permutations of the multiset $\{l \cdot a, \ m \cdot b, \ n \cdot c\}$ have the property that, as we read the permutation from left to right, the number of c's never exceeds the number of b's, and the number of b's never exceeds the number of a's? (For example, $a\ a\ b\ c\ a\ b\ b\ c\ a\ c\ a$ is such a permutation.)

16. [*M08*] In how many ways can the partial ordering represented by (39) be sorted topologically?

17. [*HM25*] Let

$$g(x_1, x_2, \ldots, x_n; \ y) = x_1 \, \Delta(x_1{+}y, x_2, \ldots, x_n) + x_2 \, \Delta(x_1, x_2{+}y, \ldots, x_n)$$
$$+ \cdots + x_n \, \Delta(x_1, x_2, \ldots, x_n{+}y).$$

Prove that

$$g(x_1, x_2, \ldots, x_n; \ y) = \left(x_1 + x_2 + \cdots + x_n + \binom{n}{2} y\right) \Delta(x_1, x_2, \ldots, x_n).$$

[*Hint:* The polynomial g is homogeneous (all terms have the same total degree); and it is antisymmetric in the x's (interchanging x_i and x_j changes the sign of g).]

18. [*HM30*] Generalizing exercise 17, evaluate the sum

$$x_1^m \, \Delta(x_1{+}y, x_2, \ldots, x_n) + x_2^m \, \Delta(x_1, x_2{+}y, \ldots, x_n) + \cdots + x_n^m \, \Delta(x_1, x_2, \ldots, x_n{+}y),$$

when $m \geq 0$.

19. [*M40*] Find a formula for the number of ways to fill an array that is like a tableau but with two boxes removed at the left of row 1; for example,

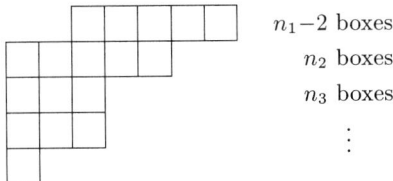

n_1-2 boxes

n_2 boxes

n_3 boxes

$\vdots$

is such a shape. (The rows and columns are to be in increasing order, as in ordinary tableaux.)

In other words, how many tableaux of shape $(n_1, n_2, \ldots, n_m)$ on the elements $\{1, 2, \ldots, n_1 + \cdots + n_m\}$ have both of the elements 1 and 2 in the first row?

▶ **20.** [*M24*] Prove that the number of ways to label the nodes of a given tree with the elements $\{1, 2, \ldots, n\}$, such that the label of each node is less than that of its descendants, is $n!$ divided by the product of the subtree sizes (the number of nodes in each subtree). For example, the number of ways to label the nodes of

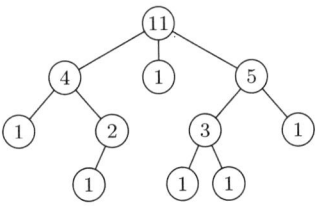

is $11!/(11 \cdot 4 \cdot 1 \cdot 5 \cdot 1 \cdot 2 \cdot 3 \cdot 1 \cdot 1 \cdot 1 \cdot 1) = 10 \cdot 9 \cdot 8 \cdot 7 \cdot 6$. (Compare with Theorem H.)

21. [*HM31*] (R. M. Thrall.) Let $n_1 > n_2 > \cdots > n_m$ specify the shape of a "shifted tableau" where row $i+1$ starts one position to the right of row i; for example, a shifted tableau of shape $(7, 5, 4, 1)$ has the form of the diagram

12	11	8	7	5	4	1
	9	6	5	3	2	
		5	4	2	1	
			1			

Prove that the number of ways to put the integers $1, 2, \ldots, n = n_1 + n_2 + \cdots + n_m$ into shifted tableaux of shape $(n_1, n_2, \ldots, n_m)$, so that rows and columns are in increasing order, is $n!$ divided by the product of the "generalized hook lengths"; a generalized hook of length 11, corresponding to the cell in row 1 column 2, has been shaded in the diagram above. (Hooks in the "inverted staircase" portion of the array, at the left, have a U-shape, tilted 90°, instead of an L-shape.) Thus there are

$$17!/(12 \cdot 11 \cdot 8 \cdot 7 \cdot 5 \cdot 4 \cdot 1 \cdot 9 \cdot 6 \cdot 5 \cdot 3 \cdot 2 \cdot 5 \cdot 4 \cdot 2 \cdot 1 \cdot 1)$$

ways to fill the shape with rows and columns in increasing order.

22. [*M39*] In how many ways can an array of shape $(n_1, n_2, \ldots, n_m)$ be filled with elements from the set $\{1, 2, \ldots, N\}$ *with repetitions allowed*, so that the rows are nondecreasing and the columns are strictly increasing? For example, the simple m-rowed shape $(1, 1, \ldots, 1)$ can be filled in $\binom{N}{m}$ ways; the 1-rowed shape (m) can be filled in $\binom{m+N-1}{m}$ ways; the small square shape $(2, 2)$ in $\frac{1}{3}\binom{N+1}{2}\binom{N}{2}$ ways.

▶ **23.** [*HM30*] (D. André.) In how many ways, A_n, can the numbers $\{1, 2, \ldots, n\}$ be placed into the array of n cells

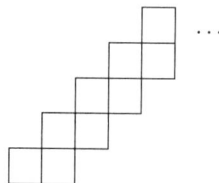

in such a way that the rows and columns are in increasing order? Find the generating function $g(z) = \sum A_n z^n/n!$.

24. [*M28*] Prove that

$$\sum_{\substack{q_1 + \cdots + q_n = t \\ 0 \leq q_1, \ldots, q_n \leq m}} \binom{m}{q_1} \cdots \binom{m}{q_n} \Delta(q_1, \ldots, q_n)^2$$

$$= n! \binom{nm - (n^2 - n)}{t - \frac{1}{2}(n^2 - n)} \binom{m}{n-1} \binom{m}{n-2} \cdots \binom{m}{0} \Delta(n-1, \ldots, 0)^2.$$

[*Hints:* Prove that $\Delta(k_1 + n - 1, \ldots, k_n) = \Delta(m - k_n + n - 1, \ldots, m - k_1)$; decompose an $n \times (m - n + 1)$ tableau in a fashion analogous to (38); and manipulate the sum as in the derivation of (36).]

25. [*M20*] Why is (42) the generating function for involutions?

26. [*HM21*] Evaluate $\int_{-\infty}^{\infty} x^t \exp(-2x^2/\sqrt{n}) \, dx$ when t is a nonnegative integer.

27. [*M24*] Let Q be a Young tableau on $\{1, 2, \ldots, n\}$; let the element i be in row r_i and column c_i. We say that i is "above" j when $r_i < r_j$.

a) Prove that, for $1 \leq i < n$, i is above $i + 1$ if and only if $c_i \geq c_{i+1}$.

b) Given that Q is such that (P, Q) corresponds to the permutation

$$\begin{pmatrix} 1 & 2 & \ldots & n \\ a_1 & a_2 & \ldots & a_n \end{pmatrix},$$

prove that i is above $i + 1$ if and only if $a_i > a_{i+1}$. (Therefore we can determine the number of runs in the permutation, knowing only Q. This result is due to M. P. Schützenberger.)

c) Prove that, for $1 \leq i < n$, i is above $i + 1$ in Q if and only if $i + 1$ is above i in Q^S.

28. [*M43*] Prove that the average length of the longest increasing subsequence of a random permutation of $\{1, 2, \ldots, n\}$ is asymptotically $2\sqrt{n}$. (This is the average length of row 1 in the correspondence of Theorem A.)

29. [*HM25*] Prove that a random permutation of n elements has an increasing subsequence of length $\geq l$ with probability $\leq \binom{n}{l}/l!$. This probability is $O(1/\sqrt{n})$ when $l = e\sqrt{n} + O(1)$, and $O(\exp(-c\sqrt{n}))$ when $l = 3\sqrt{n}$, $c = 6 \ln 3 - 6$.

30. [*M41*] (M. P. Schützenberger.) Show that the operation of going from P to P^S is a special case of an operation applicable in connection with *any* finite partially ordered set, not merely a tableau: Label the elements of a partially ordered set with the integers

$\{1, 2, \ldots, n\}$ in such a way that the partial order is consistent with the labeling. Find a dual labeling analogous to (26), by successively deleting the labels 1, 2, … while moving the other labels in a fashion analogous to Algorithm S and placing *1*, *2*, … in the vacated places. Show that this operation, when repeated on the dual labeling in reverse numerical order, yields the original labeling; and explore other properties of the operation.

31. [*HM30*] Let x_n be the number of ways to place n mutually nonattacking rooks on an $n \times n$ chessboard, where each arrangement is unchanged by reflection about both diagonals. Thus, $x_4 = 6$. (Involutions are required to be symmetrical about only one diagonal. Exercise 5.1.3–19 considers a related problem.) Find the asymptotic behavior of x_n.

32. [*HM21*] Prove that the involution number t_n is the expected value of X^n, when X is a normal deviate with mean 1 and variance 1.

33. [*M25*] (O. H. Mitchell, 1881.) True or false: $\Delta(a_1, a_2, \ldots, a_m)/\Delta(1, 2, \ldots, m)$ is an integer when $a_1, a_2, \ldots, a_m$ are integers.

34. [*25*] (T. Nakayama, 1940.) Prove that if a tableau shape contains a hook of length ab, it contains a hook of length a.

▶ **35.** [*30*] (A. P. Hillman and R. M. Grassl, 1976.) An arrangement of nonnegative integers p_{ij} in a tableau shape is called a *plane partition of m* if $\sum p_{ij} = m$ and

$$p_{i1} \geq \cdots \geq p_{in_i}, \qquad p_{1j} \geq \cdots \geq p_{n'_j j}, \qquad \text{for } 1 \leq i \leq n'_1,\, 1 \leq j \leq n_1,$$

when there are n_i cells in row i and n'_j cells in column j. It is called a *reverse plane partition* if instead

$$p_{i1} \leq \cdots \leq p_{in_i}, \qquad p_{1j} \leq \cdots \leq p_{n'_j j}, \qquad \text{for } 1 \leq i \leq n'_1,\, 1 \leq j \leq n_1.$$

Consider the following algorithm, which operates on reverse plane partitions of a given shape and constructs another array of numbers q_{ij} having the same shape:

G1. [Initialize.] Set $q_{ij} \leftarrow 0$ for $1 \leq j \leq n_i$ and $1 \leq i \leq n'_1$. Then set $j \leftarrow 1$.

G2. [Find nonzero cell.] If $p_{n'_j j} > 0$, set $i \leftarrow n'_j$, $k \leftarrow j$, and go on to step G3. Otherwise if $j < n_1$, increase j by 1 and repeat this step. Otherwise stop (the p array is now zero).

G3. [Decrease p.] Decrease p_{ik} by 1.

G4. [Move up or right.] If $i > 1$ and $p_{(i-1)k} > p_{ik}$, decrease i by 1 and return to G3. Otherwise if $k < n_i$, increase k by 1 and return to G3.

G5. [Increase q.] Increase q_{ij} by 1 and return to G2. ∎

Prove that this construction defines a one-to-one correspondence between reverse plane partitions of m and solutions of the equation

$$m = \sum h_{ij} q_{ij},$$

where the numbers h_{ij} are the hook lengths of the shape, by designing an algorithm that recomputes the p's from the q's.

36. [*HM27*] (R. P. Stanley, 1971.) (a) Prove that the number of reverse plane partitions of m in a given shape is $[z^m]\, 1/\prod(1 - z^{h_{ij}})$, where the numbers h_{ij} are the hook lengths of the shape. (b) Derive Theorem H from this result. [*Hint:* What is the asymptotic number of partitions as $m \to \infty$?]

37. [*M20*] (P. A. MacMahon, 1912.) What is the generating function for all plane partitions? (The coefficient of z^m should be the total number of plane partitions of m when the tableau shape is unbounded.)

▶ **38.** [*M30*] (Greene, Nijenhuis, and Wilf, 1979.) We can construct a directed acyclic graph on the cells T of any given tableau shape by letting arcs run from each cell to the other cells in its hook; the out-degree of cell (i,j) will then be $d_{ij} = h_{ij} - 1$, where h_{ij} is the hook length. Suppose we generate a random path in this digraph by choosing a random starting cell (i,j) and choosing further arcs at random, until coming to a corner cell from which there is no exit. Each random choice is made uniformly.

a) Let (a,b) be a corner cell of T, and let $I = \{i_0,\dots,i_k\}$ and $J = \{j_0,\dots,j_l\}$ be sets of rows and columns with $i_0 < \cdots < i_k = a$ and $j_0 < \cdots < j_l = b$. The digraph contains $\binom{k+l}{k}$ paths whose row and column sets are respectively I and J; let $P(I,J)$ be the probability that the random path is one of these. Prove that $P(I,J) = 1/(n\, d_{i_0 b} \dots d_{i_{k-1} b}\, d_{a j_0} \dots d_{a j_{l-1}})$, where $n = |T|$.

b) Let $f(T) = n!/\prod h_{ij}$. Prove that the random path ends at corner (a,b) with probability $f(T \setminus \{(a,b)\})/f(T)$.

c) Show that the result of (b) proves Theorem H and also gives us a way to generate a random tableau of shape T, with all $f(T)$ tableaux equally likely.

39. [*M38*] (I. M. Pak and A. V. Stoyanovskii, 1992.) Let P be an array of shape $(n_1,\dots,n_m)$ that has been filled with any permutation of the integers $\{1,\dots,n\}$, where $n = n_1 + \cdots + n_m$. The following procedure, which is analogous to the "siftup" algorithm in Section 5.2.3, can be used to convert P to a tableau. It also defines an array Q of the same shape, which can be used to provide a combinatorial proof of Theorem H.

P1. [Loop on (i,j).] Perform steps P2 and P3 for all cells (i,j) of the array, in reverse lexicographic order (that is, from bottom to top, and from right to left in each row); then stop.

P2. [Fix P at (i,j).] Set $K \leftarrow P_{ij}$ and perform Algorithm S' (see below).

P3. [Adjust Q.] Set $Q_{ik} \leftarrow Q_{i(k+1)} + 1$ for $j \leq k < s$, and set $Q_{is} \leftarrow i - r$. ∎

Here Algorithm S' is the same as Schützenberger's Algorithm S, except that steps S1 and S2 are generalized slightly:

S1'. [Initialize.] Set $r \leftarrow i$, $s \leftarrow j$.

S2'. [Done?] If $K \lesssim P_{(r+1)s}$ and $K \lesssim P_{r(s+1)}$, set $P_{rs} \leftarrow K$ and terminate.

(Algorithm S is essentially the special case $i = 1$, $j = 1$, $K = \infty$.)

For example, Algorithm P straightens out one particular array of shape $(3,3,2)$ in the following way, if we view the contents of arrays P and Q at the beginning of step P2, with P_{ij} in boldface type:

The final result is

$$P = \begin{array}{|c|c|c|} \hline 1 & 3 & 4 \\ \hline 2 & 5 & 8 \\ \hline 6 & 7 \\ \cline{1-2} \end{array}, \qquad Q = \begin{array}{|c|c|c|} \hline 1 & -2 & -1 \\ \hline 0 & -1 & 0 \\ \hline 1 & 0 \\ \cline{1-2} \end{array}.$$

a) If P is simply a $1 \times n$ array, Algorithm P sorts it into $\boxed{1 \;\; \cdots \;\; n}$. Explain what the Q array will contain in that case.

b) Answer the same question if P is $n \times 1$ instead of $1 \times n$.

c) Prove that, in general, we will have

$$-b_{ij} \leq Q_{ij} \leq r_{ij},$$

where b_{ij} is the number of cells below (i, j) and r_{ij} is the number of cells to the right. Thus, the number of possible values for Q_{ij} is exactly h_{ij}, the size of the (i, j)th hook.

d) Theorem H will be proved constructively if we can show that Algorithm P defines a one-to-one correspondence between the $n!$ ways to fill the original shape and the pairs of output arrays (P, Q), where P is a tableau and the elements of Q satisfy the condition of part (c). Therefore we want to find an inverse of Algorithm P. For what initial permutations does Algorithm P produce the 2×2 array $Q = \left(\begin{smallmatrix} 0 & -1 \\ 0 & 0 \end{smallmatrix}\right)$?

e) What initial permutation does Algorithm P convert into the arrays

$$P = \begin{array}{|c|c|c|c|c|c|} \hline 1 & 3 & 5 & 7 & 11 & 15 \\ \hline 2 & 6 & 8 & 14 \\ \cline{1-4} 4 & 9 & 13 \\ \cline{1-3} 10 & 12 \\ \cline{1-2} 16 \\ \cline{1-1} \end{array}, \qquad Q = \begin{array}{|c|c|c|c|c|c|} \hline -2 & -3 & -1 & -1 & 1 & 0 \\ \hline 3 & -2 & -1 & 0 \\ \cline{1-4} 0 & -1 & 0 \\ \cline{1-3} -1 & 0 \\ \cline{1-2} 0 \\ \cline{1-1} \end{array} \qquad ?$$

f) Design an algorithm that inverts Algorithm P, given any pair of arrays (P, Q) such that P is a tableau and Q satisfies the condition of part (c). [*Hint:* Construct an oriented tree whose vertices are the cells (i, j), with arcs

$$(i, j) \to (i, j - 1) \quad \text{if } P_{i(j-1)} > P_{(i-1)j};$$
$$(i, j) \to (i - 1, j) \quad \text{if } P_{i(j-1)} < P_{(i-1)j}.$$

In the example of part (e) we have the tree

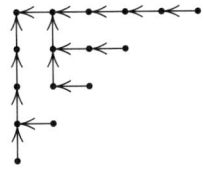

The paths of this tree hold the key to inverting Algorithm P.]

40. [*HM43*] Suppose a random Young tableau has been constructed by successively placing the numbers 1, 2, …, n in such a way that each possibility is equally likely when a new number is placed. For example, the tableau (1) would be obtained with probability $\frac{1}{1} \cdot \frac{1}{2} \cdot \frac{1}{2} \cdot \frac{1}{3} \cdot \frac{1}{3} \cdot \frac{1}{3} \cdot \frac{1}{4} \cdot \frac{1}{3} \cdot \frac{1}{3} \cdot \frac{1}{4} \cdot \frac{1}{4} \cdot \frac{1}{5} \cdot \frac{1}{4} \cdot \frac{1}{5} \cdot \frac{1}{4}$ using this procedure.

Prove that, with high probability, the resulting shape $(n_1, n_2, \ldots, n_m)$ will have $m \approx \sqrt{6n}$ and $\sqrt{k} + \sqrt{n_{k+1}} \approx \sqrt{m}$ for $0 \leq k \leq m$.

41. [*25*] (*Disorder in a library.*) Casual users of a library often put books back on the shelves in the wrong place. One way to measure the amount of disorder present in a library is to consider the minimum number of times we would have to take a book out of one place and insert it in another, before all books are restored to the correct order.

Thus let $\pi = a_1 a_2 \ldots a_n$ be a permutation of $\{1, 2, \ldots, n\}$. A "deletion-insertion operation" changes π to

$$a_1 \ldots a_{i-1} a_{i+1} \ldots a_j a_i a_{j+1} \ldots a_n \qquad \text{or} \qquad a_1 \ldots a_j a_i a_{j+1} \ldots a_{i-1} a_{i+1} \ldots a_n,$$

for some i and j. Let $\operatorname{dis}(\pi)$ be the minimum number of deletion-insertion operations that will sort π into order. Can $\operatorname{dis}(\pi)$ be expressed in terms of simpler characteristics of π?

▶ **42.** [*30*] (*Disorder in a genome.*) The DNA of *Lobelia fervens* has genes occurring in the sequence $g_7^R g_1 g_2 g_4 g_5 g_3 g_6^R$, where g_7^R stands for the left-right reflection of g_7; the same genes occur in tobacco plants, but in the order $g_1 g_2 g_3 g_4 g_5 g_6 g_7$. Show that five "flip" operations on substrings are needed to get from $g_1 g_2 g_3 g_4 g_5 g_6 g_7$ to $g_7^R g_1 g_2 g_4 g_5 g_3 g_6^R$. (A flip takes $\alpha \beta \gamma$ to $\alpha \beta^R \gamma$, when α, β, and γ are strings.)

43. [*35*] Continuing the previous exercise, show that at most $n + 1$ flips are needed to sort any rearrangement of $g_1 g_2 \ldots g_n$. Construct examples that require $n + 1$ flips, for all $n > 3$.

44. [*M37*] Show that the average number of flips required to sort a random arrangement of n genes is greater than $n - H_n$, if all $2^n n!$ genome rearrangements are equally likely.

5.2. INTERNAL SORTING

LET'S BEGIN our discussion of good "sortsmanship" by conducting a little experiment. How would you solve the following programming problem?

"Memory locations R+1, R+2, R+3, R+4, and R+5 contain five numbers. Write a computer program that rearranges these numbers, if necessary, so that they are in ascending order."

(If you already are familiar with some sorting methods, please do your best to forget about them momentarily; imagine that you are attacking this problem for the first time, without any prior knowledge of how to proceed.)

Before reading any further, you are requested to construct a solution to this problem.

. . . .

The time you spent working on the challenge problem will pay dividends as you continue to read this chapter. Chances are your solution is one of the following types:

A. *An insertion sort.* The items are considered one at a time, and each new item is inserted into the appropriate position relative to the previously-sorted items. (This is the way many bridge players sort their hands, picking up one card at a time.)

B. *An exchange sort.* If two items are found to be out of order, they are interchanged. This process is repeated until no more exchanges are necessary.

C. *A selection sort.* First the smallest (or perhaps the largest) item is located, and it is somehow separated from the rest; then the next smallest (or next largest) is selected, and so on.

D. *An enumeration sort.* Each item is compared with each of the others; an item's final position is determined by the number of keys that it exceeds.

E. *A special-purpose sort*, which works nicely for sorting five elements as stated in the problem, but does not readily generalize to larger numbers of items.

F. *A lazy attitude*, with which you ignored the suggestion above and decided not to solve the problem at all. Sorry, by now you have read too far and you have lost your chance.

G. *A new, super sorting technique* that is a definite improvement over known methods. (Please communicate this to the author at once.)

If the problem had been posed for, say, 1000 items, not merely 5, you might also have discovered some of the more subtle techniques that will be mentioned later. At any rate, when attacking a new problem it is often wise to find some fairly obvious procedure that works, and then try to improve upon it. Cases A, B, and C above lead to important classes of sorting techniques that are refinements of the simple ideas stated.

Many different sorting algorithms have been invented, and we will be discussing about 25 of them in this book. This rather alarming number of methods is actually only a fraction of the algorithms that have been devised so far; many techniques that are now obsolete will be omitted from our discussion, or mentioned only briefly. Why are there so many sorting methods? For computer programming, this is a special case of the question, "Why are there so many x methods?", where x ranges over the set of problems; and the answer is that each method has its own advantages and disadvantages, so that it outperforms the others on some configurations of data and hardware. Unfortunately, there is no known "best" way to sort; there are *many* best methods, depending on what is to be sorted on what machine for what purpose. In the words of Rudyard Kipling, "There are nine and sixty ways of constructing tribal lays, and every single one of them is right."

It is a good idea to learn the characteristics of each sorting method, so that an intelligent choice can be made for particular applications. Fortunately, it is not a formidable task to learn these algorithms, since they are interrelated in interesting ways.

At the beginning of this chapter we defined the basic terminology and notation to be used in our study of sorting: The records

$$R_1, R_2, \ldots, R_N \tag{1}$$

are supposed to be sorted into nondecreasing order of their keys $K_1, K_2, \ldots, K_N$, essentially by discovering a permutation $p(1)\,p(2)\ldots p(N)$ such that

$$K_{p(1)} \leq K_{p(2)} \leq \cdots \leq K_{p(N)}. \tag{2}$$

In the present section we are concerned with *internal sorting*, when the number of records to be sorted is small enough that the entire process can be performed in a computer's high-speed memory.

In some cases we will want the records to be physically rearranged in memory so that their keys are in order, while in other cases it may be sufficient merely to have an auxiliary table of some sort that specifies the permutation. If the records and/or the keys each take up quite a few words of computer memory, it is often better to make up a new table of link addresses that point to the records, and to manipulate these link addresses instead of moving the bulky records around. This method is called *address table sorting* (see Fig. 6). If the key is short but the satellite information of the records is long, the key may be placed with the link addresses for greater speed; this is called *keysorting*. Other sorting schemes utilize an auxiliary link field that is included in each record; these links are manipulated in such a way that, in the final result, the records are linked together to form a straight linear list, with each link pointing to the following record. This is called *list sorting* (see Fig. 7).

After sorting with an address table or list method, the records can be rearranged into increasing order as desired. Exercises 10 and 12 discuss interesting ways to do this, requiring only enough additional memory space to hold one record; alternatively, we can simply move the records into a new area capable of holding all records. The latter method is usually about twice as fast as the former, but it demands nearly twice as much storage space. Many applications can get by without moving the records at all, since the link fields are often adequate for all of the subsequent processing.

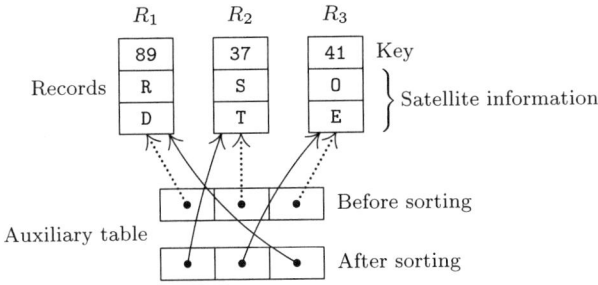

Fig. 6. Address table sorting.

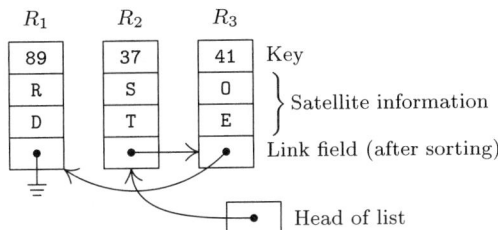

Fig. 7. List sorting.

All of the sorting methods that we shall examine in depth will be illustrated in four ways, by means of

a) an English-language description of the algorithm,

b) a flow diagram,

c) a MIX program, and

d) an example of the sorting method applied to a certain set of 16 numbers.

For convenience, the MIX programs will usually assume that the key is numeric and that it fits in a single word; sometimes we will even restrict the key to part of a word. The order relation $<$ will be ordinary arithmetic order; and the record will consist of the key alone, with no satellite information. These assumptions make the programs shorter and easier to understand, and a reader should find it fairly easy to adapt any of the programs to the general case by using address table sorting or list sorting. An analysis of the running time of each sorting algorithm will be given with the MIX programs.

Sorting by counting. As a simple example of the way in which we shall study internal sorting methods, let us consider the "counting" idea mentioned near the beginning of this section. This simple method is based on the idea that the jth key in the final sorted sequence is greater than exactly $j-1$ of the other keys. Putting this another way, if we know that a certain key exceeds exactly 27 others, and if no two keys are equal, the corresponding record should go into position 28 after sorting. So the idea is to compare every pair of keys, counting how many are less than each particular one.

The obvious way to do the comparisons is to

$$\big(\text{(compare } K_j \text{ with } K_i) \text{ for } 1 \leq j \leq N\big) \text{ for } 1 \leq i \leq N;$$

but it is easy to see that more than half of these comparisons are redundant, since it is unnecessary to compare a key with itself, and it is unnecessary to compare K_a with K_b and later to compare K_b with K_a. We need merely to

$$\big(\text{(compare } K_j \text{ with } K_i) \text{ for } 1 \leq j < i\big) \text{ for } 1 < i \leq N.$$

Hence we are led to the following algorithm.

Algorithm C (*Comparison counting*). This algorithm sorts $R_1, \ldots, R_N$ on the keys $K_1, \ldots, K_N$ by maintaining an auxiliary table COUNT[1], ..., COUNT[N] to count the number of keys less than a given key. After the conclusion of the algorithm, COUNT[j] + 1 will specify the final position of record R_j.

C1. [Clear COUNTs.] Set COUNT[1] through COUNT[N] to zero.

C2. [Loop on i.] Perform step C3, for $i = N$, $N-1$, ..., 2; then terminate the algorithm.

C3. [Loop on j.] Perform step C4, for $j = i-1$, $i-2$, ..., 1.

C4. [Compare $K_i : K_j$.] If $K_i < K_j$, increase COUNT[j] by 1; otherwise increase COUNT[i] by 1. ▌

Note that this algorithm involves no movement of records. It is similar to an address table sort, since the COUNT table specifies the final arrangement of records; but it is somewhat different because COUNT[j] tells us where to move R_j, instead of indicating which record should be moved into the place of R_j. (Thus the COUNT table specifies the *inverse* of the permutation $p(1) \ldots p(N)$; see Section 5.1.1.)

Table 1 illustrates the typical behavior of comparison counting, by applying it to 16 numbers that were chosen at random by the author on March 19, 1963. The same 16 numbers will be used to illustrate almost all of the other methods that we shall discuss later.

In our discussion preceding this algorithm we blithely assumed that no two keys were equal. This was a potentially dangerous assumption, for if equal keys corresponded to equal COUNTs the final rearrangement of records would be quite complicated. Fortunately, however, Algorithm C gives the correct result no matter how many equal keys are present; see exercise 2.

Program C (*Comparison counting*). The following MIX implementation of Algorithm C assumes that R_j is stored in location INPUT + j, and COUNT[j] in location COUNT + j, for $1 \leq j \leq N$; rI1 $\equiv i$; rI2 $\equiv j$; rA $\equiv K_i \equiv R_i$; rX $\equiv$ COUNT[i].

```
01  START  ENT1  N           1    C1. Clear COUNTs.
02         STZ   COUNT,1      N    COUNT[i] ← 0.
03         DEC1  1            N
04         J1P   *-2          N    N ≥ i > 0.
```

Table 1

SORTING BY COUNTING (ALGORITHM C)

KEYS:	503	087	512	061	908	170	897	275	653	426	154	509	612	677	765	703
COUNT (init.):	0	0	0	0	0	0	0	0	0	0	0	0	0	0	0	0
COUNT ($i = N$):	0	0	0	0	1	0	1	0	0	0	0	0	0	0	1	12
COUNT ($i = N-1$):	0	0	0	0	2	0	2	0	0	0	0	0	0	0	13	12
COUNT ($i = N-2$):	0	0	0	0	3	0	3	0	0	0	0	0	0	11	13	12
COUNT ($i = N-3$):	0	0	0	0	4	0	4	0	1	0	0	0	9	11	13	12
COUNT ($i = N-4$):	0	0	1	0	5	0	5	0	2	0	0	7	9	11	13	12
COUNT ($i = N-5$):	1	0	2	0	6	1	6	1	3	1	2	7	9	11	13	12
· · ·																
COUNT ($i = 2$):	6	1	8	0	15	3	14	4	10	5	2	7	9	11	13	12

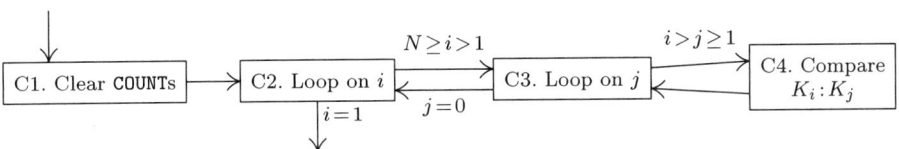

Fig. 8. Algorithm C: Comparison counting.

```
05         ENT1  N          1       C2. Loop on i.
06         JMP   1F         1
07  2H     LDA   INPUT,1    N − 1
08         LDX   COUNT,1    N − 1
09  3H     CMPA  INPUT,2    A       C4. Compare Kᵢ : Kⱼ.
10         JGE   4F         A       Jump if Kᵢ ≥ Kⱼ.
11         LD3   COUNT,2    B       COUNT[j]
12         INC3  1          B       +1
13         ST3   COUNT,2    B         → COUNT[j].
14         JMP   5F         B
15  4H     INCX  1          A − B   COUNT[i] ← COUNT[i] + 1.
16  5H     DEC2  1          A       C3. Loop on j.
17         J2P   3B         A
18         STX   COUNT,1    N − 1
19         DEC1  1          N − 1
20  1H     ENT2  -1,1       N       N ≥ i > j > 0.
21         J2P   2B         N   ∎
```

The running time of this program is $13N + 6A + 5B - 4$ units, where N is the number of records; A is the number of choices of two things from a set of N objects, namely $\binom{N}{2} = (N^2 - N)/2$; and B is the number of pairs of indices for which $j < i$ and $K_j > K_i$. Thus, B is the number of *inversions* of the permutation $K_1 \ldots K_N$; this is the quantity that was analyzed extensively in Section 5.1.1, where we found in Eqs. 5.1.1–(12) and 5.1.1–(13) that, for unequal keys in random order, we have

$$B = \left(\min 0, \ \text{ave} \ (N^2 - N)/4, \ \max \ (N^2 - N)/2, \ \text{dev} \ \sqrt{N(N-1)(N+2.5)}/6\right).$$

Hence Program C requires between $3N^2 + 10N - 4$ and $5.5N^2 + 7.5N - 4$ units of time, and the average running time lies halfway between these two extremes. For example, the data in Table 1 has $N = 16$, $A = 120$, $B = 41$, so Program C will sort it in $1129u$. See exercise 5 for a modification of Program C that has slightly different timing characteristics.

The factor N^2 that dominates this running time shows that Algorithm C is not an efficient way to sort when N is large; doubling the number of records increases the running time fourfold. Since the method requires a comparison of all distinct pairs of keys (K_i, K_j), there is no apparent way to get rid of the dependence on N^2, although we will see later in this chapter that the worst-case running time for sorting can be reduced to order $N \log N$ using other techniques. Our main interest in Algorithm C is its simplicity, not its speed. Algorithm C serves as an example of the style in which we will be describing more complex (and more efficient) methods.

There is another way to sort by counting that *is* quite important from the standpoint of efficiency; it is primarily applicable in the case that many equal keys are present, and when all keys fall into the range $u \le K_j \le v$, where $(v - u)$ is small. These assumptions appear to be quite restrictive, but in fact we shall see quite a few applications of the idea. For example, if we apply this method to the leading digits of keys instead of applying it to entire keys, the file will be partially sorted and it will be comparatively simple to complete the job.

In order to understand the principles involved, suppose that all keys lie between 1 and 100. In one pass through the file we can count how many 1s, 2s, ..., 100s are present; and in a second pass we can move the records into the appropriate place in an output area. The following algorithm spells things out in complete detail:

Algorithm D (*Distribution counting*). Assuming that all keys are integers in the range $u \le K_j \le v$ for $1 \le j \le N$, this algorithm sorts the records $R_1, \ldots, R_N$ by making use of an auxiliary table COUNT$[u], \ldots,$ COUNT$[v]$. At the conclusion of the algorithm the records are moved to an output area $S_1, \ldots, S_N$ in the desired order.

D1. [Clear COUNTs.] Set COUNT$[u]$ through COUNT$[v]$ all to zero.

D2. [Loop on j.] Perform step D3 for $1 \le j \le N$; then go to step D4.

D3. [Increase COUNT$[K_j]$.] Increase the value of COUNT$[K_j]$ by 1.

D4. [Accumulate.] (At this point COUNT$[i]$ is the number of keys that are equal to i.) Set COUNT$[i] \leftarrow$ COUNT$[i] +$ COUNT$[i-1]$, for $i = u+1, u+2, \ldots, v$.

D5. [Loop on j.] (At this point COUNT$[i]$ is the number of keys that are less than or equal to i; in particular, COUNT$[v] = N$.) Perform step D6 for $j = N$, $N - 1, \ldots, 1$; then terminate the algorithm.

D6. [Output R_j.] Set $i \leftarrow$ COUNT$[K_j]$, $S_i \leftarrow R_j$, and COUNT$[K_j] \leftarrow i - 1$. ∎

An example of this algorithm is worked out in exercise 6; a MIX program appears in exercise 9. When the range $v - u$ is small, this sorting procedure is very fast.

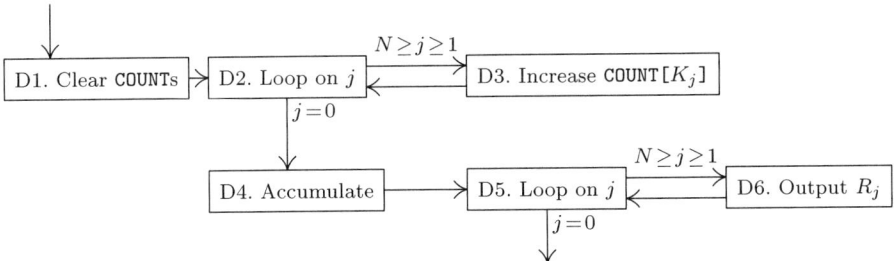

Fig. 9. Algorithm D: Distribution counting.

Sorting by comparison counting as in Algorithm C was first mentioned in print by E. H. Friend [*JACM* **3** (1956), 152], although he didn't claim it as his own invention. Distribution sorting as in Algorithm D was first developed by H. Seward in 1954 for use with radix sorting techniques that we will discuss later (see Section 5.2.5); it was also published under the name "Mathsort" by W. Feurzeig, *CACM* **3** (1960), 601.

EXERCISES

1. [*15*] Would Algorithm C still work if i varies from 2 up to N in step C2, instead of from N down to 2? What if j varies from 1 up to $i-1$ in step C3?

2. [*21*] Show that Algorithm C works properly when equal keys are present. If $K_j = K_i$ and $j < i$, does R_j come before or after R_i in the final ordering?

▸ **3.** [*21*] Would Algorithm C still work properly if the test in step C4 were changed from "$K_i < K_j$" to "$K_i \le K_j$"?

4. [*16*] Write a MIX program that "finishes" the sorting begun by Program C; your program should transfer the keys to locations OUTPUT+1 through OUTPUT+N, in ascending order. How much time does your program require?

5. [*22*] Does the following set of changes improve Program C?

      New line 08a: INCX 0,2
    Change line 10: JGE 5F
    Change line 14: DECX 1
        Delete line 15.

6. [*18*] Simulate Algorithm D by hand, showing intermediate results when the 16 records 5T, 0C, 5U, 0O, 9., 1N, 8S, 2R, 6A, 4A, 1G, 5L, 6T, 6I, 7O, 7N are being sorted. Here the numeric digit is the key, and the alphabetic information is just carried along with the records.

7. [*13*] Is Algorithm D a stable sorting method?

8. [*15*] Would Algorithm D still work properly if j were to vary from 1 up to N in step D5, instead of from N down to 1?

9. [*23*] Write a MIX program for Algorithm D, analogous to Program C and exercise 4. What is the execution time of your program, as a function of N and $(v - u)$?

10. [*25*] Design an efficient algorithm that replaces the N quantities $(R_1, \ldots, R_N)$ by $(R_{p(1)}, \ldots, R_{p(N)})$, respectively, given the values of $R_1, \ldots, R_N$ and the permutation

$p(1) \ldots p(N)$ of $\{1, \ldots, N\}$. Try to avoid using excess memory space. (This problem arises if we wish to rearrange records in memory after an address table sort, without having enough room to store $2N$ records.)

11. [*M27*] Write a MIX program for the algorithm of exercise 10, and analyze its efficiency.

▸ **12.** [*25*] Design an efficient algorithm suitable for rearranging the records $R_1, \ldots, R_N$ into sorted order, after a list sort (Fig. 7) has been completed. Try to avoid using excess memory space.

▸ **13.** [*27*] Algorithm D requires space for $2N$ records $R_1, \ldots, R_N$ and $S_1, \ldots, S_N$. Show that it is possible to get by with only N records $R_1, \ldots, R_N$, if a new unshuffling procedure is substituted for steps D5 and D6. (Thus the problem is to design an algorithm that rearranges $R_1, \ldots, R_N$ in place, based on the values of COUNT[u], $\ldots$, COUNT[v] after step D4, without using additional memory space; this is essentially a generalization of the problem considered in exercise 10.)

5.2.1. Sorting by Insertion

One of the important families of sorting techniques is based on the "bridge player" method mentioned near the beginning of Section 5.2: Before examining record R_j, we assume that the preceding records $R_1, \ldots, R_{j-1}$ have already been sorted; then we insert R_j into its proper place among the previously sorted records. Several interesting variations on this basic theme are possible.

Straight insertion. The simplest insertion sort is the most obvious one. Assume that $1 < j \leq N$ and that records $R_1, \ldots, R_{j-1}$ have been rearranged so that

$$K_1 \leq K_2 \leq \cdots \leq K_{j-1}.$$

(Remember that, throughout this chapter, K_j denotes the key portion of R_j.) We compare the new key K_j with K_{j-1}, K_{j-2}, $\ldots$, in turn, until discovering that R_j should be inserted between records R_i and R_{i+1}; then we move records $R_{i+1}, \ldots, R_{j-1}$ up one space and put the new record into position $i + 1$. It is convenient to combine the comparison and moving operations, interleaving them as shown in the following algorithm; since R_j "settles to its proper level" this method of sorting has often been called the *sifting* or *sinking* technique.

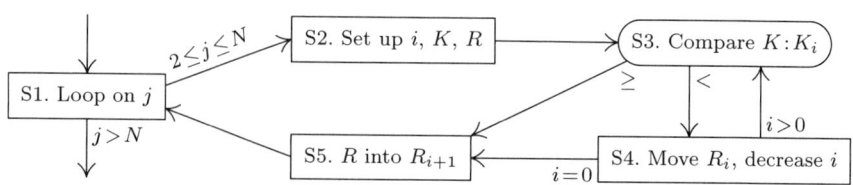

Fig. 10. Algorithm S: Straight insertion.

Algorithm S (*Straight insertion sort*). Records $R_1, \ldots, R_N$ are rearranged in place; after sorting is complete, their keys will be in order, $K_1 \leq \cdots \leq K_N$.

S1. [Loop on j.] Perform steps S2 through S5 for $j = 2, 3, \ldots, N$; then terminate the algorithm.

S2. [Set up i, K, R.] Set $i \leftarrow j - 1$, $K \leftarrow K_j$, $R \leftarrow R_j$. (In the following steps we will attempt to insert R into the correct position, by comparing K with K_i for decreasing values of i.)

S3. [Compare $K : K_i$.] If $K \geq K_i$, go to step S5. (We have found the desired position for record R.)

S4. [Move R_i, decrease i.] Set $R_{i+1} \leftarrow R_i$, then $i \leftarrow i - 1$. If $i > 0$, go back to step S3. (If $i = 0$, K is the smallest key found so far, so record R belongs in position 1.)

S5. [R into R_{i+1}.] Set $R_{i+1} \leftarrow R$. ∎

Table 1 shows how our sixteen example numbers are sorted by Algorithm S. This method is extremely easy to implement on a computer; in fact the following MIX program is the shortest decent sorting routine in this book.

Table 1

EXAMPLE OF STRAIGHT INSERTION

503 : 087																
087	503 : 512															
087	503	512 : 061														
061	087	503	512 : 908													
061	087	503	512	908 : 170												
061	087	170	503	512	908 : 897											

. . . .

061	087	154	170	275	426	503	509	512	612	653	677	765	897	908 : 703	
061	087	154	170	275	426	503	509	512	612	653	677	703	765	897	908

Program S (*Straight insertion sort*). The records to be sorted are in locations INPUT+1 through INPUT+N; they are sorted in place in the same area, on a full-word key. $rI1 \equiv j - N$; $rI2 \equiv i$; $rA \equiv R \equiv K$; assume that $N \geq 2$.

01	START	ENT1 2-N	1	*S1. Loop on j.* $j \leftarrow 2$.
02	2H	LDA INPUT+N,1	$N - 1$	*S2. Set up i, K, R.*
03		ENT2 N-1,1	$N - 1$	$i \leftarrow j - 1$.
04	3H	CMPA INPUT,2	$B + N - 1 - A$	*S3. Compare $K : K_i$.*
05		JGE 5F	$B + N - 1 - A$	To S5 if $K \geq K_i$.
06	4H	LDX INPUT,2	B	*S4. Move R_i, decrease i.*
07		STX INPUT+1,2	B	$R_{i+1} \leftarrow R_i$.
08		DEC2 1	B	$i \leftarrow i - 1$.
09		J2P 3B	B	To S3 if $i > 0$.
10	5H	STA INPUT+1,2	$N - 1$	*S5. R into R_{i+1}.*
11		INC1 1	$N - 1$	
12		J1NP 2B	$N - 1$	$2 \leq j \leq N$. ∎

The running time of this program is $9B + 10N - 3A - 9$ units, where N is the number of records sorted, A is the number of times i decreases to zero in step S4, and B is the number of moves. Clearly A is the number of times $K_j < \min(K_1, \ldots, K_{j-1})$ for $1 < j \leq N$; this is one less than the number of left-to-right minima, so A is equivalent to the quantity that was analyzed carefully in Section 1.2.10. Some reflection shows us that B is also a familiar quantity: The number of moves for fixed j is the number of inversions of K_j, so B is the total number of inversions of the permutation $K_1 K_2 \ldots K_N$. Hence by Eqs. 1.2.10–(16), 5.1.1–(12), and 5.1.1–(13), we have

$$A = \left(\min 0, \text{ ave } H_N - 1, \text{ max } N - 1, \text{ dev } \sqrt{H_N - H_N^{(2)}}\, \right);$$

$$B = \left(\min 0, \text{ ave } (N^2 - N)/4, \text{ max } (N^2 - N)/2, \text{ dev } \sqrt{N(N-1)(N+2.5)}/6\right);$$

and the average running time of Program S, assuming that the input keys are distinct and randomly ordered, is $(2.25N^2 + 7.75N - 3H_N - 6)\,u$. Exercise 33 explains how to improve this slightly.

The example data in Table 1 involves 16 items; there are two changes to the left-to-right minimum, namely 087 and 061; and there are 41 inversions, as we have seen in the previous section. Hence $N = 16$, $A = 2$, $B = 41$, and the total sorting time is $514u$.

Binary insertion and two-way insertion. While the jth record is being processed during a straight insertion sort, we compare its key with about $j/2$ of the previously sorted keys, on the average; therefore the total number of comparisons performed comes to roughly $(1 + 2 + \cdots + N)/2 \approx N^2/4$, and this gets very large when N is only moderately large. In Section 6.2.1 we shall study "binary search" techniques, which show where to insert the jth item after only about $\lg j$ well-chosen comparisons have been made. For example, when inserting the 64th record we can start by comparing K_{64} with K_{32}; if it is less, we compare it with K_{16}, but if it is greater we compare it with K_{48}, etc., so that the proper place to insert R_{64} will be known after making only six comparisons. The total number of comparisons for inserting all N items comes to about $N \lg N$, a substantial improvement over $\frac{1}{4}N^2$; and Section 6.2.1 shows that the corresponding program need not be much more complicated than a program for straight insertion. This method is called *binary insertion*; it was mentioned by John Mauchly as early as 1946, in the first published discussion of computer sorting.

The unfortunate difficulty with binary insertion is that it solves only half of the problem; after we have found where record R_j is to be inserted, we still need to move about $\frac{1}{2}j$ of the previously sorted records in order to make room for R_j, so the total running time is still essentially proportional to N^2. Some early computers such as the IBM 705 had a built-in "tumble" instruction that did such move operations at high speed, and modern machines can do the moves even faster with special hardware attachments; but as N increases, the dependence on N^2 eventually takes over. For example, an analysis by H. Nagler [*CACM* **3**

(1960), 618–620] indicated that binary insertion could not be recommended for sorting more than about $N = 128$ records on the IBM 705, when each record was 80 characters long, and similar analyses apply to other machines.

Of course, a clever programmer can think of various ways to reduce the amount of moving that is necessary; the first such trick, proposed early in the 1950s, is illustrated in Table 2. Here the first item is placed in the center of an output area, and space is made for subsequent items by moving to the right or to the left, whichever is most convenient. This saves about half the running time of ordinary binary insertion, at the expense of a somewhat more complicated program. It is possible to use this method without using up more space than required for N records (see exercise 6); but we shall not dwell any longer on this "two-way" method of insertion, since considerably more interesting techniques have been developed.

Table 2

TWO-WAY INSERTION

				503			
			087	503			
			087	503	512		
		061	087	503	512		
		061	087	503	512	908	
	061	087	170	503	512	908	
	061	087	170	503	512	897	908
061	087	170	275	503	512	897	908

Shell's method. If we have a sorting algorithm that moves items only one position at a time, its average time will be, at best, proportional to N^2, since each record must travel an average of about $\frac{1}{3}N$ positions during the sorting process (see exercise 7). Therefore, if we want to make substantial improvements over straight insertion, we need some mechanism by which the records can take long leaps instead of short steps.

Such a method was proposed in 1959 by Donald L. Shell [*CACM* **2**, 7 (July 1959), 30–32], and it became known as *shellsort*. Table 3 illustrates the general idea behind the method: First we divide the 16 records into 8 groups of two each, namely $(R_1, R_9), (R_2, R_{10}), \ldots, (R_8, R_{16})$. Sorting each group of records separately takes us to the second line of Table 3; this is called the "first pass." Notice that 154 has changed places with 512; 908 and 897 have both jumped to the right. Now we divide the records into 4 groups of four each, namely $(R_1, R_5, R_9, R_{13}), \ldots, (R_4, R_8, R_{12}, R_{16})$, and again each group is sorted separately; this "second pass" takes us to line 3. A third pass sorts two groups of eight records, then a fourth pass completes the job by sorting all 16 records. Each of the intermediate sorting processes involves either a comparatively short file or a file that is comparatively well ordered, so straight insertion can be used

Table 3

SHELLSORT WITH INCREMENTS 8, 4, 2, 1

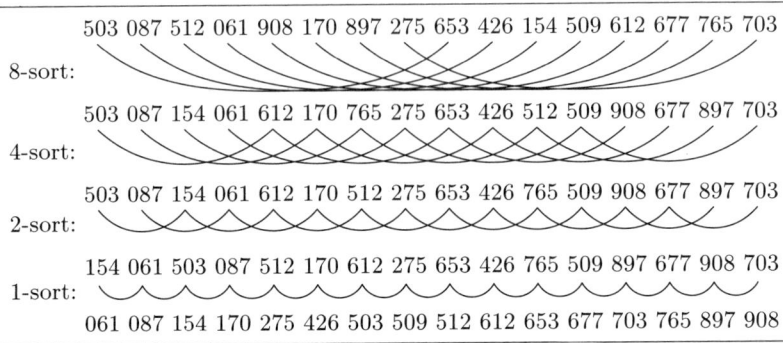

| 503 087 512 061 908 170 897 275 653 426 154 509 612 677 765 703 |

8-sort:

503 087 154 061 612 170 765 275 653 426 512 509 908 677 897 703

4-sort:

503 087 154 061 612 170 512 275 653 426 765 509 908 677 897 703

2-sort:

154 061 503 087 512 170 612 275 653 426 765 509 897 677 908 703

1-sort:

061 087 154 170 275 426 503 509 512 612 653 677 703 765 897 908

for each sorting operation. In this way the records tend to converge quickly to their final destinations.

Shellsort is also known as the "diminishing increment sort," since each pass is defined by an increment h such that we sort the records that are h units apart. The sequence of increments 8, 4, 2, 1 is not sacred; indeed, *any* sequence h_{t-1}, $h_{t-2}, \ldots, h_0$ can be used, so long as the last increment h_0 equals 1. For example, Table 4 shows the same data sorted with increments 7, 5, 3, 1. Some sequences are much better than others; we will discuss the choice of increments later.

Algorithm D (*Shellsort*). Records $R_1, \ldots, R_N$ are rearranged in place; after sorting is complete, their keys will be in order, $K_1 \leq \cdots \leq K_N$. An auxiliary sequence of increments $h_{t-1}, h_{t-2}, \ldots, h_0$ is used to control the sorting process, where $h_0 = 1$; proper choice of these increments can significantly decrease the sorting time. This algorithm reduces to Algorithm S when $t = 1$.

D1. [Loop on s.] Perform step D2 for $s = t - 1, t - 2, \ldots, 0$; then terminate the algorithm.

D2. [Loop on j.] Set $h \leftarrow h_s$, and perform steps D3 through D6 for $h < j \leq N$. (We will use a straight insertion method to sort elements that are h positions apart, so that $K_i \leq K_{i+h}$ for $1 \leq i \leq N - h$. Steps D3 through D6 are essentially the same as steps S2 through S5, respectively, in Algorithm S.)

D3. [Set up i, K, R.] Set $i \leftarrow j - h$, $K \leftarrow K_j$, $R \leftarrow R_j$.

D4. [Compare $K : K_i$.] If $K \geq K_i$, go to step D6.

D5. [Move R_i, decrease i.] Set $R_{i+h} \leftarrow R_i$, then $i \leftarrow i - h$. If $i > 0$, go back to step D4.

D6. [R into R_{i+h}.] Set $R_{i+h} \leftarrow R$. ∎

The corresponding MIX program is not much longer than our program for straight insertion. Lines 08–19 of the following code are a direct translation of Program S into the more general framework of Algorithm D.

Program D (*Shellsort*). We assume that the increments are stored in an auxiliary table, with h_s in location H + s; all increments are less than N. Register

Table 4

SHELLSORT WITH INCREMENTS 7, 5, 3, 1

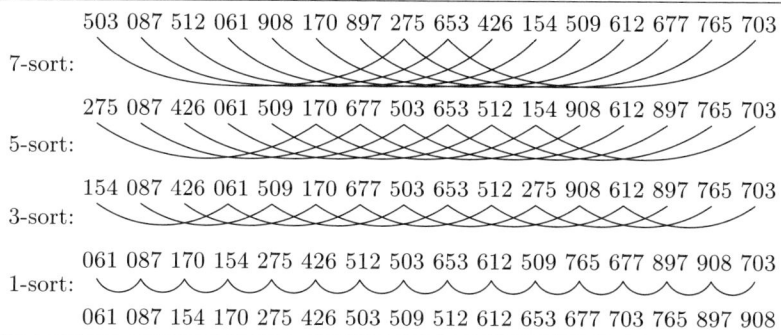

503 087 512 061 908 170 897 275 653 426 154 509 612 677 765 703

7-sort:

275 087 426 061 509 170 677 503 653 512 154 908 612 897 765 703

5-sort:

154 087 426 061 509 170 677 503 653 512 275 908 612 897 765 703

3-sort:

061 087 170 154 275 426 512 503 653 612 509 765 677 897 908 703

1-sort:

061 087 154 170 275 426 503 509 512 612 653 677 703 765 897 908

assignments: rI1 $\equiv j - N$; rI2 $\equiv i$; rA $\equiv R \equiv K$; rI3 $\equiv s$; rI4 $\equiv h$. Note that this program modifies itself, in order to obtain efficient execution of the inner loop.

01	START	ENT3	T-1	1	D1. Loop on s. $s \leftarrow t - 1$.
02	1H	LD4	H,3	T	D2. Loop on j. $h \leftarrow h_s$.
03		ENT1	INPUT,4	T	Modify the addresses of three
04		ST1	5F(0:2)	T	instructions in the main loop.
05		ST1	6F(0:2)	T	
06		ENN1	-N,4	T	rI1 $\leftarrow N - h$.
07		ST1	3F(0:2)	T	
08		ENT1	1-N,4	T	$j \leftarrow h + 1$.
09	2H	LDA	INPUT+N,1	$NT - S$	D3. Set up i, K, R.
10	3H	ENT2	N-H,1	$NT - S$	$i \leftarrow j - h$. [Instruction modified]
11	4H	CMPA	INPUT,2	$B+NT-S-A$	D4. Compare $K : K_i$.
12		JGE	6F	$B+NT-S-A$	To D6 if $K \geq K_i$.
13		LDX	INPUT,2	B	D5. Move R_i, decrease i.
14	5H	STX	INPUT+H,2	B	$R_{i+h} \leftarrow R_i$. [Instruction modified]
15		DEC2	0,4	B	$i \leftarrow i - h$.
16		J2P	4B	B	To D4 if $i > 0$.
17	6H	STA	INPUT+H,2	$NT - S$	D6. R into R_{i+h}. [Instruction modified]
18	7H	INC1	1	$NT - S$	$j \leftarrow j + 1$.
19		J1NP	2B	$NT - S$	To D3 if $j \leq N$.
20		DEC3	1	T	
21		J3NN	1B	T	$t > s \geq 0$. ▌

*Analysis of shellsort. In order to choose a good sequence of increments $h_{t-1}, \ldots, h_0$ for use in Algorithm D, we need to analyze the running time as a function of those increments. This leads to some fascinating mathematical problems, not yet completely resolved; nobody has been able to determine the best possible sequence of increments for large values of N. Yet a good many interesting facts are known about the behavior of shellsort, and we will summarize them here; details appear in the exercises below. [Readers who are not mathematically inclined should skim over the next few pages, continuing with the discussion of list insertion following (12).]

The frequency counts shown with Program D indicate that five factors determine the execution time: the size of the file, N; the number of passes (that is, the number of increments), $T = t$; the sum of the increments,

$$S = h_0 + \cdots + h_{t-1};$$

the number of comparisons, $B + NT - S - A$; and the number of moves, B. As in the analysis of Program S, A is essentially the number of left-to-right minima encountered in the intermediate sorting operations, and B is the number of inversions in the subfiles. The factor that governs the running time is B, so we shall devote most of our attention to it. For purposes of analysis we shall assume that the keys are distinct and initially in random order.

Let us call the operation of step D2 "h-sorting," so that shellsort consists of h_{t-1}-sorting, followed by h_{t-2} sorting, ..., followed by h_0-sorting. A file in which $K_i \leq K_{i+h}$ for $1 \leq i \leq N - h$ will be called "h-ordered."

Consider first the simplest generalization of straight insertion, when there are just two increments, $h_1 = 2$ and $h_0 = 1$. In this case the second pass begins with a 2-ordered sequence of keys, $K_1 K_2 \ldots K_N$. It is easy to see that the number of permutations $a_1 a_2 \ldots a_n$ of $\{1, 2, \ldots, n\}$ having $a_i \leq a_{i+2}$ for $1 \leq i \leq n - 2$ is

$$\binom{n}{\lfloor n/2 \rfloor},$$

since we obtain exactly one 2-ordered permutation for each choice of $\lfloor n/2 \rfloor$ elements to put in the even-numbered positions $a_2 a_4 \ldots$, while the remaining $\lceil n/2 \rceil$ elements occupy the odd-numbered positions. Each 2-ordered permutation is equally likely after a random file has been 2-sorted. What is the average number of inversions among all such permutations?

Let A_n be the total number of inversions among all 2-ordered permutations of $\{1, 2, \ldots, n\}$. Clearly $A_1 = 0$, $A_2 = 1$, $A_3 = 2$; and by considering the six cases

$$1\,3\,2\,4 \qquad 1\,2\,3\,4 \qquad 1\,2\,4\,3 \qquad 2\,1\,3\,4 \qquad 2\,1\,4\,3 \qquad 3\,1\,4\,2$$

we find that $A_4 = 1 + 0 + 1 + 1 + 2 + 3 = 8$. One way to investigate A_n in general is to consider the "lattice diagram" illustrated in Fig. 11 for $n = 15$. A 2-ordered permutation of $\{1, 2, \ldots, n\}$ can be represented as a path from the upper left corner point $(0,0)$ to the lower right corner point $(\lceil n/2 \rceil, \lfloor n/2 \rfloor)$, if we make the kth step of the path go downwards or to the right, respectively, according as k appears in an odd or an even position in the permutation. This rule defines a one-to-one correspondence between 2-ordered permutations and n-step paths from corner to corner of the lattice diagram; for example, the path shown by the heavy line in Fig. 11 corresponds to the permutation

$$2\ 1\ 3\ 4\ 6\ 5\ 7\ 10\ 8\ 11\ 9\ 12\ 14\ 13\ 15. \tag{1}$$

Furthermore, we can attach "weights" to the vertical lines of the path, as Fig. 11 shows; a line from (i, j) to $(i+1, j)$ gets weight $|i - j|$. A little study will convince the reader that the sum of these weights along each path is equal to the number of inversions of the corresponding permutation; this sum also equals the number

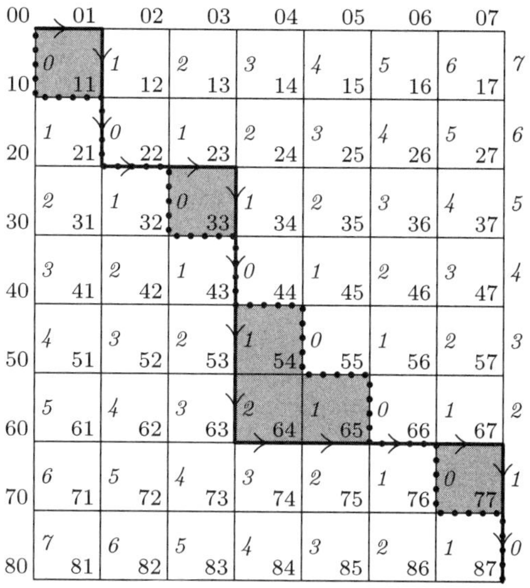

Fig. 11. Correspondence between 2-ordering and paths in a lattice. Italicized numbers are weights that yield the number of inversions in the 2-ordered permutation.

of shaded squares between the given path and the staircase path indicated by heavy dots in the figure. (See exercise 12.) Thus, for example, (1) has $1 + 0 + 1 + 0 + 1 + 2 + 1 + 0 = 6$ inversions.

When $a \le a'$ and $b \le b'$, the number of relevant paths from (a, b) to (a', b') is the number of ways to mix $a' - a$ vertical lines with $b' - b$ horizontal lines, namely

$$\binom{a' - a + b' - b}{a' - a};$$

hence the number of permutations whose corresponding path traverses the vertical line segment from (i, j) to $(i+1, j)$ is

$$\binom{i + j}{i}\binom{n - i - j - 1}{\lfloor n/2 \rfloor - j}.$$

Multiplying by the associated weight and summing over all segments gives

$$A_{2n} = \sum_{\substack{0 \le i \le n \\ 0 \le j \le n}} |i - j| \binom{i + j}{i}\binom{2n - i - j - 1}{n - j};$$

$$A_{2n+1} = \sum_{\substack{0 \le i \le n \\ 0 \le j \le n}} |i - j| \binom{i + j}{i}\binom{2n - i - j}{n - j}. \tag{2}$$

The absolute value signs in these sums make the calculations somewhat tricky, but exercise 14 shows that A_n has the surprisingly simple form $\lfloor n/2 \rfloor 2^{n-2}$. Hence the average number of inversions in a random 2-ordered permutation is

$$\lfloor n/2 \rfloor 2^{n-2} \Big/ \binom{n}{\lfloor n/2 \rfloor} \, ;$$

by Stirling's approximation this is asymptotically $\sqrt{\pi/128}\, n^{3/2} \approx 0.15 n^{3/2}$. The maximum number of inversions is easily seen to be

$$\binom{\lfloor n/2 \rfloor + 1}{2} \approx \frac{1}{8} n^2 .$$

It is instructive to study the distribution of inversions more carefully, by examining the generating functions

$$\begin{aligned}
h_1(z) &= 1, \\
h_2(z) &= 1 + z, \\
h_3(z) &= 1 + 2z, \\
h_4(z) &= 1 + 3z + z^2 + z^3, \qquad \dots,
\end{aligned} \tag{3}$$

as in exercise 15. In this way we find that the standard deviation is also proportional to $n^{3/2}$, so the distribution is not extremely stable about the mean.

Now let us consider the general two-pass case of Algorithm D, when the increments are h and 1:

Theorem H. *The average number of inversions in an h-ordered permutation of $\{1, 2, \dots, n\}$ is*

$$f(n, h) = \frac{2^{2q-1} q!\, q!}{(2q+1)!} \left(\binom{h}{2} q(q+1) + \binom{r}{2}(q+1) - \frac{1}{2} \binom{h-r}{2} q \right), \tag{4}$$

where $q = \lfloor n/h \rfloor$ and $r = n \bmod h$.

This theorem is due to Douglas H. Hunt [Bachelor's thesis, Princeton University (April 1967)]. Note that when $h \geq n$ the formula correctly gives $f(n, h) = \frac{1}{2}\binom{n}{2}$.

Proof. An h-ordered permutation contains r sorted subsequences of length $q+1$, and $h - r$ of length q. Each inversion comes from a pair of distinct subsequences, and a given pair of distinct subsequences in a random h-ordered permutation defines a random 2-ordered permutation. The average number of inversions is therefore the sum of the average number of inversions between each pair of distinct subsequences, namely

$$\binom{r}{2} \frac{A_{2q+2}}{\binom{2q+2}{q+1}} + r(h-r) \frac{A_{2q+1}}{\binom{2q+1}{q}} + \binom{h-r}{2} \frac{A_{2q}}{\binom{2q}{q}} = f(n, h). \quad \blacksquare$$

Corollary H. *If the sequence of increments $h_{t-1}, \dots, h_1, h_0$ satisfies the condition*

$$h_{s+1} \bmod h_s = 0, \qquad \text{for } t - 1 > s \geq 0, \tag{5}$$

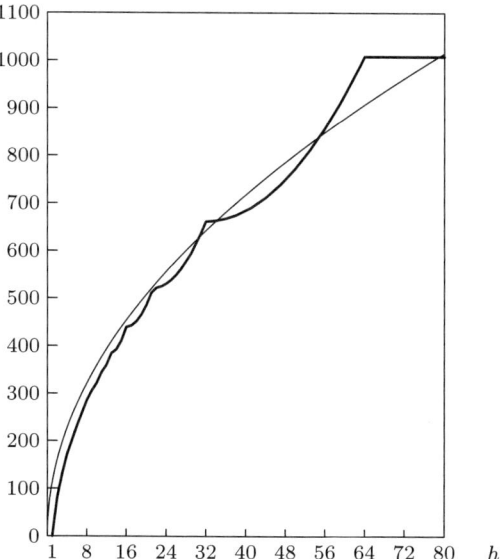

Fig. 12. The average number, $f(n, h)$, of inversions in an h-ordered file of n elements, shown for $n = 64$.

then the average number of move operations in Algorithm D is

$$\sum_{t > s \geq 0} \left(r_s f(q_s + 1, h_{s+1}/h_s) + (h_s - r_s) f(q_s, h_{s+1}/h_s) \right), \tag{6}$$

where $r_s = N \bmod h_s$, $q_s = \lfloor N/h_s \rfloor$, $h_t = Nh_{t-1}$, and f is defined in (4).

Proof. The process of h_s-sorting consists of a straight insertion sort on r_s (h_{s+1}/h_s)-ordered subfiles of length $q_s + 1$, and on $(h_s - r_s)$ such subfiles of length q_s. The divisibility condition implies that each of these subfiles is a random (h_{s+1}/h_s)-ordered permutation, in the sense that each (h_{s+1}/h_s)-ordered permutation is equally likely, since we are assuming that the original input was a random permutation of distinct elements.   ∎

Condition (5) in this corollary is always satisfied for *two-pass* shellsorts, when the increments are h and 1. If $q = \lfloor N/h \rfloor$ and $r = N \bmod h$, the quantity B in Program D will have an average value of

$$r f(q+1, N) + (h - r) f(q, N) + f(N, h) = \frac{r}{2} \binom{q+1}{2} + \frac{h-r}{2} \binom{q}{2} + f(N, h).$$

To a first approximation, the function $f(n, h)$ equals $(\sqrt{\pi}/8) n^{3/2} h^{1/2}$; we can, for example, compare it to the smooth curve in Fig. 12 when $n = 64$. Hence the running time for a two-pass Program D is approximately proportional to

$$2N^2/h + \sqrt{\pi N^3 h}.$$

The best choice of h is therefore approximately $\sqrt[3]{16N/\pi} \approx 1.72 \sqrt[3]{N}$; and with this choice of h we get an average running time proportional to $N^{5/3}$.

Thus we can make a substantial improvement over straight insertion, from $O(N^2)$ to $O(N^{1.667})$, just by using shellsort with two increments. Clearly we can do even better when more increments are used. Exercise 18 discusses the optimum choice of $h_{t-1}, \ldots, h_0$ when t is fixed and when the h's are constrained by the divisibility condition; the running time decreases to $O(N^{1.5+\epsilon/2})$, where $\epsilon = 1/(2^t - 1)$, for large N. We cannot break the $N^{1.5}$ barrier by using the formulas above, since the last pass always contributes

$$f(N, h_1) \approx (\sqrt{\pi}/8)N^{3/2}h_1^{1/2}$$

inversions to the sum.

But our intuition tells us that we can do even better when the increments $h_{t-1}, \ldots, h_0$ do *not* satisfy the divisibility condition (5). For example, 8-sorting followed by 4-sorting followed by 2-sorting does not allow any interaction between keys in even and odd positions; therefore the final 1-sorting pass is inevitably faced with $\Theta(N^{3/2})$ inversions, on the average. By contrast, 7-sorting followed by 5-sorting followed by 3-sorting jumbles things up in such a way that the final 1-sorting pass cannot encounter more than $2N$ inversions! (See exercise 26.) Indeed, an astonishing phenomenon occurs:

Theorem K. *If a k-ordered file is h-sorted, it remains k-ordered.*

Thus a file that is first 7-sorted, then 5-sorted, becomes both 7-ordered and 5-ordered. And if we 3-sort it, the result is ordered by 7s, 5s, and 3s. Examples of this remarkable property can be seen in Table 4 on page 85.

Proof. Exercise 20 shows that Theorem K is a consequence of the following fact:

Lemma L. *Let m, n, r be nonnegative integers, and let $(x_1, \ldots, x_{m+r})$ and $(y_1, \ldots, y_{n+r})$ be any sequences of numbers such that*

$$y_1 \leq x_{m+1}, \qquad y_2 \leq x_{m+2}, \qquad \ldots, \qquad y_r \leq x_{m+r}. \tag{7}$$

If the x's and y's are sorted independently, so that $x_1 \leq \cdots \leq x_{m+r}$ and $y_1 \leq \cdots \leq y_{n+r}$, the relations (7) will still be valid.

Proof. All but m of the x's are known to dominate (that is, to be greater than or equal to) some y, where distinct x's dominate distinct y's. Let $1 \leq j \leq r$. Since x_{m+j} after sorting dominates $m + j$ of the x's, it dominates at least j of the y's; therefore it dominates the *smallest* j of the y's; hence $x_{m+j} \geq y_j$ after sorting. ∎ ∎

Theorem K suggests that it is desirable to sort with relatively prime increments, but it does not lead directly to exact estimates of the number of moves made in Algorithm D. Moreover, the number of permutations of $\{1, 2, \ldots, n\}$ that are both h-ordered and k-ordered is not always a divisor of $n!$, so we can see that Theorem K does not tell the whole story; some k- and h-ordered files are obtained more often than others after k- and h-sorting. Therefore the average-case analysis of Algorithm D for general increments $h_{t-1}, \ldots, h_0$ has baffled everyone so far when $t > 3$. There is not even an obvious way to find the *worst* case, when N and $(h_{t-1}, \ldots, h_0)$ are given. We can, however, derive several facts about the approximate maximum running time when the increments have certain forms:

Theorem P. *The running time of Algorithm D is $O(N^{3/2})$, when $h_s = 2^{s+1} - 1$ for $0 \le s < t = \lfloor \lg N \rfloor$.*

Proof. It suffices to bound B_s, the number of moves in pass s, in such a way that $B_{t-1} + \cdots + B_0 = O(N^{3/2})$. During the first $t/2$ passes, for $t > s \ge t/2$, we may use the obvious bound $B_s = O\bigl(h_s(N/h_s)^2\bigr)$; and for subsequent passes we may use the result of exercise 23, $B_s = O(Nh_{s+2}h_{s+1}/h_s)$. Consequently $B_{t-1} + \cdots + B_0 = O\bigl(N(2 + 2^2 + \cdots + 2^{t/2} + 2^{t/2} + \cdots + 2)\bigr) = O(N^{3/2})$. ∎

This theorem is due to A. A. Papernov and G. V. Stasevich, *Problemy Peredachi Informatsii* **1**, 3 (1965), 81–98. It gives an upper bound on the *worst-case* running time of the algorithm, not merely a bound on the *average* running time. The result is not trivial since the maximum running time when the h's satisfy the divisibility constraint (5) is of order N^2; and exercise 24 shows that the exponent $3/2$ cannot be lowered.

An interesting improvement of Theorem P was discovered by Vaughan Pratt in 1969: *If the increments are chosen to be the set of all numbers of the form $2^p 3^q$ that are less than N, the running time of Algorithm D is of order $N(\log N)^2$.* In this case we can also make several important simplifications to the algorithm; see exercises 30 and 31. However, even with these simplifications, Pratt's method requires a substantial overhead because it makes quite a few passes over the data. Therefore his increments don't actually sort faster than those of Theorem P in practice, unless N is astronomically large. The best sequences for real-world N appear to satisfy $h_s \approx \rho^s$, where the ratio $\rho \approx h_{s+1}/h_s$ is roughly independent of s but may depend on N.

We have observed that it is unwise to choose increments in such a way that each is a divisor of all its predecessors; but we should not conclude that the best increments are relatively prime to all of their predecessors. Indeed, every element of a file that is gh-sorted and gk-sorted with $h \perp k$ has at most $\frac{1}{2}(h-1)(k-1)$ inversions when we are g-sorting. (See exercise 21.) Pratt's sequence $\{2^p 3^q\}$ wins as $N \to \infty$ by exploiting this fact, but it grows too slowly for practical use.

Janet Incerpi and Robert Sedgewick [*J. Comp. Syst. Sci.* **31** (1985), 210–224; see also *Lecture Notes in Comp. Sci.* **1136** (1996), 1–11] have found a way to have the best of both worlds, by showing how to construct a sequence of increments for which $h_s \approx \rho^s$ yet each increment is the gcd of two of its predecessors. Given any number $\rho > 1$, they start by defining a *base sequence* $a_1, a_2, \ldots$, where a_k is the least integer $\ge \rho^k$ such that $a_j \perp a_k$ for $1 \le j < k$. If $\rho = 2.5$, for example, the base sequence is

$$a_1, a_2, a_3, \ldots = 3, 7, 16, 41, 101, 247, 613, 1529, 3821, 9539, \ldots .$$

Now they define the increments by setting $h_0 = 1$ and

$$h_s = h_{s-r} a_r \qquad \text{for} \quad \binom{r}{2} < s \le \binom{r+1}{2}. \tag{8}$$

Thus the sequence of increments starts

$$1; \; a_1; \; a_2, \, a_1a_2; \; a_1a_3, \, a_2a_3, \, a_1a_2a_3; \; \ldots.$$

For example, when $\rho = 2.5$ we get

$$1, \, 3, \, 7, \, 21, \, 48, \, 112, \, 336, \, 861, \, 1968, \, 4592, \, 13776, \, 33936, \, 86961, \, 198768, \, \ldots.$$

The crucial point is that we can turn recurrence (8) around:

$$h_s = h_{r+s}/a_r = h_{\binom{r}{2}}/a_{\binom{r}{2}-s} \qquad \text{for } \binom{r-1}{2} \le s < \binom{r}{2}. \tag{9}$$

Therefore, by the argument in the previous paragraph, the number of inversions per element when we are h_0-sorting, h_1-sorting, $\ldots$ is at most

$$b(a_2, a_1); b(a_3, a_2), b(a_3, a_1); b(a_4, a_3), b(a_4, a_2), b(a_4, a_1); \ldots \tag{10}$$

where $b(h, k) = \frac{1}{2}(h-1)(k-1)$. If $\rho^{t-1} \le N < \rho^t$, the total number B of moves is at most N times the sum of the first t elements of this sequence. Therefore (see exercise 41) we can prove that the worst-case running time is much better than order $N^{1.5}$:

Theorem I. *The running time for Algorithm D is $O(Ne^{c\sqrt{\ln N}})$ when the increments h_s are defined by (8). Here $c = \sqrt{8 \ln \rho}$ and the constant implied by O depends on ρ.* ∎

This asymptotic upper bound is not especially important as $N \to \infty$, because Pratt's sequence does better. The main point of Theorem I is that a sequence of increments with the practical growth rate $h_s \approx \rho^s$ can have a running time that is guaranteed to be $O(N^{1+\epsilon})$ for arbitrarily small $\epsilon > 0$, when any value $\rho > 1$ is given.

Let's consider practical sizes of N more carefully by looking at the *total* running time of Program D, namely $(9B + 10NT + 13T - 10S - 3A + 1)u$. Table 5 shows the average running time for various sequences of increments when $N = 8$. For this small value of N, bookkeeping operations are the most significant part of the cost, and the best results are obtained when $t = 1$; hence for $N = 8$ we are better off using simple straight insertion. (The average running time of Program S when $N = 8$ is only $191.85u$.) Curiously, the best two-pass algorithm occurs when $h_1 = 6$, since a large value of S is more important here than a small value of B. Similarly, the three increments 3 2 1 minimize the average number of moves, but they do not lead to the best three-pass sequence. It may be of interest to record here some "worst-case" permutations that maximize the number of moves, since the general construction of such permutations is still unknown:

$$h_2 = 5, \quad h_1 = 3, \quad h_0 = 1: \qquad 8\,5\,2\,6\,3\,7\,4\,1 \qquad (19 \text{ moves})$$
$$h_2 = 3, \quad h_1 = 2, \quad h_0 = 1: \qquad 8\,3\,5\,7\,2\,4\,6\,1 \qquad (17 \text{ moves})$$

Table 5

ANALYSIS OF ALGORITHM D WHEN $N = 8$

Increments	A_{ave}	B_{ave}	S	T	MIX time
1	1.718	14.000	1	1	$204.85u$
2 1	2.667	9.657	3	2	$235.91u$
3 1	2.917	9.100	4	2	$220.15u$
4 1	3.083	10.000	5	2	$217.75u$
5 1	2.601	10.000	6	2	$209.20u$
6 1	2.135	10.667	7	2	$206.60u$
7 1	1.718	12.000	8	2	$209.85u$
4 2 1	3.500	8.324	7	3	$274.42u$
5 3 1	3.301	8.167	9	3	$253.60u$
3 2 1	3.320	7.829	6	3	$280.50u$

As N grows larger we have a slightly different picture. Table 6 shows the approximate number of moves for various sequences of increments when $N = 1000$. The first few entries satisfy the divisibility constraints (5), so that formula (6) and exercise 19 can be used; empirical tests were used to get approximate average values for the other cases. Ten thousand random files of 1000 elements were generated, and they each were sorted with each of the sequences of increments. The standard deviation of the number of left-to-right minima A was usually about 15; the standard deviation of the number of moves B was usually about 300.

Some patterns are evident in this data, but the behavior of Algorithm D still remains very obscure. Shell originally suggested using the increments $\lfloor N/2 \rfloor$, $\lfloor N/4 \rfloor$, $\lfloor N/8 \rfloor$, ..., but this is undesirable when the binary representation of N contains a long string of zeros. Lazarus and Frank [*CACM* **3** (1960), 20–22] suggested using essentially the same sequence, but adding 1 when necessary, to make all increments odd. Hibbard [*CACM* **6** (1963), 206–213] suggested using increments of the form $2^k - 1$; Papernov and Stasevich suggested the form $2^k + 1$. Other natural sequences investigated in Table 6 involve the numbers $\left(2^k - (-1)^k\right)/3$ and $(3^k - 1)/2$, as well as Fibonacci numbers and the Incerpi–Sedgewick sequences (8) for $\rho = 2.5$ and $\rho = 2$. Pratt-like sequences $\{5^p 11^q\}$ and $\{7^p 13^q\}$ are also shown, because they retain the asymptotic $O\left(N(\log N)^2\right)$ behavior but have lower overhead costs for small N. The final examples in Table 6 come from another sequence devised by Sedgewick, based on slightly different heuristics [*J. Algorithms* **7** (1986), 159–173]:

$$h_s = \begin{cases} 9 \cdot 2^s - 9 \cdot 2^{s/2} + 1, & \text{if } s \text{ is even;} \\ 8 \cdot 2^s - 6 \cdot 2^{(s+1)/2} + 1, & \text{if } s \text{ is odd.} \end{cases} \tag{11}$$

When these increments $(h_0, h_1, h_2, \dots) = (1, 5, 19, 41, 109, 209, \dots)$ are used, Sedgewick proved that the worst-case running time is $O(N^{4/3})$.

The minimum number of moves, about 6750, was observed for increments of the form $2^k + 1$, and also in the Incerpi–Sedgewick sequence for $\rho = 2$. But it is important to realize that the number of moves is not the only consideration,

Table 6

APPROXIMATE BEHAVIOR OF ALGORITHM D WHEN $N = 1000$

Increments													A_{ave}	B_{ave}	T
												1	6	249750	1
											17	1	65	41667	2
										60	6	1	158	26361	3
									140	20	4	1	262	21913	4
								256	64	16	4	1	362	20459	5
							576	192	48	16	4	1	419	20088	6
						729	243	81	27	9	3	1	378	18533	7
			512	256	128	64	32	16	8	4	2	1	493	16435	10
				500	250	125	62	31	15	7	3	1	516	7655	9
				501	251	125	63	31	15	7	3	1	558	7370	9
				511	255	127	63	31	15	7	3	1	559	7200	9
					255	127	63	31	15	7	3	1	436	7445	8
						127	63	31	15	7	3	1	299	8170	7
							63	31	15	7	3	1	190	9860	6
								31	15	7	3	1	114	13615	5
			513	257	129	65	33	17	9	5	3	1	561	6745	10
				257	129	65	33	17	9	5	3	1	440	6995	9
					129	65	33	17	9	5	3	1	304	7700	8
						65	33	17	9	5	3	1	197	9300	7
							33	17	9	5	3	1	122	12695	6
			683	341	171	85	43	21	11	5	3	1	511	7365	10
				341	171	85	43	21	11	5	3	1	490	7490	9
							255	63	15	7	3	1	373	8620	6
							257	65	17	5	3	1	375	8990	6
							341	85	21	5	3	1	410	9345	6
377	233	144	89	55	34	21	13	8	5	3	2	1	518	7400	13
	233	144	89	55	34	21	13	8	5	3	2	1	432	7610	12
						377	144	55	21	8	3	1	456	8795	7
						365	122	41	14	5	2	1	440	8085	7
							364	121	40	13	4	1	437	8900	6
								121	40	13	4	1	268	9790	5
						336	112	48	21	7	3	1	432	7840	7
				306	170	90	45	18	10	5	2	1	465	6755	9
							169	91	49	13	7	1	349	8698	6
					275	125	121	55	25	11	5	1	446	6788	8
						190	84	37	16	7	3	1	359	7201	7
					929	505	209	109	41	19	5	1	512	7725	8
						505	209	109	41	19	5	1	519	7790	7
							209	109	41	19	5	1	382	8165	6

even though it dominates the asymptotic running time. Since Program D takes $9B + 10(NT - S) + \cdots$ units of time, we see that saving one pass is about as desirable as saving $\frac{10}{9}N$ moves; when $N = 1000$ we are willing to add 1111 moves if we can save one pass. (The first pass is very quick, however, if h_{t-1} is near N, because $NT - S = (N - h_{t-1}) + \cdots + (N - h_0)$.)

Empirical tests conducted by M. A. Weiss [*Comp. J.* **34** (1991), 88–91] suggest strongly that the average number of moves performed by Algorithm D with increments $2^k - 1$, ..., 15, 7, 3, 1 is approximately proportional to $N^{5/4}$. More precisely, Weiss found that $B_{\text{ave}} \approx 1.55N^{5/4} - 4.48N + O(N^{3/4})$ for $100 \leq N \leq 12000000$ when these increments are used; the empirical standard deviation was approximately $.065N^{5/4}$. On the other hand, subsequent tests by Marcin Ciura show that Sedgewick's sequence (11) apparently makes $B_{\text{ave}} = O(N(\log N)^2)$ or better. The standard deviation for sequence (11) is amazingly small for $N \leq 10^6$, but it mysteriously begins to "explode" when N passes 10^7.

Table 7 shows typical breakdowns of moves per pass obtained in three random experiments, using increments of the forms $2^k - 1$, $2^k + 1$, and (11). The same file of numbers was used in each case. The total number of moves, $\sum_s B_s$, comes to 346152, 329532, 248788 in the three cases, so sequence (11) is clearly superior in this example.

Table 7

MOVES PER PASS: EXPERIMENTS WITH $N = 20000$

h_s	B_s	h_s	B_s	h_s	B_s
4095	19458	4097	19459	3905	20714
2047	15201	2049	14852	2161	13428
1023	16363	1025	15966	929	18206
511	18867	513	18434	505	16444
255	23232	257	22746	209	21405
127	28034	129	27595	109	19605
63	33606	65	34528	41	26604
31	40350	33	45497	19	23441
15	66037	17	48717	5	38941
7	43915	9	38560	1	50000
3	24191	5	20271		
1	16898	3	9448		
		1	13459		

Although Algorithm D is gradually becoming better understood, more than three decades of research have failed to turn up any grounds for making strong assertions about what sequences of increments make it work best. If N is less than 1000, a simple rule such as

Let $h_0 = 1$, $h_{s+1} = 3h_s + 1$, and stop with h_{t-1} when $h_{t+1} > N$ (12)

seems to be about as good as any other. For larger values of N, Sedgewick's sequence (11) can be recommended. Still better results, possibly even of order $N \log N$, have been reported by N. Tokuda using the quantity $\lfloor 2.25h_s \rfloor$ in place of $3h_s$ in (12); see *Information Processing 92* **1** (1992), 449–457.

List insertion. Let us now leave shellsort and consider other types of improvements over straight insertion. One of the most important general ways to improve on a given algorithm is to examine its data structures carefully, since a reorganization of data structures to avoid unnecessary operations often leads to substantial savings. Further discussion of this general idea appears in Section 2.4, where a rather complex algorithm is studied; let us consider how it applies to a very simple algorithm like straight insertion. What is the most appropriate data structure for Algorithm S?

Straight insertion involves two basic operations:

i) scanning an ordered file to find the largest key less than or equal to a given key; and

ii) inserting a new record into a specified part of the ordered file.

The file is obviously a linear list, and Algorithm S handles this list by using sequential allocation (Section 2.2.2); therefore it is necessary to move roughly half of the records in order to accomplish each insertion operation. On the other hand, we know that linked allocation (Section 2.2.3) is ideally suited to insertion, since only a few links need to be changed; and the other operation, sequential scanning, is about as easy with linked allocation as with sequential allocation. Only one-way linkage is needed, since we always scan the list in the same direction. Therefore we conclude that the right data structure for straight insertion is a one-way, linked linear list. It also becomes convenient to revise Algorithm S so that the list is scanned in increasing order:

Algorithm L (*List insertion*). Records $R_1, \ldots, R_N$ are assumed to contain keys $K_1, \ldots, K_N$, together with link fields $L_1, \ldots, L_N$ capable of holding the numbers 0 through N; there is also an additional link field L_0, in an artificial record R_0 at the beginning of the file. This algorithm sets the link fields so that the records are linked together in ascending order. Thus, if $p(1) \ldots p(N)$ is the stable permutation that makes $K_{p(1)} \leq \cdots \leq K_{p(N)}$, this algorithm will yield

$$L_0 = p(1); \qquad L_{p(i)} = p(i+1), \quad \text{for} \quad 1 \leq i < N; \qquad L_{p(N)} = 0. \qquad (13)$$

L1. [Loop on j.] Set $L_0 \leftarrow N$, $L_N \leftarrow 0$. (Link L_0 acts as the "head" of the list, and 0 acts as a null link; hence the list is essentially circular.) Perform steps L2 through L5 for $j = N-1, N-2, \ldots, 1$; then terminate the algorithm.

L2. [Set up p, q, K.] Set $p \leftarrow L_0$, $q \leftarrow 0$, $K \leftarrow K_j$. (In the following steps we will insert R_j into its proper place in the linked list, by comparing K with the previous keys in ascending order. The variables p and q act as pointers to the current place in the list, with $p = L_q$ so that q is one step behind p.)

L3. [Compare $K : K_p$.] If $K \leq K_p$, go to step L5. (We have found the desired position for record R, between R_q and R_p in the list.)

L4. [Bump p, q.] Set $q \leftarrow p$, $p \leftarrow L_q$. If $p > 0$, go back to step L3. (If $p = 0$, K is the largest key found so far; hence record R belongs at the end of the list, between R_q and R_0.)

L5. [Insert into list.] Set $L_q \leftarrow j$, $L_j \leftarrow p$. ∎

This algorithm is important not only because it is a simple sorting method, but also because it occurs frequently as part of other list-processing algorithms.

Table 8 shows the first few steps that occur when our sixteen example numbers are sorted; exercise 32 gives the final link setting.

Table 8
EXAMPLE OF LIST INSERTION

j:	0	1	2	3	4	5	6	7	8	9	10	11	12	13	14	15	16
K_j:	−	503	087	512	061	908	170	897	275	653	426	154	509	612	677	765	703
L_j:	16	−	−	−	−	−	−	−	−	−	−	−	−	−	−	−	0
L_j:	16	−	−	−	−	−	−	−	−	−	−	−	−	−	−	0	15
L_j:	14	−	−	−	−	−	−	−	−	−	−	−	−	−	16	0	15

Program L (*List insertion*). We assume that K_j is stored in INPUT$+j$ (0:3), and L_j is stored in INPUT$+j$ (4:5). rI1 $\equiv j$; rI2 $\equiv p$; rI3 $\equiv q$; rA(0:3) $\equiv K$.

01	KEY	EQU	0:3		
02	LINK	EQU	4:5		
03	START	ENT1	N	1	*L1. Loop on j.* $j \leftarrow N$.
04		ST1	INPUT(LINK)	1	$L_0 \leftarrow N$.
05		STZ	INPUT+N(LINK)	1	$L_N \leftarrow 0$.
06		JMP	6F	1	Go to decrease j.
07	2H	LD2	INPUT(LINK)	$N-1$	*L2. Set up p, q, K.* $p \leftarrow L_0$.
08		ENT3	0	$N-1$	$q \leftarrow 0$.
09		LDA	INPUT,1	$N-1$	$K \leftarrow K_j$.
10	3H	CMPA	INPUT,2(KEY)	$B+N-1-A$	*L3. Compare $K : K_p$.*
11		JLE	5F	$B+N-1-A$	To L5 if $K \le K_p$.
12	4H	ENT3	0,2	B	*L4. Bump p, q.* $q \leftarrow p$.
13		LD2	INPUT,3(LINK)	B	$p \leftarrow L_q$.
14		J2P	3B	B	To L3 if $p > 0$.
15	5H	ST1	INPUT,3(LINK)	$N-1$	*L5. Insert into list.* $L_q \leftarrow j$.
16		ST2	INPUT,1(LINK)	$N-1$	$L_j \leftarrow p$.
17	6H	DEC1	1	N	
18		J1P	2B	N	$N > j \ge 1$. ∎

The running time of this program is $7B + 14N - 3A - 6$ units, where N is the length of the file, $A + 1$ is the number of right-to-left maxima, and B is the number of inversions in the original permutation. (See the analysis of Program S. Note that Program L does not rearrange the records in memory; this can be done as in exercise 5.2–12, at a cost of about $20N$ additional units of time.) Program S requires $(9B + 10N - 3A - 9)u$, and since B is about $\frac{1}{4}N^2$, we can see that the extra memory space used for the link fields has saved about 22 percent of the execution time. Another 22 percent can be saved by careful programming (see exercise 33), but the running time remains proportional to N^2.

To summarize what we have done so far: We started with Algorithm S, a simple and natural sorting algorithm that does about $\frac{1}{4}N^2$ comparisons and $\frac{1}{4}N^2$ moves. We improved it in one direction by considering binary insertion, which does about $N \lg N$ comparisons and $\frac{1}{4}N^2$ moves. Changing the data

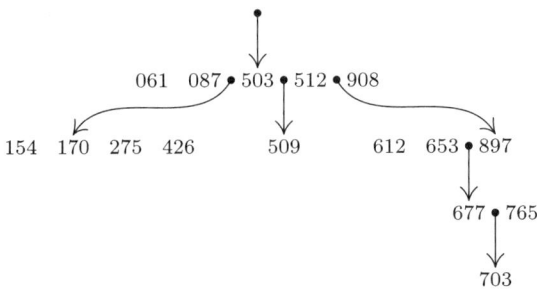

Fig. 13. Example of Wheeler's tree insertion scheme.

structure slightly with "two-way insertion" cuts the number of moves down to about $\frac{1}{8}N^2$. Shellsort cuts the number of comparisons and moves to about $N^{7/6}$, for N in a practical range; as $N \to \infty$ this number can be lowered to order $N(\log N)^2$. Another way to improve on Algorithm S, using a linked data structure, gave us the list insertion method, which does about $\frac{1}{4}N^2$ comparisons, 0 moves, and $2N$ changes of links.

Is it possible to marry the best features of these methods, reducing the number of comparisons to order $N \log N$ as in binary insertion, yet reducing the number of moves as in list insertion? The answer is yes, by going to a tree-structured arrangement. This possibility was first explored about 1957 by D. J. Wheeler, who suggested using two-way insertion until it becomes necessary to move some data; then instead of moving the data, a pointer to another area of memory is inserted, and the same technique is applied recursively to all items that are to be inserted into this new area of memory. Wheeler's original method [see A. S. Douglas, *Comp. J.* **2** (1959), 5] was a complicated combination of sequential and linked memory, with nodes of varying size; for our 16 example numbers the tree of Fig. 13 would be formed. A similar but simpler tree-insertion scheme, using binary trees, was devised by C. M. Berners-Lee about 1958 [see *Comp. J.* **3** (1960), 174, 184]. Since the binary tree method and its refinements are quite important for searching as well as sorting, they are discussed at length in Section 6.2.2.

Still another way to improve on straight insertion is to consider inserting several things at a time. For example, if we have a file of 1000 items, and if 998 of them have already been sorted, Algorithm S makes two more passes through the file (first inserting R_{999}, then R_{1000}). We can obviously save time if we compare K_{999} with K_{1000}, to see which is larger, then insert them *both* with one look at the file. A combined operation of this kind involves about $\frac{2}{3}N$ comparisons and moves (see exercise 3.4.2–5), instead of two passes each with about $\frac{1}{2}N$ comparisons and moves.

In other words, it is generally a good idea to "batch" operations that require long searches, so that multiple operations can be done together. If we carry this idea to its natural conclusion, we rediscover the method of sorting by merging, which is so important it is discussed in Section 5.2.4.

Address calculation sorting. Surely by now we have exhausted all possible ways to improve on the simple method of straight insertion; but let's look again! Suppose you want to arrange several dozen books on your bookshelves, in order by authors' names, when the books are given to you in random order. You'll naturally try to estimate the final position of each book as you put it in place, thereby reducing the number of comparisons and moves that you'll have to make. And the whole process will be somewhat more efficient if you start with a little more shelf space than is absolutely necessary. This method was first suggested for computer sorting by Isaac and Singleton, *JACM* **3** (1956), 169–174, and it was developed further by Tarter and Kronmal, *Proc. ACM National Conference* **21** (1966), 331–337.

Address calculation sorting usually requires additional storage space proportional to N, either to leave enough room so that excessive moving is not required, or to maintain auxiliary tables that account for irregularities in the distribution of keys. (See the "distribution counting" sort, Algorithm 5.2D, which is a form of address calculation.) We can probably make the best use of this additional memory space if we devote it to link fields, as in the list insertion method. In this way we can also avoid having separate areas for input and output; everything can be done in the same area of memory.

These considerations suggest that we generalize list insertion so that *several* lists are kept, not just one. Each list is used for certain ranges of keys. We make the important assumption that the keys are pretty evenly distributed, not "bunched up" irregularly: The set of all possible values of the keys is partitioned into M parts, and we assume a probability of $1/M$ that a given key falls into a given part. Then we provide additional storage for M list heads, and each list is maintained as in simple list insertion.

It is not necessary to give the algorithm in great detail here; the method simply begins with all list heads set to Λ. As each new item enters, we first decide which of the M parts its key falls into, then we insert it into the corresponding list as in Algorithm L.

To illustrate this approach, suppose that the 16 keys used in our examples are divided into the $M = 4$ ranges 0–249, 250–499, 500–749, 750–999. We obtain the following configurations as the keys $K_1, K_2, \ldots, K_{16}$ are successively inserted:

	After 4 items:	After 8 items:	After 12 items:	Final state:
List 1:	061, 087	061, 087, 170	061, 087, 154, 170	061, 087, 154, 170
List 2:		275	275, 426	275, 426
List 3:	503, 512	503, 512	503, 509, 512, 653	503, 509, 512, 612, 653, 677, 703
List 4:		897, 908	897, 908	765, 897, 908

(Program M below actually inserts the keys in reverse order, $K_{16}, \ldots, K_2, K_1$, but the final result is the same.) Because linked memory is used, the varying-length lists cause no storage allocation problem. All lists can be combined into a single list at the end, if desired (see exercise 35).

Program M (*Multiple list insertion*). In this program we make the same assumptions as in Program L, except that the keys must be *nonnegative*, thus

$$0 \le K_j < (\text{BYTESIZE})^3.$$

The program divides this range into M equal parts by multiplying each key by a suitable constant. The list heads are in locations HEAD+1 through HEAD+M.

```
01 KEY   EQU  1:3
02 LINK  EQU  4:5
03 START ENT2 M                   1
04       STZ  HEAD,2              M        HEAD[p] ← Λ.
05       DEC2 1                   M
06       J2P  *-2                 M        M ≥ p ≥ 1.
07       ENT1 N                   1        j ← N.
08 2H    LDA  INPUT,1(KEY)        N
09       MUL  =M(1:3)=            N        rA ← ⌊M · K_j / BYTESIZE³⌋.
10       STA  *+1(1:2)            N
11       ENT4 0                   N        rI4 ← rA.
12       ENT3 HEAD+1-INPUT,4      N        q ← LOC(HEAD[rA]).
13       LDA  INPUT,1             N        K ← K_j.
14       JMP  4F                  N        Jump to set p.
15 3H    CMPA INPUT,2(KEY)    B+N-A
16       JLE  5F              B+N-A        Jump to insert, if K ≤ K_p.
17       ENT3 0,2                 B        q ← p.
18 4H    LD2  INPUT,3(LINK)     B+N        p ← LINK(q).
19       J2P  3B               B+N        Jump if not end of list.
20 5H    ST1  INPUT,3(LINK)       N        LINK(q) ← LOC(R_j).
21       ST2  INPUT,1(LINK)       N        LINK(LOC(R_j)) ← p.
22 6H    DEC1 1                   N
23       J1P  2B                  N        N ≥ j ≥ 1.  ∎
```

This program is written for general M, but it would be better to fix M at some convenient value; for example, we might choose $M = \text{BYTESIZE}$, so that the list heads could be cleared with a single MOVE instruction and the multiplication sequence of lines 08–11 could be replaced by the single instruction LD4 INPUT,1(1:1). The most notable contrast between Program L and Program M is the fact that Program M must consider the case of an empty list, when no comparisons are to be made.

How much time do we save by having M lists? The total running time of Program M is $7B + 31N - 3A + 4M + 2$ units, where M is the number of lists and N is the number of records sorted; A and B respectively count the right-to-left maxima and the inversions present among the keys belonging to each list. (In contrast to other time analyses of this section, the rightmost element of a nonempty permutation is included in the count A.) We have already studied A and B for $M = 1$, when their average values are respectively H_N and $\frac{1}{2}\binom{N}{2}$. By our assumption about the distribution of keys, the probability that a given list contains precisely n items at the conclusion of sorting is the "binomial" probability

$$\binom{N}{n}\left(\frac{1}{M}\right)^n\left(1 - \frac{1}{M}\right)^{N-n}. \tag{14}$$

Therefore the average values of A and B in the general case are

$$A_{\text{ave}} = M \sum_n \binom{N}{n} \left(\frac{1}{M}\right)^n \left(1 - \frac{1}{M}\right)^{N-n} H_n; \tag{15}$$

$$B_{\text{ave}} = M \sum_n \binom{N}{n} \left(\frac{1}{M}\right)^n \left(1 - \frac{1}{M}\right)^{N-n} \binom{n}{2} \Big/ 2. \tag{16}$$

Using the identity

$$\binom{N}{n}\binom{n}{2} = \binom{N}{2}\binom{N-2}{n-2},$$

which is a special case of Eq. 1.2.6–(20), we can easily evaluate the sum in (16):

$$B_{\text{ave}} = \frac{1}{2M}\binom{N}{2}. \tag{17}$$

And exercise 37 derives the standard deviation of B. But the sum in (15) is more difficult. By Theorem 1.2.7A, we have

$$\sum_n \binom{N}{n}(M-1)^{-n} H_n = \left(1 - \frac{1}{M}\right)^{-N}(H_N - \ln M) + \epsilon,$$

$$0 < \epsilon = \sum_{n>N} \frac{1}{n}\left(1 - \frac{1}{M}\right)^{n-N} < \frac{M-1}{N+1};$$

hence

$$A_{\text{ave}} = M(H_N - \ln M) + \delta, \qquad 0 < \delta < \frac{M^2}{N+1}\left(1 - \frac{1}{M}\right)^{N+1}. \tag{18}$$

(This formula is practically useless when $M \approx N$; exercise 40 gives a more detailed analysis of the asymptotic behavior of A_{ave} when $M = N/\alpha$.)

By combining (17) and (18) we can deduce the total running time of Program M, for fixed M as $N \to \infty$:

min $31N + M + 2,$

ave $1.75N^2/M + 31N - 3MH_N + 3M \ln M + 4M - 3\delta - 1.75N/M + 2,$

max $3.50N^2 + 24.5N + 4M + 2.$ \tag{19}

Notice that when M is not too large we are speeding up the average time by a factor of M; $M = 10$ will sort about ten times as fast as $M = 1$. However, the maximum time is much larger than the average time; this reiterates the assumption we have made about a fairly equal distribution of keys, since the worst case occurs when all records pile onto the same list.

If we set $M = N$, the average running time of Program M is approximately $34.36N$ units; when $M = \frac{1}{2}N$ it is slightly more, approximately $34.52N$; and when $M = \frac{1}{10}N$ it is approximately $48.04N$. The additional cost of the supplementary program in exercise 35, which links all M lists together in a single list, raises these times respectively to $44.99N$, $41.95N$, and $52.74N$. (Note that

10N of these `MIX` time units are spent in the multiplication instruction alone!)
*We have achieved a sorting method of order N, provided only that the keys are
reasonably well spread out over their range.*

Improvements to multiple list insertion are discussed in Section 5.2.5.

EXERCISES

1. [*10*] Is Algorithm S a stable sorting algorithm?

2. [*11*] Would Algorithm S still sort numbers correctly if the relation "$K \geq K_i$" in
step S3 were replaced by "$K > K_i$"?

▸ **3.** [*30*] Is Program S the shortest possible sorting program that can be written for
`MIX`, or is there a shorter program that achieves the same effect?

▸ **4.** [*M20*] Find the minimum and maximum running times for Program S, as a
function of N.

▸ **5.** [*M27*] Find the generating function $g_N(z) = \sum_{k \geq 0} p_{Nk} z^k$ for the total running
time of Program S, where p_{Nk} is the probability that Program S takes exactly k units
of time, given a random permutation of $\{1, 2, \ldots, N\}$ as input. Also calculate the
standard deviation of the running time, given N.

6. [*23*] The two-way insertion method illustrated in Table 2 seems to imply that
there is an output area capable of holding up to $2N + 1$ records, in addition to the
input area containing N records. Show that two-way insertion can be done using only
enough space for $N + 1$ records, including both input and output.

7. [*M20*] If $a_1 a_2 \ldots a_n$ is a random permutation of $\{1, 2, \ldots, n\}$, what is the average
value of $|a_1 - 1| + |a_2 - 2| + \cdots + |a_n - n|$? (This is n times the average net distance
traveled by a record during a sorting process.)

8. [*10*] Is Algorithm D a stable sorting algorithm?

9. [*20*] What are the quantities A and B, and the total running time of Program D,
corresponding to Tables 3 and 4? Discuss the relative merits of shellsort versus straight
insertion in this case.

▸ **10.** [*22*] If $K_j \geq K_{j-h}$ when we begin step D3, Algorithm D specifies a lot of actions
that accomplish nothing. Show how to modify Program D so that this redundant
computation can be avoided, and discuss the merits of such a modification.

11. [*M10*] What path in a lattice like that of Fig. 11 corresponds to the permutation
1 2 5 3 7 4 8 6 9 11 10 12?

12. [*M20*] Prove that the area between a lattice path and the staircase path (as shown
in Fig. 11) equals the number of inversions in the corresponding 2-ordered permutation.

▸ **13.** [*M16*] Explain how to put weights on the *horizontal* line segments of a lattice,
instead of the vertical segments, so that the sum of the horizontal weights on a lattice
path is the number of inversions in the corresponding 2-ordered permutation.

14. [*M28*] (a) Show that, in the sums defined by Eq. (2), we have $A_{2n+1} = 2A_{2n}$.
(b) The general identity of exercise 1.2.6–26 simplifies to

$$\sum_k \binom{2k+s}{k} z^k = \frac{1}{\sqrt{1-4z}} \left(\frac{1 - \sqrt{1-4z}}{2z} \right)^s$$

if we set $r = s$, $t = -2$. By considering the sum $\sum_n A_{2n} z^n$, show that

$$A_{2n} = n \cdot 4^{n-1}.$$

▶ **15.** [*HM33*] Let $g_n(z)$, $\hat{g}_n(z)$, $h_n(z)$, and $\hat{h}_n(z)$ be $\sum z^{\text{total weight of path}}$ summed over all lattice paths of length $2n$ from $(0,0)$ to (n,n), where the weight is defined as in Fig. 11, subject to certain restrictions on the vertices on the paths: For $h_n(z)$, there is no restriction, but for $g_n(z)$ the path must avoid all vertices (i,j) with $i > j$; $h_n(z)$ and $\hat{g}_n(z)$ are defined similarly, except that all vertices (i,i) are also excluded, for $0 < i < n$. Thus

$$g_0(z) = 1, \qquad g_1(z) = z, \qquad g_2(z) = z^3 + z^2; \qquad \hat{g}_1(z) = z, \qquad \hat{g}_2(z) = z^3;$$

$$h_0(z) = 1, \qquad h_1(z) = z + 1, \qquad h_2(z) = z^3 + z^2 + 3z + 1;$$

$$\hat{h}_1(z) = z + 1, \qquad \hat{h}_2(z) = z^3 + z.$$

Find recurrence relations defining these functions, and use these relations to prove that

$$h_n''(1) + h_n'(1) = \frac{7n^3 + 4n^2 + 4n}{30}\binom{2n}{n}.$$

(The exact formula for the variance of the number of inversions in a random 2-ordered permutation of $\{1, 2, \ldots, 2n\}$ is therefore easily found; it is asymptotically $(\frac{7}{30} - \frac{\pi}{16})n^3$.)

16. [*M24*] Find a formula for the maximum number of inversions in an h-ordered permutation of $\{1, 2, \ldots, n\}$. What is the maximum possible number of moves in Algorithm D when the increments satisfy the divisibility condition (5)?

17. [*M21*] Show that, when $N = 2^t$ and $h_s = 2^s$ for $t > s \geq 0$, there is a unique permutation of $\{1, 2, \ldots, N\}$ that maximizes the number of move operations performed by Algorithm D. Find a simple way to describe this permutation.

18. [*HM24*] For large N the sum (6) can be estimated as

$$\frac{1}{4}\frac{N^2}{h_{t-1}} + \frac{\sqrt{\pi}}{8}\left(\frac{N^{3/2}h_{t-1}^{1/2}}{h_{t-2}} + \cdots + \frac{N^{3/2}h_1^{1/2}}{h_0}\right).$$

What real values of $h_{t-1}, \ldots, h_0$ minimize this expression when N and t are fixed and $h_0 = 1$?

▶ **19.** [*M25*] What is the average value of the quantity A in the timing analysis of Program D, when the increments satisfy the divisibility condition (5)?

20. [*M22*] Show that Theorem K follows from Lemma L.

21. [*M25*] Let h and k be relatively prime positive integers, and say that an integer is *generable* if it equals $xh + yk$ for some nonnegative integers x and y. Show that n is generable if and only if $hk - h - k - n$ is not generable. (Since 0 is the smallest generable integer, the largest nongenerable integer must therefore be $hk - h - k$. It follows that $K_i \leq K_j$ whenever $j - i \geq (h-1)(k-1)$, in any file that is both h-ordered and k-ordered.)

22. [*M30*] Prove that all integers $\geq 2^s(2^s - 1)$ can be represented in the form

$$a_0(2^s - 1) + a_1(2^{s+1} - 1) + a_2(2^{s+2} - 1) + \cdots,$$

where the a_j's are nonnegative integers; but $2^s(2^s - 1) - 1$ cannot be so represented. Furthermore, exactly $2^{s-1}(2^s + s - 3)$ positive integers are unrepresentable in this form.

Find analogous formulas when the quantities $2^k - 1$ are replaced by $2^k + 1$ in the representations.

▶ **23.** [*M22*] Prove that if h_{s+2} and h_{s+1} are relatively prime, the number of moves that occur while Algorithm D is using the increment h_s is $O(Nh_{s+2}h_{s+1}/h_s)$. *Hint:* See exercise 21.

24. [*M42*] Prove that Theorem P is best possible, in the sense that the exponent $3/2$ cannot be lowered.

▶ **25.** [*M22*] How many permutations of $\{1, 2, \ldots, N\}$ are both 3-ordered and 2-ordered? What is the maximum number of inversions in such a permutation? What is the total number of inversions among all such permutations?

26. [*M35*] Can a file of N elements have more than N inversions if it is 3-, 5-, and 7-ordered? Estimate the maximum number of inversions when N is large.

27. [*M41*] (Bjorn Poonen.) (a) Prove that there is a constant c such that if m of the increments h_s in Algorithm D are less than $N/2$, the running time is $\Omega(N^{1+c/\sqrt{m}})$ in the worst case. (b) Consequently the worst-case running time is $\Omega(N(\log N/\log\log N)^2)$ for all sequences of increments.

28. [*15*] Which sequence of increments shown in Table 6 is best from the standpoint of Program D, considering the average total running time?

29. [*40*] For $N = 1000$ and various values of t, find empirical values of $h_{t-1}, \ldots, h_1, h_0$ for which the average number of moves, B_{ave}, is as small as you can make it.

30. [*M23*] (V. Pratt.) If the set of increments in shellsort is $\{2^p 3^q \mid 2^p 3^q < N\}$, show that the number of passes is approximately $\frac{1}{2}(\log_2 N)(\log_3 N)$, and the number of moves per pass is at most $N/2$. In fact, if $K_{j-h} > K_j$ on any pass, we will always have $K_{j-3h}, K_{j-2h} \le K_j < K_{j-h} \le K_{j+h}, K_{j+2h}$; so we may simply interchange K_{j-h} and K_j and increase j by $2h$, saving two of the comparisons of Algorithm D. *Hint:* See exercise 25.

▶ **31.** [*25*] Write a MIX program for Pratt's sorting algorithm (exercise 30). Express its running time in terms of quantities A, B, S, T, N analogous to those in Program D.

32. [*10*] What would be the final contents of $L_0 L_1 \ldots L_{16}$ if the list insertion sort in Table 8 were carried through to completion?

▶ **33.** [*25*] Find a way to improve on Program L so that its running time is dominated by $5B$ instead of $7B$, where B is the number of inversions. Discuss corresponding improvements to Program S.

34. [*M10*] Verify formula (14).

35. [*21*] Write a MIX program to follow Program M, so that all lists are combined into a single list. Your program should set the LINK fields exactly as they would have been set by Program L.

36. [*18*] Assume that the byte size of MIX is 100, and that the sixteen example keys in Table 8 are actually 503000, 087000, 512000, $\ldots$, 703000. Determine the running time of Programs L and M on this data, when $M = 4$.

37. [*M25*] Let $g_n(z)$ be the probability generating function for inversions in a random permutation of n objects, Eq. 5.1.1–(11). Let $g_{NM}(z)$ be the corresponding generating function for the quantity B in Program M. Show that

$$\sum_{N \ge 0} g_{NM}(z) \frac{M^N w^N}{N!} = \left(\sum_{n \ge 0} g_n(z) \frac{w^n}{n!} \right)^M,$$

and use this formula to derive the variance of B.

38. [*HM23*] (R. M. Karp.) Let $F(x)$ be a distribution function for a probability distribution, with $F(0) = 0$ and $F(1) = 1$. Given that the keys $K_1, K_2, \ldots, K_N$ are independently chosen at random from this distribution, and that $M = cN$, where c is constant and $N \to \infty$, prove that the average running time of Program M is $O(N)$ when F is sufficiently smooth. (A key K is inserted into list j when $\lfloor MK \rfloor = j - 1$; this occurs with probability $F(j/M) - F((j-1)/M)$. Only the case $F(x) = x$, $0 \leq x \leq 1$, is treated in the text.)

39. [*HM16*] If a program runs in approximately $A/M + B$ units of time and uses $C + M$ locations in memory, what choice of M gives the minimum time × space?

▶ **40.** [*HM24*] Find the asymptotic value of the average number of right-to-left maxima that occur in multiple list insertion, Eq. (15), when $M = N/\alpha$ for fixed α as $N \to \infty$. Carry out the expansion to an absolute error of $O(N^{-1})$, expressing your answer in terms of the *exponential integral* function $E_1(z) = \int_z^\infty e^{-t}\, dt/t$.

41. [*HM26*] (a) Prove that the sum of the first $\binom{k}{2}$ elements of (10) is $O(\rho^{2k})$. (b) Now prove Theorem I.

42. [*HM43*] Analyze the average behavior of shellsort when there are $t = 3$ increments h, g, and 1, assuming that $h \perp g$. The first pass, h-sorting, obviously does a total of $\frac{1}{4}N^2/h + O(N)$ moves.

a) Prove that the second pass, g-sorting, does $\frac{\sqrt{\pi}}{8}(\sqrt{h} - 1/\sqrt{h})N^{3/2}/g + O(hN)$ moves.

b) Prove that the third pass, 1-sorting, does $\psi(h,g)N + O(g^3h^2)$ moves, where

$$\psi(h,g) = \frac{1}{2} \sum_{d=1}^{g-1} \sum_j \binom{h-1}{j} \left(\frac{d}{g}\right)^j \left(1 - \frac{d}{g}\right)^{h-1-j} \left| j - \left\lfloor \frac{hd}{g} \right\rfloor \right|.$$

▶ **43.** [*25*] Exercise 33 uses a sentinel to speed up Algorithm S, by making the test "$i > 0$" unnecessary in step S4. This trick does not apply to Algorithm D. Nevertheless, show that there is an easy way to avoid testing "$i > 0$" in step D5, thereby speeding up the inner loop of shellsort.

44. [*M25*] If $\pi = a_1 \ldots a_n$ and $\pi' = a_1' \ldots a_n'$ are permutations of $\{1, \ldots, n\}$, say that $\pi \leq \pi'$ if the ith-largest element of $\{a_1, \ldots, a_j\}$ is less than or equal to the ith-largest element of $\{a_1', \ldots, a_j'\}$, for $1 \leq i \leq j \leq n$. (In other words, $\pi \leq \pi'$ if straight insertion sorting of π is componentwise less than or equal to straight insertion sorting of π' after the first j elements have been inserted, for all j.)

a) If π is above π' in the sense of exercise 5.1.1–12, does it follow that $\pi \leq \pi'$?

b) If $\pi \leq \pi'$, does it follow that $\pi^R \geq \pi'^R$?

c) If $\pi \leq \pi'$, does it follow that π is above π'?

5.2.2. Sorting by Exchanging

We come now to the second family of sorting algorithms mentioned near the beginning of Section 5.2: "exchange" or "transposition" methods that systematically interchange pairs of elements that are out of order until no more such pairs exist.

The process of straight insertion, Algorithm 5.2.1S, can be viewed as an exchange method: We take each new record R_j and essentially exchange it with its neighbors to the left until it has been inserted into the proper place. Thus the classification of sorting methods into various families such as "insertion,"

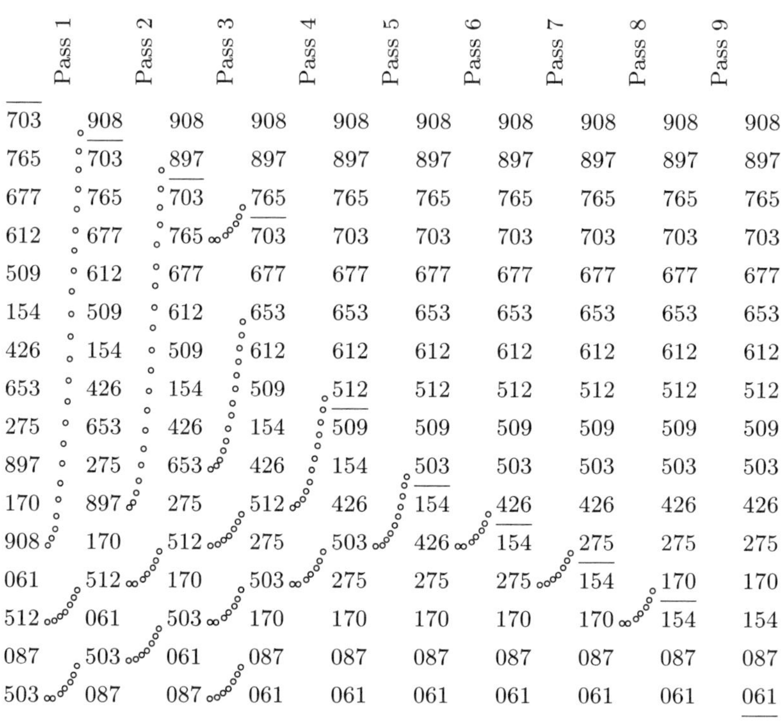

	Pass 1	Pass 2	Pass 3	Pass 4	Pass 5	Pass 6	Pass 7	Pass 8	Pass 9
703	908	908	908	908	908	908	908	908	908
765	703	897	897	897	897	897	897	897	897
677	765	703	765	765	765	765	765	765	765
612	677	765	703	703	703	703	703	703	703
509	612	677	677	677	677	677	677	677	677
154	509	612	653	653	653	653	653	653	653
426	154	509	612	612	612	612	612	612	612
653	426	154	509	512	512	512	512	512	512
275	653	426	154	509	509	509	509	509	509
897	275	653	426	154	503	503	503	503	503
170	897	275	512	426	154	426	426	426	426
908	170	512	275	503	426	154	275	275	275
061	512	170	503	275	275	275	154	170	170
512	061	503	170	170	170	170	170	154	154
087	503	061	087	087	087	087	087	087	087
503	087	087	061	061	061	061	061	061	061

Fig. 14. The bubble sort in action.

"exchange," "selection," etc., is not always clear-cut. In this section, we shall discuss four types of sorting methods for which exchanging is a dominant characteristic: *exchange selection* (the "bubble sort"); *merge exchange* (Batcher's parallel sort); *partition exchange* (Hoare's "quicksort"); and *radix exchange*.

The bubble sort. Perhaps the most obvious way to sort by exchanges is to compare K_1 with K_2, interchanging R_1 and R_2 if the keys are out of order; then do the same to records R_2 and R_3, R_3 and R_4, etc. During this sequence of operations, records with large keys tend to move to the right, and in fact the record with the largest key will move up to become R_N. Repetitions of the process will get the appropriate records into positions R_{N-1}, R_{N-2}, etc., so that all records will ultimately be sorted.

Figure 14 shows this sorting method in action on the sixteen keys 503 087 512 ... 703; it is convenient to represent the file of numbers vertically instead of horizontally, with R_N at the top and R_1 at the bottom. The method is called "bubble sorting" because large elements "bubble up" to their proper position, by contrast with the "sinking sort" (that is, straight insertion) in which elements sink down to an appropriate level. The bubble sort is also known by more prosaic names such as "exchange selection" or "propagation."

After each pass through the file, it is not hard to see that all records above and including the last one to be exchanged must be in their final position, so they need not be examined on subsequent passes. Horizontal lines in Fig. 14 show the progress of the sorting from this standpoint; notice, for example, that five more elements are known to be in final position as a result of Pass 4. On the final pass, no exchanges are performed at all. With these observations we are ready to formulate the algorithm.

Algorithm B (*Bubble sort*). Records $R_1, \ldots, R_N$ are rearranged in place; after sorting is complete their keys will be in order, $K_1 \leq \cdots \leq K_N$.

B1. [Initialize BOUND.] Set BOUND $\leftarrow N$. (BOUND is the highest index for which the record is not known to be in its final position; thus we are indicating that nothing is known at this point.)

B2. [Loop on j.] Set $t \leftarrow 0$. Perform step B3 for $j = 1, 2, \ldots,$ BOUND $- 1$, and then go to step B4. (If BOUND $= 1$, this means go directly to B4.)

B3. [Compare/exchange $R_j : R_{j+1}$.] If $K_j > K_{j+1}$, interchange $R_j \leftrightarrow R_{j+1}$ and set $t \leftarrow j$.

B4. [Any exchanges?] If $t = 0$, terminate the algorithm. Otherwise set BOUND $\leftarrow t$ and return to step B2. ∎

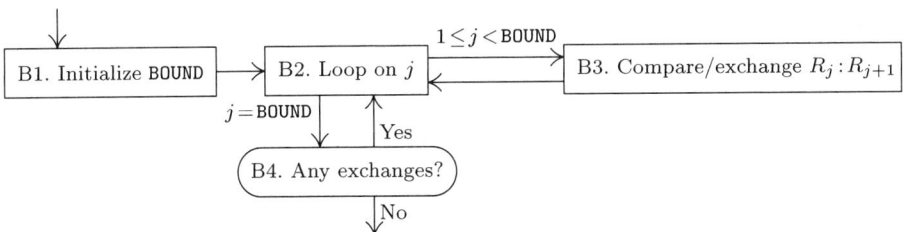

Fig. 15. Flow chart for bubble sorting.

Program B (*Bubble sort*). As in previous MIX programs of this chapter, we assume that the items to be sorted are in locations INPUT+1 through INPUT+N. $\text{rI1} \equiv t$; $\text{rI2} \equiv j$.

01	START	ENT1	N	1	*B1. Initialize BOUND.* $t \leftarrow N$.
02	1H	ST1	BOUND(1:2)	A	BOUND $\leftarrow t$.
03		ENT2	1	A	*B2. Loop on j.* $j \leftarrow 1$.
04		ENT1	0	A	$t \leftarrow 0$.
05		JMP	BOUND	A	Exit if $j \geq$ BOUND.
06	3H	LDA	INPUT,2	C	*B3. Compare/exchange $R_j : R_{j+1}$.*
07		CMPA	INPUT+1,2	C	
08		JLE	2F	C	No exchange if $K_j \leq K_{j+1}$.
09		LDX	INPUT+1,2	B	R_{j+1}
10		STX	INPUT,2	B	$\rightarrow R_j$.
11		STA	INPUT+1,2	B	(old R_j) $\rightarrow R_{j+1}$.
12		ENT1	0,2	B	$t \leftarrow j$.
13	2H	INC2	1	C	$j \leftarrow j + 1$.
14	BOUND	ENTX	-*,2	A + C	rX $\leftarrow j -$ BOUND. [Instruction modified]
15		JXN	3B	A + C	Do step B3 for $1 \leq j <$ BOUND.
16	4H	J1P	1B	A	*B4. Any exchanges?* To B2 if $t > 0$. ∎

Analysis of the bubble sort. It is quite instructive to analyze the running time of Algorithm B. Three quantities are involved in the timing: the number of passes, A; the number of exchanges, B; and the number of comparisons, C. If the input keys are distinct and in random order, we may assume that they form a random permutation of $\{1, 2, \ldots, n\}$. The idea of *inversion tables* (Section 5.1.1) leads to an easy way to describe the effect of each pass in a bubble sort.

Theorem I. *Let $a_1 a_2 \ldots a_n$ be a permutation of $\{1, 2, \ldots, n\}$, and let $b_1 b_2 \ldots b_n$ be the corresponding inversion table. If one pass of the bubble sort, Algorithm B, changes $a_1 a_2 \ldots a_n$ to the permutation $a_1' a_2' \ldots a_n'$, the corresponding inversion table $b_1' b_2' \ldots b_n'$ is obtained from $b_1 b_2 \ldots b_n$ by decreasing each nonzero entry by 1.*

Proof. If a_i is preceded by a larger element, the largest preceding element is exchanged with it, so b_{a_i} decreases by 1. But if a_i is not preceded by a larger element, it is never exchanged with a larger element, so b_{a_i} remains 0. ∎

Thus we can see what happens during a bubble sort by studying the sequence of inversion tables between passes. For example, the successive inversion tables corresponding to Fig. 14 are

$$
\begin{array}{ll}
& 3\ 1\ 8\ 3\ 4\ 5\ 0\ 4\ 0\ 3\ 2\ 2\ 3\ 2\ 1\ 0 \\
\text{Pass 1} & \\
& 2\ 0\ 7\ 2\ 3\ 4\ 0\ 3\ 0\ 2\ 1\ 1\ 2\ 1\ 0\ 0 \\
\text{Pass 2} & \\
& 1\ 0\ 6\ 1\ 2\ 3\ 0\ 2\ 0\ 1\ 0\ 0\ 1\ 0\ 0\ 0 \\
\text{Pass 3} & \\
& 0\ 0\ 5\ 0\ 1\ 2\ 0\ 1\ 0\ 0\ 0\ 0\ 0\ 0\ 0\ 0
\end{array}
\tag{1}
$$

and so on. If $b_1 b_2 \ldots b_n$ is the inversion table of the input permutation, we must therefore have

$$A = 1 + \max(b_1, b_2, \ldots, b_n), \tag{2}$$

$$B = b_1 + b_2 + \cdots + b_n, \tag{3}$$

$$C = c_1 + c_2 + \cdots + c_A, \tag{4}$$

where c_j is the value of BOUND -1 at the beginning of pass j. In terms of the inversion table,

$$c_j = \max\{b_i + i \mid b_i \geq j - 1\} - j \tag{5}$$

(see exercise 5). In example (1) we therefore have $A = 9$, $B = 41$, $C = 15 + 14 + 13 + 12 + 7 + 5 + 4 + 3 + 2 = 75$. The total MIX sorting time for Fig. 14 is $960u$.

The distribution of B (the total number of inversions in a random permutation) is very well-known to us by now; so we are left with A and C to be analyzed.

The probability that $A \leq k$ is $1/n!$ times the number of inversion tables having no components $\geq k$, namely $k^{n-k}k!$, when $1 \leq k \leq n$. Hence the probability that exactly k passes are required is

$$A_k = \frac{1}{n!}\left(k^{n-k}k! - (k-1)^{n-k+1}(k-1)!\right). \tag{6}$$

The mean value $\sum k A_k$ can now be calculated; summing by parts, it is

$$A_{\text{ave}} = n + 1 - \sum_{k=0}^{n} \frac{k^{n-k} k!}{n!} = n + 1 - P(n), \qquad (7)$$

where $P(n)$ is the function whose asymptotic value was found to be $\sqrt{\pi n/2} - \frac{2}{3} + O(1/\sqrt{n})$ in Eq. 1.2.11.3–(24). Formula (7) was stated without proof by E. H. Friend in *JACM* **3** (1956), 150; a proof was given by Howard B. Demuth [Ph.D. Thesis (Stanford University, October 1956), 64–68]. For the standard deviation of A, see exercise 7.

The total number of comparisons, C, is somewhat harder to handle, and we will consider only C_{ave}. For fixed n, let $f_j(k)$ be the number of inversion tables $b_1 \ldots b_n$ such that for $1 \le i \le n$ we have either $b_i < j - 1$ or $b_i + i - j \le k$; then

$$f_j(k) = (j + k)! \, (j - 1)^{n-j-k}, \qquad \text{for } 0 \le k \le n - j. \qquad (8)$$

(See exercise 8.) The average value of c_j in (5) is $\left(\sum k\big(f_j(k) - f_j(k-1)\big)\right)/n!$; summing by parts and then summing on j leads to the formula

$$C_{\text{ave}} = \binom{n+1}{2} - \frac{1}{n!} \sum_{\substack{1 \le j \le n \\ 0 \le k \le n-j}} f_j(k) = \binom{n+1}{2} - \frac{1}{n!} \sum_{0 \le r < s \le n} s! \, r^{n-s}. \qquad (9)$$

Here the asymptotic value is not easy to determine, and we shall return to it at the end of this section.

To summarize our analysis of the bubble sort, the formulas derived above and below may be written as follows:

$$A = \big(\min 1, \text{ ave } N - \sqrt{\pi N/2} + O(1), \text{ max } N\big); \qquad (10)$$

$$B = \big(\min 0, \text{ ave } \tfrac{1}{4}(N^2 - N), \text{ max } \tfrac{1}{2}(N^2 - N)\big); \qquad (11)$$

$$C = \big(\min N - 1, \text{ ave } \tfrac{1}{2}\big(N^2 - N \ln N - (\gamma + \ln 2 - 1)N\big) + O\big(\sqrt{N}\big),$$
$$\text{max } \tfrac{1}{2}(N^2 - N)\big). \qquad (12)$$

In each case the minimum occurs when the input is already in order, and the maximum occurs when it is in reverse order; so the MIX running time is $8A + 7B + 8C + 1 = \big(\min 8N + 1, \text{ ave } 5.75N^2 + O(N \log N), \text{ max } 7.5N^2 + 0.5N + 1\big)$.

Refinements of the bubble sort. It took a good deal of work to analyze the bubble sort; and although the techniques used in the calculations are instructive, the results are disappointing since they tell us that the bubble sort isn't really very good at all. Compared to straight insertion (Algorithm 5.2.1S), bubble sorting requires a more complicated program and takes more than twice as long!

Some of the bubble sort's deficiencies are easy to spot. For example, in Fig. 14, the first comparison in Pass 4 is redundant, as are the first two in Pass 5 and the first three in Passes 6 and 7. Notice also that elements can never move to the left more than one step per pass; so if the smallest item happens to be initially at the far right we are forced to make the maximum number of

703	908	908	908	908	908	908	908
765	703	765	897	897	897	897	897
677	765	703	765	765	765	765	765
612	677	677	703	703	703	703	703
509	612	612	677	677	677	677	677
154	509	509	612	612	653	653	653
426	154	426	509	509	612	612	612
653	426	653	426	653	509	512	512
275	653	275	653	426	512	509	509
897	275	897	275	512	426	503	503
170	897	170	512	275	503	426	426
908	170	512	170	503	275	275	275
061	512	154	503	170	170	170	170
512	061	503	154	154	154	154	154
087	503	087	087	087	087	087	087
503	087	061	061	061	061	061	061

Fig. 16. The cocktail-shaker short [shic].

comparisons. This suggests the "cocktail-shaker sort," in which alternate passes go in opposite directions (see Fig. 16). The average number of comparisons is slightly reduced by this approach. K. E. Iverson [*A Programming Language* (Wiley, 1962), 218–219] made an interesting observation in this regard: If j is an index such that R_j and R_{j+1} are not exchanged with each other on two consecutive passes in opposite directions, then R_j and R_{j+1} must be in their final position, and they need not enter into any subsequent comparisons. For example, traversing 4 3 2 1 8 6 9 7 5 from left to right yields 3 2 1 4 6 8 7 5 9; no interchange occurred between R_4 and R_5. When we traverse the latter permutation from right to left, we find R_4 still less than (the new) R_5, so we may immediately conclude that R_4 and R_5 need not participate in any further comparisons.

But none of these refinements lead to an algorithm better than straight insertion; and we already know that straight insertion isn't suitable for large N. Another idea is to eliminate most of the exchanges; since most elements simply shift left one step during an exchange, we could achieve the same effect by viewing the array differently, shifting the origin of indexing! But the resulting algorithm is no better than straight *selection*, Algorithm 5.2.3S, which we shall study later.

In short, the bubble sort seems to have nothing to recommend it, except a catchy name and the fact that it leads to some interesting theoretical problems.

Batcher's parallel method. If we are going to have an exchange algorithm whose running time is faster than order N^2, we need to select some *nonadjacent* pairs of keys (K_i, K_j) for comparisons; otherwise we will need as many exchanges as the original permutation has inversions, and the average number of inversions is $\frac{1}{4}(N^2 - N)$. An ingenious way to program a sequence of comparisons, looking for potential exchanges, was discovered in 1964 by K. E. Batcher [see *Proc. AFIPS Spring Joint Computer Conference* **32** (1968), 307–314]. His method is not at all obvious; in fact, a fairly intricate proof is needed just to show that it is valid, since comparatively few comparisons are made. We shall discuss two proofs, one in this section and another in Section 5.3.4.

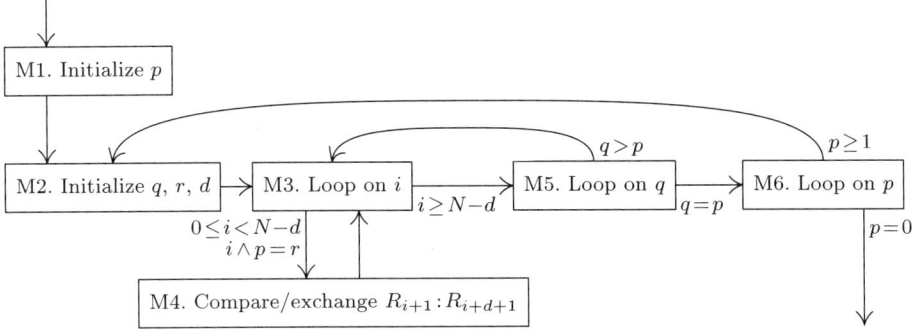

Fig. 17. Algorithm M.

Batcher's sorting scheme is similar to shellsort, but the comparisons are done in a novel way so that no propagation of exchanges is necessary. We can, for instance, compare Table 1 (on the next page) to Table 5.2.1–3; Batcher's method achieves the effect of 8-sorting, 4-sorting, 2-sorting, and 1-sorting, but the comparisons do not overlap. Since Batcher's algorithm essentially merges pairs of sorted subsequences, it may be called the "merge exchange sort."

Algorithm M (*Merge exchange*). Records $R_1, \ldots, R_N$ are rearranged in place; after sorting is complete their keys will be in order, $K_1 \leq \cdots \leq K_N$. We assume that $N \geq 2$.

M1. [Initialize p.] Set $p \leftarrow 2^{t-1}$, where $t = \lceil \lg N \rceil$ is the least integer such that $2^t \geq N$. (Steps M2 through M5 will be performed for $p = 2^{t-1}, 2^{t-2}, \ldots, 1$.)

M2. [Initialize q, r, d.] Set $q \leftarrow 2^{t-1}$, $r \leftarrow 0$, $d \leftarrow p$.

M3. [Loop on i.] For all i such that $0 \leq i < N - d$ and $i \,\&\, p = r$, do step M4. Then go to step M5. (Here $i \,\&\, p$ means the "bitwise and" of the binary representations of i and p; each bit of the result is zero except where both i and p have 1-bits in corresponding positions. Thus $13 \,\&\, 21 = (1101)_2 \,\&\, (10101)_2 = (00101)_2 = 5$. At this point, d is an odd multiple of p, and p is a power of 2, so that $i \,\&\, p \neq (i+d) \,\&\, p$; it follows that the actions of step M4 can be done for all relevant i in any order, even simultaneously.)

M4. [Compare/exchange $R_{i+1}:R_{i+d+1}$.] If $K_{i+1} > K_{i+d+1}$, interchange the records $R_{i+1} \leftrightarrow R_{i+d+1}$.

M5. [Loop on q.] If $q \neq p$, set $d \leftarrow q - p$, $q \leftarrow q/2$, $r \leftarrow p$, and return to M3.

M6. [Loop on p.] (At this point the permutation $K_1 K_2 \ldots K_N$ is p-ordered.) Set $p \leftarrow \lfloor p/2 \rfloor$. If $p > 0$, go back to M2. ∎

Table 1
MERGE-EXCHANGE SORTING (BATCHER'S METHOD)

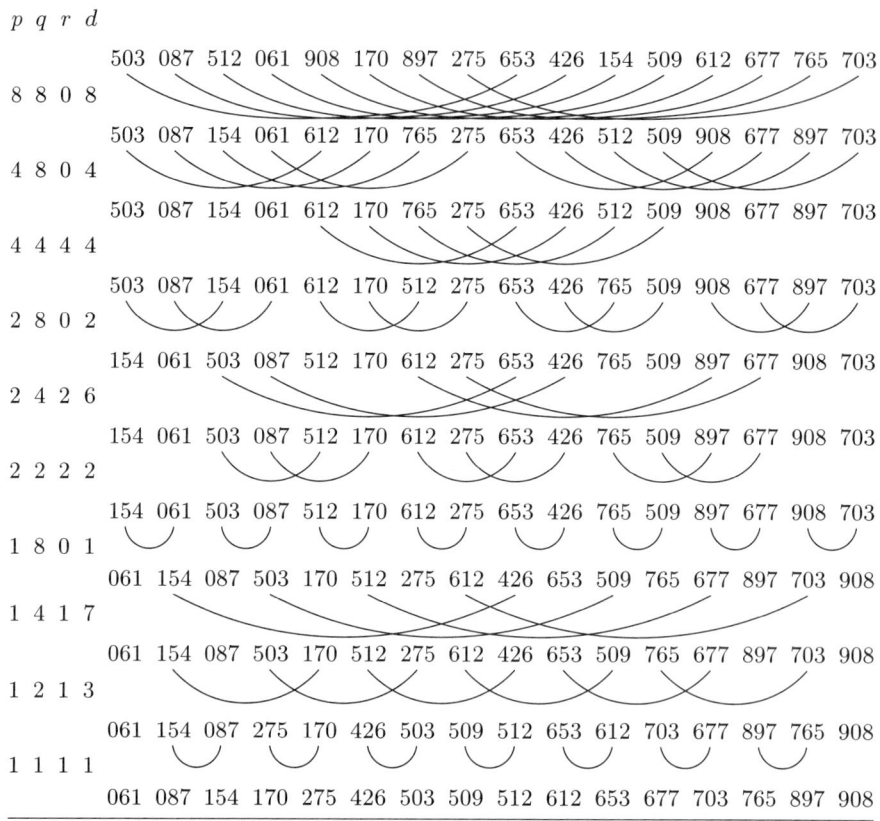

```
p q r d
          503 087 512 061 908 170 897 275 653 426 154 509 612 677 765 703
8 8 0 8
          503 087 154 061 612 170 765 275 653 426 512 509 908 677 897 703
4 8 0 4
          503 087 154 061 612 170 765 275 653 426 512 509 908 677 897 703
4 4 4 4
          503 087 154 061 612 170 512 275 653 426 765 509 908 677 897 703
2 8 0 2
          154 061 503 087 512 170 612 275 653 426 765 509 897 677 908 703
2 4 2 6
          154 061 503 087 512 170 612 275 653 426 765 509 897 677 908 703
2 2 2 2
          154 061 503 087 512 170 612 275 653 426 765 509 897 677 908 703
1 8 0 1
          061 154 087 503 170 512 275 612 426 653 509 765 677 897 703 908
1 4 1 7
          061 154 087 503 170 512 275 612 426 653 509 765 677 897 703 908
1 2 1 3
          061 154 087 275 170 426 503 509 512 653 612 703 677 897 765 908
1 1 1 1
          061 087 154 170 275 426 503 509 512 612 653 677 703 765 897 908
```

Table 1 illustrates the method for $N = 16$. Notice that the algorithm sorts N elements essentially by sorting $R_1, R_3, R_5, \ldots$ and $R_2, R_4, R_6, \ldots$ independently; then we perform steps M2 through M5 for $p = 1$, in order to merge the two sorted sequences together.

In order to prove that the magic sequence of comparison/exchanges specified in Algorithm M actually will sort all possible input files $R_1 R_2 \ldots R_N$, we must show only that steps M2 through M5 will merge all 2-ordered files $R_1 R_2 \ldots R_N$ when $p = 1$. For this purpose we can use the lattice-path method of Section 5.2.1 (see Fig. 11 on page 87); each 2-ordered permutation of $\{1, 2, \ldots, N\}$ corresponds uniquely to a path from $(0,0)$ to $(\lceil N/2 \rceil, \lfloor N/2 \rfloor)$ in a lattice diagram. Figure 18(a) shows an example for $N = 16$, corresponding to the permutation 1 3 2 4 10 5 11 6 13 7 14 8 15 9 16 12. When we perform step M3 with $p = 1$, $q = 2^{t-1}$, $r = 0$, $d = 1$, the effect is to compare (and possibly exchange) $R_1 : R_2$, $R_3 : R_4$, etc. This operation corresponds to a simple transformation of the lattice path, "folding" it about the diagonal if necessary so that it never goes above the diagonal. (See Fig. 18(b) and the proof in exercise 10.) The next iterations of step M3 have $p = r = 1$, and $d = 2^{t-1} - 1, 2^{t-2} - 1, \ldots, 1$; their effect is to compare/exchange $R_2\!:\!R_{2+d}$, $R_4\!:\!R_{4+d}$, etc., and again there is a simple lattice interpretation: The path is "folded" about a line $\frac{1}{2}(d+1)$ units below the diagonal. See Fig. 18(c) and (d); eventually we get to the path in Fig. 18(e), which corresponds to a completely sorted permutation. This completes a "geometric proof" that Batcher's algorithm is valid; we might call it sorting by folding!

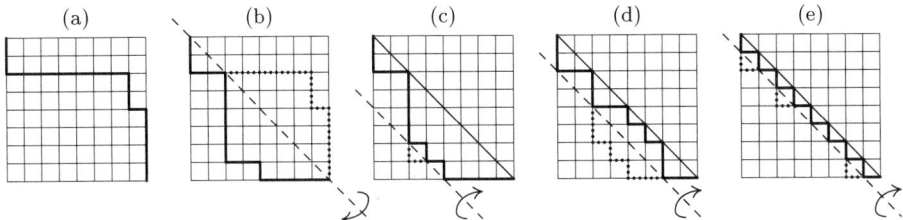

Fig. 18. A geometric interpretation of Batcher's method, $N = 16$.

A MIX program for Algorithm M appears in exercise 12. Unfortunately the amount of bookkeeping needed to control the sequence of comparisons is rather large, so the program is less efficient than other methods we have seen. But it has one important redeeming feature: All comparison/exchanges specified by a given iteration of step M3 can be done *simultaneously*, on computers or networks that allow parallel computations. With such parallel operations, sorting is completed in $\frac{1}{2}\lceil \lg N \rceil (\lceil \lg N \rceil + 1)$ steps, and this is about as fast as any general method known. For example, *1024 elements can be sorted in only 55 parallel steps by Batcher's method*. The nearest competitor is Pratt's method (see exercise 5.2.1–30), which uses either 40 or 73 steps, depending on how we count; if we are willing to allow overlapping comparisons as long as no overlapping exchanges are necessary, Pratt's method requires only 40 comparison/exchange cycles to sort 1024 elements. For further comments, see Section 5.3.4.

Quicksort. The sequence of comparisons in Batcher's method is predetermined; we compare the same pairs of keys each time, regardless of what we may have learned about the file from previous comparisons. The same is largely true of the bubble sort, although Algorithm B does make limited use of previous knowledge in order to reduce its work at the right end of the file. Let us now turn to a quite different strategy, which uses the result of each comparison to determine what keys are to be compared next. Such a strategy is inappropriate for parallel computations, but on computers that work serially it can be quite fruitful.

The basic idea of the following method is to take one record, say R_1, and to move it to the final position that it should occupy in the sorted file, say position s. While determining this final position, we will also rearrange the other records so that there will be none with greater keys to the left of position s, and none with smaller keys to the right. Thus the file will have been partitioned in such a way

that the original sorting problem is reduced to two simpler problems, namely
to sort $R_1 \ldots R_{s-1}$ and (independently) to sort $R_{s+1} \ldots R_N$. We can apply the
same technique to each of these subfiles, until the job is done.

There are several ways to achieve such a partitioning into left and right
subfiles; the following scheme due to R. Sedgewick seems to be best, for reasons
that will become clearer when we analyze the algorithm: Keep two pointers,
i and j, with $i = 2$ and $j = N$ initially. If R_i is eventually supposed to be
part of the left-hand subfile after partitioning (we can tell this by comparing
K_i with K_1), increase i by 1, and continue until encountering a record R_i that
belongs to the right-hand subfile. Similarly, decrease j by 1 until encountering
a record R_j belonging to the left-hand subfile. If $i < j$, exchange R_i with R_j;
then move on to process the next records in the same way, "burning the candle
at both ends" until $i \geq j$. The partitioning is finally completed by exchanging
R_j with R_1. For example, consider what happens to our file of sixteen numbers:

$$\begin{array}{c} i \\ \downarrow \end{array} \qquad\qquad\qquad\qquad\qquad\qquad\qquad\qquad\qquad\qquad \begin{array}{c} j \\ \downarrow \end{array}$$

Initial file: [503 **087** 512 061 908 170 897 275 653 426 154 509 612 677 765 **703**]

1st exchange: 503 087 **512** 061 908 170 897 275 653 426 **154** 509 612 677 765 703

2nd exchange: 503 087 154 061 **908** 170 897 275 653 **426** 512 509 612 677 765 703

3rd exchange: 503 087 154 061 426 170 **897 275** 653 908 512 509 612 677 765 703

Pointers cross: 503 087 154 061 426 170 **275 897** 653 908 512 509 612 677 765 703

Partitioned file:[275 087 154 061 426 170] **503** [**897** 653 908 512 509 612 677 765 703]

$$\qquad\qquad\qquad\qquad\qquad\qquad\qquad \begin{array}{cc} \uparrow & \uparrow \\ j & i \end{array}$$

(In order to indicate the positions of i and j, keys K_i and K_j are shown here in
boldface type.)

Table 2 shows how our example file gets completely sorted by this approach,
in 11 stages. Brackets indicate subfiles that still need to be sorted; double
brackets identify the subfile of current interest. Inside a computer, the current
subfile can be represented by boundary values (l, r), and the other subfiles by
a stack of additional pairs (l_k, r_k). Whenever a file is subdivided, we put the
longer subfile on the stack and commence work on the shorter one, until we reach
trivially short files; this strategy guarantees that the stack will never contain
more than $\lg N$ entries (see exercise 20).

The sorting procedure just described may be called *partition-exchange sorting*; it is due to C. A. R. Hoare, whose interesting paper [*Comp. J.* **5** (1962),
10–15] contains one of the most comprehensive accounts of a sorting method that
has ever been published. Hoare dubbed his method "quicksort," and that name
is not inappropriate, since the inner loops of the computation are extremely fast
on most computers. All comparisons during a given stage are made against the
same key, so this key may be kept in a register. Only a single index needs to
be changed between comparisons. Furthermore, the amount of data movement

Table 2

QUICKSORTING

	(l,r)	Stack
⟦503 087 512 061 908 170 897 275 653 426 154 509 612 677 765 703⟧	(1,16)	–
⟦275 087 154 061 426 170⟧ 503 ⟦897 653 908 512 509 612 677 765 703⟧	(1,6)	(8,16)
⟦170 087 154 061⟧ 275 426 503 ⟦897 653 908 512 509 612 677 765 703⟧	(1,4)	(8,16)
⟦061 087 154⟧ 170 275 426 503 ⟦897 653 908 512 509 612 677 765 703⟧	(1,3)	(8,16)
061 ⟦087 154⟧ 170 275 426 503 ⟦897 653 908 512 509 612 677 765 703⟧	(2,3)	(8,16)
061 087 154 170 275 426 503 ⟦897 653 908 512 509 612 677 765 703⟧	(8,16)	–
061 087 154 170 275 426 503 ⟦765 653 703 512 509 612 677⟧ 897 908	(8,14)	–
061 087 154 170 275 426 503 ⟦677 653 703 512 509 612⟧ 765 897 908	(8,13)	–
061 087 154 170 275 426 503 ⟦509 653 612 512⟧ 677 703 765 897 908	(8,11)	–
061 087 154 170 275 426 503 509 ⟦653 612 512⟧ 677 703 765 897 908	(9,11)	–
061 087 154 170 275 426 503 509 ⟦512 612⟧ 653 677 703 765 897 908	(9,10)	–
061 087 154 170 275 426 503 509 512 612 653 677 703 765 897 908	–	–

is quite reasonable; the computation in Table 2, for example, makes only 17 exchanges.

The bookkeeping required to control i, j, and the stack is not difficult, but it makes the quicksort partitioning procedure most suitable for fairly large N. Therefore the following algorithm uses another strategy after the subfiles have become short.

Algorithm Q (*Quicksort*). Records $R_1, \ldots, R_N$ are rearranged in place; after sorting is complete their keys will be in order, $K_1 \leq \cdots \leq K_N$. An auxiliary stack with at most $\lfloor \lg N \rfloor$ entries is needed for temporary storage. This algorithm follows the quicksort partitioning procedure described in the text above, with slight modifications for extra efficiency:

a) We assume the presence of artificial keys $K_0 = -\infty$ and $K_{N+1} = +\infty$ such that

$$K_0 \leq K_i \leq K_{N+1} \qquad \text{for } 1 \leq i \leq N. \tag{13}$$

(Equality is allowed.)

b) Subfiles of M or fewer elements are left unsorted until the very end of the procedure; then a single pass of straight insertion is used to produce the final ordering. Here $M \geq 1$ is a parameter that should be chosen as described in the text below. (This idea, due to R. Sedgewick, saves some of the overhead that would be necessary if we applied straight insertion directly to each small subfile, unless locality of reference is significant.)

c) Records with equal keys are exchanged, although it is not strictly necessary to do so. (This idea, due to R. C. Singleton, keeps the inner loops fast and helps to split subfiles nearly in half when equal elements are present; see exercise 18.)

Q1. [Initialize.] If $N \leq M$, go to step Q9. Otherwise set the stack empty, and set $l \leftarrow 1$, $r \leftarrow N$.

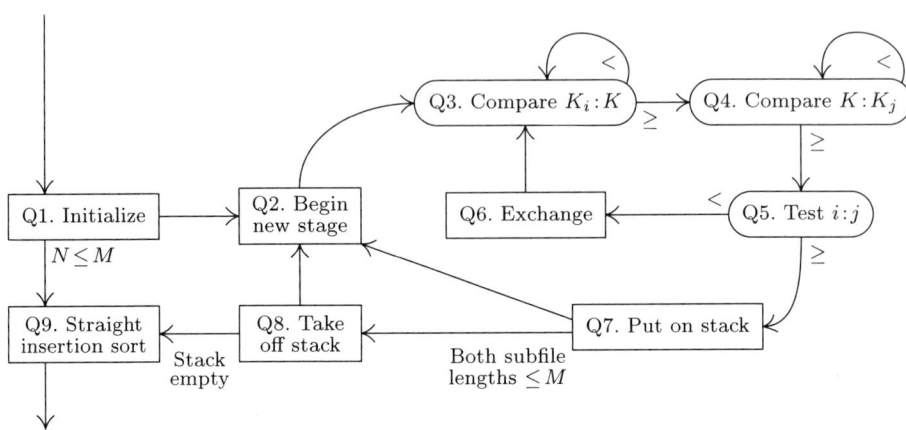

Fig. 19. Partition-exchange sorting (quicksort).

Q2. [Begin new stage.] (We now wish to sort the subfile $R_l \ldots R_r$; from the nature of the algorithm, we have $r \geq l + M$, and $K_{l-1} \leq K_i \leq K_{r+1}$ for $l \leq i \leq r$.) Set $i \leftarrow l$, $j \leftarrow r+1$; and set $K \leftarrow K_l$. (The text below discusses alternative choices for K that might be better.)

Q3. [Compare $K_i : K$.] (At this point the file has been rearranged so that

$$K_k \leq K \quad \text{for } l-1 \leq k \leq i, \qquad K \leq K_k \quad \text{for } j \leq k \leq r+1; \qquad (14)$$

and $l \leq i < j$.) Increase i by 1; then if $K_i < K$, repeat this step. (Since $K_j \geq K$, the iteration must terminate with $i \leq j$.)

Q4. [Compare $K : K_j$.] Decrease j by 1; then if $K < K_j$, repeat this step. (Since $K \geq K_{i-1}$, the iteration must terminate with $j \geq i-1$.)

Q5. [Test $i : j$.] (At this point, (14) holds except for $k = i$ and $k = j$; also $K_i \geq K \geq K_j$, and $r \geq j \geq i-1 \geq l$.) If $j \leq i$, interchange $R_l \leftrightarrow R_j$ and go to step Q7.

Q6. [Exchange.] Interchange $R_i \leftrightarrow R_j$ and go back to step Q3.

Q7. [Put on stack.] (Now the subfile $R_l \ldots R_j \ldots R_r$ has been partitioned so that $K_k \leq K_j$ for $l-1 \leq k \leq j$ and $K_j \leq K_k$ for $j \leq k \leq r+1$.) If $r-j \geq j-l > M$, insert $(j+1, r)$ on top of the stack, set $r \leftarrow j-1$, and go to Q2. If $j-l > r-j > M$, insert $(l, j-1)$ on top of the stack, set $l \leftarrow j+1$, and go to Q2. (Each entry (a, b) on the stack is a request to sort the subfile $R_a \ldots R_b$ at some future time.) Otherwise if $r-j > M \geq j-l$, set $l \leftarrow j+1$ and go to Q2; or if $j-l > M \geq r-j$, set $r \leftarrow j-1$ and go to Q2.

Q8. [Take off stack.] If the stack is nonempty, remove its top entry (l', r'), set $l \leftarrow l'$, $r \leftarrow r'$, and return to step Q2.

Q9. [Straight insertion sort.] For $j = 2, 3, \ldots, N$, if $K_{j-1} > K_j$ do the following operations: Set $K \leftarrow K_j$, $R \leftarrow R_j$, $i \leftarrow j-1$; then set $R_{i+1} \leftarrow R_i$ and $i \leftarrow i-1$ one or more times until $K_i \leq K$; then set $R_{i+1} \leftarrow R$. (This is Algorithm 5.2.1S, modified as suggested in exercise 5.2.1–10 and answer 5.2.1–33. Step Q9 may be omitted if $M = 1$. *Caution:* The final straight insertion might conceal bugs in steps Q1–Q8; don't trust an implementation just because it gives the correct answers!) ∎

The corresponding MIX program is rather long, but not complicated; in fact, a large part of the coding is devoted to step Q7, which just fools around with the variables in a very straightforward way.

Program Q (*Quicksort*). Records to be sorted appear in locations INPUT+1 through INPUT+N; assume that locations INPUT and INPUT+N+1 contain, respectively, the smallest and largest values possible in MIX. The stack is kept in locations STACK+1, STACK+2, ...; see exercise 20 for the exact number of locations to set aside for the stack. $rI2 \equiv l$, $rI3 \equiv r$, $rI4 \equiv i$, $rI5 \equiv j$, $rI6 \equiv$ size of stack, $rA \equiv K \equiv R$. We assume that $N > M$.

	A	EQU	2:3		First component of stack entry.
	B	EQU	4:5		Second component of stack entry.
01	START	ENT6	0	1	*Q1. Initialize.* Set stack empty.
02		ENT2	1	1	$l \leftarrow 1$.
03		ENT3	N	1	$r \leftarrow N$.
04	2H	ENT5	1,3	A	*Q2. Begin new stage.* $j \leftarrow r+1$.
05		LDA	INPUT,2	A	$K \leftarrow K_l$.
06		ENT4	1,2	A	$i \leftarrow l+1$.
07		JMP	0F	A	To Q3 omitting "$i \leftarrow i+1$".
08	6H	LDX	INPUT,4	B	*Q6. Exchange.*
09		ENT1	INPUT,4	B	
10		MOVE	INPUT,5	B	
11		STX	INPUT,5	B	$R_i \leftrightarrow R_j$.
12	3H	INC4	1	$C'-A$	*Q3. Compare $K_i:K$.* $i \leftarrow i+1$.
13	0H	CMPA	INPUT,4	C'	
14		JG	3B	C'	Repeat if $K > K_i$.
15	4H	DEC5	1	$C-C'$	*Q4. Compare $K:K_j$.* $j \leftarrow j-1$.
16		CMPA	INPUT,5	$C-C'$	
17		JL	4B	$C-C'$	Repeat if $K < K_j$.
18	5H	ENTX	0,5	$B+A$	*Q5. Test $i:j$.*
19		DECX	0,4	$B+A$	
20		JXP	6B	$B+A$	To Q6 if $j > i$.
21		LDX	INPUT,5	A	
22		STX	INPUT,2	A	$R_l \leftarrow R_j$.
23		STA	INPUT,5	A	$R_j \leftarrow R$.
24	7H	ENT4	0,3	A	*Q7. Put on stack.*
25		DEC4	M,5	A	$rI4 \leftarrow r-j-M$.
26		ENT1	0,5	A	
27		DEC1	M,2	A	$rI1 \leftarrow j-l-M$.
28		ENTA	0,4	A	
29		DECA	0,1	A	
30		JANN	1F	A	Jump if $r-j \geq j-l$.
31		J1NP	8F	A'	To Q8 if $M \geq j-l > r-j$.
32		J4NP	3F	$S'+A''$	Jump if $j-l > M \geq r-j$.

33		INC6 1	S'	(Now $j - l > r - j > M$.)
34		ST2 STACK,6(A)	S'	
35		ENTA -1,5	S'	
36		STA STACK,6(B)	S'	$(l, j{-}1) \Rightarrow$ stack.
37	4H	ENT2 1,5	$S' + A'''$	$l \leftarrow j + 1$.
38		JMP 2B	$S' + A'''$	To Q2.
39	1H	J4NP 8F	$A - A'$	To Q8 if $M \geq r - j \geq j - l$.
40		J1NP 4B	$S - S' + A'''$	Jump if $r - j > M \geq j - l$.
41		INC6 1	$S - S'$	(Now $r - j \geq j - l > M$.)
42		ST3 STACK,6(B)	$S - S'$	
43		ENTA 1,5	$S - S'$	
44		STA STACK,6(A)	$S - S'$	$(j{+}1, r) \Rightarrow$ stack.
45	3H	ENT3 -1,5	$S - S' + A''$	$r \leftarrow j - 1$.
46		JMP 2B	$S - S' + A''$	To Q2.
47	8H	LD2 STACK,6(A)	$S + 1$	Q8. Take off stack.
48		LD3 STACK,6(B)	$S + 1$	
49		DEC6 1	$S + 1$	$(l, r) \Leftarrow$ stack.
50		J6NN 2B	$S + 1$	To Q2 if stack wasn't empty.
51	9H	ENT5 2-N	1	Q9. Straight insertion sort. $j \leftarrow 2$.
52	2H	LDA INPUT+N,5	$N - 1$	$K \leftarrow K_j$, $R \leftarrow R_j$.
53		CMPA INPUT+N-1,5	$N - 1$	(In this loop, rI5 $\equiv j - N$.)
54		JGE 6F	$N - 1$	Jump if $K \geq K_{j-1}$.
55	3H	ENT4 N-1,5	D	$i \leftarrow j - 1$.
56	4H	LDX INPUT,4	E	
57		STX INPUT+1,4	E	$R_{i+1} \leftarrow R_i$.
58		DEC4 1	E	$i \leftarrow i - 1$.
59		CMPA INPUT,4	E	
60		JL 4B	E	Repeat if $K < K_i$.
61	5H	STA INPUT+1,4	D	$R_{i+1} \leftarrow R$.
62	6H	INC5 1	$N - 1$	
63		J5NP 2B	$N - 1$	$2 \leq j \leq N$. ∎

Analysis of quicksort. The timing information shown with Program Q is not hard to derive using Kirchhoff's conservation law (Section 1.3.3) and the fact that everything put onto the stack is eventually removed again. Kirchhoff's law applied at Q2 also shows that

$$A = 1 + (S' + A''') + (S - S' + A'') + S = 2S + 1 + A'' + A''', \qquad (15)$$

hence the total running time comes to

$$24A + 11B + 4C + 3D + 8E + 7N + 9S \text{ units},$$

where

A = number of partitioning stages;
B = number of exchanges in step Q6;
C = number of comparisons made while partitioning;
D = number of times $K_{j-1} > K_j$ during straight insertion (step Q9);
E = number of inversions removed by straight insertion;
S = number of times an entry is put on the stack. $\qquad (16)$

By analyzing these six quantities, we will be able to make an intelligent choice of the parameter M that specifies the "threshold" between straight insertion and partitioning. The analysis is particularly instructive because the algorithm is rather complex; the unraveling of this complexity makes a particularly good illustration of important techniques. However, nonmathematical readers are advised to skip to Eq. (25).

As in most other analyses of this chapter, we shall assume that the keys to be sorted are distinct; exercise 18 indicates that equalities between keys do not seriously harm the efficiency of Algorithm Q, and in fact they seem to help it. Since the method depends only on the relative order of the keys, we may as well assume that they are simply $\{1, 2, \ldots, N\}$ in some order.

We can attack this problem by considering the behavior of the very first partitioning stage, which takes us to Q7 for the first time. Once this partitioning has been achieved, *both of the subfiles $R_1 \ldots R_{j-1}$ and $R_{j+1} \ldots R_N$ will be in random order if the original file was in random order*, since the relative order of elements in these subfiles has no effect on the partitioning algorithm. Therefore the contribution of subsequent partitionings can be determined by induction on N. (This is an important observation, since some alternative algorithms that violate this property have turned out to be significantly slower; see *Computing Surveys* **6** (1974), 287–289.)

Let s be the value of the first key, K_1, and assume that exactly t of the first s keys $\{K_1, \ldots, K_s\}$ are greater than s. (Remember that the keys being sorted are the integers $\{1, 2, \ldots, N\}$.) If $s = 1$, it is easy to see what happens during the first stage of partitioning: Step Q3 is performed once, step Q4 is performed N times, and then step Q5 takes us to Q7. So the contributions of the first stage in this case are $A = 1$, $B = 0$, $C = N + 1$. A similar but slightly more complicated argument when $s > 1$ (see exercise 21) shows that the contributions of the first stage to the total running time are, in general,

$$A = 1, \; B = t, \; C = N + 1, \qquad \text{for } 1 \le s \le N. \tag{17}$$

To this we must add the contributions of the later stages, which sort subfiles of $s - 1$ and $N - s$ elements, respectively.

If we assume that the original file is in random order, it is now possible to write down formulas that define the generating functions for the probability distributions of $A, B, \ldots, S$ (see exercise 22). But for simplicity we shall consider here only the *average* values of these quantities, $A_N, B_N, \ldots, S_N$, as functions of N. Consider, for example, the average number of comparisons, C_N, that occur during the partitioning process. When $N \le M$, $C_N = 0$. Otherwise, since any given value of s occurs with probability $1/N$, we have

$$C_N = \frac{1}{N} \sum_{s=1}^{N} (N + 1 + C_{s-1} + C_{N-s})$$

$$= N + 1 + \frac{2}{N} \sum_{0 \le k < N} C_k, \qquad \text{for } N > M. \tag{18}$$

Similar formulas hold for other quantities A_N, B_N, D_N, E_N, S_N (see exercise 23).

There is a simple way to solve recurrence relations of the form

$$x_n = f_n + \frac{2}{n} \sum_{0 \le k < n} x_k, \qquad \text{for } n \ge m. \qquad (19)$$

The first step is to get rid of the summation sign: Since

$$(n+1)x_{n+1} = (n+1)f_{n+1} + 2 \sum_{0 \le k \le n} x_k,$$

$$nx_n = nf_n + 2 \sum_{0 \le k < n} x_k,$$

we may subtract, obtaining

$$(n+1)x_{n+1} - nx_n = g_n + 2x_n, \qquad \text{where } g_n = (n+1)f_{n+1} - nf_n.$$

Now the recurrence takes the much simpler form

$$(n+1)x_{n+1} = (n+2)x_n + g_n, \qquad \text{for } n \ge m. \qquad (20)$$

Any recurrence relation that has the general form

$$a_n x_{n+1} = b_n x_n + g_n \qquad (21)$$

can be reduced to a summation if we multiply both sides by the "summation factor" $a_0\, a_1 \ldots a_{n-1}/b_0\, b_1 \ldots b_n$; we obtain

$$y_{n+1} = y_n + c_n, \qquad \text{where} \quad y_n = \frac{a_0 \ldots a_{n-1}}{b_0 \ldots b_{n-1}} x_n, \qquad c_n = \frac{a_0 \ldots a_{n-1}}{b_0\, b_1 \ldots b_n} g_n. \qquad (22)$$

In our case (20), the summation factor is simply $n!/(n+2)! = 1/(n+1)(n+2)$, so we find that the simple relation

$$\frac{x_{n+1}}{n+2} = \frac{x_n}{n+1} + \frac{(n+1)f_{n+1} - nf_n}{(n+1)(n+2)}, \qquad \text{for } n \ge m, \qquad (23)$$

is a consequence of (19).

For example, if we set $f_n = 1/n$, we get the unexpected result $x_n/(n+1) = x_m/(m+1)$ for all $n \ge m$. If we set $f_n = n+1$, we get

$$x_n/(n+1) = 2/(n+1) + 2/n + \cdots + 2/(m+2) + x_m/(m+1)$$
$$= 2\,(H_{n+1} - H_{m+1}) + x_m/(m+1),$$

for all $n \ge m$. Thus we obtain the solution to (18) by setting $m = M + 1$ and $x_n = 0$ for $n \le M$; the required formula is

$$C_N = (N+1)\,(2H_{N+1} - 2H_{M+2} + 1)$$

$$\approx 2\,(N+1)\ln\left(\frac{N+1}{M+2}\right), \qquad \text{for } N > M. \qquad (24)$$

Exercise 6.2.2–8 proves that, when $M = 1$, the standard deviation of C_N is asymptotically $\sqrt{(21 - 2\pi^2)/3\,N}$; this is reasonably small compared to (24).

The other quantities can be found in a similar way (see exercise 23); when $N > M$ we have

$$A_N = 2\,(N+1)/(M+2) - 1,$$

$$B_N = \tfrac{1}{6}\,(N+1)\bigl(2H_{N+1} - 2H_{M+2} + 1 - 6/(M+2)\bigr) + \tfrac{1}{2},$$

$$D_N = (N+1)\bigl(1 - 2H_{M+1}/(M+2)\bigr),$$

$$E_N = \tfrac{1}{6}\,(N+1)M(M-1)/(M+2);$$

$$S_N = (N+1)/(2M+3) - 1, \qquad \text{for } N > 2M + 1. \tag{25}$$

The discussion above shows that it is possible to carry out an exact analysis of the average running time of a fairly complex program, by using techniques that we have previously applied only to simpler cases.

Formulas (24) and (25) can be used to determine the best value of M on a particular computer. In MIX's case, Program Q requires $(35/3)(N+1)H_{N+1} + \tfrac{1}{6}(N+1)f(M) - 34.5$ units of time on the average, for $N > 2M + 1$, where

$$f(M) = 8M - 70H_{M+2} + 71 - 36\,\frac{H_{M+1}}{M+2} + \frac{270}{M+2} + \frac{54}{2M+3}. \tag{26}$$

We want to choose M so that $f(M)$ is a minimum, and a simple computer calculation shows that $M = 9$ is best. The average running time of Program Q is approximately $11.667(N+1)\ln N - 1.74N - 18.74$ units when $M = 9$, for large N.

So Program Q is quite fast, on the average, considering that it requires very little memory space. Its speed is primarily due to the fact that the inner loops, in steps Q3 and Q4, are extremely short — only three MIX instructions each (see lines 12–14 and 15–17). The number of exchanges, in step Q6, is only about $1/6$ of the number of comparisons in steps Q3 and Q4; hence we have saved a significant amount of time by not comparing i to j in the inner loops.

But what is the *worst* case of Algorithm Q? Are there some inputs that it does not handle efficiently? The answer to this question is quite embarrassing: If the original file is already in order, with $K_1 < K_2 < \cdots < K_N$, each "partitioning" operation is almost useless, since it reduces the size of the subfile by only one element! So this situation (which ought to be easiest of all to sort) makes quicksort anything but quick; the sorting time becomes proportional to N^2 instead of $N \lg N$. (See exercise 25.) Unlike the other sorting methods we have seen, Algorithm Q *likes* a disordered file.

Hoare suggested two ways to remedy the situation, in his original paper, by choosing a better value of the test key K that governs the partitioning. One of his recommendations was to choose a *random* integer q between l and r in the last part of step Q2; we can change the instruction "$K \leftarrow K_l$" to

$$K \leftarrow K_q, \qquad R \leftarrow R_q, \qquad R_q \leftarrow R_l, \qquad R_l \leftarrow R \tag{27}$$

in that step. (The last assignment "$R_l \leftarrow R$" is necessary; otherwise step Q4 would stop with $j = l - 1$ when K is the smallest key of the subfile being

partitioned.) According to Eqs. (25), such random integers need to be calculated
only $2(N+1)/(M+2)-1$ times on the average, so the additional running time
is not substantial; and the random choice gives good protection against the
occurrence of the worst case. Even a mildly random choice of q should be safe.
Exercise 42 proves that, with truly random q, the probability of more than, say,
$20N \ln N$ comparisons will surely be less than 10^{-8}.

Hoare's second suggestion was to look at a small sample of the file and to
choose a median value of the sample. This approach was adopted by R. C.
Singleton [*CACM* **12** (1969), 185–187], who suggested letting K_q be the median
of the three values

$$K_l, \qquad K_{\lfloor (l+r)/2 \rfloor}, \qquad K_r. \qquad (28)$$

Singleton's procedure cuts the number of comparisons down from $2N \ln N$ to
about $\frac{12}{7} N \ln N$ (see exercise 29). It can be shown that B_N is asymptotically
$C_N/5$ instead of $C_N/6$ in this case, so the median method slightly increases the
amount of time spent in transferring the data; the total running time therefore
decreases by roughly 8 percent. (See exercise 56 for a detailed analysis.) The
worst case is still of order N^2, but such slow behavior will hardly ever occur.

W. D. Frazer and A. C. McKellar [*JACM* **17** (1970), 496–507] have suggested
taking a much larger sample consisting of $2^k - 1$ records, where k is chosen so
that $2^k \approx N/\ln N$. The sample can be sorted by the usual quicksort method,
then inserted among the remaining records by taking k passes over the file
(partitioning it into 2^k subfiles, bounded by the elements of the sample). Finally
the subfiles are sorted. The average number of comparisons required by such
a "samplesort" procedure is about the same as in Singleton's median method,
when N is in a practical range, but it decreases to the asymptotic value $N \lg N$
as $N \to \infty$.

An absolute guarantee of $O(N \log N)$ sorting time in the worst case, together
with fast running time on the average, can be obtained by combining quicksort
with other schemes. For example, D. R. Musser [*Software Practice & Exper.* **27**
(1997), 983–993] has suggested adding a "depth of partitioning" component to
each entry on quicksort's stack. If any subfile is found to have been subdivided
more than, say, $2 \lg N$ times, we can abandon Algorithm Q and switch to Algorithm 5.2.3H. The inner loop time remains unchanged, so the average total
running time remains almost the same as before.

Robert Sedgewick has analyzed a number of optimized variants of quicksort
in *Acta Informatica* **7** (1977), 327–356, and in *CACM* **21** (1978), 847–857,
22 (1979), 368. See also J. L. Bentley and M. D. McIlroy, *Software Practice
& Exper.* **23** (1993), 1249–1265, for a version of quicksort that has been tuned
up to fit the UNIX® software library, based on 15 further years of experience.

Radix exchange. We come now to a method that is quite different from
any of the sorting schemes we have seen before; it makes use of the *binary
representation* of the keys, so it is intended only for binary computers. Instead
of comparing two keys with each other, this method inspects individual bits of

the keys, to see if they are 0 or 1. In other respects it has the characteristics of exchange sorting, and, in fact, it is rather similar to quicksort. Since it depends on radix 2 representations, we call it "radix exchange sorting." The algorithm can be described roughly as follows:

i) Sort the sequence on its *most significant binary bit*, so that all keys that have a leading 0 come before all keys that have a leading 1. This sorting is done by finding the leftmost key K_i that has a leading 1, and the rightmost key K_j with a leading 0. Then R_i and R_j are exchanged and the process is repeated until $i > j$.

ii) Let F_0 be the elements with leading bit 0, and let F_1 be the others. Apply the radix exchange sorting method to F_0 (starting now at the *second* bit from the left instead of the most significant bit), until F_0 is completely sorted; then do the same for F_1.

For example, Table 3 shows how the radix exchange sort acts on our 16 random numbers, which have been converted to octal notation. Stage 1 in the table shows the initial input, and after exchanging on the first bit we get to stage 2. Stage 2 sorts the first group on bit 2, and stage 3 works on bit 3. (The reader should mentally convert the octal notation to 10-bit binary numbers. For example, *0232* stands for $(0\,010\,011\,010)_2$.) When we reach stage 5, after sorting on bit 4, we find that each group remaining has but a single element, so this part of the file need not be further examined. The notation "$^4[0232\ 0252]$" means that the subfile *0232 0252* is waiting to be sorted on bit 4 from the left. In this particular case, no progress occurs when sorting on bit 4; we need to go to bit 5 before the items are separated.

The complete sorting process shown in Table 3 takes 22 stages, somewhat more than the comparable number for quicksort (Table 2). Similarly, the number of bit inspections, 82, is rather high; but we shall see that the number of bit inspections for large N is actually less than the number of comparisons made by quicksort, assuming a uniform distribution of keys. The total number of exchanges in Table 3 is 17, which is quite reasonable. Note that bit inspections never have to go past bit 7 here, although 10-bit numbers are being sorted.

As in quicksort, we can use a stack to keep track of the "boundary line information" for waiting subfiles. Instead of sorting the smallest subfile first, it is convenient simply to go from left to right, since the stack size in this case can never exceed the number of bits in the keys being sorted. In the following algorithm the stack entry (r, b) is used to indicate the right boundary r of a subfile waiting to be sorted on bit b; the left boundary need not actually be recorded in the stack — it is implicit because of the left-to-right nature of the procedure.

Algorithm R (*Radix exchange sort*). Records $R_1, \ldots, R_N$ are rearranged in place; after sorting is complete, their keys will be in order, $K_1 \leq \cdots \leq K_N$. Each key is assumed to be a nonnegative m-bit binary number, $(a_1\,a_2 \ldots a_m)_2$; the ith most significant bit, a_i, is called "bit i" of the key. An auxiliary stack with room for at most $m - 1$ entries is needed for temporary storage. This algorithm

Table 3

RADIX EXCHANGE SORTING

Stage																	l	r	b	Stack
1	$^{1}[$0767	0127	1000	0075	1614	0252	1601	1215	0423	0652	0232	0775	1144	1245	1375	1277$]$	1	16	1	—
2	$^{2}[$0767	0127	0775	0075	0232	0252	0652	0423$]$	$^{2}[$1215	1601	1614	1000	1144	1245	1375	1277$]$	1	8	2	(16,2)
3	$^{3}[$0252	0127	0232	0075$]$	$^{3}[$0775	0767	0652	0423$]$	$^{2}[$1215	1601	1614	1000	1144	1245	1375	1277$]$	1	4	3	(8,3)(16,2)
4	$^{4}[$0075	0127$]$	$^{4}[$0232	0252$]$	$^{3}[$0775	0767	0652	0423$]$	$^{2}[$1215	1601	1614	1000	1144	1245	1375	1277$]$	1	2	4	(4,4)(8,3)(16,2)
5	0075	0127	$^{4}[$0232	0252$]$	$^{3}[$0775	0767	0652	0423$]$	$^{2}[$1215	1601	1614	1000	1144	1245	1375	1277$]$	3	4	4	(8,3)(16,2)
6	0075	0127	$^{5}[$0232	0252$]$	$^{3}[$0775	0767	0652	0423$]$	$^{2}[$1215	1601	1614	1000	1144	1245	1375	1277$]$	3	4	5	(8,3)(16,2)
7	0075	0127	0232	0252	$^{3}[$0775	0767	0652	0423$]$	$^{2}[$1215	1601	1614	1000	1144	1245	1375	1277$]$	5	8	3	(16,2)
8	0075	0127	0232	0252	0423	$^{4}[$0767	0652	0775$]$	$^{2}[$1215	1601	1614	1000	1144	1245	1375	1277$]$	6	8	4	(16,2)
9	0075	0127	0232	0252	0423	0652	$^{5}[$0767	0775$]$	$^{2}[$1215	1601	1614	1000	1144	1245	1375	1277$]$	7	8	5	(16,2)
10	0075	0127	0232	0252	0423	0652	$^{6}[$0767	0775$]$	$^{2}[$1215	1601	1614	1000	1144	1245	1375	1277$]$	7	8	6	(16,2)
11	0075	0127	0232	0252	0423	0652	$^{7}[$0767	0775$]$	$^{2}[$1215	1601	1614	1000	1144	1245	1375	1277$]$	7	8	7	(16,2)
12	0075	0127	0232	0252	0423	0652	0767	0775	$^{2}[$1215	1601	1614	1000	1144	1245	1375	1277$]$	9	16	2	—
13	0075	0127	0232	0252	0423	0652	0767	0775	$^{3}[$1215	1277	1375	1000	1144	1245$]$	$^{3}[$1614	1601$]$	9	14	3	(16,3)
14	0075	0127	0232	0252	0423	0652	0767	0775	$^{4}[$1144	1000$]$	$^{4}[$1375	1277	1215	1245$]$	$^{3}[$1614	1601$]$	9	10	4	(14,4)(16,3)
15	0075	0127	0232	0252	0423	0652	0767	0775	1000	1144	$^{4}[$1375	1277	1215	1245$]$	$^{3}[$1614	1601$]$	11	14	4	(16,3)
16	0075	0127	0232	0252	0423	0652	0767	0775	1000	1144	$^{5}[$1245	1277	1215$]$	1375	$^{3}[$1614	1601$]$	11	13	5	(16,3)
17	0075	0127	0232	0252	0423	0652	0767	0775	1000	1144	1215	$^{6}[$1277	1245$]$	1375	$^{3}[$1614	1601$]$	12	13	6	(16,3)
18	0075	0127	0232	0252	0423	0652	0767	0775	1000	1144	1215	1245	1277	1375	$^{3}[$1614	1601$]$	15	16	3	—
19	0075	0127	0232	0252	0423	0652	0767	0775	1000	1144	1215	1245	1277	1375	$^{4}[$1614	1601$]$	15	16	4	—
20	0075	0127	0232	0252	0423	0652	0767	0775	1000	1144	1215	1245	1277	1375	$^{5}[$1614	1601$]$	15	16	5	—
21	0075	0127	0232	0252	0423	0652	0767	0775	1000	1144	1215	1245	1277	1375	$^{6}[$1614	1601$]$	15	16	6	—
22	0075	0127	0232	0252	0423	0652	0767	0775	1000	1144	1215	1245	1277	1375	$^{7}[$1614	1601$]$	15	16	7	—
23	0075	0127	0232	0252	0423	0652	0767	0775	1000	1144	1215	1245	1277	1375	1601	1614	17	—	—	—

The radix exchange method looks precisely once at every bit that is needed to determine the final order of the keys.

essentially follows the radix exchange partitioning procedure described in the
text above; certain improvements in its efficiency are possible, as described in
the text and exercises below.

R1. [Initialize.] Set the stack empty, and set $l \leftarrow 1$, $r \leftarrow N$, $b \leftarrow 1$.

R2. [Begin new stage.] (We now wish to sort the subfile $R_l \ldots R_r$ on bit b; from the nature of the algorithm, we have $l \leq r$.) If $l = r$, go to step R10 (since a one-word file is already sorted). Otherwise set $i \leftarrow l$, $j \leftarrow r$.

R3. [Inspect K_i for 1.] Examine bit b of K_i. If it is a 1, go to step R6.

R4. [Increase i.] Increase i by 1. If $i \leq j$, return to step R3; otherwise go to step R8.

R5. [Inspect K_{j+1} for 0.] Examine bit b of K_{j+1}. If it is a 0, go to step R7.

R6. [Decrease j.] Decrease j by 1. If $i \leq j$, go to step R5; otherwise go to step R8.

R7. [Exchange R_i, R_{j+1}.] Interchange records $R_i \leftrightarrow R_{j+1}$; then go to step R4.

R8. [Test special cases.] (At this point a partitioning stage has been completed; $i = j + 1$, bit b of keys $K_l, \ldots, K_j$ is 0, and bit b of keys $K_i, \ldots, K_r$ is 1.) Increase b by 1. If $b > m$, where m is the total number of bits in the keys, go to step R10. (In such a case, the subfile $R_l \ldots R_r$ has been sorted. This test need not be made if there is no chance of having equal keys present in the file.) Otherwise if $j < l$ or $j = r$, go back to step R2 (all bits examined were 1 or 0, respectively). Otherwise if $j = l$, increase l by 1 and go to step R2 (there was only one 0 bit).

R9. [Put on stack.] Insert the entry (r, b) on top of the stack; then set $r \leftarrow j$ and go to step R2.

R10. [Take off stack.] If the stack is empty, we are done sorting; otherwise set $l \leftarrow r + 1$, remove the top entry (r', b') of the stack, set $r \leftarrow r'$, $b \leftarrow b'$, and return to step R2. ∎

Program R (*Radix exchange sort*). The following MIX code uses essentially the same conventions as Program Q. We have rI1 ≡ $l - r$, rI2 ≡ r, rI3 ≡ i, rI4 ≡ j, rI5 ≡ $m - b$, rI6 ≡ size of stack, except that it proves convenient for certain instructions (designated below) to leave rI3 = $i - j$ or rI4 = $j - i$. Because of the binary nature of radix exchange, this program uses the operations SRB (shift right AX binary), JAE (jump A even), and JAO (jump A odd), defined in Section 4.5.2. We assume that $N \geq 2$.

01	START	ENT6	0	1	*R1. Initialize.* Set stack empty.
02		ENT1	1-N	1	$l \leftarrow 1$.
03		ENT2	N	1	$r \leftarrow N$.
04		ENT5	M-1	1	$b \leftarrow 1$.
05		JMP	1F	1	To R2 (omit testing $l = r$).
06	9H	INC6	1	S	*R9. Put on stack.* [rI4 = $j-l$]
07		ST2	STACK,6(A)	S	
08		ST5	STACK,6(B)	S	$(r, b) \Rightarrow$ stack.

09		ENN1	0,4	S	$\text{rI1} \leftarrow l - j$.
10		ENT2	-1,3	S	$r \leftarrow j$.
11	1H	ENT3	0,1	A	<u>R2. Begin new stage.</u> [rI3 $= i-j$]
12		ENT4	0,2	A	$i \leftarrow l$, $j \leftarrow r$. [rI3 $= i-j$]
13	3H	INC3	0,4	C'	<u>R3. Inspect K_i for 1.</u>
14		LDA	INPUT,3	C'	
15		SRB	0,5	C'	units bit of rA $\leftarrow$ bit b of K_i.
16		JAE	4F	C'	To R4 if it is 0.
17	6H	DEC4	1,3	$C'' + X$	<u>R6. Decrease j.</u> $j \leftarrow j - 1$. [rI4 $= j-i$]
18		J4N	8F	$C'' + X$	To R8 if $j < i$. [rI4 $= j-i$]
19	5H	INC4	0,3	C''	<u>R5. Inspect K_{j+1} for 0.</u>
20		LDA	INPUT+1,4	C''	
21		SRB	0,5	C''	units bit of rA $\leftarrow$ bit b of K_{j+1}.
22		JAO	6B	C''	To R6 if it is 1.
23	7H	LDA	INPUT+1,4	B	<u>R7. Exchange R_i, R_{j+1}.</u>
24		LDX	INPUT,3	B	
25		STX	INPUT+1,4	B	
26		STA	INPUT,3	B	
27	4H	DEC3	-1,4	$C' - X$	<u>R4. Increase i.</u> $i \leftarrow i + 1$. [rI3 $= i-j$]
28		J3NP	3B	$C' - X$	To R3 if $i \leq j$. [rI3 $= i-j$]
29		INC3	0,4	$A - X$	$\text{rI3} \leftarrow i$.
30	8H	J5Z	0F	A	<u>R8. Test special cases.</u> [rI4 unknown]
31		DEC5	1	$A - G$	To R10 if $b = m$, else $b \leftarrow b + 1$.
32		ENT4	-1,3	$A - G$	$\text{rI4} \leftarrow j$.
33		DEC4	0,2	$A - G$	$\text{rI4} \leftarrow j - r$.
34		J4Z	1B	$A - G$	To R2 if $j = r$.
35		DEC4	0,1	$A - G - R$	$\text{rI4} \leftarrow j - l$.
36		J4N	1B	$A - G - R$	To R2 if $j < l$.
37		J4NZ	9B	$A-G-L-R$	To R9 if $j \neq l$.
38		INC1	1	K	$l \leftarrow l + 1$.
39	2H	J1NZ	1B	$K + S$	Jump if $l \neq r$.
40	0H	ENT1	1,2	$S + 1$	<u>R10. Take off stack.</u>
41		LD2	STACK,6(A)	$S + 1$	
42		DEC1	0,2	$S + 1$	
43		LD5	STACK,6(B)	$S + 1$	stack $\Rightarrow (r, b)$.
44		DEC6	1	$S + 1$	
45		J6NN	2B	$S + 1$	To R2 if stack was nonempty. ∎

The running time of this radix exchange program depends on

A = number of stages encountered with $l < r$;

B = number of exchanges;

$C = C' + C''$ = number of bit inspections;

G = number of times $b > m$ in step R8;

K = number of times $b \leq m$, $j = l$ in step R8; (29)

L = number of times $b \leq m$, $j < l$ in step R8;

R = number of times $b \leq m$, $j = r$ in step R8;

S = number of times things are entered onto the stack;

X = number of times $j < i$ in step R6.

By Kirchhoff's law, $S = A - G - K - L - R$; so the total running time comes to $27A + 8B + 8C - 23G - 14K - 17L - 19R - X + 13$ units. The bit-inspection loops can be made somewhat faster, as shown in exercise 34, at the expense of a more complicated program. It is also possible to increase the speed of radix exchange by using straight insertion whenever $r - l$ is sufficiently small, as we did in Algorithm Q; but we shall not dwell on these refinements.

In order to analyze the running time of radix exchange, two kinds of input data suggest themselves. We can

i) assume that $N = 2^m$ and that the keys to be sorted are simply the integers $0, 1, 2, \ldots, 2^m - 1$ in random order; or

ii) assume that $m = \infty$ (unlimited precision) and that the keys to be sorted are independent uniformly distributed real numbers in $[0 \mathbin{.\,.} 1)$.

The analysis of case (i) is relatively easy, so it has been left as an exercise for the reader (see exercise 35). Case (ii) is comparatively difficult, so it has *also* been left as an exercise (see exercise 38). The following table shows crude approximations to the results of these analyses:

Quantity	Case (i)	Case (ii)
A	N	αN
B	$\frac{1}{4} N \lg N$	$\frac{1}{4} N \lg N$
C	$N \lg N$	$N \lg N$
G	$\frac{1}{2} N$	0
K	0	$\frac{1}{2} N$
L	0	$\frac{1}{2}(\alpha - 1)N$
R	0	$\frac{1}{2}(\alpha - 1)N$
S	$\frac{1}{2} N$	$\frac{1}{2} N$
X	$\frac{1}{2} N$	$\frac{1}{2} N$ (30)

Here $\alpha = 1/\ln 2 \approx 1.4427$. Notice that the average number of exchanges, bit inspections, and stack accesses is essentially the same for both kinds of data, even though case (ii) takes about 44 percent more stages. Our MIX program takes approximately $14.4\, N \ln N$ units of time, on the average, to sort N items in case (ii), and this could be cut to about $11.5\, N \ln N$ using the suggestion of exercise 34; the corresponding figure for Program Q is $11.7\, N \ln N$, which can be decreased to about $10.6\, N \ln N$ using Singleton's median-of-three suggestion.

Thus radix exchange sorting takes about as long as quicksort, on the average, when sorting uniformly distributed data; on some machines it is actually a little quicker than quicksort. Exercise 53 indicates to what extent the process slows down for a nonuniform distribution. It is important to note that our entire analysis is predicated on the assumption that keys are distinct; *radix exchange as defined above is not especially efficient when equal keys are present*, since it goes through several time-consuming stages trying to separate sets of identical keys before b becomes $> m$. One plausible way to remedy this defect is suggested in the answer to exercise 40.

Both radix exchange and quicksort are essentially based on the idea of partitioning. Records are exchanged until the file is split into two parts: a left-hand subfile, in which all keys are $\leq K$, for some K, and a right-hand subfile in which all keys are $\geq K$. Quicksort chooses K to be an actual key in the file, while radix exchange essentially chooses an artificial key K based on binary representations. From a historical standpoint, radix exchange was discovered by P. Hildebrandt, H. Isbitz, H. Rising, and J. Schwartz [*JACM* **6** (1959), 156–163], about a year earlier than quicksort. Other partitioning schemes are also possible; for example, John McCarthy has suggested setting $K \approx \frac{1}{2}(u + v)$, if all keys are known to lie between u and v. Yihsiao Wang has suggested that the mean of three key values such as (28) be used as the threshold for partitioning; he has proved that the number of comparisons required to sort uniformly distributed random data will then be asymptotic to $1.082 N \lg N$.

Still another partitioning strategy has been proposed by M. H. van Emden [*CACM* **13** (1970), 563–567]: Instead of choosing K in advance, we "learn" what a good K might be, by keeping track of $K' = \max(K_l, \ldots, K_i)$ and $K'' = \min(K_j, \ldots, K_r)$ as partitioning proceeds. We may increase i until encountering a key greater than K', then decrease j until encountering a key less than K'', then exchange and/or adjust K' and K''. Empirical tests on this "interval-exchange sort" method indicate that it is slightly slower than quicksort; its running time appears to be so difficult to analyze that an adequate theoretical explanation will never be found, especially since the subfiles after partitioning are no longer in random order.

A generalization of radix exchange to radices higher than 2 is discussed in Section 5.2.5.

*Asymptotic methods. The analysis of exchange sorting algorithms leads to some particularly instructive mathematical problems that enable us to learn more about how to find the asymptotic behavior of functions. For example, we came across the function

$$W_n = \frac{1}{n!} \sum_{0 \leq r < s \leq n} s!\, r^{n-s} \tag{31}$$

in (9), during our analysis of the bubble sort; what is its asymptotic value?

We can proceed as in our study of the number of involutions, Eq. 5.1.4–(41); the reader will find it helpful to review the discussion at the end of Section 5.1.4 before reading further.

Inspection of (31) shows that the contribution for $s = n$ is larger than that for $s = n - 1$, etc.; this suggests replacing s by $n - s$. In fact, we soon discover that it is most convenient to use the substitutions $t = n - s + 1$, $m = n + 1$, so that (31) becomes

$$\frac{1}{m} W_{m-1} = \frac{1}{m!} \sum_{1 \leq t < m} (m - t)! \sum_{0 \leq r < m-t} r^{t-1}. \tag{32}$$

The inner sum has a well-known asymptotic series obtained from Euler's summation formula, namely

$$\sum_{0 \le r < N} r^{t-1} = \frac{N^t}{t} - \frac{1}{2}(N^{t-1} - \delta_{t1}) + \frac{B_2}{2!}(t-1)(N^{t-2} - \delta_{t2}) + \cdots$$

$$= \frac{1}{t}\sum_{j=0}^{k}\binom{t}{j} B_j (N^{t-j} - \delta_{tj}) + O(N^{t-k}) \qquad (33)$$

(see exercise 1.2.11.2–4); hence our problem reduces to studying sums of the form

$$\frac{1}{m!}\sum_{1 \le t < m}(m-t)!\,(m-t)^t t^k, \qquad k \ge -1. \qquad (34)$$

As in Section 5.1.4 we can show that the value of this summand is negligible, $O\big(\exp(-n^\delta)\big)$, whenever t is greater than $m^{1/2+\epsilon}$; hence we may put $t = O(m^{1/2+\epsilon})$ and replace the factorials by Stirling's approximation:

$$\frac{(m-t)!\,(m-t)^t}{m!}$$

$$= \sqrt{1 - \frac{t}{m}}\,\exp\left(\frac{t}{12m^2} - \left(\frac{t^2}{2m} + \frac{t^3}{3m^2} + \frac{t^4}{4m^3} + \frac{t^5}{5m^4}\right) + O(m^{-2+6\epsilon})\right).$$

We are therefore interested in the asymptotic value of

$$r_k(m) = \sum_{1 \le t < m} e^{-t^2/2m} t^k, \qquad k \ge -1. \qquad (35)$$

The sum could also be extended to the full range $1 \le t < \infty$ without changing its asymptotic value, since the values for $t > m^{1/2+\epsilon}$ are negligible.

Let $g_k(x) = x^k e^{-x^2}$ and $f_k(x) = g_k(x/\sqrt{2m})$. When $k \ge 0$, Euler's summation formula tells us that

$$\sum_{0 \le t < m} f_k(t) = \int_0^m f_k(x)\,dx + \sum_{j=1}^{p}\frac{B_j}{j!}\big(f_k^{(j-1)}(m) - f_k^{(j-1)}(0)\big) + R_p,$$

$$R_p = \frac{(-1)^{p+1}}{p!}\int_0^m B_p(\{x\})f_k^{(p)}(x)\,dx$$

$$= \left(\frac{1}{\sqrt{2m}}\right)^p O\left(\int_0^\infty |g_k^{(p)}(y)|\,dy\right) = O(m^{-p/2}); \qquad (36)$$

hence we can get an asymptotic series for $r_k(m)$ whenever $k \ge 0$ by using essentially the same ideas we have used at the end of Section 5.1.4. But when $k = -1$ the method breaks down, since $f_{-1}(0)$ is undefined; we can't merely sum from 1 to m either, because the remainders don't give smaller and smaller powers of m when the lower limit is 1. (This is the crux of the matter, and the reader should pause to appreciate the problem before proceeding further.)

To resolve the dilemma we can define $g_{-1}(x) = (e^{-x^2} - 1)/x$ and $f_{-1}(x) = g_{-1}(x/\sqrt{2m})$; then $f_{-1}(0) = 0$, and $r_{-1}(m)$ can be obtained from $\sum_{0 \le t < m} f_{-1}(t)$ in a simple way. Equation (36) is now valid for $k = -1$, and the remaining integral is well known,

$$\frac{2}{\sqrt{2m}} \int_0^m f_{-1}(x)\, dx = 2 \int_0^m \frac{e^{-x^2/2m} - 1}{x}\, dx = \int_0^{m/2} \frac{e^{-y} - 1}{y}\, dy$$

$$= \int_0^1 \frac{e^{-y} - 1}{y}\, dy + \int_1^{m/2} \frac{e^{-y}}{y}\, dy - \ln \frac{m}{2}$$

$$= -\gamma - \ln m + \ln 2 + O(e^{-m/2}),$$

by exercise 43.

Now we have enough facts and formulas to grind out the answer,

$$W_n = \tfrac{1}{2} m \ln m + \tfrac{1}{2}(\gamma + \ln 2)m - \tfrac{2}{3}\sqrt{2\pi m} + \tfrac{49}{36} + O(n^{-1/2}), \quad m = n + 1, \quad (37)$$

as shown in exercise 44. This completes our analysis of the bubble sort.

For the analysis of radix exchange sorting, we need to know the asymptotic value of the finite sum

$$U_n = \sum_{k \ge 2} \binom{n}{k} (-1)^k \frac{1}{2^{k-1} - 1} \qquad (38)$$

as $n \to \infty$. This question turns out to be harder than any of the other asymptotic problems we have met so far; the elementary methods of power series expansions, Euler's summation formula, etc., turn out to be inadequate. The following derivation has been suggested by N. G. de Bruijn.

To get rid of the cancellation effects of the large factors $\binom{n}{k}(-1)^k$ in (38), we start by rewriting the sum as an infinite series

$$U_n = \sum_{k \ge 2} \binom{n}{k} (-1)^k \sum_{j \ge 1} \left(\frac{1}{2^{k-1}}\right)^j = \sum_{j \ge 1} \left(2^j (1 - 2^{-j})^n - 2^j + n\right). \qquad (39)$$

If we set $x = n/2^j$, the summand is

$$2^j (1 - 2^{-j})^n - 2^j + n = \frac{n}{x}\left(\left(1 - \frac{x}{n}\right)^n - 1 + x\right).$$

When $x \le n^\epsilon$, we have

$$\left(1 - \frac{x}{n}\right)^n = \exp\left(n \ln\left(1 - \frac{x}{n}\right)\right) = \exp(-x + x^2 O(n^{-1})), \qquad (40)$$

and this suggests approximating (39) by

$$T_n = \sum_{j \ge 1} \left(2^j e^{-n/2^j} - 2^j + n\right). \qquad (41)$$

To justify this approximation, we have $U_n - T_n = X_n + Y_n$, where

$$X_n = \sum_{\substack{j \geq 1 \\ 2^j < n^{1-\epsilon}}} \left(2^j(1 - 2^{-j})^n - 2^j e^{-n/2^j}\right) \qquad \text{[the terms for } x > n^\epsilon]$$

$$= \sum_{\substack{j \geq 1 \\ 2^j < n^{1-\epsilon}}} O(n e^{-n/2^j}) \qquad \text{[since } 0 < 1 - 2^{-j} < e^{-2^{-j}}]$$

$$= O(n \log n \, e^{-n^\epsilon}) \qquad \text{[since there are } O(\log n) \text{ terms];}$$

and

$$Y_n = \sum_{\substack{j \geq 1 \\ 2^j \geq n^{1-\epsilon}}} \left(2^j(1 - 2^{-j})^n - 2^j e^{-n/2^j}\right) \qquad \text{[the terms for } x \leq n^\epsilon]$$

$$= \sum_{\substack{j \geq 1 \\ 2^j \geq n^{1-\epsilon}}} \left(e^{-n/2^j} \frac{n}{2^j} O(1)\right) \qquad \text{[by (40)].}$$

Our discussion below will demonstrate that the latter sum is $O(1)$; consequently $U_n - T_n = O(1)$. (See exercise 47.)

So far we haven't applied any techniques that are really different from those we have used before. But the study of T_n requires a new idea, based on simple principles of complex variable theory: If x is any positive number, we have

$$e^{-x} = \frac{1}{2\pi i} \int_{1/2 - i\infty}^{1/2 + i\infty} \Gamma(z) x^{-z} \, dz = \frac{1}{2\pi} \int_{-\infty}^{\infty} \Gamma(\tfrac{1}{2} + it) x^{-(1/2+it)} \, dt. \qquad (42)$$

To prove this identity, consider the path of integration shown in Fig. 20(a), where N, N', and M are large. The value of the integral along this contour is the sum of the residues inside, namely

$$\sum_{0 \leq k < M} x^{-(-k)} \lim_{z \to -k} (z + k)\Gamma(z) = \sum_{0 \leq k < M} x^k \frac{(-1)^k}{k!}.$$

The integral on the top line is $O\left(\int_{-\infty}^{1/2} |\Gamma(t + iN)| x^{-t} \, dt\right)$, and we have the well-known bound

$$\Gamma(t + iN) = O\left(|t + iN|^{t-1/2} e^{-t - \pi N/2}\right) \qquad \text{as } N \to \infty.$$

[For properties of the gamma function see, for example, Erdélyi, Magnus, Oberhettinger, and Tricomi, *Higher Transcendental Functions* **1** (New York: McGraw–Hill, 1953), Chapter 1.] Therefore the top line integral is quite negligible, $O\left(e^{-\pi N/2} \int_{-\infty}^{1/2} (N/xe)^t \, dt\right)$. The bottom line integral has a similar innocuous behavior. For the integral along the left line we use the fact that

$$\Gamma(\tfrac{1}{2} + it - M) = \Gamma(\tfrac{1}{2} + it) / (-M + \tfrac{1}{2} + it) \cdots (-1 + \tfrac{1}{2} + it)$$

$$= \Gamma(\tfrac{1}{2} + it) O\left(1/(M-1)!\right);$$

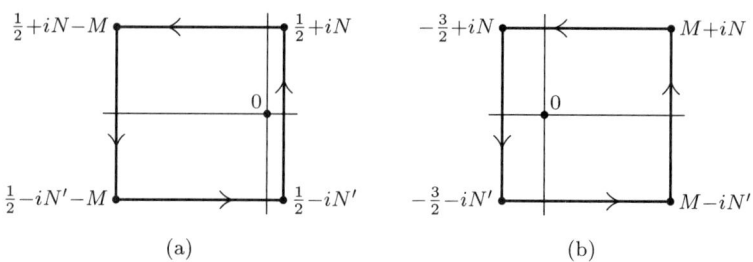

Fig. 20. Contours of integration for gamma-function identities.

hence the left-hand integral is $O\big(x^{M-1/2}/(M-1)!\big)\int_{-\infty}^{\infty}\big|\Gamma(\tfrac{1}{2}+it)\big|\,dt$. Therefore as M, N, $N' \to \infty$, only the right-hand integral survives, and this proves (42). In fact, (42) remains valid if we replace $\tfrac{1}{2}$ by any positive number.

The same argument can be used to derive many other useful relations involving the gamma function. We can replace x^{-z} by other functions of z; or we can replace the constant $\tfrac{1}{2}$ by other quantities. For example,

$$\frac{1}{2\pi i}\int_{-3/2-i\infty}^{-3/2+i\infty}\Gamma(z)x^{-z}\,dz = e^{-x}-1+x, \tag{43}$$

and this is the critical quantity in our formula (41) for T_n:

$$T_n = n\sum_{j\ge 1}\frac{1}{2\pi i}\int_{-3/2-i\infty}^{-3/2+i\infty}\Gamma(z)(n/2^j)^{-1-z}\,dz. \tag{44}$$

The sum may be placed inside the integrals, since its convergence is absolutely well-behaved; we have

$$\sum_{j\ge 1}(n/2^j)^w = n^w\sum_{j\ge 1}(1/2^w)^j = n^w/(2^w-1), \qquad \text{when } \Re(w)>0,$$

because $|2^w| = 2^{\Re(w)}>1$. Therefore

$$T_n = \frac{n}{2\pi i}\int_{-3/2-i\infty}^{-3/2+i\infty}\frac{\Gamma(z)\,n^{-1-z}}{2^{-1-z}-1}\,dz, \tag{45}$$

and it remains to evaluate the latter integral.

This time we integrate along a path that extends far to the *right*, as in Fig. 20(b). The top line integral is $O(n^{1/2}e^{-\pi N/2}\int_{-3/2}^{M}|M+iN|^t\,dt)$, if $2^{iN}\ne 1$, and the bottom line integral is equally negligible, when N and N' are much larger than M. The right-hand line integral is $O(n^{-1-M}\int_{-\infty}^{\infty}|\Gamma(M+it)|\,dt)$. Fixing M and letting N, $N' \to \infty$ shows that $-T_n/n$ is $O(n^{-1-M})$ plus the sum of the residues in the region $-3/2 < \Re(z) < M$. The factor $\Gamma(z)$ has simple poles at $z=-1$ and $z=0$, while n^{-1-z} has no poles, and $1/(2^{-1-z}-1)$ has simple poles when $z=-1+2\pi ik/\ln 2$.

The double pole at $z = -1$ is the hardest to handle. We can use the well-known relation

$$\Gamma(z+1) = \exp(-\gamma z + \zeta(2)z^2/2 - \zeta(3)z^3/3 + \zeta(4)z^4/4 - \cdots),$$

where $\zeta(s) = 1^{-s} + 2^{-s} + 3^{-s} + \cdots = H_\infty^{(s)}$, to deduce the following expansions when $w = z + 1$ is small:

$$\Gamma(z) = \frac{\Gamma(w+1)}{w(w-1)} = -w^{-1} + (\gamma - 1) + O(w),$$

$$n^{-1-z} = 1 - w \ln n + O(w^2),$$

$$1/(2^{-1-z} - 1) = -w^{-1}/\ln 2 - \tfrac{1}{2} + O(w).$$

The residue at $z = -1$ is the coefficient of w^{-1} in the product of these three formulas, namely $\frac{1}{2} - (\ln n + \gamma - 1)/\ln 2$. Adding the other residues gives the formula

$$\frac{T_n}{n} = \frac{\ln n + \gamma - 1}{\ln 2} - \frac{1}{2} + \delta(n) + \frac{2}{n} + O(n^{-M}), \tag{46}$$

for arbitrarily large M, where $\delta(n)$ is a rather strange function,

$$\delta(n) = \frac{2}{\ln 2} \sum_{k \geq 1} \Re\big(\Gamma(-1 - 2\pi i k/\ln 2) \exp(2\pi i k \lg n)\big). \tag{47}$$

Notice that $\delta(n) = \delta(2n)$. The average value of $\delta(n)$ is zero, since the average value of each term is zero. (We may assume that $(\lg n) \bmod 1$ is uniformly distributed, in view of the results about floating point numbers in Section 4.2.4.) Furthermore, since $|\Gamma(-1+it)| = |\pi/(t(1+t^2)\sinh \pi t)|^{1/2}$, it is not difficult to show that

$$|\delta(n)| < 0.000000173; \tag{48}$$

thus we may safely ignore the "wobbles" of $\delta(n)$ for practical purposes. For theoretical purposes, however, we can't obtain a valid asymptotic expansion of U_n without it; that is why U_n is a comparatively difficult function to analyze. From the definition of T_n in (41) we can see immediately that

$$\frac{T_{2n}}{2n} = \frac{T_n}{n} + 1 - \frac{1}{n} + \frac{e^{-n}}{n}. \tag{49}$$

Therefore the error term $O(n^{-M})$ in (46) is essential; it cannot be replaced by zero. However, exercise 54 presents another approach to the analysis, which avoids such error terms by deriving a rather peculiar convergent series.

In summary, we have deduced the behavior of the difficult sum (38):

$$U_n = n \lg n + n \left(\frac{\gamma - 1}{\ln 2} - \frac{1}{2} + \delta(n) \right) + O(1). \tag{50}$$

The gamma-function method we have used to obtain this result is a special case of the general technique of *Mellin transforms*, which are extremely useful in the study of radix-oriented recurrence relations. Other examples of this approach can be found in exercises 51–53 and in Section 6.3. An excellent introduction to Mellin transforms and their applications to algorithmic analysis has been presented by P. Flajolet, X. Gourdon, and P. Dumas in *Theoretical Computer Science* **144** (1995), 3–58.

EXERCISES

1. [*M20*] Let $a_1 \ldots a_n$ be a permutation of $\{1, \ldots, n\}$, and let i and j be indices such that $i < j$ and $a_i > a_j$. Let $a_1' \ldots a_n'$ be the permutation obtained from $a_1 \ldots a_n$ by interchanging a_i and a_j. Can $a_1' \ldots a_n'$ have more inversions than $a_1 \ldots a_n$?

▶ **2.** [*M25*] (a) What is the minimum number of exchanges that will sort the permutation $3\,7\,6\,9\,8\,1\,4\,5\,2$? (b) In general, given any permutation $\pi = a_1 \ldots a_n$ of $\{1, \ldots, n\}$, let $\mathrm{xch}(\pi)$ be the minimum number of exchanges that will sort π into increasing order. Express $\mathrm{xch}(\pi)$ in terms of "simpler" characteristics of π. (See exercise 5.1.4–41 for another way to measure the disorder of a permutation.)

3. [*10*] Is the bubble sort Algorithm B a stable sorting algorithm?

4. [*M23*] If $t = 1$ in step B4, we could actually terminate Algorithm B immediately, because the subsequent step B2 will do nothing useful. What is the probability that $t = 1$ will occur in step B4 when sorting a random permutation?

5. [*M25*] Let $b_1 b_2 \ldots b_n$ be the inversion table for the permutation $a_1 a_2 \ldots a_n$. Show that the value of BOUND after r passes of the bubble sort is $\max \{b_i + i \mid b_i \geq r\} - r$, for $0 \leq r \leq \max (b_1, \ldots, b_n)$.

6. [*M22*] Let $a_1 \ldots a_n$ be a permutation of $\{1, \ldots, n\}$ and let $a_1' \ldots a_n'$ be its inverse. Show that the number of passes to bubble-sort $a_1 \ldots a_n$ is $1 + \max (a_1' - 1, a_2' - 2, \ldots, a_n' - n)$.

7. [*M28*] Calculate the standard deviation of the number of passes for the bubble sort, and express it in terms of n and the function $P(n)$. [See Eqs. (6) and (7).]

8. [*M24*] Derive Eq. (8).

9. [*M48*] Analyze the number of passes and the number of comparisons in the cocktail-shaker sorting algorithm. *Note:* See exercise 5.4.8–9 for partial information.

10. [*M26*] Let $a_1 a_2 \ldots a_n$ be a 2-ordered permutation of $\{1, 2, \ldots, n\}$.
a) What are the coordinates of the endpoints of the a_ith step of the corresponding lattice path? (See Fig. 11 on page 87.)
b) Prove that the comparison/exchange of $a_1 : a_2$, $a_3 : a_4$, $\ldots$ corresponds to folding the path about the diagonal, as in Fig. 18(b).
c) Prove that the comparison/exchange of $a_2 : a_{2+d}$, $a_4 : a_{4+d}$, $\ldots$ corresponds to folding the path about a line m units below the diagonal, as in Figs. 18(c), (d), and (e), when $d = 2m - 1$.

▶ **11.** [*M25*] What permutation of $\{1, 2, \ldots, 16\}$ maximizes the number of exchanges done by Batcher's algorithm?

12. [*24*] Write a MIX program for Algorithm M, assuming that MIX is a binary computer with the operations AND, SRB. How much time does your program take to sort the sixteen records in Table 1?

13. [*10*] Is Batcher's method a stable sorting algorithm?

14. [*M21*] Let $c(N)$ be the number of key comparisons used to sort N elements by Batcher's method; this is the number of times step M4 is performed.
   a) Show that $c(2^t) = 2c(2^{t-1}) + (t-1)2^{t-1} + 1$, for $t \geq 1$.
   b) Find a simple expression for $c(2^t)$ as a function of t. *Hint:* Consider the sequence $x_t = c(2^t)/2^t$.

15. [*M38*] The object of this exercise is to analyze the function $c(N)$ of exercise 14, and to find a formula for $c(N)$ when $N = 2^{e_1} + 2^{e_2} + \cdots + 2^{e_r}$, $e_1 > e_2 > \cdots > e_r \geq 0$.
   a) Let $a(N) = c(N+1) - c(N)$. Prove that $a(2n) = a(n) + \lfloor \lg(2n) \rfloor$, and $a(2n+1) = a(n) + 1$; hence

$$a(N) = \binom{e_1 + 1}{2} - r(e_1 - 1) + (e_1 + e_2 + \cdots + e_r).$$

   b) Let $x(n) = a(n) - a(\lfloor n/2 \rfloor)$, so that $a(n) = x(n) + x(\lfloor n/2 \rfloor) + x(\lfloor n/4 \rfloor) + \cdots$. Let $y(n) = x(1) + x(2) + \cdots + x(n)$; and let $z(2n) = y(2n) - a(n)$, $z(2n+1) = y(2n+1)$. Prove that $c(N+1) = z(N) + 2z(\lfloor N/2 \rfloor) + 4z(\lfloor N/4 \rfloor) + \cdots$.
   c) Prove that $y(N) = N + (\lfloor N/2 \rfloor + 1)(e_1 - 1) - 2^{e_1} + 2$.
   d) Now put everything together and find a formula for $c(N)$ in terms of the exponents e_j, holding r fixed.

16. [*HM42*] Find the asymptotic value of the *average* number of exchanges occurring when Batcher's method is applied to a random permutation of N distinct elements, assuming that N is a power of two.

▸ **17.** [*20*] Where in Algorithm Q do we use the fact that K_0 and K_{N+1} have the values postulated in (13)?

▸ **18.** [*20*] Explain how the computation proceeds in Algorithm Q when all of the input keys are equal. What would happen if the "<" signs in steps Q3 and Q4 were changed to "≤" instead?

19. [*15*] Would Algorithm Q still work properly if a queue (first-in-first-out) were used instead of a stack (last-in-first-out)?

20. [*M20*] What is the largest possible number of elements that will ever be on the stack at once in Algorithm Q, as a function of M and N?

21. [*20*] Explain why the first partitioning phase of Algorithm Q takes the number of comparisons and exchanges specified in (17), when the keys are distinct.

22. [*M25*] Let p_{kN} be the probability that the quantity A in (16) will equal k, when Algorithm Q is applied to a random permutation of $\{1, 2, \ldots, N\}$, and let $A_N(z) = \sum_k p_{kN} z^k$ be the corresponding generating function. Prove that $A_N(z) = 1$ for $N \leq M$, and $A_N(z) = z(\sum_{1 \leq s \leq N} A_{s-1}(z) A_{N-s}(z))/N$ for $N > M$. Find similar recurrence relations defining the other probability distributions $B_N(z)$, $C_N(z)$, $D_N(z)$, $E_N(z)$, $S_N(z)$.

23. [*M23*] Let A_N, B_N, D_N, E_N, S_N be the average values of the corresponding quantities in (16), when sorting a random permutation of $\{1, 2, \ldots, N\}$. Find recurrence relations for these quantities, analogous to (18); and solve these recurrences to obtain (25).

24. [*M21*] Algorithm Q obviously does a few more comparisons than it needs to, since we can have $i = j$ in step Q3 and even $i > j$ in step Q4. How many comparisons C_N would be done on the average if we avoided all comparisons when $i \geq j$?

25. [*M20*] When the input keys are the numbers $1\,2\,\ldots\,N$ in order, what are the exact values of the quantities A, B, C, D, E, and S in the timing of Program Q? (Assume that $N > M$.)

▶ **26.** [*M24*] Construct an input file that makes Program Q go even more slowly than it does in exercise 25. (Try to find a really bad case.)

27. [*M28*] (R. Sedgewick.) Consider the *best* case of Algorithm Q: Find a permutation of $\{1, 2, \ldots, 23\}$ that takes the least time to be sorted when $N = 23$ and $M = 3$.

28. [*M26*] Find the recurrence relation analogous to (20) that is satisfied by the average number of comparisons in Singleton's modification of Algorithm Q (choosing s as the median of $\{K_1, K_{\lfloor (N+1)/2 \rfloor}, K_N\}$ instead of $s = K_1$). Ignore the comparisons made when computing the median value s.

29. [*HM40*] Continuing exercise 28, find the asymptotic value of the number of comparisons in Singleton's "median of three" method.

▶ **30.** [*25*] (P. Shackleton.) When *multiword keys* are being sorted, many sorting methods become progressively slower as the file gets closer to its final order, since equal and nearly-equal keys require an inspection of several words to determine the proper lexicographic order. (See exercise 5–5.) Files that arise in practice often involve such keys, so this phenomenon can have a significant impact on the sorting time.

Explain how Algorithm Q can be extended to avoid this difficulty; within a subfile in which the leading k words are known to have constant values for all keys, only the $(k+1)$st words of the keys should be inspected.

▶ **31.** [*20*] (C. A. R. Hoare.) Suppose that, instead of sorting an entire file, we only want to determine the mth smallest of a given set of n elements. Show that quicksort can be adapted to this purpose, avoiding many of the computations required to do a complete sort.

32. [*M40*] Find a simple closed form expression for C_{nm}, the average number of key comparisons required to select the mth smallest of n elements by the "quickfind" method of exercise 31. (For simplicity, let $M = 1$; that is, don't assume the use of a special technique for short subfiles.) What is the asymptotic behavior of $C_{(2m-1)m}$, the average number of comparisons needed to find the median of $2m - 1$ elements by Hoare's method?

▶ **33.** [*15*] Design an algorithm that rearranges all the numbers in a given table so that all *negative* values precede all nonnegative ones. (The items need not be sorted completely, just separated between negative and nonnegative.) Your algorithm should use the minimum possible number of exchanges.

34. [*20*] How can the bit-inspection loops of radix exchange (in steps R3 through R6) be speeded up?

35. [*M23*] Analyze the values of the frequencies A, B, C, G, K, L, R, S, and X that arise in radix exchange sorting using "case (i) input."

36. [*M27*] Given a sequence of numbers $\langle a_n \rangle = a_0, a_1, a_2, \ldots$, define its *binomial transform* $\langle \hat{a}_n \rangle = \hat{a}_0, \hat{a}_1, \hat{a}_2, \ldots$ by the rule

$$\hat{a}_n = \sum_k \binom{n}{k} (-1)^k a_k.$$

a) Prove that $\langle \hat{\hat{a}}_n \rangle = \langle a_n \rangle$.
b) Find the binomial transforms of the sequences $\langle 1 \rangle$; $\langle n \rangle$; $\langle \binom{n}{m} \rangle$, for fixed m; $\langle a^n \rangle$, for fixed a; $\langle \binom{n}{m} a^n \rangle$, for fixed a and m.

c) Suppose that a sequence $\langle x_n \rangle$ satisfies the relation

$$x_n = a_n + 2^{1-n} \sum_{k \geq 2} \binom{n}{k} x_k, \qquad \text{for } n \geq 2; \qquad x_0 = x_1 = a_0 = a_1 = 0.$$

Prove that the solution to this recurrence is

$$x_n = \sum_{k \geq 2} \binom{n}{k} (-1)^k \frac{2^{k-1} \hat{a}_k}{2^{k-1} - 1} = a_n + \sum_{k \geq 2} \binom{n}{k} (-1)^k \frac{\hat{a}_k}{2^{k-1} - 1}.$$

37. [*M28*] Determine all sequences $\langle a_n \rangle$ such that $\langle \hat{a}_n \rangle = \langle a_n \rangle$, in the sense of exercise 36.

▶ **38.** [*M30*] Find A_N, B_N, C_N, G_N, K_N, L_N, R_N, and X_N, the average values of the quantities in (29), when radix exchange is applied to "case (ii) input." Express your answers in terms of N and the quantities

$$U_n = \sum_{k \geq 2} \binom{n}{k} \frac{(-1)^k}{2^{k-1} - 1} \qquad V_n = \sum_{k \geq 2} \binom{n}{k} \frac{(-1)^k k}{2^{k-1} - 1} = n(U_n - U_{n-1}).$$

[*Hint:* See exercise 36.]

39. [*20*] The results shown in (30) indicate that radix exchange sorting involves about $1.44N$ partitioning stages when it is applied to random input. Prove that quicksort will never require more than N stages; and explain why radix exchange often does.

40. [*21*] Explain how to modify Algorithm R so that it works with reasonable efficiency when sorting files containing numerous equal keys.

▶ **41.** [*30*] Devise a good way to exchange records $R_l \ldots R_r$ so that they are partitioned into three blocks, with (i) $K_k < K$ for $l \leq k < i$; (ii) $K_k = K$ for $i \leq k \leq j$; (iii) $K_k > K$ for $j < k \leq r$. Schematically, the final arrangement should be

$< K$	$= K$	$> K$
l	i	j	r

42. [*HM32*] For any real number $c > 0$, prove that the probability is less than e^{-c} that Algorithm Q will make more than $(c + 1)(N + 1)H_N$ comparisons when sorting random data. (This upper bound is especially interesting when c is, say, N^{ϵ}.)

43. [*HM21*] Prove that $\int_0^1 y^{-1}(e^{-y} - 1) \, dy + \int_1^\infty y^{-1} e^{-y} \, dy = -\gamma$. [*Hint:* Consider $\lim_{a \to 0+} y^{a-1}$.]

44. [*HM24*] Derive (37) as suggested in the text.

45. [*HM20*] Explain why (43) is true, when $x > 0$.

46. [*HM20*] What is the value of $(1/2\pi i) \int_{a-i\infty}^{a+i\infty} \Gamma(z) n^{s-z} \, dz / (2^{s-z} - 1)$, given that s is a positive integer and $0 < a < s$?

47. [*HM21*] Prove that $\sum_{j \geq 1} (n/2^j) e^{-n/2^j}$ is a bounded function of n.

48. [*HM24*] Find the asymptotic value of the quantity V_n defined in exercise 38, using a method analogous to the text's study of U_n, obtaining terms up to $O(1)$.

49. [*HM24*] Extend the asymptotic formula (47) for U_n to $O(n^{-1})$.

50. [*HM24*] Find the asymptotic value of the function

$$U_{mn} = \sum_{k \geq 2} \binom{n}{k} (-1)^k \frac{1}{m^{k-1} - 1},$$

when m is any fixed number greater than 1. (When m is an integer greater than 2, this quantity arises in the study of generalizations of radix exchange, as well as the trie memory search algorithms of Section 6.3.)

▶ **51.** [*HM28*] Show that the gamma-function approach to asymptotic problems can be used instead of Euler's summation formula to derive the asymptotic expansion of the quantity $r_k(m)$ in (35). (This gives us a uniform method for studying $r_k(m)$ for all k, without relying on tricks such as the text's introduction of $g_{-1}(x) = (e^{-x^2} - 1)/x$.)

52. [*HM35*] (N. G. de Bruijn.) What is the asymptotic behavior of the sum

$$S_n = \sum_{t \geq 1} \binom{2n}{n+t} d(t),$$

where $d(t)$ is the number of divisors of t? (Thus, $d(1) = 1$, $d(2) = d(3) = 2$, $d(4) = 3$, $d(5) = 2$, etc. This question arises in connection with the analysis of a tree traversal algorithm, exercise 2.3.1–11.) Find the value of $S_n / \binom{2n}{n}$ to terms of $O(n^{-1})$.

53. [*HM42*] Analyze the average number of bit inspections and exchanges done by radix exchange when the input data consists of infinite-precision binary numbers in $[0\,..\,1)$, each of whose bits is independently equal to 1 with probability p. (Only the case $p = \frac{1}{2}$ is discussed in the text; the methods we have used can be generalized to arbitrary p.) Consider in particular the case $p = 1/\phi = .61803\ldots$.

54. [*HM24*] (S. O. Rice.) Show that U_n can be written

$$U_n = (-1)^n \frac{n!}{2\pi i} \oint_C \frac{dz}{z(z-1)\ldots(z-n)} \frac{1}{2^{z-1}-1},$$

where C is a skinny closed curve encircling the points $2, 3, \ldots, n$. Changing C to an arbitrarily large circle centered at the origin, derive the convergent series

$$U_n = \frac{(H_{n-1} - 1)n}{\ln 2} - \frac{n}{2} + 2 + \frac{2}{\ln 2} \sum_{m \geq 1} \Re\left(B(n+1, -1+ibm)\right),$$

where $b = 2\pi/\ln 2$, and $B(n+1, -1+ibm) = \Gamma(n+1)\Gamma(-1+ibm)/\Gamma(n+ibm) = n!/\prod_{k=0}^{n}(k-1+ibm)$.

▶ **55.** [*22*] Show how to modify Program Q so that the partitioning element is the median of the three keys (28), assuming that $M > 1$.

56. [*M43*] Analyze the average behavior of the quantities that occur in the running time of Algorithm Q when the program has been modified to take the median of three elements as in exercise 55. (See exercise 29.)

5.2.3. Sorting by Selection

Another important family of sorting techniques is based on the idea of repeated selection. The simplest selection method is perhaps the following:

i) Find the smallest key; transfer the corresponding record to the output area; then replace the key by the value ∞ (which is assumed to be higher than any actual key).

ii) Repeat step (i). This time the second smallest key will be selected, since the smallest key has been replaced by ∞.

iii) Continue repeating step (i) until N records have been selected.

A selection method requires all of the input items to be present before sorting may proceed, and it generates the final outputs one by one in sequence. This is essentially the opposite of insertion, where the inputs are received sequentially but we do not know any of the final outputs until sorting is completed.

Step (i) involves $N-1$ comparisons each time a new record is selected, and it also requires a separate output area in memory. But we can obviously do better: We can move the selected record into its proper final position, by exchanging it with the record currently occupying that position. Then we need not consider that position again in future selections, and we need not deal with infinite keys. This idea yields our first selection sorting algorithm.

Algorithm S (*Straight selection sort*). Records $R_1, \ldots, R_N$ are rearranged in place; after sorting is complete, their keys will be in order, $K_1 \leq \cdots \leq K_N$. Sorting is based on the method indicated above, except that it proves to be more convenient to select the *largest* element first, then the second largest, etc.

S1. [Loop on j.] Perform steps S2 and S3 for $j = N, N-1, \ldots, 2$.

S2. [Find $\max(K_1, \ldots, K_j)$.] Search through keys $K_j, K_{j-1}, \ldots, K_1$ to find a maximal one; let it be K_i, where i is as large as possible.

S3. [Exchange with R_j.] Interchange records $R_i \leftrightarrow R_j$. (Now records $R_j, \ldots, R_N$ are in their final position.) ▮

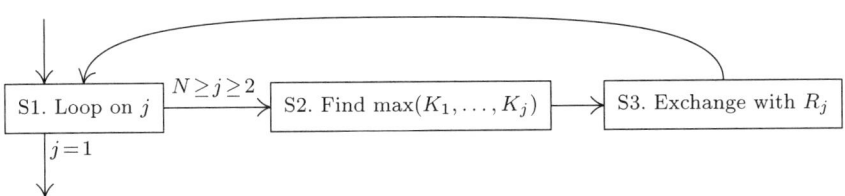

Fig. 21. Straight selection sorting.

Table 1 shows this algorithm in action on our sixteen example keys. Elements that are candidates for the maximum during the right-to-left search in step S2 are shown in boldface type.

Table 1

STRAIGHT SELECTION SORTING

503	087	512	061	**908**	170	**897**	275	653	426	154	509	612	677	**765**	**703**|
503	087	512	061	703	170	**897**	275	653	426	154	509	612	677	**765**|908	
503	087	512	061	703	170	**765**	275	653	426	154	509	612	**677**|897	908	
503	087	512	061	**703**	170	677	275	**653**	426	154	509	**612**|765	897	908	
503	087	512	061	612	170	**677**	275	**653**	426	154	**509**|703	765	897	908	
503	087	512	061	612	170	509	275	**653**	**426**	**154**|677	703	765	897	908	

$\cdots$

061\|087   154   170   275   426   503   509   512   612   653   677   703   765   897   908

The corresponding MIX program is quite simple:

Program S (*Straight selection sort*). As in previous programs of this chapter, the records in locations INPUT+1 through INPUT+N are sorted in place, on a full-word key. rA ≡ current maximum, rI1 ≡ $j - 1$, rI2 ≡ k (the current search position), rI3 ≡ i. Assume that $N \geq 2$.

```
01  START  ENT1  N-1             1        S1. Loop on j. j ← N.
02  2H     ENT2  0,1            N-1       S2. Find max(K₁,...,Kⱼ). k ← j - 1.
03         ENT3  1,1            N-1       i ← j.
04         LDA   INPUT,3        N-1       rA ← Kᵢ.
05  8H     CMPA  INPUT,2         A
06         JGE   *+3             A        Jump if Kᵢ ≥ Kₖ.
07         ENT3  0,2             B        Otherwise set i ← k,
08         LDA   INPUT,3         B          rA ← Kᵢ.
09         DEC2  1               A        k ← k - 1.
10         J2P   8B              A        Repeat if k > 0.
11         LDX   INPUT+1,1      N-1       S3. Exchange with Rⱼ.
12         STX   INPUT,3        N-1       Rᵢ ← Rⱼ.
13         STA   INPUT+1,1      N-1       Rⱼ ← rA.
14         DEC1  1              N-1
15         J1P   2B             N-1       N ≥ j ≥ 2. ▮
```

The running time of this program depends on the number of items, N; the number of comparisons, A; and the number of changes to right-to-left maxima, B. It is easy to see that

$$A = \binom{N}{2} = \frac{1}{2}N(N - 1),\qquad\qquad (1)$$

regardless of the values of the input keys; hence only B is variable. In spite of the simplicity of straight selection, this quantity B is not easy to analyze precisely. Exercises 3 through 6 show that

$$B = \left(\min\ 0,\ \text{ave}\ (N + 1)H_N - 2N,\ \max\ \lfloor N^2/4 \rfloor\right);\qquad (2)$$

in this case the maximum value turns out to be particularly interesting. The standard deviation of B is of order $N^{3/4}$; see exercise 7.

Thus the average running time of Program S is $2.5N^2 + 3(N + 1)H_N + 3.5N - 11$ units, just slightly slower than straight insertion (Program 5.2.1S). It is interesting to compare Algorithm S to the bubble sort (Algorithm 5.2.2B), since bubble sorting may be regarded as a selection algorithm that sometimes selects more than one element at a time. For this reason bubble sorting usually does fewer comparisons than straight selection and it may seem to be preferable; but in fact Program 5.2.2B is more than twice as slow as Program S! Bubble sorting is handicapped by the fact that it does so many exchanges, while straight selection involves very little data movement.

Refinements of straight selection. Is there any way to improve on the selection method used in Algorithm S? For example, take the search for a maximum in step S2; is there a substantially faster way to find a maximum? The answer to the latter question is *no*!

Lemma M. *Every algorithm for finding the maximum of n elements, based on comparing pairs of elements, must make at least $n - 1$ comparisons.*

Proof. If we have made fewer than $n - 1$ comparisons, there will be at least two elements that have never been found to be less than any others. Therefore we do not know which of these two elements is larger, and we cannot have determined the maximum. ∎

Thus, any selection process that finds the largest element must perform at least $n - 1$ comparisons; and we might suspect that all sorting methods based on n repeated selections are doomed to require $\Omega(n^2)$ operations. But fortunately Lemma M applies only to the *first* selection step; subsequent selections can make use of previously gained information. For example, exercises 8 and 9 show that a comparatively simple change to Algorithm S will cut the average number of comparisons in half.

Consider the 16 numbers in Table 1; one way to save time on repeated selections is to regard them as four groups of four. We can start by determining the largest in each group, namely the respective keys

$$512, 908, 653, 765;$$

the largest of these four elements, 908, is then the largest of the entire file. To get the second largest we need only look at 512, 653, 765, and the other three elements of the group containing 908; the largest of $\{170, 897, 275\}$ is 897, and the largest of

$$512, 897, 653, 765$$

is 897. Similarly, to get the third largest element we determine the largest of $\{170, 275\}$ and then the largest of

$$512, 275, 653, 765.$$

Each selection after the first takes at most 5 additional comparisons. In general, if N is a perfect square, we can divide the file into $\sqrt{N}$ groups of $\sqrt{N}$ elements each; each selection after the first takes at most $\sqrt{N} - 2$ comparisons within the group of the previously selected item, plus $\sqrt{N} - 1$ comparisons among the "group leaders." This idea is called *quadratic selection*; its total execution time is $O(N\sqrt{N})$, which is substantially better than order N^2.

Quadratic selection was first published by E. H. Friend [*JACM* **3** (1956), 152–154], who pointed out that the same idea can be generalized to cubic, quartic, and higher degrees of selection. For example, cubic selection divides the file into $\sqrt[3]{N}$ large groups, each containing $\sqrt[3]{N}$ small groups, each containing $\sqrt[3]{N}$ records; the execution time is proportional to $N\sqrt[3]{N}$. If we carry this idea to its ultimate conclusion we arrive at what Friend called "nth degree selecting," based on a binary tree structure. This method has an execution time proportional to $N \log N$; we shall call it *tree selection*.

Tree selection. The principles of tree selection sorting are easy to understand in terms of matches in a typical "knockout tournament." Consider, for example, the results of the ping-pong contest shown in Fig. 22; at the bottom level, Kim beats Sandy and Chris beats Lou, then in the next round Chris beats Kim, etc.

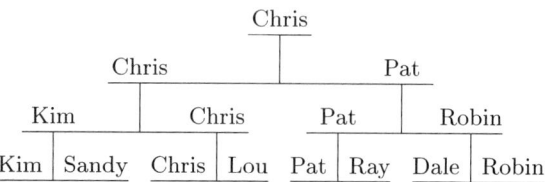

Fig. 22. A ping-pong tournament.

Figure 22 shows that Chris is the champion of the eight players, and $8-1 = 7$ matches/comparisons were required to determine this fact. Pat is not necessarily the second-best player; any of the people defeated by Chris, including the first-round loser Lou, might possibly be second best. We can determine the second-best player by having Lou play Kim, and the winner of that match plays Pat; only two additional matches are required to find the second-best player, because of the structure we have remembered from the earlier games.

In general, we can "output" the player at the root of the tree, and replay the tournament as if that player had been sick and unable to play a good game. Then the original second-best player will rise to the root; and to recalculate the winners in the upper levels of the tree, only one path must be changed. It follows that fewer than $\lceil \lg N \rceil$ further comparisons are needed to select the second-best player. The same procedure will find the third-best, etc.; hence the total time for such a selection sort will be roughly proportional to $N \log N$, as claimed above.

Figure 23 shows tree selection sorting in action, on our 16 example numbers. Notice that we need to know where the key at the root came from, in order to know where to insert the next "$-\infty$". Therefore each branch node of the tree should actually contain a pointer or index specifying the position of the relevant key, instead of the key itself. It follows that we need memory space for N input records, $N - 1$ pointers, and N output records or pointers to those records. (If the output goes to tape or disk, of course, we don't need to retain the output records in high-speed memory.)

The reader should pause at this point and work exercise 10, because a good understanding of the basic principles of tree selection will make it easier to appreciate the remarkable improvements we are about to discuss.

One way to modify tree selection, essentially introduced by K. E. Iverson [*A Programming Language* (Wiley, 1962), 223–227], does away with the need for pointers by "looking ahead" in the following way: When the winner of a match in the bottom level of the tree is moved up, the winning value can be replaced immediately by $-\infty$ at the bottom level; and whenever a winner moves up from one branch to another, we can replace the corresponding value by the one that should eventually move up into the vacated place (namely the larger of the two keys below). Repeating this operation as often as possible converts Fig. 23(a) into Fig. 24.

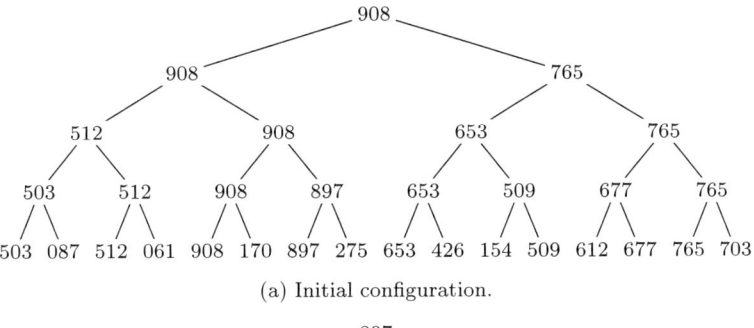

(a) Initial configuration.

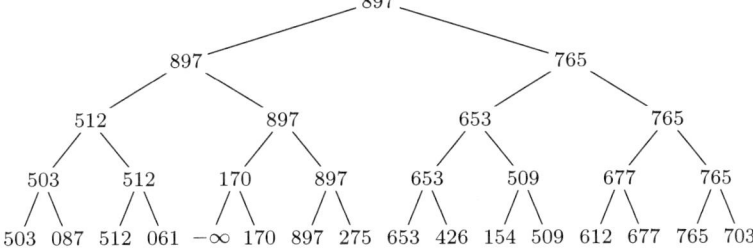

(b) Key 908 is replaced by $-\infty$, and the second highest element moves up to the root.

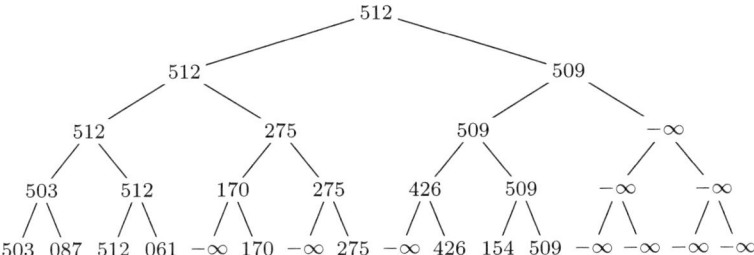

(c) Configuration after 908, 897, 765, 703, 677, 653, and 612 have been output.

Fig. 23. An example of tree selection sorting.

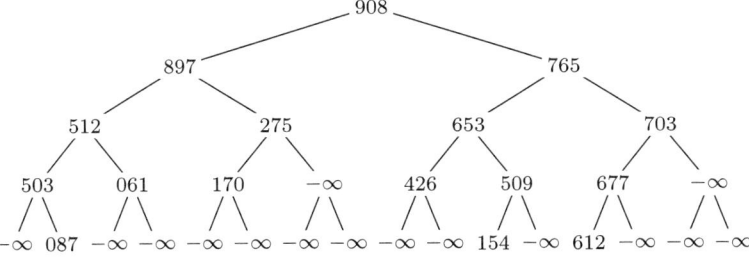

Fig. 24. The Peter Principle applied to sorting. Everyone rises to their level of incompetence in the hierarchy.

Once the tree has been set up in this way we can proceed to sort by a "top-down" method, instead of the "bottom up" method of Fig. 23: We output the root, then move up its largest descendant, then move up the latter's largest descendant, and so forth. The process begins to look less like a ping-pong tournament and more like a corporate system of promotions.

The reader should be able to see that this top-down method has the advantage that redundant comparisons of $-\infty$ with $-\infty$ can be avoided. (The bottom-up approach finds $-\infty$ omnipresent in the latter stages of sorting, but the top-down approach can stop modifying the tree during each stage as soon as a $-\infty$ has been stored.)

Figures 23 and 24 are *complete binary trees* with 16 terminal nodes (see Section 2.3.4.5), and it is convenient to represent such trees in consecutive locations as shown in Fig. 25. Note that the parent of node number k is node $\lfloor k/2 \rfloor$, and its children are nodes $2k$ and $2k+1$. This leads to another advantage of the top-down approach, since it is often considerably simpler to go top-down from node k to nodes $2k$ and $2k+1$ than bottom-up from node k to nodes $k \oplus 1$ and $\lfloor k/2 \rfloor$. (Here $k \oplus 1$ stands for $k+1$ or $k-1$, according as k is even or odd.)

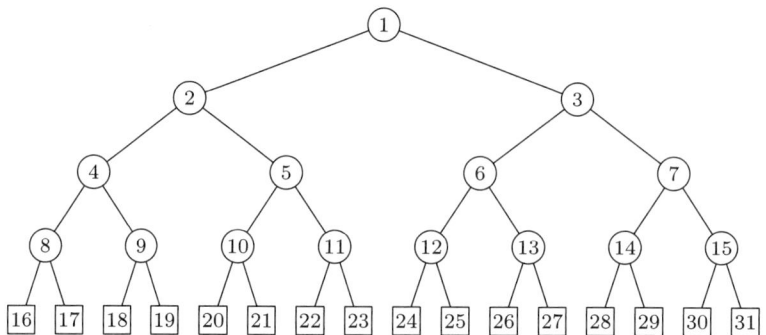

Fig. 25. Sequential storage allocation for a complete binary tree.

Our examples of tree selection so far have more or less assumed that N is a power of 2; but actually we can work with arbitrary N, since the complete binary tree with N terminal nodes is readily constructed for any N.

Now we come to the crucial question: Can't we do the top-down method without using $-\infty$ at all? Wouldn't it be nice if the important information of Fig. 24 were all in locations 1 through 16 of the complete binary tree, without the useless "holes" containing $-\infty$? Some reflection shows that it is indeed possible to achieve this goal, not only eliminating $-\infty$ but also avoiding the need for an auxiliary output area. This line of thinking leads us to an important sorting algorithm that was christened "heapsort" by its discoverer J. W. J. Williams [*CACM* **7** (1964), 347–348].

Heapsort. Let us say that a file of keys $K_1, K_2, \ldots, K_N$ is a *heap* if

$$K_{\lfloor j/2 \rfloor} \geq K_j \qquad \text{for } 1 \leq \lfloor j/2 \rfloor < j \leq N. \tag{3}$$

Thus, $K_1 \geq K_2$, $K_1 \geq K_3$, $K_2 \geq K_4$, etc.; this is exactly the condition that holds in Fig. 24, and it implies in particular that the largest key appears "on top of the heap,"

$$K_1 = \max(K_1, K_2, \ldots, K_N). \tag{4}$$

If we can somehow transform an arbitrary input file into a heap, we can sort the elements by using a top-down selection procedure as described above.

An efficient approach to heap creation has been suggested by R. W. Floyd [*CACM* **7** (1964), 701]. Let us assume that we have been able to arrange the file so that

$$K_{\lfloor j/2 \rfloor} \geq K_j \qquad \text{for } l < \lfloor j/2 \rfloor < j \leq N, \tag{5}$$

where l is some number ≥ 1. (In the original file this condition holds vacuously for $l = \lfloor N/2 \rfloor$, since no subscript j satisfies the condition $\lfloor N/2 \rfloor < \lfloor j/2 \rfloor < j \leq N$.) It is not difficult to see how to transform the file so that the inequalities in (5) are extended to the case $l = \lfloor j/2 \rfloor$, working entirely in the subtree whose root is node l. Then we can decrease l by 1, until condition (3) is finally achieved. These ideas of Williams and Floyd lead to the following elegant algorithm, which merits careful study:

Algorithm H (*Heapsort*). Records $R_1, \ldots, R_N$ are rearranged in place; after sorting is complete, their keys will be in order, $K_1 \leq \cdots \leq K_N$. First we rearrange the file so that it forms a heap, then we repeatedly remove the top of the heap and transfer it to its proper final position. Assume that $N \geq 2$.

H1. [Initialize.] Set $l \leftarrow \lfloor N/2 \rfloor + 1$, $r \leftarrow N$.

H2. [Decrease l or r.] If $l > 1$, set $l \leftarrow l - 1$, $R \leftarrow R_l$, $K \leftarrow K_l$. (If $l > 1$, we are in the process of transforming the input file into a heap; on the other hand if $l = 1$, the keys $K_1 K_2 \ldots K_r$ presently constitute a heap.) Otherwise set $R \leftarrow R_r$, $K \leftarrow K_r$, $R_r \leftarrow R_1$, and $r \leftarrow r - 1$; if this makes $r = 1$, set $R_1 \leftarrow R$ and terminate the algorithm.

H3. [Prepare for siftup.] Set $j \leftarrow l$. (At this point we have

$$K_{\lfloor k/2 \rfloor} \geq K_k \qquad \text{for } l < \lfloor k/2 \rfloor < k \leq r; \tag{6}$$

and record R_k is in its final position for $r < k \leq N$. Steps H3–H8 are called the *siftup algorithm*; their effect is equivalent to setting $R_l \leftarrow R$ and then rearranging $R_l, \ldots, R_r$ so that condition (6) holds also for $l = \lfloor k/2 \rfloor$.)

H4. [Advance downward.] Set $i \leftarrow j$ and $j \leftarrow 2j$. (In the following steps we have $i = \lfloor j/2 \rfloor$.) If $j < r$, go right on to step H5; if $j = r$, go to step H6; and if $j > r$, go to H8.

H5. [Find larger child.] If $K_j < K_{j+1}$, then set $j \leftarrow j + 1$.

H6. [Larger than K?] If $K \geq K_j$, then go to step H8.

H7. [Move it up.] Set $R_i \leftarrow R_j$, and go back to step H4.

H8. [Store R.] Set $R_i \leftarrow R$. (This terminates the siftup algorithm initiated in step H3.) Return to step H2. ∎

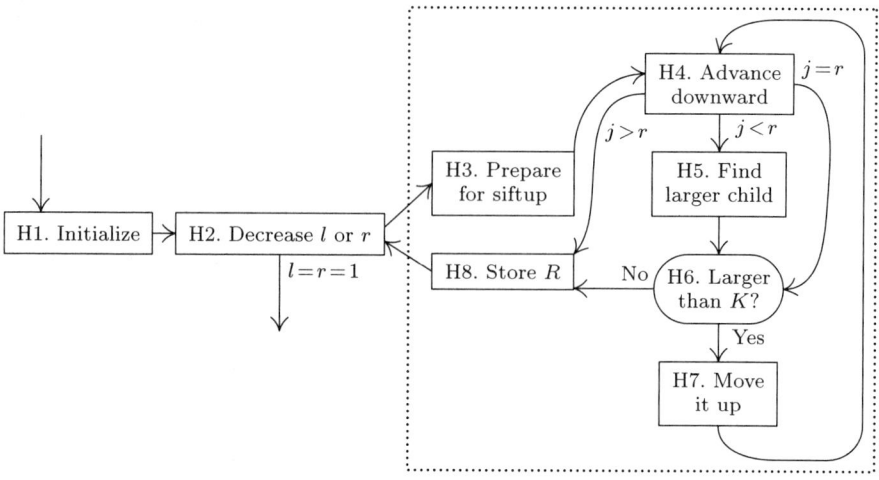

Fig. 26. Heapsort; dotted lines enclose the siftup algorithm.

Heapsort has sometimes been described as the ϕ algorithm, because of the motion of l and r. The upper triangle represents the heap-creation phase, when $r = N$ and l decreases to 1; and the lower triangle represents the selection phase, when $l = 1$ and r decreases to 1. Table 2 shows the process of heapsorting our sixteen example numbers. (Each line in that table shows the state of affairs at the beginning of step H2, and brackets indicate the position of l and r.)

Program H (*Heapsort*). The records in locations INPUT+1 through INPUT+N are sorted by Algorithm H, with the following register assignments: $\text{rI1} \equiv l - 1$, $\text{rI2} \equiv r - 1$, $\text{rI3} \equiv i$, $\text{rI4} \equiv j$, $\text{rI5} \equiv r - j$, $\text{rA} \equiv K \equiv R$, $\text{rX} \equiv R_j$.

01	START	ENT1	N/2	1	*H1. Initialize.* $l \leftarrow \lfloor N/2 \rfloor + 1$.
02		ENT2	N-1	1	$r \leftarrow N$.
03	1H	DEC1	1	$\lfloor N/2 \rfloor$	$l \leftarrow l - 1$.
04		LDA	INPUT+1,1	$\lfloor N/2 \rfloor$	$R \leftarrow R_l, K \leftarrow K_l$.
05	3H	ENT4	1,1	P	*H3. Prepare for siftup.* $j \leftarrow l$.
06		ENT5	0,2	P	
07		DEC5	0,1	P	$\text{rI5} \leftarrow r - j$.
08		JMP	4F	P	To H4.
09	5H	LDX	INPUT,4	$B + A - D$	*H5. Find larger child.*
10		CMPX	INPUT+1,4	$B + A - D$	
11		JGE	6F	$B + A - D$	Jump if $K_j \geq K_{j+1}$.
12		INC4	1	C	Otherwise set $j \leftarrow j + 1$.
13		DEC5	1	C	
14	9H	LDX	INPUT,4	$C + D$	$\text{rX} \leftarrow R_j$.
15	6H	CMPA	INPUT,4	$B + A$	*H6. Larger than K?*
16		JGE	8F	$B + A$	To H8 if $K \geq K_j$.
17	7H	STX	INPUT,3	B	*H7. Move it up.* $R_i \leftarrow R_j$.
18	4H	ENT3	0,4	$B + P$	*H4. Advance downward.* $i \leftarrow j$.
19		DEC5	0,4	$B + P$	$\text{rI5} \leftarrow \text{rI5} - j$.
20		INC4	0,4	$B + P$	$j \leftarrow j + j$.

Table 2

EXAMPLE OF HEAPSORT

K_1	K_2	K_3	K_4	K_5	K_6	K_7	K_8	K_9	K_{10}	K_{11}	K_{12}	K_{13}	K_{14}	K_{15}	K_{16}	l	r
503	087	512	061	908	170	897	275	[653	426	154	509	612	677	765	703]	9	16
503	087	512	061	908	170	897	[703	653	426	154	509	612	677	765	275]	8	16
503	087	512	061	908	170	[897	703	653	426	154	509	612	677	765	275]	7	16
503	087	512	061	908	[612	897	703	653	426	154	509	170	677	765	275]	6	16
503	087	512	061	[908	612	897	703	653	426	154	509	170	677	765	275]	5	16
503	087	512	[703	908	612	897	275	653	426	154	509	170	677	765	061]	4	16
503	087	[897	703	908	612	765	275	653	426	154	509	170	677	512	061]	3	16
503	[908	897	703	426	612	765	275	653	087	154	509	170	677	512	061]	2	16
[908	703	897	653	426	612	765	275	503	087	154	509	170	677	512	061]	1	16
[897	703	765	653	426	612	677	275	503	087	154	509	170	061	512]	908	1	15
[765	703	677	653	426	612	512	275	503	087	154	509	170	061]	897	908	1	14
[703	653	677	503	426	612	512	275	061	087	154	509	170]	765	897	908	1	13
[677	653	612	503	426	509	512	275	061	087	154	170]	703	765	897	908	1	12
[653	503	612	275	426	509	512	170	061	087	154]	677	703	765	897	908	1	11
[612	503	512	275	426	509	154	170	061	087]	653	677	703	765	897	908	1	10
[512	503	509	275	426	087	154	170	061]	612	653	677	703	765	897	908	1	9
[509	503	154	275	426	087	061	170]	512	612	653	677	703	765	897	908	1	8
[503	426	154	275	170	087	061]	509	512	612	653	677	703	765	897	908	1	7
[426	275	154	061	170	087]	503	509	512	612	653	677	703	765	897	908	1	6
[275	170	154	061	087]	426	503	509	512	612	653	677	703	765	897	908	1	5
[170	087	154	061]	275	426	503	509	512	612	653	677	703	765	897	908	1	4
[154	087	061]	170	275	426	503	509	512	612	653	677	703	765	897	908	1	3
[087	061]	154	170	275	426	503	509	512	612	653	677	703	765	897	908	1	2

21		J5P	5B	$B + P$	To H5 if $j < r$.
22		J5Z	9B	$P - A + D$	To H6 if $j = r$.
23	8H	STA	INPUT,3	P	H8. Store R. $R_i \leftarrow R$.
24	2H	J1P	1B	P	H2. Decrease l or r.
25		LDA	INPUT+1,2	$N - 1$	If $l = 1$, set $R \leftarrow R_r$, $K \leftarrow K_r$.
26		LDX	INPUT+1	$N - 1$	
27		STX	INPUT+1,2	$N - 1$	$R_r \leftarrow R_1$.
28		DEC2	1	$N - 1$	$r \leftarrow r - 1$.
29		J2P	3B	$N - 1$	To H3 if $r > 1$.
30		STA	INPUT+1	1	$R_1 \leftarrow R$. ∎

Although this program is only about twice as long as Program S, it is much more efficient when N is large. Its running time depends on

$P = N + \lfloor N/2 \rfloor - 2$, the number of siftup passes;

A, the number of siftup passes in which the key K finally lands in an interior node of the heap;

B, the total number of keys promoted during siftups;

C, the number of times $j \leftarrow j + 1$ in step H5; and

D, the number of times $j = r$ in step H4.

These quantities are analyzed below; in practice they show comparatively little fluctuation about their average values,

$$A \approx 0.349N, \qquad\qquad B \approx N \lg N - 1.87N,$$
$$C \approx \tfrac{1}{2} N \lg N - 0.94N, \qquad D \approx \lg N. \qquad\qquad (7)$$

For example, when $N = 1000$, four experiments on random input gave, respectively, $A = 371$, 351, 341, 340; $B = 8055$, 8072, 8094, 8108; $C = 4056$, 4087, 4017, 4083; and $D = 12$, 14, 8, 13. The total running time,

$$7A + 14B + 4C + 20N - 2D + 15\lfloor N/2 \rfloor - 28,$$

is therefore approximately $16N \lg N + 0.01N$ units on the average.

A glance at Table 2 makes it hard to believe that heapsort is very efficient; large keys migrate to the left before we stash them at the right! It is indeed a strange way to sort, when N is small; the sorting time for the 16 keys in Table 2 is $1068u$, while the simple method of straight insertion (Program 5.2.1S) takes only $514u$. Straight selection (Program S) takes $853u$.

For larger N, Program H is more efficient. It invites comparison with shellsort (Program 5.2.1D) and quicksort (Program 5.2.2Q), since all three programs sort by comparisons of keys and use little or no auxiliary storage. When $N = 1000$, the approximate average running times on MIX are

$$160000u \text{ for heapsort,}$$
$$130000u \text{ for shellsort,}$$
$$80000u \text{ for quicksort.}$$

(MIX is a typical computer, but particular machines will of course yield somewhat different relative values.) As N gets larger, heapsort will be superior to shellsort, but its asymptotic running time $16N \lg N \approx 23.08N \ln N$ will never beat quicksort's $11.67N \ln N$. A modification of heapsort discussed in exercise 18 will speed up the process by substantially reducing the number of comparisons, but even this improvement falls short of quicksort.

On the other hand, quicksort is efficient only on the average, and its worst case is of order N^2. Heapsort has the interesting property that its worst case isn't much worse than the average: We always have

$$A \leq 1.5N, \qquad B \leq N\lfloor \lg N \rfloor, \qquad C \leq N\lfloor \lg N \rfloor, \qquad\qquad (8)$$

so Program H will take no more than $18N\lfloor \lg N \rfloor + 38N$ units of time, regardless of the distribution of the input data. Heapsort is the first sorting method we have seen that is *guaranteed* to be of order $N \log N$. Merge sorting, discussed in Section 5.2.4 below, also has this property, but it requires more memory space.

Largest in, first out. We have seen in Chapter 2 that linear lists can often be classified in a meaningful way by the nature of the insertion and deletion operations that make them grow and shrink. A *stack* has last-in-first-out behavior, in the sense that every deletion removes the youngest item in the list — the item that was inserted most recently of all items currently present. A simple *queue* has first-in-first-out behavior, in the sense that every deletion removes the oldest remaining item. In more complex situations, such as the elevator simulation of Section 2.2.5, we want a smallest-in-first-out list, where every deletion removes the item having the smallest key. Such a list may be called a *priority queue*, since the key of each item reflects its relative ability to get out of the list quickly. Selection sorting is a special case of a priority queue in which we do N insertions followed by N deletions.

Priority queues arise in a wide variety of applications. For example, some numerical iterative schemes are based on repeated selection of an item having the largest (or smallest) value of some test criterion; parameters of the selected item are changed, and it is reinserted into the list with a new test value, based on the new values of its parameters. Operating systems often make use of priority queues for the scheduling of jobs. Exercises 15, 29, and 36 mention other typical applications of priority queues, and many other examples will appear in later chapters.

How shall we implement priority queues? One of the obvious methods is to maintain a sorted list, containing the items in order of their keys. Inserting a new item is then essentially the same problem we have treated in our study of insertion sorting, Section 5.2.1. Another even more obvious way to deal with priority queues is to keep the list of elements in arbitrary order, selecting the appropriate element each time a deletion is required by finding the largest (or smallest) key. The trouble with both of these obvious approaches is that they require $\Omega(N)$ steps either for insertion or deletion, when there are N entries in the list, so they are very time-consuming when N is large.

In his original paper on heapsorting, Williams pointed out that heaps are ideally suited to large priority queue applications, since we can insert or delete elements from a heap in $O(\log N)$ steps; furthermore, all elements of the heap are compactly located in consecutive memory locations. The selection phase of Algorithm H is a sequence of deletion steps of a *largest-in-first-out* process: To delete the largest element K_1 we remove it and sift K_N up into a new heap of $N - 1$ elements. (If we want a smallest-in-first-out algorithm, as in the elevator simulation, we can obviously change the definition of heap so that "$\geq$" becomes "$\leq$" in (3); for convenience, we shall consider only the largest-in-first-out case here.) In general, if we want to delete the largest item and then insert a new element x, we can do the siftup procedure with

$$l = 1, \qquad r = N, \qquad \text{and} \qquad K = x.$$

If we wish to insert an element x without a prior deletion, we can use the bottom-up procedure of exercise 16.

A linked representation for priority queues. An efficient way to represent priority queues as linked binary trees was discovered in 1971 by Clark A. Crane [Technical Report STAN-CS-72-259 (Computer Science Department, Stanford University, 1972)]. His method requires two link fields and a small count in every record, but it has the following advantages over a heap:

i) When the priority queue is being treated as a stack, the insertion and deletion operations take a fixed time independent of the queue size.

ii) The records never move, only the pointers change.

iii) Two disjoint priority queues, having a total of N elements, can easily be merged into a single priority queue, in only $O(\log N)$ steps.

Crane's original method, slightly modified, is illustrated in Fig. 27, which shows a special kind of binary tree structure. Each node contains a KEY field, a DIST field, and two link fields LEFT and RIGHT. The DIST field is always set to the length of a shortest path from that node to the null link Λ; in other words, it is the distance from that node to the nearest empty subtree. If we define DIST$(\Lambda) = 0$ and KEY$(\Lambda) = -\infty$, the KEY and DIST fields in the tree satisfy the following properties:

$$\text{KEY(P)} \geq \text{KEY(LEFT(P))}, \qquad \text{KEY(P)} \geq \text{KEY(RIGHT(P))}; \tag{9}$$

$$\text{DIST(P)} = 1 + \min(\text{DIST(LEFT(P))}, \text{DIST(RIGHT(P))}); \tag{10}$$

$$\text{DIST(LEFT(P))} \geq \text{DIST(RIGHT(P))}. \tag{11}$$

Relation (9) is analogous to the heap condition (3); it guarantees that the root of the tree has the largest key. Relation (10) is just the definition of the DIST fields as stated above. Relation (11) is the interesting innovation: It implies that a shortest path to Λ may always be obtained by moving to the right. We shall say that a binary tree with this property is a *leftist tree*, because it tends to lean so heavily to the left.

It is clear from these definitions that DIST$(\text{P}) = n$ implies the existence of at least 2^n empty subtrees below P; otherwise there would be a shorter path from P to Λ. Thus, if there are N nodes in a leftist tree, the path leading downward from the root towards the right contains at most $\lfloor \lg(N + 1) \rfloor$ nodes. It is possible to insert a new node into the priority queue by traversing this path (see exercise 33); hence only $O(\log N)$ steps are needed in the worst case. The best case occurs when the tree is linear (all RIGHT links are Λ), and the worst case occurs when the tree is perfectly balanced.

To remove the node at the root, we simply need to merge its two subtrees. The operation of merging two disjoint leftist trees, pointed to respectively by P and Q, is conceptually simple: If KEY$(\text{P}) \geq$ KEY(Q) we take P as the root and merge Q with P's right subtree; then DIST(P) is updated, and LEFT(P) is interchanged with RIGHT(P) if necessary. A detailed description of this process is not difficult to devise (see exercise 33).

Comparison of priority queue techniques. When the number of nodes, N, is small, it is best to use one of the straightforward linear list methods to maintain a priority queue; but when N is large, a $\log N$ method using heaps or leftist trees is obviously much faster. In Section 6.2.3 we shall discuss the representation of linear lists as *balanced trees*, and this leads to a third $\log N$ method suitable for priority queue implementation. It is therefore appropriate to compare these three techniques.

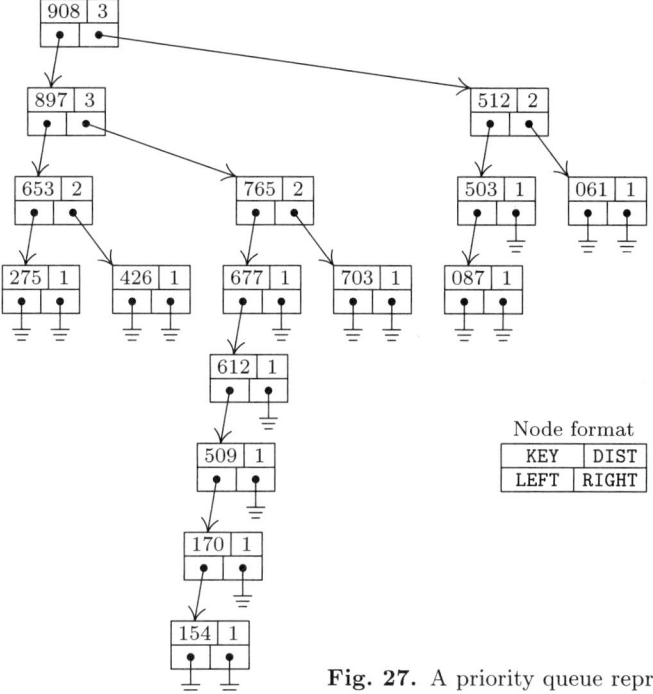

Fig. 27. A priority queue represented as a leftist tree.

We have seen that leftist tree operations tend to be slightly faster than heap operations, although heaps consume less memory space because they have no link fields. Balanced trees take about the same space as leftist trees, perhaps slightly less; the operations are slower than heaps, and the programming is more complicated, but the balanced tree structure is considerably more flexible in several ways. When using a heap or a leftist tree we cannot predict very easily what will happen to two items with equal keys; it is impossible to guarantee that items with equal keys will be treated in a last-in-first-out or first-in-first-out manner, unless the key is extended to include an additional "serial number of insertion" field so that no equal keys are really present. With balanced trees, on the other hand, we can easily stipulate consistent conventions about equal keys, and we can also do things such as "insert x immediately before (or after) y." Balanced trees are symmetrical, so that we can delete either the largest or the smallest element at any time, while heaps and leftist trees must be oriented one way or the other. (See exercise 31, however, which shows how to construct *symmetrical* heaps.) Balanced trees can be used for searching as well as for sorting; and we can rather quickly remove consecutive blocks of elements from a balanced tree. But $\Omega(N)$ steps are needed in general to merge two balanced trees, while leftist trees can be merged in only $O(\log N)$ steps.

In summary, heaps use minimum memory; leftist trees are great for merging disjoint priority queues; and the flexibility of balanced trees is available, if necessary, at reasonable cost.

◈ *Many new ways to represent priority queues have been discovered since the
pioneering work of Williams and Crane discussed above. Programmers now
have a large menu of options to ponder, besides simple lists, heaps, leftist or
balanced trees:*
  - stratified trees, which provide symmetrical priority queue operations in only
    $O(\log \log M)$ steps when all keys lie in a given range $0 \le K < M$ [P. van
    Emde Boas, R. Kaas, and E. Zijlstra, *Math. Systems Theory* **10** (1977),
    99–127];
  - binomial queues [J. Vuillemin, *CACM* **21** (1978), 309–315; M. R. Brown,
    SICOMP **7** (1978), 298–319];
  - pagodas [J. Françon, G. Viennot, and J. Vuillemin, *FOCS* **19** (1978), 1–7];
  - pairing heaps [M. L. Fredman, R. Sedgewick, D. D. Sleator, and R. E. Tarjan,
    Algorithmica **1** (1986), 111–129; J. T. Stasko and J. S. Vitter, *CACM* **30**
    (1987), 234–249; M. L. Fredman, *JACM* **46** (1999), 473–501];
  - skew heaps [D. D. Sleator and R. E. Tarjan, *SICOMP* **15** (1986), 52–59];
  - Fibonacci heaps [M. L. Fredman and R. E. Tarjan, *JACM* **34** (1987), 596–
    615] and the more general AF-heaps [M. L. Fredman and D. E. Willard,
    J. Computer and System Sci. **48** (1994), 533–551];
  - calendar queues [R. Brown, *CACM* **31** (1988), 1220–1227; G. A. Davison,
    CACM **32** (1989), 1241–1243];
  - relaxed heaps [J. R. Driscoll, H. N. Gabow, R. Shrairman, and R. E. Tarjan,
    CACM **31** (1988), 1343–1354];
  - fishspear [M. J. Fischer and M. S. Paterson, *JACM* **41** (1994), 3–30];
  - hot queues [B. V. Cherkassky, A. V. Goldberg, and C. Silverstein, *SICOMP*
    28 (1999), 1326–1346];

*etc. Not all of these methods will survive the test of time; leftist trees are in fact
already obsolete, except for applications with a strong tendency towards last-in-
first-out behavior. Detailed implementations and expositions of binomial queues
and Fibonacci heaps can be found in D. E. Knuth, The Stanford GraphBase
(New York: ACM Press, 1994), 475–489.*

*Analysis of heapsort. Algorithm H is rather complicated, so it probably will
never submit to a complete mathematical analysis; but several of its properties
can be deduced without great difficulty. Therefore we shall conclude this section
by studying the anatomy of a heap in some detail.

Figure 28 shows the shape of a heap with 26 elements; each node has been
labeled in binary notation corresponding to its subscript in the heap. Asterisks
in this diagram denote the *special nodes*, those that lie on the path from 1 to N.

One of the most important attributes of a heap is the collection of its subtree
sizes. For example, in Fig. 28 the sizes of the subtrees rooted at $1, 2, \ldots, 26$ are,
respectively,

$$26^*, 15, 10^*, 7, 7, 6^*, 3, 3, 3, 3, 3, 3, 2^*, 1, 1, 1, 1, 1, 1, 1, 1, 1, 1, 1, 1, 1^*. \qquad (12)$$

Asterisks denote *special subtrees*, rooted at the special nodes; exercise 20 shows
that if the binary representation of N is

$$N = (b_n b_{n-1} \ldots b_1 b_0)_2, \qquad n = \lfloor \lg N \rfloor, \qquad (13)$$

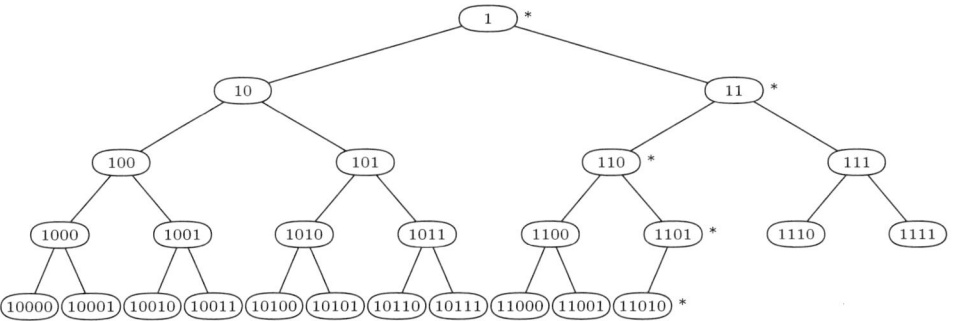

Fig. 28. A heap of $26 = (11010)_2$ elements looks like this.

then the special subtree sizes are always

$$(1b_{n-1}\ldots b_1 b_0)_2,\ (1b_{n-2}\ldots b_1 b_0)_2,\ \ldots,\ (1b_1 b_0)_2,\ (1b_0)_2,\ (1)_2. \qquad (14)$$

Nonspecial subtrees are always perfectly balanced, so their size is always of the form $2^k - 1$. Exercise 21 shows that the nonspecial sizes consist of exactly

$$\left\lfloor \frac{N-1}{2} \right\rfloor \text{ 1s,} \quad \left\lfloor \frac{N-2}{4} \right\rfloor \text{ 3s,} \quad \left\lfloor \frac{N-4}{8} \right\rfloor \text{ 7s,} \quad \ldots, \quad \left\lfloor \frac{N-2^{n-1}}{2^n} \right\rfloor (2^n - 1)\text{s.} \qquad (15)$$

For example, Fig. 28 contains twelve nonspecial subtrees of size 1, six of size 3, two of size 7, and one of size 15.

Let s_l be the size of the subtree whose root is l, and let M_N be the multiset $\{s_1, s_2, \ldots, s_N\}$ of all these sizes. We can calculate M_N easily for any given N by using (14) and (15). Exercise 5.1.4–20 tells us that the total number of ways to arrange the integers $\{1, 2, \ldots, N\}$ into a heap is

$$N!/s_1 s_2 \ldots s_N = N! \Big/ \prod \{s \mid s \in M_N\}. \qquad (16)$$

For example, the number of ways to place the 26 letters $\{A, B, C, \ldots, Z\}$ into Fig. 28 so that vertical lines preserve alphabetic order is

$$26!/(26 \cdot 10 \cdot 6 \cdot 2 \cdot 1 \cdot 1^{12} \cdot 3^6 \cdot 7^2 \cdot 15^1).$$

We are now in a position to analyze the heap-creation phase of Algorithm H, namely the computations that take place before the condition $l = 1$ occurs for the first time in step H2. Fortunately we can reduce the study of heap creation to the study of independent siftup operations, because of the following theorem.

Theorem H. *If Algorithm H is applied to a random permutation of $\{1, 2, \ldots, N\}$, each of the $N!/\prod \{s \mid s \in M_N\}$ possible heaps is an equally likely outcome of the heap-creation phase. Moreover, each of the $\lfloor N/2 \rfloor$ siftup operations performed during this phase is uniform, in the sense that each of the s_l possible values of i is equally likely when step H8 is reached.*

Proof. We can apply what numerical analysts might call a "backwards analysis"; given a possible result $K_1 \ldots K_N$ of the siftup operation rooted at l, we see that there are exactly s_l prior configurations $K'_1 \ldots K'_N$ of the file that will sift up to that result. Each of these prior configurations has a different value of K'_l; hence, working backwards, there are exactly $s_l\, s_{l+1} \ldots s_N$ input permutations of $\{1, 2, \ldots, N\}$ that yield the configuration $K_1 \ldots K_N$ after the siftup at position l has been completed.

The case $l = 1$ is typical: Let $K_1 \ldots K_N$ be a heap, and let $K'_1 \ldots K'_N$ be a file that is transformed by siftup into $K_1 \ldots K_N$ when $l = 1$, $K = K'_1$. If $K = K_i$, we must have $K'_i = K_{\lfloor i/2 \rfloor}$, $K'_{\lfloor i/2 \rfloor} = K_{\lfloor i/4 \rfloor}$, etc., while $K'_j = K_j$ for all j not on the path from 1 to i. Conversely, for each i this construction yields a file $K'_1 \ldots K'_N$ such that (a) siftup transforms $K'_1 \ldots K'_N$ into $K_1 \ldots K_N$, and (b) $K_{\lfloor j/2 \rfloor} \geq K_j$ for $2 \leq \lfloor j/2 \rfloor < j \leq N$. Therefore exactly N such files $K'_1 \ldots K'_N$ are possible, and the siftup operation is uniform. (An example of the proof of this theorem appears in exercise 22.) ∎

Referring to the quantities A, B, C, D in the analysis of Program H, we can see that a uniform siftup operation on a subtree of size s contributes $\lfloor s/2 \rfloor / s$ to the average value of A; it contributes

$$\frac{1}{s}(0 + 1 + 1 + 2 + \cdots + \lfloor \lg s \rfloor) = \frac{1}{s}\sum_{k=1}^{s} \lfloor \lg k \rfloor = \frac{1}{s}\left((s+1)\lfloor \lg s \rfloor - 2^{\lfloor \lg s \rfloor + 1} + 2\right)$$

to the average value of B (see exercise 1.2.4–42); and it contributes either $2/s$ or 0 to the average value of D, according as s is even or odd. The corresponding contribution to C is somewhat more difficult to determine, so it has been left to the reader (see exercise 26). Summing over all siftups, we find that the average value of A during heap creation is

$$A'_N = \sum \{\lfloor s/2 \rfloor / s \mid s \in M_N\}, \tag{17}$$

and similar formulas hold for B, C, and D. It is therefore possible to compute these average values exactly without great difficulty, and the following table shows typical results:

N	A'_N	B'_N	C'_N	D'_N
99	19.18	68.35	42.95	0.00
100	19.93	69.39	42.71	1.84
999	196.16	734.66	464.53	0.00
1000	196.94	735.80	464.16	1.92
9999	1966.02	7428.18	4695.54	0.00
10000	1966.82	7429.39	4695.06	1.97
10001	1966.45	7430.07	4695.84	0.00
10002	1967.15	7430.97	4695.95	1.73

Asymptotically speaking, we may ignore the special subtree sizes in M_N, and we find for example that

$$A'_N = \frac{N}{2} \cdot \frac{0}{1} + \frac{N}{4} \cdot \frac{1}{3} + \frac{N}{8} \cdot \frac{3}{7} + \cdots + O(\log N) = \left(1 - \tfrac{1}{2}\alpha\right)N + O(\log N), \tag{18}$$

where

$$\alpha = \sum_{k \geq 1} \frac{1}{2^k - 1} = 1.60669\,51524\,15291\,76378\,33015\,23190\,92458\,04806-. \quad (19)$$

(This value was first computed to high precision by J. W. Wrench, Jr., using the series transformation of exercise 27. Paul Erdős has proved that α is irrational [*J. Indian Math. Soc.* **12** (1948), 63–66], and Peter Borwein has demonstrated the irrationality of many similar constants [*Proc. Camb. Phil. Soc.* **112** (1992), 141–146].) For large N, we may use the approximate formulas

$$\begin{aligned}
A'_N &\approx 0.1967N + (-1)^N 0.3; \\
B'_N &\approx 0.74403N - 1.3\ln N; \\
C'_N &\approx 0.47034N - 0.8\ln N; \\
D'_N &\approx (1.8 \pm 0.2)[N \text{ even}].
\end{aligned} \quad (20)$$

The minimum and maximum values are also readily determined. Only $O(N)$ steps are needed to create the heap (see exercise 23).

This theory nicely explains the heap-creation phase of Algorithm H. But the selection phase is another story, which remains to be written! Let A''_N, B''_N, C''_N, and D''_N denote the average values of A, B, C, and D during the selection phase when N elements are being heapsorted. The behavior of Algorithm H on random input is subject to comparatively little fluctuation about the empirically determined average values

$$\begin{aligned}
A''_N &\approx 0.152N; \\
B''_N &\approx N\lg N - 2.61N; \\
C''_N &\approx \tfrac{1}{2}N\lg N - 1.41N; \\
D''_N &\approx \lg N \pm 2;
\end{aligned} \quad (21)$$

but no adequate theoretical explanation for the behavior of D''_N or for the conjectured constants 0.152, 2.61, or 1.41 has yet been found. The leading terms of B''_N and C''_N have, however, been established in an elegant manner by R. Schaffer and R. Sedgewick; see exercise 30. Schaffer has also proved that the minimum and maximum possible values of C''_N are respectively asymptotic to $\frac{1}{4}N\lg N$ and $\frac{3}{4}N\lg N$.

EXERCISES

1. [*10*] Is straight selection (Algorithm S) a stable sorting method?

2. [*15*] Why does it prove to be more convenient to select the largest key, then the second-largest, etc., in Algorithm S, instead of first finding the smallest, then the second-smallest, etc.?

3. [*M21*] (a) Prove that if the input to Algorithm S is a random permutation of $\{1, 2, \ldots, N\}$, then the first iteration of steps S2 and S3 yields a random permutation of $\{1, 2, \ldots, N-1\}$ followed by N. (In other words, the presence of each permutation of $\{1, 2, \ldots, N-1\}$ in $K_1 \ldots K_{N-1}$ is equally likely.) (b) Therefore if B_N denotes the average value of the quantity B in Program S, given randomly ordered input, we have $B_N = H_N - 1 + B_{N-1}$. [*Hint:* See Eq. 1.2.10–(16).]

▶ **4.** [*M25*] Step S3 of Algorithm S accomplishes nothing when $i = j$; is it a good idea to test whether or not $i = j$ before doing step S3? What is the average number of times the condition $i = j$ will occur in step S3 for random input?

5. [*20*] What is the value of the quantity B in the analysis of Program S, when the input is $N \ldots 3\,2\,1$?

6. [*M29*] (a) Let $a_1 a_2 \ldots a_N$ be a permutation of $\{1, 2, \ldots, N\}$ having C cycles, I inversions, and B changes to the right-to-left maxima when sorted by Program S. Prove that $2B \le I + N - C$. [*Hint:* See exercise 5.2.2–1.] (b) Show that $I + N - C \le \lfloor N^2/2 \rfloor$; hence B can never exceed $\lfloor N^2/4 \rfloor$.

7. [*M41*] Find the variance of the quantity B in Program S, as a function of N, assuming random input.

▶ **8.** [*24*] Show that if the search for $\max(K_1, \ldots, K_j)$ in step S2 is carried out by examining keys in left-to-right order K_1, K_2, $\ldots$, K_j, instead of going from right to left as in Program S, it is often possible to reduce the number of comparisons needed on the next iteration of step S2. Write a MIX program based on this observation.

9. [*M25*] What is the average number of comparisons performed by the algorithm of exercise 8, for random input?

10. [*12*] What will be the configuration of the tree in Fig. 23 after 14 of the original 16 items have been output?

11. [*10*] What will be the configuration of the tree in Fig. 24 after the element 908 has been output?

12. [*M20*] How many times will $-\infty$ be compared with $-\infty$ when the bottom-up method of Fig. 23 is used to sort a file of 2^n elements into order?

13. [*20*] (J. W. J. Williams.) Step H4 of Algorithm H distinguishes between the three cases $j < r$, $j = r$, and $j > r$. Show that if $K \ge K_{r+1}$ it would be possible to simplify step H4 so that only a two-way branch is made. How could the condition $K \ge K_{r+1}$ be ensured throughout the heapsort process, by modifying step H2?

14. [*10*] Show that simple queues are special cases of priority queues. (Explain how keys can be assigned to the elements so that a largest-in-first-out procedure is equivalent to first-in-first-out.) Is a stack also a special case of a priority queue?

▶ **15.** [*M22*] (B. A. Chartres.) Design a high-speed algorithm that builds a table of the prime numbers $\le N$, making use of a priority queue to avoid division operations. [*Hint:* Let the smallest key in the priority queue be the least odd nonprime number greater than the last odd number considered as a prime candidate. Try to minimize the number of elements in the queue.]

16. [*20*] Design an efficient algorithm that inserts a new key into a given heap of n elements, producing a heap of $n + 1$ elements.

17. [*20*] The algorithm of exercise 16 can be used for heap creation, instead of the "decrease l to 1" method used in Algorithm H. Do both methods create the same heap when they begin with the same input file?

▶ **18.** [*21*] (R. W. Floyd.) During the selection phase of heapsort, the key K tends to be quite small, so that nearly all of the comparisons in step H6 find $K < K_j$. Show how to modify the algorithm so that K is not compared with K_j in the main loop of the computation, thereby nearly cutting the average number of comparisons in half.

19. [*21*] Design an algorithm that *deletes* a given element of a heap of length N, producing a heap of length $N - 1$.

20. [*M20*] Prove that (14) gives the special subtree sizes in a heap.

21. [*M24*] Prove that (15) gives the nonspecial subtree sizes in a heap.

▸ **22.** [*20*] What permutations of $\{1, 2, 3, 4, 5\}$ are transformed into 5 3 4 1 2 by the heap-creation phase of Algorithm H?

23. [*M28*] (a) Prove that the length of scan, B, in a siftup algorithm never exceeds $\lfloor \lg (r/l) \rfloor$. (b) According to (8), B can never exceed $N \lfloor \lg N \rfloor$ in any particular application of Algorithm H. Find the maximum value of B as a function of N, taken over all possible input files. (You must prove that an input file exists such that B takes on this maximum value.)

24. [*M24*] Derive an exact formula for the standard deviation of B'_N (the total length of scan during the heap-creation phase of Algorithm H).

25. [*M20*] What is the average value of the contribution to C made during the siftup pass when $l = 1$ and $r = N$, if $N = 2^{n+1} - 1$?

26. [*M30*] Solve exercise 25, (a) for $N = 26$, (b) for general N.

27. [*M25*] (T. Clausen, 1828.) Prove that

$$\sum_{n \geq 1} \frac{x^n}{1 - x^n} = \sum_{n \geq 1} \frac{1 + x^n}{1 - x^n} x^{n^2}.$$

(Setting $x = \frac{1}{2}$ gives a very rapidly converging series for the evaluation of (19).)

28. [*35*] Explore the idea of *ternary heaps*, based on complete ternary trees instead of binary trees. Do ternary heaps sort faster than binary heaps?

29. [*26*] (W. S. Brown.) Design an algorithm for multiplication of polynomials or power series $(a_1 x^{i_1} + a_2 x^{i_2} + \cdots)(b_1 x^{j_1} + b_2 x^{j_2} + \cdots)$, in which the coefficients of the answer $c_1 x^{i_1 + j_1} + \cdots$ are generated in order as the input coefficients are being multiplied. [*Hint:* Use an appropriate priority queue.]

▸ **30.** [*HM35*] (R. Schaffer and R. Sedgewick.) Let h_{nm} be the number of heaps on the elements $\{1, 2, \ldots, n\}$ for which the selection phase of heapsort does exactly m promotions. Prove that $h_{nm} \leq 2^m \prod_{k=2}^{n} \lg k$, and use this relation to show that the average number of promotions performed by Algorithm H is $N \lg N + O(N \log \log N)$.

31. [*37*] (J. W. J. Williams.) Show that if two heaps are placed "back to back" in a suitable way, it is possible to maintain a structure in which either the smallest or the largest element can be deleted at any time in $O(\log n)$ steps. (Such a structure may be called a *priority deque*.)

32. [*M28*] Prove that the number of heapsort promotions, B, is always at least $\frac{1}{2} N \lg N + O(N)$, if the keys being sorted are distinct. *Hint:* Consider the movement of the largest $\lceil N/2 \rceil$ keys.

33. [*21*] Design an algorithm that merges two disjoint priority queues, represented as leftist trees, into one. (In particular, if one of the given queues contains a single element, your algorithm will insert it into the other queue.)

34. [*M41*] How many leftist trees with N nodes are possible, ignoring the KEY values? The sequence begins 1, 1, 2, 4, 8, 17, 38, 87, 203, 482, 1160, ...; show that the number is asymptotically $ab^N N^{-3/2}$ for suitable constants a and b, using techniques like those of exercise 2.3.4.4–4.

35. [*26*] If UP links are added to a leftist tree (see the discussion of triply linked trees in Section 6.2.3), it is possible to delete an arbitrary node P from within the priority queue as follows: Replace P by the merger of LEFT(P) and RIGHT(P); then adjust the DIST fields of P's ancestors, possibly swapping left and right subtrees, until either reaching the root or reaching a node whose DIST is unchanged.

Prove that this process never requires changing more than $O(\log N)$ of the DIST fields, if there are N nodes in the tree, even though the tree may contain very long upward paths.

36. [*18*] (*Least-recently-used page replacement.*) Many operating systems make use of the following type of algorithm: A collection of nodes is subjected to two operations, (i) "using" a node, and (ii) replacing the least-recently-used node by a new node. What data structure makes it easy to ascertain the least-recently-used node?

37. [*HM32*] Let $e_N(k)$ be the expected treewise distance of the kth-largest element from the root, in a random heap of N elements, and let $e(k) = \lim_{N \to \infty} e_N(k)$. Thus $e(1) = 0$, $e(2) = 1$, $e(3) = 1.5$, and $e(4) = 1.875$. Find the asymptotic value of $e(k)$ to within $O(k^{-1})$.

38. [*M21*] Find a simple recurrence relation for the multiset M_N of subtree sizes in a heap or in a complete binary tree with N internal nodes.

5.2.4. Sorting by Merging

Merging (or *collating*) means the combination of two or more ordered files into a single ordered file. For example, we can merge the two files 503 703 765 and 087 512 677 to obtain 087 503 512 677 703 765. A simple way to accomplish this is to compare the two smallest items, output the smallest, and then repeat the same process. Starting with

$$\begin{cases} 503 \ 703 \ 765 \\ 087 \ 512 \ 677 \end{cases}$$

we obtain

$$087 \begin{cases} 503 \ 703 \ 765 \\ 512 \ 677 \end{cases}$$

then

$$087 \ 503 \begin{cases} 703 \ 765 \\ 512 \ 677 \end{cases}$$

and

$$087 \ 503 \ 512 \begin{cases} 703 \ 765 \\ 677 \end{cases}$$

and so on. Some care is necessary when one of the two files becomes exhausted; a detailed description of the process appears in the following algorithm:

Algorithm M (*Two-way merge*). This algorithm merges nonempty ordered files $x_1 \leq x_2 \leq \cdots \leq x_m$ and $y_1 \leq y_2 \leq \cdots \leq y_n$ into a single file $z_1 \leq z_2 \leq \cdots \leq z_{m+n}$.

M1. [Initialize.] Set $i \leftarrow 1$, $j \leftarrow 1$, $k \leftarrow 1$.

M2. [Find smaller.] If $x_i \leq y_j$, go to step M3, otherwise go to M5.

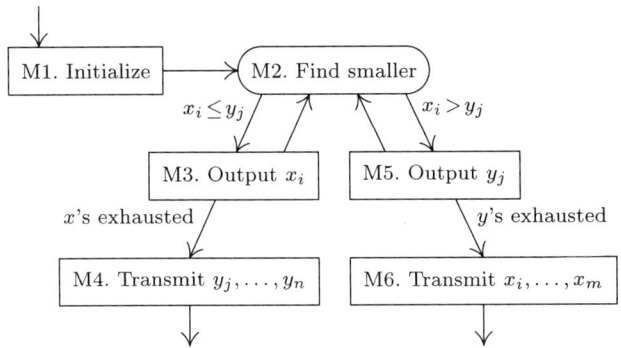

Fig. 29. Merging $x_1 \le \cdots \le x_m$ with $y_1 \le \cdots \le y_n$.

M3. [Output x_i.] Set $z_k \leftarrow x_i$, $k \leftarrow k+1$, $i \leftarrow i+1$. If $i \le m$, return to M2.

M4. [Transmit $y_j, \ldots, y_n$.] Set $(z_k, \ldots, z_{m+n}) \leftarrow (y_j, \ldots, y_n)$ and terminate the algorithm.

M5. [Output y_j.] Set $z_k \leftarrow y_j$, $k \leftarrow k+1$, $j \leftarrow j+1$. If $j \le n$, return to M2.

M6. [Transmit $x_i, \ldots, x_m$.] Set $(z_k, \ldots, z_{m+n}) \leftarrow (x_i, \ldots, x_m)$ and terminate the algorithm. ∎

We shall see in Section 5.3.2 that this straightforward procedure is essentially the best possible way to merge on a conventional computer, when $m \approx n$. (On the other hand, when m is much smaller than n, it is possible to devise more efficient merging algorithms, although they are rather complicated in general.) Algorithm M could be made slightly simpler without much loss of efficiency by placing sentinel elements $x_{m+1} = y_{n+1} = \infty$ at the end of the input files, stopping just before ∞ is output. For an analysis of Algorithm M, see exercise 2.

The total amount of work involved in Algorithm M is essentially proportional to $m + n$, so it is clear that merging is a simpler problem than sorting. Furthermore, we can reduce the problem of sorting to merging, because we can repeatedly merge longer and longer subfiles until everything is in sort. We may consider this to be an extension of the idea of insertion sorting: Inserting a new element into a sorted file is the special case $n = 1$ of merging. If we want to speed up the insertion process we can consider inserting several elements at a time, "batching" them, and this leads naturally to the general idea of merge sorting. From a historical point of view, merge sorting was one of the very first methods proposed for computer sorting; it was suggested by John von Neumann as early as 1945 (see Section 5.5).

We shall study merging in considerable detail in Section 5.4, with regard to external sorting algorithms; our main concern in the present section is the somewhat simpler question of merge sorting within a high-speed random-access memory.

Table 1 shows a merge sort that "burns the candle at both ends" in a manner similar to the scanning procedure we have used in quicksort and radix exchange: We examine the input from the left and from the right, working towards the middle. Ignoring the top line of the table for a moment, let us consider the transformation from line 2 to line 3. At the left we have the ascending run 503 703 765; at the right, reading leftwards, we have the run 087 512 677. Merging these two sequences leads to 087 503 512 677 703 765, which is placed at the left of line 3. Then the keys 061 612 908 in line 2 are merged with 170 509 897, and the result (061 170 509 612 897 908) is recorded at the *right* end of line 3. Finally, 154 275 426 653 is merged with 653 — discovering the overlap before it causes any harm — and the result is placed at the left, following the previous run. Line 2 of the table was formed in the same way from the original input in line 1.

Table 1

NATURAL TWO-WAY MERGE SORTING

503	087	512	061	908	170	897	275	653	426	154	509	612	677	765	703
503	703	765	061	612	908	154	275	426	653	897	509	170	677	512	087
087	503	512	677	703	765	154	275	426	653	908	897	612	509	170	061
061	087	170	503	509	512	612	677	703	765	897	908	653	426	275	154
061	087	154	170	275	426	503	509	512	612	653	677	703	765	897	908

Vertical lines in Table 1 represent the boundaries between runs. They are the so-called *stepdowns*, where a smaller element follows a larger one in the direction of reading. We generally encounter an ambiguous situation in the middle of the file, when we read the same key from both directions; this causes no problem if we are a little bit careful as in the following algorithm. The method is traditionally called a "natural" merge because it makes use of the runs that occur naturally in its input.

Algorithm N (*Natural two-way merge sort*). Records $R_1, \ldots, R_N$ are sorted using two areas of memory, each of which is capable of holding N records. For convenience, we shall say that the records of the second area are $R_{N+1}, \ldots, R_{2N}$, although it is not really necessary that R_{N+1} be adjacent to R_N. The initial contents of $R_{N+1}, \ldots, R_{2N}$ are immaterial. After sorting is complete, the keys will be in order, $K_1 \leq \cdots \leq K_N$.

N1. [Initialize.] Set $s \leftarrow 0$. (When $s = 0$, we will be transferring records from the $(R_1, \ldots, R_N)$ area to the $(R_{N+1}, \ldots, R_{2N})$ area; when $s = 1$, we will be going the other way.)

N2. [Prepare for pass.] If $s = 0$, set $i \leftarrow 1$, $j \leftarrow N$, $k \leftarrow N + 1$, $l \leftarrow 2N$; if $s = 1$, set $i \leftarrow N + 1$, $j \leftarrow 2N$, $k \leftarrow 1$, $l \leftarrow N$. (Variables i, j, k, l point to the current positions in the "source files" being read and the "destination files" being written.) Set $d \leftarrow 1$, $f \leftarrow 1$. (Variable d gives the current direction of output; f is set to zero if future passes are necessary.)

N3. [Compare $K_i : K_j$.] If $K_i > K_j$, go to step N8. If $i = j$, set $R_k \leftarrow R_i$ and go to N13.

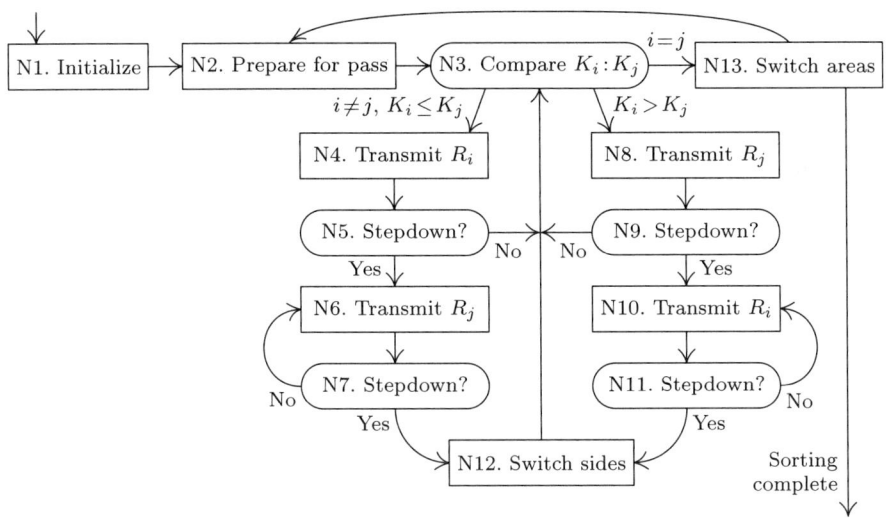

Fig. 30. Merge sorting.

N4. [Transmit R_i.] (Steps N4–N7 are analogous to steps M3–M4 of Algorithm M.) Set $R_k \leftarrow R_i$, $k \leftarrow k + d$.

N5. [Stepdown?] Increase i by 1. Then if $K_{i-1} \leq K_i$, go back to step N3.

N6. [Transmit R_j.] Set $R_k \leftarrow R_j$, $k \leftarrow k + d$.

N7. [Stepdown?] Decrease j by 1. Then if $K_{j+1} \leq K_j$, go back to step N6; otherwise go to step N12.

N8. [Transmit R_j.] (Steps N8–N11 are dual to steps N4–N7.) Set $R_k \leftarrow R_j$, $k \leftarrow k + d$.

N9. [Stepdown?] Decrease j by 1. Then if $K_{j+1} \leq K_j$, go back to step N3.

N10. [Transmit R_i.] Set $R_k \leftarrow R_i$, $k \leftarrow k + d$.

N11. [Stepdown?] Increase i by 1. Then if $K_{i-1} \leq K_i$, go back to step N10.

N12. [Switch sides.] Set $f \leftarrow 0$, $d \leftarrow -d$, and interchange $k \leftrightarrow l$. Return to step N3.

N13. [Switch areas.] If $f = 0$, set $s \leftarrow 1 - s$ and return to N2. Otherwise sorting is complete; if $s = 0$, set $(R_1, \ldots, R_N) \leftarrow (R_{N+1}, \ldots, R_{2N})$. (This last copying operation is unnecessary if it is acceptable to have the output in $(R_{N+1}, \ldots, R_{2N})$ about half of the time.) ∎

This algorithm contains one tricky feature that is explained in exercise 5.

It would not be difficult to program Algorithm N for MIX, but we can deduce the essential facts of its behavior without constructing the entire program. The number of ascending runs in the input will be about $\frac{1}{2}N$, under random conditions, since we have $K_i > K_{i+1}$ with probability $\frac{1}{2}$; detailed information about the number of runs, under slightly different hypotheses, has been derived in Section 5.1.3. Each pass cuts the number of runs in half (except in unusual cases such as the situation in exercise 6). So the number of passes will usually be about $\lg \frac{1}{2} N = \lg N - 1$. Each pass requires us to transmit each of the N records, and by exercise 2 most of the time is spent in steps N3, N4, N5, N8, N9. We can sketch the time in the inner loop as follows, if we assume that there is low probability of equal keys:

Step	Operations	Time
N3	CMPA, JG, JE	$3.5u$

$$\text{Either} \begin{cases} \text{N4} \\ \text{N5} \end{cases}$$

N4	STA, INC	$3u$
N5	INC, LDA, CMPA, JGE	$6u$

$$\text{Or} \begin{cases} \text{N8} \\ \text{N9} \end{cases}$$

N8	STX, INC	$3u$
N9	DEC, LDX, CMPX, JGE	$6u$

Thus about $12.5u$ is spent on each record in each pass, and the total running time will be asymptotically $12.5N \lg N$, for both the average case and the worst case. This is slower than quicksort's average time, and it may not be enough better than heapsort to justify taking twice as much memory space, since the asymptotic running time of Program 5.2.3H is never more than $18N \lg N$.

The boundary lines between runs are determined in Algorithm N entirely by stepdowns. This has the possible advantage that input files with a preponderance of increasing order can be handled very quickly, and so can input files with a preponderance of decreasing order; but it slows down the main loop of the calculation. Instead of testing stepdowns, we can determine the length of runs artificially, by saying that all runs in the input have length 1, all runs after the first pass (except possibly the last run) have length 2, ..., all runs after k passes (except possibly the last run) have length 2^k. This is called a *straight* two-merge, as opposed to the "natural" merge in Algorithm N.

Straight two-way merging is very similar to Algorithm N, and it has essentially the same flow chart; but things are sufficiently different that we had better write down the whole algorithm again:

Algorithm S (*Straight two-way merge sort*). Records $R_1, \ldots, R_N$ are sorted using two memory areas as in Algorithm N.

S1. [Initialize.] Set $s \leftarrow 0$, $p \leftarrow 1$. (For the significance of variables s, i, j, k, l, and d, see Algorithm N. Here p represents the size of ascending runs to be merged on the current pass; further variables q and r will keep track of the number of unmerged items in a run.)

S2. [Prepare for pass.] If $s = 0$, set $i \leftarrow 1$, $j \leftarrow N$, $k \leftarrow N$, $l \leftarrow 2N+1$; if $s = 1$, set $i \leftarrow N+1$, $j \leftarrow 2N$, $k \leftarrow 0$, $l \leftarrow N+1$. Then set $d \leftarrow 1$, $q \leftarrow p$, $r \leftarrow p$.

S3. [Compare $K_i : K_j$.] If $K_i > K_j$, go to step S8.

S4. [Transmit R_i.] Set $k \leftarrow k + d$, $R_k \leftarrow R_i$.

S5. [End of run?] Set $i \leftarrow i + 1$, $q \leftarrow q - 1$. If $q > 0$, go back to step S3.

S6. [Transmit R_j.] Set $k \leftarrow k + d$. Then if $k = l$, go to step S13; otherwise set $R_k \leftarrow R_j$.

Table 2

STRAIGHT TWO-WAY MERGE SORTING

503 | 087 | 512 | 061 | 908 | 170 | 897 | 275 **❙** 653 | 426 | 154 | 509 | 612 | 677 | 765 | 703
503   703 | 512   677 | 509   908 | 426   897 **❙** 653   275 | 170   154 | 612   061 | 765   087
087   503   703   765 | 154   170   509   908 **❙** 897   653   426   275 | 677   612   512   061
061   087   503   512   612   677   703   765 **❙** 908   897   653   509   426   275   170   154
061   087   154   170   275   426   503   509   512   612   653   677   703   765   897   908

S7. [End of run?] Set $j \leftarrow j - 1$, $r \leftarrow r - 1$. If $r > 0$, go back to step S6; otherwise go to S12.

S8. [Transmit R_j.] Set $k \leftarrow k + d$, $R_k \leftarrow R_j$.

S9. [End of run?] Set $j \leftarrow j - 1$, $r \leftarrow r - 1$. If $r > 0$, go back to step S3.

S10. [Transmit R_i.] Set $k \leftarrow k + d$. Then if $k = l$, go to step S13; otherwise set $R_k \leftarrow R_i$.

S11. [End of run?] Set $i \leftarrow i + 1$, $q \leftarrow q - 1$. If $q > 0$, go back to step S10.

S12. [Switch sides.] Set $q \leftarrow p$, $r \leftarrow p$, $d \leftarrow -d$, and interchange $k \leftrightarrow l$. If $j - i < p$, return to step S10; otherwise return to S3.

S13. [Switch areas.] Set $p \leftarrow p + p$. If $p < N$, set $s \leftarrow 1 - s$ and return to S2. Otherwise sorting is complete; if $s = 0$, set

$$(R_1, \ldots, R_N) \leftarrow (R_{N+1}, \ldots, R_{2N}).$$

(The latter copying operation will be done if and only if $\lceil \lg N \rceil$ is odd, or in the trivial case $N = 1$, regardless of the distribution of the input. Therefore it is possible to predict the location of the sorted output in advance, and copying will usually be unnecessary.) ▮

An example of this algorithm appears in Table 2. It is somewhat amazing that the method works properly when N is not a power of 2; the runs being merged are not all of length 2^k, yet no provision has apparently been made for the exceptions! (See exercise 8.) The former tests for stepdowns have been replaced by decrementing q or r and testing the result for zero; this reduces the asymptotic MIX running time to $11N \lg N$ units, slightly faster than we were able to achieve with Algorithm N.

In practice it would be worthwhile to combine Algorithm S with straight insertion; we can sort groups of, say, 16 items using straight insertion, in place of the first four passes of Algorithm S, thereby avoiding the comparatively wasteful bookkeeping operations involved in short merges. As we saw with quicksort, such a combination of methods does not affect the asymptotic running time, but it gives us a reasonable improvement nevertheless.

Let us now study Algorithms N and S from the standpoint of data structures. Why did we need $2N$ record locations instead of N? The reason is comparatively simple: We were dealing with four lists of varying size (two source lists and two destination lists on each pass); and we were using the standard "growing

together" idea discussed in Section 2.2.2, for each pair of sequentially allocated
lists. But half of the memory space was always unused, and a little reflection
shows that we could really make use of a *linked* allocation for the four lists. If
we add one link field to each of the N records, we can do everything required
by the merging algorithms using simple link manipulations, without moving the
records at all! Adding N link fields is generally better than adding the space
needed for N more records, and the reduced record movement may also save
us time, unless our computer memory is especially good at sequential reading
and writing. Therefore we ought to consider also a merging algorithm like the
following one:

Algorithm L (*List merge sort*). Records $R_1, \ldots, R_N$ are assumed to contain
keys $K_1, \ldots, K_N$, together with link fields $L_1, \ldots, L_N$ capable of holding the
numbers $-(N+1)$ through $(N+1)$. There are two auxiliary link fields L_0 and
L_{N+1} in artificial records R_0 and R_{N+1} at the beginning and end of the file. This
algorithm is a "list sort" that sets the link fields so that the records are linked
together in ascending order. After sorting is complete, L_0 will be the index of
the record with the smallest key; and L_k, for $1 \le k \le N$, will be the index of the
record that follows R_k, or $L_k = 0$ if R_k is the record with the largest key. (See
Eq. 5.2.1–(13).)

During the course of this algorithm, R_0 and R_{N+1} serve as list heads for two
linear lists whose sublists are being merged. A negative link denotes the end of
a sublist known to be ordered; a zero link denotes the end of the entire list. We
assume that $N \ge 2$.

The notation "$|L_s| \leftarrow p$" means "Set L_s to p or $-p$, retaining the previous
sign of L_s." This operation is well-suited to MIX, but unfortunately not to most
computers; it is possible to modify the algorithm in straightforward ways to
obtain an equally efficient method for most other machines.

L1. [Prepare two lists.] Set $L_0 \leftarrow 1$, $L_{N+1} \leftarrow 2$, $L_i \leftarrow -(i+2)$ for $1 \le i \le N-2$,
and $L_{N-1} \leftarrow L_N \leftarrow 0$. (We have created two lists containing $R_1, R_3, R_5, \ldots$
and $R_2, R_4, R_6, \ldots$, respectively; the negative links indicate that each ordered sublist consists of one element only. For another way to do this step,
taking advantage of ordering that may be present in the initial data, see
exercise 12.)

L2. [Begin new pass.] Set $s \leftarrow 0$, $t \leftarrow N+1$, $p \leftarrow L_s$, $q \leftarrow L_t$. If $q = 0$, the
algorithm terminates. (During each pass, p and q traverse the lists being
merged; s usually points to the most recently processed record of the current
sublist, while t points to the end of the previously output sublist.)

L3. [Compare $K_p : K_q$.] If $K_p > K_q$, go to L6.

L4. [Advance p.] Set $|L_s| \leftarrow p$, $s \leftarrow p$, $p \leftarrow L_p$. If $p > 0$, return to L3.

L5. [Complete the sublist.] Set $L_s \leftarrow q$, $s \leftarrow t$. Then set $t \leftarrow q$ and $q \leftarrow L_q$, one
or more times, until $q \le 0$. Finally go to L8.

L6. [Advance q.] (Steps L6 and L7 are dual to L4 and L5.) Set $|L_s| \leftarrow q$, $s \leftarrow q$,
$q \leftarrow L_q$. If $q > 0$, return to L3.

Table 3
LIST MERGE SORTING

j	0	1	2	3	4	5	6	7	8	9	10	11	12	13	14	15	16	17
K_j	–	503	087	512	061	908	170	897	275	653	426	154	509	612	677	765	703	–
L_j	1	−3	−4	−5	−6	−7	−8	−9	−10	−11	−12	−13	−14	−15	−16	0	0	2
L_j	2	−6	1	−8	3	−10	5	−11	7	−13	9	12	−16	14	0	0	15	4
L_j	4	3	1	−11	2	−13	8	5	7	0	12	10	9	14	16	0	15	6
L_j	4	3	6	7	2	0	8	5	1	14	12	10	13	9	16	0	15	11
L_j	4	12	11	13	2	0	8	5	10	14	1	6	3	9	16	7	15	0

L7. [Complete the sublist.] Set $L_s \leftarrow p$, $s \leftarrow t$. Then set $t \leftarrow p$ and $p \leftarrow L_p$, one or more times, until $p \leq 0$.

L8. [End of pass?] (At this point, $p \leq 0$ and $q \leq 0$, since both pointers have moved to the end of their respective sublists.) Set $p \leftarrow -p$, $q \leftarrow -q$. If $q = 0$, set $|L_s| \leftarrow p$, $|L_t| \leftarrow 0$ and return to L2. Otherwise return to L3. ∎

An example of this algorithm in action appears in Table 3, where we can see the link settings each time step L2 is encountered. It is possible to rearrange the records $R_1, \ldots, R_N$ at the end of this algorithm so that their keys are in order, using the method of exercise 5.2–12. There is an interesting similarity between list merging and the addition of sparse polynomials (see Algorithm 2.2.4A).

Let us now construct a MIX program for Algorithm L, to see whether the list manipulation is advantageous from the standpoint of speed as well as space:

Program L (*List merge sort*). For convenience, we assume that records are one word long, with L_j in the $(0:2)$ field and K_j in the $(3:5)$ field of location INPUT $+ j$; rI1 $\equiv p$, rI2 $\equiv q$, rI3 $\equiv s$, rI4 $\equiv t$, rA $\equiv K_q$; $N \geq 2$.

01	L	EQU	0:2		Definition of field names
02	ABSL	EQU	1:2		
03	KEY	EQU	3:5		
04	START	ENT1	N-2	1	*L1. Prepare two lists.*
05		ENNA	2,1	$N-2$	
06		STA	INPUT,1(L)	$N-2$	$L_i \leftarrow -(i+2)$.
07		DEC1	1	$N-2$	
08		J1P	*-3	$N-2$	$N-2 \geq i > 0$.
09		ENTA	1	1	
10		STA	INPUT(L)	1	$L_0 \leftarrow 1$.
11		ENTA	2	1	
12		STA	INPUT+N+1(L)	1	$L_{N+1} \leftarrow 2$.
13		STZ	INPUT+N-1(L)	1	$L_{N-1} \leftarrow 0$.
14		STZ	INPUT+N(L)	1	$L_N \leftarrow 0$.
15		JMP	L2	1	To L2.
16	L3Q	LDA	INPUT,2	$C'' + B'$	*L3. Compare $K_p:K_q$.*
17	L3P	CMPA	INPUT,1(KEY)	C	
18		JL	L6	C	To L6 if $K_q < K_p$.
19	L4	ST1	INPUT,3(ABSL)	C'	*L4. Advance p.* $|L_s| \leftarrow p$.
20		ENT3	0,1	C'	$s \leftarrow p$.
21		LD1	INPUT,1(L)	C'	$p \leftarrow L_p$.
22		J1P	L3P	C'	To L3 if $p > 0$.

23	L5	ST2	INPUT,3(L)	B'	*L5. Complete the sublist.* $L_s \leftarrow q$.
24		ENT3	0,4	B'	$s \leftarrow t$.
25		ENT4	0,2	D'	$t \leftarrow q$.
26		LD2	INPUT,2(L)	D'	$q \leftarrow L_q$.
27		J2P	*-2	D'	Repeat if $q > 0$.
28		JMP	L8	B'	To L8.
29	L6	ST2	INPUT,3(ABSL)	C''	*L6. Advance q.* $|L_s| \leftarrow q$.
30		ENT3	0,2	C''	$s \leftarrow q$.
31		LD2	INPUT,2(L)	C''	$q \leftarrow L_q$.
32		J2P	L3Q	C''	To L3 if $q > 0$.
33	L7	ST1	INPUT,3(L)	B''	*L7. Complete the sublist.* $L_s \leftarrow p$.
34		ENT3	0,4	B''	$s \leftarrow t$.
35		ENT4	0,1	D''	$t \leftarrow p$.
36		LD1	INPUT,1(L)	D''	$p \leftarrow L_p$.
37		J1P	*-2	D''	Repeat if $p > 0$.
38	L8	ENN1	0,1	B	*L8. End of pass?* $p \leftarrow -p$.
39		ENN2	0,2	B	$q \leftarrow -q$.
40		J2NZ	L3Q	B	To L3 if $q \neq 0$.
41		ST1	INPUT,3(ABSL)	A	$|L_s| \leftarrow p$.
42		STZ	INPUT,4(ABSL)	A	$|L_t| \leftarrow 0$.
43	L2	ENT3	0	$A+1$	*L2. Begin new pass.* $s \leftarrow 0$.
44		ENT4	N+1	$A+1$	$t \leftarrow N+1$.
45		LD1	INPUT(L)	$A+1$	$p \leftarrow L_s$.
46		LD2	INPUT+N+1(L)	$A+1$	$q \leftarrow L_t$.
47		J2NZ	L3Q	$A+1$	To L3 if $q \neq 0$. ∎

The running time of this program can be deduced using techniques we have seen many times before (see exercises 13 and 14); it comes to approximately $(10N \lg N + 4.92N)u$ on the average, with a small standard deviation of order $\sqrt{N}$. Exercise 15 shows that the running time can in fact be reduced to about $(8N \lg N)u$, at the expense of a substantially longer program.

Thus we have a clear victory for linked-memory techniques over sequential allocation, when internal merging is being done: Less memory space is required, and the program runs about 10 to 20 percent faster. Similar algorithms have been published by L. J. Woodrum [*IBM Systems J.* **8** (1969), 189–203] and A. D. Woodall [*Comp. J.* **13** (1970), 110–111].

EXERCISES

1. [*21*] Generalize Algorithm M to a *k-way merge* of the input files $x_{i1} \leq \cdots \leq x_{im_i}$ for $i = 1, 2, \ldots, k$.

2. [*M24*] Assuming that each of the $\binom{m+n}{m}$ possible arrangements of m x's among n y's is equally likely, find the mean and standard deviation of the number of times step M2 is performed during Algorithm M. What are the maximum and minimum values of this quantity?

▶ **3.** [*20*] (*Updating.*) Given records $R_1, \ldots, R_M$ and $R'_1, \ldots, R'_N$ whose keys are distinct and in order, so that $K_1 < \cdots < K_M$ and $K'_1 < \cdots < K'_N$, show how to modify Algorithm M to obtain a merged file in which records R_i of the first file have been *discarded* if their keys appear also in the second file.

4. [*21*] The text observes that merge sorting may be regarded as a generalization of insertion sorting. Show that merge sorting is also strongly related to tree selection sorting as depicted in Fig. 23.

▶ **5.** [*21*] Prove that i can never be equal to j in steps N6 or N10. (Therefore it is unnecessary to test for a possible jump to N13 in those steps.)

6. [*22*] Find a permutation $K_1 K_2 \ldots K_{16}$ of $\{1, 2, \ldots, 16\}$ such that

$$K_2 > K_3, \quad K_4 > K_5, \quad K_6 > K_7, \quad K_8 > K_9, \quad K_{10} < K_{11}, \quad K_{12} < K_{13}, \quad K_{14} < K_{15},$$

yet Algorithm N will sort the file in only two passes. (Since there are eight or more runs, we would expect to have at least four runs after the first pass, two runs after the second pass, and sorting would ordinarily not be complete until after at least three passes. How can we get by with only two passes?)

7. [*16*] Give a formula for the exact number of passes required by Algorithm S, as a function of N.

8. [*22*] During Algorithm S, the variables q and r are supposed to represent the lengths of the unmerged elements in the runs currently being processed; q and r both start out equal to p, while the runs are not always this long. How can this possibly work?

9. [*24*] Write a MIX program for Algorithm S. Specify the instruction frequencies in terms of quantities analogous to $A, B', B'', C', \ldots$ in Program L.

10. [*25*] (D. A. Bell.) Show that sequentially allocated straight two-way merging can be done with at most $\frac{3}{2} N$ memory locations, instead of $2N$ as in Algorithm S.

11. [*21*] Is Algorithm L a stable sorting method?

▶ **12.** [*22*] Revise step L1 of Algorithm L so that the two-way merge is "natural," taking advantage of ascending runs that are initially present. (In particular, if the input is already sorted, step L2 should terminate the algorithm immediately after your step L1 has acted.)

▶ **13.** [*M34*] Give an analysis of the average running time of Program L, in the style of other analyses in this chapter: Interpret the quantities $A, B, B', \ldots$, and explain how to compute their exact average values. How long does Program L take to sort the 16 numbers in Table 3?

14. [*M24*] Let the binary representation of N be $2^{e_1} + 2^{e_2} + \cdots + 2^{e_t}$, where $e_1 > e_2 > \cdots > e_t \geq 0$, $t \geq 1$. Prove that the maximum number of key comparisons performed by Algorithm L is $1 - 2^{e_t} + \sum_{k=1}^{t} (e_k + k - 1) 2^{e_k}$.

15. [*20*] Hand simulation of Algorithm L reveals that it occasionally does redundant operations; the assignments $|L_s| \leftarrow p$, $|L_s| \leftarrow q$ in steps L4 and L6 are unnecessary about half of the time, since we have $L_s = p$ (or q) each time step L4 (or L6) returns to L3. How can Program L be improved so that this redundancy disappears?

16. [*28*] Design a list merging algorithm like Algorithm L but based on three-way merging.

17. [*20*] (J. McCarthy.) Let the binary representation of N be as in exercise 14, and assume that we are given N records arranged in t ordered subfiles of respective sizes $2^{e_1}, 2^{e_2}, \ldots, 2^{e_t}$. Show how to maintain this state of affairs when a new $(N+1)$st record is added and $N \leftarrow N+1$. (The resulting algorithm may be called an *online merge sort*.)

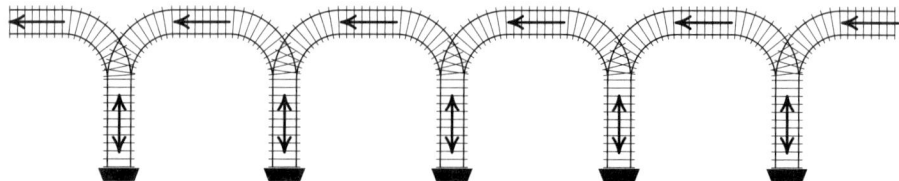

Fig. 31. A railway network with five "stacks."

18. [*40*] (M. A. Kronrod.) Given a file of N records containing only two runs,

$$K_1 \leq \cdots \leq K_M \qquad \text{and} \qquad K_{M+1} \leq \cdots \leq K_N,$$

is it possible to sort the file with $O(N)$ operations in a random-access memory, *using only a small fixed amount of additional memory space* regardless of the sizes of M and N? (All of the merging algorithms described in this section make use of extra memory space proportional to N.)

19. [*26*] Consider a railway switching network with n "stacks," as shown in Fig. 31 when $n = 5$; we considered one-stack networks in exercises 2.2.1–2 through 2.2.1–5. If N railroad cars enter at the right, we observed that only comparatively few of the $N!$ permutations of those cars could appear at the left, in the one-stack case.

In the n-stack network, assume that 2^n cars enter at the right. Prove that each of the $2^n!$ possible permutations of these cars *is* achievable at the left, by a suitable sequence of operations. (Each stack is actually much bigger than indicated in the illustration — big enough to accommodate all the cars, if necessary.)

20. [*47*] In the notation of exercise 2.2.1–4, at most a_N^n permutations of N elements can be produced with an n-stack railway network; hence the number of stacks needed to obtain all $N!$ permutations is at least $\log N!/\log a_N \approx \log_4 N$. Exercise 19 shows that at most $\lceil \lg N \rceil$ stacks are needed. What is the true rate of growth of the necessary number of stacks, as $N \to \infty$?

21. [*23*] (A. J. Smith.) Explain how to extend Algorithm L so that, in addition to sorting, it computes the number of *inversions* present in the input permutation.

22. [*28*] (J. K. R. Barnett.) Develop a way to speed up merge sorting on multiword keys. (Exercise 5.2.2–30 considers the analogous problem for quicksort.)

23. [*M30*] Exercises 13 and 14 analyze a "bottom-up" or iterative version of merge sort, where the cost $c(N)$ of sorting N items satisfies the recurrence

$$c(N) = c(2^k) + c(N - 2^k) + f(2^k, N - 2^k) \qquad \text{for } 2^k < N \leq 2^{k+1}$$

and $f(m, n)$ is the cost of merging m things with n. Study the "top-down" or divide-and-conquer recurrence

$$c(N) = c(\lceil N/2 \rceil) + c(\lfloor N/2 \rfloor) + f(\lceil N/2 \rceil, \lfloor N/2 \rfloor) \qquad \text{for } N > 1,$$

which arises when merge sort is programmed recursively.

5.2.5. Sorting by Distribution

We come now to an interesting class of sorting methods that are essentially the exact *opposite* of merging, when considered from a standpoint we shall discuss in Section 5.4.7. These methods were used to sort punched cards for many years, long before electronic computers existed. The same approach can be adapted to computer programming, and it is generally known as "bucket sorting," "radix sorting," or "digital sorting," because it is based on the digits of the keys.

Suppose we want to sort a 52-card deck of playing cards. We may define

$$\mathsf{A} < 2 < 3 < 4 < 5 < 6 < 7 < 8 < 9 < 10 < \mathsf{J} < \mathsf{Q} < \mathsf{K},$$

as an ordering of the face values, and for the suits we may define

$$\clubsuit < \diamondsuit < \heartsuit < \spadesuit.$$

One card is to precede another if either (i) its suit is less than the other suit, or (ii) its suit equals the other suit but its face value is less. (This is a particular case of *lexicographic ordering* between ordered pairs of objects; see exercise 5–2.) Thus

$$\mathsf{A}\clubsuit < 2\clubsuit < \cdots < \mathsf{K}\clubsuit < \mathsf{A}\diamondsuit < \cdots < \mathsf{Q}\spadesuit < \mathsf{K}\spadesuit.$$

We could sort the cards by any of the methods already discussed. Card players often use a technique somewhat analogous to the idea behind radix exchange: First they divide the cards into four piles, according to suit, then they fiddle with each individual pile until everything is in order.

But there is a faster way to do the trick! First deal the cards face up into 13 piles, one for each face value. Then collect these piles by putting the aces on the bottom, the 2s face up on top of them, then the 3s, etc., finally putting the kings (face up) on top. Turn the deck face down and deal again, this time into four piles for the four suits. (Again you turn the cards face up as you deal them.) By putting the resulting piles together, with clubs on the bottom, then diamonds, hearts, and spades, you'll get the deck in perfect order.

The same idea applies to the sorting of numbers and alphabetic data. Why does it work? Because (in our playing card example) if two cards go into different piles in the final deal, they have different suits, so the one with the lower suit is lowest. But if two cards have the same suit (and consequently go into the same pile), they are already in proper order because of the previous sorting. In other words, the face values will be in increasing order, on each of the four piles, as we deal the cards on the second pass. The same proof can be abstracted to show that any lexicographic ordering can be sorted in this way; for details, see the answer to exercise 5–2, at the beginning of this chapter.

The sorting method just described is not immediately obvious, and it isn't clear who first discovered the fact that it works so conveniently. A 19-page pamphlet entitled "The Inventory Simplified," published by the Tabulating Machines Company division of IBM in 1923, presented an interesting Digit Plan method for forming sums of products on their Electric Sorting Machine: Suppose, for example, that we want to multiply the number punched in columns 1–10 by the number punched in columns 23–25, and to sum all of these products for a large number of cards. We can sort first on column 25, then use the Tabulating Machine to find the quantities $a_1, a_2, \ldots, a_9$, where a_k is the total of columns 1–10 summed over all cards having k in column 25. Then we can sort on column 24, finding the analogous totals $b_1, b_2, \ldots, b_9$; also on column 23, obtaining $c_1, c_2, \ldots, c_9$. The desired sum of products is easily seen to be

$$a_1 + 2a_2 + \cdots + 9a_9 + 10b_1 + 20b_2 + \cdots + 90b_9 + 100c_1 + 200c_2 + \cdots + 900c_9.$$

This punched-card tabulating method leads naturally to the discovery of least-significant-digit-first radix sorting, so it probably became known to the machine operators. The first published reference to this principle for sorting appears in L. J. Comrie's early discussion of punched-card equipment [*Transactions of the Office Machinery Users' Assoc., Ltd.* (1929), 25–37, especially page 28].

In order to handle radix sorting inside a computer, we must decide what to do with the piles. Suppose that there are M piles; we could set aside M areas of memory, moving each record from an input area into its appropriate pile area. But this is unsatisfactory, since each area must be large enough to hold N items, and $(M + 1)N$ record spaces would be required. Therefore most people rejected the idea of radix sorting within a computer, until H. H. Seward [Master's thesis, M.I.T. Digital Computer Laboratory Report R-232 (1954), 25–28] pointed out that we can achieve the same effect with only $2N$ record areas and M count fields. We simply count how many elements will lie in each of the M piles, by making a preliminary pass over the data; this tells us precisely how to allocate memory for the piles. We have already made use of the same idea in the "distribution counting sort," Algorithm 5.2D.

Thus radix sorting can be carried out as follows: Start with a distribution sort based on the *least significant digit* of the keys (in radix M notation), moving records from the input area to an auxiliary area. Then do another distribution sort, on the next least significant digit, moving the records back into the original input area; and so on, until the final pass (on the most significant digit) puts all records into the desired order.

If we have a decimal computer with 12-digit keys, and if N is rather large, we can choose $M = 1000$ (considering three decimal digits as one radix-1000 digit); then sorting will be complete in four passes, regardless of the size of N. Similarly, if we have a binary computer and a 40-bit key, we can set $M = 1024 = 2^{10}$ and complete the sorting in four passes. Actually each pass consists of three parts (counting, allocating, moving); E. H. Friend [*JACM* **3** (1956), 151] suggested combining two of those parts at the expense of M more memory locations, by accumulating the counts for pass $k + 1$ while moving the records on pass k.

Table 1 shows how such a radix sort can be applied to our 16 example numbers, with $M = 10$. Radix sorting is generally not useful for such small N, so a small example like this is intended to illustrate the sufficiency rather than the efficiency of the method.

An alert, "modern" reader will note, however, that the whole idea of making digit counts for the storage allocation is tied to old-fashioned ideas about sequential data representation. We know that *linked* allocation is specifically designed to handle a set of tables of variable size, so it is natural to choose a linked data structure for radix sorting. Since we traverse each pile serially, all

Table 1

RADIX SORTING

Input area contents:	503 087 512 061 908 170 897 275 653 426 154 509 612 677 765 703
Counts for units digit distribution:	1 1 2 3 1 2 1 3 1 1
Storage allocations based on these counts:	1 2 4 7 8 10 11 14 15 16
Auxiliary area contents:	170 061 512 612 503 653 703 154 275 765 426 087 897 677 908 509
Counts for tens digit distribution:	4 2 1 0 0 2 2 3 1 1
Storage allocations based on these counts:	4 6 7 7 7 9 11 14 15 16
Input area contents:	503 703 908 509 512 612 426 653 154 061 765 170 275 677 087 897
Counts for hundreds digit distribution:	2 2 1 0 1 3 3 2 1 1
Storage allocations based on these counts:	2 4 5 5 6 9 12 14 15 16
Auxiliary area contents:	061 087 154 170 275 426 503 509 512 612 653 677 703 765 897 908

we need is a single link from each item to its successor. Furthermore, we never
need to move the records; we merely adjust the links and proceed merrily down
the lists. The amount of memory required is $(1 + \epsilon)N + 2\epsilon M$ records, where ϵ
is the amount of space taken up by a link field. Formal details of this procedure
are rather interesting since they furnish an excellent example of typical data
structure manipulations, combining sequential and linked allocation:

Algorithm R (*Radix list sort*). Records $R_1, \ldots, R_N$ are each assumed to contain
a LINK field. Their keys are assumed to be p-tuples

$$(a_1, a_2, \ldots, a_p), \qquad 0 \le a_i < M, \tag{1}$$

where the order is defined lexicographically so that

$$(a_1, a_2, \ldots, a_p) < (b_1, b_2, \ldots, b_p) \tag{2}$$

if and only if for some j, $1 \le j \le p$, we have

$$a_i = b_i \quad \text{for all } i < j, \qquad \text{but} \qquad a_j < b_j. \tag{3}$$

The keys may, in particular, be thought of as numbers written in radix M
notation,

$$a_1 M^{p-1} + a_2 M^{p-2} \cdots + a_{p-1} M + a_p, \tag{4}$$

and in this case lexicographic order corresponds to the normal ordering of nonnegative numbers. The keys may also be strings of alphabetic letters, etc.

Sorting is done by keeping M "piles" of records, in a manner that exactly
parallels the action of a card sorting machine. The piles are really queues in the
sense of Chapter 2, since we link them together so that they are traversed in a
first-in-first-out manner. There are two pointer variables TOP$[i]$ and BOTM$[i]$
for each pile, $0 \le i < M$, and we assume as in Chapter 2 that

$$\text{LINK}(\text{LOC}(\text{BOTM}[i])) \equiv \text{BOTM}[i]. \tag{5}$$

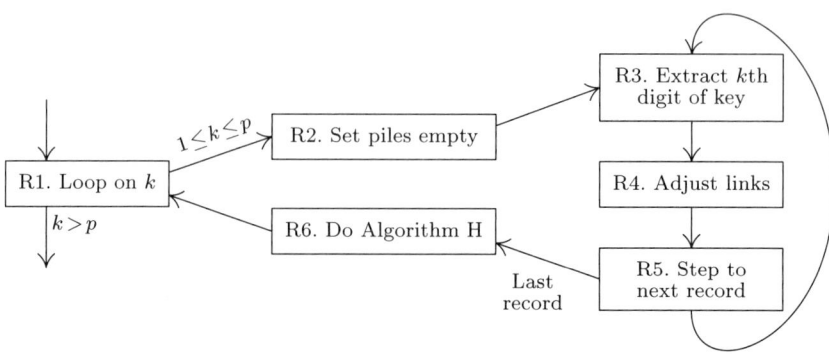

Fig. 32. Radix list sort.

R1. [Loop on k.] In the beginning, set P $\leftarrow$ LOC(R_N), a pointer to the last record. Then perform steps R2 through R6 for $k = 1, 2, \ldots, p$. (Steps R2 through R6 constitute one "pass.") Then the algorithm terminates, with P pointing to the record with the smallest key, LINK(P) to the record with next smallest, then LINK(LINK(P)), etc.; the LINK in the final record will be Λ.

R2. [Set piles empty.] Set TOP[i] $\leftarrow$ LOC(BOTM[i]) and BOTM[i] $\leftarrow$ Λ, for $0 \le i < M$.

R3. [Extract kth digit of key.] Let KEY(P), the key in the record referenced by P, be $(a_1, a_2, \ldots, a_p)$; set $i \leftarrow a_{p+1-k}$, the kth least significant digit of this key.

R4. [Adjust links.] Set LINK(TOP[i]) $\leftarrow$ P, then set TOP[i] $\leftarrow$ P.

R5. [Step to next record.] If $k = 1$ (the first pass) and if P = LOC(R_j), for some $j \ne 1$, set P $\leftarrow$ LOC(R_{j-1}) and return to R3. If $k > 1$ (subsequent passes), set P $\leftarrow$ LINK(P), and return to R3 if P $\ne \Lambda$.

R6. [Do Algorithm H.] (We are now done distributing all elements onto the piles.) Perform Algorithm H below, which "hooks together" the individual piles into one list, in preparation for the next pass. Then set P $\leftarrow$ BOTM[0], a pointer to the first element of the hooked-up list. (See exercise 3.) ∎

Algorithm H (*Hooking-up of queues*). Given M queues, linked according to the conventions of Algorithm R, this algorithm adjusts at most M links so that a single queue is created, with BOTM[0] pointing to the first element, and with pile 0 preceding pile 1 ... preceding pile $M-1$.

H1. [Initialize.] Set $i \leftarrow 0$.

H2. [Point to top of pile.] Set P $\leftarrow$ TOP[i].

H3. [Next pile.] Increase i by 1. If $i = M$, set LINK(P) $\leftarrow$ Λ and terminate the algorithm.

H4. [Is pile empty?] If BOTM[i] $= \Lambda$, go back to H3.

H5. [Tie piles together.] Set LINK(P) $\leftarrow$ BOTM[i]. Return to H2. ∎

Figure 33 shows the contents of the piles after each of the three passes, when our 16 example numbers are sorted with $M = 10$. Algorithm R is very easy to program for MIX, once a suitable way to treat the pass-by-pass variation of steps R3 and R5 has been found. The following program does this without sacrificing any speed in the inner loop, by overlaying two of the instructions. Note that TOP[i] and BOTM[i] can be packed into the same word.

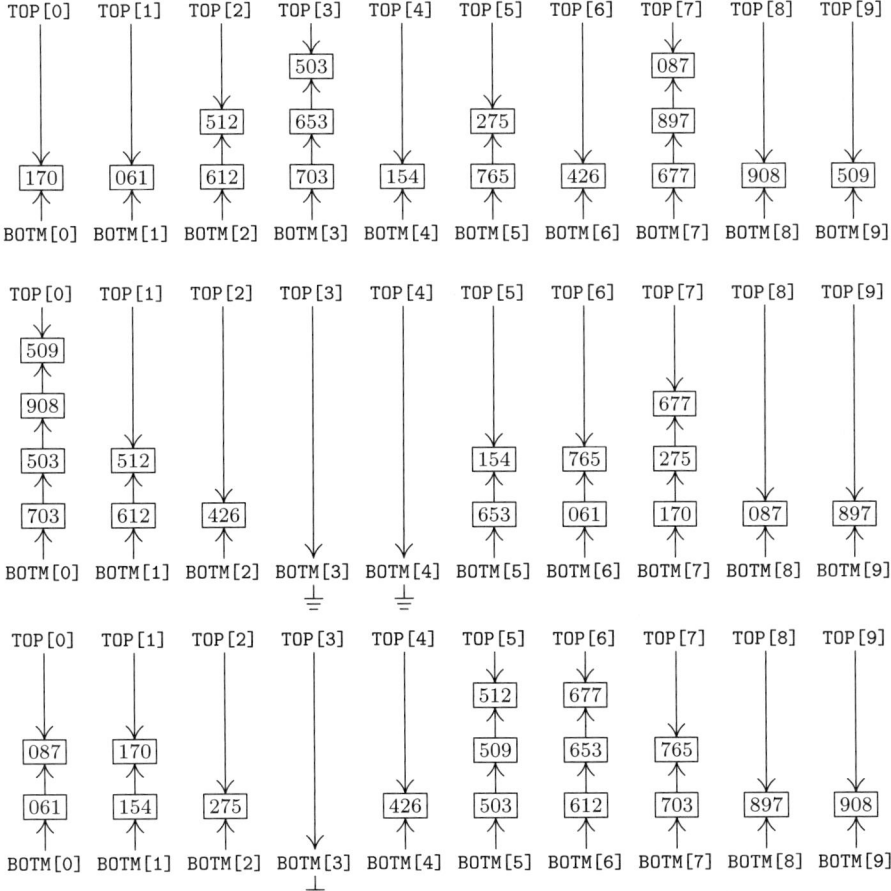

Fig. 33. Radix sort using linked allocation: contents of the ten piles after each pass.

Program R (*Radix list sort*). The given records in locations INPUT+1 through INPUT+N are assumed to have $p = 3$ components (a_1, a_2, a_3) stored respectively in the (1:1), (2:2), and (3:3) fields. (Thus M is assumed to be less than or equal to the byte size of MIX.) The (4:5) field of each record is its LINK. We let TOP[i] $\equiv$ PILES $+ i(1:2)$ and BOTM[i] $\equiv$ PILES $+ i(4:5)$, for $0 \le i < M$. It is convenient to make links relative to location INPUT, so that LOC(BOTM[i]) = PILES$+i-$INPUT; to avoid negative links we therefore want the PILES table to be in higher locations than the INPUT table. Index registers are assigned as follows: rI1 ≡ P, rI2 ≡ i, rI3 ≡ $3 - k$, rI4 ≡ TOP[i]; during Algorithm H, rI2 ≡ $i - M$.

01	LINK	EQU	4:5		
02	TOP	EQU	1:2		
03	START	ENT1	N	1	*R1. Loop on k.* P = LOC(R_N).
04		ENT3	2	1	$k \leftarrow 1$.
05	2H	ENT2	M-1	3	*R2. Set piles empty.*
06		ENTA	PILES-INPUT,2	3M	LOC(BOTM[i])
07		STA	PILES,2(TOP)	3M	→ TOP[i].
08		STZ	PILES,2(LINK)	3M	BOTM[i] ← Λ.
09		DEC2	1	3M	
10		J2NN	*-4	3M	$M > i \geq 0$.
11		LDA	R3SW,3	3	
12		STA	3F	3	Modify instructions for pass k.
13		LDA	R5SW,3	3	
14		STA	5F	3	
15	3H	[LD2	INPUT,1(3:3)]		*R3. Extract kth digit of key.*
16	4H	LD4	PILES,2(TOP)	3N	*R4. Adjust links.*
17		ST1	INPUT,4(LINK)	3N	LINK(TOP[i]) ← P.
18		ST1	PILES,2(TOP)	3N	TOP[i] ← P.
19	5H	[DEC1	1]		*R5. Step to next record.*
20		J1NZ	3B	3N	To R3 if end of pass.
21	6H	ENN2	M	3	*R6. Do Algorithm H.*
22		JMP	7F	3	To H2 with $i \leftarrow 0$.
23	R3SW	LD2	INPUT,1(1:1)	N	Instruction for R3 when $k = 3$.
24		LD2	INPUT,1(2:2)	N	Instruction for R3 when $k = 2$.
25		LD2	INPUT,1(3:3)	N	Instruction for R3 when $k = 1$.
26	R5SW	LD1	INPUT,1(LINK)	N	Instruction for R5 when $k = 3$.
27		LD1	INPUT,1(LINK)	N	Instruction for R5 when $k = 2$.
28		DEC1	1	N	Instruction for R5 when $k = 1$.
29	9H	LDA	PILES+M,2(LINK)	3M−3	*H4. Is pile empty?*
30		JAZ	8F	3M−3	To H3 if BOTM[i] = Λ.
31		STA	INPUT,1(LINK)	3M−3−E	*H5. Tie piles together.*
32	7H	LD1	PILES+M,2(TOP)	3M − E	*H2. Point to top of pile.*
33	8H	INC2	1	3M	*H3. Next pile.* $i \leftarrow i + 1$.
34		J2NZ	9B	3M	To H4 if $i \neq M$.
35		STZ	INPUT,1(LINK)	3	LINK(P) ← Λ.
36		LD1	PILES(LINK)	3	P ← BOTM[0].
37		DEC3	1	3	
38		J3NN	2B	3	Loop for $1 \leq k \leq 3$. ∎

The running time of Program R is $32N + 48M + 38 - 4E$, where N is the number of input records, M is the radix (the number of piles), and E is the number of occurrences of empty piles. This compares very favorably with other programs we have constructed based on similar assumptions (Programs 5.2.1M, 5.2.4L). A p-pass version of the program would take $(11p - 1)N + O(pM)$ units of time; the critical factor in the timing is the inner loop, which involves five references to memory and one branch. On a typical computer we will have $M = b^r$ and $p = \lceil t/r \rceil$, where t is the number of radix-b digits in the keys;

increasing r will decrease p, so the formulas can be used to determine a best value of r.

The only variable in the timing is E, the number of empty piles observed in step H4. If we consider each of the M^N sequences of radix-M digits to be equally probable, we know from our study of the "poker test" in Section 3.3.2D that there are $M - r$ empty piles with probability

$$\frac{M(M - 1) \ldots (M - r + 1)}{M^N} \left\{ {N \atop r} \right\} \tag{6}$$

on each pass, where $\left\{ {N \atop r} \right\}$ is a Stirling number of the second kind. By exercise 6,

$$E = \left(\min \ \max(M - N, 0)p, \quad \text{ave} \ M\left(1 - \frac{1}{M}\right)^N p, \quad \max \ (M - 1)p \right). \tag{7}$$

An ever-increasing number of "pipeline" or "number-crunching" computers have appeared in recent years. These machines have multiple arithmetic units and look-ahead circuitry so that memory references and computation can be highly overlapped; but their efficiency deteriorates noticeably in the presence of conditional branch instructions unless the branch almost always goes the same way. The inner loop of a radix sort is well adapted to such machines, because it is a straight iterative calculation of typical number-crunching form. Therefore *radix sorting is usually more efficient than any other known method for internal sorting on such machines*, provided that N is not too small and the keys are not too long.

Of course, radix sorting is not very efficient when the keys are extremely long. For example, imagine sorting 60-digit decimal numbers with 20 passes of a radix sort, using $M = 10^3$; very few pairs of numbers will tend to have identical keys in their leading 9 digits, so the first 17 passes accomplish very little. In our analysis of radix exchange sorting, we found that it was unnecessary to inspect many bits of the key, when we looked at the keys from the left instead of the right. Let us therefore reconsider the idea of a radix sort that starts at the most significant digit (MSD) instead of the least significant digit (LSD).

We have already remarked that an MSD-first radix method suggests itself naturally; in fact, it is not hard to see why the post office uses such a method to sort mail. A large collection of letters can be sorted into separate bags for different geographical areas; each of these bags then contains a smaller number of letters that can be sorted independently of the other bags, into finer and finer geographical divisions. (Indeed, bags of letters can be transported nearer to their destinations before they are sorted further, or as they are being sorted further.) This principle of "divide and conquer" is quite appealing, and the only reason it doesn't work especially well for sorting punched cards is that it ultimately spends too much time fussing with very small piles. Algorithm R is relatively efficient, even though it considers LSD first, since we never have more than M piles, and the piles need to be hooked together only p times. On the other hand, it is not difficult to design an MSD-first radix method using linked memory, with negative links as in Algorithm 5.2.4L to denote the boundaries between piles. (See exercise 10.) The main difficulty is that empty piles tend to proliferate and to consume a great deal of time in an MSD-first method.

Perhaps the best compromise has been suggested by M. D. MacLaren [*JACM* **13** (1966), 404–411], who recommends an LSD-first sort as in Algorithm R, but *applied only to the most significant digits*. This does not completely sort the file, but it usually brings the file very nearly into order so that very few inversions remain; therefore straight insertion can be used to finish up. Our analysis of Program 5.2.1M applies also to this situation, so that if the keys are uniformly distributed we will have an average of $\frac{1}{4}N(N-1)M^{-p}$ inversions remaining in the file after sorting on the leading p digits. (See Eq. 5.2.1–(17) and exercise 5.2.1–38.) MacLaren has computed the average number of memory references per item sorted, and the optimum choice of M and p (assuming that M is a power of 2, that the keys are uniformly distributed, and that $N/M^p \leq 0.1$ so that deviations from uniformity are tolerable) turns out to be given by the following table:

$N =$	100	1000	10000	100000	1000000	10^7	10^8	10^9
best $M =$	32	128	512	1024	8192	2^{15}	2^{17}	2^{19}
best $p =$	2	2	2	2	2	2	2	2
$\beta(N) =$	19.3	18.5	18.2	18.1	18.0	18.0	18.0	18.0

Here $\beta(N)$ denotes the average number of memory references per item sorted,

$$\beta(N) = 5p + 8 + \frac{2pM}{N} + \frac{N-1}{2M^p} - \frac{H_N}{N};\tag{8}$$

it is bounded as $N \to \infty$, if we take $p = 2$ and $M > \sqrt{N}$, so the average sorting time is actually $O(N)$ instead of order $N \log N$. This method is an improvement over multiple list insertion (Program 5.2.1M), which is essentially the case $p = 1$. Exercise 12 gives MacLaren's interesting procedure for final rearrangement of a partially list-sorted file.

It is also possible to avoid the link fields, using the methods of Algorithm 5.2D and exercise 5.2–13, so that only $O(\sqrt{N})$ memory locations are needed in addition to the space required for the records themselves. The average sorting time is proportional to N if the input records are uniformly distributed.

W. Dobosiewicz obtained good results by using an MSD-first distribution sort until reaching short subfiles, with the distribution process constrained so that the first $M/2$ piles were guaranteed to receive between 25% and 75% of the records [see *Inf. Proc. Letters* **7** (1978), 1–6; **8** (1979), 170–172]; this ensured that the average time to sort uniform keys would be $O(N)$ while the worst case would be $O(N \log N)$. His papers inspired several other researchers to devise new address calculation algorithms, of which the most instructive is perhaps the following 2-level scheme due to Markku Tamminen [*J. Algorithms* **6** (1985), 138–144]: Assume that all keys are fractions in the interval $[0..1)$. First distribute the N records into $\lfloor N/8 \rfloor$ bins by mapping key K into bin $\lfloor KN/8 \rfloor$. Then suppose bin k has received N_k records; if $N_k \leq 16$, sort it by straight insertion, otherwise sort it by a MacLaren-like distribution-plus-insertion sort into M^2 bins, where $M^2 \approx 10N_k$. Tamminen proved the following remarkable result:

Theorem T. *There is a constant T such that the sorting method just described performs at most TN operations on the average, whenever the keys are independent random numbers whose density function $f(x)$ is bounded and Riemann-integrable for $0 \le x \le 1$.* (The constant T does not depend on f.)

Proof. See exercise 18. Intuitively, the first distribution into $N/8$ piles finds intervals in which f is approximately constant; the second distribution will then make the expected bin size approximately constant. ∎

Several versions of radix sort that have been well tuned for sorting large arrays of alphabetic strings are described in an instructive article by P. M. McIlroy, K. Bostic, and M. D. McIlroy, *Computing Systems* **6** (1993), 5–27.

EXERCISES

▶ **1.** [*20*] The algorithm of exercise 5.2–13 shows how to do a distribution sort with only N record areas (and M count fields), instead of $2N$ record areas. Does this lead to an improvement over the radix sorting algorithm illustrated in Table 1?

2. [*13*] Is Algorithm R a stable sorting method?

3. [*15*] Explain why Algorithm H makes BOTM[0] point to the first record in the "hooked-up" queue, *even though pile 0 might be empty.*

▶ **4.** [*23*] Algorithm R keeps the M piles linked together as queues (first-in-first-out). Explore the idea of linking the piles as *stacks* instead. (The arrows in Fig. 33 would go downward instead of upward, and the BOTM table would be unnecessary.) Show that if the piles are "hooked together" in an appropriate order, it is possible to achieve a valid sorting method. Does this lead to a simpler or a faster algorithm?

5. [*20*] What changes are necessary to Program R so that it sorts eight-byte keys instead of three-byte keys? Assume that the most significant bytes of K_i are stored in location KEY$+i$ (1:5), while the three least significant bytes are in location INPUT$+i$ (1:3) as presently. What is the running time of the program, after these changes have been made?

6. [*M24*] Let $g_{MN}(z) = \sum p_{MNk}z^k$, where p_{MNk} is the probability that exactly k empty piles are present after a random radix-sort pass puts N elements into M piles.
a) Show that $g_{M(N+1)}(z) = g_{MN}(z) + ((1 - z)/M)g'_{MN}(z)$.
b) Use this relation to find simple expressions for the mean and variance of this probability distribution, as a function of M and N.

7. [*20*] Discuss the similarities and differences between Algorithm R and radix exchange sorting (Algorithm 5.2.2R).

▶ **8.** [*20*] The radix-sorting algorithms discussed in the text assume that all keys being sorted are nonnegative. What changes should be made to the algorithms when the keys are numbers expressed in *two's complement* or *ones' complement* notation?

9. [*20*] Continuing exercise 8, what changes should be made to the algorithms when the keys are numbers expressed in *signed magnitude* notation?

10. [*30*] Design an efficient most-significant-digit-first radix-sorting algorithm that uses linked memory. (As the size of the subfiles decreases, it is wise to decrease M, and to use a nonradix method on the really short subfiles.)

11. [*16*] The sixteen input numbers shown in Table 1 start with 41 inversions; after sorting is complete, of course, there are no inversions remaining. How many inversions would be present in the file if we omitted pass 1, doing a radix sort only on the tens and hundreds digits? How many inversions would be present if we omitted both pass 1 and pass 2?

12. [*24*] (M. D. MacLaren.) Suppose that Algorithm R has been applied only to the p leading digits of the actual keys; thus the file is nearly sorted when we read it in the order of the links, but keys that agree in their first p digits may be out of order. Design an algorithm that rearranges the records in place so that their keys are in order, $K_1 \leq K_2 \leq \cdots \leq K_N$. [*Hint:* The special case that the file is perfectly sorted appears in the answer to exercise 5.2–12; it is possible to combine this with straight insertion without loss of efficiency, since few inversions remain in the file.]

13. [*40*] Implement the internal sorting method suggested in the text at the close of this section, producing a subroutine that sorts random data in $O(N)$ units of time with only $O(\sqrt{N})$ additional memory locations.

14. [*22*] The sequence of playing cards

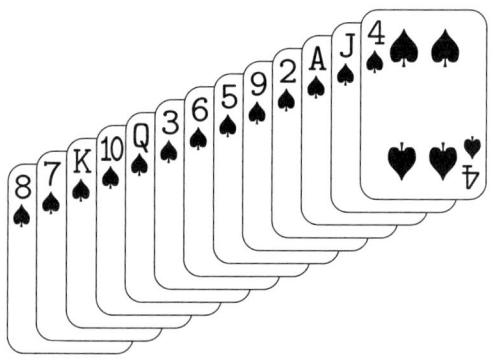

can be sorted into increasing order A 2 ... J Q K from top to bottom in two passes, using just two piles for intermediate storage: Deal the cards face down into two piles containing respectively A 2 9 3 10 and 4 J 5 6 Q K 7 8 (from bottom to top); then put the second pile on the first, turn the deck face up, and deal into two piles A 2 3 4 5 6 7 8, 9 10 J Q K. Combine these piles, turn them face up, and you're done.

Prove that this sequence of cards cannot be sorted into *decreasing* order K Q J ... 2 A from top to bottom in two passes, even if you are allowed to use up to three piles for intermediate storage. (Dealing must always be from the top of the deck, turning the cards face down as they are dealt. Top to bottom is right to left in the illustration.)

15. [*M25*] Consider the problem of exercise 14 when all cards must be dealt face up instead of face down. Thus, one pass can be used to convert increasing order into decreasing order. How many passes are required?

▶ **16.** [*25*] Design an algorithm to sort strings $\alpha_1, \ldots, \alpha_n$ on an m-letter alphabet into lexicographic order. The total running time of your algorithm should be $O(m+n+N)$, where $N = |\alpha_1| + \cdots + |\alpha_n|$ is the total length of all the strings.

17. [*15*] In the two-level distribution sort proposed by Tamminen (see Theorem T), why is a MacLaren-like method used for the second level of distribution but not the first level?

18. [*HM26*] Prove Theorem T. *Hint:* Show first that MacLaren's distribution-plus-insertion algorithm does $O(BN)$ operations, on the average, when it is applied to independent random keys whose probability density function satisfies $f(x) \leq B$ for $0 \leq x \leq 1$.

> *For sorting the roots and words*
> *we had the use of 1100 lozenge boxes,*
> *and used trays for the forms.*
> — GEORGE V. WIGRAM (1843)

5.3. OPTIMUM SORTING

Now THAT WE have analyzed a great many methods for internal sorting, it is time to turn to a broader question: *What is the best possible way to sort?* Can we place limits on the maximum sorting speeds that will ever be achievable, no matter how clever a programmer might be?

Of course there *is* no best possible way to sort; we must define precisely what is meant by "best," and there is no best possible way to define "best." We have discussed similar questions about the theoretical optimality of algorithms in Sections 4.3.3, 4.6.3, and 4.6.4, where high-precision multiplication and polynomial evaluation were considered. In each case it was necessary to formulate a rather simple definition of a "best possible" algorithm, in order to give sufficient structure to the problem to make it workable. And in each case we ran into interesting problems that are so difficult they still haven't been completely resolved. The same situation holds for sorting; some very interesting discoveries have been made, but many fascinating questions remain unanswered.

Studies of the inherent complexity of sorting have usually been directed towards minimizing the number of times we make comparisons between keys while sorting n items, or merging m items with n, or selecting the tth largest of an unordered set of n items. Sections 5.3.1, 5.3.2, and 5.3.3 discuss these questions in general, and Section 5.3.4 deals with similar issues under the interesting restriction that the pattern of comparisons must essentially be fixed in advance. Several other types of interesting theoretical questions related to optimum sorting appear in the exercises for Section 5.3.4, and in the discussion of external sorting (Sections 5.4.4, 5.4.8, and 5.4.9).

> As soon as an Analytical Engine exists,
> it will necessarily guide the future course of the science.
> Whenever any result is sought by its aid,
> the question will then arise —
> By what course of calculation can these
> results be arrived at by the machine
> in the shortest time?
> — CHARLES BABBAGE (1864)

5.3.1. Minimum-Comparison Sorting

The minimum number of key comparisons needed to sort n elements is obviously *zero*, because we have seen radix methods that do no comparisons at all. In fact, it is possible to write MIX programs that are able to sort, although they contain no conditional jump instructions at all! (See exercise 5–8 at the beginning of this chapter.) We have also seen several sorting methods that are based essentially on comparisons of keys, yet their running time in practice is dominated by other considerations such as data movement, housekeeping operations, etc.

Therefore it is clear that comparison counting is not the only way to measure the effectiveness of a sorting method. But it is fun to scrutinize the number of comparisons anyway, since a theoretical study of this subject gives us a good

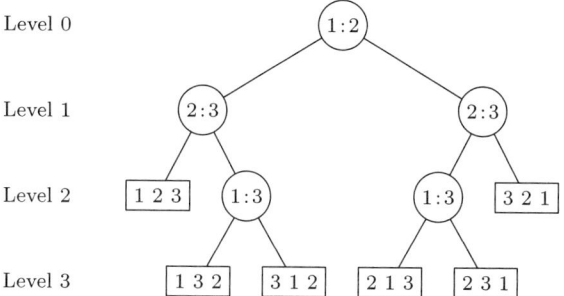

Level 0

Level 1

Level 2

Level 3

Fig. 34. A comparison tree for sorting three elements.

deal of useful insight into the nature of sorting processes, and it also helps us to sharpen our wits for the more mundane problems that confront us at other times.

In order to rule out radix-sorting methods, which do no comparisons at all, we shall restrict our discussion to sorting techniques that are based solely on an abstract linear ordering relation "<" between keys, as discussed at the beginning of this chapter. For simplicity, we shall also confine our discussion to the case of *distinct* keys, so that there are only two possible outcomes of any comparison of K_i versus K_j: either $K_i < K_j$ or $K_i > K_j$. (For an extension of the theory to the general case where equal keys are allowed, see exercises 3 through 12. For bounds on the worst-case running time that is needed to sort integers without the restriction to comparison-based methods, see Fredman and Willard, *J. Computer and Syst. Sci.* **47** (1993), 424–436; Ben-Amram and Galil, *J. Comp. Syst. Sci.* **54** (1997), 345–370; Thorup, *SODA* **9** (1998), 550–555.)

The problem of sorting by comparisons can also be expressed in other equivalent ways. Given a set of n distinct weights and a balance scale, we can ask for the least number of weighings necessary to completely rank the weights in order of magnitude, when the pans of the balance scale can each accommodate only one weight. Alternatively, given a set of n players in a tournament, we can ask for the smallest number of games that suffice to rank all contestants, assuming that the strengths of the players can be linearly ordered (with no ties).

All n-element sorting methods that satisfy the constraints above can be represented in terms of an extended binary tree structure such as that shown in Fig. 34. Each *internal node* (drawn as a circle) contains two indices "$i:j$" denoting a comparison of K_i versus K_j. The left subtree of this node represents the subsequent comparisons to be made if $K_i < K_j$, and the right subtree represents the actions to be taken when $K_i > K_j$. Each *external node* of the tree (drawn as a box) contains a permutation $a_1 a_2 \ldots a_n$ of $\{1, 2, \ldots, n\}$, denoting the fact that the ordering

$$K_{a_1} < K_{a_2} < \cdots < K_{a_n}$$

has been established. (If we look at the path from the root to this external node, each of the $n-1$ relationships $K_{a_i} < K_{a_{i+1}}$ for $1 \le i < n$ will be the result of some comparison $a_i : a_{i+1}$ or $a_{i+1} : a_i$ on this path.)

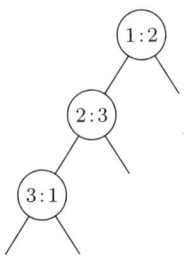

Fig. 35. Example of a redundant comparison.

Thus Fig. 34 represents a sorting method that first compares K_1 with K_2; if $K_1 > K_2$, it goes on (via the right subtree) to compare K_2 with K_3, and then if $K_2 < K_3$ it compares K_1 with K_3; finally if $K_1 > K_3$ it knows that $K_2 < K_3 < K_1$. An actual sorting algorithm will usually also move the keys around in the file, but we are interested here only in the comparisons, so we ignore all data movement. A comparison of K_i with K_j in this tree always means the *original* keys K_i and K_j, not the keys that might currently occupy the ith and jth positions of the file after the records have been shuffled around.

It is possible to make redundant comparisons; for example, in Fig. 35 there is no reason to compare $3:1$, since $K_1 < K_2$ and $K_2 < K_3$ implies that $K_1 < K_3$. No permutation can possibly correspond to the left subtree of node $3:1$ in Fig. 35; consequently that part of the algorithm will never be performed! Since we are interested in minimizing the number of comparisons, we may assume that no redundant comparisons are made. Hence we have an extended binary tree structure in which every external node corresponds to a permutation. All permutations of the input keys are possible, and every permutation defines a unique path from the root to an external node; it follows that *there are exactly $n!$ external nodes in a comparison tree that sorts n elements with no redundant comparisons.*

The best worst case.   The first problem that arises naturally is to find comparison trees that minimize the *maximum* number of comparisons made. (Later we shall consider the *average* number of comparisons.)

Let $S(n)$ be the minimum number of comparisons that will suffice to sort n elements. If all the internal nodes of a comparison tree are at levels $< k$, it is obvious that there can be at most 2^k external nodes in the tree. Hence, letting $k = S(n)$, we have

$$n! \leq 2^{S(n)}.$$

Since $S(n)$ is an integer, we can rewrite this formula to obtain the lower bound

$$S(n) \geq \lceil \lg n! \rceil. \tag{1}$$

Stirling's approximation tells us that

$$\lceil \lg n! \rceil = n \lg n - n/\ln 2 + \tfrac{1}{2} \lg n + O(1), \tag{2}$$

hence roughly $n \lg n$ comparisons are needed.

Relation (1) is often called the *information-theoretic lower bound*, since cognoscenti of information theory would say that $\lg n!$ "bits of information" are being acquired during a sorting process; each comparison yields at most one bit of information. Trees such as Fig. 34 have also been called "questionnaires"; their mathematical properties were first explored systematically in Claude Picard's book *Théorie des Questionnaires* (Paris: Gauthier-Villars, 1965).

Of all the sorting methods we have seen, the three that require fewest comparisons are binary insertion (see Section 5.2.1), tree selection (see Section 5.2.3), and straight two-way merging (see Algorithm 5.2.4L). The maximum number of comparisons for binary insertion is readily seen to be

$$B(n) = \sum_{k=1}^{n} \lceil \lg k \rceil = n \lceil \lg n \rceil - 2^{\lceil \lg n \rceil} + 1, \tag{3}$$

by exercise 1.2.4–42, and the maximum number of comparisons in two-way merging is given in exercise 5.2.4–14. We will see in Section 5.3.3 that tree selection has the same bound on its comparisons as either binary insertion or two-way merging, depending on how the tree is set up. In all three cases we achieve an asymptotic value of $n \lg n$; combining these lower and upper bounds for $S(n)$ proves that

$$\lim_{n\to\infty} \frac{S(n)}{n \lg n} = 1. \tag{4}$$

Thus we have an approximate formula for $S(n)$, but it is desirable to obtain more precise information. The following table gives exact values of the lower and upper bounds discussed above, for small n:

$n =$	1	2	3	4	5	6	7	8	9	10	11	12	13	14	15	16	17
$\lceil \lg n! \rceil =$	0	1	3	5	7	10	13	16	19	22	26	29	33	37	41	45	49
$B(n) =$	0	1	3	5	8	11	14	17	21	25	29	33	37	41	45	49	54
$L(n) =$	0	1	3	5	9	11	14	17	25	27	30	33	38	41	45	49	65

Here $B(n)$ and $L(n)$ refer respectively to binary insertion and two-way list merging. It can be shown that $B(n) \le L(n)$ for all n (see exercise 2).

From the table above, we can see that $S(4) = 5$, but $S(5)$ might be either 7 or 8. This brings us back to a problem stated at the beginning of Section 5.2: What is the best way to sort five elements? Can five elements be sorted using only seven comparisons?

The answer is yes, but a seven-step procedure is not especially easy to discover. We begin by first comparing $K_1 : K_2$, then $K_3 : K_4$, then the larger elements of these pairs. This produces a configuration that may be diagrammed

$$\tag{5}$$

to indicate that $a < b < d$ and $c < d$. (It is convenient to represent known ordering relations between elements by drawing directed graphs such as this, where x is known to be less than y if and only if there is a path from x to y in the graph.) At this point we insert the fifth element $K_5 = e$ into its proper place among $\{a, b, d\}$; only two comparisons are needed, since we may compare it first with b and then with a or d. This leaves one of four possibilities,

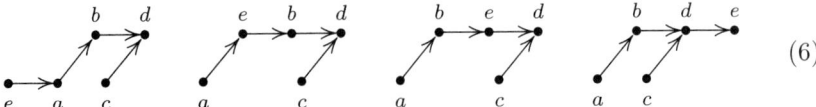

$$(6)$$

and in each case we can insert c among the remaining elements less than d in one or two more comparisons. This method for sorting five elements was first found by H. B. Demuth [Ph.D. thesis, Stanford University (1956), 41–43].

Merge insertion. A pleasant generalization of the method above has been discovered by Lester Ford, Jr. and Selmer Johnson. Since it involves some aspects of merging and some aspects of insertion, we shall call it *merge insertion*. For example, consider the problem of sorting 21 elements. We start by comparing the ten pairs $K_1:K_2, K_3:K_4, \ldots, K_{19}:K_{20}$; then we sort the ten larger elements of the pairs, using merge insertion. As a result we obtain the configuration

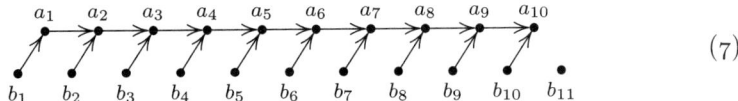

$$(7)$$

analogous to (5). The next step is to insert b_3 among $\{b_1, a_1, a_2\}$, then b_2 among the other elements less than a_2; we arrive at the configuration

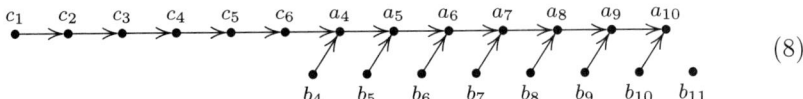

$$(8)$$

Let us call the upper-line elements the *main chain*. We can insert b_5 into its proper place in the main chain, using three comparisons (first comparing it to c_4, then c_2 or c_6, etc.); then b_4 can be moved into the main chain in three more steps, leading to

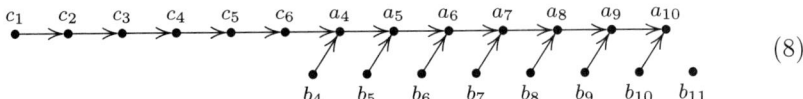

$$(9)$$

The next step is crucial; is it clear what to do? We insert b_{11} (*not* b_7) into the main chain, using only four comparisons. Then $b_{10}, b_9, b_8, b_7, b_6$ (in this order) can also be inserted into their proper places in the main chain, using at most four comparisons each.

A careful count of the comparisons involved here shows that the 21 elements have been sorted in at most $10 + S(10) + 2 + 2 + 3 + 3 + 4 + 4 + 4 + 4 + 4 = 66$ steps. Since

$$2^{65} < 21! < 2^{66},$$

we also know that no fewer than 66 would be possible in any event; hence

$$S(21) = 66. \tag{10}$$

(Binary insertion would have required 74 comparisons.)

In general, merge insertion proceeds as follows for n elements:

i) Make pairwise comparisons of $\lfloor n/2 \rfloor$ disjoint pairs of elements. (If n is odd, leave one element out.)

ii) Sort the $\lfloor n/2 \rfloor$ larger numbers, found in step (i), by merge insertion.

iii) Name the elements $a_1, a_2, \ldots, a_{\lfloor n/2 \rfloor}, b_1, b_2, \ldots, b_{\lceil n/2 \rceil}$ as in (7), where $a_1 \leq a_2 \leq \cdots \leq a_{\lfloor n/2 \rfloor}$ and $b_i \leq a_i$ for $1 \leq i \leq \lfloor n/2 \rfloor$; call b_1 and the a's the "main chain." Insert the remaining b's into the main chain, using binary insertion, in the following order, leaving out all b_j for $j > \lceil n/2 \rceil$:

$$b_3, b_2; \ b_5, b_4; \ b_{11}, b_{10}, \ldots, b_6; \ \ldots; \ b_{t_k}, b_{t_k-1}, \ldots, b_{t_{k-1}+1}; \ \ldots \tag{11}$$

We wish to define the sequence $(t_1, t_2, t_3, t_4, \ldots) = (1, 3, 5, 11, \ldots)$, which appears in (11), in such a way that each of $b_{t_k}, b_{t_k-1}, \ldots, b_{t_{k-1}+1}$ can be inserted into the main chain with at most k comparisons. Generalizing (7), (8), and (9), we obtain the diagram

where the main chain up to and including a_{t_k-1} contains $2t_{k-1} + (t_k - t_{k-1} - 1)$ elements. This number must be less than 2^k; our best bet is to set it equal to $2^k - 1$, so that

$$t_{k-1} + t_k = 2^k. \tag{12}$$

Since $t_1 = 1$, we may set $t_0 = 1$ for convenience, and we find that

$$t_k = 2^k - t_{k-1} = 2^k - 2^{k-1} + t_{k-2} = \cdots = 2^k - 2^{k-1} + \cdots + (-1)^k 2^0$$
$$= \left(2^{k+1} + (-1)^k\right)/3 \tag{13}$$

by summing a geometric series. (Curiously, this same sequence arose in our study of an algorithm for calculating the greatest common divisor of two integers; see exercise 4.5.2–36.)

Let $F(n)$ be the number of comparisons required to sort n elements by merge insertion. Clearly

$$F(n) = \lfloor n/2 \rfloor + F(\lfloor n/2 \rfloor) + G(\lceil n/2 \rceil), \tag{14}$$

where G represents the amount of work involved in step (iii). If $t_{k-1} \leq m \leq t_k$, we have

$$G(m) = \sum_{j=1}^{k-1} j(t_j - t_{j-1}) + k(m - t_{k-1}) = km - (t_0 + t_1 + \cdots + t_{k-1}), \tag{15}$$

summing by parts. Let us set

$$w_k = t_0 + t_1 + \cdots + t_{k-1} = \lfloor 2^{k+1}/3 \rfloor, \tag{16}$$

so that $(w_0, w_1, w_2, w_3, w_4, \dots) = (0, 1, 2, 5, 10, 21, \dots)$. Exercise 13 shows that

$$F(n) - F(n-1) = k \qquad \text{if and only if} \qquad w_k < n \le w_{k+1}, \tag{17}$$

and the latter condition is equivalent to

$$\frac{2^{k+1}}{3} < n \le \frac{2^{k+2}}{3},$$

or $k + 1 < \lg 3n \le k + 2$; hence

$$F(n) - F(n-1) = \left\lceil \lg \tfrac{3}{4} n \right\rceil. \tag{18}$$

(This formula is due to A. Hadian [Ph.D. thesis, Univ. of Minnesota (1969), 38–42].) It follows that $F(n)$ has a remarkably simple expression,

$$F(n) = \sum_{k=1}^{n} \left\lceil \lg \tfrac{3}{4} k \right\rceil, \tag{19}$$

quite similar to the corresponding formula (3) for binary insertion. A closed form for this sum appears in exercise 14.

Equation (19) makes it easy to construct a table of $F(n)$; we have

$n =$	1	2	3	4	5	6	7	8	9	10	11	12	13	14	15	16	17
$\lceil \lg n! \rceil =$	0	1	3	5	7	10	13	16	19	22	26	29	33	37	41	45	49
$F(n) =$	0	1	3	5	7	10	13	16	19	22	26	30	34	38	42	46	50

$n =$	18	19	20	21	22	23	24	25	26	27	28	29	30	31	32	33
$\lceil \lg n! \rceil =$	53	57	62	66	70	75	80	84	89	94	98	103	108	113	118	123
$F(n) =$	54	58	62	66	71	76	81	86	91	96	101	106	111	116	121	126

Notice that $F(n) = \lceil \lg n! \rceil$ for $1 \le n \le 11$ and for $20 \le n \le 21$, so we know that merge insertion is optimum for those n:

$$S(n) = \lceil \lg n! \rceil = F(n) \qquad \text{for } n = 1, \dots, 11, 20, \text{ and } 21. \tag{20}$$

Hugo Steinhaus posed the problem of finding $S(n)$ in the second edition of his classic book *Mathematical Snapshots* (Oxford University Press, 1950), 38–39. He described the method of binary insertion, which is the best possible way to sort n objects if we start by sorting $n - 1$ of them first before the nth is considered; and he conjectured that binary insertion would be optimum in general. Several years later [*Calcutta Math. Soc. Golden Jubilee Commemoration* **2** (1959), 323–327], he reported that two of his colleagues, S. Trybuła and P. Czen, had "recently" disproved his conjecture, and that they had determined $S(n)$ for $n \le 11$. Trybuła and Czen may have independently discovered the method of merge insertion, which was published soon afterwards by Ford and Johnson [*AMM* **66** (1959), 387–389].

After the discovery of merge insertion, the first unknown value of $S(n)$ was $S(12)$. Table 1 shows that 12! is quite close to 2^{29}, hence the existence of a

Table 1

VALUES OF FACTORIALS IN BINARY NOTATION

$$(1)_2 = 1!$$
$$(10)_2 = 2!$$
$$(110)_2 = 3!$$
$$(11000)_2 = 4!$$
$$(1111000)_2 = 5!$$
$$(1011010000)_2 = 6!$$
$$(1001110110000)_2 = 7!$$
$$(1001110110000000)_2 = 8!$$
$$(1011000100110000000)_2 = 9!$$
$$(11011101011111100000000)_2 = 10!$$
$$(100110000100010101000000000)_2 = 11!$$
$$(1110010001100111111000000000000)_2 = 12!$$
$$(1011100110010100011001100000000000)_2 = 13!$$
$$(101000100110000111011001010000000000000)_2 = 14!$$
$$(100110000011101110111011101011000000000000000)_2 = 15!$$
$$(1001100000111011101110111010110000000000000000000)_2 = 16!$$
$$(1010000110111111011110111011001101100000000000000000000)_2 = 17!$$
$$(101101011111011110110011001010011100110000000000000000000000)_2 = 18!$$
$$(1101100000010101110010011000001101000100100000000000000000000000)_2 = 19!$$
$$(100001110000110110011101111100100000101011010000000000000000000000000)_2 = 20!$$

29-step sorting procedure for 12 elements is somewhat unlikely. An exhaustive search (about 60 hours on a Maniac II computer) was therefore carried out by Mark Wells, who discovered that $S(12) = 30$ [*Proc. IFIP Congress 65* **2** (1965), 497–498; *Elements of Combinatorial Computing* (Pergamon, 1971), 213–215]. Thus the merge insertion procedure turns out to be optimum for $n = 12$ as well.

*A slightly deeper analysis. In order to study $S(n)$ more carefully, let us look more closely at partial ordering diagrams such as (5). After several comparisons have been made, we can represent the knowledge we have gained in terms of a directed graph. This directed graph contains no cycles, in view of the transitivity of the $<$ relation, so we can draw it in such a way that all arcs go from left to right; it is therefore convenient to leave arrows off the diagram. In this way (5) becomes

$$(21)$$

If G is such a directed graph, let $T(G)$ be the number of permutations consistent with G, that is, the number of ways to assign the integers $\{1, 2, \ldots, n\}$ to the vertices of G so that the number on vertex x is less than the number on vertex y whenever $x \to y$ in G. For example, one of the permutations consistent with (21) has $a = 1$, $b = 4$, $c = 2$, $d = 5$, $e = 3$. We have studied $T(G)$ for various G in Section 5.1.4, where we observed that $T(G)$ is the number of ways in which G can be sorted topologically.

If G is a graph on n elements that can be obtained after k comparisons, we define the *efficiency* of G to be

$$E(G) = \frac{n!}{2^k T(G)}. \qquad (22)$$

(This idea is due to Frank Hwang and Shen Lin.) Strictly speaking, the efficiency is not a function of the graph G alone, it depends on the way we arrived at G during a sorting process, but it is convenient to be a little careless in our language. After making one more comparison, between elements i and j, we obtain two graphs G_1 and G_2, one for the case $K_i < K_j$ and one for the case $K_i > K_j$. Clearly

$$T(G) = T(G_1) + T(G_2).$$

If $T(G_1) \geq T(G_2)$, we have

$$T(G) \leq 2T(G_1),$$

$$E(G_1) = \frac{n!}{2^{k+1} T(G_1)} = \frac{E(G)T(G)}{2T(G_1)} \leq E(G). \qquad (23)$$

Therefore each comparison leads to at least one graph of less or equal efficiency; we can't improve the efficiency by making further comparisons.

When G has no arcs at all, we have $k = 0$ and $T(G) = n!$, so the initial efficiency is 1. At the other extreme, when G is a graph representing the final result of sorting, G looks like a straight line and $T(G) = 1$. Thus, for example, if we want to find a sorting procedure that sorts five elements in at most seven steps, we must obtain the linear graph •—•—•—•—•, whose efficiency is $5!/(2^7 \times 1) = 120/128 = 15/16$. It follows that all of the graphs arising in the sorting procedure must have efficiency $\geq \frac{15}{16}$; if any less efficient graph were to appear, at least one of its descendants would also be less efficient, and we would ultimately reach a linear graph whose efficiency is $< \frac{15}{16}$. In general, this argument proves that all graphs corresponding to the tree nodes of a sorting procedure for n elements must have efficiency $\geq n!/2^l$, where l is the number of levels of the tree (not counting external nodes). This is another way to prove that $S(n) \geq \lceil \lg n! \rceil$, although the argument is not really much different from what we said before.

The graph (21) has efficiency 1, since $T(G) = 15$ and since G has been obtained in three comparisons. In order to see what vertices should be compared next, we can form the *comparison matrix*

$$C(G) = \begin{array}{c} \\ a \\ b \\ c \\ d \\ e \end{array} \overset{\begin{array}{ccccc} a & b & c & d & e \end{array}}{\begin{pmatrix} 0 & 15 & 10 & 15 & 11 \\ 0 & 0 & 5 & 15 & 7 \\ 5 & 10 & 0 & 15 & 9 \\ 0 & 0 & 0 & 0 & 3 \\ 4 & 8 & 6 & 12 & 0 \end{pmatrix}}, \qquad (24)$$

where C_{ij} is $T(G_1)$ for the graph G_1 obtained by adding the arc $i \to j$ to G. For example, if we compare K_c with K_e, the 15 permutations consistent with G

split up into $C_{ec} = 6$ having $K_e < K_c$ and $C_{ce} = 9$ having $K_c < K_e$. The latter graph would have efficiency $15/(2 \times 9) = \frac{5}{6} < \frac{15}{16}$, so it could not lead to a seven-step sorting procedure. The next comparison *must* be $K_b : K_e$ in order to keep the efficiency $\geq \frac{15}{16}$.

The concept of efficiency is especially useful when we consider the connected components of graphs. Consider for example the graph

$$G = \qquad \overset{a \qquad b}{\underset{c}{\diagdown}} \qquad \overset{d \qquad e}{\underset{f \quad g}{\diagup}} \quad ;$$

it has two components

$$G' = \quad \overset{a \qquad b}{\underset{c}{\diagdown}} \qquad \text{and} \qquad G'' = \quad \overset{d \qquad e}{\underset{f \quad g}{\diagup}}$$

with no arcs connecting G' to G'', so it has been formed by making some comparisons entirely within G' and others entirely within G''. In general, assume that $G = G' \oplus G''$ has no arcs between G' and G'', where G' and G'' have respectively n' and n'' vertices; it is easy to see that

$$T(G) = \binom{n' + n''}{n'} T(G')T(G''), \tag{25}$$

since each consistent permutation of G is obtained by choosing n' elements to assign to G' and then making consistent permutations within G' and G'' independently. If k' comparisons have been made within G' and k'' within G'', we have the basic result

$$E(G) = \frac{(n' + n'')!}{2^{k'+k''}T(G)} = \frac{n'!}{2^{k'}T(G')} \frac{n''!}{2^{k''}T(G'')} = E(G')E(G''), \tag{26}$$

showing that the efficiency of a graph is related in a simple way to the efficiency of its components. Therefore we may restrict consideration to graphs having only one component.

Now suppose that G' and G'' are one-component graphs, and suppose that we want to hook them together by comparing a vertex x of G' with a vertex y of G''. We want to know how efficient this will be. For this purpose we need a function that can be denoted by

$$\binom{p \quad < \quad q}{m \qquad n}, \tag{27}$$

defined to be the number of permutations consistent with the graph

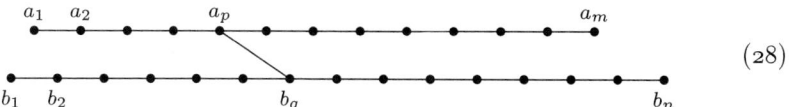

$$\tag{28}$$

Thus $\left(\begin{smallmatrix}p&<&q\\m&&n\end{smallmatrix}\right)$ is $\binom{m+n}{m}$ times the probability that the pth smallest of a set of m numbers is less than the qth smallest of an independently chosen set of n numbers. Exercise 17 shows that we can express $\left(\begin{smallmatrix}p&<&q\\m&&n\end{smallmatrix}\right)$ in two ways in terms of binomial coefficients,

$$\left(\begin{matrix}p&<&q\\m&&n\end{matrix}\right) = \sum_{0\le k<q} \binom{m-p+n-k}{m-p}\binom{p-1+k}{p-1}$$

$$= \sum_{p\le j\le m} \binom{n-q+m-j}{n-q}\binom{q-1+j}{q-1}. \tag{29}$$

(Incidentally, it is by no means obvious on algebraic grounds that these two sums of products of binomial coefficients should come out to be equal.) We also have the formulas

$$\left(\begin{matrix}p&<&q\\m&&n\end{matrix}\right) + \left(\begin{matrix}q&<&p\\n&&m\end{matrix}\right) = \binom{m+n}{m}; \tag{30}$$

$$\left(\begin{matrix}q&<&p\\n&&m\end{matrix}\right) = \left(\begin{matrix}m+1-p&<&n+1-q\\m&&n\end{matrix}\right); \tag{31}$$

$$\left(\begin{matrix}p&<&q\\m&&n\end{matrix}\right) = \left(\begin{matrix}p&<&q\\m-1&&n\end{matrix}\right) + \left(\begin{matrix}p&<&q\\m&&n-1\end{matrix}\right) + [p\le m][q=n]\binom{m+n-1}{m}. \tag{32}$$

For definiteness, let us now consider the two graphs

$$\tag{33}$$

It is not hard to show by direct enumeration that $T(G') = 42$ and $T(G'') = 5$; so if G is the 11-vertex graph having G' and G'' as components, we have $T(G) = \binom{11}{4} \cdot 42 \cdot 5 = 69300$ by Eq. (25). This is a formidable number of permutations to list, if we want to know how many of them have $x_i < y_j$ for each i and j. But the calculation can be done by hand, in less than an hour, as follows. We form the matrices $A(G')$ and $A(G'')$, where A_{ik} is the number of consistent permutations of G' (or G'') in which x_i (or y_i) is equal to k. Thus the number of permutations of G in which x_i is less than y_j is the (i,p) element of $A(G')$ times $\left(\begin{smallmatrix}p&<&q\\7&&4\end{smallmatrix}\right)$ times the (j,q) element of $A(G'')$, summed over $1 \le p \le 7$ and $1 \le q \le 4$. In other words, we want to form the matrix product $A(G') \cdot L \cdot A(G'')^T$, where $L_{pq} = \left(\begin{smallmatrix}p&<&q\\7&&4\end{smallmatrix}\right)$. This comes to

$$\begin{pmatrix} 21 & 16 & 5 & 0 & 0 & 0 & 0 \\ 0 & 5 & 10 & 12 & 10 & 5 & 0 \\ 21 & 16 & 5 & 0 & 0 & 0 & 0 \\ 0 & 0 & 12 & 18 & 12 & 0 & 0 \\ 0 & 0 & 0 & 0 & 5 & 16 & 21 \\ 0 & 5 & 10 & 12 & 10 & 5 & 0 \\ 0 & 0 & 0 & 0 & 5 & 16 & 21 \end{pmatrix} \begin{pmatrix} 210 & 294 & 322 & 329 \\ 126 & 238 & 301 & 325 \\ 70 & 175 & 265 & 315 \\ 35 & 115 & 215 & 295 \\ 15 & 65 & 155 & 260 \\ 5 & 29 & 92 & 204 \\ 1 & 8 & 36 & 120 \end{pmatrix} \begin{pmatrix} 2 & 3 & 0 & 0 \\ 2 & 2 & 0 & 1 \\ 1 & 0 & 2 & 2 \\ 0 & 0 & 3 & 2 \end{pmatrix} = \begin{pmatrix} 48169 & 42042 & 66858 & 64031 \\ 22825 & 16005 & 53295 & 46475 \\ 48169 & 42042 & 66858 & 64031 \\ 22110 & 14850 & 54450 & 47190 \\ 5269 & 2442 & 27258 & 21131 \\ 22825 & 16005 & 53295 & 46475 \\ 5269 & 2442 & 27258 & 21131 \end{pmatrix}.$$

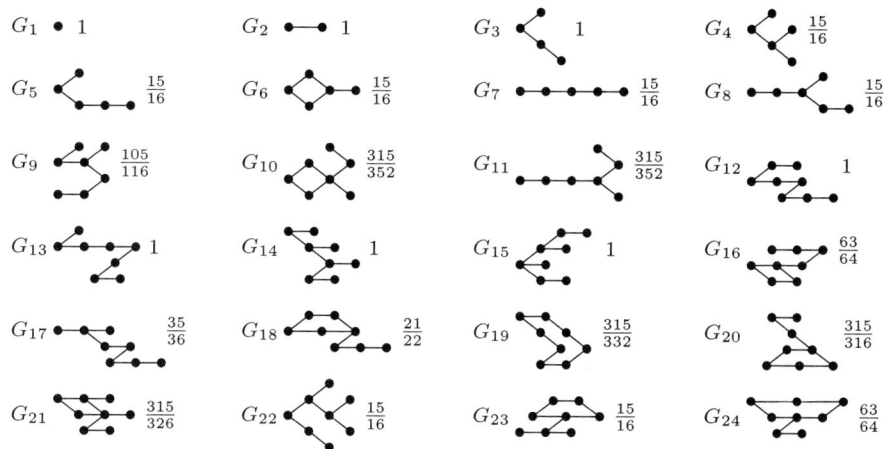

Fig. 36. Some graphs and their efficiencies, obtained at the beginning of a long proof that $S(12) > 29$.

Thus the "best" way to hook up G' and G'' is to compare x_1 with y_2; this gives 42042 cases with $x_1 < y_2$ and $69300 - 42042 = 27258$ cases with $x_1 > y_2$. (By symmetry, we could also compare x_3 with y_2, x_5 with y_3, or x_7 with y_3, leading to essentially the same results.) The efficiency of the resulting graph for $x_1 < y_2$ is

$$\frac{69300}{84084} E(G') E(G''),$$

which is none too good; hence it is probably a bad idea to hook G' up with G'' in any sorting method. The point of this example is that we are able to make such a decision without excessive calculation.

These ideas can be used to provide independent confirmation of Mark Wells's proof that $S(12) = 30$. Starting with a graph containing one vertex, we can repeatedly try to add a comparison to one of our graphs G or to $G' \oplus G''$ (a pair of graph components G' and G'') in such a way that the two resulting graphs have 12 or fewer vertices and efficiency $\geq 12!/2^{29} \approx 0.89221$. Whenever this is possible, we take the resulting graph of least efficiency and add it to our set, unless one of the two graphs is isomorphic to a graph we already have included. If both of the resulting graphs have the same efficiency, we arbitrarily choose one of them. A graph can be identified with its dual (obtained by reversing the order), so long as we consider adding comparisons to $G' \oplus \text{dual}(G'')$ as well as to $G' \oplus G''$. A few of the smallest graphs obtained in this way are displayed in Fig. 36 together with their efficiencies.

Exactly 1649 graphs were generated, by computer, before this process terminated. Since the graph •–•–•–•–•–•–•–•–•–•–•–• was not obtained, we may conclude that $S(12) > 29$. It is plausible that a similar experiment could be performed to deduce that $S(22) > 70$ in a fairly reasonable amount of time, since $22!/2^{70} \approx 0.952$ requires extremely high efficiency to sort in 70 steps. (Only 91 of the 1649 graphs found on 12 or fewer vertices had such high efficiency.)

Marcin Peczarski [see *Algorithmica* **40** (2004), 133–145; *Information Proc. Letters* **101** (2007), 126–128] extended Wells's method and proved that $S(13) = 34$, $S(14) = 38$, $S(15) = 42$, $S(22) = 71$; thus merge insertion is optimum in those cases as well. Intuitively, it seems likely that $S(16)$ will some day be shown to be less than $F(16)$, since $F(16)$ involves no fewer steps than sorting ten elements with $S(10)$ comparisons and then inserting six others by binary insertion, one at a time. There must be a way to improve upon this! But at present, the smallest case where $F(n)$ is definitely known to be nonoptimum is $n = 47$: After sorting 5 and 42 elements with $F(5) + F(42) = 178$ comparisons, we can merge the results with 22 further comparisons, using a method due to J. Schulte Mönting, *Theoretical Comp. Sci.* **14** (1981), 19–37; this strategy beats $F(47) = 201$. (Glenn K. Manacher [*JACM* **26** (1979), 441–456] had previously proved that infinitely many n exist with $S(n) < F(n)$, starting with $n = 189$.)

The average number of comparisons. So far we have been considering procedures that are best possible in the sense that their worst case isn't bad; in other words, we have looked for "minimax" procedures that minimize the *maximum* number of comparisons. Now let us look for a "minimean" procedure that minimizes the *average* number of comparisons, assuming that the input is random so that each permutation is equally likely.

Consider once again the tree representation of a sorting procedure, as shown in Fig. 34. The average number of comparisons in that tree is

$$\frac{2+3+3+3+3+2}{6} = 2\tfrac{2}{3},$$

averaging over all permutations. In general, the average number of comparisons in a sorting method is the *external path length* of the tree divided by $n!$. (Recall that the external path length is the sum of the distances from the root to each of the external nodes; see Section 2.3.4.5.) It is easy to see from the considerations of Section 2.3.4.5 that the minimum external path length occurs in a binary tree with N external nodes if there are $2^q - N$ external nodes at level $q - 1$ and $2N - 2^q$ at level q, where $q = \lceil \lg N \rceil$. (The root is at level zero.) The minimum external path length is therefore

$$(q-1)(2^q - N) + q(2N - 2^q) = (q+1)N - 2^q. \tag{34}$$

The minimum path length can also be characterized in another interesting way: *An extended binary tree has minimum external path length for a given number of external nodes if and only if there is a number l such that all external nodes appear on levels l and $l + 1$.* (See exercise 20.)

If we set $q = \lg N + \theta$, where $0 \le \theta < 1$, the formula for minimum external path length becomes

$$N(\lg N + 1 + \theta - 2^\theta). \tag{35}$$

The function $1 + \theta - 2^\theta$ is shown in Fig. 37; for $0 < \theta < 1$ it is positive but very small, never exceeding

$$1 - (1 + \ln\ln 2)/\ln 2 = 0.08607\ 13320\ 55934+. \tag{36}$$

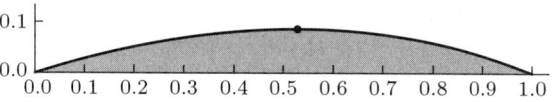

Fig. 37. The function $1 + \theta - 2^\theta$.

Thus the minimum possible average number of comparisons, obtained by dividing (35) by N, is never less than $\lg N$ and never more than $\lg N + 0.0861$. [This result was first obtained by A. Gleason in an internal IBM memorandum (1956).]

Now if we set $N = n!$, we get a lower bound for the average number of comparisons in any sorting scheme. Asymptotically speaking, this lower bound is

$$\lg n! + O(1) = n \lg n - n/\ln 2 + O(\log n). \tag{37}$$

Let $\bar{F}(n)$ be the average number of comparisons performed by the merge insertion algorithm; we have

$n =$	1	2	3	4	5	6	7	8
lower bound (34) $=$	0	2	16	112	832	6896	62368	619904
$n!\,\bar{F}(n) =$	0	2	16	112	832	6912	62784	623232

Thus merge insertion is optimum in both senses for $n \le 5$, but for $n = 6$ it averages $6912/720 = 9.6$ comparisons while our lower bound says that an average of $6896/720 = 9.577777\ldots$ comparisons might be possible. A moment's reflection shows why this is true: Some "fortunate" permutations of six elements are sorted by merge insertion after only eight comparisons, so the comparison tree has external nodes appearing on three levels instead of two. This forces the overall path length to be higher. Exercise 24 shows that it is possible to construct a six-element sorting procedure that requires nine or ten comparisons in each case; it follows that this method is superior to merge insertion, on the average, and no worse than merge insertion in its worst case.

When $n = 7$, Y. Césari [Thesis (Univ. of Paris, 1968), page 37] has shown that no sorting method can attain the lower bound 62368 on external path length. (It is possible to prove this fact without a computer, using the results of exercise 22.) On the other hand, he has constructed procedures that do achieve the lower bound (34) when $n = 9$ or 10. In general, the problem of minimizing the average number of comparisons turns out to be substantially more difficult than the problem of determining $S(n)$. It may even be true that, for some n, all methods that minimize the *average* number of comparisons require *more* than $S(n)$ comparisons in their worst case.

EXERCISES

1. [*20*] Draw the comparison trees for sorting four elements using the method of (a) binary insertion; (b) straight two-way merging. What are the external path lengths of these trees?

2. [*M24*] Prove that $B(n) \le L(n)$, and find all n for which equality holds.

3. [*M22*] (*Weak orderings.*) When equality between keys is allowed, there are 13 possible outcomes when sorting three elements:

$$
\begin{array}{ccc}
K_1 = K_2 = K_3, & K_1 = K_2 < K_3, & K_1 = K_3 < K_2, \\
K_2 = K_3 < K_1, & K_1 < K_2 = K_3, & K_2 < K_1 = K_3, \\
K_3 < K_1 = K_2, & K_1 < K_2 < K_3, & K_1 < K_3 < K_2, \\
\end{array}
$$
$$
K_2 < K_1 < K_3, \quad K_2 < K_3 < K_1, \quad K_3 < K_1 < K_2, \quad K_3 < K_2 < K_1.
$$

Let P_n denote the number of possible outcomes when n elements are sorted with ties allowed, so that $(P_0, P_1, P_2, P_3, P_4, P_5, \ldots) = (1, 1, 3, 13, 75, 541, \ldots)$. Prove that the generating function $P(z) = \sum_{n \geq 0} P_n z^n / n!$ is equal to $1/(2 - e^z)$. *Hint:* Show that

$$
P_n = \sum_{k > 0} \binom{n}{k} P_{n-k} \qquad \text{when } n > 0.
$$

4. [*HM27*] (O. A. Gross.) Determine the asymptotic value of the numbers P_n of exercise 3, as $n \to \infty$. [*Possible hint:* Consider the partial fraction expansion of $\cot z$.]

5. [*16*] When keys can be equal, each comparison may have three results instead of two: $K_i < K_j$, $K_i = K_j$, $K_i > K_j$. Sorting algorithms for this general situation can be represented as extended *ternary* trees, in which each internal node $i{:}j$ has three subtrees; the left, middle, and right subtrees correspond respectively to the three possible outcomes of the comparison.

Draw an extended ternary tree that defines a sorting algorithm for $n = 3$, when equal keys are allowed. There should be 13 external nodes, corresponding to the 13 possible outcomes listed in exercise 3.

▶ **6.** [*M22*] Let $S'(n)$ be the minimum number of comparisons necessary to sort n elements and to determine all equalities between keys, when each comparison has three outcomes as in exercise 5. The information-theoretic argument of the text can readily be generalized to show that $S'(n) \geq \lceil \log_3 P_n \rceil$, where P_n is the function studied in exercises 3 and 4; but prove that, in fact, $S'(n) = S(n)$.

7. [*20*] Draw an extended ternary tree in the sense of exercise 5 for sorting four elements, when it is known that all keys are either 0 or 1. (Thus if $K_1 < K_2$ and $K_3 < K_4$, we know that $K_1 = K_3$ and $K_2 = K_4$!) Use the minimum average number of comparisons, assuming that the 2^4 possible inputs are equally likely. Be sure to determine all equalities that are present; for example, don't stop sorting when you know only that $K_1 \leq K_2 \leq K_3 \leq K_4$.

8. [*26*] Draw an extended ternary tree as in exercise 7 for sorting four elements, when it is known that all keys are either -1, 0, or $+1$. Use the minimum average number of comparisons, assuming that the 3^4 possible inputs are equally likely.

9. [*M20*] When sorting n elements as in exercise 7, knowing that all keys are 0 or 1, what is the minimum number of comparisons in the worst case?

▶ **10.** [*M25*] When sorting n elements as in exercise 7, knowing that all keys are 0 or 1, what is the minimum *average* number of comparisons as a function of n?

11. [*HM27*] When sorting n elements as in exercise 5, and knowing that all keys are members of the set $\{1, 2, \ldots, m\}$, let $S_m(n)$ be the minimum number of comparisons needed in the worst case. [Thus by exercise 6, $S_n(n) = S(n)$.] Prove that, for fixed m, $S_m(n)$ is asymptotically $n \lg m + O(1)$ as $n \to \infty$.

▶ **12.** [*M25*] (W. G. Bouricius, circa 1954.) Suppose that equal keys may occur, but we merely want to sort the elements $\{K_1, K_2, \ldots, K_n\}$ so that a permutation $a_1 a_2 \ldots a_n$ is determined with $K_{a_1} \leq K_{a_2} \leq \cdots \leq K_{a_n}$; we do not need to know whether or not equality occurs between K_{a_i} and $K_{a_{i+1}}$.

Let us say that a comparison tree sorts a sequence of keys *strongly* if it will sort the sequence in the stated sense no matter which branch is taken below the nodes $i\!:\!j$ for which $K_i = K_j$. (The tree is binary, not ternary.)

a) Prove that a comparison tree with no redundant comparisons sorts every sequence of keys strongly if and only if it sorts every sequence of distinct keys.

b) Prove that a comparison tree sorts every sequence of keys strongly if and only if it sorts every sequence of zeros and ones strongly.

13. [*M28*] Prove (17).

14. [*M24*] Find a closed form for the sum (19).

15. [*M21*] Determine the asymptotic behavior of $B(n)$ and $F(n)$ up to $O(\log n)$. [*Hint:* Show that in both cases the coefficient of n involves the function shown in Fig. 37.]

16. [*HM26*] (F. Hwang and S. Lin.) Prove that $F(n) > \lceil \lg n! \rceil$ for $n \geq 22$.

17. [*M20*] Prove (29).

18. [*20*] If the procedure whose first steps are shown in Fig. 36 had produced the linear graph •——•—•—•—•—•—•—•—•——• with efficiency $12!/2^{29}$, would this have proved that $S(12) = 29$?

19. [*40*] Experiment with the following heuristic rule for deciding which pair of elements to compare next while designing a comparison tree: At each stage of sorting $\{K_1, \ldots, K_n\}$, let u_i be the number of keys known to be $\leq K_i$ as a result of the comparisons made so far, and let v_i be the number of keys known to be $\geq K_i$, for $1 \leq i \leq n$. Renumber the keys in terms of increasing u_i/v_i, so that $u_1/v_1 \leq u_2/v_2 \leq \cdots \leq u_n/v_n$. Now compare $K_i\!:\!K_{i+1}$ for some i that minimizes $|u_i v_{i+1} - u_{i+1} v_i|$. (Although this method is based on far less information than a full comparison matrix as in (24), it appears to give optimum results in many cases.)

▶ **20.** [*M26*] Prove that an extended binary tree has minimum external path length if and only if there is a number l such that all external nodes appear on levels l and $l+1$ (or perhaps all on a single level l).

21. [*M21*] The *height* of an extended binary tree is the maximum level number of its external nodes. If x is an internal node of an extended binary tree, let $t(x)$ be the number of external nodes below x, and let $l(x)$ denote the root of x's left subtree. If x is an external node, let $t(x) = 1$. Prove that an extended binary tree has minimum height among all binary trees with the same number of nodes if

$$\big|t(x) - 2t(l(x))\big| \leq 2^{\lceil \lg t(x) \rceil} - t(x)$$

for all internal nodes x.

22. [*M24*] Continuing exercise 21, prove that a binary tree has minimum external path length among all binary trees with the same number of nodes if and only if

$$\big|t(x) - 2t(l(x))\big| \leq 2^{\lceil \lg t(x) \rceil} - t(x) \qquad \text{and} \qquad \big|t(x) - 2t(l(x))\big| \leq t(x) - 2^{\lfloor \lg t(x) \rfloor}$$

for all internal nodes x. [Thus, for example, if $t(x) = 67$, we must have $t(l(x)) = 32$, 33, 34, or 35. If we merely wanted to minimize the height of the tree we could have $3 \leq t(l(x)) \leq 64$, by the preceding exercise.]

23. [*10*] The text proves that the average number of comparisons made by any sorting method for n elements must be at least $\lceil \lg n! \rceil \approx n \lg n$. But multiple list insertion (Program 5.2.1M) takes only $O(n)$ units of time on the average. How can this be?

24. [*27*] (C. Picard.) Find a sorting tree for six elements such that all external nodes appear on levels 10 and 11.

25. [*11*] If there were a sorting procedure for seven elements that achieves the minimum average number of comparisons predicted by the use of Eq. (34), how many external nodes would there be on level 13?

26. [*M42*] Find a sorting procedure for seven elements that minimizes the average number of comparisons performed.

▶ **27.** [*20*] Suppose it is known that the configurations $K_1 < K_2 < K_3$, $K_1 < K_3 < K_2$, $K_2 < K_1 < K_3$, $K_2 < K_3 < K_1$, $K_3 < K_1 < K_2$, $K_3 < K_2 < K_1$ occur with respective probabilities .01, .25, .01, .24, .25, .24. Find a comparison tree that sorts these three elements with the smallest average number of comparisons.

28. [*40*] Write a MIX program that sorts five one-word keys in the minimum possible amount of time, and halts. (See the beginning of Section 5.2 for ground rules.)

29. [*M25*] (S. M. Chase.) Let $a_1 a_2 \ldots a_n$ be a permutation of $\{1, 2, \ldots, n\}$. Prove that any algorithm that decides whether this permutation is even or odd (that is, whether it has an even or odd number of inversions), based solely on comparisons between the a's, must make at least $n \lg n$ comparisons, even though the algorithm has only two possible outcomes.

30. [*M23*] (*Optimum exchange sorting.*) Every exchange sorting algorithm as defined in Section 5.2.2 can be represented as a *comparison-exchange tree*, namely a binary tree structure whose internal nodes have the form $i : j$ for $i < j$, interpreted as the following operation: "If $K_i \leq K_j$, continue by taking the left branch of the tree; if $K_i > K_j$, continue by interchanging records i and j and then taking the right branch of the tree." When an external node is encountered, it must be true that $K_1 \leq K_2 \leq \cdots \leq K_n$. Thus, a comparison-exchange tree differs from a comparison tree in that it specifies data movement as well as comparison operations.

Let $S_e(n)$ denote the minimum number of comparison-exchanges needed, in the worst case, to sort n elements by means of a comparison-exchange tree. Prove that $S_e(n) \leq S(n) + n - 1$.

31. [*M38*] Continuing exercise 30, prove that $S_e(5) = 8$.

32. [*M42*] Continuing exercise 31, investigate $S_e(n)$ for small values of $n > 5$.

33. [*M30*] (T. N. Hibbard.) A *real-valued search tree* of order x and resolution δ is an extended binary tree in which all nodes contain a nonnegative real value such that (i) the value in each external node is $\leq \delta$, (ii) the value in each internal node is at most the sum of the values in its two children, and (iii) the value in the root is x. The *weighted path length* of such a tree is defined to be the sum, over all external nodes, of the level of that node times the value it contains.

Prove that a real-valued search tree of order x and resolution 1 has minimum weighted path length, taken over all such trees of the same order and resolution, if and only if equality holds in (ii) and the following further conditions hold for all pairs of values x_0 and x_1 that are contained in sibling nodes: (iv) There is no integer $k \geq 0$ such that $x_0 < 2^k < x_1$ or $x_1 < 2^k < x_0$. (v) $\lceil x_0 \rceil - x_0 + \lceil x_1 \rceil - x_1 < 1$. (In particular if x is an integer, condition (v) implies that all values in the tree are integers, and condition (iv) is equivalent to the result of exercise 22.)

Also prove that the corresponding minimum weighted path length is $x\lceil \lg x\rceil + \lceil x\rceil - 2^{\lceil \lg x\rceil}$.

34. [*M50*] Determine the exact value of $S(n)$ for infinitely many n.

35. [*49*] Determine the exact value of $S(16)$.

36. [*M50*] (S. S. Kislitsyn, 1968.) Prove or disprove: Any directed acyclic graph G with $T(G) > 1$ has two vertices u and v such that the digraphs G_1 and G_2 obtained from G by adding the arcs $u \leftarrow v$ and $u \rightarrow v$ are acyclic and satisfy $1 \le T(G_1)/T(G_2) \le 2$. (Thus $T(G_1)/T(G)$ always lies between $\frac{1}{3}$ and $\frac{2}{3}$, for some u and v.)

*5.3.2. Minimum-Comparison Merging

Let us now consider a related question: What is the best way to merge an ordered set of m elements with an ordered set of n? Denoting the elements to be merged by

$$A_1 < A_2 < \cdots < A_m \quad \text{and} \quad B_1 < B_2 < \cdots < B_n, \tag{1}$$

we shall assume as in Section 5.3.1 that the $m + n$ elements are distinct. The A's may appear among the B's in $\binom{m+n}{m}$ ways, so the arguments we have used for the sorting problem tell us immediately that at least

$$\left\lceil \lg\binom{m+n}{m}\right\rceil \tag{2}$$

comparisons are required. If we set $m = \alpha n$ and let $n \to \infty$, while α is fixed, Stirling's approximation tells us that

$$\lg\binom{\alpha n + n}{\alpha n} = n\big((1+\alpha)\lg(1+\alpha) - \alpha\lg\alpha\big) - \tfrac{1}{2}\lg n + O(1). \tag{3}$$

The normal merging procedure, Algorithm 5.2.4M, takes $m+n-1$ comparisons in its worst case.

Let $M(m, n)$ denote the function analogous to $S(n)$, namely the minimum number of comparisons that will always suffice to merge m things with n. By the observations we have just made,

$$\left\lceil \lg\binom{m+n}{m}\right\rceil \le M(m,n) \le m+n-1 \quad \text{for all } m, n \ge 1. \tag{4}$$

Formula (3) shows how far apart this lower bound and upper bound can be. When $\alpha = 1$ (that is, $m = n$), the lower bound is $2n - \frac{1}{2}\lg n + O(1)$, so both bounds have the right order of magnitude but the difference between them can be arbitrarily large. When $\alpha = 0.5$ (that is, $m = \frac{1}{2}n$), the lower bound is

$$\tfrac{3}{2}n(\lg 3 - \tfrac{2}{3}) + O(\log n),$$

which is about $\lg 3 - \frac{2}{3} \approx 0.918$ times the upper bound. And as α decreases, the bounds get farther and farther apart, since the standard merging algorithm is primarily designed for files with $m \approx n$.

When $m = n$, the merging problem has a fairly simple solution; it turns out that the *lower* bound of (4), not the upper bound, is at fault. The following theorem was discovered independently by R. L. Graham and R. M. Karp about 1968:

Theorem M. For all $m \geq 1$, we have $M(m, m) = 2m - 1$.

Proof. Consider any algorithm that merges $A_1 < \cdots < A_m$ with $B_1 < \cdots < B_m$. When it compares $A_i : B_j$, take the branch $A_i < B_j$ if $i < j$, the branch $A_i > B_j$ if $i \geq j$. Merging must eventually terminate with the configuration

$$B_1 < A_1 < B_2 < A_2 < \cdots < B_m < A_m, \tag{5}$$

since this is consistent with all the branches taken. And each of the $2m - 1$ comparisons

$$B_1 : A_1, \quad A_1 : B_2, \quad B_2 : A_2, \quad \ldots, \quad B_m : A_m$$

must have been made explicitly, or else there would be at least two configurations consistent with the known facts. For example, if A_1 has not been compared to B_2, the configuration

$$B_1 < B_2 < A_1 < A_2 < \cdots < B_m < A_m$$

is indistinguishable from (5). ∎

A simple modification of this proof yields the companion formula

$$M(m, m+1) = 2m, \qquad \text{for } m \geq 0. \tag{6}$$

Constructing lower bounds. Theorem M shows that the "information theoretic" lower bound (2) can be arbitrarily far from the true value; thus the technique used to prove Theorem M gives us another way to discover lower bounds. Such a proof technique is often viewed as the creation of an *adversary*, a pernicious being who tries to make algorithms run slowly. When an algorithm for merging decides to compare $A_i : B_j$, the adversary determines the fate of the comparison so as to force the algorithm down the more difficult path. If we can invent a suitable adversary, as in the proof of Theorem M, we can ensure that every valid merging algorithm will have to make quite a few comparisons.

We shall make use of *constrained adversaries*, whose power is limited with regard to the outcomes of certain comparisons. A merging method that is under the influence of a constrained adversary does not know about the constraints, so it must make the necessary comparisons even though their outcomes have been predetermined. For example, in our proof of Theorem M we constrained all outcomes by condition (5), yet the merging algorithm was unable to make use of that fact in order to avoid any of the comparisons.

The constraints we shall use in the following discussion apply to the left and right ends of the files. Left constraints are symbolized by

. (meaning no left constraint),

\ (meaning that all outcomes must be consistent with $A_1 < B_1$),

/ (meaning that all outcomes must be consistent with $A_1 > B_1$);

similarly, right constraints are symbolized by

. (meaning no right constraint),

\\ (meaning that all outcomes must be consistent with $A_m < B_n$),

/ (meaning that all outcomes must be consistent with $A_m > B_n$).

There are nine kinds of adversaries, denoted by $\lambda M \rho$, where λ is a left constraint and ρ is a right constraint. For example, a $\backslash M \backslash$ adversary must say that $A_1 < B_j$ and $A_i < B_n$; a $.M.$ adversary is unconstrained. For small values of m and n, constrained adversaries of certain kinds are impossible; when $m = 1$ we obviously can't have a $\backslash M/$ adversary.

Let us now construct a rather complicated, but very formidable, adversary for merging. It does not always produce optimum results, but it gives lower bounds that cover a lot of interesting cases. Given m, n, and the left and right constraints λ and ρ, suppose the adversary is asked which is the greater of A_i or B_j. Six strategies can be used to reduce the problem to cases of smaller $m+n$:

Strategy A(k,l), *for* $i \le k \le m$ *and* $1 \le l \le j$. Say that $A_i < B_j$, and require that subsequent operations merge $\{A_1, \ldots, A_k\}$ with $\{B_1, \ldots, B_{l-1}\}$ and $\{A_{k+1}, \ldots, A_m\}$ with $\{B_l, \ldots, B_n\}$. Thus future comparisons $A_p : B_q$ will result in $A_p < B_q$ if $p \le k$ and $q \ge l$; $A_p > B_q$ if $p > k$ and $q < l$; they will be handled by a $(k, l-1, \lambda, .)$ adversary if $p \le k$ and $q < l$; they will be handled by an $(m-k, n+1-l, ., \rho)$ adversary if $p > k$ and $q \ge l$.

Strategy B(k,l), *for* $i \le k \le m$ *and* $1 \le l < j$. Say that $A_i < B_j$, and require that subsequent operations merge $\{A_1, \ldots, A_k\}$ with $\{B_1, \ldots, B_l\}$ and $\{A_{k+1}, \ldots, A_m\}$ with $\{B_l, \ldots, B_n\}$, stipulating that $A_k < B_l < A_{k+1}$. (Note that B_l appears in both lists to be merged. The condition $A_k < B_l < A_{k+1}$ ensures that merging one group gives no information that could help to merge the other.) Thus future comparisons $A_p : B_q$ will result in $A_p < B_q$ if $p \le k$ and $q \ge l$; $A_p > B_q$ if $p > k$ and $q \le l$; they will be handled by a $(k, l, \lambda, \backslash)$ adversary if $p \le k$ and $q \le l$; by an $(m-k, n+1-l, /, \rho)$ adversary if $p > k$ and $q \ge l$.

Strategy C(k,l), *for* $i < k \le m$ *and* $1 \le l \le j$. Say that $A_i < B_j$, and require that subsequent operations merge $\{A_1, \ldots, A_k\}$ with $\{B_1, \ldots, B_{l-1}\}$ and $\{A_k, \ldots, A_m\}$ with $\{B_l, \ldots, B_n\}$, stipulating that $B_{l-1} < A_k < B_l$. (Analogous to Strategy B, interchanging the roles of A and B.)

Strategy A$'(k,l)$, *for* $1 \le k \le i$ *and* $j \le l \le n$. Say that $A_i > B_j$, and require the merging of $\{A_1, \ldots, A_{k-1}\}$ with $\{B_1, \ldots, B_l\}$ and $\{A_k, \ldots, A_m\}$ with $\{B_{l+1}, \ldots, B_n\}$. (Analogous to Strategy A.)

Strategy B$'(k,l)$, *for* $1 \le k \le i$ *and* $j < l \le n$. Say that $A_i > B_j$, and require the merging of $\{A_1, \ldots, A_{k-1}\}$ with $\{B_1, \ldots, B_l\}$ and $\{A_k, \ldots, A_m\}$ with $\{B_l, \ldots, B_n\}$, subject to $A_{k-1} < B_l < A_k$. (Analogous to Strategy B.)

Strategy C$'(k,l)$, *for* $1 \le k < i$ *and* $j \le l \le n$. Say that $A_i > B_j$, and require the merging of $\{A_1, \ldots, A_k\}$ with $\{B_1, \ldots, B_l\}$ and $\{A_k, \ldots, A_m\}$ with $\{B_{l+1}, \ldots, B_n\}$, subject to $B_l < A_k < B_{l+1}$. (Analogous to Strategy C.)

Because of the constraints, the strategies above cannot be used in certain cases summarized here:

Strategy	Must be omitted when
$A(k,1)$, $B(k,1)$, $C(k,1)$	$\lambda = /$
$A'(1,l)$, $B'(1,l)$, $C'(1,l)$	$\lambda = \backslash$
$A(m,l)$, $B(m,l)$, $C(m,l)$	$\rho = /$
$A'(k,n)$, $B'(k,n)$, $C'(k,n)$	$\rho = \backslash$

Let $\lambda M\rho(m,n)$ denote the maximum lower bound for merging that is obtainable by an adversary of the class described above. Each strategy, when applicable, gives us an inequality relating these nine functions, when the first comparison is $A_i : B_j$, namely,

$A(k,l)$: $\lambda M\rho(m,n) \geq 1 + \lambda M.(k,l-1) + .M\rho(m-k,n+1-l)$;

$B(k,l)$: $\lambda M\rho(m,n) \geq 1 + \lambda M\backslash(k,l) + /M\rho(m-k,n+1-l)$;

$C(k,l)$: $\lambda M\rho(m,n) \geq 1 + \lambda M/(k,l-1) + \backslash M\rho(m+1-k,n+1-l)$;

$A'(k,l)$: $\lambda M\rho(m,n) \geq 1 + \lambda M.(k-1,l) + .M\rho(m+1-k,n-l)$;

$B'(k,l)$: $\lambda M\rho(m,n) \geq 1 + \lambda M\backslash(k-1,l) + /M\rho(m+1-k,n+1-l)$;

$C'(k,l)$: $\lambda M\rho(m,n) \geq 1 + \lambda M/(k,l) + \backslash M\rho(m+1-k,n-l)$.

For fixed i and j, the adversary will adopt a strategy that maximizes the lower bound given by all possible right-hand sides, when k and l lie in the ranges permitted by i and j. Then we define $\lambda M\rho(m,n)$ to be the minimum of these lower bounds taken over $1 \leq i \leq m$ and $1 \leq j \leq n$. When m or n is zero, $\lambda M\rho(m,n)$ is zero.

For example, consider the case $m = 2$ and $n = 3$, and suppose that our adversary is unconstrained. If the first comparison is $A_1 : B_1$, the adversary may adopt strategy $A'(1,1)$, requiring $.M.(0,1) + .M.(2,2) = 3$ further comparisons. If the first comparison is $A_1 : B_3$, the adversary may adopt strategy $B(1,2)$, requiring $.M\backslash(1,2) + /M.(1,2) = 4$ further comparisons. No matter what comparison $A_i : B_j$ is made first, the adversary can guarantee that at least three further comparisons must be made. Hence $.M.(2,3) = 4$.

It isn't easy to do these calculations by hand, but a computer can grind out tables of $\lambda M\rho$ functions rather quickly. There are obvious symmetries, such as

$$/M.(m,n) = .M\backslash(m,n) = \backslash M.(n,m) = .M/(n,m), \tag{7}$$

by means of which we can reduce the nine functions to just four,

$$.M.(m,n), \qquad /M.(m,n), \qquad /M\backslash(m,n), \qquad \text{and} \qquad /M/(m,n).$$

Table 1 shows the resulting values for all $m,n \leq 10$; our merging adversary has been defined in such a way that

$$.M.(m,n) \leq M(m,n) \qquad \text{for all} \qquad m,n \geq 0. \tag{8}$$

Table 1

LOWER BOUNDS FOR MERGING, FROM THE "ADVERSARY"

$.M.(m,n)$	1	2	3	4	5	6	7	8	9	10	n	$/M.(m,n)$	1	2	3	4	5	6	7	8	9	10	
1	1	2	2	3	3	3	3	4	4	4			1	2	2	3	3	3	3	4	4	4	1
2	2	3	4	5	5	6	6	6	7	7			1	3	4	4	5	5	6	6	7	7	2
3	2	4	5	6	7	7	8	8	9	9			1	3	5	6	7	7	8	8	9	9	3
4	3	5	6	7	8	9	10	10	11	11			1	4	5	7	8	9	9	10	10	11	4
5	3	5	7	8	9	10	11	12	12	13			1	4	6	8	9	10	11	12	12	13	5
6	3	6	7	9	10	11	12	13	14	15			1	4	6	8	10	11	12	13	14	14	6
7	3	6	8	10	11	12	13	14	15	16			1	4	7	9	10	12	13	14	15	16	7
8	4	6	8	10	12	13	14	15	16	17			1	5	7	9	11	13	14	15	16	17	8
9	4	7	9	11	12	14	15	16	17	18			1	5	8	10	11	13	15	16	17	18	9
10	4	7	9	11	13	15	16	17	18	19			1	5	8	10	12	14	15	17	18	19	10

m																							m
$/M\backslash(m,n)$												$/M/(m,n)$											
1	$-\infty$	2	2	3	3	3	3	4	4	4			1	1	1	1	1	1	1	1	1	1	1
2	$-\infty$	2	4	4	5	5	6	6	7	7			1	3	3	4	4	4	4	5	5	5	2
3	$-\infty$	2	4	6	6	7	8	8	8	9			1	3	5	5	6	6	7	7	8	8	3
4	$-\infty$	2	5	6	8	8	9	10	10	11			1	4	5	7	7	8	9	9	9	10	4
5	$-\infty$	2	5	7	8	10	10	11	12	13			1	4	6	7	9	9	10	11	11	12	5
6	$-\infty$	2	5	7	9	10	12	13	14	14			1	4	6	8	9	11	11	12	13	14	6
7	$-\infty$	2	5	8	10	11	12	14	15	16			1	4	7	9	10	11	13	14	15	15	7
8	$-\infty$	2	6	8	10	12	13	15	16	17			1	5	7	9	11	12	14	15	16	17	8
9	$-\infty$	2	6	9	10	12	14	16	17	18			1	5	8	9	11	13	15	16	17	18	9
10	$-\infty$	2	6	9	11	13	15	16	18	19			1	5	8	10	12	14	15	17	18	19	10
	1	2	3	4	5	6	7	8	9	10	n		1	2	3	4	5	6	7	8	9	10	

This relation includes Theorem M as a special case, because our adversary will use the simple strategy of that theorem when $|m - n| \leq 1$.

Let us now consider some simple relations satisfied by the M function:

$$M(m,n) = M(n,m); \tag{9}$$

$$M(m,n) \leq M(m,n{+}1); \tag{10}$$

$$M(k{+}m,n) \leq M(k,n) + M(m,n); \tag{11}$$

$$M(m,n) \leq \max\big(M(m,n{-}1) + 1, \ M(m{-}1,n) + 1\big), \quad \text{for } m \geq 1, \ n \geq 1; \tag{12}$$

$$M(m,n) \leq \max\big(M(m,n{-}2) + 1, \ M(m{-}1,n) + 2\big), \quad \text{for } m \geq 1, \ n \geq 2. \tag{13}$$

Relation (12) comes from the usual merging procedure, if we first compare $A_1 : B_1$. Relation (13) is derived similarly, by first comparing $A_1 : B_2$; if $A_1 > B_2$, we need $M(m,n{-}2)$ more comparisons, but if $A_1 < B_2$, we can insert A_1 into its proper place and merge $\{A_2, \ldots, A_m\}$ with $\{B_1, \ldots, B_n\}$. Generalizing, we can see that if $m \geq 1$ and $n \geq k$ we have

$$M(m,n) \leq \max\big(M(m,n{-}k) + 1, \ M(m{-}1,n) + 1 + \lceil \lg k \rceil\big), \tag{14}$$

by first comparing $A_1 : B_k$ and using binary search if $A_1 < B_k$.

It turns out that $M(m,n) = .M.(m,n)$ for all $m, n \leq 10$, so Table 1 actually gives the optimum values for merging. This can be proved by using (9)–(14) together with special constructions for $(m,n) = (2,8)$, $(3,6)$, and $(5,9)$ given in exercises 8, 9, and 10.

On the other hand, our adversary doesn't always give the best possible lower bounds; the simplest example is $m = 3$, $n = 11$, when $.M.(3, 11) = 9$ but $M(3, 11) = 10$. To see where the adversary has "failed" in this case, we must study the reasons for its decisions. Further scrutiny reveals that if $(i, j) \neq (2, 6)$, the adversary can find a strategy that demands 10 comparisons; but when $(i, j) = (2, 6)$, no strategy beats Strategy $A(2, 4)$, leading to the lower bound $1 + .M.(2, 3) + .M.(1, 8) = 9$. It is necessary but not sufficient to finish by merging $\{A_1, A_2\}$ with $\{B_1, B_2, B_3\}$ and $\{A_3\}$ with $\{B_4, \ldots, B_{11}\}$, so the lower bound fails to be sharp in this case.

Similarly it can be shown that $.M.(2, 38) = 10$ while $M(2, 38) = 11$, so our adversary isn't even good enough to solve the case $m = 2$. But there is an infinite class of values for which it excels:

Theorem K. $M(m, m+2) = 2m + 1,$ for $m \geq 2$;

$M(m, m+3) = 2m + 2,$ for $m \geq 4$;

$M(m, m+4) = 2m + 3,$ for $m \geq 6$.

Proof. We can in fact prove the result with M replaced by $.M.$; for small m the results have been obtained by computer, so we may assume that m is sufficiently large. We may also assume that the first comparison is $A_i : B_j$ where $i \leq \lceil m/2 \rceil$. If $j \leq i$ we use strategy $A'(i, i)$, obtaining

$$.M.(m, m+d) \geq 1 + .M.(i-1, i) + .M.(m+1-i, m+d-i) = 2m + d - 1$$

by induction on d, for $d \leq 4$. If $j > i$ we use strategy $A(i, i+1)$, obtaining

$$.M.(m, m+d) \geq 1 + .M.(i, i) + .M.(m-i, m+d-i) = 2m + d - 1$$

by induction on m.   ∎

The first two parts of Theorem K were obtained by F. K. Hwang and S. Lin in 1969. Paul Stockmeyer and Frances Yao showed several years later that the pattern evident in these three formulas holds in general, namely that the lower bounds derived by the adversarial strategies above suffice to establish the values $M(m, m+d) = 2m + d - 1$ for $m \geq 2d - 2$. [*SICOMP* **9** (1980), 85–90.]

Upper bounds. Now let us consider *upper* bounds for $M(m, n)$; good upper bounds correspond to efficient merging algorithms.

When $m = 1$ the merging problem is equivalent to an insertion problem, and there are $n + 1$ places in which A_1 might fall among $B_1, \ldots, B_n$. For this case it is easy to see that *any* extended binary tree with $n + 1$ external nodes is the tree for some merging method! (See exercise 2.) Hence we may choose an optimum binary tree, realizing the information-theoretic lower bound

$$1 + \lfloor \lg n \rfloor = M(1, n) = \lceil \lg(n + 1) \rceil. \tag{15}$$

Binary search (Section 6.2.1) is, of course, a simple way to attain this value.

The case $m = 2$ is extremely interesting, but considerably harder. It has been solved completely by R. L. Graham, F. K. Hwang, and S. Lin (see exercises

11, 12, and 13), who proved the general formula

$$M(2,n) = \left\lceil \lg \tfrac{7}{12}(n+1) \right\rceil + \left\lceil \lg \tfrac{14}{17}(n+1) \right\rceil. \tag{16}$$

We have seen that the usual merging procedure is optimum when $m = n$, while the rather different binary search procedure is optimum when $m = 1$. What we need is an in-between method that combines the normal merging algorithm with binary search in such a way that the best features of both are retained. Formula (14) suggests the following algorithm, due to F. K. Hwang and S. Lin [*SICOMP* **1** (1972), 31–39]:

Algorithm H (*Binary merging*).

H1. [If not done, choose t.] If m or n is zero, stop. Otherwise, if $m > n$, set $t \leftarrow \lfloor \lg(m/n) \rfloor$ and go to step H4. Otherwise set $t \leftarrow \lfloor \lg(n/m) \rfloor$.

H2. [Compare.] Compare $A_m : B_{n+1-2^t}$. If A_m is smaller, set $n \leftarrow n - 2^t$ and return to step H1.

H3. [Insert.] Using binary search (which requires exactly t more comparisons), insert A_m into its proper place among $\{B_{n+1-2^t}, \ldots, B_n\}$. If k is maximal such that $B_k < A_m$, set $m \leftarrow m - 1$ and $n \leftarrow k$. Return to H1.

H4. [Compare.] (Steps H4 and H5 are like H2 and H3, interchanging the roles of m and n, A and B.) If $B_n < A_{m+1-2^t}$, set $m \leftarrow m - 2^t$ and return to step H1.

H5. [Insert.] Insert B_n into its proper place among the A's. If k is maximal such that $A_k < B_n$, set $m \leftarrow k$ and $n \leftarrow n - 1$. Return to H1. ∎

As an example of this algorithm, Table 2 shows the process of merging the three keys $\{087, 503, 512\}$ with thirteen keys $\{061, 154, \ldots, 908\}$; eight comparisons are required in this example. The elements compared at each step are shown in boldface type.

Table 2

EXAMPLE OF BINARY MERGING

A	B	Output
087 503 **512**	061 154 170 275 426 509 612 653 677 **703** 765 897 908	
087 503 **512**	061 154 170 275 426 509 612 **653** 677	703 765 897 908
087 503 **512**	061 154 170 275 426 **509** 612	653 677 703 765 897 908
087 503 **512**	061 154 170 275 426 509 **612**	653 677 703 765 897 908
087 **503**	061 154 170 275 **426** 509	512 612 653 677 703 765 897 908
087 **503**	061 154 170 275 426 **509**	512 612 653 677 703 765 897 908
087	061 **154** 170 275 426	503 509 512 612 653 677 703 765 897 908
087	**061** 154 170 275 426 503 509 512 612 653 677 703 765 897 908	
	061 087 154 170 275 426 503 509 512 612 653 677 703 765 897 908	

Let $H(m, n)$ be the maximum number of comparisons required by Hwang and Lin's algorithm. To calculate $H(m, n)$, we may assume that $k = n$ in step H3 and $k = m$ in step H5, since we shall prove that $H(m-1, n) \leq H(m-1, n+1)$

for all $n \geq m - 1$ by induction on m. Thus when $m \leq n$ we have

$$H(m, n) = \max\bigl(H(m, n-2^t)+1,\ H(m-1, n)+t+1\bigr), \qquad (17)$$

for $2^t m \leq n < 2^{t+1} m$. Replace n by $2n + \epsilon$, with $\epsilon = 0$ or 1, to get

$$H(m, 2n+\epsilon) = \max\bigl(H(m, 2n+\epsilon-2^{t+1}) + 1,\ H(m-1, 2n+\epsilon)+t+2\bigr),$$

for $2^t m \leq n < 2^{t+1} m$; and it follows by induction on n that

$$H(m, 2n+\epsilon) = H(m, n) + m, \qquad \text{for } m \leq n \text{ and } \epsilon = 0 \text{ or } 1. \qquad (18)$$

It is also easy to see that $H(m, n) = m + n - 1$ when $m \leq n < 2m$; hence a repeated application of (18) yields the general formula

$$H(m, n) = m + \lfloor n/2^t \rfloor - 1 + tm, \quad \text{for} \quad m \leq n, \quad t = \lfloor \lg(n/m) \rfloor. \qquad (19)$$

This implies that $H(m, n) \leq H(m, n+1)$ for all $n \geq m$, verifying our inductive hypothesis about step H3.

Setting $m = \alpha n$ and $\theta = \lg(n/m) - t$ gives

$$H(\alpha n, n) = \alpha n(1 + 2^\theta - \theta - \lg \alpha) + O(1), \qquad (20)$$

as $n \to \infty$. We know by Eq. 5.3.1–(36) that $1.9139 < 1 + 2^\theta - \theta \leq 2$; hence (20) may be compared with the information-theoretic lower bound (3). Hwang and Lin have proved (see exercise 17) that

$$H(m, n) < \left\lceil \lg \binom{m + n}{m} \right\rceil + \min(m, n). \qquad (21)$$

The Hwang–Lin binary merging algorithm does not always give optimum results, but it has the great virtue that it can be programmed rather easily. It reduces to "uncentered binary search" when $m = 1$, and it reduces to the usual merging procedure when $m \approx n$, so it represents an excellent compromise between those two methods. Furthermore, it *is* optimum in many cases (see exercise 16). Improved algorithms have been found by F. K. Hwang and D. N. Deutsch, *JACM* **20** (1973), 148–159; G. K. Manacher, *JACM* **26** (1979), 434–440; and most notably by C. Christen, *FOCS* **19** (1978), 259–266. Christen's merging procedure, called *forward-testing-backward-insertion*, saves about $m/3$ comparisons over Algorithm H when $n/m \to \infty$. Moreover, Christen's procedure achieves the lower bound $.M.(m, n) = \lfloor (11m + n - 3)/4 \rfloor$ when $5m - 3 \leq n \leq 7m + 2[m \text{ even}]$; hence it is optimum in such cases (and, remarkably, so is our adversarial lower bound).

Formula (18) suggests that the M function itself might satisfy

$$M(m, n) \leq M(m, \lfloor n/2 \rfloor) + m. \qquad (22)$$

This is actually true (see exercise 19). Tables of $M(m, n)$ suggest several other plausible relations, such as

$$M(m+1, n) \geq 1 + M(m, n) \geq M(m, n+1), \qquad \text{for } m \leq n; \qquad (23)$$

$$M(m+1, n + 1) \geq 2 + M(m, n); \qquad (24)$$

but no proof of these inequalities is known.

EXERCISES

1. [15] Find an interesting relation between $M(m, n)$ and the function S defined in Section 5.3.1. [*Hint:* Consider $S(m + n)$.]

▸ **2.** [22] When $m = 1$, every merging algorithm without redundant comparisons defines an extended binary tree with $\binom{m+n}{m} = n + 1$ external nodes. Prove that, conversely, every extended binary tree with $n + 1$ external nodes corresponds to some merging algorithm with $m = 1$.

3. [M24] Prove that $.M.(1, n) = M(1, n)$ for all n.

4. [M42] Is $.M.(m, n) \geq \lceil \lg \binom{m+n}{m} \rceil$ for all m and n?

5. [M30] Prove that $.M.(m, n) \leq .M\backslash(m, n+1)$.

6. [M26] The stated proof of Theorem K requires that a lot of cases be verified by computer. How can the number of such cases be drastically reduced?

7. [21] Prove (11).

▸ **8.** [24] Prove that $M(2, 8) \leq 6$, by finding an algorithm that merges two elements with eight others using at most six comparisons.

9. [27] Prove that three elements can be merged with six in at most seven steps.

10. [33] Prove that five elements can be merged with nine in at most twelve steps. [*Hint:* Experience with the adversary suggests first comparing $A_1:B_2$, then trying $A_5:B_8$ if $A_1 < B_2$.]

11. [M40] (F. K. Hwang, S. Lin.) Let $g_{2k} = \lfloor \frac{17}{14} 2^k \rfloor$ and $g_{2k+1} = \lfloor \frac{12}{7} 2^k \rfloor$, for $k \geq 0$, so that $(g_0, g_1, g_2, \dots) = (1, 1, 2, 3, 4, 6, 9, 13, 19, 27, 38, 54, 77, \dots)$. Prove that it takes more than t comparisons to merge two elements with g_t elements, in the worst case; but two elements can be merged with $g_t - 1$ in at most t steps. [*Hint:* Show that if $n = g_t$ or $n = g_t - 1$ and if we want to merge $\{A_1, A_2\}$ with $\{B_1, B_2, \dots, B_n\}$ in t comparisons, we can't do better than to compare $A_2 : B_{g_{t-1}}$ on the first step.]

12. [M21] Let $R_n(i, j)$ be the least number of comparisons required to sort the distinct objects $\{\alpha, \beta, X_1, \dots, X_n\}$, given the relations

$$\alpha < \beta, \qquad X_1 < X_2 < \dots < X_n, \qquad \alpha < X_{i+1}, \qquad \beta > X_{n-j}.$$

(The condition $\alpha < X_{i+1}$ or $\beta > X_{n-j}$ becomes vacuous when $i \geq n$ or $j \geq n$. Therefore $R_n(n, n) = M(2, n)$.)

Clearly, $R_n(0, 0) = 0$. Prove that

$$R_n(i, j) = 1 + \min\left(\min_{1 \leq k \leq i} \max(R_n(k-1, j), R_{n-k}(i-k, j)), \right.$$
$$\left. \min_{1 \leq k \leq j} \max(R_n(i, k-1), R_{n-k}(i, j-k)) \right)$$

for $0 \leq i \leq n$, $0 \leq j \leq n$, $i + j > 0$.

13. [M42] (R. L. Graham.) Show that the solution to the recurrence in exercise 12 may be expressed as follows. Define the function $G(x)$, for $0 < x < \infty$, by the rules

$$G(x) = \begin{cases} 1, & \text{if } 0 < x \leq \frac{5}{7}; \\ \frac{1}{2} + \frac{1}{8} G(8x - 5), & \text{if } \frac{5}{7} < x \leq \frac{3}{4}; \\ \frac{1}{2} G(2x - 1), & \text{if } \frac{3}{4} < x \leq 1; \\ 0, & \text{if } 1 < x < \infty. \end{cases}$$

(See Fig. 38.) Since $R_n(i,j) = R_n(j,i)$ and since $R_n(0,j) = M(1,j)$, we may assume that $1 \le i \le j \le n$. Let $p = \lfloor \lg i \rfloor$, $q = \lfloor \lg j \rfloor$, $r = \lfloor \lg n \rfloor$, and let $t = n - 2^r + 1$. Then

$$R_n(i,j) = p + q + S_n(i,j) + T_n(i,j),$$

where S_n and T_n are functions that are either 0 or 1:

$$S_n(i,j) = 1 \quad \text{if and only if} \quad q < r \text{ or } (i - 2^p \ge u \text{ and } j - 2^r \ge u),$$
$$T_n(i,j) = 1 \quad \text{if and only if} \quad p < r \text{ or } (t > \tfrac{6}{7} 2^{r-2} \text{ and } i - 2^r \ge v),$$

where $u = 2^p G(t/2^p)$ and $v = 2^{r-2} G(t/2^{r-2})$.

(This may be the most formidable recurrence relation that will ever be solved!)

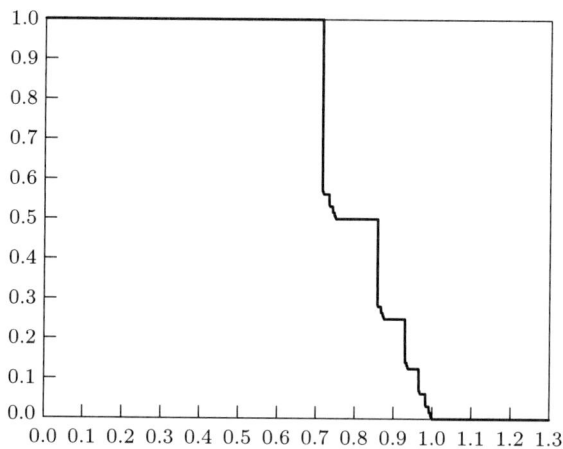

Fig. 38. Graham's function (see exercise 13).

14. [*41*] (F. K. Hwang.) Let $h_{3k} = \lfloor \tfrac{43}{28} 2^k \rfloor - 1$, $h_{3k+1} = h_{3k} + 3 \cdot 2^{k-3}$, $h_{3k+2} = \lfloor \tfrac{17}{7} 2^k - \tfrac{6}{7} \rfloor$ for $k \ge 3$, and let the initial values be defined so that

$$(h_0, h_1, h_2, \dots) = (1, 1, 2, 2, 3, 4, 5, 7, 9, 11, 14, 18, 23, 29, 38, 48, 60, 76, \dots).$$

Prove that $M(3, h_t) > t$ and $M(3, h_t - 1) \le t$ for all t, thereby establishing the exact values of $M(3, n)$ for all n.

15. [*12*] Step H1 of the binary merge algorithm may require the calculation of the expression $\lfloor \lg(n/m) \rfloor$, for $n \ge m$. Explain how to compute this easily without division or calculation of a logarithm.

16. [*18*] For which m and n is Hwang and Lin's binary merging algorithm optimum, for $1 \le m \le n \le 10$?

17. [*M25*] Prove (21). [*Hint:* The inequality isn't very tight.]

18. [*M40*] Study the *average* number of comparisons used by binary merge.

▶ **19.** [*23*] Prove that the M function satisfies (22).

20. [*20*] Show that if $M(m, n+1) \le M(m+1, n)$ for all $m \le n$, then $M(m, n+1) \le 1 + M(m, n)$ for all $m \le n$.

21. [*M47*] Prove or disprove (23) and (24).

22. [*M43*] Study the minimum *average* number of comparisons needed to merge m things with n.

23. [*M31*] (E. Reingold.) Let $\{A_1, \ldots, A_n\}$ and $\{B_1, \ldots, B_n\}$ be sets containing n elements each. Consider an algorithm that attempts to test *equality* of these two sets solely by making comparisons for equality between elements. Thus, the algorithm asks questions of the form "Is $A_i = B_j$?" for certain i and j, and it branches depending on the answer.

By defining a suitable adversary, prove that any such algorithm must make at least $\frac{1}{2}n(n+1)$ comparisons in its worst case.

24. [*22*] (E. L. Lawler.) What is the maximum number of comparisons needed by the following algorithm for merging m elements with $n \geq m$ elements? "Set $t \leftarrow \lfloor \lg(n/m) \rfloor$ and use Algorithm 5.2.4M to merge $A_1, A_2, \ldots, A_m$ with $B_{2^t}, B_{2 \cdot 2^t}, \ldots, B_{q \cdot 2^t}$, where $q = \lfloor n/2^t \rfloor$. Then insert each A_j into its proper place among the B_k."

▶ **25.** [*25*] Suppose (x_{ij}) is an $m \times n$ matrix with nondecreasing rows and columns: $x_{ij} \leq x_{(i+1)j}$ for $1 \leq i < m$ and $x_{ij} \leq x_{i(j+1)}$ for $1 \leq j < n$. Show that $M(m, n)$ is the minimum number of comparisons needed to determine whether a given number x is present in the matrix, if all comparisons are between x and some matrix element.

*5.3.3. Minimum-Comparison Selection

A similar class of interesting problems arises when we look for best possible procedures to select the tth largest of n elements.

The history of this question goes back to Rev. C. L. Dodgson's amusing (though serious) essay on lawn tennis tournaments, which appeared in *St. James's Gazette*, August 1, 1883, pages 5–6. Dodgson — who is of course better known as Lewis Carroll — was concerned about the unjust manner in which prizes were awarded in tennis tournaments. Consider, for example, Fig. 39, which shows a typical "knockout tournament" between 32 players labeled *01, 02, ..., 32*. In the finals, player *01* defeats player *05*, so it is clear that player *01* is the champion and deserves the first prize. The inequity arises because player *05* usually gets second prize, although someone else might well be the second best. You can win second prize even if you are worse than half of the players in the competition! In fact, as Dodgson observed, the second-best player wins second prize if and only if the champion and the next-best are originally in opposite halves of the tournament; this occurs with probability $2^{n-1}/(2^n - 1)$, when there are 2^n competitors, so the wrong player receives second prize almost half of the time. If the losers of the semifinal round (players *25* and *17* in Fig. 39) compete for third prize, it is highly unlikely that the third-best player receives third prize.

Dodgson therefore set out to design a tournament that determines the true second- and third-best players, assuming a transitive ranking. (In other words, if player A beats player B and B beats C, Dodgson assumed that A would beat C.) He devised a procedure in which losers are allowed to play further games until they are known to be definitely inferior to three other players. An example of Dodgson's scheme appears in Fig. 40, which is a supplementary tournament to be run in conjunction with Fig. 39. He tried to pair off players whose records in previous rounds were equivalent; he also tried to avoid matches in which both players had been defeated by the same person. In this particular example, *16* loses to *11* and *13* loses to *12* in Round 1; after *13* beats *16* in the second round, we can eliminate *16*, who is now known to be inferior to *11*, *12*, and *13*. In Round 3 Dodgson did not allow *19* to play with *21*, since they have both been defeated by *18* and we could not automatically eliminate the loser of *19* versus *21*.

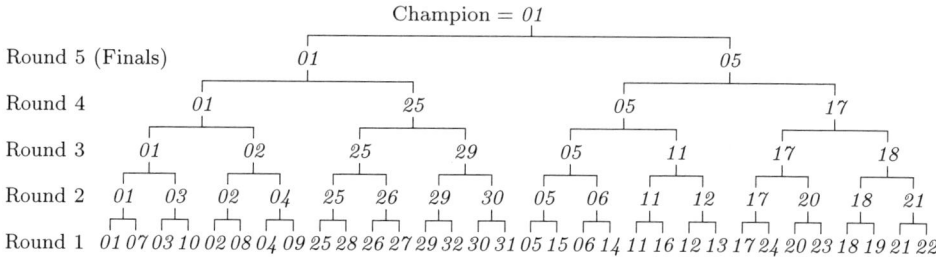

Fig. 39. A knockout tournament with 32 players.

It would be nice to report that Lewis Carroll's tournament turns out to be optimal, but unfortunately that is not the case. His diary entry for July 23, 1883, says that he composed the essay in about six hours, and he felt "we are now so late in the [tennis] season that it is better it should appear soon than be written well." His procedure makes more comparisons than necessary, and it is not formulated precisely enough to qualify as an algorithm. On the other hand, it has some rather interesting aspects from the standpoint of parallel computation. And it appears to be an excellent plan for a tennis tournament, because he built in some dramatic effects; for example, he specified that the two finalists should sit out round 5, playing an extended match during rounds 6 and 7. But tournament directors presumably thought the proposal was too logical, and so Carroll's system has apparently never been tried. Instead, a method of "seeding" is used to keep the supposedly best players in different parts of the tree.

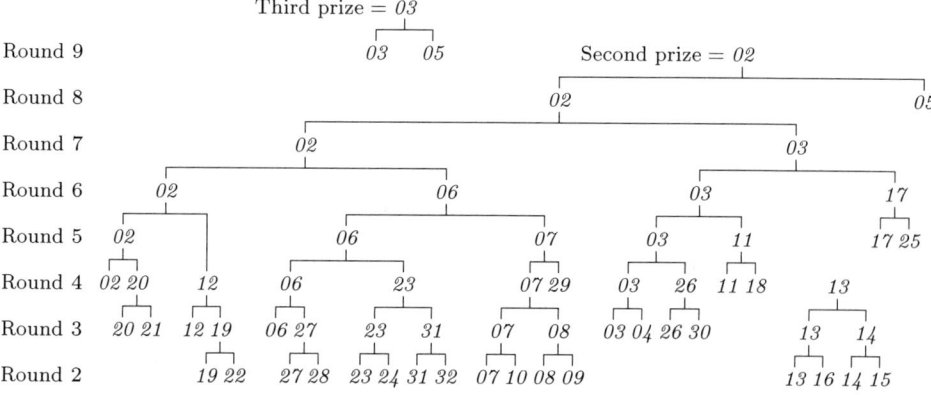

Fig. 40. Lewis Carroll's lawn tennis tournament (played in conjunction with Fig. 39).

In a mathematical seminar during 1929–1930, Hugo Steinhaus posed the problem of finding the *minimum* number of tennis matches required to determine the first and second best players in a tournament, when there are $n \geq 2$ players in all. J. Schreier [*Mathesis Polska* **7** (1932), 154–160] gave a procedure that requires at most $n - 2 + \lceil \lg n \rceil$ matches, using essentially the same method as the first two stages in what we have called tree selection sorting (see Section 5.2.3, Fig. 23), avoiding redundant comparisons that involve $-\infty$. Schreier also claimed that $n - 2 + \lceil \lg n \rceil$ is best possible, but his proof was incorrect, as was another attempted proof by J. Słupecki [*Colloquium Mathematicum* **2** (1951), 286–290]. Thirty-two years went by before a correct, although rather complicated, proof was finally published by S. S. Kislitsyn [*Sibirskiĭ Mat. Zhurnal* **5** (1964), 557–564].

Let $V_t(n)$ denote the minimum number of comparisons needed to determine the tth largest of n elements, for $1 \leq t \leq n$, and let $W_t(n)$ be the minimum number required to determine the largest, second largest, ..., and the tth largest, collectively. By symmetry, we have

$$V_t(n) = V_{n+1-t}(n), \qquad (1)$$

and it is obvious that

$$V_1(n) = W_1(n), \qquad (2)$$

$$V_t(n) \leq W_t(n), \qquad (3)$$

$$W_n(n) = W_{n-1}(n) = S(n). \qquad (4)$$

We have observed in Lemma 5.2.3M that

$$V_1(n) = n - 1. \qquad (5)$$

In fact, there is an astonishingly simple proof of this fact, since everyone in a tournament except the champion must lose at least one game! By extending this idea and using an "adversary" as in Section 5.3.2, we can prove the Schreier–Kislitsyn theorem without much difficulty:

Theorem S. $V_2(n) = W_2(n) = n - 2 + \lceil \lg n \rceil$, for $n \geq 2$.

Proof. Assume that n players have participated in a tournament that has determined the second-best player by some given procedure, and let a_j be the number of players who have lost j or more matches. The total number of matches played is then $a_1 + a_2 + a_3 + \cdots$. We cannot determine the second-best player without also determining the champion (see exercise 2), so our previous argument shows that $a_1 = n - 1$. To complete the proof, we will show that there is always some sequence of outcomes of the matches that makes $a_2 \geq \lceil \lg n \rceil - 1$.

Suppose that at the end of the tournament the champion has played (and beaten) p players; one of these is the second best, and the others must have lost at least one other time, so $a_2 \geq p - 1$. Therefore we can complete the proof by constructing an adversary who decides the results of the games in such a way that the champion must play at least $\lceil \lg n \rceil$ other people.

Let the adversary declare A to be better than B if A is previously undefeated and B has lost at least once, or if both are undefeated and B has won fewer matches than A at that time. In other circumstances the adversary may make an arbitrary decision consistent with some partial ordering.

Consider the outcome of a complete tournament whose matches have been decided by such an adversary. Let us say that "A supersedes B" if and only if $A = B$ or A supersedes the player who first defeated B. (Only a player's first defeat is relevant in this relation; a loser's subsequent games are ignored. According to the mechanism of the adversary, any player who *first* defeats another must be previously unbeaten.) It follows that a player who won the first p matches supersedes at most 2^p players on the basis of those p contests. (This is clear for $p = 0$, and for $p > 0$ the pth match was against someone who was either previously beaten or who supersedes at most 2^{p-1} players.) Hence the champion, who supersedes everyone, must have played at least $\lceil \lg n \rceil$ matches. ∎

Theorem S completely resolves the problem of finding the second-best player, in the minimax sense. Exercise 6 shows, in fact, that it is possible to give a simple formula for the minimum number of comparisons needed to find the second largest element of a set when an *arbitrary* partial ordering of the elements is known beforehand.

What if $t > 2$? In the paper cited above, Kislitsyn went on to consider larger values of t, proving that

$$W_t(n) \le n - t + \sum_{n+1-t < j \le n} \lceil \lg j \rceil, \qquad \text{for } n \ge t. \tag{6}$$

For $t = 1$ and $t = 2$ we have seen that equality actually holds in this formula; for $t = 3$ it can be slightly improved (see exercise 21).

We shall prove Kislitsyn's theorem by showing that the first t stages of *tree selection* require at most $n - t + \sum_{n+1-t<j\le n} \lceil \lg j \rceil$ comparisons, ignoring all of the comparisons that involve $-\infty$. It is interesting to note that, by Eq. 5.3.1–(3), the right-hand side of (6) equals $B(n)$ when $t = n$, and also when $t = n - 1$; hence tree selection and binary insertion yield the same upper bound for the sorting problem, although they are quite different methods.

Let α be an extended binary tree with n external nodes, and let π be a permutation of $\{1, 2, \ldots, n\}$. Place the elements of π into the external nodes, from left to right in symmetric order, and fill in the internal nodes according to the rules of a knockout tournament as in tree selection. When the resulting tree is subjected to repeated selection operations, it defines a sequence $c_{n-1} c_{n-2} \ldots c_1$, where c_j is the number of comparisons required to bring element j to the root of the tree when element $j + 1$ has been replaced by $-\infty$. For example, if α is the tree

$$\tag{7}$$

and if $\pi = 5\ 3\ 1\ 4\ 2$, we obtain the successive trees

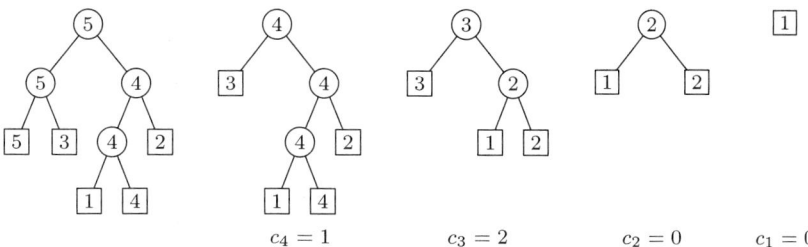

$$c_4 = 1 \qquad\qquad c_3 = 2 \qquad\qquad c_2 = 0 \qquad\qquad c_1 = 0$$

If π had been $3\ 1\ 5\ 4\ 2$, the sequence $c_4\,c_3\,c_2\,c_1$ would have been 2 1 1 0 instead. It is not difficult to see that c_1 is always zero.

Let $\mu(\alpha, \pi)$ be the multiset $\{c_{n-1}, c_{n-2}, \ldots, c_1\}$ determined by α and π. If

$$\alpha = \overset{\bigcirc}{\underset{\alpha'\quad\alpha''}{\diagdown}}$$

and if elements 1 and 2 do not both appear in α' or both in α'', it is easy to see that

$$\mu(\alpha, \pi) = \big(\mu(\alpha', \pi') + 1\big) \uplus \big(\mu(\alpha'', \pi'') + 1\big) \uplus \{0\} \qquad (8)$$

for appropriate permutations π' and π'', where $\mu+1$ denotes the multiset obtained by adding 1 to each element of μ. (See exercise 7.) On the other hand, if elements 1 and 2 both appear in α', we have

$$\mu(\alpha, \pi) = \big(\mu(\alpha', \pi') + \epsilon\big) \uplus \big(\mu(\alpha'', \pi'') + 1\big) \uplus \{0\},$$

where $\mu + \epsilon$ denotes a multiset obtained by adding 1 to some elements of μ and 0 to the others. A similar formula holds when 1 and 2 both appear in α''. Let us say that multiset μ_1 *dominates* μ_2 if both μ_1 and μ_2 contain the same number of elements, and if the kth largest element of μ_1 is greater than or equal to the kth largest element of μ_2 for all k; and let us define $\mu(\alpha)$ to be the dominant $\mu(\alpha, \pi)$, taken over all permutations π, in the sense that $\mu(\alpha)$ dominates $\mu(\alpha, \pi)$ for all π and $\mu(\alpha) = \mu(\alpha, \pi)$ for some π. The formulas above show that

$$\mu(\square) = \emptyset, \qquad \mu\Big(\underset{\alpha'\ \alpha''}{\overset{\bigcirc}{\diagdown}}\Big) = \big(\mu(\alpha') + 1\big) \uplus \big(\mu(\alpha'') + 1\big) \uplus \{0\}; \qquad (9)$$

hence $\mu(\alpha)$ *is the multiset of all distances from the root to the internal nodes of* α.

The reader who has followed this train of thought will now see that we are ready to prove Kislitsyn's theorem (6). Indeed, $W_t(n)$ is less than or equal to $n - 1$ plus the $t - 1$ largest elements of $\mu(\alpha)$, where α is any tree being used in tree selection sorting. We may take α to be the complete binary tree with n external nodes (see Section 2.3.4.5), when

$$\mu(\alpha) = \big\{ \lfloor \lg 1 \rfloor, \lfloor \lg 2 \rfloor, \ldots, \lfloor \lg(n-1) \rfloor \big\}$$
$$= \big\{ \lceil \lg 2 \rceil - 1, \lceil \lg 3 \rceil - 1, \ldots, \lceil \lg n \rceil - 1 \big\}. \qquad (10)$$

Formula (6) follows when we consider the $t - 1$ largest elements of this multiset.

Kislitsyn's theorem gives a good upper bound for $W_t(n)$; he remarked that $V_3(5) = 6 < W_3(5) = 7$, but he was unable to find a better bound for $V_t(n)$ than for $W_t(n)$. A. Hadian and M. Sobel discovered a way to do this using *replacement selection* instead of tree selection; their formula [Univ. of Minnesota, Dept. of Statistics Report 121 (1969)],

$$V_t(n) \leq n - t + (t-1)\lceil \lg(n+2-t)\rceil, \qquad n \geq t, \qquad (11)$$

is similar to Kislitsyn's upper bound for $W_t(n)$ in (6), except that each term in the sum has been replaced by the smallest term.

Hadian and Sobel's theorem (11) can be proved by using the following construction: First set up a binary tree for a knockout tournament on $n - t + 2$ items. (This takes $n - t + 1$ comparisons.) The largest item is greater than $n - t + 1$ others, so it can't be tth largest. Replace it, where it appears at an external node of the tree, by one of the $t - 2$ elements held in reserve, and find the largest element of the resulting $n - t + 2$; this requires at most $\lceil \lg(n+2-t)\rceil$ comparisons, because we need to recompute only one path in the tree. Repeat this operation $t - 2$ times in all, for each element held in reserve. Finally, replace the currently largest element by $-\infty$, and determine the largest of the remaining $n + 1 - t$; this requires at most $\lceil \lg(n+2-t)\rceil - 1$ comparisons, and it brings the tth largest element of the original set to the root of the tree. Summing the comparisons yields (11).

In relation (11) we should of course replace t by $n + 1 - t$ on the right-hand side whenever $n+1-t$ gives a better value (as when $n = 6$ and $t = 3$). Curiously, the formula gives a smaller bound for $V_7(13)$ than it does for $V_6(13)$. The upper bound in (11) is exact for $n \leq 6$, but as n and t get larger it is possible to obtain much better estimates of $V_t(n)$.

For example, the following elegant method (due to David G. Doren) can be used to show that $V_4(8) \leq 12$. Let the elements be $X_1, \ldots, X_8$; first compare $X_1 : X_2$ and $X_3 : X_4$ and the two winners, and do the same to $X_5 : X_6$ and $X_7 : X_8$ and their winners. Relabel elements so that $X_1 < X_2 < X_4 > X_3$, $X_5 < X_6 < X_8 > X_7$, then compare $X_2 : X_6$; by symmetry assume that $X_2 < X_6$, so that we have the configuration

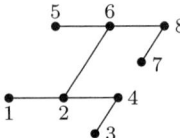

(Now X_1 and X_8 are out of contention and we must find the third largest of $\{X_2, \ldots, X_7\}$.) Compare $X_2 : X_7$, and discard the smaller; in the worst case we have $X_2 < X_7$ and we must find the third largest of

$$5 \bullet\!\!-\!\!-\!\!\bullet 6$$
$$\bullet 7$$
$$3 \bullet\!\!-\!\!-\!\!\bullet 4$$

This can be done in $V_3(5) - 2 = 4$ more steps, since the procedure of (11) that achieves $V_3(5) = 6$ begins by comparing two disjoint pairs of elements.

Table 1

VALUES OF $V_t(n)$ FOR SMALL n

n	$V_1(n)$	$V_2(n)$	$V_3(n)$	$V_4(n)$	$V_5(n)$	$V_6(n)$	$V_7(n)$	$V_8(n)$	$V_9(n)$	$V_{10}(n)$
1	0									
2	1	1								
3	2	3	2							
4	3	4	4	3						
5	4	6	6	6	4					
6	5	7	8	8	7	5				
7	6	8	10	10*	10	8	6			
8	7	9	11	12	12	11	9	7		
9	8	11	12	14	14*	14	12	11	8	
10	9	12	14*	15	16**	16**	15	14*	12	9

* Exercises 10–12 give constructions that improve on Eq. (11) in these cases.
** See K. Noshita, *Trans. of the IECE of Japan* **E59**, 12 (December 1976), 17–18.

Other tricks of this kind can be used to produce the results shown in Table 1; no general method is evident as yet. The values listed for $V_4(9) = V_6(9)$ and $V_5(10) = V_6(10)$ were proved optimum in 1996 by W. Gasarch, W. Kelly, and W. Pugh [*SIGACT News* **27**, 2 (June 1996), 88–96], using a computer search.

A fairly good lower bound for the selection problem when t is small was obtained by David G. Kirkpatrick [*JACM* **28** (1981), 150–165]: If $2 \le t \le (n+1)/2$, we have

$$V_t(n) \ge n + t - 3 + \sum_{j=0}^{t-2} \left\lceil \lg \frac{n-t+2}{t+j} \right\rceil . \tag{12}$$

In his Ph.D. thesis [U. of Toronto, 1974], Kirkpatrick also proved that

$$V_3(n) \le n + 1 + \left\lceil \lg \frac{n-1}{4} \right\rceil + \left\lceil \lg \frac{n-1}{5} \right\rceil ; \tag{13}$$

this upper bound matches the lower bound (12) for $\lg \frac{5}{3} \approx 74\%$ of all integers n, and it exceeds (12) by at most 1. Kirkpatrick's analysis made it natural to conjecture that equality holds in (13) for all $n > 4$, but Jutta Eusterbrock found the surprising counterexample $V_3(22) = 28$ [*Discrete Applied Math.* **41** (1993), 131–137]. Improved lower bounds for larger values of t were found by S. W. Bent and J. W. John (see exercise 27):

$$V_t(n) \ge n + m - 2\lceil \sqrt{m} \rceil, \qquad m = 2 + \left\lceil \lg \left(\binom{n}{t} \middle/ (n+1-t) \right) \right\rceil . \tag{14}$$

This formula proves in particular that

$$V_{\alpha n}(n) \ge \left(1 + \alpha \lg \frac{1}{\alpha} + (1-\alpha) \lg \frac{1}{1-\alpha} \right) n + O(\sqrt{n}). \tag{15}$$

A linear method. When n is odd and $t = \lceil n/2 \rceil$, the tth largest (and tth smallest) element is called the median. According to (11), we can find the median of n elements in $\approx \frac{1}{2} n \lg n$ comparisons; but this is only about twice as fast as sorting, even though we are asking for much less information. For several years, concerted efforts were made by a number of people to find an improvement over (11) when t and n are large. Finally in 1971, Manuel Blum discovered a method that needed only $O(n \log \log n)$ steps. Blum's approach to the problem suggested a new class of techniques, which led to the following construction due to R. Rivest and R. Tarjan [*J. Comp. and Sys. Sci.* **7** (1973), 448–461]:

Theorem L. *If $n > 32$ and $1 \le t \le n$, we have $V_t(n) \le 15n - 163$.*

Proof. The theorem is trivial when n is small, since $V_t(n) \le S(n) \le 10n \le 15n - 163$ for $32 < n \le 2^{10}$. By adding at most 13 dummy $-\infty$ elements, we may assume that $n = 7(2q + 1)$ for some integer $q \ge 73$. The following method may now be used to select the tth largest:

Step 1. Divide the elements into $2q + 1$ groups of seven elements each, and sort each of the groups. This takes at most $13(2q + 1)$ comparisons.

Step 2. Find the median of the $2q + 1$ median elements obtained in Step 1, and call it x. By induction on q, this takes at most $V_{q+1}(2q + 1) \le 30q - 148$ comparisons.

Step 3. The $n - 1$ elements other than x have now been partitioned into three sets (see Fig. 41):

$4q + 3$ elements known to be greater than x (Region B);

$4q + 3$ elements known to be less than x (Region C);

$6q$ elements whose relation to x is unknown (Regions A and D).

By making $4q$ additional comparisons, we can tell exactly which of the elements in regions A and D are less than x. (We first test x against the middle element of each triple.)

Step 4. We have now found r elements greater than x and $n - 1 - r$ elements less than x, for some r. If $t = r + 1$, x is the answer; if $t < r + 1$, we need to find the tth largest of the r large elements; and if $t > r + 1$, we need to find the $(t-1-r)$th largest of the $n - 1 - r$ small elements. The point is that r and $n - 1 - r$ are both less than or equal to $10q + 3$ (the size of regions A and D, plus either B or C). By induction on q this step therefore requires at most $15(10q + 3) - 163$ comparisons.

The total number of comparisons comes to at most

$$13(2q + 1) + 30q - 148 + 4q + 15(10q + 3) - 163 = 15(14q - 6) - 163.$$

Since we started with at least $14q - 6$ elements, the proof is complete. ∎

Theorem L shows that selection can always be done in linear time, namely that $V_t(n) = O(n)$. Of course, the method used in this proof is rather crude, since it throws away good information in Step 4. Deeper study of the problem

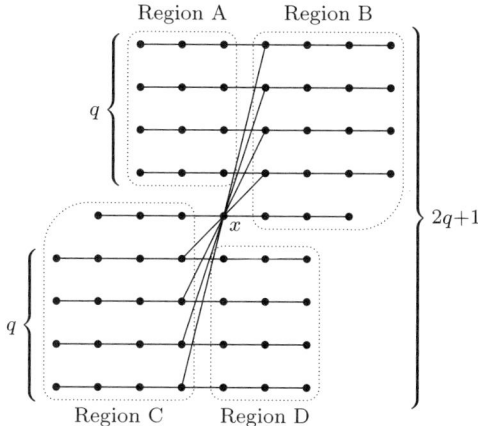

Fig. 41. The selection algorithm of Rivest and Tarjan ($q = 4$).

has led to much sharper bounds; for example, A. Schönhage, M. Paterson, and N. Pippenger [*J. Comp. Sys. Sci.* **13** (1976), 184–199] proved that the maximum number of comparisons required to find the median is at most $3n + O(n \log n)^{3/4}$. See exercise 23 for a lower bound and for references to more recent results.

The average number. Instead of minimizing the *maximum* number of comparisons, we can ask instead for an algorithm that minimizes the *average* number of comparisons, assuming random order. As usual, the minimean problem is considerably harder than the minimax problem; indeed, the minimean problem is still unsolved even in the case $t = 2$. Claude Picard mentioned the problem in his book *Théorie des Questionnaires* (1965), and an extensive exploration was undertaken by Milton Sobel [Univ. of Minnesota, Dept. of Statistics Reports 113 and 114 (November 1968); *Revue Française d'Automatique, Informatique et Recherche Opérationnelle* **6**, R-3 (December 1972), 23–68].

Sobel constructed the procedure of Fig. 42, which finds the second largest of six elements using only $6\frac{1}{2}$ comparisons on the average. In the worst case, 8 comparisons are required, and this is worse than $V_2(6) = 7$; in fact, an exhaustive computer search by D. Hoey has shown that the best procedure for this problem, if restricted to at most 7 comparisons, uses $6\frac{26}{45}$ comparisons on the average. Thus no procedure that finds the second largest of six elements can be optimum in both the minimax and the minimean senses simultaneously.

Let $\overline{V}_t(n)$ denote the minimum average number of comparisons needed to find the tth largest of n elements. Table 2 shows the exact values for small n, as computed by D. Hoey.

R. W. Floyd discovered in 1970 that the median of n elements can be found with only $\frac{3}{2}n + O(n^{2/3} \log n)$ comparisons, on the average. He and R. L. Rivest refined this method a few years later and constructed an elegant algorithm to prove that

$$\overline{V}_t(n) \leq n + \min(t, n-t) + O(\sqrt{n \log n}). \tag{16}$$

(See exercises 13 and 24.)

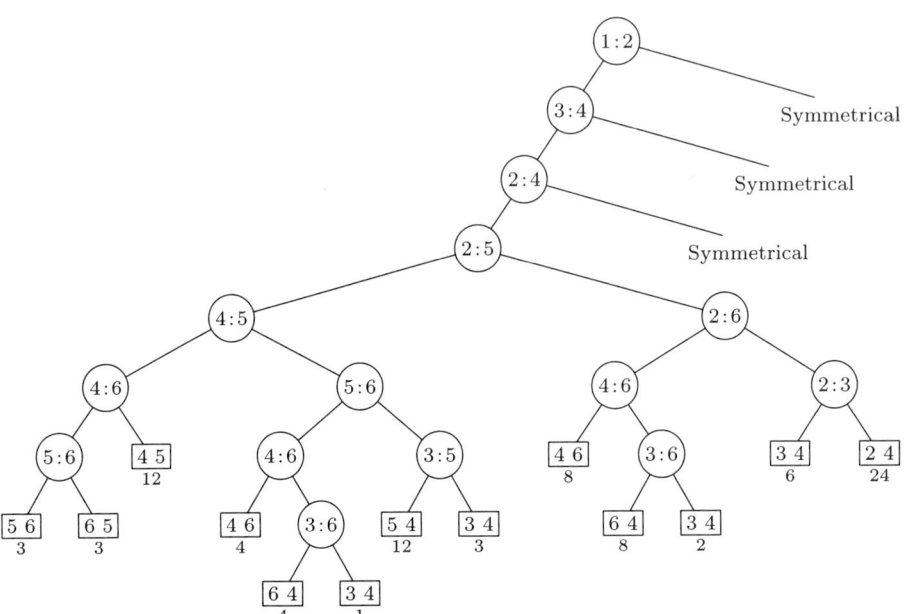

Fig. 42. A procedure that selects the second largest of $\{X_1, X_2, X_3, X_4, X_5, X_6\}$, using $6\frac{1}{2}$ comparisons on the average. Each "symmetrical" branch is identical to its sibling, with names permuted in some appropriate manner. External nodes contain "$j\ k$" when X_j is known to be the second largest and X_k the largest; the number of permutations leading to such a node appears immediately below it.

Using another approach, based on a generalization of one of Sobel's constructions for $t = 2$, David W. Matula [Washington Univ. Tech. Report AMCS-73-9 (1973)] showed that

$$\overline{V}_t(n) \leq n + t\lceil \lg t \rceil (11 + \ln \ln n). \tag{17}$$

Thus, for fixed t the average amount of work can be reduced to $n + O(\log \log n)$ comparisons. An elegant lower bound on $\overline{V}_t(n)$ appears in exercise 25.

The sorting and selection problems are special cases of the much more general problem of finding a permutation of n given elements that is consistent with a given partial ordering. A. C. Yao [*SICOMP* **18** (1989), 679–689] has shown that, if the partial ordering is defined by an acyclic digraph G on n vertices with k connected components, the minimum number of comparisons necessary to solve such problems is always $\Theta\big(\lg\big(n!/T(G)\big) + n - k\big)$, in both the worst case and on the average, where $T(G)$ is the total number of permutations consistent with the partial ordering (the number of topological sortings of G).

EXERCISES

1. [*15*] In Lewis Carroll's tournament (Figs. 39 and 40), why was player *13* eliminated in spite of winning in Round 3?

Table 2

MINIMUM AVERAGE COMPARISONS FOR SELECTION

n	$\bar{V}_1(n)$	$\bar{V}_2(n)$	$\bar{V}_3(n)$	$\bar{V}_4(n)$	$\bar{V}_5(n)$	$\bar{V}_6(n)$	$\bar{V}_7(n)$
1	0						
2	1	1					
3	2	$2\frac{2}{3}$	2				
4	3	4	4	3			
5	4	$5\frac{4}{15}$	$5\frac{13}{15}$	$5\frac{4}{15}$	4		
6	5	$6\frac{1}{2}$	$7\frac{7}{18}$	$7\frac{7}{18}$	$6\frac{1}{2}$	5	
7	6	$7\frac{149}{210}$	$8\frac{509}{630}$	$9\frac{32}{105}$	$8\frac{509}{630}$	$7\frac{149}{210}$	6

▸ **2.** [*M25*] Prove that after we have found the tth largest of n elements by a sequence of comparisons, we also know which $t-1$ elements are greater than it, and which $n-t$ elements are less than it.

3. [*20*] Prove that $V_t(n) > V_t(n-1)$ and $W_t(n) > W_t(n-1)$, for $1 \le t < n$.

▸ **4.** [*M25*] (F. Fussenegger and H. N. Gabow.) Prove that $W_t(n) \ge n - t + \lceil \lg n \frac{t-1}{} \rceil$.

5. [*10*] Prove that $W_3(n) \le V_3(n) + 1$.

▸ **6.** [*M26*] (R. W. Floyd.) Given n distinct elements $\{X_1, \ldots, X_n\}$ and a set of relations $X_i < X_j$ for certain pairs (i, j), we wish to find the second largest element. If we know that $X_i < X_j$ and $X_i < X_k$ for $j \ne k$, X_i cannot possibly be the second largest, so it can be eliminated. The resulting relations now have a form such as

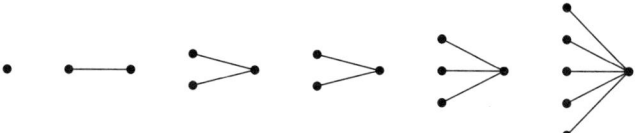

namely, m groups of elements that can be represented by a multiset $\{l_1, l_2, \ldots, l_m\}$; the jth group contains $l_j + 1$ elements, one of which is known to be greater than the others. For example, the configuration above can be described by the multiset $\{0, 1, 2, 2, 3, 5\}$; when no relations are known we have a multiset of n zeros.

Let $f(l_1, l_2, \ldots, l_m)$ be the minimum number of comparisons needed to find the second largest element of such a partially ordered set. Prove that

$$f(l_1, l_2, \ldots, l_m) = m - 2 + \lceil \lg(2^{l_1} + 2^{l_2} + \cdots + 2^{l_m}) \rceil.$$

[*Hint:* Show that the best strategy is always to compare the largest elements of the two smallest groups, until reducing m to unity; use induction on $l_1 + l_2 + \cdots + l_m + 2m$.]

7. [*M20*] Prove (8).

8. [*M21*] Kislitsyn's formula (6) is based on tree selection sorting using the complete binary tree with n external nodes. Would a tree selection method based on some *other* tree give a better bound, for any t and n?

▸ **9.** [*20*] Draw a comparison tree that finds the median of five elements in at most six steps, using the replacement-selection method of Hadian and Sobel [see (11)].

10. [*35*] Show that the median of seven elements can be found in at most 10 steps.

11. [*38*] (K. Noshita.) Show that the median of nine elements can be found in at most 14 steps, of which the first seven are identical to Doren's method.

12. [*21*] (Hadian and Sobel.) Prove that $V_3(n) \leq V_3(n-1) + 2$. [*Hint:* Start by discarding the smallest of $\{X_1, X_2, X_3, X_4\}$.]

▶ **13.** [*HM28*] (R. W. Floyd.) Show that if we start by finding the median element of $\{X_1, \ldots, X_{n^{2/3}}\}$, using a recursively defined method, we can go on to find the median of $\{X_1, \ldots, X_n\}$ with an average of $\frac{3}{2}n + O(n^{2/3} \log n)$ comparisons.

▶ **14.** [*20*] (M. Sobel.) Let $U_t(n)$ be the minimum number of comparisons needed to find the t largest of n elements, without necessarily knowing their relative order. Show that $U_2(5) \leq 5$.

15. [*22*] (I. Pohl.) Suppose that we are interested in minimizing space instead of time. What is the minimum number of data words needed in memory in order to compute the tth largest of n elements, if each element fills one word and if the elements are input one at a time into a single register?

▶ **16.** [*25*] (I. Pohl.) Show that we can find both the maximum and the minimum of a set of n elements, using at most $\lceil \frac{3}{2}n \rceil - 2$ comparisons; and the latter number cannot be lowered. [*Hint:* Any stage in such an algorithm can be represented as a quadruple (a, b, c, d), where a elements have never been compared, b have won but never lost, c have lost but never won, d have both won and lost. Construct an adversary.]

17. [*20*] (R. W. Floyd.) Show that it is possible to select, in order, both the k largest and the l smallest elements of a set of n elements, using at most $\lceil \frac{3}{2}n \rceil - k - l + \sum_{n+1-k<j\leq n} \lceil \lg j \rceil + \sum_{n+1-l<j\leq n} \lceil \lg j \rceil$ comparisons.

18. [*M20*] If groups of size 5, not 7, had been used in the proof of Theorem L, what theorem would have been obtained?

19. [*M42*] Extend Table 2 to $n = 8$.

20. [*M47*] What is the asymptotic value of $\overline{V}_2(n) - n$, as $n \to \infty$?

21. [*32*] (P. V. Ramanan and L. Hyafil.) Prove that $W_t(2^k + 2^{k+1-t}) \leq 2^k + 2^{k+1-t} + (t-1)(k-1)$, when $k \geq t \geq 2$; also show that equality holds for infinitely many k and t, because of exercise 4. [*Hint:* Maintain two knockout trees and merge their results cleverly.]

22. [*24*] (David G. Kirkpatrick.) Show that when $4 \cdot 2^k < n - 1 \leq 5 \cdot 2^k$, the upper bound (11) for $V_3(n)$ can be reduced by 1 as follows: (i) Form four knockout trees of size 2^k. (ii) Find the minimum of the four maxima, and discard all 2^k elements of its tree. (iii) Using the known information, build a single knockout tree of size $n - 1 - 2^k$. (iv) Continue as in the proof of (11).

23. [*M49*] What is the asymptotic value of $V_{\lceil n/2 \rceil}(n)$, as $n \to \infty$?

24. [*HM40*] Prove that $\overline{V}_t(n) \leq n + t + O(\sqrt{n \log n})$ for $t \leq \lceil n/2 \rceil$. *Hint:* Show that with this many comparisons we can in fact find both the $\lfloor t - \sqrt{t \ln n} \rfloor$th and $\lceil t + \sqrt{t \ln n} \rceil$th elements, after which the tth is easily located.

▶ **25.** [*M35*] (W. Cunto and J. I. Munro.) Prove that $\overline{V}_t(n) \geq n + t - 2$ when $t \leq \lceil n/2 \rceil$.

26. [*M32*] (A. Schönhage, 1974.) (a) In the notation of exercise 14, prove that $U_t(n) \geq \min(2 + U_t(n-1), 2 + U_{t-1}(n-1))$ for $n \geq 3$. [*Hint:* Construct an adversary by reducing from n to $n-1$ as soon as the current partial ordering is not composed entirely of components having the form • or •——•.] (b) Similarly, prove that

$$U_t(n) \geq \min(2 + U_t(n-1), 3 + U_{t-1}(n-1), 3 + U_t(n-2))$$

for $n \geq 5$, by constructing an adversary that deals with components •, ⟶, ➤,
⟿. (c) Therefore we have $U_t(n) \geq n + t + \min(\lfloor(n-t)/2\rfloor, t) - 3$ for $1 \leq t \leq n/2$.
[The inequalities in (a) and (b) apply also when V or W replaces U, thereby establishing
the optimality of several entries in Table 1.]

▶ **27.** [*M34*] A *randomized adversary* is an adversary algorithm that is allowed to flip
coins as it makes decisions.

   a) Let A be a randomized adversary and let $\Pr(l)$ be the probability that A reaches
     leaf l of a given comparison tree. Show that if $\Pr(l) \leq p$ for all l, the height of the
     comparison tree is $\geq \lg(1/p)$.

   b) Consider the following adversary for the problem of selecting the tth largest of n
     elements, given integer parameters q and r to be selected later:

     A1. Choose a random set T of t elements; all $\binom{n}{t}$ possibilities are equally likely.
       (We will ensure that the $t - 1$ largest elements belong to T.) Let $S =$
       $\{1, \ldots, n\} \setminus T$ be the other elements, and set $S_0 \leftarrow S$, $T_0 \leftarrow T$; S_0 and T_0 will
       represent elements that might become the tth largest.

     A2. While $|T_0| > r$, decide all comparisons $x:y$ as follows: If $x \in S$ and $y \in T$, say
       that $x < y$. If $x \in S$ and $y \in S$, flip a coin to decide, and remove the smaller
       element from S_0 if it was in S_0. If $x \in T$ and $y \in T$, flip a coin to decide, and
       remove the larger element from T_0 if it was in T_0.

     A3. As soon as $|T_0| = r$, partition the elements into three classes P, Q, R as follows:
       If $|S_0| < q$, let $P = S$, $Q = T_0$, $R = T \setminus T_0$. Otherwise, for each $y \in T_0$, let
       $C(y)$ be the elements of S already compared with y, and choose y_0 so that
       $|C(y_0)|$ is minimum. Let $P = (S \setminus S_0) \cup C(y_0)$, $Q = (S_0 \setminus C(y_0)) \cup \{y_0\}$,
       $R = T \setminus \{y_0\}$. Decide all future comparisons $x:y$ by saying that elements of P
       are less than elements of Q, and elements of Q are less than elements of R;
       flip a coin when x and y are in the same class. ∎

     Prove that if $1 \leq r \leq t$ and if $|C(y_0)| \leq q - r$ at the beginning of step A3, each
     leaf is reached with probability $\leq (n + 1 - t)/(2^{n-q}\binom{n}{t})$. *Hint:* Show that at least
     $n - q$ coin flips are made.

   c) Continuing (b), show that we have

$$V_t(n) \geq \min\bigl(n - 1 + (r - 1)(q + 1 - r), \; n - q + \lg(\binom{n}{t}/(n + 1 - t))\bigr),$$

     for all integers q and r.

   d) Establish (14) by choosing q and r.

*5.3.4. Networks for Sorting

In this section we shall study a constrained type of sorting that is particularly
interesting because of its applications and its rich underlying theory. The new
constraint is to insist on an *oblivious* sequence of comparisons, in the sense that
whenever we compare K_i versus K_j the subsequent comparisons for the case
$K_i < K_j$ are exactly the same as for the case $K_i > K_j$, but with i and j
interchanged.

    Figure 43(a) shows a comparison tree in which this homogeneity condition is
satisfied. Notice that every level has the same number of comparisons, so there
are 2^m outcomes after m comparisons have been made. But $n!$ is not a power
of 2; some of the comparisons must therefore be redundant, in the sense that

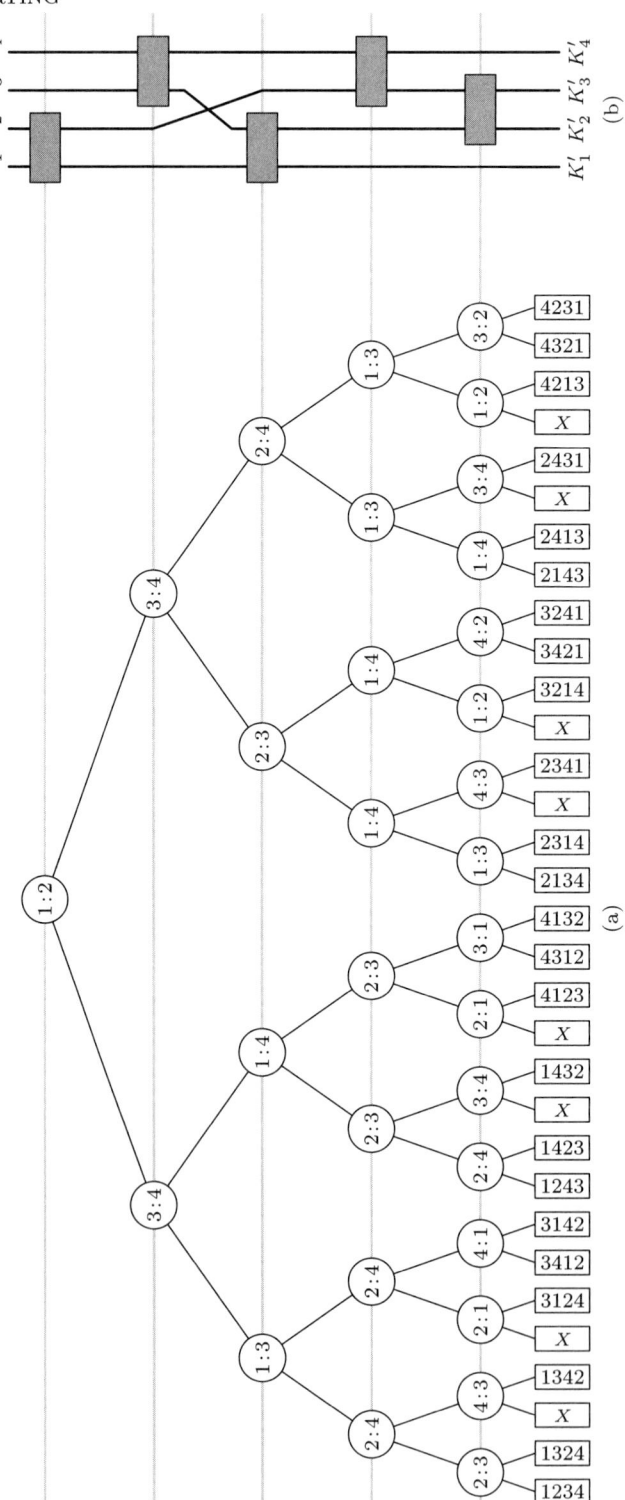

Fig. 43. (a) An oblivious comparison tree. (b) The corresponding network.

one of their subtrees can never arise in practice. In other words, some branches of the tree must make more comparisons than necessary, in order to ensure that all of the corresponding branches of the tree will sort properly.

Since each path from top to bottom of such a tree determines the entire tree, such a sorting scheme is most easily represented as a *network*; see Fig. 43(b). The boxes in such a network represent "comparator modules" that have two inputs (represented as lines coming into the module from above) and two outputs (represented as lines leading downward); the left-hand output is the smaller of the two inputs, and the right-hand output is the larger. At the bottom of the network, K_1' is the smallest of $\{K_1, K_2, K_3, K_4\}$, K_2' the second smallest, etc. It is not difficult to prove that any sorting network corresponds to an oblivious comparison tree in the sense above, and that any oblivious tree corresponds to a network of comparator modules.

Incidentally, we may note that comparator modules are fairly easy to manu-facture, from an engineering point of view. For example, assume that the lines contain binary numbers, where one bit enters each module per unit time, most significant bit first. Each comparator module has three states, and behaves as follows:

	Time t		Time $(t+1)$
State	Inputs	State	Outputs
0	0 0	0	0 0
0	0 1	1	0 1
0	1 0	2	0 1
0	1 1	0	1 1
1	$x\ y$	1	$x\ y$
2	$x\ y$	2	$y\ x$

Initially all modules are in state 0 and are outputting 0 0. A module enters either state 1 or state 2 as soon as its inputs differ. Numbers that begin to be transmitted at the top of Fig. 43(b) at time t will begin to be output at the bottom, in sorted order, at time $t + 3$, if a suitable delay element is attached to the K_1' and K_4' lines.

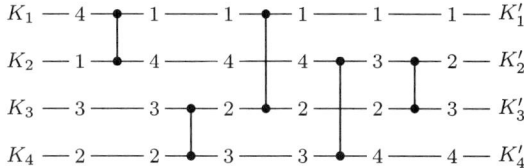

Fig. 44. Another way to represent the network of Fig. 43, as it sorts the sequence of four numbers $\langle 4, 1, 3, 2 \rangle$.

In order to develop the theory of sorting networks it is convenient to repre-sent them in a slightly different way, illustrated in Fig. 44. Here numbers enter at the *left*, and comparator modules are represented by vertical connections between two lines; each comparator causes an interchange of its inputs, if necessary, so that the larger number sinks to the *lower* line after passing the comparator. At the right of the diagram all the numbers are in order from top to bottom.

Our previous studies of optimal sorting have concentrated on minimizing the number of comparisons, with little or no regard for any underlying data movement or for the complexity of the decision structure that may be necessary. In this respect sorting networks have obvious advantages, since the data can be maintained in n locations and the decision structure is "straight line" — there is no need to remember the results of previous comparisons, since the plan is immutably fixed in advance. Another important advantage of sorting networks is that we can usually overlap several of the operations, performing them simultaneously (on a suitable machine). For example, the five steps in Figs. 43 and 44 can be collapsed into three when simultaneous nonoverlapping comparisons are allowed, since the first two and the second two can be combined. We shall exploit this property of sorting networks later in this section. Thus sorting networks can be very useful, although it is not at all obvious that efficient n-element sorting networks can be constructed for large n; we may find that many additional comparisons are needed in order to keep the decision structure oblivious.

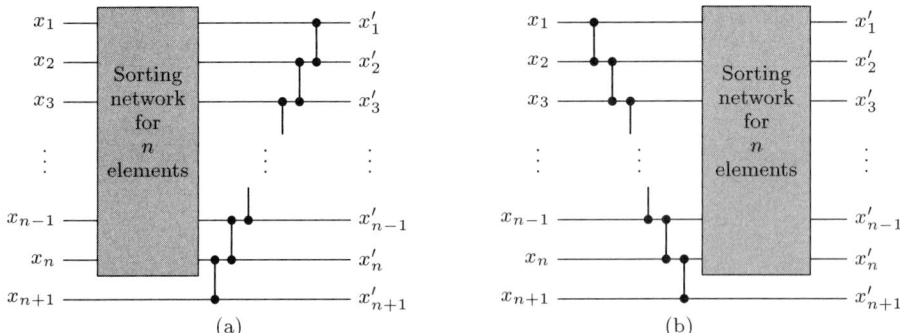

Fig. 45. Making $(n+1)$-sorters from n-sorters: (a) insertion, (b) selection.

There are two simple ways to construct a sorting network for $n+1$ elements when an n-element network is given, using either the principle of *insertion* or the principle of *selection*. Figure 45(a) shows how the $(n+1)$st element can be inserted into its proper place after the first n elements have been sorted; and part (b) of the figure shows how the largest element can be selected before we proceed to sort the remaining ones. Repeated application of Fig. 45(a) gives the network analog of straight insertion sorting (Algorithm 5.2.1S), and repeated application of Fig. 45(b) yields the network analog of the bubble sort (Algorithm 5.2.2B). Figure 46 shows the corresponding six-element networks.

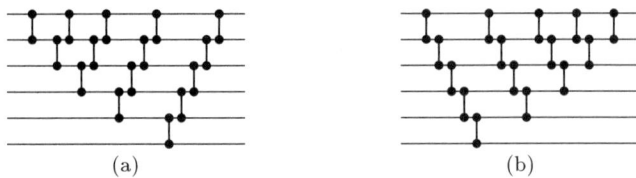

(a)   (b)

Fig. 46. Network analogs of elementary internal sorting schemes, obtained by applying the constructions of Fig. 45 repeatedly: (a) straight insertion, (b) bubble sort.

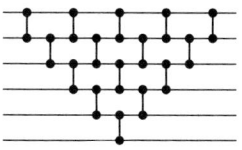

Fig. 47. With parallelism, straight insertion = bubble sort!

Notice that when we collapse either network together to allow simultaneous operations, both methods actually reduce to the same "triangular" $(2n - 3)$-stage procedure (Fig. 47).

It is easy to prove that the network of Figs. 43 and 44 will sort any set of four numbers into order, since the first four comparators route the smallest and the largest elements to the correct places, and the last comparator puts the remaining two elements in order. But it is not always so easy to tell whether or not a given network will sort all possible input sequences; for example, both

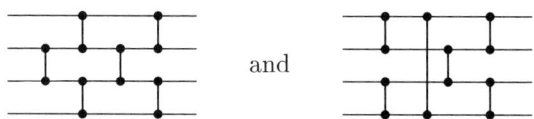

are valid 4-element sorting networks, but the proofs of their validity are not trivial. It would be sufficient to test each n-element network on all $n!$ permutations of n distinct numbers, but in fact we can get by with far fewer tests:

Theorem Z (*Zero-one principle*). *If a network with n input lines sorts all 2^n sequences of 0s and 1s into nondecreasing order, it will sort any arbitrary sequence of n numbers into nondecreasing order.*

Proof. (This is a special case of Bouricius's theorem, exercise 5.3.1–12.) If $f(x)$ is any monotonic function, with $f(x) \le f(y)$ whenever $x \le y$, and if a given network transforms $\langle x_1, \dots, x_n \rangle$ into $\langle y_1, \dots, y_n \rangle$, then it is easy to see that the network will transform $\langle f(x_1), \dots, f(x_n) \rangle$ into $\langle f(y_1), \dots, f(y_n) \rangle$. If $y_i > y_{i+1}$ for some i, consider the monotonic function f that takes all numbers $< y_i$ into 0 and all numbers $\ge y_i$ into 1; this defines a sequence $\langle f(x_1), \dots, f(x_n) \rangle$ of 0s and 1s that is not sorted by the network. Hence if all 0–1 sequences are sorted, we have $y_i \le y_{i+1}$ for $1 \le i < n$. ∎

The zero-one principle is quite helpful in the construction of sorting networks. As a nontrivial example, we can derive a generalized version of Batcher's "merge exchange" sort (Algorithm 5.2.2M). The idea is to sort $m+n$ elements by (i) sorting the first m and the last n independently, then (ii) applying an (m, n)-*merging network* to the result. An (m, n)-merging network can be constructed inductively as follows:

a) If $m = 0$ or $n = 0$, the network is empty. If $m = n = 1$, the network is a single comparator module.

b) If $mn > 1$, let the sequences to be merged be $\langle x_1, \dots, x_m \rangle$ and $\langle y_1, \dots, y_n \rangle$. Merge the "odd sequences" $\langle x_1, x_3, \dots, x_{2\lceil m/2 \rceil - 1} \rangle$ and $\langle y_1, y_3, \dots, y_{2\lceil n/2 \rceil - 1} \rangle$,

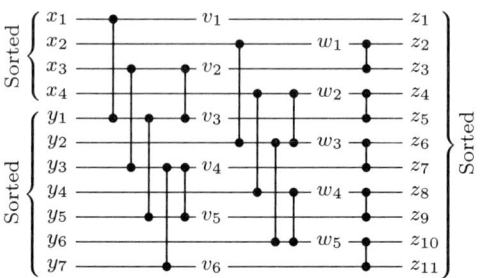

Fig. 48. The odd-even merge, when $m = 4$ and $n = 7$.

obtaining the sorted result $\langle v_1, v_2, \ldots, v_{\lceil m/2 \rceil + \lceil n/2 \rceil} \rangle$; also merge the "even sequences" $\langle x_2, x_4, \ldots, x_{2\lfloor m/2 \rfloor} \rangle$ and $\langle y_2, y_4, \ldots, y_{2\lfloor n/2 \rfloor} \rangle$, obtaining the sorted result $\langle w_1, w_2, \ldots, w_{\lfloor m/2 \rfloor + \lfloor n/2 \rfloor} \rangle$. Finally, apply the comparison-interchange operations

$$w_1 : v_2, \quad w_2 : v_3, \quad w_3 : v_4, \quad \ldots, \quad w_{\lfloor m/2 \rfloor + \lfloor n/2 \rfloor} : v^* \tag{1}$$

to the sequence

$$\langle v_1, w_1, v_2, w_2, v_3, w_3, \ldots, v_{\lfloor m/2 \rfloor + \lfloor n/2 \rfloor}, w_{\lfloor m/2 \rfloor + \lfloor n/2 \rfloor}, v^*, v^{**} \rangle; \tag{2}$$

the result will be sorted(!). Here $v^* = v_{\lfloor m/2 \rfloor + \lfloor n/2 \rfloor + 1}$ does not exist if both m and n are even, and $v^{**} = v_{\lfloor m/2 \rfloor + \lfloor n/2 \rfloor + 2}$ does not exist unless both m and n are odd; the total number of comparator modules indicated in (1) is $\lfloor (m+n-1)/2 \rfloor$.

Batcher's (m, n)-merging network is called the *odd-even merge*. A $(4, 7)$-merge constructed according to these principles is illustrated in Fig. 48.

To prove that this rather strange merging procedure actually works, when $mn > 1$, we use the zero-one principle, testing it on all sequences of 0s and 1s. After the initial m-sort and n-sort, the sequence $\langle x_1, \ldots, x_m \rangle$ will consist of k 0s followed by $m - k$ 1s, and the sequence $\langle y_1, \ldots, y_n \rangle$ will be l 0s followed by $n - l$ 1s, for some k and l. Hence the sequence $\langle v_1, v_2, \ldots \rangle$ will consist of exactly $\lceil k/2 \rceil + \lceil l/2 \rceil$ 0s, followed by 1s; and $\langle w_1, w_2, \ldots \rangle$ will consist of $\lfloor k/2 \rfloor + \lfloor l/2 \rfloor$ 0s, followed by 1s. Now here's the point:

$$\big(\lceil k/2 \rceil + \lceil l/2 \rceil\big) - \big(\lfloor k/2 \rfloor + \lfloor l/2 \rfloor\big) = 0, 1, \text{ or } 2. \tag{3}$$

If this difference is 0 or 1, the sequence (2) is already in order, and if the difference is 2 one of the comparison-interchanges in (1) will fix everything up. This completes the proof. (Note that the zero-one principle reduces the merging problem from a consideration of $\binom{m+n}{m}$ cases to only $(m+1)(n+1)$, represented by the two parameters k and l.)

Let $C(m, n)$ be the number of comparator modules used in the odd-even merge for m and n, not counting the initial m-sort and n-sort; we have

$$C(m, n) = \begin{cases} mn, & \text{if } mn \le 1; \\ C\big(\lceil m/2 \rceil, \lceil n/2 \rceil\big) + C\big(\lfloor m/2 \rfloor, \lfloor n/2 \rfloor\big) + \lfloor (m+n-1)/2 \rfloor, & \text{if } mn > 1. \end{cases} \tag{4}$$

This is not an especially simple function of m and n, in general, but by noting that $C(1, n) = n$ and that

$$C(m + 1, n + 1) - C(m, n)$$
$$= 1 + C\big(\lfloor m/2 \rfloor + 1, \lfloor n/2 \rfloor + 1\big) - C\big(\lfloor m/2 \rfloor, \lfloor n/2 \rfloor\big), \quad \text{if } mn \geq 1,$$

we can derive the relation

$$C(m + 1, n + 1) - C(m, n) = \lfloor \lg m \rfloor + 2 + \lfloor n/2^{\lfloor \lg m \rfloor + 1} \rfloor, \quad \text{if } n \geq m \geq 1. \quad (5)$$

Consequently

$$C(m, m + r) = B(m) + m + R_m(r), \qquad \text{for } m \geq 0 \text{ and } r \geq 0, \qquad (6)$$

where $B(m)$ is the "binary insertion" function $\sum_{k=1}^{m} \lceil \lg k \rceil$ of Eq. 5.3.1–(3), and where $R_m(r)$ denotes the sum of the first m terms of the series

$$\left\lfloor \frac{r+0}{1} \right\rfloor + \left\lfloor \frac{r+1}{2} \right\rfloor + \left\lfloor \frac{r+2}{4} \right\rfloor + \left\lfloor \frac{r+3}{4} \right\rfloor + \left\lfloor \frac{r+4}{8} \right\rfloor + \cdots + \left\lfloor \frac{r+j}{2^{\lfloor \lg j \rfloor + 1}} \right\rfloor + \cdots. \quad (7)$$

In particular, when $r = 0$ we have the important special case

$$C(m, m) = B(m) + m. \qquad (8)$$

Furthermore if $t = \lceil \lg m \rceil$,

$$R_m(r + 2^t) = R_m(r) + 1 \cdot 2^{t-1} + 2 \cdot 2^{t-2} + \cdots + 2^{t-1} \cdot 2^0 + m$$
$$= R_m(r) + m + t \cdot 2^{t-1}.$$

Hence $C(m, n + 2^t) - C(m, n)$ has a simple form, and

$$C(m, n) = \left(\frac{t}{2} + \frac{m}{2^t} \right) n + O(1), \qquad \text{for } m \text{ fixed}, n \to \infty, t = \lceil \lg m \rceil; \quad (9)$$

the $O(1)$ term is an eventually periodic function of n, with period length 2^t. As $n \to \infty$ we have $C(n, n) = n \lg n + O(n)$, by Eq. (8) and exercise 5.3.1–15.

Minimum-comparison networks. Let $\hat{S}(n)$ be the minimum number of comparators needed in a sorting network for n elements; clearly $\hat{S}(n) \geq S(n)$, where $S(n)$ is the minimum number of comparisons needed in a not-necessarily-oblivious sorting procedure (see Section 5.3.1). We have $\hat{S}(4) = 5 = S(4)$, so the new constraint causes no loss of efficiency when $n = 4$; but already when $n = 5$ it turns out that $\hat{S}(5) = 9$ while $S(5) = 7$. The problem of determining $\hat{S}(n)$ seems to be even harder than the problem of determining $S(n)$; even the asymptotic behavior of $\hat{S}(n)$ is known only in a very weak sense.

It is interesting to trace the history of this problem, since each step was forged with some difficulty. Sorting networks were first explored by P. N. Armstrong, R. J. Nelson, and D. G. O'Connor, about 1954 [see *U.S. Patent 3029413*]; in the words of their patent attorney, "By the use of skill, it is possible to design economical n-line sorting switches using a reduced number of two-line sorting switches." After observing that $\hat{S}(n + 1) \leq \hat{S}(n) + n$, they gave special constructions for $4 \leq n \leq 8$, using 5, 9, 12, 18, and 19 comparators, respectively.

Then Nelson worked together with R. C. Bose to show that $\hat{S}(2^n) \leq 3^n - 2^n$ for all n; hence $\hat{S}(n) = O(n^{\lg 3}) = O(n^{1.585})$. Bose and Nelson published their interesting method in *JACM* **9** (1962), 282–296, where they conjectured that it was best possible; T. N. Hibbard [*JACM* **10** (1963), 142–150] found a similar but slightly simpler construction that used the same number of comparisons, thereby reinforcing the conjecture.

In 1964, R. W. Floyd and D. E. Knuth found a new way to approach the problem, leading to an asymptotic bound of the form $\hat{S}(n) = O(n^{1 + c/\sqrt{\log n}})$. Working independently, K. E. Batcher discovered the general merging strategy outlined above. Using a number of comparators defined by the recursion

$$c(1) = 0, \quad c(n) = c(\lceil n/2 \rceil) + c(\lfloor n/2 \rfloor) + C(\lceil n/2 \rceil, \lfloor n/2 \rfloor) \quad \text{for } n \geq 2, \quad (10)$$

he proved (see exercise 5.2.2–14) that

$$c(2^t) = (t^2 - t + 4)2^{t-2} - 1;$$

consequently $\hat{S}(n) = O(n(\log n)^2)$. Neither Floyd and Knuth nor Batcher published their constructions until some time later [*Notices of the Amer. Math. Soc.* **14** (1967), 283; *Proc. AFIPS Spring Joint Computer Conf.* **32** (1968), 307–314].

Several people have found ways to reduce the number of comparators used by Batcher's merge-exchange construction; the following table shows the best upper bounds currently known for $\hat{S}(n)$:

$$
\begin{array}{rcccccccccccccccccc}
n &=& 1 & 2 & 3 & 4 & 5 & 6 & 7 & 8 & 9 & 10 & 11 & 12 & 13 & 14 & 15 & 16 \\
c(n) &=& 0 & 1 & 3 & 5 & 9 & 12 & 16 & 19 & 26 & 31 & 37 & 41 & 48 & 53 & 59 & 63 \\
\hat{S}(n) &\leq& 0 & 1 & 3 & 5 & 9 & 12 & 16 & 19 & 25 & 29 & 35 & 39 & 45 & 51 & 56 & 60
\end{array}
\qquad (11)
$$

Since $\hat{S}(n) < c(n)$ for $8 < n \leq 16$, merge exchange is nonoptimal for all $n > 8$. When $n \leq 8$, merge exchange uses the same number of comparators as the construction of Bose and Nelson. Floyd and Knuth proved in 1964–1966 that the values listed for $\hat{S}(n)$ are *exact* when $n \leq 8$ [see *A Survey of Combinatorial Theory* (North-Holland, 1973), 163–172]; the values of $\hat{S}(n)$ for $n > 8$ are still not known.

Constructions that lead to the values in (11) are shown in Fig. 49. The network for $n = 9$, based on an interesting three-way merge, was found by R. W. Floyd in 1964; its validity can be established by using the general principle described in exercise 27. The network for $n = 10$ was discovered by A. Waksman in 1969, by regarding the inputs as permutations of $\{1, 2, \ldots, 10\}$ and trying to reduce as much as possible the number of values that can appear on each line at a given stage, while maintaining some symmetry.

The network shown for $n = 13$ has quite a different pedigree: Hugues Juillé [*Lecture Notes in Comp. Sci.* **929** (1995), 246–260] used a computer program to construct it, by simulating an evolutionary process of genetic breeding. The network exhibits no obvious rhyme or reason, but it works — and it's shorter than any other construction devised so far by human ratiocination.

A 62-comparator sorting network for 16 elements was found by G. Shapiro in 1969, and this was rather surprising since Batcher's method (63 comparisons)

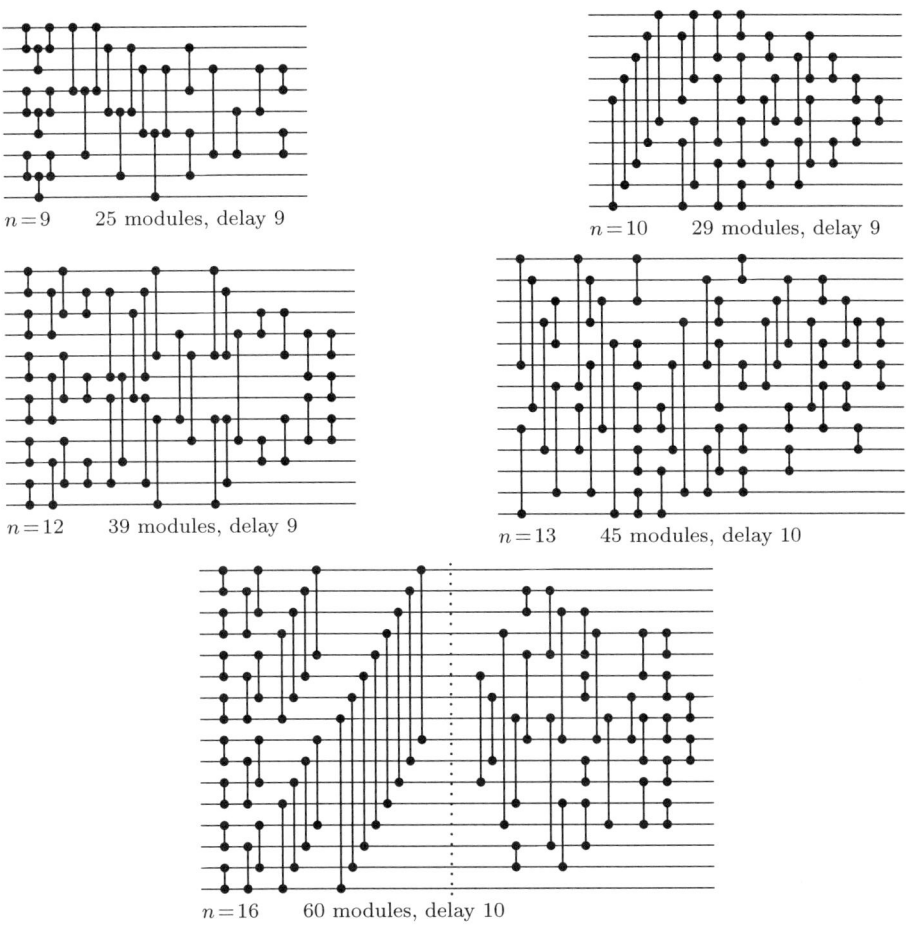

Fig. 49. Efficient sorting networks.

would appear to be at its best when n is a power of 2. Soon after hearing of Shapiro's construction, M. W. Green tripled the amount of surprise by finding the 60-comparison sorter in Fig. 49. The first portion of Green's construction is fairly easy to understand; after the 32 comparison/interchanges to the left of the dotted line have been made, the lines can be labeled with the 16 subsets of $\{a, b, c, d\}$, in such a way that the line labeled s is known to contain a number less than or equal to the contents of the line labeled t whenever s is a subset of t. The state of the sort at this point is discussed further in exercise 32. Comparisons made on subsequent levels of Green's network become increasingly mysterious, however, and as yet nobody has seen how to generalize the construction in order to obtain correspondingly efficient networks for higher values of n.

Shapiro and Green also discovered the network shown for $n = 12$. When $n = 11$, 14, or 15, good networks can be found by removing the bottom line of the network for $n + 1$, together with all comparators touching that line.

The best sorting network currently known for 256 elements, due to D. Van Voorhis, shows that $\hat{S}(256) \leq 3651$, compared to 3839 by Batcher's method. [See R. L. Drysdale and F. H. Young, *SICOMP* **4** (1975), 264–270.] As $n \to \infty$, it turns out in fact that $\hat{S}(n) = O(n \log n)$; this astonishing upper bound was proved by Ajtai, Komlós, and Szemerédi in *Combinatorica* **3** (1983), 1–19. The networks they constructed are not of practical interest, since many comparators were introduced just to save a factor of $\log n$; Batcher's method is much better, unless n exceeds the total memory capacity of all computers on earth! But the theorem of Ajtai, Komlós, and Szemerédi does establish the true asymptotic growth rate of $\hat{S}(n)$, up to a constant factor.

Minimum-time networks. In physical realizations of sorting networks, and on parallel computers, it is possible to do nonoverlapping comparison-exchanges at the same time; therefore it is natural to try to minimize the delay time. A moment's reflection shows that the delay time of a sorting network is equal to the maximum number of comparators in contact with any "path" through the network, if we define a path to consist of any left-to-right route that possibly switches lines at the comparators. We can put a sequence number on each comparator indicating the earliest time it can be executed; this is one higher than the maximum of the sequence numbers of the comparators that occur earlier on its input lines. (See Fig. 50(a); part (b) of the figure shows the same network redrawn so that each comparison is done at the earliest possible moment.)

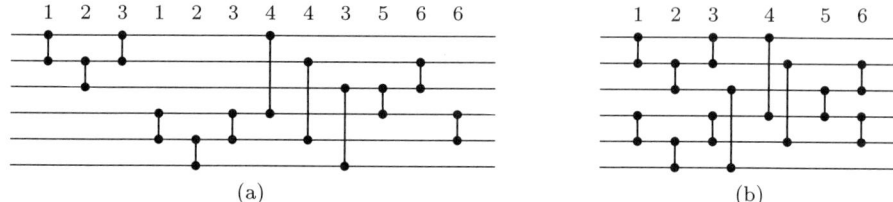

Fig. 50. Doing each comparison at the earliest possible time.

Batcher's odd-even merging network described above takes $T_B(m, n)$ units of time, where $T_B(m, 0) = T_B(0, n) = 0$, $T_B(1, 1) = 1$, and

$$T_B(m, n) = 1 + \max\big(T_B(\lfloor m/2 \rfloor, \lfloor n/2 \rfloor), T_B(\lceil m/2 \rceil, \lceil n/2 \rceil)\big) \quad \text{for } mn \geq 2.$$

We can use these relations to prove that $T_B(m, n+1) \geq T_B(m, n)$, by induction; hence $T_B(m, n) = 1 + T_B(\lceil m/2 \rceil, \lceil n/2 \rceil)$ for $mn \geq 2$, and it follows that

$$T_B(m, n) = 1 + \lceil \lg \max(m, n) \rceil, \qquad \text{for } mn \geq 1. \tag{12}$$

Exercise 5 shows that Batcher's sorting method therefore has a delay time of

$$\binom{1 + \lceil \lg n \rceil}{2}. \tag{13}$$

Let $\hat{T}(n)$ be the minimum achievable delay time in any sorting network for n elements. It is possible to improve some of the networks described above so

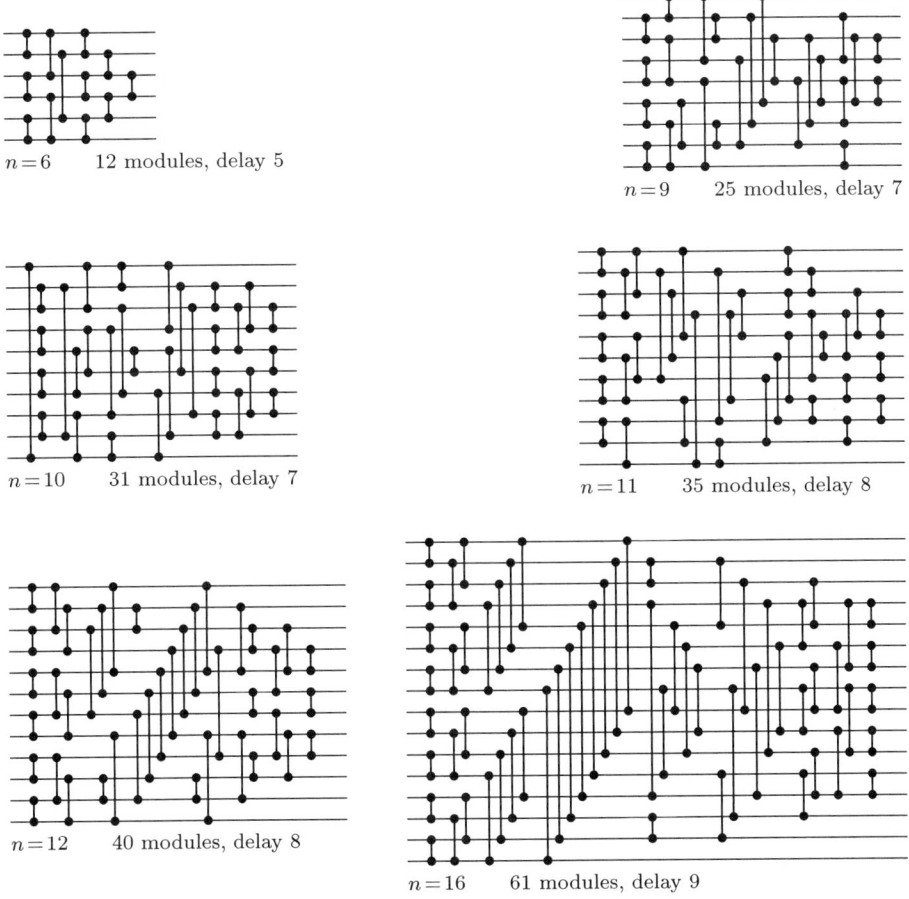

$n=6$ 12 modules, delay 5

$n=9$ 25 modules, delay 7

$n=10$ 31 modules, delay 7

$n=11$ 35 modules, delay 8

$n=12$ 40 modules, delay 8

$n=16$ 61 modules, delay 9

Fig. 51. Sorting networks that are the fastest known, when comparisons are performed in parallel.

that they have smaller delay time but use no more comparators, as shown for $n = 6$, $n = 9$, and $n = 11$ in Fig. 51, and for $n = 10$ in exercise 7. Still smaller delay time can be achieved if we add one or two extra comparator modules, as shown in the remarkable networks for $n = 10$, 12, and 16 in Fig. 51. These constructions yield the following upper bounds on $\hat{T}(n)$ for small n:

$$
\begin{array}{llllllllllllllllll}
n & = & 1 & 2 & 3 & 4 & 5 & 6 & 7 & 8 & 9 & 10 & 11 & 12 & 13 & 14 & 15 & 16 \\
\hat{T}(n) & \leq & 0 & 1 & 3 & 3 & 5 & 5 & 6 & 6 & 7 & 7 & 8 & 8 & 9 & 9 & 9 & 9
\end{array} \tag{14}
$$

For $n \leq 10$ the values given here are known to be exact (see exercise 4). The networks in Fig. 51 merit careful study, because it is by no means obvious that they always sort. Some of these networks were discovered in 1969–1971 by G. Shapiro ($n = 6$, 12) and D. Van Voorhis ($n = 10$, 16); the others were found in 2001 by Loren Schwiebert, using genetic methods ($n = 9$, 11).

Merging networks. Let $\hat{M}(m, n)$ denote the minimum number of comparator modules needed in a network that merges m elements $x_1 \leq \cdots \leq x_m$ with n elements $y_1 \leq \cdots \leq y_n$ to form the sorted sequence $z_1 \leq \cdots \leq z_{m+n}$. At present no merging networks have been discovered that are superior to the odd-even merge described above; hence the function $C(m, n)$ in (6) represents the best upper bound known for $\hat{M}(m, n)$.

R. W. Floyd has discovered an interesting way to find *lower* bounds for this merging problem.

Theorem F. *For all $n \geq 1$, we have $\hat{M}(2n, 2n) \geq 2\hat{M}(n, n) + n$.*

Proof. Consider a network with $\hat{M}(2n, 2n)$ comparator modules, capable of sorting all input sequences $\langle z_1, \ldots, z_{4n} \rangle$ such that $z_1 \leq z_3 \leq \cdots \leq z_{4n-1}$ and $z_2 \leq z_4 \leq \cdots \leq z_{4n}$. We may assume that each module replaces (z_i, z_j) by $\big(\min(z_i, z_j), \max(z_i, z_j)\big)$, for some $i < j$ (see exercise 16). The comparators can therefore be divided into three classes:

a) $i \leq 2n$ and $j \leq 2n$.

b) $i > 2n$ and $j > 2n$.

c) $i \leq 2n$ and $j > 2n$.

Class (a) must contain at least $\hat{M}(n, n)$ comparators, since $z_{2n+1}, z_{2n+2}, \ldots, z_{4n}$ may be already in their final position when the merge starts; similarly, there are at least $\hat{M}(n, n)$ comparators in class (b). Furthermore the input sequence $\langle 0, 1, 0, 1, \ldots, 0, 1 \rangle$ shows that class (c) contains at least n comparators, since n zeros must move from $\{z_{2n+1}, \ldots, z_{4n}\}$ to $\{z_1, \ldots, z_{2n}\}$. ▮

Repeated use of Theorem F proves that $\hat{M}(2^m, 2^m) \geq \frac{1}{2}(m + 2)2^m$; hence $\hat{M}(n, n) \geq \frac{1}{2}n \lg n + O(n)$. We know from Theorem 5.3.2M that merging *without* the network restriction requires only $M(n, n) = 2n - 1$ comparisons; hence we have proved that merging with networks is intrinsically harder than merging in general.

The odd-even merge shows that

$$\hat{M}(m, n) \leq C(m, n) = \tfrac{1}{2}(m + n) \lg \min(m, n) + O(m + n).$$

P. B. Miltersen, M. Paterson, and J. Tarui [*JACM* **43** (1996), 147–165] have improved Theorem F by establishing the lower bound

$$\hat{M}(m, n) \geq \tfrac{1}{2}\big((m + n)\lg(m + 1) - m/\ln 2\big) \qquad \text{for } 1 \leq m \leq n.$$

Consequently $\hat{M}(m, n) = \frac{1}{2}(m + n) \lg \min(m, n) + O(m + n)$.

The exact formula $\hat{M}(2, n) = C(2, n) = \lceil \frac{3}{2}n \rceil$ has been proved by A. C. Yao and F. F. Yao [*JACM* **23** (1976), 566–571]. The value of $\hat{M}(m, n)$ is also known to equal $C(m, n)$ for $m = n \leq 5$; see exercise 9.

Bitonic sorting. When simultaneous comparisons are allowed, we have seen in Eq. (12) that the odd-even merge uses $\lceil \lg(2n) \rceil$ units of delay time, when $1 \leq m \leq n$. Batcher has devised another type of network for merging, called a

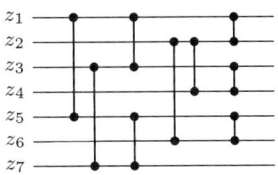

Fig. 52. Batcher's bitonic sorter of order 7.

bitonic sorter, which lowers the delay time to $\lceil \lg(m+n) \rceil$ although it requires more comparator modules. [See *U.S. Patent 3428946* (1969).]

Let us say that a sequence $\langle z_1, \ldots, z_p \rangle$ of p numbers is *bitonic* if $z_1 \geq \cdots \geq z_k \leq \cdots \leq z_p$ for some k, $1 \leq k \leq p$. (Compare this with the ordinary definition of "monotonic" sequences.) A bitonic sorter of order p is a comparator network that is capable of sorting any bitonic sequence of length p into nondecreasing order. The problem of merging $x_1 \leq \cdots \leq x_m$ with $y_1 \leq \cdots \leq y_n$ is a special case of the bitonic sorting problem, since merging can be done by applying a bitonic sorter of order $m+n$ to the sequence $\langle x_m, \ldots, x_1, y_1, \ldots, y_n \rangle$.

Notice that when a sequence $\langle z_1, \ldots, z_p \rangle$ is bitonic, so are all of its sub-sequences. Shortly after Batcher discovered the odd-even merging networks, he observed that we can construct a bitonic sorter of order p in an analogous way, by first sorting the bitonic subsequences $\langle z_1, z_3, z_5, \ldots \rangle$ and $\langle z_2, z_4, z_6, \ldots \rangle$ independently, then comparing and interchanging $z_1 : z_2$, $z_3 : z_4$, $\ldots$. (See exercise 10 for a proof.) If $C'(p)$ is the corresponding number of comparator modules, we have

$$C'(p) = C'\big(\lceil p/2 \rceil\big) + C'\big(\lfloor p/2 \rfloor\big) + \lfloor p/2 \rfloor, \qquad \text{for } p \geq 2; \qquad (15)$$

and the delay time is clearly $\lceil \lg p \rceil$. Figure 52 shows the bitonic sorter of order 7 constructed in this way: It can be used as a $(3,4)$- as well as a $(2,5)$-merging network, with three units of delay; the odd-even merge for $m = 2$ and $n = 5$ saves one comparator but adds one more level of delay.

Batcher's bitonic sorter of order 2^t is particularly interesting; it consists of t levels of 2^{t-1} comparators each. If we number the input lines $z_0, z_1, \ldots, z_{2^t-1}$, element z_i is compared to z_j on level l if and only if i and j differ only in the lth most significant bit of their binary representations. This simple structure leads to parallel sorting networks that are as fast as merge exchange, Algorithm 5.2.2M, but considerably easier to implement. (See exercises 11 and 13.)

Bitonic merging is optimum, in the sense that no parallel merging method based on simultaneous disjoint comparisons can sort in fewer than $\lceil \lg(m+n) \rceil$ stages, whether it works obliviously or not. (See exercise 46.) Another way to achieve this optimum time, with fewer comparisons but a slightly more complicated control logic, is discussed in exercise 57.

When $1 \leq m \leq n$, the nth smallest output of an (m,n)-merging network depends on $2m + [m < n]$ of the inputs (see exercise 29). If it can be computed by comparators with l levels of delay, it involves at most 2^l of the inputs; hence $2^l \geq 2m + [m < n]$, and $l \geq \lceil \lg(2m + [m < n]) \rceil$. Batcher has shown [Report GER-14122 (Akron, Ohio: Goodyear Aerospace Corporation, 1968)] that this

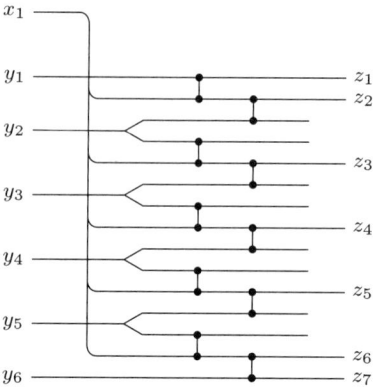

Fig. 53. Merging one item with six others, with multiple fanout, in order to achieve the minimum possible delay time.

minimum delay time is achievable if we allow "multiple fanout" in the network, namely the splitting of lines so that the same number is fed to many modules at once. For example, one of his networks, capable of merging one item with n others after only two levels of delay, is illustrated for $n = 6$ in Fig. 53. Of course, networks with multiple fanout do not conform to our conventions, and it is fairly easy to see that any $(1, n)$-merging network without multiple fanout must have a delay time of $\lg(n + 1)$ or more. (See exercise 45.)

Selection networks. We can also use networks to approach the problem of Section 5.3.3. Let $\hat{U}_t(n)$ denote the minimum number of comparators required in a network that moves the t largest of n distinct inputs into t specified output lines; the numbers are allowed to appear in any order on these output lines. Let $\hat{V}_t(n)$ denote the minimum number of comparators required to move the tth largest of n distinct inputs into a specified output line; and let $\hat{W}_t(n)$ denote the minimum number of comparators required to move the t largest of n distinct inputs into t specified output lines in nondecreasing order. It is not difficult to deduce (see exercise 17) that

$$\hat{U}_t(n) \le \hat{V}_t(n) \le \hat{W}_t(n). \tag{16}$$

Suppose first that we have $2t$ elements $\langle x_1, \ldots, x_{2t} \rangle$ and we wish to select the largest t. V. E. Alekseev [*Kibernetika* **5**, 5 (1969), 99–103] has observed that we can do the job by first sorting $\langle x_1, \ldots, x_t \rangle$ and $\langle x_{t+1}, \ldots, x_{2t} \rangle$, then comparing and interchanging

$$x_1 : x_{2t}, \qquad x_2 : x_{2t-1}, \qquad \ldots, \qquad x_t : x_{t+1}. \tag{17}$$

Since none of these pairs can contain more than one of the largest t elements (why?), Alekseev's procedure must select the largest t elements.

If we want to select the t largest of nt elements, we can apply Alekseev's procedure $n - 1$ times, eliminating t elements each time; hence

$$\hat{U}_t(nt) \le (n - 1)\big(2\hat{S}(t) + t\big). \tag{18}$$

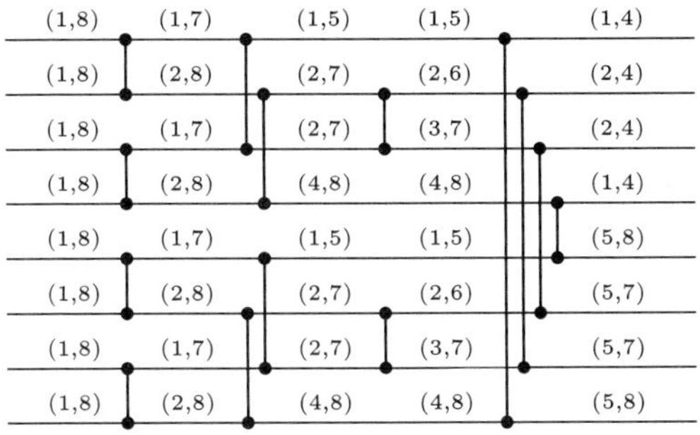

(1,8)	(1,7)	(1,5)	(1,5)	(1,4)
(1,8)	(2,8)	(2,7)	(2,6)	(2,4)
(1,8)	(1,7)	(2,7)	(3,7)	(2,4)
(1,8)	(2,8)	(4,8)	(4,8)	(1,4)
(1,8)	(1,7)	(1,5)	(1,5)	(5,8)
(1,8)	(2,8)	(2,7)	(2,6)	(5,7)
(1,8)	(1,7)	(2,7)	(3,7)	(5,7)
(1,8)	(2,8)	(4,8)	(4,8)	(5,8)

Fig. 54. Separating the largest four from the smallest four. (Numbers on these lines are used in the proof of Theorem A.)

Alekseev also derived an interesting *lower* bound for the selection problem:

Theorem A. $\hat{U}_t(n) \geq (n-t)\lceil \lg(t+1) \rceil$.

Proof. It is most convenient to consider the equivalent problem of selecting the *smallest* t elements. We can attach numbers (l, u) to each line of a comparator network, as shown in Fig. 54, where l and u denote respectively the minimum and maximum values that can appear at that position when the input is a permutation of $\{1, 2, \ldots, n\}$. Let l_i and l_j be the lower bounds on lines i and j before a comparison of $x_i : x_j$, and let l_i' and l_j' be the corresponding lower bounds after the comparison. It is obvious that $l_i' = \min(l_i, l_j)$; exercise 24 proves the (nonobvious) relation

$$l_j' \leq l_i + l_j. \tag{19}$$

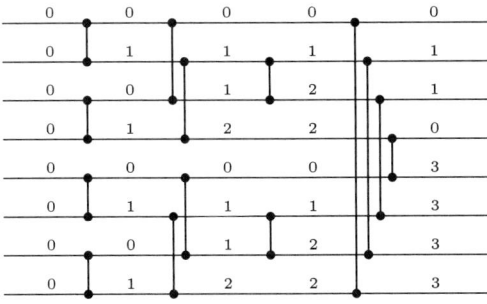

Fig. 55. Another interpretation for the network of Fig. 54.

Now let us reinterpret the network operations in another way (see Fig. 55): All input lines are assumed to contain zero, and each "comparator" now places the smaller of its inputs on the upper line and the larger *plus one* on the lower line. The resulting numbers $\langle m_1, m_2, \ldots, m_n \rangle$ have the property that

$$2^{m_i} \geq l_i \tag{20}$$

Table 1

COMPARISONS NEEDED IN SELECTION NETWORKS $(\hat{U}_t(n),\ \hat{V}_t(n),\ \hat{W}_t(n))$

	$t=1$	$t=2$	$t=3$	$t=4$	$t=5$	$t=6$
$n=1$	$(0,0,0)$					
$n=2$	$(1,1,1)$	$(0,1,1)$				
$n=3$	$(2,2,2)$	$(2,3,3)$	$(0,2,3)$			
$n=4$	$(3,3,3)$	$(4,5,5)$	$(3,5,5)$	$(0,3,5)$		
$n=5$	$(4,4,4)$	$(6,7,7)$	$(6,7,8)$	$(4,7,9)$	$(0,4,9)$	
$n=6$	$(5,5,5)$	$(8,9,9)$	$(8,10,10)$	$(8,10,12)$	$(5,9,12)$	$(0,5,12)$

throughout the network, since this holds initially and it is preserved by each comparator because of (19). Furthermore, the final value of

$$m_1 + m_2 + \cdots + m_n$$

is the total number of comparators in the network, since each comparator adds unity to this sum.

If the network selects the smallest t numbers, $n - t$ of the l_i are $\geq t + 1$; hence $n - t$ of the m_i must be $\geq \lceil \lg(t+1) \rceil$. ∎

The lower bound in Theorem A turns out to be exact when $t = 1$ and when $t = 2$ (see exercise 19). Table 1 gives some values of $\hat{U}_t(n)$, $\hat{V}_t(n)$, and $\hat{W}_t(n)$ for small t and n. Andrew Yao [Ph.D. thesis, U. of Illinois (1975)] determined the asymptotic behavior of $\hat{U}_t(n)$ for fixed t, by showing that $\hat{U}_3(n) = 2n + \lg n + O(1)$ and $\hat{U}_t(n) = n\lceil \lg(t+1) \rceil + O\big((\log n)^{\lfloor \lg t \rfloor}\big)$ as $n \to \infty$; the minimum delay time is $\lg n + \lfloor \lg t \rfloor \lg \lg n + O(\log \log \log n)$. N. Pippenger [*SICOMP* **20** (1991), 878–887] has proved by nonconstructive methods that for any $\epsilon > 0$ there exist selection networks with $\hat{U}_{\lceil n/2 \rceil}(n) \leq (2+\epsilon)n \lg n$, whenever n is sufficiently large (depending on ϵ).

EXERCISES — First Set

Several of the following exercises develop the theory of sorting networks in detail, and it is convenient to introduce some notation. We let $[i:j]$ stand for a comparison/interchange module. A network with n inputs and r comparator modules is written $[i_1:j_1][i_2:j_2]\ldots[i_r:j_r]$, where each of the i's and j's is $\leq n$; we shall call it an *n-network* for short. A network is called *standard* if $i_q < j_q$ for $1 \leq q \leq r$. Thus, for example, Fig. 44 on page 221 depicts a standard 4-network, denoted by the comparator sequence $[1:2][3:4][1:3][2:4][2:3]$.

The text's convention for drawing network diagrams represents only standard networks; all comparators $[i:j]$ are represented by a line from i to j, where $i < j$. When nonstandard networks must be drawn, we can use an *arrow* from i to j, indicating that the larger number goes to the point of the arrow. For example, Fig. 56 illustrates a nonstandard network for 16 elements, whose comparators are $[1:2][4:3][5:6][8:7]\ldots$. Exercise 11 proves that Fig. 56 is a sorting network.

If $x = \langle x_1, \ldots, x_n \rangle$ is an n-vector and α is an n-network, we write $x\alpha$ for the vector of numbers $\langle (x\alpha)_1, \ldots, (x\alpha)_n \rangle$ produced by the network. For brevity, we also let $a \vee b = \max(a,b)$, $a \wedge b = \min(a,b)$, $\bar{a} = 1-a$. Thus $(x[i:j])_i = x_i \wedge x_j$, $(x[i:j])_j = x_i \vee x_j$,

Stage 1 Stage 2   Stage 3   Stage 4

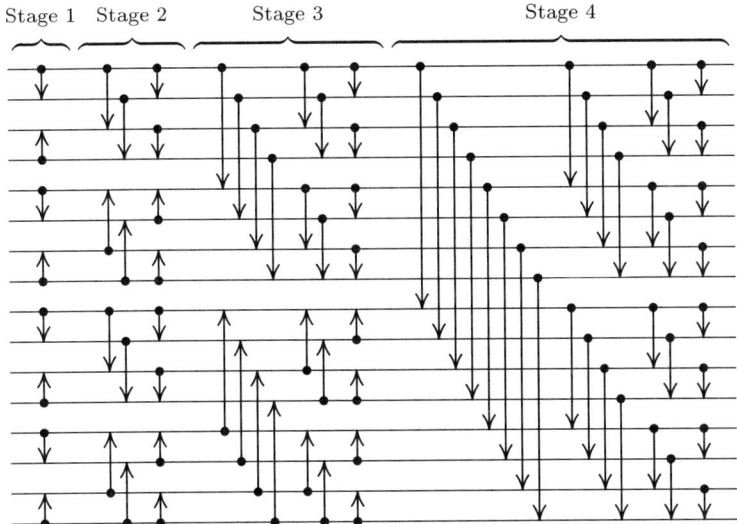

Fig. 56. A nonstandard sorting network based on bitonic sorting.

and $(x[i:j])_k = x_k$ when $i \neq k \neq j$. We say α is a *sorting network* if $(x\alpha)_i \leq (x\alpha)_{i+1}$ for all x and for $1 \leq i < n$.

The symbol $e^{(i)}$ stands for a vector that has 1 in position i, 0 elsewhere; thus $(e^{(i)})_j = \delta_{ij}$. The symbol D_n stands for the set of all 2^n n-place vectors of 0s and 1s, and P_n stands for the set of all $n!$ vectors that are permutations of $\{1, 2, \ldots, n\}$. We write $x \wedge y$ and $x \vee y$ for the vectors $\langle x_1 \wedge y_1, \ldots, x_n \wedge y_n \rangle$ and $\langle x_1 \vee y_1, \ldots, x_n \vee y_n \rangle$, and we write $x \subseteq y$ if $x_i \leq y_i$ for all i. Thus $x \subseteq y$ if and only if $x \vee y = y$ if and only if $x \wedge y = x$. If x and y are in D_n, we say that x *covers* y if $x = (y \vee e^{(i)}) \neq y$ for some i. Finally for all x in D_n we let $\nu(x)$ be the number of 1s in x, and $\zeta(x)$ the number of 0s; thus $\nu(x) + \zeta(x) = n$.

1. [*20*] Draw a network diagram for the odd-even merge when $m = 3$ and $n = 5$.

2. [*22*] Show that V. Pratt's sorting algorithm (exercise 5.2.1–30) leads to a sorting network for n elements that has approximately $(\log_2 n)(\log_3 n)$ levels of delay. Draw the corresponding network for $n = 12$.

3. [*M20*] (K. E. Batcher.) Find a simple relation between $C(m, m-1)$ and $C(m, m)$.

▶ **4.** [*M23*] Prove that $\hat{T}(6) = 5$.

5. [*M16*] Prove that (13) is the delay time associated with the sorting network outlined in (10).

6. [*28*] Let $T(n)$ be the minimum number of stages needed to sort n distinct numbers by making *simultaneous disjoint comparisons* (without necessarily obeying the network constraint); such comparisons can be represented as a node containing a set of pairs $\{i_1 : j_1, i_2 : j_2, \ldots, i_r : j_r\}$ where $i_1, j_1, i_2, j_2, \ldots, i_r, j_r$ are distinct, with 2^r branches below this node for the respective cases

$$\langle K_{i_1} < K_{j_1}, K_{i_2} < K_{j_2}, \ldots, K_{i_r} < K_{j_r} \rangle,$$
$$\langle K_{i_1} > K_{j_1}, K_{i_2} < K_{j_2}, \ldots, K_{i_r} < K_{j_r} \rangle, \qquad \text{etc.}$$

Prove that $T(5) = T(6) = 5$.

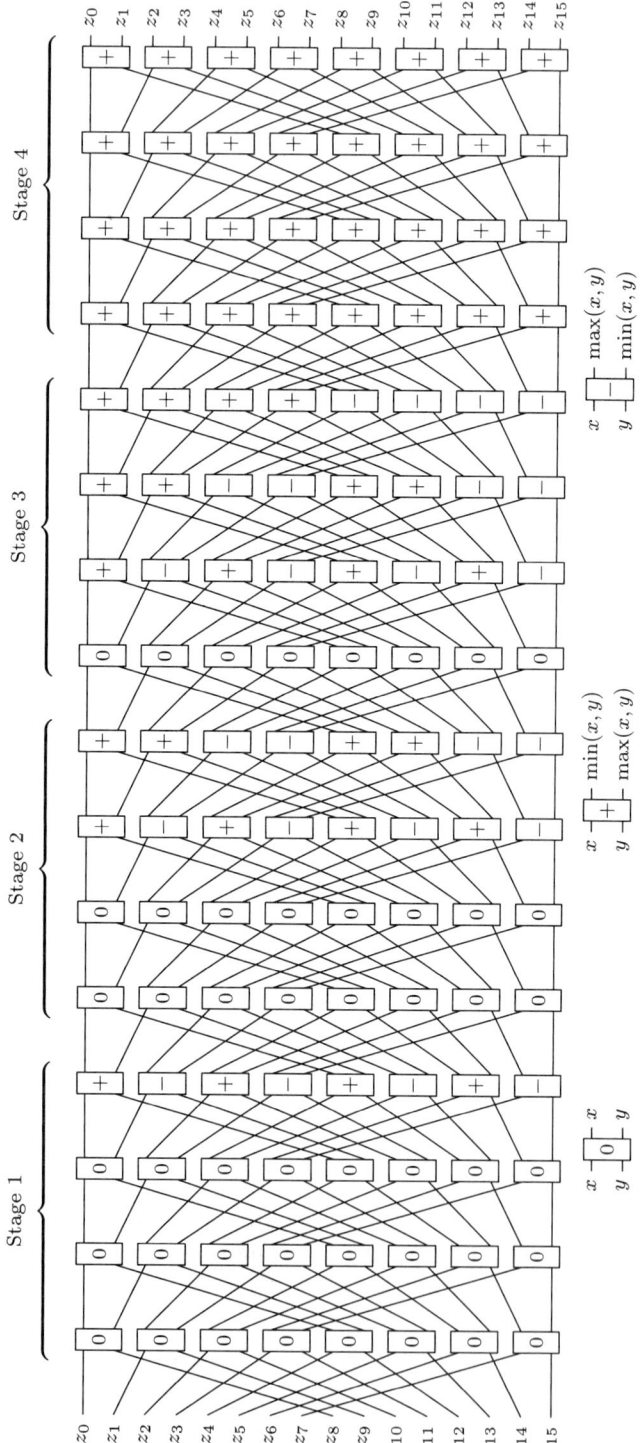

Fig. 57. Sorting 16 elements with perfect shuffles.

7. [*25*] Show that if the final three comparators of the network for $n = 10$ in Fig. 49 are replaced by the "weaker" sequence $[5:6][4:5][6:7]$, the network will still sort.

8. [*M20*] Prove that $\hat{M}(m_1+m_2, n_1+n_2) \geq \hat{M}(m_1, n_1) + \hat{M}(m_2, n_2) + \min(m_1, n_2)$, for $m_1, m_2, n_1, n_2 \geq 0$.

9. [*M25*] (R. W. Floyd.) Prove that $\hat{M}(3,3) = 6$, $\hat{M}(4,4) = 9$, $\hat{M}(5,5) = 13$.

10. [*M22*] Prove that Batcher's bitonic sorter, as defined in the remarks preceding (15), is valid. [*Hint:* It is only necessary to prove that all sequences consisting of k 1s followed by l 0s followed by $n - k - l$ 1s will be sorted.]

11. [*M23*] Prove that Batcher's bitonic sorter of order 2^t will not only sort sequences $\langle z_0, z_1, \ldots, z_{2^t-1} \rangle$ for which $z_0 \geq \cdots \geq z_k \leq \cdots \leq z_{2^t-1}$, it also will sort any sequence for which $z_0 \leq \cdots \leq z_k \geq \cdots \geq z_{2^t-1}$. [As a consequence, the network in Fig. 56 will sort 16 elements, since each stage consists of bitonic sorters or reverse-order bitonic sorters, applied to sequences that have been sorted in opposite directions.]

12. [*M20*] Prove or disprove: If x and y are bitonic sequences of the same length, so are $x \vee y$ and $x \wedge y$.

▶ **13.** [*24*] (H. S. Stone.) Show that a sorting network for 2^t elements can be constructed by following the pattern illustrated for $t = 4$ in Fig. 57. Each of the t^2 steps in this scheme consists of a "perfect shuffle" of the first 2^{t-1} elements with the last 2^{t-1}, followed by simultaneous operations performed on 2^{t-1} pairs of adjacent elements. Each of the latter operations is either "0" (no operation), "+" (a standard comparator module), or "−" (a reverse comparator module). The sorting proceeds in t stages of t steps each; during the last stage all operations are "+". During stage s, for $s < t$, we do $t - s$ steps in which all operations are "0", followed by s steps in which the operations within step q consist alternately of 2^{q-1} "+" followed by 2^{q-1} "−", for $q = 1, 2, \ldots, s$.

[Note that this sorting scheme could be performed by a fairly simple device whose circuitry performs one "shuffle-and-operate" step and feeds the output lines back into the input. The first three steps in Fig. 57 could of course be eliminated; they have been retained only to make the pattern clear. Stone notes that the same pattern "shuffle/operate" occurs in several other algorithms, such as the fast Fourier transform (see 4.6.4–(40)).]

▶ **14.** [*M27*] (V. E. Alekseev.) Let $\alpha = [i_1:j_1] \ldots [i_r:j_r]$ be an n-network; for $1 \leq s \leq r$ we define $\alpha^s = [i'_1:j'_1] \ldots [i'_{s-1}:j'_{s-1}][i_s:j_s] \ldots [i_r:j_r]$, where the i'_k and j'_k are obtained from i_k and j_k by changing i_s to j_s and changing j_s to i_s wherever they appear. For example, if $\alpha = [1:2][3:4][1:3][2:4][2:3]$, then $\alpha^4 = [1:4][3:2][1:3][2:4][2:3]$.

a) Prove that $D_n\alpha = D_n(\alpha^s)$.

b) Prove that $(\alpha^s)^t = (\alpha^t)^s$.

c) A *conjugate* of α is any network of the form $(\ldots((\alpha^{s_1})^{s_2})\ldots)^{s_k}$. Prove that α has at most 2^{r-1} conjugates.

d) Let $g_\alpha(x) = [x \in D_n\alpha]$, and let $f_\alpha(x) = (\bar{x}_{i_1} \vee x_{j_1}) \wedge \cdots \wedge (\bar{x}_{i_r} \vee x_{j_r})$. Prove that $g_\alpha(x) = \bigvee \{f_{\alpha'}(x) \mid \alpha' \text{ is a conjugate of } \alpha\}$.

e) Let G_α be the directed graph with vertices $\{1, \ldots, n\}$ and with arcs $i_s \to j_s$ for $1 \leq s \leq r$. Prove that α is a sorting network if and only if $G_{\alpha'}$ has an oriented path from i to $i + 1$ for $1 \leq i < n$ and for all α' conjugate to α. [This condition is somewhat remarkable, since G_α does not depend on the order of the comparators in α.]

15. [*20*] Find a nonstandard sorting network for four elements that has only five comparator modules.

16. [*M22*] Prove that the following algorithm transforms any sorting network $[i_1\!:\!j_1]$ $\ldots [i_r\!:\!j_r]$ into a standard sorting network of the same length:

> **T1.** Let q be the smallest index such that $i_q > j_q$. If no such index exists, stop.
>
> **T2.** Change all occurrences of i_q to j_q, and all occurrences of j_q to i_q, in all comparators $[i_s\!:\!j_s]$ for $q \leq s \leq r$. Return to T1. ∎

Thus, $[4\!:\!1][3\!:\!2][1\!:\!3][2\!:\!4][1\!:\!2][3\!:\!4]$ is first transformed into $[1\!:\!4][3\!:\!2][4\!:\!3][2\!:\!1][4\!:\!2][3\!:\!1]$, then $[1\!:\!4][2\!:\!3][4\!:\!2][3\!:\!1][4\!:\!3][2\!:\!1]$, then $[1\!:\!4][2\!:\!3][2\!:\!4][3\!:\!1][2\!:\!3][4\!:\!1]$, etc., until the standard network $[1\!:\!4][2\!:\!3][2\!:\!4][1\!:\!3][1\!:\!2][3\!:\!4]$ is obtained.

17. [*M25*] Let D_{tn} be the set of all $\binom{n}{t}$ sequences $\langle x_1, \ldots, x_n \rangle$ of 0s and 1s having exactly t 1s. Show that $\hat{U}_t(n)$ is the minimum number of comparators needed in a network that sorts all the elements of D_{tn}; $\hat{V}_t(n)$ is the minimum number needed to sort $D_{tn} \cup D_{(t-1)n}$; and $\hat{W}_t(n)$ is the minimum number needed to sort $\bigcup_{0 \leq k \leq t} D_{kn}$.

▶ **18.** [*M20*] Prove that a network that finds the median of $2t - 1$ elements requires at least $(t-1)\lceil \lg(t+1) \rceil + \lceil \lg t \rceil$ comparator modules. [*Hint:* See the proof of Theorem A.]

19. [*M22*] Prove that $\hat{U}_2(n) = 2n - 4$ and $\hat{V}_2(n) = 2n - 3$, for all $n \geq 2$.

20. [*28*] Prove that (a) $\hat{V}_3(5) = 7$; (b) $\hat{U}_4(n) \leq 3n - 10$ for $n \geq 6$.

21. [*21*] True or false: Inserting a new standard comparator into any standard sorting network yields another standard sorting network.

22. [*M17*] Let α be any n-network, and let x and y be n-vectors.
a) Prove that $x \subseteq y$ implies that $x\alpha \subseteq y\alpha$.
b) Prove that $x \cdot y \leq (x\alpha) \cdot (y\alpha)$, where $x \cdot y$ denotes the dot product $x_1 y_1 + \cdots + x_n y_n$.

23. [*M18*] Let α be an n-network. Prove that there is a permutation $p \in P_n$ such that $(p\alpha)_i = j$ if and only if there are vectors x and y in D_n such that x covers y, $(x\alpha)_i = 1$, $(y\alpha)_i = 0$, and $\zeta(y) = j$.

▶ **24.** [*M21*] (V. E. Alekseev.) Let α be an n-network, and for $1 \leq k \leq n$ let

$$l_k = \min\{(p\alpha)_k \mid p \in P_n\}, \qquad u_k = \max\{(p\alpha)_k \mid p \in P_n\}$$

denote the lower and upper bounds on the range of values that may appear in line k of the output. Let l_k' and u_k' be defined similarly for the network $\alpha' = \alpha[i\!:\!j]$. Prove that

$$l_i' = l_i \wedge l_j, \qquad l_j' \leq l_i + l_j, \qquad u_i' \geq u_i + u_j - (n+1), \qquad u_j' = u_i \vee u_j.$$

[*Hint:* Given vectors x and y in D_n with $(x\alpha)_i = (y\alpha)_j = 0$, $\zeta(x) = l_i$, and $\zeta(y) = l_j$, find a vector z in D_n with $(z\alpha')_j = 0$, $\zeta(z) \leq l_i + l_j$.]

25. [*M30*] Let l_k and u_k be as defined in exercise 24. Prove that all integers between l_k and u_k inclusive are in the set $\{(p\alpha)_k \mid p \text{ in } P_n\}$.

26. [*M24*] (R. W. Floyd.) Let α be an n-network. Prove that one can determine the set $D_n\alpha = \{x\alpha \mid x \text{ in } D_n\}$ from the set $P_n\alpha = \{p\alpha \mid p \text{ in } P_n\}$; conversely, $P_n\alpha$ can be determined from $D_n\alpha$.

▶ **27.** [*M20*] Let x and y be vectors, and let $x\alpha$ and $y\alpha$ be sorted. Prove that $(x\alpha)_i \leq (y\alpha)_j$ if and only if, for every choice of j elements from y, we can choose i elements from x such that every chosen x element is $\leq$ some chosen y element. Use this principle to prove that *if we sort the rows of any matrix, then sort the columns, the rows will remain in order.*

▶ **28.** [*M20*] The following diagram illustrates the fact that we can systematically write down formulas for the contents of all lines in a sorting network in terms of the inputs:

$$
\begin{array}{llll}
a \;-\!\!\!-\; a \wedge b \;-\!\!\!-\; & (a \wedge b) \wedge (c \wedge d) \;-\!\!\!-\; & (a \wedge b) \wedge (c \wedge d) \\
b \;-\!\!\!-\; a \vee b \;-\!\!\!-\; & (a \vee b) \wedge (c \vee d) \;-\!\!\!-\; & ((a \vee b) \wedge (c \vee d)) \wedge ((a \wedge b) \vee (c \wedge d)) \\
c \;-\!\!\!-\; c \wedge d \;-\!\!\!-\; & (a \wedge b) \vee (c \wedge d) \;-\!\!\!-\; & ((a \vee b) \wedge (c \vee d)) \vee ((a \wedge b) \vee (c \wedge d)) \\
d \;-\!\!\!-\; c \vee d \;-\!\!\!-\; & (a \vee b) \vee (c \vee d) \;-\!\!\!-\; & (a \vee b) \vee (c \vee d)
\end{array}
$$

Using the commutative laws $x \wedge y = y \wedge x$, $x \vee y = y \vee x$, the associative laws $x \wedge (y \wedge z) = (x \wedge y) \wedge z$, $x \vee (y \vee z) = (x \vee y) \vee z$, the distributive laws $x \wedge (y \vee z) = (x \wedge y) \vee (x \wedge z)$, $x \vee (y \wedge z) = (x \vee y) \wedge (x \vee z)$, the absorption laws $x \wedge (x \vee y) = x \vee (x \wedge y) = x$, and the idempotent laws $x \wedge x = x \vee x = x$, we can reduce the formulas at the right of this network to $(a \wedge b \wedge c \wedge d)$, $(a \wedge b \wedge c) \vee (a \wedge b \wedge d) \vee (a \wedge c \wedge d) \vee (b \wedge c \wedge d)$, $(a \wedge b) \vee (a \wedge c) \vee (a \wedge d) \vee (b \wedge c) \vee (b \wedge d) \vee (c \wedge d)$, and $a \vee b \vee c \vee d$, respectively.

Prove that, in general, the tth largest element of $\{x_1, \ldots, x_n\}$ is given by the "elementary symmetric function"

$$
\sigma_t(x_1, \ldots, x_n) = \bigvee \{x_{i_1} \wedge x_{i_2} \wedge \cdots \wedge x_{i_t} \mid 1 \le i_1 < i_2 < \cdots < i_t \le n\}.
$$

[There are $\binom{n}{t}$ terms being $\vee$'d together. Thus the problem of finding minimum-cost sorting networks is equivalent to the problem of computing the elementary symmetric functions with a minimum of "and/or" circuits, where at every stage we are required to replace two quantities ϕ and ψ by $\phi \wedge \psi$ and $\phi \vee \psi$.]

29. [*M20*] Given that $x_1 \le x_2 \le x_3$ and $y_1 \le y_2 \le y_3 \le y_4 \le y_5$, and that $z_1 \le z_2 \le \cdots \le z_8$ is the result of merging the x's with the y's, find formulas for each of the z's in terms of the x's and the y's, using the operators $\wedge$ and $\vee$.

30. [*HM24*] Prove that any formula involving $\wedge$ and $\vee$ and the independent variables $\{x_1, \ldots, x_n\}$ can be reduced using the identities in exercise 28 to a "canonical" form $\tau_1 \vee \tau_2 \vee \cdots \vee \tau_k$, where $k \ge 1$, each τ_i has the form $\bigwedge \{x_j \mid j \text{ in } S_i\}$ where S_i is a subset of $\{1, 2, \ldots, n\}$, and no set S_i is included in S_j for $i \ne j$. Prove also that two such canonical forms are equal for all $x_1, \ldots, x_n$ if and only if they are identical (up to order).

31. [*M24*] (R. Dedekind, 1897.) Let δ_n be the number of distinct canonical forms on $x_1, \ldots, x_n$ in the sense of exercise 30. Thus $\delta_1 = 1$, $\delta_2 = 4$, and $\delta_3 = 18$. What is δ_4?

32. [*M28*] (M. W. Green.) Let $G_1 = \{00, 01, 11\}$, and let G_{t+1} be the set of all strings $\theta\phi\psi\omega$ such that θ, ϕ, ψ, ω have length 2^{t-1} and $\theta\phi$, $\psi\omega$, $\theta\psi$, and $\phi\omega$ are in G_t. Let α be the network consisting of the first four levels of the 16-sorter shown in Fig. 49. Show that $D_{16}\alpha = G_4$, and prove that it has exactly $\delta_4 + 2$ elements. (See exercise 31.)

▶ **33.** [*M22*] Not all δ_n of the functions of $\langle x_1, \ldots, x_n \rangle$ in exercise 31 can appear in comparator networks. In fact, prove that the function $(x_1 \wedge x_2) \vee (x_2 \wedge x_3) \vee (x_3 \wedge x_4)$ cannot appear as an output of any comparator network on $\langle x_1, \ldots, x_n \rangle$.

34. [*23*] Is the following a sorting network?

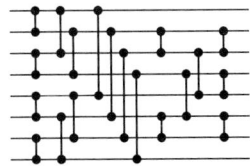

35. [20] Prove that any standard sorting network must contain each of the *adjacent* comparators $[i:i+1]$, for $1 \le i < n$, at least once.

▶ **36.** [22] The network of Fig. 47 involves only adjacent comparisons $[i:i+1]$; let us call such a network *primitive*.

  a) Prove that a primitive sorting network for n elements must have at least $\binom{n}{2}$ comparators. [*Hint:* Consider the inversions of a permutation.]

  b) (R. W. Floyd, 1964.) Let α be a primitive network for n elements, and let x be a vector such that $(x\alpha)_i > (x\alpha)_j$ for some $i < j$. Prove that $(y\alpha)_i > (y\alpha)_j$, where y is the vector $\langle n, n-1, \ldots, 1 \rangle$.

  c) As a consequence of (b), a primitive network is a sorting network if and only if it sorts the single vector $\langle n, n-1, \ldots, 1 \rangle$.

37. [M22] The *odd-even transposition sort* for n numbers, $n \ge 3$, is a network n levels deep with $\frac{1}{2}n(n-1)$ comparators, arranged in a brick-like pattern as shown in Fig. 58. (When n is even, there are two possibilities.) Such a sort is especially easy to implement in hardware, since only two kinds of actions are performed alternatively. Prove that such a network is, in fact, a valid sorting network. [*Hint:* See exercise 36.]

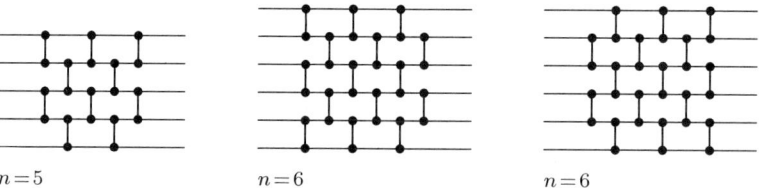

$n=5$ $n=6$ $n=6$

Fig. 58. The odd-even transposition sort.

▶ **38.** [43] Let $N = \binom{n}{2}$. Find a one-to-one correspondence between Young tableaux of shape $(n-1, n-2, \ldots, 1)$ and primitive sorting networks $[i_1:i_1+1] \ldots [i_N:i_N+1]$. [Consequently by Theorem 5.1.4H there are exactly

$$\frac{N!}{1^{n-1}\, 3^{n-2}\, 5^{n-3} \ldots (2n-3)^1}$$

such sorting networks.] *Hint:* Exercise 36(c) shows that primitive networks without redundant comparators correspond to paths from $1\,2\ldots n$ to $n\ldots 2\,1$ in polyhedra like Fig. 1 in Section 5.1.1.

39. [25] Suppose that a primitive comparator network on n lines is known to sort the single input $1\,0\,1\,0\,\ldots\,1\,0$ correctly. (See exercise 36; assume that n is even.) Show that its "middle third," consisting of all comparators that involve only lines $\lceil n/3 \rceil$ through $\lceil 2n/3 \rceil$ inclusive, will sort *all* inputs.

40. [HM44] Comparators $[i_1:i_1+1][i_2:i_2+1] \ldots [i_r:i_r+1]$ are chosen at random, with each value of $i_k \in \{1, 2, \ldots, n-1\}$ equally likely; the process stops when the network contains a bubble sort configuration like that of Fig. 47 as a subnetwork. Prove that $r \le 4n^2 + O(n^{3/2} \log n)$, except with probability $O(n^{-1000})$.

41. [M47] Comparators $[i_1:j_1][i_2:j_2] \ldots [i_r:j_r]$ are chosen at random, with each *irredundant* choice $1 \le i_k < j_k \le n$ equally likely; the process stops when a sorting network has been obtained. Estimate the expected value of r; is it $O(n^{1+\epsilon})$ for all $\epsilon > 0$?

▶ **42.** [25] (D. Van Voorhis.) Prove that $\hat{S}(n) \ge \hat{S}(n-1) + \lceil \lg n \rceil$.

43. [*48*] Find an (m,n)-merging network with fewer than $C(m,n)$ comparators, or prove that no such network exists.

44. [*50*] Find the exact value of $\hat{S}(n)$ for some $n > 8$.

45. [*M20*] Prove that any $(1,n)$-merging network without multiple fanout must have at least $\lceil \lg(n+1) \rceil$ levels of delay.

▶ **46.** [*30*] (M. Aigner.) Show that the minimum number of stages needed to merge m elements with n, using any algorithm that does simultaneous disjoint comparisons as in exercise 6, is at least $\lceil \lg(m+n) \rceil$; hence the bitonic merging network has optimum delay.

47. [*47*] Is the function $T(n)$ of exercise 6 strictly less than $\hat{T}(n)$ for some n?

▶ **48.** [*26*] We can interpret sorting networks in another way, letting each line carry a multiset of m numbers instead of a single number; under this interpretation, the operation $[i\!:\!j]$ replaces x_i and x_j, respectively, by $x_i \wedge x_j$ and $x_i \vee x_j$, the least m and the greatest m of the $2m$ numbers $x_i \uplus x_j$. (For example, the diagram

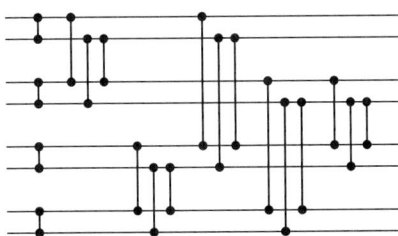

illustrates this interpretation when $m = 2$; each comparator merges its inputs and separates the lower half from the upper half.)

If a and b are multisets of m numbers each, we say that $a \ll b$ if and only if $a \wedge b = a$ (equivalently, $a \vee b = b$; the largest element of a is less than or equal to the smallest of b). Thus $a \wedge b \ll a \vee b$.

Let α be an n-network, and let $x = \langle x_1, \ldots, x_n \rangle$ be a vector in which each x_i is a multiset of m elements. Prove that if $(x\alpha)_i$ is not $\ll (x\alpha)_j$ in the interpretation above, there is a vector y in D_n such that $(y\alpha)_i = 1$ and $(y\alpha)_j = 0$. [Consequently, a sorting network for n elements becomes a sorting network for mn elements if we replace each comparison by a merge network with $\hat{M}(m,m)$ modules. Figure 59 shows an 8-element sorter constructed from a 4-element sorter by using this observation.]

Fig. 59. An 8-sorter constructed from a 4-sorter, by using the merging interpretation.

49. [*M23*] Show that, in the notation of exercise 48, $(x \wedge y) \wedge z = x \wedge (y \wedge z)$ and $(x \vee y) \vee z = x \vee (y \vee z)$; however $(x \vee y) \wedge z$ is *not* always equal to $(x \wedge z) \vee (y \wedge z)$, and $(x \wedge y) \vee (x \wedge z) \vee (y \wedge z)$ does *not* always equal the middle m elements of $x \uplus y \uplus z$. Find a correct formula, in terms of x, y, z and the $\wedge$ and $\vee$ operations, for those middle elements.

50. [*HM46*] Explore the properties of the $\bigwedge$ and $\bigvee$ operations defined in exercise 48. Is it possible to characterize all of the identities in this algebra in some nice way, or to derive them all from a finite set of identities? In this regard, identities such as $x \bigwedge x \bigwedge x = x \bigwedge x$, or $x \bigwedge (x \bigvee (x \bigwedge (x \bigvee y))) = x \bigwedge (x \bigvee y)$, which hold only for $m \leq 2$, are of comparatively little interest; consider only the identities that are true for all m.

▶ **51.** [*M25*] (R. L. Graham.) The comparator $[i:j]$ is called *redundant* in the network $\alpha_1[i:j]\alpha_2$ if either $(x\alpha_1)_i \leq (x\alpha_1)_j$ for all vectors x, or $(x\alpha_1)_i \geq (x\alpha_1)_j$ for all vectors x. Prove that if α is a network with r irredundant comparators, there are at least r distinct ordered pairs (i,j) of distinct indices such that $(x\alpha)_i \leq (x\alpha)_j$ for all vectors x. (Consequently, a network with no redundant comparators contains at most $\binom{n}{2}$ modules.)

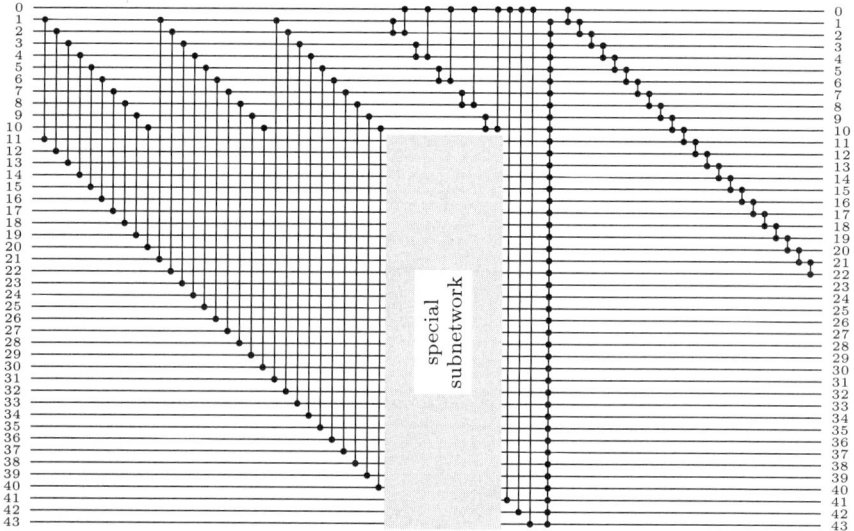

Fig. 60. A family of networks whose ability to sort is difficult to verify, illustrated for $m = 3$ and $n = 5$. (See exercise 52.)

▶ **52.** [*32*] (M. O. Rabin, 1980.) Prove that it is intrinsically difficult to decide in general whether a sequence of comparators defines a sorting network, by considering networks of the form sketched in Fig. 60. It is convenient to number the inputs x_0 to x_N, where $N = 2mn + m + 2n$; the positive integers m and n are parameters. The first comparators are $[j:j+2nk]$ for $1 \leq j \leq 2n$ and $1 \leq k \leq m$. Then we have $[2j-1:2j][0:2j]$ for $1 \leq j \leq n$, in parallel with a special subnetwork that uses only indices $> 2n$. Next we compare $[0:2mn+2n+j]$ for $1 \leq j \leq m$. And finally there is a complete sorting network for $\langle x_1, \ldots, x_N \rangle$, followed by $[0:1][1:2] \ldots [N-t-1:N-t]$, where $t = mn + n + 1$.

a) Describe all inputs $\langle x_0, x_1, \ldots, x_N \rangle$ that are *not* sorted by such a network, in terms of the behavior of the special subnetwork.

b) Given a set of clauses such as $(y_1 \lor y_2 \lor \bar{y}_3) \land (\bar{y}_2 \lor y_3 \lor \bar{y}_4) \land \ldots$, explain how to construct a special subnetwork such that Fig. 60 sorts all inputs if and only if the clauses are unsatisfiable. [Hence the task of deciding whether a comparator sequence forms a sorting network is co-NP-complete, in the sense of Section 7.9.]

53. [*30*] (*Periodic sorting networks.*) The following two 16-networks illustrate general recursive constructions of t-level networks for $n = 2^t$ in the case $t = 4$:

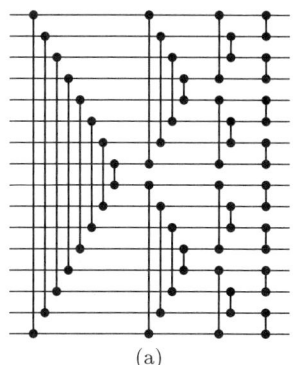 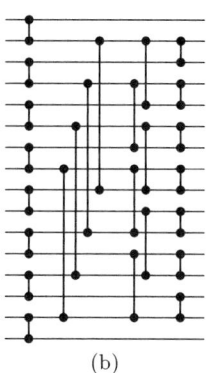

(a)   (b)

If we number the input lines from 0 to $2^t - 1$, the lth level in case (a) has comparators $[i\!:\!j]$ where $i \bmod 2^{t+1-l} < 2^{t-l}$ and $j = i \oplus (2^{t+1-l} - 1)$; there are $t2^{t-1}$ comparators altogether, as in the bitonic merge. In case (b) the first-level comparators are $[2j\!:\!2j\!+\!1]$ for $0 \le j < 2^{t-1}$, and the lth-level comparators for $2 \le l \le t$ are $[2j + 1\!:\!2j + 2^{t+1-l}]$ for $0 \le j < 2^{t-1} - 2^{t-l}$; there are $(t - 1)2^{t-1} + 1$ comparators altogether, as in the odd-even merge.

  If the input numbers are 2^k-ordered in the sense of Theorem 5.2.1H, for some $k \ge 1$, prove that both networks yield outputs that are 2^{k-1}-ordered. Therefore we can sort 2^t numbers by passing them through either network t times. [When t is large, these sorting networks use roughly twice as many comparisons as Algorithm 5.2.2M; but the total delay time is the same as in Fig. 57, and the implementation is simpler because the same network is used repeatedly.]

54. [*42*] Study the properties of sorting networks made from m-sorter modules instead of 2-sorters. (For example, G. Shapiro has constructed the network

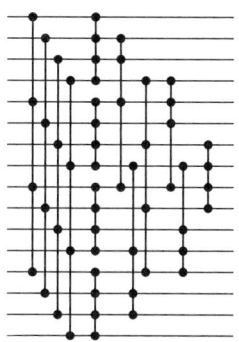

which sorts 16 elements using fourteen 4-sorters. Is this the best possible? Prove that m^2 elements can be sorted with at most 16 levels of m-sorters, when m is sufficiently large.)

55. [*23*] A *permutation network* is a sequence of modules $[i_1\!:\!j_1] \dots [i_r\!:\!j_r]$ where each module $[i\!:\!j]$ can be set by external controls to pass its inputs unchanged or to switch x_i and x_j (irrespective of the values of x_i and x_j), and such that each permutation of the inputs is achievable on the output lines by some setting of the modules. Every sorting network is clearly a permutation network, but the converse is not true: Find a permutation network for five elements that has only eight modules.

▶ **56.** [*25*] Suppose the bit vector $x \in D_n$ is not sorted. Show that there is a standard n-network α_x that fails to sort x, although it sorts all other elements of D_n.

57. [*M35*] The *even-odd merge* is similar to Batcher's odd-even merge, except that when $mn > 2$ it recursively merges the sequence $\langle x_{m \bmod 2+1}, \ldots, x_{m-3}, x_{m-1} \rangle$ with $\langle y_1, y_3, \ldots, y_{2\lceil n/2 \rceil - 1} \rangle$ and $\langle x_{(m+1) \bmod 2+1}, \ldots, x_{m-2}, x_m \rangle$ with $\langle y_2, y_4, \ldots, y_{2\lfloor n/2 \rfloor} \rangle$ before making a set of $\lceil m/2 \rceil + \lceil n/2 \rceil - 1$ comparison-interchanges analogous to (1). Show that the even-odd merge achieves the optimum delay time $\lceil \lg(m+n) \rceil$ of bitonic merging, without making more comparisons than the bitonic method. In fact, prove that the number of comparisons $A(m, n)$ made by even-odd merging satisfies $C(m, n) \leq A(m, n) < \frac{1}{2}(m+n) \lg \min(m, n) + m + \frac{3}{2}n$.

EXERCISES — Second Set

The following exercises deal with several different types of optimality questions related to sorting. The first few problems are based on an interesting "multihead" generalization of the bubble sort, investigated by P. N. Armstrong and R. J. Nelson as early as 1954. [See *U.S. Patents 3029413, 3034102*.] Let $1 = h_1 < h_2 < \cdots < h_m = n$ be an increasing sequence of integers; we shall call it a "head sequence" of length m and span n, and we shall use it to define a special kind of sorting method. The sorting of records $R_1 \ldots R_N$ proceeds in several passes, and each pass consists of $N + n - 1$ steps. On step j, for $j = 1 - n, 2 - n, \ldots, N - 1$, the records $R_{j+h[1]}, R_{j+h[2]}, \ldots, R_{j+h[m]}$ are examined and rearranged if necessary so that their keys are in order. (We say that $R_{j+h[1]}, \ldots, R_{j+h[m]}$ are "under the read-write heads." When $j + h[k]$ is < 1 or $> N$, record $R_{j+h[k]}$ is left out of consideration; in effect, the keys $K_0, K_{-1}, K_{-2}, \ldots$ are treated as $-\infty$ and $K_{N+1}, K_{N+2}, \ldots$ are treated as $+\infty$. Therefore step j is actually trivial when $j \leq -h[m-1]$ or $j > N - h[2]$.)

For example, the following table shows one pass of a sort when $m = 3$, $N = 9$, and $h_1 = 1$, $h_2 = 2$, $h_3 = 4$:

	K_{-2}	K_{-1}	K_0	K_1	K_2	K_3	K_4	K_5	K_6	K_7	K_8	K_9	K_{10}	K_{11}	K_{12}
$j = -3$	—	—	3	1	4	5	9	2	6	8	7				
$j = -2$		—	—	3	1	4	5	9	2	6	8	7			
$j = -1$			—	3	1	4	5	9	2	6	8	7			
$j = 0$				1	3	4	5	9	2	6	8	7			
$j = 1$				1	3	4	5	9	2	6	8	7			
$j = 2$				1	3	2	4	9	5	6	8	7			
$j = 3$				1	3	2	4	6	5	9	8	7			
$j = 4$				1	3	2	4	5	6	9	8	7			
$j = 5$				1	3	2	4	5	6	7	8	9			
$j = 6$				1	3	2	4	5	6	7	8	9	—		
$j = 7$				1	3	2	4	5	6	7	8	9	—		
$j = 8$				1	3	2	4	5	6	7	8	9	—	—	

When $m = 2$, $h_1 = 1$, and $h_2 = 2$, this multihead method reduces to the bubble sort (Algorithm 5.2.2B).

58. [*21*] (James Dugundji.) Prove that if $h[k+1] = h[k] + 1$ for some k, $1 \le k < m$, the multihead sorter defined above will eventually sort any input file in a finite number of passes. But if $h[k+1] \ge h[k] + 2$ for $1 \le k < m$, the input might *never* become sorted.

▶ **59.** [*30*] (Armstrong and Nelson.) Given that $h[k+1] \le h[k] + k$ for $1 \le k < m$, and $N \ge n - 1$, prove that the largest $n - 1$ elements always move to their final destination on the first pass. [*Hint:* Use the zero-one principle; when sorting 0s and 1s, with fewer than n 1s, prove that it is impossible to have all heads sensing a 1 unless all 0s lie to the left of the heads.]

Prove that sorting will be complete in at most $\lceil (N-1)/(n-1) \rceil$ passes when the heads satisfy the given conditions. Is there an input file that requires this many passes?

60. [*26*] If $n = N$, prove that the first pass can be guaranteed to place the smallest key into position R_1 if and only if $h[k+1] \le 2h[k]$ for $1 \le k < m$.

61. [*34*] (J. Hopcroft.) A "perfect sorter" for N elements is a multihead sorter with $N = n$ that always finishes in one pass. Exercise 59 proves that the sequence $\langle h_1, h_2, h_3, h_4, \ldots, h_m \rangle = \langle 1, 2, 4, 7, \ldots, 1 + \binom{m}{2} \rangle$ gives a perfect sorter for $N = \binom{m}{2} + 1$ elements, using $m = (\sqrt{8N - 7} + 1)/2$ heads. For example, the head sequence $\langle 1, 2, 4, 7, 11, 16, 22 \rangle$ is a perfect sorter for 22 elements.

Prove that, in fact, the head sequence $\langle 1, 2, 4, 7, 11, 16, 23 \rangle$ is a perfect sorter for 23 elements.

62. [*49*] Study the largest N for which m-head perfect sorters exist, given m. Is $N = O(m^2)$?

63. [*23*] (V. Pratt.) When each head h_k is in position 2^{k-1} for $1 \le k \le m$, how many passes are necessary to sort the sequence $z_1 z_2 \ldots z_{2^m-1}$ of 0s and 1s where $z_j = 0$ if and only if j is a power of 2?

64. [*24*] (*Uniform sorting.*) The tree of Fig. 34 in Section 5.3.1 makes the comparison 2:3 in both branches on level 1, and on level 2 it compares 1:3 in each branch unless that comparison would be redundant. In general, we can consider the class of all sorting algorithms whose comparisons are uniform in that way; assuming that the $M = \binom{N}{2}$ pairs $\{(a, b) \mid 1 \le a < b \le N\}$ have been arranged into a sequence

$$(a_1, b_1), (a_2, b_2), \ldots, (a_M, b_M),$$

we can successively make each of the comparisons $K_{a_1} : K_{b_1}$, $K_{a_2} : K_{b_2}$, ... whose outcome is not already known. Each of the $M!$ arrangements of the (a, b) pairs defines a uniform sorting algorithm. The concept of uniform sorting is due to H. L. Beus [*JACM* **17** (1970), 482–495], whose work has suggested the next few exercises.

It is convenient to define uniform sorting formally by means of graph theory. Let G be the directed graph on the vertices $\{1, 2, \ldots, N\}$ having no arcs. For $i = 1, 2, \ldots, M$ we add arcs to G as follows:

Case 1. G contains a path from a_i to b_i. Add the arc $a_i \to b_i$ to G.

Case 2. G contains a path from b_i to a_i. Add the arc $b_i \to a_i$ to G.

Case 3. G contains no path from a_i to b_i or b_i to a_i. Compare $K_{a_i} : K_{b_i}$; then add the arc $a_i \to b_i$ to G if $K_{a_i} \le K_{b_i}$, the arc $b_i \to a_i$ if $K_{a_i} > K_{b_i}$.

We are concerned primarily with the number of key comparisons made by a uniform sorting algorithm, not with the mechanism by which redundant comparisons are actually avoided. Thus the graph G need not be constructed explicitly; it is used here merely to help define the concept of uniform sorting.

We shall also consider *restricted uniform sorting*, in which only paths of length 2 are counted in cases 1, 2, and 3 above. (A restricted uniform sorting algorithm may make some redundant comparisons, but exercise 65 shows that the analysis is somewhat simpler in the restricted case.)

Prove that the restricted uniform algorithm is the same as the uniform algorithm when the sequence of pairs is taken in lexicographic order

$$(1,2)(1,3)(1,4)\ldots(1,N)(2,3)(2,4)\ldots(2,N)\ldots(N-1,N).$$

Show in fact that both algorithms are equivalent to quicksort (Algorithm 5.2.2Q) when the keys are distinct and when quicksort's redundant comparisons are removed as in exercise 5.2.2–24. (Disregard the order in which the comparisons are actually made in quicksort; consider only which pairs of keys are compared.)

65. [*M38*] Given a pair sequence $(a_1, b_1)\ldots(a_M, b_M)$ as in exercise 64, let c_i be the number of pairs (j, k) such that $j < k < i$ and (a_i, b_i), (a_j, b_j), (a_k, b_k) forms a triangle.

  a) Prove that the average number of comparisons made by the restricted uniform sorting algorithm is $\sum_{i=1}^{M} 2/(c_i + 2)$.

  b) Use the results of (a) and exercise 64 to determine the average number of irredundant comparisons performed by quicksort.

  c) The following pair sequence is inspired by (but not equivalent to) merge sorting:

$$(1,2)(3,4)(5,6)\ldots(1,3)(1,4)(2,3)(2,4)(5,7)\ldots(1,5)(1,6)(1,7)(1,8)(2,5)\ldots$$

Does the uniform method based on this sequence do more or fewer comparisons than quicksort, on the average?

66. [*M29*] In the worst case, quicksort does $\binom{N}{2}$ comparisons. Do all restricted uniform sorting algorithms (in the sense of exercise 64) perform $\binom{N}{2}$ comparisons in their worst case?

67. [*M48*] (H. L. Beus.) Does quicksort have the minimum average number of comparisons, over all (restricted) uniform sorting algorithms?

68. [*25*] The Ph.D. thesis "Electronic Data Sorting" by Howard B. Demuth (Stanford University, October 1956) was perhaps the first publication to deal in any detail with questions of computational complexity. Demuth considered several abstract models for sorting devices, and established lower and upper bounds on the mean and maximum execution times achievable with each model. His simplest model, the "circular nonreversible memory" (Fig. 61), is the subject of this exercise.

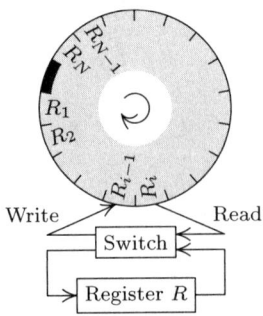

Fig. 61. A device for which the bubble-sort strategy is optimum.

Consider a machine that sorts $R_1 R_2 \ldots R_N$ in a number of passes, where each pass contains the following $N + 1$ steps:

Step 1. Set $R \leftarrow R_1$. (R is an internal machine register.)

Step i, for $1 < i \le N$. Either (i) set $R_{i-1} \leftarrow R$, $R \leftarrow R_i$, or (ii) set $R_{i-1} \leftarrow R_i$, leaving R unchanged.

Step $N+1$. Set $R_N \leftarrow R$.

The problem is to find a way to choose between alternatives (i) and (ii) each time, in order to minimize the number of passes required to sort.

Prove that the "bubble sort" technique is optimum for this model. In other words, show that the strategy that selects alternative (i) whenever $R \le R_i$ and alternative (ii) whenever $R > R_i$ will achieve the minimum number of passes.

They that weave networks shall be confounded.

— *Isaiah 19:9*

5.4. EXTERNAL SORTING

NOW IT IS TIME for us to study the interesting problems that arise when the
number of records to be sorted is larger than our computer can hold in its
high-speed internal memory. External sorting is quite different from internal
sorting, even though the problem in both cases is to sort a given file into
nondecreasing order, since efficient storage accessing on external files is rather
severely limited. The data structures must be arranged so that comparatively
slow peripheral memory devices (tapes, disks, drums, etc.) can quickly cope with
the requirements of the sorting algorithm. Consequently most of the internal
sorting techniques we have studied (insertion, exchange, selection) are virtually
useless for external sorting, and it is necessary to reconsider the whole question.

Suppose, for example, that we are supposed to sort a file of five million
records $R_1 R_2 \ldots R_{5000000}$, and that each record R_i is 20 words long (although
the keys K_i are not necessarily this long). If only one million of these records
will fit in the internal memory of our computer at one time, what shall we do?

One fairly obvious solution is to start by sorting each of the five subfiles
$R_1 \ldots R_{1000000}$, $R_{1000001} \ldots R_{2000000}$, $\ldots$, $R_{4000001} \ldots R_{5000000}$ independently,
then to merge the resulting subfiles together. Fortunately the process of merging
uses only very simple data structures, namely linear lists that are traversed in
a sequential manner as stacks or as queues; hence merging can be done without
difficulty on the least expensive external memory devices.

The process just described — internal sorting followed by external merging —
is very commonly used, and we shall devote most of our study of external sorting
to variations on this theme.

The ascending sequences of records that are produced by the initial internal
sorting phase are often called *strings* in the published literature about sorting;
this terminology is fairly widespread, but it unfortunately conflicts with even
more widespread usage in other branches of computer science, where "strings"
are *arbitrary* sequences of symbols. Our study of permutations has already given
us a perfectly good name for the sorted segments of a file, which are conventionally called ascending runs or simply *runs*. Therefore we shall consistently use
the word "runs" to describe sorted portions of a file. In this way it is possible to
distinguish between "strings of runs" and "runs of strings" without ambiguity.
(Of course, "runs of a program" means something else again; we can't have
everything.)

Let us consider first the process of external sorting when *magnetic tapes*
are used for auxiliary storage. Perhaps the simplest and most appealing way to
merge with tapes is the *balanced two-way merge* following the central idea that
was used in Algorithms 5.2.4N, S, and L. We use four "working tapes" in this
process. During the first phase, ascending runs produced by internal sorting are
placed alternately on Tapes 1 and 2, until the input is exhausted. Then Tapes 1
and 2 are rewound to their beginnings, and we merge the runs from these tapes,
obtaining new runs that are twice as long as the original ones; the new runs
are written alternately on Tapes 3 and 4 as they are being formed. (If Tape
1 contains one more run than Tape 2, an extra "dummy" run of length 0 is

assumed to be present on Tape 2.) Then all tapes are rewound, and the contents of Tapes 3 and 4 are merged into quadruple-length runs recorded alternately on Tapes 1 and 2. The process continues, doubling the length of runs each time, until only one run is left (namely the entire sorted file). If S runs were produced during the internal sorting phase, and if $2^{k-1} < S \leq 2^k$, this balanced two-way merge procedure makes exactly $k = \lceil \lg S \rceil$ merging passes over all the data.

For example, in the situation above where 5000000 records are to be sorted with an internal memory capacity of 1000000, we have $S = 5$. The initial distribution phase of the sorting process places five runs on tape as follows:

$$
\begin{array}{ll}
\text{Tape 1} & R_1 \ldots R_{1000000}; \; R_{2000001} \ldots R_{3000000}; \; R_{4000001} \ldots R_{5000000}. \\
\text{Tape 2} & R_{1000001} \ldots R_{2000000}; \; R_{3000001} \ldots R_{4000000}. \\
\text{Tape 3} & \text{(empty)} \\
\text{Tape 4} & \text{(empty)}
\end{array}
\tag{1}
$$

The first pass of merging then produces longer runs on Tapes 3 and 4, as it reads Tapes 1 and 2, as follows:

$$
\begin{array}{ll}
\text{Tape 3} & R_1 \ldots R_{2000000}; \; R_{4000001} \ldots R_{5000000}. \\
\text{Tape 4} & R_{2000001} \ldots R_{4000000}.
\end{array}
\tag{2}
$$

(A dummy run has implicitly been added at the end of Tape 2, so that the last run $R_{4000001} \ldots R_{5000000}$ on Tape 1 is merely copied onto Tape 3.) After all tapes are rewound, the next pass over the data produces

$$
\begin{array}{ll}
\text{Tape 1} & R_1 \ldots R_{4000000}. \\
\text{Tape 2} & R_{4000001} \ldots R_{5000000}.
\end{array}
\tag{3}
$$

(Again that run $R_{4000001} \ldots R_{5000000}$ was simply copied; but if we had started with 8000000 records, Tape 2 would have contained $R_{4000001} \ldots R_{8000000}$ at this point.) Finally, after another spell of rewinding, $R_1 \ldots R_{5000000}$ is produced on Tape 3, and the sorting is complete.

Balanced merging can easily be generalized to the case of T tapes, for any $T \geq 3$. Choose any number P with $1 \leq P < T$, and divide the T tapes into two "banks," with P tapes on the left bank and $T - P$ on the right. Distribute the initial runs as evenly as possible onto the P tapes in the left bank; then do a P-way merge from the left to the right, followed by a $(T - P)$-way merge from the right to the left, etc., until sorting is complete. The best choice of P usually turns out to be $\lceil T/2 \rceil$ (see exercises 3 and 4).

Balanced two-way merging is the special case $T = 4$, $P = 2$. Let us reconsider the example above using more tapes, taking $T = 6$ and $P = 3$. The initial distribution now gives us

$$
\begin{array}{ll}
\text{Tape 1} & R_1 \ldots R_{1000000}; \; R_{3000001} \ldots R_{4000000}. \\
\text{Tape 2} & R_{1000001} \ldots R_{2000000}; \; R_{4000001} \ldots R_{5000000}. \\
\text{Tape 3} & R_{2000001} \ldots R_{3000000}.
\end{array}
\tag{4}
$$

And the first merging pass produces

  Tape 4 $R_1 \ldots R_{3000000}$.

  Tape 5 $R_{3000001} \ldots R_{5000000}$.   (5)

  Tape 6   (empty)

(A dummy run has been assumed on Tape 3.) The second merging pass completes the job, placing $R_1 \ldots R_{5000000}$ on Tape 1. In this special case $T = 6$ is essentially the same as $T = 5$, since the sixth tape is used only when $S \geq 7$.

Three-way merging requires more computer processing than two-way merging; but this is generally negligible compared to the cost of reading, writing, and rewinding the tapes. We can get a fairly good estimate of the running time by considering only the amount of tape motion. The example in (4) and (5) required only two passes over the data, compared to three passes when $T = 4$, so the merging takes only about two-thirds as long when $T = 6$.

Balanced merging is quite simple, but if we look more closely, we find immediately that it isn't the *best* way to handle the particular cases treated above. Instead of going from (1) to (2) and rewinding all of the tapes, we should have stopped the first merging pass after Tapes 3 and 4 contained $R_1 \ldots R_{2000000}$ and $R_{2000001} \ldots R_{4000000}$, respectively, with Tape 1 poised ready to read the records $R_{4000001} \ldots R_{5000000}$. Then Tapes 2, 3, 4 could be rewound and we could complete the sort by doing a three-way merge onto Tape 2. The total number of records read from tape during this procedure would be only $4000000 + 5000000 = 9000000$, compared to $5000000 + 5000000 + 5000000 = 15000000$ in the balanced scheme. A smart computer would be able to figure this out.

Indeed, when we have five runs and four tapes we can do even better by distributing them as follows:

  Tape 1 $R_1 \ldots R_{1000000}$; $R_{3000001} \ldots R_{4000000}$.

  Tape 2 $R_{1000001} \ldots R_{2000000}$; $R_{4000001} \ldots R_{5000000}$.

  Tape 3 $R_{2000001} \ldots R_{3000000}$.

  Tape 4   (empty)

Then a three-way merge to Tape 4, followed by a rewind of Tapes 3 and 4, followed by a three-way merge to Tape 3, would complete the sort with only $3000000 + 5000000 = 8000000$ records read.

And, of course, if we had six tapes we could put the initial runs on Tapes 1 through 5 and complete the sort in one pass by doing a five-way merge to Tape 6. These considerations indicate that simple balanced merging isn't the best, and it is interesting to look for improved merging patterns.

Subsequent portions of this chapter investigate external sorting more deeply. In Section 5.4.1, we will consider the internal sorting phase that produces the initial runs; of particular interest is the technique of "replacement selection," which takes advantage of the order present in most data to produce long initial runs that actually exceed the internal memory capacity by a significant amount. Section 5.4.1 also discusses a suitable data structure for multiway merging.

The most important merging patterns are discussed in Sections 5.4.2 through 5.4.5. It is convenient to have a rather naïve conception of tape sorting as we learn the characteristics of these patterns, before we come to grips with the harsh realities of real tape drives and real data to be sorted. For example, we may blithely assume (as we did above) that the original input records appear magically during the initial distribution phase; in fact, these input records might well occupy one of our tapes, and they may even fill several tape reels since tapes aren't of infinite length! It is best to ignore such mundane considerations until after an academic understanding of the classical merging patterns has been gained. Then Section 5.4.6 brings the discussion down to earth by discussing real-life constraints that strongly influence the choice of a pattern. Section 5.4.6 compares the basic merging patterns of Sections 5.4.2 through 5.4.5, using a variety of assumptions that arise in practice.

Some other approaches to external sorting, *not* based on merging, are discussed in Sections 5.4.7 and 5.4.8. Finally Section 5.4.9 completes our survey of external sorting by treating the important problem of sorting on bulk memories such as disks and drums.

When this book was first written, magnetic tapes were abundant and disk drives were expensive. But disks became enormously better during the 1980s, and by the late 1990s they had almost completely replaced magnetic tape units on most of the world's computer systems. Therefore the once-crucial topic of patterns for tape merging has become of limited relevance to current needs.

Yet many of the patterns are quite beautiful, and the associated algorithms reflect some of the best research done in computer science during its early years; the techniques are just too nice to be discarded abruptly onto the rubbish heap of history. Indeed, the ways in which these methods blend theory with practice are especially instructive. Therefore merging patterns are discussed carefully and completely below, in what may be their last grand appearance before they accept a final curtain call.

> *For all we know now,*
> *these techniques may well become crucial once again.*
> — PAVEL CURTIS (1997)

EXERCISES

1. [15] The text suggests internal sorting first, followed by external merging. Why don't we do away with the internal sorting phase, simply merging the records into longer and longer runs right from the start?

2. [10] What will the sequence of tape contents be, analogous to (1) through (3), when the example records $R_1 R_2 \ldots R_{5000000}$ are sorted using a 3-tape balanced method with $P = 2$? Compare this to the 4-tape merge; how many passes are made over all the data, after the initial distribution of runs?

3. [20] Show that the balanced $(P, T-P)$-way merge applied to S initial runs takes $2k$ passes, when $P^k(T - P)^{k-1} < S \leq P^k(T - P)^k$; and it takes $2k + 1$ passes, when $P^k(T - P)^k < S \leq P^{k+1}(T - P)^k$.

Give simple formulas for (a) the exact number of passes, as a function of S, when $T = 2P$; and (b) the approximate number of passes, as $S \to \infty$, for general P and T.

4. [HM15] What value of P, for $1 \leq P < T$, makes $P(T - P)$ a maximum?

5.4.1. Multiway Merging and Replacement Selection

In Section 5.2.4, we studied internal sorting methods based on two-way merging, the process of combining two ordered sequences into a single ordered sequence. It is not difficult to extend this to the notion of P-way merging, where P runs of input are combined into a single run of output.

Let's assume that we have been given P ascending runs, that is, sequences of records whose keys are in nondecreasing order. The obvious way to merge them is to look at the first record of each run and to select the record whose key is smallest; this record is transferred to the output and removed from the input, and the process is repeated. At any given time we need to look at only P keys (one from each input run) and select the smallest. If two or more keys are smallest, an arbitrary one is selected.

When P isn't too large, it is convenient to make this selection by simply doing $P - 1$ comparisons to find the smallest of the current keys. But when P is, say, 8 or more, we can save work by using a *selection tree* as described in Section 5.2.3; then only about $\lg P$ comparisons are needed each time, once the tree has been set up.

Consider, for example, the case of four-way merging, with a two-level selection tree:

$$
\textit{Step 1.} \qquad\qquad 087 \begin{cases} 087 \begin{cases} 087\ 503\ \infty \\ 170\ 908\ \infty \end{cases} \\ 154 \begin{cases} 154\ 426\ 653\ \infty \\ 612\ \infty \end{cases} \end{cases}
$$

$$
\textit{Step 2.} \qquad\qquad 087\ 154 \begin{cases} 170 \begin{cases} 503\ \infty \\ 170\ 908\ \infty \end{cases} \\ 154 \begin{cases} 154\ 426\ 653\ \infty \\ 612\ \infty \end{cases} \end{cases}
$$

$$
\textit{Step 3.} \qquad\qquad 087\ 154\ 170 \begin{cases} 170 \begin{cases} 503\ \infty \\ 170\ 908\ \infty \end{cases} \\ 426 \begin{cases} 426\ 653\ \infty \\ 612\ \infty \end{cases} \end{cases}
$$

$$
\vdots
$$

$$
\textit{Step 9.} \quad 087\ 154\ 170\ 426\ 503\ 612\ 653\ 908\ \infty \begin{cases} \infty \begin{cases} \infty \\ \infty \end{cases} \\ \infty \begin{cases} \infty \\ \infty \end{cases} \end{cases}
$$

An additional key "∞" has been placed at the end of each run in this example, so that the merging terminates gracefully. Since external merging generally deals with very long runs, the addition of records with ∞ keys does not add substantially to the length of the data or to the amount of work involved in merging, and such sentinel records frequently serve as a useful way to delimit the runs on a file.

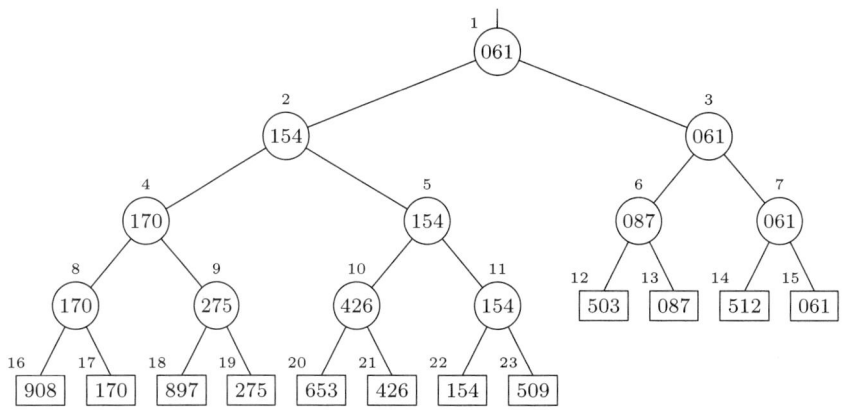

Fig. 62. A tournament to select the smallest key, using a complete binary tree whose nodes are numbered from 1 to 23.

Each step after the first in this process consists of replacing the smallest element by the succeeding element in its run, and changing the corresponding path in the selection tree. Thus the three positions of the tree that contain 087 in Step 1 are changed in Step 2; the three positions containing 154 in Step 2 are changed in Step 3; and so on. The process of replacing one key by another in the selection tree is called *replacement selection*.

We can look at this four-way merge in several ways. From one standpoint it is equivalent to three two-way merges performed concurrently as coroutines; each node in the selection tree represents one of the sequences involved in concurrent merging processes. The selection tree is also essentially operating as a priority queue, with a smallest-in-first-out discipline.

As in Section 5.2.3 we could implement the priority queue by using a heap instead of a selection tree. (The heap would, of course, be arranged so that the *smallest* element appears at the top, instead of the largest, reversing the order of Eq. 5.2.3–(3).) Since a heap does not have a fixed size, we could therefore avoid the use of ∞ keys; merging would be complete when the heap becomes empty. On the other hand, external sorting applications usually deal with comparatively long records and keys, so that the heap is filled with pointers to keys instead of the keys themselves; we shall see below that selection trees can be represented by pointers in such a convenient manner that they are probably superior to heaps in this situation.

A tree of losers. Figure 62 shows the complete binary tree with 12 external (rectangular) nodes and 11 internal (circular) nodes. The external nodes have been filled with keys, and the internal nodes have been filled with the "winners," if the tree is regarded as a tournament to select the smallest key. The smaller numbers above each node show the traditional way to allocate consecutive storage positions for complete binary trees.

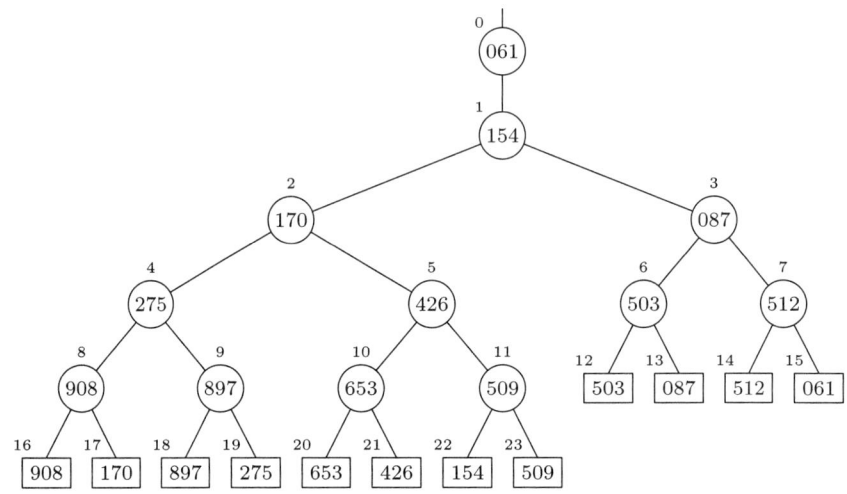

Fig. 63. The same tournament as Fig. 62, but showing the losers instead of the winners; the champion appears at the very top.

When the smallest key, 061, is to be replaced by another key in the selection tree of Fig. 62, we will have to look at the keys 512, 087, and 154, and no other existing keys, in order to determine the new state of the selection tree. Considering the tree as a tournament, these three keys are the losers in the matches played by 061. This suggests that the *loser* of a match should actually be stored in each internal node of the tree, instead of the winner; then the information required for updating the tree will be readily available.

Figure 63 shows the same tree as Fig. 62, but with the losers represented instead of the winners. An extra node number 0 has been appended at the top of the tree, to indicate the champion of the tournament. Each key except the champion is a loser exactly once (see Section 5.3.3), so each key appears just once in an external node and once in an internal node.

In practice, the external nodes at the bottom of Fig. 63 will represent fairly long records stored in computer memory, and the internal nodes will represent pointers to those records. Note that P-way merging calls for exactly P external nodes and P internal nodes, each in consecutive positions of memory, hence several efficient methods of storage allocation suggest themselves. It is not difficult to see how to use a loser-oriented tree for replacement selection; we shall discuss the details later.

Initial runs by replacement selection. The technique of replacement selection can be used also in the *first* phase of external sorting, if we essentially do a P-way merge of the input data with itself! In this case we take P to be quite large, so that the internal memory is essentially filled. When a record is output, it is replaced by the next record from the input. If the new record has a smaller key than the one just output, we cannot include it in the current run; but

Table 1

EXAMPLE OF FOUR-WAY REPLACEMENT SELECTION

Memory contents				Output
503	087	512	061	061
503	087	512	908	087
503	170	512	908	170
503	897	512	908	503
(275)	897	512	908	512
(275)	897	653	908	653
(275)	897	(426)	908	897
(275)	(154)	(426)	908	908
(275)	(154)	(426)	(509)	(end of run)
275	154	426	509	154
275	612	426	509	275
		etc.		

otherwise we can enter it into the selection tree in the usual way and it will form part of the run currently being produced. Thus the runs can contain more than P records each, even though we never have more than P in the selection tree at any time. Table 1 illustrates this process for $P = 4$; parenthesized numbers are waiting for inclusion in the following run.

This important method of forming initial runs was first described by Harold H. Seward [Master's Thesis, Digital Computer Laboratory Report R-232 (Mass. Inst. of Technology, 1954), 29–30], who gave reason to believe that the runs would contain more than $1.5P$ records when applied to random data. A. I. Dumey had also suggested the idea about 1950 in connection with a special sorting device planned by Engineering Research Associates, but he did not publish it. The name "replacement selecting" was coined by E. H. Friend [*JACM* **3** (1956), 154], who remarked that "the expected length of the sequences produced eludes formulation but experiment suggests that $2P$ is a reasonable expectation."

A clever way to show that $2P$ is indeed the expected run length was discovered by E. F. Moore, who compared the situation to a snowplow on a circular track [*U.S. Patent 2983904* (1961), columns 3–4]. Consider the situation shown in Fig. 64: Flakes of snow are falling uniformly on a circular road, and a lone snowplow is continually clearing the snow. Once the snow has been plowed off the road, it disappears from the system. Points on the road may be designated by real numbers x, $0 \le x < 1$; a flake of snow falling at position x represents an input record whose key is x, and the snowplow represents the output of replacement selection. The ground speed of the snowplow is inversely proportional to the height of snow it encounters, and the situation is perfectly balanced so that the total amount of snow on the road at all times is exactly P. A new run is formed in the output whenever the plow passes point 0.

After this system has been in operation for awhile, it is intuitively clear that it will approach a stable situation in which the snowplow runs at constant speed (because of the circular symmetry of the track). This means that the snow is at

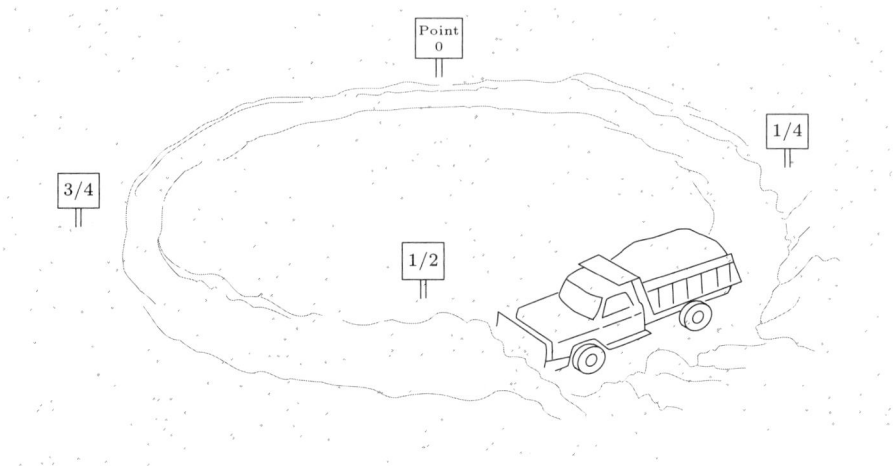

Fig. 64. The perpetual plow on its ceaseless cycle.

constant height when it meets the plow, and the height drops off linearly in front
of the plow as shown in Fig. 65. It follows that the volume of snow removed in
one revolution (namely the run length) is twice the amount present at any one
time (namely P).

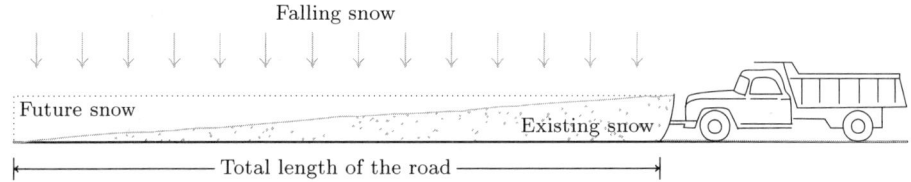

Fig. 65. Cross-section, showing the varying height of snow in front of the plow when
the system is in its steady state.

In many commercial applications the input data is *not* completely random;
it already has a certain amount of existing order. Therefore the runs produced by
replacement selection will tend to contain even more than $2P$ records. We shall
see that the time required for external merge sorting is largely governed by the
number of runs produced by the initial distribution phase, so that replacement
selection becomes especially desirable; other types of internal sorting would produce about twice as many initial runs because of the limitations on memory size.

Let us now consider the process of creating initial runs by replacement
selection in detail. The following algorithm is due to John R. Walters, James
Painter, and Martin Zalk, who used it in a merge-sort program for the Philco
2000 in 1958. It incorporates a rather nice way to initialize the selection tree
and to distinguish records belonging to different runs, as well as to flush out the
last run, with comparatively simple and uniform logic. (The proper handling
of the last run produced by replacement selection turns out to be a bit tricky,

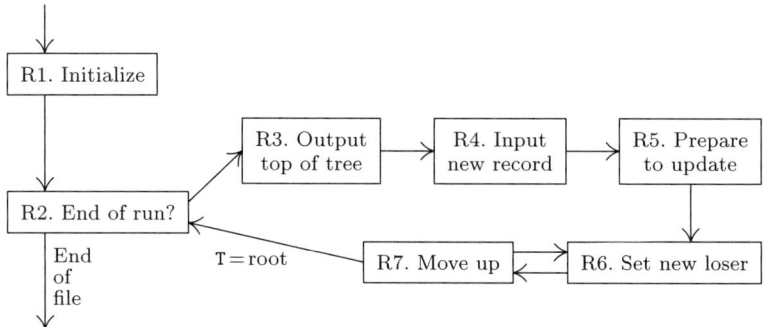

Fig. 66. Making initial runs by replacement selection.

and it has tended to be a stumbling block for programmers.) The principal idea is to consider each key as a pair (S, K), where K is the original key and S is the run number to which this record belongs. When such extended keys are lexicographically ordered, with S as major key and K as minor key, we obtain the output sequence produced by replacement selection.

The algorithm below uses a data structure containing P nodes to represent the selection tree; the jth node $X[j]$ is assumed to contain c words beginning in $\texttt{LOC}(X[j]) = L_0 + cj$, for $0 \le j < P$, and it represents both internal node number j and external node number $P + j$ in Fig. 63. There are several named fields in each node:

> $\texttt{KEY}$ = the key stored in this external node;

> $\texttt{RECORD}$ = the record stored in this external node (including $\texttt{KEY}$ as a subfield);

> $\texttt{LOSER}$ = pointer to the "loser" stored in this internal node;

> $\texttt{RN}$ = run number of the record stored in this external node;

> $\texttt{PE}$ = pointer to internal node above this external node in the tree;

> $\texttt{PI}$ = pointer to internal node above this internal node in the tree.

For example, when $P = 12$, internal node number 5 and external node number 17 of Fig. 63 would both be represented in $X[5]$, by the fields $\texttt{KEY} = 170$, $\texttt{LOSER} = L_0 + 9c$ (the address of external node number 21), $\texttt{PE} = L_0 + 8c$, $\texttt{PI} = L_0 + 2c$.

The $\texttt{PE}$ and $\texttt{PI}$ fields have constant values, so they need not appear explicitly in memory; however, the initial phase of external sorting sometimes has trouble keeping up with the I/O devices, and it might be worthwhile to store these redundant values with the data instead of recomputing them each time.

Algorithm R (*Replacement selection*). This algorithm reads records sequentially from an input file and writes them sequentially onto an output file, producing $\texttt{RMAX}$ runs whose length is P or more (except for the final run). There are $P \ge 2$ nodes, $X[0], \ldots, X[P-1]$, having fields as described above.

R1. [Initialize.] Set $\texttt{RMAX} \leftarrow 0$, $\texttt{RC} \leftarrow 0$, $\texttt{LASTKEY} \leftarrow \infty$, and $\texttt{Q} \leftarrow \texttt{LOC}(X[0])$. (Here $\texttt{RC}$ is the number of the current run and $\texttt{LASTKEY}$ is the key of the

last record output. The initial setting of LASTKEY should be larger than any
possible key; see exercise 8.) For $0 \le j < P$, set the initial contents of $X[j]$
as follows:

$$J \leftarrow \text{LOC}(X[j]); \qquad \text{LOSER(J)} \leftarrow J; \qquad \text{RN(J)} \leftarrow 0;$$

$$\text{PE(J)} \leftarrow \text{LOC}(X[\lfloor (P+j)/2 \rfloor]); \qquad \text{PI(J)} \leftarrow \text{LOC}(X[\lfloor j/2 \rfloor]).$$

(The settings of LOSER(J) and RN(J) are artificial ways to get the tree
initialized by considering a fictitious run number 0 that is never output.
This is tricky; see exercise 10.)

R2. [End of run?] If RN(Q) = RC, go on to step R3. (Otherwise RN(Q) = RC + 1
and we have just completed run number RC; any special actions required by
a merging pattern for subsequent passes of the sort would be done at this
point.) If RC = RMAX, stop; otherwise set RC ← RC + 1.

R3. [Output top of tree.] (Now Q points to the "champion," and RN(Q) = RC.)
If RC ≠ 0, output RECORD(Q) and set LASTKEY ← KEY(Q).

R4. [Input new record.] If the input file is exhausted, set RN(Q) ← RMAX + 1
and go on to step R5. Otherwise set RECORD(Q) to the next record from the
input file. If KEY(Q) < LASTKEY (so that this new record does not belong to
the current run), set RMAX ← RN(Q) ← RC + 1.

R5. [Prepare to update.] (Now Q points to a new record.) Set T ← PE(Q).
(Variable T is a pointer that will move up the tree.)

R6. [Set new loser.] Set L ← LOSER(T). If RN(L) < RN(Q) or if RN(L) = RN(Q)
and KEY(L) < KEY(Q), then set LOSER(T) ← Q and Q ← L. (Variable Q
keeps track of the current winner.)

R7. [Move up.] If T = LOC(X[1]) then go back to R2, otherwise set T ← PI(T)
and return to R6. ∎

Algorithm R speaks of input and output of records one at a time, while in
practice it is best to read and write relatively large blocks of records. Therefore
some input and output buffers are actually present in memory, behind the scenes,
effectively lowering the size of P. We shall illustrate this in Section 5.4.6.

*Delayed reconstitution of runs. A very interesting way to improve on
replacement selection has been suggested by R. J. Dinsmore [*CACM* **8** (1965),
48] using a concept that we shall call *degrees of freedom.* As we have seen,
each block of records on tape within a run is in nondecreasing order, so that its
first element is the lowest and its last element is the highest. In the ordinary
process of replacement selection, the lowest element of each block within a run
is never less than the highest element of the preceding block in that run; this is
"1 degree of freedom." Dinsmore suggests relaxing this condition to "m degrees
of freedom," where the lowest element of each block may be less than the highest
element of the preceding block so long as it is *not less than the highest elements
in m different preceding blocks of the same run.* Records within individual blocks
are ordered, as before, but adjacent blocks need not be in order.

For example, suppose that there are just two records per block; the following sequence of blocks is a run with three degrees of freedom:

$$| \ 08 \ 50 \ | \ 06 \ 90 \ | \ 17 \ 27 \ | \ 42 \ 67 \ | \ 51 \ 89 \ | \qquad (1)$$

A subsequent block that is to be part of the same run must begin with an element not less than the third largest element of $\{50, 90, 27, 67, 89\}$, namely 67. The sequence (1) would not be a run if there were only two degrees of freedom, since 17 is less than both 50 and 90.

A run with m degrees of freedom can be "reconstituted" while it is being read during the next phase of sorting, so that for all practical purposes it is a run in the ordinary sense. We start by reading the first m blocks into m buffers, and doing an m-way merge on them; when one buffer is exhausted, we replace it with the $(m+1)$st block, and so on. In this way we can recover the run as a single sequence, for the first word of every newly read block must be greater than or equal to the last word of the just-exhausted block (lest it be less than the highest elements in m different blocks that precede it). This method of reconstituting the run is essentially like an m-way merge using a single tape unit for all the input blocks! The reconstitution procedure acts as a coroutine that is called upon to deliver one record of the run at a time. We could be reconstituting different runs from different tape units with different degrees of freedom, and merging the resulting runs, all at the same time, in essentially the same way as the four-way merge illustrated at the beginning of this section may be thought of as several two-way merges going on at once.

This ingenious idea is difficult to analyze precisely, but T. O. Espelid has shown how to extend the snowplow analogy to obtain an approximate formula for the behavior [BIT **16** (1976), 133–142]. According to his approximation, which agrees well with empirical tests, the run length will be about

$$2P + (m - 1.5) \left(\frac{2P + (m-2)b}{2P + (2m-3)b} \right) b,$$

when b is the block size and $m \geq 2$. Such an increase may not be enough to justify the added complication; on the other hand, it may be advantageous when there is room for a rather large number of buffers during the second phase of sorting.

*Natural selection.** Another way to increase the run lengths produced by replacement selection has been explored by W. D. Frazer and C. K. Wong [$CACM$ **15** (1972), 910–913]. Their idea is to proceed as in Algorithm R, except that a new record is not placed in the tree when its key is less than LASTKEY; it is output into an external *reservoir* instead, and another new record is read in. This process continues until the reservoir is filled with a certain number of records, P'; then the remainder of the current run is output from the tree, and the reservoir items are used as input for the next run.

The use of a reservoir tends to produce longer runs than replacement selection, because it reroutes the "dead" records that belong to the next run instead of letting them clutter up the tree; but it requires extra time for input and output

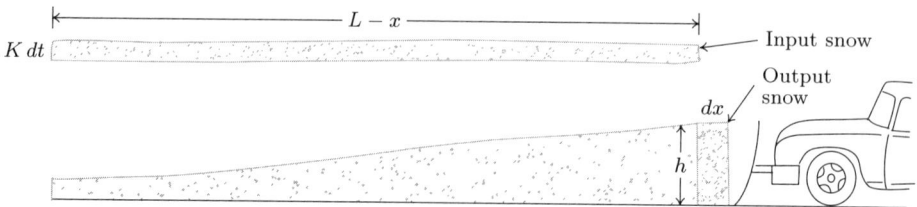

Fig. 67. Equal amounts of snow are input and output; the plow moves dx in time dt.

to and from the reservoir. When $P' > P$ it is possible that some records will be placed into the reservoir twice, but when $P' \leq P$ this will never happen.

Frazer and Wong made extensive empirical tests of their method, noticing that when P is reasonably large (say $P \geq 32$) and $P' = P$ the average run length for random data is approximately given by eP, where $e \approx 2.718$ is the base of natural logarithms. This phenomenon, and the fact that the method is an evolutionary improvement over simple replacement selection, naturally led them to call their method *natural selection.*

The "natural" law for run lengths can be proved by considering the snowplow of Fig. 64 again, and applying elementary calculus. Let L be the length of the track, and let $x(t)$ be the position of the snowplow at time t, for $0 \leq t \leq T$. The reservoir is assumed to be full at time T, when the snow stops temporarily while the plow returns to its starting position (clearing the P units of snow remaining in its path). The situation is the same as before except that the "balance condition" is different; instead of P units of snow on the road at all times, we have P units of snow in front of the plow, and the reservoir (behind the plow) gets up to $P' = P$ units. The snowplow advances by dx during a time interval dt if $h(x,t)\,dx$ records are output, where $h(x,t)$ is the height of the snow at time t and position $x = x(t)$, measured in suitable units; hence $h(x,t) = h(x,0) + Kt$ for all x, where K is the rate of snowfall. Since the number of records in memory stays constant, $h(x,t)\,dx$ is also the number of records that are input *ahead* of the plow, namely $K\,dt\,(L-x)$ (see Fig. 67). Thus

$$\frac{dx}{dt} = \frac{K(L-x)}{h(x,t)}. \tag{2}$$

Fortunately, it turns out that $h(x,t)$ is constant, equal to KT, whenever $x = x(t)$ and $0 \leq t \leq T$, since the snow falls steadily at position $x(t)$ for $T-t$ units of time after the plow passes that point, plus t units of time before it comes back. In other words, the plow sees all snow at the same height on its journey, assuming that a steady state has been reached where each journey is the same. Hence the total amount of snow cleared (the run length) is LKT; and the amount of snow in memory is the amount cleared after time T, namely $KT\bigl(L-x(T)\bigr)$. The solution to (2) such that $x(0) = 0$ is

$$x(t) = L\bigl(1 - e^{-t/T}\bigr); \tag{3}$$

hence $P = LKTe^{-1} = (\text{run length})/e$; and this is what we set out to prove.

Exercises 21 through 23 show that this analysis can be extended to the case of general P'; for example, when $P' = 2P$ the average run length turns out to be $e^\theta (e - \theta)P$, where $\theta = (e - \sqrt{e^2 - 4})/2$, a result that probably wouldn't have been guessed offhand! Table 2 shows the dependence of run length on reservoir size; the usefulness of natural selection in a given computer environment can be estimated by referring to this table. The table entries for reservoir size $< P$ use an improved technique that is discussed in exercise 27.

The ideas of delayed run reconstitution and natural selection can be combined, as discussed by T. C. Ting and Y. W. Wang in *Comp. J.* **20** (1977), 298–301.

Table 2
RUN LENGTHS BY NATURAL SELECTION

Reservoir size	Run length	$k + \theta$	Reservoir size	Run length	$k + \theta$
$0.10000P$	$2.15780P$	0.32071	$0.00000P$	$2.00000P$	0.00000
$0.50000P$	$2.54658P$	0.69952	$0.43428P$	$2.50000P$	0.65348
$1.00000P$	$2.71828P$	1.00000	$1.30432P$	$3.00000P$	1.15881
$2.00000P$	$3.53487P$	1.43867	$1.95014P$	$3.50000P$	1.42106
$3.00000P$	$4.16220P$	1.74773	$2.72294P$	$4.00000P$	1.66862
$4.00000P$	$4.69446P$	2.01212	$4.63853P$	$5.00000P$	2.16714
$5.00000P$	$5.16369P$	2.24938	$21.72222P$	$10.00000P$	4.66667
$10.00000P$	$7.00877P$	3.17122	$5.29143P$	$5.29143P$	2.31329

The quantity $k + \theta$ is defined in exercise 22, or (when $k = 0$) in exercise 27.

*Analysis of replacement selection.** Let us now return to the case of replacement selection without an auxiliary reservoir. The snowplow analogy gives us a fairly good indication of the average length of runs obtained by replacement selection in the steady-state limit, but it is possible to get much more precise information about Algorithm R by applying the facts about runs in permutations that we have studied in Section 5.1.3. For this purpose it is convenient to assume that the input file is an arbitrarily long sequence of independent random real numbers between 0 and 1.

Let

$$g_P(z_1, z_2, \ldots, z_k) = \sum_{l_1, l_2, \ldots, l_k \geq 0} a_P(l_1, l_2, \ldots, l_k) z_1^{l_1} z_2^{l_2} \ldots z_k^{l_k}$$

be the generating function for run lengths produced by P-way replacement selection on such a file, where $a_P(l_1, l_2, \ldots, l_k)$ is the probability that the first run has length l_1, the second has length l_2, ..., the kth has length l_k. The following "independence theorem" is basic, since it reduces the analysis to the case $P = 1$:

Theorem K. $g_P(z_1, z_2, \ldots, z_k) = g_1(z_1, z_2, \ldots, z_k)^P$.

Proof. Let the input keys be $X_1, X_2, X_3, \ldots$. Algorithm R partitions them into P subsequences, according to which external node position they occupy in the tree; the subsequence containing X_n is determined by the values of $X_1, \ldots, X_{n-1}$. Each of these subsequences is therefore an independent sequence of independent random numbers between 0 and 1. Furthermore, the output of replacement selection is precisely what would be obtained by doing a P-way merge on these subsequences; an element belongs to the jth run of a subsequence if and only if it belongs to the jth run produced by replacement selection (since LASTKEY and KEY(Q) belong to the same subsequence in step R4).

In other words, we might just as well assume that Algorithm R is being applied to P independent random input files, and that step R4 reads the next record from the file corresponding to external node Q; in this sense, the algorithm is equivalent to a P-way merge, with "stepdowns" marking the ends of the runs.

Thus the output has runs of lengths $(l_1, \ldots, l_k)$ if and only if the subsequences have runs of respective lengths $(l_{11}, \ldots, l_{1k}), \ldots, (l_{P1}, \ldots, l_{Pk})$, where the l_{ij} are some nonnegative integers satisfying $\sum_{1 \le i \le P} l_{ij} = l_j$ for $1 \le j \le k$. It follows that

$$a_P(l_1, \ldots, l_k) = \sum_{\substack{l_{11} + \cdots + l_{P1} = l_1 \\ \vdots \\ l_{1k} + \cdots + l_{Pk} = l_k}} a_1(l_{11}, \ldots, l_{1k}) \ldots a_1(l_{P1}, \ldots, l_{Pk}),$$

and this is equivalent to the desired result. ∎

We have discussed the average length L_k of the kth run, when $P = 1$, in Section 5.1.3, where the values are tabulated in Table 5.1.3–2. Theorem K implies that the average length of the kth run for general P is P times as long as the average when $P = 1$, namely $L_k P$; and the variance is also P times as large, so the standard deviation of the run length is proportional to $\sqrt{P}$. These results were first derived by B. J. Gassner about 1958.

Thus the first run produced by Algorithm R will be about $(e-1)P \approx 1.718P$ records long, for random data; the second run will be about $(e^2 - 2e)P \approx 1.952P$ records long; the third, about $1.996P$; and subsequent runs will be very close to $2P$ records long until we get to the last two runs (see exercise 14). The standard deviation of most of these run lengths is approximately $\sqrt{(4e - 10)P} \approx 0.934\sqrt{P}$ [*CACM* **6** (1963), 685–688]. Furthermore, exercise 5.1.3–10 shows that the *total* length of the first k runs will be fairly close to $(2k - \frac{1}{3})P$, with a standard deviation of $((\frac{2}{3}k + \frac{2}{9})P)^{1/2}$. The generating functions $g_1(z, z, \ldots, z)$ and $g_1(1, \ldots, 1, z)$ are derived in exercises 5.1.3–9 and 11.

The analysis above has assumed that the input file is infinitely long, but the proof of Theorem K shows that the same probability $a_p(l_1, \ldots, l_k)$ would be obtained in any random input sequence containing at least $l_1 + \cdots + l_k + P$ elements. So the results above are applicable for, say, files of size $N > (2k+1)P$, in view of the small standard deviation.

We will be seeing some applications in which the merging pattern wants some of the runs to be ascending and some to be descending. Since the residue accumulated in memory at the end of an ascending run tends to contain numbers somewhat smaller on the average than random data, a change in the direction of ordering decreases the average length of the runs. Consider, for example, a snowplow that must make a U-turn every time it reaches an end of a straight road; it will go very speedily over the area just plowed. The run lengths when directions are reversed vary between $1.5P$ and $2P$ for random data (see exercise 24).

EXERCISES

▶ **1.** [*10*] What is Step 4, in the example of four-way merging at the beginning of this section?

2. [*12*] What changes would be made to the tree of Fig. 63 if the key 061 were replaced by 612?

3. [*16*] (E. F. Moore.) What output is produced by four-way replacement selection when it is applied to successive words of the following sentence:

> fourscore and seven years ago our fathers brought forth
> on this continent a new nation conceived in liberty and
> dedicated to the proposition that all men are created equal.

(Use ordinary alphabetic order, treating each word as one key.)

4. [*16*] Apply four-way *natural* selection to the sentence in exercise 3, using a reservoir of capacity 4.

5. [*00*] True or false: Replacement selection using a tree works only when P is a power of 2 or the sum of two powers of 2.

6. [*15*] Algorithm R specifies that P must be ≥ 2; what comparatively small changes to the algorithm would make it valid for all $P \geq 1$?

7. [*17*] What does Algorithm R do when there is no input at all?

8. [*20*] Algorithm R makes use of an artificial key "∞" that must be larger than any possible key. Show that the algorithm might fail if an actual key were equal to ∞, and explain how to modify the algorithm in case the implementation of a true ∞ is inconvenient.

▶ **9.** [*23*] How would you modify Algorithm R so that it causes certain specified runs (depending on RC) to be output in ascending order, and others in descending order?

10. [*26*] The initial setting of the LOSER pointers in step R1 usually doesn't correspond to any actual tournament, since external node $P + j$ may not lie in the subtree below internal node j. Explain why Algorithm R works anyway. [*Hint:* Would the algorithm work if {LOSER(LOC($X[0]$)), ..., LOSER(LOC($X[P-1]$))} were set to an *arbitrary* permutation of {LOC($X[0]$), ..., LOC($X[P-1]$)} in step R1?]

11. [*M20*] True or false: The probability that KEY(Q) < LASTKEY in step R4 is approximately 50%, assuming random input.

12. [*M46*] Carry out a detailed analysis of the number of times each portion of Algorithm R is executed; for example, how often does step R6 set LOSER ← Q?

13. [*13*] Why is the second run produced by replacement selection usually longer than the first run?

▶ **14.** [*HM25*] Use the snowplow analogy to estimate the average length of the *last two runs* produced by replacement selection on a long sequence of input data.

15. [20] True or false: The final run produced by replacement selection never contains more than P records. Discuss your answer.

16. [M26] Find a "simple" necessary and sufficient condition that a file $R_1 R_2 \ldots R_N$ will be completely sorted in one pass by P-way replacement selection. What is the probability that this happens, as a function of P and N, when the input is a random permutation of $\{1, 2, \ldots, N\}$?

17. [20] What is output by Algorithm R when the input keys are in decreasing order, $K_1 \geq K_2 \geq \cdots \geq K_N$?

▶ **18.** [22] What happens if Algorithm R is applied *again* to an output file that was produced by Algorithm R?

19. [HM22] Use the snowplow analogy to prove that the first run produced by replacement selection is approximately $(e - 1)P$ records long.

20. [HM24] Approximately how long is the first run produced by natural selection, when $P = P'$?

▶ **21.** [HM23] Determine the approximate length of runs produced by natural selection when $P' < P$.

22. [HM40] The purpose of this exercise is to determine the average run length obtained in natural selection, when $P' > P$. Let $\kappa = k + \theta$ be a real number ≥ 1, where $k = \lfloor \kappa \rfloor$ and $\theta = \kappa \bmod 1$, and consider the function $F(\kappa) = F_k(\theta)$, where $F_k(\theta)$ is the polynomial defined by the generating function

$$\sum_{k \geq 0} F_k(\theta) z^k = e^{-\theta z} / (1 - z e^{1-z}).$$

Thus, $F_0(\theta) = 1$, $F_1(\theta) = e - \theta$, $F_2(\theta) = e^2 - e - e\theta + \frac{1}{2}\theta^2$, etc.

Suppose that a snowplow starts out at time 0 to simulate the process of natural selection, and suppose that after T units of time exactly P snowflakes have fallen behind it. At this point a second snowplow begins on the same journey, occupying the same position at time $t + T$ as the first snowplow did at time t. Finally, at time κT, exactly P' snowflakes have fallen behind the first snowplow; it instantaneously plows the rest of the road and disappears.

Using this model to represent the process of natural selection, show that a run length equal to $e^\theta F(\kappa)P$ is obtained when

$$P'/P = k + 1 + e^\theta \left(\kappa F(\kappa) - \sum_{j=0}^{k} F(\kappa - j) \right).$$

23. [HM35] The preceding exercise analyzes natural selection when the records from the reservoir are always read in the same order as they were written, first-in-first-out. Find the approximate run length that would be obtained if the reservoir contents from the preceding run were read in completely *random* order, as if the records in the reservoir had been thoroughly shuffled between runs.

24. [HM39] The purpose of this exercise is to analyze the effect caused by haphazardly changing the direction of runs in replacement selection.

a) Let $g_P(z_1, z_2, \ldots, z_k)$ be a generating function defined as in Theorem K, but with each of the k runs specified as to whether it is to be ascending or descending.

For example, we might say that all odd-numbered runs are ascending, all even-numbered runs are descending. Show that Theorem K is valid for each of the 2^k generating functions of this type.

b) As a consequence of (a), we may assume that $P = 1$. We may also assume that the input is a uniformly distributed sequence of independent random numbers between 0 and 1. Let

$$a(x, y) = \begin{cases} e^{1-x} - e^{y-x}, & \text{if } x \le y; \\ e^{1-x}, & \text{if } x > y. \end{cases}$$

Given that $f(x)\,dx$ is the probability that a certain ascending run begins with x, prove that $\left(\int_0^1 a(x, y)f(x)\,dx\right) dy$ is the probability that the following run begins with y. [*Hint:* Consider, for each $n \ge 0$, the probability that $x \le X_1 \le \cdots \le X_n > y$, when x and y are given.]

c) Consider runs that change direction with probability p; in other words, the direction of each run after the first is randomly chosen to be the same as that of the previous run, $q = (1 - p)$ of the time, but it is to be in the opposite direction p of the time. (Thus when $p = 0$, all runs have the same direction; when $p = 1$, the runs alternate in direction; and when $p = \frac{1}{2}$, the runs are independently random.) Let

$$f_1(x) = 1, \qquad f_{n+1}(y) = p\int_0^1 a(x, y)f_n(1 - x)\,dx + q\int_0^1 a(x, y)f_n(x)\,dx.$$

Show that the probability that the nth run begins with x is $f_n(x)\,dx$ when the $(n - 1)$st run is ascending, $f_n(1 - x)\,dx$ when the $(n - 1)$st run is descending.

d) Find a solution f to the steady-state equations

$$f(y) = p\int_0^1 a(x, y)f(1 - x)\,dx + q\int_0^1 a(x, y)f(x)\,dx, \qquad \int_0^1 f(x)\,dx = 1.$$

[*Hint:* Show that $f''(x)$ is independent of x.]

e) Show that the sequence $f_n(x)$ in part (c) converges rather rapidly to the function $f(x)$ in part (d).

f) Show that the average length of an ascending run starting with x is e^{1-x}.

g) Finally, put all these results together to prove the following theorem: *If the directions of consecutive runs are independently reversed with probability p in replacement selection, the average run length approaches* $(6/(3 + p))P$.

(The case $p = 1$ of this theorem was first derived by Knuth [*CACM* **6** (1963), 685–688]; the case $p = \frac{1}{2}$ was first proved by A. G. Konheim in 1970.)

25. [*HM40*] Consider the following procedure:

N1. Read a record into a one-word "reservoir." Then read another record, R, and let K be its key.

N2. Output the reservoir, set LASTKEY to its key, and set the reservoir empty.

N3. If K < LASTKEY then output R and set LASTKEY ← K and go to N5.

N4. If the reservoir is nonempty, return to N2; otherwise enter R into the reservoir.

N5. Read in a new record, R, and let K be its key. Go to N3. ∎

This is essentially equivalent to natural selection with $P = 1$ and with $P' = 1$ or 2 (depending on whether you choose to empty the reservoir at the moment it fills or at the moment it is about to overfill), except that it produces *descending* runs, and it never stops. The latter anomalies are convenient and harmless assumptions for the purposes of this problem.

Proceeding as in exercise 24, let $f_n(x, y)\, dy\, dx$ be the probability that x and y are the respective values of LASTKEY and K just after the nth time step N2 is performed. Prove that there is a function $g_n(x)$ of one variable such that $f_n(x, y) = g_n(x)$ when $x < y$, and $f_n(x, y) = g_n(x) - e^{-y}(g_n(x) - g_n(y))$ when $x > y$. This function $g_n(x)$ is defined by the relations $g_1(x) = 1$,

$$g_{n+1}(x) = \int_0^x e^u g_n(u)\, du + \int_0^x dv\,(v+1) \int_v^1 du\, ((e^v - 1)g_n(u) + g_n(v))$$

$$+ x \int_x^1 dv \int_v^1 du\, ((e^v - 1)g_n(u) + g_n(v)).$$

Show further that the expected length of the nth run is

$$\int_0^1 dx \int_0^x dy\, (g_n(x)(e^y - 1) + g_n(y))(2 - \tfrac{1}{2}y^2) + \int_0^1 dx\,(1 - x)g_n(x)e^x.$$

[*Note:* The steady-state solution to these equations appears to be very complicated; it has been obtained numerically by J. McKenna, who showed that the run lengths approach a limiting value ≈ 2.61307209. Theorem K does not apply to natural selection, so the case $P = 1$ does not carry over to other P.]

26. [*M33*] Considering the algorithm in exercise 25 as a definition of natural selection when $P' = 1$, find the expected length of the *first* run when $P' = r$, for any $r \geq 0$, as follows.

a) Show that the first run has length n with probability

$$(n+r)\left[{n+r \atop n}\right]\Big/(n+r+1)!.$$

b) Define "associated Stirling numbers" $\left[\!\left[{n \atop m}\right]\!\right]$ by the rules

$$\left[\!\left[{0 \atop m}\right]\!\right] = \delta_{m0}, \quad \left[\!\left[{n \atop m}\right]\!\right] = (n+m-1)\left(\left[\!\left[{n-1 \atop m}\right]\!\right] + \left[\!\left[{n-1 \atop m-1}\right]\!\right]\right) \qquad \text{for } n > 0.$$

Prove that

$$\left[{n+r \atop n}\right] = \sum_{k=0}^r \binom{n+r}{k+r}\left[\!\left[{r \atop k}\right]\!\right].$$

c) Prove that the average length of the first run is therefore $c_r e - r - 1$, where

$$c_r = \sum_{k=0}^r \left[\!\left[{r \atop k}\right]\!\right]\frac{r+k+1}{(r+k)!}.$$

▶ **27.** [*HM30*] (W. Dobosiewicz.) When natural selection is used with $P' < P$, we need not stop forming a run when the reservoir becomes full; we can store records that do not belong to the current run in the main priority queue, as in replacement selection, until only P' records of the current run are left. Then we can flush them to the output and replace them with the reservoir contents.

How much better is this method than the simpler approach analyzed in exercise 21?

28. [*25*] The text considers only the case that all records to be sorted have a fixed size. How can replacement selection be done reasonably well on *variable-length* records?

29. [*22*] Consider the 2^k nodes of a complete binary tree that has been right-threaded, illustrated here when $k = 3$:

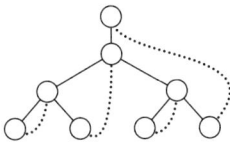

(Compare with 2.3.1–(10); the top node is the list head, and the dotted lines are thread links. In this exercise we are not concerned with sorting but rather with the structure of complete binary trees when a list-head-like node 0 has been added above node 1, as in the "tree of losers," Fig. 63.)

Show how to assign the 2^{n+k} internal nodes of a large tree of losers onto these 2^k host nodes so that (i) every host node holds exactly 2^n nodes of the large tree; (ii) adjacent nodes in the large tree either are assigned to the same host node or to host nodes that are adjacent (linked); and (iii) no two pairs of adjacent nodes in the large tree are separated by the same link in the host tree. [Multiple virtual processors in a large binary tree network can thereby be mapped to actual processors without undue congestion in the communication links.]

30. [*M29*] Prove that if $n \geq k \geq 1$, the construction in the preceding exercise is optimum, in the sense that *any* 2^k-node host graph satisfying (i), (ii), and (iii) must have at least $2^k + 2^{k-1} - 1$ edges (links) between nodes.

*5.4.2. The Polyphase Merge

Now that we have seen how initial runs can be built up, we shall consider various patterns that can be used to distribute them onto tapes and to merge them together until only a single run remains.

Let us begin by assuming that there are three tape units, T1, T2, and T3, available; the technique of "balanced merging," described near the beginning of Section 5.4, can be used with $P = 2$ and $T = 3$, when it takes the following form:

B1. Distribute initial runs alternately on tapes T1 and T2.

B2. Merge runs from T1 and T2 onto T3; then stop if T3 contains only one run.

B3. Copy the runs of T3 alternately onto T1 and T2, then return to B2.   ▮

If the initial distribution pass produces S runs, the first merge pass will produce $\lceil S/2 \rceil$ runs on T3, the second will produce $\lceil S/4 \rceil$, etc. Thus if, say, $17 \leq S \leq 32$, we will have 1 distribution pass, 5 merge passes, and 4 copy passes; in general, if $S > 1$, the number of passes over all the data is $2\lceil \lg S \rceil$.

The copying passes in this procedure are undesirable, since they do not reduce the number of runs. Half of the copying can be avoided if we use a *two-phase* procedure:

A1. Distribute initial runs alternately on tapes T1 and T2.

A2. Merge runs from T1 and T2 onto T3; then stop if T3 contains only one run.

A3. Copy *half* of the runs from T3 onto T1.

A4. Merge runs from T1 and T3 onto T2; then stop if T2 contains only one run.

A5. Copy *half* of the runs from T2 onto T1. Return to A2.   ▮

The number of passes over the data has been reduced to $\frac{3}{2}\lceil \lg S\rceil + \frac{1}{2}$, since steps A3 and A5 do only "half a pass"; about 25 percent of the time has therefore been saved.

The copying can actually be eliminated *entirely*, if we start with F_n runs on T1 and F_{n-1} runs on T2, where F_n and F_{n-1} are consecutive Fibonacci numbers. Consider, for example, the case $n = 7$, $S = F_n + F_{n-1} = 13 + 8 = 21$:

Phase	Contents of T1	Contents of T2	Contents of T3	Remarks
1	1,1,1,1,1,1,1,1,1,1,1,1,1	1,1,1,1,1,1,1,1		Initial distribution
2	1,1,1,1,1	—	2,2,2,2,2,2,2,2	Merge 8 runs to T3
3	—	3,3,3,3,3	2,2,2	Merge 5 runs to T2
4	5,5,5	3,3	—	Merge 3 runs to T1
5	5	—	8,8	Merge 2 runs to T3
6	—	13	8	Merge 1 run to T2
7	21	—	—	Merge 1 run to T1

Here, for example, "2,2,2,2,2,2,2,2" denotes eight runs of relative length 2, considering each initial run to be of relative length 1. Fibonacci numbers are omnipresent in this chart!

Only phases 1 and 7 are complete passes over the data; phase 2 processes only 16/21 of the initial runs, phase 3 only 15/21, etc., and so the total number of "passes" comes to $(21 + 16 + 15 + 15 + 16 + 13 + 21)/21 = 5\frac{4}{7}$ if we assume that the initial runs have approximately equal length. By comparison, the two-phase procedure above would have required 8 passes to sort these 21 initial runs. We shall see that in general this "Fibonacci" pattern requires approximately $1.04 \lg S + 0.99$ passes, making it competitive with a *four*-tape balanced merge although it requires only three tapes.

The same idea can be generalized to T tapes, for any $T \geq 3$, using $(T-1)$-way merging. We shall see, for example, that the four-tape case requires only about $.703 \lg S + 0.96$ passes over the data. The generalized pattern involves generalized Fibonacci numbers. Consider the following six-tape example:

Phase	T1	T2	T3	T4	T5	T6	Initial runs processed
1	1^{31}	1^{30}	1^{28}	1^{24}	1^{16}	—	$31 + 30 + 28 + 24 + 16 = 129$
2	1^{15}	1^{14}	1^{12}	1^{8}	—	5^{16}	$16 \times 5 = 80$
3	1^{7}	1^{6}	1^{4}	—	9^{8}	5^{8}	$8 \times 9 = 72$
4	1^{3}	1^{2}	—	17^{4}	9^{4}	5^{4}	$4 \times 17 = 68$
5	1^{1}	—	33^{2}	17^{2}	9^{2}	5^{2}	$2 \times 33 = 66$
6	—	65^{1}	33^{1}	17^{1}	9^{1}	5^{1}	$1 \times 65 = 65$
7	129^{1}	—	—	—	—	—	$1 \times 129 = 129$

Here 1^{31} stands for 31 runs of relative length 1, etc.; five-way merges have been used throughout. This general pattern was developed by R. L. Gilstad [*Proc. Eastern Joint Computer Conf.* **18** (1960), 143–148], who called it the *polyphase merge*. The three-tape case had been discovered earlier by B. K. Betz [unpublished memorandum, Minneapolis–Honeywell Regulator Co. (1956)].

In order to make polyphase merging work as in the examples above, we need to have a "perfect Fibonacci distribution" of runs on the tapes after each phase. By reading the table above from bottom to top, we can see that the first seven perfect Fibonacci distributions when $T = 6$ are $\{1,0,0,0,0\}$, $\{1,1,1,1,1\}$, $\{2,2,2,2,1\}$, $\{4,4,4,3,2\}$, $\{8,8,7,6,4\}$, $\{16,15,14,12,8\}$, and $\{31,30,28,24,16\}$. The big questions now facing us are

1. What is the rule underlying these perfect Fibonacci distributions?

2. What do we do if S does not correspond to a perfect Fibonacci distribution?

3. How should we design the initial distribution pass so that it produces the desired configuration on the tapes?

4. How many "passes" over the data will a T-tape polyphase merge require, as a function of S (the number of initial runs)?

We shall discuss these four questions in turn, first giving "easy answers" and then making a more intensive analysis.

The perfect Fibonacci distributions can be obtained by running the pattern backwards, cyclically rotating the tape contents. For example, when $T = 6$ we have the following distribution of runs:

Level	T1	T2	T3	T4	T5	Total	Final output will be on
0	1	0	0	0	0	1	T1
1	1	1	1	1	1	5	T6
2	2	2	2	2	1	9	T5
3	4	4	4	3	2	17	T4
4	8	8	7	6	4	33	T3
5	16	15	14	12	8	65	T2
6	31	30	28	24	16	129	T1
7	61	59	55	47	31	253	T6
8	120	116	108	92	61	497	T5
$\cdots$							
n	a_n	b_n	c_n	d_n	e_n	t_n	T(k)
$n+1$	$a_n + b_n$	$a_n + c_n$	$a_n + d_n$	$a_n + e_n$	a_n	$t_n + 4a_n$	T($k-1$)
$\cdots$							

$$\text{(1)}$$

(Tape T6 will always be empty after the initial distribution.)

The rule for going from level n to level $n + 1$ shows that the condition

$$a_n \geq b_n \geq c_n \geq d_n \geq e_n \tag{2}$$

will hold in every level. In fact, it is easy to see from (1) that

$$
\begin{aligned}
e_n &= a_{n-1}, \\
d_n &= a_{n-1} + e_{n-1} = a_{n-1} + a_{n-2}, \\
c_n &= a_{n-1} + d_{n-1} = a_{n-1} + a_{n-2} + a_{n-3}, \\
b_n &= a_{n-1} + c_{n-1} = a_{n-1} + a_{n-2} + a_{n-3} + a_{n-4}, \\
a_n &= a_{n-1} + b_{n-1} = a_{n-1} + a_{n-2} + a_{n-3} + a_{n-4} + a_{n-5},
\end{aligned}
\tag{3}
$$

where $a_0 = 1$ and where we let $a_n = 0$ for $n = -1, -2, -3, -4$.

The *pth-order Fibonacci numbers* $F_n^{(p)}$ are defined by the rules

$$
\begin{aligned}
F_n^{(p)} &= F_{n-1}^{(p)} + F_{n-2}^{(p)} + \cdots + F_{n-p}^{(p)}, \quad \text{for } n \geq p; \\
F_n^{(p)} &= 0, \quad \text{for } 0 \leq n \leq p-2; \qquad F_{p-1}^{(p)} = 1.
\end{aligned} \tag{4}
$$

In other words, we start with $p-1$ 0s, then 1, and then each number is the sum of the preceding p values. When $p = 2$, this is the usual Fibonacci sequence, and when $p = 3$ it has been called the Tribonacci sequence. Such sequences were apparently first studied for $p > 2$ by Nārāyaṇa Paṇḍita in 1356 [see P. Singh, *Historia Mathematica* **12** (1985), 229–244], then many years later by V. Schlegel in *El Progreso Matemático* **4** (1894), 173–174. Schlegel derived the generating function

$$
\sum_{n \geq 0} F_n^{(p)} z^n = \frac{z^{p-1}}{1 - z - z^2 - \cdots - z^p} = \frac{z^{p-1} - z^p}{1 - 2z + z^{p+1}}. \tag{5}
$$

The last equation of (3) shows that the number of runs on T1 during a six-tape polyphase merge is a fifth-order Fibonacci number: $a_n = F_{n+4}^{(5)}$.

In general, if we set $P = T-1$, the polyphase merge distributions for T tapes will correspond to Pth order Fibonacci numbers in the same way. The kth tape gets

$$
F_{n+P-2}^{(P)} + F_{n+P-3}^{(P)} + \cdots + F_{n+k-2}^{(P)}
$$

initial runs in the perfect nth level distribution, for $1 \leq k \leq P$, and the total number of initial runs on all tapes is therefore

$$
t_n = P F_{n+P-2}^{(P)} + (P-1) F_{n+P-3}^{(P)} + \cdots + F_{n-1}^{(P)}. \tag{6}
$$

This settles the issue of "perfect Fibonacci distributions." But what should we do if S is not exactly equal to t_n, for any n? And how do we get the runs onto the tapes in the first place?

When S isn't perfect (and so few values are), we can do just as we did in balanced P-way merging, adding artificial "dummy runs" so that we can pretend S is perfect after all. There are several ways to add the dummy runs, and we aren't ready yet to analyze the "best" way of doing this. We shall discuss first a method of distribution and dummy-run assignment that isn't strictly optimal, although it has the virtue of simplicity and appears to be better than all other equally simple methods.

Algorithm D (*Polyphase merge sorting with "horizontal" distribution*). This algorithm takes initial runs and disperses them to tapes, one run at a time, until the supply of initial runs is exhausted. Then it specifies how the tapes are to be merged, assuming that there are $T = P + 1 \geq 3$ available tape units, using P-way merging. Tape T may be used to hold the input, since it does not receive any initial runs. The following tables are maintained:

A[j], $1 \leq j \leq T$: The perfect Fibonacci distribution we are striving for.

D[j], $1 \leq j \leq T$: Number of dummy runs assumed to be present at the beginning of logical tape unit number j.

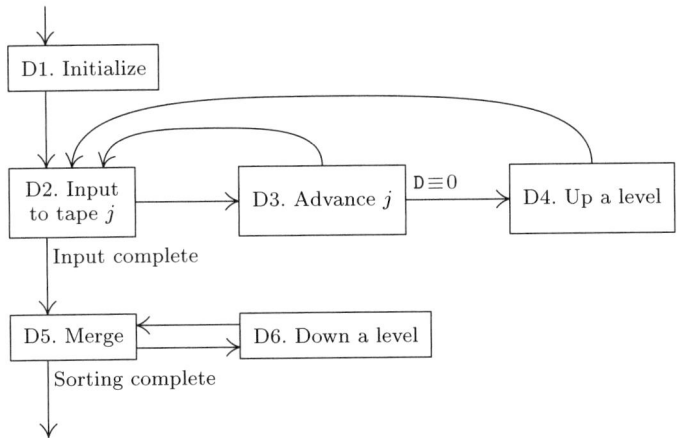

Fig. 68. Polyphase merge sorting.

TAPE[j], $1 \le j \le T$: Number of the physical tape unit corresponding to logical
tape unit number j.

(It is convenient to deal with "logical tape unit numbers" whose assignment to
physical tape units varies as the algorithm proceeds.)

D1. [Initialize.] Set A[j] ← D[j] ← 1 and TAPE[j] ← j, for $1 \le j < T$. Set
A[T] ← D[T] ← 0 and TAPE[T] ← T. Then set $l \leftarrow 1$, $j \leftarrow 1$.

D2. [Input to tape j.] Write one run on tape number j, and decrease D[j] by 1.
Then if the input is exhausted, rewind all the tapes and go to step D5.

D3. [Advance j.] If D[j] < D[$j+1$], increase j by 1 and return to D2.
Otherwise if D[j] = 0, go on to D4. Otherwise set $j \leftarrow 1$ and return to D2.

D4. [Up a level.] Set $l \leftarrow l + 1$, $a \leftarrow$ A[1], and then for $j = 1, 2, \ldots, P$ (in
this order) set D[j] ← $a +$ A[$j+1$] − A[j] and A[j] ← $a +$ A[$j+1$].
(See (1) and note that A[$P+1$] is always zero. At this point we will have
D[1] ≥ D[2] ≥ $\cdots$ ≥ D[T].) Now set $j \leftarrow 1$ and return to D2.

D5. [Merge.] If $l = 0$, sorting is complete and the output is on TAPE[1]. Otherwise, merge runs from TAPE[1],...,TAPE[P] onto TAPE[T] until TAPE[P]
is empty and D[P] = 0. The merging process should operate as follows,
for each run merged: If D[j] > 0 for all j, $1 \le j \le P$, then increase D[T]
by 1 and decrease each D[j] by 1 for $1 \le j \le P$; otherwise merge one run
from each TAPE[j] such that D[j] = 0, and decrease D[j] by 1 for each
other j. (Thus the dummy runs are imagined to be at the *beginning* of the
tape instead of at the ending.)

D6. [Down a level.] Set $l \leftarrow l - 1$. Rewind TAPE[P] and TAPE[T]. (Actually the
rewinding of TAPE[P] could have been initiated during step D5, just after
its last block was input.) Then set (TAPE[1],TAPE[2],...,TAPE[T]) ←
(TAPE[T],TAPE[1],...,TAPE[$T-1$]), (D[1],D[2],...,D[T]) ← (D[T],
D[1],...,D[$T-1$]), and return to step D5. ∎

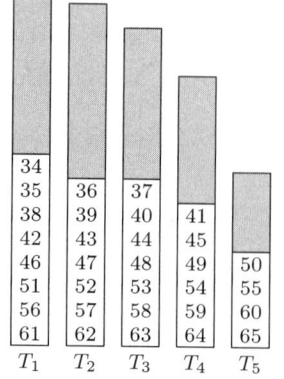

Fig. 69. The order in which runs 34 through 65 are distributed to tapes, when advancing from level 4 to level 5. (See the table of perfect distributions, Eq. (1).) Shaded areas represent the first 33 runs that were distributed when level 4 was reached. The bottom row corresponds to the beginning of each tape.

The distribution rule that is stated so succinctly in step D3 of this algorithm is intended to equalize the number of dummies on each tape as well as possible. Figure 69 illustrates the order of distribution when we go from level 4 (33 runs) to level 5 (65 runs) in a six-tape sort; if there were only, say, 53 initial runs, all runs numbered 54 and higher would be treated as dummies. (The runs are actually being written at the end of the tape, but it is best to imagine them being written at the beginning, since the dummies are assumed to be at the beginning.)

We have now discussed the first three questions listed above, and it remains to consider the number of "passes" over the data. Comparing our six-tape example to the table (1), we see that the total number of initial runs processed when $S = t_6$ was $a_5t_1 + a_4t_2 + a_3t_3 + a_2t_4 + a_1t_5 + a_0t_6$, excluding the initial distribution pass. Exercise 4 derives the generating functions

$$a(z) = \sum_{n \geq 0} a_n z^n = \frac{1}{1 - z - z^2 - z^3 - z^4 - z^5},$$

$$t(z) = \sum_{n \geq 1} t_n z^n = \frac{5z + 4z^2 + 3z^3 + 2z^4 + z^5}{1 - z - z^2 - z^3 - z^4 - z^5}. \tag{7}$$

It follows that, in general, the number of initial runs processed when $S = t_n$ is exactly the coefficient of z^n in $a(z)t(z)$, plus t_n (for the initial distribution pass). This makes it possible to calculate the asymptotic behavior of polyphase merging, as shown in exercises 5 through 7, and we obtain the following results:

Table 1

APPROXIMATE BEHAVIOR OF POLYPHASE MERGE SORTING

Tapes	Phases	Passes	Pass/phase	Growth ratio
3	$2.078 \ln S + 0.672$	$1.504 \ln S + 0.992$	72%	1.6180340
4	$1.641 \ln S + 0.364$	$1.015 \ln S + 0.965$	62%	1.8392868
5	$1.524 \ln S + 0.078$	$0.863 \ln S + 0.921$	57%	1.9275620
6	$1.479 \ln S - 0.185$	$0.795 \ln S + 0.864$	54%	1.9659482
7	$1.460 \ln S - 0.424$	$0.762 \ln S + 0.797$	52%	1.9835828
8	$1.451 \ln S - 0.642$	$0.744 \ln S + 0.723$	51%	1.9919642
10	$1.445 \ln S - 1.017$	$0.728 \ln S + 0.568$	50%	1.9980295
20	$1.443 \ln S - 2.170$	$0.721 \ln S - 0.030$	50%	1.9999981

In Table 1, the "growth ratio" is $\lim_{n\to\infty} t_{n+1}/t_n$, the approximate factor by which the number of runs increases at each level. "Passes" denotes the average number of times each record is processed, namely $1/S$ times the total number of initial runs processed during the distribution and merge phases. The stated number of passes and phases is correct in each case up to $O(S^{-\epsilon})$, for some $\epsilon > 0$, for perfect distributions as $S \to \infty$.

Figure 70 shows the average number of times each record is merged, as a function of S, when Algorithm D is used to handle the case of nonperfect numbers. Note that with three tapes there are "peaks" of relative inefficiency occurring just after the perfect distributions, but this phenomenon largely disappears when there are four or more tapes. The use of eight or more tapes gives comparatively little improvement over six or seven tapes.

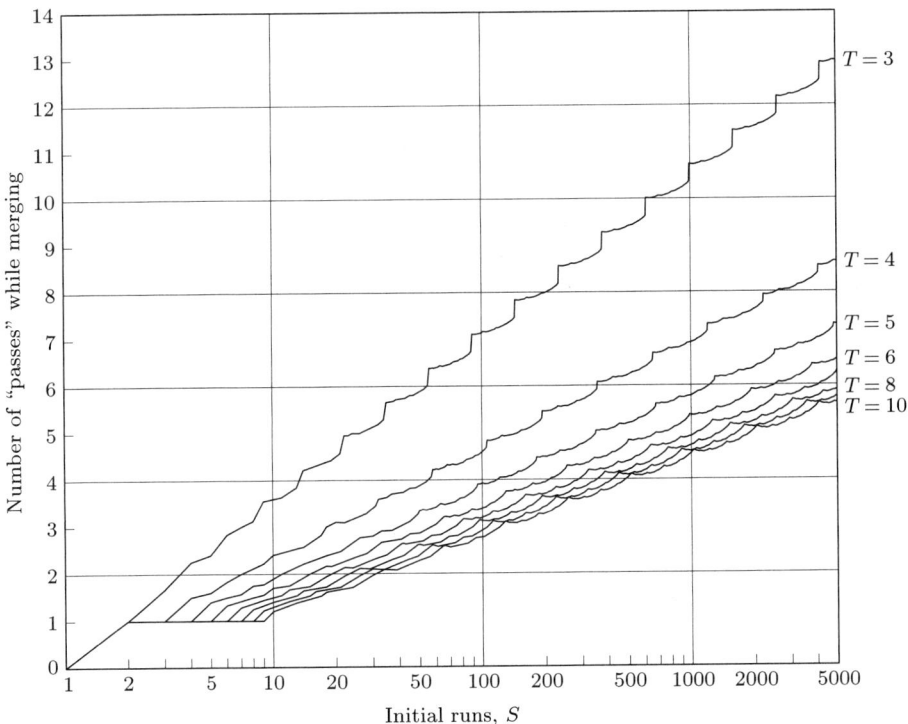

Fig. 70. Efficiency of polyphase merge using Algorithm D.

A closer look. In a balanced merge requiring k passes, every record is processed exactly k times during the course of the sort. But the polyphase procedure does not have this lack of bias; some records may get processed many more times than others, and we can gain speed if we arrange to put dummy runs into the oft-processed positions.

Let us therefore study the polyphase distribution more closely; instead of merely looking at the number of runs on each tape, as in (1), let us associate with each run its *merge number*, the number of times it will be processed during the complete polyphase sort. We get the following table in place of (1):

Level	T1	T2	T3	T4	T5
0	0	—	—	—	—
1	1	1	1	1	1
2	21	21	21	21	2
3	3221	3221	3221	322	32
4	43323221	43323221	4332322	433232	4332
5	5443433243323221	544343324332322	54434332433232	544343324332	54434332
. . .	. . .	. . .	. . .	. . .	. . .
n	A_n	B_n	C_n	D_n	E_n
$n+1$	$(A_n+1)B_n$	$(A_n+1)C_n$	$(A_n+1)D_n$	$(A_n+1)E_n$	A_n+1
. . .	. . .	. . .	. . .	. . .	. . .

$$(8)$$

Here A_n is a string of a_n values representing the merge numbers for each run on T1, if we begin with the level n distribution; B_n is the corresponding string for T2; etc. The notation "$(A_n + 1)B_n$" means "A_n with all values increased by 1, followed by B_n."

Figure 71(a) shows A_5, B_5, C_5, D_5, E_5 tipped on end, showing how the merge numbers for each run appear on tape; notice, for example, that the run at the beginning of each tape will be processed five times, while the run at the end of T1 will be processed only once. This discriminatory practice of the polyphase merge makes it much better to put a dummy run at the beginning of the tape than at the end. Figure 71(b) shows an optimum order in which to distribute runs for a five-level polyphase merge, placing each new run into a position with the smallest available merge number. Algorithm D is not quite as good (see Fig. 69), since it fills some "4" positions before all of the "3" positions are used up.

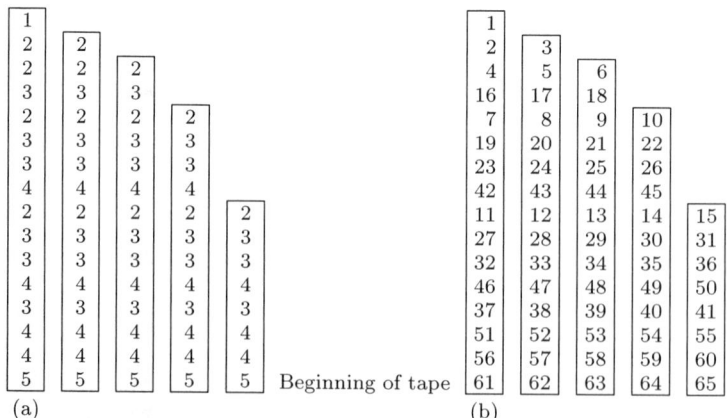

Fig. 71. Analysis of the fifth-level polyphase distribution for six tapes: (a) merge numbers, (b) optimum distribution order.

The recurrence relations (8) show that each of B_n, C_n, D_n, and E_n are initial substrings of A_n. In fact, we can use (8) to derive the formulas

$$
\begin{aligned}
E_n &= (A_{n-1}) + 1, \\
D_n &= (A_{n-1}A_{n-2}) + 1, \\
C_n &= (A_{n-1}A_{n-2}A_{n-3}) + 1, \\
B_n &= (A_{n-1}A_{n-2}A_{n-3}A_{n-4}) + 1, \\
A_n &= (A_{n-1}A_{n-2}A_{n-3}A_{n-4}A_{n-5}) + 1,
\end{aligned}
\tag{9}
$$

generalizing Eqs. (3), which treated only the lengths of these strings. Furthermore, the rule defining the A's implies that essentially the same structure is present at the beginning of every level; we have

$$
A_n = n - Q_n,
\tag{10}
$$

where Q_n is a string of a_n values defined by the law

$$
\begin{aligned}
&Q_n = Q_{n-1}(Q_{n-2}+1)(Q_{n-3}+2)(Q_{n-4}+3)(Q_{n-5}+4), \quad \text{for } n \geq 1; \\
&Q_0 = 0; \qquad Q_n = \epsilon \quad \text{(the empty string)} \quad \text{for } n < 0.
\end{aligned}
\tag{11}
$$

Since Q_n begins with Q_{n-1}, we can consider the *infinite* string Q_∞, whose first a_n elements are equal to Q_n; this string Q_∞ essentially characterizes all the merge numbers in polyphase distribution. In the six-tape case,

$$
Q_\infty = 0112122312232334123233423334341122323342334344523343445344545 12232\cdots.
\tag{12}
$$

Exercise 11 contains an interesting interpretation of this string.

Given that A_n is the string $m_1 m_2 \ldots m_{a_n}$, let

$$
A_n(x) = x^{m_1} + x^{m_2} + \cdots + x^{m_{a_n}}
$$

be the corresponding generating function that counts the number of times each merge number appears; and define $B_n(x)$, $C_n(x)$, $D_n(x)$, $E_n(x)$ similarly. For example, $A_4(x) = x^4 + x^3 + x^3 + x^2 + x^3 + x^2 + x^2 + x = x^4 + 3x^3 + 3x^2 + x$. Relations (9) tell us that

$$
\begin{aligned}
E_n(x) &= x\big(A_{n-1}(x)\big), \\
D_n(x) &= x\big(A_{n-1}(x) + A_{n-2}(x)\big), \\
C_n(x) &= x\big(A_{n-1}(x) + A_{n-2}(x) + A_{n-3}(x)\big), \\
B_n(x) &= x\big(A_{n-1}(x) + A_{n-2}(x) + A_{n-3}(x) + A_{n-4}(x)\big), \\
A_n(x) &= x\big(A_{n-1}(x) + A_{n-2}(x) + A_{n-3}(x) + A_{n-4}(x) + A_{n-5}(x)\big),
\end{aligned}
\tag{13}
$$

for $n \geq 1$, where $A_0(x) = 1$ and $A_n(x) = 0$ for $n = -1, -2, -3, -4$. Hence

$$
\sum_{n \geq 0} A_n(x) z^n = \frac{1}{1 - x(z + z^2 + z^3 + z^4 + z^5)} = \sum_{k \geq 0} x^k (z + z^2 + z^3 + z^4 + z^5)^k.
\tag{14}
$$

Considering the runs on all tapes, we let

$$T_n(x) = A_n(x) + B_n(x) + C_n(x) + D_n(x) + E_n(x), \qquad n \geq 1; \qquad (15)$$

from (13) we immediately have

$$T_n(x) = 5A_{n-1}(x) + 4A_{n-2}(x) + 3A_{n-3}(x) + 2A_{n-4}(x) + A_{n-5}(x),$$

hence

$$\sum_{n \geq 1} T_n(x) z^n = \frac{x(5z + 4z^2 + 3z^3 + 2z^4 + z^5)}{1 - x(z + z^2 + z^3 + z^4 + z^5)}. \qquad (16)$$

The form of (16) shows that it is easy to compute the coefficients of $T_n(x)$:

	z	z^2	z^3	z^4	z^5	z^6	z^7	z^8	z^9	z^{10}	z^{11}	z^{12}	z^{13}	z^{14}
x	5	4	3	2	1	0	0	0	0	0	0	0	0	0
x^2	0	5	9	12	14	15	10	6	3	1	0	0	0	0
x^3	0	0	5	14	26	40	55	60	57	48	35	20	10	4
x^4	0	0	0	5	19	45	85	140	195	238	260	255	220	170
x^5	0	0	0	0	5	24	69	154	294	484	703	918	1088	1168

(17)

The columns of this tableau give $T_n(x)$; for example, $T_4(x) = 2x + 12x^2 + 14x^3 + 5x^4$. After the first row, each entry in the tableau is the sum of the five entries just above and to the left in the previous row.

The number of runs in a "perfect" nth level distribution is $T_n(1)$, and the total amount of processing as these runs are merged is the derivative, $T_n'(1)$. Now

$$\sum_{n \geq 1} T_n'(x) z^n = \frac{5z + 4z^2 + 3z^3 + 2z^4 + z^5}{\left(1 - x(z + z^2 + z^3 + z^4 + z^5)\right)^2}; \qquad (18)$$

setting $x = 1$ in (16) and (18) gives a result in agreement with our earlier demonstration that the merge processing for a perfect nth level distribution is the coefficient of z^n in $a(z)t(z)$; see (7).

We can use the functions $T_n(x)$ to determine the work involved when dummy runs are added in an optimum way. Let $\Sigma_n(m)$ be the sum of the smallest m merge numbers in an nth level distribution. These values are readily calculated by looking at the columns of (17), and we find that $\Sigma_n(m)$ is given by

$m =$	1	2	3	4	5	6	7	8	9	10	11	12	13	14	15	16	17	18	19	20	21
$n = 1$	1	2	3	4	5	∞	∞	∞	∞	∞	∞	∞	∞	∞	∞	∞	∞	∞	∞	∞	∞
$n = 2$	1	2	3	4	6	8	10	12	14	∞	∞	∞	∞	∞	∞	∞	∞	∞	∞	∞	∞
$n = 3$	1	2	3	5	7	9	11	13	15	17	19	21	24	27	30	33	36	∞	∞	∞	∞
$n = 4$	1	2	4	6	8	10	12	14	16	18	20	22	24	26	29	32	35	38	41	44	47
$n = 5$	1	3	5	7	9	11	13	15	17	19	21	23	25	27	29	32	35	38	41	44	47
$n = 6$	2	4	6	8	10	12	14	16	18	20	22	24	26	28	30	33	36	39	42	45	48
$n = 7$	2	4	6	8	10	12	14	16	18	20	23	26	29	32	35	38	41	44	47	50	53

(19)

For example, if we wish to sort 17 runs using a level-3 distribution, the total amount of processing is $\Sigma_3(17) = 36$; but if we use a level-4 or level-5 distribution

Table 2

NUMBER OF RUNS FOR WHICH A GIVEN LEVEL IS OPTIMUM

Level	$T = 3$	$T = 4$	$T = 5$	$T = 6$	$T = 7$	$T = 8$	$T = 9$	$T = 10$	
1	2	2	2	2	2	2	2	2	M_1
2	3	4	5	6	7	8	9	10	M_2
3	4	6	8	10	12	14	16	18	M_3
4	6	10	14	14	17	20	23	26	M_4
5	9	18	23	29	20	24	28	32	M_5
6	14	32	35	43	53	27	32	37	M_6
7	22	55	76	61	73	88	35	41	M_7
8	35	96	109	154	98	115	136	44	M_8
9	56	173	244	216	283	148	171	199	M_9
10	90	280	359	269	386	168	213	243	M_{10}
11	145	535	456	779	481	640	240	295	M_{11}
12	234	820	1197	1034	555	792	1002	330	M_{12}
13	378	1635	1563	1249	1996	922	1228	1499	M_{13}
14	611	2401	4034	3910	2486	1017	1432	1818	M_{14}
15	988	4959	5379	4970	2901	4397	1598	2116	M_{15}
16	1598	7029	6456	5841	10578	5251	1713	2374	M_{16}
17	2574	14953	18561	19409	13097	5979	8683	2576	M_{17}
18	3955	20583	22876	23918	15336	6499	10069	2709	M_{18}
19	6528	44899	64189	27557	17029	30164	11259	15787	M_{19}

and position the dummy runs optimally, the total amount of processing during the merge phases is only $\Sigma_4(17) = \Sigma_5(17) = 35$. It is better to use level 4, even though 17 corresponds to a "perfect" level-3 distribution! Indeed, as S gets large it turns out that the optimum number of levels is many more than that used in Algorithm D.

Exercise 14 proves that there is a nondecreasing sequence of numbers M_n such that level n is optimum for $M_n \leq S < M_{n+1}$, but not for $S \geq M_{n+1}$. In the six-tape case the table of $\Sigma_n(m)$ we have just calculated shows that

$$M_0 = 0, \qquad M_1 = 2, \qquad M_2 = 6, \qquad M_3 = 10, \qquad M_4 = 14.$$

The discussion above treats only the case of six tapes, but it is clear that the same ideas apply to polyphase merging with T tapes for any $T \geq 3$; we simply replace 5 by $P = T - 1$ in all appropriate places. Table 2 shows the sequences M_n obtained for various values of T. Table 3 and Fig. 72 indicate the total number of initial runs that are processed after making an optimum distribution of dummy runs. (The formulas that appear at the bottom of Table 3 should be taken with a grain of salt, since they are least-squares fits over the range $1 \leq S \leq 5000$, or $1 \leq S \leq 10000$ for $T = 3$; this leads to somewhat erratic behavior because the given range of S values is not equally favorable for all T. As $S \to \infty$, the number of initial runs processed after an optimum polyphase distribution is asymptotically $S \log_P S$, but convergence to this asymptotic limit is extremely slow.)

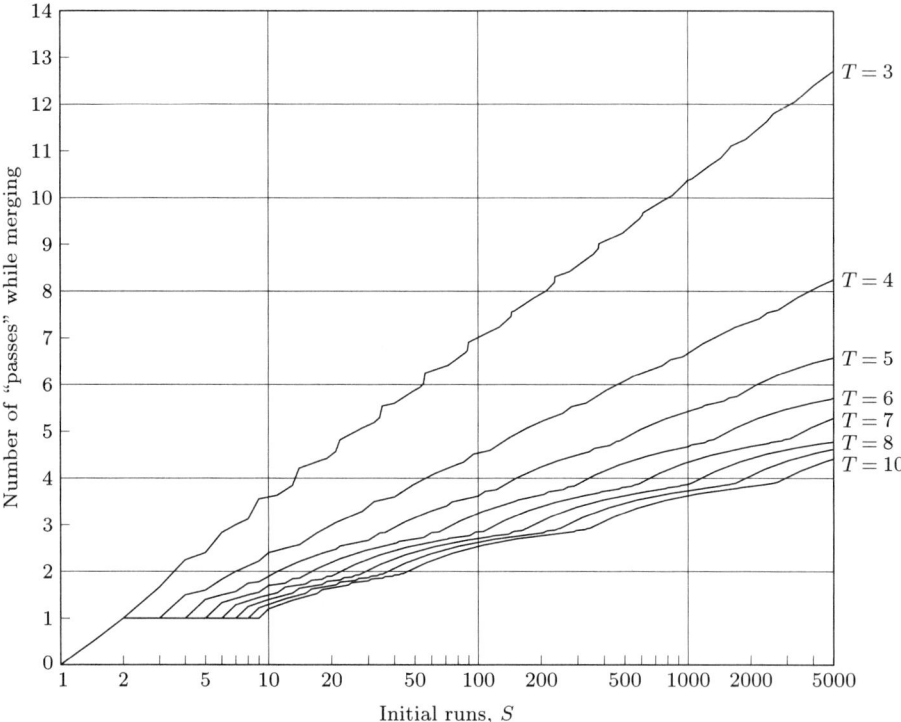

Fig. 72. Efficiency of polyphase merge with optimum initial distribution, using the same assumptions as Fig. 70.

Table 3
INITIAL RUNS PROCESSED DURING AN OPTIMUM POLYPHASE MERGE

S	T = 3	T = 4	T = 5	T = 6	T = 7	T = 8	T = 9	T = 10
10	36	24	19	17	15	14	13	12
20	90	60	49	44	38	36	34	33
50	294	194	158	135	128	121	113	104
100	702	454	362	325	285	271	263	254
500	4641	3041	2430	2163	1904	1816	1734	1632
1000	10371	6680	5430	4672	4347	3872	3739	3632
5000	63578	41286	32905	28620	26426	23880	23114	22073

$$S \begin{cases} (1.51 & 0.951 & 0.761 & 0.656 & 0.589 & 0.548 & 0.539 & 0.488) \times S \ln S + \\ (-.11 & +.14 & +.16 & +.19 & +.21 & +.20 & +.02 & +.18) \times S \end{cases}$$

Table 4 shows how the distribution method of Algorithm D compares with the results of optimum distribution in Table 3. It is clear that Algorithm D is not very close to the optimum when S and T become large; but it is not clear

Table 4

INITIAL RUNS PROCESSED DURING THE STANDARD POLYPHASE MERGE

S	$T=3$	$T=4$	$T=5$	$T=6$	$T=7$	$T=8$	$T=9$	$T=10$
10	36	24	19	17	15	14	13	12
20	90	62	49	44	41	37	34	33
50	294	194	167	143	134	131	120	114
100	714	459	393	339	319	312	292	277
500	4708	3114	2599	2416	2191	2100	2047	2025
1000	10730	6920	5774	5370	4913	4716	4597	4552
5000	64740	43210	36497	32781	31442	29533	28817	28080

how to do much better than Algorithm D without considerable complication in such cases, especially if we do not know S in advance. Fortunately, we rarely have to worry about large S (see Section 5.4.6), so Algorithm D is not too bad in practice; in fact, it's pretty good.

Polyphase sorting was first analyzed mathematically by W. C. Carter [*Proc. IFIP Congress* (1962), 62–66]. Many of the results stated above about optimal dummy run placement are due originally to B. Sackman and T. Singer ["A vector model for merge sort analysis," an unpublished paper presented at the ACM Sort Symposium (November 1962), 21 pages]. Sackman later suggested the horizontal method of distribution used in Algorithm D. Donald Shell [*CACM* **14** (1971), 713–719; **15** (1972), 28] developed the theory independently, noted relation (10), and made a detailed study of several different distribution algorithms. Further instructive developments and refinements have been made by Derek A. Zave [*SICOMP* **6** (1977), 1–39]; some of Zave's results are discussed in exercises 15 through 17. The generating function (16) was first investigated by W. Burge [*Proc. IFIP Congress* (1971), **1**, 454–459].

But what about rewind time? So far we have taken "initial runs processed" as the sole measure of efficiency for comparing tape merge strategies. But after each of phases 2 through 6, in the examples at the beginning of this section, it is necessary for the computer to wait for two tapes to rewind; both the previous output tape and the new current output tape must be repositioned at the beginning, before the next phase can proceed. This can cause a significant delay, since the previous output tape generally contains a significant percentage of the records being sorted (see the "pass/phase" column in Table 1). It is a shame to have the computer twiddling its thumbs during all these rewind operations, since useful work could be done with the other tapes if we used a different merging pattern.

A simple modification of the polyphase procedure will overcome this problem, although it requires at least five tapes [see Y. Césari, Thesis, U. of Paris (1968), 25–27, where the idea is credited to J. Caron]. Each phase in Caron's scheme merges runs from $T - 3$ tapes onto another tape, while the remaining two tapes are rewinding.

For example, consider the case of six tapes and 49 initial runs. In the following tableau, R denotes rewinding during the phase, and T5 is assumed to contain the original input:

Phase	T1	T2	T3	T4	T5	T6	Write time	Rewind time
1	1^{11}	1^{17}	1^{13}	1^8	—	(R)	49	17
2	(R)	1^9	1^5	—	R	3^8	$8 \times 3 = 24$	$49 - 17 = 32$
3	1^6	1^4	—	R	3^5	R	$5 \times 3 = 15$	$\max(8, 24)$
4	1^2	—	R	5^4	R	3^4	$4 \times 5 = 20$	$\max(13, 15)$
5	—	R	7^2	R	3^3	3^2	$2 \times 7 = 14$	$\max(17, 20)$
6	R	11^2	R	5^2	3^1	—	$2 \times 11 = 22$	$\max(11, 14)$
7	15^1	R	7^1	5^1	—	R	$1 \times 15 = 15$	$\max(22, 24)$
8	R	11^1	7^0	—	R	23^1	$1 \times 23 = 23$	$\max(15, 15)$
9	15^1	11^1	—	R	33^0	R	$0 \times 33 = 0$	$\max(20, 23)$
10	(15^0)	—	R	49^1	(R)	(23^0)	$1 \times 49 = 49$	14

Here all the rewind time is essentially overlapped, except in phase 9 (a "dummy phase" that prepares for the final merge), and after the initial distribution phase (when all tapes are rewound). If t is the time to merge the number of records in one initial run, and if r is the time to rewind over one initial run, this process takes about $182t + 40r$ plus the time for initial distribution and final rewind. The corresponding figures for standard polyphase using Algorithm D are $140t + 104r$, which is slightly worse when $r = \frac{3}{4}t$, slightly better when $r = \frac{1}{2}t$.

Everything we have said about standard polyphase can be adapted to Caron's polyphase; for example, the sequence a_n now satisfies the recurrence

$$a_n = a_{n-2} + a_{n-3} + a_{n-4} \tag{20}$$

instead of (3). The reader will find it instructive to analyze this method in the same way we analyzed standard polyphase, since it will enhance an understanding of both methods. (See, for example, exercises 19 and 20.)

Table 5 gives statistics about Polyphase Caron that are analogous to the facts about Polyphase Ordinaire in Table 1. Notice that Caron's method actually becomes *superior* to polyphase on eight or more tapes, in the number of runs processed as well as in the rewind time, even though it does $(T - 3)$-way merging instead of $(T - 1)$-way merging!

Table 5

APPROXIMATE BEHAVIOR OF CARON'S POLYPHASE MERGE SORTING

Tapes	Phases	Passes	Pass/phase	Growth ratio
5	$3.556 \ln S + 0.158$	$1.463 \ln S + 1.016$	41%	1.3247180
6	$2.616 \ln S - 0.166$	$0.951 \ln S + 1.014$	36%	1.4655712
7	$2.337 \ln S - 0.472$	$0.781 \ln S + 1.001$	33%	1.5341577
8	$2.216 \ln S - 0.762$	$0.699 \ln S + 0.980$	32%	1.5701473
9	$2.156 \ln S - 1.034$	$0.654 \ln S + 0.954$	30%	1.5900054
10	$2.124 \ln S - 1.290$	$0.626 \ln S + 0.922$	29%	1.6013473
20	$2.078 \ln S - 3.093$	$0.575 \ln S + 0.524$	28%	1.6179086

This may seem paradoxical until we realize that *a high order of merge does not necessarily imply an efficient sort*. As an extreme example, consider placing one run on T1 and n runs on T2, T3, T4, T5; if we alternately do five-way merging to T6 and T1 until T2, T3, T4, T5 are empty, the processing time is $(2n^2 + 3n)$ initial run lengths, essentially proportional to S^2 instead of $S \log S$, although five-way merging was done throughout.

Tape splitting. Efficient overlapping of rewind time is a problem that arises in many applications, not just sorting, and there is a general approach that can often be used. Consider an iterative process that uses two tapes in the following way:

	T1	T2
Phase 1	Output 1	—
	Rewind	—
Phase 2	Input 1	Output 2
	Rewind	Rewind
Phase 3	Output 3	Input 2
	Rewind	Rewind
Phase 4	Input 3	Output 4
	Rewind	Rewind

and so on, where "Output k" means write the kth output file and "Input k" means read it. The rewind time can be avoided when three tapes are used, as suggested by C. Weisert [*CACM* **5** (1962), 102]:

	T1	T2	T3
Phase 1	Output 1.1	—	—
	Output 1.2	—	—
	Rewind	Output 1.3	—
Phase 2	Input 1.1	Output 2.1	—
	Input 1.2	Rewind	Output 2.2
	Rewind	Input 1.3	Output 2.3
Phase 3	Output 3.1	Input 2.1	Rewind
	Output 3.2	Rewind	Input 2.2
	Rewind	Output 3.3	Input 2.3
Phase 4	Input 3.1	Output 4.1	Rewind
	Input 3.2	Rewind	Output 4.2
	Rewind	Input 3.3	Output 4.3

and so on. Here "Output $k.j$" means write the jth third of the kth output file, and "Input $k.j$" means read it. Virtually all of the rewind time will be eliminated if rewinding is at least twice as fast as the read/write speed. Such a procedure, in which the output of each phase is divided between tapes, is called "tape splitting."

R. L. McAllester [*CACM* **7** (1964), 158–159] has shown that tape splitting leads to an efficient way of overlapping the rewind time in a polyphase merge. His method can be used with four or more tapes, and it does $(T-2)$-way merging.

Assuming once again that we have six tapes, let us try to design a merge pattern that operates as follows, splitting the output on each level, where "I", "O", and "R", respectively, denote input, output, and rewinding:

Level	T1	T2	T3	T4	T5	T6	Number of runs output
7	I	I	I	I	R	O	u_7
	I	I	I	I	O	R	v_7
6	I	I	I	R	O	I	u_6
	I	I	I	O	R	I	v_6
5	I	I	R	O	I	I	u_5
	I	I	O	R	I	I	v_5
4	I	R	O	I	I	I	u_4
	I	O	R	I	I	I	v_4
3	R	O	I	I	I	I	u_3
	O	R	I	I	I	I	v_3
2	O	I	I	I	I	R	u_2
	R	I	I	I	I	O	v_2
1	I	I	I	I	R	O	u_1
	I	I	I	I	O	R	v_1
0	I	I	I	R	O	I	u_0
	I	I	I	O	R	I	v_0

$$(21)$$

In order to end with one run on T4 and all other tapes empty, we need to have

$$v_0 = 1,$$
$$u_0 + v_1 = 0,$$
$$u_1 + v_2 = u_0 + v_0,$$
$$u_2 + v_3 = u_1 + v_1 + u_0 + v_0,$$
$$u_3 + v_4 = u_2 + v_2 + u_1 + v_1 + u_0 + v_0,$$
$$u_4 + v_5 = u_3 + v_3 + u_2 + v_2 + u_1 + v_1 + u_0 + v_0,$$
$$u_5 + v_6 = u_4 + v_4 + u_3 + v_3 + u_2 + v_2 + u_1 + v_1,$$

etc.; in general, the requirement is that

$$u_n + v_{n+1} = u_{n-1} + v_{n-1} + u_{n-2} + v_{n-2} + u_{n-3} + v_{n-3} + u_{n-4} + v_{n-4} \quad (22)$$

for all $n \geq 0$, if we regard $u_j = v_j = 0$ for all $j < 0$.

There is no unique solution to these equations; indeed, if we let all the u's be zero, we get the usual polyphase merge with one tape wasted! But if we choose $u_n \approx v_{n+1}$, the rewind time will be satisfactorily overlapped.

McAllester suggested taking

$$u_n = v_{n-1} + v_{n-2} + v_{n-3} + v_{n-4},$$
$$v_{n+1} = u_{n-1} + u_{n-2} + u_{n-3} + u_{n-4},$$

so that the sequence

$$\langle x_0, x_1, x_2, x_3, x_4, x_5, \ldots \rangle = \langle v_0, u_0, v_1, u_1, v_2, u_2, \ldots \rangle$$

satisfies the uniform recurrence $x_n = x_{n-3} + x_{n-5} + x_{n-7} + x_{n-9}$. However, it turns out to be better to let

$$\begin{aligned} v_{n+1} &= u_{n-1} + v_{n-1} + u_{n-2} + v_{n-2}, \\ u_n &= u_{n-3} + v_{n-3} + u_{n-4} + v_{n-4}; \end{aligned} \qquad (23)$$

this sequence not only leads to a slightly better merging time, it also has the great virtue that its merging time can be analyzed mathematically. McAllester's choice is extremely difficult to analyze because runs of different lengths may occur during a single phase; we shall see that this does not happen with (23).

We can deduce the number of runs on each tape on each level by working backwards in the pattern (21), and we obtain the following sorting scheme:

Level	T1	T2	T3	T4	T5	T6	Write time	Rewind time
	1^{23}	1^{21}	1^{17}	1^{10}	—	1^{11}	82	23
7	1^{19}	1^{17}	1^{13}	1^6	R	$1^{11}4^4$	$4 \times 4 = 16$	$82 - 23$
	1^{13}	1^{11}	1^7	—	4^6	R	$6 \times 4 = 24$	27
6	1^{10}	1^8	1^4	R	4^9	$1^8 4^4$	$3 \times 4 = 12$	10
	1^6	1^4	—	4^4	R	$1^4 4^4$	$4 \times 4 = 16$	36
5	1^5	1^3	R	$4^4 7^1$	4^8	$1^3 4^4$	$1 \times 7 = 7$	17
	1^2	—	7^3	R	4^5	4^4	$3 \times 7 = 21$	23
4	1^1	R	$7^3 13^1$	$4^3 7^1$	4^4	4^3	$1 \times 13 = 13$	21
	—	13^1	R	$4^2 7^1$	4^3	4^2	$1 \times 13 = 13$	34
3	R	$13^1 19^1$	$7^2 13^1$	$4^1 7^1$	4^2	4^1	$1 \times 19 = 19$	23
	19^1	R	$7^1 13^1$	7^1	4^1	—	$1 \times 19 = 19$	32
2	$19^1 31^0$	$13^1 19^1$	$7^1 13^1$	7^1	4^1	R	$0 \times 31 = 0$	27
	R	$13^0 19^1$	13^1	7^0	—	31^1	$1 \times 31 = 31$	19
1	$19^1 31^0$	$13^0 19^1$	13^1	7^0	R	$31^1 52^0$	$0 \times 52 = 0$	$\left.\rule{0pt}{20pt}\right\}$
	$19^1 31^0$	19^1	13^1	—	52^0	R	$0 \times 52 = 0$	$\max(36, 31, 23)$
0	$19^1 31^0$	19^1	13^1	R	$52^0 82^0$	$31^1 52^0$	$0 \times 82 = 0$	
	(31^0)	(19^0)	—	82^1	(R)	$(31^0 52^0)$	$1 \times 82 = 82$	0

Unoverlapped rewinding occurs in three places: when the input tape T5 is being rewound (82 units), during the first half of the level 2 phase (27 units), and during the final "dummy merge" phases in levels 1 and 0 (36 units). So we may estimate the time as $273t + 145r$; the corresponding amount for Algorithm D, $268t + 208r$, is almost always inferior.

Exercise 23 proves that the run lengths output during each phase are successively

$$4, 4, 7, 13, 19, 31, 52, 82, 133, \ldots, \qquad (24)$$

a sequence $\langle t_1, t_2, t_3, \ldots \rangle$ satisfying the law

$$t_n = t_{n-2} + 2t_{n-3} + t_{n-4} \qquad (25)$$

if we regard $t_n = 1$ for $n \le 0$. We can also analyze the optimum placement of dummy runs, by looking at strings of merge numbers as we did for standard polyphase in Eq. (8):

Level	T1	T2	T3	T4	T6	Final output on
1	1	1	1	1	—	T5
2	1	1	1	—	1	T4
3	21	21	2	2	1	T3
4	2221	222	222	22	2	T2
5	23222	23222	2322	23	222	T1
6	333323222	33332322	333323	3333	2322	T6
n	A_n	B_n	C_n	D_n	E_n	$T(k)$
$n+1$	$(A_n''E_n+1)B_n$	$(A_n''E_n+1)C_n$	$(A_n''E_n+1)D_n$	$A_n''E_n+1$	A_n'	$T(k-1)$ $\quad(26)$

where $A_n = A_n'A_n''$, and A_n'' consists of the last u_n merge numbers of A_n. The rule above for going from level n to level $n+1$ is valid for *any* scheme satisfying (22). When we define the u's and v's by (23), the strings $A_n, \ldots, E_n$ can be expressed in the following rather simple way analogous to (9):

$$
\begin{aligned}
A_n &= (W_{n-1}W_{n-2}W_{n-3}W_{n-4}) + 1, \\
B_n &= (W_{n-1}W_{n-2}W_{n-3}) + 1, \\
C_n &= (W_{n-1}W_{n-2}) + 1, \\
D_n &= (W_{n-1}) + 1, \\
E_n &= (W_{n-2}W_{n-3}) + 1,
\end{aligned}
\tag{27}
$$

where

$$
\begin{aligned}
W_n &= (W_{n-3}W_{n-4}W_{n-2}W_{n-3}) + 1 \quad \text{for } n > 0, \\
W_0 &= 0, \quad \text{and} \quad W_n = \epsilon \quad \text{for } n < 0.
\end{aligned}
\tag{28}
$$

From these relations it is easy to make a detailed analysis of the six-tape case.

In general, when there are $T \geq 5$ tapes, we let $P = T - 2$, and we define the sequences $\langle u_n \rangle$, $\langle v_n \rangle$ by the rules

$$
\begin{aligned}
v_{n+1} &= u_{n-1} + v_{n-1} + \cdots + u_{n-r} + v_{n-r}, \\
u_n &= u_{n-r-1} + v_{n-r-1} + \cdots + u_{n-P} + v_{n-P}, \quad \text{for } n \geq 0,
\end{aligned}
\tag{29}
$$

where $r = \lfloor P/2 \rfloor$; $v_0 = 1$, and $u_n = v_n = 0$ for $n < 0$. So if $w_n = u_n + v_n$, we have

$$
w_n = w_{n-2} + \cdots + w_{n-r} + 2w_{n-r-1} + w_{n-r-2} + \cdots + w_{n-P}, \quad \text{for } n > 0; \tag{30}
$$

$w_0 = 1$; and $w_n = 0$ for $n < 0$. The initial distribution on tapes for level $n + 1$ places $w_n + w_{n-1} + \cdots + w_{n-P+k}$ runs on tape k, for $1 \leq k \leq P$, and $w_{n-1} + \cdots + w_{n-r}$ on tape T; tape $T - 1$ is used for input. Then u_n runs are merged to tape T while $T - 1$ is being rewound; v_n are merged to $T - 1$ while T is rewinding; u_{n-1} to $T - 1$ while $T - 2$ is rewinding; etc.

Table 6 shows the approximate behavior of this procedure when S is not too small. The "pass/phase" column indicates approximately how much of the entire file is being rewound during each half of a phase, and approximately how much of the file is being written during each full phase. *The tape splitting method is superior to standard polyphase on six or more tapes,* and probably also on five, at least for large S.

Table 6

APPROXIMATE BEHAVIOR OF POLYPHASE MERGE WITH TAPE SPLITTING

Tapes	Phases	Passes	Pass/phase	Growth ratio
4	$2.885 \ln S + 0.000$	$1.443 \ln S + 1.000$	50%	1.4142136
5	$2.078 \ln S + 0.232$	$0.929 \ln S + 1.022$	45%	1.6180340
6	$2.078 \ln S - 0.170$	$0.752 \ln S + 1.024$	36%	1.6180340
7	$1.958 \ln S - 0.408$	$0.670 \ln S + 1.007$	34%	1.6663019
8	$2.008 \ln S - 0.762$	$0.624 \ln S + 0.994$	31%	1.6454116
9	$1.972 \ln S - 0.987$	$0.595 \ln S + 0.967$	30%	1.6604077
10	$2.013 \ln S - 1.300$	$0.580 \ln S + 0.941$	29%	1.6433803
20	$2.069 \ln S - 3.164$	$0.566 \ln S + 0.536$	27%	1.6214947

When $T = 4$ the procedure above would become essentially equivalent to balanced two-way merging, *without* overlapping the rewind time, since w_{2n+1} would be 0 for all n. So the entries in Table 6 for $T = 4$ have been obtained by making a slight modification, letting $v_2 = 0$, $u_1 = 1$, $v_1 = 0$, $u_0 = 0$, $v_0 = 1$, and $v_{n+1} = u_{n-1} + v_{n-1}$, $u_n = u_{n-2} + v_{n-2}$ for $n \geq 2$. This leads to a very interesting sorting scheme (see exercises 25 and 26).

EXERCISES

1. [*16*] Figure 69 shows the order in which runs 34 through 65 are distributed to five tapes with Algorithm D; in what order are runs 1 through 33 distributed?

▶ **2.** [*21*] True or false: After two merge phases in Algorithm D (that is, on the second time we reach step D6), all dummy runs have disappeared.

▶ **3.** [*22*] Prove that the condition $D[1] \geq D[2] \geq \cdots \geq D[T]$ is always satisfied at the conclusion of step D4. Explain why this condition is important, in the sense that the mechanism of steps D2 and D3 would not work properly otherwise.

4. [*M20*] Derive the generating functions (7).

5. [*HM26*] (E. P. Miles, Jr., 1960.) For all $p \geq 2$, prove that the polynomial $f_p(z) = z^p - z^{p-1} - \cdots - z - 1$ has p distinct roots, of which exactly one has magnitude greater than unity. [*Hint:* Consider the polynomial $z^{p+1} - 2z^p + 1$.]

6. [*HM24*] The purpose of this exercise is to consider how Tables 1, 5, and 6 were prepared. Assume that we have a merging pattern whose properties are characterized by polynomials $p(z)$ and $q(z)$ in the following way: (i) The number of initial runs present in a "perfect distribution" requiring n merging phases is $[z^n] p(z)/q(z)$. (ii) The number of initial runs processed during these n merging phases is $[z^n] p(z)/q(z)^2$. (iii) There is a "dominant root" α of $q(z^{-1})$ such that $q(\alpha^{-1}) = 0$, $q'(\alpha^{-1}) \neq 0$, $p(\alpha^{-1}) \neq 0$, and $q(\beta^{-1}) = 0$ implies that $\beta = \alpha$ or $|\beta| < |\alpha|$.

Prove that there is a number $\epsilon > 0$ such that, if S is the number of runs in a perfect distribution requiring n merging phases, and if ρS initial runs are processed during those phases, we have $n = a \ln S + b + O(S^{-\epsilon})$ and $\rho = c \ln S + d + O(S^{-\epsilon})$, where

$$a = (\ln \alpha)^{-1}, \qquad b = -a \ln \left(\frac{p(\alpha^{-1})}{-q'(\alpha^{-1})} \right) - 1, \qquad c = a \, \frac{\alpha}{-q'(\alpha^{-1})},$$

$$d = \frac{(b+1)\alpha - p'(\alpha^{-1})/p(\alpha^{-1}) + q''(\alpha^{-1})/q'(\alpha^{-1})}{-q'(\alpha^{-1})}.$$

7. [*HM22*] Let α_p be the dominant root of the polynomial $f_p(z)$ in exercise 5. What is the asymptotic behavior of α_p as $p \to \infty$?

8. [*M20*] (E. Netto, 1901.) Let $N_m^{(p)}$ be the number of ways to express m as an ordered sum of the integers $\{1, 2, \ldots, p\}$. For example, when $p = 3$ and $m = 5$, there are 13 ways, namely $1+1+1+1+1 = 1+1+1+2 = 1+1+2+1 = 1+1+3 = 1+2+1+1 = 1+2+2 = 1+3+1 = 2+1+1+1 = 2+1+2 = 2+2+1 = 2+3 = 3+1+1 = 3+2$. Show that $N_m^{(p)}$ is a generalized Fibonacci number.

9. [*M20*] Let $K_m^{(p)}$ be the number of sequences of m 0s and 1s such that there are no p consecutive 1s. For example, when $p = 3$ and $m = 5$ there are 24 such sequences: 00000, 00001, 00010, 00011, 00100, 00101, 00110, 01000, 01001, ..., 11011. Show that $K_m^{(p)}$ is a generalized Fibonacci number.

10. [*M27*] (*Generalized Fibonacci number system.*) Prove that every nonnegative integer n has a unique representation as a sum of distinct pth order Fibonacci numbers $F_j^{(p)}$, for $j \geq p$, subject to the condition that no p consecutive Fibonacci numbers are used.

11. [*M24*] Prove that the nth element of the string Q_∞ in (12) is equal to the number of distinct Fibonacci numbers in the fifth-order Fibonacci representation of $n - 1$. [See exercise 10.]

▶ **12.** [*M18*] Find a connection between powers of the matrix $\begin{pmatrix} 0 & 1 & 0 & 0 & 0 \\ 0 & 0 & 1 & 0 & 0 \\ 0 & 0 & 0 & 1 & 0 \\ 0 & 0 & 0 & 0 & 1 \\ 1 & 1 & 1 & 1 & 1 \end{pmatrix}$ and the perfect Fibonacci distributions in (1).

▶ **13.** [*22*] Prove the following rather odd property of perfect Fibonacci distributions: When the final output will be on tape number T, the number of runs on each other tape is *odd*; when the final output will be on some tape other than T, the number of runs will be *odd* on that tape, and it will be *even* on the others. [See (1).]

14. [*M35*] Let $T_n(x) = \sum_{k \geq 0} T_{nk} x^k$, where $T_n(x)$ is the polynomial defined in (16).
a) Show that for each k there is a number $n(k)$ such that $T_{1k} \leq T_{2k} \leq \cdots \leq T_{n(k)k} > T_{(n(k)+1)k} \geq \cdots$.
b) Given that $T_{n'k'} < T_{nk'}$ and $n' < n$, prove that $T_{n'k} \leq T_{nk}$ for all $k \geq k'$.
c) Prove that there is a nondecreasing sequence $\langle M_n \rangle$ such that $\Sigma_n(S) = \min_{j \geq 1} \Sigma_j(S)$ when $M_n \leq S < M_{n+1}$, but $\Sigma_n(S) > \min_{j \geq 1} \Sigma_j(S)$ when $S \geq M_{n+1}$. [See (19).]

15. [*M43*] Prove or disprove: $\Sigma_{n-1}(m) < \Sigma_n(m)$ implies that $\Sigma_n(m) \leq \Sigma_{n+1}(m) \leq \Sigma_{n+2}(m) \leq \cdots$. [Such a result would greatly simplify the calculation of Table 2.]

16. [*HM43*] Determine the asymptotic behavior of the polyphase merge with optimum distribution of dummy runs.

17. [*32*] Prove or disprove: There is a way to disperse runs for an optimum polyphase distribution in such a way that the distribution for $S + 1$ initial runs is formed by adding one run (on an appropriate tape) to the distribution for S initial runs.

18. [*30*] Does the optimum polyphase distribution produce the best possible merging pattern, in the sense that the total number of initial runs processed is minimized, if we insist that the initial runs be placed on at most $T-1$ of the tapes? (Ignore rewind time.)

19. [*21*] Make a table analogous to (1), for Caron's polyphase sort on six tapes.

20. [*M24*] What generating functions for Caron's polyphase sort on six tapes correspond to (7) and to (16)? What relations, analogous to (9) and (27), define the strings of merge numbers?

21. [*11*] What should appear on level 7 in (26)?

22. [*M21*] Each term of the sequence (24) is approximately equal to the sum of the previous two. Does this phenomenon hold for the remaining numbers of the sequence? Formulate and prove a theorem about $t_n - t_{n-1} - t_{n-2}$.

▶ **23.** [*29*] What changes would be made to (25), (27), and (28), if (23) were changed to $v_{n+1} = u_{n-1} + v_{n-1} + u_{n-2}$, $u_n = v_{n-2} + u_{n-3} + v_{n-3} + u_{n-4} + v_{n-4}$?

24. [*HM41*] Compute the asymptotic behavior of the tape-splitting polyphase procedure, when v_{n+1} is defined to be the sum of the first q terms of $u_{n-1} + v_{n-1} + \cdots + u_{n-P} + v_{n-P}$, for various $P = T - 2$ and for $0 \le q \le 2P$. (The text treats only the case $q = 2\lfloor P/2 \rfloor$; see exercise 23.)

25. [*19*] Show how the tape-splitting polyphase merge on four tapes, mentioned at the end of this section, would sort 32 initial runs. (Give a phase-by-phase analysis like the 82-run six-tape example in the text.)

26. [*M21*] Analyze the behavior of the tape-splitting polyphase merge on four tapes, when $S = 2^n$ and when $S = 2^n + 2^{n-1}$. (See exercise 25.)

27. [*23*] Once the initial runs have been distributed to tapes in a perfect distribution, the polyphase strategy is simply to "merge until empty": We merge runs from all nonempty input tapes until one of them has been entirely read; then we use that tape as the next output tape, and let the previous output tape serve as an input.

Does this merge-until-empty strategy always sort, no matter how the initial runs are distributed, as long as we distribute them onto at least two tapes? (One tape will, of course, be left empty so that it can be the first output tape.)

28. [*M26*] The previous exercise defines a rather large family of merging patterns. Show that polyphase is the *best* of them, in the following sense: If there are six tapes, and if we consider the class of all initial distributions (a, b, c, d, e) such that the merge-until-empty strategy requires at most n phases to sort, then $a + b + c + d + e \le t_n$, where t_n is the corresponding value for polyphase sorting (1).

29. [*M47*] Exercise 28 shows that the polyphase distribution is optimal among all merge-until-empty patterns in the minimum-phase sense. But is it optimal also in the minimum-pass sense?

Let a be relatively prime to b, and assume that $a + b$ is the Fibonacci number F_n. Prove or disprove the following conjecture due to R. M. Karp: The number of initial runs processed during the merge-until-empty pattern starting with distribution (a, b) is greater than or equal to $((n-5)F_{n+1} + (2n+2)F_n)/5$. (The latter figure is achieved when $a = F_{n-1}$, $b = F_{n-2}$.)

30. [*42*] Prepare a table analogous to Table 2, for the tape-splitting polyphase merge.

31. [*M22*] (R. Kemp.) Let $K_d(n)$ be the number of n-node ordered trees in which every leaf is at distance d from the root. For example, $K_3(8) = 7$ because of the trees

Show that $K_d(n)$ is a generalized Fibonacci number, and find a one-to-one correspondence between such trees and the ordered partitions considered in exercise 8.

*5.4.3. The Cascade Merge

Another basic pattern, called the "cascade merge," was actually discovered before polyphase [B. K. Betz and W. C. Carter, *ACM National Meeting* **14** (1959), Paper 14]. This approach is illustrated for six tapes and 190 initial runs in the following table, using the notation developed in Section 5.4.2:

	T1	T2	T3	T4	T5	T6	Initial runs processed
Pass 1	1^{55}	1^{50}	1^{41}	1^{29}	1^{15}	—	190
Pass 2	—	$*1^{5}$	2^{9}	3^{12}	4^{14}	5^{15}	190
Pass 3	15^{5}	14^{4}	12^{3}	9^{2}	$*5^{1}$	—	190
Pass 4	—	$*15^{1}$	29^{1}	41^{1}	50^{1}	55^{1}	190
Pass 5	190^{1}	—	—	—	—	—	190

A cascade merge, like polyphase, starts out with a "perfect distribution" of runs on tapes, although the rule for perfect distributions is somewhat different from those in Section 5.4.2. Each line in the table represents a complete pass over *all* the data. Pass 2, for example, is obtained by doing a five-way merge from $\{T1, T2, T3, T4, T5\}$ to T6, until T5 is empty (this puts 15 runs of relative length 5 on T6), then a four-way merge from $\{T1, T2, T3, T4\}$ to T5, then a three-way merge to T4, a two-way merge to T3, and finally a one-way merge (a copying operation) from T1 to T2. Pass 3 is obtained in the same way, first doing a five-way merge until one tape becomes empty, then a four-way merge, and so on. (Perhaps the present section of this book should be numbered 5.4.3.2.1 instead of 5.4.3!)

It is clear that the copying operations are unnecessary, and they could be omitted. Actually, however, in the six-tape case this copying takes only a small percentage of the total time. The items marked with an asterisk in the table above are those that were simply copied; only 25 of the 950 runs processed are of this type. Most of the time is devoted to five-way and four-way merging.

Table 1
APPROXIMATE BEHAVIOR OF CASCADE MERGE SORTING

Tapes	Passes (with copying)	Passes (without copying)	Growth ratio
3	$2.078 \ln S + 0.672$	$1.504 \ln S + 0.992$	1.6180340
4	$1.235 \ln S + 0.754$	$1.102 \ln S + 0.820$	2.2469796
5	$0.946 \ln S + 0.796$	$0.897 \ln S + 0.800$	2.8793852
6	$0.796 \ln S + 0.821$	$0.773 \ln S + 0.808$	3.5133371
7	$0.703 \ln S + 0.839$	$0.691 \ln S + 0.822$	4.1481149
8	$0.639 \ln S + 0.852$	$0.632 \ln S + 0.834$	4.7833861
9	$0.592 \ln S + 0.861$	$0.587 \ln S + 0.845$	5.4189757
10	$0.555 \ln S + 0.869$	$0.552 \ln S + 0.854$	6.0547828
20	$0.397 \ln S + 0.905$	$0.397 \ln S + 0.901$	12.4174426

At first it may seem that the cascade pattern is a rather poor choice, by comparison with polyphase, since standard polyphase uses $(T - 1)$-way merging throughout while the cascade uses $(T-1)$-way, $(T-2)$-way, $(T-3)$-way, etc. But in fact it is asymptotically *better* than polyphase, on six or more tapes! As we have observed in Section 5.4.2, a high order of merge is not a guarantee of efficiency. Table 1 shows the performance characteristics of cascade merge, by analogy with the similar tables in Section 5.4.2.

The "perfect distributions" for a cascade merge are easily derived by working backwards from the final state $(1, 0, \ldots, 0)$. With six tapes, they are

Level	T1	T2	T3	T4	T5
0	1	0	0	0	0
1	1	1	1	1	1
2	5	4	3	2	1
3	15	14	12	9	5
4	55	50	41	29	15
5	190	175	146	105	55

$$\cdots \cdots \cdots \cdots \cdots \cdots \cdots$$

n	a_n	b_n	c_n	d_n	e_n	
$n+1$	$a_n+b_n+c_n+d_n+e_n$	$a_n+b_n+c_n+d_n$	$a_n+b_n+c_n$	a_n+b_n	a_n	(1)

It is interesting to note that the relative magnitudes of these numbers appear also in the diagonals of a regular $(2T-1)$-sided polygon. For example, the five diagonals in the hendecagon of Fig. 73 have relative lengths very nearly equal to 190, 175, 146, 105, and 55! We shall prove this remarkable fact later in this section, and we shall also see that the relative amount of time spent in $(T-1)$-way merging, $(T-2)$-way merging, $\ldots$, 1-way merging is approximately proportional to the *squares* of the lengths of these diagonals.

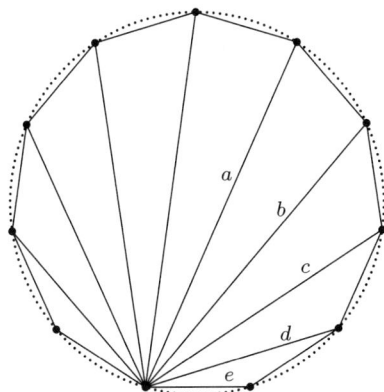

Fig. 73. Geometrical interpretation of cascade numbers.

Initial distribution of runs. When the actual number of initial runs isn't perfect, we can insert dummy runs as usual. A superficial analysis of this situation would indicate that the method of dummy run assignment is immaterial,

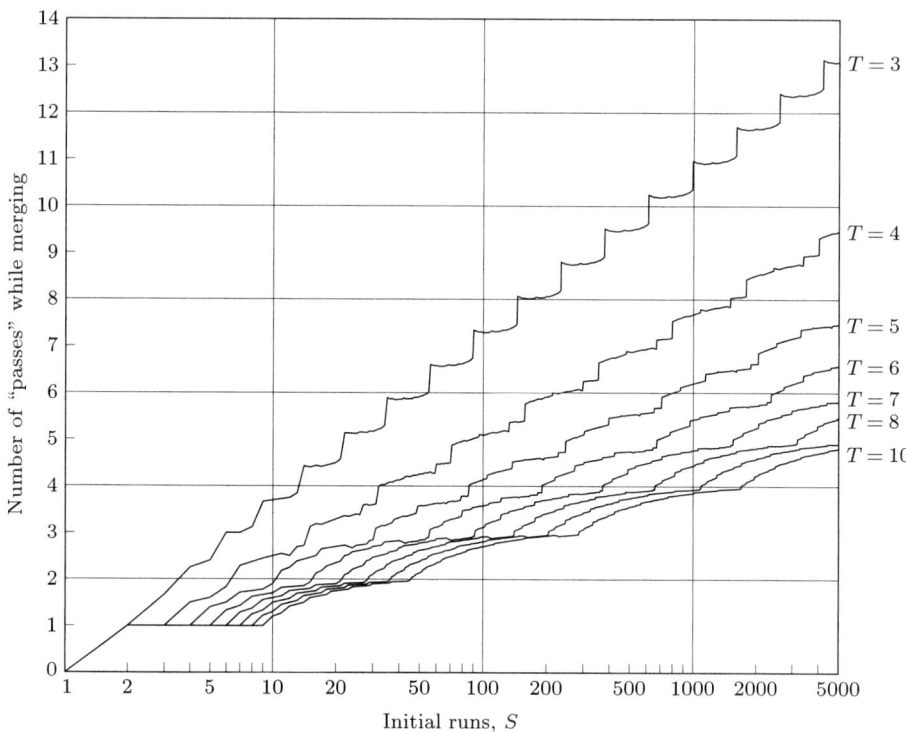

Fig. 74. Efficiency of cascade merge with the distribution of Algorithm D.

since cascade merging operates by complete passes; if we have 190 initial runs, each record is processed five times as in the example above, but if there are 191 we must apparently go up a level so that every record is processed six times. Fortunately this abrupt change is not actually necessary; David E. Ferguson has found a way to distribute initial runs so that many of the operations during the first merge pass reduce to copying the contents of a tape. When such copying relations are bypassed (by simply changing "logical" tape unit numbers relative to the "physical" numbers as in Algorithm 5.4.2D), we obtain a relatively smooth transition from level to level, as shown in Fig. 74.

Suppose that (a, b, c, d, e) is a perfect distribution, where $a \geq b \geq c \geq d \geq e$. By redefining the correspondence between logical and physical tape units, we can imagine that the distribution is actually (e, d, c, b, a), with a runs on T5, b on T4, etc. The next perfect distribution is $(a+b+c+d+e, a+b+c+d, a+b+c, a+b, a)$; and if the input is exhausted before we reach this next level, let us assume that the tapes contain, respectively, $(D_1, D_2, D_3, D_4, D_5)$ dummy runs, where

$$D_1 \leq a+b+c+d, \quad D_2 \leq a+b+c, \quad D_3 \leq a+b, \quad D_4 \leq a, \quad D_5 = 0;$$
$$D_1 \geq D_2 \geq D_3 \geq D_4 \geq D_5. \tag{2}$$

We are free to imagine that the dummy runs appear in any convenient place on the tapes. The first merge pass is supposed to produce a runs by five-way merging, then b by four-way merging, etc., and our goal is to arrange the dummies so as to replace merging by copying. It is convenient to do the first merge pass as follows:

1. If $D_4 = a$, subtract a from each of D_1, D_2, D_3, D_4 and pretend that T5 is the result of the merge. If $D_4 < a$, merge a runs from tapes T1 through T5, using the minimum possible number of dummies on tapes T1 through T5 so that the new values of D_1, D_2, D_3, D_4 will satisfy

$$D_1 \leq b + c + d, \quad D_2 \leq b + c, \quad D_3 \leq b, \quad D_4 = 0;$$
$$D_1 \geq D_2 \geq D_3 \geq D_4. \tag{3}$$

Thus, if D_2 was originally $\leq b + c$, we use no dummies from it at this step, while if $b + c < D_2 \leq a + b + c$ we use exactly $D_2 - b - c$ of them.

2. (This step is similar to step 1, but "shifted.") If $D_3 = b$, subtract b from each of D_1, D_2, D_3 and pretend that T4 is the result of the merge. If $D_3 < b$, merge b runs from tapes T1 through T4, reducing the number of dummies if necessary in order to make

$$D_1 \leq c + d, \quad D_2 \leq c, \quad D_3 = 0; \qquad D_1 \geq D_2 \geq D_3.$$

3. And so on.

Table 2
EXAMPLE OF CASCADE DISTRIBUTION STEPS

	Add to T1	Add to T2	Add to T3	Add to T4	Add to T5	"Amount saved"
Step (1,1)	9	0	0	0	0	15+14+12+5
Step (2,2)	3	12	0	0	0	15+14+9+5
Step (2,1)	9	0	0	0	0	15+14+5
Step (3,3)	2	2	14	0	0	15+12+5
Step (3,2)	3	12	0	0	0	15+9+5
Step (3,1)	9	0	0	0	0	15+5
Step (4,4)	1	1	1	15	0	14+5
Step (4,3)	2	2	14	0	0	12+5
Step (4,2)	3	12	0	0	0	9+5
Step (4,1)	9	0	0	0	0	5

Ferguson's method of distributing runs to tapes can be illustrated by considering the process of going from level 3 to level 4 in (1). Assume that "logical" tapes (T1, ..., T5) contain respectively (5, 9, 12, 14, 15) runs and that we want eventually to bring this up to (55, 50, 41, 29, 15). The procedure can be summarized as shown in Table 2. We first put nine runs on T1, then (3, 12) on T1 and T2, etc. If the input becomes exhausted during, say, Step (3,2), then the "amount saved" is $15 + 9 + 5$, meaning that the five-way merge of 15 runs, the two-way merge of 9 runs, and the one-way merge of 5 runs are avoided by the dummy run assignment. In other words, $15 + 9 + 5$ of the runs present at level 3 are not processed during the first merge phase.

The following algorithm defines the process in detail.

Algorithm C (*Cascade merge sorting with special distribution*). This algorithm takes initial runs and disperses them to tapes, one run at a time, until the supply of initial runs is exhausted. Then it specifies how the tapes are to be merged, assuming that there are $T \geq 3$ available tape units, using at most $(T-1)$-way merging and avoiding unnecessary one-way merging. Tape T may be used to hold the input, since it does not receive any initial runs. The following tables are maintained:

A[j], $1 \leq j \leq T$: The perfect cascade distribution we have most recently reached.

AA[j], $1 \leq j \leq T$: The perfect cascade distribution we are striving for.

D[j], $1 \leq j \leq T$: Number of dummy runs assumed to be present on logical tape unit number j.

M[j], $1 \leq j < T$: Maximum number of dummy runs desired on logical tape unit number j.

TAPE[j], $1 \leq j \leq T$: Number of the physical tape unit corresponding to logical tape unit number j.

C1. [Initialize.] Set A[k] ← AA[k] ← D[k] ← 0 for $2 \leq k \leq T$; and set A[1] ← 0, AA[1] ← 1, D[1] ← 1. Set TAPE[k] ← k for $1 \leq k \leq T$. Finally set $i \leftarrow T-2$, $j \leftarrow 1$, $k \leftarrow 1$, $l \leftarrow 0$, $m \leftarrow 1$, and go to step C5. (This maneuvering is one way to get everything started, by jumping right into the inner loop with appropriate settings of the control variables.)

C2. [Begin new level.] (We have just reached a perfect distribution, and since there is more input we must get ready for the next level.) Increase l by 1. Set A[k] ← AA[k], for $1 \leq k \leq T$; then set AA[$T-k$] ← AA[$T-k+1$]+A[k], for $k = 1, 2, \ldots, T-1$ in this order. Set (TAPE[1],...,TAPE[$T-1$]) ← (TAPE[$T-1$],...,TAPE[1]), and set D[k] ← AA[$k+1$] for $1 \leq k < T$. Finally set $i \leftarrow 1$.

C3. [Begin ith sublevel.] Set $j \leftarrow i$. (The variables i and j represent "Step (i, j)" in the example shown in Table 2.)

C4. [Begin Step (i, j).] Set $k \leftarrow j$ and $m \leftarrow$ A[$T-j-1$]. If $m = 0$ and $i = j$, set $i \leftarrow T-2$ and return to C3; if $m = 0$ and $i \neq j$, return to C2. (Variable m represents the number of runs to be written onto TAPE[k]; $m = 0$ occurs only when $l = 1$.)

C5. [Input to TAPE[k].] Write one run on tape number TAPE[k], and decrease D[k] by 1. Then if the input is exhausted, rewind all the tapes and go to step C7.

C6. [Advance.] Decrease m by 1. If $m > 0$, return to C5. Otherwise decrease k by 1; if $k > 0$, set $m \leftarrow$ A[$T-j-1$] − A[$T-j$] and return to C5 if $m > 0$. Otherwise decrease j by 1; if $j > 0$, go to C4. Otherwise increase i by 1; if $i < T-1$, return to C3. Otherwise go to C2.

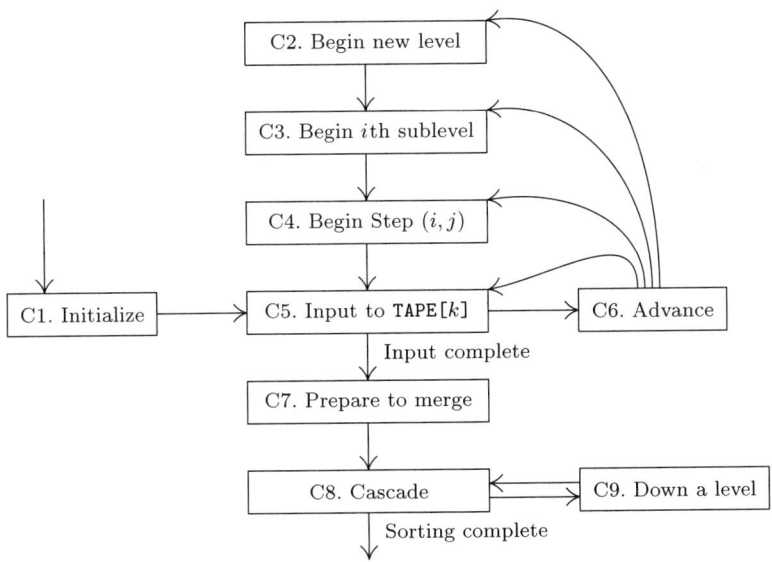

Fig. 75. The cascade merge, with special distribution.

C7. [Prepare to merge.] (At this point the initial distribution is complete, and the AA, D, and TAPE tables describe the present states of the tapes.) Set $M[k] \leftarrow AA[k+1]$ for $1 \le k < T$, and set FIRST $\leftarrow 1$. (Variable FIRST is nonzero only during the first merge pass.)

C8. [Cascade.] If $l = 0$, stop; sorting is complete and the output is on TAPE[1]. Otherwise, for $p = T - 1, T - 2, \ldots, 1$, in this order, do a p-way merge from TAPE[1], ..., TAPE[p] to TAPE[$p+1$] as follows:

If $p = 1$, simulate the one-way merge by simply rewinding TAPE[2], then interchanging TAPE[1] $\leftrightarrow$ TAPE[2].

Otherwise if FIRST $= 1$ and $D[p-1] = M[p-1]$, simulate the p-way merge by simply interchanging TAPE[p] $\leftrightarrow$ TAPE[$p+1$], rewinding TAPE[p], and subtracting $M[p-1]$ from each of $D[1], \ldots, D[p-1], M[1], \ldots, M[p-1]$.

Otherwise, subtract $M[p-1]$ from each of $M[1], \ldots, M[p-1]$. Then merge one run from each TAPE[j] such that $1 \le j \le p$ and $D[j] \le M[j]$; subtract one from each $D[j]$ such that $1 \le j \le p$ and $D[j] > M[j]$; and put the output run on TAPE[$p+1$]. Continue doing this until TAPE[p] is empty. Then rewind TAPE[p] and TAPE[$p+1$].

C9. [Down a level.] Decrease l by 1, set FIRST $\leftarrow 0$, and set (TAPE[1], ..., TAPE[T]) $\leftarrow$ (TAPE[T], ..., TAPE[1]). (At this point all D's and M's are zero and will remain so.) Return to C8. ∎

Steps C1–C6 of this algorithm do the distribution, and steps C7–C9 do the merging; the two parts are fairly independent of each other, and it would be possible to store $M[k]$ and $AA[k+1]$ in the same memory locations.

Analysis of cascade merging. The cascade merge is somewhat harder to analyze than polyphase, but the analysis is especially interesting because so many remarkable formulas are present. Readers who enjoy discrete mathematics are urged to study the cascade distribution for themselves, *before reading further*, since the numbers have extraordinary properties that are a pleasure to discover. We shall discuss here one of the many ways to approach the analysis, emphasizing the way in which the results might be discovered.

For convenience, let us consider the six-tape case, looking for formulas that generalize to all T. Relations (1) lead to the first basic pattern:

$$
\begin{aligned}
a_n &= a_n & &= \tbinom{0}{0} a_n, \\
b_n &= a_n - e_{n-1} & & \\
&= a_n - a_{n-2} & &= \tbinom{1}{0} a_n - \tbinom{2}{2} a_{n-2}, \\
c_n &= b_n - d_{n-1} & & \\
&= b_n - a_{n-2} - b_{n-2} & &= \tbinom{2}{0} a_n - \tbinom{3}{2} a_{n-2} + \tbinom{4}{4} a_{n-4}, \\
d_n &= c_n - c_{n-1} & & \\
&= c_n - a_{n-2} - b_{n-2} - c_{n-2} & &= \tbinom{3}{0} a_n - \tbinom{4}{2} a_{n-2} + \tbinom{5}{4} a_{n-4} - \tbinom{6}{6} a_{n-6}, \\
e_n &= d_n - b_{n-1} & & \\
&= d_n - a_{n-2} - b_{n-2} - c_{n-2} - d_{n-2} & &= \tbinom{4}{0} a_n - \tbinom{5}{2} a_{n-2} + \tbinom{6}{4} a_{n-4} - \tbinom{7}{6} a_{n-6} + \tbinom{8}{8} a_{n-8}.
\end{aligned}
$$

$$(4)$$

Let $A(z) = \sum_{n \geq 0} a_n z^n$, $\ldots$, $E(z) = \sum_{n \geq 0} e_n z^n$, and define the polynomials

$$
q_m(z) = \binom{m}{0} - \binom{m+1}{2} z^2 + \binom{m+2}{4} z^4 - \cdots
$$

$$
= \sum_{k} \binom{m+k}{2k} (-1)^k z^{2k} = \sum_{k=0}^{m} \binom{2m-k}{k} (-1)^{m-k} z^{2m-2k}. \qquad (5)
$$

The result of (4) can be summarized by saying that the generating functions $B(z) - q_1(z)A(z)$, $C(z) - q_2(z)A(z)$, $D(z) - q_3(z)A(z)$, and $E(z) - q_4(z)A(z)$ reduce to finite sums, corresponding to the values of $a_{-1}, a_{-2}, a_{-3}, \ldots$ that appear in (4) for small n but do not appear in $A(z)$. In order to supply appropriate boundary conditions, let us run the recurrence backwards to negative levels, through level -8:

n	a_n	b_n	c_n	d_n	e_n
0	1	0	0	0	0
-1	0	0	0	0	1
-2	1	-1	0	0	0
-3	0	0	0	-1	2
-4	2	-3	1	0	0
-5	0	0	1	-4	5
-6	5	-9	5	-1	0
-7	0	-1	6	-14	14
-8	14	-28	20	-7	1

(On seven tapes the table would be similar, with entries for odd n shifted right one column.) The sequence $a_0, a_{-2}, a_{-4}, \ldots = 1, 1, 2, 5, 14, \ldots$ is a dead giveaway for computer scientists, since it occurs in connection with so many recursive algorithms (see, for example, exercise 2.2.1–4 and Eq. 2.3.4.4–(14)); therefore we conjecture that in the T-tape case

$$a_{-2n} = \binom{2n}{n}\frac{1}{n+1}, \qquad \text{for } 0 \le n \le T - 2; \tag{6}$$

$$a_{-2n-1} = 0, \qquad \text{for } 0 \le n \le T - 3.$$

To verify that this choice is correct, it suffices to show that (6) and (4) yield the correct results for levels 0 and 1. On level 1 this is obvious, and on level 0 we have to verify that

$$\binom{m}{0}a_0 - \binom{m+1}{2}a_{-2} + \binom{m+2}{4}a_{-4} - \binom{m+3}{6}a_{-6} + \cdots$$

$$= \sum_{k \ge 0}\binom{m+k}{2k}\binom{2k}{k}\frac{(-1)^k}{k+1} = \delta_{m0} \tag{7}$$

for $0 \le m \le T - 2$. Fortunately this sum can be evaluated by standard techniques; it is, in fact, Example 2 in Section 1.2.6.

Now we can compute the coefficients of $B(z) - q_1(z)A(z)$, etc. For example, consider the coefficient of z^{2m} in $D(z) - q_3(z)A(z)$: It is

$$\sum_{k \ge 0}\binom{3+m+k}{2m+2k}(-1)^{m+k}a_{-2k} = \sum_{k \ge 0}\binom{3+m+k}{2m+2k}\binom{2k}{k}\frac{(-1)^{m+k}}{k+1}$$

$$= (-1)^m\left(\binom{2+m}{2m-1} - \binom{3+m}{2m}\right)$$

$$= (-1)^{m+1}\binom{2+m}{2m},$$

by the result of Example 3 in Section 1.2.6. Therefore we have deduced that

$$A(z) = q_0(z)A(z),$$
$$B(z) = q_1(z)A(z) - q_0(z), \qquad C(z) = q_2(z)A(z) - q_1(z),$$
$$D(z) = q_3(z)A(z) - q_2(z), \qquad E(z) = q_4(z)A(z) - q_3(z). \tag{8}$$

Furthermore we have $e_{n+1} = a_n$; hence $zA(z) = E(z)$, and

$$A(z) = q_3(z)/(q_4(z) - z). \tag{9}$$

The generating functions have now been derived in terms of the q polynomials, and so we want to understand the q's better. Exercise 1.2.9–15 is useful in this regard, since it gives us a closed form that may be written

$$q_m(z) = \frac{\left((\sqrt{4 - z^2} + iz)/2\right)^{2m+1} + \left((\sqrt{4 - z^2} - iz)/2\right)^{2m+1}}{\sqrt{4 - z^2}}. \tag{10}$$

Everything simplifies if we now set $z = 2\sin\theta$:

$$q_m(2\sin\theta) = \frac{(\cos\theta + i\sin\theta)^{2m+1} + (\cos\theta - i\sin\theta)^{2m+1}}{2\cos\theta} = \frac{\cos(2m+1)\theta}{\cos\theta}. \quad (11)$$

(This coincidence leads us to suspect that the polynomial $q_m(z)$ is well known in mathematics; and indeed, a glance at appropriate tables will show that $q_m(z)$ is essentially a Chebyshev polynomial of the second kind, namely $(-1)^m U_{2m}(z/2)$ in conventional notation.)

We can now determine the roots of the denominator in (9): The equation $q_4(2\sin\theta) = 2\sin\theta$ reduces to

$$\cos 9\theta = 2\sin\theta\cos\theta = \sin 2\theta.$$

We can obtain solutions to this relation whenever $\pm 9\theta = 2\theta + (2n - \frac{1}{2})\pi$; and all such θ yield roots of the denominator in (9) provided that $\cos\theta \neq 0$. (When $\cos\theta = 0$, $q_m(\pm 2) = (2m+1)$ is never equal to ± 2.) The following eight distinct roots for $q_4(z) - z = 0$ are therefore obtained:

$$2\sin\tfrac{-5}{14}\pi,\ 2\sin\tfrac{-1}{14}\pi,\ 2\sin\tfrac{3}{14}\pi;\ 2\sin\tfrac{-7}{22}\pi,\ 2\sin\tfrac{-3}{22}\pi,\ 2\sin\tfrac{1}{22}\pi,\ 2\sin\tfrac{5}{22}\pi,\ 2\sin\tfrac{9}{22}\pi.$$

Since $q_4(z)$ is a polynomial of degree 8, this accounts for all the roots. The first three of these values make $q_3(z) = 0$, so $q_3(z)$ and $q_4(z) - z$ have a polynomial of degree three as a common factor. The other five roots govern the asymptotic behavior of the coefficients of $A(z)$, if we expand (9) in partial fractions.

Considering the general T-tape case, let $\theta_k = (4k+1)\pi/(4T - 2)$. The generating function $A(z)$ for the T-tape cascade distribution numbers takes the form

$$\frac{4}{2T-1} \sum_{-T/2 < k < \lfloor T/2 \rfloor} \frac{\cos^2\theta_k}{1 - z/(2\sin\theta_k)} \quad (12)$$

(see exercise 8); hence

$$a_n = \frac{4}{2T-1} \sum_{-T/2 < k < \lfloor T/2 \rfloor} \cos^2\theta_k \left(\frac{1}{2\sin\theta_k}\right)^n. \quad (13)$$

The equations in (8) now lead to the similar formulas

$$b_n = \frac{4}{2T-1} \sum_{-T/2 < k < \lfloor T/2 \rfloor} \cos\theta_k \cos 3\theta_k \left(\frac{1}{2\sin\theta_k}\right)^n,$$

$$c_n = \frac{4}{2T-1} \sum_{-T/2 < k < \lfloor T/2 \rfloor} \cos\theta_k \cos 5\theta_k \left(\frac{1}{2\sin\theta_k}\right)^n, \quad (14)$$

$$d_n = \frac{4}{2T-1} \sum_{-T/2 < k < \lfloor T/2 \rfloor} \cos\theta_k \cos 7\theta_k \left(\frac{1}{2\sin\theta_k}\right)^n,$$

and so on. Exercise 9 shows that these equations hold for all $n \geq 0$, not only for large n. In each sum the term for $k = 0$ dominates all the others, especially when n is reasonably large; therefore the "growth ratio" is

$$\frac{1}{2\sin\theta_0} = \frac{2}{\pi}T - \frac{1}{\pi} + \frac{\pi}{48T} + O(T^{-2}). \tag{15}$$

Cascade sorting was first analyzed by W. C. Carter [*Proc. IFIP Congress* (1962), 62–66], who obtained numerical results for small T, and by David E. Ferguson [see *CACM* **7** (1964), 297], who discovered the first two terms in the asymptotic behavior (15) of the growth ratio. During the summer of 1964, R. W. Floyd discovered the explicit form $1/(2\sin\theta_0)$ of the growth ratio, so that exact formulas could be used for all T. An intensive analysis of the cascade numbers was independently carried out by G. N. Raney [*Canadian J. Math.* **18** (1966), 332–349], who came across them in quite another way having nothing to do with sorting. Raney observed the "ratio of diagonals" principle of Fig. 73, and derived many other interesting properties of the numbers. Floyd and Raney used matrix manipulations in their proofs (see exercise 6).

Modifications of cascade sorting. If one more tape is added, it is possible to overlap nearly all of the rewind time during a cascade sort. For example, we can merge T1–T5 to T7, then T1–T4 to T6, then T1–T3 to T5 (which by now is rewound), then T1–T2 to T4, and the next pass can begin when the comparatively short data on T4 has been rewound. The efficiency of this process can be predicted from the analysis of cascading. (See Section 5.4.6 for further information.)

A "compromise merge" scheme, which includes both polyphase and cascade as special cases, was suggested by D. E. Knuth in *CACM* **6** (1963), 585–587. Each phase consists of $(T-1)$-way, $(T-2)$-way, ..., P-way merges, where P is any fixed number between 1 and $T-1$. When $P = T-1$, this is polyphase, and when $P = 1$ it is pure cascade; when $P = 2$ it is cascade without copy phases. Analyses of this scheme have been made by C. E. Radke [*IBM Systems J.* **5** (1966), 226–247] and by W. H. Burge [*Proc. IFIP Congress* (1971), **1**, 454–459]. Burge found the generating function $\sum T_n(x)z^n$ for each (P,T) compromise merge, generalizing Eq. 5.4.2–(16); he showed that the best value of P, from the standpoint of fewest initial runs processed as a function of S as $S \to \infty$ (using a straightforward distribution scheme and ignoring rewind time), is respectively $(2,3,3,4,4,4,3,3,4)$ for $T = (3,4,5,6,7,8,9,10,11)$. These values of P lean more towards cascade than polyphase as T increases; and it turns out that the compromise merge is never substantially better than cascade itself. On the other hand, with an optimum choice of levels and optimum distribution of dummy runs, as described in Section 5.4.2, pure polyphase seems to be best of all the compromise merges; unfortunately the optimum distribution is comparatively difficult to implement.

Th. L. Johnsen [*BIT* **6** (1966), 129–143] has studied a combination of balanced and polyphase merging; a rewind-overlap variation of balanced merging has been proposed by M. A. Goetz [*Digital Computer User's Handbook*, edited by M. Klerer and G. A. Korn (New York: McGraw–Hill, 1967), 1.311–1.312]; and many other hybrid schemes can be imagined.

EXERCISES

1. [*10*] Using Table 1, compare cascade merging with the tape-splitting version of polyphase described in Section 5.4.2. Which is better? (Ignore rewind time.)

▶ **2.** [*22*] Compare cascade sorting on three tapes, using Algorithm C, to polyphase sorting on three tapes, using Algorithm 5.4.2D. What similarities and differences can you find?

3. [*23*] Prepare a table that shows what happens when 100 initial runs are sorted on six tapes using Algorithm C.

4. [*M20*] (G. N. Raney.) An "nth level cascade distribution" is a multiset defined as follows (in the case of six tapes): $\{1, 0, 0, 0, 0\}$ is a 0th level cascade distribution; and if $\{a, b, c, d, e\}$ is an nth level cascade distribution, $\{a+b+c+d+e,\ a+b+c+d, a+b+c,\ a+b,\ a\}$ is an $(n + 1)$st level cascade distribution. (A multiset is unordered, hence up to 5! different $(n + 1)$st level distributions can be formed from a single nth level distribution.)

    a) Prove that *any* multiset $\{a, b, c, d, e\}$ of relatively prime integers is an nth level cascade distribution, for some n.

    b) Prove that the distribution defined for cascade sorting is *optimum*, in the sense that, if $\{a, b, c, d, e\}$ is any nth level distribution with $a \geq b \geq c \geq d \geq e$, we have $a \leq a_n, b \leq b_n, c \leq c_n, d \leq d_n, e \leq e_n$, where $(a_n, b_n, c_n, d_n, e_n)$ is the distribution defined in (1).

▶ **5.** [*20*] Prove that the cascade numbers defined in (1) satisfy the law

$$a_k a_{n-k} + b_k b_{n-k} + c_k c_{n-k} + d_k d_{n-k} + e_k e_{n-k} = a_n, \qquad \text{for } 0 \leq k \leq n.$$

[*Hint:* Interpret this relation by considering how many runs of various lengths are output during the kth pass of a complete cascade sort.]

6. [*M20*] Find a 5×5 matrix Q such that the first row of Q^n contains the six-tape cascade numbers $a_n\, b_n\, c_n\, d_n\, e_n$ for all $n \geq 0$.

7. [*M20*] Given that cascade merge is being applied to a perfect distribution of a_n initial runs, find a formula for the amount of processing saved when one-way merging is suppressed.

8. [*HM23*] Derive (12).

9. [*HM26*] Derive (14).

▶ **10.** [*M28*] Instead of using the pattern (4) to begin the study of the cascade numbers, start with the identities

$$e_n = a_{n-1} \qquad\qquad\qquad = \tbinom{1}{1}a_{n-1},$$
$$d_n = 2a_{n-1} - e_{n-2} \qquad\quad = \tbinom{2}{1}a_{n-1} - \tbinom{3}{3}a_{n-3},$$
$$c_n = 3a_{n-1} - d_{n-2} - 2e_{n-2} = \tbinom{3}{1}a_{n-1} - \tbinom{4}{3}a_{n-3} - \tbinom{5}{5}a_{n-5},$$

etc. Letting

$$r_m(z) = \binom{m}{1}z - \binom{m+1}{3}z^3 + \binom{m+2}{5}z^5 - \cdots,$$

express $A(z)$, $B(z)$, etc. in terms of these r polynomials.

11. [*M38*] Let

$$f_m(z) = \sum_{k=0}^{m} \binom{\lfloor (m+k)/2 \rfloor}{k} (-1)^{\lceil k/2 \rceil} z^k.$$

Prove that the generating function $A(z)$ for the T-tape cascade numbers is equal to $f_{T-3}(z)/f_{T-1}(z)$, where the numerator and denominator in this expression have no common factor.

12. [*M40*] Prove that Ferguson's distribution scheme is optimum, in the sense that no method of placing the dummy runs, satisfying (2), will cause fewer initial runs to be processed during the first pass, *provided* that the strategy of steps C7–C9 is used during this pass.

13. [*40*] The text suggests overlapping most of the rewind time, by adding an extra tape. Explore this idea. (For example, the text's scheme involves waiting for T4 to rewind; would it be better to omit T4 from the first merge phase of the next pass?)

*5.4.4. Reading Tape Backwards

Many magnetic tape units have the ability to read tape in the opposite direction from which it was written. The merging patterns we have encountered so far always write information onto tape in the "forward" direction, then rewind the tape, read it forwards, and rewind again. The tape files therefore behave as queues, operating in a first-in-first-out manner. Backwards reading allows us to eliminate both of these rewind operations: We write the tape forwards and read it backwards. In this case the files behave as stacks, since they are used in a last-in-first-out manner.

The balanced, polyphase, and cascade merge patterns can all be adapted to backward reading. The main difference is that *merging reverses the order of the runs* when we read backwards and write forwards. If two runs are in ascending order on tape, we can merge them while reading backwards, but this produces descending order. The descending runs produced in this way will subsequently become ascending on the next pass; so the merging algorithms must be capable of dealing with runs in either order. Programmers who are confronted with read-backwards for the first time often feel like they are standing on their heads!

As an example of backwards reading, consider the process of merging 8 initial runs, using a *balanced* merge on four tapes. The operations can be summarized as follows:

	T1	T2	T3	T4	
Pass 1	$A_1A_1A_1A_1$	$A_1A_1A_1A_1$	—	—	Initial distribution
Pass 2	—	—	D_2D_2	D_2D_2	Merge to T3 and T4
Pass 3	A_4	A_4	—	—	Merge to T1 and T2
Pass 4	—	—	D_8	—	Final merge to T3

Here A_r stands for a run of relative length r that appears on tape in ascending order, if the tape is read forwards as in our previous examples; D_r is the corresponding notation for a descending run of length r. During Pass 2 the ascending runs become descending: They appear to be descending in the input, since we are reading T1 and T2 backwards. Then the runs switch orientation again on Pass 3.

Notice that the process above finishes with the result on tape T3, in *descending* order. If this is bad (depending on whether the output is to be read backwards, or to be dismounted and put away for future use), we could copy it to another tape, reversing the direction. A faster way would be to rewind T1 and T2 after Pass 3, producing A_8 during Pass 4. Still faster would be to start with eight *descending* runs during Pass 1, since this would interchange all the A's and D's. However, the balanced merge on 16 initial runs would require the initial runs to be ascending; and we usually don't know in advance how many initial runs will be formed, so it is necessary to choose one consistent direction. Therefore the idea of rewinding after Pass 3 is probably best.

The *cascade* merge carries over in the same way. For example, consider sorting 14 initial runs on four tapes:

	T1	T2	T3	T4
Pass 1	$A_1 A_1 A_1 A_1 A_1 A_1$	$A_1 A_1 A_1 A_1 A_1$	$A_1 A_1 A_1$	—
Pass 2	—	D_1	$D_2 D_2$	$D_3 D_3 D_3$
Pass 3	A_6	A_5	A_3	—
Pass 4	—	—	—	D_{14}

Again, we could produce A_{14} instead of D_{14}, if we rewound T1, T2, T3 just before the final pass. This tableau illustrates a "pure" cascade merge, in the sense that all of the one-way merges have been performed explicitly. If we had suppressed the copying operations, as in Algorithm 5.4.3C, we would have been confronted with the situation

$$A_1 \qquad\qquad — \qquad\qquad D_2 D_2 \qquad\qquad D_3 D_3 D_3$$

after Pass 2, and it would have been impossible to continue with a three-way merge since we cannot merge runs that are in opposite directions! The operation of copying T1 to T2 could be avoided if we rewound T1 and proceeded to read it forward during the next merge phase (while reading T3 and T4 backwards). But it would then be necessary to rewind T1 again after merging, so this trick trades one copy for two rewinds.

Thus the distribution method of Algorithm 5.4.3C does not work as efficiently for read-backwards as for read-forwards; the amount of time required jumps rather sharply every time the number of initial runs passes a "perfect" cascade distribution number. Another dispersion technique can be used to give a smoother transition between perfect cascade distributions (see exercise 17).

Read-backward polyphase. At first glance (and even at second and third glance), the polyphase merge scheme seems to be totally unfit for reading backwards. For example, suppose that we have 13 initial runs and three tapes:

	T1	T2	T3
Phase 1	$A_1 A_1 A_1 A_1 A_1$	$A_1 A_1 A_1 A_1 A_1 A_1 A_1 A_1$	—
Phase 2	—	$A_1 A_1 A_1$	$D_2 D_2 D_2 D_2 D_2$

Now we're stuck; we could rewind either T2 or T3 and then read it forwards, while reading the other tape backwards, but this would jumble things up and we would have gained comparatively little by reading backwards.

An ingenious idea that saves the situation is to *alternate the direction of runs on each tape*. Then the merging can proceed in perfect synchronization:

	T1	T2	T3
	$A_1 D_1 A_1 D_1 A_1$	$D_1 A_1 D_1 A_1 D_1 A_1 D_1 A_1$	—
Phase 1	$A_1 D_1 A_1 D_1 A_1$	$D_1 A_1 D_1 A_1 D_1 A_1 D_1 A_1$	—
Phase 2	—	$D_1 A_1 D_1$	$D_2 A_2 D_2 A_2 D_2$
Phase 3	$A_3 D_3 A_3$	—	$D_2 A_2$
Phase 4	A_3	$D_5 A_5$	—
Phase 5	—	D_5	D_8
Phase 6	A_{13}	—	—

This principle was mentioned briefly by R. L. Gilstad in his original article on polyphase merging, and he described it more fully in *CACM* **6** (1963), 220–223.

The *ADA*... technique works properly for polyphase merging on *any* number of tapes; for we can show that the A's and D's will be properly synchronized at each phase, provided only that the initial distribution pass produces alternating A's and D's on each tape and that each tape ends with A (or each tape ends with D): Since the last run written on the output file during one phase is in the opposite direction from the last runs used from the input files, the next phase always finds its runs in the proper orientation. Furthermore we have seen in exercise 5.4.2–13 that most of the perfect Fibonacci distributions call for an *odd* number of runs on one tape (the eventual output tape), and an *even* number of runs on each other tape. If T1 is designated as the final output tape, we can therefore guarantee that all tapes end with an A run, if we start T1 with an A and let the remaining tapes start with a D. A distribution method analogous to Algorithm 5.4.2D can be used, modified so that the distributions on each level have T1 as the final output tape. (We skip levels 1, $T+1$, $2T+1$, ..., since they are the levels in which the initially empty tape is the final output tape.) For example, in the six-tape case, we can use the following distribution numbers in place of 5.4.2–(1):

Level	T1	T2	T3	T4	T5	Total	Final output will be on
0	1	0	0	0	0	1	T1
2	1	2	2	2	2	9	T1
3	3	4	4	4	2	17	T1
4	7	8	8	6	4	33	T1 (1)
5	15	16	14	12	8	65	T1
6	31	30	28	24	16	129	T1
8	61	120	116	108	92	497	T1

Thus, T1 always gets an odd number of runs, while T2 through T5 get the even numbers, in decreasing order for flexibility in dummy run assignment. Such a distribution has the advantage that the final output tape is known in advance, regardless of the number of initial runs that happen to be present. It turns out (see exercise 3) that the output will always appear in *ascending* order on T1 when this scheme is used.

Another way to handle the distribution for read-backward polyphase has been suggested by D. T. Goodwin and J. L. Venn [*CACM* **7** (1964), 315]. We can distribute runs almost as in Algorithm 5.4.2D, beginning with a D run on each tape. When the input is exhausted, a dummy A run is imagined to be at the beginning of the unique "odd" tape, unless a distribution with all odd numbers has been reached. Other dummies are imagined at the end of the tapes, or grouped into pairs in the middle. The question of optimum placement of dummy runs is analyzed in exercise 5 below.

Optimum merge patterns. So far we have been discussing various patterns for merging on tape, without asking for "best possible" methods. It appears to be quite difficult to determine the optimal patterns, especially in the read-forward case where the interaction of rewind time with merge time is hard to handle. On the other hand, when merging is done by reading backwards and writing forwards, all rewinding is essentially eliminated, and it is possible to get a fairly good characterization of optimal ways to merge. Richard M. Karp has introduced some very interesting approaches to this problem, and we shall conclude this section by discussing the theory he has developed.

In the first place we need a more satisfactory way to describe merging patterns, instead of the rather mysterious tape-content tableaux that have been used above. Karp has suggested two ways to do this, the *vector representation* and the *tree representation* of a merge pattern. Both forms of representation are useful in practice, so we shall describe them in turn.

The vector representation of a merge pattern consists of a sequence of "merge vectors" $y^{(m)} \ldots y^{(1)} y^{(0)}$, each of which has T components. The ith-last merge step is represented by $y^{(i)}$ in the following way:

$$y_j^{(i)} = \begin{cases} +1, & \text{if tape number } j \text{ is an input to the merge;} \\ 0, & \text{if tape number } j \text{ is not used in the merge;} \\ -1, & \text{if tape number } j \text{ gets the output of the merge.} \end{cases} \qquad (2)$$

Thus, exactly one component of $y^{(i)}$ is -1, and the other components are 0s and 1s. The final vector $y^{(0)}$ is special; it is a unit vector, having 1 in position j if the final sorted output appears on unit j, and 0 elsewhere. These definitions imply that the vector sum

$$v^{(i)} = y^{(i)} + y^{(i-1)} + \cdots + y^{(0)} \qquad (3)$$

represents the distribution of runs on tape just before the ith-last merge step, with $v_j^{(i)}$ runs on tape j. In particular, $v^{(m)}$ tells how many runs the initial distribution pass places on each tape.

It may seem awkward to number these vectors backwards, with $y^{(m)}$ coming first and $y^{(0)}$ last, but this peculiar viewpoint turns out to be advantageous for developing the theory. One good way to search for an optimal method is to start with the sorted output and to imagine "unmerging" it to various tapes, then unmerging these, etc., considering the successive distributions $v^{(0)}$, $v^{(1)}$, $v^{(2)}$, ... in the reverse order from which they actually occur during the sorting process.

In fact that is essentially the approach we have taken already in our analysis of polyphase and cascade merging.

The three merge patterns described in tabular form earlier in this section have the following vector representations:

Balanced $(T = 4, S = 8)$

$$v^{(7)} = (4,4,0,0)$$
$$y^{(7)} = (+1,+1,-1,0)$$
$$y^{(6)} = (+1,+1,0,-1)$$
$$y^{(5)} = (+1,+1,-1,0)$$
$$y^{(4)} = (+1,+1,0,-1)$$
$$y^{(3)} = (-1,0,+1,+1)$$
$$y^{(2)} = (0,-1,+1,+1)$$
$$y^{(1)} = (+1,+1,-1,0)$$
$$y^{(0)} = (0,0,1,0)$$

Cascade $(T = 4, S = 14)$

$$v^{(10)} = (6,5,3,0)$$
$$y^{(10)} = (+1,+1,+1,-1)$$
$$y^{(9)} = (+1,+1,+1,-1)$$
$$y^{(8)} = (+1,+1,+1,-1)$$
$$y^{(7)} = (+1,+1,-1,0)$$
$$y^{(6)} = (+1,+1,-1,0)$$
$$y^{(5)} = (+1,-1,0,0)$$
$$y^{(4)} = (-1,+1,+1,+1)$$
$$y^{(3)} = (0,-1,+1,+1)$$
$$y^{(2)} = (0,0,-1,+1)$$
$$y^{(1)} = (+1,+1,+1,-1)$$
$$y^{(0)} = (0,0,0,1)$$

Polyphase $(T = 3, S = 13)$

$$v^{(12)} = (5,8,0)$$
$$y^{(12)} = (+1,+1,-1)$$
$$y^{(11)} = (+1,+1,-1)$$
$$y^{(10)} = (+1,+1,-1)$$
$$y^{(9)} = (+1,+1,-1)$$
$$y^{(8)} = (+1,+1,-1)$$
$$y^{(7)} = (-1,+1,+1)$$
$$y^{(6)} = (-1,+1,+1)$$
$$y^{(5)} = (-1,+1,+1)$$
$$y^{(4)} = (+1,-1,+1)$$
$$y^{(3)} = (+1,-1,+1)$$
$$y^{(2)} = (+1,+1,-1)$$
$$y^{(1)} = (-1,+1,+1)$$
$$y^{(0)} = (1,0,0)$$

Every merge pattern obviously has a vector representation. Conversely, it is easy to see that the sequence of vectors $y^{(m)} \ldots y^{(1)} y^{(0)}$ corresponds to an actual merge pattern if and only if the following three conditions are satisfied:

i) $y^{(0)}$ is a unit vector.

ii) $y^{(i)}$ has exactly one component equal to -1, all other components equal to 0 or $+1$, for $m \geq i \geq 1$.

iii) All components of $y^{(i)} + \cdots + y^{(1)} + y^{(0)}$ are nonnegative, for $m \geq i \geq 1$.

The tree representation of a merge pattern gives another picture of the same information. We construct a tree with one external leaf node for each initial run, and one internal node for each run that is merged, in such a way that the descendants of each internal node are the runs from which it was fabricated. Each internal node is labeled with the step number on which the corresponding run was formed, numbering steps backwards as in the vector representation; furthermore, the line just above each node is labeled with the name of the tape on which that run appears. For example, the three merge patterns above have the tree representations depicted in Fig. 76, if we call the tapes A, B, C, D instead of T1, T2, T3, T4.

This representation displays many of the relevant properties of the merge pattern in convenient form; for example, if the run on level 0 of the tree (the root) is to be ascending, then the runs on level 1 must be descending, those on level 2 must be ascending, etc.; an initial run is ascending if and only if the corresponding external node is on an even-numbered level. Furthermore the total number of initial runs processed during the merging (not including the initial distribution) is exactly equal to the *external path length* of the tree, since each initial run on level k is processed exactly k times.

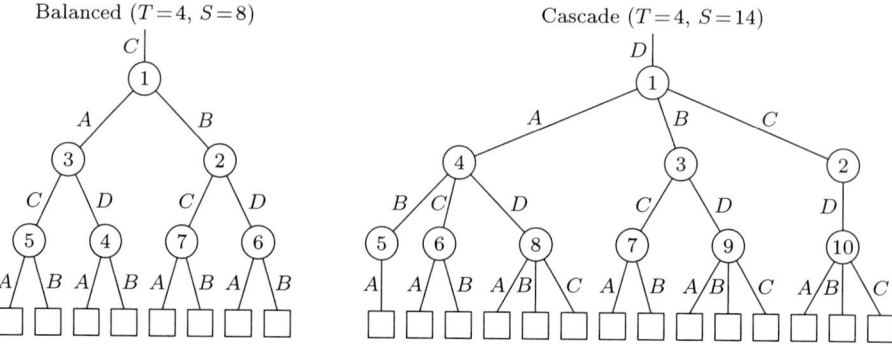

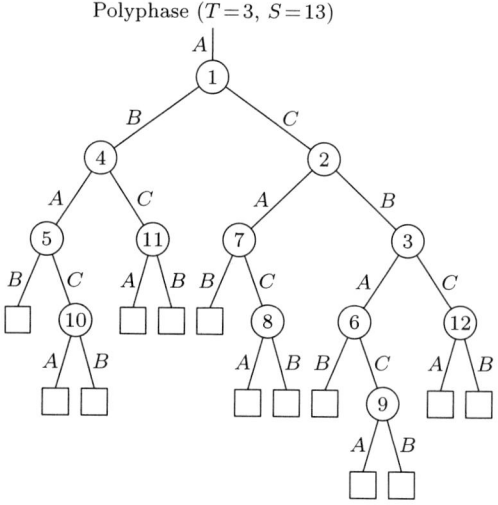

Fig. 76. Tree representations of three merge patterns.

Every merge pattern has a tree representation, but not every tree defines a merge pattern. A tree whose internal nodes have been labeled with the numbers 1 through m, and whose lines have been labeled with tape names, represents a valid read-backward merge pattern if and only if

a) no two lines adjacent to the same internal node have the same tape name;

b) if $i > j$, and if A is a tape name, the tree does not contain the configuration

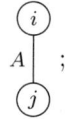 ;

c) if $i < j < k < l$, and if A is a tape name, the tree does not contain

both $A\begin{smallmatrix}i\\ \\k\end{smallmatrix}$ and $A\begin{smallmatrix}j\\ \\l\end{smallmatrix}$ or   both $A\begin{smallmatrix}i\\ \\k\end{smallmatrix}$ and $A\begin{smallmatrix}j\\ \\\square\end{smallmatrix}$.   (4)

Condition (a) is self-evident, since the input and output tapes in a merge must be distinct; similarly, (b) is obvious. The "no crossover" condition (c) mirrors the last-in-first-out restriction that characterizes read-backward operations on tape: The run formed at step k must be removed before any runs formed previously on that same tape; hence the configurations in (4) are impossible. It is not difficult to verify that any labeled tree satisfying conditions (a), (b), (c) does indeed correspond to a read-backward merge pattern.

If there are T tape units, condition (a) implies that the degree of each internal node is $T - 1$ or less. It is not always possible to attach suitable labels to all such trees; for example, when $T = 3$ there is no merge pattern whose tree has the shape

$$(5)$$

This shape would lead to an optimal merge pattern if we could attach step numbers and tape names in a suitable way, since it is the only way to achieve the minimum external path length in a tree having four external nodes. But there is essentially only one way to do the labeling according to conditions (a) and (b), because of the symmetries of the diagram, namely,

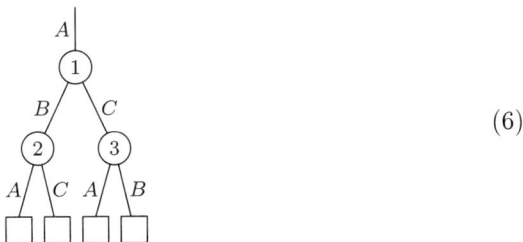

$$(6)$$

and this violates condition (c). A shape that *can* be labeled according to the conditions above, using at most T tape names, is called a *T-lifo* tree.

Another way to characterize all labeled trees that can arise from merge patterns is to consider how all such trees can be "grown." Start with some tape name, say A, and with the seedling

Step number i in the tree's growth consists of choosing distinct tape names $B, B_1, B_2, \ldots, B_k$, and changing the *most recently formed* external node corresponding to B

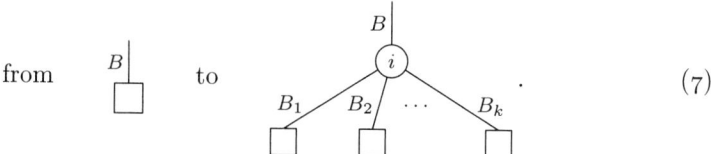

$$\text{from} \quad \text{to} \qquad (7)$$

This "last formed, first grown on" rule explains how the tree representation can be constructed directly from the vector representation.

The determination of strictly optimum T-tape merge patterns — that is, of T-lifo trees whose path length is minimum for a given number of external nodes — seems to be quite difficult. For example, the following nonobvious pattern turns out to be an optimum way to merge seven initial runs on four tapes, reading backwards:

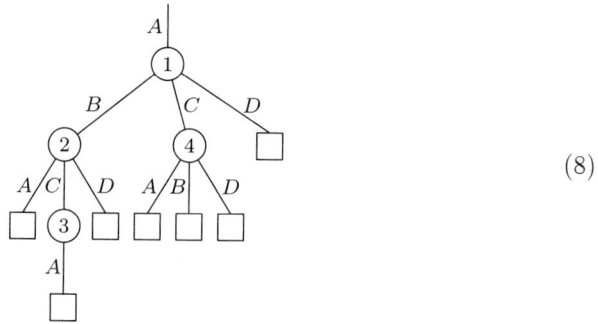

$$(8)$$

A one-way merge is actually necessary to achieve the optimum! (See exercise 8.) On the other hand, it is not so difficult to give constructions that are *asymptotically* optimal, for any fixed T.

Let $K_T(n)$ be the minimum external path length achievable in a T-lifo tree with n external nodes. From the theory developed in Section 2.3.4.5, it is not difficult to prove that

$$K_T(n) \geq nq - \lfloor ((T-1)^q - n)/(T-2) \rfloor, \qquad q = \lceil \log_{T-1} n \rceil, \tag{9}$$

since this is the minimum external path length of *any* tree with n external nodes and all nodes of degree $< T$. At the present time comparatively few values of $K_T(n)$ are known exactly. Here are some upper bounds that are probably exact:

$n =$	1	2	3	4	5	6	7	8	9	10	11	12	13	14	15	
$K_3(n) \leq$	0	2	5	9	12	16	21	25	30	34	39	45	50	56	61	(10)
$K_4(n) \leq$	0	2	3	6	8	11	14	17	20	24	27	31	33	37	40	

Karp discovered that *any* tree whose internal nodes have degrees $< T$ is *almost* T-lifo, in the sense that it can be made T-lifo by changing some of the external nodes to one-way merges. In fact, the construction of a suitable labeling is fairly simple. Let A be a particular tape name, and proceed as follows:

Step 1. Attach tape names to the lines of the tree diagram, in any manner consistent with condition (a) above, provided that the special name A is used only in the leftmost line of a branch.

Step 2. Replace each external node of the form

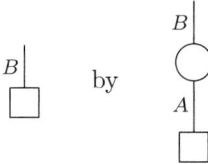

whenever $B \neq A$.

Step 3. Number the internal nodes of the tree in *preorder*. The result will be a labeling satisfying conditions (a), (b), and (c).

For example, if we start with the tree

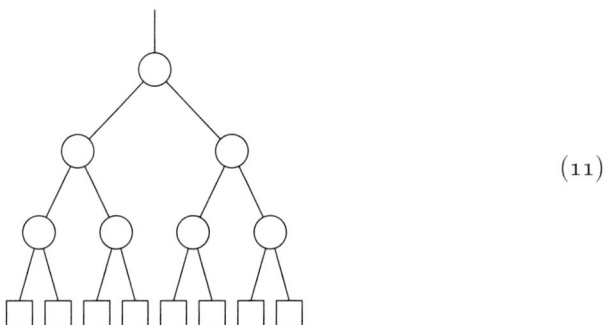

$$(11)$$

and three tapes, this procedure might assign labels as follows:

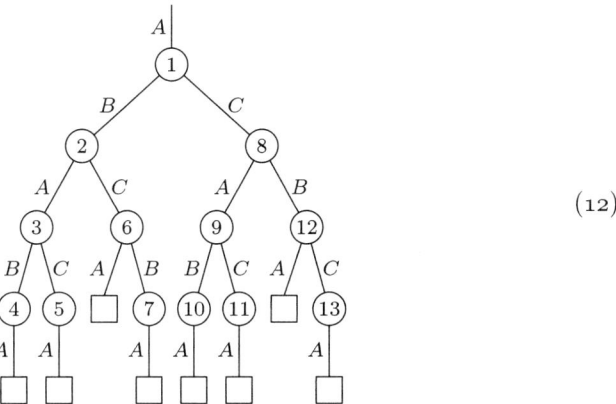

$$(12)$$

It is not difficult to verify that Karp's construction satisfies the "last formed, first grown on" discipline, because of the nature of preorder (see exercise 12).

The result of this construction is a merge pattern for which all of the initial runs appear on tape A. This suggests the following distribution and sorting scheme, which we may call the *preorder merge:*

P1. Distribute initial runs onto Tape A until the input is exhausted. Let S be the total number of initial runs.

P2. Carry out the construction above, using a minimum-path-length $(T-1)$-ary tree with S external nodes, obtaining a T-lifo tree whose external path length is within S of the lower bound in (9).

P3. Merge the runs according to this pattern.   ▌

This scheme will produce its output on any desired tape. But *it has one serious flaw*—does the reader see what will go wrong? The problem is that the merge pattern requires some of the runs initially on tape A to be ascending, and some to be descending, depending on whether the corresponding external node appears on an odd or an even level. This problem can be resolved without knowing S in advance, by copying runs that should be descending onto an auxiliary tape or tapes, just before they are needed. Then the total amount of processing, in terms of initial run lengths, comes to

$$S \log_{T-1} S + O(S). \tag{13}$$

Thus the preorder merge is definitely better than polyphase or cascade, as $S \to \infty$; indeed, it is asymptotically *optimum*, since (9) shows that $S \log_{T-1} S + O(S)$ is the best we could ever hope to achieve on T tapes. On the other hand, for the comparatively small values of S that usually arise in practice, the preorder merge is rather inefficient; polyphase or cascade methods are simpler and faster, when S is reasonably small. Perhaps it will be possible to invent a simple distribution-and-merge scheme that is competitive with polyphase and cascade for small S, and that is asymptotically optimum for large S.

The second set of exercises below shows how Karp has formulated the question of *read-forward* merging in a similar way. The theory turns out to be rather more complicated in this case, although some very interesting results have been discovered.

EXERCISES — First Set

1. [*17*] It is often convenient, during read-forward merging, to mark the end of each run on tape by including an artificial sentinel record whose key is $+\infty$. How should this practice be modified, when reading backwards?

2. [*20*] Will the columns of an array like (1) always be nondecreasing, or is there a chance that we will have to "subtract" runs from some tape as we go from one level to the next?

▶ **3.** [*20*] Prove that when read-backward polyphase merging is used with the perfect distributions of (1), we will always obtain an A run on tape T1 when sorting is complete, if T1 originally starts with $ADA\ldots$ and T2 through T5 start with $DAD\ldots$.

4. [*M22*] Is it a good idea to do read-backward polyphase merging after distributing all runs in *ascending* order, imagining all the D positions to be initially filled with dummies?

▶ **5.** [*23*] What formulas for the strings of merge numbers replace (8), (9), (10), and (11) of Section 5.4.2, when read-backward polyphase merging is used? Show the

merge numbers for the fifth level distribution on six tapes, by drawing a diagram
like Fig. 71(a).

6. [*07*] What is the vector representation of the merge pattern whose tree representation is (8)?

7. [*16*] Draw the tree representation for the read-backward merge pattern defined
by the following sequence of vectors:

$$
\begin{aligned}
v^{(33)} &= (\ 20, \quad 9, \quad 5) & y^{(16)} &= (+1, +1, -1) \\
y^{(33)} &= (+1, -1, +1) & y^{(15)} &= (+1, +1, -1) \\
y^{(32)} &= (+1, +1, -1) & y^{(14)} &= (+1, -1, +1) \\
y^{(31)} &= (+1, +1, -1) & y^{(13)} &= (+1, -1, +1) \\
y^{(30)} &= (+1, +1, -1) & y^{(12)} &= (-1, +1, +1) \\
y^{(29)} &= (+1, -1, +1) & y^{(11)} &= (+1, +1, -1) \\
y^{(28)} &= (-1, +1, +1) & y^{(10)} &= (+1, +1, -1) \\
y^{(27)} &= (+1, -1, +1) & y^{(9)} &= (+1, -1, +1) \\
y^{(26)} &= (+1, -1, +1) & y^{(8)} &= (+1, +1, -1) \\
y^{(25)} &= (+1, +1, -1) & y^{(7)} &= (+1, +1, -1) \\
y^{(24)} &= (+1, -1, +1) & y^{(6)} &= (+1, +1, -1) \\
y^{(23)} &= (+1, -1, +1) & y^{(5)} &= (-1, +1, +1) \\
y^{(22)} &= (+1, -1, +1) & y^{(4)} &= (+1, -1, +1) \\
y^{(21)} &= (-1, +1, +1) & y^{(3)} &= (-1, +1, +1) \\
y^{(20)} &= (+1, +1, -1) & y^{(2)} &= (+1, -1, +1) \\
y^{(19)} &= (-1, +1, +1) & y^{(1)} &= (-1, +1, +1) \\
y^{(18)} &= (+1, +1, -1) & y^{(0)} &= (\ 1, \quad 0, \quad 0) \\
y^{(17)} &= (+1, +1, -1)
\end{aligned}
$$

8. [*23*] Prove that (8) is an optimum way to merge, reading backwards, when $S = 7$
and $T = 4$, and that all methods that avoid one-way merging are inferior.

9. [*M22*] Prove the lower bound (9).

10. [*41*] Prepare a table of the exact values of $K_T(n)$, using a computer.

▶ **11.** [*20*] True or false: Any read-backward merge pattern that uses nothing but
$(T - 1)$-way merging must always have the runs alternating $ADAD\ldots$ on each tape;
it will not work if two adjacent runs appear in the same order.

12. [*22*] Prove that Karp's preorder construction always yields a labeled tree satisfying conditions (a), (b), and (c).

13. [*16*] Make (12) more efficient, by removing as many of the one-way merges as
possible so that preorder still gives a valid labeling of the internal nodes.

14. [*40*] Devise an algorithm that carries out the preorder merge without explicitly
representing the tree in steps P2 and P3, using only $O(\log S)$ words of memory to
control the merging pattern.

15. [*M39*] Karp's preorder construction in the text yields trees with one-way merges at
several terminal nodes. Prove that when $T = 3$ it is possible to construct asymptotically
optimal 3-lifo trees in which two-way merging is used throughout.

In other words, let $\hat{K}_T(n)$ be the minimum external path length over all T-lifo
trees with n external nodes, such that every internal node has degree $T - 1$. Prove that
$\hat{K}_3(n) = n\lg n + O(n)$.

16. [*M46*] In the notation of exercise 15, is $\hat{K}_T(n) = n\log_{T-1} n + O(n)$ for *all* $T \geq 3$,
when $n \equiv 1$ (modulo $T - 2$)?

▶ **17.** [*28*] (Richard D. Pratt.) To achieve ascending order in a read-backward cascade merge, we could insist on an *even* number of merging passes; this suggests a technique of initial distribution that is somewhat different from Algorithm 5.4.3C.

a) Change 5.4.3–(1) so that it shows only the perfect distributions that require an even number of merging passes.

b) Design an initial distribution scheme that interpolates between these perfect distributions. (Thus, if the number of initial runs falls between perfect distributions, it is desirable to merge some, but not all, of the runs twice, in order to reach a perfect distribution.)

▶ **18.** [*M38*] Suppose that T tape units are available, for some $T \geq 3$, and that T1 contains N records while the remaining tapes are empty. Is it possible to reverse the order of the records on T1 in fewer than $\Omega(N \log N)$ steps, *without* reading backwards? (The operation is, of course, trivial if backwards reading is allowed.) See exercise 5.2.5–14 for a class of such algorithms that *do* require order $N \log N$ steps.

EXERCISES — Second Set

The following exercises develop the theory of tape merging on read-forward tapes; in this case each tape acts as a queue instead of as a stack. A merge pattern can be represented as a sequence of vectors $y^{(m)} \dots y^{(1)} y^{(0)}$ exactly as in the text, but when we convert the vector representation to a tree representation we change "last formed, first grown on" to "*first* formed, first grown on." Thus the invalid configurations (4) would be changed to

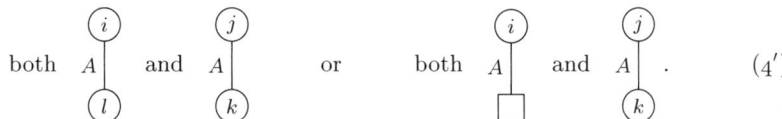

$$ \text{both } A \begin{smallmatrix} i \\ | \\ l \end{smallmatrix} \text{ and } A \begin{smallmatrix} j \\ | \\ k \end{smallmatrix} \quad \text{or} \quad \text{both } A \begin{smallmatrix} i \\ | \\ \square \end{smallmatrix} \text{ and } A \begin{smallmatrix} j \\ | \\ k \end{smallmatrix}. \tag{4'} $$

A tree that can be labeled so as to represent a read-forward merge on T tapes is called *T-fifo*, analogous to the term "*T-lifo*" in the read-backward case.

When tapes can be read backwards, they make very good stacks. But unfortunately they don't make very good general-purpose queues. If we randomly write and read, in a first-in-first-out manner, we waste a lot of time moving from one part of the tape to another. Even worse, we will soon run off the end of the tape! We run into the same problem as the queue overrunning memory in 2.2.2–(4) and (5), but the solution in 2.2.2–(6) and (7) doesn't apply to tapes since they aren't circular loops. Therefore we shall call a tree *strongly T-fifo* if it can be labeled so that the corresponding merge pattern makes each tape follow the special queue discipline "write, rewind, read all, rewind; write, rewind, read all, rewind; etc."

▶ **19.** [*22*] (R. M. Karp.) Find a binary tree that is not 3-fifo.

▶ **20.** [*22*] Formulate the condition "strongly T-fifo" in terms of a fairly simple rule about invalid configurations of tape labels, analogous to (4′).

21. [*18*] Draw the tree representation for the read-forwards merge pattern defined by the vectors in exercise 7. Is this tree strongly 3-fifo?

22. [*28*] (R. M. Karp.) Show that the tree representations for polyphase and cascade merging with perfect distributions are exactly the same for both the read-backward and the read-forward case, except for the numbers that label the internal nodes. Find a larger class of vector representations of merging patterns for which this is true.

23. [*24*] (R. M. Karp.) Let us say that a segment $y^{(q)} \ldots y^{(r)}$ of a merge pattern is a *stage* if no output tape is subsequently used as an input tape — that is, if there do not exist i, j, k with $q \geq i > k \geq r$, $y_j^{(i)} = -1$, and $y_j^{(k)} = +1$. The purpose of this exercise is to prove that *cascade merge minimizes the number of stages*, over all merge patterns having the same number of tapes and initial runs.

It is convenient to define some notation. Let us write $v \to w$ if v and w are T-vectors such that w reduces to v in the first stage of some merge pattern. (Thus there is a merge pattern $y^{(m)} \ldots y^{(0)}$ such that $y^{(m)} \ldots y^{(l+1)}$ is a stage, $w = y^{(m)} + \cdots + y^{(0)}$, and $v = y^{(l)} + \cdots + y^{(0)}$.) Let us write $v \preceq w$ if v and w are T-vectors such that the sum of the largest k elements of v is $\leq$ the sum of the largest k elements of w, for $1 \leq k \leq T$. Thus, for example, $(2, 1, 2, 2, 2, 1) \preceq (1, 2, 3, 0, 3, 1)$, since $2 \leq 3$, $2+2 \leq 3+3$, $\ldots$, $2 + 2 + 2 + 2 + 1 + 1 \leq 3 + 3 + 2 + 1 + 1 + 0$. Finally, if $v = (v_1, \ldots, v_T)$, let $C(v) = (s_T, s_{T-2}, s_{T-3}, \ldots, s_1, 0)$ where s_k is the sum of the largest k elements of v.

a) Prove that $v \to C(v)$.

b) Prove that $v \preceq w$ implies $C(v) \preceq C(w)$.

c) Assuming the result of exercise 24, prove that cascade merge minimizes the number of stages.

24. [*M35*] In the notation of exercise 23, prove that $v \to w$ implies $w \preceq C(v)$.

25. [*M36*] (R. M. Karp.) Let us say that a segment $y^{(q)} \ldots y^{(r)}$ of a merge pattern is a *phase* if no tape is used both for input and for output — that is, if there do not exist i, j, k with $q \geq i \geq r$, $q \geq k \geq r$, $y_j^{(i)} = +1$, and $y_j^{(k)} = -1$. The purpose of this exercise is to investigate merge patterns that minimize the number of phases. We shall write $v \Rightarrow w$ if w can be reduced to v in one phase (a similar notation was introduced in exercise 23); and we let

$$D_k(v) = (s_k + t_{k+1}, \ s_k + t_{k+2}, \ \ldots, \ s_k + t_T, \ 0, \ \ldots, \ 0),$$

where t_j denotes the jth largest element of v and $s_k = t_1 + \cdots + t_k$.

a) Prove that $v \Rightarrow D_k(v)$ for $1 \leq k < T$.

b) Prove that $v \preceq w$ implies $D_k(v) \preceq D_k(w)$, for $1 \leq k < T$.

c) Prove that $v \Rightarrow w$ implies $w \preceq D_k(v)$, for some k, $1 \leq k < T$.

d) Consequently, a merge pattern that sorts the maximum number of initial runs on T tapes in q phases can be represented by a sequence of integers $k_1 k_2 \ldots k_q$, such that the initial distribution is $D_{k_q}(\ldots(D_{k_2}(D_{k_1}(u)))\ldots)$, where $u = (1, 0, \ldots, 0)$. This minimum-phase strategy has a strongly T-fifo representation, and it also belongs to the class of patterns in exercise 22. When $T = 3$ it is the *polyphase* merge, and for $T = 4$, 5, 6, 7 it is a variation of the *balanced* merge.

26. [*M46*] (R. M. Karp.) Is the optimum sequence $k_1 k_2 \ldots k_q$ mentioned in exercise 25 equal to $1 \lceil T/2 \rceil \lfloor T/2 \rfloor \lceil T/2 \rceil \lfloor T/2 \rfloor \ldots$, for all $T \geq 4$ and all sufficiently large q?

*5.4.5. The Oscillating Sort

A somewhat different approach to merge sorting was introduced by Sheldon Sobel in *JACM* **9** (1962), 372–375. Instead of starting with a distribution pass where all the initial runs are dispersed to tapes, he proposed an algorithm that oscillates back and forth between distribution and merging, so that much of the sorting takes place before the input has been completely examined.

Suppose, for example, that there are five tapes available for merging. Sobel's method would sort 16 initial runs as follows:

	Operation	T1	T2	T3	T4	T5	Cost
Phase 1	Distribute	A_1	A_1	A_1	A_1	—	4
Phase 2	Merge	—	—	—	—	D_4	4
Phase 3	Distribute	—	A_1	A_1	A_1	$D_4 A_1$	4
Phase 4	Merge	D_4	—	—	—	D_4	4
Phase 5	Distribute	$D_4 A_1$	—	A_1	A_1	$D_4 A_1$	4
Phase 6	Merge	D_4	D_4	—	—	D_4	4
Phase 7	Distribute	$D_4 A_1$	$D_4 A_1$	—	A_1	$D_4 A_1$	4
Phase 8	Merge	D_4	D_4	D_4	—	D_4	4
Phase 9	Merge	—	—	—	A_{16}	—	16

Here, as in Section 5.4.4, we use A_r and D_r to stand respectively for ascending and descending runs of relative length r. The method begins by writing an initial run onto each of four tapes, and merges them (reading backwards) onto the fifth tape. Distribution resumes again, this time cyclically shifted one place to the right with respect to the tapes, and a second merge produces another run D_4. When four D_4's have been formed in this way, an additional merge creates A_{16}. We could go on to create three more A_{16}'s, merging them into a D_{64}, and so on until the input is exhausted. It isn't necessary to know the length of the input in advance.

When the number of initial runs, S, is 4^m, it is not difficult to see that this method processes each record exactly $m+1$ times: once during the distribution, and m times during a merge. When S is between 4^{m-1} and 4^m, we could assume that dummy runs are present, bringing S up to 4^m; hence the total sorting time would essentially amount to $\lceil \log_4 S \rceil + 1$ passes over all the data. This is just what would be achieved by a balanced sort on *eight* tapes; in general, oscillating sort with T work tapes is equivalent to balanced merging with $2(T-1)$ tapes, since it makes

$$\lceil \log_{T-1} S \rceil + 1$$

passes over the data. When S is a power of $T-1$, this is the best *any* T-tape method could possibly do, since it achieves the lower bound in Eq. 5.4.4–(9). On the other hand, when S is

$$(T-1)^{m-1} + 1,$$

just one higher than a power of $T-1$, the method wastes nearly a whole pass.

Exercise 2 shows how to eliminate part of this penalty for non-perfect-powers S, by using a special ending routine. A further refinement was discovered in 1966 by Dennis L. Bencher, who called his procedure the "criss-cross merge" [see H. Wedekind, *Datenorganisation* (Berlin: W. de Gruyter, 1970), 164–166; see also *U.S. Patent 3540000* (1970)]. The main idea is to delay merging until more knowledge of S has been gained. We shall discuss a slightly modified form of Bencher's original scheme.

This improved oscillating sort proceeds as follows:

	Operation	T1	T2	T3	T4	T5	Cost
Phase 1	Distribute	—	A_1	A_1	A_1	A_1	4
Phase 2	Distribute	—	A_1	$A_1 A_1$	$A_1 A_1$	$A_1 A_1$	3
Phase 3	Merge	D_4	—	A_1	A_1	A_1	4
Phase 4	Distribute	$D_4 A_1$	—	A_1	$A_1 A_1$	$A_1 A_1$	3
Phase 5	Merge	D_4	D_4	—	A_1	A_1	4
Phase 6	Distribute	$D_4 A_1$	$D_4 A_1$	—	A_1	$A_1 A_1$	3
Phase 7	Merge	D_4	D_4	D_4	—	A_1	4
Phase 8	Distribute	$D_4 A_1$	$D_4 A_1$	$D_4 A_1$	—	A_1	3
Phase 9	Merge	D_4	D_4	D_4	D_4	—	4

We do not merge the D_4's into an A_{16} at this point (unless the input happens to be exhausted); only after building up to

Phase 15	Merge	$D_4 D_4$	$D_4 D_4$	$D_4 D_4$	D_4	—	4

will we get

Phase 16	Merge	D_4	D_4	D_4	—	A_{16}	16

The second A_{16} will occur after three more D_4's have been made,

Phase 22	Merge	$D_4 D_4$	$D_4 D_4$	D_4	—	$A_{16} D_4$	4
Phase 23	Merge	D_4	D_4	—	A_{16}	A_{16}	16

and so on (compare with Phases 1–5). The advantage of Bencher's scheme can be seen for example if there are only five initial runs: Oscillating sort as modified in exercise 2 would do a four-way merge (in Phase 2) followed by a two-way merge, for a total cost of $4 + 4 + 1 + 5 = 14$, while Bencher's scheme would do a two-way merge (in Phase 3) followed by a four-way merge, for a total cost of $4 + 1 + 2 + 5 = 12$. Both methods also involve a small additional cost, namely one unit of rewind before the final merge.

A precise description of Bencher's method appears in Algorithm B below. Unfortunately it seems to be a procedure that is harder to understand than to code; it is much easier to explain the technique to a computer than to a computer scientist! This is partly because it is an inherently recursive method that has been expressed in iterative form and then optimized somewhat; the reader may find it necessary to trace through the operation of this algorithm several times before discovering what is really going on.

Algorithm B (*Oscillating sort with "criss-cross" distribution*). This algorithm takes initial runs and disperses them to tapes, occasionally interrupting the distribution process in order to merge some of the tape contents. The algorithm uses P-way merging, assuming that $T = P + 1 \geq 3$ tape units are available — *not* counting the unit that may be necessary to hold the input data. The tape units must allow reading in both forward and backward directions, and they are designated by the numbers $0, 1, \ldots, P$. The following tables are maintained:

$D[j]$, $0 \le j \le P$: Number of dummy runs assumed to be present at the end of tape j.

$A[l, j]$, $0 \le l \le L$, Here L is a number such that at most P^{L+1} initial runs will $0 \le j \le P$ be input. When $A[l, j] = k \ge 0$, a run of nominal length P^k is present on tape j, corresponding to "level l" of the algorithm's operation. This run is ascending if k is even, descending if k is odd. When $A[l, j] < 0$, level l does not use tape j.

The statement "Write an initial run on tape j" is an abbreviation for the following operations:

Set $A[l, j] \leftarrow 0$. If the input is exhausted, increase $D[j]$ by 1; otherwise write an initial run (in ascending order) onto tape j.

The statement "Merge to tape j" is an abbreviation for the following operations:

If $D[i] > 0$ for all $i \ne j$, decrease $D[i]$ by 1 for all $i \ne j$ and increase $D[j]$ by 1. Otherwise merge one run to tape j, from all tapes $i \ne j$ such that $D[i] = 0$, and decrease $D[i]$ by 1 for all other $i \ne j$.

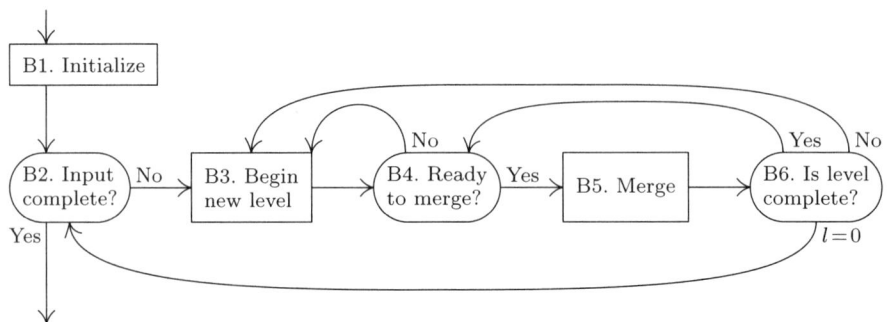

Fig. 77. Oscillating sort, with a "criss-cross" distribution.

B1. [Initialize.] Set $D[j] \leftarrow 0$ for $0 \le j \le P$. Set $A[0,0] \leftarrow -1$, $l \leftarrow 0$, $q \leftarrow 0$. Then write an initial run on tape j, for $1 \le j \le P$.

B2. [Input complete?] (At this point tape q is empty and the other tapes contain at most one run each.) If there is more input, go on to step B3. But if the input is exhausted, rewind all tapes $j \ne q$ such that $A[0, j]$ is even; then merge to tape q, reading forwards on tapes just rewound, and reading backwards on the other tapes. This completes the sort, with the output in ascending order on tape q.

B3. [Begin new level.] Set $l \leftarrow l + 1$, $r \leftarrow q$, $s \leftarrow 0$, and $q \leftarrow (q + 1) \bmod T$. Write an initial run on tape $(q + j) \bmod T$, for $1 \le j \le T - 2$. (Thus an initial run is written onto each tape except tapes q and r.) Set $A[l, q] \leftarrow -1$ and $A[l, r] \leftarrow -2$.

B4. [Ready to merge?] If $A[l-1, q] \ne s$, go back to step B3.

B5. [Merge.] (At this point $A[l-1,q] = A[l,j] = s$ for all $j \neq q$, $j \neq r$.) Merge to tape r, reading backwards. (See the definition of this operation above.) Then set $s \leftarrow s+1$, $l \leftarrow l-1$, $A[l,r] \leftarrow s$, and $A[l,q] \leftarrow -1$. Set $r \leftarrow (2q-r) \bmod T$. (In general, we have $r = (q-1) \bmod T$ when s is even, $r = (q+1) \bmod T$ when s is odd.)

B6. [Is level complete?] If $l = 0$, go to B2. Otherwise if $A[l,j] = s$ for all $j \neq q$ and $j \neq r$, go to B4. Otherwise return to B3. ∎

We can use a "recursion induction" style of proof to show that this algorithm is valid, just as we have done for Algorithm 2.3.1T. Suppose that we begin at step B3 with $l = l_0$, $q = q_0$, $s_+ = A[l_0, (q_0+1) \bmod T]$, and $s_- = A[l_0, (q_0-1) \bmod T]$; and assume furthermore that either $s_+ = 0$ or $s_- = 1$ or $s_+ = 2$ or $s_- = 3$ or $\cdots$. It is possible to verify by induction that the algorithm will eventually get to step B5 without changing rows 0 through l_0 of A, and with $l = l_0 + 1$, $q = q_0 \pm 1$, $r = q_0$, and $s = s_+$ or s_-, where we choose the $+$ sign if $s_+ = 0$ or ($s_+ = 2$ and $s_- \neq 1$) or ($s_+ = 4$ and $s_- \neq 1, 3$) or $\cdots$, and we choose the $-$ sign if ($s_- = 1$ and $s_+ \neq 0$) or ($s_- = 3$ and $s_+ \neq 0, 2$) or $\cdots$. The proof sketched here is not very elegant, but the algorithm has been stated in a form more suited to implementation than to verification.

Figure 78 shows the efficiency of Algorithm B, in terms of the average number of times each record is merged as a function of the number S of initial runs, assuming that the initial runs are approximately equal in length. (Corresponding graphs for polyphase and cascade sort have appeared in Figs. 70 and 74.) A slight improvement, mentioned in exercise 3, has been used in preparing this chart.

A related method called the *gyrating sort* was developed by R. M. Karp, based on the theory of preorder merging that we have discussed in Section 5.4.4; see *Combinatorial Algorithms*, edited by Randall Rustin (Algorithmics Press, 1972), 21–29.

Reading forwards. The oscillating sort pattern appears to require a read-backwards capability, since we need to store long runs somewhere as we merge newly input short runs. However, M. A. Goetz [*Proc. AFIPS Spring Joint Comp. Conf.* **25** (1964), 599–607] has discovered a way to perform an oscillating sort using only forward reading and simple rewinding. His method is radically different from the other schemes we have seen in this chapter, in two ways:

a) Data is sometimes written at the front of the tape, with the understanding that the existing data in the *middle* of the tape is not destroyed.

b) All initial runs have a fixed maximum length.

Condition (a) violates the first-in-first-out property we have assumed to be characteristic of forward reading, but it can be implemented reliably if a sufficient amount of blank tape is left between runs and if parity errors are ignored at appropriate times. Condition (b) tends to be somewhat incompatible with an efficient use of replacement selection.

Goetz's read-forward oscillating sort has the somewhat dubious distinction of being one of the first algorithms to be patented as an algorithm instead of as a physical device [*U.S. Patent 3380029* (1968)]; between 1968 and 1988, no one in the U.S.A. could legally use the algorithm in a program without permission of the patentee. Bencher's read-backward oscillating sort technique was patented by IBM several years later. [Alas, we have reached the end of the era when the joy of discovering a new algorithm was satisfaction enough! Fortunately the oscillating sort isn't especially good; let's hope that community-minded folks who invent the best algorithms continue to make their ideas freely available. Of course the specter of people keeping new techniques completely secret is far worse than the public appearance of algorithms that are proprietary for a limited time.]

The central idea in Goetz's method is to arrange things so that each tape begins with a run of relative length 1, followed by one of relative length P, then P^2, etc. For example, when $T = 5$ the sort begins as follows, using "." to indicate the current position of the read-write head on each tape:

	Operation	T1	T2	T3	T4	T5	"Cost"	Remarks
Phase 1	Distribute	$.A_1$	$.A_1$	$.A_1$	$.A_1$	$A_1.$	5	[T5 not rewound]
Phase 2	Merge	$\not{A}_1.$	$\not{A}_1.$	$\not{A}_1.$	$\not{A}_1.$	$A_1\,A_4.$	4	[Now rewind all]
Phase 3	Distribute	$.A_1$	$.A_1$	$.A_1$	$A_1.$	$.A_1\,A_4$	4	[T4 not rewound]
Phase 4	Merge	$\not{A}_1.$	$\not{A}_1.$	$\not{A}_1.$	$A_1\,A_4.$	$\not{A}_1.A_4$	4	[Now rewind all]
Phase 5	Distribute	$.A_1$	$.A_1$	$A_1.$	$.A_1\,A_4$	$.A_1\,A_4$	4	[T3 not rewound]
Phase 6	Merge	$\not{A}_1.$	$\not{A}_1.$	$A_1\,A_4.$	$\not{A}_1.A_4$	$\not{A}_1.A_4$	4	[Now rewind all]
Phase 7	Distribute	$.A_1$	$A_1.$	$.A_1\,A_4$	$.A_1\,A_4$	$.A_1\,A_4$	4	[T2 not rewound]
Phase 8	Merge	$\not{A}_1.$	$A_1\,A_4.$	$\not{A}_1.A_4$	$\not{A}_1.A_4$	$\not{A}_1.A_4$	4	[Now rewind all]
Phase 9	Distribute	$A_1.$	$.A_1\,A_4$	$.A_1\,A_4$	$.A_1\,A_4$	$.A_1\,A_4$	4	[T1 not rewound]
Phase 10	Merge	$A_1A_4.$	$\not{A}_1.A_4$	$\not{A}_1.A_4$	$\not{A}_1.A_4$	$\not{A}_1.A_4$	4	[No rewinding]
Phase 11	Merge	$A_1A_4A_{16}.$	$\not{A}_1\,\not{A}_4.$	$\not{A}_1\,\not{A}_4.$	$\not{A}_1\,\not{A}_4.$	$\not{A}_1\,\not{A}_4.$	16	[Now rewind all]

And so on. During Phase 1, T1 was rewinding while T2 was receiving its input, then T2 was rewinding while T3 was receiving input, etc. Eventually, when the input is exhausted, dummy runs will start to appear, and we will sometimes need to imagine that they were written explicitly on the tape at full length. For example, if $S = 18$, the A_1's on T4 and T5 would be dummies during Phase 9; we would have to skip forwards on T4 and T5 while merging from T2 and T3 to T1 during Phase 10, because we have to get to the A_4's on T4 and T5 in preparation for Phase 11. On the other hand, the dummy A_1 on T1 need not appear explicitly. Thus the "endgame" is a bit tricky.

Another example of this method appears in the next section.

EXERCISES

1. [*22*] The text illustrates Sobel's original oscillating sort for $T = 5$ and $S = 16$. Give a precise specification of an algorithm that generalizes the procedure, sorting $S = P^L$ initial runs on $T = P + 1 \geq 3$ tapes. Strive for simplicity.

2. [*24*] If $S = 6$ in Sobel's original method, we could pretend that $S = 16$ and that 10 dummy runs were present. Then Phase 3 in the text's example would put dummy runs A_0 on T4 and T5; Phase 4 would merge the A_1's on T2 and T3 into a D_2 on T1; Phases 5–8 would do nothing; and Phase 9 would produce A_6 on T4. It would be better

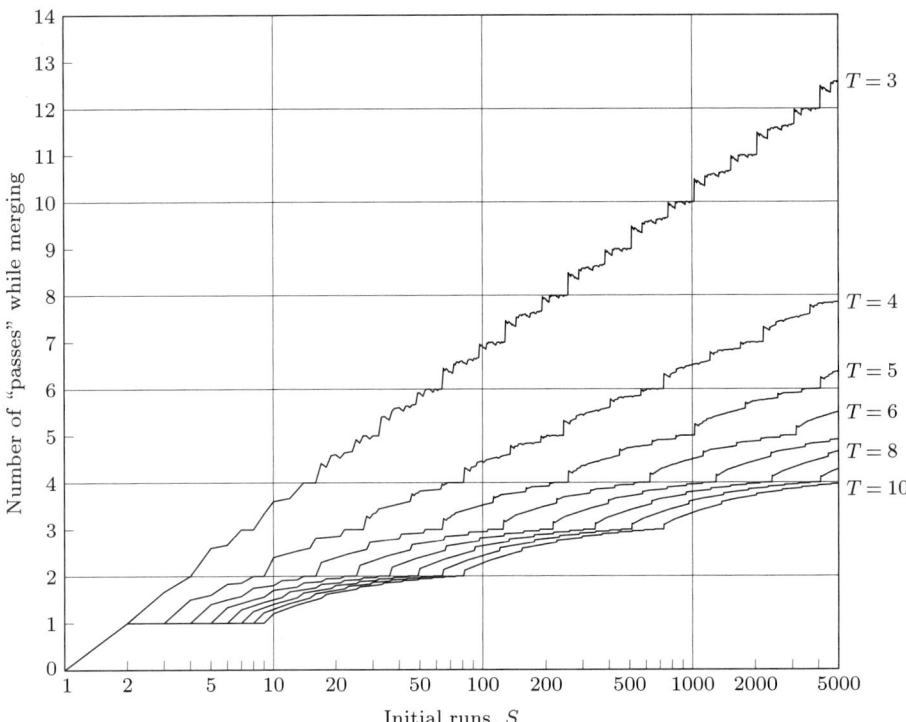

Fig. 78. Efficiency of oscillating sort, using the technique of Algorithm B and exercise 3.

to rewind T2 and T3 just after Phase 3, then to produce A_6 immediately on T4 by three-way merging.

Show how to modify the algorithm of exercise 1, so that an improved ending like this is obtained when S is not a perfect power of P.

▶ **3.** [*29*] Prepare a chart showing the behavior of Algorithm B when $T = 3$, assuming that there are nine initial runs. Show that the procedure is obviously inefficient in one place, and prescribe corrections to Algorithm B that will remedy the situation.

4. [*21*] Step B3 sets A[l, q] and A[l, r] to negative values. Show that one of these two operations is always superfluous, since the corresponding A table entry is never looked at.

5. [*M25*] Let S be the number of initial runs present in the input to Algorithm B. Which values of S require *no rewinding* in step B2?

*5.4.6. Practical Considerations for Tape Merging

Now comes the nitty-gritty: We have discussed the various families of merge patterns, so it is time to see how they actually apply to real configurations of computers and magnetic tapes, and to compare them in a meaningful way. Our study of internal sorting showed that we can't adequately judge the efficiency of a sorting method merely by counting the number of comparisons it performs; similarly we can't properly evaluate an external sorting method by simply knowing the number of passes it makes over the data.

In this section we shall discuss the characteristics of typical tape units, and the way they affect initial distribution and merging. In particular we shall study some schemes for buffer allocation, and the corresponding effects on running time. We also shall consider briefly the construction of *sort generator* programs.

How tape works. Different manufacturers have provided tape units with widely varying characteristics. For convenience, we shall define a hypothetical MIXT tape unit, which is reasonably typical of the equipment that was being manufactured at the time this book was first written. MIXT reads and writes 800 characters per inch of tape, at a rate of 75 inches per second. This means that one character is read or written every $\frac{1}{60}$ ms, or $16\frac{2}{3}$ microseconds, when the tape is active. Actual tape units that were available in 1970 had densities ranging from 200 to 1600 characters per inch, and tape speeds ranging from $37\frac{1}{2}$ to 150 inches per second, so their effective speed varied from 1/8 to 4 times as fast as MIXT.

Of course, we observed near the beginning of Section 5.4 that magnetic tapes in general are now pretty much obsolete. But many lessons were learned during the decades when tape sorting was of major importance, and those lessons are still valuable. Thus our main concern here is not to obtain particular answers; it is to learn how to combine theory and practice in a reasonable way. Methodology is much more important than phenomenology, because the principles of problem solving remain useful despite technological changes. Readers will benefit most from this material by transplanting themselves temporarily into the mindset of the 1970s. *Let us therefore pretend that we still live in that bygone era.*

One of the important considerations to keep in mind, as we adopt the perspective of the early days, is the fact that individual tapes have a strictly limited capacity. Each reel contains 2400 feet of tape or less; hence there is room for at most 23,000,000 or so characters per reel of MIXT tape, and it takes about $23000000/3600000 \approx 6.4$ minutes to read them all. If larger files must be sorted, it is generally best to sort one reelful at a time, and then to merge the individually sorted reels, in order to avoid excessive tape handling. This means that the number of initial runs, S, actually present in the merge patterns we have been studying is never extremely large. We will never find $S > 5000$, even with a very small internal memory that produces initial runs only 5000 characters long. Consequently the formulas that give asymptotic efficiency of the algorithms as $S \to \infty$ are primarily of academic interest.

Data appears on tape in *blocks* (Fig. 79), and each read/write instruction transmits a single block. Tape blocks are often called "records," but we shall avoid that terminology because it conflicts with the fact that we are sorting a file of "records" in another sense. Such a distinction was unnecessary on many of the early sorting programs written during the 1950s, since one record was written per block; but we shall see that it is usually advantageous to have quite a few records in every block on the tape.

An *interblock gap*, 480 character positions long, appears between adjacent blocks, in order to allow the tape to stop and to start between individual read or write commands. The effect of interblock gaps is to decrease the number of

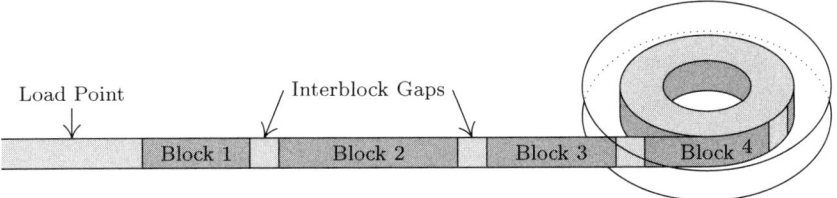

Fig. 79. Magnetic tape with variable-size blocks.

characters per reel of tape, depending on the number of characters per block (see Fig. 80); and the average number of characters transmitted per second decreases in the same way, since tape moves at a fairly constant speed.

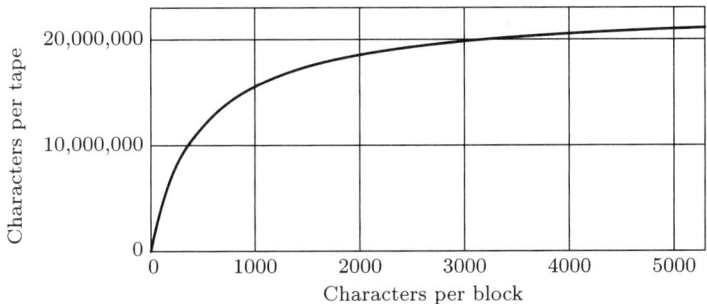

Fig. 80. The number of characters per reel of MIXT tape, as a function of the block size.

Many old-fashioned computers had fixed block sizes that were rather small; their design was reflected in the MIX computer as defined in Chapter 1, which always reads and writes 100-word blocks. But MIX's convention corresponds to about 500 characters per block, and 480 characters per gap, hence almost half the tape is wasted! Most machines of the 1970s therefore allowed the block size to be variable; we shall discuss the choice of appropriate block sizes below.

At the end of a read or write operation, the tape unit "coasts" at full speed over the first 66 characters (or so) of the gap. If the next operation for the same tape is initiated during this time, the tape motion continues without interruption. But if the next operation doesn't come soon enough, the tape will stop and it will also require some time to accelerate to full speed on the next operation. The combined stop/start time delay is 5 ms, 2 for the stop and 3 for the start (see Fig. 81). Thus if we just miss the chance to have continuous full-speed reading, the effect on running time is essentially the same as if there were 780 characters instead of 480 in the interblock gap.

Now let us consider the operation of *rewinding*. Unfortunately, the exact time needed to rewind over a given number n of characters is not easy to characterize. On some machines there is a high-speed rewind that applies only when n is greater than 5 million or so; for smaller values of n, rewinding goes at

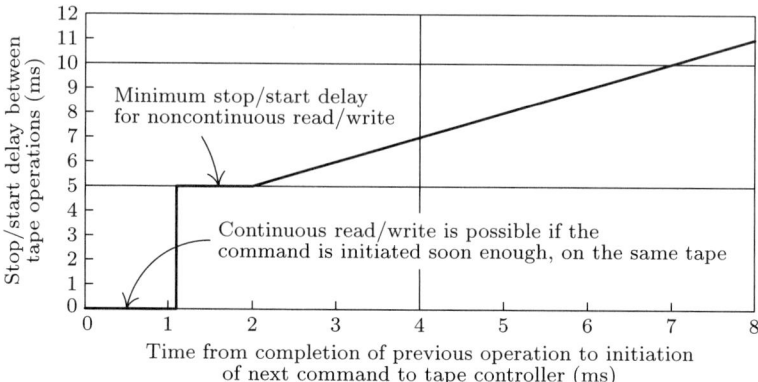

Fig. 81. How to compute the stop/start delay time. (This gets added to the time used for reading or writing the blocks and the gaps.)

normal read/write speed. On other machines a special motor is used to control all of the rewind operations; it gradually accelerates the tape reel to a certain number of revolutions per minute, then puts on the brakes when it is time to stop, and the actual tape speed varies with the fullness of the reel. For simplicity, we shall assume that MIXT requires $\max(30, n/150)$ ms to rewind over n character positions (including gaps), roughly two-fifths as long as it took to write them. This is a reasonably good approximation to the behavior of many actual tape units, where the ratio of read/write time to rewind time is generally between 2 and 3, but it does not adequately model the effect of combined low-speed and high-speed rewind that is present on many other machines. (See Fig. 82.)

Initial loading and/or rewinding will position a tape at "load point," and an extra 110 ms are necessary for any read or write operation initiated at load point. When the tape is not at load point, it may be read backwards; an extra 32 ms is added to the time of any backward operation following a forward operation or any forward operation following a backward one.

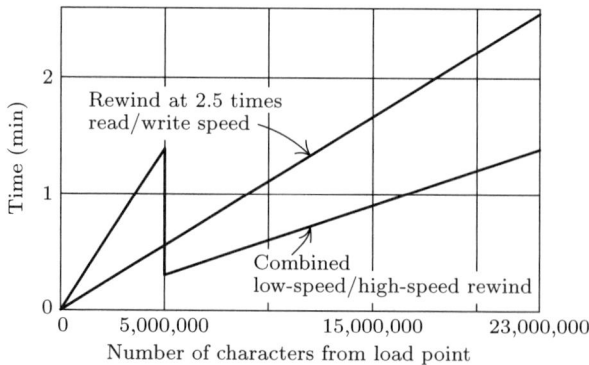

Fig. 82. Approximate running time for two commonly used rewind techniques.

Merging revisited. Let us now look again at the process of P-way merging, with an emphasis on input and output activities, assuming that $P+1$ tape units are being used for the input files and the output file. Our goal is to overlap the input/output operations as much as possible with each other and with the computations of the program, so that the overall merging time is minimized.

It is instructive to consider the following special case, in which serious restrictions are placed on the amount of simultaneity possible. Suppose that

a) at most one tape may be written on at any one time;

b) at most one tape may be read from at any one time;

c) reading, writing, and computing may take place simultaneously only when the read and write operations have been initiated simultaneously.

It turns out that a system of $2P$ input buffers and 2 output buffers is sufficient to keep the tape moving at essentially its maximum speed, even though these three restrictions are imposed, unless the computer is unusually slow. Note that condition (a) is not really a restriction, since there is only one output tape. Furthermore the amount of input is equal to the amount of output, so there is only one tape being read, on the average, at any given time; if condition (b) is not satisfied, there will necessarily be periods when no input at all is occurring. Thus we can minimize the merging time if we keep the output tape busy.

An important technique called *forecasting* leads to the desired effect. While we are doing a P-way merge, we generally have P *current input buffers*, which are being used as the source of data; some of them are more full than others, depending on how much of their data has already been scanned. If all of them become empty at about the same time, we will need to do a lot of reading before we can proceed further, unless we have foreseen this eventuality in advance. Fortunately it is always possible to tell which buffer will empty first, by simply looking at the *last* record in each buffer. The buffer whose last record has the smallest key will always be the first one empty, regardless of the values of any other keys; so we always know which file should be the source of our next input command. The following algorithm spells out this principle in detail.

Algorithm F (*Forecasting with floating buffers*). This algorithm controls the buffering during a P-way merge of long input files, for $P \geq 2$. Assume that the input tapes and files are numbered $1, 2, \ldots, P$. The algorithm uses $2P$ input buffers I[1], ..., I[2P]; two output buffers O[0] and O[1]; and the following auxiliary tables:

A[j], $1 \leq j \leq 2P$: 0 if I[j] is available for input, 1 otherwise.

B[i], $1 \leq i \leq P$:   Index of the buffer holding the last block read so far from file i.

C[i], $1 \leq i \leq P$:   Index of the buffer currently being used for the input from file i.

L[i], $1 \leq i \leq P$:   The last key read so far from file i.

S[j], $1 \leq j \leq 2P$: Index of the buffer to use when I[j] becomes empty.

The algorithm described here does not terminate; an appropriate way to shut it off is discussed below.

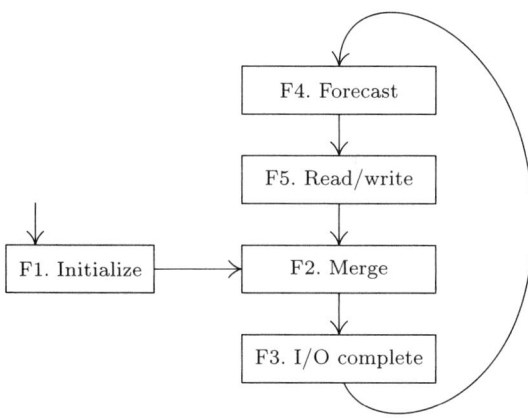

Fig. 83. Forecasting with floating buffers.

F1. [Initialize.] Read the first block from tape i into buffer $I[i]$, set $A[i] \leftarrow 1$, $A[P + i] \leftarrow 0$, $B[i] \leftarrow i$, $C[i] \leftarrow i$, and set $L[i]$ to the key of the final record in buffer $I[i]$, for $1 \leq i \leq P$. Then find m such that $L[m] = \min\{L[1],\dots,L[P]\}$; and set $t \leftarrow 0$, $k \leftarrow P + 1$. Begin to read from tape m into buffer $I[k]$.

F2. [Merge.] Merge records from buffers $I[C[1]],\dots,I[C[P]]$ to $O[t]$, until $O[t]$ is full. If during this process an input buffer, say $I[C[i]]$, becomes empty and $O[t]$ is not yet full, set $A[C[i]] \leftarrow 0$, $C[i] \leftarrow S[C[i]]$, and continue to merge.

F3. [I/O complete.] Wait until the previous read (or read/write) operation is complete. Then set $A[k] \leftarrow 1$, $S[B[m]] \leftarrow k$, $B[m] \leftarrow k$, and set $L[m]$ to the key of the final record in $I[k]$.

F4. [Forecast.] Find m such that $L[m] = \min\{L[1],\dots,L[P]\}$, and find k such that $A[k] = 0$.

F5. [Read/write.] Begin to read from tape m into buffer $I[k]$, and to write from buffer $O[t]$ onto the output tape. Then set $t \leftarrow 1 - t$ and return to F2. ∎

The example in Fig. 84 shows how forecasting works when $P = 2$, assuming that each block on tape contains only two records. The input buffer contents are illustrated each time we get to the beginning of step F2. Algorithm F essentially forms P *queues of buffers*, with $C[i]$ pointing to the front and $B[i]$ to the rear of the ith queue, and with $S[j]$ pointing to the successor of buffer $I[j]$; these pointers are shown as arrows in Fig. 84. Line 1 illustrates the state of affairs after initialization: There is one buffer for each input file, and another block is being read from File 1 (since $03 < 05$). Line 2 shows the status of things after the first block has been merged: We are outputting a block containing $\boxed{01\ \ 02}$, and inputting the next block from File 2 (since $05 < 09$). Note that in line 3, three of the four input buffers are essentially committed to File 2, since we are reading from that file and we already have a full buffer and a partly full buffer in its

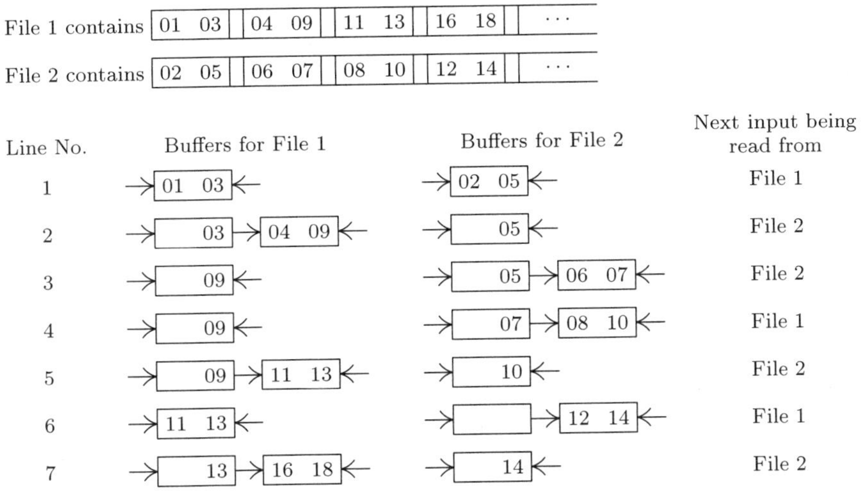

File 1 contains | 01 03 | | 04 09 | | 11 13 | | 16 18 | | · · ·

File 2 contains | 02 05 | | 06 07 | | 08 10 | | 12 14 | | · · ·

Line No.	Buffers for File 1	Buffers for File 2	Next input being read from
1	→ 01 03 ←	→ 02 05 ←	File 1
2	→ [03] → 04 09 ←	→ [05] ←	File 2
3	→ [09] ←	→ [05] → 06 07 ←	File 2
4	→ [09] ←	→ [07] → 08 10 ←	File 1
5	→ [09] → 11 13 ←	→ [10] ←	File 2
6	→ 11 13 ←	→ [ ] → 12 14 ←	File 1
7	→ [13] → 16 18 ←	→ [14] ←	File 2

Fig. 84. Buffer queuing, according to Algorithm F.

queue. This floating-buffer arrangement is an important feature of Algorithm F, since we would be unable to proceed in line 4 if we had chosen File 1 instead of File 2 for the input on line 3.

In order to prove that Algorithm F is valid, we must show two things:

i) There is always an input buffer available (that is, we can always find a k in step F4).

ii) If an input buffer is exhausted while merging, its successor is already present in memory (that is, S[C[i]] is meaningful in step F2).

Suppose (i) is false, so that all buffers are unavailable at some point when we reach step F4. Each time we get to that step, the total amount of unprocessed data among all the buffers is exactly P bufferloads, just enough data to fill P buffers if it were redistributed, since we are inputting and outputting data at the same rate. Some of the buffers are only partially full; but at most one buffer for each file is partially full, so at most P buffers are in that condition. By hypothesis all $2P$ of the buffers are unavailable; therefore at least P of them must be completely full. This can happen only if P are full and P are empty, otherwise we would have too much data. But at most one buffer can be unavailable and empty at any one time; hence (i) cannot be false.

Suppose (ii) is false, so that we have no unprocessed records in memory, for some file, but the current output buffer is not yet full. By the principle of forecasting, we must have no more than one block of data for each of the other files, since we do not read in a block for a file unless that block will be needed before the buffers on any other file are exhausted. Therefore the total number of unprocessed records amounts to at most $P-1$ blocks; adding the unfilled output buffer leads to less than P bufferloads of data in memory, a contradiction.

This argument establishes the validity of Algorithm F; and it also indicates the possibility of pathological circumstances under which the algorithm just barely avoids disaster. An important subtlety that we have not mentioned, regarding the possibility of equal keys, is discussed in exercise 5. See also exercise 4, which considers the case $P = 1$.

One way to terminate Algorithm F gracefully is to set L[m] to ∞ in step F3 if the block just read is the last of a run. (It is customary to indicate the end of a run in some special way.) After all of the data on all of the files has been read, we will eventually find all of the L's equal to ∞ in step F4; then it is usually possible to begin reading the first blocks of the next run on each file, beginning initialization of the next merge phase as the final $P + 1$ blocks are output.

Thus we can keep the output tape going at essentially full speed, without reading more than one tape at a time. An exception to this rule occurs in step F1, where it would be beneficial to read several tapes at once in order to get things going in the beginning; but step F1 can usually be arranged to overlap with the preceding part of the computation.

The idea of looking at the last record in each block, to predict which buffer will empty first, was discovered in 1953 by F. E. Holberton. The technique was first published by E. H. Friend [*JACM* **3** (1956), 144–145, 165]. His rather complicated algorithm used $3P$ input buffers, with three dedicated to each input file; Algorithm F improves the situation by making use of floating buffers, allowing any single file to claim as many as $P + 1$ input buffers at once, yet never needing more than $2P$ in all. A discussion of merging with fewer than $2P$ input buffers appears at the end of this section. Some interesting improvements to Algorithm F are discussed in Section 5.4.9.

Comparative behavior of merge patterns. Let us now use what we know about tapes and merging to compare the effectiveness of the various merge patterns that we have studied in Sections 5.4.2 through 5.4.5. It is very instructive to work out the details when each method is applied to the same task. Consider therefore the problem of sorting a file whose records each contain 100 characters, when there are 100,000 character positions of memory available for data storage — not counting the space needed for the program and its auxiliary variables, or the space occupied by links in a selection tree. (Remember that we are pretending to live in the days when memories were small.) The input appears in random order on tape, in blocks of 5000 characters each, and the output is to appear in the same format. There are five scratch tapes to work with, in addition to the unit containing the input tape.

The total number of records to be sorted is 100,000, but this information is not known in advance to the sorting algorithm.

The foldout illustration in Chart A summarizes the actions that transpire when ten different merging schemes are applied to this data. The best way to look at this important illustration is to imagine that you are actually watching the sort take place: Scan each line slowly from left to right, pretending that you can actually see six tapes reading, writing, rewinding, and/or reading backwards, as indicated on the diagram. During a P-way merge the input tapes will be moving only $1/P$ times as often as the output tape. When the original input tape has been completely read (and rewound "with lock"), Chart A assumes that a skilled computer operator dismounts it and replaces it with a scratch tape, in just 30 seconds. In examples 2, 3, and 4 this is "critical path time" when the computer is idly waiting for the operator to finish; but in the remaining examples, the dismount-reload operation is overlapped by other processing.

Example 1. Read-forward balanced merge. Let's review the specifications of the problem: The records are 100 characters long, there is enough internal memory to hold 1000 records at a time, and each block on the input tape contains 5000 characters (50 records). There are 100,000 records ($= 10,000,000$ characters $= 2000$ blocks) in all.

We are free to choose the block size for intermediate files. A six-tape balanced merge uses three-way merging, so the technique of Algorithm F calls for 8 buffers; we may therefore use blocks containing $1000/8 = 125$ records ($= 12500$ characters) each.

The initial distribution pass can make use of replacement selection (Algorithm 5.4.1R), and in order to keep the tapes running smoothly we may use two input buffers of 50 records each, plus two output buffers of 125 records each. This leaves room for 650 records in the replacement selection tree. Most of the initial runs will therefore be about 1300 records long (10 or 11 blocks); it turns out that 78 initial runs are produced in Chart A, the last one being rather short.

The first merge pass indicated shows nine runs merged to tape 4, instead of alternating between tapes 4, 5, and 6. This makes it possible to do useful work while the computer operator is loading a scratch tape onto unit 6; since the total number S of runs is known once the initial distribution has been completed, the algorithm knows that $\lceil S/9 \rceil$ runs should be merged to tape 4, then $\lceil (S-3)/9 \rceil$ to tape 5, then $\lceil (S-6)/9 \rceil$ to tape 6.

The entire sorting procedure for this example can be summarized in the following way, using the notation introduced in Section 5.4.2:

$$
\begin{array}{cccccc}
1^{26} & 1^{26} & 1^{26} & - & - & - \\
- & - & - & 3^9 & 3^9 & 3^8 \\
9^3 & 9^3 & 9^2 6^1 & - & - & - \\
- & - & - & 27^1 & 27^1 & 24^1 \\
78^1 & - & - & - & - & -
\end{array}
$$

Example 2. Read-forward polyphase merge. The second example in Chart A carries out the polyphase merge, according to Algorithm 5.4.2D. In this case we do five-way merging, so the memory is split into 12 buffers of 83 records each. During the initial replacement selection we have two 50-record input buffers and two 83-record output buffers, leaving 734 records in the tree; so the initial runs this time are about 1468 records long (17 or 18 blocks). The situation illustrated shows that $S = 70$ initial runs were obtained, the last two actually being only four blocks and one block long, respectively. The merge pattern can be summarized thus:

$0^{13}1^{18}$	$0^{13}1^{17}$	$0^{13}1^{15}$	$0^{12}1^{12}$	0^81^8	—
1^{15}	1^{14}	1^{12}	1^8	—	$0^81^42^15^3$
1^7	1^6	1^4	—	4^8	$1^42^15^3$
1^3	1^2	—	8^4	4^4	2^15^3
1^1	—	16^119^1	8^2	4^2	5^2
—	34^1	19^1	8^1	4^1	5^1
70^1	—	—	—	—	—

Curiously, polyphase actually took about 25 seconds *longer* than the far less sophisticated balanced merge! There are two main reasons for this:

1) Balanced merge was particularly lucky in this case, since $S = 78$ is just less than a perfect power of 3. If 82 initial runs had been produced, the balanced merge would have needed an extra pass.

2) Polyphase merge wasted 30 seconds while the input tape was being changed, and a total of more than 5 minutes went by while it was waiting for rewind operations to be completed. By contrast the balanced merge needed comparatively little rewind time. In the second phase of the polyphase merge, 13 seconds were saved because the 8 dummy runs on tape 6 could be assumed present even while that tape was rewinding; but no other rewind overlap occurred. Therefore polyphase lost out even though it required significantly less read/write time.

Example 3. Read-forward cascade merge. This case is analogous to the preceding, but using Algorithm 5.4.3C. The merging may be summarized thus:

1^{14}	1^{15}	1^{12}	1^{14}	1^{15}	—
1^5	1^9	—	1^{14}	1^{15}	$1^32^33^6$
5^16^3	5^3	5^36^2	—	1^1	2^2
—	12^1	6^1	18^1	18^1	16^1
70^1	—	—	—	—	—

(Remember to watch each of these examples in action, by scanning Chart A in the foldout illustration.)

Example 4. Tape-splitting polyphase merge. This procedure, described at the end of Section 5.4.2, allows most of the rewind time to be overlapped. It uses four-way merging, so we divide the memory into ten 100-record buffers; there are 700 records in the replacement selection tree, so it turns out that 72 initial runs are formed. The last run, again, is very short. A distribution scheme analogous to Algorithm 5.4.2D has been used, followed by a simple but somewhat ad hoc method of placing dummy runs:

1^{21}	1^{19}	1^{15}	1^8	—	$0^2 1^9$
$0^2 1^{17}$	$0^2 1^{15}$	$0^2 1^{11}$	$0^2 1^4$	—	$0^2 1^9 4^4$
1^{13}	1^{11}	1^7	—	$0^2 4^4$	$0^2 1^9 4^4$
1^{10}	1^8	1^4	—	$0^2 4^4 3^2 4^1$	$1^8 4^4$
1^6	1^4	—	4^4	$0^2 4^4 3^2 4^1$	$1^4 4^4$
1^5	1^3	—	$4^4 3^1$	$0^1 4^4 3^2 4^1$	$1^3 4^4$
1^2	—	$3^1 7^2$	$4^4 3^1$	$4^2 3^2 4^1$	4^4
1^1	—	$3^1 7^2 13^1$	$4^3 3^1$	$4^1 3^2 4^1$	4^3
—	13^1	$3^1 7^2 13^1$	$4^2 3^1$	$3^2 4^1$	4^2
—	$13^1 14^1$	$7^2 13^1$	$4^1 3^1$	$3^1 4^1$	4^1
18^1	$13^1 14^1$	$7^1 13^1$	3^1	4^1	—
18^1	14^1	13^1	—	—	27^1
—	—	—	72^1	—	—

This turns out to give the best running time of all the examples in Chart A that do not read backwards. Since S will never be very large, it would be possible to develop a more complicated algorithm that places dummy runs in an even better way; see Eq. 5.4.2–(26).

Example 5. Cascade merge with rewind overlap. This procedure runs almost as fast as the previous example, although the algorithm governing it is much simpler. We simply use the cascade sort method as in Algorithm 5.4.3C for the initial distribution, but with $T = 5$ instead of $T = 6$. Then each phase of each "cascade" staggers the tapes so that we ordinarily don't write on a tape until after it has had a chance to be rewound. The pattern, very briefly, is

1^{21}	1^{22}	1^{19}	1^{10}	—	—
1^4	1^7	—	—	$1^2 2^2 3^5$	4^{10}
7^2	—	8^3	$7^2 8^2$	—	4^1
—	26^1	—	8^1	22^1	16^1
72^1	—	—	—	—	—

Example 6. Read-backward balanced merge. This is like example 1 but with all the rewinding eliminated:

A_1^{26}	A_1^{26}	A_1^{26}	—	—	—
—	—	—	D_3^9	D_3^9	D_3^8
A_9^3	A_9^3	$A_9^2 A_6^1$	—	—	—
—	—	—	D_{24}^1	D_{27}^1	D_{27}^1
A_{78}^1	—	—	—	—	—

Since there was comparatively little rewinding in example 1, this scheme is not a great deal better than the read-forward case. In fact, it turns out to be slightly slower than tape-splitting polyphase, in spite of the fortunate value $S = 78$.

Example 7. Read-backward polyphase merge. In this example only five of the six tapes are used, in order to eliminate the time for rewinding and changing the input tape. Thus, the merging is only four-way, and the buffer allocation is like that in examples 4 and 5. A distribution like Algorithm 5.4.2D is used, but with alternating directions of runs, and with tape 1 fixed as the final output tape. First an ascending run is written on tape 1; then descending runs on tapes 2, 3, 4; then ascending runs on 2, 3, 4; then descending on 1, 2, 3; etc. Each time we switch direction, replacement selection usually produces a shorter run, so it turns out that 77 initial runs are formed instead of the 72 in examples 4 and 5.

This procedure results in a distribution of (22, 21, 19, 15) runs, and the next perfect distribution is (29, 56, 52, 44). Exercise 5.4.4–5 shows how to generate strings of merge numbers that can be used to place dummy runs in optimum positions; such a procedure is feasible in practice because the finiteness of a tape reel ensures that S is never too large. Therefore the example in Chart A has been constructed using such a method for dummy run placement (see exercise 7). This turns out to be the fastest of all the examples illustrated.

Example 8. Read-backward cascade merge. As in example 7, only five tapes are used here. This procedure follows Algorithm 5.4.3C, using rewind and forward read to avoid one-way merging (since rewinding is more than twice as fast as reading on MIXT units). Distribution is therefore the same as in example 5. The pattern may be summarized briefly as follows, using $\downarrow$ to denote rewinding:

$$
\begin{array}{ccccc}
A_1^{21} & A_1^{22} & A_1^{19} & A_1^{10} & - \\[4pt]
A_1^4\!\downarrow & A_1^7\!\downarrow & - & D_1^2 D_2^2 D_3^5 & D_4^{10} \\[4pt]
A_8 A_7^2 & A_5^2 & A_9^4 & - & D_4^1\!\downarrow \\[4pt]
- & D_{17} & A_9\!\downarrow & D_{25} & D_{21} \\[4pt]
A_{72} & - & - & - & -
\end{array}
$$

Example 9. Read-backward oscillating sort. Oscillating sort with $T = 5$ (Algorithm 5.4.5B) can use buffer allocation as in examples 4, 5, 7, and 8, since it does four-way merging. However, replacement selection does not behave in the same way, since a run of length 700 (not 1400 or so) is output just before entering each merge phase, in order to clear the internal memory. Consequently 85 runs are produced in this example, instead of 72. Some of the key steps in the process are

$$
\begin{array}{ccccc}
- & A_1 & A_1 A_1 & A_1 A_1 & A_1 A_1 \\[4pt]
D_4 & - & A_1 & A_1 & A_1
\end{array}
$$

$$\cdots \cdots \cdots \cdots \cdots \cdots \cdots \cdots \cdots \cdots \cdots$$

$D_4 D_4$	$D_4 D_4$	$D_4 D_4$	D_4	—
D_4	D_4	D_4	—	A_{16}
. . .	. . .	. . .	. . .	. . .
D_4	$A_{16} D_4 D_4$	$A_{16} D_4$	$A_{16} D_4 A_1$	A_{16}
D_4	$A_{16} D_4 D_4$	$A_{16} D_4 D_1$	$A_{16} D_4$	A_{16}
—	$A_{16} D_4$	$A_{16} D_4$	A_{16}	$A_{16} A_{13}$
—	$A_{16} D_4$	A_{16}	$A_{16} A_4$	$A_{16} A_{13}$
—	A_{16}	$A_{16} A_4$	$A_{16} A_4$	$A_{16} A_{13}$
D_{37}	—	$A_{16}{\downarrow}$	$A_{16}{\downarrow}$	$A_{16}{\downarrow}$
—	A_{85}	—	—	—

Example 10. Read-forward oscillating sort. In the final example, replacement selection is not used because all initial runs must be the same length. Therefore full core loads of 1000 records are sorted internally whenever an initial run is required; this makes $S = 100$. Some key steps in the process are

A_1	A_1	A_1	A_1	A_1
—	—	—	—	$A_1 A_4$
. . .	. . .	. . .	. . .	. . .
A_1	A_1	A_1	A_1	$A_1 A_4$
—	—	—	$A_1 A_4$	$\cancel{A}_1 A_4$
A_1	A_1	A_1	$A_1 A_4$	$A_1 A_4$
. . .	. . .	. . .	. . .	. . .
A_1	$A_1 A_4$	$A_1 A_4$	$A_1 A_4$	$A_1 A_4$
$A_1 A_4$	$\cancel{A}_1 A_4$	$\cancel{A}_1 A_4$	$\cancel{A}_1 A_4$	$\cancel{A}_1 A_4$
$A_1 A_4 A_{16}$	—	—	—	—
. . .	. . .	. . .	. . .	. . .
—	$A_1 A_4$	$A_1 A_4$	$A_1 A_4$	$A_1 A_4 A_{16} A_{64}$
A_4	$\cancel{A}_1 A_4$	$\cancel{A}_1 A_4$	$\cancel{A}_1 A_4$	$\cancel{A}_1 A_4 A_{16} A_{64}$
$A_4 A_{16}$	—	—	—	$\cancel{A}_1 \cancel{A}_4 A_{16} A_{64}$
$\cancel{A}_4 A_{16}$	A_4	—	—	$\cancel{A}_1 \cancel{A}_4 A_{16} A_{64}$
—	—	—	A_{36}	$\cancel{A}_1 \cancel{A}_4 \cancel{A}_{16} A_{64}$
A_{100}	—	—	—	—

This routine turns out to be slowest of all, partly because it does not use replacement selection, but mostly because of its rather awkward ending (a two-way merge).

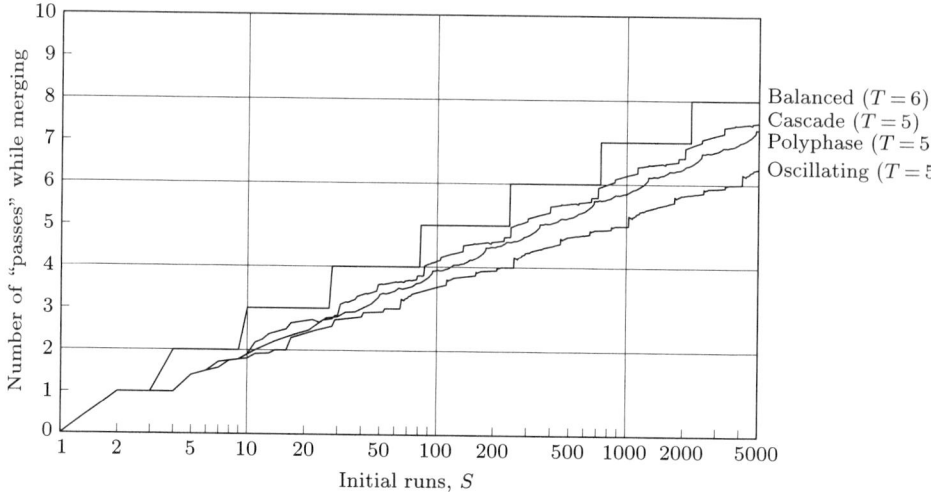

Fig. 85. A somewhat misleading way to compare merge patterns.

Estimating the running time. Let's see now how to figure out the approximate execution time of a sorting method using MIXT tapes. Could we have predicted the outcomes shown in Chart A without carrying out a detailed simulation?

One way that has traditionally been used to compare different merge patterns is to superimpose graphs such as we have seen in Figs. 70, 74, and 78. These graphs show the effective number of passes over the data, as a function of the number of initial runs, assuming that each initial run has approximately the same length. (See Fig. 85.) But this is *not* a very realistic comparison, because we have seen that different methods lead to different numbers of initial runs; furthermore there is a different overhead time caused by the relative frequency of interblock gaps, and the rewind time also has significant effects. All of these machine-dependent features make it impossible to prepare charts that provide a valid machine-independent comparison of the methods. On the other hand, Fig. 85 does show us that, except for balanced merge, the effective number of passes can be reasonably well approximated by smooth curves of the form $\alpha \ln S + \beta$. Therefore we can make a fairly good comparison of the methods in any particular situation, by studying formulas that approximate the running time. Our goal, of course, is to find formulas that are simple yet sufficiently realistic.

Let us now attempt to develop such formulas, in terms of the following parameters:

N = number of records to be sorted,

C = number of characters per record,

M = number of character positions available in the internal memory (assumed to be a multiple of C),

τ = number of seconds to read or write one character,

$\rho\tau$ = number of seconds to rewind over one character,

$\sigma\tau$ = number of seconds for stop/start time delay,

γ = number of characters per interblock gap,

δ = number of seconds for operator to dismount and replace input tape,

B_i = number of characters per block in the unsorted input,

B_o = number of characters per block in the sorted output.

For MIXT we have $\tau = 1/60000$, $\rho = 2/5$, $\sigma = 300$, $\gamma = 480$. The example application treated above has $N = 100000$, $C = 100$, $M = 100000$, $\delta = 30$, $B_i = B_o = 5000$. These parameters are usually the machine and data characteristics that affect sorting time most critically (although rewind time is often given by a more complicated expression than a simple ratio ρ). Given the parameters above and a merge pattern, we shall compute further quantities such as

P = maximum order of merge in the pattern,

P' = number of records in replacement selection tree,

S = number of initial runs,

$\pi = \alpha \ln S + \beta$ = approximate average number of times each character is read and written, not counting the initial distribution or the final merge,

$\pi' = \alpha' \ln S + \beta'$ = approximate average number of times rewinding over each character during intermediate merge phases,

B = number of characters per block in the intermediate merge phases,

$\omega_i, \omega, \omega_o$ = "overhead ratio," the effective time required to read or write a character (due to gaps and stop/start) divided by the hardware time τ.

The examples of Chart A have chosen block and buffer sizes according to the formula

$$B = \left\lfloor \frac{M}{C(2P+2)} \right\rfloor C, \tag{1}$$

so that the blocks can be as large as possible consistent with the buffering scheme of Algorithm F. (In order to avoid trouble during the final pass, P should be small enough that (1) makes $B \geq B_o$.) The size of the tree during replacement selection is then

$$P' = (M - 2B_i - 2B)/C. \tag{2}$$

For random data the number of initial runs S can be estimated as

$$S \approx \left\lceil \frac{N}{2P'} + \frac{7}{6} \right\rceil, \tag{3}$$

using the results of Section 5.4.1. Assuming that $B_i < B$ and that the input tape can be run at full speed during the distribution (see below), it takes about $NC\omega_i\tau$ seconds to distribute the initial runs, where

$$\omega_i = (B_i + \gamma)/B_i. \qquad (4)$$

While merging, the buffering scheme allows simultaneous reading, writing, and computing, but the frequent switching between input tapes means that we must add the stop/start time penalty; therefore we set

$$\omega = (B + \gamma + \sigma)/B, \qquad (5)$$

and the merge time is approximately

$$(\pi + \rho\pi')NC\omega\tau. \qquad (6)$$

This formula penalizes rewind slightly, since ω includes stop/start time, but other considerations, such as rewind interlock and the penalty for reading from load point, usually compensate for this. The final merge pass, assuming that $B_o \leq B$, is constrained by the overhead ratio

$$\omega_o = (B_o + \gamma)/B_o. \qquad (7)$$

We may estimate the running time of the final merge and rewind as

$$NC(1 + \rho)\omega_o\tau;$$

in practice it might take somewhat longer due to the presence of unequal block lengths (input and output are not synchronized as in Algorithm F), but the running time will be pretty much the same for all merge patterns.

Before going into more specific formulas for individual patterns, let us try to justify two of the assumptions made above.

a) *Can replacement selection keep up with the input tape?* In the examples of Chart A it probably can, since it takes about ten iterations of the inner loop of Algorithm 5.4.1R to select the next record, and we have $C\omega_i\tau > 1667$ microseconds in which to do this. With careful programming of the replacement selection loop, this can be done on most machines (even in the 1970s). Notice that the situation is somewhat less critical while merging: The computation time per record is almost always less than the tape time per record during a P-way merge, since P isn't very large.

b) *Should we really choose B to be the maximum possible buffer size, as in* (1)? A large buffer size cuts down the overhead ratio ω in (5); but it also increases the number of initial runs S, since P' is decreased. It is not immediately clear which factor is more important. Considering the merging time as a function of $x = CP'$, we can express it in the approximate form

$$\left(\theta_1 \ln\left(\frac{N}{x} + \frac{7}{6}\right) + \theta_2\right)\left(\frac{\theta_3 - x}{\theta_4 - x}\right) \qquad (8)$$

for some appropriate constants $\theta_1, \theta_2, \theta_3, \theta_4$, with $\theta_3 > \theta_4$. Differentiating with respect to x shows that there is some N_0 such that for all $N \geq N_0$ it does not pay to increase x at the expense of buffer size. In the sorting application of Chart A, for example, N_0 turns out to be roughly 10000; when sorting more than 10000 records the large buffer size is superior.

Note, however, that with balanced merge the number of passes jumps sharply when S passes a power of P. If an approximation to N is known in advance, the buffer size should be chosen so that S will most likely be slightly less than a power of P. For example, the buffer size for the first line of Chart A was 12500; since $S = 78$, this was very satisfactory, but if S had turned out to be 82 it would have been much better to decrease the buffer size a little.

Formulas for the ten examples. Returning to Chart A, let us try to give formulas that approximate the running time in each of the ten methods. In most cases the basic formula

$$NC\omega_i\tau + (\pi + \rho\pi')NC\omega\tau + (1+\rho)NC\omega_o\tau \qquad (9)$$

will be a sufficiently good approximation to the overall sorting time, once we have specified the number of intermediate merge passes $\pi = \alpha \ln S + \beta$ and the number of intermediate rewind passes $\pi' = \alpha' \ln S + \beta'$. Sometimes it is necessary to add a further correction to (9); details for each method can be worked out as follows:

Example 1. Read-forward balanced merge. The formulas

$$\pi = \lceil \ln S/\ln P \rceil - 1, \qquad \pi' = \lceil \ln S/\ln P \rceil/P$$

may be used for P-way merging on $2P$ tapes.

Example 2. Read-forward polyphase merge. We may take $\pi' \approx \pi$, since every phase is usually followed by a rewind of about the same length as the previous merge. From Table 5.4.2–1 we get the values $\alpha \approx 0.795$, $\beta \approx 0.864 - 2$, in the case of six tapes. (We subtract 2 because the table entry includes the initial and final passes as well as the intermediate ones.) The time for rewinding the input tape after the initial distribution, namely $\rho NC\omega_i\tau + \delta$, should be added to (9).

Example 3. Read-forward cascade merge. Table 5.4.3–1 gives the values $\alpha \approx 0.773$, $\beta \approx 0.808 - 2$. Rewind time is comparatively difficult to estimate; perhaps setting $\pi' \approx \pi$ is accurate enough. As in example 2, we need to add the initial rewind time to (9).

Example 4. Tape-splitting polyphase merge. Table 5.4.2–6 tells us that $\alpha \approx 0.752$, $\beta \approx 1.024 - 2$. The rewind time is almost overlapped except after the initialization ($\rho NC\omega_i\tau + \delta$) and two phases near the end ($2\rho NC\omega\tau$ times 36 percent). We may also subtract 0.18 from β since the first half phase is overlapped by the initial rewind.

Example 5. Cascade merge with rewind overlap. In this case we use Table 5.4.3–1 for $T = 5$, to get $\alpha \approx 0.897$, $\beta \approx 0.800 - 2$. Nearly all of the unoverlapped rewind occurs just after the initial distribution and just after each two-way merge. After a perfect initial distribution, the longest tape contains about $1/g$ of the data, where g is the "growth ratio." After each two-way merge the amount of rewind in the six-tape case is $d_k d_{n-k}$ (see exercise 5.4.3–5), hence the amount of rewind after two-way merges in the T-tape case can be shown to be approximately

$$\bigl(2/(2T-1)\bigr)\bigl(1 - \cos\bigl(4\pi/(2T-1)\bigr)\bigr)$$

of the file. In our case, $T = 5$, this is $\frac{2}{9}(1 - \cos 80°) \approx 0.184$ of the file, and the number of times it occurs is $0.946 \ln S + 0.796 - 2$.

Example 6. Read-backward balanced merge. This is like example 1, except that most of the rewinding is eliminated. The change in direction from forward to backward causes some delays, but they are not significant. There is a 50-50 chance that rewinding will be necessary before the final pass, so we may take $\pi' = 1/(2P)$.

Example 7. Read-backward polyphase merge. Since replacement selection in this case produces runs that change direction about every P times, we must replace (3) by another formula for S. A reasonably good approximation, suggested by exercise 5.4.1–24, is $S = \lceil N(3 + 1/P)/(6P') \rceil + 1$. All rewind time is eliminated, and Table 5.4.2–1 gives $\alpha \approx 0.863$, $\beta \approx 0.921 - 2$.

Example 8. Read-backward cascade merge. From Table 5.4.3–1 we have $\alpha \approx 0.897$, $\beta \approx 0.800 - 2$. The rewind time can be estimated as twice the difference between "passes with copying" minus "passes without copying" in that table, plus $1/(2P)$ in case the final merge must be preceded by rewinding to get ascending order.

Example 9. Read-backward oscillating sort. In this case replacement selection has to be started and stopped many times; bursts of $P - 1$ to $2P - 1$ runs are distributed at a time, averaging P in length; the average length of runs therefore turns out to be approximately $P'(2P - 4/3)/P$, and we may estimate $S = \lceil N/\bigl((2 - 4/(3P))P'\bigr) \rceil + 1$. A little time is used to switch from merging to distribution and vice-versa; this is approximately the time to read in P' records from the input tape, namely $P'C\omega_i\tau$, and it occurs about S/P times. Rewind time and merging time may be estimated as in example 6.

Example 10. Read-forward oscillating sort. This method is not easy to analyze, because the final "cleanup" phases performed after the input is exhausted are not as efficient as the earlier phases. Ignoring this troublesome aspect, and simply calling it one extra pass, we can estimate the merging time by setting $\alpha = 1/\ln P$, $\beta = 0$, and $\pi' = \pi/P$. The distribution of runs is somewhat different in this case, since replacement selection is not used; we set $P' = M/C$ and $S = \lceil N/P' \rceil$. With care we will be able to overlap computing, reading, and writing during the distribution, with an additional factor of about $(M+2B)/M$ in the overhead. The "mode-switching" time mentioned in example 9 is not needed in the present case because it is overlapped by rewinding. So the estimated sorting time in this case is (9) plus $2BNC\omega_i\tau/M$.

Table 1

SUMMARY OF SORTING TIME ESTIMATES

Ex.	P	B	P'	S	ω	α	β	α'	β'	(9)	Additions to (9)	Est. total	Actual total
1	3	12500	650	79	1.062	0.910	−1.000	0.303	0.000	1064		1064	1076
2	5	8300	734	70	1.094	0.795	−1.136	0.795	−1.136	1010	$\rho NC\omega_i\tau + \delta$	1113	1103
3	5	8300	734	70	1.094	0.773	−1.192	0.773	−1.192	972	$\rho NC\omega_i\tau + \delta$	1075	1127
4	4	10000	700	73	1.078	0.752	−0.994	0.000	0.720	844	$\rho NC\omega_i\tau + \delta$	947	966
5	4	10000	700	73	1.078	0.897	−1.200	0.173	0.129	972		972	992
6	3	12500	650	79	1.062	0.910	−1.000	0.000	0.167	981		981	980
7	4	10000	700	79	1.078	0.863	−1.079	0.000	0.000	922		922	907
8	4	10000	700	73	1.078	0.897	−1.200	0.098	0.117	952		952	949
9	4	10000	700	87	1.078	0.721	−1.000	0.000	0.125	846	$P'SC\omega_i\tau/P$	874	928
10	4	10000	—	100	1.078	0.721	0.000	0.180	0.000	1095	$2BNC\omega_i\tau/M$	1131	1158

Table 1 shows that the estimates are not too bad in these examples, although in a few cases there is a discrepancy of 50 seconds or so. The formulas in examples 2 and 3 indicate that cascade merge should be preferable to polyphase on six tapes, yet in practice polyphase was better. The reason is that graphs like Fig. 85 (which shows the five-tape case) are more nearly straight lines for the polyphase algorithm; cascade is superior to polyphase on six tapes for $14 \leq S \leq 15$ and $43 \leq S \leq 55$, near the "perfect" cascade numbers 15 and 55, but the polyphase distribution of Algorithm 5.4.2D is equal or better for all other $S \leq 100$. Cascade will win over polyphase as $S \to \infty$, but S doesn't actually approach ∞. The underestimate in example 9 is due to similar circumstances; polyphase was superior to oscillating even though the asymptotic theory tells us that oscillating will be better for large S.

Some miscellaneous remarks. It is now appropriate to make a few more or less random observations about tape merging.

• The formulas above show that the cost of tape sorting is essentially a function of N times C, not of N and C independently. Except for a few relatively minor considerations (such as the fact that B was taken to be a multiple of C), our formulas say that it takes about as long to sort one million records of 10 characters each as to sort 100,000 records of 100 characters each. Actually there may be a difference, not revealed in our formulas, because of the space used by link fields during replacement selection. In any event the size of the *key* makes hardly any difference, unless keys get so long and complicated that internal computation cannot keep up with the tapes.

With long records and short keys it is tempting to "detach" the keys, sort them first, and then somehow rearrange the records as a whole. But this idea doesn't really work; it merely postpones the agony, because the final rearrangement procedure takes about as long as a conventional merge sort would take.

• When writing a sort routine that is to be used repeatedly, it is wise to estimate the running time very carefully and to compare the theory with actual observed performance. Since the theory of sorting has been fairly well developed, this procedure has been known to turn up bugs in the input/output hardware or software on existing systems; the service was substantially slower than it should have been, yet nobody had noticed it until the sorting routine ran too slowly!

• Our analysis of replacement selection has been carried out for "random" files, but the files that actually arise in practice very often have a good deal of existing order. (In fact, sometimes people will sort a file that is already in order, just to be sure.) Therefore experience has shown that replacement selection is preferable to other kinds of internal sort, even more so than our formulas indicate. This advantage is slightly mitigated in the case of read-backward polyphase sorting, since a number of descending runs must be produced; indeed, R. L. Gilstad (who first published the polyphase merge) originally rejected the read-backward technique for that reason. But he noticed later that alternating directions will still pick up long ascending runs. Furthermore, read-backward polyphase is the only standard technique that likes descending input files as well as ascending ones.

• Another advantage of replacement selection is that it allows simultaneous reading, writing, and computing. If we merely did the internal sort in an obvious way — filling the memory, sorting it, then writing it out as it becomes filled with the next load — the distribution pass would take about twice as long.

The only other internal sort we have discussed that appears to be amenable to simultaneous reading, writing, and computing is heapsort. Suppose for convenience that the internal memory holds 1000 records, and that each block on tape holds 100. Example 10 of Chart A was prepared with the following strategy, letting $B_1 B_2 \ldots B_{10}$ stand for the contents of memory divided into ten 100-record blocks:

Step 0. Fill memory, and make the elements of $B_2 \ldots B_{10}$ satisfy the inequalities for a heap (with smallest element at the root).

Step 1. Make $B_1 \ldots B_{10}$ into a heap, then select out the least 100 records and move them to B_{10}.

Step 2. Write out B_{10}, while selecting the smallest 100 records of $B_1 \ldots B_9$ and moving them to B_9.

Step 3. Read into B_{10}, and write out B_9, while selecting the smallest 100 records of $B_1 \ldots B_8$ and moving them to B_8.

$\vdots$

Step 9. Read into B_4, and write out B_3, while selecting the smallest 100 records of $B_1 B_2$ and moving them to B_2 and while making the heap inequalities valid in $B_5 \ldots B_{10}$.

Step 10. Read into B_3, and write out B_2, while sorting B_1 and while making the heap inequalities valid in $B_4 \ldots B_{10}$.

Step 11. Read into B_2, and write out B_1, while making the heap inequalities valid in $B_3 \ldots B_{10}$.

Step 12. Read into B_1, while making the heap inequalities valid in $B_2 \ldots B_{10}$. Return to step 1. ∎

• We have been assuming that the number N of records to be sorted is not known in advance. Actually in most computer applications it would be possible to keep track of the number of records in all files at all times, and we could assume that our computer system is capable of telling us the value of N. How much help would this be? Unfortunately, not very much! We have seen that replacement selection is very advantageous, but it leads to an unpredictable number of initial runs. In a balanced merge we could use information about N to set the buffer size B in such a way that S will probably be just less than a power of P; and in a polyphase distribution with optimum placement of dummy runs we could use information about N to decide what level to shoot for (see Table 5.4.2–2).

• Tape drives tend to be the least reliable part of a computer. Therefore *the original input tape should never be destroyed until it is known that the entire sort has been satisfactorily completed.* The "operator dismount time" is annoying in some of the examples of Chart A, but it would be too risky to overwrite the input in view of the probability that something might go wrong during a long sort.

• When changing from forward write to backward read, we could save some time by never writing the last bufferload onto tape; it will just be read back in again anyway. But Chart A shows that this trick actually saves comparatively little time, except in the oscillating sort where directions are reversed frequently.

• Although a large computer system might have lots of tape units, we might be better off not using them all. The percentage difference between $\log_P S$ and $\log_{P+1} S$ is not very great when P is large, and a higher order of merge usually implies a smaller block size. (Consider also the poor computer operator who has to mount all those scratch tapes.) On the other hand, exercise 12 describes an interesting way to make use of additional tape units, grouping them so as to overlap input/output time without increasing the order of merge.

• On machines like MIX, which have fixed rather small block sizes, hardly any internal memory is needed while merging. Oscillating sort then becomes more attractive, because it becomes possible to maintain the replacement selection tree in memory while merging. In fact we can improve on oscillating sort in this case (as suggested by Colin J. Bell in 1962), merging a new initial run into the output every time we merge from the working tapes.

• We have observed that multireel files should be sorted one reel at a time, in order to avoid excessive tape handling. This is sometimes called a "reel time" application. Actually a balanced merge on six tapes can sort *three* reelfuls, up until the time of the final merge, if it has been programmed carefully.

To merge a fairly large number of individually sorted reels, a minimum-path-length merging tree will be fastest (see Section 5.4.4). This construction was first made by E. H. Friend [*JACM* **3** (1956), 166–167]; then W. H. Burge [*Information and Control* **1** (1958), 181–197] pointed out that an optimum way to merge runs of given (possibly unequal) lengths is obtained by constructing a tree with minimum *weighted* path length, using the run lengths as weights (see Sections 2.3.4.5 and 5.4.9), if we ignore tape handling time.

• Our discussions have blithely assumed that we have direct control over the input/output instructions for tape units, and that no complicated operating system keeps us from using tape as efficiently as the tape designers intended. These idealistic assumptions give us insights into the tape merging problem, and may give some insights into the proper design of operating system interfaces, but we should realize that multiprogramming and multiprocessing can make the situation considerably more complicated.

• The issues we have studied in this section were first discussed in print by E. H. Friend [*JACM* **3** (1956), 134–168], W. Zoberbier [*Elektronische Daten-verarbeitung* **5** (1960), 28–44], and M. A. Goetz [*Digital Computer User's Hand-book* (New York: McGraw–Hill, 1967), 1.292–1.320].

Summary. We can sum up what we have learned about the relative efficiencies of different approaches to tape sorting in the following way:

Theorem A. *It is difficult to decide which merge pattern is best in a given situation.* ∎

The examples we have seen in Chart A show how 100,000 randomly ordered 100-character records (or 1 million 10-character records) might be sorted using six tapes under realistic assumptions. This much data fills about half of a tape, and it can be sorted in about 15 to 19 minutes on the MIXT tapes. However, there is considerable variation in available tape equipment, and running times for such a job could vary between about four minutes and about two hours on different machines of the 1970s. In our examples, about 3 minutes of the total time were used for initial distribution of runs and internal sorting; about $4\frac{1}{2}$ minutes were used for the final merge and rewinding the output tape; and about $7\frac{1}{2}$ to $11\frac{1}{2}$ minutes were spent in intermediate stages of merging.

Given six tapes that cannot read backwards, the best sorting method under our assumptions was the "tape-splitting polyphase merge" (example 4); and for tapes that do allow backward reading, the best method turned out to be read-backward polyphase with a complicated placement of dummy runs (example 7). Oscillating sort (example 9) was a close second. In both cases the cascade merge provided a simpler alternative that was only slightly slower (examples 5 and 8). In the read-forward case, a straightforward balanced merge (example 1) was surprisingly effective, partly by luck in this particular example but partly also because it spends comparatively little time rewinding.

The situation would change somewhat if we had a different number of available tapes.

Sort generators. Given the wide variability of data and equipment charac-teristics, it is almost impossible to write a single external sorting program that is satisfactory in a variety of different applications. And it is also rather difficult to prepare a program that really handles tapes efficiently. Therefore the preparation of sorting software is a particularly challenging job. A *sort generator* is a program that produces machine code specially tailored to particular sorting applications, based on parameters that describe the data format and the hardware configuration. Such a program is often tied to high-level languages such as COBOL or PL/I.

One of the features normally provided by a sort generator is the ability to insert the user's "own coding," a sequence of special instructions to be incorporated into the first and last passes of the sorting routine. First-pass own coding is usually used to edit the input records, often shrinking them or slightly expanding them into a form that is easier to sort. For example, suppose that the input records are to be sorted on a nine-character key that represents a date in month-day-year format:

JUL041776   OCT311517   NOV051605   JUL141789   NOV071917

On the first pass the three-letter month code can be looked up in a table, and the month codes can be replaced by numbers with the most significant fields at the left:

17760704   15171031   16051105   17890714   19171107

This decreases the record length and makes subsequent comparisons much simpler. (An even more compact code could also be substituted.) Last-pass own coding can be used to restore the original format, and/or to make other desired changes to the file, and/or to compute some function of the output records. The merging algorithms we have studied are organized in such a way that it is easy to distinguish the last pass from other merges. Notice that when own coding is present there must be at least two passes over the file even if it is initially in order. Own coding that changes the record size can make it difficult for the oscillating sort to overlap some of its input/output operations.

Sort generators also take care of system details like tape label conventions, and they often provide for "hash totals" or other checks to make sure that none of the data has been lost or altered. Sometimes there are provisions for stopping the sort at convenient places and resuming later. The fanciest generators allow records to have dynamically varying lengths [see D. J. Waks, *CACM* **6** (1963), 267–272].

*Merging with fewer buffers. We have seen that $2P + 2$ buffers are sufficient to keep tapes moving rapidly during a P-way merge. Let us conclude this section by making a mathematical analysis of the merging time when *fewer* than $2P + 2$ buffers are present.

Two output buffers are clearly desirable, since we can be writing from one while forming the next block of output in the other. Therefore we may ignore the output question entirely, and concentrate only on the input.

Suppose there are $P + Q$ input buffers, where $1 \leq Q \leq P$. We shall use the following approximate model of the situation, as suggested by L. J. Woodrum [*IBM Systems J.* **9** (1970), 118–144]: It takes one unit of time to read a block of tape. During this time there is a probability p_0 that no input buffers have been emptied, p_1 that one has been emptied, $p_{\geq 2}$ that two or more have been, etc. When completing a tape read we are in one of $Q + 1$ states:

State 0. Q buffers are empty; we begin to read a block into one of them from the appropriate file, using the forecasting technique explained earlier in this section. After one unit of time we go to state 1 with probability p_0, otherwise we remain in state 0.

State 1. $Q - 1$ buffers are empty; we begin to read into one of them, forecasting the appropriate file. After one unit of time we go to state 2 with probability p_0, to state 1 with probability p_1, and to state 0 with probability $p_{\geq 2}$.

$$\vdots$$

State $Q - 1$. One buffer is empty; we begin to read into it, forecasting the appropriate file. After one unit of time we go to state Q with probability p_0, to state $Q - 1$ with probability p_1, ..., to state 1 with probability p_{Q-1}, and to state 0 with probability $p_{\geq Q}$.

State Q. All buffers are filled. Tape reading stops for an average of μ units of time and then we go to state $Q - 1$.

We start in state 0. This model of the situation corresponds to a *Markov process* (see exercise 2.3.4.2–26), which can be analyzed via generating functions in the following interesting way: Let z be an arbitrary parameter, and assume that each time we have a chance to read from tape we make a decision to do so with probability z, but we decide to terminate the algorithm with probability $1 - z$. Now let $g_Q(z) = \sum_{n \geq 0} a_n^{(Q)} z^n (1 - z)$ be the average number of times that state Q occurs in such a process; it follows that $a_n^{(Q)}$ is the average number of times state Q occurs when exactly n blocks have been read. Then $n + a_n^{(Q)} \mu$ is the average total time for input plus computation. If we had perfect overlap, as in the $(2P + 2)$-buffer algorithm, the total time would be only n units, so $a_n^{(Q)} \mu$ represents the "reading hangup" time.

Let A_{ij} be the probability that we go from state i to state j in this process, for $0 \leq i, j \leq Q + 1$, where $Q + 1$ is a new "stopped" state. For example, the A-matrix takes the following forms for small Q:

$$Q = 1: \quad \begin{pmatrix} p_{\geq 1}z & p_0 z & 1 - z \\ 1 & 0 & 0 \\ 0 & 0 & 0 \end{pmatrix},$$

$$Q = 2: \quad \begin{pmatrix} p_{\geq 1}z & p_0 z & 0 & 1 - z \\ p_{\geq 2}z & p_1 z & p_0 z & 1 - z \\ 0 & 1 & 0 & 0 \\ 0 & 0 & 0 & 0 \end{pmatrix},$$

$$Q = 3: \quad \begin{pmatrix} p_{\geq 1}z & p_0 z & 0 & 0 & 1 - z \\ p_{\geq 2}z & p_1 z & p_0 z & 0 & 1 - z \\ p_{\geq 3}z & p_2 z & p_1 z & p_0 z & 1 - z \\ 0 & 0 & 1 & 0 & 0 \\ 0 & 0 & 0 & 0 & 0 \end{pmatrix}.$$

Exercise 2.3.4.2–26(b) tells us that $g_Q(z) = \text{cofactor}_{Q0}(I - A)/\det(I - A)$. Thus for example when $Q = 1$ we have

$$g_1(z) = \det \begin{pmatrix} 0 & -p_0 z & z - 1 \\ 1 & 0 & 0 \\ 0 & 0 & 1 \end{pmatrix} \bigg/ \det \begin{pmatrix} 1 - p_{\geq 1}z & -p_0 z & z - 1 \\ -1 & 1 & 0 \\ 0 & 0 & 1 \end{pmatrix}$$

$$= \frac{p_0 z}{1 - p_{\geq 1}z - p_0 z} = \frac{p_0 z}{1 - z} = \sum_{n \geq 0} n p_0 z^n (1 - z),$$

so $a_n^{(1)} = np_0$. This of course was obvious *a priori*, since the problem is very simple when $Q = 1$. A similar calculation when $Q = 2$ (see exercise 14) gives the less obvious formula

$$a_n^{(2)} = \frac{p_0^2 n}{1 - p_1} - \frac{p_0^2(1 - p_1^n)}{(1 - p_1)^2}. \tag{10}$$

In general we can show that $a_n^{(Q)}$ has the form $\alpha^{(Q)}n + O(1)$ as $n \to \infty$, where the constant $\alpha^{(Q)}$ is not terribly difficult to calculate. (See exercise 15.) It turns out that $\alpha^{(3)} = p_0^3 / ((1 - p_1)^2 - p_0 p_2)$.

The nature of merging makes it fairly reasonable to assume that $\mu = 1/P$ and that we have a binomial distribution

$$p_k = \binom{P}{k} \left(\frac{1}{P}\right)^k \left(\frac{P - 1}{P}\right)^{P-k}.$$

For example, when $P = 5$ we have $p_0 = .32768$, $p_1 = .4096$, $p_2 = .2048$, $p_3 = .0512$, $p_4 = .0064$, and $p_5 = .00032$; hence $\alpha^{(1)} \approx 0.328$, $\alpha^{(2)} \approx 0.182$, and $\alpha^{(3)} \approx 0.125$. In other words, if we use $5 + 3$ input buffers instead of $5 + 5$, we can expect an additional "reading hangup" time of about $0.125/5 \approx 2.5$ percent.

Of course this model is only a very rough approximation; we know that when $Q = P$ there is no hangup time at all, but the model says that there is. The extra reading hangup time for smaller Q just about counterbalances the savings in overhead gained by having larger blocks, so the simple scheme with $Q = P$ seems to be vindicated.

EXERCISES

1. [*13*] Give a formula for the exact number of characters per tape, when every block on the tape contains n characters. Assume that the tape could hold exactly 23000000 characters if there were no interblock gaps.

2. [*15*] Explain why the first buffer for File 2, in line 6 of Fig. 84, is completely blank.

3. [*20*] Would Algorithm F work properly if there were only $2P - 1$ input buffers instead of $2P$? If so, prove it; if not, give an example where it fails.

4. [*20*] How can Algorithm F be changed so that it works also when $P = 1$?

▶ **5.** [*21*] When equal keys are present on different files, it is necessary to be very careful in the forecasting process. Explain why, and show how to avoid difficulty by defining the merging and forecasting operations of Algorithm F more precisely.

6. [*22*] What changes should be made to Algorithm 5.4.3C in order to convert it into an algorithm for cascade merge *with rewind overlap*, on $T + 1$ tapes?

▸ **7.** [*26*] The initial distribution in example 7 of Chart A produces

$$(A_1 D_1)^{11} \qquad D_1 (A_1 D_1)^{10} \qquad D_1 (A_1 D_1)^9 \qquad D_1 (A_1 D_1)^7$$

on tapes 1–4, where $(A_1 D_1)^7$ means $A_1 D_1 A_1 D_1 A_1 D_1 A_1 D_1 A_1 D_1 A_1 D_1 A_1 D_1$. Show how to insert additional A_0's and D_0's in a "best possible" way (in the sense that the overall number of initial runs processed while merging is minimized), bringing the distribution up to

$$A(DA)^{14} \qquad (DA)^{28} \qquad (DA)^{26} \qquad (DA)^{22}.$$

Hint: To preserve parity it is necessary to insert many of the A_0's and D_0's as adjacent pairs. The merge numbers for each initial run may be computed as in exercise 5.4.4–5; some simplification occurs since adjacent runs always have adjacent merge numbers.

8. [*20*] Chart A shows that most of the schemes for initial distribution of runs (with the exception of the initial distribution for the cascade merge) tend to put consecutive runs onto different tapes. If consecutive runs went onto the same tape we could save the stop/start time; would it therefore be a good idea to modify the distribution algorithms so that they switch tapes less often?

▸ **9.** [*22*] Estimate how long the read-backward polyphase algorithm would have taken in Chart A, if we had used all $T = 6$ tapes for sorting, instead of $T = 5$ as in example 7. Was it wise to avoid using the input tape?

10. [*M23*] Use the analyses in Sections 5.4.2 and 5.4.3 to show that the length of each rewind during a standard six-tape polyphase or cascade merge is rarely more than about 54 percent of the file (except for the initial and final rewinds, which cover the entire file).

11. [*23*] By modifying the appropriate entries in Table 1, estimate how long the first nine examples of Chart A would have taken if we had a combined low speed/high speed rewind. Assume that $\rho = 1$ when the tape is less than about one-fourth full, and that the rewind time for fuller tapes is approximately five seconds plus the time that would be obtained for $\rho = \frac{1}{5}$. Change example 8 so that it uses cascade merge *with* copying, since rewinding and reading forward is slower than copying in this case. [*Hint:* Use the result of exercise 10.]

12. [*40*] Consider partitioning six tapes into three pairs of tapes, with each pair playing the role of a single tape in a polyphase merge with $T = 3$. One tape of each pair will contains blocks $1, 3, 5, \ldots$ and the other tape will contain blocks $2, 4, 6, \ldots$; in this way we can essentially have two input tapes and two output tapes active at all times while merging, effectively doubling the merging speed.

   a) Find an appropriate way to extend Algorithm F to this situation. How many buffers should there be?

   b) Estimate the total running time that would be obtained if this method were used to sort 100,000 100-character records, considering both the read-forward and read-backward cases.

13. [*20*] Can a five-tape oscillating sort, as defined in Algorithm 5.4.5B, be used to sort four reelfuls of input data, up until the time of the final merge?

14. [*M19*] Derive (10).

15. [*HM29*] Prove that $g_Q(z) = h_Q(z)/(1-z)$, where $h_Q(z)$ is a rational function of z having no singularities inside the unit circle; hence $a_n^{(Q)} = h_Q(1)n + O(1)$ as $n \to \infty$. In particular, show that

$$h_3(1) = \det \begin{pmatrix} 0 & -p_0 & 0 & 0 \\ 0 & 1-p_1 & -p_0 & 0 \\ 0 & -p_2 & 1-p_1 & -p_0 \\ 1 & 0 & 0 & 0 \end{pmatrix} \Big/ \det \begin{pmatrix} 1 & -p_0 & 0 & 0 \\ 1 & 1-p_1 & -p_0 & 0 \\ 1 & -p_2 & 1-p_1 & -p_0 \\ 0 & 0 & -1 & 1 \end{pmatrix}.$$

16. [*41*] Carry out detailed studies of the problem of sorting 100,000 100-character records, drawing charts such as those in Chart A, assuming that 3, 4, or 5 tapes are available.

*5.4.7. External Radix Sorting

The previous sections have discussed the process of tape sorting by merging; but there is another way to sort with tapes, based on the radix sorting principle that was once used in mechanical card sorters (see Section 5.2.5). This method is sometimes called distribution sorting, column sorting, pocket sorting, digital sorting, separation sorting, etc.; it turns out to be essentially the *opposite* of merging!

Suppose, for example, that we have four tapes and that there are only eight possible keys: 0, 1, 2, 3, 4, 5, 6, 7. If the input data is on tape T1, we can begin by transferring all even keys to T3, all odd keys to T4:

	T1	T2	T3	T4
Given	$\{0, 1, 2, 3, 4, 5, 6, 7\}$	—	—	—
Pass 1	—	—	$\{0, 2, 4, 6\}$	$\{1, 3, 5, 7\}$

Now we rewind, and read T3 and then T4, putting $\{0, 1, 4, 5\}$ on T1 and $\{2, 3, 6, 7\}$ on T2:

	T1	T2	T3	T4
Pass 2	$\{0,4\}\{1,5\}$	$\{2,6\}\{3,7\}$	—	—

(The notation "$\{0, 4\}\{1, 5\}$" stands for a file that contains some records whose keys are all 0 or 4 followed by records whose keys are all 1 or 5. Notice that T1 now contains those keys whose middle binary digit is 0.) After rewinding again and distributing 0, 1, 2, 3 to T3 and 4, 5, 6, 7 to T4, we have

	T1	T2	T3	T4
Pass 3			$\{0\}\{1\}\{2\}\{3\}$	$\{4\}\{5\}\{6\}\{7\}$

Now we can finish up by copying T4 to the end of T3. In general, if the keys range from 0 to $2^k - 1$, we could sort the file in an analogous way using k passes, followed by a final collection phase that copies about half of the data from one tape to another. With six tapes we could use radix 3 representations in a similar way, to sort keys from 0 to $3^k - 1$ in k passes.

Partial-pass methods can also be used. For example, suppose that there are ten possible keys $\{0, 1, \ldots, 9\}$, and consider the following procedure due to

R. L. Ashenhurst [*Theory of Switching*, Progress Report BL-7 (Harvard Univ. Comp. Laboratory: May 1954), I.1–I.76]:

Phase	T1	T2	T3	T4	passes
	$\{0,1,\ldots,9\}$	—	—	—	
1	—	$\{0,2,4,7\}$	$\{1,5,6\}$	$\{3,8,9\}$	1.0
2	$\{0\}$	—	$\{1,5,6\}\{2,7\}$	$\{3,8,9\}\{4\}$	0.4
3	$\{0\}\{1\}\{2\}$	$\{6\}\{7\}$	—	$\{3,8,9\}\{4\}\{5\}$	0.5
4	$\{0\}\{1\}\{2\}\{3\}$	$\{6\}\{7\}\{8\}$	$\{9\}$	$\{4\}\{5\}$	0.3
C	$\{0\}\{1\}\{2\}\{3\}\{4\}\ldots\{9\}$				0.6
					2.8

Here C represents the collection phase. If each key value occurs about one-tenth of the time, the procedure above takes only 2.8 passes to sort ten keys, while the first example required 3.5 passes to sort only eight keys. Therefore we find that a clever distribution pattern can make a significant difference, for radix sorting as well as for merging.

The distribution patterns in the examples above can conveniently be represented as tree structures:

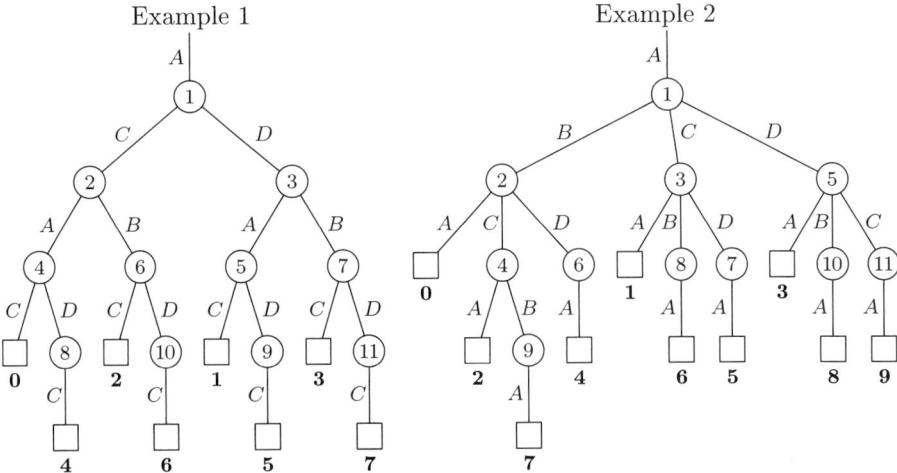

The circular internal nodes of these trees are numbered 1, 2, 3, ..., corresponding to steps 1, 2, 3, ... of the process. Tape names A, B, C, D (instead of T1, T2, T3, T4) have been placed next to the lines of the trees, in order to show where the records go. Square external nodes represent portions of a file that contain only one key, and that key is shown in boldface type just below the node. The lines just above square nodes all carry the name of the output tape (C in the first example, A in the second).

Thus, step 3 of example 1 consists of reading from tape D and writing 1s and 5s on tape A, 3s and 7s on tape B. It is not difficult to see that the number of passes performed is equal to the *external path length* of the tree divided by the number of external nodes, if we assume that each key occurs equally often.

Because of the sequential nature of tape, and the first-in-first-out discipline of forwards reading, we can't simply use *any* labeled tree as the basis of a distribution pattern. In the tree of example 1, data gets written on tape A during step 2 and step 3; it is necessary to use the data written during step 2 before we use the data written during step 3. In general if we write onto a tape during steps i and j, where $i < j$, we must use the data written during step i first; when the tree contains two branches of the form

$$
\begin{array}{cc}
\textcircled{i} & \textcircled{j} \\
A| & A| \\
\textcircled{k} & \textcircled{l}
\end{array}
\quad , \qquad i < j,
$$

we must have $k < l$. Furthermore we cannot write anything onto tape A *between* steps k and l, because we must rewind between reading and writing.

The reader who has worked the exercises of Section 5.4.4 will now immediately perceive that the allowable trees for read-forward radix sorting on T tapes are precisely the *strongly T-fifo trees*, which characterize read-forward *merge* sorting on T tapes! (See exercise 5.4.4–20.) The only difference is that all of the external nodes on the trees we are considering here have the same tape labels. We could remove this restriction by assuming a final collection phase that transfers all records to an output tape, or we could add that restriction to the rules for T-fifo trees by requiring that the initial distribution pass of a merge sort be explicitly represented in the corresponding merge tree.

In other words, *every merge pattern corresponds to a distribution pattern, and every distribution pattern corresponds to a merge pattern.* A moment's reflection shows why this is so, if we consider the actions of a merge sort and imagine that time could run backwards: The final output is "unmerged" into subfiles, which are unmerged into others, etc.; at time zero the output has been unmerged into S runs. Such a pattern is possible with tapes if and only if the corresponding radix sort distribution pattern, for S keys, is possible. This duality between merging and distribution is almost perfect; it breaks down only in one respect, namely that the input tape must be saved at different times.

The eight-key example treated at the beginning of this section is clearly dual to a balanced merge on four tapes. The ten-key example with partial passes corresponds to the following ten-run merge pattern (if we suppress the copy phases, steps 6–11 in the tree):

	T1	T2	T3	T4
Initial distribution	1^4	1^3	1^1	1^2
Tree step 5	1^3	1^2	—	$1^2 3^1$
Tree step 4	1^2	1^1	2^1	$1^2 3^1$
Tree step 3	1^1	—	$2^1 3^1$	$1^1 3^1$
Tree step 2	—	4^1	3^1	3^1
Tree step 1	10^1	—	—	—

If we compare this to the radix sort, we see that the methods have essentially the same structure but are reversed in time, with the tape contents also reversed from back to front: $1^2 3^1$ (two runs each of length 1 followed by one of length 3) corresponds to $\{3,8,9\}\{4\}\{5\}$ (two subfiles containing one key each, preceded by one subfile containing three).

Going the other way, we can in principle construct a radix sort dual to polyphase merge, another one dual to cascade merge, etc. For example, the 21-run polyphase merge on three tapes, illustrated at the beginning of Section 5.4.2, corresponds to the following interesting radix sort:

Phase	T1	T2	T3
	$\{0,1,\dots,20\}$	—	—
1	—	$\{0,2,4,5,7,9,10,12,13,15,17,18,20\}$	$\{1,3,6,8,11,14,16,19\}$
2	$\{0,5,10,13,18\}$	—	$\{1,3,6,8,11,14,16,19\}$ $\{2,4,7,9,12,15,17,20\}$
3	$\{0,5,10,13,18\}\{1,6,11,14,19\}$ $\{2,7,12,15,20\}$	$\{3,8,16\}\{4,9,17\}$	—
4	—	$\{3,8,16\}\{4,9,17\}\{5,10,18\}$ $\{6,11,19\}\{7,12,20\}$	$\{0,13\}\{1,14\}\{2,15\}$
5	$\{8\}\{9\}\{10\}\{11\}\{12\}$	—	$\{0,13\}\{1,14\}\{2,15\}$ $\{3,16\}\dots\{7,20\}$
6	$\{8\}\{9\}\{10\}\{11\}\{12\}\{13\}\dots\{20\}$	$\{0\}\{1\}\dots\{7\}$	—

The distribution rule used here to decide which keys go on which tapes at each step appears to be magic, but in fact it has a simple connection with the Fibonacci number system. (See exercise 2.)

Reading backwards. Duality between radix sorting and merging applies also to algorithms that read tapes backwards. We have defined "T-lifo trees" in Section 5.4.4, and it is easy to see that they correspond to radix sorts as well as to merge sorts.

A read-backward radix sort was actually considered by John Mauchly already in 1946, in one of the first papers ever to be published about sorting (see Section 5.5); Mauchly essentially gave the following construction:

Phase	T1	T2	T3	T4
	—	$\{0,1,2,\dots,9\}$	—	—
1	$\{4,5\}$	—	$\{2,3,6,7\}$	$\{0,1,8,9\}$
2	$\{4,5\}\{2,7\}$	$\{3,6\}$	—	$\{0,1,8,9\}$
3	$\{4,5\}\{2,7\}\{0,9\}$	$\{3,6\}\{1,8\}$	—	—
4	$\{4,5\}\{2,7\}$	$\{3,6\}\{1,8\}$	$\{9\}$	$\{0\}$
$\cdots$	$\cdots$	$\cdots$	$\cdots$	$\cdots$
8	—	—	$\{9\}\{8\}\{7\}\{6\}\{5\}$	$\{0\}\{1\}\{2\}\{3\}\{4\}$
C	—	—	—	$\{0\}\{1\}\{2\}\{3\}\{4\}\{5\}\dots\{9\}$

His scheme is not the most efficient one possible, but it is interesting because it shows that partial pass methods were considered for radix sorting already in 1946, although they did not appear in the literature for merging until about 1960.

An efficient construction of read-backward distribution patterns has been suggested by A. Bayes [*CACM* **11** (1968), 491–493]: Given $P+1$ tapes and S keys, divide the keys into P subfiles each containing $\lfloor S/P \rfloor$ or $\lceil S/P \rceil$ keys, and apply this procedure recursively to each subfile. When $S < 2P$, one subfile should consist of the smallest key alone, and it should be written onto the output file. (R. M. Karp's general preorder construction, which appears at the end of Section 5.4.4, includes this method as a special case.)

Backward reading makes merging a little more complicated because it reverses the order of runs. There is a corresponding effect on radix sorting: The outcome is stable or "anti-stable" depending on what level is reached in the tree. After a read-backward radix sort in which some of the external nodes are at odd levels and some are at even levels, the relative order of different records with equal keys will be the *same* as the original order for some keys, but it will be the *opposite* of the original order for the other keys. (See exercise 6.)

Oscillating merge sorts have their counterparts too, under duality. In an *oscillating radix sort* we continue to separate out the keys until reaching subfiles that have only one key or are small enough to be internally sorted; such subfiles are sorted and written onto the output tape, then the separation process is resumed. For example, if we have three work tapes and one output tape, and if the keys are binary numbers, we may start by putting keys of the form $0x$ on tape T1, keys $1x$ on T2. If T1 receives more than one memory load, we scan it again and put $00x$ on T2 and $01x$ on T3. Now if the $00x$ subfile is short enough to be internally sorted, we do so and output the result, then continue by processing the $01x$ subfile. Such a method was called a "cascading pseudo-radix sort" by E. H. Friend [*JACM* **3** (1956), 157–159]; it was developed further by H. Nagler [*JACM* **6** (1959), 459–468], who gave it the colorful name "amphisbaenic sort," and by C. H. Gaudette [*IBM Tech. Disclosure Bull.* **12** (April 1970), 1849–1853].

Does radix sorting beat merging? One important consequence of the duality principle is that *radix sorting is usually inferior to merge sorting.* This happens because the technique of replacement selection gives merge sorting a definite advantage; there is no apparent way to arrange radix sorts so that we can make use of internal sorts encompassing more than one memory load at a time. Indeed, the oscillating radix sort will often produce subfiles that are somewhat smaller than one memory load, so the distribution pattern will correspond to a tree with many more external nodes than would be present if merging and replacement selection were used. Consequently the external path length of the tree — the sorting time — will be increased. (See exercise 5.3.1–33.)

On the other hand, external radix sorting does have its uses. Suppose, for example, that we have a file containing the names of all employees of a large corporation, in alphabetic order; the corporation has 10 divisions, and it is desired to sort the file by division, *retaining* the alphabetic order of the employees in each division. This is a perfect situation in which to apply a stable radix sort, if the file is long, since the number of records that belong to each of the 10 divisions is likely to be more than the number of records that would be obtained in initial runs produced by replacement selection. In general, if the range of key values is so small that the collection of records having a given key is expected to fill the internal memory more than twice, it is wise to use a radix sort technique.

We have seen in Section 5.2.5 that *internal* radix sorting is superior to merging, on certain high-speed computers, because the inner loop of the radix sort algorithm avoids complicated branching. If the external memory is especially fast, it may be impossible for such machines to merge data rapidly enough to keep up with the input/output equipment. Radix sorting may therefore turn out to be superior to merging in such a situation, especially if the keys are known to be uniformly distributed.

EXERCISES

1. [*20*] The general T-tape balanced merge with parameter P, $1 \leq P < T$, was defined near the beginning of Section 5.4. Show that this corresponds to a radix sort based on a mixed-radix number system.

2. [*M28*] The text illustrates the three-tape polyphase radix sort for 21 keys. Generalize to the case of F_n keys; explain what keys appear on what tapes at the end of each phase. [*Hint:* Consider the Fibonacci number system, exercise 1.2.8–34.]

3. [*M35*] Extend the results of exercise 2 to the polyphase radix sort on four or more tapes. (See exercise 5.4.2–10.)

4. [*M23*] Prove that Ashenhurst's distribution pattern is the best way to sort 10 keys on four tapes without reading backwards, in the sense that the associated tree has minimum external path length over all strongly 4-fifo trees. (Thus, it is essentially the best method if we ignore rewind time.)

5. [*15*] Draw the 4-lifo tree corresponding to Mauchly's read-backwards radix sort for 10 keys.

▶ **6.** [*20*] A certain file contains two-digit keys 00, 01, ..., 99. After performing Mauchly's radix sort on the least significant digits, we can repeat the same scheme on the most significant digits, interchanging the roles of tapes T2 and T4. In what order will the keys finally appear on T2?

7. [*21*] Does the duality principle apply also to multireel files?

*5.4.8. Two-Tape Sorting

Since we need three tapes to carry out a merge process without excessive tape motion, it is interesting to speculate about how we could perform a reasonable external sort using only two tapes.

One approach, suggested by H. B. Demuth in 1956, is sort of a combined replacement-selection and bubble sort. Assume that the input is on tape T1, and begin by reading $P + 1$ records into memory. Now output the record whose key is smallest, to tape T2, and replace it by the next input record. Continue outputting a record whose key is currently the smallest in memory, maintaining a selection tree or a priority queue of $P + 1$ elements. When the input is finally exhausted, the largest P keys of the file will be present in memory; output them in ascending order. Now rewind both tapes and repeat the process by reading from T2 and writing to T1; each such pass puts at least P more records into their proper place. A simple test can be built into the program that determines when the entire file is in sort. At most $\lceil (N - 1)/P \rceil$ passes will be necessary.

A few moments' reflection shows that each pass of this procedure is essentially equivalent to P consecutive passes of the bubble sort (Algorithm 5.2.2B). If an element has P or more inversions, it will be smaller than everything in the tree when it is input, so it will be output immediately — thereby losing P inversions. If an element has fewer than P inversions, it will go into the selection tree and will be output before all greater keys — thereby losing all its inversions. When $P = 1$, this is exactly what happens in the bubble sort, by Theorem 5.2.2I.

The total number of passes will therefore be $\lceil I/P \rceil$, where I is the maximum number of inversions of any element. By the theory developed in Section 5.2.2, the average value of I is $N - \sqrt{\pi N/2} + 2/3 + O(1/\sqrt{N})$.

If the file is not too much larger than the memory size, or if it is nearly in order to begin with, this order-P bubble sort will be fairly rapid; in fact, such a method might be advantageous even when extra tape units are available, because scratch tapes must be mounted by a human operator. But a two-tape bubble sort will run quite slowly on fairly long, randomly ordered files, since its average running time will be approximately proportional to N^2.

Let us consider how this method might be implemented for the 100,000-record example of Section 5.4.6. We need to choose P intelligently, in order to compensate for interblock gaps while doing simultaneous reading, writing, and computing. Since the example assumes that each record is 100 characters long and that 100,000 characters will fit into memory, we can make room for two input buffers and two output buffers of size B by setting

$$100(P + 1) + 4B = 100000. \tag{1}$$

Using the notation of Section 5.4.6, the running time for each pass will be about

$$NC\omega\tau(1 + \rho), \qquad \omega = (B + \gamma)/B. \tag{2}$$

Since the number of passes is inversely proportional to P, we want to choose B to be a multiple of 100 that minimizes the quantity ω/P. Elementary calculus shows that this occurs when B is approximately $\sqrt{24975\gamma + \gamma^2} - \gamma$, so we take $B = 3000$, $P = 879$. Setting $N = 100000$ in the formulas above shows that the number of passes $\lceil I/P \rceil$ will be about 114, and the total estimated running time will be approximately 8.57 hours (assuming for convenience that the initial input and the final output also have $B = 3000$). This represents approximately 0.44 reelfuls of data; a full reel would take about five times as long. Some improvements could be made if the algorithm were interrupted periodically, writing the records with largest keys onto an auxiliary tape that is dismounted, since such records are merely copied back and forth once they have been put into order.

Application of quicksort. Another internal sorting method that traverses the data in a nearly sequential manner is the partition exchange or quicksort procedure, Algorithm 5.2.2Q. Can we adapt it to two tapes? [N. B. Yoash, *CACM* **8** (1965), 649.]

It is not difficult to see how this can indeed be done, using backward reading. Assume that the two tapes are numbered 0 and 1, and imagine that the file is laid out as follows:

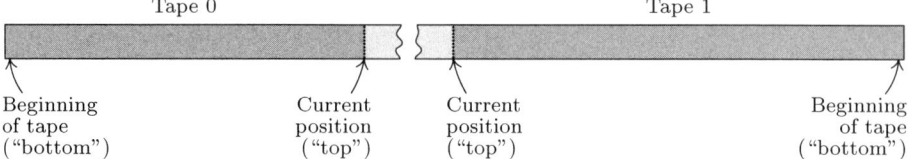

Beginning
of tape
("bottom")

Current
position
("top")

Current
position
("top")

Beginning
of tape
("bottom")

Each tape serves as a stack; putting them together like this makes it possible to view the file as a linear list in which we can move the current position left or right by copying from one stack to the other. The following recursive subroutines define a suitable sorting procedure:

• SORT00 [Sort the top subfile on tape 0 and return it to tape 0].
If the subfile fits in the internal memory, sort it internally and return it to tape. Otherwise select one record R from the subfile, and let its key be K. Reading backwards on tape 0, copy all records whose key is $> K$, forming a new subfile on the top of tape 1. Now read forward on tape 0, copying all records whose key is $= K$ onto tape 1. Then read backwards again, copying all records whose key is $< K$ onto tape 1. Complete the sort by executing SORT10 on the $< K$ keys, then copying the $= K$ keys to tape 0, and finally executing SORT10 on the $> K$ keys.

• SORT01 [Sort the top subfile on tape 0 and write it on tape 1].
Same as SORT00, but the final "SORT10" is changed to "SORT11" followed by copying the $\leq K$ keys to tape 1.

• SORT10 [Sort the top subfile on tape 1 and write it on tape 0].
Same as SORT01, interchanging 0 with 1 and $<$ with $>$.

• SORT11 [Sort the top subfile on tape 1 and return it to tape 1].
Same as SORT00, interchanging 0 with 1 and $<$ with $>$.

The recursive nature of these subroutines can be handled without difficulty by storing appropriate control information on the tapes.

The running time for this algorithm can be estimated as follows, if we assume that the data are in random order, with negligible probability of equal keys. Let M be the number of records that fit into internal memory. Let X_N be the average number of records read while applying SORT00 or SORT11 to a subfile of N records, when $N > M$, and let Y_N be the corresponding quantity for SORT01 or SORT10. Then we have

$$X_N = \begin{cases} 0, & \text{if } N \leq M; \\ 3N + 1 + \frac{1}{N} \sum_{0 \leq k < N} (Y_k + Y_{N-1-k}), & \text{if } N > M; \end{cases}$$

$$Y_N = \begin{cases} 0, & \text{if } N \leq M; \\ 3N + 2 + \frac{1}{N} \sum_{0 \leq k < N} (Y_k + X_{N-1-k} + k), & \text{if } N > M. \end{cases} \tag{3}$$

The solution to these recurrences (see exercise 2) shows that the total amount of tape reading during the external partitioning phases will be $6\frac{2}{3} N \ln N + O(N)$, on the average, as $N \to \infty$. We also know from Eq. 5.2.2–(25) that the average number of internal sort phases will be $2(N+1)/(M+2) - 1$.

If we apply this analysis to the 100,000-record example of Section 5.4.6, using 25,000-character buffers and assuming that the sorting time is $2nC\omega\tau$ for a subfile of $n \le M = 1000$ records, we obtain an average sorting time of approximately 103 minutes (including the final rewind as in Chart A). Thus the quicksort method isn't bad, on the average; but of course its *worst* case turns out to be even more awful than the bubble sort discussed above. Randomization will make the worst case extremely unlikely.

Radix sorting. The radix exchange method (Algorithm 5.2.2R) can be adapted to two-tape sorting in a similar way, since it is so much like quicksort. The trick that makes both of these methods work is the idea of reading a file more than once, something we never did in our previous tape algorithms.

The same trick can be used to do a conventional least-significant-digit-first radix sort on two tapes. Given the input data on T1, we copy all records onto T2 whose key ends with 0 in binary notation; then after rewinding T1 we read it again, copying the records whose key ends with 1. Now both tapes are rewound and a similar pair of passes is made, interchanging the roles of T1 and T2, and using the *second* least significant binary digit. At this point T1 will contain all records whose keys are $(\dots 00)_2$, followed by those whose keys are $(\dots 01)_2$, then $(\dots 10)_2$, then $(\dots 11)_2$. If the keys are b bits long, we need only $2b$ passes over the file in order to complete the sort.

Such a radix sort could be applied only to the *leading* b bits of the keys, for some judiciously chosen number b; that would reduce the number of inversions by a factor of about 2^b, if the keys were uniformly distributed, so a few passes of the P-way bubble sort could then be used to complete the job. This approach reads tape in the forward direction only.

A novel but somewhat more complicated approach to two-tape distribution sorting has been suggested by A. I. Nikitin and L. I. Sholmov [*Kibernetika* **2**, 6 (1966), 79–84]. Counts are made of the number of keys having each possible configuration of leading bits, and artificial keys $\kappa_1, \kappa_2, \dots, \kappa_M$ based on these counts are constructed so that the number of actual keys lying between κ_i and κ_{i+1} is between predetermined limits P_1 and P_2, for each i. Thus, M lies between $\lceil N/P_2 \rceil$ and $\lceil N/P_1 \rceil$. If the leading bit counts do not give sufficient information to determine such $\kappa_1, \kappa_2, \dots, \kappa_M$, one or more further passes are made to count the frequency of less significant bit patterns, for certain configurations of most significant bits. After the table of artificial keys $\kappa_1, \kappa_2, \dots, \kappa_M$ has been constructed, $2\lceil \lg M \rceil$ further passes will suffice to complete the sort. (This method requires memory space proportional to N, so it can't be used for external sorting as $N \to \infty$. In practice we would not use the technique for multireel files, so M will be comparatively small and the table of artificial keys will fit comfortably in memory.)

Simulation of more tapes. F. C. Hennie and R. E. Stearns have devised a general technique for simulating k tapes on only two tapes, in such a way that the tape motion required is increased by a factor of only $O(\log L)$, where L is the maximum distance to be traveled on any one tape [*JACM* **13** (1966), 533–546].

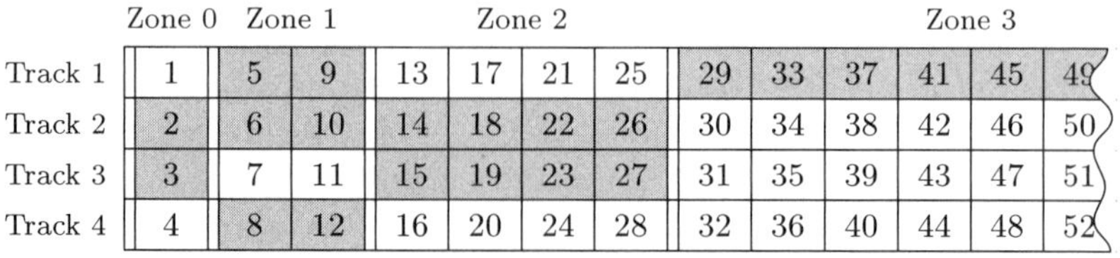

	Zone 0	Zone 1		Zone 2				Zone 3					
Track 1	1	5	9	13	17	21	25	29	33	37	41	45	49
Track 2	2	6	10	14	18	22	26	30	34	38	42	46	50
Track 3	3	7	11	15	19	23	27	31	35	39	43	47	51
Track 4	4	8	12	16	20	24	28	32	36	40	44	48	52

Fig. 86. Layout of tape T1 in the Hennie–Stearns construction; nonblank zones are shaded.

Their construction can be simplified slightly in the case of sorting, as in the following method suggested by R. M. Karp.

We shall simulate an ordinary four-tape balanced merge, using two tapes T1 and T2. The first of these, T1, holds the simulated tape contents in a way that may be diagrammed as in Fig. 86; we imagine that the data is written in four "tracks," one for each simulated tape. (In actual fact the tape doesn't have such tracks; blocks 1, 5, 9, 13, ... are thought of as Track 1, blocks 2, 6, 10, 14, ... as Track 2, etc.) The other tape, T2, is used only for auxiliary storage, to help move things around on T1.

The blocks of each track are divided into *zones*, containing, respectively, $1, 2, 4, 8, \ldots, 2^k, \ldots$ blocks per zone. Zone k on each track is either filled with exactly 2^k blocks of data, or it is completely blank. In Fig. 86, for example, Track 1 has data in zones 1 and 3; Track 2 in zones 0, 1, 2; Track 3 in zones 0 and 2; Track 4 in zone 1; and the other zones are blank.

Suppose that we are merging data from Tracks 1 and 2 to Track 3. The internal computer memory contains two buffers used for input to a two-way merge, plus a third buffer for output. When the input buffer for Track 1 becomes empty, we can refill it as follows: Find the first nonempty zone on Track 1, say zone k, and copy its first block into the input buffer; then copy the other $2^k - 1$ blocks of data onto T2, and move them to zones $0, 1, \ldots, k-1$ of Track 1. (Zones $0, 1, \ldots, k-1$ are now full and zone k is blank.) An analogous procedure is used to refill the input buffer for Track 2, whenever it becomes empty. When the output buffer is ready to be written on Track 3, we reverse the process, scanning across T1 to find the first *blank* zone on Track 3, say zone k, while copying the data from zones $0, 1, \ldots, k-1$ onto T2. The data on T2, augmented by the contents of the output buffer, is now used to fill zone k of Track 3.

This procedure requires the ability to write in the middle of tape T1, without destroying subsequent information on that tape. As in the case of read-forward oscillating sort (Section 5.4.5), it is possible to do this reliably if suitable precautions are taken.

The amount of tape motion required to bring $2^l - 1$ blocks of Track 1 into memory is $\sum_{0 \le k < l} 2^{l-1-k} \cdot c \cdot 2^k = c l 2^{l-1}$, for some constant c, since we scan up to zone k only once in every 2^k steps. Thus each merge pass requires $O(N \log N)$ steps. Since there are $O(\log N)$ passes in a balanced merge, the total time to sort is guaranteed to be $O\bigl(N(\log N)^2\bigr)$ in the worst case; this is asymptotically much better than the worst case of quicksort.

But this method wouldn't work very well if we applied it to the 100,000-record example of Section 5.4.6, since the information specified for tape T1 would overflow the contents of one tape reel. Even if we ignore this fact, and if we use optimistic assumptions about read/write/compute overlap and interblock gap lengths, etc., we find that roughly 37 hours would be required to complete the sort! So this method is purely of academic interest; the constant in $O\bigl(N(\log N)^2\bigr)$ is much too high to be satisfactory when N is in a practical range.

One-tape sorting. Could we live with only one tape? It is not difficult to see that the order-P bubble sort described above could be converted into a one-tape sort, but the result would be ghastly.

H. B. Demuth [Ph.D. thesis (Stanford University, 1956), 85] observed that a computer with bounded internal memory cannot reduce the number of inversions of a permutation by more than a bounded amount as it moves a bounded distance on tape; hence every one-tape sorting algorithm must take at least $N^2 d$ units of time on the average, for some positive constant d that depends on the computer configuration.

R. M. Karp has pursued this topic in a very interesting way, discovering an essentially *optimum* way to sort with one tape. It is convenient to discuss Karp's algorithm by reformulating the problem as follows: *What is the fastest way to transport people between floors using a single elevator?* [See *Combinatorial Algorithms*, edited by Randall Rustin (Algorithmics Press, 1972), 17–21.]

Consider a building with n floors, having room for exactly b people on each floor. The building contains no doors, windows, or stairs, but it does have an elevator that can stop on each floor. There are bn people in the building, and exactly b of them want to be on each particular floor. The elevator holds at most m people, and it takes one unit of time to go from floor i to floor $i \pm 1$. We wish to find the quickest way to get all the people onto the proper floors, if the elevator is required to start and finish on floor 1.

The connection between this elevator problem and one-tape sorting is not hard to see: The people are the records and the building is the tape. The floors are individual blocks on the tape, and the elevator is the internal computer memory. A computer program has more flexibility than an elevator operator (it can, for example, duplicate people, or temporarily chop them into two parts on different floors, etc.); but the solution below solves the problem in the fastest conceivable time without doing such operations.

The following two auxiliary tables are required by Karp's algorithm.

$$u_k,\ 1 \le k \le n: \text{Number of people on floors } \le k \text{ whose destination is } > k;$$
$$d_k,\ 1 \le k \le n: \text{Number of people on floors } \ge k \text{ whose destination is } < k. \tag{4}$$

When the elevator is empty, we always have $u_k = d_{k+1}$ for $1 \le k < n$, since there are b people on every floor; the number of misfits on floors $\{1, \ldots, k\}$ must equal the corresponding number on floors $\{k+1, \ldots, n\}$. By definition, $u_n = d_1 = 0$.

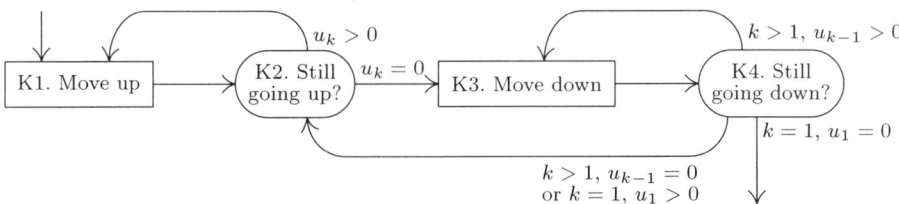

Fig. 87. Karp's elevator algorithm.

It is clear that the elevator must make at least $\lceil u_k/m \rceil$ trips from floor k to floor $k+1$, for $1 \leq k < n$, since only m passengers can ascend on each trip. Similarly it must make at least $\lceil d_k/m \rceil$ trips from floor k to floor $k-1$. Therefore the elevator must necessarily take at least

$$\sum_{k=1}^{n}\left(\lceil u_k/m \rceil + \lceil d_k/m \rceil\right) \tag{5}$$

units of time on any correct schedule. Karp discovered that this lower bound can actually be achieved, when $u_1, \ldots, u_{n-1}$ are nonzero.

Theorem K. *If $u_k > 0$ for $1 \leq k < n$, there is an elevator schedule that delivers everyone to the correct floor in the minimum time* (5).

Proof. Assume that there are m extra people in the building; they start in the elevator and their destination floor is artificially set to 0. The elevator can operate according to the following algorithm, starting with k (the current floor) equal to 1:

K1. [Move up.] From among the $b+m$ people currently in the elevator or on floor k, those m with the highest destinations get into the elevator, and the others remain on floor k.

Let there be u people now in the elevator whose destination is $> k$, and d whose destination is $\leq k$. (It will turn out that $u = \min(m, u_k)$; if $u_k < m$ we may therefore be transporting some people away from their destination. This represents their sacrifice to the common good.) Decrease u_k by u, increase d_{k+1} by d, and then increase k by 1.

K2. [Still going up?] If $u_k > 0$, return to step K1.

K3. [Move down.] From among the $b+m$ people currently in the elevator or on floor k, those m with the lowest destinations get into the elevator, and the others remain on floor k.

Let there be u people now in the elevator whose destination is $\geq k$, and d whose destination is $< k$. (It will always turn out that $u = 0$ and $d = m$, but the algorithm is described here in terms of general u and d in order to make the proof a little clearer.) Decrease d_k by d, increase u_{k-1} by u, and then decrease k by 1.

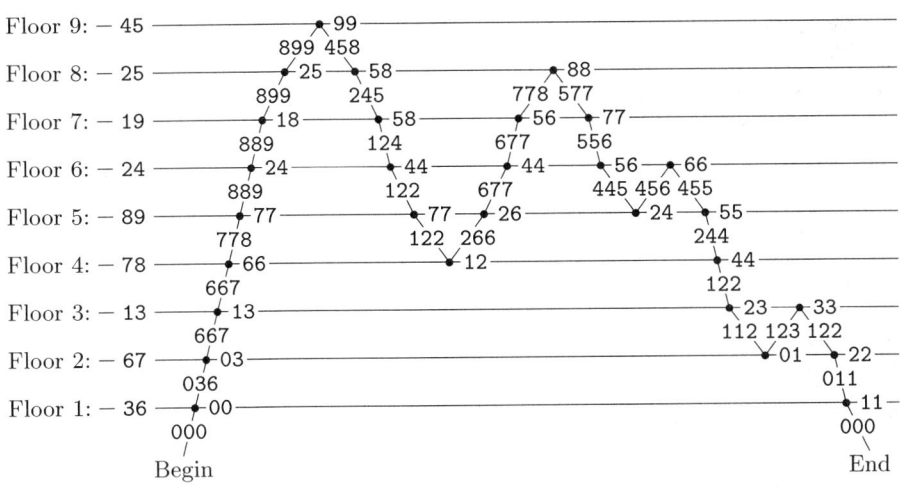

Fig. 88. An optimum way to rearrange people using a small, slow elevator. (People are each represented by the number of their destination floor.)

K4. [Still going down?] If $k > 1$ and $u_{k-1} > 0$, return to step K3. If $k = 1$ and $u_1 = 0$, terminate the algorithm (everyone has arrived safely and the m "extras" are back in the elevator). Otherwise return to step K2.

Figure 88 shows an example of this algorithm, with a nine-floor building and $b = 2$, $m = 3$. Note that one of the 6s is temporarily transported to floor 7, in spite of the fact that the elevator travels the minimum possible distance. The idea of testing u_{k-1} in step K4 is the crux of the algorithm, as we shall see.

To verify the validity of this algorithm, we note that steps K1 and K3 always keep the u and d tables (4) up to date, if we regard the people in the elevator as being on the "current" floor k. It is now possible to prove by induction that the following properties hold at the beginning of each step:

$$u_l = d_{l+1}, \qquad \text{for } k \le l < n; \tag{6}$$

$$u_l = d_{l+1} - m, \qquad \text{for } 1 \le l < k; \tag{7}$$

$$u_{l+1} = 0, \qquad \text{if } u_l = 0 \text{ and } k \le l < n. \tag{8}$$

Furthermore, at the beginning of step K1, the $\min(u_k, m)$ people with highest destinations, among all people on floors $\le k$ with destination $> k$, are in the elevator or on floor k. At the beginning of step K3, the $\min(d_k, m)$ people with lowest destinations, among all people on floors $\ge k$ with destination $< k$, are in the elevator or on floor k.

From these properties it follows that the parenthesized remarks in steps K1 and K3 are valid. Each execution of step K1 therefore decreases $\lceil u_k/m \rceil$ by 1 and leaves $\lceil d_{k+1}/m \rceil$ unchanged; each execution of K3 decreases $\lceil d_k/m \rceil$ by 1 and leaves $\lceil u_{k-1}/m \rceil$ unchanged. The algorithm must therefore terminate in a finite number of steps, and everybody must then be on the correct floor because of (6) and (8). ∎

When $u_k = 0$ and $u_{k+1} > 0$ we have a "disconnected" situation; the elevator must journey up to floor $k + 1$ in order to rearrange the people up there, even though nobody wants to move from floors $\leq k$ to floors $\geq k + 1$. Without loss of generality, we may assume that $u_{n-1} > 0$; then every valid elevator schedule must include at least

$$2 \sum_{1 \leq k < n} \max\left(1, \lceil u_k/m \rceil\right) \tag{9}$$

moves, since we require the elevator to return to floor 1. A schedule achieving this lower bound is readily constructed (exercise 4).

EXERCISES

1. [*20*] The order-P bubble sort discussed in the text uses only forward reading and rewinding. Can the algorithm be modified to take advantage of *backward* reading?

2. [*M26*] Find explicit closed-form solutions for the numbers X_N, Y_N defined in (3). [*Hint:* Study the solution to Eq. 5.2.2–(19).]

3. [*38*] Is there a two-tape sorting method, based only on comparisons of keys (not digital properties), whose tape motion is $O(N \log N)$ in the worst case, when sorting N records? [Quicksort achieves this on the average, but not in the worst case, and the Hennie–Stearns method (Fig. 86) achieves $O(N(\log N)^2)$.]

4. [*M23*] In the elevator problem, suppose there are indices p and q, with $q \geq p + 2$, $u_p > 0$, $u_q > 0$, and $u_{p+1} = \cdots = u_{q-1} = 0$. Explain how to construct a schedule requiring at most (9) units of time.

▶ **5.** [*M23*] True or false: After step K1 of the algorithm in Theorem K, nobody on the elevator has a lower destination than any person on floors $< k$.

6. [*M30*] (R. M. Karp.) Generalize the elevator problem (Fig. 88) to the case that there are b_j passengers initially on floor j, and b'_j passengers whose destination is floor j, for $1 \leq j \leq n$. Show that a schedule exists that takes $2\sum_{k=1}^{n-1} \max(1, \lceil u_k/m \rceil, \lceil d_{k+1}/m \rceil)$ units of time, never allowing more than $\max(b_j, b'_j)$ passengers to be on floor j at any one time. [*Hint:* Introduce fictitious people, if necessary, to make $b_j = b'_j$ for all j.]

7. [*M40*] (R. M. Karp.) Generalize the problem of exercise 6, replacing the linear path of an elevator by a network of roads to be traveled by a bus, given that the network forms any *free tree*. The bus has finite capacity, and the goal is to transport passengers to their destinations in such a way that the bus travels a minimum distance.

8. [*M32*] Let $b = 1$ in the elevator problem treated in the text. How many permutations of the n people on the n floors will make $u_k \leq 1$ for $1 \leq k \leq n$ in (4)? [For example, 3 1 4 5 9 2 6 8 7 is such a permutation.]

▶ **9.** [*M25*] Find a significant connection between the "cocktail-shaker sort" described in Section 5.2.2, Fig. 16, and the numbers $u_1, u_2, \ldots, u_n$ of (4) in the case $b = 1$.

10. [*20*] How would you sort a multireel file with only two tapes?

*5.4.9. Disks and Drums

So far we have considered tapes as the vehicles for external sorting, but more flexible types of mass storage devices are generally available. Although such "bulk memory" or "direct-access storage" units come in many different forms, they may be roughly characterized by the following properties:

  i) Any specified part of the stored information can be accessed quickly.

 ii) Blocks of consecutive words can be transmitted rapidly between the internal
and external memory.

Magnetic tape satisfies (ii) but not (i), because it takes a long time to get from
one end of a tape to the other.

    Every external memory unit has idiosyncrasies that ought to be studied
carefully before major programs are written for it; but technology changes so
rapidly, it is impossible to give a complete discussion here of all the available
varieties of hardware. Therefore we shall consider only some typical memory
devices that illustrate useful approaches to the sorting problem.

    One of the most common types of external memories satisfying (i) and (ii) is
a disk device (see Fig. 89). Data is kept on a number of rapidly rotating circular
disks, covered with magnetic material; a comb-like access arm, containing one
or more "read/write heads" for each disk surface, is used to store and retrieve
the information. Each individual surface is divided into concentric rings called
tracks, so that an entire track of data passes a read/write head every time the
disk completes one revolution. The access arm can move in and out, shifting
the read/write heads from track to track; but this motion takes time. A set
of tracks that can be read or written without repositioning the access arm is
called a *cylinder*. For example, Fig. 89 illustrates a disk unit that has just one
read/write head per surface; the light gray circles show one of the cylinders,
consisting of all tracks currently being scanned by the read/write heads.

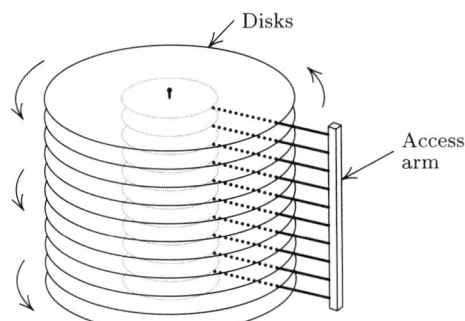

Fig. 89. A disk device.

To fix the ideas, let us consider hypothetical MIXTEC disk units, for which

$$1 \text{ track} = 5000 \text{ characters}$$
$$1 \text{ cylinder} = 20 \text{ tracks}$$
$$1 \text{ disk unit} = 200 \text{ cylinders}$$

Such a disk unit contains 20 million characters, slightly less than the amount
of data that can be stored on a single MIXT magnetic tape. On some machines,
tracks near the center have fewer characters than tracks near the rim; this tends

to make the programming much more complicated, and `MIXTEC` fortunately avoids such problems. (See Section 5.4.6 for a discussion of `MIXT` tapes. As in that section, we are studying classical techniques by considering machine characteristics that were typical of the early 1970s; modern disks are much bigger and faster.)

The amount of time required to read or write on a disk device is essentially the sum of three quantities:

• seek time (the time to move the access arm to the proper cylinder);

• latency time (rotational delay until the read/write head reaches the right spot);

• transmission time (rotational delay while the data passes the read/write head).

On `MIXTEC` devices the seek time required to go from cylinder i to cylinder j is $25 + \frac{1}{2}|i - j|$ milliseconds. If i and j are randomly selected integers between 1 and 200, the average value of $|i - j|$ is $2\binom{201}{3}/200^2 \approx 66.7$, so the average seek time is about 60 ms. `MIXTEC` disks rotate once every 25 ms, so the latency time averages about 12.5 ms. The transmission time for n characters is $(n/5000) \times 25\,\text{ms} = 5n\,\mu\text{s}$. (This is about $3\frac{1}{3}$ times as fast as the transmission rate of the `MIXT` tapes that were used in the examples of Section 5.4.6.)

Thus the main differences between `MIXTEC` disks and `MIXT` tapes are these:

a) Tapes can only be accessed sequentially.

b) Individual disk operations tend to require significantly more overhead (seek time + latency time compared to stop/start time).

c) The disk transmission rate is faster.

By using clever merge patterns on tape, we were able to compensate somewhat for disadvantage (a). Our goal now is to think of some clever algorithms for disk sorting that will compensate for disadvantage (b).

Overcoming latency time. Let us consider first the problem of minimizing the delays caused by the fact that the disks aren't always positioned properly when we want to start an I/O command. We can't make the disk spin faster, but we can still apply some tricks that reduce or even eliminate all of the latency time. The addition of more access arms would obviously help, but that would be an expensive hardware modification. Here are some software ideas:

• If we read or write several tracks of a cylinder at a time, we avoid the latency time (*and* the seek time) on all tracks but the first. In general it is often possible to synchronize the computing time with the disk movement in such a way that a sequence of input/output instructions can be carried out without latency delays.

• Consider the problem of reading half a track of data (Fig. 90): If the read command begins when the heads are at axis A, there is no latency delay, and the total time for reading is just the transmission time, $\frac{1}{2} \times 25\,\text{ms}$. If the command begins with the heads at B, we need $\frac{1}{4}$ of a revolution for latency and $\frac{1}{2}$ for transmission, totalling $\frac{3}{4} \times 25\,\text{ms}$. The most interesting case occurs when the

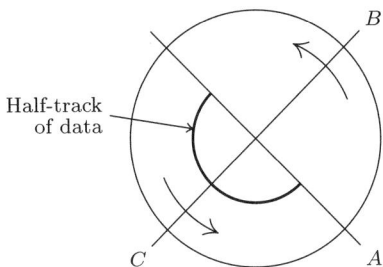

Fig. 90. Analysis of the latency time when reading half of a track.

heads are initially at C: With proper hardware and software we need *not* waste $\frac{3}{4}$ of a revolution for latency delay. Reading can begin immediately, into the second half of the input buffer; then after a $\frac{1}{2} \times 25$ ms pause, reading can resume into the first half of the buffer, so that the instruction is completed when axis C is reached again. In a similar manner, we can ensure that the total latency plus transmission time will never exceed the time for one revolution, regardless of the initial position of the disk. The average amount of latency delay is reduced by this scheme from half a revolution to $\frac{1}{2}(1 - x^2)$ of a revolution, if we are reading or writing a given fraction x of a track, for $0 < x \leq 1$. When an entire track is being read or written ($x = 1$), this technique eliminates *all* the latency time.

Drums: The no-seek case. Some external memory units, traditionally called drum memories, eliminate the seek time by having one read/write head for every track. If the technique of Fig. 90 is employed on such devices, both seek time and latency time reduce to zero, provided that we always read or write a track at a time; this is the ideal situation in which transmission time is the only limiting factor.

Let us consider again the example application of Section 5.4.6, sorting 100,000 records of 100 characters each, with a 100,000-character internal memory. The total amount of data to be sorted fills half of a MIXTEC disk. It is usually impossible to read and write simultaneously on a single disk unit; we shall assume that two disks are available, so that reading and writing can overlap each other. For the moment we shall assume, in fact, that the disks are actually drums, containing 4000 tracks of 5000 characters each, with no seek time required.

What sorting algorithm should be used? The method of merging is a fairly natural choice; other methods of internal sorting do not lend themselves so well to a disk implementation, except for the radix techniques of Section 5.2.5. The considerations of Section 5.4.7 show that radix sorting is usually inferior to merging for general-purpose applications, because the duality theorem of that section applies to disks as well as to tapes. Radix sorting does have a strong advantage, however, when the keys are uniformly distributed and many disks can be used in parallel, because an initial distribution by the most significant digits of the keys will divide the work up into independent subproblems that need no further communication. (See, for example, R. C. Agarwal, *SIGMOD Record* **25**, 2 (June 1996), 240–246.)

We will concentrate on merge sorting in the following discussion. To begin a merge sort for the stated problem we can use replacement selection, with two 5000-character input buffers and two 5000-character output buffers. In fact, it is possible to reduce this to *three* 5000-character buffers, if records in the current input buffer are replaced by records that come off the selection tree. That leaves 85,000 characters (850 records) for a selection tree, so one pass over our example data will form about 60 initial runs. (See Eq. 5.4.6–(3).) This pass takes only about 50 seconds, if we assume that the internal processing time is fast enough to keep up with the input/output rate, with one record moving to the output buffer every 500 microseconds. If the input to be sorted appeared on a MIXT tape, instead of a drum, this pass would be slower, governed by the tape speed.

With two drums and full-track reading/writing, it is not hard to see that the total transmission time for P-way merging is minimized if we let P be as large as possible. Unfortunately we can't simply do a 60-way merge on all of the initial runs, since there isn't room for 60 buffers in memory. (A buffer of fewer than 5000 characters would introduce unwanted latency time. Remember that we are still pretending to be living in the 1970s, when internal memory space was significantly limited.) If we do P-way merges, passing all the data from one drum to the other so that reading and writing are overlapped, the number of merge passes is $\lceil \log_P 60 \rceil$, so we may complete the job in two passes if $8 \leq P \leq 59$. The smallest such P reduces the amount of internal computing, so we choose $P = 8$; if 65 initial runs had been formed we would take $P = 9$. If 82 or more initial runs had been formed, we could take $P = 10$, but since there is room for only 18 input buffers and 2 output buffers there would be a possibility of hangup during the merge (see Algorithm 5.4.6F); it may be better in such a case to do two partial passes over a small portion of the data, reducing the number of initial runs to 81 or less.

Under our assumptions, both of the merging passes will take about 50 seconds, so the entire sort in this ideal situation will be completed in just 2.5 minutes (plus a few seconds for bookkeeping, initialization, etc.). This is six times faster than the best six-tape sort considered in Section 5.4.6; the reasons for this speedup are the improved external/internal transmission rate (3.5 times faster), the higher order of merge (we can't do an eight-way tape merge unless we have nine or more tapes), and the fact that the output was left on disk (no final rewind, etc., was necessary). If the initial input and sorted output were required to be on MIXT tapes, with the drums used for merging only, the corresponding sorting time would have been about 8.2 minutes.

If only one drum were available instead of two, the input-output time would take twice as long, since reading and writing must be done separately. (In fact, the input-output operations might take *three times* as long, since we would be overwriting the initial input data; in such a case it is prudent to follow each write by a "read-back check" operation, lest some of the input data be irretrievably lost, if the hardware does not provide automatic verification of written information.) But some of this excess time can be recovered because we can use partial pass methods that process some data records more often than others. The two-drum case requires all data to be processed an even number or an odd number of times, but the one-drum case can use more general merge patterns.

We observed in Section 5.4.4 that merge patterns can be represented by trees, and that the transmission time corresponding to a merge pattern is proportional to the external path length of its tree. Only certain trees (T-lifo or strongly T-fifo) could be used as efficient tape merging patterns, because some runs get buried in the middle of a tape as the merging proceeds. But *on disks or drums, all trees define usable merge patterns* if the degrees of their internal nodes are not too large for the available internal memory size.

Therefore we can minimize transmission time by choosing a tree with minimum external path length, such as a complete P-ary tree where P is as large as possible. By Eq. 5.4.4–(9), the external path length of such a tree is equal to

$$qS - \lfloor (P^q - S)/(P-1) \rfloor, \qquad q = \lceil \log_P S \rceil, \tag{1}$$

if there are S external nodes (leaves).

It is particularly easy to design an algorithm that merges according to the complete P-ary tree pattern. See, for example, Fig. 91, which shows the case $P = 3$, $S = 6$. First we add dummy runs, if necessary, to make $S \equiv 1$ (modulo $P - 1$); then we combine runs according to a first-in-first-out discipline, at every stage merging the P oldest runs at the front of the queue into a single run that is placed at the rear.

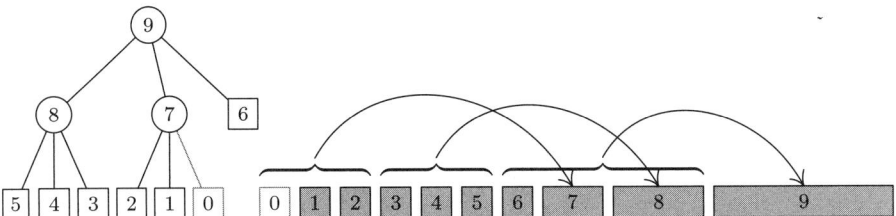

Fig. 91. Complete ternary tree with six leaves, and the corresponding merge pattern.

The complete P-ary tree gives an optimum pattern if all of the initial runs are the same length, but we can often do better if some runs are longer than others. An optimum pattern for this general situation can be constructed without difficulty by using Huffman's method (exercise 2.3.4.5–10), which may be stated in merging language as follows: "First add $(1 - S) \bmod (P - 1)$ dummy runs of length 0. Then repeatedly merge together the P *shortest* existing runs until only one run is left." When all initial runs have the same length this method reduces to the FIFO discipline described above.

In our 100,000-record example we can do nine-way merging, since 18 input buffers and two output buffers will fit in memory and Algorithm 5.4.6F will overlap all compute time. The complete 9-ary tree with 60 leaves corresponds to a merging pattern with $1\frac{29}{30}$ passes, if all initial runs have the same length. The total sorting time with one drum, using read-back check after every write, therefore comes to about 7.4 minutes. A higher value of P may reduce this running time slightly; but the situation is complicated because "reading hangup" might occur when the buffers become too full or too empty.

The influence of seek time. Our discussion shows that it is relatively easy to construct optimum merging patterns for drums, because seek time and latency time can be essentially nonexistent. But when disks are used with small buffers we often spend more time seeking information than reading it, so the seek time has a considerable influence on the sorting strategy. Decreasing the order of merge, P, makes it possible to use larger buffers, so fewer seeks are required; this often compensates for the extra transmission time demanded by the smaller value of P.

Seek time depends on the distance traveled by the access arm, and we could try to arrange things so that this distance is minimized. For example, it may be wise to sort the records within cylinders first. However, large-scale merging requires a good deal of jumping around between cylinders (see exercise 2). Furthermore, the multiprogramming capability of modern operating systems means that users tend to lose control over the position of disk access arms. We are often justified, therefore, in assuming that each disk command involves a "random" seek.

Our goal is to discover a merge pattern that achieves the best balance between seek time and transmission time. For this purpose we need some way to estimate the goodness of any particular tree with respect to a particular hardware configuration. Consider, for example, the tree in Fig. 92; we want to estimate how long it will take to carry out the corresponding merge, so that we can compare this tree to other trees.

In the following discussion we shall make some simple assumptions about disk merging, in order to illustrate some of the general ideas. Let us suppose that (i) it takes $72.5 + 0.005n$ milliseconds to read or write n characters; (ii) 100,000 characters of internal memory are available for working storage; (iii) an average of 0.004 milliseconds of computation time are required to transmit each character from input to output; (iv) there is to be *no overlap* between reading, writing, or computing; and (v) the buffer size used on output need not be the same as the buffer size used to read the data on the following pass. An analysis of the sorting problem under these simple assumptions will give us some insights when we turn to more complicated situations.

If we do a P-way merge, we can divide the internal working storage into $P+1$ buffer areas, P for input and one for output, with $B = 100000/(P+1)$ characters per buffer. Suppose the files being merged contain a total of L characters; then we will do approximately L/B output operations and about the same number of input operations, so the total merging time under our assumptions will be approximately

$$2\left(72.5\frac{L}{B} + 0.005L\right) + 0.004L = (0.00145P + 0.01545)L \qquad (2)$$

milliseconds.

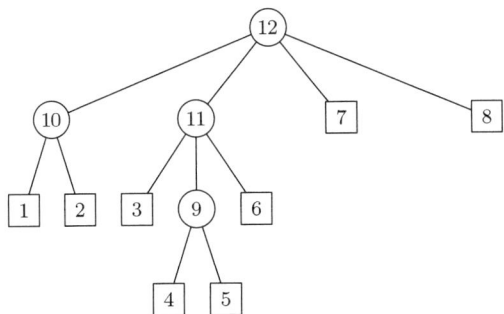

Fig. 92. A tree whose external path length is 16 and whose degree path length is 52.

In other words, a P-way merge of L characters takes about $(\alpha P + \beta)L$ units of time, for some constants α and β depending on the seek time, latency time, compute time, and memory size. This formula leads to an interesting way to construct good merge patterns for disks. Consider Fig. 92, for example, and assume that all initial runs (represented by square leaf nodes) have length L_0. Then the merges at nodes 9 and 10 each take $(2\alpha + \beta)(2L_0)$ units of time, the merge at node 11 takes $(3\alpha + \beta)(4L_0)$, and the final merge at node 12 takes $(4\alpha + \beta)(8L_0)$. The total merging time therefore comes to $(52\alpha + 16\beta)L_0$ units. The coefficient "16" here is well-known to us, it is simply the external path length of the tree. The coefficient "52" of α is, however, a new concept, which we may call the *degree path length* of the tree; it is the sum, taken over all leaf nodes, of the internal-node degrees on the path from the leaf to the root. For example, in Fig. 92 the degree path length is

$$(2+4) + (2+4) + (3+4) + (2+3+4) + (2+3+4) + (3+4) + (4) + (4)$$
$$= 52.$$

If $\mathcal{T}$ is any tree, let $D(\mathcal{T})$ and $E(\mathcal{T})$ denote its degree path length and its external path length, respectively. Our analysis may be summarized as follows:

Theorem H. *If the time required to do a P-way merge on L characters has the form $(\alpha P + \beta)L$, and if there are S equal-length runs to be merged, the best merge pattern corresponds to a tree $\mathcal{T}$ for which $\alpha D(\mathcal{T}) + \beta E(\mathcal{T})$ is a minimum, over all trees having S leaves.* ∎

(This theorem was implicitly contained in an unpublished paper that George U. Hubbard presented at the ACM National Conference in 1963.)

Let α and β be fixed constants; we shall say a tree is *optimal* if it has the minimum value of $\alpha D(\mathcal{T}) + \beta E(\mathcal{T})$ over all trees, $\mathcal{T}$, with the same number of leaves. It is not difficult to see that *all subtrees of an optimal tree are optimal*, and therefore we can construct optimal trees with n leaves by piecing together optimal trees with $< n$ leaves.

Theorem K. *Let the sequence of numbers $A_m(n)$ be defined for $1 \leq m \leq n$ by the rules*

$$A_1(1) = 0; \tag{3}$$

$$A_m(n) = \min_{1 \leq k \leq n/m} \big(A_1(k) + A_{m-1}(n-k)\big), \qquad \text{for } 2 \leq m \leq n; \tag{4}$$

$$A_1(n) = \min_{2 \leq m \leq n} \big(\alpha mn + \beta n + A_m(n)\big), \qquad \text{for } n \geq 2. \tag{5}$$

Then $A_1(n)$ is the minimum value of $\alpha D(\mathcal{T}) + \beta E(\mathcal{T})$, over all trees $\mathcal{T}$ with n leaves.

Proof. Equation (4) implies that $A_m(n)$ is the minimum value of $A_1(n_1) + \cdots + A_1(n_m)$ taken over all positive integers $n_1, \ldots, n_m$ such that $n_1 + \cdots + n_m = n$. The result now follows by induction on n. ∎

The recurrence relations (3), (4), (5) can also be used to construct the optimal trees themselves: Let $k_m(n)$ be a value for which the minimum occurs in the definition of $A_m(n)$. Then we can construct an optimal tree with n leaves by joining $m = k_1(n)$ subtrees at the root; the subtrees are optimal trees with $k_m(n)$, $k_{m-1}\big(n - k_m(n)\big)$, $k_{m-2}\big(n - k_m(n) - k_{m-1}(n - k_m(n))\big)$, $\ldots$ leaves, respectively.

For example, Table 1 illustrates this construction when $\alpha = \beta = 1$. A compact specification of the corresponding optimal trees appears at the right of the table; the entry "4:9:9" when $n = 22$ means, for example, that an optimal tree $\mathcal{T}_{22}$ with 22 leaves may be obtained by combining $\mathcal{T}_4$, $\mathcal{T}_9$, and $\mathcal{T}_9$ (see Fig. 93). Optimal trees are not unique; for instance, 5:8:9 would be just as good as 4:9:9.

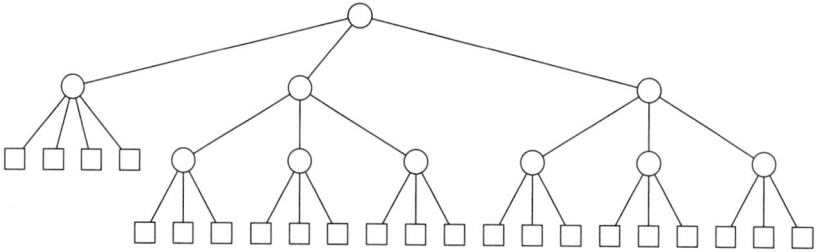

Fig. 93. An optimum way to merge 22 initial runs of equal length, when $\alpha = \beta$ in Theorem H. This pattern minimizes the seek time, under the assumptions leading to Eq. (2) in the text.

Our derivation of (2) shows that the relation $\alpha \leq \beta$ will hold whenever $P + 1$ equal buffer areas are used. The limiting case $\alpha = \beta$, shown in Table 1 and Fig. 93, occurs when the seek time itself is to be minimized without regard to transmission time.

Returning to our original application, we still haven't considered how to get the initial runs in the first place; without read/write/compute overlap, replacement selection loses some of its advantages. Perhaps we should fill the entire internal memory, sort it, and output the results; such input and output

Table 1

OPTIMAL TREE CHARACTERISTICS $A_m(n)$, $k_m(n)$ WHEN $\alpha = \beta = 1$

						m								
n	1	2	3	4	5	6	7	8	9	10	11	12	Tree	n
1	0,0												—	1
2	6,2	0,1											1:1	2
3	12,3	6,1	0,1										1:1:1	3
4	20,4	12,1	6,1	0,1									1:1:1:1	4
5	30,5	18,2	12,1	6,1	0,1								1:1:1:1:1	5
6	42,2	24,3	18,1	12,1	6,1	0,1							3:3	6
7	52,3	32,3	24,1	18,1	12,1	6,1	0,1						1:3:3	7
8	62,3	40,4	30,2	24,1	18,1	12,1	6,1	0,1					2:3:3	8
9	72,3	50,4	36,3	30,1	24,1	18,1	12,1	6,1	0,1				3:3:3	9
10	84,3	60,5	44,3	36,1	30,1	24,1	18,1	12,1	6,1	0,1			3:3:4	10
11	96,3	72,4	52,3	42,2	36,1	30,1	24,1	18,1	12,1	6,1	0,1		3:4:4	11
12	108,3	82,4	60,4	48,3	42,1	36,1	30,1	24,1	18,1	12,1	6,1	0,1	4:4:4	12
13	121,4	92,4	70,4	56,3	48,1	42,1	36,1	30,1	24,1	18,1	12,1	6,1	3:3:3:4	13
14	134,4	102,5	80,4	64,3	54,2	48,1	42,1	36,1	30,1	24,1	18,1	12,1	3:3:4:4	14
15	147,4	114,5	90,4	72,3	60,3	54,1	48,1	42,1	36,1	30,1	24,1	18,1	3:4:4:4	15
16	160,4	124,7	102,4	80,4	68,3	60,1	54,1	48,1	42,1	36,1	30,1	24,1	4:4:4:4	16
17	175,4	134,8	112,4	90,4	76,3	66,2	60,1	54,1	48,1	42,1	36,1	30,1	4:4:4:5	17
18	190,4	144,9	122,4	100,4	84,3	72,3	66,1	60,1	54,1	48,1	42,1	36,1	4:4:5:5	18
19	205,4	156,9	132,5	110,4	92,3	80,3	72,1	66,1	60,1	54,1	48,1	42,1	4:5:5:5	19
20	220,4	168,9	144,4	120,5	100,4	88,3	78,2	72,1	66,1	60,1	54,1	48,1	5:5:5:5	20
21	236,5	180,9	154,4	132,4	110,4	96,3	84,3	78,1	72,1	66,1	60,1	54,1	4:4:4:4:5	21
22	252,3	192,10	164,4	142,4	120,4	104,3	92,3	84,1	78,1	72,1	66,1	60,1	4:9:9	22
23	266,3	204,11	174,5	152,4	130,4	112,3	100,3	90,2	84,1	78,1	72,1	66,1	5:9:9	23
24	282,3	216,12	186,5	162,5	140,4	120,4	108,3	96,3	90,1	84,1	78,1	72,1	5:9:10	24
25	296,3	229,12	196,7	174,4	150,5	130,4	116,3	104,3	96,1	90,1	84,1	78,1	7:9:9	25

operations can each be done with one seek. Or perhaps we are better off using, say, 20 percent of the memory as a combination input/output buffer, and doing replacement selection. This requires five times as many seeks (an extra 60 seconds or so!), but it reduces the number of initial runs from 100 to 64; the reduction would be more dramatic if the input file were pretty much in order already.

If we decide not to use replacement selection, the optimum tree for $S = 100$, $\alpha = 0.00145$, $\beta = 0.01545$ [see (2)] turns out to be rather prosaic: It is simply a 10-way merge, completed in two passes over the data. Allowing 30 seconds for internal sorting (100 quicksorts, say), the initial distribution pass takes about 2.5 minutes, and the merge passes each take almost 5 minutes, for a total of 12.4 minutes. If we decide to use replacement selection, the optimal tree for $S = 64$ turns out to be equally uninteresting (two 8-way merge passes); the initial distribution pass takes about 3.5 minutes, the merge passes each take about 4.5 minutes, and the estimated total time comes to 12.6 minutes. Remember that both of these methods give up virtually all read/write/compute overlap in order to have larger buffers, reducing seek time. None of these estimated times includes the time that might be necessary for read-back check operations.

In practice the final merge pass tends to be quite different from the others; for example, the output is often expanded and/or written onto tape. In such cases the tree pattern should be chosen using a different optimality criterion at the root.

*A closer look at optimal trees. It is interesting to examine the extreme case $\beta = 0$ in Theorems H and K, even though practical situations usually lead to parameters with $0 \leq \alpha \leq \beta$. What tree with n leaves has the smallest possible degree path length? Curiously it turns out that three-way merging is best.

Theorem L. *The degree path length of a tree with n leaves is never less than*

$$f(n) = \begin{cases} 3qn + 2(n - 3^q), & \text{if } 2 \cdot 3^{q-1} \leq n \leq 3^q; \\ 3qn + 4(n - 3^q), & \text{if } 3^q \leq n \leq 2 \cdot 3^q. \end{cases} \tag{6}$$

Ternary trees $\mathcal{T}_n$ defined by the rules

$$\mathcal{T}_1 = \square , \qquad \mathcal{T}_2 = \quad , \qquad \mathcal{T}_n = \quad \tag{7}$$

$$\mathcal{T}_{\left\lfloor \frac{n}{3} \right\rfloor} \quad \mathcal{T}_{\left\lfloor \frac{n+1}{3} \right\rfloor} \quad \mathcal{T}_{\left\lfloor \frac{n+2}{3} \right\rfloor}$$

have the minimum degree path length.

Proof. It is important to observe that $f(n)$ is a *convex function*, namely that

$$f(n + 1) - f(n) \geq f(n) - f(n - 1) \qquad \text{for all } n \geq 2. \tag{8}$$

The relevance of this property is due to the following lemma, which is dual to the result of exercise 2.3.4.5–17.

Lemma C. *A function $g(n)$ defined on the positive integers satisfies*

$$\min_{1 \leq k < n} \big(g(k) + g(n - k)\big) = g\big(\lfloor n/2 \rfloor\big) + g\big(\lceil n/2 \rceil\big), \qquad n \geq 2, \tag{9}$$

if and only if it is convex.

Proof. If $g(n + 1) - g(n) < g(n) - g(n - 1)$ for some $n \geq 2$, we have $g(n + 1) + g(n - 1) < g(n) + g(n)$, contradicting (9). Conversely, if (8) holds for g, and if $1 \leq k < n - k$, we have $g(k + 1) + g(n - k - 1) \leq g(k) + g(n - k)$ by convexity. ∎

The latter part of Lemma C's proof can be extended for any $m \geq 2$ to show that

$$\min_{\substack{n_1 + \cdots + n_m = n \\ n_1, \ldots, n_m \geq 1}} \big(g(n_1) + \cdots + g(n_m)\big)$$

$$= g\big(\lfloor n/m \rfloor\big) + g\big(\lfloor (n + 1)/m \rfloor\big) + \cdots + g\big(\lfloor (n + m - 1)/m \rfloor\big) \tag{10}$$

whenever g is convex. Let

$$f_m(n) = f\big(\lfloor n/m \rfloor\big) + f\big(\lfloor (n + 1)/m \rfloor\big) + \cdots + f\big(\lfloor (n + m - 1)/m \rfloor\big); \tag{11}$$

the proof of Theorem L is completed by proving that $f_3(n) + 3n = f(n)$ and $f_m(n) + mn \geq f(n)$ for all $m \geq 2$. (See exercise 11.) ∎

It would be very nice if optimal trees could always be characterized neatly as in Theorem L. But the results we have seen for $\alpha = \beta$ in Table 1 show that the function $A_1(n)$ is not always convex. In fact, Table 1 is sufficient to disprove most simple conjectures about optimal trees! We can, however, salvage part of Theorem L in the general case; M. Schlumberger and J. Vuillemin have shown that *large* orders of merge can always be avoided:

Theorem M. *Given α and β as in Theorem H, there exists an optimal tree in which the degree of every node is at most*

$$d(\alpha,\beta) = \left\lceil \min_{k\geq 1} \left(k + \left(1+\frac{1}{k}\right)\left(1+\frac{\beta}{\alpha}\right)\right)\right\rceil. \tag{12}$$

Proof. Let $n_1,\ldots,n_m$ be positive integers such that $n_1+\cdots+n_m = n$, $A(n_1)+\cdots+A(n_m) = A_m(n)$, and $n_1 \leq \cdots \leq n_m$, and assume that $m \geq d(\alpha,\beta)+1$. Let k be the value that minimizes (12); we shall show that

$$\alpha n(m-k) + \beta n + A_{m-k}(n) \leq \alpha nm + \beta n + A_m(n), \tag{13}$$

hence the minimum value in (5) is always achieved for some $m \leq d(\alpha,\beta)$.

By definition, since $m \geq k+2$, we must have

$$\begin{aligned}
A_{m-k}(n) &\leq A_1(n_1+\cdots+n_{k+1})+A_1(n_{k+2})+\cdots+A_1(n_m)\\
&\leq \alpha(n_1+\cdots+n_{k+1})(k+1)+\beta(n_1+\cdots+n_{k+1})+A_1(n_1)+\cdots+A_1(n_m)\\
&= \big(\alpha(k+1)+\beta\big)(n_1+\cdots+n_{k+1})+A_m(n)\\
&\leq \big(\alpha(k+1)+\beta\big)(k+1)n/m+A_m(n),
\end{aligned}$$

and (13) now follows easily. (Careful inspection of this proof shows that (12) is best possible, in the sense that some optimal trees must have nodes of degree $d(\alpha,\beta)$; see exercise 13.) ∎

The construction in Theorem K needs $O(N^2)$ memory cells and $O(N^2\log N)$ steps to evaluate $A_m(n)$ for $1 \leq m \leq n \leq N$; Theorem M shows that only $O(N)$ cells and $O(N^2)$ steps are needed. Schlumberger and Vuillemin have discovered several more very interesting properties of optimal trees [*Acta Informatica* **3** (1973), 25–36]. Furthermore the asymptotic value of $A_1(n)$ can be worked out as shown in exercise 9.

*Another way to allocate buffers. David E. Ferguson [*CACM* **14** (1971), 476–478] pointed out that seek time can be reduced if we don't make all buffers the same size. The same idea occurred at about the same time to several other people [S. J. Waters, *Comp. J.* **14** (1971), 109–112; Ewing S. Walker, *Software Age* **4** (August–September, 1970), 16–17].

Suppose we are doing a four-way merge on runs of equal length L_0, with M characters of memory. If we divide the memory into equal buffers of size $B = M/5$, we need about L_0/B seeks on each input file and $4L_0/B$ seeks for the output, totalling $8L_0/B = 40L_0/M$ seeks. But if we use four input buffers of size $M/6$ and one output buffer of size $M/3$, we need only about $4\times(6L_0/M)+4\times(3L_0/M) = 36L_0/M$ seeks! The transmission time is the same in both cases, so we haven't lost anything by the change.

In general, suppose that we want to merge sorted files of lengths $L_1,\ldots,L_P$ into a sorted file of length

$$L_{P+1} = L_1 + \cdots + L_P,$$

and assume that a buffer of size B_k is being used for the kth file. Thus

$$B_1 + \cdots + B_P + B_{P+1} = M, \tag{14}$$

where M is the total size of available internal memory. The number of seeks will be approximately

$$\frac{L_1}{B_1} + \cdots + \frac{L_P}{B_P} + \frac{L_{P+1}}{B_{P+1}}. \tag{15}$$

Let's try to minimize this quantity, subject to condition (14), assuming for convenience that the B_k's don't have to be integers. If we increase B_j by δ and decrease B_k by the same amount, the number of seeks changes by

$$\frac{L_j}{B_j + \delta} - \frac{L_j}{B_j} + \frac{L_k}{B_k - \delta} - \frac{L_k}{B_k} = \left(\frac{L_k}{B_k(B_k - \delta)} - \frac{L_j}{B_j(B_j + \delta)} \right) \delta,$$

so the allocation can be improved if $L_j/B_j^2 \neq L_k/B_k^2$. Therefore we get the minimum number of seeks only if

$$\frac{L_1}{B_1^2} = \cdots = \frac{L_P}{B_P^2} = \frac{L_{P+1}}{B_{P+1}^2}. \tag{16}$$

Since a minimum does exist it must occur when

$$B_k = \sqrt{L_k}\, M / (\sqrt{L_1} + \cdots + \sqrt{L_{P+1}}), \qquad 1 \le k \le P + 1; \tag{17}$$

these are the only values of $B_1, \ldots, B_{P+1}$ that satisfy both (14) and (16). Plugging (17) into (15) gives a fairly simple formula for the total number of seeks,

$$(\sqrt{L_1} + \cdots + \sqrt{L_{P+1}})^2/M, \tag{18}$$

which may be compared with the number $(P + 1)(L_1 + \cdots + L_{P+1})/M$ obtained if all buffers are equal in length. By exercise 1.2.3–31, the improvement is

$$\sum_{1 \le j < k \le P+1} (\sqrt{L_j} - \sqrt{L_k})^2/M.$$

Unfortunately formula (18) does not lend itself to an easy determination of optimum merge patterns as in Theorem K (see exercise 14).

The use of chaining. M. A. Goetz [*CACM* **6** (1963), 245–248] has suggested an interesting way to avoid seek time on output, by linking individual tracks together. His idea requires a fairly fancy set of disk storage management routines, but it applies to many problems besides sorting, and it may therefore be a very worthwhile technique for general-purpose use.

The concept is simple: Instead of allocating tracks sequentially within cylinders of the disk, we link them together and maintain lists of available space, one for each cylinder. When it is time to output a track of information, we write it on the current cylinder (wherever the access arm happens to be), unless that cylinder is full. In this way the seek time usually disappears.

The catch is that we can't store a link-to-next-track within the track itself, since the necessary information isn't known at the right time. (We could store a link-to-previous-track and read the file backwards on the next pass, if that were suitable.) A table of link addresses for the tracks of each file can be maintained separately, because it requires comparatively little space. The available space lists can be represented compactly by using bit tables, with 1000 bits specifying the availability or unavailability of 1000 tracks.

Forecasting revisited. Algorithm 5.4.6F shows that we can forecast which input buffer of a P-way merge will empty first, by looking at the last keys in each buffer. Therefore we can be reading and computing at the same time. That algorithm uses floating input buffers, not dedicated to a particular file; so the buffers must all be the same size, and the buffer allocation technique above cannot be used. But the restriction to a uniform buffer size is no great loss, since computers now have much larger internal memories than they used to. Nowadays a natural buffer size, such as the capacity of a full disk track, often suggests itself.

Let us therefore imagine that the P runs to be merged each consist of a sequence of data *blocks*, where each block (except possibly the last) contains exactly B records. D. L. Whitlow and A. Sasson developed an interesting algorithm called SyncSort [*U.S. Patent 4210961* (1980)], which improves on Algorithm 5.4.6F by needing only three buffers of size B together with a memory pool holding PB records and PB pointers. By contrast, Algorithm 5.4.6F requires $2P$ input buffers and 2 output buffers, but no pointers.

SyncSort begins by reading the first block of each run and putting these PB records into the memory pool. Each record in the memory pool is linked to its successor in the run it belongs to, except that the final record in each block has no successor as yet. The smallest of the keys in those final records determines the run that will need to replenished first, so we begin to read the second block of that run into the first buffer. Merging begins as soon as that second block has been read; by looking at its final key we can accurately forecast the next relevant block, and we can continue in the same way to prefetch exactly the right blocks to input, just before they are needed.

The three SyncSort buffers are arranged in a circle. As merging proceeds, the computer is processing data in the current buffer, while input is being read into the next buffer and output is being written from the third. The merging algorithm exchanges each record in the current buffer with the next record of output, namely the record in the memory pool that has the smallest key. The selection tree and the successor links are also updated appropriately as we make each exchange. Once the end of the current buffer is reached, we are ready to rotate the buffer circle: The reading buffer becomes current, the writing buffer is used for reading, and we begin to write from the former current buffer.

Many extensions of this basic idea are possible, depending on hardware capabilities. For example, we might use two disks, one for reading and one for writing, so that input and output and merging can all take place simultaneously. Or we might be able to overlap seek time by extending the circle to four or more buffers, as in Fig. 26 of Section 1.4.4, and deviating from the forecast input order.

Using several disks. Disk devices once were massive both in size and weight, but they became dramatically smaller, lighter, and less expensive during the late 1980s — although they began to hold more data than ever before. Therefore people began to design algorithms for once-unimaginable clusters of 5 or 10 or 50 disk devices or for even larger disk farms.

One easy way to gain speed with additional disks is to use the technique of *disk striping* for large files. Suppose we have D disk units, numbered 0, 1, ..., $D - 1$, and consider a file that consists of L blocks $a_0 a_1 \ldots a_{L-1}$. Striping this file on D disks means that we put block a_j on disk number $j \bmod D$; thus, disk 0 holds $a_0 a_D a_{2D} \ldots$, disk 1 holds $a_1 a_{D+1} a_{2D+1} \ldots$, etc. Then we can perform D reads or D writes simultaneously on D-block groups $a_0 a_1 \ldots a_{D-1}$, $a_D a_{D+1} \ldots a_{2D-1}$, ..., which are called *superblocks*. The individual blocks of each superblock should be on corresponding cylinders on different disks so that the seek time will be the same on each unit. In essence, we are acting as if we had a single disk unit with blocks and buffers of size DB, but the input and output operations run up to D times faster.

An elegant improvement on superblock striping can be used when we're doing 2-way merging, or in general whenever we want to match records with equal keys in two files that are in order by keys. Suppose the blocks $a_0 a_1 a_2 \ldots$ of the first file are striped on D disks as above, but the blocks $b_0 b_1 b_2 \ldots$ of the other file are striped in the reverse direction, with block b_j on disk $(D - 1 - j) \bmod D$. For example, if $D = 5$ the blocks a_j appear respectively on disks 0, 1, 2, 3, 4, 0, 1, ..., while the blocks b_j for $j \geq 0$ appear on 4, 3, 2, 1, 0, 4, 3, ... Let α_j be the last key of block a_j and let β_j be the last key of block b_j. By examining the α's and β's we can forecast the sequence in which we will want to read the data blocks; this sequence might, for example, be

$$a_0 b_0 a_1 a_2 b_1 \quad a_3 a_4 b_2 a_5 a_6 \quad a_7 a_8 b_3 b_4 b_5 \quad b_6 b_7 b_8 b_9 b_{10} \quad \ldots.$$

These blocks appear respectively on disks

$$0 \ 4 \ 1 \ 2 \ 3 \quad 3 \ 4 \ 2 \ 0 \ 1 \quad 2 \ 3 \ 1 \ 0 \ 4 \quad 3 \ 2 \ 1 \ 0 \ 4 \quad \ldots$$

when $D = 5$, and if we read them five at a time we will be inputting successively from disks $\{0, 4, 1, 2, 3\}$, $\{3, 4, 2, 0, 1\}$, $\{2, 3, 1, 0, 4\}$, $\{3, 2, 1, 0, 4\}$, ...; there will never be a conflict in which we need to read two blocks from the same disk at the same time! In general, with D disks we can read D at a time without conflict, because the first group will have k blocks $a_0 \ldots a_{k-1}$ on disks 0 through $k-1$ and $D - k$ blocks $b_0 \ldots b_{D-k-1}$ on disks $D - 1$ through k, for some k; then we will be poised to continue in the same way but with disk numbers shifted cyclically by k.

This trick is well known to card magicians, who call it the *Gilbreath principle*; it was invented during the 1960s by Norman Gilbreath [see Martin Gardner, *Mathematical Magic Show* (New York: Knopf, 1977), Chapter 7; N. Gilbreath, *Genii* **52** (1989), 743–744]. We need to know the α's and β's, to decide what blocks should be read next, but that information takes up only a small fraction of the space needed by the a's and b's, and it can be kept in separate files. Therefore we need fewer buffers to keep the input going at full speed (see exercise 23).

Randomized striping. If we want to do P-way merging with D disks when P and D are large, we cannot keep reading the information simultaneously from D disks without conflict unless we have a large number of buffers, because there is no analog of the Gilbreath principle when $P > 2$. No matter how we allocate the blocks of a file to disks, there will be a chance that we might need to read many blocks into memory before we are ready to use them, because the blocks that we really need might all happen to reside on the same disk.

Suppose, for example, that we want to do 8-way merging on 5 disks, and suppose that the blocks $a_0 a_1 a_2 \dots$, $b_0 b_1 b_2 \dots$, $\dots$, $h_0 h_1 h_2 \dots$ of 8 runs have been striped with a_j on disk $j \bmod D$, b_j on disk $(j+1) \bmod D$, $\dots$, h_j on disk $(j+7) \bmod D$. We might need to access these blocks in the order

$$a_0 b_0 c_0 d_0 e_0 \; f_0 g_0 h_0 d_1 e_1 \; d_2 e_2 d_3 a_1 f_1 \; b_1 g_1 a_2 f_2 e_3 \; d_4 c_1 h_1 b_2 g_2 \; a_3 f_3 e_4 d_5 d_6 \; \dots; \quad (19)$$

then they appear on the respective disks

$$0\;1\;2\;3\;4\;\;0\;1\;2\;4\;0\;\;0\;1\;1\;1\;1\;\;2\;2\;2\;2\;2\;\;2\;3\;3\;3\;3\;\;3\;3\;3\;3\;4\;\dots, \quad (20)$$

so our best bet is to input them as follows:

Time 1	Time 2	Time 3	Time 4	Time 5
$a_0 b_0 c_0 d_0 e_0$	$f_0 g_0 h_0 c_1 d_1$	$e_1 e_2 b_1 h_1 d_6$	$d_2 d_3 g_1 b_2$?	? $a_1 a_2 g_2$?

Time 6	Time 7	Time 8	Time 9	
? $f_1 f_2 a_3$?	? ? $e_3 f_3$?	? ? $d_4 e_4$?	? ? ? d_5 ?	(21)

By the time we are able to look at block d_5, we need to have read d_6 as well as 15 blocks of future data denoted by "?", because of congestion on disk 3. And we will not yet be done with the seven buffers containing remnants of a_3, b_2, c_1, e_4, f_3, g_2, and h_1; so we will need buffer space for at least $(16 + 8 + 5)B$ input records in this particular example.

The simple superblock approach to disk striping would proceed instead to read blocks $a_0 a_1 a_2 a_3 a_4$ at time 1, $b_0 b_1 b_2 b_3 b_4$ at time 2, $\dots$, $h_0 h_1 h_2 h_3 h_4$ at time 8, then $d_5 d_6 d_7 d_8 d_9$ at time 9 (since $d_5 d_6 d_7 d_8 d_9$ is the superblock needed next), and so on. Using the SyncSort strategy, it would require buffers for $(P+3)DB$ records and PDB pointers in memory. The more versatile approach indicated above can be shown to need only about half as much buffer space; but the memory requirement is still approximately proportional to PDB when P and D are large (see exercise 24).

R. D. Barve, E. F. Grove, and J. S. Vitter [*Parallel Computing* **23** (1997), 601–631] showed that a slight modification of the independent-block approach leads to an algorithm that keeps the disk input/output running at nearly its full speed while needing only $O(P + D \log D)$ buffer blocks instead of $\Omega(PD)$. Their technique of *randomized striping* puts block j of run k on disk $(x_k + j) \bmod D$, where x_k is a random integer selected just before run k is first written. Instead of insisting that D blocks are constantly being input, one from each disk, they introduced a simple mechanism for holding back when there isn't enough space to keep reading ahead on certain disks, and they proved that their method is asymptotically optimal.

To do P-way merging on D disks with randomized striping, we can maintain $2D + P + Q - 1$ floating input buffers, each holding a block of B records. Input is typically being read into D of these buffers, called *active read buffers*, while P of the others contain the leading blocks from which records are currently being merged; these are called *active merge buffers*. The remaining $D + Q - 1$ "scratch buffers" are either empty or they hold prefetched data that will be needed later; Q is a nonnegative parameter that can be increased in order to lessen the chance that reading will be held back on any of the disks.

The blocks of all runs can be arranged into *chronological order* as in (19): First we list block 0 of each run, then we list the others by determining the order in which active merge buffers will become empty. As explained above, this order is determined by the final keys in each block, so we can readily forecast which blocks ought to be prefetched first.

Let's consider example (19) again, with $P = 8$, $D = 5$, and $Q = 4$. Now we will have only $2D + P + Q - 1 = 21$ input buffer blocks to work with instead of the 29 that were needed above for maximum-speed reading. We will use the offsets

$$x_1 = 3, \ x_2 = 1, \ x_3 = 4, \ x_4 = 1, \ x_5 = 0, \ x_6 = 4, \ x_7 = 2, \ x_8 = 1 \qquad (22)$$

(suggested by the decimal digits of π) for runs a, b, $\ldots$, h; thus the respective disks contain

Disk	Blocks									
0:		e_0			f_1	a_2	$d_4 c_1$			$\ldots$
1:	b_0 d_0		h_0 e_1			f_2		a_3	d_5	$\ldots$
2:		g_0 d_1	e_2		b_1		h_1	f_3	$d_6 \ldots$	(23)
3:	a_0		d_2		g_1	e_3	b_2			$\ldots$
4:		c_0 f_0		$d_3 a_1$			g_2	e_4		$\ldots$

if we list their blocks in chronological order. The "random" offsets of (22), together with sequential striping within each run, will tend to minimize the congestion of any particular chronological sequence. The actual processing now goes like this:

	Active reading	Active merging	Scratch	Waiting for	
Time 1	$e_0 b_0 g_0 a_0 c_0$	$-------$	$(---------)$	a_0	
Time 2	$f_1 d_0 d_1 d_2 f_0$	$a_0 -------$	$b_0 c_0 (e_0 g_0 ----)$	d_0	
Time 3	$a_2 h_0 e_2 g_1 d_3$	$a_0 b_0 c_0 d_0 ----$	$e_0 f_0 g_0 (d_1 d_2 f_1 --)$	h_0	
Time 4	$a_2 e_1 b_1 g_1 a_1$	$a_0 b_0 c_0 d_0 e_0 f_0 g_0 h_0$	$d_1 (d_2 e_2 d_3 f_1 g_1 a_2 -)$	e_1	(24)
Time 5	$d_4 f_2 h_1 e_3 g_2$	$a_0 b_0 c_0 d_1 e_1 f_0 g_0 h_0$	$d_2 e_2 d_3 a_1 f_1 b_1 g_1 a_2 ()$	f_2	
Time 6	$c_1 a_3 f_3 b_2 e_4$	$a_2 b_1 c_0 d_3 e_2 f_2 g_1 h_0$	$e_3 d_4 (h_1 g_2 ----)$	c_1	
Time 7	$? d_5 d_6 ? \ ?$	$a_2 b_1 c_1 d_4 e_3 f_2 g_1 h_0$	$h_1 b_2 g_2 a_3 f_3 e_4 (--)$	d_5	

At each unit of time we are waiting for the chronologically first block that is not yet merged and not yet in a scratch buffer; this is one of the blocks that is currently being input to an active read buffer. We assume that the computer is much faster than the disks; thus, all blocks before the one we are waiting for will have already entered the merging process before input is complete. We also assume that sufficient output buffers are available so that merging will not be delayed by the lack of a place to place the output (see exercise 26). When a round of input is complete, the block we were waiting for is immediately classified as an active merge buffer, and the empty merge buffer it replaces will be used for the next active reading. The other $D-1$ active read buffers now trade places with the $D-1$ least important scratch buffers; scratch buffers are ranked by chronological order of their contents. On the next round we will wait for the first unmerged block that isn't present in the scratch buffers. Any scratch buffers preceding that block in chronological order will become part of the active merge before the next input cycle, but the others — shown in parentheses above — will be carried over and they will remain as scratch buffers on the next round. However, at most Q of the buffers in parentheses can be carried over, because we will need to convert $D-1$ scratch buffers to active read status immediately after the input is ready. Any additional scratch buffers are effectively blanked out, as if they hadn't been read. This blanking-out occurs at Time 4 in (24): We cannot carry all six of the blocks $d_2 e_2 d_3 f_1 g_1 a_2$ over to Time 5, because $Q = 4$, so we reread g_1 and a_2. Otherwise the reading operations in this example take place at full speed.

Exercise 29 proves that, given any chronological sequence of runs to be merged, the method of randomized striping will achieve the minimum number of disk reads within a factor of $r(D, Q+2)$, on the average, where the function r is tabulated in Table 2. For example, if $D = 4$ and $Q = 18$, the average time to do a P-way merge on L blocks of data with 4 disks and $P + 25$ input buffers will be at most the time to read $r(4, 20)L/D \approx 1.785L/4$ blocks on a single disk. This theoretical upper bound is quite conservative; in practice the performance is even better, very near the optimum time $L/4$.

Table 2
GUARANTEES ON THE PERFORMANCE OF RANDOMIZED STRIPING

	$r(d,d)$	$r(d,2d)$	$r(d,3d)$	$r(d,4d)$	$r(d,5d)$	$r(d,6d)$	$r(d,7d)$	$r(d,8d)$	$r(d,9d)$	$r(d,10d)$
$d = 2$	1.500	1.500	1.499	1.467	1.444	1.422	1.393	1.370	1.353	1.339
$d = 4$	2.460	2.190	1.986	1.888	1.785	1.724	1.683	1.633	1.597	1.570
$d = 8$	3.328	2.698	2.365	2.183	2.056	1.969	1.889	1.836	1.787	1.743
$d = 16$	4.087	3.103	2.662	2.434	2.277	2.156	2.067	1.997	1.933	1.890
$d = 32$	4.503	3.392	2.917	2.654	2.458	2.319	2.218	2.130	2.062	2.005
$d = 64$	5.175	3.718	3.165	2.847	2.613	2.465	2.346	2.249	2.174	2.107
$d = 128$	5.431	3.972	3.356	2.992	2.759	2.603	2.459	2.358	2.273	2.201
$d = 256$	5.909	4.222	3.536	3.155	2.910	2.714	2.567	2.464	2.363	2.289
$d = 512$	6.278	4.455	3.747	3.316	3.024	2.820	2.675	2.556	2.450	2.375
$d = 1024$	6.567	4.689	3.879	3.434	3.142	2.937	2.780	2.639	2.536	2.452

Will keysorting help? When records are long and keys are short, it is very tempting to create a new file consisting simply of the keys together with a serial number specifying their original file location. After sorting this key file, we can replace the keys by the successive numbers $1, 2, \ldots$; the new file can then be sorted by original file location and we will have a convenient specification of how to unshuffle the records for the final rearrangement. Schematically, the process has the following form:

i)	Original file	$(K_1, I_1)(K_2, I_2)\ldots(K_N, I_N)$	long
ii)	Key file	$(K_1, 1)(K_2, 2)\ldots(K_N, N)$	short
iii)	Sorted (ii)	$(K_{p_1}, p_1)(K_{p_2}, p_2)\ldots(K_{p_N}, p_N)$	short
iv)	Edited (iii)	$(1, p_1)(2, p_2)\ldots(N, p_N)$	short
v)	Sorted (iv)	$(q_1, 1)(q_2, 2)\ldots(q_N, N)$	short
vi)	Edited (i)	$(q_1, I_1)(q_2, I_2)\ldots(q_N, I_N)$	long

Here $p_j = k$ if and only if $q_k = j$. The two sorting processes in (iii) and (v) are comparatively fast (perhaps even internal sorts), since the records aren't very long. In stage (vi) we have reduced the problem to sorting a file whose keys are simply the numbers $\{1, 2, \ldots, N\}$; each record now specifies exactly where it is to be moved.

The external rearrangement problem that remains after stage (vi) seems trivial, at first glance; but in fact it is rather difficult, and no really good algorithms (significantly better than sorting) have yet been found. We could obviously do the rearrangement in N steps, moving one record at a time; for large enough N this is better than the $N \log N$ of a sorting method. But N is never that large; N is, however, sufficiently large that N seeks are unthinkable.

A radix sorting method can be used efficiently on the edited records of (vi), since their keys have a perfectly uniform distribution. On modern computers, the processing time for an eight-way distribution is much faster than the processing time for an eight-way merge; hence a distribution sort is probably the best procedure. (See Section 5.4.7, and see also exercise 19.)

On the other hand, it seems wasteful to do a full sort after the keys have already been sorted. One reason the external rearrangement problem is unexpectedly difficult has been discovered by R. W. Floyd, who found a nontrivial lower bound on the number of seeks required to rearrange records on a disk device [*Complexity of Computer Computations* (New York: Plenum, 1972), 105–109].

It is convenient to describe Floyd's result in terms of the elevator problem of Section 5.4.8; but this time we want to find an elevator schedule that minimizes the number of *stops*, instead of minimizing the distance traveled. Minimizing the number of stops is not precisely equivalent to finding the minimum-seek rearrangement algorithm, since a stop combines input to the elevator with output from the elevator; but the stop-minimization criterion is close enough to indicate the basic ideas.

We shall make use of the "discrete entropy" function

$$F(n) = \sum_{1 < k \leq n} \left(\lceil \lg k \rceil + 1 \right) = B(n) + n - 1 = n\lceil \lg n \rceil - 2^{\lceil \lg n \rceil} + n, \qquad (25)$$

where $B(n)$ is the binary insertion function, Eq. 5.3.1–(3). By Eq. 5.3.1–(34), $F(n)$ is the minimum external path length of a binary tree with n leaves, and

$$n \lg n \leq F(n) \leq n \lg n + 0.0861n. \qquad (26)$$

Since $F(n)$ is convex and satisfies $F(n) = n + F(\lfloor n/2 \rfloor) + F(\lceil n/2 \rceil)$, we know by Lemma C above that

$$F(n) \leq F(k) + F(n - k) + n, \qquad \text{for } 0 \leq k \leq n. \tag{27}$$

This relation is also evident from the external path length characterization of F; it is the crucial fact we need in the following argument.

As in Section 5.4.8 we shall assume that each floor holds b people, the elevator holds m people, and there are n floors. Let s_{ij} be the number of people currently on floor i whose destination is floor j. The *togetherness rating* of any configuration of people in the building is defined to be the sum $\sum_{1 \leq i,j \leq n} F(s_{ij})$.

For example, assume that $b = m = n = 6$ and that the 36 people are initially scattered among the floors as follows:

```
ⳙⳙⳙⳙⳙⳙ
123456   123456   123456   123456   123456   123456
```
(28)

The elevator is empty, sitting on floor 1; "⌴" denotes a vacant position. Each floor contains one person with each possible destination, so all s_{ij} are 1 and the togetherness rating is zero. If the elevator now transports six people to floor 2, we have the configuration

```
         123456
ⳙⳙⳙⳙⳙⳙ   123456   123456   123456   123456   123456
```
(29)

and the togetherness rating becomes $6F(0) + 24F(1) + 6F(2) = 12$. Suppose the elevator now carries 1, 1, 2, 3, 3, and 4 to floor 3:

```
         112334
ⳙⳙⳙⳙⳙⳙ   245566   123456   123456   123456   123456
```
(30)

The togetherness rating has jumped to $4F(2) + 2F(3) = 18$. When all people have finally been transported to their destinations, the togetherness rating will be $6F(6) = 96$.

Floyd observed that the togetherness rating can never increase by more than $b+m$ at each stop, since a set of s equal-destination people joining with a similar set of size s' improves the rating by $F(s + s') - F(s) - F(s') \leq s + s'$. Therefore we have the following result.

Theorem F. *Let t be the togetherness rating of an initial configuration of bn people, in terms of the definitions above. The elevator must make at least*

$$\lceil (F(b)n - t)/(b + m) \rceil$$

stops in order to bring them all to their destinations. ∎

Translating this result into disk terminology, let there be bn records, with b per block, and suppose the internal memory can hold m records at a time. Every disk read brings one block into memory, every disk write stores one block, and s_{ij} is the number of records in block i that belong in block j. If $n \geq b$, there are initial configurations in which all the s_{ij} are ≤ 1; so $t = 0$ and at least $f(b)n/(b+m) \approx (bn \lg b)/m$ block-reading operations are necessary to rearrange the records. (The factor $\lg b$ makes this lower bound nontrivial when b is large.) Exercise 17 derives a substantially stronger lower bound for the common case that m is substantially larger than b.

EXERCISES

1. [*M22*] The text explains a method by which the average latency time required to read a fraction x of a track is reduced from $\frac{1}{2}$ to $\frac{1}{2}(1 - x^2)$ revolutions. This is the minimum possible value, when there is one access arm. What is the corresponding minimum average latency time if there are *two* access arms, 180° apart, assuming that only one arm can transmit data at any one time?

2. [*M30*] (A. G. Konheim.) The purpose of this problem is to investigate how far the access arm of a disk must move while merging files that are allocated "orthogonally" to the cylinders. Suppose there are P files, each containing L blocks of records, and assume that the first block of each file appears on cylinder 1, the second on cylinder 2, etc. The relative order of the last keys in each block governs the access arm motion during the merge, hence we may represent the situation in the following mathematically tractable way: Consider a set of PL ordered pairs

$$
\begin{array}{cccc}
(a_{11}, 1) & (a_{21}, 1) & \cdots & (a_{P1}, 1) \\
(a_{12}, 2) & (a_{22}, 2) & \cdots & (a_{P2}, 2) \\
\vdots & \vdots & & \vdots \\
(a_{1L}, L) & (a_{2L}, L) & \cdots & (a_{PL}, L)
\end{array}
$$

where the set $\{a_{ij} \mid 1 \le i \le P,\ 1 \le j \le L\}$ consists of the numbers $\{1, 2, \ldots, PL\}$ in some order, and where $a_{ij} < a_{i(j+1)}$ for $1 \le j < L$. (Rows represent cylinders, columns represent input files.) Sort the pairs on their first components and let the resulting sequence be $(1, j_1)(2, j_2)\ldots(PL, j_{PL})$. Show that, if each of the $(PL)!/L!^P$ choices of the a_{ij} is equally likely, the average value of

$$
|j_2 - j_1| + |j_3 - j_2| + \cdots + |j_{PL} - j_{PL-1}|
$$

is

$$
(L - 1)\left(1 + (P - 1)2^{2L-2}\Big/\binom{2L}{L}\right).
$$

[*Hint:* See exercise 5.2.1–14.] Notice that as $L \to \infty$ this value is asymptotically equal to $\frac{1}{4}(P - 1)L\sqrt{\pi L} + O(PL)$.

3. [*M15*] Suppose the internal memory is limited so that 10-way merging is not feasible. How can recurrence relations (3), (4), (5) be modified so that $A_1(n)$ is the minimum value of $\alpha D(\mathcal{T}) + \beta E(\mathcal{T})$, over all n-leaved trees $\mathcal{T}$ having no internal nodes of degree greater than 9?

▶ **4.** [*M21*] Consider a modified form of the square root buffer allocation scheme, in which all P of the input buffers have equal length, but the output buffer size should be chosen so as to minimize seek time.

 a) Derive a formula corresponding to (2), for the running time of an L-character P-way merge.

 b) Show that the construction in Theorem K can be modified in order to obtain a merge pattern that is optimal according to your formula from part (a).

5. [*M20*] When two disks are being used, so that reading on one is overlapped with writing on the other, we cannot use merge patterns like that of Fig. 93 since some leaves are at even levels and some are at odd levels. Show how to modify the construction of Theorem K in order to produce trees that are optimal subject to the constraint that all leaves appear on even levels or all on odd levels.

▸ **6.** [*22*] Find a tree that is optimum in the sense of exercise 5, when $n = 23$ and $\alpha = \beta = 1$. (You may wish to use a computer.)

▸ **7.** [*M24*] When the initial runs are not all the same length, the best merge pattern (in the sense of Theorem H) minimizes $\alpha D(\mathcal{T}) + \beta E(\mathcal{T})$, where $D(\mathcal{T})$ and $E(\mathcal{T})$ now represent *weighted* path lengths: Weights $w_1, \ldots, w_n$ (corresponding to the lengths of the initial runs) are attached to each leaf of the tree, and the degree sums and path lengths are multiplied by the appropriate weights. For example, if $\mathcal{T}$ is the tree of Fig. 92, we would have $D(\mathcal{T}) = 6w_1 + 6w_2 + 7w_3 + 9w_4 + 9w_5 + 7w_6 + 4w_7 + 4w_8$, $E(\mathcal{T}) = 2w_1 + 2w_2 + 2w_3 + 3w_4 + 3w_5 + 2w_6 + w_7 + w_8$.

Prove that there is always an optimal pattern in which the *shortest* k runs are merged first, for some k.

8. [*49*] Is there an algorithm that finds optimal trees for given α, β and weights $w_1, \ldots, w_n$, in the sense of exercise 7, taking only $O(n^c)$ steps for some c?

9. [*HM39*] (L. Hyafil, F. Prusker, J. Vuillemin.) Prove that, for fixed α and β,

$$A_1(n) = \left(\min_{m \geq 2} \frac{\alpha m + \beta}{\log m} \right) n \log n + O(n)$$

as $n \to \infty$, where the $O(n)$ term is ≥ 0.

10. [*HM44*] (L. Hyafil, F. Prusker, J. Vuillemin.) Prove that when α and β are fixed, $A_1(n) = \alpha mn + \beta n + A_m(n)$ for all sufficiently large n, if m minimizes the coefficient in exercise 9.

11. [*M29*] In the notation of (6) and (11), prove that $f_m(n) + mn \geq f(n)$ for all $m \geq 2$ and $n \geq 2$, and determine all m and n for which equality holds.

12. [*25*] Prove that, for all $n > 0$, there is a tree with n leaves and minimum degree path length (6), with all leaves at the same level.

13. [*M24*] Show that for $2 \leq n \leq d(\alpha, \beta)$, where $d(\alpha, \beta)$ is defined in (12), the unique best merge pattern in the sense of Theorem H is an n-way merge.

14. [*40*] Using the square root method of buffer allocation, the seek time for the merge pattern in Fig. 92 would be proportional to $(\sqrt{2} + \sqrt{4} + \sqrt{1} + \sqrt{1} + \sqrt{8})^2 + (\sqrt{1} + \sqrt{1} + \sqrt{2})^2 + (\sqrt{1} + \sqrt{2} + \sqrt{1} + \sqrt{4})^2 + (\sqrt{1} + \sqrt{1} + \sqrt{2})^2$; this is the sum, over each internal node, of $(\sqrt{n_1} + \cdots + \sqrt{n_m} + \sqrt{n_1 + \cdots + n_m})^2$, where that node's respective subtrees have $(n_1, \ldots, n_m)$ leaves. Write a computer program that generates minimum-seek time trees having 1, 2, 3, ... leaves, based on this formula.

15. [*M22*] Show that Theorem F can be improved slightly if the elevator is initially empty and if $F(b)n \neq t$: At least $\lceil (F(b)n + m - t)/(b + m) \rceil$ stops are necessary in such a case.

16. [*23*] (R. W. Floyd.) Find an elevator schedule that transports all the people of (28) to their destinations in at most 12 stops. (Configuration (29) shows the situation after one stop, not two.)

▸ **17.** [*HM25*] (R. W. Floyd, 1980.) Show that the lower bound of Theorem F can be improved to

$$\frac{n(b \ln n - \ln b - 1)}{\ln n + b\big(1 + \ln(1 + m/b)\big)},$$

in the sense that some initial configuration must require at least this many stops. [*Hint:* Count the configurations that can be obtained after s stops.]

18. [*HM26*] Let L be the lower bound of exercise 17. Show that the average number of elevator stops needed to take all people to their desired floors is at least $L - 1$, when the $(bn)!$ possible permutations of people into bn desks are equally likely.

▸ **19.** [*25*] (B. T. Bennett and A. C. McKellar.) Consider the following approach to keysorting, illustrated on an example file with 10 keys:

   i) Original file: $(50, I_0)(08, I_1)(51, I_2)(06, I_3)(90, I_4)(17, I_5)(89, I_6)(27, I_7)(65, I_8)(42, I_9)$
  ii) Key file: $(50, 0)(08, 1)(51, 2)(06, 3)(90, 4)(17, 5)(89, 6)(27, 7)(65, 8)(42, 9)$
 iii) Sorted (ii): $(06, 3)(08, 1)(17, 5)(27, 7)(42, 9)(50, 0)(51, 2)(65, 8)(89, 6)(90, 4)$
 iv) Bin assignments (see below): $(2, 1)(2, 3)(2, 5)(2, 7)(2, 8)(2, 9)(1, 0)(1, 2)(1, 4)(1, 6)$
  v) Sorted (iv): $(1, 0)(2, 1)(1, 2)(2, 3)(1, 4)(2, 5)(1, 6)(2, 7)(2, 8)(2, 9)$
 vi) (i) distributed into bins using (v):
      Bin 1: $(50, I_0)(51, I_2)(90, I_4)(89, I_6)$
      Bin 2: $(08, I_1)(06, I_3)(17, I_5)(27, I_7)(65, I_8)(42, I_9)$
vii) The result of replacement selection, reading first bin 2, then bin 1:
      $(06, I_3)(08, I_1)(17, I_5)(27, I_7)(42, I_9)(50, I_0)(51, I_2)(65, I_8)(89, I_6)(90, I_4)$

The assignment of bin numbers in step (iv) is made by doing *replacement selection* on (iii), *from right to left*, in *decreasing* order of the second component. The bin number is the run number. The example above uses replacement selection with only two elements in the selection tree; the same size tree should be used for replacement selection in both (iv) and (vii). Notice that the bin contents are not necessarily in sorted order!

Prove that this method will sort, namely that the replacement selection in (vii) will produce only one run. (This technique reduces the number of bins needed in a conventional keysort by distribution, especially if the input is largely in order already.)

▸ **20.** [*25*] Modern hardware/software systems provide programmers with a *virtual memory:* Programs are written as if there were a very large internal memory, able to contain all of the data. This memory is divided into *pages*, only a few of which are in the actual internal memory at any one time; the others are on disks or drums. Programmers need not concern themselves with such details, since the system takes care of everything; new pages are automatically brought into memory when needed.

It would seem that the advent of virtual memory technology makes external sorting methods obsolete, since the job can simply be done using the techniques developed for internal sorting. Discuss this situation; in what ways might a hand-tailored external sorting method be better than the application of a general-purpose paging technique to an internal sorting method?

▸ **21.** [*M15*] How many blocks of an L-block file go on disk j when the file is striped on D disks?

22. [*22*] If you are merging two files with the Gilbreath principle and you want to store the keys α_j with the a blocks and the keys β_j with the b blocks, in which block should α_j be placed in order to have the information available when it is needed?

▸ **23.** [*20*] How much space is needed for input buffers to keep input going continuously when two-way merging is done by (a) superblock striping? (b) the Gilbreath principle?

24. [*M36*] Suppose P runs have been striped on D disks so that block j of run k appears on disk $(x_k + j) \bmod D$. A P-way merge will read those blocks in some chronological order such as (19). If groups of D blocks are to be input continuously, we will read at time t the chronologically tth block stored on each disk, as in (21). What is the minimum number of buffer records needed in memory to hold input data that has not yet been merged, regardless of the chronological order? Explain how to choose the offsets $x_1, x_2, \ldots, x_P$ so that the fewest buffers are needed in the worst case.

25. [*23*] Rework the text's example of randomized striping for the case $Q = 3$ instead of $Q = 4$. What buffer contents would occur in place of (24)?

26. [*26*] How many output buffers will guarantee that a P-way merge with randomized striping will never have to pause for lack of a place in internal memory to put newly merged output? Assume that the time to write a block equals the time to read a block.

27. [*HM27*] (*The cyclic occupancy problem.*) Suppose n empty urns have been arranged in a circle and assigned the numbers $0, 1, \ldots, n - 1$. For $k = 1, 2, \ldots, p$, we throw m_k balls into urns $(X_k + j) \bmod n$ for $j = 0, 1, \ldots, m_k - 1$, where the integers X_k are chosen at random. Let $S_n(m_1, \ldots, m_p)$ be the number of balls in urn 0, and let $E_n(m_1, \ldots, m_p)$ be the expected number of balls in the fullest urn.

 a) Prove that $E_n(m_1, \ldots, m_p) \le \sum_{t=1}^{m} \min\bigl(1, n \Pr(S_n(m_1, \ldots, m_p) \ge t)\bigr)$, where $m = m_1 + \cdots + m_p$.

 b) Use the tail inequality, Eq. 1.2.10–(25), to prove that

$$E_n(m_1, \ldots, m_p) \le \sum_{t=1}^{m} \min\left(1, \; \frac{n(1 + \alpha_t/n)^m}{(1 + \alpha_t)^t}\right)$$

 for any nonnegative real numbers $\alpha_1, \alpha_2, \ldots, \alpha_m$. What values of $\alpha_1, \ldots, \alpha_m$ give the best upper bound?

28. [*HM47*] Continuing exercise 27, is $E_n(m_1, \ldots, m_p) \ge E_n(m_1 + m_2, m_3, \ldots, m_p)$?

▸ **29.** [*M30*] The purpose of this exercise is to derive an upper bound on the average time needed to input any sequence of blocks in chronological order by the randomized striping procedure, when the blocks represent P runs and D disks. We say that the block being waited for at each time step as the algorithm proceeds (see (24)) is "marked"; thus the total input time is proportional to the number of marked blocks. Marking depends only on the chronological sequence of disk accesses (see (20)).

 a) Prove that if $Q + 1$ consecutive blocks in chronological order have N_j blocks on disk j, then at most $\max(N_0, N_1, \ldots, N_{D-1})$ of those blocks are marked.

 b) Strengthen the result of (a) by showing that it holds also for $Q + 2$ consecutive blocks.

 c) Now use the cyclic occupancy problem of exercise 27 to obtain an upper bound on the average running time in terms of a function $r(D, Q + 2)$ as in Table 2, given any chronological order.

30. [*HM30*] Prove that the function $r(d, m)$ of exercise 29 satisfies $r(d, sd \log d) = 1 + O(1/\sqrt{s})$ for fixed d as $s \to \infty$.

31. [*HM48*] Analyze randomized striping to determine its true average behavior, not merely an upper bound, as a function of P, Q, and D. (Even the case $Q = 0$, which needs an average of $\Theta(L/\sqrt{D})$ read cycles, is interesting.)

5.5. SUMMARY, HISTORY, AND BIBLIOGRAPHY

NOW THAT WE have nearly reached the end of this enormously long chapter, we had better "sort out" the most important facts that we have studied.

An algorithm for sorting is a procedure that rearranges a file of records so that the keys are in ascending order. This orderly arrangement is useful because it brings equal-key records together, it allows efficient processing of several files that are sorted on the same key, it leads to efficient retrieval algorithms, and it makes computer output look less chaotic.

Internal sorting is used when all of the records fit in the computer's high speed internal memory. We have studied more than two dozen algorithms for internal sorting, in various degrees of detail; and perhaps we would be happier if we didn't know so many different approaches to the problem! It was fun to learn all the techniques, but now we must face the horrible prospect of actually deciding which method ought to be used in a given situation.

It would be nice if only one or two of the sorting methods would dominate all of the others, regardless of the application or the computer being used. But in fact, each method has its own peculiar virtues. For example, the bubble sort (Algorithm 5.2.2B) has no apparent redeeming features, since there is always a better way to do what it does; but even this technique, suitably generalized, turns out to be useful for two-tape sorting (see Section 5.4.8). Thus we find that nearly all of the algorithms deserve to be remembered, since there are some applications in which they turn out to be best.

The following brief survey gives the highlights of the most significant algorithms we have encountered for internal sorting. As usual, N stands for the number of records in the given file.

1. *Distribution counting*, Algorithm 5.2D, is very useful when the keys have a small range. It is stable (doesn't affect the order of records with equal keys), but requires memory space for counters and for $2N$ records. A modification that saves N of these record spaces at the cost of stability appears in exercise 5.2–13.

2. *Straight insertion*, Algorithm 5.2.1S, is the simplest method to program, requires no extra space, and is quite efficient for small N (say $N \leq 25$). For large N it is unbearably slow unless the input is nearly in order.

3. *Shellsort*, Algorithm 5.2.1D, is also quite easy to program, and uses minimum memory space; and it is reasonably efficient for moderately large N (say $N \leq 1000$).

4. *List insertion*, Algorithm 5.2.1L, uses the same basic idea as straight insertion, so it is suitable only for small N. Like the other list sorting methods described below, it saves the cost of moving long records by manipulating links; this is particularly advantageous when the records have variable length or are part of other data structures.

5. *Address calculation* techniques are efficient when the keys have a known (usually uniform) distribution; the principal variants of this approach are *multiple list insertion* (Program 5.2.1M), and MacLaren's combined radix-insertion

method (discussed at the close of Section 5.2.5). The latter can be done with only $O(\sqrt{N})$ cells of additional memory. A two-pass method that learns a nonuniform distribution is discussed in Theorem 5.2.5T.

6. *Merge exchange*, Algorithm 5.2.2M (Batcher's method) and its cousin the *bitonic sort* (exercise 5.3.4–10) are useful when a large number of comparisons can be made simultaneously.

7. *Quicksort*, Algorithm 5.2.2Q (Hoare's method) is probably the most useful general-purpose technique for internal sorting, because it requires very little memory space and its average running time on most computers beats that of its competitors when it is well implemented. It can run *very* slowly in its worst case, however, so a careful choice of the partitioning elements should be made whenever nonrandom data are likely. Choosing the median of three elements, as suggested in exercise 5.2.2–55, makes the worst-case behavior extremely unlikely and also improves the average running time slightly.

8. *Straight selection*, Algorithm 5.2.3S, is a simple method especially suitable when special hardware is available to find the smallest element of a list rapidly.

9. *Heapsort*, Algorithm 5.2.3H, requires minimum memory and is guaranteed to run pretty fast; its average time and its maximum time are both roughly twice the average running time of quicksort.

10. *List merging*, Algorithm 5.2.4L, is a list sort that, like heapsort, is guaranteed to be rather fast even in its worst case; moreover, it is stable with respect to equal keys.

11. *Radix sorting*, using Algorithm 5.2.5R, is a list sort especially appropriate for keys that are either rather short or that have an unusual lexicographic collating sequence. The method of distribution counting (point 1 above) can also be used, as an alternative to linking; such a procedure requires $2N$ record spaces, plus a table of counters, but the simple form of its inner loop makes it especially good for ultra-fast, "number-crunching" computers that have look-ahead control. *Caution:* Radix sorting should not be used for small N!

12. *Merge insertion*, see Section 5.3.1, is especially suitable for very small values of N, in a "straight-line-coded" routine; for example, it would be the appropriate method in an application that requires the sorting of numerous five- or six-record groups.

13. Hybrid methods, combining one or more of the techniques above, are also possible. For example, merge insertion could be used for sorting short subfiles that arise in quicksort.

14. Finally, an unnamed method appearing in the answer to exercise 5.2.1–3 seems to require the shortest possible sorting program. But its average running time, proportional to N^3, makes it the slowest sorting routine in this book!

Table 1 summarizes the speed and space characteristics of many of these methods, when programmed for MIX. It is important to realize that the figures in this table are only rough indications of the relative sorting times; they apply to one computer only, and the assumptions made about input data are not

Table 1

A COMPARISON OF INTERNAL SORTING METHODS USING THE MIX COMPUTER

Method	Reference	Stable?	Length of MIX code	Space	Running Time				Notes
					Average	Maximum	$N = 16$	$N = 1000$	
Comparison counting	Ex. 5.2-5	Yes	22	$N(1+\epsilon)$	$4N^2 + 10N$	$5.5N^2$	1065	3992432	c
Distribution counting	Ex. 5.2-9	Yes	26	$2N + 1000\epsilon$	$22N + 10010$	$22N$	10362	32010	a
Straight insertion	Ex. 5.2.1-33	Yes	10	$N+1$	$1.5N^2 + 9.5N$	$3N^2$	412	1491928	
Shellsort	Prog. 5.2.1D	No	21	$N + \epsilon \lg N$	$3.9N^{7/6} + 10N \lg N + 166N$	$cN^{4/3}$	567	128758	d, h
List insertion	Ex. 5.2.1-33	Yes	19	$N(1+\epsilon)$	$1.25N^2 + 13.25N$	$2.5N^2$	433	1248615	b, c
Multiple list insertion	Prog. 5.2.1M	No	18	$N + \epsilon(N + 100)$	$.0175N^2 + 18N$	$3.5N^2$	645	35246	b, c, f, i
Merge exchange	Ex. 5.2.2-12	No	35	N	$2.875N(\lg N)^2$	$4N(\lg N)^2$	939	284366	
Quicksort	Prog. 5.2.2Q	No	63	$N + 2\epsilon \lg N$	$11.67N \ln N - 1.74N$	$\geq 2N^2$	470	81486	
Median-of-3 quicksort	Ex. 5.2.2-55	No	100	$N + 2\epsilon \lg N$	$10.63N \ln N + 2.12N$	$\geq N^2$	487	74574	e
Radix exchange	Prog. 5.2.2R	No	45	$N + 68\epsilon$	$14.43N \ln N + 23.9N$	$272N$	1135	137614	g, i, j
Straight selection	Prog. 5.2.3S	No	15	N	$2.5N^2 + 3N \ln N$	$3.25N^2$	853	2525287	j
Heapsort	Prog. 5.2.3H	No	30	N	$23.08N \ln N + 0.01N$	$24.5N \ln N$	1068	159714	h, j
List merge	Prog. 5.2.4L	Yes	44	$N(1+\epsilon)$	$14.43N \ln N + 4.92N$	$14.4N \ln N$	761	104716	b, c, j
Radix list sort	Prog. 5.2.5R	Yes	36	$N + \epsilon(N + 200)$	$32N + 4838$	$32N$	4250	36838	b, c

a: Three-digit keys only.

b: Six-digit (that is, three-byte) keys only.

c: Output not rearranged; final sequence is specified implicitly by links or counters.

d: Increments chosen as in 5.2.1–(11); a slightly better sequence appears in exercise 5.2.1–29.

e: $M = 9$, using SRB; for the version with DIV, add $1.60N$ to the average running time.

f: $M = 100$ (the byte size).

g: $M = 34$, since $2^{34} > 10^{10} > 2^{33}$.

h: The average time is based on an empirical estimate, since the theory is incomplete.

i: The average time is based on the assumption of uniformly distributed keys.

j: Further refinements, mentioned in the text and exercises accompanying this program, would reduce the running time.

completely consistent for all programs. Comparative tables such as this have been given by many authors, with no two people reaching the same conclusions. On the other hand, the timings do give at least an indication of the kind of speed to be expected from each algorithm, when sorting a rather small array of one-word records, since MIX is a fairly typical computer.

The "space" column in Table 1 gives some information about the amount of auxiliary memory used by each program, in units of record length. Here ϵ denotes the fraction of a record needed for one link field; thus, for example, $N(1 + \epsilon)$ means that the method requires space for N records plus N link fields.

The asymptotic average and maximum times appearing in Table 1 give only the leading terms that dominate for large N, assuming random input; c denotes an unspecified constant. These formulas can often be misleading, so actual total running times have also been listed, for sample runs of the program on two particular sequences of input data. The case $N = 16$ refers to the sixteen keys that appear in so many of the examples of Section 5.2; and the case $N = 1000$ refers to the sequence $K_1, K_2, \ldots, K_{1000}$ defined by

$$K_{1001} = 0; \qquad K_{n-1} = (3141592621 K_n + 2113148651) \bmod 10^{10}.$$

A MIX program of reasonably high quality has been used to represent each algorithm in the table, often incorporating improvements that have been suggested in the exercises. The byte size for these runs was 100.

External sorting techniques are different from internal sorting, because they must use comparatively primitive data structures, and because there is a great emphasis on minimizing their input/output time. Section 5.4.6 summarizes the interesting methods that have been developed for tape merging, and Section 5.4.9 discusses the use of disks and drums.

Of course, sorting isn't the whole story. While studying all of these sorting techniques, we have learned a good deal about how to handle data structures, how to deal with external memories, and how to analyze algorithms; and perhaps we have even learned a little about how to discover new algorithms.

Early developments. A search for the origin of today's sorting techniques takes us back to the nineteenth century, when the first machines for sorting were invented. The United States conducts a census of all its citizens every ten years, and by 1880 the problem of processing the voluminous census data was becoming very acute; in fact, the total number of single (as opposed to married) people was never tabulated that year, although the necessary information had been gathered. Herman Hollerith, a 20-year-old employee of the Census Bureau, devised an ingenious electric tabulating machine to meet the need for better statistics-gathering, and about 100 of his machines were successfully used to tabulate the 1890 census rolls.

Figure 94 shows Hollerith's original battery-driven apparatus; of chief interest to us is the "sorting box" at the right, which has been opened to show half of the 26 inner compartments. The operator would insert a $6\frac{5}{8}'' \times 3\frac{1}{4}''$ punched card into the "press" and lower the handle; this caused spring-actuated pins in the upper plate to make contact with pools of mercury in the lower plate, wherever a hole was punched in the card. The corresponding completed circuits would cause associated dials on the panel to advance by one unit; and furthermore, one of the 26 lids of the sorting box would pop open. At this point the operator would reopen the press, put the card into the open compartment, and close the lid. One man reportedly ran 19071 cards through this machine in a single $6\frac{1}{2}$-hour working day, an average of about 49 cards per minute! (A typical operator would work at about one-third this speed.)

Fig. 94. Hollerith's original tabulating and sorting machine. (Photo courtesy of IBM archives.)

Population continued its inexorable growth, and the original tabulator-sorters were not fast enough to handle the 1900 census; so Hollerith devised another machine to stave off another data processing crisis. His new device (patented in 1901 and 1904) had an automatic card feed, and in fact it looked essentially like modern card sorters. The story of Hollerith's early machines has been told in interesting detail by Leon E. Truesdell, *The Development of Punch Card Tabulation* (Washington: U.S. Bureau of the Census, 1965); see also the contemporary accounts in *Columbia College School of Mines Quarterly* **10** (1889), 238–255; *J. Franklin Inst.* **129** (1890), 300–306; *The Electrical Engineer* **12** (November 11, 1891), 521–530; *J. Amer. Statistical Assn.* **2** (1891), 330–341, **4** (1895), 365; *J. Royal Statistical Soc.* **55** (1892), 326–327; *Allgemeines statistisches Archiv* **2** (1892), 78–126; *J. Soc. Statistique de Paris* **33** (1892), 87–96; *U.S. Patents 395781* (1889), *685608* (1901), *777209* (1904). Hollerith and another former Census Bureau employee, James Powers, went on to found rival companies that eventually became part of IBM and Remington Rand corporations, respectively.

Hollerith's sorting machine is, of course, the basis for radix sorting methods now used in digital computers. His patent mentions that two-column numerical items are to be sorted "separately for each column," but he didn't say whether the units or the tens columns should be considered first. Patent number 518240 by John K. Gore in 1894, which described another early machine for sorting cards, suggested starting with the tens column. The nonobvious trick of using the units column first was presumably discovered by some anonymous machine operator and passed on to others (see Section 5.2.5); it appears in the earliest extant IBM sorter manual (1936). The first known mention of this right-to-left technique is in a book by Robert Feindler, *Das Hollerith-Lochkarten-Verfahren* (Berlin: Reimar Hobbing, 1929), 126–130; it was also mentioned at about the same time in an article by L. J. Comrie, *Transactions of the Office Machinery Users' Association* (London: 1929–1930), 25–37. Incidentally, Comrie was the first person to make the important observation that tabulating machines could fruitfully be employed in scientific calculations, even though they were originally designed for statistical and accounting applications. His article is especially interesting because it gives a detailed description of the tabulating equipment available in England in 1930. Sorting machines at that time processed 360 to 400 cards per minute, and could be rented for £9 per month.

The idea of merging goes back to another card-walloping machine, the *collator*, which was a much later invention (1936). With its two feeding stations, it could merge two sorted decks of cards into one, in only one pass; the technique for doing this was clearly explained in the first IBM collator manual (April 1939). [See Ralph E. Page, *U.S. Patent 2359670* (1944).]

Then computers arrived on the scene, and sorting was intimately involved in this development; in fact, there is evidence that a sorting routine was the first program ever written for a stored-program computer. The designers of EDVAC were especially interested in sorting, because it epitomized the potential nonnumerical applications of computers; they realized that a satisfactory order code should not only be capable of expressing programs for the solution of difference equations, it must also have enough flexibility to handle the combinatorial "decision-making" aspects of algorithms. John von Neumann therefore prepared programs for internal merge sorting in 1945, in order to test the adequacy of some instruction codes he was proposing for the EDVAC computer. The existence of efficient special-purpose sorting machines provided a natural standard by which the merits of his proposed computer organization could be evaluated. Details of this interesting development have been described in an article by D. E. Knuth, *Computing Surveys* **2** (1970), 247–260; see also von Neumann's *Collected Works* **5** (New York: Macmillan, 1963), 196–214, for the final polished form of his original sorting programs.

In Germany, K. Zuse independently constructed a program for straight insertion sorting in 1945, as one of the simplest examples of linear list operations in his

"Plankalkül" language. (This pioneering work remained unpublished for nearly 30 years; see *Berichte der Gesellschaft für Mathematik und Datenverarbeitung* **63** (Bonn: 1972), part 4, 84–85.)

The limited internal memory size planned for early computers made it natural to think of external sorting as well as internal sorting, and a "Progress Report on the EDVAC" prepared by J. P. Eckert and J. W. Mauchly of the Moore School of Electrical Engineering (30 September 1945) pointed out that a computer augmented with magnetic wire or tape devices could simulate the operations of card equipment, achieving a faster sorting speed. This progress report described balanced two-way radix sorting, and balanced two-way merging (called "collating"), using four magnetic wire or tape units, reading or writing "at least 5000 pulses per second."

John Mauchly lectured on "Sorting and Collating" at the special session on computing presented at the Moore School in 1946, and the notes of his lecture constitute the first published discussion of computer sorting [*Theory and Techniques for the Design of Electronic Digital Computers*, edited by G. W. Patterson, **3** (1946), 22.1–22.20]. Mauchly began his presentation with an interesting remark: "To ask that a single machine combine the abilities to compute and to sort might seem like asking that a single device be able to perform both as a can opener and a fountain pen." Then he observed that machines capable of carrying out sophisticated mathematical procedures must also have the ability to sort and classify data, and he showed that sorting may even be useful in connection with numerical calculations. He described straight insertion and binary insertion, observing that the former method uses about $N^2/4$ comparisons on the average, while the latter never needs more than about $N \lg N$. Yet binary insertion requires a rather complex data structure, and he went on to show that two-way merging achieves the same low number of comparisons using only sequential accessing of lists. The last half of his lecture notes were devoted to a discussion of partial-pass radix sorting methods that simulate digital card sorting on four tapes, using fewer than four passes per digit (see Section 5.4.7).

Shortly afterwards, Eckert and Mauchly started a company that produced some of the earliest electronic computers, the BINAC (for military applications) and the UNIVAC (for commercial applications). Again the U.S. Census Bureau played a part in this development, receiving the first UNIVAC. At this time it was not at all clear that computers would be economically profitable; computing machines could sort faster than card equipment, but they cost more. Therefore the UNIVAC programmers, led by Frances E. Snyder, put considerable effort into the design of high-speed external sorting routines, and their preliminary programs also influenced the hardware design. According to their estimates, 100 million 10-word records could be sorted on UNIVAC in 9000 hours, or 375 days.

UNIVAC I, officially dedicated in July 1951, had an internal memory of 1000 12-character (72-bit) words. It was designed to read and write 60-word blocks on tapes, at a rate of 500 words per second; reading could be either forward or backward, and simultaneous reading, writing, and computing was possible. In 1948, Snyder devised an interesting way to do two-way merging with perfect overlap of reading, writing, and computing, using six input buffers: Let there be one "current buffer" and two "auxiliary buffers" for each input file; it is possible to merge in such a way that, whenever it is time to output one block, the two current input buffers contain a total of exactly one block's worth of unprocessed records. Therefore exactly one input buffer becomes empty while each output block is being formed, and we can arrange to have three of the four auxiliary buffers full at all times while we are reading into the other. This method is slightly faster than the forecasting method of Algorithm 5.4.6F, since it is not necessary to inspect the result of one input before initiating the next. [See *Collation Methods for the UNIVAC System* (Eckert–Mauchly Computer Corp., 1950), 2 volumes.]

The culmination of this work was a sort generator program, which was the first major software routine ever developed for automatic programming. The user would specify the record size, the positions of up to five keys in partial fields of each record, and the sentinel keys that mark file's end; then the sort generator would produce a copyrighted sorting program for one-reel files. The first pass of this program was an internal sort of 60-word blocks, using comparison counting (Algorithm 5.2C); then came a number of balanced two-way merge passes, reading backwards and avoiding tape interlock as described above. [See "Master Generating Routine for 2-way Sorting" (Eckert–Mauchly Division of Remington Rand, 1952); the first draft of this report was entitled "Master Prefabrication Routine for 2-way Collation." See also Frances E. [Snyder] Holberton, *Symposium on Automatic Programming* (Office of Naval Research, 1954), 34–39.]

By 1952, many approaches to internal sorting were well known in the programming folklore, but comparatively little theory had been developed. Daniel Goldenberg ["Time analyses of various methods of sorting data," Digital Computer Laboratory memo M-1680 (Mass. Inst. of Tech., 17 October 1952)] coded five different methods for the Whirlwind computer, and made best-case and worst-case analyses of each program. When sorting one hundred 15-bit words on an 8-bit key, he found that the fastest method was to use a 256-word table, storing each record into a unique position corresponding to its key, then compressing the table. But this technique had an obvious disadvantage, since it would eliminate a record whenever a subsequent one had the same key. The other four methods he analyzed were ranked as follows: Straight two-way merging beat radix-2 sorting beat straight selection beat bubble sort.

Goldenberg's results were extended by Harold H. Seward in his 1954 Master's thesis ["Information sorting in the application of electronic digital computers to business operations," Digital Computer Lab. report R-232 (Mass. Inst. of Tech., 24 May 1954; 60 pages)]. Seward introduced the ideas of distribution counting and replacement selection; he showed that the first run in a random permutation has an average length of $e-1$; and he analyzed external sorting as well as internal sorting, on various types of bulk memories as well as tapes.

An even more noteworthy thesis — a Ph.D. thesis in fact — was written by Howard B. Demuth in 1956 ["Electronic Data Sorting" (Stanford University, October 1956), 92 pages; *IEEE Trans.* **C-34** (1985), 296–310]. This work helped to lay the foundations of computational complexity theory. It considered three abstract models of the sorting problem, using cyclic, linear, and random-access memories; and optimal or near-optimal methods were developed for each model. (See exercise 5.3.4–68.) Although no practical consequences flowed immediately from Demuth's thesis, it established important ideas about how to link theory with practice.

Thus the history of sorting has been closely associated with many "firsts" in computing: the first data-processing machines, the first stored programs, the first software, the first buffering methods, the first work on algorithmic analysis and computational complexity.

None of the computer-related documents mentioned so far actually appeared in the "open literature"; in fact, most of the early history of computing appears in comparatively inaccessible reports, because comparatively few people were involved with computers at the time. Literature about sorting finally broke into print in 1955–1956, in the form of three major survey articles.

The first paper was prepared by J. C. Hosken [*Proc. Eastern Joint Computer Conference* **8** (1955), 39–55]. He began with an astute observation: "To lower costs per unit of output, people usually increase the size of their operations. But under these conditions, the unit cost of sorting, instead of falling, rises." Hosken surveyed all the available special-purpose equipment then being marketed, as well as the methods of sorting on computers. His bibliography of 54 items was based mostly on manufacturers' brochures.

The comprehensive paper "Sorting on Electronic Computer Systems" by E. H. Friend [*JACM* **3** (1956), 134–168] was a major milestone in the development of sorting. Although numerous techniques have been developed since 1956, this paper is still remarkably up-to-date in many respects. Friend gave careful descriptions of quite a few internal and external sorting algorithms, and he paid special attention to buffering techniques and the characteristics of magnetic tape units. He introduced some new methods (for example, tree selection, amphisbaenic sorting, and forecasting), and developed some of the mathematical properties of the older methods.

The third survey of sorting to appear about this time was prepared by D. W. Davies [*Proc. Inst. Elect. Engineers* **103B**, Supplement 1 (1956), 87–93]. In the following years several other notable surveys were published, by D. A. Bell [*Comp. J.* **1** (1958), 71–77]; A. S. Douglas [*Comp. J.* **2** (1959), 1–9]; D. D. McCracken, H. Weiss, and T. Lee [*Programming Business Computers* (New York: Wiley, 1959), Chapter 15, pages 298–332]; I. Flores [*JACM* **8** (1961), 41–80]; K. E. Iverson [*A Programming Language* (New York: Wiley, 1962), Chapter 6, 176–245]; C. C. Gotlieb [*CACM* **6** (1963), 194–201]; T. N. Hibbard [*CACM* **6** (1963), 206–213]; M. A. Goetz [*Digital Computer User's Handbook*, edited by M. Klerer and G. A. Korn (New York: McGraw–Hill, 1967), Chapter 1.10, pages 1.292–1.320]. A symposium on sorting was sponsored by ACM in November 1962; most of the papers presented at that symposium were published in the May 1963 issue of *CACM*, and they constitute a good representation of the state of the art at that time. C. C. Gotlieb's survey of contemporary sort generators,

T. N. Hibbard's survey of minimal storage internal sorting, and G. U. Hubbard's early exploration of disk file sorting are particularly noteworthy articles in this collection.

New sorting methods were being discovered throughout this period: Address calculation (1956), merge insertion (1959), radix exchange (1959), cascade merge (1959), shellsort (1959), polyphase merge (1960), tree insertion (1960), oscillating sort (1962), Hoare's quicksort (1962), Williams's heapsort (1964), Batcher's merge exchange (1964). The history of each individual algorithm has been traced in the particular section of this chapter where that method is described. The late 1960s saw an intensive development of the corresponding theory.

A complete bibliography of all papers on sorting examined by the author as this chapter was first being written, compiled with the help of R. L. Rivest, appeared in *Computing Reviews* **13** (1972), 283–289.

Later developments. Dozens of sorting algorithms have been invented since 1970, although nearly all of them are variations on earlier themes. *Multikey quicksort*, which is discussed in the answer to exercise 5.2.2–30, is an excellent example of such more recent methods.

Another trend, primarily of theoretical interest so far, has been to study sorting schemes that are *adaptive*, in the sense that they are guaranteed to run faster when the input is already pretty much in order according to various criteria. See, for example, H. Mannila, *IEEE Transactions* **C-34** (1985), 318–325; V. Estivill-Castro and D. Wood, *Computing Surveys* **24** (1992), 441–476; C. Levcopoulos and O. Petersson, *Journal of Algorithms* **14** (1993), 395–413; A. Moffat, G. Eddy, and O. Petersson, *Software Practice & Experience* **26** (1996), 781–797.

Changes in computer hardware have prompted many interesting studies of the efficiency of sorting algorithms when the cost criteria change; see, for example, the discussion of virtual memory in exercise 5.4.9–20. The effect of hardware caches on internal sorting has been studied by A. LaMarca and R. E. Ladner, *J. Algorithms* **31** (1999), 66–104. One of their conclusions is that step Q9 of Algorithm 5.2.2Q is a bad idea on modern machines (although it worked well on traditional computers like MIX): Instead of finishing quicksort with a straight insertion sort, it is now better to sort the short subfiles earlier, while their keys are still in the cache.

What is the current state of the art for sorting large amounts of data? One popular benchmark since 1985 has been the task of sorting one million 100-character records that have uniformly random 10-character keys. The input and output are supposed to reside on disk, and the objective is to minimize the total elapsed time, including the time it takes to launch the program. R. C. Agarwal [*SIGMOD Record* **25**, 2 (June 1996), 240–246] used a desktop RISC computer, the IBM RS/6000 model 39H, to implement radix sorting with files that were striped on 8 disk units, and he finished this task in 5.1 seconds. Input/output was the main bottleneck; indeed, the processor needed only 0.6 seconds to control the actual sorting! Even faster times have been achieved when several processors are

available: A network of 32 UltraSPARC I workstations, each with two internal
disks, can sort a million records in 2.41 seconds using a hybrid method called
NOW-Sort [A. C. Arpaci-Dusseau, R. H. Arpaci-Dusseau, D. E. Culler, J. M.
Hellerstein, and D. A. Patterson, *SIGMOD Record* **26**, 2 (June 1997), 243–254].

Such advances mean that the million-record benchmark has become mostly
a test of startup and shutdown time; larger data sets are needed to give more
meaningful results. For example, the present world record for *terabyte sorting* —
10^{10} records of 100 characters each — is 2.5 hours, achieved in September 1997 on
a Silicon Graphics Origin2000 system with 32 processors, 8 gigabytes of internal
memory, and 559 disks of 4 gigabytes each. This record was set by a commercially
available sorting routine called Nsort™, developed by C. Nyberg, C. Koester, and
J. Gray using methods that have not yet been published.

Perhaps even the terabyte benchmark will be considered too small some day.
The best current candidate for a benchmark that will live forever is *MinuteSort*:
How many 100-character records can be sorted in 60 seconds? As this book
went to press, the current record holder for this task was NOW-Sort; 95 workstations needed only 59.21 seconds to put 90.25 million records into order, on 30
March 1997. But present-day methods are not yet pushing up against any truly
fundamental limitations on speed.

In summary, the problem of efficient sorting remains just as fascinating today
as it ever was.

EXERCISES

1. [*05*] Summarize the contents of this chapter by stating a generalization of Theorem 5.4.6A.

2. [*20*] Based on the information in Table 1, what is the best list-sorting method for
six-digit keys, for use on the MIX computer?

3. [*37*] (*Stable sorting in minimum storage.*) A sorting algorithm is said to require
minimum storage if it uses only $O((\log N)^2)$ bits of memory space for its variables
besides the space needed to store the N records. The algorithm must be general in
the sense that it works for all N, not just for a particular value of N, assuming that
a sufficient amount of random access memory has been made available whenever the
algorithm is actually called upon to sort.

Many of the sorting methods we have studied violate this minimum-storage requirement; in particular, the use of N link fields is forbidden. Quicksort (Algorithm
5.2.2Q) satisfies the minimum-storage requirement, but its worst case running time is
proportional to N^2. Heapsort (Algorithm 5.2.3H) is the only $O(N \log N)$ algorithm we
have studied that uses minimum storage, although another such algorithm could be
formulated using the idea of exercise 5.2.4–18.

The fastest general algorithm we have considered that sorts keys in a *stable* manner
is the list merge sort (Algorithm 5.2.4L), but it does not use minimum storage. In fact,
the only stable minimum-storage sorting algorithms we have seen are $\Omega(N^2)$ methods
(straight insertion, bubble sorting, and a variant of straight selection).

Design a stable minimum-storage sorting algorithm that needs only $O(N(\log N)^2)$
units of time in its worst case. [*Hint:* It is possible to do stable minimum-storage merging — namely, sorting when there are at most two runs — in $O(N \log N)$ units of time.]

▶ **4.** [*28*] A sorting algorithm is called *parsimonious* if it makes decisions entirely by comparing keys, and if it never makes a comparison whose outcome could have been predicted from the results of previous comparisons. Which of the methods listed in Table 1 are parsimonious?

5. [*46*] It is much more difficult to sort nonrandom data with numerous equal keys than to sort uniformly random data. Devise a sorting benchmark that (i) is interesting now and will probably be interesting 100 years from now; (ii) does not involve uniformly random keys; and (iii) does not use data sets that change with time.

I shall have accomplished my purpose if I have sorted and put in logical order the gist of the great volume of material which has been generated about sorting over the past few years.

— J. C. HOSKEN (1955)

CHAPTER SIX

SEARCHING

Let's look at the record.
— AL SMITH (1928)

THIS CHAPTER might have been given the more pretentious title "Storage and Retrieval of Information"; on the other hand, it might simply have been called "Table Look-Up." We are concerned with the process of collecting information in a computer's memory, in such a way that the information can subsequently be recovered as quickly as possible. Sometimes we are confronted with more data than we can really use, and it may be wisest to forget and to destroy most of it; but at other times it is important to retain and organize the given facts in such a way that fast retrieval is possible.

Most of this chapter is devoted to the study of a very simple search problem: how to find the data that has been stored with a given identification. For example, in a numerical application we might want to find $f(x)$, given x and a table of the values of f; in a nonnumerical application, we might want to find the English translation of a given Russian word.

In general, we shall suppose that a set of N records has been stored, and the problem is to locate the appropriate one. As in the case of sorting, we assume that each record includes a special field called its *key*; this terminology is especially appropriate, because many people spend a great deal of time every day searching for their keys. We generally require the N keys to be distinct, so that each key uniquely identifies its record. The collection of all records is called a *table* or *file*, where the word "table" is usually used to indicate a small file, and "file" is usually used to indicate a large table. A large file or a group of files is frequently called a *database*.

Algorithms for searching are presented with a so-called *argument*, K, and the problem is to find which record has K as its key. After the search is complete, two possibilities can arise: Either the search was *successful*, having located the unique record containing K; or it was *unsuccessful*, having determined that K is nowhere to be found. After an unsuccessful search it is sometime desirable to enter a new record, containing K, into the table; a method that does this is called a *search-and-insertion* algorithm. Some hardware devices known as *associative memories* solve the search problem automatically, in a way that might resemble the functioning of a human brain; but we shall study techniques for searching on a conventional general-purpose digital computer.

Although the goal of searching is to find the information stored in the record associated with K, the algorithms in this chapter generally ignore everything but the keys themselves. In practice we can find the associated data once we have located K; for example, if K appears in location TABLE $+ i$, the associated data (or a pointer to it) might be in location TABLE $+ i + 1$, or in DATA $+ i$, etc. It is therefore convenient to gloss over the details of what should be done after K has been successfully found.

Searching is the most time-consuming part of many programs, and the substitution of a good search method for a bad one often leads to a substantial increase in speed. In fact we can often arrange the data or the data structure so that searching is eliminated entirely, by ensuring that we always know just where to find the information we need. Linked memory is a common way to achieve this; for example, a doubly linked list makes it unnecessary to search for the predecessor or successor of a given item. Another way to avoid searching occurs if we are allowed to choose the keys freely, since we might as well let them be the numbers $\{1, 2, \ldots, N\}$; then the record containing K can simply be placed in location TABLE $+ K$. Both of these techniques were used to eliminate searching from the topological sorting algorithm discussed in Section 2.2.3. However, searches would have been necessary if the objects in the topological sorting algorithm had been given symbolic names instead of numbers. Efficient algorithms for searching turn out to be quite important in practice.

Search methods can be classified in several ways. We might divide them into internal versus external searching, just as we divided the sorting algorithms of Chapter 5 into internal versus external sorting. Or we might divide search methods into static versus dynamic searching, where "static" means that the contents of the table are essentially unchanging (so that it is important to minimize the search time without regard for the time required to set up the table), and "dynamic" means that the table is subject to frequent insertions and perhaps also deletions. A third possible scheme is to classify search methods according to whether they are based on comparisons between keys or on digital properties of the keys, analogous to the distinction between sorting by comparison and sorting by distribution. Finally we might divide searching into those methods that use the actual keys and those that work with transformed keys.

The organization of this chapter is essentially a combination of the latter two modes of classification. Section 6.1 considers "brute force" sequential methods of search, then Section 6.2 discusses the improvements that can be made based on comparisons between keys, using alphabetic or numeric order to govern the decisions. Section 6.3 treats digital searching, and Section 6.4 discusses an important class of methods called hashing techniques, based on arithmetic transformations of the actual keys. Each of these sections treats both internal and external searching, in both the static and the dynamic case; and each section points out the relative advantages and disadvantages of the various algorithms.

Searching and sorting are often closely related to each other. For example, consider the following problem: *Given two sets of numbers, $A = \{a_1, a_2, \ldots, a_m\}$ and $B = \{b_1, b_2, \ldots, b_n\}$, determine whether or not $A \subseteq B$.* Three solutions suggest themselves:

1. Compare each a_i sequentially with the b_j's until finding a match.

2. Sort the a's and b's, then make one sequential pass through both files, checking the appropriate condition.

3. Enter the b_j's in a table, then search for each of the a_i.

Each of these solutions is attractive for a different range of values of m and n. Solution 1 will take roughly $c_1 mn$ units of time, for some constant c_1, and solution 2 will take about $c_2(m \lg m + n \lg n)$ units, for some (larger) constant c_2. With a suitable hashing method, solution 3 will take roughly $c_3 m + c_4 n$ units of time, for some (still larger) constants c_3 and c_4. It follows that solution 1 is good for very small m and n, but solution 2 soon becomes better as m and n grow larger. Eventually solution 3 becomes preferable, until n exceeds the internal memory size; then solution 2 is usually again superior until n gets much larger still. Thus we have a situation where sorting is sometimes a good substitute for searching, and searching is sometimes a good substitute for sorting.

More complicated search problems can often be reduced to the simpler case considered here. For example, suppose that the keys are words that might be slightly misspelled; we might want to find the correct record in spite of this error. If we make two copies of the file, one in which the keys are in normal lexicographic order and another in which they are ordered from right to left (as if the words were spelled backwards), a misspelled search argument will probably agree up to half or more of its length with an entry in one of these two files. The search methods of Sections 6.2 and 6.3 can therefore be adapted to find the key that was probably intended.

A related problem has received considerable attention in connection with airline reservation systems, and in other applications involving people's names when there is a good chance that the name will be misspelled due to poor handwriting or voice transmission. The goal is to transform the argument into some code that tends to bring together all variants of the same name. The following contemporary form of the "Soundex" method, a technique that was originally developed by Margaret K. Odell and Robert C. Russell [see *U.S. Patents 1261167* (1918), *1435663* (1922)], has often been used for encoding surnames:

1. Retain the first letter of the name, and drop all occurrences of a, e, h, i, o, u, w, y in other positions.

2. Assign the following numbers to the remaining letters after the first:

b, f, p, v → 1	l → 4
c, g, j, k, q, s, x, z → 2	m, n → 5
d, t → 3	r → 6

3. If two or more letters with the same code were adjacent in the original name (before step 1), or adjacent except for intervening h's and w's, omit all but the first.

4. Convert to the form "letter, digit, digit, digit" by adding trailing zeros (if there are less than three digits), or by dropping rightmost digits (if there are more than three).

For example, the names Euler, Gauss, Hilbert, Knuth, Lloyd, Lukasiewicz, and Wachs have the respective codes E460, G200, H416, K530, L300, L222, W200. Of course this system will bring together names that are somewhat different, as well as names that are similar; the same seven codes would be obtained for Ellery, Ghosh, Heilbronn, Kant, Liddy, Lissajous, and Waugh. And on the other hand a few related names like Rogers and Rodgers, or Sinclair and St. Clair, or Tchebysheff and Chebyshev, remain separate. But by and large the Soundex code greatly increases the chance of finding a name in one of its disguises. [For further information, see C. P. Bourne and D. F. Ford, *JACM* **8** (1961), 538–552; Leon Davidson, *CACM* **5** (1962), 169–171; *Federal Population Censuses 1790–1890* (Washington, D.C.: National Archives, 1971), 90.]

When using a scheme like Soundex, we need not give up the assumption that all keys are distinct; we can make lists of all records with equivalent codes, treating each list as a unit.

Large databases tend to make the retrieval process more complex, since people often want to consider many different fields of each record as potential keys, with the ability to locate items when only part of the key information is specified. For example, given a large file about stage performers, a producer might wish to find all unemployed actresses between 25 and 30 with dancing talent and a French accent; given a large file of baseball statistics, a sportswriter may wish to determine the total number of runs scored by the Chicago White Sox in 1964, during the seventh inning of night games, against left-handed pitchers. Given a large file of data about anything, people like to ask arbitrarily complicated questions. Indeed, we might consider an entire library as a database, and a searcher may want to find everything that has been published about information retrieval. An introduction to the techniques for such *secondary key* (multi-attribute) retrieval problems appears below in Section 6.5.

Before entering into a detailed study of searching, it may be helpful to put things in historical perspective. During the pre-computer era, many books of logarithm tables, trigonometry tables, etc., were compiled, so that mathematical calculations could be replaced by searching. Eventually these tables were transferred to punched cards, and used for scientific problems in connection with collators, sorters, and duplicating punch machines. But when stored-program computers were introduced, it soon became apparent that it was now cheaper to recompute $\log x$ or $\cos x$ each time, instead of looking up the answer in a table.

Although the problem of sorting received considerable attention already in the earliest days of computers, comparatively little was done about algorithms for searching. With small internal memories, and with nothing but sequential media like tapes for storing large files, searching was either trivially easy or almost impossible.

But the development of larger and larger random-access memories during the 1950s eventually led to the recognition that searching was an interesting problem in its own right. After years of complaining about the limited amounts of space in the early machines, programmers were suddenly confronted with larger amounts of memory than they knew how to use efficiently.

The first surveys of the searching problem were published by A. I. Dumey, *Computers & Automation* **5**, 12 (December 1956), 6–9; W. W. Peterson, *IBM J. Research & Development* **1** (1957), 130–146; A. D. Booth, *Information and Control* **1** (1958), 159–164; A. S. Douglas, *Comp. J.* **2** (1959), 1–9. More extensive treatments were given later by Kenneth E. Iverson, *A Programming Language* (New York: Wiley, 1962), 133–158, and by Werner Buchholz, *IBM Systems J.* **2** (1963), 86–111.

During the early 1960s, a number of interesting new search procedures based on tree structures were introduced, as we shall see; and research about searching is still actively continuing at the present time.

6.1. SEQUENTIAL SEARCHING

"Begin at the beginning, and go on till you find the right key; then stop." This sequential procedure is the obvious way to search, and it makes a useful starting point for our discussion of searching because many of the more intricate algorithms are based on it. We shall see that sequential searching involves some very interesting ideas, in spite of its simplicity.

The algorithm might be formulated more precisely as follows:

Algorithm S (*Sequential search*). Given a table of records $R_1, R_2, \ldots, R_N$, whose respective keys are $K_1, K_2, \ldots, K_N$, this algorithm searches for a given argument K. We assume that $N \geq 1$.

S1. [Initialize.] Set $i \leftarrow 1$.

S2. [Compare.] If $K = K_i$, the algorithm terminates successfully.

S3. [Advance.] Increase i by 1.

S4. [End of file?] If $i \leq N$, go back to S2. Otherwise the algorithm terminates unsuccessfully. ∎

Notice that this algorithm can terminate in two different ways, *successfully* (having located the desired key) or *unsuccessfully* (having established that the given argument is not present in the table). The same will be true of most other algorithms in this chapter.

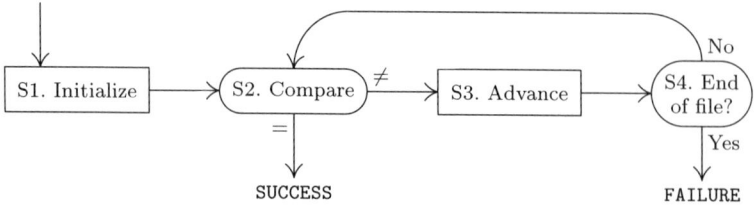

Fig. 1. Sequential or "house-to-house" search.

A MIX program can be written down immediately.

Program S (*Sequential search*). Assume that K_i appears in location KEY $+ i$, and that the remainder of record R_i appears in location INFO $+ i$. The following program uses rA $\equiv K$, rI1 $\equiv i - N$.

01	START	LDA	K	1	*S1. Initialize.*
02		ENT1	1-N	1	$i \leftarrow 1$.
03	2H	CMPA	KEY+N,1	C	*S2. Compare.*
04		JE	SUCCESS	C	Exit if $K = K_i$.
05		INC1	1	$C - S$	*S3. Advance.*
06		J1NP	2B	$C - S$	*S4. End of file?*
07	FAILURE	EQU	*	$1 - S$	Exit if not in table.

At location SUCCESS, the instruction "LDA INFO+N,1" will now bring the desired information into rA. ∎

The analysis of this program is straightforward; it shows that the running time of Algorithm S depends on two things,

$$C = \text{the number of key comparisons;}$$
$$S = 1 \text{ if successful, 0 if unsuccessful.} \tag{1}$$

Program S takes $5C - 2S + 3$ units of time. If the search successfully finds $K = K_i$, we have $C = i$, $S = 1$; hence the total time is $(5i + 1)u$. On the other hand if the search is unsuccessful, we have $C = N$, $S = 0$, for a total time of $(5N + 3)u$. If every input key occurs with equal probability, the average value of C in a successful search will be

$$\frac{1 + 2 + \cdots + N}{N} = \frac{N + 1}{2}; \tag{2}$$

the standard deviation is, of course, rather large, about $0.289N$ (see exercise 1).

The algorithm above is surely familiar to all programmers. But too few people know that it is *not* always the right way to do a sequential search! A straightforward change makes the algorithm faster, unless the list of records is quite short:

Algorithm Q (*Quick sequential search*). This algorithm is the same as Algorithm S, except that it assumes the presence of a dummy record R_{N+1} at the end of the file.

Q1. [Initialize.] Set $i \leftarrow 1$, and set $K_{N+1} \leftarrow K$.

Q2. [Compare.] If $K = K_i$, go to Q4.

Q3. [Advance.] Increase i by 1 and return to Q2.

Q4. [End of file?] If $i \leq N$, the algorithm terminates successfully; otherwise it terminates unsuccessfully $(i = N + 1)$. ∎

Program Q (*Quick sequential search*). rA $\equiv K$, rI1 $\equiv i - N$.

01	START	LDA	K	1	*Q1. Initialize.*
02		STA	KEY+N+1	1	$K_{N+1} \leftarrow K$.

```
03              ENT1  -N              1          i ← 0.
04              INC1  1          C + 1 − S   Q3. Advance.
05              CMPA  KEY+N,1    C + 1 − S   Q2. Compare.
06              JNE   *-2        C + 1 − S   To Q3 if Kᵢ ≠ K.
07              J1NP  SUCCESS         1        Q4. End of file?
08  FAILURE EQU  *              1 − S        Exit if not in table.  ▌
```

In terms of the quantities C and S in the analysis of Program S, the running
time has decreased to $(4C - 4S + 10)u$; this is an improvement whenever $C \geq 6$
in a successful search, and whenever $N \geq 8$ in an unsuccessful search.

The transition from Algorithm S to Algorithm Q makes use of an important speed-up principle: When an inner loop of a program tests two or more
conditions, we should try to reduce the testing to just one condition.

Another technique will make Program Q *still* faster.

Program Q′ (*Quicker sequential search*). rA ≡ K, rI1 ≡ $i - N$.

```
01  START  LDA  K                 1              Q1. Initialize.
02         STA  KEY+N+1           1              K_{N+1} ← K.
03         ENT1 -1-N              1              i ← −1.
04  3H     INC1 2          ⌊(C − S + 2)/2⌋   Q3. Advance. (twice)
05         CMPA KEY+N,1    ⌊(C − S + 2)/2⌋   Q2. Compare.
06         JE   4F         ⌊(C − S + 2)/2⌋   To Q4 if K = Kᵢ.
07         CMPA KEY+N+1,1  ⌊(C − S + 1)/2⌋   Q2. Compare. (next)
08         JNE  3B         ⌊(C − S + 1)/2⌋   To Q3 if K ≠ K_{i+1}.
09         INC1 1          (C − S) mod 2     Advance i.
10  4H     J1NP SUCCESS           1          Q4. End of file?
11  FAILURE EQU  *               1 − S       Exit if not in table.  ▌
```

The inner loop has been duplicated; this avoids about half of the "$i \leftarrow i + 1$"
instructions, so it reduces the running time to

$$3.5C - 3.5S + 10 + \frac{(C - S) \bmod 2}{2}$$

units. We have saved 30 percent of the running time of Program S, when large
tables are being searched; many existing programs can be improved in this way.
The same ideas apply to programming in high-level languages. [See, for example,
D. E. Knuth, *Computing Surveys* **6** (1974), 266–269.]

A slight variation of the algorithm is appropriate if we know that the keys
are in increasing order:

Algorithm T (*Sequential search in ordered table*). Given a table of records
$R_1, R_2, \ldots, R_N$ whose keys are in increasing order $K_1 < K_2 < \cdots < K_N$,
this algorithm searches for a given argument K. For convenience and speed,
the algorithm assumes that there is a dummy record R_{N+1} whose key value is
$K_{N+1} = \infty > K$.

T1. [Initialize.] Set $i \leftarrow 1$.

T2. [Compare.] If $K \leq K_i$, go to T4.

T3. [Advance.] Increase i by 1 and return to T2.

T4. [Equality?] If $K = K_i$, the algorithm terminates successfully. Otherwise it terminates unsuccessfully. ∎

If all input keys are equally likely, this algorithm takes essentially the same average time as Algorithm Q, for a successful search. But unsuccessful searches are performed about twice as fast, since the absence of a record can be established more quickly.

Each of the algorithms above uses subscripts to denote the table entries. It is convenient to describe the methods in terms of these subscripts, but the same search procedures can be used for tables that have a *linked* representation, since the data is being traversed sequentially. (See exercises 2, 3, and 4.)

Frequency of access. So far we have been assuming that every argument occurs as often as every other. This is not always a realistic assumption; in a general situation, key K_j will occur with probability p_j, where $p_1 + p_2 + \cdots + p_N = 1$. The time required to do a successful search is essentially proportional to the number of comparisons, C, which now has the average value

$$\bar{C}_N = p_1 + 2p_2 + \cdots + Np_N. \tag{3}$$

If we have the option of putting the records into the table in any desired order, this quantity $\bar{C}_N$ is smallest when

$$p_1 \geq p_2 \geq \cdots \geq p_N, \tag{4}$$

that is, when the most frequently used records appear near the beginning.

Let's look at several probability distributions, in order to see how much of a saving is possible when the records are arranged in the optimal manner specified in (4). If $p_1 = p_2 = \cdots = p_N = 1/N$, formula (3) reduces to $\bar{C}_N = (N+1)/2$; we have already derived this in Eq. (2). Suppose, on the other hand, that

$$p_1 = \frac{1}{2}, \quad p_2 = \frac{1}{4}, \quad \ldots, \quad p_{N-1} = \frac{1}{2^{N-1}}, \quad p_N = \frac{1}{2^{N-1}}. \tag{5}$$

Then $\bar{C}_N = 2 - 2^{1-N}$, by exercise 7; the average number of comparisons is *less than two*, for this distribution, if the records appear in the proper order within the table.

Another probability distribution that suggests itself is

$$p_1 = Nc, \quad p_2 = (N-1)c, \quad \ldots, \quad p_N = c, \quad \text{where } c = \frac{2}{N(N+1)}. \tag{6}$$

This wedge-shaped distribution is not as dramatic a departure from uniformity as (5). In this case we find

$$\bar{C}_N = c \sum_{k=1}^{N} k(N+1-k) = \frac{N+2}{3}; \tag{7}$$

the optimum arrangement saves about one-third of the search time that would have been obtained if the records had appeared in random order.

Of course the probability distributions in (5) and (6) are rather artificial, and they may never be a very good approximation to reality. A more typical sequence of probabilities, called "Zipf's law," has

$$p_1 = c/1, \quad p_2 = c/2, \quad \ldots, \quad p_N = c/N, \qquad \text{where } c = 1/H_N. \qquad (8)$$

This distribution was popularized by G. K. Zipf, who observed that the nth most common word in natural language text seems to occur with a frequency approximately proportional to $1/n$. [*The Psycho-Biology of Language* (Boston, Mass.: Houghton Mifflin, 1935); *Human Behavior and the Principle of Least Effort* (Reading, Mass.: Addison–Wesley, 1949).] He observed the same phenomenon in census tables, when metropolitan areas are ranked in order of decreasing population. If Zipf's law governs the frequency of the keys in a table, we have immediately

$$\bar{C}_N = N/H_N; \qquad (9)$$

searching such a file is about $\frac{1}{2} \ln N$ times faster than searching the same file with randomly ordered records. [See A. D. Booth, L. Brandwood, and J. P. Cleave, *Mechanical Resolution of Linguistic Problems* (New York: Academic Press, 1958), 79.]

Another approximation to realistic distributions is the "80-20" rule of thumb that has commonly been observed in commercial applications [see, for example, W. P. Heising, *IBM Systems J.* **2** (1963), 114–115]. This rule states that 80 percent of the transactions deal with the most active 20 percent of a file; and the same rule applies in fractal fashion to the top 20 percent, so that 64 percent of the transactions deal with the most active 4 percent, etc. In other words,

$$\frac{p_1 + p_2 + \cdots + p_{.20n}}{p_1 + p_2 + p_3 + \cdots + p_n} \approx .80 \qquad \text{for all } n. \qquad (10)$$

One distribution that satisfies this rule exactly whenever n is a multiple of 5 is

$$p_1 = c, \quad p_2 = (2^\theta - 1)c, \quad p_3 = (3^\theta - 2^\theta)c, \quad \ldots, \quad p_N = \left(N^\theta - (N-1)^\theta\right)c, \quad (11)$$

where

$$c = 1/N^\theta, \qquad \theta = \frac{\log .80}{\log .20} \approx 0.1386, \qquad (12)$$

since $p_1 + p_2 + \cdots + p_n = cn^\theta$ for all n in this case. It is not especially easy to work with the probabilities in (11); we have, however, $n^\theta - (n-1)^\theta = \theta n^{\theta-1}\left(1 + O(1/n)\right)$, so there is a simpler distribution that approximately fulfills the 80-20 rule, namely

$$p_1 = c/1^{1-\theta}, \quad p_2 = c/2^{1-\theta}, \quad \ldots, \quad p_N = c/N^{1-\theta}, \qquad \text{where } c = 1/H_N^{(1-\theta)}. \quad (13)$$

Here $\theta = \log .80 / \log .20$ as before, and $H_N^{(s)}$ is the Nth harmonic number of order s, namely $1^{-s} + 2^{-s} + \cdots + N^{-s}$. Notice that this probability distribution is very similar to that of Zipf's law (8); as θ varies from 1 to 0, the probabilities vary from a uniform distribution to a Zipfian one. Applying (3) to (13) yields

$$\bar{C}_N = H_N^{(-\theta)}/H_N^{(1-\theta)} = \frac{\theta N}{\theta+1} + O(N^{1-\theta}) \approx 0.122N \tag{14}$$

as the mean number of comparisons for the 80-20 law (see exercise 8).

A study of word frequencies carried out by E. S. Schwartz [see the interesting graph on page 422 of *JACM* **10** (1963)] suggests that distribution (13) with a slightly *negative* value of θ gives a better fit to the data than Zipf's law (8). In this case the mean value

$$\bar{C}_N = H_N^{(-\theta)}/H_N^{(1-\theta)} = \frac{N^{1+\theta}}{(1+\theta)\zeta(1-\theta)} + O(N^{1+2\theta}) \tag{15}$$

is substantially smaller than (9) as $N \to \infty$.

Distributions like (11) and (13) were first studied by Vilfredo Pareto in connection with disparities of personal income and wealth [*Cours d'Économie Politique* **2** (Lausanne: Rouge, 1897), 304–312]. If p_k is proportional to the wealth of the kth richest individual, the probability that a person's wealth exceeds or equals x times the wealth of the poorest individual is k/N when $x = p_k/p_N$. Thus, when $p_k = ck^{\theta-1}$ and $x = (k/N)^{\theta-1}$, the stated probability is $x^{-1/(1-\theta)}$; this is now called a *Pareto distribution* with parameter $1/(1-\theta)$.

Curiously, Pareto didn't understand his own distribution; he believed that a value of θ near 0 would correspond to a more egalitarian society than a value near 1! His error was corrected by Corrado Gini [*Atti della III Riunione della Società Italiana per il Progresso delle Scienze* (1910), reprinted in his *Memorie di Metodologia Statistica* **1** (Rome: 1955), 3–120], who was the first person to formulate and explain the significance of ratios like the 80-20 law (10). People still tend to misunderstand such distributions; they often speak about a "75-25 law" or a "90-10 law" as if an a-b law makes sense only when $a+b = 100$, while (12) shows that the sum $80 + 20$ is quite irrelevant.

Another discrete distribution analogous to (11) and (13) was introduced by G. Udny Yule when he studied the increase in biological species as a function of time, assuming various models of evolution [*Philos. Trans.* **B213** (1924), 21–87]. Yule's distribution applies when $\theta < 2$:

$$p_1 = c,\ p_2 = \frac{c}{2-\theta},\ p_3 = \frac{2c}{(3-\theta)(2-\theta)},\ \dots,\ p_N = \frac{(N-1)!\,c}{(N-\theta)\dots(2-\theta)} = \frac{c}{\binom{N-\theta}{N-1}};$$

$$c = \frac{\theta}{1-\theta}\frac{\binom{N-\theta}{N}}{1-\binom{N-\theta}{N}}. \tag{16}$$

The limiting value $c = 1/H_N$ or $c = 1/N$ is used when $\theta = 0$ or $\theta = 1$.

A "self-organizing" file. These calculations with probabilities are very nice, but in most cases we don't know what the probabilities are. We could keep a count in each record of how often it has been accessed, reallocating the records on the basis of those counts; the formulas derived above suggest that this procedure would often lead to a worthwhile savings. But we probably don't want to devote so much memory space to the count fields, since we can make better use of that memory by using one of the nonsequential search techniques that are explained later in this chapter.

A simple scheme, which has been in use for many years although its origin is unknown, can be used to keep the records in a pretty good order without auxiliary count fields: Whenever a record has been successfully located, it is moved to the front of the table.

The idea behind this "self-organizing" technique is that the oft-used items will tend to be located fairly near the beginning of the table, when we need them. If we assume that the N keys occur with respective probabilities $\{p_1, p_2, \ldots, p_N\}$, with each search being completely *independent* of previous searches, it can be shown that the average number of comparisons needed to find an item in such a self-organizing file tends to the limiting value

$$\widetilde{C}_N = 1 + 2 \sum_{1 \le i < j \le N} \frac{p_i p_j}{p_i + p_j} = \frac{1}{2} + \sum_{i,j} \frac{p_i p_j}{p_i + p_j}. \tag{17}$$

(See exercise 11.) For example, if $p_i = 1/N$ for $1 \le i \le N$, the self-organizing table is always in completely random order, and this formula reduces to the familiar expression $(N + 1)/2$ derived above. In general, the average number of comparisons (17) is always less than twice the optimal value (3), since $\widetilde{C}_N \le 1 + 2\sum_{j=1}^{N}(j-1)p_j = 2\bar{C}_N - 1$. In fact, $\widetilde{C}_N$ is always less than $\pi/2$ times the optimal value $\bar{C}_N$ [Chung, Hajela, and Seymour, *J. Comp. Syst. Sci.* **36** (1988), 148–157]; this ratio is the best possible constant in general, since it is approached when p_j is proportional to $1/j^2$.

Let us see how well the self-organizing procedure works when the key probabilities obey Zipf's law (8). We have

$$\widetilde{C}_N = \frac{1}{2} + \sum_{1 \le i, j \le N} \frac{(c/i)(c/j)}{c/i + c/j} = \frac{1}{2} + c \sum_{1 \le i, j \le N} \frac{1}{i + j}$$

$$= \frac{1}{2} + c \sum_{i=1}^{N} (H_{N+i} - H_i) = \frac{1}{2} + c \sum_{i=1}^{2N} H_i - 2c \sum_{i=1}^{N} H_i$$

$$= \tfrac{1}{2} + c\big((2N + 1)H_{2N} - 2N - 2(N + 1)H_N + 2N\big)$$

$$= \tfrac{1}{2} + c\big(N \ln 4 - \ln N + O(1)\big) \approx 2N/\lg N, \tag{18}$$

by Eqs. 1.2.7–(8) and 1.2.7–(3). This is substantially better than $\frac{1}{2}N$, when N is reasonably large, and it is only about $\ln 4 \approx 1.386$ times as many comparisons as would be obtained in the optimum arrangement; see (9).

Computational experiments involving actual compiler symbol tables indicate that the self-organizing method works even better than our formulas predict, because successive searches are not independent (small groups of keys tend to occur in bunches).

This self-organizing scheme was first analyzed by John McCabe [*Operations Research* **13** (1965), 609–618], who established (17). McCabe also introduced another interesting scheme, under which each successfully located key that is not already at the beginning of the table is simply *interchanged with the preceding key*, instead of being moved all the way to the front. He conjectured that the limiting average search time for this method, assuming independent searches, never exceeds (17). Several years later, Ronald L. Rivest proved in fact that the transposition method uses strictly *fewer* comparisons than the move-to-front method, in the long run, except of course when $N \leq 2$ or when all the nonzero probabilities are equal [*CACM* **19** (1976), 63–67]. However, convergence to the asymptotic limit is much slower than for the move-to-front heuristic, so move-to-front is better unless the process is prolonged [J. R. Bitner, *SICOMP* **8** (1979), 82–110]. Moreover, J. L. Bentley, C. C. McGeoch, D. D. Sleator, and R. E. Tarjan have proved that the move-to-front method never makes more than four times the total number of memory accesses made by any algorithm on linear lists, given any sequence of accesses whatever to the data — even if the algorithm knows the future; the frequency-count and transposition methods do not have this property [*CACM* **28** (1985), 202–208, 404–411]. See *SODA* **8** (1997), 53–62, for an interesting empirical study of more than 40 heuristics for self-organizing lists, carried out by R. Bachrach and R. El-Yaniv.

Tape searching with unequal-length records. Now let's give the problem still another twist: Suppose the table we are searching is stored on tape, and the individual records have varying lengths. For example, in an old-fashioned operating system, the "system library tape" was such a file; standard system programs such as compilers, assemblers, loading routines, and report generators were the "records" on this tape, and most user jobs would start by searching down the tape until the appropriate routine had been input. This setup makes our previous analysis of Algorithm S inapplicable, since step S3 takes a variable amount of time each time we reach it. The number of comparisons is therefore not the only criterion of interest.

Let L_i be the length of record R_i, and let p_i be the probability that this record will be sought. The average running time of the search method will now be approximately proportional to

$$p_1 L_1 + p_2 (L_1 + L_2) + \cdots + p_N (L_1 + L_2 + L_3 + \cdots + L_N). \qquad (19)$$

When $L_1 = L_2 = \cdots = L_N = 1$, this reduces to (3), the case already studied.

It seems logical to put the most frequently needed records at the beginning of the tape; but this is sometimes a bad idea! For example, assume that the tape contains just two programs, A and B, where A is needed twice as often as B but it is four times as long. Thus,

$$N = 2, \quad p_A = \tfrac{2}{3}, \quad L_A = 4, \quad p_B = \tfrac{1}{3}, \quad L_B = 1.$$

If we place A first on tape, according to the "logical" principle stated above, the average running time is $\tfrac{2}{3} \cdot 4 + \tfrac{1}{3} \cdot 5 = \tfrac{13}{3}$; but if we use an "illogical" idea, placing B first, the average running time is reduced to $\tfrac{1}{3} \cdot 1 + \tfrac{2}{3} \cdot 5 = \tfrac{11}{3}$.

The optimum arrangement of programs on a library tape may be determined as follows.

Theorem S. *Let L_i and p_i be as defined above. The arrangement of records in the table is optimal if and only if*

$$p_1/L_1 \geq p_2/L_2 \geq \cdots \geq p_N/L_N. \tag{20}$$

In other words, the minimum value of

$$p_{a_1} L_{a_1} + p_{a_2}(L_{a_1} + L_{a_2}) + \cdots + p_{a_N}(L_{a_1} + \cdots + L_{a_N}),$$

over all permutations $a_1 a_2 \ldots a_N$ of $\{1, 2, \ldots, N\}$, is equal to (19) if and only if (20) holds.

Proof. Suppose that R_i and R_{i+1} are interchanged on the tape; the cost (19) changes from

$$\cdots + p_i(L_1 + \cdots + L_{i-1} + L_i) + p_{i+1}(L_1 + \cdots + L_{i+1}) + \cdots$$

to

$$\cdots + p_{i+1}(L_1 + \cdots + L_{i-1} + L_{i+1}) + p_i(L_1 + \cdots + L_{i+1}) + \cdots,$$

a net change of $p_i L_{i+1} - p_{i+1} L_i$. Therefore if $p_i/L_i < p_{i+1}/L_{i+1}$, such an interchange will improve the average running time, and the given arrangement is not optimal. It follows that (20) holds in any optimal arrangement.

Conversely, assume that (20) holds; we need to prove that the arrangement is optimal. The argument just given shows that the arrangement is "locally optimal" in the sense that adjacent interchanges make no improvement; but there may conceivably be a long, complicated sequence of interchanges that leads to a better "global optimum." We shall consider two proofs, one that uses computer science and one that uses a mathematical trick.

First proof. Assume that (20) holds. We know that any permutation of the records can be sorted into the order $R_1 R_2 \ldots R_N$ by using a sequence of interchanges of adjacent records. Each of these interchanges replaces $\ldots R_j R_i \ldots$ by $\ldots R_i R_j \ldots$ for some $i < j$, so it decreases the search time by the nonnegative amount $p_i L_j - p_j L_i$. Therefore the order $R_1 R_2 \ldots R_N$ must have minimum search time.

Second proof. Replace each probability p_i by

$$p_i(\epsilon) = p_i + \epsilon^i - (\epsilon^1 + \epsilon^2 + \cdots + \epsilon^N)/N, \tag{21}$$

where ϵ is an extremely small positive number. When ϵ is sufficiently small, we will never have $x_1 p_1(\epsilon) + \cdots + x_N p_N(\epsilon) = y_1 p_1(\epsilon) + \cdots + y_N p_N(\epsilon)$ unless $x_1 = y_1$, $\ldots$, $x_N = y_N$; in particular, equality will not hold in (20). Consider now the $N!$ permutations of the records; at least one of them is optimum, and we know that it satisfies (20). But only one permutation satisfies (20) because there are no equalities. Therefore (20) uniquely characterizes the optimum arrangement of records in the table for the probabilities $p_i(\epsilon)$, whenever ϵ is sufficiently small. By continuity, the same arrangement must also be optimum when ϵ is set equal to zero. (This "tie-breaking" type of proof is often useful in connection with combinatorial optimization.) ∎

Theorem S is due to W. E. Smith, *Naval Research Logistics Quarterly* **3** (1956), 59–66. The exercises below contain further results about optimum file arrangements.

EXERCISES

1. [*M20*] When all the search keys are equally probable, what is the standard deviation of the number of comparisons made in a successful sequential search through a table of N records?

2. [*15*] Restate the steps of Algorithm S, using linked-memory notation instead of subscript notation. (If P points to a record in the table, assume that KEY(P) is the key, INFO(P) is the associated information, and LINK(P) is a pointer to the next record. Assume also that FIRST points to the first record, and that the last record points to Λ.)

3. [*16*] Write a MIX program for the algorithm of exercise 2. What is the running time of your program, in terms of the quantities C and S in (1)?

▶ **4.** [*17*] Does the idea of Algorithm Q carry over from subscript notation to linked-memory notation? (See exercise 2.)

5. [*20*] Program Q′ is, of course, noticeably faster than Program Q, when C is large. But are there any small values of C and S for which Program Q′ actually takes more time than Program Q?

▶ **6.** [*20*] Add three more instructions to Program Q′, reducing its running time to about $(3.33C + \text{constant})u$.

7. [*M20*] Evaluate the average number of comparisons, (3), using the "binary" probability distribution (5).

8. [*HM22*] Find an asymptotic series for $H_n^{(x)}$ as $n \to \infty$, when $x \neq 1$.

▶ **9.** [*HM28*] The text observes that the probability distributions given by (11), (13), and (16) are roughly equivalent when $0 < \theta < 1$, and that the mean number of comparisons using (13) is $\frac{\theta}{\theta+1}N + O(N^{1-\theta})$.

    a) Is the mean number of comparisons equal to $\frac{\theta}{\theta+1}N + O(N^{1-\theta})$ also when the probabilities of (11) are used?

    b) What about (16)?

    c) How do (11) and (16) compare to (13) when $\theta < 0$?

10. [*M20*] The best arrangement of records in a sequential table is specified by (4); what is the *worst* arrangement? Show that the average number of comparisons in the worst arrangement has a simple relation to the average number of comparisons in the best arrangement.

11. [*M30*] The purpose of this exercise is to analyze the limiting behavior of a self-organizing file with the move-to-front heuristic. First we need to define some notation: Let $f_m(x_1, x_2, \ldots, x_m)$ be the infinite sum of all distinct ordered products $x_{i_1} x_{i_2} \ldots x_{i_k}$ such that $1 \leq i_1, \ldots, i_k \leq m$, where each of $x_1, x_2, \ldots, x_m$ appears in every term. For example,

$$f_2(x, y) = \sum_{j,k \geq 0} (x^{1+j}y(x+y)^k + y^{1+j}x(x+y)^k) = \frac{xy}{1-x-y}\left(\frac{1}{1-x} + \frac{1}{1-y}\right).$$

Given a set X of n variables $\{x_1, \ldots, x_n\}$, let

$$P_{nm} = \sum_{1 \le j_1 < \cdots < j_m \le n} f_m(x_{j_1}, \ldots, x_{j_m}); \qquad Q_{nm} = \sum_{1 \le j_1 < \cdots < j_m \le n} \frac{1}{1 - x_{j_1} - \cdots - x_{j_m}}.$$

For example, $P_{32} = f_2(x_1, x_2) + f_2(x_1, x_3) + f_2(x_2, x_3)$ and $Q_{32} = 1/(1 - x_1 - x_2) + 1/(1 - x_1 - x_3) + 1/(1 - x_2 - x_3)$. By convention we set $P_{n0} = Q_{n0} = 1$.

a) Assume that the text's self-organizing file has been servicing requests for item R_i with probability p_i. After the system has been running a long time, show that R_i will be the mth item from the front with limiting probability $p_i P_{(N-1)(m-1)}$, where the set of variables X is $\{p_1, \ldots, p_{i-1}, p_{i+1}, \ldots, p_N\}$.

b) By summing the result of (a) for $m = 1, 2, \ldots$, we obtain the identity

$$P_{nn} + P_{n(n-1)} + \cdots + P_{n0} = Q_{nn}.$$

Prove that, consequently,

$$P_{nm} + \binom{n - m + 1}{1} P_{n(m-1)} + \cdots + \binom{n - m + m}{m} P_{n0} = Q_{nm};$$

$$Q_{nm} - \binom{n - m + 1}{1} Q_{n(m-1)} + \cdots + (-1)^m \binom{n - m + m}{m} Q_{n0} = P_{nm}.$$

c) Compute the limiting average distance $d_i = \sum_{m \ge 1} m p_i P_{(N-1)(m-1)}$ of R_i from the front of the list; then evaluate $\widetilde{C}_N = \sum_{i=1}^{N} p_i d_i$.

12. [*M23*] Use (17) to evaluate the average number of comparisons needed to search the self-organizing file when the search keys have the binary probability distribution (5).

13. [*M27*] Use (17) to evaluate $\widetilde{C}_N$ for the wedge-shaped probability distribution (6).

14. [*M21*] Given two sequences $\langle x_1, x_2, \ldots, x_n \rangle$ and $\langle y_1, y_2, \ldots, y_n \rangle$ of real numbers, what permutation $a_1 a_2 \ldots a_n$ of the subscripts will make $\sum_i x_i y_{a_i}$ a maximum? What permutation will make it a minimum?

▶ **15.** [*M22*] The text shows how to arrange programs optimally on a system library tape, when only one program is being sought. But another set of assumptions is more appropriate for a *subroutine* library tape, from which we may wish to load various subroutines called for in a user's program.

For this case let us suppose that subroutine j is desired with probability P_j, independently of whether or not other subroutines are desired. Then, for example, the probability that no subroutines at all are needed is $(1 - P_1)(1 - P_2) \ldots (1 - P_N)$; and the probability that the search will end just after loading the jth subroutine is $P_j(1 - P_{j+1}) \ldots (1 - P_N)$. If L_j is the length of subroutine j, the average search time will therefore be essentially proportional to

$$L_1 P_1 (1 - P_2) \ldots (1 - P_N) + (L_1 + L_2) P_2 (1 - P_3) \ldots (1 - P_N) + \cdots + (L_1 + \cdots + L_N) P_N.$$

What is the optimum arrangement of subroutines on the tape, under these assumptions?

16. [*M22*] (H. Riesel.) We often need to test whether or not n given conditions are all simultaneously true. (For example, we may want to test whether both $x > 0$ and $y < z^2$, and it is not immediately clear which condition should be tested first.) Suppose that the testing of condition j costs T_j units of time, and that the condition will be true with probability p_j, independent of the outcomes of all the other conditions. In what order should we make the tests?

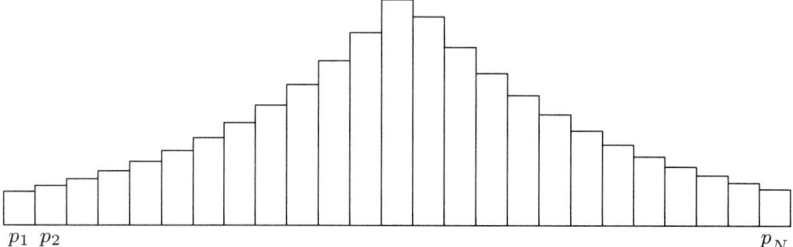

Fig. 2. An "organ-pipe arrangement" of probabilities minimizes the average seek time in a catenated search.

17. [*M23*] (J. R. Jackson.) Suppose you have to do n jobs; the jth job takes T_j units of time, and it has a *deadline* D_j. In other words, the jth job is supposed to be finished after at most D_j units of time have elapsed. What schedule $a_1 a_2 \ldots a_n$ for processing the jobs will minimize the *maximum tardiness*, namely

$$\max(T_{a_1} - D_{a_1}, T_{a_1} + T_{a_2} - D_{a_2}, \ldots, T_{a_1} + T_{a_2} + \cdots + T_{a_n} - D_{a_n})\,?$$

18. [*M30*] (*Catenated search.*) Suppose that N records are located in a linear array $R_1 \ldots R_N$, with probability p_j that record R_j will be sought. A search process is called "catenated" if each search begins where the last one left off. If consecutive searches are independent, the average time required will be $\sum_{1 \le i,j \le N} p_i p_j d(i,j)$, where $d(i,j)$ represents the amount of time to do a search that starts at position i and ends at position j. This model can be applied, for example, to disk file seek time, if $d(i,j)$ is the time needed to travel from cylinder i to cylinder j.

The object of this exercise is to characterize the optimum placement of records for catenated searches, whenever $d(i,j)$ is an increasing function of $|i - j|$, that is, whenever we have $d(i,j) = d_{|i-j|}$ for $d_1 < d_2 < \cdots < d_{N-1}$. (The value of d_0 is irrelevant.) Prove that in this case the records are optimally placed, among all $N!$ permutations, if and only if either $p_1 \le p_N \le p_2 \le p_{N-1} \le \cdots \le p_{\lfloor N/2 \rfloor + 1}$ or $p_N \le p_1 \le p_{N-1} \le p_2 \le \cdots \le p_{\lceil N/2 \rceil}$. (Thus, an "organ-pipe arrangement" of probabilities is best, as shown in Fig. 2.) *Hint:* Consider any arrangement where the respective probabilities are $q_1 q_2 \ldots q_k \, s \, r_k \ldots r_2 r_1 t_1 \ldots t_m$, for some $m \ge 0$ and $k > 0$; $N = 2k + m + 1$. Show that the rearrangement $q_1' q_2' \ldots q_k' \, s \, r_k' \ldots r_2' r_1' t_1 \ldots t_m$ is better, where $q_i' = \min(q_i, r_i)$ and $r_i' = \max(q_i, r_i)$, except when $q_i' = q_i$ and $r_i' = r_i$ for all i or when $q_i' = r_i$ and $r_i' = q_i$ and $t_j = 0$ for all i and j. The same holds true when s is not present and $N = 2k + m$.

19. [*M20*] Continuing exercise 18, what are the optimal arrangements for catenated searches when the function $d(i,j)$ has the property that $d(i,j) + d(j,i) = c$ for all $i \ne j$? [This situation occurs, for example, on tapes without read-backwards capability, when we do not know the appropriate direction to search; for $i < j$ we have, say, $d(i,j) = a + b(L_{i+1} + \cdots + L_j)$ and $d(j,i) = a + b(L_{j+1} + \cdots + L_N) + r + b(L_1 + \cdots + L_i)$, where r is the rewind time.]

20. [*M28*] Continuing exercise 18, what are the optimal arrangements for catenated searches when the function $d(i,j)$ is $\min(d_{|i-j|}, d_{n-|i-j|})$, for $d_1 < d_2 < \cdots$? [This situation occurs, for example, in a two-way linked circular list, or in a two-way shift-register storage device.]

21. [*M28*] Consider an n-dimensional cube whose vertices have coordinates $(d_1,\ldots,d_n)$ with $d_j = 0$ or 1; two vertices are called *adjacent* if they differ in exactly one coordinate. Suppose that a set of 2^n numbers $x_0 \le x_1 \le \cdots \le x_{2^n-1}$ is to be assigned to the 2^n vertices in such a way that $\sum_{i,j} |x_i - x_j|$ is minimized, where the sum is over all i and j such that x_i and x_j have been assigned to adjacent vertices. Prove that this minimum will be achieved if, for all j, x_j is assigned to the vertex whose coordinates are the binary representation of j.

▶ **22.** [*20*] Suppose you want to search a large file, not for equality but to find the 1000 records that are *closest* to a given key, in the sense that these 1000 records have the smallest values of $d(K_j, K)$ for some given distance function d. What data structure is most appropriate for such a sequential search?

Attempt the end, and never stand to doubt;
Nothing's so hard, but search will find it out.

— ROBERT HERRICK, *Seeke and finde* (1648)

6.2. SEARCHING BY COMPARISON OF KEYS

IN THIS SECTION we shall discuss search methods that are based on a linear ordering of the keys, such as alphabetic order or numeric order. After comparing the given argument K to a key K_i in the table, the search continues in three different ways, depending on whether $K < K_i$, $K = K_i$, or $K > K_i$. The sequential search methods of Section 6.1 were essentially limited to a two-way decision ($K = K_i$ versus $K \neq K_i$), but if we free ourselves from the restriction of sequential access we are able to make effective use of an order relation.

6.2.1. Searching an Ordered Table

What would you do if someone handed you a large telephone directory and told you to find the name of the person whose number is 795-6841? There is no better way to tackle this problem than to use the sequential methods of Section 6.1. (Well, you might try to dial the number and talk to the person who answers; or you might know how to obtain a special directory that is sorted by number instead of by name.) The point is that it is much easier to find an entry by the party's name, instead of by number, although the telephone directory contains all the information necessary in both cases. When a large file must be searched, sequential scanning is almost out of the question, but an ordering relation simplifies the job enormously.

With so many sorting methods at our disposal (Chapter 5), we will have little difficulty rearranging a file into order so that it may be searched conveniently. Of course, if we need to search the table only once, a sequential search would be faster than to do a complete sort of the file; but if we need to make repeated searches in the same file, we are better off having it in order. Therefore in this section we shall concentrate on methods that are appropriate for searching a table whose keys satisfy

$$K_1 < K_2 < \cdots < K_N,$$

assuming that we can easily access the key in any given position. After comparing K to K_i in such a table, we have either

	• $K < K_i$	$[R_i, R_{i+1}, \ldots, R_N$ are eliminated from consideration];
or	• $K = K_i$	[the search is done];
or	• $K > K_i$	$[R_1, R_2, \ldots, R_i$ are eliminated from consideration].

In each of these three cases, substantial progress has been made, unless i is near one of the ends of the table; this is why the ordering leads to an efficient algorithm.

Binary search. Perhaps the first such method that suggests itself is to start by comparing K to the middle key in the table; the result of this probe tells which half of the table should be searched next, and the same procedure can be used again, comparing K to the middle key of the selected half, etc. After at most about $\lg N$ comparisons, we will have found the key or we will have established

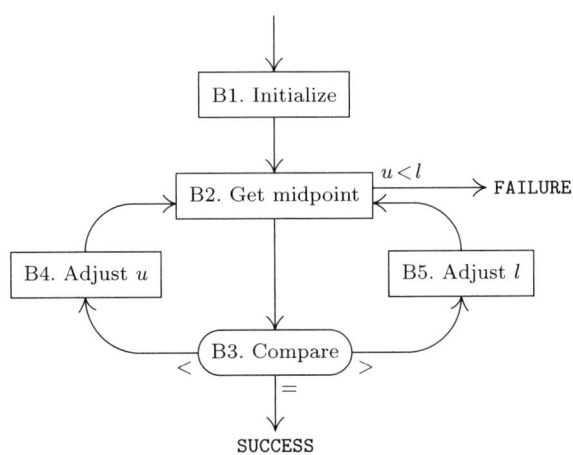

Fig. 3. Binary search.

that it is not present. This procedure is sometimes known as "logarithmic search" or "bisection," but it is most commonly called *binary search*.

Although the basic idea of binary search is comparatively straightforward, the details can be surprisingly tricky, and many good programmers have done it wrong the first few times they tried. One of the most popular correct forms of the algorithm makes use of two pointers, l and u, that indicate the current lower and upper limits for the search, as follows:

Algorithm B (*Binary search*). Given a table of records $R_1, R_2, \ldots, R_N$ whose keys are in increasing order $K_1 < K_2 < \cdots < K_N$, this algorithm searches for a given argument K.

B1. [Initialize.] Set $l \leftarrow 1$, $u \leftarrow N$.

B2. [Get midpoint.] (At this point we know that if K is in the table, it satisfies $K_l \leq K \leq K_u$. A more precise statement of the situation appears in exercise 1 below.) If $u < l$, the algorithm terminates unsuccessfully. Otherwise, set $i \leftarrow \lfloor (l+u)/2 \rfloor$, the approximate midpoint of the relevant table area.

B3. [Compare.] If $K < K_i$, go to B4; if $K > K_i$, go to B5; and if $K = K_i$, the algorithm terminates successfully.

B4. [Adjust u.] Set $u \leftarrow i - 1$ and return to B2.

B5. [Adjust l.] Set $l \leftarrow i + 1$ and return to B2. ∎

Figure 4 illustrates two cases of this binary search algorithm: first to search for the argument 653, which is present in the table, and then to search for 400, which is absent. The brackets indicate l and u, and the underlined key represents K_i. In both examples the search terminates after making four comparisons.

a) Searching for 653:

[061 087 154 170 275   426 503 <u>509</u> 512 612 653   677 703 765 897 908]
061 087 154 170 275   426 503 509 [512 612 653   <u>677</u> 703 765 897 908]
061 087 154 170 275   426 503 509 [512 <u>612</u> 653] 677 703 765 897 908
061 087 154 170 275   426 503 509 512 612 [653] 677 703 765 897 908

b) Searching for 400:

[061 087 154 170 275   426 503 <u>509</u> 512 612 653   677 703 765 897 908]
[061 087 154 <u>170</u> 275   426 503] 509 512 612 653   677 703 765 897 908
061 087 154 170 [275   <u>426</u> 503] 509 512 612 653   677 703 765 897 908
061 087 154 170 [<u>275</u>] 426 503 509 512 612 653   677 703 765 897 908
061 087 154 170 275] [426 503 509 512 612 653   677 703 765 897 908

Fig. 4. Examples of binary search.

Program B (*Binary search*). As in the programs of Section 6.1, we assume here that K_i is a full-word key appearing in location KEY$+i$. The following code uses rI1 $\equiv l$, rI2 $\equiv u$, rI3 $\equiv i$.

01	START	ENT1	1	1	*B1. Initialize.* $l \leftarrow 1$.
02		ENT2	N	1	$u \leftarrow N$.
03		JMP	2F	1	To B2.
04	5H	JE	SUCCESS	$C1$	Jump if $K = K_i$.
05		ENT1	1,3	$C1-S$	*B5. Adjust l.* $l \leftarrow i+1$.
06	2H	ENTA	0,1	$C+1-S$	*B2. Get midpoint.*
07		INCA	0,2	$C+1-S$	rA $\leftarrow l+u$.
08		SRB	1	$C+1-S$	rA $\leftarrow \lfloor$rA$/2\rfloor$. (rX changes too.)
09		STA	TEMP	$C+1-S$	
10		CMP1	TEMP	$C+1-S$	
11		JG	FAILURE	$C+1-S$	Jump if $u < l$.
12		LD3	TEMP	C	$i \leftarrow$ midpoint.
13	3H	LDA	K	C	*B3. Compare.*
14		CMPA	KEY,3	C	
15		JGE	5B	C	Jump if $K \geq K_i$.
16		ENT2	-1,3	$C2$	*B4. Adjust u.* $u \leftarrow i-1$.
17		JMP	2B	$C2$	To B2. ∎

This procedure doesn't blend with MIX quite as smoothly as the other algorithms we have seen, because MIX does not allow much arithmetic in index registers. The running time is $(18C - 10S + 12)u$, where $C = C1 + C2$ is the number of comparisons made (the number of times step B3 is performed), and $S = [$outcome is successful$]$. The operation on line 08 of this program is "shift right binary 1," which is legitimate only on binary versions of MIX; for general byte size, this instruction should be replaced by "MUL =1//2+1=", increasing the running time to $(26C - 18S + 20)u$.

A tree representation. In order to really understand what is happening in Algorithm B, our best bet is to think of the procedure as a binary decision tree, as shown in Fig. 5 for the case $N = 16$.

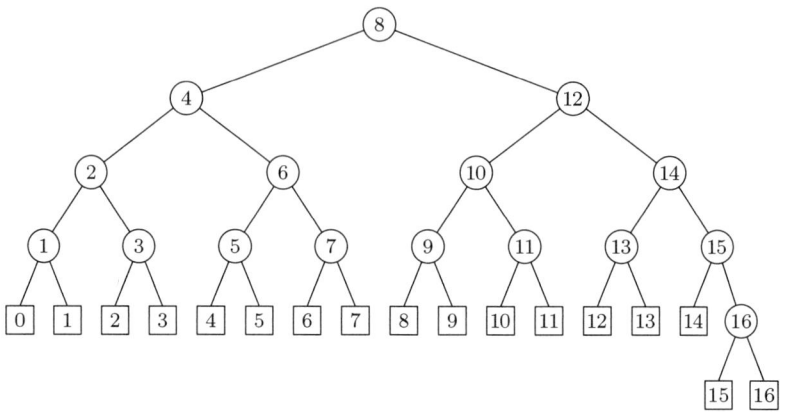

Fig. 5. A comparison tree that corresponds to binary search when $N = 16$.

When N is 16, the first comparison made by the algorithm is $K : K_8$; this is represented by the root node ⑧ in the figure. Then if $K < K_8$, the algorithm follows the left subtree, comparing K to K_4; similarly if $K > K_8$, the right subtree is used. An unsuccessful search will lead to one of the external square nodes numbered ⎕0⎕ through ⎕N⎕; for example, we reach node ⎕6⎕ if and only if $K_6 < K < K_7$.

The binary tree corresponding to a binary search on N records can be constructed as follows: If $N = 0$, the tree is simply ⎕0⎕. Otherwise the root node is

$$\left(\lceil N/2 \rceil\right),$$

the left subtree is the corresponding binary tree with $\lceil N/2 \rceil - 1$ nodes, and the right subtree is the corresponding binary tree with $\lfloor N/2 \rfloor$ nodes and with all node numbers increased by $\lceil N/2 \rceil$.

In an analogous fashion, *any* algorithm for searching an ordered table of length N by means of comparisons can be represented as an N-node binary tree in which the nodes are labeled with the numbers 1 to N (unless the algorithm makes redundant comparisons). Conversely, any binary tree corresponds to a valid method for searching an ordered table; we simply label the nodes

$$\boxed{0}\quad ①\quad \boxed{1}\quad ②\quad \boxed{2}\quad \cdots\quad \boxed{N-1}\quad ⓝ\quad \boxed{N}\qquad (1)$$

in symmetric order, from left to right.

If the search argument input to Algorithm B is K_{10}, the algorithm makes the comparisons $K > K_8$, $K < K_{12}$, $K = K_{10}$. This corresponds to the path from the root to ⑩ in Fig. 5. Similarly, the behavior of Algorithm B on other keys corresponds to the other paths leading from the root of the tree. The method of constructing the binary trees corresponding to Algorithm B therefore makes it easy to prove the following result by induction on N:

Theorem B. *If $2^{k-1} \le N < 2^k$, a successful search using Algorithm B requires* (min 1, max k) *comparisons. If $N = 2^k - 1$, an unsuccessful search requires*

k comparisons; and if $2^{k-1} \leq N < 2^k - 1$, an unsuccessful search requires either $k-1$ or k comparisons.   ∎

Further analysis of binary search. (Nonmathematical readers should skip to Eq. (4).) The tree representation shows us also how to compute the *average* number of comparisons in a simple way. Let C_N be the average number of comparisons in a successful search, assuming that each of the N keys is an equally likely argument; and let C_N' be the average number of comparisons in an *un*successful search, assuming that each of the $N + 1$ intervals between and outside the extreme values of the keys is equally likely. Then we have

$$C_N = 1 + \frac{\text{internal path length of tree}}{N}, \qquad C_N' = \frac{\text{external path length of tree}}{N + 1},$$

by the definition of internal and external path length. We saw in Eq. 2.3.4.5–(3) that the external path length is always $2N$ more than the internal path length. Hence there is a rather unexpected relationship between C_N and C_N':

$$C_N = \left(1 + \frac{1}{N}\right)C_N' - 1. \tag{2}$$

This formula, which is due to T. N. Hibbard [*JACM* **9** (1962), 16–17], holds for all search methods that correspond to binary trees; in other words, it holds for all methods that are based on nonredundant comparisons. The variance of successful-search comparisons can also be expressed in terms of the corresponding variance for unsuccessful searches (see exercise 25).

From the formulas above we can see that the "best" way to search by comparisons is one whose tree has minimum external path length, over all binary trees with N internal nodes. Fortunately it can be proved that *Algorithm B is optimum* in this sense, for all N; for we have seen (exercise 5.3.1–20) that a binary tree has minimum path length if and only if its external nodes all occur on at most two adjacent levels. It follows that the external path length of the tree corresponding to Algorithm B is

$$(N + 1)(\lfloor \lg N \rfloor + 2) - 2^{\lfloor \lg N \rfloor + 1}. \tag{3}$$

(See Eq. 5.3.1–(34).) From this formula and (2) we can compute the exact average number of comparisons, assuming that all search arguments are equally probable.

$N =$	1	2	3	4	5	6	7	8	9	10	11	12	13	14	15	16
$C_N =$	1	$1\frac{1}{2}$	$1\frac{2}{3}$	2	$2\frac{1}{5}$	$2\frac{2}{6}$	$2\frac{3}{7}$	$2\frac{5}{8}$	$2\frac{7}{9}$	$2\frac{9}{10}$	3	$3\frac{1}{12}$	$3\frac{2}{13}$	$3\frac{3}{14}$	$3\frac{4}{15}$	$3\frac{6}{16}$
$C_N' =$	1	$1\frac{2}{3}$	2	$2\frac{2}{5}$	$2\frac{4}{6}$	$2\frac{6}{7}$	3	$3\frac{2}{9}$	$3\frac{4}{10}$	$3\frac{6}{11}$	$3\frac{8}{12}$	$3\frac{10}{13}$	$3\frac{12}{14}$	$3\frac{14}{15}$	4	$4\frac{2}{17}$

In general, if $k = \lfloor \lg N \rfloor$, we have

$$
\begin{aligned}
C_N &= k + 1 - (2^{k+1} - k - 2)/N &&= \lg N - 1 + \epsilon + (k + 2)/N, \\
C_N' &= k + 2 - 2^{k+1}/(N + 1) &&= \lg(N + 1) + \epsilon'
\end{aligned}
\tag{4}
$$

where $0 \leq \epsilon, \epsilon' < 0.0861$; see Eq. 5.3.1–(35).

To summarize: Algorithm B never makes more than $\lfloor \lg N \rfloor + 1$ comparisons, and it makes about $\lg N - 1$ comparisons in an average successful search. No search method based on comparisons can do better than this. The average running time of Program B is approximately

$$(18 \lg N - 16)u \qquad \text{for a successful search,}$$
$$(18 \lg N + 12)u \qquad \text{for an unsuccessful search,} \tag{5}$$

if we assume that all outcomes of the search are equally likely.

An important variation. Instead of using three pointers l, i, and u in the search, it is tempting to use only two, namely the current position i and its rate of change, δ; after each unequal comparison, we could then set $i \leftarrow i \pm \delta$ and $\delta \leftarrow \delta/2$ (approximately). It is possible to do this, but only if extreme care is paid to the details, as in the following algorithm. Simpler approaches are doomed to failure!

Algorithm U (*Uniform binary search*). Given a table of records $R_1, R_2, \ldots, R_N$ whose keys are in increasing order $K_1 < K_2 < \cdots < K_N$, this algorithm searches for a given argument K. If N is even, the algorithm will sometimes refer to a dummy key K_0 that should be set to $-\infty$ (or any value less than K). We assume that $N \geq 1$.

U1. [Initialize.] Set $i \leftarrow \lceil N/2 \rceil$, $m \leftarrow \lfloor N/2 \rfloor$.

U2. [Compare.] If $K < K_i$, go to U3; if $K > K_i$, go to U4; and if $K = K_i$, the algorithm terminates successfully.

U3. [Decrease i.] (We have pinpointed the search to an interval that contains either m or $m-1$ records; i points just to the right of this interval.) If $m = 0$, the algorithm terminates unsuccessfully. Otherwise set $i \leftarrow i - \lceil m/2 \rceil$; then set $m \leftarrow \lfloor m/2 \rfloor$ and return to U2.

U4. [Increase i.] (We have pinpointed the search to an interval that contains either m or $m-1$ records; i points just to the left of this interval.) If $m = 0$, the algorithm terminates unsuccessfully. Otherwise set $i \leftarrow i + \lceil m/2 \rceil$; then set $m \leftarrow \lfloor m/2 \rfloor$ and return to U2. ∎

Figure 6 shows the corresponding binary tree for the search, when $N = 10$. In an unsuccessful search, the algorithm may make a redundant comparison just before termination; those nodes are shaded in the figure. We may call the search process *uniform* because the difference between the number of a node on level l and the number of its ancestor on level $l - 1$ has a constant value δ for all nodes on level l.

The theory underlying Algorithm U can be understood as follows: Suppose that we have an interval of length $n - 1$ to search; a comparison with the middle element (for n even) or with one of the two middle elements (for n odd) leaves us with two intervals of lengths $\lfloor n/2 \rfloor - 1$ and $\lceil n/2 \rceil - 1$. After repeating this process k times, we obtain 2^k intervals, of which the smallest has length $\lfloor n/2^k \rfloor - 1$ and the largest has length $\lceil n/2^k \rceil - 1$. Hence the lengths of two intervals at the same

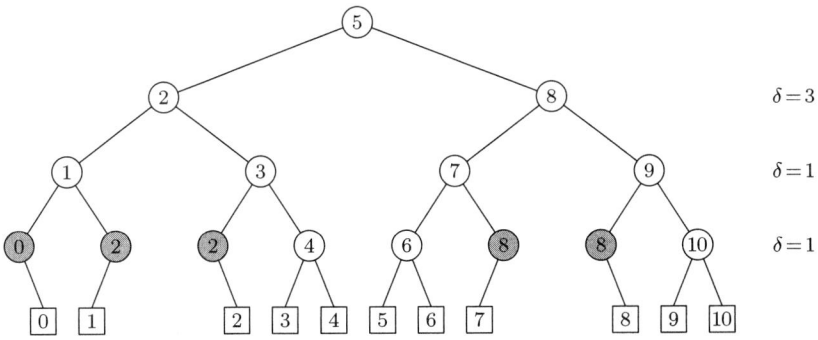

Fig. 6. The comparison tree for a "uniform" binary search, when $N = 10$.

level differ by at most unity; this makes it possible to choose an appropriate
"middle" element, without keeping track of the exact lengths.

The principal advantage of Algorithm U is that we need not maintain the
value of m at all; we need only refer to a short table of the various δ to use at
each level of the tree. Thus the algorithm reduces to the following procedure,
which is equally good on binary or decimal computers:

Algorithm C (*Uniform binary search*). This algorithm is just like Algorithm U,
but it uses an auxiliary table in place of the calculations involving m. The table
entries are

$$\text{DELTA}[j] = \left\lfloor \frac{N + 2^{j-1}}{2^j} \right\rfloor, \qquad \text{for } 1 \le j \le \lfloor \lg N \rfloor + 2. \tag{6}$$

C1. [Initialize.] Set $i \leftarrow \text{DELTA}[1]$, $j \leftarrow 2$.

C2. [Compare.] If $K < K_i$, go to C3; if $K > K_i$, go to C4; and if $K = K_i$, the
algorithm terminates successfully.

C3. [Decrease i.] If $\text{DELTA}[j] = 0$, the algorithm terminates unsuccessfully.
Otherwise, set $i \leftarrow i - \text{DELTA}[j]$, $j \leftarrow j + 1$, and go to C2.

C4. [Increase i.] If $\text{DELTA}[j] = 0$, the algorithm terminates unsuccessfully.
Otherwise, set $i \leftarrow i + \text{DELTA}[j]$, $j \leftarrow j + 1$, and go to C2. ∎

Exercise 8 proves that this algorithm refers to the artificial key $K_0 = -\infty$
only when N is even.

Program C (*Uniform binary search*). This program does the same job as
Program B, using Algorithm C with $rA \equiv K$, $rI1 \equiv i$, $rI2 \equiv j$, $rI3 \equiv \text{DELTA}[j]$.

01	START	ENT1 N+1/2	1	*C1. Initialize.* $i \leftarrow \lfloor (N+1)/2 \rfloor$.
02		ENT2 2	1	$j \leftarrow 2$.
03		LDA K	1	
04		JMP 2F	1	
05	3H	JE SUCCESS	$C1$	Jump if $K = K_i$.
06		J3Z FAILURE	$C1 - S$	Jump if $\text{DELTA}[j] = 0$.
07		DEC1 0,3	$C1 - S - A$	*C3. Decrease i.*

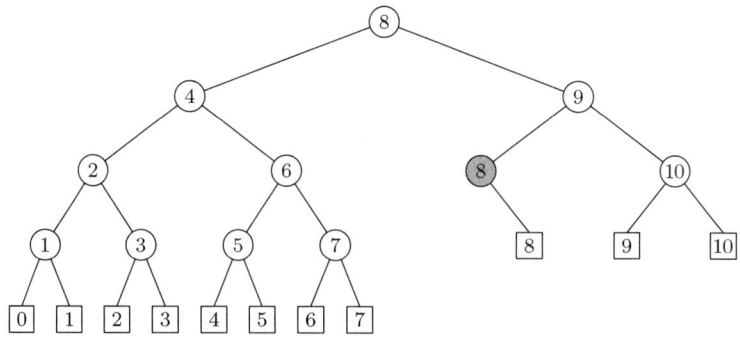

Fig. 7. The comparison tree for Shar's almost uniform search, when $N = 10$.

08	5H	INC2 1	$C-1$	$j \leftarrow j + 1$.
09	2H	LD3 DELTA,2	C	*C2. Compare.*
10		CMPA KEY,1	C	
11		JLE 3B	C	Jump if $K \leq K_i$.
12		INC1 0,3	$C2$	*C4. Increase i.*
13		J3NZ 5B	$C2$	Jump if DELTA[j] $\neq 0$.
14	FAILURE	EQU *	$1-S$	Exit if not in table. ∎

In a successful search, this algorithm corresponds to a binary tree with the same internal path length as the tree of Algorithm B, so the average number of comparisons C_N is the same as before. In an unsuccessful search, Algorithm C always makes exactly $\lfloor \lg N \rfloor + 1$ comparisons. The total running time of Program C is not quite symmetrical between left and right branches, since $C1$ is weighted more heavily than $C2$, but exercise 11 shows that we have $K < K_i$ roughly as often as $K > K_i$; hence Program C takes approximately

$$(8.5 \lg N - 6)u \qquad \text{for a successful search,}$$
$$(8.5 \lfloor \lg N \rfloor + 12)u \qquad \text{for an unsuccessful search.} \tag{7}$$

This is more than twice as fast as Program B, without using any special properties of binary computers, even though the running times (5) for Program B assume that MIX has a "shift right binary" instruction.

Another modification of binary search, suggested in 1971 by L. E. Shar, will be still faster on some computers, because it is uniform after the first step, and it requires no table. The first step is to compare K with K_i, where $i = 2^k$, $k = \lfloor \lg N \rfloor$. If $K < K_i$, we use a uniform search with the δ's equal to 2^{k-1}, 2^{k-2}, ..., 1, 0. On the other hand, if $K > K_i$ we reset i to $i' = N + 1 - 2^l$, where $l = \lceil \lg(N - 2^k + 1) \rceil$, and pretend that the first comparison was actually $K > K_{i'}$, using a uniform search with the δ's equal to 2^{l-1}, 2^{l-2}, ..., 1, 0.

Shar's method is illustrated for $N = 10$ in Fig. 7. Like the previous algorithms, it never makes more than $\lfloor \lg N \rfloor + 1$ comparisons; hence it makes at most one more than the minimum possible average number of comparisons, in spite of the fact that it occasionally goes through several redundant steps in succession (see exercise 12).

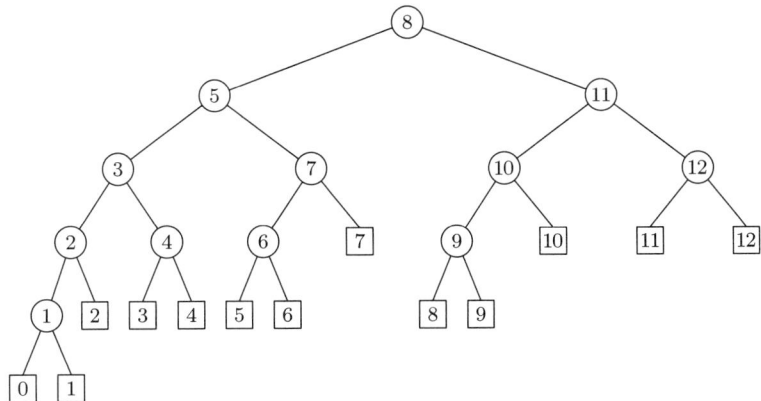

Fig. 8. The Fibonacci tree of order 6.

Still another modification of binary search, which increases the speed of *all* the methods above when N is extremely large, is discussed in exercise 23. See also exercise 24, for a method that is faster yet.

*Fibonaccian search. In the polyphase merge we have seen that the Fibonacci numbers can play a role analogous to the powers of 2. A similar phenomenon occurs in searching, where Fibonacci numbers provide us with an alternative to binary search. The resulting method is preferable on some computers, because it involves only addition and subtraction, not division by 2. The procedure we are about to discuss should be distinguished from an important numerical procedure called "Fibonacci search," which is used to locate the maximum of a unimodal function [see *Fibonacci Quarterly* **4** (1966), 265–269]; the similarity of names has led to some confusion.

The Fibonaccian search technique looks very mysterious at first glance, if we simply take the program and try to explain what is happening; it seems to work by magic. But the mystery disappears as soon as the corresponding search tree is displayed. Therefore we shall begin our study of the method by looking at *Fibonacci trees.*

Figure 8 shows the Fibonacci tree of order 6. It looks somewhat more like a real-life shrub than the other trees we have been considering, perhaps because many natural processes satisfy a Fibonacci law. In general, the Fibonacci tree of order k has $F_{k+1} - 1$ internal (circular) nodes and F_{k+1} external (square) nodes, and it is constructed as follows:

If $k = 0$ or $k = 1$, the tree is simply $\boxed{0}$.

If $k \geq 2$, the root is F_k; the left subtree is the Fibonacci tree of order $k - 1$; and the right subtree is the Fibonacci tree of order $k - 2$ with all numbers increased by F_k.

Except for the external nodes, the numbers on the two children of each internal node differ from their parent's number by the same amount, and this amount is a Fibonacci number. For example, $5 = 8 - F_4$ and $11 = 8 + F_4$ in Fig. 8. When the difference is F_j, the corresponding Fibonacci difference for the next branch on the left is F_{j-1}, while on the right it skips down to F_{j-2}. For example, $3 = 5 - F_3$ while $10 = 11 - F_2$.

If we combine these observations with an appropriate mechanism for recognizing the external nodes, we arrive at the following method:

Algorithm F (*Fibonaccian search*). Given a table of records R_1, R_2, ..., R_N whose keys are in increasing order $K_1 < K_2 < \cdots < K_N$, this algorithm searches for a given argument K.

For convenience in description, we assume that $N + 1$ is a perfect Fibonacci number, F_{k+1}. It is not difficult to make the method work for arbitrary N, if a suitable initialization is provided (see exercise 14).

F1. [Initialize.] Set $i \leftarrow F_k$, $p \leftarrow F_{k-1}$, $q \leftarrow F_{k-2}$. (Throughout the algorithm, p and q will be consecutive Fibonacci numbers.)

F2. [Compare.] If $K < K_i$, go to step F3; if $K > K_i$, go to F4; and if $K = K_i$, the algorithm terminates successfully.

F3. [Decrease i.] If $q = 0$, the algorithm terminates unsuccessfully. Otherwise set $i \leftarrow i - q$, and set $(p, q) \leftarrow (q, p-q)$; then return to F2.

F4. [Increase i.] If $p = 1$, the algorithm terminates unsuccessfully. Otherwise set $i \leftarrow i + q$, $p \leftarrow p - q$, then $q \leftarrow q - p$, and return to F2. ∎

The following MIX implementation gains speed by making two copies of the inner loop, one in which p is in rI2 and q in rI3, and one in which the registers are reversed; this simplifies step F3. In fact, the program actually keeps $p - 1$ and $q - 1$ in the registers, instead of p and q, in order to simplify the test "$p = 1$?" in step F4.

Program F (*Fibonaccian search*). We follow the previous conventions, with rA ≡ K, rI1 ≡ i, (rI2 or rI3) ≡ $p - 1$, (rI3 or rI2) ≡ $q - 1$.

01	START	LDA	K	1	*F1. Initialize.*
02		ENT1	F_k	1	$i \leftarrow F_k$.
03		ENT2	F_{k-1}-1	1	$p \leftarrow F_{k-1}$.
04		ENT3	F_{k-2}-1	1	$q \leftarrow F_{k-2}$.
05		JMP	F2A	1	To step F2.
06	F4A	INC1	1,3	$C2 - S - A$	*F4. Increase i.* $i \leftarrow i + q$.
07		DEC2	1,3	$C2 - S - A$	$p \leftarrow p - q$.
08		DEC3	1,2	$C2 - S - A$	$q \leftarrow q - p$.
09	F2A	CMPA	KEY,1	C	*F2. Compare.*
10		JL	F3A	C	To F3 if $K < K_i$.
11		JE	SUCCESS	$C2$	Exit if $K = K_i$.
12		J2NZ	F4A	$C2 - S$	To F4 if $p \neq 1$.
13		JMP	FAILURE	A	Exit if not in table.
14	F3A	DEC1	1,3	$C1$	*F3. Decrease i.* $i \leftarrow i - q$.
15		DEC2	1,3	$C1$	$p \leftarrow p - q$.
16		J3NN	F2B	$C1$	Swap registers if $q > 0$.
17		JMP	FAILURE	$1 - S - A$	Exit if not in table.

18	F4B	INC1 1,2		(Lines 18–29 are parallel to 06–17.)
19		DEC3 1,2		
20		DEC2 1,3		
21	F2B	CMPA KEY,1		
22		JL	F3B	
23		JE	SUCCESS	
24		J3NZ F4B		
25		JMP	FAILURE	
26	F3B	DEC1 1,2		
27		DEC3 1,2		
28		J2NN F2A		
29		JMP	FAILURE	▮

The running time of this program is analyzed in exercise 18. Figure 8 shows, and the analysis proves, that a left branch is taken somewhat more often than a right branch. Let C, $C1$, and $(C2 - S)$ be the respective number of times steps F2, F3, and F4 are performed. Then we have

$$C = (\text{ave} \quad \phi k/\sqrt{5} + O(1), \quad \max \ k - 1),$$
$$C1 = (\text{ave} \quad k/\sqrt{5} + O(1), \quad \max \ k - 1), \tag{8}$$
$$C2 - S = (\text{ave} \ \phi^{-1}k/\sqrt{5} + O(1), \quad \max \ \lfloor k/2 \rfloor).$$

Thus the left branch is taken about $\phi \approx 1.618$ times as often as the right branch (a fact that we might have guessed, since each probe divides the remaining interval into two parts, with the left part about ϕ times as large as the right). The total average running time of Program F therefore comes to approximately

$$\tfrac{1}{5}\big((18 + 4\phi)k + 31 - 26\phi\big)u \approx (7.050 \lg N + 1.08)u \tag{9}$$

for a successful search, plus $(9 - 3\phi)u \approx 4.15u$ for an unsuccessful search. This is faster than Program C, although the worst-case running time (roughly $8.6 \lg N$) is slightly slower.

Interpolation search. Let's forget computers for a moment, and consider how people actually carry out a search. Sometimes everyday life provides us with clues that lead to good algorithms.

Imagine yourself looking up a word in a dictionary. You probably *don't* begin by looking first at the middle page, then looking at the 1/4 or 3/4 point, etc., as in a binary search. It's even less likely that you use a Fibonaccian search!

If the word you want starts with the letter A, you probably begin near the front of the dictionary. In fact, many dictionaries have thumb indexes that show the starting page or the middle page for the words beginning with a fixed letter. This thumb-index technique can readily be adapted to computers, and it will speed up the search; such algorithms are explored in Section 6.3.

Yet even after the initial point of search has been found, your actions still are not much like the methods we have discussed. If you notice that the desired word is alphabetically much greater than the words on the page being examined, you will turn over a fairly large chunk of pages before making the next reference.

This is quite different from the algorithms above, which make no distinction between "much greater" and "slightly greater."

Such considerations suggest an algorithm that might be called *interpolation search:* When we know that K lies between K_l and K_u, we can choose the next probe to be about $(K - K_l)/(K_u - K_l)$ of the way between l and u, assuming that the keys are numeric and that they increase in a roughly constant manner throughout the interval.

Interpolation search is asymptotically superior to binary search. One step of binary search essentially reduces the amount of uncertainty from n to $\frac{1}{2}n$, while one step of interpolation search essentially reduces it to $\sqrt{n}$, when the keys in the table are randomly distributed. Hence interpolation search takes about $\lg \lg N$ steps, on the average, to reduce the uncertainty from N to 2. (See exercise 22.)

However, computer simulation experiments show that interpolation search does not decrease the number of comparisons enough to compensate for the extra computing time involved, unless the table is rather large. Typical files aren't sufficiently random, and the difference between $\lg \lg N$ and $\lg N$ is not substantial unless N exceeds, say, $2^{16} = 65{,}536$. Interpolation is most successful in the early stages of searching a large possibly external file; after the range has been narrowed down, binary search finishes things off more quickly. (Note that dictionary lookup by hand is essentially an external, not an internal, search. We shall discuss external searching later.)

History and bibliography. The earliest known example of a long list of items that was sorted into order to facilitate searching is the remarkable Babylonian reciprocal table of Inakibit-Anu, dating from about 200 B.C. This clay tablet contains more than 100 pairs of values, which appear to be the beginning of a list of approximately 500 multiple-precision sexagesimal numbers and their reciprocals, sorted into lexicographic order. For example, the list included the following sequence of entries:

01 13 09 34 29 08 08 53 20	49 12 27
01 13 14 31 52 30	49 09 07 12
01 13 43 40 48	48 49 41 15
01 13 48 40 30	48 46 22 59 25 25 55 33 20
01 14 04 26 40	48 36

The task of sorting 500 entries like this, given the technology available at that time, must have been phenomenal. [See D. E. Knuth, *Selected Papers on Computer Science* (Cambridge Univ. Press, 1996), Chapter 11, for further details.]

It is fairly natural to sort numerical values into order, but an order relation between letters or words does not suggest itself so readily. Yet a collating sequence for individual letters was present already in the most ancient alphabets. For example, many of the Biblical psalms have verses that follow a strict alphabetic sequence, the first verse starting with aleph, the second with beth, etc.; this was an aid to memory. Eventually the standard sequence of letters was used by Semitic and Greek peoples to denote numerals; for example, α, β, γ stood for 1, 2, 3, respectively.

The use of alphabetic order for entire words seems to be a much later invention; it is something we might think is obvious, yet it has to be taught to children, and at some point in history it was necessary to teach it to adults. Several lists from about 300 B.C. have been found on the Aegean Islands, giving the names of people in certain religious cults; these lists have been alphabetized, but only by the first letter, thus representing only the first pass of a left-to-right radix sort. Some Greek papyri from the years A.D. 134–135 contain fragments of ledgers that show the names of taxpayers alphabetized by the first two letters. Apollonius Sophista used alphabetic order on the first two letters, and often on subsequent letters, in his lengthy concordance of Homer's poetry (first century A.D.). A few examples of more perfect alphabetization are known, notably Galen's *Hippocratic Glosses* (c. 200), but they are very rare. Words were arranged by their first letter only in the *Etymologiarum* of St. Isidorus (c. 630, Book x); and the *Corpus Glossary* (c. 725) used only the first two letters of each word. The latter two works were perhaps the largest nonnumerical files of data to be compiled during the Middle Ages.

It is not until Giovanni di Genoa's *Catholicon* (1286) that we find a specific description of true alphabetical order. In his preface, Giovanni explained that

amo	precedes	*bibo*
abeo	precedes	*adeo*
amatus	precedes	*amor*
imprudens	precedes	*impudens*
iusticia	precedes	*iustus*
polisintheton	precedes	*polissenus*

(thereby giving examples of situations in which the ordering is determined by the 1st, 2nd, ..., 6th letters), "and so in like manner." He remarked that strenuous effort was required to devise these rules. "I beg of you, therefore, good reader, do not scorn this great labor of mine and this order as something worthless."

A detailed study of the development of alphabetic order, up to the time printing was invented, has been made by Lloyd W. Daly [*Collection Latomus* **90** (1967), 100 pages]. He found some interesting old manuscripts that were evidently used as worksheets while sorting words by their first letters (see pages 89–90 of his monograph).

The first dictionary of English, Robert Cawdrey's *Table Alphabeticall* (London, 1604), contains the following instructions:

Nowe if the word, which thou art desirous to finde, beginne with (a) then looke in the beginning of this Table, but if with (v) looke towards the end. Againe, if thy word beginne with (ca) looke in the beginning of the letter (c) but if with (cu) then looke toward the end of that letter. And so of all the rest. &c.

Cawdrey seems to have been teaching *himself* how to alphabetize as he prepared his dictionary; numerous misplaced words appear on the first few pages, but the alphabetic order in the last part is not as bad.

Binary search was first mentioned by John Mauchly, in what was perhaps the first published discussion of nonnumerical programming methods [*Theory and Techniques for the Design of Electronic Digital Computers*, edited by G. W. Patterson, **1** (1946), 9.7–9.8; **3** (1946), 22.8–22.9]. The method became well known to programmers, but nobody seems to have worked out the details of what should be done when N does not have the special form $2^n - 1$. [See A. D. Booth, *Nature* **176** (1955), 565; A. I. Dumey, *Computers and Automation* **5** (December 1956), 7, where binary search is called "Twenty Questions"; Daniel D. McCracken, *Digital Computer Programming* (Wiley, 1957), 201–203; and M. Halpern, *CACM* **1**, 1 (February 1958), 1–3.]

D. H. Lehmer [*Proc. Symp. Appl. Math.* **10** (1960), 180–181] was apparently the first to publish a binary search algorithm that works for all N. The next step was taken by H. Bottenbruch [*JACM* **9** (1962), 214], who presented an interesting variation of Algorithm B that avoids a separate test for equality until the very end: Using

$$i \leftarrow \lceil (l + u)/2 \rceil$$

instead of $i \leftarrow \lfloor (l + u)/2 \rfloor$ in step B2, he set $l \leftarrow i$ whenever $K \geq K_i$; then $u - l$ decreases at every step. Eventually, when $l = u$, we have $K_l \leq K < K_{l+1}$, and we can test whether or not the search was successful by making one more comparison. (He assumed that $K \geq K_1$ initially.) This idea speeds up the inner loop slightly on many computers, and the same principle can be used with all of the algorithms we have discussed in this section; but a successful search will require about one more iteration, on the average, because of (2). Since the inner loop is performed only about $\lg N$ times, this tradeoff between an extra iteration and a faster loop does not save time unless n is extremely large. (See exercise 23.) On the other hand Bottenbruch's algorithm will find the rightmost occurrence of a given key when the table contains duplicates, and this property is occasionally important.

K. E. Iverson [*A Programming Language* (Wiley, 1962), 141] gave the procedure of Algorithm B, but without considering the possibility of an unsuccessful search. D. E. Knuth [*CACM* **6** (1963), 556–558] presented Algorithm B as an example used with an automated flowcharting system. The uniform binary search, Algorithm C, was suggested to the author by A. K. Chandra of Stanford University in 1971.

Fibonaccian searching was invented by David E. Ferguson [*CACM* **3** (1960), 648]. Binary trees similar to Fibonacci trees appeared in the pioneering work of the Norwegian mathematician Axel Thue as early as 1910 (see exercise 28). A Fibonacci tree without labels was also exhibited as a curiosity in the first edition of Hugo Steinhaus's popular book *Mathematical Snapshots* (New York: Stechert, 1938), page 28; he drew it upside down and made it look like a real tree, with right branches twice as long as left branches so that all the leaves would occur at the same level.

Interpolation searching was suggested by W. W. Peterson [*IBM J. Res. & Devel.* **1** (1957), 131–132]. A correct analysis of its average behavior was not discovered until many years later (see exercise 22).

EXERCISES

▶ **1.** [21] Prove that if $u < l$ in step B2 of the binary search, we have $u = l - 1$ and $K_u < K < K_l$. (Assume by convention that $K_0 = -\infty$ and $K_{N+1} = +\infty$, although these artificial keys are never really used by the algorithm so they need not be present in the actual table.)

▶ **2.** [22] Would Algorithm B still work properly when K is present in the table if we (a) changed step B5 to "$l \leftarrow i$" instead of "$l \leftarrow i+1$"? (b) changed step B4 to "$u \leftarrow i$" instead of "$u \leftarrow i - 1$"? (c) made both of these changes?

3. [15] What searching method corresponds to the tree 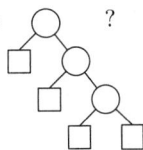 ?

What is the average number of comparisons made in a successful search? in an unsuccessful search?

4. [20] If a search using Program 6.1S (sequential search) takes exactly 638 units of time, how long does it take with Program B (binary search)?

5. [M24] For what values of N is Program B actually *slower* than a sequential search (Program 6.1Q′) on the average, assuming that the search is successful?

6. [28] (K. E. Iverson.) Exercise 5 suggests that it would be best to have a hybrid method, changing from binary search to sequential search when the remaining interval has length less than some judiciously chosen value. Write an efficient MIX program for such a search and determine the best changeover value.

▶ **7.** [M22] Would Algorithm U still work properly if we changed step U1 so that
a) both i and m are set equal to $\lfloor N/2 \rfloor$?
b) both i and m are set equal to $\lceil N/2 \rceil$?
[*Hint:* Suppose the first step were "Set $i \leftarrow 0$, $m \leftarrow N$ (or $N + 1$), go to U4."]

8. [M20] Let $\delta_j = \text{DELTA}[j]$ be the jth increment in Algorithm C, as defined in (6).
a) What is the sum $\sum_{j=0}^{\lfloor \lg N \rfloor + 2} \delta_j$?
b) What are the minimum and maximum values of i that can occur in step C2?

9. [20] Is there any value of $N > 1$ for which Algorithm B and C are exactly equivalent, in the sense that they will both perform the same sequence of comparisons for all search arguments?

10. [21] Explain how to write a MIX program for Algorithm C containing approximately $7 \lg N$ instructions and having a running time of about $4.5 \lg N$ units.

11. [M26] Find exact formulas for the average values of $C1$, $C2$, and A in the frequency analysis of Program C, as a function of N and S.

12. [20] Draw the binary search tree corresponding to Shar's method when $N = 12$.

13. [M24] Tabulate the average number of comparisons made by Shar's method, for $1 \le N \le 16$, considering both successful and unsuccessful searches.

14. [21] Explain how to extend Algorithm F so that it will apply for all $N \ge 1$.

15. [M19] For what values of k does the Fibonacci tree of order k define an optimal search procedure, in the sense that the fewest comparisons are made on the average?

16. [*21*] Figure 9 shows the lineal chart of the rabbits in Fibonacci's original rabbit problem (see Section 1.2.8). Is there a simple relationship between this and the Fibonacci tree discussed in the text?

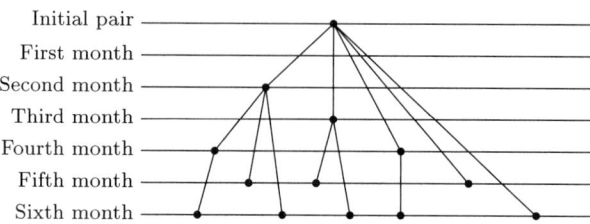

Fig. 9. Pairs of rabbits breeding by Fibonacci's rule.

17. [*M21*] From exercise 1.2.8–34 (or exercise 5.4.2–10) we know that every positive integer n has a unique representation as a sum of Fibonacci numbers

$$n = F_{a_1} + F_{a_2} + \cdots + F_{a_r},$$

where $r \geq 1$, $a_j \geq a_{j+1} + 2$ for $1 \leq j < r$, and $a_r \geq 2$. Prove that in the Fibonacci tree of order k, the path from the root to node $\text{(}n\text{)}$ has length $k + 1 - r - a_r$.

18. [*M30*] Find exact formulas for the average values of $C1$, $C2$, and A in the frequency analysis of Program F, as a function of k, F_k, F_{k+1}, and S.

19. [*M42*] Carry out a detailed analysis of the average running time of the algorithm suggested in exercise 14.

20. [*M22*] The number of comparisons required in a binary search is approximately $\log_2 N$, and in the Fibonaccian search it is roughly $(\phi/\sqrt{5}) \log_\phi N$. The purpose of this exercise is to show that these formulas are special cases of a more general result.

Let p and q be positive numbers with $p + q = 1$. Consider a search algorithm that, given a table of N numbers in increasing order, starts by comparing the argument with the (pN)th key, and iterates this procedure on the smaller blocks. (The binary search has $p = q = 1/2$; the Fibonaccian search has $p = 1/\phi$, $q = 1/\phi^2$.)

If $C(N)$ denotes the average number of comparisons required to search a table of size N, it approximately satisfies the relations

$$C(1) = 0; \qquad C(N) = 1 + pC(pN) + qC(qN) \quad \text{for } N > 1.$$

This happens because there is probability p (roughly) that the search reduces to a pN-element search, and probability q that it reduces to a qN-element search, after the first comparison. When N is large, we may ignore the small-order effect caused by the fact that pN and qN aren't exactly integers.

a) Show that $C(N) = \log_b N$ satisfies these relations exactly, for a certain choice of b. For binary and Fibonaccian search, this value of b agrees with the formulas derived earlier.

b) Consider the following argument: "With probability p, the size of the interval being scanned in this algorithm is divided by $1/p$; with probability q, the interval size is divided by $1/q$. Therefore the interval is divided by $p \cdot (1/p) + q \cdot (1/q) = 2$ on the average, so the algorithm is exactly as good as the binary search, regardless of p and q." Is there anything wrong with this reasoning?

21. [20] Draw the binary tree corresponding to interpolation search when $N = 10$.

22. [M41] (A. C. Yao and F. F. Yao.) Show that an appropriate formulation of interpolation search requires asymptotically $\lg \lg N$ comparisons, on the average, when applied to N independent uniform random keys that have been sorted. Furthermore *all* search algorithms on such tables must make asymptotically $\lg \lg N$ comparisons, on the average.

▶ **23.** [25] The binary search algorithm of H. Bottenbruch, mentioned at the close of this section, avoids testing for equality until the very end of the search. (During the algorithm we know that $K_l \leq K < K_{u+1}$, and the case of equality is not examined until $l = u$.) Such a trick would make Program B run a little bit faster for large N, since the "JE" instruction could be removed from the inner loop. (However, the idea wouldn't really be practical since $\lg N$ is always rather small; we would need $N > 2^{66}$ in order to compensate for the extra work necessary on a successful search, because the running time $(18 \lg N - 16)u$ of (5) is "decreased" to $(17.5 \lg N + 17)u$!)

Show that *every* search algorithm corresponding to a binary tree can be adapted to a search algorithm that uses two-way branching ($<$ versus $\geq$) at the internal nodes of the tree, in place of the three-way branching ($<$, $=$, or $>$) used in the text's discussion. In particular, show how to modify Algorithm C in this way.

▶ **24.** [23] We have seen in Sections 2.3.4.5 and 5.2.3 that the complete binary tree is a convenient way to represent a minimum-path-length tree in consecutive locations. Devise an efficient search method based on this representation. [*Hint:* Is it possible to use multiplication by 2 instead of division by 2 in a binary search?]

▶ **25.** [M25] Suppose that a binary tree has a_k internal nodes and b_k external nodes on level k, for $k = 0, 1, \ldots$ (The root is at level zero.) Thus in Fig. 8 we have $(a_0, a_1, \ldots, a_5) = (1, 2, 4, 4, 1, 0)$ and $(b_0, b_1, \ldots, b_5) = (0, 0, 0, 4, 7, 2)$.

a) Show that a simple algebraic relationship holds between the generating functions $A(z) = \sum_k a_k z^k$ and $B(z) = \sum_k b_k z^k$.

b) The probability distribution for a successful search in a binary tree has the generating function $g(z) = zA(z)/N$, and for an unsuccessful search the generating function is $h(z) = B(z)/(N+1)$. (Thus in the text's notation we have $C_N = \text{mean}(g)$, $C_N' = \text{mean}(h)$, and Eq. (2) gives a relation between these quantities.) Find a relation between $\text{var}(g)$ and $\text{var}(h)$.

26. [22] Show that Fibonacci trees are related to polyphase merge sorting on three tapes.

27. [M30] (H. S. Stone and John Linn.) Consider a search process that uses k processors simultaneously and that is based solely on comparisons of keys. Thus at every step of the search, k indices $i_1, \ldots, i_k$ are specified, and we perform k simultaneous comparisons; if $K = K_{i_j}$ for some j, the search terminates successfully, otherwise the search proceeds to the next step based on the 2^k possible outcomes $K < K_{i_j}$ or $K > K_{i_j}$, for $1 \leq j \leq k$.

Prove that such a process must always take at least approximately $\log_{k+1} N$ steps on the average, as $N \to \infty$, assuming that each key of the table is equally likely as a search argument. (Hence the potential increase in speed over 1-processor binary search is only a factor of $\lg(k+1)$, not the factor of k we might expect. In this sense it is more efficient to assign each processor to a different, independent search problem, instead of making them cooperate on a single search.)

28. [*M23*] Define *Thue trees* T_n by means of algebraic expressions in a binary operator $*$ as follows: $T_0(x) = x * x$, $T_1(x) = x$, $T_{n+2}(x) = T_{n+1}(x) * T_n(x)$.
   a) The number of leaves of T_n is the number of occurrences of x when $T_n(x)$ is written out in full. Express this number in terms of Fibonacci numbers.
   b) Prove that if the binary operator $*$ satisfies the axiom

$$((x * x) * x) * ((x * x) * x) = x,$$

then $T_m(T_n(x)) = T_{m+n-1}(x)$ for all $m \geq 0$ and $n \geq 1$.

▶ **29.** [*22*] (Paul Feldman, 1985.) Instead of assuming that $K_1 < K_2 < \cdots < K_N$, assume only that $K_{p(1)} < K_{p(2)} < \cdots < K_{p(N)}$ where the permutation $p(1)p(2)\ldots p(N)$ is an involution, and $p(j) = j$ for all even values of j. Show that we can locate any given key K, or determine that K is not present, by making at most $2\lfloor \lg N \rfloor + 1$ comparisons.

30. [*27*] (*Involution coding.*) Using the idea of the previous exercise, find a way to arrange N distinct keys in such a way that their relative order implicitly encodes an arbitrarily given array of t-bit numbers x_1, x_2, $\ldots$, x_m, when $m \leq N/4 + 1 - 2^t$. With your arrangement it should be possible to determine the leading k bits of x_j by making only k comparisons, for any given j, as well as to look up an arbitrary key with $\leq 2\lfloor \lg N \rfloor + 1$ comparisons. (This result is used in theoretical studies of data structures that are asymptotically efficient in both time and space.)

6.2.2. Binary Tree Searching

In the preceding section, we learned that an implicit binary tree structure makes the behavior of binary search and Fibonaccian search easier to understand. For a given value of N, the tree corresponding to binary search achieves the theoretical minimum number of comparisons that are necessary to search a table by means of key comparisons. But the methods of the preceding section are appropriate mainly for fixed-size tables, since the sequential allocation of records makes insertions and deletions rather expensive. If the table is changing dynamically, we might spend more time maintaining it than we save in binary-searching it.

The use of an *explicit* binary tree structure makes it possible to insert and delete records quickly, as well as to search the table efficiently. As a result, we essentially have a method that is useful both for searching and for sorting. This gain in flexibility is achieved by adding two link fields to each record of the table.

Techniques for searching a growing table are often called *symbol table algorithms*, because assemblers and compilers and other system routines generally use such methods to keep track of user-defined symbols. For example, the key of each record within a compiler might be a symbolic identifier denoting a variable in some FORTRAN or C program, and the rest of the record might contain information about the type of that variable and its storage allocation. Or the key might be a symbol in a `MIXAL` program, with the rest of the record containing the equivalent of that symbol. The tree search and insertion routines to be described in this section are quite efficient for use as symbol table algorithms, especially in applications where it is desirable to print out a list of the symbols in alphabetic order. Other symbol table algorithms are described in Sections 6.3 and 6.4.

Figure 10 shows a binary search tree containing the names of eleven signs of the zodiac. If we now search for the twelfth name, SAGITTARIUS, starting at the

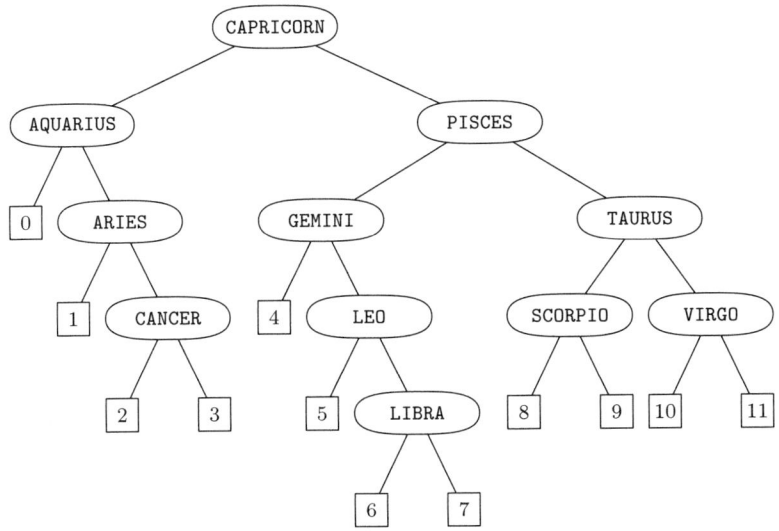

Fig. 10. A binary search tree.

root or apex of the tree, we find it is greater than CAPRICORN, so we move to the
right; it is greater than PISCES, so we move right again; it is less than TAURUS, so
we move left; and it is less than SCORPIO, so we arrive at external node $\boxed{8}$. The
search was unsuccessful; we can now *insert* SAGITTARIUS at the place the search
ended, by linking it into the tree in place of the external node $\boxed{8}$. In this way
the table can grow without the necessity of moving any of the existing records.
Figure 10 was formed by starting with an empty tree and successively inserting
the keys CAPRICORN, AQUARIUS, PISCES, ARIES, TAURUS, GEMINI, CANCER, LEO,
VIRGO, LIBRA, SCORPIO, in this order.

All of the keys in the left subtree of the root in Fig. 10 are alphabetically
less than CAPRICORN, and all keys in the right subtree are alphabetically greater.
A similar statement holds for the left and right subtrees of every node. It follows
that the keys appear in strict alphabetic sequence from left to right,

AQUARIUS,   ARIES,   CANCER,   CAPRICORN,   GEMINI,   LEO,   ...,   VIRGO

if we traverse the tree in *symmetric order* (see Section 2.3.1), since symmetric
order is based on traversing the left subtree of each node just before that node,
then traversing the right subtree.

The following algorithm spells out the searching and insertion processes in
detail.

Algorithm T (*Tree search and insertion*). Given a table of records that form a
binary tree as described above, this algorithm searches for a given argument K.
If K is not in the table, a new node containing K is inserted into the tree in the
appropriate place.

The nodes of the tree are assumed to contain at least the following fields:

$$\text{KEY(P)} = \text{key stored in NODE(P)};$$
$$\text{LLINK(P)} = \text{pointer to left subtree of NODE(P)};$$
$$\text{RLINK(P)} = \text{pointer to right subtree of NODE(P)}.$$

Null subtrees (the external nodes in Fig. 10) are represented by the null pointer Λ. The variable ROOT points to the root of the tree. For convenience, we assume that the tree is not empty (that is, ROOT $\neq \Lambda$), since the necessary operations are trivial when ROOT $= \Lambda$.

T1. [Initialize.] Set P $\leftarrow$ ROOT. (The pointer variable P will move down the tree.)

T2. [Compare.] If $K <$ KEY(P), go to T3; if $K >$ KEY(P), go to T4; and if $K =$ KEY(P), the search terminates successfully.

T3. [Move left.] If LLINK(P) $\neq \Lambda$, set P $\leftarrow$ LLINK(P) and go back to T2. Otherwise go to T5.

T4. [Move right.] If RLINK(P) $\neq \Lambda$, set P $\leftarrow$ RLINK(P) and go back to T2.

T5. [Insert into tree.] (The search is unsuccessful; we will now put K into the tree.) Set Q $\Leftarrow$ AVAIL, the address of a new node. Set KEY(Q) $\leftarrow$ K, LLINK(Q) $\leftarrow$ RLINK(Q) $\leftarrow \Lambda$. (In practice, other fields of the new node should also be initialized.) If K was less than KEY(P), set LLINK(P) $\leftarrow$ Q, otherwise set RLINK(P) $\leftarrow$ Q. (At this point we could set P $\leftarrow$ Q and terminate the algorithm successfully.) ▮

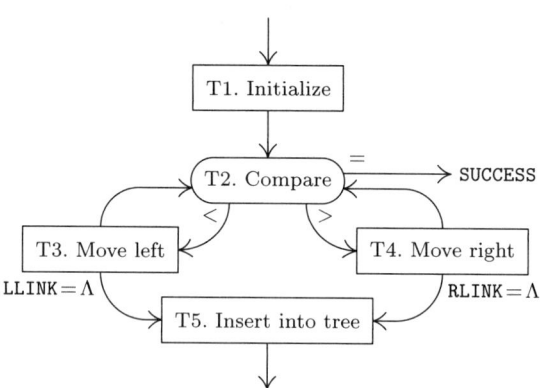

Fig. 11. Tree search and insertion.

This algorithm lends itself to a convenient machine language implementation. We may assume, for example, that the tree nodes have the form

$$\begin{array}{|c|c|c|c|} \hline + & 0 & \text{LLINK} & \text{RLINK} \\ \hline \multicolumn{4}{|c|}{\text{KEY}} \\ \hline \end{array} \qquad (1)$$

followed perhaps by additional words of INFO. Using an AVAIL list for the free storage pool, as in Chapter 2, we can write the following MIX program:

Program T (*Tree search and insertion*).   rA $\equiv K$, rI1 $\equiv$ P, rI2 $\equiv$ Q.

01	LLINK	EQU	2:3		
02	RLINK	EQU	4:5		
03	START	LDA	K	1	*T1. Initialize.*
04		LD1	ROOT	1	P ← ROOT.
05		JMP	2F	1	
06	4H	LD2	0,1(RLINK)	$C2$	*T4. Move right.* Q ← RLINK(P).
07		J2Z	5F	$C2$	To T5 if Q = Λ.
08	1H	ENT1	0,2	$C-1$	P ← Q.
09	2H	CMPA	1,1	C	*T2. Compare.*
10		JG	4B	C	To T4 if $K >$ KEY(P).
11		JE	SUCCESS	$C1$	Exit if $K =$ KEY(P).
12		LD2	0,1(LLINK)	$C1-S$	*T3. Move left.* Q ← LLINK(P).
13		J2NZ	1B	$C1-S$	To T2 if Q ≠ Λ.
14	5H	LD2	AVAIL	$1-S$	*T5. Insert into tree.*
15		J2Z	OVERFLOW	$1-S$	
16		LDX	0,2(RLINK)	$1-S$	
17		STX	AVAIL	$1-S$	Q ⇐ AVAIL.
18		STA	1,2	$1-S$	KEY(Q) ← K.
19		STZ	0,2	$1-S$	LLINK(Q) ← RLINK(Q) ← Λ.
20		JL	1F	$1-S$	Was $K <$ KEY(P)?
21		ST2	0,1(RLINK)	A	RLINK(P) ← Q.
22		JMP	*+2	A	
23	1H	ST2	0,1(LLINK)	$1-S-A$	LLINK(P) ← Q.
24	DONE	EQU	*	$1-S$	Exit after insertion. ∎

The first 13 lines of this program do the search; the last 11 lines do the insertion. The running time for the searching phase is $(7C + C1 - 3S + 4)u$, where

$$C = \text{number of comparisons made};$$
$$C1 = \text{number of times } K \leq \text{KEY(P)};$$
$$C2 = \text{number of times } K > \text{KEY(P)};$$
$$S = [\text{search is successful}].$$

On the average we have $C1 = \frac{1}{2}(C + S)$, since $C1 + C2 = C$ and $C1 - S$ has the same probability distribution as $C2$; so the running time is about $(7.5C - 2.5S + 4)u$. This compares favorably with the binary search algorithms that use an implicit tree (see Program 6.2.1C). By duplicating the code as in Program 6.2.1F we could effectively eliminate line 08 of Program T, reducing the running time to $(6.5C - 2.5S + 5)u$. If the search is unsuccessful, the insertion phase of the program costs an extra $14u$ or $15u$.

Algorithm T can conveniently be adapted to *variable-length keys* and variable-length records. For example, if we allocate the available space sequentially, in a last-in-first-out manner, we can easily create nodes of varying size; the first word of (1) could indicate the size. Since this is an efficient use of storage, symbol table algorithms based on trees are often especially attractive for use in compilers, assemblers, and loaders.

But what about the worst case? Programmers are often skeptical of Algorithm T when they first see it. If the keys of Fig. 10 had been entered into the tree in alphabetic order AQUARIUS, ..., VIRGO instead of the calendar order CAPRICORN, ..., SCORPIO, the algorithm would have built a degenerate tree that essentially specifies a *sequential* search. All LLINKs would be null. Similarly, if the keys come in the uncommon order

> AQUARIUS, VIRGO, ARIES, TAURUS, CANCER, SCORPIO,
>
> CAPRICORN, PISCES, GEMINI, LIBRA, LEO

we obtain a "zigzag" tree that is just as bad. (Try it!)

On the other hand, the particular tree in Fig. 10 requires only $3\frac{2}{11}$ comparisons, on the average, for a successful search; this is just a little higher than the minimum possible average number of comparisons, 3, achievable in the best possible binary tree.

When we have a fairly balanced tree, the search time is roughly proportional to $\log N$, but when we have a degenerate tree, the search time is roughly proportional to N. Exercise 2.3.4.5–5 proves that the average search time would be roughly proportional to $\sqrt{N}$ if we considered each N-node binary tree to be equally likely. What behavior can we really expect from Algorithm T?

Fortunately, it turns out that tree search will require only about $2 \ln N \approx 1.386 \lg N$ comparisons, if the keys are inserted into the tree in random order; well-balanced trees are common, and degenerate trees are very rare.

There is a surprisingly simple proof of this fact. Let us assume that each of the $N!$ possible orderings of the N keys is an equally likely sequence of insertions for building the tree. The number of comparisons needed to find a key is exactly one more than the number of comparisons that were needed when that key was entered into the tree. Therefore if C_N is the average number of comparisons involved in a successful search and C_N' is the average number in an unsuccessful search, we have

$$C_N = 1 + \frac{C_0' + C_1' + \cdots + C_{N-1}'}{N}. \tag{2}$$

But the relation between internal and external path length tells us that

$$C_N = \left(1 + \frac{1}{N}\right) C_N' - 1; \tag{3}$$

this is Eq. 6.2.1–(2). Putting (3) together with (2) yields

$$(N+1)C_N' = 2N + C_0' + C_1' + \cdots + C_{N-1}'. \tag{4}$$

This recurrence is easy to solve. Subtracting the equation

$$NC_{N-1}' = 2(N-1) + C_0' + C_1' + \cdots + C_{N-2}',$$

we obtain

$$(N+1)C_N' - NC_{N-1}' = 2 + C_{N-1}', \qquad \text{hence} \qquad C_N' = C_{N-1}' + 2/(N+1).$$

Since $C_0' = 0$, this means that

$$C_N' = 2H_{N+1} - 2. \tag{5}$$

Applying (3) and simplifying yields the desired result

$$C_N = 2\left(1 + \frac{1}{N}\right)H_N - 3. \tag{6}$$

Exercises 6, 7, and 8 below give more detailed information; it is possible to compute the exact probability distribution of C_N and C_N', not merely the average values.

Tree insertion sorting. Algorithm T was developed for searching, but it can also be used as the basis of an internal *sorting* algorithm; in fact, we can view it as a natural generalization of list insertion, Algorithm 5.2.1L. When properly programmed, its average running time will be only a little slower than some of the best algorithms we discussed in Chapter 5. After the tree has been constructed for all keys, a symmetric tree traversal (Algorithm 2.3.1T) will visit the records in sorted order.

A few precautions are necessary, however. Something different needs to be done if $K = \text{KEY(P)}$ in step T2, since we are sorting instead of searching. One solution is to treat $K = \text{KEY(P)}$ exactly as if $K > \text{KEY(P)}$; this leads to a stable sorting method. (Equal keys will not necessarily be adjacent in the tree; they will only be adjacent in symmetric order.) But if many duplicate keys are present, this method will cause the tree to get badly unbalanced, and the sorting will slow down. Another idea is to keep a list, for each node, of all records having the same key; this requires another link field, but it will make the sorting faster when a lot of equal keys occur.

Thus if we are interested only in sorting, not in searching, Algorithm T isn't the best, but it isn't bad. And if we have an application that combines searching with sorting, the tree method can be warmly recommended.

It is interesting to note that there is a strong relation between the analysis of tree insertion sorting and the analysis of quicksort, although the methods are superficially dissimilar. If we successively insert N keys into an initially empty tree, we make the same average number of comparisons between keys as Algorithm 5.2.2Q does, with minor exceptions. For example, in tree insertion every key gets compared with K_1, and then every key less than K_1 gets compared with the first key less than K_1, etc.; in quicksort, every key gets compared to the first partitioning element K and then every key less than K gets compared to a particular element less than K, etc. The average number of comparisons needed in both cases is $NC_N - N$. (However, Algorithm 5.2.2Q actually makes a few more comparisons, in order to speed up the inner loops.)

Deletions. Sometimes we want to make the computer forget one of the table entries it knows. We can easily delete a node in which either LLINK or RLINK $= \Lambda$; but when both subtrees are nonempty, we have to do something special, since we can't point two ways at once.

For example, consider Fig. 10 again; how could we delete the root node, CAPRICORN? One solution is to delete the alphabetically *next* node, which always has a null LLINK, then reinsert it in place of the node we really wanted to delete. For example, in Fig. 10 we could delete GEMINI, then replace CAPRICORN by GEMINI. This operation preserves the essential left-to-right order of the table entries. The following algorithm gives a detailed description of such a deletion process.

Algorithm D (*Tree deletion*). Let Q be a variable that points to a node of a binary search tree represented as in Algorithm T. This algorithm deletes that node, leaving a binary search tree. (In practice, we will have either Q ≡ ROOT or Q ≡ LLINK(P) or RLINK(P) in some node of the tree. This algorithm resets the value of Q in memory, to reflect the deletion.)

D1. [Is RLINK null?] Set T ← Q. If RLINK(T) = Λ, set Q ← LLINK(T) and go to D4. (For example, if Q ≡ RLINK(P) for some P, we would set RLINK(P) ← LLINK(T).)

D2. [Find successor.] Set R ← RLINK(T). If LLINK(R) = Λ, set LLINK(R) ← LLINK(T), Q ← R, and go to D4.

D3. [Find null LLINK.] Set S ← LLINK(R). Then if LLINK(S) ≠ Λ, set R ← S and repeat this step until LLINK(S) = Λ. (At this point S will be equal to Q$, the symmetric successor of Q.) Finally, set LLINK(S) ← LLINK(T), LLINK(R) ← RLINK(S), RLINK(S) ← RLINK(T), Q ← S.

D4. [Free the node.] Set AVAIL ⇐ T, thus returning the deleted node to the free storage pool. ∎

The reader may wish to try this algorithm by deleting AQUARIUS, CANCER, and CAPRICORN from Fig. 10; each case is slightly different. An alert reader may have noticed that no special test has been made for the case RLINK(T) ≠ Λ, LLINK(T) = Λ; we will defer the discussion of this case until later, since the algorithm as it stands has some very interesting properties.

Since Algorithm D is quite unsymmetrical between left and right, it stands to reason that a sequence of deletions will make the tree get way out of balance, so that the efficiency estimates we have made will be invalid. But deletions don't actually make the trees degenerate at all!

Theorem H (T. N. Hibbard, 1962). *After a random element is deleted from a random tree by Algorithm D, the resulting tree is still random.*

[Nonmathematical readers, please skip to (10).] This statement of the theorem is admittedly quite vague. We can summarize the situation more precisely as follows: Let T be a tree of n elements, and let $P(T)$ be the probability that T occurs if its keys are inserted in random order by Algorithm T. Some trees are more probable than others. Let $Q(T)$ be the probability that T will occur if $n+1$ elements are inserted in random order by Algorithm T and then one of these elements is chosen at random and deleted by Algorithm D. In calculating $P(T)$, we assume that the $n!$ permutations of the keys are equally likely; in calculating

$Q(T)$, we assume that the $(n + 1)! \, (n + 1)$ permutations of keys and selections of the doomed key are equally likely. The theorem states that $P(T) = Q(T)$ for all T.

Proof. We are faced with the fact that permutations are equally probable, not trees, and therefore we shall prove the result by considering *permutations* as the random objects. We shall define a deletion from a permutation, and then we will prove that "a random element deleted from a random permutation leaves a random permutation."

Let $a_1 \, a_2 \ldots a_{n+1}$ be a permutation of $\{1, 2, \ldots, n+1\}$; we want to define the operation of deleting a_i, so as to obtain a permutation $b_1 \, b_2 \ldots b_n$ of $\{1, 2, \ldots, n\}$. This operation should correspond to Algorithms T and D, so that if we start with the tree constructed from the sequence of insertions $a_1, a_2, \ldots, a_{n+1}$ and delete a_i, renumbering the keys from 1 to n, we obtain the tree constructed from $b_1 \, b_2 \ldots b_n$.

It is not hard to define such a deletion operation. There are two cases:

Case 1: $a_i = n + 1$, or $a_i + 1 = a_j$ for some $j < i$. (This is essentially the condition "RLINK$(a_i) = \Lambda$.") Remove a_i from the sequence, and subtract unity from each element greater than a_i.

Case 2: $a_i + 1 = a_j$ for some $j > i$. Replace a_i by a_j, remove a_j from its original place, and subtract unity from each element greater than a_i.

For example, suppose we have the permutation 4 6 1 3 5 2. If we circle the element to be deleted, we have

$$④\,6\ 1\ 3\ 5\ 2 = 4\ 5\ 1\ 3\ 2 \qquad 4\ 6\ 1\ ③\ 5\ 2 = 3\ 5\ 1\ 4\ 2$$

$$4\ ⑥\ 1\ 3\ 5\ 2 = 4\ 1\ 3\ 5\ 2 \qquad 4\ 6\ 1\ 3\ ⑤\ 2 = 4\ 5\ 1\ 3\ 2$$

$$4\ 6\ ①\ 3\ 5\ 2 = 3\ 5\ 1\ 2\ 4 \qquad 4\ 6\ 1\ 3\ 5\ ②= 3\ 5\ 1\ 2\ 4$$

Since there are $(n + 1)! \, (n + 1)$ possible deletion operations, the theorem will be established if we can show that every permutation of $\{1, 2, \ldots, n\}$ is the result of exactly $(n + 1)^2$ deletions.

Let $b_1 \, b_2 \ldots b_n$ be a permutation of $\{1, 2, \ldots, n\}$. We shall define $(n + 1)^2$ deletions, one for each pair i, j with $1 \le i, j \le n + 1$, as follows:

If $i < j$, the deletion is

$$b'_1 \, \ldots \, b'_{i-1} \, ⓑ_i \, b'_{i+1} \, \ldots \, b'_{j-1} \, (b_i{+}1) \, b'_j \, \ldots \, b'_n. \tag{7}$$

Here, as below, b'_k stands for either b_k or $b_k + 1$, depending on whether or not b_k is less than the circled element. This deletion corresponds to Case 2.

If $i > j$, the deletion is

$$b'_1 \ldots b'_{i-1} \, ⓑ_j \, b'_i \ldots b'_n; \tag{8}$$

this deletion fits the definition of Case 1.

Finally, if $i = j$, we have another Case 1 deletion, namely

$$b'_1 \ldots b'_{i-1} \, ⓝ{+}① \, b'_i \ldots b'_n. \tag{9}$$

As an example, let $n = 4$ and consider the 25 deletions that map into 3 1 4 2:

	$i = 1$	$i = 2$	$i = 3$	$i = 4$	$i = 5$
$j = 1$	⑤3 1 4 2	4 ③1 5 2	4 1 ③5 2	4 1 5 ③2	4 1 5 2 ③
$j = 2$	③4 1 5 2	3 ⑤1 4 2	4 2 ①5 3	4 2 5 ①3	4 2 5 3 ①
$j = 3$	③1 4 5 2	4 ①2 5 3	3 1 ⑤4 2	3 1 5 ④2	3 1 5 2 ④
$j = 4$	③1 5 4 2	4 ①5 2 3	3 1 ④5 2	3 1 4 ⑤2	4 1 5 3 ②
$j = 5$	③1 5 2 4	4 ①5 3 2	3 1 ④2 5	4 1 5 ②3	3 1 4 2 ⑤

The circled element is always in position i, and for fixed i we have constructed $n+1$ different deletions, one for each j; hence $(n+1)^2$ different deletions have been constructed for each permutation $b_1 b_2 \ldots b_n$. Since only $(n+1)^2 n!$ deletions are possible, we must have found all of them. ∎

The proof of Theorem H not only tells us about the result of deletions, it also helps us analyze the running time in an average deletion. Exercise 12 shows that we can expect to execute step D2 slightly less than half the time, on the average, when deleting a random element from a random table.

Let us now consider how often the loop in step D3 needs to be performed: Suppose that we are deleting a node on level l, and that the *external* node immediately following in symmetric order is on level k. For example, if we are deleting CAPRICORN from Fig. 10, we have $l = 0$ and $k = 3$ since node 4 is on level 3. If $k = l + 1$, we have RLINK(T) $= \Lambda$ in step D1; and if $k > l + 1$, we will set S $\leftarrow$ LLINK(R) exactly $k - l - 2$ times in step D3. The average value of l is (internal path length)$/N$; the average value of k is

(external path length $-$ distance to leftmost external node)$/N$.

The distance to the leftmost external node is the number of left-to-right minima in the insertion sequence, so it has the average value H_N by the analysis of Section 1.2.10. Since external path length minus internal path length is $2N$, the average value of $k - l - 2$ is $-H_N/N$. Adding to this the average number of times that $k - l - 2$ is -1, we see that *the operation* S $\leftarrow$ LLINK(R) *in step D3 is performed only*

$$\tfrac{1}{2} + \left(\tfrac{1}{2} - H_N\right)/N \qquad (10)$$

times, on the average, in a random deletion. This is reassuring, since the worst case can be pretty slow (see exercise 11).

Although Theorem H is rigorously true, in the precise form we have stated it, it *cannot* be applied, as we might expect, to a sequence of deletions followed by insertions. The shape of the tree is random after deletions, but the relative distribution of values in a given tree shape may change, and it turns out that the first random insertion after deletion actually *destroys* the randomness property on the shapes. This startling fact, first observed by Gary Knott in 1972, must be seen to be believed (see exercise 15). Even more startling is the empirical evidence gathered by J. L. Eppinger [*CACM* **26** (1983), 663–669, **27** (1984),

235], who found that the path length decreases slightly when a few random deletions and insertions are made, but then it *increases* until reaching a steady state after about N^2 deletion/insertion operations have been performed. This steady state is *worse* than the behavior of a random tree, when N is greater than about 150. Further study by Culberson and Munro [*Comp. J.* **32** (1989), 68–75; *Algorithmica* **5** (1990), 295–311] has led to a plausible conjecture that the average search time in the steady state is asymptotically $\sqrt{2N/9\pi}$. However, Eppinger also devised a simple modification that alternates between Algorithm D and a left-right reflection of the same algorithm; he found that this leads to an excellent steady state in which the path length is reduced to about 88% of its normal value for random trees. A theoretical explanation for this behavior is still lacking.

As mentioned above, Algorithm D does not test for the case LLINK(T) = Λ, although this is one of the easy cases for deletion. We could add a new step between D1 and D2, namely,

D1.5. [Is LLINK null?] If LLINK(T) = Λ, set Q $\leftarrow$ RLINK(T) and go to D4.

Exercise 14 shows that Algorithm D with this extra step always leaves a tree that is at least as good as the original Algorithm D, in the path-length sense, and sometimes the result is even better. When this idea is combined with Eppinger's symmetric deletion strategy, the steady-state path length for repeated random deletion/insertion operations decreases to about 86% of its insertion-only value.

Frequency of access. So far we have assumed that each key was equally likely as a search argument. In a more general situation, let p_k be the probability that we will search for the kth element inserted, where $p_1 + \cdots + p_N = 1$. Then a straightforward modification of Eq. (2), if we retain the assumption of random order so that the shape of the tree stays random and Eq. (5) holds, shows that the average number of comparisons in a successful search will be

$$1 + \sum_{k=1}^{N} p_k(2H_k - 2) = 2\sum_{k=1}^{N} p_k H_k - 1. \tag{11}$$

For example, if the probabilities obey Zipf's law, Eq. 6.1–(8), the average number of comparisons reduces to

$$H_N - 1 + H_N^{(2)}/H_N \tag{12}$$

if we insert the keys in decreasing order of importance. (See exercise 18.) This is about half as many comparisons as predicted by the equal-frequency analysis, and it is fewer than we would make using binary search.

Figure 12 shows the tree that results when the most common 31 words of English are entered in decreasing order of frequency. The relative frequency is shown with each word, using statistics from *Cryptanalysis* by H. F. Gaines (New York: Dover, 1956), 226. The average number of comparisons for a successful search in this tree is 4.042; the corresponding binary search, using Algorithm 6.2.1B or 6.2.1C, would require 4.393 comparisons.

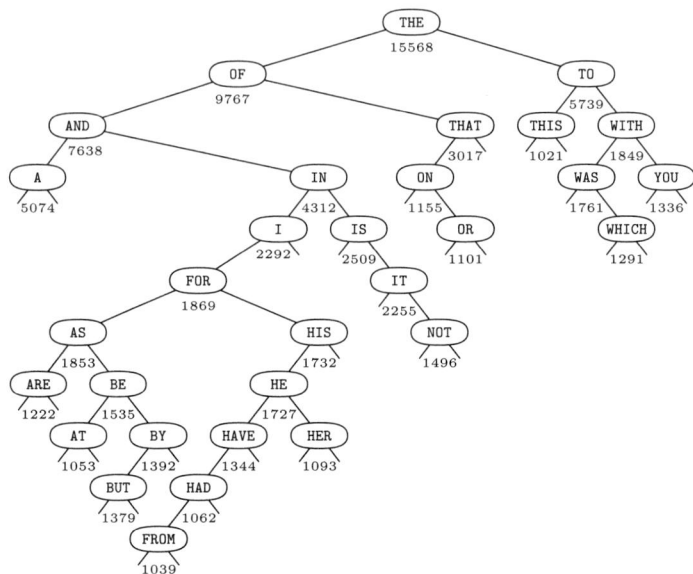

Fig. 12. The 31 most common English words, inserted in decreasing order of frequency.

Optimum binary search trees. These considerations make it natural to ask about the best possible tree for searching a table of keys with given frequencies. For example, the optimum tree for the 31 most common English words is shown in Fig. 13; it requires only 3.437 comparisons for an average successful search.

Let us now explore the problem of finding the optimum tree. When $N = 3$, for example, let us assume that the keys $K_1 < K_2 < K_3$ have respective probabilities p, q, r. There are five possible trees:

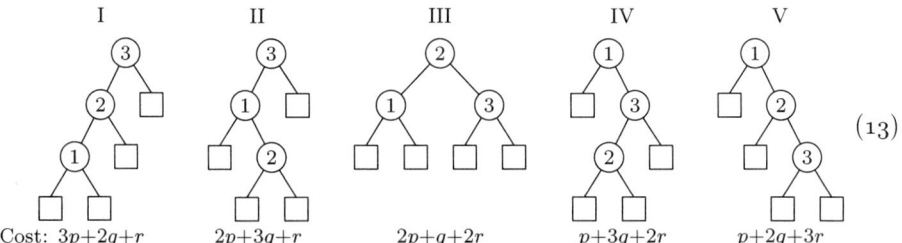

$$\tag{13}$$

Figure 14 shows the ranges of p, q, r for which each tree is optimum; the balanced tree is best about 45 percent of the time, if we choose p, q, r at random (see exercise 21).

Unfortunately, when N is large there are

$$\binom{2N}{N} \Big/ (N + 1) \approx 4^N / \left(\sqrt{\pi}\, N^{3/2} \right)$$

binary trees, so we can't just try them all and see which is best. Let us therefore study the properties of optimum binary search trees more closely, in order to discover a better way to find them.

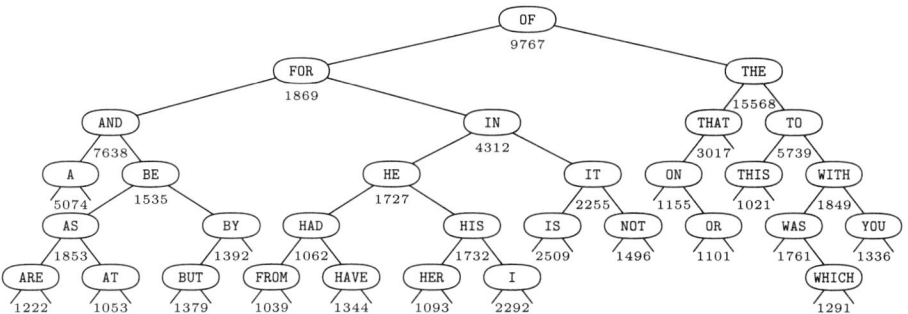

Fig. 13. An optimum search tree for the 31 most common English words.

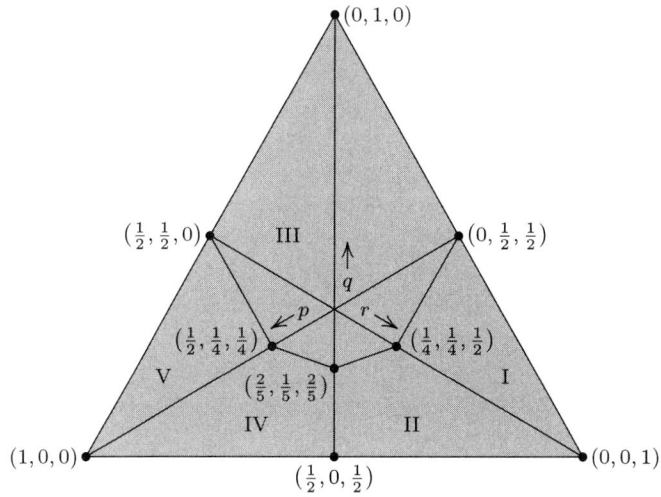

Fig. 14. If the relative frequencies of (K_1, K_2, K_3) are (p, q, r), this graph shows which of the five trees in (13) is best. The fact that $p + q + r = 1$ makes the graph two-dimensional although there are three coordinates.

So far we have considered only the probabilities for a successful search; in practice, the unsuccessful case must usually be considered as well. For example, the 31 words in Fig. 13 account for only about 36 percent of typical English text; the other 64 percent will certainly influence the structure of the optimum search tree.

Therefore let us set the problem up in the following way: We are given $2n+1$ probabilities $p_1, p_2, \ldots, p_n$ and $q_0, q_1, \ldots, q_n$, where

$\quad p_i =$ probability that K_i is the search argument;

$\quad q_i =$ probability that the search argument lies between K_i and K_{i+1}.

(By convention, q_0 is the probability that the search argument is less than K_1, and q_n is the probability that the search argument is greater than K_n.) Thus,

$p_1 + p_2 + \cdots + p_n + q_0 + q_1 + \cdots + q_n = 1$, and we want to find a binary tree that minimizes the expected number of comparisons in the search, namely

$$\sum_{j=1}^{n} p_j \left(\text{level}(\textcircled{\scriptsize j}) + 1 \right) + \sum_{k=0}^{n} q_k \, \text{level}(\boxed{k}), \qquad (14)$$

where $\textcircled{\scriptsize j}$ is the jth internal node in symmetric order and $\boxed{k}$ is the $(k+1)$st external node, and where the root has level zero. Thus the expected number of comparisons for the binary tree

$$(15)$$

is $2q_0 + 2p_1 + 3q_1 + 3p_2 + 3q_2 + p_3 + q_3$. Let us call this the *cost* of the tree; and let us say that a minimum-cost tree is *optimum*. In this definition there is no need to require that the p's and q's sum to unity; we can ask for a minimum-cost tree with any given sequence of "weights" $(p_1, \ldots, p_n; q_0, \ldots, q_n)$.

We have studied Huffman's procedure for constructing trees with minimum weighted path length, in Section 2.3.4.5; but that method requires all the p's to be zero, and the tree it produces will usually not have the external node weights $(q_0, \ldots, q_n)$ in the proper symmetric order from left to right. Therefore we need another approach.

What saves us is that *all subtrees of an optimum tree are optimum.* For example, if (15) is an optimum tree for the weights $(p_1, p_2, p_3; q_0, q_1, q_2, q_3)$, then the left subtree of the root must be optimum for $(p_1, p_2; q_0, q_1, q_2)$; any improvement to a subtree leads to an improvement in the whole tree.

This principle suggests a computation procedure that systematically finds larger and larger optimum subtrees. We have used much the same idea in Section 5.4.9 to construct optimum merge patterns; the general approach is known as "dynamic programming," and we shall consider it further in Section 7.7.

Let $c(i, j)$ be the cost of an optimum subtree with weights $(p_{i+1}, \ldots, p_j; q_i, \ldots, q_j)$; and let $w(i, j) = p_{i+1} + \cdots + p_j + q_i + \cdots + q_j$ be the sum of all those weights; thus $c(i, j)$ and $w(i, j)$ are defined for $0 \le i \le j \le n$. It follows that

$$c(i, i) = 0,$$
$$c(i, j) = w(i, j) + \min_{i < k \le j} \left(c(i, k-1) + c(k, j) \right), \qquad \text{for } i < j, \qquad (16)$$

since the minimum possible cost of a tree with root $\textcircled{\scriptsize k}$ is $w(i, j) + c(i, k-1) + c(k, j)$. When $i < j$, let $R(i, j)$ be the set of all k for which the minimum is achieved in (16); this set specifies the possible roots of the optimum trees.

Equation (16) makes it possible to evaluate $c(i, j)$ for $j - i = 1, 2, \ldots, n$; there are about $\frac{1}{2}n^2$ such values, and the minimization operation is carried out for about $\frac{1}{6}n^3$ values of k. This means we can determine an optimum tree in $O(n^3)$ units of time, using $O(n^2)$ cells of memory.

A factor of n can actually be removed from the running time if we make use of a monotonicity property. Let $r(i,j)$ denote an element of $R(i,j)$; we need not compute the entire set $R(i,j)$, a single representative is sufficient. Once we have found $r(i,j-1)$ and $r(i+1,j)$, the result of exercise 27 proves that we may always assume that

$$r(i,j-1) \leq r(i,j) \leq r(i+1,j) \tag{17}$$

when the weights are nonnegative. This limits the search for the minimum, since only $r(i+1,j) - r(i,j-1) + 1$ values of k need to be examined in (16) instead of $j - i$. The total amount of work when $j - i = d$ is now bounded by the telescoping series

$$\sum_{\substack{d \leq j \leq n \\ i = j - d}} \big(r(i+1,j) - r(i,j-1) + 1\big) = r(n-d+1, n) - r(0, d-1) + n - d + 1 < 2n;$$

hence the total running time is reduced to $O(n^2)$.

The following algorithm describes this procedure in detail.

Algorithm K (*Find optimum binary search trees*). Given $2n + 1$ nonnegative weights $(p_1, \ldots, p_n; q_0, \ldots, q_n)$, this algorithm constructs binary trees $t(i,j)$ that have minimum cost for the weights $(p_{i+1}, \ldots, p_j; q_i, \ldots, q_j)$ in the sense defined above. Three arrays are computed, namely

$$c[i,j], \qquad \text{for } 0 \leq i \leq j \leq n, \qquad \text{the cost of } t(i,j);$$
$$r[i,j], \qquad \text{for } 0 \leq i < j \leq n, \qquad \text{the root of } t(i,j);$$
$$w[i,j], \qquad \text{for } 0 \leq i \leq j \leq n, \qquad \text{the total weight of } t(i,j).$$

The results of the algorithm are specified by the r array: If $i = j$, $t(i,j)$ is null; otherwise its left subtree is $t(i, r[i,j]-1)$ and its right subtree is $t(r[i,j], j)$.

K1. [Initialize.] For $0 \leq i \leq n$, set $c[i,i] \leftarrow 0$ and $w[i,i] \leftarrow q_i$ and $w[i,j] \leftarrow w[i,j-1] + p_j + q_j$ for $j = i+1, \ldots, n$. Then for $1 \leq j \leq n$ set $c[j-1,j] \leftarrow w[j-1,j]$ and $r[j-1,j] \leftarrow j$. (This determines all the 1-node optimum trees.)

K2. [Loop on d.] Do step K3 for $d = 2, 3, \ldots, n$, then terminate the algorithm.

K3. [Loop on j.] (We have already determined the optimum trees of fewer than d nodes. This step determines all the d-node optimum trees.) Do step K4 for $j = d, d+1, \ldots, n$.

K4. [Find $c[i,j]$, $r[i,j]$.] Set $i \leftarrow j - d$. Then set

$$c[i,j] \leftarrow w[i,j] + \min_{r[i,j-1] \leq k \leq r[i+1,j]}\big(c[i, k-1] + c[k,j]\big),$$

and set $r[i,j]$ to a value of k for which the minimum occurs. (Exercise 22 proves that $r[i,j-1] \leq r[i+1,j]$.) ∎

As an example of Algorithm K, consider Fig. 15, which is based on a "keyword-in-context" (KWIC) indexing application. The titles of all articles in the first ten volumes of the *Journal of the ACM* were sorted to prepare a concordance in which there was one line for every word of every title. However, certain words like "THE" and "EQUATION" were felt to be sufficiently uninformative that they were left out of the index. These special words and their frequency of occurrence are shown in the internal nodes of Fig. 15. Notice that a title such as "On the solution of an equation for a certain new problem" would be so uninformative, it wouldn't appear in the index at all! The idea of KWIC indexing is due to H. P. Luhn, *Amer. Documentation* **11** (1960), 288–295. (See W. W. Youden, *JACM* **10** (1963), 583–646, where the full KWIC index appears.)

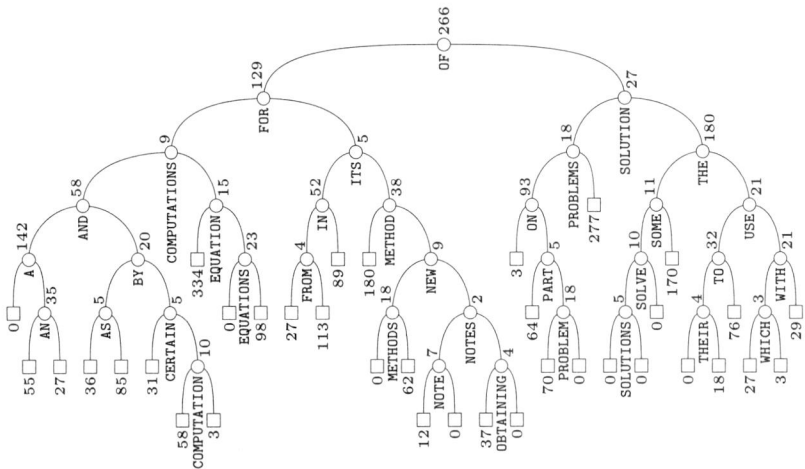

Fig. 15. An optimum binary search tree for a KWIC indexing application.

When preparing a KWIC index file for sorting, we might want to use a binary search tree in order to test whether or not each particular word is to be indexed. The other words fall between two of the unindexed words, with the frequencies shown in the external nodes of Fig. 15; thus, exactly 277 words that are alphabetically between "PROBLEMS" and "SOLUTION" appeared in the *JACM* titles during 1954–1963.

Figure 15 shows the optimum tree obtained by Algorithm K, with $n = 35$. The computed values of $r[0, j]$ for $j = 1, 2, \ldots, 35$ are $(1, 1, 2, 3, 3, 3, 3, 8, 8, 8, 8, 8, 8, 11, 11, \ldots, 11, 21, 21, 21, 21, 21, 21)$; the values of $r[i, 35]$ for $i = 0, 1, \ldots, 34$ are $(21, 21, \ldots, 21, 25, 25, 25, 25, 25, 25, 25, 26, 26, 26, 30, 30, 30, 30, 30, 30, 30, 33, 33, 33, 35, 35)$.

The "betweenness frequencies" q_j have a noticeable effect on the optimum tree structure; Fig. 16(a) shows the optimum tree that would have been obtained with the q_j set to zero. Similarly, the internal frequencies p_i are important; Fig. 16(b) shows the optimum tree when the p_i are set to zero. Considering the full set of frequencies, the tree of Fig. 15 requires only 4.15 comparisons, on the average, while the trees of Fig. 16 require, respectively, 4.69 and 4.72.

a)

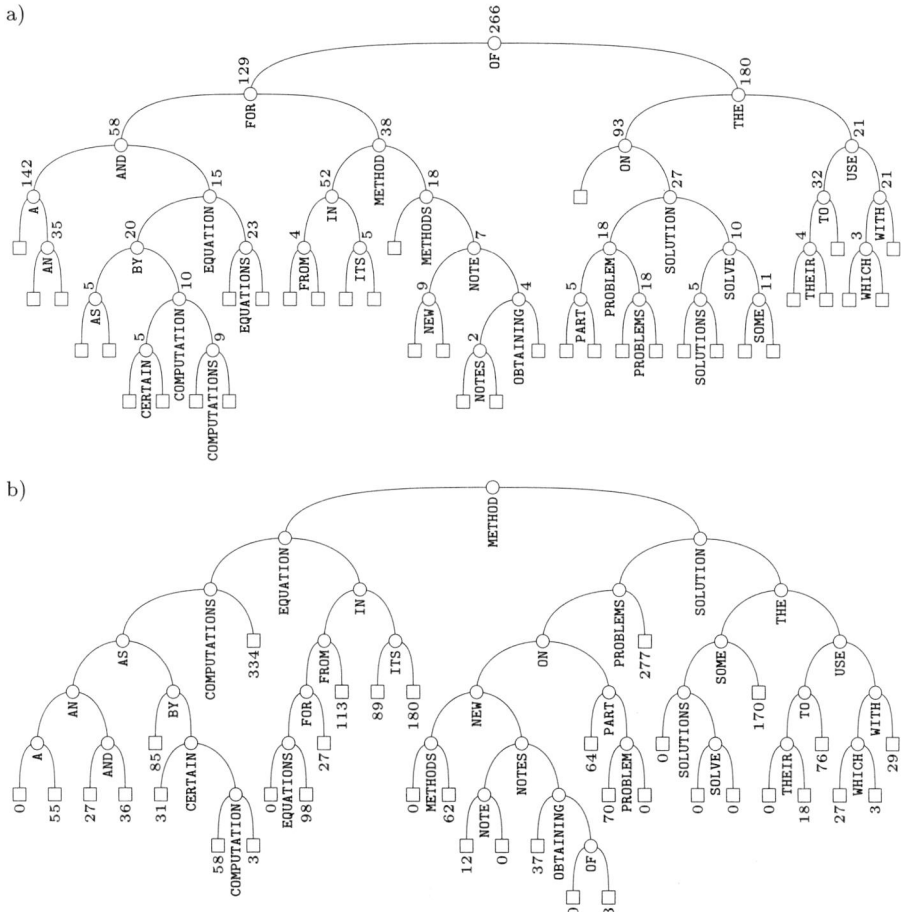

b)

Fig. 16. Optimum binary search trees based on half of the data of Fig. 15: (a) external frequencies suppressed; (b) internal frequencies suppressed.

Since Algorithm K requires time and space proportional to n^2, it becomes impractical when n is very large. Of course we may not really want to use binary search trees for large n, in view of the other search techniques to be discussed later in this chapter; but let's assume anyway that we want to find an optimum or nearly optimum tree when n is large.

We have seen that the idea of inserting the keys in order of decreasing frequency can tend to make a fairly good tree, on the average; but it can also be very bad (see exercise 20), and it is not usually very near the optimum, since it makes no use of the q_j weights. Another approach is to choose the root k so that the resulting maximum subtree weight, $\max\bigl(w(0, k-1), w(k, n)\bigr)$, is as small as possible. This approach can also be fairly poor, because it may choose a node with very small p_k to be the root; however, Theorem M below shows that the resulting tree will not be extremely far from the optimum.

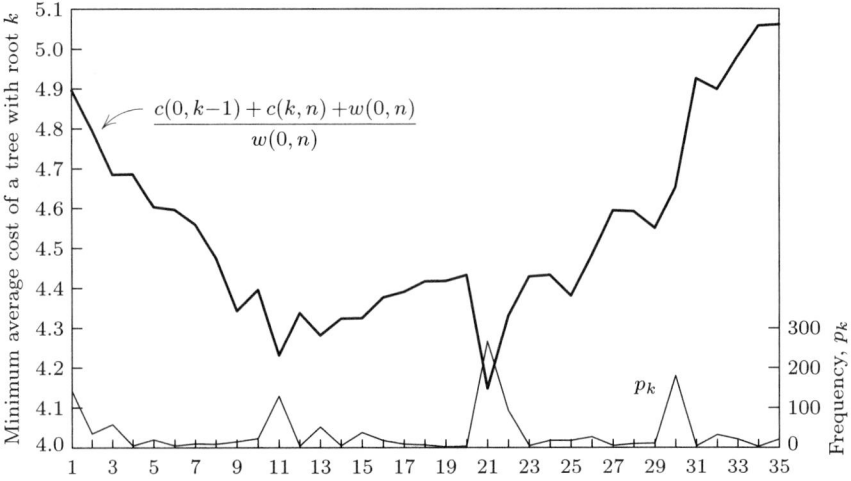

Fig. 17. Behavior of the cost as a function of the root, k.

A more satisfactory procedure can be obtained by combining these two methods, as suggested by W. A. Walker and C. C. Gotlieb [*Graph Theory and Computing* (Academic Press, 1972), 303–323]: Try to equalize the left-hand and right-hand weights, but be prepared to move the root a few steps to the left or right to find a node with relatively large p_k. Figure 17 shows why this method is reasonable: If we plot $c(0, k-1) + c(k, n)$ as a function of k, for the KWIC data of Fig. 15, we see that the result is quite sensitive to the magnitude of p_k.

A top-down method such as this can be used for large n to choose the root and then to work on the left and the right subtrees. When we get down to a sufficiently small subtree we can apply Algorithm K. The resulting method yields fairly good trees (reportedly within 2 or 3 percent of the optimum), and it requires only $O(n)$ units of space, $O(n \log n)$ units of time. In fact, M. Fredman has shown that $O(n)$ units of time suffice, if suitable data structures are used [*STOC* **7** (1975), 240–244]; see K. Mehlhorn, *Data Structures and Algorithms* **1** (Springer, 1984), Section 4.2.

Optimum trees and entropy. The minimum cost is closely related to a mathematical concept called *entropy*, which was introduced by Claude Shannon in his seminal work on information theory [*Bell System Tech. J.* **27** (1948), 379–423, 623–656]. If $p_1, p_2, \ldots, p_n$ are probabilities with $p_1 + p_2 + \cdots + p_n = 1$, we define the entropy $H(p_1, p_2, \ldots, p_n)$ by the formula

$$H(p_1, p_2, \ldots, p_n) = \sum_{k=1}^{n} p_k \lg \frac{1}{p_k}. \tag{18}$$

Intuitively, if n events are possible and the kth event occurs with probability p_k, we can imagine that we have received $\lg(1/p_k)$ bits of information when the kth event has occurred. (An event of probability $\frac{1}{32}$ gives 5 bits of information, etc.) Then $H(p_1, p_2, \ldots, p_n)$ is the expected number of bits of information in a random event. If $p_k = 0$, we define $p_k \lg(1/p_k) = 0$, because

$$\lim_{\epsilon \to 0+} \epsilon \lg \frac{1}{\epsilon} = \lim_{m \to \infty} \frac{1}{m} \lg m = 0.$$

This convention allows us to use (18) when some of the probabilities are zero.

The function $x \lg(1/x)$ is concave; that is, its second derivative, $-1/(x \ln 2)$, is negative. Therefore the maximum value of $H(p_1, p_2, \ldots, p_n)$ occurs when $p_1 = p_2 = \cdots = p_n = 1/n$, namely

$$H\left(\frac{1}{n}, \frac{1}{n}, \ldots, \frac{1}{n}\right) = \lg n. \tag{19}$$

In general, if we specify $p_1, \ldots, p_{n-k}$ but allow the other probabilities $p_{n-k+1}, \ldots, p_n$ to vary, we have

$$H(p_1, \ldots, p_{n-k}, p_{n-k+1}, \ldots, p_n) \leq H\left(p_1, \ldots, p_{n-k}, \frac{q}{k}, \ldots, \frac{q}{k}\right)$$

$$= H(p_1, \ldots, p_{n-k}, q) + q \lg k, \tag{20}$$

$$H(p_1, \ldots, p_{n-k}, p_{n-k+1}, \ldots, p_n) \geq H(p_1, \ldots, p_{n-k}, q, 0, \ldots, 0)$$

$$= H(p_1, \ldots, p_{n-k}, q), \tag{21}$$

where $q = 1 - (p_1 + \cdots + p_{n-k})$.

Consider any not-necessarily-binary tree in which probabilities have been assigned to the leaves, say

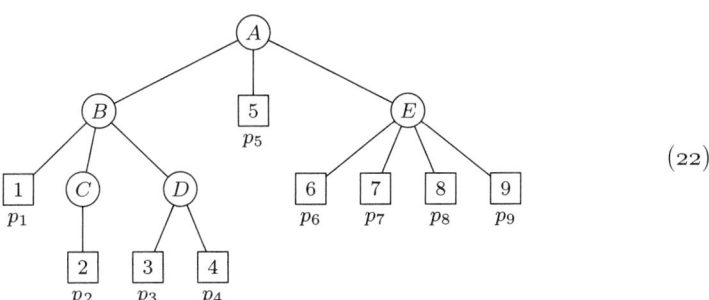

$$\tag{22}$$

Here p_k represents the probability that a search procedure will end at leaf $\boxed{k}$. Then the branching at each internal (nonleaf) node corresponds to a local probability distribution based on the sums of leaf probabilities below each branch. For example, at node $\textcircled{A}$ the first, second, and third branches are taken with the respective probabilities

$$(p_1 + p_2 + p_3 + p_4, \ p_5, \ p_6 + p_7 + p_8 + p_9),$$

and at node $\textcircled{B}$ the probabilities are

$$(p_1, p_2, p_3 + p_4)/(p_1 + p_2 + p_3 + p_4).$$

Let us say that each internal node has the entropy of its local probability distribution; thus

$$H(A) = (p_1+p_2+p_3+p_4) \lg \frac{1}{p_1+p_2+p_3+p_4}$$

$$+ p_5 \lg \frac{1}{p_5} + (p_6+p_7+p_8+p_9) \lg \frac{1}{p_6+p_7+p_8+p_9},$$

$$H(B) = \frac{p_1}{p_1+p_2+p_3+p_4} \lg \frac{p_1+p_2+p_3+p_4}{p_1} + \frac{p_2}{p_1+p_2+p_3+p_4} \lg \frac{p_1+p_2+p_3+p_4}{p_2}$$

$$+ \frac{p_3+p_4}{p_1+p_2+p_3+p_4} \lg \frac{p_1+p_2+p_3+p_4}{p_3+p_4},$$

$$H(C) = \frac{p_2}{p_2} \lg \frac{p_2}{p_2},$$

$$H(D) = \frac{p_3}{p_3+p_4} \lg \frac{p_3+p_4}{p_3} + \frac{p_4}{p_3+p_4} \lg \frac{p_3+p_4}{p_4},$$

$$H(E) = \frac{p_6}{p_6+p_7+p_8+p_9} \lg \frac{p_6+p_7+p_8+p_9}{p_6} + \frac{p_7}{p_6+p_7+p_8+p_9} \lg \frac{p_6+p_7+p_8+p_9}{p_7}$$

$$+ \frac{p_8}{p_6+p_7+p_8+p_9} \lg \frac{p_6+p_7+p_8+p_9}{p_8} + \frac{p_9}{p_6+p_7+p_8+p_9} \lg \frac{p_6+p_7+p_8+p_9}{p_9}.$$

Lemma E.   *The sum of $p(\alpha)H(\alpha)$ over all internal nodes α of a tree, where $p(\alpha)$ is the probability of reaching node α and $H(\alpha)$ is the entropy of α, equals the entropy of the probability distribution on the leaves.*

Proof. It is easy to establish this identity by induction from bottom to top. For example, we have

$$H(A)+(p_1+p_2+p_3+p_4)H(B)+p_2 H(C)+(p_3+p_4)H(D)+(p_6+p_7+p_8+p_9)H(E)$$

$$= p_1 \lg \frac{1}{p_1} + p_2 \lg \frac{1}{p_2} + \cdots + p_9 \lg \frac{1}{p_9}$$

with respect to the formulas above; all terms involving $\lg(p_1 + p_2 + p_3 + p_4)$, $\lg(p_3 + p_4)$, and $\lg(p_6 + p_7 + p_8 + p_9)$ cancel out. ∎

As a consequence of Lemma E, we can use entropy to establish a convenient lower bound on the cost of any binary tree.

Theorem B.   *Let $(p_1,\ldots,p_n; q_0,\ldots,q_n)$ be nonnegative weights as in Algorithm K, normalized so that $p_1+\cdots+p_n+q_0+\cdots+q_n = 1$, and let $P = p_1+\cdots+p_n$ be the probability of a successful search. Let*

$$H = H(p_1,\ldots,p_n,q_0,\ldots,q_n)$$

be the entropy of the corresponding probability distribution, and let C be the minimum cost, (14). Then if $H \geq 2P/e$ we have

$$C \geq H - P \lg \frac{eH}{2P}. \tag{23}$$

Proof. Take a binary tree of cost C and assign the probabilities q_k to its leaves. Also add a middle branch below each internal node, leading to a new leaf that has probability p_k. Then $C = \sum p(\alpha)$, summed over the internal nodes α of the resulting ternary tree, and $H = \sum p(\alpha)H(\alpha)$ by Lemma E.

The entropy $H(\alpha)$ corresponds to a three-way distribution, where one of the probabilities is $p_j/p(\alpha)$ if α is internal node (j). Exercise 35 proves that

$$H(p,q,r) \leq p \lg x + 1 + \lg\left(1 + \frac{1}{2x}\right) \tag{24}$$

for all $x > 0$, whenever $p + q + r = 1$. Therefore we have the inequality

$$H = \sum_{\alpha} p(\alpha)H(\alpha) \leq \sum_{j=1}^{n} p_j \lg x + \left(1 + \lg\left(1 + \frac{1}{2x}\right)\right)C$$

for all positive x. Choosing $2x = H/P$ now leads to the desired result, since

$$
\begin{aligned}
C &\geq \frac{1}{1 + \lg(1 + P/H)}\left(H - P\lg\frac{H}{2P}\right) \\
&= \frac{1}{1 + \lg(1 + P/H)}(H + P\lg e) - \frac{P}{1 + \lg(1 + P/H)}\lg\frac{eH}{2P} \\
&\geq H - P\lg\frac{eH}{2P},
\end{aligned}
$$

using the fact that $\lg(1 + y) \leq y \lg e$ for all $y > 0$. $\blacksquare$

Equation (23) does not necessarily hold when the entropy is extremely low. But the restriction to cases where $H \geq 2P/e$ is not severe, since the value of H is usually near $\lg n$; see exercise 37. Notice that the proof doesn't actually use the left-to-right order of the nodes; the lower bound (23) holds for any binary search tree that has internal node probabilities p_j and external node probabilities q_k in any order.

Entropy calculations also yield an upper bound that is not too far from (23), even when we do stick to the left-to-right order:

Theorem M. *Under the assumptions of Theorem B, we also have*

$$C \leq H + 2 - P. \tag{25}$$

Proof. Form the $n+1$ sums $s_0 = \frac{1}{2}q_0$, $s_1 = q_0+p_1+\frac{1}{2}q_1$, $s_2 = q_0+p_1+q_1+p_2+\frac{1}{2}q_2$, $\ldots$, $s_n = q_0+p_1+\cdots+q_{n-1}+p_n+\frac{1}{2}q_n$; we may assume that $s_0 < s_1 < \cdots < s_n$ (see exercise 38). Express each s_k as a binary fraction, writing $s_n = (.111\ldots)_2$ if $s_n = 1$. Then let the string σ_k be the leading bits of s_k, retaining just enough bits to distinguish s_k from s_j for $j \neq k$. For example, we might have $n = 3$ and

$$
\begin{array}{ll}
s_0 = (.0000001)_2 & \sigma_0 = 00000 \\
s_1 = (.0000101)_2 & \sigma_1 = 00001 \\
s_2 = (.0001011)_2 & \sigma_2 = 0001 \\
s_3 = (.1100000)_2 & \sigma_3 = 1
\end{array}
$$

Construct a binary tree with $n+1$ leaves, in such a way that σ_k corresponds to the path from the root to $\boxed{k}$ for $0 \le k \le n$, where '0' denotes a left branch and '1' denotes a right branch. Also, if σ_{k-1} has the form $\alpha_k 0 \beta_k$ and σ_k has the form $\alpha_k 1 \gamma_k$ for some α_k, β_k, and γ_k, let the internal node $\widehat{k}$ correspond to the path α_k. Thus we would have

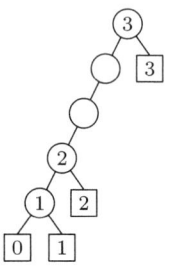

in the example above. There may be some internal nodes that are still nameless; replace each of them by their one and only child. The cost of the resulting tree is at most $\sum_{k=1}^{n} p_k(|\alpha_k| + 1) + \sum_{k=0}^{n} q_k |\sigma_k|$.

We have

$$p_k \le \tfrac{1}{2}q_{k-1} + p_k + \tfrac{1}{2}q_k = s_k - s_{k-1} \le 2^{-|\alpha_k|}, \qquad (26)$$

because $s_k \le (.\alpha_k)_2 + 2^{-|\alpha_k|}$ and $s_{k-1} \ge (.\alpha_k)_2$. Furthermore, if $q_k \ge 2^{-t}$ we have $s_k \ge s_{k-1} + 2^{-t-1}$ and $s_{k+1} \ge s_k + 2^{-t-1}$, hence $|\sigma_k| \le t+1$. It follows that $q_k < 2^{-|\sigma_k|+2}$, and we have constructed a binary tree of cost

$$\le \sum_{k=1}^{n} p_k(1 + |\alpha_k|) + \sum_{k=0}^{n} q_k |\sigma_k| \le \sum_{k=1}^{n} p_k \left(1 + \lg \frac{1}{p_k}\right) + \sum_{k=0}^{n} q_k \left(2 + \lg \frac{1}{q_k}\right)$$

$$= P + 2(1 - P) + H = H + 2 - P. \quad \blacksquare$$

In the KWIC indexing application of Fig. 15, we have $P = 1304/3288 \approx 0.39659$, and $H(p_1, \ldots, p_{35}, q_0, \ldots, q_{35}) \approx 5.00635$. Therefore Theorem B tells us that $C \ge 3.3800$, and Theorem M tells us that $C < 6.6098$.

*The Garsia–Wachs algorithm. An amazing improvement on Algorithm K is possible in the special case that $p_1 = \cdots = p_n = 0$. This case, in which only the leaf probabilities $(q_0, q_1, \ldots, q_n)$ are relevant, is especially important because it arises in several significant applications. Let us therefore assume in the remainder of this section that the probabilities p_j are zero. Notice that Theorems B and M reduce to the inequalities

$$H(q_0, q_1, \ldots, q_n) \le C(q_0, q_1, \ldots, q_n) < H(q_0, q_1, \ldots, q_n) + 2 \qquad (27)$$

in this case, because we cannot have $C = H + 2 - P$ unless $P = 1$; and the cost function (14) simplifies to

$$C = \sum_{k=0}^{n} q_k l_k, \qquad l_k = \text{the level of } \boxed{k}. \qquad (28)$$

A simpler algorithm is possible because of the following key property:

Lemma W. *If $q_{k-1} > q_{k+1}$ then $l_k \leq l_{k+1}$ in every optimum tree. If $q_{k-1} = q_{k+1}$ then $l_k \leq l_{k+1}$ in some optimum tree.*

Proof. Suppose $q_{k-1} \geq q_{k+1}$ and consider a tree in which $l_k > l_{k+1}$. Then $\boxed{k}$ must be a right child, and its left sibling L is a subtree of weight $w \geq q_{k-1}$. Replace the parent of $\boxed{k}$ by L; replace $\boxed{k+1}$ by a node whose children are $\boxed{k}$ and $\boxed{k+1}$. This changes the overall cost by $-w - q_k(l_k - l_{k+1} - 1) + q_{k+1} \leq q_{k+1} - q_{k-1}$. So the given tree was not optimum if $q_{k-1} > q_{k+1}$, and an optimum tree has been transformed into another optimum tree if $q_{k-1} = q_{k+1}$. In the latter case we have found an optimum tree in which $l_k = l_{k+1}$. ∎

A deeper analysis of the structure tells us considerably more.

Lemma X. *Suppose j and k are indices such that $j < k$ and we have*
  i) $q_{i-1} > q_{i+1}$ *for* $1 \leq i < k$;
 ii) $q_{k-1} \leq q_{k+1}$;
iii) $q_i < q_{k-1} + q_k$ *for* $j \leq i < k - 1$; *and*
 iv) $q_{j-1} \geq q_{k-1} + q_k$.
Then there is an optimum tree in which $l_{k-1} = l_k$ and either
  a) $l_j = l_k - 1$, *or*
  b) $l_j = l_k$ *and* $\boxed{j}$ *is a left child.*

Proof. By reversing left and right in Lemma W, we see that (ii) implies the existence of an optimum tree in which $l_{k-1} \geq l_k$. But Lemma W and (i) also imply that $l_1 \leq l_2 \leq \cdots \leq l_k$. Therefore $l_{k-1} = l_k$.

Suppose $l_s < l_k - 1 \leq l_{s+1}$ for some s with $j \leq s < k - 1$. Let t be the smallest index $< k$ such that $l_t = l_k$. Then $l_i = l_k - 1$ for $s < i < t$, and $\boxed{s+1}$ is a left child; possibly $s + 1 = t$. Furthermore $\boxed{t}$ and $\boxed{t+1}$ are siblings. Replace their parent by $\boxed{t+1}$; replace $\boxed{i}$ by $\boxed{i+1}$ for $s < i < t$; and replace the external node $\boxed{s}$ by an internal node whose children are $\boxed{s}$ and $\boxed{s+1}$. This change increases the cost by $\leq q_s - q_t - q_{t+1} \leq q_s - q_{k-1} - q_k$, so it is an improvement if $q_s < q_{k-1} + q_k$. Therefore, by (iii), $l_j \geq l_k - 1$.

We still have not used hypothesis (iv). If $l_j = l_k$ and $\boxed{j}$ is not a left child, $\boxed{j}$ must be the right sibling of $\boxed{j-1}$. Replace their parent by $\boxed{j-1}$; then replace leaf $\boxed{i}$ by $\boxed{i-1}$ for $j < i < k$; and replace the external node $\boxed{k}$ by an internal node whose children are $\boxed{k-1}$ and $\boxed{k}$. The cost increases by $-q_{j-1} + q_{k-1} + q_k \leq 0$, so we obtain an optimum tree satisfying (a) or (b). ∎

Lemma Y. *Let j and k be as in Lemma X, and consider the modified probabilities $(q'_0, \ldots, q'_{n-1}) = (q_0, \ldots, q_{j-1}, q_{k-1} + q_k, q_j, \ldots, q_{k-2}, q_{k+1}, \ldots, q_n)$ obtained by removing q_{k-1} and q_k and inserting $q_{k-1} + q_k$ after q_{j-1}. Then*

$$C(q'_0, \ldots, q'_{n-1}) \leq C(q_0, \ldots, q_n) - (q_{k-1} + q_k). \qquad (29)$$

Proof. It suffices to show that any optimum tree for $(q_0, \ldots, q_n)$ can be transformed into a tree of the same cost in which $\boxed{k-1}$ and $\boxed{k}$ are siblings and the leaves appear in the permuted order

$$\boxed{0} \quad \cdots \quad \boxed{j-1} \quad \boxed{k-1} \quad \boxed{k} \quad \boxed{j} \quad \cdots \quad \boxed{k-2} \quad \boxed{k+1} \quad \cdots \quad \boxed{n}. \qquad (30)$$

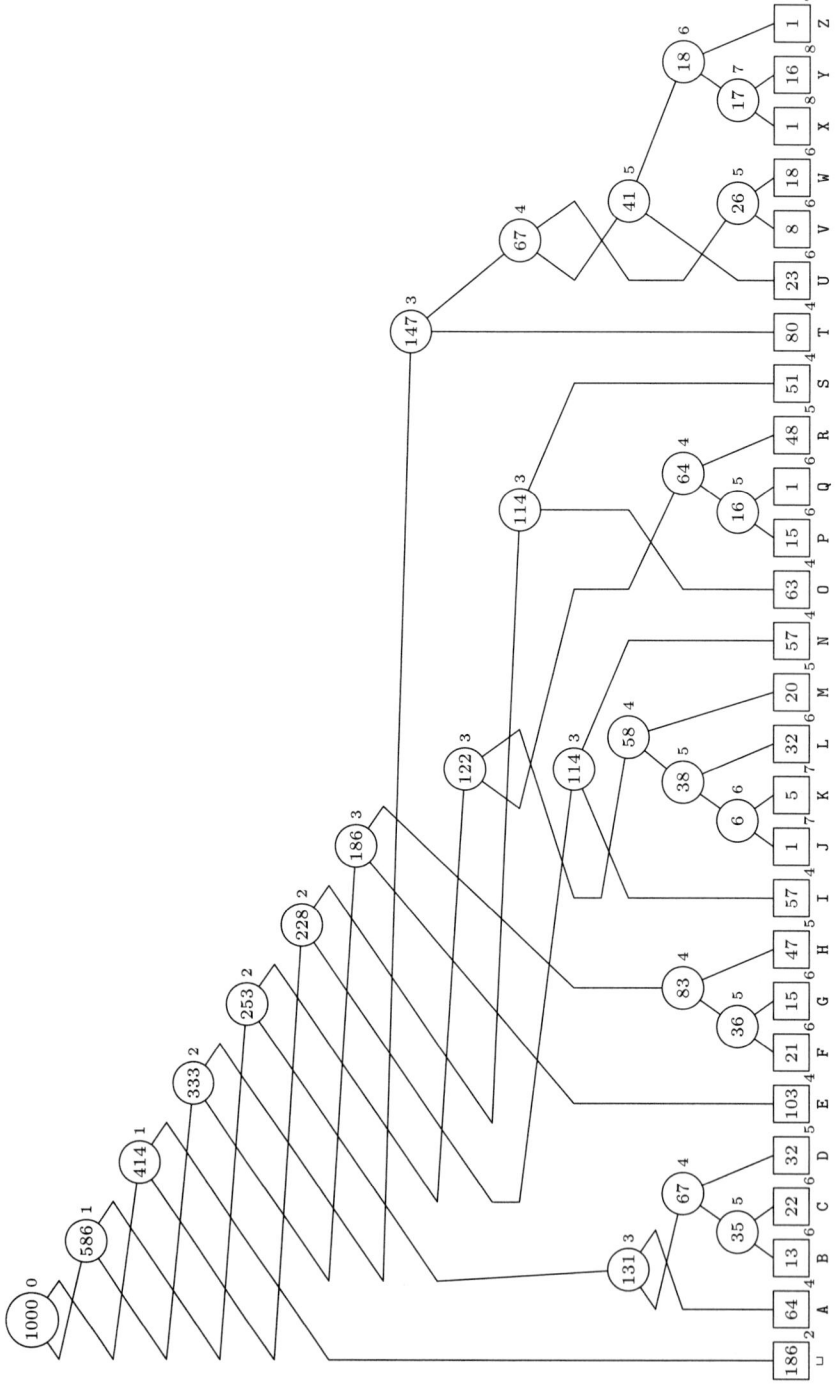

Fig. 18. The Garsia–Wachs algorithm applied to alphabetic frequency data: Phases 1 and 2.

We start with the tree constructed in Lemma X. If it is of type (b), we simply rename the leaves, sliding $\boxed{k{-}1}$ and $\boxed{k}$ to the left by $k-1-j$ places. If it is of type (a), suppose $l_{s-1} = l_k - 1$ and $l_s = l_k$; we proceed as follows: First slide $\boxed{k{-}1}$ and $\boxed{k}$ left by $k-1-s$ places; then replace their (new) parent by $\boxed{s{-}1}$; finally replace $\boxed{j}$ by a node whose children are $\boxed{k{-}1}$ and $\boxed{k}$, and replace node $\boxed{i}$ by $\boxed{i{-}1}$ for $j < i < s$. ∎

Lemma Z. *Under the hypotheses of Lemma Y, equality holds in* (29).

Proof. Every tree for $(q'_0, \ldots, q'_{n-1})$ corresponds to a tree with leaves (30) in which the two out-of-order leaf nodes $\boxed{k{-}1}$ and $\boxed{k}$ are siblings. Let internal node $\textcircled{x}$ be their parent. We want to show that any optimum tree of that type can be converted to a tree of the same cost in which the leaves appear in normal order $\boxed{0} \ldots \boxed{n}$.

There is nothing to prove if $j = k - 1$. Otherwise we have $q'_{i-1} > q'_{i+1}$ for $j \leq i < k - 1$, because $q_{j-1} \geq q_{k-1} + q_k > q_j$. Therefore by Lemma W we have $l_x \leq l_j \leq \cdots \leq l_{k-2}$, where l_x is the level of $\textcircled{x}$ and l_i is the level of $\boxed{i}$ for $j \leq i < k - 1$. If $l_x = l_{k-2}$, we simply slide node $\textcircled{x}$ to the right, replacing the sequence $\textcircled{x} \boxed{j} \ldots \boxed{k{-}2}$ by $\boxed{j} \ldots \boxed{k{-}2} \textcircled{x}$; this straightens out the leaves as desired.

Otherwise suppose $l_s = l_x$ and $l_{s+1} > l_x$. We first replace $\textcircled{x} \boxed{j} \ldots \boxed{s}$ by $\boxed{j} \ldots \boxed{s} \textcircled{x}$; this makes $l \leq l_{s+1} \leq \cdots \leq l_{k-2}$, where $l = l_x + 1$ is the common level of nodes $\boxed{k{-}1}$ and $\boxed{k}$. Finally replace nodes

$$\boxed{k{-}1}\ \boxed{k}\ \boxed{s{+}1}\ \ldots\ \boxed{k{-}2}$$

by the cyclically shifted sequence

$$\boxed{s{+}1}\ \ldots\ \boxed{k{-}2}\ \boxed{k{-}1}\ \boxed{k}.$$

Exercise 40 proves that these changes decrease the cost, unless $l_{k-2} = l$. But the cost cannot decrease, because of Lemma Y. Therefore $l_{k-2} = l$, and the proof is complete. ∎

These lemmas show that the problem for $n + 1$ weights $q_0, q_1, \ldots, q_n$ can be reduced to an n-weight problem: We first find the smallest index k with $q_{k-1} \leq q_{k+1}$; then we find the largest $j < k$ with $q_{j-1} \geq q_{k-1} + q_k$; then we remove q_{k-1} and q_k from the list, and insert the sum $q_{k-1} + q_k$ just after q_{j-1}. In the special cases $j = 0$ or $k = n$, the proofs show that we should proceed as if infinite weights q_{-1} and q_{n+1} were present at the left and right. The proofs also show that any optimum tree T' that is obtained from the new weights $(q'_0, \ldots, q'_{n-1})$ can be rearranged into a tree T that has the original weights $(q_0, \ldots, q_n)$ in the correct left-to-right order; moreover, each weight will appear at the same level in both T and T'.

For example, Fig. 18 illustrates the construction when the weights q_k are the relative frequencies of the characters ␣, A, B, ..., Z in English text. The first few weights are

$$186, 64, 13, 22, 32, 103, \ldots$$

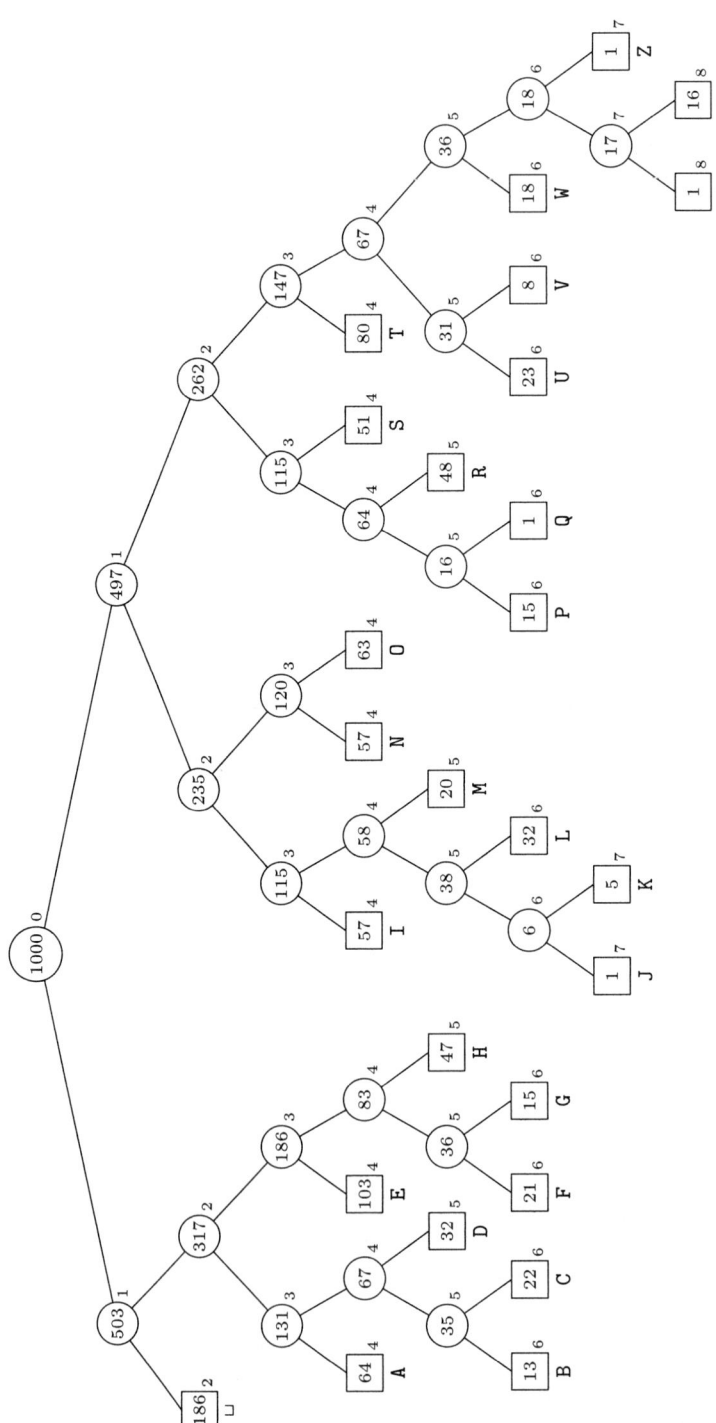

Fig. 19. The Garsia–Wachs algorithm applied to alphabetic frequency data: Phase 3.

BINARY TREE SEARCHING   451

and we have $186 > 13$, $64 > 22$, $13 \leq 32$; therefore we replace "$13, 22$" by 35. In the new sequence

$$186, \ 64, \ 35, \ 32, \ 103, \ \ldots$$

we replace "$35, 32$" by 67 and slide 67 to the left of 64, obtaining

$$186, \ 67, \ 64, \ 103, \ \ldots .$$

Then "$67, 64$" becomes 131, and we begin to examine the weights that follow 103. After the 27 original weights have been combined into the single weight 1000, the history of successive combinations specifies a binary tree whose weighted path length is the solution to the original problem.

But the leaves of the tree in Fig. 18 are not at all in the correct order, because they get tangled up when we slide $q_{k-1} + q_k$ to the left (see exercise 41). Still, the proof of Lemma Z guarantees that there is a tree whose leaves are in the correct order and on exactly the same levels as in the tangled tree. This untangled tree, Fig. 19, is therefore optimum; it is the binary tree output by the Garsia–Wachs algorithm.

Algorithm G (*Garsia–Wachs algorithm for optimum binary trees*). Given a sequence of nonnegative weights w_0, w_1, ..., w_n, this algorithm constructs a binary tree with n internal nodes for which $\sum_{k=0}^{n} w_k l_k$ is minimum, where l_k is the distance of external node $\boxed{k}$ from the root. It uses an array of $2n + 2$ nodes whose addresses are X_k for $0 \leq k \leq 2n + 1$; each node has four fields called WT, LLINK, RLINK, and LEVEL. The leaves of the constructed tree will be nodes $X_0 \ldots X_n$; the internal nodes will be $X_{n+1} \ldots X_{2n}$; the root will be X_{2n}; and X_{2n+1} is used as a temporary sentinel. The algorithm also maintains a working array of pointers P_0, P_1, ..., P_t, where $t \leq n + 1$.

G1. [Begin phase 1.] Set $\text{WT}(X_k) \leftarrow w_k$ and $\text{LLINK}(X_k) \leftarrow \text{RLINK}(X_k) \leftarrow \Lambda$ for $0 \leq k \leq n$. Also set $P_0 \leftarrow X_{2n+1}$, $\text{WT}(P_0) \leftarrow \infty$, $P_1 \leftarrow X_0$, $t \leftarrow 1$, $m \leftarrow n$. Then perform step G2 for $r = 1, 2, \ldots, n$, and go to G3.

G2. [Absorb w_r.] (At this point we have the basic condition

$$\text{WT}(P_{i-1}) > \text{WT}(P_{i+1}) \qquad \text{for } 1 \leq i < t; \tag{31}$$

in other words, the weights in the working array are "2-descending.") If $\text{WT}(P_{t-1}) \leq w_r$, set $k \leftarrow t$, perform Subroutine C below, and repeat step G2. Otherwise set $t \leftarrow t + 1$ and $P_t \leftarrow X_r$.

G3. [Finish phase 1.] While $t > 1$, set $k \leftarrow t$ and perform Subroutine C below.

G4. [Do phase 2.] (Now $P_1 = X_{2n}$ is the root of a binary tree, and $\text{WT}(P_1) = w_0 + \cdots + w_n$.) Set l_k to the distance of node X_k from node P_1, for $0 \leq k \leq n$. (See exercise 43. An example is shown in Fig. 18, where level numbers appear at the right of each node.)

G5. [Do phase 3.] By changing the links of $X_{n+1}, \ldots, X_{2n}$, construct a new binary tree having the same level numbers l_k, but with the leaf nodes in symmetric order $X_0, \ldots, X_n$. (See exercise 44; an example appears in Fig. 19.) ∎

Subroutine C (*Combination*). This recursive subroutine is the heart of the Garsia–Wachs algorithm. It combines two weights, shifts them left as appropriate, and maintains the 2-descending condition (31). Variables j and w are local, but variables k, m, and t are global.

C1. [Create a new node.] (At this point we have $k \geq 2$.) Set $m \leftarrow m + 1$, $\texttt{LLINK}(\texttt{X}_m) \leftarrow \texttt{P}_{k-1}$, $\texttt{RLINK}(\texttt{X}_m) \leftarrow \texttt{P}_k$, $\texttt{WT}(\texttt{X}_m) \leftarrow w \leftarrow \texttt{WT}(\texttt{P}_{k-1}) + \texttt{WT}(\texttt{P}_k)$.

C2. [Shift the following nodes left.] Set $t \leftarrow t - 1$, then $\texttt{P}_j \leftarrow \texttt{P}_{j+1}$ for $k \leq j \leq t$.

C3. [Shift the preceding nodes right.] Set $j \leftarrow k - 2$; then while $\texttt{WT}(\texttt{P}_j) < w$ set $\texttt{P}_{j+1} \leftarrow \texttt{P}_j$ and $j \leftarrow j - 1$.

C4. [Insert the new node.] Set $\texttt{P}_{j+1} \leftarrow \texttt{X}_m$.

C5. [Done?] If $j = 0$ or $\texttt{WT}(\texttt{P}_{j-1}) > w$, exit the subroutine.

C6. [Restore (31).] Set $k \leftarrow j$, $j \leftarrow t-j$, and call Subroutine C recursively. Then reset $j \leftarrow t - j$ (note that t may have changed!) and return to step C5. ∎

Subroutine C might need $\Omega(n)$ steps to create and insert a new node, because it uses sequential memory instead of linked lists. Therefore the total running time of Algorithm G might be $\Omega(n^2)$. But more elaborate data structures can be used to guarantee that phase 1 will require at most $O(n \log n)$ steps (see exercise 45). Phases 2 and 3 need only $O(n)$ steps.

Kleitman and Saks [*SIAM J. Algeb. Discr. Methods* **2** (1981), 142–146] proved that the optimum weighted path length never exceeds the value of the optimum weighted path length that occurs when the q's have been rearranged in "sawtooth order":

$$q_0 \leq q_2 \leq q_4 \leq \cdots \leq q_{2\lfloor n/2 \rfloor} \leq q_{2\lceil n/2 \rceil - 1} \leq \cdots \leq q_3 \leq q_1. \qquad (32)$$

(This is the inverse of the organ-pipe order discussed in exercise 6.1–18.) In the latter case the Garsia–Wachs algorithm essentially reduces to Huffman's algorithm on the weights $q_0 + q_1$, $q_2 + q_3$, $\ldots$, because the weights in the working array will actually be nonincreasing (not merely "2-descending" as in (31)). Therefore we can improve the upper bound of Theorem M without knowing the order of the weights.

The optimum binary tree in Fig. 19 has an important application to coding theory as well as to searching: Using 0 to stand for a left branch in the tree and 1 to stand for a right branch, we obtain the following variable-length codewords:

⊔	00	I	1000	R	11001
A	0100	J	1001000	S	1101
B	010100	K	1001001	T	1110
C	010101	L	100101	U	111100
D	01011	M	10011	V	111101
E	0110	N	1010	W	111110
F	011100	O	1011	X	11111100
G	011101	P	110000	Y	11111101
H	01111	Q	110001	Z	1111111

(33)

Thus a message like "RIGHT ON" would be encoded by the string

$$11001100001110101111111000101111010.$$

Decoding from left to right is easy, in spite of the variable length of the codewords, because the tree structure tells us when one codeword ends and another begins. This method of coding preserves the alphabetical order of messages, and it uses an average of about 4.2 bits per letter. Thus the code could be used to compress data files, without destroying lexicographic order of alphabetic information. (The figure of 4.2 bits per letter is minimum over all binary tree codes, although it could be reduced to 4.1 bits per letter if we disregarded the alphabetic ordering constraint. A further reduction, preserving alphabetic order, could be achieved if pairs of letters instead of single letters were encoded.)

History and bibliography. The tree search methods of this section were discovered independently by several people during the 1950s. In an unpublished memorandum dated August 1952, A. I. Dumey described a primitive form of tree insertion in the following way:

> Consider a drum with 2^n item storages in it, each having a binary address.
>
> Follow this program:
>
> 1. Read in the first item and store it in address 2^{n-1}, i.e., at the halfway storage place.
> 2. Read in the next item. Compare it with the first.
> 3. If it is larger, put it in address $2^{n-1} + 2^{n-2}$. If it is smaller, put it at 2^{n-2}. ...

Another early form of tree insertion was introduced by D. J. Wheeler, who actually allowed multiway branching similar to what we shall discuss in Section 6.2.4; and a binary tree insertion technique was devised by C. M. Berners-Lee [see *Comp. J.* **2** (1959), 5].

The first published descriptions of tree insertion were by P. F. Windley [*Comp. J.* **3** (1960), 84–88], A. D. Booth and A. J. T. Colin [*Information and Control* **3** (1960), 327–334], and Thomas N. Hibbard [*JACM* **9** (1962), 13–28]. Each of these authors seems to have developed the method independently of the others, and each paper derived the average number of comparisons (6) in a different way. The individual authors also went on to treat different aspects of the algorithm: Windley gave a detailed discussion of tree insertion sorting; Booth and Colin discussed the effect of preconditioning by making the first $2^n - 1$ elements form a perfectly balanced tree (see exercise 4); Hibbard introduced the idea of deletion and showed the connection between the analysis of tree insertion and the analysis of quicksort.

The idea of *optimum* binary search trees was first developed for the special case $p_1 = \cdots = p_n = 0$, in the context of alphabetic binary encodings like (33). A very interesting paper by E. N. Gilbert and E. F. Moore [*Bell System Tech. J.* **38** (1959), 933–968] discussed this problem and its relation to other coding problems. Gilbert and Moore proved Theorem M in the special case

$P = 0$, and observed that an optimum tree could be constructed in $O(n^3)$ steps, using a method like Algorithm K but without making use of the monotonicity relation (17). K. E. Iverson [*A Programming Language* (Wiley, 1962), 142–144] independently considered the *other* case, when all the q's are zero. He suggested that an optimum tree would be obtained if the root is chosen so as to equalize the left and right subtree probabilities as much as possible; unfortunately we have seen that this idea doesn't work. D. E. Knuth [*Acta Informatica* **1** (1971), 14–25, 270] subsequently considered the case of general p and q weights and proved that the algorithm could be reduced to $O(n^2)$ steps; he also presented an example from a compiler application, where the keys in the tree are "reserved words" in an ALGOL-like language. T. C. Hu had been studying his own algorithm for the case $p_j = 0$ for several years; a rigorous proof of the validity of that algorithm was difficult to find because of the complexity of the problem, but he eventually obtained a proof jointly with A. C. Tucker [*SIAM J. Applied Math.* **21** (1971), 514–532]. Simplifications leading to Algorithm G were found several years later by A. M. Garsia and M. L. Wachs, *SICOMP* **6** (1977), 622–642, although their proof was still rather complicated. Lemmas W, X, Y, and Z above are due to J. H. Kingston, *J. Algorithms* **9** (1988), 129–136. Further properties have been found by M. Karpinski, L. L. Larmore, and W. Rytter, *Theoretical Comp. Sci.* **180** (1997), 309–324. See also the paper by Hu, Kleitman, and Tamaki, *SIAM J. Applied Math.* **37** (1979), 246–256, for an elementary proof of the Hu–Tucker algorithm and some generalizations to other cost functions.

Theorem B is due to Paul J. Bayer, report MIT/LCS/TM-69 (Mass. Inst. of Tech., 1975), who also proved a slightly weaker form of Theorem M. The stronger form above is due to K. Mehlhorn, *SICOMP* **6** (1977), 235–239.

EXERCISES

1. [*15*] Algorithm T has been stated only for nonempty trees. What changes should be made so that it works properly for the empty tree too?

2. [*20*] Modify Algorithm T so that it works with *right-threaded* trees. (See Section 2.3.1; symmetric traversal is easier in such trees.)

▶ **3.** [*20*] In Section 6.1 we found that a slight change to the sequential search Algorithm 6.1S made it faster (Algorithm 6.1Q). Can a similar trick be used to speed up Algorithm T?

4. [*M24*] (A. D. Booth and A. J. T. Colin.) Given N keys in random order, suppose that we use the first $2^n - 1$ to construct a perfectly balanced tree, placing 2^k keys on level k for $0 \le k < n$; then we use Algorithm T to insert the remaining keys. What is the average number of comparisons in a successful search? [*Hint:* Modify Eq. (2).]

▶ **5.** [*M25*] There are $11! = 39,916,800$ different orders in which the names CAPRICORN, AQUARIUS, etc. could have been inserted into a binary search tree.
a) How many of these arrangements will produce Fig. 10?
b) How many of these arrangements will produce a *degenerate* tree, in which LLINK or RLINK is Λ in each node?

6. [*M26*] Let P_{nk} be the number of permutations $a_1 a_2 \ldots a_n$ of $\{1, 2, \ldots, n\}$ such that, if Algorithm T is used to insert $a_1, a_2, \ldots, a_n$ successively into an initially empty tree, exactly k comparisons are made when a_n is inserted. (In this problem, we will ignore the comparisons made when $a_1, \ldots, a_{n-1}$ were inserted. In the notation of the text, we have $C'_{n-1} = (\sum_k k P_{nk})/n!$, since this is the average number of comparisons made in an unsuccessful search of a tree containing $n-1$ elements.)

   a) Prove that $P_{(n+1)k} = 2P_{n(k-1)} + (n-1)P_{nk}$. [*Hint:* Consider whether or not a_{n+1} falls below a_n in the tree.]
   b) Find a simple formula for the generating function $G_n(z) = \sum_k P_{nk} z^k$, and use your formula to express P_{nk} in terms of Stirling numbers.
   c) What is the *variance* of this distribution?

   7. [*M25*] (S. R. Arora and W. T. Dent.) After n elements have been inserted into an initially empty tree, in random order, what is the average number of comparisons needed by Algorithm T to find the mth largest element, given the key of that element?

   8. [*M38*] Let $p(n, k)$ be the probability that k is the total internal path length of a tree built by Algorithm T from n randomly ordered keys. (The internal path length is the number of comparisons made by tree insertion sorting as the tree is being built.)
   a) Find a recurrence relation that defines the corresponding generating function.
   b) Compute the variance of this distribution. [Several of the exercises in Section 1.2.7 may be helpful here.]

   9. [*41*] We have proved that tree search and insertion requires only about $2 \ln N$ comparisons when the keys are inserted in random order; but in practice, the order may not be random. Make empirical studies to see how suitable tree insertion really is for symbol tables within a compiler and/or assembler. Do the identifiers used in typical large programs lead to fairly well-balanced binary search trees?

▶ **10.** [*22*] (R. W. Floyd.) Perhaps we are not interested in the sorting property of Algorithm T, but we expect that the input will come in nonrandom order. Devise a way to keep tree search efficient, by making the input "appear to be" in random order.

   11. [*20*] What is the maximum number of times the assignment S ← LLINK(R) might be performed in step D3, when deleting a node from a tree of size N?

   12. [*M22*] When making a random deletion from a random tree of N items, how often does step D1 go to D4, on the average? (See the proof of Theorem H.)

▶ **13.** [*M23*] If the root of a random tree is deleted by Algorithm D, is the resulting tree still random?

▶ **14.** [*22*] Prove that the path length of the tree produced by Algorithm D with step D1.5 added is never more than the path length of the tree produced without that step. Find a case where step D1.5 actually decreases the path length.

   15. [*23*] Let $a_1 a_2 a_3 a_4$ be a permutation of $\{1, 2, 3, 4\}$, and let $j = 1, 2,$ or 3. Take the one-element tree with key a_1 and insert a_2, a_3 using Algorithm T; then delete a_j using Algorithm D; then insert a_4 using Algorithm T. How many of the $4! \times 3$ possibilities produce trees of shape I, II, III, IV, V, respectively, in (13)?

▶ **16.** [*25*] Is the deletion operation *commutative*? That is, if Algorithm D is used to delete X and then Y, is the resulting tree the same as if Algorithm D is used to delete Y and then X?

   17. [*25*] Show that if the roles of left and right are completely reversed in Algorithm D, it is easy to extend the algorithm so that it deletes a given node from a *right-threaded* tree, preserving the necessary threads. (See exercise 2.)

   18. [*M21*] Show that Zipf's law yields (12).

19. [*M23*] What is the approximate average number of comparisons, (11), when the input probabilities satisfy the 80-20 law defined in Eq. 6.1–(11)?

20. [*M20*] Suppose we have inserted keys into a tree in order of decreasing frequency $p_1 \geq p_2 \geq \cdots \geq p_n$. Can this tree be substantially worse than the optimum search tree?

21. [*M20*] If p, q, r are probabilities chosen at random, subject to the condition that $p + q + r = 1$, what are the probabilities that trees I, II, III, IV, V of (13) are optimal, respectively? (Consider the relative areas of the regions in Fig. 14.)

22. [*M20*] Prove that $r[i, j-1]$ is never greater than $r[i+1, j]$ when step K4 of Algorithm K is performed.

▶ **23.** [*M23*] Find an optimum binary search tree for the case $N = 40$, with weights $p_1 = 9$, $p_2 = p_3 = \cdots = p_{40} = 1$, $q_0 = q_1 = \cdots = q_{40} = 0$. (Don't use a computer.)

24. [*M25*] Given that $p_n = q_n = 0$ and that the other weights are nonnegative, prove that an optimum tree for $(p_1, \ldots, p_n; q_0, \ldots, q_n)$ may be obtained by replacing

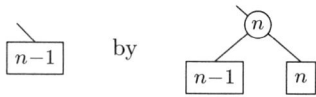

in any optimum tree for $(p_1, \ldots, p_{n-1}; q_0, \ldots, q_{n-1})$.

25. [*M20*] Let A and B be nonempty sets of real numbers, and define $A \leq B$ if the following property holds:

$$(a \in A, \ b \in B, \ \text{and} \ b < a) \qquad \text{implies} \qquad (a \in B \ \text{and} \ b \in A).$$

a) Prove that this relation is transitive on nonempty sets.
b) Prove or disprove: $A \leq B$ if and only if $A \leq A \cup B \leq B$.

26. [*M22*] Let $(p_1, \ldots, p_n; q_0, \ldots, q_n)$ be nonnegative weights, where $p_n + q_n = x$. Prove that as x varies from 0 to ∞, while $(p_1, \ldots, p_{n-1}; q_0, \ldots, q_{n-1})$ are held constant, the cost $c(0, n)$ of an optimum binary search tree is a concave, continuous, piecewise linear function of x with integer slopes. In other words, prove that there exist positive integers $l_0 > l_1 > \cdots > l_m$ and real constants $0 = x_0 < x_1 < \cdots < x_m < x_{m+1} = \infty$ and $y_0 < y_1 \cdots < y_m$ such that $c(0, n) = y_h + l_h x$ when $x_h \leq x \leq x_{h+1}$, for $0 \leq h \leq m$.

27. [*M33*] The object of this exercise is to prove that the sets of roots $R(i, j)$ of optimum binary search trees satisfy

$$R(i, j-1) \leq R(i, j) \leq R(i+1, j), \qquad \text{for } j - i \geq 2,$$

in terms of the relation defined in exercise 25, when the weights $(p_1, \ldots, p_n; q_0, \ldots, q_n)$ are nonnegative. The proof is by induction on $j - i$; our task is to prove that $R(0, n-1) \leq R(0, n)$, assuming that $n \geq 2$ and that the stated relation holds for $j - i < n$. [By left-right symmetry it follows that $R(0, n) \leq R(1, n)$.]

a) Prove that $R(0, n-1) \leq R(0, n)$ if $p_n = q_n = 0$. (See exercise 24.)
b) Let $p_n + q_n = x$. In the notation of exercise 26, let R_h be the set $R(0, n)$ of optimum roots when $x_h < x < x_{h+1}$, and let R'_h be the set of optimum roots when $x = x_h$. Prove that

$$R'_0 \leq R_0 \leq R'_1 \leq R_1 \leq \cdots \leq R'_m \leq R_m.$$

Hence by part (a) and exercise 25 we have $R(0, n-1) \leq R(0, n)$ for all x. [*Hint:* Consider the case $x = x_h$, and assume that both the trees

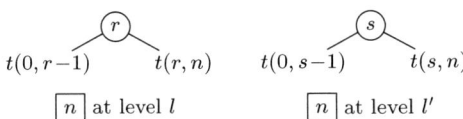

$$t(0, r-1) \qquad t(r, n) \qquad t(0, s-1) \qquad t(s, n)$$

$\boxed{n}$ at level l $\qquad\qquad$ $\boxed{n}$ at level l'

are optimum, with $s < r$ and $l \geq l'$. Use the induction hypothesis to prove that there is an optimum tree with root (r) such that $\boxed{n}$ is at level l', and an optimum tree with root (s) such that $\boxed{n}$ is at level l.]

28. [*24*] Use some macro language to define an "optimum binary search" macro, whose parameter is a nested specification of an optimum binary tree.

29. [*40*] What is the *worst* possible binary search tree for the 31 most common English words, using the frequency data of Fig. 12?

30. [*M34*] Prove that the costs of optimum binary search trees satisfy the "quadrangle inequality" $c(i, j) - c(i, j-1) \geq c(i+1, j) - c(i+1, j-1)$ when $j \geq i + 2$.

31. [*M35*] (K. C. Tan.) Prove that, among all possible sets of probabilities $(p_1, \ldots, p_n; q_0, \ldots, q_n)$ with $p_1 + \cdots + p_n + q_0 + \cdots + q_n = 1$, the most expensive minimum-cost tree occurs when $p_i = 0$ for all i, $q_j = 0$ for all even j, and $q_j = 1/\lceil n/2 \rceil$ for all odd j.

▶ **32.** [*M25*] Let $n + 1 = 2^m + k$, where $0 \leq k \leq 2^m$. There are exactly $\binom{2^m}{k}$ binary trees in which all external nodes appear on levels m and $m + 1$. Show that, among all these trees, we obtain one with the minimum cost for the weights $(p_1, \ldots, p_n; q_0, \ldots, q_n)$ if we apply Algorithm K to the weights $(p_1, \ldots, p_n; M+q_0, \ldots, M+q_n)$ for sufficiently large M.

33. [*M41*] In order to find the binary search tree that minimizes the running time of Program T, we should minimize the quantity $7C + C1$ instead of simply minimizing the number of comparisons C. Develop an algorithm that finds optimum binary search trees when different costs are associated with left and right branches in the tree. (Incidentally, when the right cost is twice the left cost, and the node frequencies are all equal, the Fibonacci trees turn out to be optimum; see L. E. Stanfel, *JACM* **17** (1970), 508–517. On machines that cannot make three-way comparisons at once, a program for Algorithm T will have to make two comparisons in step T2, one for equality and one for less-than; B. Sheil and V. R. Pratt have observed that these comparisons need not involve the same key, and it may well be best to have a binary tree whose internal nodes specify either an equality test *or* a less-than test but not both. This situation would be interesting to explore as an alternative to the stated problem.)

34. [*HM21*] Show that the asymptotic value of the multinomial coefficient

$$\binom{N}{p_1 N, \; p_2 N, \; \ldots, \; p_n N}$$

as $N \to \infty$ is related to the entropy $H(p_1, p_2, \ldots, p_n)$.

35. [*HM22*] Complete the proof of Theorem B by establishing the inequality (24).

▶ **36.** [*HM25*] (Claude Shannon.) Let X and Y be random variables with finite ranges $\{x_1, \ldots, x_m\}$ and $\{y_1, \ldots, y_n\}$, and let $p_i = \Pr(X = x_i)$, $q_j = \Pr(Y = y_j)$, $r_{ij} = \Pr(X = x_i \text{ and } Y = y_j)$. Let $H(X) = H(p_1, \ldots, p_m)$ and $H(Y) = H(q_1, \ldots, q_n)$ be the respective entropies of the variables singly, and let $H(XY) = H(r_{11}, \ldots, r_{mn})$ be the entropy of their joint distribution. Prove that

$$H(X) \leq H(XY) \leq H(X) + H(Y).$$

[*Hint:* If f is any concave function, we have $\mathrm{E}\, f(X) \leq f(\mathrm{E}\, X)$.]

37. [*HM26*] (P. J. Bayer, 1975.) Suppose $(P_1, \ldots, P_n)$ is a random probability distribution, namely a random point in the $(n-1)$-dimensional simplex defined by $P_k \geq 0$ for $1 \leq k \leq n$ and $P_1 + \cdots + P_n = 1$. (Equivalently, $(P_1, \ldots, P_n)$ is a set of random *spacings*, in the sense of exercise 3.3.2–26.) What is the expected value of the entropy $H(P_1, \ldots, P_n)$?

38. [*M20*] Explain why Theorem M holds in general, although we have only proved it in the case $s_0 < s_1 < s_2 < \cdots < s_n$.

▶ **39.** [*M25*] Let $w_1, \ldots, w_n$ be nonnegative weights with $w_1 + \cdots + w_n = 1$. Prove that the weighted path length of the Huffman tree constructed in Section 2.3.4.5 is less than $H(w_1, \ldots, w_n) + 1$. *Hint:* See the proof of Theorem M.

40. [*M26*] Complete the proof of Lemma Z.

41. [*21*] Figure 18 shows the construction of a tangled binary tree. List its leaves in left-to-right order.

42. [*23*] Explain why Subroutine C preserves the 2-descending condition (31).

43. [*20*] Explain how to implement phase 2 of the Garsia–Wachs algorithm efficiently.

▶ **44.** [*25*] Explain how to implement phase 3 of the Garsia–Wachs algorithm efficiently: Construct a binary tree, given the levels $l_0, l_1, \ldots, l_n$ of its leaves in symmetric order.

▶ **45.** [*30*] Explain how to implement Subroutine C so that the total running time of the Garsia–Wachs algorithm is at most $O(n \log n)$.

46. [*M30*] (C. K. Wong and Shi-Kuo Chang.) Consider a scheme whereby a binary search tree is constructed by Algorithm T, except that whenever the number of nodes reaches a number of the form $2^n - 1$ the tree is reorganized into a perfectly balanced uniform tree, with 2^k nodes on level k for $0 \leq k < n$. Prove that the total number of comparisons made while constructing such a tree is $N \lg N + O(N)$ on the average. (It is not difficult to show that the amount of time needed for the reorganizations is $O(N)$.)

47. [*M40*] Generalize Theorems B and M from binary trees to t-ary trees. If possible, also allow the branching costs to be nonuniform as in exercise 33.

48. [*M47*] Carry out a rigorous analysis of the steady state of a binary search tree subjected to random insertions and deletions.

49. [*HM42*] Analyze the average height of a random binary search tree.

6.2.3. Balanced Trees

The tree insertion algorithm we have just learned will produce good search trees, when the input data is random, but there is still the annoying possibility that a degenerate tree will occur. Perhaps we could devise an algorithm that keeps the tree optimum at all times; but unfortunately that seems to be very difficult. Another idea is to keep track of the total path length, and to reorganize the tree completely whenever its path length exceeds $5N \lg N$, say. But such an approach might require about $\sqrt{N/2}$ reorganizations as the tree is being built.

A very pretty solution to the problem of maintaining a good search tree was discovered in 1962 by two Russian mathematicians, G. M. Adelson-Velsky and E. M. Landis [*Doklady Akademii Nauk SSSR* **146** (1962), 263–266; English translation in *Soviet Math. Doklady* **3** (1962), 1259–1263]. Their method requires only two extra bits per node, and it never uses more than $O(\log N)$ operations to search the tree or to insert an item. In fact, we shall see that their approach also leads to a general technique that is good for representing arbitrary *linear lists* of length N, so that each of the following operations can be done in only $O(\log N)$ units of time:

i) Find an item having a given key.

ii) Find the kth item, given k.

iii) Insert an item at a specified place.

iv) Delete a specified item.

If we use sequential allocation for linear lists, operations (i) and (ii) are efficient but operations (iii) and (iv) take order N steps; on the other hand, if we use linked allocation, operations (iii) and (iv) are efficient but operations (i) and (ii) take order N steps. A tree representation of linear lists can do *all four* operations in $O(\log N)$ steps. And it is also possible to do other standard operations with comparable efficiency, so that, for example, we can concatenate a list of M elements with a list of N elements in $O\big(\log(M + N)\big)$ steps.

The method for achieving all this involves what we shall call *balanced trees*. (Many authors also call them *AVL trees*, where the AV stands for Adelson-Velsky and the L stands for Landis.) The preceding paragraph is an advertisement for balanced trees, which makes them sound like a universal panacea that makes all other forms of data representation obsolete; but of course we ought to have a balanced attitude about balanced trees! In applications that do not involve all four of the operations above, we may be able to get by with substantially less overhead and simpler programming. Furthermore, there is no advantage to balanced trees unless N is reasonably large; thus if we have an efficient method that takes $64 \lg N$ units of time and an inefficient method that takes $2N$ units of time, we should use the inefficient method unless N is greater than 256. On the other hand, N shouldn't be too large, either; balanced trees are appropriate chiefly for *internal* storage of data, and we shall study better methods for external direct-access files in Section 6.2.4. Since internal memories seem to be getting larger and larger as time goes by, balanced trees are becoming more and more important.

The *height* of a tree is defined to be its maximum level, the length of the longest path from the root to an external node. A binary tree is called *balanced* if the height of the left subtree of every node never differs by more than ±1 from the height of its right subtree. Figure 20 shows a balanced tree with 17 internal nodes and height 5; the *balance factor* within each node is shown as +, •, or − according as the right subtree height minus the left subtree height is +1, 0, or −1. The Fibonacci tree in Fig. 8 (Section 6.2.1) is another balanced binary tree of height 5, having only 12 internal nodes; most of the balance factors in that tree

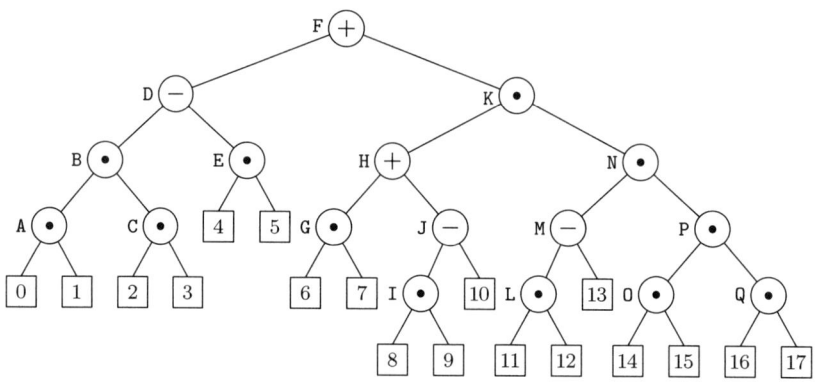

Fig. 20. A balanced binary tree.

are -1. The zodiac tree in Fig. 10 (Section 6.2.2) is *not* balanced, because the height restriction on subtrees fails at both the AQUARIUS and GEMINI nodes.

This definition of balance represents a compromise between *optimum* binary trees (with all external nodes required to be on two adjacent levels) and *arbitrary* binary trees (unrestricted). It is therefore natural to ask how far from optimum a balanced tree can be. The answer is that its search paths will never be more than 45 percent longer than the optimum:

Theorem A (Adelson-Velsky and Landis). *The height of a balanced tree with N internal nodes always lies between $\lg(N+1)$ and $1.4405 \lg(N+2) - 0.3277$.*

Proof. A binary tree of height h obviously cannot have more than 2^h external nodes; so $N + 1 \le 2^h$, that is, $h \ge \lceil \lg(N+1) \rceil$ in any binary tree.

In order to find the maximum value of h, let us turn the problem around and ask for the minimum number of nodes possible in a balanced tree of height h. Let T_h be such a tree with fewest possible nodes; then one of the subtrees of the root, say the left subtree, has height $h - 1$, and the other subtree has height $h - 1$ or $h - 2$. Since we want T_h to have the minimum number of nodes, we may assume that the left subtree of the root is T_{h-1}, and that the right subtree is T_{h-2}. This argument shows that the *Fibonacci tree* of order $h + 1$ has the fewest possible nodes among all possible balanced trees of height h. (See the definition of Fibonacci trees in Section 6.2.1.) Thus

$$N \ge F_{h+2} - 1 > \phi^{h+2}/\sqrt{5} - 2,$$

and the stated result follows as in the corollary to Theorem 4.5.3F. ∎

The proof of this theorem shows that a search in a balanced tree will require more than 25 comparisons only if the tree contains at least $F_{28} - 1 = 317{,}810$ nodes.

Consider now what happens when a new node is inserted into a balanced tree using tree insertion (Algorithm 6.2.2T). In Fig. 20, the tree will still be balanced if the new node takes the place of $\boxed{4}$, $\boxed{5}$, $\boxed{6}$, $\boxed{7}$, $\boxed{10}$, or $\boxed{13}$, but

some adjustment will be needed if the new node falls elsewhere. The problem
arises when we have a node with a balance factor of $+1$ whose right subtree
got higher after the insertion; or, dually, if the balance factor is -1 and the left
subtree got higher. It is not difficult to see that trouble arises only in two cases:

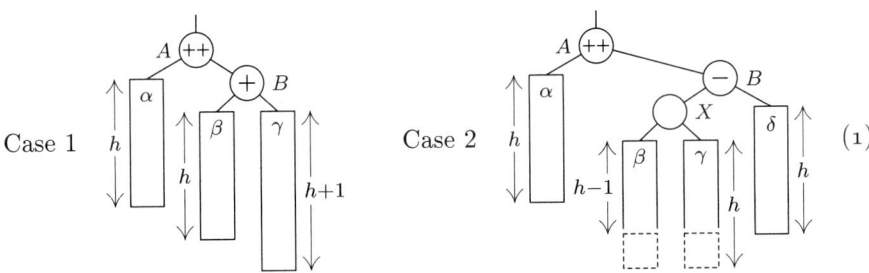

(Two other essentially identical cases occur if we reflect these diagrams, interchanging left and right.) In these diagrams the large rectangles α, β, γ, δ
represent subtrees having the respective heights shown. Case 1 occurs when a
new element has just increased the height of node B's right subtree from h to
$h + 1$, and Case 2 occurs when the new element has increased the height of B's
left subtree. In the second case, we have either $h = 0$ (so that X itself was the
new node), or else node X has two subtrees of respective heights $(h-1, h)$ or
$(h, h-1)$.

Simple transformations will restore balance in both of these cases, while
preserving the symmetric order of the tree nodes:

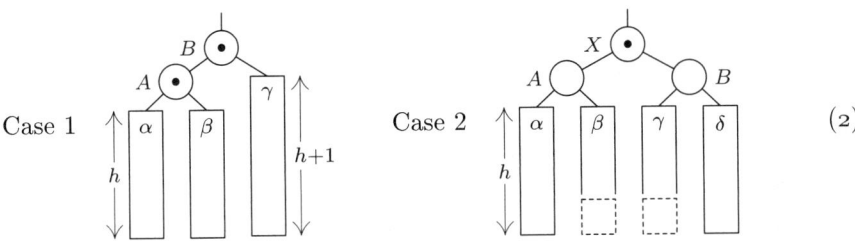

In Case 1 we simply "rotate" the tree to the left, attaching β to A instead of B.
This transformation is like applying the associative law to an algebraic formula,
replacing $\alpha(\beta\gamma)$ by $(\alpha\beta)\gamma$. In Case 2 we use a double rotation, first rotating
(X, B) right, then (A, X) left. In both cases only a few links of the tree need to
be changed. Furthermore, the new trees have height $h + 2$, which is exactly the
height that was present before the insertion; hence the rest of the tree (if any)
that was originally above node A always remains balanced.

For example, if we insert a new node into position $\boxed{17}$ of Fig. 20 we obtain
the balanced tree shown in Fig. 21, after a single rotation (Case 1). Notice that
several of the balance factors have changed.

The details of this insertion procedure can be worked out in several ways.
At first glance an auxiliary stack seems to be necessary, in order to keep track
of which nodes will be affected, but the following algorithm gains some speed by

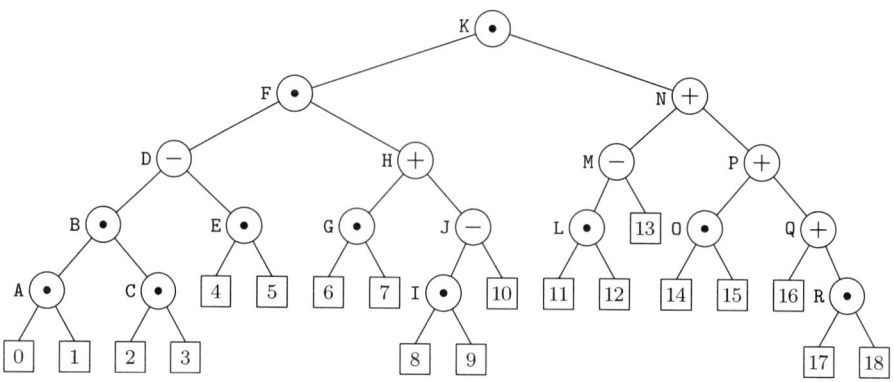

Fig. 21. The tree of Fig. 20, rebalanced after a new key R has been inserted.

exploiting the fact that the balance factor of node B in (1) was zero before the
insertion.

Algorithm A (*Balanced tree search and insertion*). Given a table of records
that form a balanced binary tree as described above, this algorithm searches for
a given argument K. If K is not in the table, a new node containing K is inserted
into the tree in the appropriate place and the tree is rebalanced if necessary.

The nodes of the tree are assumed to contain KEY, LLINK, and RLINK fields
as in Algorithm 6.2.2T. We also have a new field

$$\text{B(P)} = \text{balance factor of NODE(P)},$$

the height of the right subtree minus the height of the left subtree; this field
always contains either $+1$, 0, or -1. A special header node also appears at the
top of the tree, in location HEAD; the value of RLINK(HEAD) is a pointer to the
root of the tree, and LLINK(HEAD) is used to keep track of the overall height of
the tree. (Knowledge of the height is not really necessary for this algorithm, but
it is useful in the concatenation procedure discussed below.) We assume that
the tree is *nonempty*, namely that RLINK(HEAD) $\neq \Lambda$.

For convenience in description, the algorithm uses the notation LINK(a,P)
as a synonym for LLINK(P) if $a = -1$, and for RLINK(P) if $a = +1$.

A1. [Initialize.] Set T $\leftarrow$ HEAD, S $\leftarrow$ P $\leftarrow$ RLINK(HEAD). (The pointer variable P
will move down the tree; S will point to the place where rebalancing may
be necessary, and T always points to the parent of S.)

A2. [Compare.] If $K < $ KEY(P), go to A3; if $K > $ KEY(P), go to A4; and if
$K = $ KEY(P), the search terminates successfully.

A3. [Move left.] Set Q $\leftarrow$ LLINK(P). If Q $= \Lambda$, set Q $\Leftarrow$ AVAIL and LLINK(P) $\leftarrow$ Q
and go to step A5. Otherwise if B(Q) $\neq 0$, set T $\leftarrow$ P and S $\leftarrow$ Q. Finally
set P $\leftarrow$ Q and return to step A2.

A4. [Move right.] Set Q $\leftarrow$ RLINK(P). If Q $= \Lambda$, set Q $\Leftarrow$ AVAIL and RLINK(P) $\leftarrow$ Q
and go to step A5. Otherwise if B(Q) $\neq 0$, set T $\leftarrow$ P and S $\leftarrow$ Q. Finally set

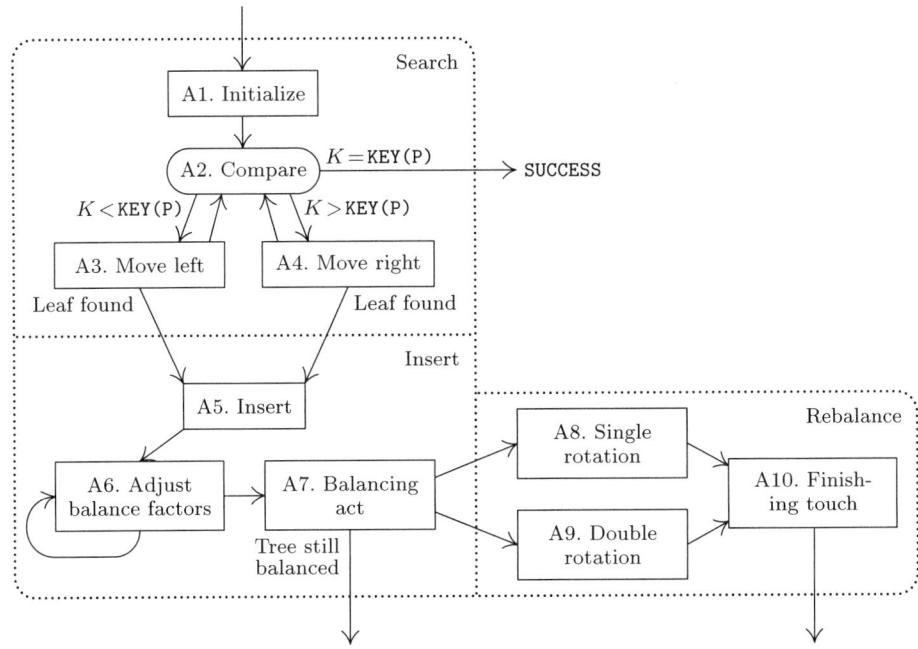

Fig. 22. Balanced tree search and insertion.

P ← Q and return to step A2. (The last part of this step may be combined
with the last part of step A3.)

A5. [Insert.] (We have just linked a new node, NODE(Q), into the tree, and its
fields need to be initialized.) Set KEY(Q) ← K, LLINK(Q) ← RLINK(Q) ← Λ,
and B(Q) ← 0.

A6. [Adjust balance factors.] (Now the balance factors on nodes between S
and Q need to be changed from zero to ±1.) If $K <$ KEY(S) set $a \leftarrow -1$,
otherwise set $a \leftarrow +1$. Then set R ← P ← LINK(a,S), and repeatedly do
the following operations zero or more times until P = Q: If $K <$ KEY(P) set
B(P) ← −1 and P ← LLINK(P); if $K >$ KEY(P), set B(P) ← +1 and P ←
RLINK(P). (If $K =$ KEY(P), then P = Q and we proceed to the next step.)

A7. [Balancing act.] Several cases now arise:
    i) If B(S) = 0 (the tree has grown higher), set B(S) ← a, LLINK(HEAD)
      ← LLINK(HEAD) + 1, and terminate the algorithm.
    ii) If B(S) = $-a$ (the tree has gotten more balanced), set B(S) ← 0 and
      terminate the algorithm.
    iii) If B(S) = a (the tree has gotten out of balance), go to step A8 if
      B(R) = a, to A9 if B(R) = $-a$.
      (Case (iii) corresponds to the situations depicted in (1) when $a = +1$;
      S and R point, respectively, to nodes A and B, and LINK($-a$,S) points
      to α, etc.)

A8. [Single rotation.] Set P ← R, LINK(a,S) ← LINK($-a$,R), LINK($-a$,R) ← S, B(S) ← B(R) ← 0. Go to A10.

A9. [Double rotation.] Set P ← LINK($-a$,R), LINK($-a$,R) ← LINK(a,P), LINK(a,P) ← R, LINK(a,S) ← LINK($-a$,P), LINK($-a$,P) ← S. Now set

$$(B(S), B(R)) \leftarrow \begin{cases} (-a, 0), & \text{if } B(P) = a; \\ (0, 0), & \text{if } B(P) = 0; \\ (0, a), & \text{if } B(P) = -a; \end{cases} \tag{3}$$

and then set B(P) ← 0.

A10. [Finishing touch.] (We have completed the rebalancing transformation, taking (1) to (2), with P pointing to the new subtree root and T pointing to the parent of the old subtree root S.) If S = RLINK(T) then set RLINK(T) ← P, otherwise set LLINK(T) ← P. ∎

This algorithm is rather long, but it divides into three simple parts: Steps A1–A4 do the search, steps A5–A7 insert a new node, and steps A8–A10 rebalance the tree if necessary. Essentially the same method can be used if the tree is *threaded* (see exercise 6.2.2–2), since the balancing act never needs to make difficult changes to thread links.

We know that the algorithm takes about $C \log N$ units of time, for some C, but it is important to know the approximate value of C so that we can tell how large N should be in order to make balanced trees worth all the trouble. The following MIX implementation gives some insight into this question.

Program A (*Balanced tree search and insertion*). This program for Algorithm A uses tree nodes having the form

$$\begin{array}{|c|c|c|} \hline B & \text{LLINK} & \text{RLINK} \\ \hline \multicolumn{3}{|c|}{\text{KEY}} \\ \hline \end{array} \;; \tag{4}$$

rA ≡ K, rI1 ≡ P, rI2 ≡ Q, rI3 ≡ R, rI4 ≡ S, rI5 ≡ T. The code for steps A7–A9 is duplicated so that the value of a appears implicitly (not explicitly) in the program.

```
01 B     EQU  0:1
02 LLINK EQU  2:3
03 RLINK EQU  4:5
04 START LDA  K            1      A1. Initialize.
05       ENT5 HEAD         1      T ← HEAD.
06       LD2  0,5(RLINK)   1      Q ← RLINK(HEAD).
07       JMP  2F           1      To A2 with S ← P ← Q.
08 4H    LD2  0,1(RLINK)   C2     A4. Move right. Q ← RLINK(P).
09       J2Z  5F           C2     To A5 if Q = Λ.
10 1H    LDX  0,2(B)       C-1    rX ← B(Q).
11       JXZ  *+3          C-1    Jump if B(Q) = 0.
12       ENT5 0,1          D-1    T ← P.
```

13	2H	ENT4	0,2	D	S ← Q.
14		ENT1	0,2	C	P ← Q.
15		CMPA	1,1	C	_A2. Compare._
16		JG	4B	C	To A4 if $K >$ KEY(P).
17		JE	SUCCESS	$C1$	Exit if $K =$ KEY(P).
18		LD2	0,1(LLINK)	$C1-S$	_A3. Move left._ Q ← LLINK(P).
19		J2NZ	1B	$C1-S$	Jump if Q $\neq \Lambda$.
20	5H	LD2	AVAIL	$1-S$	_A5. Insert._
21		J2Z	OVERFLOW	$1-S$	
22		LDX	0,2(RLINK)	$1-S$	
23		STX	AVAIL	$1-S$	Q $\Leftarrow$ AVAIL.
24		STA	1,2	$1-S$	KEY(Q) ← K.
25		STZ	0,2	$1-S$	LLINK(Q) ← RLINK(Q) ← Λ.
26		JL	1F	$1-S$	Was $K <$ KEY(P)?
27		ST2	0,1(RLINK)	A	RLINK(P) ← Q.
28		JMP	*+2	A	
29	1H	ST2	0,1(LLINK)	$1-S-A$	LLINK(P) ← Q.
30	6H	CMPA	1,4	$1-S$	_A6. Adjust balance factors._
31		JL	*+3	$1-S$	Jump if $K <$ KEY(S).
32		LD3	0,4(RLINK)	E	R ← RLINK(S).
33		JMP	*+2	E	
34		LD3	0,4(LLINK)	$1-S-E$	R ← LLINK(S).
35		ENT1	0,3	$1-S$	P ← R.
36		ENTX	-1	$1-S$	rX ← -1.
37		JMP	1F	$1-S$	To comparison loop.
38	4H	JE	7F	$F2+1-S$	To A7 if $K =$ KEY(P).
39		STX	0,1(1:1)	$F2$	B(P) ← $+1$ (it was +0).
40		LD1	0,1(RLINK)	$F2$	P ← RLINK(P).
41	1H	CMPA	1,1	$F+1-S$	
42		JGE	4B	$F+1-S$	Jump if $K \geq$ KEY(P).
43		STX	0,1(B)	$F1$	B(P) ← -1.
44		LD1	0,1(LLINK)	$F1$	P ← LLINK(P).
45		JMP	1B	$F1$	To comparison loop.
46	7H	LD2	0,4(B)	$1-S$	_A7. Balancing act._ rI2 ← B(S).
47		STZ	0,4(B)	$1-S$	B(S) ← 0.
48		CMPA	1,4	$1-S$	
49		JG	A7R	$1-S$	To $a = +1$ routine if $K >$ KEY(S).
50	A7L	J2P	DONE	$U1$	Exit if rI2 = $-a$.
51		J2Z	7F	$G1+J1$	Jump if B(S) was zero.
52		ENT1	0,3	$G1$	P ← R.
53		LD2	0,3(B)	$G1$	rI2 ← B(R).
54		J2N	A8L	$G1$	To A8 if rI2 = a.
55	A9L	LD1	0,3(RLINK)	$H1$	_A9. Double rotation._
56		LDX	0,1(LLINK)	$H1$	LINK(a,P ← LINK($-a$,R))
57		STX	0,3(RLINK)	$H1$	→ LINK($-a$,R).
58		ST3	0,1(LLINK)	$H1$	LINK(a,P) ← R.
59		LD2	0,1(B)	$H1$	rI2 ← B(P).
60		LDX	T1,2	$H1$	$-a$, 0, or 0
61		STX	0,4(B)	$H1$	→ B(S).

62		LDX	T2,2	$H1$	$0, 0$, or a
63		STX	0,3(B)	$H1$	$\to$ B(R).
64	A8L	LDX	0,1(RLINK)	$G1$	*A8. Single rotation.*
65		STX	0,4(LLINK)	$G1$	LINK(a,S) $\gets$ LINK($-a$,P).
66		ST4	0,1(RLINK)	$G1$	LINK($-a$,P) $\gets$ S.
67		JMP	8F	$G1$	Join up with the other branch.
68	A7R	J2N	DONE	$U2$	Exit if rI2 $= -a$.
69		J2Z	6F	$G2 + J2$	Jump if B(S) was zero.
70		ENT1	0,3	$G2$	P $\gets$ R.
71		LD2	0,3(B)	$G2$	rI2 $\gets$ B(R).
72		J2P	A8R	$G2$	To A8 if rI2 $= a$.
73	A9R	LD1	0,3(LLINK)	$H2$	*A9. Double rotation.*
74		LDX	0,1(RLINK)	$H2$	LINK(a,P $\gets$ LINK($-a$,R))
75		STX	0,3(LLINK)	$H2$	$\to$ LINK($-a$,R).
76		ST3	0,1(RLINK)	$H2$	LINK(a,P) $\gets$ R.
77		LD2	0,1(B)	$H2$	rI2 $\gets$ B(P).
78		LDX	T2,2	$H2$	$-a, 0$, or 0
79		STX	0,4(B)	$H2$	$\to$ B(S).
80		LDX	T1,2	$H2$	$0, 0$, or a
81		STX	0,3(B)	$H2$	$\to$ B(R).
82	A8R	LDX	0,1(LLINK)	$G2$	*A8. Single rotation.*
83		STX	0,4(RLINK)	$G2$	LINK(a,S) $\gets$ LINK($-a$,P).
84		ST4	0,1(LLINK)	$G2$	LINK($-a$,P) $\gets$ S.
85	8H	STZ	0,1(B)	G	B(P) $\gets 0$.
86	A10	CMP4	0,5(RLINK)	G	*A10. Finishing touch.*
87		JNE	*+3	G	Jump if RLINK(T) $\neq$ S.
88		ST1	0,5(RLINK)	$G3$	RLINK(T) $\gets$ P.
89		JMP	DONE	$G3$	Exit.
90		ST1	0,5(LLINK)	$G4$	LLINK(T) $\gets$ P.
91		JMP	DONE	$G4$	Exit.
92		CON	+1		
93	T1	CON	0		Table for (3).
94	T2	CON	0		
95		CON	-1		
96	6H	ENTX	+1	$J2$	rX $\gets +1$.
97	7H	STX	0,4(B)	J	B(S) $\gets a$.
98		LDX	HEAD(LLINK)	J	LLINK(HEAD)
99		INCX	1	J	$+ 1$
100		STX	HEAD(LLINK)	J	$\to$ LLINK(HEAD).
101	DONE	EQU	*	$1 - S$	Insertion is complete. ∎

Analysis of balanced tree insertion. [Nonmathematical readers, please skip to (10).] In order to figure out the running time of Algorithm A, we would like to know the answers to the following questions:

- How many comparisons are made during the search?
- How far apart will nodes S and Q be? (In other words, how much adjustment is needed in step A6?)
- How often do we need to do a single or double rotation?

It is not difficult to derive upper bounds on the worst-case running time, using Theorem A, but of course in practice we want to know the average behavior. No theoretical determination of the average behavior has been successfully completed as yet, since the algorithm appears to be quite complicated, but several interesting theoretical and empirical results have been obtained.

In the first place we can ask about the number B_{nh} of balanced binary trees with n internal nodes and height h. It is not difficult to compute the generating function $B_h(z) = \sum_{n\geq 0} B_{nh} z^n$ for small h, from the relations

$$B_0(z) = 1, \qquad B_1(z) = z, \qquad B_{h+1}(z) = zB_h(z)\big(B_h(z) + 2B_{h-1}(z)\big). \quad (5)$$

(See exercise 6.) Thus

$$B_2(z) = 2z^2 + z^3,$$
$$B_3(z) = \qquad\quad 4z^4 + 6z^5 + 4z^6 + z^7,$$
$$B_4(z) = \qquad\qquad\qquad\quad 16z^7 + 32z^8 + 44z^9 + \cdots + 8z^{14} + z^{15},$$

and in general $B_h(z)$ has the form

$$2^{F_{h+1}-1} z^{F_{h+2}-1} + 2^{F_{h+1}-2} L_{h-1} z^{F_{h+2}} + \text{complicated terms} + 2^{h-1} z^{2^h-2} + z^{2^h-1} \quad (6)$$

for $h \geq 3$, where $L_k = F_{k+1} + F_{k-1}$. (This formula generalizes Theorem A.) The total number of balanced trees with height h is $B_h = B_h(1)$, which satisfies the recurrence

$$B_0 = B_1 = 1, \qquad B_{h+1} = B_h^2 + 2B_h B_{h-1}, \quad (7)$$

so that $B_2 = 3$, $B_3 = 3 \cdot 5$, $B_4 = 3^2 \cdot 5 \cdot 7$, $B_5 = 3^3 \cdot 5^2 \cdot 7 \cdot 23$; and, in general,

$$B_h = A_0^{F_h} A_1^{F_{h-1}} \cdots A_{h-1}^{F_1} A_h^{F_0}, \quad (8)$$

where $A_0 = 1$, $A_1 = 3$, $A_2 = 5$, $A_3 = 7$, $A_4 = 23$, $A_5 = 347$, ..., $A_h = A_{h-1}B_{h-2} + 2$. The sequences B_h and A_h grow very rapidly; in fact, they are *doubly exponential*: Exercise 7 shows that there is a real number $\theta \approx 1.43687$ such that

$$B_h = \lfloor \theta^{2^h} \rfloor - \lfloor \theta^{2^{h-1}} \rfloor + \lfloor \theta^{2^{h-2}} \rfloor - \cdots + (-1)^h \lfloor \theta^{2^0} \rfloor. \quad (9)$$

If we consider each of the B_h trees to be equally likely, exercise 8 shows that the average number of nodes in a tree of height h is

$$B_h'(1)/B_h(1) \approx (0.70118)2^h - 1. \quad (10)$$

This indicates that the height of a balanced tree with N nodes is usually much closer to $\log_2 N$ than to $\log_\phi N$.

Unfortunately, these results don't really have much to do with Algorithm A, since the mechanism of that algorithm makes some trees significantly more probable than others. For example, consider the case $N = 7$, where 17 balanced trees are possible. There are $7! = 5040$ possible orderings in which seven keys can be inserted, and the perfectly balanced "complete" tree

$$(11)$$

is obtained 2160 times. By contrast, the Fibonacci tree

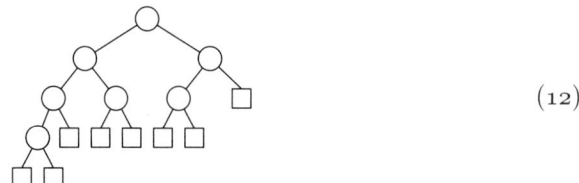

$$(12)$$

occurs only 144 times, and the similar tree

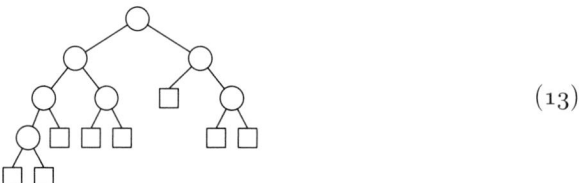

$$(13)$$

occurs 216 times. Replacing the left subtrees of (12) and (13) by arbitrary four-node balanced trees, and then reflecting left and right, yields 16 different trees; the eight generated from (12) each occur 144 times, and those generated from (13) each occur 216 times. It is surprising that (13) is more common than (12).

The fact that the perfectly balanced tree is obtained with such high probability — together with (10), which corresponds to the case of equal probabilities — makes it plausible that the average search time for a balanced tree should be about $\lg N + c$ comparisons for some small constant c. But R. W. Floyd has observed that the coefficient of $\lg N$ is unlikely to be exactly 1, because the root of the tree would then be near the median, and the roots of its two subtrees would be near the quartiles; then single and double rotation could not easily keep the root near the median. Empirical tests indicate that the true average number of comparisons needed to insert the Nth item is approximately $1.01 \lg N + 0.1$, except when N is small.

In order to study the behavior of the insertion and rebalancing phases of Algorithm A, we can classify the external nodes of balanced trees as shown in Fig. 23. The path leading up from an external node can be specified by a sequence of +'s and −'s (+ for a right link, − for a left link); we write down the link specifications until reaching the first node with a nonzero balance factor, or until reaching the root, if there is no such node. Then we write A or B according as the new tree will be balanced or unbalanced when an internal node is inserted in the given place. Thus the path up from ⬛3 is ++−B, meaning "right link, right link, left link, unbalance." A specification ending in A requires

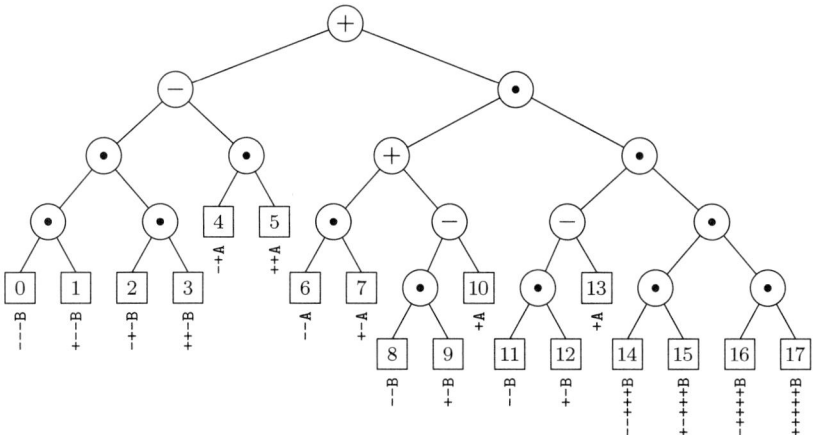

Fig. 23. Classification codes that specify the behavior of Algorithm A after insertion.

no rebalancing after insertion of a new node; a specification ending in ++B or --B requires a single rotation; and a specification ending in +-B or -+B requires a double rotation. When k links appear in the specification, step A6 has to adjust exactly $k-1$ balance factors. Thus the specifications give the essential facts that govern the running time of steps A6 to A10.

Empirical tests on random numbers for $100 \le N \le 2000$ gave the approximate probabilities shown in Table 1 for paths of various types; apparently these probabilities rapidly approach limiting values as $N \to \infty$. Table 2 gives the exact probabilities corresponding to Table 1 when $N = 10$, considering the 10! permutations of the input as equally probable. (The probabilities that show up as .143 in Table 1 are actually equal to $1/7$, for all $N \ge 7$; see exercise 11. Single and double rotations are equally likely when $N \le 15$, but double rotations occur slightly less often when $N \ge 16$.)

Table 1

APPROXIMATE PROBABILITIES FOR INSERTING THE NTH ITEM

Path length k	No rebalancing	Single rotation	Double rotation
1	.143	.000	.000
2	.152	.143	.143
3	.092	.048	.048
4	.060	.024	.024
5	.036	.010	.010
> 5	.051	.009	.008
ave 2.78	total .534	.233	.232

From Table 1 we can see that k is ≤ 2 with probability about $.143 + .152 + .143 + .143 = .581$; thus, step A6 is quite simple almost 60 percent of the time. The average number of balance factors changed from 0 to ± 1 in that step is

Table 2

EXACT PROBABILITIES FOR INSERTING THE 10TH ITEM

Path length k	No rebalancing	Single rotation	Double rotation
1	1/7	0	0
2	6/35	1/7	1/7
3	4/21	2/35	2/35
4	0	1/21	1/21
ave 247/105	53/105	26/105	26/105

about 1.8. The average number of balanced factors changed from ±1 to 0 in steps A7 through A10 is approximately $.534+2(.233+.232) \approx 1.5$; thus, inserting one new node adds about $1.8 - 1.5 = 0.3$ unbalanced nodes, on the average. This agrees with the fact that about 68 percent of all nodes were found to be balanced in random trees built by Algorithm A.

An approximate model of the behavior of Algorithm A has been proposed by C. C. Foster [*Proc. ACM Nat. Conf.* **20** (1965), 192–205.] This model is not rigorously accurate, but it is close enough to the truth to give some insight. Let us assume that p is the probability that the balance factor of a given node in a large tree built by Algorithm A is 0; then the balance factor is $+1$ with probability $\frac{1}{2}(1-p)$, and it is -1 with the same probability $\frac{1}{2}(1-p)$. Let us assume further (without justification) that the balance factors of all nodes are independent. Then the probability that step A6 sets exactly $k-1$ balance factors nonzero is $p^{k-1}(1-p)$, so the average value of k is $1/(1-p)$. The probability that we need to rotate part of the tree is $q \approx \frac{1}{2}$. Inserting a new node should increase the number of balanced nodes by p, on the average; this number is actually increased by 1 in step A5, by $-p/(1-p)$ in step A6, by q in step A7, and by $2q$ in step A8 or A9, so we should have

$$p = 1 - p/(1-p) + 3q \approx 5/2 - p/(1-p).$$

Solving for p yields fair agreement with Table 1:

$$p \approx \frac{9 - \sqrt{41}}{4} \approx 0.649; \qquad 1/(1-p) \approx 2.851. \tag{14}$$

The running time of the search phase of Program A (lines 01–19) is

$$10C + C1 + 2D + 2 - 3S, \tag{15}$$

where C, $C1$, S are the same as in previous algorithms of this chapter and D is the number of unbalanced nodes encountered on the search path. Empirical tests show that we may take $D \approx \frac{1}{3}C$, $C1 \approx \frac{1}{2}(C+S)$, $C+S \approx 1.01 \lg N + 0.1$, so the average search time is approximately $11.3 \lg N + 3 - 13.7S$ units. (If searching is done much more often than insertion, we could of course use a separate, faster program for searching, since it would be unnecessary to look at the balance factors; the average running time for a successful search would then be only about $(6.6 \lg N - 3.4)u$, and the worst case running time would in fact be better than the average running time obtained with Program 6.2.2T.)

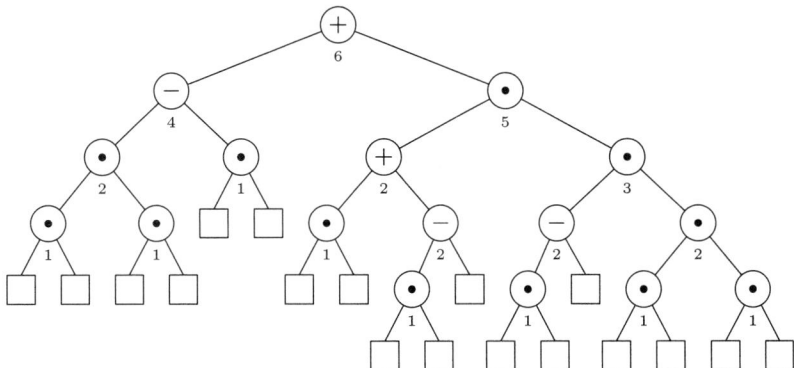

Fig. 24. RANK fields, used for searching by position.

The running time of the insertion phase of Program A (lines 20–45) is $8F + 26 + (0, 1, \text{ or } 2)$ units, when the search is unsuccessful. The data of Table 1 indicate that $F \approx 1.8$ on the average. The rebalancing phase (lines 46–101) takes either 16.5, 8, 27.5, or 45.5 (± 0.5) units, depending on whether we increase the total height, or simply exit without rebalancing, or do a single or double rotation. The first case almost never occurs, and the others occur with the approximate probabilities .534, .233, .232, so the average running time of the combined insertion-rebalancing portion of Program A is about $63u$.

These figures indicate that maintenance of a balanced tree in memory is reasonably fast, even though the program is rather lengthy. If the input data are random, the simple tree insertion algorithm of Section 6.2.2 is roughly $50u$ faster per insertion; but the balanced tree algorithm is guaranteed to be reliable even with nonrandom input data.

One way to compare Program A with Program 6.2.2T is to consider the worst case of the latter. If we study the amount of time necessary to insert N keys in increasing order into an initially empty tree, it turns out that Program A is slower for $N \le 26$ and faster for $N \ge 27$.

Linear list representation. Now let us return to the claim made at the beginning of this section, that balanced trees can be used to represent linear lists in such a way that we can insert items rapidly (overcoming the difficulty of sequential allocation), yet we can also perform random accesses to list items (overcoming the difficulty of linked allocation).

The idea is to introduce a new field in each node, called the RANK field. The field indicates the relative position of that node in its subtree, namely one plus the number of nodes in its left subtree. Figure 24 shows the RANK values for the binary tree of Fig. 23. We can eliminate the KEY field entirely; or, if desired, we can have both KEY and RANK fields, so that it is possible to retrieve items either by their key value or by their relative position in the list.

Using such a RANK field, retrieval by position is a straightforward modification of the search algorithms we have been studying.

Algorithm B (*Tree search by position*). Given a linear list represented as a binary tree, this algorithm finds the kth element of the list (the kth node of the tree in symmetric order), given k. The binary tree is assumed to have LLINK and RLINK fields and a header as in Algorithm A, plus a RANK field as described above.

B1. [Initialize.] Set $M \leftarrow k$, $P \leftarrow$ RLINK(HEAD).

B2. [Compare.] If $P = \Lambda$, the algorithm terminates unsuccessfully. (This can happen only if k was greater than the number of nodes in the tree, or $k \leq 0$.) Otherwise if $M <$ RANK(P), go to B3; if $M >$ RANK(P), go to B4; and if $M =$ RANK(P), the algorithm terminates successfully (P points to the kth node).

B3. [Move left.] Set $P \leftarrow$ LLINK(P) and return to B2.

B4. [Move right.] Set $M \leftarrow M -$ RANK(P) and $P \leftarrow$ RLINK(P) and return to B2. ∎

The only new point of interest in this algorithm is the manipulation of M in step B4. We can modify the insertion procedure in a similar way, although the details are somewhat trickier:

Algorithm C (*Balanced tree insertion by position*). Given a linear list represented as a balanced binary tree, this algorithm inserts a new node just before the kth element of the list, given k and a pointer Q to the new node. If $k = N+1$, the new node is inserted just after the last element of the list.

The binary tree is assumed to be nonempty and to have LLINK, RLINK and B fields and a header, as in Algorithm A, plus a RANK field as described above. This algorithm is merely a transcription of Algorithm A; the difference is that it uses and updates the RANK fields instead of the KEY fields.

C1. [Initialize.] Set $T \leftarrow$ HEAD, $S \leftarrow P \leftarrow$ RLINK(HEAD), $U \leftarrow M \leftarrow k$.

C2. [Compare.] If $M \leq$ RANK(P), go to C3, otherwise go to C4.

C3. [Move left.] Set RANK(P) $\leftarrow$ RANK(P) $+ 1$ (we will be inserting a new node to the left of P). Set $R \leftarrow$ LLINK(P). If $R = \Lambda$, set LLINK(P) $\leftarrow$ Q and go to C5. Otherwise if B(R) $\neq 0$ set $T \leftarrow P$, $S \leftarrow R$, and $U \leftarrow M$. Finally set $P \leftarrow R$ and return to C2.

C4. [Move right.] Set $M \leftarrow M -$ RANK(P), and $R \leftarrow$ RLINK(P). If $R = \Lambda$, set RLINK(P) $\leftarrow$ Q and go to C5. Otherwise if B(R) $\neq 0$ set $T \leftarrow P$, $S \leftarrow R$, and $U \leftarrow M$. Finally set $P \leftarrow R$ and return to C2.

C5. [Insert.] Set RANK(Q) $\leftarrow 1$, LLINK(Q) $\leftarrow$ RLINK(Q) $\leftarrow \Lambda$, B(Q) $\leftarrow 0$.

C6. [Adjust balance factors.] Set $M \leftarrow U$. (This restores the former value of M when P was S; all RANK fields are now properly set.) If $M <$ RANK(S), set $R \leftarrow P \leftarrow$ LLINK(S) and $a \leftarrow -1$; otherwise set $R \leftarrow P \leftarrow$ RLINK(S), $a \leftarrow +1$, and $M \leftarrow M -$ RANK(S). Then repeatedly do the following operations until $P =$ Q: If $M <$ RANK(P), set B(P) $\leftarrow -1$ and $P \leftarrow$ LLINK(P); if $M >$ RANK(P), set B(P) $\leftarrow +1$ and $M \leftarrow M -$ RANK(P) and $P \leftarrow$ RLINK(P). (If $M =$ RANK(P), then $P =$ Q and we proceed to the next step.)

C7. [Balancing act.] Several cases now arise.

i) If B(S) = 0, set B(S) ← a, LLINK(HEAD) ← LLINK(HEAD) + 1, and
   terminate the algorithm.

ii) If B(S) = −a, set B(S) ← 0 and terminate the algorithm.

iii) If B(S) = a, go to step C8 if B(R) = a, to C9 if B(R) = −a.

C8. [Single rotation.] Set P←R, LINK(a,S) ← LINK(−a,R), LINK(−a,R) ← S,
B(S) ← B(R) ← 0. If a = +1, set RANK(R) ← RANK(R) + RANK(S); if
a = −1, set RANK(S) ← RANK(S) − RANK(R). Go to C10.

C9. [Double rotation.] Do all the operations of step A9 (Algorithm A). Then
if a = +1, set RANK(R) ← RANK(R) − RANK(P), RANK(P) ← RANK(P) +
RANK(S); if a = −1, set RANK(P) ← RANK(P) + RANK(R), then RANK(S) ←
RANK(S) − RANK(P).

C10. [Finishing touch.] If S = RLINK(T) then set RLINK(T) ← P, otherwise set
LLINK(T) ← P. ∎

*Deletion, concatenation, etc. It is possible to do many other things to
balanced trees and maintain the balance, but the algorithms are sufficiently
lengthy that the details are beyond the scope of this book. We shall discuss
the general ideas here, and an interested reader will be able to fill in the details
without much difficulty.

The problem of deletion can be solved in $O(\log N)$ steps if we approach it
correctly [C. C. Foster, "A Study of AVL Trees," Goodyear Aerospace Corp.
report GER-12158 (April 1965)]. In the first place we can reduce deletion of
an arbitrary node to the simple deletion of a node P for which LLINK(P) or
RLINK(P) is Λ, as in Algorithm 6.2.2D. The algorithm should also be modified
so that it constructs a list of pointers that specify the path to node P, namely

$$(P_0, a_0), \qquad (P_1, a_1), \qquad \ldots, \qquad (P_l, a_l), \qquad (16)$$

where $P_0 =$ HEAD, $a_0 = +1$; LINK$(a_i, P_i) = P_{i+1}$, for $0 \le i < l$; $P_l =$ P; and
LINK$(a_l, P_l) = \Lambda$. This list can be placed on an auxiliary stack as we search down
the tree. The process of deleting node P sets LINK$(a_{l-1}, P_{l-1}) \leftarrow$ LINK$(-a_l, P_l)$,
and we must adjust the balance factor at node P_{l-1}. Suppose that we need to
adjust the balance factor at node P_k, because the a_k subtree of this node has
just decreased in height; the following adjustment procedure should be used: If
$k = 0$, set LLINK(HEAD) ← LLINK(HEAD) − 1 and terminate the algorithm, since
the whole tree has decreased in height. Otherwise look at the balance factor
B(P_k); there are three cases:

i) B$(P_k) = a_k$. Set B$(P_k) \leftarrow 0$, decrease k by 1, and repeat the adjustment
   procedure for this new value of k.

ii) B$(P_k) = 0$. Set B(P_k) to $-a_k$ and terminate the deletion algorithm.

iii) B$(P_k) = -a_k$. Rebalancing is required!

The situations that require rebalancing are almost the same as we met in the
insertion algorithm; referring again to (1), A is node P_k, and B is the node
LINK$(-a_k, P_k)$, on the *opposite* branch from where the deletion has occurred.
The only new feature is that node B might be balanced; this leads to a new

Case 3, which is like Case 1 except that β has height $h + 1$. In the former cases, rebalancing as in (2) means that we decrease the height, so we set LINK(a_{k-1}, P_{k-1}) to the root of (2), decrease k by 1, and restart the adjustment procedure for this new value of k. In Case 3 we do a single rotation, and this leaves the balance factors of both A and B nonzero without changing the overall height; after making LINK(a_{k-1}, P_{k-1}) point to node B, we therefore terminate the algorithm.

The important difference between deletion and insertion is that deletion might require up to $\log N$ rotations, while insertion never needs more than one. The reason for this becomes clear if we try to delete the rightmost node of a Fibonacci tree (see Fig. 8 in Section 6.2.1). But empirical tests show that only about 0.21 rotations per deletion are actually needed, on the average.

The use of balanced trees for linear list representation suggests also the need for a *concatenation* algorithm, where we want to insert an entire tree L_2 to the right of tree L_1, without destroying the balance. An elegant algorithm for concatenation was first devised by Clark A. Crane: Assume that height(L_1) $\geq$ height(L_2); the other case is similar. Delete the first node of L_2, calling it the *juncture node* J, and let L'_2 be the new tree for $L_2 \setminus \{J\}$. Now go down the right links of L_1 until reaching a node P such that

$$\text{height}(P) - \text{height}(L'_2) = 0 \text{ or } 1;$$

this is always possible, since the height changes by 1 or 2 each time we go down one level. Then replace $\overset{\frown}{P}$ by

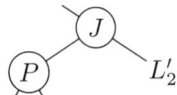

and proceed to adjust L_1 as if the new node J had just been inserted by Algorithm A.

Crane also solved the more difficult inverse problem, to *split* a list into two parts whose concatenation would be the original list. Consider, for example, the problem of splitting the list in Fig. 20 to obtain two lists, one containing $\{A, \ldots, I\}$ and the other containing $\{J, \ldots, Q\}$; a major reassembly of the subtrees is required. In general, when we want to split a tree at some given node P, the path to P will be something like that in Fig. 25. We wish to construct a left tree that contains the nodes of $\alpha_1, P_1, \alpha_4, P_4, \alpha_6, P_6, \alpha_7, P_7, \alpha, P$ in symmetric order, and a right tree that contains $\beta, P_8, \beta_8, P_5, \beta_5, P_3, \beta_3, P_2, \beta_2$. This can be done by a sequence of concatenations: First insert P at the right of α, then concatenate β with β_8 using P_8 as juncture node, concatenate α_7 with αP using P_7 as juncture node, α_6 with $\alpha_7 P_7 \alpha P$ using P_6, $\beta P_8 \beta_8$ with β_5 using P_5, etc.; the nodes $P_8, P_7, \ldots, P_1$ on the path to P are used as juncture nodes. Crane proved that this splitting algorithm takes only $O(\log N)$ units of time, when the original tree contains N nodes; the essential reason is that concatenation using a given juncture node takes $O(k)$ steps, where k is the difference in heights between the

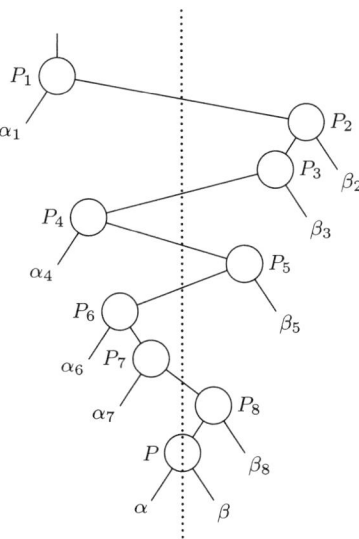

Fig. 25. The problem of splitting a list.

trees being concatenated, and the values of k that must be summed essentially form a telescoping series for both the left and right trees being constructed.

All of these algorithms can be used with either KEY or RANK fields or both, although in the case of concatenation the keys of L_2 must all be greater than the keys of L_1. For general purposes it is often preferable to use a *triply linked tree*, with UP links as well as LLINKs and RLINKs, together with a new one-bit field that specifies whether a node is the left or right child of its parent. The triply linked tree representation simplifies the algorithms slightly, and allows us to specify nodes in the tree without explicitly tracing the path to that node; we can write a subroutine to delete NODE(P), given P, or to delete the node that follows NODE(P) in symmetric order, or to find the list containing NODE(P), etc. In the deletion algorithm for triply linked trees it is unnecessary to construct the list (16), since the UP links provide the information we need. Of course, a triply linked tree requires us to change a few more links when insertions, deletions, and rotations are being performed. The use of a triply linked tree instead of a doubly linked tree is analogous to the use of two-way linking instead of one-way: We can start at any point and go either forward or backward. A complete description of list algorithms based on triply linked balanced trees appears in Clark A. Crane's Ph.D. thesis (Stanford University, 1972).

Alternatives to AVL trees. Many other ways have been proposed to organize trees so that logarithmic accessing time is guaranteed. For example, C. C. Foster [*CACM* **16** (1973), 513–517] considered the binary trees that arise when we allow the height difference of subtrees to be at most k. Such structures have been called HB(k) (meaning "height-balanced"), so that ordinary balanced trees represent the special case HB(1).

The interesting concept of *weight-balanced trees* has been studied by J. Nievergelt, E. Reingold, and C. K. Wong. Instead of considering the height of trees, they stipulate that the subtrees of all nodes must satisfy

$$\sqrt{2} - 1 < \frac{\text{left weight}}{\text{right weight}} < \sqrt{2} + 1, \qquad (17)$$

where the left and right weights count the number of *external* nodes in the left and right subtrees, respectively. It is possible to show that weight balance can be maintained under insertion, using only single and double rotations for rebalancing as in Algorithm A (see exercise 25). However, it may be necessary to do several rebalancings during a single insertion. It is possible to relax the conditions of (17), decreasing the amount of rebalancing at the expense of increased search time.

Weight-balanced trees may seem at first glance to require more memory than plain balanced trees, but in fact they sometimes require slightly less! If we already have a RANK field in each node, for the linear list representation, this is precisely the left weight, and it is possible to keep track of the corresponding right weights as we move down the tree. But it appears that the bookkeeping required for maintaining weight balance takes more time than Algorithm A, and the elimination of two bits per node is probably not worth the trouble.

> *Why don't you pair 'em up in threes?*
> — attributed to YOGI BERRA (c. 1970)

Another interesting alternative to AVL trees, called "2-3 trees," was introduced by John Hopcroft in 1970 [see Aho, Hopcroft, and Ullman, *The Design and Analysis of Computer Algorithms* (Reading, Mass.: Addison–Wesley, 1974), Chapter 4]. The idea is to have either 2-way or 3-way branching at each node, and to stipulate that all external nodes appear on the same level. Every internal node contains either one or two keys, as shown in Fig. 26.

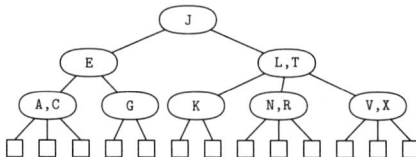

Fig. 26. A 2-3 tree.

Insertion into a 2-3 tree is somewhat easier to explain than insertion into an AVL tree: If we want to put a new key into a node that contains just one key, we simply insert it as the second key. On the other hand, if the node already contains two keys, we divide it into two one-key nodes, and insert the middle key into the parent node. This may cause the parent node to be divided in a similar way, if it already contains two keys. Figure 27 shows the process of inserting a new key into the 2-3 tree of Fig. 26.

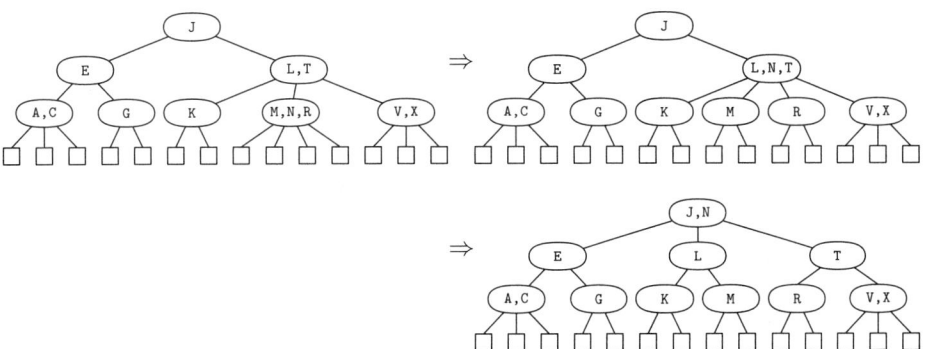

Fig. 27. Inserting the new key "M" into the 2-3 tree of Fig. 26.

Hopcroft observed that deletion, concatenation, and splitting can all be done with 2-3 trees, in a reasonably straightforward manner analogous to the corresponding operations with AVL trees.

R. Bayer [*Proc. ACM–SIGFIDET Workshop* (1971), 219–235] proposed an interesting binary tree representation for 2-3 trees. See Fig. 28, which shows the binary tree representation of Fig. 26; one bit in each node is used to distinguish "horizontal" RLINKs from "vertical" ones. Note that the keys of the tree appear from left to right in symmetric order, just as in any binary search tree. It turns out that the transformations we need to perform on such a binary tree, while inserting a new key as in Fig. 27, are precisely the single and double rotations used while inserting a new key into an AVL tree, although we need just one version of each rotation, not the left-right reflections needed by Algorithms A and C.

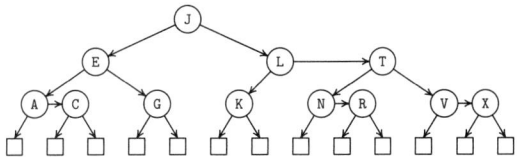

Fig. 28. The 2-3 tree of Fig. 26 represented as a binary search tree.

Elaboration of these ideas has led to many additional flavors of balanced trees, most notably the *red-black trees*, also called symmetric binary *B*-trees or half-balanced trees [R. Bayer, *Acta Informatica* **1** (1972), 290–306; L. Guibas and R. Sedgewick, *FOCS* **19** (1978), 8–21; H. J. Olivié, *RAIRO Informatique Théorique* **16** (1982), 51–71; R. E. Tarjan, *Inf. Proc. Letters* **16** (1983), 253–257; T. H. Cormen, C. E. Leiserson, and R. L. Rivest, *Introduction to Algorithms* (MIT Press, 1990), Chapter 14; R. Sedgewick, *Algorithms in C* (Addison–Wesley, 1997), §13.4]. There is also a strongly related family called hysterical *B*-trees or (a, b)-trees, notably $(2, 4)$-trees [D. Maier and S. C. Salveter, *Inf. Proc. Letters* **12** (1981), 199–202; S. Huddleston and K. Mehlhorn, *Acta Informatica* **17** (1982), 157–184].

When some keys are accessed much more frequently than others, we want the important ones to be relatively close to the root, as in the optimum binary search trees of Section 6.2.2. Dynamic trees that make it possible to maintain weighted balance within a constant factor of the optimum, called *biased trees*, have been developed by S. W. Bent, D. D. Sleator, and R. E. Tarjan, *SICOMP* **14** (1985), 545–568; J. Feigenbaum and R. E. Tarjan, *Bell System Tech. J.* **62** (1983), 3139–3158. The algorithms are, however, quite complicated.

A much simpler self-adjusting data structure called a *splay tree* was developed subsequently by D. D. Sleator and R. E. Tarjan [*JACM* **32** (1985), 652–686], based on ideas like the move-to-front and transposition heuristics discussed in Section 6.1; similar techniques had previously been explored by B. Allen and I. Munro [*JACM* **25** (1978), 526–535] and by J. Bitner [*SICOMP* **8** (1979), 82–110]. Splay trees, like the other kinds of balanced trees already mentioned, support the operations of concatenation and splitting as well as insertion and deletion, and in a particularly simple way. Moreover, the time needed to access data in a splay tree is known to be at most a small constant multiple of the access time of a statically optimum tree, when amortized over any series of operations. Indeed, Sleator and Tarjan conjectured that the total splay tree access time is at most a constant multiple of the optimum time to access data and to perform rotations dynamically by any binary tree algorithm whatsoever.

Randomization leads to methods that appear to be even simpler and faster than splay trees. Jean Vuillemin [*CACM* **23** (1980), 229–239] introduced *Cartesian trees*, in which every node has two keys (x, y). The x parts are ordered from left to right as in binary search trees; the y parts are ordered from top to bottom as in the priority queue trees of Section 5.2.3. C. R. Aragon and R. G. Seidel gave this data structure the more colorful name *treap*, because it neatly combines the notions of trees and heaps. Exactly one treap can be formed with n given key pairs (x_1, y_1), ..., (x_n, y_n), if the x's and y's are distinct. One way to obtain it is to insert the x's by Algorithm 6.2.2T according to the order of the y's; but there is also a simple algorithm that inserts any new key pair directly into any treap. Aragon and Seidel observed [*FOCS* **30** (1989), 540–546] that if the x's are ordinary keys while the y's are chosen at random, we can be sure that the treap has the shape of a random binary search tree. In particular, a treap with random y values will always be reasonably well balanced, except with exponentially small probability (see exercise 5.2.2–42). Aragon and Seidel also showed that treaps can readily be biased so that, for example, a key x with relative frequency f will appear suitably near the root when it is associated with $y = U^{1/f}$, where U is a random number between 0 and 1. Treaps performed consistently better than splay trees in some experiments conducted by D. E. Knuth relating to the calculation of convex hulls [*Lecture Notes in Comp. Sci.* **606** (1992), 53–55].

▲ *A new Section 6.2.5 devoted to randomized data structures is planned for the next edition of the present book. It will discuss "skip lists" [W. Pugh, CACM* **33** *(1990), 668–676] and "randomized binary search trees" [S. Roura and C. Martínez, JACM* **45** *(1998), 288–323] as well as treaps.*

EXERCISES

1. [*01*] In Case 2 of (1), why isn't it a good idea to restore the balance by simply interchanging the left subtrees of A and B?

2. [*16*] Explain why the tree has gotten one level higher if we reach step A7 with B(S) = 0.

▶ **3.** [*M25*] Prove that a balanced tree with N internal nodes never contains more than $(\phi - 1)N \approx 0.61803N$ nodes whose balance factor is nonzero.

4. [*M22*] Prove or disprove: Among all balanced trees with $F_{h+1} - 1$ internal nodes, the Fibonacci tree of order h has the greatest internal path length.

▶ **5.** [*M25*] Prove or disprove: If Algorithm A is used to insert the keys $K_2, \ldots, K_N$ successively in increasing order into a tree that initially contains only the single key K_1, where $K_1 < K_2 < \cdots < K_N$, then the tree produced is always *optimum* (that is, it has minimum internal path length over all N-node binary trees).

6. [*M21*] Prove that Eq. (5) defines the generating function for balanced trees of height h.

7. [*M27*] (A. V. Aho and N. J. A. Sloane.) Prove the remarkable formula (9) for the number of balanced trees of height h. [*Hint:* Let $C_n = B_n + B_{n-1}$, and use the fact that $\log(C_{n+1}/C_n^2)$ is exceedingly small for large n.]

8. [*M24*] (L. A. Khizder.) Show that there is a constant β such that $B'_h(1)/B_h(1) = 2^h \beta - 1 + O(2^h/B_{h-1})$ as $h \to \infty$.

9. [*HM44*] What is the asymptotic number of balanced binary trees with n internal nodes, $\sum_{h\geq0} B_{nh}$? What is the asymptotic average height, $\sum_{h\geq0} hB_{nh} / \sum_{h\geq0} B_{nh}$?

▶ **10.** [*27*] (R. C. Richards.) Show that the shape of a balanced tree can be constructed uniquely from the list of its balance factors B(1)B(2)...B(N) in symmetric order.

11. [*M24*] (Mark R. Brown.) Prove that when $n \geq 6$ the average number of external nodes of each of the types +A, -A, ++B, +-B, -+B, --B is exactly $(n+1)/14$, in a random balanced tree of n internal nodes constructed by Algorithm A.

▶ **12.** [*24*] What is the maximum possible running time of Program A when the eighth node is inserted into a balanced tree? What is the minimum possible running time for this insertion?

13. [*05*] Why is it better to use RANK fields as defined in the text, instead of simply to store the index of each node as its key (calling the first node "1", the second node "2", and so on)?

14. [*11*] Could Algorithms 6.2.2T and 6.2.2D be adapted to work with linear lists, using a RANK field, just as the balanced tree algorithms of this section have been so adapted?

15. [*18*] (C. A. Crane.) Suppose that an ordered linear list is being represented as a binary tree, with both KEY and RANK fields in each node. Design an algorithm that searches the tree for a given key, K, and determines the position of K in the list; that is, it finds the number m such that K is the mth smallest key.

▶ **16.** [*20*] Draw the balanced tree that is obtained after node E and the root node F are deleted from Fig. 20, using the deletion algorithm suggested in the text.

▶ **17.** [*21*] Draw the balanced trees that are obtained after the Fibonacci tree (12) is concatenated (a) to the right, (b) to the left, of the tree in Fig. 20, using the concatenation algorithm suggested in the text.

18. [*22*] Draw the balanced trees that are obtained after Fig. 20 is split into two parts {A, ..., I} and {J, ..., Q}, using the splitting algorithm suggested in the text.

▶ **19.** [*26*] Find a way to transform a given balanced tree so that the balance factor at the root is not −1. Your transformation should preserve the symmetric order of the nodes; and it should produce another balanced tree in $O(1)$ units of time, regardless of the size of the original tree.

20. [*40*] Explore the idea of using the restricted class of balanced trees whose nodes all have balance factors of 0 or +1. (Then the length of the B field can be reduced to one bit.) Is there a reasonably efficient insertion procedure for such trees?

▶ **21.** [*30*] (*Perfect balancing.*) Design an algorithm to construct N-node binary trees that are optimum in the sense of exercise 5. Your algorithm should use $O(N)$ steps and it should be "online," in the sense that it inputs the nodes one by one in increasing order and builds partial trees as it goes, without knowing the final value of N in advance. (It would be appropriate to use such an algorithm when restructuring a badly balanced tree, or when merging the keys of two trees into a single tree.)

22. [*M20*] What is the analog of Theorem A, for weight-balanced trees?

23. [*M20*] (E. Reingold.) Demonstrate that there is no simple relation between height-balanced trees and weight-balanced trees:
   a) Prove that there exist height-balanced trees that have an arbitrarily small ratio (left weight)/(right weight) in the sense of (17).
   b) Prove that there exist weight-balanced trees that have an arbitrarily large difference between left and right subtree heights.

24. [*M22*] (E. Reingold.) Prove that if we strengthen condition (17) to

$$\frac{1}{2} < \frac{\text{left weight}}{\text{right weight}} < 2,$$

the only binary trees that satisfy this condition are perfectly balanced trees with $2^n - 1$ internal nodes. (In such trees, the left and right weights are exactly equal at all nodes.)

25. [*27*] (J. Nievergelt, E. Reingold, C. Wong.) Show that it is possible to design an insertion algorithm for weight-balanced trees so that condition (17) is preserved, making at most $O(\log N)$ rotations per insertion.

26. [*40*] Explore the properties of balanced t-ary trees, for $t > 2$.

▶ **27.** [*M23*] Estimate the maximum number of comparisons needed to search in a 2-3 tree with N internal nodes.

28. [*41*] Prepare efficient implementations of 2-3 tree algorithms.

29. [*M47*] Analyze the average behavior of 2-3 trees under random insertions.

30. [*26*] (E. McCreight.) Section 2.5 discusses several strategies for dynamic storage allocation, including best-fit (choosing an available area as small as possible from among all those that fulfill the request) and first-fit (choosing the available area with lowest address among all those that fulfill the request). Show that if the available space is linked together as a balanced tree in an appropriate way, it is possible to do (a) best-fit (b) first-fit allocation in only $O(\log n)$ units of time, where n is the number of available areas. (The algorithms given for those methods in Section 2.5 take order n steps.)

31. [*34*] (M. L. Fredman, 1975.) Invent a representation of linear lists with the property that insertion of a new item between positions $m - 1$ and m, given m, takes $O(\log m)$ units of time.

32. [*M27*] Given two n-node binary trees, T and T', let us say that $T \preceq T'$ if T' can be obtained from T by a sequence of zero or more rotations to the right. Prove that $T \preceq T'$ if and only if $r_k \leq r'_k$ for $1 \leq k \leq n$, where r_k and r'_k denote the respective sizes of the right subtrees of the kth nodes of T and T' in symmetric order.

▶ **33.** [*25*] (A. L. Buchsbaum.) Explain how to encode the balance factors of an AVL tree implicitly, thus saving two bits per node, at the expense of additional work when the tree is accessed.

> *Samuel considered the nation of Israel, tribe by tribe,*
> *and the tribe of Benjamin was picked by lot.*
> *Then he considered the tribe of Benjamin, family by family,*
> *and the family of Matri was picked by lot.*
> *Then he considered the family of Matri, man by man,*
> *and Saul son of Kish was picked by lot.*
> *But when they looked for Saul he could not be found.*
> *— 1 Samuel 10:20–21*

6.2.4. Multiway Trees

The tree search methods we have been discussing were developed primarily for internal searching, when we want to look at a table that is contained entirely within a computer's high-speed internal memory. Let's now consider the problem of *external* searching, when we want to retrieve information from a very large file that appears on direct access storage units such as disks or drums. (An introduction to disks and drums appears in Section 5.4.9.)

Tree structures lend themselves nicely to external searching, if we choose an appropriate way to represent the tree. Consider the large binary search tree shown in Fig. 29, and imagine that it has been stored in a disk file. (The LLINKs and RLINKs of the tree are now disk addresses instead of internal memory addresses.) If we search this tree in a naïve manner, simply applying the algorithms we have learned for internal tree searching, we will have to make about $\lg N$ disk accesses before our search is complete. When N is a million, this means we will need 20 or so seeks. But suppose we divide the table into 7-node "pages," as shown by the dotted lines in Fig. 29; if we access one page at a time, we need only about one third as many seeks, so the search goes about three times as fast!

Grouping the nodes into pages in this way essentially changes the tree from a binary tree to an octonary tree, with 8-way branching at each page-node. If we let the pages be still larger, with 128-way branching after each disk access, we can find any desired key in a million-entry table after looking at only three pages. We can keep the root page in the internal memory at all times, so that only two references to the disk are required even though the internal memory never needs to hold more than 254 keys at any time.

Of course we don't want to make the pages arbitrarily large, since the internal memory size is limited and also since it takes a long time to read a large page. For example, suppose that it takes $72.5 + 0.05m$ milliseconds to read a page that allows m-way branching. The internal processing time per page will

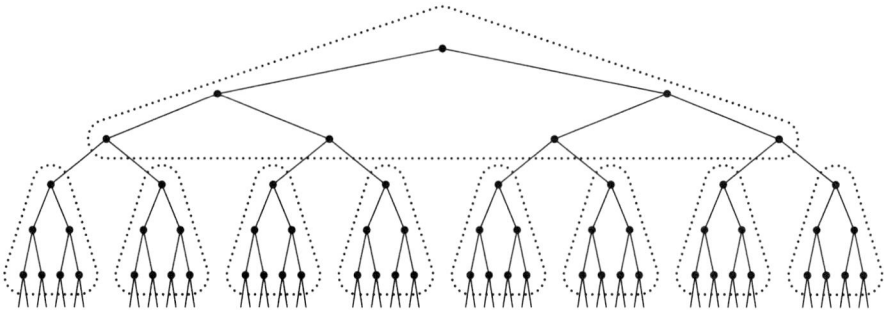

Fig. 29. A large binary search tree can be divided into "pages."

be about $a + b \lg m$, where a is small compared to $72.5\,\mathrm{ms}$, so the total amount of time needed for searching a large table is approximately proportional to $\lg N$ times

$$(72.5 + 0.05m)/\lg m + b.$$

This quantity achieves a minimum when $m \approx 307$; actually the minimum is very "broad" — a nearly optimum value is achieved for all m between 200 and 500. In practice there will be a similar range of good values for m, based on the characteristics of particular external memory devices and on the length of the records in the table.

W. I. Landauer [*IEEE Trans.* **EC-12** (1963), 863–871] suggested building an m-ary tree by requiring level l to become nearly full before anything is allowed to appear on level $l + 1$. This scheme requires a rather complicated rotation method, since we may have to make major changes throughout the tree just to insert a single new item; Landauer was assuming that we need to search for items in the tree much more often than we need to insert or delete them.

When a file is stored on disk, and is subject to comparatively few insertions and deletions, a three-level tree is appropriate, where the first level of branching determines what cylinder is to be used, the second level of branching determines the appropriate track on that cylinder, and the third level contains the records themselves. This method is called *indexed-sequential* file organization [see *JACM* **16** (1969), 569–571].

R. Muntz and R. Uzgalis [*Proc. Princeton Conf. on Inf. Sciences and Systems* **4** (1970), 345–349] suggested modifying the tree search and insertion method, Algorithm 6.2.2T, so that all insertions go onto nodes belonging to the same page as their parent node, whenever possible; if that page is full, a new page is started, whenever possible. If the number of pages is unlimited, and if the data arrives in random order, it can be shown that the average number of page accesses is approximately $H_N/(H_m - 1)$, only slightly more than we would obtain in the best possible m-ary tree. (See exercise 8.)

B-trees. A new approach to external searching by means of multiway tree branching was discovered in 1970 by R. Bayer and E. McCreight [*Acta Informa-*

tica **1** (1972), 173–189], and independently at about the same time by M. Kaufman [unpublished]. Their idea, based on a versatile new kind of data structure called a *B-tree*, makes it possible both to search and to update a large file with guaranteed efficiency, in the worst case, using comparatively simple algorithms.

A *B-tree of order m* is a tree that satisfies the following properties:

i) Every node has at most m children.

ii) Every node, except for the root and the leaves, has at least $m/2$ children.

iii) The root has at least 2 children (unless it is a leaf).

iv) All leaves appear on the same level, and carry no information.

v) A nonleaf node with k children contains $k-1$ keys.

(As usual, a "leaf" is a terminal node, one with no children. Since the leaves carry no information, we may regard them as external nodes that aren't really in the tree, so that Λ is a pointer to a leaf.)

Figure 30 shows a *B*-tree of order 7. Each node (except for the root and the leaves) has between $\lceil 7/2 \rceil$ and 7 children, so it contains 3, 4, 5, or 6 keys. The root node is allowed to contain from 1 to 6 keys; in this case it has 2. All of the leaves are at level 3. Notice that (a) the keys appear in increasing order from left to right, using a natural extension of the concept of symmetric order; and (b) the number of leaves is exactly one greater than the number of keys.

B-trees of order 1 or 2 are obviously uninteresting, so we will consider only the case $m \geq 3$. The 2-3 trees defined at the close of Section 6.2.3 are equivalent to *B*-trees of order 3. (Bayer and McCreight considered only the case that m is odd; some authors consider a *B*-tree of order m to be what we are calling a *B*-tree of order $2m+1$.)

A node that contains j keys and $j+1$ pointers can be represented as

$$\overset{\text{P}}{\downarrow} \left(\text{P}_0, K_1, \text{P}_1, K_2, \text{P}_2, \ldots, \text{P}_{j-1}, K_j, \text{P}_j \right) \qquad (1)$$

where $K_1 < K_2 < \cdots < K_j$ and P_i points to the subtree for keys between K_i and K_{i+1}. Therefore searching in a *B*-tree is quite straightforward: After node (1) has been fetched into the internal memory, we search for the given argument among the keys $K_1, K_2, \ldots, K_j$. (When j is large, we probably do a binary search; but when j is smallish, a sequential search is best.) If the search is successful, we have found the desired key; but if the search is unsuccessful because the argument lies between K_i and K_{i+1}, we fetch the node indicated by P_i and continue the process. The pointer P_0 is used if the argument is less than K_1, and P_j is used if the argument is greater than K_j. If $\text{P}_i = \Lambda$, the search is unsuccessful.

The nice thing about *B*-trees is that insertion is also quite simple. Consider Fig. 30, for example; every leaf corresponds to a place where a new insertion might happen. If we want to insert the new key 337, we simply change the

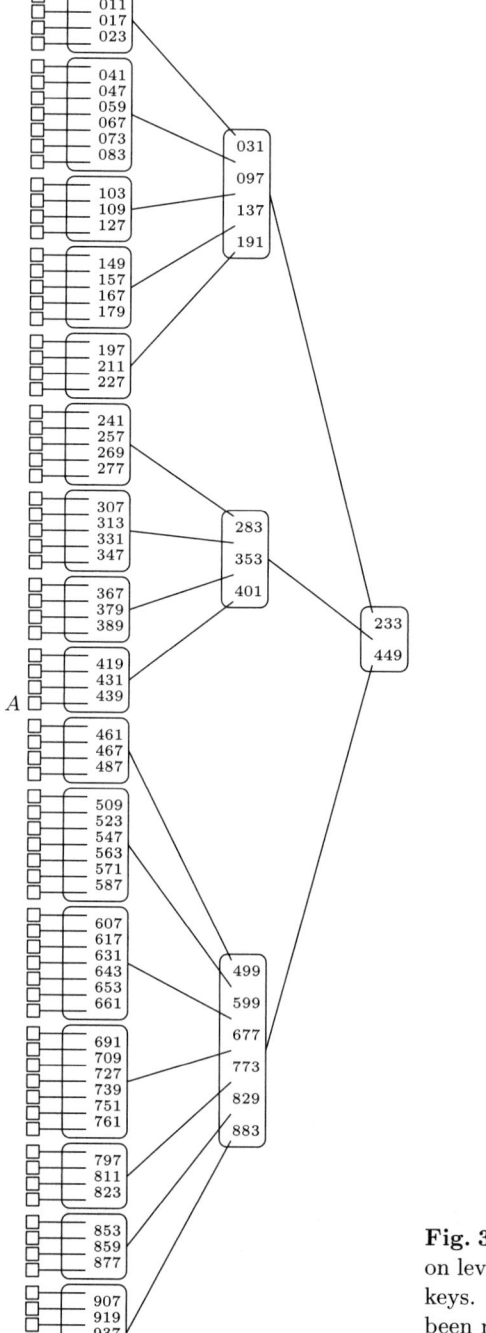

Fig. 30. A *B*-tree of order 7, with all leaves on level 3. Every node contains 3, 4, 5, or 6 keys. The leaf that precedes key 449 has been marked *A*; see (8).

appropriate node from

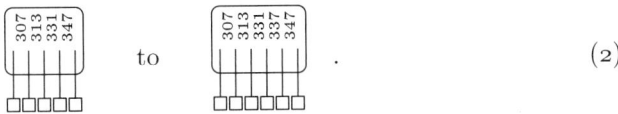
to   . (2)

On the other hand, if we want to insert the new key 071, there is no room since the corresponding node on level 2 is already "full." This case can be handled by splitting the node into two parts, with three keys in each part, and passing the middle key up to level 1:

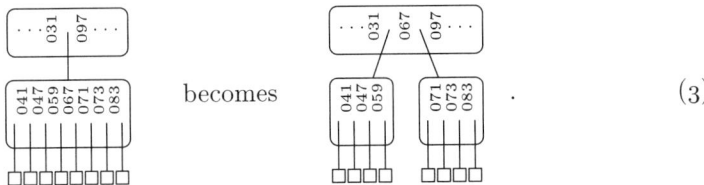
becomes   . (3)

In general, if we want to insert a new item into a B-tree of order m, when all the leaves are at level l, we insert the new key into the appropriate node on level $l - 1$. If that node now contains m keys, so that it has the form (1) with $j = m$, we split it into two nodes

$$\overbrace{\left(P_0, K_1, P_1, \ldots, K_{\lceil m/2 \rceil - 1}, P_{\lceil m/2 \rceil - 1} \right)}^{P} \quad \overbrace{\left(P_{\lceil m/2 \rceil}, K_{\lceil m/2 \rceil + 1}, P_{\lceil m/2 \rceil + 1}, \ldots, K_m, P_m \right)}^{P'} \quad (4)$$

and insert the key $K_{\lceil m/2 \rceil}$ into the parent of the original node. (Thus the pointer P in the parent node is replaced by the sequence P, $K_{\lceil m/2 \rceil}$, P$'$.) This insertion may cause the parent node to contain m keys, and if so, it should be split in the same way. (Figure 27 in the previous section illustrates the case $m = 3$.) If we need to split the root node, which has no parent, we simply create a new root node containing the single key $K_{\lceil m/2 \rceil}$; the tree gets one level taller in this case.

This insertion procedure neatly preserves all of the B-tree properties; in order to appreciate the full beauty of the idea, the reader should work exercise 1. The tree essentially grows up from the top, instead of down from the bottom, since it gains in height only when the root splits.

Deletion from B-trees is only slightly more complicated than insertion (see exercise 6).

Upper bounds on the running time. Let us now see how many nodes have to be accessed in the worst case, while searching in a B-tree of order m. Suppose that there are N keys, and that the $N + 1$ leaves appear on level l. Then the number of nodes on levels $1, 2, 3, \ldots$ is at least $2, 2\lceil m/2 \rceil, 2\lceil m/2 \rceil^2, \ldots$; hence

$$N + 1 \geq 2\lceil m/2 \rceil^{l-1}. \tag{5}$$

In other words,

$$l \leq 1 + \log_{\lceil m/2 \rceil}\left(\frac{N+1}{2} \right); \tag{6}$$

this means, for example, that if $N = 1,999,998$ and $m = 199$, then l is at most 3. Since we need to access at most l nodes during a search, this formula guarantees that the running time is quite small.

When a new key is being inserted, we may have to split as many as l nodes. However, the average number of nodes that need to be split is much less, since the total number of splittings that occur while the entire tree is being constructed is just the total number of internal nodes in the tree, minus l. If there are p internal nodes, there are at least $1 + (\lceil m/2 \rceil - 1)(p - 1)$ keys; hence

$$p \le 1 + \frac{N - 1}{\lceil m/2 \rceil - 1}. \tag{7}$$

It follows that $(p - l)/N$, the average number of times we need to split a node while building a tree of N keys, is less than $1/(\lceil m/2 \rceil - 1)$ split per insertion.

Refinements and variations. There are several ways to improve upon the basic B-tree structure defined above, by breaking the rules a little.

In the first place, we note that all of the pointers in the level $l - 1$ nodes are Λ, and none of the pointers in the other levels are Λ. This often represents a significant amount of wasted space, so we can save both time and space by eliminating all the Λ's and using a different value of m for all of the "bottom" nodes. This use of two different m's does not foul up the insertion algorithm, since both halves of a node that is being split remain on the same level as the original node. We could in fact define a generalized B-tree of orders $m_1, m_2, m_3, \ldots$ by requiring all nonroot nodes on level $l - k$ to have between $m_k/2$ and m_k children; such a B-tree has different m's on each level, yet the insertion algorithm still works essentially as before.

To carry the idea in the preceding paragraph even further, we might use a completely different node format in each level of the tree, and we might also store information in the leaves. Sometimes the keys form only a small part of the records in a file, and in such cases it is a mistake to store the entire records in the branch nodes near the root of the tree; this would make m too small for efficient multiway branching.

We can therefore reconsider Fig. 30, imagining that all the records of the file are now stored in the leaves, and that only a few of the keys have been duplicated in the branch nodes. Under this interpretation, the leftmost leaf contains all records whose key is ≤ 011; the leaf marked A contains all records whose key satisfies

$$439 < K \le 449; \tag{8}$$

and so on. Under this interpretation the leaf nodes grow and split just as the branch nodes do, except that a record is never passed up from a leaf to the next level. Thus the leaves are always at least half filled to capacity. A new key enters the nonleaf part of the tree whenever a leaf splits. If each leaf is linked to its successor in symmetric order, we gain the ability to traverse the file both sequentially and randomly in an efficient and convenient manner. This variant has become known as a B^+-tree.

Some calculations by S. P. Ghosh and M. E. Senko [*JACM* **16** (1969), 569–579] suggest that it might be a good idea to make the leaves fairly large, say up to about 10 consecutive pages long. By linear interpolation in the known range of keys for each leaf, we can guess which of the 10 pages probably contains a given search argument. If our guess is wrong, we lose time, but experiments indicate that this loss might be less than the time we save by decreasing the size of the tree.

T. H. Martin [unpublished] has pointed out that the idea underlying B-trees can be used also for *variable-length* keys. We need not put bounds $[m/2 .. m]$ on the number of children of each node; instead we can say merely that each node should be at least about half full of data. The insertion and splitting mechanism still works fine, even though the exact number of keys per node depends on whether the keys are long or short. However, the keys shouldn't be allowed to get extremely long, or they can mess things up. (See exercise 5.)

Another important modification to the basic B-tree scheme is the idea of *overflow* introduced by Bayer and McCreight. The idea is to improve the insertion algorithm by resisting its temptation to split nodes so often; a local rotation is used instead. Suppose we have a node that is over-full because it contains m keys and $m + 1$ pointers; instead of splitting it, we can look first at its sibling node on the right, which has say j keys and $j + 1$ pointers. In the parent node there is a key $\overline{K}_f$ that separates the keys of the two siblings; schematically,

$$(9)$$

If $j < m - 1$, a simple rearrangement makes splitting unnecessary: We leave $\lfloor (m+j)/2 \rfloor$ keys in the left node, we replace $\overline{K}_f$ by $K_{\lfloor (m+j)/2 \rfloor + 1}$ in the parent node, and we put the $\lceil (m+j)/2 \rceil$ remaining keys (including $\overline{K}_f$) and the corresponding pointers into the right node. Thus the full node "flows over" into its sibling node. On the other hand, if the sibling node is already full ($j = m-1$), we can split *both* of the nodes, making three nodes each about two-thirds full, containing, respectively, $\lfloor (2m - 2)/3 \rfloor$, $\lfloor (2m - 1)/3 \rfloor$, and $\lfloor 2m/3 \rfloor$ keys:

$$(10)$$

If the original node has no right sibling, we can look at its left sibling in essentially the same way. (If the original node has both a right and a left sibling, we could even refrain from splitting off a new node unless *both* left and right siblings are full.) Finally if the original node to be split has no siblings at all, it must be the root; we can change the definition of B-tree, allowing the root to contain as many as $2\lfloor(2m-2)/3\rfloor$ keys, so that when the root splits it produces two nodes of $\lfloor(2m-2)/3\rfloor$ keys each.

The effect of all the technicalities in the preceding paragraph is to produce a superior breed of tree, say a B^*-tree of order m, which can be defined as follows:

i) Every node except the root has at most m children.

ii) Every node, except for the root and the leaves, has at least $(2m-1)/3$ children.

iii) The root has at least 2 and at most $2\lfloor(2m-2)/3\rfloor+1$ children.

iv) All leaves appear on the same level.

v) A nonleaf node with k children contains $k-1$ keys.

The important change is condition (ii), which asserts that we utilize at least two-thirds of the available space in every node. This change not only uses space more efficiently, it also makes the search process faster, since we may replace $\lceil m/2 \rceil$ by $\lceil (2m-1)/3 \rceil$ in (6) and (7). However, the insertion process gets slower, because nodes tend to need more attention as they fill up; see B. Zhang and M. Hsu, *Acta Informatica* **26** (1989), 421–438, for an approximate analysis of the tradeoffs involved.

At the other extreme, it is sometimes better to let nodes become less than half full in a tree that changes quite frequently, especially if insertions tend to outnumber deletions. This situation has been analyzed by T. Johnson and D. Shasha, *J. Comput. Syst. Sci.* **47** (1993), 45–76.

Perhaps the reader has been skeptical of B-trees because the degree of the root can be as low as 2. Why should we waste a whole disk access on merely a 2-way decision?! A simple buffering scheme, called *least-recently-used page replacement*, overcomes this objection; we can keep several bufferloads of information in the internal memory, so that input commands can be avoided when the corresponding page is already present. Under this scheme, the algorithms for searching or insertion issue "virtual read" commands that are translated into actual input instructions only when the necessary page is not in memory; a subsequent "release" command is issued when the buffer has been read and possibly modified by the algorithm. When an actual read is required, the buffer that has least recently been released is chosen; we write out that buffer, if its contents have changed since they were read in, then we read the desired page into the chosen buffer.

Since the number of levels in the tree is generally small compared to the number of buffers, this paging scheme will ensure that the root page is always present in memory; and if the root has only 2 or 3 children, the first-level pages will almost surely stay there too. Any pages that might need to be split during an insertion are automatically present in memory when they are needed, because they will be remembered from the immediately preceding search.

Experiments by E. McCreight have shown that this policy is quite successful. For example, he found that with 10 buffers and $m=121$, the process of inserting

100,000 keys in ascending order required only 22 actual read commands, and only 857 actual write commands; thus most of the activity took place in the internal memory. Furthermore the tree contained only 835 nodes, just one higher than the minimum possible value $\lceil 100000/(m-1)\rceil = 834$; thus the storage utilization was nearly 100 percent. For this experiment he used the overflow technique, but with only 2-way node splitting as in (4), not 3-way splitting as in (10). (See exercise 3.)

In another experiment, again with 10 buffers and $m = 121$ and the overflow technique, he inserted 5000 keys into an initially empty tree, in *random* order; this produced a 2-level tree with 48 nodes (87 percent storage utilization), after making 2762 actual reads and 2739 actual writes. Then 1000 random searches required 786 actual reads. The same experiment *without* the overflow feature produced a 2-level tree with 62 nodes (67 percent storage utilization), after making 2743 actual reads and 2800 actual writes; 1000 subsequent random searches required 836 actual reads. This shows not only that the paging scheme is effective but also that it is wise to handle overflows locally before deciding to split a node.

Andrew Yao has proved that the average number of nodes after random insertions without the overflow feature will be

$$N/(m \ln 2) + O(N/m^2),$$

for large N and m, so the storage utilization will be approximately $\ln 2 = 69.3$ percent [*Acta Informatica* **9** (1978), 159–170]. See also the more detailed analyses by B. Eisenbarth, N. Ziviani, G. H. Gonnet, K. Mehlhorn, and D. Wood, *Information and Control* **55** (1982), 125–174; R. A. Baeza-Yates, *Acta Informatica* **26** (1989), 439–471.

B-trees became popular soon after they were invented. See, for example, the article by Douglas Comer in *Computing Surveys* **11** (1979), 121–137, 412, which discusses early developments and describes a widely used system called VSAM (Virtual Storage Access Method) developed by IBM Corporation. One of the innovations of VSAM was to replicate blocks on a disk track so that latency time was minimized.

Two of the most interesting developments of the basic *B*-tree strategy have unfortunately been given almost identical names: "*SB*-trees" and "SB-trees." The *SB*-tree of P. E. O'Neil [*Acta Inf.* **29** (1992), 241–265] is designed to minimize disk I/O time by allocating nearby records to the same track or cylinder, maintaining efficiency in applications where many consecutive records need to be accessed at the same time; in this case "*SB*" is in italic type and the *S* connotes "sequential." The SB-tree of P. Ferragina and R. Grossi [*STOC* **27** (1995), 693–702; *SODA* **7** (1996), 373–382] is an elegant combination of *B*-tree structure with the Patricia trees that we will consider in Section 6.3; in this case "SB" is in roman type and the S connotes "string." SB-trees have many applications to large-scale text processing, and they provide a basis for efficient sorting of variable-length strings on disk [see Arge, Ferragina, Grossi, and Vitter, *STOC* **29** (1997), 540–548].

EXERCISES

1. [*10*] What *B*-tree of order 7 is obtained after the key 613 is inserted into Fig. 30? (Do not use the overflow technique.)

2. [*15*] Work exercise 1, but use the overflow technique, with 3-way splitting as in (10).

▶ **3.** [*23*] Suppose we insert the keys 1, 2, 3, ... in ascending order into an initially empty *B*-tree of order 101. Which key causes the leaves to be on level 4 for the first time
   a) when we use no overflow?
   b) when we use overflow and only 2-way splitting as in (4)?
   c) when we use a B^*-tree of order 101, with overflow and 3-way splitting as in (10)?

4. [*21*] (Bayer and McCreight.) Explain how to handle insertions into a generalized *B*-tree so that all nodes except the root and leaves will be guaranteed to have at least $\frac{3}{4}m - \frac{1}{2}$ children.

▶ **5.** [*21*] Suppose that a node represents 1000 character positions of external memory. If each pointer occupies 5 characters, and if the keys are variable in length, between 5 and 50 characters long but always a multiple of 5 characters, what is the minimum number of character positions occupied in a node after it splits during an insertion? (Consider only a simple splitting procedure analogous to that described in the text for fixed-length-key *B*-trees, without overflowing; move up the key that makes the remaining two parts most nearly equal in size.)

6. [*23*] Design a deletion algorithm for *B*-trees.

7. [*28*] Design a concatenation algorithm for *B*-trees (see Section 6.2.3).

▶ **8.** [*HM37*] Consider the generalization of tree insertion suggested by Muntz and Uzgalis, where each page can hold M keys. After N random items have been inserted into such a tree, so that there are $N+1$ external nodes, let $b_{Nk}^{(j)}$ be the probability that an unsuccessful search requires k page accesses and that it ends at an external node whose parent node belongs to a page containing j keys. If $B_N^{(j)}(z) = \sum b_{Nk}^{(j)} z^k$ is the corresponding generating function, prove that we have $B_1^{(j)}(z) = \delta_{j1} z$ and

$$B_N^{(j)}(z) = \frac{N-j-1}{N+1} B_{N-1}^{(j)}(z) + \frac{j+1}{N+1} B_{N-1}^{(j-1)}(z), \qquad \text{for } 1 < j < M;$$

$$B_N^{(1)}(z) = \frac{N-2}{N+1} B_{N-1}^{(1)}(z) + \frac{2z}{N+1} B_{N-1}^{(M)}(z);$$

$$B_N^{(M)}(z) = \frac{N-1}{N+1} B_{N-1}^{(M)}(z) + \frac{M+1}{N+1} B_{N-1}^{(M-1)}(z).$$

Find the asymptotic behavior of $C_N' = \sum_{j=1}^{M} B_N^{(j)'}(1)$, the average number of page accesses per unsuccessful search. [*Hint:* Express the recurrence in terms of the matrix

$$W(z) = \begin{pmatrix} -3 & 0 & \cdots & 0 & 2z \\ 3 & -4 & \cdots & 0 & 0 \\ 0 & 4 & \cdots & 0 & 0 \\ \vdots & \vdots & & \vdots & \vdots \\ 0 & 0 & \cdots & -M-1 & 0 \\ 0 & 0 & \cdots & M+1 & -2 \end{pmatrix},$$

and relate C_N' to an Nth degree polynomial in $W(1)$.]

9. [*22*] Can the *B*-tree idea be used to retrieve items of a linear list by position instead of by key value? (See Algorithm 6.2.3B.)

▶ **10.** [*35*] Discuss how a large file, organized as a *B*-tree, can be used for concurrent accessing and updating by a large number of simultaneous users, in such a way that users of different pages rarely interfere with each other.

> *Little is known, even for otherwise equivalent algorithms,*
> *about the optimization of storage allocation,*
> *minimization of the number of required operations,*
> *and so on. This area of investigation*
> *must draw upon the most powerful resources*
> *of both pure and applied mathematics*
> *for further progress.*
>
> — ANTHONY G. OETTINGER (1961)

6.3. DIGITAL SEARCHING

INSTEAD OF BASING a search method on comparisons between keys, we can make use of their representation as a sequence of digits or alphabetic characters. Consider, for example, the thumb index on a large dictionary; from the first letter of a given word, we can immediately locate the pages that contain all words beginning with that letter.

If we pursue the thumb-index idea to one of its logical conclusions, we come up with a searching scheme based on repeated "subscripting" as illustrated in Table 1. Suppose that we want to test a given search argument to see whether it is one of the 31 most common words of English (see Figs. 12 and 13 in Section 6.2.2). The data is represented in Table 1 as a *trie structure*; this name was suggested by E. Fredkin [*CACM* **3** (1960), 490–499] because it is a part of information re*trie*val. A trie — pronounced "try" — is essentially an M-ary tree, whose nodes are M-place vectors with components corresponding to digits or characters. Each node on level l represents the set of all keys that begin with a certain sequence of l characters called its *prefix*; the node specifies an M-way branch, depending on the $(l + 1)$st character.

For example, the trie of Table 1 has 12 nodes; node (1) is the root, and we look up the first letter here. If the first letter is, say, N, the table tells us that our word must be NOT (or else it isn't in the table). On the other hand, if the first letter is W, node (1) tells us to go on to node (9), looking up the second letter in the same way; node (9) says that the second letter should be A, H, or I. The prefix of node (10) is HA. Blank entries in the table stand for null links.

The node vectors in Table 1 are arranged according to MIX character code. This means that a trie search will be quite fast, since we are merely fetching words of an array by using the characters of our keys as subscripts. Techniques for making quick multiway decisions by subscripting have been called "table look-at" as opposed to "table look-up" [see P. M. Sherman, *CACM* **4** (1961), 172–173, 175].

Algorithm T (*Trie search*). Given a table of records that form an M-ary trie, this algorithm searches for a given argument K. The nodes of the trie are vectors whose subscripts run from 0 to $M - 1$; each component of these vectors is either a key or a link (possibly null).

T1. [Initialize.] Set the link variable P so that it points to the root of the trie.

T2. [Branch.] Set k to the next character of the input argument, K, from left to right. (If the argument has been completely scanned, we set k to a "blank" or end-of-word symbol. The character should be represented as a number in the range $0 \le k < M$.) Let X be table entry number k in NODE(P). If X is a link, go to T3; but if X is a key, go to T4.

T3. [Advance.] If $X \ne \Lambda$, set P $\leftarrow$ X and return to step T2; otherwise the algorithm terminates unsuccessfully.

T4. [Compare.] If $X = K$, the algorithm terminates successfully; otherwise it terminates unsuccessfully. ∎

Table 1

A TRIE FOR THE 31 MOST COMMON ENGLISH WORDS

	(1)	(2)	(3)	(4)	(5)	(6)	(7)	(8)	(9)	(10)	(11)	(12)
⊔		A				I					HE	
A	(2)				(10)				WAS			THAT
B	(3)											
C												
D										HAD		
E			BE		(11)							THE
F	(4)						OF					
G												
H	(5)							(12)	WHICH			
I	(6)			HIS					WITH			THIS
Δ												
J												
K												
L												
M												
N	NOT	AND				IN	ON					
O	(7)			FOR			TO					
P												
Q												
R		ARE		FROM			OR				HER	
Σ												
Π												
S		AS				IS						
T	(8)	AT				IT						
U			BUT									
V										HAVE		
W	(9)											
X												
Y	YOU		BY									
Z												

Notice that if the search is unsuccessful, the *longest match* has been found. This property is occasionally useful in applications.

In order to compare the speed of this algorithm to the others in this chapter, we can write a short MIX program assuming that the characters are bytes and that the keys are at most five bytes long.

Program T (*Trie search*). This program assumes that all keys are represented in one MIX word, with blank spaces at the right whenever the key has less than five characters. Since we use MIX character code, each byte of the search argument is assumed to contain a number less than 30. Links are represented as negative numbers in the 0:2 field of a node word. $rI1 \equiv P$, $rX \equiv$ unscanned part of K.

01	START	LDX	K	1 *T1. Initialize.*
02		ENT1	ROOT	1 P ← pointer to root of trie.
03	2H	SLAX	1	C *T2. Branch.*
04		STA	*+1(2:2)	C Extract next character, k.
05		ENT2	0,1	C Q ← P + k.
06		LD1N	0,2(0:2)	C P = LINK(Q).
07		J1P	2B	C *T3. Advance.* To T2 if P is a link $\neq \Lambda$.

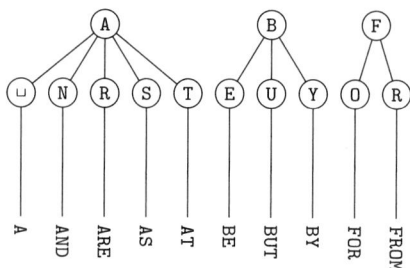

Fig. 31. The trie of Table 1,
converted into a "forest."

```
08              LDA  0,2      1    T4. Compare. rA ← KEY(Q).
09              CMPA K        1
10              JE   SUCCESS  1    Exit successfully if rA = K.
11  FAILURE EQU *                  Exit if not in the trie.  ▮
```

The running time of this program is $8C + 8$ units, where C is the number of characters examined. Since $C \leq 5$, the search never needs more than 48 units of time.

If we now compare the efficiency of this program (using the trie of Table 1) to Program 6.2.2T (using the *optimum* binary search tree of Fig. 13), we can make the following observations.

1. The trie takes much more memory space; we are using 360 words just to represent 31 keys, while the binary search tree uses only 62 words of memory. (However, exercise 4 shows that, with some fiddling around, we can actually fit the trie of Table 1 into only 49 words.)

2. A successful search takes about 26 units of time for both programs. But an unsuccessful search will go faster in the trie, slower in the binary search tree. For this data the search will be unsuccessful more often than it is successful, so the trie is preferable from the standpoint of speed.

3. If we consider the KWIC indexing application of Fig. 15 instead of the 31 commonest English words, the trie loses its advantage because of the nature of the data. For example, a trie requires 12 iterations to distinguish between COMPUTATION and COMPUTATIONS. In this case it would be better to build the trie so that words are scanned from right to left instead of from left to right.

The abstract concept of a trie to represent a family of strings was introduced by Axel Thue, in a paper about strings that do not contain adjacent repeated substrings [*Skrifter udgivne af Videnskabs-Selskabet i Christiania*, Mathematisk-Naturvidenskabelig Klasse (1912), No. 1; reprinted in Thue's *Selected Mathematical Papers* (Oslo: Universitetsforlaget, 1977), 413–477].

Trie memory for computer searching was first recommended by René de la Briandais [*Proc. Western Joint Computer Conf.* **15** (1959), 295–298]. He pointed out that we can save memory space at the expense of running time if we use a linked list for each node vector, since most of the entries in the vectors tend to be empty. In effect, this idea amounts to replacing the trie of Table 1 by the forest of trees shown in Fig. 31. Searching in such a forest proceeds by finding the root that matches the first character, then finding the child node of that root that matches the second character, etc.

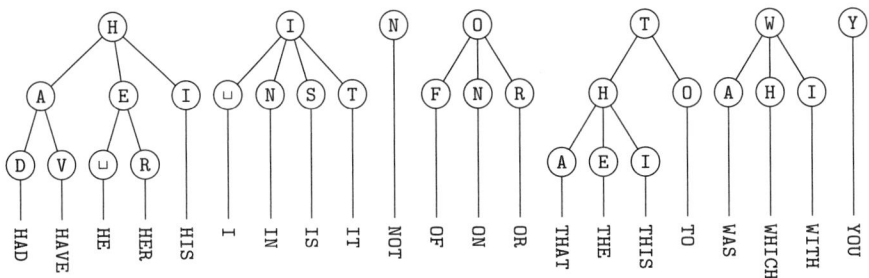

In his article, de la Briandais did not actually stop the tree branching exactly as shown in Table 1 or Fig. 31; instead, he continued to represent each key, character by character, until reaching the end-of-word delimiter. Thus he would actually have used

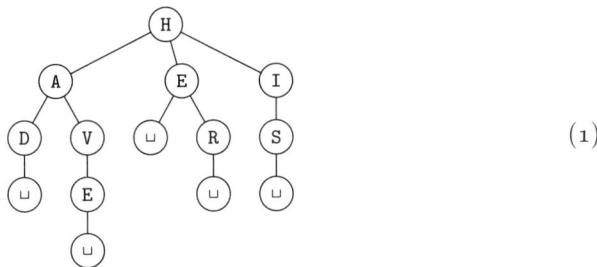

$$(1)$$

in place of the "H" tree in Fig. 31. This representation requires more storage, but it makes the processing of variable-length data especially easy. If we use two link fields per character, dynamic insertions and deletions can be handled in a simple manner.

If we use the normal way of representing trees as binary trees, (1) becomes the binary tree

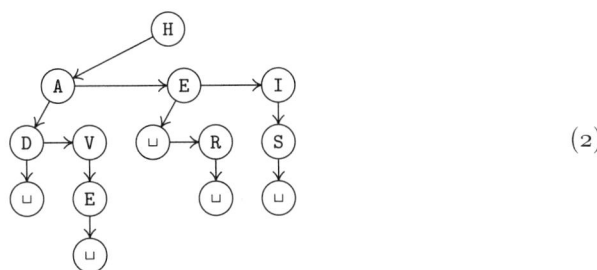

$$(2)$$

(In the representation of the full forest, Fig. 31, we would also have a pointer leading to the right from H to its neighboring root I.) The search in this binary tree proceeds by comparing a character of the argument to the character in the tree, and following RLINKs until finding a match; then the LLINK is taken and we treat the next character of the argument in the same way.

With such a binary tree, we are more or less doing a search by comparison, with equal-unequal branching instead of less-greater branching. The elementary theory of Section 6.2.1 tells that we must make at least $\lg N$ comparisons, on the average, to distinguish between N keys; the average number of tests made when searching a tree like that of Fig. 31 must be at least as many as we make when doing a binary search using the techniques of Section 6.2.

On the other hand, the trie in Table 1 is capable of making an M-way branch all at once; we shall see that the average search time for large N involves only about

$$\log_M N = \lg N / \lg M$$

iterations, if the input data is random. We shall also see that a "pure" trie scheme like that in Algorithm T requires a total of approximately $N/\ln M$ nodes to distinguish between N random inputs; hence the total amount of space is proportional to $MN/\ln M$.

From these considerations it is clear that the trie idea pays off only in the first few levels of the tree. We can get better performance by mixing two strategies, using a trie for the first few characters and then switching to some other technique. For example, E. H. Sussenguth, Jr. [*CACM* **6** (1963), 272–279] suggested using a character-by-character scheme until we reach part of the tree where only, say, six or fewer keys of the file are possible, and then we can sequentially run through the short list of remaining keys. We shall see that this mixed strategy decreases the number of trie nodes by roughly a factor of six, without substantially changing the running time.

An interesting way to store large, growing tries in external memory was suggested by S. Y. Berkovich in *Doklady Akademii Nauk SSSR* **202** (1972), 298–299 [English translation in *Soviet Physics–Doklady* **17** (1972), 20–21].

T. N. Turba [*CACM* **25** (1982), 522–526] points out that it is sometimes most convenient to search for variable-length keys by having one search tree or trie for each different length.

The binary case. Let us now consider the special case $M = 2$, in which we scan the search argument one bit at a time. Two interesting methods have been developed that are especially appropriate for this case.

The first method, which we call *digital tree search*, is due to E. G. Coffman and J. Eve [*CACM* **13** (1970), 427–432, 436]. The idea is to store full keys in the nodes just as we did in the tree search algorithm of Section 6.2.2, but to use bits of the argument (instead of results of the comparisons) to govern whether to take the left or right branch at each step. Figure 32 shows the binary tree constructed by this method when we insert the 31 most common English words in order of decreasing frequency. In order to provide binary data for this illustration, the words have been expressed in MIX character code, and the codes have been converted into binary numbers with 5 bits per byte. Thus, the word WHICH is represented as the bit sequence 11010 01000 01001 00011 01000.

To search for this word WHICH in Fig. 32, we compare it first with the word THE at the root of the tree. Since there is no match and since the first bit of WHICH is 1, we move to the right and compare with OF. Since there is no match and since the second bit of WHICH is 1, we move to the right and compare with WITH; and so on. Alphabetic order of the keys in a digital search tree no longer corresponds to symmetric order of the nodes.

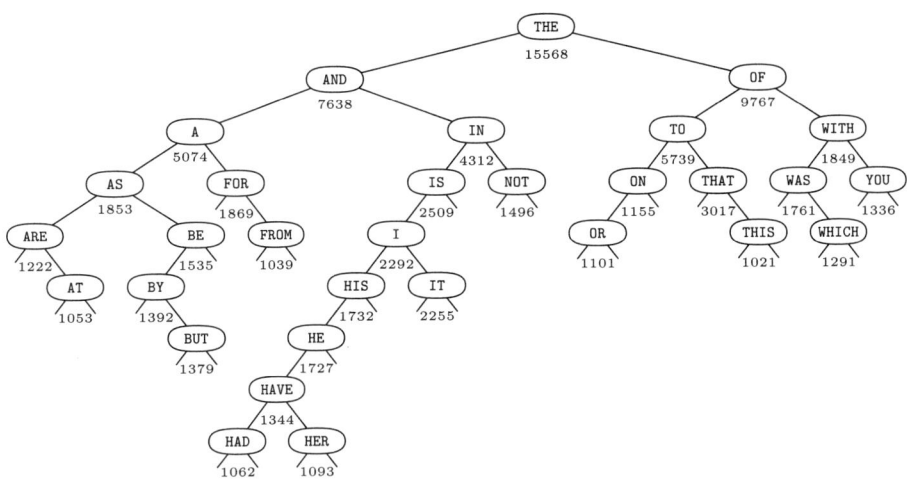

Fig. 32. A digital search tree for the 31 most common English words, inserted in decreasing order of frequency.

It is interesting to note the contrast between Fig. 32 and Fig. 12 in Section 6.2.2, since the latter tree was formed in the same way but using comparisons instead of key bits for the branching. If we consider the given frequencies, the digital search tree of Fig. 32 requires an average of 3.42 comparisons per successful search; this is somewhat better than the 4.04 comparisons needed by Fig. 12, although of course the computing time per comparison will probably be different.

Algorithm D (*Digital tree search and insertion*).   Given a table of records that form a binary tree as described above, this algorithm searches for a given argument K. If K is not in the table, a new node containing K is inserted into the tree in the appropriate place.

This algorithm assumes that the tree is nonempty and that its nodes have KEY, LLINK, and RLINK fields just as in Algorithm 6.2.2T. In fact, the two algorithms are almost identical, as the reader may verify.

D1. [Initialize.] Set P ← ROOT, and $K' ← K$.

D2. [Compare.] If K = KEY(P), the search terminates successfully. Otherwise set b to the leading bit of K', and shift K' left one place (thereby removing that bit and introducing a 0 at the right). If $b = 0$, go to D3, otherwise go to D4.

D3. [Move left.]   If LLINK(P) ≠ Λ, set P ← LLINK(P) and go back to D2. Otherwise go to D5.

D4. [Move right.] If RLINK(P) ≠ Λ, set P ← RLINK(P) and go back to D2.

D5. [Insert into tree.] Set Q ⇐ AVAIL, KEY(Q) ← K, LLINK(Q) ← RLINK(Q) ← Λ. If $b = 0$ set LLINK(P) ← Q, otherwise set RLINK(P) ← Q. ∎

Although the tree search of Algorithm 6.2.2T is inherently binary, it is not difficult to see that the present algorithm could be extended to an M-ary digital search for any $M \geq 2$ (see exercise 13).

Donald R. Morrison [*JACM* **15** (1968), 514–534] has discovered a very pretty way to form N-node search trees based on the binary representation of keys, *without* storing keys in the nodes. His method, called "Patricia" (Practical Algorithm To Retrieve Information Coded In Alphanumeric), is especially suitable for dealing with extremely long, variable-length keys such as titles or phrases stored within a large bulk file. A closely related algorithm was published at almost exactly the same time in Germany by G. Gwehenberger, *Elektronische Rechenanlagen* **10** (1968), 223–226.

Patricia's basic idea is to build a binary trie, but to avoid one-way branching by including in each node the number of bits to skip over before making the next test. There are several ways to exploit this idea; perhaps the simplest to explain is illustrated in Fig. 33. We have a TEXT array of bits, which is usually quite long; it may be stored as an external direct-access file, since each search accesses TEXT only once. Each key to be stored in our table is specified by a starting place in the text, and it can be imagined to go from this starting place all the way to the end of the text. (Patricia does not search for strict equality between key and argument; instead, it will determine whether or not there exists a key *beginning* with the argument.)

T H I S ␣ I S ␣ T H E ␣ H O U S E ␣ T H A T ␣ J A C K ␣ B U I L T ?
10111010001001101100000001001101100000010111010000010100000010001000011000101100010100000101110100000110111000000101100010001011000000000101100001001011011111111

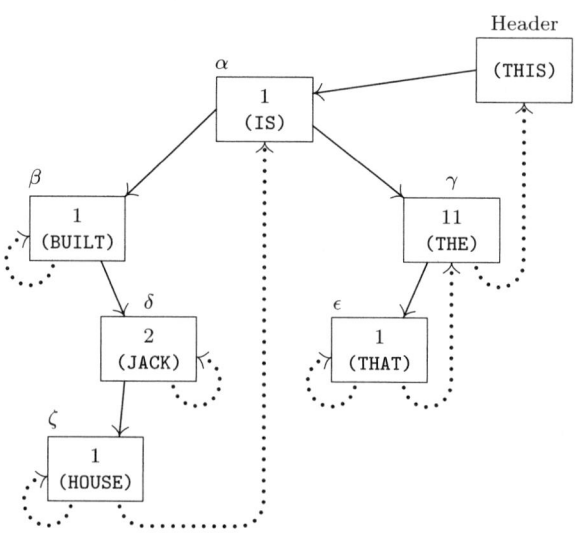

Fig. 33. An example of Patricia's tree and TEXT.

The situation depicted in Fig. 33 involves seven keys, one starting at each word, namely "THIS IS THE HOUSE THAT JACK BUILT?" and "IS THE HOUSE THAT

JACK BUILT?" and ... and "BUILT?". There is one important restriction, namely that *no one key may be a prefix of another*; this restriction can be met if we end the text with a unique end-of-text code (in this case "?") that appears nowhere else. The same restriction was implicit in the trie scheme of Algorithm T, where "␣" was the termination code.

The tree that Patricia uses for searching should be contained in random-access memory, or it should be arranged on pages as suggested in Section 6.2.4. It consists of a header and $N - 1$ nodes, where the nodes contain several fields:

KEY, a pointer to the text. This field must be at least $\lg C$ bits long, if the text contains C characters. In Fig. 33 the words shown within each node would really be represented by pointers to the text; for example, instead of "(JACK)" the node would contain the number 24 (which indicates the starting place of "JACK BUILT?" in the text string).

LLINK and RLINK, pointers within the tree. These fields must be at least $\lg N$ bits long.

LTAG and RTAG, one-bit fields that tell whether or not LLINK and RLINK, respectively, are pointers to children or to ancestors of the node. The dotted lines in Fig. 33 correspond to pointers whose TAG bit is 1.

SKIP, a number that tells how many bits to skip when searching, as explained below. This field should be large enough to hold the largest number k such that all keys with prefix σ agree in the next k bits following σ, for some string σ that is a prefix of at least two different keys; in practice, we may usually assume that k isn't too large, and an error indication can be given if the size of the SKIP field is exceeded. The SKIP fields are shown as numbers within each non-header node of Fig. 33.

The header contains only KEY, LLINK, and LTAG fields.

A search in Patricia's tree is carried out as follows: Suppose we are looking up the word THE (bit pattern 10111 01000 00101). We start by looking at the SKIP field of the root node α, which tells us to examine bit 1 of the argument. That bit is 1, so we move to the right. The SKIP field in the next node, γ, tells us to look at the $1 + 11 = 12$th bit of the argument. It is 0, so we move to the left. The SKIP field of the next node, ϵ, tells us to look at the $(12 + 1)$st bit, which is 1; now we find RTAG $= 1$, so we go back to node γ, which refers us to the TEXT. The search path we have taken would occur for any argument whose bit pattern is 1xxxx xxxxx x01..., and we must check to see if it matches the unique key beginning with that pattern, namely THE.

Suppose, on the other hand, that we are looking for any or all keys starting with TH. The search process begins as above, but it eventually tries to look at the (nonexistent) 12th bit of the 10-bit argument. At this point we compare the argument to the TEXT at the point specified in the current node (in this case node γ). If it does not match, the argument is not the beginning of any key; but if it does match, the argument is the beginning of every key represented by dotted links in node γ and its descendants (namely THIS, THAT, THE).

The search process can be spelled out more precisely in the following way.

Algorithm P (*Patricia*). Given a TEXT array and a tree with KEY, LLINK, RLINK, LTAG, RTAG, and SKIP fields, as described above, this algorithm determines whether or not there is a key in the TEXT that begins with a specified argument K. (If r such keys exist, for $r \geq 1$, it is subsequently possible to locate them all in $O(r)$ steps; see exercise 14.) We assume that at least one key is present.

P1. [Initialize.] Set P ← HEAD and j ← 0. (Variable P is a pointer that will move down the tree, and j is a counter that will designate bit positions of the argument.) Set n ← number of bits in K.

P2. [Move left.] Set Q ← P and P ← LLINK(Q). If LTAG(Q) = 1, go to P6.

P3. [Skip bits.] (At this point we know that if the first j bits of K match any key whatsoever, they match the key that starts at KEY(P).) Set j ← j+SKIP(P). If $j > n$, go to P6.

P4. [Test bit.] (At this point we know that if the first $j - 1$ bits of K match any key, they match the key starting at KEY(P).) If the jth bit of K is 0, go to P2, otherwise go to P5.

P5. [Move right.] Set Q ← P and P ← RLINK(Q). If RTAG(Q) = 0, go to P3.

P6. [Compare.] (At this point we know that if K matches any key, it matches the key starting at KEY(P).) Compare K to the key that starts at position KEY(P) in the TEXT array. If they are equal (up to n bits, the length of K), the algorithm terminates successfully; if unequal, it terminates unsuccessfully. ∎

Exercise 15 shows how Patricia's tree can be built in the first place. We can also add to the text and insert new keys, provided that the new text material always ends with a unique delimiter (for example, an end-of-text symbol followed by a serial number).

Patricia is a little tricky, and she requires careful scrutiny before all of her beauties are revealed.

Analyses of the algorithms. We shall conclude this section by making a mathematical study of tries, digital search trees, and Patricia. A summary of the main consequences of these analyses appears at the very end.

Let us consider first the case of binary tries, namely tries with $M = 2$. Figure 34 shows the binary trie that is formed when the sixteen keys from the sorting examples of Chapter 5 are treated as 10-bit binary numbers. (The keys are shown in octal notation, so that for example *1144* represents the 10-bit number $612 = (1001100100)_2$.) As in Algorithm T, we use the trie to store information about the leading bits of the keys until we get to the first point where the key is uniquely identified; then the key is recorded in full.

If Fig. 34 is compared to Table 5.2.2–3, an amazing relationship between trie memory and radix exchange sorting is revealed. (Then again, perhaps this relationship is obvious.) The 22 nodes of Fig. 34 correspond precisely to the 22

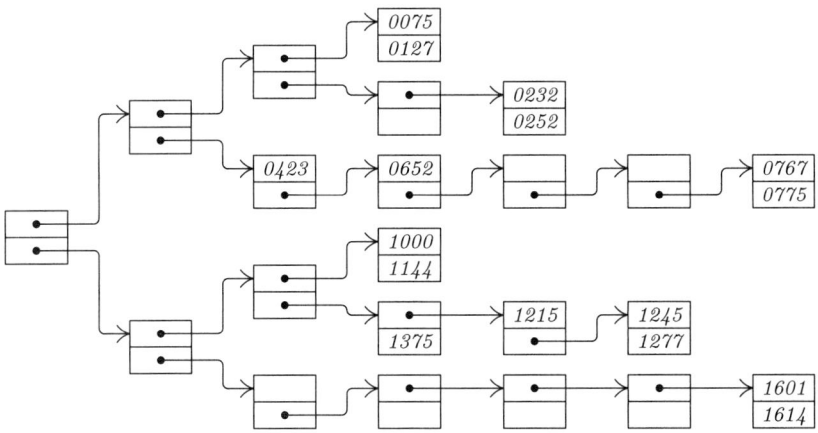

Fig. 34. Example of a random binary trie.

partitioning stages in Table 5.2.2–3, with the pth node in preorder corresponding
to Stage p. The number of bit inspections in a partitioning stage is equal to the
number of keys within the corresponding node and its subtries; consequently we
may state the following result.

Theorem T. *If N distinct binary numbers are put into a binary trie as described
above, then* (i) *the number of nodes of the trie is equal to the number of
partitioning stages required if these numbers are sorted by radix exchange; and*
(ii) *the average number of bit inspections required to retrieve a key by means of
Algorithm T is $1/N$ times the number of bit inspections required by the radix
exchange sort.* ▮

Because of this theorem, we can make use of all the mathematical machinery
that was developed for radix exchange in Section 5.2.2. For example, if we
assume that our keys are infinite-precision random uniformly distributed real
numbers between 0 and 1, the number of bit inspections needed for retrieval will
be $\lg N + \gamma/\ln 2 + 1/2 + \delta(N) + O(N^{-1})$, and the number of trie nodes will be
$N/\ln 2 + N\bar{\delta}(N) + O(1)$. Here $\delta(N)$ and $\bar{\delta}(N)$ are complicated functions that
may be neglected since their absolute value is always less than 10^{-6} (see exercises
5.2.2–38 and 5.2.2–48).

Of course there is still more work to be done, since we need to generalize
from binary tries to M-ary tries. We shall describe only the starting point of
the investigations here, leaving the instructive details as exercises.

Let A_N be the average number of internal nodes in a random M-ary search
trie that contains N keys. Then $A_0 = A_1 = 0$, and for $N \geq 2$ we have

$$A_N = 1 + \sum_{k_1 + \cdots + k_M = N} \left(\frac{N!}{k_1! \ldots k_M!} M^{-N} \right) (A_{k_1} + \cdots + A_{k_M}), \qquad (3)$$

since $N!\,M^{-N}/k_1!\ldots k_M!$ is the probability that k_1 of the keys are in the first subtrie, $\ldots$, k_M in the Mth. This equation can be rewritten

$$A_N = 1 + M^{1-N} \sum_{k_1+\cdots+k_M=N} \left(\frac{N!}{k_1!\ldots k_M!}\right) A_{k_1}$$

$$= 1 + M^{1-N} \sum_k \binom{N}{k} (M-1)^{N-k} A_k, \qquad \text{for } N \geq 2, \qquad (4)$$

by using symmetry and then summing over $k_2, \ldots, k_M$. Similarly, if C_N denotes the average total number of digit inspections needed to look up all N keys in the trie, we find $C_0 = C_1 = 0$ and

$$C_N = N + M^{1-N} \sum_k \binom{N}{k} (M-1)^{N-k} C_k \qquad \text{for } N \geq 2. \qquad (5)$$

Exercise 17 shows how to deal with general recurrences of this type, and exercises 18–25 work out the corresponding theory of random tries. [The analysis of A_N was first approached from another point of view by L. R. Johnson and M. H. McAndrew, *IBM J. Res. and Devel.* **8** (1964), 189–193, in connection with an equivalent hardware-oriented sorting algorithm.]

If we now turn to a study of digital search trees, we find that the formulas are similar, yet different enough that it is not easy to see how to deduce the asymptotic behavior. For example, if $\bar{C}_N$ denotes the average total number of digit inspections made when looking up all N keys in an M-ary digital search tree, it is not difficult to deduce as above that $\bar{C}_0 = \bar{C}_1 = 0$, and

$$\bar{C}_{N+1} = N + M^{1-N} \sum_k \binom{N}{k} (M-1)^{N-k} \bar{C}_k \qquad \text{for } N \geq 0. \qquad (6)$$

This is almost identical to Eq. (5); but the appearance of $N+1$ instead of N on the left-hand side of this equation is enough to change the entire character of the recurrence, so the methods we have used to study (5) are wiped out.

Let's consider the binary case first. Figure 35 shows the digital search tree corresponding to the sixteen example keys of Fig. 34, when they have been inserted in the order used in the examples of Chapter 5. If we want to determine the average number of bit inspections made in a random successful search, this is just the internal path length of the tree divided by N, since we need l bit inspections to find a node on level l. Notice, however, that the average number of bit inspections made in a random *unsuccessful* search is *not* simply related to the external path length of the tree, since unsuccessful searches are more likely to occur at external nodes near the root; thus, the probability of reaching the left sub-branch of node *0075* in Fig. 35 is $\frac{1}{8}$ (assuming infinitely precise keys), and the left sub-branch of node *0232* will be encountered with probability only $\frac{1}{32}$. For this reason, digital search trees tend to stay better balanced than the binary search trees of Algorithm 6.2.2T, when the keys are uniformly distributed.

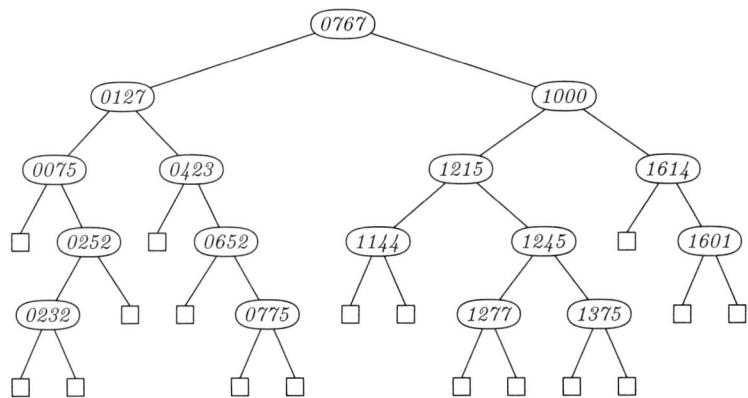

Fig. 35. A random digital search tree constructed by Algorithm D.

We can use a generating function to describe the pertinent characteristics of a digital search tree. If there are a_l internal nodes on level l, consider the generating function $a(z) = \sum_l a_l z^l$; for example, the generating function corresponding to Fig. 35 is $a(z) = 1 + 2z + 4z^2 + 5z^3 + 4z^4$. If there are b_l external nodes on level l, and if $b(z) = \sum_l b_l z^l$, we have

$$b(z) = 1 + (2z - 1)a(z) \tag{7}$$

by exercise 6.2.1–25. For example, $1 + (2z - 1)(1 + 2z + 4z^2 + 5z^3 + 4z^4) = 3z^3 + 6z^4 + 8z^5$. The average number of bit inspections made in a random successful search is $a'(1)/a(1)$, since $a'(1)$ is the internal path length of the tree and $a(1)$ is the number of internal nodes. The average number of bit inspections made in a random *unsuccessful* search is $\sum_l lb_l 2^{-l} = \frac{1}{2}b'(\frac{1}{2}) = a(\frac{1}{2})$, since we end up at a given external node on level l with probability 2^{-l}. The number of comparisons is the same as the number of bit inspections, plus one in a successful search. For example, in Fig. 35, a successful search will take $2\frac{9}{16}$ bit inspections and $3\frac{9}{16}$ comparisons, on the average; an unsuccessful search will take $3\frac{7}{8}$ of each.

Now let $g_N(z)$ be the "average" $a(z)$ for trees with N nodes; in other words, $g_N(z)$ is the sum $\sum p_T a_T(z)$ over all binary digital search trees T with N internal nodes, where $a_T(z)$ is the generating function for the internal nodes of T and p_T is the probability that T occurs when N random numbers are inserted using Algorithm D. Then the average number of bit inspections will be $g'_N(1)/N$ in a successful search, $g_N(\frac{1}{2})$ in an unsuccessful search.

We can compute $g_N(z)$ by mimicking the tree construction process, as follows. If $a(z)$ is the generating function for a tree of N nodes, we can form $N+1$ trees from it by making the next insertion into any one of the external node positions. The insertion goes into a given external node on level l with probability 2^{-l}; hence the sum of the generating functions for the $N+1$ new trees, multiplied by the probability of occurrence, is $a(z) + b(\frac{1}{2}z) = a(z) + 1 + (z - 1)a(\frac{1}{2}z)$.

Averaging over all trees for N nodes, it follows that

$$g_{N+1}(z) = g_N(z) + 1 + (z-1)g_N\left(\tfrac{1}{2}z\right); \qquad g_0(z) = 0. \tag{8}$$

The corresponding generating function for external nodes,

$$h_N(z) = 1 + (2z-1)g_N(z),$$

is somewhat easier to work with, because (8) is equivalent to the formula

$$h_{N+1}(z) = h_N(z) + (2z-1)h_N\left(\tfrac{1}{2}z\right); \qquad h_0(z) = 1. \tag{9}$$

Applying this rule repeatedly, we find that

$$h_{N+1}(z) = h_{N-1}(z) + 2(2z-1)h_{N-1}\left(\tfrac{1}{2}z\right) + (2z-1)(z-1)h_{N-1}\left(\tfrac{1}{4}z\right)$$
$$= h_{N-2}(z) + 3(2z-1)h_{N-2}\left(\tfrac{1}{2}z\right) + 3(2z-1)(z-1)h_{N-2}\left(\tfrac{1}{4}z\right)$$
$$+ (2z-1)(z-1)\left(\tfrac{1}{2}z-1\right)h_{N-2}\left(\tfrac{1}{8}z\right)$$

and so on, so that eventually we have

$$h_N(z) = \sum_k \binom{N}{k} \prod_{j=0}^{k-1}(2^{1-j}z - 1); \tag{10}$$

$$g_N(z) = \sum_{k\geq 0} \binom{N}{k+1} \prod_{j=0}^{k-1}(2^{-j}z - 1). \tag{11}$$

For example, $g_4(z) = 4 + 6(z-1) + 4(z-1)\left(\tfrac{1}{2}z-1\right) + (z-1)\left(\tfrac{1}{2}z-1\right)\left(\tfrac{1}{4}z-1\right)$.
These formulas make it possible to express the quantities we are looking for as
sums of products:

$$\bar{C}_N = g_N'(1) = \sum_{k\geq 0} \binom{N}{k+2} \prod_{j=1}^{k}(2^{-j} - 1); \tag{12}$$

$$g_N\left(\tfrac{1}{2}\right) = \sum_{k\geq 0} \binom{N}{k+1} \prod_{j=1}^{k}(2^{-j} - 1) = \bar{C}_{N+1} - \bar{C}_N. \tag{13}$$

It is not at all obvious that this formula for $\bar{C}_N$ satisfies (6)!

Unfortunately, these expressions are not suitable for calculation or for finding
an asymptotic expansion, since $2^{-j} - 1$ is negative; we get large terms and a lot
of cancellation. A more useful formula for $\bar{C}_N$ can be obtained by applying the
partition identities of exercise 5.1.1–16. We have

$$\bar{C}_N = \left(\prod_{j\geq 1}(1 - 2^{-j})\right)\sum_{k\geq 0} \binom{N}{k+2}(-1)^k \prod_{l\geq 0}(1 - 2^{-l-k-1})^{-1}$$

$$= \left(\prod_{j\geq 1}(1 - 2^{-j})\right)\sum_{k\geq 0} \binom{N}{k+2}(-1)^k \sum_{m\geq 0}(2^{-k-1})^m \prod_{r=1}^{m}(1 - 2^{-r})^{-1}$$

$$= \sum_{m \geq 0} 2^m \left(\sum_k \binom{N}{k}(-2^{-m})^k - 1 + 2^{-m}N \right) \prod_{j \geq 0}(1 - 2^{-j-m-1})$$

$$= \sum_{m \geq 0} 2^m \left((1-2^{-m})^N - 1 + 2^{-m}N \right) \sum_{n \geq 0}(-2^{-m-1})^n \frac{2^{-n(n-1)/2}}{\prod_{r=1}^{n}(1 - 2^{-r})}. \quad (14)$$

This may not seem at first glance to be an improvement over Eq. (12), but it has the great advantage that the sum on m converges rapidly for each fixed n. A precisely analogous situation occurred for the trie case in Eqs. 5.2.2–(38) and 5.2.2–(39); in fact, if we consider only the terms of (14) with $n = 0$, we have exactly $N - 1$ plus the number of bit inspections in a binary trie. We can now proceed to get the asymptotic value in essentially the same way as before; see exercise 27. [The derivation above is largely based on an approach suggested by A. J. Konheim and D. J. Newman, *Discrete Mathematics* **4** (1973), 57–63.]

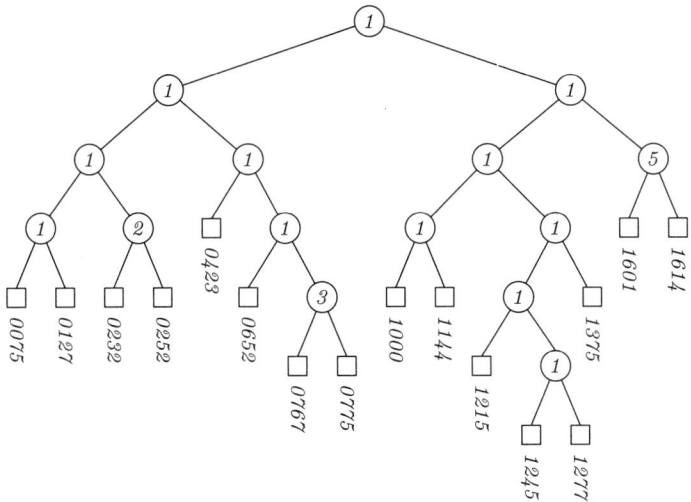

Fig. 36. Patricia constructs this tree instead of Fig. 34.

Finally let us take a mathematical look at Patricia. In her case the binary tree is like the corresponding binary trie on the same keys, but squashed together (because the SKIP fields eliminate 1-way branching), so that there are always exactly $N-1$ internal nodes and N external nodes. Figure 36 shows the Patrician tree corresponding to the sixteen keys in the trie of Fig. 34. The number shown in each branch node is the amount of SKIP; the keys are indicated with the external nodes, although the external node is not explicitly present (there is actually a tagged link to an internal node that references the TEXT, in place of each external node). For the purposes of analysis, we may assume that external nodes exist as shown.

Since successful searches with Patricia end at external nodes, the average number of bit inspections made in a random successful search will be the external path length, divided by N. If we form the generating function $b(z)$ for external nodes as above, this will be $b'(1)/b(1)$. An *unsuccessful* search with Patricia also ends at an external node, but weighted with probability 2^{-l} for external nodes on level l, so the average number of bit inspections is $\frac{1}{2}b'\left(\frac{1}{2}\right)$. For example, in Fig. 36 we have $b(z) = 3z^3 + 8z^4 + 3z^5 + 2z^6$; therefore there are $4\frac{1}{4}$ bit inspections per successful search and $3\frac{25}{32}$ per unsuccessful search, on the average.

Let $h_n(z)$ be the "average" $b(z)$ for a Patrician tree constructed with n external nodes, using uniformly distributed keys. The recurrence relation

$$h_n(z) = 2^{1-n}\sum_k \binom{n}{k} h_k(z)\big(z + \delta_{kn}(1-z)\big), \quad h_0(z) = 0, \quad h_1(z) = 1 \quad (15)$$

appears to have no simple solution. But fortunately, there is a simple recurrence for the average external path length $h'_n(1)$, since

$$h'_n(1) = 2^{1-n}\sum_k \binom{n}{k} h'_k(1) + 2^{1-n}\sum_k \binom{n}{k} k(1-\delta_{kn})$$

$$= n - 2^{1-n}n + 2^{1-n}\sum_k \binom{n}{k} h'_k(1). \quad (16)$$

Since this has the form of (6), we can use the methods already developed to solve for $h'_n(1)$, which turns out to be exactly n less than the corresponding number of bit inspections in a random binary trie. Thus, the SKIP fields save us about one bit inspection per successful search, on random data. (See exercise 31.) The redundancy of typical real data will lead to greater savings.

When we try to find the average number of bit inspections for a random *unsuccessful* search by Patricia, we obtain the recurrence

$$a_n = 1 + \frac{1}{2^n - 2}\sum_{k<n} \binom{n}{k} a_k, \quad \text{for } n \ge 2; \qquad a_0 = a_1 = 0. \quad (17)$$

Here $a_n = \frac{1}{2}h'_n\left(\frac{1}{2}\right)$. This does *not* have the form of any recurrence we have studied, nor is it easily transformed into such a recurrence. The theory of Mellin transforms, introduced in Section 5.2.2 and the references cited there, provides a high-level way to deal with recurrences that have a digital character. It turns out that the solution to (17) involves the Bernoulli numbers:

$$\frac{na_{n-1}}{2} - n + 2 = \sum_{k=2}^{n-1} \binom{n}{k} \frac{B_k}{2^{k-1}-1}, \quad \text{for } n \ge 2. \quad (18)$$

This formula is probably the hardest asymptotic nut we have yet had to crack; the solution in exercise 34 is an instructive review of many things we have done before, with some slightly different twists.

Summary of the analyses. As a result of all the complicated mathematics in this section, the following facts are perhaps the most noteworthy:

a) The number of nodes needed to store N random keys in an M-ary trie, with the trie branching terminated for subfiles of $\le s$ keys, is approximately $N/(s \ln M)$. This approximation is valid for large N, small s, and small M.

Since a trie node involves M link fields, we will need only about $N/\ln M$ link fields if we choose $s = M$.

b) The number of digits or characters examined during a random search is approximately $\log_M N$ for all methods considered. When $M = 2$, the various analyses give us the following more accurate approximations to the number of bit inspections:

	Successful	Unsuccessful
Trie search	$\lg N + 1.33275$	$\lg N - 0.10995$
Digital tree search	$\lg N - 1.71665$	$\lg N - 0.27395$
Patricia	$\lg N + 0.33275$	$\lg N - 0.31875$

(These approximations can all be expressed in terms of fundamental mathematical constants; for example, 0.31875 stands for $(\ln \pi - \gamma)/\ln 2 - 1/2$.)

c) "Random" data here means that the M-ary digits are uniformly distributed, as if the keys were real numbers between 0 and 1 expressed in M-ary notation. Digital search methods are insensitive to the order in which keys are entered into the file (except for Algorithm D, which is only slightly sensitive to the order); but they are very sensitive to the distribution of digits. For example, if 0-bits are much more common than 1-bits, the trees will become much more skewed than they would be for random data as considered in the analyses cited above. Exercise 5.2.2–53 works out one example of what happens when the data is biased in this way.

EXERCISES

1. [*00*] If a tree has leaves, what does a trie have?

2. [*20*] Design an algorithm for the insertion of a new key into an M-ary trie, using the conventions of Algorithm T.

3. [*21*] Design an algorithm for the deletion of a key from an M-ary trie, using the conventions of Algorithm T.

▶ **4.** [*21*] Most of the 360 entries in Table 1 are blank (null links). But we can compress the table into only 49 entries, by overlapping nonblank entries with blank ones as follows:

Position	1	2	3	4	5	6	7	8	9	10	11	12	13	14	15	16	17	18	19	20	21	22	23	24	25
Entry		(10)	WAS	THAT	(11)	OF	BE	THE	HIS	WHICH	WITH	THIS	(12)	ON	I	HE	A	OR	(2)	(3)	TO	HAD			

Position	26	27	28	29	30	31	32	33	34	35	36	37	38	39	40	41	42	43	44	45	46	47	48	49
Entry	(4)	BUT	(5)	(6)	FOR	BY	IN	FROM	AND	NOT	(7)	HER	ARE	IS	IT	AS	AT	(8)		HAVE	(9)		YOU	

(Nodes (1), (2), ..., (12) of Table 1 begin, respectively, at positions 20, 19, 3, 14, 1, 17, 1, 7, 3, 20, 18, 4 within this compressed table.)

Show that if the compressed table is substituted for Table 1, Program T will still work, but not quite as fast.

▶ **5.** [*M26*] (Y. N. Patt.) The trees of Fig. 31 have their letters arranged in alphabetic order within each family. This order is not necessary, and if we rearrange the order of nodes within the families before constructing binary tree representations such as (2) we may get a faster search. What rearrangement of Fig. 31 is optimum from this standpoint? (Use the frequency assumptions of Fig. 32, and find the forest that minimizes the successful search time when it has been represented as a binary tree.)

6. [*15*] What digital search tree is obtained if the fifteen 4-bit binary keys 0001, 0010, 0011, ..., 1111 are inserted in increasing order by Algorithm D? (Start with 0001 at the root and then do fourteen insertions.)

▶ **7.** [*M26*] If the fifteen keys of exercise 6 are inserted in a different order, we might get a different tree. Of all the 15! possible permutations of these keys, which is the *worst*, in the sense that it produces a tree with the greatest internal path length?

8. [*20*] Consider the following changes to Algorithm D, which have the effect of eliminating variable K': Change "K'" to "K" in both places in step D2, and delete the operation "$K' \leftarrow K$" from step D1. Will the resulting algorithm still be valid for searching and insertion?

9. [*21*] Write a MIX program for Algorithm D, and compare it to Program 6.2.2T. You may use binary operations such as SLB (shift left AX binary), JAE (jump if A even), etc.; and you may also use the idea of exercise 8 if it helps.

10. [*23*] Given a file in which all the keys are n-bit binary numbers, and given a search argument $K = b_1 b_2 \ldots b_n$, suppose we want to find the maximum value of k such that there is a key in the file beginning with the bit pattern $b_1 b_2 \ldots b_k$. How can we do this efficiently if the file is represented as
  a) a binary search tree (Algorithm 6.2.2T)?
  b) a binary trie (Algorithm T)?
  c) a binary digital search tree (Algorithm D)?

11. [*21*] Can Algorithm 6.2.2D be used without change to delete a node from a digital search tree?

12. [*25*] After a random element is deleted from a random digital search tree constructed by Algorithm D, is the resulting tree still random? (See exercise 11 and Theorem 6.2.2H.)

13. [*20*] (*M-ary digital searching.*) Explain how Algorithms T and D can be combined into a generalized algorithm that is essentially the same as Algorithm D when $M = 2$. What changes would be made to Table 1, if your algorithm is used for $M = 30$?

▶ **14.** [*25*] Design an efficient algorithm that can be performed just after Algorithm P has terminated successfully, to locate *all* places where K appears in the TEXT.

15. [*28*] Design an efficient algorithm that can be used to construct the tree used by Patricia, or to insert new TEXT references into an existing tree. Your insertion algorithm should refer to the TEXT array at most twice.

16. [*22*] Why is it desirable for Patricia to make the restriction that no key is a prefix of another?

17. [*M25*] Find a way to express the solution of the recurrence

$$x_0 = x_1 = 0, \qquad x_n = a_n + m^{1-n} \sum_k \binom{m}{k} (m-1)^{n-k} x_k, \qquad n \geq 2,$$

in terms of binomial transforms, by generalizing the technique of exercise 5.2.2–36.

18. [*M21*] Use the result of exercise 17 to express the solutions to (4) and (5) in terms of functions U_n and V_n analogous to those defined in exercise 5.2.2–38.

19. [*HM23*] Find the asymptotic value of the function

$$K(n, s, m) = \sum_{k \geq 2} \binom{n}{k}\binom{k}{s} \frac{(-1)^k}{m^{k-1} - 1}$$

to $O(1)$ as $n \to \infty$, for fixed $s \geq 0$ and $m > 1$. [The case $s = 0$ has already been solved in exercise 5.2.2–50, and the case $s = 1$, $m = 2$ has been solved in exercise 5.2.2–48.]

▶ **20.** [*M30*] Consider M-ary trie memory in which we use a sequential search whenever reaching a subfile of s or fewer keys. (Algorithm T is the special case $s = 1$.) Apply the results of the preceding exercises to analyze
  a) the average number of trie nodes;
  b) the average number of digit or character inspections in a successful search; and
  c) the average number of comparisons made in a successful search.
State your answers as asymptotic formulas as $N \to \infty$, for fixed M and s; the answer for (a) should be correct to within $O(1)$, and the answers for (b) and (c) should be correct to within $O(N^{-1})$. [When $M = 2$, this analysis applies also to the modified radix exchange sort, in which subfiles of size $\leq s$ are sorted by insertion.]

21. [*M25*] How many of the nodes, in a random M-ary trie containing N keys, have a null pointer in table entry 0? (For example, 9 of the 12 nodes in Table 1 have a null pointer in the "␣" position. "Random" in this exercise means as usual that the digits of the keys are uniformly distributed between 0 and $M - 1$.)

22. [*M25*] How many trie nodes are on level l of a random M-ary trie containing N keys, for $l = 0, 1, 2, \ldots$?

23. [*M26*] How many digit inspections are made on the average during an *unsuccessful* search in an M-ary trie containing N random keys?

24. [*M30*] Consider an M-ary trie that has been represented as a forest (see Fig. 31). Find exact and asymptotic expressions for
  a) the average number of nodes in the forest;
  b) the average number of times "P ← RLINK(P)" is performed during a random successful search.

▶ **25.** [*M24*] The mathematical derivations of asymptotic values in this section have been quite difficult, involving complex variable theory, because it is desirable to get more than just the leading term of the asymptotic behavior (and the second term is intrinsically complicated). The purpose of this exercise is to show that elementary methods are good enough to deduce some of the results in weaker form.
  a) Prove by induction that the solution to (4) satisfies $A_N \leq M(N - 1)/(M - 1)$.
  b) Let $D_N = C_N - NH_{N-1}/\ln M$, where C_N is defined by (5). Prove that $D_N = O(N)$; hence $C_N = N \log_M N + O(N)$. [*Hint:* Use (a) and Theorem 1.2.7A.]

26. [*23*] Determine the value of the infinite product

$$\left(1 - \tfrac{1}{2}\right)\left(1 - \tfrac{1}{4}\right)\left(1 - \tfrac{1}{8}\right)\left(1 - \tfrac{1}{16}\right)\cdots$$

correct to five decimal places, by hand calculation. [*Hint:* See exercise 5.1.1–16.]

27. [*HM31*] What is the asymptotic value of $\bar{C}_N$, as given by (14), to within $O(1)$?

28. [*HM26*] Find the asymptotic average number of digit inspections when searching in a random M-ary digital search tree, for general $M \geq 2$. Consider both successful and unsuccessful search, and give your answer to within $O(N^{-1})$.

29. [*HM40*] What is the asymptotic average number of nodes, in an M-ary digital search tree, for which all M links are null? (We might save memory space by eliminating such nodes; see exercise 13.)

30. [*M24*] Show that the Patrician generating function $h_n(z)$ defined in (15) can be expressed in the rather horrible form

$$n \sum_{m \geq 1} z^m \left(\sum_{\substack{a_1 + \cdots + a_m = n-1 \\ a_1, \ldots, a_m \geq 1}} \binom{n-1}{a_1, \ldots, a_m} \frac{1}{(2^{a_1} - 1)(2^{a_1 + a_2} - 1) \ldots (2^{a_1 + \cdots + a_m} - 1)} \right).$$

[Thus, if there is a simple formula for $h_n(z)$, we will be able to simplify this rather ungainly expression.]

31. [*M21*] Solve the recurrence (16).

32. [*M21*] What is the average value of the sum of all SKIP fields in a random Patrician tree with $N - 1$ internal nodes?

33. [*M30*] Prove that (18) is a solution to the recurrence (17). [*Hint:* Consider the generating function $A(z) = \sum_{n \geq 0} a_n z^n / n!$.]

34. [*HM40*] The purpose of this exercise is to find the asymptotic behavior of (18).
a) Prove that, if $n \geq 2$,

$$\frac{1}{n} \sum_{2 \leq k < n} \binom{n}{k} \frac{B_k}{2^{k-1} - 1} = \sum_{j \geq 1} \left(\frac{1^{n-1} + 2^{n-1} + \cdots + (2^j - 1)^{n-1}}{2^{j(n-1)}} - \frac{2^j}{n} + \frac{1}{2} \right).$$

b) Show that the summand in (a) is approximately $1/(e^x - 1) - 1/x + 1/2$, where $x = n/2^j$; the resulting sum equals the original sum plus $O(n^{-1})$.
c) Show that

$$\frac{1}{e^x - 1} - \frac{1}{x} + \frac{1}{2} = \frac{1}{2\pi i} \int_{-\frac{1}{2} - i\infty}^{-\frac{1}{2} + i\infty} \zeta(z) \Gamma(z) x^{-z} dz, \qquad \text{for real } x > 0.$$

d) Therefore the sum equals

$$\frac{1}{2\pi i} \int_{-\frac{1}{2} - i\infty}^{-\frac{1}{2} + i\infty} \frac{\zeta(z) \Gamma(z) n^{-z}}{2^{-z} - 1} dz + O(n^{-1});$$

evaluate this integral.

▶ **35.** [*M20*] What is the probability that Patricia's tree on five keys will be

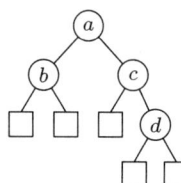

with the SKIP fields a, b, c, d as shown? (Assume that the keys have independent random bits, and give your answer as a function of a, b, c, and d.)

36. [*M25*] There are five binary trees with three internal nodes. If we consider how frequently each particular one of these occurs as the search tree in various algorithms, for random data, we find the following different probabilities:

Tree search (Algorithm 6.2.2T)	$\frac{1}{6}$	$\frac{1}{6}$	$\frac{1}{3}$	$\frac{1}{6}$	$\frac{1}{6}$
Digital tree search (Algorithm D)	$\frac{1}{8}$	$\frac{1}{8}$	$\frac{1}{2}$	$\frac{1}{8}$	$\frac{1}{8}$
Patricia (Algorithm P)	$\frac{1}{7}$	$\frac{1}{7}$	$\frac{3}{7}$	$\frac{1}{7}$	$\frac{1}{7}$

(Notice that the digital search tree tends to be balanced more often than the others.) In exercise 6.2.2–5 we found that the probability of a tree in the tree search algorithm was $\prod\bigl(1/s(x)\bigr)$, where the product is over all internal nodes x, and $s(x)$ is the number of internal nodes in the subtree rooted at x. Find similar formulas for the probability of a tree in the case of (a) Algorithm D; (b) Algorithm P.

▶ **37.** [*M22*] Consider a binary tree with b_l external nodes on level l. The text observes that the running time for unsuccessful searching in digital search trees is not directly related to the external path length $\sum lb_l$, but instead it is essentially proportional to the *modified external path length* $\sum lb_l2^{-l}$. Prove or disprove: The smallest modified external path length, over all trees with N external nodes, occurs when all of the external nodes appear on at most two adjacent levels. (See exercise 5.3.1–20.)

38. [*M40*] Develop an algorithm to find the n-node tree having the minimum value of $\alpha \cdot$ (internal path length) $+ \beta \cdot$ (modified external path length), given α and β, in the sense of exercise 37.

39. [*M43*] Develop an algorithm to find optimum digital search trees, analogous to the optimum binary search trees considered in Section 6.2.2.

▶ **40.** [*25*] Let $a_0\,a_1\,a_2\ldots$ be a periodic binary sequence with $a_{N+k} = a_k$ for all $k \geq 0$. Show that there is a way to represent any fixed sequence of this type in $O(N)$ memory locations, so that the following operation can be done in only $O(N)$ steps: Given any binary pattern $b_0\,b_1\ldots b_{n-1}$, determine how often the pattern occurs in the period (thus, find how many values of p exist with $0 \leq p < N$ and $b_k = a_{p+k}$ for $0 \leq k < n$). The length n of the pattern is variable as well as the pattern itself. Assume that each memory location can hold arbitrary integers between 0 and N. [*Hint:* See exercise 14.]

41. [*HM28*] This is an application to group theory. Let G be the free group on the letters $\{a_1,\ldots,a_n\}$, namely the set of all strings $\alpha = b_1\ldots b_r$, where each b_i is one of the a_j or a_j^- and no adjacent pair $a_j a_j^-$ or $a_j^- a_j$ occurs. The inverse of α is $b_r^-\ldots b_1^-$, and we multiply two such strings by concatenating them and canceling adjacent inverse pairs. Let H be the subgroup of G generated by the strings $\{\beta_1,\ldots,\beta_p\}$, namely the set of all elements of G that can be written as products of the β's and their inverses. According to a well-known theorem of Jakob Nielsen (see Marshall Hall, *The Theory of Groups* (New York: Macmillan, 1959), Chapter 7), we can always find generators $\theta_1,\ldots,\theta_m$

of H, with $m \leq p$, having the property that the middle character of θ_i (or at least one of the two central characters of θ_i if it has even length) is never canceled in the expressions $\theta_i \theta_j^e$ or $\theta_j^e \theta_i$, $e = \pm 1$, unless $j = i$ and $e = -1$. This property implies that there is a simple algorithm for testing whether an arbitrary element of G is in H: Record the $2m$ keys $\theta_1, \ldots, \theta_m, \theta_1^-, \ldots, \theta_m^-$ in a character-oriented search tree, using the $2n$ letters $a_1, \ldots, a_n, a_1^-, \ldots, a_n^-$. Let $\alpha = b_1 \ldots b_r$ be a given element of G; if $r = 0$, α is obviously in H. Otherwise look up α, finding the longest prefix $b_1 \ldots b_k$ that matches a key. If there is more than one key beginning with $b_1 \ldots b_k$, α is not in H; otherwise let the unique such key be $b_1 \ldots b_k c_1 \ldots c_l = \theta_i^e$, and replace α by $\theta_i^{-e} \alpha = c_l^- \ldots c_1^- b_{k+1} \ldots b_r$. If this new value of α is longer than the old (that is, if $l > k$), α is not in H; otherwise repeat the process on the new value of α. The Nielsen property implies that this algorithm will always terminate. If α is eventually reduced to the null string, we can reconstruct the representation of the original α as a product of θ's.

For example, let $\{\theta_1, \theta_2, \theta_3\} = \{bbb,\ b^- a^- b^-,\ ba^- b\}$ and $\alpha = bbabaab$. The forest

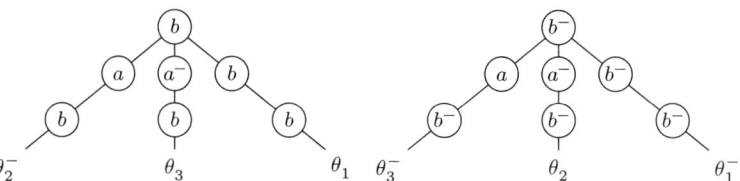

can be used with the algorithm above to deduce that $\alpha = \theta_1 \theta_3^- \theta_1 \theta_3^- \theta_2^-$. Implement this algorithm, given the θ's as input to your program.

42. [23] (*Front and rear compression.*) When a set of binary keys is being used as an index, to partition a larger file, we need not store the full keys. For example, if the sixteen keys of Fig. 34 are used, they can be truncated at the right, as soon as enough digits have been given to identify them uniquely: 0000, 0001, 00100, 00101, 010, ..., 1110001. These truncated keys can be used to partition a file into seventeen parts, where for example the fifth part consists of all keys beginning with 0011 or 010, and the last part contains all keys beginning with 111001, 11101, or 1111. The truncated keys can be represented more compactly if we suppress all leading digits common to the previous key: 0000, ◇◇◇1, ◇◇100, ◇◇◇◇1, ◇10, ..., ◇◇◇◇◇◇◇1. The bit following a ◇ is always 1, so it may be suppressed. A large file will have many ◇'s, and we need store only the number of ◇'s and the values of the following bits.

Show that the total number of bits in the compressed file, excluding ◇'s and the following 1-bits, is always equal to the number of nodes in the binary trie for the keys.

(Consequently the average total number of such bits in the entire index is about $N/\ln 2$, only 1.44 bits per key. This compression technique was shown to the author by A. Heller and R. L. Johnsen. Still further compression is possible, since we need only represent the trie structure; see Theorem 2.3.1A.)

43. [HM42] Analyze the height of a random M-ary trie that has N keys and cutoff parameter s as in exercise 20. (When $s = 1$, this is the length of the longest common prefix of N long random words in an M-ary alphabet.)

▶ **44.** [30] (J. L. Bentley and R. Sedgewick.) Explore a ternary representation of tries, in which left and right links correspond to the horizontal branches of (2) while middle links correspond to the downward branches.

▶ **45.** [M25] If the seven keys of Fig. 33 are inserted in random order by the algorithm of exercise 15, what is the probability of obtaining the tree shown?

6.4. HASHING

SO FAR WE HAVE CONSIDERED search methods based on comparing the given
argument K to the keys in the table, or using its digits to govern a branching
process. A third possibility is to avoid all this rummaging around by doing some
arithmetical calculation on K, computing a function $f(K)$ that is the location
of K and the associated data in the table.

For example, let's consider again the set of 31 English words that we have
subjected to various search strategies in Sections 6.2.2 and 6.3. Table 1 shows
a short MIX program that transforms each of the 31 keys into a unique number
$f(K)$ between -10 and 30. If we compare this method to the MIX programs
for the other methods we have considered (for example, binary search, optimal
tree search, trie memory, digital tree search), we find that it is superior from
the standpoint of both space and speed, except that binary search uses slightly
less space. In fact, the average time for a successful search, using the program
of Table 1 with the frequency data of Fig. 12, is only about $17.8u$, and only 41
table locations are needed to store the 31 keys.

Unfortunately, such functions $f(K)$ aren't very easy to discover. There are
$41^{31} \approx 10^{50}$ possible functions from a 31-element set into a 41-element set, and
only $41 \cdot 40 \cdot \ldots \cdot 11 = 41!/10! \approx 10^{43}$ of them will give distinct values for each
argument; thus only about one of every 10 million functions will be suitable.

Functions that avoid duplicate values are surprisingly rare, even with a fairly
large table. For example, the famous "birthday paradox" asserts that if 23 or
more people are present in a room, chances are good that two of them will have
the same month and day of birth! In other words, if we select a random function
that maps 23 keys into a table of size 365, the probability that no two keys map
into the same location is only 0.4927 (less than one-half). Skeptics who doubt
this result should try to find the birthday mates at the next large parties they
attend. [The birthday paradox was discussed informally by mathematicians in
the 1930s, but its origin is obscure; see I. J. Good, *Probability and the Weighing
of Evidence* (Griffin, 1950), 38. See also R. von Mises, *İstanbul Üniversitesi
Fen Fakültesi Mecmuası* **4** (1939), 145–163, and W. Feller, *An Introduction to
Probability Theory* (New York: Wiley, 1950), Section 2.3.]

On the other hand, the approach used in Table 1 is fairly flexible [see
M. Greniewski and W. Turski, *CACM* **6** (1963), 322–323], and for a medium-
sized table a suitable function can be found after about a day's work. In
fact it is rather amusing to solve a puzzle like this. Suitable techniques have
been discussed by many people, including for example R. Sprugnoli, *CACM* **20**
(1977), 841–850, **22** (1979), 104, 553; R. J. Cichelli, *CACM* **23** (1980), 17–19;
T. J. Sager, *CACM* **28** (1985), 523–532, **29** (1986), 557; B. S. Majewski, N. C.
Wormald, G. Havas, and Z. J. Czech, *Comp. J.* **39** (1996), 547–554; Czech,
Havas, and Majewski, *Theoretical Comp. Sci.* **182** (1997), 1–143. See also the
article by J. Körner and K. Marton, *Europ. J. Combinatorics* **9** (1988), 523–530,
for theoretical limitations on perfect hash functions.

Of course this method has a serious flaw, since the contents of the table
must be known in advance; adding one more key will probably ruin everything,

Table 1

TRANSFORMING A SET OF KEYS INTO UNIQUE ADDRESSES

Instruction	A	AND	ARE	AS	AT	BE	BUT	BY	FOR	FROM	HAD	HAVE	HE	HER
LD1N K(1:1)	−1	−1	−1	−1	−1	−2	−2	−2	−6	−6	−8	−8	−8	−8
LD2 K(2:2)	−1	−1	−1	−1	−1	−2	−2	−2	−6	−6	−8	−8	−8	−8
INC1 -8,2	−9	6	10	13	14	−5	14	18	2	5	−15	−15	−11	−11
J1P *+2	−9	6	10	13	14	−5	14	18	2	5	−15	−15	−11	−11
INC1 16,2	7	.	.	.	.	16	.	.	.	.	2	2	10	10
LD2 K(3:3)	7	6	10	13	14	16	14	18	2	5	2	2	10	10
J2Z 9F	7	6	10	13	14	16	14	18	2	5	2	2	10	10
INC1 -28,2	.	−18	−13	.	.	.	9	.	−7	−7	−22	−1	.	1
J1P 9F	.	−18	−13	.	.	.	9	.	−7	−7	−22	−1	.	1
INC1 11,2	.	−3	3	.	.	.	.	.	23	20	−7	35	.	.
LDA K(4:4)	.	−3	3	.	.	.	.	.	23	20	−7	35	.	.
JAZ 9F	.	−3	3	.	.	.	.	.	23	20	−7	35	.	.
DEC1 -5,2	.	.	.	.	.	.	.	.	.	9	.	15	.	.
J1N 9F	.	.	.	.	.	.	.	.	.	9	.	15	.	.
INC1 10	.	.	.	.	.	.	.	.	.	19	.	25	.	.
9H LDA K	7	−3	3	13	14	16	9	18	23	19	−7	25	10	1
CMPA TABLE,1	7	−3	3	13	14	16	9	18	23	19	−7	25	10	1
JNE FAILURE	7	−3	3	13	14	16	9	18	23	19	−7	25	10	1

making it necessary to start over almost from scratch. We can obtain a much more versatile method if we give up the idea of uniqueness, permitting different keys to yield the same value $f(K)$, and using a special method to resolve any ambiguity after $f(K)$ has been computed.

These considerations lead to a popular class of search methods commonly known as *hashing* or *scatter storage* techniques. The verb "to hash" means to chop something up or to make a mess out of it; the idea in hashing is to scramble some aspects of the key and to use this partial information as the basis for searching. We compute a *hash address* $h(K)$ and begin searching there.

The birthday paradox tells us that there will probably be distinct keys $K_i \neq K_j$ that hash to the same value $h(K_i) = h(K_j)$. Such an occurrence is called a *collision*, and several interesting approaches have been devised to handle the collision problem. In order to use a hash table, programmers must make two almost independent decisions: They must choose a hash function $h(K)$, and they must select a method for collision resolution. We shall now consider these two aspects of the problem in turn.

Hash functions. To make things more explicit, let us assume throughout this section that our hash function h takes on at most M different values, with

$$0 \leq h(K) < M, \tag{1}$$

for all keys K. The keys in actual files that arise in practice usually have a great deal of redundancy; we must be careful to find a hash function that breaks up clusters of almost identical keys, in order to reduce the number of collisions.

Contents of rI1 after executing the instruction, given a particular key K

HIS	I	IN	IS	IT	NOT	OF	ON	OR	THAT	THE	THIS	TO	WAS	WHICH	WITH	YOU
−8	−9	−9	−9	−9	−15	−16	−16	−16	−23	−23	−23	−23	−26	−26	−26	−28
−8	−9	−9	−9	−9	−15	−16	−16	−16	−23	−23	−23	−23	−26	−26	−26	−28
−7	−17	−2	5	6	−7	−18	−9	−5	−23	−23	−23	−15	−33	−26	−25	−20
−7	−17	−2	5	6	−7	−18	−9	−5	−23	−23	−23	−15	−33	−26	−25	−20
18	−1	29	.	.	25	4	22	30	1	1	1	17	−16	−2	0	12
18	−1	29	5	6	25	4	22	30	1	1	1	17	−16	−2	0	12
18	−1	29	5	6	25	4	22	30	1	1	1	17	−16	−2	0	12
12	.	.	.	.	20	.	.	.	−26	−22	−18	.	−22	−21	−5	8
12	.	.	.	.	20	.	.	.	−26	−22	−18	.	−22	−21	−5	8
.	.	.	.	.	.	.	.	.	−14	−6	2	.	11	−1	29	.
.	.	.	.	.	.	.	.	.	−14	−6	2	.	11	−1	29	.
.	.	.	.	.	.	.	.	.	−14	−6	2	.	11	−1	29	.
.	.	.	.	.	.	.	.	.	−10	.	−2	.	.	−5	11	.
.	.	.	.	.	.	.	.	.	−10	.	−2	.	.	−5	11	.
.	.	.	.	.	.	.	.	.	.	.	.	.	.	.	21	.
12	−1	29	5	6	20	4	22	30	−10	−6	−2	17	11	−5	21	8
12	−1	29	5	6	20	4	22	30	−10	−6	−2	17	11	−5	21	8
12	−1	29	5	6	20	4	22	30	−10	−6	−2	17	11	−5	21	8

It is theoretically impossible to define a hash function that creates truly random data from the nonrandom data in actual files. But in practice it is not difficult to produce a pretty good imitation of random data, by using simple arithmetic as we have discussed in Chapter 3. And in fact we can often do even better, by exploiting the nonrandom properties of actual data to construct a hash function that leads to fewer collisions than truly random keys would produce.

Consider, for example, the case of 10-digit keys on a decimal computer. One hash function that suggests itself is to let $M = 1000$, say, and to let $h(K)$ be three digits chosen from somewhere near the middle of the 20-digit product $K \times K$. This would seem to yield a fairly good spread of values between 000 and 999, with low probability of collisions. Experiments with actual data show, in fact, that this "middle square" method isn't bad, provided that the keys do not have a lot of leading or trailing zeros; but it turns out that there are safer and saner ways to proceed, just as we found in Chapter 3 that the middle square method is not an especially good random number generator.

Extensive tests on typical files have shown that two major types of hash functions work quite well. One is based on division, and the other is based on multiplication.

The division method is particularly easy; we simply use the remainder modulo M:

$$h(K) = K \bmod M. \tag{2}$$

In this case, some values of M are obviously much better than others. For example, if M is an even number, $h(K)$ will be even when K is even and odd when K is odd, and this will lead to a substantial bias in many files. It would be even worse to let M be a power of the radix of the computer, since $K \bmod M$ would then be simply the least significant digits of K (independent of the other digits). Similarly we can argue that M probably shouldn't be a multiple of 3; for if the keys are alphabetic, two keys that differ only by permutation of letters would then differ in numeric value by a multiple of 3. (This occurs because $2^{2n} \bmod 3 = 1$ and $10^n \bmod 3 = 1$.) In general, we want to avoid values of M that divide $r^k \pm a$, where k and a are small numbers and r is the radix of the alphabetic character set (usually $r = 64$, 256, or 100), since a remainder modulo such a value of M tends to be largely a simple superposition of the key digits. Such considerations suggest that we *choose M to be a prime number* such that $r^k \not\equiv \pm a$ (modulo M) for small k and a. This choice has been found to be quite satisfactory in most cases.

For example, on the MIX computer we could choose $M = 1009$, computing $h(K)$ by the sequence

$$
\begin{array}{lll}
\texttt{LDX} & \texttt{K} & \text{rX} \leftarrow K. \\
\texttt{ENTA} & \texttt{0} & \text{rA} \leftarrow 0. \\
\texttt{DIV} & \texttt{=1009=} & \text{rX} \leftarrow K \bmod 1009.
\end{array}
\tag{3}
$$

The multiplicative hashing scheme is equally easy to do, but it is slightly harder to describe because we must imagine ourselves working with fractions instead of with integers. Let w be the word size of the computer, so that w is usually 10^{10} or 2^{30} for MIX; we can regard an integer A as the fraction A/w if we imagine the radix point to be at the left of the word. The method is to choose some integer constant A relatively prime to w, and to let

$$
h(K) = \left\lfloor M \left(\left(\frac{A}{w} K \right) \bmod 1 \right) \right\rfloor.
\tag{4}
$$

In this case we usually let M be a power of 2 on a binary computer, so that $h(K)$ consists of the leading bits of the least significant half of the product AK.

In MIX code, if we let $M = 2^m$ and assume a binary radix, the multiplicative hash function is

$$
\begin{array}{lll}
\texttt{LDA} & \texttt{K} & \text{rA} \leftarrow K. \\
\texttt{MUL} & \texttt{A} & \text{rAX} \leftarrow AK. \\
\texttt{ENTA} & \texttt{0} & \text{rAX} \leftarrow AK \bmod w. \\
\texttt{SLB} & m & \text{Shift rAX } m \text{ bits to the left.}
\end{array}
\tag{5}
$$

Now $h(K)$ appears in register A. Since MIX has rather slow multiplication and shift instructions, this sequence takes exactly as long to compute as (3); but on many machines multiplication is significantly faster than division.

In a sense this method can be regarded as a generalization of (3), since we could for example take A to be an approximation to $w/1009$; multiplying by the reciprocal of a constant is often faster than dividing by that constant. The technique of (5) is almost a "middle square" method, but there is one important difference: We shall see that multiplication by a suitable constant has demonstrably good properties.

One of the nice features of the multiplicative scheme is that no information is lost when we blank out the A register in (5); we could determine K again, given only the contents of rAX after (5) has finished. The reason is that A is relatively prime to w, so Euclid's algorithm can be used to find a constant A' with $AA' \bmod w = 1$; this implies that $K = \bigl(A'(AK \bmod w)\bigr) \bmod w$. In other words, if $f(K)$ denotes the contents of register X just before the SLB instruction in (5), then

$$K_1 \neq K_2 \qquad \text{implies} \qquad f(K_1) \neq f(K_2). \tag{6}$$

Of course $f(K)$ takes on values in the range 0 to $w-1$, so it isn't any good as a hash function, but it can be very useful as a *scrambling function*, namely a function satisfying (6) that tends to randomize the keys. Such a function can be very useful in connection with the tree search algorithms of Section 6.2.2, if the order of keys is unimportant, since it removes the danger of degeneracy when keys enter the tree in increasing order. (See exercise 6.2.2–10.) A scrambling function is also useful in connection with the digital tree search algorithm of Section 6.3, if the bits of the actual keys are biased.

Another feature of the multiplicative hash method is that it makes good use of the nonrandomness found in many files. Actual sets of keys often have a preponderance of arithmetic progressions, where $\{K, K+d, K+2d, \ldots, K+td\}$ all appear in the file; for example, consider alphabetic names like $\{$PART1, PART2, PART3$\}$ or $\{$TYPEA, TYPEB, TYPEC$\}$. The multiplicative hash method converts an arithmetic progression into an approximate arithmetic progression $h(K)$, $h(K+d)$, $h(K+2d)$, $\ldots$ of distinct hash values, reducing the number of collisions from what we would expect in a random situation. The division method has this same property.

Figure 37 illustrates this aspect of multiplicative hashing in a particularly interesting case. Suppose that A/w is approximately the golden ratio $\phi^{-1} = (\sqrt{5}-1)/2 \approx 0.6180339887$; then the successive values $h(K)$, $h(K+1)$, $h(K+2)$, $\ldots$ have essentially the same behavior as the successive hash values $h(0)$, $h(1)$, $h(2)$, $\ldots$, so the following experiment suggests itself: Starting with the line

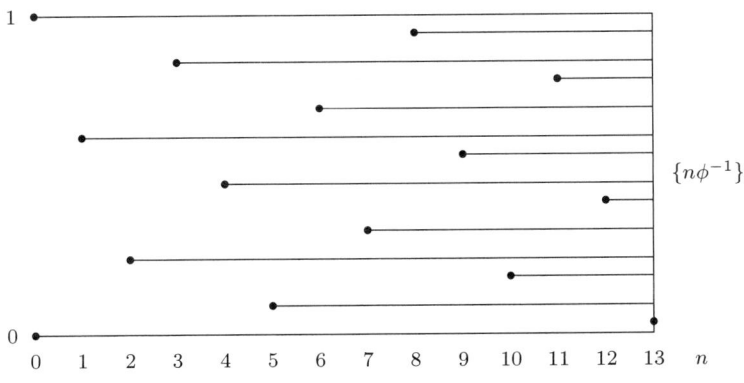

Fig. 37. Fibonacci hashing.

segment $[0 \mathinner{.\,.} 1]$, we successively mark off the points $\{\phi^{-1}\}$, $\{2\phi^{-1}\}$, $\{3\phi^{-1}\}$, ...,
where $\{x\}$ denotes the fractional part of x (namely $x - \lfloor x \rfloor$, or $x \bmod 1$). As shown
in Fig. 37, these points stay very well separated from each other; in fact, each
newly added point falls into one of the largest remaining intervals, and divides
it in the golden ratio! [This phenomenon was observed long ago by botanists
Louis and Auguste Bravais, *Annales des Sciences Naturelles* **7** (1837), 42–110,
who gave an illustration equivalent to Fig. 37 and related it to the Fibonacci
sequence. See also S. Świerczkowski, *Fundamenta Math.* **46** (1958), 187–189.]

The remarkable scattering property of the golden ratio is actually just a
special case of a very general result, originally conjectured by Hugo Steinhaus
and first proved by Vera Turán Sós [*Acta Math. Acad. Sci. Hung.* **8** (1957),
461–471; *Ann. Univ. Sci. Budapest. Eötvös Sect. Math.* **1** (1958), 127–134]:

Theorem S. *Let θ be any irrational number. When the points $\{\theta\}$, $\{2\theta\}$, ...,
$\{n\theta\}$ are placed in the line segment $[0 \mathinner{.\,.} 1]$, the $n + 1$ line segments formed have
at most three different lengths. Moreover, the next point $\{(n+1)\theta\}$ will fall in
one of the largest existing segments.* ∎

Thus, the points $\{\theta\}, \{2\theta\}, \dots, \{n\theta\}$ are spread out very evenly between 0 and 1.
If θ is rational, the same theorem holds if we give a suitable interpretation to
the segments of length 0 that appear when n is greater than or equal to the
denominator of θ. A proof of Theorem S, together with a detailed analysis of
the underlying structure of the situation, appears in exercise 8; it turns out that
the segments of a given length are created and destroyed in a first-in-first-out
manner. Of course, some θ's are better than others, since for example a value
that is near 0 or 1 will start out with many small segments and one large segment.
Exercise 9 shows that the two numbers ϕ^{-1} and $\phi^{-2} = 1 - \phi^{-1}$ lead to the "most
uniformly distributed" sequences, among all numbers θ between 0 and 1.

The theory above suggests *Fibonacci hashing*, where we choose the constant
A to be the nearest integer to $\phi^{-1}w$ that is relatively prime to w. For example
if MIX were a decimal computer we would take

$$A = \boxed{+\ |\ 61\ |\ 80\ |\ 33\ |\ 98\ |\ 87\ } . \tag{7}$$

This multiplier will spread out alphabetic keys like LIST1, LIST2, LIST3 very
nicely. But notice what happens when we have an arithmetic series in the
fourth character position, as in the keys SUM1␣, SUM2␣, SUM3␣: The effect is
as if Theorem S were being used with $\theta = \{100A/w\} = .80339887$ instead of
$\theta = .6180339887 = A/w$. The resulting behavior is still all right, in spite of the
fact that this value of θ is not quite as good as ϕ^{-1}. On the other hand, if the
progression occurs in the second character position, as in A1␣␣␣, A2␣␣␣, A3␣␣␣,
the effective θ is .9887, and this is probably too close to 1.

Therefore we might do better with a multiplier like

$$A = \boxed{+\ |\ 61\ |\ 61\ |\ 61\ |\ 61\ |\ 61\ }$$

in place of (7); such a multiplier will separate out consecutive sequences of keys
that differ in *any* character position. Unfortunately this choice suffers from

another problem analogous to the difficulty of dividing by $r^k \pm 1$: Keys such
as XY and YX will tend to hash to the same location! One way out of this
difficulty is to look more closely at the structure underlying Theorem S. For
short progressions of keys, only the first few partial quotients of the continued
fraction representation of θ are relevant, and small partial quotients correspond
to good distribution properties. Therefore we find that the best values of θ lie
in the ranges

$$\tfrac{1}{4} < \theta < \tfrac{3}{10}, \qquad \tfrac{1}{3} < \theta < \tfrac{3}{7}, \qquad \tfrac{4}{7} < \theta < \tfrac{2}{3}, \qquad \tfrac{7}{10} < \theta < \tfrac{3}{4}.$$

A value of A can be found so that each of its bytes lies in a good range and is
not too close to the values of the other bytes or their complements, for example

$$A = \boxed{+\ \vert\ 61\ \vert\ 25\ \vert\ 42\ \vert\ 33\ \vert\ 71\ } . \tag{8}$$

Such a multiplier can be recommended. (These ideas about multiplicative hashing are due largely to R. W. Floyd.)

A good hash function should satisfy two requirements:

a) Its computation should be very fast.
b) It should minimize collisions.

Property (a) is machine-dependent, and property (b) is data-dependent. If the
keys were truly random, we could simply extract a few bits from them and use
those bits for the hash function; but in practice we nearly always need to have a
hash function that depends on all bits of the key in order to satisfy (b).

So far we have considered how to hash one-word keys. Multiword or variable-length keys can be handled by multiple-precision extensions of the methods
above, but it is generally adequate to speed things up by combining the individual
words together into a single word, then doing a single multiplication or division
as above. The combination can be done by addition mod w, or by exclusive-or
on a binary computer; both of these operations have the advantage that they are
invertible, namely that they depend on all bits of both arguments, and exclusive-
or is sometimes preferable because it avoids arithmetic overflow. However, both
of these operations are commutative, hence (X, Y) and (Y, X) will hash to the
same address; G. D. Knott has suggested avoiding this problem by doing a cyclic
shift just before adding or exclusive-oring.

An even better way to hash l-character or l-word keys $K = x_1 x_2 \ldots x_l$ is to
compute

$$h(K) = \bigl(h_1(x_1) + h_2(x_2) + \cdots + h_l(x_l)\bigr) \bmod M, \tag{9}$$

where each h_j is an independent hash function. This idea, introduced by J. L.
Carter and M. N. Wegman in 1977, is especially efficient when each x_j is a single
character, because we can then use a precomputed array for each h_j. Such arrays
make multiplication unnecessary. If M is a power of 2, we can avoid the division
in (9) by substituting exclusive-or for addition; this gives a different, but equally
good, hash function. Therefore (9) certainly satisfies property (a). Moreover,
Carter and Wegman proved that if the h_j are chosen at random, property (b)
will hold *regardless of the input data*. (See exercise 72.)

Many more methods for hashing have been suggested, but none of them have proved to be superior to the simple methods described above. For a survey of several approaches together with detailed statistics on their performance with actual files, see the article by V. Y. Lum, P. S. T. Yuen, and M. Dodd, *CACM* **14** (1971), 228–239.

Of all the other hash methods that have been tried, perhaps the most interesting is a technique based on algebraic coding theory; the idea is analogous to the division method above, but we divide by a polynomial modulo 2 instead of dividing by an integer. (As observed in Section 4.6, this operation is analogous to division, just as addition is analogous to exclusive-or.) For this method, M should be a power of 2, say $M = 2^m$, and we make use of an mth degree polynomial $P(x) = x^m + p_{m-1}x^{m-1} + \cdots + p_0$. An n-digit binary key $K = (k_{n-1} \ldots k_1 k_0)_2$ can be regarded as the polynomial $K(x) = k_{n-1}x^{n-1} + \cdots + k_1 x + k_0$, and we compute the remainder

$$K(x) \bmod P(x) = h_{m-1}x^{m-1} + \cdots + h_1 x + h_0$$

using polynomial arithmetic modulo 2; then $h(K) = (h_{m-1} \ldots h_1 h_0)_2$. If $P(x)$ is chosen properly, this hash function can be guaranteed to avoid collisions between nearly equal keys. For example if $n = 15$, $m = 10$, and

$$P(x) = x^{10} + x^8 + x^5 + x^4 + x^2 + x + 1, \tag{10}$$

it can be shown that $h(K_1)$ will be unequal to $h(K_2)$ whenever K_1 and K_2 are distinct keys that differ in fewer than seven bit positions. (See exercise 7 for further information about this scheme; it is, of course, more suitable for hardware or microprogramming implementation than for software.)

It is often convenient to use the constant hash function $h(K) = 0$ when debugging a program, since all keys will be stored together; an efficient $h(K)$ can be substituted later.

Collision resolution by "chaining." We have observed that some hash addresses will probably be burdened with more than their share of keys. Perhaps the most obvious way to solve this problem is to maintain M linked lists, one for each possible hash code. A LINK field should be included in each record, and there will also be M list heads, numbered say from 1 through M. After hashing the key, we simply do a sequential search in list number $h(K) + 1$. (See exercise 6.1–2. The situation is very similar to multiple-list-insertion sorting, Program 5.2.1M.)

Figure 38 illustrates this simple chaining scheme when $M = 9$, for the sequence of seven keys

$$K = \text{EN, TO, TRE, FIRE, FEM, SEKS, SYV} \tag{11}$$

(the numbers 1 through 7 in Norwegian), having the respective hash codes

$$h(K) + 1 = 3,\ 1,\ 4,\ 1,\ 5,\ 9,\ 2. \tag{12}$$

The first list has two elements, and three of the lists are empty.

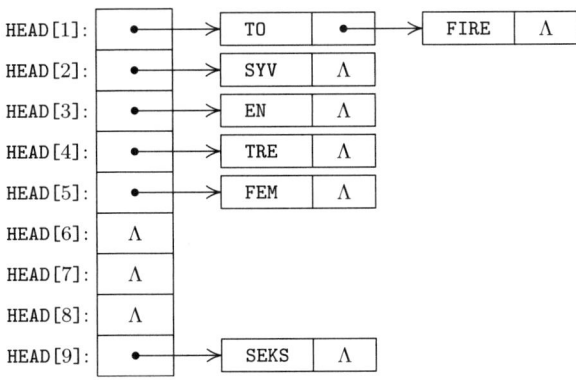

Fig. 38. Separate chaining.

Chaining is quite fast, because the lists are short. If 365 people are gathered together in one room, there will probably be many pairs having the same birthday, but the average number of people with any given birthday will be only 1! In general, if there are N keys and M lists, the average list size is N/M; thus hashing decreases the average amount of work needed for sequential searching by roughly a factor of M. (A precise formula is worked out in exercise 34.)

This method is a straightforward combination of techniques we have discussed before, so we do not need to formulate a detailed algorithm for chained hash tables. It is often a good idea to keep the individual lists in order by key, so that unsuccessful searches — which must precede insertions — go faster. Thus if we choose to make the lists ascending, the TO and FIRE nodes of Fig. 38 would be interchanged, and all the Λ links would be replaced by pointers to a dummy record whose key is ∞. (See Algorithm 6.1T.) Alternatively we could make use of the "self-organizing" concept discussed in Section 6.1; instead of keeping the lists in order by key, they may be kept in order according to the time of most recent occurrence.

For the sake of speed we would like to make M rather large. But when M is large, many of the lists will be empty and much of the space for the M list heads will be wasted. This suggests another approach, when the records are small: We can overlap the record storage with the list heads, making room for a total of M records and M links instead of for N records and $M + N$ links. Sometimes it is possible to make one pass over all the data to find out which list heads will be used, then to make another pass inserting all the "overflow" records into the empty slots. But this is often impractical or impossible, and we'd rather have a technique that processes each record only once when it first enters the system. The following algorithm, due to F. A. Williams [*CACM* **2**, 6 (June 1959), 21–24], is a convenient way to solve the problem.

Algorithm C (*Chained hash table search and insertion*). This algorithm looks for a given key K in an M-node table. If K is not in the table and the table is not full, K is inserted.

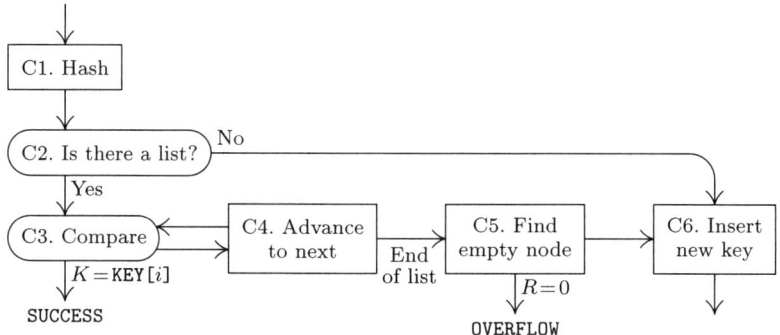

Fig. 39. Chained hash table search and insertion.

The nodes of the table are denoted by TABLE[i], for $0 \le i \le M$, and they are of two distinguishable types, *empty* and *occupied*. An occupied node contains a key field KEY[i], a link field LINK[i], and possibly other fields.

The algorithm makes use of a hash function $h(K)$. An auxiliary variable R is also used, to help find empty spaces; when the table is empty, we have $R = M + 1$, and as insertions are made it will always be true that TABLE[j] is occupied for all j in the range $R \le j \le M$. By convention, TABLE[0] will always be empty.

C1. [Hash.] Set $i \leftarrow h(K) + 1$. (Now $1 \le i \le M$.)

C2. [Is there a list?] If TABLE[i] is empty, go to C6. (Otherwise TABLE[i] is occupied; we will look at the list of occupied nodes that starts here.)

C3. [Compare.] If $K = $ KEY[i], the algorithm terminates successfully.

C4. [Advance to next.] If LINK[i] $\ne 0$, set $i \leftarrow$ LINK[i] and go back to step C3.

C5. [Find empty node.] (The search was unsuccessful, and we want to find an empty position in the table.) Decrease R one or more times until finding a value such that TABLE[R] is empty. If $R = 0$, the algorithm terminates with overflow (there are no empty nodes left); otherwise set LINK[i] $\leftarrow R$, $i \leftarrow R$.

C6. [Insert new key.] Mark TABLE[i] as an occupied node, with KEY[i] $\leftarrow K$ and LINK[i] $\leftarrow 0$. ∎

This algorithm allows several lists to coalesce, so that records need not be moved after they have been inserted into the table. For example, see Fig. 40, where SEKS appears in the list containing TO and FIRE since the latter had already been inserted into position 9.

In order to see how Algorithm C compares with others in this chapter, we can write the following MIX program. The analysis worked out below indicates that the lists of occupied cells tend to be short, and the program has been designed with this fact in mind.

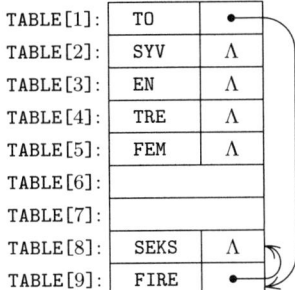

Fig. 40. Coalesced chaining.

Program C (*Chained hash table search and insertion*). For convenience, the keys are assumed to be only three bytes long, and nodes are represented as follows:

empty node $\boxed{-\;|\;1\;|\;0\;|\;0\;|\;0\;|\;0}$;

occupied node $\boxed{+\;|\;\text{LINK}\;|\;\text{KEY}}$.

(13)

The table size M is assumed to be prime; TABLE$[i]$ is stored in location TABLE$+i$. rI1 $\equiv i$, rA $\equiv K$; rI2 $\equiv$ LINK$[i]$ and/or R.

```
01  KEY    EQU  3:5
02  LINK   EQU  0:2
03  START  LDX  K              1          C1. Hash.
04         ENTA 0              1
05         DIV  =M=            1
06         STX  *+1(0:2)       1
07         ENT1 *              1          i ← h(K)
08         INC1 1              1                + 1.
09         LDA  K              1
10         LD2  TABLE,1(LINK)  1          C2. Is there a list?
11         J2N  6F             1          To C6 if TABLE[i] empty.
12         CMPA TABLE,1(KEY)   A          C3. Compare.
13         JE   SUCCESS        A          Exit if K = KEY[i].
14         J2Z  5F             A − S1     To C5 if LINK[i] = 0.
15  4H     ENT1 0,2            C − 1      C4. Advance to next.
16         CMPA TABLE,1(KEY)   C − 1      C3. Compare.
17         JE   SUCCESS        C − 1      Exit if K = KEY[i].
18         LD2  TABLE,1(LINK)  C − 1 − S2
19         J2NZ 4B             C − 1 − S2 Advance if LINK[i] ≠ 0.
20  5H     LD2  R              A − S      C5. Find empty node.
21         DEC2 1              T          R ← R − 1.
22         LDX  TABLE,2        T
23         JXNN *-2            T          Repeat until TABLE[R] empty.
24         J2Z  OVERFLOW       A − S      Exit if no empty nodes left.
25         ST2  TABLE,1(LINK)  A − S      LINK[i] ← R.
26         ENT1 0,2            A − S      i ← R.
```

27		ST2	R	$A - S$	Update R in memory.
28	6H	STZ	TABLE,1(LINK)	$1 - S$	*C6. Insert new key.* LINK$[i] \leftarrow 0.$
29		STA	TABLE,1(KEY)	$1 - S$	KEY$[i] \leftarrow K.$ ∎

The running time of this program depends on

C = number of table entries probed while searching;

A = [initial probe found an occupied node];

S = [search was successful];

T = number of table entries probed while looking for an empty space.

Here $S = S1 + S2$, where $S1 = 1$ if successful on the first try. The total running time for the searching phase of Program C is $(7C + 4A + 17 - 3S + 2S1)u$, and the insertion of a new key when $S = 0$ takes an additional $(8A + 4T + 4)u$.

Suppose there are N keys in the table at the start of this program, and let

$$\alpha = N/M = \text{load factor of the table.} \qquad (14)$$

Then the average value of A in an unsuccessful search is obviously α, if the hash function is random; and exercise 39 proves that the average value of C in an unsuccessful search is

$$C'_N = 1 + \frac{1}{4}\left(\left(1 + \frac{2}{M}\right)^N - 1 - \frac{2N}{M}\right) \approx 1 + \frac{e^{2\alpha} - 1 - 2\alpha}{4}. \qquad (15)$$

Thus when the table is half full, the average number of probes made in an unsuccessful search is about $\frac{1}{4}(e + 2) \approx 1.18$; and even when the table gets completely full, the average number of probes made just before inserting the final item will be only about $\frac{1}{4}(e^2 + 1) \approx 2.10$. The standard deviation is also small, as shown in exercise 40. These statistics prove that *the lists stay short even though the algorithm occasionally allows them to coalesce*, when the hash function is random. Of course C can be as high as N, if the hash function is bad or if we are extremely unlucky.

In a successful search, we always have $A = 1$. The average number of probes during a successful search may be computed by summing the quantity $C + A$ over the first N unsuccessful searches and dividing by N, if we assume that each key is equally likely. Thus we obtain

$$C_N = \frac{1}{N}\sum_{0 \leq k < N}\left(C'_k + \frac{k}{M}\right) = 1 + \frac{1}{8}\frac{M}{N}\left(\left(1 + \frac{2}{M}\right)^N - 1 - \frac{2N}{M}\right) + \frac{1}{4}\frac{N-1}{M}$$

$$\approx 1 + \frac{e^{2\alpha} - 1 - 2\alpha}{8\alpha} + \frac{\alpha}{4} \qquad (16)$$

as the average number of probes in a random successful search. Even a full table will require only about 1.80 probes, on the average, to find an item! Similarly (see exercise 42), the average value of $S1$ turns out to be

$$S1_N = 1 - \frac{1}{2}\big((N - 1)/M\big) \approx 1 - \frac{1}{2}\alpha. \qquad (17)$$

At first glance it may appear that step C5 is inefficient, since it has to search sequentially for an empty position. But actually the total number of table probes made in step C5 as a table is being built will never exceed the number of items in the table; so we make an average of at most one of these probes per insertion. Exercise 41 proves that T is approximately αe^{α} in a random unsuccessful search.

It would be possible to modify Algorithm C so that no two lists coalesce, but then it would become necessary to move records around. For example, consider the situation in Fig. 40 just before we wanted to insert SEKS into position 9; in order to keep the lists separate, it would be necessary to move FIRE, and for this purpose it would be necessary to discover which node points to FIRE. We could solve this problem without providing two-way linkage by hashing FIRE and searching down its list, as suggested by D. E. Ferguson, since the lists are short. Exercise 34 shows that the average number of probes, when lists aren't coalesced, is reduced to

$$C_N' = 1 + \frac{N(N-1)}{2M^2} \approx 1 + \frac{\alpha^2}{2} \quad \text{(unsuccessful search)}, \tag{18}$$

$$C_N = 1 + \frac{N-1}{2M} \approx 1 + \frac{\alpha}{2} \quad \text{(successful search)}. \tag{19}$$

This is not enough of an improvement over (15) and (16) to warrant changing the algorithm.

On the other hand, Butler Lampson has observed that most of the space that is occupied by links can actually be saved in the chaining method, if we avoid coalescing the lists. This leads to an interesting algorithm that is discussed in exercise 13. Lampson's method introduces a tag bit in each entry, and causes the average number of probes needed in an unsuccessful search to decrease slightly, from (18) to

$$\left(1 - \frac{1}{M}\right)^N + \frac{N}{M} \approx e^{-\alpha} + \alpha. \tag{18'}$$

Separate chaining as in Fig. 38 can be used when $N > M$, so overflow is not a serious problem in that case. When the lists coalesce as in Fig. 40 and Algorithm C, we can link extra items into an auxiliary storage pool; L. Guibas has proved that the average number of probes to insert the $(M + L + 1)$st item is then $\left(L/2M + \frac{1}{4}\right)\left((1 + 2/M)^M - 1\right) + \frac{1}{2}$. However, it is usually preferable to use an alternative scheme that puts the first colliding elements into an auxiliary storage area, allowing lists to coalesce only when this auxiliary area has filled up; see exercise 43.

Collision resolution by "open addressing." Another way to resolve the problem of collisions is to do away with links entirely, simply looking at various entries of the table one by one until either finding the key K or finding an empty position. The idea is to formulate some rule by which every key K determines a "probe sequence," namely a sequence of table positions that are to be inspected whenever K is inserted or looked up. If we encounter an empty position while searching for K, using the probe sequence determined by K, we can conclude that K is not in the table, since the same sequence of probes will be made every time K is processed. This general class of methods was named *open addressing* by W. W. Peterson [*IBM J. Research & Development* **1** (1957), 130–146].

The simplest open addressing scheme, known as *linear probing*, uses the cyclic probe sequence

$$h(K), h(K) - 1, \ldots, 0, M - 1, M - 2, \ldots, h(K) + 1 \qquad (20)$$

as in the following algorithm.

Algorithm L (*Linear probing and insertion*). This algorithm searches an M-node table, looking for a given key K. If K is not in the table and the table is not full, K is inserted.

The nodes of the table are denoted by TABLE[i], for $0 \le i < M$, and they are of two distinguishable types, *empty* and *occupied*. An occupied node contains a key, called KEY[i], and possibly other fields. An auxiliary variable N is used to keep track of how many nodes are occupied; this variable is considered to be part of the table, and it is increased by 1 whenever a new key is inserted.

This algorithm makes use of a hash function $h(K)$, and it uses the linear probing sequence (20) to address the table. Modifications of that sequence are discussed below.

L1. [Hash.] Set $i \leftarrow h(K)$. (Now $0 \le i < M$.)

L2. [Compare.] If TABLE[i] is empty, go to step L4. Otherwise if KEY[i] = K, the algorithm terminates successfully.

L3. [Advance to next.] Set $i \leftarrow i - 1$; if now $i < 0$, set $i \leftarrow i + M$. Go back to step L2.

L4. [Insert.] (The search was unsuccessful.) If $N = M - 1$, the algorithm terminates with overflow. (This algorithm considers the table to be full when $N = M - 1$, not when $N = M$; see exercise 15.) Otherwise set $N \leftarrow N + 1$, mark TABLE[i] occupied, and set KEY[i] $\leftarrow K$. ∎

Figure 41 shows what happens when the seven example keys (11) are inserted by Algorithm L, using the respective hash codes 2, 7, 1, 8, 2, 8, 1: The last three keys, FEM, SEKS, and SYV, have been displaced from their initial locations $h(K)$.

0	FEM
1	TRE
2	EN
3	
4	
5	SYV
6	SEKS
7	TO
8	FIRE

Fig. 41. Linear open addressing.

Program L (*Linear probing and insertion*). This program deals with full-word keys; but a key of 0 is not allowed, since 0 is used to signal an empty position in the table. (Alternatively, we could require the keys to be nonnegative, letting empty positions contain -1.) The table size M is assumed to be prime, and TABLE[i] is stored in location TABLE $+ i$ for $0 \le i < M$. For speed in the inner loop, location TABLE $- 1$ is assumed to contain 0. Location VACANCIES is assumed to contain the value $M - 1 - N$; and rA $\equiv K$, rI1 $\equiv i$.

In order to speed up the inner loop of this program, the test "$i < 0$" has been removed from the loop so that only the essential parts of steps L2 and L3 remain. The total running time for the searching phase comes to $(7C + 9E + 21 - 4S)u$, and the insertion after an unsuccessful search adds an extra $8u$.

01	START	LDX	K	1	*L1. Hash.*
02		ENTA	0	1	
03		DIV	=M=	1	
04		STX	*+1(0:2)	1	
05		ENT1	*	1	$i \leftarrow h(K)$.
06		LDA	K	1	
07		JMP	2F	1	
08	8H	INC1	M+1	E	*L3. Advance to next.*
09	3H	DEC1	1	$C + E - 1$	$i \leftarrow i - 1$.
10	2H	CMPA	TABLE,1	$C + E$	*L2. Compare.*
11		JE	SUCCESS	$C + E$	Exit if $K = $ KEY[i].
12		LDX	TABLE,1	$C + E - S$	
13		JXNZ	3B	$C + E - S$	To L3 if TABLE[i] nonempty.
14		J1N	8B	$E + 1 - S$	To L3 with $i \leftarrow M$ if $i = -1$.
15	4H	LDX	VACANCIES	$1 - S$	*L4. Insert.*
16		JXZ	OVERFLOW	$1 - S$	Exit with overflow if $N = M - 1$.
17		DECX	1	$1 - S$	
18		STX	VACANCIES	$1 - S$	Increase N by 1.
19		STA	TABLE,1	$1 - S$	TABLE[i] $\leftarrow K$. ∎

As in Program C, the variable C denotes the number of probes, and S tells whether or not the search was successful. We may ignore the variable E, which is 1 only if a spurious probe of TABLE[-1] has been made, since its average value is $(C - 1)/M$.

Experience with linear probing shows that the algorithm works fine until the table begins to get full; but eventually the process slows down, with long drawn-out searches becoming increasingly frequent. The reason for this behavior can be understood by considering the following hypothetical hash table in which $M = 19$ and $N = 9$:

$$(21)$$

Shaded squares represent occupied positions. The next key K to be inserted into the table will go into one of the ten empty spaces, but these are not equally likely; in fact, K will be inserted into position 11 if $11 \le h(K) \le 15$, while it will fall into position 8 only if $h(K) = 8$. Therefore position 11 is five times as likely as position 8; long lists tend to grow even longer.

This phenomenon isn't enough by itself to account for the relatively poor behavior of linear probing, since a similar thing occurs in Algorithm C. (A list of length 4 is four times as likely to grow in Algorithm C as a list of length 1.) The real problem occurs when a cell like 4 or 16 becomes occupied in (21); then two separate lists are combined, while the lists in Algorithm C never grow by more than one step at a time. Consequently the performance of linear probing degrades rapidly when N approaches M.

We shall prove later in this section that the average number of probes needed by Algorithm L is approximately

$$C'_N \approx \frac{1}{2}\left(1 + \left(\frac{1}{1-\alpha}\right)^2\right) \quad \text{(unsuccessful search)}, \qquad (22)$$

$$C_N \approx \frac{1}{2}\left(1 + \frac{1}{1-\alpha}\right) \qquad \text{(successful search)}, \qquad (23)$$

where $\alpha = N/M$ is the load factor of the table. Therefore Program L is almost as fast as Program C, when the table is less than 75 percent full, in spite of the fact that Program C deals with unrealistically short keys. On the other hand, when α approaches 1 the best thing we can say about Program L is that it works, slowly but surely. In fact, when $N = M - 1$, there is only one vacant space in the table, so the average number of probes in an unsuccessful search is $(M + 1)/2$; we shall also prove that the average number of probes in a successful search is approximately $\sqrt{\pi M/8}$ when the table is full.

The pileup phenomenon that makes linear probing costly on a nearly full table is aggravated by the use of division hashing, if consecutive key values $\{K, K+1, K+2, \ldots\}$ are likely to occur, since these keys will have consecutive hash codes. Multiplicative hashing will break up these clusters satisfactorily.

Another way to protect against the consecutive hash code problem is to set $i \leftarrow i - c$ in step L3, instead of $i \leftarrow i - 1$. Any positive value of c will do, so long as it is *relatively prime* to M, since the probe sequence will still examine every position of the table in this case. Such a change would make Program L a bit slower, because of the test for $i < 0$. Decreasing by c instead of by 1 won't alter the pileup phenomenon, since groups of c-apart records will still be formed; equations (22) and (23) will still apply. But the appearance of consecutive keys $\{K, K+1, K+2, \ldots\}$ will now actually be a help instead of a hindrance.

Although a fixed value of c does not reduce the pileup phenomenon, we can improve the situation nicely by letting c depend on K. This idea leads to an important modification of Algorithm L, first introduced by Guy de Balbine [Ph.D. thesis, Calif. Inst. of Technology (1968), 149–150]:

Algorithm D (*Open addressing with double hashing*). This algorithm is almost identical to Algorithm L, but it probes the table in a slightly different fashion by making use of two hash functions $h_1(K)$ and $h_2(K)$. As usual $h_1(K)$ produces a value between 0 and $M - 1$, inclusive; but $h_2(K)$ must produce a value between

1 and $M-1$ that is *relatively prime* to M. (For example, if M is prime, $h_2(K)$ can be any value between 1 and $M-1$ inclusive; or if $M = 2^m$, $h_2(K)$ can be any *odd* value between 1 and $2^m - 1$.)

D1. [First hash.] Set $i \leftarrow h_1(K)$.

D2. [First probe.] If TABLE[i] is empty, go to D6. Otherwise if KEY[i] = K, the algorithm terminates successfully.

D3. [Second hash.] Set $c \leftarrow h_2(K)$.

D4. [Advance to next.] Set $i \leftarrow i - c$; if now $i < 0$, set $i \leftarrow i + M$.

D5. [Compare.] If TABLE[i] is empty, go to D6. Otherwise if KEY[i] = K, the algorithm terminates successfully. Otherwise go back to D4.

D6. [Insert.] If $N = M - 1$, the algorithm terminates with overflow. Otherwise set $N \leftarrow N + 1$, mark TABLE[i] occupied, and set KEY[i] $\leftarrow K$. ∎

Several possibilities have been suggested for computing $h_2(K)$. If M is prime and $h_1(K) = K \bmod M$, we might let $h_2(K) = 1 + (K \bmod (M-1))$; but since $M-1$ is even, it would be better to let $h_2(K) = 1 + (K \bmod (M-2))$. This suggests choosing M so that M and $M-2$ are "twin primes" like 1021 and 1019. Alternatively, we could set $h_2(K) = 1 + (\lfloor K/M \rfloor \bmod (M-2))$, since the quotient $\lfloor K/M \rfloor$ might be available in a register as a by-product of the computation of $h_1(K)$.

If $M = 2^m$ and we are using multiplicative hashing, $h_2(K)$ can be computed simply by shifting left m more bits and "oring in" a 1, so that the coding sequence in (5) would be followed by

$$\begin{array}{lll} \text{ENTA} & 0 & \text{Clear rA.} \\ \text{SLB} & m & \text{Shift rAX } m \text{ bits left.} \\ \text{OR} & \text{=1=} & \text{rA} \leftarrow \text{rA} \mid 1. \end{array} \qquad (24)$$

This is faster than the division method.

In each of the techniques suggested above, $h_1(K)$ and $h_2(K)$ are essentially independent, in the sense that different keys will yield the same values for both h_1 and h_2 with probability approximately proportional to $1/M^2$ instead of to $1/M$. Empirical tests show that the behavior of Algorithm D with independent hash functions is essentially indistinguishable from the number of probes that would be required if the keys were inserted at random into the table; there is practically no "piling up" or "clustering" as in Algorithm L.

It is also possible to let $h_2(K)$ depend on $h_1(K)$, as suggested by Gary Knott in 1968; for example, if M is prime we could let

$$h_2(K) = \begin{cases} 1, & \text{if } h_1(K) = 0; \\ M - h_1(K), & \text{if } h_1(K) > 0. \end{cases} \qquad (25)$$

This would be faster than doing another division, but we shall see that it does cause a certain amount of *secondary clustering*, requiring slightly more probes because of the increased chance that two or more keys will follow the same path. The formulas derived below can be used to determine whether the gain in hashing time outweighs the loss of probing time.

Algorithms L and D are very similar, yet there are enough differences that it is instructive to compare the running time of the corresponding MIX programs.

Program D (*Open addressing with double hashing*).   Since this program is substantially like Program L, it is presented without comments. rI2 ≡ $c - 1$.

01	START	LDX	K	1	15	3H DEC1	1,2	$C-1$
02		ENTA	0	1	16	J1NN	*+2	$C-1$
03		DIV	=M=	1	17	INC1	M	B
04		STX	*+1(0:2)	1	18	CMPA	TABLE,1	$C-1$
05		ENT1	*	1	19	JE	SUCCESS	$C-1$
06		LDX	TABLE,1	1	20	LDX	TABLE,1	$C-1-S2$
07		CMPX	K	1	21	JXNZ	3B	$C-1-S2$
08		JE	SUCCESS	1	22	4H LDX	VACANCIES	$1-S$
09		JXZ	4F	$1-S1$	23	JXZ	OVERFLOW	$1-S$
10		SRAX	5	$A-S1$	24	DECX	1	$1-S$
11		DIV	=M-2=	$A-S1$	25	STX	VACANCIES	$1-S$
12		STX	*+1(0:2)	$A-S1$	26	LDA	K	$1-S$
13		ENT2	*	$A-S1$	27	STA	TABLE,1	$1-S$
14		LDA	K	$A-S1$				

The frequency counts A, C, $S1$, $S2$ in this program have a similar interpretation to those in Program C above. The other variable B will be about $(C-1)/2$ on the average. (If we restricted the range of $h_2(K)$ to, say, $1 \le h_2(K) \le M/2$, B would be only about $(C-1)/4$; this increase of speed will probably *not* be offset by a noticeable increase in the number of probes.) When there are $N = \alpha M$ keys in the table, the average value of A is, of course, α in an unsuccessful search, and $A = 1$ in a successful search. As in Algorithm C, the average value of $S1$ in a successful search is $1 - \frac{1}{2}\big((N-1)/M\big) \approx 1 - \frac{1}{2}\alpha$. The average number of probes is difficult to determine exactly, but empirical tests show good agreement with formulas derived below for "uniform probing," namely

$$C_N' = \frac{M+1}{M+1-N} \qquad \approx (1-\alpha)^{-1} \qquad \text{(unsuccessful search),} \quad (26)$$

$$C_N = \frac{M+1}{N}(H_{M+1}-H_{M+1-N}) \approx -\alpha^{-1}\ln(1-\alpha) \quad \text{(successful search),} \qquad (27)$$

when $h_1(K)$ and $h_2(K)$ are independent. When $h_2(K)$ depends on $h_1(K)$ as in (25), the secondary clustering causes (26) and (27) to be increased to

$$C_N' = \frac{M+1}{M+1-N} - \frac{N}{M+1} + H_{M+1} - H_{M+1-N} + O(M^{-1})$$

$$\approx (1-\alpha)^{-1} - \alpha - \ln(1-\alpha); \quad (28)$$

$$C_N = 1 + H_{M+1} - H_{M+1-N} - \frac{N}{2(M+1)} - (H_{M+1}-H_{M+1-N})/N + O(N^{-1})$$

$$\approx 1 - \ln(1-\alpha) - \tfrac{1}{2}\alpha. \qquad (29)$$

(See exercise 44.) Note that as the table gets full, these values of C_N approach $H_{M+1} - 1$ and $H_{M+1} - \frac{1}{2}$, respectively, when $N = M$; this is much better than we observed in Algorithm L, but not as good as in the chaining methods.

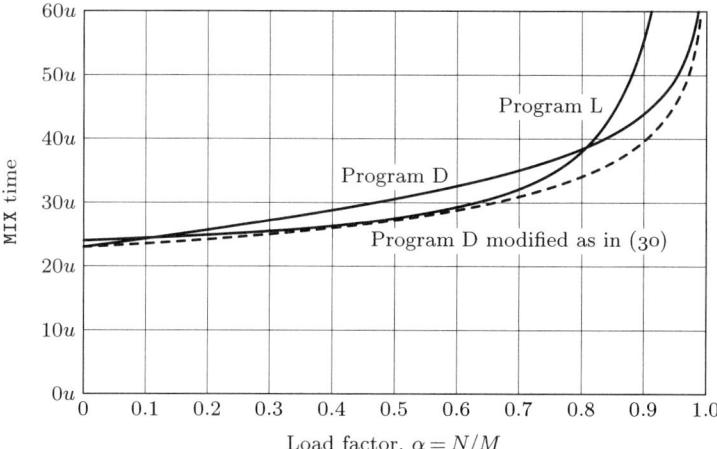

Fig. 42. The running time for successful searching by three open addressing schemes.

Since each probe takes slightly less time in Algorithm L, double hashing is advantageous only when the table gets full. Figure 42 compares the average running time of Program L, Program D, and a modified Program D that involves secondary clustering, replacing the rather slow calculation of $h_2(K)$ in lines 10–13 by the following three instructions:

$$
\begin{array}{lll}
\texttt{ENN2} & \texttt{1-M,1} & c \leftarrow M - i. \\
\texttt{J1NZ} & \texttt{*+2} & \\
\texttt{ENT2} & \texttt{0} & \text{If } i = 0,\, c \leftarrow 1.
\end{array}
\tag{30}
$$

Program D takes a total of $8C + 19A + B + 26 - 13S - 17S1$ units of time; modification (30) saves about $15(A - S1) \approx 7.5\alpha$ of these in a successful search. In this case, secondary clustering is preferable to independent double hashing.

On a binary computer, we could speed up the computation of $h_2(K)$ in another way, if M is prime greater than, say, 512, replacing lines 10–13 by

$$
\begin{array}{lll}
\texttt{AND} & \texttt{=511=} & \text{rA} \leftarrow \text{rA mod } 512. \\
\texttt{STA} & \texttt{*+1(0:2)} & \\
\texttt{ENT2} & \texttt{*} & c \leftarrow \text{rA} + 1.
\end{array}
\tag{31}
$$

This idea (suggested by Bell and Kaman, *CACM* **13** (1970), 675–677, who discovered Algorithm D independently) avoids secondary clustering without the expense of another division.

Many other probe sequences have been proposed as improvements on Algorithm L, but none seem to be superior to Algorithm D except possibly the method described in exercise 20.

By using the relative order of keys we can reduce the average running time for unsuccessful searches by Algorithms L or D to the average running time for successful search; see exercise 66. This technique can be important in applications for which unsuccessful searches are common; for example, TEX uses such an algorithm when looking for exceptions to its hyphenation rules.

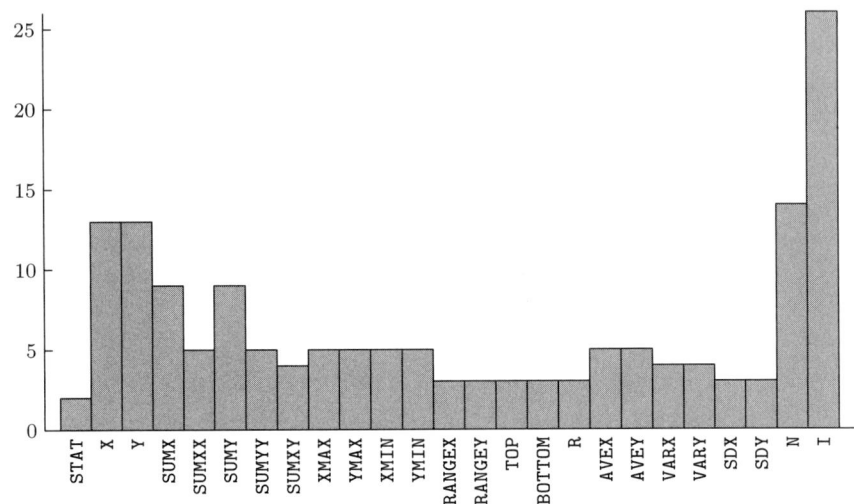

Fig. 43. The number of times a compiler typically searches for variable names. The names are listed from left to right in order of their first appearance.

Brent's Variation. Richard P. Brent has discovered a way to modify Algorithm D so that the average successful search time remains bounded as the table gets full. His method [*CACM* **16** (1973), 105–109] is based on the fact that successful searches are much more common than insertions, in many applications; therefore he proposes doing more work when inserting an item, moving records in order to reduce the expected retrieval time.

For example, Fig. 43 shows the number of times each identifier was actually found to appear, in a typical PL/I procedure. This data indicates that a PL/I compiler that uses a hash table to keep track of variable names will be looking up many of the names five or more times but inserting them only once. Similarly, Bell and Kaman found that a COBOL compiler used its symbol table algorithm 10988 times while compiling a program, but made only 735 insertions into the table; this is an average of about 14 successful searches per unsuccessful search. Sometimes a table is actually created only once (for example, a table of symbolic opcodes in an assembler), and it is used thereafter purely for retrieval.

Brent's idea is to change the insertion process in Algorithm D as follows. Suppose an unsuccessful search has probed locations $p_0, p_1, \ldots, p_{t-1}, p_t$, where $p_j = \big(h_1(K) - jh_2(K)\big) \bmod M$ and TABLE$[p_t]$ is empty. If $t \leq 1$, we insert K in position p_t as usual; but if $t \geq 2$, we compute $c_0 = h_2(K_0)$, where $K_0 = $ KEY$[p_0]$, and see if TABLE$[(p_0 - c_0) \bmod M]$ is empty. If it is, we set it to TABLE$[p_0]$ and then insert K in position p_0. This increases the retrieval time for K_0 by one step, but it decreases the retrieval time for K by $t \geq 2$ steps, so it results in a net improvement. Similarly, if TABLE$[(p_0 - c_0) \bmod M]$ is occupied and $t \geq 3$, we try TABLE$[(p_0 - 2c_0) \bmod M]$; if that is full too, we compute $c_1 = h_2($KEY$[p_1])$ and try TABLE$[(p_1 - c_1) \bmod M]$; etc. In general, let $c_j = h_2($KEY$[p_j])$ and

$p_{j,k} = (p_j - kc_j) \bmod M$; if we have found `TABLE`$[p_{j,k}]$ occupied for all indices j and k such that $j+k < r$, and if $t \geq r+1$, we look at `TABLE`$[p_{0,r}]$, `TABLE`$[p_{1,r-1}]$, ..., `TABLE`$[p_{r-1,1}]$. If the first empty space occurs at position $p_{j,r-j}$ we set `TABLE`$[p_{j,r-j}] \leftarrow$ `TABLE`$[p_j]$ and insert K in position p_j.

Brent's analysis indicates that the average number of probes per successful search is reduced to the levels shown in Fig. 44, on page 545, with a maximum value of about 2.49.

The number $t+1$ of probes in an unsuccessful search is not reduced by Brent's variation; it remains at the level indicated by Eq. (26), approaching $\frac{1}{2}(M+1)$ as the table gets full. The average number of times h_2 needs to be computed per insertion is $\alpha^2 + \alpha^5 + \frac{1}{3}\alpha^6 + \cdots$, according to Brent's analysis, eventually approaching $\Theta(\sqrt{M})$; and the number of additional table positions probed while deciding how to make the insertion is about $\alpha^2 + \alpha^4 + \frac{4}{3}\alpha^5 + \alpha^6 + \cdots$.

E. G. Mallach [*Comp. J.* **20** (1977), 137–140] has experimented with refinements of Brent's variation, and further results have been obtained by Gaston H. Gonnet and J. Ian Munro [*SICOMP* **8** (1979), 463–478].

Deletions. Many computer programmers have great faith in algorithms, and they are surprised to find that *the obvious way to delete records from a hash table doesn't work.* For example, if we try to delete the key `EN` from Fig. 41, we can't simply mark that table position empty, because another key `FEM` would suddenly be forgotten! (Recall that `EN` and `FEM` both hashed to the same location. When looking up `FEM`, we would find an empty place, indicating an unsuccessful search.) A similar problem occurs with Algorithm C, due to the coalescing of lists; imagine the deletion of both `TO` and `FIRE` from Fig. 40.

In general, we can handle deletions by putting a special code value in the corresponding cell, so that there are three kinds of table entries: empty, occupied, and deleted. When searching for a key, we should skip over deleted cells, as if they were occupied. If the search is unsuccessful, the key can be inserted in place of the first deleted or empty position that was encountered.

But this idea is workable only when deletions are very rare, because the entries of the table never become empty again once they have been occupied. After a long sequence of repeated insertions and deletions, all of the empty spaces will eventually disappear, and every unsuccessful search will take M probes! Furthermore the time per probe will be increased, since we will have to test whether i has returned to its starting value in step D4; and the number of probes in a successful search will drift upward from C_N to C_N'.

When linear probing is being used (Algorithm L), we can make deletions in a way that avoids such a sorry state of affairs, if we are willing to do some extra work for the deletion.

Algorithm R (*Deletion with linear probing*). Assuming that an open hash table has been constructed by Algorithm L, this algorithm deletes the record from a given position `TABLE`$[i]$.

R1. [Empty a cell.] Mark `TABLE`$[i]$ empty, and set $j \leftarrow i$.

R2. [Decrease i.] Set $i \leftarrow i - 1$, and if this makes i negative set $i \leftarrow i + M$.

R3. [Inspect TABLE[i].] If TABLE[i] is empty, the algorithm terminates. Otherwise set $r \leftarrow h(\text{KEY}[i])$, the original hash address of the key now stored at position i. If $i \leq r < j$ or if $r < j < i$ or $j < i \leq r$ (in other words, if r lies cyclically between i and j), go back to R2.

R4. [Move a record.] Set TABLE[j] $\leftarrow$ TABLE[i], and return to step R1. ▮

Exercise 22 shows that this algorithm causes no degradation in performance; in other words, the average number of probes predicted in Eqs. (22) and (23) will remain the same. (A weaker result for tree insertion was proved in Theorem 6.2.2H.) But the validity of Algorithm R depends heavily on the fact that linear probing is involved, and no analogous deletion procedure for use with Algorithm D is possible. The average running time of Algorithm R is analyzed in exercise 64.

Of course when chaining is used with separate lists for each possible hash value, deletion causes no problems since it is simply a deletion from a linked linear list. Deletion with Algorithm C is discussed in exercise 23.

Algorithm R may move some of the table entries, and this is undesirable if they are being pointed to from elsewhere. Another approach to deletions is possible by adapting some of the ideas used in garbage collection (see Section 2.3.5): We might keep a reference count with each key telling how many other keys collide with it; then it is possible to convert unoccupied cells to empty status when their reference drops to zero. Alternatively we might go through the entire table whenever too many deleted entries have accumulated, changing all the unoccupied positions to empty and then looking up all remaining keys, in order to see which unoccupied positions still require "deleted" status. These procedures, which avoid relocation and work with any hash technique, were originally suggested by T. Gunji and E. Goto [*J. Information Proc.* **3** (1980), 1–12].

*Analysis of the algorithms. It is especially important to know the average behavior of a hashing method, because we are committed to trusting in the laws of probability whenever we hash. The worst case of these algorithms is almost unthinkably bad, so we need to be reassured that the average behavior is very good.

Before we get into the analysis of linear probing, etc., let us consider an approximate model of the situation, called *uniform probing*. In this model, which was suggested by W. W. Peterson [*IBM J. Research & Devel.* **1** (1957), 135–136], we assume that each key is placed in a completely random location of the table, so that each of the $\binom{M}{N}$ possible configurations of N occupied cells and $M-N$ empty cells is equally likely. This model ignores any effect of primary or secondary clustering; the occupancy of each cell in the table is essentially independent of all the others. Then the probability that any permutation of table positions needs exactly r probes to insert the $(N+1)$st item is the number of configurations in which $r-1$ given cells are occupied and another is empty, divided by $\binom{M}{N}$, namely

$$P_r = \binom{M-r}{N-r+1} \Big/ \binom{M}{N} ;$$

therefore the average number of probes for uniform probing is

$$C_N' = \sum_{r=1}^{M} r P_r = M + 1 - \sum_{r=1}^{M} (M + 1 - r) P_r$$

$$= M + 1 - \sum_{r=1}^{M} (M + 1 - r) \binom{M - r}{M - N - 1} \Big/ \binom{M}{N}$$

$$= M + 1 - \sum_{r=1}^{M} (M - N) \binom{M + 1 - r}{M - N} \Big/ \binom{M}{N}$$

$$= M + 1 - (M - N) \binom{M + 1}{M - N + 1} \Big/ \binom{M}{N}$$

$$= M + 1 - (M - N) \frac{M + 1}{M - N + 1} = \frac{M + 1}{M - N + 1}, \quad \text{for } 1 \le N < M. \quad (32)$$

(We have already solved essentially the same problem in connection with random sampling, in exercise 3.4.2–5.) Setting $\alpha = N/M$, this exact formula for C_N' is approximately equal to

$$\frac{1}{1 - \alpha} = 1 + \alpha + \alpha^2 + \alpha^3 + \cdots, \quad (33)$$

a series that has a rough intuitive interpretation: With probability α we need more than one probe, with probability α^2 we need more than two, etc. The corresponding average number of probes for a successful search is

$$C_N = \frac{1}{N} \sum_{k=0}^{N-1} C_k' = \frac{M + 1}{N} \left(\frac{1}{M + 1} + \frac{1}{M} + \cdots + \frac{1}{M - N + 2} \right)$$

$$= \frac{M + 1}{N} (H_{M+1} - H_{M-N+1}) \approx \frac{1}{\alpha} \ln \frac{1}{1 - \alpha}. \quad (34)$$

As remarked above, extensive tests show that Algorithm D with two independent hash functions behaves essentially like uniform probing, for all practical purposes. In fact, double hashing is asymptotically equivalent to uniform probing, in the limit as $M \to \infty$ (see exercise 70).

This completes our analysis of uniform probing. In order to study linear probing and other types of collision resolution, we need to set up the theory in a different, more realistic way. The probabilistic model we shall use for this purpose assumes that each of the M^N possible "hash sequences"

$$a_1 a_2 \ldots a_N, \qquad 0 \le a_j < M, \quad (35)$$

is equally likely, where a_j denotes the initial hash address of the jth key inserted into the table. The average number of probes in a successful search, given any particular searching algorithm, will be denoted by C_N as above; this is assumed to be the average number of probes needed to find the kth key, averaged over $1 \le k \le N$ with each key equally likely, and averaged over all hash sequences (35) with each sequence equally likely. Similarly, the average number of probes needed when the Nth key is inserted, considering all sequences (35) to be equally likely, will be denoted by C'_{N-1}; this is the average number of probes in an unsuccessful search starting with $N-1$ elements in the table. When open addressing is used,

$$C_N = \frac{1}{N} \sum_{k=0}^{N-1} C'_k, \qquad (36)$$

so that we can deduce one quantity from the other as we have done in (34).

Strictly speaking, there are two defects even in this more accurate model. In the first place, the different hash sequences aren't all equally probable, because the keys themselves are distinct. This makes the probability that $a_1 = a_2$ slightly less than $1/M$; but the difference is usually negligible since the set of all possible keys is typically very large compared to M. (See exercise 24.) Furthermore a good hash function will exploit the nonrandomness of typical data, making it even less likely that $a_1 = a_2$; as a result, our estimates for the number of probes will be pessimistic. Another inaccuracy in the model is indicated in Fig. 43: Keys that occur earlier are (with some exceptions) more likely to be looked up than keys that occur later. Therefore our estimate of C_N tends to be doubly pessimistic, and the algorithms should perform slightly better in practice than our analysis predicts.

With these precautions, we are ready to make an "exact" analysis of linear probing.* Let $f(M, N)$ be the number of hash sequences (35) such that position 0 of the table will be empty after the keys have been inserted by Algorithm L. The circular symmetry of linear probing implies that position 0 is empty just as often as any other position, so it is empty with probability $1 - N/M$; in other words

$$f(M, N) = \left(1 - \frac{N}{M}\right) M^N. \qquad (37)$$

By convention we also set $f(0,0) = 1$. Now let $g(M, N, k)$ be the number of hash sequences (35) such that the algorithm leaves position 0 empty, positions 1 through k occupied, and position $k + 1$ empty. We have

$$g(M, N, k) = \binom{N}{k} f(k+1, k) f(M-k-1, N-k), \qquad (38)$$

because all such hash sequences are composed of two subsequences, one (containing k elements $a_i \le k$) that leaves position 0 empty and positions 1 through k occupied and one (containing $N - k$ elements $a_j \ge k + 1$) that leaves position $k + 1$ empty; there are $f(k+1, k)$ subsequences of the former type and $f(M-k-1, N-k)$ of the latter type, and there are $\binom{N}{k}$ ways to intersperse two such subsequences. Finally let P_k be the probability that exactly $k + 1$ probes will be needed when the $(N + 1)$st key is inserted; it follows (see exercise 25)

---

* The author cannot resist inserting a biographical note at this point: I first formulated the following derivation in 1962, shortly after beginning work on *The Art of Computer Programming*. Since this was the first nontrivial algorithm I had ever analyzed satisfactorily, it had a strong influence on the structure of these books. Ever since that day, the analysis of algorithms has in fact been one of the major themes of my life.

that

$$P_k = M^{-N}\big(g(M, N, k) + g(M, N, k+1) + \cdots + g(M, N, N)\big). \qquad (39)$$

Now $C'_N = \sum_{k=0}^{N} (k + 1)P_k$; putting this equation together with (36)–(39) and simplifying yields the following result.

Theorem K. *The average number of probes needed by Algorithm L, assuming that all M^N hash sequences (35) are equally likely, is*

$$C_N = \tfrac{1}{2}\big(1 + Q_0(M, N-1)\big) \quad \text{(successful search)}, \qquad (40)$$

$$C'_N = \tfrac{1}{2}\big(1 + Q_1(M, N)\big) \qquad \text{(unsuccessful search)}, \qquad (41)$$

where

$$Q_r(M, N) = \binom{r}{0} + \binom{r+1}{1}\frac{N}{M} + \binom{r+2}{2}\frac{N(N-1)}{M^2} + \cdots$$

$$= \sum_{k \geq 0}\binom{r+k}{k}\frac{N}{M}\frac{N-1}{M}\cdots\frac{N-k+1}{M}. \qquad (42)$$

Proof. Details of the calculation are worked out in exercise 27. (For the variance, see exercises 28, 67, and 68.) ∎

The rather strange-looking function $Q_r(M, N)$ that appears in this theorem is really not hard to deal with. We have

$$N^k - \binom{k}{2}N^{k-1} \leq N(N-1)\ldots(N-k+1) \leq N^k;$$

hence if $N/M = \alpha$,

$$\sum_{k\geq 0}\binom{r+k}{k}\left(N^k - \binom{k}{2}N^{k-1}\right)\Big/M^k \leq Q_r(M, N) \leq \sum_{k\geq 0}\binom{r+k}{k}N^k/M^k,$$

$$\sum_{k\geq 0}\binom{r+k}{k}\alpha^k - \frac{\alpha}{M}\sum_{k\geq 0}\binom{r+k}{k}\binom{k}{2}\alpha^{k-2} \leq Q_r(M, \alpha M) \leq \sum_{k\geq 0}\binom{r+k}{k}\alpha^k;$$

that is,

$$\frac{1}{(1-\alpha)^{r+1}} - \frac{1}{M}\binom{r+2}{2}\frac{\alpha}{(1-\alpha)^{r+3}} \leq Q_r(M, \alpha M) \leq \frac{1}{(1-\alpha)^{r+1}}. \qquad (43)$$

This relation gives us a good estimate of $Q_r(M, N)$ when M is large and α is not too close to 1. (The lower bound is a better approximation than the upper bound.) When α approaches 1, these formulas become useless, but fortunately $Q_0(M, M-1)$ is the function $Q(M)$ whose asymptotic behavior was studied in great detail in Section 1.2.11.3; and $Q_1(M, M-1)$ is simply equal to M (see exercise 50). In terms of the standard notation for hypergeometric functions, Eq. 1.2.6–(39), we have $Q_r(M, N) = F(r+1, -N; ; -1/M) = F\big(\begin{smallmatrix} r+1, -N, 1 \\ 1 \end{smallmatrix} \big| -\frac{1}{M}\big)$.

Another approach to the analysis of linear probing was taken in the early days by G. Schay, Jr. and W. G. Spruth [*CACM* **5** (1962), 459–462]. Although their method yielded only an approximation to the exact formulas in Theorem K, it sheds further light on the algorithm, so we shall sketch it briefly here. First let us consider a surprising property of linear probing that was first noticed by W. W. Peterson in 1957:

Theorem P. *The average number of probes in a successful search by Algorithm L is independent of the order in which the keys were inserted; it depends only on the number of keys that hash to each address.*

In other words, any rearrangement of a hash sequence $a_1 a_2 \ldots a_N$ yields a hash sequence with the same average displacement of keys from their hash addresses. (We are assuming, as stated earlier, that all keys in the table have equal importance. If some keys are more frequently accessed than others, the proof can be extended to show that an optimal arrangement occurs if we insert them in decreasing order of frequency, using the method of Theorem 6.1S.)

Proof. It suffices to show that the total number of probes needed to insert keys for the hash sequence $a_1 a_2 \ldots a_N$ is the same as the total number needed for $a_1 \ldots a_{i-1} a_{i+1} a_i a_{i+2} \ldots a_N$, $1 \le i < N$. There is clearly no difference unless the $(i+1)$st key in the second sequence falls into the position occupied by the ith in the first sequence. But then the ith and $(i+1)$st merely exchange places, so the number of probes for the $(i+1)$st is decreased by the same amount that the number for the ith is increased. ∎

Theorem P tells us that the average search length for a hash sequence $a_1 a_2 \ldots a_N$ can be determined from the numbers $b_0 b_1 \ldots b_{M-1}$, where b_j is the number of a's that equal j. From this sequence we can determine the "carry sequence" $c_0 c_1 \ldots c_{M-1}$, where c_j is the number of keys for which both locations j and $j-1$ are probed as the key is inserted. This sequence is determined by the rule

$$c_j = \begin{cases} 0, & \text{if } b_j = c_{(j+1) \bmod M} = 0; \\ b_j + c_{(j+1) \bmod M} - 1, & \text{otherwise.} \end{cases} \qquad (44)$$

For example, let $M = 10$, $N = 8$, and $b_0 \ldots b_9 = 0\ 3\ 2\ 0\ 1\ 0\ 0\ 0\ 0\ 2$; then $c_0 \ldots c_9 = 2\ 3\ 1\ 0\ 0\ 0\ 0\ 1\ 2\ 3$, since one key needs to be "carried over" from position 2 to position 1, three from position 1 to position 0, two of these from position 0 to position 9, etc. We have $b_0 + b_1 + \cdots + b_{M-1} = N$, and the average number of probes needed for retrieval of the N keys is

$$1 + (c_0 + c_1 + \cdots + c_{M-1})/N. \qquad (45)$$

Rule (44) seems to be a circular definition of the c's in terms of themselves, but actually there is a unique solution to the stated equations whenever $N < M$ (see exercise 32).

Schay and Spruth used this idea to determine the probability q_k that $c_j = k$, in terms of the probability p_k that $b_j = k$. (These probabilities are independent of j.) Thus

$$q_0 = p_0 q_0 + p_1 q_0 + p_0 q_1,$$
$$q_1 = p_2 q_0 + p_1 q_1 + p_0 q_2, \tag{46}$$
$$q_2 = p_3 q_0 + p_2 q_1 + p_1 q_2 + p_0 q_3,$$

etc., since, for example, the probability that $c_j = 2$ is the probability that $b_j + c_{(j+1) \bmod M} = 3$. Let $B(z) = \sum p_k z^k$ and $C(z) = \sum q_k z^k$ be the generating functions for these probability distributions; the equations (46) are equivalent to

$$B(z)C(z) = p_0 q_0 + (q_0 - p_0 q_0)z + q_1 z^2 + \cdots = p_0 q_0 (1 - z) + z C(z).$$

Since $B(1) = 1$, we may write $B(z) = 1 + (z-1)D(z)$, and it follows that

$$C(z) = \frac{p_0 q_0}{1 - D(z)} = \frac{1 - D(1)}{1 - D(z)}, \tag{47}$$

since $C(1) = 1$. The average number of probes needed for retrieval, according to (45), will therefore be

$$1 + \frac{M}{N}C'(1) = 1 + \frac{M}{N}\frac{D'(1)}{1 - D(1)} = 1 + \frac{M}{2N}\frac{B''(1)}{1 - B'(1)}. \tag{48}$$

Since we are assuming that each hash sequence $a_1 \ldots a_N$ is equally likely, we have

$$p_k = \Pr(\text{exactly } k \text{ of the } a_i \text{ are equal to } j, \text{ for fixed } j)$$
$$= \binom{N}{k}\left(\frac{1}{M}\right)^k\left(1 - \frac{1}{M}\right)^{N-k}; \tag{49}$$

hence

$$B(z) = \left(1 + \frac{z-1}{M}\right)^N, \quad B'(1) = \frac{N}{M}, \quad B''(1) = \frac{N(N-1)}{M^2}, \tag{50}$$

and the average number of probes according to (48) will be

$$C_N = \frac{1}{2}\left(1 + \frac{M-1}{M-N}\right). \tag{51}$$

Can the reader spot the incorrect reasoning that has caused this answer to be different from the correct result in Theorem K? (See exercise 33.)

*Optimality considerations. We have seen several examples of probe sequences for open addressing, and it is natural to ask for one that can be proved *best possible* in some meaningful sense. This problem has been set up in the following interesting way by J. D. Ullman [*JACM* **19** (1972), 569–575]: Instead of computing a hash address $h(K)$, we map each key K into an entire permutation of $\{0, 1, \ldots, M-1\}$, which represents the probe sequence to use for K. Each of the $M!$ permutations is assigned a probability, and the generalized hash function is supposed to select each permutation with that probability. The question is, "What assignment of probabilities to permutations gives the best performance, in the sense that the corresponding average number of probes C_N or C'_N is minimized?"

For example, if we assign the probability $1/M!$ to each permutation, it is easy to see that we have exactly the behavior of *uniform probing* that we have analyzed above in (32) and (34). However, Ullman found an example with $M = 4$ and $N = 2$ for which C'_N is smaller than the value $\frac{5}{3}$ obtained with uniform probing. His construction assigns zero probability to all but the following six permutations:

Permutation	Probability	Permutation	Probability	
0 1 2 3	$(1+2\epsilon)/6$	1 0 3 2	$(1+2\epsilon)/6$	
2 0 1 3	$(1-\epsilon)/6$	2 1 0 3	$(1-\epsilon)/6$	(52)
3 0 1 2	$(1-\epsilon)/6$	3 1 0 2	$(1-\epsilon)/6$	

Roughly speaking, the first probe tends to be either 2 or 3, but the second probe is always 0 or 1. The average number of probes needed to insert the third item, C'_2, turns out to be $\frac{5}{3} - \frac{1}{9}\epsilon + O(\epsilon^2)$, so we can improve on uniform probing by taking ϵ to be a small positive value.

However, the corresponding value of C'_1 for these probabilities is $\frac{23}{18} + O(\epsilon)$, which is larger than $\frac{5}{4}$ (the uniform probing value). Ullman proved that any assignment of probabilities such that $C'_N < (M+1)/(M+1-N)$ for some N always implies that $C'_n > (M+1)/(M+1-n)$ for some $n < N$; you can't win all the time over uniform probing.

Actually the number of probes C_N for a *successful* search is a better measure than C'_N. The permutations in (52) do not lead to an improved value of C_N for any N, and indeed Ullman conjectured that no assignment of probabilities will be able to make C_N less than the uniform value $((M+1)/N)(H_{M+1}-H_{M+1-N})$. Andrew Yao proved an asymptotic form of this conjecture by showing that the limiting cost when $N = \alpha M$ and $M \to \infty$ is always $\geq \frac{1}{\alpha}\ln\frac{1}{1-\alpha}$ [*JACM* **32** (1985), 687–693].

The strong form of Ullman's conjecture appears to be very difficult to prove, especially because there are many ways to assign probabilities to achieve the effect of uniform probing; we do not need to assign $1/M!$ to each permutation. For example, the following assignment for $M = 4$ is equivalent to uniform probing:

Permutation	Probability	Permutation	Probability	
0 1 2 3	1/6	0 2 1 3	1/12	
1 2 3 0	1/6	1 3 2 0	1/12	(53)
2 3 0 1	1/6	2 0 3 1	1/12	
3 0 1 2	1/6	3 1 0 2	1/12	

with zero probability assigned to the other 16 permutations.

The following theorem characterizes *all* assignments that produce the behavior of uniform probing.

Theorem U. *An assignment of probabilities to permutations will make each of the $\binom{M}{N}$ configurations of empty and occupied cells equally likely after N*

insertions, for $0 < N < M$, if and only if the sum of probabilities assigned to all permutations whose first N elements are the members of a given N-element set is $1/\binom{M}{N}$, for all N and for all N-element sets.

For example, the sum of probabilities assigned to each of the $3!\,(M-3)!$ permutations beginning with the numbers $\{0, 1, 2\}$ in some order must be $1/\binom{M}{3} = 3!\,(M-3)!/M!$. Observe that the condition of this theorem holds in (53), because $1/6 + 1/12 = 1/4$.

Proof. Let $A \subseteq \{0, 1, \ldots, M-1\}$, and let $\Pi(A)$ be the set of all permutations whose first $|A|$ elements are members of A; also let $S(A)$ be the sum of the probabilities assigned to those permutations. Let $P_k(A)$ be the probability that the first $|A|$ insertions of the open addressing procedure occupy the locations specified by A, and that the last insertion required exactly k probes. Finally, let $P(A) = P_1(A) + P_2(A) + \cdots$. The proof is by induction on $N \geq 1$, assuming that

$$P(A) = S(A) = 1 \Big/ \binom{M}{n}$$

for all sets A with $|A| = n < N$. Let B be any N-element set. Then

$$P_k(B) = \sum_{\substack{A \subseteq B \\ |A| = k}} \sum_{\pi \in \Pi(A)} \Pr(\pi) P\big(B \setminus \{\pi_k\}\big),$$

where $\Pr(\pi)$ is the probability assigned to permutation π and π_k is its kth element. By induction

$$P_k(B) = \sum_{\substack{A \subseteq B \\ |A| = k}} \frac{1}{\binom{M}{N-1}} \sum_{\pi \in \Pi(A)} \Pr(\pi),$$

which equals

$$\binom{N}{k} \Big/ \binom{M}{N-1}\binom{M}{k}, \qquad \text{if } k < N;$$

hence

$$P(B) = \frac{1}{\binom{M}{N-1}} \left(S(B) + \sum_{k=1}^{N-1} \frac{\binom{N}{k}}{\binom{M}{k}} \right),$$

and this can be equal to $1/\binom{M}{N}$ if and only if $S(B)$ has the correct value. $\blacksquare$

External searching. Hashing techniques lend themselves well to external searching on direct-access storage devices like disks or drums. For such applications, as in Section 6.2.4, we want to minimize the number of accesses to the file, and this has two major effects on the choice of algorithms:

1) It is reasonable to spend more time computing the hash function, since the penalty for bad hashing is much greater than the cost of the extra time needed to do a careful job.

2) The records are usually grouped into pages or *buckets*, so that several records are fetched from the external memory each time.

The file is divided into M buckets containing b records each. Collisions now cause no problem unless more than b keys have the same hash address. The following three approaches to collision resolution seem to be best:

A) *Chaining with separate lists.* If more than b records fall into the same bucket, a link to an overflow record can be inserted at the end of the first bucket. These overflow records are kept in a special overflow area. There is usually no advantage in having buckets in the overflow area, since comparatively few overflows occur; thus, the extra records are usually linked together so that the $(b+k)$th record of a list requires $1+k$ accesses. It is usually a good idea to leave some room for overflows on each cylinder of a disk file, so that most accesses are to the same cylinder.

Although this method of handling overflows seems inefficient, the number of overflows is statistically small enough that the average search time is very good. See Tables 2 and 3, which show the average number of accesses required as a function of the load factor

$$\alpha = N/Mb, \qquad (54)$$

for fixed α as M, $N \to \infty$. Curiously when $\alpha = 1$ the asymptotic number of accesses for an unsuccessful search increases with increasing b.

Table 2
AVERAGE ACCESSES IN AN UNSUCCESSFUL SEARCH BY SEPARATE CHAINING

Bucket size, b	Load factor, α									
	10%	20%	30%	40%	50%	60%	70%	80%	90%	95%
1	1.0048	1.0187	1.0408	1.0703	1.1065	1.1488	1.197	1.249	1.307	1.34
2	1.0012	1.0088	1.0269	1.0581	1.1036	1.1638	1.238	1.327	1.428	1.48
3	1.0003	1.0038	1.0162	1.0433	1.0898	1.1588	1.252	1.369	1.509	1.59
4	1.0001	1.0016	1.0095	1.0314	1.0751	1.1476	1.253	1.394	1.571	1.67
5	1.0000	1.0007	1.0056	1.0225	1.0619	1.1346	1.249	1.410	1.620	1.74
10	1.0000	1.0000	1.0004	1.0041	1.0222	1.0773	1.201	1.426	1.773	2.00
20	1.0000	1.0000	1.0000	1.0001	1.0028	1.0234	1.113	1.367	1.898	2.29
50	1.0000	1.0000	1.0000	1.0000	1.0000	1.0007	1.018	1.182	1.920	2.70

Table 3
AVERAGE ACCESSES IN A SUCCESSFUL SEARCH BY SEPARATE CHAINING

Bucket size, b	Load factor, α									
	10%	20%	30%	40%	50%	60%	70%	80%	90%	95%
1	1.0500	1.1000	1.1500	1.2000	1.2500	1.3000	1.350	1.400	1.450	1.48
2	1.0063	1.0242	1.0520	1.0883	1.1321	1.1823	1.238	1.299	1.364	1.40
3	1.0010	1.0071	1.0215	1.0458	1.0806	1.1259	1.181	1.246	1.319	1.36
4	1.0002	1.0023	1.0097	1.0257	1.0527	1.0922	1.145	1.211	1.290	1.33
5	1.0000	1.0008	1.0046	1.0151	1.0358	1.0699	1.119	1.186	1.268	1.32
10	1.0000	1.0000	1.0002	1.0015	1.0070	1.0226	1.056	1.115	1.206	1.27
20	1.0000	1.0000	1.0000	1.0000	1.0005	1.0038	1.018	1.059	1.150	1.22
50	1.0000	1.0000	1.0000	1.0000	1.0000	1.0000	1.001	1.015	1.083	1.16

B) *Chaining with coalescing lists.* Instead of providing a separate overflow area, we can adapt Algorithm C to external files. A doubly linked list of available space can be maintained for each cylinder, linking together each bucket that is not yet full. Under this scheme, every bucket contains a count of how many record positions are empty, and the bucket is removed from the doubly linked list only when its count becomes zero. A "roving pointer" can be used to distribute overflows (see exercise 2.5–6), so that different chains tend to use different overflow buckets. This method has not yet been analyzed, but it might prove to be quite useful.

C) *Open addressing.* We can also do without links, using an "open" method. Linear probing is probably better than random probing when we consider external searching, because the increment c can often be chosen so that it minimizes latency delays between consecutive accesses. The approximate theoretical model of linear probing that was worked out above can be generalized to account for the influence of buckets, and it shows that linear probing is indeed satisfactory unless the table has gotten very full. For example, see Table 4; when the load factor is 90 percent and the bucket size is 50, the average number of accesses in a successful search is only 1.04. This is actually *better* than the 1.08 accesses required by the chaining method (A) with the same bucket size!

Table 4

AVERAGE ACCESSES IN A SUCCESSFUL SEARCH BY LINEAR PROBING

Bucket size, b	Load factor, α									
	10%	20%	30%	40%	50%	60%	70%	80%	90%	95%
1	1.0556	1.1250	1.2143	1.3333	1.5000	1.7500	2.167	3.000	5.500	10.50
2	1.0062	1.0242	1.0553	1.1033	1.1767	1.2930	1.494	1.903	3.147	5.64
3	1.0009	1.0066	1.0201	1.0450	1.0872	1.1584	1.286	1.554	2.378	4.04
4	1.0001	1.0021	1.0085	1.0227	1.0497	1.0984	1.190	1.386	2.000	3.24
5	1.0000	1.0007	1.0039	1.0124	1.0307	1.0661	1.136	1.289	1.777	2.77
10	1.0000	1.0000	1.0001	1.0011	1.0047	1.0154	1.042	1.110	1.345	1.84
20	1.0000	1.0000	1.0000	1.0000	1.0003	1.0020	1.010	1.036	1.144	1.39
50	1.0000	1.0000	1.0000	1.0000	1.0000	1.0000	1.001	1.005	1.040	1.13

The analysis of methods (A) and (C) involves some very interesting mathematics; we shall merely summarize the results here, since the details are worked out in exercises 49 and 55. The formulas involve two functions strongly related to the Q-functions of Theorem K, namely

$$R(\alpha, n) = \frac{n}{n+1} + \frac{n^2\alpha}{(n+1)(n+2)} + \frac{n^3\alpha^2}{(n+1)(n+2)(n+3)} + \cdots, \qquad (55)$$

and

$$t_n(\alpha) = e^{-n\alpha}\left(\frac{(\alpha n)^n}{(n+1)!} + 2\frac{(\alpha n)^{n+1}}{(n+2)!} + 3\frac{(\alpha n)^{n+2}}{(n+3)!} + \cdots\right)$$

$$= \frac{e^{-n\alpha}n^n\alpha^n}{n!}\left(1 - (1-\alpha)R(\alpha, n)\right). \qquad (56)$$

In terms of these functions, the average number of accesses made by the chaining method (A) in an unsuccessful search is

$$C'_N = 1 + \alpha b t_b(\alpha) + O\left(\frac{1}{M}\right) \tag{57}$$

as $M, N \to \infty$, and the corresponding number in a successful search is

$$C_N = 1 + \frac{e^{-b\alpha} b^b \alpha^b}{2b!}\left(2 + (\alpha - 1)b + \left(\alpha^2 + (\alpha - 1)^2(b - 1)\right)R(\alpha, b)\right) + O\left(\frac{1}{M}\right). \tag{58}$$

The limiting values of these formulas are the quantities shown in Tables 2 and 3.

Since chaining method (A) requires a separate overflow area, we need to estimate how many overflows will occur. The average number of overflows will be $M(C'_N - 1) = N t_b(\alpha)$, since $C'_N - 1$ is the average number of overflows in any given list. Therefore Table 2 can be used to deduce the amount of overflow space required. For fixed α, the standard deviation of the total number of overflows will be roughly proportional to $\sqrt{M}$ as $M \to \infty$.

Asymptotic values for C'_N and C_N appear in exercise 53, but the approximations aren't very good when b is small or α is large; fortunately the series for $R(\alpha, n)$ converges rather rapidly even when α is large, so the formulas can be evaluated to any desired precision without much difficulty. The maximum values occur for $\alpha = 1$, when

$$\max C'_N = 1 + \frac{e^{-b} b^{b+1}}{b!} = \sqrt{\frac{b}{2\pi}} + 1 + O(b^{-1/2}), \tag{59}$$

$$\max C_N = 1 + \frac{e^{-b} b^b}{2b!}\left(R(b) + 1\right) = \frac{5}{4} + \sqrt{\frac{2}{9\pi b}} + O(b^{-1}), \tag{60}$$

as $b \to \infty$, by Stirling's approximation and the analysis of the function $R(n) = R(1, n) - 1$ in Section 1.2.11.3.

The average number of accesses in a successful external search with *linear probing* has the remarkably simple expression

$$C_N \approx 1 + t_b(\alpha) + t_{2b}(\alpha) + t_{3b}(\alpha) + \cdots, \tag{61}$$

which can be understood as follows: The average total number of accesses to look up all N keys is $N C_N$, and this is $N + T_1 + T_2 + \cdots$, where T_k is the average number of keys that require more than k accesses. Theorem P says that we can enter the keys in any order without affecting C_N, and it follows that T_k is the average number of overflow records that would occur in the chaining method if we had M/k buckets of size kb, namely $N t_{kb}(\alpha)$ by what we said above. Further justification of Eq. (61) appears in exercise 55.

An excellent early discussion of practical considerations involved in the design of external hash tables was given by Charles A. Olson, *Proc. ACM Nat. Conf.* **24** (1969), 539–549. He included several worked examples and pointed out that the number of overflow records will increase substantially if the file is subject to frequent insertion/deletion activity without relocating records. He also presented an analysis of this situation that was obtained jointly with J. A. de Peyster.

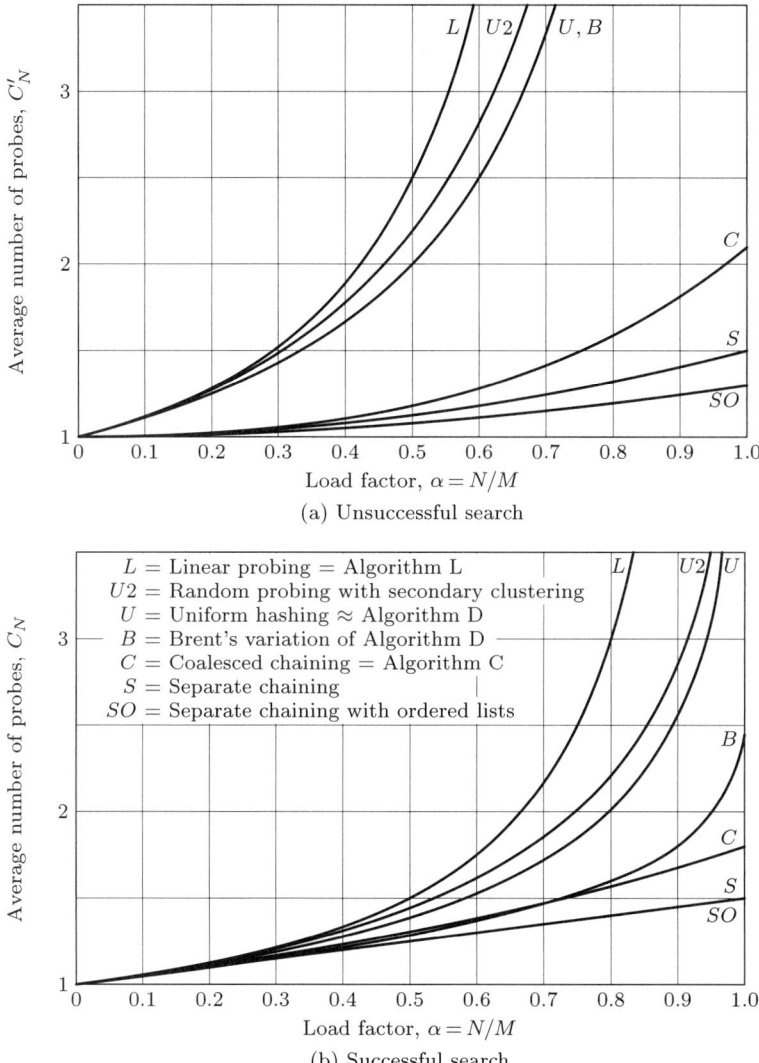

Fig. 44. Comparison of collision resolution methods: limiting values of the average number of probes as $M \to \infty$.

Comparison of the methods. We have now studied a large number of techniques for searching; how can we select the right one for a given application? It is difficult to summarize in a few words all the relevant details of the trade-offs involved in the choice of a search method, but the following things seem to be of primary importance with respect to the speed of searching and the requisite storage space.

Figure 44 summarizes the analyses of this section, showing that the various methods for collision resolution lead to different numbers of probes. But probe counting does not tell the whole story, since the time per probe varies in different methods, and the latter variation has a noticeable effect on the running time (as we have seen in Fig. 42). Linear probing accesses the table more frequently than the other methods shown in Fig. 44, but it has the advantage of simplicity. Furthermore, even linear probing isn't terribly bad: When the table is 90 percent full, Algorithm L requires fewer than 5.5 probes, on the average, to locate a random item in the table. (However, a 90-percent-full table does require about 50.5 probes for every *new* item inserted by Algorithm L.)

Figure 44 shows that the chaining methods are quite economical with respect to the number of probes, but the extra memory space needed for link fields sometimes makes open addressing more attractive for small records. For example, if we have to choose between a chained hash table of capacity 500 and an open hash table of capacity 1000, the latter is clearly preferable, since it allows efficient searching when 500 records are present and it is capable of absorbing twice as much data. On the other hand, sometimes the record size and format will allow space for link fields at virtually no extra cost. (See exercise 65.)

How do hash methods compare with the other search strategies we have studied in this chapter? From the standpoint of speed we can argue that they are better, when the number of records is large, because the average search time for a hash method stays bounded as $N \to \infty$ if we stipulate that the table never gets too full. For example, Program L will take only about 55 units of time for a successful search when the table is 90 percent full; this beats the fastest MIX binary search routine we have seen (exercise 6.2.1–24) when N is greater than 600 or so, at the cost of only 11 percent in storage space. Moreover the binary search is suitable only for fixed tables, while a hash table allows efficient insertions.

We can also compare Program L to the tree-oriented search methods that allow dynamic insertions. Program L with a 90-percent-full table is faster than Program 6.2.2T when N is greater than about 90, and faster than Program 6.3D (exercise 6.3–9) when N is greater than about 75.

Only one search method in this chapter is efficient for successful searching with virtually no storage overhead, namely Brent's variation of Algorithm D. His method allows us to put N records into a table of size $M = N + 1$, and to find any record in about 2.5 probes on the average. No extra space for link fields or tag bits is needed; however, an unsuccessful search will be very slow, requiring about $N/2$ probes.

Thus hashing has several advantages. On the other hand, there are three important respects in which hash table searching is inferior to other methods:

a) After an unsuccessful search in a hash table, we know only that the desired key is not present. Search methods based on comparisons always yield more information; they allow us to find the largest key $\leq K$ and/or the smallest key $\geq K$. This is important in many applications; for example, it allows us to interpolate function values from a stored table. We can also use comparison-based algorithms to locate all keys that lie *between* two given values K and K'. Furthermore the tree search algorithms of Section 6.2 make it easy to traverse the contents of a table in ascending order, without sorting it separately.

b) The storage allocation for hash tables is often somewhat difficult; we have to dedicate a certain area of the memory for use as the hash table, and it may not be obvious how much space should be allotted. If we provide too much memory, we may be wasting storage at the expense of other lists or other computer users; but if we don't provide enough room, the table will overflow. By contrast, the tree search and insertion algorithms deal with trees that grow no larger than necessary. In a virtual memory environment we can keep memory accesses localized if we use tree search or digital tree search, instead of creating a large hash table that requires the operating system to access a new page nearly every time we hash a key.

c) Finally, we need a great deal of faith in probability theory when we use hashing methods, since they are efficient only on the average, while their worst case is terrible! As in the case of random number generators, we can never be completely sure that a hash function will perform properly when it is applied to a new set of data. Therefore hash tables are inappropriate for certain real-time applications such as air traffic control, where people's lives are at stake; the balanced tree algorithms of Sections 6.2.3 and 6.2.4 are much safer, since they provide guaranteed upper bounds on the search time.

History. The idea of hashing appears to have been originated by H. P. Luhn, who wrote an internal IBM memorandum in January 1953 that suggested the use of chaining; in fact, his suggestion was one of the first applications of linked linear lists. He pointed out the desirability of using buckets that contain more than one element, for external searching. Shortly afterwards, A. D. Lin carried Luhn's analysis further, and suggested a technique for handling overflows that used "degenerative addresses"; for example, the overflows from primary bucket 2748 were put in secondary bucket 274; overflows from that bucket went to tertiary bucket 27, and so on, assuming the presence of 10000 primary buckets, 1000 secondary buckets, 100 tertiary buckets, etc. The hash functions originally suggested by Luhn were digital in nature; for example, he combined adjacent pairs of key digits by adding them mod 10, so that 31415926 would be compressed to 4548.

At about the same time the idea of hashing occurred independently to another group of IBMers: Gene M. Amdahl, Elaine M. Boehm, N. Rochester, and Arthur L. Samuel, who were building an assembly program for the IBM 701. In order to handle the collision problem, Amdahl originated the idea of open addressing with linear probing. [See also Derr and Luke, *JACM* **3** (1956), 303.]

Hash coding was first described in the open literature by Arnold I. Dumey, *Computers and Automation* **5**, 12 (December 1956), 6–9. He was the first to mention the idea of dividing by a prime number and using the remainder as the hash address. Dumey's interesting article mentions chaining but not open addressing. A. P. Ershov of Russia independently discovered linear open addressing in 1957 [*Doklady Akad. Nauk SSSR* **118** (1958), 427–430]; he published empirical results about the number of probes, conjecturing correctly that the average number of probes per successful search is < 2 when $N/M < 2/3$.

A classic article by W. W. Peterson, *IBM J. Research & Development* **1** (1957), 130–146, was the first major paper dealing with the problem of searching in large files. Peterson defined open addressing in general, analyzed the performance of uniform probing, and gave numerous empirical statistics about the behavior of linear open addressing with various bucket sizes, noting the degradation in performance that occurred when items were deleted. Another comprehensive survey of the subject was published six years later by Werner Buchholz [*IBM Systems J.* **2** (1963), 86–111], who gave an especially good discussion of hash functions. Correct analyses of Algorithm L were first published by A. G. Konheim and B. Weiss, *SIAM J. Appl. Math.* **14** (1966), 1266–1274; V. Podderjugin, *Wissenschaftliche Zeitschrift der Technischen Universität Dresden* **17** (1968), 1087–1089.

Up to this time linear probing was the only type of open addressing scheme that had appeared in the literature, but another scheme based on repeated random probing by independent hash functions had independently been developed by several people (see exercise 48). During the next few years hashing became very widely used, but hardly anything more was published about it. Then Robert Morris wrote a very influential survey of the subject [*CACM* **11** (1968), 38–44], in which he introduced the idea of random probing with secondary clustering. Morris's paper touched off a flurry of activity that culminated in Algorithm D and its refinements.

It is interesting to note that the word "hashing" apparently never appeared in print, with its present meaning, until the late 1960s, although it had already become common jargon in several parts of the world by that time. The first published appearance of the word seems to have been in H. Hellerman's book *Digital Computer System Principles* (New York: McGraw–Hill, 1967), 152; the only previous occurrence among approximately 60 relevant documents studied by the author as this section was being written was in an unpublished memorandum written by W. W. Peterson in 1961. Somehow the verb "to hash" magically became standard terminology for key transformation during the mid-1960s, yet nobody was rash enough to use such an undignified word in print until 1967!

Later developments. Many advances in the theory and practice of hashing have been made since the author first prepared this chapter in 1972, although the basic ideas discussed above still remain useful for ordinary applications. For example, the book *Design and Analysis of Coalesced Hashing* by J. S. Vitter and W.-C. Chen (New York: Oxford Univ. Press, 1987) discusses and analyzes several instructive variants of Algorithm C.

From a practical standpoint, the most important hash technique invented in the late 1970s is probably the method that Witold Litwin called *linear hashing* [*Proc. 6th International Conf. on Very Large Databases* (1980), 212–223]. Linear hashing — which incidentally has nothing to do with the classical technique of linear probing — allows the number of hash addresses to grow and/or contract gracefully as items are inserted and/or deleted. An excellent discussion of linear hashing, including comparisons with other methods for internal searching, has been given by Per-Åke Larson in *CACM* **31** (1988), 446–457; see also W. G. Griswold and G. M. Townsend, *Software Practice & Exp.* **23** (1993), 351–367, for improvements when many large and/or small tables are present simultaneously. Linear hashing can also be used for huge databases that are distributed between many different sites on a network [see Litwin, Neimat, and Schneider, *ACM Trans. Database Syst.* **21** (1996), 480–525]. An alternative scheme called *extendible hashing*, which has the property that at most two references to external pages are needed to retrieve any record, was proposed at about the same time by R. Fagin, J. Nievergelt, N. Pippenger, and H. R. Strong [*ACM Trans. Database Syst.* **4** (1979), 315–344]; related ideas had been explored by G. D. Knott, *Proc. ACM-SIGFIDET Workshop on Data Description, Access and Control* (1971), 187–206. Both linear hashing and extendible hashing are preferable to the *B*-trees of Section 6.2.4, when the order of keys is unimportant.

In the theoretical realm, more complicated methods have been devised by which it is possible to guarantee $O(1)$ maximum time per access, with $O(1)$ average amortized time per insertion and deletion, regardless of the keys being examined; moreover, the total storage used at any time is bounded by a constant times the number of items currently present, plus another additive constant. This result, which builds on ideas of Fredman, Komlós, and Szemerédi [*JACM* **31** (1984), 538–544], is due to Dietzfelbinger, Karlin, Mehlhorn, Meyer auf der Heide, Rohnert, and Tarjan [*SICOMP* **23** (1994), 738–761].

EXERCISES

1. [*20*] When the instruction 9H in Table 1 is reached, how small and how large can the contents of rI1 possibly be, assuming that bytes 1, 2, 3 of K each contain alphabetic character codes less than 30?

2. [*20*] Find a reasonably common English word not in Table 1 that could be added to that table without changing the program.

3. [*23*] Explain why no program beginning with the five instructions

```
LD1  K(1:1)   or   LD1N  K(1:1)
LD2  K(2:2)   or   LD2N  K(2:2)
INC1 a,2
LD2  K(3:3)
J2Z  9F
```

could be used in place of the more complicated program in Table 1, for any constant a, since unique addresses would not be produced for the given keys.

4. [*M30*] How many people should be invited to a party in order to make it likely that there are *three* with the same birthday?

5. [*15*] Mr. B. C. Dull was writing a FORTRAN compiler using a decimal MIX computer, and he needed a symbol table to keep track of the names of variables in the FORTRAN program being compiled. These names were restricted to be at most ten characters in length. He decided to use a hash table with $M = 100$, and to use the fast hash function $h(K) = $ leftmost byte of K. Was this a good idea?

6. [*15*] Would it be wise to change the first two instructions of (3) to LDA K; ENTX 0?

7. [*HM30*] (*Polynomial hashing.*) The purpose of this exercise is to consider the construction of polynomials $P(x)$ such as (10), which convert n-bit keys into m-bit addresses, in such a way that distinct keys differing in t or fewer bits will hash to different addresses. Given n and $t \leq n$, and given an integer k such that n divides $2^k - 1$, we shall construct a polynomial whose degree m is a function of n, t, and k. (Usually n is increased, if necessary, so that k can be chosen to be reasonably small.)

Let S be the smallest set of integers such that $\{1, 2, \ldots, t\} \subseteq S$ and $(2j)$ mod $n \in S$ for all $j \in S$. For example, when $n = 15$, $k = 4$, and $t = 6$, we have $S = \{1, 2, 3, 4, 5, 6, 8, 10, 12, 9\}$. We now define the polynomial $P(x) = \prod_{j \in S}(x - \alpha^j)$, where α is an element of order n in the finite field $\mathrm{GF}(2^k)$, and where the coefficients of $P(x)$ are computed in this field. The degree m of $P(x)$ is the number of elements of S. Since α^{2j} is a root of $P(x)$ whenever α^j is a root, it follows that the coefficients p_i of $P(x)$ satisfy $p_i^2 = p_i$, so they are 0 or 1.

Prove that if $R(x) = r_{n-1}x^{n-1} + \cdots + r_1 x + r_0$ is any nonzero polynomial modulo 2, with at most t nonzero coefficients, then $R(x)$ is not a multiple of $P(x)$ modulo 2. [It follows that the corresponding hash function behaves as advertised.]

8. [*M34*] (*The three-distance theorem.*) Let θ be an irrational number between 0 and 1, whose regular continued fraction representation in the notation of Section 4.5.3 is $\theta = /\!/a_1, a_2, a_3, \ldots /\!/$. Let $q_0 = 0$, $p_0 = 1$, $q_1 = 1$, $p_1 = 0$, and $q_{k+1} = a_k q_k + q_{k-1}$, $p_{k+1} = a_k p_k + p_{k-1}$ for $k \geq 1$. Let $\{x\}$ denote x mod $1 = x - \lfloor x \rfloor$, and let $\{x\}^+$ denote $x - \lceil x \rceil + 1$. As the points $\{\theta\}, \{2\theta\}, \{3\theta\}, \ldots$ are successively inserted into the interval $[0 .. 1]$, let the line segments be numbered as they appear in such a way that the first segment of a given length is number 0, the next is number 1, etc. Prove that the following statements are all true: Interval number s of length $\{t\theta\}$, where $t = rq_k + q_{k-1}$ and $0 \leq r < a_k$ and k is even and $0 \leq s < q_k$, has left endpoint $\{s\theta\}$ and right endpoint $\{(s+t)\theta\}^+$. Interval number s of length $1 - \{t\theta\}$, where $t = rq_k + q_{k-1}$ and $0 \leq r < a_k$ and k is odd and $0 \leq s < q_k$, has left endpoint $\{(s + t)\theta\}$ and right endpoint $\{s\theta\}^+$. Every positive integer n can be uniquely represented as $n = rq_k + q_{k-1} + s$ for some $k \geq 1$, $1 \leq r \leq a_k$, and $0 \leq s < q_k$. In terms of this representation, just before the point $\{n\theta\}$ is inserted the n intervals present are

the first s intervals (numbered 0, $\ldots$, $s - 1$) of length $\{(-1)^k(rq_k + q_{k-1})\theta\}$;

the first $n - q_k$ intervals (numbered 0, $\ldots$, $n - q_k - 1$) of length $\{(-1)^{k+1}q_k\theta\}$;

the last $q_k - s$ intervals (numbered s, $\ldots$, $q_k - 1$) of length $\{(-1)^k((r-1)q_k + q_{k-1})\theta\}^+$.

The operation of inserting $\{n\theta\}$ removes interval number s of the third type and converts it into interval number s of the first type, number $n - q_k$ of the second type.

9. [*M30*] When we successively insert the points $\{\theta\}$, $\{2\theta\}$, $\ldots$ into the interval $[0 .. 1]$, Theorem S asserts that each new point always breaks up one of the largest remaining intervals. If the interval $[a .. c]$ is thereby broken into two parts $[a .. b]$, $[b .. c]$, we may call it a *bad break* if one of these parts is more than twice as long as the other, namely if $b - a > 2(c - b)$ or $c - b > 2(b - a)$.

Prove that bad breaks will occur for some $\{n\theta\}$ unless θ mod $1 = \phi^{-1}$ or ϕ^{-2}; and the latter values of θ *never* produce bad breaks.

10. [*M38*] (R. L. Graham.) If $\theta, \alpha_1, \ldots, \alpha_d$ are real numbers with $\alpha_1 = 0$, and if $n_1, \ldots, n_d$ are positive integers, and if the points $\{n\theta + \alpha_j\}$ are inserted into the interval $[0 .. 1]$ for $0 \leq n < n_j$ and $1 \leq j \leq d$, prove that the resulting $n_1 + \cdots + n_d$ (possibly empty) intervals have at most $3d$ different lengths.

11. [*16*] Successful searches are often more frequent than unsuccessful ones. Would it therefore be a good idea to interchange lines 12–13 of Program C with lines 10–11?

▶ **12.** [*21*] Show that Program C can be rewritten so that there is only one conditional jump instruction in the inner loop. Compare the running time of the modified program with the original.

▶ **13.** [*24*] (*Abbreviated keys.*) Let $h(K)$ be a hash function, and let $q(K)$ be a function of K such that K can be determined once $h(K)$ and $q(K)$ are given. For example, in division hashing we may let $h(K) = K \bmod M$ and $q(K) = \lfloor K/M \rfloor$; in multiplicative hashing we may let $h(K)$ be the leading bits of $(AK/w) \bmod 1$, and $q(K)$ can be the other bits.

Show that when chaining is used without overlapping lists, we need only store $q(K)$ instead of K in each record. (This almost saves the space needed for the link fields.) Modify Algorithm C so that it allows such abbreviated keys by avoiding overlapping lists, yet uses no auxiliary storage locations for overflow records.

14. [*24*] (E. W. Elcock.) Show that it is possible to let a large hash table *share memory* with any number of other linked lists. Let every word of the list area have a 2-bit TAG field and two link fields called LINK and AUX, with the following interpretation:

TAG(P) = 0 indicates a word in the list of available space; LINK(P) points to the next entry in this list, and AUX(P) is unused.

TAG(P) = 1 indicates a word in use where P is not the hash address of any key in the hash table; the other fields of the word in location P may have any desired format.

TAG(P) = 2 indicates that P is the hash address of at least one key; AUX(P) points to a linked list specifying all such keys, and LINK(P) points to another word in the list memory. Whenever a word with TAG(P) = 2 is accessed during the processing of any list, we set P ← LINK(P) repeatedly until reaching a word with TAG(P) ≤ 1. (For efficiency we might also then change prior links so that it will not be necessary to skip over the same entries again and again.)

Define suitable algorithms for inserting and retrieving keys in such a hash table.

15. [*16*] Why is it a good idea for Algorithm L and Algorithm D to signal overflow when $N = M - 1$ instead of when $N = M$?

16. [*10*] Program L says that K should not be zero. But doesn't it actually work even when K is zero?

17. [*15*] Why not simply define $h_2(K) = h_1(K)$ in (25), when $h_1(K) \neq 0$?

▶ **18.** [*21*] Is (31) better or worse than (30), as a substitute for lines 10–13 of Program D? Give your answer on the basis of the average values of A, $S1$, and C.

19. [*40*] Empirically test the effect of restricting the range of $h_2(K)$ in Algorithm D, so that (a) $1 \le h_2(K) \le r$ for $r = 1, 2, 3, \ldots, 10$; (b) $1 \le h_2(K) \le \rho M$ for $\rho = \frac{1}{10}, \frac{2}{10}, \ldots, \frac{9}{10}$.

20. [*M25*] (R. Krutar.) Change Algorithm D as follows, avoiding the hash function $h_2(K)$: In step D3, set $c \leftarrow 0$; and at the beginning of step D4, set $c \leftarrow c + 1$. Prove that if $M = 2^m$, the corresponding probe sequence $h_1(K), (h_1(K) - 1) \bmod M$, $\ldots, \left(h_1(K) - \binom{M}{2}\right) \bmod M$ will be a permutation of $\{0, 1, \ldots, M-1\}$. When this "quadratic probing" method is programmed for MIX, how does it compare with the three programs considered in Fig. 42, assuming that the algorithm behaves like random probing with secondary clustering?

▶ **21.** [*20*] Suppose that we wish to delete a record from a table constructed by Algorithm D, marking it "deleted" as suggested in the text. Should we also decrease the variable N that is used to govern Algorithm D?

22. [*27*] Prove that Algorithm R leaves the table exactly as it would have been if KEY[i] had never been inserted in the first place.

▶ **23.** [*33*] Design an algorithm analogous to Algorithm R, for deleting entries from a chained hash table that has been constructed by Algorithm C.

24. [*M20*] Suppose that the set of all possible keys that can occur has MP elements, where exactly P keys hash to any given address. (In practical cases, P is very large; for example, if the keys are arbitrary 10-digit numbers and if $M = 10^3$, we have $P = 10^7$.) Assume that $M \geq 7$ and $N = 7$. If seven distinct keys are selected at random from the set of all possible keys, what is the exact probability that the hash sequence 1 2 6 2 1 6 1 will be obtained (namely that $h(K_1) = 1$, $h(K_2) = 2$, ..., $h(K_7) = 1$), as a function of M and P?

25. [*M19*] Explain why Eq. (39) is true.

26. [*M20*] How many hash sequences $a_1 a_2 \ldots a_9$ yield the pattern of occupied cells (21), using linear probing?

27. [*M27*] Complete the proof of Theorem K. [*Hint:* Let

$$s(n, x, y) = \sum_k \binom{n}{k} (x + k)^{k+1} (y - k)^{n-k-1} (y - n);$$

use Abel's binomial theorem, Eq. 1.2.6–(16), to prove that $s(n, x, y) = x(x + y)^n + ns(n-1, x+1, y-1)$.]

28. [*M30*] In the old days when computers were much slower than they are now, it was possible to watch the lights flashing and see how fast Algorithm L was running. When the table began to fill up, some entries would be processed very quickly, while others took a great deal of time.

This experience suggests that the standard deviation of the number of probes in an unsuccessful search is rather high, when linear probing is used. Find a formula that expresses the variance in terms of the Q_r functions defined in Theorem K, and estimate the variance when $N = \alpha M$ as $M \to \infty$.

29. [*M21*] (*The parking problem.*) A certain one-way street has m parking spaces in a row, numbered 1 through m. A man and his dozing wife drive by, and suddenly she wakes up and orders him to park immediately. He dutifully parks at the first available space; but if there are no places left that he can get to without backing up (that is, if his wife awoke when the car approached space k, but spaces k, $k + 1$, ..., m are all full), he expresses his regrets and drives on.

Suppose, in fact, that this happens for n different cars, where the jth wife wakes up just in time to park at space a_j. In how many of the sequences $a_1 \ldots a_n$ will all of the cars get safely parked, assuming that the street is initially empty and that nobody leaves after parking? For example, when $m = n = 9$ and $a_1 \ldots a_9 = 3\ 1\ 4\ 1\ 5\ 9\ 2\ 6\ 5$, the cars get parked as follows:

[*Hint:* Use the analysis of linear probing.]

30. [*M38*] When $n = m$ in the parking problem of exercise 29, show that all cars get parked if and only if there exists a permutation $p_1 p_2 \ldots p_n$ of $\{1, 2, \ldots, n\}$ such that $a_j \leq p_j$ for all j.

31. [*M40*] When $n = m$ in the parking problem of exercise 29, the number of solutions turns out to be $(n+1)^{n-1}$; and from exercise 2.3.4.4–22 we know that this is the same as the number of free trees on $n+1$ labeled vertices! Find an interesting connection between parking sequences and trees.

32. [*M27*] Prove that the system of equations (44) has a unique solution $(c_0, c_1, \ldots, c_{M-1})$, whenever $b_0, b_1, \ldots, b_{M-1}$ are nonnegative integers whose sum is less than M. Design an algorithm to find that solution.

▶ **33.** [*M23*] Explain why (51) is only an approximation to the true average number of probes made by Algorithm L. What was there about the derivation of (51) that wasn't rigorously exact?

▶ **34.** [*M23*] The purpose of this exercise is to investigate the average number of probes in a chained hash table when the lists are kept separate as in Fig. 38.
  a) What is P_{Nk}, the probability that a given list has length k, when the M^N hash sequences (35) are equally likely?
  b) Find the generating function $P_n(z) = \sum_{k \geq 0} P_{Nk} z^k$.
  c) Express the average number of probes for a successful search in terms of this generating function.
  d) Deduce the average number of probes in an *unsuccessful* search, considering variants of the data structure in which the following conventions are used: (i) hashing is always to a list head (see Fig. 38); (ii) hashing is to a table position (see Fig. 40), but all keys except the first of a list go into a separate overflow area; (iii) hashing is to a table position and all entries appear in the hash table.

35. [*M24*] Continuing exercise 34, what is the average number of probes in an unsuccessful search when the individual lists are kept in order by their key values? Consider data structures (i), (ii), and (iii).

36. [*M23*] Continuing exercise 34(d), find the *variance* of the number of probes when the search is unsuccessful, using data structures (i) and (ii).

▶ **37.** [*M29*] Equation (19) gives the average number of probes in separate chaining when the search is successful; what is the *variance* of that number of probes?

38. [*M32*] (*Tree hashing.*) A clever programmer might try to use binary search trees instead of linear lists in the chaining method, thereby combining Algorithm 6.2.2T with hashing. Analyze the average number of probes that would be required by this compound algorithm, for both successful and unsuccessful searches. [*Hint:* See Eq. 5.2.1–(15).]

39. [*M28*] Let $c_N(k)$ be the total number of lists of length k formed when Algorithm C is applied to all M^N hash sequences (35). Find a recurrence relation on the numbers $c_N(k)$ that makes it possible to determine a simple formula for the sum
$$S_N = \sum_k \binom{k}{2} c_N(k).$$

How is S_N related to the number of probes in an unsuccessful search by Algorithm C?

40. [*M33*] Equation (15) gives the average number of probes used by Algorithm C in an unsuccessful search; what is the *variance* of that number of probes?

41. [*M40*] Analyze T_N, the average number of times the index R is decreased by 1 when the $(N + 1)$st item is being inserted by Algorithm C.

▶ **42.** [*M20*] Derive (17), the probability that Algorithm C succeeds immediately.

43. [*HM44*] Analyze a modification of Algorithm C that uses a table of size $M' \geq M$. Only the first M locations are used for hashing, so the first $M' - M$ empty nodes found in step C5 will be in the extra locations of the table. For fixed M', what choice of M in the range $1 \leq M \leq M'$ leads to the best performance?

44. [*M43*] (*Random probing with secondary clustering.*) The object of this exercise is to determine the expected number of probes in the open addressing scheme with probe sequence

$$h(K), \quad (h(K) + p_1) \bmod M, \quad (h(K) + p_2) \bmod M, \quad \ldots, \quad (h(K) + p_{M-1}) \bmod M,$$

where $p_1 \, p_2 \ldots p_{M-1}$ is a randomly chosen permutation of $\{1, 2, \ldots, M-1\}$ that depends on $h(K)$. In other words, all keys with the same value of $h(K)$ follow the same probe sequence, and the $(M - 1)!^M$ possible choices of M probe sequences with this property are equally likely.

This situation can be modeled accurately by the following experimental procedure performed on an initially empty linear array of size m. Do the following operation n times: "With probability p, occupy the leftmost empty position. Otherwise (that is, with probability $q = 1 - p$), select any table position except the one at the extreme left, with each of these $m - 1$ positions equally likely. If the selected position is empty, occupy it; otherwise select *any* empty position (including the leftmost) and occupy it, considering each of the empty positions equally likely."

For example, when $m = 5$ and $n = 3$, the array configuration after such an experiment will be (occupied, occupied, empty, occupied, empty) with probability

$$\tfrac{7}{192}qqq + \tfrac{1}{6}pqq + \tfrac{1}{6}qpq + \tfrac{11}{64}qqp + \tfrac{1}{3}ppq + \tfrac{1}{4}pqp + \tfrac{1}{4}qpp.$$

(This procedure corresponds to random probing with secondary clustering, when $p = 1/m$, since we can renumber the table entries so that a particular probe sequence is 0, 1, 2, ... and all the others are random.)

Find a formula for the average number of occupied positions at the left of the array (namely 2 in the example above). Also find the asymptotic value of this quantity when $p = 1/m$, $n = \alpha(m + 1)$, and $m \to \infty$.

45. [*M43*] Solve the analog of exercise 44 with *tertiary clustering*, when the probe sequence begins $h_1(K)$, $((h_1(K) + h_2(K)) \bmod M$, and the succeeding probes are randomly chosen depending only on $h_1(K)$ and $h_2(K)$. (Thus the $(M-2)!^{M(M-1)}$ possible choices of $M(M - 1)$ probe sequences with this property are considered to be equally likely.) Is this procedure asymptotically equivalent to uniform probing?

46. [*M42*] Determine C_N' and C_N for the open addressing method that uses the probe sequence

$$h(K), \; 0, \; 1, \; \ldots, \; h(K) - 1, \; h(K) + 1, \; \ldots, \; M - 1.$$

47. [*M25*] Find the average number of probes needed by open addressing when the probe sequence is

$$h(K), \; h(K) - 1, \; h(K) + 1, \; h(K) - 2, \; h(K) + 2, \; \ldots.$$

This probe sequence was once suggested because all the distances between consecutive probes are distinct when M is even. [*Hint:* Find the trick and this problem is easy.]

▶ **48.** [*M21*] Analyze the open addressing method that probes locations $h_1(K)$, $h_2(K)$, $h_3(K), \ldots$, given an infinite sequence of mutually independent random hash functions $\langle h_n(K) \rangle$. In this setup it is possible to probe the same location twice, for example if $h_1(K) = h_2(K)$, but such coincidences are rather unlikely until the table gets full.

49. [*HM24*] Generalizing exercise 34 to the case of b records per bucket, determine the average number of probes (external memory accesses) C_N and C'_N, for chaining with separate lists, assuming that a list containing k elements requires $\max(1, k - b + 1)$ probes in an unsuccessful search. Instead of using the exact probability P_{Nk} as in exercise 34, use the *Poisson approximation*

$$\binom{N}{k}\left(\frac{1}{M}\right)^k\left(1 - \frac{1}{M}\right)^{N-k} = \frac{N}{M}\frac{N-1}{M}\cdots\frac{N-k+1}{M}\left(1 - \frac{1}{M}\right)^N\left(1 - \frac{1}{M}\right)^{-k}\frac{1}{k!}$$

$$= \frac{e^{-\rho}\rho^k}{k!}(1 + O(k^2/M)),$$

which is valid for $N = \rho M$ and $k \le \sqrt{M}$ as $M \to \infty$; derive formulas (57) and (58).

50. [*M20*] Show that $Q_1(M, N) = M - (M - N - 1)Q_0(M, N)$, in the notation of (42). [*Hint:* Prove first that $Q_1(M, N) = (N + 1)Q_0(M, N) - NQ_0(M, N-1)$.]

51. [*HM17*] Express the function $R(\alpha, n)$ defined in (55) in terms of the function Q_0 defined in (42).

52. [*HM20*] Prove that $Q_0(M, N) = \int_0^\infty e^{-t}(1 + t/M)^N\, dt$.

53. [*HM20*] Prove that the function $R(\alpha, n)$ can be expressed in terms of the incomplete gamma function, and use the result of exercise 1.2.11.3–9 to find the asymptotic value of $R(\alpha, n)$ to $O(n^{-2})$ as $n \to \infty$, for fixed $\alpha < 1$.

54. [*HM28*] Show that when $b = 1$, Eq. (61) is equivalent to Eq. (23). *Hint:* We have

$$t_n(\alpha) = \frac{(-1)^{n-1}}{n!\,\alpha} \sum_{m>n} \frac{(-n\alpha)^m}{m(m-1)(m-n-1)!}.$$

55. [*HM43*] Generalize the Schay–Spruth model, discussed after Theorem P, to the case of M buckets of size b. Prove that $C(z)$ is equal to $Q(z)/(B(z) - z^b)$, where $Q(z)$ is a polynomial of degree b and $Q(1) = 0$. Show that the average number of probes is

$$1 + \frac{M}{N}C'(1) = 1 + \frac{1}{b}\left(\frac{1}{1 - q_1} + \cdots + \frac{1}{1 - q_{b-1}} - \frac{1}{2}\frac{B''(1) - b(b-1)}{B'(1) - b}\right),$$

where $q_1, \ldots, q_{b-1}$ are the roots of $Q(z)/(z - 1)$. Replacing the binomial probability distribution $B(z)$ by the Poisson approximation $P(z) = e^{b\alpha(z-1)}$, where $\alpha = N/Mb$, and using Lagrange's inversion formula (see Eq. 2.3.4.4–(21) and exercise 4.7–8), reduce your answer to Eq. (61).

56. [*HM43*] Generalize Theorem K, obtaining an exact analysis of linear probing with buckets of size b. What is the asymptotic number of probes in a successful search when the table is full ($N = Mb$)?

57. [*M47*] Does the uniform assignment of probabilities to probe sequences give the minimum value of C_N, over all open addressing methods?

58. [*M21*] (S. C. Johnson.) Find ten permutations on $\{0, 1, 2, 3, 4\}$ that are equivalent to uniform probing in the sense of Theorem U.

59. [*M25*] Prove that if an assignment of probabilities to permutations is equivalent to uniform probing, in the sense of Theorem U, the number of permutations with nonzero probabilities exceeds M^a for any fixed exponent a, when M is sufficiently large.

60. [*M47*] Let us say that an open addressing scheme involves *single hashing* if it uses exactly M probe sequences, one beginning with each possible value of $h(K)$, each of which occurs with probability $1/M$.

Are the best single-hashing schemes (in the sense of minimum C_N) asymptotically better than the random ones described by (29)? In particular, is $C_{\alpha M} \geq 1 + \frac{1}{2}\alpha + \frac{1}{2}\alpha^2 + O(\alpha^3)$ as $M \to \infty$?

61. [*M46*] Is the method analyzed in exercise 46 the worst possible single-hashing scheme, in the sense of exercise 60?

62. [*M49*] A single hashing scheme is called *cyclic* if the increments $p_1 p_2 \ldots p_{M-1}$ in the notation of exercise 44 are fixed for all K. (Examples of such methods are linear probing and the sequences considered in exercises 20 and 47.) An *optimum* single hashing scheme is one for which C_M is minimum, over all $(M-1)!^M$ single hashing schemes for a given M. When $M \leq 5$ the best single hashing schemes are cyclic. Is this true for all M?

63. [*M25*] If repeated random insertions and deletions are made in a hash table, how many independent insertions are needed on the average before all M locations have become occupied at one time or another? (This is the mean time to failure of the deletion method that simply marks cells "deleted.")

64. [*M41*] Analyze the expected behavior of Algorithm R (deletion with linear probing). How many times will step R4 be performed, on the average?

▶ **65.** [*20*] (*Variable-length keys.*) Many applications of hash tables deal with keys that can be any number of characters long. In such cases we can't simply store the key in the table as in the programs of this section. What would be a good way to deal with variable-length keys in a hash table on the MIX computer?

▶ **66.** [*25*] (Ole Amble, 1973.) Is it possible to insert keys into an open hash table making use also of their numerical or alphabetic order, so that a search with Algorithm L or Algorithm D is known to be unsuccessful whenever a key *smaller* than the search argument is encountered?

67. [*M41*] If Algorithm L inserts N keys with respective hash addresses $a_1 a_2 \ldots a_N$, let d_j be the displacement of the jth key from its home address a_j; then $C_N = 1 + (d_1 + d_2 + \cdots + d_N)/N$. Theorem P tells us that permutation of the a's has no effect on the sum $d_1 + d_2 + \cdots + d_N$. However, such permutation might drastically change the sum $d_1^2 + d_2^2 + \cdots + d_N^2$. For example, the hash sequence $1\ 2\ \ldots\ N{-}1\ N{-}1$ makes $d_1 d_2 \ldots d_{N-1} d_N = 0\ 0\ \ldots\ 0\ N{-}1$ and $\sum d_j^2 = (N-1)^2$, while its reflection $N{-}1\ N{-}1\ \ldots\ 2\ 1$ leads to much more civilized displacements $0\ 1\ \ldots\ 1\ 1$ for which $\sum d_j^2 = N - 1$.

a) Which rearrangement of $a_1 a_2 \ldots a_N$ minimizes $\sum d_j^2$?

b) Explain how to modify Algorithm L so that it maintains a least-variance set of displacements after every insertion.

c) Determine the average value of $\sum d_j^2$ with and without this modification.

68. [*M41*] What is the variance of the average number of probes in a successful search by Algorithm L? In particular, what is the average of $(d_1+d_2+\cdots+d_N)^2$ in the notation of exercise 67?

69. [*M25*] (Andrew Yao.) Prove that all cyclic single hashing schemes in the sense of exercise 62 satisfy the inequality $C'_{\alpha M} \geq \frac{1}{2}(1 + 1/(1 - \alpha))$. [*Hint:* Show that an unsuccessful search takes exactly k probes with probability $p_k \leq (M - N)/M$.]

70. [*HM43*] Prove that the expected number of probes that are needed to insert the $(\alpha M + 1)$st item with double hashing is at most the expected number needed to insert the $(\alpha M + \sqrt{O(\log M)/M})$th item with uniform probing.

71. [*40*] Experiment with the behavior of Algorithm C when it has been adapted to external searching as described in the text.

▶ **72.** [*M28*] (*Universal hashing.*) Imagine a gigantic matrix H that has one column for every possible key K. The entries of H are numbers between 0 and $M - 1$; the rows of H represent hash functions. We say that H defines a *universal family of hash functions* if any two columns agree in at most R/M rows, where R is the total number of rows.

    a) Prove that if H is universal in this sense, and if we select a hash function h by choosing a row of H at random, then the expected size of the list containing any given key K in the method of separate chaining (Fig. 38) will be $\leq 1 + N/M$, after we have inserted any set of N distinct keys $K_1, K_2, \ldots, K_N$.

    b) Suppose each h_j in (9) is a randomly chosen mapping from the set of all characters to the set $\{0, 1, \ldots, M - 1\}$. Show that this corresponds to a universal family of hash functions.

    c) Would the result of (b) still be true if $h_j(0) = 0$ for all j, but $h_j(x)$ is random for $x \neq 0$?

73. [*M26*] (Carter and Wegman.) Show that part (b) of the previous exercise holds even when the h_j are not completely random functions, but they have either of the following special forms: (i) Let x_j be the binary number $(b_{j(n-1)} \ldots b_{j1} b_{j0})_2$. Then $h_j(x_j) = (a_{j(n-1)} b_{j(n-1)} + \cdots + a_{j1} b_{j1} + a_{j0} b_{j0}) \bmod M$, where each a_{jk} is chosen randomly modulo M. (ii) Let M be prime and assume that $0 \leq x_j < M$. Then $h_j(x_j) = (a_j x_j + b_j) \bmod M$, where a_j and b_j are chosen randomly modulo M.

74. [*M29*] Let H define a universal family of hash functions. Prove or disprove: Given any N distinct columns, and any row chosen at random, the expected number of zeros in those columns is $O(1) + O(N/M)$. [Thus, every list in the method of separate chaining will have this expected size.]

75. [*M26*] Prove or disprove the following statements about the hash function h of (9), when the h_j are independent random functions:

    a) The probability that $h(K) = m$ is $1/M$, for all $0 \leq m < M$.

    b) If $K \neq K'$, the probability that $h(K) = m$ and $h(K') = m'$ is $1/M^2$, for all $0 \leq m, m' < M$.

    c) If K, K', and K'' are distinct, the probability that $h(K) = m$, $h(K') = m'$, and $h(K'') = m''$ is $1/M^3$, for all $0 \leq m, m', m'' < M$.

    d) If K, K', K'', and K''' are distinct, the probability that $h(K) = m$, $h(K') = m'$, $h(K'') = m''$, and $h(K''') = m'''$ is $1/M^4$, for all $0 \leq m, m', m'', m''' < M$.

▶ **76.** [*M21*] Suggest a way to modify (9) for keys with variable length, preserving the properties of universal hashing.

77. [*M22*] Let H define a universal family of hash functions from 32-bit keys to 16-bit keys. (Thus H has 2^{32} columns, and $M = 2^{16}$, in the notation of exercise 72.) A 256-bit key can be regarded as the concatenation of eight 32-bit parts $x_1 x_2 x_3 x_4 x_5 x_6 x_7 x_8$; we can map it into a 16-bit address with the hash function

$$h_4\big(h_3\big(h_2(h_1(x_1)h_1(x_2))h_2(h_1(x_3)h_1(x_4))\big)h_3\big(h_2(h_1(x_5)h_1(x_6))h_2(h_1(x_7)h_1(x_8))\big)\big),$$

where h_1, h_2, h_3, and h_4 are randomly and independently chosen rows of H. (Here, for example, $h_1(x_1)h_1(x_2)$ stands for the 32-bit number obtained by concatenating $h_1(x_1)$ with $h_1(x_2)$.) Prove that the probability is less than 2^{-14} that two distinct keys hash to the same address. [This scheme requires substantially fewer random choices than (9).]

▶ **78.** [*M26*] (P. Woelfel.) If $0 \le x < 2^n$, let $h_{a,b}(x) = \lfloor (ax + b)/2^k \rfloor \bmod 2^{n-k}$. Show that the set $\{h_{a,b} \mid 0 < a < 2^n,\ a\text{ odd, and }0 \le b < 2^k\}$ is a universal family of hash functions from n-bit keys to $(n - k)$-bit keys. (These functions are particularly easy to implement on a binary computer.)

She made a hash of the proper names, to be sure.
— GRANT ALLEN, *The Tents of Shem* (1889)

HASH, x. There is no definition
for this word —
nobody knows what hash is.
— AMBROSE BIERCE, *The Devil's Dictionary* (1906)

6.5. RETRIEVAL ON SECONDARY KEYS

WE HAVE NOW COMPLETED our study of searching for *primary keys*, namely for keys that uniquely specify a record in a file. But it is sometimes necessary to conduct a search based on the values of other fields in the records besides the primary key; these other fields are often called *secondary keys* or *attributes* of the record. For example, in an enrollment file that contains information about the students at a university, it may be desirable to search for all sophomores from Ohio who are not majoring in mathematics or statistics; or to search for all unmarried French-speaking graduate student women; etc.

In general, we assume that each record contains several attributes, and we want to search for all records that have certain values of certain attributes. The specification of the desired records is called a *query*. Queries are usually restricted to at most the following three types:

a) A *simple query* that gives a specific value of a specific attribute; for example, "MAJOR = MATHEMATICS", or "RESIDENCE.STATE = OHIO".

b) A *range query* that gives a specific range of values for a specific attribute; for example, "COST < \$18.00", or "21 < AGE ≤ 23".

c) A *Boolean query* that consists of the previous types combined with the operations AND, OR, NOT; for example,

> "(CLASS = SOPHOMORE) AND (RESIDENCE.STATE = OHIO)
> AND NOT ((MAJOR = MATHEMATICS) OR (MAJOR = STATISTICS))".

The problem of discovering efficient search techniques for these three types of queries is already quite difficult, and therefore queries of more complicated types are usually not considered. For example, a railroad company might have a file giving the current status of all its freight cars; a query such as "find all empty refrigerator cars within 500 miles of Seattle" would not be explicitly allowed, unless "distance from Seattle" were an attribute stored within each record instead of a complicated function to be deduced from other attributes. And the use of logical quantifiers, in addition to AND, OR, and NOT, would introduce further complications, limited only by the imagination of the query-poser; given a file of baseball statistics, for example, we might ask for the longest consecutive hitting streak in night games. These examples are complicated, but they can still be handled by taking one pass through a suitably arranged file. Other queries are even more difficult — for example, to find all pairs of records that have the same values on five or more attributes (without specifying which attributes must match). Such queries may be regarded as general programming tasks that are beyond the scope of this discussion, although they can often be broken down into subproblems of the kind considered here.

Before we begin to study the various techniques for secondary key retrieval, it is important to put the subject in a proper economic context. Although a vast number of applications fit into the general framework of the three types of queries outlined above, not many of these applications are really suited to the sophisticated techniques we shall be studying, and some of them are better done by hand than by machine! People climb Mt. Everest "because it is there" and because tools have been developed that make the climb possible; similarly, when faced with a mountain of data, people are tempted to use a computer to find the answer to the most difficult queries they can dream up, in an online real-time environment, without properly balancing the cost. The desired calculations are possible, but they're not right for everyone's application.

For example, consider the following simple approach to secondary key retrieval: After *batching* a number of queries, we can do a sequential search through the entire file, retrieving all the relevant records. ("Batching" means that we accumulate a number of queries before doing anything about them.) This method is quite satisfactory if the file isn't too large and if the queries don't have to be handled immediately. It can be used even with tape files, and it only ties up the computer at odd intervals, so it will tend to be very economical in terms of equipment costs. Moreover, it will even handle computational queries of the "distance to Seattle" type discussed above.

Another simple way to facilitate secondary key retrieval is to let *people* do part of the work, by providing them with suitable printed indexes to the information. This method is often the most reasonable and economical way to proceed (provided, of course, that the old paper is recycled whenever a new index is printed), especially because people tend to notice interesting patterns when they have convenient access to masses of data.

The applications that are not satisfactorily handled by the simple schemes given above involve very large files for which quick responses to queries are important. Such a situation would occur, for example, if the file were continuously being queried by a number of simultaneous users, or if the queries were being generated by machine instead of by people. Our goal in this section will be to see how well we can do secondary key retrieval with conventional computers, under various assumptions about the file structure. Fortunately, the methods we will discuss are becoming more and more feasible in practice, as the cost of computation continues to decrease dramatically.

A lot of good ideas have been developed for dealing with the problem, but (as the reader will have guessed from all these precautionary remarks) the algorithms are by no means as good as those available for primary key retrieval. Because of the wide variety of files and applications, we will not be able to give a complete discussion of all the possibilities that have been considered, or to analyze the behavior of each algorithm in typical environments. The remainder of this section presents the basic approaches that have been proposed, and it is left to the reader's imagination to decide what combination of techniques is most appropriate in each particular case.

Inverted files. The first important class of techniques for secondary key retrieval is based on the idea of an *inverted file*. This does not mean that the file is turned upside down; it means that the roles of records and attributes are reversed. Instead of listing the attributes of a given record, we list the records having a given attribute.

We encounter inverted files (under other names) quite often in our daily lives. For example, the inverted file corresponding to a Russian-English dictionary is an English-Russian dictionary. The inverted file corresponding to this book is the index that appears at the close of the book. Accountants traditionally use "double-entry bookkeeping," where all transactions are entered both in a cash account and in a customer account, so that the current cash position and the current customer liability are both readily accessible.

In general, an inverted file usually doesn't stand by itself; it is to be used together with the original uninverted file. It provides duplicate, redundant information in order to speed up secondary key retrieval. The components of an inverted file are called *inverted lists*, namely the lists of all records having a given value of some attribute.

Like all lists, the inverted lists can be represented in many ways within a computer, and different modes of representation are appropriate at different times. Some secondary key fields have only two values (for example, "SEX"), and the corresponding inverted lists are quite long; but other fields typically have a great many values with few duplications (for example, "PHONENUMBER").

Imagine that we want to store the information in a telephone directory so that all entries can be retrieved on the basis of either name, phone number, or residence address. One solution is simply to make three separate files, oriented to retrieval on each type of key. Another idea is to combine the files, for example by making three hash tables that serve as the list heads for the chaining method. In the latter scheme, each record of the file would be an element of three lists, and it would therefore contain three link fields; this is the so-called *multilist* method illustrated in Fig. 13 of Section 2.2.6 and discussed further below. A third possibility is to combine the three files into one super file, by analogy with library card catalogues in which author cards, title cards, and subject cards are all alphabetized together.

A consideration of the format used in the index to this book leads to further ideas on inverted list representation. For secondary key fields in which there are typically five or so entries per attribute value, we can simply make a short sequential list of the record locations (analogous to page locations in a book index), following the key value. If related records tend to be clustered consecutively, a range specification code (for example, pages 559–582) is useful. If the records in the file tend to be reallocated frequently, it may be better to use primary keys instead of record locations in the inverted files, so that no updating needs to be done when the locations change; for example, references to Bible passages are always given by chapter and verse, and the index to some books is based on paragraph numbers instead of page numbers.

None of these ideas is especially appropriate for the case of a two-valued attribute like "SEX". In such a case only one inverted list is needed, of course, since the non-males will be female and conversely. If each value relates to about half the items of the file, the inverted list will be horribly long, but we can solve the problem rather nicely on a binary computer by using a bit string representation, with each bit specifying the value of a particular record. Thus the bit string 01001011101 . . . might mean that the first record in the file refers to a male, the second female, the next two male, etc.

Such methods suffice to handle simple queries about specific attribute values. A slight extension makes it possible to treat range queries, except that a comparison-based search scheme (Section 6.2) must be used instead of hashing.

For Boolean queries like "(MAJOR = MATHEMATICS) AND (RESIDENCE.STATE = OHIO)", we need to intersect two inverted lists. This can be done in several ways; for example, if both lists are ordered, one pass through each will pick out all common entries. Alternatively, we could select the *shortest* list and look up each of its records, checking the other attributes; but this method works only for AND's, not for OR's, and it is unattractive on external files because it requires many accesses to records that will not satisfy the query.

The same considerations show that a multilist organization as described above is inefficient for Boolean queries on an external file, since it implies many unnecessary accesses. For example, imagine what would happen if the index to this book were organized in a multilist manner: Each entry of the index would refer only to the last page on which its particular subject was mentioned; then on every page there would be a further reference, for each subject on that page, to the previous occurrence of that subject. In order to find all pages relevant to "[Analysis of algorithms] and [(External sorting) or (External searching)]", we would need to turn many pages. On the other hand, the same query can be resolved by looking at only two pages of the real index as it actually appears, doing simple operations on the inverted lists in order to find the small subset of pages that satisfy the query.

When an inverted list is represented as a bit string, Boolean combinations of simple queries are, of course, easily performed, because computers can manipulate bit strings at relatively high speed. For mixed queries in which some attributes are represented as sequential lists of record numbers while other attributes are represented as bit strings, it is not difficult to convert the sequential lists into bit strings, then to perform the Boolean operations on these bit strings.

A quantitative example of a hypothetical application may be helpful at this point. Assume that we have 1,000,000 records of 40 characters each, and that our file is stored on MIXTEC disks, as described in Section 5.4.9. The file itself therefore fills two disk units, and the inverted lists will probably fill several more. Each track contains 5000 characters = 30,000 bits, so an inverted list for a particular attribute will take up at most 34 tracks. (This maximum number of tracks occurs when the bitstring representation is the shortest possible one.) Suppose that we have a rather involved query that refers to a Boolean combination of 10 inverted lists; in the worst case we will have to read 340 tracks of information from the inverted file, for a total read time of $340 \times 25\,\text{ms} = 8.5\,\text{sec}$. The average latency delay will be about one half of the read time, but by careful programming we may be able to eliminate the latency. By storing the first track of each bitstring list in one cylinder, and the second track of each list in the next, etc., most of the seek time will be eliminated, so we can estimate the maximum seek time as about $34 \times 26\,\text{ms} \approx 0.9\,\text{sec}$ (or twice this if two independent disk units are involved). Finally, if q records satisfy the query, we will need about $q \times \big(60\,\text{ms (seek)} + 12.5\,\text{ms (latency)} + 0.2\,\text{ms (read)}\big)$ extra time to fetch each one for subsequent processing. Thus an optimistic estimate of the total expected time to process this rather complicated query is roughly $(10 + .073q)$ seconds. This may be contrasted with about 210 seconds to read through the entire file at top speed under the same assumptions without using any inverted lists.

This example shows that space optimization is closely related to time optimization in a disk memory; the time to process the inverted lists is roughly the time needed to seek and to read them.

The discussion above has more or less assumed that the file is not growing or shrinking as we query it; what should we do if frequent updates are necessary? In many applications it is sufficient to batch a number of requests for updates, and to take care of them in dull moments when no queries need to be answered. Alternatively, if updating the file has high priority, the method of B-trees (Section 6.2.4) is attractive. The entire collection of inverted lists could be made into one huge B-tree, with special conventions for the leaves so that the branch nodes contain key values while the leaves contain both keys and lists of pointers of records. File updates can also be handled by other methods that we shall discuss below.

Geometric data. A great many applications deal with points, lines, and shapes in spaces of two or more dimensions. One of the first approaches to distance-oriented queries was the "post-office tree" proposed in 1972 by Bruce McNutt. Suppose, for example, that we wish to handle queries like "What is the nearest city to point x?", given the value of x. Each node of McNutt's tree corresponds to a city y and a "test radius" r; the left subtree of this node corresponds to all cities z entered subsequently into this part of the tree such that the distance from y to z is $\leq r + \delta$, and the right subtree similarly is for distances $\geq r - \delta$. Here δ is a given tolerance; cities between $r - \delta$ and $r + \delta$ away from y must be entered in *both* subtrees. Searching in such a tree makes it possible to locate all cities within distance δ of a given point. (See Fig. 45.)

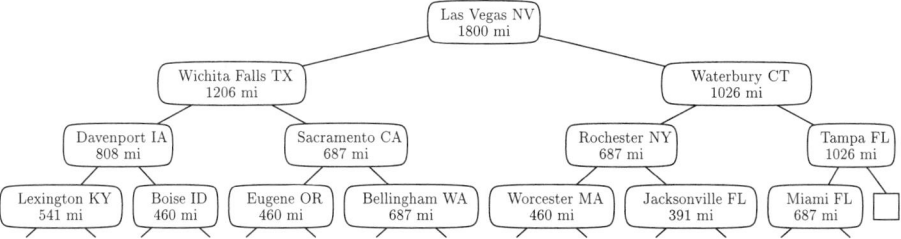

Fig. 45. The top levels of an example "post-office tree." To search for all cities near a given point x, start at the root: If x is within 1800 miles of Las Vegas, go left, otherwise go to the right; then repeat the process until encountering a terminal node. The method of tree construction ensures that all cities within 20 miles of x will be encountered during this search.

Several experiments based on this idea were conducted by McNutt and Edward Pring, using the 231 most populous cities in the continental United States in random order as an example database. They let the test radii shrink in a regular manner, replacing r by $0.67r$ when going to the left, and by $0.57r$ when going to the right, except that r was left unchanged when taking the second of two consecutive right branches. The result was that 610 nodes were required in the tree for $\delta = 20$ miles, and 1600 nodes were required for $\delta = 35$ miles. The top levels of their smaller tree are shown in Fig. 45. (In the remaining levels of this tree, Orlando FL appeared below both Jacksonville and Miami. Some cities occurred quite often; for example, 17 of the nodes were for Brockton MA!)

The rapid file growth as δ increases indicates that post-office trees probably have limited utility. We can do better by working directly with the *coordinates* of each point, regarding the coordinates as attributes or secondary keys; then we can make Boolean queries based on ranges of the keys. For example, suppose that the records of the file refer to North American cities, and that the query asks for all cities with

$$(21.49° \leq \text{LATITUDE} \leq 37.41°) \text{ AND } (70.34° \leq \text{LONGITUDE} \leq 75.72°).$$

Reference to a map will show that many cities satisfy this LATITUDE range, and many satisfy the LONGITUDE range, but hardly any cities lie in both ranges. One approach to such *orthogonal range queries* is to partition the set of all possible LATITUDE and LONGITUDE values rather coarsely, with only a few classes per attribute (for example, by truncating to the next lower multiple of $5°$), then to have one inverted list for each combined (LATITUDE, LONGITUDE) class. This is like having maps with one page for each local region. Using $5°$ intervals, the query above would refer to eight pages, namely $(20°, 70°)$, $(25°, 70°)$, $\ldots$, $(35°, 75°)$. The range query needs to be processed for each of these pages, either by going to a finer partition within the page or by direct reference to the records themselves, depending on the number of records corresponding to that page. In a sense this is a tree structure with two-dimensional branching at each internal node.

A substantial elaboration of this approach, called a *grid file*, was developed by J. Nievergelt, H. Hinterberger, and K. C. Sevcik [*ACM Trans. Database Systems* **9** (1984), 38–71]. If each point x has k coordinates $(x_1, \ldots, x_k)$, they divide the ith coordinate values into ranges

$$-\infty = g_{i0} < g_{i1} < \cdots < g_{ir_i} = +\infty \tag{1}$$

and locate x by determining indices $(j_1, \ldots, j_k)$ such that

$$0 \leq j_i < r_i, \qquad g_{ij_i} \leq x_i < g_{i(j_i+1)} \qquad \text{for } 1 \leq i \leq k. \tag{2}$$

All points that have a given value of $(j_1, \ldots, j_k)$ are called *cells*. Records for points in the same cell are stored in the same bucket in an external memory. Buckets are also allowed to contain points from several adjacent cells, provided that each bucket corresponds to a k-dimensional rectangular region or "super-cell." Various strategies for updating the grid boundary values g_{ij} and for splitting or combining buckets are possible; see, for example, K. Hinrichs, *BIT* **25**

(1985), 569–592. The characteristics of grid files with random data have been analyzed by M. Regnier, *BIT* **25** (1985), 335–357; P. Flajolet and C. Puech, *JACM* **33** (1986), 371–407, §4.2.

A simpler way to deal with orthogonal range queries was introduced by J. L. Bentley and R. A. Finkel, using structures called *quadtrees* [*Acta Informatica* **4** (1974), 1–9]. In the two-dimensional case of their construction, every node of such a tree represents a rectangle and also contains one of the points in that rectangle; there are four subtrees, corresponding to the four quadrants of the original rectangle relative to the coordinates of the given point. Similarly, in three dimensions there is eight-way branching, and the trees are sometimes called *octrees*. A k-dimensional quadtree has 2^k-way branching.

The mathematical analysis of random quadtrees is quite difficult, but in 1988 the asymptotic form of the expected insertion time for the N-th node in a random k-dimensional quadtree was determined to be

$$\frac{2}{k} \ln N + O(1), \tag{3}$$

by two groups of researchers working independently: See L. Devroye and L. Laforest, *SICOMP* **19** (1990), 821–832; P. Flajolet, G. Gonnet, C. Puech, and J. M. Robson, *Algorithmica* **10** (1993), 473–500. Notice that when $k = 1$, this result agrees with the well-known formula for insertion into a binary search tree, Eq. 6.2.2–(5). Further work by P. Flajolet, G. Labelle, L. Laforest, and B. Salvy showed in fact that the average internal path length can be expressed in the surprisingly elegant form

$$\sum_{l \geq 2} \binom{N}{l} (-1)^l \prod_{j=3}^{l} \left(1 - \frac{2^k}{j^k} \right), \tag{4}$$

and further analysis of random quadtrees was therefore possible with the help of hypergeometric functions [see *Random Structures & Algorithms* **7** (1995), 117–144].

Bentley went on to simplify the quadtree representation even further by introducing "k-d trees," which have only two-way branching at each node [*CACM* **18** (1975), 509–517; *IEEE Transactions* **SE-5** (1979), 333–340]. A 1-d tree is just an ordinary binary search tree, as in Section 6.2.2; a 2-d tree is similar, but the nodes on even levels compare x-coordinates and the nodes on odd levels compare y-coordinates when branching. In general, a k-d tree has nodes with k coordinates, and the branching on each level is based on only one of the coordinates; for example, we might branch on coordinate number $(l \bmod k) + 1$ on level l. A tie-breaking rule based on a record's serial number or location in memory can be used to ensure that no two records agree in any coordinate position. Randomly grown k-d trees turn out to have exactly the same average path length and shape distribution as ordinary binary search trees, because the assumptions underlying their growth are the same as in the one-dimensional case (see exercise 6.2.2–6).

If the file is not changing dynamically, we can balance any N-node k-d tree so that its height is $\approx \lg N$, by choosing a median value for branching at each node. Then we can be sure that several fundamental types of queries will be handled efficiently. For example, Bentley proved that we can identify all records that have t specified coordinates in $O(N^{1-t/k})$ steps. We can also find all records that lie in a given rectangular region in at most $O(tN^{1-1/k} + q)$ steps, if t of the coordinates are restricted to subranges and there are q such records altogether [D. T. Lee and C. K. Wong, *Acta Informatica* **23** (1977), 23–29]. In fact, if the given region is nearly cubical and q is small, and if the coordinate chosen for branching at each node has the greatest spread of attribute values, Friedman, Bentley, and Finkel [*ACM Trans. Math. Software* **3** (1977), 209–226] showed that the average time for such a region query will be only $O(\log N + q)$. The same formula applies when searching such k-d trees for the nearest neighbor of a given point in k-dimensional space.

When k-d trees are random instead of perfectly balanced, the average running time for partial matches of t specified coordinates increases slightly to $\Theta(N^{1-t/k+f(t/k)})$; here the function f is defined implicitly by the equation

$$\left(f(x) + 3 - x\right)^x \left(f(x) + 2 - x\right)^{1-x} = 2, \tag{5}$$

and it is quite small: We have

$$0 \le f(x) < 0.06329\,33881\,23738\,85718\,14011\,27797\,33590\,58170-, \tag{6}$$

and the maximum occurs when x is near 0.585. [See P. Flajolet and C. Puech, *JACM* **33** (1986), 371–407, §3.]

Because of the aesthetic appeal and great significance of geometric algorithms, there has been an enormous growth in techniques for solving higher-dimensional search problems and related questions of many kinds. Indeed, a new subfield of mathematics and computer science called Computational Geometry has developed rapidly since the 1970s. The *Handbook of Discrete and Computational Geometry*, edited by J. E. Goodman and J. O'Rourke (Boca Raton, Florida: CRC Press, 1997), is an excellent reference to the state of the art in that field as of 1997.

A comprehensive survey of data structures and algorithms for the important special cases of two- and three-dimensional objects has been prepared by Hanan Samet in a pair of complementary books, *The Design and Analysis of Spatial Data Structures* and *Applications of Spatial Data Structures* (Addison–Wesley, 1990). Samet points out that the original quadtrees of Bentley and Finkel are now more properly called "point quadtrees"; the name "quadtree" itself has become a generic term for any hierarchical decomposition of geometric data.

Compound attributes. It is possible to combine two or more attributes into one super-attribute. For example, a (`CLASS`, `MAJOR`) attribute could be created by combining the `CLASS` and `MAJOR` fields of a university enrollment file. In this way queries can often be satisfied by taking the union of disjoint, short lists instead of the intersection of longer lists.

The idea of attribute combination was developed further by V. Y. Lum [*CACM* **13** (1970), 660–665], who suggested ordering the inverted lists of combined attributes lexicographically from left to right, and making multiple copies, with the individual attributes permuted in a clever way. For example, suppose that we have three attributes A, B, and C; we can form three compound attributes

$$(\text{A}, \text{B}, \text{C}), \qquad (\text{B}, \text{C}, \text{A}), \qquad (\text{C}, \text{A}, \text{B}) \qquad (7)$$

and construct ordered inverted lists for each of these. (Thus in the first list, the records occur in order of their A values, with all records of the same A value in order by B and then by C.) This organization makes it possible to satisfy queries based on any combination of the three attributes; for example, all records having specified values for A and C will appear consecutively in the third list.

Similarly, from four attributes A, B, C, D, we can form the six combined attributes

$$(\text{A},\text{B},\text{C},\text{D}),\ (\text{B},\text{C},\text{D},\text{A}),\ (\text{B},\text{D},\text{A},\text{C}),\ (\text{C},\text{A},\text{D},\text{B}),\ (\text{C},\text{D},\text{A},\text{B}),\ (\text{D},\text{A},\text{B},\text{C}), \qquad (8)$$

which suffice to answer all combinations of simple queries relating to the simultaneous values of one, two, three, or four of the attributes. There is a general procedure for constructing $\binom{n}{k}$ combined attributes from n attributes, where $k \leq \frac{1}{2}n$, such that all records having specified combinations of at most k or at least $n - k$ of the attribute values will appear consecutively in one of the combined attribute lists (see exercise 1). Alternatively, we can get by with fewer combinations when some attributes have a limited number of values. For example, if D is simply a two-valued attribute, the three combinations

$$(\text{D},\text{A},\text{B},\text{C}), \qquad (\text{D},\text{B},\text{C},\text{A}), \qquad (\text{D},\text{C},\text{A},\text{B}) \qquad (9)$$

obtained by placing D in front of (7) will be almost as good as (8) with only half the redundancy, since queries that do not depend on D can be treated by looking in just two places in one of the lists.

Binary attributes. It is instructive to consider the special case in which all attributes are two-valued. In a sense this is the *opposite* of combining attributes, since we can represent any value as a binary number and regard the individual bits of that number as separate attributes. Table 1 shows a typical file involving "yes-no" attributes; in this case the records stand for selected cookie recipes, and the attributes specify which ingredients are used. For example, Almond Lace Wafers are made from butter, flour, milk, nuts, and granulated sugar. If we think of Table 1 as a matrix of zeros and ones, the transpose of the matrix is the inverted file, in bitstring form.

The right-hand column of Table 1 is used to indicate special items that occur only rarely. These can be coded in a more efficient way than to devote an entire column to each one; and the "Cornstarch" column could be treated similarly. Dually, we could find a more efficient way to encode the "Flour" column, since flour occurs in everything except Meringues. For the present, however, let us sidestep these considerations and simply ignore the "Special ingredients" column.

Table 1
A FILE WITH BINARY ATTRIBUTES

Recipe	Allspice	Anise seed	Baking powder	Baking soda	Butter	Cardamom	Chocolate	Cinnamon	Cloves	Coconut	Coffee	Cornstarch	Dates	Egg whites	Egg yolk	Flour	Ginger	Lemon juice	Lemon peel	Milk	Molasses	Nutmeg	Nuts	Oatmeal	Raisins	Salt	Sugar, brown	Sugar, granulated	Sugar, powdered	Vanilla extract	Special ingredients
Almond Lace Wafers	0	0	0	0	1	0	0	0	0	0	0	0	0	0	0	1	0	0	0	1	0	0	1	0	0	0	0	1	0	0	—
Applesauce-Spice Squares	0	0	0	1	1	0	0	1	1	0	0	0	0	0	1	1	0	0	0	0	0	1	1	0	1	1	1	0	0	1	Applesauce
Banana-Oatmeal Cookies	0	0	1	1	1	0	0	1	0	0	0	0	0	0	1	1	0	0	0	0	0	0	1	1	0	1	0	1	0	1	Bananas
Chocolate Chip Cookies	0	0	0	1	1	0	1	0	0	0	0	0	0	0	1	1	0	0	0	0	0	0	1	0	0	1	1	1	0	1	—
Coconut Macaroons	0	0	0	0	0	0	0	0	0	1	0	0	0	1	0	0	0	0	0	0	0	0	0	0	0	0	0	1	0	1	—
Cream-Cheese Cookies	0	0	1	0	1	0	0	0	0	0	0	0	0	1	1	1	0	1	1	0	0	0	0	0	0	0	0	1	0	1	Cream cheese
Delicious Prune Bars	0	0	1	0	1	0	0	1	1	0	0	0	0	0	1	1	0	0	0	0	0	1	1	0	0	1	0	1	0	0	Oranges, prunes
Double-Chocolate Drops	0	0	0	0	1	0	1	0	0	0	0	0	0	0	1	1	0	0	0	0	0	0	1	0	0	1	0	1	0	1	—
Dream Bars	0	0	1	0	1	0	0	0	0	1	0	0	0	0	1	1	0	0	0	0	0	0	1	0	0	1	1	0	1	0	—
Filled Turnovers	0	0	1	0	1	0	0	0	0	0	0	0	1	1	0	1	0	0	0	0	0	0	0	0	0	1	0	1	0	1	—
Finska Kakor	0	0	0	0	1	0	0	0	0	0	0	0	0	0	1	1	0	0	0	0	0	0	1	0	0	0	0	0	1	0	Almond extract
Glazed Gingersnaps	0	0	0	1	1	0	0	1	1	0	0	0	0	0	0	1	1	0	0	0	1	0	0	0	0	1	0	1	0	0	Vinegar
Hermits	1	0	0	1	1	0	0	1	1	0	0	0	0	0	1	1	0	0	0	0	0	1	1	0	1	1	1	0	0	1	Apricots
Jewel Cookies	0	0	0	0	1	0	0	0	0	0	0	0	0	0	1	1	0	0	0	0	0	0	0	0	0	1	0	0	1	1	Currant jelly
Jumbles	0	0	1	0	1	0	0	0	0	0	0	0	0	1	1	1	0	0	0	1	0	0	1	0	0	1	0	1	0	1	Salad oil
Kris Kringles	0	0	0	0	1	0	0	0	0	0	0	0	0	0	1	1	0	0	0	0	0	0	0	0	0	1	0	0	1	1	—
Lebkuchen Rounds	1	0	0	0	0	0	0	1	1	0	0	0	0	0	0	1	1	0	1	0	1	1	1	0	0	1	0	0	0	0	Honey
Meringues	0	0	0	0	0	0	0	0	0	0	0	0	0	1	0	0	0	0	0	0	0	0	0	0	0	0	0	1	0	1	Candied cherries
Moravian Spice Cookies	1	0	0	1	0	0	0	1	1	0	0	0	0	0	0	1	1	0	0	0	1	1	0	0	0	1	1	0	0	0	—
Oatmeal-Date Bars	0	0	1	0	1	0	0	0	0	0	0	0	1	0	1	1	0	0	0	0	0	0	1	1	0	1	0	1	0	1	—
Old-Fashioned Sugar Cookies	0	0	1	0	1	0	0	0	0	0	0	0	0	0	1	1	0	0	0	1	0	0	0	0	0	1	0	1	0	1	Sour cream
Peanut-Butter Pinwheels	0	0	1	0	1	0	0	0	0	0	0	0	0	1	0	1	0	0	0	1	0	0	0	0	0	1	0	1	0	1	Peanut butter
Petticoat Tails	0	0	0	0	1	0	0	0	0	0	0	0	0	0	1	1	0	0	0	1	0	0	0	0	0	1	0	0	1	1	—
Pfeffernuesse	1	1	1	0	0	0	0	1	1	0	0	0	0	0	0	1	1	0	1	0	0	1	0	0	0	1	1	0	1	0	Citron, mace, pepper
Scotch Oatmeal Shortbread	0	0	0	0	1	0	0	0	0	0	0	0	0	0	0	1	0	0	0	0	0	0	0	1	0	1	0	0	1	0	—
Shortbread Stars	0	0	0	0	1	0	0	0	0	0	0	0	0	0	0	1	0	0	0	0	0	0	0	0	0	1	0	0	1	0	—
Springerle	0	1	1	0	0	0	0	0	0	0	0	0	0	0	1	1	0	0	0	0	0	0	0	0	0	0	0	0	1	0	—
Spritz Cookies	0	0	0	0	1	0	0	0	0	0	0	0	0	1	1	1	0	0	0	0	0	0	0	0	0	0	0	1	0	1	—
Swedish Kringler	0	0	1	0	1	0	0	0	0	0	0	0	0	1	0	1	0	0	0	1	0	0	0	0	0	1	0	1	0	1	—
Swiss-Cinnamon Crisps	0	0	0	0	1	0	0	1	0	0	0	0	0	0	0	1	0	0	0	0	0	0	0	0	0	1	0	1	0	1	—
Toffee Bars	0	0	0	0	1	0	1	0	0	0	0	0	0	0	0	1	0	0	0	0	0	0	1	0	0	0	1	0	0	1	—
Vanilla-Nut Icebox Cookies	0	0	1	0	1	0	0	0	0	0	0	0	0	0	1	1	0	0	0	0	0	0	1	0	0	1	0	1	0	1	—

Let us define a *basic query* in a binary attribute file as a request for all records having 0's in certain columns, 1's in other columns, and arbitrary values in the remaining columns. Using "∗" to stand for an arbitrary value, we can represent any basic query as a sequence of 0's, 1's, and ∗'s. For example, consider a man who is in the mood for some coconut cookies, but he is allergic to chocolate, hates anise, and has run out of vanilla extract; he can formulate the query

$$* 0 * * * * 0 * * 1 * * * * * * * * * * * * * * * * * * * 0. \qquad (10)$$

Table 1 now says that Delicious Prune Bars are just the thing.

Before we consider the general problem of organizing a file for basic queries, it is important to look at the special case where no 0's are specified, only 1's and ∗'s. This may be called an *inclusive query*, because it asks for all records that include a certain set of attributes, if we assume that 1's denote attributes that are present and 0's denote attributes that are absent. For example, the recipes in Table 1 that call for both baking powder and baking soda are Glazed Gingersnaps and Old-Fashioned Sugar Cookies.

In some applications it is sufficient to provide for the special case of inclusive queries. This occurs, for example, in the case of many manual card-filing systems, such as "edge-notched cards" or "feature cards." An edge-notched card system corresponding to Table 1 would have one card for every recipe, with holes cut out for each ingredient (see Fig. 46). In order to process an inclusive query, the file of cards is arranged into a neat deck and needles are put in each column position corresponding to an attribute that is to be included. After raising the needles, all cards having the appropriate attributes will drop out.

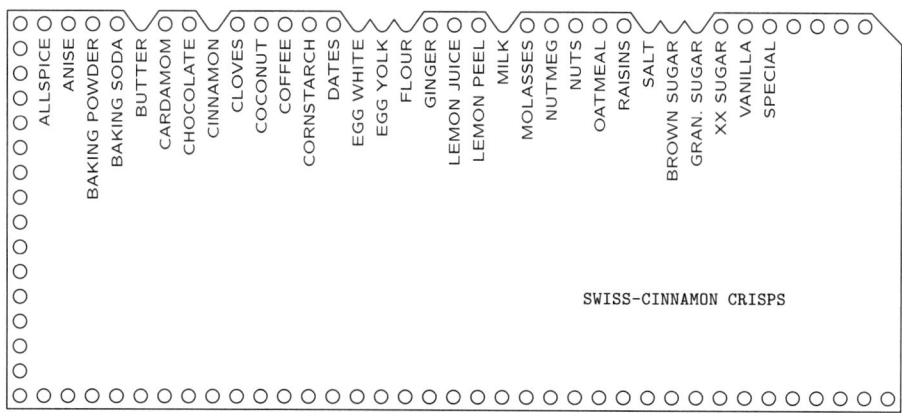

Fig. 46. An edge-notched card.

A feature-card system works on the inverse file in a similar way. In this case there is one card for every attribute, and holes are punched in designated positions on the surface of the card for every record possessing that attribute. An ordinary 80-column card can therefore be used to tell which of $12 \times 80 = 960$

records have a given attribute. To process an inclusive query, the feature cards for the specified attributes are selected and put together; then light will shine through all positions corresponding to the desired records. This operation is analogous to the treatment of Boolean queries by intersecting inverted bit strings as explained above.

Table 2
AN EXAMPLE OF SUPERIMPOSED CODING

Codes for individual flavorings

Almond extract	0100000001	Dates	1000000100
Allspice	0000100001	Ginger	0000110000
Anise seed	0000011000	Honey	0000000011
Applesauce	0010010000	Lemon juice	1000100000
Apricots	1000010000	Lemon peel	0011000000
Bananas	0000100010	Mace	0000010100
Candied cherries	0000101000	Molasses	1001000000
Cardamom	1000000001	Nutmeg	0000010010
Chocolate	0010001000	Nuts	0000100100
Cinnamon	1000000010	Oranges	0100000100
Citron	0100000010	Peanut butter	0000000101
Cloves	0001100000	Pepper	0010000100
Coconut	0001010000	Prunes	0010000010
Coffee	0001000100	Raisins	0101000000
Currant jelly	0010000001	Vanilla extract	0000001001

Superimposed codes

Almond Lace Wafers	0000100100	Lebkuchen Rounds	1011110111
Applesauce-Spice Squares	1111111111	Meringues	1000101100
Banana-Oatmeal Cookies	1000111111	Moravian Spice Cookies	1001110011
Chocolate Chip Cookies	0010101101	Oatmeal-Date Bars	1000100100
Coconut Macaroons	0001111101	Old-Fashioned Sugar Cookies	0000011011
Cream-Cheese Cookies	0010001001	Peanut-Butter Pinwheels	0010001101
Delicious Prune Bars	0111110110	Petticoat Tails	0000001001
Double-Chocolate Drops	0010101100	Pfeffernuesse	1111111111
Dream Bars	0001111101	Scotch Oatmeal Shortbread	0000001001
Filled Turnovers	1011101101	Shortbread Stars	0000000000
Finska Kakor	0100100101	Springerle	0011011000
Glazed Gingersnaps	1001110010	Spritz Cookies	0000001001
Hermits	1101010110	Swedish Kringler	0000000000
Jewel Cookies	0010101101	Swiss-Cinnamon Crisps	1000000010
Jumbles	1000001011	Toffee Bars	0010101101
Kris Kringles	1011100101	Vanilla-Nut Icebox Cookies	0000101101

Superimposed coding. The reason these manual card systems are of special interest to us is that ingenious schemes have been devised to save space on edge-notched cards; the same principles can be applied in the representation of computer files. Superimposed coding is a technique similar to hashing, and it was actually invented several years before hashing itself was discovered. The idea is to map attributes into random k-bit codes in an n-bit field, and to superimpose the codes for each attribute that is present in a record. An inclusive query for some set of attributes can be converted into an inclusive query for the corresponding superimposed bit codes. A few extra records may satisfy this query, but the number of such "false drops" can be statistically controlled. [See Calvin N. Mooers, *Amer. Chem. Soc. Meeting* **112** (September 1947), 14E–15E; *American Documentation* **2** (1951), 20–32.]

As an example of superimposed coding, let's consider Table 1 again, but only the flavorings instead of the basic ingredients like baking powder, shortening, eggs, and flour. Table 2 shows what happens if we assign random 2-bit codes in a 10-bit field to each of the flavoring attributes and superimpose the coding. For example, the entry for Chocolate Chip Cookies is obtained by superimposing the codes for chocolate, nuts, and vanilla:

$$0010001000 \mid 0000100100 \mid 0000001001 = 0010101101.$$

The superimposition of these codes also yields some spurious attributes, in this case allspice, candied cherries, currant jelly, peanut butter, and pepper; these will cause false drops to occur on certain queries (and they also suggest the creation of a new recipe called False Drop Cookies!).

Superimposed coding actually doesn't work very well in Table 2, because that table is a small example with lots of attributes present. In fact, Applesauce-Spice Squares will drop out for *every* query, since it was obtained by superimposing seven codes that cover all ten positions; and Pfeffernuesse is even worse, obtained by superimposing twelve codes. On the other hand Table 2 works surprisingly well in some respects; for example, if we try the query "Vanilla extract", only the record for Pfeffernuesse comes out as a false drop.

A more appropriate example of superimposed coding occurs if we have, say, a 32-bit field and a set of $\binom{32}{3} = 4960$ different attributes, where each record is allowed to possess up to six attributes and each attribute is encoded by specifying 3 of the 32 bits. In this situation, if we assume that each record has six randomly selected attributes, the probability of a false drop in an inclusive query

on one attribute is	.07948358;	
on two attributes is	.00708659;	
on three attributes is	.00067094;	(11)
on four attributes is	.00006786;	
on five attributes is	.00000728;	
on six attributes is	.00000082.	

Thus if there are M records that do not actually satisfy a two-attribute query, about $.007M$ will have a superimposed code that spuriously matches all code bits of the two specified attributes. (These probabilities are computed in exercise 4.) The total number of bits needed in the inverted file is only 32 times the number of records, which is less than half the number of bits needed to specify the attributes themselves in the original file.

If carefully selected nonrandom codes are used, it is possible to avoid false drops entirely in superimposed coding, as shown by W. H. Kautz and R. C. Singleton, *IEEE Trans.* **IT-10** (1964), 363–377; one of their constructions appears in exercise 16.

Malcolm C. Harrison [*CACM* **14** (1971), 777–779] has observed that superimposed coding can be used to speed up *text searching*. Assume that we want to locate all occurrences of a particular string of characters in a long body of text, without building an extensive table as in Algorithm 6.3P; and assume, for example, that the text is divided into individual lines $c_1 c_2 \ldots c_{50}$ of 50 characters each. Harrison suggests encoding each of the 49 pairs $c_1 c_2$, $c_2 c_3$, $\ldots$, $c_{49} c_{50}$ by hashing each of them into a number between 0 and 127, say; then the "signature" of the line $c_1 c_2 \ldots c_{50}$ is the string of 128 bits $b_0 b_1 \ldots b_{127}$, where $b_i = 1$ if and only if $h(c_j c_{j+1}) = i$ for some j.

If now we want to search for all occurrences of the word NEEDLE in a large text file called HAYSTACK, we simply look for all lines whose signature contains 1-bits in positions $h(\text{NE})$, $h(\text{EE})$, $h(\text{ED})$, $h(\text{DL})$, and $h(\text{LE})$. Assuming that the hash function is random, the probability that a random line contains all these bits in its signature is only 0.00341 (see exercise 4); hence the intersection of five inverted-list bit strings will rapidly identify all the lines containing NEEDLE, together with a few false drops.

The assumption of randomness is not really justified in this application, since typical text has so much redundancy; the distribution of adjacent letter pairs in English words is highly biased. For example, it will probably be very helpful to discard all pairs $c_j c_{j+1}$ containing a blank character, since blanks are usually much more common than any other symbol.

Another interesting application of superimposed coding to search problems has been suggested by Burton H. Bloom [*CACM* **13** (1970), 422–426]; his method actually applies to *primary* key retrieval, although it is most appropriate for us to discuss it in this section. Imagine a search application with a large database in which no calculation needs to be done if the search was unsuccessful. For example, we might want to check somebody's credit rating or passport number, and if no record for that person appears in the file we don't have to investigate further. Similarly in an application to computerized typesetting, we might have a simple algorithm that hyphenates most words correctly, but it fails on some 50,000 exceptional words; if we don't find the word in the exception file we are free to use the simple algorithm.

In such situations it is possible to maintain a bit table in internal memory so that most keys not in the file can be recognized as absent without making *any* references to the external memory. Here's how: Let the internal bit table be $b_0 b_1 \ldots b_{M-1}$, where M is rather large. For each key K_j in the file, compute k independent hash functions $h_1(K_j), \ldots, h_k(K_j)$, and set the corresponding k b's equal to 1. (These k values need not be distinct.) Thus $b_i = 1$ if and only if $h_l(K_j) = i$ for some j and l. Now to determine if a search argument K is in the external file, first test whether or not $b_{h_l(K)} = 1$ for $1 \leq l \leq k$; if not, there is no need to access the external memory, but if so, a conventional search will probably find K if k and M have been chosen properly. The chance of a false drop when there are N records in the file is approximately $(1 - e^{-kN/M})^k$. In a sense, Bloom's method treats the entire file as one record, with the primary keys as the attributes that are present, and with superimposed coding in a huge M-bit field.

Still another variation of superimposed coding has been developed by Richard A. Gustafson [Ph.D. thesis (Univ. South Carolina, 1969)]. Suppose that we have N records and that each record possesses six attributes chosen from a set of 10,000 possibilities. The records may, for example, stand for technical articles and the attributes may be keywords describing the article. Let h be a hash function that maps each attribute into a number between 0 and 15. If a record has attributes $a_1, a_2, \ldots, a_6$, Gustafson suggests mapping the record into the 16-bit number $b_0 b_1 \ldots b_{15}$, where $b_i = 1$ if and only if $h(a_j) = i$ for some j; and furthermore if this method results in only k of the b's equal to 1, for $k < 6$, another $6 - k$ 1s are supplied by some random method (not necessarily depending on the record itself). There are $\binom{16}{6} = 8008$ sixteen-bit codes in which exactly six 1-bits are present, and with luck about $N/8008$ records will be mapped into each value. We can keep 8008 lists of records, directly calculating the address corresponding to $b_0 b_1 \ldots b_{15}$ using a suitable formula. In fact, if the 1s occur in positions $0 \leq p_1 < p_2 < \cdots < p_6$, the function

$$\binom{p_1}{1} + \binom{p_2}{2} + \cdots + \binom{p_6}{6}$$

will convert each string $b_0 b_1 \ldots b_{15}$ into a unique number between 0 and 8007, as we have seen in exercises 1.2.6–56 and 2.2.6–7.

Now if we want to find all records having three particular attributes A_1, A_2, A_3, we compute $h(A_1)$, $h(A_2)$, $h(A_3)$; assuming that these three values are distinct, we need only look at the records stored in the $\binom{13}{3} = 286$ lists whose bit code $b_0 b_1 \ldots b_{15}$ contains 1s in those three positions. In other words, only $286/8008 \approx 3.5$ percent of the records need to be examined in the search.

See the article by C. S. Roberts, *Proc. IEEE* **67** (1979), 1624–1642, for an excellent exposition of superimposed coding, together with an application to a large database of telephone-directory listings. An application to spelling-check software is discussed by J. K. Mullin and D. J. Margoliash, *Software Practice & Exper.* **20** (1990), 625–630.

Combinatorial hashing. The idea underlying Gustafson's method just described is to find some way to map the records into memory locations so that comparatively few locations are relevant to a particular query. But his method applies only to inclusive queries when the individual records possess few attributes. Another type of mapping, designed to handle arbitrary basic queries like (10) consisting of 0's, 1's, and *'s, was discovered by Ronald L. Rivest in 1971. [See *SICOMP* **5** (1976), 19–50.]

Suppose first that we wish to construct a crossword-puzzle dictionary for all six-letter words of English; a typical query asks for all words of the form N**D*E, say, and gets the reply {NEEDLE, NIDDLE, NODDLE, NOODLE, NUDDLE}. We can solve this problem nicely by keeping 2^{12} lists, putting the word NEEDLE into list number

$$h(\text{N})\,h(\text{E})\,h(\text{E})\,h(\text{D})\,h(\text{L})\,h(\text{E}).$$

Here h is a hash function taking each letter into a 2-bit value, and we get a 12-bit list address by putting the six bit-pairs together. Then the query N**D*E can be answered by looking through just 64 of the 4096 lists.

Similarly let's suppose that we have 1,000,000 records each containing 10 secondary keys, where each secondary key has a fairly large number of possible values. We can map the records whose secondary keys are $(K_1, K_2, \ldots, K_{10})$ into the 20-bit number

$$h(K_1)\,h(K_2)\,\ldots\,h(K_{10}), \tag{12}$$

where h is a hash function taking each secondary key into a 2-bit value, and (12) stands for the juxtaposition of these ten pairs of bits. This scheme maps 1,000,000 records into $2^{20} = 1{,}048{,}576$ possible values, and we can consider the total mapping as a hash function with $M = 2^{20}$; chaining can be used to resolve collisions. If we want to retrieve all records having specified values of any five secondary keys, we need to look at only 2^{10} lists, corresponding to the five unspecified bit pairs in (12); thus only about $1000 = \sqrt{N}$ records need to be examined on the average. (A similar approach was suggested by M. Arisawa, *J. Inf. Proc. Soc. Japan* **12** (1971), 163–167, and by B. Dwyer (unpublished). Dwyer suggested using a more flexible mapping than (12), namely

$$\bigl(h_1(K_1) + h_2(K_2) + \cdots + h_{10}(K_{10})\bigr) \bmod M,$$

where M is any convenient number, and the h_i are arbitrary hash functions possibly of the form $w_i K_i$ for "random" w_i.)

Rivest has developed this idea further so that in many cases we have the following situation. Assume that there are $N \approx 2^n$ records, each having m secondary keys. Each record is mapped into an n-bit hash address, in such a way that a query that leaves the values of k keys unspecified corresponds to approximately $N^{k/m}$ hash addresses. All the other methods we have discussed in this section (except Gustafson's) require order N steps for retrieval, although the constant of proportionality is small; for large enough N, Rivest's method will be faster, and it requires no inverted files.

But we have to define an appropriate mapping before we can apply this technique. Here is an example with small parameters, when $m = 4$ and $n = 3$ and when all secondary keys are binary-valued; we can map 4-bit records into eight addresses as follows:

$$
\begin{array}{llll}
* \ 0 \ 0 \ 1 \to 0 & \qquad & * \ 1 \ 1 \ 0 \to 4 & \\
0 \ * \ 0 \ 0 \to 1 & \qquad & 1 \ * \ 1 \ 1 \to 5 & \\
1 \ 0 \ * \ 0 \to 2 & \qquad & 0 \ 1 \ * \ 1 \to 6 & \qquad (13) \\
1 \ 1 \ 0 \ * \to 3 & \qquad & 0 \ 0 \ 1 \ * \to 7 &
\end{array}
$$

An examination of this table reveals that all records corresponding to the query 0 * * * are mapped into locations 0, 1, 4, 6, and 7; and similarly *any* basic query with three *'s corresponds to exactly five locations. The basic queries

with two *'s correspond to three locations each; and the basic queries with one *
correspond to either one or two locations, $(8 \times 1 + 24 \times 2)/32 = 1.75$ on the
average. Thus we have

Number of unspecified bits in the query	Number of locations to search	
4	$8 = 8^{4/4}$	
3	$5 \approx 8^{3/4}$	(14)
2	$3 \approx 8^{2/4}$	
1	$1.75 \approx 8^{1/4}$	
0	$1 = 8^{0/4}$	

Of course this is such a small example, we could handle it more easily by
brute force. But it leads to nontrivial applications, since we can use it also
when $m = 4r$ and $n = 3r$, mapping $4r$-bit records into $2^{3r} \approx N$ locations by
dividing the secondary keys into r groups of 4 bits each and applying (13) in each
group. The resulting mapping has the desired property: *A query that leaves k
of the m bits unspecified will correspond to approximately $N^{k/m}$ locations.* (See
exercise 6.)

A. E. Brouwer [*SICOMP* **28** (1999), 1970–1971] has found an attractive
way to compress 8 bits to 5, with a mapping analogous to (13). Every 8-bit byte
belongs to exactly one of the following 32 classes:

$$
\begin{array}{llll}
0*000*0* & 01*0**11 & 00*11**1 & *11**101 \\
1*000*0* & 11*0**11 & 10*11**1 & *11**010 \\
0*010*0* & 01*1**11 & 00*0*01* & *10*0*10 \\
1*010*0* & 11*1**11 & 10*0*01* & *10*1*01 \\
0*10*1*0 & 0*1*000* & *01*01*1 & *0*1001* \\
1*10*1*0 & 1*1*000* & *10*10*0 & *0*0100* \\
0*11*1*0 & 0*0*11*0 & *00*011* & *0*011*1 \\
1*11*1*0 & 1*0*11*0 & *11*100* & *0*110*0
\end{array} \qquad (15)
$$

The *'s in this design are arranged in such a way that there are 3 in each row
and 12 in each column. Exercise 18 explains how to obtain similar schemes that
will compress records having, say, $m = 4^r$ bits into addresses having $n = 3^r$ bits.
In practice, buckets of size b would be used, and we would take $N \approx 2^n b$; the
case $b = 1$ has been used in the discussion above for simplicity in exposition.

Rivest has also suggested another simple way to handle basic queries. Suppose we have, say, $N \approx 2^{10}$ records of 30 bits each, where we wish to answer
arbitrary 30-bit basic queries like (10). Then we can simply divide the 30 bits
into three 10-bit fields, and keep three separate hash tables of size $M = 2^{10}$. Each
record is stored thrice, in lists corresponding to its bit configurations in the three
fields. Under suitable conditions, each list will contain about one element. Given
a basic query with k unspecified bits, at least one of the fields will have $\lfloor k/3 \rfloor$ or
fewer bits unspecified; hence we need to look in at most $2^{\lfloor k/3 \rfloor} \approx N^{k/30}$ of the
lists to find all answers to the query. Or we could use any other technique for
handling basic queries in the selected field.

Generalized tries. Rivest went on to suggest yet another approach, based on a data structure like the tries in Section 6.3. We can let each internal node of a generalized binary trie specify which bit of the record it represents. For example, in the data of Table 1 we could let the root of the trie represent Vanilla extract; then the left subtrie would correspond to those 16 cookie recipes that omit Vanilla extract, while the right subtrie would be for the 16 that use it. This 16–16 split nicely bisects the file; and we can handle each subfile in a similar way. When a subfile becomes suitably small, we represent it by a terminal node.

To process a basic query, we start at the root of the trie. When searching a generalized trie whose root specifies an attribute where the query has 0 or 1, we search the left or right subtrie, respectively; and if the query has * in that bit position, we search both subtries.

Suppose the attributes are not binary, but they are represented in binary notation. We can build a trie by looking first at the first bit of attribute 1, then the first bit of attribute 2, ..., the first bit of attribute m, then the second bit of attribute 1, etc. Such a structure is called an "m-d trie," by analogy with m-d trees (which branch by comparisons instead of by bit inspections). P. Flajolet and C. Puech have shown that the average time to answer a partial match query in a random m-d trie of N nodes is $\Theta(N^{k/m})$ when k/m of the attributes are unspecified [*JACM* **33** (1986), 371–407, §4.1]; the variance has been calculated by W. Schachinger, *Random Structures & Algorithms* **7** (1995), 81–95.

Similar algorithms can be developed for m-dimensional versions of the digital search trees and Patricia trees of Section 6.3. These structures, which tend to be slightly better balanced than m-d tries, have been analyzed by P. Kirschenhofer and H. Prodinger, *Random Structures & Algorithms* **5** (1994), 123–134.

*Balanced filing schemes. Another combinatorial approach to information retrieval, based on *balanced incomplete block designs*, has been the subject of considerable investigation. Although the subject is quite interesting from a mathematical point of view, it has unfortunately not yet proved to be more useful than the other methods described above. A brief introduction to the theory will be presented here in order to indicate the flavor of the results, in hopes that readers might think of good ways to put the ideas to practical use.

A *Steiner triple system* is an arrangement of v objects into unordered triples in such a way that every pair of objects occurs in exactly one triple. For example, when $v = 7$ there is essentially only one Steiner triple system, namely

Triple	Pairs included	
$\{1,2,4\}$	$\{1,2\}, \{1,4\}, \{2,4\}$	
$\{2,3,5\}$	$\{2,3\}, \{2,5\}, \{3,5\}$	
$\{3,4,6\}$	$\{3,4\}, \{3,6\}, \{4,6\}$	
$\{4,5,0\}$	$\{0,4\}, \{0,5\}, \{4,5\}$	(16)
$\{5,6,1\}$	$\{1,5\}, \{1,6\}, \{5,6\}$	
$\{6,0,2\}$	$\{0,2\}, \{0,6\}, \{2,6\}$	
$\{0,1,3\}$	$\{0,1\}, \{0,3\}, \{1,3\}$	

Since there are $\frac{1}{2}v(v-1)$ pairs of objects and three pairs per triple, there must be $\frac{1}{6}v(v-1)$ triples in all; and since each object must be paired with $v-1$ others, each object must appear in exactly $\frac{1}{2}(v-1)$ triples. These conditions imply that a Steiner triple system can't exist unless $\frac{1}{6}v(v-1)$ and $\frac{1}{2}(v-1)$ are integers, and this is equivalent to saying that v is odd and not congruent to 2 modulo 3; thus

$$v \bmod 6 = 1 \text{ or } 3. \qquad (17)$$

Conversely, T. P. Kirkman proved in 1847 that Steiner triple systems do exist for all $v \geq 1$ such that (17) holds. His interesting construction is given in exercise 10.

Steiner triple systems can be used to reduce the redundancy of combined inverted file indexes. For example, consider again the cookie recipe file of Table 1, and convert the rightmost column into a 31st attribute that is 1 if any special ingredients are necessary, 0 otherwise. Assume that we want to answer all inclusive queries on pairs of attributes, such as "What recipes use both coconut and raisins?" We could make up an inverted list for each of the $\binom{31}{2} = 465$ possible queries. But it would turn out that this takes a lot of space since Pfeffernuesse (for example) would appear in $\binom{17}{2} = 136$ of the lists, and a record with all 31 attributes would appear in every list! A Steiner triple system can be used to make a slight improvement in this situation. There is a Steiner triple system on 31 objects, with 155 triples and each pair of objects occurring in exactly one of the triples. We can associate four lists with each triple $\{a,b,c\}$, one list for all records having attributes a, b, $\bar{c}$ (that is, a and b but not c); another for a, $\bar{b}$, c; another for $\bar{a}$, b, c; and another for records having all three attributes a, b, c. This guarantees that no record will be included in more than 155 of the inverted lists, and it saves space whenever a record has three attributes that correspond to a triple of the system.

Triple systems are special cases of block designs that have blocks of three or more objects. For example, there is a way to arrange 31 objects into sextuples so that every pair of objects appears in exactly one sextuple:

$$\{0,4,16,21,22,24\}, \{1,5,17,22,23,25\}, \ldots, \{30,3,15,20,21,23\} \qquad (18)$$

(This design is formed from the first block by addition mod 31. To verify that it has the stated property, note that the 30 values $(a_i - a_j) \bmod 31$, for $i \neq j$, are distinct, where $(a_1, a_2, \ldots, a_6) = (0,4,16,21,22,24)$. To find the sextuple containing a pair (x,y), choose i and j such that $a_i - a_j \equiv x - y$ (modulo 31); now if $k = (x - a_i) \bmod 31$, we have $(a_i + k) \bmod 31 = x$ and $(a_j + k) \bmod 31 = y$.)

We can use the design above to store the inverted lists in such a way that no record can appear more than 31 times. Each sextuple $\{a,b,c,d,e,f\}$ is associated with 57 lists, for the various possibilities of records having two or more of the attributes a, b, c, d, e, f, namely $(a,b,\bar{c},\bar{d},\bar{e},\bar{f})$, $(a,\bar{b},c,\bar{d},\bar{e},\bar{f})$, $\ldots$, (a,b,c,d,e,f); and the answer to each inclusive 2-attribute query is the disjoint union of 16 appropriate lists in the appropriate sextuple. For this design, Pfeffernuesse would be stored in 29 of the 31 blocks, since that record has two of the six attributes in all but blocks $\{19,23,4,9,10,12\}$ and $\{13,17,29,3,4,6\}$ if we number the columns from 0 to 30.

The theory of block designs and related patterns is developed in detail in Marshall Hall, Jr.'s book *Combinatorial Theory* (Waltham, Mass.: Blaisdell, 1967). Although such combinatorial configurations are very beautiful, their main application to information retrieval so far has been to decrease the redundancy incurred when compound inverted lists are being used; and David K. Chow [*Information and Control* **15** (1969), 377–396] has observed that this type of decrease can be obtained even without using combinatorial designs.

A short history and bibliography. The first published article dealing with a technique for secondary key retrieval was by L. R. Johnson in *CACM* **4** (1961), 218–222. The multilist system was developed independently by Noah S. Prywes, H. J. Gray, W. I. Landauer, D. Lefkowitz, and S. Litwin at about the same time; see *IEEE Trans. on Communication and Electronics* **82** (1963), 488–492. Another rather early publication that influenced later work was by D. R. Davis and A. D. Lin, *CACM* **8** (1965), 243–246.

Since then a large literature on the subject grew up rapidly, but much of it dealt with the user interface and with programming language considerations, which are not within the scope of this book. In addition to the papers already cited, the following published articles were found to be most helpful to the author as this section was first being written in 1972: Jack Minker and Jerome Sable, *Ann. Rev. of Information Science and Technology* **2** (1967), 123–160; Robert E. Bleier, *Proc. ACM Nat. Conf.* **22** (1967), 41–49; Jerome A. Feldman and Paul D. Rovner, *CACM* **12** (1969), 439–449; Burton H. Bloom, *Proc. ACM Nat. Conf.* **24** (1969), 83–95; H. S. Heaps and L. H. Thiel, *Information Storage and Retrieval* **6** (1970), 137–153; Vincent Y. Lum and Huei Ling, *Proc. ACM Nat. Conf.* **26** (1971), 349–356. A good survey of manual card-filing systems appears in *Methods of Information Handling* by C. P. Bourne (New York: Wiley, 1963), Chapter 5. Balanced filing schemes were originally developed by C. T. Abraham, S. P. Ghosh, and D. K. Ray-Chaudhuri in 1965; see the article by R. C. Bose and Gary G. Koch, *SIAM J. Appl. Math.* **17** (1969), 1203–1214.

Most of the classical algorithms for multi-attribute data that are known to be of practical importance have been discussed above; but a few more topics are planned for the next edition of this book, including the following:

- E. M. McCreight introduced *priority search trees* [*SICOMP* **14** (1985), 257–276], which are specially designed to represent intersections of dynamically changing families of intervals, and to handle range queries of the form "Find all records with $x_0 \le x \le x_1$ and $y \le y_1$." (Notice that the lower bound on y must be $-\infty$, but x can be bounded on both sides.)

- M. L. Fredman has proved several fundamental lower bounds, which show that a sequence of N intermixed insertions, deletions, and k-dimensional range queries must take $\Omega(N(\log N)^k)$ operations in the worst case, regardless of the data structure being used. See *JACM* **28** (1981), 696–705; *SICOMP* **10** (1981), 1–10; *J. Algorithms* **2** (1981), 77–87.

Basic algorithms for pattern matching and approximate pattern matching in text strings will be discussed in Chapter 9.

It is interesting to note that the human brain is much better at secondary key retrieval than computers are; in fact, people find it rather easy to recognize faces or melodies from only fragmentary information, while computers have barely been able to do this at all. Therefore it is not unlikely that a completely new approach to machine design will someday be discovered that solves the problem of secondary key retrieval once and for all, making this entire section obsolete.

EXERCISES

▶ **1.** [*M27*] Let $0 \le k \le n/2$. Prove that the following construction produces $\binom{n}{k}$ permutations of $\{1, 2, \ldots, n\}$ such that every t-element subset of $\{1, 2, \ldots, n\}$ appears as the first t elements of at least one of the permutations, for $t \le k$ or $t \ge n - k$: Consider a path in the plane from $(0,0)$ to (n, r) where $r \ge n - 2k$, in which the ith step is from $(i-1, j)$ to $(i, j+1)$ or to $(i, j-1)$; the latter possibility is allowed only if $j \ge 1$, so that the path never goes below the x axis. There are exactly $\binom{n}{k}$ such paths. For each path of this kind, a permutation is constructed as follows, using three lists that are initially empty: For $i = 1, 2, \ldots, n$, if the ith step of the path goes up, put the number i into list B; if the step goes down, put i into list A and move the currently largest element of list B into list C. The resulting permutation is equal to the final contents of list A, then list B, then list C, each list in increasing order.

For example, when $n = 4$ and $k = 2$, the six paths and permutations defined by this procedure are

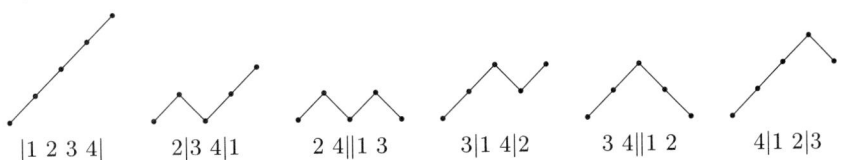

|1 2 3 4| 2|3 4|1   2 4||1 3   3|1 4|2   3 4||1 2   4|1 2|3

(Vertical lines show the division between lists A, B, and C. These six permutations correspond to the compound attributes in (8).)

Hint: Represent each t-element subset S by a path that goes from $(0,0)$ to $(n, n-2t)$, whose ith step runs from $(i-1, j)$ to $(i, j+1)$ if $i \notin S$ and to $(i, j-1)$ if $i \in S$. Convert every such path into an appropriate path having the special form stated above.

2. [*M25*] (Sakti P. Ghosh.) Find the minimum possible length l of a list $r_1 r_2 \ldots r_l$ of references to records, such that the set of all responses to any of the inclusive queries **1, *1*, 1**, *11, 1*1, 11*, 111 on three binary-valued secondary keys will appear in consecutive locations $r_i \ldots r_j$.

3. [*19*] In Table 2, what inclusive queries will cause (a) Old-Fashioned Sugar Cookies, (b) Oatmeal-Date Bars, to be obtained among the false drops?

4. [*M30*] Find exact formulas for the probabilities in (11), assuming that each record has r distinct attributes chosen randomly from among the $\binom{n}{k}$ k-bit codes in an n-bit field and that the query involves q distinct but otherwise random attributes. (Don't be alarmed if the formulas do not simplify.)

5. [*40*] Experiment with various ways to avoid the redundancy of text when using Harrison's technique for substring searching.

▶ **6.** [*M20*] The total number of m-bit basic queries with t bits specified is $s = \binom{m}{t} 2^t$. If a combinatorial hashing function like that in (13) converts these queries into l_1, l_2,

..., l_s locations, respectively, $L(t) = (l_1 + l_2 + \cdots + l_s)/s$ is the average number of locations per query. [For example, in (13) we have $L(3) = 1.75$.]

Consider now a composite hash function on an $(m_1 + m_2)$-bit field, formed by mapping the first m_1 bits with one hash function and the remaining m_2 with another, where $L_1(t)$ and $L_2(t)$ are the corresponding average numbers of locations per query. Find a formula that expresses $L(t)$, for the composite function, in terms of L_1 and L_2.

7. [*M24*] (R. L. Rivest.) Find the functions $L(t)$, as defined in the previous exercise, for the following combinatorial hash functions:

(a) $m = 3$, $n = 2$

$$0\ 0\ * \to 0$$
$$1\ *\ 0 \to 1$$
$$*\ 1\ 1 \to 2$$
$$1\ 0\ 1 \to 3$$
$$0\ 1\ 0 \to 3$$

(b) $m = 4$, $n = 2$

$$0\ 0\ *\ * \to 0$$
$$*\ 1\ *\ 0 \to 1$$
$$*\ 1\ 1\ 1 \to 2$$
$$1\ 0\ 1\ * \to 2$$
$$*\ 1\ 0\ 1 \to 3$$
$$1\ 0\ 0\ * \to 3$$

8. [*M32*] (R. L. Rivest.) Consider the set $Q_{t,m}$ of all $2^t \binom{m}{t}$ basic m-bit queries like (10) in which there are exactly t specified bits. Given a set S of m-bit records, let $f_t(S)$ denote the number of queries in $Q_{t,m}$ whose answer contains a member of S; and let $f_t(s, m)$ be the minimum $f_t(S)$ over all such sets S having s elements, for $0 \le s \le 2^m$. By convention, $f_t(0, 0) = 0$ and $f_t(1, 0) = \delta_{t0}$.

a) Prove that, for all $t \ge 1$ and $m \ge 1$, and for $0 \le s \le 2^m$,

$$f_t(s, m) = f_t(\lceil s/2 \rceil, m - 1) + f_{t-1}(\lceil s/2 \rceil, m - 1) + f_{t-1}(\lfloor s/2 \rfloor, m - 1).$$

b) Consider any combinatorial hash function h from the 2^m possible records to 2^n lists, with each list corresponding to 2^{m-n} records. If each of the queries in $Q_{t,m}$ is equally likely, the average number of lists that need to be examined per query is $1/2^t \binom{m}{t}$ times

$$\sum_{Q \in Q_{t,m}} (\text{lists examined for } Q) = \sum_{\text{lists } S} (\text{queries of } Q_{t,m} \text{ relevant to } S) \ge 2^n f_t(2^{m-n}, m).$$

Show that h is optimal, in the sense that this lower bound is achieved, when each of the lists is a "subcube"; in other words, show that equality holds in the case when each list corresponds to a set of records that satisfies some basic query with exactly n specified bits.

9. [*M20*] Prove that when $v = 3^n$, the set of all triples of the form

$$\{(a_1 \ldots a_{k-1}\, 0\, b_1 \ldots b_{n-k})_3, (a_1 \ldots a_{k-1}\, 1\, c_1 \ldots c_{n-k})_3, (a_1 \ldots a_{k-1}\, 2\, d_1 \ldots d_{n-k})_3\},$$

$1 \le k \le n$, forms a Steiner triple system, where the a's, b's, c's, and d's range over all combinations of 0s, 1s, and 2s such that $b_j + c_j + d_j \equiv 0$ (modulo 3) for $1 \le j \le n - k$.

10. [*M32*] (Thomas P. Kirkman, *Cambridge and Dublin Math. Journal* **2** (1847), 191–204.) Let us say that a *Kirkman triple system* of order v is an arrangement of $v + 1$ objects $\{x_0, x_1, \ldots, x_v\}$ into triples such that every pair $\{x_i, x_j\}$ for $i \ne j$ occurs in exactly one triple, except that the v pairs $\{x_i, x_{(i+1) \bmod v}\}$ do not ever occur in the same triple, for $0 \le i < v$. For example,

$$\{x_0, x_2, x_4\},\ \{x_1, x_3, x_4\}$$

is a Kirkman triple system of order 4.

a) Prove that a Kirkman triple system can exist only when $v \bmod 6 = 0$ or 4.

b) Given a Steiner triple system S on v objects $\{x_1, \ldots, x_v\}$, prove that the following construction yields another Steiner system S' on $2v + 1$ objects and a Kirkman triple system K' of order $2v - 2$: The triples of S' are those of S plus

   i) $\{x_i, y_j, y_k\}$ where $j + k \equiv i$ (modulo v) and $j < k$, $1 \le i, j, k \le v$;

   ii) $\{x_i, y_j, z\}$ where $2j \equiv i$ (modulo v), $1 \le i, j \le v$.

   The triples of K' are those of S' minus all those containing y_1 and/or y_v.

c) Given a Kirkman triple system K on $\{x_0, x_1, \ldots, x_v\}$, where $v = 2u$, prove that the following construction yields a Steiner triple system S' on $2v + 1$ objects and a Kirkman triple system K' of order $2v - 2$: The triples of S' are those of K plus

   i) $\{x_i, x_{(i+1) \bmod v}, y_{i+1}\}$, $0 \le i < v$;

   ii) $\{x_i, y_j, y_k\}$, $j + k \equiv 2i + 1$ (modulo $v-1$), $1 \le j < k - 1 \le v - 2$, $1 \le i \le v - 2$;

   iii) $\{x_i, y_j, y_v\}$, $2j \equiv 2i + 1$ (modulo $v-1$), $1 \le j \le v - 1$, $1 \le i \le v - 2$;

   iv) $\{x_0, y_{2j}, y_{2j+1}\}$, $\{x_{v-1}, y_{2j-1}, y_{2j}\}$, $\{x_v, y_j, y_{v-j}\}$, for $1 \le j < u$;

   v) $\{x_v, y_u, y_v\}$.

   The triples of K' are those of S' minus all those containing y_1 and/or y_{v-1}.

d) Use the preceding results to prove that Kirkman triple systems of order v exist for all $v \ge 0$ of the form $6k$ or $6k + 4$, and Steiner triple systems on v objects exist for all $v \ge 1$ of the form $6k + 1$ or $6k + 3$.

11. [*M25*] The text describes the use of Steiner triple systems in connection with inclusive queries; in order to extend this to all basic queries it is natural to define the following concept. A *complemented triple system* of order v is an arrangement of $2v$ objects $\{x_1, \ldots, x_v, \bar{x}_1, \ldots, \bar{x}_v\}$ into triples such that every pair of objects occurs together in exactly one triple, except that complementary pairs $\{x_i, \bar{x}_i\}$ never occur together. For example,

$$\{x_1, x_2, x_3\}, \quad \{x_1, \bar{x}_2, \bar{x}_3\}, \quad \{\bar{x}_1, x_2, \bar{x}_3\}, \quad \{\bar{x}_1, \bar{x}_2, x_3\}$$

is a complemented triple system of order three.

Prove that complemented triple systems of order v exist for all $v \ge 0$ not of the form $3k + 2$.

12. [*M23*] Continuing exercise 11, construct a complemented *quadruple* system of order 7.

13. [*M25*] Construct quadruple systems with $v = 4^n$ elements, analogous to the triple system of exercise 9.

14. [*28*] Discuss the problem of deleting nodes from quadtrees, k-d trees, and post-office trees like Fig. 45.

15. [*HM30*] (P. Elias.) Given a large collection of m-bit records, suppose we want to find a record closest to a given search argument, in the sense that it agrees in the most bits. Devise an algorithm for solving this problem efficiently, assuming that an m-bit t-error-correcting code of 2^n elements is given, and that each record has been hashed onto one of 2^n lists corresponding to the nearest codeword.

▶ **16.** [*25*] (W. H. Kautz and R. C. Singleton.) Show that a Steiner triple system of order v can be used to construct $v(v - 1)/6$ codewords of v bits each such that no codeword is contained in the superposition of any two others.

▶ **17.** [*M30*] Consider the following way to reduce $(2n+1)$-bit keys $a_{-n} \ldots a_0 \ldots a_n$ to $(n+1)$-bit bucket addresses $b_0 \ldots b_n$:

$$b_0 \leftarrow a_0;$$
$$\text{if } b_{k-1} = 0 \text{ then } b_k \leftarrow a_{-k} \text{ else } b_k \leftarrow a_k, \text{ for } 1 \le k \le n.$$

a) Describe the keys that appear in bucket $b_0 \ldots b_n$.

b) What is the largest number of buckets that need to be examined, in a basic query that has t bits specified?

▶ **18.** [*M35*] (*Associative block designs.*) A set of m-tuples like (13), with exactly $m-n$ *'s in each of 2^n rows, is called an ABD(m,n) if every column contains the same number of *'s and if every pair of rows has a "mismatch" (0 versus 1) in some column. Every m-bit binary number will then match exactly one row. For example, (13) is an ABD$(4,3)$.

a) Prove that an ABD(m,n) is impossible unless m is a divisor of $2^{n-1}n$ and $n^2 \ge 2m(1-2^{-n})$.

b) A row of an ABD is said to have *odd parity* if it contains an odd number of 1s. Show that, for every choice of $m-n$ columns in an ABD(m,n), the number of odd-parity rows with *'s in these columns equals the number of even-parity rows. In particular, each pattern of asterisks must occur in an even number of rows.

c) Find an ABD$(4,3)$ that cannot be obtained from (13) by permuting and/or complementing columns.

d) Construct an ABD$(16,9)$.

e) Construct an ABD$(16,10)$. Start with the ABD$(16,9)$ of part (d), instead of the ABD$(8,5)$ of (15).

19. [*M22*] Analyze the ABD$(8,5)$ of (15), as (13) has been analyzed in (14): How many of the 32 locations must be searched for an average query with k bits unspecified? How many must be searched in the worst case?

20. [*M47*] Find all ABD(m,n) when $n=5$ or $n=6$.

A new Section 6.6 devoted to "persistent data structures" is planned for the next edition of the present book. Persistent structures are able to represent changing information in such a way that the past history can be reconstructed efficiently. In other words, we might do many insertions and deletions, but we can still conduct searches as if the updates after a given time had not been made. Relevant early references to this topic include the following papers:

- J. K. Mullin, *Comp. J.* **24** (1981), 367–373;
- M. H. Overmars, *Lecture Notes in Comp. Sci.* **156** (1983), Chapter 9;
- E. W. Myers, *ACM Symp. Principles of Prog. Lang.* **11** (1984), 66–75;
- B. Chazelle, *Information and Control* **63** (1985), 77–99;
- D. Dobkin and J. I. Munro, *J. Algorithms* **6** (1985), 455–465;
- R. Cole, *J. Algorithms* **7** (1986), 202–220;
- D. Field, *Information Processing Letters* **24** (1987), 95–96;
- C. W. Fraser and E. W. Myers, *ACM Trans. Prog. Lang. and Systems* **9** (1987), 277–295;
- J. R. Driscoll, N. Sarnak, D. D. Sleator, and R. E. Tarjan, *J. Comp. Syst. Sci.* **38** (1989), 86–124;
- R. B. Dannenberg, *Software Practice & Experience* **20** (1990), 109–132;
- J. R. Driscoll, D. D. K. Sleator, and R. E. Tarjan, *JACM* **41** (1994), 943–959.

*Instruction tables [programs] will have to be made up
by mathematicians with computing experience
and perhaps a certain puzzle solving ability.
There will probably be a great deal of work of this kind to be done,
for every known process has got to be
translated into instruction table form at some stage. ...
This process of constructing instruction tables should be very fascinating.
There need be no real danger of it ever becoming a drudge,
for any processes that are quite mechanical
may be turned over to the machine itself.*

— ALAN M. TURING (1945)

ANSWERS TO EXERCISES

"I have answered three questions, and that is enough,"
Said his father, "don't give yourself airs!
"Do you think I can listen all day to such stuff?
Be off, or I'll kick you down stairs!"
— LEWIS CARROLL, *Alice's Adventures Under Ground* (1864)

NOTES ON THE EXERCISES

1. An average problem for a mathematically inclined reader.

3. See W. J. LeVeque, *Topics in Number Theory* **2** (Reading, Mass.: Addison–Wesley, 1956), Chapter 3; P. Ribenboim, *13 Lectures on Fermat's Last Theorem* (New York: Springer-Verlag, 1979); A. Wiles, *Annals of Mathematics* (2) **141** (1995), 443–551.

SECTION 5

1. Let $p(1)\ldots p(N)$ and $q(1)\ldots q(N)$ be different permutations satisfying the conditions, and let i be minimal with $p(i) \neq q(i)$. Then $p(i) = q(j)$ for some $j > i$, and $q(i) = p(k)$ for some $k > i$. Since $K_{p(i)} \leq K_{p(k)} = K_{q(i)} \leq K_{q(j)} = K_{p(i)}$ we have $K_{p(i)} = K_{q(i)}$; hence by stability $p(i) < p(k) = q(i) < q(j) = p(i)$, a contradiction.

2. Yes, if the sorting operations were all stable. (If they were not stable we cannot say.) Alice and Chris certainly have the same result; and so does Bill, since the stability shows that equal major keys in his result are accompanied by minor keys in nondecreasing order.

Formally, assume that Bill obtains $R_{p(1)}\ldots R_{p(N)} = R'_1 \ldots R'_N$ after sorting the minor keys, then $R'_{q(1)}\ldots R'_{q(N)} = R_{p(q(1))}\ldots R_{p(q(N))}$ after sorting the major keys; we want to show that

$$\left(K_{p(q(i))}, k_{p(q(i))}\right) \leq \left(K_{p(q(i+1))}, k_{p(q(i+1))}\right)$$

for $1 \leq i < N$. If $K_{p(q(i))} \neq K_{p(q(i+1))}$, we have $K_{p(q(i))} < K_{p(q(i+1))}$; and if $K_{p(q(i))} = K_{p(q(i+1))}$, then $K'_{q(i)} = K'_{q(i+1)}$, hence $q(i) < q(i + 1)$, hence $k'_{q(i)} \leq k'_{q(i+1)}$; that is, $k_{p(q(i))} \leq k_{p(q(i+1))}$.

3. We can always bring all records with equal keys together, preserving their relative order, treating these groups of records as a unit in further operations; hence we may assume that all keys are distinct. Let $a < b < c < a$; then we can arrange things so that the first three keys are *abc*, *bca*, or *cab*. Now if $N - 1$ distinct keys can be sorted in three ways, so can N; for if $K_1 < \cdots < K_{N-1} > K_N$ we always have either $K_{i-1} < K_N < K_i$ for some i, or $K_N < K_1$.

4. First compare words without case distinction, then use case to break ties. More precisely, replace each word α by the pair (α', α) where α' is obtained from α by mapping A $\to$ a, ..., Z $\to$ z; then sort the pairs lexicographically. This procedure gives, for example, tex < Tex < TeX < TEX < text.

Dictionaries must also deal with accented letters, prefixes, suffixes, and abbreviations; for example,

$$a < A < Å < a\text{-} < a. < \text{-}a < A\text{-} < A. < aa < a.a.$$
$$< \bar{a}a < \bar{a}\bar{a} < AA < A.A. < AAA < \cdots < zz < Zz. < ZZ < zzz < ZZZ.$$

In this more general situation we obtain α' by mapping $\bar{a} \to$ a, $Å \to$ a, etc., and dropping the hyphens and periods.

5. Let $\rho(0) = 0$ and $\rho((1\alpha)_2) = 1\rho(|\alpha|)\alpha$; here $(1\alpha)_2$ is the ordinary binary representation of a positive integer, and $|\alpha|$ is the length of the string α. We have $\rho(1) = 10$, $\rho(2) = 1100$, $\rho(3) = 1101$, $\rho(4) = 1110000$, ..., $\rho(1009) = 111101001111110001$, ..., $\rho(65536) = 1^5 0^{24}$, ..., $\rho(2^{65536}) = 1^6 0^{65560}$, etc. The length of $\rho(n)$ is

$$|\rho(n)| = \lambda(n) + \lambda(\lambda(n)) + \lambda(\lambda(\lambda(n))) + \cdots + \lg^* n + 1,$$

where $\lambda(0) = 0$, $\lambda(n) = \lfloor \lg n \rfloor$ for $n \geq 1$, and $\lg^* n$ is the least integer $m \geq 0$ such that $\lambda^{[m]}(n) = 0$. [This construction is due to V. I. Levenshtein, *Problemy Kibernetiki* **20** (1968), 173–179; see also D. E. Knuth in *The Mathematical Gardner*, edited by D. A. Klarner (Belmont, California: Wadsworth International, 1981), 310–325.]

6. Overflow is possible, and it can lead to a false equality indication. He should have written, "LDA A; CMPA B" and tested the comparison indicator. (The inability to make full-word comparisons by subtraction is a problem on essentially all computers; it is the chief reason for including CMPA, ..., CMPX in MIX's repertoire.)

7.
```
COMPARE STJ  9F                    DEC1 1
   1H      LDX  A,1                J1P  1B
           CMPX B,1            9H  JMP  *  ▌
           JNE  9F
```

8. *Solution 1*, based on the identity $\min(a, b) = \frac{1}{2}(a + b - |a - b|)$:

```
SOL1 LDA  A                        SRAX 1
     SRAX 5                        ADD  AB1
     DIV  =2=                      ENTX 1
     STA  A1    a = 2a₁ + a₂       SLAX 5
     STX  A2    |a₂| ≤ 1           MUL  AB2
     LDA  B                        STX  AB3    (a₂ − b₂) sign(a − b)
     SRAX 5                        LDA  A2
     DIV  =2=                      ADD  B2
     STA  B1    b = 2b₁ + b₂       SUB  AB3
     STX  B2    |b₂| ≤ 1           SRAX 5
     LDA  A1                       DIV  =2=
     SUB  B1    no overflow possible  ADD  A1
     STA  AB1   a₁ − b₁            ADD  B1    no overflow possible
     LDA  A2                       SUB  AB1(1:5)
     SUB  B2                       STA  C  ▌
     STA  AB2   a₂ − b₂
```

Solution 2, based on the fact that indexing can cause interchanges in a tricky way:

```
SOL2 LDA  A
     STA  C
     STA  TA
     LDA  B
     STA  TB
```

Now duplicate the following code k times, where $2^k > 10^{10}$:

```
     LDA  TA
     SRAX 5
     DIV  =2=
     STX  TEMP
     LD1  TEMP
     STA  TA
     LDA  TB
     SRAX 5
     DIV  =2=
     STX  TEMP
     LD2  TEMP
     STA  TB
     INC1 0,2
     INC1 0,2
     INC1 0,2
     LD3  TMIN,1
     LDA  0,3
     STA  C
```

(This scans the binary representations of a and b from right to left, preserving their signs.) The program concludes with a table:

```
     HLT
     CON  C    -1   -1
     CON  B     0   -1
     CON  B    +1   -1
     CON  A    -1    0
TMIN CON  C     0    0
     CON  B     1    0
     CON  A    -1    1
     CON  A     0    1
     CON  C     1    1   ▌
```

9. $\sum_j \binom{r+j-1}{j}(-1)^j \binom{N}{r+j} x^{r+j}$, by the method of inclusion and exclusion (exercise 1.3.3–26). This can also be written $r\binom{N}{r} \int_0^x t^{r-1}(1-t)^{N-r}\,dt$, a beta distribution.

10. Sort the tape contents, then count. (Some sorting methods make it convenient to drop records whose keys appear more than once as the sorting progresses.)

11. Assign each person an identification number, which must appear on all forms concerning that individual. Sort the information forms and the tax forms separately, with this identification number as the key. Denote the sorted tax forms by $R_1, \ldots, R_N$, with keys $K_1 < \cdots < K_N$. (There should be no two tax forms with equal keys.) Add a new $(N+1)$st record whose key is ∞, and set $i \leftarrow 1$. Then, for each record in the information file, check if it has been reported, as follows: Let K denote the key on the information form being processed.

a) If $K > K_i$, increase i by 1 and repeat this step.

b) If $K < K_i$, or if $K = K_i$ and the information is not reflected on tax form R_i, signal an error.

Try to do all this processing without wasting the taxpayers' money.

12. One way is to attach the key (j, i) to the entry $a_{i,j}$ and to sort using lexicographic order, then omit the keys. (A similar idea can be used to obtain *any* desired reordering of information, when a simple formula for the reordering can be given.)

In the special case considered in this problem, the method of "balanced two-way merge sorting" treats the keys in such a simple manner that it is unnecessary to write any keys explicitly on the tapes. Given an $n \times n$ matrix, we may proceed as follows: First put odd-numbered rows on tape 1, even-numbered rows on tape 2, etc., obtaining

Tape 1: $a_{11}\, a_{12} \ldots a_{1n}\, a_{31}\, a_{32} \ldots a_{3n}\, a_{51}\, a_{52} \ldots a_{5n} \ldots$

Tape 2: $a_{21}\, a_{22} \ldots a_{2n}\, a_{41}\, a_{42} \ldots a_{4n}\, a_{61}\, a_{62} \ldots a_{6n} \ldots$

Then rewind these tapes, and process them synchronously, to obtain

Tape 3: $a_{11}\, a_{21}\, a_{12}\, a_{22} \ldots a_{1n}\, a_{2n}\, a_{51}\, a_{61}\, a_{52}\, a_{62} \ldots a_{5n}\, a_{6n} \ldots$

Tape 4: $a_{31}\, a_{41}\, a_{32}\, a_{42} \ldots a_{3n}\, a_{4n}\, a_{71}\, a_{81}\, a_{72}\, a_{82} \ldots a_{7n}\, a_{8n} \ldots$

Rewind these tapes, and process them synchronously, to obtain

Tape 1: $a_{11}\, a_{21}\, a_{31}\, a_{41}\, a_{12} \ldots a_{42} \ldots a_{4n}\, a_{9,1} \ldots$

Tape 2: $a_{51}\, a_{61}\, a_{71}\, a_{81}\, a_{52} \ldots a_{82} \ldots a_{8n}\, a_{13,1} \ldots$

And so on, until the desired transpose is obtained after $\lceil \lg n \rceil + 1$ passes.

13. One way is to attach random distinct key values, sort on those keys, then discard the keys. (See exercise 12; a similar method for obtaining a random *sample* was discussed in Section 3.4.2.) Another technique, involving about the same amount of work but apparently not straining the accuracy of the random number generator as much, is to attach a random integer in the range $0 \le K_i \le N - i$ to R_i, then rearrange using the technique of exercise 5.1.1–5.

14. With a character-conversion table, you can design a lexicographic comparison routine that simulates the order used on the other machine. Alternatively, you could create artificial keys, different from the actual characters but giving the desired ordering. The latter method has the advantage that it needs to be done only once; but it takes more space and requires conversion of the entire key. The former method can often determine the result of a comparison by converting only one or two letters of the keys; during later stages of sorting, the comparison will be between nearly equal keys, however, and the former method may find it advantageous to check for equality of letters before converting them.

15. For this problem, just run through the file once keeping 50 or so individual counts. But if "city" were substituted for "state," and if the total number of cities were quite large, it would be a good idea to sort on the city name.

16. As in exercise 15, it depends on the size of the problem. If the total number of cross-reference entries fits into high-speed memory, the best approach is probably to use a symbol table algorithm (Chapter 6) with each identifier associated with the head of a linked list of references. For larger problems, create a file of records, one record for each cross-reference citation to be put in the index, and sort it.

17. Carry along with each card a "shadow key" that, sorted lexicographically in the usual simple way, will define the desired ordering. This key is to be supplied by library personnel and attached to the catalog data when it first enters the system, although it is not visible to normal users. A possible key uses the following two-letter codes to separate words from each other:

␣0	end of key;
␣1	end of cross-reference card;
␣2	end of surname;
␣3	hyphen of multiple surname;
␣4	end of author name;
␣5	end of place name;
␣6	end of subject heading;
␣7	end of book title;
␣8	space between words.

The given example would come out as follows (showing only the first 25 characters):

```
ACCADEMIA␣8NAZIONALE␣8DEI          I␣8HA␣8EHAD␣7␣0
ACHTZEHNHUNDERTZWOLF␣8EIN          IA␣8A␣8LOVE␣8STORY␣7␣0
BIBLIOTHEQUE␣8D␣8HISTOIRE          INTERNATIONAL␣8BUSINESS␣8
BIBLIOTHEQUE␣8DES␣8CURIOS          KHUWARIZMI␣2MUHAMMAD␣8IBN
BROWN␣2J␣8CROSBY␣4␣0               LABOR␣7A␣8MAGAZINE␣8FOR␣8
BROWN␣2JOHN␣4␣0                    LABOR␣8RESEARCH␣8ASSOCIAT
BROWN␣2JOHN␣4MATHEMATICIA          LABOUR␣1␣0
BROWN␣2JOHN␣4OF␣8BOSTON␣0          MACCALLS␣8COOKBOOK␣7␣0
BROWN␣2JOHN␣41715␣0                MACCARTHY␣2JOHN␣41927␣0
BROWN␣2JOHN␣41715␣6␣0              MACHINE␣8INDEPENDENT␣8COM
BROWN␣2JOHN␣41761␣0                MACMAHON␣2PERCY␣8ALEXANDE
BROWN␣2JOHN␣41810␣0                MISTRESS␣8DALLOWAY␣7␣0
BROWN␣3WILLIAMS␣2REGINALD          MISTRESS␣8OF␣8MISTRESSES␣
BROWN␣8AMERICA␣7␣0                 ROYAL␣8SOCIETY␣8OF␣8LONDO
BROWN␣8AND␣8DALLISONS␣8NE          SAINT␣8PETERSBURGER␣8ZEIT
BROWNJOHN␣2ALAN␣4␣0                SAINT␣8SAENS␣2CAMILLE␣418
DEN␣2VLADIMIR␣8EDUARDOVIC          SAINTE␣8MARIE␣2GASTON␣8P␣
DEN␣7␣0                            SEMINUMERICAL␣8ALGORITHMS
DEN␣8LIEBEN␣8LANGEN␣8TAG␣          UNCLE␣8TOMS␣8CABIN␣7␣0
DIX␣2MORGAN␣41827␣0                UNITED␣8STATES␣8BUREAU␣8O
DIX␣8HUIT␣8CENT␣8DOUZE␣80          VANDERMONDE␣2ALEXANDER␣8T
DIX␣8NEUVIEME␣8SIECLE␣8FR          VANVALKENBURG␣2MAC␣8ELWYN
EIGHTEEN␣8FORTY␣8SEVEN␣8I          VONNEUMANN␣2JOHN␣41903␣0
EIGHTEEN␣8TWELVE␣8OVERTUR          WHOLE␣8ART␣8OF␣8LEGERDEMA
I␣8AM␣8A␣8MATHEMATICIAN␣7          WHOS␣8AFRAID␣8OF␣8VIRGINI
I␣8B␣8M␣8JOURNAL␣8OF␣8RES          WIJNGAARDEN␣2ADRIAAN␣8VAN
```

This auxiliary key should be followed by the card data, so that unequal cards having the same auxiliary key (e.g., Sir John = John) are distinguished properly. Notice that "Saint-Saëns" is a hyphenated name but not a compound name. The birth year of al-Khuwārizmī should be given as, say, ␣40779 with a leading zero. (This scheme will work until the year 9999, after which the world will face a huge software crisis.)

Careful study of this example reveals how to deal with many other unusual types of order that are needed in human-computer interaction.

18. For example, we can make two files containing values of $(u^6 + v^6 + w^6) \bmod m$ and $(z^6 - x^6 - y^6) \bmod m$ for $u \le v \le w$, $x \le y \le z$, where m is the word size of our computer. Sort these and look for duplicates, then subject the duplicates to further tests. (Some congruences modulo small primes might also be used to place further restrictions on u, v, w, x, y, z.)

19. In general, to find all pairs of numbers $\{x_i, x_j\}$ with $x_i + x_j = c$, where c is given: Sort the file so that $x_1 < x_2 < \cdots < x_N$. Set $i \leftarrow 1$, $j \leftarrow N$, and then repeat the following operation until $j \le i$:

> If $x_i + x_j = c$, output $\{x_i, x_j\}$, set $i \leftarrow i + 1$, $j \leftarrow j - 1$;
> If $x_i + x_j < c$, set $i \leftarrow i + 1$;
> If $x_i + x_j > c$, set $j \leftarrow j - 1$.

Finally if $j = i$ and $2x_i = c$, output $\{x_i, x_i\}$. This process is like the method of exercise 18: We are essentially making two sorted files, one containing $x_1, \ldots, x_N$ and the other containing $c - x_N, \ldots, c - x_1$, and checking for duplicates. But the second file doesn't need to be explicitly formed in this case. Another approach, suggested by Jiang Ling, is to sort on a key such as $(x > c/2 \Rightarrow x, \ x \le c/2 \Rightarrow c - x)$.

A similar algorithm can be used to find $\max\{x_i + x_j \mid x_i + x_j \le c\}$; or to find, say, $\min\{x_i + y_j \mid x_i + y_j > t\}$ given t and two sorted files $x_1 \le \cdots \le x_m$, $y_1 \le \cdots \le y_n$.

20. Some of the alternatives are: (a) For each of the 499,500 pairs i, j, with $1 \le i < j \le 1000$, set $y_1 \leftarrow x_i \oplus x_j$, $y_2 \leftarrow y_1 \ \& \ (y_1 - 1)$, $y_3 \leftarrow y_2 \ \& \ (y_2 - 1)$; then print (x_i, x_j) if and only if $y_3 = 0$. Here $\oplus$ denotes "exclusive or" and $\&$ denotes "bitwise and". (b) Create a file with 31,000 entries, forming 31 entries from each original word x_i by including x_i and the 30 words that differ from x_i in one position. Sort this file and look for duplicates. (c) Do a test analogous to (a) on

  i) all pairs of words that agree in their first 10 bits;

 ii) all pairs of words that agree in their middle 10 bits, but not the first 10;

iii) all pairs of words that agree in their last 10 bits, but neither the first nor middle 10.

This involves three sorts of the data, using a specified 10-bit key each time. The expected number of pairs in each of the three cases is at most $499500/2^{10}$, which is less than 500, if the original words are randomly distributed.

21. First prepare a file containing all five-letter English words. (Be sure to consider adding suffixes such as -ED, -ER, -ERS, -S to shorter words.) Now take each five-letter word α and sort its letters into ascending order, obtaining the sorted five-letter sequence α'. Finally sort all pairs (α', α) to bring all anagrams together.

Experiments by Kim D. Gibson in 1967 showed that the second longest set of commonly known five-letter anagrams is LEAST, SLATE, STALE, STEAL, TAELS, TALES, TEALS. But if he had been able to use larger dictionaries, he would have been able to catapult this set into first place, by adding the words ALETS (steel shoulderplates), ASTEL (a splinter), ATLES (intends), LAETS (people who rank between slaves and freemen), LASET (an ermine), LATES (a Nile perch), LEATS (watercourses), SALET (a mediæval helmet), SETAL (pertaining to setae), SLEAT (to incite), STELA (a column), and TESLA (a unit of magnetic flux density). Together with the old spellings SATEL, TASEL, and TASLE for "settle" and "teasel," we obtain 22 mutually permutable words, none of which needs to be spelled with an uppercase letter. And with a bit more daring we might add the Old English *tæsl*, German *altes*, and Madame de Staël! The set {LAPSE, LEAPS, PALES, PEALS, PLEAS, SALEP, SEPAL} can also be extended to at least 14 words when we turn to unabridged dictionaries. [See H. E. Dudeney, *Strand* **65** (1923), 208, 312, and his *300 Best Word Puzzles*, edited by Martin Gardner (1968), Puzzles 190 and 194; Ross Eckler, *Making the Alphabet Dance* (St. Martin's Griffin, 1997), Fig. 46c.]

The first and last sets of three or more five-letter English anagrams are {ALBAS, BALAS, BALSA, BASAL} and {STRUT, STURT, TRUST}, if proper names are not allowed. However, the proper names Alban, Balan, Laban, and Nabal lead to an earlier set {ALBAN, BALAN, BANAL, LABAN, NABAL, NABLA} if that restriction is dropped. The most striking example of longer anagram words in common English is perhaps the amazingly mathematical set {ALERTING, ALTERING, INTEGRAL, RELATING, TRIANGLE}.

A faster way to proceed is to compute $f(\alpha) = (h(a_1) + h(a_2) + \cdots + h(a_5)) \bmod m$, where $a_1, \ldots, a_5$ are numerical codes for the individual letters in α, and $(h(1), h(2), \ldots)$ are 26 randomly selected constants; here m is, say, $2^{\lfloor 2 \lg N \rfloor}$ when there are N words. Sorting the file $(f(\alpha), \alpha)$ with two passes of Algorithm 5.2.5R will bring anagrams together; afterwards when $f(\alpha) = f(\beta)$ we must make sure that we have a true anagram with $\alpha' = \beta'$. The value $f(\alpha)$ can be calculated more rapidly than α', and this method avoids the determination of α' for most of the words α in the file.

Note: A similar technique can be used when we want to bring together all sets of records that have equal multiword keys $(a_1, \ldots, a_n)$. Suppose that we don't care about the order of the file, except that records with equal keys are to be brought together; it is sometimes faster to sort on the one-word key $(a_1 x^{n-1} + a_2 x^{n-2} + \cdots + a_n) \bmod m$, where x is any fixed value, instead of sorting on the original multiword key.

22. Find isomorphic invariants of the graphs (functions that take equal values on isomorphic directed graphs) and sort on these invariants, to separate "obviously nonisomorphic" graphs from each other. Examples of isomorphic invariants: (a) Represent vertex v_i by (a_i, b_i), where a_i is its in-degree and b_i is its out-degree; then sort the pairs (a_i, b_i) into lexicographic order. The resulting file is an isomorphic invariant. (b) Represent an arc from v_i to v_j by (a_i, b_i, a_j, b_j), and sort these quadruples into lexicographic order. (c) Separate the directed graph into connected components (see Algorithm 2.3.3E), determine invariants of each component, and sort the components into order of their invariants in some way. See also the discussion in exercise 21.

After sorting the directed graphs on their invariants, it will still be necessary to make secondary tests to see whether directed graphs with identical invariants are in fact isomorphic. The invariants are helpful for these tests too. In the case of free trees it is possible to find "characteristic" or "canonical" invariants that completely characterize the tree, so that secondary testing is unnecessary [see J. Hopcroft and R. E. Tarjan, in *Complexity of Computer Computations* (New York: Plenum, 1972), 140–142].

23. One way is to form a file containing all three-person cliques, then transform it into a file containing all four-person cliques, etc.; if there are no large cliques, this method will be quite satisfactory. (On the other hand, if there is a clique of size n, there are at least $\binom{n}{k}$ cliques of size k; so this method can blow up even when n is only 25 or so.)

Given a file that lists all $(k-1)$-person cliques, in the form $(a_1, \ldots, a_{k-1})$ where $a_1 < \cdots < a_{k-1}$, we can find the k-person cliques by (i) creating a new file containing the entries $(b, c, a_1, \ldots, a_{k-2})$ for each pair of $(k-1)$-person cliques of the respective forms $(a_1, \ldots, a_{k-2}, b)$, $(a_1, \ldots, a_{k-2}, c)$ with $b < c$; (ii) sorting this file on its first two components; (iii) for each entry $(b, c, a_1, \ldots, a_{k-2})$ in this new file that matches a pair (b, c) of acquaintances in the originally given file, output the k-person clique $(a_1, \ldots, a_{k-2}, b, c)$.

24. (Solution by Norman Hardy, c. 1967.) Make another copy of the input file; sort one copy on the first components and the other on the second. Passing over these files in sequence now allows us to create a new file containing all pairs (x_i, x_{i+2}) for $1 \le i \le N - 2$, and to identify (x_{N-1}, x_N). The pairs $(N-1, x_{N-1})$ and (N, x_N) should be written on still another file.

The process continues inductively. Assume that file F contains all pairs (x_i, x_{i+t}) for $1 \le i \le N - t$, in random order, and that file G contains all pairs (i, x_i) for $N - t < i \le N$ in order of the second components. Let H be a copy of file F, and sort H by first components, F by second. Now go through F, G, and H, creating two new files F' and G', as follows. If the current records of files F, G, H are, respectively (x, x'), (y, y'), (z, z'), then:

  i) If $x' = z$, output (x, z') to F' and advance files F and H.

 ii) If $x' = y'$, output $(y-t, x)$ to G' and advance files F and G.

iii) If $x' > y'$, advance file G.

iv) If $x' > z$, advance file H.

When file F is exhausted, sort G' by second components and merge G with it; then replace t by $2t$, F by F', G by G'.

Thus t takes the values $2, 4, 8, \ldots$; and for fixed t we do $O(\log N)$ passes over the data to sort it. Hence the total number of passes is $O((\log N)^2)$. Eventually $t \ge N$, so F is empty; then we simply sort G on its *first* components.

25. (An idea due to D. Shanks.) Prepare two files, one containing $a^{mn} \bmod p$ and the other containing $ba^{-n} \bmod p$ for $0 \le n < m$. Sort these files and find a common entry.

Note: This reduces the worst-case running time from $\Theta(p)$ to $\Theta(\sqrt{p}\log p)$. Significant further improvements are often possible; for example, we can easily determine if n is even or odd, in $\log p$ steps, by testing whether $b^{(p-1)/2} \bmod p = 1$ or $(p-1)$. In general if f is any divisor of $p - 1$ and d is any divisor of $\gcd(f, n)$, we can similarly determine $(n/d) \bmod f$ by looking up the value of $b^{(p-1)/f}$ in a table of length f/d. If $p - 1$ has the prime factors $q_1 \le q_2 \le \cdots \le q_t$ and if q_t is small, we can therefore compute n rapidly by finding the digits from right to left in its mixed-radix representation, for radices $q_1, \ldots, q_t$. (This idea is due to R. L. Silver, 1964; see also S. C. Pohlig and M. Hellman, *IEEE Transactions* **IT-24** (1978), 106–110.)

John M. Pollard discovered an elegant way to compute discrete logs with about $O(\sqrt{p})$ operations mod p, requiring very little memory, based on the theory of random mappings. See *Math. Comp.* **32** (1978), 918–924, where he also suggests another method based on numbers $n_j = r^j \bmod p$ that have only small prime factors.

Asymptotically faster methods are discussed in exercise 4.5.4–46.

SECTION 5.1.1

1. 205223000; 27354186.

2. $b_1 = (m - 1) \bmod n$; $b_{j+1} = (b_j + m - 1) \bmod (n - j)$.

3. $\bar{a}_j = a_{n+1-j}$ (the "reflected" permutation). This idea was used by O. Terquem [*Journ. de Math.* **3** (1838), 559–560] to prove that the average number of inversions in a random permutation is $\frac{1}{2}\binom{n}{2}$.

4. C1. Set $x_0 \leftarrow 0$. (It is possible to let x_j share memory with b_j in what follows, for $1 \le j \le n$.)

   C2. For $k = n$, $n-1$, $\ldots$, 1 (in this order) do the following: Set $j \leftarrow 0$; then set $j \leftarrow x_j$ exactly b_k times; then set $x_k \leftarrow x_j$ and $x_j \leftarrow k$.

   C3. Set $j \leftarrow 0$.

C4. For $k = 1, 2, \ldots, n$ (in this order), do the following: Set $a_k \leftarrow x_j$; then set $j \leftarrow x_j$. ∎

To save memory space, see exercise 5.2–12.

5. Let α be a string $[m_1, n_1] \ldots [m_k, n_k]$ of ordered pairs of nonnegative integers; we write $|\alpha| = k$, the length of α. Let ϵ denote the empty (length 0) string. Consider the binary operation $\circ$ defined recursively on pairs of such strings as follows:

$$\epsilon \circ \alpha = \alpha \circ \epsilon = \alpha;$$

$$([m,n]\,\alpha) \circ ([m',n']\,\beta) = \begin{cases} [m,n]\,(\alpha \circ ([m'-m,n']\,\beta)), & \text{if } m \le m', \\ [m',n']\,(((m-m'-1,n]\,\alpha) \circ \beta), & \text{if } m > m'. \end{cases}$$

It follows that the computation time required to evaluate $\alpha \circ \beta$ is proportional to $|\alpha \circ \beta| = |\alpha| + |\beta|$. Furthermore, we can prove that $\circ$ is associative and that $[b_1, 1] \circ [b_2, 2] \circ \cdots \circ [b_n, n] = [0, a_1][0, a_2] \ldots [0, a_n]$. The expression on the left can be evaluated in $\lceil \lg n \rceil$ passes, each pass combining pairs of strings, for a total of $O(n \log n)$ steps.

Example: Starting from (2), we want to evaluate $[2,1] \circ [3,2] \circ [6,3] \circ [4,4] \circ [0,5] \circ [2,6] \circ [2,7] \circ [1,8] \circ [0,9]$. The first pass reduces this to $[2,1][1,2] \circ [4,4][1,3] \circ [0,5][2,6] \circ [1,8][0,7] \circ [0,9]$. The second pass reduces it to $[2,1][1,2][1,4][1,3] \circ [0,5][1,8][0,6][0,7] \circ [0,9]$. The third pass yields $[0,5][1,1][0,8][0,2][0,6][0,4][0,7][0,3] \circ [0,9]$. The fourth pass yields (1).

Motivation: A string such as $[4,4][1,3]$ stands for "␣␣␣␣4␣3␣$^\infty$", where "␣" denotes a blank; the operation $\alpha \circ \beta$ inserts the blanks and nonblanks of β into the blanks of α. Note that, together with exercise 2, we obtain an algorithm for the Josephus problem that is $O(n \log n)$ instead of $O(mn)$, partially answering a question raised in exercise 1.3.2–22.

Another $O(n \log n)$ solution to this problem, using a random-access memory, follows from the use of balanced trees in a straightforward manner.

6. Start with $b_1 = b_2 = \cdots = b_n = 0$. For $k = \lfloor \lg n \rfloor, \lfloor \lg n \rfloor - 1, \ldots, 0$ do the following: Set $x_s \leftarrow 0$ for $0 \le s \le n/2^{k+1}$; then for $j = 1, 2, \ldots, n$ do the following: Set $r \leftarrow \lfloor a_j / 2^k \rfloor \bmod 2$, $s \leftarrow \lfloor a_j / 2^{k+1} \rfloor$ (these are essentially bit extractions); if $r = 0$, set $b_{a_j} \leftarrow b_{a_j} + x_s$, and if $r = 1$ set $x_s \leftarrow x_s + 1$.

Another solution appears in exercise 5.2.4–21.

7. $B_j < j$ and $C_j \le n - j$, since a_j has $j - 1$ elements to its left and $n - j$ elements to its right. To reconstruct $a_1 a_2 \ldots a_n$ from $B_1 B_2 \ldots B_n$, start with the element 1; then for $k = 2, \ldots, n$ add one to each element $\ge k - B_k$ and append $k - B_k$ at the right. (See Method 2 in Section 1.2.5). A similar procedure works for the C's. Alternatively, we could use the result of the following exercise. [The c inversion table was discussed by Rodrigues, *J. de Math.* **4** (1839), 236–240. The C inversion table was used by Rothe in 1800; see also Netto's *Lehrbuch der Combinatorik* (1901), §5.]

8. $b' = C$, $c' = B$, $B' = c$, $C' = b$, since each inversion (a_i, a_j) of $a_1 \ldots a_n$ corresponds to the inversion (j, i) of $a'_1 \ldots a'_n$. Some further relations: (a) $c_j = j - 1$ if and only if $(b_i > b_j$ for all $i < j$); (b) $b_j = n - j$ if and only if $(c_i > c_j$ for all $i > j$); (c) $b_j = 0$ if and only if $(c_i - i < c_j - j$ for all $i > j$); (d) $c_j = 0$ if and only if $(b_i + i < b_j + j$ for all $i < j$); (e) $b_i \le b_{i+1}$ if and only if $a'_i < a'_{i+1}$, if and only if $c_i \ge c_{i+1}$; (f) $a_j = j + C_j - B_j$; $a'_j = j + b_j - c_j$.

9. $b = C = b'$ is equivalent to $a = a'$.

10. $\sqrt{10}$. (One way to coordinatize the truncated octahedron lets the respective vectors $(1,0,0)$, $(0,1,0)$, $\frac{1}{2}(1,1,\sqrt{2})$, $\frac{1}{2}(1,-1,\sqrt{2})$, $\frac{1}{2}(-1,1,\sqrt{2})$, $\frac{1}{2}(-1,-1,\sqrt{2})$ stand for adjacent interchanges of the respective pairs $2\bar{1}$, $4\bar{3}$, $4\bar{1}$, $3\bar{1}$, $4\bar{2}$, $3\bar{2}$. The sum of these vectors gives $(1,1,2\sqrt{2})$ as the difference between vertices 4321 and 1234.)

A more symmetric solution is to represent vertex π in *four* dimensions by

$$\sum \{\mathbf{e}_u - \mathbf{e}_v \mid (u,v) \text{ is an inversion of } \pi\},$$

where $\mathbf{e}_1 = (1,0,0,0)$, $\mathbf{e}_2 = (0,1,0,0)$, $\mathbf{e}_3 = (0,0,1,0)$, $\mathbf{e}_4 = (0,0,0,1)$. Thus, $1234 \leftrightarrow (0,0,0,0)$; $1243 \leftrightarrow (0,0,-1,1)$; $\ldots$; $4321 \leftrightarrow (-3,-1,1,3)$. All points lie on the three-dimensional subspace $\{(w,x,y,z) \mid w+x+y+z = 0\}$; the distance between adjacent vertices is $\sqrt{2}$. Equivalently (see answer 8(f)) we may represent $\pi = a_1\,a_2\,a_3\,a_4$ by the vector (a_1', a_2', a_3', a_4'), where $a_1'\,a_2'\,a_3'\,a_4'$ is the inverse permutation. (This 4-D representation of the truncated octahedron with permutations as coordinates was discussed together with its n-dimensional generalization by C. Howard Hinton in *The Fourth Dimension* (London, 1904), Chapter 10. Further properties were found many years later by Guilbaud and Rosenstiehl, who called Fig. 1 the "permutahedron"; see exercise 12.)

Replicas of the truncated octahedron will fill three-dimensional space in what has been called the simplest possible way [see H. Steinhaus, *Mathematical Snapshots* (Oxford, 1960), 200–203; C. S. Smith, *Scientific American* **190**, 1 (January 1954), 58–64]. Book V of Pappus's *Collection* (c. A.D. 300) mentions the truncated octahedron as one of 13 special solid figures studied by Archimedes. Illustrations of the Archimedean solids — the nonprism polyhedra that have symmetries taking any vertex into any other, and whose faces are regular polygons but not all identical — can be found, for example, in books by W. W. Rouse Ball, *Mathematical Recreations and Essays*, revised by H. S. M. Coxeter (Macmillan, 1939), Chapter 5; H. Martyn Cundy and A. P. Rollett, *Mathematical Models* (Oxford, 1952), 94–109.

11. (a) Obvious. (b) Construct a directed graph with vertices $\{1, 2, \ldots, n\}$ and arcs $x \to y$ if either $x > y$ and $(x,y) \in E$ or $x < y$ and $(y,x) \in \bar{E}$. If there are no oriented cycles, this directed graph can be topologically sorted, and the resulting linear order is the desired permutation. If there is an oriented cycle, the shortest has length 3, since there are none of length 1 or 2 and since a longer cycle $a_1 \to a_2 \to a_3 \to a_4 \to \cdots \to a_1$ can be shortened (either $a_1 \to a_3$ or $a_3 \to a_1$). But an oriented cycle of length 3 contains two arcs of either E or $\bar{E}$, and proves that E or $\bar{E}$ is not transitive after all.

12. [G. T. Guilbaud and P. Rosenstiehl, *Math. et Sciences Humaines* **4** (1963), 9–33.] Suppose that $(a,b) \in \bar{E}$, $(b,c) \in \bar{E}$, $(a,c) \notin \bar{E}$. Then for some $k \geq 1$ we have $a = x_0 > x_1 > \cdots > x_k = c$, where $(x_i, x_{i+1}) \in E(\pi_1) \cup E(\pi_2)$ for $0 \leq i < k$. Consider a counterexample of this type where k is minimal. Since $(a,b) \notin E(\pi_1)$ and $(b,c) \notin E(\pi_1)$, we have $(a,c) \notin E(\pi_1)$, and similarly $(a,c) \notin E(\pi_2)$; hence $k > 1$. But if $x_1 > b$, then $(x_1, b) \in \bar{E}$ contradicts the minimality of k, while $(x_1, b) \in E$ implies that $(a,b) \in E$. Similarly, if $x_1 < b$, both $(b, x_1) \in \bar{E}$ and $(b, x_1) \in E$ are impossible.

13. For any fixed choice of b_1, $\ldots$, b_{n-m}, b_{n-m+2}, $\ldots$, b_n in the inversion table, the total $\sum_j b_j$ will assume each possible residue modulo m exactly once as b_{n-m+1} runs through its possible values $0, 1, \ldots, m-1$.

14. The hinted construction takes pairs of distinct-part partitions into each other, except in the two cases $j = k = p_k$ and $j = k = p_k - 1$. In the exceptional cases, n is $(2j-1) + \cdots + j = (3j^2 - j)/2$ and $(2j) + \cdots + (j+1) = (3j^2 + j)/2$, respectively, and there is a unique unpaired partition with j parts. [*Comptes Rendus Acad. Sci.* **92** (Paris, 1881), 448–450. Euler's original proof, in *Novi Comment. Acad. Sci. Pet.* **5**

(1754), 75–83, was also very interesting. He showed by simple manipulations that the infinite product equals s_1, if we define s_n as the power series $1 - z^{2n-1} - z^{3n-1}s_{n+1}$, for $n \geq 1$. Finite versions of Euler's infinite sum are discussed by Knuth and Paterson in *Fibonacci Quarterly* **16** (1978), 198–212.]

15. Transpose the dot diagram, to go from the p's to the P's. The generating function for the P's is easily obtained, since we first choose any number of 1s $\big($generating function $1/(1-z)\big)$, then independently choose any number of 2s $\big($generating function $1/(1-z^2)\big)$, ..., finally any number of n's.

16. The coefficient of $z^n q^m$ in the first identity is the number of partitions of m into at most n parts. In the second identity it is the number of partitions of m into n distinct nonnegative parts, namely sums of the form $m = p_1 + p_2 + \cdots + p_n$, where $p_1 > p_2 > \cdots > p_n \geq 0$. This is the same as $m - \binom{n}{2} = q_1 + q_2 + \cdots + q_n$, where $q_1 \geq q_2 \geq \cdots \geq q_n \geq 0$, under the correspondence $q_i = p_i - n + i$. [*Commentarii Academiæ Scientiarum Petropolitanæ* **13** (1741), 64–93.]

Notes: The second identity is the limit as $n \to \infty$ of the q-nomial theorem, exercise 1.2.6–58. The first identity, similarly, is the limit as $r \to \infty$ of the dual form of that theorem, proved in the answer to that exercise.

Let $n!_q = \prod_{k=1}^{n}(1 + q + \cdots + q^{k-1})$, and let $\exp_q(z) = \sum_{n=0}^{\infty} z^n/n!_q$. The first identity tells us that $\exp_q(z)$ is equal to $1/\prod_{k=0}^{\infty}(1 - q^k z(1-q))$ when $|q| < 1$; the second tells us that it equals $\prod_{k=0}^{\infty}(1 + q^{-k}z(1-q^{-1}))$ when $|q| > 1$. The resulting formal power series identity $\exp_q(z)\exp_{q^{-1}}(-z) = 1$ is equivalent to the formula

$$\sum_{k=0}^{n} \frac{(-1)^k q^{k(k-1)/2}}{(1-q)\ldots(1-q^k)(1-q)\ldots(1-q^{n-k})} = \delta_{n0}, \qquad \text{integer } n \geq 0,$$

which is a consequence of the q-nomial theorem with $x = -1$.

17.

0 0 0 0	0 1 0 0	0 0 1 0	0 0 0 1
1 1 0 1	1 2 0 1	1 0 2 1	1 0 1 2
1 0 1 0	0 1 1 0	0 1 2 0	0 1 0 2
1 0 1 1	0 1 1 1	0 1 2 1	0 1 1 2
1 0 0 1	0 1 0 1	0 0 1 1	0 0 1 2
2 0 1 2	0 2 1 2	0 1 2 2	0 1 2 3

18. Let $q = 1 - p$. The sum $\sum \Pr(\alpha)$ over all instances α of inversions may be evaluated by summing on k, where $0 \leq k < n$ is the exact number of leftmost bit positions in which there is equality between i and j as well as between X_i and X_j, in an inversion $X_i \oplus i > X_j \oplus j$ for $i < j$. In this way we obtain the formula $\sum_{0 \leq k < n} 2^k(p^2 + q^2)^k(p^2 2^{n-k-1} 2^{n-k-1} + 2pq 2^{n-k-1}(2^{n-k-1} - 1))$; summing and simplifying yields $2^{n-1}(p(2-p)(2^n - (p^2+q^2)^n)/(2-p^2-q^2) + (p^2+q^2)^n - 1)$.

19. The number of inversions is $\sum_{0 < i < j < n}(\lfloor mj/n \rfloor - \lfloor mi/n \rfloor - \lfloor m(j-i)/n \rfloor) = \sum_{0 < i < j < n}[mj \bmod n < mi \bmod n] = \sum_{0 < r < n}\lfloor mr/n \rfloor(r - (n-r) - (n-r-1))$, which can be transformed to $\frac{1}{4}(n-1)(n-2) - \frac{1}{4}n\sigma(m,n,0)$. [*Crelle* **198** (1957), 162–166.]

20. See J. J. Sylvester, *Amer. J. Math.* **5** (1882), 251–330, **6** (1883), 334–336, §57–§68; E. M. Wright, *J. London Math. Soc.* **40** (1965), 55–57; and J. Zolnowsky, *Discrete Math.* **9** (1974), 293–298.

Jacobi's identity can be proved rapidly as follows. Since

$$\prod_{k=1}^{n}(1 - u^k v^{k-1}) = (-1)^n u^{\binom{n+1}{2}} v^{\binom{n}{2}} \prod_{k=1}^{n}(1 - u^{-k} v^{1-k}),$$

the q-nomial theorem of exercise 1.2.6–58 with $q = uv$ tells us that

$$\prod_{k=1}^{n}(1 - u^k v^{k-1})(1 - u^{k-1}v^k) = (-1)^n u^{\binom{n+1}{2}} v^{\binom{n}{2}} \prod_{k=-n+1}^{n}(1 - u^{k-1}v^k)$$

$$= (-1)^n u^{\binom{n+1}{2}} v^{\binom{n}{2}} \sum_{j}\binom{2n}{j}_{uv}(uv)^{\binom{j}{2}}(-u^{-n}v^{1-n})^j$$

$$= \sum_{j}\binom{2n}{n+j}_{uv}(-1)^j u^{\binom{j}{2}}v^{\binom{j+1}{2}}.$$

Multiply both sides by $\prod_{k=1}^{n}(1 - u^k v^k) = \prod_{k=1}^{n}(1 - q^k)$ and note that, for fixed j, we have $\binom{2n}{n+j}_q \prod_{k=1}^{n}(1 - q^k) = 1 + O(q^{n+1-|j|})$. Jacobi's identity follows as $n \to \infty$.

21. Interpret C_j as the number of elements on the stack after the jth output. (See exercise 2.3.3–19 for characterizations of the b and B tables of stack permutations.)

22. (a) Arrange the numbers $\{1, 2, \ldots, n\}$ in a circle as on the face of a clock, and point at 1. Then for $j = n, n - 1, \ldots, 1$ (in this order), move the pointer counterclockwise $h_j + 1$ steps, remove the number pointed to from the circle, and call it a_j.

(b) Each i is counted as often as the sequence $a_i a_{i+1} \ldots a_n$ wraps around; this is the number of times that $a_j > a_{j+1}$ for $j \geq i$. Therefore each j with $a_j > a_{j+1}$ corresponds to the indices $1, \ldots, j$ being counted once. [Guo-Niu Han, *Advances in Math.* **105** (1994), 28–29; an equivalent result had been obtained by Rawlings, in the context of the next exercise.]

23. Suppose, for example, that $n = 5$ and $a_1 a_2 a_3 a_4 a_5 = 3\,1\,4\,2\,5$. The number of missed shots before each death must then be $2 + 5k_1$, $2 + 4k_2$, $1 + 3k_3$, $1 + 2k_2$, k_5, for some nonnegative integers k_j. Note that the dual permutation $1\,4\,2\,5\,3$ has h-table $0\,1\,1\,2\,2$ in the notation of the previous exercise. In general, the probability of obtaining $a_1 a_2 \ldots a_n$ will be

$$\sum_{k_1,\ldots,k_n \geq 0}(q_1^{h_n+nk_1}p_1)(q_2^{h_{n-1}+(n-1)k_2}p_2)\ldots(q_n^{h_1+k_n}p_n)$$

$$= \frac{1 - q_1}{1 - q_1^n}\frac{1 - q_2}{1 - q_2^{n-1}}\cdots\frac{1 - q_n}{1 - q_n^1}q_1^{h_n}q_2^{h_{n-1}}\cdots q_n^{h_1},$$

where $p_j = 1 - q_j$ is the probability of fatality after $j - 1$ deaths, and $h_1 h_2 \ldots h_n$ corresponds to the dual of $a_1 a_2 \ldots a_n$. In particular, when $p_1 = \cdots = p_n = p = 1 - q$, the probability is $q^{h_1 + \cdots + h_n}/G_n(q)$. The least likely order is therefore $n \ldots 2\,1$. [J. Treadway and D. Rawlings, *Math. Mag.* **67** (1994), 345–354; Rawlings generalized the process to multiset permutations in *Int. J. Math. & Math. Sci.* **15** (1992), 291–312.]

24. Let $a_0 = 0$, and say that a *generalized descent* occurs at $j < n$ if $a_j > t(a_{j+1})$. Inserting n between a_{j-1} and a_j causes a new generalized descent if and only if $a_{j-1} \leq t(a_j) < n$. Suppose this occurs when j has the values $j_1 > j_2 > \cdots > j_k > 0$; let the other values of j be $j_n > j_{n-1} > \cdots > j_{k+1}$. Then $j_n = n$, and it can be shown that the generalized index increases by $n - k$ when n is inserted just before a_{j_k}. [The special case in which $t(j) = j + d$ for some $d \geq 0$ is due to D. Rawlings, *J. Combinatorial Theory* **A31** (1981), 175–183; he generalized this special case to multiset permutations in *Linear and Multilinear Algebra* **10** (1981), 253–260.]

This exercise defines $n!$ different statistics on permutations, each of which has the generating function $G_n(z)$ that appears in (7) and (8). We can define many more such statistics by generalizing Russian roulette as follows: After $j - 1$ deaths, the person who begins the next round of shooting is $f_j(a_1, \ldots, a_{j-1})$, where f_j is an arbitrary function taking values in $\{1, \ldots, n\} \setminus \{a_1, \ldots, a_{j-1}\}$. [See Guo-Niu Han, *Calcul Denertien* (Thesis, Univ. Strasbourg, 1992), Part 1.3, §7.]

25. (a) If $a_1 < a_n$, $h(\alpha)$ has exactly as many inversions as α, because the elements of α_j now invert x_j instead of a_n. But if $a_1 > a_n$, $h(\alpha)$ has $n-1$ fewer inversions, because x_j loses its inversion of a_n and of each element in α_j. Therefore if we set $x_n = a_n$ and recursively let $x_1 \ldots x_{n-1} = f(h(\alpha))$, the permutation $f(\alpha) = x_1 \ldots x_n$ has the desired properties. We have $f(198263745) = 912638745$, and $f^{[-1]}(198263745) = 192687345$.

(b) The key point is that $\mathrm{inv}(\alpha) = \mathrm{inv}(\alpha^-)$ and $\mathrm{ind}(\alpha^-) = \mathrm{ind}(f(\alpha)^-)$, when α^- is the inverse of α. Therefore if $\alpha_1 = \alpha^-$, $\alpha_2 = f(\alpha_1)$, $\alpha_3 = \alpha_2^-$, $\alpha_4 = f^{[-1]}(\alpha_3)$, and $\alpha_5 = \alpha_4^-$, we have

$$\mathrm{inv}(\alpha_5) = \mathrm{inv}(\alpha_4) = \mathrm{ind}(\alpha_3) = \mathrm{ind}(\alpha_2^-) = \mathrm{ind}(\alpha_1^-) = \mathrm{ind}(\alpha);$$
$$\mathrm{ind}(\alpha_5) = \mathrm{ind}(\alpha_4^-) = \mathrm{ind}(\alpha_3^-) = \mathrm{ind}(\alpha_2) = \mathrm{inv}(\alpha_1) = \mathrm{inv}(\alpha).$$

[*Math. Nachrichten* **83** (1978), 143–159.]

26. (Solution by Doron Zeilberger.) The average of $\mathrm{inv}(\alpha)\,\mathrm{ind}(\alpha)$ is

$$\frac{1}{n!} \sum_{\alpha} \sum_{1 \le j < k \le n} \sum_{1 \le l < n} [a_j > a_k]\, l\, [a_l > a_{l+1}],$$

which is a polynomial in n of degree ≤ 4. Evaluating this sum for $1 \le n \le 5$ gives the respective values $0, \frac{1}{2}, \frac{6}{2}, \frac{21}{2}, \frac{55}{2}$; so the polynomial must be $\frac{1}{8}n(n-1) + \frac{1}{16}n^2(n-1)^2$. Subtracting $\mathrm{mean}(g_n)^2$ and dividing by $\mathrm{var}(g_n)$ gives the answer $9/(2n+5)$ for $n \ge 2$, by (12) and (13).

27. We have $\mathrm{inv}(a_1 a_2 \ldots a_n) = \mathrm{inv}(q_n \ldots q_2 q_1)$, when $q_n \ldots q_2 q_1$ is regarded as a permutation of a multiset (see Section 5.1.2). It follows that

$$\frac{H_n(w,z)}{(1-z)\ldots(1-z^n)} = \sum_{a_1 \ldots a_n} w^{\mathrm{inv}(a_1 \ldots a_n)}\, z^{\mathrm{ind}(a_1 \ldots a_n)} \sum_{p_1 \ge \cdots \ge p_n \ge 0} z^{p_1 + \cdots + p_n}$$

$$= \sum_{q_1, q_2, \ldots, q_n \ge 0} w^{\mathrm{inv}(q_n \ldots q_2 q_1)}\, z^{q_1 + q_2 + \cdots + q_n}$$

$$= \sum_{k_0 + k_1 + k_2 + \cdots = n} \binom{n}{k_0, k_1, k_2, \ldots}_w z^{k_1 + 2k_2 + \cdots}$$

$$= n!_w\, [u^n] \sum_{k_0, k_1, k_2, \ldots} \prod_{j=0}^{\infty} \frac{(z^j u)^{k_j}}{k_j!_w}$$

$$= n!_w\, [u^n] \prod_{j=0}^{\infty} \exp_w(z^j u)$$

$$= n!_w\, [u^n] \prod_{j=0}^{\infty} \prod_{k=0}^{\infty} \frac{1}{1 - z^j w^k u(1-w)},$$

using the notation of answer 16 and the result of exercise 5.1.2–16. Thus we have the elegant identity

$$\prod_{j,k \ge 0} \frac{1}{1 - w^j z^k u} = \sum_{n \ge 0} \frac{H_n(w,z)\, u^n}{(1-w)(1-w^2)\ldots(1-w^n)(1-z)(1-z^2)\ldots(1-z^n)},$$

which was established for the generating function $H_n(w, z) = \sum_\alpha w^{\mathrm{ind}(\alpha^-)} z^{\mathrm{ind}(\alpha)}$ by D. P. Roselle in *Proc. Amer. Math. Soc.* **45** (1974), 144–150. Exercise 25 shows that the same bivariate generating function counts indexes and inversions. The proof given here is due to Garsia and Gessel [*Advances in Math.* **31** (1979), 288–305], who went on to obtain considerably more general results.

Setting $m = \infty$ in exercise 4.7–27 leads to the recurrence

$$H_n(w, z) = \sum_{k=1}^{n} \binom{n}{k}_w z^{n-k} \left(\prod_{j=1}^{k-1} (1 - z^{n-j}) \right) H_{n-k}(w, z).$$

28. Interchanging two adjacent elements changes the total displacement by 0 or ± 2; hence $\mathrm{td}(a_1 a_2 \ldots a_n) \le 2 \,\mathrm{inv}(a_1 a_2 \ldots a_n)$.

We can also prove that $\mathrm{td}(a_1 a_2 \ldots a_n) \ge \mathrm{inv}(a_1 a_2 \ldots a_n)$. Suppose j is the smallest element out of place, and let $a_k = j$. Let l be maximum with $l < k$ and $a_l \ge k$. Interchanging a_l with a_k reduces the inversions by $2(k-l)-1$, and reduces the total displacement by $2(k-l)$. Therefore if m repetitions of this algorithm are needed to sort a given permutation $a_1 a_2 \ldots a_n$, we have $\mathrm{td}(a_1 a_2 \ldots a_n) = \mathrm{inv}(a_1 a_2 \ldots a_n) + m$.

The average total displacement of a random permutation is $(n^2 - 1)/3$; see exercise 5.2.1–7. The generating function for total displacement does not appear to have a simple form. *References:* C. Spearman, *British J. Psychology* **2** (1906), 89–108; P. Diaconis and R. L. Graham, *J. Royal Stat. Soc.* **B39** (1977), 262–268.

29. We can obtain π as a product of $\mathrm{inv}(\pi)$ transpositions τ_j, where τ_j interchanges j and $j + 1$. For example, the path $1234 \to 1324 \to 1342 \to 3142$ in Fig. 1 corresponds to τ_2, then τ_3, then τ_1; hence $3142 = \tau_1 \tau_3 \tau_2$. Therefore $\pi\pi'$ is obtainable from π' by making $\mathrm{inv}(\pi)$ transpositions, each of which changes the number of inversions by ± 1. It follows that $\mathrm{inv}(\pi\pi') \le \mathrm{inv}(\pi) + \mathrm{inv}(\pi')$. If equality holds, each transposition adds a new inversion, hence $E(\pi\pi') \supseteq E(\pi')$.

Conversely, if $E(\pi\pi') \supseteq E(\pi')$, we want to show that some sequence of $|E(\pi\pi')| - |E(\pi')| = \mathrm{inv}(\pi\pi') - \mathrm{inv}(\pi')$ transpositions will transform π' to $\pi\pi'$. Such transpositions define π, so this will prove that $\mathrm{inv}(\pi) \le \mathrm{inv}(\pi\pi') - \mathrm{inv}(\pi')$; hence equality must hold. Suppose, for example, that $\pi' = 314592687$ and that $E(\pi\pi') \supseteq E(\pi')$. If $E(\pi\pi')$ does not contain $(4, 1)$ or $(5, 4)$ or $(9, 5)$ or $(6, 2)$ or $(8, 6)$, then $\pi\pi'$ must be equal to π'. Otherwise $E(\pi\pi')$ contains one of them, say $(9, 5)$; then $E(\pi\pi')$ contains $E(\tau_4 \pi') = E(314952687)$. In this way we can prove the result by induction on $|E(\pi\pi')| - |E(\pi')|$.

SECTION 5.1.2

1. False, because of a reasonably important technicality. If you said "true," you probably didn't know the definition of $M_1 \cup M_2$ given in Section 4.6.3, which has the property that $M_1 \cup M_2$ is a set whenever M_1 and M_2 are sets. Actually, $\alpha \top \beta$ is a permutation of $M_1 \uplus M_2$.

2. $b \, c \, a \, d \, d \, a \, d \, a \, d \, b$.

3. Certainly not, since we may have $\alpha = \beta$. (The unique factorization theorem shows that there aren't too many possibilities, however.)

4. $(d) \top (b \, c \, d) \top (b \, b \, c \, a \, d) \top (b \, a \, b \, c \, d) \top (d)$.

5. The number of occurrences of the pair $\ldots x x \ldots$ is equal to the number of $\frac{x}{x}$ columns, minus 0 or 1. When x is the smallest element, the numbers of occurrences are equal if and only if x is not first in the permutation.

6. Counting the associated number of two-line arrays is easy: $\binom{m}{k}\binom{n}{k}$.

7. Using part (a) of Theorem B, a derivation like that of (20) gives

$$\binom{A-1}{A-k-m-1}\binom{B}{m}\binom{C}{k}\binom{B+k}{B-l}\binom{C-k}{l};$$

$$\binom{A-1}{A-k-m}\binom{B}{m}\binom{C}{k}\binom{B+k-1}{B-l-1}\binom{C-k}{l};$$

$$\binom{A-1}{A-k-m}\binom{B}{m}\binom{C}{k}\binom{B+k-1}{B-l}\binom{C-k}{l}.$$

8. The complete factorization into primes is $(d)_\top(b\ c\ d)_\top(b)_\top(a\ d\ b\ c)_\top(a\ b)_\top(b\ c\ d)_\top(d)$, which is unique since no adjacent pairs commute. So there are eight solutions, with $\alpha = \epsilon, (d), (d)_\top(b\ c\ d), \ldots$.

10. False, but true in interesting cases. Given any linear ordering of the primes, there is at least one factorization of the stated form, since whenever the condition is violated we can make an interchange that reduces the number of "inversions" in the factorization. So the condition fails only because some permutations have more than one such factorization.

Let $\rho \sim \sigma$ mean that ρ commutes with σ. The following condition is necessary and sufficient for the uniqueness of the factorization as stated:

$$\rho \sim \sigma \sim \tau \quad \text{and} \quad \rho \prec \sigma \prec \tau \quad \text{implies} \quad \rho \sim \tau.$$

Proof. If $\rho \sim \sigma \sim \tau$ and $\rho \prec \sigma \prec \tau$ and $\rho \not\sim \tau$, we would have two factorizations $\sigma_\top\tau_\top\rho = \tau_\top\rho_\top\sigma$; hence the condition is necessary. Conversely, to show that it is sufficient for uniqueness, let $\rho_1 {}_\top \cdots {}_\top \rho_n = \sigma_1 {}_\top \cdots {}_\top \sigma_n$ be two distinct factorizations satisfying the condition. We may assume that $\sigma_1 \prec \rho_1$, and hence $\sigma_1 = \rho_k$ for some $k > 1$; furthermore $\sigma_1 \sim \rho_j$ for $1 \le j < k$. Since $\rho_{k-1} \sim \sigma_1 = \rho_k$, we have $\rho_{k-1} \prec \sigma_1$; hence $k > 2$. Let j be such that $\sigma_1 \prec \rho_j$ and $\rho_i \prec \sigma_1$ for $j < i < k$. Then $\rho_{j+1} \sim \sigma_1 \sim \rho_j$ and $\rho_{j+1} \prec \sigma_1 \prec \rho_j$ implies that $\rho_{j+1} \sim \rho_j$; hence $\rho_j \prec \rho_{j+1}$, a contradiction.

Therefore if we are given an ordering relation on a set S of primes, satisfying the condition above, and if we know that all prime factors of a permutation π belongs to S, we can conclude that π has a unique factorization of the stated type. Such a condition holds, for example, when S is the set of cycles in (29).

But the set of *all* primes cannot be so ordered. For if we have, say, $(a\ b) \prec (d\ e)$, then we are forced to define

$$(a\ b) \prec (d\ e) \succ (b\ c) \prec (e\ a) \succ (c\ d) \prec (a\ b) \succ (d\ e),$$

a contradiction. (See also the following exercise.)

11. We wish to show that, if $p(1)\ldots p(t)$ is a permutation of $\{1,\ldots,t\}$, the permutation $x_{p(1)}\ldots x_{p(t)}$ is topologically sorted if and only if we have $\sigma_{p(1)}{}_\top\cdots{}_\top\sigma_{p(t)} = \sigma_1{}_\top\cdots{}_\top\sigma_t$ and $p(i) < p(j)$ whenever $\sigma_{p(i)} = \sigma_{p(j)}$ for $i < j$. We also want to show that, if $x_{p(1)}\ldots x_{p(t)}$ and $x_{q(1)}\ldots x_{q(t)}$ are distinct topological sortings, we have $\sigma_{p(j)} \ne \sigma_{q(j)}$ for some j. The first property follows by observing that $x_{p(1)}$ can be first in a topological sort if and only if $\sigma_{p(1)}$ commutes with (yet is distinct from) $\sigma_{p(1)-1},\ldots,\sigma_1$; and this condition implies that $\sigma_{p(2)}{}_\top\cdots{}_\top\sigma_{p(t)} = \sigma_1{}_\top\cdots{}_\top\sigma_{p(1)-1}{}_\top\sigma_{p(1)+1}{}_\top\cdots{}_\top\sigma_t$, so induction can be used. The second property follows because if j is minimal with $p(j) \ne q(j)$, we have, say, $p(j) < q(j)$ and $x_{p(j)} \not\prec x_{q(j)}$ by definition of topological sorting; hence $\sigma_{p(j)}$ has no letters in common with $\sigma_{q(j)}$.

To get an arbitrary partial ordering, let the cycle σ_k consist of all ordered pairs (i, j) such that $x_i \prec x_j$ and either $i = k$ or $j = k$; these ordered pairs are to appear in some arbitrary order as individual elements of the cycle. Thus the cycles for the partial ordering $x_1 \prec x_2$, $x_3 \prec x_4$, $x_1 \prec x_4$ would be $\sigma_1 = ((1,2)(1,4))$, $\sigma_2 = ((1,2))$, $\sigma_3 = ((3,4))$, $\sigma_4 = ((1,4)(3,4))$.

12. No other cycles can be formed, since, for example, the original permutation contains no $\begin{smallmatrix}a\\c\end{smallmatrix}$ columns. If $(a\ b\ c\ d)$ occurs s times, then $(a\ b)$ must occur $A - r - s$ times, since there are $A - r$ columns $\begin{smallmatrix}a\\b\end{smallmatrix}$, and only two kinds of cycles contribute to such columns.

13. In the two-line notation, first place $A - t$ columns of the form $\begin{smallmatrix}d\\a\end{smallmatrix}$, then put the other t a's in the second line, then place the b's, and finally the remaining letters.

14. Since the elements below any given letter in the two-line notation for π^- are in nondecreasing order, we do not always have $(\pi^-)^- = \pi$; but it is true that $((\pi^-)^-)^- = \pi^-$. In fact, the identity

$$(\alpha_\top \beta)^- = ((\alpha^-_\top \beta^-)^-)^-$$

holds for all α and β. (See exercise 5–2.)

Given a multiset whose distinct letters are $x_1 < \cdots < x_m$, we can characterize its self-inverse permutations by observing that they each have a unique prime factorization of the form $\beta_{1\top}\cdots_\top\beta_m$, where β_j has zero or more prime factors $(x_j)_\top\cdots_\top(x_j)_\top(x_j x_{k_1})_\top$ $\cdots_\top(x_j x_{k_t})$, $j < k_1 \le \cdots \le k_t$. For example, $(a)_\top(a\ b)_\top(a\ b)_\top(b\ c)_\top(c)$ is a self-inverse permutation. The number of self-inverse permutations of $\{m \cdot a, n \cdot b\}$ is therefore $\min(m, n) + 1$; and the corresponding number for $\{l \cdot a, m \cdot b, n \cdot c\}$ is the number of solutions of the inequalities $x + y \le l$, $x + z \le m$, $y + z \le n$ in nonnegative integers x, y, z. The number of self-inverse permutations of a *set* is considered in Section 5.1.4.

The number of permutations of $\{n_1 \cdot x_1, \ldots, n_m \cdot x_m\}$ having n_{ij} occurrences of $\begin{smallmatrix}x_i\\x_j\end{smallmatrix}$ in their two-line notation is $\prod_i n_i! / \prod_{i,j} n_{ij}!$, the same as the number having n_{ij} occurrences of $\begin{smallmatrix}x_j\\x_i\end{smallmatrix}$ in the two-line notation. Hence there ought to be a better way to define the inverse of a multiset permutation. For example, if the prime factorization of π is $\sigma_{1\top}\sigma_{2\top}\cdots_\top\sigma_t$ as in Theorem C, we can define $\pi^- = \sigma_t^-\top\cdots_\top\sigma_2^-\top\sigma_1^-$, where $(x_1\ldots x_n)^- = (x_n \ldots x_1)$.

Dominique Foata and Guo-Niu Han have observed that it would be even more desirable to define inverses in such a way that π and π^- have the same number of inversions, because the generating function for inversions given the numbers n_{ij} is $\prod_i n_i!_z / \prod_{i,j} n_{ij}!_z$ times a power of z; see exercise 16. However, there does not seem to be any natural way to define an involution having that property.

15. See Theorem 2.3.4.2D and Lemma 2.3.4.2E. Removing one arc of the directed graph must leave an oriented tree.

16. If $x_1 < x_2 < \cdots$, the inversion table entries for the x_j's must have the form $b_{j1} \le \cdots \le b_{jn_j}$ where b_{jn_j} (the number of inversions of the rightmost x_j) is at most $n_{j+1} + n_{j+2} + \cdots$. So the generating function for the jth part of the inversion table is the generating function for partitions into at most n_j parts, no part exceeding $n_{j+1} + n_{j+2} + \cdots$. The generating function for partitions into at most m parts, no part exceeding n, is the z-nomial coefficient $\binom{m+n}{m}_z$; this is readily proved by induction, and it can also be proved by means of an ingenious construction due to F. Franklin [*Amer. J. Math.* **5** (1882), 268–269; see also Pólya and Alexanderson, *Elemente der Mathematik* **26** (1971), 102–109]. Multiplying the generating functions for $j = 1, 2, \ldots$ gives the

desired formula for inversions of multiset permutations, which MacMahon published in
Proc. London Math. Soc. (2) **15** (1916), 314–321.

17. Let $h_n(z) = (n!_z)/n!$; then the desired probability generating function is

$$g(z) = h_n(z)/h_{n_1}(z)h_{n_2}(z) \cdots .$$

The mean of $h_n(z)$ is $\frac{1}{2}\binom{n}{2}$, by Eq. 5.1.1–(12), so the mean of g is

$$\frac{1}{2}\left(\binom{n}{2} - \binom{n_1}{2} - \binom{n_2}{2} - \cdots\right) = \frac{1}{4}(n^2 - n_1^2 - n_2^2 - \cdots) = \frac{1}{2}\sum_{i<j} n_i n_j.$$

The variance is, similarly,

$$\frac{1}{72}\big(n(n-1)(2n+5) - n_1(n_1-1)(2n_1+5) - \cdots\big)$$
$$= \frac{1}{36}(n^3 - n_1^3 - n_2^3 - \cdots) + \frac{1}{24}(n^2 - n_1^2 - n_2^2 - \cdots).$$

18. Yes; the construction of exercise 5.1.1–25 can be extended in a straightforward
way. Alternatively we can generalize the proof following 5.1.1–(14), by constructing
a one-to-one correspondence between m-tuples $(q_1, \ldots, q_m)$ where q_j is a multiset
containing n_j nonnegative integers, on the one hand, and ordered pairs of n-tuples
$((a_1, \ldots, a_n), (p_1, \ldots, p_n))$ on the other hand, where $a_1 \ldots a_n$ is a permutation of
$\{n_1 \cdot 1, \ldots, n_m \cdot m\}$, and $p_1 \geq \cdots \geq p_n \geq 0$. This correspondence is defined as before,
giving all elements of q_j the subscript j; it satisfies the condition

$$\Sigma(q_1) + \cdots + \Sigma(q_m) = \mathrm{ind}(a_1 \ldots a_n) + (p_1 + \cdots + p_n)$$

where $\Sigma(q_j)$ denotes the sum of the elements of q_j. [For a further generalization of the
technique used in this proof and in the derivation of Eq. 5.1.3–(8), see D. E. Knuth,
Math. Comp. **24** (1970), 955–961. See also the comprehensive treatment by Richard P.
Stanley in *Memoirs Amer. Math. Soc.* **119** (1972).]

19. (a) Let $S = \{\sigma \mid \sigma \text{ is prime, } \sigma \text{ is a left factor of } \pi\}$. If S has k elements, the left
factors λ of π such that $\mu(\lambda) \neq 0$ are precisely the 2^k intercalations of the subsets of S
(see the proof of Theorem C); hence $\sum \mu(\lambda) = \prod_{\sigma \in S}(1 + \mu(\sigma)) = 0$, since $\mu(\sigma) = -1$
and S is nonempty. (b) Clearly $\epsilon(i_1 \ldots i_n) = \mu(\pi) = 0$ if $i_j = i_k$ for some $j \neq k$.
Otherwise $\epsilon(i_1 \ldots i_n) = (-1)^r$ where $i_1 \ldots i_n$ has r inversions; this is $(-1)^s$, where
$i_1 \ldots i_n$ has s even cycles; and this is $(-1)^{n+t}$ where $i_1 \ldots i_n$ has t cycles.

20. (a) Obvious, by definition of intercalation. (b) By definition,

$$\det(b_{ij}) = \sum_{1 \leq i_1, \ldots, i_m \leq m} \epsilon(i_1 \ldots i_m)\, b_{1i_1} \ldots b_{mi_m}.$$

Setting $b_{ij} = \delta_{ij} - a_{ij}x_j$ and applying exercise 19(b), we obtain

$$\sum_{n \geq 0} \sum_{1 \leq i_1, \ldots, i_n \leq m} x_{i_1} \ldots x_{i_n} \mu(x_{i_1} \ldots x_{i_n})\nu(x_{i_1} \ldots x_{i_n}),$$

since $\mu(\pi)$ is usually zero.

(c) Use exercise 19(a) to show that $D \top G = 1$ when we regard the products of x's
as permutations of noncommutative variables, using the natural algebraic convention
$(\alpha + \beta)\top\pi = \alpha\top\pi + \beta\top\pi$.

A succinct rendition of this combinatorial proof and similar proofs of other important theorems has been given by D. Zeilberger, *Discrete Math.* **56** (1985), 61–72.

21. $\prod_{k=1}^{m} \binom{n_k + \cdots + n_{k-d}}{n_k}$, if we let $n_k = 0$ for $k \leq 0$, since there are $\binom{n_m + \cdots + n_{m-d}}{n_m}$ ways to insert the m's into such a permutation of $\{n_1 \cdot 1, \ldots, n_{m-1} \cdot (m-1)\}$.

22. (a) The left-right reversal of $l(\pi)$ is in $P_0(0^k 1^{n_1} \ldots t^{n_t})$, for some k; but instead of reversing $l(\pi)$, we will give it a two-line form by placing 0 last instead of first in the top line. The number k of 0s in $l(\pi)$ and $r(\pi)$ is the number of columns $\frac{j}{k}$ in the two-line form of π for which $j \leq t < k$; this is also the number of columns with $k \leq t < j$. We can easily reconstruct π from the two-line forms of $l(\pi)$ and $r(\pi)$, because each column $\frac{j}{k}$ with $j, k \leq t$ occurs in $l(\pi)$, each column with $t < j, k$ occurs in $r(\pi)$, and the remaining columns are obtained by merging $\frac{j}{0}$ or $\frac{0}{k}$ of $l(\pi)$ with $\frac{0}{k}$ or $\frac{j}{0}$ of $r(\pi)$ from left to right.

(b) Let π be a permutation of the stated form, and let σ be any permutation of $P_0(0^{n_0} 1^{n_1} \ldots m^{n_m})$. Construct λ as follows: Delete the first n_0 entries of σ; then replace the 0s by x's, subscripted with the first n_0 entries of π; replace the other elements by y's, subscripted with the remaining nonzero entries of π. Also construct ρ as follows: Delete the 0s of σ, and replace the n_j occurrences of j with x_j or y_j according as the columns $\frac{j}{k}$ of π have $k = 0$ or $k \neq 0$, from left to right. For example, if $\pi = \binom{00000011111222233333}{23131302310102032010}$ and $\sigma = \binom{00000011111222233333}{32313201103201300201}$, we have $\lambda = x_2 y_2 y_3 x_3 y_1 y_1 x_1 y_2 y_3 x_3 x_1 y_2 x_3 y_1$ and $\rho = y_3 y_2 y_3 x_1 x_3 x_2 y_1 y_1 y_3 y_2 y_1 x_3 x_2 x_1$. Conversely, we can reconstruct π and σ from λ and ρ.

(c) We have $w(\pi) = w(l(\pi)) w(r(\pi))$ in the construction of (a), because column $\frac{j}{k}$ of π either becomes $\frac{j}{k}$ of weight w_j / w_k in $l(\pi)$ or $r(\pi)$, or it is factored into columns $\frac{j}{0}$ and $\frac{0}{k}$ having weights z_j / z_0 and z_0 / z_k. If $l(\pi)$ has p_j columns $\frac{0}{j}$ and q_j columns $\frac{j}{0}$, its weight is $\prod_{j=1}^{t} (z_j^{q_j} w_j^{n_j - q_j} / z_j^{p_j} w_j^{n_j - p_j}) = \prod_{j=1}^{t} (w_j / z_j)^{p_j - q_j}$. Now $\prod_{j=1}^{t} (w_j / z_j)^{-q_j}$ is the complex conjugate of $\prod_{j=1}^{t} (w_j / z_j)^{q_j}$; so the sum of weights over all elements of $P_0(0^k 1^{n_1} \ldots t^{n_t})$ simplifies to

$$\frac{k! (n_1 + \cdots + n_t - k)!}{n_1! \ldots n_t!} \left| \sum_{p_1 + \cdots + p_t = k} \binom{n_1}{p_1} \cdots \binom{n_t}{p_t} \left(\frac{w_1}{z_1}\right)^{p_1} \cdots \left(\frac{w_t}{z_t}\right)^{p_t} \right|^2 .$$

Similar remarks apply to $r(\pi)$. The stated sum is positive because the term for $k = 0$ is nonzero.

23. We can assume that the original strand was sorted. Let $t = 2$, $m = 4$, $w_1 = w_3 = z_1 = z_2 = +1$, $w_2 = w_4 = z_3 = z_4 = -1$ in part (c) of the previous exercise. Then $w(\pi) = (-1)^d$, where d is the number of columns $\frac{j}{k}$ with $j \neq k$. [See Gillis and Zeilberger, *European J. Comb.* **4** (1983), 221–223. This result was first proved in a completely different way by Askey, Ismail, and Koornwinder, *J. Comb. Theory* **A25** (1978), 277–287, who found intriguing connections between multiset permutations and integrals of products of the Laguerre polynomials $L_n^\alpha(x) = \sum_{k=0}^{n} \binom{n+\alpha}{n-k} (-x)^k / k!$.] The analogous result for a five-letter alphabet is false, because the 5! permutations of $\{1, 2, 3, 4, 5\}$ include $1 + 10 + 45$ with an even number of differences, $0 + 20 + 44$ with an odd number.

24. (a) Transposing $\begin{smallmatrix} w & x \\ y & z \end{smallmatrix}$ twice restores $\begin{smallmatrix} w & x \\ y & z \end{smallmatrix}$. Given $\mathrm{sort}\binom{x_1 \ \cdots \ x_n}{y_1 \ \cdots \ y_n} = \binom{x_1' \ \cdots \ x_n'}{y_1' \ \cdots \ y_n'}$, unsort it by finding the leftmost x in the top row and transposing it to the left. This brings out the proper y. (The value of $\mathrm{sort}\binom{x_2' \ \cdots \ x_n'}{y_2' \ \cdots \ y_n'}$ is also uniquely determined.)

(b) We are essentially expressing the two-line notation of π in the form

$$\pi = \mathrm{sort} \left(\begin{matrix} y_1 \ \cdots \ x_{1n_1} & y_2 \ \cdots \ x_{2n_2} & \cdots & y_t \ \cdots \ x_{tn_t} \\ x_{11} \cdots \ y_1 & x_{21} \cdots \ y_2 & \cdots & x_{t1} \cdots \ y_t \end{matrix} \right),$$

and part (a) provides us with precisely the tools we need. [When R preserves certain statistics of the two-line notation, this construction provides combinatorial proofs of interesting theorems. See Guo-Niu Han, *Advances in Math.* **105** (1994), 26–41.]

SECTION 5.1.3

1. We must only show that this value makes (11) valid for $x = k$, when $k \geq 1$. Using (7), the formula becomes

$$k^n = \sum_{r=0}^{k} \left\langle {n \atop r-1} \right\rangle \binom{k+n-r}{n} = \sum_{0 \leq j \leq r \leq k} (-1)^j (r-j)^n \binom{n+1}{j} \binom{n+k-r}{n}$$

$$= \sum_{s=0}^{k} s^n \sum_{j=0}^{k-s} (-1)^j \binom{n+1}{j} \binom{n+k-s-j}{n}.$$

For $s < k$, the sum on j can be extended to the range $0 \leq j \leq n+1$, and it is zero (the $(n+1)$st difference of an nth-degree polynomial in j).

2. (a) The number of sequences $a_1 a_2 \ldots a_n$ containing each of the elements $(1, 2, \ldots, q)$ at least once is $\left\{ {n \atop q} \right\} q!$, by exercise 1.2.6–64; the number of such sequences satisfying the analog of (10), for $m = q$, is $\binom{n-k}{n-q}$, since we must choose $n - q$ of the possible $=$ signs. (b) Add the results of (a) for $q = n - m$ and $q = n - m + 1$.

3. $\sum_n \dfrac{x^n}{n!} \sum_k \left\langle {n \atop k} \right\rangle (-1)^k = \dfrac{2}{e^{-2x}+1} = \dfrac{1}{x} \left(\dfrac{(-4x)}{e^{-4x}-1} - \dfrac{(-2x)}{e^{-2x}-1} \right)$ by (20), hence the result is $(-1)^{n+1} B_{n+1} 2^{n+1} (2^{n+1} - 1)/(n+1)$. Alternatively, the identity $2/(e^{-2x}+1) = 1 + \tanh x$ lets us express the answer as $(-1)^{(n-1)/2} T_n$ when n is odd, where T_n denotes the tangent number defined by the formula

$$\tan z = T_1 z + T_3 z^3/3! + T_5 z^5/5! + \cdots.$$

When $n > 0$ is even, the sum obviously vanishes, by (7). Incidentally, (18) now yields the curious Stirling number identity $\sum_k \left\{ {n \atop k} \right\} k!/(-2)^k = 2B_{n+1}(1 - 2^{n+1})/(n+1)$.

4. $(-1)^{n+m} \left\langle {n \atop m} \right\rangle$. (Consider the coefficient of z^{m+1} in (18).)

5. $\left\langle {p \atop k} \right\rangle \equiv (k+1)^p - k^p \equiv (k+1) - k \equiv 1$ (modulo p) for $0 \leq k < p$, by formula (13), exercise 1.2.6–10, and Theorem 1.2.4F.

6. Summing first on k is not allowed, because the terms are nonzero for arbitrarily large j and k, and the sum of the absolute values is infinite.

For a simpler example of the fallacy, let $a_{jk} = (k-j) [|j-k| = 1]$. Then

$$\sum_{j \geq 0} \left(\sum_{k \geq 0} a_{jk} \right) = \sum_{j \geq 0} (\delta_{j0}) = +1, \quad \text{while} \quad \sum_{k \geq 0} \left(\sum_{j \geq 0} a_{jk} \right) = \sum_{k \geq 0} (-\delta_{k0}) = -1.$$

7. Yes. [F. N. David and D. E. Barton, *Combinatorial Chance* (1962), 150–154; see also the answer to exercise 25.]

8. [*Combinatory Analysis* **1** (1915), 190.] By inclusion and exclusion. For example, $1/(l_1 + l_2)! \, l_3! \, (l_4 + l_5 + l_6)!$ is the probability that $x_1 < \cdots < x_{l_1+l_2}$, $x_{l_1+l_2+1} < \cdots < x_{l_1+l_2+l_3}$, and $x_{l_1+l_2+l_3+1} < \cdots < x_{l_1+l_2+l_3+l_4+l_5+l_6}$.

A simple $O(n^2)$ algorithm to count the number of permutations of $\{1, \ldots, n\}$ having respective run lengths $(l_1, \ldots, l_k)$ has been given by N. G. de Bruijn, *Nieuw Archief voor Wiskunde* (3) **18** (1970), 61–65.

9. $p_{km} = q_{km} - q_{k(m+1)}$ in (23). Since $\sum_{k,m} q_{km} z^m x^k = \frac{x}{1-x} g(x, z)$ and $g(x, 0) = 1$, we have

$$h(z, x) = \sum h_k(z) x^k = \frac{x}{1-x} g(x, z)(1 - z^{-1}) + \frac{x}{1-x} z^{-1} = \frac{(1 - z^{-1})x}{e^{(x-1)z} - x} + \frac{z^{-1} x}{1-x}.$$

Thus $h_1(z) = e^z - (e^z - 1)/z$; $h_2(z) = (e^{2z} - ze^z) + e^z - (e^{2z} - 1)/z$.

10. Let $M_n = L_1 + \cdots + L_n$ be the mean; then $\sum M_n x^n = h'(1, x)$, where the derivative is taken with respect to z, and this is $x/(e^{x-1} - x) - x/(1-x) = M(x)$, say. By the residue theorem

$$\frac{1}{2\pi i} \oint M(z) z^{-n-1} \, dz = M_n - 2(n + \tfrac{1}{3}) + 1 + \frac{z_1^{-n}}{z_1 - 1} + \frac{\bar{z}_1^{-n}}{\bar{z}_1 - 1},$$

if we integrate around a circle of radius r where $|z_1| < r < |z_2|$. (Note the double pole at $z = 1$.) Furthermore, the absolute value of this integral is less than $\oint |M(z)| \, r^{-n-1} \, dz = O(r^{-n})$. Integrating over larger and larger circles gives the convergent series $M_n = 2n - \tfrac{1}{3} + \sum_{k \geq 1} 2\Re(1/z_k^n (1 - z_k))$.

To find the variance, we have $h''(1, x) = -2h'(1, x) - 2x(x - 1)e^{x-1}/(e^{x-1} - x)^2$. An argument similar to that used for the mean, this time with a triple pole, shows that the coefficients of $h''(1, x)$ are asymptotically $4n^2 + \tfrac{4}{3}n - 2M_n$ plus smaller terms; this leads to the asymptotic formula $\tfrac{2}{3}n + \tfrac{2}{9}$ (plus exponentially smaller terms) for the variance.

11. $P_{kn} = \sum_{t_1 \geq 1, \ldots, t_{k-1} \geq 1} D(t_1, \ldots, t_{k-1}, n, 1)$, where $D(l_1, l_2, \ldots, l_k)$ is MacMahon's determinant of exercise 8. Evaluating this determinant by its first row, we find $P_{kn} = c_0 P_{(k-1)n} + c_1 P_{(k-2)n} + \cdots + c_{k-2} P_{1n} - E_k(n)$, where c_j and E_k are defined as follows:

$$c_j = (-1)^j \sum_{t_1, \ldots, t_{j+1} \geq 1} \frac{1}{(t_1 + \cdots + t_{j+1})!} = (-1)^j \sum_{m \geq 0} \binom{m}{j} \frac{1}{(m+1)!}$$

$$= (-1)^j \sum_{r, m \geq 0} \binom{-1}{j-r} \binom{m+1}{r} \frac{1}{(m+1)!} = -1 + e\left(\frac{1}{0!} - \frac{1}{1!} + \cdots + (-1)^j \frac{1}{j!} \right);$$

$$E_1(n) = 1/(n+1)! - 1/n!; \qquad E_2(n) = [n > 0]/(n+1)!;$$

$$E_k(n) = (-1)^k \sum_{m \geq 0} \binom{m}{k-3} \frac{[n > 0]}{(n+2+m)!}, \qquad k \geq 3.$$

Let $P_{0n} = 0$, $C(z) = \sum c_j z^j = (e^{1-z} - 1)/(1 - z)$, and let

$$E(z, x) = \sum_{n,k} E_{k+1}(n) z^n x^k = \frac{ez^2 x^2 - e^x(1 - x + zx)(z + x - 1) - e^{z+x}(1 - z)^2(1 - x)^2}{e^x z (z + x - 1)(1 - x)^2}.$$

The recurrence relation we have derived is equivalent to the formula $C(x)H(z, x) = H(z, x)/x + E(z, x)$; hence $H(z, x) = E(z, x)x(1 - x)/(xe^{1-x} - 1)$. Expanding this power series gives $H_1(z) = h_1(z)$ (see exercise 9); $H_2(z) = eh_1(z) + 1 - e^z$.

[*Note:* The generating functions for the first three runs were derived by Knuth, *CACM* **6** (1963), 685–688. Barton and Mallows, *Ann. Math. Statistics* **36** (1965), 249, stated the formula $1 - H_{n+1}(z) = (1 - H_n(z))/(1 - z) - L_n h_1(z)$ for $n \geq 1$, together with (25). Another way to attack this problem is illustrated in exercise 23. Because adjacent runs are not independent, there is no simple relation between the problem solved here and the simpler (probably more useful) result of exercise 9.]

12. [*Combinatory Analysis* **1** (1915), 209–211.] The number of ways to put the multiset into t distinguishable boxes is

$$N_t = \binom{t + n_1 - 1}{n_1}\binom{t + n_2 - 1}{n_2} \cdots \binom{t + n_m - 1}{n_m},$$

since there are $\binom{t+n_1-1}{n_1}$ ways to place the 1s, etc. If we require that no box be empty, the method of inclusion and exclusion tells us that the number of ways is

$$M_t = N_t - \binom{t}{1}N_{t-1} + \binom{t}{2}N_{t-2} - \cdots.$$

Let P_k be the number of permutations having k runs; if we put $k - 1$ vertical lines between the runs, and $t - k$ additional vertical lines in any of the $n - k$ remaining places, we get one of the M_t ways to divide the multiset into t nonempty distinguishable parts. Hence

$$M_t = P_t + \binom{n - t + 1}{1}P_{t-1} + \binom{n - t + 2}{2}P_{t-2} + \cdots.$$

Equating the two values of M_t allows us to determine $P_1, P_2, \ldots$ successively in terms of $N_1, N_2, \ldots$. (A more direct proof would be desirable.)

13. $1 + \frac{1}{2}13 \times 3 = 20.5$.

14. By Foata's correspondence the given permutation corresponds to

$$(3\,1)\,\top\,(1)\,\top\,\cdots\,\top\,(4) = \begin{pmatrix} 1\ 1\ 1\ 1\ 2\ 2\ 2\ 2\ 3\ 3\ 3\ 3\ 4\ 4\ 4\ 4 \\ 3\ 1\ 1\ 2\ 3\ 4\ 3\ 2\ 1\ 1\ 3\ 4\ 2\ 2\ 4\ 4 \end{pmatrix};$$

by (33) this corresponds to

$$\begin{pmatrix} 1\ 1\ 1\ 1\ 2\ 2\ 2\ 2\ 3\ 3\ 3\ 3\ 4\ 4\ 4\ 4 \\ 2\ 4\ 4\ 3\ 3\ 3\ 1\ 1\ 4\ 4\ 2\ 1\ 2\ 1\ 2\ 3 \end{pmatrix},$$

which corresponds to $2\,3\,4\,2\,3\,4\,1\,4\,2\,1\,4\,3\,2\,1\,3\,1$ with 9 runs.

15. The number of alternating runs is 1 plus the number of j such that $1 < j < n$ and either $a_{j-1} < a_j > a_{j+1}$ or $a_{j-1} > a_j < a_{j+1}$. For fixed j, the probability is $\frac{2}{3}$; hence the average, for $n \geq 2$, is $1 + \frac{2}{3}(n - 2)$.

16. Each permutation of $\{1, 2, \ldots, n-1\}$, having k alternating runs, yields k permutations with k such runs, 2 with $k + 1$, and $n - k - 2$ with $k + 2$, when the new element n is inserted in all possible places. Hence

$$\left\langle\!\!\left\langle{n \atop k}\right\rangle\!\!\right\rangle = k\left\langle\!\!\left\langle{n - 1 \atop k}\right\rangle\!\!\right\rangle + 2\left\langle\!\!\left\langle{n - 1 \atop k - 1}\right\rangle\!\!\right\rangle + (n - k)\left\langle\!\!\left\langle{n - 1 \atop k - 2}\right\rangle\!\!\right\rangle.$$

It is convenient to let $\left\langle\!\!\left\langle{1 \atop k}\right\rangle\!\!\right\rangle = \delta_{k0}$, $G_1(z) = 1$. Then

$$G_n(z) = \frac{z}{n}\big((1 - z^2)G'_{n-1}(z) + (2 + (n - 2)z)G_{n-1}(z)\big).$$

Differentiation leads to the recurrence

$$x_n = \frac{1}{n}\big((n - 2)x_{n-1} + 2n - 2\big)$$

for $x_n = G'_n(1)$, and this has the solution $x_n = \frac{2}{3}n - \frac{1}{3}$ for $n \geq 2$. Another differentiation leads to the recurrence

$$y_n = \frac{1}{n}\big((n - 4)y_{n-1} + \tfrac{8}{3}n^2 - \tfrac{26}{3}n + 6\big)$$

for $y_n = G''_n(1)$. Set $y_n = \alpha n^2 + \beta n + \gamma$ and solve for α, β, γ to get $y_n = \frac{4}{9}n^2 - \frac{14}{15}n + \frac{11}{90}$ for $n \geq 4$. Hence $\text{var}(g_n) = \frac{1}{90}(16n - 29)$, $n \geq 4$.

These formulas for the mean and variance are due to J. Bienaymé, who stated them without proof [*Bull. Soc. Math. de France* **2** (1874), 153–154; *Comptes Rendus Acad. Sci.* **81** (Paris, 1875), 417–423, see also Bertrand's remarks on p. 458]. The recurrence relation for $\left\langle\!\!{n \atop k}\!\!\right\rangle$ is due to D. André [*Comptes Rendus Acad. Sci.* **97** (Paris, 1883), 1356–1358; *Annales Scientifiques de l'École Normale Supérieure* (3) **1** (1884), 121–134]. André noted that $G_n(-1) = 0$ for $n \geq 4$; thus, the number of permutations with an even number of alternating runs is $n!/2$. He also proved the formula for the mean, and determined the number of permutations that have the maximum number of alternating runs (see exercise 5.1.4–23). It can be shown that

$$G_n(z) = \left(\frac{1+z}{2}\right)^{n-1}(1+w)^{n+1}g_n\left(\frac{1-w}{1+w}\right), \qquad w = \sqrt{\frac{1-z}{1+z}}, \qquad n \geq 2,$$

where $g_n(z)$ is the generating function (18) for ascending runs. [See David and Barton, *Combinatorial Chance* (London: Griffin, 1962), 157–162.]

17. $\binom{n+1}{2k-1}$; $\binom{n}{2k-2}$ end with 0, $\binom{n}{2k-1}$ end with 1.

18. (a) Let the given sequence be an inversion table as in Section 5.1.1. If it has k descents, the inverse of the corresponding permutation has k descents (see answer 5.1.1–8(e)); hence the answer is $\left\langle\!\!{n \atop k}\!\!\right\rangle$. (b) This quantity satisfies $f(n,k) = kf(n-1,k) + (n-k+1)f(n-1,k-1)$, so it must be $\left\langle\!\!{n \atop k-1}\!\!\right\rangle$. [See D. Dumont, *Duke Math. J.* **41** (1974), 313–315.]

19. (a) $\left\langle\!\!{n \atop k}\!\!\right\rangle$, by the correspondence of Theorem 5.1.2B. (b) There are $(n-k)!$ ways to put $n-k$ further nonattacking rooks on the entire board; hence the answer is $1/(n-k)!$ times $\sum_{j\geq 0} a_{nj}\binom{j}{k}$, where $a_{nj} = \left\langle\!\!{n \atop j}\!\!\right\rangle$ by part (a). This comes to $\left\{\!\!{n \atop n-k}\!\!\right\}$, by exercise 2.

A direct proof of this result, due to E. A. Bender, associates each partition of $\{1,2,\ldots,n\}$ into k nonempty disjoint subsets with an arrangement of $n-k$ rooks: Let the partition be $\{1,2,\ldots,n\} = \{a_{11}, a_{12}, \ldots, a_{1n_1}\} \cup \cdots \cup \{a_{k1}, \ldots, a_{kn_k}\}$, where $a_{ij} < a_{i(j+1)}$ for $1 \leq j < n_i$, $1 \leq i \leq k$. The corresponding arrangement puts rooks in column a_{ij} of row $a_{i(j+1)}$, for $1 \leq j < n_i$, $1 \leq i \leq k$. For example, the configuration illustrated in Fig. 4 corresponds to the partition $\{1,3,8\} \cup \{2\} \cup \{4,6\} \cup \{5\} \cup \{7\}$. [*Duke Math. J.* **13** (1946), 259–268. Sections 2.3 and 2.4 of Richard Stanley's *Enumerative Combinatorics* **1** (1986) discuss rook placement in general.]

20. The number of readings is the number of runs in the inverse permutation. The first run corresponds to the first reading, etc.

21. It has $n + 1 - k$ runs and requires $n + 1 - j$ readings.

22. [*J. Combinatorial Theory* **1** (1966), 350–374.] If $rs < n$, some reading will pick up $t > r$ elements, $a_{i_1} = j + 1$, ..., $a_{i_t} = j + t$, where $i_1 < \cdots < i_t$. We cannot have $a_m > a_{m+1}$ for all m in the range $i_k \leq m < i_{k+1}$, so the permutation contains at least $t - 1$ places with $a_m < a_{m+1}$; it therefore has at most $n - t + 1$ runs.

On the other hand, consider the permutation $\alpha_r \ldots \alpha_2\, \alpha_1$, where block α_j contains the numbers $\equiv j$ (modulo r), in decreasing order; for example, when $n = 9$ and $r = 4$, this permutation is $8\,4\,7\,3\,6\,2\,9\,5\,1$. If $n \geq 2r - 1$, this permutation has $r - 1$ ascents, so it has $n + 1 - r$ runs. Moreover, it requires exactly $n + 1 - \lceil n/r \rceil$ readings, if $r > 1$. We can rearrange the elements of $\{kr+1, \ldots, kr+r\}$ arbitrarily without changing the number of runs, thereby reducing the number of readings to any desired value $\geq \lceil n/r \rceil$.

Now suppose $rs \geq n$ and $r + s \leq n+1$ and $r, s \geq 1$. By exercises 20 and 21 we can assume that $r \leq s$, since the reflection of the inverse of a permutation with $n + 1 - r$ runs and s readings has $n + 1 - s$ runs and r readings. Then the construction in the preceding paragraph handles all cases except those where $s > n+1 - \lceil n/r \rceil$ and $r \geq 2$. To complete the proof we may use a permutation of the form

$$2k+1 \ 2k-1 \ \ldots \ 1 \ n+2-r \ n+1-r \ \ldots \ 2k+2 \ 2k \ \ldots \ 2 \ n+3-r \ \ldots \ n-1 \ n,$$

which has $n + 1 - r$ runs and $n + 1 - r - k$ readings, for $0 \leq k \leq \frac{1}{2}(n - r)$.

23. [*SIAM Review* **3** (1967), 121–122.] Assume that the infinite permutation consists of independent samples from the uniform distribution. Let $f_k(x)\,dx$ be the probability that the kth long run begins with x; and let $g(u, x)\,dx$ be the probability that a long run begins with x, when the preceding long run begins with u. Then $f_1(x) = 1$, $f_{k+1}(x) = \int_0^1 f_k(u)g(u, x)\,du$. We have $g(u, x) = \sum_{m \geq 1} g_m(u, x)$, where

$$\begin{aligned}
g_m(u, x) &= \Pr(u < X_1 < \cdots < X_m > x \ \text{ or } \ u > X_1 > \cdots > X_m < x) \\
&= \Pr(u < X_1 < \cdots < X_m) + \Pr(u > X_1 > \cdots > X_m) \\
&\quad - \Pr(u < X_1 < \cdots < X_m < x) - \Pr(u > X_1 > \cdots > X_m > x) \\
&= (u^m + (1 - u)^m - |u - x|^m)/m! \, ;
\end{aligned}$$

hence $g(u, x) = e^u + e^{1-u} - 1 - e^{|u-x|}$, and we find $f_2(x) = 2e - 1 - e^x - e^{1-x}$. One can show that $f_k(x)$ approaches the limiting value $(2\cos(x - \frac{1}{2}) - \sin\frac{1}{2} - \cos\frac{1}{2})/(3\sin\frac{1}{2} - \cos\frac{1}{2})$. The average length of a run starting with x is $e^x + e^{1-x} - 1$; hence the length $\mathcal{L}_k$ of the kth long run is $\int_0^1 f_k(x)(e^x + e^{1-x} - 1)\,dx$; $\mathcal{L}_1 = 2e - 3 \approx 2.43656$; $\mathcal{L}_2 = 3e^2 - 8e + 2 \approx 2.42091$. See Section 5.4.1 for similar results.

24. Arguing as before, the result is

$$1 + \sum_{0 \leq k < n} 2^k (p^2 + q^2)^k (p^2 + 2pq(2^{n-k-1} - 1 + q^2((2pq)^{n-k-1} - 1)/(2pq - 1)));$$

carrying out the sum and simplifying yields

$$2^n (p^2 + q^2)^n (p(p - q)/(p^2 + q^2 - pq) - \tfrac{1}{2}) + (2pq)^n pq^3/(p^2 + q^2)(p^2 + q^2 - pq)$$
$$+ q^2/(p^2 + q^2) + 2^{n-1}.$$

25. Let $V_j = (U_1 + \cdots + U_j) \bmod 1$; then $V_1, \ldots, V_n$ are independent uniform random numbers in $[0 \mathinner{.\,.} 1)$, forming a permutation that has k descents if and only if $\lfloor U_1 + \cdots + U_n \rfloor = k$. Hence the answer is $\left\langle {n \atop k} \right\rangle / n!$, a property first noticed by S. Tanny [*Duke Math. J.* **40** (1973), 717–722]; see also W. Meyer and R. von Randow, *Math. Annalen* **193** (1971), 315–321.

26. For example, $\vartheta^5 (1 - z)^{-1} = (z + 26z^2 + 66z^3 + 26z^4 + z^5)/(1 - z)^6$.

27. The following rule defines a one-to-one correspondence that takes a permutation $a_1 a_2 \ldots a_n$ with k descents into an n-node increasing forest with $k + 1$ leaves: The first root is a_1, and its descendants are the forest corresponding to $a_2 \ldots a_k$, where k is minimal such that $a_{k+1} < a_1$ or $k = n$. [R. P. Stanley, *Enumerative Combinatorics* **1** (Wadsworth, 1986), Proposition 1.3.16.]

28. The poles of $L(z)$ are the values of $T(1/e)$, where $T(z)$ is the (multivalued) tree function defined by $T(z) = ze^{T(z)}$. Thus for $m > 0$ we have the convergent series

$$z_m = -\sigma_m + \sum_{n \geq 0} \frac{1}{\sigma_m^n} \sum_k (-1)^k \begin{bmatrix} n \\ k \end{bmatrix} \frac{(\ln \sigma_m)^{n+1-k}}{(n + 1 - k)!}, \qquad \sigma_m = -1 - (2m + 1)\pi i$$

[Corless, Gonnet, Hare, Jeffrey, and Knuth, *Advances in Computational Mathematics* **5** (1996), 329–359, formula (4.18)]; in particular, we have $z_m = (2m + \frac{1}{2})\pi i + \ln(2\pi em) + (\frac{1}{4} - \frac{i}{2\pi} \ln(2\pi em))/m + O((\log m)^2/m^2)$.

Let $P(z) = \sum_{m=0}^{\infty}(z/(z - z_m) + z/(z - \bar{z}_m))$. It follows that $P(x) - P(-x) = \sum_{m=0}^{\infty} 4\Re(xz_m/(x^2 - z_m^2)) = \sum_{m=1}^{\infty} O((x \log m)/(x^2 + m^2)) = \sum_{m=1}^{x} O((x \log x)/x^2) + \sum_{m=x+1}^{\infty} O((x \log m)/m^2) = O(\log x)$ for $x > 1$. But we know that $L(x) + P(x) = cx$ for some c; hence $2cx = L(x) - L(-x) + O(\log x)$, and by letting $x \to \infty$ in (25) we find $c = -1/2$. Hence $L_1 = \sum_{m=0}^{\infty} 2r_m^{-1} \cos \theta_m - 1/2$. (This result is due to Svante Janson.)

29. (a) If $a_1 \ldots a_n$ has $2k$ alternating runs and k peaks, $(n+1-a_1)\ldots(n+1-a_n)$ has $k-1$ peaks. (b,c) See L. W. Shapiro, W.-J. Woan, and S. Getu, *SIAM J. Algebraic and Discrete Methods* **4** (1983), 459–466.

SECTION 5.1.4

1.

1	2	3	8
4	5	7	
6	9		

1	3	5	8
2	4	9	
6	7		

$\begin{pmatrix} 1 & 3 & 4 & 5 & 7 & 8 & 9 \\ 5 & 9 & 2 & 4 & 8 & 1 & 7 \end{pmatrix}$.

2. When p_i is inserted into column t, let the element in column $t - 1$ be p_j. Then (q_j, p_j) is in class $t-1$, $q_j < q_i$, and $p_j < p_i$; so, by induction, indices $i_1, \ldots, i_t$ exist with the property. Conversely, if $q_j < q_i$ and $p_j < p_i$ and if (q_j, p_j) is in class $t-1$, then column $t - 1$ contains an element $< p_i$ when p_i is inserted, so (q_i, p_i) is in class $\geq t$.

3. The columns are the bumping sequences (9) when p_i is inserted. Lines 1 and 2 reflect the operations on row 1, see (14). If we remove columns in which line 2 has ∞ entries, lines 0 and 2 constitute the bumped array, as in (15). The stated method for going from line k to line $k + 1$ is just the class-determination algorithm of the text.

4. (a) Use a case analysis, by induction on the size of the tableau, considering first the effect on row 1 and then the effect on the sequence of elements bumped from row 1. (b) Admissible interchanges can simulate the operations of Algorithm I, with the tableau represented as a canonical permutation before and after the algorithm. For example, we can transform

17 11 4 13 14 2 6 10 15 1 3 5 9 12 16 8   into   17 11 13 4 10 14 2 6 9 15 1 3 5 8 12 16

by a sequence of admissible interchanges (see (4) and (5)).

5. Admissible interchanges are symmetrical between left and right, and the canonical permutation for P obviously goes into P^T when the insertion order is reversed.

6. Let there be t classes in all; exactly k of them have an odd number of elements, since the elements of a class have the form

$$(p_{i_k}, p_{i_1}), \qquad (p_{i_{k-1}}, p_{i_2}), \qquad \ldots, \qquad (p_{i_1}, p_{i_k}).$$

(See (18) and (22).) The bumped two-line array has exactly $t - k$ fixed points, because of the way it is constructed; hence by induction the tableau minus its first row has $t - k$ columns of odd length. So the t elements in the first row lead to k odd-length columns in the whole tableau.

7. The number of columns, namely the length of row 1, is the number of classes (exercise 2). The number of rows is the number of columns of P^T, so exercise 5 (or Theorem D) completes the proof.

8. With more than n^2 elements, the corresponding P tableau must either have more than n rows or more than n columns. But there are $n \times n$ tableaux. [This result was originally proved in *Compositio Math.* **2** (1935), 463–470.]

9. Such permutations are in 1–1 correspondence with pairs of tableaux of shape $(n, n, \ldots, n)$; so by (34) the answer is

$$\left(\frac{n^2!\,\Delta(2n-1, 2n-2, \ldots, n)}{(2n-1)!\,(2n-2)!\ldots n!}\right)^2 = \left(\frac{n^2!}{(2n-1)(2n-2)^2 \ldots n^n (n-1)^{n-1} \ldots 1^1}\right)^2.$$

The existence of such a simple formula for this problem is truly amazing. We can also count the number of permutations of $\{1, 2, \ldots, mn\}$ with no increasing subsequences longer than m, no decreasing subsequences longer than n.

10. We prove inductively that, at step S3, $P_{(r-1)s}$ and $P_{r(s-1)}$ are both less than $P_{(r+1)s}$ and $P_{r(s+1)}$.

11. We also need to know, of course, the element that was originally P_{11}. Then it is possible to restore things using an algorithm remarkably similar to Algorithm S.

12. $\binom{n_1+1}{2} + \binom{n_2+2}{2} + \cdots + \binom{n_m+m}{2} - \binom{m+1}{3}$, the total distance traveled. The minimum is the sum of the first n terms of the sequence 1, 2, 2, 3, 3, 3, 4, 4, 4, 4, 5, 5, 5, 5, 5, $\ldots$ of exercise 1.2.4–41; this sum is approximately $\sqrt{8/9}\,n^{3/2}$. (Nearly all tableaux on n elements come reasonably close to this lower bound, according to exercise 29, so the average number of times is $\Theta(n^{3/2})$.)

13. Assume that the elements permuted are $\{1, 2, \ldots, n\}$, so that $a_i = 1$; and assume that $a_j = 2$. *Case 1: $j < i$.* Then 1 bumps 2, so row 1 of the tableau corresponding to $a_1 \ldots a_{i-1} a_{i+1} \ldots a_n$ is row 1 of P^S; and the bumped permutation is the former bumped permutation except for its smallest element, 2, so we may use induction on n. *Case 2: $j > i$.* Apply Case 1 to P^T, in view of exercise 5 and the fact that $(P^T)^S = (P^S)^T$.

15. As in (37), the example permutation corresponds to the tableau

1	2	5	9	11
3	6	7		
4	8	10		

;

hence the number is $f(l, m, n) = (l+m+n)!\,(l-m+1)(l-n+2)(m-n+1)/(l+2)!\,(m+1)!\,(n)!$, provided, of course, that $l \geq m \geq n$.

16. By Theorem H, 80080.

17. Since g is antisymmetric in the x's, it is zero when $x_i = x_j$, so it is divisible by $x_i - x_j$ for all $i < j$. Hence $g(x_1, \ldots, x_n; y) = h(x_1, \ldots, x_n; y)\Delta(x_1, \ldots, x_n)$. Here h must be homogeneous in $x_1, \ldots, x_n, y$, of total degree 1, and symmetric in $x_1, \ldots, x_n$; so $h(x_1, \ldots, x_n; y) = a(x_1 + \cdots + x_n) + by$ for some a, b depending only on n. We can evaluate a by setting $y = 0$; we can evaluate b by taking the partial derivative with respect to y and then setting $y = 0$. We have

$$\frac{\partial}{\partial y}\Delta(x_1, \ldots, x_i+y, \ldots, x_n)|_{y=0} = \frac{\partial}{\partial x_i}\Delta(x_1, \ldots, x_n) = \Delta(x_1, \ldots, x_n)\sum_{j \neq i}\frac{1}{x_i - x_j}.$$

Finally, $\sum_i \sum_{j \neq i}(x_i/(x_i - x_j)) = \sum_i \sum_{j < i}(x_i/(x_i - x_j) + x_j/(x_j - x_i)) = \binom{n}{2}$.

18. It must be $\Delta(x_1, \ldots, x_n) \cdot (b_0 + b_1 y + \cdots + b_m y^m)$, where each b_k is a homogeneous symmetric polynomial of degree $m - k$ in the x's. We have

$$\frac{\partial^k}{k!\,\partial y^k}\Delta(x_1, \ldots, x_i+y, \ldots, x_n)|_{y=0} = \Delta(x_1, \ldots, x_n)\sum\left(1\Big/\prod_{l=1}^k (x_i - x_{j_l})\right)$$

summed over all $\binom{n-1}{k}$ choices of distinct indices $j_1, \ldots, j_k \neq i$. Now, in the expression $b_k = \sum x_i^m / \prod_{l=1}^{k} (x_i - x_{j_l})$, we may combine those groups of $k+1$ terms having a given set of indices $\{i, j_1, \ldots, j_k\}$; for example, when $k = 2$, we group sets of three terms of the form $a^m/(a - b)(a - c) + b^m/(b - a)(b - c) + c^m/(c - a)(c - b)$. The sum of every such group is $[z^{m-k}] 1/(1 - x_i z)(1 - x_{j_1} z) \ldots (1 - x_{j_k} z)$, by exercise 1.2.3–33. We find therefore that

$$b_k = \sum_j \binom{n-j}{k+1-j} \sum s(p_1, \ldots, p_j),$$

where $s(p_1, \ldots, p_j)$ is the monomial symmetric function consisting of all distinct terms having the form $x_{i_1}^{p_1} \ldots x_{i_j}^{p_j}$, for distinct indices $i_1, \ldots, i_j \in \{1, \ldots, n\}$; and the inner sum is over all partitions of $m - k$ into exactly j parts, namely $p_1 \geq \cdots \geq p_j \geq 1$, $p_1 + \cdots + p_j = m - k$. (This result was obtained jointly with E. A. Bender in 1969.)

When $m = 2$ the answer is $\left(s(2) + (n-1)s(1)y + \binom{n}{3}y^2\right) \Delta(x_1, \ldots, x_n)$; for $m = 3$ we get $\left(s(3) + ((n-1)s(2) + s(1,1))y + \binom{n-1}{2}s(1)y^2 + \binom{n}{4}y^3\right) \Delta(x_1, \ldots, x_n)$; etc.

Another expression gives b_k as the coefficient of z^m in

$$\left(\binom{n}{k+1}z^k - \binom{n-1}{k+1}e_1 z^{k+1} + \binom{n-2}{k+1}e_2 z^{k+2} - \cdots\right) \Big/ (1 - e_1 z + e_2 z^2 - \cdots),$$

where $e_l = \sum_{1 \leq i_1 < \cdots < i_l \leq n} x_{i_1} \ldots x_{i_l}$ is an elementary symmetric function. Multiplying by y^k and summing on k gives the answer as the coefficient of z^m in

$$\frac{1}{yz} \left(\frac{(1 + z(y - x_1)) \ldots (1 + z(y - x_n))}{(1 - zx_1) \ldots (1 - zx_n)} - 1\right) \Delta(x_1, \ldots, x_n).$$

19. Let the shape of the transposed tableau be $(n_1', n_2', \ldots, n_r')$; the answer is

$$\frac{1}{2} f(n_1, n_2, \ldots, n_m) \left(\frac{(\sum n_i^2 - \sum n_j'^2)}{n(n-1)} + 1\right),$$

where $n = \sum n_i = \sum n_j'$. (This formula can be expressed in a less symmetrical form using the relation $\sum i n_i = \frac{1}{2}(n + \sum n_j'^2)$.)

Note: W. Feit [*Proc. Amer. Math. Soc.* **4** (1953), 740–744] showed that the number of ways to place the integers $\{1, 2, \ldots, n\}$ into an array that is the "difference" of two tableau shapes $(n_1, \ldots, n_m) \setminus (l_1, \ldots, l_m)$, where $0 \leq l_j \leq n_j$ and $n = \sum(n_j - l_j)$, is $n! \det(1/((n_j - j) - (l_i - i))!)$.

20. The fallacious argument in the discussion following Theorem H is actually valid for this case (the corresponding probabilities *are* independent).

Note: If we consider all $n!$ ways to label the nodes, the labelings considered here are those having no "inversions." Inversions in permutations are the same as inversions in tree labelings, in the special case when the tree is simply a path. See A. Björner and M. L. Wachs, *J. Combinatorial Theory* **A52** (1989), 165–187.

21. [*Michigan Math. J.* **1** (1952), 81–88.] Let $g(n_1, \ldots, n_m) = (n_1 + \cdots + n_m)! \Delta(n_1, \ldots, n_m)/n_1! \ldots n_m! \sigma(n_1, \ldots, n_m)$, where $\sigma(x_1, \ldots, x_m) = \prod_{1 \leq i < j \leq m} (x_i + x_j)$. To prove that $g(n_1, \ldots, n_m)$ is the number of ways to fill the shifted tableau, we must prove that $g(n_1, \ldots, n_m) = g(n_1 - 1, \ldots, n_m) + \cdots + g(n_1, \ldots, n_m - 1)$. The identity corresponding to exercise 17 is $x_1 \Delta(x_1 + y, \ldots, x_n)/\sigma(x_1 + y, \ldots, x_n) + \cdots + x_n \Delta(x_1, \ldots, x_n + y)/\sigma(x_1, \ldots, x_n + y) = (x_1 + \cdots + x_n)\Delta(x_1, \ldots, x_n)/\sigma(x_1, \ldots, x_n)$, independent of y; for if we calculate the derivative as in exercise 17, we find that $2x_i x_j/(x_j^2 - x_i^2) + 2x_j x_i/(x_i^2 - x_j^2) = 0$.

22. Assume that $m = N$, by adding 0s to the shape if necessary; if $m > N$ and $n_m > 0$, the number of ways is clearly zero. When $m = N$ the answer is

$$\det \begin{pmatrix} \binom{n_1 + m - 1}{m - 1} & \binom{n_2 + m - 2}{m - 1} & \cdots & \binom{n_m}{m - 1} \\ \vdots & \vdots & & \vdots \\ \binom{n_1 + m - 1}{0} & \binom{n_2 + m - 2}{0} & \cdots & \binom{n_m}{0} \end{pmatrix}.$$

Proof. We may assume that $n_m = 0$, for if $n_m > 0$, the first n_m columns of the array must be filled with i in row i, and we may consider the remaining shape $(n_1 - n_m, \ldots, n_m - n_m)$. By induction on m, the number of ways is

$$\sum_{\substack{n_2 \le k_1 \le n_1 \\ \vdots \\ n_m \le k_{m-1} \le n_{m-1}}} \det \begin{pmatrix} \binom{k_1 + m - 2}{m - 2} & \binom{k_2 + m - 3}{m - 2} & \cdots & \binom{k_{m-1}}{m - 2} \\ \vdots & \vdots & & \vdots \\ \binom{k_1 + m - 2}{0} & \binom{k_2 + m - 3}{0} & \cdots & \binom{k_{m-1}}{0} \end{pmatrix},$$

where $n_j - k_j$ represents the number of m's in row j. The sum on each k_j may be carried out independently, giving

$$\det \begin{pmatrix} \binom{n_1+m-1}{m-1} - \binom{n_2+m-2}{m-1} & \binom{n_2+m-2}{m-1} - \binom{n_3+m-3}{m-1} & \cdots & \binom{n_{m-1}+1}{m-1} - \binom{n_m}{m-1} \\ \vdots & \vdots & & \vdots \\ \binom{n_1+m-1}{1} - \binom{n_2+m-2}{1} & \binom{n_2+m-2}{1} - \binom{n_3+m-3}{1} & \cdots & \binom{n_{m-1}+1}{1} - \binom{n_m}{1} \end{pmatrix},$$

which is the desired answer since $n_m = 0$. The answer can be converted into a Vandermonde determinant by row operations, giving $\Delta(n_1+m-1, n_2+m-2, \ldots, n_m)/(m-1)!\,(m-2)!\ldots 0!$. [The answer to this exercise, in connection with an equivalent problem in group theory, appears in D. E. Littlewood's *Theory of Group Characters* (Oxford, 1940), 189.]

23. [*Journal de Math.* (3) **7** (1881), 167–184.] (This is a special case of exercise 5.1.3–8, with all runs of length 2 except that the final run might have length 1.) When $n \ge 2$, element n must appear in one of the rightmost positions of a row; once it has been placed in the rightmost box on row k from the bottom, we have $\binom{n-1}{2k-1} E_{2k-1} E_{n-2k}$ ways to complete the job. Let

$$h(z) = \sum_{n \ge 1} E_{2n-1} z^{2n-1}/(2n-1)! = \tfrac{1}{2}(g(z) - g(-z));$$

then

$$h(z)g(z) = \sum_{k,n \ge 1} \binom{n}{2k-1} E_{2k-1} E_{n-2k+1} z^n/n! = \left(\sum_{n \ge 0} E_{n+1} z^n/n! \right) - 1 = g'(z) - 1.$$

Replace z by $-z$ and add, obtaining $h(z)^2 = h'(z) - 1$; hence $h(z) = \tan z$. Setting $k(z) = g(z) - h(z)$, we have $h(z)k(z) = k'(z)$; hence $k(z) = \sec z$ and $g(z) = \sec z + \tan z = \tan(\tfrac{1}{2}z + \tfrac{1}{4}\pi)$. The coefficients E_n are called *Euler numbers*; with odd index, E_{2n-1} is the tangent number $T_{2n-1} = (-1)^{n-1} 4^n (4^n - 1) B_{2n}/(2n)$. Tables of these numbers appear in *Math. Comp.* **21** (1967), 663–688; the sequence begins $(E_0, E_1, E_2, \ldots) = (1, 1, 1, 2, 5, 16, 61, 272, 1385, 7936, \ldots)$. The easiest way to compute

Euler numbers is probably to form the triangular array

$$
\begin{array}{ccccccc}
1 \\
0 & 1 \\
1 & 1 & 0 \\
0 & 1 & 2 & 2 \\
5 & 5 & 4 & 2 & 0 \\
0 & 5 & 10 & 14 & 16 & 16 \\
61 & 61 & 56 & 46 & 32 & 16 & 0
\end{array}
$$

in which partial sums are alternately formed from left to right and right to left [L. Seidel, *Sitzungsberichte math.-phys. Classe Akademie Wissen. München* **7** (1877), 157–187].

25. In general, if u_{nk} is the number of permutations on $\{1, 2, \ldots, n\}$ having no cycles of length $> k$, $\sum u_{nk} z^n/n! = \exp(z + z^2/2 + \cdots + z^k/k)$; this is proved by multiplying $\exp(z) \times \cdots \times \exp(z^k/k)$, obtaining

$$
\sum_n z^n \left(\sum_{j_1 + 2j_2 + \cdots + kj_k = n} \frac{1}{1^{j_1} j_1! \, 2^{j_2} j_2! \, \ldots} \right);
$$

see also exercise 1.3.3–21. Similarly, $\exp(\sum_{s \in S} z^s/s)$ is the corresponding generating function for permutations whose cycle lengths are all members of a given set S.

26. The integral from 0 to ∞ is $n^{(t+1)/4} \Gamma((t+1)/2)/2^{(t+3)/2}$, by the gamma function integral (exercise 1.2.5–20, $t = 2x^2/\sqrt{n}$). So, from $-\infty$ to ∞, we get 0 when t is odd, otherwise $n^{(t+1)/4} \sqrt{\pi} \, t!/2^{(3t+1)/2} (t/2)!$.

27. (a) If $r_i < r_{i+1}$ and $c_i < c_{i+1}$, the condition $i < Q_{r_i c_{i+1}} < i + 1$ is impossible. If $r_i \geq r_{i+1}$ and $c_i \geq c_{i+1}$, we certainly cannot have $i + 1 \leq Q_{r_i c_{i+1}} \leq i$. (b) Prove, by induction on the number of rows in the tableau for $a_1 \ldots a_i$, that $a_i < a_{i+1}$ implies $c_i < c_{i+1}$, and $a_i > a_{i+1}$ implies $c_i \geq c_{i+1}$. (Consider row 1 and the "bumped" sequences.) (c) This follows from Theorem D(c).

28. This result is due to A. M. Vershik and S. V. Kerov, *Dokl. Akad. Nauk SSSR* **233** (1977), 1024–1028; see also B. F. Logan and L. A. Shepp, *Advances in Math.* **26** (1977), 206–222. [J. Baik, P. Deift, and K. Johansson, *J. Amer. Math. Soc.* **12** (1999), 1119–1178, showed that the standard deviation is $\Theta(n^{1/6})$; moreover, the probability that the length is less than $2\sqrt{n} + tn^{1/6}$ approaches $\exp(-\int_t^\infty (x - t)u^2(x)\,dx)$, where $u''(x) = 2u^3(x) + xu(x)$ and $u(x)$ is asymptotic to the Airy function $\text{Ai}(x)$ as $x \to \infty$.]

29. $\binom{n}{l}/l!$ is the average number of increasing subsequences of length l. (By exercises 8 and 29, the probability is $O(1/\sqrt{n})$ that the largest increasing sequence has length $\geq e\sqrt{n}$ or $\leq \sqrt{n}/e$.) [J. D. Dixon, *Discrete Math.* **12** (1975), 139–142.]

30. [*Discrete Math.* **2** (1972), 73–94; a simplified proof has been given by Marc van Leeuwen, *Electronic J. Combinatorics* **3**, 2 (1996), paper #R15.]

31. $x_n = a_{\lfloor n/2 \rfloor}$ where $a_0 = 1$, $a_1 = 2$, $a_n = 2a_{n-1} + (2n - 2)a_{n-2}$; $\sum a_n z^n/n! = \exp(2z + z^2) = (\sum t_n z^n/n!)^2$; $x_n \approx \exp(\frac{1}{4}n \ln n - \frac{1}{4}n + \sqrt{n} - \frac{1}{2} - \frac{1}{2}\ln 2)$ for n even. [See E. Lucas, *Théorie des Nombres* (1891), 217–223.]

32. Let $m_n = \int_{-\infty}^{\infty} t^n e^{-(t-1)^2/2} dt/\sqrt{2\pi}$. Then $m_0 = m_1 = 1$, and $m_{n+1} - m_n = nm_{n-1}$ if we integrate by parts. So $m_n = t_n$ by (40).

33. True; it is $\det_{i,j=1}^m \binom{a_i}{j-1}$. [Mitchell, in *Amer. J. Math.* **4** (1881), 341–344, showed that it is the number of terms in the expansion of a certain symmetric function, now called a Schur function. Indeed, if $0 < a_1 < \cdots < a_m$, it is the number of terms in $S_{n_1 n_2 \ldots n_m}(x_1, x_2, \ldots, x_m)$ where $n_1 = a_m - m$, $n_2 = a_{m-1} - (m-1)$, $\ldots$, $n_m = a_1 - 1$.

This Schur function is the sum over all generalized tableaux of shape $(n_1, \ldots, n_m)$ with elements in $\{1, \ldots, m\}$ of the products of x_j for all j in the tableau, where a generalized tableau is like an ordinary tableau except that equal elements are allowed in the rows. In this definition we allow the parameters n_k to be zero. For example, $S_{210}(x_1, x_2, x_3) = x_1^2 x_2 + x_1^2 x_3 + x_1 x_2^2 + x_1 x_2 x_3 + x_1 x_2 x_3 + x_1 x_3^2 + x_2^2 x_3 + x_2 x_3^2$, because of the generalized tableaux $\frac{11}{2}, \frac{11}{3}, \frac{12}{2}, \frac{12}{3}, \frac{13}{2}, \frac{13}{3}, \frac{22}{3}, \frac{23}{3}$. The number of such tableaux is $\Delta(1, 3, 5)/\Delta(1, 2, 3) = 8$. By extending Algorithms I and D to generalized tableaux [*Pacific J. Math.* **34** (1970), 709–727], we can obtain combinatorial proofs of the remarkable identities

$$\sum_\lambda S_\lambda(x_1, \ldots, x_m) S_\lambda(y_1, \ldots, y_n) = \prod_{i=1}^m \prod_{j=1}^n \frac{1}{1 - x_i y_j},$$

$$\sum_\lambda S_\lambda(x_1, \ldots, x_m) S_{\lambda^T}(y_1, \ldots, y_n) = \prod_{i=1}^m \prod_{j=1}^n (1 + x_i y_j);$$

here the sum is over all possible shapes λ, and λ^T denotes the transposed shape. These identities were first discovered by D. E. Littlewood, *Proc. London Math. Soc.* (2) **40** (1936), 40–70, Theorem V.]

Notes: It follows, for example, that any product of consecutive binomial coefficients $\binom{a}{k}\binom{a+1}{k} \ldots \binom{a+l}{k}$ is divisible by $\binom{k}{k}\binom{k+1}{k} \ldots \binom{k+l}{k}$, since the ratio is $\Delta(a + l, \ldots, a + 1, a, k - 1, \ldots, 1, 0)/\Delta(k + l, \ldots, 1, 0)$. The value of $\Delta(k, \ldots, 1, 0) = k! \ldots 2! \, 1!$ is sometimes called a "superfactorial."

34. The length of a hook is also the length of any zigzag path from the hook's bottom left cell (i, j) to its top right cell (i', j'). We prove a stronger result: If there is a hook of length $a + b$, then there is either a hook of length a or a hook of length b. Consider the cells $(i, j) = (i_1, j_1), (i_2, j_2), \ldots, (i_{a+b}, j_{a+b}) = (i', j')$ that hug the bottom of the shape. If $j_{a+1} = j_a$, the cell (i_a, j_1) has a hook of length a; otherwise (i_{a+b}, j_{a+1}) has a hook of length b. [*Reference: Japanese J. Math.* **17** (1940), 165–184, 411–423. Nakayama was the first to consider hooks in the study of permutation groups, and he came close to discovering Theorem H.]

35. The execution of steps G3–G5 decreases exactly h_{ij} elements of the p array by 1 when q_{ij} is increased, because the algorithm follows a zigzag path from $p_{n'_j j}$ to $p_{i n_i}$. The next execution of those steps either starts with a larger value of j or stays above or equal to the preceding zigzag. Therefore the q array is filled from left to right and bottom to top; to reverse the process we proceed from right to left and top to bottom:

H1. [Initialize.] Set $p_{ij} \leftarrow 0$ for $1 \le j \le n_i$ and $1 \le i \le n'_1$. Then set $i \leftarrow 1$ and $j \leftarrow n_1$.

H2. [Find nonzero cell.] If $q_{ij} > 0$, go on to step H3. Otherwise if $i < n'_j$, increase i by 1 and repeat this step. Otherwise if $j > 1$, decrease j by 1, set $i \leftarrow 1$, and repeat this step. Otherwise stop (the q array is now zero).

H3. [Decrease q, prepare for zigzag.] Decrease q_{ij} by 1 and set $l \leftarrow i$, $k \leftarrow n_i$.

H4. [Increase p.] Increase p_{lk} by 1.

H5. [Move down or left.] If $l < n'_k$ and $p_{lk} > p_{(l+1)k}$, increase l by 1 and return to H4. Otherwise if $k > j$, decrease k by 1 and return to H4. Otherwise return to H2. ▮

The first zigzag path for a given column j ends by incrementing $p_{n'_j j}$, because $p_{1j} \le \cdots \le p_{n'_j j}$ implies that $p_{n'_j j} > 0$. Each subsequent path for column j stays below or equal to the previous one, so it also ends at $p_{n'_j j}$. The inequalities encountered on the way show that this algorithm inverts the other. [*J. Combinatorial Theory* **A21** (1976), 216–221.]

36. (a) The stated coefficient of z^m is the number of solutions to $m = \sum h_{ij} q_{ij}$, so we can apply the result of the previous exercise. (b) If $a_1, \ldots, a_k$ are any positive integers, we can prove by induction on k that

$$[z^m]\, 1/(1 - z)(1 - z^{a_1}) \ldots (1 - z^{a_k}) = \binom{m}{k}\Big/ a_1 \ldots a_k + O(m^{k-1}).$$

The number of partitions of m with at most n parts is therefore $\binom{m}{n-1}/n! + O(m^{n-2})$ for fixed n, by exercise 5.1.1–15. This is also the asymptotic number of partitions $m = p_1 + \cdots + p_n$ with *distinct* parts $p_1 > \cdots > p_n > 0$ (see exercise 5.1.1–16). So the number of reverse plane partitions is asymptotically $N\binom{m}{n-1}/n! + O(m^{n-2})$ when there are N tableaux of a given n-cell shape. By part (a) this is also $\binom{m}{n-1}/\prod h_{ij} + O(m^{n-2})$. [*Studies in Applied Math.* **50** (1971), 167–188, 259–279.]

37. Plane partitions in a rectangle are equivalent to reverse plane partitions, so the hook lengths tell us the generating function $1/\prod_{i=1}^{r} \prod_{j=1}^{c} (1 - z^{i+j-1})$ in an $r \times c$ rectangle. Letting $r, c \to \infty$ yields the elegant answer $1/(1 - z)(1 - z^2)^2(1 - z^3)^3 \cdots$. [MacMahon's original derivation in *Philosophical Transactions* **A211** (1912), 75–110, 345–373, was extremely complicated. The first reasonably simple proof was found by Leonard Carlitz, *Acta Arithmetica* **13** (1967), 29–47.]

38. (a) The probability is $1/n$ when $k = l = 1$; otherwise it is

$$\frac{nP(I \setminus \{i_0\}, J) + nP(I, J \setminus \{j_0\})}{n\, d_{i_0 j_0}} = \frac{(d_{i_0 b} + d_{a j_0})/(n\, d_{i_0 b} \ldots d_{i_{k-1} b}\, d_{a j_0} \ldots d_{a j_{l-1}})}{d_{i_0 b} + d_{a j_0}},$$

by induction on $k + l$.

(b) Summing over all I and J gives

$$n^{-1}(1 + d_{1b}^{-1}) \ldots (1 + d_{(a-1)b}^{-1})\,(1 + d_{a1}^{-1}) \ldots (1 + d_{a(b-1)}^{-1}),$$

which is easily seen to equal $f(T \setminus \{(a, b)\})/f(T)$.

(c) The sum over all corners yields 1, because every path ends at a corner. Therefore $\sum f(T \setminus \{(a, b)\}) = f(T)$, and this proves Theorem H by induction on n. Furthermore, if we put n into the corner cell at the end of the random path and repeat the process on the remaining $n - 1$ cells, we get each tableau with probability $1/f(T)$. [*Advances in Math.* **31** (1979), 104–109.]

39. (a) $Q_{11} \ldots Q_{1n}$ will be $b_1 \ldots b_n$, the inversion table of the original permutation $P_{11} \ldots P_{1n}$. (See Section 5.1.1.)

(b) $Q_{11} \ldots Q_{n1}$ is the negated inversion table $(-C_1) \ldots (-C_n)$ of exercise 5.1.1–7.

(c) This condition is clearly preserved by step P3.

(d) $\binom{1\,4}{2\,3} \to (\binom{1\,3}{2\,4}, \binom{0\;-1}{0\;\;0})$; $\binom{4\,3}{1\,2} \to (\binom{1\,2}{3\,4}, \binom{0\;-1}{0\;\;0})$. This example shows that we cannot run step P3 backwards without looking at the array P.

(e)

12	10	8	14	15	11
9	13	7	1		
6	4	5			
16	3				
2					

ANSWERS TO EXERCISES 5.1.4

(f) The following algorithm is correct, but not obviously so.

Q1. [Loop on (i,j).] Perform steps Q2 and Q3 for all cells (i,j) of the array in lexicographic order (that is, from top to bottom, and from left to right in each row); then stop.

Q2. [Adjust Q.] Find the "first candidate" (r,s) by the rule below. Then set $Q_{i(k+1)} \leftarrow Q_{ik} - 1$ for $j \le k < s$.

Q3. [Unfix P at (i,j).] Set $K \leftarrow P_{rs}$. Then do the following operations until $(r,s) = (i,j)$: If $P_{(r-1)s} > P_{r(s-1)}$, set $P_{rs} \leftarrow P_{(r-1)s}$ and $r \leftarrow r-1$; otherwise set $P_{rs} \leftarrow P_{r(s-1)}$ and $s \leftarrow s-1$. Finally set $P_{ij} \leftarrow K$. ∎

In step Q2, cell (r,s) is a *candidate* when $s \ge j$ and $Q_{is} \le 0$ and $r = i - Q_{is}$. Let T be the oriented tree of the hint. One of the basic invariants of Algorithm Q is that there will be a path from (r,s) to (i,j) in T whenever (r,s) is a candidate in step Q2. The reverse of that path can be encoded by a sequence of letters D, Q, and R, meaning that we start at (i,j), then go down (D) or to the right (R) or quit (Q). The *first candidate* is the one whose code is lexicographically first in alphabetic order; intuitively, it is the candidate with the "leftmost and bottommost" path.

For example, the candidates when $(i,j) = (1,1)$ in the example of part (e) are $(3,1)$, $(4,2)$, $(2,3)$, $(2,4)$, and $(1,6)$. Their respective codes are DDQ, DDDRQ, RDRQ, RDRRQ, and RRRRRQ; so the first is $(4,2)$.

Algorithm P is a slightly simplified version of a construction stated without proof in *Funkts. Analiz i Ego Priloz.* **26**, 3 (1992), 80–82. The proof of correctness is nontrivial; a proof was given by J.-C. Novelli, I. Pak, and A. V. Stoyanovskii in *Disc. Math. and Theoretical Comp. Sci.* **1** (1997), 53–67.

40. An equivalent process was analyzed by H. Rost, *Zeitschrift für Wahrscheinlichkeitstheorie und verwandte Gebiete* **58** (1981), 41–53.

41. (Solution by R. W. Floyd.) A deletion-insertion operation essentially moves only a_i. In a sequence of such operations, unmoved elements retain their relative order. Therefore if π can be sorted with k deletion-insertions, it has an increasing subsequence of length $n - k$; and conversely. Hence $\mathrm{dis}(\pi) = n - $ (length of longest increasing subsequence of π) $= n - $ (length of row 1 in Theorem A).

M. L. Fredman has proved that the minimum number of comparisons needed to compute this length is $n \lg n - n \lg \lg n + O(n)$ [*Discrete Math.* **11** (1975), 29–35].

42. Construct a multigraph that has vertices $\{0_R, 1_L, 1_R, \dots, n_L, n_R, (n+1)_L\}$ and edges $k_R - (k+1)_L$ for $0 \le k \le n$; also include the edges $0_R - 7_R$, $7_L - 1_L$, $1_R - 2_L$, $2_R - 4_L$, $4_R - 5_L$, $5_R - 3_L$, $3_R - 6_L$, $6_L - 8_L$, which define the "bonds" of *Lobelia fervens*. Exactly two edges touch each vertex, so the connected components are cycles: $(0_R\, 1_L\, 7_L\, 6_R\, 3_R\, 4_L\, 2_R\, 3_L\, 5_R\, 6_L\, 8_L\, 7_R)(1_R\, 2_L)(4_R\, 5_L)$. Any flip operation changes the number of cycles by -1, 0, or $+1$. Therefore we need at least five flips to reach the eight cycles $(0_R\, 1_L)(1_R\, 2_L)\dots(7_R\, 8_L)$. [J. Kececioglu and D. Sankoff, *Algorithmica* **13** (1995), 180–210.]

The first flip must break the bond $6_L - 8_L$, because we get no new cycle when we break two bonds that have the same left-to-right orientation in the linear arrangement. This leaves five possibilities after one flip, namely $g_7^R g_6 g_3^R g_5^R g_4^R g_2^R g_1^R$, $g_7^R g_1 g_2 g_4 g_5 g_3 g_6$, $g_7^R g_1 g_2 g_6 g_3^R g_5^R g_4^R$, $g_7^R g_1 g_2 g_4 g_5 g_6 g_3^R$, and $g_6 g_3^R g_5^R g_4^R g_2^R g_1^R g_7$; four more flips suffice to sort all but the second of these.

Incidentally, there are $2^7 \cdot 7! = 645120$ different possible arrangements of $g_1 \dots g_7$, and 179904 of them are at distance ≤ 5 from tobacco order.

[An efficient algorithm to find the best way to sort any signed permutation by reversals was first developed by S. Hannenhalli and P. Pevzner, *JACM* **46** (1999), 1–27. Improvements that solve the problem in $O(n^{1.5}\sqrt{\log n})$ time were subsequently found by H. Kaplan and E. Verbin, *J. Comp. Syst. Sci.* **70** (2005), 321–341; E. Tannier, A. Bergeron, and M.-F. Sagot, *Discrete Applied Math.* **155** (2007), 881–888.]

43. Denote an arrangement like $g_7^R g_1 g_2 g_4 g_5 g_3 g_6^R$ by the signed permutation $\overline{7}12453\overline{6}$. If there is a negated element, say $\overline{k}$ is present but not $\overline{k-1}$, one flip will create the 2-cycle $((k-1)_R k_L)$. Similarly, if $\overline{k}$ is present but not $\overline{k+1}$, a single flip creates $(k_R (k+1)_L)$. And if all flips of that special kind remove all negated elements, a single flip creates two 2-cycles. If no negated elements are present and the permutation isn't sorted, some flip will preserve the number of cycles. Hence we can sort in $\leq n$ flips if the given permutation has a negated element, $\leq n+1$ otherwise.

When n is even, the permutation $n(n-1)\dots 1$ requires $n+1$ flips, because it has one cycle after the first flip. When $n > 3$ is odd, the permutation $213n(n-1)\dots 4$ requires $n+1$ by a similar argument.

44. Let c_k be the number of cycles of length $2k$ in the multigraph of the previous answers. An upper bound on the average value of c_k can be found as follows: The total number of potential $2k$-cycles is $2^k(n+1)^{\underline{k}}/(2k)$, because we can choose a sequence of k distinct edges from $\{0_R - 1_L, \dots, n_R - (n+1)_L\}$ in $(n+1)^{\underline{k}}$ ways and orient them in 2^k ways; this counts each cycle $2k$ times, including impossible cases like $(1_R 2_L 2_R 3_L)$ or $(1_R 2_L 3_L 2_R 3_R 4_L)$ or $(1_R 2_L 6_R 7_L 4_L 3_R 2_R 3_L 6_L 5_R)$. When $k \leq n$, every possible $2k$-cycle occurs in exactly $2^{n-k}(n-k)!$ signed permutations. For example, consider the case $k = 5$, $n = 9$, and the cycle $(0_R 1_L 9_L 8_R 7_R 8_L 1_R 2_L 5_L 4_R)$. This cycle occurs in the multigraph if and only if the signed permutation begins with $\overline{4}$ and contains the substrings $\overline{9}18\overline{7}$ and $\overline{2}5$ or their reverses; we obtain all solutions by finding all signed permutations of $\{1,2,3,6\}$ and replacing 1 by $\overline{9}18\overline{7}$, 2 by $\overline{2}5$. Therefore $\mathrm{E}\,c_k \leq 1/(2k)\, 2^k(n+1)^{\underline{k}}2^{n-k}(n-k)!/2^n n! = \frac{1}{2}(1/k + 1/(n+1-k))$. It follows that $\mathrm{E}\,c = \sum_{k=1}^{n} \mathrm{E}\,c_k + \mathrm{E}\,c_{n+1} < H_n + 1$. Since $n+1-c$ is a lower bound on the number of flips, we need $\geq n+1-\mathrm{E}\,c > n - H_n$ of them.

[This proof uses ideas of V. Bafna and P. Pevzner, *SICOMP* **25** (1996), 272–289, who studied the more difficult problem of sorting *unsigned* permutations by reversals. In that problem, an interesting permutation that can be written as the product of non-disjoint cycles $(1\,2\,3)(3\,4\,5)(5\,6\,7)\dots$, ending with either $(n-1\,n)$ or $(n-2\,n-1\,n)$ depending on whether n is even or odd, turns out to be the hardest to sort.]

SECTION 5.2

1. Yes; i and j may run through the set of values $1 \leq j < i \leq N$ in any order, possibly in parallel and/or as records are being read in.

2. The sorting is *stable* in the sense defined at the beginning of this chapter, because the algorithm is essentially sorting by lexicographic order on the *distinct* key-pairs $(K_1, 1), (K_2, 2), \dots, (K_N, N)$. (If we think of each key as extended on the right by its location in the file, no equal keys are present, and the sorting is stable.)

3. It would sort, but not in a stable manner; if $K_j = K_i$ and $j < i$, R_j will come *after* R_i in the final ordering. This change would also make Program C run more slowly.

4.

```
    ENT1 N          1        STA  OUTPUT+1,2  N
    LD2  COUNT,1    N        DEC1 1           N
    LDA  INPUT,1    N        J1P  *-4         N
```

5. The running time is decreased by $A + 1 - N - B$ units, and this is almost always an improvement.

6. $u = 0$, $v = 9$.

```
After D1,   COUNT =  0  0  0  0  0  0  0  0  0  0
After D2,   COUNT =  2  2  1  0  1  3  3  2  1  1
After D4,   COUNT =  2  4  5  5  6  9 12 14 15 16
During D5,  COUNT =  2  3  5  5  5  8  9 12 15 16        j = 8
            OUTPUT = -- -- -- 1G -- 4A -- -- 5L 6A 6T 6I 70 7N -- --
After D5,   OUTPUT = 0C 00 1N 1G 2R 4A 5T 5U 5L 6A 6T 6I 70 7N 8S 9.
```

7. Yes; note that $\mathtt{COUNT}[K_j]$ is decreased in step D6, and j decreases.

8. It would sort, but not in a stable manner (see exercise 7).

9. Let $M = v - u$; assume that $|u|$ and $|v|$ fit in two bytes. $\mathtt{LOC}(R_j) \equiv \mathtt{INPUT} + j$; $\mathtt{LOC}(\mathtt{COUNT}[j]) \equiv \mathtt{COUNT} + j$; $\mathtt{LOC}(S_j) \equiv \mathtt{OUTPUT} + j$; rI1 $\equiv i$; rI2 $\equiv j$; rI3 $\equiv i - v$ or rI3 $\equiv K_j$.

M	EQU	V-U		
KEY	EQU	0:2		(Satellite information is in bytes 3:5)
1H	ENN3	M	1	D1. Clear COUNTs.
	STZ	COUNT+V,3	$M + 1$	COUNT$[v - k] \leftarrow 0$.
	INC3	1	$M + 1$	
	J3NP	*-2	$M + 1$	$u \leq i \leq v$.
2H	ENT2	N	1	D2. Loop on j.
3H	LD3	INPUT,2(KEY)	N	D3. Increase COUNT$[K_j]$.
	LDA	COUNT,3	N	
	INCA	1	N	
	STA	COUNT,3	N	
	DEC2	1	N	
	J2P	3B	N	$N \geq j > 0$.
	ENN3	M-1	1	D4. Accumulate.
	LDA	COUNT+U	1	rA $\leftarrow$ COUNT$[i - 1]$.
4H	ADD	COUNT+V,3	M	COUNT$[i - 1]$ + COUNT$[i]$
	STA	COUNT+V,3	M	$\rightarrow$ COUNT$[i]$.
	INC3	1	M	
	J3NP	4B	M	$u \leq i \leq v$.
5H	ENT2	N	1	D5. Loop on j.
6H	LD3	INPUT,2(KEY)	N	D6. Output R_j.
	LD1	COUNT,3	N	$i \leftarrow$ COUNT$[K_j]$.
	LDA	INPUT,2	N	rA $\leftarrow R_j$.
	STA	OUTPUT,1	N	$S_i \leftarrow$ rA.
	DEC1	1	N	
	ST1	COUNT,3	N	COUNT$[K_j] \leftarrow i - 1$.
	DEC2	1	N	
	J2P	6B	N	$N \geq j > 0$. ∎

The running time is $(10M + 22N + 10)u$.

10. In order to avoid using N extra "tag" bits [see Section 1.3.3 and *Cybernetics* **1** (1965), 95], yet keep the running time essentially proportional to N, we may use the following algorithm based on the cycle structure of the permutation:

P1. [Loop on i.] Do step P2 for $1 \leq i \leq N$; then terminate the algorithm.

P2. [Is $p(i) = i$?] Do steps P3 through P5, if $p(i) \neq i$.

P3. [Begin cycle.] Set $t \leftarrow R_i$, $j \leftarrow i$.

P4. [Fix R_j.] Set $k \leftarrow p(j)$, $R_j \leftarrow R_k$, $p(j) \leftarrow j$, $j \leftarrow k$. If $p(j) \neq i$, repeat this step.

P5. [End cycle.] Set $R_j \leftarrow t$, $p(j) \leftarrow j$. ∎

This algorithm changes $p(i)$, since the sorting application lets us assume that $p(i)$ is stored in memory. On the other hand, there are applications such as matrix transposition where $p(i)$ is a function of i that is to be computed (not tabulated) in order to save memory space. In such a case we can use the following method, performing steps B1 through B3 for $1 \leq i \leq N$.

B1. Set $k \leftarrow p(i)$.

B2. If $k > i$, set $k \leftarrow p(k)$ and repeat this step.

B3. If $k < i$, do nothing; but if $k = i$ (this means that i is smallest in its cycle), we permute the cycle containing i as follows: Set $t \leftarrow R_i$; then while $p(k) \neq i$ repeatedly set $R_k \leftarrow R_{p(k)}$ and $k \leftarrow p(k)$; finally set $R_k \leftarrow t$. ∎

This algorithm is similar to the procedure of J. Boothroyd [*Comp. J.* **10** (1967), 310], but it requires less data movement; some refinements have been suggested by I. D. G. MacLeod [*Australian Comp. J.* **2** (1970), 16–19]. For random permutations the analysis in exercise 1.3.3–14 shows that step B2 is performed $(N+1)H_N - N$ steps on the average. See also the references in the answer to exercise 1.3.3–12. Similar algorithms can be designed to replace $(R_{p(1)}, \ldots, R_{p(N)})$ by $(R_1, \ldots, R_N)$, for example if the rearrangement in exercise 4 were to be done with OUTPUT = INPUT.

11. Let rI1 ≡ i; rI2 ≡ j; rI3 ≡ k; rX ≡ t.

1H	ENT1	N	1	*P1. Loop on i.*
2H	CMP1	P,1	N	*P2. Is $p(i) = i$?*
	JE	8F	N	Jump if $p(i) = i$.
3H	LDX	INPUT,1	$A - B$	*P3. Begin cycle.* $t \leftarrow R_i$.
	ENT2	0,1	$A - B$	$j \leftarrow i$.
4H	LD3	P,2	$N - A$	*P4. Fix R_j.* $k \leftarrow p(j)$.
	LDA	INPUT,3	$N - A$	
	STA	INPUT,2	$N - A$	$R_j \leftarrow R_k$.
	ST2	P,2	$N - A$	$p(j) \leftarrow j$.
	ENT2	0,3	$N - A$	$j \leftarrow k$.
	CMP1	P,2	$N - A$	
	JNE	4B	$N - A$	Repeat if $p(j) \neq i$.
5H	STX	INPUT,2	$A - B$	*P5. End cycle.* $R_j \leftarrow t$.
	ST2	P,2	$A - B$	$p(j) \leftarrow j$.
8H	DEC1	1	N	
	J1P	2B	N	$N \geq i \geq 1$. ∎

The running time is $(17N - 5A - 7B + 1)u$, where A is the number of cycles in the permutation $p(1) \ldots p(N)$ and B is the number of fixed points (1-cycles). We have

$$A = \left(\min 1, \text{ ave } H_N, \text{ max } N, \text{ dev } \sqrt{H_N - H_N^{(2)}} \right) \text{ and } B = (\min 0, \text{ ave } 1, \text{ max } N, \text{ dev } 1),$$

for $N \geq 2$, by Eqs. 1.3.3–(21) and 1.3.3–(28).

12. The obvious way is to run through the list, replacing the link of the kth element by the number k, and then to rearrange the elements in a second pass. The following more direct method, due to M. D. MacLaren, is shorter and faster if the records are not too long. (Assume for convenience that $0 \leq \text{LINK(P)} \leq N$, for $1 \leq \text{P} \leq N$, where $\Lambda \equiv 0$.)

> **M1.** [Initialize.] Set $\text{P} \leftarrow \text{HEAD}$, $k \leftarrow 1$.
>
> **M2.** [Done?] If $\text{P} = \Lambda$ (or equivalently if $k = N + 1$), the algorithm terminates.
>
> **M3.** [Ensure $\text{P} \geq k$.] If $\text{P} < k$, set $\text{P} \leftarrow \text{LINK(P)}$ and repeat this step.
>
> **M4.** [Exchange.] Interchange R_k and $R[\text{P}]$. (Assume that $\text{LINK}(k)$ and LINK(P) are also interchanged in this process.) Then set $\text{Q} \leftarrow \text{LINK}(k)$, $\text{LINK}(k) \leftarrow \text{P}$, $\text{P} \leftarrow \text{Q}$, $k \leftarrow k + 1$, and return to step M2. ∎

A proof that MacLaren's method is valid can be based on an inductive verification of the following property that holds at the beginning of step M2: The entries that are $\geq k$ in the sequence $\text{P}, \text{LINK(P)}, \text{LINK(LINK(P))}, \ldots, \Lambda$ are $a_1, a_2, \ldots, a_{N+1-k}$, where $R_1 \leq \cdots \leq R_{k-1} \leq R_{a_1} \leq \cdots \leq R_{a_{N+1-k}}$ is the desired final order of the records. Furthermore $\text{LINK}(j) \geq j$ for $1 \leq j < k$, so that $\text{LINK}(j) = \Lambda$ implies $j \geq k$.

It is quite interesting to analyze MacLaren's algorithm; one of its remarkable properties is that it can be run backwards, reconstructing the original set of links from the final values of $\text{LINK}(1) \ldots \text{LINK}(N)$. Each of the $N!$ possible output configurations with $j \leq \text{LINK}(j) \leq N$ corresponds to exactly one of the $N!$ possible input configurations. If A is the number of times $\text{P} \leftarrow \text{LINK(P)}$ in step M3, then $N - A$ is the number of j such that $\text{LINK}(j) = j$ at the conclusion of the algorithm; this occurs if and only if j was largest in its cycle; hence $N - A$ is the number of cycles in the permutation, and $A = (\min 0, \text{ave } N - H_N, \max N - 1)$.

References: M. D. MacLaren, *JACM* **13** (1966), 404–411; D. Gries and J. F. Prins, *Science of Computer Programming* **8** (1987), 139–145.

13. **D5′.** Set $r \leftarrow N$.

> **D6′.** If $r = 0$, stop. Otherwise, if $\text{COUNT}[K_r] < r$ set $r \leftarrow r - 1$ and repeat this step; if $\text{COUNT}[K_r] = r$, decrease both $\text{COUNT}[K_r]$ and r by 1 and repeat this step. Otherwise set $R \leftarrow R_r$, $j \leftarrow \text{COUNT}[K_r]$, $\text{COUNT}[K_r] \leftarrow j - 1$.
>
> **D7′.** Set $S \leftarrow R_j$, $k \leftarrow \text{COUNT}[K_j]$, $\text{COUNT}[K_j] \leftarrow k - 1$, $R_j \leftarrow R$, $R \leftarrow S$, $j \leftarrow k$. Then if $j \neq r$ repeat this step; if $j = r$ set $R_j \leftarrow R$, $r \leftarrow r - 1$, and go back to D6′. ∎

To prove that this procedure is valid, observe that at the beginning of step D6′ all records R_j such that $j > r$ that are not in their final resting place must move to the left; when $r = 0$ there can't be any such records since *somebody* must move right. The algorithm is elegant but not stable for equal keys. It is intimately related to Foata's construction in Theorem 5.1.2B.

SECTION 5.2.1

1. Yes; equal elements are never moved across each other.

2. Yes. But the running time would be slower when equal elements are present, and the sorting would be just the opposite of stable.

3. The following eight-liner is conjectured to be the shortest MIX sorting routine, although it is not recommended for speed. We assume that the numbers appear in locations $1, \ldots, N$ (that is, INPUT EQU 0); otherwise another line of code is necessary.

```
2H       LDA  0,1    B
         CMPA 1,1    B
         JLE  1F     B
         MOVE 1,1    A
         STA  0,1    A
START    ENT1 N      A + 1
1H       DEC1 1      B + 1
         J1P  2B     B + 1     ▌
```

Note: To estimate the running time of this program, note that A is the number of inversions. The quantity B is a reasonably simple function of the inversion table, and (assuming distinct inputs in random order) it has the generating function

$$z^{N-1}(1+z)(1+z^2+z^{2+1})$$
$$\times (1+z^3+z^{3+2}+z^{3+2+1})\ldots(1+z^{N-1}+z^{2N-3}+\cdots+z^{N(N-1)/2})/N!.$$

The mean value of B is $N - 1 + \sum_{k=1}^{N}(k-1)(2k-1)/6 = (N-1)(4N^2+N+36)/36$; hence the average running time of this program is roughly $\frac{7}{9}N^3 u$.

4. Consider the inversion table $B_1 \ldots B_N$ of the given input permutation, in the sense of exercise 5.1.1–7. Then A is one less than the number of B_j's that are equal to $j-1$, and B is the sum of the B_j's. Hence both $B - A$ and B are maximized when the input permutation is $N \ldots 2\ 1$; they both are minimized when the input is $1\ 2 \ldots N$. The minimum achievable time therefore occurs for $A = 0$ and $B = 0$, namely $(10N - 9)u$; the maximum occurs for $A = N - 1$ and $B = \binom{N}{2}$, namely $(4.5N^2 + 2.5N - 6)u$.

5. The generating function is z^{10N-9} times the generating function for $9B - 3A$. By considering the inversion table as in the previous exercise, remembering that individual entries of the inversion table are independent of each other, the desired generating function is $z^{10N-9}\prod_{1<j\le N}((1+z^9+\cdots+z^{9j-18}+z^{9j-12})/j)$. The variance comes to $2.25N^3 + 3.375N^2 - 32.625N + 36H_N - 9H_N^{(2)}$.

6. Treat the input area as a circular list, with position N adjacent to position 1. Take new elements to be inserted from either the left or the right of the current segment of unsorted elements, according as the previously inserted element fell to the right or left of the center of the sorted elements, respectively. Afterwards it will usually be necessary to "rotate" the area, moving each record k places around the circle for some fixed k; this can be done efficiently as in exercise 1.3.3–34.

7. The average value of $|a_j - j|$ is

$$\frac{1}{n}(|1-j|+|2-j|+\cdots+|n-j|) = \frac{1}{n}\left(\binom{j}{2}+\binom{n-j+1}{2}\right);$$

summing on j gives $\frac{1}{n}\left(\binom{n+1}{3}+\binom{n+1}{3}\right) = \frac{1}{3}(n^2-1)$. Incidentally, the *variance* of the stated sum can be shown to equal $[n>1](2n^2+7)(n+1)/45$.

8. No; for example, consider the keys 2 1 1 1 1 1 1 1 1 1 1.

9. For Table 3, $A = 3+0+2+1 = 6$, $B = 3+1+4+21 = 29$; in Table 4, $A = 4+2+2+0 = 8$, $B = 4+3+8+10 = 25$; hence the running time of Program D comes to $786u$ and $734u$, respectively. Although the number of moves has been cut from 41 to 25, the running time is not competitive with Program S since the bookkeeping time for four passes is wasted when $N = 16$. When sorting 16 items we will be better off using only two passes; a two-pass Program D begins to beat Program S at about $N = 13$, although they are fairly equal for awhile (and for such small N the length of the program is perhaps significant).

10. Insert "`INC1 INPUT; ST1 OF(0:2)`" between lines 07 and 08, and change lines 10–17 to:

```
OH CMPA INPUT+N-H,1       NT − S
   JGE  7F                NT − S
3H ENT2 N-H,1             NT − S − C
4H LDX  INPUT,2             B
5H STX  INPUT+H,2           B
   DEC2 0,4                 B
   J2NP 6F                  B
   CMPA INPUT,2           B − A
   JL   4B                B − A
6H STA  INPUT+H,2        NT − S − C
```

For a net increase of four instructions, this saves $3(C - T)$ units of time, where C is the number of times $K_j \geq K_{j-h}$. In Tables 3 and 4 the time savings is approximately 87 and 88, respectively; empirically the value of $C/(NT - S)$ seems to be about 0.4 when $h_{s+1}/h_s \approx 2$ and about 0.3 when $h_{s+1}/h_s \approx 3$, so the improvement is worth while. (On the other hand, the analogous change to Program S is not desirable, since the savings in that case is only proportional to $\log N$ unless the input is known to be pretty well ordered.)

11.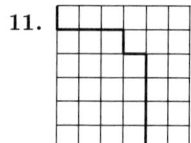

12. Changing $\llcorner$ to $\urcorner$ always changes the number of inversions by ±1, depending on whether the change is above or below the diagonal.

13. Put the weight $|i - j|$ on the segment from $(i, j-1)$ to (i, j).

14. (a) Interchange i and j in the sum for A_{2n} and add the two sums. (b) Taking half of this result, we see that

$$A_{2n} = \sum_{0 \leq i \leq j} (j - i) \binom{i+j}{i} \binom{2n-i-j}{n-j} = \sum_{i,k \geq 0} k \binom{2i+k}{i} \binom{2n-2i-k}{n-i-k};$$

hence $\sum A_{2n} z^n = \sum_{k \geq 0} k z^k \alpha^{2k}/(1 - 4z) = z/(1 - 4z)^2$, where $\alpha = (1 - \sqrt{1 - 4z})/2z$.

The proof above was suggested to the author by Leonard Carlitz. Another proof can be based on interplay between horizontal and vertical weights (see exercise 13), and still another by the identity in the answer to exercise 5.2.2–16 with $f(k) = k$; but no simple combinatorial derivation of the formula $A_n = \lfloor n/2 \rfloor 2^{n-2}$ is apparent.

15. For $n > 0$,

$$\hat{g}_n(z) = z^n g_{n-1}(z); \qquad \hat{h}_n(z) = \hat{g}_n(z) + z^{-n} \hat{g}_n(z);$$

$$g_n(z) = \sum_{k=1}^{n} \hat{g}_k(z) g_{n-k}(z); \qquad h_n(z) = \sum_{k=1}^{n} \hat{h}_k(z) h_{n-k}(z).$$

Letting $G(w, z) = \sum_n g_n(z) w^n$, we find that $wzG(w, z)G(wz, z) = G(w, z) - 1$. From this representation we can deduce that, if $t = \sqrt{1 - 4w} = 1 - 2w - 2w^2 - 4w^3 - \cdots$, we have $G(w, 1) = (1 - t)/(2w)$; $G_{\prime}(w, 1) = 1/(wt) - (1 - t)/(2w^2)$; $G'(w, 1) = 1/(2t^2) - 1/(2t)$; $G_{\prime\prime}(w, 1) = 2/(wt^3) - 2/(w^2 t) + (1-t)/w^3$; $G_{\prime}'(w, 1) = 2/t^4 - 1/t^3$; and

$G''(w, 1) = 1/t^3 - (1 - 2w)/t^4 + 10w^2/t^5$. Here lower primes denote differentiation with respect to the first parameter, and upper primes denote differentiation with respect to the second parameter. Similarly, from the formula

$$w(zG(wz, z) + G(w, z))H(w, z) = H(w, z) - 1$$

we deduce that

$$H'(w, 1) = w/t^4, \qquad H''(w, 1) = -w/t^3 - w/t^4 + 2w/t^5 + (2w^2 + 20w^3)/t^7.$$

The formula manipulation summarized here was originally done by hand, but today it can readily be done by computer. In principle all moments of the distribution are obtainable in this way.

The generating function $g_n(z)$ also represents $\sum z^{\text{internal path length}}$ over all trees with $n + 1$ nodes; see exercise 2.3.4.5–5. It is interesting to note that $G(w, z)$ is equal to $F(-wz, z)/F(-w, z)$, where $F(z, q) = \sum_{n \geq 0} z^n q^{n^2}/\prod_{k=1}^{n}(1 - q^k)$; the coefficient of $q^m z^n$ in $F(z, q)$ is the number of partitions $m = p_1 + \cdots + p_n$ such that $p_j \geq p_{j+1} + 2$ for $1 \leq j < n$ and $p_n > 0$ (see exercise 5.1.1–16).

16. For $h = 2$ the maximum clearly occurs for the path that goes through the upper right corner of the lattice diagram, namely

$$\binom{\lfloor n/2 \rfloor + 1}{2}.$$

For general h the corresponding number is

$$\hat{f}(n, h) = \binom{h}{2}\binom{q+1}{2} + \binom{r}{2}(q + 1),$$

where q and r are defined in Theorem H; the permutation with

$$a_{i+jh} = 1 + q(h - i) + (r - i)[i \leq r] \qquad \text{for } 1 \leq i \leq h \text{ and } j \geq 0$$

maximizes the number of inversions between each of the $\binom{h}{2}$ pairs of sorted subsequences. The maximum number of moves is obtained if we replace f by $\hat{f}$ in (6).

17. The only two-ordered permutation of $\{1, 2, \ldots, 2n\}$ that has as many as $\binom{n+1}{2}$ inversions is $n+1 \; 1 \; n+2 \; 2 \; \ldots \; 2n \; n$. Using this idea recursively, we obtain the permutation defined by adding unity to each element of the sequence $(2^t - 1)^R \ldots 1^R 0^R$, where R denotes the operation of writing an integer as a t-bit binary number and reversing the left-to-right order of the bits(!).

18. Take out a common factor and let $h_t = 4N/\pi$; we want to minimize the sum $\sum_{s=1}^{t} h_s^{1/2}/h_{s-1}$, when $h_0 = 1$. Differentiation yields $h_s^3 = 4h_{s-1}^2 h_{s+1}$, and we find $(2^t - 1)\lg h_1 = 2^{t+1} - 2(t + 1) + \lg h_t$. The minimum value of the stated estimate comes to $(1 - 2^{-t})\pi^{(2^{t-1}-1)/(2^t-1)} N^{1+2^{t-1}/(2^t-1)}/2^{1+(t-1)/(2^t-1)}$, which rapidly approaches the limiting value $N\sqrt{\pi N}/2$ as $t \to \infty$.

Typical examples of "optimum" h's when $N = 1000$ (see also Table 6) are:

$$h_2 \approx 57.64, \qquad h_1 \approx 6.13, \qquad h_0 = 1;$$
$$h_3 \approx 135.30, \qquad h_2 \approx 22.05, \qquad h_1 \approx 4.45, \qquad h_0 = 1;$$
$$h_4 \approx 284.46, \qquad h_3 \approx 67.23, \qquad h_2 \approx 16.34, \qquad h_1 \approx 4.03, \qquad h_0 = 1;$$
$$h_9 \approx 9164.74, \quad h_8 \approx 12294.05, \quad h_7 \approx 7119.55, \quad h_6 \approx 2708.95, \quad h_5 \approx 835.50,$$
$$h_4 \approx 232.00, \quad h_3 \approx 61.13, \quad h_2 \approx 15.69, \quad h_1 \approx 3.97, \quad h_0 = 1.$$

19. Let $g(n,h) = H_r - 1 + \sum_{r < j \le h} q/(qj + r)$, where q and r are defined in Theorem H; then replace f by g in (6).

20. (This is much harder to write down than to understand.) Assume that a k-ordered file $R_1, \ldots, R_N$ has been h-sorted, and let $1 \le i \le N - k$; we want to show that $K_i \le K_{i+k}$. Find u, v such that $i \equiv u$ and $i + k \equiv v$ (modulo h), $1 \le u, v \le h$; and apply Lemma L with $x_j = K_{v+(j-1)h}$, $y_j = K_{u+(j-1)h}$. Then the first r elements K_u, K_{u+h}, $\ldots$, $K_{u+(r-1)h}$ of the y's are respectively $\le$ the last r elements K_{u+k}, K_{u+k+h}, $\ldots$, $K_{u+k+(r-1)h}$ of the x's, where r is the greatest integer such that $u + k + (r-1)h \le N$.

21. If $xh + yk = x'h + y'k$, we have $(x - x')h = (y' - y)k$, so $x' = x + tk$ and $y' = y - th$ for some integer t. Let $h'h + k'k = 1$; then $n = (nh')h + (nk')k$, so every integer n has a unique representation of the form $n = xh + yk$ where $0 \le x < k$, and n is generable if and only if $y \ge 0$. Let, similarly, $hk - h - k - n = x'h + y'k$; then $(x + x')h + (y + y')k = hk - h - k$. Hence $x + x' \equiv k - 1$ (modulo k) and we must have $x + x' = k - 1$. Hence $y + y' = -1$, and $y \ge 0$ if and only if $y' < 0$.

The symmetry of this result shows that exactly $\frac{1}{2}(h-1)(k-1)$ positive integers are unrepresentable in the stated form, a result originally due to Sylvester [*Mathematical Questions, with their Solutions, from the 'Educational Times'* **41** (1884), 21].

22. To avoid cumbersome notation, consider $s = 4$, which is representative of the general case. Let n_k be the smallest number that is congruent to k (modulo 15) and representable in the form $15a_0 + 31a_1 + \cdots$; then we find easily that

$$
\begin{array}{ccccccccccccccccc}
k & = & 0 & 1 & 2 & 3 & 4 & 5 & 6 & 7 & 8 & 9 & 10 & 11 & 12 & 13 & 14 \\
n_k & = & 0 & 31 & 62 & 63 & 94 & 125 & 126 & 127 & 158 & 189 & 190 & 221 & 252 & 253 & 254.
\end{array}
$$

Hence $239 = 2^4(2^4 - 1) - 1$ is the largest unrepresentable number, and the total number of unrepresentables is

$$
\begin{aligned}
x_4 &= (n_1 - 1 + n_2 - 2 + \cdots + n_{14} - 14)/15 \\
&= (2 + 4 + 4 + 6 + 8 + 8) + 8 + (10 + 12 + 12 + 14 + 16 + 16) + 16 \\
&= 2x_3 + 8 \cdot 9;
\end{aligned}
$$

in general, $x_s = 2x_{s-1} + 2^{s-1}(2^{s-1} + 1)$.

For the other problem the answers are $2^{2s} + 2^s + 2$ and $2^{s-1}(2^s + s - 1) + 2$, respectively.

23. Each of the N numbers has at most $\lceil (h_{s+2} - 1)(h_{s+1} - 1)/h_s \rceil$ inversions in its subfile.

24. (Solution obtained jointly with V. Pratt.) Construct the "h-recidivous permutation" of $\{1, 2, \ldots, N\}$ as follows. Start with $a_1 \ldots a_N$ blank; then for $j = 2, 3, 4, \ldots$ do Step j: Fill in all blank positions a_i from left to right, using the smallest number that has not yet appeared in the permutation, whenever $(2^h - 1)j - i$ is a positive integer representable as in exercise 22. Continue until all positions are filled. Thus the 2-recidivous permutation for $N = 20$ is

6 2 1 9 4 3 12 7 5 15 10 8 17 13 11 19 16 14 20 18.

The h-recidivous permutation is $(2^k - 1)$-ordered for all $k \ge h$. When $2^h < j \le N/(2^h - 1)$, exactly $2^h - 1$ positions are filled during step j; the $(k+1)$st of them adds at least $2^{h-1} - 2k$ to the number of moves required to $(2^{h-1} - 1)$-sort the permutation. Hence the number of moves to sort the h-recidivous permutation with increments $h_s = 2^s - 1$ when $N = 2^{h+1}(2^h - 1)$ is $> 2^{3h-4} > \frac{1}{64}N^{3/2}$. Pratt generalized this construction to a large family of similar sequences, including (12), in his Ph.D. thesis (Stanford University, 1972). Heuristics that find permutations needing even more moves are discussed by H. Erkiö, *BIT* **20** (1980), 130–136. See also Weiss and Sedgewick, *J. Algorithms* **11** (1990), 242–251, for improvements on Pratt's construction.

25. F_{N+1} [this result is due to H. B. Mann, *Econometrica* **13** (1945), 256]; for the permutation must begin with either 1 or 2 1. There are at most $\lfloor N/2 \rfloor$ inversions; and the total number of inversions is

$$\frac{N-1}{5} F_N + \frac{2N}{5} F_{N-1}.$$

(See exercise 1.2.8–12.) Note that the F_{N+1} permutations can conveniently be represented by "Morse code" sequences of dots and dashes, where a dash corresponds to an inversion; see exercise 4.5.3–32. Hence we have found the total number of dashes among all Morse code sequences of length N.

Our derivation shows that a random 3- and 2-ordered permutation has roughly $\frac{1}{5}(\phi^{-1} + 2\phi^{-2})N = \phi^{-1}N/\sqrt{5} \approx .276N$ inversions. But if a random permutation is 3-sorted, then 2-sorted, exercise 42 shows that it has $\approx N/4$ inversions; if it is 2-sorted, then 3-sorted, it has $\approx N/3$.

26. Yes; a shortest example is 4 1 3 7 2 6 8 5, which has nine inversions. In general, the construction $a_{3k+s} = 3k + 4s$ for $-1 \le s \le 1$ yields files that are 3-, 5-, and 7-ordered, having approximately $\frac{4}{3}N$ inversions. When $N \bmod 3 = 2$ this construction is best possible.

27. (a) See *J. Algorithms* **15** (1993), 101–124. A simpler proof, which shows that c can be any constant $< \frac{1}{2}$, was found independently by C. G. Plaxton and T. Suel, *J. Algorithms* **23** (1997), 221–240. (b) This is obvious if $m > \frac{1}{4}c^2(\ln N/\ln\ln N)^2$. Otherwise $N^{1+c/\sqrt{m}} \ge N(\ln N)^2$. R. E. Cypher [*SICOMP* **22** (1993), 62–71] has proved the slightly stronger bound $\Omega(N(\log N)^2/\log\log N)$ when the increments satisfy $h_{s+1} > h_s$ for all s and when a sorting network is constructed as in exercise 5.3.4–2. No nontrivial lower bounds are yet known for the asymptotic *average* running time.

28. 209 109 41 19 5 1, from (11). But better sequences are possible; see exercise 29.

29. Experiments by C. Tribolet in 1971 resulted in the choices 373 137 53 19 7 3 1 ($B_{ave} \approx 7210$) and 317 101 31 11 3 1 ($B_{ave} \approx 8170$). [The first of these yields a sorting time of $\approx 127720u$, compared to $\approx 128593u$ when the same data are sorted using increments (11).] In general Tribolet suggests letting h_s be the nearest prime number to $N^{s/t}$. Experiments by Shelby Siegel in 1972 indicate that the best number of increments in such a method, for $N \le 10000$, is $t \approx \frac{4}{3}\ln(N/5.75)$. On the other hand, Marcin Ciura's experiments [*Lect. Notes Comp. Sci.* **2138** (2001), 106–117] indicate that the minimum 7-pass B_{ave} (≈ 6879) is obtained with increments 229 96 41 19 10 4 1, while the sequence 737 176 69 27 10 4 1 yields the smallest total sorting time ($\approx 125077u$).

The best three-increment sequence, according to extensive tests by Carole M. McNamee, appears to be 45 7 1 ($B_{ave} \approx 18240$). For four increments, 91 23 7 1 was the winner in her tests ($B_{ave} \approx 11865$), but a rather broad range of increments gave roughly the same performance.

30. The number of integer points in the triangular region

$$\{x\ln 2 + y\ln 3 < \ln N,\ x \ge 0,\ y \ge 0\} \qquad \text{is} \qquad \tfrac{1}{2}(\log_2 N)(\log_3 N) + O(\log N).$$

While we are h-sorting, the file is already $2h$-ordered and $3h$-ordered, by Theorem K; hence exercise 25 applies.

31.

01	START	ENT3	T	1
02	1H	LD4	H,3	T
03		ENN2	-INPUT-N,4	T
04		ST2	6F(0:2)	T
05		ST2	7F(0:2)	T
06		ST2	4F(0:2)	T
07		ENT2	0,4	T
08		JMP	9F	T
09	2H	LDA	INPUT+N,1	$NT - S - B + A$
10	4H	CMPA	INPUT+N-H,1	$NT - S - B + A$
11		JGE	8F	$NT - S - B + A$
12	6H	LDX	INPUT+N-H,1	B
13		STX	INPUT+N,1	B
14	7H	STA	INPUT+N-H,1	B
15		INC1	0,4	B
16	8H	INC1	0,4	$NT - B + A$
17		J1NP	2B	$NT - B + A$
18		DEC2	1	S
19	9H	ENT1	-N,2	$T + S$
20		J2P	8B	$T + S$
21		DEC3	1	T
22		J3P	1B	T ▌

Here A is related to right-to-left maxima in the same way that A in Program D is related to left-to-right minima; both quantities have the same statistical behavior. The simplifications in the inner loop have cut the running time to $7NT + 7A - 2S + 1 + 15T$ units, curiously independent of B!

When $N = 8$ the increments are 6, 4, 3, 2, 1, and we have $A_{\mathrm{ave}} = 3.892$, $B_{\mathrm{ave}} = 6.762$; the average total running time is $276.24u$. (Compare with Table 5.) Both A and B are maximized in the permutation 7 3 8 4 5 1 6 2. When $N = 1000$ there are 40 increments, $972, 864, 768, 729, \ldots, 8, 6, 4, 3, 2, 1$; empirical tests like those in Table 6 give $A \approx 875$, $B \approx 4250$, and a total time of about $268000u$ (more than twice as long as Program D with the increments of exercise 28).

Instead of storing the increments in an auxiliary table, it is convenient to generate them as follows on a binary machine:

P1. Set $m \leftarrow 2^{\lceil \lg N \rceil - 1}$, the largest power of 2 less than N.

P2. Set $h \leftarrow m$.

P3. Use h as the increment for one sorting pass.

P4. If h is even, set $h \leftarrow h + h/2$; then if $h < N$, return to P3.

P5. Set $m \leftarrow \lfloor m/2 \rfloor$ and if $m \geq 1$ return to P2. ▌

Although the increments are not being generated in descending order, the order specified here is sufficient to make the sorting algorithm valid.

32. 4 12 11 13 2 0 8 5 10 14 1 6 3 9 16 7 15.

33. Two types of improvements can be made. First, by assuming that the artificial key K_0 is ∞, we can omit testing whether or not $p > 0$. (This idea has been used, for example, in Algorithm 2.2.4A.) Secondly, a standard optimization technique: We can make two copies of the inner loop with the register assignments for p and q interchanged; this avoids the assignment $q \leftarrow p$. (This idea has been used in exercise 1.1–3.)

Thus we assume that location INPUT contains the largest possible value in its $(0:3)$ field, and we replace lines 07 and following of Program L by:

```
07  8H  LD3   INPUT,2(LINK)    B'   p ← L_q. (Here p ≡ rI3, q ≡ rI2.)
08      CMPA  INPUT,3(KEY)     B'
09      JG    4F               B'   To L4 with q ↔ p if K > K_p.
10  7H  ST1   INPUT,2(LINK)    N'   L_q ← j.
11      ST3   INPUT,1(LINK)    N'   L_j ← p.
12      JMP   6F               N'   Go to decrease j.
13  4H  LD2   INPUT,3(LINK)    B''  p ← L_q. (Here p ≡ rI2, q ≡ rI3.)
14      CMPA  INPUT,2(KEY)     B''
15      JG    8B               B''  To L4 with q ↔ p if K > K_p.
16  5H  ST1   INPUT,3(LINK)    N''  L_q ← j.
17      ST2   INPUT,1(LINK)    N''  L_j ← p.
18  6H  DEC1  1                N    j ← j − 1.
19      ENT3  0                N    q ← 0.
20      LDA   INPUT,1          N    K ← K_j.
21      J1P   4B               N    N > j ≥ 1.  ∎
```

Here $B' + B'' = B + N - 1$, $N' + N'' = N - 1$, so the total running time is $5B + 14N + N' - 3$ units. Since N' is the number of elements with an odd number of lesser elements to their right, it has the statistics

$$\left(\min 0, \ \text{ave} \ \frac{1}{2}N + \frac{1}{4}H_{\lfloor N/2 \rfloor} - \frac{1}{2}H_N, \ \max N - 1\right).$$

The ∞ trick also speeds up Program S; the following code suggested by J. H. Halperin uses this idea and the MOVE instruction to reduce the running time to $(6B + 11N - 10)u$, assuming that location INPUT+N+1 already contains the largest possible one-word value:

```
01  START  ENT2  N-1           1
02  2H     LDA   INPUT,2        N − 1
03         ENT1  INPUT,2        N − 1
04         JMP   3F             N − 1
05  4H     MOVE  1,1(1)         B
06  3H     CMPA  1,1            B + N − 1
07         JG    4B             B + N − 1
08  5H     STA   0,1            N − 1
09         DEC2  1              N − 1
10         J2P   2B             N − 1    ∎
```

Doubling up the inner loop would save an additional $B/2$ or so units of time.

34. There are $\binom{N}{n}$ sequences of N choices in which the given list is chosen n times; every such sequence has probability $(1/M)^n(1-1/M)^{N-n}$ of occurring, since the given list is chosen with probability $1/M$.

35.
```
24      ENT1  0                    1    29      ENT1  0,3               N
25      ENT2  1-M                  1    30      LD3   INPUT,1(LINK)     N
26  7H  LD3   HEAD+M,2             M    31      J3P   *-2               N
27      J3Z   8F                   M    32  8H  INC2  1                 M
28      ST3   INPUT,1(LINK)   M − E     33      J2NP  7B                M  ∎
```

Note: If Program M were modified to keep track of the current end of each list, by inserting "ST1 END,4" between lines 19 and 20, we could save time by hooking the lists together as in Algorithm 5.2.5H.

36. Program L: $A = 3$, $B = 41$, $N = 16$, time $= 496u$. Program M: $A = 2 + 1 + 1 + 3 = 7$, $B = 2+0+3+3 = 8$, $N = 16$, time $= 549u$. (We should also add the time needed by exercise 35, $94u$, in order to make a strictly fair comparison. The multiplications are slow! Notice also that the improved Program L in exercise 33 takes only $358u$.)

37. The stated identity is equivalent to

$$g_{NM}(z) = M^{-N} \sum_{n_1 + \cdots + n_M = N} \left(\frac{N!}{n_1! \ldots n_M!} \right) g_{n_1}(z) \ldots g_{n_M}(z),$$

which is proved as in exercise 34. It may be of interest to tabulate some of these generating functions, to indicate the trend for increasing M:

$$g_{41}(z) = (216 + 648z + 1080z^2 + 1296z^3 + 1080z^4 + 648z^5 + 216z^6)/5184,$$
$$g_{42}(z) = (945 + 1917z + 1485z^2 + 594z^3 + 135z^4 + 81z^5 + 27z^6)/5184,$$
$$g_{43}(z) = (1704 + 2264z + 840z^2 + 304z^3 + 40z^4 + 24z^5 + 8z^6)/5184.$$

If $G_M(w, z)$ is the stated double generating function, differentiation by z gives

$$G'_M(w, z) = M \left(\sum_{n \geq 0} g_n(z) \frac{w^n}{n!} \right)^{M-1} \sum_{n \geq 0} g'_n(z) \frac{w^n}{n!},$$

hence

$$\sum_{N \geq 0} g'_{NM}(1) \frac{M^N w^N}{N!} = Me^{(M-1)w} \left(\frac{w^2}{4} e^w \right) = \frac{M}{4} w^2 e^{Mw};$$

similarly, the formula $g''_n(1) = \frac{3}{2} \binom{n}{4} + \frac{5}{3} \binom{n}{3}$ yields

$$\sum_{N \geq 0} g''_{NM}(1) \frac{M^N w^N}{N!} = M(M - 1) e^{(M-2)w} \left(\frac{w^2}{4} e^w \right)^2 + Me^{(M-1)w} \left(\frac{w^4}{16} + \frac{5w^3}{18} \right) e^w.$$

Equating coefficients of w^N gives $g'_{NM}(1) = \frac{1}{2} \binom{N}{2} M^{-1}$, $g''_{NM}(1) = \left(\frac{3}{2} \binom{N}{4} + \frac{5}{3} \binom{N}{3} \right) M^{-2}$, and the variance is $\left(\frac{1}{6} \binom{N}{3} + \frac{2M-1}{4} \binom{N}{2} \right) M^{-2}$.

38. $\sum_{j,n} \binom{N}{n} p_j^n (1 - p_j)^{N-n} \binom{n}{2} = \binom{N}{2} \sum_j p_j^2$; setting $p_j = F(j/M) - F((j-1)/M)$, and $F'(x) = f(x)$, this is asymptotic to $\binom{N}{2}/M$ times $\int_0^1 f(x)^2 \, dx$ when F is reasonably well behaved. [However, $\int_0^1 f(x)^2 \, dx$ might be quite large. See Theorem 5.2.5T for a refinement that applies to *all* bounded integrable densities.]

39. To minimize $AC/M + BM$ we need $M = \sqrt{AC/B}$, so M is one of the integers just above or below this quantity. (In the case of Program M we would choose M proportional to N.)

40. The asymptotic series for

$$\sum_{n > N} n^{-1} (1 - \alpha/N)^{n-N} = -N^{-1} + \sum_{k \geq 0} (N + k)^{-1} (1 - \alpha/N)^k$$

can be obtained by restricting k to $O(N^{1+\epsilon})$, expanding $(1 - \alpha/N)^k$ as $e^{-\alpha k/N}$ times $(1 - k\alpha^2/2N^2 + \cdots)$, and using Euler's summation formula; it begins with the terms $e^\alpha E_1(\alpha)(1 + \alpha^2/2N) - (1 + \alpha)/2N + O(N^{-2})$. Hence the asymptotic value of (15) is

$N(\ln\alpha+\gamma+E_1(\alpha))/\alpha+(1-e^{-\alpha}(1+\alpha))/2\alpha+O(N^{-1})$. [The coefficient of N is ≈ 0.7966, 0.6596, 0.2880, respectively, for $\alpha=1,2,10$.] Note that we have $\ln\alpha+\gamma+E_1(\alpha)=\int_0^\alpha(1-e^{-t})t^{-1}\,dt$, by exercise 5.2.2–43.

41. (a) We have $a_k=O(\rho^k)$, because the prime number theorem implies that the number of primes between ρ^k and ρ^{k+1} is $(\rho^{k+1}/(k+1)-\rho^k/k)/\ln\rho+O(\rho^k/k^2)$; this is positive for all sufficiently large k. Therefore the sum of the first $\binom{k}{2}$ elements of (10) is $\sum_{1\le i<j\le k}b(a_i,a_j)=\sum_{1\le i<j\le k}O(\rho^{i+j})$; and we have

$$\sum_{1\le i<j\le k}\rho^{i+j}=\frac{\rho^3(\rho^k-1)(\rho^{k-1}-1)}{(\rho^2-1)(\rho-1)}\,.$$

(b) If $\binom{k-1}{2}<\log_\rho N\le\binom{k}{2}$ we have $(k-2)^2<2\log_\rho N$, hence $\rho^{2k}=O(\exp c\sqrt{\ln N})$.

Notice that as $\rho\to 1$, the base sequence $a_1,a_2,\dots$ becomes equal to the sequence of prime numbers, and the bound in Theorem I reduces to $O\bigl(N(\log N)^4(\log\log N)^{-2}\bigr)$.

42. (a) [A. C. Yao, *J. Algorithms* **1** (1980), 14–50.] We can show that each of the $\binom{h}{2}$ pairs of lists contributes $\frac{\sqrt\pi}{4}g^{-2}h^{-3/2}N^{3/2}+O(N/gh)$ inversions to each subfile $(K_a,K_{a+g},K_{a+2g},\dots)$, $1\le a\le g$. For example, suppose $h=12$, $g=5$, $a=1$, and consider inversions where the lists $K_3<K_{15}<K_{27}<\cdots$ and $K_7<K_{19}<K_{31}<\cdots$ intersect the subfile $(K_1,K_6,K_{11},\dots)$. After the first pass, $(K_3,K_7,K_{15},K_{19},K_{27},K_{31},\dots)$ is a random 2-ordered permutation. The elements K_j of concern to us have $j\equiv 1$ (modulo 5) and $j\equiv 3$ or 7 (modulo 12); hence $j\equiv 51$ or 31 (modulo 60), and we want to compute the average value of $g(51,31)$ where

$$g(x,y)=\sum_{j<k}\bigl([K_{x+ghj}>K_{y+ghk}]+[K_{y+ghj}>K_{x+ghk}]\bigr)+r(x,y)\,,$$

$$r(x,y)=\sum_j[K_{\min(x,y)+ghj}>K_{\max(x,y)+ghj}]<N/gh+1\,.$$

If $|p|\le g$ and $|q|\le g$ we have

$$[K_{j+ph-gh}>K_{k+qh+gh}]\le[K_j>K_k]\le[K_{j+ph+gh}>K_{k+qh-gh}]\,;$$

hence

$$[K_{x+ghj}>K_{y+ghk}]+[K_{y+ghj}>K_{x+ghk}]$$
$$\le[K_{x+ph+gh(j+1)}>K_{y+qh+gh(k-1)}]+[K_{y+qh+gh(j+1)}>K_{x+ph+gh(k-1)}]$$

and it follows that $g(x,y)\le g(x+ph,y+qh)+8N/gh$. Similarly we find $g(x,y)\ge g(x+ph,y+qh)-8N/gh$. But the sum of $g(x,y)$ over all g^2 pairs (x,y) such that $x\bmod h=b$ and $y\bmod h=c$, for any given $b\ne c$, is the total number of inversions in a random 2-ordered permutation of $2N/h$ elements. Therefore by exercise 14, the average value of $g(x,y)$ is $g^{-2}\sqrt{\pi/128}\,(2N/h)^{3/2}+O(N/gh)$.

(b) See S. Janson and D. E. Knuth, *Random Structures & Algorithms* **10** (1997), 125–142. For large g and h we have $\psi(h,g)=\sqrt{\pi h/128}\,g+O(g^{-1/2}h^{1/2})+O(gh^{-1/2})$.

43. If $K<K_l$ after step D3, set $(K_l,\dots,K_{j-h},K_j)\leftarrow(K,K_l,\dots,K_{j-h})$; otherwise do steps D4 and D5 until $K\ge K_i$. Here $l=1$ when $j=h+1$, and $l\leftarrow l+1-h[l=h]$ when j increases by 1. [See H. W. Thimbleby, *Software Practice & Exper.* **19** (1989), 303–307.] However, with a decent sequence of increments the inner loop is not performed often enough to make this change desirable.

Another idea for speeding up the program [see W. Dobosiewicz, *Inf. Proc. Letters* **11** (1980), 5–6] is to sort only partially when $h > 1$, not attempting to propagate K_j further left than position $j - h$; but that approach seems to require more increments.

44. (a) Yes. This is clear whenever π' is one step above π, and exercise 5.1.1–29 shows that there is a path of adjacent transpositions from π to any permutation above it.

(b) Yes. Similarly, if π is above π', π^R is below π'^R.

(c) No; $2\,1\,3$ is neither above nor below $3\,1\,2$, but $2\,1\,3 \leq 3\,1\,2$.

[The partial ordering $\pi \leq \pi'$ was first discussed by C. Ehresmann, *Annals of Math.* (2) **35** (1934), 396–443, §20, in the context of algebraic topology. Many mathematicians now call it the "Bruhat order" of permutations, while aboveness is called the "weak Bruhat order" — although aboveness is actually a stronger condition, because it holds less often. Only the weak order defines a lattice.]

SECTION 5.2.2

1. No; it has $2m+1$ *fewer* inversions, where $m \geq 0$ is the number of elements a_k such that $i < k < j$ and $a_i > a_k > a_j$. (Hence *all* exchange-sorting methods will eventually converge to a sorted permutation.)

2. (a) 6. (b) [A. Cayley, *Philosophical Mag.* (3) **34** (1849), 527–529.] Consider the cycle representation of π. Any exchange of elements in the *same* cycle increases the number of cycles by 1; any exchange of elements in *different* cycles decreases the number by 1. (This is essentially the content of exercise 2.2.4–3.) A completely sorted permutation is characterized by having n cycles. Hence $\mathrm{xch}(\pi)$ is n minus the number of cycles in π. (Algorithm 5.2.3S does exactly $\mathrm{xch}(\pi)$ exchanges; see exercise 5.2.3–4.)

3. Yes; equal elements are never moved across each other.

4. It is the probability that $b_1 > \max(b_2, \ldots, b_n)$ in the inversion table, namely

$$\left(\sum_{1 \leq k < n} k!\, k^{n-k-1} \right) \Big/ n! = \sqrt{\pi/2n} + O(n^{-1}) = \text{negligible}.$$

5. We may assume that $r > 0$. Let $b'_i = (b_i - r + 1)[b_i \geq r]$ be the inversion table after $r - 1$ passes. If $b'_i > 0$, element i is preceded by b'_i larger elements, the largest of which will bubble up at least to position $b'_i + i$, because there are i elements $\leq i$. Furthermore if element j is the rightmost to be exchanged, we have $b'_j > 0$ and $\mathtt{BOUND} = b'_j + j - 1$ after the rth pass.

6. *Solution 1:* An element displaced farthest to the right of its final position moves one step left on each pass except the last. *Solution 2* (higher level): By exercise 5.1.1–8, answer (f), $a'_i - i = b_i - c_i$, for $1 \leq i \leq n$, where $c_1 c_2 \ldots c_n$ is the dual inversion table. If $b_j = \max(b_1, \ldots, b_n)$ then $c_j = 0$.

7. $(2(n + 1)(1 + P(n) - P(n + 1)) - P(n) - P(n)^2)^{1/2} = \sqrt{(2 - \pi/2)n} + O(1)$.

8. For $i < k + 2$ there are $j + k - i + 1$ choices for b_i; for $k + 2 \leq i < n - j + 2$ there are $j - 1$ choices; and for $i \geq n - j + 2$ there are $n - i + 1$.

10. (a) If $i = 2k - 1$, from $(k - 1, a_i - k)$ to $(k, a_i - k)$. If $i = 2k$, from $(a_i - k, k - 1)$ to $(a_i - k, k)$. (b) Step a_{2k-1} is above the diagonal $\iff k \leq a_{2k-1} - k \iff a_{2k-1} \geq 2k \iff a_{2k-1} > a_{2k} \iff a_{2k} \leq 2k - 1 \iff a_{2k} - k \leq k - 1 \iff$ step a_{2k} is above the diagonal. Exchanging them interchanges horizontal and vertical steps. (c) Step a_{2k+d} is at least m below the diagonal $\iff k + m - 1 \geq a_{2k+d} - (k + m) + m \iff a_{2k+d} < 2k + m \iff a_{2k} \geq 2k + m \iff a_{2k} - k \geq k + m \iff$ step a_{2k} is at least m

below the diagonal. (If $a_{2k+d} < 2k+m$ and $a_{2k} < 2k+m$, there are at least $(k+m)+k$ elements less than $2k+m$; that's impossible. If $a_{2k+d} \geq 2k+m$ and $a_{2k} \geq 2k+m$, one of the $\geq$ must be $>$; but we can't fit all of the elements $\leq 2k+m$ into fewer than $(k+m)+k$ positions. Hence $a_{2k+2m-1} < a_{2k}$ if and only if $a_{2k+2m-1} < 2k+m$ if and only if $2k+m \leq a_{2k}$. A rather unexpected result!)

11. 16 10 13 5 14 6 9 2 15 8 11 3 12 4 7 1 (61 exchanges), by considering the lattice diagram. The situation becomes more complicated when N is larger; in general, the set $\{K_2, K_4, \dots\}$ should be $\{1, 2, \dots, M-1, M, M+2, M+4, \dots, 2\lfloor N/2 \rfloor - M\}$, permuted so as to maximize the exchanges for $\lfloor N/2 \rfloor$ elements. Here $M = \lceil 2^k/3 \rceil$, where k maximizes $k\lfloor N/2 \rfloor - \frac{1}{9}((3k-2)2^{k-1}+(-1)^k)$. The maximum total number of exchanges is $1 - 2\lg\lg N/\lg N + O(1/\log N)$ times the number of comparisons [R. Sedgewick, *SICOMP* **7** (1978), 239–272].

12. The following program by W. Panny avoids the AND instruction by noting that step M4 is performed for $i = r + 2kp + s$, $k \geq 0$, and $0 \leq s < p$. Here $\text{TT} \equiv 2^{t-1}$, $p \equiv \text{rI1}$, $r \equiv \text{rI2}$, $i \equiv \text{rI3}$, $i + d - N \equiv \text{rI4}$, and $p - 1 - s \equiv \text{rI5}$; we assume that $N \geq 2$.

01	START	ENT1	TT	1	M1. Initialize p. $p \leftarrow 2^{t-1}$.
02	2H	ENT2	TT	T	M2. Initialize q, r, d.
03		ST2	Q(1:2)	T	$q \leftarrow 2^{t-1}$.
04		ENT2	0	T	$r \leftarrow 0$.
05		ENT4	0,1	T	$\text{rI4} \leftarrow d$.
06	3H	ENT3	0,2	A	M3. Loop on i. $i \leftarrow r$.
07		INC4	-N,3	A	$\text{rI4} \leftarrow i + d - N$.
08	8H	ENT5	-1,1	$D+E$	$s \leftarrow 0$.
09	4H	LDA	INPUT+1,3	C	M4. Compare/exchange $R_{i+1}:R_{i+d+1}$.
10		CMPA	INPUT+N+1,4	C	
11		JLE	*+4	C	Jump if $K_{i+1} \leq K_{i+d+1}$.
12		LDX	INPUT+N+1,4	B	
13		STX	INPUT+1,3	B	$R_{i+1} \leftrightarrow R_{i+d+1}$.
14		STA	INPUT+N+1,4	B	
15		J5Z	7F	C	Jump if $s = p - 1$.
16		DEC5	1	$C-D$	$s \leftarrow s + 1$.
17		INC3	1	$C-D$	$i \leftarrow i + 1$.
18		INC4	1	$C-D$	
19		J4N	4B	$C-D$	Repeat loop if $i + d < N$.
20		JMP	5F	E	Otherwise go to M5.
21	7H	INC3	1,1	D	$i \leftarrow i + p + 1$.
22		INC4	1,1	D	
23		J4N	4B	D	Repeat loop if $i + d < N$.
24	5H	ENT2	0,1	A	M5. Loop on q. $r \leftarrow p$.
25	Q	ENT4	*	A	$\text{rI4} \leftarrow q$.
26		ENTA	0,4	A	
27		SRB	1	A	
28		STA	Q(1:2)	A	$q \leftarrow q/2$.
29		DEC4	0,1	A	$\text{rI4} \leftarrow d$.
30		J4P	3B	A	To M3 if $d \neq 0$.
31	6H	ENTA	0,1	T	M6. Loop on p.
32		SRB	1	T	
33		STA	*+1(1:2)	T	

34	ENT1 *	T	$p \leftarrow \lfloor p/2 \rfloor$.
35	J1NZ 2B	T	To M2 if $p \neq 0$. ∎

The running time depends on six quantities, only one of which depends on the input data (the remaining five are functions of N alone): $T = t$, the number of "major cycles"; $A = t(t+1)/2$, the number of passes or "minor cycles"; $B =$ the (variable) number of exchanges; $C =$ the number of comparisons; $D =$ the number of blocks of consecutive comparisons; and $E =$ the number of incomplete blocks. When $N = 2^t$, it is not difficult to prove that $D = (t-2)N + t + 2$ and $E = 0$. For Table 1, we have $T = 4$, $A = 10$, $B = 3 + 0 + 1 + 4 + 0 + 0 + 8 + 0 + 4 + 5 = 25$, $C = 63$, $D = 38$, $E = 0$, so the total running time is $11A + 6B + 10C + 2E + 12T + 1 = 939u$.

In general when $N = 2^{e_1} + \cdots + 2^{e_r}$, Panny has shown that $D = e_1(N+1) - 2(2^{e_1} - 1)$, $E = \binom{e_1 - e_r}{2} + (e_1 + e_2 + \cdots + e_{r-1}) - (e_1 - 1)(r - 1)$.

13. No, nor are Algorithms Q or R.

14. (a) When $p = 1$ we do $(2^{t-1} - 0) + (2^{t-1} - 1) + (2^{t-1} - 2) + (2^{t-1} - 4) + \cdots + (2^{t-1} - 2^{t-2}) = (t-1)2^{t-1} + 1$ comparisons for the final merge. (b) $x_t = x_{t-1} + \frac{1}{2}(t-1) + 2^{-t} = \cdots = x_0 + \sum_{0 \le k < t} (\frac{1}{2}k + 2^{-k-1}) = \frac{1}{2}\binom{t}{2} + 1 - 2^{-t}$. Hence $c(2^t) = 2^{t-2}(t^2 - t + 4) - 1$.

15. (a) Consider the number of comparisons such that $i + d = N$; then use induction on r. (b) If $b(n) = c(n+1)$, we have $b(2n) = a(1) + \cdots + a(2n) = a(0) + a(1) + a(1) + \cdots + a(n-1) + a(n) + x(1) + x(2) + \cdots + x(2n) = 2b(n) + y(2n) - a(n)$; similarly $b(2n+1) = 2b(n) + y(2n+1)$. (c) See exercise 1.2.4–42. (d) A rather laborious calculation of $(z(N) + 2z(\lfloor N/2 \rfloor) + \cdots) - a(N)$, using formulas such as

$$\sum_{k=0}^{n} 2^k(n-k) = 2^{n+1} - n - 2, \qquad \sum_{k=0}^{n} 2^k \binom{n-k}{2} = 2^{n+1} - \binom{n+2}{2} - 1,$$

leads to the result

$$c(N) = N\left(\frac{1}{2}\binom{e_1}{2} + 2e_1 - 1\right) - 2^{e_1}(e_1 - 1) - 1$$

$$+ \sum_{j=1}^{r} 2^{e_j}\left(e_1 + \cdots + e_{j-1} - j(e_1 - 1) + \frac{1}{2}\binom{e_1 - e_j}{2}\right).$$

16. Consider the $\binom{2n}{n}$ lattice paths from $(0,0)$ to (n,n) as in Figs. 11 and 18, and attach weight $f(i - j)$ if $i \geq j$, $f(j - i - 1) + 1$ if $i < j$, to the line from (i,j) to $(i+1,j)$; here $f(k)$ is the number of bit variations $b_r \neq b_{r+1}$ in the binary expansion $k = (\ldots b_2 b_1 b_0)_2$. The total number of exchanges on the final merge when $N = 2n$ is then $\sum_{0 \le j \le i < n}(2f(j) + 1)\binom{2i-j}{i-j}\binom{2n-2i+j-1}{n-i-1}$. R. Sedgewick showed that this sum simplifies, for general f, to $\frac{n}{2}\binom{2n}{n} + 2\sum_{k \ge 1}\binom{2n}{n-k}\sum_{0 \le j < k} f(j)$; then he used the gamma function method to obtain the asymptotic formula

$$\binom{2n}{n}\left(\frac{1}{4}n \lg n + \left(\lg \frac{\Gamma(1/4)^2}{2\pi} + \frac{1}{4} + \frac{\gamma + 2}{4 \ln 2} + \delta(n)\right)n + O(\sqrt{n} \log n)\right),$$

where $\delta(n)$ is a periodic function of $\lg n$ with magnitude bounded by .0005. Hence about $1/4$ of the comparisons lead to exchanges, on the average, as $n \to \infty$. [*SICOMP* **7** (1978), 239–272; see also Flajolet and Odlyzko, *SIAM J. Discrete Math.* **3** (1990), 238–239.]

17. K_{N+1} is inspected when we are sorting a subfile with $r = N$ and K_l the largest key. K_0 is inspected during step Q9 if left-to-right minima sink to position R_1.

18. Steps Q3 and Q4 make only a single change to i and j before exiting to Q5; the partitioning process for $R_l \ldots R_r$ ends with $j = \lceil (l+r)/2 \rceil$ in step Q7, bisecting the subfile as perfectly as possible. Quantitatively speaking, we replace (17) by $A = 1$, $B = \lfloor (N-1)/2 \rfloor$, $C = N + (N \bmod 2)$; this puts us essentially in the *best* case of the algorithm (see exercise 27), except that $B \approx \frac{1}{2}C$. If the "<" signs in steps Q3 and Q4 are changed to "$\leq$," the algorithm won't sort any more; even if we assume "<" signs in (13), it will interchange R_0 with R_1, then the third partitioning phase will move the original R_0 to position R_2, etc. — a real catastrophe.

19. Yes, the other subfiles may be processed in any order. But the queue will contain $\Omega(N/\sqrt{\log N})$ items when each partitioning step divides the file equally, while a stack is guaranteed to stay much smaller than this (see the next exercise).

20. $\max(0, \lfloor \lg(N+2)/(M+2) \rfloor)$. (The worst case occurs when $N = 2^k(M+2) - 1$ and all subfiles are perfectly bisected when they are partitioned.)

21. Exactly t records move to the area $R_{s+1} \ldots R_N$ in step Q6, hence $B = t$. The partitioning phase ends with $j = s$, hence $C - C' = N + 1 - s$ is the number of times j decreases. We must also have $i = s + 1$ in step Q7 when the keys are distinct, since $i = j$ implies $K_j = K$; thus $C' = s$.

22. The stated relations for $A_N(z)$ follow because $A_{s-1}(z)A_{N-s}(z)$ is the generating function for the value of A after independently sorting randomly and independently ordered files of sizes $s - 1$ and $N - s$. Similarly, we obtain the relations

$$B_N(z) = \sum_{s=1}^{N} \sum_{t=0}^{s} b_{stN} z^t B_{s-1}(z) B_{N-s}(z),$$

$$C_N(z) = \frac{1}{N} \sum_{s=1}^{N} z^{N+1} C_{s-1}(z) C_{N-s}(z),$$

$$D_N(z) = \frac{1}{N} \sum_{s=1}^{N} D_{s-1}(z) D_{N-s}(z),$$

$$E_N(z) = \frac{1}{N} \sum_{s=1}^{N} E_{s-1}(z) E_{N-s}(z),$$

$$S_N(z) = \frac{1}{N} \sum_{s=1}^{N} z^{[M+1 < s < N-M]} S_{s-1}(z) S_{N-s}(z),$$

for $N > M$. Here b_{stN} is the probability that s and t have given values in a file of length N, namely

$$\binom{s-1}{t} \binom{N-s}{t} \Big/ N \binom{N-1}{s-1},$$

which is $(1/N!)$ times the $(s-1)!$ ways to permute $\{1, \ldots, s-1\}$ times the $(N-s)!$ ways to permute $\{s+1, \ldots, N\}$ times the $\binom{s-1}{t}\binom{N-s}{t}$ patterns with t displaced elements on each side. For $0 \leq N \leq M$, we have $B_N(z) = C_N(z) = S_N(z) = 1$; $D_N(z) = \prod_{k=1}^{N}((1 + (k-1)z)/k)$; and $E_N(z) = \prod_{k=1}^{N}((1 + z + \cdots + z^{k-1})/k)$.

[It is interesting to consider the behavior of these generating functions when N is large; a sequence analogous to $C_N(z)$, but with z^{N+1} replaced by z^{N-1}, is known to converge to a non-normal probability distribution that has not yet been fully analyzed.

See the articles by P. Hennequin, M. Regnier, and U. Rösler in *RAIRO Theoretical Informatics and Applications* **23** (1989), 317–333; **23** (1989), 335–343; **25** (1991), 85–100.]

23. When $N > M$, $A_N = 1 + (2/N)\sum_{0 \le k < N} A_k$; $B_N = \sum_{0 \le t < s \le N} b_{stN}(t + B_{s-1} + B_{N-s}) = (1/N)\sum_{s=1}^{N}((s-1)(N-s)/(N-1) + B_{s-1} + B_{N-s}) = (N-2)/6 + (2/N)\sum_{0 \le k < N} B_k$ [see exercise 22]; $D_N = (2/N)\sum_{0 \le k < N} D_k$; E_N is similar. When $N > 2M + 1$, $S_N = (2/N)\sum_{0 \le k < N} S_k + (N - 2M - 2)/N$. Each of these recurrences has the form (19) for some function f_n.

24. The recurrence $C_N = N - 1 + (2/N)\sum_{0 \le k < N} C_k$, for $N > M$, has the solution $(N+1)(2H_{N+1} - 2H_{M+2} + 1 - 4/(M+2) + 2/(N+1))$, for $N > M$. (So we could save about $4N/M$ comparisons. But each comparison takes longer if it must be followed by a test of i versus j, so we lose, unless the cost of a key comparison exceeds $\frac{1}{2}M\ln N$ times the cost of a register comparison. Many texts on sorting fail to realize that such an "improvement" makes quicksort significantly less quick!)

25. (Use (17) repeatedly with $s = 1$.) $A = N - M$, $B = 0$, $C = \binom{N+2}{2} - \binom{M+2}{2}$, $D = E = S = 0$.

26. Actually you can't do worse than to sort

$$1 \ 2 \ 3 \ \ldots \ N{-}M \ N \ N{-}1 \ \ldots \ N{-}M{+}1;$$

the subtler answer $N \ M{-}1 \ M{-}2 \ \ldots \ 1 \ M \ M{+}1 \ \ldots \ N{-}1$ is an equally bad case. This is only a little worse than exercise 25, because it makes $D = M - 1$, $E = \binom{M}{2}$.

27. 12 2 3 1 8 6 7 5 9 10 11 4 16 14 15 13 20 18 19 17 21 22 23, which requires $546u$. It can be shown that the best case for $N = 3(M+1)2^k - 1$ occurs when the subfiles are bisected by each partitioning until reaching size $3M + 2$; then a trisection is performed to avoid stack-pushing overhead. We have $A = 3 \cdot 2^k - 1$, $C = (k + \frac{5}{3})(N + 1)$, $S = 2^k - 1$, $B = D = E = 0$. (The behavior of the best case for general M and N makes an interesting but complex pattern.)

28. The recurrence

$$C_n = n + 1 + \frac{2}{\binom{n}{3}} \sum_{k=1}^{n}(k-1)(n-k)C_{k-1}$$

can be transformed into

$$\binom{n}{3}C_n - 2\binom{n-1}{3}C_{n-1} + \binom{n-2}{3}C_{n-2} = 2(n-1)(n-2) + 2(n-2)C_{n-2}.$$

29. In general, consider the recurrence

$$C_n = n + 1 + \frac{2}{\binom{n}{2t+1}} \sum_{k=1}^{n}\binom{k-1}{t}\binom{n-k}{t}C_{k-1},$$

which arises when the median of $2t + 1$ elements governs the partitioning. Letting $C(z) = \sum_n C_n z^n$, the recurrence can be transformed to $(1-z)^{t+1}C^{(2t+1)}(z)/(2t+2)! = 1/(1-z)^{t+2} + C^{(t)}(z)/(t+1)!$. Let $f(x) = C^{(t)}(1-x)$; then $p_t(\vartheta)f(x) = (2t+2)!/x^{t+2}$, where ϑ denotes the operator $x(d/dx)$, and $p_t(x) = (t-x)^{\underline{t+1}} - (2t+2)^{\underline{t+1}}$. The general solution to $(\vartheta - \alpha)g(x) = x^\beta$ is $g(x) = x^\beta/(\beta - \alpha) + Cx^\alpha$, for $\alpha \neq \beta$; $g(x) = x^\beta(\ln x + C)$ for $\alpha = \beta$. We have $p_t(-t-2) = 0$; so the general solution to our differential equation is

$$C^{(t)}(z) = (2t+2)! \ln(1-z)/p_t'(-t-2)(1-z)^{t+2} + \sum_{j=0}^{t} c_j(1-z)^{\alpha_j}$$

where $\alpha_0, \ldots, \alpha_t$ are the roots of $p_t(x) = 0$, and the constants c_i depend on the initial values $C_t, \ldots, C_{2t}$. The handy identity

$$\frac{1}{(1-z)^{m+1}} \ln\left(\frac{1}{1-z}\right) = \sum_{n \geq 0} (H_{n+m} - H_m)\binom{n+m}{m} z^n, \qquad m \geq 0,$$

now leads to the surprisingly simple *closed form solution*

$$C_n = \frac{H_{n+1} - H_{t+1}}{H_{2t+2} - H_{t+1}}(n+1) + \frac{1}{n!}\sum_{j=0}^{t} c_j(-\alpha_j)^{\overline{n-t}},$$

from which the asymptotic formula is easily deduced. (The leading term $n \ln n/ (H_{2t+2} - H_{t+1})$ was discovered by M. H. van Emden [*CACM* **13** (1970), 563–567] using an information-theoretic approach. In fact, suppose we wish to analyze any partitioning process such that the left subfile contains at most xN elements with asymptotic probability $\int_0^x f(x)\,dx$, as $N \to \infty$, for $0 \leq x \leq 1$; van Emden proved that the average number of comparisons required to sort the file completely is asymptotic to $\alpha^{-1}n \ln n$, where $\alpha = -1/\int_0^1 (f(x) + f(1-x))x \ln x\,dx$. This formula applies to radix exchange as well as to quicksort and various other methods. See also H. Hurwitz, *CACM* **14** (1971), 99–102.)

30. *Solution 1* (of historic interest): Each subfile may be identified by four quantities (l, r, k, X), where l and r are the boundaries (as presently), k indicates the number of words of the keys that are known to be equal throughout the subfile, and X is a lower bound for the $(k+1)$st words of the key. Assuming nonnegative keys, we have $(l, r, k, X) = (1, N, 0, 0)$ initially. When partitioning a file, we let K be the $(k+1)$st word of the test key K_q. If $K > X$, partitioning takes place with all keys $\geq K$ at the right and all keys $< K$ at the left (looking only at the $(k+1)$st word of the key each time); the partitioned subfiles get the respective identifications $(l, j-1, k, X)$ and (j, r, k, K). But if $K = X$, partitioning takes place with all keys $> K$ at the right and all keys $\leq K$ [actually $= K$] at the left; the partitioned subfiles get the respective identifications $(l, j, k+1, 0)$ and $(j+1, r, k, K)$. In both cases we are unsure that R_j is in its final position since we haven't looked at the $(k+2)$nd words. Obvious further changes are made to handle boundary conditions properly. By adding a fifth "upper bound" component, the method could be made symmetrical between left and right.

    Solution 2, by Bentley and Sedgewick [*SODA* **8** (1997), 360–369]: In a subfile identified by (l, r, k), let K be word $k+1$ of K_q as in solution 1, but use the algorithm of exercise 41 to tripartition the subfile into $(l, i-1, k)$, $(i, j, k+1)$, $(j+1, r, k)$ for the cases $<K$, $=K$, $>K$. This approach, which the authors call *multikey quicksort*, is significantly better than solution 1, and it is competitive with the fastest known methods for sorting strings of characters.

31. Go through a normal partitioning process, with R_1 finally falling into position R_s. If $s = m$, stop; if $s < m$, use the same technique to find the $(m-s)$th smallest element of the right-hand subfile; and if $s > m$, find the mth smallest element of the left-hand subfile. [*CACM* **4** (1961), 321–322; **14** (1971), 39–45.]

R. G. Dromey [*Software Practice & Experience* **16** (1986), 981–986] has observed that fewer comparisons and exchanges are needed if we stop each partitioning stage as soon as i or j has reached position m.

32. The recurrence is $C_{11} = 0$ and $C_{nm} = n + 1 + (A_{nm} + B_{nm})/n$ for $n > 1$, where

$$A_{nm} = \sum_{1 \le s < m} C_{(n-s)(m-s)} \quad \text{and} \quad B_{nm} = \sum_{m < s \le n} C_{(s-1)m},$$

for $1 \le m \le n$. Since $A_{(n+1)(m+1)} = A_{nm} + C_{nm}$ and $B_{(n+1)m} = B_{nm} + C_{nm}$, we can first find a formula for the quantity $D_n = (n+1)C_{(n+1)(m+1)} - nC_{nm}$, then sum this to obtain the answer $2((n+1)H_n - (n+2-m)H_{n+1-m} - (m+1)H_m + n + \frac{5}{3}) - \frac{1}{3}\delta_{mn} - \frac{1}{3}\delta_{m1} - \frac{2}{3}\delta_{mn}\delta_{m1}$. When $n = 2m - 1$, it becomes $4m(H_{2m-1} - H_m) + 4m - 4H_m + \frac{4}{3}(1 - \delta_{m1}) = (4 + 4\ln 2)m - 4\ln m - 4\gamma - \frac{5}{3} + O(m^{-1}) \approx 3.39n$. [See D. E. Knuth, *Proc. IFIP Congress* (1971), 19–27.]

Another solution follows from the theory of Section 6.2.2: Suppose the keys are $\{1, 2, \ldots, n\}$, and let X_{jk} be the number of common ancestors of nodes j and k in the binary search tree corresponding to quicksort. Then the number of comparisons made by the algorithm of exercise 31 can be shown to be $\sum_{j=1}^n X_{jm} + X_{mm} - 2[\text{node } m \text{ is a leaf}]$. The probability that node i is a common ancestor of nodes j and k in a random binary search tree is $1/(\max(i,j,k) - \min(i,j,k) + 1)$. We obtain the average number of comparisons from the facts that $\mathrm{E}\,X_{jk} = H_k + H_{n+1-j} + 1 - 2H_{k-j+1}$ for $1 \le j \le k$, and $\Pr(\text{node } m \text{ is a leaf}) = \Pr(m \text{ isn't followed by } m \pm 1 \text{ in a random permutation}) = \frac{1}{3} + \frac{1}{6}\delta_{m1} + \frac{1}{6}\delta_{mn} + \frac{1}{3}\delta_{m1}\delta_{mn}$. [See R. Raman, *SIGACT News* **25**, 2 (June 1994), 86–89.]

For an analysis of a similar selection algorithm that uses median-of-three partitioning, see Kirschenhofer, Prodinger, and Martínez, *Random Structures & Algorithms* **10** (1997), 143–156. Asymptotically faster methods are discussed in exercise 5.3.3–24.

33. Proceed as in the first stage of radix exchange, using the sign instead of bit 1.

34. We can avoid testing whether or not $i \le j$, as soon as we have found at least one 0 bit and at least one 1 bit in each stage — that is, after making the first exchange in each stage. This saves approximately $2C$ units of time in Program R.

35. $A = N - 1$, $B = (\min 0, \text{ave } \frac{1}{4}N \lg N, \max \frac{1}{2}N \lg N)$, $C = N \lg N$, $G = \frac{1}{2}N$, $K = L = R = 0$, $S = \frac{1}{2}N - 1$, $X = (\min 0, \text{ave } \frac{1}{2}(N-1), \max N - 1)$. In general, the quantities A, C, G, K, L, R, and S depend only on the set of keys in the file, not on their initial order; only B and X are influenced by the initial order of the keys.

36. (a) $\sum \binom{n}{k}\binom{k}{j}(-1)^{k+j}a_j = \sum \binom{n}{j}\binom{n-j}{k-j}(-1)^{k-j}a_j = \sum \binom{n}{j}\delta_{nj}a_j = a_n$. (b) $\langle\delta_{n0}\rangle$; $\langle-\delta_{n1}\rangle$; $\langle(-1)^m\delta_{nm}\rangle$; $\langle(1-a)^n\rangle$; $\langle\binom{n}{m}(-a)^m(1-a)^{n-m}\rangle$. (c) Writing the relations to be proved as $x_n = y_n = a_n + z_n$, we have $y_n = a_n + z_n$ by part (a); also $2^{1-n}\sum_{k \ge 2}\binom{n}{k}y_k = z_n$, so y_n satisfies the same recurrence as x_n. [See exercises 53 and 6.3–17 for some generalizations of this result. It does not appear to be easy to prove *directly* that $\hat{x}_n = \hat{a}_n 2^{n-1}/(2^{n-1} - 1)$.]

37. $\langle\sum_m c_m \binom{n}{2m}2^{-n}\rangle$ for an arbitrary sequence of constants $c_0, c_1, c_2, \ldots$. [This answer, although correct, does not reveal immediately that $\langle 1/(n+1)\rangle$ and $\langle n - \delta_{n1}\rangle$ are such sequences! Sequences having the form $\langle a_n + \hat{a}_n\rangle$ are always self-dual. Notice that, in terms of the generating function $A(z) = \sum a_n z^n/n!$, we have $\hat{A}(z) = e^z A(-z)$; hence $A = \hat{A}$ is equivalent to saying that $A(z)e^{-z/2}$ is an even function.]

38. A partitioning stage that yields a left subfile of size s and a right subfile of size $N - s$ makes the following contributions to the total running time:

$$A = 1, \quad B = t, \quad C = N, \quad K = \delta_{s1}, \quad L = \delta_{s0}, \quad R = \delta_{sN}, \quad X = h,$$

where t is the number of keys $K_1, \ldots, K_s$ with bit b equal to 1, and h is bit b of K_{s+1}; if $s = N$, then $h = 0$. (See (17).) This leads to recurrence equations such as

$$B_N = 2^{-N} \sum_{0 \le t \le s \le N} \binom{s}{t} \binom{N-s}{t} (t + B_s + B_{N-s})$$

$$= \frac{1}{4}(N - 1) + 2^{1-N} \sum_{s \ge 2} \binom{N}{s} B_s, \quad \text{for } N \ge 2; \qquad B_0 = B_1 = 0.$$

(See exercise 23.) Solving these recurrences by the method of exercise 36 yields the formulas $A_N = V_N - U_N + 1$, $B_N = \frac{1}{4}(U_N + N - 1)$, $C_N = V_N + N$, $K_N = N/2$, $L_N = R_N = \frac{1}{2}(V_N - U_N - N) + 1$, $X_N = \frac{1}{2} A_N$. Clearly $G_N = 0$.

39. Each stage of quicksort puts at least one element into its final position, but this need not happen during radix exchange (see Table 3).

40. If we switch to straight insertion whenever $r - l < M$ in step R2, the problem doesn't arise unless more than M equal elements occur. If the latter is a likely prospect, we can test whether or not $K_l = \cdots = K_r$ whenever $j < l$ or $j = r$ in step R8.

41. Lutz M. Wegner [*IEEE Trans.* **C-34** (1985), 362–367] has discussed several approaches, of which the following (as simplified by Bentley and McIlroy in *Software Practice & Exp.* **23** (1993), 1256–1258) appears to be best in practice. The basic idea is to work with the five-part array

$= K$	$< K$	?	$> K$	$= K$
l	a	b	c	d

until the middle part is empty, then swap the two ends into the middle.

D1. [Initialize.] Set $a \leftarrow b \leftarrow l$, $c \leftarrow d \leftarrow r$.

D2. [Increase b until $K_b > K$.] If $b \le c$ and $K_b < K$, increase b by 1 and repeat this step. If $b \le c$ and $K_b = K$, exchange $R_a \leftrightarrow R_b$, increase a and b by 1, and repeat this step.

D3. [Decrease c until $K_c < K$.] If $b \le c$ and $K_c > K$, decrease c by 1 and repeat this step. If $b \le c$ and $K_c = K$, exchange $R_c \leftrightarrow R_d$, decrease c and d by 1, and repeat this step.

D4. [Exchange.] If $b < c$, exchange $R_b \leftrightarrow R_c$, increase b by 1, decrease c by 1, and return to D2.

D5. [Cleanup.] Exchange $R_{l+k} \leftrightarrow R_{c-k}$ for $0 \le k < \min(a-l, b-a)$; also exchange $R_{b+k} \leftrightarrow R_{r-k}$ for $0 \le k < \min(d - c, r - d)$. Finally set $i \leftarrow l + b - a$, $j \leftarrow r - d + c$. ∎

Straightforward modifications to step D1 will handle degenerate cases efficiently and ensure that $a < b$ and $c < d$ before we get to D2. Then the tests "$b \le c$" in D2 and D3 will be unnecessary; see exercise 24. Furthermore, this change will keep those steps from needlessly exchanging records with themselves.

One of the main applications of sorting is to bring records with equal keys together. Therefore this tripartitioning scheme is often preferable to the bipartitioning of Algorithm Q. The exchanges in step D5 are efficient because all records with keys equal to K are now in their final resting place.

This exercise is due to W. H. J. Feijen, who called it the "Dutch national flag problem": Given a set of red, white, and blue tokens arranged randomly in a column, decide how to swap pairs of tokens so that the red ones will all be at the top and the blue ones all at the bottom, while looking at each token only once and using only a few auxiliary variables to control the process. [See E. W. Dijkstra, *A Discipline of Programming* (Prentice–Hall, 1976), Chapter 14.]

42. This is a special case of a general theorem due to R. M. Karp; see *JACM* **41** (1994), 1136–1150, §2.8. Significantly sharper asymptotic bounds for tails of the quicksort distribution have been obtained by McDiarmid and Hayward, *J. Algorithms* **21** (1996), 476–507.

43. As $a \to 0+$, we have $\int_0^1 y^{a-1}(e^{-y} - 1)\,dy + \int_1^\infty y^{a-1}e^{-y}\,dy = \Gamma(a) - 1/a = (\Gamma(a+1) - \Gamma(1))/a \to \Gamma'(1) = -\gamma$, by exercise 1.2.7–24.

44. For $k \ge 0$, we have $r_k(m) \sim \frac{1}{2}(2m)^{(k+1)/2}\Gamma((k+1)/2) - \delta_{k0} - \sum_{j\ge0}(-1)^j B_{k+2j+1}/((k+2j+1)j!\,(2m)^j)$. When $k = -1$, the contributions from $f_k^{(j-1)}(m)$ in (36) cancel with similar terms in the expansion of H_{m-1}, and we have $r_{-1}(m) = H_{m-1} + (1/\sqrt{2m})\sum_{t\ge0} f_{-1}(t) \sim \frac{1}{2}(\ln(2m) + \gamma) - \sum_{j\ge1}(-1)^j B_{2j}/((2j)j!\,(2m)^j)$. Therefore the contribution to W_{m-1} from the term N^t/t of (33) is obtained from the sum $m\sum_{t\ge1} t^{-1}\exp(-t^2/2m)(1 - t^3/3m^2 + t^6/18m^4)(1 - t^4/4m^3)(1 - t/2m - t^2/8m^2) + O(m^{-1/2}) = \frac{1}{2}m\ln m + \frac{1}{2}(\ln 2 + \gamma)m - \frac{5}{12}\sqrt{2\pi m} + \frac{4}{9} + O(m^{-1/2})$. The term $-\frac{1}{2}N^{t-1}$ contributes $-\frac{1}{2}\sum_{t\ge1}\exp(-t^2/2m)(1 - t^3/3m^2)(1 - t/2m)(1 + t/m) + O(m^{-1/2}) = -\frac{1}{4}\sqrt{2\pi m} + \frac{1}{3}$. The term $\frac{1}{2}\delta_{t1}$ yields $\frac{1}{2}$. And finally the term $\frac{1}{2}(t-1)B_2 N^{t-2}$ contributes $\frac{1}{12}m^{-1}\sum_{t\ge1} t\exp(-t^2/2m) + O(m^{-1/2}) = \frac{1}{12} + O(m^{-1/2})$.

45. The argument used to derive (42) is also valid for (43), except that we leave out the residues at $z = -1$ and $z = 0$.

46. Proceeding as we did with (45), we obtain $(s - 1)!/\ln 2 + \delta_s(n)$, where

$$\delta_s(n) = \frac{2}{\ln 2}\sum_{k\ge1}\Re(\Gamma(s - 2\pi ik/\ln 2)\exp(2\pi ik\lg n)).$$

[Note that $|\Gamma(s + it)|^2 = (\prod_{0\le k<s}(k^2 + t^2))\pi/(t\sinh \pi t)$, for integer $s \ge 0$, so we can bound $\delta_s(n)$.]

47. In fact, $\sum_{j\ge1} e^{-n/2^j}(n/2^j)^s$ equals the integral in exercise 46, for all $s > 0$.

48. Making use of the intermediate identity

$$1 - e^{-x} = \frac{-1}{2\pi i}\int_{-1/2-i\infty}^{-1/2+i\infty}\Gamma(z)x^{-z}\,dz,$$

we proceed as in the text, with $1 - e^{-x}$ playing the role of $e^{-x} - 1 + x$; $V_{n+1}/(n+1) = (-1/2\pi i)\int_{-1/2-i\infty}^{-1/2+i\infty}\Gamma(z)n^{-z}\,dz/(2^{-z} - 1) + O(n^{-1})$, and the integral equals $\lg n + \gamma/\ln 2 - \frac{1}{2} - \delta_0(n) + O(n^{-100})$ in the notation of exercise 46. [Thus the quantity A_N in exercise 38 is $N(1/\ln 2 - \delta_0(N - 1) - \delta_{-1}(N)) + O(1)$.]

49. The right-hand side of Eq. (40) can be improved to the estimate $e^{-x}(1 - \frac{1}{2}x^2/n + O((x^3+x^4)n^{-2}))$. The effect is to subtract half the sum in exercise 47, replacing $O(1)$ in (50) by $2 - \frac{1}{2}(1/\ln 2 + \delta_1(n)) + O(n^{-1})$. (The "2" comes from the "2/n" in (46).)

50. $U_{mn} = n \log_m n + n((\gamma-1)/\ln m - \frac{1}{2} + \delta_{-1}(n)) + m/(m-1) - 1/(2\ln m) - \frac{1}{2}\delta_1(n) + O(n^{-1})$, with $\delta_s(n)$ as in exercise 46 but replacing $\ln 2$ and $\lg$ by $\ln m$ and $\log_m$. [*Note:* For $m = 2, 3, 4, 5, 10, 100, 1000$, and 10^6 we have $\delta_{-1}(n) < .000000172501, .000041227, .0002963, .0008501433, .0062704, .06797, .1525$, and $.348$, respectively.]

51. Let $N = 2m$. We may extend the sum (35) over all $t \geq 1$, when it equals

$$\sum_{t \geq 1} \frac{1}{2\pi i} \int_{a-i\infty}^{a+i\infty} \Gamma(z)(t^2/N)^{-z} t^k \, dz = \frac{1}{2\pi i} \int_{a-i\infty}^{a+i\infty} \Gamma(z) N^z \zeta(2z-k) \, dz,$$

provided that $a > (k+1)/2$. So we need to know properties of the zeta function. When $\Re(w) \geq -q$, we have $\zeta(w) = O(|w|^{q+1})$ as $|w| \to \infty$; hence we can shift the line of integration to the left as far as we please if we only take the residues into account. The factor $\Gamma(z)$ has poles at $0, -1, -2, \ldots$, and $\zeta(2z-k)$ has a pole only at $z = (k+1)/2$. The residue at $z = -j$ is $N^{-j}(-1)^j \zeta(-2j-k)/j!$, and $\zeta(-n) = (-1)^n B_{n+1}/(n+1)$. The residue at $z = (k+1)/2$ is $\frac{1}{2}\Gamma((k+1)/2)N^{(k+1)/2}$. But when $k = -1$ there is a double pole at $z = 0$; and $\zeta(z) = 1/(z-1) + \gamma + O(|z-1|)$, so the residue at 0 in this case is $\gamma + \frac{1}{2}\ln N - \frac{1}{2}\gamma$. We therefore obtain the asymptotic series mentioned in the answer to exercise 44.

52. Set $x = t/n$; then

$$\binom{2n}{n+t} \Big/ \binom{2n}{n} = \exp(-2n(x^2/1\cdot2 + x^4/3\cdot4 + \cdots) + (x^2/2 + x^4/4 + \cdots)$$
$$- (1/6n)(x^2 - x^4 + \cdots) + \cdots);$$

the desired sum can now be expressed in terms of $\sum_{t\geq1} t^k d(t) e^{-t^2/n}$, for various k. Proceeding as in exercise 51, since $\zeta(z)^2 = \sum_{t\geq1} d(t)t^{-z}$, we wish to evaluate the residues of $\Gamma(z)n^z\zeta(2z-k)^2$ when $k \geq 0$. At $z = -j$ the residue is

$$n^{-j}(-1)^j(B_{2j+k+1}/(2j+k+1))^2/j!,$$

and at $z = (k+1)/2$ it is $n^{(k+1)/2}\Gamma((k+1)/2)(\gamma + \frac{1}{4}\ln n + \frac{1}{4}\psi((k+1)/2))$, where $\psi(z) = \Gamma'(z)/\Gamma(z) = H_{z-1} - \gamma$; thus, for example, when $k = 0$, $\sum_{t\geq1} e^{-t^2/n}d(t) = \frac{1}{4}\sqrt{\pi n}\ln n + (\frac{3}{4}\gamma - \frac{1}{2}\ln 2)\sqrt{\pi n} + \frac{1}{4} + O(n^{-M})$ for all M. For $S_n/\binom{2n}{n}$, add $(\frac{1}{32}\ln n + \frac{3}{32}\gamma + \frac{1}{24} - \frac{1}{16}\ln 2)\sqrt{\pi/n} + O(n^{-1})$ to this quantity. (See exercises 1.2.7–23 and 1.2.9–19.)

53. Let $q = 1 - p$. Generalizing exercise 36(c), if

$$x_n = a_n + \sum_{k\geq2} \binom{n}{k}(p^k q^{n-k} + q^k p^{n-k})x_k,$$

then

$$x_n = a_n + \sum_{k\geq2} \binom{n}{k}(-1)^k \hat{a}_k(p^k + q^k)/(1 - p^k - q^k).$$

We can therefore find B_N and C_N as before; the factor $\frac{1}{4}$ in B_N should be replaced by pq. The asymptotic examination of U_N proceeds essentially as in the text, with

$$T_n = \sum_{r\geq1,\, s\geq0} \binom{r}{s}(e^{-np^s q^{r-s}} - 1 + np^s q^{r-s})$$

$$= \frac{1}{2\pi i}\int_{-3/2-i\infty}^{-3/2+i\infty} \Gamma(z)n^{-z}(p^{-z} + q^{-z})\,dz/(1 - p^{-z} - q^{-z})$$

$$= (n/h_p)(\ln n + \gamma - 1 + h_p^{(2)}/2h_p - h_p + \delta(n)) + O(1),$$

where $h_p = -(p \ln p + q \ln q)$, $h_p^{(2)} = p(\ln p)^2 + q(\ln q)^2$, and $\delta(n) = \sum \Gamma(z)n^{-1-z}/h_p$ summed over all complex $z \neq 1$ such that $p^{-z} + q^{-z} = 1$. The latter set of points seems to be difficult to analyze in general; but when $p = \phi^{-1}$, $q = \phi^{-2}$, the solutions are $z = (-1)^{k+1} + k\pi i/\ln \phi$. The dominant term, $(n \ln n)/h_p$, could also have been obtained from van Emden's general formula quoted in the answer to exercise 29. For $p = \phi^{-1}$ we have $1/h_p \approx 1.503718$, compared to $1/h_{1/2} \approx 1.442695$.

54. Let C be a circle of radius $(M+\frac{1}{2})b$, so that the integral vanishes on C as $M \to \infty$. (The asymptotic form of U_n can now be derived in a new way, expanding $\Gamma(n+1)/\Gamma(n+ibm)$. The method of this exercise applies to *all* sums of the form

$$\sum_k \binom{n}{k}(-1)^{n-k} f(k) = \frac{-1}{2\pi i} \oint B(n+1, -z) f(z)\, dz,$$

when f is reasonably well behaved. The latter formula can be found in N. E. Nörlund's *Vorlesungen über Differenzenrechnung* (Berlin: Springer, 1924), §103.)

55. Replace lines 04–06 of Program Q by

2H	ENTA	0,2		STA	INPUT,3	$c \leq b < a$	JGE 5F
	INCA	0,3		STX	INPUT,2		CMPX INPUT,4 $a<b,c$
	SRB	1		5H LDA	INPUT,4	$rA \leftarrow b$	JGE 5B
	STA	*+1(0:2)		JMP	6F		LDA INPUT,3 $a<c<b$
	ENT4	*		4H LDA	INPUT,3	$b<c\leq a$	LDX INPUT,4
	LDA	INPUT,2 $rA \leftarrow a$		LDX	INPUT,2		STX INPUT,3
	LDX	INPUT,3 $rX \leftarrow c$		STX	INPUT,3		JMP 6F
	CMPA	INPUT,3		JMP	5F		5H LDX INPUT,4 $b\leq a<c$
	JL	1F		3H STX	INPUT,2	$c\leq a\leq b$	STX INPUT,2
	CMPA	INPUT,4 $rA:b$		LDX	INPUT,4		6H LDX INPUT+1,2
	JLE	3F		STX	INPUT,3		STX INPUT,4
	CMPX	INPUT,4 $rX:b$		JMP	6F		ENT4 2,2
	JG	4F		1H CMPA	INPUT,4		ENT5 0,3

followed by 'STA INPUT+1,2' (see the remark after (27)); and change the instruction in line 22 to 'STX INPUT+1,2'. The first three of these instructions should be replaced by 'ENTX 0,2; INCX 0,3; ENTA 0; DIV =2=' if binary shifting is not available.

This program essentially exchanges R_{l+1} with $R_{\lfloor (l+r)/2 \rfloor}$ and sorts the three records R_l, R_{l+1}, R_r, then applies normal partitioning to $R_{l+1} \ldots R_{r-1}$. It is tempting to save a few lines of code by simply putting the median element in rA, moving R_l to the median's former place, and using Program Q as it stands. But such an approach has bad consequences, since it requires order N^2 steps to sort the file N $N-1$ $\ldots$ 1. (This amazing result, first noticed by D. B. Coldrick, has to be seen to be believed — try it!) The technique recommended above, due to R. Sedgewick, appears to be free of such simple worst-case anomalies, and runs faster too.

With this median-of-three partitioning scheme, the algorithm does not look at K_{N+1}, but it still might examine K_0 in step Q9.

56. We can solve the recurrence $\binom{n}{3}x_n = b_n + 2\sum_{k=1}^{n}(k-1)(n-k)x_{k-1}$, for $n > m$, by letting $y_n = nx_n$, $u_n = ny_{n+1} - (n+2)y_n$, $v_n = nu_{n+1} - (n-5)u_n$; it follows that $v_n = 6(b_{n+2} - 2b_{n+1} + b_n)$, for $n > m$. *Example:* Let $x_n = \delta_{n1}$ for $n \leq m$, and let $b_n \equiv 0$. Then $v_n = 0$ for all $n > m$, hence $n^{\underline{5}}u_{n+1} = m^{\underline{5}}u_{m+1}$. Since $y_{m+1} = 12/m$ and $y_{m+2} = 12/(m+1)$, we ultimately find $x_n = \frac{48}{7}(n+1)/m(m+1)(m+2) + \frac{36}{7}(m-1)^{\underline{4}}/n^{\underline{6}}$, for $n > m$. In general, let $f_n = (12/(n-1)(n-2))\sum_{k=1}^{n}(k-1)(n-k)x_{k-1}$; the solution for $n > m$ when b_n is identically zero is

$$x_n = (n+1)\frac{(m+1)f_{m+2} - (m-4)f_{m+1}}{7(m+1)(m+2)} - \frac{((m+1)f_{m+2} - (m+3)f_{m+1})m^{\underline{5}}}{7n^{\underline{6}}}.$$

When $b_n = \binom{n}{3}/n^{\underline{p}}$ and $x_n = 0$ for $n \le m$, the solution is

$$\frac{x_n}{n+1} = \frac{(p-3)(p-2)}{(p-6)(p+1)(n+1)^{\underline{p+1}}} + \frac{12}{7}\frac{1}{(p+1)(m+2)^{\underline{p+1}}} - \frac{12}{7}\frac{(m+1-p)^{\underline{6-p}}}{(p-6)(n+1)^{\underline{7}}},$$

for $n > m$; except that when $p = -1$ we have $x_n/(n+1) = \frac{12}{7}(H_{n+1} - H_{m+2}) + \frac{37}{49} + \frac{12}{49}(m+2)^{\underline{7}}/(n+1)^{\underline{7}}$, and when $p = 6$, $x_n/(n+1) = -\frac{12}{7}(H_{n-6} - H_{m-5})/(n+1)^{\underline{7}} + \frac{12}{49}/(m+2)^{\underline{7}} + \frac{37}{49}/(n+1)^{\underline{7}}$.

Arguing as in exercises 21–23, we find that the first partitioning phase now contributes 1 to A, t to B, and $N-1$ to C, where t is defined as before but *after* the rearrangement made in exercise 55. Under the new assumptions we find $b_{stN} = 6\binom{s-2}{t}\binom{N-s-1}{t}/N\binom{N-1}{s-1}$; hence the recurrence stated above arises in the following ways:

	Value for $N \le M$	$b_N/\binom{N}{3}$ for $N > M$	Solution for $N > M$
A_N	0	1	$(N+1)(\frac{12}{7}/(M+2)) - 1 + O(N^{-6})$
B_N	0	$(N-4)/5$	$(C_N - 3A_N)/5$
C_N	0	$N-1$	$(N+1)(\frac{12}{7}(H_{N+1} - H_{M+2}) + \frac{37}{49} - \frac{24}{7}/(M+2)) + 2 + O(N^{-6})$
D_N	$N - H_N$	0	$(N+1)(1 - \frac{12}{7}H_{M+1}/(M+2) - \frac{4}{7}/(M+2)) + O(N^{-6})$
E_N	$N(N-1)/4$	0	$(N+1)(\frac{6}{35}M - \frac{17}{35} + \frac{6}{7}/(M+2)) + O(N^{-6})$

Similarly $S_N = \frac{3}{7}(N+1)(5M+3)/(2M+3)(2M+1) - 1 + O(N^{-6})$. The total average running time of the program in exercise 55 is $53\frac{1}{2}A_N + 11B_N + 4C_N + 3D_N + 8E_N + 9S_N + 7N$; the choice $M = 9$ is very slightly better than $M = 10$, producing an average time of approximately $10\frac{22}{35}N \ln N + 2.116N$ [*Acta Inf.* **7** (1977), 336–341]. With DIV instead of SRB, add $11A_N$ to the average running time and take $M = 10$.

SECTION 5.2.3

1. No; consider the case $K_1 > K_2 = \cdots = K_N$. But the method using ∞ (described just before Algorithm S) is stable.

2. Traversing a linear list stored sequentially in memory is often slightly faster if we scan the list from higher indices to lower, since it is usually easier for a computer to test if an index is zero than to test if it exceeds N. (For the same reason, the search in step S2 runs from j down to 1; but see exercise 8!)

3. (a) The permutation $a_1 \ldots a_{N-1}N$ occurs for inputs

$$N\, a_2 \ldots a_{N-1}\, a_1, \quad a_1\, N\, a_3 \ldots a_{N-1}\, a_2, \quad \ldots, \quad a_1\, a_2 \ldots a_{N-2}\, N\, a_{N-1}, \quad a_1 \ldots a_{N-1}N.$$

(b) The average number of times the maximum is changed during the first iteration of step S2 is $H_N - 1$, as shown in Section 1.2.10. [Hence B_N can be found from Eq. 1.2.7–(8).]

4. If the input is a permutation of $\{1, 2, \ldots, N\}$, the number of times $i = j$ in step S3 is exactly one less than the number of cycles in the permutation. (Indeed, it is not hard to show that steps S2 and S3 simply remove element j from its cycle; hence S3 is inactive only when j was the smallest element in its cycle.) By Eq. 1.3.3–(21) we could save $H_N - 1$ of the $N - 1$ executions of step S3, on the average.

Thus it is inefficient to insert an extra test "$i = j$?" before step S3. Instead of testing i versus j, however, we could lengthen the program for S2 slightly, duplicating part of the code, so that S3 never is encountered if the initial guess K_j is not changed during the search for the maximum; this would make Program S a wee bit faster.

5. $(N - 1) + (N - 3) + \cdots = \lfloor N^2/4 \rfloor$.

6. (a) If $i \neq j$ in step S3, that step decreases the number of inversions by $2m - 1$, where m is one more than the number of keys in $K_{i+1} \ldots K_{j-1}$ that lie between K_i and K_j; clearly m is not less than the contribution to B on the previous step S2. Now apply the observation of exercise 4, connecting cycles to the condition $i = j$. (b) Every permutation can be obtained from $N \ldots 2\ 1$ by successive interchanges of adjacent elements that are out of order. (Apply, in reverse sequence, the interchanges that sort the permutation into decreasing order.) Every such operation decreases I by one and changes C by ± 1. Hence no permutation has a value of $I - C$ exceeding the corresponding value for $N \ldots 2\ 1$. [By exercise 5 the inequality $B \leq \lfloor N^2/4 \rfloor$ is best possible.]

7. A. C. Yao, "On straight selection sort," Computer Science Technical Report 185 (Princeton University, 1988), showed that the variance is $\alpha N^{1.5} + O(N^{1.495} \log N)$, where $\alpha = \frac{4}{3}\sqrt{\pi} \ln \frac{4}{e} \approx 0.9129$; he also conjectured that the actual error term is significantly smaller.

8. We can start the next iteration of step S2 at position K_i, provided that we have remembered $\max(K_1, \ldots, K_{i-1})$. One way to keep all of this auxiliary information is to use a link table $L_1 \ldots L_N$ such that K_{L_k} is the previous boldface element whenever K_k is boldface; $L_1 = 0$. [We could also get by with less auxiliary storage, at the expense of some redundant comparisons.]

The following MIX program uses address modification so that the inner loop is fast. $\text{rI1} \equiv j$, $\text{rI2} \equiv k - j$, $\text{rI3} \equiv i$, $\text{rA} \equiv K_i$.

01	START	ENT1	N	1	$j \leftarrow N$.	
02		STZ	LINK+1	1		
03		JMP	9F	1		
04	1H	ST1	6F(0:2)	$N - D$	Modify addresses in loop.	
05		ENT4	INPUT,1	$N - D$		
06		ST4	7F(0:2)	$N - D$		
07		ENT4	LINK,1	$N - D$		
08		ST4	8F(0:2)	$N - D$		
09	7H	CMPA	INPUT+J,2	A		[Address modified]
10		JGE	*+4	A	Jump if $K_i \geq K_k$.	
11	8H	ST3	LINK+J,2	$N + 1 - C$	Otherwise $L_k \leftarrow i$,	[Address modified]
12	6H	ENT3	J,2	$N + 1 - C$	$i \leftarrow k$.	[Address modified]
13		LDA	INPUT,3	$N + 1 - C$		
14		INC2	1	A	$k \leftarrow k + 1$.	
15		J2NP	7B	A	Jump if $k \leq j$.	
16	4H	LDX	INPUT,1	N		
17		STX	INPUT,3	N	$R_i \leftarrow R_j$.	
18		STA	INPUT,1	N	$R_j \leftarrow$ former R_i.	
19		DEC1	1	N	$j \leftarrow j - 1$.	
20		ENT2	0,3	N	$\text{rI2} \leftarrow i$.	

21		LD3	LINK,3	N	$i \leftarrow L_i$.
22		J3NZ	5F	N	If $i > 0$, k will start at i.
23	9H	ENT3	1	C	Otherwise $i \leftarrow 1$.
24		ENT2	2	C	k will start at 2.
25	5H	DEC2	0,1	$N+1$	
26		LDA	INPUT,3	$N+1$	$rA \leftarrow K_i$.
27		J2NP	1B	$N+1$	Jump if $k \leq j$.
28		J1P	4B	$D+1$	Jump if $j > 0$. ∎

9. $N - 1 + \sum_{N \geq k \geq 2}\left((k-1)/2 - 1/k\right) = \frac{1}{2}\binom{N}{2} + N - H_N$. [The average values of C and D are, respectively, $H_N + 1$ and $H_N - \frac{1}{2}$; hence the average running time of the program is $(1.25N^2 + 31.75N - 15H_N + 14.5)u$.] Program H is much better.

10.

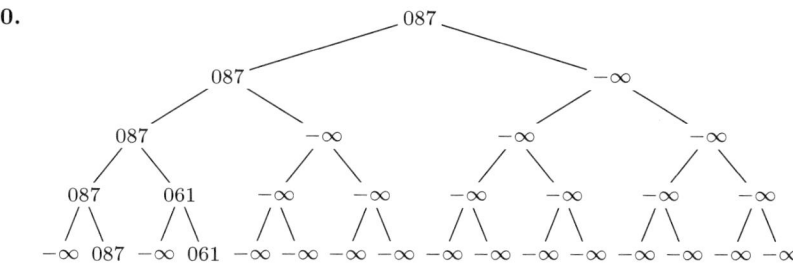

11.

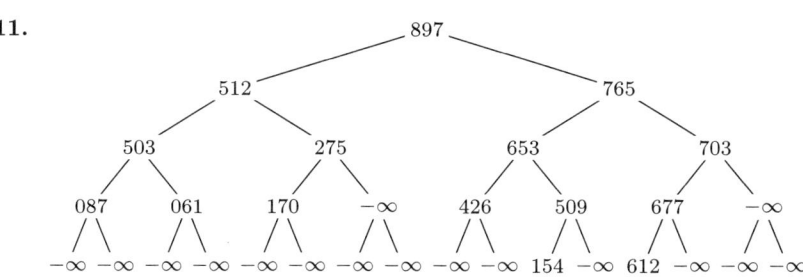

12. $2^n - 1$, once for each $-\infty$ in a branch node.

13. If $K \geq K_{r+1}$, then step H4 may go to step H5 if $j = r$. (Step H5 is inactive unless $K_r < K_{r+1}$, when step H6 will go to H8 anyway.) To ensure that $K \geq K_{r+1}$ throughout the algorithm, we may start with $K_{N+1} \leq \min(K_1, \ldots, K_N)$; instead of setting $R_r \leftarrow R_1$ in step H2, set $R_{r+1} \leftarrow R_{N+1}$ and $R_{N+1} \leftarrow R_1$; also set $R_2 \leftarrow R_{N+1}$ after $r = 1$. (This trick does not speed up the algorithm nor does it make Program H any shorter.)

14. When inserting an element, give it a key that is less (or greater) than all previously assigned keys, to get the effect of a simple queue (or stack, respectively).

15. For efficiency, the following solution is a little bit tricky, avoiding all multiples of 3 [*CACM* **10** (1967), 570].

> **P1.** [Initialize.] Set $p[1] \leftarrow 2$, $p[2] \leftarrow 3$, $k \leftarrow 2$, $n \leftarrow 5$, $d \leftarrow 2$, $r \leftarrow 1$, $t \leftarrow 25$, and place $(25, 10, 30)$ in the priority queue. (In this algorithm, $p[i] = i$th prime; k = number of primes found so far; n = prime candidate; d = distance to next candidate; r = number of elements in the queue; $t = p[r+2]^2$, the next n for which we should increase r. The queue entries have the form $(u, v, 6p)$, where p is a prime divisor of u, $v = 2p$ or $4p$, and $u + v$ is not a multiple of 3.)

P2. [Advance q.] Let (q, q', q'') be a queue element with the smallest first component. Replace it in the queue by $(q + q', q'' - q', q'')$. (This denotes the next multiple of $q''/6$ that must be excluded.) If $n > q$, repeat this step until $n \leq q$.

P3. [Check for prime n.] If $n > N$, terminate the algorithm. Otherwise, if $n < q$, set $k \leftarrow k + 1$, $p[k] \leftarrow n$, $n \leftarrow n + d$, $d \leftarrow 6 - d$, and repeat this step.

P4. [Check for prime $\sqrt{n}$.] (Now $n = q$ is not prime.) If $n = t$, set $r \leftarrow r + 1$, $u \leftarrow p[r + 2]$, $t \leftarrow u^2$, and insert $(t, 2u, 6u)$ or $(t, 4u, 6u)$ into the queue according as $u \bmod 3 = 2$ or $u \bmod 3 = 1$.

P5. [Advance n.] Set $n \leftarrow n + d$, $d \leftarrow 6 - d$, and return to P2. ∎

Thus the computation begins as follows:

Queue contents	Primes found
(25, 10, 30)	5, 7, 11, 13, 17, 19, 23
(35, 20, 30)(49, 28, 42)	29, 31
(49, 28, 42)(55, 10, 30)	37, 41, 43, 47
(55, 10, 30)(77, 14, 42)(121, 22, 66)	53

If the queue is maintained as a heap, we can find all primes $\leq N$ in $O(N \log N \log \log N)$ steps; the length of the heap is at most the number of primes $\leq \sqrt{N}$, and the entry for p is updated $O(N/p)$ times. The sieve of Eratosthenes, as implemented in exercise 4.5.4–8, is a $O(N \log \log N)$ method requiring considerably more random access storage. More efficient implementations are discussed in Section 7.1.3.

16. I1. [Make a new leaf j.] Set $K \leftarrow$ key to be inserted; $j \leftarrow n + 1$.

I2. [Find parent of j.] Set $i \leftarrow \lfloor j/2 \rfloor$.

I3. [Done?] If $i = 0$ or $K_i \geq K$, set $K_j \leftarrow K$ and terminate the algorithm.

I4. [Sift and move j up.] Set $K_j \leftarrow K_i$, $j \leftarrow i$, and return to I2. ∎

[T. Porter and I. Simon showed in *IEEE Trans.* **SE-1** (1975), 292–298, that if A_{n+1} denotes the average number of times step 4 is executed, given a random heap of uniformly random numbers, we have $A_n = \lfloor \lg n \rfloor + (1 - n^{-1})A_{n'}$ for $n > 1$, where $n = (1b_{l-1}b_{l-2} \ldots b_0)_2$ implies $n' = (1b_{l-2} \ldots b_0)_2$. If $l = \lfloor \lg n \rfloor$, this value is always $\geq A_{2^{l+1}-1} = (2^{l+1} - 2)/(2^{l+1} - 1)$, and always $\leq A_{2^l} < \alpha$, where α is the constant in (19).]

17. The file 1 2 3 goes into the heap 3 2 1 with Algorithm H, but into 3 1 2 with exercise 16. [*Note:* The latter method of heap creation has a worst case of order $N \log N$; but empirical tests have shown that the average number of iterations of step 2 during the creation of a heap is less than about $2.28N$, for random input. R. Hayward and C. McDiarmid [*J. Algorithms* **12** (1991), 126–153] have proved rigorously that the constant of proportionality lies between 2.2778 and 2.2994.]

18. Delete step H6, and replace H8 by:

H8'. [Move back up.] Set $j \leftarrow i$, $i \leftarrow \lfloor j/2 \rfloor$.

H9'. [Does K fit?] If $K \leq K_i$ or $j = l$, set $R_j \leftarrow R$ and return to H2. Otherwise set $R_j \leftarrow R_i$ and return to H8'. ∎

The method is essentially the same as in exercise 16, but with a different starting place in the heap. The net change to the file is the same as in Algorithm H. Empirical tests on this method show that the number of times $R_j \leftarrow R_i$ occurs per siftup during the selection phase is $(0, 1, 2)$ with respective probabilities $(.837, .135, .016)$. This method makes Program H somewhat longer but improves its asymptotic speed to $(13N \lg N + O(N))u$. A MIX instruction to halve the value of an index register would be desirable.

C. J. H. McDiarmid and B. A. Reed [*J. Algorithms* **10** (1989), 352–365] have proved that this modification also saves an average of $(3\beta - 8)N \approx 0.232N$ comparisons during the heap-creation phase, where β is defined in the answer to exercise 27. For further analysis of Floyd's improvement, see I. Wegener, *Theoretical Comp. Sci.* **118** (1993), 81–98.

J. Wu and H. Zhu [*J. Comp. Sci. and Tech.* **9** (1994), 261–266] have observed that binary search can also be used, so that each siftup of the selection phase involves at most $\lg N + \lg \lg N$ comparisons and $\lg N$ moves.

19. Proceed as in the revised siftup algorithm of exercise 18, with $K = K_N$, $l = 1$, and $r = N - 1$, starting with a given value of j in step H3.

20. For $0 \le k \le n$, the number of positive integers $\le N$ whose binary representation has the form $(b_n \ldots b_k a_1 \ldots a_q)_2$ for some $q \ge 0$ is clearly $(b_{k-1} \ldots b_0)_2 + 1 + \sum_{0 \le q < k} 2^q = (1 b_{k-1} \ldots b_0)_2$.

21. Let $j = (c_r \ldots c_0)_2$ be in the range $\lfloor N/2^{k+1} \rfloor = (b_n \ldots b_{k+1})_2 < j < (b_n \ldots b_k)_2 = \lfloor N/2^k \rfloor$. Then s_j is the number of positive integers $\le N$ whose binary representation has the form $(c_r \ldots c_0 a_1 \ldots a_q)_2$ for some $q \ge 0$, namely $\sum_{0 \le q \le k} 2^q = 2^{k+1} - 1$. Hence the number of nonspecial subtrees of size $2^{k+1} - 1$ is

$$\lfloor N/2^k \rfloor - \lfloor N/2^{k+1} \rfloor - 1 = \lfloor (N - 2^k)/2^{k+1} \rfloor.$$

[To prove the latter identity, use the replicative law in exercise 1.2.4–38 with $n = 2$ and $x = N/2^{k+1}$.]

22. The five possibilities before $l = 1$ are $5\,3\,4\,1\,2$, $3\,5\,4\,1\,2$, $4\,3\,5\,1\,2$, $1\,5\,4\,3\,2$, and $2\,5\,4\,1\,3$. Each of these possibilities $a_1 a_2 a_3 a_4 a_5$ leads to three possible permutations $a_1 a_2 a_3 a_4 a_5$, $a_1 a_4 a_3 a_2 a_5$, $a_1 a_5 a_3 a_4 a_2$ before $l = 2$.

23. (a) After B iterations, $j \ge 2^B l$; hence $2^B l \le r$. (b) We have $\sum_{l=1}^{n} \lfloor \log_2 (N/l) \rfloor = (\lfloor N/2 \rfloor - \lfloor N/4 \rfloor) + 2(\lfloor N/4 \rfloor - \lfloor N/8 \rfloor) + 3(\lfloor N/8 \rfloor - \lfloor N/16 \rfloor) + \cdots = \lfloor N/2 \rfloor + \lfloor N/4 \rfloor + \lfloor N/8 \rfloor + \cdots = N - \nu(N)$, where $\nu(N)$ is the number of ones in the binary representation of N. Also by exercise 1.2.4–42 we have $\sum_{r=1}^{N-1} \lfloor \lg r \rfloor = N \lfloor \lg N \rfloor - 2^{\lfloor \lg N \rfloor + 1} + 2$. We know by Theorem H that this upper bound on B is best possible during the heap-creation phase. Furthermore it is interesting to note that there is a unique heap containing the keys $\{1, 2, \ldots, N\}$ such that K is identically equal to 1 throughout the selection phase of Algorithm H. (For example, when $N = 7$ that heap is $7\ 5\ 6\ 2\ 4\ 3\ 1$; it is not difficult to pass from N to $N + 1$.) This heap gives the maximum value of B (as well as the maximum value of $\lceil N/2 \rceil - 1$ of D) for the selection phase of heapsort, so the best possible upper bound on B for the entire sort is $N - \nu(N) + N \lfloor \lg N \rfloor - 2^{\lfloor \lg N \rfloor + 1} + 2$.

24. $\sum_{k=1}^{N} \lfloor \lg k \rfloor^2 = (N + 1 - 2^n)n^2 + \sum_{0 \le k < n} k^2 2^k = (N + 1)n^2 - (2n - 3)2^{n+1} - 6$, where $n = \lfloor \lg N \rfloor$ (see exercise 4.5.2–22); hence the variance of the last siftup is $\beta_N = ((N + 1)n^2 - (2n - 3)2^{n+1} - 6)/N - ((N + 1)n + 2 - 2^{n+1})^2/N^2 = O(1)$. The standard deviation of B'_N is $(\sum \{\beta_s \mid s \in M_N\})^{1/2} = O(\sqrt{N})$.

25. The siftup is "uniform," and each comparison $K_j : K_{j+1}$ has probability $\frac{1}{2}$ of coming out $<$. The average contribution to C in this case is just one-half the sum of the average contributions to A and B, namely $((2n - 1)2^{n-1} + \frac{1}{2})/(2^{n+1} - 1)$.

26. (a) $(\frac{10}{25} + \frac{1}{2} + 1\frac{3}{9} + \frac{1}{2} + 1\frac{1}{2} + 1\frac{2}{5} + 2\frac{1}{2} + \frac{1}{2} + 1\frac{1}{2} + 1\frac{1}{2} + 2\frac{1}{2} + 1\frac{1}{2} + 2 + 2 + 3 + 0 + 1 + 1 + 2 + 1 + 2 + 2 + 3 + 1 + 2 + 2)/26 = 1189/780 \approx 1.524$.

(b) $\left(\sum_{k=1}^{N} \nu(k) - N + \frac{1}{2}\lfloor N/2\rfloor - \frac{1}{2}n + \sum_{k=1}^{n-1} \min(\alpha_{k-1}, \alpha_k - \alpha_{k-1} - 1)/(\alpha_k - 1)\right)/N$, where $\nu(k)$ is the number of one bits in the binary representation of k, and $\alpha_k = (1b_k \ldots b_0)_2$. If $N = 2^{e_1} + 2^{e_2} + \cdots + 2^{e_t}$, with $e_1 > e_2 > \cdots > e_t \geq 0$, it can be shown that $\sum_{k=0}^{N} \nu(k) = \frac{1}{2}((e_1 + 2)2^{e_1} + (e_2 + 4)2^{e_2} + \cdots + (e_t + 2t)2^{e_t}) + t - N$. [The asymptotic properties of such sums can be analyzed perspicuously with the help of Mellin transforms; see Flajolet, Grabner, Kirschenhofer, Prodinger, and Tichy, *Theoretical Comp. Sci.* **123** (1994), 291–314.]

27. J. W. Wrench, Jr. has observed that the general Lambert series $\sum_{n\geq 1} a_n x^n/(1-x^n)$ can be expanded as $\sum_{N\geq 1}\left(\sum_{d\backslash N} a_d\right)x^N = \sum_{m\geq 1}\left(a_m + \sum_{k\geq 1}(a_m + a_{m+k})x^{km}\right)x^{m^2}$.

[The cases $a_n = 1$ and $a_n = n$ were introduced by J. H. Lambert in his *Anlage zur Architectonic* **2** (Riga: 1771), §875; Clausen stated his formula for the case $a_n = 1$ in *Crelle* **3** (1828), 95, and H. F. Scherk presented a proof in *Crelle* **9** (1832), 162–163. When $a_n = n$ and $x = \frac{1}{2}$ we obtain the relation

$$\beta = \sum_{n\geq 1}\frac{n}{2^n - 1} = \sum_{m\geq 1}\left(m\left(\frac{2^m + 1}{2^m - 1}\right) + \frac{2^m}{(2^m - 1)^2}\right)2^{-m^2}$$

$$= 2.74403\,38887\,59488\,36048\,02148\,91492\,27216\,43114+;$$

this constant arises in (20), where we have $B_N' \sim (\beta - 2)N$ and $C_N' \sim (\frac{1}{2}\beta - \frac{1}{4}\alpha - \frac{1}{2})N$.]

Incidentally, if we set $q = x$ and $z = xy$ in the first identity of exercise 5.1.1–16, then evaluate $\frac{\partial}{\partial y}$ at $y = 1$, we get the interesting identity

$$\sum_{n\geq 1}\frac{x^n}{1 - x^n} = \sum_{k\geq 1}kx^k(1 - x^{k+1})(1 - x^{k+2})\ldots.$$

28. The children of node k are nodes $3k-1$, $3k$, and $3k+1$; the parent is $\lfloor(k+1)/3\rfloor$. A MIX program analogous to Program H takes asymptotically $21\frac{2}{3}N\log N \approx 13.7N\lg N$ units of time. Using the idea of exercise 18 lowers this to $18\frac{2}{3}N\log_3 N \approx 11.8N\lg N$, although the division by 3 will add a large $\Theta(N)$ term.

For further information about t-ary heaps, see S. Okoma, *Lecture Notes in Comp. Sci.* **88** (1980), 439–451.

30. Suppose $n = 2^t - 1 + r$, where $t = \lfloor\lg n\rfloor$ and $1 \leq r \leq 2^t$. Then $h_{2m} = [m=0]$ and

$$h_{(n+1)m} \leq \sum_{j=0}^{t-2}(2^j - 1)h_{n(m-j)} + 2^{t-1}h_{n(m-t+1)} + rh_{n(m-t)} \qquad \text{for } n \geq 2,$$

by considering the number of elements on level j that could be the final resting place of K_{n+1} after it has been sifted up in place of K_1. Therefore, if $g_{nm} = h_{nm}/2^m$, we have

$$g_{(n+1)m} \leq \sum_{j=0}^{t-2}\frac{2^j - 1}{2^j}g_{n(m-j)} + g_{n(m-t+1)} + \frac{r}{2^t}g_{n(m-t)} \leq \big(\lg(n+1)\big)\max_{m\geq 0}g_{nm},$$

and it follows by induction that $g_{nm} \leq L_n = \prod_{k=2}^{n}\lg k$.

The average total number of promotions during the selection phase is $B_N'' = h_N^{-1}\sum_{m\geq 0}mh_{Nm}$, where $h_N = \sum_{m\geq 0}h_{Nm}$ is the total number of possible heaps (Theorem H). We know that $B_N'' \leq N\lceil\lg N\rceil$. On the other hand, we have $B_N'' \geq m - h_N^{-1}\sum_{k=1}^{m}(m-k)h_{Nk} \geq m - h_N^{-1}L_N\sum_{k=1}^{m}(m-k)2^k > m - 2^{m+1}h_N^{-1}L_N$, for all m. Choosing $m = \lg(h_N/L_N) + O(1)$ now gives $B_N'' \geq \lg(h_N/L_N) + O(1)$.

The number of comparisons needed to create a heap is at most $2N$, by exercise 23(b); hence $h_N \geq N!/2^{2N}$. Clearly $L_N \leq (\lg N)^N$, so we have $\lg(h_N/L_N) \geq N \lg N - N \lg\lg N + O(N)$. [*J. Algorithms* **15** (1993), 76–100.]

31. (Solution by J. Edighoffer, 1981.) Let A be an array of $2n$ elements such that $A[2\lfloor i/2 \rfloor] \leq A[2i]$ and $A[2\lfloor i/2 \rfloor - 1] \geq A[2i-1]$ for $1 < i \leq n$; furthermore we require that $A[2i-1] \geq A[2i]$ for $1 \leq i \leq n$. (The latter condition holds for all i if and only if it holds for $n/2 < i \leq n$, because of the heap structure.) This "twin heap" contains $2n$ elements; to handle an odd number of elements, we simply keep one element off to the side. Appropriate modifications of the other algorithms in this section can be used to maintain twin heaps, and it is interesting to work out the details. This idea was independently discovered and developed further by J. van Leeuwen and D. Wood [*Comp. J.* **36** (1993), 209–216], who called the structure an "interval heap."

32. In any heap of N distinct elements, the largest $m = \lceil N/2 \rceil$ elements form a subtree. At least $\lfloor m/2 \rfloor$ of them must be nonleaves of that subtree, since a binary tree with k leaves has at least $k-1$ nonleaves. Therefore at least $\lfloor m/2 \rfloor$ of the largest m elements appear in the first $\lfloor N/2 \rfloor$ positions of the heap. Those elements must be promoted to the root position before reaching their final destinations; so their movement contributes at least $\sum_{k=1}^{\lfloor m/2 \rfloor} \lfloor \lg k \rfloor = \frac{1}{2}m \lg m + O(m)$ to B, by exercise 1.2.4–42. Thus $B_{\min}(N) \geq \frac{1}{4}N \lg N + O(N) + B_{\min}(\lfloor N/2 \rfloor)$, and the result follows by induction on N. [I. Wegener, *Theoretical Comp. Sci.* **118** (1993), 81–98, Theorem 5.1. Schaffer and Sedgewick, and independently Bollobás, Fenner, and Frieze, have constructed permutations that require no more than $\frac{1}{2}N \lg N + O(N \log\log N)$ promotions; see *J. Algorithms* **15** (1993), 76–100; **20** (1996), 205–217. Such permutations are quite rare, by the result of exercise 30.]

33. Let P and Q point to the given priority queues. The following algorithm uses the convention $\mathrm{DIST}(\Lambda) = 0$, as in the text, although Λ isn't really a node.

M1. [Initialize.] Set R ← Λ.

M2. [List merge.] If Q $= \Lambda$, set D ← DIST(P) and go to M3. If P $= \Lambda$, set P ← Q, D ← DIST(P), and go to M3. Otherwise if KEY(P) $\geq$ KEY(Q), set T ← RIGHT(P), RIGHT(P) ← R, R ← P, P ← T and repeat step M2. If KEY(P) $<$ KEY(Q), set T ← RIGHT(Q), RIGHT(Q) ← R, R ← Q, Q ← T and repeat step M2. (This step essentially merges the two "right lists" of the given trees, temporarily inserting upward pointers into the RIGHT fields.)

M3. [Done?] If R $= \Lambda$, terminate the algorithm; P points to the answer.

M4. [Fix DISTs.] Set Q ← RIGHT(R). If DIST(LEFT(R)) $<$ D, then set D ← DIST(LEFT(R)) $+ 1$, RIGHT(R) ← LEFT(R), LEFT(R) ← P; otherwise set D ← D $+ 1$, RIGHT(R) ← P. Finally set DIST(R) ← D, P ← R, R ← Q, and return to M3. ∎

34. Starting with the recurrence

$$L_1(z) = z, \qquad L_{m+1}(z) = L_m(z)\left(L(z) - \sum_{k=1}^{m-1} L_k(z) \right),$$

for parts of the overall generating function $L(z) = \sum_{n \geq 0} l_n z^n = \sum_{m \geq 1} L_m(z)$, where $L_m(z) = z^{2^{m-1}} + \cdots$ generates leftist trees with shortest path length m from root to Λ, Rainer Kemp has proved that $L(z) = z + \frac{1}{2}L(z)^2 + \frac{1}{2}\sum_{m \geq 1} L_m(z)^2$, and that $a \approx 0.25036$ and $b \approx 2.7494879$ [*Inf. Proc. Letters* **25** (1987), 227–232; *Random Graphs '87* (1990), 103–130]. Luis Trabb Pardo noticed in 1978 that the generating function $G(z) = zL(z)$ satisfies the elegant relation $G(z) = z + G(zG(z))$.

35. Let the DIST field of the deleted node be d_0, and let the DIST field of the merged subtrees be d_1. If $d_0 = d_1$, we need not go up at all. If $d_0 > d_1$, then $d_1 = d_0 - 1$; and if we go up n levels, the new DIST fields of the ancestors of P must be, respectively, $d_1 + 1, d_1 + 2, \ldots, d_1 + n$. If $d_0 < d_1$, the upward path must go only leftwards.

36. Instead of a general priority queue, it is simplest to use a doubly linked list; move nodes to one end of the list whenever they are used, and delete nodes from the other end. [See the discussion of self-organizing files in Section 6.1.]

37. In an infinite heap, the kth-largest element is equally likely to appear in the left or the right subheap of its larger ancestors. Thus we can use the theory of digital search trees, obtaining $e(k) = \overline{C}_k - \overline{C}_{k-1}$ in the notation of Eq. 6.3–(13). By exercise 6.3–28 we have $e(k) = \lg k + \gamma/(\ln 2) + \frac{1}{2} - \alpha + \delta_0(k) + O(k^{-1}) \approx \lg k - .274$, where α is defined in (19) and $\delta_0(k)$ is a periodic function of $\lg k$. [P. V. Poblete, *BIT* **33** (1993), 411–412.]

38. $M_0 = \emptyset$; $M_1 = \{1\}$; $M_N = \{N\} \uplus M_{2^k - 1} \uplus M_{N - 2^k}$ for $N > 1$, where $k = \lfloor \lg(2N/3) \rfloor$.

SECTION 5.2.4

1. Start with $i_1 = \cdots = i_k = 1$, $j = 1$. Repeatedly find $\min(x_{1i_1}, \ldots, x_{ki_k}) = x_{ri_r}$, and set $z_j = x_{ri_r}$, $j \leftarrow j + 1$, $i_r \leftarrow i_r + 1$. (In this case the use of $x_{i(m_i+1)} = \infty$ is a decided convenience.)

When k is moderately large, it is desirable to keep the keys $x_{1i_1}, \ldots, x_{ki_k}$ in a tree structure suited to repeated selection, as discussed in Section 5.2.3, so that only $\lfloor \lg k \rfloor$ comparisons are needed to find the new minimum each time after the first. Indeed, this is a typical application of the principle of "smallest in, first out" in a priority queue. The keys can be maintained as a heap, and ∞ can be avoided entirely. See the further discussion in Section 5.4.1.

2. Let C be the number of comparisons; we have $C = m + n - S$, where S is the number of elements transmitted in step M4 or M6. The probability that $S \geq s$ is easily seen to be

$$q_s = \left(\binom{m + n - s}{m} + \binom{m + n - s}{n} \right) \bigg/ \binom{m + n}{m}$$

for $1 \leq s \leq m + n$; $q_s = 0$ for $s > m + n$. Hence the mean of S is $\mu_{mn} = q_1 + q_2 + \cdots = m/(n+1) + n/(m+1)$ [see exercises 3.4.2–5, 6], and the variance is $\sigma_{mn}^2 = (q_1 + 3q_2 + 5q_3 + \cdots) - \mu_{mn}^2 = m(2m+n)/(n+1)(n+2) + (m+2n)n/(m+1)(m+2) - \mu_{mn}^2$. Thus

$$C = (\min \ \min(m, n), \quad \text{ave} \ m + n - \mu_{mn}, \quad \max \ m + n - 1, \quad \text{dev} \ \sigma_{mn}).$$

When $m = n$ the average was first computed by H. Nagler, *CACM* **3** (1960), 618–620; it is asymptotically $2n - 2 + O(n^{-1})$, with a standard deviation of $\sqrt{2} + O(n^{-1})$. Thus C hovers close to its maximum value.

3. **M2'.** If $K_i < K'_j$, go to M3'; if $K_i = K'_j$, go to M7'; if $K_i > K'_j$, go to M5'.

   M7'. Set $K''_k \leftarrow K'_j$, $k \leftarrow k+1$, $i \leftarrow i+1$, $j \leftarrow j+1$. If $i > M$, go to M4'; otherwise if $j > N$, go to M6'; otherwise return to M2'.   ∎

(Appropriate modifications are made to other steps of Algorithm M. Again many special cases disappear if we insert artificial keys $K_{M+1} = K'_{N+1} = \infty$ at the end of the files.)

4. The sequence of elements that appears at a fixed internal node of the selection tree, as time passes, is obtained by merging the sequences of elements that appear at the children of that node. (The discussion in Section 5.2.3 is based on selecting the *largest* element, but it could equally well have reversed the order.) So the operations involved in tree selection are essentially the same as those involved in merging, but they are performed in a different sequence and using different data structures.

Another relation between merging and tree selection is indicated in exercise 1. Note that an N-way merge of one-element files is a selection sort; compare also four-way merging of (A, B, C, D) to two-way merging of (A, B), (C, D), then (AB, CD).

5. In step N6 we always have $K_i < K_{i-1} \le K_j$; in N10, $K_j < K_{j+1} < K_i$.

6. For example, 2 6 4 10 8 14 12 16 15 11 13 7 9 3 5 1; after one pass, two of the expected stepdowns disappear: 1 2 5 6 7 8 13 14 16 15 12 11 10 9 4 3. This possibility was first noted by D. A. Bell, *Comp. J.* **1** (1958), 74. Quirks like this make it almost hopeless to carry out a precise analysis of Algorithm N.

7. $\lceil \lg N \rceil$, if $N > 1$. (Consider how many times p must be doubled until it is $\ge N$.)

8. If N is not a multiple of $2p$, there is one short run on the pass, and it is always near the middle; letting its length be t, we have $0 \le t < p$. Step S12 handles the cases where the short run is to be "merged" with an empty run, or where $t = 0$; otherwise we have essentially $x_1 \le x_2 \le \cdots \le x_p \mid y_t \ge \cdots \ge y_1$. If $x_p \le y_t$, the left-hand run is exhausted first, and step S6 will take us to S13 after x_p has been transmitted. On the other hand, if $x_p > y_t$, the right-hand side will be artificially exhausted, but $K_j = x_p$ will never be $< K_i$ in step S3! Thus S6 will eventually take us to S13 in all cases.

10. For example, Algorithm M can merge elements $x_{j+1} \ldots x_{j+m}$ with $x_{j+m+1} \cdots x_{j+m+n}$ into positions $x_1 \ldots x_{m+n}$ of an array without conflict, if $j \ge n$. With care we can exploit this idea so that $N + 2^{\lfloor \lg N \rfloor - 1}$ locations are required for an entire sort. But the program seems to be rather complicated compared to Algorithm S. [*Comp. J.* **1** (1958), 75; see also L. S. Lozinskii, *Kibernetika* **1**, 3 (1965), 58–62.]

11. Yes. This can be seen, for example, by considering the relation to tree selection mentioned in exercise 4. But Algorithms N and S are obviously not stable.

12. Set $L_0 \leftarrow 1$, $t \leftarrow N + 1$; then for $p = 1, 2, \ldots, N - 1$, do the following:

If $K_p \le K_{p+1}$ set $L_p \leftarrow p + 1$; otherwise set $L_t \leftarrow -(p+1)$, $t \leftarrow p$.

Finally, set $L_t \leftarrow 0$, $L_N \leftarrow 0$, $L_{N+1} \leftarrow |L_{N+1}|$.

(Stability is preserved. The number of passes is $\lceil \lg r \rceil$, where r is the number of ascending runs in the input; the exact distribution of r is analyzed in Section 5.1.3. We may conclude that natural merging is preferable to straight merging when linked allocation is being used, although it was inferior for sequential allocation.)

13. The running time for $N \ge 3$ is $(11A + 6B + 3B' + 9C + 2C'' + 4D + 5N + 9)u$, where A is the number of passes; $B = B' + B''$ is the number of subfile-merge operations performed, where B' is the number of such merges in which the p subfile was exhausted first; $C = C' + C''$ is the number of comparisons performed, where C' is the number of such comparisons with $K_p \le K_q$; $D = D' + D''$ is the number of elements remaining in subfiles when the other subfile has been exhausted, where D' is the number of such elements belonging to the q subfile. In Table 3 we have $A = 4$, $B' = 6$, $B'' = 9$, $C' = 22$, $C'' = 22$, $D' = 10$, $D'' = 10$, total time $= 761u$. (The comparable Program 5.2.1L takes only $433u$, when improved as in exercise 5.2.1–33, so we can see that merging isn't especially efficient when N is small.)

Algorithm L does a sequence of merges on subfiles whose sizes (m, n) can be determined as follows: Let $N - 1 = (b_k \ldots b_1 b_0)_2$ in binary notation. There are

$(b_k \ldots b_{j+1})_2$ "ordinary" merges with $(m, n) = (2^j, 2^j)$, for $0 \le j < k$; and there are "special" merges with $(m, n) = (2^j, 1 + (b_{j-1} \ldots b_0)_2)$ whenever $b_j = 1$, for $0 \le j \le k$. For example, when $N = 14$ there are six ordinary $(1, 1)$ merges, three ordinary $(2, 2)$ merges, one ordinary $(4, 4)$ merge, and the special merges deal with subfiles of sizes $(1, 1)$, $(4, 2)$, $(8, 6)$. The multiset M_N of merge sizes (m, n) can also be described by the recurrence relations

$$M_1 = \emptyset; \qquad M_{2^k + r} = \{(2^k, r)\} \uplus M_{2^k} \uplus M_r \quad \text{for } 0 < r \le 2^k.$$

It follows that, regardless of the input distribution, we have $A = \lceil \lg N \rceil$, $B = N - 1$, $C' + D'' = \sum_{j=0}^{k} b_j 2^j (1 + \frac{1}{2} j)$, $C'' + D' = \sum_{j=0}^{k} b_j (1 + 2^j (\frac{1}{2} j + b_{j+1} + \cdots + b_k))$; hence only B', C', D' need to be analyzed further.

If the input to Algorithm L is random, each of the merging operations satisfies the conditions of exercise 2, and is independent of the behavior of the other merges; so the distribution of B', C', D' is the convolution of their individual distributions for each subfile merge. The average values for such a merge are $B' = n/(m + n)$, $C' = mn/(n + 1)$, $D' = n/(m + 1)$. Sum these over all relevant (m, n) to get the exact average values.

When $N = 2^k$ we have, of course, the simplest situation; $B'_{\text{ave}} = \frac{1}{2} B$, $C'_{\text{ave}} = \frac{1}{2} C_{\text{ave}}$, $C + D = kN$, and $D_{\text{ave}} = \sum_{j=1}^{k} (2^{k-j} 2^j / (2^{j-1} + 1)) = \alpha' N + O(1)$, where

$$\alpha' = \sum_{n \ge 0} \frac{1}{2^n + 1} = \alpha + \frac{1}{2} - 2 \sum_{n \ge 1} \frac{1}{4^n - 1}$$

$$= 1.26449\ 97803\ 48444\ 20919\ 13197\ 47255\ 49848\ 25577-$$

can be evaluated to high precision as in exercise 5.2.3–27. This special case was first analyzed by A. Gleason [unpublished, 1956] and H. Nagler [*CACM* **3** (1960), 618–620].

14. Set $D = B$ in exercise 13 to maximize C. [A detailed analysis of Algorithm L has been carried out by W. Panny and H. Prodinger, *Algorithmica* **14** (1995), 340–354.]

15. Make extra copies of steps L3, L4, L6 for the cases that L_s is known to equal p or q. [A *further* improvement can also be made, removing the assignment $s \leftarrow p$ (or $s \leftarrow q$) from the inner loop, by simply renaming the registers! For example, change lines 20 and 21 to 'LD3 INPUT,1(L)' and continue with p in rI3, s in rI1 and L_s known to equal p. With eighteen copies of the inner loop, corresponding to the different permutations of (p, q, s) with respect to (rI1, rI2, rI3), and to different knowledge about L_s, we can cut the average running time to $(8N \lg N + O(N))u$.]

16. (The result will be slightly faster than Algorithm L; see exercise 5.2.3–28.)

17. Consider the new record as a subfile of length 1. Repeatedly merge the smallest two subfiles if they have the same length. (The resulting sorting algorithm is essentially the same as Algorithm L, but the subfiles are merged at different relative times.)

18. Yes, but it seems to be a complicated job. The first solution to be found used the following ingenious construction [*Doklady Akad. Nauk SSSR* **186** (1969), 1256–1258]: Let n be $\approx \sqrt{N}$. Divide the file into $m + 2$ "zones" $Z_1 \ldots Z_m\ Z_{m+1}\ Z_{m+2}$, where Z_{m+2} contains $N \bmod n$ records while each other zone contains exactly n records. Interchange the records of Z_{m+1} with the zone containing R_M; the file now takes the form $Z_1 \ldots Z_m\ A$, where each of the $Z_1 \ldots Z_m$ contains exactly n records in order and where A is an auxiliary area containing s records, for some s in the range $n \le s < 2n$.

Find the zone with smallest leading element, and exchange that entire zone with Z_1; if more than one zone has the smallest leading element, choose one that has the smallest trailing element. (This takes $O(m + n)$ operations.) Then find the zone with the next smallest leading and trailing elements, and exchange it with Z_2, etc. Finally in $O(m(m + n)) = O(N)$ operations we will have rearranged the m zones so that their leading elements are in order. Furthermore, because of our original assumptions about the file, each of the keys in $Z_1 \ldots Z_m$ will now have fewer than n inversions.

We can merge Z_1 with Z_2, using the following trick: Interchange Z_1 with the first n elements A' of A; then merge Z_2 with A' in the usual way but exchanging elements with the elements of $Z_1 Z_2$ as they are output. For example, if $n = 3$ and $x_1 < y_1 < x_2 < y_2 < x_3 < y_3$, we have

	Zone 1			Zone 2			Auxiliary		
Initial contents:	x_1	x_2	x_3	y_1	y_2	y_3	a_1	a_2	a_3
Exchange Z_1:	a_1	a_2	a_3	y_1	y_2	y_3	x_1	x_2	x_3
Exchange x_1:	x_1	a_2	a_3	y_1	y_2	y_3	a_1	x_2	x_3
Exchange y_1:	x_1	y_1	a_3	a_2	y_2	y_3	a_1	x_2	x_3
Exchange x_2:	x_1	y_1	x_2	a_2	y_2	y_3	a_1	a_3	x_3
Exchange y_2:	x_1	y_1	x_2	y_2	a_2	y_3	a_1	a_3	x_3
Exchange x_3:	x_1	y_1	x_2	y_2	x_3	y_3	a_1	a_3	a_2

(The merge is always complete when the nth element of the auxiliary area has been exchanged; this method generally permutes the auxiliary records.)

The trick above is used to merge Z_1 with Z_2, then Z_2 with Z_3, $\ldots$, Z_{m-1} with Z_m, requiring a total of $O(mn) = O(N)$ operations. Since no element has more than n inversions, the $Z_1 \ldots Z_m$ portion of the file has been completely sorted.

For the final "cleanup," we sort $R_{N+1-2s} \ldots R_N$ by insertion, in $O(s^2) = O(N)$ steps; this brings the s largest elements into area A. Then we merge $R_1 \ldots R_{N-2s}$ with $R_{N+1-2s} \ldots R_{N-s}$, using the trick above with auxiliary storage area A (but interchanging the roles of right and left, less and greater, throughout). Finally, we sort $R_{N+1-s} \ldots R_N$ by insertion.

Subsequent refinements are discussed by J. Katajainen, T. Pasanen, and J. Teuhola in *Nordic J. Computing* **3** (1996), 27–40. See answer 5.5–3 for the problem of *stable* merging in place.

19. We may number the input cars so that the final permutation has them in order, $1\ 2\ \ldots\ 2^n$; so this is essentially a sorting problem. First move the first 2^{n-1} cars through $n - 1$ stacks, putting them in decreasing order, and transfer them to the nth stack so that the smallest is on top. Then move the other 2^{n-1} cars through $n - 1$ stacks, putting them into increasing order and leaving them positioned just before the nth stack. Finally, merge the two sequences together in the obvious way.

20. For further information, see R. E. Tarjan, *JACM* **19** (1972), 341–346.

22. See *Information Processing Letters* **2** (1973), 127–128.

23. The merges can be represented by a binary tree that has all external nodes on levels $\lfloor \lg N \rfloor$ and $\lceil \lg N \rceil$. Therefore the maximum number of comparisons is the minimum external path length of a binary tree with N external nodes, Eq. 5.3.1–(34), minus $N - 1$, since $f(m, n) = m + n - 1$ gives the maximum and there are $N - 1$ merges. (See also Eq. 5.4.9–(1).)

General techniques for studying the asymptotic properties of such recurrences with the help of Mellin transforms have been presented by P. Flajolet and M. Golin in *Acta Informatica* **31** (1994), 673–696; in particular, they show that the average number of comparisons is $N \lg N - \theta N + \delta(\lg N)N + O(1)$ and the variance is $\approx .345N$, where δ is a continuous function of period 1 and average value 0, and

$$\theta = \frac{1}{\ln 2} - \frac{1}{2} + \frac{1}{\ln 2} \sum_{m=1}^{\infty} \frac{2}{(m+1)(m+2)} \ln \frac{2m+1}{2m}$$

$$= 1.24815\ 20420\ 99653\ 84890\ 29565\ 64329\ 53240\ 16127+.$$

The total number of comparisons is well approximated by a normal distribution as $N \to \infty$; see the complementary analyses by H.-K. Hwang and M. Cramer in *Random Structures & Algorithms* **8** (1996), 319–336; **11** (1997), 81–96.

SECTION 5.2.5

1. No, because radix sorting doesn't work at all unless the distribution sorting is stable, after the first pass. (But the suggested distribution sort *could* be used in a most-significant-digit-first radix sorting method, generalizing radix exchange, as suggested in the last paragraph of the text.)

2. It is "anti-stable," just the opposite; elements with equal keys appear in reverse order, since the first pass goes through the records from R_N to R_1. (This proves to be convenient because of lines 28 and 20 of Program R, equating Λ with 0; but of course it is not necessary to make the first pass go backwards.)

3. If pile 0 is not empty, `BOTM[0]` already points to the first element; if it is empty, we set `P ← LOC(BOTM[0])` and later make `LINK(P)` point to the bottom of the first nonempty pile.

4. When there are an even number of passes remaining, take pile 0 first (top to bottom), followed by pile 1, ..., pile $(M-1)$; the result will be in order with respect to the digits examined so far. When there are an odd number of passes remaining, take pile $(M-1)$ first, then pile $(M-2)$, ..., pile 0; the result will be in *reverse* order with respect to the digits examined so far. (This rule was apparently first published by E. H. Friend [*JACM* **3** (1956), 156, 165–166].)

5. Change line 04 to '`ENT3 7`', and change the R3SW and R5SW tables to:

```
R3SW    LD2    KEY,1(1:1)
        LD2    KEY,1(2:2)
        LD2    KEY,1(3:3)
        LD2    KEY,1(4:4)
        LD2    KEY,1(5:5)
        LD2    INPUT,1(1:1)
        LD2    INPUT,1(2:2)
        LD2    INPUT,1(3:3)
R5SW    LD1    INPUT,1(LINK)
         ⋮     (repeat the previous line six more times)
        DEC1   1          ▌
```

The new running time is found by changing "3" to "8" everywhere; it amounts to $(11p-1)N + 16pM + 12p - 4E + 2$, for $p = 8$.

6. (a) Consider placing an $(N+1)$st element. The recurrence

$$p_{M(N+1)k} = \frac{k+1}{M} p_{MN(k+1)} + \frac{M-k}{M} p_{MNk}$$

is equivalent to the stated formula. (b) The nth derivative satisfies $g_{M(N+1)}^{(n)}(z) = (1 - n/M)g_{MN}^{(n)}(z) + ((1 - z)/M)g_{MN}^{(n+1)}(z)$, by induction on n. Setting $z = 1$, we find $g_{MN}^{(n)}(1) = (1 - n/M)^N M^{\underline{n}}$, since $g_{M0}(z) = z^M$. Hence $\text{mean}(g_{MN}) = (1 - 1/M)^N M$, $\text{var}(g_{MN}) = (1 - 2/M)^N M(M - 1) + (1 - 1/M)^N M - (1 - 1/M)^{2N} M^2$. (Notice that the generating function for E in Program R is $g_{MN}(z)^p$.)

7. Let R = radix sort, RX = radix exchange. Some of the important similarities and differences: RX goes from most significant digit to least significant, while R goes the other way. Both methods sort by digit inspections, without making comparisons of keys. RX always has $M = 2$ (but see exercise 1). The running time for R is almost unvarying, while RX is sensitive to the distribution of the digits. In both cases the running time is $O(N \log K)$, where K is the range of keys, but the constant of proportionality is higher for RX; on the other hand, when the keys are uniformly distributed in their leading digits, RX has an average running time of $O(N \log N)$ regardless of the size of K. R requires link fields while RX runs in minimal space. The inner loop of R is more suited to pipeline computers.

8. On the final pass, the piles should be hooked together in another order; for example, if $M = 256$, pile $(10000000)_2$ comes first, then pile $(10000001)_2$, ..., pile $(11111111)_2$, pile $(00000000)_2$, pile $(00000001)_2$, ..., pile $(01111111)_2$. This change in hooking order can be done easily by modifying Algorithm H, or (in Table 1) by changing the storage allocation strategy, on the last pass.

9. We could first separate the negative keys from the positive keys, as in exercise 5.2.2–33; or we could change the keys to complement notation on the first pass. Alternatively, after the last pass we could separate the positive keys from the negative ones, reversing the order of the latter, although the method of exercise 5.2.2–33 no longer applies.

11. Without the first pass the method would still sort perfectly, because (by coincidence) 503 already precedes 509. Without the first two passes, the number of inversions would be $1 + 1 + 0 + 0 + 0 + 1 + 1 + 1 + 0 + 0 = 5$.

12. After exchanging R_k with $R[P]$ in step M4 (exercise 5.2–12), we can compare K_k to K_{k-1}. If K_k is less, we compare it to K_{k-2}, K_{k-3}, ..., until finding $K_k \geq K_j$. Then set $(R_{j+1}, \ldots, R_{k-1}, R_k) \leftarrow (R_k, R_{j+1}, \ldots, R_{k-1})$, *without* changing the LINK fields. It is convenient to place an artificial key K_0, which is $\leq$ all other keys, at the left of the file.

14. If the original permutation of the cards requires k readings, in the sense of exercise 5.1.3–20, and if we use m piles per pass, we must make at least $\lceil \log_m k \rceil$ passes. (Consider going back from a sorted deck to the original one; the number of readings increases by at most a factor of m on each pass.) The given permutation requires 4 increasing readings, 10 decreasing readings; hence decreasing order requires 4 passes with two piles or 3 passes with three piles.

Conversely, this optimum number of passes can be achieved: Number the cards from 0 to $k - 1$ according to which reading it belongs to, and use a radix sort (least significant digit first in radix m). [See *Martin Gardner's Sixth Book of Mathematical Games* (San Francisco: W. H. Freeman, 1971), 111–112.]

15. Let there be k readings and m piles. The order is reversed on each pass; if there are k readings in one order, the number of readings in the opposite order is $n + 1 - k$. The minimum number of passes is either the smallest even number greater than or equal to $\log_m k$ or the smallest odd number greater than or equal to $\log_m(n + 1 - k)$. (Going backwards, there are at most m decreasing readings after one pass, m^2 increasing readings after two passes, etc.) The example can be sorted into increasing order in $\min(2,5) = 2$ passes, into decreasing order in $\min(3,4) = 3$ passes, using only two piles.

16. Assume that each string is followed by a special null character that is less than any letter of the alphabet. Perform a left-to-right radix sort by starting with all strings linked together in a single block of data. Then for $k = 1, 2, \ldots$, refine every block that contains more than one distinct string by splitting it into subblocks based on the kth letter of each string, meanwhile keeping the blocks sorted by their already-examined prefixes. When a block has only one item, or when its kth characters are all null (so that its keys are identical), we can arrange to avoid examining it again. [R. Paige and R. E. Tarjan, *SICOMP* **16** (1987), 973–989, §2.] This process is essentially that of constructing a trie as in Section 6.3. A simpler but slightly less efficient algorithm based on right-to-left radix sort was given for this problem by Aho, Hopcroft, and Ullman, *The Design and Analysis of Computer Algorithms* (Addison–Wesley, 1974), 79–84. The methods of McIlroy, Bostic, and McIlroy, cited in the text, are faster yet in practice.

17. MacLaren's method speeds up the second level, but it cannot be used at the top level because it does not compute the numbers N_k.

18. First we prove the hint: Let $p_k = \int_{k/CN}^{(k+1)/CN} f(x)\,dx$ be the probability that a key falls into bin k when there are CN bins. The time needed to distribute the records is $O(N)$, and the average number of inversions remaining after distribution is $\frac{1}{2}\sum_{k=0}^{CN-1}\sum_j \binom{N}{j}p_k^j(1-p_k)^{N-j}\binom{j}{2} = \frac{1}{2}\sum_{k=0}^{CN-1}\binom{N}{2}p_k^2 \le \frac{N-1}{4}\sum_{k=0}^{CN-1}p_k B/C$, because $p_k \le B/CN$.

Now consider two levels of distribution, with cN top-level bins, and let $b_k = \sup\{f(x) \mid k/cN \le x < (k+1)/cN\}$. Then the average total running time is $O(N)$ plus $\sum_{k=0}^{cN-1} T_k$, where T_k is the average time needed by MacLaren's method to sort N_k keys having the density function $f_k(x) = f((k+x)/cN)/cNp_k$. By the hint, we have $T_k = \mathrm{E}\,O(b_k N_k/cNp_k)$, because $f_k(x)$ is bounded by b_k/cNp_k. But $\mathrm{E}\,N_k = Np_k$, so $T_k = O(b_k/c)$. And as $N \to \infty$ we have $\sum_{k=0}^{cN-1} b_k \to N\int_0^1 f(x)\,dx = N$, by the definition of Riemann integrability.

SECTION 5.3.1

1. (a)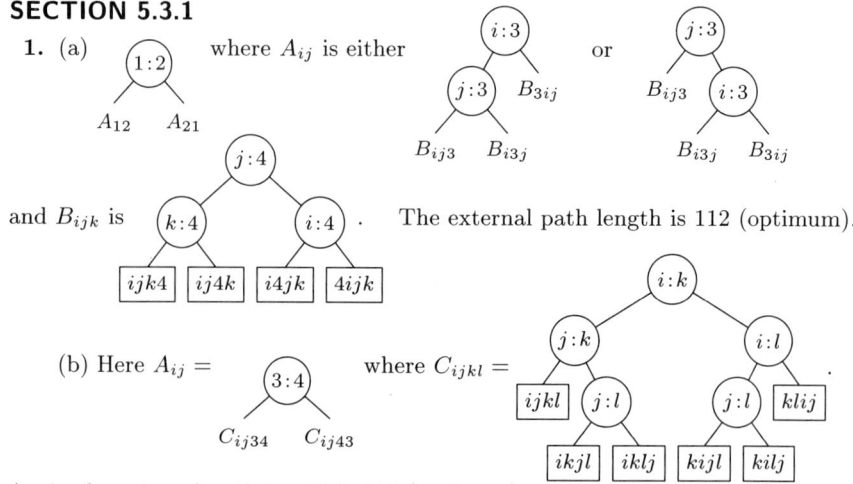

and B_{ijk} is . The external path length is 112 (optimum).

(b) Here $A_{ij} =$ where $C_{ijkl} =$.

Again the external path length is 112 (optimum).

2. In the notation of exercise 5.2.4–14,

$$L(n) - B(n) = \sum_{k=1}^{t}((e_k + k - 1)2^{e_k} - (e_1 + 1)2^{e_k}) + 2^{e_1+1} - 2^{e_t}$$

$$= 2^{e_1} - 2^{e_t} - \sum_{k=2}^{t}(e_1 - e_k + 2 - k)2^{e_k}$$

$$\geq 2^{e_1} - (2^{e_1-1} + \cdots + 2^{e_1-t+1} + 2^{e_t}) \geq 0,$$

with equality if and only if $n = 2^k - 2^j$ for some $k > j \geq 0$. [When merging is done "top-down" as in exercise 5.2.4–23, the maximum number of comparisons is $B(n)$.]

3. When $n > 0$, the number of outcomes such that the smallest key appears exactly k times is $\binom{n}{k}P_{n-k}$. Thus $2P_n = \sum_k \binom{n}{k}P_{n-k}$, for $n > 0$, and we have $2P(z) = e^z P(z) + 1$ by Eq. 1.2.9–(10).

Another proof comes from the fact that $P_n = \sum_{k\geq 0}\{{n \atop k}\}k!$, since $\{{n \atop k}\}$ is the number of ways to partition n elements into k nonempty parts and these parts can be permuted in $k!$ ways. Thus $\sum_{n\geq 0}P_n z^n/n! = \sum_{k\geq 0}(e^z - 1)^k = 1/(2 - e^z)$ by Eq. 1.2.9–(23).

Still *another* proof, perhaps the most interesting, arises if we arrange the elements in sequence in a stable manner, so that K_i precedes K_j if and only if $K_i < K_j$ or ($K_i = K_j$ and $i < j$). Among all P_n outcomes, a given arrangement $K_{a_1}\ldots K_{a_n}$ now occurs exactly 2^k times if the permutation $a_1 \ldots a_n$ contains k ascents; hence P_n can be expressed in terms of the Eulerian numbers, $P_n = \sum_k \langle{n \atop k}\rangle 2^k$. Eq. 5.1.3–(20) with $z = 2$ now establishes the desired result.

This generating function was obtained by A. Cayley [*Phil. Mag.* (4) **18** (1859), 374–378] in connection with the enumeration of an imprecisely defined class of trees. See also P. A. MacMahon, *Proc. London Math. Soc.* **22** (1891), 341–344; J. Touchard, *Ann. Soc. Sci. Bruxelles* **53** (1933), 21–31; and O. A. Gross, *AMM* **69** (1962), 4–8, who gave the interesting formula $P_n = \sum_{k\geq 1}k^n/2^{1+k}$, $n \geq 1$.

4. The representation

$$2P(z) = \frac{1}{2}\left(1 - i\cot\frac{i(z - \ln 2)}{2}\right) = \frac{1}{2} - \frac{1}{z - \ln 2} - \sum_{k\geq 1}\left(\frac{1}{z - \ln 2 - 2\pi ik} + \frac{1}{z - \ln 2 + 2\pi ik}\right)$$

yields the convergent series $P_n/n! = \frac{1}{2}(\ln 2)^{-n-1} + \sum_{k\geq 1}\Re((\ln 2 + 2\pi ik)^{-n-1})$.

5.

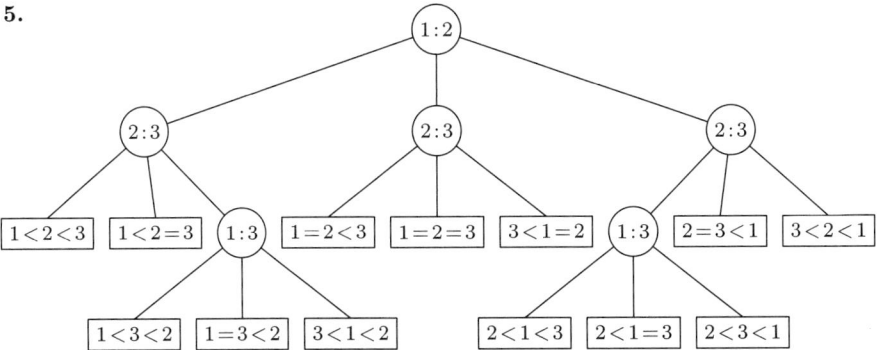

6. $S'(n) \geq S(n)$, since the keys might all be distinct; thus we must show that $S'(n) \leq S(n)$. Given a sorting algorithm that takes $S(n)$ steps on distinct keys, we can construct a sorting algorithm for the general case by defining the = branch to be identical to the

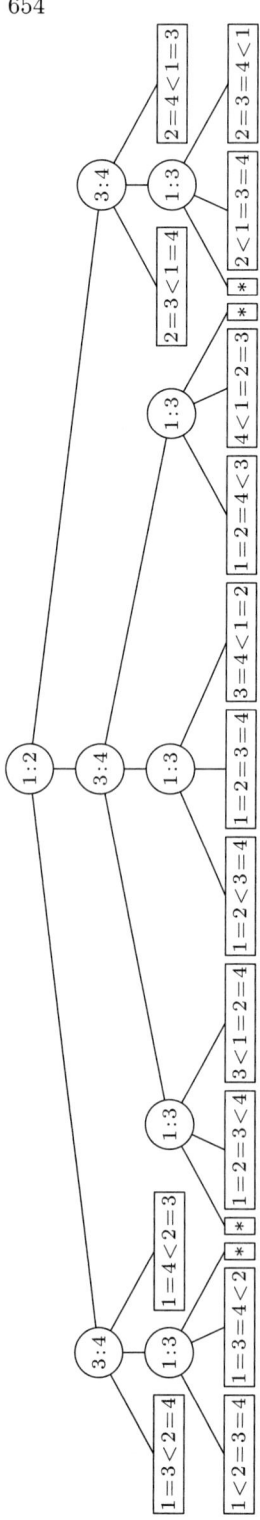

Fig. A–1. Solution to exercise 7. ("*" denotes an impossible case.)

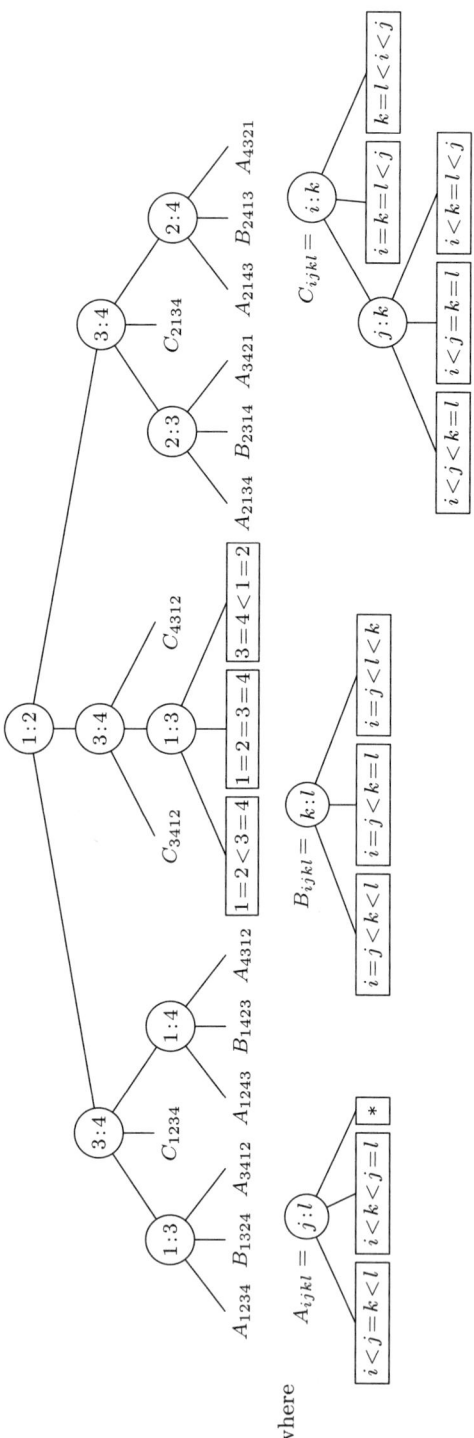

Fig. A–2. Solution to exercise 8.

< branch, removing redundancies. When an external node appears, we know all of the equality relations, since we have $K_{a_1} \leq K_{a_2} \leq \cdots \leq K_{a_n}$ and an explicit comparison $K_{a_i} : K_{a_{i+1}}$ has been made for $1 \leq i < n$.

M. Paterson observes that if the multiplicities of keys are $(n_1, \ldots, n_m)$, the number of comparisons can be reduced to $n \lg n - \sum n_j \lg n_j + O(n)$; see *SICOMP* **5** (1976), 2. This lower bound can almost be reached without substantial auxiliary memory by adapting heapsort to equal keys as suggested by Munro and Raman in *Lecture Notes in Comp. Sci.* **519** (1991), 473–480.

7. See Fig. A–1. The average number of comparisons is $(2 + 3 + 3 + 2 + 3 + 3 + 3 + 2 \cdot 3 + 3 + 3 + 3 + 2 + 3 + 3 + 2)/16 = 2\frac{3}{4}$.

8. See Fig. A–2. The average number of comparisons is $3\frac{56}{81}$.

9. We need at least $n - 1$ comparisons to discover that all keys are equal, if they are. Conversely, $n - 1$ comparisons always suffice, since we can always deduce the final ordering after comparing K_1 with all of the other keys.

10. Let $f(n)$ be the desired function, and let $g(n)$ be the minimum average number of comparisons needed to sort $n+k$ elements when $k > 0$ and exactly k of the elements have known values (0 or 1). Then $f(0) = f(1) = g(0) = 0$, $g(1) = 1$; $f(n) = 1 + \frac{1}{2}f(n-1) + \frac{1}{2}g(n-2)$, $g(n) = 1 + \min(g(n-1), \frac{1}{2}g(n-1) + \frac{1}{2}g(n-2)) = 1 + \frac{1}{2}g(n-1) + \frac{1}{2}g(n-2)$, for $n \geq 2$. (Thus the best strategy is to compare two unknown elements whenever possible.) It follows that $f(n) - g(n) = \frac{1}{2}(f(n-1) - g(n-1))$ for $n \geq 2$, and $g(n) = \frac{2}{3}(n + \frac{1}{3}(1 - (-\frac{1}{2})^n))$ for $n \geq 0$. Hence the answer is

$$\tfrac{2}{3}n + \tfrac{2}{9} - \tfrac{2}{9}(-\tfrac{1}{2})^n - (\tfrac{1}{2})^{n-1}, \quad \text{for } n \geq 1.$$

(This exact formula may be compared with the information-theoretic lower bound, $\log_3(2^n - 1) \approx 0.6309n$.)

11. Binary insertion proves that $S_m(n) \leq B(m) + (n - m)\lceil \lg(m + 1) \rceil$, for $n \geq m$. On the other hand $S_m(n) \geq \lceil \lg \sum_{k=1}^{m} \{ {n \atop k} \} k! \rceil$, and this is asymptotically $n \lg m + O(((m - 1)/m)^n)$; see Eq. 1.2.6–(53).

12. (a) If there are no redundant comparisons, we can arbitrarily assign an order to keys that are actually equal, when they are first compared, since no order can be deduced from previously made comparisons. (b) Assume that the tree strongly sorts every sequence of zeros and ones; we shall prove that it strongly sorts every permutation of $\{1, 2, \ldots, n\}$. Suppose it doesn't; then there is a permutation for which it claims that $K_{a_1} \leq K_{a_2} \leq \cdots \leq K_{a_n}$, whereas in fact $K_{a_i} > K_{a_{i+1}}$ for some i. Replace all elements $< K_{a_i}$ by 0 and all elements $\geq K_{a_i}$ by 1; by assumption the method will now sort when we take the path that leads to $K_{a_1} \leq K_{a_2} \leq \cdots \leq K_{a_n}$, a contradiction.

13. If n is even, $F(n) - F(n-1) = 1 + F(\lfloor n/2 \rfloor) - F(\lfloor n/2 \rfloor - 1)$ so we must prove that $w_{k-1} < \lfloor n/2 \rfloor \leq w_k$; this is obvious since $w_{k-1} = \lfloor w_k/2 \rfloor$. If n is odd, $F(n) - F(n-1) = G(\lceil n/2 \rceil) - G(\lfloor n/2 \rfloor)$, so we must prove that $t_{k-1} < \lceil n/2 \rceil \leq t_k$; this is obvious since $t_{k-1} = \lceil w_k/2 \rceil$.

14. By exercise 1.2.4–42, the sum is $n\lceil \lg \frac{3}{4}n \rceil - (w_1 + \cdots + w_j)$ where $w_j < n \leq w_{j+1}$. The latter sum is $w_{j+1} - \lfloor j/2 \rfloor - 1$. We can therefore express $F(n)$ in the form $n\lceil \lg \frac{3}{4}n \rceil - \lfloor 2^{\lfloor \lg(6n) \rfloor}/3 \rfloor + \lfloor \frac{1}{2} \lg(6n) \rfloor$ (and in many other ways).

15. If $\lceil \lg \frac{3}{4}n \rceil = \lg(\frac{3}{4}n) + \theta$, $F(n) = n \lg n - (3 - \lg 3)n + n(\theta + 1 - 2^\theta) + O(\log n)$. If $\lceil \lg n \rceil = \lg n + \theta$, $B(n) = n \lg n - n + n(\theta + 1 - 2^\theta) + O(\log n)$. [Note that $\lg n! = n \lg n - n/(\ln 2) + O(\log n)$; $1/(\ln 2) \approx 1.443$; $3 - \lg 3 \approx 1.415$.]

17. The number of cases with $b_k < a_p < b_{k+1}$ is

$$\binom{m-p+n-k}{m-p}\binom{p-1+k}{p-1},$$

and the number of cases with $a_j < b_q < a_{j+1}$ is

$$\binom{n-q+m-j}{n-q}\binom{q-1+j}{q-1}.$$

18. No, since we are considering only the less efficient branch of the tree below each comparison. One of the more efficient branches might turn out to be harder to handle.

20. Let L be the maximum level on which an external node appears, and let l be the minimum such level. If $L \geq l + 2$, we can remove two nodes from level L and place them below a node at level l; this decreases the external path length by $l + 2L - (L - 1 + 2(l+1)) = L - l - 1 \geq 1$. Conversely, if $L \leq l + 1$, let there be k external nodes on level l and $N - k$ on level $l + 1$, where $0 < k \leq N$. By exercise 2.3.4.5–3, $k2^{-l} + (N-k)2^{-l-1} = 1$; hence $N + k = 2^{l+1}$. The inequalities $2^l \leq N < 2^{l+1}$ now show that $l = \lfloor \lg N \rfloor$; this defines k and yields the external path length (34).

21. Let $r(x)$ be the root of x's right subtree. All subtrees have minimum height if and only if $\lceil \lg t(l(x)) \rceil \leq \lceil \lg t(x) \rceil - 1$ and $\lceil \lg t(r(x)) \rceil \leq \lceil \lg t(x) \rceil - 1$ for all x. The first condition is equivalent to $2t(l(x)) - t(x) \leq 2^{\lceil \lg t(x) \rceil} - t(x)$, and the second condition is equivalent to $t(x) - 2t(l(x)) \leq 2^{\lceil \lg t(x) \rceil} - t(x)$.

22. By exercise 20, the four conditions $\lfloor \lg t(l(x)) \rfloor$, $\lfloor \lg t(r(x)) \rfloor \geq \lfloor \lg t(x) \rfloor - 1$ and $\lceil \lg t(l(x)) \rceil$, $\lceil \lg t(r(x)) \rceil \leq \lceil \lg t(x) \rceil - 1$ are necessary and sufficient. Arguing as in exercise 21, we can prove them equivalent to the stated conditions. [Martin Sandelius, *AMM* **68** (1961), 133–134.] See exercise 33 for a generalization.

23. Multiple list insertion assumes that the keys are uniformly distributed in a known range, so it isn't a "pure comparison" method satisfying the restrictions considered in this section.

24. First proceed as if sorting five elements, until after five comparisons we reach one of the configurations in (6). In the first three cases, complete sorting the five elements in two more comparisons, then insert the sixth element f. In the other case, first compare $f:b$, insert f into the main chain, then insert c. [Picard, *Théorie des Questionnaires*, page 116.]

25. Since $N = 7! = 5040$ and $q = 13$, there would be $8192 - 5040 = 3152$ external nodes on level 12 and $5040 - 3152 = 1888$ on level 13.

26. Ľ. Kollár [*Lecture Notes in Comp. Sci.* **233** (1986), 449–457] has presented an excellent way to verify that the optimum method has an external path length of 62416.

27.

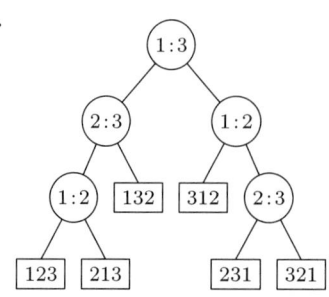

is the *only* way to recognize the two most frequent permutations with two comparisons, even though the first comparison produces a .27/.73 split!

28. Lun Kwan has constructed an 873-line program whose average running time is $38.925u$. Its maximum running time is $43u$; the latter appears to be optimal since it is the time for 7 compares, 7 tests, 6 loads, 5 stores.

29. We must make at least $S(n)$ comparisons, because it is impossible to know whether a permutation is even or odd unless we have made enough comparisons to determine it uniquely. For we can assume that enough comparisons have been made to narrow things down to two possibilities that depend on whether or not a_i is less than a_j, for some i and j; one of the two possibilities is even, the other is odd. [On the other hand there *is* an $O(n)$ algorithm for this problem, which simply counts the number of cycles and uses no comparisons at all; see exercise 5.2.2–2.]

30. Start with an optimal comparison tree of height $S(n)$; repeatedly interchange $i \leftrightarrow j$ in the right subtree of a node labeled $i:j$, from top to bottom. Interpreting the result as a comparison-exchange tree, every terminal node defines a unique permutation that can be sorted by at most $n-1$ more comparison-exchanges (by exercise 5.2.2–2).

[The idea of a comparison-exchange tree is due to T. N. Hibbard.]

31. At least 8 are required, since every tree of height 7 will produce the configuration

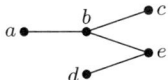

(or its dual) in some branch after 4 steps, with $a \neq 1$. This configuration cannot be sorted in 3 more comparison/exchange operations. On the other hand the following tree achieves the desired bound (and perhaps also the minimum *average* number of comparison/exchanges):

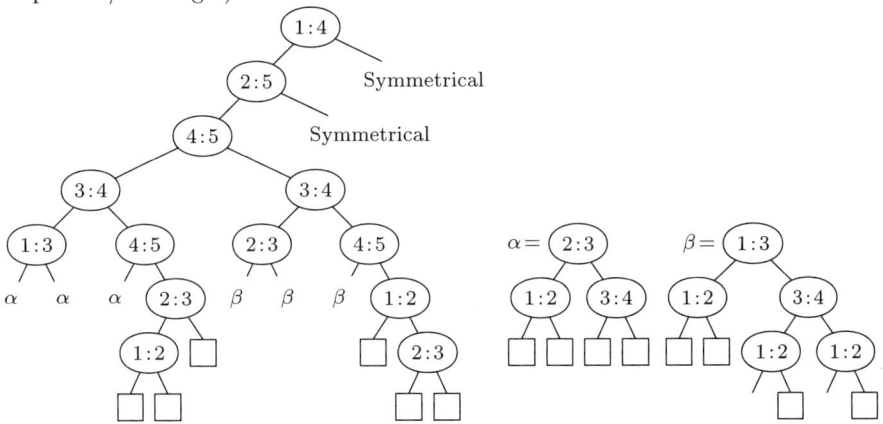

33. Simple operations applied to any tree of order x and resolution 1 can be applied to yield another whose weighted path length is no greater, where all external nodes lie on levels k and $k-1$ for some k, and at most one external node is noninteger. Furthermore, the noninteger external node lies on level k, if such a node is present. The weighted path length of any such tree has the stated value, so this must be minimal. Conversely, if (iv) and (v) hold in any real-valued search tree it is possible to show by induction that the weighted path length has the stated value, since there is a simple formula for the weighted path length of a tree in terms of the weighted path lengths of the two subtrees of the root.

36. [*Mat. Zametki* **4** (1968), 511–518.] See S. Felsner and W. T. Trotter, *Combinatorics, Paul Erdős is Eighty* **1** (1993), 145–157, for a summary of progress on this problem, and for a proof that we can always achieve

$$1 \le T(G_1)/T(G_2) \le \rho,$$

where the constant ρ is slightly less than $8/3$.

SECTION 5.3.2

1. $S(m+n) \le S(m) + S(n) + M(m,n)$.

2. The internal node that is kth in symmetric order corresponds to the comparison $A_1 : B_k$.

3. Strategy $B(1,l)$ is no better than strategy $A(1,l+1)$, and strategy $B'(1,l)$ no better than $A'(1,l-1)$; hence we must solve the recurrence

$$.M.(1,n) = \min_{1 \le j \le n} \max\Big(\max_{1 \le l \le j} (1 + .M.(1,l-1)), \max_{j \le l \le n} (1 + .M.(1,n-l)) \Big), \quad n \ge 1;$$

$$.M.(1,0) = 0.$$

It is not difficult to verify that $\lceil \lg(n+1) \rceil$ satisfies this recurrence.

4. No. [C. Christen, *FOCS* **19** (1978), 259–266.]

6. Strategy $A'(i, i+1)$ can be used when $j = i + 1$, except when $i \le 2$. And we can use strategy $A(i, i+2)$ when $j \ge i + 2$.

7. To insert $k + m$ elements among n others, independently insert k elements and m elements. (When k and m are large, an improved procedure is possible; see exercise 19.)

8, 9. In the following diagrams, $i:j$ denotes the comparison $A_i : B_j$, M_{ij} denotes merging i elements with j in $M(i,j)$ steps, and A denotes sorting the pattern .↗. or .↘. in three steps.

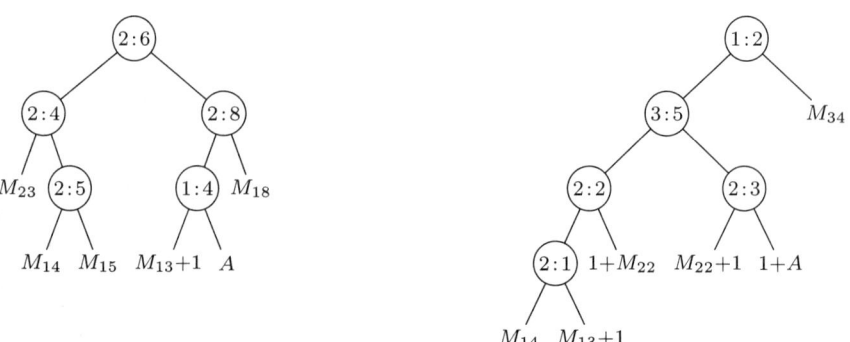

10.

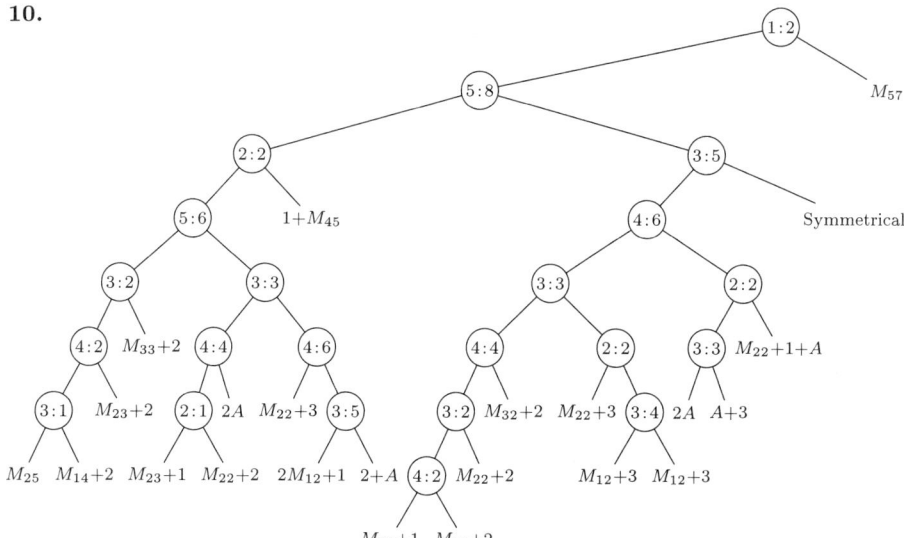

11. Let $n = g_t$ as in the hint. We may assume that $t \geq 6$. Without loss of generality let $A_2 : B_j$ be the first comparison. If $j > g_{t-1}$, the outcome $A_2 < B_j$ will require $\geq t$ more steps. If $j \leq g_{t-1}$, the outcome $A_2 < B_j$ would be no problem, so only the case $A_2 > B_j$ needs study, and we get the most information when $j = g_{t-1}$. If $t = 2k + 1$, we might have to merge A_2 with the $g_t - g_{t-1} = 2^{k-1}$ elements $> B_{g_{t-1}}$, and merge A_1 with the g_{t-1} others, but this requires $k + (k+1) = t$ further steps. On the other hand if $n = g_t - 1$, we could merge A_2 with $2^{k-1} - 1$ elements, then A_1 with n elements, in $(k-1) + (k+1)$ further steps, hence $M(2, g_t - 1) \leq t$.

    The case $t = 2k$ is considerably more difficult; note that $g_t - g_{t-1} \geq 2^{k-2}$. After $A_2 > B_{g_{t-1}}$, suppose we compare $A_1 : B_j$. If $j > 2^{k-1}$ the outcome $A_1 < B_j$ requires $k + (k-1)$ further comparisons (too many). If $j \leq 2^{k-1}$, we can argue as before that $j = 2^{k-1}$ gives most information. After $A_1 > B_{2^{k-1}}$, the next comparisons with A_1 might as well be with $B_{2^{k-1}+2^{k-2}}$, then $B_{2^{k-1}+2^{k-2}+2^{k-3}}$; since $2^{k-1} + 2^{k-2} + 2^{k-3} > g_{t-1}$, the remaining problem is to merge $\{A_1, A_2\}$ with $n - (2^{k-1} + 2^{k-2} + 2^{k-3})$ elements. Of course we needn't make any comparisons with A_1 right away; we could instead compare $A_2 : B_{n+1-j}$. If $j \leq 2^{k-3}$, we consider the case $A_2 < B_{n+1-j}$, while if $j > 2^{k-3}$ we consider $A_2 > B_{n+1-j}$. The latter case requires at least $(k-2) + (k+1)$ more steps. Continuing, we find that the *only* potentially fruitful line is $A_2 > B_{g_{t-1}}$, $A_2 < B_{n+1-2^{k-3}}$, $A_1 > B_{2^{k-1}}$, $A_1 > B_{2^{k-1}+2^{k-2}}$, $A_1 > B_{2^{k-1}+2^{k-2}+2^{k-3}}$, but then we have exactly g_{t-5} elements left! Conversely, if $n = g_t - 1$, this line works. [*Acta Informatica* **1** (1971), 145–158.]

12. The first comparison must be either $\alpha : X_k$ for $1 \leq k \leq i$, or (symmetrically) $\beta : X_{n-k}$ for $1 \leq k \leq j$. In the former case the response $\alpha < X_k$ leaves us with $R_n(k-1, j)$ more comparisons to make; the response $\alpha > X_k$ leaves us with the problem of sorting $\alpha < \beta$, $Y_1 < \cdots < Y_{n-k}$, $\alpha < Y_{i-k+1}$, $\beta > Y_{n-k-j}$, where $Y_r = X_{r-k}$.

13. [*Computers in Number Theory* (New York: Academic Press, 1971), 263–269.]

14. [*SICOMP* **9** (1980), 298–320. The complete solution for $M(4, n)$ was obtained shortly afterwards by J. Schulte Mönting, who also gave a conjectured solution for $M(5, n)$, in *Theor. Comp. Sci.* **14** (1981), 19–37.]

15. Double m until it exceeds n. This involves $\lfloor \lg(n/m) \rfloor + 1$ doublings.

16. All except $(m, n) = (2, 8)$, $(3, 6)$, $(3, 8)$, $(3, 10)$, $(4, 8)$, $(4, 10)$, $(5, 9)$, $(5, 10)$, when it's one over.

17. Assume that $m \leq n$ and let $t = \lg(n/m) - \theta$. Then $\lg \binom{m+n}{m} > \lg n^m - \lg m! \geq m \lg n - (m \lg m - m + 1) = m(t + \theta) + m - 1 = H(m, n) + \theta m - \lfloor 2^\theta m \rfloor \geq H(m, n) + \theta m - 2^\theta m \geq H(m, n) - m$. (The inequality $m! \leq m^m 2^{1-m}$ is a consequence of the fact that $k(m - k) \leq (m/2)^2$ for $1 \leq k < m$.)

19. First merge $\{A_1, \ldots, A_m\}$ with $\{B_2, B_4, \ldots, B_{2\lfloor n/2 \rfloor}\}$. Then we must insert the odd elements B_{2i-1} among a_i of the A's for $1 \leq i \leq \lceil n/2 \rceil$, where $a_1 + a_2 + \cdots + a_{\lceil n/2 \rceil} \leq m$. The latter operation requires at most a_i operations for each i, so at most m more comparisons will finish the job.

20. Apply (12).

22. R. Michael Tanner [*SICOMP* **7** (1978), 18–38] has shown that a "fractile insertion" algorithm makes at most $1.06 \lg \binom{m+n}{m}$ comparisons on the average. Ľ. Kollár [*Computers and Artificial Int.* **5** (1986), 335–344] has studied the average behavior of Algorithm H.

23. The adversary keeps an $n \times n$ matrix X whose entries x_{ij} are initially all 1. When the algorithm asks if $A_i = B_j$, the adversary sets x_{ij} to 0. The answer is "No," unless the permanent of X has just become zero. In the latter case, the adversary answers "Yes" (as it must, lest the algorithm terminate immediately!), and deletes row i and column j from X; the resulting $(n-1) \times (n-1)$ matrix will have a nonzero permanent. The adversary continues in this way until only a 0×0 matrix is left.

If the permanent is about to become zero, we can rearrange rows and columns so that $i = j = 1$ and the matrix has all 1s on the diagonal, yet its permanent vanishes when $x_{11} \leftarrow 0$; then we must have $x_{1k} x_{k1} = 0$ for all $k > 1$. It follows that at least n zeros are deleted when the adversary first answers "Yes," and $n - 1$ the second time, etc. The algorithm will terminate only after receiving n "Yes" answers to nonredundant questions, and after asking at least $n + (n - 1) + \cdots + 1$ questions [*JACM* **19** (1972), 649–659]. A similar argument shows that $n + (n - 1) + \cdots + (n - m + 1)$ questions are needed to determine that $A \subseteq B$ when $|A| = m \leq n = |B|$.

24. The coarse preliminary merge needs at most $m + q - 1$ comparisons, and the subsequent insertions need at most t each. These upper bounds cannot be decreased. So the maximum is the same as for Algorithm H (see (19)).

25. The general problem is as hard as the special case where each x_{ij} is 0 or 1 and $x = \frac{1}{2}$. Then each comparison is equivalent to looking at the bit x_{ij}, and we want to determine the entire matrix by inspecting the fewest bits. Any merging problem (1) corresponds to such a 0–1 matrix if we set $x_{ij} = [A_i > B_{n+1-j}]$. (N. Linial and M. Saks, in *J. Algorithms* **6** (1985), 86–103, attribute this observation to J. Shearer. A similar result connects searching and sorting with respect to any partial order.)

SECTION 5.3.3

1. Player *11* lost to *05*; so *13* was known to be worse than *05*, *11*, and *12*.

2. Let x be the tth largest, and let S be the set of all elements y such that the comparisons made are insufficient to prove either that $x < y$ or $y < x$. There are permutations, consistent with all the comparisons made, in which all elements of S are less than x; for we can stipulate that all elements of S are less than x and embed the resulting partial ordering in a linear ordering. Similarly there are consistent permutations in which all elements of S are greater than x. Hence we don't know the rank of x unless S is empty.

3. An adversary may regard the loser of the first comparison as the worst player of all.

4. Suppose the largest $t-1$ elements are $\{a_1, \ldots, a_{t-1}\}$. Any path in the comparison tree to determine the largest t elements, consistent with this assumption, must include at least $n-t$ comparisons to determine the largest of the remaining $n-t+1$ elements. Such paths have at least $n-t$ binary choice points, so there are at least 2^{n-t} of them. Thus, each of the $n^{\underline{t-1}}$ choices for the largest $t-1$ elements must appear in at least 2^{n-t} leaves of the tree.

5. In fact, $W_t(n) \leq V_t(n) + S(t-1)$, by exercise 2.

6. Let $g(l_1, l_2, \ldots, l_m) = m - 2 + \lceil \lg(2^{l_1} + 2^{l_2} + \cdots + 2^{l_m}) \rceil$, and assume that $f = g$ whenever $l_1 + l_2 + \cdots + l_m + 2m < N$. We shall prove that $f = g$ when $l_1 + l_2 + \cdots + l_m + 2m = N$. We may assume that $l_1 \geq l_2 \geq \cdots \geq l_m$. There are only a few possible ways to make the first comparison:

Strategy A(j, k), for $j < k$. Compare the largest element of group j with the largest of group k. This gives the relation

$$f(l_1, \ldots, l_m) \leq 1 + g(l_1, \ldots, l_{j-1}, l_j + 1, l_{j+1}, \ldots, l_{k-1}, l_{k+1}, \ldots, l_m)$$
$$= g(l_1, \ldots, l_{j-1}, l_j, l_{j+1}, \ldots, l_{k-1}, l_j, l_{k+1}, \ldots, l_m) \geq g(l_1, \ldots, l_m).$$

Strategy B(j, k), for $l_k > 0$. Compare the largest element of group j with one of the small elements of group k. This gives the relation

$$f(l_1, \ldots, l_m) \leq 1 + \max(\alpha, \beta) = 1 + \beta,$$

where

$$\alpha = g(l_1, \ldots, l_{j-1}, l_{j+1}, \ldots, l_m) \leq g(l_1, \ldots, l_m) - 1,$$
$$\beta = g(l_1, \ldots, l_{k-1}, l_k - 1, l_{k+1}, \ldots, l_m) \geq g(l_1, \ldots, l_m) - 1.$$

Strategy C(j, k), for $j \leq k$, $l_j > 0$, $l_k > 0$. Compare a small element from group j with a small element from group k. The corresponding relation is

$$f(l_1, \ldots, l_m) \leq 1 + g(l_1, \ldots, l_{k-1}, l_k - 1, l_{k+1}, \ldots, l_m) \geq g(l_1, \ldots, l_m).$$

The value of $f(l_1, \ldots, l_m)$ is found by taking the minimum right-hand side over all these strategies; hence $f(l_1, \ldots, l_m) \geq g(l_1, \ldots, l_m)$. When $m > 1$, Strategy A$(m-1, m)$ shows that $f(l_1, \ldots, l_m) \leq g(l_1, \ldots, l_m)$, since $g(l_1, \ldots, l_{m-1}, l_m) = g(l_1, \ldots, l_{m-1}, l_{m-1})$ when $l_1 \geq \cdots \geq l_m$. (*Proof:* $\lceil \lg(M + 2^a) \rceil = \lceil \lg(M + 2^b) \rceil$ for $0 \leq a \leq b$, when M is a positive multiple of 2^b.) When $m = 1$, use Strategy C$(1, 1)$.

[S. S. Kislitsyn's paper determined the optimum strategy A$(m-1, m)$ and evaluated $f(l, l, \ldots, l)$ in closed form; the general formula for f and this simplified proof were discovered by Floyd in 1970.]

7. For $j > 1$, if $j + 1$ is in α', c_j is 1 plus the number of comparisons needed to select the next largest element of α'. Similar reasoning applies if $j + 1$ is in α''; and c_1 is always 0, since the tree always looks the same at the end.

8. In other words, is there an extended binary tree with n external nodes such that the sum of the distances to the $t - 1$ farthest internal nodes from the root is less than the corresponding sum for the complete binary tree? The answer is no, since it is not hard to show that the kth largest element of $\mu(\alpha)$ is at least $\lfloor \lg(n - k) \rfloor$ for all α.

9. (All paths use six comparisons, yet the procedure is not optimum for $\bar{V}_3(5)$.)

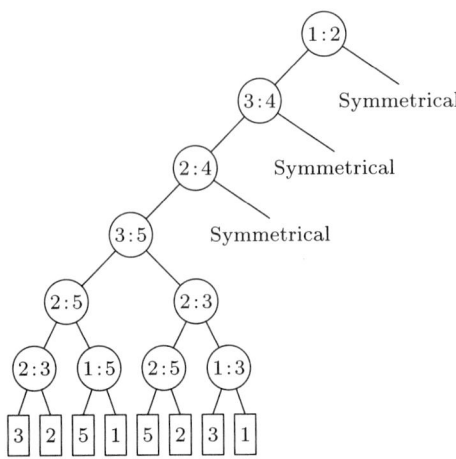

10. (Found manually by trial and error, using exercise 6 to help find fruitful lines.)

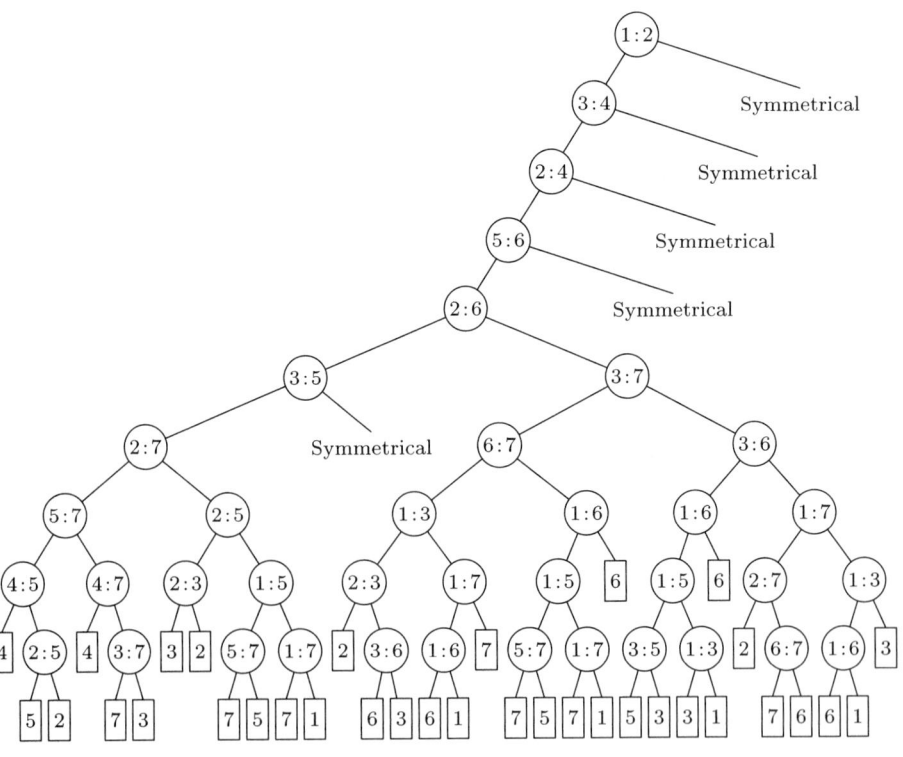

11. See *Information Processing Letters* **3** (1974), 8–12.

12. After discarding the smallest of $\{X_1, X_2, X_3, X_4\}$, we have the configuration •—•
plus $n-3$ isolated elements; the third largest of them can be found in $V_3(n-1)-1$
further steps.

13. After finding the median of the first $f(n)$ elements, say X_j, compare it to each of the others; this splits the elements into approximately $n/2 - k$ less than X_j and $n/2 + k$ greater than X_j, for some k. It remains to find the $|k|$th largest or smallest element of the bigger set, which requires $n/2 + O(|k| \log n)$ further comparisons. The average value of $|k|$ (consider points uniformly distributed in $[0 .. 1]$) is $O(1/\sqrt{n}) + O(n/\sqrt{f(n)})$. Let $T(n)$ be the average number of comparisons when $f(n) = n^{2/3}$; then $T(n) - n = T(n^{2/3}) - n^{2/3} + n/2 + O(n^{2/3})$, and the result follows.

It is interesting to note that when $n = 5$, this method requires only $5\frac{13}{15}$ comparisons on the average, slightly better than the tree of exercise 9.

14. In general, the t largest can be found in $U_t(n) \le V_t(n-1) + 1$ comparisons, by finding the tth largest of $\{X_1, \ldots, X_{n-1}\}$ and comparing it with X_n, because of exercise 2. (Kirkpatrick actually proved that (12) is a lower bound for $U_t(n+1) - 1$. For larger t, an improved bound for $U_t(n)$ was found by J. W. John, *SICOMP* **17** (1988), 640–647.)

15. $\min(t, n+1-t)$. Assuming that $t \le n + 1 - t$, if we don't save each of the first t words when they are first read in, we may have forgotten the tth largest, depending on the subsequent values still unknown to us. Conversely, t locations are sufficient, since we can compare a newly input item with the previous tth largest, storing the register if and only if it is greater.

16. The algorithm starts with $(a, b, c, d) = (n, 0, 0, 0)$ and ends with $(0, 1, 1, n-2)$. If the adversary avoids "surprising" outcomes, the only transitions possible after each comparison are from (a, b, c, d) to itself or to

$$
\begin{aligned}
(a-2,\ b+1,\ c+1,\ d), &\qquad \text{if } a \ge 2; \\
(a-1,\ b,\ c+1,\ d) \text{ or } (a-1,\ b+1,\ c,\ d), &\qquad \text{if } a \ge 1; \\
(a,\ b-1,\ c,\ d+1), &\qquad \text{if } b \ge 2; \\
(a,\ b,\ c-1,\ d+1), &\qquad \text{if } c \ge 2.
\end{aligned}
$$

It follows that $\lceil \frac{3}{2}a \rceil + b + c - 2$ comparisons are needed to get from (a, b, c, d) to $(0, 1, 1, a+b+c+d-2)$. [*Reference: CACM* **15** (1972), 462–464. In *FOCS* **16** (1975), 71–74, Pohl proved that the algorithm also minimizes the *average* number of comparisons.]

17. Use (6) first for the largest, then for the smallest, noting that $\lfloor n/2 \rfloor$ of the comparisons are common to both.

18. $V_t(n) \le 18n - 151$, for all sufficiently large n.

21. Step 0. Build two knockout trees of sizes 2^k and 2^{k-t+1}.

Step j, for $1 \le j \le t$. (At this point we have output the largest $j-1$ elements. The remaining elements, together with a set of dummy placeholders that each equal $-\infty$, now appear in two knockout trees A and B, where A has 2^k leaves and B has 2^{k-t+j}.) Let a be the champion of A, and assume that a has beaten $a_0, a_1, \ldots, a_{k-1}$, where a_l is a champion of 2^l elements. Similarly, let b and $b_0, b_1, \ldots, b_{k-t+j-1}$ be the champion and subchampions of B. If $j = t$, output $\max(a, b)$ and stop. Otherwise, "grow" another level at the bottom of B by introducing 2^{k-t+j} dummies who each have lost their first game to the players of B. (Our strategy will be to merge B into A, if possible, by exchanging it with the subtree A' of A that contains $a_0, a_1, \ldots, a_{k-t+j}$; notice that A', like the newly enlarged B, is a knockout tree with $2^{k-t+j+1}$ leaves.) Compare b to $a_{k-t+j+1}$, then compare the winner to $a_{k-t+j+2}$, etc., until $c = \max(b, a_{k-t+j-1}, \ldots, a_{k-1})$ has been found. Case 1, $b < c$: Output a and interchange

B with A'. Case 2, $b = c$ and $b < a$: Output a and interchange B with A'. Case 3, $b = c$ and $b > a$: Output b. After handling these three cases we are left with (possibly new) knockout trees A and B in which the champion of B has just been output. Remove that element from B and replace it by $-\infty$, making any necessary comparisons to restore the knockout tournament structure (as in tree selection). This completes Step j.

Step 0 makes $2^k - 1 + 2^{k+1-t} - 1$ comparisons, and Step t makes 1. Steps 1, 2, $\ldots$, $t - 1$ each make at most $k - 1$ comparisons, except in Case 2 when there might be k. But whenever Case 2 occurs, we'll save one comparison the next time we're in Case 1 or Case 2, because a_0 will then be $-\infty$. Thus the first $t - 1$ steps make at most $(t - 1)(k - 1) + 1$ comparisons altogether.

By exercise 3 we have $W_t(n) \le n + (t - 1)(k - 1)$ for all $n \le 2^k + 2^{k+1-t}$, when $k \ge t \ge 2$. If $n \ge 2^k + t - 2$, exercise 4 says that $W_t(n) \ge n - t + \lceil \lg(2^k + t - 2) \frac{t-1}{t} \rceil$, which is $n - t + (t - 1)k + 1$ if $t \ge 3$. Thus the method is optimum for $2^k + t - 2 \le n \le 2^k + 2^{k+1-t}$ when $k \ge t \ge 3$. (Also for several smaller values of n, if t is large.)

A similar method, which uses a reserved element instead of $-\infty$ when rebuilding B at the end of steps 1, $\ldots$, $t - 2$ (see the proof of (11)), proves that $V_t(n) \le n + (t-1)(k-1)$ when $n \le 2^k + 2^{k+1-t} + t - 2$ and $k \ge t \ge 3$. [See J. *Algorithms* **5** (1984), 557–578.]

22. In general when $2^r \cdot 2^k < n + 2 - t \le (2^r + 1) \cdot 2^k$ and $t < 2^r \le 2t$, this procedure starting with $t + 1$ knockout trees of size 2^k will yield $\lfloor (t - 1)/2 \rfloor$ fewer comparisons than (11), since at least this many of the comparisons that were used to find the minimum in (ii) can be "reused" in (iii).

23. According to (15), the quantity $V_{\lceil n/2 \rceil}(n)/n$ is bounded below by 2 as $n \to \infty$. But D. Dor and U. Zwick have shown that the actual lower limit is strictly greater than 2, while the upper limit is less than 2.942 [*SICOMP* **28** (1999), 1722–1758; **14** (2001), 312–325]. They also have proved an asymptotic upper bound

$$V_{\alpha n}(n) \le \left(1 + \alpha \lg \frac{1}{\alpha} + O\left(\alpha \log \log \frac{1}{\alpha}\right)\right) n,$$

which is not extremely far from (15) when α is small [*Combinatorica* **16** (1996), 41–58].

24. Since $W_t(n) = n + O(t \log n)$ by Eq. (6), the statement in the hint is surely true when $t \le \sqrt{n/\ln n}$. Suppose that statement holds for n, and let u and v have ranks $t_- = \lfloor t - \sqrt{t \ln n} \rfloor$ and $t_+ = \lceil t + \sqrt{t \ln n} \rceil$ in the first n of $2n$ randomly ordered elements. (The smallest element has rank 1.) Compare the other n elements to v, and compare those less than v also to u. The probability p_s that an element x of rank t in the first n has rank s overall is $\binom{s-1}{t-1}\binom{2n-s}{n-t} / \binom{2n}{n}$. The average value of s is $\sum sp_s = \frac{2n+1}{n+1}t$; this is the average number of elements $< x$, hence the average number of comparisons to u is $\binom{n}{n+1}t_+ = t + O(n \log n)^{1/2}$. Let u and v have ranks s_- and s_+ among all $2n$ elements, and let $T_- = \lfloor 2t - \sqrt{2t \ln 2n} \rfloor$, $T_+ = \lceil 2t + \sqrt{2t \ln 2n} \rceil$. If $s_- \le T_-$ and $s_+ \ge T_+$, we can find the elements of ranks T_- and T_+ by selecting from the $s_+ - s_- + 1$ elements between u and v. We will prove that it's very unlikely to have $s_- > T_-$ or $s_- < T_- - 2\sqrt{n \ln n}$ or $s_+ < T_+$ or $s_+ > T_+ + 2\sqrt{n \ln n}$; therefore $O(n \log n)^{1/2}$ further comparisons will almost always suffice. The hint will follow by induction on n if we can show that "very unlikely" means "with probability $O(n^{-1-\epsilon})$ for all sufficiently large n."

Notice that $p_{s+1}/p_s = s(n - s + t)/(s + 1 - t)(2n - s)$ decreases as s increases from t to $n + t$, and it is ≤ 1 if and only if $s \ge 2n(t - 1)/(n - 1)$; it is $\le 1 - \frac{1}{2}cn^{-1/2} + O(n^{-1})$ when $s = \bar{s}(c) = 2t + ct(n - t)/n^{3/2}$. Therefore the probability that $s \ge \bar{s}(c)$ is $\le 2c^{-1}n^{1/2}p_{\bar{s}(c)}(1 + O(n^{-1/2}))$. Similarly, $p_{s-1}/p_s < 1 - \frac{1}{2}cn^{-1/2} - O(n^{-1})$

when $s = \underline{s}(c) = 2t - 1 - c(t - 1)(n + 1 - t)/n^{3/2}$, so $s \leq \underline{s}(c)$ with probability $\leq 2c^{-1}n^{1/2}p_{\underline{s}(c)}(1 + O(n^{-1/2}))$. In the cases we need, the relevant values of c are $\geq .55n^{3/2}(\ln n)^{1/2}t^{-1/2}(n - t)^{-1}$ for all large n, and Stirling's approximation implies that $p_{\bar{s}(c)}$ and $p_{\underline{s}(c)}$ are both

$$O(n^{1/2}s^{-1/2}(2n - s)^{-1/2})\exp(-2sc^2(n - t)^2/n^3 - 2(2n - s)c^2t^2/n^3)$$
$$\leq O(t^{-1/2}\exp(-4t(n - t)c^2/n^2)) \leq O(t^{-1/2}n^{-1.2}).$$

Thus the probability $O(n^{-1.2}(\log n)^{1/2})$ is indeed very unlikely. [A similar construction appeared in *CACM* **18** (1975), 165–172, but the analysis was incorrect.]

25. Given a selection algorithm and a permutation π of $\{1, \ldots, n\}$, let's charge each comparison $\pi_i : \pi_j$ to π_i if $|\pi_i - t| > |\pi_j - t|$; if $|\pi_i - t| = |\pi_j - t|$, we charge $\frac{1}{2}$ to each. A charge to π_i is called *useful* if $\pi_i < \pi_j \leq t$ or $\pi_i > \pi_j \geq t$; otherwise it's *useless*. Let x_k be the total charge to k. Then the total number of comparisons is $x_1 + \cdots + x_n$. Clearly $x_t = 0$; but $x_k \geq 1$ for all $k \neq t$, because every element other than t has a useful charge. We will prove that $\mathrm{E}\, x_{t+k} + \mathrm{E}\, x_{t-k} \geq 3$ for $0 < k < t$.

Let $A_k(\pi) = $ [the first charge to $t + k$ was useless]. Then $A_k(\pi) = 1 - A_{-k}(\pi')$, where π' is like π but with the elements $(t - k, \ldots, t + k - 1, t + k)$ replaced respectively by $(t - k + 1, \ldots, t + k, t - k)$. Therefore $\mathrm{E}\, A_k + \mathrm{E}\, A_{-k} = 1$.

Let $B_k(\pi) = $ [the first charge to both $t + k$ and $t - k$ was $\frac{1}{2}$, and $t + k$ received its second charge before $t - k$ did]. Also let $C_k(\pi) = [x_{t+k} \geq 2 + A_k]$. Then $B_k(\pi) \leq C_k(\pi')$, where π' is like π but with the elements $(t - k, t - k + 1, \ldots, t + k - 1)$ replaced by $(t + k - 1, t - k, \ldots, t + k - 2)$. Similarly, $B_{-k}(\pi) \leq C_{-k}(\pi'')$, where π'' is obtained from π by changing $(t - k + 1, \ldots, t + k - 1, t + k)$ to $(t - k + 2, \ldots, t + k, t - k + 1)$. It follows that $\mathrm{E}\, B_k \leq \mathrm{E}\, C_k$ and $\mathrm{E}\, B_{-k} \leq \mathrm{E}\, C_{-k}$.

The proof is completed by observing that $x_{t-k} + x_{t+k} \geq 2 + A_k + A_{-k} - B_k - B_{-k} + C_k + C_{-k}$. [See *JACM* **36** (1989), 270–279, for further results.]

The upper bound in (17) also has a matching lower bound: Andrew and Frances Yao proved that $\bar{V}_t(n) \geq n + \frac{1}{2}t(\ln\ln n - \ln t - 9)$ for $t > 1$ and $n \geq (8t)^{18t}$, in *SICOMP* **11** (1982), 428–447.

26. (a) Let the vertices of the two types of components be designated a; $b < c$. The adversary acts as follows on nonredundant comparisons: Case 1, $a : a'$, make an arbitrary decision. Case 2, $x : b$, say that $x > b$; all future comparisons $y : b$ with this particular b will result in $y > b$, otherwise the comparisons are decided by an adversary for $U_t(n - 1)$, yielding $\geq 2 + U_t(n - 1)$ comparisons in all. This reduction will be abbreviated "let $b = \min; 2 + U_t(n - 1)$." Case 3, $x : c$, let $c = \max; 2 + U_{t-1}(n - 1)$.

(b) Let the new types of vertices be designated $d_1, d_2 < e$; $f < g < h > i$. Case 1, $a : a'$ or $c : c'$, arbitrary decision. Case 2, $a : c$, say that $a < c$. Case 3, $x : b$, let $b = \min$; $2 + U_t(n - 1)$. Case 4, $x : d$, let $d = \min$; $2 + U_t(n - 1)$. Case 5, $x : e$, let $e = \max$; $3 + U_{t-1}(n-1)$. Case 6, $x : f$, let $f = \min$; $2 + U_t(n-1)$. Case 7, $x : g$, let f and $g = \min$; $3 + U_t(n - 2)$. Case 8, $x : h$, let $h = \max$; $3 + U_{t-1}(n - 1)$. Case 9, $x : i$, let $i = \min$; $2 + U_t(n - 1)$.

(c) For $t = 1$ we have $U_t(n) = n - 1$, so the inequality holds. For $1 < t \leq n/2 - 1$, use induction and (b). For $t = (n - 1)/2$, use induction and (a). For $t = n/2$, $U_t(n - 1) = U_{t-1}(n - 1)$; use induction and (a).

27. (a) The height h satisfies $2^h \geq \sum_l 1 \geq \sum_l \Pr(l)/p = 1/p$.

(b) If $r \leq t$, we reach A3 after at least $n - |S_0| - |T_0| = n - |S_0| - r$ flips. The tth largest element will be either the smallest or largest element of Q, and the elements of

Q have not yet been compared to each other, so we will need at least $|Q| - 1$ more flips. If $|S_0| < q$ we have $|Q| = r$, and if not we have $|Q| \geq |S_0| - |C(y_0)| + 1 \geq |S_0| - (q - r) + 1$; so in both cases at least $n - q$ flips will be made. There are $n + 1 - t$ sets T containing the $t - 1$ largest elements determined by a given leaf, and for every such T the probability of reaching that leaf is either zero or $2^{-f} / \binom{n}{t}$, where $f \geq n - q$ is the number of flips corresponding to T. [This adversary is implicit in the paper of Bent and John, *STOC* **17** (1985), 213–216.]

(c) If $t < r$, change t to $n + 1 - t$; this will make $t \geq r$ when r maximizes the right-hand side, since r will be $O(\sqrt{n})$. If it is possible to reach A3 with $|C(y)| > q - r$ for all $y \in T_0$, the algorithm will make $n - 1$ comparisons to relate the tth largest element to all the others, in addition to at least $(r - 1)(q - r + 1)$ comparisons that it made between S and $T \setminus \{y_0\}$.

(d) Choose $r = \lceil \sqrt{m} \rceil$ and $q = 2r - 2$. (It is slightly better to let $q = r + \lfloor \sqrt{m} + \frac{1}{2} \rfloor - 2$; this choice maximizes the lower bound derived in (c).)

SECTION 5.3.4

1. (When $m = 2k - 1$ is odd it is best to have v_k followed by v_{k+1}, w_{k+1}, v_{k+2}, $\ldots$ instead of by w_{k+1}, v_{k+1}, w_{k+2}, $\ldots$ in the diagram. This change is valid because the swapped lines are being compared to each other.)

(3,5) odd-even merge

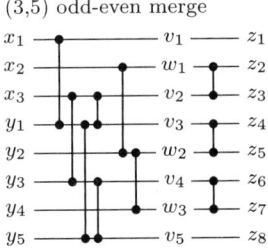

Pratt eight-sort

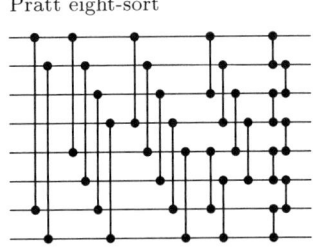

2. The increment h needs $2 - \lceil 2h \geq n \rceil$ levels; see the diagram above for $n = 8$.

3. $C(m, m-1) = C(m, m) - 1$, for $m \geq 1$.

4. If $\hat{T}(6) = 4$, there would be three comparators acting at each time, since $\hat{S}(6) = 12$. But then removing the bottom line and its four comparators would give $\hat{S}(5) \leq 8$, a contradiction. [The same argument yields $\hat{T}(7) = \hat{T}(8) = 6$. Ian Parberry has shown by exhaustive computer search that $\hat{T}(9) = \hat{T}(10) = 7$; see *Math. Systems Theory* **24** (1991), 101–116.]

5. Let $f(n) = f(\lceil n/2 \rceil) + 1 + \lceil \lg \lceil n/2 \rceil \rceil$, if $n \geq 2$. Then $f(n) = (1 + \lceil \lg n \rceil) \lceil \lg n \rceil / 2$ by induction on n.

6. We may assume that each stage makes $\lfloor n/2 \rfloor$ comparisons (extra comparisons can't hurt). Since $\hat{T}(6) = 5$, it suffices to show that $T(5) = 5$. After two stages when $n = 5$, we cannot avoid the partial orderings ⤻ or ⤞, which cannot be sorted in two more stages.

7. Assume that the input keys are $\{1, 2, \ldots, 10\}$. The key fact is that after the first 16 comparators, lines 2, 3, 4, and 6 cannot contain 8 or 9, nor can they contain both 6 and 7. (Notice that the modified network has delay 8.)

8. Straightforward generalization of Theorem F.

9. $\hat{M}(3,3) \geq \hat{S}(6) - 2\hat{S}(3)$; $\hat{M}(4,4) \geq \hat{S}(8) - 2\hat{S}(4)$; $\hat{M}(5,5) \geq 2\hat{M}(2,3) + 3$ by exercise 8; and $\hat{M}(2,3) \geq \hat{S}(5) - \hat{S}(2) - \hat{S}(3)$. Similarly $\hat{M}(3,4) = 8$. But what are $\hat{M}(3,5)$ and $\hat{M}(4,5)$?

10. The hint follows by the method of proof in Theorem Z. Hence the number of 0s in the even subsequence minus the number of 0s in the odd subsequence is ± 1 or 0.

11. (Solution by M. W. Green.) The network is symmetric in the sense that, whenever z_i is compared to z_j, there is a corresponding comparison of $z_{2^t-1-j} : z_{2^t-1-i}$. Any symmetric network capable of sorting a sequence $\langle z_0, \ldots, z_{2^t-1} \rangle$ will also sort the sequence $\langle -z_{2^t-1}, \ldots, -z_0 \rangle$.

Batcher has observed that the network will actually sort any cyclic shift $\langle z_j, z_{j+1}, \ldots, z_{2^t-1}, z_0, \ldots, z_{j-1} \rangle$ of a bitonic sequence. This is a consequence of the 0–1 principle.

[These results do *not* hold for bitonic sorters when the order is not a power of 2. For example, Fig. 52 does not sort $\langle 0, 0, 0, 0, 0, 1, 0 \rangle$. Batcher's original definition of bitonic sequences was more complicated and less useful than the definition adopted here.]

12. $x \vee y$ is (consider 0–1 sequences), but not $x \wedge y$ (consider $\langle 3, 1, 4, 5 \rangle \wedge \langle 6, 7, 8, 2 \rangle$).

13. A perfect shuffle has the effect of replacing z_i by z_j, where the binary representation of j is that of i rotated cyclically to the right one place (see exercise 3.4.2–13). Consider shuffling the comparators instead of the lines; then the first column of comparators acts on the pairs $z[i]$ and $z[i \oplus 2^{r-1}]$, the next column on $z[i]$ and $z[i \oplus 2^{r-2}]$, ..., the tth column on $z[i]$ and $z[i \oplus 1]$, the $(t+1)$st column on $z[i]$ and $z[i \oplus 2^{r-1}]$ again, etc. Here $\oplus$ denotes exclusive-or on the binary representation. This shows that Fig. 57 is equivalent to Fig. 56; after s stages we have groups of 2^s elements that are alternatively sorted and reverse-sorted.

C. G. Plaxton and T. Suel [*Math. Systems Theory* **27** (1994), 491–508] have shown that any such network requires at least $\Omega((\log n)^2/\log \log n)$ levels of delay.

14. (a) Let $y_{i_s} = x_{j_s}$, $y_{j_s} = x_{i_s}$, $y_k = x_k$ for $i_s \neq k \neq j_s$; then $y\alpha^s = x\alpha$. (b) This is obvious unless the set $\{i_s, j_s, i_t, j_t\}$ has only three distinct elements; suppose that $i_s = i_t$. Then if $s < t$ the first $s - 1$ comparators have (i_s, j_s, j_t) replaced, respectively, by (j_s, j_t, i_s) in both $(\alpha^s)^t$ and $(\alpha^t)^s$. (c) $(\alpha^s)^s = \alpha$, and $\alpha^1 = \alpha$, so we can assume that $s_1 > s_2 > \cdots > s_k > 1$. (d) Let $\beta = \alpha[i:j]$; then $g_\beta(x_1, \ldots, x_n) = (\bar{x}_i \vee x_j) \wedge (g_\alpha(x_1, \ldots, x_i, \ldots, x_j, \ldots, x_n) \vee g_\alpha(x_1, \ldots, x_j, \ldots, x_i, \ldots, x_n))$. Iterating this identity yields the result. (e) $f_\alpha(x) = 1$ if and only if no path in G_α goes from i to j where $x_i > x_j$. If α is a sorting network, the conjugates of α are also; and $f_\alpha(x) = 0$ for all x with $x_i > x_{i+1}$. Take $x = e^{(i)}$; this shows that G has an arc from i to k_1 for some $k_1 \neq i$. If $k_1 \neq i+1$, $x = e^{(i)} \vee e^{(k_1)}$ shows that G has an arc from i or k_1 to k_2 for some $k_2 \notin \{i, k_1\}$. If $k_2 \neq i+1$, continue in the same way until finding a path in G from i to $i+1$. Conversely if α is not a sorting network, let x be a vector with $x_i > x_{i+1}$ and $g_\alpha(x) = 1$. Some conjugate α' has $f_{\alpha'}(x) = 1$, so $G_{\alpha'}$ can have no path from i to $i+1$. [In general, $(x\alpha)_i \leq (x\alpha)_j$ for all x if and only if $G_{\alpha'}$ has an oriented path from i to j for all α' conjugate to α.]

15. $[1:4][3:2][1:3][2:4][2:3]$.

16. The process clearly terminates. Each execution of step T2 has the effect of interchanging the i_qth and j_qth outputs, so the result of the algorithm is to permute the output lines in some way. Since the resulting (standard) network makes no change to the input $\langle 1, 2, \ldots, n \rangle$, the output lines must have been returned to their original position.

17. Make the network standard by the algorithm of exercise 16; then by considering the input sequence $\langle 1, 2, \ldots, n \rangle$, we see that standard selection networks must take the

t largest elements into the t highest-numbered lines; and a $\hat{V}_t(n)$ network must take the tth largest into line $n + 1 - t$. Apply the zero-one principle.

18. The proof in Theorem A shows that $\hat{V}_t(n) \geq (n - t)\lceil \lg(t + 1)\rceil + \lceil \lg t \rceil$.

19. The network $[1\!:\!n][2\!:\!n]\dots[1\!:\!3][2\!:\!3]$ selects the smallest two elements with $2n - 4$ comparators; add $[1\!:\!2]$ for $\hat{V}_2(n)$. The lower bounds come from the proof of Theorem A (see the previous answer).

20. (a) First note that $\hat{V}_3(n) \geq \hat{V}_3(n - 1) + 2$ when $n \geq 4$: By symmetry the first comparator may be assumed to be $[1\!:\!n]$; after this must come a network to select the third largest of $\langle x_2, x_3, \dots, x_n \rangle$, and another comparator touching line 1. On the other hand, $\hat{V}_3(5) \leq 7$, since four comparators find the min and max of $\{x_1, x_2, x_3, x_4\}$, then we sort the other three.

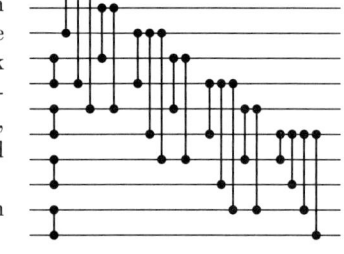

(b) A subtle construction by M. W. Green, shown for $n = 11$, does the job. (Equality probably holds.)

21. False; consider, for example, the two networks $[1\!:\!2][3\!:\!4][2\!:\!3][1\!:\!4][1\!:\!2][3\!:\!4]$ and $[1\!:\!2][3\!:\!4][2\!:\!3][3\!:\!4][1\!:\!4][1\!:\!2][3\!:\!4]$. (However, N. G. de Bruijn proved in *Discrete Math.* **9** (1974), 337, that new comparators do not mess up sorting networks that are *primitive* in the sense of exercise 36.)

22. (a) By induction on the length of α, since $x_i \leq y_i$ and $x_j \leq y_j$ implies that $x_i \wedge x_j \leq y_i \wedge y_j$ and $x_i \vee x_j \leq y_i \vee y_j$. (b) By induction on the length of α, since $(x_i \wedge x_j)(y_i \wedge y_j) + (x_i \vee x_j)(y_i \vee y_j) \geq x_i y_i + x_j y_j$. [Consequently $\nu(x \wedge y) \leq \nu(x\alpha \wedge y\alpha)$, an observation due to W. Shockley.]

23. Let $x_k = 1$ if and only if $p_k \geq j$, $y_k = 1$ if and only if $p_k > j$; then $(x\alpha)_k = 1$ if and only if $(p\alpha)_k \geq j$, etc.

24. The formula for l_i' is obvious and for l_j' take $z = x \wedge y$ as in the hint and observe that $(z\alpha)_i = (z\alpha)_j = 0$ by exercise 21. Adding additional 1s to z shows the existence of a permutation p with $(p\alpha')_j \leq \zeta(z)$, by exercise 23. The relations for u_i' and u_j' follow by reversing the order.

25. (Solution by H. Shapiro.) Let p and q be permutations with $(p\alpha)_k = l_k$ and $(q\alpha)_k = u_k$. We can transform p into q by repeatedly interchanging pairs $(i, i + 1)$ of adjacent integers; such an interchange in the input affects the kth output by at most ± 1.

26. There is a one-to-one correspondence that takes the element $\langle p_1, \dots, p_n \rangle$ of $P_n \alpha$ into the "covering sequence" $x^{(0)}$ covers $x^{(1)}$ covers $\dots$ covers $x^{(n)}$, where the $x^{(i)}$ are in $D_n \alpha$; in this correspondence, $x^{(i-1)} = x^{(i)} \vee e^{(j)}$ if and only if $p_j = i$. For example, $\langle 3, 1, 4, 2 \rangle$ corresponds to the sequence $\langle 1, 1, 1, 1 \rangle$ covers $\langle 1, 0, 1, 1 \rangle$ covers $\langle 1, 0, 1, 0 \rangle$ covers $\langle 0, 0, 1, 0 \rangle$ covers $\langle 0, 0, 0, 0 \rangle$. [Andrew Yao observes that consequently it suffices to test a sorting network on $\binom{n}{\lfloor n/2 \rfloor} - 1$ suitably chosen permutations. For example, any 4-network that sorts $\langle 4, 1, 2, 3 \rangle$, $\langle 3, 1, 4, 2 \rangle$, $\langle 3, 4, 1, 2 \rangle$, $\langle 2, 4, 1, 3 \rangle$, and $\langle 2, 3, 4, 1 \rangle$ sorts everything. See exercise 6.5–1; see also exercise 56.]

27. The principle holds because $(x\alpha)_i$ is the ith smallest element of x. If x and y denote different columns of a matrix whose rows are sorted, so that $x_i \leq y_i$ for all i, and if $x\alpha$ and $y\alpha$ denote the result of sorting the columns, the stated principle shows that $(x\alpha)_i \leq (y\alpha)_i$ for all i, since we can choose i elements of x in the same rows as any i given elements of y. [We have used this principle to prove the invariance property of shellsort, Theorem 5.2.1K. Further exploitation of the idea appears in an interesting paper by David Gale and R. M. Karp, *J. Computer and System Sciences* **6** (1972), 103–115. The fact that column sorting does not mess up sorted rows was apparently first observed in connection with the manipulation of tableaux; see Hermann Boerner, *Darstellung von Gruppen* (Springer, 1955), Chapter V, §5.]

28. If $\{x_{i_1}, \ldots, x_{i_t}\}$ are the t largest elements, then $x_{i_1} \wedge \ldots \wedge x_{i_t}$ is the tth largest. If $\{x_{i_1}, \ldots, x_{i_t}\}$ are *not* the t largest, then $x_{i_1} \wedge \ldots \wedge x_{i_t}$ is *less than* the tth largest.

29. $\langle x_1 \wedge y_1, (x_2 \wedge y_1) \vee (x_1 \wedge y_2), (x_3 \wedge y_1) \vee (x_2 \wedge y_2) \vee (x_1 \wedge y_3), y_1 \vee (x_3 \wedge y_2) \vee (x_2 \wedge y_3) \vee (x_1 \wedge y_4), y_2 \vee (x_3 \wedge y_3) \vee (x_2 \wedge y_4) \vee (x_1 \wedge y_5), y_3 \vee (x_3 \wedge y_4) \vee (x_2 \wedge y_5) \vee x_1, y_4 \vee (x_3 \wedge y_5) \vee x_2, y_5 \vee x_3 \rangle$.

30. Applying the distributive and associative laws reduces any formula to $\vee$'s of $\wedge$'s; then the commutative, idempotent, and absorption laws lead to canonical form. The S_i are precisely those sets S such that the formula is 1 when $x_j = [j \in S]$ while the formula is 0 when $x_j = [j \in S']$ for any proper subset S' of S.

31. $\delta_4 = 166$. R. Church [*Duke Math. J.* **6** (1940), 732–734] found $\delta_5 = 7579$, M. Ward [*Bull. Amer. Math. Soc.* **52** (1946), 423] found $\delta_6 = 7828352$, and the next values are $\delta_7 = 2414682040996$, $\delta_8 = 56130437228687557907786$ [R. Church, *Notices Amer. Math. Soc.* **12** (1965), 724; J. Berman and P. Köhler, *Mitteilungen Math. Seminar Gießen* **121** (1976), 103–124; D. Wiedemann, *Order* **8** (1991), 5–6]. The asymptotic formula $\delta_{2m} = \exp\left(\binom{2m-1}{m} \ln 2 + \binom{2m}{m+1}/2^{m+1} + \frac{1}{16}(m-1)\sqrt{m/\pi} + O(m^{-1/2})\right)$ has been established by A. D. Korshunov and A. A. Sapozhenko, with a similar formula for δ_{2m+1}; see *Russian Math. Surveys* **58** (2003), 929–1001, Theorem 1.8.

32. G_{t+1} is also the set of all strings $\theta\psi$ where θ and ψ are in G_t and $\theta \subseteq \psi$ as vectors of 0s and 1s. It follows that G_t is the set of all strings $z_0 \ldots z_{2^t-1}$ of 0s and 1s having the property that $z_i \le z_j$ whenever the binary representation of i is "$\subseteq$" the binary representation of j in the 0–1 vector sense. Each element $z_0 \ldots z_{2^t-1}$ of G_t, except $00\ldots0$ and $11\ldots1$, represents a $\wedge$–$\vee$ function $f(x_1, \ldots, x_t)$ from D_{2^t} into $\{0,1\}$, under the correspondence $f(x_1, \ldots, x_t) = z_{(x_1 \ldots x_t)_2}$.

33. If such a network existed we would have $(x_1 \wedge x_2) \vee (x_2 \wedge x_3) \vee (x_3 \wedge x_4) = f(x_1 \wedge x_2, x_1 \vee x_2, x_3, x_4)$ or $f(x_1 \wedge x_3, x_2, x_1 \vee x_3, x_4)$ or $\ldots$ or $f(x_1, x_2, x_3 \wedge x_4, x_3 \vee x_4)$ for some function f. The choices $\langle x_1, x_2, x_3, x_4 \rangle = \langle x, \bar{x}, 1, 0 \rangle$, $\langle x, 0, \bar{x}, 1 \rangle$, $\langle x, 1, 0, \bar{x} \rangle$, $\langle 1, x, \bar{x}, 0 \rangle$, $\langle 1, x, 0, \bar{x} \rangle$, $\langle 0, 1, x, \bar{x} \rangle$ show that no such f exists.

34. Yes; after proving this, you are ready to tackle the network for $n = 16$ in Fig. 49 (unless you simply checked all 2^n bit vectors by brute force using Theorem Z).

35. Otherwise the permutation in which only i and $i+1$ are misplaced would never be sorted. Let D_k be the number of comparators $[i:i+k]$ in a standard sorting network. Then $D_1 + 2D_2 + D_3 \ge 2(n-2)$ since there must be two comparators from $\{i, i+1\}$ to $\{i+2, i+3\}$, for $1 \le i \le n-3$, as well as $[1:2]$ and $[n-1:n]$. Similarly $D_1 + 2D_2 + \cdots + kD_k + (k-1)D_{k+1} + \cdots + D_{2k-1} \ge k(n-k)$, a formula suggested by J. M. Pollard. We can also prove that $2D_1 + D_2 \ge 3n-4$: If we strike out the first comparators of the form $[j:j+1]$ for all j there must be at least one more comparator lying within $\{i, i+1, i+2\}$, for $1 \le i \le n-2$. Similarly $kD_1 + (k-1)D_2 + \cdots + D_k \ge S(k+1)(n-k) + k(k-1)$.

36. (a) Each adjacent comparator reduces the number of inversions by 0 or 1, and $\langle n, n-1, \ldots, 1 \rangle$ has $\binom{n}{2}$ inversions. (b) Let $\alpha = \beta[p:p+1]$, and argue by induction on the length of α. If $p = i$, then $j > p+1$, and $(x\beta)_p > (x\beta)_j$, $(x\beta)_{p+1} > (x\beta)_j$; hence $(y\beta)_p > (y\beta)_j$ and $(y\beta)_{p+1} > (y\beta)_j$. If $p = i - 1$, then either $(x\beta)_p$ or $(x\beta)_{p+1}$ is $> (x\beta)_j$; hence either $(y\beta)_p$ or $(y\beta)_{p+1}$ is $> (y\beta)_j$. If $p = j - 1$ or j, the arguments are similar. For other p the argument is trivial.

Notes: If α is a primitive sorting network, so is α^R (the comparators in reverse order). For generalizations and another proof of (c), see N. G. de Bruijn, *Discrete Mathematics* **9** (1974), 333–339; *Indagationes Math.* **45** (1983), 125–132. In the latter paper, de Bruijn proved that a primitive network sorts all permutations of the multiset $\{n_1 \cdot 1, \ldots, n_m \cdot m\}$ if and only if it sorts the single permutation $m^{c_m} \ldots 1^{c_1}$. The relation $x \preceq y$, defined for permutations x and y to mean that there exists a standard network α such that $x = y\alpha$, is called *Bruhat order*; the analogous relation restricted to primitive α is *weak Bruhat order* (see the answer to exercise 5.2.1–44).

37. It suffices to show that if each comparator is replaced by an *interchange* operation we obtain a "reflection network" that transforms $\langle x_1, \ldots, x_n \rangle$ into $\langle x_n, \ldots, x_1 \rangle$. But in this interpretation it is not difficult to trace the route of x_k. Note that the permutation $\pi = (1\ 2)(3\ 4) \ldots (2n{-}1\ 2n)(2\ 3)(4\ 5) \ldots (2n{-}2\ 2n{-}1) = (1\ 3\ 5\ \ldots\ 2n{-}1\ 2n\ 2n{-}2\ \ldots\ 2)$ satisfies $\pi^n = (1\ 2n)(2\ 2n{-}1) \ldots (n{-}1\ n)$. The odd-even transposition sort was mentioned briefly by H. Seward in 1954; it has been discussed by A. Grasselli [*IRE Trans.* **EC-11** (1962), 483] and by Kautz, Levitt, and Waksman [*IEEE Trans.* **C-17** (1968), 443–451]. The reflective property of this network was introduced much earlier by H. E. Dudeney in one of his "frog puzzles" [*Strand* **46** (1913), 352, 472; *Amusements in Mathematics* (1917), 193].

38. Insert the elements $i_1, \ldots, i_N$ into an initially empty tableau using Algorithm 5.1.4I but with one crucial change: Set $P_{ij} \leftarrow x_i$ in step I3 only if $x_i \ne P_{i(j-1)}$. It can be proved that x_i will equal $P_{i(j-1)}$ in that step only if $x_i + 1 = P_{ij}$, when the inputs $i_1 \ldots i_N$ define a primitive sorting network. (The parenthesized assertions of the algorithm need to be modified.) After i_j has been inserted into P, set $Q_{st} \leftarrow j$ as in Theorem 5.1.4A. After N steps, the tableau P will always contain $(r, r{+}1, \ldots, n{-}1)$ in row r, while Q will be a tableau from which the sequence $i_1 \ldots i_N$ can be reconstructed by working backwards.

For example, when $n = 6$ the sequence $i_1 \ldots i_N = 4\,1\,3\,2\,4\,3\,5\,4\,3\,1\,2\,3\,5\,1\,4$ corresponds to

$$P = \begin{array}{|c|c|c|c|c|}
\hline 1 & 2 & 3 & 4 & 5 \\ \hline
\end{array}$$

$$
P = \begin{array}{ccccc}
\boxed{1}\boxed{2}\boxed{3}\boxed{4}\boxed{5} \\
\boxed{2}\boxed{3}\boxed{4}\boxed{5} \\
\boxed{3}\boxed{4}\boxed{5} \\
\boxed{4}\boxed{5} \\
\boxed{5}
\end{array}
\quad , \quad
Q = \begin{array}{cccc}
\boxed{1}\boxed{4}\boxed{5}\boxed{8}\boxed{13} \\
\boxed{2}\boxed{6}\boxed{7}\boxed{15} \\
\boxed{3}\boxed{9}\boxed{12} \\
\boxed{10}\boxed{11} \\
\boxed{14}
\end{array} \quad .
$$

The transpose of Q corresponds to the complementary network $[n{-}i_1{:}n{-}i_1{+}1] \ldots [n{-}i_N{:}n{-}i_N{+}1]$.

References: A. Lascoux and M. P. Schützenberger, *Comptes Rendus Acad. Sci.* (I) **295** (Paris, 1982), 629–633; R. P. Stanley, *Eur. J. Combinatorics* **5** (1984), 359–372; P. H. Edelman and C. Greene, *Advances in Math.* **63** (1987), 42–99. The diagrams of primitive sorting networks also correspond to arrangements of pseudolines and to other abstractions of two-dimensional convexity; see D. E. Knuth, *Lecture Notes in Comp. Sci.* **606** (1992), for further information.

39. When $n = 8$, for example, such a network must include the comparators shown here; all other comparators are ineffective on 10101010. Then lines $\lceil n/3 \rceil \mathinner{.\,.} \lceil 2n/3 \rceil = 3 \mathinner{.\,.} 6$ sort 4 elements, as in exercise 37. (This exercise is based on an idea of David B. Wilson.)

Notes: There is a one-to-one correspondence between minimal-length primitive networks that sort a given bit string and Young tableaux whose shape is bounded by the zigzag path defined by that bit string. Thus, exercise 38 yields a one-to-one correspondence between primitive networks of $\binom{n/2+1}{2}$ comparators that sort $(10)^{n/2}$ and primitive networks of $\binom{n/2+1}{2}$ comparators that sort $n/2 + 1$ arbitrary numbers. If a primitive network sorts the bit string $1^{n/2}0^{n/2}$, we can make a stronger statement: All of its "halves," consisting of the subnetworks on lines k through $k+n/2$ inclusive, are sorting networks, for $1 \le k \le n/2$. (See also de Bruijn's theorem, cited in the answer to exercise 36.)

40. This follows by applying the tail inequalities to the interesting construction in Proposition 7 of a paper by H. Rost, *Zeitschrift für Wahrscheinlichkeitstheorie und verwandte Gebiete* **58** (1981), 41–53, setting $b = \frac{1}{2}$, $a = \frac{1}{4}$, and $t = 4n + \sqrt{n}\,\ln n$.

Experiments show that the expected time to reach *any* primitive sorting network — not necessarily the bubble sort — is very nearly $2n^2$. Curiously, R. P. Stanley and S. V. Fomin have proved that if the comparators $[i_k:i_k+1]$ are chosen nonuniformly in such a way that $i_k = j$ occurs with probability $j/\binom{n}{2}$, the corresponding expected time comes to exactly $\binom{n}{2}H_{\binom{n}{2}}$.

42. There must exist a path of length $\lceil \lg n \rceil$ or more, from some input to the largest output (consider m_n in Theorem A); when that input is set to ∞, the comparators on this path have a predetermined behavior, and the remaining network must be an $(n-1)$-sorter. [*IEEE Trans.* **C-21** (1972), 612–613.]

45. After l levels the input x_1 can be in at most 2^l different places. After merging is complete, x_1 can be in $n + 1$ different places.

46. [*J. Algorithms* **3** (1982), 79–88; the following alternative proof is due to V. S. Grinberg.] We may assume that $1 \le m \le n$ and that every stage makes m comparisons. Let $l = \lceil (n-m)/2 \rceil$ and suppose we are merging $x_1 \le \cdots \le x_m$ with $y_1 \le \cdots \le y_n$. An adversary can force $\lceil \lg(m+n) \rceil$ stages as follows: In the first stage some x_j is compared to an element y_k where we have either $k \le l$ or $k \ge l + m$. The adversary decides that $x_{j-1} < y_1$ and $x_{j+1} > y_n$; also that $x_j > y_k$ if $k \le l$, $x_j < y_k$ if $k \ge l+m$. The remaining task is essentially to merge x_j with either $y_{k+1} \le \cdots \le y_n$ and $k \le l$ or $y_1 \le \cdots \le y_{k-1}$ and $k \ge l + m$; so at least $\min(n-l+1, l+m) = \lceil (m+n)/2 \rceil$ outcomes remain. At least $\lceil \lg \lceil (m+n)/2 \rceil \rceil = \lceil \lg(m+n) \rceil - 1$ subsequent stages are therefore necessary.

48. Let u be the smallest element of $(x\alpha)_j$, and let $y^{(0)}$ be any vector in D_n such that $(y^{(0)})_k = 0$ implies $(x\alpha)_k$ contains an element $\le u$, $(y^{(0)})_k = 1$ implies $(x\alpha)_k$ contains an element $> u$. If $\alpha = \beta[p:q]$, it is possible to find a vector $y^{(1)}$ satisfying the same conditions but with α replaced by β, and such that $y^{(1)}[p:q] = y^{(0)}$. Starting with $(y^{(0)})_i = 1$, $(y^{(0)})_j = 0$, we eventually reach $y = y^{(r)}$ satisfying the desired condition.

G. Baudet and D. Stevenson have observed that exercises 37 and 48 combine to yield a simple sorting method with $(n \ln n)/k + O(n)$ comparison cycles on k processors: First sort k subfiles of size $\le \lceil n/k \rceil$, then merge them in k passes using the "odd-even transposition merge" of order k. [*IEEE Trans.* **C-27** (1978), 84–87.]

49. Both $(x \bigvee y) \bigvee z$ and $x \bigvee (y \bigvee z)$ represent the largest m elements of the multiset $x \uplus y \uplus z$; $(x \bigwedge y) \bigwedge z$ and $x \bigwedge (y \bigwedge z)$ represent the smallest m. If $x = y = z = \{0,1\}$, $(x \bigwedge z) \bigvee (y \bigwedge z) = (x \bigwedge y) \bigvee (x \bigwedge z) \bigvee (y \bigwedge z) = \{0,0\}$, but the middle elements of $\{0,0,0,1,1,1\}$ are $\{0,1\}$. Sorting networks for three elements and the result of exercise 48 imply that the middle elements of $x \uplus y \uplus z$ may be expressed either as $((x \bigvee y) \bigwedge z) \bigvee (x \bigwedge y)$ or $((x \bigwedge y) \bigvee z) \bigwedge (x \bigvee y)$ or any other formula obtained by permuting x, y, z in these expressions. (There seems to be no symmetrical formula for the middle elements.)

50. Equivalently by Theorem Z, we must find all identities satisfied by the operations

$$x \lor\!\!\!\lor y = \min(x+y, 1), \qquad x \land\!\!\!\land y = \max(0, x+y-1)$$

on rational values x, y in $[0\mathbin{.\,.}1]$. [This is the operation of pouring as much liquid as possible from a glass that is x full into another that is y full, as observed by J. M. Pollard.] All such identities can be obtained from a system of four axioms and a rule of inference for multivalued logic due to Lukasiewicz; see Rose and Rosser, *Trans. Amer. Math. Soc.* **87** (1958), 1–53.

51. Let $\alpha' = \alpha[i:j]$, and let k be an index $\neq i, j$. If $(x\alpha)_i \leq (x\alpha)_k$ for all x, then $(x\alpha')_i \leq (x\alpha')_k$; if $(x\alpha)_k \leq (x\alpha)_i$ and $(x\alpha)_k \leq (x\alpha)_j$ for all x, the same holds when α is replaced by α'; if $(x\alpha)_k \leq (x\alpha)_i$ for all x, then $(x\alpha')_k \leq (x\alpha')_j$. In this way we see that α' has at least as many known relations as α, plus one more if $[i:j]$ isn't redundant. [*Bell System Tech. J.* **49** (1970), 1627–1644.]

52. (a) Consider sorting 0s and 1s; let $w = x_0 + x_1 + \cdots + x_N$. The network fails if and only if $w \leq t$ and $x_0 = 1$ before the complete N-sort. If $x_0 = 1$ at this point, it must have been 1 initially, and for $1 \leq j \leq n$ we must have had initially either $x_{2j-1+2nk} = 1$ for $0 \leq k \leq m$ or $x_{2j+2nk} = 1$ for $0 \leq k \leq m$; therefore $w \geq 1+(m+1)n = t$. So failure implies that $w = t$ and $x_j = x_{j+2nk}$ for $1 \leq k \leq m$ and $x_{2j} = \bar{x}_{2j-1}$ for $1 \leq j \leq n$. Furthermore the special subnetwork must transform such inputs so that $x_{2m+2n+j} = 1$ for $1 \leq j \leq m$.

(b) For example, the special subnetwork for $(y_1 \lor y_2 \lor \bar{y}_3) \land (\bar{y}_2 \lor y_3 \lor \bar{y}_4) \land \dots$ could be

$$[1 + 2n:2mn + 2n + 1][3 + 2n:2mn + 2n + 1][6 + 2n:2mn + 2n + 1]$$
$$[4 + 4n:2mn + 2n + 2][5 + 4n:2mn + 2n + 2][8 + 4n:2mn + 2n + 2]\dots,$$

using $x_{2j-1+2kn}$ and x_{2j+2kn} to represent y_j and $\bar{y}_j$ in the kth clause, and $x_{2m+2n+k}$ to represent that clause itself.

53. Paint the lines red or blue according to the following rule:

if $i \bmod 4$ is	then line i in case (a) is	and in case (b) it is
0	red	red;
1	blue	red;
2	blue	blue;
3	red	blue.

Now observe that the first $t - 1$ levels of the network consist of two separate networks, one for the 2^{t-1} red lines and another for the 2^{t-1} blue lines. The comparators on the tth level complete a merging network, as in the bitonic or odd-even merge. This establishes the desired result for $k = 1$.

The red-blue decomposition also establishes the case $k = 2$. For if the input is 4-ordered, the red lines contain 2^{t-1} numbers that are 2-ordered, and so do the blue lines, so we are left with

$$x_0 y_0 y_1 x_1 x_2 y_2 y_3 x_3 \dots \text{ (case (a))} \qquad \text{or} \qquad x_0 x_1 y_0 y_1 x_2 x_3 y_2 y_3 \dots \text{ (case (b))}$$

after $t - 1$ levels; the final result

$$(x_0 \land y_0)(x_0 \lor y_0)(y_1 \land x_1)(y_1 \lor x_1) \dots \qquad \text{or} \qquad x_0(x_1 \land y_0)(x_1 \lor y_0)(y_1 \land x_2)(y_1 \lor x_2) \dots$$

is clearly 2-ordered.

Now for $k \geq 2$, we can assume that $k \leq t$. The first $t - k + 2$ levels decompose into 2^{k-2} separate networks of size 2^{t-k+2}, which each are 2-ordered by the case $k = 2$; hence the lines are 2^{k-1}-ordered after $t - k + 2$ levels. The subsequent levels clearly preserve 2^{k-1}-ordering, because they have a "vertical" periodicity of order 2^{k-2}. (We can imagine $-\infty$ on lines $-1, -2, \ldots$ and $+\infty$ on lines $2^t, 2^t + 1, \ldots$.)

References: Network (a) was introduced by M. Dowd, Y. Perl, L. Rudolph, and M. Saks, *JACM* **36** (1989), 738–757; network (b) by E. R. Canfield and S. G. Williamson, *Linear and Multilinear Algebra* **29** (1991), 43–51. It is interesting to note that in case (a) we have $D_n \alpha = G_t$, where G_t is defined in exercise 32 [Dowd et al., Theorem 17]; thus the image of D_n is not enough by itself to characterize the behavior of a periodic network.

54. The following construction by Ajtai, Komlós, and Szemerédi [*FOCS* **33** (1992), 686–692] shows how to sort m^3 elements with four levels of m^2-sorters: We may suppose that the elements being sorted are 0s and 1s; let the lines be numbered $(a, b, c) = am^2 + bm + c$ for $0 \leq a, b, c < m$. The first level sorts the lines $\{(a, b, (b + k) \bmod m) \mid 0 \leq a, b < m\}$ for $0 \leq k < m$; let a_k be the number of 1s in the kth group of m^2 lines. The second level sorts $\{(a, b, k) \mid 0 \leq a, b < m\}$ for $0 \leq k < m$; the number of 1s in the kth group is then

$$b_k = \sum_{j=0}^{m^2-1} \left\lfloor \frac{a_{(k-j) \bmod m} + j}{m^2} \right\rfloor,$$

and it follows that $b_0 \leq b_1 + 1, b_1 \leq b_2 + 1, \ldots, b_{m-1} \leq b_0 + 1$. In the third level we sort $\{(k, a, b) \mid 0 \leq a, b < m\}$ for $0 \leq k < m$; the number of 1s in the kth group is

$$c_k = \sum_{i=0}^{m-1} \sum_{j=0}^{m-1} \left\lfloor \frac{b_i + km + j}{m^2} \right\rfloor.$$

If $0 < c_{k+1} < m^2$ we have $c_k \leq \binom{m-1}{2}$ and $c_j = 0$ for $j < k$. Similarly, if $0 < c_k < m^2$ we have $c_{k+1} \geq m^2 - \binom{m-1}{2}$ and $c_j = 0$ for $j > k + 1$. Consequently a fourth level that sorts lines $m^2k - \binom{m-1}{2} .. m^2k + \binom{m-1}{2} - 1$ for $0 < k < m$ will complete the sorting.

It follows that four levels of m-sorters will sort $f(m) = \lfloor \sqrt{m} \rfloor^3$ elements, and 16 levels will sort $f(f(m))$ elements. This proves the stated result, since $f(f(m)) > m^2$ when $m > 24$. (The construction is not "tight," so we can probably do the job with substantially fewer than 16 levels.)

55. [If $P(n)$ denotes the minimum number of switches needed in a permutation network, it is clear that $P(n) \geq \lceil \lg n! \rceil$. By slightly extending a construction due to L. J. Goldstein and S. W. Leibholz, *IEEE Trans.* **EC-16** (1967), 637–641, one can show that $P(n) \leq P(\lfloor n/2 \rfloor) + P(\lceil n/2 \rceil) + n - 1$, hence $P(n) \leq B(n)$ for all n, where $B(n)$ is the binary insertion function of Eq. 5.3.1–(3). M. W. Green has proved (unpublished) that $P(5) = 8$.]

56. In fact we can construct α_x inductively so that $x\alpha_x = 0^{k-1}101^{n-k-1}$, when x has k zeros. The base case, α_{10}, is empty. Otherwise at least one of the following four cases applies, where y is not sorted: (1) $x = y0$, $\alpha_x = \alpha_y[n-1:n][n-2:n-1]\ldots[1:2]$. (2) $x = y1$, $\alpha_x = \alpha_y[1:n][2:n]\ldots[n-1:n]$. (3) $x = 0y$, $\alpha_x = \alpha_y^+[1:n][1:n-1]\ldots[1:2]$. (4) $x = 1y$, $\alpha_x = \alpha_y^+[1:2][2:3]\ldots[n-1:n]$. The network α^+ is obtained from α by changing each comparator $[i:j]$ to $[i+1:j+1]$. [See M. J. Chung and B. Ravikumar,

Discrete Math. **81** (1990), 1–9.] This construction uses $\binom{n}{2} - 1$ comparators; can it be done with substantially fewer?

57. [See H. Zhu and R. Sedgewick, *STOC* **14** (1982), 296–302.] The stated delay time is easily verified by induction. But the problem of analyzing the recurrence

$$A(m,n) = A(\lfloor m/2 \rfloor, \lceil n/2 \rceil) + A(\lceil m/2 \rceil, \lfloor n/2 \rfloor) + \lceil m/2 \rceil + \lceil n/2 \rceil - 1,$$

when $A(0,n) = A(m,0) = 0$, is more difficult.

A bitonic merge makes $B(m,n) = C'(m+n)$ comparisons; see (15). Therefore we can use the fact that $\{\lfloor m/2 \rfloor + \lceil n/2 \rceil, \lceil m/2 \rceil + \lfloor n/2 \rfloor\} = \{\lfloor (m+n)/2 \rfloor, \lceil (m+n)/2 \rceil\}$ to show that $B(m,n) = B(\lfloor m/2 \rfloor, \lceil n/2 \rceil) + B(\lceil m/2 \rceil, \lfloor n/2 \rfloor) + \lfloor (m+n)/2 \rfloor$. Then $A(m,n) \le B(m,n)$ by induction.

Let $D(m,n) = C(m+1,n+1) + C(m,n) - C(m+1,n) - C(m,n+1)$. We have $D(0,n) = D(m,0) = 1$, and $D(m,n) = 1$ when $m+n$ is odd. Otherwise $m+n$ is even and $mn \ge 1$, and we have $D(m,n) = D(\lfloor m/2 \rfloor, \lfloor n/2 \rfloor) - 1$. Consequently $D(m,n) \le 1$ for all $m,n \ge 0$.

The recurrence for A is equivalent to the recurrence for C except when m and n are both odd. And in that case we have $A(m,n) \ge C(\lfloor m/2 \rfloor, \lceil n/2 \rceil) + C(\lceil m/2 \rceil, \lfloor n/2 \rfloor) + \lceil m/2 \rceil + \lceil n/2 \rceil - 1 = C(m,n) + 1 - D(\lfloor m/2 \rfloor, \lfloor n/2 \rfloor) \ge C(m,n)$ by induction.

Let $l = \lceil \lg \min(m,n) \rceil$. On level k of the even-odd recursion, for $0 \le k < l$, we perform 2^k merges of the respective sizes $(m_{jk}, n_{jk}) = (\lfloor (m+j)/2^k \rfloor, \lfloor (n+2^k - 1 - j)/2^k \rfloor)$ for $0 \le j < 2^k$. The cost of recursion, $\sum_j (\lceil m_{jk}/2 \rceil + \lceil n_{jk}/2 \rceil - 1)$, is $f_k(m) + f_k(n) - 2^k$; we can write $f_k(n) = \max(n'_k, n - n'_k)$, where $n'_k = 2^k \lfloor n/2^{k+1} + 1/2 \rfloor$ is the multiple of 2^k that is nearest to $n/2$. Since $0 \le f_k(n) - n/2 \le 2^{k-1}$, the total cost of recursion for levels 0 to $l-1$ lies between $\frac{1}{2}(m+n)l - 2^l$ and $\frac{1}{2}(m+n)l$.

Finally, if $m \le n$, the 2^l merges (m_{jl}, n_{jl}) on level l have $m_{jl} = 0$ for $0 \le j < 2^l - m$, and $m_{jl} = 1$ for the other m values of j. Since $A(1,n) = n$, the total cost of level l is $\sum_{k=n}^{m+n-1} \lfloor k/2^l \rfloor \le \sum_{k=n}^{m+n-1} k/m = \frac{m-1}{2} + n$.

Thus even-odd merging, unlike bitonic merging, is within $O(m+n)$ of the optimum number of comparisons $\hat{M}(m,n)$. Our derivation shows in fact that $A(m,n) = \sum_{k=0}^{l-1}(f_k(m) + f_k(n) - 2^k) + g_l(m+n) - g_l(\max(m,n))$, where $g_l(n)$ can be expressed in the form $\sum_{k=0}^{n-1} \lfloor k/2^l \rfloor = \lfloor n/2^l \rfloor (n - 2^{l-1}(\lfloor n/2^l \rfloor + 1))$.

58. If $h[k+1] = h[k] + 1$ and the file is not in order, something must happen to it on the next pass; this decreases the number of inversions, by exercise 5.2.2–1, hence the file will eventually become sorted. But if $h[k+1] \ge h[k] + 2$ for $1 \le k < m$, the smallest key will never move into its proper place if it is initially in R_2.

59. We use the hint, and also regard $K_{N+1} = K_{N+2} = \cdots = 1$. If $K_{h[1]+j} = \cdots = K_{h[m]+j} = 1$ at step j, and if $K_i = 0$ for some $i > h[1] + j$, we must have $i < h[m] + j$ since there are fewer than n 1s. Suppose k and i are minimal such that $h[k] + j < i < h[k+1] + j$ and $K_i = 0$. Let $s = h[k+1] + j - i$; we have $s < h[k+1] - h[k] \le k$. At step $j - s$, at least $k + 1$ 0s must have been under the heads, since $K_i = K_{h[k+1]+j-s}$ was set to zero at that step; s steps later, there are at least $k + 1 - s \ge 2$ 0s remaining between $K_{h[1]+j}$ and K_i, inclusive, contradicting the minimality of i.

The second pass gets the next $n - 1$ elements into place, etc. If we start with the permutation $N\ N{-}1\ \ldots\ 2\ 1$, the first pass changes it to

$$N{+}1{-}n\ N{-}n\ \ldots\ 1\ N{+}2{-}n\ \ldots\ N{-}1\ N,$$

since $K_{h[1]+j} > K_{h[m]+j}$ whenever $1 \le h[1] + j$ and $h[m] + j \le N$; therefore the bound is best possible.

60. Suppose that $h[k+1] - s > h[k]$ and $h[k] \leq s$; the smallest key ends in position R_i for $i > 1$ if it starts in R_{n-s}. Therefore $h[k+1] \leq 2h[k]$ is necessary; it is also sufficient, by the special case $t = 0$ of the following result:

Theorem. *If $n = N$ and if $K_1 \ldots K_N$ is a permutation of $\{1, 2, \ldots, n\}$, a single sorting pass will set $K_i = i$ for $1 \leq i \leq t+1$, if $h[k+1] \leq h[k] + h[k-i] + i$ for $1 \leq k < m$ and $0 \leq i \leq t$. (By convention, let $h[k] = k$ when $k \leq 0$.)*

Proof. By induction on t; if step t does not find the key $t+1$ under the heads, we may assume that it appears in position $R_{h[k+1]+t-s}$ for some $s > 0$, where $h[k+1] - s < h[k]$; hence $h[k-t] + t - s > 0$. But this is impossible if we consider step $t - s$, which presumably placed the element $t + 1$ into position $R_{h[k+1]+t-s}$ although there were at least $t + 1$ lower heads active. $\blacksquare$

(The condition is necessary for $t = 0$ and $t = 1$, but not for $t = 2$.)

61. If the numbers $\{1, \ldots, 23\}$ are being sorted, the theorem in the previous exercise shows that $\{1, 2, 3, 4\}$ find their true destination. When 0s and 1s are being sorted one can verify that it is impossible to have all heads reading 0 while all positions not under the heads contain 1s, at steps -2, -1, and 0; hence the proof in the previous exercise can be extended to show that $\{5, 6, 7\}$ find their true destination. Finally $\{8, \ldots, 23\}$ must be sorted, by the argument in exercise 59.

63. When $r \leq m-2$, the heads take the string $0^p 1^1 0 1^3 0 1^7 0 \ldots 0 1^{2^r - 1} 0 1^q$ into the string $0^{p+1} 1^1 0 1^3 0 1^7 0 \ldots 0 1^{2^{r-1} - 1} 0 1^{2^r - 1 + q}$; hence $m-2$ passes are necessary. [When the heads are at positions $1, 2, 3, 5, \ldots, 1 + 2^{m-2}$, Pratt has discovered a similar result: The string $0^p 1^a 0 1^{2^b - 1} 0 1^{2^{b+1} - 1} 0 \ldots 0 1^{2^r - 1} 0 1^q$, $1 \leq a \leq 2^{b-1}$, goes into $0^{p+1} 1^{a-1} 0 1^{2^b - 1} 0 1^{2^{b+1} - 1} 0 \ldots 0 1^{2^{r-1} - 1} 0 1^{2^r + q}$, hence at least $m - \lceil \log_2 m \rceil - 1$ passes are necessary in the worst case for this sequence of heads. The latter head sequence is of special interest since it has been used as the basis of a very ingenious sorting device invented by P. N. Armstrong [see *U.S. Patent 3399383* (1965)]. Pratt conjectures that these input sequences provide the true worst case, over all inputs.]

64. During quicksort, each key $K_2, \ldots, K_N$ is compared with K_1; let $A = \{i \mid K_i < K_1\}$, $B = \{j \mid K_j > K_1\}$. Subsequent operations quicksort A and B independently; all comparisons $K_i : K_j$ for i in A and j in B are suppressed, by both quicksort and the restricted uniform algorithm, and no other comparisons are suppressed by the unrestricted uniform algorithm.

In this case we could restrict the algorithm even further, omitting cases 1 and 2 so that arcs are added to G only when comparisons are explicitly made, yet considering only paths of length 2 when testing for redundancy. Another way to solve this problem is to consider the equivalent tree insertion sorting algorithm of Section 6.2.2, which makes precisely the same comparisons as the uniform algorithm in the same order.

65. (a) The probability that K_{a_i} is compared with K_{b_i} is the probability that c_i other specified keys do not lie between K_{a_i} and K_{b_i}; this is the probability that two numbers chosen at random from $\{1, 2, \ldots, c_i + 2\}$ are consecutive, namely $2/(c_i + 2)$.

(b) The first $n - 1$ values of c_i are zero, then come $(n - 2)$ 1s, $(n - 3)$ 2s, etc.; hence the average is $2 \sum_{k=1}^{n} (n - k)/(k + 1) = 2 \sum_{k=1}^{n} ((n + 1)/(k + 1) - 1) = 2(n + 1)(H_{n+1} - 1) - 2n$.

(c) The "bipartite" nature of merging shows that the restricted uniform algorithm is the same as the uniform algorithm for this sequence. The pairs involving vertex N

have c's equal to $0, 1, \ldots, N-2$, respectively; so the average number of comparisons is exactly the same as quicksort.

66. No; when $N = 5$ every pair sequence beginning with $(1,2)(2,3)(3,4)(4,5)(1,5)$ will avoid at least one subsequent comparison. [An interesting research problem: For all N, find a (restricted) uniform sorting method whose worst case is as good as possible.]

67. Suppose $c_i = j$ for exactly t_j values of i. For the restricted case we need to prove that $\sum_j t_j/(2 + j)$ is minimized when $(t_0, t_1, \ldots, t_{N-2}) = (N-1, \ldots, 2, 1)$. Gil Kalai has shown that the achievable vectors $(t_0, t_1, \ldots, t_{N-2})$ are always lexicographically $\geq (N-1, \ldots, 2, 1)$; see *Graphs and Combinatorics* **1** (1985), 65–79.

68. An item can lose at most one inversion per pass, so the minimum number of passes is at least the maximum number of inversions of any item in the input permutation. The bubble sort strategy achieves this bound, since each pass decreases the inversion count of every inverted item by one (see exercise 5.2.2–1). An additional pass may be needed to determine whether or not sorting is complete, but the wording of this exercise allows us to overlook such considerations.

It is perhaps unfortunate that the first theorem in the study of computational complexity via automata established the "optimality" of a sorting method that is so poor from a programming standpoint! The situation is analogous to the history of random number generation, which took several backward steps when generators that are "optimum" from one particular point of view were recommended for general use. (See the comments following Eq. 3.3.3–(39).) The moral is that optimality results are often heavily dependent on the abstract model; the results are quite interesting, but they must be applied wisely in practice.

[Demuth went on to consider a generalization to an r-register machine (saving a factor of r), and to a Turing-like machine in which the direction of scan could oscillate between left-right and right-left at will. He observed that the latter type of machine can do the straight insertion and the cocktail-shaker sorts; but any such 1-register machine must go through at least $\frac{1}{4}(N^2 - N)$ steps on the average, since each step reduces the total number of inversions by at most one. Finally he considered r-register random-access machines and the question of minimum-comparison sorting. These portions of his thesis have been reprinted in *IEEE Transactions* **C-34** (1985), 296–310.]

SECTION 5.4

1. We could omit the internal sorting phase, but that would generally be much slower since it would increase the number of times each piece of data is read and written on the external memory.

2. The runs are distributed as in (1), then Tape 3 is set to $R_1 \ldots R_{2000000}$; $R_{2000001} \ldots R_{4000000}$; $R_{4000001} \ldots R_{5000000}$. After all tapes are rewound, a "one-way merge" sets T_1 and T_2 to the respective contents of T_3 and T_4 in (2). Then T_1 and T_2 are merged to T_3, and the information is copied back and merged once again, for a total of five passes. In general, the procedure is like the four-tape balanced merge, but with copy passes between each of the merge passes, so one less than twice as many passes are performed.

3. (a) $\lceil \log_P S \rceil$. (b) $\log_B S$, where $B = \sqrt{P(T - P)}$ is called the "effective power of the merge." When $T = 2P$ the effective power is P; when $T = 2P - 1$ the effective power is $\sqrt{P(P - 1)} = P - \frac{1}{2} - \frac{1}{8}P^{-1} + O(P^{-2})$, slightly less than $\frac{1}{2}T$.

4. $\frac{1}{2}T$. If T is odd and P must be an integer, both $\lceil T/2 \rceil$ and $\lfloor T/2 \rfloor$ give the same maximum value. It is best to have $P \geq T - P$, according to exercise 3, so we should choose $P = \lceil T/2 \rceil$ for balanced merging.

SECTION 5.4.1

1. 087 154 170 426 $\begin{cases} 503 \begin{cases} 503 & \infty \\ 908 & \infty \end{cases} \\ 426 \begin{cases} 426 \ 653 & \infty \\ 612 & \infty \end{cases} \end{cases}$

2. The path $\boxed{061}$—$\boxed{512}$—$\boxed{087}$—$\boxed{154}$—$\boxed{061}$ would be changed to $\boxed{612}$—$\boxed{612}$—$\boxed{512}$—$\boxed{154}$—$\boxed{087}$. (We are essentially doing a "bubble sort" along the path!)

3. and fourscore our seven years/ ago brought fathers forth on this/ a conceived continent in liberty nation new the to/ and dedicated men proposition that/ all are created equal.

4. (The problem is slightly ambiguous; in this interpretation we do not clear the internal memory until the reservoir is about to overflow.)

   and fourscore on our seven this years/ ago brought continent fathers forth in liberty nation new to/ a and conceived dedicated men proposition that the/ all are created equal.

5. False; the complete binary tree with P external nodes is defined for all $P \geq 1$.

6. Insert "If T = LOC($X[0]$) then go to R2, otherwise" at the beginning of step R6, and delete the similar clause from step R7.

7. There is no output, and RMAX stays equal to 0.

8. If any of the first P actual keys were ∞, their records would be lost. To avoid ∞, we can make two almost-identical copies of the program; the first copy omits the test involving LASTKEY in step R4, and it jumps to the second copy when RC $\neq 0$ in step R3 for the first time. The second copy needs no step R1, and it never needs to test RC in step R3. (Further optimization is possible because of answer 10.)

9. Assume, for example, that the current run is ascending, while the next should be descending. Then the steps of Algorithm R will work properly except for one change: In step R6, if RN(L) = RN(Q) > RC, reverse the test on KEY(L) versus KEY(Q).
   When RC changes, the key tests of steps R4 and R6 should change appropriately.

10. Let $\cdot j \equiv$ LOC($X[j]$), and suppose we add the unnecessary assignment 'LOSER($\cdot 0$) $\leftarrow$ Q' at the beginning of step R3. The mechanism of Algorithm R ensures that the following conditions are true just after we've done that assignment: The values of LOSER($\cdot 0$), ..., LOSER($\cdot(P-1)$) are a permutation of $\{\cdot 0, \cdot 1, \ldots, \cdot(P-1)\}$; and there exists a permutation of the pointers $\{$LOSER($\cdot j$) $\mid$ RN(LOSER($\cdot j$)) $= 0\}$ that corresponds to an actual tournament. In other words, when RN($\cdot j$) is zero, the value of KEY($\cdot j$) is irrelevant; we may permute such "winners" among themselves. After P iterations all RN($\cdot j$) will be nonzero, so the entire tree will be consistent. (The answer to the hint is "yes.")
   David P. Kanter observes that we can go directly from R6 to R4 as soon as RN(Q) = 0, thereby avoiding all comparisons that involve uninitialized keys when $N \geq P$.

11. True. (The proof of Theorem K notes that both keys belong to the same subsequence.)

13. The keys left in memory when the first run has ended tend to be smaller than average, since they didn't make it into the first run. Thus the second run can output more of the smaller keys.

14. Assume that the snow suddenly stops when the snowplow is at a random point u, $0 \le u < 1$, after it has reached its steady state. Then the next-to-last run contains $(1 + 2u - u^2)P$ records, and the last run contains $u^2 P$. Integrating this times du yields an average time of $(2 - \frac{1}{3})P$ records in the penultimate run, $\frac{1}{3}P$ in the last.

15. False; the last run can be arbitrarily long, whenever all records in memory belong to the same run at the moment the input is exhausted (for example, in a one-pass sort).

16. If and only if each element has fewer than P inversions. (See Sections 5.1.1, 5.4.8.) The probability is 1 when $N \le P$, $P^{N-P}P!/N!$ when $N \ge P$, by considering inversion tables. (In actual practice, however, a one-pass sort is not too uncommon, since people tend to sort a file even when they suspect it might be in order, as a precautionary measure.)

17. Exactly $\lceil N/P \rceil$ runs, all but the last having length P. (The "worst case.")

18. Nothing changes on the second pass, since it is possible to show that the kth record of a run is less than at least $P + 1 - k$ records of the preceding run, for $1 \le k \le P$. (However, there seems to be no simple way to characterize the result of P-way replacement selection followed by P'-way replacement selection when $P' > P$.)

19. Argue as in the derivation of (2) that $h(x,t)\,dx = KL\,dt$, where this time $h(x,t) = I + Kt$ for all x, and $P = LI$. This implies $x(t) = L\ln((I + Kt)/I)$, so that when $x(T) = L$ we have $KT = (e - 1)I$. The amount of snowfall since $t = 0$ is therefore $(e - 1)LI = (e - 1)P$.

20. As in exercise 19, we have $(I + Kt)\,dx = K(L - x)\,dt$; hence $x(t) = LKt/(I + Kt)$. The snow in the reservoir is $LI = P = P' = \int_0^T x(t)K\,dt = L(KT - I\ln((I + KT)/I))$; hence $KT = \alpha I$, where $\alpha \approx 2.14619$ is the root of $1 + \alpha = e^{\alpha - 1}$. The run length is the total amount of snowfall during $0 \le t \le T$, namely $LKT = \alpha P$.

21. Proceed as in the text, but after each run wait for $P - P'$ snowflakes to fall before the plow starts out again. This means that $h(x(t), t)$ is now KT_1, instead of KT, where $T_1 - T$ is the amount of time taken by the extra snowfall. The run length is LKT_1, $x(t) = L(1 - e^{-t/T_1})$, $P = LKT_1 e^{-T/T_1}$, and $P' = \int_0^T x(t)K\,dt = P + LK(T - T_1)$. In other words, a run length of $e^\theta P$ is obtained when $P' = (1 - (1 - \theta)e^\theta)P$, for $0 \le \theta \le 1$.

22. For $0 \le t \le (\kappa - 1)T$, $dx \cdot h = K\,dt\,(x(t + T) - x(t))$, and for $(\kappa - 1)T \le t \le T$, $dx \cdot h = K\,dt\,(L - x(t))$, where h is seen to be constantly equal to KT at the position of the plows. It follows that for $0 \le j \le k$, $0 \le u \le 1$, and $t = (\kappa - j - u)T$, we have $x(t) = L(1 - e^{u-\theta}F_j(u)/F(\kappa))$. The run length is LKT, the amount of snowfall between the times that consecutive snowplows leave point 0 in the steady state; P is the amount cleared during each snowplow's last burst of speed, namely $KT(L - x(\kappa T)) = LKTe^{-\theta}/F(\kappa)$; and $P' = \int_0^{\kappa T} x(t)K\,dt$ can be shown to have the stated form.

Notes: It turns out that the stated formulas are valid also for $k = 0$. When $k \ge 1$ the number of elements per run that go into the reservoir *twice* is $P'' = \int_0^{(\kappa-1)T} x(t)K\,dt$, and it is easy to show that (run length) $- P' + P'' = (e - 1)P$, a phenomenon noticed by Frazer and Wong. Is it a coincidence that the generating function for $F_k(\theta)$ is so similar to the generating function in exercise 5.1.3–11?

23. Let $P = pP'$ and $q = 1 - p$. For the first T_1 units of time the snowfall comes from the qP' elements remaining in the reservoir after the first pP' have been initially removed in random order; and when the old reservoir is empty, uniform snow begins to fall again. We choose T_1 so that $LKT_1 = qP'$. For $0 \le t \le T_1$, $h(x, t) = (p + qt/T_1)g(x)$, where $g(x)$ is the height of snow put into the reservoir from position x; for $T_1 \le t \le T$, $h(x, t) = g(x) + (t - T_1)K$. For $0 \le t \le T_1$, $g(x(t))$ is $(q(T_1 - t)/T_1)g(x(t)) + (T - T_1)K$; and for $T_1 \le t \le T$, $g(x(t)) = (T - t)K$. Hence $h(x(t), t) = (T - T_1)K$ for $0 \le t \le T$, and $x(t) = L(1 - \exp(-t/(T - T_1)))$. The total run length is $LK(T - T_1)$; the total amount "recycled" from the reservoir back again (see exercise 22) is LKT_1; and the total amount cleared after time T is $P = KT(L - x(T))$.

So the assumptions of this exercise give runs of length $(e^s/s)P$ when the reservoir size is $(1 + (s - 1)e^s/s)P$. This is considerably worse than the results of exercise 22, since the reservoir contents are being used in a more advantageous order in that case.

(The fact that $h(x(t), t)$ is constant in so many of these problems is not surprising, since it is equivalent to saying that the elements of each run obtained during a steady state of the system are uniformly distributed.)

24. (a) Essentially the same proof works; each of the subsequences has runs in the same direction as the output runs. (b) The stated probability is the probability that the run has length $n + 1$ and is followed by y; it equals $(1 - x)^n/n!$ when $x > y$, and it is $(1 - x)^n/n! - (y - x)^n/n!$ when $x \le y$. (c) Induction. For example, if the nth run is ascending, the $(n-1)$st was descending with probability p, so the first integral applies. (d) We find that $f'(x) = f(x) - c - pf(1 - x) - qf(x)$, then $f''(x) = -2pc$, which ultimately leads to $f(x) = c(1 - qx - px^2)$, $c = 6/(3 + p)$. (e) If $p > eq$ then $pe^x + qe^{1-x}$ is monotone increasing for $0 \le x \le 1$, and $\int_0^1 |pe^x + qe^{1-x} - e^{1/2}| \, dx = (p - q)(e^{1/2} - 1)^2 < 0.43$. If $q \le p < eq$ then $pe^x + qe^{1-x}$ lies between $2\sqrt{pqe}$ and $p + qe$, so $\int_0^1 |pe^x + qe^{1-x} - \frac{1}{2}(p + qe + 2\sqrt{pqe})| \, dx \le \frac{1}{2}(\sqrt{p} - \sqrt{qe})^2 < 0.4$; and if $p < q$ we may use a symmetrical argument. Thus for all p and q there is a constant C such that $\int_0^1 |pe^x + qe^{1-x} - C| \, dx < 0.43$. Let $\delta_n(x) = f_n(x) - f(x)$. Then $\delta_{n+1}(y) = (1 - e^{y-1}) \int_0^1 (pe^x + qe^{1-x} - C)\delta_n(x) \, dx + p \int_0^{1-y} e^{y-1+x}\delta_n(x) \, dx + q \int_y^1 e^{y-x}\delta_n(x) \, dx$; hence if $\delta_n(y) \le \alpha_n$, $|\delta_{n+1}(y)| \le (1 - e^{y-1}) \cdot 1.43\alpha_n < 0.91\alpha_n$. (f) For all $n \ge 0$, $(1-x)^n/n!$ is the probability that the run length exceeds n. (g) $\int_0^1 (pe^x + qe^{1-x})f(x) \, dx = 6/(3 + p)$.

26. (a) Consider the number of permutations with $n + r + 1$ elements and n left-to-right minima, where the rightmost element is not the smallest. (b) Use the fact that

$$\sum_{1 \le k < n} \begin{bmatrix} k \\ k - r \end{bmatrix} k = \begin{bmatrix} n \\ n - r - 1 \end{bmatrix},$$

by the definition of Stirling numbers in Appendix B. (c) Add $r + 1$ to the mean, using the fact that $\sum_{n \ge 0} \begin{bmatrix} n+r \\ n \end{bmatrix}(n + r)/(n + r + 1)! = 1$, to get $\sum_{n \ge 0} \begin{bmatrix} n+r \\ n \end{bmatrix}/(n + r - 1)!$.

The formula in (b) is due to P. Appell, *Archiv der Math. und Physik* **65** (1880), 171–175. We have, incidentally, $[\begin{bmatrix} r \\ k \end{bmatrix}] = (r + k)! [x^k z^r] e^{zf(z)}$, where $f(z) = z/2 + z^2/3 + \cdots = -z^{-1}\ln(1 - z) - 1$; hence $c_r = [z^r](r + 1 + f(z))e^{f(z)}$. The number of derangements of n objects having k cycles, sometimes denoted by $\begin{bmatrix} n \\ k \end{bmatrix}_{\ge 2}$, is $[[\begin{smallmatrix} n-k \\ k \end{smallmatrix}]]$; see J. Riordan, *An Introduction to Combinatorial Analysis* (Wiley, 1958), §4.4.

27. When $P'/P = 2(e^{-\theta} - 1 + \theta)/(1 - 2\theta + \theta^2 + 2\theta e^{-\theta})$, for $0 \le \theta \le 1$, the steady-state average run length will be $2P/(1 - 2\theta + \theta^2 + 2\theta e^{-\theta})$. [See *Information Processing Letters* **21** (1985), 239–243.]

Dobosiewicz has also observed that we can continue the replacement selection mechanism even longer, because we can be inputting from the front of the reservoir queue while outputting to its rear. For example, if $P' = .5P$ and we continue replacement selection until the current run contains $.209P$ records, the average run length increases from about $2.55P$ to about $2.61P$ with this modification. If $P' = P$ and we continue replacement selection until only $.314P$ records remain in the current run, the average run length increases from eP to about $3.034P$. [See *Comp. J.* **27** (1984), 334–339, where an even more efficient method called "merge replacement" is also presented.]

28. For multiway merging there is comparatively little problem, since P stays constant and records are processed sequentially on each file; but when forming initial runs, we would like to vary the number of records in memory depending on their lengths. We could keep a heap of as many records as will fit in memory, using dynamic storage allocation as described in Section 2.5. M. A. Goetz [*Proc. AFIPS Joint Computer Conf.* **25** (1964), 602–604] has suggested another approach, breaking each record into fixed-size parts that are linked together; they occupy space at the leaves of the tree, but only the leading part participates in the tournament.

29. The top 2^k loser nodes go into the corresponding host positions. The remaining loser nodes consist of 2^k subtrees of $2^n - 1$ nodes each; they are assigned to host nodes in symmetric order — the leftmost subtree into the leftmost host node, etc. [See K. Efe and N. Eleser, *Acta Informatica* **34** (1997), 429–447.]

30. Suppose t of the host nodes hold a *connected* 2^n-node subgraph of the complete 2^{n+k}-node loser tree. That tree has one node at level 0 and 2^{l-1} nodes at level l for $1 \leq l \leq n + k$. A subtree rooted at level $l \geq 1$ has $2^{n+k+1-l} - 1$ nodes; therefore the roots of t disjoint 2^n-node subtrees must all be on levels $\leq k$. And each of these subtrees must contain at least one node on level k, because there are only $2^{k-1} < 2^n$ nodes on levels $< k$. It follows that $t \leq 2^{k-1}$. But the number of edges in the host graph is at least $t + 2(2^k - t) - 1$, by (ii) and (iii), since there are at least this many loser nodes whose parent has a different image in the host.

[The hypothesis $n \geq k$ is necessary: When $n = k - 1$ there is a suitable host graph with $2^k + 2^{k-1} - 2$ edges.]

SECTION 5.4.2

1.

2. After the first merge phase, all remaining dummies are on tape T, and there are at most $a_n - a_{n-1} \leq a_{n-1}$ of them. Therefore they all disappear during the second merge phase.

3. We have $(\text{D}[1], \text{D}[2], \ldots, \text{D}[T]) = (a_n - a_{n-P}, a_n - a_{n-P+1}, \ldots, a_n - a_n)$, so the condition follows from the fact that the a's are nondecreasing. The condition is important to the validity of the algorithm, since steps D2 and D3 never decrease $\text{D}[j+1]$ more often than $\text{D}[j]$.

4. $(1 - z - \cdots - z^5)a(z) = 1$ because of (3). And $t(z) = \sum_{n\geq 1}(a_n + b_n + c_n + d_n + e_n)z^n = (z + \cdots + z^5)a(z) + (z + \cdots + z^4)a(z) + \cdots + za(z) = (5z + 4z^2 + 3z^3 + 2z^4 + z^5)a(z)$.

5. Let $g_p(z) = (z-1)f_p(z) = z^{p+1} - 2z^p + 1$, and let $h_p(z) = z^{p+1} - 2z^p$. Rouché's theorem [*J. École Polytechnique* **21**, 37 (1858), 1–34] tells us that $h_p(z)$ and $g_p(z)$ have the same number of roots inside the circle $|z| = 1 + \epsilon$, provided $|h_p(z)| > |h_p(z) - g_p(z)| = 1$ on the circle. If $\phi^{-1} > \epsilon > 0$ we have $|h_p(z)| \geq (1+\epsilon)^p(1-\epsilon) > (1+\phi^{-1})^2(1-\phi^{-1}) = 1$. Hence g_p has p roots of magnitude ≤ 1. They are distinct, since $\gcd(g_p(z), g_p'(z)) = \gcd(g_p(z), (p+1)z - 2p) = 1$. [*AMM* **67** (1960), 745–752.]

6. Let $c_0 = -\alpha p(\alpha^{-1})/q'(\alpha^{-1})$. Then $p(z)/q(z) - c_0/(1 - \alpha z)$ is analytic in $|z| \leq R$ for some $R > |\alpha|^{-1}$; hence $[z^n]\, p(z)/q(z) = c_0\alpha^n + O(R^{-n})$. Thus, $\ln S = n \ln \alpha + \ln c_0 + O((\alpha R)^{-n})$; and $n = (\ln S/\ln \alpha) + O(1)$ implies that $O((\alpha R)^{-n}) = O(S^{-\epsilon})$. Similarly, let $c_1 = \alpha^2 p(\alpha^{-1})/q'(\alpha^{-1})^2$ and $c_2 = -\alpha p'(\alpha^{-1})/q'(\alpha^{-1})^2 + \alpha p(\alpha^{-1})q''(\alpha^{-1})/q'(\alpha^{-1})^3$, and consider $p(z)/q(z)^2 - c_1/(1 - \alpha z)^2 - c_2/(1 - \alpha z)$.

7. Let $\alpha_p = 2x$ and $z = -1/2^{p+1}$. Then $x^{p+1} = x^p + z$, so we have the convergent series $\alpha_p = 2\sum_{k\geq 0} \binom{1-kp}{k} z^k/(1 - kp) = 2 - 2^{-p} - p2^{-2p-1} + O(p^2 2^{-3p})$ by Eq. 1.2.6–(25).

Note: It follows that the quantity ρ in exercise 6 becomes approximately $\log_4 S$ as p increases. Similarly, for both Table 5 and Table 6, the coefficient c approaches $1/((\phi + 2)\ln\phi)$ on a large number of tapes.

8. Evidently $N_0^{(p)} = 1$, $N_m^{(p)} = 0$ for $m < 0$, and by considering the different possibilities for the first summand we have $N_m^{(p)} = N_{m-1}^{(p)} + \cdots + N_{m-p}^{(p)}$ when $m > 0$. Hence $N_m^{(p)} = F_{m+p-1}^{(p)}$. [*Lehrbuch der Combinatorik* (Leipzig: Teubner, 1901), 136–137.]

9. Consider the position of the leftmost 0, if there is one; we find $K_m^{(p)} = F_{m+p}^{(p)}$. *Note:* There is a simple one-to-one correspondence between such sequences of 0s and 1s and the representations of $m+1$ considered in exercise 8: Place a 0 at the right end of the sequence, and look at the positions of all the 0s.

10. *Lemma:* If $n = F_{j_1}^{(p)} + \cdots + F_{j_m}^{(p)}$ is such a representation, with $j_1 > \cdots > j_m \geq p$, we have $n < F_{j_1+1}^{(p)}$. *Proof:* The result is obvious if $m < p$; otherwise let k be minimal with $j_k > j_{k+1} + 1$; we have $k < p$, and by induction $F_{j_{k+1}}^{(p)} + \cdots + F_{j_m}^{(p)} < F_{j_k-1}^{(p)}$, hence $n < F_{j_1}^{(p)} + \cdots + F_{j_1-k-1}^{(p)} \leq F_{j_1+1}^{(p)}$.

The stated result can now be proved, by induction on n. If $n > 0$ let j be maximal such that $F_j^{(p)} \leq n$. The lemma shows that each representation of n must consist of $F_j^{(p)}$ plus a representation of $n - F_j^{(p)}$. By induction, $n - F_j^{(p)}$ has a unique representation of the desired form, and this representation does not include all of the numbers $F_{j-1}^{(p)}, \ldots, F_{j-p+1}^{(p)}$ because j is maximal.

Notes: This number system was implicitly known in 14th-century India (see Section 7.2.1.7). We have considered the case $p = 2$ in exercise 1.2.8–34. There is a simple algorithm to go from the representation of n to that of $n+1$, working on the sequence $c_j \ldots c_1 c_0$ of 0s and 1s such that $n = \sum c_j F_{j+p}^{(p)}$: For example, if $p = 3$, we look at the rightmost digits, changing $\ldots 0$ to $\ldots 1$, $\ldots 01$ to $\ldots 10$, $\ldots 011$ to $\ldots 100$; then we "carry" to the left if necessary, replacing $\ldots 0111 \ldots$ by $\ldots 1000 \ldots$. (See the sequences of 0s and 1s in exercise 9, in the order listed.) A similar number system has been studied by W. C. Lynch [*Fibonacci Quarterly* **8** (1970), 6–22], who found a very interesting way to make it govern both the distribution and merge phases of a polyphase sort.

12. The kth power contains the perfect distributions for levels $k - 4$ through k, on successive rows, with the largest elements to the right.

13. By induction on the level.

14. (a) $n(1) = 1$, so assume that $k > 1$. The law $T_{nk} = T_{(n-1)(k-1)} + \cdots + T_{(n-P)(k-1)}$ shows that $T_{nk} \leq T_{(n+1)k}$ if and only if $T_{(n-P)(k-1)} \leq T_{n(k-1)}$. Let r be any positive integer, and let n' be minimal such that $T_{(n'-r)(k-1)} > T_{n'(k-1)}$; then $T_{(n-r)(k-1)} \geq T_{n(k-1)}$ for all $n \geq n'$, since this relation is trivial for $n \geq n(k-1) + r$ and otherwise $T_{(n-r)(k-1)} \geq T_{(n'-r)(k-1)} \geq T_{n'(k-1)} \geq T_{n(k-1)}$. (b) The same argument with $r = n - n'$ shows that $T_{n'k'} < T_{nk'}$ implies $T_{(n'-j)k} \leq T_{(n-j)k'}$ for all $j \geq 0$; hence the recurrence implies that $T_{(n'-j)k} \leq T_{(n-j)k}$ for all $j \geq 0$ and $k \geq k'$. (c) Let $\ell(S)$ be the least n such that $\Sigma_n(S)$ assumes its minimum value. The sequence M_n exists as desired if and only if $\ell(S) \leq \ell(S + 1)$ for all S. Suppose $n = \ell(S) > \ell(S + 1) = n'$, so that $\Sigma_n(S) < \Sigma_{n'}(S)$ and $\Sigma_n(S+1) \geq \Sigma_{n'}(S+1)$. There is some smallest S' such that $\Sigma_n(S') < \Sigma_{n'}(S')$, and we have $m = \Sigma_n(S') - \Sigma_n(S' - 1) < \Sigma_{n'}(S') - \Sigma_{n'}(S' - 1) = m'$. Then $\sum_{k=1}^{m} T_{n'k} < S' \leq \sum_{k=1}^{m} T_{nk}$; hence there is some $k' \leq m$ such that $T_{n'k'} < T_{nk'}$. Similarly we have $l = \Sigma_n(S+1) - \Sigma_n(S) > \Sigma_{n'}(S+1) - \Sigma_{n'}(S) = l'$; hence $\sum_{k=1}^{l'} T_{n'k} \geq S + 1 > \sum_{k=1}^{l'} T_{nk}$. Since $l' \geq m' > m$, there is some $k > m$ such that $T_{n'k} > T_{nk}$. But this contradicts part (b).

15. This theorem has been proved by D. A. Zave, whose article was cited in the text.

16. D. A. Zave has shown that the number of records input (and output) is $S \log_{T-1} S + \frac{1}{2} S \log_{T-1} \log_{T-1} S + O(S)$.

17. Let $T = 3$; $A_{11}(x) = 6x^6 + 35x^7 + 56x^8 + \cdots$, $B_{11}(x) = x^6 + 15x^7 + 35x^8 + \cdots$, $T_{11}(x) = 7x^6 + 50x^7 + 91x^8 + 64x^9 + 19x^{10} + 2x^{11}$. The optimum distribution for $S = 144$ requires 55 runs on T2, and this forces a nonoptimum distribution for $S = 145$. D. A. Zave has studied near-optimum procedures of this kind.

18. Let $S = 9$, $T = 3$, and consider the following two patterns.

Optimum Polyphase:

T1	T2	T3	Cost
$0^2 1^6$	$0^2 1^3$	—	
1^3	—	$0^2 2^3$	6
—	$1^2 3^1$	2^2	5
3^2	3^1	—	6
3^1	—	6^1	6
—	9^1	—	9
			32

Alternative:

T1	T2	T3	Cost
$0^1 1^6$	$0^1 1^3$	—	
1^3	—	$0^1 2^3$	6
—	$1^1 3^2$	2^1	7
3^1	3^2	—	3
—	3^1	6^1	6
9^1	—	—	9
			31

(Still another way to improve on "optimum" polyphase is to reconsider where dummy runs appear on the output tape of every merge phase. For example, the result of merging $0^2 1^3$ with $0^2 1^3$ might be regarded as $2^1 0^1 2^1 0^1 2^1$ instead of $0^2 2^3$. Thus, many unresolved questions of optimality remain.)

19.

Level	T1	T2	T3	T4	Total	Final output on
0	1	0	0	0	1	T1
1	0	1	1	1	3	T6
2	1	1	1	0	3	T5
3	1	2	1	1	5	T4
4	2	2	2	1	7	T3
5	2	4	3	2	11	T2
6	4	5	4	2	15	T1
7	5	8	6	4	23	T6
$\cdot\cdot\cdot$						
n	a_n	b_n	c_n	d_n	t_n	T(k)
$n+1$	b_n	$c_n + a_n$	$d_n + a_n$	a_n	t_n+2a_n	T($k-1$)

20. $a(z) = 1/(1 - z^2 - z^3 - z^4)$, $t(z) = (3z + 3z^2 + 2z^3 + z^4)/(1 - z^2 - z^3 - z^4)$, $\sum_{n \geq 1} T_n(x)z^n = x(3z + 3z^2 + 2z^3 + z^4)/(1 - x(z^2 + z^3 + z^4))$. $D_n = A_{n-1} + 1$, $C_n = A_{n-1}A_{n-2} + 1$, $B_n = A_{n-1}A_{n-2}A_{n-3} + 1$, $A_n = A_{n-2}A_{n-3}A_{n-4} + 1$.

21. 333343333332322 3333433333323 33334333333 3333433 333323 T5

22. $t_n - t_{n-1} - t_{n-2} = -1 + 3[n \bmod 3 = 1]$. (This Fibonacci-like relation follows from the fact that $1 - z^2 - 2z^3 - z^4 = (1 - \phi z)(1 - \hat{\phi}z)(1 - \omega z)(1 - \overline{\omega}z)$, where $\omega^3 = 1$.)

23. In place of (25), the run lengths during the first half of the nth merge phase are s_n, and on the second half they are t_n, where

$$s_n = t_{n-2} + t_{n-3} + s_{n-3} + s_{n-4}, \qquad t_n = t_{n-2} + s_{n-2} + s_{n-3} + s_{n-4}.$$

Here we regard $s_n = t_n = 1$ for $n \leq 0$. [In general, if v_{n+1} is the sum of the first $2r$ terms of $u_{n-1}+\cdots+v_{n-P}$, we have $s_n = t_n = t_{n-2}+\cdots+t_{n-r}+2t_{n-r-1}+t_{n-r-2}+\cdots+t_{n-P}$; if v_{n+1} is the sum of the first $2r-1$, we have $s_n = t_{n-2}+\cdots+t_{n-r-1}+s_{n-r-1}+\cdots+s_{n-P}$, $t_n = t_{n-2} + \cdots + t_{n-r} + s_{n-r} + \cdots + s_{n-P}$.]

In place of (27) and (28), $A_n = (U_{n-1}V_{n-1}U_{n-2}V_{n-2}U_{n-3}V_{n-3}U_{n-4}V_{n-4}) + 1$, $\dots, D_n = (U_{n-1}V_{n-1}) + 1$, $E_n = (U_{n-2}V_{n-2}U_{n-3}) + 1$; $V_{n+1} = (U_{n-1}V_{n-1}U_{n-2}) + 1$, $U_n = (V_{n-2}U_{n-3}V_{n-3}U_{n-4}V_{n-4}) + 1$.

25.

1^{16}	1^8	—	1^8
1^{12}	1^4	R	$1^8 2^4$
1^8	—	2^4	R

$\cdot\cdot\cdot$			
R	$8^1 16^1$	8^1	8^0
16^0	R	8^1	—
16^1	16^1	8^0	R
R	16^1	—	24^0
16^1	16^1	R	$24^0 32^0$
16^0	16^0	32^1	(R)

26. When 2^n are sorted, $n \cdot 2^n$ initial runs are processed while merging; each half phase (with a few exceptions) merges 2^{n-2} and rewinds 2^{n-1}. When $2^n + 2^{n-1}$ are sorted, $n \cdot 2^n + (n-1) \cdot 2^{n-1}$ initial runs are processed while merging; each half phase (with a few exceptions) merges 2^{n-2} or 2^{n-1} and rewinds $2^{n-1} + 2^{n-2}$.

27. It works if and only if the gcd of the distribution numbers is 1. For example, let there be six tapes; if we distribute (a, b, c, d, e) to T1 through T5, where $a \geq b \geq c \geq d \geq e > 0$, the first phase leaves a distribution $(a-e, b-e, c-e, d-e, e)$, and

$\gcd(a-e, b-e, c-e, d-e, e) = \gcd(a, b, c, d, e)$, since any common divisor of one set of numbers divides the others too. The process decreases the number of runs at each phase until $\gcd(a, b, c, d, e)$ runs are left on a single tape.

[Nonpolyphase distributions sometimes turn out to be superior to polyphase under certain configurations of dummy runs, as shown in exercise 18. This phenomenon was first observed by B. Sackman about 1963.]

28. We get any such (a, b, c, d, e) by starting with $(1, 0, 0, 0, 0)$ and doing the following operation exactly n times: Choose x in $\{a, b, c, d, e\}$, and add x to each of the other four elements of (a, b, c, d, e).

To show that $a+b+c+d+e \leq t_n$, we shall prove that if $a \geq b \geq c \geq d \geq e$ on level n, we always have $a \leq a_n$, $b \leq b_n$, $c \leq c_n$, $d \leq d_n$, $e \leq e_n$. The proof follows by induction, since the level $n + 1$ distributions are $(b+a, c+a, d+a, e+a, a)$, $(a+b, c+b, d+b, e+b, b)$, $(a+c, b+c, d+c, e+c, c)$, $(a+d, b+d, c+d, e+d, d)$, $(a+e, b+e, c+e, d+e, e)$.

30. The following table has been computed by J. A. Mortenson.

Level	$T = 5$	$T = 6$	$T = 7$	$T = 8$	$T = 9$	$T = 10$	
1	2	2	2	2	2	2	M_1
2	4	5	6	7	8	9	M_2
3	4	5	6	7	8	9	M_3
4	8	8	10	12	14	16	M_4
5	10	14	18	17	20	23	M_5
6	18	20	26	27	32	31	M_6
7	26	32	46	47	56	42	M_7
8	44	53	74	82	92	92	M_8
9	68	83	122	111	138	139	M_9
10	112	134	206	140	177	196	M_{10}
11	178	197	317	324	208	241	M_{11}
12	290	350	401	488	595	288	M_{12}
13	466	566	933	640	838	860	M_{13}
14	756	917	1371	769	1064	1177	M_{14}
15	1220	1481	1762	2078	1258	1520	M_{15}
16	1976	2313	4060	2907	3839	1821	M_{16}

31. [*Random Structures & Algorithms* **5** (1994), 102–104.] $K_d(n) = F_{n-2}^{(d)} = N_{n-d-1}^{(d)}$. We have $n - d - 1 = a_1 + \cdots + a_r$ if the tree has $r + 1$ leaves and the $(k + 1)$st leaf has $a_k - 1$ ancestors distinct from the ancestors of the first k leaves. (The seven example trees correspond respectively to $1 + 1 + 1 + 1$, $1 + 1 + 2$, $1 + 2 + 1$, $1 + 3$, $2 + 1 + 1$, $2 + 2$, and $3 + 1$.)

SECTION 5.4.3

1. The tape-splitting polyphase is superior with respect to the average number of times each record is processed (Table 5.4.2–6), when there are 6, 7, or 8 tapes.

2. The methods are essentially identical when the number of initial runs is a Fibonacci number; but the manner of distributing dummy runs in other cases is better with polyphase. The cascade algorithm puts 1 on T1, then 1 on T2, 1 on T1, 2 on T2, 3 on T1, 5 on T2, etc., and step C8 never finds $D[p - 1] = M[p - 1]$ when $p = 2$. In effect, all dummies are on one tape, and this is less efficient than the method of Algorithm 5.4.2D.

3. (Distribution stops after putting 12 runs on T3 during Step $(3,3)$.)

T1	T2	T3	T4	T5	T6
1^{26}	1^{21}	1^{24}	1^{14}	1^{15}	—
1^5	—	1^{12}	$1^2 2^7$	1^{15}	$2^2 4^{12}$
8^4	$6^2 9^3$	5^2	6^3	1^1	—
—	9^1	23^1	17^1	25^1	26^1
100^1	—	—	—	—	—

4. Induction. (See exercise 5.4.2–28.)

5. When there are a_n initial runs, the kth pass outputs a_{n-k} runs of length a_k, then b_{n-k} of length b_k, etc.

6.

$$\begin{pmatrix} 1 & 1 & 1 & 1 & 1 \\ 1 & 1 & 1 & 1 & 0 \\ 1 & 1 & 1 & 0 & 0 \\ 1 & 1 & 0 & 0 & 0 \\ 1 & 0 & 0 & 0 & 0 \end{pmatrix}.$$

7. We save $e_2 e_{n-2} + e_3 e_{n-3} + \cdots + e_n e_0$ initial run lengths (see exercise 5), which may also be written $a_1 a_{n-3} + a_2 a_{n-4} + \cdots + a_{n-2} a_0$; it is $[z^{n-2}] (A(z)^2 - A(z))$.

8. The denominator of $A(z)$ has distinct roots and greater degree than the numerator, hence $A(z) = \sum q_3(\rho)/(1 - \rho z)\rho(1 - q_4'(\rho))$ summed over all roots ρ of $q_4(\rho) = \rho$. The special form of ρ is helpful in evaluating $q_3(\rho)$ and $q_4'(\rho)$.

9. The formulas hold for all *large* n, by (8) and (12), in view of the value of $q_m(2 \sin \theta_k)$. To show that they hold for all n we need to know that $q_{m-1}(z)$ is the quotient when $q_{r-1}(z) q_m(z)$ is divided by $q_r(z) - z$, for $0 \le m < r$. This can be proved either by using (10) and noting that cancellations bring down the degree of the polynomial $q_{r-1}(z) q_m(z) - q_r(z) q_{m-1}(z)$, or by noting that $A(z)^2 + B(z)^2 + \cdots + E(z)^2 \to 0$ as $z \to \infty$ (see exercise 5), or by finding explicit formulas for the numerators of $B(z)$, $C(z)$, etc.

10. $E(z) = r_1(z) A(z)$; $D(z) = r_2(z) A(z) - r_1(z)$; $C(z) = r_3(z) A(z) - r_2(z)$; $B(z) = r_4(z) A(z) - r_3(z)$; $A(z) = r_5(z) A(z) + 1 - r_4(z)$. Thus $A(z) = (1 - r_4(z))/(1 - r_5(z))$. [Notice that $r_m(2 \sin \theta) = \sin(2m\theta)/\cos \theta$; hence $r_m(z)$ is the Chebyshev polynomial $(-1)^{m+1} U_{2m-1}(z/2)$.]

11. Prove that $f_m(z) = q_{\lfloor m/2 \rfloor}(z) - r_{\lceil m/2 \rceil}(z)$ and that $f_m(z) f_{m-1}(z) = 1 - r_m(z)$. Then use the result of exercise 10. (This explicit form for the denominator was first discovered by David E. Ferguson.)

13. See exercise 5.4.6–6.

SECTION 5.4.4

1. When writing an ascending run, *first* write a sentinel record containing $-\infty$ before outputting the run. (And a $+\infty$ sentinel should be written at the end of the run as well, if the output is ever going to be read forward, as on the final pass.) For descending runs, interchange the roles of $-\infty$ and $+\infty$.

2. The smallest number on level $n + 1$ is equal to the largest on level n; hence the columns are nondecreasing, regardless of the way we permute the numbers in any particular row.

3. In fact, during the merge process the first run on T2–T6 will always be descending, and the first on T1 will always be ascending. (By induction.)

4. It requires several "copy" operations on the second and third phases; the approximate extra cost is $(\log 2)/(\log \rho)$ passes, where ρ is the "growth ratio" in Table 5.4.2–1.

5. If α is a string, let α^R denote its left-right reversal.

Level	T1	T2	T3	T4	T5
0	0	—	—	—	—
1	1	1	1	1	1
2	12	12	12	12	2
3	1232	1232	1232	232	32
4	12323432	12323432	2323432	323432	3432
. . .	. . .	. . .	. . .	. . .	. . .
n	A_n	B_n	C_n	D_n	E_n
$n+1$	$B_n(A_n^R+1)$	$C_n(A_n^R+1)$	$D_n(A_n^R+1)$	$E_n(A_n^R+1)$	A_n^R+1

Staircase of merge numbers:

```
2
3 2
4 3 2
3 4 3
4 3 4 2
5 4 3 3
4 5 4 4
3 4 5 3
2 3 4 4 2
3 2 3 5 3
4 3 2 4 4
3 4 3 3 3
2 3 4 2 4
3 2 3 3 5
2 3 2 4 4
1 2 3 3 3
```

We have
$$E_n = A_{n-1}^R + 1,$$
$$D_n = A_{n-2}^R A_{n-1}^R + 1,$$
$$C_n = A_{n-3}^R A_{n-2}^R A_{n-1}^R + 1,$$
$$B_n = A_{n-4}^R A_{n-3}^R A_{n-2}^R A_{n-1}^R + 1, \quad \text{and}$$
$$A_n = A_{n-5}^R A_{n-4}^R A_{n-3}^R A_{n-2}^R A_{n-1}^R + 1$$
$$= n - Q_n,$$

where

$$Q_n^R = Q_{n-1}(Q_{n-2}+1)(Q_{n-3}+2)(Q_{n-4}+3)(Q_{n-5}+4), \qquad n \geq 1,$$

$Q_0 = 0$, and $Q_n = \epsilon$ for $n < 0$.

These strings A_n, B_n, ... contain the same entries as the corresponding strings in Section 5.4.2, but in another order. Note that adjacent merge numbers always differ by 1. An initial run must be A if and only if its merge number is even, D if and only if odd. Simple distribution schemes such as Algorithm 5.4.2D are not quite as effective at placing dummies into high-merge-number positions; therefore it is probably advantageous to compute Q_n between phases 1 and 2, in order to help control dummy run placement.

6. $y^{(4)} = (+1, +1, -1, +1)$
$y^{(3)} = (+1, \ \ 0, -1, \ \ 0)$
$y^{(2)} = (+1, -1, +1, +1)$
$y^{(1)} = (-1, +1, +1, +1)$
$y^{(0)} = (\ \ 1, \ \ 0, \ \ 0, \ \ 0)$

7. (See exercise 15.)

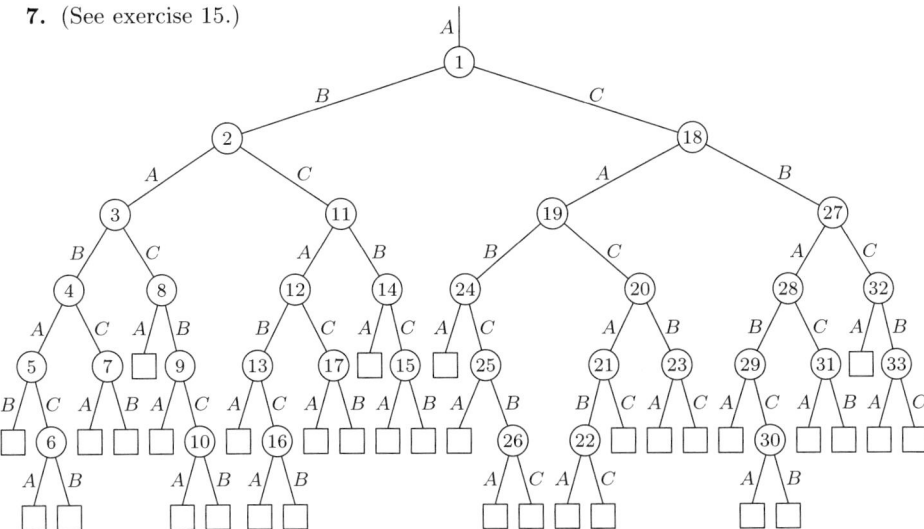

Incidentally, 34 is apparently the smallest Fibonacci number F_n for which polyphase doesn't produce the optimum read-backward merge for F_n initial runs on three tapes. This tree has external path length 178, which beats polyphase's 176.

8. For $T = 4$, the tree with external path length 13 is not T-lifo, and every tree with external path length 14 includes a one-way merge.

9. We may consider a complete $(T-1)$-ary tree, by the result of exercise 2.3.4.5–6; the degree of the "last" internal node is between 2 and $T - 1$. When there are $(T-1)^q - m$ external nodes, $\lfloor m/(T-2) \rfloor$ of them are on level $q - 1$, and the rest are on level q.

11. True by induction on the number of initial runs. If there is a valid distribution with S runs and two adjacent runs in the same direction, then there is one with fewer than S runs; but there is none when $S = 1$.

12. Conditions (a) and (b) are obvious. If either configuration in (4) is present, for some tape name A and some $i < j < k$, node j must be in a subtree below node i and to the left of node k, by the definition of preorder. Hence the case "$j - l$" can't be present, and A must be the "special" name since it appears on an external branch. But this contradicts the fact that the special name is supposed to be on the leftmost branch below node i.

13. Nodes now numbered 4, 7, 11, 13 could be external instead of one-way merges. (This gives an external path length one higher than the polyphase tree.)

15. Let the tape names be A, B, and C. We shall construct several species of trees, botanically identified by their root and leaf (external node) structure:

Type $r(A)$	Root A
Type $s(A,C)$	Root A, no C leaves
Type $t(A)$	Root A, no A leaves
Type $u(A,C)$	Root A, no C leaves, no compound B leaves
Type $v(A,C)$	Root A, no C leaves, no compound A leaves
Type $w(A,C)$	Root A, no A leaves, no compound C leaves

A "compound leaf" is a leaf whose sibling is not a leaf. We can grow a 3-lifo type $r(A)$ tree by first growing its left subtree as a type $s(B,C)$, then growing the right subtree as type $r(C)$. Similarly, type $s(A,C)$ comes from a type $s(B,C)$ then $t(C)$; type $u(A,C)$ from $v(B,C)$ and $w(C,B)$; type $v(A,C)$ from $u(B,C)$ and $w(C,A)$. We can grow a 3-lifo type $t(A)$ tree whose left subtree is type $u(B,A)$ and whose right subtree is type $s(C,A)$, by first letting the left subtree grow except for its (non-compound) C leaves and its right subtree; at this point the left subtree has only A and B leaves, so we can grow the right subtree of the whole tree, then grow off the A leaves of the left left subtree, and finally grow the left right subtree. Similarly, a type $w(A,C)$ tree can be fabricated from a $u(B,A)$ and a $v(C,A)$. [The tree of exercise 7 is an $r(A)$ tree constructed in this manner.]

Let $r(n),\ldots,w(n)$ denote the minimum external path length over all n-leaf trees of the relevant type, when they are constructed by such a procedure. We have $r(1) = s(1) = u(1) = 0$, $r(2) = t(2) = w(2) = 2$, $t(1) = v(1) = w(1) = s(2) = u(2) = v(2) = \infty$; and for $n \geq 3$,

$$r(n) = n + \min_k\big(s(k) + r(n-k)\big), \qquad u(n) = n + \min_k\big(v(k) + w(n-k)\big),$$
$$s(n) = n + \min_k\big(s(k) + t(n-k)\big), \qquad v(n) = n + \min_k\big(u(k) + w(n-k)\big),$$
$$t(n) = n + \min_k\big(u(k) + s(n-k)\big), \qquad w(n) = n + \min_k\big(u(k) + v(n-k)\big).$$

It follows that $r(n) \leq s(n) \leq u(n)$, $s(n) \leq v(n)$, and $r(n) \leq t(n) \leq w(n)$ for all n; furthermore $s(2n) = t(2n+1) = \infty$. (The latter is evident a priori.)

Let $A(n)$ be the function defined by the laws $A(1) = 0$, $A(2n) = 2n + 2A(n)$, $A(2n+1) = 2n+1+A(n)+A(n+1)$; then $A(2n) = 2n + A(n-1) + A(n+1) - (0 \text{ or } 1)$ for all $n \geq 2$. Let C be a constant such that, for $4 \leq n \leq 8$,

i) n even implies that $w(n) \leq A(n) + Cn - 1$.

ii) n odd implies that $u(n)$ and $v(n)$ are $\leq A(n) + Cn - 1$.

(This actually works for all $C \geq \frac{5}{6}$.) Then an inductive argument, choosing k to be $\lfloor n/2 \rfloor \pm 1$ as appropriate, shows that the relations are valid for all $n \geq 4$. But $A(n)$ is the lower bound in (9) when $T = 3$, and $r(n) \leq \min(u(n), v(n), w(n))$, hence we have proved that $A(n) \leq \hat{K}_3(n) \leq r(n) \leq A(n) + \frac{5}{6}n - 1$. [The constant $\frac{5}{6}$ can be improved.]

17. [The following method was used in the UNIVAC III sort program, and presented at the 1962 ACM Sort Symposium.]

Level	T1	T2	T3	T4	T5
0	1	0	0	0	0
1	5	4	3	2	1
2	55	50	41	29	15
$\cdots$	$\cdots$	$\cdots$	$\cdots$	$\cdots$	$\cdots$
n	a_n	b_n	c_n	d_n	e_n
$n+1$	$5a_n+4b_n+$ $3c_n+2d_n+e_n$	$4a_n+4b_n+$ $3c_n+2d_n+e_n$	$3a_n+3b_n+$ $3c_n+2d_n+e_n$	$2a_n+2b_n+$ $2c_n+2d_n+e_n$	a_n+b_n+ $c_n+d_n+e_n$

To get from level n to level $n+1$ during the initial distribution, insert k_1 "sublevels" with $(4,4,3,2,1)$ runs added respectively to tapes (T1, T2, ..., T5), k_2 "sublevels" with $(4,3,3,2,1)$ runs added, k_3 with $(3,3,2,2,1)$, k_4 with $(2,2,2,1,1)$, k_5 with $(1,1,1,1,0)$, where $k_1 \leq a_n$, $k_2 \leq b_n$, $k_3 \leq c_n$, $k_4 \leq d_n$, $k_5 \leq e_n$. [If $(k_1,\ldots,k_5) = (a_n,\ldots,e_n)$ we have reached level $n+1$.] Add dummy runs if necessary to fill out a sublevel. Then merge $k_1 + k_2 + k_3 + k_4 + k_5$ runs from (T1, ..., T5) to T6, merge $k_1 + \cdots + k_4$ from (T1, ..., T4) to T5, ..., merge k_1 from T1 to T2; and merge k_1 from (T2, ..., T6) to T1, k_2 from (T3, ..., T6) to T2, ..., k_5 from T6 to T5.

18. (Solution by M. S. Paterson.) Suppose record j is written on the sequence of tape numbers τ_j. At most $C|\tau|$ records can have a given sequence τ, where C depends on the internal memory size (see Section 5.4.8). Hence $|\tau_1| + \cdots + |\tau_N| = \Omega(N \log_T N)$.

19.

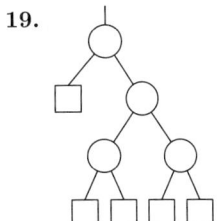

20. A strongly T-fifo tree has a T-fifo labeling in which there are no three branches having the respective forms

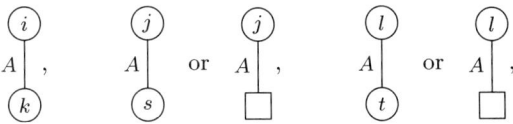

for some tape name A and some $i < j < k < l < s$. Informally, when we grow on an A, we must grow on all other A's before creating any new A's.

21. It is very weakly fifo:

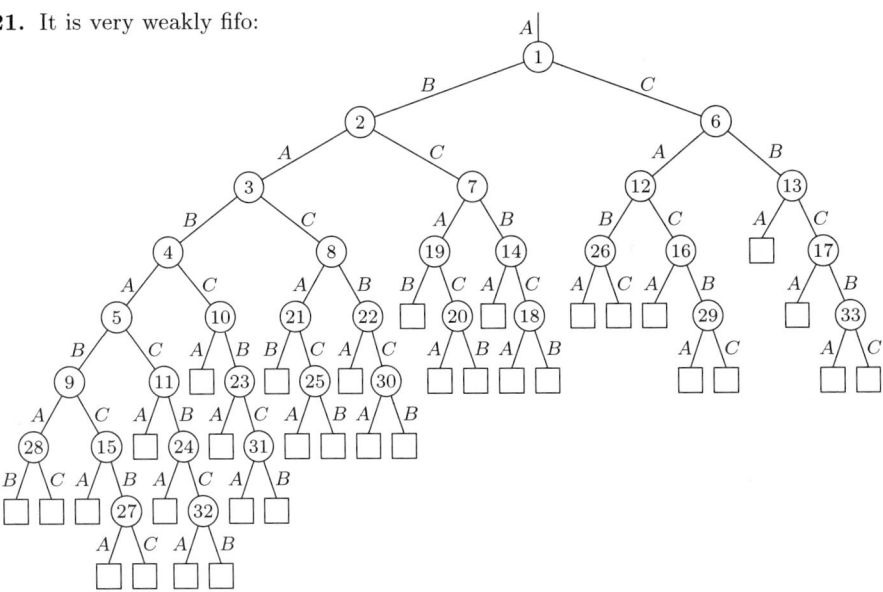

22. This occurs for any tree representations formed by successively replacing all occurrences of, for example,

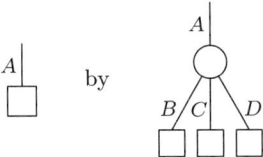

for some fixed tape names A, B, C, D. Since all occurrences are replaced by the same pattern, the lifo or fifo order makes no difference in the structure of the tree.

Stating the condition in terms of the vector model: Whenever $(y^{(k+1)} \neq y^{(k)}$ or $k = m)$ and $y_j^{(k)} = -1$, we have $y_j^{(k)} + \cdots + y_j^{(1)} + y_j^{(0)} = 0$.

23. (a) Assume that $v_1 \leq v_2 \leq \cdots \leq v_T$; the "cascade" stage

$$(1,\ldots,1,-1)^{v_T}(1,\ldots,1,-1,0)^{v_T-1}\ldots(1,-1,0,\ldots,0)^{v_2}$$

takes $C(v)$ into v. (b) Immediate, since $C(v)_k \leq C(w)_k$ for all k. (c) If v is obtained in q stages, we have $u \to u^{(1)} \to \cdots \to u^{(q)} = v$ for some unit vector u, and some other vectors $u^{(1)}, \ldots, u^{(q-1)}$. Hence $u^{(1)} \preceq C(u)$, $u^{(2)} \preceq C(C(u))$, $\ldots$, $v \preceq C^{[q]}(u)$. Hence $v_1 + \cdots + v_T$ is less than or equal to the sum of the elements of $C^{[q]}(u)$; and the latter is obtained in cascade merge. [This theorem generalizes the result of exercise 5.4.3–4. Unfortunately the concept of "stage" as defined here doesn't seem to have any practical significance.]

24. Let $y^{(m)}\ldots y^{(l+1)}$ be a stage that reduces w to v. If we have $y_j^{(i)} = -1$, $y_j^{(i-1)} = 0$, $\ldots$, $y_j^{(k+1)} = 0$, and $y_j^{(k)} = -1$, for some $k < i - 1$, we can insert $y^{(k)}$ between $y^{(i)}$ and $y^{(i-1)}$. Repeat this operation until all (-1)'s in each column are adjacent. Then if $y_j^{(i)} = 0$ and $y_j^{(i-1)} \neq 0$ it is possible to set $y_j^{(i)} \leftarrow 1$; ultimately each column consists of $+1$'s followed by -1's followed by 0s, and we have constructed a stage that reduces w' to v for some $w' \succeq w$. Permuting the columns, this stage takes the form $(1,\ldots,1,-1)^{a_T}\ldots(1,-1,0,\ldots,0)^{a_2}(-1,0,\ldots,0)^{a_1}$. The sequence of $T - 1$ relations

$$(x_1,\ldots,x_T) \preceq (x_1+x_T,\ldots,x_{T-1}+x_T,0)$$
$$\preceq (x_1+x_{T-1}+x_T,\ldots,x_{T-2}+x_{T-1}+x_T,x_T,0)$$
$$\preceq (x_1+x_{T-2}+x_{T-1}+x_T,\ldots,x_{T-3}+x_{T-2}+x_{T-1}+x_T,x_{T-1}+x_T,x_T,0)$$
$$\preceq \cdots$$
$$\preceq (x_1+x_2+x_3+\cdots+x_T,x_3+\cdots+x_T,\ldots,x_{T-1}+x_T,x_T,0)$$

now shows that the best choice of the a's is $a_T = v_T$, $a_{T-1} = v_{T-1}$, $\ldots$, $a_2 = v_2$, $a_1 = 0$. And the result is best if we permute columns so that $v_1 \leq \cdots \leq v_T$.

25. (a) Assume that $v_{T-k+1} \geq \cdots \geq v_T \geq v_1 \geq \cdots \geq v_{T-k}$ and use

$$(1,\ldots,1,-1,0,\ldots,0)^{v_{T-k+1}}\ldots(1,\ldots,1,0,\ldots,0,-1)^{v_T}.$$

(b) The sum of the l largest elements of $D_k(v)$ is $(l-1)s_k + s_{k+l}$ for $1 \leq l \leq T - k$. (c) If $v \Rightarrow w$ in a phase that uses k output tapes, we may obviously assume that the phase has the form $(1,\ldots,1,-1,0,\ldots,0)^{a_1}\ldots(1,\ldots,1,0,\ldots,0,-1)^{a_k}$, with each of the other $T - k$ tapes used as input in each operation. Choosing $a_1 = v_{T-k+1}, \ldots$, $a_k = v_T$ is best. (d) See exercise 22(c). We always have $k_1 = 1$; and $k = T - 2$ always beats $k = T - 1$ since we assume that at least one component of v is zero. Hence for $T = 3$ we have $k_1\ldots k_q = 1^q$ and the initial distribution $(F_{q+1}, F_q, 0)$. For $T = 4$ the undominated strategies and their corresponding distributions are found to be

$$
\begin{aligned}
q &= 2 \quad 12 \ (3,2,0,0) \\
q &= 3 \quad 121 \ (5,3,3,0); \ 122 \ (5,5,0,0) \\
q &= 4 \quad 1211 \ (8,8,5,0); \ 1222 \ (10,10,0,0); \ 1212 \ (11,8,0,0) \\
q &= 5 \quad 12121 \ (19,11,11,0); \ 12222 \ (20,20,0,0); \ 12112 \ (21,16,0,0) \\
q &= 6 \quad 122222 \ (40,40,0,0); \ 121212 \ (41,30,0,0) \\
q &\geq 7 \quad 12^{q-1} \ (5 \cdot 2^{q-3}, 5 \cdot 2^{q-3}, 0, 0)
\end{aligned}
$$

So for $T = 4$ and $q \geq 6$, the minimum-phase merge is like balanced merge, with a slight twist at the very end (going from $(3, 2, 0, 0)$ to $(1, 0, 1, 1)$ instead of to $(0, 0, 2, 1)$).

When $T = 5$ the undominated strategies are $1(32)^{n-1}2$, $1(32)^{n-1}3$ for $q = 2n \geq 2$; $1(32)^{n-1}32$, $1(32)^{n-1}22$, $1(32)^{n-1}23$ for $q = 2n + 1 \geq 3$. (The first strategy listed has most runs in its distribution.) On six tapes they are 13 or 14, 142 or 132 or 133, 1333 or 1423, then 13^{q-1} for $q \geq 5$.

SECTION 5.4.5

1. The following algorithm is controlled by a table $A[L-1] \ldots A[1]A[0]$ that essentially represents a number in radix P notation. As we repeatedly add unity to this number, the carries tell us when to merge. Tapes are numbered from 0 to P.

    O1. [Initialize.] Set $(A[L-1], \ldots, A[0]) \leftarrow (0, \ldots, 0)$ and $q \leftarrow 0$. (During this algorithm, q will equal $(A[L-1] + \cdots + A[0]) \bmod T$.)

    O2. [Distribute.] Write an initial run on tape q, in ascending order. Set $l \leftarrow 0$.

    O3. [Add one.] If $l = L$, stop; the output is on tape $(-L) \bmod T$, in ascending order if and only if L is even. Otherwise set $A[l] \leftarrow A[l]+1$, $q \leftarrow (q+1) \bmod T$.

    O4. [Carry?] If $A[l] < P$, return to O2. Otherwise merge to tape $(q - l) \bmod T$, set $A[l] \leftarrow 0$ and $q \leftarrow (q + 1) \bmod T$, increase l by 1, and return to O3. ∎

2. Keep track of how many runs are on each tape. When the input is exhausted, add dummy runs if necessary and continue merging until reaching a situation with at most one run on each tape and at least one tape empty. Then finish the sort in one more merge, rewinding some tapes first if necessary. (It is possible to deduce the orientation of the runs from the A table.)

3.

Op	T0	T1	T2		Op	T0	T1	T2
Dist	—	A_1	A_1A_1		Dist	D_2A_1	A_1	A_4
Merge	D_2	—	A_1		Merge	D_2	—	A_4D_2
Dist	D_2A_1	—	A_1		Merge	—	A_4	A_4
Merge	D_2	D_2	—		Dist	—	A_4	A_4A_1
Dist	D_2	D_2A_1	A_1		Copy	—	A_4D_1	A_4
Merge	D_2D_2	D_2	—		Copy	—	A_4	A_4A_1
Merge	D_2	—	A_4		Merge	D_5	—	A_4

At this point T2 would be rewound and a final merge would complete the sort.

To avoid useless copying in which runs are simply shifted back and forth, we can say "If the input is exhausted, go to B7" at the end of B3, and add the following new step:

    B7. [Do the endgame.] Set $s \leftarrow -1$, and go to B2 after repeating the following operations until $l = 0$: Set $s' \leftarrow A[l-1, q]$, and set q' and r' to the indices such that $A[l-1, q'] = -1$ and $A[l-1, r'] = -2$. (We will have $q' = r$, and $s' \leq A[l-1, j] \leq s' + 1$ for $j \neq q'$, $j \neq r'$.) If $s' - s$ is odd, promote level l, otherwise demote it (see below). Then merge to tape r, reading backwards; set $l \leftarrow l - 1$, $A[l, q] \leftarrow -1$, $A[l, r] \leftarrow s' + 1$, $r \leftarrow r'$, and repeat.

Here "promotion" means to repeat the following operation until $(q+(-1)^s) \bmod T = r$: Set $p \leftarrow (q+(-1)^s) \bmod T$ and copy one run from tape p to tape q, then set $A[l, q] \leftarrow s + 1$, $A[l, p] \leftarrow -1$, $q \leftarrow p$. And "demotion" means to repeat the following until $(q-(-1)^s) \bmod T = r$: Set $p \leftarrow (q-(-1)^s) \bmod T$ and copy one run from tape p to tape q, then set $A[l, q] \leftarrow s$, $A[l, p] \leftarrow -1$, $q \leftarrow p$. The copy operation reads backwards on tape p, hence it reverses the direction of the run being copied. If $\mathtt{D}[p] > 0$ when copying from p to q, we simply decrease $\mathtt{D}[p]$ and increase $\mathtt{D}[q]$ instead of copying.

[The basic idea is that, once the input is exhausted, we want to reduce to at most one run on each tape. The parity of each nonnegative entry $\mathtt{A}[l,j]$ tells us whether a run is ascending or descending. The smallest S for which this change makes any difference is $P^3 + 1$. When P is large, the change hardly ever makes much difference, but it does keep the computer from looking too foolish in some circumstances. The algorithm should also be changed to handle the case $S = 1$ more efficiently.]

4. We can, in fact, omit setting $\mathtt{A}[0,0]$ in step B1, $\mathtt{A}[l,q]$ in steps B3 and B5. [But $\mathtt{A}[l,r]$ *must* be set in step B3.] The new step B7 in the previous answer does need the value of $\mathtt{A}[l,q]$ (unless it explicitly uses the fact that $q' = r$, as noted there).

5. $P^{2k} - (P-1)P^{2k-2} < S \leq P^{2k}$ for some $k > 0$.

SECTION 5.4.6

1. $\lfloor 23000480/(n+480) \rfloor n$.

2. At the instant shown, all the records in that buffer have been moved to the output. Step F2 insists that the test "Is output buffer full?" precede the test "Is input buffer empty?" while merging, otherwise we would have trouble (unless the changes of exercise 4 were made).

3. No; for example, we might reach a state with P buffers $1/P$ full and $P-1$ buffers full, if file i contains the keys i, $i+P$, $i+2P$, ..., for $1 \leq i \leq P$. This example shows that $2P$ input buffers would be necessary for continuous output even if we allowed simultaneous reading, unless we reallocated memory for partial buffers. [Well, we don't really need $2P$ buffers if the blocks contain fewer than $P-1$ records; but that is unlikely.]

4. Set up S sooner (in steps F1 and F4 instead of F3).

5. If, for example, all keys of all files were equal, we couldn't simply make arbitrary decisions while forecasting; the forecast must be compatible with decisions made by the merging process. One safe way is to find the smallest possible m in steps F1 and F4, namely to consider a record from file $\mathtt{C}[i]$ to be less than all records having the same key on file $\mathtt{C}[j]$ whenever $i < j$. (In essence, the file number is appended to the key.)

6. In step C1 also set $\mathtt{TAPE}[T+1] \leftarrow T+1$. In step C8 the merge should be to $\mathtt{TAPE}[p+2]$ instead of $\mathtt{TAPE}[p+1]$. In step C9, set $(\mathtt{TAPE}[1],\ldots,\mathtt{TAPE}[T+1]) \leftarrow (\mathtt{TAPE}[T+1],\ldots,\mathtt{TAPE}[1])$.

7. The method used in Chart A is $(A_1D_1)^4 A_0 D_0 A_1 D_1 (A_0 D_0 (A_1 D_1)^3)^2 A_0$, $D_1 (A_1 D_1)^2$ $A_0 D_0 (A_1 D_1)^3 A_0 D_0 \alpha A_0 D_0 A_0$, $D_1 A_0 D_0 (A_1 D_1)^3 A_0 D_0 \alpha A_1 D_1 A_0$, $D_1 A_1 D_1 \alpha A_1 D_1 A_0$, where $\alpha = (A_0 D_0)^2 A_1 D_1 A_0 D_0 (A_1 D_1)^2 (A_0 D_0)^7 A_1 D_1 (A_0 D_0)^3 A_1 D_1 A_0 D_0$. The first merge phase writes $D_0 A_3 D_3 A_1 D_1 A_4 D_4 A_0 D_0 A_1 D_1 A_1 D_1 A_4 D_4 A_0 D_0 A_1 D_1 A_0 D_0 (A_1 D_1)^4$ on tape 5; the next writes $A_4 D_4 A_4 D_4 A_1 D_1 A_4 D_4 A_0 D_0 A_1 D_1 A_1 D_1 A_7$ on tape 1; the next, $D_{13} A_4 D_4 A_4 D_4 A_0 D_0 A_{10}$ on tape 4. The final phases are

$$
\begin{array}{ccccc}
A_4 D_4 A_4 & - & D_{19} A_3 D_3 A_{12} & D_{13} A_4 D_4 A_4 & D_0 A_3 \\
A_4 & D_{23} A_{11} & D_{19} A_3 & D_{13} A_4 & - \\
- & D_{23} & D_{19} & D_{13} & D_{22} \\
A_{77} & - & - & - & -
\end{array}
$$

8. No, since at most S stop/starts are saved, and since the speed of the input tape (not the output tapes) tends to govern the initial distribution time anyway. The other advantages of the distribution schemes used in Chart A outweigh this minuscule disadvantage.

9. $P = 5$, $B = 8300$, $B' = 734$, $S = \lceil (3 + 1/P)N/(6P') \rceil + 1 = 74$, $\omega \approx 1.094$, $\alpha \approx 0.795$, $\beta \approx -1.136$, $\alpha' = \beta' = 0$; Eq. (9) ≈ 855 seconds, to which we add the time for initial rewind, for a total of 958 seconds. The savings of about one minute in the merging time does not compensate for the loss of time due to the initial rewinding and tape changing (unless perhaps we are in a multiprogramming environment).

10. The rewinds during standard polyphase merge involve about 54 percent of the file (the "pass/phase" column in Table 5.4.2–1), and the longest rewinds during standard cascade merge involve approximately $a_k a_{n-k}/a_n \approx (4/(2T-1)) \cos^2(\pi/(4T-2)) < \frac{4}{11}$ of the file, by exercise 5.4.3–5 and Eq. 5.4.3–(13).

11. Only initial and final rewinds get to make use of the high-speed feature, since the reel is only a little more than 10/23 full when it contains the whole example file. Using $\pi = \lceil .946 \ln S - 1.204 \rceil$, $\pi' = 1/8$ in example 8, we get the following estimated totals for examples 1–9, respectively:

$$1115, \ 1296, \ 1241, \ 1008, \ 1014, \ 967, \ 891, \ 969, \ 856.$$

12. (a) An obvious solution with $4P+4$ buffers simply reads and writes simultaneously from paired tapes. But note that three output buffers are sufficient: At a given moment we can be performing the second half of a write from one, the first half of a write from another, and outputting into a third. This approach suggests a corresponding improvement in the input buffer situation. It turns out that $3P$ input buffers and 3 output buffers are necessary and sufficient, using a slightly weakened forecasting technique. A simpler and superior approach, suggested by J. Sue, adds a "lookahead key" to each block, specifying the final key of the subsequent block. Sue's method requires $2P+1$ input buffers and 4 output buffers, and it is a straightforward modification of Algorithm F. (See also Section 5.4.9.)

(b) In this case the high value of α means that we must do between five and six passes over the data, which wipes out the advantage of double-quick merging. The idea works out much better on eight or nine tapes.

13. No; consider, for example, the situation just before $A_{16}A_{16}A_{16}A_{16}$. But two reelfuls *can* be handled.

14. $\det \begin{pmatrix} 0 & -p_0 z & 0 & z-1 \\ 0 & 1 - p_1 z & -p_0 z & z-1 \\ 1 & 0 & 0 & 0 \\ 0 & 0 & 0 & 1 \end{pmatrix} \Bigg/ \det \begin{pmatrix} 1 - p_{\geq 1} z & -p_0 z & 0 & z-1 \\ -p_{\geq 2} z & 1 - p_1 z & -p_0 z & z-1 \\ 0 & -1 & 1 & 0 \\ 0 & 0 & 0 & 1 \end{pmatrix}.$

15. The A matrix has the form

$$A = \begin{pmatrix} B_{10}z & B_{11}z & \cdots & B_{1n}z & 1-z \\ \vdots & & & & \vdots \\ B_{n0}z & B_{n1}z & \cdots & B_{nn}z & 1-z \\ 0 \cdots 0 & 1 & 0 & 0 \\ 0 \cdots 0 & 0 & 0 & 0 \end{pmatrix},$$

$$\begin{aligned} B_{10} + B_{11} + \cdots + B_{1n} &= 1, \\ &\vdots \\ B_{n0} + B_{n1} + \cdots + B_{nn} &= 1. \end{aligned} \qquad (11)$$

Therefore

$$\det(I - A) = \det \begin{pmatrix} 1 - B_{10}z & -B_{11}z & \cdots & -B_{1(n-1)}z & -B_{1n}z \\ \vdots & & & & \vdots \\ -B_{n0}z & -B_{n1}z & \cdots & 1 - B_{n(n-1)}z & -B_{nn}z \\ 0 & 0 & \cdots & -1 & 1 \end{pmatrix}$$

and we can add all columns to the first column, then factor out $(1 - z)$. Consequently $g_Q(z)$ has the form $h_Q(z)/(1 - z)$, and $\alpha^{(Q)} = h_Q(1)$ because we have $h_Q(1) \neq 0$ and $\det(I - A) \neq 0$ for $|z| < 1$.

SECTION 5.4.7

1. Sort from least significant digit to most significant digit in the number system whose radices are alternately P and $T - P$. (If pairs of digits are grouped, we have essentially the pure radix $P \cdot (T - P)$. Thus, if $P = 2$ and $T = 7$, the number system is "biquinary," related to decimal notation in a simple way.)

2. If K is a key between 0 and $F_n - 1$, let the Fibonacci representation of $F_n - 1 - K$ be $a_{n-2}F_{n-1} + \cdots + a_1 F_2$, where the a_j are 0 or 1, and no two consecutive 1s appear. After phase j, tape $(j + 1) \bmod 3$ contains the keys with $a_j = 0$, and tape $(j - 1) \bmod 3$ contains those with $a_j = 1$, in decreasing order of $a_{j-1} \ldots a_1$.

[Imagine a card sorter with two pockets, "0" and "1", and consider the procedure of sorting F_n cards that have been punched with the keys $a_{n-2} \ldots a_1$ in $n - 2$ columns. The conventional procedure for sorting these into decreasing order, starting at the least significant digit, can be simplified since we know that everything in the "1" pocket at the end of one pass will go into the "0" pocket on the following pass.]

4. If there were an external node on level 2 we could not construct such a good tree. Otherwise there are at most three external nodes on level 3, and six on level 4, since each external node is supposed to appear on the same tape.

5.

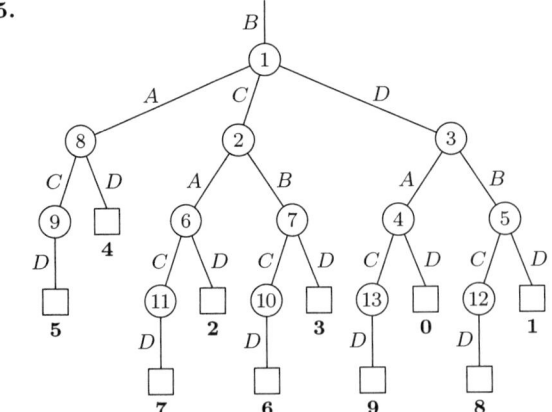

6. 09, 08, ..., 00, 19, ..., 10, 29, ..., 20, 39, ..., 30, 40, 41, ..., 49, 59, ..., 50, 60, 61, ..., 99.

7. Yes; first distribute the records into smaller and smaller subfiles until obtaining one-reel files that can be sorted individually. This is dual to the process of sorting one-reel files and then merging them into larger and larger multireel files.

SECTION 5.4.8

1. Yes. If we alternately use ascending and descending order in the selection tree, we have in effect an order-P cocktail-shaker sort. (See exercise 9.)

2. Let $Z_N = Y_N - X_N$, and solve the recurrence for Z_N by noting that

$$(N + 1)N Z_{N+1} = N(N - 1)Z_N + N^2 + N;$$

hence

$$Z_N = \tfrac{1}{3}(N+1) + \binom{M+2}{3} \Big/ N(N-1), \qquad \text{for } N > M.$$

Now eliminate Y_N and obtain

$$\frac{X_N}{N+1} = \frac{20}{3}(H_{N+1} - H_{M+2}) + 2\left(\frac{1}{N+1} - \frac{1}{M+2}\right)$$

$$- \frac{2}{3}\binom{M+2}{3}\left(\frac{1}{(N+1)N(N-1)} - \frac{1}{(M+2)(M+1)M}\right) + \frac{3M+4}{M+2}, \quad N > M.$$

3. Yes; find a median element in $O(N)$ steps, using a construction like that of Theorem 5.3.3L, and use it to partition the file. Another interesting approach, due to R. W. Floyd and A. J. Smith, is to merge two runs of N items in $O(N)$ units of time as follows: Spread the items out on the tapes, with spaces between them, then successively fill each space with a number specifying the final position of the item just preceding that space.

4. It is possible to piece together a schedule for floors $\{1, \ldots, p+1\}$ with a schedule for floors $\{q, \ldots, n\}$: When the former schedule first reaches floor $p+1$, go up to floor q and carry out the latter schedule (using the current elevator contents as if they were the "extras" in the algorithm of Theorem K). After finishing that schedule, go back to floor $p+1$ and resume the previous schedule.

5. Consider $b = 2$, $m = 4$ and the following behavior of the algorithm:

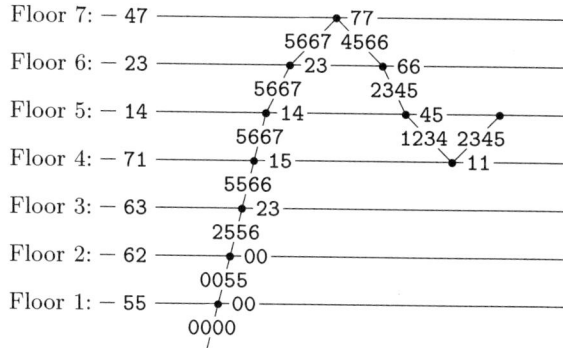

Now 2 (in the elevator) is less than 3 (on floor 3).

    [After constructing an example such as this, the reader should be able to see how to demonstrate the weaker property required in the proof of Theorem K.]

6. Let i and j be minimal with $b_i < b'_i$ and $b_j > b'_j$. Introduce a new person who wants to go from i to j. This doesn't increase $\max(u_k, d_{k+1}, 1)$ or $\max(b_k, b'_k)$ for any k. Continue this until $b_j = b'_j$ for all j. Now observe that the algorithm in the text works also with b replaced by b_k in steps K1 and K3.

8. Let the number be P_n, and let Q_n be the number of permutations such that $u_k = 1$ for $1 \le k < n$. Then $P_n = Q_1 P_{n-1} + Q_2 P_{n-2} + \cdots + Q_n P_0$, $P_0 = 1$. It can be shown that $Q_n = 3^{n-2}$ for $n \ge 2$ (see below), hence a generating function argument yields

$$\sum P_n z^n = (1 - 3z)/(1 - 4z + 2z^2) = 1 + z + 2z^2 + 6z^3 + 20z^4 + 68z^5 + \cdots;$$

$$2P_n = (2 + \sqrt{2})^{n-1} + (2 - \sqrt{2})^{n-1}.$$

To prove that $Q_n = 3^{n-2}$, consider a ternary sequence $x_1 x_2 \ldots x_n$ such that $x_1 = 2$, $x_n = 0$, and $0 \le x_k \le 2$ for $1 < k < n$. The following rule defines a one-to-one correspondence between such sequences and the desired permutations $a_1 a_2 \ldots a_n$:

$$a_k = \begin{cases} \max\{j \mid (j < k \text{ and } x_j = 0) \text{ or } j = 1\}, & \text{if } x_k = 0; \\ k, & \text{if } x_k = 1; \\ \min\{j \mid (j > k \text{ and } x_j = 2) \text{ or } j = n\}, & \text{if } x_k = 2. \end{cases}$$

(This correspondence was obtained by the author jointly with E. A. Bender.)

9. The number of passes of the cocktail-shaker sort is $2 \max(u_1, \ldots, u_n) - (0 \text{ or } 1)$, since each pair of passes (left-right-left) reduces each of the nonzero u's by 1.

10. Begin with a distribution method (quicksort or radix exchange) until one-reel files are obtained. And be patient.

SECTION 5.4.9

1. $\frac{1}{4} - (x \bmod \frac{1}{2})^2$ revolutions.

2. The probability that $k = a_{iq}$ and $k + 1 = a_{i'r}$ for fixed k, q, r, and $i \ne i'$ is $f(q, r, k) L! L! (PL - 2L)! / (PL)!$, where

$$f(q, r, k) = \binom{k-1}{q-1}\binom{k-q}{r-1}\binom{PL-k-1}{L-q}\binom{PL-k-1-L+q}{L-r}$$
$$= \binom{k-1}{q+r-2}\binom{q+r-2}{q-1}\binom{PL-k-1}{2L-q-r}\binom{2L-q-r}{L-q};$$

and

$$\sum_{\substack{1 \le k < PL \\ 1 \le q, r \le L}} |q - r| f(q, r, k) = \sum_{1 \le q, r \le L} |q - r|\binom{PL-1}{2L-1}\binom{q+r-2}{q-1}\binom{2L-q-r}{L-q} = \binom{PL-1}{2L-1} A_{2L-1}.$$

The probability that $k = a_{iq}$ and $k + 1 = a_{i(q+1)}$ for fixed k, q, and i is

$$g(k, q)\bigg/\binom{PL}{L}, \quad \text{where} \quad g(k, q) = \binom{k-1}{q-1}\binom{PL-k-1}{L-q-1};$$

and

$$\sum_{\substack{1 \le k < PL \\ 1 \le q < L}} g(k, q) = \sum_{1 \le q < L} \binom{PL-1}{L-1} = (L-1)\binom{PL-1}{L-1}.$$

[*SICOMP* **1** (1972), 161–166.]

3. Take the minimum in (5) over the range $2 \le m \le \min(9, n)$.

4. (a) $(0.000725(\sqrt{P} + 1)^2 + 0.014)L$. (b) Change "$\alpha mn + \beta n$" in formula (5) to "$(0.000725(\sqrt{m} + 1)^2 + 0.014)n$." [Computer experiments show that the optimal trees defined by this new recurrence are very similar to those defined by Theorem K with $\alpha = 0.00145$, $\beta = 0.01545$; in fact, trees exist that are optimal for both recurrences, when $30 \le n \le 100$. The change suggested in this exercise saves about 10 percent of the merging time, when $n = 64$ or 100 as in the text's example. This style of buffer allocation was considered already in 1954 by H. Seward, who found that four-way merging minimizes the seek time.]

5. Let $A_m(n)$ and $B_m(n)$ be the cost of optimum sets of m trees whose n leaves are all at (even, odd) levels, respectively. Then $A_1(1) = 0$, $B_1(1) = \alpha + \beta$; $A_m(n)$ and $B_m(n)$ are defined as in (4) when $m \geq 2$; $A_1(n) = \min_{1 \leq m \leq n}(\alpha mn + \beta n + B_m(n))$, $B_1(n) = \min_{1 \leq m \leq n}(\alpha mn + \beta n + A_m(n))$. The latter equations are well-defined in spite of the fact that $A_1(n)$ and $B_1(n)$ are defined in terms of each other!

6.

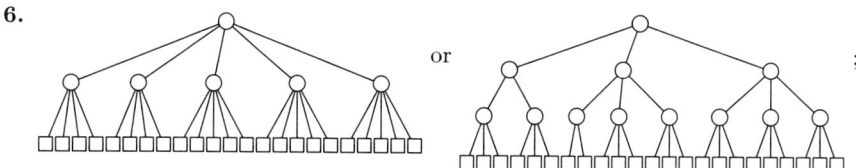

$A_1(23) = B_1(23) = 268$. [Curiously, $n = 23$ is the only value ≤ 50 for which no equal-parity tree with n leaves is optimal in the unrestricted-parity case. Perhaps it is the *only* such value, when $\alpha = \beta$.]

7. Consider the quantities $\alpha d_1 + \beta e_1, \ldots, \alpha d_n + \beta e_n$ in any tree, where d_j is the degree sum and e_j is the path length for the jth leaf. An optimum tree for weights $w_1 \leq \cdots \leq w_n$ will have $\alpha d_1 + \beta e_1 \geq \cdots \geq \alpha d_n + \beta e_n$. It is always possible to reorder the indices so that $\alpha d_1 + \beta e_1 = \cdots = \alpha d_k + \beta e_k$ where the first k leaves are merged together.

9. Let d minimize $(\alpha m + \beta)/\ln m$. A simple induction using convexity shows that $A_1(n) \geq (\alpha d + \beta)n \log_d n$, with equality when $n = d^t$. A suitable upper bound comes from complete d-ary trees, since these have $D(\mathcal{T}) = dE(\mathcal{T})$, $E(\mathcal{T}) = tn + dr$ for $n = d^t + (d-1)r$, $0 \leq r \leq d^t$.

10. See *STOC* **6** (1974), 216–229.

11. Using exercise 1.2.4–38, $f_m(n) = 3qn + 2(n - 3^q m)$, when $2 \cdot 3^{q-1} \leq n/m \leq 3^q$; $f_m(n) = 3qn + 4(n - 3^q m)$, when $3^q \leq n/m \leq 2 \cdot 3^q$. Thus $f_2(n) + 2n \geq f(n)$, with equality if and only if $4 \cdot 3^{q-1} \leq n \leq 2 \cdot 3^q$; $f_3(n) + 3n = f(n)$; $f_4(n) + 4n \geq f(n)$, with equality if and only if $n = 4 \cdot 3^q$; and $f_m(n) + mn > f(n)$ for all $m \geq 5$.

12. Use the specifications $-$, 1:1, 1:1:1, 1:1:1:1 or 2:2, 2:3, 2:2:2, $\ldots$, $\lfloor n/3 \rfloor : \lfloor (n+1)/3 \rfloor$: $\lfloor (n+2)/3 \rfloor$, $\ldots$; this gives trees with all leaves at level $q + 2$, for $4 \cdot 3^q \leq n \leq 4 \cdot 3^{q+1}$. (When $n = 4 \cdot 3^q$, two such trees are formed.)

14. The following tree specifications were found for $n = 1, 2, 3, \ldots$ by exhaustively examining all partitions of n: $-$, 1:1, 1:1:1, 1:1:1:1, 1:1:1:1:1, 1:1:1:1:1:1, 1:1:1:1:3, 1:1:3:3, 3:3:3, 1:3:3:3, 3:4:4, 3:3:3:3, 3:3:3:4, 3:3:4:4, 3:4:4:4, 4:4:4:4, $\ldots$, 5:6:6:6:12, 6:6:6:6:12, 6:6:6:6:13, $\ldots$. (The degrees seem to be always ≤ 6, but such a result appears to be quite difficult to prove.)

15. If a people initially got on the elevator, the togetherness rating increases by at most $a + b$ at the first stop. When it next stops at the initial floor, the rating increases by at most $b + m - a$. Hence the rating increases at most $kb + (k-1)m$ after k stops.

16. Eleven stops: 123456 to floor 2, 334466 to 3, 444666 to 4, 256666 to 5, 466666 to 6, 123445 to 4, 112335 to 5, 222333 to 3, 122225 to 2, 111555 to 5, 111111 to 1. [This is minimal, for a 10-stop solution with any elevator capacity can, by symmetry, be arranged to stop on floors 2, 3, 4, 5, 6, p_2, p_3, p_4, p_5, 1 in that order, where $p_2 p_3 p_4 p_5$ is a permutation of $\{2, 3, 4, 5\}$; such schedules are possible only when $b \geq 8$. See Martin Gardner, *Knotted Doughnuts* (New York: Freeman, 1986), Chapter 10.]

17. There are at least $(bn)!/b!^n$ configurations; and the number that can be obtained from a given one after s stops is at most $\left((n-1)\binom{b+m}{b}\right)^{s-1}$, which is less than $\left(n((b+m)e/b)^b\right)^s$ by exercise 1.2.6–67. Hence some configuration requires

$$s\left(\ln n + b(1 + \ln(1 + m/b))\right) > \ln(bn)! - n\ln b! > bn\ln bn - bn - n((b+1)\ln b - b + 1)$$

by exercise 1.2.5–24.

Notes: Using the fact that $1/(x+y) \geq \frac{1}{2}\min(1/x, 1/y)$ when x and y are positive, we can express this lower bound in the convenient form

$$\Omega\left(\min\left(nb,\ \frac{n\log(1+n)}{\log(1+m/b)}\right)\right).$$

Related results have been obtained by A. Aggarwal and J. S. Vitter, *CACM* **31** (1988), 1116–1127, who also established the matching upper bound

$$O\left(\min\left(nb,\ \frac{n\log(1+n)}{\log(1+m/b)}\right)\right).$$

See also M. H. Nodine and J. S. Vitter, *ACM Symposium on Parallel Algorithms and Architectures* **5** (1993), 120–129, for extensions to several disks.

18. The expected number of stops is $\sum_{s\geq1} p_s$, where p_s is the probability that at least s stops are needed. Let $q_s = 1 - p_{s+1}$ be the probability that at most s stops are needed. Then exercise 17 shows that $q_s \leq f(s-1+[s=0])$, where $f(s) = b!^n \alpha^s/(bn)!$ and $\alpha = n((b+m)e/b)^b$. If $f(t-1) < 1 \leq f(t)$ then $\sum_{s\geq1} p_s \geq p_1 + \cdots + p_t = t - (q_0 + \cdots + q_{t-1}) \geq t - (f(0) + f(0) + \cdots + f(t-2)) \geq t - (\alpha^{1-t} + \alpha^{1-t} + \cdots + \alpha^{-1}) \geq t - 1 \geq L - 1$.

19. Consider doing step (vii) backwards, distributing the records into bin 1, then bin 2. This operation is precisely what step (iv) is simulating on the key file. [*Princeton Conference on Information Sciences and Systems* **6** (1972), 140–144.]

20. The internal sort must be carefully chosen, with paging in mind; methods such as shellsort, address calculation, heapsort, and list sorting can be disastrous if the actual internal memory is small, since they require a large "working set" of pages. Quicksort, radix exchange, and sequentially allocated merge or radix sorting are much better suited to a paging environment.

Some things the designer of an external sort can do that are virtually impossible to include in an automatically paged method are: (i) Forecasting the input file that should be read next, so that the data is available when it is required; (ii) choosing the buffer sizes and the order of merge according to hardware and data characteristics.

On the other hand a virtual machine is considerably easier to program, and it can give results that aren't bad, if the programmer is careful and knows the properties of the underlying actual machine. The first substantial study of this question was made by Brawn, Gustavson, and Mankin [*CACM* **13** (1970), 483–494.]

21. $\lceil (L-j)/D \rceil$; see *CMath*, Eq. (3.24).

22. After reading a group of D blocks that contains a_j, we might need to know α_{j+D-1} before reading the next group of D blocks. And if we store α_{j+D-1} with a_j, we also need the values $\alpha_0, \ldots, \alpha_{D-2}$ in some sort of file header to get the process started.

But with this scheme we cannot write blocks $a_0 \ldots a_{D-1}$ until we have computed $a_D \ldots a_{2D-2}$, so we will need $3D - 1$ output buffers instead of $2D$ to keep writing continuously. It is therefore better to put the α's in a separate (short) file. [The same analysis applies to randomized striping.]

23. (a) Algorithm 5.4.6F needs 4 input buffers, each of superblock size DB. (If we count output buffers as well, we have a total of $6DB$ buffer records in memory with Algorithm 5.4.6F and $5DB$ with SyncSort.)

(b) While we are reading a group of D blocks we need buffer space for the previous D blocks and one unfinished block, for a total of $(2D+1)B$ records. (Output requires another $2DB$. But many data processing operations that do 2-way merging on input actually produce comparatively little output.)

24. Let the lth block in chronological order be block j_l of run k_l; in particular, $j_l = 0$ and $k_l = l$ for $1 \le l \le P$. We will read that block at time $t_l = \sum_{k=1}^{P} t_{lkd}$, where

$$t_{lkd} = \big|\{r \mid 1 \le r \le l \text{ and } k_r = k \text{ and } (x_k + j_r) \bmod D = d\}\big|$$

is the number of blocks of run k on disk d that are chronologically $\le l$, and $d = (x_{k_l} + j_l) \bmod D$. Let $u_{lk} = \big|\{r \mid 1 \le r \le l \text{ and } k_r = k\}\big|$; then

$$t_{lkd} = \left\lceil \frac{u_{lk} - (d - x_k) \bmod D}{D} \right\rceil,$$

because j_r runs through the values $0, 1, \ldots, u_{lk} - 1$ when $1 \le r \le l$ and $k_r = k$. The sequence t_l for the example of (19), (20), and (21) is

$$11111\ 22223\ 43456\ 34567\ 82345\ 67893\ \ldots .$$

If $l > P$, the number of buffer blocks we need as we begin to merge from the lth block in chronological order is $I_l + D + P$, where I_l is the number of "inversions-with-equality" of t_l, namely $\big|\{r \mid r > l \text{ and } t_r \le t_l\}\big|$, the number of bufferfuls that we've read but aren't ready to use; D represents the buffers into which the next input is going, and P represents the partially full buffers from which we are currently merging. (With special care, using links as in SyncSort, we could reduce the latter requirement from P to $P - 1$, but the extra complication is probably not worthwhile.)

So the problem boils down to getting an upper bound on I_l. We may assume that the input runs are infinitely long. Suppose s of the elements $\{t_1, \ldots, t_l\}$ are greater than t_l; then t_l has $t_l D - l + s$ inversions-with-equality, because exactly $t_l D$ elements are $\le t_l$. It follows that the maximum I_l occurs when $s = 0$ and t_l is a left-to-right maximum. We have $\sum_{k=1}^{P} u_{lk} = l$; hence by the formulas for t_l above,

$$I_l \le \max_{l > P}(t_l D - l) \le \sum_{k=1}^{P}\big(u_{lk} - (d - x_k) \bmod D + D - 1 - u_{lk}\big)$$

$$= P(D-1) - \sum_{k=1}^{P}(d - x_k) \bmod D$$

$$\le P(D-1) - \min_{0 \le d < D} \sum_{k=1}^{P}(d - x_k) \bmod D,$$

and there exist chronological orders for which this upper bound is attained.

Suppose r_t of the x_k are equal to t. We want to choose the x_k so that $\min_{0 \le d < D} s_d$ is maximized, where $s_d = \sum_{k=1}^{P}(d - x_k) \bmod D = \sum_{t=0}^{D-1}((d-t) \bmod D)r_t$. We can assume that the minimum occurs at $d = 0$. Then $s_1 = s_0 + P - r_1 D$, $s_2 = s_1 + P - r_2 D$, $\ldots$, hence we have $r_1 \le \lfloor P/D \rfloor$, $r_1 + r_2 \le \lfloor 2P/D \rfloor$, $\ldots$; it follows that the minimum is

$$s_0 = (D-1)r_1 + (D-2)r_2 + \cdots + r_{D-1} \le \sum_{k=1}^{D-1}\lfloor kP/D \rfloor = \frac{1}{2}\big((P-1)(D-1) + \gcd(P,D) - 1\big),$$

by exercise 1.2.4–37. This bound is achieved when $x_j = \lceil jD/P \rceil - 1$ for $1 \le j \le P$.

With such x_j we can handle every chronological sequence at full speed if we have $I_{\max} + D + P = \frac{1}{2}PD + \frac{3}{2}D + \frac{1}{2}P + \frac{1}{2}\gcd(P, D) - 1$ input buffers containing B records each. (This is pretty good when $D = 2$ or 3.)

25. Notice that at Time 4, we go back to reading f_1 on disk 0:

	Active reading	Active merging	Scratch	Waiting for
Time 1	$e_0\,b_0\,g_0\,a_0\,c_0$	$-\,-\,-\,-\,-\,-\,-\,-$	$(-\,-\,-\,-\,-\,-\,-)$	a_0
Time 2	$f_1\,d_0\,d_1\,d_2\,f_0$	$a_0\,-\,-\,-\,-\,-\,-\,-$	$b_0\,c_0\,(e_0\,g_0\,-\,-\,-)$	d_0
Time 3	$a_2\,h_0\,e_2\,g_1\,d_3$	$a_0\,b_0\,c_0\,d_0\,-\,-\,-\,-$	$e_0\,f_0\,g_0\,(d_1\,d_2\,f_1\,-)$	h_0
Time 4	$f_1\,e_1\,b_1\,g_1\,a_1$	$a_0\,b_0\,c_0\,d_0\,e_0\,f_0\,g_0\,h_0$	$d_1\,(d_2\,e_2\,d_3\,f_1\,g_1\,a_2)$	e_1
Time 5	$a_2\,f_2\,h_1\,e_3\,g_2$	$a_0\,b_0\,c_0\,d_1\,e_1\,f_0\,g_0\,h_0$	$d_2\,e_2\,d_3\,a_1\,f_1\,b_1\,g_1\,()$	a_2
Time 6	$d_4\,a_3\,f_3\,b_2\,e_4$	$a_2\,b_1\,c_0\,d_3\,e_2\,f_1\,g_1\,h_0$	$f_2\,e_3\,(h_1\,g_2\,-\,-\,-)$	d_4
Time 7	$c_1\,a_3\,f_3$? e_4	$a_2\,b_1\,c_0\,d_4\,e_3\,f_2\,g_1\,h_0$	$(h_1\,b_2\,g_2\,a_3\,f_3\,e_4\,-)$	c_1
Time 8	? $d_5\,d_6$? ?	$a_2\,b_1\,c_1\,d_4\,e_3\,f_2\,g_1\,h_0$	$h_1\,b_2\,g_2\,a_3\,f_3\,e_4\,(?)$	d_5

26. While D blocks are being read and D are being written, the merging procedure might generate up to $P + Q - 1$ blocks of output, under the assumptions of (24). (Not $P + Q$, since only one merge buffer becomes totally empty.) Reading is as fast as writing, so $D + P + Q - 1$ output buffers are necessary and sufficient to prevent output hangup.

However, at most D blocks are output for every D blocks of input, on the average, so about $3D$ output buffers should be adequate in practice.

27. (a) $E_n(m_1, \ldots, m_p) = \sum_{t=1}^{m} q_t$, where q_t is the probability that some urn contains at least t balls. Clearly $q_t \le 1$ and

$$q_t \le \sum_{k=0}^{n-1} \Pr(\text{urn } k \text{ contains at least } t \text{ balls}) = n\Pr(S_n(m_1, \ldots, m_p) \ge t).$$

(b) The probability generating function of $S_n(m_1, \ldots, m_p)$ is

$$p(z) = \prod_{k=1}^{p} z^{q_k}\left(1 + (z-1)r_k/n\right),$$

where $q_k = \lfloor m_k/n \rfloor$ and $r_k = m_k \bmod n$. Now $1 + \alpha \le (1 + \alpha/n)^n$ and $1 + \alpha r/n \le (1 + \alpha/n)^r$ when $\alpha \ge 0$; hence we have $\Pr(S_n(m_1, \ldots, m_p) \ge t) \le (1+\alpha)^{-t}p(1+\alpha) \le (1+\alpha)^{-t}\prod_{k=1}^{p}(1 + \alpha/n)^{m_k} = (1+\alpha)^{-t}(1 + \alpha/n)^m$.

If $t \le m/n$, we use the "1" term in the stated minimum. If $t > m/n$, the quantity $(1+\alpha)^{-t}(1 + \alpha/n)^m$ takes its minimum value $(n-1)^{m-t}m^m/(n^m t^t(m-t)^{m-t})$ when $\alpha = (nt - m)/(m - t)$.

28. Numerical evidence seems to support this natural conjecture. For example, we have

$$
\begin{array}{lll}
E_{10}(1,1,1,1,1,1,1) = 2.3993180, & E_{10}(2,2,2,2) = 2.178, & E_{10}(4,3,1) = 2.00, \\
E_{10}(2,1,1,1,1,1,1) = 2.364540, & E_{10}(3,2,2,1) = 2.166, & E_{10}(5,2,1) = 1.98, \\
E_{10}(2,2,1,1,1,1) = 2.32076, & E_{10}(3,3,1,1) = 2.152, & E_{10}(6,1,1) = 1.94, \\
E_{10}(3,1,1,1,1,1) = 2.29958, & E_{10}(4,2,1,1) = 2.138, & E_{10}(4,4) = 1.7, \\
E_{10}(2,2,2,1,1) = 2.2628, & E_{10}(5,1,1,1) = 2.090, & E_{10}(5,3) = 1.7, \\
E_{10}(3,2,1,1,1) = 2.2460, & E_{10}(3,3,2) = 2.02, & E_{10}(6,2) = 1.7, \\
E_{10}(4,1,1,1,1) = 2.2076, & E_{10}(4,2,2) = 2.01, & E_{10}(7,1) = 1.7.
\end{array}
$$

29. (a) At time t, all disks are reading blocks that occur no earlier than the block marked at time t. The next Q blocks are never removed from the scratch buffers once they have been read. Thus the relevant blocks on disk j all are read by time $\leq t + N_j$; they must all participate in the merge by time $t + \max(N_0, \ldots, N_{D-1})$.

(b) If the $(Q+1)$st block after a marked block is not removed, the same argument applies. Otherwise the previous Q are not marked, and the $Q+2$ blocks cannot all be on different disks.

(c) Divide the chronological order of blocks into groups of size $Q+2$, and consider any particular group. If there are M_k blocks from run k, then the numbers N_j are equivalent to the number of balls in the jth urn, in a cyclic occupancy problem with $n = D$ and $m = Q + 2$. Thus the expected number of marked cells in any group is at most the upper bound in exercise 27(b). Calling that upper bound $e_n(m)$, we may take $r(d, m) = (d/m)e_d(m)$.

[Actually this function $r(2, m)$ is not monotonic in m when m is small. Therefore the entries listed for $r(2,4)$ and $r(2,12)$ in Table 2 are actually the values of $r(2,3)$ and $r(2,11)$; additional buffers cannot increase the number of marked blocks.]

30. Let $l = \lceil (s + \sqrt{2s}) \ln d \rceil$, $\alpha = \sqrt{2/s}$. Then

$$e_d(sd \ln d) < l + \sum_{t>l} d(1 + \alpha/d)^{sd \ln d}/(1 + \alpha)^t$$
$$= l + d(1 + \alpha/d)^{sd \ln d}/\alpha(1 + \alpha)^l$$
$$\leq l + \alpha^{-1} \exp((\ln d)(1 + s\alpha - (s + \sqrt{2s}) \ln(1 + \alpha))),$$

and $(s + \sqrt{2s}) \ln(1 + \alpha) > s\alpha + 1 - \alpha/3$. Therefore

$$1 \leq r(d, sd \ln d) = \frac{e_d(sd \ln d)}{s \ln d} < 1 + \sqrt{\frac{2}{s}} + \frac{1}{\sqrt{2s} \ln d}\left(1 + \sqrt{\frac{2}{9s}} \ln d + O(s^{-1}(\log d)^2)\right),$$

if $s/(\log d)^2 \to \infty$. Convergence to this asymptotic behavior is rather slow (see Table 2).

31. (When $Q = 0$, we mark the first block and then repeatedly mark the next block that shares a disk with one of the blocks in the group starting with the previously marked block. For example, if the chronological order of disk accesses is 112020121210122, the marking would be $\bar{1}\bar{1}20\bar{2}01\bar{2}1\bar{2}10\bar{1}2\bar{2}$. Therefore as $P \to \infty$, we read an average of $Q(D)n$ blocks during n units of time, where Q is Ramanujan's function, defined in Eq. 1.2.11.3–(2). By contrast, $r(d,2) = (d+1)/2$ gives a much more pessimistic estimate.)

SECTION 5.5

1. It is difficult to decide which sorting algorithm is best in a given situation. ∎

2. For small N, list insertion; for medium N, say $N = 64$, list merge; for large N, radix list sort.

3. (Solution by V. Pratt.) Given two nondecreasing runs α and β to be merged, determine in a straightforward way the subruns $\alpha_1\alpha_2\alpha_3\beta_1\beta_2\beta_3$ such that α_2 and β_2 contain precisely the keys of α and β having the median value of the entire file. By successive "reversals," first forming $\alpha_1\alpha_2\beta_1^R\alpha_3^R\beta_2\beta_3$, then $\alpha_1\beta_1\alpha_2^R\beta_2^R\alpha_3\beta_3$, then $\alpha_1\beta_1\alpha_2\beta_2\alpha_3\beta_3$, we can reduce the problem to the merging of subfiles $\alpha_1\beta_1$ and $\alpha_3\beta_3$ that are of length $\leq N/2$.

A considerably more complicated algorithm due to L. Trabb Pardo provides the best possible asymptotic answer to this problem: We can do stable merging in $O(N)$ time and stable sorting in $O(N \log N)$ time, using only $O(\log N)$ bits of auxiliary memory for a fixed number of index variables, without transforming the records being sorted in any way [*SICOMP* **6** (1977), 351–372]. The same time and space bounds have been achieved with much smaller constant factors by B.-C. Huang and M. A. Langston, *Comp. J.* **35** (1992), 643–650. See also A. Symvonis, *Comp. J.* **38** (1995), 681–690, for stable merging of M items with N when M is much smaller than N.

4. Only straight insertion, list insertion, and list merge. The variants of quicksort could be made parsimonious, but only at the expense of extra work in the inner loops (see exercise 5.2.2–24).

Parsimonious methods are especially useful when the result of a comparison is not 100% reliable; see D. E. Knuth, *Lecture Notes in Comp. Sci.* **606** (1992), 61–67.

SECTION 6.1

1. $\sqrt{(N^2-1)/12}$; see Eq. 1.2.10–(22).

2. S1$'$. [Initialize.] Set P ← FIRST.

S2$'$. [Compare.] If $K = \mathrm{KEY}(\mathrm{P})$, the algorithm terminates successfully.

S3$'$. [Advance.] Set P ← LINK(P).

S4$'$. [End of file?] If P $\neq$ Λ, go back to S2$'$. Otherwise the algorithm terminates unsuccessfully. ∎

3.

KEY	EQU	3:5		JE	SUCCESS	C
LINK	EQU	1:2		LD1	0,1(LINK)	$C - S$
START	LDA	K	1	J1NZ	2B	$C - S$
	LD1	FIRST	1	FAILURE EQU	*	$1 - S$ ∎
2H	CMPA	0,1(KEY)	C			

The running time is $(6C - 3S + 4)u$.

4. Yes, if we have a way to set "$\mathrm{KEY}(\Lambda)$" equal to K. [But the technique of loop duplication used in Program Q$'$ has no effect in this case.]

5. No; Program Q always does at least as many operations as Program Q$'$.

6. Replace line 08 by JE *+4; CMPA KEY+N+2,1; JNE 3B; INC1 1; and change lines 03–04 to ENT1 -2-N; 3H INC1 3.

7. Note that $\bar{C}_N = \frac{1}{2}\bar{C}_{N-1} + 1$.

8. Euler's summation formula gives

$$H_n^{(x)} = \zeta(x) + \frac{n^{1-x}}{(1-x)} + \frac{1}{2}n^{-x} - \frac{B_2 x}{2!}n^{-1-x} + \frac{B_3 x(x+1)}{3!}n^{-2-x} - O(n^{-3-x}).$$

[Complex variable theory tells us that

$$\zeta(x) = 2^x \pi^{x-1} \sin(\tfrac{1}{2}\pi x)\Gamma(1-x)\zeta(1-x),$$

a formula that is particularly useful when $x < 0$.]

9. (a) Yes: $\bar{C}_N = N - N^{-\theta}H_{N-1}^{(-\theta)} = N + 1 - N^{-\theta}H_N^{(-\theta)} = \frac{\theta}{1+\theta}N + \frac{1}{2} + O(N^{-\theta})$.

(b) $\bar{C}_N = \frac{\theta}{1+\theta}\left(1 + N/\left(1 - \binom{N-\theta}{N}\right)\right) = \frac{\theta}{1+\theta}(N + N^{1-\theta}/\Gamma(1-\theta) + 1) + O(N^{1-2\theta})$.

(c) When $\theta < 0$, (11) is not a probability distribution; (16) gives the estimate $\bar{C}_N = -\frac{\theta}{1+\theta}\Gamma(1-\theta)N^{1+\theta} + O(N^{1+2\theta}) + O(1)$ instead of (15).

10. $p_1 \leq \cdots \leq p_N$; (maximum $\bar{C}_N$) $= (N+1) -$ (minimum $\bar{C}_N$). [Similarly in the unequal-length case, the maximum average search time is $L_1(1+p_1) + \cdots + L_N(1+p_N)$ minus the minimum average search time.]

11. (a) The terms of $f_{m-1}(x_{i_1}, \ldots, x_{i_{m-1}})p_i$ are just the probabilities of the possible sequences of requests that could have preceded, leaving R_i in position m. (b) The second identity comes from summing $\binom{n}{m}$ cases of the first, on the different m-subsets of X, noting the number of times each P_{nk} occurs. The third identity is a consequence of the second, by inversion. [Alternatively, the principle of inclusion and exclusion could be used.] (c) $\sum_{m \geq 0} m P_{nm} = n Q_{nn} - Q_{n(n-1)}$; hence

$$d_i = 1 + (N-1) - p_i \sum_{j \neq i} \frac{1}{p_i + p_j};$$

$$\sum_i p_i d_i = N - \sum_{i<j} \frac{p_i^2 + p_j^2}{p_i + p_j} = N - \sum_{i<j} \left(p_i + p_j - \frac{2p_i p_j}{p_i + p_j} \right) = \text{Eq. (17)}.$$

Notes: W. J. Hendricks [*J. Applied Probability* **9** (1972), 231–233] found a simple formula for the steady-state probability of each permutation of the records. For example, when $N = 4$ the sequence will be $R_3 R_1 R_4 R_2$ with limiting probability

$$\frac{p_3}{p_3 + p_1 + p_4 + p_2} \frac{p_1}{p_1 + p_4 + p_2} \frac{p_4}{p_4 + p_2} \frac{p_2}{p_2}.$$

In fact, this distribution had already been obtained by M. L. Tsetlin in his Ph.D. thesis at Moscow University in 1964, and published in Chapter 1 of his Russian book *Studies in Automata Theory and Simulation of Biological Systems* (1969).

James Bitner [*SICOMP* **8** (1979), 82–85] proved that, if the list is originally in random order, the expected search time after t random requests exceeds $\widetilde{C}_N$ by the quantity $\frac{1}{4} \sum_{i,j} (p_i - p_j)^2 (1 - p_i - p_j)^t / (p_i + p_j)$. Thus, t searches require fewer than $t\widetilde{C}_N + \frac{1}{4} \sum_{i,j} (p_i - p_j)^2 / (p_i + p_j)^2 < t\widetilde{C}_N + \frac{1}{2}\binom{N}{2}$ comparisons altogether, on the average. See P. Flajolet, D. Gardy, and L. Thimonier, *Discrete Applied Math.* **39** (1992), 207–229, §6, for instructive proofs via generating functions.

12. $\widetilde{C}_N = 2^{1-N} + 2\sum_{n=0}^{N-2} 1/(2^n + 1)$, which converges rapidly to $2\alpha' \approx 2.5290$; exercise 5.2.4–13 gives the value of α' to 40 decimal places.

13. After evaluating the rather tedious sum

$$\sum_{k=1}^{n} k^2 H_{n+k} = \frac{n(n+1)(2n+1)}{6}(2H_{2n} - H_n) - \frac{n(n+1)(10n-1)}{36},$$

we obtain the answer

$$\widetilde{C}_N = \tfrac{4}{3}N - \tfrac{2}{3}(2N+1)(H_{2n} - H_n) + \tfrac{5}{6} - \tfrac{1}{3}(N+1)^{-1} \approx .409N.$$

14. We may assume that $x_1 \leq x_2 \leq \cdots \leq x_n$; then the maximum value occurs when $y_{a_1} \leq y_{a_2} \leq \cdots \leq y_{a_n}$, and the minimum when $y_{a_1} \geq \cdots \geq y_{a_n}$, by an argument like that of Theorem S.

15. Arguing as in Theorem S, the arrangement $R_1 R_2 \ldots R_N$ is optimum if and only if

$$P_1/L_1(1 - P_1) \geq \cdots \geq P_N/L_N(1 - P_N).$$

16. The expected time $T_1 + p_1 T_2 + p_1 p_2 T_3 + \cdots + p_1 p_2 \cdots p_{N-1} T_N$ is minimized if and only if $T_1/(1 - p_1) \leq \cdots \leq T_N/(1 - p_N)$. [*BIT* **3** (1963), 255–256; some interesting extensions have been obtained by James R. Slagle, *JACM* **11** (1964), 253–264.]

17. Do the jobs in order of increasing deadlines, regardless of the respective times T_j! [Management Science Research Report 43, UCLA (1955). Of course in practice some jobs are more important than others, and we may want to minimize the maximum *weighted* tardiness. Or we may wish to minimize the sum $\sum_{i=1}^{n} \max(T_{a_1} + \cdots + T_{a_i} - D_{a_i}, 0)$. Neither of these problems appears to have a simple solution.]

18. Let $h = [s \text{ is present}]$. Let $A = \{j \mid q_j < r_j\}$, $B = \{j \mid q_j = r_j\}$, $C = \{j \mid q_j > r_j\}$, $D = \{j \mid t_j > 0\}$; then the sum $\sum_{i,j} p_i p_j d_{|i-j|}$ for the (q, r) arrangement minus the corresponding sum for the (q', r') arrangement is equal to

$$2 \sum_{i \in A,\, j \in C} (q_i - r_i)(q_j - r_j)(d_{|i-j|} - d_{h+1+2k-i-j}) + 2 \sum_{i \in C,\, j \in D} (q_i - r_i) t_j (d_{h+2k-i+j} - d_{i-1+j}).$$

This is positive unless $C = \emptyset$ or $A \cup D = \emptyset$. The desired result now follows because the organ-pipe arrangements are the only permutations that are not improved by this construction and its left-right dual when $m = 0, 1$.

[This result is essentially due to G. H. Hardy, J. E. Littlewood, and G. Pólya, *Proc. London Math. Soc.* (2), **25** (1926), 265–282, who showed, in fact, that the minimum of $\sum_{i,j} p_i q_j d_{|i-j|}$ is achieved, under all independent arrangements of the p's and q's, when both p's and q's are in a consistent organ-pipe order. For further commentary and generalizations, see their book *Inequalities* (Cambridge University Press, 1934), Chapter 10.]

19. All arrangements are equally good. Assuming that $d(j, j) = 0$, we have

$$\sum_{i,j} p_i p_j\, d(i, j) = \tfrac{1}{2} \sum_{i,j} p_i p_j \big(d(i, j) + d(j, i)\big)[i \neq j] = \tfrac{1}{2}(1 - p_1^2 - \cdots - p_N^2)c.$$

[The special case $d(i, j) = 1 + (j - i) \bmod N$ for $i \neq j$ is due to K. E. Iverson, *A Programming Language* (New York: Wiley, 1962), 138. R. L. Baber, *JACM* **10** (1963), 478–486, has studied some other problems associated with tape searching when a tape can read forward, rewind, or backspace k blocks without reading. W. D. Frazer observes that it is possible to make significant reductions in the search time if we are allowed to *replicate* some of the information in the file; see E. B. Eichelberger, W. C. Rodgers, and E. W. Stacy, *IBM J. Research & Development* **12** (1968), 130–139, for an empirical solution to a similar problem.]

20. Going from (q, r) to (q', r') as in exercise 18, with $m = 0$ or $m = h = 1$, gives a net change of

$$\sum_{i \in A,\, j \in C} (q_i - r_i)(q_j - r_j)\big(d_{|i-j|} - \min(d_{h+1+2k-i-j}, d_{i+j-1})\big),$$

which is positive unless A or C is $\emptyset$. By circular symmetry it follows that the only optimal arrangements are cyclic shifts of the organ-pipe configurations. [For a different class of problems with the same answer, see T. S. Motzkin and E. G. Straus, *Proc. Amer. Math. Soc.* **7** (1956), 1014–1021.]

21. This problem was essentially first solved by L. H. Harper, *SIAM J. Appl. Math.* **12** (1964), 131–135. For generalizations and references to other work, see *J. Applied Probability* **4** (1967), 397–401.

22. A priority queue of size 1000 (represented as, say, a heap, see Section 5.2.3). Insert the first 1000 records into this queue, with the element of *greatest* $d(K_j, K)$ at the front. For each subsequent K_j with $d(K_j, K) < d(\text{front of queue}, K)$, replace the front element by R_j and readjust the queue.

SECTION 6.2.1

1. Prove inductively that $K_{l-1} < K < K_{u+1}$ whenever we reach step B2; and that $l \leq i \leq u$ whenever we reach B3.

2. (a, c) No; it loops if $l = u - 1$ and $K > K_u$. (b) Yes, it does work. But when K is absent, there will often be a loop with $l = u$ and $K < K_u$.

3. This is Algorithm 6.1T with $N = 3$. In a successful search, that algorithm makes $(N+1)/2$ comparisons, on the average; in an unsuccessful search it makes $N/2 + 1 - 1/(N+1)$.

4. It must be an unsuccessful search with $N = 127$; hence by Theorem B the answer is $138u$.

5. Program 6.1Q′ has an average running time of $1.75N + 8.5 - (N \bmod 2)/4N$; this beats Program B if and only if $N \leq 44$. [It beats Program C only for $N \leq 11$.]

7. (a) Certainly not. (b) The parenthesized remarks in Algorithm U will hold true, so it will work, but only if $K_0 = -\infty$ and $K_{N+1} = +\infty$ are both present when N is odd.

8. (a) N. It is interesting to prove this by induction, observing that exactly one of the δ's increases if we replace N by $N+1$. [See *AMM* **77** (1970), 884 for a generalization.] (b) Maximum $= \sum_j \delta_j = N$; minimum $= 2\delta_1 - \sum_j \delta_j = N \bmod 2$.

9. If and only if $N = 2^k - 1$.

10. Use a "macro-expanded" program with the DELTA's included; thus, for $N = 10$:

```
       START  ENT1  5
              LDA   K
              CMPA  KEY,1
              JL    C3A
       C4A    JE    SUCCESS        C3A  EQU   *
              INC1  3                   DEC1  3
              CMPA  KEY,1               CMPA  KEY,1
              JL    C3B                 JGE   C4B
       C4B    JE    SUCCESS        C3B  EQU   *
              INC1  1                   DEC1  1
              CMPA  KEY,1               CMPA  KEY,1
              JL    C3C                 JGE   C4C
       C4C    JE    SUCCESS        C3C  EQU   *
              INC1  1                   DEC1  1
              CMPA  KEY,1               CMPA  KEY,1
              JE    SUCCESS             JE    SUCCESS
              JMP   FAILURE             JMP   FAILURE  ▮
```

[Exercise 23 shows that most of the "JE" instructions may be eliminated, yielding a program about $6 \lg N$ lines long that takes only about $4 \lg N$ units of time; but that program will be faster only for $N \geq 1000$ (approximately).]

11. Consider the corresponding tree, such as Fig. 6: When N is odd, the left subtree of the root is a mirror image of the right subtree, so $K < K_i$ occurs just as often as $K > K_i$; on the average $C1 = \frac{1}{2}(C + S)$ and $C2 = \frac{1}{2}(C - S)$, $A = \frac{1}{2}(1 - S)$. When N is even, the tree is the same as the tree for $N + 1$ with all labels decreased by 1, except that ⓪ becomes redundant; on the average, letting $k = \lfloor \lg N \rfloor$, we have

$$C1 = \frac{C+1}{2} - \frac{k}{2N}, \qquad C2 = \frac{C-1}{2} + \frac{k}{2N}, \qquad A = 0, \qquad \text{if } S = 1;$$

$$C1 = \frac{(k+1)N}{2(N+1)}, \qquad C2 = \frac{(k+1)(N+2)}{2(N+1)}, \qquad A = \frac{N}{2(N+1)}, \quad \text{if } S = 0.$$

(The average value of C is stated in the text.)

12.

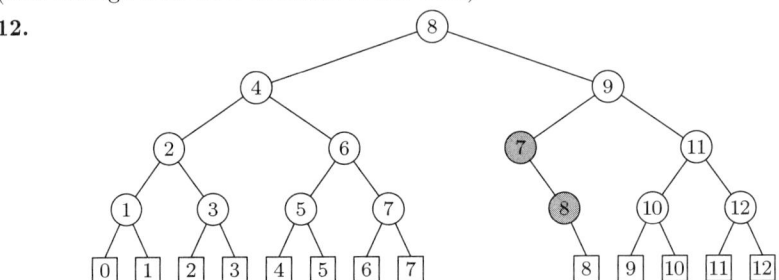

13.

$N =$	1	2	3	4	5	6	7	8	9	10	11	12	13	14	15	16
$C_N =$	1	$1\frac{1}{2}$	$1\frac{2}{3}$	$2\frac{1}{4}$	$2\frac{1}{5}$	$2\frac{2}{6}$	$2\frac{3}{7}$	$3\frac{1}{8}$	3	3	3	$3\frac{2}{12}$	$3\frac{3}{13}$	$3\frac{3}{14}$	$3\frac{4}{15}$	$4\frac{1}{16}$
$C'_N =$	1	$1\frac{2}{3}$	2	$2\frac{3}{5}$	$2\frac{4}{6}$	3	3	$3\frac{6}{9}$	$3\frac{6}{10}$	$3\frac{8}{11}$	$3\frac{8}{12}$	4	4	4	4	$4\frac{13}{17}$

14. One idea is to find the least $M \geq 0$ such that $N + M$ has the form $F_{k+1} - 1$, then to start with $i \leftarrow F_k - M$ in step F1, and to insert "If $i \leq 0$, go to F4" at the beginning of F2. A better solution would be to adapt Shar's idea to the Fibonaccian case: If the result of the very first comparison is $K > K_{F_k}$, set $i \leftarrow i - M$ and go to F4 (proceeding normally from then on). This avoids extra time in the inner loop.

15. The external nodes appear on levels $\lfloor k/2 \rfloor$ through $k - 1$; the difference between these levels is greater than unity except when $k = 0, 1, 2, 3, 4$.

16. The Fibonacci tree of order k, with left and right reversed, is the binary tree corresponding to the lineal chart up to the kth month, under the "natural correspondence" of Section 2.3.2, if we remove the topmost node of the lineal chart.

17. Let the path length be $k - A(n)$; then $A(F_j) = j$ and $A(F_j + m) = 1 + A(m)$ when $0 < m < F_{j-1}$.

18. Successful search: $A_k = 0$, $C_k = (3kF_{k+1} + (k-4)F_k)/5(F_{k+1} - 1) - 1$, $C1_k = C_{k-1}(F_k - 1)/(F_{k+1} - 1)$. Unsuccessful search: $A'_k = F_k/F_{k+1}$, $C'_k = (3kF_{k+1} + (k-4)F_k)/5F_{k+1}$, $C1'_k = C'_{k-1}F_k/F_{k+1} + F_{k-1}/F_{k+1}$. $C2 = C - C1$. (See exercise 1.2.8–12 for the solution to related recurrences.)

20. (a) $b = p^{-p}q^{-q}$. (b) There are at least *two* errors. The first blunder is that division is not a linear function, so it can't be simply "averaged over." Actually with probability p we get pN elements remaining, and with probability q we get qN, so we can expect to get $(p^2 + q^2)N$; thus the average reduction factor is really $1/(p^2 + q^2)$. Now the reduction factor after k iterations is $1/(p^2 + q^2)^k$, but we cannot conclude that $b = 1/(p^2 + q^2)$ since the number of iterations needed to locate some of the items is much more than to locate others. This is a second fallacy. [It is very easy to make plausible but fallacious probability arguments, and we must always be on our guard against such pitfalls!]

21. It's impossible, since the method depends on the key values.

22. *FOCS* **17** (1976), 173–177. See also Y. Perl, A. Itai, and H. Avni, *CACM* **21** (1978), 550–554; G. H. Gonnet, L. D. Rogers, and J. A. George, *Acta Informatica* **13** (1980), 39–52; G. Louchard, *RAIRO Inform. Théor.* **17** (1983), 365–385; *Computing* **46** (1991), 193–222. The variance is $O(\log \log N)$. Extensive empirical tests by G. Marsaglia and B. Narasimhan, *Computers and Math.* **26**, 8 (1993), 31–42, show that the average number of table accesses is very close to $\lg \lg N$, plus about 0.7 if the search is unsuccessful. When $N = 2^{20}$, for example, a random successful search in a random table takes about 4.29 accesses, while a random unsuccessful search takes about 5.05.

23. Go to the right on $\geq$, to the left on $<$; when reaching node $\boxed{i}$ it follows from (1) that $K_i \leq K < K_{i+1}$, so a final test for equality will distinguish between success or failure. (The key $K_0 = -\infty$ should always be present.)

Algorithm C would be changed to go to C4 if $K = K_i$ in step C2. In C3 if DELTA$[j] = 0$, set $i \leftarrow i - 1$ and go to C5. In C4 if DELTA$[j] = 0$, go directly to C5. Add a new step C5: "If $K = K_i$, the algorithm terminates successfully, otherwise it terminates unsuccessfully." [This would not speed up Program C unless $N > 2^{26}$; the average successful search time changes from $(8.5 \lg N - 6)u$ to $(8 \lg N + 7)u$.]

24. The keys can be arranged so that we first set $i \leftarrow 1$, then $i \leftarrow 2i$ or $2i + 1$ according as $K < K_i$ or $K > K_i$; the search is unsuccessful when $i > N$. For example when $N = 12$ the necessary key arrangement is

$$K_8 < K_4 < K_9 < K_2 < K_{10} < K_5 < K_{11} < K_1 < K_{12} < K_6 < K_3 < K_7.$$

When programmed for MIX this method will take only about $6 \lg N$ units of time, so it is faster than Program C. The only disadvantage is that it is a little tricky to set up the table in the first place.

25. (a) Since $a_0 = 1 - b_0$, $a_1 = 2a_0 - b_1$, $a_2 = 2a_1 - b_2$, etc., we have $A(z) + B(z) = 1 + 2zA(z)$. Several of the formulas derived in Section 2.3.4.5 follow immediately from this relation by considering $A(1)$, $B(1)$, $B(\frac{1}{2})$, $A'(1)$, and $B'(1)$. If we use two variables to distinguish left and right steps of a path we obtain the more general result $A(x, y) + B(x, y) = 1 + (x + y)A(x, y)$, a special case of a formula that holds in t-ary trees [see R. M. Karp, *IRE Transactions* **IT-7** (1961), 27–38].

(b) $\mathrm{var}\,(g) = ((N + 1)/N)\,\mathrm{var}\,(h) - ((N + 1)/N^2)\,\mathrm{mean}(h)^2 + 2$.

26. The merge tree for the three-tape polyphase merge with a perfect level k distribution is the Fibonacci tree of order $k + 1$ if we permute left and right appropriately. (Redraw the polyphase tree of Fig. 76 in Section 5.4.4, with the left and right subtrees of A and C reversed, obtaining Fig. 8.)

27. At most $k + 1$ of the 2^k outcomes will ever occur, since we may order the indices in such a way that $K_{i_1} < K_{i_2} < \cdots < K_{i_k}$. Thus the search can be described by a tree with at most $(k + 1)$-way branching at each node. The number of items that can be found on the mth step is at most $k(k + 1)^{m-1}$; hence the average number of comparisons is at least N^{-1} times the sum of the smallest N elements of the multiset $\{k{\cdot}1, k(k + 1){\cdot}2, k(k + 1)^2{\cdot}3, \ldots\}$. When $N \geq (k + 1)^n - 1$, the average number of comparisons is $\geq ((k + 1)^n - 1)^{-1} \sum_{m=1}^{n} k(k + 1)^{m-1}m > n - 1/k$.

28. [*Skrifter udgivne af Videnskabs-Selskabet i Christiania,* Mathematisk-Naturviden-skabelig Klasse (1910), No. 8; reprinted in Thue's *Selected Mathematical Papers* (Oslo: Universitetsforlaget, 1977), 273–310.] (a) T_n has $F_{n+1}+F_{n-1} = F_{2n}/F_n$ leaves. (This is the so-called Lucas number $L_n = \phi^n + \hat{\phi}^n$.) (b) The axiom says that $T_0(T_2(x)) = T_1(x)$, and we obviously have $T_m(T_n(x)) = T_{m+n-1}(x)$ when $m = 1$ or $n = 1$. By induction on n, the result holds when $m = 0$; for example, $T_0(T_3(x)) = T_0(T_2(x) * T_1(x)) = T_0(T_1(T_2(x)) * T_0(T_2(x))) = T_0(T_2(T_2(x))) = T_2(x)$. Finally we can use induction on m.

29. Assume that $K_0 = -\infty$ and $K_{N+1} = K_{N+2} = \infty$. First do a binary search on $K_2 < K_4 < \cdots$; this takes at most $\lfloor \lg N \rfloor$ comparisons. If unsuccessful, it determines an interval with $K_{2j-2} < K < K_{2j}$; and K is not present if $2j = N + 2$. Otherwise, a binary search for K_{2j-1} will determine i such that $K_{2i-2} < K_{2j-1} < K_{2i}$. Then either $K = K_{2i-1}$ or K is not present. [See *Theor. Comp. Sci.* **58** (1988), 67.]

30. Let $n = \lfloor N/4 \rfloor$. Starting with $K_1 < K_2 < \cdots < K_N$, we can put K_1, K_3, ..., K_{2n-1} into any desired order by swapping them with a permutation of K_{2n+1}, K_{2n+3}, ..., K_{4n-1}; this arrangement satisfies the conditions of the previous exercise. Now we let $K_1 < K_3 < \cdots < K_{2^{t+1}-3}$ represent the boundaries between all possible t-bit numbers, and we insert $K_{2^{t+1}-1}, K_{2^{t+1}+1}, \ldots, K_{2^{t+1}+2m-3}$ between these "fence-posts" according to the values of $x_1, x_2, \ldots, x_m$. For example, if $m = 4$, $t = 3$, $x_1 = (001)_2$, $x_2 = (111)_2$, and $x_3 = x_4 = (100)_2$, the desired order is

$$K_1 < K_{15} < K_3 < K_5 < K_7 < K_{19} < K_{21} < K_9 < K_{11} < K_{13} < K_{17}.$$

(We could also let K_{21} precede K_{19}.) A binary search for $K_{2^{t+1}+2j-3}$ in the subarray $K_1 < K_3 < \cdots < K_{2^{t+1}-3}$ will now find the bits of x_j from left to right. [See Fiat, Munro, Naor, Schäffer, Schmidt, and Siegel, *J. Comp. Syst. Sci.* **43** (1991), 406–424.]

SECTION 6.2.2

1. Use a header node, with say ROOT $\equiv$ RLINK(HEAD); start the algorithm at step T4 with P $\leftarrow$ HEAD. Step T5 should act as if $K >$ KEY(HEAD). [Thus, change lines 04 and 05 of Program T to "ENT1 ROOT; CMPA K".]

2. In step T5, set RTAG(Q) $\leftarrow$ 1. Also, when inserting to the left, set RLINK(Q) $\leftarrow$ P; when inserting to the right, set RLINK(Q) $\leftarrow$ RLINK(P) and RTAG(P) $\leftarrow$ 0. In step T4, change the test "RLINK(P) $\neq \Lambda$" to "RTAG(P) $= 0$". [If nodes are inserted into successively increasing locations Q, and if all deletions are last-in-first-out, the RTAG fields can be eliminated since RTAG(P) will be 1 if and only if RLINK(P) $<$ P. Similar remarks apply with simultaneous left and right threading.]

3. We could replace Λ by a valid address, and set KEY(Λ) $\leftarrow K$ at the beginning of the algorithm; then the tests for LLINK or RLINK $= \Lambda$ could be removed from the inner loop. However, in order to do a proper insertion we need to introduce another pointer variable that follows P; this can be done without losing the stated speed advantage, by duplicating the code as in Program 6.2.1F. Thus the MIX time would be reduced to about $5.5C$ units.

4. $C_N = 1 + \left(0 \cdot 1 + 1 \cdot 2 + \cdots + (n-1)2^{n-1} + C'_{2^n-1} + \cdots + C'_{N-1}\right)/N = (1 + 1/N)C'_N - 1$, for $N \geq 2^n - 1$. The solution to these equations is $C'_N = 2(H_{N+1} - H_{2^n}) + n$ for $N \geq 2^n - 1$, a savings of $2H_{2^n} - n - 2 \approx n(\ln 4 - 1)$ comparisons. The actual improvement for $n = 1, 2, 3, 4$ is, respectively 0, $\frac{1}{6}$, $\frac{61}{140}$, $\frac{274399}{360360}$; thus comparatively little is gained for small fixed n. [See Frazer and McKellar, *JACM* **17** (1970), 502, for a more detailed derivation related to an equivalent sorting problem.]

5. (a) The first element must be `CAPRICORN`; then we multiply the number of ways to produce the left subtree by the number of ways to produce the right subtree, times $\binom{10}{3}$, the number of ways to shuffle those two sequences together. Thus the answer comes to

$$\binom{10}{3}\binom{2}{0}\binom{1}{0}\binom{0}{0}\binom{6}{3}\binom{2}{0}\binom{1}{0}\binom{0}{0}\binom{2}{1}\binom{0}{0}\binom{0}{0} = 4800.$$

[In general, the answer is the product, over all nodes, of $\binom{l+r}{r}$, where l and r stand for the sizes of the left and right subtrees of the node. This is equal to $N!$ divided by the product of the subtree sizes. It is the same formula as in exercise 5.1.4–20; indeed, there is an obvious one-to-one correspondence between the permutations that yield a particular search tree and the "topological" permutations counted in that exercise, if we replace a_k in the search tree by k (using the notation of exercise 6).] (b) $2^{N-1} = 1024$; at each step but the last, insert either the smallest or largest remaining key.

6. (a) For each of the P_{nk} permutations $a_1 \ldots a_{n-1}a_n$ whose cost is k, construct $n+1$ permutations $a'_1 \ldots a'_{n-1}m\,a'_n$, where $a'_j = a_j$ or a_j+1, according as $a_j < m$ or $a_j \geq m$. [See Section 1.2.5, Method 2.] If $m = a_n$ or a_n+1, this permutation has a cost of $k+1$, otherwise it has a cost of k. (b) $G_n(z) = (2z+n-2)(2z+n-3)\ldots(2z)$. Hence

$$P_{nk} = \begin{bmatrix} n-1 \\ k \end{bmatrix} 2^k.$$

This generating function was, in essence, obtained by W. C. Lynch, *Comp. J.* **7** (1965), 299–302. (c) The generating function for probabilities is $g_n(z) = G_n(z)/n!$. This is a product of simple probability generating functions, so the variance of C'_{n-1} is

$$\text{var}(g_n) = \sum_{k=0}^{n-2} \text{var}\left(\frac{2z+k}{2+k}\right) = \sum_{k=0}^{n-2}\left(\frac{2}{k+2} - \frac{4}{(k+2)^2}\right) = 2H_n - 4H_n^{(2)} + 2.$$

[By exercise 6.2.1–25(b) we can use the mean and variance of C'_n to compute the variance of C_n, which is $(2+10/n)H_n - 4(1+1/n)(H_n^{(2)} + H_n^2/n) + 4$; this formula is due to G. D. Knott.]

7. A comparison with the kth largest element will be made if and only if that element occurs before the mth and before all those between the kth and mth; this happens with probability $1/(|m-k|+1)$. Summing over k gives the answer $H_m+H_{n+1-m}-1$. [*CACM* **12** (1969), 77–80; see also L. Guibas, *Acta Informatica* **4** (1975), 293–298.]

8. (a) $g_n(z) = z^{n-1}\sum_{k=1}^{n} g_{k-1}(z)g_{n-k}(z)/n$, $g_0(z) = 1$.

(b) $7n^2 - 4(n+1)^2 H_n^{(2)} - 2(n+1)H_n + 13n$. [P. F. Windley, *Comp. J.* **3** (1960), 86, gave recurrence relations from which this variance could be computed numerically, but he did not obtain the solution. Notice that this result is *not* simply related to the variance of C_n stated in the answer to exercise 6.]

10. For example, each word x of the key could be replaced by $ax \bmod m$, where m is the computer word size and a is a random multiplier relatively prime to m. A value near to $(\phi-1)m$ can be recommended (see Section 6.4). The flexible storage allocation of a tree method may make it more attractive than a hash coding scheme.

11. $N-2$; but this occurs with probability $1/(N\,N!)$, only in the deletion

① $N\ N{-}1\ \ldots\ 2.$

12. $\frac{1}{2}(n+1)(n+2)$ of the deletions in the proof of Theorem H belong to Case 1, so the answer is $(N+1)/2N$.

13. Yes. In fact, the proof of Theorem H shows that if we delete the kth element inserted, for any fixed k, the result is random. (G. D. Knott [Ph.D. thesis, Stanford, 1975] showed that the result is random after an arbitrary sequence of random insertions followed by successive deletion of the $(k_1, \ldots, k_d)$th elements inserted, for any fixed sequence $k_1, \ldots, k_d$.)

14. Let NODE(T) be on level k, and let LLINK(T) $= \Lambda$, RLINK(T) $= R_1$, LLINK(R_1) $= R_2$, $\ldots$, LLINK(R_d) $= \Lambda$, where $R_d \ne \Lambda$ and $d \ge 1$. Let NODE(R_i) have n_i internal nodes in its right subtree, for $1 \le i \le d$. With step D1.5 the internal path length decreases by $k + d + n_1 + \cdots + n_d$; without that step it decreases by $k + d + n_d$.

15. 11, 13, 25, 11, 12. [If a_j is the (smallest, middle, largest) of $\{a_1, a_2, a_3\}$, the tree is obtained $(4, 2, 3) \times 4$ times after the deletion.]

16. Yes; even the deletion operation on permutations, as defined in the proof of Theorem H, is commutative (if we omit the renumbering aspect). If there is an element between X and Y, deletion is obviously commutative since the operation is affected only by the relative positions of X, Y, and their successors and there is no interaction between the deletion of X and the deletion of Y. On the other hand, if Y is the successor of X, and Y is the largest element, both orders of deletion have the effect of simply removing X and Y. If Y is the successor of X and Z the successor of Y, both orders of deletion have the effect of replacing the *first* occurrence of X, Y, or Z by Z and deleting the second and third occurrences of these elements within the permutation.

18. Use exercise 1.2.7–14.

19. $2H_N - 1 - 2\sum_{k=1}^{N}(k-1)^\theta/kN^\theta = 2H_N - 1 - 2/\theta + O(N^{-\theta})$. [The Pareto distribution 6.1–(13) also gives the same asymptotic result, to within $O(n^{-\theta}\log n)$.]

20. Yes indeed. Assume that $K_1 < \cdots < K_N$, so that the tree built by Algorithm T is degenerate; if, say, $p_k = \bigl(1 + ((N+1)/2 - k)\epsilon\bigr)/N$, the average number of comparisons is $(N + 1)/2 - (N^2 - 1)\epsilon/12$, while the optimum tree requires fewer than $\lceil \lg N \rceil$ comparisons.

21. $\frac{1}{8}$, $\frac{3}{20}$, $\frac{9}{20}$, $\frac{3}{20}$, $\frac{1}{8}$. (Most of the angles are 30°, 60°, or 90°.)

22. This is obvious when $d = 2$, and for $d > 2$ we had $r[i, j-1] \le r[i+1, j-1] \le r[i+1, j]$.

23.

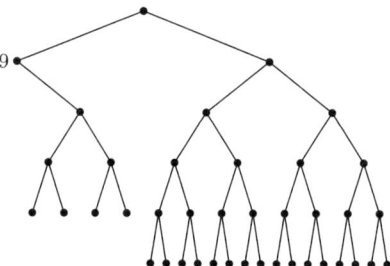

[Increasing the weight of the first node will eventually make it move to the root position; this suggests that dynamically maintaining a perfectly optimum tree is hard.]

24. Let c be the cost of a tree obtained by deleting the nth node of an optimum tree. Then $c(0, n-1) \le c \le c(0, n) - q_{n-1}$, since the deletion operation always moves $\boxed{n-1}$ up one level. Also $c(0, n) \le c(0, n-1) + q_{n-1}$, since the stated replacement yields a tree of the latter cost. It follows that $c(0, n-1) = c = c(0, n) - q_{n-1}$.

25. (a) Assume that $A \leq B$ and $B \leq C$, and let $a \in A$, $b \in B$, $c \in C$, $c < a$. If $c \leq b$ then $c \in B$; hence $c \in A$ and $a \in B$; hence $a \in C$. If $c > b$, then $a \in B$; hence $a \in C$ and $c \in B$; hence $c \in A$. (b) Not hard to prove.

26. The cost of every tree has the form $y + lx$ for some real $y \geq 0$ and integer $l > 0$. The minimum of a finite number of such functions (taken over all trees) always has the form described.

27. (a) The answer to exercise 24 (especially the fact that $c = c(0, n-1)$) implies that $R(0, n-1) = R(0, n) \setminus \{n\}$.

(b) If $l = l'$, the result in the hint is trivial. Otherwise let the paths to $\boxed{n}$ be

$$\boxed{r_0}, \boxed{r_1}, \ldots, \boxed{r_l} \qquad \text{and} \qquad \boxed{s_0}, \boxed{s_1}, \ldots, \boxed{s_{l'}}.$$

Since $r = r_0 > s_0 = s$ and $r_{l'} < s_{l'} = n$, we can find a level $k \geq 0$ such that $r_k > s_k$ and $r_{k+1} \leq s_{k+1}$. We have $r_{k+1} \in R(r_k, n)$, $s_{k+1} \in R(s_k, n)$, and $R(s_k, n) \leq R(r_k, n)$ by induction, hence $r_{k+1} \in R(s_k, n)$ and $s_{k+1} \in R(r_k, n)$; the result in the hint follows.

Now to prove that $R'_h \leq R_h$, let $r \in R'_h$, $s \in R_h$, $s < r$, and consider the optimum trees shown when $x = x_h$; we must have $l \geq l_h$ and we may assume that $l' = l_h$. To prove that $R_h \leq R'_{h+1}$, let $r \in R_h$, $s \in R'_{h+1}$, $s < r$, and consider the optimum trees shown when $x = x_{h+1}$; we must have $l' \leq l_h$ and we may assume that $l = l_h$.

29. It is a degenerate tree (see exercise 5) with YOU at the top, THE at the bottom, needing 19.158 comparisons on the average.

Douglas A. Hamilton has proved that some degenerate tree is always worst. Therefore an $O(n^2)$ algorithm exists to find pessimal binary search trees.

30. See R. L. Wessner, *Information Processing Letters* **4** (1976), 90–94; F. F. Yao, *SIAM J. Algebraic and Discrete Methods* **3** (1982), 532–540.

31. See *Acta Informatica* **1** (1972), 307–310.

32. When M is large enough, the optimum tree must have the stated form and the minimum cost must be M times the minimum external path length plus the solution to the stated problem.

[*Notes:* The paper by Wessner cited in answer 30 explains how to find optimum binary search trees of height $\leq L$. In the special case $p_1 = \cdots = p_n = 0$, the stated result is due to T. C. Hu and K. C. Tan, MRC Report 1111 (Univ. of Wisconsin, 1970). A. M. Garsia and M. L. Wachs proved that in this case all external nodes will appear on at most two levels if $\min_{k=1}^{n}(q_{k-1} + q_k) \geq \max_{k=0}^{n} q_k$, and they presented an algorithm that needs only $O(n)$ steps to find an optimum two-level tree.]

33. For the stated problem, see A. Itai, *SICOMP* **5** (1976), 9–18. For the alternatives, see D. Spuler, *Acta Informatica* **31** (1994), 729–740.

34. It equals $2^{H(p_1, \ldots, p_n)N} (2\pi N)^{(1-n)/2} (p_1 \ldots p_n)^{-1/2} (1 + O(1/N))$, if $p_1 \ldots p_n \neq 0$, by Stirling's approximation.

35. The minimum value of the right-hand side occurs when $2x = (1 - p)/p$, and it equals $1 - p + H(p, 1 - p)$. But $H(p, q, r) \leq 1 - p + H(p, 1 - p)$, by (20) with $k = 2$.

36. First we prove the hint, which is due to Jensen [*Acta Math.* **30** (1906), 175–193]. If f is concave, the function $g(p) = f(px + (1 - p)y) - pf(x) - (1 - p)f(y)$ is concave and satisfies $g(0) = g(1) = 0$. If $g(p) < 0$ and $0 < p < 1$ there must be a value $p_0 < p$ with $g'(p_0) < 0$ and a value $p_1 > p$ with $g'(p_1) > 0$, by the mean value theorem; but this contradicts concavity. Therefore $f(px + (1 - p)y) \geq pf(x) + (1 - p)f(y)$ for $0 \leq p \leq 1$, a fact that is also geometrically obvious. Now we can prove by induction that $f(p_1x_1 + \cdots + p_nx_n) \geq p_1f(x_1) + \cdots + p_nf(x_n)$, since $f(p_1x_1 + \cdots + p_nx_n) \geq p_1f(x_1) + \cdots + p_{n-2}f(x_{n-2}) + (p_{n-1} + p_n)f((p_{n-1}x_{n-1} + p_nx_n)/(p_{n-1} + p_n))$ if $n > 2$.

By Lemma E we have

$$H(XY) = H(X) + \sum_{i=1}^{m} p_i H(r_{i1}/p_i, \ldots, r_{in}/p_i);$$

and the latter sum is $\sum_{j=1}^{n} \sum_{i=1}^{m} p_i f(r_{ij}/p_i) \leq \sum_{j=1}^{n} f(\sum_{i=1}^{m} r_{ij}) = H(Y)$, where $f(x) = x \lg(1/x)$ is concave.

37. By part (a) of exercise 3.3.2–26, we have $\Pr(P_1 \geq s) = (1 - s)^{n-1}$. Therefore $E\, H(P_1, \ldots, P_n) = n\, E\, P_1 \lg(1/P_1) = n \int_0^1 (1 - s)^{n-1} d(s \lg(1/s)) = -(A + B)/\ln 2$, where $A = n \int_0^1 (1 - s)^{n-1} ds = 1$ and

$$B = n \int_0^1 (1 - s)^{n-1} \ln s \, ds = \sum_{k=1}^{n} \binom{n}{k} (-1)^k s^k \left(\frac{1}{k} - \ln s \right) \Big|_0^1 = -H_n$$

by exercise 1.2.7–13. Thus the answer is $(H_n - 1)/\ln 2$. (This is $\lg n + (\gamma - 1)/\ln 2 + O(n^{-1})$, very near the maximum entropy $H(\frac{1}{n}, \ldots, \frac{1}{n}) = \lg n$. Therefore $H(p_1, \ldots, p_n)$ is $\Omega(\log n)$ with high probability.)

38. If $s_{k-1} = s_k$ we have $q_{k-1} = p_k = q_k = 0$; see (26). Construct a tree for the $n - 1$ probabilities $(p_1, \ldots, p_{k-1}, p_{k+1}, \ldots, p_n; q_0, \ldots, q_{k-1}, q_{k+1}, \ldots, q_n)$, and replace leaf $\boxed{k-1}$ by a 2-leaf subtree.

39. We can argue as in Theorem M, if $0 < w_1 \leq w_2 \leq \cdots \leq w_n$ and $s_k = w_1 + \cdots + w_k$, because $w_k \geq 2^{-t}$ implies that $s_{k-1} + 2^{-t} \leq s_k \leq s_{k+1} - 2^{-t}$ when the weights are ordered; hence we have $|\sigma_k| < 1 + \lg(1/w_k)$. [This result, together with the matching lower bound $H(w_1, \ldots, w_n)$, was Theorem 9 in Shannon's original paper of 1948.]

40. If $k = s + 3$, the stated rearrangement changes the cost from $q_{k-1}l + q_kl + q_{k-2}l_{k-2}$ to $q_{k-2}l + q_{k-1}l + q_kl_{k-2}$, so the net change is $(q_{k-2} - q_k)(l - l_{k-2})$; this is negative if $l < l_{k-2}$, because $q_{k-2} > q_k$.

Similarly, if $k \geq s + 4$ the rearrangement changes the cost by

$$\delta = q_{s+1}(l - l_{s+1}) + q_{s+2}(l - l_{s+2}) + q_{s+3}(l_{s+1} - l_{s+3}) + \cdots + q_{k-2}(l_{k-4} - l_{k-2})$$
$$+ q_{k-1}(l_{k-3} - l) + q_k(l_{k-2} - l).$$

We have $q_{s+1} > q_{s+3}, q_{s+2} > q_{s+4}, \ldots, q_{k-2} > q_k$. Therefore we find

$$\delta \leq (q_{k-2} - q_k)(l - l_{k-2}) + (q_{k-3} - q_{k-1})(l - l_{k-3}) \leq 0;$$

for example, when $k - s$ is even we have

$$\delta \leq q_{k-3}(l - l_{s+1}) + q_{k-2}(l - l_{s+2}) + q_{k-3}(l_{s+1} - l_{s+3}) + \cdots + q_{k-2}(l_{k-4} - l_{k-2})$$
$$+ q_{k-1}(l_{k-3} - l) + q_k(l_{k-2} - l)$$

and a similar derivation works when $k - s$ is odd. It follows that δ is negative unless $l_{k-2} = l$.

41. E F G H T U X Y Z V W B C D A P Q R J K L M I N O S ␣.

42. Let $q_j = \mathtt{WT}(P_j)$. Steps C1–C4, which move $q_{k-1} + q_k$ into position between q_{j-1} and q_j, can spoil (31) only at the point $i = j - 1$.

43. Invoke the recursive procedure $mark(P_1, 0)$, where $mark(P, l)$ means the following:

> LEVEL(P) $\leftarrow l$;
> if LLINK(P) $\neq \Lambda$ then $mark$(LLINK(P), $l + 1$);
> if RLINK(P) $\neq \Lambda$ then $mark$(RLINK(P), $l + 1$).

44. Set the global variables $t \leftarrow 0$, $m \leftarrow 2n$, and invoke the recursive subroutine $build(1)$, where $build(l)$ means the following:

> Set $j \leftarrow m$;
> if LEVEL(X_t) $= l$ then set LLINK(X_j) $\leftarrow X_t$ and $t \leftarrow t + 1$,
>   otherwise set $m \leftarrow m - 1$, LLINK(X_j) $\leftarrow X_m$, and $build(l + 1)$;
> if LEVEL(X_t) $= l$ then set RLINK(X_j) $\leftarrow X_t$ and $t \leftarrow t + 1$,
>   otherwise set $m \leftarrow m - 1$, RLINK(X_j) $\leftarrow X_m$, and $build(l + 1)$.

The variable j is local to the $build$ routine. [This elegant solution is due to R. E. Tarjan, *SICOMP* **6** (1977), 639.] Caution: If the numbers l_0, ..., l_n do not correspond to any binary tree, the algorithm will loop forever.

45. Maintain the working array P_0, ..., P_t as a doubly linked list that also has the links of a balanced tree (see Section 6.2.3). If the 2-descending weights are q_0, ..., q_t, with q_h at the root of the tree, we can decide whether to proceed left or right in the tree based on the values of q_h and q_{h+1}; the double linking provides instant access to q_{h+1}. (No RANK fields are needed; rotation preserves symmetric order, so it does not require any changes to the double links.)

     Several families of weights for which the problem can be solved in $O(n)$ time have been presented by Hu and Morgenthaler, *Lecture Notes in Comp. Sci.* **1120** (1996), 234–243; it is unknown whether $O(n)$ steps are sufficient in general.

46. See *IEEE Trans.* **C-23** (1974), 268–271; see also exercise 6.2.3–21.

47. See Altenkamp and Mehlhorn, *JACM* **27** (1980), 412–427.

48. Don't let the complicated analyses of the cases $N = 3$ [Jonassen and Knuth, *J. Comp. Syst. Sci.* **16** (1978), 301–322] or $N = 4$ [Baeza-Yates, *BIT* **29** (1989), 378–394] scare you; think big! Some progress has been reported by Louchard, Randrianarimanana, and Schott, *Theor. Comp. Sci.* **93** (1992), 201–225.

49. This question was first investigated by J. M. Robson [*Australian Comp. J.* **11** (1979), 151–153], B. Pittel [*J. Math. Anal. Applic.* **103** (1984), 461–480], and Luc Devroye [*JACM* **33** (1986), 489–498; *Acta Inf.* **24** (1987), 277–298], who obtained limit formulas that hold with probability $\to 1$ as $n \to \infty$; see the exposition by H. M. Mahmoud, *Evolution of Random Search Trees* (Wiley, 1992), Chapter 2. Sharper results were subsequently found by Bruce Reed [*JACM* **50** (2003), 306–332] and Michael Drmota [*JACM* **50** (2003), 333–374], who proved that the average height is $\alpha \ln n - (3\alpha \ln \ln n)/(2\alpha - 2) + O(1)$ and the variance is $O(1)$, where

$$\alpha = 1/T(\frac{1}{2e}) \approx 4.31107\,04070\,01005\,03504\,70760\,96446\,89027\,83916-$$

and $T(z) = \sum_{n=1}^{\infty} n^{n-1} z^n / n!$ is the tree function.

SECTION 6.2.3

1. The symmetric order of nodes must be preserved by the transformation, otherwise we wouldn't have a binary search tree.

2. B(S) $= 0$ can happen only when S points to the root of the tree (it has never been changed in steps A3 or A4), and all nodes from S to the point of insertion were balanced.

3. Let ρ_h be the largest possible ratio of unbalanced nodes in balanced trees of height h. Thus $\rho_1 = 0$, $\rho_2 = \frac{1}{2}$, $\rho_3 = \frac{1}{2}$. We will prove that $\rho_h = (F_{h+1} - 1)/(F_{h+2} - 1)$. Let T_h be a tree that maximizes ρ_h; then we may assume that its left subtree has height $h - 1$ and its right subtree has height $h - 2$, for if both subtrees had height $h - 1$ the ratio would be less than ρ_{h-1}. Thus the ratio for T_h is at most $(\rho_{h-1}N_l + \rho_{h-2}N_r + 1)/(N_l + N_r + 1)$, where there are (N_l, N_r) nodes in the (left, right) subtree. This formula takes its maximum value when (N_l, N_r) take their minimum values; hence we may assume that T_h is a Fibonacci tree. And $\rho_h < \phi - 1$ by exercise 1.2.8–28.

4. When $h = 7$,

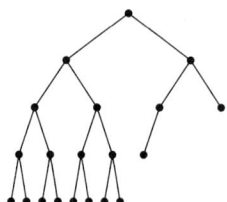

has greater path length. [*Note:* C. C. Foster, *Proc. ACM Nat. Conf.* **20** (1965), 197–198, gave an incorrect procedure for constructing N-node balanced trees of maximum path length; Edward Logg has observed that Foster's Fig. 3 gives a nonoptimal result after 24 steps (node number 22 can be removed in favor of number 25).]

The Fibonacci tree of order h does, however, minimize the value of $(h + a)N -$ (external path length(T)) over all balanced trees T of height $h - 1$, when a is any nonnegative constant; this is readily proved by induction on h. Its external path length is $\frac{3}{5}hF_{h-1} + \frac{4}{5}(h-1)F_h = (\phi/\sqrt{5})hF_{h+1} + O(F_{h+1}) = \Theta(h\phi^h)$. Consequently the path length of any N-node balanced tree is at most

$$\min_h (hN - \Theta(h\phi^h) + O(N)) \le N \log_\phi N - N \log_\phi \log_\phi N + O(N).$$

Moreover, if N is large and $k = \lceil \lg N \rceil$, $h = \lfloor k/\lg \phi - \log_\phi k \rfloor = \log_\phi N - \log_\phi \log_\phi N + O(1)$, we can construct a balanced tree of path length $hN + O(N)$ as follows: Write $N + 1 = F_h + F_{h-1} + \cdots + F_{k+1} + N' = F_{h+2} - F_{k+2} + N'$, and construct a complete binary tree on N' nodes; then successively join it with Fibonacci trees of orders k, $k+1$, $\ldots$, $h - 1$. [See R. Klein and D. Wood, *Theoretical Comp. Sci.* **72** (1990), 251–264.]

5. This can be proved by induction; if T_N denotes the tree constructed, we have

$$T_N = \begin{cases} \begin{array}{c} \bigcirc \\ \diagup \quad \diagdown \\ T_{2^{n-1}-1} \quad T_{N-2^{n-1}} \end{array}, & \text{if } 2^n \le N < 2^n + 2^{n-1}; \\[2em] \begin{array}{c} \bigcirc \\ \diagup \quad \diagdown \\ T_{2^n-1} \quad T_{N-2^n} \end{array}, & \text{if } 2^n + 2^{n-1} \le N < 2^{n+1}. \end{cases}$$

6. The coefficient of z^n in $zB_j(z)B_k(z)$ is the number of n-node binary trees whose left subtree is a balanced binary tree of height j and whose right subtree is a balanced binary tree of height k.

7. $C_{n+1} = C_n^2 + 2B_{n-1}B_{n-2}$; hence if we let $\alpha_0 = \ln 2$, $\alpha_1 = 0$, and $\alpha_{n+2} = \ln(1 + 2B_{n+1}B_n/C_{n+2}^2) = O(1/B_nC_{n+2})$, and $\theta = \exp(\alpha_0/2 + \alpha_1/4 + \alpha_2/8 + \cdots)$, we find that $0 \leq \theta^{2^n} - C_n = C_n(\exp(\alpha_n/2 + \alpha_{n+1}/4 + \cdots) - 1) < 1$; thus $C_n = \lfloor \theta^{2^n} \rfloor$. For general results on doubly exponential sequences, see *Fibonacci Quarterly* **11** (1973), 429–437. The expression for θ converges rapidly to the value

$$\theta = 1.43687\,28483\,94461\,87580\,04279\,84335\,54862\,92481+.$$

8. Let $b_h = B_h'(1)/B_h(1) + 1$, and let $\epsilon_h = 2B_hB_{h-1}(b_h - b_{h-1})/B_{h+1}$. Then $b_1 = 2$, $b_{h+1} = 2b_h - \epsilon_h$, and $\epsilon_h = O(b_h/B_{h-1})$; hence $b_h = 2^h\beta + r_h$, where

$$\beta = 1 - \tfrac{1}{4}\epsilon_1 - \tfrac{1}{8}\epsilon_2 - \cdots = 0.70117\,98151\,02026\,33972\,44868\,92779\,46053\,74616+$$

and $r_h = \epsilon_h/2 + \epsilon_{h+1}/4 + \cdots$ is extremely small for large h. [*Zhurnal Vychisl. Matem. i Matem. Fiziki* **6**, 2 (1966), 389–394. Analogous results for 2-3 trees were obtained by E. M. Reingold, *Fib. Quart.* **17** (1979), 151–157.]

9. Andrew Odlyzko has shown that the number of balanced trees is asymptotically

$$c^n f(\log_{(\sqrt{10}+2)/3} n)/n,$$

where $c \approx 1.916067$ and $f(x) = f(x + 1)$. His techniques will also yield the average height. [See *Congressus Numerantium* **42** (1984), 27–52, a paper in which he also discusses the enumeration of 2-3 trees.]

10. [*Inf. Proc. Letters* **17** (1983), 17–20.] Let $X_1, \ldots, X_N$ be nodes whose balance factors $\text{B}(X_k)$ are given. To construct the tree, set $k \leftarrow 0$ and compute $\text{TREE}(\infty)$, where $\text{TREE}(hmax)$ is the following recursive procedure with local variables h, h', and Q: Set $h \leftarrow 0$, $\text{Q} \leftarrow \Lambda$; then while $h < hmax$ and $k < N$ set $k \leftarrow k + 1$, $h' \leftarrow h + \text{B}(X_k)$, $\text{LEFT}(X_k) \leftarrow \text{Q}$, $\text{RIGHT}(X_k) \leftarrow \text{TREE}(h')$, $h \leftarrow \max(h, h') + 1$, $\text{Q} \leftarrow X_k$; return Q. (Tree Q has height h and corresponds to the balance factors that have been read since entry to the procedure.) The algorithm works even if $|\text{B}(X_k)| > 1$.

11. Clearly there are as many +A's as --B's and +-B's, when $n \geq 2$, and there is symmetry between + and -. If there are M nodes of types +A or -A, consideration of all possible cases when $n \geq 1$ shows that the next random insertion results in $M - 1$ such nodes with probability $3M/(n+1)$, otherwise it results in $M + 1$ such nodes. The result follows. [*SICOMP* **8** (1979), 33–41; Kurt Mehlhorn extended the analysis to deletions in *SICOMP* **11** (1982), 748–780. See R. A. Baeza-Yates, *Computing Surveys* **27** (1995), 109–119, for a summary of later developments in such "fringe analyses," which typically use the methods illustrated in exercise 6.2.4–8.]

12. The maximum occurs when inserting into the second external node of (12); $C = 4$, $C1 = 3$, $D = 3$, $A = C2 = F = G1 = H1 = U1 = 1$, for a total time of $132u$. The minimum occurs when inserting into the third-last external node of (13); $C = 2$, $C1 = C2 = 1$, $D = 2$, for a total time of $61u$. [The corresponding figures for Program 6.2.2T are $74u$ and $26u$.]

13. When the tree changes, only $O(\log N)$ RANK values need to be updated; the "simple" system might require very extensive changes.

14. Yes. (But typical operations on lists are sufficiently nonrandom that degenerate trees would probably occur.)

15. Use Algorithm 6.2.2T with m set to zero in step T1, and $m \leftarrow m + \text{RANK}(P)$ whenever $K \geq \text{KEY}(P)$ in step T2.

16. Delete E; do Case 3 rebalancing at D. Delete G; replace F by G; do Case 2 rebalancing at H; adjust balance factor at K.

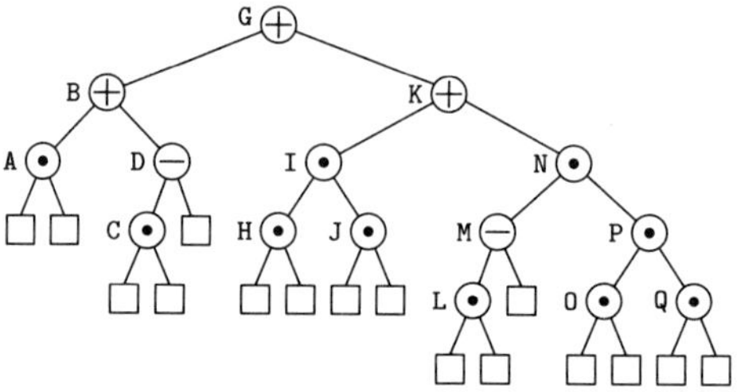

17. (a)

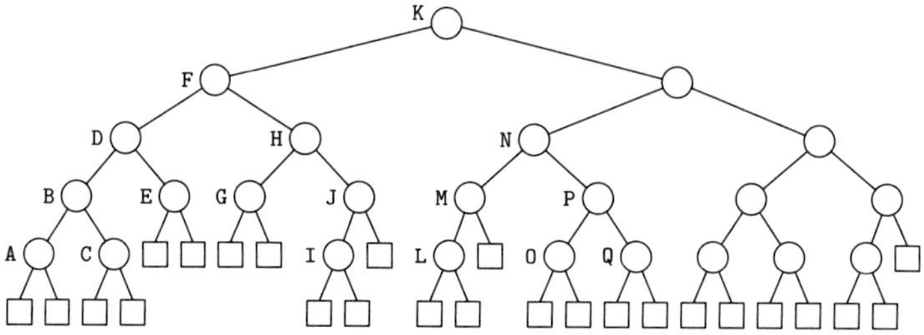

(b)

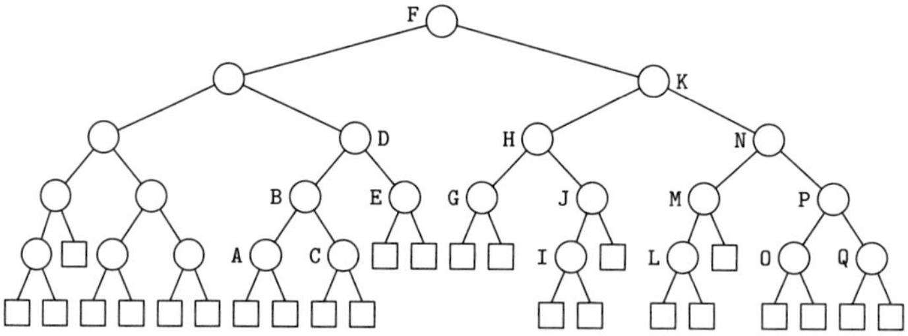

18.

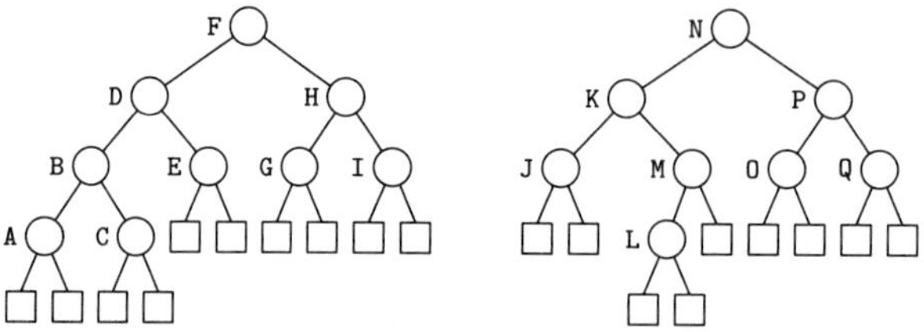

19. (Solution by Clark Crane.) There is one case that can't be handled by a single or double rotation at the root, namely

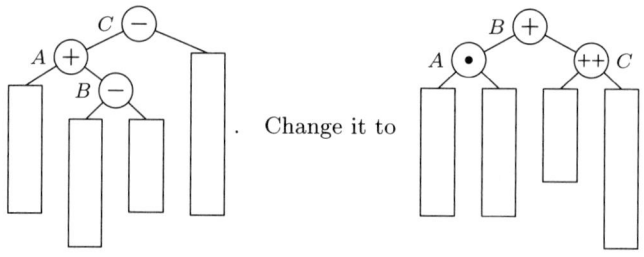

. Change it to

and then resolve the imbalance by applying a single or double rotation at C.

20. It is difficult to insert a new node at the extreme left of the tree

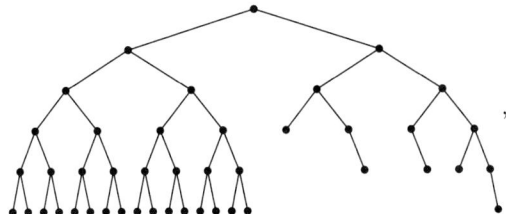

,

but K.-J. Räihä and S. H. Zweben have devised a general insertion algorithm that takes $O(\log N)$ steps. [*CACM* **22** (1979), 508–512.]

21. Algorithm A does the job in order $N \log N$ steps (see exercise 5); the following algorithm creates the same trees in $O(N)$ steps, using an interesting iterative rendition of a recursive method. We use three auxiliary lists:

$D_1, \ldots, D_l$ (a binary counter that essentially controls the recursion);

$J_1, \ldots, J_l$ (a list of pointers to juncture nodes);

$T_1, \ldots, T_l$ (a list of pointers to trees).

Here $l = \lceil \lg(N+1) \rceil$. For convenience the algorithm also sets $D_0 \leftarrow 1$, $J_0 \leftarrow J_{l+1} \leftarrow \Lambda$.

G1. [Initialize.] Set $l \leftarrow 0$, $J_0 \leftarrow J_1 \leftarrow \Lambda$, $D_0 \leftarrow 1$.

G2. [Get next item.] Let P point to the next input node. (We may invoke another coroutine in order to obtain P.) If there is no more input, go to G5. Otherwise, set $k \leftarrow 1$, $Q \leftarrow \Lambda$, and interchange P $\leftrightarrow J_1$.

G3. [Carry.] If $k > l$ (or, equivalently, if P $= \Lambda$), set $l \leftarrow l + 1$, $D_k \leftarrow 1$, $T_k \leftarrow Q$, $J_{k+1} \leftarrow \Lambda$, and return to G2. Otherwise set $D_k \leftarrow 1 - D_k$, interchange $Q \leftrightarrow T_k$, P $\leftrightarrow J_{k+1}$, and increase k by 1. If now $D_{k-1} = 0$, repeat this step.

G4. [Concatenate.] Set LLINK(P) $\leftarrow T_k$, RLINK(P) $\leftarrow Q$, B(P) $\leftarrow 0$, $T_k \leftarrow$ P, and return to G2.

G5. [Finish up.] Set LLINK(J_k) $\leftarrow T_k$, RLINK(J_k) $\leftarrow J_{k-1}$, B(J_k) $\leftarrow 1 - D_{k-1}$, for $1 \le k \le l$. Then terminate the algorithm; J_l points to the root of the desired tree. ∎

Step G3 is executed $2N - \nu(N)$ times, where $\nu(N)$ is the number of 1s in the binary representation of N.

22. The height of a weight-balanced tree with N internal nodes always lies between $\lg(N + 1)$ and $2\lg(N + 1)$. To get this upper bound, note that the heavier subtree of the root has at most $(N + 1)/\sqrt{2}$ external nodes.

23. (a) Form a tree whose right subtree is a complete binary tree with $2^n - 1$ nodes, and whose left subtree is a Fibonacci tree with $F_{n+1} - 1$ nodes. (b) Form a weight-balanced tree whose right subtree is about $2\lg N$ levels high and whose left subtree is about $\lg N$ levels high (see exercise 22).

24. Consider a smallest tree that satisfies the condition but is not perfectly balanced. Then its left and right subtrees are perfectly balanced, so they have 2^l and 2^r external nodes, respectively, where $l \ne r$. But this contradicts the stated condition.

25. After inserting a node at the bottom of the tree, we work up from the bottom to check the weight balance at each node on the search path. Suppose imbalance occurs at node A in (1), after we have inserted a new node in the right subtree, where B and its subtrees are weight-balanced. Then a single rotation will restore the balance unless $(|\alpha| + |\beta|)/|\gamma| > \sqrt{2} + 1$, where $|x|$ denotes the number of external nodes in a tree x. But in this case it can be shown that a double rotation will suffice. [See *SICOMP* **2** (1973), 33–43.]

27. It is sometimes necessary to make two comparisons in nodes that contain two keys. The worst case occurs in a tree like the following, which sometimes needs $2 \lg(N+2) - 2$ comparisons:

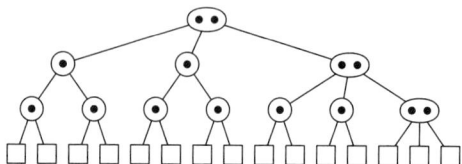

29. Partial solution by A. Yao: With $N \geq 6$ keys the lowest level will contain an average of $\frac{2}{7}(N + 1)$ one-key nodes and $\frac{1}{7}(N + 1)$ two-key nodes. The average total number of nodes lies between $0.70N$ and $0.79N$, for large N. [*Acta Informatica* **9** (1978), 159–170.]

30. For best-fit, arrange the records in order of size, with an arbitrary rule to break ties in case of equality. (See exercise 2.5–9.) For first fit, arrange the records in order of location, with an extra field in each node telling the size of the largest area in the subtree rooted at that node. This extra field can be maintained under insertions and deletions. (Although the running time is $O(\log n)$, it probably still doesn't beat the "ROVER" method of exercise 2.5–6 in practice; but the memory distribution may be better without ROVER, since there will usually be a nice large empty region for emergencies.)

An improved method has been developed by R. P. Brent, *ACM Trans. Prog. Languages and Systems* **11** (1989), 388–403.

31. Use a nearly balanced tree, with additional upward links for the leftmost part, plus a stack of postponed balance factor adjustments along this path. (Each insertion does a bounded number of these adjustments.)

This problem can be generalized to require $O(\log m)$ steps to find, insert, and/or delete items that are m steps away from any given "finger," where any key once located can serve as a finger in later operations. [See S. Huddleston and K. Mehlhorn, *Acta Inf.* **17** (1982), 157–184.]

32. Each right rotation increases one of the r's and leaves the others unchanged; hence $r_k \leq r_k'$ is necessary. To show that it is sufficient, suppose $r_j = r_j'$ for $1 \leq j < k$ but $r_k < r_k'$. Then there is a right rotation that increases r_k to a value $\leq r_k'$, because the numbers $r_1 r_2 \ldots r_n$ satisfy the condition of exercise 2.3.3–19(a).

Notes: This partial ordering, first introduced by D. Tamari in 1951, has many interesting properties. Any two trees have a greatest lower bound $T \wedge T'$, determined by the right-subtree sizes $\min(r_1, r_1') \min(r_2, r_2') \ldots \min(r_n, r_n')$, as well as a least upper bound $T \vee T'$ determined by the left-subtree sizes $\min(l_1, l_1') \min(l_2, l_2') \ldots \min(l_n, l_n')$. The left-subtree sizes are, of course, one less than the RANK fields of Algorithms B and C. For further information, see H. Friedman and D. Tamari, *J. Combinatorial Theory* **2** (1967), 215–242, **4** (1968), 201; C. Greene, *Europ. J. Combinatorics* **9** (1988), 225–240; D. D. Sleator, R. E. Tarjan, and W. P. Thurston, *J. Amer. Math. Soc.* **1** (1988), 647–681; J. M. Pallo, *Theoretical Informatics and Applic.* **27** (1993), 341–348; M. K.

Bennett and G. Birkhoff, *Algebra Universalis* **32** (1994), 115–144; P. H. Edelman and
V. Reiner, *Mathematika* **43** (1996), 127–154.

33. First, we can reduce the storage to one bit A(P) in each node P, so that B(P) =
A(RLINK(P)) − A(LLINK(P)) whenever LLINK(P) and RLINK(P) are both nonnull; oth-
erwise B(P) is known already. Moreover, we can assume that A(P) = 0 whenever
LLINK(P) and RLINK(P) are both null. Then A(P) can be eliminated in all other nodes
by swapping LLINK(P) with RLINK(P) whenever A(P) = 1; a comparison of KEY(P) with
KEY(LLINK(P)) or KEY(RLINK(P)) will determine A(P).

Of course, on machines for which pointers are always even, two unused bits are
present already in every node. Further economies are possible as in exercise 2.3.1–37.

SECTION 6.2.4

1. Two nodes split:

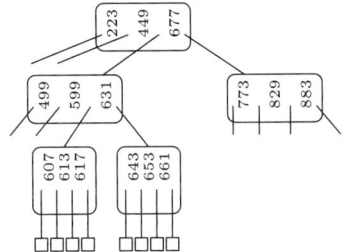

2. Altered nodes:

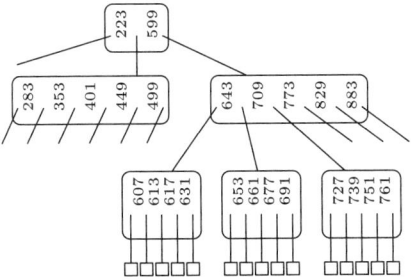

(Of course a B^*-tree would have no nonroot 3-key nodes, although Fig. 30 does.)

3. (a) $1 + 2 \cdot 50 + 2 \cdot 51 \cdot 50 + 2 \cdot 51 \cdot 51 \cdot 50 = 2 \cdot 51^3 - 1 = 265301$.
    (b) $1 + 2 \cdot 50 + (2 \cdot 51 \cdot 100 - 100) + ((2 \cdot 51 \cdot 101 - 100) \cdot 100 - 100) = 101^3 = 1030301$.
    (c) $1 + 2 \cdot 66 + (2 \cdot 67 \cdot 66 + 2) + (2 \cdot 67 \cdot 67 \cdot 66 + 2 \cdot 67) = 601661$. (Less than (b)!)

4. Before splitting a nonroot node, make sure that it has two full siblings, then
split these three nodes into four. The root should split only when it has more than
$3\lfloor (3m - 3)/4 \rfloor$ keys.

5. Interpretation 1, trying to maximize the stated minimum: 450. (The worst case
occurs if we have 1005 characters and the key to be passed to the parent must be 50
characters long: 445 chars + ptr + 50-char key + ptr + 50-char key + ptr + 445 chars.)

Interpretation 2, trying to equalize the number of keys after splitting, in order to
keep branching factors high: 155 (15 short keys followed by 16 long ones).

See E. M. McCreight, *CACM* **20** (1977), 670–674, for further comments.

6. If the key to be deleted is not on level $l − 1$, replace it by its successor and delete
the successor. To delete a key on level $l − 1$, we simply erase it; if this makes the node

too empty, we look at its right (or left) sibling, and "underflow," that is, move keys in from the sibling so that both nodes have approximately the same amount of data. This underflow operation will fail only if the sibling was minimally full, but in that case the two nodes can be collapsed into one (together with one key from their parent); such collapsing may cause the parent in turn to underflow, etc. With variable-length keys as in exercise 5, a parent node may need to split when one of its keys becomes longer.

8. Given a tree $\mathcal{T}$ with N internal nodes, let there be $a_k^{(j)}$ external nodes that require k accesses and whose parent node belongs to a page containing j keys; and let $A^{(j)}(z)$ be the corresponding generating function. Thus $A^{(1)}(1) + \cdots + A^{(M)}(1) = N + 1$. (Note that $a_k^{(j)}$ is a multiple of $j + 1$, for $1 \le j < M$.) The next random insertion leads to $N + 1$ equally probable trees, whose generating functions are obtained by decreasing some coefficient $a_k^{(j)}$ by $j + 1$ and adding $j + 2$ to $a_k^{(j+1)}$; or (if $j = M$) by decreasing some $a_k^{(M)}$ by 1 and adding 2 to $a_{k+1}^{(1)}$. Now $B_N^{(j)}(z)$ is $(N+1)^{-1}$ times the sum, over all trees $\mathcal{T}$, of the generating function $A^{(j)}(z)$ for $\mathcal{T}$ times the probability that $\mathcal{T}$ occurs; the stated recurrence relations follow.

The recurrence has the form

$$\left(B_N^{(1)}(z), \ldots, B_N^{(M)}(z)\right)^T = \left(I + (N+1)^{-1}W(z)\right)\left(B_{N-1}^{(1)}(z), \ldots, B_{N-1}^{(M)}(z)\right)^T$$
$$= \cdots = g_N\big(W(z)\big)(0, \ldots, 0, 1)^T,$$

where

$$g_n(x) = \left(1 + \frac{x}{n+1}\right) \cdots \left(1 + \frac{x}{2}\right) = \frac{1}{x+1}\binom{x+n+1}{n+1}.$$

It follows that $C_N' = (1, \ldots, 1)\left(B_N^{(1)\prime}(1), \ldots, B_N^{(M)\prime}(1)\right)^T = 2B_{N-1}^{(M)}(1)/(N+1) + C_{N-1}' = 2f_N(W)_{MM}$, where $f_n(x) = g_{n-1}(x)/(n+1) + \cdots + g_0(x)/2 = (g_n(x) - 1)/x$, and $W = W(1)$. (The subscript MM denotes the lower right corner element of the matrix.) Now $W = S^{-1} \operatorname{diag}(\lambda_1, \ldots, \lambda_M)S$, for some matrix S, where $\operatorname{diag}(\lambda_1, \ldots, \lambda_M)$ denotes the diagonal matrix whose entries are the roots of $\chi(\lambda) = (\lambda+2) \ldots (\lambda+M+1) - (M+1)!$. (The roots are distinct, since $\chi(\lambda) = \chi'(\lambda) = 0$ implies $1/(\lambda+2) + \cdots + 1/(\lambda+M+1) = 0$; the latter can hold only when λ is real, and $-M - 1 < \lambda < -2$, which implies that $|\lambda + 2| \ldots |\lambda + M + 1| < (M + 1)!$, a contradiction.) If $p(x)$ is any polynomial, $p(W) = p(S^{-1} \operatorname{diag}(\lambda_1, \ldots, \lambda_M)S) = S^{-1} \operatorname{diag}(p(\lambda_1), \ldots, p(\lambda_M))S$; hence the lower right corner element of $p(W)$ has the form $c_1 p(\lambda_1) + \cdots + c_M p(\lambda_M)$ for some constants $c_1, \ldots, c_M$ independent of p. These constants may be evaluated by setting $p(\lambda) = \chi(\lambda)/(\lambda - \lambda_j)$; since $(W^k)_{MM} = (-2)^k$ for $0 \le k \le M-1$, we have $p(W)_{MM} = p(-2) = (M+1)!/(\lambda_j+2) = c_j p(\lambda_j) = c_j \chi'(\lambda_j) = c_j(M+1)!\left(1/(\lambda_j+2) + \cdots + 1/(\lambda_j+M+1)\right)$; hence $c_j = (\lambda_j + 2)^{-1}\left(1/(\lambda_j + 2) + \cdots + 1/(\lambda_j + M + 1)\right)^{-1}$. This yields an "explicit" formula $C_N' = \sum_{j=1}^M 2c_j f_N(\lambda_j)$; and it remains to study the roots λ_j. Note that $|\lambda_j + M + 1| \le M + 1$ for all j, otherwise we would have $|\lambda_j + 2| \ldots |\lambda_j + M + 1| > (M + 1)!$. Taking $\lambda_1 = 0$, this implies that $\Re(\lambda_j) < 0$ for $2 \le j \le M$. By Eq. 1.2.5–(15), $g_n(x) \sim (n+1)^x/\Gamma(x+2)$ as $n \to \infty$; hence $g_n(\lambda_j) \to 0$ for $2 \le j \le M$. Consequently $C_N' = 2c_1 f_N(0) + O(1) = H_N/(H_{M+1} - 1) + O(1)$.

Notes: The analysis above is relevant also to the "samplesort" algorithm discussed briefly in Section 5.2.2. The calculations may readily be extended to show that $B_N^{(j)}(1) \sim (H_{M+1} - 1)^{-1}/(j+2)$ for $1 \le j < M$, $B_N^{(M)}(1) \sim (H_{M+1} - 1)^{-1}/2$. Hence the total number of interior nodes on unfilled pages is approximately

$$\left(\frac{1}{3 \times 2} + \frac{2}{4 \times 3} + \cdots + \frac{M-1}{(M+1) \times M}\right)\frac{N}{H_{M+1} - 1} = \left(1 - \frac{M}{(M+1)(H_{M+1} - 1)}\right)N;$$

and the total number of pages used is approximately

$$\left(\frac{1}{3\times 2}+\frac{1}{4\times 3}+\cdots+\frac{1}{(M+1)\times M}+\frac{1}{M+1}\right)\frac{N}{H_{M+1}-1}=\frac{N}{2(H_{M+1}-1)},$$

yielding an asymptotic storage utilization of $2(H_{M+1}-1)/M$.

This analysis has been extended by Mahmoud and Pittel [*J. Algorithms* **10** (1989), 52–75], who discovered that the variance of the storage utilization undergoes a surprising phase transition: When $M \leq 25$, the variance is $\Theta(N)$; but when $M \geq 26$ it is asymptotically $f(N)N^{1+2\alpha}$ where $f(e^{\pi/\beta}N) = f(N)$, if $-\frac{1}{2}+\alpha+\beta i$ and $-\frac{1}{2}+\alpha-\beta i$ are the nonzero roots λ_j with largest real part.

The height of such trees has been analyzed by L. Devroye [*Random Structures & Algorithms* **1** (1990), 191–203]; see also B. Pittel, *Random Structures & Algorithms* **5** (1994), 337–347.

9. Yes; for example we could replace each K_i in (1) by i plus the number of keys in subtrees $P_0, \ldots, P_{i-1}$. The search, insertion, and deletion algorithms can be modified appropriately.

10. Brief sketch: Extend the paging scheme so that exclusive access to buffers is given to one user at a time; the search, insertion, and deletion algorithms must be carefully modified so that such exclusive access is granted only for a limited time when absolutely necessary, and in such a way that no deadlocks can occur. For details, see B. Samadi, *Inf. Proc. Letters* **5** (1976), 107–112; R. Bayer and M. Schkolnick, *Acta Inf.* **9** (1977), 1–21; Y. Sagiv, *J. Comp. Syst. Sci.* **33** (1986), 275–296.

SECTION 6.3

1. Lieves (the plural of "lief").

2. Perform Algorithm T using the new key as argument; it will terminate unsuccessfully in either step T3 or T4. If in T3, simply set table entry k of NODE(P) to K and terminate the insertion algorithm. Otherwise set this table entry to the address of a new node Q $\Leftarrow$ AVAIL, containing only null links, then set P $\leftarrow$ Q. Now set k and k' to the respective next characters of K and X; if $k \neq k'$, store K in position k of NODE(P) and store X in position k', but if $k = k'$ again make the k position point to a new node Q $\Leftarrow$ AVAIL, set P $\leftarrow$ Q, and repeat the process until eventually $k \neq k'$. (We must assume that no key is a prefix of another.)

3. Replace the key by a null link, in the node where it appears. If this node is now useless because all its entries are null except one that is a key X, delete the node and replace the corresponding pointer in its parent by X. If the parent node is now useless, delete it in the same way.

4. Successful searches take place exactly as with the full table, but unsuccessful searches in the compressed table may go through several additional iterations. For example, an input argument such as TRASH will make Program T take *six* iterations (more than five!); this is the worst case. It is necessary to verify that no infinite looping on blank sequences is possible. (This remarkable 49-place packing is due to J. Scot Fishburn, who also showed that 48 places do not suffice.)

A slower but more versatile way to economize on trie storage has been proposed by Kurt Maly, *CACM* **19** (1976), 409–415.

In general, if we want to compress n sparse tables containing respectively x_1, ..., x_n nonzero entries, a first-fit method that offsets the jth table by the minimum amount r_j that will not conflict with the previously placed tables will have $r_j \leq (x_1 + \cdots + x_{j-1})x_j$, since each previous nonzero entry can block at most x_j offsets. This worst-case estimate gives $r_j \leq 93$ for the data in Table 1, guaranteeing that any twelve tables of length 30 containing respectively 10, 5, 4, 3, 3, 3, 3, 3, 2, 2, 2, 2 nonzero entries can be packed into $93 + 30$ consecutive locations regardless of the pattern of the nonzeros. Further refinements of this method have been developed by R. E. Tarjan and A. C. Yao, *CACM* **22** (1979), 606–611. A dynamic implementation of compressed tries, due to F. M. Liang, is used for hyphenation tables in the TEX typesetting system; see D. E. Knuth, *CACM* **29** (1986), 471–478; *Literate Programming* (1992), 206–233.

5. In each family, test for the most probable outcome first, by arranging the letters from left to right in decreasing order of probability. The optimality of this arrangement can be proved as in Theorem 6.1S. [See *CACM* **12** (1969), 72–76.]

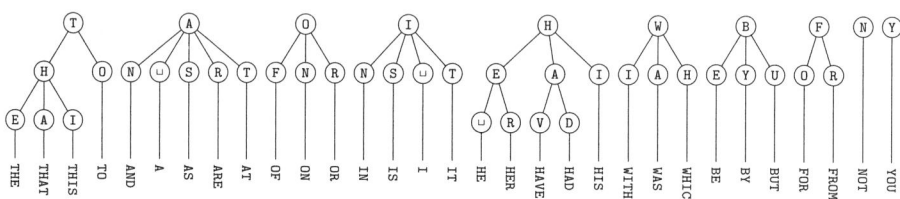

6.

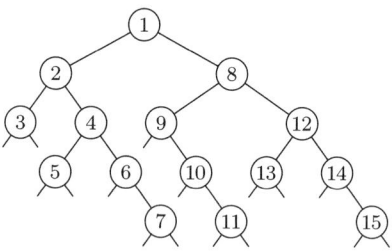

7. For example, 8, 4, 1, 2, 3, 5, 6, 7, 12, 9, 10, 11, 13, 14, 15. (No matter what sequence is used, the left subtree cannot contain more than two nodes on level 4, nor can the right subtree.) Even this "worst" tree is within 4 of the best possible tree, so we see that digital search trees aren't very sensitive to the order of insertion.

8. Yes. The KEY fields now contain only a truncated key; leading bits implied by the node position are chopped off. (A similar modification of Algorithm T is possible.)

```
9. START LDX   K              1      D1. Initialize. (rX ≡ K)
         LD1   ROOT           1      P ← ROOT.     (rI1 ≡ P)
         JMP   2F             1
   4H    LD2   0,1(RLINK)     C2     D4. Move right. Q ← RLINK(P).
         J2Z   5F             C2     To D5 if Q = Λ.
   1H    ENT1  0,2            C − 1  P ← Q.
   2H    CMPX  1,1            C      D2. Compare.
         JE    SUCCESS        C      Exit if K = KEY(P).
         SLB   1              C − S  Shift K left one bit.
         JAO   4B             C − S  To D4 if the detached bit was 1.
         LD2   0,1(LLINK)     C1     D3. Move left. Q ← LLINK(P).
         J2NZ  1B             C1     To D2 with P ← Q if Q ≠ Λ.
   5H    Continue as in Program 6.2.2T, interchanging the roles of rA and rX.   ∎
```

The running time for the searching phase of this program is $(10C - 3S + 4)u$, where $C - S$ is the number of bit inspections. For random data, the approximate average running times are therefore:

	Successful	Unsuccessful
Program 6.2.2T	15 ln N − 12.34	15 ln N − 2.34
This program	14.4 ln N − 6.17	14.4 ln N + 1.26

(Consequently Program 6.2.2T is a shade faster unless N is very large.)

10. Let $\oplus$ denote the exclusive or operation on n-bit numbers, and let $f(x) = n - \lceil \lg(x + 1) \rceil$ be the number of leading zero bits of x. One solution: (b) If a search via Algorithm T ends unsuccessfully in step T3, K is one less than the number of bit inspections made so far; otherwise if the search ends in step T4, $k = f(K \oplus X)$. (a, c) Do a regular search, but also keep track of the minimum value, x, of $K \oplus \texttt{KEY(P)}$ over all $\texttt{KEY(P)}$ compared with K during the search. Then $k = f(x)$. (Prove that no other key can have more bits in common with K than those compared to K. In case (a), the maximum k occurs for either the largest key $\leq K$ or the smallest key $> K$.)

11. No; eliminating a node with only one empty subtree will "forget" one bit in the keys of the nonempty subtree. To delete a node, we should replace it by one of its *terminal* descendants, for example by searching to the right whenever possible.

12. Insert three random numbers α, β, γ between 0 and 1 into an initially empty tree; then delete α with probability p, β with probability q, γ with probability r, using the algorithm suggested in the previous exercise. The tree

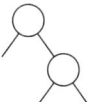

is obtained with probability $\frac{1}{4}p + \frac{1}{2}q + \frac{1}{2}r$, and this is $\frac{1}{2}$ only if $p = 0$.

13. Add a KEY field to each node, and compare K with this key before looking at the vector element in step T2. Table 1 would change as follows: Nodes (1), ..., (12) would contain the respective keys THE, AND, BE, FOR, HIS, IN, OF, TO, WITH, HAVE, HE, THAT (if we inserted them in order of decreasing frequency), and these keys would be deleted from their previous positions. [The corresponding program would be slower and more complicated than Program T, in this case. A more direct M-ary generalization of Algorithm D would create a tree with N nodes, having one key and M links per node.]

14. If $j \leq n$, there is only one place, namely KEY(P). But if $j > n$, the set of all occurrences is found by traversing the subtree of node P: If there are r occurrences, this subtree contains $r - 1$ nodes (including node P), and so it has r link fields with TAG = 1; these link fields point to all the nodes that reference TEXT positions matching K. (It isn't necessary to check the TEXT again at all.)

15. To begin forming the tree, set KEY(HEAD) to the first TEXT reference, and set LLINK(HEAD) ← HEAD, LTAG(HEAD) ← 1. Further TEXT references can be entered into the tree using the following insertion algorithm:

Set K to the new key that we wish to enter. (This is the first reference the insertion algorithm makes to the TEXT array.) Perform Algorithm P; it must terminate unsuccessfully, since no key is allowed to be a prefix of another. (Step P6 makes the second reference to the TEXT; no more references will be needed!) Now suppose that the key located in step P6 agrees with the argument K in the first l bits, but differs from it in position $l+1$, where K has the digit b and the key has $1-b$. (Even though the search in Algorithm P might have let j get much greater than l, it is possible to prove that the procedure specified here will find the longest match between K and *any* existing key. Thus, *all* keys of the text that start with the first l bits of K have $1-b$ as their $(l+1)$st bit.) Now repeat Algorithm P with K replaced by these leading l bits (thus, $n \leftarrow l$). This time the search will be successful, so we needn't perform step P6. Now set $R \Leftarrow \text{AVAIL}$, $\text{KEY(R)} \leftarrow$ position of the new key in TEXT. If $\text{LLINK(Q)} = P$, set $\text{LLINK(Q)} \leftarrow R$, $t \leftarrow \text{LTAG(Q)}$, $\text{LTAG(Q)} \leftarrow 0$; otherwise set $\text{RLINK(Q)} \leftarrow R$, $t \leftarrow \text{RTAG(Q)}$, $\text{RTAG(Q)} \leftarrow 0$. If $b = 0$, set $\text{LTAG(R)} \leftarrow 1$, $\text{LLINK(R)} \leftarrow R$, $\text{RTAG(R)} \leftarrow t$, $\text{RLINK(R)} \leftarrow P$; otherwise set $\text{RTAG(R)} \leftarrow 1$, $\text{RLINK(R)} \leftarrow R$, $\text{LTAG(R)} \leftarrow t$, $\text{LLINK(R)} \leftarrow P$. If $t = 1$, set $\text{SKIP(R)} \leftarrow 1+l-j$; otherwise set $\text{SKIP(R)} \leftarrow 1+l-j+\text{SKIP(P)}$ and $\text{SKIP(P)} \leftarrow j-l-1$.

16. The tree setup requires precisely one dotted link coming from below a node to that node; it comes from that part of the tree where this key first differs from all others. If there is no such part of the tree, the algorithms break down. We could simply drop keys that are prefixes of others, but then the algorithm of exercise 14 wouldn't have enough data to find *all* occurrences of the argument.

17. If we define $a_0 = a_1 = 0$, then

$$x_n = a_n + \sum_{k \geq 2} \binom{n}{k}(-1)^k \hat{a}_k/(m^{k-1}-1) = \sum_{k \geq 2} \binom{n}{k}(-1)^k \hat{a}_k m^{k-1}/(m^{k-1}-1).$$

18. To solve (4) we need the transform of $a_n = [n > 1]$, namely $\hat{a}_n = [n=0] - 1 + n$; hence for $N \geq 2$ we obtain $A_N = 1 - U_N + V_N$, where $U_N = K(N, 0, M)$ and $V_N = K(N, 1, M)$ in the notation of exercise 19. Similarly, to solve (5), take $a_n = n - [n=1] = \hat{a}_n$ and obtain $C_N = N + V_N$ for $N \geq 2$.

19. For $s = 1$, we have $V_n = K(n, 1, m) = n((\ln n + \gamma)/\ln m - \frac{1}{2} - \delta_0(n-1)) + O(1)$, and for $s \geq 2$ we have $K(n, s, m) = (-1)^s n(1/\ln m + \delta_{s-1}(n-s))/s(s-1) + O(1)$, where

$$\delta_s(n) = \frac{2}{\ln m} \sum_{k \geq 1} \Re(\Gamma(s - 2\pi ik/\ln m) \exp(2\pi ik \log_m n))$$

is a periodic function of $\log n$. [In this derivation we have

$$K(n+s, s, m)/(-1)^s \binom{n+s}{s} = \frac{n^{-s+1}}{2\pi i} \int_{1/2-i\infty}^{1/2+i\infty} \frac{\Gamma(z)n^{s-1-z}}{m^{s-1-z}-1}\, dz + O(n^{-s}).$$

For small m and s, the δ's will be negligibly small; see exercise 5.2.2–46. Note that $\delta_s(n-a) = \delta_s(n) + O(n^{-1})$ for fixed a.]

20. For (a), let $a_n = [n > s] = 1 - \sum_{k=0}^{s}[n=k]$; for (b), let $a_n = n - \sum_{k=0}^{s} k[n=k]$; and for (c), we want to solve the recurrence

$$y_n = \begin{cases} m^{1-n} \sum_k \binom{n}{k}(m-1)^{n-k} y_k & \text{for } n > s, \\ \binom{n+1}{2} & \text{for } n \leq s. \end{cases}$$

Setting $x_n = y_n - n$ yields a recurrence of the form of exercise 17, with

$$a_n = (1 - M^{-1}) \sum_{k=0}^{s} \binom{k}{2}[n=k].$$

Therefore, in the notation of previous exercises, the answers are (a) $1 - K(N, 0, M) + K(N, 1, M) - \cdots + (-1)^{s-1} K(N, s, M) = N/(s \ln M) - N(\delta_{-1}(N) + \delta_0(N-1) +$

$\delta_1(N-2)/2{\cdot}1 + \cdots + \delta_{s-1}(N-s)/s(s-1)) + O(1)$; (b) $N^{-1}(N + K(N,1,M) - 2K(N,2,M) + \cdots + (-1)^{s-1}sK(N,s,M)) = (\ln N + \gamma - H_{s-1})/\ln M + 1/2 - (\delta_0(N-1)+\delta_1(N-2)/1+\cdots+\delta_{s-1}(N-s)/(s-1))+O(N^{-1})$; (c) $N^{-1}(N+(1-M^{-1}) \times \sum_{k=2}^{s}(-1)^k\binom{k}{2}K(N,k,M)) = 1 + \frac{1}{2}(1 - M^{-1})((s-1)/\ln M + \delta_1(N-2) + \cdots + \delta_{s-1}(N-s)) + O(N^{-1})$.

21. Let there be A_N nodes in all. The number of nonnull pointers is $A_N - 1$, and the number of nonpointers is N, so the total number of null pointers is $MA_N - A_N + 1 - N$. To get the average number of null pointers in any fixed position, divide by M. [The average value of A_N appears in exercise 20(a).]

22. There is a node for each of the M^l sequences of leading bits such that at least two keys have this bit pattern. The probability that exactly k keys have a particular bit pattern is

$$\binom{N}{k}M^{-lk}(1 - M^{-l})^{N-k},$$

so the average number of trie nodes on level l is $M^l(1 - (1 - M^{-l})^N) - N(1 - M^{-l})^{N-1}$.

23. More generally, consider the case of arbitrary s as in exercise 20. If there are a_l nodes on level l, they contain a_{l+1} links and $Ma_l - a_{l+1}$ places where the search might be unsuccessful. The average number of digit inspections will therefore be $\sum_{l\geq 0}(l+1)M^{-l-1}(Ma_l - a_{l+1}) = \sum_{l\geq 0} M^{-l}a_l$. Using the formula for a_l in a random trie, this equals

$$1 + \frac{K(N+1,1,M) - 2K(N+1,2,M) + \cdots + (-1)^s(s+1)K(N+1,s+1,M)}{N+1}$$

$$= \frac{\ln N + \gamma - H_s}{\ln M} + \frac{1}{2} - \delta_0(N) - \frac{\delta_1(N-1)}{1} - \cdots - \frac{\delta_s(N-s)}{s} + O(N^{-1}).$$

24. We must solve the recurrences $x_0 = x_1 = y_0 = y_1 = 0$,

$$x_n = m^{-n}\sum_{n_1+\cdots+n_m=n}\binom{n}{n_1,\ldots,n_m}\left(x_{n_1} + \cdots + x_{n_m} + \sum_{1\leq j\leq m}[n_j\neq 0]\right)$$

$$= a_n + m^{1-n}\sum_k\binom{n}{k}x_k,$$

$$y_n = m^{-n}\sum_{n_1+\cdots+n_m=n}\binom{n}{n_1,\ldots,n_m}\left(y_{n_1} + \cdots + y_{n_m} + \sum_{1\leq i<j\leq m}[n_i\neq 0]n_j\right)$$

$$= b_n + m^{1-n}\sum_k\binom{n}{k}y_k,$$

for $n \geq 2$, where $a_n = m(1 - (1 - 1/m)^n)$ and $b_n = \frac{1}{2}(m-1)n(1 - (1 - 1/m)^{n-1})$. By exercises 17 and 18 the answers are (a) $x_N = N + V_N - U_N - [N=1] = A_N + N - 1$ (a result that could have been obtained directly, since the number of nodes in the forest is always $N - 1$ more than the number in the corresponding trie!); and (b) $y_N/N = \frac{1}{2}(M-1)V_N/N = \frac{1}{2}(M-1)((\ln N + \gamma)/\ln M - \frac{1}{2} - \delta_0(N-1)) + O(N^{-1})$.

25. (a) Let $A_N = M(N-1)/(M-1) - E_N$; then for $N \geq 2$, we have $(1 - M^{1-N})E_N = M - 1 - M(1 - 1/M)^{N-1} + M^{1-N}\sum_{0<k<N}\binom{N}{k}(M-1)^{N-k}E_k$. Since $M - 1 \geq M(1 - 1/M)^{N-1}$, we have $E_N \geq 0$ by induction. (b) By Theorem 1.2.7A with $x = 1/(M-1)$ and $n = N - 1$, we find $D_N = a_N + M^{1-N}\sum_k\binom{N}{k}(M-1)^{N-k}D_k$,

where $a_1 = 0$ and $0 < a_N < M(1 - 1/M)^N / \ln M \le (M-1)^2/M \ln M$ for $N \ge 2$. Hence $0 \le D_N \le (M-1)^2 A_N/M \ln M \le (M-1)(N-1)/\ln M$.

26. Taking $q = \frac{1}{2}$, $z = -\frac{1}{2}$ in the second identity of exercise 5.1.1–16, we get $1/3 - 1/(3\cdot 7) + 1/(3\cdot 7\cdot 15) - \cdots = 0.28879$; it's slightly faster to use $z = -\frac{1}{4}$ and take half of the result. Alternatively, Euler's formula from exercise 5.1.1–14 can be used, involving only negative powers of 2. (John Wrench has computed the value to 40 decimal digits, namely $0.28878\,80950\,86602\,42127\,88997\,21929\,23078\,00889+$.)

27. (For fun, the following derivation goes to $O(N^{-1})$.) In the notation of exercises 5.2.2–38 and 5.2.2–48, we have

$$\bar{C}_N = U_N + N - 1 + \frac{V_{N+1}}{N+1} - \alpha N - \beta + \sum_{n \ge 2} (-1)^n 2^{-n(n+1)/2} \frac{\sum_{m \ge 0} (2^{1-n})^m (1 - 2^{-m})^N}{\prod_{r=1}^n (1 - 2^{-r})},$$

where

$$\alpha = 2/(1\cdot 1) - 4/(3\cdot 3\cdot 1) + 8/(7\cdot 7\cdot 3\cdot 1) - 16/(15\cdot 15\cdot 7\cdot 3\cdot 1) + \cdots \approx 1.60670;$$
$$\beta = 2/(1\cdot 3\cdot 1) - 4/(3\cdot 7\cdot 3\cdot 1) + 8/(7\cdot 15\cdot 7\cdot 3\cdot 1) - \cdots \approx 0.60670.$$

This numerical evaluation suggests that $\alpha = \beta + 1$, a fact that is not hard to prove. Moreover, α turns out to be identical to the constant defined quite differently in 5.2.3–(19); see Karl Dilcher, *Discrete Math.* **145** (1995), 83–93. We have $V_{N+1}/(N+1) = U_{N+1} - U_N$, and the value of $\sum_{m \ge 0} (2^{1-n})^m (1 - 2^{-m})^N$ is $O(N^{1-n})$, by exercise 5.2.2–46. Hence $\bar{C}_N = U_{N+1} - (\alpha - 1)N - \alpha + O(N^{-1}) = (N+1)\lg(N+1) + N((\gamma - 1)/\ln 2 + \frac{1}{2} - \alpha + \delta_{-1}(N)) + \frac{1}{2} - 1/\ln 4 - \alpha - \frac{1}{2}\delta_1(N) + O(N^{-1})$, by exercise 5.2.2–50.

The variance of the internal path length of a digital search tree has been computed by Kirschenhofer, Prodinger, and Szpankowski, *SICOMP* **23** (1994), 598–616.

28. The derivations in the text and exercise 27 apply to general $M \ge 2$, if we substitute M for 2 in the obvious places. Hence the average number of digit inspections in a random successful search is $\bar{C}_N/N = U_{N+1} - \alpha_M + 1 + O(N^{-1}) = \log_M N + (\gamma - 1)/\ln M + \frac{1}{2} - \alpha_M + \delta_{-1}(N) + (\log_M N)/N + O(N^{-1})$; and for the unsuccessful case it is $\bar{C}_{N+1} - \bar{C}_N = V_{N+2}/(N+2) - \alpha_M + 1 + O(N^{-1}) = \log_M N + \gamma/\ln M + \frac{1}{2} - \alpha_M - \delta_0(N+1) + O(N^{-1})$. Here $\delta_s(n)$ is defined in exercise 19, and

$$\alpha_M = \sum_{j \ge 0} (-1)^j M^{j+1}/(M^{j+1} - 1)^2 (M^j - 1)\dots(M-1).$$

29. Flajolet and Sedgewick [*SICOMP* **15** (1986), 748–767] have shown that the approximate average number of such nodes is $.372N$ when $M = 2$ and $.689N$ when $M = 16$. See also the generalization by Flajolet and Richmond, *Random Structures & Algorithms* **3** (1992), 305–320.

30. By iterating the recurrence, $h_n(z)$ is the sum of all possible terms of the form

$$\binom{n}{p_1} \frac{z}{2^{p_1} - 1} \binom{p_1}{p_2} \frac{z}{2^{p_2} - 1} \cdots \frac{z}{2^{p_m} - 1} \binom{p_m}{1}, \qquad \text{for } n > p_1 > \cdots > p_m > 1.$$

31. $h_n'(1) = V_n$; see exercise 5.2.2–36(b). [For the variance and limiting distributions of M-ary generalizations of Patrician trees, see P. Kirschenhofer and H. Prodinger, *Lecture Notes in Comp. Sci.* **226** (1986), 177–185; W. Szpankowski, *JACM* **37** (1990), 691–711; B. Rais, P. Jacquet, and W. Szpankowski, *SIAM J. Discrete Math.* **6** (1993), 197–213.]

32. The sum of the SKIP fields is the number of nodes in the corresponding binary trie, so the answer is A_N (see exercise 20).

33. Here's how (18) was discovered: $A(2z) - 2A(z) = e^{2z} - 2e^z + 1 + A(z)(e^z - 1)$ can be transformed into $A(2z)/(e^{2z} - 1) = (e^z - 1)/(e^z + 1) + A(z)/(e^z - 1)$. Hence $A(z) = (e^z - 1)\sum_{j\geq1}(e^{z/2^j} - 1)/(e^{z/2^j} + 1)$. Now if $f(z) = \sum c_n z^n$, $\sum_{j\geq1} f(z/2^j) = \sum c_n z^n/(2^n - 1)$. In this case $f(z) = (e^z - 1)/(e^z + 1) = \tanh(z/2)$, which equals $1 - 2z^{-1}(z/(e^z - 1) - 2z/(e^{2z} - 1)) = \sum_{n\geq1} B_{n+1} z^n (2^{n+1} - 1)/(n + 1)!$. From this formula the route is apparent.

34. (a) Consider $\sum_{j\geq1}\sum_{k=2}^{n-1}\binom{n}{k}B_k/2^{j(k-1)}$; $1^{n-1}+\cdots+(m-1)^{n-1} = (B_n(m)-B_n)/n$ by exercise 1.2.11.2–4. (b) Let $S_n(m) = \sum_{k=1}^{m-1}(1 - k/m)^n$ and $T_n(m) = 1/(e^{n/m} - 1)$. If $k \leq m/2$ we have $e^{-kn/m} > \exp(n\ln(1 - k/m)) > \exp(-kn/m - k^2n/m^2) > e^{-kn/m}(1 - k^2/m^2)$, hence $(1 - k/m)^n = e^{-kn/m} + O(e^{-kn/m}k^2n/m^2)$. Since $S_n(m) = \sum_{k=1}^{m/2}(1 - k/m)^n + O(2^{-n})$ and $T_n(m) = \sum_{k=1}^{m/2}e^{-kn/m} + O(e^{-n/2})$, we have $S_n(m) = T_n(m)+O(e^{-n/m}n/m^2)$. The sum of $O(\exp(-n/2^j)n/2^{2j})$ is $O(n^{-1})$, because the sum for $j \leq \lg n$ is of order $n^{-1}(1 + 2/e + (2/e)^2 + \cdots)$ and the sum for $j \geq \lg n$ is of order $n^{-1}(1 + 1/4 + (1/4)^2 + \cdots)$. (c) Argue as in Section 5.2.2 when $|x| < 2\pi$, then use analytic continuation. (d) $\frac{1}{2}\lg(n/\pi) + \gamma/(2\ln 2) - \frac{3}{4} + \delta(n) + 2/n$, where

$$\delta(n) = (2/\ln 2)\sum_{k\geq1}\Re\big(\zeta(-2\pi ik/\ln 2)\Gamma(-2\pi ik/\ln 2)\exp(2\pi ik\lg n)\big)$$
$$= (1/\ln 2)\sum_{k\geq1}\Re\big(\zeta(1 + 2\pi ik/\ln 2)\exp(2\pi ik\lg(n/\pi)))/\cosh(\pi^2 k/\ln 2).$$

The variance and higher moments have been calculated by W. Szpankowski, *JACM* **37** (1990), 691–711.

35. The keys must be $\{\alpha 0\beta 0\omega_1, \alpha 0\beta 1\omega_2, \alpha 1\gamma 0\omega_3, \alpha 1\gamma 1\delta 0\omega_4, \alpha 1\gamma 1\delta 1\omega_5\}$, where $\alpha, \beta, \ldots$ are strings of 0s and 1s with $|\alpha| = a - 1$, $|\beta| = b - 1$, etc. The probability that five random keys have this form is $5!\,2^{a-1+b-1+c-1+d-1}/2^{a+b+a+b+a+c+a+c+a+c+d} = 5!/2^{4a+b+2c+d+4}$.

36. Let there be n internal nodes. (a) $(n!/2^I)\prod(1/s(x)) = n!\prod(1/2^{s(x)-1}s(x))$, where I is the internal path length of the tree. (b) $((n + 1)!/2^n)\prod(1/(2^{s(x)} - 1))$. (Consider summing the answer of exercise 35 over all a, b, c, $d \geq 1$.)

37. The smallest modified external path length is actually $2 - 1/2^{N-2}$, and it occurs only in a degenerate tree (whose external path length is *maximal*). [One can prove that the *largest* modified external path length occurs if and only if the external nodes appear on at most two adjacent levels! But it is not always true that a tree whose external path length is smaller than another has a larger modified external path length.]

38. Consider as subproblems the finding of k-node trees with parameters $(\alpha,\beta), (\alpha,\frac{1}{2}\beta)$, $\ldots, (\alpha, 2^{k-n}\beta)$.

39. See Miyakawa, Yuba, Sugito, and Hoshi, *SICOMP* **6** (1977), 201–234.

40. Let N/r be the true period length of the sequence. Form a Patricia-like tree, with $a_0 a_1 \ldots$ as the TEXT and with N/r keys starting at positions $0, 1, \ldots, N/r - 1$. (No key is a prefix of another, because of our choice of r.) Also include in each node a SIZE field, containing the number of tagged link fields in the subtree below that node. To do the specified operation, use Algorithm P; if the search is unsuccessful, the answer is 0, but if it is successful and $j \leq n$ the answer is r. Finally if it is successful and $j > n$, the answer is $r \cdot$ SIZE(P).

43. The expected height is asymptotic to $(1 + 1/s) \log_M N$, and the variance is $O(1)$. See H. Mendelson, *IEEE Transactions* **SE-8** (1982), 611–619; P. Flajolet, *Acta Informatica* **20** (1983), 345–369; L. Devroye, *Acta Informatica* **21** (1984), 229–237; B. Pittel, *Advances in Applied Probability* **18** (1986), 139–155; W. Szpankowski, *Algorithmica* **6** (1991), 256–277.

The average height of a random digital search tree with $M = 2$ is asymptotically $\lg n + \sqrt{2 \lg n}$ [Aldous and Shields, *Probability Theory and Related Fields* **79** (1988), 509–542], and the same is true for a random Patricia tree [Pittel and Rubin, *Journal of Combinatorial Theory* **A55** (1990), 292–312].

44. See *SODA* **8** (1997), 360–369; this search structure is closely related to the multikey quicksort algorithm discussed in the answer to exercise 5.2.2–30. J. Clément, P. Flajolet, and B. Vallée have shown that the ternary representation makes trie searching about three times faster than the binary representation of (2), with respect to nodes accessed [see *SODA* **9** (1998), 531–539].

45. The probability of {THAT, THE, THIS} before {BUILT, HOUSE, IS, JACK}, {HOUSE, IS, JACK} before {BUILT}, {HOUSE, IS} before {JACK}, {IS} before {HOUSE}, {THIS} before {THAT, THE}, and {THE} before {THAT} is $\frac{3}{7} \cdot \frac{3}{4} \cdot \frac{2}{3} \cdot \frac{1}{2} \cdot \frac{1}{3} \cdot \frac{1}{2} = \frac{1}{56}$.

SECTION 6.4

1. $-37 \le \text{rI1} \le 46$. Therefore the locations preceding and following TABLE must be guaranteed to contain no data that matches any given argument; for example, their first byte could be zero. It would certainly be bad to store K in this range! [Thus we might say that the method in exercise 6.3–4 uses less space, since the boundaries of that table are never exceeded.]

2. TOW. [Can the reader find ten common words of at most 5 letters that fill all the remaining gaps between -10 and 30?]

3. The alphabetic codes satisfy $\text{A} + \text{T} = \text{I} + \text{N}$ and $\text{B} - \text{E} = \text{O} - \text{R}$, so we would have either $f(\text{AT}) = f(\text{IN})$ or $f(\text{BE}) = f(\text{OR})$. Notice that instructions 4 and 5 of Table 1 resolve this dilemma rather well, while keeping rI1 from having too wide a range.

4. Consider cases with k pairs. The smallest n such that

$$m^{-n} n! \sum_k \binom{m}{n-k} \binom{n-k}{k} 2^{-k} < \frac{1}{2}, \qquad \text{for } m = 365,$$

is 88. If you invite 88 people (including yourself), the chance of a birthday trio is .511065, but if only 87 people come it is lowered to .499455. See C. F. Pinzka, *AMM* **67** (1960), 830.

5. The hash function is bad since it assumes at most 26 different values, and some of them occur much more often than the others. Even with double hashing (letting $h_2(K) = 1$ plus the second byte of K, say, and $M = 101$) the search will be slowed down more than the time saved by faster hashing. Also $M = 100$ is too small, since FORTRAN programs often have more than 100 distinct variables.

6. Not on MIX, since arithmetic overflow will almost always occur (dividend too large). [It would be nice to be able to compute $(wK) \bmod M$, especially if linear probing were being used with $c = 1$, but unfortunately most computers disallow this since the quotient overflows.]

7. If $R(x)$ is a multiple of $P(x)$, then $R(\alpha^j) = 0$ in $GF(2^k)$ for all $j \in S$. Let $R(x) = x^{a_1} + \cdots + x^{a_s}$, where $a_1 > \cdots > a_s \geq 0$ and $s \leq t$, and select $t - s$ further values $a_{s+1}, \ldots, a_t$ such that $a_1, \ldots, a_t$ are distinct nonnegative integers less than n. The Vandermonde matrix

$$\begin{pmatrix} \alpha^{a_1} & \cdots & \alpha^{a_t} \\ \alpha^{2a_1} & \cdots & \alpha^{2a_t} \\ \vdots & & \vdots \\ \alpha^{ta_1} & \cdots & \alpha^{ta_t} \end{pmatrix}$$

is singular, since the sum of its first s columns is zero. But this contradicts the fact that $\alpha^{a_1}, \ldots, \alpha^{a_t}$ are distinct elements of $GF(2^k)$. (See exercise 1.2.3–37.)

[The idea of polynomial hashing originated with M. Hanan, S. Muroga, F. P. Palermo, N. Raver, and G. Schay; see *IBM J. Research & Development* **7** (1963), 121–129; *U.S. Patent 3311888* (1967).]

8. By induction. The strong induction hypotheses can be supplemented by the fact that $\{(-1)^k(rq_k + q_{k-1})\theta\} = (-1)^k\big(r(q_k\theta - p_k) + (q_{k-1}\theta - p_{k-1})\big)$ for $0 \leq r \leq a_k$. The "record low" values of $\{n\theta\}$ occur for $n = q_1, q_2 + q_1, 2q_2 + q_1, \ldots, a_2q_2 + q_1 = 0q_4 + q_3$, $q_4 + q_3, \ldots, a_4q_4 + q_3 = 0q_6 + q_5, \ldots$; the "record high" values occur for $n = q_0$, $q_1 + q_0, \ldots, a_1q_1 + q_0 = 0q_3 + q_2, \ldots$. These are the steps when interval number 0 of a new length is formed. [Further structure can be deduced by generalizing the Fibonacci number system of exercise 1.2.8–34; see L. H. Ramshaw, *J. Number Theory* **13** (1981), 138–175.]

9. We have $\phi^{-1} = /\!/1, 1, 1, \ldots/\!/$ and $\phi^{-2} = /\!/2, 1, 1, \ldots/\!/$. Let $\theta = /\!/a_1, a_2, \ldots/\!/$ and $\theta_k = /\!/a_{k+1}, a_{k+2}, \ldots/\!/$, and let $Q_k = q_k + q_{k-1}\theta_{k-2}$ in the notation of exercise 8. If $a_1 > 2$, the very first break is bad. The three sizes of intervals in exercise 8 are, respectively, $(1 - r\theta_{k-1})/Q_k$, θ_{k-1}/Q_k, and $(1 - (r - 1)\theta_{k-1})/Q_k$, so the ratio of the first length to the second is $(a_k - r) + \theta_k$. This will be less than $\frac{1}{2}$ when $r = a_k$ and $a_{k+1} \geq 2$; hence $\{a_2, a_3, \ldots\}$ must all equal 1 if there are to be no bad breaks. [For related theorems, see R. L. Graham and J. H. van Lint, *Canadian J. Math.* **20** (1968), 1020–1024, and the references cited there.]

10. See F. M. Liang's elegant proof in *Discrete Math.* **28** (1979), 325–326.

11. There would be a problem if $K = 0$. If keys were required to be nonzero as in Program L, this change would be worthwhile, and we could also represent empty positions by 0.

12. We can store K in KEY[0], replacing lines 14–19 by

	STA	TABLE(KEY)	$A - S1$		CMPA TABLE,2(KEY)	$C - 1 - S2$

```
      STA   TABLE(KEY)      A - S1          CMPA  TABLE,2(KEY)   C - 1 - S2
      CMPA  TABLE,2(KEY)    A - S1          JNE   2B             C - 1 - S2
      JE    3F              A - S1      3H  J2Z   5F             A - S1
  2H  ENT1  0,2             C - 1 - S2      ENT1  0,2            S2
      LD2   TABLE,1(LINK)   C - 1 - S2      JMP   SUCCESS        S2
```

The time "saved" is $C - 1 - 5A + S + 4S1$ units, which is actually a net *loss* because C is rarely more than 5. (An inner loop shouldn't always be optimized!)

13. Let the table entries be of two distinguishable types, as in Algorithm C, with an additional one-bit TAG[i] field in each entry. This solution uses circular lists, following a suggestion of Allen Newell, with TAG[i] = 1 in the first word of each list.

A1. [Initialize.] Set $i \leftarrow j \leftarrow h(K) + 1$, $Q \leftarrow q(K)$.

A2. [Is there a list?] If TABLE$[i]$ is empty, set TAG$[i] \leftarrow 1$ and go to A8. Otherwise if TAG$[i] = 0$, go to A7.

A3. [Compare.] If $Q = $ KEY$[i]$, the algorithm terminates successfully.

A4. [Advance to next.] If LINK$[i] \neq j$, set $i \leftarrow$ LINK$[i]$ and go back to A3.

A5. [Find empty node.] Decrease R one or more times until finding a value such that TABLE$[R]$ is empty. If $R = 0$, the algorithm terminates with overflow; otherwise set LINK$[i] \leftarrow R$.

A6. [Prepare to insert.] Set $i \leftarrow R$, TAG$[R] \leftarrow 0$, and go to A8.

A7. [Displace a record.] Repeatedly set $i \leftarrow$ LINK$[i]$ one or more times until LINK$[i] = j$. Then do step A5. Then set TABLE$[R] \leftarrow$ TABLE$[i]$, $i \leftarrow j$, TAG$[j] \leftarrow 1$.

A8. [Insert new key.] Mark TABLE$[i]$ as an occupied node, with KEY$[i] \leftarrow Q$, LINK$[i] \leftarrow j$. ▌

(Note that if TABLE$[i]$ is occupied it is possible to determine the corresponding full key K, given only the value of i. We have $q(K) = $ KEY$[i]$, and then if we set $i \leftarrow$ LINK$[i]$ zero or more times until TAG$[i] = 1$ we will have $h(K) = i - 1$.)

14. According to the stated conventions, the notation "X $\Leftarrow$ AVAIL" of 2.2.3–(6) now stands for the following operations: "Set X $\leftarrow$ AVAIL; then set X $\leftarrow$ LINK(X) zero or more times until either X $= \Lambda$ (an OVERFLOW error) or TAG(X) $= 0$; finally set AVAIL $\leftarrow$ LINK(X)."

To insert a new key K: Set Q $\Leftarrow$ AVAIL, TAG(Q) $\leftarrow 1$, and store K in this word. [Alternatively, if all keys are short, omit this and substitute K for Q in what follows.] Then set R $\Leftarrow$ AVAIL, TAG(R) $\leftarrow 1$, AUX(R) $\leftarrow$ Q, LINK(R) $\leftarrow \Lambda$. Set P $\leftarrow h(K)$, and

if TAG(P) $= 0$, set TAG(P) $\leftarrow 2$, AUX(P) $\leftarrow$ R;

if TAG(P) $= 1$, set S $\Leftarrow$ AVAIL, CONTENTS(S) $\leftarrow$ CONTENTS(P), TAG(P) $\leftarrow 2$, AUX(P) $\leftarrow$ R, LINK(P) $\leftarrow$ S;

if TAG(P) $= 2$, set LINK(R) $\leftarrow$ AUX(P), AUX(P) $\leftarrow$ R.

To retrieve a key K: Set P $\leftarrow h(K)$, and

if TAG(P) $\neq 2$, K is not present;

if TAG(P) $= 2$, set P $\leftarrow$ AUX(P); then set P $\leftarrow$ LINK(P) zero or more times until either P $= \Lambda$, or TAG(P) $= 1$ and either AUX(P) $= K$ (if all keys are short) or AUX(P) points to a word containing K (perhaps indirectly through words with TAG $= 2$).

Elcock's original scheme [*Comp. J.* **8** (1965), 242–243] actually used TAG $= 2$ and TAG $= 3$ to distinguish between lists of length one (when we can save one word of space) and longer lists. This is a worthwhile improvement, since we presumably have such a large hash table that almost all lists have length one.

Another way to place a hash table "on top of" a large linked memory, using coalescing lists instead of separate chaining, has been suggested by J. S. Vitter [*Inf. Proc. Letters* **13** (1981), 77–79].

15. Knowing that there is always an empty node makes the inner search loop faster, since we need not maintain a counter to determine how many times step L2 is performed. The shorter program amply compensates for this one wasted cell. [On the other hand, there is a neat way to avoid the variable N and to allow the table to become completely full, in Algorithm L, without slowing down the method appreciably except when the table actually does overflow: Simply check whether $i < 0$ happens twice! This trick does not apply to Algorithm D.]

16. No: 0 always leads to SUCCESS, whether it has been inserted or not, and SUCCESS occurs with different values of i at different times.

17. The second probe would then always be to position 0.

18. The code in (31) costs about $3(A - S1)$ units more than (30), and it saves $4u$ times the difference between (26), (27), and (28), (29). For a successful search, (31) is advantageous only when the table is more than about 94 percent full, and it never saves more than about $\frac{1}{2}u$ of time. For an unsuccessful search, (31) is advantageous when the table is more than about 71 percent full.

20. We want to show that

$$\binom{j}{2} \equiv \binom{k}{2} \pmod{2^m} \qquad \text{and} \qquad 1 \le j \le k \le 2^m$$

implies $j = k$. Observe that the congruence $j(j-1) \equiv k(k-1) \pmod{2^{m+1}}$ implies $(k-j)(k+j-1) \equiv 0$. If $k - j$ is odd, $k + j - 1$ must be a multiple of 2^{m+1}, but that's impossible since $2 \le k + j - 1 \le 2^{m+1} - 2$. Hence $k - j$ is even, so $k + j - 1$ is odd, so $k - j$ is a multiple of 2^{m+1}, so $k = j$. [Conversely, if M is not a power of 2, this probe sequence does not work.]

The probe sequence has secondary clustering, and it increases the running time of Program D $\big($as modified in (30)$\big)$ by about $\frac{1}{2}(C-1)-(A-S1)$ units since $B \approx \binom{C+1}{3}/M$ will now be negligible. This is a small improvement, until the table gets about 60 percent full.

21. If N is decreased, Algorithm D can fail since it might reach a state with no empty spaces and loop indefinitely. On the other hand, if N isn't decreased, Algorithm D might signal overflow when there still is room. The latter alternative is the lesser of the two evils, because rehashing can be used to get rid of deleted cells. (In the latter case Algorithm D should increase N and test for overflow only when inserting an item into a previously *empty* position, since N represents the number of nonempty positions.) We could also maintain two counters.

22. Suppose that positions $j - 1$, $j - 2$, ..., $j - k$ are occupied and $j - k - 1$ is empty (modulo M). The keys that probe position j and find it occupied before being inserted are precisely those keys in positions $j - 1$ through $j - k$ whose hash address does not lie between $j - 1$ and $j - k$; such problematical keys appear in the order of insertion. Algorithm R moves the first such key into position j, and repeats the process on a smaller range of problematical positions until no problematical keys remain.

23. A deletion scheme for coalesced chaining devised by J. S. Vitter [*J. Algorithms* **3** (1982), 261–275] preserves the distribution of search times.

24. We have $P(P - 1)(P - 2)P(P - 1)P(P - 1)/(MP(MP - 1)\ldots(MP - 6)) = M^{-7}(1 - (5 - 21/M)P^{-1} + O(P^{-2}))$. In general, the probability of a hash sequence $a_1 \ldots a_N$ is $(\prod_{j=0}^{M-1} P^{b_j})/(MP)^{\underline{N}} = M^{-N} + O(P^{-1})$, where b_j is the number of a_i that equal j.

25. Let the $(N + 1)$st key hash to location a; P_k is M^{-N} times the number of hash sequences that leave the k locations a, $a - 1$, ..., $a - k + 1$ (modulo M) occupied and

$a - k$ empty. The number of such sequences with $a+1, \ldots, a+t$ occupied and $a+t+1$ empty is $g(M, N, t+k)$, by circular symmetry of the algorithm.

26. $\dfrac{9!}{2!\,2!\,4!\,1!}\, f(3,2)\, f(3,2)\, f(5,4)\, f(2,1) = 2^2 3^5 5^4 7 = 4252500.$

27. Following the hint,

$$s(n, x, y) = \sum_k \binom{n}{k} x(x+k)^k (y-k)^{n-k-1}(y-n) + n\sum_k \binom{n-1}{k-1}(x+k)^k(y-k)^{n-k-1}(y-n).$$

In the first sum, replace k by $n - k$ and apply Abel's formula; in the second, replace k by $k + 1$. Now

$$g(M, N, k) = \binom{N}{k}(k+1)^{k-1}(M - k - 1)^{N-k-1}(M - N - 1),$$

with $0/0 = 1$ when $k = N = M - 1$, and

$$M^N \sum (k+1)P_k = \sum_{k \geq 0} \binom{k+2}{2} g(M, N, k)$$

$$= \frac{1}{2}\left(\sum_{k \geq 0}(k+1)g(M, N, k) + \sum_{k \geq 0}(k+1)^2 g(M, N, k)\right).$$

The first sum is $M^N \sum P_k = M^N$, and the second is $s(N, 1, M-1) = M^N + 2NM^{N-1} + 3N(N - 1)M^{N-2} + \cdots = M^N Q_1(M, N)$. [See J. Riordan, *Combinatorial Identities* (New York: Wiley, 1968), 18–23, for further study of sums like $s(n, x, y)$.]

28. Let $t(n, x, y) = \sum_{k \geq 0}\binom{n}{k}(x + k)^{k+2}(y - k)^{n-k-1}(y - n)$; then as in exercise 27 we find $t(n, x, y) = xs(n, x, y) + nt(n-1, x+1, y-1)$, $t(N, 1, M-1) = M^N(3Q_3(M, N) - 2Q_2(M, N))$. Thus $\sum(k+1)^2 P_k = M^{-N}\sum(\frac{1}{3}(k+1)^3 + \frac{1}{2}(k+1)^2 + \frac{1}{6}(k+1))g(M, N, k) = Q_3(M, N) - \frac{2}{3}Q_2(M, N) + \frac{1}{2}Q_1(M, N) + \frac{1}{6}$. Subtracting $(C_N')^2$ gives the variance, which is approximately $\frac{3}{4}(1 - \alpha)^{-4} - \frac{2}{3}(1 - \alpha)^{-3} - \frac{1}{12}$. The standard deviation is often larger than the mean; for example, when $\alpha = .9$ the mean is 50.5 and the standard deviation is $\frac{1}{2}\sqrt{27333} \approx 82.7$.

29. Let $M = m+1$, $N = n$; the safe parking sequences are precisely those in which location 0 is empty when Algorithm L is applied to the hash sequence $(M - a_1)\ldots(M - a_n)$. Hence the answer is $f(m+1, n) = (m + 1)^n - n(m + 1)^{n-1}$. [This problem originated with A. G. Konheim and B. Weiss, *SIAM J. Applied Math.* **14** (1966), 1266–1274; see also R. Pyke, *Annals of Math. Stat.* **30** (1959), 568–576, Lemma 1.]

30. Obviously if the cars get parked they define such a permutation. Conversely, if $p_1 p_2 \ldots p_n$ exists, let $q_1 q_2 \ldots q_n$ be the inverse permutation ($q_i = j$ if and only if $p_j = i$), and let b_i be the number of a_j that equal i. Every car will be parked if we can prove that $b_n \leq 1$, $b_{n-1} + b_n \leq 2$, etc.; equivalently $b_1 \geq 1$, $b_1 + b_2 \geq 2$, etc. But this is clearly true, since the k elements $a_{q_1}, \ldots, a_{q_k}$ are all $\leq k$.

[Let r_j be the "left influence" of q_j, namely $r_j = k$ if and only if $q_{j-1} < q_j, \ldots,$ $q_{j-k-1} < q_j$ and either $j = k$ or $q_{j-k} > q_j$. Of all permutations $p_1 \ldots p_n$ that dominate a given wakeup sequence $a_1 \ldots a_n$, the "park immediately" algorithm finds the smallest one (in lexicographic order). Konheim and Weiss observed that the number of wakeup sequences leading to a given permutation $p_1 \ldots p_n$ is $\prod_{j=1}^n r_j$; it is remarkable that the sum of these products, taken over all permutations $q_1 \ldots q_n$, is $(n + 1)^{n-1}$.]

31. Many interesting connections are possible, and the following three are the author's favorites [see also Foata and Riordan, *Æquat. Math.* **10** (1974), 10–22]:

a) In the notation of the previous answer, the counts $b_1, b_2, \ldots, b_n$ correspond to a full parking sequence if and only if $(b_1, b_2, \ldots, b_n, 0)$ is a valid sequence of *degrees* of tree nodes in preorder. (Compare with 2.3.3–(9), which illustrates postorder.) Every such tree corresponds to $n!/b_1! \ldots b_n!$ distinct labeled free trees on $\{0, \ldots, n\}$, since we can let 0 be the label of the root, and for $k = 1, 2, \ldots, n$ we can successively choose the labels of the children of the kth node in preorder in $(b_k + \cdots + b_n)!/b_k! \, (b_{k+1} + \cdots + b_n)!$ ways from the remaining unused labels, attaching labels from left to right in increasing order. And every such sequence of counts corresponds to $n!/b_1! \ldots b_n!$ wakeup sequences.

b) Dominique Foata has given the following pretty one-to-one correspondence: Let $a_1 \ldots a_n$ be a safe parking sequence, which leaves car q_j parked in space j. A labeled free tree on $\{0, 1, \ldots, n\}$ is constructed by drawing a line from j to 0 when $a_j = 1$, and from j to $q_{a_j - 1}$ otherwise, for $1 \le j \le n$. (Think of the tree nodes as cars; car j is connected to the car that eventually winds up parked just before where wife j woke up.) For example, the wakeup times 3 1 4 1 5 9 2 6 5 lead to the free tree

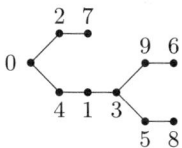

by Foata's rule. Conversely, the sequence of parked cars may be obtained from the tree by topological sorting, assuming that arrows emanate from the root 0 and choosing the smallest "source" at each step. From this sequence, $a_1 \ldots a_n$ can be reconstructed.

c) First construct an auxiliary tree by letting the parent of node k be the first element $> k$ that follows k in the permutation $q_1 \ldots q_n$; if there's no such element, let the parent be 0. Then make a copy of the auxiliary tree and relabel the nonzero nodes of the new tree by proceeding as follows, in preorder: If the label of the current node was k in the auxiliary tree, swap its current label with the label that is currently $(1 + p_k - a_k)$th smallest in its subtree. For example,

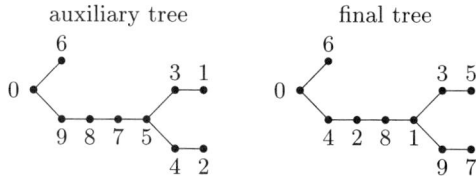

To reverse the procedure, we can reconstruct the auxiliary tree by proceeding in preorder to swap the label of each node with the largest label currently in its subtree.

Constructions (a) and (b) are strongly related, but construction (c) is quite different. It has the interesting property that the sum of displacements of cars from their preferred locations is equal to the number of *inversions* in the tree — the number of pairs of labels $a > b$ where a is an ancestor of b. This relation between parking sequences and tree inversions was first discovered by G. Kreweras [*Periodica Math. Hung.* **11** (1980), 309–320]. The fact that tree inversions are intimately related to connected graphs [Mallows and Riordan, *Bull. Amer. Math. Soc.* **74** (1968), 92–94] now makes it possible to deduce that the sum of $\binom{D(p)}{k}$ taken over all parking sequences, where $D(p) = (p_1 - a_1) + \cdots + (p_n - a_n)$, is equal to the total number of connected graphs with $n + k$ edges on the labeled vertices $\{0, 1, \ldots, n\}$. [See equations (2.11), (3.5), and

(8.13) in the paper by Janson, Łuczak, Knuth, and Pittel, *Random Struct. & Alg.* **4** (1993), 233–358.]

32. Let

$$s_j = \sum_{k=0}^{j} (b_{k \bmod M} - 1).$$

Then, as observed by Svante Janson, we have $c_j = \max_{k \geq j}(s_k - s_j)$, a quantity that is well defined because $\lim_{k \to \infty} s_k = -\infty$.

The solution can be found by defining $c_{M-1}, c_{M-2}, \ldots$ on the assumption that $c_0 = 0$; then if c_0 turns out to be greater than 0, it suffices to redefine $c_{M-1}, c_{M-2}, \ldots$ until no more changes are made.

33. The individual probabilities are not independent, since the condition $b_0 + b_1 + \cdots + b_{M-1} = N$ was not taken into account; the derivation allows a nonzero probability that $\sum b_j$ has any given nonnegative value. Equations (46) are not strictly correct; they imply, for example, that q_k is positive for all k, contradicting the fact that c_j can never exceed $N - 1$.

Gaston Gonnet and Ian Munro [*J. Algorithms* **5** (1984), 451–470] have found an interesting way to derive the exact result from the argument leading up to (51) by introducing a useful operation called the *Poisson transform* of a sequence $\langle A_{mn} \rangle$: We have $e^{-mz} \sum_n A_{mn}(mz)^n/n! = \sum_k a_k z^k$ if and only if $A_{mn} = \sum_k a_k n^{\underline{k}}/m^k$.

34. (a) There are $\binom{N}{k}$ ways to choose the set of j such that a_j has a particular value, and $(M-1)^{N-k}$ ways to assign values to the other a's. Therefore

$$P_{Nk} = \binom{N}{k}(M-1)^{N-k}/M^N.$$

(b) $P_N(z) = B(z)$ in (50). (c) Consider the total number of probes to find all keys, not counting the fetching of the pointer in the list head table of Fig. 38 if such a table is used. A list of length k contributes $\binom{k+1}{2}$ to the total; hence

$$C_N = M \sum \binom{k+1}{2} P_{Nk}/N = (M/N)(\tfrac{1}{2}P_N''(1) + P_N'(1)).$$

(d) In case (i) a list of length k requires k probes (not counting the list-head fetch), while in case (ii) it requires $k + \delta_{k0}$. Thus in case (ii) we get $C_N' = \sum(k + \delta_{k0})P_{Nk} = P_N'(1) + P_N(0) = N/M + (1 - 1/M)^N \approx \alpha + e^{-\alpha}$, while case (i) has simply $C_N' = N/M = \alpha$. The formula $MC_N' = M - N + NC_N$ applies in case (iii), since $M - N$ hash addresses will discover an empty table position while N will cause searching to the end of some list from a point within it; this yields (18).

35. (i) $\sum(1 + \tfrac{1}{2}k - (k+1)^{-1})P_{Nk} = 1 + N/(2M) - M(1 - (1 - 1/M)^{N+1})/(N+1) \approx 1 + \tfrac{1}{2}\alpha - (1 - e^{-\alpha})/\alpha$. (ii) Add $\sum \delta_{k0}P_{Nk} = (1 - 1/M)^N \approx e^{-\alpha}$ to the result of (i). (iii) Assume that when an unsuccessful search begins at the jth element of a list of length k, the given key has random order with respect to the other k elements, so the expected length of search is $(j \cdot 1 + 2 + \cdots + (k+1-j) + (k+1-j))/(k+1)$. Summing on j now gives $MC_N' = M - N + M \sum(k^3 + 9k^2 + 2k)P_{Nk}/(6k+6) = M - N + M(\tfrac{1}{6}N(N-1)/M^2 + \tfrac{3}{2}N/M - 1 + (M/(N+1))(1 - (1 - 1/M)^{N+1}))$; hence $C_N' \approx \tfrac{1}{2}\alpha + \tfrac{1}{6}\alpha^2 + (1 - e^{-\alpha})/\alpha$.

36. (i) $N/M - N/M^2$. (ii) $\sum(\delta_{k0} + k)^2 P_{Nk} = \sum(\delta_{k0} + k^2)P_{Nk} = P_N(0) + P_N''(1) + P_N'(1)$. Subtracting $(C_N')^2$ gives the answer, $(M-1)N/M^2 + (1 - 1/M)^N(1 - 2N/M - (1 - 1/M)^N) \approx \alpha + e^{-\alpha}(1 - 2\alpha - e^{-\alpha}) \leq 1 - e^{-1} - e^{-2} = 0.4968$. [For data structure (iii), a more complicated analysis like that in exercise 37 would be necessary.]

37. Let S_N be the average value of $(C - 1)^2$, considering all $M^N N$ choices of hash sequences and keys to be equally likely. Then

$$
\begin{aligned}
M^N N S_N &= \frac{1}{3} \sum \binom{N}{k_1, \ldots, k_M} \left(k_1 (k_1 - \tfrac{1}{2})(k_1 - 1) + \cdots + k_M (k_M - \tfrac{1}{2})(k_M - 1) \right) \\
&= \frac{1}{3} M \sum_k \binom{N}{k} (M - 1)^{N-k} k (k - \tfrac{1}{2})(k - 1) \\
&= \frac{1}{3} M N (N - 1)(N - 2) \sum_k \binom{N-3}{k-3} (M-1)^{N-k} \\
&\quad + \frac{1}{2} M N (N - 1) \sum_k \binom{N-2}{k-2} (M-1)^{N-k} \\
&= \frac{1}{3} M N (N-1)(N-2) M^{N-3} + \frac{1}{2} M N (N-1) M^{N-2}.
\end{aligned}
$$

The variance is $S_N - \left((N-1)/2M \right)^2 = (N-1)(N+6M-5)/12M^2 \approx \frac{1}{2}\alpha + \frac{1}{12}\alpha^2$.

See *CMath* §8.5 for interesting connections between the total variance calculated here and two other notions of variance: the variance (over random hash tables) of the average number of probes (over all items present), and the average (over random hash tables) of the variance of the number of probes (over all items present). The total variance is always the sum of the other two; and in this case the variance of the average number of probes is $(M-1)(N-1)/(2M^2N)$.

38. The average number of probes is $\sum P_{Nk}(2H_{k+1} - 2 + \delta_{k0})$ in the unsuccessful case, $(M/N) \sum P_{Nk} k(2(1 + 1/k)H_k - 3)$ in the successful case, by Eqs. 6.2.2–(5) and 6.2.2–(6). These sums are $2f(N) + 2M(1 - (1 - 1/M)^{N+1})/(N+1) + (1 - 1/M)^N - 2$ and $2(M/N)f(N) + 2f(N-1) + 2M(1 - (1 - 1/M)^N)/N - 3$, respectively, where $f(N) = \sum P_{Nk} H_k$. Exercise 5.2.1–40 tells us that $f(N) = \ln \alpha + \gamma + E_1(\alpha) + O(M^{-1})$ when $N = \alpha M$, $M \to \infty$.

[Tree hashing was first proposed by P. F. Windley, *Comp. J.* **3** (1960), 84–88. The analysis in the previous paragraph shows that tree hashing is not enough better than simple chaining to justify the extra link fields; the lists are short anyway. Moreover, when M is small, tree hashing is not enough better than pure tree search to justify the hashing time.]

39. (This approach to the analysis of Algorithm C was suggested by J. S. Vitter.) We have $c_{N+1}(k) = (M - k)c_N(k) + (k - 1)c_N(k - 1)$ for $k \geq 2$, and furthermore $\sum k c_N(k) = NM^N$. Hence

$$
\begin{aligned}
S_{N+1} &= \sum_{k \geq 2} \binom{k}{2} c_{N+1}(k) = \sum_{k \geq 2} \binom{k}{2} \left((M - k)c_N(k) + (k - 1)c_N(k - 1) \right) \\
&= \sum_{k \geq 1} \left((M + 2)\binom{k}{2} + k \right) c_N(k) = (M + 2)S_N + NM^N.
\end{aligned}
$$

Consequently $S_N = (N - 1)M^{N-1} + (N - 2)M^{N-2}(M + 2) + \cdots + M(M + 2)^{N-2} = \frac{1}{4}\left(M(M + 2)^N - M^{N+1} - 2NM^N \right)$.

Consider the total number of probes in unsuccessful searches, summed over all M values of $h(K)$; each list of length k contributes $k + \delta_{k0} + \binom{k}{2}$ to the total, hence $M^{N+1} C_N' = M^{N+1} + S_N$.

40. Define U_N to be like S_N in exercise 39, but with $\binom{k}{2}$ replaced by $\binom{k+1}{3}$. We find $U_{N+1} = (M+3)U_N + S_N + NM^N$, hence

$$U_N = \tfrac{1}{36}\left(M^N(M-6N) - 9M(M+2)^N + 8M(M+3)^N\right).$$

The variance is $2U_N/M^{N+1} + C'_N - (C'_N)^2$, which approaches

$$\tfrac{35}{144} - \tfrac{1}{12}\alpha - \tfrac{1}{4}\alpha^2 + \left(\tfrac{1}{4}\alpha - \tfrac{5}{8}\right)e^{2\alpha} + \tfrac{4}{9}e^{3\alpha} - \tfrac{1}{16}e^{4\alpha}$$

for $N = \alpha M$, $M \to \infty$. When $\alpha = 1$ this is about 2.65, so the standard deviation is bounded by 1.63. [Svante Janson (to appear) has found the asymptotic moments of all orders, also when the search is successful.]

41. Let V_N be the average length of the block of occupied cells at the "high" end of the table. The probability that this block has length k is $A_{Nk}(M-1-k)^{\underline{N-k}}/M^N$, where A_{Nk} is the number of hash sequences (35) such that Algorithm C leaves the first $N-k$ and the last k cells occupied and such that the subsequence $1\,2\ldots N-k$ appears in increasing order. Therefore

$$M^N V_N = \sum_k k A_{Nk}(M-1-k)^{\underline{N-k}} = M^{N+1} - \sum_k(M-k)A_{Nk}(M-1-k)^{\underline{N-k}}$$
$$= M^{N+1} - (M-N)\sum_k A_{Nk}(M-k)^{\underline{N-k}} = M^{N+1} - (M-N)(M+1)^N.$$

Now $T_N = (N/M)(1+V_N-T_0-\cdots-T_{N-1})$, since $T_0+\cdots+T_{N-1}$ is the average number of times R has previously decreased and N/M is the probability that it decreases on the current step. The solution to this recurrence is $T_N = (N/M)(1+1/M)^N$. (Such a simple formula deserves a simpler proof!)

42. $S1_N$ is the number of items that were inserted with $A=0$, divided by N.

43. Let $N = \alpha M'$ and $M = \beta M'$, and let $e^{-\lambda} + \lambda = 1/\beta$, $\rho = \alpha/\beta$. Then $C_N \approx 1 + \tfrac{1}{2}\rho$ and $C'_N \approx \rho + e^{-\rho}$, if $\rho \le \lambda$; $C_N \approx \tfrac{1}{8\rho}(e^{2\rho-2\lambda}-1-2\rho+2\lambda)(3-2/\beta+2\lambda)+\tfrac{1}{4}(\rho+2\lambda-\lambda^2/\rho)$ and $C'_N \approx 1/\beta + \tfrac{1}{4}(e^{2\rho-2\lambda}-1)(3-2/\beta+2\lambda) - \tfrac{1}{2}(\rho-\lambda)$, if $\rho \ge \lambda$. For $\alpha = 1$ we get the smallest $C_N \approx 1.69$ when $\beta \approx .853$; the smallest $C'_N \approx 1.79$ occurs when $\beta \approx .782$. The setting $\beta = .86$ gives near-optimal search performance for a wide range of α. So it pays to put the first collisions into an area that doesn't conflict with hash addresses, even though a smaller range of hash addresses will cause more collisions to occur. These results are due to Jeffrey S. Vitter, *JACM* **30** (1983), 231–258.

44. (The following brute-force approach was the solution found by the author in 1972; a much more elegant solution by M. S. Paterson is explained in *Mathematics for the Analysis of Algorithms* by Greene and Knuth (Birkhäuser Boston, 1980), §3.4. Paterson also found significant ways to simplify several other analyses in this section.)

Number the positions of the array from 1 to m, left to right. Considering the set of all $\binom{n}{k}$ sequences of operations with k "p steps" and $n-k$ "q steps" to be equally likely, let $g(m,n+1,k,r)$ be $\binom{n}{k}$ times the probability that the first $r-1$ positions become occupied and the rth remains empty. Thus $g(m,l,k,r)$ is $(m-1)^{-(l-1-k)}$ times the sum, over all configurations

$$1 \le a_1 < \cdots < a_k < l, \qquad (c_1,\ldots,c_{l-1-k}), \qquad 2 \le c_i \le m,$$

of the probability that the first empty location is r, when the a_jth operation is a p step and the remaining $l-1-k$ operations are q steps that begin by selecting positions $c_1,\ldots,c_{l-1-k}$, respectively. By summing over all configurations subject to the further condition that the a_jth operation occupies position b_j, given $1 \le b_1 < \cdots < b_k < r$, we obtain the recurrence

$$g(m, l, k+1, r) = \sum_{\substack{a < l \\ b < r \\ 1 \le b \le a}} \frac{(l-b-1)!}{(l-r)!} \frac{(m-r)!}{(m-b)!} (m-l+1) g(m, a, k, b);$$

$$g(m, l, 0, r) = \frac{(l-1)!}{(l-r)!} \frac{(m-r)!}{m!} (m-l+1) \left(P_l + [r \neq 1] \frac{m}{l-1}(1 - P_l) \right),$$

where $P_l = (m/(m-1))^{l-1}$. Letting $G(m, l, k) = \sum_{r=1}^{l}(m+1-r)g(m, l, k, r)$, it follows that

$$G(m, l, k+1) = \frac{m-l+1}{m-l+2} \sum_{a=1}^{l-1} G(m, a, k); \qquad G(m, l, 0) = \frac{m-l+1}{m-l+2}(m + P_l).$$

The answer to the stated problem is $m - \sum_{k=0}^{n} p^k q^{n-k} G(m, n+1, k)$, which (after some maneuvering) equals $m - ((m-n)/(m-n+1))(Q_n + mR + pSR)$, where

$$Q_j = P_{j+1} q^j,$$

$$R = \left(1 - \frac{p}{m+1}\right)\left(1 - \frac{p}{m}\right) \cdots \left(1 - \frac{p}{m-n+2}\right) = \prod_{j=0}^{n-1}\left(1 - \frac{p}{m+1-j}\right),$$

$$S = \frac{\left(1 - \frac{1}{m+1}\right)Q_0}{\left(1 - \frac{p}{m+1}\right)} + \frac{\left(1 - \frac{1}{m}\right)Q_1}{\left(1 - \frac{p}{m+1}\right)\left(1 - \frac{p}{m}\right)} + \cdots + \frac{1 - \left(\frac{1}{m-n+2}\right)Q_{n-1}}{R}$$

$$= \sum_{k=0}^{n-1} \frac{(1 - 1/(m+1-k))Q_k}{\prod_{j=0}^{k}(1 - p/(m+1-j))}.$$

When $p = 1/m$, $Q_j = 1$ for all j. Letting $w = m+1$, $n = \alpha w$, $w \to \infty$, we find $\ln R = -(H_w - H_{w(1-\alpha)})p + O(p^2)$; hence $R = 1 + w^{-1}\ln(1-\alpha) + O(w^{-2})$; and similarly $S = \alpha w + O(1)$. Thus the answer is $(1-\alpha)^{-1} - 1 - \alpha - \ln(1-\alpha) + O(w^{-1})$.

    Notes: The simpler problem "with probability p occupy the leftmost, otherwise occupy any randomly chosen empty position" is solved by taking $P_j = 1$ in the formulas above, and the answer is $m - (m+1)(m-n)R/(m-n+1)$. To get C'_N for random probing with secondary clustering, set $n = N$, $m = M$ and add 1 to the answer above.

45. Yes. See L. Guibas, *JACM* **25** (1978), 544–555.

46. Define the numbers $\left[\!\left[\begin{smallmatrix} n \\ k \end{smallmatrix}\right]\!\right]$ for $k \ge 0$ by the rule

$$\sum_k \binom{x+k}{k} \left[\!\!\left[\begin{matrix} n \\ k \end{matrix}\right]\!\!\right] = (x+n+1)^n$$

for all x and all nonnegative integers n. Setting $x = -1, -2, \ldots, -n-1$ implies that

$$\left[\!\!\left[\begin{matrix} n \\ k \end{matrix}\right]\!\!\right] = \sum_j \binom{k}{j}(-1)^j (n-j)^n \qquad \text{for } 0 \le k \le n;$$

then setting $x = 0$ implies that we may take $\left[\!\left[\begin{smallmatrix} n \\ k \end{smallmatrix}\right]\!\right] = 0$ for all $k > n$, so the two sides of the defining equation are polynomials in x of degree n that agree on $n+1$ points. It follows that the numbers $\left[\!\left[\begin{smallmatrix} n \\ k \end{smallmatrix}\right]\!\right]$ have the stated property.

Let $f(N, r)$ be the number of hash sequences $a_1 \ldots a_N$ that leave the first r locations occupied and the next one empty. There are $\binom{M-r-1}{N-r}$ possible patterns of occupied cells, and each pattern occurs as many times as there are sequences $a_1' \ldots a_N'$, $1 \le a_i' \le N$, that contain each of the numbers $r+1$, $r+2$, $\ldots$, N at least once. By inclusion-exclusion, there are $\left[\!\left[{N \atop N-r} \right]\!\right]$ such sequences; hence

$$f(N, r) = \binom{M-r-1}{N-r} \left[\!\left[{N \atop N-r} \right]\!\right].$$

Now

$$C_N' = 1 + M^{-N-1} \sum_{r=0}^{N} f(N, r) \left(\sum_{a=0}^{r-1} r + \sum_{a=r+1}^{M-1} \frac{N-r}{M-r-1}(r+1) \right)$$

$$= 1 + M^{-N-1} \sum_{r=0}^{N} f(N, r)\big(N + (N-1)r\big).$$

Let $S_n(x) = \sum_k k \binom{x+k}{k} \left[\!\left[{n \atop k} \right]\!\right]$; we have

$$(x+1)^{-1} S_n(x) + \sum_k \binom{x+k}{k} \left[\!\left[{n \atop k} \right]\!\right] = \sum_k \binom{x+1+k}{k} \left[\!\left[{n \atop k} \right]\!\right];$$

hence $S_n(x) = (x+1)\big((x+n+2)^n - (x+n+1)^n\big)$. It follows that $C_N' = N(1+1/M) - (N-1)(1-N/M)(1+1/M)^N \approx N(1 - (1-\alpha)e^\alpha)$; and $C_N = (N-1)\big((1+1/M)/2 + (1+1/M)^N\big) + (3M^2 + 6M + 2)\big((1+1/M)^N - 1\big)/N - (3M+2)(1+1/M)^N$, which is $(e - 2.5)M + O(1)$ when $N = M - 1$.

For further properties of the numbers $\left[\!\left[{n \atop k} \right]\!\right]$, see John Riordan, *Combinatorial Identities* (New York: Wiley, 1968), 228–229.

47. The analysis of Algorithm L applies, almost word for word! Any probe sequence with cyclic symmetry, and which explores only positions adjacent to those previously examined, will have the same behavior.

48. $C_N' = 1 + p + p^2 + \cdots$, where $p = N/M$ is the probability that a random location is filled; hence $C_N' = M/(M - N)$, and $C_N = N^{-1} \sum_{k=0}^{N-1} C_k' = N^{-1} M(H_M - H_{M-N})$. These values are approximately equal to those for uniform probing, but slightly higher because of the chance of repeated probes in the same place. Indeed, for $4 = N < M \le 16$, linear probing is better!

In practice we wouldn't use infinitely many hash functions; some other scheme like linear probing would ultimately be used as a last resort. This method is inferior to those described in the text, but it is of historical importance because it suggested Morris's method, which led to Algorithm D. See *CACM* **6** (1963), 101, where M. D. McIlroy credits the idea to V. A. Vyssotsky; the same technique had been discovered as early as 1956 by A. W. Holt, who used it successfully in the GPX system for the UNIVAC.

49. $C_N' - 1 = \sum_{k>b}(k - b)P_{Nk} \approx \sum_{k>b}(k - b)e^{-\alpha b}(\alpha b)^k/k! = \alpha b t_b(\alpha)$. [*Note:* We have

$$\sum_{b \ge 0} \left(\sum_{k > b}(k - b)P_k \right) z^b = \frac{P'(1)}{1-z} + \frac{z(P(z) - 1)}{(1-z)^2}$$

in general, if $P(z) = P_0 + P_1 z + \cdots$ is any probability generating function.] And

$$C_N - 1 = \frac{M}{N} \sum_{k>b} \binom{k-b+1}{2} P_{Nk}$$

$$= \frac{M}{2N} \sum_{k>b} (k(k-1) - 2k(b-1) + b(b-1)) P_{Nk}$$

$$= \tfrac{1}{2} e^{-b\alpha} (b\alpha)^b b!^{-1} (b + b\alpha - 2b + 2 + (b\alpha^2 - 2\alpha(b-1) + b - 1) R(\alpha, b)).$$

[The analysis of successful search with chaining was first carried out by W. P. Heis-ing in 1957. The simple expressions in (57) and (58) were found by J. A. van der Pool in 1971; he also considered how to minimize a function that represents the combined cost of storage space and number of accesses. We can determine the variance of C'_N and of the number of overflows per bucket, since $\sum_{k>b}(k-b)^2 P_{Nk} = (2N/M)(C_N - 1) - (C'_N - 1)$. The variance of the total number of overflows may be approximated by M times the variance in a single bucket, but this is actually too high because the total number of records is constrained to be N. The true variance can be found as in exercise 37. See also the derivation of the chi-square test in Section 3.3.1C.]

50. And next that $Q_0(M, N-1) = (M/N)(Q_0(M, N) - 1)$. In general, $rQ_r(M, N) = MQ_{r-2}(M, N) - (M - N - r)Q_{r-1}(M, N) = M(Q_{r-1}(M, N+1) - Q_{r-1}(M, N))$; $Q_r(M, N-1) = (M/N)(Q_r(M, N) - Q_{r-1}(M, N))$.

51. $R(\alpha, n) = \alpha^{-1}(n! \, e^{\alpha n}(\alpha n)^{-n} - Q_0(\alpha n, n))$.

52. See Eq. 1.2.11.3–(9) and exercise 3.1–14.

53. By Eq. 1.2.11.3–(8), $\alpha(\alpha n)^n R(\alpha, n) = e^{\alpha n} \gamma(n+1, \alpha n)$; hence by the suggested exercise $R(\alpha, n) = (1 - \alpha)^{-1} - (1 - \alpha)^{-3} n^{-1} + O(n^{-2})$. [This asymptotic formula can be obtained more directly by the method of (43), if we note that the coefficient of α^k in $R(\alpha, n)$ is

$$1 - \binom{k+2}{2} n^{-1} + O(k^4 n^{-2}).$$

In fact, the coefficient of α^k is

$$\sum_{r\geq 0} (-1)^r n^{-r} \left\{ \begin{matrix} r+k+1 \\ k+1 \end{matrix} \right\}$$

by Eq. 1.2.9–(28).]

54. Using the hint together with Eqs. 1.2.6–(53) and 1.2.6–(49), we have

$$\sum_{b\geq 1} t_b(\alpha) = \sum_{m\geq 1} \frac{\alpha^m}{(m+1)(m)m!} \sum_k \binom{m}{k} (-1)^{m-k} k^{m+1} = \sum_{m\geq 1} \alpha^m/2.$$

The hint follows from Kummer's well-known hypergeometric identity $e^{-z} F(a; b; z) = F(b - a; b; -z)$, since $(n + 1)! \, t_n(\alpha) = e^{-n\alpha}(\alpha n)^n F(2; n + 2; \alpha n)$; see *Crelle* **15** (1836), 39–83, 127–172, Eq. 26.4.

55. If $B(z)C(z) = \sum s_i z^i$, we have $c_0 = s_0 + \cdots + s_b$, $c_1 = s_{b+1}$, $c_2 = s_{b+2}$, ...; hence $B(z)C(z) = z^b C(z) + Q(z)$. Now $P(z) = z^b$ has $b-1$ roots q_j with $|q_j| < 1$, determined as the solutions to $e^{\alpha(q_j - 1)} = \omega^{-j} q_j$, $\omega = e^{2\pi i/b}$. To solve $e^{\alpha(q-1)} = \omega^{-1} q$, let $t = \alpha q$

and $z = \alpha\omega e^{-\alpha}$ so that $t = ze^t$. By Lagrange's formula we get

$$\frac{1}{1-q} = 1 + \sum_{r\geq 0} r \sum_{n\geq r} \frac{n^{n-r-1}\omega^n\alpha^{n-r}e^{-n\alpha}}{(n-r)!}$$

$$= 1 + \sum_{r\geq 1} r \sum_{m\geq 0} \frac{\alpha^m}{m!}(-1)^m \sum_{n\geq r}\binom{m}{n-r}(-1)^{n-r}\omega^n n^{m-1}.$$

By Abel's limit theorem, letting $|\omega| \to 1$ from inside the unit circle, this can be rearranged to equal

$$\frac{1-\alpha\omega}{1-\omega} + \sum_{m\geq 2}\frac{\alpha^m}{m!}(-1)^m\sum_{n\geq 0}\binom{m-2}{n}(-1)^n\omega^{n+1}(n+1)^{m-1}.$$

Now replacing ω by ω^j and summing for $1 \leq j < b$ yields

$$\frac{b-1}{2} + \alpha\frac{b-1}{2} + \sum_{m\geq 2}\alpha^m\left(-\frac{1}{2} + \frac{(-1)^m}{m!}b\sum_{n\geq 1}\binom{m-2}{nb-1}(-1)^{nb-1}(nb)^{m-1}\right)$$

and the desired result follows after some more juggling using the hint of exercise 54.

This analysis, applied to a variety of problems, was begun by N. T. J. Bailey, *J. Roy. Stat. Soc.* **B16** (1954), 80–87; M. Tainiter, *JACM* **10** (1963), 307–315; A. G. Konheim and B. Meister, *JACM* **19** (1972), 92–108.

56. See Blake and Konheim, *JACM* **24** (1977), 591–606. Alfredo Viola and Patricio Poblete [*Algorithmica* **21** (1998), 37–71] have shown that

$$C_{Mb} = 1 + \frac{M-1}{2Mb} + \frac{1}{b}\sum_{j\geq 2}\binom{bm-1}{j}m^{-j}\sum_{k\geq 1}\binom{j-2}{bk-1}(-1)^{j+bk-1}k^{j-1}$$

$$= \sqrt{\frac{\pi M}{8b}} + \frac{1}{3b} + \frac{1}{b}\sum_{j=1}^{b-1}\frac{1}{(1-T(e^{2\pi ij/b-1}))} + \frac{1}{24}\sqrt{\frac{\pi}{2b^3 M}} + O(b^{-2}M^{-1}),$$

where T is the tree function of Eq. 2.3.4.4–(30).

58. 0 1 2 3 4 and 0 2 4 1 3, plus additive shifts of 1 1 1 1 1 mod 5, each with probability $\frac{1}{10}$. Similarly, for $M = 6$ we need 30 permutations, and a solution exists starting with

$$\tfrac{1}{20}\times 0\,1\,2\,3\,4\,5, \quad \tfrac{1}{60}\times 0\,1\,3\,2\,5\,4, \quad \tfrac{1}{60}\times 0\,2\,4\,3\,1\,5, \quad \tfrac{1}{20}\times 0\,2\,3\,4\,5\,1, \quad \tfrac{1}{30}\times 0\,3\,4\,1\,2\,5.$$

For $M = 7$ we need 49, and a solution is generated by

$$\tfrac{1}{35}\times 0\,1\,2\,3\,4\,5\,6, \quad \tfrac{2}{105}\times 0\,1\,5\,3\,2\,4\,6, \quad \tfrac{1}{35}\times 0\,2\,4\,3\,5\,1\,6, \quad \tfrac{2}{105}\times 0\,2\,6\,3\,1\,4\,5,$$
$$\tfrac{1}{35}\times 0\,3\,6\,1\,4\,2\,5, \quad \tfrac{1}{105}\times 0\,3\,2\,6\,4\,1\,5, \quad \tfrac{1}{105}\times 0\,3\,1\,5\,4\,2\,6.$$

59. No permutation can have a probability larger than $1/\binom{M}{\lfloor M/2\rfloor}$, so there must be at least $\binom{M}{\lfloor M/2\rfloor} = \exp(M\ln 2 + O(\log M))$ permutations with nonzero probability.

60. Preliminary results have been obtained by Ajtai, Komlós, and Szemerédi, *Information Processing Letters* **7** (1978), 270–273.

62. See the discussion in *AMM* **81** (1974), 323–343, where the best cyclic hashing sequences are exhibited for $M \leq 9$.

63. MH_M, by exercise 3.3.2–8; the standard deviation is $\approx \pi M/\sqrt{6}$.

64. The average number of moves is equal to $\frac{1}{2}(N-1)/M + \frac{2}{3}(N-1)(N-2)/M^2 + \frac{3}{4}(N-1)(N-2)(N-3)/M^3 + \cdots \approx \frac{1}{1-\alpha} - \frac{1}{\alpha}\ln\frac{1}{1-\alpha}$. [An equivalent problem is solved in *Comp. J.* **17** (1974), 139–140.]

65. The keys can be stored in a separate table, allocated sequentially (assuming that deletions, if any, are LIFO). The hash table entries point to this "names table"; for example, TABLE[i] might have the form

			L_i	KEY[i]

where L_i is the number of words in the key stored at locations KEY[i], KEY[i] + 1, ...

The rest of the hash table entry might be used in any of several ways: (i) as a link for Algorithm C; (ii) as part of the information associated with the key; or (iii) as a "secondary hash code." The latter idea, suggested by Robert Morris, sometimes speeds up a search [we take a careful look at the key in KEY[i] only if $h_2(K)$ matches its secondary hash code, for some function $h_2(K)$].

66. Yes; and the arrangement of the records is unique. The average number of probes per unsuccessful search is reduced to C_{N-1}, although it remains C'_N when the Nth term is inserted. This important technique is called *ordered hashing*. See *Comp. J.* **17** (1974), 135–142; D. E. Knuth, *Literate Programming* (1992), 144–149, 216–217.

67. (a) If $c_j = 0$ in (44), an optimum arrangement is obtained by sorting the a's into nonincreasing "cyclic order," assuming that $j - 1 > \cdots > 0 > M - 1 > \cdots > j$. (b) Between steps L2 and L3, exchange the record-in-hand with TABLE[i] if the latter is closer to home than the former. [This algorithm, called "Robin Hood hashing" by Celis, Larson, and Munro in *FOCS* **26** (1985), 281–288, is equivalent to a variant of ordered hashing.] (c) Let $h(m, n, d)$ be the number of hash sequences that make $c_0 \le d$. It can be shown [*Comp. J.* **17** (1974), 141] that $(h(m, n, d) - h(m, n, d - 1))M$ is the total number of occurrences of displacement $d > 0$ among all M^N hash sequences, and that we can write $h(M, N, d) = a(M, N, d + 1) - Na(M, N - 1, d + 1)$ where $a(m, n, d) = \sum_{k=0}^{d}\binom{n}{k}(m+d-k)^{n-k}(k-d)^k$. An elaborate calculation using the methods of exercises 28 and 50 now shows that the average value of $\sum d_j^2$ is

$$M^{1-N}\sum_{d=1}^{N}d^2\bigl(h(M, N, d) - h(M, N, d - 1)\bigr)$$

$$= \frac{M^2}{2} + \frac{2M}{3} + \frac{N}{6} + \frac{N^2}{6M} - \frac{N}{6M} - M\left(\frac{M}{2} - \frac{N}{2} + \frac{2}{3}\right)Q_0(M, N)$$

$$= M\left(\frac{1}{2(1-\alpha)^2} - \frac{7}{6(1-\alpha)} + \frac{2}{3} + \frac{\alpha}{6} + \frac{\alpha^2}{6}\right) + O(1)$$

when $N = \alpha M$. Without the modification (see exercise 28), $\mathrm{E}\sum d_j^2$ comes to

$$\frac{M}{3}(Q_2(M, N) - Q_1(M, N)) - \frac{M}{2}(Q_0(M, N) - 1) + \frac{N}{6}$$

$$= M\left(\frac{1}{3(1-\alpha)^3} - \frac{1}{3(1-\alpha)^2} - \frac{1}{2(1-\alpha)} + \frac{1}{2} + \frac{\alpha}{6}\right) + O(1).$$

If the records all have approximately the same displacement d, and if successful searches are significantly more common than unsuccessful ones, it is advantageous to start at position $h' = h(K) + d$ and then to probe $h' - 1$, $h' + 1$, $h' - 2$, etc. P. V. Poblete, A. Viola, and J. I. Munro have shown [*Random Structures & Algorithms* **10** (1997),

221–255] that $\sum d_j^2$ can be made almost as small as in the Robin Hood method by using a much simpler approach called "last-come-first-served" hashing, in which every newly inserted key is placed in its home position; all other keys move one step away until an empty slot is found. The Robin Hood and last-come-first-served techniques apply to double hashing as well as to linear probing, but the reduction in probes does not compensate for the increased time per probe with respect to double hashing unless the table is extremely full. (See Poblete and Munro, *J. Algorithms* **10** (1989), 228–248.)

68. The average value of $(d_1 + \cdots + d_N)^2$ can be shown to equal

$$\frac{N}{12}((M-N)^3 + (N+3)(M-N)^2 + (8N+1)(M-N) + 5N^2 + 4N - 1$$
$$- ((M-N)^3 + 4(M-N)^2 + (6N+3)(M-N) + 8N)Q_0(M, N-1))$$

using the connection between the parking problem and connected graphs mentioned in the answer to exercise 31. To get the variance of the average number of probes in a successful search, divide by N^2 and subtract $\frac{1}{4}(Q_0(M, N-1)-1)^2$; this is asymptotically $\frac{1}{12}((1+2\alpha)/(1-\alpha)^4 - 1)/N + O(N^{-2})$. (See P. Flajolet, P. V. Poblete, and A. Viola, *Algorithmica* **22** (1998), 490–515; D. E. Knuth, *Algorithmica* **22** (1998), 561–568. The variance calculated here should be distinguished from the total variance, which is $E\sum d_j^2/N - \frac{1}{4}(Q_0(M, N-1) - 1)^2$; see the answers to exercises 37 and 67.)

69. Let $q_k = p_k + p_{k+1} + \cdots$; then the inequality $q_k \geq \max(0, 1 - (k-1)(M-n)/M)$ gives a lower bound on $C'_N = \sum_{k \geq 1} q_k$.

70. A remarkably simple proof by Lueker and Molodowitch [*Combinatorica* **13** (1993), 83–96] establishes a similar result but with an extra factor $(\log M)^2$ in the O-bound; the stated result follows in the same way by using sharper probability estimates. A. Siegel and J. P. Schmidt have shown, in fact, that the expected number of probes in double hashing is $1/(1-\alpha) + O(1/M)$ for fixed $\alpha = N/M$. [Computer Science Tech. Report 687 (New York: Courant Institute, 1995).]

72. [*J. Comp. Syst. Sci.* **18** (1979), 143–154.] (a) Given keys $K_1, \ldots, K_N$ and K, the probability that K_j is in the same list as K is $\leq 1/M$ if $K \neq K_j$. Hence the expected list size is $\leq 1 + (N-1)/M$.

(b) Suppose there are Q possible characters; then there are M^Q possible choices for each h_j. Choosing each h_j at random is equivalent to choosing a random row from a matrix H of M^{Ql} rows and Q^l columns, with the entry $h(x_1 \ldots x_l) = (h_1(x_1) + \cdots + h_l(x_l)) \bmod M$ in column $x_1 \ldots x_l$. In columns $K = x_1 \ldots x_l$ and $K' = x'_1 \ldots x'_l$ with $x_j \neq x'_j$ for some j, we have $h(K) = (s + h_j(x_j)) \bmod M$ and $h(K') = (s' + h_j(x'_j)) \bmod M$, where $s = \sum_{i \neq j} h_i(x_i)$ and $s' = \sum_{i \neq j} h_i(x'_i)$ are independent of h_j. The value of $h_j(x_j) - h_j(x'_j)$ is uniformly distributed modulo M; hence we have $h(K) = h(K')$ with probability $1/M$, regardless of the values of s and s'.

(c) Yes; adding any constant to $h_j(x_j)$ changes $h(x)$ by a constant, modulo M.

73. (i) This is the special case of exercise 72(c) when each key is regarded as a sequence of bits, not characters. [It was invented as early as 1970 by Alfred L. Zobrist, whose original technical report has been reprinted in *ICCA Journal* **13** (1990), 69–73.] (ii) The proof of (b) shows that it suffices to show that $h_j(x_j) - h_j(x'_j)$ is uniform modulo M when $x_j \neq x'_j$. And in fact, the probability that $h_j(x_j) = y$ and $h_j(x'_j) = y'$ is $1/M^2$, for any given y and y', because the congruences $a_j x_j + b_j \equiv y$ and $a_j x'_j + b_j \equiv y'$ have a unique solution (a_j, b_j) for any given (y, y'), modulo the prime M.

When M is not prime and p is a prime $> M$, a similar result holds if we let $h_j(x_j) = ((a_j x_j + b_j) \bmod p) \bmod M$, where a_j and b_j are chosen randomly mod p. In this case the family is not quite universal, but it comes close enough for practical purposes: The probability that different keys collide is at most $1/M + r(M-r)/Mp^2 \le 1/M + M/4p^2$, where $r = p \bmod M$.

74. The statement is false in general. For example, suppose $M = N = n^2$, and consider the matrix H with $\binom{N}{n}$ rows, one for every way to put n zeros in different columns; the nonzero entries are $1, 2, \ldots, N - n$ from left to right in each row. This matrix is universal because there are $\binom{N-2}{n-2} = \binom{N}{n}\frac{n}{N}\frac{n-1}{N-1} < \binom{N}{n}\left(\frac{n}{N}\right)^2 = R/M$ matches in every pair of columns. But the number of zeros in every row is $\sqrt{N} \ne O(1) + O(N/M)$.

Notes: This exercise points out that expected list size is quite different from the expected number of collisions when a new key is inserted. Consider letting $h(x_1 \ldots x_l) = h_1(x_1)$, where h_1 is chosen at random. This family of hash functions makes the expected size of every list N/M; yet it is certainly not universal, because a set of N keys that have the same first character x_1 will lead to one list of size N and all other lists empty. The expected number of collisions will be $N(N-1)/2$, but with a universal hash family this number is at most $N(N-1)/2M$, regardless of the set of keys.

On the other hand we *can* show that the expected size of every list is $O(1) + O(N/\sqrt{M})$ in a universal family. Suppose there are z_h zeros in row h. Then that row contains at least $\binom{z_h}{2}$ pairs of equal elements. The maximum of $\sum_{h=1}^{R} x_h$ subject to $\sum_{h=1}^{R} \binom{z_h}{2} \le \binom{N}{2}R/M$ occurs when each z_h is equal to z where $\binom{z}{2} = \binom{N}{2}/M$, namely

$$z = \frac{1}{2} + \sqrt{\frac{1}{4} + \frac{N(N-1)}{M}} < 1 + \sqrt{\frac{N(N-1)}{M}}.$$

75. (a) Obviously true, even if $h_2, \ldots, h_l$ are identically zero. (b) True, by the answer to 72(b). (c) True. The result is clear if K, K', and K'' all differ in some character position. Otherwise, say $x_j = x_j' \ne x_j''$ and $x_k \ne x_k' = x_k''$. Then the quantities $h_j(x_j) + h_k(x_k)$, $h_j(x_j) + h_k(x_k')$, and $h_j(x_j'') + h_k(x_k')$ are independent of each other, uniformly distributed, and independent of the other $l-2$ characters of the keys. (d) False. Consider, for example, the case $M = l = 2$ with 1-bit characters. Then all four keys hash to the same location with probability $1/4$.

76. Use $h(K) = \big(h_0(l) + h_1(x_1) + \cdots + h_l(x_l)\big) \bmod M$, where each h_j is chosen as in exercise 73. Generate the random coefficients for h_j (and, if desired, precompute its array of values) when a key of length $\ge j$ occurs for the first time. Since l is unbounded, the matrix H is infinite; but only a finite portion is relevant in any particular program run.

77. Let $p \le 2^{-16}$ be the probability that two 32-bit keys have the same image under H. The worst case occurs when two given keys agree in seven of their eight 32-bit subkeys; then the probability of collision is $1 - (1-p)^4 < 4p$. [See Wegman and Carter, *J. Comp. Syst. Sci.* **22** (1981), 265–279.]

78. Let $g(x) = \lfloor x/2^k \rfloor \bmod 2^{n-k}$ and $\delta(x, x') = \sum_{b=0}^{2^k-1}[g(x+b) = g(x'+b)]$. Then $\delta(x+1, x'+1) = \delta(x, x') + [g(x+2^k) = g(x'+2^k)] - [g(x) = g(x')] = \delta(x, x')$. Also $\delta(x, 0) = (2^k \dot- (x \bmod 2^n)) + (2^k \dot- ((-x) \bmod 2^n))$ when $0 < x < 2^n$, where $a \dot- b = \max(a-b, 0)$. These formulas characterize $\delta(x, x')$ when $x \not\equiv x'$ (modulo 2^n).

Now let $A = \{a \mid 0 < a < 2^n, \ a \text{ odd}\}$ and $B = \{b \mid 0 \le b < 2^k\}$. We want to show that $\sum_{a \in A}\sum_{b \in B}[g(ax+b) = g(ax'+b)] \le R/M = 2^{n-1+k}/2^{n-k} = 2^{2k-1}$ when $0 \le x < x' < 2^n$. And indeed, if $x' - x = 2^p q$ with q odd, then we have

$$\sum_{a \in A}\sum_{b \in B}[g(ax+b) = g(ax'+b)] = \sum_{a \in A}\delta(ax, ax') = 2\sum_{a \in A}(2^k \dot- ((2^p aq) \bmod 2^n))$$

$$= 2^{p+1}\sum_{j=0}^{2^{n-p-1}-1}(2^k \dot- 2^p(2j+1)) = 2^{p+1}\sum_{j=0}^{2^{k-p-1}-1}(2^k - 2^p(2j+1))[p < k] = 2^{2k-1}[p < k].$$

[See *Lecture Notes in Computer Science* **1672** (1999), 262–272.]

SECTION 6.5

1. The path described in the hint can be converted by changing each downward step that runs from $(i-1,j)$ to a "new record low" value $(i, j-1)$ into an upward step. If c such changes are made, the path ends at $(m, n-2t+2c)$, where $c \geq 0$ and $c \geq 2t-n$; hence $n-2t+2c \geq n-2k$. In the permutation corresponding to the changed path, the smallest c elements of list B correspond to the downward steps that changed, and list A contains the $t-c$ elements corresponding to downward steps that didn't change.

When $t = k$ it is not difficult to see that the construction is reversible; hence exactly $\binom{n}{k}$ permutations are constructed. Incidentally, according to this proof, the contents of lists A and C may appear in arbitrary order.

Notes: We have counted these paths in another way in exercise 2.2.1–4. When $k = \lfloor n/2 \rfloor$ this construction proves *Sperner's Theorem*, which states that it is impossible to have more than $\binom{n}{\lfloor n/2 \rfloor}$ subsets of $\{1, 2, \ldots, n\}$ with no subset contained in another. [Emanuel Sperner, *Math. Zeitschrift* **27** (1928), 544–548.] For if we have such a collection of subsets, each of the $\binom{n}{k}$ permutations can have at most one of the subsets appearing in the initial positions, yet each subset appears in some permutation. The construction used here is a disguised form of a more general construction by which N. G. de Bruijn, C. van Ebbenhorst Tengbergen, and D. Kruyswijk [*Nieuw Archief voor Wiskunde* (2) **23** (1951), 191–193] proved the multiset generalization of Sperner's Theorem: "Let M be a multiset containing n elements (counting multiplicities). The collection of all $\lfloor n/2 \rfloor$-element submultisets of M is the largest possible collection such that no submultiset is contained in another." For example, the largest such collection when $M = \{a, a, b, b, c, c\}$ consists of the seven submultisets $\{a, a, b\}$, $\{a, a, c\}$, $\{a, b, b\}$, $\{a, b, c\}$, $\{a, c, c\}$, $\{b, b, c\}$, $\{b, c, c\}$. This would correspond to seven permutations of six attributes $A_1, B_1, A_2, B_2, A_3, B_3$ in which all queries involving A_i also involve B_i. Further comments appear in a paper by C. Greene and D. J. Kleitman, *J. Combinatorial Theory* **A20** (1976), 80–88.

2. Let a_{ijk} be a list of all references to records having (i, j, k) as the respective values of the three attributes, and assume that a_{011} is the shortest of the three lists a_{011}, a_{101}, a_{110}. Then a minimum-length list is $a_{001}a_{011}a_{111}a_{101}a_{100}a_{110}a_{111}a_{011}a_{010}$. However, if a_{011} is empty and so is either of a_{001}, a_{010}, or a_{100}, the length can be shortened by deleting one of the two occurrences of a_{111} [*CACM* **15** (1972), 802–808].

3. (a) Anise seed and/or honey, possibly in combination with nutmeg and/or vanilla extract. (b) None.

4. Let p_t be the probability that the query involves exactly t bit positions, and let P_t be the probability that t given positions are all 1 in a random record. Then the answer is $\sum_t p_t P_t$, minus the probability that a particular record is a "true drop"; the latter probability is $\binom{N-q}{r-q}/\binom{N}{r}$, where $N = \binom{n}{k}$. By the principle of inclusion and exclusion,

$$P_t = \sum_{j \geq 0} (-1)^j \binom{t}{j} f(n-j, k, r) / f(n, k, r),$$

where $f(n, k, r)$ is the number of possible choices of r distinct k-bit attribute codes in an n-bit field, namely $\binom{N}{r}$ where $N = \binom{n}{k}$. And if $q = r$ we have, by exercise 1.3.3–26,

$$p_t = \sum_{l \geq 0} (-1)^l \binom{t+l}{t} \binom{n}{t+l} P_{t+l} = \binom{n}{t} \sum_{j \geq 0} (-1)^j \binom{t}{j} f(t-j, k, q) / f(n, k, q).$$

Notes: The calculations above were first carried out, in more general form, by G. Orosz and L. Takács, *J. of Documentation* **12** (1956), 231–234. The mean $\sum t p_t$ is easily shown to be $n(1 - f(n-1, k, q)/f(n, k, q))$. Another assumption, that the random attribute codes in records and queries are not necessarily distinct, as in the techniques of Harrison and Bloom, can be analyzed by the same method, setting $f(n, k, r) = \binom{n}{k}^r$. When the parameters are in appropriate ranges, we have $P_t \approx (1 - e^{-kr/n})^t$ and $\sum p_t P_t \approx P_{n(1 - \exp(-kq/n))}$.

6. $L(t) = \sum_j \binom{m_1}{j} \binom{m_2}{t-j} L_1(j) L_2(t - j) / \binom{m_1 + m_2}{t}$. [Hence if $L_1(t) \approx N_1 \alpha^{-t}$ and $L_2(t) \approx N_2 \alpha^{-t}$, then $L(t) \approx N_1 N_2 \alpha^{-t}$.]

7. (a) $L(1) = 3$, $L(2) = 1\frac{3}{4}$. (b) $L(1) = 3\frac{3}{4}$, $L(2) = 2\frac{1}{3}$, $L(3) = 1\frac{9}{16}$. [*Note:* A trivial projection mapping such as $0\,0\,*\,* \to 0$, $0\,1\,*\,* \to 1$, $1\,0\,*\,* \to 2$, $1\,1\,*\,* \to 3$, has a worse worst-case behavior; but it has a better average case, because of the exercise that follows: $L(1) = 3$, $L(2) = 2\frac{1}{6}$, $L(3) = 1\frac{1}{2}$.]

8. (a) When $S = S_0 0 \cup S_1 1$, we have $f_t(S) = f_t(S_0 \cup S_1) + f_{t-1}(S_0) + f_{t-1}(S_1)$. Therefore $f_t(s, m)$ is the minimum of $f_t(s_0, m-1) + f_{t-1}(s_0, m-1) + f_{t-1}(s_1, m-1)$ over all s_0 and s_1 such that $2^{m-1} \geq s_0 \geq s_1 \geq 0$ and $s_0 + s_1 = s$. To prove that the minimum occurs for $s_0 = \lceil s/2 \rceil$ and $s_1 = \lfloor s/2 \rfloor$, we can use induction on m, the result being clear for $m = 1$: Given $m \geq 2$, let $g_t(s) = f_t(s, m - 1)$ and $h_t(s) = f_t(s, m - 2)$. Then, by induction, $g_t(s_0) + g_{t-1}(s_0) + g_{t-1}(s_1) = h_t(\lceil s_0/2 \rceil) + h_{t-1}(\lceil s_0/2 \rceil) + h_{t-1}(\lfloor s_0/2 \rfloor) + h_{t-1}(\lceil s_0/2 \rceil) + h_{t-2}(\lceil s_0/2 \rceil) + h_{t-2}(\lfloor s_0/2 \rfloor) + h_{t-1}(\lceil s_1/2 \rceil) + h_{t-2}(\lceil s_1/2 \rceil) + h_{t-2}(\lfloor s_1/2 \rfloor)$, which is $\geq g_t(\lceil s_0/2 \rceil + \lceil s_1/2 \rceil) + g_{t-1}(\lceil s_0/2 \rceil + \lceil s_1/2 \rceil) + g_{t-1}(\lfloor s_0/2 \rfloor + \lfloor s_1/2 \rfloor)$. And if $s_0 > s_1 + 1$, we have $\lceil s_0/2 \rceil + \lceil s_1/2 \rceil < s_0$, except in the case $s_0 = 2k+1$ and $s_1 = 2k-1$. In the latter case, however, $g_t(s_0) + g_{t-1}(s_0) + g_{t-1}(s_1) \geq h_t(2k + 1) + 2h_{t-1}(2k) \geq h_t(2k) + 2h_{t-1}(2k)$.

(b) Observe that the set S containing the numbers $0, 1, \ldots, s - 1$ in binary notation has the property that $S_0 \cup S_1 = S_0$, and S_0 contains $\lceil s_0/2 \rceil$ elements. It follows, incidentally, that $f_t(2^{m-n}, m) = [z^t](1 + z)^n (1 + 2z)^{m-n}$.

10. (a) There must be $\frac{1}{6} v(v - 1)$ triples, and x_v must occur in $\frac{1}{2} v$ of them. (b) Since v is odd, there is a unique triple $\{x_i, y_j, z\}$ for each i, and so S' is readily shown to be a Steiner triple system. The pairs missing in K' are $\{z, x_2\}$, $\{x_2, y_2\}$, $\{y_2, x_3\}$, $\{x_3, y_3\}$, $\ldots$, $\{x_{v-1}, y_{v-1}\}$, $\{y_{v-1}, x_v\}$, $\{x_v, z\}$. (d) Starting with the case $v = 1$ and applying the operations $v \to 2v - 2$, $v \to 2v + 1$ yields all nonnegative numbers not of the form $3k + 2$, because the cases $6k + (0, 1, 3, 4)$ come respectively from the smaller cases $3k + (1, 0, 1, 3)$.

Incidentally, "Steiner triple systems" should not have been named after Steiner, although that name has become deeply entrenched in the literature. Steiner's publication [*Crelle* **45** (1853), 181–182] came several years after Kirkman's, and Felix Klein has noted [*Vorlesungen über die Entwicklung der Math. im 19. Jahrhundert* **1** (Springer, 1926), 128] that Steiner quoted English authors without giving them credit, during the later years of his life. Moreover, the concept had appeared already in two well-known books of J. Plücker [*System der analytischen Geometrie* (1835), 283–284; *Theorie der algebraischen Curven* (1839), 245–247]. Kirkman wrote his paper in response to a substantially more general problem posed by W. S. B. Woolhouse, namely to find the maximum number of t-element subsets of $\{1, \ldots, n\}$ in which no q-element subset appears more than once; that problem remains unsolved. [See *Lady's and Gentleman's Diary* (1844), 84; (1845), 63–64; (1846), 76, 78; (1847), 62–67.]

11. Take a Steiner triple system on $2v + 1$ objects. Call one of the objects z and name the others in such a way that the triples containing z are $\{z, x_i, \bar{x}_i\}$; delete those triples.

12. $\{k, (k+1) \bmod 14, (k+4) \bmod 14, (k+6) \bmod 14\}$, for $0 \le k < 14$, where $(k+7)$ $\bmod 14$ is the complement of k. [Complemented systems are a special case of *group divisible block designs*; see Bose, Shrikhande, and Bhattacharya, *Ann. Math. Statistics* **24** (1953), 167–195.]

14. Deletion is easiest in k-d trees (a replacement for the root can be found in about $O(N^{1-1/k})$ steps). In quadtrees, deletion seems to require rebuilding the entire subtree rooted at the node being removed (but this subtree contains only about $\log N$ nodes on the average). In post-office trees, deletion is almost hopeless.

16. Let each triple correspond to a codeword, where each codeword has exactly three 1-bits, identifying the elements of the corresponding triple. If u, v, w are distinct codewords, u has at most two 1 bits in common with the superposition of v and w, since it had at most one in common with v or w alone. [Similarly, from quadruple systems of order v we can construct $v(v-1)/12$ codewords, none of which is contained in the superposition of any three others, etc.]

17. (a) Let $c_0 = b_0$ and, for $1 \le k \le n$, let $c_k = $ (if $b_{k-1} = 0$ then $*$ else b_k), $c_{-k} = $ (if $b_{k-1} = 1$ then $*$ else b_k). Then the basic query $c_{-n} \ldots c_0 \ldots c_n$ describes the contents of bucket $b_0 \ldots b_n$. [Consequently this scheme is a special case of combinatorial hashing, and its average query time matches the lower bound in exercise 8(b).]

(b) Let $d_k = [\text{bit } k \text{ is specified}]$, for $-n \le k \le n$. We can assume that $d_{-k} \le d_k$ for $1 \le k \le n$. Then the maximum number of buckets examined occurs when the specified bits are all 0, and it may be computed as follows: Set $x \leftarrow y \leftarrow 1$. Then for $k = n, n-1, \ldots, 0$, set $(x, y) \leftarrow (x, y)M_{d_{-k}+d_k}$, where

$$M_0 = \begin{pmatrix} 1 & 1 \\ 1 & 1 \end{pmatrix}, \qquad M_1 = \begin{pmatrix} 1 & 1 \\ 1 & 0 \end{pmatrix}, \qquad M_2 = \begin{pmatrix} 1 & 1 \\ 0 & 0 \end{pmatrix}.$$

Finally, output x (which also happens to equal y, after $k = 0$).

Say that $(x, y) \succeq (x', y')$ if $x \ge x'$ and $x + y \ge x' + y'$. Then if $(x, y) \succeq (x', y')$ we have $(x, y)M_d \succeq (x', y')M_d$ for $d = 0, 1, 2$. Now

$$(x, y)M_2 M_1^j M_0 = (F_{j+3}x, F_{j+3}x),$$
$$(x, y)M_1 M_1^j M_1 = (F_{j+3}x + F_{j+2}y, F_{j+2}x + F_{j+1}y),$$
$$(x, y)M_0 M_1^j M_2 = (F_{j+2}x + F_{j+2}y, F_{j+2}x + F_{j+2}y);$$

therefore we have $(x, y)M_1 M_1^j M_1 \succeq (x, y)M_2 M_1^j M_0$, because $2y \ge x$; and similarly $(x, y)M_1 M_1^j M_1 \succeq (x, y)M_0 M_1^j M_2$, because $x \ge y$. It follows that the worst case occurs when either $d_{-k} + d_k \le 1$ for $1 \le k \le n$ or $d_{-k} + d_k \ge 1$ for $1 \le k \le n$. We also have

$$(x, y)M_0 M_1^j = (F_{j+2}x + F_{j+2}y, F_{j+1}x + F_{j+1}y),$$
$$(x, y)M_1^j M_0 = (F_{j+2}x + F_{j+1}y, F_{j+2}x + F_{j+1}y);$$
$$(x, y)M_2 M_1^j = (F_{j+2}x, F_{j+1}x),$$
$$(x, y)M_1^j M_2 = (F_{j+1}x + F_j y, F_{j+1}x + F_j y).$$

Consequently the worst case requires the following number of buckets:

$$2^{n-t}F_{t+3}, \qquad \text{if } 0 \le t \le n \qquad\qquad [\text{from } M_1^t M_0^{n+1-t}];$$
$$2^{t-n}F_{3n-2t+3}, \quad \text{if } n \le t \le \lceil 3n/2 \rceil \quad [\text{from } M_1^{3n-2t}(M_1 M_2)^{t-n}M_0];$$
$$2^{2n+1-t}, \qquad\quad \text{if } \lceil 3n/2 \rceil \le t \le 2n \quad [\text{from } M_2^{2t-3n}(M_1 M_2)^{2n-t}M_0].$$

[These results are essentially due to W. A. Burkhard, *BIT* **16** (1976), 13–31, generalized in *J. Comp. Syst. Sci.* **15** (1977), 280–299; but Burkhard's more complicated mapping from $a_0 \ldots a_{2n}$ to $b_0 \ldots b_n$ has been simplified here as suggested by P. Dubost and J.-M. Trousse, Report STAN-CS-75-511 (Stanford Univ., 1975).]

18. (a) There are $2^n(m-n)$ *'s altogether, hence $2^n n$ digits, with $2^n n/m$ digits in each column. Half of the digits in each column must be 0. Hence $2^{n-1}n/m$ is an integer, and each column contains $(2^{n-1}n/m)^2$ mismatches. Since each pair of rows has at least one mismatch, we must have $2^n(2^n-1)/2 \le (2^{n-1}n/m)^2 m$.

(b) Consider the 2^n m-bit numbers that are 0 in $m-n$ specified columns. Half of these have odd parity. A row with $*$ in any of the unspecified columns covers as many evens as odds.

(c) $*000$, $*111$, $0*10$, $1*10$, $00*1$, $10*1$, $010*$, $110*$. This one isn't as uniform as (13), because a query like $*01*$ hits four rows while $*10*$ hits only two. Notice that (13) has cyclic symmetry.

(d) Generate 4^3 rows from each row of (13) by replacing each $*$ by $****$, each 0 by any one of the first four rows, and each 1 by any one of the last four rows. (A similar construction makes an $\text{ABD}(mm', nn')$ from any $\text{ABD}(m,n)$ and $\text{ABD}(m',n')$.)

(e) Given an $\text{ABD}(16,9)$, we can encircle one $*$ in each row in such a way that there are equally many circles in each column. Then we can split each row into two rows, with the circled element replaced by 0 and 1. To show that such encirclement is possible, note that the asterisks of each column can be arbitrarily divided into 32 groups of 7 each; then the 512 rows each contain asterisks of 7 different groups, and the $32 \times 16 = 512$ groups each appear in 7 different rows. Theorem 7.5.1E (the "marriage theorem") now guarantees the existence of a perfect matching with exactly one circled element in each row and each group.

References: R. L. Rivest, *SICOMP* **5** (1976), 19–50; A. E. Brouwer, *Combinatorics*, edited by Hajnal and Sós, *Colloq. Math. Soc. János Bolyai* **18** (1978), 173–184. Brouwer went on to prove that an $\text{ABD}(2n,n)$ exists for all $n \ge 32$. The method of part (d) also yields an $\text{ABD}(32,15)$ when (13) is combined with (15).

19. By exercise 8, the average number with $8-k$ specified bits is $2^{k-3} f_{8-k}(8,8)/\binom{8}{k}$, which has the respective values $(32, 22, \frac{104}{7}, \frac{69}{7}, \frac{45}{7}, \frac{33}{8}, \frac{73}{28}, \frac{13}{8}, 1) \approx (32, 22, 14.9, 9.9, 6.4, 4.1, 2.6, 1.6, 1)$ for $8 \ge k \ge 0$. These are only slightly higher than the values of $32^{k/8} \approx (32, 20.7, 13.5, 8.7, 5.7, 3.7, 2.4, 1.5, 1)$. The worst-case numbers are $(32, 22, 18, 15, 11, 8, 4, 2, 1)$.

20. J. A. La Poutré [*Disc. Math.* **58** (1986), 205–208] showed that an $\text{ABD}(m,n)$ cannot exist when $m > \binom{n}{2}$ and $n > 3$; therefore no $\text{ABD}(16,6)$ exists. La Poutré and van Lint [*Util. Math.* **31** (1987), 219–225] proved that there is no $\text{ABD}(10,5)$. We get an $\text{ABD}(8,6)$ from an $\text{ABD}(8,5)$ or $\text{ABD}(4,3)$ using the methods of exercise 18; this produces several nonisomorphic solutions, and additional examples of $\text{ABD}(8,6)$ might also exist. The only remaining possibilities (besides the trivial $\text{ABD}(5,5)$ and $\text{ABD}(6,6)$) are $\text{ABD}(8,5)$ distinct from (15), and perhaps one or more $\text{ABD}(12,6)$.

All right — I'm glad we found it out detective fashion;
I wouldn't give shucks for any other way.

— TOM SAWYER (1884)

APPENDIX A

TABLES OF NUMERICAL QUANTITIES

Table 1

QUANTITIES THAT ARE FREQUENTLY USED IN STANDARD SUBROUTINES
AND IN ANALYSIS OF COMPUTER PROGRAMS (40 DECIMAL PLACES)

$$\sqrt{2} = 1.41421\ 35623\ 73095\ 04880\ 16887\ 24209\ 69807\ 85697-$$
$$\sqrt{3} = 1.73205\ 08075\ 68877\ 29352\ 74463\ 41505\ 87236\ 69428+$$
$$\sqrt{5} = 2.23606\ 79774\ 99789\ 69640\ 91736\ 68731\ 27623\ 54406+$$
$$\sqrt{10} = 3.16227\ 76601\ 68379\ 33199\ 88935\ 44432\ 71853\ 37196-$$
$$\sqrt[3]{2} = 1.25992\ 10498\ 94873\ 16476\ 72106\ 07278\ 22835\ 05703-$$
$$\sqrt[3]{3} = 1.44224\ 95703\ 07408\ 38232\ 16383\ 10780\ 10958\ 83919-$$
$$\sqrt[4]{2} = 1.18920\ 71150\ 02721\ 06671\ 74999\ 70560\ 47591\ 52930-$$
$$\ln 2 = 0.69314\ 71805\ 59945\ 30941\ 72321\ 21458\ 17656\ 80755+$$
$$\ln 3 = 1.09861\ 22886\ 68109\ 69139\ 52452\ 36922\ 52570\ 46475-$$
$$\ln 10 = 2.30258\ 50929\ 94045\ 68401\ 79914\ 54684\ 36420\ 76011+$$
$$1/\ln 2 = 1.44269\ 50408\ 88963\ 40735\ 99246\ 81001\ 89213\ 74266+$$
$$1/\ln 10 = 0.43429\ 44819\ 03251\ 82765\ 11289\ 18916\ 60508\ 22944-$$
$$\pi = 3.14159\ 26535\ 89793\ 23846\ 26433\ 83279\ 50288\ 41972-$$
$$1° = \pi/180 = 0.01745\ 32925\ 19943\ 29576\ 92369\ 07684\ 88612\ 71344+$$
$$1/\pi = 0.31830\ 98861\ 83790\ 67153\ 77675\ 26745\ 02872\ 40689+$$
$$\pi^2 = 9.86960\ 44010\ 89358\ 61883\ 44909\ 99876\ 15113\ 53137-$$
$$\sqrt{\pi} = \Gamma(1/2) = 1.77245\ 38509\ 05516\ 02729\ 81674\ 83341\ 14518\ 27975+$$
$$\Gamma(1/3) = 2.67893\ 85347\ 07747\ 63365\ 56929\ 40974\ 67764\ 41287-$$
$$\Gamma(2/3) = 1.35411\ 79394\ 26400\ 41694\ 52880\ 28154\ 51378\ 55193+$$
$$e = 2.71828\ 18284\ 59045\ 23536\ 02874\ 71352\ 66249\ 77572+$$
$$1/e = 0.36787\ 94411\ 71442\ 32159\ 55237\ 70161\ 46086\ 74458+$$
$$e^2 = 7.38905\ 60989\ 30650\ 22723\ 04274\ 60575\ 00781\ 31803+$$
$$\gamma = 0.57721\ 56649\ 01532\ 86060\ 65120\ 90082\ 40243\ 10422-$$
$$\ln \pi = 1.14472\ 98858\ 49400\ 17414\ 34273\ 51353\ 05871\ 16473-$$
$$\phi = 1.61803\ 39887\ 49894\ 84820\ 45868\ 34365\ 63811\ 77203+$$
$$e^\gamma = 1.78107\ 24179\ 90197\ 98523\ 65041\ 03107\ 17954\ 91696+$$
$$e^{\pi/4} = 2.19328\ 00507\ 38015\ 45655\ 97696\ 59278\ 73822\ 34616+$$
$$\sin 1 = 0.84147\ 09848\ 07896\ 50665\ 25023\ 21630\ 29899\ 96226-$$
$$\cos 1 = 0.54030\ 23058\ 68139\ 71740\ 09366\ 07442\ 97660\ 37323+$$
$$-\zeta'(2) = 0.93754\ 82543\ 15843\ 75370\ 25740\ 94567\ 86497\ 78979-$$
$$\zeta(3) = 1.20205\ 69031\ 59594\ 28539\ 97381\ 61511\ 44999\ 07650-$$
$$\ln \phi = 0.48121\ 18250\ 59603\ 44749\ 77589\ 13424\ 36842\ 31352-$$
$$1/\ln \phi = 2.07808\ 69212\ 35027\ 53760\ 13226\ 06117\ 79576\ 77422-$$
$$-\ln \ln 2 = 0.36651\ 29205\ 81664\ 32701\ 24391\ 58232\ 66946\ 94543-$$

Table 2

QUANTITIES THAT ARE FREQUENTLY USED IN STANDARD SUBROUTINES
AND IN ANALYSIS OF COMPUTER PROGRAMS (45 OCTAL PLACES)

The names at the left of the "=" signs are given in decimal notation.

$$
\begin{aligned}
0.1 &= \textit{0.06314 63146 31463 14631 46314 63146 31463 14631 46315}- \\
0.01 &= \textit{0.00507 53412 17270 24365 60507 53412 17270 24365 60510}- \\
0.001 &= \textit{0.00040 61115 64570 65176 76355 44264 16254 02030 44672}+ \\
0.0001 &= \textit{0.00003 21556 13530 70414 54512 75170 33021 15002 35223}- \\
0.00001 &= \textit{0.00000 24761 32610 70664 36041 06077 17401 56063 34417}- \\
0.000001 &= \textit{0.00000 02061 57364 05536 66151 55323 07746 44470 26033}+ \\
0.0000001 &= \textit{0.00000 00153 27745 15274 53644 12741 72312 20354 02151}+ \\
0.00000001 &= \textit{0.00000 00012 57143 56106 04303 47374 77341 01512 63327}+ \\
0.000000001 &= \textit{0.00000 00001 04560 27640 46655 12262 71426 40124 21742}+ \\
0.0000000001 &= \textit{0.00000 00000 06676 33766 35367 55653 37265 34642 01627}-
\end{aligned}
$$

$$
\begin{aligned}
\sqrt{2} &= \textit{1.32404 74631 77167 46220 42627 66115 46725 12575 17435}+ \\
\sqrt{3} &= \textit{1.56663 65641 30231 25163 54453 50265 60361 34073 42223}- \\
\sqrt{5} &= \textit{2.17067 36334 57722 47602 57471 63003 00563 55620 32021}- \\
\sqrt{10} &= \textit{3.12305 40726 64555 22444 02242 57101 41466 33775 22532}+ \\
\sqrt[3]{2} &= \textit{1.20505 05746 15345 05342 10756 65334 25574 22415 03024}+ \\
\sqrt[3]{3} &= \textit{1.34233 50444 22175 73134 67363 76133 05334 31147 60121}- \\
\sqrt[4]{2} &= \textit{1.14067 74050 61556 12455 72152 64430 60271 02755 73136}+ \\
\ln 2 &= \textit{0.54271 02775 75071 73632 57117 07316 30007 71366 53640}+ \\
\ln 3 &= \textit{1.06237 24752 55006 05227 32440 63065 25012 35574 55337}+ \\
\ln 10 &= \textit{2.23273 06735 52524 25405 56512 66542 56026 46050 50705}+ \\
1/\ln 2 &= \textit{1.34252 16624 53405 77027 35750 37766 40644 35175 04353}+ \\
1/\ln 10 &= \textit{0.33626 75425 11562 41614 52325 33525 27655 14756 06220}- \\
\pi &= \textit{3.11037 55242 10264 30215 14230 63050 56006 70163 21122}+ \\
1^\circ = \pi/180 &= \textit{0.01073 72152 11224 72344 25603 54276 63351 22056 11544}+ \\
1/\pi &= \textit{0.24276 30155 62344 20251 23760 47257 50765 15156 70067}- \\
\pi^2 &= \textit{11.67517 14467 62135 71322 25561 15466 30021 40654 34103}- \\
\sqrt{\pi} = \Gamma(1/2) &= \textit{1.61337 61106 64736 65247 47035 40510 15273 34470 17762}- \\
\Gamma(1/3) &= \textit{2.53347 35234 51013 61316 73106 47644 54653 00106 66046}- \\
\Gamma(2/3) &= \textit{1.26523 57112 14154 74312 54572 37655 60126 23231 02452}+ \\
e &= \textit{2.55760 52130 50535 51246 52773 42542 00471 72363 61661}+ \\
1/e &= \textit{0.27426 53066 13167 46761 52726 75436 02440 52371 03355}+ \\
e^2 &= \textit{7.30714 45615 23355 33460 63507 35040 32664 25356 50217}+ \\
\gamma &= \textit{0.44742 14770 67666 06172 23215 74376 01002 51313 25521}- \\
\ln \pi &= \textit{1.11206 40443 47503 36413 65374 52661 52410 37511 46057}+ \\
\phi &= \textit{1.47433 57156 27751 23701 27634 71401 40271 66710 15010}+ \\
e^\gamma &= \textit{1.61772 13452 61152 65761 22477 36553 53327 17554 21260}+ \\
e^{\pi/4} &= \textit{2.14275 31512 16162 52370 35530 11342 53525 44307 02171}- \\
\sin 1 &= \textit{0.65665 24436 04414 73402 03067 23644 11612 07474 14505}- \\
\cos 1 &= \textit{0.42450 50037 32406 42711 07022 14666 27320 70675 12321}+ \\
-\zeta'(2) &= \textit{0.74001 45144 53253 42362 42107 23350 50074 46100 27706}+ \\
\zeta(3) &= \textit{1.14735 00023 60014 20470 15613 42561 31715 10177 06614}+ \\
\ln \phi &= \textit{0.36630 26256 61213 01145 13700 41004 52264 30700 40646}+ \\
1/\ln \phi &= \textit{2.04776 60111 17144 41512 11436 16575 00355 43630 40651}+ \\
-\ln \ln 2 &= \textit{0.27351 71233 67265 63650 17401 56637 26334 31455 57005}-
\end{aligned}
$$

Several interesting constants without common names have arisen in connection with the analyses of sorting and searching algorithms. These constants have been evaluated to 40 decimal places in Eqs. 5.2.3-(19) and 6.5-(6), and in the answers to exercises 5.2.3-27, 5.2.4-13, 5.2.4-23, 6.2.2-49, 6.2.3-7, 6.2.3-8, and 6.3-26.

Table 3

VALUES OF HARMONIC NUMBERS, BERNOULLI NUMBERS,
AND FIBONACCI NUMBERS, FOR SMALL VALUES OF n

n	H_n	B_n	F_n	n
0	0	1	0	0
1	1	$-1/2$	1	1
2	3/2	1/6	1	2
3	11/6	0	2	3
4	25/12	$-1/30$	3	4
5	137/60	0	5	5
6	49/20	1/42	8	6
7	363/140	0	13	7
8	761/280	$-1/30$	21	8
9	7129/2520	0	34	9
10	7381/2520	5/66	55	10
11	83711/27720	0	89	11
12	86021/27720	$-691/2730$	144	12
13	1145993/360360	0	233	13
14	1171733/360360	7/6	377	14
15	1195757/360360	0	610	15
16	2436559/720720	$-3617/510$	987	16
17	42142223/12252240	0	1597	17
18	14274301/4084080	43867/798	2584	18
19	275295799/77597520	0	4181	19
20	55835135/15519504	$-174611/330$	6765	20
21	18858053/5173168	0	10946	21
22	19093197/5173168	854513/138	17711	22
23	444316699/118982864	0	28657	23
24	1347822955/356948592	$-236364091/2730$	46368	24
25	34052522467/8923714800	0	75025	25
26	34395742267/8923714800	8553103/6	121393	26
27	312536252003/80313433200	0	196418	27
28	315404588903/80313433200	$-23749461029/870$	317811	28
29	9227046511387/2329089562800	0	514229	29
30	9304682830147/2329089562800	8615841276005/14322	832040	30

For any x, let $H_x = \sum_{n \geq 1} \left(\dfrac{1}{n} - \dfrac{1}{n+x} \right)$. Then

$$H_{1/2} = 2 - 2\ln 2,$$

$$H_{1/3} = 3 - \tfrac{1}{2}\pi/\sqrt{3} - \tfrac{3}{2}\ln 3,$$

$$H_{2/3} = \tfrac{3}{2} + \tfrac{1}{2}\pi/\sqrt{3} - \tfrac{3}{2}\ln 3,$$

$$H_{1/4} = 4 - \tfrac{1}{2}\pi - 3\ln 2,$$

$$H_{3/4} = \tfrac{4}{3} + \tfrac{1}{2}\pi - 3\ln 2,$$

$$H_{1/5} = 5 - \tfrac{1}{2}\pi\phi^{3/2}5^{-1/4} - \tfrac{5}{4}\ln 5 - \tfrac{1}{2}\sqrt{5}\ln\phi,$$

$$H_{2/5} = \tfrac{5}{2} - \tfrac{1}{2}\pi\phi^{-3/2}5^{-1/4} - \tfrac{5}{4}\ln 5 + \tfrac{1}{2}\sqrt{5}\ln\phi,$$

$$H_{3/5} = \tfrac{5}{3} + \tfrac{1}{2}\pi\phi^{-3/2}5^{-1/4} - \tfrac{5}{4}\ln 5 + \tfrac{1}{2}\sqrt{5}\ln\phi,$$

$$H_{4/5} = \tfrac{5}{4} + \tfrac{1}{2}\pi\phi^{3/2}5^{-1/4} - \tfrac{5}{4}\ln 5 - \tfrac{1}{2}\sqrt{5}\ln\phi,$$

$$H_{1/6} = 6 - \tfrac{1}{2}\pi\sqrt{3} - 2\ln 2 - \tfrac{3}{2}\ln 3,$$

$$H_{5/6} = \tfrac{6}{5} + \tfrac{1}{2}\pi\sqrt{3} - 2\ln 2 - \tfrac{3}{2}\ln 3,$$

and, in general, when $0 < p < q$ (see exercise 1.2.9–19),

$$H_{p/q} = \frac{q}{p} - \frac{\pi}{2}\cot\frac{p}{q}\pi - \ln 2q + 2\sum_{1 \leq n < q/2} \cos\frac{2pn}{q}\pi \cdot \ln\sin\frac{n}{q}\pi.$$

APPENDIX B

INDEX TO NOTATIONS

In the following formulas, letters that are not further qualified have the following significance:

j, k	integer-valued arithmetic expression
m, n	nonnegative integer-valued arithmetic expression
x, y	real-valued arithmetic expression
z	complex-valued arithmetic expression
f	real-valued or complex-valued function
P	pointer-valued expression (either Λ or a computer address)
S, T	set or multiset
α, β	strings of symbols

Formal symbolism	Meaning	Where defined
$V \leftarrow E$	give variable V the value of expression E	1.1
$U \leftrightarrow V$	interchange the values of variables U and V	1.1
A_n or $A[n]$	the nth element of linear array A	1.1
A_{mn} or $A[m, n]$	the element in row m and column n of rectangular array A	1.1
NODE(P)	the node (group of variables that are individually distinguished by their field names) whose address is P, assuming that $\text{P} \neq \Lambda$	2.1
F(P)	the variable in NODE(P) whose field name is F	2.1
CONTENTS(P)	contents of computer word whose address is P	2.1
LOC(V)	address of variable V within a computer	2.1
P $\Leftarrow$ AVAIL	set the value of pointer variable P to the address of a new node	2.2.3
AVAIL $\Leftarrow$ P	return NODE(P) to free storage; all its fields lose their identity	2.2.3
top(S)	node at the top of a nonempty stack S	2.2.1
$X \Leftarrow$ S	pop up S to X: set $X \leftarrow$ top(S); then delete top(S) from nonempty stack S	2.2.1
S $\Leftarrow X$	push down X onto S: insert the value X as a new entry on top of stack S	2.2.1

Formal symbolism	Meaning	Where defined
$(B \Rightarrow E;\ E')$	conditional expression: denotes E if B is true, E' if B is false	
$[B]$	characteristic function of condition B: $$(B \Rightarrow 1;\ 0)$$	1.2.3
δ_{kj}	Kronecker delta: $[j = k]$	1.2.3
$[z^n]\,g(z)$	coefficient of z^n in power series $g(z)$	1.2.9
$\displaystyle\sum_{R(k)} f(k)$	sum of all $f(k)$ such that the variable k is an integer and relation $R(k)$ is true	1.2.3
$\displaystyle\prod_{R(k)} f(k)$	product of all $f(k)$ such that the variable k is an integer and relation $R(k)$ is true	1.2.3
$\displaystyle\min_{R(k)} f(k)$	minimum value of all $f(k)$ such that the variable k is an integer and relation $R(k)$ is true	1.2.3
$\displaystyle\max_{R(k)} f(k)$	maximum value of all $f(k)$ such that the variable k is an integer and relation $R(k)$ is true	1.2.3
$j\backslash k$	j divides k: $k \bmod j = 0$ and $j > 0$	1.2.4
$S \setminus T$	set difference: $\{a \mid a \text{ in } S \text{ and } a \text{ not in } T\}$	
$\gcd(j, k)$	greatest common divisor of j and k: $$\left(j = k = 0 \Rightarrow 0;\ \max_{d\backslash j,\, d\backslash k} d\right)$$	1.1
$j \perp k$	j is relatively prime to k: $\gcd(j, k) = 1$	1.2.4
A^T	transpose of rectangular array A: $$A^T[j, k] = A[k, j]$$	
α^R	left-right reversal of α	
x^y	x to the y power (when x is positive)	1.2.2
x^k	x to the kth power: $$\left(k \geq 0 \Rightarrow \prod_{0 \leq j < k} x;\ 1/x^{-k}\right)$$	1.2.2
$x^{\bar{k}}$	x to the k rising: $\Gamma(x + k)/\Gamma(x) =$ $$\left(k \geq 0 \Rightarrow \prod_{0 \leq j < k} (x + j);\ 1/(x + k)^{\overline{-k}}\right)$$	1.2.5
$x^{\underline{k}}$	x to the k falling: $x!/(x - k)! =$ $$\left(k \geq 0 \Rightarrow \prod_{0 \leq j < k} (x - j);\ 1/(x - k)^{\underline{-k}}\right)$$	1.2.5

Formal symbolism	Meaning	Where defined
$n!$	n factorial: $\Gamma(n+1) = n^{\underline{n}}$	1.2.5
$\binom{x}{k}$	binomial coefficient: $(k < 0 \Rightarrow 0;\; x^{\underline{k}}/k!)$	1.2.6
$\binom{n}{n_1, n_2, \ldots, n_m}$	multinomial coefficient (defined only when $n = n_1 + n_2 + \cdots + n_m$)	1.2.6
$\left[\begin{matrix} n \\ m \end{matrix} \right]$	Stirling number of the first kind: $$\sum_{0 < k_1 < k_2 < \cdots < k_{n-m} < n} k_1 k_2 \ldots k_{n-m}$$	1.2.6
$\left\{ \begin{matrix} n \\ m \end{matrix} \right\}$	Stirling number of the second kind: $$\sum_{1 \le k_1 \le k_2 \le \cdots \le k_{n-m} \le m} k_1 k_2 \ldots k_{n-m}$$	1.2.6
$\{a \mid R(a)\}$	set of all a such that the relation $R(a)$ is true	
$\{a_1, \ldots, a_n\}$	the set or multiset $\{a_k \mid 1 \le k \le n\}$	
$\{x\}$	fractional part (used in contexts where a real value, not a set, is implied): $x - \lfloor x \rfloor$	1.2.11.2
$[a \mathbin{..} b]$	closed interval: $\{x \mid a \le x \le b\}$	1.2.2
$(a \mathbin{..} b)$	open interval: $\{x \mid a < x < b\}$	1.2.2
$[a \mathbin{..} b)$	half-open interval: $\{x \mid a \le x < b\}$	1.2.2
$(a \mathbin{..} b]$	half-closed interval: $\{x \mid a < x \le b\}$	1.2.2
$|S|$	cardinality: the number of elements in set S	
$|x|$	absolute value of x: $(x \ge 0 \Rightarrow x;\; -x)$	
$|\alpha|$	length of α	
$\lfloor x \rfloor$	floor of x, greatest integer function: $\max_{k \le x} k$	1.2.4
$\lceil x \rceil$	ceiling of x, least integer function: $\min_{k \ge x} k$	1.2.4
$x \bmod y$	mod function: $\big(y = 0 \Rightarrow x;\; x - y\lfloor x/y \rfloor\big)$	1.2.4
$x \equiv x' \pmod{y}$	relation of congruence: $x \bmod y = x' \bmod y$	1.2.4
$O\big(f(n)\big)$	big-oh of $f(n)$, as the variable $n \to \infty$	1.2.11.1
$O\big(f(z)\big)$	big-oh of $f(z)$, as the variable $z \to 0$	1.2.11.1
$\Omega\big(f(n)\big)$	big-omega of $f(n)$, as the variable $n \to \infty$	1.2.11.1
$\Theta\big(f(n)\big)$	big-theta of $f(n)$, as the variable $n \to \infty$	1.2.11.1

Formal symbolism	Meaning	Where defined
$\log_b x$	logarithm, base b, of x (when $x > 0$, $b > 0$, and $b \neq 1$): the y such that $x = b^y$	1.2.2
$\ln x$	natural logarithm: $\log_e x$	1.2.2
$\lg x$	binary logarithm: $\log_2 x$	1.2.2
$\exp x$	exponential of x: e^x	1.2.9
$\langle X_n \rangle$	the infinite sequence $X_0, X_1, X_2, \ldots$ (here the letter n is part of the symbolism)	1.2.9
$f'(x)$	derivative of f at x	1.2.9
$f''(x)$	second derivative of f at x	1.2.10
$f^{(n)}(x)$	nth derivative: $\big(n = 0 \Rightarrow f(x);\ g'(x)\big)$, where $g(x) = f^{(n-1)}(x)$	1.2.11.2
$H_n^{(x)}$	harmonic number of order x: $\sum_{1 \leq k \leq n} 1/k^x$	1.2.7
H_n	harmonic number: $H_n^{(1)}$	1.2.7
F_n	Fibonacci number: $(n \leq 1 \Rightarrow n;\ F_{n-1} + F_{n-2})$	1.2.8
B_n	Bernoulli number: $n!\,[z^n]\,z/(e^z - 1)$	1.2.11.2
$\det(A)$	determinant of square matrix A	1.2.3
$\text{sign}(x)$	sign of x: $[x > 0] - [x < 0]$	
$\zeta(x)$	zeta function: $\lim_{n \to \infty} H_n^{(x)}$ (when $x > 1$)	1.2.7
$\Gamma(x)$	gamma function: $(x - 1)! = \gamma(x, \infty)$	1.2.5
$\gamma(x, y)$	incomplete gamma function: $\int_0^y e^{-t} t^{x-1}\, dt$	1.2.11.3
γ	Euler's constant: $\lim_{n \to \infty}(H_n - \ln n)$	1.2.7
e	base of natural logarithms: $\sum_{n \geq 0} 1/n!$	1.2.2
π	circle ratio: $4\sum_{n \geq 0}(-1)^n/(2n + 1)$	1.2.2
∞	infinity: larger than any number	
Λ	null link (pointer to no address)	2.1
ϵ	empty string (string of length zero)	
$\emptyset$	empty set (set with no elements)	
ϕ	golden ratio: $\frac{1}{2}\big(1 + \sqrt{5}\big)$	1.2.8
$\varphi(n)$	Euler's totient function: $\sum_{0 \leq k < n} [k \perp n]$	1.2.4
$x \approx y$	x is approximately equal to y	1.2.5

Formal symbolism	Meaning	Where defined
$\Pr(S(X))$	probability that statement $S(X)$ is true, for random values of X	1.2.10
$\mathrm{E}\,X$	expected value of X: $\sum_x x \Pr(X = x)$	1.2.10
$\mathrm{mean}(g)$	mean value of the probability distribution represented by generating function g: $g'(1)$	1.2.10
$\mathrm{var}(g)$	variance of the probability distribution represented by generating function g: $$g''(1) + g'(1) - g'(1)^2$$	1.2.10
$(\min x_1, \text{ave } x_2, \max x_3, \text{dev } x_4)$	a random variable having minimum value x_1, average (expected) value x_2, maximum value x_3, standard deviation x_4	1.2.10
$\Re z$	real part of z	1.2.2
$\Im z$	imaginary part of z	1.2.2
$\bar{z}$	complex conjugate: $\Re z - i\,\Im z$	1.2.2
$(\dots a_1 a_0 . a_{-1} \dots)_b$	radix-b positional notation: $\sum_k a_k b^k$	4.1
$/\!/x_1, x_2, \dots, x_n/\!/$	continued fraction: $$1/\bigl(x_1 + 1/(x_2 + 1/(\cdots + 1/(x_n)\dots)))$$	4.5.3
$\alpha \top \beta$	intercalation product	5.1.2
$S \uplus T$	multiset sum; e.g., $\{a, b\} \uplus \{a, c\} = \{a, a, b, c\}$	4.6.3
$f(x)\big|_a^b$	function growth: $f(b) - f(a)$	
∎	end of algorithm, program, or proof	1.1
␣	one blank space	1.3.1
rA	register A (accumulator) of MIX	1.3.1
rX	register X (extension) of MIX	1.3.1
rI1, $\dots$, rI6	(index) registers I1, $\dots$, I6 of MIX	1.3.1
rJ	(jump) register J of MIX	1.3.1
(L:R)	partial field of MIX word, $0 \le \text{L} \le \text{R} \le 5$	1.3.1
OP ADDRESS,I(F)	notation for MIX instruction	1.3.1, 1.3.2
u	unit of time in MIX	1.3.1
*	"self" in MIXAL	1.3.2
0F, 1F, 2F, $\dots$, 9F	"forward" local symbol in MIXAL	1.3.2
0B, 1B, 2B, $\dots$, 9B	"backward" local symbol in MIXAL	1.3.2
0H, 1H, 2H, $\dots$, 9H	"here" local symbol in MIXAL	1.3.2

INDEX TO ALGORITHMS AND THEOREMS

One of my mathematician friends told me he would be willing
to recognize computer science as a worthwhile field of study
as soon as it contains 1,000 deep theorems.
This criterion should obviously be changed to include algorithms
as well as theorems — say 500 deep theorems and 500 deep algorithms.
But even so, it is clear that computer science today doesn't measure up
to such a test, if "deep" means that a brilliant person would need
many months to discover the theorem or the algorithm.
... The potential for "1,000 deep results" is there,
but only perhaps 50 have been discovered so far.

— DONALD E. KNUTH, *Computer Science and Mathematics* (1973)

INDEX AND GLOSSARY

*If you don't find it in the Index,
look very carefully through the entire catalogue.*
— SEARS, ROEBUCK AND CO., *Consumers Guide* (1897)

When an index entry refers to a page containing a relevant exercise, see also the *answer* to that exercise for further information. An answer page is not indexed here unless it refers to a topic not included in the statement of the exercise.

$-\infty$, 4, 142–144, 156, 214, 663–664, 685, 707.
0–1 matrices, 660.
0–1 principle, 223, 224, 245, 667, 668.
1/3–2/3 conjecture, 197.
2-3 trees, 476–477, 480, 483, 715.
$(2,4)$-trees, 477.
2-d trees, 565.
2-descending sequence, 451.
2-ordered permutations, 86–88, 103, 112–113, 134.
80-20 rule, 400–401, 405, 456.
∞, 4, 138–139, 257–258, 263, 521, 624–625, 646.
  as sentinel, 159, 252, 308, 324.
$\zeta(x)$ (number of 0s), 235; *see also* Zeta function.
$\nu(x)$ (number of 1s), 235, 643, 644, 717.
π (circle ratio), 372, 520, 748–749.
  as "random" example, 17, 370, 385, 547, 552, 733.
ϕ (golden ratio), xiv, 138, 517–518, 748–749.

(a, b)-trees, 477.
Abbreviated keys, 512, 551.
Abel, Niels Henrik, binomial formula, 552.
  limit theorem, 740.
Abraham, Chacko Thakadiparambil, 578.
Absorption laws, 239.
Adaptive sorting, 389.
Addition of apples to oranges, 401.
Addition of polynomials, 165.
Addition to a list, *see* Insertion.
Address calculation sorting, 99–102, 104–105, 176–177, 380, 389, 698.
Address table sorting, 74–75, 80.
Adelson-Velsky, Georgii Maximovich (Адельсон-Вельский, Георгий Максимович), 459, 460.
Adjacent transpositions, 13, 240, 403, 404, 640, 668.
Adversaries, 198–202, 205–207, 209–210, 218, 671.
AF-heaps, 152.
Agarwal, Ramesh Chandra (रमेश चन्द्र अग्रवाल), 359, 389.
Agenda, *see* Priority queue.
Aggarwal, Alok (आलोक अग्रवाल), 698.

Aho, Alfred Vaino, 476, 479, 652.
Aigner, Martin, 241.
Airy, George Biddle, function, 611.
Ajtai, Miklós, 228, 673, 740.
al-Khwārizmī, Abū 'Abd Allāh Muḥammad ibn Mūsā (أبو عبد الله محمد بن موسى الخوارزمي), 8.
Aldous, David John, 728.
Alekseev, Vladimir Evgenievich (Алексеев, Владимир Евгеньевич), 232, 233, 237, 238.
Alexanderson, Gerald Lee, 599.
ALGOL language, 454.
Algorithms, analysis of, *see* Analysis.
  comparison of, *see* Comparison.
  proof of, *see* Proof.
Allen, Brian Richard, 478.
Allen, Charles Grant Blairfindie, 558.
Alphabetic binary encoding, 452–454.
Alphabetic order, 7, 420–421, 453.
Altenkamp, Doris, 713.
Alternating runs, 46, 607.
Amble, Ole, 556.
Amdahl, Gene Myron, 547.
American Library Association rules, 7–8.
AMM: American Mathematical Monthly, published by the Mathematical Association of America since 1894.
Amortized cost, 478, 549.
Amphisbaenic sort, 347, 388.
Anagrams, 9, *see also* Permutations of a multiset.
Analysis of algorithms, 3, 77–78, 80, 82, 85–95, 100–105, 108–109, 118–122, 140, 152–158, 161–162, 167–168, 174–177, 185–186, 255–256, 259–266, 274–279, 285–287, 294–299, 330–335, 339–343, 379, 382, 387–388, 397–408, 412–413, 424–425, 430–431, 454–458, 466–471, 479–480, 485–486, 490, 500–512, 524–525, 534–539, 543–544, 552–557, 565–566, 576, 619, *see also* Complexity analysis.
Analytical Engine, 180.
AND (bitwise and), 111, 134, 531, 589, 592, 629.
André, Antoine Désiré, 68, 605.
Anti-stable sorting, 347, 615, 650.
Antisymmetric function, 66.

759

Concave functions, 443, 456, 458.
Concurrent access, 491.
Conditional expressions, 753.
Connected graphs, 189, 733, 742.
Consecutive retrieval, 567, 579.
Convex functions, 366, 375.
Convex hulls, 478, 670.
Cookies, 567–571, 577.
Coordinates, 564–566.
Copyrights, iv, 387.
Corless, Robert Malcolm, 606.
Cormen, Thomas H., 477.
Coroutines, 259.
Cotangent, 194.
Counting, sorting by, 75–80.
Covering, 235.
Coxeter, Harold Scott MacDonald, 593.
Cramer, Gabriel, 11.
Cramer, Michael, 650.
Crane, Clark Allan, 149–150, 152, 474,
    475, 479, 716.
*Crelle: Journal für die reine und angewandte
    Mathematik*, an international journal
    founded by A. L. Crelle in 1826.
Criss-cross merge, 312–315, 317.
Cross-indexing, *see* Secondary key retrieval.
Cross-reference routine, 7.
Crossword-puzzle dictionary, 573.
Cube, *n*-dimensional, linearized, 408.
Culberson, Joseph Carl, 435.
Culler, David Ethan, 390.
Cundy, Henry Martyn, 593.
Cunto Pucci, Walter, 218.
Curtis, Pavel, 251.
Cycles of a permutation, 25–32, 62, 156,
    617, 628, 639–640, 657.
Cyclic occupancy problem, 379.
Cyclic rotation of data, 619.
Cyclic single hashing, 556–557.
Cylinders of a disk, 357, 376, 482, 489, 562.
Cypher, Robert Edward, 623.
Czech, Zbigniew Janusz, 513.
Czen Ping (成平), 186.

Daly, Lloyd William, 421.
Dannenberg, Roger Berry, 583.
Data compression, 453, 512.
Data structure, choice of, 95–96, 141,
    151–152, 163–164, 170–171, 459,
    561–567.
Database, 392.
David, Florence Nightingale, 44, 602, 605.
Davidson, Leon, 395.
Davies, Donald Watts, 388.
Davis, David Robert, 578.
Davison, Gerald A., 152.
de Balbine, Guy, 528.
de Bruijn, Nicolaas Govert, 130, 138,
    602, 668, 670, 671, 744.
de la Briandais, René Edward, 494.

de Peyster, James Abercrombie, Jr., 544.
de Staël, Madame, *see* Staël-Holstein.
Deadlines, 407.
Deadlocks, 721.
Debugging, 520.
Decision trees, 181–182, 192–197, 217,
    219–220, 411–417, 443–444.
Dedekind, Julius Wilhelm Richard, 239.
    sums, 20.
Degenerate trees, 430, 454, 711.
Degenerative addresses, 547.
Degree path length, 363–367.
Degrees of freedom, 258–259.
Deift, Percy Alec, 611.
Deletion: Removing an item.
    from a *B*-tree, 490.
    from a balanced tree, 473, 479.
    from a binary search tree, 431–435,
        455, 458.
    from a digital search trees, 508.
    from a hash table, 533–534, 548–549,
        552, 556, 741.
    from a heap, 157.
    from a leftist tree, 158.
    from a multidimensional tree, 581.
    from a trie, 507.
Demuth, Howard B., 109, 184, 246, 348,
    353, 387, 388, 676.
Den, Vladimir Eduardovich (День,
    Владимир Эдуардович), 7.
Denert, Marlene, 596.
Dent, Warren Thomas, 455.
Derangements, 679.
Derr, John Irving, 547.
Descents of a permutation, 35, 46, 47, 606.
Determinants, 11, 14, 19, 33–34.
    Vandermonde, 59, 610, 729.
Deutsch, David Nachman, 204.
Devroye, Luc Piet-Jan Arthur, 565,
    713, 721, 728.
Diaconis, Persi Warren, 597.
Diagram of a partial order, 61–62,
    183–184, 187.
Dictionaries of English, 1–2, 421, 558, 589.
Dictionary order, 5.
Dietzfelbinger, Martin Johannes, 549.
Digital search trees, 502–505, 508–511,
    576, 646.
    optimum, 511.
Digital searching, 492–512.
Digital sorting, 169, 343, *see* Radix sorting.
Digital tree search, 496–498, 517, 546–547.
Dijkstra, Edsger Wybe, 636.
Dilcher, Karl Heinrich, 726.
Diminishing increment sort, 84.
Dinsmore, Robert Johe, 258.
Direct-access memory, 356, *see* Disk storage.
Direct sum of graphs, 189–191.
Directed graphs, 9, 61–62, 184.
Discrete entropy, 374–375.
Discrete logarithms, 10.
Discrete system simulation, 149.

> *Although you may pass for*
> *an artist, computist, or analyst,*
> *yet you may not be justly esteemed*
> *a man of science.*
> — GEORGE BERKELEY, *The Analyst* (1734)

THIS BOOK was composed on a Sun SPARCstation with Computer Modern typefaces, using the TEX and METAFONT software as described in the author's books *Computers & Typesetting* (Reading, Mass.: Addison–Wesley, 1986), Volumes A–E. The illustrations were produced with John Hobby's METAPOST system. Some names in the index were typeset with additional fonts developed by Yannis Haralambous (Greek, Hebrew, Arabic), Olga G. Lapko (Cyrillic), Frans J. Velthuis (Devanagari), Masatoshi Watanabe (Japanese), and Linbo Zhang (Chinese).

Character code:

00	01	02	03	04	05	06	07	08	09	10	11	12	13	14	15	16	17	18	19	20	21	22	23	24
␣	A	B	C	D	E	F	G	H	I	Δ	J	K	L	M	N	O	P	Q	R	Σ	Π	S	T	U

00	*1*	**01**	*2*	**02**	*2*	**03**	*10*
No operation		rA ← rA + V		rA ← rA − V		rAX ← rA × V	
NOP(0)		ADD(0:5) FADD(6)		SUB(0:5) FSUB(6)		MUL(0:5) FMUL(6)	

08	*2*	**09**	*2*	**10**	*2*	**11**	*2*
rA ← V		rI1 ← V		rI2 ← V		rI3 ← V	
LDA(0:5)		LD1(0:5)		LD2(0:5)		LD3(0:5)	

16	*2*	**17**	*2*	**18**	*2*	**19**	*2*
rA ← −V		rI1 ← −V		rI2 ← −V		rI3 ← −V	
LDAN(0:5)		LD1N(0:5)		LD2N(0:5)		LD3N(0:5)	

24	*2*	**25**	*2*	**26**	*2*	**27**	*2*
M(F) ← rA		M(F) ← rI1		M(F) ← rI2		M(F) ← rI3	
STA(0:5)		ST1(0:5)		ST2(0:5)		ST3(0:5)	

32	*2*	**33**	*2*	**34**	*1*	**35**	*1 + T*
M(F) ← rJ		M(F) ← 0		Unit F busy?		Control, unit F	
STJ(0:2)		STZ(0:5)		JBUS(0)		IOC(0)	

40	*1*	**41**	*1*	**42**	*1*	**43**	*1*
rA : 0, jump		rI1 : 0, jump		rI2 : 0, jump		rI3 : 0, jump	
JA[+]		J1[+]		J2[+]		J3[+]	

48	*1*	**49**	*1*	**50**	*1*	**51**	*1*
rA ← [rA]? ± M		rI1 ← [rI1]? ± M		rI2 ← [rI2]? ± M		rI3 ← [rI3]? ± M	
INCA(0) DECA(1) ENTA(2) ENNA(3)		INC1(0) DEC1(1) ENT1(2) ENN1(3)		INC2(0) DEC2(1) ENT2(2) ENN2(3)		INC3(0) DEC3(1) ENT3(2) ENN3(3)	

56	*2*	**57**	*2*	**58**	*2*	**59**	*2*
CI ← rA(F) : V		CI ← rI1(F) : V		CI ← rI2(F) : V		CI ← rI3(F) : V	
CMPA(0:5) FCMP(6)		CMP1(0:5)		CMP2(0:5)		CMP3(0:5)	

General form:

C	t
Description	
OP(F)	

C = operation code, (5 : 5) field of instruction
F = op variant, (4 : 4) field of instruction
M = address of instruction after indexing
V = M(F) = contents of F field of location M
OP = symbolic name for operation
(F) = normal F setting
t = execution time; T = interlock time

THE ART OF
COMPUTER PROGRAMMING

DONALD E. KNUTH *Stanford University*

ADDISON–WESLEY

Volume 4A / **Combinatorial Algorithms, Part 1**

THE ART OF
COMPUTER PROGRAMMING

Upper Saddle River, NJ · Boston · Indianapolis · San Francisco
New York · Toronto · Montréal · London · Munich · Paris · Madrid
Capetown · Sydney · Tokyo · Singapore · Mexico City

The poem on page 437 is quoted from *The Golden Gate* by Vikram Seth (New York: Random House, 1986), copyright © 1986 by Vikram Seth.

The publisher offers excellent discounts on this book when ordered in quantity for bulk purposes or special sales, which may include electronic versions and/or custom covers and content particular to your business, training goals, marketing focus, and branding interests. For more information, please contact:

    U.S. Corporate and Government Sales   (800) 382-3419
    `corpsales@pearsontechgroup.com`

For sales outside the U.S., please contact:

    International Sales   `international@pearsoned.com`

Visit us on the Web: `informit.com/aw`

Library of Congress Cataloging-in-Publication Data

```
Knuth, Donald Ervin, 1938-
  The art of computer programming / Donald Ervin Knuth.
  xvi,883 p. 24 cm.
  Includes bibliographical references and index.
  Contents: v. 1. Fundamental algorithms. -- v. 2. Seminumerical
algorithms. -- v. 3. Sorting and searching. -- v. 4a. Combinatorial
algorithms, part 1.
  Contents: v. 4a. Combinatorial algorithms, part 1.
  ISBN 978-0-201-89683-1 (v. 1, 3rd ed.)
  ISBN 978-0-201-89684-8 (v. 2, 3rd ed.)
  ISBN 978-0-201-89685-5 (v. 3, 2nd ed.)
  ISBN 978-0-201-03804-0 (v. 4a)
  1. Electronic digital computers--Programming.  2. Computer
algorithms.   I. Title.
QA76.6.K64   1997
005.1--DC21                                          97-2147
```

Internet page `http://www-cs-faculty.stanford.edu/~knuth/taocp.html` contains current information about this book and related books.

See also `http://www-cs-faculty.stanford.edu/~knuth/sgb.html` for information about *The Stanford GraphBase*, including downloadable software for dealing with the graphs used in many of the examples.

And see `http://www-cs-faculty.stanford.edu/~knuth/mmix.html` for basic information about the MMIX computer.

ISBN-13 978-0-201-03804-0
ISBN-10   0-201-03804-8

Text printed in the United States at Courier Westford in Westford, Massachusetts.
Third printing, January 2012

PREFACE

To put all the good stuff into one book is patently impossible,
and attempting even to be reasonably comprehensive
about certain aspects of the subject is likely to lead to runaway growth.
— GERALD B. FOLLAND, "Editor's Corner" (2005)

THE TITLE of Volume 4 is *Combinatorial Algorithms*, and when I proposed it I was strongly inclined to add a subtitle: *The Kind of Programming I Like Best.* My editors have decided to tone down such exuberance, but the fact remains that programs with a combinatorial flavor have always been my favorites.

On the other hand I've often been surprised to find that, in many people's minds, the word "combinatorial" is linked with computational difficulty. Indeed, Samuel Johnson, in his famous dictionary of the English language (1755), said that the corresponding noun "is now generally used in an ill sense." Colleagues tell me tales of woe, in which they report that "the combinatorics of the situation defeated us." Why is it that, for me, combinatorics arouses feelings of pure pleasure, yet for many others it evokes pure panic?

It's true that combinatorial problems are often associated with humongously large numbers. Johnson's dictionary entry also included a quote from Ephraim Chambers, who had stated that the total number of words of length 24 or less, in a 24-letter alphabet, is 1,391,724,288,887,252,999,425,128,493,402,200. The corresponding number for a 10-letter alphabet is 11,111,111,110; and it's only 3905 when the number of letters is 5. Thus a "combinatorial explosion" certainly does occur as the size of the problem grows from 5 to 10 to 24 and beyond.

Computing machines have become tremendously more powerful throughout my life. As I write these words, I know that they are being processed by a "laptop" whose speed is more than 100,000 times faster than the trusty IBM Type 650 computer to which I've dedicated these books; my current machine's memory capacity is also more than 100,000 times greater. Tomorrow's computers will be even faster and more capacious. But these amazing advances have not diminished people's craving for answers to combinatorial questions; quite the contrary. Our once-unimaginable ability to compute so rapidly has raised our expectations, and whetted our appetite for more — because, in fact, the size of a combinatorial problem can increase more than 100,000-fold when n simply increases by 1.

Combinatorial algorithms can be defined informally as techniques for the high-speed manipulation of combinatorial objects such as permutations or graphs. We typically try to find patterns or arrangements that are the best possible ways to satisfy certain constraints. The number of such problems is vast, and the art of writing such programs is especially important and appealing because a single good idea can save years or even centuries of computer time.

Indeed, the fact that good algorithms for combinatorial problems can have a terrific payoff has led to terrific advances in the state of the art. Many problems that once were thought to be intractable can now be polished off with ease, and many algorithms that once were known to be good have now become better. Starting about 1970, computer scientists began to experience a phenomenon that we called "Floyd's Lemma": Problems that seemed to need n^3 operations could actually be solved in $O(n^2)$; problems that seemed to require n^2 could be handled in $O(n \log n)$; and $n \log n$ was often reducible to $O(n)$. More difficult problems saw a reduction in running time from $O(2^n)$ to $O(1.5^n)$ to $O(1.3^n)$, etc. Other problems remained difficult in general, but they were found to have important special cases that are much simpler. Many combinatorial questions that I once thought would never be answered during my lifetime have now been resolved, and those breakthroughs have been due mainly to improvements in algorithms rather than to improvements in processor speeds.

By 1975, such research was advancing so rapidly that a substantial fraction of the papers published in leading journals of computer science were devoted to combinatorial algorithms. And the advances weren't being made only by people in the core of computer science; significant contributions were coming from workers in electrical engineering, artificial intelligence, operations research, mathematics, physics, statistics, and other fields. I was trying to complete Volume 4 of *The Art of Computer Programming*, but instead I felt like I was sitting on the lid of a boiling kettle: I was confronted with a combinatorial explosion of another kind, a prodigious explosion of new ideas!

This series of books was born at the beginning of 1962, when I naïvely wrote out a list of tentative chapter titles for a 12-chapter book. At that time I decided to include a brief chapter about combinatorial algorithms, just for fun. "Hey look, most people use computers to deal with numbers, but we can also write programs that deal with patterns." In those days it was easy to give a fairly complete description of just about every combinatorial algorithm that was known. And even by 1966, when I'd finished a first draft of about 3000 handwritten pages for that already-overgrown book, fewer than 100 of those pages belonged to Chapter 7. I had absolutely no idea that what I'd foreseen as a sort of "salad course" would eventually turn out to be the main dish.

The great combinatorial fermentation of 1975 has continued to churn, as more and more people have begun to participate. New ideas improve upon the older ones, but rarely replace them or make them obsolete. So of course I've had to abandon any hopes that I once had of being able to surround the field, to write a definitive book that sets everything in order and provides one-stop shopping for everyone who has combinatorial problems to solve. The array of applicable techniques has mushroomed to the point where I can almost never discuss a subtopic and say, "Here's the final solution: end of story." Instead, I must restrict myself to explaining the most important principles that seem to underlie all of the efficient combinatorial methods that I've encountered so far.

At present I've accumulated more than twice as much raw material for Volume 4 as for all of Volumes 1–3 combined.

This sheer mass of material implies that the once-planned "Volume 4" must actually become several physical volumes. You are now looking at Volume 4A. Volumes 4B and 4C will exist someday, assuming that I'm able to remain healthy; and (who knows?) there may also be Volumes 4D, 4E, ... ; but surely not 4Z.

My plan is to go systematically through the files that I've amassed since 1962 and to tell the stories that I believe are still waiting to be told, to the best of my ability. I can't aspire to completeness, but I do want to give proper credit to all of the pioneers who have been responsible for key ideas; so I won't scrimp on historical details. Furthermore, whenever I learn something that I think is likely to remain important 50 years from now, something that can also be explained elegantly in a paragraph or two, I can't bear to leave it out. Conversely, difficult material that requires a lengthy proof is beyond the scope of these books, unless the subject matter is truly fundamental.

OK, it's clear that the field of Combinatorial Algorithms is vast, and I can't cover it all. What are the most important things that I'm leaving out? My biggest blind spot, I think, is geometry, because I've always been much better at visualizing and manipulating algebraic formulas than objects in space. Therefore I don't attempt to deal in these books with combinatorial problems that are related to computational geometry, such as close packing of spheres, or clustering of data points in n-dimensional Euclidean space, or even the Steiner tree problem in the plane. More significantly, I tend to shy away from polyhedral combinatorics, and from approaches that are based primarily on linear programming, integer programming, or semidefinite programming. Those topics are treated well in many other books on the subject, and they rely on geometrical intuition. Purely combinatorial developments are easier for me to understand.

I also must confess a bias against algorithms that are efficient only in an asymptotic sense, algorithms whose superior performance doesn't begin to "kick in" until the size of the problem exceeds the size of the universe. A great many publications nowadays are devoted to algorithms of that kind. I can understand why the contemplation of ultimate limits has intellectual appeal and carries an academic cachet; but in *The Art of Computer Programming* I tend to give short shrift to any methods that I would never consider using myself in an actual program. (There are, of course, exceptions to this rule, especially with respect to basic concepts in the core of the subject. Some impractical methods are simply too beautiful and/or too insightful to be excluded; others provide instructive examples of what *not* to do.)

Furthermore, as in earlier volumes of this series, I'm intentionally concentrating almost entirely on *sequential* algorithms, even though computers are increasingly able to carry out activities in parallel. I'm unable to judge what ideas about parallelism are likely to be useful five or ten years from now, let alone fifty, so I happily leave such questions to others who are wiser than I. Sequential methods, by themselves, already test the limits of my own ability to discern what the artful programmers of tomorrow will want to know.

The main decision that I needed to make when planning how to present this material was whether to organize it by problems or by techniques. Chapter 5 in Volume 3, for example, was devoted to a single problem, the sorting of data into order; more than two dozen techniques were applied to different aspects of that problem. Combinatorial algorithms, by contrast, involve many different problems, which tend to be attacked with a smaller repertoire of techniques. I finally decided that a mixed strategy would work better than any pure approach. Thus, for example, these books treat the problem of finding shortest paths in Section 7.3, and problems of connectivity in Section 7.4.1; but many other sections are devoted to basic techniques, such as the use of Boolean algebra (Section 7.1), backtracking (Section 7.2.2), matroid theory (Section 7.6), or dynamic programming (Section 7.7). The famous Traveling Salesrep Problem, and other classic combinatorial tasks related to covering, coloring, and packing, have no sections of their own, but they come up several times in different places as they are treated by different methods.

I've mentioned great progress in the art of combinatorial computing, but I don't mean to imply that all combinatorial problems have actually been tamed. When the running time of a computer program goes ballistic, its programmers shouldn't expect to find a silver bullet for their needs in this book. The methods described here will often work a great deal faster than the first approaches that a programmer tries; but let's face it: Combinatorial problems get huge very quickly. We can even prove rigorously that a certain small, natural problem will *never* have a feasible solution in the real world, although it is solvable in principle (see the theorem of Stockmeyer and Meyer in Section 7.1.2). In other cases we cannot prove as yet that no decent algorithm for a given problem exists, but we know that such methods are unlikely, because any efficient algorithm would yield a good way to solve thousands of other problems that have stumped the world's greatest experts (see the discussion of NP-completeness in Section 7.9).

Experience suggests that new combinatorial algorithms will continue to be invented, for new combinatorial problems and for newly identified variations or special cases of old ones; and that people's appetite for such algorithms will also continue to grow. The art of computer programming continually reaches new heights when programmers are faced with challenges such as these. Yet today's methods are also likely to remain relevant.

Most of this book is self-contained, although there are frequent tie-ins with the topics discussed in Volumes 1–3. Low-level details of machine language programming have been covered extensively in those volumes, so the algorithms in the present book are usually specified only at an abstract level, independent of any machine. However, some aspects of combinatorial programming are heavily dependent on low-level details that didn't arise before; in such cases, all examples in this book are based on the MMIX computer, which supersedes the MIX machine that was defined in early editions of Volume 1. Details about MMIX appear in a paperback supplement to that volume called *The Art of Computer Programming*, Volume 1, Fascicle 1, containing Sections 1.3.1′, 1.3.2′, etc.; they're also available on the Internet, together with downloadable assemblers and simulators.

Another downloadable resource, a collection of programs and data called *The Stanford GraphBase*, is cited extensively in the examples of this book. Readers are encouraged to play with it, in order to learn about combinatorial algorithms in what I think will be the most efficient and most enjoyable way.

Incidentally, while writing the introductory material at the beginning of Chapter 7, I was pleased to note that it was natural to mention some work of my Ph.D. thesis advisor, Marshall Hall, Jr. (1910–1990), as well as some work of *his* thesis advisor, Oystein Ore (1899–1968), as well as some work of *his* thesis advisor, Thoralf Skolem (1887–1963). Skolem's advisor, Axel Thue (1863–1922), was already present in Chapter 6.

I'm immensely grateful to the hundreds of readers who have helped me to ferret out numerous mistakes that I made in the early drafts of this volume, which were originally posted on the Internet and subsequently printed in paperback fascicles. In particular, the extensive comments of Thorsten Dahlheimer, Marc van Leeuwen, and Udo Wermuth have been especially influential. But I fear that other errors still lurk among the details collected here, and I want to correct them as soon as possible. Therefore I will cheerfully award $2.56 to the first finder of each technical, typographical, or historical error. The taocp webpage cited on page iv contains a current listing of all corrections that have been reported to me.

Stanford, California   D. E. K.
October 2010

> *In my preface to the first edition,*
> *I begged the reader not to draw attention to errors.*
> *I now wish I had not done so*
> *and am grateful to the few readers who ignored my request.*
> — STUART SUTHERLAND, *The International Dictionary of Psychology* (1996)

> *Naturally, I am responsible for the remaining errors—*
> *although, in my opinion, my friends could have caught a few more.*
> — CHRISTOS H. PAPADIMITRIOU, *Computational Complexity* (1994)

> *I like to work in a variety of fields*
> *in order to spread my mistakes more thinly.*
> — VICTOR KLEE (1999)

A note on references. Several oft-cited journals and conference proceedings have special code names, which appear in the Index and Glossary at the close of this book. But the various kinds of *IEEE Transactions* are cited by including a letter code for the type of transactions, in boldface preceding the volume number. For example, '*IEEE Trans.* **C-35**' means the *IEEE Transactions on Computers*, volume 35. The IEEE no longer uses these convenient letter codes, but the codes aren't too hard to decipher: '**EC**' once stood for "Electronic Computers," '**IT**' for "Information Theory," '**SE**' for "Software Engineering," and '**SP**' for "Signal Processing," etc.; '**CAD**' meant "Computer-Aided Design of Integrated Circuits and Systems."

A cross-reference such as 'exercise 7.10–00' points to a future exercise in Section 7.10 whose number is not yet known.

A note on notations. Simple and intuitive conventions for the algebraic representation of mathematical concepts have always been a boon to progress, especially when most of the world's researchers share a common symbolic language. The current state of affairs in combinatorial mathematics is unfortunately a bit of a mess in this regard, because the same symbols are occasionally used with completely different meanings by different groups of people; some specialists who work in comparatively narrow subfields have unintentionally spawned conflicting symbolisms. Computer science — which interacts with large swaths of mathematics — needs to steer clear of this danger by adopting internally consistent notations whenever possible. Therefore I've often had to choose among a number of competing schemes, knowing that it will be impossible to please everyone. I have tried my best to come up with notations that I believe will be best for the future, often after many years of experimentation and discussion with colleagues, often flip-flopping between alternatives until finding something that works well. Usually it has been possible to find convenient conventions that other people have not already coopted in contradictory ways.

Appendix B is a comprehensive index to all of the principal notations that are used in the present book, inevitably including several that are not (yet?) standard. If you run across a formula that looks weird and/or incomprehensible, chances are fairly good that Appendix B will direct you to a page where my intentions are clarified. But I might as well list here a few instances that you might wish to watch for when you read this book for the first time:

- Hexadecimal constants are preceded by a number sign or hash mark. For example, $^{\#}123$ means $(123)_{16}$.
- The "monus" operation $x \mathbin{\dot{-}} y$, sometimes called dot-minus or saturating subtraction, yields $\max(0, x - y)$.
- The median of three numbers $\{x, y, z\}$ is denoted by $\langle xyz \rangle$.
- A set such as $\{x\}$, which consists of a single element, is often denoted simply by x in contexts such as $X \cup x$ or $X \setminus x$.
- If n is a nonnegative integer, the number of 1-bits in n's binary representation is νn. Furthermore, if $n > 0$, the leftmost and rightmost 1-bits of n are respectively $2^{\lambda n}$ and $2^{\rho n}$. For example, $\nu 10 = 2$, $\lambda 10 = 3$, $\rho 10 = 1$.
- The Cartesian product of graphs G and H is denoted by $G \mathbin{\square} H$. For example, $C_m \mathbin{\square} C_n$ denotes an $m \times n$ torus, because C_n denotes a cycle of n vertices.

NOTES ON THE EXERCISES

THE EXERCISES in this set of books have been designed for self-study as well as for classroom study. It is difficult, if not impossible, for anyone to learn a subject purely by reading about it, without applying the information to specific problems and thereby being encouraged to think about what has been read. Furthermore, we all learn best the things that we have discovered for ourselves. Therefore the exercises form a major part of this work; a definite attempt has been made to keep them as informative as possible and to select problems that are enjoyable as well as instructive.

In many books, easy exercises are found mixed randomly among extremely difficult ones. A motley mixture is, however, often unfortunate because readers like to know in advance how long a problem ought to take — otherwise they may just skip over all the problems. A classic example of such a situation is the book *Dynamic Programming* by Richard Bellman; this is an important, pioneering work in which a group of problems is collected together at the end of some chapters under the heading "Exercises and Research Problems," with extremely trivial questions appearing in the midst of deep, unsolved problems. It is rumored that someone once asked Dr. Bellman how to tell the exercises apart from the research problems, and he replied, "If you can solve it, it is an exercise; otherwise it's a research problem."

Good arguments can be made for including both research problems and very easy exercises in a book of this kind; therefore, to save the reader from the possible dilemma of determining which are which, *rating numbers* have been provided to indicate the level of difficulty. These numbers have the following general significance:

Rating   Interpretation

00   An extremely easy exercise that can be answered immediately if the material of the text has been understood; such an exercise can almost always be worked "in your head," unless you're multitasking.

10   A simple problem that makes you think over the material just read, but is by no means difficult. You should be able to do this in one minute at most; pencil and paper may be useful in obtaining the solution.

20   An average problem that tests basic understanding of the text material, but you may need about fifteen or twenty minutes to answer it completely. Maybe even twenty-five.

30 A problem of moderate difficulty and/or complexity; this one may involve more than two hours' work to solve satisfactorily, or even more if the TV is on.

40 Quite a difficult or lengthy problem that would be suitable for a term project in classroom situations. A student should be able to solve the problem in a reasonable amount of time, but the solution is not trivial.

50 A research problem that has not yet been solved satisfactorily, as far as the author knew at the time of writing, although many people have tried. If you have found an answer to such a problem, you ought to write it up for publication; furthermore, the author of this book would appreciate hearing about the solution as soon as possible (provided that it is correct).

By interpolation in this "logarithmic" scale, the significance of other rating numbers becomes clear. For example, a rating of *17* would indicate an exercise that is a bit simpler than average. Problems with a rating of *50* that are subsequently solved by some reader may appear with a *40* rating in later editions of the book, and in the errata posted on the Internet (see page iv).

The remainder of the rating number divided by 5 indicates the amount of detailed work required. Thus, an exercise rated *24* may take longer to solve than an exercise that is rated *25*, but the latter will require more creativity.

The author has tried earnestly to assign accurate rating numbers, but it is difficult for the person who makes up a problem to know just how formidable it will be for someone else to find a solution; and everyone has more aptitude for certain types of problems than for others. It is hoped that the rating numbers represent a good guess at the level of difficulty, but they should be taken as general guidelines, not as absolute indicators.

This book has been written for readers with varying degrees of mathematical training and sophistication; as a result, some of the exercises are intended only for the use of more mathematically inclined readers. The rating is preceded by an *M* if the exercise involves mathematical concepts or motivation to a greater extent than necessary for someone who is primarily interested only in programming the algorithms themselves. An exercise is marked with the letters "*HM*" if its solution necessarily involves a knowledge of calculus or other higher mathematics not developed in this book. An "*HM*" designation does *not* necessarily imply difficulty.

Some exercises are preceded by an arrowhead, "▶"; this designates problems that are especially instructive and especially recommended. Of course, no reader/student is expected to work *all* of the exercises, so those that seem to be the most valuable have been singled out. (This distinction is not meant to detract from the other exercises!) Each reader should at least make an attempt to solve all of the problems whose rating is *10* or less; and the arrows may help to indicate which of the problems with a higher rating should be given priority.

Several sections have more than 100 exercises. How can you find your way among so many? In general the sequence of exercises tends to follow the sequence of ideas in the main text. Adjacent exercises build on each other, as in the pioneering problem books of Pólya and Szegő. The final exercises of a section often involve the section as a whole, or introduce supplementary topics.

Solutions to most of the exercises appear in the answer section. Please use them wisely; do not turn to the answer until you have made a genuine effort to solve the problem by yourself, or unless you absolutely do not have time to work this particular problem. *After* getting your own solution or giving the problem a decent try, you may find the answer instructive and helpful. The solution given will often be quite short, and it will sketch the details under the assumption that you have earnestly tried to solve it by your own means first. Sometimes the solution gives less information than was asked; often it gives more. It is quite possible that you may have a better answer than the one published here, or you may have found an error in the published solution; in such a case, the author will be pleased to know the details. Later printings of this book will give the improved solutions together with the solver's name where appropriate.

When working an exercise you may generally use the answers to previous exercises, unless specifically forbidden from doing so. The rating numbers have been assigned with this in mind; thus it is possible for exercise $n + 1$ to have a lower rating than exercise n, even though it includes the result of exercise n as a special case.

Summary of codes:		*00* Immediate
		10 Simple (one minute)
		20 Medium (quarter hour)
▶	Recommended	*30* Moderately hard
M	Mathematically oriented	*40* Term project
HM	Requiring "higher math"	*50* Research problem

EXERCISES

▶ **1.** [*00*] What does the rating "*M15*" mean?

2. [*10*] Of what value can the exercises in a textbook be to the reader?

3. [*HM45*] Prove that every simply connected, closed 3-dimensional manifold is topologically equivalent to a 3-dimensional sphere.

> *Art derives a considerable part of its beneficial exercise*
> *from flying in the face of presumptions.*
> — HENRY JAMES, "The Art of Fiction" (1884)

I am grateful to all my friends,
and record here and now my most especial appreciation
to those friends who, after a decent interval,
stopped asking me, "How's the book coming?"
— PETER J. GOMES, *The Good Book* (1996)

I at last deliver to the world a Work which I have long promised,
and of which, I am afraid, too high expectations have been raised.
The delay of its publication must be imputed, in a considerable degree,
to the extraordinary zeal which has been shown by distinguished persons
in all quarters to supply me with additional information.
— JAMES BOSWELL, *The Life of Samuel Johnson, LL.D.* (1791)

The author is especially grateful to the Addison–Wesley Publishing Company
for its patience in waiting a full decade for this manuscript
from the date the contract was signed.
— FRANK HARARY, *Graph Theory* (1969)

The average boy who abhors square root or algebra
finds delight in working puzzles which involve similar
principles, and may be led into a course of study
which would develop the mathematical and inventive bumps
in a way to astonish the family phrenologist.
— SAM LOYD, *The World of Puzzledom* (1896)

Bitte ein Bit!
— Slogan of Bitburger Brauerei (1951)

CONTENTS

Hommage à Bach.

CHAPTER SEVEN

COMBINATORIAL SEARCHING

You shall seeke all day ere you finde them,
& when you have them, they are not worth the search.
— BASSANIO, in *The Merchant of Venice* (Act I, Scene 1, Line 117)

Amid the action and reaction of so dense a swarm of humanity,
every possible combination of events may be expected to take place,
and many a little problem will be presented which may be striking and bizarre.
— SHERLOCK HOLMES, in *The Adventure of the Blue Carbuncle* (1892)

The field of combinatorial algorithms is too vast to cover
in a single paper or even in a single book.
— ROBERT E. TARJAN (1976)

While jostling against all manner of people
it has been impressed upon my mind that the successful ones
are those who have a natural faculty for solving puzzles.
Life is full of puzzles, and we are called upon
to solve such as fate throws our way.
— SAM LOYD, JR. (1926)

COMBINATORICS is the study of the ways in which discrete objects can be arranged into various kinds of patterns. For example, the objects might be $2n$ numbers $\{1, 1, 2, 2, \ldots, n, n\}$, and we might want to place them in a row so that exactly k numbers occur between the two appearances of each digit k. When $n = 3$ there is essentially only one way to arrange such "Langford pairs," namely 231213 (and its left-right reversal); similarly, there's also a unique solution when $n = 4$. Many other types of combinatorial patterns are discussed below.

Five basic types of questions typically arise when combinatorial problems are studied, some more difficult than others.

i) Existence: Are there any arrangements X that conform to the pattern?
ii) Construction: If so, can such an X be found quickly?
iii) Enumeration: How many different arrangements X exist?
iv) Generation: Can all arrangements X_1, X_2, ... be visited systematically?
v) Optimization: What arrangements maximize or minimize $f(X)$, given an objective function f?

Each of these questions turns out to be interesting with respect to Langford pairs.

1

For example, consider the question of existence. Trial and error quickly reveals that, when $n = 5$, we cannot place $\{1, 1, 2, 2, \ldots, 5, 5\}$ properly into ten positions. The two 1s must both go into even-numbered slots, or both into odd-numbered slots; similarly, the 3s and 5s must choose between two evens or two odds; but the 2s and 4s use one of each. Thus we can't fill exactly five slots of each parity. This reasoning also proves that the problem has no solution when $n = 6$, or in general whenever the number of odd values in $\{1, 2, \ldots, n\}$ is odd.

In other words, Langford pairings can exist only when $n = 4m - 1$ or $n = 4m$, for some integer m. Conversely, when n does have this form, Roy O. Davies has found an elegant way to construct a suitable placement (see exercise 1).

How many essentially different pairings, L_n, exist? Lots, when n grows:

$$
\begin{array}{ll}
L_3 = 1; & L_4 = 1; \\
L_7 = 26; & L_8 = 150; \\
L_{11} = 17{,}792; & L_{12} = 108{,}144; \\
L_{15} = 39{,}809{,}640; & L_{16} = 326{,}721{,}800; \\
L_{19} = 256{,}814{,}891{,}280; & L_{20} = 2{,}636{,}337{,}861{,}200; \\
L_{23} = 3{,}799{,}455{,}942{,}515{,}488; & L_{24} = 46{,}845{,}158{,}056{,}515{,}936.
\end{array}
\tag{1}
$$

[The values of L_{23} and L_{24} were determined by M. Krajecki, C. Jaillet, and A. Bui in 2004 and 2005; see *Studia Informatica Universalis* **4** (2005), 151–190.] A seat-of-the-pants calculation suggests that L_n might be roughly of order $(4n/e^3)^{n+1/2}$ when it is nonzero (see exercise 5); and in fact this prediction turns out to be basically correct in all known cases. But no simple formula is apparent.

The problem of Langford arrangements is a simple special case of a general class of combinatorial challenges called *exact cover problems*. In Section 7.2.2.1 we shall study an algorithm called "dancing links," which is a convenient way to generate all solutions to such problems. When $n = 16$, for example, that method needs to perform only about 3200 memory accesses for each Langford pair arrangement that it finds. Thus the value of L_{16} can be computed in a reasonable amount of time by simply generating all of the pairings and counting them.

Notice, however, that L_{24} is a *huge* number — roughly 5×10^{16}, or about 1500 MIP-years. (Recall that a "MIP-year" is the number of instructions executed per year by a machine that carries out a million instructions per second, namely 31,556,952,000,000.) Therefore it's clear that the exact value of L_{24} was determined by some technique that did *not* involve generating all of the arrangements. Indeed, there is a much, much faster way to compute L_n, using polynomial algebra. The instructive method described in exercise 6 needs $O(4^n n)$ operations, which may seem inefficient; but it beats the generate-and-count method by a whopping factor of order $\Theta((n/e^3)^{n-1/2})$, and even when $n = 16$ it runs about 20 times faster. On the other hand, the exact value of L_{100} will probably never be known, even as computers become faster and faster.

We can also consider Langford pairings that are *optimum* in various ways. For example, it's possible to arrange sixteen pairs of weights $\{1, 1, 2, 2, \ldots, 16, 16\}$ that satisfy Langford's condition and have the additional property of being "well-balanced," in the sense that they won't tip a balance beam when they are placed in the appropriate order:

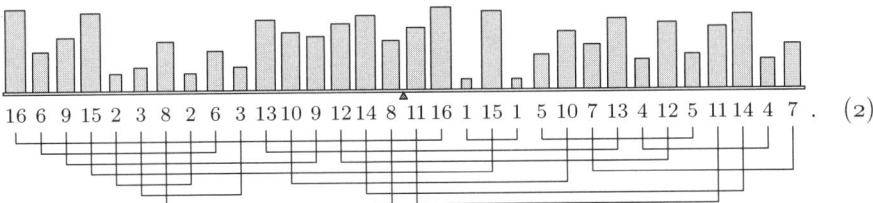

$$16\ 6\ 9\ 15\ 2\ 3\ 8\ 2\ 6\ 3\ 13\ 10\ 9\ 12\ 14\ 8\ 11\ 16\ 1\ 15\ 1\ 5\ 10\ 7\ 13\ 4\ 12\ 5\ 11\ 14\ 4\ 7\ . \quad (2)$$

In other words, $15.5 \cdot 16 + 14.5 \cdot 6 + \cdots + 0.5 \cdot 8 = 0.5 \cdot 11 + \cdots + 14.5 \cdot 4 + 15.5 \cdot 7$; and in this particular example we also have another kind of balance, $16 + 6 + \cdots + 8 = 11 + 16 + \cdots + 7$, hence also $16 \cdot 16 + 15 \cdot 6 + \cdots + 1 \cdot 8 = 1 \cdot 11 + \cdots + 15 \cdot 4 + 16 \cdot 7$.

Moreover, the arrangement in (2) has *minimum width* among all Langford pairings of order 16: The connecting lines at the bottom of the diagram show that no more than seven pairs are incomplete at any point, as we read from left to right; and one can show that a width of six is impossible. (See exercise 7.)

What arrangements $a_1 a_2 \ldots a_{32}$ of $\{1, 1, \ldots, 16, 16\}$ are the *least* balanced, in the sense that $\sum_{k=1}^{32} k a_k$ is maximized? The maximum possible value turns out to be 5268. One such pairing—there are 12,016 of them—is

$$2\ 3\ 4\ 2\ 1\ 3\ 1\ 4\ 16\ 13\ 15\ 5\ 14\ 7\ 9\ 6\ 11\ 5\ 12\ 10\ 8\ 7\ 6\ 13\ 9\ 16\ 15\ 14\ 11\ 8\ 10\ 12. \quad (3)$$

A more interesting question is to ask for the Langford pairings that are smallest and largest in lexicographic order. The answers for $n = 24$ are

$$\{\texttt{abacbdecfgdoersfpgqtuwxvjklonhmirpsjqkhltiunmwvx,}$$
$$\texttt{xvwsquntkigrdapaodgiknqsvxwutmrpohljcfbecbhmfejl}\} \quad (4)$$

if we use the letters a, b, ..., w, x instead of the numbers 1, 2, ..., 23, 24.

We shall discuss many techniques for combinatorial optimization in later sections of this chapter. Our goal, of course, will be to solve such problems without examining more than a tiny portion of the space of all possible arrangements.

Orthogonal latin squares. Let's look back for a moment at the early days of combinatorics. A posthumous edition of Jacques Ozanam's *Recreations mathematiques et physiques* (Paris: 1725) included an amusing puzzle in volume 4, page 434: "Take all the aces, kings, queens, and jacks from an ordinary deck of playing cards and arrange them in a square so that each row and each column contains all four values and all four suits." Can you do it? Ozanam's solution, shown in Fig. 1 on the next page, does even more: It exhibits the full panoply of values and of suits also on both main diagonals. (Please don't turn the page until you've given this problem a try.)

By 1779 a similar puzzle was making the rounds of St. Petersburg, and it came to the attention of the great mathematician Leonhard Euler. "Thirty-six officers of six different ranks, taken from six different regiments, want to march in a 6×6 formation so that each row and each column will contain one officer of each rank and one of each regiment. How can they do it?" Nobody was able to

Fig. 1. Disorder in the court cards: No agreement in any line of four. (This configuration is one of many ways to solve a popular eighteenth-century problem.)

find a satisfactory marching order. So Euler decided to resolve the riddle — even though he had become nearly blind in 1771 and was dictating all of his work to assistants. He wrote a major paper on the subject [eventually published in *Verhandelingen uitgegeven door het Zeeuwsch Genootschap der Wetenschappen te Vlissingen* **9** (1782), 85–239], in which he constructed suitable arrangements for the analogous task with n ranks and n regiments when $n = 1, 3, 4, 5, 7, 8, 9, 11, 12, 13, 15, 16, \ldots$; only the cases with $n \bmod 4 = 2$ eluded him.

There's obviously no solution when $n = 2$. But Euler was stumped when $n = 6$, after having examined a "very considerable number" of square arrangements that didn't work. He showed that any actual solution would lead to many others that look different, and he couldn't believe that all such solutions had escaped his attention. Therefore he said, "I do not hesitate to conclude that one cannot produce a complete square of 36 cells, and that the same impossibility extends to the cases $n = 10$, $n = 14$ ... in general to all oddly even numbers."

Euler named the 36 officers $a\alpha$, $a\beta$, $a\gamma$, $a\delta$, $a\epsilon$, $a\zeta$, $b\alpha$, $b\beta$, $b\gamma$, $b\delta$, $b\epsilon$, $b\zeta$, $c\alpha$, $c\beta$, $c\gamma$, $c\delta$, $c\epsilon$, $c\zeta$, $d\alpha$, $d\beta$, $d\gamma$, $d\delta$, $d\epsilon$, $d\zeta$, $e\alpha$, $e\beta$, $e\gamma$, $e\delta$, $e\epsilon$, $e\zeta$, $f\alpha$, $f\beta$, $f\gamma$, $f\delta$, $f\epsilon$, $f\zeta$, based on their regiments and ranks. He observed that any solution would amount to having two *separate* squares, one for Latin letters and another for Greek. Each of those squares is supposed to have distinct entries in rows and columns; so he began by studying the possible configurations for $\{a, b, c, d, e, f\}$, which he called *Latin squares*. A Latin square can be paired up with a Greek square to form a "Græco-Latin square" only if the squares are *orthogonal* to each other, meaning that no (Latin, Greek) pair of letters can be found together in more than one place when the squares are superimposed. For example, if we let $a = \mathtt{A}$, $b = \mathtt{K}$, $c = \mathtt{Q}$, $d = \mathtt{J}$, $\alpha = \clubsuit$, $\beta = \spadesuit$, $\gamma = \diamondsuit$, and $\delta = \heartsuit$, Fig. 1 is equivalent to the Latin, Greek, and Græco-Latin squares

$$\begin{pmatrix} d & a & b & c \\ c & b & a & d \\ a & d & c & b \\ b & c & d & a \end{pmatrix}, \begin{pmatrix} \gamma & \delta & \beta & \alpha \\ \beta & \alpha & \gamma & \delta \\ \alpha & \beta & \delta & \gamma \\ \delta & \gamma & \alpha & \beta \end{pmatrix}, \text{ and } \begin{pmatrix} d\gamma & a\delta & b\beta & c\alpha \\ c\beta & b\alpha & a\gamma & d\delta \\ a\alpha & d\beta & c\delta & b\gamma \\ b\delta & c\gamma & d\alpha & a\beta \end{pmatrix}. \quad (5)$$

Of course we can use *any* n distinct symbols in an $n \times n$ Latin square; all that matters is that no symbol occurs twice in any row or twice in any column. So we might as well use numeric values $\{0, 1, \ldots, n-1\}$ for the entries. Furthermore we'll just refer to "latin squares" (with a lowercase "l"), instead of categorizing a square as either Latin or Greek, because orthogonality is a symmetric relation.

Euler's assertion that two 6×6 latin squares cannot be orthogonal was verified by Thomas Clausen, who reduced the problem to an examination of 17 fundamentally different cases, according to a letter from H. C. Schumacher to C. F. Gauss dated 10 August 1842. But Clausen did not publish his analysis. The first demonstration to appear in print was by G. Tarry [*Comptes rendus, Association française pour l'avancement des sciences* **29**, part 2 (1901), 170–203], who discovered in his own way that 6×6 latin squares can be classified into 17 different families. (In Section 7.2.3 we shall study how to decompose a problem into combinatorially inequivalent classes of arrangements.)

Euler's conjecture about the remaining cases $n = 10$, $n = 14$, ... was "proved" three times, by J. Petersen [*Annuaire des mathématiciens* (Paris: 1902), 413–427], by P. Wernicke [*Jahresbericht der Deutschen Math.-Vereinigung* **19** (1910), 264–267], and by H. F. MacNeish [*Annals of Math.* (2) **23** (1922), 221–227]. Flaws in all three arguments became known, however; and the question was still unsettled when computers became available many years later. One of the very first combinatorial problems to be tackled by machine was therefore the enigma of 10×10 Græco-Latin squares: Do they exist or not?

In 1957, L. J. Paige and C. B. Tompkins programmed the SWAC computer to search for a counterexample to Euler's prediction. They selected one particular 10×10 latin square "almost at random," and their program tried to find another square that would be orthogonal to it. But the results were discouraging, and they decided to shut the machine off after five hours. Already the program had generated enough data for them to predict that at least 4.8×10^{11} hours of computer time would be needed to finish the run!

Shortly afterwards, three mathematicians made a breakthrough that put latin squares onto page one of major world newspapers: R. C. Bose, S. S. Shrikhande, and E. T. Parker found a remarkable series of constructions that yield orthogonal $n \times n$ squares for all $n > 6$ [*Proc. Nat. Acad. Sci.* **45** (1959), 734–737, 859–862; *Canadian J. Math.* **12** (1960), 189–203]. Thus, after resisting attacks for 180 years, Euler's conjecture turned out to be almost entirely wrong.

Their discovery was made without computer help. But Parker worked for UNIVAC, and he soon brought programming skills into the picture by solving the problem of Paige and Tompkins in less than an hour, on a UNIVAC 1206 Military Computer. [See *Proc. Symp. Applied Math.* **10** (1960), 71–83; **15** (1963), 73–81.]

Let's take a closer look at what the earlier programmers did, and how Parker dramatically trumped their approach. Paige and Tompkins began with the following 10×10 square L and its unknown orthogonal mate(s) M:

$$L = \begin{pmatrix} 0 & 1 & 2 & 3 & 4 & 5 & 6 & 7 & 8 & 9 \\ 1 & 8 & 3 & 2 & 5 & 4 & 7 & 6 & 9 & 0 \\ 2 & 9 & 5 & 6 & 3 & 0 & 8 & 4 & 7 & 1 \\ 3 & 7 & 0 & 9 & 8 & 6 & 1 & 5 & 2 & 4 \\ 4 & 6 & 7 & 5 & 2 & 9 & 0 & 8 & 1 & 3 \\ 5 & 0 & 9 & 4 & 7 & 8 & 3 & 1 & 6 & 2 \\ 6 & 5 & 4 & 7 & 1 & 3 & 2 & 9 & 0 & 8 \\ 7 & 4 & 1 & 8 & 0 & 2 & 9 & 3 & 5 & 6 \\ 8 & 3 & 6 & 0 & 9 & 1 & 5 & 2 & 4 & 7 \\ 9 & 2 & 8 & 1 & 6 & 7 & 4 & 0 & 3 & 5 \end{pmatrix} \quad \text{and} \quad M = \begin{pmatrix} 0 & \sqcup & \sqcup & \sqcup & \sqcup & \sqcup & \sqcup & \sqcup & \sqcup & \sqcup \\ 1 & \sqcup & \sqcup & \sqcup & \sqcup & \sqcup & \sqcup & \sqcup & \sqcup & \sqcup \\ 2 & \sqcup & \sqcup & \sqcup & \sqcup & \sqcup & \sqcup & \sqcup & \sqcup & \sqcup \\ 3 & \sqcup & \sqcup & \sqcup & \sqcup & \sqcup & \sqcup & \sqcup & \sqcup & \sqcup \\ 4 & \sqcup & \sqcup & \sqcup & \sqcup & \sqcup & \sqcup & \sqcup & \sqcup & \sqcup \\ 5 & \sqcup & \sqcup & \sqcup & \sqcup & \sqcup & \sqcup & \sqcup & \sqcup & \sqcup \\ 6 & \sqcup & \sqcup & \sqcup & \sqcup & \sqcup & \sqcup & \sqcup & \sqcup & \sqcup \\ 7 & \sqcup & \sqcup & \sqcup & \sqcup & \sqcup & \sqcup & \sqcup & \sqcup & \sqcup \\ 8 & \sqcup & \sqcup & \sqcup & \sqcup & \sqcup & \sqcup & \sqcup & \sqcup & \sqcup \\ 9 & \sqcup & \sqcup & \sqcup & \sqcup & \sqcup & \sqcup & \sqcup & \sqcup & \sqcup \end{pmatrix}. \quad (6)$$

We can assume without loss of generality that the rows of M begin with 0, 1, ..., 9, as shown. The problem is to fill in the remaining 90 blank entries, and the original SWAC program proceeded from top to bottom, left to right. The top left $\sqcup$ can't be filled with 0, since 0 has already occurred in the top row of M. And it can't be 1 either, because the pair $(1,1)$ already occurs at the left of the next row in (L, M). We can, however, tentatively insert a 2. The digit 1 can be placed next; and pretty soon we find the lexicographically smallest top row that might work for M, namely 0214365897. Similarly, the smallest rows that fit below 0214365897 are 1023456789 and 2108537946; and the smallest legitimate row below them is 3540619278. Now, unfortunately, the going gets tougher: There's no way to complete another row without coming into conflict with a previous choice. So we change 3540619278 to 3540629178 (but that doesn't work either), then to 3540698172, and so on for several more steps, until finally 3546109278 can be followed by 4397028651 before we get stuck again.

In Section 7.2.3, we'll study ways to estimate the behavior of such searches, without actually performing them. Such estimates tell us in this case that the Paige–Tompkins method essentially traverses an implicit search tree that contains about 2.5×10^{18} nodes. Most of those nodes belong to only a few levels of the tree; more than half of them deal with choices on the right half of the sixth row of M, after about 50 of the 90 blanks have been tentatively filled in. A typical node of the search tree probably requires about 75 mems (memory accesses) for processing, to check validity. Therefore the total running time on a modern computer would be roughly the time needed to perform 2×10^{20} mems.

Parker, on the other hand, went back to the method that Euler had originally used to search for orthogonal mates in 1779. First he found all of the so-called *transversals* of L, namely all ways to choose some of its elements so that there's exactly one element in each row, one in each column, and one of each value. For example, one transversal is 0859734216, in Euler's notation, meaning that we choose the 0 in column 0, the 8 in column 1, ..., the 6 in column 9. Each transversal that includes the k in L's leftmost column represents a legitimate way to place the ten k's into square M. The task of finding transversals is, in fact, rather easy, and the given matrix L turns out to have exactly 808 of them; there are respectively $(79, 96, 76, 87, 70, 84, 83, 75, 95, 63)$ transversals for $k = (0, 1, \ldots, 9)$.

Once the transversals are known, we're left with an exact cover problem of 10 stages, which is much simpler than the original 90-stage problem in (6). All we need to do is cover the square with ten transversals that don't intersect — because every such set of ten is equivalent to a latin square M that is orthogonal to L.

The particular square L in (6) has, in fact, exactly one orthogonal mate:

$$
\begin{pmatrix}
0 & 1 & 2 & 3 & 4 & 5 & 6 & 7 & 8 & 9 \\
1 & 8 & 3 & 2 & 5 & 4 & 7 & 6 & 9 & 0 \\
2 & 9 & 5 & 6 & 3 & 0 & 8 & 4 & 7 & 1 \\
3 & 7 & 0 & 9 & 8 & 6 & 1 & 5 & 2 & 4 \\
4 & 6 & 7 & 5 & 2 & 9 & 0 & 8 & 1 & 3 \\
5 & 0 & 9 & 4 & 7 & 8 & 3 & 1 & 6 & 2 \\
6 & 5 & 4 & 7 & 1 & 3 & 2 & 9 & 0 & 8 \\
7 & 4 & 1 & 8 & 0 & 2 & 9 & 3 & 5 & 6 \\
8 & 3 & 6 & 0 & 9 & 1 & 5 & 2 & 4 & 7 \\
9 & 2 & 8 & 1 & 6 & 7 & 4 & 0 & 3 & 5
\end{pmatrix}
\perp
\begin{pmatrix}
0 & 2 & 8 & 5 & 9 & 4 & 7 & 3 & 6 & 1 \\
1 & 7 & 4 & 9 & 3 & 6 & 5 & 0 & 2 & 8 \\
2 & 5 & 6 & 4 & 8 & 7 & 0 & 1 & 9 & 3 \\
3 & 6 & 9 & 0 & 4 & 5 & 8 & 2 & 1 & 7 \\
4 & 8 & 1 & 7 & 5 & 3 & 6 & 9 & 0 & 2 \\
5 & 1 & 7 & 8 & 0 & 2 & 9 & 4 & 3 & 6 \\
6 & 9 & 0 & 2 & 7 & 1 & 3 & 8 & 4 & 5 \\
7 & 3 & 5 & 1 & 2 & 0 & 4 & 6 & 8 & 9 \\
8 & 0 & 2 & 3 & 6 & 9 & 1 & 7 & 5 & 4 \\
9 & 4 & 3 & 6 & 1 & 8 & 2 & 5 & 7 & 0
\end{pmatrix}
. \qquad (7)
$$

The dancing links algorithm finds it, and proves its uniqueness, after doing only about 1.7×10^8 mems of computation, given the 808 transversals. Furthermore, the cost of the transversal-finding phase, about 5 million mems, is negligible by comparison. Thus the original running time of 2×10^{20} mems — which once was regarded as the inevitable cost of solving a problem for which there are 10^{90} ways to fill in the blanks — has been reduced by a further factor of more than $10^{12}(!)$.

We will see later that advances have also been made in methods for solving 90-level problems like (6). Indeed, (6) turns out to be representable directly as an exact cover problem (see exercise 17), which the dancing links procedure of Section 7.2.2.1 solves after expending only 1.3×10^{11} mems. Even so, the Euler–Parker approach remains about a thousand times better than the Paige–Tompkins approach. By "factoring" the problem into two separate phases, one for transversal-finding and one for transversal-combining, Euler and Parker essentially reduced the computational cost from a product, $T_1 T_2$, to a sum, $T_1 + T_2$.

The moral of this story is clear: Combinatorial problems might confront us with a huge universe of possibilities, yet we shouldn't give up too easily. A single good idea can reduce the amount of computation by many orders of magnitude.

Puzzles versus the real world. Many of the combinatorial problems we shall study in this chapter, like Langford's problem of pairs or Ozanam's problem of the sixteen honor cards, originated as amusing puzzles or "brain twisters." Some readers might be put off by this emphasis on recreational topics, which they regard as a frivolous waste of time. Shouldn't computers really be doing useful work? And shouldn't textbooks about computers be primarily concerned with significant applications to industry and/or world progress?

Well, the author of the textbook you are reading has absolutely no objections to useful work and human progress. But he believes strongly that a book such as this should stress *methods* of problem solving, together with mathematical ideas and *models* that help to solve many different problems, rather than focusing on the reasons why those methods and models might be useful. We shall learn many beautiful and powerful ways to attack combinatorial problems, and the elegance of those methods will be our main motivation for studying them. Combinatorial challenges pop up everywhere, and new ways to apply the techniques discussed in this chapter arise every day. So let's not limit our horizons by attempting to catalog in advance what the ideas are good for.

For example, it turns out that orthogonal latin squares are enormously useful, particularly in the design of experiments. Already in 1788, François Cretté de Palluel used a 4×4 latin square to study what happens when sixteen sheep — four each from four different breeds — were fed four different diets and harvested at four different times. [*Mémoires d'Agriculture* (Paris: Société Royale d'Agriculture, trimestre d'été, 1788), 17–23.] The latin square allowed him to do this with 16 sheep instead of 64; with a Græco-Latin square he could also have varied another parameter by trying, say, four different quantities of food or four different grazing paradigms.

But if we had focused our discussion on his approach to animal husbandry, we might well have gotten bogged down in details about breeding, about root vegetables versus grains and the costs of growing them, etc. Readers who aren't farmers might therefore have decided to skip the whole topic, even though latin square designs apply to a wide range of studies. (Think about testing five kinds of pills, on patients in five stages of some disease, five age brackets, and five weight groups.) Moreover, a concentration on experimental design could lead readers to miss the fact that latin squares also have important applications to discrete geometry and error-correcting codes (see exercises 18–24).

Even the topic of Langford pairing, which seems at first to be purely recreational, turns out to have practical importance. T. Skolem used Langford sequences to construct Steiner triple systems, which we have applied to database queries in Section 6.5 [see *Math. Scandinavica* **6** (1958), 273–280]; and in the 1960s, E. J. Groth of Motorola Corporation applied Langford pairs to the design of circuits for multiplication. Furthermore, the algorithms that efficiently find Langford pairs and latin square transversals, such as the method of dancing links, apply to exact cover problems in general; and the problem of exact covering has great relevance to crucial problems such as the equitable apportionment of voter precincts to electoral districts, etc.

The applications are not the most important thing, and neither are the puzzles. Our primary goal is rather to get basic concepts into our brains, like the notions of latin squares and exact covering. Such notions give us the building blocks, vocabulary, and insights that *tomorrow's* problems will need.

Still, it's foolish to discuss problem solving without actually solving any problems. We need good problems to stimulate our creative juices, to light up our grey cells in a more or less organized fashion, and to make the basic concepts familiar. Mind-bending puzzles are often ideal for this purpose, because they can be presented in a few words, needing no complicated background knowledge.

Václav Havel once remarked that the complexities of life are vast: "There is too much to know... We have to abandon the arrogant belief that the world is merely a puzzle to be solved, a machine with instructions for use waiting to be discovered, a body of information to be fed into a computer." He called for an increased sense of justice and responsibility; for taste, courage, and compassion. His words were filled with great wisdom. Yet thank goodness we do also have puzzles that *can* be solved! Puzzles deserve to be counted among the great pleasures of life, to be enjoyed in moderation like all other treats.

Of course, Langford and Ozanam directed their puzzles to human beings, not to computers. Aren't we missing the point if we merely shuffle such questions off to machines, to be solved by brute force instead of by rational thought? George Brewster, writing to Martin Gardner in 1963, expressed a widely held view as follows: "Feeding a recreational puzzle into a computer is no more than a step above dynamiting a trout stream. Succumbing to instant recreation."

Yes, but that view misses another important point: Simple puzzles often have generalizations that go beyond human ability and arouse our curiosity. The study of those generalizations often suggests instructive methods that apply to numerous other problems and have surprising consequences. Indeed, many of the key techniques that we shall study were born when people were trying to solve various puzzles. While writing this chapter, the author couldn't help relishing the fact that puzzles are now more fun than ever, as computers get faster and faster, because we keep getting more powerful dynamite to play with. [Further comments appear in the author's essay, "Are toy problems useful?", originally written in 1976; see *Selected Papers on Computer Science* (1996), 169–183.]

Puzzles do have the danger that they can be *too* elegant. Good puzzles tend to be mathematically clean and well-structured, but we also need to learn how to deal systematically with the messy, chaotic, organic stuff that surrounds us every day. Indeed, some computational techniques are important chiefly because they provide powerful ways to cope with such complexities. That is why, for example, the arcane rules of library-card alphabetization were presented at the beginning of Chapter 5, and an actual elevator system was discussed at length to illustrate simulation techniques in Section 2.2.5.

A collection of programs and data called the Stanford GraphBase (SGB) has been prepared so that experiments with combinatorial algorithms can readily be performed on a variety of real-world examples. SGB includes, for example, data about American highways, and an input-output model of the U.S. economy; it records the casts of characters in Homer's *Iliad*, Tolstoy's *Anna Karenina*, and several other novels; it encapsulates the structure of Roget's *Thesaurus* of 1879; it documents hundreds of college football scores; it specifies the gray-value pixels of Leonardo da Vinci's *Gioconda* (Mona Lisa). And perhaps most importantly, SGB contains a collection of five-letter words, which we shall discuss next.

The five-letter words of English. Many of the examples in this chapter will be based on the following list of five-letter words:

`aargh, abaca, abaci, aback, abaft, abase, abash, ..., zooms, zowie.` (8)

(There are 5757 words altogether — too many to display here; but those that are missing can readily be imagined.) It's a personal list, collected by the author between 1972 and 1992, beginning when he realized that such words would make `ideal` data for testing many kinds of combinatorial algorithms.

The list has intentionally been restricted to words that are **truly** part of the English language, in the sense that the author has encountered them in actual use. Unabridged dictionaries contain thousands of entries that are much more esoteric, like `aalii`, `abamp`, ..., `zymin`, and `zyxst`; words like that are useful primarily to Scrabble® players. But unfamiliar words tend to **spoil** the fun for anybody who doesn't know them. Therefore, for twenty years, the author systematically took note of all **words** that seemed **right** for the expository **goals** of *The Art of Computer Programming*.

Finally it was necessary to freeze the collection, in order to have a **fixed point** for reproducible experiments. The English language will always be evolving, but the 5757 SGB words will therefore always stay the same — even though the author has been tempted at times to add a few words that he didn't know in 1992, such as `chads`, `stent`, `blogs`, `ditzy`, `phish`, `bling`, and possibly `tetch`. No; `noway`. The time for any changes to SGB has long since `ended`: `finis`.

> *The following Glossary is intended to contain all well-known English words*
> *... which may be used in good Society, and which can serve as Links.*
> *... There must be a stent to the admission of spick words.*
>
> — LEWIS CARROLL, *Doublets: A Word-Puzzle* (1879)
>
> *If there is such a verb as to tetch, Mr. Lillywaite tetched.*
>
> — ROBERT BARNARD, *Corpse in a Gilded Cage* (1984)

Proper names like `Knuth` are not considered to be legitimate words. But `gauss` and `hardy` are `valid`, because "gauss" is a unit of magnetic induction and "hardy" is hardy. In fact, SGB words are composed entirely of ordinary lowercase letters; the list contains no hyphenated words, contractions, or terms like `blasé` that require an accent. Thus each word can also be regarded as a vector, which has five components in the range $[0 .. 26)$. In the vector sense, the words `yucca` and `abuzz` are furthest apart: The Euclidean distance between them is

$$\|(24, 20, 2, 2, 0) - (0, 1, 20, 25, 25)\|_2 = \sqrt{24^2 + 19^2 + 18^2 + 23^2 + 25^2} = \sqrt{2415}.$$

The entire Stanford GraphBase, including all of its programs and data sets, is easy to download from the author's website (see page iv). And the list of all SGB words is even easier to obtain, because it is in the file '`sgb-words.txt`' at the same place. That file contains 5757 lines with one word per line, beginning with '`which`' and ending with '`pupal`'. The words appear in a default order, corresponding to frequency of usage; for example, the words of rank 1000, 2000, 3000, 4000, and 5000 are respectively `ditch`, `galls`, `visas`, `faker`, and `pismo`. The notation '`WORDS`(n)' will be used in this chapter to stand for the n most common words, according to this ranking.

Incidentally, five-letter words include many plurals of *four-letter words*, and it should be noted that no Victorian-style censorship was done. Potentially offensive vocabulary has been expurgated from *The Official Scrabble® Players Dictionary*, but not from the SGB. One way to ensure that semantically unsuitable terms will not appear in a professional paper based on the SGB wordlist is to restrict consideration to WORDS(n) where n is, say, 3000.

Exercises 26–37 below can be used as warmups for initial explorations of the SGB words, which we'll see in many different combinatorial contexts throughout this chapter. For example, while covering problems are still on our minds, we might as well note that the four words 'third flock began jumps' cover 20 of the first 21 letters of the alphabet. Five words can, however, cover at most 24 different letters, as in {becks, fjord, glitz, nymph, squaw} — unless we resort to a rare non-SGB word like waqfs (Islamic endowments), which can be combined with {gyved, bronx, chimp, klutz} to cover 25.

Simple words from WORDS(400) suffice to make a *word square*:

$$
\begin{matrix}
\texttt{class} \\
\texttt{light} \\
\texttt{agree} \\
\texttt{sheep} \\
\texttt{steps}
\end{matrix} \quad . \tag{9}
$$

We need to go almost to WORDS(3000), however, to obtain a *word cube*,

$$
\begin{matrix}
\texttt{types} & \texttt{yeast} & \texttt{pasta} & \texttt{ester} & \texttt{start} \\
\texttt{yeast} & \texttt{earth} & \texttt{armor} & \texttt{stove} & \texttt{three} \\
\texttt{pasta} & \texttt{armor} & \texttt{smoke} & \texttt{token} & \texttt{arena} \\
\texttt{ester} & \texttt{stove} & \texttt{token} & \texttt{event} & \texttt{rents} \\
\texttt{start} & \texttt{three} & \texttt{arena} & \texttt{rents} & \texttt{tease}
\end{matrix} \quad , \tag{10}
$$

in which every 5×5 "slice" is a word square. With a simple extension of the basic dancing links algorithm (see Section 7.2.2.2), one can show after performing about 390 billion mems of computation that WORDS(3000) supports only three symmetric word cubes such as (10); exercise 36 reveals the other two. Surprisingly, 83,576 symmetrical cubes can be made from the full set, WORDS(5757).

Graphs from words. It's interesting and important to arrange objects into rows, squares, cubes, and other designs; but in practical applications another kind of combinatorial structure is even *more* interesting and important, namely a *graph*. Recall from Section 2.3.4.1 that a graph is a set of points called *vertices*, together with a set of lines called *edges*, which connect certain pairs of vertices. Graphs are ubiquitous, and many beautiful graph algorithms have been discovered, so graphs will naturally be the primary focus of many sections in this chapter. In fact, the Stanford GraphBase is primarily about graphs, as its name implies; and the SGB words were collected chiefly because they can be used to define interesting and instructive graphs.

Lewis Carroll blazed the trail by inventing a game that he called Word-Links or Doublets, at the end of 1877. [See Martin Gardner, *The Universe in a Handkerchief* (1996), Chapter 6.] Carroll's idea, which soon became quite popular, was to transform one word to another by changing a letter at a time:

$$
\texttt{tears} — \texttt{sears} — \texttt{stars} — \texttt{stare} — \texttt{stale} — \texttt{stile} — \texttt{smile}. \tag{11}
$$

The shortest such transformation is the shortest *path* in a graph, where the vertices of the graph are English words and the edges join pairs of words that have "Hamming distance 1" (meaning that they disagree in just one place).

When restricted to SGB words, Carroll's rule produces a graph of the Stanford GraphBase whose official name is $words(5757, 0, 0, 0)$. Every graph defined by SGB has a unique identifier called its *id*, and the graphs that are derived in Carrollian fashion from SGB words are identified by *id*s of the form $words(n, l, t, s)$. Here n is the number of vertices; l is either 0 or a list of weights, used to emphasize various kinds of vocabulary; t is a threshold so that low-weight words can be disallowed; and s is the seed for any pseudorandom numbers that might be needed to break ties between words of equal weight. The full details needn't concern us, but a few examples will give the general idea:

- $words(n, 0, 0, 0)$ is precisely the graph that arises when Carroll's idea is applied to WORDS(n), for $1 \le n \le 5757$.
- $words(1000, \{0, 0, 0, 0, 0, 0, 0, 0, 0, 0\}, 0, s)$ contains 1000 randomly chosen SGB words, usually different for different values of s.
- $words(766, \{0, 0, 0, 0, 0, 0, 0, 1, 1, 0\}, 1, 0)$ contains all of the five-letter words that appear in *The TEXbook* and *The METAFONTbook*.

There are only 766 words in the latter graph, so we can't form very many long paths like (11), although

$$\text{basic} - \text{basis} - \text{bases} - \text{based}$$
$$- \text{baked} - \text{naked} - \text{named} - \text{names} - \text{games} \qquad (12)$$

is one noteworthy example.

Of course there are many other ways to define the edges of a graph when the vertices represent five-letter words. We could, for example, require the Euclidean distance to be small, instead of the Hamming distance. Or we could declare two words to be adjacent whenever they share a subword of length four; that strategy would substantially enrich the graph, making it possible for chaos to yield peace, even when confined to the 766 words that are related to TEX:

$$\text{chaos} - \text{chose} - \text{whose} - \text{whole} - \text{holes} - \text{hopes} - \text{copes} - \text{scope}$$
$$- \text{score} - \text{store} - \text{stare} - \text{spare} - \text{space} - \text{paces} - \text{peace}. \qquad (13)$$

(In this rule we remove a letter, then insert another, possibly in a different place.) Or we might choose a totally different strategy, like putting an edge between word vectors $a_1a_2a_3a_4a_5$ and $b_1b_2b_3b_4b_5$ if and only if their dot product $a_1b_1 + a_2b_2 + a_3b_3 + a_4b_4 + a_5b_5$ is a multiple of some parameter m. Graph algorithms thrive on different kinds of data.

SGB words lead also to an interesting family of *directed* graphs, if we write $a_1a_2a_3a_4a_5 \to b_1b_2b_3b_4b_5$ when $\{a_2, a_3, a_4, a_5\} \subseteq \{b_1, b_2, b_3, b_4, b_5\}$ as multisets. (Remove the first letter, insert another, and rearrange.) With this rule we can, for example, transform words to graph via a shortest oriented path of length six:

$$\text{words} \to \text{dross} \to \text{soars} \to \text{orcas} \to \text{crash} \to \text{sharp} \to \text{graph}. \qquad (14)$$

Theory is the first term in the Taylor series of practice.
— THOMAS M. COVER (1992)

The number of systems of terminology presently used in graph theory
is equal, to a close approximation, to the number of graph theorists.
— RICHARD P. STANLEY (1986)

Graph theory: The basics. A graph G consists of a set V of vertices together
with a set E of edges, which are pairs of distinct vertices. We will assume that
V and E are *finite* sets unless otherwise specified. We write $u \,—\, v$ if u and v
are vertices with $\{u, v\} \in E$, and $u \,\not\!\!-\, v$ if u and v are vertices with $\{u, v\} \notin E$.
Vertices with $u \,—\, v$ are called "neighbors," and they're also said to be "adjacent"
in G. One consequence of this definition is that we have $u \,—\, v$ if and only if
$v \,—\, u$. Another consequence is that $v \,\not\!\!-\, v$, for all $v \in V$; that is, no vertex is
adjacent to itself. (We shall, however, discuss multigraphs below, in which loops
from a vertex to itself are permitted.)

The graph $G' = (V', E')$ is a *subgraph* of $G = (V, E)$ if $V' \subseteq V$ and $E' \subseteq E$.
It's a *spanning* subgraph of G if, in fact, $V' = V$. And it's an *induced* subgraph
of G if E' has as many edges as possible, when V' is a given subset of the
vertices. In other words, when $V' \subseteq V$ the subgraph of $G = (V, E)$ induced by
V' is $G' = (V', E')$, where

$$E' = \{ \{u, v\} \mid u \in V', v \in V', \text{ and } \{u, v\} \in E \}. \qquad (15)$$

This subgraph G' is denoted by $G \mid V'$, and often called "G restricted to V'." In
the common case where $V' = V \setminus \{v\}$, we write simply $G \setminus v$ ("G minus vertex v")
as an abbreviation for $G \mid (V \setminus \{v\})$. The similar notation $G \setminus e$ is used when
$e \in E$ to denote the subgraph $G' = (V, E \setminus \{e\})$, obtained by removing an edge
instead of a vertex. Notice that all of the SGB graphs known as $words(n, l, t, s)$,
described earlier, are induced subgraphs of the main graph $words(5757, 0, 0, 0)$;
only the vocabulary changes in those graphs, not the rule for adjacency.

A graph with n vertices and e edges is said to have *order* n and *size* e. The
simplest and most important graphs of order n are the *complete graph* K_n, the
path P_n, and the *cycle* C_n. Suppose the vertices are $V = \{1, 2, \ldots, n\}$. Then

- K_n has $\binom{n}{2} = \frac{1}{2}n(n - 1)$ edges $u \,—\, v$ for $1 \leq u < v \leq n$; every n-vertex
  graph is a spanning subgraph of K_n.
- P_n has $n - 1$ edges $v \,—\, (v+1)$ for $1 \leq v < n$, when $n \geq 1$; it is a path
  of length $n-1$ from 1 to n.
- C_n has n edges $v \,—\, ((v \bmod n)+1)$ for $1 \leq v \leq n$, when $n \geq 1$; it is a graph
  only when $n \geq 3$ (but C_1 and C_2 are multigraphs).

We could actually have defined K_n, P_n, and C_n on the vertices $\{0, 1, \ldots, n-1\}$,
or on *any* n-element set V instead of $\{1, 2, \ldots, n\}$, because two graphs that differ
only in the names of their vertices but not in the structure of their edges are
combinatorially equivalent.

Formally, we say that graphs $G = (V, E)$ and $G' = (V', E')$ are *isomorphic*
if there is a one-to-one correspondence φ from V to V' such that $u \,—\, v$ in G if

and only if $\varphi(u)$ — $\varphi(v)$ in G'. The notation $G \cong G'$ is often used to indicate that G and G' are isomorphic; but we shall often be less precise, by treating isomorphic graphs as if they were equal, and by occasionally writing $G = G'$ even when the vertex sets of G and G' aren't strictly identical.

Small graphs can be defined by simply drawing a diagram, in which the vertices are small circles and the edges are lines between them. Figure 2 illustrates several important examples, whose properties we will be studying later. The Petersen graph in Figure 2(e) is named after Julius Petersen, an early graph theorist who used it to disprove a plausible conjecture [L'*Intermédiaire des Mathématiciens* **5** (1898), 225–227]; it is, in fact, a remarkable configuration that serves as a counterexample to many optimistic predictions about what might be true for graphs in general. The Chvátal graph, Figure 2(f), was introduced by Václav Chvátal in *J. Combinatorial Theory* **9** (1970), 93–94.

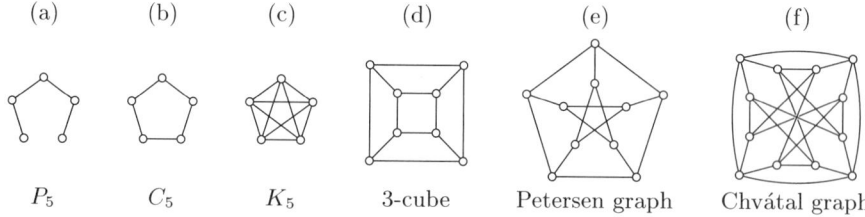

(a)	(b)	(c)	(d)	(e)	(f)
P_5	C_5	K_5	3-cube	Petersen graph	Chvátal graph

Fig. 2. Six example graphs, which have respectively $(5, 5, 5, 8, 10, 12)$ vertices and $(4, 5, 10, 12, 15, 24)$ edges.

The lines of a graph diagram are allowed to cross each other at points that aren't vertices. For example, the center point of Fig. 2(f) is *not* a vertex of Chvátal's graph. A graph is called *planar* if there's a way to draw it without any crossings. Clearly P_n and C_n are always planar; Fig. 2(d) shows that the 3-cube is also planar. But K_5 has too many edges to be planar (see exercise 46).

The *degree* of a vertex is the number of neighbors that it has. If all vertices have the same degree, the graph is said to be *regular*. In Fig. 2, for example, P_5 is irregular because it has two vertices of degree 1 and three of degree 2. But the other five graphs are regular, of degrees $(2, 4, 3, 3, 4)$ respectively. A regular graph of degree 3 is often called "cubic" or "trivalent."

There are many ways to draw a given graph, some of which are much more perspicuous than others. For example, each of the six diagrams

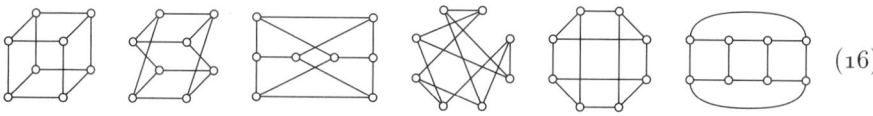   (16)

is isomorphic to the 3-cube, Fig. 2(d). The layout of Chvátal's graph that appears in Fig. 2(f) was discovered by Adrian Bondy many years after Chvátal's paper was published, thereby revealing unexpected symmetries.

The symmetries of a graph, also known as its *automorphisms*, are the permutations of its vertices that preserve adjacency. In other words, the permutation φ is an automorphism of G if we have $\varphi(u)$ — $\varphi(v)$ whenever u — v in G. A well-chosen drawing like Fig. 2(f) can reveal underlying symmetry, but a single diagram isn't always able to display all the symmetries that exist. For example, the 3-cube has 48 automorphisms, and the Petersen graph has 120. We'll study algorithms that deal with isomorphisms and automorphisms in Section 7.2.3. Symmetries can often be exploited to avoid unnecessary computations, making an algorithm almost k times faster when it operates on a graph that has k automorphisms.

Graphs that have evolved in the real world tend to be rather different from the mathematically pristine graphs of Figure 2. For example, here's a familiar graph that has no symmetry whatsoever, although it does have the virtue of being planar:

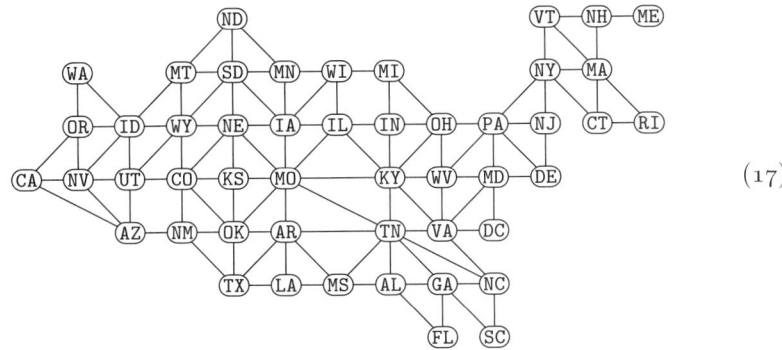

(17)

It represents the contiguous United States of America, and we'll be using it later in several examples. The 49 vertices of this diagram have been labeled with two-letter postal codes for convenience, instead of being reduced to empty circles.

Paths and cycles. A spanning path P_n of a graph is called a *Hamiltonian path*, and a spanning cycle C_n is called a *Hamiltonian cycle*, because W. R. Hamilton invented a puzzle in 1856 whose goal was to find such paths and cycles on the edges of a dodecahedron. T. P. Kirkman had independently studied the problem for polyhedra in general, in *Philosophical Transactions* **146** (1856), 413–418; **148** (1858), 145–161. [See *Graph Theory 1736–1936* by N. L. Biggs, E. K. Lloyd, and R. J. Wilson (1998), Chapter 2.] The task of finding a spanning path or cycle is, however, much older — indeed, we can legitimately consider it to be the oldest combinatorial problem of all, because paths and tours of a knight on a chessboard have a continuous history going back to ninth-century India (see Section 7.3.3). A graph is called *Hamiltonian* if it has a Hamiltonian cycle. (The Petersen graph, incidentally, is the smallest 3-regular graph that is neither planar nor Hamiltonian; see C. de Polignac, *Bull. Soc. Math. de France* **27** (1899), 142–145.)

The *girth* of a graph is the length of its shortest cycle; the girth is infinite if the graph is acyclic (containing no cycles). For example, the six graphs of Fig. 2 have girths $(\infty, 5, 3, 4, 5, 4)$, respectively. It's not difficult to prove that a graph of minimum degree k and girth 5 must have at least $k^2 + 1$ vertices. Further analysis shows in fact that this minimum value is achievable only if $k = 2$ (C_5), $k = 3$ (Petersen), $k = 7$, or perhaps $k = 57$. (See exercises 63 and 65.)

The *distance* $d(u, v)$ between two vertices u and v is the minimum length of a path from u to v in the graph; it is infinite if there's no such path. Clearly $d(v, v) = 0$, and $d(u, v) = d(v, u)$. We also have the triangle inequality

$$d(u, v) + d(v, w) \geq d(u, w). \qquad (18)$$

For if $d(u, v) = p$ and $d(v, w) = q$ and $p < \infty$ and $q < \infty$, there are paths

$$u = u_0 - u_1 - \cdots - u_p = v \quad \text{and} \quad v = v_0 - v_1 - \cdots - v_q = w, \qquad (19)$$

and we can find the least subscript r such that $u_r = v_s$ for some s. Then

$$u_0 - u_1 - \cdots - u_{r-1} - v_s - v_{s+1} - \cdots - v_q \qquad (20)$$

is a path of length $\leq p + q$ from u to w.

The *diameter* of a graph is the maximum of $d(u, v)$, over all vertices u and v. The graph is *connected* if its diameter is finite. The vertices of a graph can always be partitioned into connected *components*, where two vertices u and v belong to the same component if and only if $d(u, v) < \infty$.

In the graph $words(5757, 0, 0, 0)$, for example, we have $d(\texttt{tears}, \texttt{smile}) = 6$, because (11) is a shortest path from `tears` to `smile`. Also $d(\texttt{tears}, \texttt{happy}) = 6$, and $d(\texttt{smile}, \texttt{happy}) = 10$, and $d(\texttt{world}, \texttt{court}) = 6$. But $d(\texttt{world}, \texttt{happy}) = \infty$; the graph isn't connected. In fact, it contains 671 words like `aloof`, which have no neighbors and form connected components of order 1 all by themselves. Word pairs such as `alpha` — `aloha`, `droid` — `druid`, and `opium` — `odium` account for 103 further components of order 2. Some components of order 3, like `chain` — `chair` — `choir`, are paths; others, like {`getup`, `letup`, `setup`}, are cycles. A few more small components are also present, like the curious path

$$\texttt{login} - \texttt{logic} - \texttt{yogic} - \texttt{yogis} - \texttt{yogas} - \texttt{togas}, \qquad (21)$$

whose words have no other neighbors. But the vast majority of all five-letter words belong to a giant component of order 4493. If you can go two steps away from a given word, changing two different letters, the odds are better than 15 to 1 that your word is connected to everything in the giant component.

Similarly, the graph $words(n, 0, 0, 0)$ has a giant component of order (3825, 2986, 2056, 1186, 224) when $n = (5000, 4000, 3000, 2000, 1000)$, respectively. But if n is small, there aren't enough edges to provide much connectivity. For example, $words(500, 0, 0, 0)$ has 327 different components, none of order 15 or more.

The concept of distance can be generalized to $d(v_1, v_2, \ldots, v_k)$ for any value of k, meaning the minimum number of edges in a connected subgraph that contains the vertices $\{v_1, v_2, \ldots, v_k\}$. For example, $d(\texttt{blood}, \texttt{sweat}, \texttt{tears})$ turns out to be 15, because the subgraph

$$
\begin{array}{l}
\texttt{blood} - \texttt{brood} - \texttt{broad} - \texttt{bread} - \texttt{tread} - \texttt{treed} - \texttt{tweed} \\[4pt]
\hspace{9.6cm} | \hspace{1.3cm} | \\[2pt]
\texttt{tears} - \texttt{teams} - \texttt{trams} - \texttt{trims} - \texttt{tries} - \texttt{trees} \hspace{0.4cm} \texttt{tweet} \hspace{1cm} (22) \\[4pt]
\hspace{11cm} | \\[2pt]
\hspace{7.2cm} \texttt{sweat} - \texttt{sweet}
\end{array}
$$

has 15 edges, and there's no suitable 14-edge subgraph.

We noted in Section 2.3.4.1 that a connected graph with fewest edges is called a *free tree*. A subgraph that corresponds to the generalized distance $d(v_1, \ldots, v_k)$ will always be a free tree. It is misleadingly called a *Steiner tree*, because Jacob Steiner once mentioned the case $k = 3$ for points $\{v_1, v_2, v_3\}$ in the Euclidean plane [*Crelle* **13** (1835), 362–363]. Franz Heinen had solved that problem in *Über Systeme von Kräften* (1834); Gauss extended the analysis to $k = 4$ in a letter to Schumacher (21 March 1836).

Coloring. A graph is said to be *k-partite* or *k-colorable* if its vertices can be partitioned into k or fewer parts, with the endpoints of each edge belonging to different parts — or equivalently, if there's a way to paint its vertices with at most k different colors, never assigning the same color to two adjacent vertices. The famous Four Color Theorem, conjectured by F. Guthrie in 1852 and finally proved with massive computer aid by K. Appel, W. Haken, and J. Koch [*Illinois J. Math.* **21** (1977), 429–567], states that *every planar graph is 4-colorable*. No simple proof is known, but special cases like (17) can be colored at sight (see exercise 45); and $O(n^2)$ steps suffice to 4-color a planar graph in general [N. Robertson, D. P. Sanders, P. Seymour, and R. Thomas, *STOC* **28** (1996), 571–575].

The case of 2-colorable graphs is especially important in practice. A 2-partite graph is generally called *bipartite*, or simply a "bigraph"; every edge of such a graph has one endpoint in each part.

Theorem B. *A graph is bipartite if and only if it contains no cycle of odd length.*

Proof. [See D. König, *Math. Annalen* **77** (1916), 453–454.] Every subgraph of a k-partite graph is k-partite. Therefore the cycle C_n can be a subgraph of a bipartite graph only if C_n itself is a bigraph, in which case n must be even.

Conversely, if a graph contains no odd cycles we can color its vertices with the two colors $\{0, 1\}$ by carrying out the following procedure: Begin with all vertices uncolored. If all neighbors of colored vertices are already colored, choose an uncolored vertex w, and color it 0. Otherwise choose a colored vertex u that has an uncolored neighbor v; assign to v the opposite color. Exercise 48 proves that a valid 2-coloring is eventually obtained. ∎

The *complete bipartite graph* $K_{m,n}$ is the largest bipartite graph whose vertices have two parts of sizes m and n. We can define it on the vertex set $\{1, 2, \ldots, m+n\}$ by saying that $u \mathbin{\text{---}} v$ whenever $1 \leq u \leq m < v \leq m + n$. In other words, $K_{m,n}$ has mn edges, one for each way to choose one vertex in the first part and another in the second part. Similarly, the *complete k-partite graph* $K_{n_1, \ldots, n_k}$ has $N = n_1 + \cdots + n_k$ vertices partitioned into parts of sizes $\{n_1, \ldots, n_k\}$, and it has edges between any two vertices that don't belong to the same part. Here are some examples when $N = 6$:

$$K_{1,5} \qquad K_{3,3} \qquad K_{2,2,2} \qquad\qquad (23)$$

Notice that $K_{1,n}$ is a free tree; it is popularly called the *star graph* of order $n+1$.

From now on say "digraph" instead of "directed graph."
It is clear and short and it will catch on.
— GEORGE PÓLYA, letter to Frank Harary (c. 1954)

Directed graphs. In Section 2.3.4.2 we defined *directed graphs* (or *digraphs*), which are very much like graphs except that they have *arcs* instead of edges. An arc $u \longrightarrow v$ runs from one vertex to another, while an edge $u \relbar v$ joins two vertices without distinguishing between them. Furthermore, digraphs are allowed to have self-loops $v \longrightarrow v$ from a vertex to itself, and more than one arc $u \longrightarrow v$ may be present between the same vertices u and v.

Formally, a digraph $D = (V, A)$ of order n and size m is a set V of n vertices and a multiset A of m ordered pairs (u, v), where $u \in V$ and $v \in V$. The ordered pairs are called arcs, and we write $u \longrightarrow v$ when $(u, v) \in A$. The digraph is called *simple* if A is actually a set instead of a general multiset — namely, if there's at most one arc (u, v) for all u and v. Each arc (u, v) has an initial vertex u and a final vertex v, also called its "tip." Each vertex has an *out-degree* $d^+(v)$, the number of arcs for which v is the initial vertex, and an *in-degree* $d^-(v)$, the number of arcs for which v is the tip. A vertex with in-degree 0 is called a "source"; a vertex with out-degree 0 is called a "sink." Notice that $\sum_{v \in V} d^+(v) = \sum_{v \in V} d^-(v)$, because both sums are equal to m, the total number of arcs.

Most of the notions we've defined for graphs carry over to digraphs in a natural way, if we just insert the word "directed" or "oriented" (or the syllable "di") when it's necessary to distinguish between edges and arcs. For example, digraphs have subdigraphs, which can be spanning or induced or neither. An isomorphism between digraphs $D = (V, A)$ and $D' = (V', A')$ is a one-to-one correspondence φ from V to V' for which the number of arcs $u \longrightarrow v$ in D equals the number of arcs $\varphi(u) \longrightarrow \varphi(v)$ in D', for all $u, v \in V$.

Diagrams for digraphs use arrows between the vertices, instead of unadorned lines. The simplest and most important digraphs of order n are directed variants of the graphs K_n, P_n, and C_n, namely the *transitive tournament* $K_n^{\rightarrow}$, the *oriented path* $P_n^{\rightarrow}$, and the *oriented cycle* $C_n^{\rightarrow}$. They can be schematically indicated by the following diagrams for $n = 5$:

$$K_5^{\rightarrow} \qquad\qquad\qquad P_5^{\rightarrow} \qquad\qquad\qquad C_5^{\rightarrow} \qquad\qquad (24)$$

There's also the *complete digraph* J_n, which is the largest simple digraph on n vertices; it has n^2 arcs $u \longrightarrow v$, one for each choice of u and v.

Figure 3 shows a more elaborate diagram, for a digraph of order 17 that we might call "expressly oriented": It is the directed graph described by Hercule Poirot in Agatha Christie's novel *Murder on the Orient Express* (1934). Vertices correspond to the berths of the Stamboul–Calais coach in that story, and an arc $u \longrightarrow v$ means that the occupant of berth u has corroborated the alibi of the person in berth v. This example has six connected components, namely $\{0, 1, 3, 6, 8, 12, 13, 14, 15, 16\}$, $\{2\}$, $\{4, 5\}$, $\{7\}$, $\{9\}$, and $\{10, 11\}$, because connectivity in a digraph is determined by treating arcs as edges.

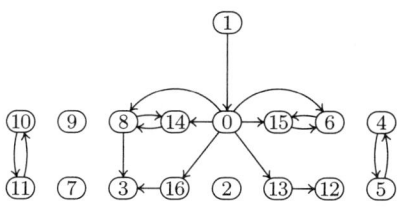

2: Samuel Edward Ratchett, the deceased American
3: Caroline Martha Hubbard, the American matron
4: Edward Henry Masterman, the British valet
5: Antonio Foscarelli, the Italian automobile salesman
6: Hector Willard MacQueen, the American secretary
7: Harvey Harris, the Englishman who didn't show up
8: Hildegarde Schmidt, the German lady's maid
9: (vacancy)
10: Greta Ohlsson, the Swedish nurse
11: Mary Hermione Debenham, the English governess
12: Helena Maria Andrenyi, the beautiful countess
13: Rudolph Andrenyi, the Hungarian count/diplomat
14: Natalia Dragomiroff, the Russian princess dowager
15: Colonel Arbuthnot, the British officer from India
16: Cyrus Bethman Hardman, the American detective

LEGEND

0: Pierre Michel, the French conductor
1: Hercule Poirot, the Belgian detective

Fig. 3. A digraph of order 17 and size 18, devised by Agatha Christie.

Two arcs are *consecutive* if the tip of the first is the initial vertex of the second. A sequence of consecutive arcs $(a_1, a_2, \ldots, a_k)$ is called a *walk* of length k; it can be symbolized by showing the vertices as well as the arcs:

$$v_0 \xrightarrow{a_1} v_1 \xrightarrow{a_2} v_2 \cdots v_{k-1} \xrightarrow{a_k} v_k. \tag{25}$$

In a simple digraph it's sufficient merely to specify the vertices; for example, $1 \rightarrow 0 \rightarrow 8 \rightarrow 14 \rightarrow 8 \rightarrow 3$ is a walk in Fig. 3. The walk in (25) is an oriented path when the vertices $\{v_0, v_1, \ldots, v_k\}$ are distinct; it's an oriented cycle when they are distinct except that $v_k = v_0$.

In a digraph, the directed distance $d(u, v)$ is the number of arcs in the shortest *oriented* path from u to v, which is also the length of the shortest walk from u to v. It may differ from $d(v, u)$; but the triangle inequality (18) remains valid.

Every graph can be regarded as a digraph, because an edge $u \relbar v$ is essentially equivalent to a matched pair of arcs, $u \rightarrow v$ and $v \rightarrow u$. The digraph obtained in this way retains all the properties of the original graph; for example, the degree of each vertex in the graph becomes its out-degree in the digraph, and also its in-degree in the digraph. Furthermore, distances remain the same.

A *multigraph* (V, E) is like a graph except that its edges E can be any *multiset* of pairs $\{u, v\}$; edges $v \relbar v$ that loop from a vertex to itself, which correspond to "multipairs" $\{v, v\}$, are also permitted. For example,

$$\overcirc{1} \relbar \overcirc{2} \relbar \overcirc{3} \tag{26}$$

is a multigraph of order 3 with six edges, $\{1, 1\}$, $\{1, 2\}$, $\{2, 3\}$, $\{2, 3\}$, $\{3, 3\}$, and $\{3, 3\}$. The vertex degrees in this example are $d(1) = d(2) = 3$ and $d(3) = 6$, because each loop contributes 2 to the degree of its vertex. An edge loop $v \relbar v$ becomes *two* arc loops $v \rightarrow v$ when a multigraph is regarded as a digraph.

Representation of graphs and digraphs. Any digraph, and therefore any graph or multigraph, is completely described by its *adjacency matrix* $A = (a_{uv})$, which has n rows and n columns when there are n vertices. Each entry a_{uv} of this matrix specifies the number of arcs from u to v. For example, the adjacency matrices for $\vec{K_3}$, $\vec{P_3}$, $\vec{C_3}$, J_3, and (26) are respectively

$$\vec{K_3} = \begin{pmatrix} 011 \\ 001 \\ 000 \end{pmatrix}, \quad \vec{P_3} = \begin{pmatrix} 010 \\ 001 \\ 000 \end{pmatrix}, \quad \vec{C_3} = \begin{pmatrix} 010 \\ 001 \\ 100 \end{pmatrix}, \quad J_3 = \begin{pmatrix} 111 \\ 111 \\ 111 \end{pmatrix}, \quad A = \begin{pmatrix} 210 \\ 102 \\ 024 \end{pmatrix}. \tag{27}$$

The powerful mathematical tools of matrix theory make it possible to prove many nontrivial results about graphs by studying their adjacency matrices; exercise 65 provides a particularly striking example of what can be done. One of the main reasons is that matrix multiplication has a simple interpretation in the context of digraphs. Consider the square of A, where the element in row u and column v is

$$(A^2)_{uv} = \sum_{w \in V} a_{uw} a_{wv}, \tag{28}$$

by definition. Since a_{uw} is the number of arcs from u to w, we see that $a_{uw} a_{wv}$ is the number of walks of the form $u \longrightarrow w \longrightarrow v$. Therefore $(A^2)_{uv}$ is the total number of walks of length 2 from u to v. Similarly, the entries of A^k tell us the total number of walks of length k between any ordered pair of vertices, for all $k \geq 0$. For example, the matrix A in (27) satisfies

$$A = \begin{pmatrix} 2 & 1 & 0 \\ 1 & 0 & 2 \\ 0 & 2 & 4 \end{pmatrix}, \qquad A^2 = \begin{pmatrix} 5 & 2 & 2 \\ 2 & 5 & 8 \\ 2 & 8 & 20 \end{pmatrix}, \qquad A^3 = \begin{pmatrix} 12 & 9 & 12 \\ 9 & 18 & 42 \\ 12 & 42 & 96 \end{pmatrix}; \tag{29}$$

there are 12 walks of length 3 from the vertex 1 of the multigraph (26) to vertex 3, and 18 such walks from vertex 2 to itself.

Reordering of the vertices changes an adjacency matrix from A to $P^- A P$, where P is a permutation matrix (a 0–1 matrix with exactly one 1 in each row and column), and $P^- = P^T$ is the matrix for the inverse permutation. Thus

$$\begin{pmatrix} 210 \\ 102 \\ 024 \end{pmatrix}, \quad \begin{pmatrix} 201 \\ 042 \\ 120 \end{pmatrix}, \quad \begin{pmatrix} 012 \\ 120 \\ 204 \end{pmatrix}, \quad \begin{pmatrix} 021 \\ 240 \\ 102 \end{pmatrix}, \quad \begin{pmatrix} 402 \\ 021 \\ 210 \end{pmatrix}, \quad \text{and} \quad \begin{pmatrix} 420 \\ 201 \\ 012 \end{pmatrix} \tag{30}$$

are all adjacency matrices for (26), and there are no others.

There are more than $2^{n(n-1)/2}/n!$ graphs of order n, when $n > 1$, and almost all of them require $\Omega(n^2)$ bits of data in their most economical encoding. Consequently the best way to represent the vast majority of all possible graphs inside a computer, from the standpoint of memory usage, is essentially to work with their adjacency matrices.

But the graphs that actually arise in practical problems have quite different characteristics from graphs that are chosen at random from the set of all possibilities. A real-life graph usually turns out to be "sparse," having say $O(n \log n)$ edges instead of $\Omega(n^2)$, unless n is rather small, because $\Omega(n^2)$ bits of data are difficult to generate. For example, suppose the vertices correspond to people, and the edges correspond to friendships. If we consider 5 billion people, few of them will have more than 10000 friends. But even if everybody had 10000 friends, on average, the graph would still have only 2.5×10^{13} edges, while almost all graphs of order 5 billion have approximately 6.25×10^{18} edges.

Thus the best way to represent a graph inside a machine usually turns out to be rather different than to record n^2 values a_{uv} of adjacency matrix elements. Instead, the algorithms of the Stanford GraphBase were developed with a data structure akin to the linked representation of sparse matrices discussed in Section 2.2.6, though somewhat simplified. That approach has proved to be not only versatile and efficient, but also easy to use.

The SGB representation of a digraph is a combination of sequential and linked allocation, using nodes of two basic types. Some nodes represent vertices, other nodes represent arcs. (There's also a third type of node, which represents an entire graph, for algorithms that deal with several graphs at once. But each graph needs only one graph node, so the vertex and arc nodes predominate.)

Here's how it works: Every SGB digraph of order n and size m is built upon a sequential array of n vertex nodes, making it easy to access vertex k for $0 \le k < n$. The m arc nodes, by contrast, are linked together within a general memory pool that is essentially unstructured. Each vertex node typically occupies 32 bytes, and each arc node occupies 20 (and the graph node occupies 220); but the node sizes can be modified without difficulty. A few fields of each node have a fixed, definite meaning in all cases; the remaining fields can be used for different purposes in different algorithms or in different phases of a single algorithm. The fixed-purpose parts of a node are called its "standard fields," and the multipurpose parts are called its "utility fields."

Every vertex node has two standard fields called NAME and ARCS. If v is a variable that points to a vertex node, we'll call it a *vertex variable*. Then NAME(v) points to a string of characters that can be used to identify the corresponding vertex in human-oriented output; for example, the 49 vertices of graph (17) have names like CA, WA, OR, ..., RI. The other standard field, ARCS(v), is far more important in algorithms: It points to an arc node, the first in a singly linked list of length $d^+(v)$, with one node for each arc that emanates from vertex v.

Every arc node has two standard fields called TIP and NEXT; a variable a that points to an arc node is called an *arc variable*. TIP(a) points to the vertex node that represents the tip of arc a; NEXT(a) points to the arc node that represents the next arc whose initial vertex agrees with that of a.

A vertex v with out-degree 0 is represented by letting ARCS$(v) = \Lambda$ (the null pointer). Otherwise if, say, the out-degree is 3, the data structure contains three arc nodes with ARCS$(v) = a_1$, NEXT$(a_1) = a_2$, NEXT$(a_2) = a_3$, and NEXT$(a_3) = \Lambda$; and the three arcs from v lead to TIP(a_1), TIP(a_2), TIP(a_3).

Suppose, for example, that we want to compute the out-degree of vertex v, and store it in a utility field called ODEG. It's easy:

> Set $a \leftarrow$ ARCS(v) and $d \leftarrow 0$.
> While $a \ne \Lambda$, set $d \leftarrow d + 1$ and $a \leftarrow$ NEXT(a).   (31)
> Set ODEG$(v) \leftarrow d$.

When a graph or a multigraph is considered to be a digraph, as mentioned above, its edges $u - v$ are each equivalent to two arcs, $u \longrightarrow v$ and $v \longrightarrow u$. These arcs are called "mates"; and they occupy two arc nodes, say a and a', where a appears in the list of arcs from u and a' appears in the list of arcs from v. Then TIP$(a) = v$ and TIP$(a') = u$. We'll also write

$$\text{MATE}(a) = a' \quad \text{and} \quad \text{MATE}(a') = a, \quad (32)$$

in algorithms that want to move rapidly from one list to another. However, we usually won't need to store an explicit pointer from an arc to its mate, or to have a utility field called MATE within each arc node, because the necessary link can be deduced *implicitly* when the data structure has been constructed cleverly.

The implicit-mate trick works like this: While creating each edge $u - v$ of an undirected graph or multigraph, we introduce *consecutive* arc nodes for $u \longrightarrow v$ and $v \longrightarrow u$. For example, if there are 20 bytes per arc node, we'll reserve 40 consecutive bytes for each new pair. We can also make sure that the memory address of the first byte is a multiple of 8. Then if the arc node a is in memory location α, its mate is in location

$$\left\{ \begin{matrix} \alpha + 20, & \text{if } \alpha \bmod 8 = 0 \\ \alpha - 20, & \text{if } \alpha \bmod 8 = 4 \end{matrix} \right\} = \alpha - 20 + \big(40 \ \& \ ((\alpha \ \& \ 4) - 1)\big). \qquad (33)$$

Such tricks are valuable in combinatorial problems, when operations might be performed a trillion times, because every way to save 3.6 nanoseconds per operation will make such a computation finish an hour sooner. But (33) isn't directly "portable" from one implementation to another. If the size of an arc node were changed from 20 to 24, for example, we would have to change the numbers 40, 20, 8, and 4 in (33) to 48, 24, 16, and 8.

The algorithms in this book will make no assumptions about node sizes. Instead, we'll adopt a convention of the C programming language and its descendants, so that if a points to an arc node, '$a + 1$' denotes a pointer to the arc node that follows it in memory. And in general

$$\texttt{LOC(NODE}(a + k)) \ = \ \texttt{LOC(NODE}(a)) + kc, \qquad (34)$$

when there are c bytes in each arc node. Similarly, if v is a vertex variable, '$v + k$' will stand for the kth vertex node following node v; the actual memory location of that node will be v plus k times the size of a vertex node.

The standard fields of a graph node g include M(g), the total number of arcs; N(g), the total number of vertices; VERTICES(g), a pointer to the first vertex node in the sequential list of all vertex nodes; ID(g), the graph's identification, which is a string like words(5757,0,0,0); and some other fields needed for the allocation and recycling of memory when the graph grows or shrinks, or for exporting a graph to external formats that interface with other users and other graph-manipulation systems. But we will rarely need to refer to any of these graph node fields, nor will it be necessary to give a complete description of SGB format here, since we shall describe almost all of the graph algorithms in this chapter by sticking to an English-language description at a fairly abstract level instead of descending to the bit level of machine programs.

A simple graph algorithm. To illustrate a medium-high-level algorithm of the kind that will appear later, let's convert the proof of Theorem B into a step-by-step procedure that paints the vertices of a given graph with two colors whenever that graph is bipartite.

Algorithm B (*Bipartiteness testing*). Given a graph represented in SGB format, this algorithm either finds a 2-coloring with COLOR$(v) \in \{0, 1\}$ in each vertex v, or it terminates unsuccessfully when no valid 2-coloring is possible. Here COLOR is a utility field in each vertex node. Another vertex utility field, LINK(v), is a vertex pointer used to maintain a stack of all colored vertices whose neighbors have not yet been examined. An auxiliary vertex variable s points to the top of this stack. The algorithm also uses variables u, v, w for vertices and a for arcs. The vertex nodes are assumed to be $v_0 + k$ for $0 \le k < n$.

B1. [Initialize.] Set $\texttt{COLOR}(v_0 + k) \leftarrow -1$ for $0 \le k < n$. (Now all vertices are uncolored.) Then set $w \leftarrow v_0 + n$.

B2. [Done?] (At this point all vertices $\ge w$ have been colored, and so have the neighbors of all colored vertices.) Terminate the algorithm successfully if $w = v_0$. Otherwise set $w \leftarrow w - 1$, the next lower vertex node.

B3. [Color w if necessary.] If $\texttt{COLOR}(w) \ge 0$, return to B2. Otherwise set $\texttt{COLOR}(w) \leftarrow 0$, $\texttt{LINK}(w) \leftarrow \Lambda$, and $s \leftarrow w$.

B4. [Stack $\Rightarrow u$.] Set $u \leftarrow s$, $s \leftarrow \texttt{LINK}(s)$, $a \leftarrow \texttt{ARCS}(u)$. (We will examine all neighbors of the colored vertex u.)

B5. [Done with u?] If $a = \Lambda$, go to B8. Otherwise set $v \leftarrow \texttt{TIP}(a)$.

B6. [Process v.] If $\texttt{COLOR}(v) < 0$, set $\texttt{COLOR}(v) \leftarrow 1 - \texttt{COLOR}(u)$, $\texttt{LINK}(v) \leftarrow s$, and $s \leftarrow v$. Otherwise if $\texttt{COLOR}(v) = \texttt{COLOR}(u)$, terminate unsuccessfully.

B7. [Loop on a.] Set $a \leftarrow \texttt{NEXT}(a)$ and return to B5.

B8. [Stack nonempty?] If $s \ne \Lambda$, return to B4. Otherwise return to B2. ∎

This algorithm is a variant of a general graph traversal procedure called "depth-first search," which we will study in detail in Section 7.4.1. Its running time is $O(m + n)$ when there are m arcs and n vertices (see exercise 70); therefore it is well adapted to the common case of sparse graphs. With small changes we can make it output an odd-length cycle whenever it terminates unsuccessfully, thereby proving the impossibility of a 2-coloring (see exercise 72).

Examples of graphs. The Stanford GraphBase includes a library of more than three dozen generator routines, capable of producing a great variety of graphs and digraphs for use in experiments. We've already discussed *words*; now let's look at a few of the others, in order to get a feeling for some of the possibilities.

- *roget*(1022, 0, 0, 0) is a directed graph with 1022 vertices and 5075 arcs. The vertices represent the categories of words or concepts that P. M. Roget and J. L. Roget included in their famous 19th-century *Thesaurus* (London: Longmans, Green, 1879). The arcs are the cross-references between categories, as found in that book. For example, typical arcs are water $\longrightarrow$ moisture, discovery $\longrightarrow$ truth, preparation $\longrightarrow$ learning, vulgarity $\longrightarrow$ ugliness, wit $\longrightarrow$ amusement.

- *book*("jean", 80, 0, 1, 356, 0, 0, 0) is a graph with 80 vertices and 254 edges. The vertices represent the characters of Victor Hugo's *Les Misérables*; the edges connect characters who encounter each other in that novel. Typical edges are Fantine — Javert, Cosette — Thénardier.

- *bi_book*("jean", 80, 0, 1, 356, 0, 0, 0) is a bipartite graph with 80+356 vertices and 727 edges. The vertices represent characters or chapters in *Les Misérables*; the edges connect characters with the chapters in which they appear (for instance, Napoleon — 2.1.8, Marius — 4.14.4).

• *plane_miles*(128, 0, 0, 0, 1, 0, 0) is a planar graph with 129 vertices and 381 edges. The vertices represent 128 cities in the United States or Canada, plus a special vertex INF for a "point at infinity." The edges define the so-called *Delaunay triangulation* of those cities, based on latitude and longitude in a plane; this means that $u - v$ if and only if there's a circle passing through u and v that does not enclose any other vertex. Edges also run between INF and all vertices that lie on the convex hull of all city locations. Typical edges are Seattle, WA — Vancouver, BC — INF; Toronto, ON — Rochester, NY.

• *plane_lisa*(360, 250, 15, 0, 360, 0, 250, 0, 22950000) is a planar graph that has 3027 vertices and 5967 edges. It is obtained by starting with a digitized image of Leonardo da Vinci's *Mona Lisa*, having 360 rows and 250 columns of pixels, then rounding the pixel intensities to 16 levels of gray from 0 (black) to 15 (white). The resulting 3027 rookwise connected regions of constant brightness are then considered to be neighbors when they share a pixel boundary. (See Fig. 4.)

 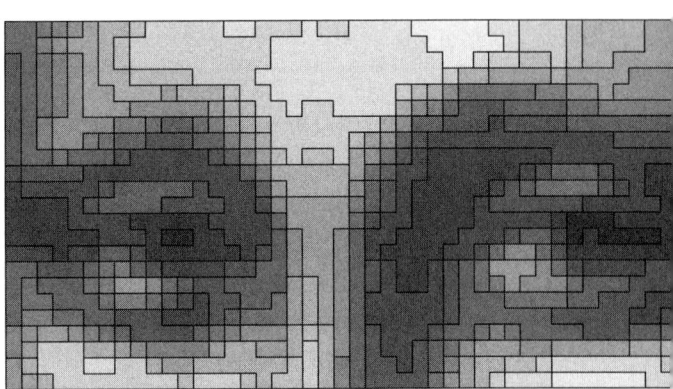

Fig. 4. A digital rendition of *Mona Lisa*, with a closeup detail (best viewed from afar).

• *bi_lisa*(360, 250, 0, 360, 0, 250, 8192, 0) is a bipartite graph with $360 + 250 = 610$ vertices and 40923 edges. It's another takeoff on Leonardo's famous painting, this time linking rows and columns where the brightness level is at least 1/8. For example, the edge r102 — c113 occurs right in the middle of Lisa's "smile."

• *raman*(31, 23, 3, 1) is a graph with quite a different nature from the SGB graphs in previous examples. Instead of being linked to language, literature, or other outgrowths of human culture, it's a so-called "Ramanujan expander graph," based on strict mathematical principles. Each of its $(23^3 - 23)/2 = 6072$ vertices has degree 32; hence it has 97152 edges. The vertices correspond to equivalence classes of 2×2 matrices that are nonsingular modulo 23; a typical edge is (2,7;1,1) — (4,6;1,3). Ramanujan graphs are important chiefly because they have unusually high girth and low diameter for their size and degree. This one has girth 4 and diameter 4.

- $raman(5, 37, 4, 1)$, similarly, is a regular graph of degree 6 with 50616 vertices and 151848 edges. It has girth 10, diameter 10, and happens also to be bipartite.

- $random\_graph(1000, 5000, 0, 0, 0, 0, 0, 0, 0, s)$ is a graph with 1000 vertices, 5000 edges, and seed s. It "evolved" by starting with no edges, then by repeatedly choosing pseudorandom vertex numbers $0 \le u, v < 1000$ and adding the edge $u \,\text{---}\, v$, unless $u = v$ or that edge was already present. When $s = 0$, all vertices belong to a giant component of order 999, except for the isolated vertex 908.

- $random\_graph(1000, 5000, 0, 0, 1, 0, 0, 0, 0, 0)$ is a digraph with 1000 vertices and 5000 arcs, obtained via a similar sort of evolution. (In fact, each of its arcs happens to be part also of $random\_graph(1000, 5000, 0, 0, 0, 0, 0, 0, 0, 0)$.)

- $subsets(5, 1, -10, 0, 0, 0, {}^{\#}1, 0)$ is a graph with $\binom{11}{5} = 462$ vertices, one for every five-element subset of $\{0, 1, \ldots, 10\}$. Two vertices are adjacent whenever the corresponding subsets are disjoint; thus, the graph is regular of degree 6, and it has 1386 edges. We can consider it to be a generalization of the Petersen graph, which has $subsets(2, 1, -4, 0, 0, 0, {}^{\#}1, 0)$ as one of its SGB names.

- $subsets(5, 1, -10, 0, 0, 0, {}^{\#}10, 0)$ has the same 462 vertices, but now they are adjacent if the corresponding subsets have four elements in common. This graph is regular of degree 30, and it has 6930 edges.

- $parts(30, 10, 30, 0)$ is another SGB graph with a mathematical basis. It has 3590 vertices, one for each partition of 30 into at most 10 parts. Two partitions are adjacent when one is obtained by subdividing a part of the other; this rule defines 31377 edges. The digraph $parts(30, 10, 30, 1)$ is similar, but its 31377 arcs point from shorter to longer partitions (for example, 13+7+7+3 $\longrightarrow$ 7+7+7+6+3).

- $simplex(10, 10, 10, 10, 10, 0, 0)$ is a graph with 286 vertices and 1320 edges. Its vertices are the integer solutions to $x_1 + x_2 + x_3 + x_4 = 10$ with $x_i \ge 0$, namely the "compositions of 10 into four nonnegative parts"; they can also be regarded as barycentric coordinates for points inside a tetrahedron. The edges, such as 3.1.4.2 — 3.0.4.3, connect compositions that are as close together as possible.

- $board(8, 8, 0, 0, 5, 0, 0)$ and $board(8, 8, 0, 0, -2, 0, 0)$ are graphs on 64 vertices whose 168 or 280 edges correspond to the moves of a knight or bishop in chess.

And zillions of further examples are obtainable by varying the parameters to the SGB graph generators. For example, Fig. 5 shows two simple variants of $board$ and $simplex$; the somewhat arcane rules of $board$ are explained in exercise 75.

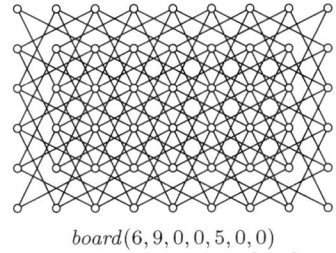

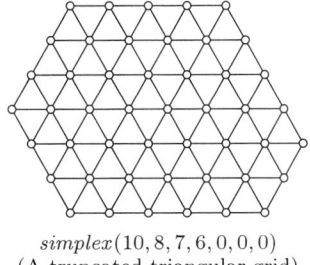

$board(6, 9, 0, 0, 5, 0, 0)$ $simplex(10, 8, 7, 6, 0, 0, 0)$
(Knight moves on a 6 × 9 chessboard)   (A truncated triangular grid)

Fig. 5. Samples of SGB graphs related to board games.

Graph algebra. We can also obtain new graphs by operating on the graphs that we already have. For example, if $G = (V, E)$ is any graph, its *complement* $\overline{G} = (V, \overline{E})$ is obtained by letting

$$u \relbar v \text{ in } \overline{G} \qquad \Longleftrightarrow \qquad u \neq v \text{ and } u \not\relbar v \text{ in } G. \qquad (35)$$

Thus, non-edges become edges, and vice versa. Notice that $\overline{\overline{G}} = G$, and that $\overline{K_n}$ has no edges. The corresponding adjacency matrices A and $\overline{A}$ satisfy

$$A + \overline{A} = J - I; \qquad (36)$$

here J is the matrix of all 1s, and I is the identity matrix, so J and $J - I$ are respectively the adjacency matrices of J_n and K_n when G has order n.

Furthermore, every graph $G = (V, E)$ leads to a *line graph* $L(G)$, whose vertices are the edges E; two edges of G are adjacent in $L(G)$ if they have a common vertex. Thus, for example, the line graph $L(K_n)$ has $\binom{n}{2}$ vertices, and it is regular of degree $2n - 4$ when $n \geq 2$ (see exercise 82). A graph is called *k-edge-colorable* when its line graph is k-colorable.

Given two graphs $G = (U, E)$ and $H = (V, F)$, their *union* $G \cup H$ is the graph $(U \cup V, E \cup F)$ obtained by combining the vertices and edges. For example, suppose G and H are the graphs of rook and bishop moves in chess; then $G \cup H$ is the graph of queen moves, and its official SGB name is

$$gunion\,(board\,(8, 8, 0, 0, -1, 0, 0), board\,(8, 8, 0, 0, -2, 0, 0), 0, 0). \qquad (37)$$

In the special case where the vertex sets U and V are disjoint, the union $G \cup H$ doesn't require the vertices to be identified in any consistent way for cross-correlation; we get a diagram for $G \cup H$ by simply drawing a diagram of G next to a diagram of H. This special case is called the "juxtaposition" or *direct sum* of G and H, and we shall denote it by $G \oplus H$. For example, it's easy to see that

$$K_m \oplus K_n \cong \overline{K_{m,n}}, \qquad (38)$$

and that every graph is the direct sum of its connected components.

Equation (38) is a special case of the general formula

$$K_{n_1} \oplus K_{n_2} \oplus \cdots \oplus K_{n_k} \cong \overline{K_{n_1, n_2, \ldots, n_k}}, \qquad (39)$$

which holds for complete k-partite graphs whenever $k \geq 2$. But (39) fails when $k = 1$, because of a scandalous fact: The standard graph-theoretic notation for complete graphs is inconsistent! Indeed, $K_{m,n}$ denotes a complete 2-partite graph, but K_n does *not* denote a complete 1-partite graph. Somehow graph theorists have been able to live with this anomaly for decades without going berserk.

Another important way to combine disjoint graphs G and H is to form their *join*, $G \relbar H$, which consists of $G \oplus H$ together with all edges $u \relbar v$ for $u \in U$ and $v \in V$. [See A. A. Zykov, *Mat. Sbornik* **24** (1949), 163–188, §I.3.] And if G and H are disjoint *digraphs*, their *directed join* $G \longrightarrow H$ is similar, but it supplements $G \oplus H$ by adding only the one-way arcs $u \longrightarrow v$ from U to V.

The direct sum of two matrices A and B is obtained by placing B diagonally below and to the right of A:

$$A \oplus B = \begin{pmatrix} A & O \\ O & B \end{pmatrix}, \tag{40}$$

where each O in this example is a matrix of all zeros, with the proper number of rows and columns to make everything line up correctly. Our notation $G \oplus H$ for the direct sum of graphs is easy to remember because the adjacency matrix for $G \oplus H$ is precisely the direct sum of the respective adjacency matrices A and B for G and H. Similarly, the adjacency matrices for G—H, $G \to H$, and $G \leftarrow H$ are

$$A—B = \begin{pmatrix} A & J \\ J & B \end{pmatrix}, \quad A \to B = \begin{pmatrix} A & J \\ O & B \end{pmatrix}, \quad A \leftarrow B = \begin{pmatrix} A & O \\ J & B \end{pmatrix}, \tag{41}$$

respectively, where J is an all-1s matrix as in (36). These operations are associative, and related by complementation:

$$A \oplus (B \oplus C) = (A \oplus B) \oplus C, \quad A—(B—C) = (A—B)—C; \tag{42}$$
$$A \to (B \to C) = (A \to B) \to C, \quad A \leftarrow (B \leftarrow C) = (A \leftarrow B) \leftarrow C; \tag{43}$$
$$\overline{A \oplus B} = \overline{A}—\overline{B}, \quad \overline{A—B} = \overline{A} \oplus \overline{B}; \tag{44}$$
$$\overline{A \to B} = \overline{A} \leftarrow \overline{B}, \quad \overline{A \leftarrow B} = \overline{A} \to \overline{B}; \tag{45}$$
$$(A \oplus B) + (A—B) = (A \to B) + (A \leftarrow B). \tag{46}$$

Notice that, by combining (39) with (42) and (44), we have

$$K_{n_1, n_2, \ldots, n_k} = \overline{K_{n_1}}—\overline{K_{n_2}}—\cdots—\overline{K_{n_k}} \tag{47}$$

when $k \geq 2$. Also

$$K_n = K_1—K_1—\cdots—K_1 \quad \text{and} \quad \vec{K_n} = K_1 \to K_1 \to \cdots \to K_1, \tag{48}$$

with n copies of K_1, showing that $K_n = K_{1,1,\ldots,1}$ is a complete n-partite graph.

Direct sums and joins are analogous to addition, because we have $\overline{K_m} \oplus \overline{K_n} = \overline{K_{m+n}}$ and $K_m—K_n = K_{m+n}$. We can also combine graphs with algebraic operations that are analogous to multiplication. For example, the *Cartesian product* operation forms a graph $G \square H$ of order mn from a graph $G = (U, E)$ of order m and a graph $H = (V, F)$ of order n. The vertices of $G \square H$ are ordered pairs (u, v), where $u \in U$ and $v \in V$; the edges are (u, v) — (u', v) when u — u' in G, together with (u, v) — (u, v') when v — v' in H. In other words, $G \square H$ is formed by replacing each vertex of G by a copy of H, and replacing each edge of G by edges between corresponding vertices of the appropriate copies:

$$\tag{49}$$

As usual, the simplest special cases of this general construction turn out to be especially important in practice. When both G and H are paths or cycles, we get "graph-paper graphs," namely the $m \times n$ *grid* $P_m \square P_n$, the $m \times n$ *cylinder* $P_m \square C_n$, and the $m \times n$ *torus* $C_m \square C_n$, illustrated here for $m = 3$ and $n = 4$:

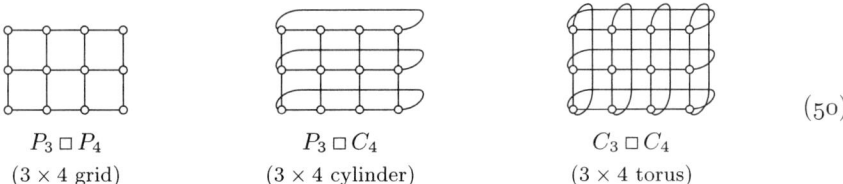

$$(50)$$

$P_3 \square P_4$ $P_3 \square C_4$ $C_3 \square C_4$

(3 × 4 grid)   (3 × 4 cylinder)   (3 × 4 torus)

Four other noteworthy ways to define products of graphs have also proved to be useful. In each case the vertices of the product graph are ordered pairs (u, v).

• The *direct product* $G \otimes H$, also called the "conjunction" of G and H, or their "categorical product," has $(u, v) \,\text{---}\, (u', v')$ when $u \,\text{---}\, u'$ in G and $v \,\text{---}\, v'$ in H.

• The *strong product* $G \boxtimes H$ combines the edges of $G \square H$ with those of $G \otimes H$.

• The *odd product* $G \bigtriangleup H$ has $(u, v) \,\text{---}\, (u', v')$ when we have either $u \,\text{---}\, u'$ in G or $v \,\text{---}\, v'$ in H, but not both.

• The *lexicographic product* $G \circ H$, also called the "composition" of G and H, has $(u, v) \,\text{---}\, (u', v')$ when $u \,\text{---}\, u'$ in G, and $(u, v) \,\text{---}\, (u, v')$ when $v \,\text{---}\, v'$ in H.

All five of these operations extend naturally to products of $k \geq 2$ graphs $G_1 = (V_1, E_1), \ldots, G_k = (V_k, E_k)$, whose vertices are the ordered k-tuples $(v_1, \ldots, v_k)$ with $v_j \in V_j$ for $1 \leq j \leq k$. For example, when $k = 3$, the Cartesian products $G_1 \square (G_2 \square G_3)$ and $(G_1 \square G_2) \square G_3$ are isomorphic, if we consider the compound vertices $(v_1, (v_2, v_3))$ and $((v_1, v_2), v_3)$ to be the same as (v_1, v_2, v_3). Therefore we can write this Cartesian product without parentheses, as $G_1 \square G_2 \square G_3$. The most important example of a Cartesian product with k factors is the k-cube,

$$P_2 \square P_2 \square \cdots \square P_2; \qquad (51)$$

its 2^k vertices $(v_1, \ldots, v_k)$ are adjacent when their Hamming distance is 1.

In general, suppose $v = (v_1, \ldots, v_k)$ and $v' = (v'_1, \ldots, v'_k)$ are k-tuples of vertices, where we have $v_j \,\text{---}\, v'_j$ in G_j for exactly a of the subscripts j, and $v_j = v'_j$ for exactly b of the subscripts. Then we have:

• $v \,\text{---}\, v'$ in $G_1 \square \cdots \square G_k$ if and only if $a = 1$ and $b = k - 1$;

• $v \,\text{---}\, v'$ in $G_1 \otimes \cdots \otimes G_k$ if and only if $a = k$ and $b = 0$;

• $v \,\text{---}\, v'$ in $G_1 \boxtimes \cdots \boxtimes G_k$ if and only if $a + b = k$ and $a > 0$;

• $v \,\text{---}\, v'$ in $G_1 \bigtriangleup \cdots \bigtriangleup G_k$ if and only if a is odd.

The lexicographic product is somewhat different, because it isn't commutative; in $G_1 \circ \cdots \circ G_k$ we have $v \,\text{---}\, v'$ for $v \neq v'$ if and only if $v_j \,\text{---}\, v'_j$, where j is the minimum subscript with $v_j \neq v'_j$.

Exercises 91–102 explore some of the basic properties of graph products. See also the book *Product Graphs* by Wilfried Imrich and Sandi Klavžar (2000), which contains a comprehensive introduction to the general theory, including algorithms for factorization of a given graph into "prime" subgraphs.

*Graphical degree sequences. A sequence $d_1 d_2 \ldots d_n$ of nonnegative integers is called *graphical* if there's at least one graph on vertices $\{1, 2, \ldots, n\}$ such that vertex k has degree d_k. We can assume that $d_1 \geq d_2 \geq \cdots \geq d_n$. Clearly $d_1 < n$ in any such graph; and the sum $m = d_1 + d_2 + \cdots + d_n$ of any graphical sequence is always even, because it is twice the number of edges. Furthermore, it's easy to see that the sequence 3311 is not graphical; therefore graphical sequences must also satisfy additional conditions. What are they?

A simple way to decide if a given sequence $d_1 d_2 \ldots d_n$ is graphical, and to construct such a graph if one exists, was discovered by V. Havel [*Časopis pro Pěstování Matematiky* **80** (1955), 477–479]. We begin with an empty tableau, having d_k cells in row k; these cells represent "slots" into which we'll place the neighbors of vertex k in the constructed graph. Let c_j be the number of cells in column j; thus $c_1 \geq c_2 \geq \cdots$, and when $1 \leq k \leq n$ we have $c_j \geq k$ if and only if $d_k \geq j$. For example, suppose $n = 8$ and $d_1 \ldots d_8 = 55544322$; then

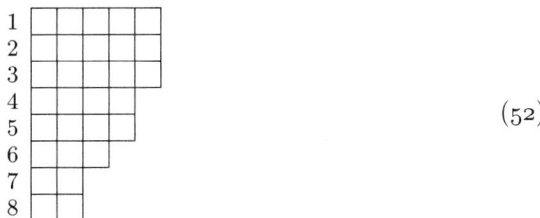

$$(52)$$

is the initial tableau, and we have $c_1 \ldots c_5 = 88653$. Havel's idea is to pair up vertex n with d_n of the highest-degree vertices. In this case, for example, we create the two edges 8 — 3 and 8 — 2, and the tableau takes the following form:

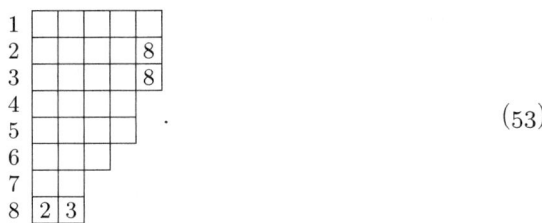

$$(53)$$

(We don't want 8 — 1, because the empty slots should continue to form a tableau shape; the cells of each column must be filled from the bottom up.) Next we set $n \leftarrow 7$ and create two further edges, 7 — 1 and 7 — 5. And then come three more, 6 — 4, 6 — 3, 6 — 2, making the tableau almost half full:

1					7
2				6	8
3				6	8
4				6	
5				7	
6	2	3	4		
7	5	1			
8	2	3			

$$(54)$$

We've reduced the problem to finding a graph with degree sequence $d_1 \ldots d_5 = 43333$; at this point we also have $c_1 \ldots c_4 = 5551$. The reader is encouraged to fill in the remaining blanks, before looking at the answer in exercise 103.

Algorithm H (*Graph generator for specified degrees*). Given $d_1 \geq \cdots \geq d_n \geq d_{n+1} = 0$, this algorithm creates edges between the vertices $\{1, \ldots, n\}$ in such a way that exactly d_k edges touch vertex k, for $1 \leq k \leq n$, unless the sequence $d_1 \ldots d_n$ isn't graphical. An array $c_1 \ldots c_{d_1}$ is used for auxiliary storage.

H1. [Set the c's.] Start with $k \leftarrow d_1$ and $j \leftarrow 0$. Then while $k > 0$ do the following operations: Set $j \leftarrow j + 1$; while $k > d_{j+1}$, set $c_k \leftarrow j$ and $k \leftarrow k - 1$. Terminate successfully if $j = 0$ (all d's are zero).

H2. [Find n.] Set $n \leftarrow c_1$. Terminate successfully if $n = 0$; terminate unsuccessfully if $d_1 \geq n > 0$.

H3. [Begin loop on j.] Set $i \leftarrow 1$, $t \leftarrow d_1$, $r \leftarrow c_t$, and $j \leftarrow d_n$.

H4. [Generate a new edge.] Set $c_j \leftarrow c_j - 1$ and $m \leftarrow c_t$. Create the edge $n - m$, and set $d_m \leftarrow d_m - 1$, $c_t \leftarrow m - 1$, $j \leftarrow j - 1$. If $j = 0$, return to step H2. Otherwise, if $m = i$, set $i \leftarrow r + 1$, $t \leftarrow d_i$, and $r \leftarrow c_t$ (see exercise 104); repeat step H4. $\blacksquare$

When Algorithm H succeeds, it certainly has constructed a graph with the desired degrees. But when it fails, how can we be sure that its mission was impossible? The key fact is based on an important concept called "majorization": If $d_1 \ldots d_n$ and $d_1' \ldots d_n'$ are two partitions of the same integer (that is, if $d_1 \geq \cdots \geq d_n$ and $d_1' \geq \cdots \geq d_n'$ and $d_1 + \cdots + d_n = d_1' + \cdots + d_n'$), we say that $d_1 \ldots d_n$ *majorizes* $d_1' \ldots d_n'$ if $d_1 + \cdots + d_k \geq d_1' + \cdots + d_k'$ for $1 \leq k \leq n$.

Lemma M. *If $d_1 \ldots d_n$ is graphical and $d_1 \ldots d_n$ majorizes $d_1' \ldots d_n'$, then $d_1' \ldots d_n'$ is also graphical.*

Proof. It is sufficient to prove the claim when $d_1 \ldots d_n$ and $d_1' \ldots d_n'$ differ in only two places,

$$d_k' = d_k - [k = i] + [k = j] \qquad \text{where } i < j, \tag{55}$$

because any sequence majorized by $d_1 \ldots d_n$ can be obtained by repeatedly performing mini-majorizations such as this. (Exercise 7.2.1.4–55 discusses majorization in detail.)

Condition (55) implies that $d_i > d_i' \geq d_{i+1}' \geq d_j' > d_j$. So any graph with degree sequence $d_1 \ldots d_n$ contains a vertex v such that $v - i$ and $v \not\!\!- j$. Deleting the edge $v - i$ and adding the edge $v - j$ yields a graph with degree sequence $d_1' \ldots d_n'$, as desired. $\blacksquare$

Corollary H. *Algorithm H succeeds whenever $d_1 \ldots d_n$ is graphical.*

Proof. We may assume that $n > 1$. Suppose G is any graph on $\{1, \ldots, n\}$ with degree sequence $d_1 \ldots d_n$, and let G' be the subgraph induced by $\{1, \ldots, n-1\}$; in other words, obtain G' by removing vertex n and the d_n edges that it touches. The degree sequence $d_1' \ldots d_{n-1}'$ of G' is obtained from $d_1 \ldots d_{n-1}$ by reducing some d_n of the entries by 1 and sorting them into nonincreasing order. By definition, $d'_1 \ldots d'_{n-1}$ is graphical. The new degree sequence $d''_1 \ldots d''_{n-1}$ produced by the strategy of steps H3 and H4 is designed to be majorized by every such $d'_1 \ldots d'_{n-1}$, because it reduces the largest possible d_n entries by 1. Thus the new $d''_1 \ldots d''_{n-1}$ is graphical. Algorithm H, which sets $d_1 \ldots d_{n-1} \leftarrow d''_1 \ldots d''_{n-1}$, will therefore succeed by induction on n. ∎

The running time of Algorithm H is roughly proportional to the number of edges generated, which can be of order n^2. Exercise 105 presents a faster method, which decides in $O(n)$ steps whether or not a given sequence $d_1 \ldots d_n$ is graphical (without constructing any graph).

Beyond graphs. When the vertices and/or arcs of a graph or digraph are decorated with additional data, we call it a *network*. For example, every vertex of *words*(5757, 0, 0, 0) has an associated rank, which corresponds to the popularity of the corresponding five-letter word. Every vertex of *plane_lisa*(360, 250, 15, 0, 360, 0, 250, 0, 22950000) has an associated pixel density, between 0 and 15. Every arc of *board*(8, 8, 0, 0, −2, 0, 0) has an associated length, which reflects the distance of a piece's motion on the board: A bishop's move from corner to corner has length 7. The Stanford GraphBase includes several further generators that were not mentioned above, because they are primarily used to generate interesting networks, rather than to generate graphs with interesting structure:

• *miles*(128, 0, 0, 0, 0, 127, 0) is a network with 128 vertices, corresponding to the same North American cities as the graph *plane_miles* described earlier. But *miles*, unlike *plane_miles*, is a complete graph with $\binom{128}{2}$ edges. Every edge has an integer length, which represents the distance that a car or truck would have needed to travel in 1949 when going from one given city to another. For example, 'Vancouver, BC' is 3496 miles from 'West Palm Beach, FL' in the *miles* network.

• *econ*(81, 0, 0, 0) is a network with 81 vertices and 4902 arcs. Its vertices represent sectors of the United States economy, and its arcs represent the flow of money from one sector to another during the year 1985, measured in millions of dollars. For example, the flow value from Apparel to Household furniture is 44, meaning that the furniture industry paid $44,000,000 to the apparel industry in that year. The sum of flows coming into each vertex is equal to the sum of flows going out. An arc appears only when the flow is nonzero. A special vertex called Users receives the flows that represent total demand for a product; a few of these end-user flows are negative, because of the way imported goods are treated by government economists.

• *games*(120, 0, 0, 0, 0, 0, 128, 0) is a network with 120 vertices and 1276 arcs. Its vertices represent football teams at American colleges and universities. Arcs run between teams that played each other during the exciting 1990 season, and they are labeled with the number of points scored. For example, the arc Stanford ⟶ California has value 27, and the arc California ⟶ Stanford has value 25, because the Stanford Cardinal defeated the U. C. Berkeley Golden Bears by a score of 27–25 on 17 November 1990.

• *risc*(16) is a network of an entirely different kind. It has 3240 vertices and 7878 arcs, which define a *directed acyclic graph* or "dag" — namely, a digraph that contains no oriented cycles. The vertices represent gates that have Boolean values; an arc such as Z45 $\longrightarrow$ R0:7~ means that the value of gate Z45 is an input to gate R0:7~. Each gate has a type code (AND, OR, XOR, NOT, latch, or external input); each arc has a length, denoting an amount of delay. The network contains the complete logic for a miniature RISC chip that is able to obey simple commands governing sixteen registers, each 16 bits wide.

Complete details about all the SGB generators can be found in the author's book *The Stanford GraphBase* (New York: ACM Press, 1994), together with dozens of short example programs that explain how to manipulate the graphs and networks that the generators produce. For example, a program called LADDERS shows how to find a shortest path between one five-letter word and another. A program called TAKE_RISC demonstrates how to put a nanocomputer through its paces by simulating the actions of a network built from the gates of *risc*(16).

Hypergraphs. Graphs and networks can be utterly fascinating, but they aren't the end of the story by any means. Lots of important combinatorial algorithms are designed to work with *hypergraphs*, which are more general than graphs because their edges are allowed to be *arbitrary* subsets of the vertices.

For example, we might have seven vertices, identified by nonzero binary strings $v = a_1 a_2 a_3$, together with seven edges, identified by bracketed nonzero binary strings $e = [b_1 b_2 b_3]$, with $v \in e$ if and only if $(a_1 b_1 + a_2 b_2 + a_3 b_3) \bmod 2 = 0$. Each of these edges contains exactly three vertices:

$$[001] = \{010, 100, 110\}; \quad [010] = \{001, 100, 101\}; \quad [011] = \{011, 100, 111\};$$
$$[100] = \{001, 010, 011\}; \quad [101] = \{010, 101, 111\};$$
$$[110] = \{001, 110, 111\}; \quad [111] = \{011, 101, 110\}. \tag{56}$$

And by symmetry, each vertex belongs to exactly three edges. (Edges that contain three or more vertices are sometimes called "hyperedges," to distinguish them from the edges of an ordinary graph. But it's OK to call them just "edges.")

A hypergraph is said to be *r-uniform* if every edge contains exactly r vertices. Thus (56) is a 3-uniform hypergraph, and a 2-uniform hypergraph is an ordinary graph. The complete r-uniform hypergraph $K_n^{(r)}$ has n vertices and $\binom{n}{r}$ edges.

Most of the basic concepts of graph theory can be extended to hypergraphs in a natural way. For example, if $H = (V, E)$ is a hypergraph and if $U \subseteq V$, the subhypergraph $H \mid U$ induced by U has the edges $\{e \mid e \in E \text{ and } e \subseteq U\}$. The complement $\overline{H}$ of an r-uniform hypergraph has the edges of $K_n^{(r)}$ that aren't edges of H. A k-coloring of a hypergraph is an assignment of colors to the vertices so that no edge is monochromatic. And so on.

Hypergraphs go by many other names, because the same properties can be formulated in many different ways. For example, every hypergraph $H = (V, E)$ is essentially a *family of sets*, because each edge is a subset of V. A 3-uniform hypergraph is also called a *triple system*. A hypergraph is also equivalent to a matrix B of 0s and 1s, with one row for each vertex v and one column for each edge e; row v and column e of this matrix contains the value $b_{ve} = [v \in e]$.

Matrix B is called the *incidence matrix* of H, and we say that "v is incident with e" when $v \in e$. Furthermore, a hypergraph is equivalent to a *bipartite graph*, with vertex set $V \cup E$ and with the edge v — e whenever v is incident with e. The hypergraph is said to be *connected* if and only if the corresponding bipartite graph is connected. A *cycle* of length k in a hypergraph is defined to be a cycle of length $2k$ in the corresponding bipartite graph.

For example, the hypergraph (56) can be defined by an equivalent incidence matrix or an equivalent bipartite graph as follows:

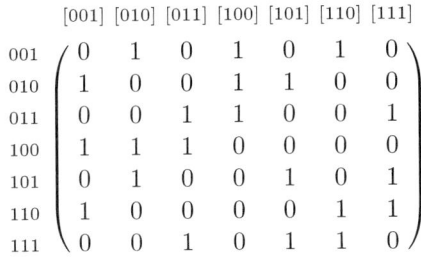 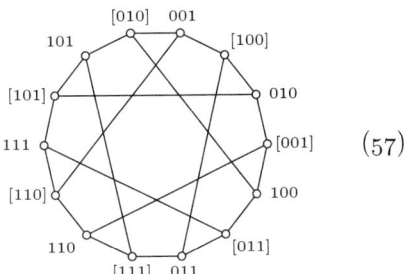

$$(57)$$

It contains 28 cycles of length 3, such as

$$[101] \text{---} 101 \text{---} [010] \text{---} 001 \text{---} [100] \text{---} 010 \text{---} [101]. \qquad (58)$$

The *dual* H^T of a hypergraph H is obtained by interchanging the roles of vertices and edges, but retaining the incidence relation. In other words, it corresponds to transposing the incidence matrix. Notice, for example, that the dual of an r-regular graph is an r-uniform hypergraph.

Incidence matrices and bipartite graphs might correspond to hypergraphs in which some edges occur more than once, because distinct columns of the matrix might be equal. When a hypergraph $H = (V, E)$ does not have any repeated edges, it corresponds also to yet another combinatorial object, namely a *Boolean function*. For if, say, the vertex set V is $\{1, 2, \ldots, n\}$, the function

$$h(x_1, x_2, \ldots, x_n) = \left[\{ j \mid x_j = 1 \} \in E \right] \qquad (59)$$

characterizes the edges of H. For example, the Boolean formula

$$(x_1 \oplus x_2 \oplus x_3) \wedge (x_2 \oplus x_4 \oplus x_6) \wedge (x_3 \oplus x_4 \oplus x_7)$$
$$\wedge (x_3 \oplus x_5 \oplus x_6) \wedge (\bar{x}_1 \vee \bar{x}_2 \vee \bar{x}_4) \qquad (60)$$

is another way to describe the hypergraph of (56) and (57).

The fact that combinatorial objects can be viewed in so many ways can be mind-boggling. But it's also extremely helpful, because it suggests different ways to solve equivalent problems. When we look at a problem from different perspectives, our brains naturally think of different ways to attack it. Sometimes we get the best insights by thinking about how to manipulate rows and columns in a matrix. Sometimes we make progress by imagining vertices and paths, or by visualizing clusters of points in space. Sometimes Boolean algebra is just the thing. If we're stuck in one domain, another might come to our rescue.

Covering and independence. If $H = (V, E)$ is a graph or hypergraph, a set U of vertices is said to *cover* H if every edge contains at least one member of U. A set W of vertices is said to be *independent* (or "stable") in H if no edge is completely contained in W.

From the standpoint of the incidence matrix, a covering is a set of rows whose sum is nonzero in every column. And in the special case that H is a graph, every column of the matrix contains just two 1s; hence an independent set in a graph corresponds to a set of rows that are mutually orthogonal—that is, a set for which the dot product of any two different rows is zero.

These concepts are opposite sides of the same coin. If U covers H, then $W = V \setminus U$ is independent in H; conversely, if W is independent in H, then $U = V \setminus W$ covers H. Both statements are equivalent to saying that the induced hypergraph $H \mid W$ has no edges.

This dual relationship between covering and independence, which was perhaps first noted by Claude Berge [*Proc. National Acad. Sci.* **43** (1957), 842–844], is somewhat paradoxical. Although it's logically obvious and easy to verify, it's also intuitively surprising. When we look at a graph and try to find a large independent set, we tend to have rather different thoughts from when we look at the same graph and try to find a small vertex cover; yet both goals are the same.

A covering set U is *minimal* if $U \setminus u$ fails to be a cover for all $u \in U$. Similarly, an independent set W is *maximal* if $W \cup w$ fails to be independent for all $w \notin W$. Here, for example, is a minimal cover of the 49-vertex graph of the contiguous United States, (17), and the corresponding maximal independent set:

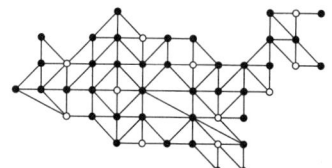 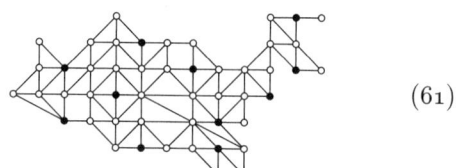

(61)

Minimal vertex cover, with 38 vertices	Maximal independent set, with 11 vertices

A covering is called *minimum* if it has the smallest possible size, and an independent set is called *maximum* if it has the largest possible size. For example, with graph (17) we can do much better than (61):

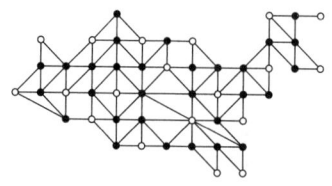 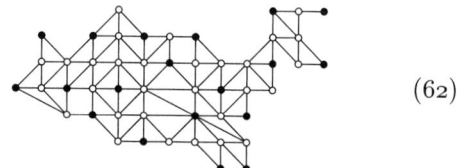

(62)

Minimum vertex cover, with 30 vertices	Maximum independent set, with 19 vertices

Notice the subtle distinction between "minimal" and "minimum" here: In general (but in contrast to most dictionaries of English), people who work with combinatorial algorithms use '-al' words like "minimal" or "optimal" to refer to combinatorial configurations that are *locally* best, in the sense that small changes don't improve them. The corresponding '-um' words, "minimum" or "optimum," are reserved for configurations that are *globally* best, considered over all possibilities. It's easy to find solutions to any optimization problem that are merely optimal, in the weak local sense, by climbing repeatedly until reaching the top of a hill. But it's usually much harder to find solutions that are truly optimum. For example, we'll see in Section 7.9 that the problem of finding a maximum independent set in a given graph belongs to a class of difficult problems that are called *NP-complete*.

Even when a problem is NP-complete, we needn't despair. We'll discuss techniques for finding minimum covers in several parts of this chapter, and those methods work fine on smallish problems; the optimum solution in (62) was found in less than a second, after examining only a tiny fraction of the 2^{49} possibilities. Furthermore, special cases of NP-complete problems often turn out to be simpler than the general case. In Sections 7.5.1 and 7.5.5 we'll see that a minimum vertex cover can be discovered quickly in any bipartite graph, or in any hypergraph that is the dual of a graph; we'll also study efficient ways to discover a maximum *matching*, which is a maximum independent set in the line graph of a given graph.

The problem of maximizing the size of an independent set occurs sufficiently often that it has acquired a special notation: If H is any hypergraph, the number

$$\alpha(H) \;=\; \max\big\{|W| \;\big|\; W \text{ is an independent set of vertices in } H\big\} \qquad (63)$$

is called the *independence number* (or the stability number) of H. Similarly,

$$\chi(H) \;=\; \min\{k \mid H \text{ is } k\text{-colorable}\} \qquad (64)$$

is called the *chromatic number* of H. Notice that $\chi(H)$ is the size of a minimum covering of H by independent sets, because the vertices that receive any particular color must be independent according to our definitions.

These definitions of $\alpha(H)$ and $\chi(H)$ apply in particular to the case when H is an ordinary graph, but of course we usually write $\alpha(G)$ and $\chi(G)$ in such situations. Graphs have another important number called their *clique number*,

$$\omega(G) \;=\; \max\big\{|X| \;\big|\; X \text{ is a clique in } G\big\}, \qquad (65)$$

where a "clique" is a set of mutually adjacent vertices. Clearly

$$\omega(G) \;=\; \alpha(\overline{G}), \qquad (66)$$

because a clique in G is an independent set in the complementary graph. Similarly we can see that $\chi(\overline{G})$ is the minimum size of a "clique cover," which is a set of cliques that exactly covers all of the vertices.

Several instances of "exact cover problems" were mentioned earlier in this section, without an explanation of exactly what such a problem really signifies. Finally we're ready for the definition: Given the incidence matrix of a hypergraph H, an *exact cover* of H is a set of rows whose sum is $(1\,1\,\ldots\,1)$. In other words, an exact cover is a set of vertices that touches each hyperedge exactly once; an ordinary cover is only required to touch each hyperedge *at least* once.

EXERCISES

1. [25] Suppose $n = 4m - 1$. Construct arrangements of Langford pairs for the numbers $\{1, 1, \ldots, n, n\}$, with the property that we also obtain a solution for $n = 4m$ by changing the first '$2m-1$' to '$4m$' and appending '$2m-1$ $4m$' at the right. *Hint:* Put the $m - 1$ even numbers $4m-4$, $4m-6$, ..., $2m$ at the left.

2. [20] For which n can $\{0, 0, 1, 1, \ldots, n-1, n-1\}$ be arranged as Langford pairs?

3. [22] Suppose we arrange the numbers $\{0, 0, 1, 1, \ldots, n-1, n-1\}$ in a *circle*, instead of a straight line, with distance k between the two k's. Do we get solutions that are essentially distinct from those of exercise 2?

4. [M20] (T. Skolem, 1957.) Show that the Fibonacci string $S_\infty = babbababbabba\ldots$ of exercise 1.2.8–36 leads directly to an infinite sequence $0012132453674\ldots$ of Langford pairs for the set of *all* nonnegative integers, if we simply replace the a's and b's independently by 0, 1, 2, etc., from left to right.

▶ **5.** [HM22] If a permutation of $\{1, 1, 2, 2, \ldots, n, n\}$ is chosen at random, what is the probability that the two k's are exactly k positions apart, given k? Use this formula to guess the size of the Langford numbers L_n in (1).

▶ **6.** [M28] (M. Godfrey, 2002.) Let $f(x_1, \ldots, x_{2n}) = \prod_{k=1}^{n}\left(x_k x_{n+k} \sum_{j=1}^{2n-k-1} x_j x_{j+k+1}\right)$.
   a) Prove that $\sum_{x_1, \ldots, x_{2n} \in \{-1, +1\}} f(x_1, \ldots, x_{2n}) = 2^{2n+1} L_n$.
   b) Explain how to evaluate this sum in $O(4^n n)$ steps. How many bits of precision are needed for the arithmetic?
   c) Gain a factor of eight by exploiting the identities

$$f(x_1, \ldots, x_{2n}) = f(-x_1, \ldots, -x_{2n}) = f(x_{2n}, \ldots, x_1) = f(x_1, -x_2, \ldots, x_{2n-1}, -x_{2n}).$$

7. [M22] Prove that every Langford pairing of $\{1, 1, \ldots, 16, 16\}$ must have seven uncompleted pairs at some point, when read from left to right.

8. [23] The simplest Langford sequence is not only well-balanced; it's *planar*, in the sense that its pairs can be connected up without crossing lines as in (2):

$$2\,3\,1\,2\,1\,3.$$

Find all of the planar Langford pairings for which $n \le 8$.

9. [24] (*Langford triples.*) In how many ways can $\{1, 1, 1, 2, 2, 2, \ldots, 9, 9, 9\}$ be arranged in a row so that consecutive k's are k apart, for $1 \le k \le 9$?

10. [M20] Explain how to construct a *magic square* directly from Fig. 1. (Convert each card into a number between 1 and 16, in such a way that the rows, columns, and main diagonals all sum to 34.)

11. [20] Extend (5) to a "Hebraic-Græco-Latin" square by appending one of the letters $\{\aleph, \beth, \gimel, \daleth\}$ to the two-letter string in each compartment. No letter pair (Latin, Greek), (Latin, Hebrew), or (Greek, Hebrew) should appear in more than one place.

▶ **12.** [M21] (L. Euler.) Let $L_{ij} = (i+j) \bmod n$ for $0 \le i, j < n$ be the addition table for integers mod n. Prove that a latin square orthogonal to L exists if and only if n is odd.

13. [M25] A 10×10 square can be divided into four quarters of size 5×5. A 10×10 latin square formed from the digits $\{0, 1, \ldots, 9\}$ has k "intruders" if its upper left quarter has exactly k elements ≥ 5. (See exercise 14(e) for an example with $k = 3$.) Prove that the square has no orthogonal mate unless there are at least three intruders.

14. [*29*] Find all orthogonal mates of the following latin squares:

(a)	(b)	(c)	(d)	(e)
3145926870	2718459036	0572164938	1680397425	7823456019
2819763504	0287135649	6051298473	8346512097	8234067195
9452307168	7524093168	4867039215	9805761342	2340178956
6208451793	1435962780	1439807652	2754689130	3401289567
8364095217.	6390718425.	8324756091.	0538976214.	4012395678.
5981274036'	4069271853'	7203941586'	4963820571'	5678912340'
4627530981	3102684597	5610473829	7192034658	6789523401
0576148329	9871546302	9148625307	6219405783	0195634782
1730689452	8956307214	2795380164	3471258906	1956740823
7093812645	5643820971	3986512740	5027143869	9567801234

15. [*50*] Find three 10×10 latin squares that are mutually orthogonal to each other.

16. [*48*] (H. J. Ryser, 1967.) A latin square is said to be of "order n" if it has n rows, n columns, and n symbols. Does every latin square of odd order have a transversal?

17. [*25*] Let L be a latin square with elements L_{ij} for $0 \le i, j < n$. Show that the problems of (a) finding all the transversals of L, and (b) finding all the orthogonal mates of L, are special cases of the general exact cover problem.

18. [*M26*] The string $x_1 x_2 \ldots x_N$ is called "n-ary" if each element x_j belongs to the set $\{0, 1, \ldots, n-1\}$ of n-ary digits. Two strings $x_1 x_2 \ldots x_N$ and $y_1 y_2 \ldots y_N$ are said to be *orthogonal* if the N pairs (x_j, y_j) are distinct for $1 \le j \le N$. (Consequently, two n-ary strings cannot be orthogonal if their length N exceeds n^2.) An n-ary matrix with m rows and n^2 columns whose rows are orthogonal to each other is called an *orthogonal array* of order n and depth m.

Find a correspondence between orthogonal arrays of depth m and lists of $m - 2$ mutually orthogonal latin squares. What orthogonal array corresponds to exercise 11?

▶ **19.** [*M25*] Continuing exercise 18, prove that an orthogonal array of order $n > 1$ and depth m is possible only if $m \le n + 1$. Show that this upper limit is achievable when n is a prime number p. Write out an example when $p = 5$.

20. [*HM20*] Show that if each element k in an orthogonal array is replaced by $e^{2\pi ki/n}$, the rows become orthogonal vectors in the usual sense (their dot product is zero).

▶ **21.** [*M21*] A *geometric net* is a system of points and lines that obeys three axioms:

   i) Each line is a set of points.

   ii) Distinct lines have at most one point in common.

   iii) If p is a point and L is a line with $p \notin L$, then there is exactly one line M such that $p \in M$ and $L \cap M = \emptyset$.

If $L \cap M = \emptyset$ we say that L is *parallel* to M, and write $L \parallel M$.

   a) Prove that the lines of a geometric net can be partitioned into equivalence classes, with two lines in the same class if and only if they are equal or parallel.

   b) Show that if there are at least two classes of parallel lines, every line contains the same number of points as the other lines in its class.

   c) Furthermore, if there are at least three classes, there are numbers m and n such that all points belong to exactly m lines and all lines contain exactly n points.

▶ **22.** [*M22*] Show that every orthogonal array can be regarded as a geometric net. Is the converse also true?

23. [*M23*] (*Error-correcting codes.*) The "Hamming distance" $d(x, y)$ between two strings $x = x_1 \ldots x_N$ and $y = y_1 \ldots y_N$ is the number of positions j where $x_j \ne y_j$. A *b-ary code with n information digits and r check digits* is a set $C(b, n, r)$ of b^n strings $x = x_1 \ldots x_{n+r}$, where $0 \le x_j < b$ for $1 \le j \le n+r$. When a codeword x is transmitted and the message y is received, $d(x, y)$ is the number of transmission errors. The code is called *t-error correcting* if we can reconstruct the value of x whenever a message y is received with $d(x, y) \le t$. The *distance* of the code is the minimum value of $d(x, x')$, taken over all pairs of codewords $x \ne x'$.

a) Prove that a code is t-error correcting if and only if its distance exceeds $2t$.

b) Prove that a single-error correcting b-ary code with 2 information digits and 2 check digits is equivalent to a pair of orthogonal latin squares of order b.

c) Furthermore, a code $C(b, 2, r)$ with distance $r+1$ is equivalent to a set of r mutually orthogonal latin squares of order b.

▶ **24.** [*M30*] A geometric net with N points and R lines leads naturally to the binary code $C(2, N, R)$ with codewords $x_1 \ldots x_N x_{N+1} \ldots x_{N+R}$ defined by the parity bits

$$x_{N+k} = f_k(x_1, \ldots, x_N) = \left(\sum \{x_j \mid \text{point } j \text{ lies on line } k\} \right) \bmod 2.$$

a) If the net has m classes of parallel lines, prove that this code has distance $m + 1$.

b) Find an efficient way to correct up to t errors with this code, assuming that $m = 2t$. Illustrate the decoding process in the case $N = 25$, $R = 30$, $t = 3$.

25. [*27*] Find a latin square whose rows and columns are five-letter words. (For this exercise you'll need to dig out the big dictionaries.)

▶ **26.** [*25*] Compose a meaningful English sentence that contains only five-letter words.

27. [*20*] How many SGB words contain exactly k distinct letters, for $1 \le k \le 5$?

28. [*20*] Are there any pairs of SGB word vectors that differ by ± 1 in each component?

29. [*20*] Find all SGB words that are *palindromes* (equal to their reflection), or mirror pairs (like `regal lager`).

▶ **30.** [*20*] The letters of `first` are in alphabetic order from left to right. What is the lexicographically *first* such five-letter word? What is the last?

31. [*21*] (C. McManus.) Find all sets of three SGB words that are in arithmetic progression but have no common letters in any fixed position. (One such example is {`power`, `slugs`, `visit`}.)

32. [*23*] Does the English language contain any 10-letter words $a_0 a_1 \ldots a_9$ for which both $a_0 a_2 a_4 a_6 a_8$ and $a_1 a_3 a_5 a_7 a_9$ are SGB words?

33. [*20*] (Scot Morris.) Complete the following list of 26 interesting SGB words:

about, bacon, faced, under, chief, ..., pizza.

▶ **34.** [*21*] For each SGB word that doesn't include the letter `y`, obtain a 5-bit binary number by changing the vowels {`a`, `e`, `i`, `o`, `u`} to 1 and the other letters to 0. What are the most common words for each of the 32 binary outcomes?

▶ **35.** [*26*] Sixteen well-chosen elements of WORDS(1000) lead to the branching pattern

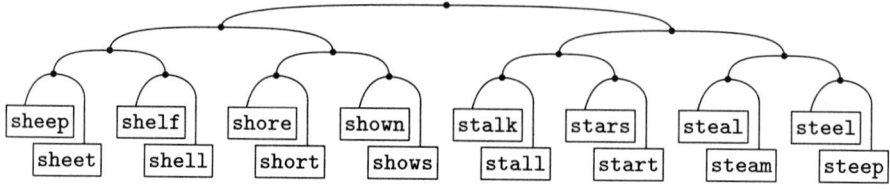

which is a complete binary trie of words that begin with the letter s. But there's no such pattern of words beginning with a, even if we consider the full collection WORDS(5757).

What letters of the alphabet can be used as the starting letter of sixteen words that form a complete binary trie within WORDS(n), given n?

36. [*M17*] Explain the symmetries that appear in the word cube (10). Also show that two more such cubes can be obtained by changing only the two words {stove, event}.

37. [*20*] Which vertices of the graph *words*(5757, 0, 0, 0) have maximum degree?

38. [*22*] Using the digraph rule in (14), change tears to smile in just three steps, *without computer assistance*.

39. [*M00*] Is $G \setminus e$ an induced subgraph of G? Is it a spanning subgraph?

40. [*M15*] How many (a) spanning (b) induced subgraphs does a graph $G = (V, E)$ have, when $|V| = n$ and $|E| = e$?

41. [*M10*] For which integers n do we have (a) $K_n = P_n$? (b) $K_n = C_n$?

42. [*15*] (D. H. Lehmer.) Let G be a graph with 13 vertices, in which every vertex has degree 5. Make a nontrivial statement about G.

43. [*23*] Are any of the following graphs the same as the Petersen graph?

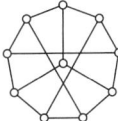  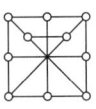 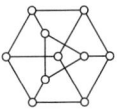

44. [*M23*] How many symmetries does Chvátal's graph have? (See Fig. 2(f).)

45. [*20*] Find an easy way to 4-color the planar graph (17). Would 3 colors suffice?

46. [*M25*] Let G be a graph with $n \geq 3$ vertices, defined by a planar diagram that is "maximal," in the sense that no additional lines can be drawn between nonadjacent vertices without crossing an existing edge.

a) Prove that the diagram partitions the plane into regions that each have exactly three vertices on their boundary. (One of these regions is the set of all points that lie outside the diagram.)

b) Therefore G has exactly $3n - 6$ edges.

47. [*M22*] Prove that the complete bigraph $K_{3,3}$ isn't planar.

48. [*M25*] Complete the proof of Theorem B by showing that the stated procedure never gives the same color to two adjacent vertices.

49. [*18*] Draw diagrams of all the cubic graphs with at most 6 vertices.

50. [*M24*] Find all bipartite graphs that can be 3-colored in exactly 24 ways.

▶ **51.** [*M22*] Given a geometric net as described in exercise 21, construct the bipartite graph whose vertices are the points p and the lines L of the net, with $p \text{ --- } L$ if and only if $p \in L$. What is the *girth* of this graph?

52. [*M16*] Find a simple inequality that relates the diameter of a graph to its girth. (How small can the diameter be, if the girth is large?)

53. [*15*] Which of the words world and happy belongs to the giant component of the graph *words*(5757, 0, 0, 0)?

▶ **54.** [*21*] The 49 postal codes in graph (17) are AL, AR, AZ, CA, CO, CT, DC, DE, FL, GA, IA, ID, IL, IN, KS, KY, LA, MA, MD, ME, MI, MN, MO, MS, MT, NC, ND, NE, NH, NJ, NM, NV, NY, OH, OK, OR, PA, RI, SC, SD, TN, TX, UT, VA, VT, WA, WI, WV, WY, in alphabetical order.

   a) Suppose we consider two states to be adjacent if their postal codes agree in one place (namely AL — AR — OR — OH, etc.). What are the components of this graph?

   b) Now form a directed graph with XY ⟶ YZ (for example, AL ⟶ LA ⟶ AR, etc.). What are the *strongly connected components* of this digraph? (See Section 2.3.4.2.)

   c) The United States has additional postal codes AA, AE, AK, AP, AS, FM, GU, HI, MH, MP, PW, PR, VI, besides those in (17). Reconsider question (b), using all 62 codes.

55. [*M20*] How many edges are in the complete k-partite graph $K_{n_1,\dots,n_k}$?

▶ **56.** [*M10*] True or false: A multigraph is a graph if and only if the corresponding digraph is simple.

57. [*M10*] True or false: Vertices u and v are in the same connected component of a directed graph if and only if either $d(u,v) < \infty$ or $d(v,u) < \infty$.

58. [*M17*] Describe all (a) graphs (b) multigraphs that are regular of degree 2.

▶ **59.** [*M23*] A *tournament* of order n is a digraph on n vertices that has exactly $\binom{n}{2}$ arcs, either $u \longrightarrow v$ or $v \longrightarrow u$ for every pair of distinct vertices $\{u,v\}$.

   a) Prove that every tournament contains an oriented spanning path $v_1 \longrightarrow \cdots \longrightarrow v_n$.

   b) Consider the tournament on vertices $\{0,1,2,3,4\}$ for which $u \longrightarrow v$ if and only if $(u - v) \bmod 5 \geq 3$. How many oriented spanning paths does it have?

   c) Is $\vec{K_n}$ the only tournament of order n that has a unique oriented spanning path?

▶ **60.** [*M22*] Let u be a vertex of greatest out-degree in a tournament, and let v be any other vertex. Prove that $d(u,v) \leq 2$.

61. [*M16*] Construct a digraph that has k walks of length k from vertex 1 to vertex 2.

62. [*M21*] A *permutation digraph* is a directed graph in which every vertex has out-degree 1 and in-degree 1; therefore its components are oriented cycles. If it has n vertices and k components, we call it *even* if $n - k$ is even, *odd* if $n - k$ is odd.

   a) Let G be a directed graph with adjacency matrix A. Prove that the number of spanning permutation digraphs of G is per A, the permanent of A.

   b) Interpret the determinant, det A, in terms of spanning permutation digraphs.

63. [*M23*] Let G be a graph of girth g in which every vertex has at least d neighbors. Prove that G has at least N vertices, where

$$N = \begin{cases} 1 + \sum_{0 \leq k < t} d(d-1)^k, & \text{if } g = 2t+1; \\ 1 + (d-1)^t + \sum_{0 \leq k < t} d(d-1)^k, & \text{if } g = 2t+2. \end{cases}$$

▶ **64.** [*M21*] Continuing exercise 63, show that there's a *unique* graph of girth 4, minimum degree d, and order $2d$, for each $d \geq 2$.

▶ **65.** [*HM31*] Suppose graph G has girth 5, minimum degree d, and $N = d^2 + 1$ vertices.

   a) Prove that the adjacency matrix A of G satisfies the equation $A^2 + A = (d-1)I + J$.

   b) Since A is a symmetric matrix, it has N orthogonal eigenvectors x_j, with corresponding eigenvalues λ_j, such that $Ax_j = \lambda_j x_j$ for $1 \leq j \leq N$. Prove that each λ_j is either d or $(-1 \pm \sqrt{4d-3})/2$.

   c) Show that if $\sqrt{4d-3}$ is irrational, then $d = 2$. *Hint:* $\lambda_1 + \cdots + \lambda_N = \text{trace}(A) = 0$.

   d) And if $\sqrt{4d-3}$ is rational, $d \in \{3, 7, 57\}$.

66. [*M30*] Continuing exercise 65, construct such a graph when $d = 7$.

67. [*M48*] Is there a regular graph of degree 57, order 3250, and girth 5?

68. [*M20*] How many different adjacency matrices does a graph G on n vertices have?

▶ **69.** [*20*] Extending (31), explain how to calculate both out-degree ODEG(v) and in-degree IDEG(v) for *all* vertices v in a graph that has been represented in SGB format.

▶ **70.** [*M20*] How often is each step of Algorithm B performed, when that algorithm successfully 2-colors a graph with m arcs and n vertices?

71. [*26*] Implement Algorithm B for the MMIX computer, using the MMIXAL assembly language. Assume that, when your program begins, register v0 points to the first vertex node and register n contains the number of vertices.

▶ **72.** [*M22*] When COLOR(v) is set in step B6, call u the *parent* of v; but when COLOR(w) is set in step B3, say that w has no parent. Define the (inclusive) *ancestors* of vertex v, recursively, to be v together with the ancestors of v's parent (if any).

   a) Prove that if v is below u in the stack during Algorithm B, the parent of v is an ancestor of u.
   b) Furthermore, if COLOR(v) = COLOR(u) in step B6, v is currently in the stack.
   c) Use these facts to extend Algorithm B so that, if the given graph is not bipartite, the names of vertices in a cycle of odd length are output.

73. [*15*] What's another name for $random\_graph(10, 45, 0, 0, 0, 0, 0, 0, 0, 0)$?

74. [*21*] What vertex of $roget(1022, 0, 0, 0)$ has the largest out-degree?

75. [*22*] The SGB graph generator $board(n_1, n_2, n_3, n_4, p, w, o)$ creates a graph whose vertices are the t-dimensional integer vectors $(x_1, \ldots, x_t)$ for $0 \le x_i < b_i$, determined by the first four parameters (n_1, n_2, n_3, n_4) as follows: Set $n_5 \leftarrow 0$ and let $j \ge 0$ be minimum such that $n_{j+1} \le 0$. If $j = 0$, set $b_1 \leftarrow b_2 \leftarrow 8$ and $t \leftarrow 2$; this is the default 8×8 board. Otherwise if $n_{j+1} = 0$, set $b_i \leftarrow n_i$ for $1 \le i \le j$ and $t \leftarrow j$. Finally, if $n_{j+1} < 0$, set $t \leftarrow |n_{j+1}|$, and set b_i to the ith element of the periodic sequence $(n_1, \ldots, n_j, n_1, \ldots, n_j, n_1, \ldots)$. (For example, the specification $(n_1, n_2, n_3, n_4) = (2, 3, 5, -7)$ is about as tricky as you can get; it produces a 7-dimensional board with $(b_1, \ldots, b_7) = (2, 3, 5, 2, 3, 5, 2)$, hence a graph with $2 \cdot 3 \cdot 5 \cdot 2 \cdot 3 \cdot 5 \cdot 2 = 1800$ vertices.)

The remaining parameters (p, w, o), for "piece, wrap, and orientation," determine the arcs of the graph. Suppose first that $w = o = 0$. If $p > 0$, we have $(x_1, \ldots, x_t) \longrightarrow (y_1, \ldots, y_t)$ if and only if $y_i = x_i + \delta_i$ for $1 \le i \le t$, where $(\delta_1, \ldots, \delta_t)$ is an integer solution to the equation $\delta_1^2 + \cdots + \delta_t^2 = |p|$. And if $p < 0$, we allow also $y_i = x_i + k\delta_i$ for $k \ge 1$, corresponding to k moves in the same direction.

If $w \ne 0$, let $w = (w_t \ldots w_1)_2$ in binary notation. Then we allow "wraparound," $y_i = (x_i + \delta_i) \bmod b_i$ or $y_i = (x_i + k\delta_i) \bmod b_i$, in each coordinate i for which $w_i = 1$.

If $o \ne 0$, the graph is directed; offsets $(\delta_1, \ldots, \delta_t)$ produce arcs only when they are lexicographically greater than $(0, \ldots, 0)$. But if $o = 0$, the graph is undirected.

Find settings of $(n_1, n_2, n_3, n_4, p, w, o)$ for which $board$ will produce the following fundamental graphs: (a) the complete graph K_n; (b) the path P_n; (c) the cycle C_n; (d) the transitive tournament $\vec{K_n}$; (e) the oriented path $\vec{P_n}$; (f) the oriented cycle $\vec{C_n}$; (g) the $m \times n$ grid $P_m \square P_n$; (h) the $m \times n$ cylinder $P_m \square C_n$; (i) the $m \times n$ torus $C_m \square C_n$; (j) the $m \times n$ rook graph $K_m \square K_n$; (k) the $m \times n$ directed torus $\vec{C_m} \square \vec{C_n}$; (l) the null graph $\overline{K_n}$; (m) the n-cube $P_2 \square \cdots \square P_2$ with 2^n vertices.

76. [*20*] Can $board(n_1, n_2, n_3, n_4, p, w, o)$ produce loops, or parallel (repeated) edges?

77. [*M20*] If graph G has diameter ≥ 3, prove that $\overline{G}$ has diameter ≤ 3.

78. [*M27*] Let $G = (V, E)$ be a graph with $|V| = n$ and $G \cong \overline{G}$. (In other words, G is *self-complementary*: There's a permutation φ of V such that $u \,\text{---}\, v$ if and only if $\varphi(u) \,\text{---}\!\!\!/\;\, \varphi(v)$ and $u \neq v$. We can imagine that the edges of K_n have been painted black or white; the white edges define a graph that's isomorphic to the graph of black edges.)
  a) Prove that $n \bmod 4 = 0$ or 1. Draw diagrams for all such graphs with $n < 8$.
  b) Prove that if $n \bmod 4 = 0$, every cycle of the permutation φ has a length that is a multiple of 4.
  c) Conversely, every permutation φ with such cycles arises in some such graph G.
  d) Extend these results to the case $n \bmod 4 = 1$.

▶ **79.** [*M22*] Given $k \geq 0$, construct a graph on the vertices $\{0, 1, \ldots, 4k\}$ that is both regular and self-complementary.

▶ **80.** [*M22*] A self-complementary graph must have diameter 2 or 3, by exercise 77. Given $k \geq 2$, construct self-complementary graphs of both possible diameters, when (a) $V = \{1, 2, \ldots, 4k\}$; (b) $V = \{0, 1, 2, \ldots, 4k\}$.

81. [*20*] The complement of a simple digraph without loops is defined by extending (35) and (36), so that we have $u \to v$ in $\overline{D}$ if and only if $u \neq v$ and $u \not\to v$ in D. What are the self-complementary digraphs of order 3?

82. [*M21*] Are the following statements about line graphs true or false?
  a) If G is contained in G', then $L(G)$ is an induced subgraph of $L(G')$.
  b) If G is a regular graph, so is $L(G)$.
  c) $L(K_{m,n})$ is regular, for all $m, n > 0$.
  d) $L(K_{m,n,r})$ is regular, for all $m, n, r > 0$.
  e) $L(K_{m,n}) \cong K_m \mathbin{\square} K_n$.
  f) $L(K_4) \cong K_{2,2,2}$.
  g) $L(P_{n+1}) \cong P_n$.
  h) The graphs G and $L(G)$ both have the same number of components.

83. [*16*] Draw the graph $\overline{L(K_5)}$.

▶ **84.** [*M21*] Is $L(K_{3,3})$ self-complementary?

85. [*M22*] (O. Ore, 1962.) For which graphs G do we have $G \cong L(G)$?

86. [*M20*] (R. J. Wilson.) Find a graph G of order 6 for which $\overline{G} \cong L(G)$.

87. [*20*] Is the Petersen graph (a) 3-colorable? (b) 3-edge-colorable?

88. [*M20*] The graph $W_n = K_1 \,\text{---}\, C_{n-1}$ is called the *wheel* of order n, when $n \geq 4$. How many cycles does it contain as subgraphs?

W_8

89. [*M20*] Prove the associative laws, (42) and (43).

▶ **90.** [*M24*] A graph is called a *cograph* if it can be constructed algebraically from 1-element graphs by means of complementation and/or direct sum operations. For example, there are four nonisomorphic graphs of order 3, and they all are cographs: $\overline{K_3} = K_1 \oplus K_1 \oplus K_1$ and its complement, K_3; $\overline{K_{1,2}} = K_1 \oplus K_2$ and its complement, $K_{1,2}$, where $K_2 = \overline{K_1 \oplus K_1}$.

  Exhaustive enumeration shows that there are 11 nonisomorphic graphs of order 4. Give algebraic formulas to prove that 10 of them are cographs. Which one isn't?

▶ **91.** [*20*] Draw diagrams for the 4-vertex graphs (a) $K_2 \mathbin{\square} K_2$; (b) $K_2 \otimes K_2$; (c) $K_2 \boxtimes K_2$; (d) $K_2 \mathbin{\triangle} K_2$; (e) $K_2 \circ K_2$; (f) $\overline{K_2} \circ K_2$; (g) $K_2 \circ \overline{K_2}$.

92. [*21*] The five types of graph products defined in the text work fine for simple digraphs as well as for ordinary graphs. Draw diagrams for the 4-vertex digraphs (a) $\vec{K_2} \mathbin{\square} \vec{K_2}$; (b) $\vec{K_2} \otimes \vec{K_2}$; (c) $\vec{K_2} \boxtimes \vec{K_2}$; (d) $\vec{K_2} \mathbin{\triangle} \vec{K_2}$; (e) $\vec{K_2} \circ \vec{K_2}$.

93. [15] Which of the five graph products takes K_m and K_n into K_{mn}?

94. [10] Are the SGB *words* graphs induced subgraphs of $P_{26} \square P_{26} \square P_{26} \square P_{26} \square P_{26}$?

95. [M20] If vertex u of G has degree d_u and vertex v of H has degree d_v, what is the degree of vertex (u, v) in (a) $G \square H$? (b) $G \otimes H$? (c) $G \boxtimes H$? (d) $G \triangle H$? (e) $G \circ H$?

▶ **96.** [M22] Let A be an $m \times m'$ matrix with $a_{uu'}$ in row u and column u'; let B be an $n \times n'$ matrix with $b_{vv'}$ in row v and column v'. The *direct product* $A \otimes B$ is an $mn \times m'n'$ matrix with $a_{uu'}b_{vv'}$ in row (u, v) and column (u', v'). Thus $A \otimes B$ is the adjacency matrix of $G \otimes H$, if A and B are the adjacency matrices of G and H.

Find analogous formulas for the adjacency matrices of (a) $G \square H$; (b) $G \boxtimes H$; (c) $G \triangle H$; (d) $G \circ H$.

97. [M25] Find as many interesting algebraic relations between graph sums and products as you can. (For example, the distributive law $(A \oplus B) \otimes C = (A \otimes C) \oplus (B \otimes C)$ for direct sums and products of matrices implies that $(G \oplus G') \otimes H = (G \otimes H) \oplus (G' \otimes H)$. We also have $\overline{K_m} \square H = H \oplus \cdots \oplus H$, with m copies of H, etc.)

98. [M20] If the graph G has k components and the graph H has l components, how many components are in the graphs $G \square H$ and $G \boxtimes H$?

99. [M20] Let $d_G(u, u')$ be the distance from vertex u to vertex u' in graph G. Prove that $d_{G \square H}((u, v), (u', v')) = d_G(u, u') + d_H(v, v')$, and find a similar formula for $d_{G \boxtimes H}((u, v), (u', v'))$.

100. [M21] For which connected graphs is $G \otimes H$ connected?

▶ **101.** [M25] Find all connected graphs G and H such that $G \square H \cong G \otimes H$.

102. [M20] What's a simple algebraic formula for the graph of *king moves* (which take one step horizontally, vertically, or diagonally) on an $m \times n$ board?

103. [20] Complete tableau (54). Also apply Algorithm H to the sequence 866444444.

104. [18] Explain the manipulation of variables i, t, and r in steps H3 and H4.

105. [M38] Suppose $d_1 \geq \cdots \geq d_n \geq 0$, and let $c_1 \geq \cdots \geq c_{d_1}$ be its conjugate as in Algorithm H. Prove that $d_1 \ldots d_n$ is graphical if and only if $d_1 + \cdots + d_n$ is even and $d_1 + \cdots + d_k \leq c_1 + \cdots + c_k - k$ for $1 \leq k \leq s$, where s is maximal such that $d_s \geq s$.

106. [20] True or false: If $d_1 = \cdots = d_n = d < n$ and nd is even, Algorithm H constructs a *connected* graph.

107. [M21] Prove that the degree sequence $d_1 \ldots d_n$ of a self-complementary graph satisfies $d_j + d_{n+1-j} = n - 1$ and $d_{2j-1} = d_{2j}$ for $1 \leq j \leq n/2$.

▶ **108.** [M23] Design an algorithm analogous to Algorithm H that constructs a *simple directed graph* on vertices $\{1, \ldots, n\}$, having specified values d_k^- and d_k^+ for the in-degree and out-degree of each vertex k, whenever at least one such graph exists.

109. [M20] Design an algorithm analogous to Algorithm H that constructs a *bipartite graph* on vertices $\{1, \ldots, m + n\}$, having specified degrees d_k for each vertex k when possible; all edges $j \!-\! k$ should have $j \leq m$ and $k > m$.

110. [M22] Without using Algorithm H, show by a direct construction that the sequence $d_1 \ldots d_n$ is graphical when $n > d_1 \geq \cdots \geq d_n \geq d_1 - 1$ and $d_1 + \cdots + d_n$ is even.

▶ **111.** [25] Let G be a graph on vertices $V = \{1, \ldots, n\}$, with d_k the degree of k and $\max(d_1, \ldots, d_n) = d$. Prove that there's an integer N with $n \leq N \leq 2n$ and a graph H on vertices $\{1, \ldots, N\}$, such that H is regular of degree d and $H \mid V = G$. Explain how to construct such a regular graph with N as small as possible.

▶ **112.** [*20*] Does the network *miles*(128, 0, 0, 0, 0, 127, 0) have three equidistant cities? If not, what three cities come closest to an equilateral triangle?

113. [*05*] When H is a hypergraph with m edges and n vertices, how many rows and columns does its incidence matrix have?

114. [*M20*] Suppose the multigraph (26) is regarded as a hypergraph. What is the corresponding incidence matrix? What is the corresponding bipartite multigraph?

▶ **115.** [*M20*] When B is the incidence matrix of a graph G, explain the significance of the symmetric matrices $B^T B$ and BB^T.

116. [*M17*] Describe the edges of the complete bipartite r-uniform hypergraph $K_{m,n}^{(r)}$.

117. [*M22*] How many nonisomorphic 1-uniform hypergraphs have m edges and n vertices? (Edges may be repeated.) List them all when $m = 4$ and $n = 3$.

118. [*M20*] A "hyperforest" is a hypergraph that contains no cycles. If a hyperforest has m edges, n vertices, and p components, what's the sum of the degrees of its vertices?

119. [*M18*] What hypergraph corresponds to (60) without the final term $(\bar{x}_1 \vee \bar{x}_2 \vee \bar{x}_4)$?

120. [*M20*] Define *directed hypergraphs*, by generalizing the concept of directed graphs.

121. [*M19*] Given a hypergraph $H = (V, E)$, let $I(H) = (V, F)$, where F is the family of all maximal independent sets of H. Express $\chi(H)$ in terms of $|V|$, $|F|$, and $\alpha(I(H)^T)$.

▶ **122.** [*M24*] Find a maximum independent set and a minimum coloring of the following triple systems: (a) the hypergraph (56); (b) the dual of the Petersen graph.

123. [*17*] Show that the optimum colorings of $K_n \square K_n$ are equivalent to the solutions of a famous combinatorial problem.

124. [*M22*] What is the chromatic number of the Chvátal graph, Fig. 2(f)?

125. [*M48*] For what values of g is there a 4-regular, 4-chromatic graph of girth g?

▶ **126.** [*M22*] Find optimum colorings of the "kingwise torus," $C_m \boxtimes C_n$, when $m, n \geq 3$.

127. [*M22*] Prove that (a) $\chi(G) + \chi(\overline{G}) \leq n + 1$ and (b) $\chi(G)\chi(\overline{G}) \geq n$ when G is a graph of order n, and find graphs for which equality holds.

128. [*M18*] Express $\chi(G \square H)$ in terms of $\chi(G)$ and $\chi(H)$, when G and H are graphs.

129. [*23*] Describe the maximal cliques of the 8×8 queen graph (37).

130. [*M20*] How many maximal cliques are in a complete k-partite graph?

131. [*M30*] Let $N(n)$ be the largest number of maximal cliques that an n-vertex graph can have. Prove that $3^{\lfloor n/3 \rfloor} \leq N(n) \leq 3^{\lceil n/3 \rceil}$.

▶ **132.** [*M20*] We call G *tightly colorable* if $\chi(G) = \omega(G)$. Prove that $\chi(G \boxtimes H) = \chi(G)\chi(H)$ whenever G and H are tightly colorable.

133. [*21*] The "musical graph" illustrated here provides a nice way to review numerous definitions that were given in this section, because its properties are easily analyzed. Determine its (a) order; (b) size; (c) girth; (d) diameter; (e) independence number, $\alpha(G)$; (f) chromatic number, $\chi(G)$; (g) edge-chromatic number, $\chi(L(G))$; (h) clique number, $\omega(G)$; (i) algebraic formula as a product of well-known smaller graphs. What is the size of (j) a minimum vertex cover? (k) a maximum matching? Is G (l) regular? (m) planar? (n) connected? (o) directed? (p) a free tree? (q) Hamiltonian?

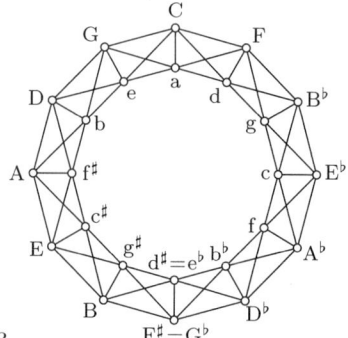

134. [*M22*] How many automorphisms does the musical graph have?

▶ **135.** [*HM26*] Suppose a composer takes a random walk in the musical graph, starting at vertex C and then making five equally likely choices at each step. Show that after an even number of steps, the walk is more likely to end at vertex C than at any other vertex. What is the exact probability of going from C to C in a 12-step walk?

136. [*HM23*] A *Cayley digraph* is a directed graph whose vertices V are the elements of a group and whose arcs are $v \longrightarrow v\alpha_j$ for $1 \leq j \leq d$ and all vertices v, where $(\alpha_1, \ldots, \alpha_d)$ are fixed elements of the group. A *Cayley graph* is a Cayley digraph that is also a graph. Is the Petersen graph a Cayley graph?

▶ **137.** [*M25*] (*Generalized toruses.*) An $m \times n$ torus can be regarded as a tiling of the plane. For example, we can imagine that infinitely many copies of the 3×4 torus in (50) have been placed together gridwise, as indicated in the left-hand illustration above; from each vertex we can move north, south, east, or west to another vertex of the torus. The vertices have been numbered here so that a northward move from v goes to $(v+4) \bmod 12$, and an eastward move to $(v+3) \bmod 12$, etc. The right-hand illustration shows the same torus, but with a differently shaped tile; *any* way to choose twelve cells numbered $\{0, 1, \ldots, 11\}$ will tile the plane, with exactly the same underlying graph.

Shifted copies of a single shape will also tile the plane if they form a *generalized torus*, in which cell (x, y) corresponds to the same vertex as cells $(x + a, y + b)$ and $(x + c, y + d)$, where (a, b) and (c, d) are integer vectors and $n = ad - bc > 0$. The generalized torus will then have n points. These vectors (a, b) and (c, d) are $(4, 0)$ and $(0, 3)$ in the 3×4 example above; and when they are respectively $(5, 2)$ and $(1, 3)$ we get

Here $n = 13$, and a northward move from v goes to $(v + 4) \bmod 13$; an eastward move goes to $(v + 1) \bmod 13$.

Prove that if $\gcd(a, b, c, d) = 1$, the vertices of such a generalized torus can always be assigned integer labels $\{0, 1, \ldots, n-1\}$ in such a way that the neighbors of v are $(v \pm p) \bmod n$ and $(v \pm q) \bmod n$, for some integers p and q.

138. [*HM27*] Continuing exercise 137, what is a good way to label k-dimensional vertices $x = (x_1, \ldots, x_k)$, when integer vectors α_j are given such that each vector x is equivalent to $x + \alpha_j$ for $1 \le j \le k$? Illustrate your method in the case $k = 3$, $\alpha_1 = (3, 1, 1)$, $\alpha_2 = (1, 3, 1)$, $\alpha_3 = (1, 1, 3)$.

▶ **139.** [*M22*] Let H be a fixed graph of order h, and let $\#(H\!:\!G)$ be the number of times that H occurs as an induced subgraph of a given graph G. If G is chosen at random from the set of all $2^{n(n-1)/2}$ graphs on the vertices $V = \{1, 2, \ldots, n\}$, what is the average value of $\#(H\!:\!G)$ when H is (a) K_h; (b) P_h, for $h > 1$; (c) C_h, for $h > 2$; (d) arbitrary?

140. [*M30*] A graph G is called *proportional* if its induced subgraph counts $\#(K_3\!:\!G)$, $\#(\overline{K_3}\!:\!G)$, and $\#(P_3\!:\!G)$ each agree with the expected values derived in exercise 139.

a) Show that the wheel graph W_8 of exercise 88 is proportional in this sense.

b) Prove that G is proportional if and only if $\#(K_3\!:\!G) = \frac{1}{8}\binom{n}{3}$ and the degree sequence $d_1 \ldots d_n$ of its vertices satisfies the identities

$$d_1 + \cdots + d_n = \binom{n}{2}, \qquad d_1^2 + \cdots + d_n^2 = \frac{n}{2}\binom{n}{2}. \qquad (*)$$

141. [*26*] The conditions of exercise 140(b) can hold only if $n \bmod 16 \in \{0, 1, 8\}$. Write a program to find all of the proportional graphs that have $n = 8$ vertices.

142. [*M30*] (S. Janson and J. Kratochvíl, 1991.) Prove that no graph G on 4 or more vertices can be "extraproportional," in the sense that its subgraph counts $\#(H\!:\!G)$ agree with the expected values in exercise 139 for each of the eleven nonisomorphic graphs H of order 4 that are considered in exercise 90. *Hint:* Observe that $(n - 3)\#(K_3\!:\!G) = 4\#(K_4\!:\!G) + 2\#(K_{1,1,2}\!:\!G) + \#(\overline{K_{1,3}}\!:\!G) + \#(\overline{K_1 \oplus K_{1,2}}\!:\!G)$.

▶ **143.** [*M25*] Let A be any matrix with $m > 1$ distinct rows, and $n \ge m$ columns. Prove that at least one column of A can be deleted, without making any two rows equal.

▶ **144.** [*21*] Let X be an $m \times n$ matrix whose entries x_{ij} are either 0, 1, or $*$. A "completion" of X is a matrix X^* in which every $*$ has been replaced by either 0 or 1. Show that the problem of finding a completion with fewest distinct rows is equivalent to the problem of finding the chromatic number of a graph.

▶ **145.** [*25*] (R. S. Boyer and J. S. Moore, 1980.) Suppose the array $a_1 \ldots a_n$ contains a *majority element*, namely a value that occurs more than $n/2$ times. Design an algorithm that finds it after making fewer than n comparisons. *Hint:* If $n \ge 3$ and $a_{n-1} \ne a_n$, the majority element of $a_1 \ldots a_n$ is also the majority element of $a_1 \ldots a_{n-2}$.

Yet now and then your men of wit
Will condescend to take a bit.
— JONATHAN SWIFT, *Cadenus and Vanessa* (1713)

If the base 2 is used the resulting units may be called binary digits,
or more briefly bits, *a word suggested by J. W. Tukey.*
— CLAUDE E. SHANNON, in *Bell System Technical Journal* (1948)

bit (bit), n ... *[A] boring tool ...*
— *Random House Dictionary of the English Language* (1987)

7.1. ZEROS AND ONES

COMBINATORIAL ALGORITHMS often require special attention to efficiency, and
the proper representation of data is an important way to gain the necessary
speed. It is therefore wise to beef up our knowledge of elementary representation
techniques before we set out to study combinatorial algorithms in detail.

Most of today's computers are based on the binary number system, instead
of working directly with the decimal numbers that human beings prefer, because
machines are especially good at dealing with the two-state on-off quantities that
we usually denote by the digits 0 and 1. But in Chapters 1 to 6 we haven't made
much use of the fact that binary computers can do several things quickly that
decimal computers cannot. A binary machine can usually perform "logical" or
"bitwise" operations just as easily as it can add or subtract; yet we have seldom
capitalized on that capability. We've seen that binary and decimal computers are
not significantly different, for many purposes, but in a sense we've been asking
a binary computer to operate with one hand tied behind its back.

The amazing ability of 0s and 1s to encode information as well as to encode
the logical relations between items, and even to encode algorithms for processing
information, makes the study of binary digits especially rich. Indeed, we not only
use bitwise operations to enhance combinatorial algorithms, we also find that the
properties of binary logic lead naturally to new combinatorial problems that are
of great interest in their own right.

Computer scientists have gradually become better and better at taming the
wild 0s and 1s of the universe and making them do useful tricks. But as bit
players on the world's stage, we'd better have a thorough understanding of the
low-level properties of binary quantities before we launch into a study of higher-
level concepts and techniques. Therefore we shall start by investigating basic
ways to combine individual bits and sequences of bits.

7.1.1. Boolean Basics

There are 16 possible functions $f(x, y)$ that transform two given bits x and y
into a third bit $z = f(x, y)$, since there are two choices for each of $f(0, 0)$, $f(0, 1)$,
$f(1, 0)$, and $f(1, 1)$. Table 1 indicates the names and notations that have traditionally been associated with these functions in studies of formal logic, assuming
that 1 corresponds to "true" and 0 to "false." The sequence of four values
$f(0,0)f(0,1)f(1,0)f(1,1)$ is customarily called the *truth table* of the function f.

Let us conceive, then, of an Algebra
in which the symbols x, y, z, &c. *admit indifferently of*
the values 0 *and* 1, *and of these values alone.*
— GEORGE BOOLE, *An Investigation of the Laws of Thought* (1854)

'Contrariwise,' continued Tweedledee, 'if it was so, it might be;
and if it were so, it would be;
but as it isn't, it ain't. That's logic.'
— LEWIS CARROLL, *Through the Looking Glass* (1871)

Such functions are often called "Boolean operations" in honor of George
Boole, who first discovered that algebraic operations on 0s and 1s could be used
to construct a calculus for logical reasoning [*The Mathematical Analysis of Logic*
(Cambridge: 1847); *An Investigation of the Laws of Thought* (London: 1854)].
But Boole never actually dealt with the "logical or" operation $\vee$; he confined
himself strictly to ordinary arithmetic operations on 0s and 1s. Thus he would
write $x + y$ to stand for disjunction, but he took pains never to use this notation
unless x and y were mutually exclusive (not both 1). If necessary, he wrote
$x + (1-x)y$ to ensure that the result of a disjunction would never be equal to 2.

When rendering the $+$ operation in English, Boole sometimes called it "and,"
sometimes "or." This practice may seem strange to modern mathematicians until
we realize that his usage was in fact normal English; we say, for example, that
"boys and girls are children," but "children are boys or girls."

Boole's calculus was extended to include the unconventional rule $x + x = x$
by W. Stanley Jevons [*Pure Logic* (London: Edward Stanford, 1864), §69], who
pointed out that $(x + y)z$ was equal to $xz + yz$ using his new $+$ operation. But
Jevons did not know the other distributive law $xy+z = (x+z)(y+z)$. Presumably
he missed this because of the notation he was using, since the second distributive
law has no familiar counterpart in arithmetic; the more symmetrical notations
$x \wedge y$, $x \vee y$ in Table 1 make it easier for us to remember both distributive laws

$$(x \vee y) \wedge z = (x \wedge z) \vee (y \wedge z); \tag{1}$$

$$(x \wedge y) \vee z = (x \vee z) \wedge (y \vee z). \tag{2}$$

The second law (2) was introduced by C. S. Peirce, who had discovered independently how to extend Boole's calculus [*Proc. Amer. Acad. Arts and Sciences* **7**
(1867), 250–261]. Incidentally, when Peirce discussed these early developments
several years later [*Amer. J. Math.* **3** (1880), 32], he referred to "the Boolian
algebra, with Jevons's addition"; his now-unfamiliar spelling of "Boolean" was
in use for many years, appearing in the Funk and Wagnalls unabridged dictionary
as late as 1963.

The notion of truth-value combination is actually much older than Boolean
algebra. Indeed, propositional logic had been developed by Greek philosophers
already in the fourth century B.C. There was considerable debate in those days
about how to assign an appropriate true-or-false value to the proposition "if x
then y" when x and y are propositions; Philo of Megara, about 300 B.C., defined

Table 1

THE SIXTEEN LOGICAL OPERATIONS ON TWO VARIABLES

Truth table	New and old notation(s)	Operator symbol ∘	Name(s)
0000	0	$\bot$	Contradiction; falsehood; antilogy; constant 0
0001	xy, $\ x \wedge y$, $\ x \,\&\, y$	$\wedge$	Conjunction; and
0010	$x \wedge \bar{y}$, $\ x \not\supset y$, $\ [x>y]$, $\ x \mathbin{\dot-} y$	$\bar{\supset}$	Nonimplication; difference; but not
0011	x	$\llcorner$	Left projection; first dictator
0100	$\bar{x} \wedge y$, $\ x \not\subset y$, $\ [x<y]$, $\ y \mathbin{\dot-} x$	$\bar{\subset}$	Converse nonimplication; not ... but
0101	y	R	Right projection; second dictator
0110	$x \oplus y$, $\ x \not\equiv y$, $\ x\char`^y$	$\oplus$	Exclusive disjunction; nonequivalence; "xor"
0111	$x \vee y$, $\ x \mid y$	$\vee$	(Inclusive) disjunction; or; and/or
1000	$\bar{x} \wedge \bar{y}$, $\ \overline{x \vee y}$, $\ x \,\bar\vee\, y$, $\ x \downarrow y$	$\bar{\vee}$	Nondisjunction; joint denial; neither ... nor
1001	$x \equiv y$, $\ x \leftrightarrow y$, $\ x \Leftrightarrow y$	$\equiv$	Equivalence; if and only if; "iff"
1010	$\bar{y}$, $\ \neg y$, $\ !y$, $\ \sim y$	$\bar{\mathsf{R}}$	Right complementation
1011	$x \vee \bar{y}$, $\ x \subset y$, $\ x \Leftarrow y$, $\ [x \geq y]$, $\ x^{y}$	$\subset$	Converse implication; if
1100	$\bar{x}$, $\ \neg x$, $\ !x$, $\ \sim x$	$\bar{\llcorner}$	Left complementation
1101	$\bar{x} \vee y$, $\ x \supset y$, $\ x \Rightarrow y$, $\ [x \leq y]$, $\ y^{x}$	$\supset$	Implication; only if; if ... then
1110	$\bar{x} \vee \bar{y}$, $\ \overline{x \wedge y}$, $\ x \,\bar\wedge\, y$, $\ x \mid y$	$\bar{\wedge}$	Nonconjunction; not both ... and; "nand"
1111	1	$\top$	Affirmation; validity; tautology; constant 1

it by the truth table shown in Table 1, which states in particular that the implication is true when both x and y are false. Much of this early work has been lost, but there are passages in the works of Galen (2nd century A.D.) that refer to both inclusive and exclusive disjunction of propositions. [See I. M. Bocheński, *Formale Logik* (1956), English translation by Ivo Thomas (1961), for an excellent survey of the development of logic from ancient times up to the 20th century.]

A function of two variables is often written $x \circ y$ instead of $f(x,y)$, using some appropriate operator symbol $\circ$. Table 1 shows the sixteen operator symbols that we shall adopt for Boolean functions of two variables; for example, $\bot$ symbolizes the function whose truth table is 0000, $\wedge$ is the symbol for 0001, $\bar{\supset}$ is the symbol for 0010, and so on. We have $x \bot y = 0$, $x \wedge y = xy$, $x \bar{\supset} y = x \mathbin{\dot-} y$, $x \llcorner y = x$, ..., $x \bar{\wedge} y = \bar{x} \vee \bar{y}$, $x \top y = 1$.

Of course the operations in Table 1 aren't all of equal importance. For example, the first and last cases are trivial, since they have a constant value independent of x and y. Four of them are functions of x alone or y alone. We write $\bar{x}$ for $1 - x$, the *complement* of x.

The four operations whose truth table contains just a single 1 are easily expressed in terms of the AND operator $\wedge$, namely $x \wedge y$, $x \wedge \bar{y}$, $\bar{x} \wedge y$, $\bar{x} \wedge \bar{y}$. Those with three 1s are easily written in terms of the OR operator $\vee$, namely $x \vee y$, $x \vee \bar{y}$, $\bar{x} \vee y$, $\bar{x} \vee \bar{y}$. The basic functions $x \wedge y$ and $x \vee y$ have proved to be more useful in practice than their complemented or half-complemented cousins, although the NOR and NAND operations $x \bar{\vee} y = \bar{x} \wedge \bar{y}$ and $x \bar{\wedge} y = \bar{x} \vee \bar{y}$ are also of interest because they are easily implemented in transistor circuits.

In 1913, H. M. Sheffer showed that all 16 of the functions can be expressed in terms of just one, starting with either $\bar{\vee}$ or $\bar{\wedge}$ as the given operation (see exercise 4). Actually C. S. Peirce had made the same discovery about 1880, but his work on the subject remained unpublished until after his death [*Collected Papers of Charles Sanders Peirce* **4** (1933), §§12–20, 264]. Table 1 indicates that NAND and NOR have occasionally been written $x \mid y$ and $x \downarrow y$; sometimes they have been called "Sheffer's stroke" and the "Peirce arrow." Nowadays it is best *not* to use Sheffer's vertical line for NAND, because $x \mid y$ denotes bitwise $x \vee y$ in programming languages like C.

So far we have discussed all but two of the functions in Table 1. The remaining two are $x \equiv y$ and $x \oplus y$, "equivalence" and "exclusive-or," which are related by the identities

$$x \equiv y \;=\; \bar{x} \oplus y \;=\; x \oplus \bar{y} \;=\; 1 \oplus x \oplus y; \tag{3}$$

$$x \oplus y \;=\; \bar{x} \equiv y \;=\; x \equiv \bar{y} \;=\; 0 \equiv x \equiv y. \tag{4}$$

Both operations are associative (see exercise 6). In propositional logic, the notion of equivalence is more important than the notion of exclusive-or, which means inequivalence; but when we consider bitwise operations on full computer words, we shall see in Section 7.1.3 that the situation is reversed: Exclusive-or turns out to be more useful than equivalence, in typical programs. The chief reason why $x \oplus y$ has significant applications, even in the one-bit case, is the fact that

$$x \oplus y \;=\; (x + y) \bmod 2. \tag{5}$$

Therefore $x \oplus y$ and $x \wedge y$ denote addition and multiplication in the field of two elements (see Section 4.6), and $x \oplus y$ naturally inherits many "clean" mathematical properties.

Basic identities. Now let's take a look at interactions between the fundamental operators $\wedge$, $\vee$, $\oplus$, and $^-$, since the other operations are easily expressed in terms of these four. Each of $\wedge$, $\vee$, $\oplus$ is associative and commutative. Besides the distributive laws (1) and (2), we also have

$$(x \oplus y) \wedge z \;=\; (x \wedge z) \oplus (y \wedge z), \tag{6}$$

as well as the *absorption laws*

$$(x \wedge y) \vee x \;=\; (x \vee y) \wedge x \;=\; x. \tag{7}$$

One of the simplest, yet most useful, identities is

$$x \oplus x \;=\; 0, \tag{8}$$

since it implies among other things that

$$(x \oplus y) \oplus x \;=\; y, \qquad (x \oplus y) \oplus y \;=\; x, \tag{9}$$

when we use the obvious fact that $x \oplus 0 = x$. In other words, given $x \oplus y$ and either x or y, it is easy to determine the other. And let us not overlook the simple *complementation law*

$$\bar{x} \;=\; x \oplus 1. \tag{10}$$

Another important pair of identities is known as *De Morgan's laws* in honor of Augustus De Morgan, who stated that "The contrary of an aggregate is the compound of the contraries of the aggregants; the contrary of a compound is the aggregate of the contraries of the components. Thus (A, B) and AB have ab and (a, b) for contraries." [*Trans. Cambridge Philos. Soc.* **10** (1858), 208.] In more modern notation, these are the rules we have implicitly derived via truth tables in connection with the operations NAND and NOR in Table 1, namely

$$\overline{x \wedge y} = \bar{x} \vee \bar{y}; \qquad\qquad (11)$$

$$\overline{x \vee y} = \bar{x} \wedge \bar{y}. \qquad\qquad (12)$$

Incidentally, W. S. Jevons knew (12) but not (11); he consistently wrote $\bar{A}B + \bar{B}A + \bar{A}\bar{B}$ instead of $\bar{A} + \bar{B}$ for the complement of AB. Yet De Morgan was not the first Englishman who enunciated the laws above. Both (11) and (12) can be found in the early 14th century writings of two scholastic philosophers, William of Ockham [*Summa Logicæ* **2** (1323)] and Walter Burley [*De Puritate Artis Logicæ* (c. 1330)].

De Morgan's laws and a few other identities can be used to express $\wedge$, $\vee$, and $\oplus$ in terms of each other:

$$x \wedge y = \overline{\bar{x} \vee \bar{y}} = x \oplus y \oplus (x \vee y); \qquad\qquad (13)$$

$$x \vee y = \overline{\bar{x} \wedge \bar{y}} = x \oplus y \oplus (x \wedge y); \qquad\qquad (14)$$

$$x \oplus y = (x \vee y) \wedge \overline{x \wedge y} = (x \wedge \bar{y}) \vee (\bar{x} \wedge y). \qquad\qquad (15)$$

According to exercise 7.1.2–77, all computations of $x_1 \oplus x_2 \oplus \cdots \oplus x_n$ that use only the operations $\wedge$, $\vee$, and $^-$ must be at least $4(n-1)$ steps long; thus, the other three operations are not an especially good substitute for $\oplus$.

Functions of n variables. A Boolean function $f(x, y, z)$ of three Boolean variables x, y, z can be defined by its 8-bit truth table $f(0,0,0) f(0,0,1) \ldots f(1,1,1)$; and in general, every n-ary Boolean function $f(x_1, \ldots, x_n)$ corresponds to a 2^n-bit truth table that lists the successive values of $f(0, \ldots, 0, 0)$, $f(0, \ldots, 0, 1)$, $f(0, \ldots, 1, 0)$, $\ldots$, $f(1, \ldots, 1, 1)$.

We needn't devise special names and notations for all these functions, since they can all be expressed in terms of the binary functions that we've already learned. For example, as observed by I. I. Zhegalkin [*Matematicheskiĭ Sbornik* **35** (1928), 311–369], we can always write

$$f(x_1, \ldots, x_n) = g(x_1, \ldots, x_{n-1}) \oplus h(x_1, \ldots, x_{n-1}) \wedge x_n \qquad\qquad (16)$$

when $n > 0$, for appropriate functions g and h, by letting

$$\begin{aligned} g(x_1, \ldots, x_{n-1}) &= f(x_1, \ldots, x_{n-1}, 0); \\ h(x_1, \ldots, x_{n-1}) &= f(x_1, \ldots, x_{n-1}, 0) \oplus f(x_1, \ldots, x_{n-1}, 1). \end{aligned} \qquad (17)$$

(The operation $\wedge$ conventionally takes precedence over $\oplus$, so we need not use parentheses to enclose the subformula '$h(x_1, \ldots, x_{n-1}) \wedge x_n$' on the right-hand side of (16).) Repeating this process recursively on g and h until we're down to

0-ary functions leaves us with an expression that involves only the operators $\oplus$, $\wedge$, and a sequence of 2^n constants. Furthermore, those constants can usually be simplified away, because we have

$$x \wedge 0 = 0 \qquad \text{and} \qquad x \wedge 1 = x \oplus 0 = x. \tag{18}$$

After applying the associative and distributive laws, we end up needing the constant 0 only if $f(x_1, \ldots, x_n)$ is identically zero, and the constant 1 only if $f(0, \ldots, 0) = 1$.

We might have, for instance,

$$\begin{aligned}
f(x, y, z) &= \big((1 \oplus 0 \wedge x) \oplus (0 \oplus 1 \wedge x) \wedge y\big) \oplus \big((0 \oplus 1 \wedge x) \oplus (1 \oplus 1 \wedge x) \wedge y\big) \wedge z \\
&= (1 \oplus x \wedge y) \oplus (x \oplus y \oplus x \wedge y) \wedge z \\
&= 1 \oplus x \wedge y \oplus x \wedge z \oplus y \wedge z \oplus x \wedge y \wedge z.
\end{aligned}$$

And by rule (5), we see that we're simply left with the polynomial

$$f(x, y, z) = (1 + xy + xz + yz + xyz) \bmod 2, \tag{19}$$

because $x \wedge y = xy$. Notice that this polynomial is linear (of degree ≤ 1) in each of its variables. In general, a similar calculation will show that *any* Boolean function $f(x_1, \ldots, x_n)$ has a unique representation such as this, called its *multilinear representation* or *exclusive normal form*, which is a sum (modulo 2) of zero or more of the 2^n possible terms 1, x_1, x_2, $x_1 x_2$, x_3, $x_1 x_3$, $x_2 x_3$, $x_1 x_2 x_3$, $\ldots$, $x_1 x_2 \ldots x_n$.

George Boole decomposed Boolean functions in a different way, which is often simpler for the kinds of functions that arise in practice. Instead of (16), he essentially wrote

$$f(x_1, \ldots, x_n) = \big(g(x_1, \ldots, x_{n-1}) \wedge \bar{x}_n\big) \vee \big(h(x_1, \ldots, x_{n-1}) \wedge x_n\big) \tag{20}$$

and called it the "law of development," where we now have simply

$$\begin{aligned}
g(x_1, \ldots, x_{n-1}) &= f(x_1, \ldots, x_{n-1}, 0), \\
h(x_1, \ldots, x_{n-1}) &= f(x_1, \ldots, x_{n-1}, 1),
\end{aligned} \tag{21}$$

instead of (17). Repeatedly iterating Boole's procedure, using the distributive law (1), and eliminating constants, leaves us with a formula that is a disjunction of zero or more *minterms*, where each minterm is a conjunction such as $x_1 \wedge \bar{x}_2 \wedge \bar{x}_3 \wedge x_4 \wedge x_5$ in which every variable or its complement is present. Notice that a minterm is a Boolean function that is true at exactly one point.

For example, let's consider the more-or-less random function $f(w, x, y, z)$ whose truth table is

$$1100\ 1001\ 0000\ 1111. \tag{22}$$

When this function is expanded by repeatedly applying Boole's law (20), we get a disjunction of eight minterms, one for each of the 1s in the truth table:

$$\begin{aligned}
f(w, x, y, z) = {}& (\bar{w} \wedge \bar{x} \wedge \bar{y} \wedge \bar{z}) \vee (\bar{w} \wedge \bar{x} \wedge \bar{y} \wedge z) \vee (\bar{w} \wedge x \wedge \bar{y} \wedge \bar{z}) \vee (\bar{w} \wedge x \wedge y \wedge z) \\
& \vee (w \wedge x \wedge \bar{y} \wedge \bar{z}) \vee (w \wedge x \wedge \bar{y} \wedge z) \vee (w \wedge x \wedge y \wedge \bar{z}) \vee (w \wedge x \wedge y \wedge z). \tag{23}
\end{aligned}$$

In general, a disjunction of minterms is called a *full disjunctive normal form*. Every Boolean function can be expressed in this way, and the result is unique — except, of course, for the order of the minterms. *Nitpick:* A special case arises when $f(x_1, \ldots, x_n)$ is identically zero. We consider '0' to be an empty disjunction, with no terms, and we also consider '1' to be an empty conjunction, for the same reasons as we defined $\sum_{k=1}^{0} a_k = 0$ and $\prod_{k=1}^{0} a_k = 1$ in Section 1.2.3.

C. S. Peirce observed, in *Amer. J. Math.* **3** (1880), 37–39, that every Boolean function also has a *full conjunctive normal form*, which is a conjunction of "min-clauses" like $\bar{x}_1 \vee x_2 \vee \bar{x}_3 \vee \bar{x}_4 \vee x_5$. A minclause is 0 at only one point; so each clause in such a conjunction accounts for a place where the truth table has a 0. For example, the full conjunctive normal form of our function in (22) and (23) is

$$f(w, x, y, z) = (w \vee x \vee \bar{y} \vee z) \wedge (w \vee x \vee \bar{y} \vee \bar{z}) \wedge (w \vee \bar{x} \vee y \vee \bar{z}) \wedge (w \vee \bar{x} \vee \bar{y} \vee z)$$
$$\wedge (\bar{w} \vee x \vee y \vee z) \wedge (\bar{w} \vee x \vee y \vee \bar{z}) \wedge (\bar{w} \vee x \vee \bar{y} \vee z) \wedge (\bar{w} \vee x \vee \bar{y} \vee \bar{z}). \quad (24)$$

Not surprisingly, however, we often want to work with disjunctions and conjunctions that *don't* necessarily involve full minterms or minclauses. Therefore, following nomenclature introduced by Paul Bernays in his *Habilitationsschrift* (1918), we speak in general of a *disjunctive normal form* or "DNF" as *any* disjunction of conjunctions,

$$\bigvee_{j=1}^{m} \bigwedge_{k=1}^{s_j} u_{jk} = (u_{11} \wedge \cdots \wedge u_{1s_1}) \vee \cdots \vee (u_{m1} \wedge \cdots \wedge u_{ms_m}), \quad (25)$$

where each u_{jk} is a *literal*, namely a variable x_i or its complement. Similarly, any conjunction of disjunctions of literals,

$$\bigwedge_{j=1}^{m} \bigvee_{k=1}^{s_j} u_{jk} = (u_{11} \vee \cdots \vee u_{1s_1}) \wedge \cdots \wedge (u_{m1} \vee \cdots \vee u_{ms_m}), \quad (26)$$

is called a *conjunctive normal form*, or "CNF" for short.

A great many electrical circuits embedded inside today's computer chips are composed of "programmable logic arrays" (PLAs), which are ORs of ANDs of possibly complemented input signals. In other words, a PLA basically computes one or more disjunctive normal forms. Such building blocks are fast, versatile, and relatively inexpensive; and indeed, DNFs have played a prominent role in electrical engineering ever since the 1950s, when switching circuits were implemented with comparatively old-fashioned devices like relays or vacuum tubes. Therefore people have long been interested in finding the simplest DNFs for classes of Boolean functions, and we can expect that an understanding of disjunctive normal forms will continue to be important as technology continues to evolve.

The terms of a DNF are often called *implicants*, because the truth of any term in a disjunction implies the truth of the whole formula. In a formula like

$$f(x, y, z) = (x \wedge \bar{y} \wedge z) \vee (y \wedge z) \vee (\bar{x} \wedge y \wedge \bar{z}),$$

for example, we know that f is true when $x \wedge \bar{y} \wedge z$ is true, namely when $(x, y, z) = (1, 0, 1)$. But notice that in this example the shorter term $x \wedge z$ also turns out to be an implicant of f, even though not written explicitly, because the additional term $y \wedge z$ makes the function true whenever $x = z = 1$, regardless of the value of y. Similarly, $\bar{x} \wedge y$ is an implicant of this particular function. So we might as well work with the simpler formula

$$f(x, y, z) = (x \wedge z) \vee (y \wedge z) \vee (\bar{x} \wedge y). \qquad (27)$$

At this point no more deletions are possible within the implicants, because neither x nor y nor z nor $\bar{x}$ is a strong enough condition to imply the truth of f.

An implicant that can't be factored further by removing any of its literals without making it too weak is called a *prime implicant*, following the terminology of W. V. Quine in *AMM* **59** (1952), 521–531.

These basic concepts can perhaps be understood most easily if we simplify the notation and adopt a more geometric viewpoint. We can write simply '$f(x)$' instead of $f(x_1, \ldots, x_n)$, and regard x as a vector, or as a binary string $x_1 \ldots x_n$ of length n. For example, the strings $wxyz$ where the function of (22) is true are

$$\{0000, 0001, 0100, 0111, 1100, 1101, 1110, 1111\}, \qquad (28)$$

and we can think of them as eight points in the 4-dimensional hypercube $2 \times 2 \times 2 \times 2$. The eight points in (28) correspond to the minterm implicants that are explicitly present in the full disjunctive normal form (23); but none of those implicants is actually prime. For example, the first two points of (28) make the subcube 000∗, and the last four points constitute the subcube 11∗∗, if we use asterisks to denote "wild cards" as we did when discussing database queries in Section 6.5; therefore $\bar{w} \wedge \bar{x} \wedge \bar{y}$ is an implicant of f, and so is $w \wedge x$. Similarly, we can see that the subcube 0∗00 accounts for two of the eight points in (28), making $\bar{w} \wedge \bar{y} \wedge \bar{z}$ an implicant.

In general, each prime implicant corresponds in this way to a *maximal* subcube that stays within the set of points that make f true. (The subcube is maximal in the sense that it isn't contained in any larger subcube with the same property; we can't replace any of its explicit bits by an asterisk. A maximal subcube has a maximal number of asterisks, hence a minimal number of constrained coordinates, hence a minimal number of variables in the corresponding implicant.) The maximal subcubes of the eight points in (28) are

$$000∗, 0∗00, ∗100, ∗111, 11∗∗; \qquad (29)$$

so the prime implicants of the function $f(w, x, y, z)$ in (23) are

$$(\bar{w} \wedge \bar{x} \wedge \bar{y}) \vee (\bar{w} \wedge \bar{y} \wedge \bar{z}) \vee (x \wedge \bar{y} \wedge \bar{z}) \vee (x \wedge y \wedge z) \vee (w \wedge x). \qquad (30)$$

The *disjunctive prime form* of a Boolean function is the disjunction of all its prime implicants. Exercise 30 contains an algorithm to find all the prime implicants of a given function, based on a list of the points where the function is true.

We can define a *prime clause* in an exactly similar way: It is a disjunctive clause that is implied by f, having no subclause with the same property. And the *conjunctive prime form* of f is the conjunction of all its prime clauses. (An example appears in exercise 19.)

In many simple cases, the disjunctive prime form is the shortest possible disjunctive normal form that a function can have. But we can often do better, because we might be able to cover all the necessary points with only a few of the maximal subcubes. For example, the prime implicant $(y \wedge z)$ is unnecessary in (27). And in expression (30) we don't need both $(\bar{w} \wedge \bar{y} \wedge \bar{z})$ and $(x \wedge \bar{y} \wedge \bar{z})$; either one is sufficient, in the presence of the other terms.

Unfortunately, we will see in Section 7.9 that the task of finding a shortest disjunctive normal form is NP-hard, thus quite difficult in general. But many useful shortcuts have been developed for sufficiently small problems, and they are well explained in the book *Introduction to the Theory of Switching Circuits* by E. J. McCluskey (New York: McGraw–Hill, 1965). For later developments, see Petr Fišer and Jan Hlavička, *Computing and Informatics* **22** (2003), 19–51.

There's an important special case for which the shortest DNF is, however, easily characterized. A Boolean function is said to be *monotone* or *positive* if its value does not change from 1 to 0 when any of its variables changes from 0 to 1. In other words, f is monotone if and only if $f(x) \leq f(y)$ whenever $x \subseteq y$, where the bit string $x = x_1 \ldots x_n$ is regarded as contained in or equal to the bit string $y = y_1 \ldots y_n$ if and only if $x_j \leq y_j$ for all j. An equivalent condition (see exercise 21) is that the function f either is constant or can be expressed entirely in terms of $\wedge$ and $\vee$, without complementation.

Theorem Q. *The shortest disjunctive normal form of a monotone Boolean function is its disjunctive prime form.*

Proof. [W. V. Quine, *Boletín de la Sociedad Matemática Mexicana* **10** (1953), 64–70.] Let $f(x_1, \ldots, x_n)$ be monotone, and let $u_1 \wedge \cdots \wedge u_s$ be one of its prime implicants. We cannot have, say, $u_1 = \bar{x}_i$, because in that case the shorter term $u_2 \wedge \cdots \wedge u_s$ would also be an implicant, by monotonicity. Therefore no prime implicant has a complemented literal.

Now if we set $u_1 \leftarrow \cdots \leftarrow u_s \leftarrow 1$ and all other variables to 0, the value of f will be 1, but all of f's other prime implicants will vanish. Thus $u_1 \wedge \cdots \wedge u_s$ must be in every shortest DNF, because every implicant of a shortest DNF is clearly prime. ∎

Corollary Q. *A disjunctive normal form is the disjunctive prime form of a monotone Boolean function if and only if it has no complemented literals and none of its implicants is contained in another.* ∎

Satisfiability. A Boolean function is said to be *satisfiable* if it is not identically zero — that is, if it has at least one implicant. The most famous unsolved problem in all of computer science is to find an efficient way to decide whether a given Boolean function is satisfiable or unsatisfiable. More precisely, we ask: Is there an algorithm that inputs a Boolean formula of length N and tests it for satisfiability, always giving the correct answer after performing at most $N^{O(1)}$ steps?

When you hear about this problem for the first time, you might be tempted to ask a question of your own in return: "What? Are you serious that computer scientists still haven't figured out how to do such a simple thing?"

Well, if you think satisfiability testing is trivial, please tell us your method. We agree that the problem isn't always difficult; if, for example, the given formula involves only 30 Boolean variables, a brute-force trial of 2^{30} cases — that's about a billion — will indeed settle the matter. But an enormous number of practical problems that still await solution can be formulated as Boolean functions with, say, 100 variables, because mathematical logic is a very powerful way to express concepts. And the solutions to those problems correspond to the vectors $x = x_1 \ldots x_{100}$ for which $f(x) = 1$. So a truly efficient solution to the satisfiability problem would be a wonderful achievement.

There is at least one sense in which satisfiability testing is a no-brainer: If the function $f(x_1, \ldots, x_n)$ has been chosen at random, so that all 2^n-bit truth tables are equally likely, then f is almost surely satisfiable, and we can find an x with $f(x) = 1$ after making fewer than 2 trials (on the average). It's like flipping a coin until it comes up heads; we rarely need to wait long. But the catch, of course, is that practical problems do not have random truth tables.

Okay, let's grant that satisfiability testing does seem to be tough, in general. In fact, satisfiability turns out to be difficult even when we try to simplify it by requiring that the Boolean function be presented as a "formula in 3CNF" — namely as a conjunctive normal form that has only *three* literals in each clause:

$$f(x_1, \ldots, x_n) = (t_1 \vee u_1 \vee v_1) \wedge (t_2 \vee u_2 \vee v_2) \wedge \cdots \wedge (t_m \vee u_m \vee v_m). \quad (31)$$

Here each t_j, u_j, and v_j is x_k or $\bar{x}_k$ for some k. The problem of deciding satisfiability for formulas in 3CNF is called "3SAT," and exercise 39 explains why it is not really easier than satisfiability in general.

We will be seeing many examples of hard-to-crack 3SAT problems, for instance in Section 7.2.2.2, where satisfiability testing will be discussed in great detail. The situation is a little peculiar, however, because a formula needs to be fairly long before we need to think twice about its satisfiability. For example, the shortest unsatisfiable formula in 3CNF is $(x \vee x \vee x) \wedge (\bar{x} \vee \bar{x} \vee \bar{x})$; but it is obviously no challenge to the intellect. We don't get into rough waters unless the three literals t_j, u_j, v_j of a clause correspond to three different variables. And in that case, each clause rules out exactly 1/8 of the possibilities, because seven different settings of (t_j, u_j, v_j) will make it true. Consequently every such 3CNF with at most seven clauses is automatically satisfiable, and a random setting of its variables will succeed with probability $\geq 1 - 7/8 = 1/8$.

The shortest interesting formula in 3CNF therefore has at least eight clauses. And in fact, an interesting 8-clause formula does exist, based on the associative block design by R. L. Rivest that we considered in 6.5–(13):

$$(x_2 \vee x_3 \vee \bar{x}_4) \wedge (x_1 \vee x_3 \vee x_4) \wedge (\bar{x}_1 \vee x_2 \vee x_4) \wedge (\bar{x}_1 \vee \bar{x}_2 \vee x_3)$$
$$\wedge (\bar{x}_2 \vee \bar{x}_3 \vee x_4) \wedge (\bar{x}_1 \vee \bar{x}_3 \vee \bar{x}_4) \wedge (x_1 \vee \bar{x}_2 \vee \bar{x}_4) \wedge (x_1 \vee x_2 \vee \bar{x}_3). \quad (32)$$

Any seven of these eight clauses are satisfiable, in exactly two ways, and they force the values of three variables; for example, the first seven imply that we have $x_1 x_2 x_3 = 001$. But the complete set of eight cannot be satisfied simultaneously.

Simple special cases. Two important classes of Boolean formulas have been identified for which the satisfiability problem does turn out to be pretty easy. These special cases arise when the conjunctive normal form being tested consists entirely of "Horn clauses" or entirely of "Krom clauses." A *Horn clause* is an OR of literals in which all or nearly all of the literals are complemented — at most one of its literals is a pure, unbarred variable. A *Krom clause* is an OR of exactly two literals. Thus, for example,

$$\bar{x} \vee \bar{y}, \qquad w \vee \bar{y} \vee \bar{z}, \qquad \bar{u} \vee \bar{v} \vee \bar{w} \vee \bar{x} \vee \bar{y} \vee z, \quad \text{and} \quad x$$

are examples of Horn clauses; and

$$x \vee x, \qquad \bar{x} \vee \bar{x}, \qquad \bar{x} \vee \bar{y}, \qquad x \vee \bar{y}, \qquad \bar{x} \vee y, \quad \text{and} \quad x \vee y$$

are examples of Krom clauses, only the last of which is not also a Horn clause. (The first example qualifies because $x \vee x = x$.) Notice that a Horn clause is allowed to contain any number of literals, but when we restrict ourselves to Krom clauses we are essentially considering the 2SAT problem. In both cases we will see that satisfiability can be decided in linear time — that is, by carrying out only $O(N)$ simple steps, when given a formula of length N.

Let's consider Horn clauses first. Why are they so easy to handle? The main reason is that a clause like $\bar{u} \vee \bar{v} \vee \bar{w} \vee \bar{x} \vee \bar{y} \vee z$ can be recast in the form $\neg(u \wedge v \wedge w \wedge x \wedge y) \vee z$, which is the same as

$$u \wedge v \wedge w \wedge x \wedge y \implies z.$$

In other words, if u, v, w, x, and y are all true, then z must also be true. For this reason, parameterized Horn clauses were chosen to be the basic underlying mechanism of the programming language called Prolog. Furthermore there is an easy way to characterize exactly which Boolean functions can be represented entirely with Horn clauses:

Theorem H. *The Boolean function* $f(x_1, \ldots, x_n)$ *is expressible as a conjunction of Horn clauses if and only if*

$$f(x_1, \ldots, x_n) = f(y_1, \ldots, y_n) = 1 \quad \text{implies} \quad f(x_1 \wedge y_1, \ldots, x_n \wedge y_n) = 1 \quad (33)$$

for all Boolean values x_j *and* y_j.

Proof. [Alfred Horn, *J. Symbolic Logic* **16** (1951), 14–21, Lemma 7.] If we have $x_0 \vee \bar{x}_1 \vee \cdots \vee \bar{x}_k = 1$ and $y_0 \vee \bar{y}_1 \vee \cdots \vee \bar{y}_k = 1$, then

$$\begin{aligned}
(x_0 \wedge y_0) &\vee \overline{x_1 \wedge y_1} \vee \cdots \vee \overline{x_k \wedge y_k} \\
&= (x_0 \vee \bar{x}_1 \vee \bar{y}_1 \vee \cdots \vee \bar{x}_k \vee \bar{y}_k) \wedge (y_0 \vee \bar{x}_1 \vee \bar{y}_1 \vee \cdots \vee \bar{x}_k \vee \bar{y}_k) \\
&\geq (x_0 \vee \bar{x}_1 \vee \cdots \vee \bar{x}_k) \wedge (y_0 \vee \bar{y}_1 \vee \cdots \vee \bar{y}_k) = 1;
\end{aligned}$$

and a similar (but simpler) calculation applies when the unbarred literals x_0 and y_0 are not present. Therefore every conjunction of Horn clauses satisfies (33).

Conversely, condition (33) implies that every prime clause of f is a Horn clause (see exercise 44). ∎

Let's say that a *Horn function* is a Boolean function that satisfies condition (33), and let's also call it *definite* if it satisfies the further condition $f(1, \ldots, 1) = 1$. It's easy to see that a conjunction of Horn clauses is definite if and only if each clause has *exactly* one unbarred literal, because only an entirely negative clause like $\bar{x} \vee \bar{y}$ will fail if all variables are true. Definite Horn functions are slightly simpler to work with than Horn functions in general, because they are obviously always satisfiable. Thus, by Theorem H, they have a unique least vector x such that $f(x) = 1$, namely the bitwise AND of all vectors that satisfy all clauses. The *core* of a definite Horn function is the set of all variables x_j that are true in this minimum vector x. Notice that the variables in the core must be true whenever f is true, so we can essentially factor them out.

Definite Horn functions arise in many ways, for example in the analysis of games (see exercises 51 and 52). Another nice example comes from compiler technology. Consider the following typical (but simplified) grammar for algebraic expressions in a programming language:

$$
\begin{aligned}
\langle \text{expression} \rangle &\to \langle \text{term} \rangle \mid \langle \text{expression} \rangle + \langle \text{term} \rangle \mid \langle \text{expression} \rangle - \langle \text{term} \rangle \\
\langle \text{term} \rangle &\to \langle \text{factor} \rangle \mid - \langle \text{factor} \rangle \mid \langle \text{term} \rangle * \langle \text{factor} \rangle \mid \langle \text{term} \rangle / \langle \text{factor} \rangle \\
\langle \text{factor} \rangle &\to \langle \text{variable} \rangle \mid \langle \text{constant} \rangle \mid (\langle \text{expression} \rangle) \\
\langle \text{variable} \rangle &\to \langle \text{letter} \rangle \mid \langle \text{variable} \rangle \langle \text{letter} \rangle \mid \langle \text{variable} \rangle \langle \text{digit} \rangle \qquad\qquad (34) \\
\langle \text{letter} \rangle &\to \text{a} \mid \text{b} \mid \text{c} \\
\langle \text{constant} \rangle &\to \langle \text{digit} \rangle \mid \langle \text{constant} \rangle \langle \text{digit} \rangle \\
\langle \text{digit} \rangle &\to \text{0} \mid \text{1}
\end{aligned}
$$

For example, the string `a/(-b0-10)+cc*cc` meets the syntax for $\langle \text{expression} \rangle$ and uses each of the grammatical rules at least once.

Suppose we want to know what pairs of characters can appear next to each other in such expressions. Definite Horn clauses provide the answer, because we can set the problem up as follows: Let the quantities Xx, xX, and xy denote Boolean "propositions," where X is one of the symbols $\{\text{E}, \text{T}, \text{F}, \text{V}, \text{L}, \text{C}, \text{D}\}$ standing respectively for $\langle \text{expression} \rangle$, $\langle \text{term} \rangle$, $\ldots$, $\langle \text{digit} \rangle$, and where x and y are symbols in the set $\{\text{+}, \text{-}, \text{*}, \text{/}, \text{(}, \text{)}, \text{a}, \text{b}, \text{c}, \text{0}, \text{1}\}$. The proposition Xx means, "X can end with x"; similarly, xX means, "X can start with x"; and xy means, "The character x can be followed immediately by y in an expression." (There are $7 \times 11 + 11 \times 7 + 11 \times 11 = 275$ propositions altogether.) Then we can write

$$
\begin{array}{lllll}
\text{xT} \Rightarrow \text{xE} & \Rightarrow \text{-T} & \text{xC} \Rightarrow \text{xF} & \text{Vx} \wedge \text{yL} \Rightarrow \text{xy} & \Rightarrow \text{Lc} \\
\text{Tx} \Rightarrow \text{Ex} & \text{xF} \Rightarrow \text{-x} & \text{Cx} \Rightarrow \text{Fx} & \text{Vx} \wedge \text{yD} \Rightarrow \text{xy} & \text{xD} \Rightarrow \text{xC} \\
\text{Ex} \Rightarrow \text{x+} & \text{Tx} \Rightarrow \text{x*} & \Rightarrow \text{(F} & \text{Dx} \Rightarrow \text{Vx} & \text{Dx} \Rightarrow \text{Cx} \\
\text{xT} \Rightarrow \text{+x} & \text{xF} \Rightarrow \text{*x} & \text{xE} \Rightarrow \text{(x} & \Rightarrow \text{aL} & \text{Cx} \wedge \text{yD} \Rightarrow \text{xy} \\
\text{Ex} \Rightarrow \text{x-} & \text{Tx} \Rightarrow \text{x/} & \text{Ex} \Rightarrow \text{x)} & \Rightarrow \text{La} & \Rightarrow \text{0D} \\
\text{xT} \Rightarrow \text{-x} & \text{xF} \Rightarrow \text{/x} & \Rightarrow \text{F)} & \Rightarrow \text{bL} & \Rightarrow \text{D0} \\
\text{xF} \Rightarrow \text{xT} & \text{xV} \Rightarrow \text{xF} & \text{xL} \Rightarrow \text{xV} & \Rightarrow \text{Lb} & \Rightarrow \text{1D} \\
\text{Fx} \Rightarrow \text{Tx} & \text{Vx} \Rightarrow \text{Fx} & \text{Lx} \Rightarrow \text{Vx} & \Rightarrow \text{cL} & \Rightarrow \text{D1}
\end{array} \qquad (35)
$$

where x and y run through the eleven terminal symbols $\{\text{+}, \ldots, \text{1}\}$. This schematic specification gives us a total of $24 \times 11 + 3 \times 11 \times 11 + 13 \times 1 = 640$ definite

Horn clauses, which we could write out formally as

$$\left(\overline{\texttt{+T}} \vee \texttt{+E}\right) \wedge \left(\overline{\texttt{-T}} \vee \texttt{-E}\right) \wedge \cdots \wedge \left(\overline{\texttt{V+}} \vee \overline{\texttt{OL}} \vee \texttt{+0}\right) \wedge \cdots \wedge \left(\texttt{D1}\right)$$

if we prefer the cryptic notation of Boolean algebra to the $\Rightarrow$ convention of (35).

Why did we do this? Because *the core of all these clauses is the set of all propositions that are true in this particular grammar.* For example, one can verify that $\texttt{-E}$ is true, hence the symbols $\texttt{(-}$ can occur next to each other within an expression; but the symbol pairs $\texttt{++}$ and $\texttt{*-}$ cannot (see exercise 46).

Furthermore, we can find the core of any given set of definite Horn clauses without great difficulty. We just start out with the propositions that appear alone, on the right-hand side of $\Rightarrow$ when the left-hand side is empty; thirteen clauses of that kind appear in (35). And once we assert the truth of those propositions, we might find one or more clauses whose left-hand sides are now known to be true. Hence their right-hand sides also belong to the core, and we can keep going in the same way. The whole procedure is pretty much like letting water run downhill until it has found its proper level. In fact, when we choose appropriate data structures, this downhill process goes quite fast, requiring only $O(N+n)$ steps, when N denotes the total length of the clauses and n is the number of propositional variables. (We assume here that all clauses have been expanded out, not abbreviated in terms of parameters like x and y above. More sophisticated techniques of theorem proving are available to deal with parameterized clauses, but they are beyond the scope of our present discussion.)

Algorithm C (*Core computation for definite Horn clauses*). Given a set P of propositional variables and a set C of clauses, each having the form

$$u_1 \wedge \cdots \wedge u_k \Rightarrow v \qquad \text{where } k \geq 0 \text{ and } \{u_1, \ldots, u_k, v\} \subseteq P, \qquad (36)$$

this algorithm finds the set $Q \subseteq P$ of all propositional variables that are necessarily true whenever all of the clauses are true.

We use the following data structures for clauses c, propositions p, and hypotheses h, where a "hypothesis" is the appearance of a proposition on the left-hand side of a clause:

CONCLUSION(c) is the proposition on the right of clause c;

COUNT(c) is the number of hypotheses of c not yet asserted;

TRUTH(p) is 1 if p is known to be true, otherwise 0;

LAST(p) is the last hypothesis in which p appears;

CLAUSE(h) is the clause for which h appears on the left;

PREV(h) is the previous hypothesis containing the proposition of h.

We also maintain a stack $S_0, S_1, \ldots, S_{s-1}$ of all propositions that are known to be true but not yet asserted.

C1. [Initialize.] Set LAST$(p) \leftarrow \Lambda$ and TRUTH$(p) \leftarrow 0$ for each proposition p. Also set $s \leftarrow 0$, so that the stack is empty. Then for each clause c, having the form (36), set CONCLUSION$(c) \leftarrow v$ and COUNT$(c) \leftarrow k$. If $k = 0$ and

TRUTH$(v) = 0$, set TRUTH$(v) \leftarrow 1$, $S_s \leftarrow v$, and $s \leftarrow s + 1$. Otherwise, for $1 \leq j \leq k$, create a hypothesis record h and set CLAUSE$(h) \leftarrow c$, PREV$(h) \leftarrow$ LAST(u_j), LAST$(u_j) \leftarrow h$.

C2. [Prepare to assert p.] Terminate the algorithm if $s = 0$; the desired core now consists of all propositions whose TRUTH has been set to 1. Otherwise set $s \leftarrow s - 1$, $p \leftarrow S_s$, and $h \leftarrow$ LAST(p).

C3. [Done with hypotheses?] If $h = \Lambda$, return to C2.

C4. [Validate h.] Set $c \leftarrow$ CLAUSE(h) and COUNT$(c) \leftarrow$ COUNT$(c) - 1$. If the new value of COUNT(c) is still nonzero, go to step C6.

C5. [Deduce CONCLUSION(c).] Set $p \leftarrow$ CONCLUSION(c). If TRUTH$(p) = 0$, set TRUTH$(p) \leftarrow 1$, $S_s \leftarrow p$, $s \leftarrow s + 1$.

C6. [Loop on h.] Set $h \leftarrow$ PREV(h) and return to C3. ∎

Notice how smoothly the data structures work together, avoiding any need to search for a place to make progress in the calculation. Algorithm C is similar in many respects to Algorithm 2.2.3T (topological sorting), which was the first example of multilinked data structures that we discussed long ago in Chapter 2; in fact, we can regard Algorithm 2.2.3T as the special case of Algorithm C in which every proposition appears on the right-hand side of exactly one clause. (See exercise 47.)

Exercise 48 shows that a slight modification of Algorithm C solves the satisfiability problem for Horn clauses in general. Further discussion can be found in papers by W. F. Dowling and J. H. Gallier, *J. Logic Programming* **1** (1984), 267–284; M. G. Scutellá, *J. Logic Programming* **8** (1990), 265–273.

We turn now to Krom functions and the 2SAT problem. Again there's a linear-time algorithm; but again, we can probably appreciate it best if we look first at a simplified-but-practical application. Let's suppose that seven comedians have each agreed to do one-night standup gigs at two of five hotels during a three-day festival, but each of them is available for only two of those days because of other commitments:

> Tomlin should do Aladdin and Caesars on days 1 and 2;
> Unwin should do Bellagio and Excalibur on days 1 and 2;
> Vegas should do Desert and Excalibur on days 2 and 3;
> Williams should do Aladdin and Desert on days 1 and 3;   (37)
> Xie should do Caesars and Excalibur on days 1 and 3;
> Yankovic should do Bellagio and Desert on days 2 and 3;
> Zany should do Bellagio and Caesars on days 1 and 2.

Is it possible to schedule them all without conflict?

To solve this problem, we can introduce seven Boolean variables $\{t, u, v, w, x, y, z\}$, where t (for example) means that Tomlin does Aladdin on day 1 and Caesars on day 2 while $\bar{t}$ means that the days booked for those hotels occur in the opposite order. Then we can set up constraints to ensure that no two comedians are booked in the same hotel on the same day:

$$\begin{array}{llll}
\neg(t \wedge w)\;[\text{A1}] & \neg(y \wedge \bar{z})\;[\text{B2}] & \neg(t \wedge z)\;[\text{C2}] & \neg(w \wedge y)\;[\text{D3}] \\
\neg(u \wedge z)\;[\text{B1}] & \neg(\bar{t} \wedge x)\;[\text{C1}] & \neg(v \wedge \bar{y})\;[\text{D2}] & \neg(\bar{u} \wedge \bar{x})\;[\text{E1}] \\
\neg(\bar{u} \wedge y)\;[\text{B2}] & \neg(\bar{t} \wedge \bar{z})\;[\text{C1}] & \neg(\bar{v} \wedge w)\;[\text{D3}] & \neg(u \wedge \bar{v})\;[\text{E2}] \\
\neg(\bar{u} \wedge \bar{z})\;[\text{B2}] & \neg(x \wedge \bar{z})\;[\text{C1}] & \neg(\bar{v} \wedge y)\;[\text{D3}] & \neg(v \wedge x)\;[\text{E3}]
\end{array} \tag{38}$$

Each of these constraints is, of course, a Krom clause; we must satisfy

$$(\bar{t}\vee \bar{w}) \wedge (\bar{u}\vee \bar{z}) \wedge (u\vee \bar{y}) \wedge (u\vee z) \wedge (\bar{y}\vee z) \wedge (t\vee \bar{x}) \wedge (t\vee z) \wedge (\bar{x}\vee z)$$
$$\wedge\; (\bar{t}\vee \bar{z}) \wedge (\bar{v}\vee y) \wedge (v\vee \bar{w}) \wedge (v\vee \bar{y}) \wedge (\bar{w}\vee \bar{y}) \wedge (u\vee x) \wedge (\bar{u}\vee v) \wedge (\bar{v}\vee \bar{x}). \tag{39}$$

Furthermore, Krom clauses (like Horn clauses) can be written as implications:

$$\begin{array}{llllllll}
t \Rightarrow \bar{w}, & u \Rightarrow \bar{z}, & \bar{u} \Rightarrow \bar{y}, & \bar{u} \Rightarrow z, & y \Rightarrow z, & \bar{t} \Rightarrow \bar{x}, & \bar{t} \Rightarrow z, & x \Rightarrow z, \\
t \Rightarrow \bar{z}, & v \Rightarrow y, & \bar{v} \Rightarrow \bar{w}, & \bar{v} \Rightarrow \bar{y}, & w \Rightarrow \bar{y}, & \bar{u} \Rightarrow x, & u \Rightarrow v, & v \Rightarrow \bar{x}.
\end{array} \tag{40}$$

And every such implication also has an alternative, "contrapositive" form:

$$\begin{array}{llllllll}
w \Rightarrow \bar{t}, & z \Rightarrow \bar{u}, & y \Rightarrow u, & \bar{z} \Rightarrow u, & \bar{z} \Rightarrow \bar{y}, & x \Rightarrow t, & \bar{z} \Rightarrow t, & \bar{z} \Rightarrow \bar{x}, \\
z \Rightarrow \bar{t}, & \bar{y} \Rightarrow \bar{v}, & w \Rightarrow v, & y \Rightarrow v, & y \Rightarrow \bar{w}, & \bar{x} \Rightarrow u, & \bar{v} \Rightarrow \bar{u}, & x \Rightarrow \bar{v}.
\end{array} \tag{41}$$

But oops — alas — there is a vicious cycle,

$$\underset{[\text{B1}]}{u \;\Rightarrow\;} \underset{[\text{B2}]}{\bar{z} \;\Rightarrow\;} \underset{[\text{D2}]}{\bar{y} \;\Rightarrow\;} \underset{[\text{E2}]}{\bar{v} \;\Rightarrow\;} \underset{[\text{B2}]}{\bar{u} \;\Rightarrow\;} \underset{[\text{C2}]}{z \;\Rightarrow\;} \underset{[\text{C1}]}{\bar{t} \;\Rightarrow\;} \underset{[\text{E1}]}{\bar{x} \;\Rightarrow\;} u. \tag{42}$$

This cycle tells that u and $\bar{u}$ must both have the same value; so there is no way to accommodate all of the conditions in (37). The festival organizers will have to renegotiate their agreement with at least one of the six comedians $\{t, u, v, x, y, z\}$, if a viable schedule is to be achieved. (See exercise 53.)

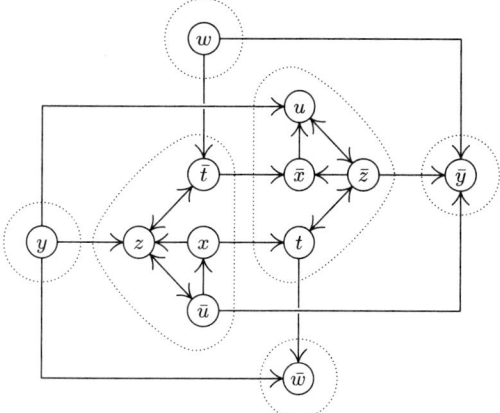

Fig. 6. The digraph corresponding to all implications of (40) and (41) that do not involve either v or $\bar{v}$. Assigning appropriate values to the literals in each strong component will solve a binary scheduling problem that is an instance of 2SAT.

The organizers might, for instance, try to leave v out of the picture temporarily. Then five of the sixteen constraints in (38) would go away and only 22 of the implications from (40) and (41) would remain, leaving the directed graph illustrated in Fig. 6. This digraph does contain cycles, like $z \Rightarrow \bar{u} \Rightarrow x \Rightarrow z$ and $t \Rightarrow \bar{z} \Rightarrow t$; but no cycle contains both a variable and its complement. Indeed, we can see from Fig. 6 that the values $tuwxyz = 110000$ do satisfy every clause of (39) that doesn't involve v or $\bar{v}$. These values give us a schedule that satisfies six of the seven original stipulations in (37), starting with (Tomlin, Unwin, Zany, Williams, Xie) at the (Aladdin, Bellagio, Caesars, Desert, Excalibur) on day 1.

In general, given any 2SAT problem with m Krom clauses that involve n Boolean variables, we can form a directed graph in the same way. There are $2n$ vertices $\{x_1, \bar{x}_1, \ldots, x_n, \bar{x}_n\}$, one for each possible literal; and there are $2m$ arcs of the form $\bar{u} \to v$ and $\bar{v} \to u$, two for each clause $u \vee v$. Two literals u and v belong to the same *strong component* of this digraph if and only if there are oriented paths from u to v and from v to u. For example, the six strong components of the digraph in Fig. 6 are indicated by dotted contours. All literals in a strong component must have the same Boolean value, in any solution to the corresponding 2SAT problem.

Theorem K. *A conjunctive normal form with two literals per clause is satisfiable if and only if no strong component of the associated digraph contains both a variable and its complement.*

Proof. [Melven Krom, *Zeitschrift für mathematische Logik und Grundlagen der Mathematik* **13** (1967), 15–20, Corollary 2.2.] If there are paths from x to $\bar{x}$ and from $\bar{x}$ to x, the formula is certainly unsatisfiable.

Conversely, assume that no such paths exist. Any digraph has at least one strong component S that is a "source," having no incoming arcs from vertices in any other strong component. Moreover, our digraph always has an attractive antisymmetry, illustrated in Fig. 6: We have $u \to v$ if and only if $\bar{v} \to \bar{u}$. Therefore the complements of the literals in S form another strong component $\overline{S} \ne S$ that is a "sink," having no *outgoing* arcs to other strong components. Hence we can assign the value 0 to all literals in S and 1 to all literals in $\overline{S}$, then remove them from the digraph and proceed in the same way until all literals have received a value. The resulting values satisfy $u \le v$ whenever $u \to v$ in the digraph; hence they satisfy $\bar{u} \vee v$ whenever $\bar{u} \vee v$ is a clause of the formula. ∎

Theorem K leads immediately to an efficient solution of the 2SAT problem, thanks to an algorithm by R. E. Tarjan that finds strong components in linear time. [See *SICOMP* **1** (1972), 146–160; D. E. Knuth, *The Stanford GraphBase* (1994), 512–519.] We shall study Tarjan's algorithm in detail in Section 7.4.1. Exercise 54 shows that the condition of Theorem K is readily checked whenever the algorithm detects a new strong component. Furthermore, the algorithm detects "sinks" first; thus, as a simple byproduct of Tarjan's procedure, we can assign values that establish satisfiability by choosing the value 1 for each literal in a strong component that occurs before its complement.

Medians. We've been focusing on Boolean binary operations like $x \vee y$ or $x \oplus y$. But there's also a significant *ternary* operation $\langle xyz \rangle$, called the *median* of x, y, and z:

$$\langle xyz \rangle = (x \wedge y) \vee (y \wedge z) \vee (x \wedge z) = (x \vee y) \wedge (y \vee z) \wedge (x \vee z). \qquad (43)$$

In fact, $\langle xyz \rangle$ is probably the most important ternary operation in the entire universe, because it has amazing properties that are continually being discovered and rediscovered.

In the first place, we can see easily that this formula for $\langle xyz \rangle$ describes the *majority* value of any three Boolean quantities x, y, and z: $\langle 000 \rangle = \langle 001 \rangle = 0$ and $\langle 011 \rangle = \langle 111 \rangle = 1$. We call $\langle xyz \rangle$ the "median" instead of the "majority" because, if x, y, and z are arbitrary *real* numbers, and if the operations $\wedge$ and $\vee$ denote min and max in (43), then

$$\langle xyz \rangle = y \qquad \text{when } x \le y \le z. \tag{44}$$

Secondly, the basic binary operations $\wedge$ and $\vee$ are special cases of medians:

$$x \wedge y = \langle x0y \rangle; \qquad\qquad x \vee y = \langle x1y \rangle. \tag{45}$$

Thus *any* monotone Boolean function can be expressed entirely in terms of the ternary median operator and the constants 0 and 1. In fact, if we lived in a median-only world, we could let $\wedge$ stand for falsehood and $\vee$ for truth; then $x \wedge y = \langle x \wedge y \rangle$ and $x \vee y = \langle x \vee y \rangle$ would be perfectly natural expressions, and we could even use Polish notation like $\langle \wedge xy \rangle$ and $\langle \vee xy \rangle$ if we wanted to! The same idea applies to extended real numbers under the min-max interpretation of $\wedge$ and $\vee$, if we take medians with respect to the constants $\wedge = -\infty$ and $\vee = +\infty$.

A Boolean function $f(x_1, x_2, \ldots, x_n)$ is called *self-dual* when it satisfies

$$\overline{f(x_1, x_2, \ldots, x_n)} = f(\bar{x}_1, \bar{x}_2, \ldots, \bar{x}_n). \tag{46}$$

We've noted that a Boolean function is monotone if and only if it can be expressed in terms of $\wedge$ and $\vee$; by De Morgan's laws (11) and (12), a monotone formula is self-dual if and only if the symbols $\wedge$ and $\vee$ can be interchanged without changing the formula's value. Thus the median operation defined in (43) is both monotone and self-dual. In fact, it is the simplest nontrivial function of that kind, since none of the binary operations in Table 1 are both monotone and self-dual except the projections $\llcorner$ and $\lrcorner$.

Furthermore, *any* expression that has been formed entirely with the median operator, without using constants, is both monotone and self-dual. For example, the function $\langle w \langle xyz \rangle \langle w \langle uvw \rangle x \rangle \rangle$ is self-dual because

$$\overline{\langle w \langle xyz \rangle \langle w \langle uvw \rangle x \rangle \rangle} = \langle \bar{w} \, \overline{\langle xyz \rangle} \, \overline{\langle w \langle uvw \rangle x \rangle} \rangle$$
$$= \langle \bar{w} \langle \bar{x}\bar{y}\bar{z} \rangle \langle \bar{w} \, \overline{\langle uvw \rangle} \, \bar{x} \rangle \rangle = \langle \bar{w} \langle \bar{x}\bar{y}\bar{z} \rangle \langle \bar{w} \langle \bar{u}\bar{v}\bar{w} \rangle \bar{x} \rangle \rangle.$$

Emil Post, while working on his Ph.D. thesis (Columbia University, 1920), proved that the converse statement is also true:

Theorem P. *Every monotone, self-dual Boolean function $f(x_1, \ldots, x_n)$ can be expressed entirely in terms of the median operation $\langle xyz \rangle$.*

Proof. [*Annals of Mathematics Studies* **5** (1941), 74–75.] Observe first that

$$\langle x_1 y \langle x_2 y \ldots y \langle x_{s-1} y x_s \rangle \ldots \rangle \rangle$$
$$= \left((x_1 \vee x_2 \vee \cdots \vee x_{s-1} \vee x_s) \wedge y\right) \vee (x_1 \wedge x_2 \wedge \cdots \wedge x_{s-1} \wedge x_s); \qquad (47)$$

this formula for repeated medianing is easily proved by induction on s.

Now suppose $f(x_1, \ldots, x_n)$ is monotone, self-dual, and has the disjunctive prime form

$$f(x_1, \ldots, x_n) = t_1 \vee \cdots \vee t_m, \qquad t_j = x_{j1} \wedge \cdots \wedge x_{js_j},$$

where no prime implicant t_j is contained in another (Corollary Q). Any two prime implicants must have at least one variable in common. For if we had, say, $t_1 = x \wedge y$ and $t_2 = u \wedge v \wedge w$, the value of f would be 1 when $x = y = 1$ and $u = v = w = 0$, as well as when $x = y = 0$ and $u = v = w = 1$, contradicting self-duality. Therefore if any t_j consists of a single variable x, it must be the only prime implicant — in which case f is the trivial function $f(x_1, \ldots, x_n) = x = \langle xxx \rangle$.

Define the functions $g_0, g_1, \ldots, g_m$ by composing medians as follows:

$$\begin{aligned} g_0(x_1, \ldots, x_n) &= x_1; \\ g_j(x_1, \ldots, x_n) &= h(x_{j1}, \ldots, x_{js_j}; g_{j-1}(x_1, \ldots, x_n)), \text{ for } 1 \le j \le m; \end{aligned} \qquad (48)$$

here $h(x_1, \ldots, x_s; y)$ denotes the function on the top line of (47). By induction on j, we can prove from (47) and (48) that $g_j(x_1, \ldots, x_n) = 1$ whenever we have $t_1 \vee \cdots \vee t_j = 1$, because $(x_{j1} \vee \cdots \vee x_{js_j}) \wedge t_k = t_k$ when $k < j$.

Finally, $f(x_1, \ldots, x_n)$ must equal $g_m(x_1, \ldots, x_n)$, because both functions are monotone and self-dual, and we have shown that $f(x_1, \ldots, x_n) \le g_m(x_1, \ldots, x_n)$ for all combinations of 0s and 1s. This inequality suffices to prove equality, because a self-dual function equals 1 in exactly half of the 2^n possible cases. ∎

One consequence of Theorem P is that we can express the median of five elements via medians of three, because the median of any odd number of Boolean variables is obviously a monotone and self-dual Boolean function. Let's write $\langle x_1 \ldots x_{2k-1} \rangle$ for such a median. Then the disjunctive prime form of $\langle vwxyz \rangle$ is

$$(v \wedge w \wedge x) \vee (v \wedge w \wedge y) \vee (v \wedge w \wedge z) \vee (v \wedge x \wedge y) \vee (v \wedge x \wedge z)$$
$$\vee (v \wedge y \wedge z) \vee (w \wedge x \wedge y) \vee (w \wedge x \wedge z) \vee (w \wedge y \wedge z) \vee (x \wedge y \wedge z);$$

so the construction in the proof of Theorem P expresses $\langle vwxyz \rangle$ as a huge formula $g_{10}(v, w, x, y, z)$ involving 2,046 median-of-3 operations. Of course this expression isn't the shortest possible one; we actually have

$$\langle vwxyz \rangle = \langle v \langle xyz \rangle \langle wx \langle wyz \rangle \rangle \rangle. \qquad (49)$$

[See H. S. Miiller and R. O. Winder, *IRE Transactions* **EC-11** (1962), 89–90.]

*Median algebras and median graphs. We noted earlier that the ternary operation $\langle xyz \rangle$ is useful when x, y, and z belong to any ordered set like the real numbers, when $\wedge$ and $\vee$ are regarded as the operators min and max. In fact, the operation $\langle xyz \rangle$ also plays a useful role in far more general circumstances.

A *median algebra* is any set M on which a ternary operation $\langle xyz \rangle$ is defined that takes elements of M into elements of M and obeys the following three axioms:

$$\langle xxy \rangle = x \quad \text{(majority law)}; \tag{50}$$

$$\langle xyz \rangle = \langle xzy \rangle = \langle yxz \rangle = \langle yzx \rangle = \langle zxy \rangle = \langle zyx \rangle \quad \text{(commutative law)}; \tag{51}$$

$$\langle xw\langle ywz \rangle \rangle = \langle \langle xwy \rangle wz \rangle \quad \text{(associative law)}. \tag{52}$$

In the Boolean case, for example, the associative law (52) holds for $w = 0$ and $w = 1$ because $\wedge$ and $\vee$ are associative. Exercises 75 and 76 prove that these three axioms imply also a *distributive law* for medians, which has both a short form

$$\langle \langle xyz \rangle uv \rangle = \langle x\langle yuv \rangle \langle zuv \rangle \rangle \tag{53}$$

and a more symmetrical long form

$$\langle \langle xyz \rangle uv \rangle = \langle \langle xuv \rangle \langle yuv \rangle \langle zuv \rangle \rangle. \tag{54}$$

No simple proof of this fact is known, but we can at least verify the special case of (53) and (54) when $y = u$ and $z = v$: We have

$$\langle \langle xyz \rangle yz \rangle = \langle xyz \rangle \tag{55}$$

because both sides equal $\langle xy\langle zyz \rangle \rangle$. In fact, the associative law (52) is just the special case $y = u$ of (53). And with (55) and (52) we can also verify the case $x = u$: $\langle \langle uyz \rangle uv \rangle = \langle vu\langle yuz \rangle \rangle = \langle \langle vuy \rangle uz \rangle = \langle \langle yuv \rangle uz \rangle = \langle \langle \langle yuv \rangle uv \rangle uz \rangle = \langle \langle yuv \rangle u\langle vuz \rangle \rangle = \langle u\langle yuv \rangle \langle zuv \rangle \rangle$.

An *ideal* in a median algebra M is a set $C \subseteq M$ for which we have

$$\langle xyz \rangle \in C \quad \text{whenever } x \in C,\ y \in C,\ \text{and } z \in M. \tag{56}$$

If u and v are any elements of M, the *interval* $[u \mathinner{\ldotp\ldotp} v]$ is defined as follows:

$$[u \mathinner{\ldotp\ldotp} v] = \{ \langle xuv \rangle \mid x \in M \}. \tag{57}$$

We say that "x is between u and v" if and only if $x \in [u \mathinner{\ldotp\ldotp} v]$. According to these definitions, u and v themselves always belong to the interval $[u \mathinner{\ldotp\ldotp} v]$.

Lemma M. *Every interval $[u \mathinner{\ldotp\ldotp} v]$ is an ideal, and $x \in [u \mathinner{\ldotp\ldotp} v] \iff x = \langle uxv \rangle$.*

Proof. Let $\langle xuv \rangle$ and $\langle yuv \rangle$ be arbitrary elements of $[u \mathinner{\ldotp\ldotp} v]$. Then

$$\langle \langle xuv \rangle \langle yuv \rangle z \rangle = \langle \langle xyz \rangle uv \rangle \in [u \mathinner{\ldotp\ldotp} v]$$

for all $z \in M$, by (51) and (53), so $[u \mathinner{\ldotp\ldotp} v]$ is an ideal. Furthermore every element $\langle xuv \rangle \in [u \mathinner{\ldotp\ldotp} v]$ satisfies $\langle xuv \rangle = \langle u\langle xuv \rangle v \rangle$ by (51) and (55). ∎

Our intervals $[u \mathinner{\ldotp\ldotp} v]$ have nice properties, because of the median laws:

$$v \in [u \mathinner{\ldotp\ldotp} u] \implies u = v; \tag{58}$$

$$x \in [u \mathinner{\ldotp\ldotp} v] \text{ and } y \in [u \mathinner{\ldotp\ldotp} x] \implies y \in [u \mathinner{\ldotp\ldotp} v]; \tag{59}$$

$$x \in [u \mathinner{\ldotp\ldotp} v] \text{ and } y \in [u \mathinner{\ldotp\ldotp} z] \text{ and } y \in [v \mathinner{\ldotp\ldotp} z] \implies y \in [x \mathinner{\ldotp\ldotp} z]. \tag{60}$$

Equivalently, $[u \mathinner{\ldotp\ldotp} u] = \{u\}$; if $x \in [u \mathinner{\ldotp\ldotp} v]$ then $[u \mathinner{\ldotp\ldotp} x] \subseteq [u \mathinner{\ldotp\ldotp} v]$; and $x \in [u \mathinner{\ldotp\ldotp} v]$ also implies that $[u \mathinner{\ldotp\ldotp} z] \cap [v \mathinner{\ldotp\ldotp} z] \subseteq [x \mathinner{\ldotp\ldotp} z]$ for all z. (See exercise 72.)

Now let's define a graph on the vertex set M, with the following edges:

$$u \,\text{---}\, v \quad \Longleftrightarrow \quad u \neq v \text{ and } \langle xuv \rangle \in \{u, v\} \text{ for all } x \in M. \tag{61}$$

In other words, u and v are adjacent if and only if the interval $[u \mathinner{\ldotp\ldotp} v]$ consists of just the two points u and v.

Theorem G. *If M is any finite median algebra, the graph defined by* (61) *is connected. Moreover, vertex x belongs to the interval $[u \mathinner{\ldotp\ldotp} v]$ if and only if x lies on a shortest path from u to v.*

Proof. If M isn't connected, choose u and v so that there is no path from u to v and the interval $[u \mathinner{\ldotp\ldotp} v]$ has as few elements as possible. Let $x \in [u \mathinner{\ldotp\ldotp} v]$ be distinct from u and v. Then $\langle xuv \rangle = x \neq v$, so $v \notin [u \mathinner{\ldotp\ldotp} x]$; similarly $u \notin [x \mathinner{\ldotp\ldotp} v]$. But $[u \mathinner{\ldotp\ldotp} x]$ and $[x \mathinner{\ldotp\ldotp} v]$ are contained in $[u \mathinner{\ldotp\ldotp} v]$, by (59). So they are smaller intervals, and there must be a path from u to x and from x to v. Contradiction.

The other half of the theorem is proved in exercise 73. ∎

Our definition of intervals implies that $\langle xyz \rangle \in [x \mathinner{\ldotp\ldotp} y] \cap [x \mathinner{\ldotp\ldotp} z] \cap [y \mathinner{\ldotp\ldotp} z]$, because $\langle xyz \rangle = \langle \langle xyz \rangle xy \rangle = \langle \langle xyz \rangle xz \rangle = \langle \langle xyz \rangle yz \rangle$ by (55). Conversely, if $w \in [x \mathinner{\ldotp\ldotp} y] \cap [x \mathinner{\ldotp\ldotp} z] \cap [y \mathinner{\ldotp\ldotp} z]$, exercise 74 proves that $w = \langle xyz \rangle$. In other words, *the intersection $[x \mathinner{\ldotp\ldotp} y] \cap [x \mathinner{\ldotp\ldotp} z] \cap [y \mathinner{\ldotp\ldotp} z]$ always contains exactly one point*, whenever x, y, and z are points of M.

Figure 7 illustrates this principle in a $4 \times 4 \times 4$ cube, where each point x has coordinates (x_1, x_2, x_3) with $0 \leq x_1, x_2, x_3 < 4$. The vertices of this cube form a median algebra because $\langle xyz \rangle = (\langle x_1 y_1 z_1 \rangle, \langle x_2 y_2 z_2 \rangle, \langle x_3 y_3 z_3 \rangle)$; furthermore, the edges of the graph in Fig. 7 are those defined in (61), running between vertices whose coordinates agree except that one coordinate changes by ± 1. Three typical intervals $[x \mathinner{\ldotp\ldotp} y]$, $[x \mathinner{\ldotp\ldotp} z]$, and $[y \mathinner{\ldotp\ldotp} z]$ are shown; the only point common to all three intervals is the vertex $\langle xyz \rangle = (2, 2, 1)$.

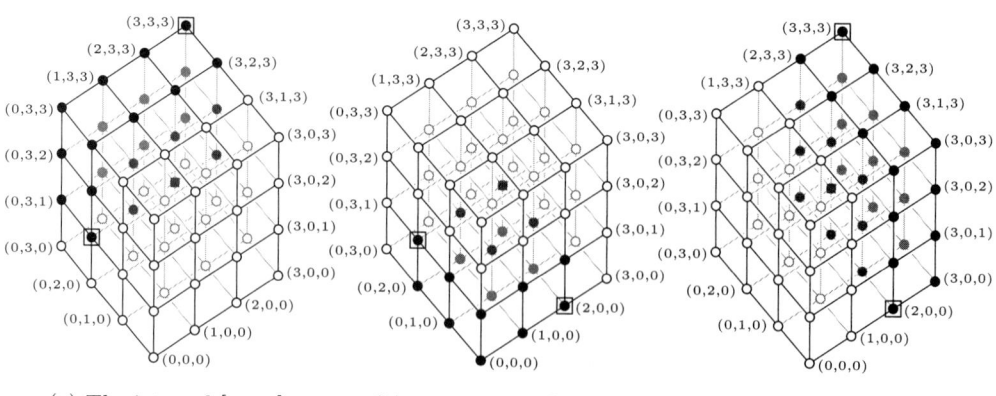

(a) The interval $[x \mathinner{\ldotp\ldotp} y]$.   (b) The interval $[x \mathinner{\ldotp\ldotp} z]$.   (c) The interval $[y \mathinner{\ldotp\ldotp} z]$.

Fig. 7. Intervals between the vertices $x = (0, 2, 1)$,
$y = (3, 3, 3)$, and $z = (2, 0, 0)$ in a $4 \times 4 \times 4$ cube.

So far we've started with a median algebra and used it to define a graph with certain properties. But we can also start with a graph that has those properties and use it to define a median algebra. If u and v are vertices of *any* graph, let us define the interval $[u \mathrel{..} v]$ to be the set of all points on shortest paths between u and v. A finite graph is said to be a *median graph* if exactly one vertex lies in the intersection $[x \mathrel{..} y] \cap [x \mathrel{..} z] \cap [y \mathrel{..} z]$ of the three intervals that tie any three given vertices x, y, and z together; and we denote that vertex by $\langle xyz \rangle$. Exercise 75 proves that the resulting ternary operation satisfies the median axioms.

Many important graphs turn out to be median graphs according to this definition. For example, any free tree is easily seen to be a median graph; and a graph like the $n_1 \times n_2 \times \cdots \times n_m$ hyperrectangle provides another simple example. Cartesian products of arbitrary median graphs also satisfy the required condition.

*Median labels. If u and v are any elements of a median algebra, the mapping $f(x)$ that takes $x \mapsto \langle xuv \rangle$ is a *homomorphism*; that is, it satisfies

$$f(\langle xyz \rangle) = \langle f(x) f(y) f(z) \rangle, \tag{62}$$

because of the long distributive law (54). This function $\langle xuv \rangle$ "projects" any given point x into the interval $[u \mathrel{..} v]$, by (57). And it is particularly interesting in the case when $u \mathrel{\text{---}} v$ is an edge of the corresponding graph, because $f(x)$ is then two-valued, essentially a Boolean mapping.

For example, consider the typical free tree shown below, with eight vertices and seven edges. We can project each vertex x onto each of the edge intervals $[u \mathrel{..} v]$ by deciding whether x is closer to u or to v:

		ac	bc	cd	de	ef	eg	dh		
a	$\mapsto$	a	c	c	d	e	e	d	0000000	
b	$\mapsto$	c	b	c	d	e	e	d	1100000	
c	$\mapsto$	c	c	c	d	e	e	d	1000000	
d	$\mapsto$	c	c	d	d	e	e	d	1010000	(63)
e	$\mapsto$	c	c	d	e	e	e	d	1011000	
f	$\mapsto$	c	c	d	e	f	e	d	1011100	
g	$\mapsto$	c	c	d	e	e	g	d	1011010	
h	$\mapsto$	c	c	d	d	e	e	h	1010001	

On the right we've reduced the projections to 0s and 1s, arbitrarily deciding that $a \mapsto 0000000$. The resulting bit strings are called *labels* of the vertices, and we write, for example, $l(b) = 1100000$. Since each projection is a homomorphism, we can calculate the median of any three points by simply taking Boolean medians in each component of their labels. For example, to compute $\langle bgh \rangle$ we find the bitwise median of $l(b) = 1100000$, $l(g) = 1011010$, and $l(h) = 1010001$, namely $1010000 = l(d)$.

When we project onto all the edges of a median graph, we might find that two columns of the binary labels are identical. This situation cannot occur with a free tree, but let's consider what would happen if the edge $g \mathrel{\text{---}} h$ were added to the tree in (63): The resulting graph would still be a median graph, but the

columns for eg and dh would become identical (except with $e \leftrightarrow d$ and $g \leftrightarrow h$).
Furthermore, the new column for gh would turn out to be equivalent to the
column for de. Redundant components should be omitted from the labels in
such cases; therefore the vertices of the augmented graph would have six-bit
labels, like $l(g) = 101101$ and $l(h) = 101001$, instead of seven-bit labels.

The elements of any median algebra can always be represented by labels in
this way. Therefore *any identity that holds in the Boolean case will be true in
all median algebras.* This "zero-one principle" makes it possible to test whether
any two given expressions built from the ternary operation $\langle xyz \rangle$ can be shown
to be equal as a consequence of axioms (50), (51), and (52) — although we do
have to check $2^{n-1} - 1$ cases when we test n-variable expressions by this method.

For example, the associative law $\langle xw\langle ywz \rangle \rangle = \langle \langle xwy \rangle wz \rangle$ suggests that
there should be a symmetrical interpretation of both sides that does not involve
nested brackets. And indeed, there is such a formula:

$$\langle xw\langle ywz \rangle \rangle = \langle \langle xwy \rangle wz \rangle = \langle xwywz \rangle, \tag{64}$$

where $\langle xwywz \rangle$ denotes the median of the five-element multiset $\{x, w, y, w, z\} = \{w, w, x, y, z\}$. We can prove this formula by using the zero-one principle, noting
also that median is the same thing as majority in the Boolean case. In a similar
way we can prove (49), and we can show that the function used by Post in (47)
can be simplified to

$$\langle x_1 y\langle x_2 y \ldots y\langle x_{s-1} y x_s \rangle \ldots \rangle \rangle = \langle x_1 y x_2 y \ldots y x_{s-1} y x_s \rangle; \tag{65}$$

it's a median of $2s - 1$ quantities, where nearly half of them are equal to y.

A set C of vertices in a graph is called *convex* if $[u \mathbin{. .} v] \subseteq C$ whenever
$u \in C$ and $v \in C$. In other words, whenever the endpoints of a shortest path
belong to C, all vertices of that path must also be present in C. (A convex
set is therefore identical to what we called an "ideal," a few pages ago; now
our language has become geometric instead of algebraic.) The *convex hull* of
$\{v_1, \ldots, v_m\}$ is defined to be the smallest convex set that contains each of the
vertices $v_1, \ldots, v_m$. Our theoretical results above have shown that every interval
$[u \mathbin{. .} v]$ is convex; hence $[u \mathbin{. .} v]$ is the convex hull of the two-point set $\{u, v\}$. But
in fact much more is true:

Theorem C. *The convex hull of $\{v_1, v_2, \ldots, v_m\}$ in a median graph is the set
of all points*

$$C = \big\{ \langle v_1 x v_2 x \ldots x v_m \rangle \mid x \in M \big\}. \tag{66}$$

Furthermore, x is in C if and only if $x = \langle v_1 x v_2 x \ldots x v_m \rangle$.

Proof. Clearly $v_j \in C$ for $1 \leq j \leq m$. Every point of C must belong to the
convex hull, because the point $x' = \langle v_2 x \ldots x v_m \rangle$ is in the hull (by induction
on m), and because $\langle v_1 x \ldots x v_m \rangle \in [v_1 \mathbin{. .} x']$. The zero-one principle proves that

$$\langle x\langle v_1 y v_2 y \ldots y v_m \rangle \langle v_1 z v_2 z \ldots z v_m \rangle \rangle = \langle v_1 \langle xyz \rangle v_2 \langle xyz \rangle \ldots \langle xyz \rangle v_m \rangle; \tag{67}$$

hence C is convex. Setting $y = x$ in this formula proves that $\langle v_1 x v_2 x \ldots x v_m \rangle$ is
the closest point of C to x, and that $\langle v_1 x v_2 x \ldots x v_m \rangle \in [x \mathbin{. .} z]$ for all $z \in C$. ∎

Corollary C. *Let the label of v_j be $v_{j1} \ldots v_{jt}$ for $1 \le j \le m$. Then the convex hull of $\{v_1, \ldots, v_m\}$ is the set of all $x \in M$ whose label $x_1 \ldots x_t$ satisfies $x_j = c_j$ whenever $v_{1j} = v_{2j} = \cdots = v_{mj} = c_j$.* ∎

For example, the convex hull of $\{c, g, h\}$ in (63) consists of all elements whose label matches the pattern 10∗∗0∗∗, namely $\{c, d, e, g, h\}$.

When a median graph contains a 4-cycle $u - x - v - y - u$, the edges $u - x$ and $v - y$ are equivalent, in the sense that projection onto $[u \mathinner{.\,.} x]$ and projection onto $[v \mathinner{.\,.} y]$ both yield the same label coordinates. The reason is that, for any z with $\langle zux \rangle = u$, we have

$$
\begin{aligned}
y = \langle uvy \rangle &= \langle \langle zux \rangle vy \rangle \\
&= \langle \langle zvy \rangle \langle uvy \rangle \langle xvy \rangle \rangle \\
&= \langle \langle zvy \rangle yv \rangle,
\end{aligned}
$$

hence $\langle zvy \rangle = y$; similarly $\langle zux \rangle = x$ implies $\langle zvy \rangle = v$. The edges $x - v$ and $y - u$ are equivalent for the same reasons. Exercise 77 shows, among other things, that two edges yield equivalent projections if and only if they can be proved equivalent by a chain of equivalences obtained from 4-cycles in this way. Therefore the number of bits in each vertex label is the number of equivalence classes of edges induced by the 4-cycles; and it follows that the reduced labels for vertices are uniquely determined, once we specify a vertex whose label is $00 \ldots 0$.

A nice way to find the vertex labels of any median graph was discovered by P. K. Jha and G. Slutzki [*Ars Combin.* **34** (1992), 75–92] and improved by J. Hagauer, W. Imrich, and S. Klavžar [*Theor. Comp. Sci.* **215** (1999), 123–136]:

Algorithm H (*Median labels*). Given a median graph G and a source vertex a, this algorithm determines the equivalence classes defined by the 4-cycles of G, and computes the labels $l(v) = v_1 \ldots v_t$ of each vertex, where t is the number of classes and $l(a) = 0 \ldots 0$.

H1. [Initialize.] Preprocess G by visiting all vertices in order of their distance from a. For each edge $u - v$, we say that u is an *early neighbor* of v if a is closer to u than to v, otherwise u is a *late neighbor*; in other words, the early neighbors of v will already have been visited when v is encountered, but the late neighbors will still be awaiting their turn. Rearrange all adjacency lists so that early neighbors are listed first. Place each edge initially in its own equivalence class; a "union-find algorithm" like Algorithm 2.3.3E will be used to merge classes when the algorithm learns that they're equivalent.

H2. [Call the subroutine.] Set $j \leftarrow 0$ and invoke Subroutine I with parameter a. (Subroutine I appears below. The global variable j will be used to create a master list of edges $r_j - s_j$ for $1 \le j < n$, where n is the total number of vertices; there will be one entry with $s_j = v$, for each vertex $v \ne a$.)

H3. [Assign the labels.] Number the equivalence classes from 1 to t. Then set $l(a)$ to the t-bit string $0 \ldots 0$. For $j = 1, 2, \ldots, n - 1$ (in this order), set $l(s_j)$ to $l(r_j)$ with bit k changed from 0 to 1, where k is the equivalence class of edge $r_j - s_j$. ∎

Subroutine I (*Process descendants of r*). This recursive subroutine, with parameter r and global variable j, does the main work of Algorithm H on the graph of all vertices currently reachable from vertex r. In the course of processing, all such vertices will be recorded on the master list, except r itself, and all edges between them will be removed from the current graph. Each vertex has four fields called its LINK, MARK, RANK, and MATE, initially null.

I1. [Loop over s.] Choose a vertex s with $r - s$. If there is no such vertex, return from the subroutine.

I2. [Record the edge.] Set $j \leftarrow j + 1$, $r_j \leftarrow r$, and $s_j \leftarrow s$.

I3. [Begin breadth-first search.] (Now we want to find and delete all edges of the current graph that are equivalent to $r - s$.) Set MARK(s) $\leftarrow s$, RANK(s) $\leftarrow 1$, LINK(s) $\leftarrow \Lambda$, and $v \leftarrow q \leftarrow s$.

I4. [Find the mate of v.] Find the early neighbor u of v for which MARK(u) $\neq s$ or RANK(u) $\neq 1$. (There will be exactly one such vertex u. Recall that early neighbors have been placed first, in step H1.) Set MATE(v) $\leftarrow u$.

I5. [Delete $u - v$.] Make the edges $u - v$ and $r - s$ equivalent by merging their equivalence classes. Remove u and v from each other's adjacency lists.

I6. [Classify the neighbors of v.] For each early neighbor u of v, do step I7; for each late neighbor u of v, do step I8. Then go to step I9.

I7. [Note a possible equivalence.] If MARK(u) $= s$ and RANK(u) $= 1$, make the edge $u - v$ equivalent to the edge MATE(u) $-$ MATE(v). Return to I6.

I8. [Rank u.] If MARK(u) $= s$ and RANK(u) $= 1$, return to I6. Otherwise set MARK(u) $\leftarrow s$ and RANK(u) $\leftarrow 2$. Set w to the first neighbor of u (it will be early). If $w = v$, reset w to u's second early neighbor; but return to I6 if u has only one early neighbor. If MARK(w) $\neq s$ or RANK(w) $\neq 2$, set RANK(u) $\leftarrow 1$, LINK(u) $\leftarrow \Lambda$, LINK(q) $\leftarrow u$, and $q \leftarrow u$. Return to I6.

I9. [Continue breadth-first search.] Set $v \leftarrow$ LINK(v). Return to I4 if $v \neq \Lambda$.

I10. [Process subgraph s.] Call Subroutine I recursively with parameter s. Then return to I1. ∎

This algorithm and subroutine have been described in terms of relatively high-level data structures; further details are left to the reader. For example, adjacency lists should be doubly linked, so that edges can readily be deleted in step I5. Any convenient method for merging equivalence classes can be used in that step.

Exercise 77 explains the theory that makes this algorithm work, and exercise 78 proves that each vertex is encountered at most $\lg n$ times in step I4. Furthermore, exercise 79 shows that a median graph has at most $O(n \log n)$ edges. Therefore the total running time of Algorithm H is $O(n(\log n)^2)$, except perhaps for the bit-setting in step H3.

The reader may wish to play through Algorithm H by hand on the median graph in Table 2, whose vertices represent the twelve monotone self-dual Boolean functions of four variables $\{w, x, y, z\}$. All such functions that actually involve all four variables can be expressed as a median of five things, like (64). With

Table 2

LABELS FOR THE FREE MEDIAN ALGEBRA ON FOUR GENERATORS

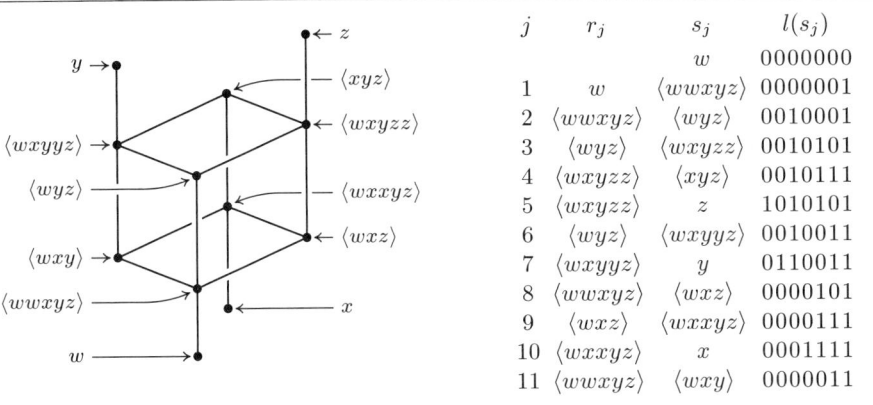

j	r_j	s_j	$l(s_j)$
		w	0000000
1	w	$\langle wwxyz \rangle$	0000001
2	$\langle wwxyz \rangle$	$\langle wyz \rangle$	0010001
3	$\langle wyz \rangle$	$\langle wxyzz \rangle$	0010101
4	$\langle wxyzz \rangle$	$\langle xyz \rangle$	0010111
5	$\langle wxyzz \rangle$	z	1010101
6	$\langle wyz \rangle$	$\langle wxyyz \rangle$	0010011
7	$\langle wxyyz \rangle$	y	0110011
8	$\langle wwxyz \rangle$	$\langle wxz \rangle$	0000101
9	$\langle wxz \rangle$	$\langle wxxyz \rangle$	0000111
10	$\langle wxxyz \rangle$	x	0001111
11	$\langle wwxyz \rangle$	$\langle wxy \rangle$	0000011

starting vertex $a = w$, the algorithm computes the master list of edges $r_j \,\text{---}\, s_j$ and the binary labels shown in the table. (The actual order of processing depends on the order in which vertices appear in adjacency lists. But the final labels will be the same under any ordering, except for permutations of the columns.)

Notice that the number of 1-bits in each label $l(v)$ is the distance of v from the starting vertex a. In fact, the uniqueness of labels tells us that *the distance between any two vertices is the number of bit positions in which their labels differ*, because we could have started at any particular vertex.

The special median graph in Table 2 could actually have been handled in a completely different way, without using Algorithm H at all, because the labels in this case are essentially the same as the *truth tables* of the corresponding functions. Here's why: We can say that the simple functions w, x, y, z have the respective truth tables $t(w) = 0000000011111111$, $t(x) = 0000111100001111$, $t(y) = 0011001100110011$, $t(z) = 0101010101010101$. Then the truth table of $\langle wwxyz \rangle$ is the bitwise majority function $\langle t(w)t(w)t(x)t(y)t(z) \rangle$, namely the string 0000000101111111; and a similar computation gives the truth tables of all the other vertices.

The last half of any self-dual function's truth table is the same as the first half, but complemented and reversed, so we can eliminate it. Furthermore the leftmost bit in each of our truth tables is always zero. We are left with the seven-bit labels shown in Table 2; and the uniqueness property guarantees that Algorithm H will produce the same result, except for possible permutation of columns, when it is presented with this particular graph.

This reasoning tells us that the edges of the graph in Table 2 correspond to pairs of functions whose truth tables are almost the same. We move between neighboring vertices by switching only two complementary bits of their truth tables. In fact, the degree of each vertex turns out to be exactly the number of prime implicants in the disjunctive prime form of the monotone self-dual function represented by that vertex (see exercises 70 and 84).

Median sets. A *median set* is a collection X of binary vectors with the property that $\langle xyz \rangle \in X$ whenever $x \in X$, $y \in X$, and $z \in X$, where the medians are computed componentwise as we've done with median labels. Thomas Schaefer noticed in 1978 that median sets provide us with an attractive counterpoint to the characterization of Horn functions in Theorem H:

Theorem S. *The Boolean function* $f(x_1, \ldots, x_n)$ *is expressible as a conjunction of Krom clauses if and only if*

$$f(x_1, \ldots, x_n) = f(y_1, \ldots, y_n) = f(z_1, \ldots, z_n) = 1$$
$$\text{implies} \quad f(\langle x_1 y_1 z_1 \rangle, \ldots, \langle x_n y_n z_n \rangle) = 1 \qquad (68)$$

for all Boolean values x_j, y_j, *and* z_j.

Proof. [*STOC* **10** (1978), 216–226, Lemma 3.1B.] If we have $x_1 \vee x_2 = y_1 \vee y_2 = z_1 \vee z_2 = 1$, say, with $x_1 \leq y_1 \leq z_1$, then $\langle x_1 y_1 z_1 \rangle \vee \langle x_2 y_2 z_2 \rangle = y_1 \vee \langle x_2 y_2 z_2 \rangle = 1$, since $y_1 = 0$ implies that $x_2 = y_2 = 1$. Thus (68) is necessary.

Conversely, if (68) holds, let $u_1 \vee \cdots \vee u_k$ be a prime clause of f, where each u_j is a literal. Then, for $1 \leq j \leq k$, the clause $u_1 \vee \cdots \vee u_{j-1} \vee u_{j+1} \vee \cdots \vee u_k$ is not a clause of f; so there's a vector $x^{(j)}$ with $f(x^{(j)}) = 1$ but with $u_i^{(j)} = 0$ for all $i \neq j$. If $k \geq 3$, the median $\langle x^{(1)} x^{(2)} x^{(3)} \rangle$ has $u_i = 0$ for $1 \leq i \leq k$; but that's impossible, because $u_1 \vee \cdots \vee u_k$ was supposedly a clause. Hence $k \leq 2$. ∎

Thus median sets are the same as "2SAT instances," the sets of points that satisfy some formula f in 2CNF.

A median set is said to be *reduced* if its vectors $x = x_1 \ldots x_t$ contain no redundant components. In other words, for each coordinate position k, a reduced median set has at least two vectors $x^{(k)}$ and $y^{(k)}$ with the property that $x_k^{(k)} = 0$ and $y_k^{(k)} = 1$ but $x_i^{(k)} = y_i^{(k)}$ for all $i \neq k$. We've seen that the labels of a median graph satisfy this condition; in fact, if coordinate k corresponds to the edge $u - v$ in the graph, we can let $x^{(k)}$ and $y^{(k)}$ be the labels of u and v. Conversely, any reduced median set X defines a median graph, with one vertex for each element of X and with adjacency defined by all-but-one equality of coordinates. The median labels of these vertices must be identical to the original vectors in X, because we know that median labels are essentially unique.

Median labels and reduced median sets can also be characterized in yet another instructive way, which harks back to the networks of *comparator modules* that we studied in Section 5.3.4. We noted in that section that such networks are useful for "oblivious sorting" of numbers, and we noted in Theorem 5.3.4Z that a network of comparators will sort all $n!$ possible input permutations if and only if it correctly sorts all 2^n combinations of 0s and 1s. When a comparator module is attached to two horizontal lines, with inputs x and y entering from the left, it outputs the same two values on the right, but with $\min(x, y) = x \wedge y$ on the upper line and $\max(x, y) = x \vee y$ on the lower line. Let's now extend the concept slightly by also allowing *inverter modules*, which change 0 to 1 and vice versa. Here, for example, is a comparator-inverter network (or CI-net, for short), which transforms the binary value 0010 into 0111:

$$
\begin{array}{llllllll}
0 & 0 & 0 & 0 & 1 & 0 & 1 & 0 \\
0 & 1 & 1 & 1 & 0 & 0 & 1 & 1 \\
1 & 0 & 1 & 1 & 0 & 1 & 1 & 1 \\
0 & 1 & 1 & 1 & 0 & 0 & 0 & 1
\end{array}
\tag{69}
$$

(A single dot denotes an inverter.) Indeed, this network transforms

$$
\begin{array}{llll}
0000 \mapsto 0110; & 0100 \mapsto 0111; & 1000 \mapsto 0111; & 1100 \mapsto 0110; \\
0001 \mapsto 0111; & 0101 \mapsto 1111; & 1001 \mapsto 0101; & 1101 \mapsto 0111; \\
0010 \mapsto 0111; & 0110 \mapsto 1111; & 1010 \mapsto 0101; & 1110 \mapsto 0111; \\
0011 \mapsto 0110; & 0111 \mapsto 0111; & 1011 \mapsto 0111; & 1111 \mapsto 0110.
\end{array}
\tag{70}
$$

Suppose a CI-net transforms the bit string $x = x_1 \ldots x_t$ into the bit string $x'_1 \ldots x'_t = f(x)$. This function f, which maps the t-cube into itself, is in fact a *graph homomorphism*. In other words, we have $f(x) \mathrel{\text{---}} f(y)$ whenever $x \mathrel{\text{---}} y$ in the t-cube: Changing one bit of x always causes exactly one bit of $f(x)$ to change, because every module in the network has this behavior. Moreover, CI-nets have a remarkable connection with median labels:

Theorem F. *Every set X of t-bit median labels can be represented by a comparator-inverter network that computes a Boolean function $f(x)$ with the property that $f(x) \in X$ for all bit vectors $x_1 \ldots x_t$, and $f(x) = x$ for all $x \in X$.*

Proof. [Tomás Feder, *Memoirs Amer. Math. Soc.* **555** (1995), 1–223, Lemma 3.37; see also the Ph. D. thesis of D. H. Wiedemann (University of Waterloo, 1986).] Consider columns i and j of the median labels, where $1 \le i < j \le t$. Any such pair of columns contains at least three of the four possibilities $\{00, 01, 10, 11\}$, if we look through the entire set of labels, because median labels have no redundant columns. Let us write $\bar{j} \to i$, $j \to i$, $i \to j$, or $i \to \bar{j}$ if the value 00, 01, 10, or 11 (respectively) is missing from those two columns; we can also note the equivalent relations $\bar{i} \to j$, $\bar{i} \to \bar{j}$, $\bar{j} \to \bar{i}$, or $j \to \bar{i}$, respectively, which involve $\bar{i}$ instead of i. For example, the labels in Table 2 give us the relations

$$
\begin{array}{ll}
1 \to \bar{2}, 3, \bar{4}, 5, \bar{6}, 7 & 2, \bar{3}, 4, \bar{5}, 6, \bar{7} \to \bar{1}; \\
2 \to 3, \bar{4}, \bar{5}, 6, 7 & \bar{3}, 4, 5, \bar{6}, \bar{7} \to \bar{2}; \\
3 \to \bar{4}, 7 & 4, \bar{7} \to \bar{3}; \\
4 \to 5, 6, 7 & \bar{5}, \bar{6}, \bar{7} \to \bar{4}; \\
5 \to 7 & \bar{7} \to \bar{5}; \\
6 \to 7 & \bar{7} \to \bar{6}.
\end{array}
\tag{71}
$$

(There is no relation between 3 and 5 because all four possibilities occur in those columns. But we have $3 \to \bar{4}$ because 11 doesn't appear in columns 3 and 4. The vertices whose label has a 1 in column 3 are those closer to $\langle wyz \rangle$ than to $\langle wwxyz \rangle$ in Table 2; they form a convex set in which column 4 of the labels is always 0, because they are also closer to $\langle wxxyz \rangle$ than to x.)

These relations between the literals $\{1, \bar{1}, 2, \bar{2}, \ldots, t, \bar{t}\}$ contain no cycles, so they can always be topologically sorted into an anti-symmetrical sequence

$u_1 \, u_2 \, \ldots \, u_{2t}$ in which u_j is the complement of u_{2t+1-j}. For example,

$$1 \; \overline{7} \; 4 \; 2 \; \overline{3} \; \overline{5} \; \overline{6} \; 6 \; 5 \; 3 \; \overline{2} \; \overline{4} \; 7 \; \overline{1} \tag{72}$$

is one such way to sort the relations in (71) topologically.

Now we proceed to construct the network, by starting with t empty lines and successively examining elements u_k and u_{k+d} in the topological sequence, for $d = 2t - 2, \, 2t - 3, \, \ldots, \, 1$ (in this order), and for $k = 1, \, 2, \, \ldots, \, t - \lceil d/2 \rceil$. If $u_k \to u_{k+d}$ is a relation between columns i and j, where $i < j$, we append new modules to lines i and j of the network as follows:

$$
\text{If } i \to j \qquad \text{If } i \to \bar{j} \qquad \text{If } \bar{\imath} \to j \qquad \text{If } \bar{\imath} \to \bar{j} \tag{73}
$$

For example, from (71) and (72) we first enforce $1 \to 7$, then $1 \to \overline{4}$, then $1 \to \overline{2}$, then $\overline{7} \to \overline{4}$ (that is, $4 \to 7$), etc., obtaining the following network:

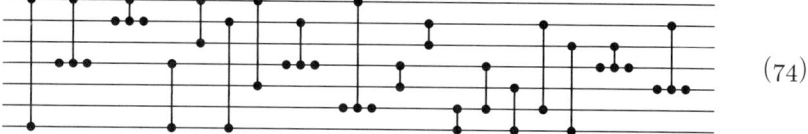

$$\tag{74}$$

(Go figure. No modules are contributed when, say, u_k is $\overline{7}$ and u_{k+d} is 3, because the relation $\overline{3} \to 7$ does not appear in (71).)

Exercise 89 proves that each new cluster of modules (73) preserves all of the previous relations and enforces a new one. Therefore, if x is any input vector, $f(x)$ satisfies all of the relations; so $f(x) \in X$ by Theorem S. Conversely, if $x \in X$, every cluster of modules in the network leaves x unchanged. $\blacksquare$

Corollary F. *Suppose the median labels in Theorem F are closed under the operations of bitwise AND and OR, so that $x \, \& \, y \in X$ and $x \mid y \in X$ whenever $x \in X$ and $y \in X$. Then there is a permutation of coordinates under which the labels are representable by a network of comparator modules only.*

Proof. The bitwise AND of all labels is $0 \ldots 0$, and the bitwise OR is $1 \ldots 1$. So the only possible relations between columns are $i \to j$ and $j \to i$. By topologically sorting and renaming the columns, we can ensure that only $i \to j$ occurs when $i < j$; and in this case the construction in the proof never uses an inverter. $\blacksquare$

In general, if G is any graph, a homomorphism f that maps the vertices of G onto a subset X of those vertices is called a *retraction* if it satisfies $f(x) = x$ for all $x \in X$; and we call X a *retract* of G when such an f exists. The importance of this concept in the theory of graphs was first pointed out by Pavol Hell [see *Lecture Notes in Math.* **406** (1974), 291–301]. One consequence, for example, is that the distance between vertices in X — the number of edges on a shortest path — remains the same even if we restrict consideration to paths that lie entirely in X. (See exercise 93.)

Theorem F demonstrates that every t-dimensional set of median labels is a retract of the t-dimensional hypercube. Conversely, exercise 94 shows that hypercube retracts are always median graphs.

Threshold functions. A particularly appealing and important class of Boolean functions $f(x_1, x_2, \ldots, x_n)$ arises when f can be defined by the formula

$$f(x_1, x_2, \ldots, x_n) = [w_1 x_1 + w_2 x_2 + \cdots + w_n x_n \geq t], \qquad (75)$$

where the constants w_1, w_2, $\ldots$, w_n are integer "weights" and t is an integer "threshold" value. For example, threshold functions are important even when all the weights are unity: We have

$$x_1 \wedge x_2 \wedge \cdots \wedge x_n = [x_1 + x_2 + \cdots + x_n \geq n]; \qquad (76)$$

$$x_1 \vee x_2 \vee \cdots \vee x_n = [x_1 + x_2 + \cdots + x_n \geq 1]; \qquad (77)$$

and $\qquad \langle x_1 x_2 \ldots x_{2t-1} \rangle = [x_1 + x_2 + \cdots + x_{2t-1} \geq t], \qquad (78)$

where $\langle x_1 x_2 \ldots x_{2t-1} \rangle$ stands for the median (or majority) value of a multiset that consists of any odd number of Boolean values $\{x_1, x_2, \ldots, x_{2t-1}\}$. In particular, the basic mappings $x \wedge y$, $x \vee y$, and $\langle xyz \rangle$ are all threshold functions, and so is

$$\bar{x} = [-x \geq 0]. \qquad (79)$$

With more general weights we get many other functions of interest, such as

$$[2^{n-1} x_1 + 2^{n-2} x_2 + \cdots + x_n \geq (t_1 t_2 \ldots t_n)_2], \qquad (80)$$

which is true if and only if the binary string $x_1 x_2 \ldots x_n$ is lexicographically greater than or equal to a given binary string $t_1 t_2 \ldots t_n$. Given a set of n objects having sizes w_1, w_2, $\ldots$, w_n, a subset of those objects will fit into a knapsack of size $t - 1$ if and only if $f(x_1, x_2, \ldots, x_n) = 0$, where $x_j = 1$ represents the presence of object j in the subset. Simple models of neurons, originally proposed by W. McCulloch and W. Pitts in *Bull. Math. Biophysics* **5** (1943), 115–133, have led to thousands of research papers about "neural networks" built from threshold functions.

We can get rid of any negative weight w_j by setting $x_j \leftarrow \bar{x}_j$, $w_j \leftarrow -w_j$, and $t \leftarrow t + |w_j|$. Thus a general threshold function can be reduced to a positive threshold function in which all weights are nonnegative. Furthermore, any positive threshold function (75) can be expressed as a special case of the median/majority-of-odd function, because we have

$$\langle 0^a 1^b x_1^{w_1} x_2^{w_2} \ldots x_n^{w_n} \rangle = [b + w_1 x_1 + w_2 x_2 + \cdots + w_n x_n \geq b + t], \qquad (81)$$

where x^m stands for m copies of x, and where a and b are defined by the rules

$$a = \max(0, 2t - 1 - w), \quad b = \max(0, w + 1 - 2t), \quad w = w_1 + w_2 + \cdots + w_n. \qquad (82)$$

For example, when all weights are 1, we have

$$\langle 0^{n-1} x_1 \ldots x_n \rangle = x_1 \wedge \cdots \wedge x_n \quad \text{and} \quad \langle 1^{n-1} x_1 \ldots x_n \rangle = x_1 \vee \cdots \vee x_n; \qquad (83)$$

we've already seen these formulas in (45) when $n = 2$. In general, either a or b is zero, and the left-hand side of (81) specifies a median of $2T - 1$ elements, where

$$T = b + t = \max(t, w_1 + w_2 + \cdots + w_n + 1 - t). \qquad (84)$$

There would be no point in letting both a and b be greater than zero, because the majority function clearly satisfies the cancellation law

$$\langle 01x_1x_2\dots x_{2t-1}\rangle = \langle x_1x_2\dots x_{2t-1}\rangle. \tag{85}$$

One important consequence of (81) is that every positive threshold function comes from the pure majority function

$$g(x_0, x_1, x_2, \dots, x_n) = \langle x_0^{a+b}x_1^{w_1}x_2^{w_2}\dots x_n^{w_n}\rangle \tag{86}$$

by setting $x_0 = 0$ or 1. In other words, we know all threshold functions of n variables if and only if we know all of the distinct median-of-odd functions of $n+1$ or fewer variables (containing no constants). Every pure majority function is monotone and self-dual; thus we've seen the pure majority functions of four variables $\{w, x, y, z\}$ in column s_j of Table 2 on page 71, namely $\langle w\rangle$, $\langle wwxyz\rangle$, $\langle wyz\rangle$, $\langle wxyzz\rangle$, $\langle xyz\rangle$, $\langle z\rangle$, $\langle wxyyz\rangle$, $\langle y\rangle$, $\langle wxz\rangle$, $\langle wxxyz\rangle$, $\langle x\rangle$, $\langle wxy\rangle$. By setting $w = 0$ or 1, we obtain all the positive threshold functions $f(x, y, z)$ of three variables:

$$\langle 0\rangle, \langle 1\rangle, \langle 00xyz\rangle, \langle 11xyz\rangle, \langle 0yz\rangle, \langle 1yz\rangle, \langle 0xyzz\rangle, \langle 1xyzz\rangle, \langle xyz\rangle, \langle z\rangle,$$

$$\langle 0xyyz\rangle, \langle 1xyyz\rangle, \langle y\rangle, \langle 0xz\rangle, \langle 1xz\rangle, \langle 0xxyz\rangle, \langle 1xxyz\rangle, \langle x\rangle, \langle 0xy\rangle, \langle 1xy\rangle. \tag{87}$$

All 150 positive threshold functions of four variables can be obtained in a similar fashion from the self-dual majority functions in the answer to exercise 84.

There are infinitely many sequences of weights $(w_1, w_2, \dots, w_n)$, but only finitely many threshold functions for any given value of n. So it is clear that many different weight sequences are equivalent. For example, consider the pure majority function

$$\langle x_1^2 x_2^3 x_3^5 x_4^7 x_5^{11} x_6^{13}\rangle,$$

in which prime numbers have been used as weights. A brute-force examination of 2^6 cases shows that

$$\langle x_1^2 x_2^3 x_3^5 x_4^7 x_5^{11} x_6^{13}\rangle = \langle x_1 x_2^2 x_3^2 x_4^3 x_5^4 x_6^5\rangle; \tag{88}$$

thus we can express the same function with substantially smaller weights. Similarly, the threshold function

$$[(x_1x_2\dots x_{20})_2 \ge (01100100100001111110)_2] = \langle 1^{225028} x_1^{524288} x_2^{262144}\dots x_{20}\rangle,$$

a special case of (80), turns out to be simply

$$\langle 1^{323} x_1^{764} x_2^{323} x_3^{323} x_4^{118} x_5^{118} x_6^{87} x_7^{31} x_8^{31} x_9^{25} x_{10}^6 x_{11}^6 x_{12}^6 x_{13}^6 x_{14}x_{15}x_{16}x_{17}x_{18}x_{19}\rangle. \tag{89}$$

Exercise 103 explains how to find a minimum set of weights without resorting to a huge brute-force search, using linear programming.

A nice indexing scheme by which a unique identifier can be assigned to any threshold function was discovered by C. K. Chow [*FOCS* **2** (1961), 34–38]. Given any Boolean function $f(x_1, \dots, x_n)$, let $N(f)$ be the number of vectors $x = (x_1, \dots, x_n)$ for which $f(x) = 1$, and let $\Sigma(f)$ be the sum of all those vectors. For example, if $f(x_1, x_2) = x_1 \vee x_2$, we have $N(f) = 3$ and $\Sigma(f) = (0, 1) + (1, 0) + (1, 1) = (2, 2)$.

Theorem T. Let $f(x_1, \ldots, x_n)$ and $g(x_1, \ldots, x_n)$ be Boolean functions with $N(f) = N(g)$ and $\Sigma(f) = \Sigma(g)$, where f is a threshold function. Then $f = g$.

Proof. Suppose there are exactly k vectors $x^{(1)}, \ldots, x^{(k)}$ such that $f(x^{(j)}) = 1$ and $g(x^{(j)}) = 0$. Since $N(f) = N(g)$, there must be exactly k vectors $y^{(1)}, \ldots, y^{(k)}$ such that $f(y^{(j)}) = 0$ and $g(y^{(j)}) = 1$. And since $\Sigma(f) = \Sigma(g)$, we must also have $x^{(1)} + \cdots + x^{(k)} = y^{(1)} + \cdots + y^{(k)}$.

Now suppose f is the threshold function (75); then we have $w \cdot x^{(j)} \geq t$ and $w \cdot y^{(j)} < t$ for $1 \leq j \leq k$. But if $f \neq g$ we have $k > 0$, and $w \cdot (x^{(1)} + \cdots + x^{(k)}) \geq kt > w \cdot (y^{(1)} + \cdots + y^{(k)})$, a contradiction. ∎

Threshold functions have many curious properties, some of which are explored in the exercises below. Their classical theory is well summarized in Saburo Muroga's book *Threshold Logic and its Applications* (Wiley, 1971).

Symmetric Boolean functions. A function $f(x_1, \ldots, x_n)$ is called *symmetric* if $f(x_1, \ldots, x_n)$ is equal to $f(x_{p(1)}, \ldots, x_{p(n)})$ for all permutations $p(1) \ldots p(n)$ of $\{1, \ldots, n\}$. When all the x_j are 0 or 1, this condition means that f depends only on the number of 1s that are present in the arguments, namely the "sideways sum" $\nu x = \nu(x_1, \ldots, x_n) = x_1 + \cdots + x_n$. The notation $S_{k_1, k_2, \ldots, k_r}(x_1, \ldots, x_n)$ is commonly used to stand for the Boolean function that is true if and only if νx is either k_1 or k_2 or $\cdots$ or k_r. For example, $S_{1,3,5}(v, w, x, y, z) = v \oplus w \oplus x \oplus y \oplus z$; $S_{3,4,5}(v, w, x, y, z) = \langle vwxyz \rangle$; $S_{4,5}(v, w, x, y, z) = \langle 00vwxyz \rangle$.

Many applications of symmetry involve the basic functions $S_k(x_1, \ldots, x_n)$ that are true only when $\nu x = k$. For example, $S_3(x_1, x_2, x_3, x_4, x_5, x_6)$ is true if and only if exactly half of the arguments $\{x_1, \ldots, x_6\}$ are true and the other half are false. In such cases we obviously have

$$S_k(x_1, \ldots, x_n) = S_{\geq k}(x_1, \ldots, x_n) \wedge \overline{S_{\geq k+1}(x_1, \ldots, x_n)}, \qquad (90)$$

where $S_{\geq k}(x_1, \ldots, x_n)$ is an abbreviation for $S_{k,k+1,\ldots,n}(x_1, \ldots, x_n)$. The functions $S_{\geq k}(x_1, \ldots, x_n)$ are, of course, the threshold functions $[x_1 + \cdots + x_n \geq k]$ that we have already studied.

More complicated cases can be treated as threshold functions of threshold functions. For example, we have

$$S_{2,3,6,8,9}(x_1, \ldots, x_{12}) = \left[\nu x \geq 2 + 4[\nu x \geq 4] + 2[\nu x \geq 7] + 5[\nu x \geq 10]\right]$$
$$= \langle 00x_1 \ldots x_{12} \langle 0^5 \bar{x}_1 \ldots \bar{x}_{12} \rangle^4 \langle 1\bar{x}_1 \ldots \bar{x}_{12} \rangle^2 \langle 1^7 \bar{x}_1 \ldots \bar{x}_{12} \rangle^5 \rangle, \qquad (91)$$

because the number of 1s in the outermost majority-of-25 turns out to be respectively $(11, 12, 13, 14, 11, 12, 13, 12, 13, 14, 10, 11, 12)$ when $x_1 + \cdots + x_{12} = (0, 1, \ldots, 12)$. A similar two-level scheme works in general [R. C. Minnick, *IRE Trans.* **EC-10** (1961), 6–16]; and with three or more levels of logic we can reduce the number of thresholding operations even further. (See exercise 113.)

A variety of ingenious tricks have been discovered for evaluating symmetric Boolean functions. For example, S. Muroga attributes the following remarkable sequence of formulas to F. Sasaki:

$$x_0 \oplus x_1 \oplus \cdots \oplus x_{2m} = \langle \bar{x}_0 s_1 s_2 \ldots s_{2m} \rangle,$$
$$\text{where} \quad s_j = \langle x_0 x_j x_{j+1} \ldots x_{j+m-1} \bar{x}_{j+m} \bar{x}_{j+m+1} \ldots \bar{x}_{j+2m-1} \rangle, \qquad (92)$$

if $m > 0$ and if we consider x_{2m+k} to be the same as x_k for $k \geq 1$. In particular, when $m = 1$ and $m = 2$ we have the identities

$$x_0 \oplus x_1 \oplus x_2 = \langle \bar{x}_0 \langle x_0 x_1 \bar{x}_2 \rangle \langle x_0 x_2 \bar{x}_1 \rangle \rangle; \tag{93}$$

$$x_0 \oplus \cdots \oplus x_4 = \langle \bar{x}_0 \langle x_0 x_1 x_2 \bar{x}_3 \bar{x}_4 \rangle \langle x_0 x_2 x_3 \bar{x}_4 \bar{x}_1 \rangle \langle x_0 x_3 x_4 \bar{x}_1 \bar{x}_2 \rangle \langle x_0 x_4 x_1 \bar{x}_2 \bar{x}_3 \rangle \rangle. \tag{94}$$

The right-hand sides are fully symmetric, but not obviously so! (See exercise 115.)

Canalizing functions. A Boolean function $f(x_1, \ldots, x_n)$ is said to be *canalizing* or "forcing" if we might be able to deduce its value by examining at most one of its variables. More precisely, f is canalizing if $n = 0$ or if there's a subscript j for which $f(x)$ either has a constant value when we set $x_j = 0$ or a constant value when we set $x_j = 1$. For example, $f(x, y, z) = (x \oplus z) \vee \bar{y}$ is canalizing because it always equals 1 when $y = 0$. (When $y = 1$ we don't know the value of f without examining also x and z; but half a loaf is better than none.) Such functions, introduced by Stuart Kauffman [*Lectures on Mathematics in the Life Sciences* **3** (1972), 63–116; *J. Theoretical Biology* **44** (1974), 167–190], have proved to be important in many applications, especially in chemistry and biology. Some of their properties are examined in exercises 125–129.

Quantitative considerations. We've been studying many different kinds of Boolean functions, so it's natural to ask: How many n-variable functions of each type actually exist? Tables 3, 4, and 5 provide the answers, at least for small values of n.

All functions are counted in Table 3. There are 2^{2^n} possibilities for each n, since there are 2^{2^n} possible truth tables. Some of these functions are self-dual, some are monotone; some are both monotone and self-dual, as in Theorem P. Some are Horn functions as in Theorem H; some are Krom functions as in Theorem S; and so on.

But in Table 4, two functions are considered identical if they differ only because the names of variables have changed. Thus only 12 different cases arise when $n = 2$, because (for example) $x \vee \bar{y}$ and $\bar{x} \vee y$ are essentially the same.

Table 5 goes a step further: It allows us to complement individual variables, and even to complement the entire function, without essentially changing it. From this perspective the 256 Boolean functions of (x, y, z) fall into only 14 different equivalence classes:

Representative	Class size	Representative	Class size	
0	2	$x \wedge (y \oplus z)$	24	
x	6	$x \oplus (y \wedge z)$	24	
$x \wedge y$	24	$(x \wedge y) \vee (\bar{x} \wedge z)$	24	
$x \oplus y$	6	$(x \vee y) \wedge (x \oplus z)$	48	(95)
$x \wedge y \wedge z$	16	$(x \oplus y) \vee (x \oplus z)$	8	
$x \oplus y \oplus z$	2	$\langle xyz \rangle$	8	
$x \wedge (y \vee z)$	48	$S_1(x, y, z)$	16	

We shall study ways to count and to list inequivalent combinatorial objects in Section 7.2.3.

Table 3

BOOLEAN FUNCTIONS OF n VARIABLES

	$n=0$	$n=1$	$n=2$	$n=3$	$n=4$	$n=5$	$n=6$
arbitrary	2	4	16	256	65,536	4,294,967,296	18,446,744,073,709,551,616
self-dual	0	2	4	16	256	65,536	4,294,967,296
monotone	2	3	6	20	168	7,581	7,828,354
both	0	1	2	4	12	81	2,646
Horn	2	4	14	122	4,960	2,771,104	151,947,502,948
Krom	2	4	16	166	4,170	224,716	24,445,368
threshold	2	4	14	104	1,882	94,572	15,028,134
symmetric	2	4	8	16	32	64	128
canalizing	2	4	14	120	3,514	1,292,276	103,071,426,294

Table 4

BOOLEAN FUNCTIONS DISTINCT UNDER PERMUTATION OF VARIABLES

	$n=0$	$n=1$	$n=2$	$n=3$	$n=4$	$n=5$	$n=6$
arbitrary	2	4	12	80	3,984	37,333,248	25,626,412,338,274,304
self-dual	0	2	2	8	32	1,088	6,385,408
monotone	2	3	5	10	30	210	16,353
both	0	1	1	2	3	7	30
Horn	2	4	10	38	368	29,328	216,591,692
Krom	2	4	12	48	308	3,028	49,490
threshold	2	4	10	34	178	1,720	590,440
canalizing	2	4	10	38	294	15,774	149,325,022

Table 5

BOOLEAN FUNCTIONS DISTINCT UNDER COMPLEMENTATION/PERMUTATION

	$n=0$	$n=1$	$n=2$	$n=3$	$n=4$	$n=5$	$n=6$
arbitrary	1	2	4	14	222	616,126	200,253,952,527,184
self-dual	0	1	1	3	7	83	109,950
threshold	1	2	3	6	15	63	567
both	0	1	1	2	3	7	21
canalizing	1	2	3	6	22	402	1,228,158

EXERCISES

1. [*15*] (Lewis Carroll.) Make sense of Tweedledee's comment, quoted near the beginning of this section. [*Hint:* See Table 1.]

2. [*17*] Logicians on the remote planet Pincus use the symbol 1 to represent "false" and 0 to represent "true." Thus, for example, they have a binary operation called "or" whose properties

$$1 \text{ or } 1 = 1, \qquad 1 \text{ or } 0 = 0, \qquad 0 \text{ or } 1 = 0, \qquad 0 \text{ or } 0 = 0$$

we associate with $\wedge$. What operations would we associate with the 16 logical operators that Pincusians respectively call "falsehood," "and," ..., "nand," "validity" (see Table 1)?

▶ **3.** [*13*] Suppose logical values were respectively -1 for falsehood and $+1$ for truth, instead of 0 and 1. What operations $\circ$ in Table 1 would then correspond to (a) $\max(x, y)$? (b) $\min(x, y)$? (c) $-x$? (d) $x \cdot y$?

4. [*24*] (H. M. Sheffer.) The purpose of this exercise is to show that all of the operations in Table 1 can be expressed in terms of NAND. (a) For each of the 16 operators $\circ$ in that table, find a formula equivalent to $x \circ y$ that uses only $\overline{\wedge}$ as an operator. Your formula should be as short as possible. For example, the answer for operation $\llcorner$ is simply "x", but the answer for $\bar{\llcorner}$ is "$x \overline{\wedge} x$". Do not use the constants 0 or 1 in your formulas. (b) Similarly, find 16 short formulas when constants *are* allowed. For example, $x \bar{\llcorner} y$ can now be expressed also as "$x \overline{\wedge} 1$".

5. [*24*] Consider exercise 4 with $\overline{\subset}$ as the basic operation instead of $\overline{\wedge}$.

6. [*21*] (E. Schröder.) (a) Which of the 16 operations in Table 1 are associative — in other words, which of them satisfy $x \circ (y \circ z) = (x \circ y) \circ z$? (b) Which of them satisfy the identity $(x \circ y) \circ (y \circ z) = x \circ z$?

7. [*20*] Which operations in Table 1 have the property that $x \circ y = z$ if and only if $y \circ z = x$?

8. [*24*] Which of the 16^2 pairs of operations $(\circ, \square)$ satisfy the left-distributive law $x \circ (y \square z) = (x \circ y) \square (x \circ z)$?

9. [*16*] True or false? (a) $(x \oplus y) \vee z = (x \vee z) \oplus (y \vee z)$; (b) $(w \oplus x \oplus y) \vee z = (w \vee z) \oplus (x \vee z) \oplus (y \vee z)$; (c) $(x \oplus y) \vee (y \oplus z) = (x \oplus z) \vee (y \oplus z)$.

10. [*17*] What is the multilinear representation of the "random" function (22)?

11. [*M25*] Is there an intuitive way to understand exactly when the multilinear representation of $f(x_1, \ldots, x_n)$ contains, say, the term $x_2 x_3 x_6 x_8$? (See (19).)

▶ **12.** [*M23*] The *integer multilinear representation* of a Boolean function extends representations like (19) to a polynomial $f(x_1, \ldots, x_n)$ with integer coefficients, in such a way that $f(x_1, \ldots, x_n)$ has the correct value (0 or 1) for all 2^n possible 0–1 vectors $(x_1, \ldots, x_n)$, *without* taking a remainder mod 2. For example, the integer multilinear representation corresponding to (19) is $1 - xy - xz - yz + 3xyz$.

a) What is the integer multilinear representation of the "random" function (22)?
b) How large can the coefficients of such a representation $f(x_1, \ldots, x_n)$ be?
c) Show that, in every integer multilinear representation, $0 \le f(x_1, \ldots, x_n) \le 1$ whenever $x_1, \ldots, x_n$ are real numbers with $0 \le x_1, \ldots, x_n \le 1$.
d) Similarly, if $f(x_1, \ldots, x_n) \le g(x_1, \ldots, x_n)$ whenever $\{x_1, \ldots, x_n\} \subseteq \{0, 1\}$, then $f(x_1, \ldots, x_n) \le g(x_1, \ldots, x_n)$ whenever $\{x_1, \ldots, x_n\} \subseteq [0 .. 1]$.
e) If f is monotone and $0 \le x_j \le y_j \le 1$ for $1 \le j \le n$, prove that $f(x) \le f(y)$.

▶ **13.** [*20*] Consider a system that consists of n units, each of which may be "working" or "failing." If x_j represents the condition "unit j is working," then a Boolean function like $x_1 \wedge (\bar{x}_2 \vee \bar{x}_3)$ represents the statement "unit 1 is working, but either unit 2 or unit 3 is failing"; and $S_3(x_1, \ldots, x_n)$ means "exactly three units are working."

Suppose each unit j is in working order with probability p_j, independent of the other units. Show that the Boolean function $f(x_1, \ldots, x_n)$ is true with probability $F(p_1, \ldots, p_n)$, where F is a polynomial in the variables $p_1, \ldots, p_n$.

14. [*20*] The probability function $F(p_1, \ldots, p_n)$ in exercise 13 is often called the *availability* of the system. Find the self-dual function $f(x_1, x_2, x_3)$ of maximum availability when the probabilities (p_1, p_2, p_3) are (a) $(.9, .8, .7)$; (b) $(.8, .6, .4)$; (c) $(.8, .6, .1)$.

▸ **15.** [*M20*] If $f(x_1, \ldots, x_n)$ is any Boolean function, show that there is a polynomial $F(x)$ with the property that $F(x)$ is an integer when x is an integer, and $f(x_1, \ldots, x_n) = F((x_n \ldots x_1)_2) \bmod 2$. *Hint:* Consider $\binom{x}{k} \bmod 2$.

16. [*13*] Can we replace each $\vee$ by $\oplus$ in a full disjunctive normal form?

17. [*10*] By De Morgan's laws, a general disjunctive normal form such as (25) is not only an OR of ANDs, it is a NAND of NANDs:

$$\overline{\overline{(u_{11} \wedge \cdots \wedge u_{1s_1})} \wedge \cdots \wedge \overline{(u_{m1} \wedge \cdots \wedge u_{ms_m})}}.$$

Both levels of logic can therefore be considered to be identical.

A student named J. H. Quick rewrote this expression in the form

$$(u_{11} \,\overline{\wedge}\, \cdots \,\overline{\wedge}\, u_{1s_1}) \,\overline{\wedge}\, \cdots \,\overline{\wedge}\, (u_{m1} \,\overline{\wedge}\, \cdots \,\overline{\wedge}\, u_{ms_m}).$$

Was that a good idea?

▸ **18.** [*20*] Let $u_1 \wedge \cdots \wedge u_s$ be an implicant in a disjunctive normal form for a Boolean function f, and let $v_1 \vee \cdots \vee v_t$ be a clause in a conjunctive normal form for the same function. Prove that $u_i = v_j$ for some i and j.

19. [*20*] What is the conjunctive prime form of the "random" function in (22)?

20. [*M21*] True or false: Every prime implicant of $f \wedge g$ can be written $f' \wedge g'$, where f' is a prime implicant of f and g' is a prime implicant of g.

21. [*M20*] Prove that a nonconstant Boolean function is monotone if and only if it can be expressed entirely in terms of the operations $\wedge$ and $\vee$.

22. [*20*] Suppose $f(x_1, \ldots, x_n) = g(x_1, \ldots, x_{n-1}) \oplus h(x_1, \ldots, x_{n-1}) \wedge x_n$ as in (16). What conditions on the functions g and h are necessary and sufficient for f to be monotone?

23. [*15*] What is the conjunctive prime form of $(v \wedge w \wedge x) \vee (v \wedge x \wedge z) \vee (x \wedge y \wedge z)$?

24. [*M20*] Consider the complete binary tree with 2^k leaves, illustrated here for $k = 3$. Operate alternately with $\wedge$ or $\vee$ on each level, using $\wedge$ at the root, obtaining for example $((x_0 \wedge x_1) \vee (x_2 \wedge x_3)) \wedge$ 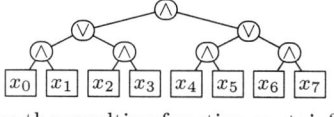 $((x_4 \wedge x_5) \vee (x_6 \wedge x_7))$. How many prime implicants does the resulting function contain?

25. [*M21*] How many prime implicants does $(x_1 \vee x_2) \wedge (x_2 \vee x_3) \wedge \cdots \wedge (x_{n-1} \vee x_n)$ have?

26. [*M23*] Let $\mathcal{F}$ and $\mathcal{G}$ be the families of index sets for the prime clauses and the prime implicants of a monotone CNF and a monotone DNF:

$$f(x) = \bigwedge_{I \in \mathcal{F}} \bigvee_{i \in I} x_i; \qquad g(x) = \bigvee_{J \in \mathcal{G}} \bigwedge_{j \in J} x_j.$$

Efficiently exhibit an x such that $f(x) \neq g(x)$ if any of the following conditions hold:

a) There is an $I \in \mathcal{F}$ and a $J \in \mathcal{G}$ with $I \cap J = \emptyset$.

b) $\bigcup_{I \in \mathcal{F}} I \neq \bigcup_{J \in \mathcal{G}} J$.

c) There's an $I \in \mathcal{F}$ with $|I| > |\mathcal{G}|$, or a $J \in \mathcal{G}$ with $|J| > |\mathcal{F}|$.

d) $\sum_{I \in \mathcal{F}} 2^{n-|I|} + \sum_{J \in \mathcal{G}} 2^{n-|J|} < 2^n$, where $n = |\bigcup_{I \in \mathcal{F}} I|$.

27. [*M31*] Continuing the previous exercise, consider the following algorithm $X(\mathcal{F}, \mathcal{G})$, which either returns a vector x with $f(x) \neq g(x)$, or returns Λ if $f = g$:

X1. [Check necessary conditions.] Return an appropriate value x if condition (a), (b), (c), or (d) in exercise 26 applies.

X2. [Done?] If $|\mathcal{F}||\mathcal{G}| \leq 1$, return Λ.

X3. [Recurse.] Compute the following reduced families, for a "best" index k:

$$\mathcal{F}_1 = \{I \mid I \in \mathcal{F}, \ k \notin I\}, \qquad \mathcal{F}_0 = \mathcal{F}_1 \cup \{I \mid k \notin I, \ I \cup \{k\} \in \mathcal{F}\};$$
$$\mathcal{G}_0 = \{J \mid J \in \mathcal{G}, \ k \notin J\}, \qquad \mathcal{G}_1 = \mathcal{G}_0 \cup \{J \mid k \notin J, \ J \cup \{k\} \in \mathcal{G}\}.$$

Delete any member of $\mathcal{F}_0$ or $\mathcal{G}_1$ that contains another member of the same family. The index k should be chosen so that the ratio $\rho = \min(|\mathcal{F}_1|/|\mathcal{F}|, |\mathcal{G}_0|/|\mathcal{G}|)$ is as small as possible. If $\mathrm{X}(\mathcal{F}_0, \mathcal{G}_0)$ returns a vector x, return the same vector extended with $x_k = 0$. Otherwise if $\mathrm{X}(\mathcal{F}_1, \mathcal{G}_1)$ returns a vector x, return the same vector extended with $x_k = 1$. Otherwise return Λ. ∎

If $N = |\mathcal{F}| + |\mathcal{G}|$, prove that step X1 is executed at most $N^{O(\log N)^2}$ times. *Hint:* Show that we always have $\rho \leq 1 - 1/\lg N$ in step X3.

28. [*21*] (W. V. Quine, 1952.) If $f(x_1, \ldots, x_n)$ is a Boolean function with prime implicants $p_1, \ldots, p_q$, let $g(y_1, \ldots, y_q) = \bigwedge_{f(x)=1} \bigvee\{y_j \mid p_j(x) = 1\}$. For example, the "random" function (22) is true at the eight points (28), and it has five prime implicants given by (29) and (30); so $g(y_1, \ldots, y_5)$ is

$$(y_1 \vee y_2) \wedge (y_1) \wedge (y_2 \vee y_3) \wedge (y_4) \wedge (y_3 \vee y_5) \wedge (y_5) \wedge (y_5) \wedge (y_4 \vee y_5)$$
$$= (y_1 \wedge y_2 \wedge y_4 \wedge y_5) \vee (y_1 \wedge y_3 \wedge y_4 \wedge y_5)$$

in this case. Prove that every shortest DNF expression for f corresponds to a prime implicant of the monotone function g.

29. [*22*] (The next several exercises are devoted to algorithms that deal with the implicants of Boolean functions by representing points of the n-cube as n-bit numbers $(b_{n-1} \ldots b_1 b_0)_2$, rather than as bit strings $x_1 \ldots x_n$.) Given a bit position j, and given n-bit values $v_0 < v_1 < \cdots < v_{m-1}$, explain how to find all pairs (k, k') such that $0 \leq k < k' < m$ and $v_{k'} = v_k \oplus 2^j$, in increasing order of k. The running time of your procedure should be $O(m)$, if bitwise operations on n-bit words take constant time.

▶ **30.** [*27*] The text points out that an implicant of a Boolean function can be regarded as a subcube such as $01*0*$, contained in the set V of all points for which the function is true. Every subcube can be represented as a pair of binary numbers $a = (a_{n-1} \ldots a_0)_2$ and $b = (b_{n-1} \ldots b_0)_2$, where a records the positions of the asterisks and b records the bits in non-$*$ positions. For example, the numbers $a = (00101)_2$ and $b = (01000)_2$ represent the subcube $c = 01*0*$. We always have $a \,\&\, b = 0$.

The "j-buddy" of a subcube is defined whenever $a_j = 0$, by changing b to $b \oplus 2^j$. For example, $01*0*$ has three buddies, namely its 4-buddy $11*0*$, its 3-buddy $00*0*$, and its 1-buddy $01*1*$. Every subcube $c \subseteq V$ can be assigned a tag value $(t_{n-1} \ldots t_0)_2$, where $t_j = 1$ if and only if the j-buddy of c is defined and contained in V. With this definition, c represents a maximal subcube (hence a prime implicant) if and only if its tag is zero.

Use these concepts to design an algorithm that finds all maximal subcubes (a, b) of a given set V, where V is represented by the n-bit numbers $v_0 < v_1 < \cdots < v_{m-1}$.

▶ **31.** [*28*] The algorithm in exercise 30 requires a complete list of all points where a Boolean function is true, and that list may be quite long. Therefore we may prefer to work directly with subcubes, never going down to the level of explicit n-tuples unless necessary. The key to such higher-level methods is the notion of *consensus* between subcubes c and c', denoted by $c \sqcup c'$ and defined to be the largest subcube c'' such that

$$c'' \subseteq c \cup c', \qquad c'' \not\subseteq c, \quad \text{and} \quad c'' \not\subseteq c'.$$

Such a c'' does not always exist. For example, if $c = 000*$ and $c' = *111$, every subcube contained in $c \cup c'$ is contained either in c or in c'.

a) Prove that the consensus, when it exists, can be computed componentwise using the following formulas in each coordinate position:

$$x \sqcup x = x \sqcup * = * \sqcup x = x \quad \text{and} \quad x \sqcup \bar{x} = * \sqcup * = *, \qquad \text{for } x = 0 \text{ and } x = 1.$$

Furthermore, $c \sqcup c'$ exists if and only if the rule $x \sqcup \bar{x} = *$ has been used in exactly one component.

b) A subcube with k asterisks is called a *k-cube*. Show that, if c is a k-cube and c' is a k'-cube, and if the consensus $c'' = c \sqcup c'$ exists, then c'' is a k''-cube where $1 \le k'' \le \min(k, k') + 1$.

c) If C and C' are families of subcubes, let

$$C \sqcup C' = \{ c \sqcup c' \mid c \in C, \, c' \in C', \text{ and } c \sqcup c' \text{ exists} \}.$$

Explain why the following algorithm works.

Algorithm E (*Find maximal subcubes*). Given a family C of subcubes of the n-cube, this algorithm outputs the maximal subcubes of $V = \bigcup_{c \in C} c$, without actually computing the set V itself.

E1. [Initialize.] Set $j \leftarrow 0$. Delete any subcube c of C that is contained in another.

E2. [Done?] (At this point, every j-cube $\subseteq V$ is contained in some element of C, and C contains no k-cubes with $k < j$.) If C is empty, the algorithm terminates.

E3. [Take consensuses.] Set $C' \leftarrow C \sqcup C$, and remove all subcubes from C' that are k-cubes for $k \le j$. While performing this computation, also output any j-cube $c \in C$ for which $c \sqcup C$ does not produce a $(j+1)$-cube of C'.

E4. [Advance.] Set $C \leftarrow C \cup C'$, but delete all j-cubes from this union. Then delete any subcube $c \in C$ that is contained in another. Set $j \leftarrow j+1$ and go to E2. ∎

(See exercise 7.1.3–142 for an efficient way to perform these computations.)

▶ **32.** [*M29*] Let $c_1, \ldots, c_m$ be subcubes of the n-cube.

a) Prove that $c_1 \cup \cdots \cup c_m$ contains at most one maximal subcube c that is not contained in $c_1 \cup \cdots \cup c_{j-1} \cup c_{j+1} \cup \cdots \cup c_m$ for any $j \in \{1, \ldots, m\}$. (If c exists, we call it the *generalized consensus* of $c_1, \ldots, c_m$, because $c = c_1 \sqcup c_2$ in the notation of exercise 31 when $m = 2$.)

b) Find a set of m subcubes for which each of the $2^m - 1$ nonempty subsets of $\{c_1, \ldots, c_m\}$ has a generalized consensus.

c) Prove that a DNF with m implicants has at most $2^m - 1$ prime implicants.

d) Find a DNF that has m implicants and $2^m - 1$ prime implicants.

33. [*M21*] Let $f(x_1, \ldots, x_n)$ be one of the $\binom{2^n}{m}$ Boolean functions that are true at exactly m points. If f is chosen at random, what is the probability that $x_1 \wedge \cdots \wedge x_k$ is (a) an implicant of f? (b) a prime implicant of f? [Give the answer to part (b) as a sum; but evaluate it in closed form when $k = n$.]

▶ **34.** [*HM37*] Continuing exercise 33, let $c(m, n)$ be the average total number of implicants, and let $p(m, n)$ be the average total number of prime implicants.

a) If $0 \le m \le 2^n/n$, show that $m \le c(m, n) \le \frac{3}{2}m + O(m/n)$ and $p(m, n) \ge me^{-1} + O(m/n)$; hence $p(m, n) = \Theta(c(m, n))$ in this range.

b) Now let $2^n/n \le m \le (1 - \epsilon)2^n$, where ϵ is a fixed positive constant. Define the numbers t and α_{mn} by the relations

$$n^{-4/3} \le \left(\frac{m}{2^n}\right)^{2^t} = \alpha_{mn} < n^{-2/3}, \qquad \text{integer } t.$$

Express the asymptotic values of $c(m, n)$ and $p(m, n)$ in terms of n, t, and α_{mn}. [*Hint:* Show that almost all of the implicants have exactly $n - t$ or $n - t - 1$ literals.]

c) Estimate $c(m, n)/p(m, n)$ when $m = 2^{n-1}$ and $n = \lfloor (\ln t - \ln \ln t)2^{2^t} \rfloor$, integer t.

d) Prove that $c(m, n)/p(m, n) = O(\log \log n / \log \log \log n)$ when $m \le (1 - \epsilon)2^n$.

▶ **35.** [*M25*] A DNF is called *orthogonal* if its implicants correspond to disjoint subcubes. Orthogonal disjunctive normal forms are particularly useful when the reliability polynomial of exercise 13 is being calculated or estimated.

The full DNF of every function is obviously orthogonal, because its subcubes are single points. But we can often find an orthogonal DNF that has significantly fewer implicants, especially when the function is monotone. For example, the function $(x_1 \wedge x_2) \vee (x_2 \wedge x_3) \vee (x_3 \wedge x_4)$ is true at eight points, and it has the orthogonal DNF

$$(x_1 \wedge x_2) \vee (\bar{x}_1 \wedge x_2 \wedge x_3) \vee (\bar{x}_2 \wedge x_3 \wedge x_4).$$

In other words, the overlapping subcubes 11**, *11*, **11 can be replaced by the disjoint subcubes 11**, 011*, *011. Using the binary notation for subcubes in exercise 30, these subcubes have asterisk codes 0011, 0001, 1000 and bit codes 1100, 0110, 0011.

Every monotone function can be defined by a list of bit codes $B_1, \ldots, B_p$, when the asterisk codes are respectively $\bar{B}_1, \ldots, \bar{B}_p$. Given such a list, let the "shadow" S_k of B_k be the bitwise OR of $B_j \,\&\, \bar{B}_k$, for all $1 \le j < k$ such that $\nu(B_j \,\&\, \bar{B}_k) = 1$:

$$S_k = \beta_{1k} \mid \cdots \mid \beta_{(k-1)k}, \quad \beta_{jk} = ((B_j \,\&\, \bar{B}_k) \oplus ((B_j \,\&\, \bar{B}_k) - 1)) \dot{-} ((B_j \,\&\, \bar{B}_k) - 1).$$

For example, when the bit codes are $(B_1, B_2, B_3) = (1100, 0110, 0011)$, we get the shadow codes $(S_1, S_2, S_3) = (0000, 1000, 0100)$.

a) Show that the asterisk codes $A'_j = \bar{B}_j - S_j$ and bit codes B_j define subcubes that cover the same points as the subcubes with asterisk codes $A_j = \bar{B}_j$.

b) A list of bit codes $B_1, \ldots, B_p$ is called a *shelling* if $B_j \,\&\, S_k$ is nonzero for all $1 \le j < k \le p$. For example, (1100, 0110, 0011) is a shelling; but if we arrange those bit codes in the order (1100, 0011, 0110) the shelling condition fails when $j = 1$ and $k = 2$, although we do have $S_3 = 1001$. Prove that the subcubes in part (a) are disjoint if and only if the list of bit codes is a shelling.

c) According to Theorem Q, every prime implicant must appear among the B's when we represent a monotone Boolean function in this way. But sometimes we need to add additional implicants if we want the subcubes to be disjoint. For example, there is no shelling for the bit codes 1100 and 0011. Show that we can, however, obtain a shelling for this function $(x_1 \wedge x_2) \vee (x_3 \wedge x_4)$ by adding one more bit code. What is the resulting orthogonal DNF?

d) Permute the bit codes $\{11000, 01100, 00110, 00011, 11010\}$ to obtain a shelling.

e) Add two bit codes to the set $\{110000, 011000, 001100, 000110, 000011\}$ in order to make a shellable list.

36. [*M21*] Continuing exercise 35, let f be any monotone function, not identically 1. Show that the set of bit vectors

$$B = \{\, x \mid f(x) = 1 \text{ and } f(x') = 0 \,\}, \qquad x' = x \,\&\, (x-1),$$

is always shellable when listed in decreasing lexicographic order. (The vector x' is obtained from x by zeroing out the rightmost 1.) For example, this method produces an orthogonal DNF for $(x_1 \wedge x_2) \vee (x_3 \wedge x_4)$ from the list $(1100, 1011, 0111, 0011)$.

▸ **37.** [*M31*] Find a shellable DNF for $(x_1 \wedge x_2) \vee (x_3 \wedge x_4) \vee \cdots \vee (x_{2n-1} \wedge x_{2n})$ that has $2^n - 1$ implicants, and prove that no orthogonal DNF for this function has fewer.

38. [*05*] Is it hard to test the satisfiability of functions in *disjunctive* normal form?

▸ **39.** [*25*] Let $f(x_1, \ldots, x_n)$ be a Boolean formula represented as an extended binary tree with N internal nodes and $N + 1$ leaves. Each leaf is labeled with a variable x_k, and each internal node is labeled with one of the sixteen binary operators in Table 1; applying the operators from bottom to top yields $f(x_1, \ldots, x_n)$ as the value of the root.

Explain how to construct a formula $F(x_1, \ldots, x_n, y_1, \ldots, y_N)$ in 3CNF, having exactly $4N + 1$ clauses, such that $f(x_1, \ldots, x_n) = \exists y_1 \ldots \exists y_N F(x_1, \ldots, x_n, y_1, \ldots, y_N)$. (Thus f is satisfiable if and only if F is satisfiable.)

40. [*23*] Given an undirected graph G, construct the following clauses on the Boolean variables $\{\, p_{uv} \mid u \neq v \,\} \cup \{\, q_{uvw} \mid u \neq v, \, u \neq w, \, v \neq w, \, u \not\!- w \,\}$, where u, v, and w denote vertices of G:

$$A = \bigwedge \{\, (p_{uv} \vee p_{vu}) \wedge (\bar{p}_{uv} \vee \bar{p}_{vu}) \mid u \neq v \,\};$$
$$B = \bigwedge \{\, (\bar{p}_{uv} \vee \bar{p}_{vw} \vee p_{uw}) \mid u \neq v, \, u \neq w, \, v \neq w \,\};$$
$$C = \bigwedge \{\, (\bar{q}_{uvw} \vee p_{uv}) \wedge (\bar{q}_{uvw} \vee p_{vw}) \wedge (q_{uvw} \vee \bar{p}_{uv} \vee \bar{p}_{vw}) \mid u \neq v, \, u \neq w, \, v \neq w, \, u \not\!- w \,\};$$
$$D = \bigwedge \{\, (\bigvee_{v \notin \{u,w\}} (q_{uvw} \vee q_{wvu})) \mid u \neq w, \, u \not\!- w \,\}.$$

Prove that the formula $A \wedge B \wedge C \wedge D$ is satisfiable if and only if G has a Hamiltonian path. *Hint:* Think of p_{uv} as the statement '$u < v$'.

41. [*20*] (*The pigeonhole principle.*) The island of San Serriffe contains m pigeons and n holes. Find a conjunctive normal form that is satisfiable if and only if each pigeon can be the sole occupant of at least one hole.

42. [*20*] Find a short, unsatisfiable CNF that is not totally trivial, although it consists entirely of Horn clauses that are also Krom clauses.

43. [*20*] Is there an efficient way to decide satisfiability of a conjunctive normal form that consists entirely of Horn clauses and/or Krom clauses (possibly mixed)?

44. [*M23*] Complete the proof of Theorem H by studying the implications of (33).

45. [*M20*] (a) Show that exactly half of the Horn functions of n variables are definite. (b) Also show that there are more Horn functions of n variables than monotone functions of n variables (unless $n = 0$).

46. [*20*] Which of the 11×11 character pairs xy can occur next to each other in the context-free grammar (34)?

47. [*20*] Given a sequence of relations $j \prec k$ with $1 \leq j, k \leq n$ as in Algorithm 2.2.3T (topological sorting), consider the clauses

$$x_{j_1} \wedge \cdots \wedge x_{j_t} \Rightarrow x_k \qquad \text{for } 1 \leq k \leq n,$$

where $\{j_1, \ldots, j_t\}$ is the set of elements such that $j_i \prec k$. Compare the behavior of Algorithm C on these clauses to the behavior of Algorithm 2.2.3T.

▶ **48.** [*21*] What's a good way to test a set of Horn clauses for satisfiability?

49. [*22*] Show that, if $f(x_1, \ldots, x_n)$ and $g(x_1, \ldots, x_n)$ are both defined by Horn clauses in CNF, there is an easy way to test if $f(x_1, \ldots, x_n) \leq g(x_1, \ldots, x_n)$ for all $x_1, \ldots, x_n$.

50. [*HM42*] There are $(n+2)2^{n-1}$ possible Horn clauses on n variables. Select $c \cdot 2^n$ of them at random, with repetition permitted, where $c > 0$; and let $P_n(c)$ be the probability that all of the selected clauses are simultaneously satisfiable. Prove that

$$\lim_{n \to \infty} P_n(c) = 1 - (1-e^{-c})(1-e^{-2c})(1-e^{-4c})(1-e^{-8c}) \ldots.$$

▶ **51.** [*22*] A great many two-player games can be defined by specifying a directed graph in which each vertex represents a game position. There are two players, Alice and Bob, who construct an oriented path by starting at a particular vertex and taking turns to extend the path, one arc at a time. Before the game starts, each vertex has either been marked A (meaning that Alice wins), or marked B (meaning that Bob wins), or marked C (meaning that the cat wins), or left unmarked.

When the path reaches a vertex v marked A or B, that player wins. The game stops without a winner if v has been visited before, with the same player to move. If v is marked C, the currently active player has the option of accepting a draw; otherwise he or she must choose an outgoing arc to extend the path, and the other player becomes active. (If v is an unmarked vertex with out-degree zero, the active player loses.)

Associating four propositional variables $A^+(v)$, $A^-(v)$, $B^+(v)$, and $B^-(v)$ with every vertex v of the graph, explain how to construct a set of definite Horn clauses such that $A^+(v)$ is in the core if and only if Alice can force a win when the path starts at v and she moves first; $A^-(v)$ is in the core if and only if Bob can force her to lose in that game; $B^+(v)$ and $B^-(v)$ are similar to $A^+(v)$ and $A^-(v)$, but with roles reversed.

52. [*25*] (*Boolean games.*) Any Boolean function $f(x_1, \ldots, x_n)$ leads to a game called "two steps forward or one step back," in the following way: There are two players, 0 and 1, who repeatedly assign values to the variables x_j; player y tries to make $f(x_1, \ldots, x_n)$ equal to y. Initially all variables are unassigned, and the position marker m is zero. Players take turns, and the currently active player either sets $m \leftarrow m + 2$ (if $m + 2 \leq n$) or $m \leftarrow m - 1$ (if $m - 1 \geq 1$), then sets

$$\begin{cases} x_m \leftarrow 0 \text{ or } 1, & \text{if } x_m \text{ was not previously assigned}; \\ x_m \leftarrow \bar{x}_m, & \text{if } x_m \text{ was previously assigned}. \end{cases}$$

The game is over as soon as a value has been assigned to all variables; then $f(x_1, \ldots, x_n)$ is the winner. A draw is declared if the same state (including the value of m) is reached twice. Notice that at most four moves are possible at any time.

Study examples of this game when $2 \leq n \leq 9$, in the following four cases:

a) $f(x_1, \ldots, x_n) = [x_1 \ldots x_n < x_n \ldots x_1]$ (in lexicographic order);
b) $f(x_1, \ldots, x_n) = x_1 \oplus \cdots \oplus x_n$;
c) $f(x_1, \ldots, x_n) = [x_1 \ldots x_n$ contains no two consecutive 1s];
d) $f(x_1, \ldots, x_n) = [(x_1 \ldots x_n)_2$ is prime].

53. [*23*] Show that the impossible comedy festival of (37) *can* be scheduled if a change is made to the requirements of only (a) Tomlin; (b) Unwin; (c) Vegas; (d) Xie; (e) Yankovic; (f) Zany.

54. [*20*] Let $S = \{u_1, u_2, \ldots, u_k\}$ be the set of literals in some strong component of a digraph that corresponds to a 2CNF formula as in Fig. 6. Show that S contains both a variable and its complement if and only if $u_j = \bar{u}_1$ for some j with $2 \leq j \leq k$.

▶ **55.** [*30*] Call $f(x_1, \ldots, x_n)$ a *renamed Horn function* if there are Boolean constants $y_1, \ldots, y_n$ such that $f(x_1 \oplus y_1, \ldots, x_n \oplus y_n)$ is a Horn function.

    a) Given $f(x_1, \ldots, x_n)$ in CNF, explain how to construct $g(y_1, \ldots, y_n)$ in 2CNF so that the clauses of $f(x_1 \oplus y_1, \ldots, x_n \oplus y_n)$ are Horn clauses if and only if $g(y_1, \ldots, y_n) = 1$.

    b) Design an algorithm that decides in $O(m)$ steps whether or not all clauses of a given CNF of length m can be converted into Horn clauses by complementing some subset of the variables.

▶ **56.** [*20*] The satisfiability problem for a Boolean function $f(x_1, x_2, \ldots, x_n)$ can be stated formally as the question of whether or not the quantified formula

$$\exists x_1 \, \exists x_2 \, \ldots \, \exists x_n \, f(x_1, x_2, \ldots, x_n)$$

is true; here '$\exists x_j \, \alpha$' means, "there exists a Boolean value x_j such that α holds."

    A much more general evaluation problem arises when we replace one or more of the existential quantifiers $\exists x_j$ by the universal quantifier $\forall x_j$, where '$\forall x_j \, \alpha$' means, "for all Boolean values x_j, α holds."

    Which of the eight quantified formulas $\exists x \, \exists y \, \exists z \, f(x, y, z)$, $\exists x \, \exists y \, \forall z \, f(x, y, z)$, $\ldots$, $\forall x \, \forall y \, \forall z \, f(x, y, z)$ are true when $f(x, y, z) = (x \vee y) \wedge (\bar{x} \vee z) \wedge (y \vee \bar{z})$?

▶ **57.** [*30*] (B. Aspvall, M. F. Plass, and R. E. Tarjan.) Continuing exercise 56, design an algorithm that decides in linear time whether or not a given fully quantified formula $f(x_1, \ldots, x_n)$ is true, when f is any formula in 2CNF (any conjunction of Krom clauses).

▶ **58.** [*37*] Continuing exercise 57, design an efficient algorithm that decides whether or not a given fully quantified conjunction of *Horn* clauses is true.

▶ **59.** [*M20*] (D. Pehoushek and R. Fraer, 1997.) If the truth table for $f(x_1, x_2, \ldots, x_n)$ has a 1 in exactly k places, show that exactly k of the fully quantified formulas $Q x_1 \, Q x_2 \, \ldots Q x_n \, f(x_1, x_2, \ldots, x_n)$ are true, when each Q is either $\exists$ or $\forall$.

60. [*12*] Which of the following expressions yield the median $\langle xyz \rangle$, as defined in (43)?
(a) $(x \wedge y) \oplus (y \wedge z) \oplus (x \wedge z)$. (b) $(x \vee y) \oplus (y \vee z) \oplus (x \vee z)$. (c) $(x \oplus y) \wedge (y \oplus z) \wedge (x \oplus z)$.
(d) $(x \equiv y) \oplus (y \equiv z) \oplus (x \equiv z)$. (e) $(x \bar{\wedge} y) \wedge (y \bar{\wedge} z) \wedge (x \bar{\wedge} z)$. (f) $(x \bar{\wedge} y) \vee (y \bar{\wedge} z) \vee (x \bar{\wedge} z)$.

61. [*13*] True or false: If ∘ is any one of the Boolean binary operations in Table 1, we have the distributive law $w \circ \langle xyz \rangle = \langle (w \circ x)(w \circ y)(w \circ z) \rangle$.

62. [*25*] (C. Schensted.) If $f(x_1, \ldots, x_n)$ is a monotone Boolean function and $n \geq 3$, prove the median expansion formula

$$f(x_1, \ldots, x_n) = \langle f(x_1, x_1, x_3, x_4, \ldots, x_n) f(x_1, x_2, x_2, x_4, \ldots, x_n) f(x_3, x_2, x_3, x_4, \ldots, x_n) \rangle.$$

63. [*20*] Equation (49) shows how to compute the median of five elements via medians of three. Conversely, can we compute $\langle xyz \rangle$ with a subroutine for medians of five?

64. [*23*] (S. B. Akers, Jr.) (a) Prove that a Boolean function $f(x_1, \ldots, x_n)$ is monotone and self-dual if and only if it satisfies the following condition:

For all $x = x_1 \ldots x_n$ and $y = y_1 \ldots y_n$ there exists k such that $f(x) = x_k$ and $f(y) = y_k$.

(b) Suppose f is undefined for certain values, but the stated condition holds whenever both $f(x)$ and $f(y)$ are defined. Show that there is a monotone self-dual Boolean function g for which $g(x) = f(x)$ whenever $f(x)$ is defined.

▶ **65.** [*M21*] Any subset X of $\{1, 2, \ldots, n\}$ corresponds to a binary vector $x = x_1 x_2 \ldots x_n$ via the rule $x_j = [j \in X]$. And any family $\mathcal{F}$ of such subsets corresponds to a Boolean function $f(x) = f(x_1, x_2, \ldots, x_n)$ of n variables, via the rule $f(x) = [X \in \mathcal{F}]$. Therefore every statement about families of subsets corresponds to a statement about Boolean functions, and vice versa.

A family $\mathcal{F}$ is called *intersecting* if $X \cap Y \neq \emptyset$ whenever $X, Y \in \mathcal{F}$. An intersecting family that loses this property whenever we try to add another subset is said to be *maximal*. Prove that $\mathcal{F}$ is a maximal intersecting family if and only if the corresponding Boolean function f is monotone and self-dual.

▸ **66.** [*M25*] A *coterie* of $\{1, \ldots, n\}$ is a family $\mathcal{C}$ of subsets called *quorums*, which have the following properties whenever $Q \in \mathcal{C}$ and $Q' \in \mathcal{C}$: (i) $Q \cap Q' \neq \emptyset$; (ii) $Q \subseteq Q'$ implies $Q = Q'$. Coterie $\mathcal{C}$ *dominates* coterie $\mathcal{C}'$ if $\mathcal{C} \neq \mathcal{C}'$ and if, for every $Q' \in \mathcal{C}'$, there is a $Q \in \mathcal{C}$ with $Q \subseteq Q'$. For example, the coterie $\{\{1,2\}, \{2,3\}\}$ is dominated by $\{\{1,2\}, \{1,3\}, \{2,3\}\}$ and also by $\{\{2\}\}$. [Coteries were introduced in classic papers by L. Lamport, *CACM* **21** (1978), 558–565; H. Garcia-Molina and D. Barbara, *JACM* **32** (1985), 841–860. They have numerous applications to distributed system protocols, including mutual exclusion, data replication, and name servers. In these applications $\mathcal{C}$ is preferred to any coterie that it dominates.]

Prove that $\mathcal{C}$ is a nondominated coterie if and only if its quorums are the index sets of variables in the prime implicants of a monotone self-dual Boolean function $f(x_1, \ldots, x_n)$. (Thus Table 2 illustrates the nondominated coteries on $\{1, 2, 3, 4\}$.)

▸ **67.** [*M30*] (J. W. Milnor and C. Schensted.) A triangular grid of order n, illustrated here for $n = 3$, contains $(n+2)(n+1)/2$ points with nonnegative "barycentric coordinates" xyz, where $x+y+z = n$. Two points are adjacent if they differ by ± 1 in exactly two coordinate positions. A point is said to lie on the x side if its x coordinate is zero, on the y side if its y coordinate is zero, or on the z side if its z coordinate is zero; thus each side contains $n+1$ points. If $n > 0$, a point lies on two different sides if and only if it occupies one of the three corner positions.

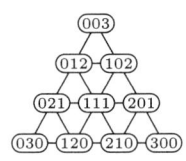

A "Y" is a connected set of points with at least one point on each side. Suppose each vertex of a triangular grid is covered with a white stone or a black stone. For example, the 52 black stones in

contain a (somewhat distorted) Y; but if any of them is changed from black to white, there is a white Y instead. A moment's thought makes it intuitively clear that, in any placement, the black stones contain a Y if and only if the white stones do not.

We can represent the color of each stone by a Boolean variable, with 0 for white and 1 for black. Let $Y(t) = 1$ if and only if there's a black Y, where t is a triangular grid comprising all the Boolean variables. This function Y is clearly monotone; and the intuitive claim made in the preceding paragraph is equivalent to saying that Y is also self-dual. The purpose of this exercise is to prove the claim rigorously, using median algebra.

Given $a, b, c \geq 0$, let t_{abc} be the triangular subgrid containing all points whose coordinates xyz satisfy $x \geq a$, $y \geq b$, $z \geq c$. For example, t_{001} denotes all points except those on the z side (the bottom row). Notice that, if $a + b + c = n$, t_{abc} is the single point with coordinates abc; and in general, t_{abc} is a triangular grid of order $n - a - b - c$.

a) If $n > 0$, let t^* be the triangular grid of order $n - 1$ defined by the rule

$$t^*_{xyz} = \langle t_{(x+1)yz} t_{x(y+1)z} t_{xy(z+1)} \rangle, \qquad \text{for } x + y + z = n - 1.$$

Prove that $Y(t) = Y(t^*)$. [In other words, t^* condenses each small triangle of stones by taking the median of their colors. Repeating this process defines a *pyramid* of stones, with the top stone black if and only if there is a black Y at the bottom. It's fun to apply this condensation principle to the twisted Y above.]

b) Prove that, if $n > 0$, $Y(t) = \langle Y(t_{100}) Y(t_{010}) Y(t_{001}) \rangle$.

68. [*46*] The just-barely-Y configuration shown in the previous exercise has 52 black stones. What is the largest number of black stones possible in such a configuration? (That is, how many variables can there be in a prime implicant of the function $Y(t)$?)

▶ **69.** [*M26*] (C. Schensted.) Exercise 67 expresses the Y function in terms of medians. Conversely, let $f(x_1, \ldots, x_n)$ be any monotone self-dual Boolean function with $m + 1$ prime implicants $p_0, p_1, \ldots, p_m$. Prove that $f(x_1, \ldots, x_n) = Y(T)$, where T is any triangular grid of order $m - 1$ in which T_{abc} is a variable common to p_a and p_{a+b+1}, for $a + b + c = m - 1$. For example, when $f(w, x, y, z) = \langle xwywz \rangle$ we have $m = 3$ and

$$f(w, x, y, z) = (w \wedge x) \vee (w \wedge y) \vee (w \wedge z) \vee (x \wedge y \wedge z) = Y\left(\begin{smallmatrix} & w & \\ & w\, w & \\ x & y & z \end{smallmatrix} \right).$$

▶ **70.** [*M20*] (A. Meyerowitz, 1989.) Given any monotone self-dual Boolean function $f(x) = f(x_1, \ldots, x_n)$, choose any prime implicant $x_{j_1} \wedge \cdots \wedge x_{j_s}$ and let

$$g(x) = (f(x) \wedge [x \neq t]) \vee [x = \bar{t}],$$

where $t = t_1 \ldots t_n$ is the bit vector that has 1s in positions $\{j_1, \ldots, j_s\}$. Prove that $g(x)$ is also monotone and self-dual. (Notice that $g(x)$ is equal to $f(x)$ except at the two points t and $\bar{t}$.)

▶ **71.** [*M21*] Given the axioms (50), (51), and (52) of a median algebra, prove that the long distributive law (54) is a consequence of the shorter law (53).

72. [*M22*] Derive (58), (59), and (60) from the median laws (50)–(53).

73. [*M32*] (S. P. Avann.) Given a median algebra M, whose intervals are defined by (57) and whose corresponding median graph is defined by (61), let $d(u, v)$ denote the distance from u to v. Also let '$[uxv]$' stand for the statement "x lies on a shortest path from u to v."

a) Prove that $[uxv]$ holds if and only if $d(u, v) = d(u, x) + d(x, v)$.

b) Suppose $x \in [u \mathbin{.\,.} v]$ and $u \in [x \mathbin{.\,.} y]$, where $x \neq u$ and $y \longrightarrow v$ is an edge of the graph. Show that $x \longrightarrow u$ is also an edge.

c) If $x \in [u \mathbin{.\,.} v]$, prove $[uxv]$, by induction on $d(u, v)$.

d) Conversely, prove that $[uxv]$ implies $x \in [u \mathbin{.\,.} v]$.

74. [*M21*] In a median algebra, show that $w = \langle xyz \rangle$ whenever we have $w \in [x \mathbin{.\,.} y]$, $w \in [x \mathbin{.\,.} z]$, and $w \in [y \mathbin{.\,.} z]$ according to definition (57).

▶ **75.** [*M36*] (M. Sholander, 1954.) Suppose M is a set of points with a betweenness relation "x lies between u and v," symbolized by $[uxv]$, which satisfies the following three axioms:

i) If $[uvu]$ then $u = v$.

ii) If $[uxv]$ and $[xyu]$ then $[vyu]$.

iii) Given x, y, and z, exactly one point $w = \langle xyz \rangle$ satisfies $[xwy]$, $[xwz]$, and $[ywz]$.

The object of this exercise is to prove that M is a median algebra.

a) Prove the majority law $\langle xxy \rangle = x$, Eq. (50).

b) Prove the commutative law $\langle xyz \rangle = \langle xzy \rangle = \cdots = \langle zyx \rangle$, Eq. (51).

c) Prove that $[uxv]$ if and only if $x = \langle uxv \rangle$.

d) If $[uxy]$ and $[uyv]$, prove that $[xyv]$.

e) If $[uxv]$ and $[uyz]$ and $[vyz]$, prove that $[xyz]$. *Hint:* Construct the points $w = \langle yuv \rangle$, $p = \langle wux \rangle$, $q = \langle wvx \rangle$, $r = \langle pxz \rangle$, $s = \langle qxz \rangle$, and $t = \langle rsz \rangle$.

f) Finally, deduce the short distributive law, Eq. (53): $\langle \langle xyz \rangle uv \rangle = \langle x \langle yuv \rangle \langle zuv \rangle \rangle$.

76. [*M33*] Derive the betweenness axioms (i), (ii), and (iii) of exercise 75, starting from the three median axioms (50), (51), and (52), letting $[uxv]$ be an abbreviation for "$x = \langle uxv \rangle$." Do not use the distributive law (53). *Hint:* See exercise 74.

77. [*M28*] Let G be a median graph containing the edge r — s. For each edge u — v, call u an *early neighbor* of v if and only if r is closer to u than to v. Partition the vertices into "left" and "right" parts, where left vertices are closer to r than to s and right vertices are closer to s than to r. Each right vertex v has a *rank*, which is the shortest distance from v to a left vertex. Similarly, each left vertex u has rank $1 - d$, where d is the shortest distance from u to a right vertex. Thus u has rank zero if it is adjacent to a right vertex, otherwise its rank is negative. Vertex r clearly has rank 0, and s has rank 1.

a) Show that every vertex of rank 1 is adjacent to exactly one vertex of rank 0.

b) Show that the set of all right vertices is convex.

c) Show that the set of all vertices with rank 1 is convex.

d) Prove that steps I3–I9 of Subroutine I correctly mark all vertices of ranks 1 and 2.

e) Prove that Algorithm H is correct.

▶ **78.** [*M26*] If the vertex v is examined k times in step I4 during the execution of Algorithm H, prove that the graph has at least 2^k vertices. *Hint:* There are k ways to start a shortest path from v to a; thus at least k 1s appear in $l(v)$.

▶ **79.** [*M27*] (R. L. Graham.) An induced *subgraph of a hypercube* is a graph whose vertices v can be labeled with bit strings $l(v)$ in such a way that u — v if and only if $l(u)$ and $l(v)$ differ in exactly one bit position. (Each label has the same length.)

a) One way to define an n-vertex subgraph of a hypercube is to let $l(v)$ be the binary representation of v, for $0 \le v < n$. Show that this subgraph has exactly $f(n) = \sum_{k=0}^{n-1} \nu(k)$ edges, where $\nu(k)$ is the sideways addition function.

b) Prove that $f(n) \le n \lceil \lg n \rceil / 2$.

c) Prove that no n-vertex subgraph of a hypercube has more than $f(n)$ edges.

80. [*27*] A *partial cube* is an "isometric" subgraph of a hypercube, namely a subgraph in which the distances between vertices are the same as they are in the full graph. The vertices of a partial cube can therefore be labeled in such a way that the distance from u to v is the "Hamming distance" between $l(u)$ and $l(v)$, namely $\nu(l(u) \oplus l(v))$. Algorithm H shows that every median graph is a partial cube.

a) Find an induced subgraph of the 4-cube that isn't a partial cube.

b) Give an example of a partial cube that isn't a median graph.

81. [*16*] Is every median graph bipartite?

82. [*25*] (*Incremental changes in service.*) Given a sequence of vertices $(v_0, v_1, \ldots, v_t)$ in a graph G, consider the problem of finding another sequence $(u_0, u_1, \ldots, u_t)$ for which $u_0 = v_0$ and the sum

$$\big(d(u_0, u_1) + d(u_1, u_2) + \cdots + d(u_{t-1}, u_t) \big) + \big(d(u_1, v_1) + d(u_2, v_2) + \cdots + d(u_t, v_t) \big)$$

is minimized, where $d(u, v)$ denotes the distance from u to v. (Each v_k can be regarded as a request for a resource needed at that vertex; a server moves to u_k as those requests are handled in sequence.) Prove that if G is a median graph, we get an optimum solution by choosing $u_k = \langle u_{k-1} v_k v_{k+1} \rangle$ for $0 < k < t$, and $u_t = v_t$.

▶ **83.** [*38*] Generalizing exercise 82, find an efficient way to minimize

$$\bigl(d(u_0, u_1) + d(u_1, u_2) + \cdots + d(u_{t-1}, u_t)\bigr) \;+\; \rho\bigl(d(u_1, v_1) + d(u_2, v_2) + \cdots + d(u_t, v_t)\bigr)$$

in a median graph, given any positive ratio ρ.

84. [*30*] Write a program to find all monotone self-dual Boolean functions of five variables. What are the edges of the corresponding median graph? (Table 2 illustrates the four-variable case.)

▶ **85.** [*M22*] Theorem S tells us that every formula in 2CNF corresponds to a median set; therefore every antisymmetric digraph such as Fig. 6 also corresponds to a median set. Precisely which of those digraphs correspond to *reduced* median sets?

86. [*15*] If v, w, x, y, and z belong to a median set X, does their five-element median $\langle vwxyz \rangle$, computed componentwise, always belong to X?

87. [*24*] What CI-net does the proof of Theorem F construct for the free tree (63)?

88. [*M21*] We can use parallel computation to condense the network (74) into

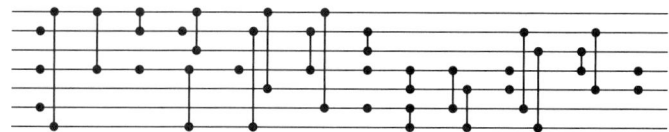

by letting each module act at the earliest possible time. Prove that, although the network constructed in the proof of Theorem F may contain $\Omega(t^2)$ modules, it always requires at most $O(t \log t)$ levels of delay.

89. [*24*] When the construction (73) appends a new cluster of modules to enforce the condition $u \to v$, for some literals u and v, prove that it preserves all previously enforced conditions $u' \to v'$.

▶ **90.** [*21*] Construct a CI-net with input bits $x_1 \ldots x_t$ and output bits $y_1 \ldots y_t$, where $y_1 = \cdots = y_{t-1} = 0$ and $y_t = x_1 \oplus \cdots \oplus x_t$. Try for only $O(\log t)$ levels of delay.

91. [*46*] Can a retraction mapping for the labels of every median graph of dimension t be computed by a CI-net that has only $O(\log t)$ levels of delay? [This question is motivated by the existence of asymptotically optimum networks for the analogous problem of sorting; see M. Ajtai, J. Komlós, and E. Szemerédi, *Combinatorica* **3** (1983), 1–19.]

92. [*46*] Can a CI-net sort n Boolean inputs with fewer modules than a "pure" sorting network that has no inverters?

93. [*M20*] Prove that every retract X of a graph G is an isometric subgraph of G. (In other words, distances in X are the same as in G; see exercise 80.)

94. [*M21*] Prove that every retract X of a hypercube is a set of median labels, if we suppress coordinates that are constant for all $x \in X$.

95. [*M25*] True or false: The set of all outputs produced by a comparator-inverter network, when the inputs range over all possible bit strings, is always a median set.

96. [*HM25*] Instead of insisting that the constants $w_1, w_2, \ldots, w_n$, and t in (75) must be integers, we could allow them to be arbitrary real numbers. Would that increase the number of threshold functions?

97. [*10*] What median/majority functions arise in (81) when $n = 2$, $w_1 = w_2 = 1$, and $t = -1$, 0, 1, 2, 3, or 4?

98. [*M23*] Prove that any self-dual threshold function can be expressed in the form

$$f(x_1, x_2, \ldots, x_n) = [v_1 y_1 + \cdots + v_n y_n > 0],$$

where each y_j is either x_j or $\bar{x}_j$. For example, $2x_1 + 3x_2 + 5x_3 + 7x_4 + 11x_5 + 13x_6 \geq 21$ if and only if $2x_1 + 3x_2 + 5x_3 - 7\bar{x}_4 + 11x_5 - 13\bar{x}_6 > 0$.

▶ **99.** [*20*] (J. E. Mezei, 1961.) Prove that

$$\langle\langle x_1 \ldots x_{2s-1} \rangle y_1 \ldots y_{2t-2}\rangle = \langle x_1 \ldots x_{2s-1} y_1^s \ldots y_{2t-2}^s\rangle.$$

100. [*20*] True or false: If $f(x_1, \ldots, x_n)$ is a threshold function, so are the functions $f(x_1, \ldots, x_n) \wedge x_{n+1}$ and $f(x_1, \ldots, x_n) \vee x_{n+1}$.

101. [*M23*] The *Fibonacci threshold function* $F_n(x_1, \ldots, x_n)$ is defined by the formula $\langle x_1^{F_1} x_2^{F_2} \ldots x_{n-1}^{F_{n-1}} x_n^{F_{n-2}}\rangle$ when $n \geq 3$; for example, $F_7(x_1, \ldots, x_7) = \langle x_1 x_2 x_3^2 x_4^3 x_5^5 x_6^8 x_7^5\rangle$.
  a) What are the prime implicants of $F_n(x_1, \ldots, x_n)$?
  b) Find an orthogonal DNF for $F_n(x_1, \ldots, x_n)$ (see exercise 35).
  c) Express $F_n(x_1, \ldots, x_n)$ in terms of the Y function (see exercises 67 and 69).

102. [*M21*] The *self-dualization* of a Boolean function is defined by the formulas

$$\hat{f}(x_0, x_1, \ldots, x_n) = (x_0 \wedge f(x_1, \ldots, x_n)) \vee (\bar{x}_0 \wedge \overline{f(\bar{x}_1, \ldots, \bar{x}_n)})$$
$$= (\bar{x}_0 \vee f(x_1, \ldots, x_n)) \wedge (x_0 \vee \overline{f(\bar{x}_1, \ldots, \bar{x}_n)}).$$

  a) If $f(x_1, \ldots, x_n)$ is any Boolean function, prove that $\hat{f}$ is self-dual.
  b) Prove that $\hat{f}$ is a threshold function if and only if f is a threshold function.

103. [*HM25*] Explain how to use linear programming to test whether or not a monotone, self-dual Boolean function is a threshold function, given a list of its prime implicants. Also, if it is a threshold function, explain how to minimize the size of its representation as a majority function $\langle x_1^{w_1} \ldots x_n^{w_n}\rangle$.

104. [*25*] Apply the method of exercise 103 to find the shortest representations of the following threshold functions as majority functions: (a) $\langle x_1^2 x_2^3 x_3^5 x_4^7 x_5^{11} x_6^{13} x_7^{17} x_8^{19}\rangle$; (b) $[(x_1 x_2 x_3 x_4)_2 \geq t]$, for $0 \leq t \leq 16$ (17 cases); (c) $\langle x_1^{29} x_2^{25} x_3^{19} x_4^{15} x_5^{12} x_6^8 x_7^8 x_8^3 x_9^3 x_{10}\rangle$.

105. [*M25*] Show that the Fibonacci threshold function in exercise 101 has no shorter representation as a majority function than the one used to define it.

▶ **106.** [*M25*] The median-of-three operation $\langle x\bar{y}\bar{z}\rangle$ is true if and only if $x \geq y + z$.
  a) Generalizing, show that we can test the condition $(x_1 x_2 \ldots x_n)_2 \geq (y_1 y_2 \ldots y_n)_2 + z$ by performing a median of $2^{n+1} - 1$ Boolean variables.
  b) Prove that no median of fewer than $2^{n+1} - 1$ will suffice for this problem.

107. [*17*] Calculate $N(f)$ and $\Sigma(f)$ for the 16 functions in Table 1. (See Theorem T.)

108. [*M21*] Let $g(x_0, x_1, \ldots, x_n)$ be a self-dual function; thus $N(g) = 2^n$ in the notation of Theorem T. Express $N(f)$ and $\Sigma(f)$ in terms of $\Sigma(g)$, when $f(x_1, \ldots, x_n)$ is (a) $g(0, x_1, \ldots, x_n)$; (b) $g(1, x_1, \ldots, x_n)$.

109. [*M25*] The binary string $\alpha = a_1 \ldots a_n$ is said to *majorize* the binary string $\beta = b_1 \ldots b_n$, written $\alpha \succeq \beta$ or $\beta \preceq \alpha$, if $a_1 + \cdots + a_k \geq b_1 + \cdots + b_k$ for $0 \leq k \leq n$.
  a) Let $\bar{\alpha} = \bar{a}_1 \ldots \bar{a}_n$. Show that $\alpha \succeq \beta$ if and only if $\bar{\beta} \succeq \bar{\alpha}$.

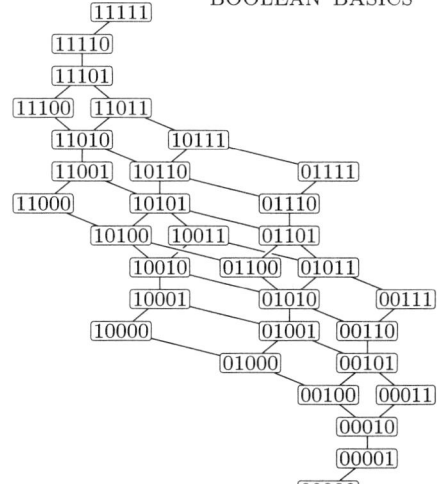

Fig. 8. The binary majorization lattice for strings of length 5. (See exercise 109.)

b) Show that any two binary strings of length n have a greatest lower bound $\alpha \wedge \beta$, which has the property that $\alpha \succeq \gamma$ and $\beta \succeq \gamma$ if and only if $\alpha \wedge \beta \succeq \gamma$. Explain how to compute $\alpha \wedge \beta$, given α and β.

c) Similarly, explain how to compute a least upper bound $\alpha \vee \beta$, with the property that $\gamma \succeq \alpha$ and $\gamma \succeq \beta$ if and only if $\gamma \succeq \alpha \vee \beta$.

d) True or false: $\alpha \wedge (\beta \vee \gamma) = (\alpha \wedge \beta) \vee (\alpha \wedge \gamma)$; $\alpha \vee (\beta \wedge \gamma) = (\alpha \vee \beta) \wedge (\alpha \vee \gamma)$.

e) Say that α *covers* β if $\alpha \succeq \beta$ and $\alpha \neq \beta$, and if $\alpha \succeq \gamma \succeq \beta$ implies that we have either $\gamma = \alpha$ or $\gamma = \beta$. For example, Fig. 8 illustrates the covering relations between binary strings of length 5. Find a simple way to describe the strings that are covered by a given binary string.

f) Show that every path $\alpha = \alpha_0, \alpha_1, \ldots, \alpha_r = 0 \ldots 0$ from a given string α to $0 \ldots 0$, where α_{j-1} covers α_j for $1 \leq j \leq r$, has the same length $r = r(\alpha)$.

g) Let $m(\alpha)$ be the number of strings β with $\beta \succeq \alpha$. Prove that $m(1\alpha) = m(\alpha)$ and $m(0\alpha) = m(\alpha) + m(\alpha')$, where α' is α with its leftmost 1 (if any) changed to 0.

h) How many strings α of length n satisfy $\bar{\alpha} \succeq \alpha$?

110. [*M23*] A Boolean function is called *regular* if $x \preceq y$ implies that $f(x) \leq f(y)$ for all vectors x and y, where $\preceq$ is the majorization relation in exercise 109. Prove or disprove the following statements:

a) Every regular function is monotone.

b) If f is a threshold function (75) for which $w_1 \geq w_2 \geq \cdots \geq w_n$, then f is regular.

c) If f is as in (b) and $\Sigma(f) = (s_1, \ldots, s_n)$, then $s_1 \geq s_2 \geq \cdots \geq s_n$.

d) Suppose f is a pure majority function, namely a threshold function of the form (86) with $a = b = 0$. Then $s_1 \geq s_2 \geq \cdots \geq s_n$ implies that $w_1 \geq w_2 \geq \cdots \geq w_n$.

111. [*M36*] An *optimum coterie* for a system with working probabilities $(p_1, \ldots, p_n)$ is a coterie that corresponds to a monotone self-dual function with maximum availability, among all monotone self-dual functions with n variables. (See exercises 14 and 66.)

a) Prove that if $1 \geq p_1 \geq \cdots \geq p_n \geq \frac{1}{2}$, at least one self-dual function with maximum availability is a regular function. Describe such a function.

b) Furthermore, it suffices to test the optimality of a regular self-dual function f at points y of the binary majorization lattice for which $f(y) = 1$ but $f(x) = 0$ for all x covered by y.

c) What coterie is optimum when some probabilities are $< \frac{1}{2}$?

▶ **112.** [*M37*] (J. Håstad.) If $f(x_1, x_2, \ldots, x_m)$ is a Boolean function, let $M(f)$ be its representation as a multilinear polynomial with integer coefficients (see exercise 12). Arrange the terms in this polynomial by using Chase's sequence $\alpha_0 = 00 \ldots 0$, $\alpha_1 = 10 \ldots 0$, $\ldots$, $\alpha_{2^m-1} = 11 \ldots 1$ to order the exponents; Chase's sequence, obtained by concatenating the sequences A_{n0}, $A_{(n-1)1}$, $\ldots$, A_{0n} of 7.2.1.3–(35), has the nice property that α_j is identical to α_{j+1} except for a slight change, either $0 \to 1$ or $01 \to 10$ or $001 \to 100$ or $10 \to 01$ or $100 \to 001$. For example, Chase's sequence is

$$0000, 1000, 0010, 0001, 0100, 1100, 1010, 1001, 0011, 0101, 0110, 1110, 1101, 1011, 0111, 1111$$

when $m = 4$, corresponding to the respective terms 1, x_1, x_3, x_4, x_2, x_1x_2, $\ldots$, $x_2x_3x_4$, $x_1x_2x_3x_4$; so the relevant representation of, say, $((x_1 \oplus \bar{x}_2) \wedge x_3) \vee (x_1 \wedge \bar{x}_3 \wedge x_4)$ is

$$x_3 - x_1x_3 + x_1x_4 - x_2x_3 + 2x_1x_2x_3 - x_1x_3x_4$$

when the terms have been arranged in this order. Now let

$$F(f) = [\text{the most significant coefficient of } M(f) \text{ is positive}].$$

For example, the most significant (final) nonzero term of $((x_1 \oplus \bar{x}_2) \wedge x_3) \vee (x_1 \wedge \bar{x}_3 \wedge x_4)$ is $-x_1x_3x_4$ in Chase's ordering, so $F(f) = 0$ in this case.

a) Determine $F(f)$ for each of the 16 functions in Table 1.

b) Show that $F(f)$ is a threshold function of the $n = 2^m$ entries $\{f_{0\ldots00}, f_{0\ldots01}, \ldots, f_{1\ldots11}\}$ of the truth table for f. Write this function out explicitly when $m = 2$.

c) Prove that, when m is large, all the weights in any threshold representation of F must be huge: Their absolute values must all exceed

$$\frac{3^{\binom{m}{3}} 7^{\binom{m}{4}} 15^{\binom{m}{5}} \ldots (2^{m-1}-1)^{\binom{m}{m}}}{n}\left(1 - O(n^{-1})\right) = 2^{mn/2 - n - 2(3/2)^m / \ln 2 + O((5/4)^m)}.$$

Hint: Consider discrete Fourier transforms of the truth table entries.

113. [*24*] Show that the following three threshold operations suffice to evaluate the function $S_{2,3,6,8,9}(x_1, \ldots, x_{12})$ in (91):

$$g_1(x_1, \ldots, x_{12}) = [\nu x \geq 6] = \langle 1 x_1 \ldots x_{12} \rangle;$$
$$g_2(x_1, \ldots, x_{12}) = [\nu x - 6g_1 \geq 2] = \langle 1^3 x_1 \ldots x_{12} \bar{g}_1^{-6} \rangle;$$
$$g_3(x_1, \ldots, x_{12}) = [-2\nu x + 13g_1 + 7g_2 \geq 1] = \langle 0^5 \bar{x}_1^2 \ldots \bar{x}_{12}^2 g_1^{13} g_2^7 \rangle.$$

Also find a four-threshold scheme that evaluates $S_{1,3,5,8}(x_1, \ldots, x_{12})$.

114. [*20*] (D. A. Huffman.) What is the function $S_{3,6}(x, x, x, x, y, y, z)$?

115. [*M22*] Explain why (92) correctly computes the parity function $x_0 \oplus x_1 \oplus \cdots \oplus x_{2m}$.

▶ **116.** [*HM28*] (B. Dunham and R. Fridshal, 1957.) By considering symmetric functions, one can prove that Boolean functions of n variables might have many prime implicants.

a) Suppose $0 \leq j \leq k \leq n$. For which symmetric functions $f(x_1, \ldots, x_n)$ is the term $x_1 \wedge \cdots \wedge x_j \wedge \bar{x}_{j+1} \wedge \cdots \wedge \bar{x}_k$ a prime implicant?

b) How many prime implicants does the function $S_{3,4,5,6}(x_1, \ldots, x_9)$ have?

c) Let $\hat{b}(n)$ be the maximum number of prime implicants, over all symmetric Boolean functions of n variables. Find a recurrence formula for $\hat{b}(n)$, and compute $\hat{b}(9)$.

d) Prove that $\hat{b}(n) = \Theta(3^n/n)$.

e) Show that, furthermore, there are symmetric functions $f(x_1, \ldots, x_n)$ for which both f and $\bar{f}$ have $\Theta(2^{3n/2}/n)$ prime implicants.

117. [*M26*] A disjunctive normal form is called *irredundant* if none of its implicants implies another. Let $b^*(n)$ be the maximum number of implicants in an irredundant DNF, over all Boolean functions of n variables. Find a simple formula for $b^*(n)$, and determine its asymptotic value.

118. [*29*] How many Boolean functions $f(x_1, x_2, x_3, x_4)$ have exactly m prime implicants, for $m = 0, 1, \ldots$?

119. [*M48*] Continuing the previous exercises, let $b(n)$ be the maximum number of prime implicants in a Boolean function of n variables. Clearly $\hat{b}(n) \leq b(n) < b^*(n)$; what is the asymptotic value of $b(n)$?

120. [*23*] What is the shortest DNF for the symmetric functions (a) $x_1 \oplus x_2 \oplus \cdots \oplus x_n$? (b) $S_{0,1,3,4,6,7}(x_1, \ldots, x_7)$? (c) Prove that every Boolean function of n variables can be expressed as a DNF with at most 2^{n-1} prime implicants.

▶ **121.** [*M23*] The function $\langle 1\,(x_1 \oplus x_2)\,y_1 y_2 y_3\rangle$ is partially symmetric, since it is symmetric in $\{x_1, x_2\}$ and in $\{y_1, y_2, y_3\}$, but not in all five variables $\{x_1, x_2, y_1, y_2, y_3\}$.

  a) Exactly how many Boolean functions $f(x_1, \ldots, x_m, y_1, \ldots, y_n)$ are symmetric in $\{x_1, \ldots, x_m\}$ and $\{y_1, \ldots, y_n\}$?
  b) How many of those functions are monotone?
  c) How many of those functions are self-dual?
  d) How many of those functions are monotone and self-dual?

122. [*M25*] Continuing exercises 110 and 121, find all Boolean functions $f(x_1, x_2, x_3, y_1, y_2, y_3, y_4, y_5, y_6)$ that are simultaneously symmetric in $\{x_1, x_2, x_3\}$, symmetric in $\{y_1, y_2, \ldots, y_6\}$, self-dual, and regular. Which of them are threshold functions?

123. [*46*] Determine the exact number of self-dual Boolean functions of ten variables that are threshold functions.

124. [*20*] Find a Boolean function of four variables that is equivalent to 767 other functions, under the ground rules of Table 5.

125. [*18*] Which of the function classes in (95) are canalizing?

126. [*23*] (a) Show that a Boolean function is canalizing if and only if its sets of prime implicants and prime clauses have a certain simple property. (b) Show that a Boolean function is canalizing if and only if its Chow parameters $N(f)$ and $\Sigma(f)$ have a certain simple property (see Theorem T). (c) Define the Boolean vectors

$$\vee(f) = \bigvee\{x \mid f(x) = 1\} \qquad \text{and} \qquad \wedge(f) = \bigwedge\{x \mid f(x) = 1\};$$

by analogy with the integer vector $\Sigma(f)$. Show that it's possible to decide whether or not f is canalizing, given only the four vectors $\vee(f)$, $\vee(\bar{f})$, $\wedge(f)$, and $\wedge(\bar{f})$.

127. [*M25*] Which canalizing functions are (a) self-dual? (b) definite Horn functions?

▶ **128.** [*20*] Find a noncanalizing $f(x_1, \ldots, x_n)$ that is true at exactly two points.

129. [*M25*] How many different canalizing functions of n variables exist?

130. [*M21*] According to Table 3, there are 168 monotone Boolean functions of four variables. But some of them, like $x \wedge y$, depend on only three variables or fewer.

  a) How many 4-variable monotone Boolean functions actually involve each variable?
  b) How many of those functions are distinct under permutation, as in Table 4?

131. [*HM42*] Table 3 makes it clear that there are many more Horn functions than Krom functions. What is the asymptotic number, as $n \to \infty$?

▸ **132.** [*HM30*] The Boolean function $g(x) = g(x_1, \ldots, x_n)$ is called *affine* if it can be
written in the form $y_0 \oplus (x_1 \wedge y_1) \oplus \cdots \oplus (x_n \wedge y_n) = (y_0 + x \cdot y) \bmod 2$ for some Boolean
constants $y_0, y_1, \ldots, y_n$.

    a) Given any Boolean function $f(x)$, show that some affine function agrees with $f(x)$
at $2^{n-1} + 2^{n/2-1}$ or more points x. *Hint:* Let $s(y) = \sum_x (-1)^{f(x)+x \cdot y}$, and prove
that $\sum_y s(y) s(y \oplus z) = 2^{2n}[z = 0 \ldots 0]$ for all n-bit vectors z.

    b) The Boolean function $f(x)$ is called *bent* if no affine function agrees with it at
more than $2^{n-1} + 2^{n/2-1}$ points. Prove that

$$(x_1 \wedge x_2) \oplus (x_3 \wedge x_4) \oplus \cdots \oplus (x_{n-1} \wedge x_n) \oplus h(x_2, x_4, \ldots, x_n)$$

is a bent function, when n is even and $h(y_1, y_2, \ldots, y_{n/2})$ is arbitrary.

    c) Prove that $f(x)$ is a bent function if and only if

$$\sum_x (f(x) \oplus f(x \oplus y)) = 2^{n-1} \qquad \text{for all } y \ne 0 \ldots 0.$$

    d) If a bent function $f(x_1, \ldots, x_n)$ is represented by a multilinear polynomial mod 2
as in (19), show that it never contains the term $x_1 \ldots x_r$ when $r > n/2 > 1$.

▸ **133.** [*20*] (Mark A. Smith, 1990.) Suppose we flip n independent coins to get n
random bits, where the kth coin produces bit 1 with probability p_k. Find a way to
choose $(p_1, \ldots, p_n)$ so that $f(x_1, \ldots, x_n) = 1$ with probability $(t_0 t_1 \ldots t_{2^n-1})_2 / (2^{2^n} - 1)$,
where $t_0 t_1 \ldots t_{2^n-1}$ is the truth table of the Boolean function f. (Thus, n suitable
random coins can generate a probability with 2^n-bit precision.)

> *By and large the minimization of switching components*
> *outweighs all other engineering considerations*
> *in designing economical logic circuits.*
>
> — H. A. CURTIS, *A New Approach to the Design of Switching Circuits* (1962)

> *He must be a great calculator indeed who succeeds.*
> *Simplify, simplify.*
>
> — HENRY D. THOREAU, *Walden; or, Life in the Woods* (1854)

7.1.2. Boolean Evaluation

Our next goal is to study the efficient evaluation of Boolean functions, much as
we studied the evaluation of polynomials in Section 4.6.4. One natural way to
investigate this topic is to consider chains of basic operations, analogous to the
polynomial chains discussed in that section.

    A *Boolean chain*, for functions of n variables $(x_1, \ldots, x_n)$, is a sequence
$(x_{n+1}, \ldots, x_{n+r})$ with the property that each step combines two of the preceding
steps:
$$x_i = x_{j(i)} \circ_i x_{k(i)}, \qquad \text{for } n + 1 \le i \le n + r, \tag{1}$$

where $1 \le j(i) < i$ and $1 \le k(i) < i$, and where $\circ_i$ is one of the sixteen binary
operators of Table 7.1.1–1. For example, when $n = 3$ the two chains

$$
\begin{array}{ll}
x_4 = x_1 \wedge x_2 & \qquad\qquad x_4 = x_2 \oplus x_3 \\
x_5 = \bar{x}_1 \wedge x_3 \qquad \text{and} & \qquad\qquad x_5 = x_1 \wedge x_4 \\
x_6 = x_4 \vee x_5 & \qquad\qquad x_6 = x_3 \oplus x_5
\end{array}
\tag{2}
$$

both evaluate the "mux" or "if-then-else" function $x_6 = (x_1? \ x_2 : x_3)$, which
takes the value x_2 or x_3 depending on whether x_1 is 1 (true) or 0 (false).

(Notice that the left-hand example in (2) uses the simplified notation '$x_5 = \bar{x}_1 \wedge x_3$' to specify the NOTBUT operation, instead of the form '$x_5 = x_1 \bar{\subset} x_3$' that appears in Table 7.1.1–1. The main point is that, regardless of notation, every step of a Boolean chain is a Boolean combination of two prior results.)

Boolean chains correspond naturally to electronic circuits, with each step in the chain corresponding to a "gate" that has two inputs and one output. Electrical engineers traditionally represent the Boolean chains of (2) by circuit diagrams such as

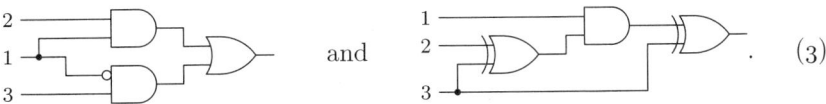

$$ (3) $$

They need to design economical circuits that are subject to various technological constraints; for example, some gates might be more expensive than others, some outputs might need to be amplified if reused, the layout might need to be planar or nearly so, some paths might need to be short. But our chief concern in this book is software, not hardware, so we don't have to worry about such things. For our purposes, all gates have equal cost, and all outputs can be reused as often as desired. (Jargonwise, our Boolean chains boil down to circuits in which all gates have fan-in 2 and unlimited fan-out.)

Furthermore we shall depict Boolean chains as binary trees such as

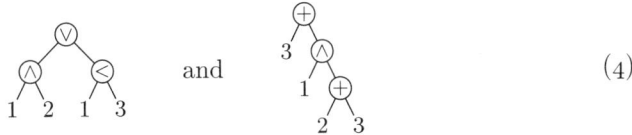

$$ (4) $$

instead of using circuit diagrams like (3). Such binary trees will have overlapping subtrees when intermediate steps of the chain are used more than once. Every internal node is labeled with a binary operator; external nodes are labeled with an integer k, representing the variable x_k. The label '$\oslash$' in the left tree of (4) stands for the NOTBUT operator, since $\bar{x} \wedge y = [x < y]$; similarly, the BUTNOT operator, $x \wedge \bar{y}$, can be represented by the node label '$\ominus$'.

Several different Boolean chains might have the same tree diagram. For example, the left-hand tree of (4) also represents the chain

$$ x_4 = \bar{x}_1 \wedge x_3, \qquad x_5 = x_1 \wedge x_2, \qquad x_6 = x_5 \vee x_4. $$

Any topological sorting of the tree nodes yields an equivalent chain.

Given a Boolean function f of n variables, we often want to find a Boolean chain such that $x_{n+r} = f(x_1, \ldots, x_n)$, where r is as small as possible. The *combinational complexity* $C(f)$ of a function f is the length of the shortest chain that computes it. To save excess verbiage, we will simply call $C(f)$ the "cost of f." The mux function in our examples above has cost 3, because one can show by exhaustive trials that it can't be produced by any Boolean chain of length 2.

The DNF and CNF representations of f, which we studied in Section 7.1.1, rarely tell us much about $C(f)$, since substantially more efficient schemes of calculation are usually possible. For example, in the discussion following 7.1.1–(30) we found that the more-or-less random function of four variables whose truth table is 1100 1001 0000 1111 has no DNF expression shorter than

$$(\bar{x}_1 \wedge \bar{x}_2 \wedge \bar{x}_3) \vee (\bar{x}_1 \wedge \bar{x}_3 \wedge \bar{x}_4) \vee (x_2 \wedge x_3 \wedge x_4) \vee (x_1 \wedge x_2). \qquad (5)$$

This formula corresponds to a Boolean chain of 10 steps. But that function can also be expressed more cleverly as

$$\bigl(((x_2 \wedge \bar{x}_4) \oplus \bar{x}_3) \wedge \bar{x}_1\bigr) \oplus x_2, \qquad (6)$$

so its complexity is at most 4.

How can nonobvious formulas like (6) be discovered? We will see that a computer can find the best chains for functions of four variables without doing an enormous amount of work. Still, the results can be quite startling, even for people who have had considerable experience with Boolean algebra. Typical examples of this phenomenon can be seen in Fig. 9, which illustrates the four-variable functions that are perhaps of greatest general interest, namely the functions that are symmetric under all permutations of their variables.

Consider, for example, the function $S_2(x_1, x_2, x_3, x_4)$, for which we have

$$
\begin{array}{lll}
x_1 & & 0000\ 0000\ 1111\ 1111 \\
x_2 & & 0000\ 1111\ 0000\ 1111 \\
x_3 & & 0011\ 0011\ 0011\ 0011 \\
x_4 & & 0101\ 0101\ 0101\ 0101 \\
x_5 = x_1 \oplus x_3 & & 0011\ 0011\ 1100\ 1100 \\
x_6 = x_1 \oplus x_2 & & 0000\ 1111\ 1111\ 0000 \\
x_7 = x_3 \oplus x_4 & & 0110\ 0110\ 0110\ 0110 \\
x_8 = x_5 \vee x_6 & & 0011\ 1111\ 1111\ 1100 \\
x_9 = x_6 \oplus x_7 & & 0110\ 1001\ 1001\ 0110 \\
x_{10} = x_8 \wedge \bar{x}_9 & & 0001\ 0110\ 0110\ 1000
\end{array} \qquad (7)
$$

according to Fig. 9. Truth tables are shown here so that we can easily verify each step of the calculation. Step x_8 yields a function that is true whenever $x_1 \neq x_2$ or $x_1 \neq x_3$; and $x_9 = x_1 \oplus x_2 \oplus x_3 \oplus x_4$ is the parity function $(x_1 + x_2 + x_3 + x_4) \bmod 2$. Therefore the final result, x_{10}, is true precisely when exactly two of $\{x_1, x_2, x_3, x_4\}$ are 1; these are the cases that satisfy x_8 and have even parity.

Several of the other computational schemes of Fig. 9 can also be justified intuitively. But some of the chains, like the one for $S_{1,4}$, are quite amazing.

Notice that the intermediate result x_6 is used twice in (7). In fact, no six-step chain for the function $S_2(x_1, x_2, x_3, x_4)$ is possible without making double use of some intermediate subexpression; the shortest algebraic formulas for S_2, including nice symmetrical ones like

$$\bigl((x_1 \wedge x_2) \vee (x_3 \wedge x_4)\bigr) \oplus \bigl((x_1 \vee x_2) \wedge (x_3 \vee x_4)\bigr), \qquad (8)$$

all have cost 7. But Fig. 9 shows that the other symmetric functions of four variables can all be evaluated optimally via "pure" binary trees, without overlapping subtrees except at external nodes (which represent the variables).

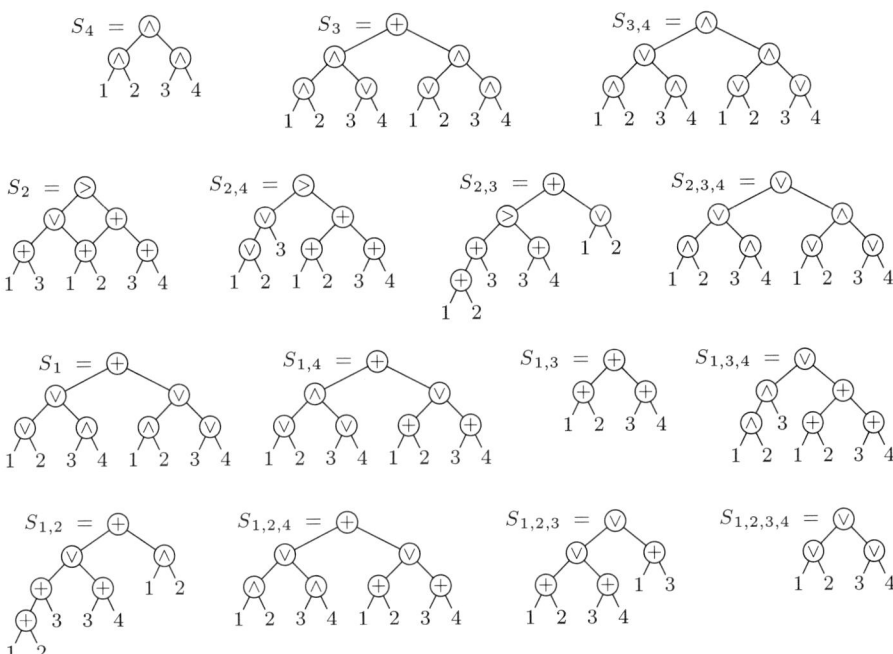

Fig. 9. Optimum Boolean chains for the symmetric functions of four variables.

In general, if $f(x_1, \ldots, x_n)$ is any Boolean function, we say that its *length* $L(f)$ is the number of binary operators in the shortest formula for f. Obviously $L(f) \geq C(f)$; and we can easily verify that $L(f) = C(f)$ whenever $n \leq 3$, by considering the fourteen basic types of 3-variable functions in 7.1.1–(95). But we have just seen that $L(S_2) = 7$ exceeds $C(S_2) = 6$ when $n = 4$, and in fact $L(f)$ is almost always substantially larger than $C(f)$ when n is large (see exercise 49).

The *depth* $D(f)$ of a Boolean function f is another important measure of its inherent complexity: We say that the depth of a Boolean chain is the length of the longest downward path in its tree diagram, and $D(f)$ is the minimum achievable depth when all Boolean chains for f are considered. All of the chains illustrated in Fig. 9 have not only the minimum cost but also the minimum depth — except in the cases $S_{2,3}$ and $S_{1,2}$, where we cannot simultaneously achieve cost 6 and depth 3. The formula

$$S_{2,3}(x_1, x_2, x_3, x_4) = \big((x_1 \wedge x_2) \oplus (x_3 \wedge x_4)\big) \vee \big((x_1 \vee x_2) \wedge (x_3 \oplus x_4)\big) \qquad (9)$$

shows that $D(S_{2,3}) = 3$, and a similar formula works for $S_{1,2}$.

Optimum chains for $n = 4$. Exhaustive computations for 4-variable functions are feasible because such functions have only $2^{16} = 65{,}536$ possible truth tables. In fact we need only consider half of those truth tables, because the complement $\bar{f}$ of any function f has the same cost, length, and depth as f itself.

Let's say that $f(x_1, \ldots, x_n)$ is *normal* if $f(0, \ldots, 0) = 0$, and in general that

$$f(x_1, \ldots, x_n) \oplus f(0, \ldots, 0) \qquad (10)$$

is the "normalization" of f. Any Boolean chain can be normalized by normalizing each of its steps and by making appropriate changes to the operators; for if $(\hat{x}_1, \ldots, \hat{x}_{i-1})$ are the normalizations of $(x_1, \ldots, x_{i-1})$ and if $x_i = x_{j(i)} \circ_i x_{k(i)}$ as in (1), then $\hat{x}_i$ is clearly a binary function of $\hat{x}_{j(i)}$ and $\hat{x}_{k(i)}$. (Exercise 7 presents an example.) Therefore we can restrict consideration to normal Boolean chains, without loss of generality.

Notice that a Boolean chain is normal if and only if each of its binary operators $\circ_i$ is normal. And there are only eight normal binary operators — three of which, namely $\bot$, $\llcorner$, and $\reflectbox{R}$, are trivial. So we can assume that all Boolean chains of interest are formed from the five operators $\wedge$, $\bar{\subset}$, $\bar{\supset}$, $\vee$, and $\oplus$, which are denoted respectively by $\circledwedge$, $\oslash$, $\ominus$, $\circledvee$, and $\oplus$ in Fig. 9. Furthermore we can assume that $j(i) < k(i)$ in each step.

There are $2^{15} = 32{,}768$ normal functions of four variables, and we can compute their lengths without difficulty by systematically enumerating all functions of length 0, 1, 2, etc. Indeed, $L(f) = r$ implies that $f = g \circ h$ for some g and h, where $L(g) + L(h) = r - 1$ and $\circ$ is one of the five nontrivial normal operators; so we can proceed as follows:

Algorithm L (*Find normal lengths*). This algorithm determines $L(f)$ for all normal truth tables $0 \le f < 2^{2^n - 1}$, by building lists of all nonzero normal functions of length r for $r \ge 0$.

L1. [Initialize.] Let $L(0) \leftarrow 0$ and $L(f) \leftarrow \infty$ for $1 \le f < 2^{2^n - 1}$. Then, for $1 \le k \le n$, set $L(x_k) \leftarrow 0$ and put x_k into list 0, where

$$x_k = (2^{2^n} - 1)/(2^{2^{n-k}} + 1) \qquad (11)$$

is the truth table for x_k. (See exercise 8.) Finally, set $c \leftarrow 2^{2^n - 1} - n - 1$; c is the number of places where $L(f) = \infty$.

L2. [Loop on r.] Do step L3 for $r = 1, 2, \ldots$; eventually the algorithm will terminate when c becomes 0.

L3. [Loop on j and k.] Do step L4 for $j = 0, 1, \ldots$, and $k = r - 1 - j$, while $j \le k$.

L4. [Loop on g and h.] Do step L5 for all g in list j and all h in list k. (If $j = k$, it suffices to restrict h to functions that *follow* g in list k.)

L5. [Loop on f.] Do step L6 for $f = g \,\&\, h$, $f = \bar{g} \,\&\, h$, $f = g \,\&\, \bar{h}$, $f = g \mid h$, and $f = g \oplus h$. (Here $g \,\&\, h$ denotes the bitwise AND of the integers g and h; we are representing truth tables by integers in binary notation.)

L6. [Is f new?] If $L(f) = \infty$, set $L(f) \leftarrow r$, $c \leftarrow c - 1$, and put f in list r. Terminate the algorithm if $c = 0$. ∎

Exercise 10 shows that a similar procedure will compute all depths $D(f)$.

With a little more work, we can in fact modify Algorithm L so that it finds better upper bounds on $C(f)$, by computing a heuristic bit vector $\phi(f)$ called

Table 1

THE NUMBER OF FOUR-VARIABLE FUNCTIONS WITH GIVEN COMPLEXITY

$C(f)$	Classes	Functions	$L(f)$	Classes	Functions	$D(f)$	Classes	Functions
0	2	10	0	2	10	0	2	10
1	2	60	1	2	60	1	2	60
2	5	456	2	5	456	2	17	1458
3	20	2474	3	20	2474	3	179	56456
4	34	10624	4	34	10624	4	22	7552
5	75	24184	5	75	24184	5	0	0
6	72	25008	6	68	24640	6	0	0
7	12	2720	7	16	3088	7	0	0

the "footprint" of f. A normal Boolean chain can begin in only $5\binom{n}{2}$ different ways, since the first step x_{n+1} must be either $x_1 \wedge x_2$ or $\bar{x}_1 \wedge x_2$ or $x_1 \wedge \bar{x}_2$ or $x_1 \vee x_2$ or $x_1 \oplus x_2$ or $x_1 \wedge x_3$ or $\cdots$ or $x_{n-1} \oplus x_n$. Suppose $\phi(f)$ is a bit vector of length $5\binom{n}{2}$ and $U(f)$ is an upper bound on $C(f)$, with the following property: Every 1 bit in $\phi(f)$ corresponds to the first step of some Boolean chain that computes f in $U(f)$ steps.

Such pairs $(U(f), \phi(f))$ can be computed by extending the basic strategy of Algorithm L. Initially we set $U(f) \leftarrow 1$ and we set $\phi(f)$ to an appropriate vector $0\ldots010\ldots0$, for all functions f of cost 1. Then, for $r = 2, 3, \ldots$, we proceed to look for functions $f = g \circ h$ where $U(g) + U(h) = r - 1$, as before, but with two changes: (1) If the footprints of g and h have at least one element in common, namely if $\phi(g) \mathbin{\&} \phi(h) \neq 0$, then we know that $C(f) \leq r - 1$, so we can decrease $U(f)$ if it was $\geq r$. (2) If the cost of $g \circ h$ is equal to (but not less than) our current upper bound $U(f)$, we can set $\phi(f) \leftarrow \phi(f) \mid (\phi(g) \mid \phi(h))$ if $U(f) = r$, $\phi(f) \leftarrow \phi(f) \mid (\phi(g) \mathbin{\&} \phi(h))$ if $U(f) = r - 1$. Exercise 11 works out the details.

It turns out that this footprint heuristic is powerful enough to find chains of optimum cost $U(f) = C(f)$ for all functions f, when $n = 4$. Moreover, we'll see later that footprints also help us solve more complicated evaluation problems.

According to Table 7.1.1–5, the $2^{16} = 65,536$ functions of four variables belong to only 222 distinct classes when we ignore minor differences due to permutation of variables and/or complementation of values. Algorithm L and its variants lead to the overall statistics shown in Table 1.

*Evaluation with minimum memory. Suppose the Boolean values $x_1, \ldots, x_n$ appear in n registers, and we want to evaluate a function by performing a sequence of operations having the form

$$x_{j(i)} \leftarrow x_{j(i)} \circ_i x_{k(i)}, \qquad \text{for } 1 \leq i \leq r, \tag{12}$$

where $1 \leq j(i) \leq n$ and $1 \leq k(i) \leq n$ and $\circ_i$ is a binary operator. At the end of the computation, the desired function value should appear in one of the registers. When $n = 3$, for example, the four-step sequence

$$
\begin{array}{ll}
x_1 \leftarrow x_1 \oplus x_2 & (x_1 = 00001111 \quad x_2 = 00110011 \quad x_3 = 01010101) \\
x_3 \leftarrow x_3 \wedge x_1 & (x_1 = 00111100 \quad x_2 = 00110011 \quad x_3 = 01010101) \\
x_2 \leftarrow x_2 \wedge \bar{x}_1 & (x_1 = 00111100 \quad x_2 = 00110011 \quad x_3 = 00010100) \\
x_3 \leftarrow x_3 \vee x_2 & (x_1 = 00111100 \quad x_2 = 00000011 \quad x_3 = 00010100) \\
& (x_1 = 00111100 \quad x_2 = 00000011 \quad x_3 = 00010111)
\end{array}
\tag{13}
$$

computes the median $\langle x_1 x_2 x_3 \rangle$ and puts it into the original position of x_3. (All eight possibilities for the register contents are shown here as truth tables, before and after each operation.)

In fact we can check the calculation by working with only one truth table at a time, instead of keeping track of all three, if we analyze the situation backwards. Let $f_l(x_1, \ldots, x_n)$ denote the function computed by steps l, $l + 1$, $\ldots$, r of the sequence, omitting the first $l - 1$ steps; thus, in our example, $f_2(x_1, x_2, x_3)$ would be the result in x_3 after the three steps $x_3 \leftarrow x_3 \wedge x_1$, $x_2 \leftarrow x_2 \wedge \bar{x}_1$, $x_3 \leftarrow x_3 \vee x_2$. Then the function computed in register x_3 by all four steps is

$$f_1(x_1, x_2, x_3) \;=\; f_2(x_1 \oplus x_2, x_2, x_3). \tag{14}$$

Similarly $f_2(x_1, x_2, x_3) = f_3(x_1, x_2, x_3 \wedge x_1)$, $f_3(x_1, x_2, x_3) = f_4(x_1, x_2 \wedge \bar{x}_1, x_3)$, $f_4(x_1, x_2, x_3) = f_5(x_1, x_2, x_3 \vee x_2)$, and $f_5(x_1, x_2, x_3) = x_3$. We can therefore go back from f_5 to f_4 to $\cdots$ to f_1 by operating on truth tables in an appropriate way.

For example, suppose $f(x_1, x_2, x_3)$ is a function whose truth table is

$$t \;=\; a_0 a_1 a_2 a_3 a_4 a_5 a_6 a_7;$$

then the truth table for $g(x_1, x_2, x_3) = f(x_1 \oplus x_2, x_2, x_3)$ is

$$u \;=\; a_0 a_1 a_6 a_7 a_4 a_5 a_2 a_3,$$

obtained by replacing a_x by $a_{x'}$, where

$$x = (x_1 x_2 x_3)_2 \qquad \text{implies} \qquad x' = ((x_1 {\oplus} x_2) x_2 x_3)_2.$$

Similarly the truth table for, say, $h(x_1, x_2, x_3) = f(x_1, x_2, x_3 \wedge x_1)$ is

$$v \;=\; a_0 a_0 a_2 a_2 a_4 a_5 a_6 a_7.$$

And we can use bitwise operations to compute u and v from t (see 7.1.3–(83)):

$$u = t \oplus \big((t \oplus (t \gg 4)) \oplus (t \ll 4)\big) \,\&\, (00110011)_2); \tag{15}$$

$$v = t \oplus \big((t \oplus (t \gg 1)) \,\&\, (01010000)_2\big). \tag{16}$$

Let $C_m(f)$ be the length of a shortest minimum-memory computation for f. The backward-computation principle tells us that, if we know the truth tables of all functions f with $C_m(f) < r$, we can readily find all the truth tables of functions with $C_m(f) = r$. Namely, we can restrict consideration to normal functions as before. Then, for all normal g such that $C_m(g) = r - 1$, we can construct the $5n(n - 1)$ truth tables for

$$g(x_1, \ldots, x_{j-1}, x_j \circ x_k, x_{j+1}, \ldots, x_n) \tag{17}$$

and mark them with cost r if they haven't previously been marked. Exercise 14 shows that those truth tables can all be computed by performing simple bitwise operations on the truth table for g.

When $n = 4$, all but 13 of the 222 basic function types turn out to have $C_m(f) = C(f)$, so they can be evaluated in minimum memory without increasing the cost. In particular, all of the symmetric functions have this property — although that fact is not at all obvious from Fig. 9. Five classes of functions have $C(f) = 5$ but $C_m(f) = 6$; eight classes have $C(f) = 6$ but $C_m(f) = 7$. The most interesting example of the latter type is probably the function $(x_1 \vee x_2) \oplus (x_3 \vee x_4) \oplus (x_1 \wedge x_2 \wedge x_3 \wedge x_4)$, which has cost 6 because of the formula

$$x_1 \oplus (x_3 \vee x_4) \oplus \big(x_2 \wedge (\bar{x}_1 \vee (x_3 \wedge x_4))\big), \tag{18}$$

but it has no minimum-memory chain of length less than 7. (See exercise 15.)

*__Determining the minimum cost.__ The exact value of $C(f)$ can be found by observing that all optimum Boolean chains $(x_{n+1}, \ldots, x_{n+r})$ for f obviously satisfy at least one of three conditions:

  i) $x_{n+r} = x_j \circ x_k$, where x_j and x_k use no common intermediate results;
  ii) $x_{n+1} = x_j \circ x_k$, where either x_j or x_k is not used in steps $x_{n+2}, \ldots, x_{n+r}$;
  iii) Neither of the above, even when the intermediate steps are renumbered.

In case (i) we have $f = g \circ h$, where $C(g) + C(h) = r - 1$, and we can call this a "top-down" construction. In case (ii) we have $f(x_1, \ldots, x_n) = g(x_1, \ldots, x_{j-1}, x_j \circ x_k, x_{j+1}, \ldots, x_n)$, where $C(g) = r-1$; we call this construction "bottom-up."

The best chains that recursively use only top-down constructions correspond to minimum formula length, $L(f)$. The best chains that recursively use only bottom-up constructions correspond to minimum-memory calculations, of length $C_m(f)$. We can do better yet, by mixing top-down constructions with bottom-up constructions; but we still won't know that we've found $C(f)$, because a special chain belonging to case (iii) might be shorter.

Fortunately such special chains are rare, because they must satisfy rather strong conditions, and they can be exhaustively listed when n and r aren't too large. For example, exercise 19 proves that no special chains exist when $r < n+2$; and when $n = 4$, $r = 6$, there are only 25 essentially different special chains that cannot be shortened in an obvious way:

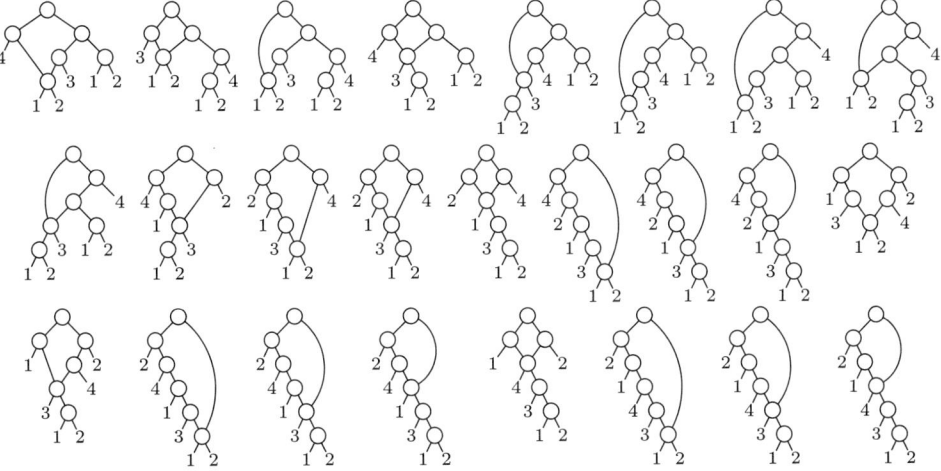

By systematically trying 5^r possibilities in every special chain, one for each way to assign a normal operator to the internal nodes of the tree, we will find at least one function f in every equivalence class for which the minimum cost $C(f)$ is achievable only in case (iii).

In fact, when $n = 4$ and $r = 6$, these $25 \cdot 5^6 = 390{,}625$ trials yield only one class of functions that can't be computed in 6 steps by any top-down-plus-bottom-up chain. The missing class, typified by the partially symmetric function $(\langle x_1 x_2 x_3 \rangle \vee x_4) \oplus (x_1 \wedge x_2 \wedge x_3)$, can be reached in six steps by appropriately specializing any of the first five chains illustrated above; for example, one way is

$$x_5 = x_1 \wedge x_2, \quad x_6 = x_1 \vee x_2, \quad x_7 = x_3 \oplus x_5,$$
$$x_8 = x_4 \wedge \bar{x}_5, \quad x_9 = x_6 \wedge x_7, \quad x_{10} = x_8 \vee x_9, \qquad (19)$$

corresponding to the first special chain. Since all other functions have $L(f) \leq 7$, these trial calculations have established the true minimum cost in all cases.

Historical notes: The first concerted attempts to evaluate all Boolean functions $f(w, x, y, z)$ optimally were reported in *Annals of the Computation Laboratory of Harvard University* **27** (1951), where Howard Aiken's staff presented heuristic methods and extensive tables of the best switching circuits they were able to construct. Their cost measure $V(f)$ was different from the cost $C(f)$ that we've been considering, because it was based on "control grids" of vacuum tubes: They had four kinds of gates, $\text{NOT}(f)$, $\text{NAND}(f, g)$, $\text{OR}(f_1, \ldots, f_k)$, and $\text{AND}(f_1, \ldots, f_k)$, respectively costing 1, 2, k, and 0. Every input to NOT, NAND, or OR could be either a variable, or the complement of a variable, or the result of a previous gate; every input to AND had to be the output of either NOT or NAND that wasn't also used elsewhere.

With those cost criteria, a function might not have the same cost as its complement. One could, for instance, evaluate $x \wedge y$ as $\text{AND}\big(\text{NOT}(\bar{x}), \text{NOT}(\bar{y})\big)$, with cost 2; but the cost of $\bar{x} \vee (\bar{y} \wedge \bar{z}) = \text{NAND}(x, \text{OR}(y, z))$ was 4 while its complement $x \wedge (y \vee z) = \text{AND}\big(\text{NOT}(\bar{x}), \text{NAND}(\bar{y}, \bar{z})\big)$ cost only 3. Therefore the Harvard researchers needed to consider 402 essentially different classes of 4-variable functions instead of 222 (see the answer to exercise 7.1.1–125). Of course in those days they worked mostly by hand. They found $V(f) < 20$ in all cases, except for the 64 functions equivalent to $S_{0,1}(w, x, y, z) \vee \big(S_2(w, x, y) \wedge z\big)$, which they evaluated with 20 control grids as follows:

$$g_1 = \text{AND}(\text{NOT}(\bar{w}), \text{NOT}(\bar{x})), \ \ g_2 = \text{NAND}(\bar{y}, z),$$
$$g_3 = \text{AND}(\text{NOT}(w), \text{NOT}(x));$$
$$f = \text{AND}\big(\text{NAND}(g_1, g_2), \text{NAND}(g_3, \text{AND}(\text{NOT}(\bar{y}), \text{NOT}(\bar{z}))),$$
$$\text{NOT}(\text{AND}(\text{NOT}(g_3), \text{NOT}(\bar{y}), \text{NOT}(z))),$$
$$\text{NOT}(\text{AND}(\text{NOT}(g_1), \text{NOT}(g_2), \text{NOT}(g_3)))\big). \qquad (20)$$

The first computer program to find provably optimum circuits was written by Leo Hellerman [*IEEE Transactions* **EC-12** (1963), 198–223], who determined the fewest NOR gates needed to evaluate any given function $f(x, y, z)$. He required every input of every gate to be either an uncomplemented variable or the output of a previous gate; fan-in and fan-out were limited to at most 3. When two circuits had the same gate count, he preferred the one with smallest

Table 2

THE NUMBER OF FIVE-VARIABLE FUNCTIONS WITH GIVEN COMPLEXITY

$C(f)$	Classes	Functions	$L(f)$	Classes	Functions	$D(f)$	Classes	Functions
0	2	12	0	2	12	0	2	12
1	2	100	1	2	100	1	2	100
2	5	1140	2	5	1140	2	17	5350
3	20	11570	3	20	11570	3	1789	6702242
4	93	109826	4	93	109826	4	614316	4288259592
5	389	995240	5	366	936440	5	0	0
6	1988	8430800	6	1730	7236880	6	0	0
7	11382	63401728	7	8782	47739088	7	0	0
8	60713	383877392	8	40297	250674320	8	0	0
9	221541	1519125536	9	141422	955812256	9	0	0
10	293455	2123645248	10	273277	1945383936	10	0	0
11	26535	195366784	11	145707	1055912608	11	0	0
12	1	1920	12	4423	31149120	12	0	0

sum-of-inputs. For example, he computed $\bar{x} = \text{NOR}(x)$ with cost 1; $x \vee y \vee z = \text{NOR}(\text{NOR}(x, y, z))$ with cost 2; $\langle xyz \rangle = \text{NOR}(\text{NOR}(x, y), \text{NOR}(x, z), \text{NOR}(y, z))$ with cost 4; $S_1(x, y, z) = \text{NOR}\big(\text{NOR}(x, y, z), \langle xyz \rangle\big)$ with cost 6; etc. Since he limited the fan-out to 3, he found that every function of three variables could be evaluated with cost 7 or less, except for the parity function $x \oplus y \oplus z = (x \equiv y) \equiv z$, where $x \equiv y$ has cost 4 because it is $\text{NOR}(\text{NOR}(x, \text{NOR}(x, y)), \text{NOR}(y, \text{NOR}(x, y)))$.

Electrical engineers continued to explore other cost criteria; but four-variable functions seemed out of reach until 1977, when Frank M. Liang established the values of $C(f)$ shown in Table 1. Liang's unpublished derivation was based on a study of all chains that cannot be reduced by the bottom-up construction.

The case $n = 5$. There are 616,126 classes of essentially different functions $f(x_1, x_2, x_3, x_4, x_5)$, according to Table 7.1.1–5. Computers are now fast enough that this number is no longer frightening; so the author decided while writing this section to investigate $C(f)$ for all Boolean functions of five variables. Thanks to a bit of good luck, complete results could indeed be obtained, leading to the statistics shown in Table 2.

For this calculation Algorithm L and its variants were modified to deal with class representatives, instead of with the entire set of 2^{31} normal truth tables. The method of exercise 7.2.1.2–20 made it easy to generate all functions of a class, given any one of them, resulting in a thousand-fold speedup. The bottom-up method was enhanced slightly, allowing it to deduce for example that $f(x_1 \wedge x_2, x_1 \vee x_2, x_3, x_4, x_5)$ has cost $\leq r$ if $C(f) = r - 2$. After all classes of cost 10 had been found, the top-down and bottom-up methods were able to find chains of length ≤ 11 for all but seven classes of functions. Then the time-consuming part of the computation began, in which approximately 53 million special chains with $n = 5$ and $r = 11$ were generated; every such chain led to $5^{11} = 48{,}828{,}125$ functions, some of which would hopefully fall into the seven remaining mystery classes. But only six of those classes were found to have 11-step solutions. The lone survivor, whose truth table is `169ae443` in hexadecimal notation, is the unique class for which $C(f) = 12$, and it also has $L(f) = 12$.

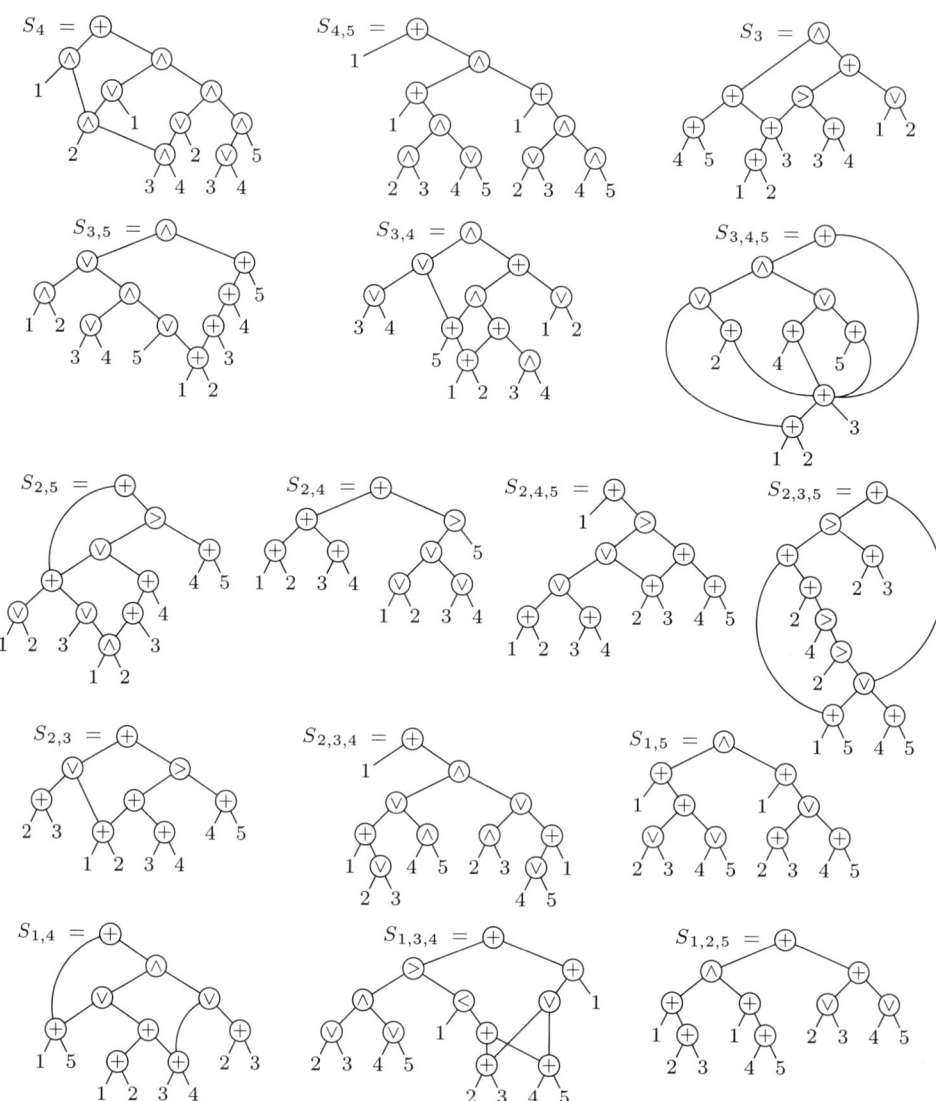

Fig. 10. Boolean chains of minimum cost
for symmetric functions of five variables.

The resulting constructions of symmetric functions are shown in Fig. 10. Some of them are astonishingly beautiful; some of them are beautifully simple; and others are simply astonishing. (Look, for example, at the 8-step computation of $S_{2,3}(x_1, x_2, x_3, x_4, x_5)$, or the elegant formula for $S_{2,3,4}$, or the nonmonotonic chains for $S_{4,5}$ and $S_{3,4,5}$.) Incidentally, Table 2 shows that all 5-variable functions have depth ≤ 4, but no attempt to minimize depth has been made in Fig. 10.

It turns out that all of these symmetric functions can be evaluated in minimum memory without increasing the cost. No simple reason is known.

Multiple outputs. We often want to evaluate several different Boolean functions $f_1(x_1, \ldots, x_n)$, $\ldots$, $f_m(x_1, \ldots, x_n)$ at the same input values x_1, $\ldots$, x_n; in other words, we often want to evaluate a multibit function $y = f(x)$, where $y = f_1 \ldots f_m$ is a binary vector of length m and $x = x_1 \ldots x_n$ is a binary vector of length n. With luck, much of the work involved in the computation of one component value $f_j(x_1, \ldots, x_n)$ can be shared with the operations that are needed to evaluate the other component values $f_k(x_1, \ldots, x_n)$.

Let $C(f) = C(f_1 \ldots f_m)$ be the length of a shortest Boolean chain that computes all of the nontrivial functions f_j. More precisely, the chain $(x_{n+1}, \ldots, x_{n+r})$ should have the property that, for $1 \leq j \leq m$, either $f_j(x_1, \ldots, x_n) = x_{l(j)}$ or $f_j(x_1, \ldots, x_n) = \bar{x}_{l(j)}$, for some $l(j)$ with $0 \leq l(j) \leq n+r$, where $x_0 = 0$. Clearly $C(f) \leq C(f_1) + \cdots + C(f_m)$, but we might be able to do much better.

For example, suppose we want to compute the functions z_1 and z_0 defined by

$$(z_1 z_0)_2 = x_1 + x_2 + x_3, \qquad (21)$$

the two-bit binary sum of three Boolean variables. We have

$$z_1 = \langle x_1 x_2 x_3 \rangle \qquad \text{and} \qquad z_0 = x_1 \oplus x_2 \oplus x_3, \qquad (22)$$

so the individual costs are $C(z_1) = 4$ and $C(z_0) = 2$. But it's easy to see that the combined cost $C(z_1 z_0)$ is at most 5, because $x_1 \oplus x_2$ is a suitable first step in the evaluation of each bit z_j:

$$x_4 = x_1 \oplus x_2, \quad z_0 = x_5 = x_3 \oplus x_4;$$
$$x_6 = x_3 \wedge x_4, \quad x_7 = x_1 \wedge x_2, \quad z_1 = x_8 = x_6 \vee x_7. \qquad (23)$$

Furthermore, exhaustive calculations show that $C(z_1 z_0) > 4$; hence $C(z_1 z_0) = 5$.

Electrical engineers traditionally call a circuit for (21) a *full adder*, because n such building blocks can be hooked together to add two n-bit numbers. The special case of (22) in which $x_3 = 0$ is also important, although it boils down simply to

$$z_1 = x_1 \wedge x_2 \qquad \text{and} \qquad z_0 = x_1 \oplus x_2 \qquad (24)$$

and has complexity 2; engineers call it a "half adder" in spite of the fact that the cost of a full adder exceeds the cost of two half adders.

The general problem of radix-2 addition

$$\begin{aligned} (x_{n-1} \ldots x_1 x_0)_2 \\ (y_{n-1} \ldots y_1 y_0)_2 \\ \hline (z_n z_{n-1} \ldots z_1 z_0)_2 \end{aligned} \qquad (25)$$

is to compute $n + 1$ Boolean outputs $z_n \ldots z_1 z_0$ from the $2n$ Boolean inputs $x_{n-1} \ldots x_1 x_0 y_{n-1} \ldots y_1 y_0$; and it is readily solved by the formulas

$$c_{j+1} = \langle x_j y_j c_j \rangle, \qquad z_j = x_j \oplus y_j \oplus c_j, \qquad \text{for } 0 \leq j < n, \qquad (26)$$

where the c_j are "carry bits" and we have $c_0 = 0$, $z_n = c_n$. Therefore we can use a half adder to compute c_1 and z_0, followed by $n - 1$ full adders to compute the other c's and z's, accumulating a total cost of $5n - 3$. And in fact N. P. Red'kin [*Problemy Kibernetiki* **38** (1981), 181–216] has proved that $5n - 3$ steps are actually necessary, by constructing an elaborate 35-page proof by induction, which concludes with Case 2.2.2.3.1.2.3.2.4.3(!). But the depth of this circuit, $2n-1$, is far too large for practical parallel computation, so a great deal of effort has gone into the task of devising circuits for addition that have depth $O(\log n)$ as well as reasonable cost. (See exercises 41–44.)

Now let's extend (21) and try to compute a general "sideways sum"

$$(z_{\lfloor \lg n \rfloor} \ldots z_1 z_0)_2 = x_1 + x_2 + \cdots + x_n. \tag{27}$$

If $n = 2k+1$, we can use k full adders to reduce the sum to $(x_1 + \cdots + x_n) \bmod 2$ plus k bits of weight 2, because each full adder decreases the number of weight-1 bits by 2. For example, if $n = 9$ and $k = 4$ the computation is

$$x_{10} = x_1 \oplus x_2 \oplus x_3, \quad x_{11} = x_4 \oplus x_5 \oplus x_6, \quad x_{12} = x_7 \oplus x_8 \oplus x_9, \quad x_{13} = x_{10} \oplus x_{11} \oplus x_{12},$$
$$y_1 = \langle x_1 x_2 x_3 \rangle, \quad\quad y_2 = \langle x_4 x_5 x_6 \rangle, \quad\quad y_3 = \langle x_7 x_8 x_9 \rangle, \quad\quad y_4 = \langle x_{10} x_{11} x_{12} \rangle,$$

and we have $x_1 + \cdots + x_9 = x_{13} + 2(y_1 + y_2 + y_3 + y_4)$. If $n = 2k$ is even, a similar reduction applies but with a half adder at the end. The bits of weight 2 can then be summed in the same way; so we obtain the recurrence

$$s(n) = 5\lfloor n/2 \rfloor - 3[n \text{ even}] + s(\lfloor n/2 \rfloor), \qquad s(0) = 0, \tag{28}$$

for the total number of gates needed to compute $z_{\lfloor \lg n \rfloor} \ldots z_1 z_0$. (A closed formula for $s(n)$ appears in exercise 30.) We have $s(n) < 5n$, and the first values

$$n \; = \; 1 \;\; 2 \;\; 3 \;\; 4 \;\; 5 \;\;\; 6 \;\;\; 7 \;\;\; 8 \;\;\; 9 \;\;\; 10 \;\; 11 \;\; 12 \;\; 13 \;\; 14 \;\; 15 \;\; 16 \;\; 17 \;\; 18 \;\; 19 \;\; 20$$
$$s(n) = 0 \;\; 2 \;\; 5 \;\; 9 \;\; 12 \;\; 17 \;\; 20 \;\; 26 \;\; 29 \;\; 34 \;\; 37 \;\; 44 \;\; 47 \;\; 52 \;\; 55 \;\; 63 \;\; 66 \;\; 71 \;\; 74 \;\; 81$$

show that the method is quite efficient even for small n. For example, when $n = 5$ it produces

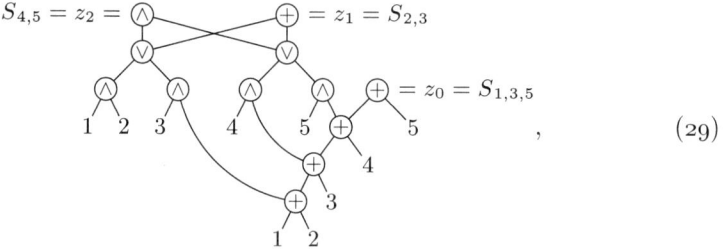

$$\tag{29}$$

which computes three different symmetric functions $z_2 = S_{4,5}(x_1, \ldots, x_5)$, $z_1 = S_{2,3}(x_1, \ldots, x_5)$, $z_0 = S_{1,3,5}(x_1, \ldots, x_5)$ in just 12 steps. The 10-step computation of $S_{4,5}$ is optimum, according to Fig. 10; of course the 4-step computation of $S_{1,3,5}$ is also optimum. Furthermore, although $C(S_{2,3}) = 8$, the function $S_{2,3}$ is computed here in a clever 10-step way that shares all but one gate with $S_{4,5}$.

Notice that we can now compute *any* symmetric function efficiently, because every symmetric function of $\{x_1, \ldots, x_n\}$ is a Boolean function of $z_{\lfloor \lg n \rfloor} \ldots z_1 z_0$. We know, for example, that any Boolean function of four variables has complexity ≤ 7; therefore any symmetric function $S_{k_1, \ldots, k_t}(x_1, \ldots, x_{15})$ costs at most $s(15) + 7 = 62$. Surprise: The symmetric functions of n variables were among the hardest of all to evaluate, when n was small, but they're among the easiest when $n \geq 10$.

We can also compute *sets* of symmetric functions efficiently. If we want, say, to evaluate all $n + 1$ symmetric functions $S_k(x_1, \ldots, x_n)$ for $0 \leq k \leq n$ with a single Boolean chain, we simply need to evaluate the first $n+1$ *minterms* of z_0, z_1, $\ldots$, $z_{\lfloor \lg n \rfloor}$. For example, when $n = 5$ the minterms that give us all functions S_k are respectively $S_0 = \bar{z}_0 \wedge \bar{z}_1 \wedge \bar{z}_2$, $S_1 = \bar{z}_0 \wedge \bar{z}_1 \wedge z_2$, $\ldots$, $S_5 = z_0 \wedge \bar{z}_1 \wedge z_2$.

How hard is it to compute all 2^n minterms of n variables? Electrical engineers call this function an n-to-2^n *binary decoder*, because it converts n bits $x_1 \ldots x_n$ into a sequence of 2^n bits $d_0 d_1 \ldots d_{2^n-1}$, exactly one of which is 1. The principle of "divide and conquer" suggests that we first evaluate all minterms on the first $\lceil n/2 \rceil$ variables, as well as all minterms on the last $\lfloor n/2 \rfloor$; then 2^n AND gates will finish the job. The cost of this method is $t(n)$, where

$$t(0) = t(1) = 0; \qquad t(n) = 2^n + t(\lceil n/2 \rceil) + t(\lfloor n/2 \rfloor) \quad \text{for } n \geq 2. \tag{30}$$

So $t(n) = 2^n + O(2^{n/2})$; there's roughly one gate per minterm. (See exercise 32.)

Functions with multiple outputs often help us build larger functions with single outputs. For example, we've seen that the sideways adder (27) allows us to compute symmetric functions; and an n-to-2^n decoder also has many applications, in spite of the fact that 2^n can be huge when n is large. A case in point is the 2^m-*way multiplexer* $M_m(x_1, \ldots, x_m; y_0, y_1, \ldots, y_{2^m-1})$, also known as the m-bit *storage access function*, which has $n = m + 2^m$ inputs and takes the value y_k when $(x_1 \ldots x_m)_2 = k$. By definition we have

$$M_m(x_1, \ldots, x_m; y_0, y_1, \ldots, y_{2^m-1}) = \bigvee_{k=0}^{2^m-1} (d_k \wedge y_k), \tag{31}$$

where d_k is the kth output of an m-to-2^m binary decoder; thus, by (30), we can evaluate M_m with $2^m + (2^m-1) + t(m) = 3n + O(\sqrt{n})$ gates. But exercise 39 shows that we can actually reduce the cost to only $2n + O(\sqrt{n})$. (See also exercise 79.)

Asymptotic facts. When the number of variables is small, our exhaustive-search methods have turned up lots of cases where Boolean functions can be evaluated with stunning efficiency. So it's natural to expect that, when more variables are present, even more opportunities for ingenious evaluations will arise. But the truth is exactly the opposite, at least from a statistical standpoint:

Theorem S. *The cost of almost every Boolean function $f(x_1, \ldots, x_n)$ exceeds $2^n/n$. More precisely, if $c(n, r)$ Boolean functions have complexity $\leq r$, we have*

$$(r - 1)! \, c(n, r) \leq 2^{2r+1}(n + r - 1)^{2r}. \tag{32}$$

Proof. If a function can be computed in $r - 1$ steps, it is also computable by an r-step chain. (This statement is obvious when $r = 1$; otherwise we can let $x_{n+r} = x_{n+r-1} \wedge x_{n+r-1}$.) We will show that there aren't very many r-step chains, hence we can't compute very many different functions with cost $\leq r$.

Let π be a permutation of $\{1, \ldots, n + r\}$ that takes $1 \mapsto 1$, $\ldots$, $n \mapsto n$, and $n+r \mapsto n+r$; there are $(r-1)!$ such permutations. Suppose $(x_{n+1}, \ldots, x_{n+r})$ is a

Boolean chain in which each of the intermediate steps $x_{n+1}, \ldots, x_{n+r-1}$ is used in at least one subsequent step. Then the permuted chains defined by the rule

$$x_i = x_{j'(i)} \circ_i' x_{k'(i)} = x_{j(i\pi)\pi^-} \circ_{i\pi} x_{k(i\pi)\pi^-}, \qquad \text{for } n < i \le n+r, \qquad (33)$$

are distinct for different π. (If π takes $a \mapsto b$, we write $b = a\pi$ and $a = b\pi^-$.) For example, if π takes $5 \mapsto 6 \mapsto 7 \mapsto 8 \mapsto 9 \mapsto 5$, the chain (7) becomes

$$
\begin{array}{ll}
\text{Original} & \text{Permuted} \\[4pt]
x_5 = x_1 \oplus x_3, & x_5 = x_1 \oplus x_2, \\
x_6 = x_1 \oplus x_2, & x_6 = x_3 \oplus x_4, \\
x_7 = x_3 \oplus x_4, & x_7 = x_9 \vee x_5, \\
x_8 = x_5 \vee x_6, & x_8 = x_5 \oplus x_6, \\
x_9 = x_6 \oplus x_7, & x_9 = x_1 \oplus x_3, \\
x_{10} = x_8 \wedge \bar{x}_9; & x_{10} = x_7 \wedge \bar{x}_8.
\end{array}
\qquad (34)
$$

Notice that we might have $j'(i) \ge k'(i)$ or $j'(i) > i$ or $k'(i) > i$, contrary to our usual rules. But the permuted chain computes the same function x_{n+r} as before, and it doesn't have any cycles by which an entry is defined indirectly in terms of itself, because the permuted x_i is the original $x_{i\pi}$.

We can restrict consideration to *normal* Boolean chains, as remarked earlier. So the $c(n,r)/2$ normal Boolean functions of cost $\le r$ lead to $(r-1)!\,c(n,r)/2$ different permuted chains, where the operator $\circ_i$ in each step is either $\wedge$, $\vee$, $\bar{}$, or $\oplus$. And there are at most $4^r(n+r-1)^{2r}$ such chains, because there are four choices for $\circ_i$ and $n+r-1$ choices for each of $j(i)$ and $k(i)$, for $n < i \le n+r$. Equation (32) follows; and we obtain the opening statement of the theorem by setting $r = \lfloor 2^n/n \rfloor$. (See exercise 46.) ∎

On the other hand, there's also good news for infinity-minded people: We can actually evaluate every Boolean function of n variables with only slightly more than $2^n/n$ steps of computation, even if we avoid $\oplus$ and $\equiv$, using a technique devised by C. E. Shannon and improved by O. B. Lupanov [*Bell System Tech. J.* **28** (1949), 59–98, Theorem 6; *Isvestiia VUZov, Radiofizika* **1** (1958), 120–140].

In fact, the Shannon–Lupanov approach leads to useful results even when n is small, so let's get acquainted with it by studying a small example. Consider

$$f(x_1, x_2, x_3, x_4, x_5, x_6) = \bigl[(x_1 x_2 x_3 x_4 x_5 x_6)_2 \text{ is prime}\bigr], \qquad (35)$$

a function that identifies all 6-bit prime numbers. Its truth table has $2^6 = 64$ bits, and we can work with it conveniently by using a 4×16 array to look at those bits instead of confining ourselves to one dimension:

$$
\begin{array}{l}
x_3 = 0\;0\;0\;0\;0\;0\;0\;0\;1\;1\;1\;1\;1\;1\;1\;1 \\
x_4 = 0\;0\;0\;0\;1\;1\;1\;1\;0\;0\;0\;0\;1\;1\;1\;1 \\
x_5 = 0\;0\;1\;1\;0\;0\;1\;1\;0\;0\;1\;1\;0\;0\;1\;1 \\
x_6 = 0\;1\;0\;1\;0\;1\;0\;1\;0\;1\;0\;1\;0\;1\;0\;1
\end{array}
$$

$$
\begin{array}{ll}
x_1 x_2 = 00 & \boxed{0\;0\;1\;1\;0\;1\;0\;1\;0\;0\;0\;1\;0\;1\;0\;0} \left.\right\} \text{ Group 1} \\
x_1 x_2 = 01 & 0\;1\;0\;1\;0\;0\;0\;1\;0\;0\;0\;0\;0\;1\;0\;1 \\
x_1 x_2 = 10 & 0\;0\;0\;0\;0\;1\;0\;0\;0\;1\;0\;1\;0\;0\;0\;1 \left.\right\} \text{ Group 2} \\
x_1 x_2 = 11 & 0\;0\;0\;0\;0\;1\;0\;0\;0\;0\;0\;1\;0\;1\;0\;0
\end{array}
\qquad (36)
$$

The rows have been divided into two groups of two rows each; and each group of rows has 16 columns, which are of four basic types, namely $\begin{smallmatrix}0\\0\end{smallmatrix}$, $\begin{smallmatrix}0\\1\end{smallmatrix}$, $\begin{smallmatrix}1\\0\end{smallmatrix}$, or $\begin{smallmatrix}1\\1\end{smallmatrix}$. Thus we see that the function can be expressed as

$$
\begin{aligned}
f(x_1,\ldots,x_6) = \quad & \big([x_1x_2 \in \{00\}] && \wedge [x_3x_4x_5x_6 \in \{0010,0101,1011\}]\big) \\
\vee\ & \big([x_1x_2 \in \{01\}] && \wedge [x_3x_4x_5x_6 \in \{0001,1111\}]\big) \\
\vee\ & \big([x_1x_2 \in \{00,01\}] && \wedge [x_3x_4x_5x_6 \in \{0011,0111,1101\}]\big) \\
\vee\ & \big([x_1x_2 \in \{10\}] && \wedge [x_3x_4x_5x_6 \in \{1001,1111\}]\big) \\
\vee\ & \big([x_1x_2 \in \{11\}] && \wedge [x_3x_4x_5x_6 \in \{1101\}]\big) \\
\vee\ & \big([x_1x_2 \in \{10,11\}] && \wedge [x_3x_4x_5x_6 \in \{0101,1011\}]\big).
\end{aligned}
\tag{37}
$$

(The first line corresponds to group 1, type $\begin{smallmatrix}1\\0\end{smallmatrix}$, then comes group 1, type $\begin{smallmatrix}0\\1\end{smallmatrix}$, etc.; the last line corresponds to group 2 and type $\begin{smallmatrix}1\\1\end{smallmatrix}$.) A function like $[x_3x_4x_5x_6 \in \{0010,0101,1011\}]$ is the OR of three minterms of $\{x_3, x_4, x_5, x_6\}$.

In general we can view the truth table as a $2^k \times 2^{n-k}$ array, with l groups of rows having either $\lfloor 2^k/l \rfloor$ or $\lceil 2^k/l \rceil$ rows in each group. A group of size m will have columns of 2^m basic types. We form a conjunction $(g_{it}(x_1,\ldots,x_k) \wedge h_{it}(x_{k+1},\ldots,x_n))$ for each group i and each nonzero type t, where g_{it} is the OR of all minterms of $\{x_1,\ldots,x_k\}$ for the rows of the group where t has a 1, while h_{it} is the OR of all minterms of $\{x_{k+1},\ldots,x_n\}$ for the columns having type t in group i. The OR of all these conjunctions $(g_{it} \wedge h_{it})$ gives $f(x_1,\ldots,x_n)$.

Once we've chosen the parameters k and l, with $1 \le k \le n-2$ and $1 \le l \le 2^k$, the computation starts by computing all the minterms of $\{x_1,\ldots,x_k\}$ and all the minterms of $\{x_{k+1},\ldots,x_n\}$, in $t(k) + t(n-k)$ steps (see (30)). Then, for $1 \le i \le l$, we let group i consist of rows for the values of $(x_1,\ldots,x_k)$ such that $(i-1)2^k/l \le (x_1\ldots x_k)_2 < i2^k/l$; it contains $m_i = \lceil i2^k/l \rceil - \lceil (i-1)2^k/l \rceil$ rows. We form all functions g_{it} for $t \in S_i$, the family of $2^{m_i} - 1$ nonempty subsets of those rows; $2^{m_i} - m_i - 1$ ORs of previously computed minterms will accomplish that task. We also form all functions h_{it} representing columns of nonzero type t; for this purpose we'll need at most 2^{n-k} OR operations in each group i, since we can OR each minterm into the h function of the appropriate type t. Finally we compute $f = \bigvee_{i=1}^{l} \bigvee_{t \in S_i}(g_{it} \wedge h_{it})$; each AND operation is compensated by an unnecessary first OR into h_{it}. So the total cost is at most

$$
t(k) + t(n-k) + (l-1) + \sum_{i=1}^{l}\big((2^{m_i} - m_i - 1) + 2^{n-k} + (2^{m_i} - 2)\big);
\tag{38}
$$

we want to choose k and l so that this upper bound is minimized. Exercise 52 discusses the best choice when n is small. And when n is large, a good choice yields a provably near-optimum chain, at least for most functions:

Theorem L. *Let $C(n)$ denote the cost of the most expensive Boolean functions of n variables. Then as $n \to \infty$ we have*

$$
C(n) \ge \frac{2^n}{n}\left(1 + \frac{\lg n}{n} + O\!\left(\frac{1}{n}\right)\right);
\tag{39}
$$

$$
C(n) \le \frac{2^n}{n}\left(1 + 3\frac{\lg n}{n} + O\!\left(\frac{1}{n}\right)\right).
\tag{40}
$$

Proof. Exercise 48 shows that the lower bound (39) is a consequence of Theorem S. For the upper bound, we set $k = \lfloor 2 \lg n \rfloor$ and $l = \lceil 2^k/(n - 3 \lg n) \rceil$ in Lupanov's method; see exercise 53. ∎

Synthesizing a good chain. Formula (37) isn't the best way to implement a 6-bit prime detector, but it does suggest a decent strategy. For example, we needn't let variables x_1 and x_2 govern the rows: Exercise 51 shows that a better chain results if the rows are based on $x_5 x_6$ while the columns come from $x_1 x_2 x_3 x_4$, and in general there are many ways to partition a truth table by playing k of the variables against the other $n - k$.

Furthermore, we can improve on (37) by using our complete knowledge of all 4-variable functions; there's no need to evaluate a function like $[x_3 x_4 x_5 x_6 \in \{0010, 0101, 1011\}]$ by first computing the minterms of $\{x_3, x_4, x_5, x_6\}$, if we know the best way to evaluate every such function from scratch. On the other hand, we do need to evaluate several 4-variable functions simultaneously, so the minterm approach might not be such a bad idea after all. Can we really improve on it?

Let's try to find a good way to synthesize a Boolean chain that computes a given set of 4-variable functions. The six functions of $x_3 x_4 x_5 x_6$ in (37) are rather tame (see exercise 54), so we'll learn more by considering a more interesting example chosen from everyday life.

A *seven-segment display* is a now-ubiquitous way to represent a 4-bit number $(x_1 x_2 x_3 x_4)_2$ in terms of seven cleverly positioned segments that are either visible or invisible. The segments are traditionally named (a, b, c, d, e, f, g) as shown; we get a '0' by turning on segments (a, b, c, d, e, f), but a '1' uses only segments (b, c). (Incidentally, the idea for such displays was invented by F. W. Wood, *U.S. Patent 974943* (1910), although Wood's original design used eight segments because he thought that a '4' requires a diagonal stroke.) Seven-segment displays usually support only the decimal digits '0', '1', ..., '9'; but of course a computer scientist's digital watch should display also hexadecimal digits. So we shall design seven-segment logic that displays the sixteen digits

$$\texttt{0123456789AbcdEF} \tag{41}$$

when given the respective inputs $x_1 x_2 x_3 x_4 = 0000, 0001, 0010, \ldots, 1111$.

In other words, we want to evaluate seven Boolean functions whose truth tables are respectively

$$
\begin{aligned}
a &= 1011\ 0111\ 1110\ 0011, \\
b &= 1111\ 1001\ 1110\ 0100, \\
c &= 1101\ 1111\ 1111\ 0100, \\
d &= 1011\ 0110\ 1101\ 1110, \\
e &= 1010\ 0010\ 1011\ 1111, \\
f &= 1000\ 1111\ 1111\ 0011, \\
g &= 0011\ 1110\ 1111\ 1111.
\end{aligned}
\tag{42}
$$

If we simply wanted to evaluate each function separately, several methods that we've already discussed would tell us how to do it with minimum costs $C(a) = 5$, $C(b) = C(c) = C(d) = 6$, $C(e) = C(f) = 5$, and $C(g) = 4$; the total cost for all seven functions would then be 37. But we want to find a single Boolean chain that contains them all, and the shortest such chain is presumably much more efficient. How can we discover it?

Well, the task of finding a truly optimum chain for $\{a, b, c, d, e, f, g\}$ is probably infeasible from a computational standpoint. But a surprisingly good solution can be found with the help of the "footprint" idea explained earlier. Namely, we know how to compute not only a function's minimum cost, but also the set of all first steps consistent with that minimum cost in a normal chain. Function e, for example, has cost 5, but only if we evaluate it by starting with one of the instructions

$$x_5 = x_1 \oplus x_4 \qquad \text{or} \qquad x_5 = x_2 \wedge \bar{x}_3 \qquad \text{or} \qquad x_5 = x_2 \vee x_3.$$

Fortunately, one of the desirable first steps belongs to four of the seven footprints: Functions c, d, f, and g can all be evaluated optimally by starting with $x_5 = x_2 \oplus x_3$. So that is a natural choice; it essentially saves us three steps, because we know that at most 33 of the original 37 steps will be needed to finish.

Now we can recompute the costs and footprints of all 2^{16} functions, proceeding as before but also initializing the cost of the new function x_5 to zero. The costs of functions c, d, f, and g decrease by 1 as a result, and the footprints change too. For example, function a still has cost 5, but its footprint has increased from $\{x_1 \oplus x_3, x_2 \wedge x_3\}$ to $\{x_1 \oplus x_3, x_1 \wedge x_4, \bar{x}_1 \wedge x_4, x_2 \wedge x_3, \bar{x}_2 \wedge x_4, x_2 \oplus x_4, x_4 \wedge x_5, x_4 \oplus x_5\}$ when the function $x_5 = x_2 \oplus x_3$ is available for free.

In fact, $x_6 = \bar{x}_1 \wedge x_4$ is common to four of the new footprints, so again we have a natural way to proceed. And when everything is recalculated with zero cost given to both x_5 and x_6, the subsequent step $x_7 = x_3 \wedge \bar{x}_6$ turns out to be desirable in five of the newest footprints. Continuing in this "greedy" fashion, we aren't always so lucky, but a chain of 22 steps does emerge; and David Stevenson has shown that only 21 steps are actually needed if we choose x_{10} non-greedily:

$$
\begin{aligned}
&x_5 = x_2 \oplus x_3, &\quad &x_{12} = x_1 \wedge x_2, &\quad &\bar{a} = x_{19} = x_{15} \oplus x_{18}, \\
&x_6 = \bar{x}_1 \wedge x_4, & &x_{13} = x_9 \wedge \bar{x}_{12}, & &\bar{b} = x_{20} = x_{11} \wedge \bar{x}_{13}, \\
&x_7 = x_3 \wedge \bar{x}_6, & &x_{14} = \bar{x}_3 \wedge x_{13}, & &\bar{c} = x_{21} = \bar{x}_8 \wedge x_{11}, \\
&x_8 = x_1 \oplus x_2, & &x_{15} = x_5 \oplus x_{14}, & &\bar{d} = x_{22} = x_9 \wedge \bar{x}_{16}, &\quad (43) \\
&x_9 = x_4 \oplus x_5, & &x_{16} = x_1 \oplus x_7, & &\bar{e} = x_{23} = x_6 \vee x_{14}, \\
&x_{10} = x_3 \vee x_9, & &x_{17} = x_1 \vee x_5, & &\bar{f} = x_{24} = \bar{x}_8 \wedge x_{15}, \\
&x_{11} = x_6 \oplus x_{10}, & &x_{18} = x_6 \oplus x_{13}, & &g = x_{25} = x_7 \vee x_{17}.
\end{aligned}
$$

(This is a *normal* chain, so it contains the normalizations $\{\bar{a}, \bar{b}, \bar{c}, \bar{d}, \bar{e}, \bar{f}, g\}$ instead of $\{a, b, c, d, e, f, g\}$. Simple changes will produce the unnormalized functions without changing the cost.)

Partial functions. In practice the output value of a Boolean function is often specified only at certain inputs $x_1 \ldots x_n$, and the outputs in other cases don't really matter. We might know, for example, that some of the input combinations will never arise. In such cases, we place an asterisk into the corresponding positions of the truth table, instead of specifying 0 or 1 everywhere.

The seven-segment display provides a case in point, because most of its applications involve only the ten binary-coded decimal inputs for which we have $(x_1x_2x_3x_4)_2 \leq 9$. We don't care what segments are visible in the other six cases. So the truth tables of (42) actually become

$$
\begin{aligned}
a &= 1011\ 0111\ 11**\ ****, \\
b &= 1111\ 1001\ 11**\ ****, \\
c &= 1101\ 1111\ 11**\ ****, \\
d &= 1011\ 0110\ 11**\ ****, \\
e &= 1010\ 0010\ 10**\ ****, \\
f &= 1000\ 111*\ 11**\ ****, \\
g &= 0011\ 1110\ 11**\ ****.
\end{aligned}
\qquad (44)
$$

(Function f here has an asterisk also in position $x_1x_2x_3x_4 = 0111$, because a '7' can be displayed as either ˥ or ˥. Both of these styles appeared about equally often in the display units available to the author when this section was written. Truncated variants of the 6 and the 9 were sometimes seen in olden days, but they have thankfully disappeared.)

Asterisks in truth tables are generally known as *don't-cares* — a quaint term that could only have been invented by an electrical engineer. Table 3 shows that the freedom to choose arbitrary outputs is advantageous. For example, there are $\binom{16}{3}2^{13} = 4{,}587{,}520$ truth tables with 3 don't-cares; 69% of them cost 4 or less, even though only 21% of the asterisk-free truth tables permit such economy. On the other hand, don't-cares don't save us as much as we might hope; exercise 63 proves that a random function with, say, 30% don't-cares in its truth table tends to save only about 30% of the cost of a fully specified function.

What is the shortest Boolean chain that evaluates the seven partially specified functions in (44)? Our greedy-footprint method adapts itself readily to the presence of don't-cares, because we can OR together the footprints of all 2^d functions that match a pattern with d asterisks. The initial costs to evaluate each function separately are now reduced to $C(a) = 3$, $C(b) = C(c) = 2$, $C(d) = 5$, $C(e) = 2$, $C(f) = 3$, $C(g) = 4$, totalling just 21 instead of 37. Function g hasn't gotten cheaper, but it does have a larger footprint. Proceeding as before, but taking advantage of the don't-cares, we now can find a suitable chain of length only 11 — a chain with fewer than 1.6 operations per output(!):

$$
\begin{aligned}
x_5 &= x_1 \lor x_2, & \bar{d} = \ x_9 &= x_6 \oplus x_8, & \bar{c} &= x_{13} = \bar{x}_4 \land x_{10}, \\
x_6 &= x_3 \oplus x_5, & \bar{f} = \ x_{10} &= \bar{x}_5 \land x_8, & \bar{e} &= x_{14} = x_4 \lor x_9, \\
x_7 &= \bar{x}_2 \land x_6, & \bar{b} = \ x_{11} &= x_2 \land \bar{x}_9, & g &= x_{15} = x_6 \lor x_{11}. \\
x_8 &= x_4 \lor x_7, & \bar{a} = \ x_{12} &= \bar{x}_3 \land x_9, & &
\end{aligned}
\qquad (45)
$$

This amazing chain, found by Corey Plover in 2011, chooses x_7 non-greedily.

Tic-tac-toe. Let's turn now to a slightly larger problem, based on a popular children's game. Two players take turns filling the cells of a 3×3 grid. One player writes ✗'s and the other writes ○'s, continuing until there either are three

Table 3
THE NUMBER OF 4-VARIABLE FUNCTIONS WITH d DON'T-CARES AND COST c

	$c=0$	$c=1$	$c=2$	$c=3$	$c=4$	$c=5$	$c=6$	$c=7$
$d=0$	10	60	456	2474	10624	24184	25008	2720
$d=1$	160	960	7296	35040	131904	227296	119072	2560
$d=2$	1200	7200	52736	221840	700512	816448	166144	
$d=3$	5600	33600	228992	831232	2045952	1381952	60192	
$d=4$	18200	108816	666528	2034408	3505344	1118128	3296	
$d=5$	43680	257472	1367776	3351488	3491648	433568	32	
$d=6$	80080	455616	2015072	3648608	1914800	86016		
$d=7$	114400	606944	2115648	2474688	533568	12032		
$d=8$	128660	604756	1528808	960080	71520	896		
$d=9$	114080	440960	707488	197632	4160			
$d=10$	78960	224144	189248	20160				
$d=11$	41440	72064	25472	800				
$d=12$	15480	12360	1280					
$d=13$	3680	800						
$d=14$	480							
$d=15$	32							
$d=16$	1							

X's or three O's in a straight line (in which case that player wins) or all nine cells are filled without a winner (in which case it's a "cat's game" or tie). For example, the game might proceed thus:

$$ \#\quad \#\quad \#\quad \#\quad \#\quad \#\quad \#\quad \#\ ; \tag{46} $$

X has won. Our goal is to design a machine that plays tic-tac-toe optimally — making a winning move from each position in which a forced victory is possible, and never making a losing move from a position in which defeat is avoidable.

More precisely, we will set things up so that there are 18 Boolean variables x_1, ..., x_9, o_1, ..., o_9, which govern lamps to illuminate cells of the current position. The cells are numbered $\begin{smallmatrix}1|2|3\\4|5|6\\7|8|9\end{smallmatrix}$ as on a telephone dial. Cell j displays an X if $x_j = 1$, an O if $o_j = 1$, or remains blank if $x_j = o_j = 0$.* We never have $x_j = o_j = 1$, because that would display '⊗'. We shall assume that the variables $x_1 \ldots x_9 o_1 \ldots o_9$ have been set to indicate a legal position in which nobody has won; the computer plays the X's, and it is the computer's turn to move. For this purpose we want to define nine functions y_1, ..., y_9, where y_j means "change x_j from 0 to 1." If the current position is a cat's game, we should make $y_1 = \cdots = y_9 = 0$; otherwise exactly one y_j should be equal to 1, and of course the output value $y_j = 1$ should occur only if $x_j = o_j = 0$.

With 18 variables, each of our nine functions y_j will have a truth table of size $2^{18} = 262{,}144$. It turns out that only 4520 legal inputs $x_1 \ldots x_9 o_1 \ldots o_9$ are

---

* This setup is based on an exhibit from the early 1950s at the Museum of Science and Industry in Chicago, where the author was first introduced to the magic of switching circuits. The machine in Chicago, designed circa 1940 by W. Keister at Bell Telephone Laboratories, allowed me to go first; yet I soon discovered that there was no way to defeat it. Therefore I decided to move as stupidly as possible, hoping that the designer had not anticipated such bizarre behavior. In fact I allowed the machine to reach a position where it had two winning moves; and it seized *both* of them! Moving twice is of course a flagrant violation of the rules, so I had won a moral victory even though the machine announced that I had lost.

> *I commenced an examination of a game called "tit-tat-to" ...*
> *to ascertain what number of combinations were required*
> *for all the possible variety of moves and situations.*
> *I found this to be comparatively insignificant.*
> *... A difficulty, however, arose of a novel kind.*
> *When the automaton had to move, it might occur that there were*
> *two different moves, each equally conducive to his winning the game.*
> *... Unless, also, some provision were made,*
> *the machine would attempt two contradictory motions.*
> — CHARLES BABBAGE, *Passages from the Life of a Philosopher* (1864)

possible, so those truth tables are 98.3% filled with don't-cares. Still, 4520 is
uncomfortably large if we hope to design and understand a Boolean chain that
makes sense intuitively. Section 7.1.4 will discuss alternative ways to represent
Boolean functions, by which it is often possible to deal with hundreds of variables
even though the associated truth tables are impossibly large.

Most functions of 18 variables require more than $2^{18}/18$ gates, but let's hope
we can do better. Indeed, a plausible strategy for making suitable moves in
tic-tac-toe suggests itself immediately, in terms of several conditions that aren't
hard to recognize:

w_j, an ✗ in cell j will win, completing a line of ✗'s;
b_j, an ○ in cell j would lose, completing a line of ○'s;
f_j, an ✗ in cell j will give ✗ two ways to win;
d_j, an ○ in cell j would give ○ two ways to win.

For example, ✗'s move to the center in (46) was needed to block ○, so it was of
type b_5; fortunately it was also of type f_5, forcing a win on the next move.

Let $L = \{\{1,2,3\},\{4,5,6\},\{7,8,9\},\{1,4,7\},\{2,5,8\},\{3,6,9\},\{1,5,9\},\{3,5,7\}\}$
be the set of winning lines. Then we have

$$m_j = \bar{x}_j \wedge \bar{o}_j; \qquad\qquad\qquad \text{[moving in cell } j \text{ is legal]} \quad (47)$$

$$w_j = m_j \wedge \textstyle\bigvee_{\{i,j,k\}\in L}(x_i \wedge x_k); \qquad \text{[moving in cell } j \text{ wins]} \quad (48)$$

$$b_j = m_j \wedge \textstyle\bigvee_{\{i,j,k\}\in L}(o_i \wedge o_k); \qquad \text{[moving in cell } j \text{ blocks]} \quad (49)$$

$$f_j = m_j \wedge S_2\big(\{\alpha_{ik} \mid \{i,j,k\} \in L\}\big); \qquad \text{[moving in cell } j \text{ forks]} \quad (50)$$

$$d_j = m_j \wedge S_2\big(\{\beta_{ik} \mid \{i,j,k\} \in L\}\big); \qquad \text{[moving in cell } j \text{ defends]} \quad (51)$$

here α_{ik} and β_{ik} denote a single ✗ or ○ together with a blank, namely

$$\alpha_{ik} = (x_i \wedge m_k) \vee (m_i \wedge x_k), \qquad \beta_{ik} = (o_i \wedge m_k) \vee (m_i \wedge o_k). \quad (52)$$

For example, $b_1 = m_1 \wedge \big((o_2 \wedge o_3) \vee (o_4 \wedge o_7) \vee (o_5 \wedge o_9)\big)$; $f_2 = m_2 \wedge S_2(\alpha_{13}, \alpha_{58}) = m_2 \wedge \alpha_{13} \wedge \alpha_{58}$; $d_5 = m_5 \wedge S_2(\beta_{19}, \beta_{28}, \beta_{37}, \beta_{46})$.

With these definitions we might try rank-ordering our moves thus:

$$\{w_1,\ldots,w_9\} > \{b_1,\ldots,b_9\} > \{f_1,\ldots,f_9\} > \{d_1,\ldots,d_9\} > \{m_1,\ldots,m_9\}. \quad (53)$$

"Win if you can; otherwise block if you can; otherwise fork if you can; otherwise
defend if you can; otherwise make a legal move." Furthermore, when choosing

between legal moves it seems sensible to use the ordering

$$m_5 > m_1 > m_3 > m_9 > m_7 > m_2 > m_6 > m_8 > m_4, \qquad (54)$$

because 5, the middle cell, occurs in four winning lines, while a corner move to 1, 3, 9, or 7 occurs in three, and a side cell 2, 6, 8, or 4 occurs in only two. We might as well adopt this ordering of subscripts within all five groups of moves $\{w_j\}$, $\{b_j\}$, $\{f_j\}$, $\{d_j\}$, and $\{m_j\}$ in (53).

To ensure that at most one move is chosen, we define w_j', b_j', f_j', d_j', m_j' to mean "a prior choice is better." Thus, $w_5' = 0$, $w_1' = w_5$, $w_3' = w_1 \lor w_1'$, ..., $w_4' = w_8 \lor w_8'$, $b_5' = w_4 \lor w_4'$, $b_1' = b_5 \lor b_5'$, ..., $m_4' = m_8 \lor m_8'$. Then we can complete the definition of a tic-tac-toe automaton by letting

$$y_j = (w_j \wedge \overline{w_j'}) \lor (b_j \wedge \overline{b_j'}) \lor (f_j \wedge \overline{f_j'}) \lor (d_j \wedge \overline{d_j'}) \lor (m_j \wedge \overline{m_j'}), \quad \text{for } 1 \le j \le 9. \quad (55)$$

So we've constructed 9 gates for the m's, 48 for the w's, 48 for the b's, 144 for the α's and β's, 35 for the f's (with the help of Fig. 9), 35 for the d's, 43 for the primed variables, and 80 for the y's. Furthermore we can use our knowledge of partial 4-variable functions to reduce the six operations in (52) to only four,

$$\alpha_{ik} = (x_i \oplus x_k) \lor \overline{(o_i \oplus o_k)}, \qquad \beta_{ik} = \overline{(x_i \oplus x_k)} \lor (o_i \oplus o_k). \quad (56)$$

This trick saves 48 gates; so our design has cost 396 gates altogether.

The strategy for tic-tac-toe in (47)–(56) works fine in most cases, but it also has some glaring glitches. For example, it loses ignominiously in the game

$\qquad (57)$

the second X move is d_3, defending against a fork by O, yet it actually forces O to fork in the opposite corner! Another failure arises, for example, after position , when move m_5 leads to the cat's game , instead of to the victory for X that appeared in (46). Exercise 65 patches things up and obtains a fully correct Boolean tic-tac-toe player that needs just 445 gates.

*Functional decomposition. If the function $f(x_1, \ldots, x_n)$ can be written in the form $g(x_1, \ldots, x_k, h(x_{k+1}, \ldots, x_n))$, it's usually a good idea to evaluate $y = h(x_{k+1}, \ldots, x_n)$ first and then to compute $g(x_1, \ldots, x_k, y)$. Robert L. Ashenhurst inaugurated the study of such decompositions in 1952 [see *Annals Computation Lab. Harvard University* **29** (1957), 74–116], and observed that there's an easy way to recognize when f has this special property: If we write the truth table for f in a $2^k \times 2^{n-k}$ array as in (36), with rows for each setting of $x_1 \ldots x_k$ and columns for each setting of $x_{k+1} \ldots x_n$, then the desired subfunctions g and h exist if and only if the columns of this array have at most two different values. For example, the truth table for the function $\langle x_1 x_2 \langle x_3 x_4 x_5 \rangle \rangle$ is

$$
\begin{array}{cccccccc}
0 & 0 & 0 & 0 & 0 & 0 & 0 & 0 \\
0 & 0 & 0 & 1 & 0 & 1 & 1 & 1 \\
0 & 0 & 0 & 1 & 0 & 1 & 1 & 1 \\
1 & 1 & 1 & 1 & 1 & 1 & 1 & 1
\end{array}
$$

when expressed in this two-dimensional form. One type of column corresponds to the case $h(x_{k+1}, \ldots, x_n) = 0$; the other corresponds to $h(x_{k+1}, \ldots, x_n) = 1$.

In general the variables $X = \{x_1, \ldots, x_n\}$ might be partitioned into any two disjoint subsets $Y = \{y_1, \ldots, y_k\}$ and $Z = \{z_1, \ldots, z_{n-k}\}$, and we might have $f(x) = g(y, h(z))$. We could test for a (Y, Z) decomposition by looking at the columns of the $2^k \times 2^{n-k}$ truth table whose rows correspond to values of y. But there are 2^n such ways to partition X; and all of them are potential winners, except for trivial cases when $|Y| = 0$ or $|Z| \leq 1$. How can we avoid examining such a humungous number of possibilities?

A practical way to proceed was discovered by V. Y.-S. Shen, A. C. McKellar, and P. Weiner [*IEEE Transactions* **C-20** (1971), 304–309], whose method usually needs only $O(n^2)$ steps to identify any potentially useful partition (Y, Z) that may exist. The basic idea is simple: Suppose $x_i \in Z$, $x_j \in Z$, and $x_m \in Y$. Define eight binary vectors δ_l for $l = (l_1 l_2 l_3)_2$, where δ_l has (l_1, l_2, l_3) respectively in components (i, j, m), and zeros elsewhere. Consider any randomly chosen vector $x = x_1 \ldots x_n$, and evaluate $f_l = f(x \oplus \delta_l)$ for $0 \leq l \leq 7$. Then the four pairs

$$\begin{pmatrix} f_0 \\ f_1 \end{pmatrix} \quad \begin{pmatrix} f_2 \\ f_3 \end{pmatrix} \quad \begin{pmatrix} f_4 \\ f_5 \end{pmatrix} \quad \begin{pmatrix} f_6 \\ f_7 \end{pmatrix} \tag{58}$$

will appear in a 2×4 submatrix of the $2^k \times 2^{n-k}$ truth table. So a decomposition is impossible if these pairs are distinct, or if they contain three different values.

Let's call the pairs "good" if they're all equal, or if they have only two different values. Otherwise they're "bad." If f has essentially random behavior, we'll soon find bad pairs if we do this experiment with several different randomly chosen vectors x, because only 88 of the 256 possibilities for $f_0 f_1 \ldots f_7$ correspond to a good set of pairs; the probability of finding good pairs ten times in a row is only $(\frac{88}{256})^{10} \approx .00002$. And when we do discover bad pairs, we can conclude that

$$x_i \in Z \quad \text{and} \quad x_j \in Z \implies x_m \in Z, \tag{59}$$

because the alternative $x_m \in Y$ is impossible.

Suppose, for example, that $n = 9$ and that f is the function whose truth table $11001001000011 \ldots 00101$ consists of the 512 most significant bits of π, in binary notation. (This is the "more-or-less random function" that we studied for $n = 4$ in (5) and (6) above.) Bad pairs for this π function are quickly found in each of the cases (i, j, m) for which $m \neq i < j \neq m$. Indeed, in the author's experiments, 170 of those 252 cases were decided immediately; the average number of random x vectors per case was only 1.52; and only one case needed as many as eight x's before bad pairs appeared. Thus (59) holds for all relevant (i, j, m), and the function is clearly indecomposable. In fact, exercise 73 points out that we needn't make 252 tests to establish the indecomposability of this π function; only $\binom{n}{2} = 36$ of them would have been sufficient.

Turning to a less random function, let $f(x_1, \ldots, x_9) = (\det X) \bmod 2$, where

$$X = \begin{pmatrix} x_1 & x_2 & x_3 \\ x_4 & x_5 & x_6 \\ x_7 & x_8 & x_9 \end{pmatrix}. \tag{60}$$

This function does not satisfy condition (59) when $i = 1$, $j = 2$, and $m = 3$, because there are no bad pairs in that case. But it does satisfy (59) for $4 \le m \le 9$ when $\{i, j\} = \{1, 2\}$. We can denote this behavior by the convenient abbreviation '$12 \Rightarrow 456789$'; the full set of implications, for all pairs $\{i, j\}$, is

$12 \Rightarrow 456789$	$18 \Rightarrow 34569$	$27 \Rightarrow 34569$	$37 \Rightarrow 24568$	$48 \Rightarrow 12369$	$67 \Rightarrow 12358$
$13 \Rightarrow 456789$	$19 \Rightarrow 24568$	$28 \Rightarrow 134679$	$38 \Rightarrow 14567$	$49 \Rightarrow 12358$	$68 \Rightarrow 12347$
$14 \Rightarrow 235689$	$23 \Rightarrow 456789$	$29 \Rightarrow 14567$	$39 \Rightarrow 124578$	$56 \Rightarrow 123789$	$69 \Rightarrow 124578$
$15 \Rightarrow 36789$	$24 \Rightarrow 36789$	$34 \Rightarrow 25789$	$45 \Rightarrow 123789$	$57 \Rightarrow 12369$	$78 \Rightarrow 123456$
$16 \Rightarrow 25789$	$25 \Rightarrow 134679$	$35 \Rightarrow 14789$	$46 \Rightarrow 123789$	$58 \Rightarrow 134679$	$79 \Rightarrow 123456$
$17 \Rightarrow 235689$	$26 \Rightarrow 14789$	$36 \Rightarrow 124578$	$47 \Rightarrow 235689$	$59 \Rightarrow 12347$	$89 \Rightarrow 123456$

(see exercise 69). Bad pairs are a little more difficult to find when we probe this function at random: The average number of x's needed in the author's experiments rose to about 3.6, when bad pairs did exist. And of course there was a need to limit the testing, by choosing a tolerance threshold t and then giving up when t consecutive trials failed to find any bad pairs. Choosing $t = 10$ would have found all but 8 of the 198 implications listed above.

Implications like (59) are Horn clauses, and we know from Section 7.1.1 that it's easy to make further deductions from Horn clauses. Indeed, the method of exercise 74 will deduce that the only possible partition with $|Z| > 1$ is the trivial one $(Y = \emptyset, Z = \{x_1, \ldots, x_9\})$, after looking at fewer than 50 cases (i, j, m).

Similar results occur when $f(x_1, \ldots, x_9) = [\mathrm{per}\, X > 0]$, where per denotes the *permanent* function. (In this case f tells us if there is a perfect matching in the bipartite subgraph of $K_{3,3}$ whose edges are specified by the variables $x_1 \ldots x_9$.) Now there are just 180 implications,

$12 \Rightarrow 456789$	$18 \Rightarrow 3459$	$27 \Rightarrow 3459$	$37 \Rightarrow 2468$	$48 \Rightarrow 1269$	$67 \Rightarrow 1358$
$13 \Rightarrow 456789$	$19 \Rightarrow 2468$	$28 \Rightarrow 134679$	$38 \Rightarrow 1567$	$49 \Rightarrow 1358$	$68 \Rightarrow 2347$
$14 \Rightarrow 235689$	$23 \Rightarrow 456789$	$29 \Rightarrow 1567$	$39 \Rightarrow 124578$	$56 \Rightarrow 123789$	$69 \Rightarrow 124578$
$15 \Rightarrow 3678$	$24 \Rightarrow 3678$	$34 \Rightarrow 2579$	$45 \Rightarrow 123789$	$57 \Rightarrow 1269$	$78 \Rightarrow 123456$
$16 \Rightarrow 2579$	$25 \Rightarrow 134679$	$35 \Rightarrow 1489$	$46 \Rightarrow 123789$	$58 \Rightarrow 134679$	$79 \Rightarrow 123456$
$17 \Rightarrow 235689$	$26 \Rightarrow 1489$	$36 \Rightarrow 124578$	$47 \Rightarrow 235689$	$59 \Rightarrow 2347$	$89 \Rightarrow 123456$,

only 122 of which would have been discovered with $t = 10$ as the cutoff threshold. (The best choice of t is not clear; perhaps it should vary dynamically.) Still, those 122 Horn clauses were more than enough to establish indecomposability.

What about a decomposable function? With $f = \langle x_2 x_3 x_6 x_9 \langle x_1 x_4 x_5 x_7 x_8 \rangle \rangle$ we get $i \wedge j \Rightarrow m$ for all $m \notin \{i, j\}$, except when $\{i, j\} \subseteq \{1, 4, 5, 7, 8\}$; in the latter case, m must also belong to $\{1, 4, 5, 7, 8\}$. Although only 185 of these 212 implications were discovered with tolerance $t = 10$, the partition $Y = \{x_2, x_3, x_6, x_9\}$, $Z = \{x_1, x_4, x_5, x_7, x_8\}$ emerged quickly as a strong possibility.

Whenever a potential decomposition is supported by the evidence, we need to verify that the corresponding $2^k \times 2^{n-k}$ truth table does indeed have only one or two distinct columns. But we're happy to spend 2^n units of time on that verification, because we've greatly simplified the evaluation of f.

The comparison function $f = \left\lceil (x_1 x_2 x_3 x_4)_2 \geq (x_5 x_6 x_7 x_8)_2 + x_9 \right\rceil$ is another interesting case. Its 184 potentially deducible implications are

$12 \Rightarrow 3456789$	$18 \Rightarrow 2345679$	$27 \Rightarrow 34689$	$37 \Rightarrow 489$	$48 \Rightarrow 9$	$67 \Rightarrow 23489$
$13 \Rightarrow 2456789$	$19 \Rightarrow 2345678$	$28 \Rightarrow 34679$	$38 \Rightarrow 479$	$49 \Rightarrow 8$	$68 \Rightarrow 23479$
$14 \Rightarrow 2356789$	$23 \Rightarrow 46789$	$29 \Rightarrow 34678$	$39 \Rightarrow 478$	$56 \Rightarrow 1234789$	$69 \Rightarrow 23478$
$15 \Rightarrow 2346789$	$24 \Rightarrow 36789$	$34 \Rightarrow 789$	$45 \Rightarrow 1236789$	$57 \Rightarrow 1234689$	$78 \Rightarrow 349$
$16 \Rightarrow 2345789$	$25 \Rightarrow 1346789$	$35 \Rightarrow 1246789$	$46 \Rightarrow 23789$	$58 \Rightarrow 1234679$	$79 \Rightarrow 348$
$17 \Rightarrow 2345689$	$26 \Rightarrow 34789$	$36 \Rightarrow 24789$	$47 \Rightarrow 389$	$59 \Rightarrow 1234678$	$89 \Rightarrow 4,$

and 145 of them were found when $t = 10$. Three decompositions reveal themselves in this case, having $Z = \{x_4, x_8, x_9\}$, $Z = \{x_3, x_4, x_7, x_8, x_9\}$, and $Z = \{x_2, x_3, x_4, x_6, x_7, x_8, x_9\}$, respectively. Ashenhurst proved that we can reduce f immediately as soon as we find a nontrivial decomposition; the other decompositions will show up later, when we try to reduce the simpler functions g and h.

*Decomposition of partial functions. When the function f is only partially specified, a decomposition with partition (Y, Z) hinges on being able to assign values to the don't-cares so that at most two different columns appear in the corresponding $2^k \times 2^{n-k}$ truth table.

Two vectors $u_1 \ldots u_m$ and $v_1 \ldots v_m$ consisting of 0s, 1s, and $*$s are said to be *incompatible* if either $u_j = 0$ and $v_j = 1$ or $u_j = 1$ and $v_j = 0$, for some j — equivalently, if the subcubes of the m-cube specified by u and v have no points in common. Consider the graph whose vertices are the columns of a truth table with don't-cares, where $u \longrightarrow v$ if and only if u and v are incompatible. We can assign values to the $*$s to achieve at most two distinct columns if and only if this graph is *bipartite*. For if $u_1, \ldots, u_l$ are mutually compatible, their generalized consensus $u_1 \sqcup \cdots \sqcup u_l$, defined in exercise 7.1.1–32, is compatible with all of them. [See S. L. Hight, *IEEE Trans.* **C-22** (1973), 103–110; E. Boros, V. Gurvich, P. L. Hammer, T. Ibaraki, and A. Kogan, *Discrete Applied Math.* **62** (1995), 51–75.] Since a graph is bipartite if and only if it contains no odd cycles, we can easily test this condition with a depth-first search (see Section 7.4.1).

Consequently the method of Shen, McKellar, and Weiner works also when don't-cares are present: The four pairs in (58) are considered bad if and only if three of them are mutually incompatible. We can operate almost as before, although bad pairs will naturally be harder to find when there are lots of $*$s (see exercise 72). However, Ashenhurst's theorem no longer applies. When several decompositions exist, they all should be explored further, because they might use different settings of the don't-cares, and some might be better than the others.

Although most functions $f(x)$ have no simple decomposition $g(y, h(z))$, we needn't give up hope too quickly, because other forms like $g(y, h_1(z), h_2(z))$ might well lead to an efficient chain. If, for example, f is symmetric in three of its variables $\{z_1, z_2, z_3\}$, we can always write $f(x) = g\big(y, S_{1,2}(z_1, z_2, z_3), S_{1,3}(z_1, z_2, z_3)\big)$, since $S_{1,2}(z_1, z_2, z_3)$ and $S_{1,3}(z_1, z_2, z_3)$ characterize the value of $z_1 + z_2 + z_3$. (Notice that just four steps will suffice to compute both $S_{1,2}$ and $S_{1,3}$.)

In general, as observed by H. A. Curtis [*JACM* **8** (1961), 484–496], $f(x)$ can be expressed in the form $g(y, h_1(z), \ldots, h_r(z))$ if and only if the $2^k \times 2^{n-k}$ truth table corresponding to Y and Z has at most 2^r different columns. And when don't-cares are present, the same result holds if and only if the incompatibility graph for Y and Z can be colored with at most 2^r colors.

For example, the function $f(x) = (\det X) \bmod 2$ considered above turns out to have eight distinct columns when $Z = \{x_4, x_5, x_6, x_7, x_8, x_9\}$; that's a surprisingly small number, considering that the truth table has 8 rows and 64 columns. From this fact we might be led to discover how to expand a determinant by cofactors of the first row,

$$f(x) = x_1 \wedge h_1(x_4, \ldots, x_9) \oplus x_2 \wedge h_2(x_4, \ldots, x_9) \oplus x_3 \wedge h_3(x_4, \ldots, x_9),$$

if we didn't already know such a rule.

When there are $d \leq 2^r$ different columns, we can think of $f(x)$ as a function of y and $h(z)$, where h takes each binary vector $z_1 \ldots z_{n-k}$ into one of the values $\{0, 1, \ldots, d-1\}$. Thus $(h_1, \ldots, h_r)$ is essentially an encoding of the different column types, and we hope to find very simple functions $h_1, \ldots, h_r$ that provide such an encoding. Moreover, if d is strictly less than 2^r, the function $g(y, h_1, \ldots, h_r)$ will have many don't-cares that may well decrease its cost.

The distinct columns might also suggest a function g for which the h's have don't-cares. For example, we can use $g(y_1, y_2, h_1, h_2) = (y_1 \oplus (h_1 \wedge y_2)) \wedge h_2$ when all columns are either $(0, 0, 0, 0)^T$ or $(0, 0, 1, 1)^T$ or $(0, 1, 1, 0)^T$; then the value of $h_1(z)$ is arbitrary when z corresponds to an all-zero column. H. A. Curtis has explained how to exploit this idea when $|Y| = 1$ and $|Z| = n - 1$ [see *IEEE Transactions* **C-25** (1976), 1033–1044].

For a comprehensive discussion of decomposition techniques, see Richard M. Karp, *J. Society for Industrial and Applied Math.* **11** (1963), 291–335.

Larger values of n. We've been considering only rather tiny examples of Boolean functions. Theorem S tells us that large, random examples are inherently difficult; but practical examples might well be highly nonrandom. So it makes sense to search for simplifications using heuristic methods.

When n grows, the best ways currently known for dealing with Boolean functions generally start with a Boolean chain — not with a huge truth table — and they try to improve that chain via "local changes." The chain can be specified by a set of equations. Then, if an intermediate result is used in comparatively few subsequent steps, we can try to eliminate it, temporarily making those subsequent steps into functions of three variables, and reformulating those functions in order to make a better chain when possible.

For example, suppose the gate $x_i = x_j \circ x_k$ is used only once, in the gate $x_l = x_i \mathbin{\square} x_m$, so that $x_l = (x_j \circ x_k) \mathbin{\square} x_m$. Other gates might already exist, by which we have computed other functions of x_j, x_k, and x_m; and the definitions of x_j, x_k, and x_m may imply that some of the joint values of (x_j, x_k, x_m) are impossible. Thus we might be able to compute x_l from other gates by doing just one further operation. For example, if $x_i = x_j \wedge x_k$ and $x_l = x_i \vee x_m$, and if the values $x_j \vee x_m$ and $x_k \vee x_m$ appear elsewhere in the chain, we can set $x_l = (x_j \vee x_m) \wedge (x_k \vee x_m)$; this eliminates x_i and reduces the cost by 1. Or if, say, $x_j \wedge (x_k \oplus x_m)$ appears elsewhere and we know that $x_j x_k x_m \neq 101$, we can set $x_l = x_m \oplus (x_j \wedge (x_k \oplus x_m))$.

If x_i is used only in x_l and x_l is used only in x_p, then gate x_p depends on four variables, and we might be able to reduce the cost by using our total knowledge of four-variable functions, obtaining x_p in a better way while eliminating x_i and x_l. Similarly, if x_i appears only in x_l and x_p, we can eliminate x_i if we find a better way to evaluate two different functions of four variables, possibly with don't-cares and with other functions of those four variables available for free. Again, we know how to solve such problems, using the footprint method discussed above.

When no local changes are able to decrease the cost, we can also try local changes that preserve or even increase the cost, in order to discover different kinds of chains that might simplify in other ways. We shall discuss such local search methods extensively in Section 7.10.

Excellent surveys of techniques for Boolean optimization, which electrical engineers call the problem of "multilevel logic synthesis," have been published by R. K. Brayton, G. D. Hachtel, and A. L. Sangiovanni-Vincentelli, *Proceedings of the IEEE* **78** (1990), 264–300, and in the book *Synthesis and Optimization of Digital Circuits* by G. De Micheli (McGraw–Hill, 1994).

Lower bounds. Theorem S tells us that nearly every Boolean function of $n \geq 12$ variables is hard to evaluate, requiring a chain whose length exceeds $2^n/n$. Yet modern computers, which are built from logic circuits involving electric signals that represent thousands of Boolean variables, happily evaluate zillions of Boolean functions every microsecond. Evidently there are plenty of important functions that can be evaluated quickly, in spite of Theorem S. Indeed, the proof of that theorem was indirect; we simply counted the cases of low cost, so we learned absolutely nothing about any particular examples that might arise in practice. When we want to compute a given function and we can only think of a laborious way to do the job, how can we be sure that there's no tricky shortcut?

The answer to that question is almost scandalous: After decades of concentrated research, computer scientists have been unable to find *any* explicit family of functions $f(x_1, \ldots, x_n)$ whose cost is inherently nonlinear, as n increases. The true behavior is $2^n/n$, but no lower bound as strong as $n \log \log \log n$ has yet been proved! Of course we could rig up artificial examples, such as "the lexicographically smallest truth table of length 2^n that isn't achievable by any Boolean chain of length $\lfloor 2^n/n \rfloor - 1$"; but such functions are surely not explicit. The truth table of an explicit function $f(x_1, \ldots, x_n)$ should be computable in at most, say, 2^{cn} units of time for some constant c; that is, the time needed to specify all of the function values should be polynomial in the length of the truth table. Under those ground rules, no family of single-output functions is currently known to have a combinational complexity that exceeds $3n + O(1)$ as $n \to \infty$. [See N. Blum, *Theoretical Computer Science* **28** (1984), 337–345.]

The picture is not totally bleak, because several interesting *linear* lower bounds have been proved for functions of practical importance. A basic way to obtain such results was introduced by N. P. Red'kin in 1970: Suppose we have an optimum chain of cost r for $f(x_1, \ldots, x_n)$. By setting $x_n \leftarrow 0$ or $x_n \leftarrow 1$, we obtain reduced chains for the functions $g(x_1, \ldots, x_{n-1}) = f(x_1, \ldots, x_{n-1}, 0)$ and $h(x_1, \ldots, x_{n-1}) = f(x_1, \ldots, x_{n-1}, 1)$, having cost $r - u$ if x_n was used as an input to u different gates. Moreover, if x_n is used in a "canalizing" gate $x_i = x_n \circ x_k$, where the operator $\circ$ is neither $\oplus$ nor $\equiv$, some setting of x_n will force x_i to be constant, thereby further reducing the chain for g or h. Lower bounds on g and/or h therefore lead to a lower bound on f. (See exercises 77–81.)

But where are the proofs of nonlinear lower bounds? Almost every problem with a yes-no answer can be formulated as a Boolean function, so there's no shortage of explicit functions that we don't know how to evaluate in linear time, or even in polynomial time. For example, any directed graph G with vertices $\{v_1, \ldots, v_m\}$ can be represented by its adjacency matrix X, where $x_{ij} = [v_i \to v_j]$; then

$$f(x_{12}, \ldots, x_{1m}, \ldots, x_{m1}, \ldots, x_{m(m-1)}) = [G \text{ has a Hamiltonian path}] \quad (61)$$

is a Boolean function of $n = m(m-1)$ variables. We would dearly love to be able to evaluate this function in, say, n^4 steps. We do know how to compute the truth table for f in $O(m!\,2^n) = 2^{n+O(\sqrt{n}\,\log n)}$ steps, since only $m!$ potential Hamiltonian paths exist; thus f is indeed "explicit." But nobody knows how to evaluate f in polynomial time, or how to prove that there isn't a $4n$-step chain.

For all we know, short Boolean chains for f might exist, for each n. After all, Figs. 9 and 10 reveal the existence of fiendishly clever chains even in the cases of 4 and 5 variables. Efficient chains for all of the larger problems that we ever will need to solve might well be "out there" — yet totally beyond our grasp, because we don't have time to find them. Even if an omniscient being revealed the simple chains to us, we might find them incomprehensible, because the shortest proof of their correctness might be longer than the number of cells in our brains.

Theorem S rules out such a scenario for most Boolean functions. But fewer than 2^{100} Boolean functions will ever be of practical importance in the entire history of the world, and Theorem S tells us zilch about them.

In 1974, Larry Stockmeyer and Albert Meyer were, however, able to construct a Boolean function f whose complexity is provably huge. Their f isn't "explicit," in the precise sense described above, but it isn't artificial either; it arises naturally in mathematical logic. Consider symbolic statements such as

$$048+1015 \neq 1063 \, ; \quad (62)$$

$$\forall m \exists n\,(m{<}n{+}1) \, ; \quad (63)$$

$$\forall n \exists m\,(m{+}1{<}n) \, ; \quad (64)$$

$$\forall a \forall b\,(b{\geq}a{+}2{\to}\exists ab\,(a{<}ab{\land}ab{<}b)) \, ; \quad (65)$$

$$\forall A \forall B\,(A{\equiv}B{\leftrightarrow}\neg\exists n\,(n{\in}A{\land}n{\notin}B{\lor}n{\in}B{\land}n{\notin}A)) \, ; \quad (66)$$

$$\forall A\,(\exists n\,(n{\in}A){\to}\exists m\,(m{\in}A{\land}\forall n\,(n{\in}A{\to}m{\leq}n))) \, ; \quad (67)$$

$$\forall A\,(\exists n\,(n{\in}A){\to}\exists m\,(m{\in}A{\land}\forall n\,(n{\in}A{\to}m{\geq}n))) \, ; \quad (68)$$

$$\exists P \forall a\,((a{\in}P{\leftrightarrow}a{+}3{\notin}P){\leftrightarrow}a{<}1000) \, ; \quad (69)$$

$$\forall A \forall B\,(\forall C \forall c\,(C{\equiv}A{\land}c{=}1{\lor}C{\equiv}B{\land}c{=}0{\to}(\forall n\,(n{\in}C{\leftrightarrow}n{+}1{\in}C){\leftrightarrow}c{=}1)){\to}\neg A{\equiv}B) \, . \quad (70)$$

Stockmeyer and Meyer defined a language L by using the 63-character alphabet

∀∃¬()≡∈∉+∧∨⇸⇹<≤=≠≥>abcdefghijklmnopqABCDEFGHIJKLMNOPQ0123456789

and giving conventional meanings to these symbols. Strings of lowercase letters within the sentences of L, like 'ab' in (65), represent numeric variables, restricted to nonnegative integers; strings of uppercase letters represent set variables, restricted to finite sets of such numbers. For example, (66) means, "For all finite sets A and B, we have $A = B$ if and only if there doesn't exist a number n that is in A but not in B, or in B but not in A." Some of these statements are true; others are false. (See exercise 82.)

All of the strings (62)–(70) belong to L, but the language is actually quite restricted: The only arithmetic operation allowed on a number is to add a constant; we can write 'a+13' but not 'a+b'. The only relation allowed between a number and a set is elementhood ($\in$ or $\notin$). The only relation allowed between sets is equality ($\equiv$). Furthermore all variables must be quantified by $\exists$ or $\forall$.*

Every sentence of L that has length $k \leq n$ can be represented by a binary vector of length $6n$, with zeros in the last $6(n-k)$ bits. Let $f(x)$ be a Boolean function of $6n$ variables such that $f(x) = 1$ whenever x represents a true sentence of L, and $f(x) = 0$ whenever x represents a sentence that is false; the value of $f(x)$ is unspecified when x doesn't represent a meaningful sentence. The truth table for such a function f can be constructed in a finite number of steps, according to theorems of Büchi and Elgot [*Zeitschrift für math. Logik und Grundlagen der Math.* **6** (1960), 66–92; *Transactions of the Amer. Math. Soc.* **98** (1961), 21–51]. But "finite" does not mean "feasible": Stockmeyer and Meyer proved that

$$C(f) > 2^{r-5} \qquad \text{whenever } n \geq 460 + .302r + 5.08 \ln r \text{ and } r > 36. \qquad (71)$$

In particular, we have $C(f) > 2^{426} > 10^{128}$ when $n = 621$. *A Boolean chain with that many gates could never be built*, since 10^{128} is a generous upper bound on the number of protons in the universe. So this is a fairly small, finite problem that will never be solved.

Details of Stockmeyer and Meyer's proof appear in *JACM* **49** (2002), 753–784. The basic idea is that the language L, though limited, is rich enough to describe truth tables and the complexity of Boolean chains, using fairly short sentences; hence f has to deal with inputs that essentially refer to themselves.

*For further reading. Thousands of significant papers have been written about networks of Boolean gates, because such networks underlie so many aspects of theory and practice. We have focused in this section chiefly on topics that are relevant to computer programming for sequential machines. But other topics have also been extensively investigated, of primary relevance to parallel computation, such as the study of small-depth circuits in which gates can have any number of inputs ("unlimited fan-in"). Ingo Wegener's book *The Complexity of*

---

* Technically speaking, the sentences of L belong to "weak second-order monadic logic with one successor." Weak second-order logic allows quantification over finite sets; monadic logic with k successors is the theory of unlabeled k-ary trees.

Boolean Functions (Teubner and Wiley, 1987) provides a good introduction to the entire subject.

We have mostly considered Boolean chains in which all binary operators have equal importance. For our purposes, gates such as $\oplus$ or $\overline{\subset}$ are neither more nor less desirable than gates such as $\wedge$ or $\vee$. But it's natural to wonder if we can get by with only the monotone operators $\wedge$ and $\vee$ when we are computing a monotone function. Alexander Razborov has developed striking proof techniques to show that, in fact, monotone operators by themselves have inherently limited capabilities. He proved, for example, that all AND-OR chains to determine whether the permanent of an $n \times n$ matrix of 0s and 1s is zero or nonzero must have cost $n^{\Omega(\log n)}$. [See *Doklady Akademii Nauk SSSR* **281** (1985), 798–801; *Matematicheskie Zametki* **37** (1985), 887–900.] By contrast, we will see in Section 7.5.1 that this problem, equivalent to "bipartite matching," is solvable in only $O(n^{2.5})$ steps. Furthermore, the efficient methods in that section can be implemented as Boolean chains of only slightly larger cost, when we allow negation or other Boolean operations in addition to $\wedge$ and $\vee$. (Vaughan Pratt has called this "the power of negative thinking.") An introduction to Razborov's methods appears in exercises 85 and 86.

EXERCISES

1. [*24*] The "random" function in formula (6) corresponds to a Boolean chain of cost 4 and depth 4. Find a formula of depth 3 that has the same cost.

2. [*21*] Show how to compute (a) $w \oplus \langle xyz \rangle$ and (b) $w \wedge \langle xyz \rangle$ with formulas that have depth 3 and cost 5.

3. [*M23*] (B. I. Finikov, 1957.) If the Boolean function $f(x_1, \ldots, x_n)$ is true at exactly k points, prove that $L(f) < 2n + (k-2)2^{k-1}$. *Hint:* Think of $k = 3$ and $n = 10^6$.

4. [*M28*] Prove that the minimum depth and formula length of a Boolean function satisfy $\lg L(f) < D(f) \le \alpha \lg L(f)$ when $L(f) > 1$, where $\alpha = 1/\lg \chi \approx 2.464965$ is related to the "plastic constant" χ of Eq. 7.1.4–(90). *Hint:* If f contains a subformula g, we have $f = g$? f_1: f_0 for suitable f_1 and f_0.

▶ **5.** [*21*] The Fibonacci threshold function $F_n(x_1, \ldots, x_n) = \langle x_1^{F_1} x_2^{F_2} \ldots x_{n-1}^{F_{n-1}} x_n^{F_{n-2}} \rangle$ was analyzed in exercise 7.1.1–101, when $n \ge 3$. Is there an efficient way to evaluate it?

6. [*20*] True or false: A Boolean function $f(x_1, \ldots, x_n)$ is normal if and only if it satisfies the general distributive law $f(x_1, \ldots, x_n) \wedge y = f(x_1 \wedge y, \ldots, x_n \wedge y)$.

7. [*20*] Convert the Boolean chain '$x_5 = x_1 \,\overline{\vee}\, x_4$, $x_6 = \bar{x}_2 \vee x_5$, $x_7 = \bar{x}_1 \wedge \bar{x}_3$, $x_8 = x_6 \equiv x_7$' to an equivalent chain $(\hat{x}_5, \hat{x}_6, \hat{x}_7, \hat{x}_8)$ in which every step is normal.

▶ **8.** [*20*] Explain why (11) is the truth table of variable x_k.

9. [*20*] Algorithm L determines the lengths of shortest formulas for all functions f, but it gives no further information. Extend the algorithm so that it also provides actual minimum-length formulas like (6).

▶ **10.** [*20*] Modify Algorithm L so that it computes $D(f)$ instead of $L(f)$.

▶ **11.** [*22*] Modify Algorithm L so that, instead of lengths $L(f)$, it computes upper bounds $U(f)$ and footprints $\phi(f)$ as described in the text.

12. [*15*] What Boolean chain is equivalent to the minimum-memory scheme (13)?

13. [*16*] What are the truth tables of f_1, f_2, f_3, f_4, and f_5 in example (13)?

14. [*22*] What's a convenient way to compute the $5n(n-1)$ truth tables of (17), given the truth table of g? (Use bitwise operations as in (15) and (16).)

15. [*28*] Find short-as-possible ways to evaluate the following Boolean functions using minimum memory: (a) $S_1(x_1, x_2, x_3)$; (b) $S_2(x_1, x_2, x_3, x_4)$; (c) $S_1(x_1, x_2, x_3, x_4)$; (d) the function in (18).

16. [*HM33*] Prove that fewer than 2^{118} of the 2^{128} Boolean functions $f(x_1, \ldots, x_7)$ are computable in minimum memory.

▶ **17.** [*25*] (M. S. Paterson, 1977.) Although Boolean functions $f(x_1, \ldots, x_n)$ cannot always be evaluated in n registers, prove that $n+1$ registers are always sufficient. In other words, show that there is always a sequence of operations like (13) to compute $f(x_1, \ldots, x_n)$ if we allow $0 \le j(i), k(i) \le n$.

▶ **18.** [*35*] Investigate optimum minimum-memory computations for $f(x_1, x_2, x_3, x_4, x_5)$: How many classes of five-variable functions have $C_m(f) = r$, for $r = 0, 1, 2, \ldots$?

19. [*M22*] If a Boolean chain uses n variables and has length $r < n+2$, prove that it must be either a "top-down" or a "bottom-up" construction.

▶ **20.** [*40*] (R. Schroeppel, 2004.) A Boolean chain is *canalizing* if it does not use the operators $\oplus$ or $\equiv$. Find the optimum cost, length, and depth of all 4-variable functions under this constraint. Does the footprint heuristic still give optimum results?

21. [*46*] For how many four-variable functions did the Harvard researchers discover an optimum vacuum-tube circuit in 1951?

22. [*21*] Explain the chain for S_3 in Fig. 10, by noting that it incorporates the chain for $S_{2,3}$ in Fig. 9. Find a similar chain for $S_2(x_1, x_2, x_3, x_4, x_5)$.

▶ **23.** [*23*] Figure 10 illustrates only 16 of the 64 symmetric functions on five elements. Explain how to write down optimum chains for the others.

24. [*47*] Does every symmetric function f have $C_m(f) = C(f)$?

▶ **25.** [*17*] Suppose we want a Boolean chain that includes *all* functions of n variables: Let $f_k(x_1, \ldots, x_n)$ be the function whose truth table is the binary representation of k, for $0 \le k < m = 2^{2^n}$. What is $C(f_0 f_1 \ldots f_{m-1})$?

26. [*25*] True or false: If $f(x_0, \ldots, x_n) = (x_0 \wedge g(x_1, \ldots, x_n)) \oplus h(x_1, \ldots, x_n)$, where g and h are nontrivial Boolean functions whose joint cost is $C(gh)$, then $C(f) = 2 + C(gh)$.

▶ **27.** [*23*] Can a full adder (22) be implemented in five steps using only minimum memory (that is, completely inside three one-bit registers)?

28. [*26*] Prove that $C(u'v') = C(u''v'') = 5$ for the two-output functions defined by

$$(u'v')_2 = (x + y - (uv)_2) \bmod 4, \qquad (u''v'')_2 = (-x - y - (uv)_2) \bmod 4.$$

Use these functions to evaluate $[(x_1 + \cdots + x_n) \bmod 4 = 0]$ in fewer than $2.5n$ steps.

29. [*M28*] Prove that the text's circuit for sideways addition (27) has depth $O(\log n)$.

30. [*M25*] Solve the binary recurrence (28) for the cost $s(n)$ of sideways addition.

31. [*21*] If $f(x_1, \ldots, x_n)$ is symmetric, prove that $C(f) \le 5n + O(n/\log n)$.

32. [*HM16*] Why does the solution to (30) satisfy $t(n) = 2^n + O(2^{n/2})$?

33. [*HM22*] True or false: If $1 \le N \le 2^n$, the first N minterms of $\{x_1, \ldots, x_n\}$ can all be evaluated in $N + O(\sqrt{N})$ steps, as $n \to \infty$ and $N \to \infty$.

▶ **34.** [*22*] A *priority encoder* has $n = 2^m - 1$ inputs $x_1 \ldots x_n$ and m outputs $y_1 \ldots y_m$, where $(y_1 \ldots y_m)_2 = k$ if and only if $k = \max\{j \mid j = 0 \text{ or } x_j = 1\}$. Design a priority encoder that has cost $O(n)$ and depth $O(m)$.

35. [*23*] If $n > 1$, show that the conjunctions $x_1 \wedge \cdots \wedge x_{k-1} \wedge x_{k+1} \wedge \cdots \wedge x_n$ for $1 \le k \le n$ can all be computed from $(x_1, \ldots, x_n)$ with total cost $\le 3n - 6$.

▶ **36.** [*M28*] (R. E. Ladner and M. J. Fischer, 1980.) Let y_k be the "prefix" $x_1 \wedge \cdots \wedge x_k$ for $1 \le k \le n$. Clearly $C(y_1 \ldots y_n) = n - 1$ and $D(y_1 \ldots y_n) = \lceil \lg n \rceil$; but we can't simultaneously minimize both cost and depth. Find a chain of optimum depth $\lceil \lg n \rceil$ that has cost $< 4n$.

37. [*M28*] (Marc Snir, 1986.) Given $n \ge m \ge 1$, consider the following algorithm:

S1. [Upward loop.] For $t \leftarrow 1, 2, \ldots, \lceil \lg m \rceil$, set $x_{\min(m, 2^t k)} \leftarrow x_{2^t(k-1/2)} \wedge x_{\min(m, 2^t k)}$ for $k \ge 1$ and $2^t(k - 1/2) < m$.

S2. [Downward loop.] For $t \leftarrow \lceil \lg m \rceil - 1, \lceil \lg m \rceil - 2, \ldots, 1$, set $x_{2^t(k+1/2)} \leftarrow x_{2^t k} \wedge x_{2^t(k+1/2)}$ for $k \ge 1$ and $2^t(k + 1/2) < m$.

S3. [Extension.] For $k \leftarrow m + 1, m + 2, \ldots, n$, set $x_k \leftarrow x_{k-1} \wedge x_k$. ▮

a) Prove that this algorithm solves the prefix problem of exercise 36: It transforms $(x_1, x_2, \ldots, x_n)$ into $(x_1, x_1 \wedge x_2, \ldots, x_1 \wedge x_2 \wedge \cdots \wedge x_n)$.
b) Let $c(m, n)$ and $d(m, n)$ be the cost and depth of the corresponding Boolean chain. Prove for fixed m that, if n is sufficiently large, $c(m, n) + d(m, n) = 2n - 2$.
c) Given $n > 1$, what is $d(n) = \min_{1 \le m \le n} d(m, n)$? Show that $d(n) < 2 \lg n$.
d) Prove that there's a Boolean chain of cost $2n - 2 - d$ and depth d for the prefix problem whenever $d(n) \le d < n$. (This cost is optimum, by exercise 81.)

38. [*25*] In Section 5.3.4 we studied *sorting networks*, by which $\hat{S}(n)$ comparator modules are able to sort n numbers $(x_1, x_2, \ldots, x_n)$ into ascending order. If the inputs x_j are 0s and 1s, each comparator module is equivalent to two gates $(x \wedge y, x \vee y)$; so a sorting network corresponds to a certain kind of Boolean chain, which evaluates n particular functions of $(x_1, x_2, \ldots, x_n)$.
a) What are the n functions $f_1 f_2 \ldots f_n$ that a sorting network computes?
b) Show that those functions $\{f_1, f_2, \ldots, f_n\}$ can be computed in $O(n)$ steps with a chain of depth $O(\log n)$. (Hence sorting networks aren't asymptotically optimal, Booleanwise.)

▶ **39.** [*M21*] (M. S. Paterson and P. Klein, 1980.) Implement the 2^m-way multiplexer $M_m(x_1, \ldots, x_m; y_0, y_1, \ldots, y_{2^m - 1})$ of (31) with an efficient chain that simultaneously establishes the upper bounds $C(M_m) \le 2n + O(\sqrt{n})$ and $D(M_m) \le m + O(\log m)$.

40. [*25*] If $n \ge k \ge 1$, let $f_{nk}(x_1, \ldots, x_n)$ be the "k in a row" function,

$$(x_1 \wedge \cdots \wedge x_k) \vee (x_2 \wedge \cdots \wedge x_{k+1}) \vee \cdots \vee (x_{n+1-k} \wedge \cdots \wedge x_n).$$

Show that the cost $C(f_{nk})$ of this function is less than $4n - 3k$.

41. [*M23*] (*Conditional-sum adders.*) One way to accomplish binary addition (25) with depth $O(\log n)$ is based on the multiplexer trick of exercise 4: If $(xx')_2 + (yy')_2 = (zz')_2$, where $|x'| = |y'| = |z'|$, we have either $(x)_2 + (y)_2 = (z)_2$ and $(x')_2 + (y')_2 = (z')_2$, or $(x)_2 + (y)_2 + 1 = (z)_2$ and $(x')_2 + (y')_2 = (1z')_2$. To save time, we can compute *both* $(x)_2 + (y)_2$ and $(x)_2 + (y)_2 + 1$ simultaneously as we compute $(x')_2 + (y')_2$. Afterwards, when we know whether or not the less significant part $(x')_2 + (y')_2$ produces a carry, we can use multiplexers to select the correct bits for the most significant part.

If this method is used recursively to build $2n$-bit adders from n-bit adders, how many gates are needed when $n = 2^m$? What is the corresponding depth?

42. [*30*] In the binary addition (25), let $u_k = x_k \wedge y_k$ and $v_k = x_k \oplus y_k$ for $0 \le k < n$.
a) Show that $z_k = v_k \oplus c_k$, where the carry bits c_k satisfy

$$c_k = u_{k-1} \vee (v_{k-1} \wedge (u_{k-2} \vee (v_{k-2} \wedge (\cdots (v_1 \wedge u_0) \cdots)))).$$

b) Let $U_k^k = 0$, $V_k^k = 1$, and $U_j^{k+1} = u_k \vee (v_k \wedge U_j^k)$, $V_j^{k+1} = v_k \wedge V_j^k$, for $k \ge j$. Prove that $c_k = U_0^k$, and that $U_i^k = U_j^k \vee (V_j^k \wedge U_i^j)$, $V_i^k = V_j^k \wedge V_i^j$ for $i \le j \le k$.

c) Let $h(m) = 2^{m(m-1)/2}$. Show that when $n = h(m)$, the carries $c_1, \ldots, c_n$ can all be evaluated with depth $(m+1)m/2 \approx \lg n + \sqrt{2 \lg n}$ and with total cost $O(2^m n)$.

▶ **43.** [*28*] A *finite-state transducer* is an abstract machine with a finite input alphabet A, a finite output alphabet B, and a finite set of internal states Q. One of those states, q_0, is called the "initial state." Given a string $\alpha = a_1 \ldots a_n$, where each $a_j \in A$, the machine computes a string $\beta = b_1 \ldots b_n$, where each $b_j \in B$, as follows:

T1. [Initialize.] Set $j \leftarrow 1$ and $q \leftarrow q_0$.

T2. [Done?] Terminate the algorithm if $j > n$.

T3. [Output b_j.] Set $b_j \leftarrow c(q, a_j)$.

T4. [Advance j.] Set $q \leftarrow d(q, a_j)$, $j \leftarrow j + 1$, and return to step T2. ∎

The machine has built-in instructions that specify $c(q, a) \in B$ and $d(q, a) \in Q$ for every state $q \in Q$ and every character $a \in A$. The purpose of this exercise is to show that, if the alphabets A and B of any finite state transducer are encoded in binary, the string β can be computed from α by a Boolean chain of size $O(n)$ and depth $O(\log n)$.
a) Consider the problem of changing a binary vector $a_1 \ldots a_n$ to $b_1 \ldots b_n$ by setting

$$b_j \leftarrow a_j \oplus [a_j = a_{j-1} = \cdots = a_{j-k} = 1 \text{ and } a_{j-k-1} = 0, \text{ where } k \ge 1 \text{ is odd}],$$

assuming that $a_0 = 0$. For example, $\alpha = 1100100100011111101101010 \mapsto \beta = 1000100100010101001001010$. Prove that this transformation can be carried out by a finite state transducer with $|A| = |B| = |Q| = 2$.
b) Suppose a finite state transducer with $|Q| = 2$ is in state q_j after reading $a_1 \ldots a_{j-1}$. Explain how to compute the sequence $q_1 \ldots q_n$ with a Boolean chain of cost $O(n)$ and depth $O(\log n)$, using the construction of Ladner and Fischer in exercise 36. (From this sequence $q_1 \ldots q_n$ it is easy to compute $b_1 \ldots b_n$, since $b_j = c(q_j, a_j)$.)
c) Apply the method of (b) to the problem in (a).

▶ **44.** [*26*] (R. E. Ladner and M. J. Fischer, 1980.) Show that the problem of binary addition (25) can be viewed as a finite state transduction. Describe the Boolean chain that results from the construction of exercise 43 when $n = 2^m$, and compare it to the conditional-sum adder of exercise 41.

45. [*HM20*] Why doesn't the proof of Theorem S simply argue that the number of ways to choose $j(i)$ and $k(i)$ so that $1 \le j(i), k(i) < i$ is $n^2(n+1)^2 \ldots (n+r-1)^2$?

▶ **46.** [*HM21*] Let $\alpha(n) = c(n, \lfloor 2^n/n \rfloor)/2^{2^n}$ be the fraction of n-variable Boolean functions $f(x_1, \ldots, x_n)$ for which $C(f) \le 2^n/n$. Prove that $\alpha(n) \to 0$ rapidly as $n \to \infty$.

47. [*M23*] Extend Theorem S to functions with n inputs and m outputs.

48. [*HM23*] Find the smallest integer $r = r(n)$ such that $(r-1)! \, 2^{2^n} \le 2^{2r+1}(n+r-1)^{2r}$, (a) exactly when $1 \le n \le 16$; (b) asymptotically when $n \to \infty$.

49. [*HM25*] Prove that, as $n \to \infty$, almost all Boolean functions $f(x_1, \ldots, x_n)$ have minimum formula length $L(f) > 2^n / \lg n - 2^{n+2}/(\lg n)^2$.

50. [*24*] What are the prime implicants and prime clauses of the prime-number function (35)? Express that function in (a) DNF (b) CNF of minimum length.

51. [*20*] What representation of the prime-number detector replaces (37), if rows of the truth table are based on $x_5 x_6$ instead of $x_1 x_2$?

52. [*23*] What choices of k and l minimize the upper bound (38) when $5 \le n \le 16$?

53. [*HM22*] Estimate (38) when $k = \lfloor 2 \lg n \rfloor$ and $l = \lceil 2^k / (n - 3 \lg n) \rceil$ and $n \to \infty$.

54. [*29*] Find a short Boolean chain to evaluate all six of the functions $f_j(x) = [x_1 x_2 x_3 x_4 \in A_j]$, where $A_1 = \{0010, 0101, 1011\}$, $A_2 = \{0001, 1111\}$, $A_3 = \{0011, 0111, 1101\}$, $A_4 = \{1001, 1111\}$, $A_5 = \{1101\}$, $A_6 = \{0101, 1011\}$. (These six functions appear in the prime-number detector (37).) Compare your chain to the minterm-first evaluation scheme of Lupanov's general method.

55. [*34*] Show that the cost of the 6-bit prime-detecting function is at most 14.

▶ **56.** [*16*] Explain why all functions with 14 or more don't-cares in Table 3 have cost 0.

57. [*19*] What seven-segment "digits" are displayed when $(x_1 x_2 x_3 x_4)_2 > 9$ in (45)?

▶ **58.** [*30*] A 4×4-bit *S-box* is a permutation of the 4-bit vectors $\{0000, 0001, \ldots, 1111\}$; such permutations are used as components of well-known cryptographic systems such as the USSR All-Union standard GOST 28147 (1989). Every 4×4-bit S-box corresponds to a sequence of four functions $f_1(x_1, x_2, x_3, x_4), \ldots, f_4(x_1, x_2, x_3, x_4)$, which transform $x_1 x_2 x_3 x_4 \mapsto f_1 f_2 f_3 f_4$.

Find all 4×4-bit S-boxes for which $C(f_1) = C(f_2) = C(f_3) = C(f_4) = 7$.

59. [*29*] One of the S-boxes satisfying the conditions of exercise 58 takes $(0, \ldots, \mathtt{f}) \mapsto (0, 6, 5, \mathtt{b}, 3, 9, \mathtt{f}, \mathtt{e}, \mathtt{c}, 4, 7, 8, \mathtt{d}, 2, \mathtt{a}, 1)$; in other words, the truth tables of (f_1, f_2, f_3, f_4) are respectively $(\mathtt{179a}, \mathtt{63e8}, \mathtt{5b26}, \mathtt{3e29})$. Find a Boolean chain that evaluates these four "maximally difficult" functions in fewer than 20 steps.

60. [*23*] (Frank Ruskey.) Suppose $z = (x+y) \bmod 3$, where $x = (x_1 x_2)_2$, $y = (y_1 y_2)_2$, $z = (z_1 z_2)_2$, and each two-bit value is required to be either 00, 01, or 10. Compute z_1 and z_2 from x_1, x_2, y_1, and y_2 in six Boolean steps.

61. [*34*] Continuing exercise 60, find a good way to compute $z = (x+y) \bmod 5$, using the three-bit values 000, 001, 010, 011, 100.

62. [*HM23*] Consider a random Boolean partial function of n variables that has $2^n c$ "cares" and $2^n d$ "don't-cares," where $c + d = 1$. Prove that the cost of almost all such partial functions exceeds $2^n c/n$.

63. [*HM35*] (L. A. Sholomov, 1969.) Continuing exercise 62, prove that all such functions have cost $\le 2^n c/n (1 + O(n^{-1} \log n))$. *Hint:* There is a set of $2^m(1+k)$ vectors $x_1 \ldots x_k$ that intersects every $(k - m)$-dimensional subcube of the k-cube.

64. [*25*] (*Magic Fifteen.*) Two players alternately select digits from 1 to 9, using no digit twice; the winner, if any, is the first to get three digits that sum to 15. What's a good strategy for playing this game?

▶ **65.** [*35*] Modify the tic-tac-toe strategy of (47)–(56) so that it always plays correctly.

66. [*20*] Criticize the moves chosen in exercise 65. Are they always optimum?

▶ **67.** [*40*] Instead of simply finding one correct move for each position in tic-tac-toe, we might prefer to find them all. In other words, given $x_1 \ldots x_9 o_1 \ldots o_9$, we could try to compute nine outputs $g_1 \ldots g_9$, where $g_j = 1$ if and only if a move into cell j is legal and minimizes X's worst-case outcome. For example, exclamation marks indicate all of the right moves for X in the following typical positions:

[tic-tac-toe board diagrams]

A machine that chooses randomly among these possibilities is more fun to play against than a machine that has only one fixed strategy.

One attractive way to solve the all-good-moves problem is to use the fact that tic-tac-toe has eight symmetries. Imagine a chip that has 18 inputs $x_1 \ldots x_9 o_1 \ldots o_9$ and three outputs (c, s, m), for "corner," "side," and "middle," with the property that the desired functions g_j can be computed by hooking together eight of the chips appropriately:

$$g_1 = c(x_1x_2x_3x_4x_5x_6x_7x_8x_9o_1o_2o_3o_4o_5o_6o_7o_8o_9)$$
$$\vee\ c(x_1x_4x_7x_2x_5x_8x_3x_6x_9o_1o_4o_7o_2o_5o_8o_3o_6o_9),$$
$$g_2 = s(x_1x_2x_3x_4x_5x_6x_7x_8x_9o_1o_2o_3o_4o_5o_6o_7o_8o_9)$$
$$\vee\ s(x_3x_2x_1x_6x_5x_4x_9x_8x_7o_3o_2o_1o_6o_5o_4o_9o_8o_7),$$
$$g_3 = c(x_3x_2x_1x_6x_5x_4x_9x_8x_7o_3o_2o_1o_6o_5o_4o_9o_8o_7)$$
$$\vee\ c(x_3x_6x_9x_2x_5x_8x_1x_4x_7o_3o_6o_9o_2o_5o_8o_1o_4o_7),$$
$$g_4 = s(x_1x_4x_7x_2x_5x_8x_3x_6x_9o_1o_4o_7o_2o_5o_8o_3o_6o_9)$$
$$\vee\ s(x_7x_4x_1x_8x_5x_2x_9x_6x_3o_7o_4o_1o_8o_5o_2o_9o_6o_3),\qquad \ldots$$
$$g_9 = c(x_9x_8x_7x_6x_5x_4x_3x_2x_1o_9o_8o_7o_6o_5o_4o_3o_2o_1)$$
$$\vee\ c(x_9x_6x_3x_8x_5x_2x_7x_4x_1o_9o_6o_3o_8o_5o_2o_7o_4o_1),$$

and g_5 is the OR of the m outputs from all eight chips.

Design the logic for such a chip, using fewer than 2000 gates.

68. [*M25*] Consider the n-bit π function $\pi_n(x_1 \ldots x_n)$, whose value is the $(x_1 \ldots x_n)_2$th bit to the right of the most significant bit in the binary representation of π. Does the method of exercise 4.3.1–39, which describes an efficient way to compute arbitrary bits of π, prove that $C(\pi_n) < 2^n/n$ for sufficiently large n?

69. [*M24*] Let the multilinear representation of f be

$$\alpha_{000} \oplus \alpha_{001}x_m \oplus \alpha_{010}x_j \oplus \alpha_{011}x_jx_m \oplus \alpha_{100}x_i \oplus \alpha_{101}x_ix_m \oplus \alpha_{110}x_ix_j \oplus \alpha_{111}x_ix_jx_m,$$

where each coefficient α_l is a function of the variables $\{x_1, \ldots, x_n\} \setminus \{x_i, x_j, x_m\}$.

a) Prove that the pairs (58) are "good" if and only if the coefficients satisfy

$$\alpha_{010}\alpha_{101} = \alpha_{011}\alpha_{100}, \quad \alpha_{101}\alpha_{110} = \alpha_{100}\alpha_{111}, \quad \text{and} \quad \alpha_{110}\alpha_{011} = \alpha_{111}\alpha_{010}.$$

b) For which values (i, j, m) are the pairs bad, when $f = (\det X) \bmod 2$? (See (60).)

▶ **70.** [*M27*] Let X be the 3×3 Boolean matrix (60). Find efficient chains for the Boolean functions (a) $(\det X) \bmod 2$; (b) $[\operatorname{per} X > 0]$; (c) $[\det X > 0]$.

▶ **71.** [*M26*] Suppose $f(x)$ is equal to 0 with probability p at each point $x = x_1 \ldots x_n$, independent of its value at other points.

a) What is the probability that the pairs (58) are good?
b) What is the probability that bad pairs (58) exist?
c) What is the probability that bad pairs (58) are found in at most t random trials?
d) What is the expected time to test case (i, j, m), as a function of p, t, and n?

72. [*M24*] Extend the previous exercise to the case of partial functions, where $f(x) = 0$ with probability p, $f(x) = 1$ with probability q, and $f(x) = *$ with probability r.

▶ **73.** [*20*] If bad pairs (58) exist for all (i, j, m) with $m \neq i \neq j \neq m$, show that the indecomposability of f can be deduced after testing only $\binom{n}{2}$ well-chosen triples (i, j, m).

74. [*25*] Extend the idea in the previous exercise, suggesting a strategy for choosing successive triples (i, j, m) when using the method of Shen, McKellar, and Weiner.

75. [*20*] What happens when the text's decomposition procedure is applied to the "all-equal" function $S_{0,n}(x_1, \ldots, x_n)$?

▶ **76.** [*M26*] (D. Uhlig, 1974.) The purpose of this exercise is to prove the amazing fact that, for certain functions f, the best chain to evaluate the Boolean function

$$F(u_1, \ldots, u_n, v_1, \ldots, v_n) = f(u_1, \ldots, u_n) \vee f(v_1, \ldots, v_n)$$

costs *less* than $2C(f)$; hence functional decomposition is *not* always a good idea.

We let $n = m + 2^m$ and write $f(i_1, \ldots, i_m, x_0, \ldots, x_{2^m-1}) = f_i(x)$, where i is regarded as the number $(i_1 \ldots i_m)_2$. Then $(u_1, \ldots, u_n) = (i_1, \ldots, i_m, x_0, \ldots, x_{2^m-1})$, $(v_1, \ldots, v_n) = (j_1, \ldots, j_m, y_0, \ldots, y_{2^m-1})$, and $F(u, v) = f_i(x) \vee f_j(y)$.

a) Prove that a chain of cost $O(n^2)$ suffices to evaluate the $2^m + 1$ functions

$$z_l = x \oplus (([l \leq i] \oplus [i \leq j]) \wedge (x \oplus y)), \qquad 0 \leq l \leq 2^m,$$

from given vectors i, j, x, and y; each z_l is a vector of length 2^m, and the one-bit quantity $([l \leq i] \oplus [i \leq j])$ is ANDed with each component of $x \oplus y$.

b) Let $g_i(x) = f_i(x) \oplus f_{i-1}(x)$ for $0 \leq i \leq 2^m$, where $f_{-1}(x) = f_{2^m}(x) = 0$. Estimate the cost of computing the $2^m + 1$ values $c_l = g_l(z_l)$, given the vectors z_l, for $0 \leq l \leq 2^m$.

c) Let $c'_l = c_l \wedge ([i \leq j] \equiv [l \leq i])$ and $c''_l = c_l \wedge ([i \leq j] \equiv [j > l])$. Prove that

$$f_i(x) = c'_0 \oplus c'_1 \oplus \cdots \oplus c'_{2^m}, \qquad f_j(y) = c''_0 \oplus c''_1 \oplus \cdots \oplus c''_{2^m}.$$

d) Conclude that $C(F) \leq 2^n/n + O(2^n(\log n)/n^2)$. (When n is sufficiently large, this cost is definitely less than $2^{n+1}/n$, but functions f exist with $C(f) > 2^n/n$.)

e) For clarity, write out the chain for F when $m = 1$ and $f(i, x_0, x_1) = (i \wedge x_0) \vee x_1$.

▶ **77.** [*35*] (N. P. Red'kin, 1970.) Suppose a Boolean chain uses only the operations AND, OR, or NOT; thus, every step is either $x_i = x_{j(i)} \wedge x_{k(i)}$ or $x_i = x_{j(i)} \vee x_{k(i)}$ or $x_i = \bar{x}_{j(i)}$. Prove that if such a chain computes either the "odd parity" function $f_n(x_1, \ldots, x_n) = x_1 \oplus \cdots \oplus x_n$ or the "even parity" function $\bar{f}_n(x_1, \ldots, x_n) = 1 \oplus x_1 \oplus \cdots \oplus x_n$, where $n \geq 2$, the length of the chain is at least $4(n-1)$.

78. [*26*] (W. J. Paul, 1977.) Let $f(x_1, \ldots, x_m, y_0, \ldots, y_{2^m-1})$ be any Boolean function that equals y_k whenever $(x_1 \ldots x_m)_2 = k \in S$, for some given set $S \subseteq \{0, 1, \ldots, 2^m - 1\}$; we don't care about the value of f at other points. Show that $C(f) \geq 2\|S\| - 2$ whenever S is nonempty. (In particular, when $S = \{0, 1, \ldots, 2^m - 1\}$, the multiplexer chain of exercise 39 is asymptotically optimum.)

79. [*32*] (C. P. Schnorr, 1976.) Say that variables u and v are "mates" in a Boolean chain if there is exactly one simple path between them in the corresponding binary tree diagram. Two variables can be mates only if they are each used only once in the chain; but this necessary condition is not sufficient. For example, variables 2 and 4 are mates in the chain for $S_{1,2,3}$ in Fig. 9, but they are not mates in the chain for S_2.

a) Prove that a Boolean chain on n variables with no mates has cost $\geq 2n - 2$.

b) Prove that $C(f) = 2n - 3$ when f is the all-equal function $S_{0,n}(x_1, \ldots, x_n)$.

▶ **80.** [*M29*] (L. J. Stockmeyer, 1977.) Another notation for symmetric functions is sometimes convenient: If $\alpha = a_0 a_1 \dots a_n$ is any binary string, let $S_\alpha(x) = a_{\nu x}$. For example, $\langle x_1 x_2 x_3 \rangle = S_{0011}$ and $x_1 \oplus x_2 \oplus x_3 = S_{0101}$ in this notation. Notice that $S_\alpha(0, x_2, \dots, x_n) = S_{\alpha'}(x_2, \dots, x_n)$ and $S_\alpha(1, x_2, \dots, x_n) = S_{'\alpha}(x_2, \dots, x_n)$, where α' and $'\alpha$ stand respectively for α with its last or first element deleted. Also,

$$S_\alpha(f(x_3, \dots, x_n), \bar{f}(x_3, \dots, x_n), x_3, \dots, x_n) = S_{'\alpha'}(x_3, \dots, x_n)$$

when f is any Boolean function of $n-2$ variables.

a) A parity function has $a_0 \neq a_1 \neq a_2 \neq \dots \neq a_n$. Assume that $n \geq 2$. Prove that if S_α is not a parity function and $S_{'\alpha'}$ isn't constant, then

$$C(S_\alpha) \geq \max(C(S_{\alpha'})+2, C(S_{'\alpha})+2, \min(C(S_{\alpha'})+3, C(S_{'\alpha})+3, C(S_{'\alpha'})+5)).$$

b) What lower bounds on $C(S_k)$ and $C(S_{\geq k})$ follow from this result, when $0 \leq k \leq n$?

81. [*23*] (M. Snir, 1986.) Show that any chain of cost c and depth d for the prefix problem of exercise 36 has $c + d \geq 2n - 2$.

▶ **82.** [*M23*] Explain the logical sentences (62)–(70). Which of them are true?

83. [*21*] If there's a Boolean chain for $f(x_1, \dots, x_n)$ that contains p canalizing operations, show that $C(f) < (p+1)(n+p/2)$.

84. [*M20*] A *monotone Boolean chain* is a Boolean chain in which every operator $\circ_i$ is monotone. The length of a shortest monotone chain for f is denoted by $C^+(f)$. If there's a monotone Boolean chain for $f(x_1, \dots, x_n)$ that contains p occurrences of $\wedge$ and q occurrences of $\vee$, show that $C^+(f) < \min((p+1)(n+p/2), (q+1)(n+q/2))$.

▶ **85.** [*M28*] Let M_n be the set of all monotone functions of n variables. If L is a family of functions contained in M_n, let

$$x \sqcup y = \bigwedge \{z \in L \mid z \supseteq x \vee y\} \quad \text{and} \quad x \sqcap y = \bigvee \{z \in L \mid z \subseteq x \wedge y\}.$$

We call L "legitimate" if it includes the constant functions 0 and 1 as well as the projection functions x_j for $1 \leq j \leq n$, and if $x \sqcup y \in L$, $x \sqcap y \in L$ whenever $x, y \in L$.

a) When $n = 3$ we can write $M_3 = \{$00, 01, 03, 05, 11, 07, 13, 15, 0f, 33, 55, 17, 1f, 37, 57, 3f, 5f, 77, 7f, ff$\}$, representing each function by its hexadecimal truth table. There are 2^{15} families L such that $\{$00, 0f, 33, 55, ff$\} \subseteq L \subseteq M_3$; how many of them are legitimate?

b) If A is a subset of $\{1, \dots, n\}$, let $\lceil A \rceil = \bigvee_{a \in A} x_a$; also let $\lceil \infty \rceil = 1$. Suppose $\mathcal{A}$ is a family of subsets of $\{1, \dots, n\}$ that contains all sets of size ≤ 1 and is closed under intersection; in other words, $A \cap B \in \mathcal{A}$ whenever $A \in \mathcal{A}$ and $B \in \mathcal{A}$. Prove that the family $L = \{\lceil A \rceil \mid A \in \mathcal{A} \cup \infty\}$ is legitimate.

c) Let $(x_{n+1}, \dots, x_{n+r})$ be a monotone Boolean chain (1). Suppose $(\hat{x}_{n+1}, \dots, \hat{x}_{n+r})$ is obtained from the same Boolean chain, but with every operator $\wedge$ changed to $\sqcap$ and with every operator $\vee$ changed to $\sqcup$, with respect to some legitimate family L. Prove that, for $n+1 \leq l \leq n+r$, we must have

$$\hat{x}_l \subseteq x_l \vee \bigvee_{i=n+1}^{l} \{\hat{x}_i \oplus (\hat{x}_{j(i)} \vee \hat{x}_{k(i)}) \mid \circ_i = \vee\};$$

$$x_l \subseteq \hat{x}_l \vee \bigvee_{i=n+1}^{l} \{\hat{x}_i \oplus (\hat{x}_{j(i)} \wedge \hat{x}_{k(i)}) \mid \circ_i = \wedge\}.$$

86. [*HM37*] A graph G on vertices $\{1,\ldots,n\}$ can be defined by $N = \binom{n}{2}$ Boolean variables x_{uv} for $1 \le u < v \le n$, where $x_{uv} = [u\text{---}v \text{ in } G]$. Let f be the function $f(x) = [G \text{ contains a triangle}]$; for example, when $n = 4$, $f(x_{12}, x_{13}, x_{14}, x_{23}, x_{24}, x_{34}) = (x_{12} \wedge x_{13} \wedge x_{23}) \vee (x_{12} \wedge x_{14} \wedge x_{24}) \vee (x_{13} \wedge x_{14} \wedge x_{34}) \vee (x_{23} \wedge x_{24} \wedge x_{34})$. The purpose of this exercise is to prove that the monotone complexity $C^+(f)$ is $\Omega(n/\log n)^3$.

a) If $u_j \text{---} v_j$ for $1 \le j \le r$ in a graph G, call $S = \{\{u_1, v_1\}, \ldots, \{u_r, v_r\}\}$ an r-*family*, and let $\Delta(S) = \bigcup_{1 \le i < j \le r}(\{u_i, v_i\} \cap \{u_j, v_j\})$ be the elements of its pairwise intersections. Say that G is r-*closed* if we have $u \text{---} v$ whenever $\Delta(S) \subseteq \{u, v\}$ for some r-family S. It is *strongly* r-*closed* if, in addition, we have $|\Delta(S)| \ge 2$ for all r-families S. Prove that a strongly r-closed graph is also strongly $(r + 1)$-closed.

b) Prove that the complete bigraph $K_{m,n}$ is strongly r-closed when $r > \max(m, n)$.

c) Prove that a strongly r-closed graph has at most $(r - 1)^2$ edges.

d) Let L be the family of functions $\{1\} \cup \{\lceil G \rceil \mid G \text{ is a strongly } r\text{-closed graph on } \{1, \ldots, n\}\}$. (See exercise 85(b); we regard G as a set of edges. For example, when the edges are $1\text{---}3$, $1\text{---}4$, $2\text{---}3$, $2\text{---}4$, we have $\lceil G \rceil = x_{13} \vee x_{14} \vee x_{23} \vee x_{24}$.) Is L legitimate?

e) Let $x_{N+1}, \ldots, x_{N+p+q} = f$ be a monotone Boolean chain with p $\wedge$-steps and q $\vee$-steps, and consider the modified chain $\hat{x}_{N+1}, \ldots, \hat{x}_{N+p+q} = \hat{f}$ based on the family L in (d). If $\hat{f} \ne 1$, show that $2(r-1)^3 p + (r-1)^2(n-2) \ge \binom{n}{3}$. *Hint:* Use the second formula in exercise 85(c).

f) Furthermore, if $\hat{f} = 1$ we must have $r^2 q \ge 2^{r+1}$. *Hint:* Now use the first formula.

g) Therefore $p = \Omega(n/\log n)^3$. *Hint:* Let $r \approx 6 \lg n$ and apply exercise 84.

87. [*M22*] Show that when nonmonotonic operations are permitted, the triangle function of exercise 86 has cost $C(f) = O(n^{\lg 7}(\log n)^2) = O(n^{2.81})$. *Hint:* A graph has a triangle if and only if the cube of its adjacency matrix has a nonzero diagonal.

88. [*40*] A *median chain* is analogous to a Boolean chain, but it uses median-of-three steps $x_i = \langle x_{j(i)} x_{k(i)} x_{l(i)} \rangle$ for $n+1 \le i \le n+r$, instead of the binary operations in (1).

Study the optimum length, depth, and cost of median chains, for all self-dual monotone Boolean functions of 7 variables. What is the shortest chain for $\langle x_1 x_2 x_3 x_4 x_5 x_6 x_7 \rangle$?

> Lady Caroline.   *Psha! that's such a hack!*
>
> Sir Simon.   *A hack, Lady Caroline, that*
> *the knowing ones have warranted sound.*
>
> — GEORGE COLMAN, *John Bull*, Act 3, Scene 1 (1803)

7.1.3. Bitwise Tricks and Techniques

Now comes the fun part: We get to use Boolean operations in our programs.

People are more familiar with arithmetic operations like addition, subtraction, and multiplication than they are with bitwise operations such as "and," "exclusive-or," and so on, because arithmetic has a very long history. But we will see that Boolean operations on binary numbers deserve to be much better known. Indeed, they're an important component of every good programmer's toolkit.

Early machine designers provided fullword bitwise operations in their computers primarily because such instructions could be included in a machine's repertoire almost for free. Binary logic seemed to be potentially useful, although only a few applications were originally foreseen. For example, the EDSAC computer, completed in 1949, included a "collate" command that essentially performed the operation $z \leftarrow z + (x \& y)$, where z was the accumulator, x was the multiplier register, and y was a specified word in memory; it was used for unpacking data. The Manchester Mark I computer, built at about the same time, included not only bitwise AND, but also OR and XOR. When Alan Turing wrote the first programming manual for the Mark I in 1950, he remarked that bitwise NOT can be obtained by using XOR (denoted '$\neq$') in combination with a row of 1s. R. A. Brooker, who extended Turing's manual in 1952 when the Mark II computer was being designed, remarked further that OR could be used "to round off a number by forcing 1 into its least significant digit position." By this time the Mark II, which was to become the prototype of the Ferranti Mercury, had also acquired new instructions for sideways addition and for the position of the most significant 1.

Keith Tocher published an unusual application of AND and OR in 1954, which has subsequently been reinvented frequently (see exercise 85). And during the ensuing decades, programmers have gradually discovered that bitwise operations can be amazingly useful. Many of these tricks have remained part of the folklore; the time is now ripe to take advantage of what has been learned.

A *trick* is a clever idea that can be used once, while a *technique* is a mature trick that can be used at least twice. We will see in this section that tricks tend to evolve naturally into techniques.

Enriched arithmetic. Let's begin by officially defining bitwise operations on integers so that, if $x = (\dots x_2 x_1 x_0)_2$, $y = (\dots y_2 y_1 y_0)_2$, and $z = (\dots z_2 z_1 z_0)_2$ in binary notation, we have

$$x \& y = z \iff x_k \wedge y_k = z_k, \qquad \text{for all } k \geq 0; \tag{1}$$

$$x \mid y = z \iff x_k \vee y_k = z_k, \qquad \text{for all } k \geq 0; \tag{2}$$

$$x \oplus y = z \iff x_k \oplus y_k = z_k, \qquad \text{for all } k \geq 0. \tag{3}$$

(It would be tempting to write '$x \wedge y$' instead of $x \& y$, and '$x \vee y$' instead of $x \mid y$; but when we study optimization problems we'll find it better to reserve the notations $x \wedge y$ and $x \vee y$ for $\min(x, y)$ and $\max(x, y)$, respectively.) Thus, for example,

$$5 \& 11 = 1, \qquad 5 \mid 11 = 15, \qquad \text{and} \qquad 5 \oplus 11 = 14,$$

since $5 = (0101)_2$, $11 = (1011)_2$, $1 = (0001)_2$, $15 = (1111)_2$, and $14 = (1110)_2$. Negative integers are to be thought of in this connection as infinite-precision numbers in two's complement notation, having infinitely many 1s at the left; for example, -5 is $(\dots 1111011)_2$. Such infinite-precision numbers are a special case of *2-adic integers*, which are discussed in exercise 4.1–31, and in fact the operators $\&$, $\mid$, $\oplus$ make perfect sense when they are applied to arbitrary 2-adic numbers.

Mathematicians have never paid much attention to the properties of $\&$ and $\mid$ as operations on integers. But the third operation, $\oplus$, has a venerable history, because it describes a winning strategy in the game of nim (see exercises 8–16). For this reason $x \oplus y$ has often been called the "nim sum" of the integers x and y.

All three of the basic bitwise operations turn out to have many useful properties. For example, every relation between $\wedge$, $\vee$, and $\oplus$ that we studied in Section 7.1.1 is automatically inherited by $\&$, $|$, and $\oplus$ on integers, since the relation holds in every bit position. We might as well recap the main identities here:

$$x \mathbin{\&} y = y \mathbin{\&} x, \qquad x \mid y = y \mid x, \qquad x \oplus y = y \oplus x; \tag{4}$$

$$(x \mathbin{\&} y) \mathbin{\&} z = x \mathbin{\&} (y \mathbin{\&} z), \quad (x \mid y) \mid z = x \mid (y \mid z), \quad (x \oplus y) \oplus z = x \oplus (y \oplus z); \tag{5}$$

$$(x \mid y) \mathbin{\&} z = (x \mathbin{\&} z) \mid (y \mathbin{\&} z), \qquad (x \mathbin{\&} y) \mid z = (x \mid z) \mathbin{\&} (y \mid z); \tag{6}$$

$$(x \oplus y) \mathbin{\&} z = (x \mathbin{\&} z) \oplus (y \mathbin{\&} z); \tag{7}$$

$$(x \mathbin{\&} y) \mid x = x, \qquad (x \mid y) \mathbin{\&} x = x; \tag{8}$$

$$(x \mathbin{\&} y) \oplus (x \mid y) = x \oplus y; \tag{9}$$

$$x \mathbin{\&} 0 = 0, \qquad x \mid 0 = x, \qquad x \oplus 0 = x; \tag{10}$$

$$x \mathbin{\&} x = x, \qquad x \mid x = x, \qquad x \oplus x = 0; \tag{11}$$

$$x \mathbin{\&} -1 = x, \qquad x \mid -1 = -1, \qquad x \oplus -1 = \bar{x}; \tag{12}$$

$$x \mathbin{\&} \bar{x} = 0, \qquad x \mid \bar{x} = -1, \qquad x \oplus \bar{x} = -1; \tag{13}$$

$$\overline{x \mathbin{\&} y} = \bar{x} \mid \bar{y}, \qquad \overline{x \mid y} = \bar{x} \mathbin{\&} \bar{y}, \qquad \overline{x \oplus y} = \bar{x} \oplus y = x \oplus \bar{y}. \tag{14}$$

The notation $\bar{x}$ in (12), (13), and (14) stands for bitwise *complementation* of x, namely $(\dots \bar{x}_2 \bar{x}_1 \bar{x}_0)_2$, also written $\sim x$. Notice that (12) and (13) aren't quite the same as 7.1.1–(10) and 7.1.1–(18); we must now use $-1 = (\dots 1111)_2$ instead of $1 = (\dots 0001)_2$ in order to make the formulas bitwise correct.

We say that x is *contained in* y, written $x \subseteq y$ or $y \supseteq x$, if the individual bits of x and y satisfy $x_k \le y_k$ for all $k \ge 0$. Thus

$$x \subseteq y \iff x \mathbin{\&} y = x \iff x \mid y = y \iff x \mathbin{\&} \bar{y} = 0. \tag{15}$$

Of course we needn't use bitwise operations only in connection with each other; we can combine them with all the ordinary operations of arithmetic. For example, from the relation $x + \bar{x} = (\dots 1111)_2 = -1$ we can deduce the formula

$$-x = \bar{x} + 1, \tag{16}$$

which turns out to be extremely important. Replacing x by $x - 1$ gives also

$$-x = \overline{x - 1}; \tag{17}$$

and in general we can reduce subtraction to complementation and addition:

$$\overline{x - y} = \bar{x} + y. \tag{18}$$

We often want to shift binary numbers to the left or right. These operations are equivalent to multiplication and division by powers of 2, with appropriate rounding, but it is convenient to have special notations for them:

$$x \ll k = x \text{ shifted left } k \text{ bits} = \lfloor 2^k x \rfloor; \tag{19}$$

$$x \gg k = x \text{ shifted right } k \text{ bits} = \lfloor 2^{-k} x \rfloor. \tag{20}$$

Here k can be any integer, possibly negative. In particular we have

$$x \ll (-k) = x \gg k \qquad \text{and} \qquad x \gg (-k) = x \ll k, \tag{21}$$

for every infinite-precision number x. Also $(x \mathbin{\&} y) \ll k = (x \ll k) \mathbin{\&} (y \ll k)$, etc.

When bitwise operations are combined with addition, subtraction, multiplication, and/or shifting, extremely intricate results can arise, even when the formulas are quite short. A taste of the possibilities can be seen, for example, in Fig. 11. Furthermore, such formulas do not merely produce purposeless, chaotic behavior: A famous chain of operations known as "Gosper's hack," first published in 1972, opened people's eyes to the fact that a large number of useful and nontrivial functions can be computed rapidly (see exercise 20). Our goal in this section is to explore how such efficient constructions might be discovered.

Fig. 11. A small portion of the patchwork quilt defined by the bitwise function $f(x, y) = ((x \oplus \bar{y}) \mathbin{\&} ((x - 350) \gg 3))^2$; the square cell in row x and column y is painted white or black according as the value of $((f(x, y) \gg 12) \mathbin{\&} 1)$ is 0 or 1. (Design by D. Sleator, 1976; see also exercise 18.)

Packing and unpacking. We studied algorithms for multiple-precision arithmetic in Section 4.3.1, dealing with situations where integers are too large to fit in a single word of memory or a single computer register. But the opposite situation, when integers are significantly *smaller* than the capacity of one computer word, is actually much more common; D. H. Lehmer called this "fractional precision." We can often deal with several integers at once, by packing them into a single word.

For example, a date x that consists of a year number y, a month number m, and a day number d, can be represented by using 4 bits for m and 5 bits for d:

$$x = (((y \ll 4) + m) \ll 5) + d. \tag{22}$$

We'll see below that many operations can be performed directly on dates in this packed form. For example, $x < x'$ when date x precedes date x'. But if necessary the individual components (y, m, d) can readily be unpacked when x is given:

$$d = x \bmod 32, \qquad m = (x \gg 5) \bmod 16, \qquad y = x \gg 9. \tag{23}$$

And these "mod" operations do not require division, because of the important law

$$x \bmod 2^n = x \mathbin{\&} (2^n - 1) \tag{24}$$

for any integer $n \geq 0$. We have, for instance, $d = x \mathbin{\&} 31$ in (22) and (23).

Such packing of data obviously saves space in memory, and it also saves time: We can more quickly move or copy items of data from one place to another when

they've been packed together. Moreover, computers run considerably faster when
they operate on numbers that fit into a cache memory of limited size.

The ultimate packing density is achieved when we have 1-bit items, because
we can then cram 64 of them into a single 64-bit word. Suppose, for example,
that we want a table of all odd prime numbers less than 1024, so that we can
easily decide the primality of a small integer. No problem; only eight 64-bit
numbers are required:

$P_0 = $ 0111011011010011001011010010011001011001010010001011011010000001,
$P_1 = $ 0100110000110010010100100110000110110000010000010110100110000100,
$P_2 = $ 1001001100101100001000000101101000000100100001101001000100100101,
$P_3 = $ 0010001010001000011000011001010010001011010000010001010001010010,
$P_4 = $ 0000110000000010010000100100110010000100100110010010110000010000,
$P_5 = $ 1101001001100000101001000100001000100001000100100100101000100101000,
$P_6 = $ 1010000001000010000011000011011000010000001011010000001011010000,
$P_7 = $ 0000010100010000100010100100100000010100100100010010000010100110.

To test whether $2k + 1$ is prime, for $0 \le k < 512$, we simply compute

$$P_{\lfloor k/64 \rfloor} \ll (k \,\&\, 63) \tag{25}$$

in a 64-bit register, and see if the leftmost bit is 1. For example, the following
MMIX instructions will do the job, if register pbase holds the address of P_0:

SRU	$0,k,3	$0 \leftarrow \lfloor k/8 \rfloor$ (i.e., $k \gg 3$).	
LDOU	$1,pbase,$0	$1 \leftarrow P_{\lfloor \$0/8 \rfloor}$ (i.e., $P_{\lfloor k/64 \rfloor}$).	
AND	$0,k,#3f	$0 \leftarrow k \bmod 64$ (i.e., $k \,\&\, {}^\#3f$).	(26)
SLU	$1,$1,$0	$1 \leftarrow (\$1 \ll \$0) \bmod 2^{64}$.	
BN	$1,PRIME	Branch to PRIME if $s(\$1) < 0$. ∎	

Notice that the leftmost bit of a register is 1 if and only if the register contents
are negative.

We could equally well pack the bits from right to left in each word:

$Q_0 = $ 1000000101101101000100101001101001100100101101001100101101101110,
$Q_1 = $ 0010000110010110100000100000110110000110010010100100110000110010,
$Q_2 = $ 1010010010001001011000010010000001011010000001000011010011001001,
$Q_3 = $ 0100101000101000100000101101000100101001100001100001000101000100,
$Q_4 = $ 0000100000110100100110010010000100110010010000100100000000110000,
$Q_5 = $ 0001010010001010010010001000100010001000100100101000001100100101011,
$Q_6 = $ 0000101101000000101101000000100001101100001100000100001000000101,
$Q_7 = $ 0110010100000100100010010010100000010010010100010000100010100000;

here $Q_j = P_j^R$. Instead of shifting left as in (25), we now shift right,

$$Q_{\lfloor k/64 \rfloor} \gg (k \,\&\, 63), \tag{27}$$

and look at the *rightmost* bit of the result. The last two lines of (26) become

SRU	$1,$1,$0	$1 \leftarrow \$1 \gg \$0$.	(28)
BOD	$1,PRIME	Branch to PRIME if $1 is odd. ∎	

(And of course we use qbase instead of pbase.) Either way, the classic *sieve of
Eratosthenes* will readily set up the basic table entries P_j or Q_j (see exercise 24).

Table 1

THE BIG-ENDIAN VIEW OF A 32-BYTE MEMORY

octa 0							
tetra 0				tetra 4			
wyde 0		wyde 2		wyde 4		wyde 6	
byte 0	byte 1	byte 2	byte 3	byte 4	byte 5	byte 6	byte 7
$a_0 \dots a_7$	$a_8 \dots a_{15}$	$a_{16} \dots a_{23}$	$a_{24} \dots a_{31}$	$a_{32} \dots a_{39}$	$a_{40} \dots a_{47}$	$a_{48} \dots a_{55}$	$a_{56} \dots a_{63}$

octa 8							
tetra 8				tetra 12			
wyde 8		wyde 10		wyde 12		wyde 14	
byte 8	byte 9	byte 10	byte 11	byte 12	byte 13	byte 14	byte 15
$a_{64} \dots a_{71}$	$a_{72} \dots a_{79}$	$a_{80} \dots a_{87}$	$a_{88} \dots a_{95}$	$a_{96} \dots a_{103}$	$a_{104} \dots a_{111}$	$a_{112} \dots a_{119}$	$a_{120} \dots a_{127}$

octa 16							
tetra 16				tetra 20			
wyde 16		wyde 18		wyde 20		wyde 22	
byte 16	byte 17	byte 18	byte 19	byte 20	byte 21	byte 22	byte 23
$a_{128} \dots a_{135}$	$a_{136} \dots a_{143}$	$a_{144} \dots a_{151}$	$a_{152} \dots a_{159}$	$a_{160} \dots a_{167}$	$a_{168} \dots a_{175}$	$a_{176} \dots a_{183}$	$a_{184} \dots a_{191}$

octa 24							
tetra 24				tetra 28			
wyde 24		wyde 26		wyde 28		wyde 30	
byte 24	byte 25	byte 26	byte 27	byte 28	byte 29	byte 30	byte 31
$a_{192} \dots a_{199}$	$a_{200} \dots a_{207}$	$a_{208} \dots a_{215}$	$a_{216} \dots a_{223}$	$a_{224} \dots a_{231}$	$a_{232} \dots a_{239}$	$a_{240} \dots a_{247}$	$a_{248} \dots a_{255}$

Big-endian and little-endian conventions. Whenever we pack bits or bytes into words, we must decide whether to place them from left to right or from right to left. The left-to-right convention is called "big-endian," because the initial items go into the most significant positions; thus they will have bigger significance than their successors, when numbers are compared. The right-to-left convention is called "little-endian"; it puts the first items where little numbers go.

A big-endian approach seems more natural in many cases, because we're accustomed to reading and writing from left to right. But a little-endian placement has advantages too. For example, let's consider the prime number problem again; let $a_k = [2k+1$ is prime]. Our table entries $\{P_0, P_1, \dots, P_7\}$ are big-endian, and we can regard them as the representation of a single multiple-precision integer that is 512 bits long:

$$(P_0 P_1 \dots P_7)_{2^{64}} = (a_0 a_1 \dots a_{511})_2. \tag{29}$$

Similarly, our little-endian table entries represent the multiprecise integer

$$(Q_7 \dots Q_1 Q_0)_{2^{64}} = (a_{511} \dots a_1 a_0)_2. \tag{30}$$

The latter integer is mathematically nicer than the former, because it is

$$\sum_{k=0}^{511} 2^k a_k = \sum_{k=0}^{511} 2^k [2k+1 \text{ is prime}] = \left(\sum_{k=0}^{\infty} 2^k [2k+1 \text{ is prime}] \right) \bmod 2^{512}. \tag{31}$$

Table 2

THE LITTLE-ENDIAN VIEW OF A 32-BYTE MEMORY

octa 24							
tetra 28				tetra 24			
wyde 30		wyde 28		wyde 26		wyde 24	
byte 31	byte 30	byte 29	byte 28	byte 27	byte 26	byte 25	byte 24
$a_{255}\ldots a_{248}$	$a_{247}\ldots a_{240}$	$a_{239}\ldots a_{232}$	$a_{231}\ldots a_{224}$	$a_{223}\ldots a_{216}$	$a_{215}\ldots a_{208}$	$a_{207}\ldots a_{200}$	$a_{199}\ldots a_{192}$

octa 16							
tetra 20				tetra 16			
wyde 22		wyde 20		wyde 18		wyde 16	
byte 23	byte 22	byte 21	byte 20	byte 19	byte 18	byte 17	byte 16
$a_{191}\ldots a_{184}$	$a_{183}\ldots a_{176}$	$a_{175}\ldots a_{168}$	$a_{167}\ldots a_{160}$	$a_{159}\ldots a_{152}$	$a_{151}\ldots a_{144}$	$a_{143}\ldots a_{136}$	$a_{135}\ldots a_{128}$

octa 8							
tetra 12				tetra 8			
wyde 14		wyde 12		wyde 10		wyde 8	
byte 15	byte 14	byte 13	byte 12	byte 11	byte 10	byte 9	byte 8
$a_{127}\ldots a_{120}$	$a_{119}\ldots a_{112}$	$a_{111}\ldots a_{104}$	$a_{103}\ldots a_{96}$	$a_{95}\ldots a_{88}$	$a_{87}\ldots a_{80}$	$a_{79}\ldots a_{72}$	$a_{71}\ldots a_{64}$

octa 0							
tetra 4				tetra 0			
wyde 6		wyde 4		wyde 2		wyde 0	
byte 7	byte 6	byte 5	byte 4	byte 3	byte 2	byte 1	byte 0
$a_{63}\ldots a_{56}$	$a_{55}\ldots a_{48}$	$a_{47}\ldots a_{40}$	$a_{39}\ldots a_{32}$	$a_{31}\ldots a_{24}$	$a_{23}\ldots a_{16}$	$a_{15}\ldots a_{8}$	$a_{7}\ldots a_{0}$

Notice, however, that we used $(Q_7 \ldots Q_1 Q_0)_{2^{64}}$ to get this simple result, not $(Q_0 Q_1 \ldots Q_7)_{2^{64}}$. The other number,

$$(Q_0 Q_1 \ldots Q_7)_{2^{64}} = (a_{63} \ldots a_1 a_0 a_{127} \ldots a_{65} a_{64} a_{191} \ldots a_{385} a_{384} a_{511} \ldots a_{449} a_{448})_2$$

is in fact quite weird, and it has no really nice formula. (See exercise 25.)

Endianness has important consequences, because most computers allow individual bytes of the memory to be addressed as well as register-sized units. MMIX has a big-endian architecture; therefore if register x contains the 64-bit number #0123456789abcdef, and if we use the commands 'STOU x,0; LDBU y,1' to store x into octabyte location 0 and read back the byte in location 1, the result in register y will be #23. On machines with a little-endian architecture, the analogous commands would set y ← #cd instead; #23 would be byte 6.

Tables 1 and 2 illustrate the competing "world views" of big-endian and little-endian aficionados. The big-endian approach is basically top-down, with bit 0 and byte 0 at the top left; the little-endian approach is basically bottom-up, with bit 0 and byte 0 at the bottom right. Because of this difference, great care is necessary when transmitting data from one kind of computer to another, or when writing programs that are supposed to give equivalent results in both cases. On the other hand, our example of the Q table for primes shows that we can perfectly well use a little-endian packing convention on a big-endian computer like `MMIX`, or vice versa. The difference is noticeable only when data is loaded and stored in different-sized chunks, or passed between machines.

Working with the rightmost bits. Big-endian and little-endian approaches aren't readily interchangeable in general, because the laws of arithmetic send signals leftward from the bits that are "least significant." Some of the most important bitwise manipulation techniques are based on this fact.

If x is almost any nonzero 2-adic integer, we can write its bits in the form

$$x = (\alpha\, 01^a 10^b)_2; \qquad (32)$$

in other words, x consists of some arbitrary (but infinite) binary string α, followed by a 0, which is followed by $a + 1$ ones, and followed by b zeros, for some $a \geq 0$ and $b \geq 0$. (The exceptions occur when $x = -2^b$; then $a = \infty$.) Consequently

$$\bar{x} = (\bar{\alpha}\, 10^a 01^b)_2, \qquad (33)$$
$$x - 1 = (\alpha\, 01^a 01^b)_2, \qquad (34)$$
$$-x = (\bar{\alpha}\, 10^a 10^b)_2; \qquad (35)$$

and we see that $\bar{x} + 1 = -x = \overline{x - 1}$, in agreement with (16) and (17). With two operations we can therefore compute relatives of x in several useful ways:

$$x \mathbin{\&} (x{-}1) = (\ \alpha\ 01^a 00^b)_2 \quad [\text{remove the rightmost 1}]; \qquad (36)$$
$$x \mathbin{\&} -x = (0^\infty 00^a 10^b)_2 \quad [\text{extract the rightmost 1}]; \qquad (37)$$
$$x \mathbin{|} -x = (1^\infty 11^a 10^b)_2 \quad [\text{smear the rightmost 1 to the left}]; \qquad (38)$$
$$x \oplus -x = (1^\infty 11^a 00^b)_2 \quad [\text{remove and smear it to the left}]; \qquad (39)$$
$$x \mathbin{|} (x{-}1) = (\ \alpha\ 01^a 11^b)_2 \quad [\text{smear the rightmost 1 to the right}]; \qquad (40)$$
$$x \oplus (x{-}1) = (0^\infty 00^a 11^b)_2 \quad [\text{extract and smear it to the right}]; \qquad (41)$$
$$\bar{x} \mathbin{\&} (x{-}1) = (0^\infty 00^a 01^b)_2 \quad [\text{extract, remove, and smear it to the right}]. \qquad (42)$$

And two further operations produce yet another variant:

$$((x{|}(x{-}1)){+}1) \mathbin{\&} x = (\ \alpha\ 00^a 00^b)_2 \quad [\text{remove the rightmost run of 1s}]. \qquad (43)$$

When $x = 0$, five of these formulas produce 0, the other three give -1. [Formula (36) is due to Peter Wegner, *CACM* **3** (1960), 322; and (43) is due to H. Tim Gladwin, *CACM* **14** (1971), 407–408. See also Henry S. Warren, Jr., *CACM* **20** (1977), 439–441.]

The quantity b in these formulas, which specifies the number of trailing zeros in x, is called the *ruler function* of x and written ρx, because it is related to the lengths of the tick marks that are often used to indicate fractions of an inch: '⊓⊓⊓⊓⊓⊓⊓⊓⊓⊓⊓⊓⊓⊓⊓'. In general, ρx is the largest integer k such that 2^k divides x, when $x \neq 0$; and we define $\rho 0 = \infty$. The recurrence relations

$$\rho(2x + 1) = 0, \qquad \rho(2x) = \rho(x) + 1 \qquad (44)$$

also serve to define ρx for nonzero x. Another handy relation is worthy of note,

$$\rho(x - y) = \rho(x \oplus y). \qquad (45)$$

The elegant formula $x \mathbin{\&} -x$ in (37) allows us to *extract* the rightmost 1 bit very nicely, but we often want to identify exactly which bit it is. The ruler function can be computed in many ways, and the best method often depends heavily on the computer that is being used. For example, a two-instruction sequence due to J. Dallos does the job quickly and easily on MMIX (see (42)):

$$\text{SUBU t,x,1; \quad SADD rho,t,x.} \tag{46}$$

(See exercise 30 for the case $x = 0$.) We shall discuss here two approaches that do not rely on exotic commands like SADD; and later, after learning a few more techniques, we'll consider a third way.

The first general-purpose method makes use of "magic mask" constants μ_k that prove to be useful in many other applications, namely

$$
\begin{aligned}
\mu_0 &= (\ldots 10101010101010101010101010101010101)_2 = -1/3, \\
\mu_1 &= (\ldots 1001100110011001100110011001100110011)_2 = -1/5, \\
\mu_2 &= (\ldots 1000011110000111100001111000011111)_2 = -1/17,
\end{aligned} \tag{47}
$$

and so on. In general μ_k is the infinite 2-adic fraction $-1/(2^{2^k}+1)$, because $(2^{2^k}+1)\mu_k = (\mu_k \ll 2^k) + \mu_k = (\ldots 11111)_2 = -1$. On a computer that has 2^d-bit registers we don't need infinite precision, of course, so we use the truncated constants

$$\mu_{d,k} = (2^{2^d}-1)/(2^{2^k}+1) \qquad \text{for } 0 \le k < d. \tag{48}$$

These constants are familiar from our study of Boolean evaluation, because they are the truth tables of the projection functions x_{d-k} (see, for example, 7.1.2–(7)).

When x is a power of 2, we can use these masks to compute

$$\rho x = [x \mathbin{\&} \mu_0 = 0] + 2[x \mathbin{\&} \mu_1 = 0] + 4[x \mathbin{\&} \mu_2 = 0] + 8[x \mathbin{\&} \mu_3 = 0] + \cdots, \tag{49}$$

because $[2^j \mathbin{\&} \mu_k = 0] = j_k$ when $j = (\ldots j_3 j_2 j_1 j_0)_2$. Thus, on a 2^d-bit computer, we can start with $\rho \leftarrow 0$ and $y \leftarrow x \mathbin{\&} -x$; then set $\rho \leftarrow \rho + 2^k$ if $y \mathbin{\&} \mu_{d,k} = 0$, for $0 \le k < d$. This procedure gives $\rho = \rho x$ when $x \ne 0$. (It also gives $\rho 0 = 2^d - 1$, an anomalous value that may need to be corrected; see exercise 30.)

For example, the corresponding MMIX program might look like this:

```
m0 GREG #5555555555555555  ;m1 GREG #3333333333333333;
m2 GREG #0f0f0f0f0f0f0f0f  ;m3 GREG #00ff00ff00ff00ff;
m4 GREG #0000ffff0000ffff  ;m5 GREG #00000000ffffffff;
NEGU y,x; AND y,x,y; AND q,y,m5; ZSZ rho,q,32;
AND q,y,m4; ADD t,rho,16; CSZ rho,q,t;
AND q,y,m3; ADD t,rho,8;  CSZ rho,q,t;
AND q,y,m2; ADD t,rho,4;  CSZ rho,q,t;
AND q,y,m1; ADD t,rho,2;  CSZ rho,q,t;
AND q,y,m0; ADD t,rho,1;  CSZ rho,q,t;
```
(50)

total time $= 19\upsilon$. Or we could replace the last three lines by

$$\text{SRU y,y,rho; \quad LDB t,rhotab,y; \quad ADD rho,rho,t} \tag{51}$$

where **rhotab** points to the beginning of an appropriate 129-byte table (only eight of whose entries are actually used). The total time would then be $\mu + 13\upsilon$.

The second general-purpose approach to the computation of ρx is quite different. On a 64-bit machine it starts as before, with $y \leftarrow x \,\&\, -x$; but then it simply sets

$$\rho \leftarrow decode\left[((a \cdot y) \bmod 2^{64}) \gg 58\right], \tag{52}$$

where a is a suitable multiplier and $decode$ is a suitable 64-byte table. The constant $a = (a_{63} \ldots a_1 a_0)_2$ must have the property that its 64 substrings

$$a_{63}a_{62} \ldots a_{58}, \; a_{62}a_{61} \ldots a_{57}, \; \ldots, \; a_5a_4 \ldots a_0, \; a_4a_3a_2a_1a_00, \; \ldots, \; a_000000$$

are distinct. Exercise 2.3.4.2–23 shows that many such "de Bruijn cycles" exist; for example, we can use M. H. Martin's constant $\#\text{03f79d71b4ca8b09}$, which is discussed in exercise 3.2.2–17. The decoding table $decode[0], \ldots, decode[63]$ is then

$$\begin{aligned}
&00, 01, 56, 02, 57, 49, 28, 03, 61, 58, 42, 50, 38, 29, 17, 04,\\
&62, 47, 59, 36, 45, 43, 51, 22, 53, 39, 33, 30, 24, 18, 12, 05,\\
&63, 55, 48, 27, 60, 41, 37, 16, 46, 35, 44, 21, 52, 32, 23, 11,\\
&54, 26, 40, 15, 34, 20, 31, 10, 25, 14, 19, 09, 13, 08, 07, 06.
\end{aligned} \tag{53}$$

[This technique was devised in 1967 by Luther Woodrum of IBM's Systems Development Division (unpublished); many other programmers have subsequently discovered it independently.]

Working with the leftmost bits. The function $\lambda x = \lfloor \lg x \rfloor$, which is dual to ρx because it locates the *leftmost* 1 when $x > 0$, was introduced in Eq. 4.6.3–(6). It satisfies the recurrence

$$\lambda 1 = 0; \qquad \lambda(2x) = \lambda(2x+1) = \lambda(x) + 1 \quad \text{for } x > 0; \tag{54}$$

and it is undefined when x is not a positive integer. What is a good way to compute it? Once again MMIX provides a quick-but-tricky solution:

```
FLOTU y,ROUND_DOWN,x;  SUB y,y,fone;  SR lam,y,52        (55)
```

where $\mathtt{fone} = \#\text{3ff0000000000000}$ is the floating point representation of 1.0. (Total time $6v$.) This code floats x, then extracts the exponent.

But if floating point conversion is not readily available, a binary reduction strategy works fairly well on a 2^d-bit machine. We can start with $\lambda \leftarrow 0$ and $y \leftarrow x$; then we set $\lambda \leftarrow \lambda + 2^k$ and $y \leftarrow y \gg 2^k$ if $y \gg 2^k \neq 0$, for $k = d - 1$, $\ldots$, 1, 0 (or until k is reduced to the point where a short table can be used to finish up). The MMIX code analogous to (50) and (51) is now

```
SRU y,x,32;  ZSNZ lam,y,32;
ADD t,lam,16;  SRU y,x,t;  CSNZ lam,y,t;
ADD t,lam,8;  SRU y,x,t;  CSNZ lam,y,t;
SRU y,x,lam;  LDB t,lamtab,y;  ADD lam,lam,t;
```
$$(56)$$

and the total time is $\mu + 11v$. In this case table $\mathtt{lamtab}$ has 256 entries, namely λx for $0 \le x < 256$. Notice that the "conditional set" (CS) and "zero or set" (ZS) instructions have been used here and in (50) instead of branch instructions.

There appears to be no simple way to extract the leftmost 1 bit that appears
in a register, analogous to the trick by which we extracted the rightmost 1 in (37).
For this purpose we could compute $y \leftarrow \lambda x$ and then $1 \ll y$, if $x \neq 0$; but a binary
"smearing right" method is somewhat shorter and faster:

$$\text{Set } y \leftarrow x, \text{ then } y \leftarrow y \mid (y \gg 2^k) \text{ for } 0 \le k < d.$$
$$\text{The leftmost 1 bit of } x \text{ is then } y - (y \gg 1). \tag{57}$$

[These non-floating-point methods have been suggested by H. S. Warren, Jr.]

Other operations at the left of a register, like removing the leftmost run of
1s, are harder yet; see exercise 39. But there is a remarkably simple, machine-
independent way to determine whether or not $\lambda x = \lambda y$, given unsigned integers
x and y, in spite of the fact that we can't compute λx or λy quickly:

$$\lambda x = \lambda y \qquad \text{if and only if} \qquad x \oplus y \le x \,\&\, y. \tag{58}$$

[See exercise 40. This elegant relation was discovered by W. C. Lynch in 2006.]
We will use (58) below, to devise another way to compute λx.

Sideways addition. Binary n-bit numbers $x = (x_{n-1} \ldots x_1 x_0)_2$ are often used
to represent subsets X of the n-element universe $\{0, 1, \ldots, n-1\}$, with $k \in X$
if and only if $2^k \subseteq x$. The functions λx and ρx then represent the largest and
smallest elements of X. The function

$$\nu x = x_{n-1} + \cdots + x_1 + x_0, \tag{59}$$

which is called the "sideways sum" or "population count" of x, also has obvious
importance in this connection, because it represents the cardinality $|X|$, namely
the number of elements in X. This function, which we considered in 4.6.3–(7),
satisfies the recurrence

$$\nu 0 = 0; \qquad \nu(2x) = \nu(x) \quad \text{and} \quad \nu(2x+1) = \nu(x) + 1, \quad \text{for } x \ge 0. \tag{60}$$

It also has an interesting connection with the ruler function (exercise 1.2.5–11),

$$\rho x = 1 + \nu(x-1) - \nu x; \qquad \text{equivalently,} \qquad \sum_{k=1}^{n} \rho k = n - \nu n. \tag{61}$$

The first textbook on programming, *The Preparation of Programs for an
Electronic Digital Computer* by Wilkes, Wheeler, and Gill, second edition (Reading, Mass.: Addison–Wesley, 1957), 155, 191–193, presented an interesting subroutine for sideways addition due to D. B. Gillies and J. C. P. Miller. Their
method was devised for the 35-bit numbers of the EDSAC, but it is readily
converted to the following 64-bit procedure for νx when $x = (x_{63} \ldots x_1 x_0)_2$:

Set $y \leftarrow x - ((x \gg 1) \,\&\, \mu_0)$. (Now $y = (u_{31} \ldots u_1 u_0)_4$, where $u_j = x_{2j+1} + x_{2j}$.)
Set $y \leftarrow (y \,\&\, \mu_1) + ((y \gg 2) \,\&\, \mu_1)$. (Now $y = (v_{15} \ldots v_1 v_0)_{16}$, $v_j = u_{2j+1} + u_{2j}$.)
Set $y \leftarrow (y + (y \gg 4)) \,\&\, \mu_2$. (Now $y = (w_7 \ldots w_1 w_0)_{256}$, $w_j = v_{2j+1} + v_{2j}$.)
Finally $\nu \leftarrow ((a \cdot y) \bmod 2^{64}) \gg 56$, where $a = (11111111)_{256}$. $\qquad (62)$

The last step cleverly computes $y \bmod 255 = w_7 + \cdots + w_1 + w_0$ via multiplication,
using the fact that the sum fits comfortably in eight bits. [David Muller had
programmed a similar method for the ILLIAC I machine in 1954.]

If x is expected to be "sparse," having at most a few 1-bits, we can use a faster method [P. Wegner, *CACM* **3** (1960), 322]:

Set $\nu \leftarrow 0$, $y \leftarrow x$. Then while $y \neq 0$, set $\nu \leftarrow \nu + 1$, $y \leftarrow y \,\&\, (y-1)$.   (63)

A similar approach, using $y \leftarrow y \,|\, (y+1)$, works when x is expected to be "dense."

Bit reversal. For our next trick, let's change $x = (x_{63} \dots x_1 x_0)_2$ to its left-right mirror image, $x^R = (x_0 x_1 \dots x_{63})_2$. Anybody who has been following the developments so far, seeing methods like (50), (56), (57), and (62), will probably think, "Aha—once again we can divide by 2 and conquer! If we've already discovered how to reverse 32-bit numbers, we can reverse 64-bit numbers almost as fast, because $(xy)^R = y^R x^R$. All we have to do is apply the 32-bit method in parallel to both halves of the register, then swap the left half with the right half."

Right. For example, we can reverse an 8-bit string in three easy steps:

$$
\begin{array}{ll}
\text{Given} & x_7 x_6 x_5 x_4 x_3 x_2 x_1 x_0 \\
\text{Swap bits} & x_6 x_7 x_4 x_5 x_2 x_3 x_0 x_1 \\
\text{Swap nyps} & x_4 x_5 x_6 x_7 x_0 x_1 x_2 x_3 \\
\text{Swap nybbles} & x_0 x_1 x_2 x_3 x_4 x_5 x_6 x_7
\end{array}
\tag{64}
$$

And six such easy steps will reverse 64 bits. Fortunately, each of the swapping operations turns out to be quite simple with the help of the magic masks μ_k:

$$
\begin{aligned}
y &\leftarrow (x \gg 1) \,\&\, \mu_0, & z &\leftarrow (x \,\&\, \mu_0) \ll 1, & x &\leftarrow y \,|\, z; \\
y &\leftarrow (x \gg 2) \,\&\, \mu_1, & z &\leftarrow (x \,\&\, \mu_1) \ll 2, & x &\leftarrow y \,|\, z; \\
y &\leftarrow (x \gg 4) \,\&\, \mu_2, & z &\leftarrow (x \,\&\, \mu_2) \ll 4, & x &\leftarrow y \,|\, z; \\
y &\leftarrow (x \gg 8) \,\&\, \mu_3, & z &\leftarrow (x \,\&\, \mu_3) \ll 8, & x &\leftarrow y \,|\, z; \\
y &\leftarrow (x \gg 16) \,\&\, \mu_4, & z &\leftarrow (x \,\&\, \mu_4) \ll 16, & x &\leftarrow y \,|\, z; \\
\end{aligned}
$$
$$
x \leftarrow (x \gg 32) \,|\, ((x \ll 32) \bmod 2^{64}).
\tag{65}
$$

[Christopher Strachey foresaw some aspects of this construction in *CACM* **4** (1961), 146, and a similar *ternary* method was devised in 1973 by Bruce Baumgart (see exercise 49). The mature algorithm (65) was presented by Henry S. Warren, Jr., in *Hacker's Delight* (Addison–Wesley, 2002), 102.]

But MMIX is once again able to trump this general-purpose technique with less traditional commands that do the job much faster. Consider

```
rev GREG #0102040810204080; MOR x,x,rev; MOR x,rev,x;     (66)
```

the first MOR instruction reverses the bytes of x from big-endian to little-endian or vice versa, while the second reverses the bits within each byte.

Bit swapping. Suppose we only want to interchange two bits within a register, $x_i \leftrightarrow x_j$, where $i > j$. What would be a good way to proceed? (Dear reader, please pause for a moment and solve this problem in your head, or with pencil and paper—without looking at the answer below.)

Let $\delta = i - j$. Here is one solution (but don't peek until you're ready):

$$
y \leftarrow (x \gg \delta) \,\&\, 2^j, \quad z \leftarrow (x \,\&\, 2^j) \ll \delta, \quad x \leftarrow (x \,\&\, m) \,|\, y \,|\, z, \quad \text{where } \overline{m} = 2^i | 2^j. \tag{67}
$$

It uses two shifts and five bitwise Boolean operations, assuming that i and j are given constants. It is like each of the first lines of (65), except that a new mask m is needed because y and z don't account for all of the bits of x.

We can, however, do better, saving one operation and one constant:

$$y \leftarrow (x \oplus (x \gg \delta)) \mathbin{\&} 2^j, \qquad x \leftarrow x \oplus y \oplus (y \ll \delta). \tag{68}$$

The first assignment now puts $x_i \oplus x_j$ into position j; the second changes x_i to $x_i \oplus (x_i \oplus x_j)$ and x_j to $x_j \oplus (x_i \oplus x_j)$, as desired. In general it's often wise to convert a problem of the form "change x to $f(x)$" into a problem of the form "change x to $x \oplus g(x)$," since the bit-difference $g(x)$ might be easy to calculate.

On the other hand, there's a sense in which (67) might be preferable to (68), because the assignments to y and z in (67) can sometimes be performed simultaneously. When expressed as a circuit, (67) has a depth of 4 while (68) has depth 5.

Operation (68) can of course be used to swap several pairs of bits simultaneously, when we use a mask θ that's more general than 2^j:

$$y \leftarrow (x \oplus (x \gg \delta)) \mathbin{\&} \theta, \qquad x \leftarrow x \oplus y \oplus (y \ll \delta). \tag{69}$$

Let us call this operation a "δ-swap," because it allows us to swap any non-overlapping pairs of bits that are δ places apart. The mask θ has a 1 in the rightmost position of each pair that's supposed to be swapped. For example, (69) will swap the leftmost 25 bits of a 64-bit word with the rightmost 25 bits, while leaving the 14 middle bits untouched, if we let $\delta = 39$ and $\theta = 2^{25} - 1 = {}^\#\texttt{1ffffff}$.

Indeed, there's an astonishing way to reverse 64 bits using δ-swaps, namely

$$
\begin{aligned}
&y \leftarrow (x \gg 1) \mathbin{\&} \mu_0, \quad z \leftarrow (x \mathbin{\&} \mu_0) \ll 1, \quad x \leftarrow y \mid z, \\
&y \leftarrow (x \oplus (x \gg 4)) \mathbin{\&} {}^\#\texttt{0300c0303030c303}, \quad x \leftarrow x \oplus y \oplus (y \ll 4), \\
&y \leftarrow (x \oplus (x \gg 8)) \mathbin{\&} {}^\#\texttt{00c0300c03f0003f}, \quad x \leftarrow x \oplus y \oplus (y \ll 8), \\
&y \leftarrow (x \oplus (x \gg 20)) \mathbin{\&} {}^\#\texttt{00000ffc00003fff}, \quad x \leftarrow x \oplus y \oplus (y \ll 20), \\
&x \leftarrow (x \gg 34) \mid ((x \ll 30) \bmod 2^{64}),
\end{aligned} \tag{70}
$$

saving two of the bitwise operations in (65) even though (65) looks "optimum."

*Bit permutation in general. The methods we've just seen can be extended to obtain an *arbitrary* permutation of the bits in a register. In fact, there always exist masks $\theta_0, \ldots, \theta_5, \hat{\theta}_4, \ldots, \hat{\theta}_0$ such that the following operations transform $x = (x_{63} \ldots x_1 x_0)_2$ into any desired rearrangement $x^\pi = (x_{63\pi} \ldots x_{1\pi} x_{0\pi})_2$ of its bits:

$$
\begin{aligned}
&x \leftarrow 2^k\text{-swap of } x \text{ with mask } \theta_k, \text{ for } k = 0, 1, 2, 3, 4, 5; \\
&x \leftarrow 2^k\text{-swap of } x \text{ with mask } \hat{\theta}_k, \text{ for } k = 4, 3, 2, 1, 0.
\end{aligned} \tag{71}
$$

In general, a permutation of 2^d bits can be achieved with $2d - 1$ such steps, using appropriate masks θ_k and $\hat{\theta}_k$, where the swap distances are respectively 2^0, 2^1, $\ldots, 2^{d-1}, \ldots, 2^1, 2^0$.

To prove this fact, we can use a special case of the permutation networks discovered independently by A. M. Duguid and J. Le Corre in 1959, based on earlier work of D. Slepian [see V. E. Beneš, *Mathematical Theory of Connecting Networks and Telephone Traffic* (New York: Academic Press, 1965), Section 3.3].

Figure 12 shows a permutation network $P(2n)$ for $2n$ elements constructed from two permutation networks for n elements, when $n = 4$. Each '⦙' connection between two lines represents a *crossbar module* that either leaves the line contents unaltered or interchanges them, as the data flows from left to right. To start the recursion when $n = 1$, we let $P(2)$ consist of a single crossbar. Every setting of the individual crossbars clearly causes $P(2n)$ to produce a permutation of its inputs; conversely, we will show that any permutation of the $2n$ inputs can be achieved if we are clever enough to set the crossbars appropriately.

The construction of Fig. 12 is best understood by considering an example. Suppose we want to route the inputs $(0, 1, 2, 3, 4, 5, 6, 7)$ to $(3, 2, 4, 1, 6, 0, 5, 7)$, respectively. The first job is to determine the contents of the lines just after the first column of crossbars and just before the last column, since we can then use a similar method to set the crossbars in the inner $P(4)$'s. Thus, in the network

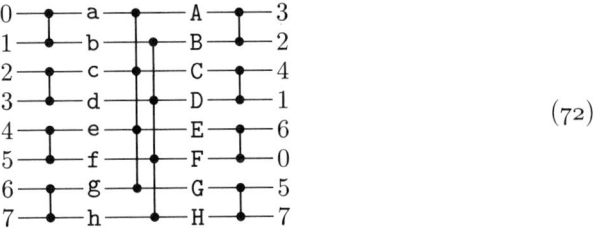

$$(72)$$

we want to find permutations abcdefgh and ABCDEFGH such that $\{a, b\} = \{0, 1\}$, $\{c, d\} = \{2, 3\}$, ..., $\{g, h\} = \{6, 7\}$, $\{a, c, e, g\} = \{A, C, E, G\}$, $\{b, d, f, h\} = \{B, D, F, H\}$, $\{A, B\} = \{3, 2\}$, $\{C, D\} = \{4, 1\}$, ..., $\{G, H\} = \{5, 7\}$. Starting at the bottom, let us choose $h = 7$, because we don't wish to disturb the contents of that line unless necessary. Then the following choices are *forced*:

$$H = 7;\ G = 5;\ e = 5;\ f = 4;\ D = 4;\ C = 1;\ a = 1;\ b = 0;\ F = 0;\ E = 6;\ g = 6. \quad (73)$$

If we had chosen $h = 6$, the forcing pattern would have been similar but reversed,

$$F = 6;\ E = 0;\ a = 0;\ b = 1;\ D = 1;\ C = 4;\ e = 4;\ f = 5;\ H = 5;\ G = 7;\ g = 7. \quad (74)$$

Options (73) and (74) can both be completed by choosing either $d = 3$ (hence $B = 3$, $A = 2$, $c = 2$) or $d = 2$ (hence $B = 2$, $A = 3$, $c = 3$).

In general the forcing pattern will go in cycles, no matter what permutation we begin with. To see this, consider the graph on eight vertices {ab, cd, ef, gh, AB, CD, EF, GH} that has an edge from uv to UV whenever the pair of inputs connected to uv has an element in common with the pair of outputs connected to UV. Thus, in our example the edges are ab — EF, ab — CD, cd — AB, cd — AB, ef — CD, ef — GH, gh — EF, gh — GH. We have a "double bond" between cd and AB, since the inputs connected to c and d are exactly the outputs connected to A and B; subject to this slight bending of the strict definition of a graph, we see that each vertex is adjacent to exactly two other vertices, and lowercase vertices are always adjacent to uppercase ones. Therefore the graph

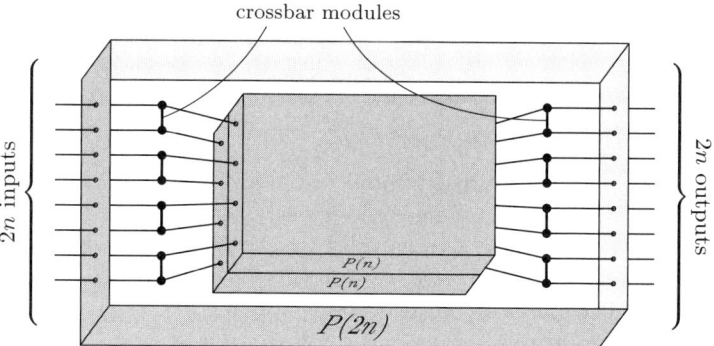

Fig. 12. The inside of a black box $P(2n)$ that permutes $2n$ elements in all possible ways, when $n > 1$. (Illustrated for $n = 4$.)

always consists of disjoint cycles of even length. In our example, the cycles are

$$\text{ab} \underset{\text{CD} - \text{ef}}{\overset{\text{EF} - \text{gh}}{\diagdown\diagup}} \text{GH} \qquad \text{cd} = \text{AB}, \qquad (75)$$

where the longer cycle corresponds to (73) and (74). If there are k different cycles, there will be 2^k different ways to specify the behavior of the first and last columns of crossbars.

To complete the network, we can process the inner 4-element permutations in the same way; and *any* 2^d-element permutation is achievable in this same recursive fashion. The resulting crossbar settings determine the masks θ_j and $\hat\theta_j$ of (71). Some choices of crossbars may lead to a mask that is entirely zero; then we can eliminate the corresponding stage of the computation.

If the input and output are identical on the bottom lines of the network, our construction shows how to ensure that none of the crossbars touching those lines are active. For example, the 64-bit algorithm in (71) could be used also with a 60-bit register, without needing the four extra bits for any intermediate results.

Of course we can often beat the general procedure of (71) in special cases. For example, exercise 52 shows that method (71) needs nine swapping steps to transpose an 8×8 matrix, but in fact three swaps suffice:

Given	7-swap	14-swap	28-swap
00 01 02 03 04 05 06 07	00 **10** 02 **12** 04 **14** 06 **16**	00 10 **20 30** 04 14 **24 34**	00 10 20 30 **40 50 60 70**
10 11 12 13 14 15 16 17	**01** 11 **03** 13 **05** 15 **07** 17	01 11 **21 31** 05 15 **25 35**	01 11 21 31 **41 51 61 71**
20 21 22 23 24 25 26 27	20 **30** 22 **32** 24 **34** 26 **36**	**02 12** 22 32 **06 16** 26 36	02 12 22 32 **42 52 62 72**
30 31 32 33 34 35 36 37	**21** 31 **23** 33 **25** 35 **27** 37	**03 13** 23 33 **07 17** 27 37	03 13 23 33 **43 53 63 73**
40 41 42 43 44 45 46 47	40 **50** 42 **52** 44 **54** 46 **56**	40 50 **60 70** 44 54 **64 74**	**04 14 24 34** 44 54 64 74
50 51 52 53 54 55 56 57	**41** 51 **43** 53 **45** 55 **47** 57	41 51 **61 71** 45 55 **65 75**	**05 15 25 35** 45 55 65 75
60 61 62 63 64 65 66 67	60 **70** 62 **72** 64 **74** 66 **76**	**42 52** 62 72 **46 56** 66 76	**06 16 26 36** 46 56 66 76
70 71 72 73 74 75 76 77	**61** 71 **63** 73 **65** 75 **67** 77	**43 53** 63 73 **47 57** 67 77	**07 17 27 37** 47 57 67 77

The "perfect shuffle" is another bit permutation that arises frequently in practice. If $x = (\dots x_2 x_1 x_0)_2$ and $y = (\dots y_2 y_1 y_0)_2$ are any 2-adic integers, we define $x \ddagger y$ ("x zip y," the *zipper function* of x and y) by interleaving their bits:

$$x \ddagger y = (\dots x_2 y_2 x_1 y_1 x_0 y_0)_2. \qquad (76)$$

This operation has important applications to the representation of 2-dimensional data, because a small change in either x or y usually causes only a small change in $x \ddagger y$ (see exercise 86). Notice also that the magic mask constants (47) satisfy

$$\mu_k \ddagger \mu_k = \mu_{k+1}. \tag{77}$$

If x appears in the left half of a register and y appears in the right half, a perfect shuffle is the permutation that changes the register contents to $x \ddagger y$.

A sequence of $d-1$ swapping steps will perfectly shuffle a 2^d-bit register; in fact, exercise 53 shows that there are several ways to achieve this. Once again, therefore, we are able to improve on the $(2d-1)$-step method of (71) and Fig. 12.

Conversely, suppose we're given the shuffled value $z = x \ddagger y$ in a 2^d-bit register; is there an efficient way to extract the original value of y? Sure: If the $d-1$ swaps that do a perfect shuffle are performed in reverse order, they'll undo the shuffle and recover both x and y. But if only y is wanted, we can save half of the work: Start with $y \leftarrow z \,\&\, \mu_0$; then set $y \leftarrow (y + (y \gg 2^{k-1})) \,\&\, \mu_k$ for $k = 1$, $\ldots$, $d-1$. For example, when $d = 3$ this procedure goes $(0y_3 0y_2 0y_1 0y_0)_2 \mapsto (00y_3y_2 00y_1y_0)_2 \mapsto (0000y_3y_2y_1y_0)_2$. "Divide and conquer" conquers again.

Consider now a more general problem, where we want to extract and compress an *arbitrary* subset of a register's bits. Suppose we're given a 2^d-bit word $z = (z_{2^d-1} \ldots z_1 z_0)_2$ and a mask $\chi = (\chi_{2^d-1} \ldots \chi_1 \chi_0)_2$ that has s 1-bits; thus $\nu\chi = s$. The problem is to assemble the compact subword

$$y = (y_{s-1} \ldots y_1 y_0)_2 = (z_{j_{s-1}} \ldots z_{j_1} z_{j_0})_2, \tag{78}$$

where $j_{s-1} > \cdots > j_1 > j_0$ are the indices where $\chi_j = 1$. For example, if $d = 3$ and $\chi = (10110010)_2$, we want to transform $z = (y_3 x_3 y_2 y_1 x_2 x_1 y_0 x_0)_2$ into $y = (y_3 y_2 y_1 y_0)_2$. (The problem of going from $x \ddagger y$ to y, considered above, is the special case $\chi = \mu_0$.) We know from (71) that y can be found by δ-swapping, at most $2d-1$ times; but in this problem the relevant data always moves to the right, so we can speed things up by doing *shifts* instead of swaps.

Let's say that a δ-shift of x with mask θ is the operation

$$x \leftarrow x \oplus \big((x \oplus (x \gg \delta)) \,\&\, \theta\big), \tag{79}$$

which changes bit x_j to $x_{j+\delta}$ if θ has 1 in position j but leaves x_j unchanged otherwise. Guy Steele discovered that there always exist masks $\theta_0, \theta_1, \ldots, \theta_{d-1}$ so that the general extraction problem (78) can be solved with a few δ-shifts:

$$\begin{aligned} &\text{Start with } x \leftarrow z; \text{ then do a } 2^k\text{-shift of } x \text{ with mask } \theta_k,\\ &\text{for } k = 0, 1, \ldots, d-1; \text{ finally set } y \leftarrow x. \end{aligned} \tag{80}$$

In fact, the idea for finding appropriate masks is surprisingly simple. Every bit that wants to move a total of exactly $l = (l_{d-1} \ldots l_1 l_0)_2$ places to the right should be transported in the 2^k-shifts for which $l_k = 1$.

For example, suppose $d = 3$ and $\chi = (10110010)_2$. (We must assume that $\chi \neq 0$.) Remembering that some 0s need to be shifted in from the left, we can set $\theta_0 = (00011001)_2$, $\theta_1 = (00000110)_2$, $\theta_2 = (11111000)_2$; then (80) maps

$(y_3 x_3 y_2 y_1 x_2 x_1 y_0 x_0)_2 \mapsto (y_3 x_3 y_2 y_2 y_1 x_1 y_0 y_0)_2 \mapsto (y_3 x_3 y_2 y_2 y_1 y_2 y_1 y_0)_2 \mapsto (0000 y_3 y_2 y_1 y_0$

Exercise 69 proves that the bits being extracted will never interfere with each other during their journey. Furthermore, there's a slick way to compute suitable masks θ_k dynamically from χ, in $O(d^2)$ steps (see exercise 70).

A "sheep-and-goats" or "grouping" operation has been suggested for computer hardware, extending (78) to produce the general unshuffled word

$$(x_{r-1} \ldots x_1 x_0 y_{s-1} \ldots y_1 y_0)_2 = (z_{i_{r-1}} \ldots z_{i_1} z_{i_0} z_{j_{s-1}} \ldots z_{j_1} z_{j_0})_2; \qquad (81)$$

here $i_{r-1} > \cdots > i_1 > i_0$ are the indices where $\chi_i = 0$. But another operation called "gather-flip," which reverses the order of the unmasked bits and gives

$$(x_0 x_1 \ldots x_{r-1} y_{s-1} \ldots y_1 y_0)_2 = (z_{i_0} z_{i_1} \ldots z_{i_{r-1}} z_{j_{s-1}} \ldots z_{j_1} z_{j_0})_2, \qquad (81')$$

turns out to be more useful and easier to implement. Any permutation of 2^d bits is achievable by using either operation, at most d times (see exercises 72 and 73).

Shifting also allows us to go beyond permutations, to arbitrary *mappings* of bits within a register. Suppose we want to transform

$$x = (x_{2^d-1} \ldots x_1 x_0)_2 \quad \mapsto \quad x^\varphi = (x_{(2^d-1)\varphi} \ldots x_{1\varphi} x_{0\varphi})_2, \qquad (82)$$

where φ is any of the $(2^d)^{2^d}$ functions from the set $\{0, 1, \ldots, 2^d - 1\}$ into itself. K. M. Chung and C. K. Wong [*IEEE Transactions* **C-29** (1980), 1029–1032] introduced an attractive way to do this in $O(d)$ steps by using *cyclic δ-shifts*, which are like (79) except that we set

$$x \leftarrow x \oplus \big((x \oplus (x \gg \delta) \oplus (x \ll (2^d - \delta))) \,\&\, \theta\big). \qquad (83)$$

Their idea is to let c_l be the number of indices j such that $j\varphi = l$, for $0 \le l < 2^d$. Then they find masks θ_0, θ_1, ..., θ_{d-1} with the property that a cyclic 2^k-shift of x with mask θ_k, done successively for $0 \le k < d$, will transform x into a number x' that contains exactly c_l copies of bit x_l for each l. Finally the general permutation procedure (71) can be used to change $x' \mapsto x^\varphi$.

For example, suppose $d = 3$ and $x^\varphi = (x_3 x_1 x_1 x_0 x_3 x_7 x_5 x_5)_2$. Then we have $(c_0, c_1, c_2, c_3, c_4, c_5, c_6, c_7) = (1, 2, 0, 2, 0, 2, 0, 1)$. Using masks $\theta_0 = (00011100)_2$, $\theta_1 = (00001000)_2$, and $\theta_2 = (01100000)_2$, three cyclic 2^k-shifts now take $x = (x_7 x_6 x_5 x_4 x_3 x_2 x_1 x_0)_2 \mapsto (x_7 x_6 x_5 x_5 x_4 x_3 x_1 x_0)_2 \mapsto (x_7 x_6 x_5 x_5 x_5 x_3 x_1 x_0)_2 \mapsto (x_7 x_3 x_1 x_5 x_5 x_3 x_1 x_0)_2 = x'$. Then, some δ-swaps: $x' \mapsto (x_3 x_7 x_5 x_1 x_3 x_5 x_1 x_0)_2 \mapsto (x_3 x_1 x_5 x_7 x_3 x_5 x_1 x_0)_2 \mapsto (x_3 x_1 x_1 x_0 x_3 x_5 x_5 x_7)_2 \mapsto (x_3 x_1 x_1 x_0 x_3 x_7 x_5 x_5)_2 = x^\varphi$; we're done! Of course any 8-bit mapping can be achieved more quickly by brute force, one bit at a time; the method of Chung and Wong becomes much more impressive in a 256-bit register. Even with MMIX's 64-bit registers it's pretty good, needing at most 96 cycles in the worst case.

To find θ_0, we use the fact that $\sum c_l = 2^d$, and we look at $\Sigma_{\text{even}} = \sum c_{2l}$ and $\Sigma_{\text{odd}} = \sum c_{2l+1}$. If $\Sigma_{\text{even}} = \Sigma_{\text{odd}} = 2^{d-1}$, we can set $\theta_0 = 0$ and omit the cyclic 1-shift. But if, say, $\Sigma_{\text{even}} < \Sigma_{\text{odd}}$, we find an even l with $c_l = 0$. Cyclically shifting into bits $l, l+1, \ldots, l+t$ (modulo 2^d) for some t will produce new counts $(c'_0, \ldots, c'_{2^d-1})$ for which $\Sigma'_{\text{even}} = \Sigma'_{\text{odd}} = 2^{d-1}$; so $\theta_0 = 2^l + \cdots + 2^{(l+t) \bmod 2^d}$. Then we can deal with the bits in even and odd positions separately, using the same method, until getting down to 1-bit subwords. Exercise 74 has the details.

Working with fragmented fields. Instead of extracting bits from various parts of a word and gathering them together, we can often manipulate those bits directly in their original positions.

For example, suppose we want to run through all subsets of a given set U, where (as usual) the set is specified by a mask χ such that $[k \in U] = (\chi \gg k) \,\&\, 1$. If $x \subseteq \chi$ and $x \neq \chi$, there's an easy way to calculate the next largest subset of U in lexicographic order, namely the smallest integer $x' > x$ such that $x' \subseteq \chi$:

$$x' = (x - \chi) \,\&\, \chi. \tag{84}$$

In the special case when $x = 0$ and $\chi \neq 0$, we've already seen in (37) that this formula produces the rightmost bit of χ, which corresponds to the lexicographically smallest nonempty subset of U.

Why does formula (84) work? Imagine adding 1 to the number $x \mid \bar{\chi}$, which has 1s wherever χ is 0. A carry will propagate through those 1s until it reaches the rightmost bit position where x has a 0 and χ has a 1; furthermore all bits to the right of that position will become zero. Therefore $x' = ((x \mid \bar{\chi}) + 1) \,\&\, \chi$. But we have $(x \mid \bar{\chi}) + 1 = (x + \bar{\chi}) + 1 = x + (\bar{\chi} + 1) = x - \chi$ when $x \subseteq \chi$. QED.

Notice further that $x' = 0$ if and only if $x = \chi$. So we'll know when we've found the largest subset. Exercise 79 shows how to go back to x, given x'.

We might also want to run through all elements of a *subcube* — for example, to find all bit patterns that match a specification like $*10*1*01$, consisting of 0s, 1s, and $*$s (don't-cares). Such a specification can be represented by asterisk codes $a = (a_{n-1} \ldots a_0)_2$ and bit codes $b = (b_{n-1} \ldots b_0)_2$, as in exercise 7.1.1–30; our example corresponds to $a = (10010100)_2$, $b = (01001001)_2$. The problem of enumerating all subsets of a set is the special case where $a = \chi$ and $b = 0$. In the more general subcube problem, the successor of a given bit pattern x is

$$x' = ((x - (a + b)) \,\&\, a) + b. \tag{85}$$

Suppose the bits of $z = (z_{n-1} \ldots z_0)_2$ have been stitched together from two subwords $x = (x_{r-1} \ldots x_0)_2$ and $y = (y_{s-1} \ldots y_0)_2$, where $r + s = n$, using an arbitrary mask χ for which $\nu\chi = s$ to govern the stitching. For example, $z = (y_2 x_4 x_3 y_1 x_2 y_0 x_1 x_0)_2$ when $n = 8$ and $\chi = (10010100)_2$. We can think of z as a "scattered accumulator," in which alien bits x_i lurk among friendly bits y_j. From this viewpoint the problem of finding successive elements of a subcube is essentially the problem of computing $y + 1$ inside a scattered accumulator z, without changing the value of x. The sheep-and-goats operation (81) would untangle x and y; but it's expensive, and (85) shows that we can solve the problem without it. We can, in fact, compute $y + y'$ when $y' = (y'_{s-1} \ldots y'_0)_2$ is *any* value inside a scattered accumulator z', if y and y' both appear in the positions specified by χ: Consider $t = z \,\&\, \chi$ and $t' = z' \,\&\, \chi$. If we form the sum $(t \mid \bar{\chi}) + t'$, all carries that occur in a normal addition $y + y'$ will propagate through the blocks of 1s in $\bar{\chi}$, just as if the scattered bits were adjacent. Thus

$$((z \,\&\, \chi) + (z' \mid \bar{\chi})) \,\&\, \chi \tag{86}$$

is the sum of y and y', modulo 2^s, scattered according to the mask χ.

Tweaking several bytes at once. Instead of concentrating on the data in one field within a word, we often want to deal simultaneously with two or more subwords, performing calculations on each of them in parallel. For example, many applications need to process long sequences of bytes, and we can gain speed by acting on eight bytes at a time; we might as well use all 64 bits that our machine provides. General multibyte techniques were introduced by Leslie Lamport in *CACM* **18** (1975), 471–475, and subsequently extended by many programmers.

Suppose first that we simply wish to take two sequences of bytes and find their sum, regarding them as coordinates of vectors, doing arithmetic modulo 256 in each byte. Algebraically speaking, we're given 8-byte vectors $x = (x_7 \ldots x_1 x_0)_{256}$ and $y = (y_7 \ldots y_1 y_0)_{256}$; we want to compute $z = (z_7 \ldots z_1 z_0)_{256}$, where $z_j = (x_j + y_j) \bmod 256$ for $0 \le j < 8$. Ordinary addition of x to y doesn't quite work, because we need to prevent carries from propagating between bytes. So we extract the high-order bits and deal with them separately:

$$z \leftarrow (x \oplus y) \mathbin{\&} h, \qquad \text{where } h = {}^{\#}8080808080808080;$$
$$z \leftarrow ((x \mathbin{\&} \bar{h}) + (y \mathbin{\&} \bar{h})) \oplus z. \tag{87}$$

The total time for MMIX to do this is 6υ, plus $3\mu + 3\upsilon$ if we also count the time to load x, load y, and store z. By contrast, eight one-byte additions (LDBU, LDBU, ADDU, and STBU, repeated eight times) would cost $8 \times (3\mu + 4\upsilon) = 24\mu + 32\upsilon$. Parallel *subtraction* of bytes is just as easy (see exercise 88).

We can also compute bytewise *averages*, with $z_j = \lfloor (x_j + y_j)/2 \rfloor$ for each j:

$$z \leftarrow ((x \oplus y) \mathbin{\&} \bar{l}) \gg 1, \qquad \text{where } l = {}^{\#}0101010101010101;$$
$$z \leftarrow (x \mathbin{\&} y) + z. \tag{88}$$

This elegant trick, suggested by H. G. Dietz, is based on the well-known formula

$$x + y = (x \oplus y) + ((x \mathbin{\&} y) \ll 1) \tag{89}$$

for radix-2 addition. (We can implement (88) with four MMIX instructions, not five, because a single MOR operation will change $x \oplus y$ to $((x \oplus y) \mathbin{\&} \bar{l}) \gg 1$.)

Exercises 88–93 and 100–104 develop these ideas further, showing how to do mixed-radix arithmetic, as well as such things as the addition and subtraction of vectors whose components are treated modulo m when m needn't be a power of 2.

In essence, we can regard the bits, bytes, or other subfields of a register as if they were elements of an array of independent microprocessors, acting independently on their own subproblems yet tightly synchronized, and communicating with each other via shift instructions and carry bits. Computer designers have been interested for many years in the development of parallel processors with a so-called SIMD architecture, namely a "Single Instruction stream with Multiple Data streams"; see, for example, S. H. Unger, *Proc. IRE* **46** (1958), 1744–1750. The increased availability of 64-bit registers has meant that programmers of ordinary sequential computers are now able to get a taste of SIMD processing. Indeed, computations such as (87), (88), and (89) are called SWAR methods — "SIMD Within A Register," a name coined by R. J. Fisher and H. G. Dietz [see *Lecture Notes in Computer Science* **1656** (1999), 290–305]. See also R. B. Lee, *IEEE Micro* **16**, 4 (August 1996), 51–59.

Of course bytes often contain alphabetic data as well as numbers, and one of the most common programming tasks is to search through a long string of characters in order to find the first appearance of some particular byte value. For example, strings are often represented as a sequence of nonzero bytes terminated by 0. In order to locate the end of a string quickly, we need a fast way to determine whether all eight bytes of a given word x are nonzero (because they usually are). Several fairly good solutions to this problem were found by Lamport and others; but Alan Mycroft discovered in 1987 that *three* instructions actually suffice:

$$t \leftarrow h \mathbin{\&} (x - l) \mathbin{\&} \bar{x}, \tag{90}$$

where h and l appear in (87) and (88). If each byte x_j is nonzero, t will be zero; for $(x_j - 1) \mathbin{\&} \bar{x}_j$ will be $2^{\rho x_j} - 1$, which is always less than ${}^\#80 = 2^7$. But if $x_j = 0$, while its right neighbors $x_{j-1}, \ldots, x_0$ (if any) are all nonzero, the subtraction $x - l$ will produce ${}^\#\mathtt{ff}$ in byte j, and t will be nonzero. In fact, ρt will be $8j + 7$.

Caution: Although the computation in (90) pinpoints the *rightmost* zero byte of x, we cannot deduce the position of the *leftmost* zero byte from the value of t alone. (See exercise 94.) In this respect the little-endian convention proves to be preferable to the corresponding big-endian behavior. An application that needs to locate the leftmost zero byte can use (90) to skip quickly over nonzeros, but then it must fall back on a slower method when the search has been narrowed down to eight finalists. The following 4-operation formula produces a completely precise test value $t = (t_7 \ldots t_1 t_0)_{256}$, in which $t_j = 128[x_j = 0]$ for each j:

$$t \leftarrow h \mathbin{\&} {\sim}(x \mid ((x \mid h) - l)). \tag{91}$$

The leftmost zero byte of x is now x_j, where $\lambda t = 8j + 7$.

Incidentally, the single MMIX instruction 'BDIF t,1,x' solves the zero-byte problem immediately by setting each byte t_j of t to $[x_j = 0]$, because $1 \mathbin{\dot{-}} x = [x = 0]$. But we are primarily interested here in fairly universal techniques that don't rely on exotic hardware; MMIX's special features will be discussed later.

Now that we know a fast way to find the first 0, we can use the same ideas to search for *any* desired byte value. For example, to test if any byte of x is the newline character (${}^\#\mathtt{a}$), we simply look for a zero byte in $x \oplus {}^\#\mathtt{0a0a0a0a0a0a0a0a}$.

And these techniques also open up many other doors. Suppose, for instance, that we want to compute $z = (z_7 \ldots z_1 z_0)_{256}$ from x and y, where $z_j = x_j$ when $x_j = y_j$ but $z_j = \text{'*'}$ when $x_j \neq y_j$. (Thus if $x = \mathtt{"beaching"}$ and $y = \mathtt{"belching"}$, we're supposed to set $z \leftarrow \mathtt{"be*ching"}$.) It's easy:

$$\begin{aligned} t &\leftarrow h \mathbin{\&} ((x \oplus y) \mid (((x \oplus y) \mid h) - l)); \\ m &\leftarrow (t \ll 1) - (t \gg 7); \\ z &\leftarrow x \oplus ((x \oplus \mathtt{"********"}) \mathbin{\&} m). \end{aligned} \tag{92}$$

The first step uses a variant of (91) to flag the high-order bits in each byte where $x_j \neq y_j$. The next step creates a mask to highlight those bytes: ${}^\#\mathtt{00}$ if $x_j = y_j$, otherwise ${}^\#\mathtt{ff}$. And the last step, which could also be written $z \leftarrow (x \mathbin{\&} \overline{m}) \mid (\mathtt{"********"} \mathbin{\&} m)$, sets $z_j \leftarrow x_j$ or $z_j \leftarrow \text{'*'}$, depending on the mask.

Operations (90) and (91) were originally designed as tests for bytes that are zero; but a closer look reveals that we can more wisely regard them as tests for bytes that are less than 1. Indeed, if we replace l by $c \cdot l = (cccccccc)_{256}$ in either formula, where c is any positive constant ≤ 128, we can use (90) or (91) to see if x contains any bytes that are less than c. Furthermore the comparison values c need not be the same in every byte position; and with a bit more work we can also do bytewise comparison in the cases where $c > 128$. Here's an 8-step formula that sets $t_j \leftarrow 128[x_j < y_j]$ for each byte position j in the test word t:

$$t \leftarrow h \mathbin{\&} \mathord{\sim}\langle x\bar{y}z\rangle, \qquad \text{where } z = (x \mid h) - (y \mathbin{\&} \bar{h}). \tag{93}$$

(See exercise 96.) The median operation in this general formula can often be simplified; for example, (93) reduces to (91) when $y = l$, because $\langle x(-1)z\rangle = x \mid z$.

Once we've found a nonzero t in (90) or (91) or (93), we might want to compute ρt or λt in order to discover the index j of the rightmost or leftmost byte that has been flagged. The problem of calculating ρ or λ is now simpler than before, since t can take on only 256 different values. Indeed, the operation

$$j \leftarrow \textit{table}[((a \cdot t) \bmod 2^{64}) \gg 56], \quad \text{where } a = \frac{2^{56} - 1}{2^7 - 1}, \tag{94}$$

now suffices to compute j, given an appropriate 256-byte table. And the multiplication here can often be performed faster by doing three shift-and-add operations, "$t \leftarrow t + (t \ll 7)$, $t \leftarrow t + (t \ll 14)$, $t \leftarrow t + (t \ll 28)$," instead.

Broadword computing. We've now seen more than a dozen ways in which a computer's bitwise operations can produce astonishing results at high speed, and the exercises below contain many more such surprises.

Elwyn Berlekamp has remarked that computer chips containing N flip-flops continue to be built with ever larger values of N, yet in practice only $O(\log N)$ of those components are flipping or flopping at any given moment. The surprising effectiveness of bitwise operations suggests that computers of the future might make use of this untapped potential by having enhanced memory units that are able to do efficient n-bit computations for fairly large values of n. To prepare for that day, we ought to have a good name for the concept of manipulating "wide words." Lyle Ramshaw has suggested the pleasant term *broadword*, so that we can speak of n-bit quantities as broadwords of width n.

Many of the methods we've discussed are *2-adic*, in the sense that they work correctly with binary numbers that have arbitrary (even infinite) precision. For example, the operation $x \mathbin{\&} -x$ always extracts $2^{\rho x}$, the least significant 1 bit of any nonzero 2-adic integer x. But other methods have an inherently broadword nature, such as the methods that use $O(d)$ steps to perform sideways addition or bit permutation of 2^d-bit words. Broadword computing is the art of dealing with n-bit words, when n is a parameter that is not extremely small.

Some broadword algorithms are of theoretical interest only, because they are efficient only in an asymptotic sense when n exceeds the size of the universe. But others are eminently practical even when $n = 64$. And in general, a broadword mindset often suggests good techniques.

One fascinating-but-impractical fact about broadword operations is the discovery by M. L. Fredman and D. E. Willard that $O(1)$ broadword steps suffice to evaluate the function $\lambda x = \lfloor \lg x \rfloor$ for any nonzero n-bit number x, no matter how big n is. Here is their remarkable scheme, when $n = g^2$ and g is a power of 2:

$$
\begin{aligned}
&t_1 \leftarrow h \,\&\, (x \mid ((x \mid h) - l)), \quad \text{where } h = 2^{g-1}l \text{ and } l = (2^n - 1)/(2^g - 1); \\
&y \leftarrow (((a \cdot t_1) \bmod 2^n) \gg (n - g)) \cdot l, \quad \text{where } a = (2^{n-g} - 1)/(2^{g-1} - 1); \\
&t_2 \leftarrow h \,\&\, (y \mid ((y \mid h) - b)), \quad \text{where } b = (2^{n+g} - 1)/(2^{g+1} - 1); \\
&m \leftarrow (t_2 \ll 1) - (t_2 \gg (g - 1)), \quad m \leftarrow m \oplus (m \gg g); \qquad\qquad (95) \\
&z \leftarrow (((l \cdot (x \,\&\, m)) \bmod 2^n) \gg (n - g)) \cdot l; \\
&t_3 \leftarrow h \,\&\, (z \mid ((z \mid h) - b)); \\
&\lambda \leftarrow ((l \cdot ((t_2 \gg (2g - \lg g - 1)) + (t_3 \gg (2g - 1)))) \bmod 2^n) \gg (n - g).
\end{aligned}
$$

(See exercise 106.) The method fails to be practical because five of these 29 steps are multiplications, so they aren't really "bitwise" operations. In fact, we'll prove later that multiplication by a constant requires at least $\Omega(\log n)$ bitwise steps.

A multiplication-free way to find λx, with only $O(\log \log n)$ bitwise broadword operations, was discovered in 1997 by Gerth Brodal, whose method is even more remarkable than (95). It is based on a formula analogous to (49),

$$
\lambda x \;=\; [\lambda x = \lambda(x \,\&\, \bar\mu_0)] + 2[\lambda x = \lambda(x \,\&\, \bar\mu_1)] + 4[\lambda x = \lambda(x \,\&\, \bar\mu_2)] + \cdots, \quad (96)
$$

and the fact that the relation $\lambda x = \lambda y$ is easily tested (see (58)):

Algorithm B (*Binary logarithm*). This algorithm uses n-bit operations to compute $\lambda x = \lfloor \lg x \rfloor$, assuming that $0 < x < 2^n$ and $n = d \cdot 2^d$.

B1. [Scale down.] Set $\lambda \leftarrow 0$. Then set $\lambda \leftarrow \lambda + 2^k$ and $x \leftarrow x \gg 2^k$ if $x \geq 2^{2^k}$, for $k = \lceil \lg n \rceil - 1, \lceil \lg n \rceil - 2, \ldots, d$.

B2. [Replicate.] (At this point $0 < x < 2^{2^d}$; the remaining task is to increase λ by $\lfloor \lg x \rfloor$. We will replace x by d copies of itself, in 2^d-bit fields.) Set $x \leftarrow x \mid (x \ll 2^{d+k})$ for $0 \leq k < \lceil \lg d \rceil$.

B3. [Change leading bits.] Set $y \leftarrow x \,\&\, \sim(\mu_{d,d-1} \cdots \mu_{d,1} \mu_{d,0})_{2^{2^d}}$. (See (48).)

B4. [Compare all fields.] Set $t \leftarrow h \,\&\, (y \mid ((y \mid h) - (x \oplus y)))$, where $h = (2^{2^d - 1} \cdots 2^{2^d - 1} 2^{2^d - 1})_{2^{2^d}}$.

B5. [Compress bits.] Set $t \leftarrow (t + (t \ll (2^{d+k} - 2^k))) \bmod 2^n$ for $0 \leq k < \lceil \lg d \rceil$.

B6. [Finish.] Finally, set $\lambda \leftarrow \lambda + (t \gg (n - d))$. ∎

This algorithm is almost competitive with (56) when $n = 64$ (see exercise 107).

Another surprisingly efficient broadword algorithm was discovered in 2006 by M. S. Paterson and the author, who considered the problem of identifying all occurrences of the pattern 01^r in a given n-bit binary string. This problem, which is related to finding r contiguous free blocks when allocating storage, is equivalent to computing

$$
q \;=\; \bar x \,\&\, (x \ll 1) \,\&\, (x \ll 2) \,\&\, (x \ll 3) \,\&\, \cdots \,\&\, (x \ll r) \qquad (97)
$$

when $x = (x_{n-1} \ldots x_1 x_0)_2$ is given. For example, when $n = 16$, $r = 3$, and $x = (1110111101100111)_2$, we have $q = (0001000000001000)_2$. One might expect intuitively that $\Omega(\log r)$ bitwise operations would be needed. But in fact the following 20-step computation does the job for all $n > r > 0$: Let $s = \lceil r/2 \rceil$, $l = \sum_{k \geq 0} 2^{ks} \bmod 2^n$, $h = (2^{s-1} l) \bmod 2^n$, and $a = \left(\sum_{k \geq 0} (-1)^{k+1} 2^{2ks} \right) \bmod 2^n$.

$$
\begin{aligned}
&y \leftarrow h \mathbin{\&} x \mathbin{\&} ((x \mathbin{\&} \bar{h}) + l); \\
&t \leftarrow (x + y) \mathbin{\&} \bar{x} \mathbin{\&} -2^r; \\
&u \leftarrow t \mathbin{\&} a, \; v \leftarrow t \mathbin{\&} \bar{a}; \\
&m \leftarrow (u - (u \gg r)) \mid (v - (v \gg r)); \\
&q \leftarrow t \mathbin{\&} ((x \mathbin{\&} m) + ((t \gg r) \mathbin{\&} \sim(m \ll 1))).
\end{aligned}
\tag{98}
$$

Exercise 111 explains why these machinations are valid. The method has little or no practical value; there's an easy way to evaluate (97) in $2\lceil \lg r \rceil + 2$ steps, so (98) is not advantageous until $r > 512$. But (98) is another indication of the unexpected power of broadword methods.

Lower bounds. Indeed, the existence of so many tricks and techniques makes it natural to wonder whether we've only been scratching the surface. Are there many more incredibly fast methods, still waiting to be discovered? A few theoretical results are known by which we can derive certain limitations on what is possible, although such studies are still in their infancy.

Let's say that a *2-adic chain* is a sequence $(x_0, x_1, \ldots, x_r)$ of 2-adic integers in which each element x_i for $i > 0$ is obtained from its predecessors via bitwise manipulation. More precisely, we want the steps of the chain to be defined by binary operations

$$
x_i = x_{j(i)} \circ_i x_{k(i)} \quad \text{or} \quad c_i \circ_i x_{k(i)} \quad \text{or} \quad x_{j(i)} \circ_i c_i, \tag{99}
$$

where each $\circ_i$ is one of the operators $\{+, -, \mathbin{\&}, \mid, \oplus, \equiv, \subset, \supset, \bar{\subset}, \bar{\supset}, \wedge, \vee, \ll, \gg\}$ and each c_i is a constant. Furthermore, when the operator $\circ_i$ is a left shift or right shift, the amount of shift must be a positive integer constant; operations such as $x_{j(i)} \ll x_{k(i)}$ or $c_i \gg x_{k(i)}$ are *not* permitted. (Without the latter restriction we couldn't derive meaningful lower bounds, because *every* 0–1 valued function of a nonnegative integer x would be computable in two steps as "$(c \gg x) \mathbin{\&} 1$" for some constant c.)

Similarly, a *broadword chain* of width n, also called an n-bit broadword chain, is a sequence $(x_0, x_1, \ldots, x_r)$ of n-bit numbers subject to essentially the same restrictions, where n is a parameter and all operations are performed modulo 2^n. Broadword chains behave like 2-adic chains in many ways, but subtle differences can arise because of the information loss that occurs at the left of n-bit computations (see exercise 113).

Both types of chains compute a function $f(x) = x_r$ when we start them out with a given value $x = x_0$. Exercise 114 shows that an mn-bit broadword chain is able to do m essentially simultaneous evaluations of any function that is computable with an n-bit chain. Our goal is to study the *shortest* chains that are able to evaluate a given function f.

Any 2-adic or broadword chain $(x_0, x_1, \ldots, x_r)$ has a sequence of "shift sets" $(S_0, S_1, \ldots, S_r)$ and "bounds" $(B_0, B_1, \ldots, B_r)$, defined as follows: Start with $S_0 = \{0\}$ and $B_0 = 1$; then for $i \geq 1$, let

$$S_i = \begin{cases} S_{j(i)} \cup S_{k(i)}, \\ S_{k(i)}, \\ S_{j(i)}, \\ S_{j(i)} + c_i, \\ S_{j(i)} - c_i, \end{cases} \quad \text{and} \quad B_i = \begin{cases} M_i B_{j(i)} B_{k(i)}, & \text{if } x_i = x_{j(i)} \circ_i x_{k(i)}, \\ M_i B_{k(i)}, & \text{if } x_i = c_i \circ_i x_{k(i)}, \\ M_i B_{j(i)}, & \text{if } x_i = x_{j(i)} \circ_i c_i, \\ B_{j(i)}, & \text{if } x_i = x_{j(i)} \gg c_i, \\ B_{j(i)}, & \text{if } x_i = x_{j(i)} \ll c_i, \end{cases} \quad (100)$$

where $M_i = 2$ if $\circ_i \in \{+, -\}$ and $M_i = 1$ otherwise, and these formulas assume that $\circ_i \notin \{\ll, \gg\}$. For example, consider the following 7-step chain:

$$
\begin{array}{ccc}
x_i & S_i & B_i \\
x_0 = x & \{0\} & 1 \\
x_1 = x_0 \mathbin{\&} -2 & \{0\} & 1 \\
x_2 = x_1 + 2 & \{0\} & 2 \\
x_3 = x_2 \gg 1 & \{1\} & 2 \\
x_4 = x_2 + x_3 & \{0,1\} & 8 \\
x_5 = x_4 \gg 4 & \{4,5\} & 8 \\
x_6 = x_4 + x_5 & \{0,1,4,5\} & 128 \\
x_7 = x_6 \gg 4 & \{4,5,8,9\} & 128 \\
\end{array}
\qquad (101)
$$

(We encountered this chain in exercise 4.4–9, which proved that these operations will yield $x_7 = \lfloor x/10 \rfloor$ for $0 \leq x < 160$ when performed with 8-bit arithmetic.)

To begin a theory of lower bounds, let's notice first that the high-order bits of $x = x_0$ cannot influence any low-order bits unless we shift them to the right.

Lemma A. *Given a 2-adic or broadword chain, let the binary representation of x_i be $(\ldots x_{i2} x_{i1} x_{i0})_2$. Then bit x_{ip} can depend on bit x_{0q} only if $q \leq p + \max S_i$.*

Proof. By induction on i we can in fact show that, if $B_i = 1$, bit x_{ip} can depend on bit x_{0q} only if $q - p \in S_i$. Addition and subtraction, which force $B_i > 1$, allow any particular bit of their operands to affect all bits that lie to the left in the sum or difference, but not those that lie to the right. ∎

Corollary I. *The function $x \mathbin{\dot{-}} 1$ cannot be computed by a 2-adic chain, nor can any function for which at least one bit of $f(x)$ depends on an unbounded number of bits of x.* ∎

Corollary W. *An n-bit function $f(x)$ can be computed by an n-bit broadword chain without shifts if and only if $x \equiv y \pmod{2^p}$ implies $f(x) \equiv f(y) \pmod{2^p}$ for $0 \leq p < n$.*

Proof. If there are no shifts we have $S_i = \{0\}$ for all i. Thus bit x_{rp} cannot depend on bit x_{0q} unless $q \leq p$. In other words we must have $x_r \equiv y_r \pmod{2^p}$ whenever $x_0 \equiv y_0 \pmod{2^p}$.

Conversely, all such functions are achievable by a sufficiently long chain. Exercise 119 gives shift-free n-bit chains for the functions

$$f_{py}(x) = 2^p[x \bmod 2^{p+1} = y], \qquad \text{when } 0 \leq p < n \text{ and } 0 \leq y < 2^{p+1}, \quad (102)$$

from which all the relevant functions arise by addition. [H. S. Warren, Jr., generalized this result to functions of m variables in *CACM* **20** (1977), 439–441.] ∎

Shift sets S_i and bounds B_i are important chiefly because of a fundamental lemma that is our principal tool for proving lower bounds:

Lemma B. *Let* $X_{pqr} = \{x_r \mathbin{\&} \lfloor 2^p - 2^q \rfloor \mid x_0 \in V_{pqr}\}$ *in an* n-*bit broadword chain, where*

$$V_{pqr} = \{x \mid x \mathbin{\&} \lfloor 2^{p+s} - 2^{q+s} \rfloor = 0 \text{ for all } s \in S_r\} \tag{103}$$

and $p > q$. *Then* $|X_{pqr}| \le B_r$. *(Here* p *and* q *are integers, possibly negative.)*

This lemma states that at most B_r different bit patterns $x_{r(p-1)} \dots x_{rq}$ can occur within $f(x)$, when certain intervals of bits in x are constrained to be zero.

Proof. The result certainly holds when $r = 0$. Otherwise if, for example, $x_r = x_j + x_k$, we know by induction that $|X_{pqj}| \le B_j$ and $|X_{pqk}| \le B_k$. Furthermore $V_{pqr} = V_{pqj} \cap V_{pqk}$, since $S_r = S_j \cup S_k$. Thus at most $B_j B_k$ possibilities for $(x_j + x_k) \mathbin{\&} \lfloor 2^p - 2^q \rfloor$ arise when there's no carry into position q, and at most $B_j B_k$ when there is a carry, making a grand total of at most $B_r = 2B_j B_k$ possibilities altogether. Exercise 122 considers the other cases. ∎

We now can prove that the ruler function needs $\Omega(\log \log n)$ steps.

Theorem R. *If* $n = d \cdot 2^d$, *every* n-*bit broadword chain that computes* ρx *for* $0 < x < 2^n$ *has more than* $\lg d$ *steps that are not shifts.*

Proof. If there are l nonshift steps, we have $|S_r| \le 2^l$ and $B_r \le 2^{2^l-1}$. Apply Lemma B with $p = d$ and $q = 0$, and suppose $|X_{d0r}| = 2^d - t$. Then there are t values of $k < 2^d$ such that

$$\{2^k, 2^{k+2^d}, 2^{k+2\cdot 2^d}, \dots, 2^{k+(d-1)2^d}\} \cap V_{d0r} = \emptyset.$$

But V_{d0r} excludes at most $2^l d$ of the n possible powers of 2; so $t \le 2^l$.

If $l \le \lg d$, Lemma B tells us that $2^d - t \le B_r \le 2^{d-1}$; hence $2^{d-1} \le t \le 2^l \le d$. But this is impossible unless $d \le 2$, when the theorem clearly holds. ∎

The same proof works also for the binary logarithm function:

Corollary L. *If* $n = d \cdot 2^d > 2$, *every* n-*bit broadword chain that computes* λx *for* $0 < x < 2^n$ *has more than* $\lg d$ *steps that are not shifts.* ∎

By using Lemma B with $q > 0$ we can derive the stronger lower bound $\Omega(\log n)$ for bit reversal, and hence for bit permutation in general.

Theorem P. *If* $2 \le g \le n$, *every* n-*bit broadword chain that computes the* g-*bit reversal* x^R *for* $0 \le x < 2^g$ *has at least* $\lfloor \frac{1}{3} \lg g \rfloor$ *steps that are not shifts.*

Proof. Assume as above that there are l nonshifts. Let $h = \lfloor \sqrt[3]{g} \rfloor$ and suppose that $l < \lfloor \lg(h+1) \rfloor$. Then S_r is a set of at most $2^l \le \frac{1}{2}(h+1)$ shift amounts s. We shall apply Lemma B with $p = q+h$, where $p \le g$ and $q \ge 0$, thus in $g-h+1$ cases altogether. The key observation is that $x^R \mathbin{\&} \lfloor 2^p - 2^q \rfloor$ is independent of $x \mathbin{\&} \lfloor 2^{p+s} - 2^{q+s} \rfloor$ whenever there are no indices j and k such that $0 \le j, k < h$ and $g - 1 - q - j = q + s + k$. The number of "bad" choices of q for which such indices exist is at most $\frac{1}{2}(h+1)h^2 \leq g - h$; therefore at least one "good" choice of q yields $|X_{pqr}| = 2^h$. But then Lemma B leads to a contradiction, because we obviously cannot have $2^h \leq B_r \leq 2^{(h-1)/2}$. ∎

Corollary M. *Multiplication by certain constants, modulo 2^n, requires $\Omega(\log n)$ steps in an n-bit broadword chain.*

Proof. In Hack 167 of the classic memorandum HAKMEM (M.I.T. A.I. Laboratory, 1972), Richard Schroeppel observed that the operations

$$t \leftarrow ((ax) \bmod 2^n) \,\&\, b, \quad y \leftarrow ((ct) \bmod 2^n) \gg (n-g) \qquad (104)$$

compute $y = x^R$ whenever $n = g^2$ and $0 \leq x < 2^g$, using the constants $a = (2^{n+g} - 1)/(2^{g+1} - 1)$, $b = 2^{g-1}(2^n - 1)/(2^g - 1)$, and $c = (2^{n-g} - 1)/(2^{g-1} - 1)$. (See exercise 123.) ∎

At this point the reader might well be thinking, "Okay, I agree that broadword chains sometimes have to be asymptotically long. But programmers needn't be shackled by such chains; we can use other techniques, like conditional branches or references to precomputed tables, which go beyond those restrictions."

Right. And we're in luck, because broadword theory can also be extended to more general models of computation. Consider, for example, the following idealization of an abstract reduced-instruction-set computer, called a *basic RAM*: The machine has n-bit registers $r_1, \ldots, r_l$, and n-bit memory words $\{M[0], \ldots, M[2^m - 1]\}$. It can perform the instructions

$$\begin{aligned} r_i \leftarrow r_j \pm r_k, \quad r_i \leftarrow r_j \circ r_k, \quad r_i \leftarrow r_j \gg r_k, \quad r_i \leftarrow c, \\ r_i \leftarrow M[r_j \bmod 2^m], \quad M[r_j \bmod 2^m] \leftarrow r_i, \end{aligned} \qquad (105)$$

where $\circ$ is any bitwise Boolean operator, and where r_k in the shift instruction is treated as a signed integer in two's complement notation. The machine is also able to branch if $r_i \leq r_j$, treating r_i and r_j as unsigned integers. Its *state* is the entire contents of all registers and memory, together with a "program counter" that points to the current instruction. Its program begins in a designated state, which may include precomputed tables in memory, and with an n-bit input value x in register r_1. This initial state is called $Q(x, 0)$, and $Q(x, t)$ denotes the state after t instructions have been performed. When the machine stops, r_1 will contain some n-bit value $f(x)$. Given a function $f(x)$, we want to find a lower bound on the least t such that r_1 is equal to $f(x)$ in state $Q(x, t)$, for $0 \leq x < 2^n$.

Theorem R′. *Let $\epsilon = 2^{-e}$. A basic n-bit RAM with memory parameter $m \leq n^{1-\epsilon}$ requires at least $\lg \lg n - e$ steps to evaluate the ruler function ρx, as $n \to \infty$.*

Proof. Let $n = 2^{2^{e+f}}$, so that $m \leq 2^{2^{e+f} - 2^f}$. Exercise 124 explains how an omniscient observer can construct a broadword chain from a certain class of inputs x, in such a way that each x causes the RAM to take the same branches, use the same shift amounts, and refer to the same memory locations. Our earlier methods can then be used to show that this chain has length $\geq f$. ∎

A skeptical reader may still object that Theorem R′ has no practical value, because $\lg \lg n$ never exceeds 6 in the real world. To this argument there is no rebuttal. But the following result is slightly more relevant:

Theorem P′. *A basic n-bit RAM requires at least $\frac{1}{3}\lg g$ steps to compute the g-bit reversal x^R for $0 \le x < 2^g$, if $g \le n$ and*

$$\max(m, 1 + \lg n) \;<\; \frac{h+1}{2\lfloor \lg(h+1) \rfloor - 2}, \qquad h = \lfloor \sqrt[3]{g} \rfloor. \tag{106}$$

Proof. An argument like the proof of Theorem R′ appears in exercise 125. ∎

Lemma B and Theorems R, P, R′, P′ and their corollaries are due to A. Brodnik, P. B. Miltersen, and J. I. Munro, *Lecture Notes in Comp. Sci.* **1272** (1997), 426–439, based on earlier work of Miltersen in *Lecture Notes in Comp. Sci.* **1099** (1996), 442–453.

Many unsolved questions remain (see exercises 126–130). For example, does sideways addition require $\Omega(\log n)$ steps in an n-bit broadword chain? Can the parity function $(\nu x) \bmod 2$, or the majority function $[\nu x > n/2]$, be computed substantially faster than νx itself, broadwordwise?

An application to directed graphs. Now let's use some of what we've learned, by implementing a simple algorithm. Given a digraph on a set of vertices V, we write $u \longrightarrow v$ when there's an arc from u to v. The *reachability problem* is to find all vertices that lie on oriented paths beginning in a specified set $Q \subseteq V$; in other words, we seek the set

$$R \;=\; \{v \mid u \longrightarrow^* v \text{ for some } u \in Q\}, \tag{107}$$

where $u \longrightarrow^* v$ means that there is a sequence of t arcs

$$u = u_0 \longrightarrow u_1 \longrightarrow \cdots \longrightarrow u_t = v, \qquad \text{for some } t \ge 0. \tag{108}$$

This problem arises frequently in practice. For example, we encountered it in Section 2.3.5 when marking all elements of Lists that are not "garbage."

If the number of vertices is small, say $|V| \le 64$, we may want to approach the reachability problem in quite a different way than we did before, by working directly with subsets of vertices. Let

$$S[u] \;=\; \{v \mid u \longrightarrow v\} \tag{109}$$

be the set of successors of vertex u, for all $u \in V$. Then the following algorithm is almost completely different from Algorithm 2.3.5E, yet it solves the same abstract problem:

Algorithm R (*Reachability*). Given a simple directed graph, represented by the successor sets $S[u]$ in (109), this algorithm computes the elements R that are reachable from a given set Q.

R1. [Initialize.] Set $R \leftarrow Q$ and $X \leftarrow \emptyset$. (In the following steps, X is the subset of vertices $u \in R$ for which we've looked at $S[u]$.)

R2. [Done?] If $X = R$, the algorithm terminates.

R3. [Examine another vertex.] Let u be an element of $R \setminus X$. Set $X \leftarrow X \cup u$, $R \leftarrow R \cup S[u]$, and return to step R2. ∎

The algorithm is correct because (i) every element placed into R is reachable; (ii) every reachable element u_j in (108) is present in R, by induction on j; and (iii) termination eventually occurs, because step R3 always increases $|X|$.

To implement Algorithm R we will assume that $V = \{0, 1, \ldots, n-1\}$, with $n \leq 64$. The set X is conveniently represented by the integer $\sigma(X) = \sum \{2^u \mid u \in X\}$, and the same convention works nicely for the other sets Q, R, and $S[u]$. Notice that the bits of $S[0]$, $S[1]$, ..., $S[n-1]$ are essentially the *adjacency matrix* of the given digraph, as explained in Section 7, but in little-endian order: The "diagonal" elements, which tell us whether or not $u \in S[u]$, go from right to left. For example, if $n = 3$ and the arcs are $\{0 \to 0, 0 \to 1, 1 \to 0, 2 \to 0\}$, we have $S[0] = (011)_2$ and $S[1] = S[2] = (001)_2$, while the adjacency matrix is $\begin{pmatrix} 110 \\ 100 \\ 100 \end{pmatrix}$.

Step R3 allows us to choose any element of $R \setminus X$, so we use the ruler function $u \leftarrow \rho(\sigma(R) - \sigma(X))$ to choose the smallest. The bitwise operations require no further trickery when we adapt the algorithm to MMIX:

Program R (*Reachability*). The input set Q is given in register q, and each successor set $S[u]$ appears in octabyte $M_8[\mathtt{suc} + 8u]$. The output set R will appear in register r; other registers s, t, tt, u, and x hold intermediate results.

01	1H	SET	r,q	1	*R1. Initialize.* $\mathtt{r} \leftarrow \sigma(Q)$.
02		SET	x,0	1	$\mathtt{x} \leftarrow \sigma(\emptyset)$.
03		JMP	2F	1	To R2.
04	3H	SUBU	tt,t,1	$|R|$	*R3. Examine another vertex.* $\mathtt{tt} \leftarrow \mathtt{t} - 1$.
05		SADD	u,tt,t	$|R|$	$\mathtt{u} \leftarrow \rho(\mathtt{t})$ [see (46)].
06		SLU	s,u,3	$|R|$	$\mathtt{s} \leftarrow 8u$.
07		LDOU	s,suc,s	$|R|$	$\mathtt{s} \leftarrow \sigma(S[u])$.
08		ANDN	tt,t,tt	$|R|$	$\mathtt{tt} \leftarrow \mathtt{t}\ \&\ \sim\!\mathtt{tt} = 2^u$.
09		OR	x,x,tt	$|R|$	$X \leftarrow X \cup u$; that is, $\mathtt{x} \leftarrow \mathtt{x}\ |\ 2^u$, since $\mathtt{x} = \sigma(X)$.
10		OR	r,r,s	$|R|$	$R \leftarrow R \cup S[u]$; that is, $\mathtt{r} \leftarrow \mathtt{r}\ |\ \mathtt{s}$, since $\mathtt{r} = \sigma(R)$.
11	2H	SUBU	t,r,x	$|R|+1$	*R2. Done?* $\mathtt{t} \leftarrow \mathtt{r} - \mathtt{x} = \sigma(R \setminus X)$, since $X \subseteq R$.
12		PBNZ	t,3B	$|R|+1$	To R3 if $R \neq X$. ∎

The total running time is $(\mu + 9\upsilon)|R| + 7\upsilon$. By contrast, exercise 131 implements Algorithm R with linked lists; the overall execution time then grows to $(3S + 4|R| - 2|Q| + 1)\mu + (5S + 12|R| - 5|Q| + 4)\upsilon$, where $S = \sum_{u \in R} |S[u]|$. (But of course that program is also able to handle graphs with millions of vertices.)

Exercise 132 presents another instructive algorithm where bitwise operations work nicely on not-too-large graphs.

Application to data representation. Computers are binary, but (alas?) the world isn't. We often must find a way to encode nonbinary data into 0s and 1s. One of the most common problems of this sort is to choose an efficient representation for items that can be in exactly three different states.

Suppose we know that $x \in \{a, b, c\}$, and we want to represent x by two bits $x_l x_r$. We could, for example, map $a \mapsto 00$, $b \mapsto 01$, and $c \mapsto 10$. But there are many other possibilities — in fact, 4 choices for a, then 3 choices for b, and 2 for c, making 24 altogether. Some of these mappings might be much easier to deal with than others, depending on what we want to do with x.

Given two elements $x, y \in \{a, b, c\}$, we typically want to compute $z = x \circ y$, for some binary operation $\circ$. If $x = x_l x_r$ and $y = y_l y_r$ then $z = z_l z_r$, where

$$z_l = f_l(x_l, x_r, y_l, y_r) \qquad \text{and} \qquad z_r = f_r(x_l, x_r, y_l, y_r); \tag{110}$$

these Boolean functions f_l and f_r of four variables depend on $\circ$ and the chosen representation. We seek a representation that makes f_l and f_r easy to compute.

Suppose, for example, that $\{a, b, c\} = \{-1, 0, +1\}$ and that $\circ$ is multiplication. If we decide to use the natural mapping $x \mapsto x \bmod 3$, namely

$$0 \mapsto 00, \qquad +1 \mapsto 01, \qquad -1 \mapsto 10, \tag{111}$$

so that $x = x_r - x_l$, then the truth tables for f_l and f_r are respectively

$$f_l \leftrightarrow 000{*}001{*}010{*}{*}{*}{*}{*} \qquad \text{and} \qquad f_r \leftrightarrow 000{*}010{*}001{*}{*}{*}{*}{*}. \tag{112}$$

(There are seven "don't-cares," for cases where $x_l x_r = 11$ and/or $y_l y_r = 11$.) The methods of Section 7.1.2 tell us how to compute z_l and z_r optimally, namely

$$z_l = (x_l \oplus y_l) \wedge (x_r \oplus y_r), \qquad z_r = (x_l \oplus y_r) \wedge (x_r \oplus y_l); \tag{113}$$

unfortunately the functions f_l and f_r in (112) are independent, in the sense that they cannot both be evaluated in fewer than $C(f_l) + C(f_r) = 6$ steps.

On the other hand the somewhat less natural mapping scheme

$$+1 \mapsto 00, \qquad 0 \mapsto 01, \qquad -1 \mapsto 10 \tag{114}$$

leads to the transformation functions

$$f_l \leftrightarrow 001{*}000{*}100{*}{*}{*}{*}{*} \qquad \text{and} \qquad f_r \leftrightarrow 010{*}111{*}010{*}{*}{*}{*}{*}, \tag{115}$$

and three operations now suffice to do the desired evaluation:

$$z_r = x_r \vee y_r, \qquad z_l = (x_l \oplus y_l) \wedge \bar{z}_r. \tag{116}$$

Is there an easy way to discover such improvements? Fortunately we don't need to try all 24 possibilities, because many of them are basically alike. For example, the mapping $x \mapsto x_r x_l$ is equivalent to $x \mapsto x_l x_r$, because the new representation $x'_l x'_r = x_r x_l$ obtained by swapping coordinates makes

$$f'_l(x'_l, x'_r, y'_l, y'_r) = z'_l = z_r = f_r(x_l, x_r, y_l, y_r);$$

the new transformation functions f'_l and f'_r defined by

$$f'_l(x_l, x_r, y_l, y_r) = f_r(x_r, x_l, y_r, y_l), \qquad f'_r(x_l, x_r, y_l, y_r) = f_l(x_r, x_l, y_r, y_l) \tag{117}$$

have the same complexity as f_l and f_r. Similarly we can complement a coordinate, letting $x'_l x'_r = \bar{x}_l x_r$; then the transformation functions turn out to be

$$f'_l(x_l, x_r, y_l, y_r) = \bar{f}_l(\bar{x}_l, x_r, \bar{y}_l, y_r), \qquad f'_r(x_l, x_r, y_l, y_r) = f_r(\bar{x}_l, x_r, \bar{y}_l, y_r), \tag{118}$$

and again the complexity is essentially unchanged.

Repeated use of swapping and/or complementation leads to eight mappings that are equivalent to any given one. So the 24 possibilities reduce to only three, which we shall call classes I, II, and III:

Class I	Class II	Class III

$$
\begin{aligned}
a &\mapsto 00\;01\;10\;11\;\;00\;10\;01\;11\;\;00\;01\;10\;11\;\;00\;10\;01\;11\;\;00\;01\;10\;11\;\;00\;10\;01\;11; \\
b &\mapsto 01\;00\;11\;10\;\;10\;00\;11\;01\;\;01\;00\;11\;10\;\;10\;00\;11\;01\;\;11\;10\;01\;00\;\;11\;01\;10\;00; \quad (119) \\
c &\mapsto 10\;11\;00\;01\;\;01\;11\;00\;10\;\;11\;10\;01\;00\;\;11\;01\;10\;00\;\;01\;00\;11\;10\;\;10\;00\;11\;01.
\end{aligned}
$$

To choose a representation we need consider only one representative of each class. For example, if $a = +1$, $b = 0$, and $c = -1$, representation (111) belongs to class II, and (114) belongs to class I. Class III turns out to have cost 3, like class I. So it appears that representation (114) is as good as any, with z computed by (116), for the 3-element multiplication problem we've been studying.

Appearances can, however, be deceiving, because we need not map $\{a, b, c\}$ into *unique* two-bit codes. Consider the one-to-many mapping

$$+1 \mapsto 00, \qquad 0 \mapsto 01 \text{ or } 11, \qquad -1 \mapsto 10, \tag{120}$$

where both 01 and 11 are allowed as representations of zero. The truth tables for f_l and f_r are now quite different from (112) and (115), because all inputs are legal but some outputs can be arbitrary:

$$f_l \leftrightarrow 0*1*****1*0***** \qquad \text{and} \qquad f_r \leftrightarrow 0101111101011111. \tag{121}$$

And in fact, this approach needs just two operations, instead of the three in (116):

$$z_l = x_l \oplus y_l, \qquad z_r = x_r \vee y_r. \tag{122}$$

A moment's thought shows that indeed, these operations obviously yield the product $z = x \cdot y$ when the three elements $\{+1, 0, -1\}$ are represented as in (120).

Such nonunique mappings add 36 more possibilities to the 24 that we had before. But again, they reduce under "2-cube equivalence" to a small number of equivalence classes. First there are three classes that we call IV_a, IV_b, and IV_c, depending on which element has an ambiguous representation:

	Class IV_a	Class IV_b	Class IV_c
$a \mapsto$	0* 0* 1* 1* *0 *0 *1 *1	11 10 01 00 11 01 10 00	10 11 00 01 01 11 00 10;
$b \mapsto$	10 11 00 01 01 11 00 10	0* 0* 1* 1* *0 *0 *1 *1	11 10 01 00 11 01 10 00;
$c \mapsto$	11 10 01 00 11 01 10 00	10 11 00 01 01 11 00 10	0* 0* 1* 1* *0 *0 *1 *1.

(123)

(Representation (120) belongs to class IV_b. Classes IV_a and IV_c don't work well for $z = x \cdot y$.) Then there are three further classes with only four mappings each:

	Class V_a	Class V_b	Class V_c
$a \mapsto$	tt $t\bar{t}$ $t\bar{t}$ tt	10 11 00 01	01 00 11 10;
$b \mapsto$	01 00 11 10	tt $t\bar{t}$ $t\bar{t}$ tt	10 11 00 01;
$c \mapsto$	10 11 00 01	01 00 11 10	tt $t\bar{t}$ $t\bar{t}$ tt.

(124)

These classes are a bit of a nuisance, because the indeterminacy in their truth tables cannot be expressed simply in terms of don't-cares as we did in (121). For example, if we try

$$+1 \mapsto 00 \text{ or } 11, \qquad 0 \mapsto 01, \qquad -1 \mapsto 10, \tag{125}$$

which is the first mapping in class V_a, there are binary variables $pqrst$ such that

$$f_l \leftrightarrow p01q000010r1s01t \qquad \text{and} \qquad f_r \leftrightarrow p10q111101r0s10t. \tag{126}$$

Furthermore, mappings of classes V_a, V_b, and V_c almost never turn out to be better than the mappings of the other six classes (see exercise 138). Still, representatives of all nine classes must be examined before we can be sure that an optimal mapping has been found.

In practice we often want to perform several different operations on ternary-valued variables, not just a single operation like multiplication. For example, we might want to compute $\max(x, y)$ as well as $x \cdot y$. With representation (120), the best we can do is $z_l = x_l \wedge y_l$, $z_r = (x_l \wedge y_r) \vee (x_r \wedge (y_l \vee y_r))$; but the "natural" mapping (111) now shines, with $z_l = x_l \wedge y_l$, $z_r = x_r \vee y_r$. Class III turns out to have cost 4; other classes are inferior. To choose between classes II, III, and IV$_b$ in this case, we need to know the relative frequencies of $x \cdot y$ and $\max(x, y)$. And if we add $\min(x, y)$ to the mix, classes II, III, and IV$_b$ compute it with the respective costs 2, 5, 5; hence (111) looks better yet.

The ternary max and min operations arise also in other contexts, such as the three-valued logic developed by Jan Łukasiewicz in 1917. [See his *Selected Works*, edited by L. Borkowski (1970), 84–88, 153–178.] Consider the logical values "true," "false," and "maybe," denoted respectively by 1, 0, and $*$. Łukasiewicz defined the three basic operations of conjunction, disjunction, and implication on these values by specifying the tables

$$
x \left\{ \begin{array}{c} 0 \\ * \\ 1 \end{array} \right.
\begin{array}{|c c c|}
\hline
0 & 0 & 0 \\
0 & * & * \\
0 & * & 1 \\
\hline
\end{array}
,\qquad
x \left\{ \begin{array}{c} 0 \\ * \\ 1 \end{array} \right.
\begin{array}{|c c c|}
\hline
0 & * & 1 \\
* & * & 1 \\
1 & 1 & 1 \\
\hline
\end{array}
,\qquad
x \left\{ \begin{array}{c} 0 \\ * \\ 1 \end{array} \right.
\begin{array}{|c c c|}
\hline
1 & 1 & 1 \\
* & 1 & 1 \\
0 & * & 1 \\
\hline
\end{array}
. \qquad (127)
$$

with column headings y ($0\ *\ 1$) above each table, labeled below as $x \wedge y$, $x \vee y$, and $x \Rightarrow y$.

For these operations the methods above show that the binary representation

$$0 \mapsto 00, \qquad * \mapsto 01, \qquad 1 \mapsto 11 \qquad (128)$$

works well, because we can compute the logical operations thus:

$$x_l x_r \wedge y_l y_r = (x_l \wedge y_l)(x_r \wedge y_r), \qquad x_l x_r \vee y_l y_r = (x_l \vee y_l)(x_r \vee y_r),$$
$$x_l x_r \Rightarrow y_l y_r = ((\bar{x}_l \vee y_l) \wedge (\bar{x}_r \vee y_r))(\bar{x}_l \vee y_r). \qquad (129)$$

Of course x need not be an isolated ternary value in this discussion; we often want to deal with ternary *vectors* $x = x_1 x_2 \ldots x_n$, where each x_j is either a, b, or c. Such ternary vectors are conveniently represented by two binary vectors

$$x_l = x_{1l} x_{2l} \ldots x_{nl} \qquad \text{and} \qquad x_r = x_{1r} x_{2r} \ldots x_{nr}, \qquad (130)$$

where $x_j \mapsto x_{jl} x_{jr}$ as above. We could also pack the ternary values into two-bit fields of a single vector,

$$x = x_{1l} x_{1r} x_{2l} x_{2r} \ldots x_{nl} x_{nr}; \qquad (131)$$

that would work fine if, say, we're doing Łukasiewicz logic with the operations $\wedge$ and $\vee$ but not $\Rightarrow$. Usually, however, the two-vector approach of (130) is better, because it lets us do bitwise calculations without shifting and masking.

Applications to data structures. Bitwise operations offer many efficient ways to represent elements of data and the relationships between them. For example, chess-playing programs often use a "bit board" to represent the positions of pieces (see exercise 143).

In Chapter 8 we shall discuss an important data structure developed by Peter van Emde Boas for representing a dynamically changing subset of integers between 0 and N. Insertions, deletions, and other operations such as "find the largest element less than x" can be done in $O(\log \log N)$ steps with his methods; the general idea is to organize the full structure recursively as $\sqrt{N}$ substructures for subsets of intervals of size $\sqrt{N}$, together with an auxiliary structure that tells which of those intervals are occupied. [See *Information Processing Letters* **6** (1977), 80–82; also P. van Emde Boas, R. Kaas, and E. Zijlstra, *Math. Systems Theory* **10** (1977), 99–127.] Bitwise operations make those computations fast.

Hierarchical data can sometimes be arranged so that the links between elements are implicit rather than explicit. For example, we studied "heaps" in Section 5.2.3, where n elements of a sequential array implicitly have a binary tree structure like

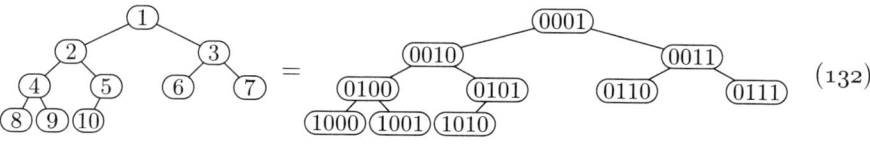 $\quad(132)$

when, say, $n = 10$. (Node numbers are shown here both in decimal and binary notation.) There is no need to store pointers in memory to relate node j of a heap to its parent (which is node $j \gg 1$ if $j \neq 1$), or to its sibling (which is node $j \oplus 1$ if $j \neq 1$), or to its children (which are nodes $j \ll 1$ and $(j \ll 1) + 1$ if those numbers don't exceed n), because a simple calculation leads directly from j to any desired neighbor.

Similarly, a *sideways heap* provides implicit links for another useful family of n-node binary tree structures, typified by

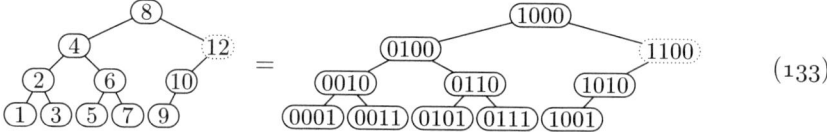 $\quad(133)$

when $n = 10$. (We sometimes need to go beyond n when moving from a node to its parent, as in the path from 10 to 12 to 8 shown here.) Heaps and sideways heaps can both be regarded as nodes 1 to n of *infinite* binary tree structures: The heap with $n = \infty$ is rooted at node 1 and has no leaves; by contrast, the sideways heap with $n = \infty$ has infinitely many leaves 1, 3, 5, ..., but no root(!).

The leaves of a sideways heap are the odd numbers, and their parents are the odd multiples of 2. The grandparents of leaves, similarly, are the odd multiples of 4; and so on. Thus the ruler function ρj tells how high node j is above leaf level.

The parent of node j in the infinite sideways heap is easily seen to be node

$$(j - k) \mid (k \ll 1), \qquad \text{where } k = j \,\&\, -j; \qquad (134)$$

this formula rounds j to the nearest odd multiple of $2^{1+\rho j}$. And the children are

$$j - (k \gg 1) \quad \text{and} \quad j + (k \gg 1) \tag{135}$$

when j is even. In general the descendants of node j form a closed interval

$$[j - 2^{\rho j} + 1 \mathrel{..} j + 2^{\rho j} - 1], \tag{136}$$

arranged as a complete binary tree of $2^{1+\rho j} - 1$ nodes. (These are the "inclusive" descendants, including j itself.) The ancestor of node j at height h is node

$$(j \mid (1 \ll h)) \mathbin{\&} -(1 \ll h) = ((j \gg h) \mid 1) \ll h \tag{137}$$

when $h \geq \rho j$. Notice that the symmetric order of the nodes, also called inorder, is just the natural order 1, 2, 3, ...

Dov Harel noted these properties in his Ph.D. thesis (U. of California, Irvine, 1980), and observed that the *nearest* common ancestor of any two nodes of a sideways heap can also be easily calculated. Indeed, if node l is the nearest common ancestor of nodes i and j, where $i \leq j$, there is a remarkable identity

$$\rho l = \max\{\rho x \mid i \leq x \leq j\} = \lambda(j \mathbin{\&} -i), \tag{138}$$

which relates the ρ and λ functions. (See exercise 146.) We can therefore use formula (137) with $h = \lambda(j \mathbin{\&} -i)$ to calculate l.

Subtle extensions of this approach lead to an asymptotically efficient algorithm that finds nearest common ancestors in *any* oriented forest whose arcs grow dynamically [D. Harel and R. E. Tarjan, *SICOMP* **13** (1984), 338–355]. Baruch Schieber and Uzi Vishkin [*SICOMP* **17** (1988), 1253–1262] subsequently discovered a much simpler way to compute nearest common ancestors in an arbitrary (but fixed) oriented forest, using an attractive and instructive blend of bitwise and algorithmic techniques that we shall consider next.

Recall that an oriented forest with m trees and n vertices is an acyclic digraph with $n - m$ arcs. There is at most one arc from each vertex; the vertices with out-degree zero are the roots of the trees. We say that v is the *parent* of u when $u \longrightarrow v$, and v is an (inclusive) *ancestor* of u when $u \longrightarrow^* v$. Two vertices have a common ancestor if and only if they belong to the same tree. Vertex w is called the nearest common ancestor of u and v when we have

$$u \longrightarrow^* z \text{ and } v \longrightarrow^* z \quad \text{if and only if} \quad w \longrightarrow^* z. \tag{139}$$

Schieber and Vishkin preprocess the given forest, mapping its vertices into a sideways heap S of size n by computing three quantities for each vertex v:

πv, the rank of v in preorder ($1 \leq \pi v \leq n$);
βv, a node of the sideways heap S ($1 \leq \beta v \leq n$);
αv, a $(1 + \lambda n)$-bit routing code ($1 \leq \alpha v < 2^{1+\lambda n}$).

If $u \longrightarrow v$ we have $\pi u > \pi v$ by the definition of preorder. Node βv is defined to be the nearest common ancestor of all sideways-heap nodes πu such that v is an ancestor of vertex u (always meaning an *inclusive* ancestor). And we define

$$\alpha v = \sum \{2^{\rho \beta w} \mid v \longrightarrow^* w\}. \tag{140}$$

For example, here's an oriented forest with ten vertices and two trees:

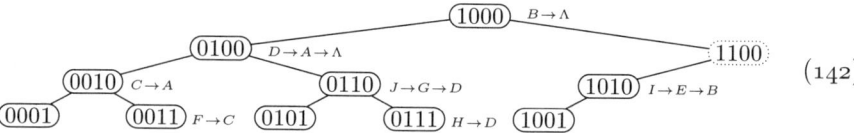

$$(141)$$

Each node has been labeled with its preorder rank, from which we can compute the β and α codes:

$$
\begin{array}{ccccccccccc}
v = & A & B & C & D & E & F & G & H & I & J \\
\pi v = & 0001 & 1000 & 0010 & 0100 & 1001 & 0011 & 0101 & 0111 & 1010 & 0110 \\
\beta v = & 0100 & 1000 & 0010 & 0100 & 1010 & 0011 & 0110 & 0111 & 1010 & 0110 \\
\alpha v = & 0100 & 1000 & 0110 & 0100 & 1010 & 0111 & 0110 & 0101 & 1010 & 0110
\end{array}
$$

Notice that, for instance, $\beta A = 4 = 0100$ because the preorder ranks of the descendants of A are $\{1, 2, 3, 4, 5, 6, 7\}$. And $\alpha H = 0101$ because the ancestors of H have β codes $\{\beta H, \beta D, \beta A\} = \{0111, 0100\}$. One can prove without difficulty that the mapping $v \mapsto \beta v$ satisfies the following key properties:

i) If $u \longrightarrow v$ in the forest, then βu is a descendant of βv in S.

ii) If several vertices have the same value of βv, they form a path in the forest.

Property (ii) holds because exactly one child u of v has $\beta u = \beta v$ when $\beta v \neq \pi v$.

Now let's imagine placing every vertex v of the forest into node βv of S:

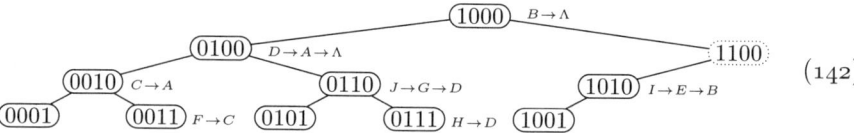

$$(142)$$

If k vertices map into node j, we can arrange them into a path

$$
v_0 \longrightarrow v_1 \longrightarrow \cdots \longrightarrow v_{k-1} \longrightarrow v_k, \qquad \text{where } \beta v_0 = \beta v_1 = \cdots = \beta v_{k-1} = j. \quad (143)
$$

These paths are illustrated in (142); for example, $J \longrightarrow G \longrightarrow D$ is a path in (141), and '$J \rightarrow G \rightarrow D$' appears with node $0110 = \beta J = \beta G$.

The preprocessing algorithm also computes a table τj for all nodes j of S, containing pointers to the vertices v_k at the tail ends of (143):

$$
\begin{array}{ccccccccccc}
j = & 0001 & 0010 & 0011 & 0100 & 0101 & 0110 & 0111 & 1000 & 1001 & 1010 \\
\tau j = & \Lambda & A & C & \Lambda & \Lambda & D & D & \Lambda & \Lambda & B
\end{array}
$$

Exercise 149 shows that all four tables πv, βv, αv, and τj can be prepared in $O(n)$ steps. And once those tables are ready, they contain just enough information to identify the nearest common ancestor of any two given vertices quickly:

Algorithm V (*Nearest common ancestors*). Suppose πv, βv, αv, and τj are known for all n vertices v of an oriented forest, and for $1 \leq j \leq n$. A dummy vertex Λ is also assumed to be present, with $\pi \Lambda = \beta \Lambda = \alpha \Lambda = 0$. This algorithm computes the nearest common ancestor z of any given vertices x and y, returning $z = \Lambda$ if x and y belong to different trees. We assume that the values $\lambda j = \lfloor \lg j \rfloor$ have been precomputed for $1 \leq j \leq n$, and that $\lambda 0 = \lambda n$.

V1. [Find common height.] If $\beta x \leq \beta y$, set $h \leftarrow \lambda(\beta y \mathrel{\&} -\beta x)$; otherwise set $h \leftarrow \lambda(\beta x \mathrel{\&} -\beta y)$. (See (138).)

V2. [Find true height.] Set $k \leftarrow \alpha x \mathrel{\&} \alpha y \mathrel{\&} -(1 \ll h)$, then $h \leftarrow \lambda(k \mathrel{\&} -k)$.

V3. [Find βz.] Set $j \leftarrow ((\beta x \gg h) \mid 1) \ll h$. (Now $j = \beta z$, if $z \neq \Lambda$.)

V4. [Find $\hat{x}$ and $\hat{y}$.] (We now seek the lowest ancestors of x and y in node j.) If $j = \beta x$, set $\hat{x} \leftarrow x$; otherwise set $l \leftarrow \lambda(\alpha x \mathrel{\&} ((1 \ll h) - 1))$ and $\hat{x} \leftarrow \tau(((\beta x \gg l) \mid 1) \ll l)$. Similarly, if $j = \beta y$, set $\hat{y} \leftarrow y$; otherwise set $l \leftarrow \lambda(\alpha y \mathrel{\&} ((1 \ll h) - 1))$ and $\hat{y} \leftarrow \tau(((\beta y \gg l) \mid 1) \ll l)$.

V5. [Find z.] Set $z \leftarrow \hat{x}$ if $\pi\hat{x} \leq \pi\hat{y}$, otherwise $z \leftarrow \hat{y}$. ∎

These artful dodges obviously exploit (137); exercise 152 explains why they work.

Sideways heaps can also be used to implement an interesting type of priority queue that J. Katajainen and F. Vitale call a "navigation pile," illustrated here for $n = 10$:

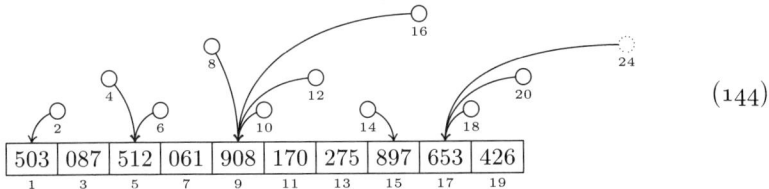

$$(144)$$

Data elements go into the leaf positions 1, 3, ..., $2n - 1$ of the sideways heap; they can be many bits wide, and they can appear in any order. By contrast, each branch position 2, 4, 6, ... contains a pointer to its largest descendant. And the novel point is that these pointers take up almost no extra space — fewer than two bits per item of data, on average — because only one bit is needed for pointers 2, 6, 10, ..., only two bits for pointers 4, 12, 20, ..., and only ρj for pointer j in general. (See exercise 153.) Thus the navigation pile requires very little memory, and it behaves nicely with respect to cache performance on a typical computer.

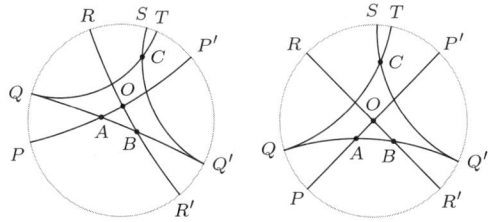

Fig. 13. Two views of five lines in the hyperbolic plane.

*Cells in the hyperbolic plane. Hyperbolic geometry suggests an instructive implicit data structure that has a rather different flavor. The *hyperbolic plane* is a fascinating example of non-Euclidean geometry that is conveniently viewed by projecting its points into the interior of a circle. Its straight lines then become circular arcs, which meet the rim at right angles. For example, the lines PP', QQ', and RR' in Fig. 13 intersect at points O, A, B, and those points form a triangle. Lines SQ' and QQ' are *parallel*: They never touch, but their points get closer and closer together. Line QT is also parallel to QQ'.

We get different views by focusing on different center points. For example, the second view in Fig. 13 puts O smack in the center. Notice that if a line passes through the very center, it remains straight after being projected; such diameter-spanning chords are the special case of a "circular arc" whose radius is infinite.

Most of Euclid's axioms for plane geometry remain valid in the hyperbolic plane. For example, exactly one line passes through any two distinct points; and if point A lies on line PP' there's exactly one line QQ' such that angle PAQ has any given value θ, for $0 < \theta < 180°$. But Euclid's famous fifth postulate does *not* hold: If point C is *not* on line QQ', there always are exactly *two* lines through C that are parallel to QQ'. Furthermore there are many pairs of lines, like RR' and SQ' in Fig. 13, that are totally disjoint or *ultraparallel*, in the sense that their points never become arbitrarily close. [These properties of the hyperbolic plane were discovered by G. Saccheri in the early 1700s, and made rigorous by N. I. Lobachevsky, J. Bolyai, and C. F. Gauss a century later.]

Quantitatively speaking, when points are projected onto the unit disk $|z| < 1$, the arc that meets the circle at $e^{i\theta}$ and $e^{-i\theta}$ has center at $\sec\theta$ and radius $\tan\theta$. The actual distance between two points whose projections are z and z' is $d(z, z') = \ln(|1 - \bar{z}z'| + |z - z'|) - \ln(|1 - \bar{z}z'| - |z - z'|)$. Thus objects far from the center appear dramatically shrunken when we see them near the circle's rim.

The sum of the angles of a hyperbolic triangle is always *less* than $180°$. For example, the angles at O, A, and B in Fig. 13 are respectively $90°$, $45°$, and $36°$. Ten such $36°$-$45°$-$90°$ triangles can be placed together to make a regular pentagon with $90°$ angles at each corner. And four such pentagons fit snugly together at their corners, allowing us to tile the entire hyperbolic plane with right regular pentagons (see Fig. 14). The edges of these pentagons form an interesting family of lines, every two of which are either ultraparallel or perpendicular; so we have a grid structure analogous to the unit squares of the ordinary plane. We call it the *pentagrid*, because each cell now has five neighbors instead of four.

There's a nice way to navigate in the pentagrid using Fibonacci numbers, based on ideas of Maurice Margenstern [see F. Herrmann and M. Margenstern, *Theoretical Comp. Sci.* **296** (2003), 345–351]. Instead of the ordinary Fibonacci sequence $\langle F_n \rangle$, however, we shall use the *negaFibonacci* numbers $\langle F_{-n} \rangle$, namely

$$F_{-1} = 1, \quad F_{-2} = -1, \quad F_{-3} = 2, \quad F_{-4} = -3, \quad \ldots, \quad F_{-n} = (-1)^{n-1} F_n. \tag{145}$$

Exercise 1.2.8–34 introduced the Fibonacci number system, in which every nonnegative integer x can be written uniquely in the form

$$x = F_{k_1} + F_{k_2} + \cdots + F_{k_r}, \qquad \text{where } k_1 \ggcurly k_2 \ggcurly \cdots \ggcurly k_r \ggcurly 0; \tag{146}$$

here '$j \ggcurly k$' means '$j \geq k+2$'. But there's also a *negaFibonacci number system*, which suits our purposes better: *Every integer x, whether positive, negative, or zero, can be written uniquely in the form*

$$x = F_{k_1} + F_{k_2} + \cdots + F_{k_r}, \qquad \text{where } k_1 \llcurly k_2 \llcurly \cdots \llcurly k_r \llcurly 1. \tag{147}$$

For example, $4 = 5 - 1 = F_{-5} + F_{-2}$ and $-2 = -3 + 1 = F_{-4} + F_{-1}$. This representation can conveniently be expressed as a binary code $\alpha = \ldots a_3 a_2 a_1$,

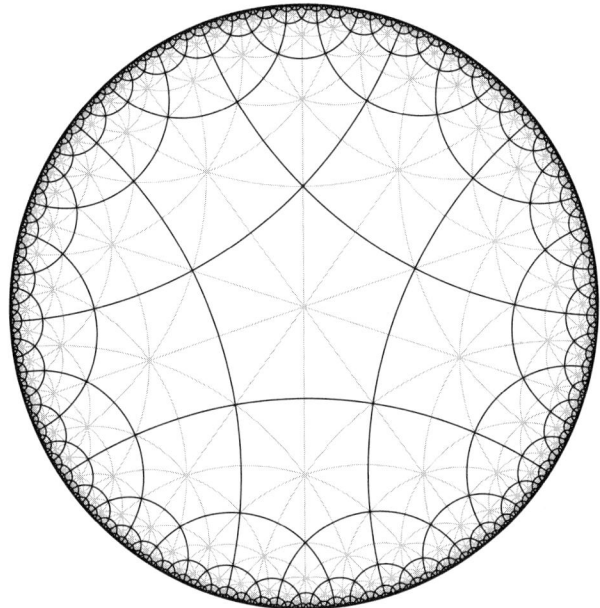

Fig. 14. The pentagrid, in which identical pentagons tile the hyperbolic plane.

A circular regular tiling, confined on all sides by infinitely small shapes, is really wonderful.
— M. C. ESCHER, letter to George Escher (9 November 1958)

standing for $N(\alpha) = \sum_k a_k F_{-k}$, with no two 1s in a row. For example, here are the negaFibonacci representation codes of all integers between -14 and $+15$:

$-14 = 10010100$	$-8 = 100000$	$-2 = 1001$	$4 = 10010$	$10 = 1001000$
$-13 = 10010101$	$-7 = 100001$	$-1 = 10$	$5 = 10000$	$11 = 1001001$
$-12 = 101010$	$-6 = 100100$	$0 = 0$	$6 = 10001$	$12 = 1000010$
$-11 = 101000$	$-5 = 100101$	$1 = 1$	$7 = 10100$	$13 = 1000000$
$-10 = 101001$	$-4 = 1010$	$2 = 100$	$8 = 10101$	$14 = 1000001$
$-9 = 100010$	$-3 = 1000$	$3 = 101$	$9 = 1001010$	$15 = 1000100$

As in the negadecimal system (see 4.1–(6) and (7)), we can tell whether x is negative or not by seeing if its representation has an even or odd number of digits.

The predecessor $\alpha-$ and successor $\alpha+$ of any negaFibonacci binary code α can be computed recursively by using the rules

$$(\alpha 01)- = \alpha 00, \quad (\alpha 000)- = \alpha 010, \quad (\alpha 100)- = \alpha 001, \quad (\alpha 10)- = (\alpha-)01,$$
$$(\alpha 10)+ = \alpha 00, \quad (\alpha 00)+ = \alpha 01, \quad (\alpha 1)+ = (\alpha-)0. \qquad (148)$$

(See exercise 157.) But ten elegant 2-adic steps do the calculation directly:

$$y \leftarrow x \oplus \bar{\mu}_0, \; z \leftarrow y \oplus (y \pm 1), \text{ where } x = (\alpha)_2;$$
$$z \leftarrow z \mid (x \mathbin{\&} (z \ll 1)); \qquad (149)$$
$$w \leftarrow x \oplus z \oplus ((z+1) \gg 2); \text{ then } w = (\alpha\pm)_2.$$

We just use $y-1$ in the top line to get the predecessor, $y+1$ to get the successor.

And now here's the point: A negaFibonacci code can be assigned to each cell of the pentagrid in such a way that the codes of its five neighbors are easy to compute. Let's call the neighbors n, s, e, w, and o, for "north," "south," "east," "west," and "other." If α is the code assigned to a given cell, we define

$$\alpha_n = \alpha \gg 2, \quad \alpha_s = \alpha \ll 2, \quad \alpha_e = \alpha_s+, \quad \alpha_w = \alpha_s-; \qquad (150)$$

thus $\alpha_{sn} = \alpha$, and also $\alpha_{en} = (\alpha 01)_n = \alpha$. The "other" direction is trickier:

$$\alpha_o = \begin{cases} \alpha_n+, & \text{if } \alpha \,\&\, 1 = 1; \\ \alpha_w-, & \text{if } \alpha \,\&\, 1 = 0. \end{cases} \qquad (151)$$

For example, $1000_o = 101001$ and $101001_o = 1000$. This mysterious interloper lies between north and east when α ends with 1, but between north and west when α ends with 0.

If we choose any cell and label it with code 0, and if we also choose an orientation so that its neighbors are n, e, s, w, and o in clockwise order, rules (150) and (151) will assign consistent labels to every cell of the pentagrid. (See exercise 160.) For example, the vicinity of a cell labeled 1000 will look like this:

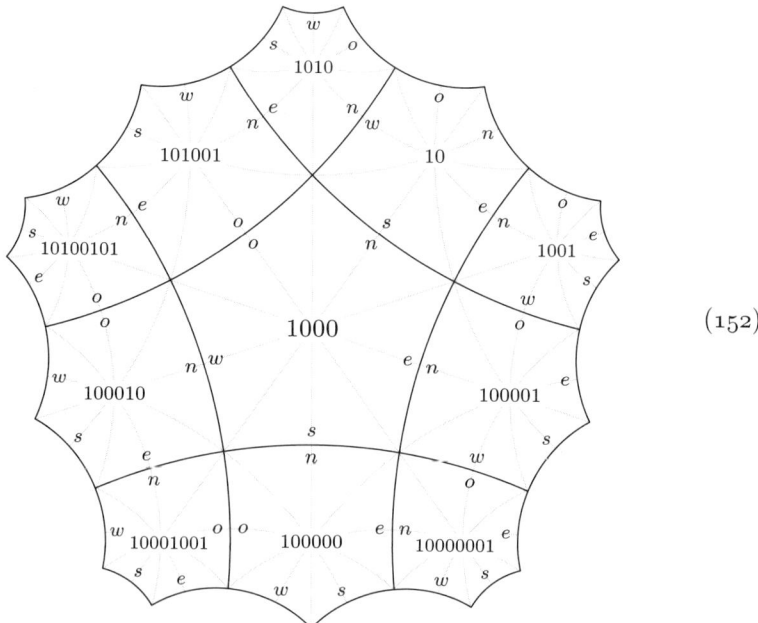

$$(152)$$

The code labels do not, however, identify cells uniquely, because infinitely many cells receive the same label. (Indeed, we clearly have $0_n = 0_s = 0$ and $1_w = 1_o = 1$.) To get a unique identifier, we attach a second coordinate so that each cell's full name has the form (α, y), where y is an integer. When y is constant and α ranges over all negaFibonacci codes, the cells (α, y) form a more-or-less hook-shaped strip whose edges take a 90° turn next to cell $(0, y)$. In general, the five neighbors of (α, y) are $(\alpha, y)_n = (\alpha_n, y + \delta_n(\alpha))$, $(\alpha, y)_s = (\alpha_s, y + \delta_s(\alpha))$,

$(\alpha, y)_e = (\alpha_e, y + \delta_e(\alpha)), (\alpha, y)_w = (\alpha_w, y + \delta_w(\alpha)),$ and $(\alpha, y)_o = (\alpha_o, y + \delta_o(\alpha)),$
where

$$\delta_n(\alpha) = [\alpha = 0], \quad \delta_s(\alpha) = -[\alpha = 0], \quad \delta_e(\alpha) = 0, \quad \delta_w(\alpha) = -[\alpha = 1];$$

$$\delta_o(\alpha) = \begin{cases} \text{sign}(\alpha_o - \alpha_n)[\alpha_o \,\&\, \alpha_n = 0], & \text{if } \alpha \,\&\, 1 = 1; \\ \text{sign}(\alpha_o - \alpha_w)[\alpha_o \,\&\, \alpha_w = 0], & \text{if } \alpha \,\&\, 1 = 0. \end{cases} \quad (153)$$

(See the illustration below.) Bitwise operations now allow us to surf the entire
hyperbolic plane with ease. On the other hand, we could also ignore the y
coordinates as we move, thereby wrapping around a "hyperbolic cylinder" of
pentagons; the α coordinates define an interesting multigraph on the set of all
negaFibonacci codes, in which every vertex has degree 5.

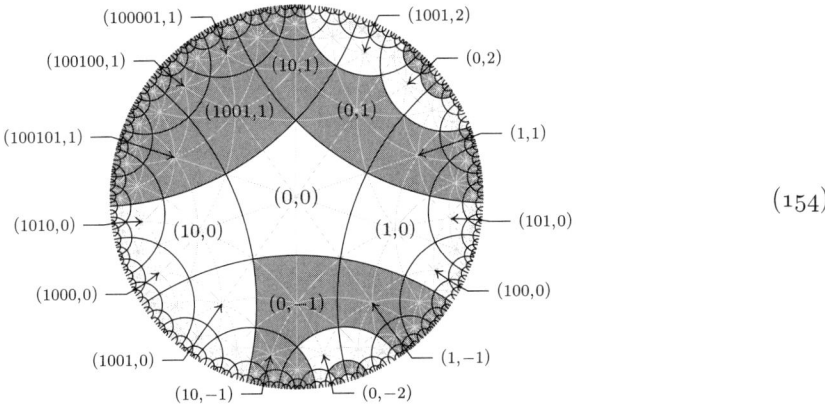

$$(154)$$

Bitmap graphics. It's fun to write programs that deal with pictures and shapes,
because they involve our left and right brains simultaneously. When image data
is involved, the results can be engrossing even if there are bugs in our code.

The book you are now reading was typeset by software that treated each
page as a gigantic matrix of 0s and 1s, called a "raster" or "bitmap," containing
millions of square picture elements called "pixels." The rasters were transmitted
to printing machines, causing tiny dots of ink to be placed wherever a 1 appeared
in the matrix. Physical properties of ink and paper caused those small clusters
of dots to look like smooth curves; but each pixel's basic squareness becomes
evident if we enlarge the images tenfold, as in the letter 'A' shown in Fig. 15(a).

With bitwise operations we can achieve special effects like "custering," in
which black pixels disappear when they're surrounded on all sides (Fig. 15(b)):

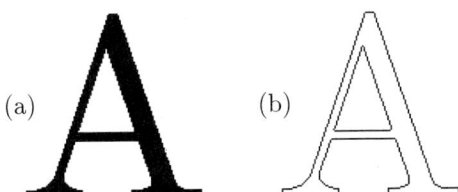

Fig. 15. The letter A,
before and after custering.

This operation, introduced by R. A. Kirsch, L. Cahn, C. Ray, and G. H. Urban [*Proc. Eastern Joint Computer Conf.* **12** (1957), 221–229], can be expressed as

$$\text{custer}(X) \;=\; X \mathbin{\&} {\sim}\bigl((X \mathbin{\veebar} 1) \mathbin{\&} (X \gg 1) \mathbin{\&} (X \ll 1) \mathbin{\&} (X \mathbin{\barwedge} 1)\bigr), \qquad (155)$$

where '$X \mathbin{\veebar} 1$' and '$X \mathbin{\barwedge} 1$' stand respectively for the result of shifting the bitmap X down or up by one row. Let us write

$$X_{\text{N}} = X \mathbin{\veebar} 1, \quad X_{\text{W}} = X \gg 1, \quad X_{\text{E}} = X \ll 1, \quad X_{\text{S}} = X \mathbin{\barwedge} 1 \qquad (156)$$

for the 1-pixel shifts of a bitmap X. Then, for example, the symbolic expression '$X_{\text{N}} \mathbin{\&} (X_{\text{S}} \mid \overline{X}_{\text{E}})$' evaluates to 1 in those pixel positions whose northern neighbor is black, and which also have either a black neighbor on the south side or a white neighbor to the east. With these abbreviations, (155) takes the form

$$\text{custer}(X) \;=\; X \mathbin{\&} {\sim}(X_{\text{N}} \mathbin{\&} X_{\text{W}} \mathbin{\&} X_{\text{E}} \mathbin{\&} X_{\text{S}}), \qquad (157)$$

which can also be expressed as $X \mathbin{\&} (\overline{X}_{\text{N}} \mid \overline{X}_{\text{W}} \mid \overline{X}_{\text{E}} \mid \overline{X}_{\text{S}})$.

Every pixel has four "rook-neighbors," with which it shares an edge at the top, left, right, or bottom. It also has eight "king-neighbors," with which it shares at least one corner point. For example, the king-neighbors that lie to the northeast of all pixels in a bitmap X can be denoted by X_{NE}, which is equivalent to $(X_{\text{N}})_{\text{E}}$ in pixel algebra. Notice that we also have $X_{\text{NE}} = (X_{\text{E}})_{\text{N}}$.

A 3×3 *cellular automaton* is an array of pixels that changes dynamically via a sequence of local transformations, all performed simultaneously: The state of each pixel at time $t + 1$ depends entirely on its state at time t and the states of its king-neighbors at that time. Thus the automaton defines a sequence of bitmaps $X^{(0)}, X^{(1)}, X^{(2)}, \ldots$ that lead from any given initial state $X^{(0)}$, where

$$X^{(t+1)} \;=\; f(X_{\text{NW}}^{(t)}, X_{\text{N}}^{(t)}, X_{\text{NE}}^{(t)}, X_{\text{W}}^{(t)}, X^{(t)}, X_{\text{E}}^{(t)}, X_{\text{SW}}^{(t)}, X_{\text{S}}^{(t)}, X_{\text{SE}}^{(t)}) \qquad (158)$$

and f is any bitwise Boolean function of nine variables. Fascinating patterns often emerge in this way. For example, after Martin Gardner introduced John Conway's game of Life to the world in 1970, more computer time was probably devoted to studying its implications than to any other computational task during the next several years — although the people paying the computer bills were rarely told! (See exercise 167.)

There are 2^{512} Boolean functions of nine variables, so there are 2^{512} different 3×3 cellular automata. Many of them are trivial, but most of them probably have such complicated behavior that they are humanly impossible to understand. Fortunately there also are many cases that do turn out to be useful in practice — and much easier to justify on economic grounds than the simulation of a game.

For example, algorithms for recognizing alphabetic characters, fingerprints, or similar patterns often make use of a "thinning" process, which removes excess black pixels and reduces each component of the image to an underlying skeleton that is comparatively simple to analyze. Several authors have proposed cellular automata for this problem, beginning with D. Rutovitz [*J. Royal Stat. Society* **A129** (1966), 512–513] who suggested a 4×4 scheme. But parallel algorithms are notoriously subtle, and flaws tended to turn up after various methods had been

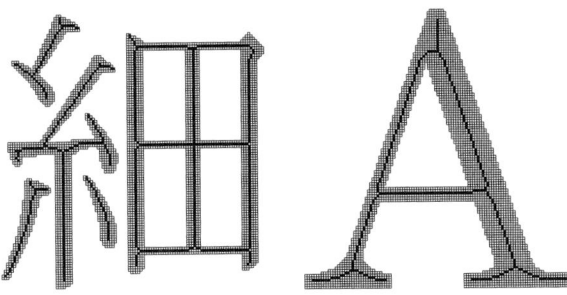

Fig. 16. Example results of Guo and Hall's 3×3 automaton for thinning the components of a bitmap. ("Hollow" pixels were originally black.)

published. For example, one, two, or three of the black pixels in a component like ▦ should be removed, yet a symmetrical scheme will erroneously erase all four.

A satisfactory solution to the thinning problem was finally found by Z. Guo and R. W. Hall [*CACM* **32** (1989), 359–373, 759], using a 3×3 automaton that invokes alternate rules on odd and even steps. Consider the function

$$f(x_{\text{NW}}, x_{\text{N}}, x_{\text{NE}}, x_{\text{W}}, x, x_{\text{E}}, x_{\text{SW}}, x_{\text{S}}, x_{\text{SE}}) = x \wedge \neg g(x_{\text{NW}}, \dots, x_{\text{W}}, x_{\text{E}}, \dots, x_{\text{SE}}), \quad (159)$$

where $g = 1$ only in the following 37 configurations surrounding a black pixel:

Then we use (158), but with $f(x_{\text{NW}}, x_{\text{N}}, x_{\text{NE}}, x_{\text{W}}, x, x_{\text{E}}, x_{\text{SW}}, x_{\text{S}}, x_{\text{SE}})$ replaced by its 180° rotation $f(x_{\text{SE}}, x_{\text{S}}, x_{\text{SW}}, x_{\text{E}}, x, x_{\text{W}}, x_{\text{NE}}, x_{\text{N}}, x_{\text{NW}})$ on even-numbered steps. The process stops when two consecutive cycles make no change.

With this rule Guo and Hall proved that the 3×3 automaton will preserve the connectivity structure of the image, in a strong sense that we will discuss below. Furthermore their algorithm obviously leaves an image intact if it is already so thin that it contains no three pixels that are king-neighbors of each other. On the other hand it usually succeeds in "removing the meat off the bones" of each black component, as shown in Fig. 16. Slightly thinner thinning is obtained in certain cases if we add four additional configurations

$$\quad (160)$$

to the 37 listed above. In either case the function g can be evaluated with a Boolean chain of length 25. (See exercises 170–172.)

In general, the black pixels of an image can be grouped into segments or components that are *kingwise connected*, in the sense that any black pixel can be reached from any other pixel of its component by a sequence of king moves through black pixels. The white pixels also form components, which are *rookwise connected*: Any two white cells of a component are mutually reachable via rook moves that touch nothing black. It's best to use different kinds of connectedness for white and black, in order to preserve the topological concepts of "inside" and "outside" that are familiar from continuous geometry [see A. Rosenfeld, *JACM* **17** (1970), 146–160]. If we imagine that the corner points of a raster are black, an infinitely thin black curve can cross between pixels at a corner, but a white curve cannot. (We could also imagine white corner points, which would lead to rookwise connectivity for black and kingwise connectivity for white.)

time = 0   time = 1   time = 3

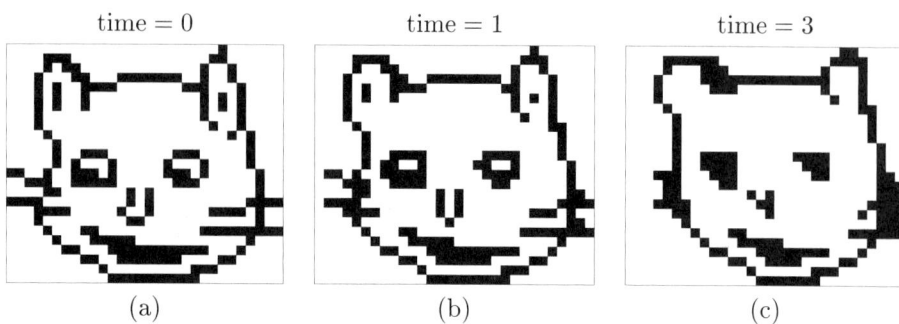

(a)   (b)   (c)

Fig. 17. The shrinking of a Cheshire cat

An amusing algorithm for shrinking a picture while preserving its connectivity, except that isolated black or white pixels disappear, was presented by S. Levialdi in *CACM* **15** (1972), 7–10; an equivalent algorithm, but with black and white reversed, had also appeared in T. Beyer's Ph.D. thesis (M.I.T., 1969). The idea is to use a cellular automaton with the simple transition function

$$f(x_{\text{NW}}, x_{\text{N}}, x_{\text{NE}}, x_{\text{W}}, x, x_{\text{E}}, x_{\text{SW}}, x_{\text{S}}, x_{\text{SE}}) = (x \wedge (x_{\text{W}} \vee x_{\text{SW}} \vee x_{\text{S}})) \vee (x_{\text{W}} \wedge x_{\text{S}}) \quad (161)$$

at each step. This formula is actually a 2×2 rule, but we still need a 3×3 window if we want to keep track of the cases when a one-pixel component goes away.

For example, the 25×30 picture of a Cheshire cat in Fig. 17(a) has seven kingwise black components: the outline of its head, the two earholes, the two eyes, the nose, and the smile. The result after one application of (161) is shown in Fig. 17(b): Seven components remain, but there's an isolated point in one ear, and the other earhole will become isolated after the next step. Hence Fig. 17(c) has only five components. After six steps the cat loses its nose, and even the smile will be gone at time 14. Sadly, the last bit of cat will vanish during step 46.

At most $M + N - 1$ transitions will wipe out any $M \times N$ picture, because the lowest visible northwest-to-southeast diagonal line moves relentlessly upward each time. Exercises 176 and 177 prove that different components will never merge together and interfere with each other.

Of course this cubic-time cellular method isn't the fastest way to count or identify the components of a picture. We can actually do that job "online," while looking at a large image one row at a time, not bothering to keep all of the previously seen rows in memory if we don't wish to look at them again.

While we're analyzing the components we might as well also record the relationships between them. Let's assume that only finitely many black pixels are present. Then there's an infinite component of white pixels called the *background*. Black components adjacent to the background constitute the main *objects* of the image. And these objects may in turn have *holes*, which may serve as a background for another level of objects, and so on. Thus the connected components of any finite picture form a hierarchy — an oriented tree, rooted at the background. Black components appear at the odd-numbered levels of this tree, and white components at the even-numbered levels, alternating between

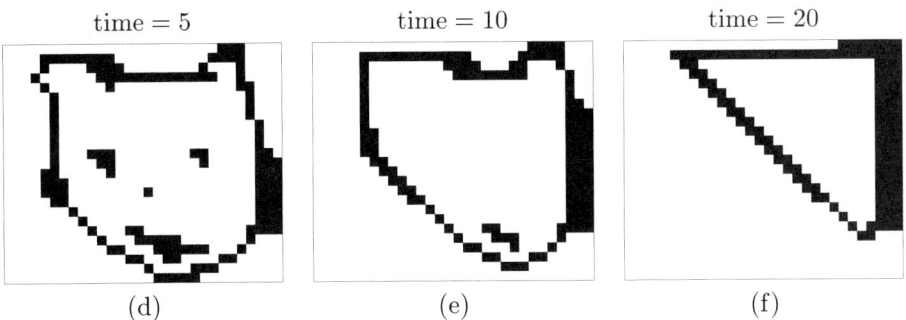

time = 5   time = 10   time = 20

(d)   (e)   (f)

by repeated application of Levialdi's transformation.

kingwise and rookwise connectedness. Each component except the background is *surrounded* by its parent. Childless components are said to be *simply connected*.

For example, here are the Cheshire cat's components, labeled with digits for white pixels and letters for the black ones, and the corresponding oriented tree:

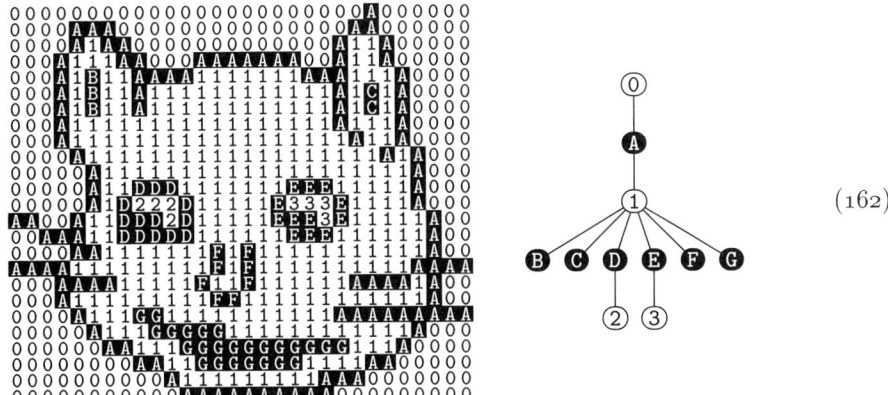

(162)

During the shrinking process of Fig. 17, components disappear in the order **C**, {**B**, ②, ③} (all at time 3), **F**, **E**, **D**, **G**, ①, **A**.

Suppose we want to analyze the components of such a picture by reading one row at a time. After we've seen four rows the result-so-far will be

(163)

and we'll be ready to scan row five. A comparison of rows four and five will then show that **B** and **C** should merge into **A**, but that new components **B** and ③ should also be launched. Exercise 179 contains full details about an instructive algorithm that properly updates the current tree as new rows are input. Additional information can also be computed on the fly: For example, we could determine the area of each component, the locations of its first and last pixels, the smallest enclosing rectangle, and/or its center of gravity.

*Filling. Let's complete our quick tour of raster graphics by considering how to fill regions that are bounded by straight lines and/or simple curves. Particularly efficient algorithms are available when the curves are built up from "conic sections" — circles, ellipses, parabolas, or hyperbolas, as in classical geometry.

In keeping with geometric tradition, we shall adopt Cartesian coordinates (x, y) in the following discussion, instead of speaking about rows or columns of pixels: An increase of x will signify a move to the right, while an increase of y will move upward. More significantly, we will focus on the *edges* between square pixels, instead of on the pixels themselves. Edges run between integer points (x, y) and (x', y') of the plane when $|x - x'| + |y - y'| = 1$. Each pixel is bounded by the four edges (x, y) — $(x-1, y)$ — $(x-1, y-1)$ — $(x, y-1)$ — (x, y). Experience has shown that algorithms for filling contours become simpler and faster when we concentrate on the edge transitions between white and black, instead of on the black pixels of a custerized boundary. (See, for example, the discussion by B. D. Ackland and N. Weste in *IEEE Trans.* **C-30** (1981), 41–48.)

Consider a continuous curve $z(t) = \big(x(t), y(t)\big)$ that is traced out as t varies from 0 to 1. We assume that the curve doesn't intersect itself for $0 \le t < 1$, and that $z(0) = z(1)$. The famous Jordan curve theorem [C. Jordan, *Cours d'analyse* **3** (1887), 587–594; O. Veblen, *Trans. Amer. Math. Soc.* **6** (1905), 83–98] states that every such curve divides the plane into two regions, called the inside and the outside. We can "digitize" $z(t)$ by forcing it to travel along edges between pixels; then we obtain an approximation in which the inside pixels are black and the outside pixels are white. This digitization process essentially replaces the original curve by the sequence of integer points

$$\text{round}(z(t)) \;=\; \big(\lfloor x(t) + \tfrac{1}{2}\rfloor, \lfloor y(t) + \tfrac{1}{2}\rfloor\big), \qquad \text{for } 0 \le t \le 1. \qquad (164)$$

The curve can be perturbed slightly, if necessary, so that $z(t)$ never passes exactly through the center of a pixel. Then the digitized curve takes discrete steps along pixel edges as t grows; and a pixel lies inside the digitization if and only if its center lies inside the original continuous curve $\{z(t) \mid 0 \le t \le 1\}$.

For example, the equations $x(t) = 20 \cos 2\pi t$ and $y(t) = 10 \sin 2\pi t$ define an ellipse. Its digitization, $\text{round}(z(t))$, starts at $(20, 0)$ when $t = 0$, then jumps to $(20, 1)$ when $t \approx .008$ and $10 \sin 2\pi t = 0.5$. Then it proceeds to the points $(20, 2)$, $(19, 2)$, $(19, 3)$, $(19, 4)$, $(18, 4)$, ..., $(20, -1)$, $(20, 0)$, as t increases through the values .024, .036, .040, .057, .062, ..., .976, .992:

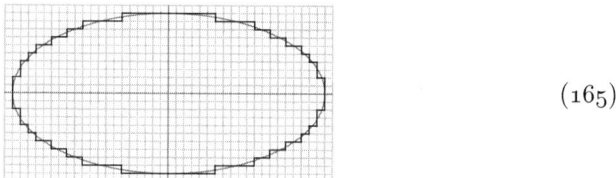

$$(165)$$

The horizontal edges of such a boundary are conveniently represented by bit vectors $H(y)$ for each y; for example, $H(10) = \ldots 000000111111111111000000 \ldots$ and $H(9) = \ldots 011111000000000000111110 \ldots$ in (165). If the ellipse is filled with black to obtain a bitmap B, the H vectors mark transitions between black and white, so we have the symbolic relation

$$H = B \oplus (B \wedge 1). \tag{166}$$

Conversely, it's easy to obtain B when the H vectors are given:

$$\begin{aligned} B(y) &= H(y_{\max}) \oplus H(y_{\max-1}) \oplus \cdots \oplus H(y+1) \\ &= H(y_{\min}) \oplus H(y_{\min+1}) \oplus \cdots \oplus H(y). \end{aligned} \tag{167}$$

Notice that $H(y_{\min}) \oplus H(y_{\min+1}) \oplus \cdots \oplus H(y_{\max})$ is the zero vector, because each bitmap is white at both top and bottom. Notice further that the analogous *vertical* edge vectors $V(x)$ are redundant: They satisfy the formulas $V = B \oplus (B \ll 1)$ and $B = V^{\oplus}$ (see exercise 36), but we need not bother to keep track of them.

Conic sections are easier to deal with than most other curves, because we can readily eliminate the parameter t. For example, the ellipse that led to (165) can be defined by the equation $(x/20)^2 + (y/10)^2 = 1$, instead of using sines and cosines. Therefore pixel (x, y) should be black if and only if its center point $(x-\frac{1}{2}, y-\frac{1}{2})$ lies inside the ellipse, if and only if $(x-\frac{1}{2})^2/400+(y-\frac{1}{2})^2/100-1 < 0$.

In general, every conic section is the set of points for which $F(x, y) = 0$, when F is an appropriate quadratic form. Therefore there's a quadratic form

$$Q(x, y) = F(x - \tfrac{1}{2}, y - \tfrac{1}{2}) = ax^2 + bxy + cy^2 + dx + ey + f \tag{168}$$

that is negative at the integer point (x, y) if and only if pixel (x, y) lies on a given side of the digitized curve.

For practical purposes we may assume that the coefficients $(a, b, \ldots, f)$ of Q are not-too-large integers. Then we're in luck, because the exact value of $Q(x, y)$ is easy to compute. In fact, as pointed out by M. L. V. Pitteway [*Comp. J.* **10** (1967), 282–289], there's a nice "three-register algorithm" by which we can quickly track the boundary points: Let x and y be integers, and suppose we've got the values of $Q(x, y)$, $Q_x(x, y)$, and $Q_y(x, y)$ in three registers (Q, Q_x, Q_y), where

$$Q_x(x, y) = 2ax + by + d \quad \text{and} \quad Q_y(x, y) = bx + 2cy + e \tag{169}$$

are $\frac{\partial}{\partial x}Q$ and $\frac{\partial}{\partial y}Q$. We can then move to any adjacent integer point, because

$$\begin{aligned} Q(x\pm1, y) &= Q(x, y)\pm Q_x(x, y)+a, & Q(x, y\pm1) &= Q(x, y)\pm Q_y(x, y)+c, \\ Q_x(x\pm1, y) &= Q_x(x, y)\pm2a, & Q_x(x, y\pm1) &= Q_x(x, y)\pm b, \\ Q_y(x\pm1, y) &= Q_y(x, y)\pm b; & Q_y(x, y\pm1) &= Q_y(x, y)\pm2c. \end{aligned} \tag{170}$$

Furthermore we can divide the contour into separate pieces, in each of which $x(t)$ and $y(t)$ are both monotonic. For example, when the ellipse (165) travels from $(20, 0)$ to $(0, 10)$, the value of x decreases while y increases; thus we need only move from (x, y) to $(x-1, y)$ or to $(x, y+1)$. If registers (Q, R, S) respectively hold $(Q, Q_x - a, Q_y + c)$, a move to $(x-1, y)$ simply sets $Q \leftarrow Q - R$, $R \leftarrow R - 2a$, and $S \leftarrow S - b$; a move to $(x, y+1)$ is just as quick. With care, this idea leads to a blindingly fast way to discover the correctly digitized edges of almost any conic curve.

For example, the quadratic form $Q(x, y)$ for ellipse (165) is $4x^2 + 16y^2 - (4x + 16y + 1595)$, when we integerize its coefficients. We have $Q(20, 0) = F(19.5, -0.5) = -75$ and $Q(21, 0) = +85$; therefore pixel $(20, 0)$, whose center is $(19.5, -0.5)$, is inside the ellipse, but pixel $(21, 0)$ isn't. Let's zoom in closer:

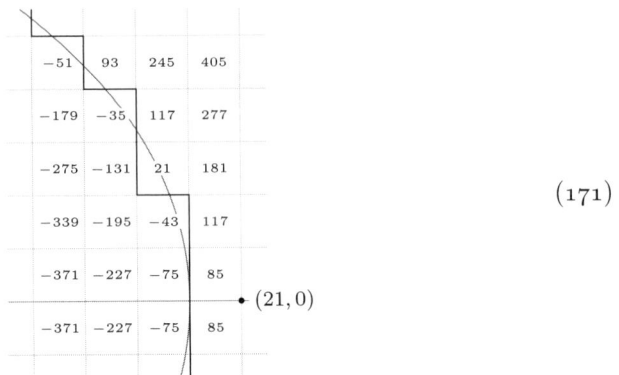

$$(171)$$

The boundary can be deduced without examining Q at very many points. In fact, we don't need to look at $Q(21, 0)$, because we know that all edges between $(20, 0)$ and $(0, 10)$ must go either upwards or to the left. First we test $Q(20, 1)$ and find it negative (-75); so we move up. Also $Q(20, 2)$ is negative (-43), so we go up again. Then we test $Q(20, 3)$, and find it positive (21); so we move left. And so on. Only the Q values -75, -43, 21, -131, -35, 93, -51, ... actually need to be examined, if we've set the three-register method up properly.

Algorithm T (*Three-register algorithm for conics*). Given two integer points (x, y) and (x', y'), and an integer quadratic form Q as in (168), this algorithm decides how to digitize a portion of the conic section defined by $F(x, y) = 0$, where $F(x, y) = Q(x + \frac{1}{2}, y + \frac{1}{2})$. It creates $|x' - x|$ horizontal edges and $|y' - y|$ vertical edges, which form a path from (x, y) to (x', y'). We assume that

i) Real-valued points (ξ, η) and (ξ', η') exist such that $F(\xi, \eta) = F(\xi', \eta') = 0$.

ii) The curve travels from (ξ, η) to (ξ', η') monotonically in both coordinates.

iii) $x = \lfloor \xi + \frac{1}{2} \rfloor$, $y = \lfloor \eta + \frac{1}{2} \rfloor$, $x' = \lfloor \xi' + \frac{1}{2} \rfloor$, and $y' = \lfloor \eta' + \frac{1}{2} \rfloor$.

iv) If we traverse the curve from (ξ, η) to (ξ', η'), we see $F < 0$ on our left.

v) No edge of the integer grid contains two roots of Q (see exercise 183).

T1. [Initialize.] If $x = x'$, go to T11; if $y = y'$, go to T10. If $x < x'$ and $y < y'$, set $Q \leftarrow Q(x{+}1, y{+}1)$, $R \leftarrow Q_x(x{+}1, y{+}1){+}a$, $S \leftarrow Q_y(x{+}1, y{+}1){+}c$, and go to T2. If $x < x'$ and $y > y'$, set $Q \leftarrow Q(x{+}1, y)$, $R \leftarrow Q_x(x{+}1, y) + a$, $S \leftarrow Q_y(x{+}1, y) - c$, and go to T3. If $x > x'$ and $y < y'$, set $Q \leftarrow Q(x, y{+}1)$, $R \leftarrow Q_x(x, y{+}1) - a$, $S \leftarrow Q_y(x, y{+}1) + c$, and go to T4. If $x > x'$ and $y > y'$, set $Q \leftarrow Q(x, y)$, $R \leftarrow Q_x(x, y) - a$, $S \leftarrow Q_y(x, y) - c$, and go to T5.

T2. [Right or up.] If $Q < 0$, do T9; otherwise do T6. Repeat until interrupted.

T3. [Down or right.] If $Q < 0$, do T7; otherwise do T9. Repeat until interrupted.

T4. [Up or left.] If $Q < 0$, do T6; otherwise do T8. Repeat until interrupted.

T5. [Left or down.] If $Q < 0$, do T8; otherwise do T7. Repeat until interrupted.

T6. [Move up.] Create the edge $(x, y) \longrightarrow (x, y+1)$, then set $y \leftarrow y+1$. Interrupt to T10 if $y = y'$; otherwise set $Q \leftarrow Q + S$, $R \leftarrow R + b$, $S \leftarrow S + 2c$.

T7. [Move down.] Create the edge $(x, y) \longrightarrow (x, y-1)$, then set $y \leftarrow y - 1$. Interrupt to T10 if $y = y'$; otherwise set $Q \leftarrow Q-S$, $R \leftarrow R-b$, $S \leftarrow S-2c$.

T8. [Move left.] Create the edge $(x, y) \longrightarrow (x-1, y)$, then set $x \leftarrow x - 1$. Interrupt to T11 if $x = x'$; otherwise set $Q \leftarrow Q-R$, $R \leftarrow R-2a$, $S \leftarrow S-b$.

T9. [Move right.] Create the edge $(x, y) \longrightarrow (x+1, y)$, then set $x \leftarrow x + 1$. Interrupt to T11 if $x = x'$; otherwise set $Q \leftarrow Q+R$, $R \leftarrow R+2a$, $S \leftarrow S+b$.

T10. [Finish horizontally.] While $x < x'$, create the edge $(x, y) \longrightarrow (x+1, y)$ and set $x \leftarrow x + 1$. While $x > x'$, create the edge $(x, y) \longrightarrow (x-1, y)$ and set $x \leftarrow x - 1$. Terminate the algorithm.

T11. [Finish vertically.] While $y < y'$, create the edge $(x, y) \longrightarrow (x, y+1)$ and set $y \leftarrow y + 1$. While $y > y'$, create the edge $(x, y) \longrightarrow (x, y-1)$ and set $y \leftarrow y - 1$. Terminate the algorithm. ∎

For example, when this algorithm is invoked with $(x, y) = (20, 0)$, $(x', y') = (0, 10)$, and $Q(x, y) = 4x^2 + 16y^2 - 4x - 16y - 1595$, it will create the edges $(20, 0)$ — $(20, 1)$ — $(20, 2)$ — $(19, 2)$ — $(19, 3)$ — $(19, 4)$ — $(18, 4)$ — $(18, 5)$ — $(17, 5)$ — $(17, 6)$ — $\cdots$ — $(6, 9)$ — $(6, 10)$, then make a beeline for $(0, 10)$. (See (165) and (171).) Exercise 182 explains why it works.

Movement to the left in step T8 is conveniently implemented by setting $H(y) \leftarrow H(y) \oplus (1 \ll (x_{\max} - x))$, using the H vectors of (166) and (167). Movement to the right is similar, but we set $x \leftarrow x + 1$ first. Step T10 could set

$$H(y) \leftarrow H(y) \oplus ((1 \ll (x_{\max} - \min(x, x'))) - (1 \ll (x_{\max} - \max(x, x')))); \quad (172)$$

but one move at a time might be just as good, because $|x' - x|$ is often small. Movement up or down needs no action, because vertical edges are redundant.

Notice that the algorithm runs somewhat faster in the special case when $b = 0$; circles always belong to this case. The even more special case of straight lines, when $a = b = c = 0$, is of course faster yet; then we have a simple *one-register* algorithm (see exercise 185).

Fig. 18. Pixels change from white to black and back again, at the edges of digitized circles.

When many contours are filled in the same image, using H vectors, the pixel values change between black and white whenever we cross an odd number of edges. Figure 18 illustrates a tiling of the hyperbolic plane by equilateral 45°-45°-45° triangles, obtained by superimposing the results of several hundred applications of Algorithm T.

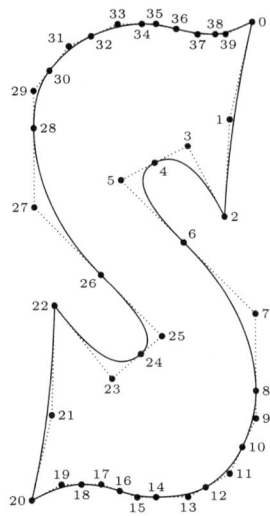

Fig. 19. Squines that define the outline contour of an '**S**'.

Algorithm T applies only to conic curves. But that's not really a limitation in practice, because just about every shape we ever need to draw can be well approximated by "piecewise conics" called quadratic Bézier splines or *squines*. For example, Fig. 19 shows a typical squine curve with 40 points $(z_0, z_1, \ldots, z_{39}, z_{40})$, where $z_{40} = z_0$. The even-numbered points $(z_0, z_2, \ldots, z_{40})$ lie on the curve; the others, $(z_1, z_3, \ldots, z_{39})$, are called "control points," because they regulate local bending and flexing. Each section $S(z_{2j}, z_{2j+1}, z_{2j+2})$ begins at point z_{2j}, traveling in direction $z_{2j+1} - z_{2j}$. It ends at point z_{2j+2}, traveling in direction $z_{2j+2} - z_{2j+1}$. Thus if z_{2j} lies on the straight line from z_{2j-1} to z_{2j+1}, the squine passes smoothly through point z_{2j} without changing direction.

Exercise 186 defines $S(z_{2j}, z_{2j+1}, z_{2j+2})$ precisely, and exercise 187 explains how to digitize any squine curve using Algorithm T. The region inside the digitized edges can then be filled with black pixels.

Incidentally, the task of *drawing* lines and curves on a bitmap turns out to be much more difficult than the task of *filling* a digitized contour, because we want diagonal strokes to have the same apparent thickness as vertical and horizontal strokes do. An excellent solution to the line-drawing problem was found by John D. Hobby, *JACM* **36** (1989), 209–229.

*Branchless computation. Modern computers tend to slow down when a program contains conditional branch instructions, because an uncertain flow of control can interfere with predictive lookahead circuitry. Therefore we've used `MMIX`'s conditional-set instructions like `CSNZ` in programs like (56). Indeed, four instructions such as 'ADD z,y,1; SR t,u,2; CSNZ x,q,z; CSNZ v,q,t' are probably faster than their three-instruction counterpart

$$\text{BZ q,@+12; ADD x,y,1; SR v,u,2} \tag{173}$$

when the actual running time is measured on a highly pipelined machine, even though the rule-of-thumb cost of (173) is only 3υ according to Table 1.3.1′–1.

Bitwise operations can help diminish the need for costly branching. For example, if MMIX didn't have a CSNZ instruction we could write

```
NEGU m,q;  OR m,m,q;   SR m,m,63;
ADD t,y,1;  XOR t,t,x;  AND t,t,m;  XOR x,x,t;          (174)
SR t,u,2;  XOR t,t,v;  AND t,t,m;  XOR v,v,t;
```

here the first line creates the mask $m = -[q \neq 0]$. On some computers these eleven branchless instructions would still run faster than the three instructions in (173).

The inner loop of a merge sort algorithm provides an instructive example. Suppose we want to do the following operations repeatedly:

> If $x_i < y_j$, set $z_k \leftarrow x_i$, $i \leftarrow i + 1$, and go to x_done if $i = i_{max}$.
> Otherwise set $z_k \leftarrow y_j$, $j \leftarrow j + 1$, and go to y_done if $j = j_{max}$.
> Then set $k \leftarrow k + 1$ and go to z_done if $k = k_{max}$.

If we implement them in the "obvious" way, four conditional branches are involved, three of which are active on each path through the loop:

```
1H CMP   t,xi,yj;  BNN  t,2F     Branch if x_i ≥ y_j.
   STO   xi,zbase,kk             z_k ← x_i.
   ADD   ii,ii,8                 i ← i + 1.
   BZ    ii,X_Done               To x_done if i = i_max.
   LDO   xi,xbase,ii             Load x_i into register xi.
   JMP   3F                      Join the other branch.
2H STO   yj,zbase,kk             z_k ← y_j.
   ADD   jj,jj,8                 j ← j + 1.
   BZ    jj,Y_Done               To y_done if j = j_max.
   LDO   yj,ybase,jj             Load y_j into register yj.
3H ADD   kk,kk,8                 k ← k + 1.
   PBNZ  kk,1B                   Repeat if k ≠ k_max.
   JMP   Z_Done                  To z_done.   ∎
```

(Here $ii = 8(i - i_{max})$, $jj = 8(j - j_{max})$, and $kk = 8(k - k_{max})$; the factor of 8 is needed because x_i, y_j, and z_k are octabytes.) Those four branches can be reduced to just one:

```
1H CMP   t,xi,yj                 t ← sign(x_i − y_j).
   CSN   yj,t,xi                 yj ← min(x_i, y_j).
   STO   yj,zbase,kk             z_k ← yj.
   AND   t,t,8                   t ← 8[x_i < y_j].
   ADD   ii,ii,t                 i ← i + [x_i < y_j].
   LDO   xi,xbase,ii             Load x_i into register xi.
   XOR   t,t,8                   t ← t ⊕ 8.
   ADD   jj,jj,t                 j ← j + [x_i ≥ y_j].
   LDO   yj,ybase,jj             Load y_j into register yj.
   ADD   kk,kk,8                 k ← k + 1.
   AND   u,ii,jj;  AND  u,u,kk   u ← ii & jj & kk.
   PBN   u,1B                    Repeat if i < i_max, j < j_max, and k < k_max.   ∎
```

When the loop stops in this version, we can readily decide whether to continue at x_done, y_done, or z_done. These instructions load both x_i and y_j from memory each time, but the redundant value will already be present in the cache.

*More applications of MOR and MXOR. Let's finish off our study of bitwise manipulation by taking a look at two operations that are specifically designed for 64-bit work. MMIX's instructions MOR and MXOR, which essentially carry out matrix multiplication on 8×8 Boolean matrices, turn out to be extremely flexible and powerful, both by themselves and in combination with other bitwise operations.

If $x = (x_7 \ldots x_1 x_0)_{256}$ is an octabyte and $a = (a_7 \ldots a_1 a_0)_2$ is a single byte, the instruction MOR t,x,a sets $t \leftarrow a_7 x_7 \mid \cdots \mid a_1 x_1 \mid a_0 x_0$, while MXOR t,x,a sets $t \leftarrow a_7 x_7 \oplus \cdots \oplus a_1 x_1 \oplus a_0 x_0$. For example, MOR t,x,2 and MXOR t,x,2 both set $t \leftarrow x_1$; MOR t,x,3 sets $t \leftarrow x_1 \mid x_0$; and MXOR t,x,3 sets $t \leftarrow x_1 \oplus x_0$.

In general, of course, MOR and MXOR are functions of octabytes. When $y = (y_7 \ldots y_1 y_0)_{256}$ is a general octabyte, the instruction MOR t,x,y produces the octabyte t whose jth byte t_j is the result of MOR applied to x and y_j.

Suppose $x = -1 = {}^{\#}\mathtt{ffffffffffffffff}$. Then MOR t,x,y computes the mask t in which byte t_j is ${}^{\#}\mathtt{ff}$ whenever $y_j \neq 0$, while t_j is zero when $y_j = 0$. This simple special case is quite useful, because it accomplishes in just one instruction what we previously needed seven operations to achieve in situations like (92).

We observed in (66) that two MORs will suffice to reverse the bits of any 64-bit word, and many other important bit permutations also become easy when MOR is in a computer's repertoire. Suppose π is a permutation of $\{0, 1, \ldots, 7\}$ that takes $0 \mapsto 0\pi$, $1 \mapsto 1\pi$, $\ldots$, $7 \mapsto 7\pi$. Then the octabyte $p = (2^{7\pi} \ldots 2^{1\pi} 2^{0\pi})_{256}$ corresponds to a permutation matrix that makes MOR do nice tricks: MOR t,x,p will *permute the bytes* of x, setting $t_j \leftarrow x_{j\pi}$. Furthermore, MOR u,p,y will *permute the bits* of each byte of y, according to the *inverse* permutation; it sets $u_j \leftarrow (a_7 \ldots a_1 a_0)_2$ when $y_j = (a_{7\pi} \ldots a_{1\pi} a_{0\pi})_2$.

With a little more skullduggery we can also expedite further permutations such as the perfect shuffle (76), which transforms a given octabyte $z = 2^{32}x + y = (x_{31} \ldots x_1 x_0 y_{31} \ldots y_1 y_0)_2$ into the "zippered" octabyte

$$w = x \ddagger y = (x_{31} y_{31} \ldots x_1 y_1 x_0 y_0)_2. \tag{175}$$

With appropriate permutation matrices p, q, and r, the intermediate results

$$t = (x_{31} x_{27} x_{30} x_{26} x_{29} x_{25} x_{28} x_{24} x_{31} y_{27} y_{30} y_{26} y_{29} y_{25} y_{28} y_{24} \cdots$$
$$x_7 x_3 x_6 x_2 x_5 x_1 x_4 x_0 y_7 y_3 y_6 y_2 y_5 y_1 y_4 y_0)_2, \tag{176}$$

$$u = (y_{27} y_{31} y_{26} y_{30} y_{25} y_{29} y_{24} y_{28} x_{27} x_{31} x_{26} x_{30} x_{25} x_{29} x_{24} x_{28} \cdots$$
$$y_3 y_7 y_2 y_6 y_1 y_5 y_0 y_4 x_3 x_7 x_2 x_6 x_1 x_5 x_0 x_4)_2 \tag{177}$$

can be computed quickly via the four instructions

$$\text{MOR t,z,p;} \quad \text{MOR t,q,t;} \quad \text{MOR u,t,r;} \quad \text{MOR u,r,u;} \tag{178}$$

see exercise 204. So there's a mask m for which 'PUT rM,m; MUX w,t,u' completes the perfect shuffle in just six cycles altogether. By contrast, the traditional method in exercise 53 requires 30 cycles (five δ-swaps).

The analogous instruction MXOR is especially useful when binary linear algebra is involved. For example, exercise 1.3.1´–37 shows that XOR and MXOR directly implement addition and multiplication in a finite field of 2^k elements, for $k \leq 8$.

The problem of *cyclic redundancy checking* provides an instructive example of another case where MXOR shines. Streams of data are often accompanied by "CRC bytes" in order to detect common types of transmission errors [see W. W. Peterson and D. T. Brown, *Proc. IRE* **49** (1961), 228–235]. One popular method, used for example in MP3 audio files, is to regard each byte $\alpha = (a_7 \ldots a_1 a_0)_2$ as if it were the polynomial

$$\alpha(x) = (a_7 \ldots a_1 a_0)_x = a_7 x^7 + \cdots + a_1 x + a_0. \qquad (179)$$

When transmitting n bytes $\alpha_{n-1} \ldots \alpha_1 \alpha_0$, we then compute the remainder

$$\beta = \big(\alpha_{n-1}(x) x^{8(n-1)} + \cdots + \alpha_1(x) x^8 + \alpha_0(x)\big) x^{16} \bmod p(x), \qquad (180)$$

where $p(x) = x^{16} + x^{15} + x^2 + 1$, using polynomial arithmetic mod 2, and append the coefficients of β as a 16-bit redundancy check.

The usual way to compute β is to process one byte at a time, according to classical methods like Algorithm 4.6.1D. The basic idea is to define the partial result $\beta_m = \big(\alpha_{n-1}(x) x^{8(n-1-m)} + \cdots + \alpha_{m+1}(x) x^8 + \alpha_m(x)\big) x^{16} \bmod p(x)$ so that $\beta_n = 0$, and then to use the recursion

$$\beta_m = ((\beta_{m+1} \ll 8) \mathbin{\&} {}^{\#}\mathtt{ff00}) \oplus crc\_table[(\beta_{m+1} \gg 8) \oplus \alpha_m] \qquad (181)$$

to decrease m by 1 until $m = 0$. Here $crc\_table[\alpha]$ is a 16-bit table entry that holds the remainder of $\alpha(x) x^{16}$, modulo $p(x)$ and mod 2, for $0 \le \alpha < 256$. [See A. Perez, *IEEE Micro* **3**, 3 (June 1983), 40–50.]

But of course we'd prefer to process 64 bits at once instead of 8. The solution is to find 8×8 matrices A and B such that

$$\alpha(x) x^{64} \equiv (\alpha A)(x) + (\alpha B)(x) x^{-8} \quad (\text{modulo } p(x) \text{ and } 2), \qquad (182)$$

for arbitrary bytes α, considering α to be a 1×8 vector of bits. Then we can pad the given data bytes $\alpha_{n-1} \ldots \alpha_1 \alpha_0$ with leading zeros so that n is a multiple of 8, and use the following efficient reduction method:

Begin with $c \leftarrow 0$, $n \leftarrow n - 8$, and $t \leftarrow (\alpha_{n+7} \ldots \alpha_n)_{256}$.
While $n > 0$, set $u \leftarrow t \cdot A$, $v \leftarrow t \cdot B$, $n \leftarrow n - 8$, $\qquad (183)$
$\quad t \leftarrow (\alpha_{n+7} \ldots \alpha_n)_{256} \oplus u \oplus (v \gg 8) \oplus (c \ll 56)$, and $c \leftarrow v \mathbin{\&} {}^{\#}\mathtt{ff}$.

Here $t \cdot A$ and $t \cdot B$ denote matrix multiplication via MXOR. The desired CRC bytes, $(tx^{16} + cx^8) \bmod p(x)$, are then readily obtained from the 64-bit quantity t and the 8-bit quantity c. Exercise 213 contains full details; the total running time for n bytes comes to only $(\mu + 10v)n/8 + O(1)$.

The exercises below contain many more instances where MOR and MXOR lead to substantial economies. New tricks undoubtedly remain to be discovered.

For further reading. The book *Hacker's Delight* by Henry S. Warren, Jr. (Addison–Wesley, 2002) discusses bitwise operations in depth, emphasizing the great variety of options that are available on real-world computers that are not as ideal as MMIX.

EXERCISES

▶ **1.** [*15*] What is the net effect of setting $x \leftarrow x \oplus y$, $y \leftarrow y \oplus (x \mathbin{\&} m)$, $x \leftarrow x \oplus y$?

2. [*16*] (H. S. Warren, Jr.) Are any of the following relations valid for all integers x and y? (i) $x \oplus y \le x \mid y$; (ii) $x \mathbin{\&} y \le x \mid y$; (iii) $|x - y| \le x \oplus y$.

3. [*M20*] If $x = (x_{n-1} \ldots x_1 x_0)_2$ with $x_{n-1} = 1$, let $x^M = (\bar{x}_{n-1} \ldots \bar{x}_1 \bar{x}_0)_2$. Thus we have 0^M, 1^M, 2^M, 3^M, $\ldots = -1, 0, 1, 0, 3, 2, 1, 0, 7, 6, \ldots$, if we let $0^M = -1$. Prove that $(x \oplus y)^M < |x - y| \le x \oplus y$ for all $x, y \ge 0$.

▶ **4.** [*M16*] Let $x^C = \bar{x}$, $x^N = -x$, $x^S = x + 1$, and $x^P = x - 1$ denote the complement, the negative, the successor, and the predecessor of an infinite-precision integer x. Then we have $x^{CC} = x^{NN} = x^{SP} = x^{PS} = x$. What are x^{CN} and x^{NC}?

5. [*M21*] Prove or disprove the following conjectured laws concerning binary shifts:
a) $(x \ll j) \ll k = x \ll (j + k)$;
b) $(x \gg j) \mathbin{\&} (y \ll k) = ((x \gg (j+k)) \mathbin{\&} y) \ll k = (x \mathbin{\&} (y \ll (j+k))) \gg j$.

6. [*M22*] Find all integers x and y such that (a) $x \gg y = y \gg x$; (b) $x \ll y = y \ll x$.

7. [*M22*] (R. Schroeppel, 1972.) Find a fast way to convert the binary number $x = (\ldots x_2 x_1 x_0)_2$ to its negabinary counterpart $x = (\ldots x'_2 x'_1 x'_0)_{-2}$, and vice versa. *Hint:* Only two bitwise operations are needed!

▶ **8.** [*M22*] Given a finite set S of nonnegative integers, the "minimal excludant" of S is defined to be

$$\mathrm{mex}(S) = \min\{\, k \mid k \ge 0 \text{ and } k \notin S \,\}.$$

Let $x \oplus S$ denote the set $\{x \oplus y \mid y \in S\}$, and let $S \oplus y$ denote $\{x \oplus y \mid x \in S\}$. Prove that if $x = \mathrm{mex}(S)$ and $y = \mathrm{mex}(T)$ then $x \oplus y = \mathrm{mex}((S \oplus y) \cup (x \oplus T))$.

9. [*M26*] (*Nim.*) Two people play a game with k piles of sticks, where there are a_j sticks in pile j. If $a_1 = \cdots = a_k = 0$ when it is a player's turn to move, that player loses; otherwise the player reduces one of the piles by any desired amount, throwing away the removed sticks, and it is the other player's turn. Prove that the player to move can force a victory if and only if $a_1 \oplus \cdots \oplus a_k \ne 0$. [*Hint:* Use exercise 8.]

10. [*HM40*] (*Nimbers*, also known as *Conway's field*.) Continuing exercise 8, define the operation $x \otimes y$ of "nim multiplication" recursively by the formula

$$x \otimes y = \mathrm{mex}\{(x \otimes j) \oplus (i \otimes y) \oplus (i \otimes j) \mid 0 \le i < x,\ 0 \le j < y\}.$$

Prove that $\oplus$ and $\otimes$ define a *field* over the set of all nonnegative integers. Prove also that if $0 \le x, y < 2^{2^n}$ then $x \otimes y < 2^{2^n}$, and $2^{2^n} \otimes y = 2^{2^n} y$. (In particular, this field contains subfields of size 2^{2^n} for all $n \ge 0$.) Explain how to compute $x \otimes y$ efficiently.

▶ **11.** [*M26*] (H. W. Lenstra, 1978.) Find a simple way to characterize all pairs of positive integers (m, n) for which $m \otimes n = mn$ in Conway's field.

12. [*M26*] Devise an algorithm for *division* of nimbers. *Hint:* If $x < 2^{2^{n+1}}$ then we have $x \otimes (x \oplus (x \gg 2^n)) < 2^{2^n}$.

13. [*M32*] (*Second-order nim.*) Extend the game of exercise 9 by allowing two kinds of moves: Either a_j is reduced for some j, as before; or a_j is reduced and a_i is replaced by an arbitrary nonnegative integer, for some $i < j$. Prove that the player to move can now force a victory if and only if the pile sizes satisfy either $a_2 \ne a_3 \oplus \cdots \oplus a_k$ or $a_1 \ne a_3 \oplus (2 \otimes a_4) \oplus \cdots \oplus ((k-2) \otimes a_k)$. For example, when $k = 4$ and $(a_1, a_2, a_3, a_4) = (7, 5, 0, 5)$, the only winning move is to $(7, 5, 6, 3)$.

14. [*M30*] Suppose each node of a complete, infinite binary tree has been labeled with 0 or 1. Such a labeling is conveniently represented as a sequence $T = (t, t_0, t_1, t_{00}, t_{01}, t_{10}, t_{11}, t_{000}, \dots)$, with one bit t_α for every binary string α; the root is labeled t, the left subtree labels are $T_0 = (t_0, t_{00}, t_{01}, t_{000}, \dots)$, and the right subtree labels are $T_1 = (t_1, t_{10}, t_{11}, t_{100}, \dots)$. Any such labeling can be used to transform a 2-adic integer $x = (\dots x_2 x_1 x_0)_2$ into the 2-adic integer $y = (\dots y_2 y_1 y_0)_2 = T(x)$ by setting $y_0 = t$, $y_1 = t_{x_0}$, $y_2 = t_{x_0 x_1}$, etc., so that $T(x) = 2T_{x_0}(\lfloor x/2 \rfloor) + t$. (In other words, x defines an infinite path in the binary tree, and y corresponds to the labels on that path, from right to left in the bit strings as we proceed from top to bottom of the tree.)

A *branching function* is the mapping $x^T = x \oplus T(x)$ defined by such a labeling. For example, if $t_{01} = 1$ and all of the other t_α are 0, we have $x^T = x \oplus 4[x \bmod 4 = 2]$.

a) Prove that every branching function is a permutation of the 2-adic integers.

b) For which integers k is $x \oplus (x \ll k)$ a branching function?

c) Let $x \mapsto x^T$ be a mapping from 2-adic integers into 2-adic integers. Prove that x^T is a branching function if and only if $\rho(x \oplus y) = \rho(x^T \oplus y^T)$ for all 2-adic x and y.

d) Prove that compositions and inverses of branching functions are branching functions. (Thus the set $\mathcal{B}$ of all branching functions is a permutation group.)

e) A branching function is *balanced* if the labels satisfy $t_\alpha = t_{\alpha 0} \oplus t_{\alpha 1}$ for all α. Show that the set of all balanced branching functions is a subgroup of $\mathcal{B}$.

▶ **15.** [*M26*] J. H. Quick noticed that $((x+2) \oplus 3) - 2 = ((x-2) \oplus 3) + 2$ for all x. Find all constants a and b such that $((x+a) \oplus b) - a = ((x-a) \oplus b) + a$ is an identity.

16. [*M31*] A function of x is called *animating* if it can be written in the form

$$((\dots((((x + a_1) \oplus b_1) + a_2) \oplus b_2) + \cdots) + a_m) \oplus b_m$$

for some integer constants $a_1, b_1, a_2, b_2, \dots, a_m, b_m$, with $m > 0$.

a) Prove that every animating function is a branching function (see exercise 14).

b) Furthermore, prove that it is balanced if and only if $b_1 \oplus b_2 \oplus \cdots \oplus b_m = 0$. *Hint:* What binary tree labeling corresponds to the animating function $((x \oplus c) - 1) \oplus c$?

c) Let $\lfloor x \rceil = x \oplus (x - 1) = 2^{\rho(x)+1} - 1$. Show that every balanced animating function can be written in the form

$$x \oplus \lfloor x \oplus p_1 \rceil \oplus \lfloor x \oplus p_2 \rceil \oplus \cdots \oplus \lfloor x \oplus p_l \rceil, \qquad p_1 < p_2 < \cdots < p_l,$$

for some integers $\{p_1, p_2, \dots, p_l\}$, where $l \geq 0$, and this representation is unique.

d) Conversely, show that every such expression defines a balanced animating function.

17. [*HM36*] The results of exercise 16 make it possible to decide whether or not any two given animating functions are equal. Is there an algorithm that decides whether *any* given expression is identically zero, when that expression is constructed from a finite number of integer variables and constants using only the binary operations $+$ and $\oplus$? What if we also allow $\&$?

18. [*M25*] The curious pixel pattern shown here has $(x^2 y \gg 11) \& 1$ in row x and column y, for $1 \leq x, y \leq 256$. Is there any simple way to explain some of its major characteristics mathematically?

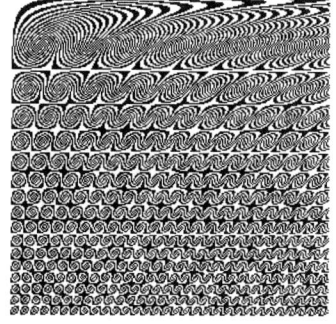

▶ **19.** [*M37*] (*Paley's rearrangement theorem.*) Given three vectors $A = (a_0, \ldots, a_{2^n-1})$, $B = (b_0, \ldots, b_{2^n-1})$, and $C = (c_0, \ldots, c_{2^n-1})$ of nonnegative numbers, let

$$f(A, B, C) = \sum_{j \oplus k \oplus l = 0} a_j b_k c_l.$$

For example, if $n = 2$ we have $f(A, B, C) = a_0 b_0 c_0 + a_0 b_1 c_1 + a_0 b_2 c_2 + a_0 b_3 c_3 + a_1 b_0 c_1 + a_1 b_1 c_0 + a_1 b_2 c_3 + \cdots + a_3 b_3 c_0$; in general there are 2^{2n} terms, one for each choice of j and k. Our goal is to prove that $f(A, B, C) \leq f(A^*, B^*, C^*)$, where A^* denotes the vector A sorted into nonincreasing order: $a_0^* \geq a_1^* \geq \cdots \geq a_{2^n-1}^*$.

a) Prove the result when all elements of A, B, and C are 0s and 1s.
b) Show that it is therefore true in general.
c) Similarly, $f(A, B, C, D) = \sum_{j \oplus k \oplus l \oplus m = 0} a_j b_k c_l d_m \leq f(A^*, B^*, C^*, D^*)$.

▶ **20.** [*21*] (*Gosper's hack.*) The following seven operations produce a useful function y of x, when x is a positive integer. Explain what this function is and why it is useful.

$$u \leftarrow x \,\&\, -x; \qquad v \leftarrow x + u; \qquad y \leftarrow v + (((v \oplus x)/u) \gg 2).$$

21. [*22*] Construct the *reverse* of Gosper's hack: Show how to compute x from y.

22. [*21*] Implement Gosper's hack efficiently with MMIX code, assuming that $x < 2^{64}$, without using division.

▶ **23.** [*27*] A sequence of nested parentheses can be represented as a binary number by putting a 1 in the position of each right parenthesis. For example, '(())()' corresponds in this way to $(001101)_2$, the number 13. Call such a number a *parenthesis trace*.

a) What are the smallest and largest parenthesis traces that have exactly m 1s?
b) Suppose x is a parenthesis trace and y is the next larger parenthesis trace with the same number of 1s. Show that y can be computed from x with a short chain of operations analogous to Gosper's hack.
c) Implement your method on MMIX, assuming that $\nu x \leq 32$.

▶ **24.** [*M30*] Program 1.3.2′P instructed MMIX to produce a table of the first five hundred prime numbers, using trial division to establish primality. Write an MMIX program that uses the "sieve of Eratosthenes" (exercise 4.5.4–8) to build a table of all odd primes that are less than N, packed into octabytes Q_0, Q_1, $\ldots$, $Q_{N/128-1}$ as in (27). Assume that $N \leq 2^{32}$, and that it's a multiple of 128. What is the running time when $N = 3584$?

▶ **25.** [*15*] Four volumes sit side by side on a bookshelf. Each of them contains exactly 500 pages, printed on 250 sheets of paper 0.1 mm thick; each book also has a front and back cover whose thicknesses are 1 mm each. A bookworm gnaws its way from page 1 of Volume 1 to page 500 of Volume 4. How far does it travel while doing so?

26. [*22*] Suppose we want random access to a table of 12 million items of 5-bit data. We could pack 12 such items into one 64-bit word, thereby fitting the table into 8 megabytes of memory. But random access then seems to require division by 12, which is rather slow; we might therefore prefer to let each item occupy a full byte, thus using 12 megabytes altogether.

Show, however, that there's a memory-efficient approach that avoids division.

27. [*21*] In the notation of Eqs. (32)–(43), how would you compute (a) $(\alpha 10^a 01^b)_2$? (b) $(\alpha 10^a 11^b)_2$? (c) $(\alpha 00^a 01^b)_2$? (d) $(0^\infty 11^a 00^b)_2$? (e) $(0^\infty 01^a 00^b)_2$? (f) $(0^\infty 11^a 11^b)_2$?

28. [*16*] What does the operation $(x+1) \,\&\, \bar{x}$ produce?

29. [*20*] (V. R. Pratt.) Express the magic mask μ_k of (47) in terms of μ_{k+1}.

30. [*20*] If $x = 0$, the MMIX instructions (46) will set $\rho \leftarrow 64$ (which is a close enough approximation to ∞). What changes to (50) and (51) will produce the same result?

▸ **31.** [*20*] A mathematician named Dr. L. I. Presume decided to calculate the ruler function with a simple loop as follows: "Set $\rho \leftarrow 0$; then while $x \,\&\, 1 = 0$, set $\rho \leftarrow \rho + 1$ and $x \leftarrow x \gg 1$." He reasoned that, when x is a random integer, the average number of right shifts is the average value of ρ, which is 1; and the standard deviation is only $\sqrt{2}$, so the loop almost always terminates quickly. Criticize his decision.

32. [*20*] What is the execution time for ρx when (52) is programmed for MMIX?

▸ **33.** [*26*] (Leiserson, Prokop, and Randall, 1998.) Show that if '58' is replaced by '49' in (52), we can use that method to identify *both* bits of the number $y = 2^j + 2^k$ quickly, when $64 > j > k \geq 0$. (Altogether $\binom{64}{2} = 2016$ cases need to be distinguished.)

34. [*M23*] Let x and y be 2-adic integers. True or false: (a) $\rho(x \,\&\, y) = \max(\rho x, \rho y)$; (b) $\rho(x \mid y) = \min(\rho x, \rho y)$; (c) $\rho x = \rho y$ if and only if $x \oplus y = (x-1) \oplus (y-1)$.

▸ **35.** [*M26*] According to Reitwiesner's theorem, exercise 4.1–34, every integer n has a unique representation $n = n^+ - n^-$ such that $n^+ \,\&\, n^- = (n^+ \mid n^-) \,\&\, ((n^+ \mid n^-) \gg 1) = 0$. Show that n^+ and n^- can be calculated quickly with bitwise operations. *Hint:* Prove the identity $(x \oplus 3x) \,\&\, ((x \oplus 3x) \gg 1) = 0$.

36. [*20*] Given $x = (x_{63} \ldots x_1 x_0)_2$, suggest efficient ways to calculate the quantities
  i) $x^{\oplus} = (x_{63}^{\oplus} \ldots x_1^{\oplus} x_0^{\oplus})_2$, where $x_k^{\oplus} = x_k \oplus \cdots \oplus x_1 \oplus x_0$ for $0 \leq k < 64$;
  ii) $x^{\&} = (x_{63}^{\&} \ldots x_1^{\&} x_0^{\&})_2$, where $x_k^{\&} = x_k \wedge \cdots \wedge x_1 \wedge x_0$ for $0 \leq k < 64$.

37. [*16*] What changes to (55) and (56) will make $\lambda 0$ come out -1?

38. [*17*] How long does the leftmost-bit-extraction procedure (57) take when implemented on MMIX?

▸ **39.** [*20*] Formula (43) shows how to remove the rightmost run of 1 bits from a given number x. How would you remove the *leftmost* run of 1 bits?

▸ **40.** [*21*] Prove (58), and find a simple way to decide if $\lambda x < \lambda y$, given x and $y \geq 0$.

41. [*M22*] What are the generating functions of the integer sequences (a) ρn, (b) λn, and (c) νn?

42. [*M21*] If $n = 2^{e_1} + \cdots + 2^{e_r}$, with $e_1 > \cdots > e_r \geq 0$, express the sum $\sum_{k=0}^{n-1} \nu k$ in terms of the exponents $e_1, \ldots, e_r$.

▸ **43.** [*20*] How sparse should x be, to make (63) faster than (62) on MMIX?

▸ **44.** [*23*] (E. Freed, 1983.) What's a fast way to evaluate the *weighted* bit sum $\sum j x_j$?

▸ **45.** [*20*] (T. Rokicki, 1999.) Explain how to test if $x^R < y^R$, without reversing x and y.

46. [*22*] Method (68) uses six operations to interchange two bits $x_i \leftrightarrow x_j$ of a register. Show that this interchange can actually be done with only *three* MMIX instructions.

47. [*10*] Can the general δ-swap (69) also be done with a method like (67)?

48. [*M21*] How many different δ-swaps are possible in an n-bit register? (When $n = 4$, a δ-swap can transform 1234 into 1234, 1243, 1324, 1432, 2134, 2143, 3214, 3412, 4231.)

▸ **49.** [*M30*] Let $s(n)$ denote the fewest δ-swaps that suffice to reverse an n-bit number.
  a) Prove that $s(n) \geq \lceil \log_3 n \rceil$ when n is odd, $s(n) \geq \lceil \log_3 3n/2 \rceil$ when n is even.
  b) Evaluate $s(n)$ when $n = 3^m$, $2 \cdot 3^m$, $(3^m + 1)/2$, and $(3^m - 1)/2$.
  c) What are $s(32)$ and $s(64)$? *Hint:* Show that $s(5n + 2) \leq s(n) + 2$.

50. [*M37*] Continuing exercise 49, prove that $s(n) = \log_3 n + O(\log \log n)$.

51. [23] Let c be a constant, $0 \le c < 2^d$. Find all sequences of masks $(\theta_0, \theta_1, \ldots, \theta_{d-1}, \hat{\theta}_{d-2}, \ldots, \hat{\theta}_1, \hat{\theta}_0)$ such that the general permutation scheme (71) takes $x \mapsto x^\pi$, where the bit permutation π is defined by either (a) $j\pi = j \oplus c$; or (b) $j\pi = (j + c) \bmod 2^d$. [The masks should satisfy $\theta_k \subseteq \mu_{d,k}$ and $\hat{\theta}_k \subseteq \mu_{d,k}$, so that (71) corresponds to Fig. 12; see (48). Notice that reversal, $x^\pi = x^R$, is the special case $c = 2^d - 1$ of part (a), while part (b) corresponds to the cyclic right shift $x^\pi = (x \gg c) + (x \ll (2^d - c))$.]

52. [22] Find hexadecimal constants $(\theta_0, \theta_1, \theta_2, \theta_3, \theta_4, \theta_5, \hat{\theta}_4, \hat{\theta}_3, \hat{\theta}_2, \hat{\theta}_1, \hat{\theta}_0)$ that cause (71) to produce the following important 64-bit permutations, based on the binary representation $j = (j_5 j_4 j_3 j_2 j_1 j_0)_2$: (a) $j\pi = (j_0 j_5 j_4 j_3 j_2 j_1)_2$; (b) $j\pi = (j_2 j_1 j_0 j_5 j_4 j_3)_2$; (c) $j\pi = (j_1 j_0 j_5 j_4 j_3 j_2)_2$; (d) $j\pi = (j_0 j_1 j_2 j_3 j_4 j_5)_2$. [Case (a) is the "perfect shuffle" (175) that takes $(x_{63} \ldots x_{33} x_{32} x_{31} \ldots x_1 x_0)_2$ into $(x_{63} x_{31} \ldots x_{33} x_1 x_{32} x_0)_2$; case (b) transposes an 8×8 matrix of bits; case (c), similarly, transposes a 4×16 matrix; and case (d) arises in connection with "fast Fourier transforms," see exercise 4.6.4–14.]

▶ **53.** [M25] The permutations in exercise 52 are said to be "induced by a permutation of index digits," because we obtain $j\pi$ by permuting the binary digits of j. Suppose $j\pi = (j_{(d-1)\psi} \ldots j_{1\psi} j_{0\psi})_2$, where ψ is a permutation of $\{0, 1, \ldots, d - 1\}$. Prove that if ψ has t cycles, the 2^d-bit permutation $x \mapsto x^\pi$ can be obtained with only $d - t$ swaps. In particular, show that this observation speeds up all four cases of exercise 52.

54. [22] (R. W. Gosper, 1985.) If an $m \times m$ bit matrix is stored in the rightmost m^2 bits of a register, show that it can be transposed by doing $(2^k(m - 1))$-swaps for $0 \le k < \lceil \lg m \rceil$. Write out the method in detail when $m = 7$.

▶ **55.** [26] Suppose an $n \times n$ bit matrix is stored in the rightmost n^2 bits of an n^3-bit register. Prove that $18d + 2$ bitwise operations suffice to multiply two such matrices, when $n = 2^d$; the matrix multiplication can be either Boolean (like MOR) or mod 2 (like MXOR).

56. [24] Suggest a way to transpose a 7×9 bit matrix in a 64-bit register.

57. [22] The network $P(2^d)$ of Fig. 12 has a total of $(2d - 1)2^{d-1}$ crossbars. Prove that any permutation of 2^d elements can be realized by some setting in which at most $d2^{d-1}$ of them are active.

▶ **58.** [M32] The first d columns of crossbar modules in the permutation network $P(2^d)$ perform a 1-swap, then a 2-swap, ..., and finally a 2^{d-1}-swap, when the network's wires are stretched into horizontal lines as shown here for $d = 3$. Let $N = 2^d$. These N lines, together with the $Nd/2$ crossbars, form a so-called "Omega router" or "inverse butterfly." The purpose of this exercise is to study the set Ω of all permutations φ such that we can obtain $(0\varphi, 1\varphi, \ldots, (N-1)\varphi)$ as outputs on the right of an Omega router when the inputs at the left are $(0, 1, \ldots, N - 1)$.

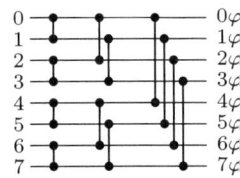

a) Prove that $|\Omega| = 2^{Nd/2}$. (Thus $\lg |\Omega| = Nd/2 \sim \frac{1}{2} \lg N!$.)

b) Prove that a permutation φ of $\{0, 1, \ldots, N - 1\}$ belongs to Ω if and only if

$$i \bmod 2^k = j \bmod 2^k \quad \text{and} \quad i\varphi \gg k = j\varphi \gg k \quad \text{implies} \quad i\varphi = j\varphi \qquad (*)$$

for all $0 \le i, j < N$ and all $0 \le k \le d$.

c) Simplify condition $(*)$ to the following, for all $0 \le i, j < N$:

$$\lambda(i\varphi \oplus j\varphi) < \rho(i \oplus j) \quad \text{implies} \quad i = j.$$

d) Let T be the set of all permutations τ of $\{0, 1, \ldots, N - 1\}$ such that $\rho(i \oplus j) = \rho(i\tau \oplus j\tau)$ for all i and j. (This is the set of branching functions considered in exercise 14, modulo 2^d; so it has 2^{N-1} members, $2^{N/2+d-1}$ of which are the animating functions modulo 2^d.) Prove that $\varphi \in \Omega$ if and only if $\tau\varphi \in \Omega$ for all $\tau \in T$.

e) Suppose φ and ψ are permutations of Ω that operate on different elements; that is, $j\varphi \neq j$ implies $j\psi = j$, for $0 \leq j < N$. Prove that $\varphi\psi \in \Omega$.

f) Prove that the permutation $0\varphi \ldots (N-1)\varphi$ is Omega-routable if and only if it is sorted by Batcher's bitonic sorting network of order N. (See Section 5.3.4.)

59. [*M30*] Given $0 \leq a < b < N = 2^d$, how many Omega-routable permutations operate only on the interval $[a \mathinner{.\,.} b]$? (Thus we want to count the number of $\varphi \in \Omega$ such that $j\varphi \neq j$ implies $a \leq j \leq b$. Exercise 58(a) is the special case $a = 0$, $b = N - 1$.)

60. [*HM28*] Given a random permutation of $\{0, 1, \ldots, 2n-1\}$, let p_{nk} be the probability that there are 2^k ways to set the crossbars in the first and last columns of the permutation network $P(2n)$ when realizing this permutation. In other words, p_{nk} is the probability that the associated graph has k cycles (see (75)). What is the generating function $\sum_{k \geq 0} p_{nk} z^k$? What are the mean and variance of 2^k?

61. [*46*] Is it NP-hard to decide whether a given permutation is realizable with at least one mask $\theta_j = 0$, using the recursive method of Fig. 12 as implemented in (71)?

▸ **62.** [*22*] Let $N = 2^d$. We can obviously represent a permutation π of $\{0, 1, \ldots, N-1\}$ by storing a table of N numbers, d bits each. With this representation we have instant access to $y = x\pi$, given x; but it takes $\Omega(N)$ steps to find $x = y\pi^-$ when y is given.

Show that, with the same amount of memory, we can represent an arbitrary permutation in such a way that $x\pi$ and $y\pi^-$ are both computable in $O(d)$ steps.

63. [*19*] For what integers w, x, y, and z does the zipper function satisfy (i) $x\ddagger y = y\ddagger x$? (ii) $(x\ddagger y) \gg z = (x \gg \lceil z/2 \rceil)\ddagger(y \gg \lfloor z/2 \rfloor)$? (iii) $(w\ddagger x)\mathbin{\&}(y\ddagger z) = (w\mathbin{\&}y)\ddagger(x\mathbin{\&}z)$?

64. [*22*] Find a "simple" expression for the zipper-of-sums $(x + x') \ddagger (y + y')$, as a function of $z = x \ddagger y$ and $z' = x' \ddagger y'$.

65. [*M16*] The binary polynomial $u(x) = u_0 + u_1 x + \cdots + u_{n-1} x^{n-1}$ (mod 2) can be represented by the integer $u = (u_{n-1} \ldots u_1 u_0)_2$. If $u(x)$ and $v(x)$ correspond to integers u and v in this way, what polynomial corresponds to $u \ddagger v$?

▸ **66.** [*M26*] Suppose the polynomial $u(x)$ has been represented as an n-bit integer u as in exercise 65, and let $v = u \oplus (u \ll \delta) \oplus (u \ll 2\delta) \oplus (u \ll 3\delta) \oplus \cdots$ for some integer δ.

a) What's a simple way to describe the polynomial $v(x)$?

b) Suppose n is large, and the bits of u have been packed into 64-bit words. How would you compute v when $\delta = 1$, using bitwise operations in 64-bit registers?

c) Consider the same question as (b), but when $\delta = 64$.

d) Consider the same question as (b), but when $\delta = 3$.

e) Consider the same question as (b), but when $\delta = 67$.

67. [*M31*] If $u(x)$ is a polynomial of degree $< n$, represented as in exercise 65, discuss the computation of $v(x) = u(x)^2 \bmod (x^n + x^m + 1)$, when $0 < m < n$ and both m and n are odd. *Hint:* This problem has an interesting connection with perfect shuffling.

68. [*20*] What three MMIX instructions implement the δ-shift operation, (79)?

69. [*25*] Prove that method (80) always extracts the proper bits when the masks θ_k have been set up properly: We never clobber any of the crucial bits y_j.

▸ **70.** [*31*] (Guy L. Steele Jr., 1994.) What's a good way to compute the masks $\theta_0, \theta_1, \ldots, \theta_{d-1}$ that are needed in the general compression procedure (80), given $\chi \neq 0$?

71. [*17*] Explain how to *reverse* the procedure of (80), going from the compact value $y = (y_{r-1} \ldots y_1 y_0)_2$ to a number $z = (z_{63} \ldots z_1 z_0)_2$ that has $z_{j_i} = y_i$ for $0 \leq i < r$.

72. [*25*] (Y. Hilewitz and R. B. Lee.) Prove that the gather-flip operation (81′) is Omega-routable in the sense of exercise 58.

73. [*22*] Prove that d well-chosen steps of (a) the sheep-and-goats operation (8_1) or (b) the gather-flip operation ($8_1'$) will implement any desired 2^d-bit permutation.

74. [*22*] Given counts $(c_0, c_1, \ldots, c_{2^d-1})$ for the Chung–Wong procedure, explain why an appropriate cyclic 1-shift can always produce new counts $(c_0', c_1', \ldots, c_{2^d-1}')$ for which $\sum c_{2l}' = \sum c_{2l+1}'$, thus allowing the recursion to proceed.

▶ **75.** [*32*] The method of Chung and Wong replicates bit l of a register exactly c_l times, but it produces results in scrambled order. For example, the case $(c_0, \ldots, c_7) = (1,2,0,2,0,2,0,1)$ illustrated in the text produces $(x_7x_3x_1x_5x_5x_3x_1x_0)_2$. In some applications this can be a disadvantage; we might prefer to have the bits retain their original order, namely $(x_7x_5x_5x_3x_3x_1x_1x_0)_2$ in that example.

Prove that the permutation network $P(2^d)$ of Fig. 12 can be modified to achieve this goal, given any sequence of counts $(c_0, c_1, \ldots, c_{2^d-1})$, if we replace the $d \cdot 2^{d-1}$ crossbar modules in the right-hand half by general 2×2 *mapping modules*. (A crossbar module with inputs (a, b) produces either (a, b) or (b, a) as output; a mapping module can also produce (a, a) or (b, b).)

76. [*47*] A *mapping network* is analogous to a sorting network or a permutation network, but it uses 2×2 mapping modules instead of comparators or crossbars, and it is supposed to be able to output all n^n possible mappings of its n inputs. Exercise 75, in conjunction with Fig. 12, shows that a mapping network for $n = 2^d$ exists with only $4d-2$ levels of delay, and with $n/2$ modules on each level; furthermore, this construction needs general 2×2 mapping modules (instead of simple crossbars) in only d of those levels.

To within $O(n)$, what is the smallest number $G(n)$ of modules that are sufficient to implement a general n-element mapping network?

77. [*26*] (R. W. Floyd and V. R. Pratt.) Design an algorithm that tests whether or not a given standard n-network is a sorting network, as defined in the exercises of Section 5.3.4. When the given network has r comparator modules, your algorithm should use $O(r)$ bitwise operations on words of length 2^n.

78. [*M27*] (*Testing disjointness.*) Suppose the binary numbers $x_1, x_2, \ldots, x_m$ each represent sets in a universe of $n - k$ elements, so that each x_j is less than 2^{n-k}. J. H. Quick (a student) decided to test whether the sets are disjoint by testing the condition

$$x_1 \mid x_2 \mid \cdots \mid x_m = (x_1 + x_2 + \cdots + x_m) \bmod 2^n.$$

Prove or disprove: Quick's test is valid if and only if $k \geq \lg(m-1)$.

▶ **79.** [*20*] If $x \neq 0$ and $x \subseteq \chi$, what is an easy way to determine the largest integer $x_{,} < x$ such that $x_{,} \subseteq \chi$? (Thus $(x_{,})' = (x')_{,} = x$, in connection with (8_4).)

80. [*20*] Suggest a fast way to find all maximal proper subsets of a set. More precisely, given χ with $\nu\chi = m$, we want to find all $x \subseteq \chi$ such that $\nu x = m - 1$.

81. [*21*] Find a formula for "scattered difference," to go with the "scattered sum" (8_6).

82. [*21*] Is it easy to shift a scattered accumulator to the left by 1, for example to change $(y_2x_4x_3y_1x_2y_0x_1x_0)_2$ to $(y_1x_4x_3y_0x_20x_1x_0)_2$?

▶ **83.** [*33*] Continuing exercise 82, find a way to shift a scattered 2^d-bit accumulator to the *right* by 1, given z and χ, in $O(d)$ steps.

84. [*25*] Given n-bit numbers $z = (z_{n-1} \ldots z_1z_0)_2$ and $\chi = (\chi_{n-1} \ldots \chi_1\chi_0)_2$, explain how to calculate the "stretched" quantities $z \leftharpoonup \chi = (z_{(n-1)\leftharpoonup\chi} \ldots z_{1\leftharpoonup\chi}z_{0\leftharpoonup\chi})_2$ and

$z \to \chi = (z_{(n-1) \to \chi} \ldots z_{1 \to \chi} z_{0 \to \chi})_2$, where

$$j \leftarrow \chi = \max\{k \mid k \leq j \text{ and } \chi_k = 1\}, \qquad j \to \chi = \min\{k \mid k \geq j \text{ and } \chi_k = 1\};$$

we let $z_{j \leftarrow \chi} = 0$ if $\chi_k = 0$ for $0 \leq k \leq j$, and $z_{j \to \chi} = 0$ if $\chi_k = 0$ for $n > k \geq j$. For example, if $n = 11$ and $\chi = (01101110010)_2$, then $z \leftarrow \chi = (z_9 z_9 z_8 z_6 z_6 z_5 z_4 z_1 z_1 z_1 0)_2$ and $z \to \chi = (0 z_9 z_8 z_8 z_6 z_5 z_4 z_4 z_4 z_1 z_1)_2$.

85. [*22*] (K. D. Tocher, 1954.) Imagine that you have a vintage 1950s computer with a drum memory for storing data, and that you need to do some computations with a $32 \times 32 \times 32$ array $a[i, j, k]$, whose subscripts are 5-bit integers in the range $0 \leq i, j, k < 32$. Unfortunately your machine has only a very small high-speed memory: You can access only 128 consecutive elements of the array in fast memory at any time. Since your application usually moves from $a[i, j, k]$ to a neighboring position $a[i', j', k']$, where $|i - i'| + |j - j'| + |k - k'| = 1$, you have decided to allocate the array so that, if $i = (i_4 i_3 i_2 i_1 i_0)_2$, $j = (j_4 j_3 j_2 j_1 j_0)_2$, and $k = (k_4 k_3 k_2 k_1 k_0)_2$, the array entry $a[i, j, k]$ is stored in drum location $(k_4 j_4 i_4 k_3 j_3 i_3 k_2 j_2 i_2 k_1 j_1 i_1 k_0 j_0 i_0)_2$. By interleaving the bits in this way, a small change to i, j, or k will cause only a small change in the address.

Discuss the implementation of this addressing function: (a) How does it change when i, j, or k changes by ± 1? (b) How would you handle a random access to $a[i, j, k]$, given i, j, and k? (c) How would you detect a "page fault" (namely, the condition that a new segment of 128 elements must be swapped into fast memory from the drum)?

86. [*M27*] An array of $2^p \times 2^q \times 2^r$ elements is to be allocated by putting $a[i, j, k]$ into a location whose bits are the $p + q + r$ bits of (i, j, k), permuted in some fashion. Furthermore, this array is to be stored in an external memory using pages of size 2^s. (Exercise 85 considers the case $p = q = r = 5$ and $s = 7$.) What allocation strategy of this kind minimizes the number of times that $a[i, j, k]$ is on a different page from $a[i', j', k']$, summed over all i, j, k, i', j', and k' such that $|i - i'| + |j - j'| + |k - k'| = 1$?

▶ **87.** [*20*] Suppose each byte of a 64-bit word x contains an ASCII code that represents either a letter, a digit, or a space. What three bitwise operations will convert all the lowercase letters to uppercase?

88. [*20*] Given $x = (x_7 \ldots x_0)_{256}$ and $y = (y_7 \ldots y_0)_{256}$, compute $z = (z_7 \ldots z_0)_{256}$, where $z_j = (x_j - y_j) \bmod 256$ for $0 \leq j < 8$. (See the addition operation in (87).)

89. [*23*] Given $x = (x_{31} \ldots x_1 x_0)_4$ and $y = (y_{31} \ldots y_1 y_0)_4$, compute $z = (z_{31} \ldots z_1 z_0)_4$, where $z_j = \lfloor x_j / y_j \rfloor$ for $0 \leq j < 32$, assuming that no y_j is zero.

90. [*20*] The bytewise averaging rule (88) always rounds downward when $x_j + y_j$ is odd. Make it less biased by rounding to the nearest odd integer in such cases.

▶ **91.** [*26*] (*Alpha channels.*) Recipe (88) is a good way to compute bytewise averages, but applications to computer graphics often require a more general blending of 8-bit values. Given three octabytes $x = (x_7 \ldots x_0)_{256}$, $y = (y_7 \ldots y_0)_{256}$, $\alpha = (a_7 \ldots a_0)_{256}$, show that bitwise operations allow us to compute $z = (z_7 \ldots z_0)_{256}$, where each byte z_j is a good approximation to $((255 - a_j) x_j + a_j y_j)/255$, *without* doing any multiplication. Implement your method with MMIX instructions.

▶ **92.** [*21*] What happens if the second line of (88) is changed to '$z \leftarrow (x \mid y) - z$'?

93. [*18*] What basic formula for subtraction is analogous to formula (89) for addition?

94. [*21*] Let $x = (x_7 \ldots x_1 x_0)_{256}$ and $t = (t_7 \ldots t_1 t_0)_{256}$ in (90). Can t_j be nonzero when x_j is nonzero? Can t_j be zero when x_j is zero?

95. [*22*] What's a bitwise way to tell if all bytes of $x = (x_7 \ldots x_1 x_0)_{256}$ are distinct?

96. [*21*] Explain (93), and find a similar formula that sets test flags $t_j \leftarrow 128[x_j \leq y_j]$.

97. [*23*] Leslie Lamport's paper in 1975 presented the following "problem taken from an actual compiler optimization algorithm": Given octabytes $x = (x_7 \ldots x_0)_{256}$ and $y = (y_7 \ldots y_0)_{256}$, compute $t = (t_7 \ldots t_0)_{256}$ and $z = (z_7 \ldots z_0)_{256}$ so that $t_j \neq 0$ if and only if $x_j \neq 0$, $x_j \neq {}$'*', and $x_j \neq y_j$; and $z_j = (x_j = 0? \ y_j : (x_j \neq {}$'*'$ \wedge x_j \neq y_j? \ $'*'$: x_j))$.

98. [*20*] Given $x = (x_7 \ldots x_0)_{256}$ and $y = (y_7 \ldots y_0)_{256}$, compute $z = (z_7 \ldots z_0)_{256}$ and $w = (w_7 \ldots w_0)_{256}$, where $z_j = \max(x_j, y_j)$ and $w_j = \min(x_j, y_j)$ for $0 \leq j < 8$.

▶ **99.** [*28*] Find hexadecimal constants a, b, c, d, e such that the six bitwise operations

$$y \leftarrow x \oplus a, \quad t \leftarrow ((((y \,\&\, b) + c) \mid y) \oplus d) \,\&\, e$$

will compute the flags $t = (f_7 \ldots f_1 f_0)_{256} \ll 7$ from any bytes $x = (x_7 \ldots x_1 x_0)_{256}$, where

$$f_0 = [x_0 = {}'!'], \ f_1 = [x_1 \neq {}'*'], \ f_2 = [x_2 < {}'A'], \ f_3 = [x_3 > {}'z'], \ f_4 = [x_4 \geq {}'a'],$$
$$f_5 = [x_5 \in \{'0', '1', \ldots, '9'\}], \ f_6 = [x_6 \leq 168], \ f_7 = [x_7 \in \{'<', '=', '>', '?'\}].$$

100. [*25*] Suppose $x = (x_{15} \ldots x_1 x_0)_{16}$ and $y = (y_{15} \ldots y_1 y_0)_{16}$ are *binary-coded decimal* numbers, where $0 \leq x_j, y_j < 10$ for each j. Explain how to compute their sum $u = (u_{15} \ldots u_1 u_0)_{16}$ and difference $v = (v_{15} \ldots v_1 v_0)_{16}$, where $0 \leq u_j, v_j < 10$ and

$$(u_{15} \ldots u_1 u_0)_{10} = ((x_{15} \ldots x_1 x_0)_{10} + (y_{15} \ldots y_1 y_0)_{10}) \bmod 10^{16},$$
$$(v_{15} \ldots v_1 v_0)_{10} = ((x_{15} \ldots x_1 x_0)_{10} - (y_{15} \ldots y_1 y_0)_{10}) \bmod 10^{16},$$

without bothering to do any radix conversion.

▶ **101.** [*22*] Two octabytes x and y contain amounts of time, represented in five fields that respectively signify days (3 bytes), hours (1 byte), minutes (1 byte), seconds (1 byte), and milliseconds (2 bytes). Can you add and subtract them quickly, without converting from this mixed-radix representation to binary and back again?

102. [*25*] Discuss routines for the addition and subtraction of polynomials modulo 5, when (a) 16 4-bit coefficients or (b) 21 3-bit coefficients are packed into a 64-bit word.

▶ **103.** [*22*] Sometimes it's convenient to represent small numbers in *unary* notation, so that $0, 1, 2, 3, \ldots, k$ appear respectively as $(0)_2, (1)_2, (11)_2, (111)_2, \ldots, 2^k - 1$ inside the computer. Then max and min are easily implemented as $\mid$ and $\&$.

Suppose the bytes of $x = (x_7 \ldots x_0)_{256}$ are such unary numbers, while the bytes of $y = (y_7 \ldots y_0)_{256}$ are all either 0 or 1. Explain how to "add" y to x or "subtract" y from x, giving $u = (u_7 \ldots u_0)_{256}$ and $v = (v_7 \ldots v_0)_{256}$ where

$$u_j = 2^{\min(8, \lg(x_j+1)+y_j)} - 1 \quad \text{and} \quad v_j = 2^{\max(0, \lg(x_j+1)-y_j)} - 1.$$

104. [*22*] Use bitwise operations to check the validity of a date represented in "year-month-day" fields (y, m, d) as in (22). You should compute a value t that is zero if and only if $1900 < y < 2100$, $1 \leq m \leq 12$, and $1 \leq d \leq max\_day(m)$, where month m has at most $max\_day(m)$ days. Can it be done in fewer than 20 operations?

105. [*30*] Given $x = (x_7 \ldots x_0)_{256}$ and $y = (y_7 \ldots y_0)_{256}$, discuss bitwise operations that will *sort* the bytes into order, so that $x_0 \leq y_0 \leq \cdots \leq x_7 \leq y_7$ afterwards.

106. [*27*] Explain the Fredman–Willard procedure (95). Also show that a simple modification of their method will compute $2^{\lambda x}$ without doing any left shifts.

▶ **107.** [*22*] Implement Algorithm B on MMIX when $d = 4$, and compare it with (56).

108. [*26*] Adapt Algorithm B to cases where n does not have the form $d \cdot 2^d$.

109. [*20*] Evaluate ρx for n-bit numbers x in $O(\log\log n)$ broadword steps.

▶ **110.** [*30*] Suppose $n = 2^{2^e}$ and $0 \le x < n$. Show how to compute $1 \ll x$ in $O(e)$ broadword steps, using only shift commands that shift by a constant amount. (Together with Algorithm B we can therefore extract the most significant bit of an n-bit number in $O(\log\log n)$ such steps.)

111. [*23*] Explain the 01^r pattern recognizer, (98).

112. [*46*] Can all occurrences of the pattern $1^r 0$ be identified in $O(1)$ broadword steps?

113. [*23*] A *strong broadword chain* is a broadword chain of a specified width n that is also a 2-adic chain, for all n-bit choices of x_0. For example, the 2-bit broadword chain (x_0, x_1) with $x_1 = x_0 + 1$ is not strong because $x_0 = (11)_2$ makes $x_1 = (00)_2$. But $(x_0, x_1, \ldots, x_4)$ is a strong broadword chain that computes $(x_0 + 1) \bmod 4$ for all $0 \le x_0 < 4$ if we set $x_1 = x_0 \oplus 1$, $x_2 = x_0 \mathbin{\&} 1$, $x_3 = x_2 \ll 1$, and $x_4 = x_1 \oplus x_3$.

     Given a broadword chain $(x_0, x_1, \ldots, x_r)$ of width n, construct a strong broadword chain $(x'_0, x'_1, \ldots, x'_{r'})$ of the same width, such that $r' = O(r)$ and $(x_0, x_1, \ldots, x_r)$ is a subsequence of $(x'_0, x'_1, \ldots, x'_{r'})$.

114. [*16*] Suppose $(x_0, x_1, \ldots, x_r)$ is a strong broadword chain of width n that computes the value $f(x) = x_r$ whenever an n-bit number $x = x_0$ is given. Construct a broadword chain $(X_0, X_1, \ldots, X_r)$ of width mn that computes $X_r = (f(\xi_1) \ldots f(\xi_m))_{2^n}$ for any given mn-bit value $X_0 = (\xi_1 \ldots \xi_m)_{2^n}$, where $0 \le \xi_1, \ldots, \xi_m < 2^n$.

▶ **115.** [*24*] Given a 2-adic integer $x = (\ldots x_2 x_1 x_0)_2$, we might want to compute $y = (\ldots y_2 y_1 y_0)_2 = f(x)$ from x by zeroing out all blocks of consecutive 1s that (a) are not immediately followed by two 0s; or (b) are followed by an odd number of 0s before the next block of 1s begins; or (c) contain an odd number of 1s. For example, if x is $(\ldots 01110111001101000110)_2$ then y is (a) $(\ldots 00000111000001000110)_2$; (b) $(\ldots 00000111000000000110)_2$; (c) $(\ldots 00000000001100000110)_2$. (Infinitely many 0s are assumed to appear at the right of x_0. Thus, in case (a) we have

$$y_j = x_j \wedge \left((\bar{x}_{j-1} \wedge \bar{x}_{j-2}) \vee (x_{j-1} \wedge \bar{x}_{j-2} \wedge \bar{x}_{j-3}) \vee (x_{j-1} \wedge x_{j-2} \wedge \bar{x}_{j-3} \wedge \bar{x}_{j-4}) \vee \cdots \right)$$

for all j, where $x_k = 0$ for $k < 0$.) Find 2-adic chains for y in each case.

116. [*HM30*] Suppose $x = (\ldots x_2 x_1 x_0)_2$ and $y = (\ldots y_2 y_1 y_0)_2 = f(x)$, where y is computable by a 2-adic chain having no shift operations. Let L be the set of all binary strings such that $y_j = [x_j \ldots x_1 x_0 \in L]$, and assume that all constants used in the chain are rational 2-adic numbers. Prove that L is a regular language. What languages L correspond to the functions in exercise 115(a) and 115(b)?

117. [*HM46*] Continuing exercise 116, is there any simple way to characterize the regular languages L that arise in shift-free 2-adic chains? (The language $L = 0^*(10^*10^*)^*$ does not seem to correspond to any such chain.)

118. [*30*] According to Lemma A, we cannot compute the function $x \gg 1$ for all n-bit numbers x by using only additions, subtractions, and bitwise Boolean operations (no shifts or branches). Show, however, that $O(n)$ such operations are necessary and sufficient if we include also the "monus" operator $y \mathbin{\dot-} z$ in our repertoire.

119. [*20*] Evaluate the function $f_{py}(x)$ in (102) with four broadword steps.

▶ **120.** [*M25*] There are $2^{n2^{mn}}$ functions that take n-bit numbers $(x_1, \ldots, x_m)$ into an n-bit number $f(x_1, \ldots, x_m)$. How many of them can be implemented with addition, subtraction, multiplication, and nonshift bitwise Boolean operations (modulo 2^n)?

▶ **121.** [*M25*] By exercise 3.1–6, a function from $[0 \mathinner{.\,.} 2^n)$ into itself is eventually periodic.

    a) Prove that if f is any n-bit broadword function that can be implemented without shift instructions, the lengths of its periods are always powers of 2.

    b) However, for every p between 1 and n, there's an n-bit broadword chain of length 3 that has a period of length p.

122. [*M22*] Complete the proof of Lemma B.

123. [*M23*] Let a_q be the constant $1 + 2^q + 2^{2q} + \cdots + 2^{(q-1)q} = (2^{q^2} - 1)/(2^q - 1)$. Using (104), show that there are infinitely many q such that the operation of multiplying by a_q, modulo 2^{q^2}, requires $\Omega(\log q)$ steps in any n-bit broadword chain with $n \geq q^2$.

124. [*M38*] Complete the proof of Theorem R′ by defining an n-bit broadword chain $(x_0, x_1, \ldots, x_f)$ and sets $(U_0, U_1, \ldots, U_f)$ such that, for $0 \leq t \leq f$, all inputs $x \in U_t$ lead to an essentially similar state $Q(x, t)$, in the following sense: (i) The current instruction in $Q(x, t)$ does not depend on x. (ii) If register r_j has a known value in $Q(x, t)$, it holds $x_{j'}$ for some definite index $j' \leq t$. (iii) If memory location $M[z]$ has been changed, it holds $x_{z''}$ for some definite index $z'' \leq t$. (The values of j' and z'' depend on j, z, and t, but not on x.) Furthermore $|U_t| \geq n/2^{2^t-1}$, and the program cannot guarantee that $r_1 = \rho x$ when $t < f$. *Hint:* Lemma B implies that a limited number of shift amounts and memory addresses need to be considered when t is small.

125. [*M33*] Prove Theorem P′. *Hint:* Lemma B remains true if we replace '= 0' by '= α_s' in (103), for any values α_s.

126. [*M46*] Does the operation of extracting the most significant bit, $2^{\lambda x}$, require $\Omega(\log \log n)$ steps in an n-bit basic RAM? (See exercise 110.)

127. [*HM40*] Prove that at least $\Omega(\log n/\log \log n)$ broadword steps are needed to compute the parity function, $(\nu x) \bmod 2$, using the theory of circuit complexity. [*Hint:* Every broadword operation is in complexity class AC$_0$.]

128. [*M46*] Can $(\nu x) \bmod 2$ be computed in $O(\log n/\log \log n)$ broadword steps?

129. [*M46*] Does sideways addition require $\Omega(\log n)$ broadword steps?

130. [*M46*] Is there an n-bit constant a such that the function $(a \ll x) \bmod 2^n$ requires $\Omega(\log n)$ n-bit broadword steps?

▶ **131.** [*23*] Write an MMIX program for Algorithm R when the graph is represented by arc lists. Vertex nodes have at least two fields, called LINK and ARCS, and arc nodes have TIP and NEXT fields, as explained in Section 7. Initially all LINK fields are zero, except in the given set of vertices Q, which is represented as a circular list. Your program should change that circular list so that it represents the set R of all reachable vertices.

▶ **132.** [*M27*] A *clique* in a graph is a set of mutually adjacent vertices; a clique is *maximal* if it's not contained in any other. The purpose of this exercise is to discuss an algorithm due to J. K. M. Moody and J. Hollis, which provides a convenient way to find every maximal clique of a not-too-large graph, using bitwise operations.

    Suppose G is a graph with n vertices $V = \{0, 1, \ldots, n-1\}$. Let $\rho_v = \sum\{2^u \mid u - v \text{ or } u = v\}$ be row v of G's reflexive adjacency matrix, and let $\delta_v = \sum\{2^u \mid u \neq v\} = 2^n - 1 - 2^v$. Every subset $U \subseteq V$ is representable as an n-bit integer $\sigma(U) = \sum_{u \in U} 2^u$; for example, $\delta_v = \sigma(V \setminus v)$. We also define the bitwise intersection

$$\tau(U) = \mathop{\&}_{0 \leq u < n} (u \in U?\ \rho_u : \delta_u).$$

For example, if $n = 5$ we have $\tau(\{0, 2\}) = \rho_0\ \&\ \delta_1\ \&\ \rho_2\ \&\ \delta_3\ \&\ \delta_4$.

a) Prove that U is a clique if and only if $\tau(U) = \sigma(U)$.

b) Show that if $\tau(U) = \sigma(T)$ then T is a clique.

c) For $1 \le k \le n$, consider the 2^k bitwise intersections

$$C_k = \left\{ \underset{0 \le u < k}{\&} (u \in U?\ \rho_u:\ \delta_u) \ \middle|\ U \subseteq \{0, 1, \ldots, k-1\} \right\},$$

and let C_k^+ be the maximal elements of C_k. Prove that U is a maximal clique if and only if $\sigma(U) \in C_n^+$.

d) Explain how to compute C_k^+ from C_{k-1}^+, starting with $C_0^+ = \{2^n - 1\}$.

▶ **133.** [20] Given a graph G, how can the algorithm of exercise 132 be used to find (a) all maximal independent sets of vertices? (b) all minimal vertex covers (sets that hit every edge)?

134. [15] Nine classes of mappings for ternary values appear in (119), (123), and (124). To which class does the representation (128) belong, if $a = 0$, $b = *$, $c = 1$?

135. [22] Łukasiewicz included a few operations besides (127) in his three-valued logic: $\neg x$ (negation) interchanges 0 with 1 but leaves $*$ unchanged; $\diamond x$ (possibility) is defined as $\neg x \Rightarrow x$; $\square x$ (necessity) is defined as $\neg \diamond \neg x$; and $x \Leftrightarrow y$ (equivalence) is defined as $(x \Rightarrow y) \wedge (y \Rightarrow x)$. Explain how to perform these operations using representation (128).

136. [29] Suggest two-bit encodings for binary operations on the set $\{a, b, c\}$ that are defined by the following "multiplication tables":

$$\text{(a)} \begin{pmatrix} a & b & c \\ b & c & c \\ c & c & c \end{pmatrix}; \qquad \text{(b)} \begin{pmatrix} a & c & b \\ c & b & a \\ b & a & c \end{pmatrix}; \qquad \text{(c)} \begin{pmatrix} a & b & a \\ a & a & c \\ a & b & c \end{pmatrix}.$$

137. [21] Show that the operation in exercise 136(c) is simpler with packed vectors like (131) than with the unpacked form (130).

138. [24] Find an example of three-state-to-two-bit encoding where class V_a is best.

139. [25] If x and y are signed bits 0, $+1$, or -1, what 2-bit encoding is good for calculating their sum $(z_1 z_2)_3 = x + y$, where z_1 and z_2 are also required to be signed bits? (This is a "half adder" for balanced ternary numbers.)

140. [27] Design an economical *full adder* for balanced ternary numbers: Show how to compute signed bits u and v such that $3u + v = x + y + z$ when $x, y, z \in \{0, +1, -1\}$.

▶ **141.** [30] The *Ulam numbers* $\langle U_1, U_2, \ldots \rangle = \langle 1, 2, 3, 4, 6, 8, 11, 13, 16, 18, 26, \ldots \rangle$ are defined for $n \ge 3$ by letting U_n be the smallest integer $> U_{n-1}$ that has a *unique* representation $U_n = U_j + U_k$ for $0 < j < k < n$. Show that a million Ulam numbers can be computed rapidly with the help of bitwise techniques.

▶ **142.** [33] A subcube such as $*10*1*01$ can be represented by asterisk codes 10010100 and bit codes 01001001, as in (85); but many other encodings are also possible. What representation scheme for subcubes works best, for finding prime implicants by the consensus-based algorithm of exercise 7.1.1–31?

143. [20] Let x be a 64-bit number that represents an 8×8 chessboard, with a 1 bit in every position where a knight is present. Find a formula for the 64-bit number $f(x)$ that has a 1 in every position reachable in one move by a knight of x. For example, the white knights at the start of a game correspond to $x = {}^{\#}42$; then $f(x) = {}^{\#}\text{a}51800$.

144. [16] What node is the sibling of node j in a sideways heap? (See (134).)

145. [17] Interpret (137) when h is *less* than the height of j.

▸ **146.** [*M20*] Prove Eq. (138), which relates the ρ and λ functions.

▸ **147.** [*M20*] What values of πv, βv, αv, and τj occur in Algorithm V when the forest is
a) the empty digraph with vertices $\{v_1, \ldots, v_n\}$ and no arcs?
b) the oriented path $v_n \longrightarrow \cdots \longrightarrow v_2 \longrightarrow v_1$?

148. [*M21*] When preprocessing for Algorithm V, is it possible to have $\beta x_3 \longrightarrow^*$ $\beta y_2 \longrightarrow^* \beta x_2 \longrightarrow^* \beta y_1 \longrightarrow^* \beta x_1$ in S when $x_3 \longrightarrow x_2 \longrightarrow x_1 \longrightarrow \Lambda$ and $y_2 \longrightarrow y_1 \longrightarrow \Lambda$ in the forest? (If so, two different trees are "entangled" in S.)

▸ **149.** [*23*] Design a preprocessing procedure for Algorithm V.

▸ **150.** [*25*] Given an array of elements $A_1, \ldots, A_n$, the *range minimum query* problem is to determine $k(i,j)$ such that $A_{k(i,j)} = \min(A_i, \ldots, A_j)$ for any given indices i and j with $1 \le i \le j \le n$. Prove that Algorithm V will solve this problem, after $O(n)$ steps of preprocessing on the array A have prepared the necessary tables $(\pi, \beta, \alpha, \tau)$. *Hint:* Consider the binary search tree constructed from the sequence of keys $(p(1), p(2), \ldots, p(n))$, where p is a permutation of $\{1, 2, \ldots, n\}$ such that $A_{p(1)} \le A_{p(2)} \le \cdots \le A_{p(n)}$.

151. [*22*] Conversely, show that any algorithm for range minimum queries can be used to find nearest common ancestors, with essentially the same efficiency.

152. [*M21*] Prove that Algorithm V is correct.

▸ **153.** [*M20*] The pointers in a navigation pile like (144) can be packed into a binary string such as

0	1	0	0	1	0	0	0	0	1	0	1	0	0	0	0	0	0	0	0	0

2	4	6	8	10	12	14	16	18	20	22	24

.

At what bit position (from the left) does the pointer for node j end?

154. [*20*] The gray lines in Fig. 14 show how each pentagon is composed of ten triangles. What decomposition of the hyperbolic plane is defined by those gray lines alone, without the black pentagon edges?

▸ **155.** [*M21*] Prove that $(x\phi) \bmod 1 = (\alpha 0)_{1/\phi}$ when α is the negaFibonacci code for x.

156. [*21*] Design algorithms (a) to convert a given integer x to its negaFibonacci code α, and (b) to convert a given negaFibonacci code α to $x = N(\alpha)$.

157. [*M21*] Explain the recursion (148) for negaFibonacci predecessor and successor.

158. [*M26*] Let $\alpha = a_n \ldots a_1$ be the binary code for $F(\alpha 0) = a_n F_{n+1} + \cdots + a_1 F_2$ in the standard Fibonacci number system (146). Develop methods analogous to (148) and (149) for incrementing and decrementing such codewords.

159. [*M34*] Exercise 7 shows that it's easy to convert between the negabinary and binary number systems. Discuss conversion between negaFibonacci codewords and the ordinary Fibonacci codes in exercise 158.

160. [*M29*] Prove that (150) and (151) yield consistent code labels for the pentagrid.

161. [*20*] The cells of a chessboard can be colored black and white, so that neighboring cells have different colors. Does the pentagrid also have this property?

▸ **162.** [*HM37*] Explain how to draw the pentagrid, Fig. 14. What circles are present?

163. [*HM41*] Devise a way to navigate through the triangles in the tiling of Fig. 18.

164. [*23*] The original definition of custerization in 1957 was not (157) but

$$\text{custer}'(X) = X \mathbin{\&} {\sim}(X_{\text{NW}} \mathbin{\&} X_{\text{N}} \mathbin{\&} X_{\text{NE}} \mathbin{\&} X_{\text{W}} \mathbin{\&} X_{\text{E}} \mathbin{\&} X_{\text{SW}} \mathbin{\&} X_{\text{S}} \mathbin{\&} X_{\text{SE}}).$$

Why is (157) preferable?

165. [*21*] (R. A. Kirsch.) Discuss the computation of the 3×3 cellular automaton with

$$X^{(t+1)} = \text{custer}(\overline{X}^{(t)}) = \sim X^{(t)} \ \& \ (X_\text{N}^{(t)} \mid X_\text{W}^{(t)} \mid X_\text{E}^{(t)} \mid X_\text{S}^{(t)}).$$

166. [*M23*] Let $f(M, N)$ be the maximum number of black pixels in an $M \times N$ bitmap X for which $X = \text{custer}(X)$. Prove that $f(M, N) = \frac{4}{5} MN + O(M + N)$.

167. [*24*] (*Life.*) If the bitmap X represents an array of cells that are either dead (0) or alive (1), the Boolean function

$$f(x_\text{NW}, \ldots, x, \ldots, x_\text{SE}) = [2 < x_\text{NW} + x_\text{N} + x_\text{NE} + x_\text{W} + \tfrac{1}{2}x + x_\text{E} + x_\text{SW} + x_\text{S} + x_\text{SE} < 4]$$

can lead to astonishing life histories when it governs a cellular automaton as in (158).

 a) Find a way to evaluate f with a Boolean chain of 26 steps or less.
 b) Let $X_j^{(t)}$ denote row j of X at time t. Show that $X_j^{(t+1)}$ can be evaluated in at most 23 broadword steps, as a function of the three rows $X_{j-1}^{(t)}$, $X_j^{(t)}$, and $X_{j+1}^{(t)}$.

▸ **168.** [*23*] To keep an image finite, we might insist that a 3×3 cellular automaton treats a $M \times N$ bitmap as a *torus*, wrapping around seamlessly between top and bottom and between left and right. The task of simulating its actions efficiently with bitwise operations is somewhat tricky: We want to minimize references to memory, yet each new pixel value depends on old values that lie on all sides. Furthermore the shifting of bits between neighboring words tends to be awkward, taxing the capacity of a register.

 Show that such difficulties can be surmounted by maintaining an array of n-bit words A_{jk} for $0 \le j \le M$ and $0 \le k \le N' = \lceil N/(n-2) \rceil$. If $j \ne M$ and $k \ne 0$, word A_{jk} should contain the pixels of row j and columns $(k-1)(n-2)$ through $k(n-2) + 1$, inclusive; the other words A_{Mk} and A_{j0} provide auxiliary buffer space. (Notice that some bits of the raster appear twice.)

169. [*22*] Continuing the previous two exercises, what happens to the Cheshire cat of Fig. 17(a) when it is subjected to the vicissitudes of Life, in a 26×31 torus?

▸ **170.** [*21*] What result does the Guo–Hall thinning automaton produce when given a solid black rectangle of M rows and N columns? How long does it take?

171. [*24*] Find a Boolean chain of length ≤ 25 to evaluate the local thinning function $g(x_\text{NW}, x_\text{N}, x_\text{NE}, x_\text{W}, x_\text{E}, x_\text{SW}, x_\text{S}, x_\text{SE})$ of (159), with or without the extra cases in (160).

172. [*M29*] Prove or disprove: If a pattern contains three black pixels that are king-neighbors of each other, the Guo–Hall procedure extended by (160) will reduce it, unless none of those pixels can be removed without destroying the connectivity.

▸ **173.** [*M30*] Raster images often need to be cleaned up if they contain noisy data. For example, accidental specks of black or white may well spoil the results when a thinning algorithm is used for optical character recognition.

 Say that a bitmap X is *closed* if every white pixel is part of a 2×2 square of white pixels, and *open* if every black pixel is part of a 2×2 square of black pixels. Let

$$X^D = \ \& \ \{Y \mid Y \supseteq X \text{ and } Y \text{ is closed}\}; \quad X^L = \mid \{Y \mid Y \subseteq X \text{ and } Y \text{ is open}\}.$$

A bitmap is called *clean* if it equals X^{DL} for some X. We might, for example, have

$$X = \ \blacksquare\text{ }; \qquad X^D = \ \blacksquare\text{ }; \qquad X^{DL} = \ \blacksquare\ .$$

In general X^D is "darker" than X, while X^L is "lighter": $X^D \supseteq X \supseteq X^L$.
 a) Prove that $(X^{DL})^{DL} = X^{DL}$. *Hint:* $X \subseteq Y$ implies $X^D \subseteq Y^D$ and $X^L \subseteq Y^L$.
 b) Show that X^D can be computed with one step of a 3×3 cellular automaton.

174. [*M46*] (M. Minsky and S. Papert.) Is there a three-dimensional shrinking algorithm that preserves connectivity, analogous to (161)?

175. [*15*] How many *rookwise* connected black components does the Cheshire cat have?

176. [*M24*] Let G be the graph whose vertices are the black pixels of a given bitmap X, with $u \!-\! v$ when u and v are a king move apart. Let G' be the corresponding graph after the shrinking transformation (161) has been applied. The purpose of this exercise is to show that the number of connected components of G' is the number of components of G minus the number of isolated vertices of G.

Let $N_{(i,j)} = \{(i,j),(i-1,j),(i-1,j+1),(i,j+1)\}$ be pixel (i,j) together with its north and/or east neighbors. For each $v \in G$ let $S(v) = \{v' \in G' \mid v' \in N_v\}$.

a) Prove that $S(v)$ is empty if and only if v is isolated in G.
b) If $u \!-\! v$ in G, $u' \in S(u)$, and $v' \in S(v)$, prove that $u' \!-\!\!\!-^* v'$ in G'.
c) For each $v' \in G'$ let $S'(v') = \{v \in G \mid v' \in N_v\}$. Is $S'(v')$ always nonempty?
d) If $u' \!-\! v'$ in G', $u \in S'(u')$, and $v \in S'(v')$, prove that $u \!-\!\!\!-^* v$ in G.
e) Hence there's a one-to-one correspondence between the nontrivial components of G and the components of G'.

177. [*M22*] Continuing exercise 176, prove an analogous result for the white pixels.

178. [*20*] If X is an $M \times N$ bitmap, let X^* be the $M \times (2N+1)$ bitmap $X \ddagger (X \mid (X \ll 1))$. Show that the kingwise connected components of X^* are also rookwise connected, and that bitmap X^* has the same "surroundedness tree" (162) as X.

▶ **179.** [*34*] Design an algorithm that constructs the surroundedness tree of a given $M \times N$ bitmap, scanning the image one row at a time as discussed in the text. (See (162) and (163).)

▶ **180.** [*M24*] Digitize the hyperbola $y^2 = x^2 + 13$ by hand, for $0 < y \le 7$.

181. [*HM20*] Explain how to subdivide a general conic (168) with rational coefficients into monotonic parts so that Algorithm T applies.

182. [*M31*] Why does the three-register method (Algorithm T) digitize correctly?

▶ **183.** [*M29*] (G. Rote.) Explain why Algorithm T might fail if condition (v) is false.

▶ **184.** [*M22*] Find a quadratic form $Q'(x,y)$ so that, when Algorithm T is applied to (x',y'), (x,y), and Q', it produces exactly the same edges as it does from (x,y), (x',y'), and Q, but in the reverse order.

▶ **185.** [*22*] Design an algorithm that properly digitizes a straight line from (ξ, η) to (ξ', η'), when ξ, η, ξ', and η' are rational numbers, by simplifying Algorithm T.

186. [*HM22*] Given three complex numbers (z_0, z_1, z_2), consider the curve traced out by

$$B(t) = (1-t)^2 z_0 + 2(1-t)t z_1 + t^2 z_2, \qquad \text{for } 0 \le t \le 1.$$

a) What is the approximate behavior of $B(t)$ when t is near 0 or 1?
b) Let $S(z_0, z_1, z_2) = \{B(t) \mid 0 \le t \le 1\}$. Prove that all points of $S(z_0, z_1, z_2)$ lie on or inside the triangle whose vertices are z_0, z_1, and z_2.
c) True or false? $S(w + \zeta z_0, w + \zeta z_1, w + \zeta z_2) = w + \zeta S(z_0, z_1, z_2)$.
d) Prove that $S(z_0, z_1, z_2)$ is part of a straight line if and only if z_0, z_1, and z_2 are collinear; otherwise it is part of a parabola.

e) Prove that if $0 \le \theta \le 1$, we have the recurrence

$$S(z_0, z_1, z_2) = S(z_0, (1-\theta)z_0 + \theta z_1, B(\theta)) \cup S(B(\theta), (1-\theta)z_1 + \theta z_2, z_2).$$

187. [*M29*] Continuing exercise 186, show how to digitize $S(z_0, z_1, z_2)$ using the three-register method (Algorithm T). For best results, the digitizations of $S(z_2, z_1, z_0)$ and $S(z_0, z_1, z_2)$ should produce the same edges, but in reverse order.

▶ **188.** [*25*] Bitmap images can often be viewed conveniently using pixels that are *shades of gray* instead of just black or white. Such gray levels typically are 8-bit values that range from 0 (black) to 255 (white); notice that the black/white convention is traditionally *reversed* with respect to the 1-bit case. An $m \times n$ bitmap whose resolution is 600 dots per inch corresponds nicely to the $(m/8) \times (n/8)$ grayscale image with 75 pixels per inch that is obtained by mapping each 8×8 subarray of 1-bit pixels into the gray level $\lfloor 255(1 - k/64)^{1/\gamma} + \frac{1}{2} \rfloor$, where $\gamma = 1.3$ and k is the number of 1s in the subarray.

Write an MMIX routine that converts a given $m \times n$ array BITMAP into the corresponding $(m/8) \times (n/8)$ image GRAYMAP, assuming that $m = 8m'$ and $n = 64n'$.

189. [*25*] Given a 64×64 bitmap, what's a good way (a) to transpose it, or (b) to rotate it by $90°$, using operations on 64-bit numbers?

190. [*23*] A *parity pattern* of length m and width n is an $m \times n$ matrix of 0s and 1s with the property that each element is the sum of its rook-neighbors, mod 2. For example,

$$
\begin{array}{cccccc}
11 & 0011 & & 100 & & 01110 \\
00, & 0100 & 01010 & 110 & & 10101 \\
 & 1101, & 11011, & 101, & \text{and} & 11011 \\
11 & 0101 & 01010 & 011 & & 10101 \\
 & & & 001 & & 01110
\end{array}
$$

are parity patterns of sizes 3×2, 4×4, 3×5, 5×3, and 5×5.

a) If the binary vectors $\alpha_1, \alpha_2, \ldots, \alpha_m$ are the rows of a parity pattern, show that $\alpha_2, \ldots, \alpha_m$ can all be computed from the top row α_1 by using bitwise operations. Thus at most one $m \times n$ parity pattern can begin with any given bit vector.

b) True or false: The sum (mod 2) of two $m \times n$ parity patterns is a parity pattern.

c) A parity pattern is called *perfect* if it contains no all-zero row or column. For example, three of the matrices above are perfect, but the 3×2 and 3×5 examples are not. Show that every $m \times n$ parity pattern contains a perfect parity pattern as a submatrix. Furthermore, all such submatrices have the same size, $m' \times n'$, where $m' + 1$ is a divisor of $m + 1$ and $n' + 1$ is a divisor $n + 1$.

d) There's a perfect parity pattern whose first row is 0011, but there is no such pattern beginning with 01010. Is there a simple way to decide whether a given binary vector is the top row of a perfect parity pattern?

e) Prove that there's a unique perfect parity pattern that begins with $1\overbrace{0\ldots0}^{n-1}$.

191. [*M30*] A *wraparound parity pattern* is analogous to the parity patterns of exercise 190, except that the leftmost and rightmost elements of each row are also neighbors.

a) Find a simple relation between the parity pattern of width n that begins with α and the wraparound parity pattern of width $2n + 2$ that begins with $0\alpha 0\alpha^R$.

b) The Fibonacci polynomials $F_j(x)$ are defined by the recurrence

$$F_0(x) = 0, \qquad F_1(x) = 1, \qquad \text{and} \qquad F_{j+1}(x) = xF_j(x) + F_{j-1}(x) \quad \text{for } j \ge 1.$$

Show that there's a simple relation between the wraparound parity patterns that begin with $10\ldots0$ ($N-1$ zeros) and the Fibonacci polynomials modulo $x^N + 1$. *Hint:* Consider $F_j(x^{-1} + 1 + x)$, and do arithmetic mod 2 as well as mod $x^N + 1$.

c) If α is the binary string $a_1 \ldots a_n$, let $f_\alpha(x) = a_1 x + \cdots + a_n x^n$. Show that

$$f_{(\alpha_j 0 \alpha_j^R)}(x) = (f_\alpha(x) + f_\alpha(x^{-1}))F_j(x^{-1}+1+x) \bmod (x^N + 1) \text{ and mod } 2,$$

when $N = 2n + 2$ and α_j is row j of a width-n parity pattern that begins with α.

d) Consequently we can compute α_j from α in only $O(n^2 \log j)$ steps. *Hints:* See exercise 4.6.3–26; and use the identity $F_{m+n}(x) = F_m(x)F_{n+1}(x) + F_{m-1}(x)F_n(x)$, which generalizes Eq. 1.2.8–(6).

192. [*HM38*] The shortest parity pattern that begins with a given string can be quite long; for example, it turns out that the perfect pattern of width 120 whose first row is $10 \ldots 0$ has length 36,028,797,018,963,966(!). The purpose of this exercise is to consider how to calculate the interesting function

$$c(q) = 1 + \max\{ m \mid \text{there exists a perfect parity pattern of length } m \text{ and width } q-1\},$$

whose initial values $(1, 3, 4, 6, 5, 24, 9, 12, 28)$ for $1 \le q \le 9$ are easy to compute by hand.

a) Characterize $c(q)$ algebraically, using the Fibonacci polynomials of exercise 191.

b) Explain how to calculate $c(q)$ if we know a number M such that $c(q)$ divides M, and if we also know the prime factors of M.

c) Prove that $c(2^e) = 3 \cdot 2^{e-1}$ when $e > 0$. *Hint:* $F_{2^e}(y)$ has a simple form, mod 2.

d) Prove that when q is odd and not a multiple of 3, $c(q)$ is a divisor of $2^{2e} - 1$, where e is the order of 2 modulo q. *Hint:* $F_{2^e-1}(y)$ has a simple form, mod 2.

e) What happens when q is an odd multiple of 3?

f) Finally, explain how to handle the case when q is even.

▶ **193.** [*M21*] If a perfect $m \times n$ parity pattern exists, when m and n are odd, show that there's also a perfect $(2m+1) \times (2n+1)$ parity pattern. (Intricate fractals arise when this observation is applied repeatedly; for example, the 5×5 pattern in exercise 190 leads to Fig. 20.)

194. [*M24*] Find all $n \le 383$ for which there exists a perfect $n \times n$ parity pattern with 8-fold symmetry, such as the example in Fig. 20. *Hint:* The diagonal elements of all such patterns must be zero.

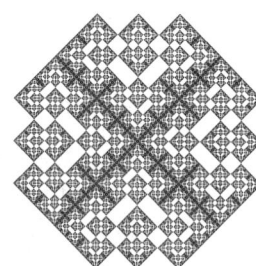

Fig. 20. A perfect 383×383 parity pattern.

▶ **195.** [*HM25*] Let A be a binary matrix having rows $\alpha_1, \ldots, \alpha_m$ of length n. Explain how to use bitwise operations to compute the rank $m - r$ of A over the binary field $\{0, 1\}$, and to find linearly independent binary vectors $\theta_1, \ldots, \theta_r$ of length m such that $\theta_j A = 0 \ldots 0$ for $1 \le j \le r$. *Hint:* See the "triangularization" algorithm for null spaces, Algorithm 4.6.2N.

196. [*21*] (K. Thompson, 1992.) Integers in the range $0 \le x < 2^{31}$ can be encoded as a string of up to six bytes $\alpha(x) = \alpha_1 \ldots \alpha_l$ in the following way: If $x < 2^7$, set $l \leftarrow 1$ and $\alpha_1 \leftarrow x$. Otherwise let $x = (x_5 \ldots x_1 x_0)_{64}$; set $l \leftarrow \lceil (\lambda x)/5 \rceil$, $\alpha_1 \leftarrow 2^8 - 2^{8-l} + x_{l-1}$, and $\alpha_j = 2^7 + x_{l-j}$ for $2 \le j \le l$. Notice that $\alpha(x)$ contains a zero byte if and only if $x = 0$.

a) What are the encodings of #a, #3a3, #7b97, and #1d141?

b) If $x \le x'$, prove that $\alpha(x) \le \alpha(x')$ in lexicographic order.

c) Suppose a sequence of values $x^{(1)} x^{(2)} \ldots x^{(n)}$ has been encoded as a byte string $\alpha(x^{(1)})\alpha(x^{(2)}) \ldots \alpha(x^{(n)})$, and let α_k be the kth byte in that string. Show that it's easy to determine the value $x^{(i)}$ from which α_k came, by looking at a few of the neighboring bytes if necessary.

197. [*22*] The Universal Character Set (UCS), also known as Unicode, is a standard mapping of characters to integer codepoints x in the range $0 \le x < 2^{20} + 2^{16}$. An encoding called UTF-16 represents such integers as one or two wydes $\beta(x) = \beta_1$ or $\beta(x) = \beta_1\beta_2$, in the following way: If $x < 2^{16}$ then $\beta(x) = x$; otherwise

$$\beta_1 = {}^\#\text{d800} + \lfloor y/2^{10} \rfloor \text{ and } \beta_2 = {}^\#\text{dc00} + (y \bmod 2^{10}), \text{ where } y = x - 2^{16}.$$

Answer questions (a), (b), and (c) of exercise 196 for this encoding.

▸ **198.** [*21*] Unicode characters are often represented as strings of bytes using a scheme called UTF-8, which is the encoding of exercise 196 restricted to integers in the range $0 \le x < 2^{20} + 2^{16}$. Notice that UTF-8 efficiently preserves the standard ASCII character set (the codepoints with $x < 2^7$), and that it is quite different from UTF-16.

Let α_1 be the first byte of a UTF-8 string $\alpha(x)$. Show that there are reasonably small integer constants a, b, and c such that only four bitwise operations

$$(a \gg ((\alpha_1 \gg b) \mathbin{\&} c)) \mathbin{\&} 3$$

suffice to determine the number $l - 1$ of bytes between α_1 and the end of $\alpha(x)$.

▸ **199.** [*23*] A person might try to encode ${}^\#$a as ${}^\#$c08a or ${}^\#$e0808a or ${}^\#$f080808a in UTF-8, because the obvious decoding algorithm produces the same result in each case. But such unnecessarily long forms are illegal, because they could lead to security holes.

Suppose α_1 and α_2 are bytes such that $\alpha_1 \ge {}^\#$80 and ${}^\#$80 $\le \alpha_2 < {}^\#$c0. Find a branchless way to decide whether α_1 and α_2 are the first two bytes of at least one legitimate UTF-8 string $\alpha(x)$.

200. [*20*] Interpret the contents of register $3 after the following three MMIX instructions have been executed: MOR $1,$0,#94; MXOR $2,$0,#94; SUBU $3,$1,$2.

201. [*20*] Suppose $x = (x_{15} \ldots x_1 x_0)_{16}$ has sixteen hexadecimal digits. What one MMIX instruction will change each nonzero digit to f, while leaving zeros untouched?

202. [*20*] What two instructions will change an octabyte's nonzero wydes to ${}^\#$ffff?

203. [*22*] Suppose we want to convert a tetrabyte $x = (x_7 \ldots x_1 x_0)_{16}$ to the octabyte $y = (y_7 \ldots y_1 y_0)_{256}$, where y_j is the ASCII code for the hexadecimal digit x_j. For example, if $x = {}^\#$1234abcd, y should represent the 8-character string "1234abcd". What clever choices of five constants a, b, c, d, and e will make the following MMIX instructions do the job?

```
MOR t,x,a;  SLU s,t,4;  XOR t,s,t;  AND t,t,b
ADD t,t,c;  MOR s,d,t;  ADD t,t,e;  ADD y,t,s
```

▸ **204.** [*22*] What are the amazing constants p, q, r, m that achieve a perfect shuffle with just six MMIX commands? (See (175)–(178).)

▸ **205.** [*22*] How would you perfectly *unshuffle* on MMIX, going from w in (175) back to z?

206. [*20*] The perfect shuffle (175) is sometimes called an "outshuffle," by comparison with the "inshuffle" that takes $z \mapsto y \ddagger x = (y_{31} x_{31} \ldots y_1 x_1 y_0 x_0)_2$; the outshuffle preserves the leftmost and rightmost bits of z, but the inshuffle has no fixed points. Can an inshuffle be performed as efficiently as an outshuffle?

207. [*22*] Use MOR to perform a 3-way perfect shuffle or "triple zip," taking $(x_{63} \ldots x_0)_2$ to $(x_{21} x_{42} x_{63} x_{20} \ldots x_2 x_{23} x_{44} x_1 x_{22} x_{43} x_0)_2$, as well as the inverse of this shuffle.

▸ **208.** [*23*] What's a fast way for MMIX to transpose an 8×8 Boolean matrix?

▸ **209.** [*21*] Is the suffix parity operation $x^{\oplus}$ of exercise 36 easy to compute with MXOR?

210. [*22*] A puzzle: Register x contains a number $8j+k$, where $0 \le j, k < 8$. Registers a and b contain arbitrary octabytes $(a_7 \ldots a_1 a_0)_{256}$ and $(b_7 \ldots b_1 b_0)_{256}$. Find a sequence of four MMIX instructions that will put a_j & b_k into register x.

▶ **211.** [*M25*] The truth table of a Boolean function $f(x_1, \ldots, x_6)$ is essentially a 64-bit number $f = (f(0,0,0,0,0,0) \ldots f(1,1,1,1,1,0)f(1,1,1,1,1,1))_2$. Show that two MOR instructions will convert f to the truth table of the least monotone Boolean function, $\hat{f}$, that is greater than or equal to f at each point.

212. [*M32*] Suppose $a = (a_{63} \ldots a_1 a_0)_2$ represents the polynomial

$$a(x) = (a_{63} \ldots a_1 a_0)_x = a_{63}x^{63} + \cdots + a_1 x + a_0.$$

Discuss using MXOR to compute the product $c(x) = a(x)b(x)$, modulo x^{64} and mod 2.

▶ **213.** [*HM26*] Implement the CRC procedure (183) on MMIX.

▶ **214.** [*HM28*] (R. W. Gosper.) Find a short, branchless MMIX computation that computes the inverse of any given 8×8 matrix X of 0s and 1s, modulo 2, if $\det X$ is odd.

▶ **215.** [*21*] What's a quick way for MMIX to test if a 64-bit number is a multiple of 3?

▶ **216.** [*M26*] Given n-bit integers $x_1, \ldots, x_m \ge 0$, $n \ge \lambda m$, compute in $O(m)$ steps the least $y > 0$ such that $y \notin \{a_1 x_1 + \cdots + a_m x_m \mid a_1, \ldots, a_m \in \{0,1\}\}$, if λx takes unit time.

217. [*40*] Explore the processing of long strings of text by packing them in a "transposed" or "sliced" manner: Represent 64 consecutive characters as a sequence of eight octabytes $w_0 \ldots w_7$, where w_k contains all 64 of their kth bits.

▶ **218.** [*M30*] (Hans Petter Selasky, 2009.) For fixed $d \ge 3$, design an algorithm to compute $a \cdot x^y \bmod 2^d$, given integers a, x, and y, where x is odd, using $O(d)$ additions and bitwise operations together with a single multiplication by y.

> *In popular usage, the term* **BDD** *almost always refers to*
> Reduced Ordered Binary Decision Diagram *(ROBDD in the literature,*
> *used when the ordering and reduction aspects need to be emphasized).*
> — WIKIPEDIA, *The Free Encyclopedia* (7 July 2007)

7.1.4. Binary Decision Diagrams

Let's turn now to an important family of data structures that have rapidly become the method of choice for representing and manipulating Boolean functions inside a computer. The basic idea is a divide-and-conquer scheme somewhat like the binary tries of Section 6.3, but with several new twists.

Figure 21 shows the binary decision diagram for a simple Boolean function of three variables, the median function $\langle x_1 x_2 x_3 \rangle$ of Eq. 7.1.1–(43). We can understand it as follows: The node at the top is called the *root*. Every internal node ⓙ, also called a *branch node*, is labeled with a name or index $j = V(ⓙ)$ that designates a variable; for example, the root node ① in Fig. 21 designates x_1. Branch nodes have two successors, indicated by descending lines. One of the successors is drawn as a dashed line and called LO; the other is drawn as a solid line and called HI. These branch nodes define a path in the diagram for any values of the Boolean variables, if we start at the root and take the LO branch from node ⓙ when $x_j = 0$, the HI branch when $x_j = 1$. Eventually this path leads to a *sink node*, which is either ⊥ (denoting FALSE) or ⊤ (denoting TRUE).

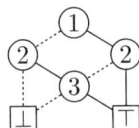

Fig. 21. The binary decision diagram (BDD)
for the majority or median function $\langle x_1 x_2 x_3 \rangle$.

In Fig. 21 it's easy to verify that this process yields the function value FALSE
when at least two of the variables $\{x_1, x_2, x_3\}$ are 0, otherwise it yields TRUE.

Many authors use $\boxed{0}$ and $\boxed{1}$ to denote the sink nodes. We use $\boxed{\perp}$ and $\boxed{\top}$
instead, hoping to avoid any confusion with the branch nodes $\textcircled{0}$ and $\textcircled{1}$.

Inside a computer, Fig. 21 would be represented as a set of four nodes in
arbitrary memory locations, where each node has three fields $\boxed{\text{V} \mid \text{LO} \mid \text{HI}}$.
The V field holds the index of a variable, while the LO and HI fields each point
to another node or to a sink:

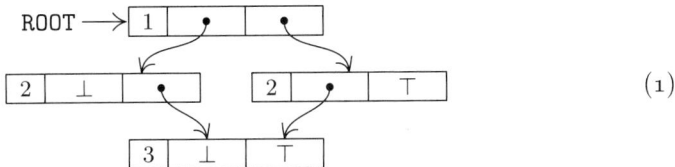

$$(1)$$

With 64-bit words, we might for example use 8 bits for V, then 28 bits for LO
and the other 28 bits for HI.

Such a structure is called a "binary decision diagram," or BDD for short.
Small BDDs can readily be drawn as actual diagrams on a piece of paper
or a computer screen. But in essence each BDD is really an abstract set of
linked nodes, which might more properly be called a "binary decision dag" — a
binary tree with shared subtrees, a directed acyclic graph in which exactly two
distinguished arcs emanate from every nonsink node.

We shall assume that every BDD obeys two important restrictions. First, it
must be *ordered*: Whenever a LO or HI arc goes from branch node $\textcircled{i}$ to branch
node $\textcircled{j}$, we must have $i < j$. Thus, in particular, no variable x_j will ever be
queried twice when the function is evaluated. Second, a BDD must be *reduced*,
in the sense that it doesn't waste space. This means that a branch node's LO
and HI pointers must never be equal, and that no two nodes are allowed to have
the same triple of values (V, LO, HI). Every node should also be accessible from
the root. For example, the diagrams

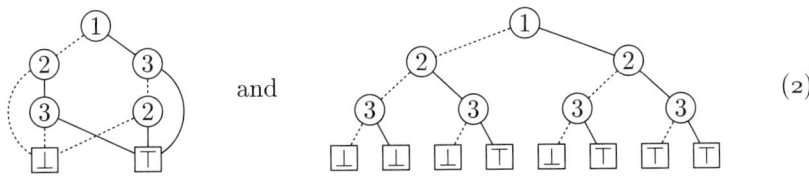

$$(2)$$

are not BDDs, because the first one isn't ordered and the other one isn't reduced.

Many other flavors of decision diagrams have been invented, and the literature of computer science now contains a rich alphabet soup of acronyms like

EVBDD, FBDD, IBDD, OBDD, OFDD, OKFDD, PBDD, ..., ZDD. In this
book we shall always use the unadorned code name "BDD" to denote a binary
decision diagram that is ordered and reduced as described above, just as we
generally use the word "tree" to denote an ordered (plane) tree, because such
BDDs and such trees are the most common in practice.

Recall from Section 7.1.1 that every Boolean function $f(x_1, \ldots, x_n)$ corresponds to a *truth table*, which is the 2^n-bit binary string that starts with
the function value $f(0, \ldots, 0)$ and continues with $f(0, \ldots, 0, 1)$, $f(0, \ldots, 0, 1, 0)$,
$f(0, \ldots, 0, 1, 1)$, ..., $f(1, \ldots, 1, 1, 1)$. For example, the truth table of the median
function $\langle x_1 x_2 x_3 \rangle$ is 00010111. Notice that this truth table is the same as the sequence of leaves in the unreduced decision tree of (2), with $0 \mapsto \boxed{\perp}$ and $1 \mapsto \boxed{\top}$.
In fact, there's an important relationship between truth tables and BDDs, which
is best understood in terms of a class of binary strings called "beads."

A truth table of order n is a binary string of length 2^n. A *bead* of order n is
a truth table β of order n that is not a square; that is, β doesn't have the form
$\alpha\alpha$ for any string α of length 2^{n-1}. (Mathematicians would say that a bead is a
"primitive string of length 2^n.") There are two beads of order 0, namely 0 and 1;
and there are two of order 1, namely 01 and 10. In general there are $2^{2^n} - 2^{2^{n-1}}$
beads of order n when $n > 0$, because there are 2^{2^n} binary strings of length 2^n
and $2^{2^{n-1}}$ of them are squares. The $16 - 4 = 12$ beads of order 2 are

$$0001, 0010, 0011, 0100, 0110, 0111, 1000, 1001, 1011, 1100, 1101, 1110; \qquad (3)$$

these are also the truth tables of all functions $f(x_1, x_2)$ that depend on x_1, in
the sense that $f(0, x_2)$ is not the same function as $f(1, x_2)$.

Every truth table τ is a power of a unique bead, called its root. For if τ has
length 2^n and isn't already a bead, it's the square of another truth table τ'; and
by induction on the length of τ, we must have $\tau' = \beta^k$ for some root β. Hence
$\tau = \beta^{2k}$, and β is the root of τ as well as τ'. (Of course k is a power of 2.)

A truth table τ of order $n > 0$ always has the form $\tau_0 \tau_1$, where τ_0 and τ_1 are
truth tables of order $n - 1$. Clearly τ represents the function $f(x_1, x_2, \ldots, x_n)$
if and only if τ_0 represents $f(0, x_2, \ldots, x_n)$ and τ_1 represents $f(1, x_2, \ldots, x_n)$.
These functions $f(0, x_2, \ldots, x_n)$ and $f(1, x_2, \ldots, x_n)$ are called *subfunctions* of f;
and their truth tables, τ_0 and τ_1, are called *subtables* of τ.

Subtables of a subtable are also considered to be subtables, and a table is
considered to be a subtable of itself. Thus, in general, a truth table of order n
has 2^k subtables of order $n - k$, for $0 \le k \le n$, corresponding to 2^k possible
settings of the first k variables $(x_1, \ldots, x_k)$. Many of these subtables often turn
out to be identical; in such cases we're able to represent τ in a compressed form.

The *beads* of a Boolean function are the subtables of its truth table that happen to be beads. For example, let's consider again the median function $\langle x_1 x_2 x_3 \rangle$,
with its truth table 00010111. The distinct subtables of this truth table are
$\{00010111, 0001, 0111, 00, 01, 11, 0, 1\}$; and all of them except 00 and 11 are
beads. Therefore the beads of $\langle x_1 x_2 x_3 \rangle$ are

$$\{00010111, 0001, 0111, 01, 0, 1\}. \qquad (4)$$

And now we get to the point: *The nodes of a Boolean function's BDD are in one-to-one correspondence with its beads.* For example, we can redraw Fig. 21 by placing the relevant bead inside of each node:

$$\begin{array}{c} \text{(00010111)} \\ \text{(0001)} \quad \text{(0111)} \\ \text{(01)} \\ \boxed{0} \quad\quad \boxed{1} \end{array} \tag{5}$$

In general, a function's truth tables of order $n + 1 - k$ correspond to its sub-functions $f(c_1, \ldots, c_{k-1}, x_k, \ldots, x_n)$ of that order; so its beads of order $n+1-k$ correspond to those subfunctions that depend on their first variable, x_k. Therefore every such bead corresponds to a branch node $\textcircled{k}$ in the BDD. And if $\textcircled{k}$ is a branch node corresponding to the truth table $\tau' = \tau'_0 \tau'_1$, its LO and HI branches point respectively to the nodes that correspond to the roots of τ'_0 and τ'_1.

This correspondence between beads and nodes proves that *every Boolean function has one and only one representation as a BDD.* The individual nodes of that BDD might, of course, be placed in different locations inside a computer.

If f is any Boolean function, let $B(f)$ denote the number of beads that it has. This is the size of its BDD — the total number of nodes, including the sinks. For example, $B(f) = 6$ when f is the median-of-three function, because (5) has size 6.

To fix the ideas, let's work out another example, the "more-or-less random" function of 7.1.1–(22) and 7.1.2–(6). Its truth table, 1100100100001111, is a bead, and so are the two subtables 11001001 and 00001111. Thus we know that the root of its BDD will be a $\textcircled{1}$ branch, and that the LO and HI nodes below the root will both be $\textcircled{2}$s. The subtables of length 4 are $\{1100, 1001, 0000, 1111\}$; here the first two are beads, but the others are squares. To get to the next level, we break the beads in half and carry over the square roots of the nonbeads, identifying duplicates; this leaves us with $\{11, 00, 10, 01\}$. Again there are two beads, and a final step produces the desired BDD:

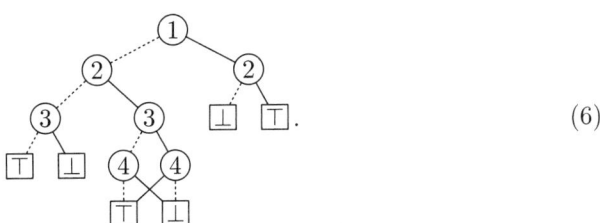

(In this diagram and others below, it's convenient to repeat the sink nodes $\boxed{\perp}$ and $\boxed{\top}$ in order to avoid excessively long connecting lines. Only one $\boxed{\perp}$ node and one $\boxed{\top}$ node are actually present; so the size of (6) is 9, not 13.)

An alert reader might well be thinking at this point, "Very nice, but what if the BDD is huge?" Indeed, functions can easily be constructed whose BDD is impossibly large; we'll study such cases later. But the wonderful thing is that a great many of the Boolean functions that are of practical importance turn out to have reasonably small values of $B(f)$. So we shall concentrate on the good news first, postponing the bad news until we've seen why BDDs have proved to be so popular.

BDD virtues. If $f(x) = f(x_1, \ldots, x_n)$ is a Boolean function whose BDD is reasonably small, we can do many things quickly and easily. For example:

• We can *evaluate* $f(x)$ in at most n steps, given any input vector $x = x_1 \ldots x_n$, by simply starting at the root and branching until we get to a sink.

• We can *find the lexicographically smallest* x such that $f(x) = 1$, by starting at the root and repeatedly taking the LO branch unless it goes directly to $\boxed{\perp}$. The solution has $x_j = 1$ only when the HI branch was necessary at $\boxed{j}$. For example, this procedure gives $x_1 x_2 x_3 = 011$ in the BDD of Fig. 21, and $x_1 x_2 x_3 x_4 = 0000$ in (6). (It locates the value of x that corresponds to the leftmost 1 in the truth table for f.) Only n steps are needed, because every branch node corresponds to a nonzero bead; we can always find a downward path to $\boxed{\top}$ without backing up. Of course this method fails when the root itself is $\boxed{\perp}$. But that happens only when f is identically zero.

• We can *count the number of solutions* to the equation $f(x) = 1$, using Algorithm C below. That algorithm does $B(f)$ operations on n-bit numbers; so its running time is $O(nB(f))$ in the worst case.

• After Algorithm C has acted, we can speedily *generate random solutions* to the equation $f(x) = 1$, in such a way that every solution is equally likely.

• We can also *generate all solutions* x to the equation $f(x) = 1$. The algorithm in exercise 16 does this in $O(nN)$ steps when there are N solutions.

• We can *solve the linear Boolean programming problem*: Find x such that

$$w_1 x_1 + \cdots + w_n x_n \text{ is maximum, subject to } f(x_1, \ldots, x_n) = 1, \qquad (7)$$

given constants $(w_1, \ldots, w_n)$. Algorithm B (below) does this in $O(n+B(f))$ steps.

• We can *compute the generating function* $a_0 + a_1 z + \cdots + a_n z^n$, where there are a_j solutions to $f(x_1, \ldots, x_n) = 1$ with $x_1 + \cdots + x_n = j$. (See exercise 25.)

• We can *calculate the reliability polynomial* $F(p_1, \ldots, p_n)$, which is the probability that $f(x_1, \ldots, x_n) = 1$ when each x_j is independently set to 1 with a given probability p_j. Exercise 26 does this in $O(B(f))$ steps.

Moreover, we will see that BDDs can be combined and modified efficiently. For example, it is not difficult to form the BDDs for $f(x_1, \ldots, x_n) \wedge g(x_1, \ldots, x_n)$ and $f(x_1, \ldots, x_{j-1}, g(x_1, \ldots, x_n), x_{j+1}, \ldots, x_n)$ from the BDDs for f and g.

Algorithms for solving basic problems with BDDs are often described most easily if we assume that the BDD is given as a sequential list of branch instructions $I_{s-1}, I_{s-2}, \ldots, I_1, I_0$, where each I_k has the form $(\bar{v}_k? \, l_k \colon h_k)$. For example, (6) might be represented as a list of $s = 9$ instructions

$$
\begin{array}{lll}
I_8 = (\bar{1}? \, 7\colon 6), & I_5 = (\bar{3}? \, 1\colon 0), & I_2 = (\bar{4}? \, 0\colon 1), \\
I_7 = (\bar{2}? \, 5\colon 4), & I_4 = (\bar{3}? \, 3\colon 2), & I_1 = (\bar{5}? \, 1\colon 1), \qquad (8) \\
I_6 = (\bar{2}? \, 0\colon 1), & I_3 = (\bar{4}? \, 1\colon 0), & I_0 = (\bar{5}? \, 0\colon 0),
\end{array}
$$

with $v_8 = 1$, $l_8 = 7$, $h_8 = 6$, $v_7 = 2$, $l_7 = 5$, $h_7 = 4$, ..., $v_0 = 5$, $l_0 = h_0 = 0$. In general the instruction '$(\bar{v}? \, l\colon h)$' means, "If $x_v = 0$, go to I_l, otherwise go to I_h," except that the last cases I_1 and I_0 are special. We require that the LO and HI branches l_k and h_k satisfy

$$l_k < k, \qquad h_k < k, \qquad v_{l_k} > v_k, \qquad \text{and} \quad v_{h_k} > v_k, \qquad \text{for } s > k \geq 2; \qquad (9)$$

in other words, all branches move downward, to variables of greater index. But the sink nodes $\boxed{\top}$ and $\boxed{\bot}$ are represented by dummy instructions I_1 and I_0, in which $l_k = h_k = k$ and the "variable index" v_k has the impossible value $n + 1$.

These instructions can be numbered in any way that respects the topological ordering of the BDD, as required by (9). The root node must correspond to I_{s-1}, and the sink nodes must correspond to I_1 and I_0, but the other index numbers aren't so rigidly prescribed. For example, (6) might also be expressed as

$$
\begin{aligned}
I'_8 &= (\bar{1}?\,7\!:\!2), & I'_5 &= (\bar{4}?\,0\!:\!1), & I'_2 &= (\bar{2}?\,0\!:\!1), \\
I'_7 &= (\bar{2}?\,4\!:\!6), & I'_4 &= (\bar{3}?\,1\!:\!0), & I'_1 &= (\bar{5}?\,1\!:\!1), \\
I'_6 &= (\bar{3}?\,3\!:\!5), & I'_3 &= (\bar{4}?\,1\!:\!0), & I'_0 &= (\bar{5}?\,0\!:\!0),
\end{aligned}
\qquad (10)
$$

and in 46 other isomorphic ways. Inside a computer, the BDD need not actually appear in consecutive locations; we can readily traverse the nodes of any acyclic digraph in topological order, when the nodes are linked as in (1). But we will imagine that they've been arranged sequentially as in (8), so that various algorithms are easier to understand.

One technicality is worth noting: If $f(x) = 1$ for all x, so that the BDD is simply the sink node $\boxed{\top}$, we let $s = 2$ in this sequential representation. Otherwise s is the size of the BDD. Then the root is always represented by I_{s-1}.

Algorithm C (*Count solutions*). Given the BDD for a Boolean function $f(x) = f(x_1, \ldots, x_n)$, represented as a sequence $I_{s-1}, \ldots, I_0$ as described above, this algorithm determines $|f|$, the number of binary vectors $x = x_1 \ldots x_n$ such that $f(x) = 1$. It also computes the table $c_0, c_1, \ldots, c_{s-1}$, where c_k is the number of 1s in the bead that corresponds to I_k.

C1. [Loop over k.] Set $c_0 \leftarrow 0$, $c_1 \leftarrow 1$, and do step C2 for $k = 2, 3, \ldots, s - 1$. Then return the answer $2^{v_{s-1}-1} c_{s-1}$.

C2. [Compute c_k.] Set $l \leftarrow l_k$, $h \leftarrow h_k$, and $c_k \leftarrow 2^{v_l - v_k - 1} c_l + 2^{v_h - v_k - 1} c_h$. ∎

For example, when presented with (8), this algorithm computes

$$c_2 \leftarrow 1, \ c_3 \leftarrow 1, \ c_4 \leftarrow 2, \ c_5 \leftarrow 2, \ c_6 \leftarrow 4, \ c_7 \leftarrow 4, \ c_8 \leftarrow 8;$$

the total number of solutions to $f(x_1, x_2, x_3, x_4) = 1$ is 8.

The integers c_k in Algorithm C satisfy

$$0 \leq c_k < 2^{n+1-v_k}, \qquad \text{for } 2 \leq k < s, \qquad (11)$$

and this upper bound is the best possible. Therefore multiprecision arithmetic may be needed when n is large. If extra storage space for high precision is problematic, one could use modular arithmetic instead, running the algorithm several times and computing $c_k \bmod p$ for various single-precision primes p; then the final answer would be deducible with the Chinese remainder algorithm, Eq. 4.3.2–(24). On the other hand, floating point arithmetic is usually sufficient in practice.

Let's look at some examples that are more interesting than (6). The BDDs

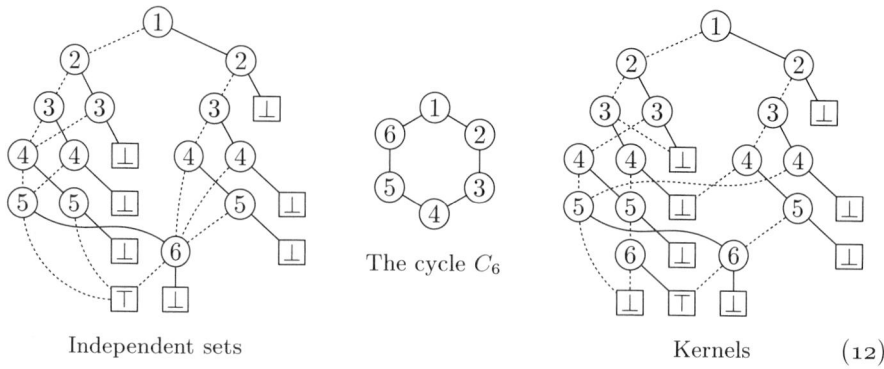

Independent sets   The cycle C_6 Kernels   (12)

represent functions of six variables that correspond to subsets of vertices in the
cycle graph C_6. In this setup a vector such as $x_1 \ldots x_6 = 100110$ stands for the
subset $\{1, 4, 5\}$; the vector 000000 stands for the empty subset; and so on. On the
left is the BDD for which we have $f(x) = 1$ when x is *independent* in C_6; on the
right is the BDD for *maximal* independent subsets, also called the *kernels* of C_6
(see exercise 12). In general, the independent subsets of C_n correspond to arrangements of 0s and 1s in a circle of length n, with no two 1s in a row; the kernels
correspond to such arrangements in which there also are no three consecutive 0s.

Algorithm C decorates a BDD with counts c_k, working from bottom to top,
where c_k is the number of ways to go from node k to $\boxed{\top}$ by choosing values for
$x_l \ldots x_n$, if l is the label of node k. When we apply that algorithm to the BDDs
in (12) we get

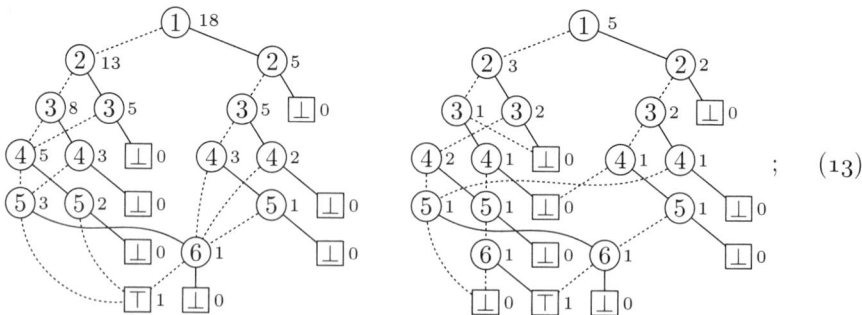

$;$ (13)

hence C_6 has 18 independent sets and 5 kernels.

These counts make it easy to generate uniformly *random* solutions. For
example, to get a random independent set vector $x_1 \ldots x_6$, we know that 13 of
the solutions in the left-hand BDD have $x_1 = 0$, while the other 5 have $x_1 = 1$.
So we set $x_1 \leftarrow 0$ with probability $13/18$, and take the LO branch; otherwise we
set $x_1 \leftarrow 1$ and take the HI branch. In the latter case, $x_1 = 1$ forces $x_2 \leftarrow 0$, but
then x_3 could go either way.

Suppose we've chosen to set $x_1 \leftarrow 1$, $x_2 \leftarrow 0$, $x_3 \leftarrow 0$, and $x_4 \leftarrow 0$; this case
occurs with probability $\frac{5}{18} \cdot \frac{5}{5} \cdot \frac{3}{5} \cdot \frac{2}{3} = \frac{2}{18}$. Then there's a branch from $\boxed{4}$ to $\boxed{6}$,

so we flip a coin and set x_5 to a completely random value. In general, a branch from (i) to (j) means that the $j - i - 1$ intermediate bits $x_{i+1} \ldots x_{j-1}$ should independently become 0 or 1 with equal probability. Similarly, a branch from (i) to $\boxed{\top}$ should assign random values to $x_{i+1} \ldots x_n$.

Of course there are simpler ways to make a random choice between 18 solutions to a combinatorial problem. Moreover, the right-hand BDD in (13) is an embarrassingly complex way to represent the five kernels of C_6: We could simply have listed them, 001001, 010010, 010101, 100100, 101010! But the point is that this same method will yield the independent sets and kernels of C_n when n is much larger. For example, the 100-cycle C_{100} has 1,630,580,875,002 kernels, yet the BDD describing them has only 855 nodes. One hundred simple steps will therefore generate a fully random kernel from this vast collection.

Boolean programming and beyond. A bottom-up algorithm analogous to Algorithm C is also able to find optimum *weighted* solutions (7) to the Boolean equation $f(x) = 1$. The basic idea is that it's easy to deduce an optimum solution for any bead of f, once we know optimum solutions for the LO and HI beads that lie directly below it.

Algorithm B (*Solutions of maximum weight*). Let $I_{s-1}, \ldots, I_0$ be a sequence of branch instructions that represents the BDD for a Boolean function f, as in Algorithm C, and let $(w_1, \ldots, w_n)$ be an arbitrary sequence of integer weights. This algorithm finds a binary vector $x = x_1 \ldots x_n$ such that $w_1 x_1 + \cdots + w_n x_n$ is maximum, over all x with $f(x) = 1$. We assume that $s > 1$; otherwise $f(x)$ is identically 0. Auxiliary integer vectors $m_1 \ldots m_{s-1}$ and $W_1 \ldots W_{n+1}$ are used in the calculations, as well as an auxiliary bit vector $t_2 \ldots t_{s-1}$.

B1. [Initialize.] Set $W_{n+1} \leftarrow 0$ and $W_j \leftarrow W_{j+1} + \max(w_j, 0)$ for $n \geq j \geq 1$.

B2. [Loop on k.] Set $m_1 \leftarrow 0$ and do step B3 for $2 \leq k < s$. Then do step B4.

B3. [Process I_k.] Set $v \leftarrow v_k$, $l \leftarrow l_k$, $h \leftarrow h_k$, $t_k \leftarrow 0$. If $l \neq 0$, set $m_k \leftarrow m_l + W_{v+1} - W_{v_l}$. Then if $h \neq 0$, compute $m \leftarrow m_h + W_{v+1} - W_{v_h} + w_v$; and if $l = 0$ or $m > m_k$, set $m_k \leftarrow m$ and $t_k \leftarrow 1$.

B4. [Compute the x's.] Set $j \leftarrow 0$, $k \leftarrow s - 1$, and do the following operations until $j = n$: While $j < v_k - 1$, set $j \leftarrow j + 1$ and $x_j \leftarrow [w_j > 0]$; if $k > 1$, set $j \leftarrow j + 1$ and $x_j \leftarrow t_k$ and $k \leftarrow (t_k = 0?\ l_k\!: h_k)$. ∎

A simple case of this algorithm is worked out in exercise 18. Step B3 does technical maneuvers that may look a bit scary, but their net effect is just to compute

$$m_k \leftarrow \max(m_l + W_{v+1} - W_{v_l}, m_h + W_{v+1} - W_{v_h} + w_v), \qquad (14)$$

and to record in t_k whether l or h is better. In fact, v_l and v_h are usually both equal to $v + 1$; then the calculation simply sets $m_k \leftarrow \max(m_l, m_h + w_v)$, corresponding to the cases $x_v = 0$ and $x_v = 1$. Technicalities arise only because we want to avoid fetching m_0, which is $-\infty$, and because v_l or v_h might exceed $v+1$.

With this algorithm we can, for example, quickly find an optimum set of kernel vertices in an n-cycle C_n, using weights based on the "Thue–Morse" sequence,

$$w_j = (-1)^{\nu j}; \qquad (15)$$

here νj denotes sideways addition, Eq. 7.1.3–(59). In other words, w_j is -1 or $+1$, depending on whether j has odd parity or even parity when expressed as a binary number. The maximum of $w_1x_1 + \cdots + w_nx_n$ occurs when the even-parity vertices 3, 5, 6, 9, 10, 12, 15, ... most strongly outnumber the odd-parity vertices 1, 2, 4, 7, 8, 11, 13, ... that appear in a kernel. It turns out that

$$\{1, 3, 6, 9, 12, 15, 18, 20, 23, 25, 27, 30, 33, 36, 39, 41, 43, 46, 48,$$
$$51, 54, 57, 60, 63, 66, 68, 71, 73, 75, 78, 80, 83, 86, 89, 92, 95, 97, 99\} \quad (16)$$

is an optimum kernel in this sense when $n = 100$; only five vertices of odd parity, namely $\{1, 25, 41, 73, 97\}$, need to be included in this set of 38 to satisfy the kernel conditions, hence $\max(w_1x_1 + \cdots + w_{100}x_{100}) = 28$. Thanks to Algorithm B, a few thousand computer instructions are sufficient to select (16) from more than a trillion possible kernels, because the BDD for all those kernels happens to be small.

Mathematically pristine problems related to combinatorial objects like cycle kernels could also be resolved efficiently with more traditional techniques, which are based on recurrences and induction. But the beauty of BDD methods is that they apply also to real-world problems that don't have any elegant structure. For example, let's consider the graph of 49 "united states" that appeared in 7–(17) and 7–(61). The Boolean function that represents all the maximal independent sets of that graph (all the kernels) has a BDD of size 780 that begins as follows:

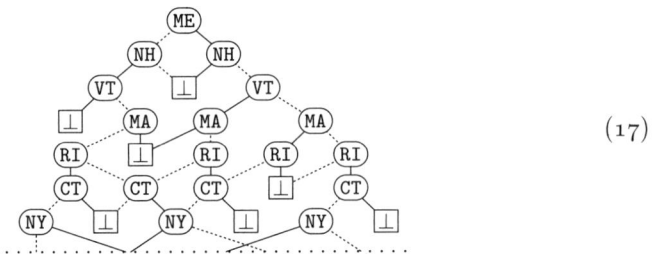

(17)

Algorithm B quickly discovers the following kernels of minimum and maximum weight, when each state vertex is simply weighted according to the sum of letters in its postal code ($w_{\mathrm{CA}} = 3 + 1$, $w_{\mathrm{DC}} = 4 + 3$, ..., $w_{\mathrm{WY}} = 23 + 25$):

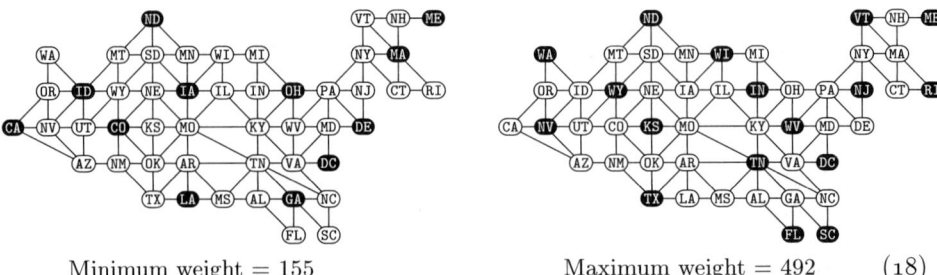

Minimum weight = 155   Maximum weight = 492 (18)

This graph has 266,137 kernels; but with Algorithm B, we needn't generate them all. In fact, the right-hand example in (18) could also be obtained with a smaller BDD of size 428, which characterizes the *independent sets*, because all weights are positive. (A kernel of maximum weight is the same thing as an independent set of maximum weight, in such cases.) There are 211,954,906 independent sets in this graph, many more than the number of kernels; yet we can find an independent set of maximum weight more quickly than a kernel of maximum weight, because the BDD is smaller.

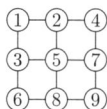

Fig. 22. The grid $P_3 \square P_3$, and a BDD for its connected subgraphs.

A quite different sort of graph-related BDD is shown in Fig. 22. This one is based on the 3×3 grid $P_3 \square P_3$; it characterizes the sets of edges that connect all vertices of the grid together. Thus, it's a function $f(x_{12}, x_{13}, \ldots, x_{89})$ of the twelve edges $1 — 2$, $1 — 3$, $\ldots$, $8 — 9$ instead of the nine vertices $\{1, \ldots, 9\}$. Exercise 55 describes one way to construct it. When Algorithm C is applied to this BDD, it tells us that exactly 431 of the $2^{12} = 4096$ spanning subgraphs of $P_3 \square P_3$ are connected.

A straightforward extension of Algorithm C (see exercise 25) will refine this total and compute the *generating function* of these solutions, namely

$$G(z) = \sum_x z^{\nu x} f(x) = 192z^8 + 164z^9 + 62z^{10} + 12z^{11} + z^{12}. \tag{19}$$

Thus $P_3 \square P_3$ has 192 spanning trees, plus 164 spanning subgraphs that are connected and have nine edges, and so on. Exercise 7.2.1.6–106(a) gives a formula for the number of spanning trees in $P_m \square P_n$ for general m and n; but the full generating function $G(z)$ contains considerably more information, and it probably has no simple formula unless $\min(m, n)$ is small.

Suppose each edge $u — v$ is present with probability p_{uv}, independent of all other edges of $P_3 \square P_3$. What is the probability that the resulting subgraph is connected? This is the *reliability polynomial*, which also goes by a variety of other names because it arises in many different applications. In general, as discussed in exercise 7.1.1–12, every Boolean function $f(x_1, \ldots, x_n)$ has a unique representation as a polynomial $F(x_1, \ldots, x_n)$ with the properties that

i) $F(x_1, \ldots, x_n) = f(x_1, \ldots, x_n)$ whenever each x_j is 0 or 1;
ii) $F(x_1, \ldots, x_n)$ is multilinear: Its degree in x_j is ≤ 1 for all j.

This polynomial F has integer coefficients and satisfies the basic recurrence

$$F(x_1, \ldots, x_n) = (1 - x_1)F_0(x_2, \ldots, x_n) + x_1 F_1(x_2, \ldots, x_n), \tag{20}$$

where F_0 and F_1 are the integer multilinear representations of $f(0, x_2, \ldots, x_n)$ and $f(1, x_2, \ldots, x_n)$. Indeed, (20) is George Boole's "law of development."

Two important things follow from recurrence (20). First, F is precisely the reliability polynomial $F(p_1, \ldots, p_n)$ mentioned earlier, because the reliability polynomial obviously satisfies the same recurrence. Second, F is easily calculated from the BDD for f, working upward from the bottom and using (20) to compute the reliability of each bead. (See exercise 26.)

The connectedness function for an 8×8 grid $P_8 \square P_8$ is, of course, much more complicated than the one for $P_3 \square P_3$; it is a Boolean function of 112 variables and its BDD has 43790 nodes, compared to only 37 in Fig. 22. Still, computations with this BDD are quite feasible, and in a second or two we can compute

$$G(z) = 12623132291249853968259481 6z^{63}$$
$$+ 10066111400354110626007613 44z^{64}$$
$$+ \cdots + 6212z^{110} + 112z^{111} + z^{112},$$

as well as the probability $F(p)$ of connectedness and its derivative $F'(p)$, when each of the edges is present with probability p (see exercise 29):

$$F(p): \quad \text{[graph]} \quad ; \qquad\qquad F'(p): \quad \text{[graph]} \quad . \qquad (21)$$

$$0 \quad p \quad 1 \qquad\qquad\qquad\qquad 0 \quad p \quad 1$$

*A sweeping generalization.** Algorithms B and C and the algorithms we've been discussing for bottom-up BDD scanning are actually special cases of a much more general scheme that can be exploited in many additional ways. Consider an abstract algebra with two associative binary operators $\circ$ and $\bullet$, satisfying the distributive laws

$$\alpha \bullet (\beta \circ \gamma) = (\alpha \bullet \beta) \circ (\alpha \bullet \gamma), \qquad (\beta \circ \gamma) \bullet \alpha = (\beta \bullet \alpha) \circ (\gamma \bullet \alpha). \qquad (22)$$

Every Boolean function $f(x_1, \ldots, x_n)$ corresponds to a *fully elaborated truth table* involving the symbols $\circ$, $\bullet$, $\perp$, and $\top$, together with $\bar{x}_j$ and x_j for $1 \le j \le n$, in a way that's best understood by considering a small example: When $n = 2$ and when the ordinary truth table for f is 0010, the fully elaborated truth table is

$$(\bar{x}_1 \bullet \bar{x}_2 \bullet \perp) \circ (\bar{x}_1 \bullet x_2 \bullet \perp) \circ (x_1 \bullet \bar{x}_2 \bullet \top) \circ (x_1 \bullet x_2 \bullet \perp). \qquad (23)$$

The meaning of such an expression depends on the meanings that we attach to the symbols $\circ$, $\bullet$, $\perp$, $\top$, and to the literals $\bar{x}_j$ and x_j; but whatever the expression means, we can compute it directly from the BDD for f.

For example, let's return to Fig. 21, the BDD for $\langle x_1 x_2 x_3 \rangle$. The elaborations of nodes $\boxed{\perp}$ and $\boxed{\top}$ are $\alpha_\perp = \perp$ and $\alpha_\top = \top$, respectively. Then the elaboration of ③ is $\alpha_3 = (\bar{x}_3 \bullet \alpha_\perp) \circ (x_3 \bullet \alpha_\top)$; the elaborations of the nodes labeled ② are $\alpha_2^l = (\bar{x}_2 \bullet (\bar{x}_3 \circ x_3) \bullet \alpha_\perp) \circ (x_2 \bullet \alpha_3)$ on the left and $\alpha_2^r = (\bar{x}_2 \bullet \alpha_3) \circ (x_2 \bullet (\bar{x}_3 \circ x_3) \bullet \alpha_\top)$ on the right; and the elaboration of node ① is $\alpha_1 = (\bar{x}_1 \bullet \alpha_2^l) \circ (x_1 \bullet \alpha_2^r)$. (Exercise 31 discusses the general procedure.) Expanding these formulas via the distributive laws (22) leads to a full elaboration with $2^n = 8$ "terms":

$$\alpha_1 = (\bar{x}_1 \bullet \bar{x}_2 \bullet \bar{x}_3 \bullet \perp) \circ (\bar{x}_1 \bullet \bar{x}_2 \bullet x_3 \bullet \perp) \circ (\bar{x}_1 \bullet x_2 \bullet \bar{x}_3 \bullet \perp) \circ (\bar{x}_1 \bullet x_2 \bullet x_3 \bullet \top)$$
$$\circ (x_1 \bullet \bar{x}_2 \bullet \bar{x}_3 \bullet \perp) \circ (x_1 \bullet \bar{x}_2 \bullet x_3 \bullet \top) \circ (x_1 \bullet x_2 \bullet \bar{x}_3 \bullet \top) \circ (x_1 \bullet x_2 \bullet x_3 \bullet \top). \quad (24)$$

Algorithm C is the special case where 'o' is addition, '•' is multiplication, '⊥' is 0, '⊤' is 1, '$\bar{x}_j$' is 1, and 'x_j' is also 1. Algorithm B arises when 'o' is the *maximum operator* and '•' is addition; the distributive laws

$$\alpha + \max(\beta, \gamma) = \max(\alpha+\beta, \alpha+\gamma), \quad \max(\beta, \gamma) + \alpha = \max(\beta+\alpha, \gamma+\alpha) \quad (25)$$

are easily checked. We interpret '⊥' as $-\infty$, '⊤' as 0, '$\bar{x}_j$' as 0, and 'x_j' as w_j. Then, for example, (24) becomes

$$\max(-\infty, -\infty, -\infty, w_2 + w_3, -\infty, w_1 + w_3, w_1 + w_2, w_1 + w_2 + w_3);$$

and in general the full elaboration under this interpretation is equivalent to the expression $\max\{w_1x_1 + \cdots + w_nx_n \mid f(x_1, \ldots, x_n) = 1\}$.

Friendly functions. Many families of functions are known to have BDDs of modest size. If f is, for example, a symmetric function of n variables, it's easy to see that $B(f) = O(n^2)$. Indeed, when $n = 5$ we can start with the triangular pattern

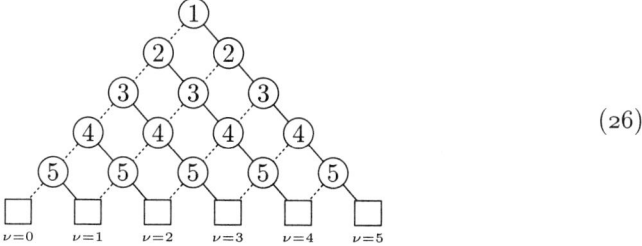

$$(26)$$

and set the leaves to $\boxed{\perp}$ or $\boxed{\top}$ depending on the respective values of f when the value of $\nu x = x_1 + \cdots + x_5$ equals 0, 1, 2, 3, 4, or 5. Then we can remove redundant or equivalent nodes, always obtaining a BDD whose size is $\binom{n+1}{2} + 2$ or less.

Suppose we take any function $f(x_1, \ldots, x_n)$ and make two adjacent variables equal:

$$g(x_1, \ldots, x_n) = f(x_1, \ldots, x_{k-1}, x_k, x_k, x_{k+2}, \ldots, x_n). \quad (27)$$

Exercise 40 proves that $B(g) \leq B(f)$. And by repeating this condensation process, we find that a function such as $f(x_1, x_1, x_3, x_3, x_3, x_6)$ has a small BDD whenever $B(f)$ is small. In particular, the threshold function $[2x_1 + 3x_3 + x_6 \geq t]$ must have a small BDD for any value of t, because it's a condensed version of the symmetric function $f(x_1, \ldots, x_6) = [x_1 + \cdots + x_6 \geq t]$. This argument shows that *any* threshold function with nonnegative integer weights,

$$f(x_1, x_2, \ldots, x_n) = [w_1x_1 + w_2x_2 + \cdots + w_nx_n \geq t], \quad (28)$$

can be obtained by condensing a symmetric function of $w_1 + w_2 + \cdots + w_n$ variables, so its BDD size is $O(w_1 + w_2 + \cdots + w_n)^2$.

Threshold functions often turn out to be easy even when the weights grow exponentially. For example, suppose $t = (t_1 t_2 \ldots t_n)_2$ and consider

$$f_t(x_1, x_2, \ldots, x_n) = [2^{n-1}x_1 + 2^{n-2}x_2 + \cdots + x_n \geq t]. \quad (29)$$

This function is true if and only if the binary string $x_1 x_2 \ldots x_n$ is lexicographically greater than or equal to $t_1 t_2 \ldots t_n$, and its BDD always has exactly $n + 2$ nodes when $t_n = 1$. (See exercise 170.)

Another kind of function with small BDD is the 2^m-way multiplexer of Eq. 7.1.2–(31), a function of $n = m + 2^m$ variables:

$$M_m(x_1, \ldots, x_m; x_{m+1}, \ldots, x_n) \;=\; x_{m+1+(x_1 \ldots x_m)_2}. \tag{30}$$

Its BDD begins with 2^{k-1} branch nodes $\boxed{k}$ for $1 \le k \le m$. But below that complete binary tree, there's just one $\boxed{k}$ for each x_k in the main block of variables with $m < k \le n$. Hence $B(M_m) = 1 + 2 + \cdots + 2^{m-1} + 2^m + 2 = 2^{m+1} + 1 < 2n$.

A linear network model of computation, illustrated in Fig. 23, helps to clarify the cases where a BDD is especially efficient. Consider an arrangement of computational modules $M_1, M_2, \ldots, M_n$, in which the Boolean variable x_k is input to module M_k; there also are wires between neighboring modules, each carrying a Boolean signal, with a_k wires from M_k to M_{k+1} and b_k wires from M_{k+1} to M_k for $1 \le k \le n$. A special wire out of M_n contains the output of the function, $f(x_1, \ldots, x_n)$. We define $a_0 = b_0 = b_n = 0$ and $a_n = 1$, so that module M_k has exactly $c_k = 1 + a_{k-1} + b_k$ input ports and exactly $d_k = a_k + b_{k-1}$ output ports for each k. It computes d_k Boolean functions of its c_k inputs.

The individual functions computed by each module can be arbitrarily complicated, but they must be *well defined* in the sense that their joint values are completely determined by the x's: Every choice of $(x_1, \ldots, x_n)$ must lead to exactly one way to set the signals on all the wires, consistent with all of the given functions.

Theorem M. *If f can be computed by such a network, then $B(f) \le \sum_{k=0}^{n} 2^{a_k 2^{b_k}}$.*

Proof. We will show that the BDD for f has at most $2^{a_{k-1} 2^{b_{k-1}}}$ branch nodes $\boxed{k}$, for $1 \le k \le n$. This is clear if $b_{k-1} = 0$, because at most $2^{a_{k-1}}$ subfunctions are possible when x_1 through x_{k-1} have any given values. So we will show that any network that has a_{k-1} forward wires and b_{k-1} backward wires between M_{k-1} and M_k can be replaced by an equivalent network that has $a_{k-1} 2^{b_{k-1}}$ forward wires and none that run backward.

For convenience, let's consider the case $k = 4$ in Fig. 23, with $a_3 = 4$ and $b_3 = 2$; we want to replace those 6 wires by 16 that run only forward. Suppose Alice is in charge of M_3 and Bob is in charge of M_4. Alice sends a 4-bit signal, a, to Bob while he sends a 2-bit signal, b, to her. More precisely, for any fixed value of $(x_1, \ldots, x_n)$, Alice computes a certain function A and Bob computes a function B, where

$$A(b) = a \qquad \text{and} \qquad B(a) = b. \tag{31}$$

Alice's function A depends on (x_1, x_2, x_3), so Bob doesn't know what it is; Bob's function B is, similarly, unknown to Alice, since it depends on $(x_4, \ldots, x_n)$. But those unknown functions have the key property that, for every choice of $(x_1, \ldots, x_n)$, there's exactly one solution (a, b) to the equations (31).

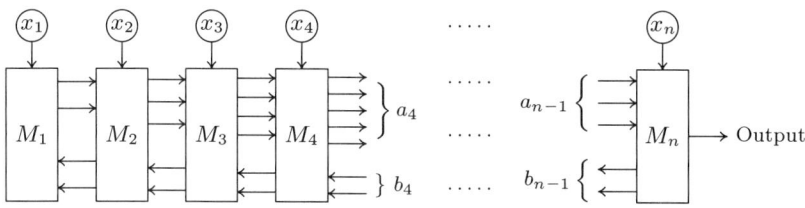

Fig. 23. A generic network of Boolean modules for which Theorem M is valid.

So Alice changes the behavior of module M_3: She sends Bob *four* 4-bit values, $A(00)$, $A(01)$, $A(10)$, and $A(11)$, thereby revealing her A function. And Bob changes the behavior of M_4: Instead of sending any feedback, he looks at those four values, together with his other inputs (namely x_4 and the b_4 bits received from M_5), and discovers the unique a and b that solve (31). His new module uses this value of a to compute the a_4 bits that he outputs to M_5. ∎

Theorem M says that the BDD size will be reasonably small if we can construct such a network with small values of a_k and b_k. Indeed, $B(f)$ will be $O(n)$ if the a's and b's are bounded, although the constant of proportionality might be huge. Let's work an example by considering the *three-in-a-row function*,

$$f(x_1, \ldots, x_n) = x_1 x_2 x_3 \vee x_2 x_3 x_4 \vee \cdots \vee x_{n-2} x_{n-1} x_n \vee x_{n-1} x_n x_1 \vee x_n x_1 x_2, \quad (32)$$

which is true if and only if a circular necklace labeled with bits x_1, ..., x_n has three consecutive 1s. One way to implement it via Boolean modules is to give M_k three inputs (u_k, v_k, w_k) from M_{k-1} and two inputs (y_k, z_k) from M_{k+1}, where

$$u_k = x_{k-1}, \quad v_k = x_{k-2} x_{k-1}, \quad w_k = x_{n-1} x_n x_1 \vee \cdots \vee x_{k-3} x_{k-2} x_{k-1};$$
$$y_k = x_n, \quad z_k = x_{n-1} x_n. \quad (33)$$

Here subscripts are treated modulo n, and appropriate changes are made at the left or right when $k = 1$ or $k \geq n - 1$. Then M_k computes the functions

$$u_{k+1} = x_k, \quad v_{k+1} = u_k x_k, \quad w_{k+1} = w_k \vee v_k x_k, \quad y_{k-1} = y_k, \quad z_{k-1} = z_k \quad (34)$$

for nearly all values of k; exercise 45 has the details. With this construction we have $a_k \leq 3$ and $b_k \leq 2$ for all k, hence Theorem M tells us that $B(f) \leq 2^{12} n = 4096n$. In fact, the truth is much sweeter: $B(f)$ is actually $< 9n$ (see exercise 46).

Shared BDDs. We often want to deal with several Boolean functions at once, and related functions often have common subfunctions. In such cases we can work with the "BDD base" for $\{f_1(x_1, \ldots, x_n), \ldots, f_m(x_1, \ldots, x_n)\}$, which is a directed acyclic graph that contains one node for every bead that occurs within the truth tables of any of the functions. The BDD base also has m "root pointers," F_j, one for each function f_j; the BDD for f_j is then the set of all nodes reachable from node F_j. Notice that node F_j itself is reachable from node F_i if and only if f_j is a subfunction of f_i.

For example, consider the problem of computing the $n + 1$ bits of the sum of two n-bit numbers,

$$(f_{n+1} f_n f_{n-1} \cdots f_1)_2 = (x_1 x_3 \ldots x_{2n-1})_2 + (x_2 x_4 \ldots x_{2n})_2. \quad (35)$$

The BDD base for those $n + 1$ bits looks like this when $n = 4$:

$$\begin{array}{c} x_1 x_3 x_5 x_7 \\ + \; x_2 x_4 x_6 x_8 \\ \hline f_5\, f_4\, f_3\, f_2\, f_1 \end{array}$$

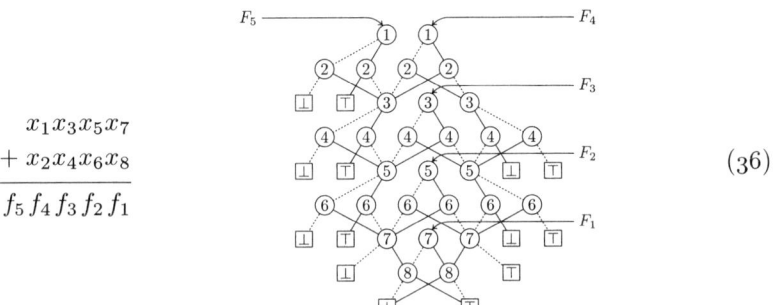

(36)

The way we've numbered the x's in (35) is important here (see exercise 51). In general there are exactly $B(f_1, \ldots, f_{n+1}) = 9n - 5$ nodes, when $n > 1$. The node just to the left of F_j, for $1 \le j \le n$, represents the subfunction for a *carry* c_j out of the jth bit position from the right; the node just to the right of F_j represents the complement of that carry, $\bar{c}_j$; and node F_{n+1} represents the final carry c_n.

Operations on BDDs. We've been talking about lots of things to do when a BDD is given. But how do we get a BDD into the computer in the first place?

One way is to start with an ordered binary decision diagram such as (26) or the right-hand example in (2), and to reduce it so that it becomes a true BDD. The following algorithm, based on ideas of D. Sieling and I. Wegener [*Information Processing Letters* **48** (1993), 139–144], shows that an arbitrary N-node binary decision diagram whose branches are properly ordered can be reduced to a BDD in $O(N + n)$ steps when there are n variables.

Of course we need some extra memory space in order to decide whether two nodes are equivalent, when doing such a reduction. Having only the three fields $(\text{V}, \text{LO}, \text{HI})$ in each node, as in (1), would give us no room to maneuver. Fortunately, only one additional pointer-size field, called AUX, is needed, together with two additional state bits. We will assume for convenience that the state bits are implicitly present in the *signs* of the LO and AUX fields, so that the algorithm needs to deal with only four fields: $(\text{V}, \text{LO}, \text{HI}, \text{AUX})$. The fact that the sign is preempted does mean that a 28-bit LO field will accommodate only 2^{27} nodes at most — about 134 million — instead of 2^{28}. (On a computer like MMIX, we might prefer to assume that all node addresses are even, and to add 1 to a field instead of complementing it as done here.)

Algorithm R (*Reduction to a BDD*). Given a binary decision diagram that is ordered but not necessarily reduced, this algorithm transforms it into a valid BDD by removing unnecessary nodes and rerouting all pointers appropriately. Each node is assumed to have four fields $(\text{V}, \text{LO}, \text{HI}, \text{AUX})$ as described above, and ROOT points to the diagram's top node. The AUX fields are initially irrelevant, except that they must be nonnegative; they will again be nonnegative at the end of the process. All deleted nodes are pushed onto a stack addressed by AVAIL, linked together by the HI fields of its nodes. (The LO fields of these nodes will be negative; their complements point to equivalent nodes that have *not* been deleted.)

The V fields of branch nodes are assumed to run from $\texttt{V(ROOT)}$ up to $v_{\max}$, in increasing order from the top downwards in the given dag. The sink nodes $\boxed{\bot}$ and $\boxed{\top}$ are assumed to be nodes 0 and 1, respectively, with nonnegative LO and HI fields. They are never deleted; in fact, they are left untouched except for their AUX fields. An auxiliary array of pointers, $\texttt{HEAD}[v]$ for $\texttt{V(ROOT)} \leq v \leq v_{\max}$, is used to create temporary lists of all nodes that have a given value of V.

R1. [Initialize.] Terminate immediately if $\texttt{ROOT} \leq 1$. Otherwise, set $\texttt{AUX}(0) \leftarrow \texttt{AUX}(1) \leftarrow \texttt{AUX(ROOT)} \leftarrow -1$, and $\texttt{HEAD}[v] \leftarrow -1$ for $\texttt{V(ROOT)} \leq v \leq v_{\max}$. (We use the fact that $-1 = \sim 0$ is the bitwise complement of 0.) Then set $s \leftarrow \texttt{ROOT}$ and do the following operations while $s \neq 0$:

Set $p \leftarrow s$, $s \leftarrow \sim\texttt{AUX}(p)$, $\texttt{AUX}(p) \leftarrow \texttt{HEAD}[\texttt{V}(p)]$, $\texttt{HEAD}[\texttt{V}(p)] \leftarrow \sim p$.
If $\texttt{AUX(LO}(p)) \geq 0$, set $\texttt{AUX(LO}(p)) \leftarrow \sim s$ and $s \leftarrow \texttt{LO}(p)$.
If $\texttt{AUX(HI}(p)) \geq 0$, set $\texttt{AUX(HI}(p)) \leftarrow \sim s$ and $s \leftarrow \texttt{HI}(p)$.

(We've essentially done a depth-first search of the dag, temporarily marking all nodes reachable from ROOT by making their AUX fields negative.)

R2. [Loop on v.] Set $\texttt{AUX}(0) \leftarrow \texttt{AUX}(1) \leftarrow 0$, and $v \leftarrow v_{\max}$.

R3. [Bucket sort.] (At this point all remaining nodes whose V field exceeds v have been properly reduced, and their AUX fields are nonnegative.) Set $p \leftarrow \sim\texttt{HEAD}[v]$, $s \leftarrow 0$, and do the following steps while $p \neq 0$:

Set $p' \leftarrow \sim\texttt{AUX}(p)$.
Set $q \leftarrow \texttt{HI}(p)$; if $\texttt{LO}(q) < 0$, set $\texttt{HI}(p) \leftarrow \sim\texttt{LO}(q)$.
Set $q \leftarrow \texttt{LO}(p)$; if $\texttt{LO}(q) < 0$, set $\texttt{LO}(p) \leftarrow \sim\texttt{LO}(q)$ and $q \leftarrow \texttt{LO}(p)$.
If $q = \texttt{HI}(p)$, set $\texttt{LO}(p) \leftarrow \sim q$, $\texttt{HI}(p) \leftarrow \texttt{AVAIL}$, $\texttt{AUX}(p) \leftarrow 0$, $\texttt{AVAIL} \leftarrow p$; otherwise if $\texttt{AUX}(q) \geq 0$, set $\texttt{AUX}(p) \leftarrow s$, $s \leftarrow \sim q$, and $\texttt{AUX}(q) \leftarrow \sim p$; otherwise set $\texttt{AUX}(p) \leftarrow \texttt{AUX}(\sim\texttt{AUX}(q))$ and $\texttt{AUX}(\sim\texttt{AUX}(q)) \leftarrow p$.
Then set $p \leftarrow p'$.

R4. [Clean up.] (Nodes with $\texttt{LO} = x \neq \texttt{HI}$ have now been linked together via their AUX fields, beginning with $\sim\texttt{AUX}(x)$.) Set $r \leftarrow \sim s$, $s \leftarrow 0$, and do the following while $r \geq 0$:

Set $q \leftarrow \sim\texttt{AUX}(r)$ and $\texttt{AUX}(r) \leftarrow 0$.
If $s = 0$ set $s \leftarrow q$; otherwise set $\texttt{AUX}(p) \leftarrow q$.
Set $p \leftarrow q$; then while $\texttt{AUX}(p) > 0$, set $p \leftarrow \texttt{AUX}(p)$.
Set $r \leftarrow \sim\texttt{AUX}(p)$.

R5. [Loop on p.] Set $p \leftarrow s$. Go to step R9 if $p = 0$. Otherwise set $q \leftarrow p$.

R6. [Examine a bucket.] Set $s \leftarrow \texttt{LO}(p)$. (At this point $p = q$.)

R7. [Remove duplicates.] Set $r \leftarrow \texttt{HI}(q)$. If $\texttt{AUX}(r) \geq 0$, set $\texttt{AUX}(r) \leftarrow \sim q$; otherwise set $\texttt{LO}(q) \leftarrow \texttt{AUX}(r)$, $\texttt{HI}(q) \leftarrow \texttt{AVAIL}$, and $\texttt{AVAIL} \leftarrow q$. Then set $q \leftarrow \texttt{AUX}(q)$. If $q \neq 0$ and $\texttt{LO}(q) = s$, repeat step R7.

R8. [Clean up again.] If $\texttt{LO}(p) \geq 0$, set $\texttt{AUX(HI}(p)) \leftarrow 0$. Then set $p \leftarrow \texttt{AUX}(p)$, and repeat step R8 until $p = q$.

R9. [Done?] If $p \neq 0$, return to R6. Otherwise, if $v > \texttt{V(ROOT)}$, set $v \leftarrow v - 1$ and return to R3. Otherwise, if $\texttt{LO(ROOT)} < 0$, set $\texttt{ROOT} \leftarrow \sim\texttt{LO(ROOT)}$. ∎

The intricate link manipulations of Algorithm R are easier to program than to explain, but they are highly instructive and not really difficult. The reader is urged to work through the example in exercise 53.

Algorithm R can also be used to compute the BDD for any *restriction* of a given function, namely for any function obtained by "hardwiring" one or more variables to a constant value. The idea is to do a little extra work between steps R1 and R2, setting $\text{HI}(p) \leftarrow \text{LO}(p)$ if variable $\text{V}(p)$ is supposed to be fixed at 0, or $\text{LO}(p) \leftarrow \text{HI}(p)$ if $\text{V}(p)$ is to be fixed at 1. We also need to recycle all nodes that become inaccessible after restriction. Exercise 57 fleshes out the details.

Synthesis of BDDs. We're ready now for the most important algorithm on binary decision diagrams, which takes the BDD for one function, f, and combines it with the BDD for another function, g, in order to obtain the BDD for further functions such as $f \wedge g$ or $f \oplus g$. Synthesis operations of this kind are the principal way to build up the BDDs for complex functions, and the fact that they can be done efficiently is the main reason why BDD data structures have become popular. We will discuss several approaches to the synthesis problem, beginning with a simple method and then speeding it up in various ways.

The basic notion that underlies synthesis is a product operation on BDD structures that we shall call *melding*. Suppose $\alpha = (v, l, h)$ and $\alpha' = (v', l', h')$ are BDD nodes, each containing the index of a variable together with LO and HI pointers. The "meld" of α and α', written $\alpha \diamond \alpha'$, is defined as follows when α and α' are not both sinks:

$$\alpha \diamond \alpha' = \begin{cases} (v,\ l \diamond l',\ h \diamond h'), & \text{if } v = v'; \\ (v,\ l \diamond \alpha',\ h \diamond \alpha'), & \text{if } v < v'; \\ (v',\ \alpha \diamond l',\ \alpha \diamond h'), & \text{if } v > v'. \end{cases} \tag{37}$$

For example, Fig. 24 shows how two small but typical BDDs are melded. The one on the left, with branch nodes $(\alpha, \beta, \gamma, \delta)$, represents $f(x_1, x_2, x_3, x_4) = (x_1 \vee x_2) \wedge (x_3 \vee x_4)$; the one in the middle, with branch nodes $(\omega, \psi, \chi, \varphi, \upsilon, \tau)$, represents $g(x_1, x_2, x_3, x_4) = (x_1 \oplus x_2) \vee (x_3 \oplus x_4)$. Nodes δ and τ are essentially the same, so we would have $\delta = \tau$ if f and g were part of a single BDD base; but melding can be applied also to BDDs that do not have common nodes. At the right of Fig. 24, $\alpha \diamond \omega$ is the root of a decision diagram that has eleven branch nodes, and it essentially represents the *ordered pair* (f, g).

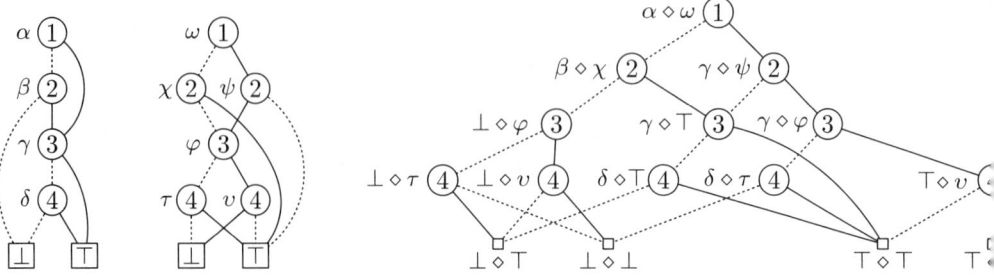

Fig. 24. Two BDDs can be melded together with the $\diamond$ operation (37).

An ordered pair of two Boolean functions can be visualized by placing the truth table of one above the truth table of the other. With this interpretation, $\alpha \diamond \omega$ stands for the ordered pair $\begin{smallmatrix}0000011101110111\\0110111111110110\end{smallmatrix}$, and $\beta \diamond \chi$ stands for $\begin{smallmatrix}00000111\\01101111\end{smallmatrix}$, etc. The melded BDD of Fig. 24 corresponds to the diagram

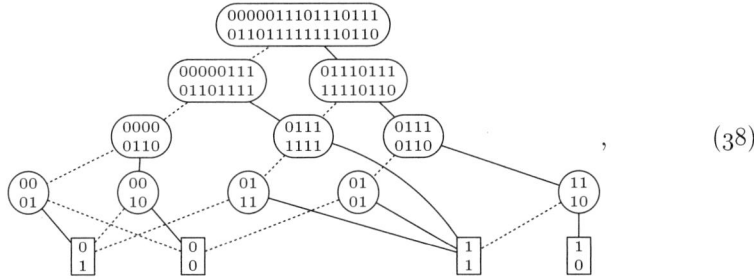

$$(38)$$

which is analogous to (5) except that each node denotes an ordered pair of functions instead of a single function. Beads and subtables are defined on ordered pairs just as before. But now we have four possible sinks instead of two, namely

$$\bot \diamond \bot, \qquad \bot \diamond \top, \qquad \top \diamond \bot, \qquad \text{and} \qquad \top \diamond \top, \qquad (39)$$

corresponding to the ordered pairs $\begin{smallmatrix}0\\0\end{smallmatrix}$, $\begin{smallmatrix}0\\1\end{smallmatrix}$, $\begin{smallmatrix}1\\0\end{smallmatrix}$, and $\begin{smallmatrix}1\\1\end{smallmatrix}$.

To compute the conjunction $f \wedge g$, we AND together the truth tables of f and g. This operation corresponds to replacing $\begin{smallmatrix}0\\0\end{smallmatrix}$, $\begin{smallmatrix}0\\1\end{smallmatrix}$, $\begin{smallmatrix}1\\0\end{smallmatrix}$, and $\begin{smallmatrix}1\\1\end{smallmatrix}$ by 0, 0, 0, and 1, respectively; so we get the BDD for $f \wedge g$ from $f \diamond g$ by replacing the respective sink nodes of (39) by $\boxed{\bot}$, $\boxed{\bot}$, $\boxed{\bot}$, and $\boxed{\top}$, then reducing the result. Similarly, the BDD for $f \oplus g$ is obtained if we replace the sinks (39) by $\boxed{\bot}$, $\boxed{\top}$, $\boxed{\top}$, and $\boxed{\bot}$. (In this particular case $f \oplus g$ turns out to be the symmetric function $S_{1,4}(x_1, x_2, x_3, x_4)$, as computed in Fig. 9 of Section 7.1.2.) The melded diagram $f \diamond g$ contains all the information needed to compute *any* Boolean combination of f and g; and the BDD for every such combination has at most $B(f \diamond g)$ nodes.

Clearly $B(f \diamond g) \leq B(f)B(g)$, because each node of $f \diamond g$ corresponds to a node of f and a node of g. Therefore the meld of small BDDs cannot be extremely large. Usually, in fact, melding produces a result that is considerably smaller than this worst-case upper bound, with something like $B(f) + B(g)$ nodes instead of $B(f)B(g)$. Exercise 60 discusses a sharper bound that sheds some light on why melds often turn out to be small. But exercises 59(b) and 63 present interesting examples where quadratic growth does occur.

Melding suggests a simple algorithm for synthesis: We can form an array of $B(f)B(g)$ nodes, with node $\alpha \diamond \alpha'$ in row α and column α' for every α in the BDD for f and every α' in the BDD for g. Then we can convert the four sink nodes (39) to $\boxed{\bot}$ or $\boxed{\top}$ as desired, and apply Algorithm R to the root node $f \diamond g$. Voilà—we've got the BDD for $f \wedge g$ or $f \oplus g$ or $f \vee \bar{g}$ or whatever.

The running time of this algorithm is clearly of order $B(f)B(g)$. We can reduce it to order $B(f \diamond g)$, because there's no need to fill in all of the matrix entries $\alpha \diamond \alpha'$; only the nodes that are reachable from $f \diamond g$ are relevant, and we can generate them on the fly when necessary. But even with this improvement in the running time, the simple algorithm is unsatisfactory because of the requirement for $B(f)B(g)$ nodes in memory. When we deal with BDDs, time is cheap but space is expensive: Attempts to solve large problems tend to fail more often because of "spaceout" than because of "timeout." That's why Algorithm R was careful to perform its machinations with only one auxiliary link field per node.

The following algorithm solves the synthesis problem with working space of order $B(f \diamond g)$; in fact, it needs only about sixteen bytes per element of the BDD for $f \diamond g$. The algorithm is designed to be used as the main engine of a "Boolean function calculator," which represents functions as BDDs in compressed form on a sequential stack. The stack is maintained at the lower end of a large array called the *pool*. Each BDD on the stack is a sequence of *nodes*, which each have three fields (V, LO, HI). The rest of the pool is available to hold temporary results called *templates*, which each have four fields $(L, H, LEFT, RIGHT)$. A node typically occupies one octabyte of memory, while a template occupies two.

The purpose of Algorithm S is to examine the top two Boolean functions on the stack, f and g, and to replace them by the Boolean combination $f \circ g$, where $\circ$ is one of the 16 possible binary operators. This operator is identified by its 4-bit truth table, op. For example, Algorithm S will form the BDD for $f \oplus g$ when op is $(0110)_2 = 6$; it will deliver $f \wedge g$ when $op = 1$.

When the algorithm begins, operand f appears in locations $[f_0 .. g_0)$ of the pool, and operand g appears in locations $[g_0 .. \text{NTOP})$. All higher locations $[\text{NTOP} .. \text{POOLSIZE})$ are available for storing the templates that the algorithm needs. Those templates will appear in locations $[\text{TBOT} .. \text{POOLSIZE})$ at the high end of the pool; the boundary markers NTOP and TBOT will change dynamically as the algorithm proceeds. The resulting BDD for $f \circ g$ will eventually be placed in locations $[f_0 .. \text{NTOP})$, taking over the space formerly occupied by f and g. We assume that a template occupies the space of two nodes. Thus, the assignments "$t \leftarrow \text{TBOT} - 2, \text{TBOT} \leftarrow t$" allocate space for a new template, pointed to by t; the assignments "$p \leftarrow \text{NTOP}, \text{NTOP} \leftarrow p + 1$" allocate a new node p. For simplicity of exposition, Algorithm S does not check that the condition $\text{NTOP} \leq \text{TBOT}$ remains valid throughout the process; but of course such tests are essential in practice. Exercise 69 remedies this oversight.

The input functions f and g are specified to Algorithm S as sequences of instructions $(I_{s-1}, \ldots, I_1, I_0)$ and $(I'_{s'-1}, \ldots, I'_1, I'_0)$, as in Algorithms B and C above. The lengths of these sequences are $s = B^+(f)$ and $s' = B^+(g)$, where

$$B^+(f) = B(f) + [f \text{ is identically } 1] \qquad (40)$$

is the number of BDD nodes when the sink $\boxed{\perp}$ is forced to be present. For example, the two BDDs at the left of Fig. 24 could be specified by the instructions

$$I_5 = (\bar{1}? \ 4: 3), \quad I_3 = (\bar{3}? \ 2: 1), \qquad \begin{aligned} I'_7 &= (\bar{1}? \ 5: 6), & I'_4 &= (\bar{3}? \ 2: 3), \\ I'_6 &= (\bar{2}? \ 1: 4), & I'_3 &= (\bar{4}? \ 1: 0), \\ I'_5 &= (\bar{2}? \ 4: 1), & I'_2 &= (\bar{4}? \ 0: 1); \end{aligned} \qquad (41)$$

$$I_4 = (\bar{2}? \ 0: 3), \quad I_2 = (\bar{4}? \ 0: 1);$$

as usual, I_1, I_0, I'_1, and I'_0 are the sinks. These instructions are packed into nodes, so that if $I_k = (\bar{v}_k? \ l_k: h_k)$ we have $V(f_0 + k) = v_k$, $LO(f_0 + k) = l_k$, and

$\text{HI}(f_0 + k) = h_k$ for $2 \leq k < s$ when Algorithm S begins. Similar conventions apply to the instructions I'_k that define g. Furthermore

$$\text{V}(f_0) = \text{V}(f_0 + 1) = \text{V}(g_0) = \text{V}(g_0 + 1) = v_{\max} + 1, \qquad (42)$$

where we assume that f and g depend only on the variables x_v for $1 \leq v \leq v_{\max}$.

Like the simple but space-hungry algorithm described earlier, Algorithm S proceeds in two phases: First it builds the BDD for $f \diamond g$, constructing templates so that every important meld $\alpha \diamond \alpha'$ is represented as a template t for which

$$\text{LEFT}(t) = \alpha, \quad \text{RIGHT}(t) = \alpha', \quad \text{L}(t) = \text{LO}(\alpha \diamond \alpha'), \quad \text{H}(t) = \text{HI}(\alpha \diamond \alpha'). \qquad (43)$$

(The L and H fields point to templates, not nodes.) Then the second phase reduces these templates, using a procedure similar to Algorithm R; it changes template t from (43) to

$$\begin{aligned} \text{LEFT}(t) &= \sim\kappa(t), \quad \text{RIGHT}(t) = \tau(t), \\ \text{L}(t) &= \tau(\text{LO}(\alpha \diamond \alpha')), \quad \text{H}(t) = \tau(\text{HI}(\alpha \diamond \alpha')), \end{aligned} \qquad (44)$$

where $\tau(t)$ is the unique template to which t has been reduced, and where $\kappa(t)$ is the "clone" of t if $\tau(t) = t$. Every reduced template t corresponds to an instruction node in the BDD of $f \circ g$, and $\kappa(t)$ is the index of this node relative to position f_0 in the stack. (Setting $\text{LEFT}(t)$ to $\sim\kappa(t)$ instead of $\kappa(t)$ is a sneaky trick that makes steps S7–S10 run faster.) Special overlapping templates are permanently reserved for sinks at the *bottom* of the pool, so that we always have

$$\text{LEFT}(0) = \sim 0, \quad \text{RIGHT}(0) = 0, \quad \text{LEFT}(1) = \sim 1, \quad \text{RIGHT}(1) = 1, \qquad (45)$$

in accord with the conventions of (42) and (44).

We needn't make a template for $\alpha \diamond \alpha'$ when the value of $\alpha \diamond \alpha'$ is obviously constant. For example, if we're computing $f \wedge g$, we know that $\alpha \diamond \alpha'$ will eventually reduce to $\boxed{\perp}$ if $\alpha = 0$ or $\alpha' = 0$. Such simplifications are discovered by a subroutine called $find\_level(f, g)$, which returns the positive integer j if the root of $f \diamond g$ begins with the branch (j), unless $f \circ g$ clearly has a constant value; in the latter case, $find\_level(f, g)$ returns the value $-(f \circ g)$, which is 0 or -1. The procedure is slightly technical, but simple, using the global truth table op:

Subroutine $find\_level(f, g)$, with local variable t:
If $f \leq 1$ and $g \leq 1$, return $-((op \gg (3 - 2f - g)) \& 1)$, which is $-(f \circ g)$.
If $f \leq 1$ and $g > 1$, set $t \leftarrow (f?\ op\ \&\ 3{:}\ op \gg 2)$; return 0 if $t = 0$, -1 if $t = 3$.
If $f > 1$ and $g \leq 1$, set $t \leftarrow (g?\ op{:}\ op \gg 1)\ \&\ 5$; return 0 if $t = 0$, -1 if $t = 5$.
Otherwise return $\min(\text{V}(f_0 + f), \text{V}(g_0 + g))$. $\qquad (46)$

The main difficulty that faces us, when generating a template for a descendant of $\alpha \diamond \alpha'$ according to (37), is to decide whether or not such a template already exists — and if so, to link to it. The best way to solve such problems is usually to use a hash table; but then we must decide where to put such a table, and how much extra space to devote to it. Alternatives such as binary search trees would be much easier to adapt to our purposes, but they would add an unwanted factor of $\log B(f \diamond g)$ to the running time. The synthesis problem can actually be solved in worst-case time and space $O(B(f \diamond g))$ by using a bucket sort method analogous to Algorithm R (see exercise 72); but that solution is complicated and somewhat awkward.

Fortunately there's a nice way out of this dilemma, requiring almost no extra memory and only modestly complex code, if we generate the templates one level at a time. Before generating the templates for level l, we'll know the number N_l of templates to be requested on that level. So we can temporarily allocate space for 2^b templates at the top of the currently free area, where $b = \lceil \lg N_l \rceil$, and put new templates there while hashing into the same area. The idea is to use chaining with separate lists, as in Fig. 38 of Section 6.4; the H and L fields of our templates and potential templates play the roles of heads and links in that illustration, while the keys appear in (LEFT, RIGHT). Here's the logic, in detail:

Subroutine $make\_template(f, g)$, with local variable t:

Set $h \leftarrow \text{HBASE} + 2(((314159257f + 271828171g) \bmod 2^d) \gg (d - b))$, where d is a convenient upper bound on the size of a pointer (usually $d = 32$). Then set $t \leftarrow \text{H}(h)$. While $t \neq \Lambda$ and either $\text{LEFT}(t) \neq f$ or $\text{RIGHT}(t) \neq g$, set $t \leftarrow \text{L}(t)$. If $t = \Lambda$, set $t \leftarrow \text{TBOT} - 2$, $\text{TBOT} \leftarrow t$, $\text{LEFT}(t) \leftarrow f$, $\text{RIGHT}(t) \leftarrow g$, $\text{L}(t) \leftarrow \text{H}(h)$, and $\text{H}(h) \leftarrow t$. Finally, return the value t.   (47)

The calling routine in steps S4 and S5 ensures that $\text{NTOP} \leq \text{HBASE} \leq \text{TBOT}$.

This breadth-first, level-at-a-time strategy for constructing the templates has an added payoff, because it promotes "locality of reference": Memory accesses tend to be confined to nearby locations that have recently been seen, hence controlled in such a way that cache misses and page faults are significantly reduced. Furthermore, the eventual BDD nodes placed on the stack will also appear in order, so that all branches on the same variable appear consecutively.

Algorithm S (*Breadth-first synthesis of BDDs*). This algorithm computes the BDD for $f \circ g$ as described above, using subroutines (46) and (47). Auxiliary arrays $\text{LSTART}[l]$, $\text{LCOUNT}[l]$, $\text{LLIST}[l]$, and $\text{HLIST}[l]$ are used for $0 \leq l \leq v_{\max}$.

S1. [Initialize.] Set $f \leftarrow g_0 - 1 - f_0$, $g \leftarrow \text{NTOP} - 1 - g_0$, and $l \leftarrow find\_level(f, g)$. See exercise 66 if $l \leq 0$. Otherwise set $\text{LSTART}[l - 1] \leftarrow \text{POOLSIZE}$, and $\text{LLIST}[k] \leftarrow \text{HLIST}[k] \leftarrow \Lambda$, $\text{LCOUNT}[k] \leftarrow 0$ for $l < k \leq v_{\max}$. Set $\text{TBOT} \leftarrow \text{POOLSIZE} - 2$, $\text{LEFT}(\text{TBOT}) \leftarrow f$, and $\text{RIGHT}(\text{TBOT}) \leftarrow g$.

S2. [Scan the level-l templates.] Set $\text{LSTART}[l] \leftarrow \text{TBOT}$ and $t \leftarrow \text{LSTART}[l - 1]$. While $t > \text{TBOT}$, schedule requests for future levels by doing the following:

> Set $t \leftarrow t - 2$, $f \leftarrow \text{LEFT}(t)$, $g \leftarrow \text{RIGHT}(t)$, $vf \leftarrow \text{V}(f_0 + f)$, $vg \leftarrow \text{V}(g_0 + g)$,
>
> $ll \leftarrow find\_level((vf \leq vg\,? \ \text{LO}(f_0 + f)\colon f), (vf \geq vg\,? \ \text{LO}(g_0 + g)\colon g))$,
> $lh \leftarrow find\_level((vf \leq vg\,? \ \text{HI}(f_0 + f)\colon f), (vf \geq vg\,? \ \text{HI}(g_0 + g)\colon g))$.
>
> If $ll \leq 0$, set $\text{L}(t) \leftarrow -ll$; otherwise set $\text{L}(t) \leftarrow \text{LLIST}[ll]$, $\text{LLIST}[ll] \leftarrow t$, $\text{LCOUNT}[ll] \leftarrow \text{LCOUNT}[ll] + 1$. If $lh \leq 0$, set $\text{H}(t) \leftarrow -lh$; otherwise set $\text{H}(t) \leftarrow \text{HLIST}[lh]$, $\text{HLIST}[lh] \leftarrow t$, $\text{LCOUNT}[lh] \leftarrow \text{LCOUNT}[lh] + 1$.

S3. [Done with phase one?] Go to S6 if $l = v_{\max}$. Otherwise set $l \leftarrow l + 1$, and return to S2 if $\text{LCOUNT}[l] = 0$.

S4. [Initialize for hashing.] Set $b \leftarrow \lceil \lg \mathtt{LCOUNT}[l] \rceil$, $\mathtt{HBASE} \leftarrow \mathtt{TBOT} - 2^{b+1}$, and $\mathtt{H}(\mathtt{HBASE} + 2k) \leftarrow \Lambda$ for $0 \leq k < 2^b$.

S5. [Make the level-l templates.] Set $t \leftarrow \mathtt{LLIST}[l]$. While $t \neq \Lambda$, set $s \leftarrow \mathtt{L}(t)$, $f \leftarrow \mathtt{LEFT}(t)$, $g \leftarrow \mathtt{RIGHT}(t)$, $vf \leftarrow \mathtt{V}(f_0 + f)$, $vg \leftarrow \mathtt{V}(g_0 + g)$, $\mathtt{L}(t) \leftarrow make\_template((vf \leq vg?\ \mathtt{LO}(f_0+f)\colon f), (vf \geq vg?\ \mathtt{LO}(g_0+g)\colon g))$, $t \leftarrow s$. (We're half done.) Then set $t \leftarrow \mathtt{HLIST}[l]$. While $t \neq \Lambda$, set $s \leftarrow \mathtt{H}(t)$, $f \leftarrow \mathtt{LEFT}(t)$, $g \leftarrow \mathtt{RIGHT}(t)$, $vf \leftarrow \mathtt{V}(f_0 + f)$, $vg \leftarrow \mathtt{V}(g_0 + g)$, $\mathtt{H}(t) \leftarrow make\_template((vf \leq vg?\ \mathtt{HI}(f_0+f)\colon f), (vf \geq vg?\ \mathtt{HI}(g_0+g)\colon g))$, $t \leftarrow s$. (Now the other half is done.) Go back to step S2.

S6. [Prepare for phase two.] (At this point it's safe to obliterate the nodes of f and g, because we've built all the templates (43). Now we'll convert them to form (44). Note that $\mathtt{V}(f_0) = \mathtt{V}(f_0 + 1) = v_{\max} + 1$.) Set $\mathtt{NTOP} \leftarrow f_0 + 2$.

S7. [Bucket sort.] Set $t \leftarrow \mathtt{LSTART}[l - 1]$. Do the following while $t > \mathtt{LSTART}[l]$:

Set $t \leftarrow t - 2$, $\mathtt{L}(t) \leftarrow \mathtt{RIGHT}(\mathtt{L}(t))$, and $\mathtt{H}(t) \leftarrow \mathtt{RIGHT}(\mathtt{H}(t))$.
If $\mathtt{L}(t) = \mathtt{H}(t)$, set $\mathtt{RIGHT}(t) \leftarrow \mathtt{L}(t)$. (This branch is redundant.)
Otherwise set $\mathtt{RIGHT}(t) \leftarrow -1$, $\mathtt{LEFT}(t) \leftarrow \mathtt{LEFT}(\mathtt{L}(t))$, $\mathtt{LEFT}(\mathtt{L}(t)) \leftarrow t$.

S8. [Restore clone addresses.] If $t = \mathtt{LSTART}[l - 1]$, set $t \leftarrow \mathtt{LSTART}[l] - 2$ and go to S9. Otherwise, if $\mathtt{LEFT}(t) < 0$, set $\mathtt{LEFT}(\mathtt{L}(t)) \leftarrow \mathtt{LEFT}(t)$. Set $t \leftarrow t + 2$ and repeat step S8.

S9. [Done with level?] Set $t \leftarrow t + 2$. If $t = \mathtt{LSTART}[l - 1]$, go to S12. Otherwise, if $\mathtt{RIGHT}(t) \geq 0$ repeat step S9.

S10. [Examine a bucket.] (Suppose $\mathtt{L}(t_1) = \mathtt{L}(t_2) = \mathtt{L}(t_3)$, where $t_1 > t_2 > t_3 = t$ and no other templates on level l have this L value. Then at this point we have $\mathtt{LEFT}(t_3) = t_2$, $\mathtt{LEFT}(t_2) = t_1$, $\mathtt{LEFT}(t_1) < 0$, and $\mathtt{RIGHT}(t_1) = \mathtt{RIGHT}(t_2) = \mathtt{RIGHT}(t_3) = -1$.) Set $s \leftarrow t$. While $s > 0$, do the following: Set $r \leftarrow \mathtt{H}(s)$, $\mathtt{RIGHT}(s) \leftarrow \mathtt{LEFT}(r)$; if $\mathtt{LEFT}(r) < 0$, set $\mathtt{LEFT}(r) \leftarrow s$; and set $s \leftarrow \mathtt{LEFT}(s)$. Finally set $s \leftarrow t$ again.

S11. [Make clones.] If $s < 0$, go back to step S9. Otherwise if $\mathtt{RIGHT}(s) \geq 0$, set $s \leftarrow \mathtt{LEFT}(s)$. Otherwise set $r \leftarrow \mathtt{LEFT}(s)$, $\mathtt{LEFT}(\mathtt{H}(s)) \leftarrow \mathtt{RIGHT}(s)$, $\mathtt{RIGHT}(s) \leftarrow s$, $q \leftarrow \mathtt{NTOP}$, $\mathtt{NTOP} \leftarrow q + 1$, $\mathtt{LEFT}(s) \leftarrow \sim(q - f_0)$, $\mathtt{LO}(q) \leftarrow \sim\mathtt{LEFT}(\mathtt{L}(s))$, $\mathtt{HI}(q) \leftarrow \sim\mathtt{LEFT}(\mathtt{H}(s))$, $\mathtt{V}(q) \leftarrow l$, $s \leftarrow r$. Repeat step S11.

S12. [Loop on l.] Set $l \leftarrow l - 1$. Return to S7 if $\mathtt{LSTART}[l] < \mathtt{POOLSIZE}$. Otherwise, if $\mathtt{RIGHT}(\mathtt{POOLSIZE} - 2) = 0$, set $\mathtt{NTOP} \leftarrow \mathtt{NTOP} - 1$ (because $f \circ g$ is identically 0). ∎

As usual, the best way to understand an algorithm like this is to trace through an example. Exercise 67 discusses what Algorithm S does when it is asked to compute $f \wedge g$, given the BDDs in (41).

Algorithm S can be used, for example, to construct the BDDs for interesting functions such as the "monotone-function function" $\mu_n(x_1, \ldots, x_{2^n})$, which is true if and only if $x_1 \ldots x_{2^n}$ is the truth table of a monotone function:

$$\mu_n(x_1, \ldots, x_{2^n}) = \bigwedge_{0 \leq i \subseteq j < 2^n} [x_{i+1} \leq x_{j+1}]. \qquad (48)$$

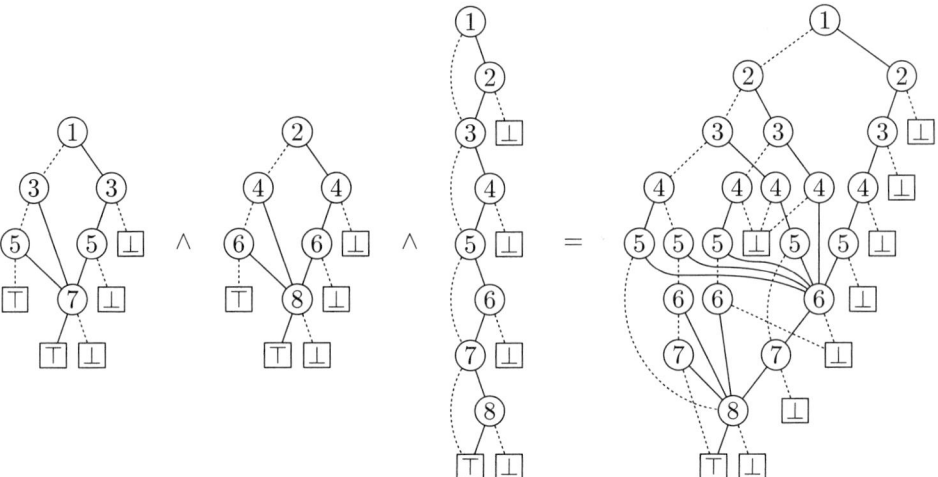

Fig. 25. $\mu_2(x_1, x_3, x_5, x_7) \wedge \mu_2(x_2, x_4, x_6, x_8) \wedge G_8(x_1, \ldots, x_8) = \mu_3(x_1, \ldots, x_8)$, as computed by Algorithm S.

Starting with $\mu_0(x_1) = 1$, this function satisfies the recursion relation

$$\mu_n(x_1, \ldots, x_{2^n}) = $$
$$\mu_{n-1}(x_1, x_3, \ldots, x_{2^n-1}) \wedge \mu_{n-1}(x_2, x_4, \ldots, x_{2^n}) \wedge G_{2^n}(x_1, \ldots, x_{2^n}), \quad (49)$$

where $G_{2^n}(x_1, \ldots, x_{2^n}) = [x_1 \leq x_2] \wedge [x_3 \leq x_4] \wedge \cdots \wedge [x_{2^n-1} \leq x_{2^n}]$. So its BDD is easy to obtain with a BDD calculator like Algorithm S: The BDDs for $\mu_{n-1}(x_1, x_3, \ldots, x_{2^n-1})$ and $\mu_{n-1}(x_2, x_4, \ldots, x_{2^n})$ are simple variants of the one for $\mu_{n-1}(x_1, x_2, \ldots, x_{2^n-1})$, and G_{2^n} has an extremely simple BDD (see Fig. 25).

Repeating this process six times will produce the BDD for μ_6, which has 103,924 nodes. There are exactly 7,828,354 monotone Boolean functions of six variables (see exercise 5.3.4–31); this BDD nicely characterizes them all, and we need only about 4.8 million memory accesses to compute it with Algorithm S. Furthermore, 6.7 billion mems will suffice to compute the BDD for μ_7, which has 155,207,320 nodes and characterizes 2,414,682,040,998 monotone functions.

We must stop there, however; the size of the next case, $B(\mu_8)$, turns out to be a whopping 69,258,301,585,604 (see exercise 77).

Synthesis in a BDD base. Another approach is called for when we're dealing with many functions at once instead of computing a single BDD on the fly. The functions of a BDD base often share common subfunctions, as in (36). Algorithm S is designed to take disjoint BDDs and to combine them efficiently, afterwards destroying the originals; but in many cases we would rather form combinations of functions whose BDDs overlap. Furthermore, after forming a new function $f \wedge g$, say, we might want to keep f and g around for future use; indeed, the new function might well share nodes with f or g or both.

Let's therefore consider the design of a general-purpose toolkit for manipulating a collection of Boolean functions. BDDs are especially attractive for this purpose because most of the necessary operations have a simple recursive formulation. We know that every nonconstant Boolean function can be written

$$f(x_1, x_2, \ldots, x_n) = (\bar{x}_v?\ f_l\colon f_h), \qquad (50)$$

where $v = f_v$ indexes the first variable on which f depends, and where we have

$$f_l = f(0, \ldots, 0, x_{v+1}, \ldots, x_n); \quad f_h = f(1, \ldots, 1, x_{v+1}, \ldots, x_n). \qquad (51)$$

This rule corresponds to branch node (v) at the top of the BDD for f; and the rest of the BDD follows by using (50) and (51) recursively, until we reach constant functions that correspond to $\boxed{\perp}$ or $\boxed{\top}$. A similar recursion defines any combination of two functions, $f \circ g$: For if f and g aren't both constant, we have

$$f(x_1, \ldots, x_n) = (\bar{x}_v?\ f_l\colon f_h) \quad \text{and} \quad g(x_1, \ldots, x_n) = (\bar{x}_v?\ g_l\colon g_h), \qquad (52)$$

where $v = \min(f_v, g_v)$ and where f_l, f_h, g_l, g_h are given by (51). Then, presto,

$$f \circ g = (\bar{x}_v?\ f_l \circ g_l\colon f_h \circ g_h). \qquad (53)$$

This important formula is another way of stating the rule by which we defined melding, Eq. (37).

Caution: The notations above need to be understood carefully, because the subfunctions f_l and f_h in (50) might not be the same as the f_l and f_h in (52). Suppose, for example, that $f = x_2 \vee x_3$ while $g = x_1 \oplus x_3$. Then Eq. (50) holds with $f_v = 2$ and $f = (\bar{x}_2?\ f_l\colon f_h)$, where $f_l = x_3$ and $f_h = 1$. We also have $g_v = 1$ and $g = (\bar{x}_1?\ x_3\colon \bar{x}_3)$. But in (52) we use the same branch variable x_v for both functions, and $v = \min(f_v, g_v) = 1$ in our example; so Eq. (52) holds with $f = (\bar{x}_1?\ f_l\colon f_h)$ and $f_l = f_h = x_2 \vee x_3$.

Every node of a BDD base represents a Boolean function. Furthermore, a BDD base is reduced; therefore two of its functions or subfunctions are equal if and only if they correspond to exactly the same node. (This convenient uniqueness property was *not* true in Algorithm S.)

Formulas (51)–(53) immediately suggest a recursive way to compute $f \wedge g$:

$$\text{AND}(f, g) = \begin{cases} \text{If } f \wedge g \text{ has an obvious value, return it.} \\ \text{Otherwise represent } f \text{ and } g \text{ as in (52);} \\ \text{compute } r_l \leftarrow \text{AND}(f_l, g_l) \text{ and } r_h \leftarrow \text{AND}(f_h, g_h); \\ \text{return the function } (\bar{x}_v?\ r_l\colon r_h). \end{cases} \qquad (54)$$

(Recursions always need to terminate when a sufficiently simple case arises. The "obvious" values in the first line correspond to the terminal cases $f \wedge 1 = f$, $1 \wedge g = g$, $f \wedge 0 = 0 \wedge g = 0$, and $f \wedge g = f$ when $f = g$.) When f and g are the functions in our example above, (54) reduces $f \wedge g$ to the computation of $(x_2 \vee x_3) \wedge x_3$ and $(x_2 \vee x_3) \wedge \bar{x}_3$. Then $(x_2 \vee x_3) \wedge x_3$ reduces to $x_3 \wedge x_3$ and $1 \wedge x_3$; etc.

But (54) is problematic if we simply implement it as stated, because every nonterminal step launches two more instances of the recursion. The computation explodes, with 2^k instances of AND when we're k levels deep!

Fortunately there's a good way to avoid that blowup. Since f has only $B(f)$ different subfunctions, at most $B(f)B(g)$ distinctly different calls of AND can arise. To keep a lid on the computations, we just need to remember what we've done before, by making a *memo* of the fact that $f \wedge g = r$ just before returning r as the computed value. Then when the same subproblem occurs later, we can retrieve the memo and say, "Hey, we've already been there and done that." Previously solved cases thereby become terminal; only distinct subproblems can generate new ones. (Chapter 8 will discuss this memoization technique in detail.)

The algorithm in (54) also glosses over another problem: It's not so easy to "return the function $(\bar{x}_v?\ r_l{:}\ r_h)$," because we must keep the BDD base reduced. If $r_l = r_h$, we should return the node r_l; and if $r_l \neq r_h$, we need to decide whether the branch node $(\bar{x}_v?\ r_l{:}\ r_h)$ already exists, before creating a new one.

Thus we need to maintain additional information, besides the BDD nodes themselves. We need to keep memos of problems already solved; we also need to be able to find a node by its content, instead of by its address. The search algorithms of Chapter 6 now come to our rescue by telling us how to do both of these things, for example by hashing. To record a memo that $f \wedge g = r$, we can hash the key '$(f, \wedge, g)$' and associate it with the value r; to record the existence of an existing node (V, LO, HI), we can hash the key '(V, LO, HI)' and associate it with that node's memory address.

The dictionary of all existing nodes (V, LO, HI) in a BDD base is traditionally called the *unique table*, because we use it to enforce the all-important uniqueness criterion that forbids duplication. Instead of putting all that information into one giant dictionary, however, it turns out to be better to maintain a collection of smaller unique tables, one for each variable V. With such separate tables we can efficiently find all nodes that branch on a particular variable.

The memos are handy, but they aren't as crucial as the unique table entries. If we happen to forget the isolated fact that $f \wedge g = r$, we can always recompute it again later. Exponential blowup won't be worrisome, if the answers to the subproblems $f_l \wedge g_l$ and $f_h \wedge g_h$ are still remembered with high probability. Therefore we can use a less expensive method to store memos, designed to do a pretty-good-but-not-perfect job of retrieval: After hashing the key '$(f, \wedge, g)$' to a table position p, we need look for a memo only in that one position, not bothering to consider collisions with other keys. If several keys all share the same hash address, position p will record only the most recent relevant memo. This simplified scheme will still be adequate in practice, as long as the hash table is large enough. We shall call such a near-perfect table the *memo cache*, because it is analogous to the hardware caches by which a computer tries to remember significant values that it has dealt with in relatively slow storage units.

Okay, let's flesh out algorithm (54) by explicitly stating how it interacts with the unique tables and the memo cache:

$$\text{AND}(f,g) = \begin{cases} \text{If } f \wedge g \text{ has an obvious value, return it.} \\ \text{Otherwise, if } f \wedge g = r \text{ is in the memo cache, return } r. \\ \text{Otherwise represent } f \text{ and } g \text{ as in (52);} \\ \text{compute } r_l \leftarrow \text{AND}(f_l, g_l) \text{ and } r_h \leftarrow \text{AND}(f_h, g_h); \\ \text{set } r \leftarrow \text{UNIQUE}(v, r_l, r_h), \text{ using Algorithm U;} \\ \text{put `} f \wedge g = r \text{' into the memo cache, and return } r. \end{cases} \quad (55)$$

Algorithm U (*Unique table lookup*). Given (v, p, q), where v is an integer while p and q point to nodes of a BDD base with variable rank $> v$, this algorithm returns a pointer to a node $\text{UNIQUE}(v, p, q)$ that represents the function $(\bar{x}_v ? \, p : q)$. A new node is added to the base if that function wasn't already present.

U1. [Easy case?] If $p = q$, return p.

U2. [Check the table.] Search variable x_v's unique table using the key (p, q). If the search successfully finds the value r, return r.

U3. [Create a node.] Allocate a new node r, and set $\text{V}(r) \leftarrow v$, $\text{LO}(r) \leftarrow p$, $\text{HI}(r) \leftarrow q$. Put r into x_v's unique table using the key (p, q). Return r.   ∎

Notice that we needn't zero out the memo cache after finishing a top-level computation of $\text{AND}(f, g)$. Each memo that we have made states a relationship between nodes of the structure; those facts are still valid, and they might be useful later when we want to compute $\text{AND}(f, g)$ for new functions f and g.

A refinement of (55) will enhance that method further, namely to swap $f \leftrightarrow g$ if we discover that $f > g$ when $f \wedge g$ isn't obvious. Then we won't have to waste time computing $f \wedge g$ when we've already computed $g \wedge f$.

With simple changes to (55), the other binary operators $\text{OR}(f, g)$, $\text{XOR}(f, g)$, $\text{BUTNOT}(f, g)$, $\text{NOR}(f, g)$, ... can also be computed readily; see exercise 81.

The combination of (55) and Algorithm U looks considerably simpler than Algorithm S. Thus one might well ask, why should anybody bother to learn the other method? Its breadth-first approach seems quite complex by comparison with the "depth-first" order of computation in the recursive structure of (55); yet Algorithm S is able to deal only with BDDs that are disjoint, while Algorithm U and recursions like (55) apply to any BDD base.

Appearances can, however, be deceiving: Algorithm S has been described at a low level, with every change to every element of its data structures spelled out explicitly. By contrast, the high-level descriptions in (55) and Algorithm U assume that a substantial infrastructure exists behind the scenes. The memo cache and the unique tables need to be set up, and their sizes need to be carefully adjusted as the BDD base grows or contracts. When all is said and done, the total length of a program that implements Algorithms (55) and U properly "from scratch" is roughly ten times the length of a similar program for Algorithm S.

Indeed, the maintenance of a BDD base involves interesting questions of dynamic storage allocation, because we want to free up memory space when nodes are no longer accessible. Algorithm S solves this problem in a last-in-first-out manner, by simply keeping its nodes and templates on sequential stacks, and by making do with a single small hash table that can easily be integrated with the other data. A general BDD base, however, requires a more intricate system.

The best way to maintain a dynamic BDD base is probably to use *reference counters*, as discussed in Section 2.3.5, because BDDs are acyclic by definition. Therefore let's assume that every BDD node has a REF field, in addition to V, LO, and HI. The REF field tells us how many references exist to this node, either from LO or HI pointers in other nodes or from external root pointers F_j as in (36). For example, the REF fields for the nodes labeled ③ in (36) are respectively 4,

1, and 2; and all of the nodes labeled ② or ④ or ⑥ in that example have REF = 1. Exercise 82 discusses the somewhat tricky issue of how to increase and decrease REF counts properly in the midst of a recursive computation.

A node becomes *dead* when its reference count becomes zero. When that happens, we should decrease the REF fields of the two nodes below it; and then they too might die in the same manner, recursively spreading the plague.

But a dead node needn't be removed from memory immediately. It still represents a potentially useful Boolean function, and we might discover that we need that function again as our computation proceeds. For example, we might find a dead node in step U2, because pointers from the unique table don't get counted as references. Likewise, in (55), we might accidentally stumble across a cache memo telling us that $f \wedge g = r$, when r is currently dead. In such cases, node r comes back to life. (And we must increase the REF counts of its LO and HI descendants, possibly resurrecting them recursively in the same fashion.)

Periodically, however, we will want to reclaim memory space by removing the deadbeats. Then we must do two things: We must purge all memos from the cache for which either f, g, or r is dead; and we must remove all dead nodes from memory and from their unique tables. See exercise 84 for typical heuristic strategies by which an automated system might decide when to invoke such cleanups and when to resize the tables dynamically.

Because of the extra machinery that is needed to support a BDD base, Algorithm U and top-down recursions like (55) cannot be expected to match the efficiency of Algorithm S on one-shot examples such as the monotone-function function μ_n in (49). The running time is approximately quadrupled when the more general approach is applied to this example, and the memory requirement grows by a factor of about 2.4.

But a BDD base really begins to shine in numerous other applications. Suppose, for example, that we want the formulas for each bit of the product of two binary numbers,

$$(z_1 \ldots z_{m+n})_2 = (x_1 \ldots x_m)_2 \times (y_1 \ldots y_n)_2. \qquad (56)$$

Clearly $z_1 \ldots z_m = 0 \ldots 0$ when $n = 0$, and the simple recurrence

$$(x_1 \ldots x_m)_2 \times (y_1 \ldots y_n y_{n+1})_2 = (z_1 \ldots z_{m+n} 0)_2 + (x_1 \ldots x_m)_2 y_{n+1} \qquad (57)$$

allows us to increase n by 1. This recurrence is easy to code for a BDD base. Here's what we get when $m = n = 3$, with subscripts chosen to match the analogous diagram for binary addition in (36):

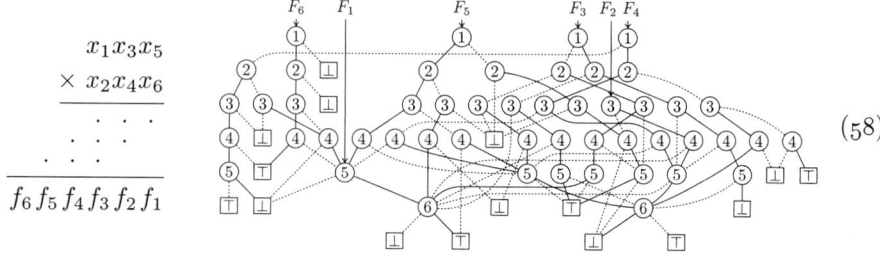

$$\begin{array}{c} x_1 x_3 x_5 \\ \times\ x_2 x_4 x_6 \\ \hline \cdot\ \cdot\ \cdot \\ \cdot\ \cdot\ \cdot \\ \hline f_6 f_5 f_4 f_3 f_2 f_1 \end{array} \qquad (58)$$

Clearly multiplication is much more complicated than addition, bitwise. (Indeed, if it weren't, factorization wouldn't be so hard.) The corresponding BDD base for binary multiplication when $m = n = 16$ is huge, with $B(f_1, \ldots, f_{32}) = 136{,}398{,}751$ nodes. It can be found after doing about 56 gigamems of calculation with Algorithm U, in 6.3 gigabytes of memory — including some 1.9 billion invocations of recursive subroutines, with hundreds of dynamic resizings of the unique tables and the memo cache, plus dozens of timely garbage collections. A similar calculation with Algorithm S would be almost unthinkable, although the individual functions in this particular example do not share many common subfunctions: It turns out that $B(f_1) + \cdots + B(f_{32}) = 168{,}640{,}131$, with the maximum occurring at the "middle bit," $B(f_{16}) = 38{,}174{,}143$.

*Ternary operations. Given three Boolean functions $f = f(x_1, \ldots, x_n)$, $g = g(x_1, \ldots, x_n)$, and $h = h(x_1, \ldots, x_n)$, not all constant, we can generalize (52) to

$$f = (\bar{x}_v? \; f_l: f_h) \quad \text{and} \quad g = (\bar{x}_v? \; g_l: g_h) \quad \text{and} \quad h = (\bar{x}_v? \; h_l: h_h), \qquad (59)$$

by taking $v = \min(f_v, g_v, h_v)$. Then, for example, (53) generalizes to

$$\langle fgh \rangle = \big(\bar{x}_v? \; \langle f_l g_l h_l \rangle: \langle f_h g_h h_h \rangle\big); \qquad (60)$$

and similar formulas hold for *any* ternary operation on f, g, and h, including

$$(\bar{f}? \; g: h) = \big(\bar{x}_v? \; (\bar{f}_l? \; g_l: h_l): (\bar{f}_h? \; g_h: h_h)\big). \qquad (61)$$

(The reader of these formulas will please forgive the two meanings of 'h' in 'h_h'.)

Now it's easy to generalize (55) to ternary combinations like multiplexing:

$$\mathrm{MUX}(f, g, h) = \begin{cases} \text{If } (\bar{f}? \; g: h) \text{ has an obvious value, return it.} \\ \text{Otherwise, if } (\bar{f}? \; g: h) = r \text{ is in the memo cache, return } r. \\ \text{Otherwise represent } f, g, \text{ and } h \text{ as in (59)}; \\ \text{compute } r_l \leftarrow \mathrm{MUX}(f_l, g_l, h_l) \text{ and } r_h \leftarrow \mathrm{MUX}(f_h, g_h, h_h); \\ \text{set } r \leftarrow \mathrm{UNIQUE}(v, r_l, r_h), \text{ using Algorithm U}; \\ \text{put } `(\bar{f}? \; g: h) = r' \text{ into the memo cache, and return } r. \end{cases} \qquad (62)$$

(See exercises 86 and 87.) The running time is $O\big(B(f)B(g)B(h)\big)$. The memo cache must now be consulted with a more complex key than before, including *three* pointers (f, g, h) instead of two, together with a code for the relevant operation. But each memo (op, f, g, h, r) can still be represented conveniently in, say, two octabytes, if the number of distinct pointer addresses is at most 2^{31}.

The ternary operation $f \wedge g \wedge h$ is an interesting special case. We could compute it with two invocations of (55), either as $\mathrm{AND}(f, \mathrm{AND}(g, h))$ or as $\mathrm{AND}(g, \mathrm{AND}(h, f))$ or as $\mathrm{AND}(h, \mathrm{AND}(f, g))$; or we could use a ternary subroutine, $\mathrm{ANDAND}(f, g, h)$, analogous to (62). This ternary routine first sorts the operands so that the pointers satisfy $f \le g \le h$. Then if $f = 0$, it returns 0; if $f = 1$ or $f = g$, it returns $\mathrm{AND}(g, h)$; if $g = h$ it returns $\mathrm{AND}(f, g)$; otherwise $1 < f < g < h$ and the operation remains ternary at the current level of recursion.

Suppose, for example, that $f = \mu_5(x_1, x_3, \ldots, x_{63})$, $g = \mu_5(x_2, x_4, \ldots, x_{64})$, and $h = G_{64}(x_1, \ldots, x_{64})$, as in Eq. (49). The computation $\mathrm{AND}(f, \mathrm{AND}(g, h))$

costs $0.2 + 6.8 = 7.0$ megamems in the author's experimental implementation; $\text{AND}(g, \text{AND}(h, f))$ costs $0.1 + 7.0 = 7.1$; $\text{AND}(h, \text{AND}(f, g))$ costs $24.4 + 5.6 = 30.0\,(!)$; and $\text{ANDAND}(f, g, h)$ costs 7.5. So in this instance the all-binary approach wins, if we don't choose a bad order of computation. But sometimes ternary ANDAND beats all three of its binary competitors (see exercise 88).

Quantifiers. If $f = f(x_1, \ldots, x_n)$ is a Boolean function and $1 \leq j \leq n$, logicians traditionally define *existential and universal quantification* by the formulas

$$\exists x_j\, f(x_1, \ldots, x_n) = f_0 \vee f_1 \quad \text{and} \quad \forall x_j\, f(x_1, \ldots, x_n) = f_0 \wedge f_1, \qquad (63)$$

where $f_c = f(x_1, \ldots, x_{j-1}, c, x_{j+1}, \ldots, x_n)$. Thus the quantifier '$\exists x_j$', pronounced "there exists x_j," changes f to the function of the remaining variables $(x_1, \ldots, x_{j-1}, x_{j+1}, \ldots, x_n)$ that is true if and only if at least one value of x_j satisfies $f(x_1, \ldots, x_n)$; the quantifier '$\forall x_j$', pronounced "for all x_j," changes f to the function that is true if and only if *both* values of x_j satisfy f.

Several quantifiers are often applied simultaneously. For example, the formula $\exists x_2\, \exists x_3\, \exists x_6\, f(x_1, \ldots, x_n)$ stands for the OR of eight terms, representing the eight functions of $(x_1, x_4, x_5, x_7, \ldots, x_n)$ that are obtained when we plug the values 0 or 1 into the variables x_2, x_3, and x_6 in all possible ways. Similarly, $\forall x_2\, \forall x_3\, \forall x_6\, f(x_1, \ldots, x_n)$ stands for the AND of those same eight terms.

One common application arises when the function $f(i_1, \ldots, i_l; j_1, \ldots, j_m)$ denotes the value in row $(i_1 \ldots i_l)_2$ and column $(j_1 \ldots j_m)_2$ of a $2^l \times 2^m$ Boolean matrix F. Then the function $h(i_1, \ldots, i_l; k_1, \ldots, k_n)$ given by

$$\exists j_1 \ldots \exists j_m \big(f(i_1, \ldots, i_l; j_1, \ldots, j_m) \wedge g(j_1, \ldots, j_m; k_1, \ldots, k_n)\big) \qquad (64)$$

represents the matrix H that is the Boolean product $F\,G$.

A convenient way to implement multiple quantification in a BDD base has been suggested by R. L. Rudell: Let $g = x_{j_1} \wedge \cdots \wedge x_{j_m}$ be a conjunction of positive literals. Then we can regard $\exists x_{j_1} \ldots \exists x_{j_m}\, f$ as the binary operation $f \mathbin{\text{E}} g$, implemented by the following variant of (55):

$$\text{EXISTS}(f, g) = \begin{cases} \text{If } f \mathbin{\text{E}} g \text{ has an obvious value, return it.} \\ \text{Otherwise represent } f \text{ and } g \text{ as in (52);} \\ \text{if } v \neq f_v, \text{ return EXISTS}(f, g_h). \\ \text{Otherwise, if } f \mathbin{\text{E}} g = r \text{ is in the memo cache, return } r. \\ \text{Otherwise, } r_l \leftarrow \text{EXISTS}(f_l, g_h) \text{ and } r_h \leftarrow \text{EXISTS}(f_h, g_h); \\ \text{if } v \neq g_v, \text{ set } r \leftarrow \text{UNIQUE}(v, r_l, r_h) \text{ using Algorithm U,} \\ \text{otherwise compute } r \leftarrow \text{OR}(r_l, r_h); \\ \text{put } `f \mathbin{\text{E}} g = r' \text{ into the memo cache, and return } r. \end{cases} \qquad (65)$$

(See exercise 94.) The E operation is undefined when g does *not* have the stated form. Notice how the memo cache nicely remembers existential computations that have gone before.

The running time of (65) is highly variable — not like (55) where we know that $O(B(f)B(g))$ is the worst possible case — because m OR operations are invoked when g specifies m-fold quantification. The worst case now can be as bad as order $B(f)^{2^m}$, if all of the quantification occurs near the root of the BDD for f; this is only $O(B(f)^2)$ if $m = 1$, but it might become unbearably large as m grows. On the other hand, if all of the quantification occurs near the sinks, the running time is simply $O(B(f))$, regardless of the size of m. (See exercise 97.)

Several other quantifiers are worthy of note, and equally easy, although they aren't as famous as $\exists$ and $\forall$. The *Boolean difference* and the *yes/no quantifiers* are defined by formulas analogous to (63):

$$\mathbb{D}x_j\, f = f_0 \oplus f_1; \qquad \bigwedge x_j\, f = \bar{f_0} \wedge f_1; \qquad \mathsf{N}x_j\, f = f_0 \wedge \bar{f_1}. \qquad (66)$$

The Boolean difference, $\mathbb{D}$, is the most important of these: $\mathbb{D}x_j\, f$ is true for all values of $\{x_1, \ldots, x_{j-1}, x_{j+1}, \ldots, x_n\}$ such that f depends on x_j. If the multilinear representation of f is $f = (x_j g + h) \bmod 2$, where g and h are multilinear polynomials in $\{x_1, \ldots, x_{j-1}, x_{j+1}, \ldots, x_n\}$, then $\mathbb{D}x_j\, f = g \bmod 2$. (See Eq. 7.1.1–(19).) Thus $\mathbb{D}$ acts like a derivative in calculus, over a finite field.

A Boolean function $f(x_1, \ldots, x_n)$ is monotone (nondecreasing) if and only if $\bigvee_{j=1}^{n} \mathsf{N}x_j\, f = 0$, which is the same as saying that $\mathsf{N}x_j\, f = 0$ for all j. However, exercise 105 presents a faster way to test a BDD for monotonicity.

Let's consider now a detailed example of existential quantification that is particularly instructive. If G is any graph, we can form Boolean functions $\text{IND}(x)$ and $\text{KER}(x)$ for its independent sets and kernels as follows, where x is a bit vector with one entry x_v for each vertex v of G:

$$\text{IND}(x) = \neg \bigvee_{u - v} (x_u \wedge x_v); \qquad (67)$$

$$\text{KER}(x) = \text{IND}(x) \wedge \bigwedge_v \left(x_v \vee \bigvee_{u-v} x_u \right). \qquad (68)$$

We can form a new graph $\mathcal{G}$ whose vertices are the kernels of G, namely the vectors x such that $\text{KER}(x) = 1$. Let's say that two kernels x and y are *adjacent* in $\mathcal{G}$ if they differ in just the two entries for u and v, where $(x_u, x_v) = (1, 0)$ and $(y_u, y_v) = (0, 1)$, in which case we'll also have $u - v$. Kernels can be considered as certain ways to place markers on vertices of G; moving a marker from one vertex to a neighboring vertex produces an adjacent kernel. Formally we define

$$\text{ADJ}(x, y) = [\nu(x \oplus y) = 2] \wedge \text{KER}(x) \wedge \text{KER}(y). \qquad (69)$$

Then $x - y$ in $\mathcal{G}$ if and only if $\text{ADJ}(x, y) = 1$.

Notice that, if $x = x_1 \ldots x_n$, the function $[\nu(x) = 2]$ is the symmetric function $S_2(x_1, \ldots, x_n)$. Furthermore $f(x \oplus y)$ has at most 3 times as many nodes as $f(x)$, if we interleave the variables zipperwise so that the branching order is $(x_1, y_1, \ldots, x_n, y_n)$. So $B(\text{ADJ})$ won't be extremely large unless $B(\text{KER})$ is large.

Quantification now makes it easy to express the condition that x is an *isolated vertex* of $\mathcal{G}$ (a vertex of degree 0, a kernel without neighbors):

$$\text{ISO}(x) = \text{KER}(x) \wedge \neg \exists y\, \text{ADJ}(x, y). \qquad (70)$$

For example, suppose G is the graph of contiguous states in the USA, as in (18). Then each kernel vector x has 49 entries x_v for $v \in \{\text{ME}, \text{NH}, \ldots, \text{CA}\}$.

The graph $\mathcal{G}$ has 266,137 vertices, and we have observed earlier that the BDD sizes for $\text{IND}(x)$ and $\text{KER}(x)$ are respectively 428 and 780 (see (17)). In this case $\text{ADJ}(x, y)$ in (69) has a BDD of only 7260 nodes, even though it's a function of 98 Boolean variables. The BDD for $\exists y\, \text{ADJ}(x, y)$, which describes all kernels x of G that have at least one neighbor, turns out to have 842 nodes; and the one for $\text{ISO}(x)$ has only 77. We find that G has exactly three isolated kernels, namely

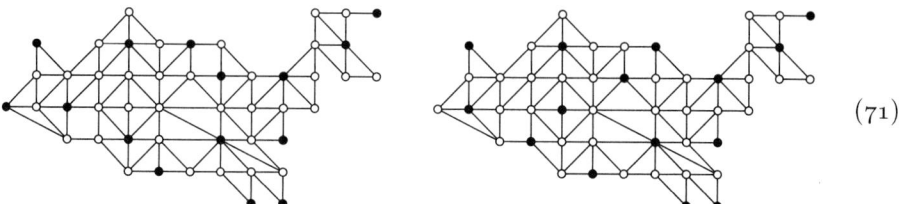

(71)

and another that is a blend of these two. Using the algorithms above, this entire calculation, starting from a list of the vertices and edges of G (not $\mathcal{G}$), can be carried out with a total cost of about 4 megamems, in about 1.6 megabytes of memory; that's only about 15 memory accesses per kernel of G.

In a similar fashion we can use BDDs to work with other "implicit graphs," which have more vertices than could possibly be represented in memory, if those vertices can be characterized as the solution vectors of Boolean functions. When the functions aren't too complicated, we can answer queries about those graphs that could never be answered by representing the vertices and arcs explicitly.

*Functional composition. The *pièce de résistance* of recursive BDD algorithms is a general procedure to compute $f(g_1, g_2, \ldots, g_n)$, where f is a given function of $\{x_1, x_2, \ldots, x_n\}$ and so is each argument g_j. Suppose we know a number $m \geq 0$ such that $g_j = x_j$ for $m < j \leq n$; then the procedure can be expressed as follows:

$$\text{COMPOSE}(f, g_1, \ldots, g_n) = \begin{cases} \text{If } f = 0 \text{ or } f = 1, \text{ return } f. \\ \text{Otherwise suppose } f = (\bar{x}_v?\ f_l\colon f_h), \text{ as in (50)}; \\ \text{if } v > m, \text{ return } f; \text{ otherwise, if } f(g_1, \ldots, g_n) = r \\ \quad \text{is in the memo cache, return } r. \\ \text{Compute } r_l \leftarrow \text{COMPOSE}(f_l, g_1, \ldots, g_n) \\ \quad \text{and } r_h \leftarrow \text{COMPOSE}(f_h, g_1, \ldots, g_n); \\ \text{set } r \leftarrow \text{MUX}(g_v, r_l, r_h) \text{ using (62)}; \\ \text{put } `f(g_1, \ldots, g_n) = r' \text{ into the cache, and return } r. \end{cases} \quad (72)$$

The representation of cache memos like '$f(g_1, \ldots, g_n) = r$' in this algorithm is a bit tricky; we will discuss it momentarily.

Although the computations here look basically the same as those we've been seeing in previous recursions, there is in fact a huge difference: The functions r_l and r_h in (72) can now involve *all* variables $\{x_1, \ldots, x_n\}$, not just the x's near the bottom of the BDDs. So the running time of (72) might actually be huge. But there also are many cases when everything works together harmoniously and efficiently. For example, the computation of $[\nu(x \oplus y) = 2]$ in (69) is no problem.

The key of a memo like '$f(g_1, \ldots, g_n) = r$' should not be a completely detailed specification of $(f, g_1, \ldots, g_n)$, because we want to hash it efficiently. Therefore we store only '$f[G] = r$', where G is an identification number for the sequence of functions $(g_1, \ldots, g_n)$. Whenever that sequence changes, we can use a new number G; and we can remember the G's for special sequences of functions that occur repeatedly in a particular computation, as long as the individual functions g_j don't die. (See also the alternative scheme in exercise 102.)

Let's return to the graph of contiguous states for one more example. That graph is planar; suppose we want to color it with four colors. Since the colors can be given 2-bit codes $\{00, 01, 10, 11\}$, it's easy to express the valid colorings as a Boolean function of 98 variables that is true if and only if the color codes ab are different for each pair of adjacent states:

$$\begin{aligned}
\text{COLOR}(a_{\text{ME}}, b_{\text{ME}}, \ldots, a_{\text{CA}}, b_{\text{CA}}) = \\
\text{IND}(a_{\text{ME}} \wedge b_{\text{ME}}, \ldots, a_{\text{CA}} \wedge b_{\text{CA}}) \wedge \text{IND}(a_{\text{ME}} \wedge \bar{b}_{\text{ME}}, \ldots, a_{\text{CA}} \wedge \bar{b}_{\text{CA}}) \qquad (73) \\
\wedge \text{IND}(\bar{a}_{\text{ME}} \wedge b_{\text{ME}}, \ldots, \bar{a}_{\text{CA}} \wedge b_{\text{CA}}) \wedge \text{IND}(\bar{a}_{\text{ME}} \wedge \bar{b}_{\text{ME}}, \ldots, \bar{a}_{\text{CA}} \wedge \bar{b}_{\text{CA}}).
\end{aligned}$$

Each of the four INDs has a BDD of 854 nodes, which can be computed via (72) with a cost of about 70 kilomems. The COLOR function turns out to have only 25579 BDD nodes. Algorithm C now quickly establishes that the total number of ways to 4-color this graph is exactly 25,623,183,458,304 — or, if we divide by 4! to remove symmetries, about 1.1 trillion. The total time needed for this computation, starting from a description of the graph, is less than 3.5 megamems, in 2.2 megabytes of memory. (We can also find *random* 4-colorings, etc.)

Nasty functions. Of course there also are functions of 98 variables that aren't nearly so nice as COLOR. Indeed, the total number of 98-variable functions is $2^{2^{98}}$; exercise 108 proves that at most $2^{2^{46}}$ of them have a BDD size less than a trillion, and that almost all Boolean functions of 98 variables actually have $B(f) \approx 2^{98}/98 \approx 3.2 \times 10^{27}$. There's just no way to compress 2^{98} bits of data into a small space, unless that data happens to be highly redundant.

What's the worst case? If f is a Boolean function of n variables, how large can $B(f)$ be? The answer isn't hard to discover, if we consider the *profile* of a given BDD, which is the sequence $(b_0, \ldots, b_{n-1}, b_n)$ when there are b_k nodes that branch on variable x_{k+1} and b_n sinks. Clearly

$$B(f) = b_0 + \cdots + b_{n-1} + b_n. \qquad (74)$$

We also have $b_0 \le 1$, $b_1 \le 2$, $b_2 \le 4$, $b_3 \le 8$, and in general

$$b_k \le 2^k, \qquad (75)$$

because each node has only two branches. Furthermore $b_n = 2$ whenever f isn't constant; and $b_{n-1} \le 2$, because there are only two legal choices for the LO and HI branches of $\text{\textcircled{n}}$. Indeed, we know that b_k is the number of *beads* of order $n - k$ in the truth table for f, namely the number of distinct subfunctions of $(x_{k+1}, \ldots, x_n)$ that depend on x_{k+1} after the values of $(x_1, \ldots, x_k)$ have been specified. Only $2^{2^m} - 2^{2^{m-1}}$ beads of order m are possible, so we must have

$$b_k \le 2^{2^{n-k}} - 2^{2^{n-k-1}}, \qquad \text{for } 0 \le k < n. \qquad (76)$$

When $n = 11$, for instance, (75) and (76) tell us that $(b_0, \ldots, b_{11})$ is at most

$$(1, 2, 4, 8, 16, 32, 64, 128, 240, 12, 2, 2). \tag{77}$$

Thus $B(f) \leq 1 + 2 + \cdots + 128 + 240 + \cdots + 2 = 255 + 256 = 511$ when $n = 11$. This upper bound is in fact obtained with the truth table

$$00000000\ 00000001\ 00000010\ \ldots\ 11111110\ 11111111, \tag{78}$$

or with any string of length 2^{11} that is a permutation of the 256 possible 8-bit bytes, because all of the 8-bit beads are clearly present, and because all of the subtables of lengths 16, 32, $\ldots$, 2^{11} are clearly beads. Similar examples can be constructed for all n (see exercise 110). Therefore the worst case is known:

Theorem U. *Every Boolean function $f(x_1, \ldots, x_n)$ has $B(f) \leq U_n$, where*

$$U_n = 2 + \sum_{k=0}^{n-1} \min(2^k, 2^{2^{n-k}} - 2^{2^{n-k-1}}) = 2^{n-\lambda(n-\lambda n)} + 2^{2^{\lambda(n-\lambda n)}} - 1. \tag{79}$$

Furthermore, explicit functions f_n with $B(f_n) = U_n$ exist for all n. ∎

If we replace λ by $\lg$, the right-hand side of (79) becomes $2^n/(n - \lg n) + 2^n/n - 1$. In general, U_n is u_n times $2^n/n$, where the factor u_n lies between 1 and $2 + O(\frac{\log n}{n})$. A BDD with about $2^{n+1}/n$ nodes needs about $n + 1 - \lg n$ bits for each of two pointers in every node, plus $\lg n$ bits to indicate the variable for branching. So the total amount of memory space taken up by the BDD for any function $f(x_1, \ldots, x_n)$ is never more than about 2^{n+2} bits, which is four times the number of bits in its truth table, even if f happens to be one of the worst possible functions from the standpoint of BDD representation.

The average case turns out to be almost the same as the worst case, if we choose the truth table for f at random from among all 2^{2^n} possibilities. Again the calculations are straightforward: The average number of $(k{+}1)$ nodes is exactly

$$\hat{b}_k = \left(2^{2^{n-k}} - 2^{2^{n-k-1}}\right)\left(2^{2^n} - (2^{2^{n-k}} - 1)^{2^k}\right)/2^{2^n}, \tag{80}$$

because there are $2^{2^{n-k}} - 2^{2^{n-k-1}}$ beads of order $n - k$ and $(2^{2^{n-k}} - 1)^{2^k}$ truth tables in which any particular bead does not occur. Exercise 112 shows that this complicated-looking quantity $\hat{b}_k$ always lies extremely close to the worst-case estimate $\min(2^k, 2^{2^{n-k}} - 2^{2^{n-k-1}})$, except for two values of k. The exceptional levels occur when $k \approx 2^{n-k}$ and the "min" has little effect. For example, the average profile $(\hat{b}_0, \ldots, \hat{b}_{n-1}, \hat{b}_n)$ when $n = 11$ is approximately

$$(1.0, 2.0, 4.0, 8.0, 16.0, 32.0, 64.0, 127.4, 151.9, 12.0, 2.0, 2.0) \tag{81}$$

when rounded to one decimal place, and these values are virtually indistinguishable from the worst case (77) except when $k = 7$ or 8.

A related concept called a *quasi-BDD*, or "QDD," is also important. Every function has a unique QDD, which is similar to its BDD except that the root node is always (1), and every (k) node for $k < n$ branches to two $(k{+}1)$ nodes; thus every path from the root to a sink has length n. To make this possible, we allow the LO and HI pointers of a QDD node to be identical. But the QDD must still be reduced, in the sense that different nodes cannot have the same two pointers (LO, HI). For example, the QDD for $\langle x_1 x_2 x_3 \rangle$ is

(82)

it has two more nodes than the corresponding BDD in Fig. 21. Notice that the V fields are redundant in a QDD, so they needn't be present in memory.

The *quasi-profile* of a function is $(q_0, \ldots, q_{n-1}, q_n)$, where q_{k-1} is the number of (k) nodes in the QDD. It's easy to see that q_k is also the number of distinct *subtables* of order $n - k$ in the truth table, just as b_k is the number of distinct beads. Every bead is a subtable, so we have

$$q_k \geq b_k, \qquad \text{for } 0 \leq k \leq n. \tag{83}$$

Furthermore, exercise 115 proves that

$$q_k \leq 1 + b_0 + \cdots + b_{k-1} \text{ and } q_k \leq b_k + \cdots + b_n, \quad \text{for } 0 \leq k \leq n. \tag{84}$$

Consequently each element of the quasi-profile is a lower bound on the BDD size:

$$B(f) \geq 2q_k - 1, \qquad \text{for } 0 \leq k \leq n. \tag{85}$$

Let $Q(f) = q_0 + \cdots + q_{n-1} + q_n$ be the total size of the QDD for f. We obviously have $Q(f) \geq B(f)$, by (83). On the other hand $Q(f)$ can't be too much bigger than $B(f)$, because (84) implies that

$$Q(f) \leq \frac{n+1}{2}\left(B(f) + 1\right). \tag{86}$$

Exercises 116 and 117 explore other basic properties of quasi-profiles.

The worst-case truth table (78) actually corresponds to a familiar function that we've already seen, the 8-way multiplexer

$$M_3(x_9, x_{10}, x_{11}; x_1, \ldots, x_8) = x_{1+(x_9 x_{10} x_{11})_2}. \tag{87}$$

But we've renumbered the variables perversely so that the multiplexing now occurs with respect to the *last* three variables (x_9, x_{10}, x_{11}), instead of the first three as in Eq. (30). This simple change to the ordering of the variables raises the BDD size of M_3 from 17 to 511; and an analogous change when $n = 2^m + m$ would cause $B(M_m)$ to make a colossal leap from $2n - 2m + 1$ to $2^{n-m+1} - 1$.

R. E. Bryant has introduced an interesting "navel-gazing" multiplexer called the *hidden weighted bit function*, defined as follows:

$$h_n(x_1, \ldots, x_n) = x_{x_1 + \cdots + x_n} = x_{\nu x}, \tag{88}$$

with the understanding that $x_0 = 0$. For example, $h_4(x_1, x_2, x_3, x_4)$ has the truth table 0000 0111 1001 1011. He proved [*IEEE Trans.* **C-40** (1991), 208–210] that h_n has a large BDD, regardless of how we might try to renumber its variables.

With the standard ordering of variables, the profile $(b_0, \ldots, b_{11})$ of h_{11} is

$$(1, 2, 4, 8, 15, 27, 46, 40, 18, 7, 2, 2); \tag{89}$$

hence $B(h_{11}) = 172$. The first half of this profile is actually the Fibonacci sequence in slight disguise, with $b_k = F_{k+4} - k - 2$. In general, h_n always has this value of b_k for $k < n/2$; thus its initial profile counts grow with order ϕ^k instead of the worst-case rate of 2^k. This growth rate slackens after k surpasses $n/2$, so that, for example, $B(h_{32})$ is only a modest 86,636. But exponential growth eventually takes over, and $B(h_{100})$ is out of sight: 17,530,618,296,680. (When $n = 100$, the maximum profile element is $b_{59} = 2{,}947{,}635{,}944{,}748$, which dwarfs $b_0 + \cdots + b_{49} = 139{,}583{,}861{,}115$.) Exercise 125 proves that $B(h_n)$ is asymptotically $c\chi^n + O(n^2)$, where

$$\chi = \frac{\sqrt[3]{27 - \sqrt{621}} + \sqrt[3]{27 + \sqrt{621}}}{\sqrt[3]{54}}$$

$$= 1.32471\,79572\,44746\,02596\,09088\,54478\,09734\,07344+ \tag{90}$$

is the so-called "plastic constant," the positive root of $\chi^3 = \chi + 1$, and the coefficient c is $7\chi - 1 + 14/(3 + 2\chi) \approx 10.75115$.

On the other hand we can do substantially better if we change the order in which the variables are tested in the BDD. If $f(x_1, \ldots, x_n)$ is any Boolean function and if π is any permutation of $\{1, \ldots, n\}$, let us write

$$f^\pi(x_1, \ldots, x_n) = f(x_{1\pi}, \ldots, x_{n\pi}). \tag{91}$$

For example, if $f(x_1, x_2, x_3, x_4) = (x_3 \vee (x_1 \wedge x_4)) \wedge (\bar{x}_2 \vee \bar{x}_4)$ and if $(1\pi, 2\pi, 3\pi, 4\pi) = (3, 2, 4, 1)$, then $f^\pi(x_1, x_2, x_3, x_4) = (x_4 \vee (x_3 \wedge x_1)) \wedge (\bar{x}_2 \vee \bar{x}_1)$; and we have $B(f) = 10$, $B(f^\pi) = 6$ because the BDDs are

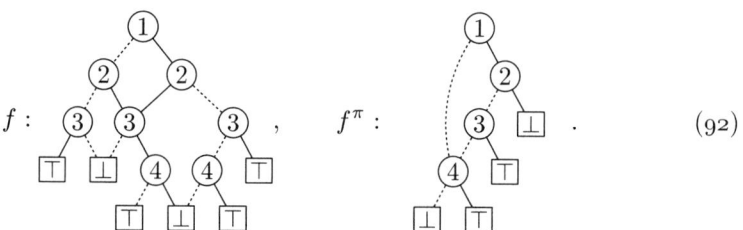

The BDD for f^π corresponds to a BDD for f that has a nonstandard ordering, in which a branch is permitted from (i) to (j) only if $i\pi < j\pi$:

$$f: \qquad\qquad\qquad\qquad\qquad \tag{93}$$

The root is (i), where $i = 1\pi^-$ is the index for which $i\pi = 1$. When the branch variables are listed from the top down, we have $(4\pi, 2\pi, 1\pi, 3\pi) = (1, 2, 3, 4)$.

Applying these ideas to the hidden weighted bit function, we have

$$h_n^\pi(x_1, \ldots, x_n) = x_{(x_1 + \cdots + x_n)\pi}, \tag{94}$$

with the understanding that $0\pi = 0$ and $x_0 = 0$. For example, $h_3^\pi(0,0,1) = 1$ if $(1\pi, 2\pi, 3\pi) = (3,1,2)$, because $x_{(x_1+x_2+x_3)\pi} = x_3 = 1$. (See exercise 120.)

Element q_k of the quasi-profile counts the number of distinct subfunctions that arise when the values of x_1 through x_k are known. Using (94), we can represent all such subfunctions by means of a *slate of options* $[r_0, \ldots, r_{n-k}]$, where r_j is the result of the subfunction when $x_{k+1} + \cdots + x_n = j$. Suppose $x_1 = c_1, \ldots, x_k = c_k$, and let $s = c_1 + \cdots + c_k$. Then $r_j = c_{(s+j)\pi}$ if $(s+j)\pi \leq k$; otherwise $r_j = x_{(s+j)\pi}$. However, we set $r_0 \leftarrow 0$ if $s\pi > k$, and $r_{n-k} \leftarrow 1$ if $(s+n-k)\pi > k$, so that the first and last options of every slate are constant.

For example, calculations show that the following permutation $1\pi \ldots 100\pi$ reduces the BDD size of h_{100} from 17.5 trillion to $B(h_{100}^\pi) = 1{,}124{,}432{,}105$:

$$\begin{array}{ccccccccccccccccccccc}
2 & 4 & 6 & 8 & 10 & 12 & 14 & 16 & 18 & 20 & 97 & 57 & 77 & 37 & 87 & 47 & 67 & 27 & 92 & 52 \\
72 & 32 & 82 & 42 & 62 & 22 & 100 & 60 & 80 & 40 & 90 & 50 & 70 & 30 & 95 & 55 & 75 & 35 & 85 & 45 \\
65 & 25 & 98 & 58 & 78 & 38 & 88 & 48 & 68 & 28 & 93 & 53 & 73 & 33 & 83 & 43 & 63 & 23 & 99 & 59 \\
79 & 39 & 89 & 49 & 69 & 29 & 94 & 54 & 74 & 34 & 84 & 44 & 64 & 24 & 96 & 56 & 76 & 36 & 86 & 46 \\
66 & 26 & 91 & 51 & 71 & 31 & 81 & 41 & 61 & 21 & 19 & 17 & 15 & 13 & 11 & 9 & 7 & 5 & 3 & 1
\end{array} \tag{95}$$

Such calculations can be based on an enumeration of all slates that can arise, for $0 \leq s \leq k \leq n$. Suppose we've tested $x_1, \ldots, x_{83}$ and found that $x_j = [j \leq 42]$, say, for $1 \leq j \leq 83$. Then $s = 42$; and the subfunction of the remaining 17 variables $(x_{84}, \ldots, x_{100})$ is given by the slate $[r_0, \ldots, r_{17}] = [c_{25}, x_{98}, c_{58}, c_{78}, c_{38}, x_{88}, c_{48}, c_{68}, c_{28}, x_{93}, c_{53}, c_{73}, c_{33}, c_{83}, c_{43}, c_{63}, c_{23}, x_{99}]$, which reduces to

$$[1, x_{98}, 0, 0, 1, x_{88}, 0, 0, 1, x_{93}, 0, 0, 1, 0, 0, 0, 1, 1]. \tag{96}$$

This is one of the 2^{14} subfunctions counted by q_{83} when $s = 42$. Exercise 124 explains how to deal similarly with the other values of k and s.

We're ready now to prove Bryant's theorem:

Theorem B. *The BDD size of h_n^π exceeds $2^{\lfloor n/5 \rfloor}$, for all permutations π.*

Proof. Observe first that two subfunctions of h_n^π are equal if and only if they have the same slate. For if $[r_0, \ldots, r_{n-k}] \neq [r_0', \ldots, r_{n-k}']$, suppose $r_j \neq r_j'$. If both r_j and r_j' are constant, the subfunctions differ when $x_{k+1} + \cdots + x_n = j$. If r_j is constant but $r_j' = x_i$, we have $0 < j < n - k$; the subfunctions differ because $x_{k+1} + \cdots + x_n$ can equal j with $x_i \neq r_j$. And if $r_j = x_i$ but $r_j' = x_{i'}$ with $i \neq i'$, we can have $x_{k+1} + \cdots + x_n = j$ with $x_i \neq x_{i'}$. (The latter case can arise only when the slates correspond to different offsets s and s'.)

Therefore q_k is the number of different slates $[r_0, \ldots, r_{n-k}]$. Exercise 123 proves that this number, for any given k, n, and s as described above, is exactly

$$\binom{w}{w-s} + \binom{w}{w-s+1} + \cdots + \binom{w}{k-s} = \binom{w}{s+w-k} + \cdots + \binom{w}{s-1} + \binom{w}{s}, \tag{97}$$

where w is the number of indices j such that $s \leq j \leq s + n - k$ and $j\pi \leq k$.

Now consider the case $k = \lfloor 3n/5 \rfloor + 1$, and let $s = k - \lceil n/2 \rceil$, $s' = \lfloor n/2 \rfloor + 1$. (Think of $n = 100$, $k = 61$, $s = 11$, $s' = 51$. We may assume that $n \geq 10$.) Then

$w + w' = k - w''$, where w'' counts the indices with $j\pi \leq k$ and either $j < s$ or $j > s' + n - k$. Since $w'' \leq (s - 1) + (k - s') = 2k - 2 - n$, we must have $w + w' \geq n + 2 - k = \lceil 2n/5 \rceil + 1$. Hence either $w > \lfloor n/5 \rfloor$ or $w' > \lfloor n/5 \rfloor$; and in both cases (97) exceeds $2^{\lfloor n/5 \rfloor - 1}$. The theorem follows from (85). ∎

Conversely, there's always a permutation π such that $B(h_n^\pi) = O(2^{0.2029n})$, although the constant hidden by O-notation is quite large. This result was proved by B. Bollig, M. Löbbing, M. Sauerhoff, and I. Wegener, *Theoretical Informatics and Applications* **33** (1999), 103–115, using a permutation like (95): The first indices, with $j\pi \leq n/5$, come alternately from $j > 9n/10$ and $j \leq n/10$; the others are ordered by reading the binary representation of $9n/10 - j$ from right to left (*colex order*).

Let's also look briefly at a much simpler example, the *permutation function* $P_m(x_1, \ldots, x_{m^2})$, which equals 1 if and only if the binary matrix with $x_{(i-1)m+j}$ in row i and column j is a permutation matrix:

$$P_m(x_1, \ldots, x_{m^2}) = \bigwedge_{i=1}^{m} S_1(x_{(i-1)m+1}, x_{(i-1)m+2}, \ldots, x_{(i-1)m+m})$$
$$\wedge \bigwedge_{j=1}^{m} S_1(x_j, x_{m+j}, \ldots, x_{m^2-m+j}). \quad (98)$$

In spite of its simplicity, this function cannot be represented with a small BDD, under any reordering of its variables:

Theorem K. *The BDD size of P_m^π exceeds $m2^{m-1}$, for all permutations π.*

Proof. [See I. Wegener, *Branching Programs and Binary Decision Diagrams* (SIAM, 2000), Theorem 4.12.3.] Given the BDD for P_m^π, notice that each of the $m!$ vectors x such that $P_m^\pi(x) = 1$ traces a path of length $n = m^2$ from the root to $\boxed{\top}$; every variable must be tested. Let $v_k(x)$ be the node from which the path for x takes its kth HI branch. This node branches on the value in row i and column j of the given matrix, for some pair $(i, j) = (i_k(x), j_k(x))$.

Suppose $v_k(x) = v_{k'}(x')$, where $x \neq x'$. Construct x'' by letting it agree with x up to $v_k(x)$ and with x' thereafter. Then $P_m^\pi(x'') = 1$; consequently we must have $k = k'$. In fact, this argument shows that we must also have

$$\{i_1(x), i_2(x), \ldots, i_{k-1}(x)\} = \{i_1(x'), i_2(x'), \ldots, i_{k-1}(x')\}$$
$$\text{and } \{j_1(x), j_2(x), \ldots, j_{k-1}(x)\} = \{j_1(x'), j_2(x'), \ldots, j_{k-1}(x')\}. \quad (99)$$

Imagine m colors of tickets, with $m!$ tickets of each color. Place a ticket of color k on node $v_k(x)$, for all k and all x. Then no node gets tickets of different colors; and no node of color k gets more than $(k - 1)! \, (m - k)!$ tickets altogether, by Eq. (99). Therefore at least $m!/((k - 1)! \, (m - k)!) = k\binom{m}{k}$ different nodes must receive tickets of color k. Summing over k gives $m2^{m-1}$ non-sink nodes. ∎

Exercise 184 shows that $B(P_m)$ is less than $m2^{m+1}$, so the lower bound in Theorem K is nearly optimum except for a factor of 4. Although the size grows exponentially, the behavior isn't hopelessly bad, because $m = \sqrt{n}$. For example, $B(P_{20})$ is only 38,797,317, even though P_{20} is a Boolean function of 400 variables.

*Optimizing the order. Let $B_{\min}(f)$ and $B_{\max}(f)$ denote the smallest and largest values of $B(f^\pi)$, taken over all permutations π that can prescribe an ordering of the variables. We've seen several cases where $B_{\min}$ and $B_{\max}$ are dramatically different; for example, the 2^m-way multiplexer has $B_{\min}(M_m) \approx 2n$ and $B_{\max}(M_m) \approx 2^n/n$, when $n = 2^m + m$. And indeed, simple functions for which a good ordering is crucial are not at all unusual. Consider, for instance,

$$f(x_1, x_2, \ldots, x_n) = (\bar{x}_1 \vee x_2) \wedge (\bar{x}_3 \vee x_4) \wedge \cdots \wedge (\bar{x}_{n-1} \vee x_n), \quad n \text{ even}; \quad (100)$$

this is the important *subset function* $[x_1 x_3 \ldots x_{n-1} \subseteq x_2 x_4 \ldots x_n]$, and we have $B(f) = B_{\min}(f) = n + 2$. But the BDD size explodes to $B(f^\pi) = B_{\max}(f) = 2^{n/2+1}$ when π is "organ-pipe order," namely the ordering for which

$$f^\pi(x_1, x_2, \ldots, x_n) = (\bar{x}_1 \vee x_n) \wedge (\bar{x}_2 \vee x_{n-1}) \wedge \cdots \wedge (\bar{x}_{n/2} \vee x_{n/2+1}). \quad (101)$$

And the same bad behavior occurs for the ordering $[x_1 \ldots x_{n/2} \subseteq x_{n/2+1} \ldots x_n]$. In these orderings the BDD must "remember" the states of $n/2$ variables, while the original formulation (100) needs very little memory.

Every Boolean function f has a *master profile chart*, which encapsulates the set of all its possible sizes $B(f^\pi)$. If f has n variables, this chart has 2^n vertices, one for each subset of the variables; and it has $n2^{n-1}$ edges, one for each pair of subsets that differ in just one element. For example, the master profile chart for the function in (92) and (93) is

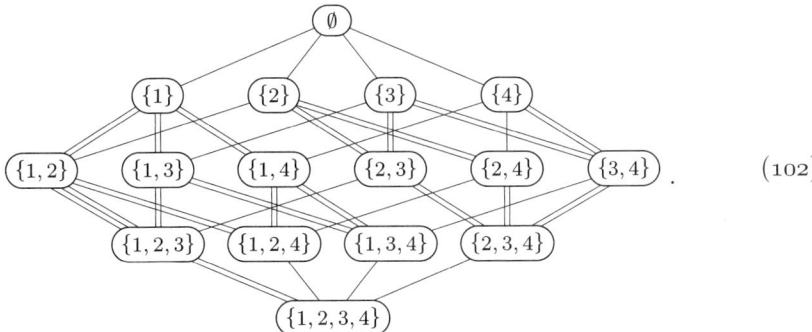

$$(102)$$

Every edge has a weight, illustrated here by the number of lines; for example, the weight between $\{1, 2\}$ and $\{1, 2, 3\}$ is 3. The chart has the following interpretation: *If X is a subset of k variables, and if $x \notin X$, then the weight between X and $X \cup x$ is the number of subfunctions of f that depend on x when the variables of X have been replaced by constants in all 2^k possible ways.* For example, if $X = \{1, 2\}$, we have $f(0, 0, x_3, x_4) = x_3$, $f(0, 1, x_3, x_4) = f(1, 1, x_3, x_4) = x_3 \wedge \bar{x}_4$, and $f(1, 0, x_3, x_4) = x_3 \vee x_4$; all three of these subfunctions depend on x_3, but only two of them depend on x_4, as shown in the weights below $\{1, 2\}$.

There are $n!$ paths of length n from $\emptyset$ to $\{1, \ldots, n\}$, and we can let the path $\emptyset \rightarrow \{a_1\} \rightarrow \{a_1, a_2\} \rightarrow \cdots \rightarrow \{a_1, \ldots, a_n\}$ correspond to the permutation π if $a_1\pi = 1$, $a_2\pi = 2$, $\ldots$, $a_n\pi = n$. Then the sum of the weights on path π is $B(f^\pi)$, if we add 2 for the sink nodes. For example, the path $\emptyset \rightarrow \{4\} \rightarrow \{2, 4\} \rightarrow \{1, 2, 4\} \rightarrow \{1, 2, 3, 4\}$ yields the only way to achieve $B(f^\pi) = 6$ as in (93).

Notice that the master profile chart is a familiar graph, the n-cube, whose edges have been decorated so that they count the number of beads in various sets of subfunctions. The graph has exponential size, $n2^{n-1}$; yet it is much smaller than the total number of permutations, $n!$. When n is, say, 25 or less, exercise 138 shows that the entire chart can be computed without great difficulty, and we can find an optimum permutation for any given function. For example, the hidden weighted bit function turns out to have $B_{\min}(h_{25}) = 2090$ and $B_{\max}(h_{25}) = 35441$; the minimum is achieved with $(1\pi,\ldots,25\pi) = (3, 5, 7, 9, 11, 13, 15, 17, 25, 24, 23, 22, 21, 20, 19, 18, 16, 14, 12, 10, 8, 6, 4, 2, 1)$, while the maximum results from a strange permutation $(22, 19, 17, 25, 15, 13, 11, 10, 9, 8, 7, 24, 6, 5, 4, 3, 2, 12, 1, 14, 23, 16, 18, 20, 21)$ that tests many "middle" variables first.

Instead of computing the entire master profile chart, we can sometimes save time by learning just enough about it to determine a path of least weight. (See exercise 140.) But when n grows and functions get more weird, we are unlikely to be able to determine $B_{\min}(f)$ exactly, because the problem of finding the best ordering is NP-complete (see exercise 137).

We've defined the profile and quasi-profile of a single Boolean function f, but the same ideas apply also to an arbitrary BDD base that contains m functions $\{f_1,\ldots,f_m\}$. Namely, the profile is $(b_0,\ldots,b_n)$ when there are b_k nodes on level k, and the quasi-profile is $(q_0,\ldots,q_n)$ when there are q_k nodes on level k of the corresponding QDD base; the truth tables of the functions have b_k different beads of order $n-k$, and q_k different subtables. For example, the profile of the $(4+4)$-bit addition functions $\{f_1, f_2, f_3, f_4, f_5\}$ in (36) is $(2, 4, 3, 6, 3, 6, 3, 2, 2)$, and the quasi-profile is worked out in exercise 144. Similarly, the concept of master profile chart applies to m functions whose variables are reordered simultaneously; and we can use it to find $B_{\min}(f_1,\ldots,f_m)$ and $B_{\max}(f_1,\ldots,f_m)$, the minimum and maximum of $b_0 + \cdots + b_n$ taken over all profiles.

*Local reordering. What happens to a BDD base when we decide to branch on x_2 first, then on $x_1, x_3, \ldots, x_n$? Figure 26 shows that the structure of the top two levels can change dramatically, but all other levels remain the same.

A closer analysis reveals, in fact, that this level-swapping process isn't difficult to understand or to implement. The ① nodes before swapping can be divided into two kinds, "tangled" and "solitary," depending on whether they have ② nodes as descendants; for example, there are three tangled nodes at the left of Fig. 26, pointed to by s_1, s_2, and s_3, while s_4 points to a solitary node. Similarly, the ② nodes before swapping are either "visible" or "hidden," depending on whether they are independent source functions or accessible only from ① nodes; all four of the ② nodes at the left of Fig. 26 are hidden.

After swapping, the solitary ① nodes simply move down one level; but the tangled nodes are transmogrified into ②s, according to a process that we shall explain shortly. The hidden ② nodes disappear, if any, and the visible ones simply move up to the top level. Additional nodes might also arise during the transmogrification process; such nodes, labeled ①, are called "newbies." For example, two newbies appear above t_2 at the right of Fig. 26. This process decreases the total number of nodes if and only if the hidden nodes outnumber the newbies.

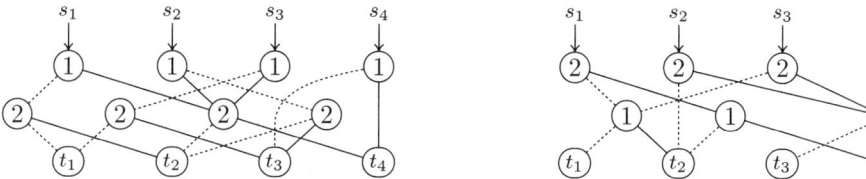

Fig. 26. Interchanging the top two levels of a BDD base. Here (s_1, s_2, s_3, s_4) are source functions; (t_1, t_2, t_3, t_4) are target nodes, representing subfunctions at lower levels.

The reverse of a swap is, of course, the same as a swap, but with the roles of ① and ② interchanged. If we begin with the diagram at the right of Fig. 26, we see that it has three tangled nodes (labeled ②) and one that's visible (labeled ①); two of its nodes are hidden, none are solitary. The swapping process in general sends (tangled, solitary, visible, hidden) nodes into (tangled, visible, solitary, newbie) nodes, respectively — after which newbies would become hidden in a reverse swap, and the originally hidden nodes would reappear as newbies.

Transmogrification is easiest to understand if we treat all nodes below the top two levels as if they were sinks, having constant values. Then every source function $f(x_1, x_2)$ depends only on x_1 and x_2; hence it takes on four values $a = f(0,0)$, $b = f(0,1)$, $c = f(1,0)$, and $d = f(1,1)$, where a, b, c, and d represent sinks. We may suppose that there are q sinks, $\boxed{1}$, $\boxed{2}$, ..., $\boxed{q}$, and that $1 \le a,b,c,d \le q$. Then $f(x_1, x_2)$ is fully described by its *extended truth table*, $f(0,0)f(0,1)f(1,0)f(1,1) = abcd$. And after swapping, we're left with $f(x_2, x_1)$, which has the extended truth table $acbd$. For example, Fig. 26 can be redrawn as follows, using extended truth tables to label its nodes:

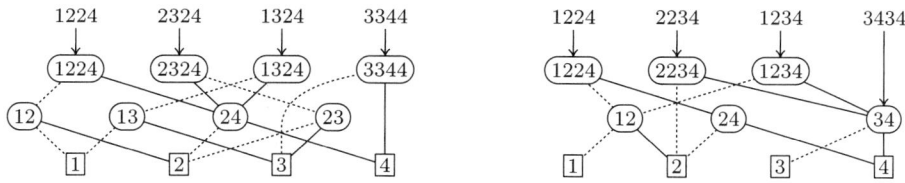

Fig. 27. Another way to represent the transformations in Fig. 26.

In these terms, the source function $abcd$ points to a solitary node when $a = b \ne c = d$, and to a visible node when $a = c \ne b = d$; otherwise it points to a tangled node (unless $a = b = c = d$, when it points directly to a sink). The tangled node $abcd$ usually has LO $= ab$ and HI $= cd$, unless $a = b$ or $c = d$; in the exceptional cases, LO or HI is a sink. After transmogrification it will have LO $= ac$ and HI $= bd$ in a similar way, where latter nodes will be either newbies or visibles or sinks (but not both sinks). One interesting case is 1224, whose children 12 and 24 on the left are hidden nodes, while the 12 and 24 on the right are newbies.

Exercise 147 discusses an efficient implementation of this transformation, which was introduced by Richard Rudell in *IEEE/ACM International Conf. Computer-Aided Design* **CAD-93** (1993), 42–47. It has the important property that no pointers need to change, except within the nodes on the top two levels:

All source nodes s_j still point to the same place in computer memory, and all sinks retain their previous identity. We have described it as a swap between ①s and ②s, but in fact the same transformation will swap ⓙs and ⓚs whenever the variables x_j and x_k correspond to branching on adjacent levels. The reason is that the upper levels of any BDD base essentially define source functions for the lower levels, which constitute a BDD base in their own right.

We know from our study of sorting that *any* reordering of the variables of a BDD base can be produced by a sequence of swaps between adjacent levels. In particular, we can use adjacent swaps to do a "jump-up" transformation, which brings a given variable x_k to the top level without disturbing the relative order of the other variables. It's easy, for instance, to jump x_4 up to the top: We simply swap ④ ↔ ③, then ④ ↔ ②, then ④ ↔ ①, because x_4 will be adjacent to x_1 after it has jumped past x_2.

Since repeated swaps can produce any ordering, they are sometimes able to make a BDD base grow until it is too big to handle. How bad can a single swap be? If exactly (s, t, v, h, ν) nodes are solitary, tangled, visible, hidden, and newbie, the top two levels end up with $s + t + v + \nu$ nodes; and this is at most $m + \nu \leq m + 2t$ when there are m source functions, because $m \geq s + t + v$. Thus the new size of those levels can't exceed twice the original, plus the number of sources.

If a single swap can double the size, a jump-up for x_k threatens to increase the size exponentially, because it does $k - 1$ swaps. Fortunately, however, jump-ups are no worse than single swaps in this regard:

Theorem J⁺. $B(f_1^\pi, \ldots, f_m^\pi) < m + 2B(f_1, \ldots, f_m)$ *after a jump-up operation.*

Proof. Let $a_1 a_2 \ldots a_{2^k-1} a_{2^k}$ be the extended truth table for a source function $f(x_1, \ldots, x_k)$, with lower-level nodes regarded as sinks. After the jump-up, the extended truth table for $f^\pi(x_1, \ldots, x_k) = f(x_{1\pi}, \ldots, x_{k\pi}) = f(x_2, \ldots, x_k, x_1)$ is $a_1 a_3 \ldots a_{2^k-1} a_2 a_4 \ldots a_{2^k}$. Thus we can see that each bead on level j of f^π is derived from some bead on level $j - 1$ of f, for $1 \leq j < k$; but every bead on level $j - 1$ of f spawns at most two beads, of half the size, in f^π. Therefore, if the respective profiles of $\{f_1, \ldots, f_m\}$ and $\{f_1^\pi, \ldots, f_m^\pi\}$ are $(b_0, \ldots, b_n)$ and $(b_0', \ldots, b_n')$, we must have $b_0' \leq m$, $b_1' \leq 2b_0$, $\ldots$, $b_{k-1}' \leq 2b_{k-2}$, $b_k' = b_k$, $\ldots$, $b_n' = b_n$. The total is therefore $\leq m + B(f_1, \ldots, f_m) + b_0 + \cdots + b_{k-2} - b_{k-1}$. ∎

The opposite of a jump-up is a "jump-down," which demotes the topmost variable by $k - 1$ levels. As before, this operation can be implemented with $k - 1$ swaps. But we have to settle for a much weaker upper bound on the resulting size:

Theorem J⁻. $B(f_1^\pi, \ldots, f_m^\pi) < B(f_1, \ldots, f_m)^2$ *after a jump-down operation.*

Proof. Now the extended truth table in the previous proof changes from $a_1 \ldots a_{2^k}$ to $a_1 \ldots a_{2^{k-1}} \ddagger a_{2^{k-1}+1} \ldots a_{2^k} = a_1 a_{2^{k-1}+1} \ldots a_{2^{k-1}} a_{2^k}$, the "zipper function" 7.1.3–(76). In this case we can identify every bead after the jump with an ordered pair of original subfunctions, as in the melding operation (37) and (38). For example, when $k = 3$ the truth table 12345678 becomes 15263748, whose bead 1526 can be regarded as the meld 12 ◇ 56. ∎

This proof indicates why quadratic growth might occur. If, for example,

$$f(x_1, \ldots, x_n) = x_1? \, M_m(x_2, \ldots, x_{m+1}; x_{2m+2}, \ldots, x_n):$$
$$M_m(x_{m+2}, \ldots, x_{2m+1}; \bar{x}_{2m+2}, \ldots, \bar{x}_n), \quad (103)$$

where $n = 1 + 2m + 2^m$, a jump-down of $2m$ levels changes $B(f) = 4n - 8m - 3$ to $B(f^{\pi}) = 2n^2 - 8m(n-m) - 2(n-2m) + 1 \approx \frac{1}{2}B(f)^2$.

Since jump-up and jump-down are inverse operations, we can also use Theorems J$^+$ and J$^-$ in reverse: *A jump-up operation might conceivably decrease the BDD size to something like its square root, but a jump-down cannot reduce the size to less than about half.* That's bad news for fans of jump-down, although they can take comfort from the knowledge that jump-downs are sometimes the only decent way to get from a given ordering to an optimum one.

Theorems J$^+$ and J$^-$ are due to B. Bollig, M. Löbbing, and I. Wegener, *Inf. Processing Letters* **59** (1996), 233–239. (See also exercise 149.)

*Dynamic reordering. In practice, a natural way to order the variables often suggests itself, based on the modules-in-a-row perspective of Fig. 23 and Theorem M. But sometimes no suitable ordering is apparent, and we can only hope to be lucky; perhaps the computer will come to our rescue and find one. Furthermore, even if we do know a good way to begin a computation, the ordering of variables that works best in the first stages of the work might turn out to be unsatisfactory in later stages. Therefore we can get better results if we don't insist on a fixed ordering. Instead, we can try to tune up the current order of branching whenever a BDD base becomes unwieldy.

For example, we might try to swap $x_{j-1} \leftrightarrow x_j$ in the order, for $1 < j \leq n$, undoing the swap if it increases the total number of nodes but letting it ride otherwise; we could keep this up until no such swap makes an improvement. That method is easy to implement, but unfortunately it's too weak; it doesn't give much of a reduction. A much better reordering technique was proposed by Richard Rudell at the same time as he introduced the swap-in-place algorithm of exercise 147. His method, called "sifting," has proved to be quite successful. The idea is simply to take a variable x_k and to try jumping it up or down to all other levels — that is, essentially to remove x_k from the ordering and then to insert it again, choosing a place for insertion that keeps the BDD size as small as possible. All of the necessary work can be done with a sequence of elementary swaps:

Algorithm J (*Sifting a variable*). This algorithm moves variable x_k into an optimum position with respect to the current ordering of the other variables $\{x_1, \ldots, x_{k-1}, x_{k+1}, \ldots, x_n\}$ in a given BDD base. It works by repeatedly calling the procedure of exercise 147 to swap adjacent variables $x_{j-1} \leftrightarrow x_j$. Throughout this algorithm, S denotes the current size of the BDD base (the total number of nodes); the swapping operation usually changes S.

J1. [Initialize.] Set $p \leftarrow 0$, $j \leftarrow k$, and $s \leftarrow S$. If $k > n/2$, go to J5.

J2. [Sift up.] While $j > 1$, swap $x_{j-1} \leftrightarrow x_j$ and set $j \leftarrow j - 1$, $s \leftarrow \min(S, s)$.

J3. [End the pass.] If $p = 1$, go to J4. Otherwise, while $j \neq k$, set $j \leftarrow j + 1$ and swap $x_{j-1} \leftrightarrow x_j$; then set $p \leftarrow 1$ and go to J5.

J4. [Finish downward.] While $s \neq S$, set $j \leftarrow j + 1$ and swap $x_{j-1} \leftrightarrow x_j$. Stop.

J5. [Sift down.] While $j < n$, set $j \leftarrow j + 1$, swap $x_{j-1} \leftrightarrow x_j$, and set $s \leftarrow \min(S, s)$.

J6. [End the pass.] If $p = 1$, go to J7. Otherwise, while $j \neq k$, swap $x_{j-1} \leftrightarrow x_j$ and set $j \leftarrow j - 1$; then set $p \leftarrow 1$ and go to J2.

J7. [Finish upward.] While $s \neq S$, swap $x_{j-1} \leftrightarrow x_j$ and set $j \leftarrow j - 1$. Stop. ∎

Whenever Algorithm J swaps $x_{j-1} \leftrightarrow x_j$, the original variable x_k is currently called either x_{j-1} or x_j. The total number of swaps varies from about n to about $2.5n$, depending on k and the optimum final position of x_k. But we can improve the running time substantially, without seriously affecting the outcome, if steps J2 and J5 are modified to proceed immediately to J3 and J6, respectively, whenever S becomes larger than, say, $1.2s$ or even $1.1s$ or even $1.05s$. In such cases, further sifting in the same direction is unlikely to decrease s.

Rudell's sifting procedure consists of applying Algorithm J exactly n times, once for each variable that is present; see exercise 151. We could continue sifting again and again until there is no more improvement; but the additional gain is usually not worth the extra effort.

Let's look at a detailed example, in order to make these ideas concrete. We've observed that when the contiguous United States are arranged in the order

$$\begin{array}{l} \text{ME NH VT MA RI CT NY NJ PA DE MD DC VA NC SC GA FL AL TN KY WV OH MI IN} \\ \text{IL WI MN IA MO AR MS LA TX OK KS NE SD ND MT WY CO NM AZ UT ID WA OR NV CA} \end{array} \quad (104)$$

as in (17), they lead to a BDD of size 428 for the independent-set function

$$\neg\bigl((x_{\text{AL}} \wedge x_{\text{FL}}) \vee (x_{\text{AL}} \wedge x_{\text{GA}}) \vee (x_{\text{AL}} \wedge x_{\text{MS}}) \vee \cdots \vee (x_{\text{UT}} \wedge x_{\text{WY}}) \vee (x_{\text{VA}} \wedge x_{\text{WV}})\bigr). \quad (105)$$

The author chose the ordering (104) by hand, starting with the historical/geographical listing of states that he had been taught as a child, then trying to minimize the size of the boundary between states-already-listed and states-to-come, so that the BDD for (105) would not need to "remember" too many partial results at any level. The resulting size, 428, is pretty good for a function of 49 variables; but sifting is able to make it even better. For example, consider WV: Some of the possibilities for altering its position, with varying sizes S, are

RI	CT	NY	NJ	PA	DE	MD	DC	VA	NC	SC	GA	FL	AL	TN	KY	OH	MI	IN	IL
424	422	417	415	414	412	411	410	412	412	415	420	421	426	425	427	428	428	436	442	453

so we can save $428 - 410 = 18$ nodes by jumping WV up to a position between MD and DC. By using Algorithm J to sift on all the variables — first on ME, then on NH, then ..., then on CA — we end up with the ordering

$$\begin{array}{l} \text{VT MA ME NH CT RI NY NJ DE PA MD WV VA DC KY OH NC GA SC AL FL MS TN IN} \\ \text{IL MI AR TX LA OK MO IA WI MN CO NE KS MT ND WY SD UT AZ NM ID CA OR WA NV} \end{array} \quad (106)$$

and the BDD size has been reduced to 345(!). That sifting process involves a total of 4663 swaps, requiring less than 4 megamems of computation altogether.

Instead of choosing an ordering carefully, let's consider a lazier alternative: We might begin with the states in alphabetic order

$$\begin{array}{l} \text{AL AR AZ CA CO CT DC DE FL GA IA ID IL IN KS KY LA MA MD ME MI MN MO MS} \\ \text{MT NC ND NE NH NJ NM NV NY OH OK OR PA RI SC SD TN TX UT VA VT WA WI WV WY} \end{array} \quad (107)$$

and proceed from there. Then the BDD for (105) turns out to have 306,214 nodes; it can be computed either via Algorithm S (with about 380 megamems of machine time) or via (55) and Algorithm U (with about 565 megamems). In this case sifting makes a dramatic difference: Those 306,214 nodes become only 2871, at a cost of 430 additional megamems. Furthermore, the sifting cost goes down from 430 Mμ to 210 Mμ if the loops of Algorithm J are aborted when $S > 1.1s$. (The more radical choice of aborting when $S > 1.05s$ would reduce the cost of sifting to 155 Mμ; but the BDD size would be reduced only to 2946 in that case.)

And we can actually do much, much better, if we sift the variables *while* evaluating (105), instead of waiting until that whole long sequence of disjunctions has been entirely computed. For example, suppose we invoke sifting automatically whenever the BDD size surpasses twice the number of nodes that were present after the previous sift. Then the evaluation of (105), starting from the alphabetic ordering (107), runs like a breeze: It automatically churns out a BDD that has only 419 nodes, after only about 60 megamems of calculation! Neither human ingenuity nor "geometric understanding" are needed to discover the ordering

$$\begin{array}{l} \text{NV OR ID WA AZ CA UT NM WY CO MT OK TX NE MO KS LA AR MS TN IA ND MN SD} \\ \text{GA FL AL NC SC KY WI MI IL OH IN WV MD VA DC PA NJ DE NY CT RI NH ME VT MA} \end{array} \quad (108)$$

which beats the author's (104). For this one, the computer just decided to invoke autosifting 39 times, on smaller BDDs.

What is the *best* ordering of states for the function (105)? The answer to that question will probably never be known for sure, but we can make a pretty good guess. First of all, a few more sifts of (108) will yield a still-better ordering

$$\begin{array}{l} \text{OR ID NV WA AZ CA UT NM WY CO MT SD MN ND IA NE OK KS TX MO LA AR MS TN} \\ \text{GA FL AL NC SC KY WI MI IL OH IN WV MD DC VA PA NJ DE NY CT RI NH ME VT MA} \end{array} \quad (109)$$

with BDD size 354. Sifting will not improve (109) further; but sifting has only limited power, because it explores only $(n-1)^2$ alternative orderings, out of $n!$ possibilities. (Indeed, exercise 134 exhibits a function of only four variables whose BDD cannot be improved by sifting, even though the ordering of its variables is not optimum.) There is, however, another arrow in our quiver: We can use *master profile charts* to optimize every window of, say, 16 consecutive levels in the BDD. There are 34 such windows; and the algorithm of exercise 139 optimizes each of them rather quickly. After about 9.6 gigamems of computation, that algorithm discovers a new champion

$$\begin{array}{l} \text{OR ID NV WA AZ CA UT NM WY CO MT SD MN ND IA NE OK KS TX MO LA AR MS WI} \\ \text{KY MI IN IL AL TN FL NC SC GA WV OH MD DC VA PA NJ DE NY CT RI NH ME VT MA} \end{array} \quad (110)$$

by cleverly rearranging 16 states within (109). This ordering, for which the BDD size is only 339, might well be optimum, because it cannot be improved either by sifting or by optimizing any window of width 25. However, such a conjecture rests on shaky ground: The ordering

AL GA FL TN NC SC VA MS AR TX LA OK KY MO NM WV MD DC PA NJ DE OH IL MI
IN IA NE KS WI SD WY ND MN MT UT CO ID CA AZ OR WA NV NY CT RI NH ME VT MA (111)

also happens to be unimprovable by sifting and by width-25 window optimization, yet its BDD has 606 nodes and is far from optimum.

   With the improved ordering (110), the 98-variable COLOR function of (73) needs only 22037 BDD nodes, instead of 25579. Sifting reduces it to 16098.

*__Read-once functions.__ Boolean functions such as $(x_1 \supset x_2) \oplus ((x_3 \equiv x_4) \wedge x_5)$, which can be expressed as formulas in which each variable occurs exactly once, form an important class for which optimum orderings of variables can easily be computed. Formally, let us say that $f(x_1, \ldots, x_n)$ is a *read-once function* if either (i) $n = 1$ and $f(x_1) = x_1$; or (ii) $f(x_1, \ldots, x_n) = g(x_1, \ldots, x_k) \circ h(x_{k+1}, \ldots, x_n)$, where $\circ$ is one of the binary operators $\{\wedge, \vee, \overline{\wedge}, \overline{\vee}, \supset, \subset, \overline{\supset}, \overline{\subset}, \oplus, \equiv\}$ and where both g and h are read-once functions. In case (i) we obviously have $B(f) = 3$. And in case (ii), exercise 163 proves that

$$B(f) = \begin{cases} B(g) + B(h) - 2, & \text{if } \circ \in \{\wedge, \vee, \overline{\wedge}, \overline{\vee}, \supset, \subset, \overline{\supset}, \overline{\subset}\}; \\ B(g) + B(h, \bar{h}) - 2, & \text{if } \circ \in \{\oplus, \equiv\}. \end{cases} \qquad (112)$$

In order to get a recurrence, we also need the similar formulas

$$B(f, \bar{f}) = \begin{cases} 4, & \text{if } n = 1; \\ 2B(g) + B(h, \bar{h}) - 4, & \text{if } \circ \in \{\wedge, \vee, \overline{\wedge}, \overline{\vee}, \supset, \subset, \overline{\supset}, \overline{\subset}\}; \\ B(g, \bar{g}) + B(h, \bar{h}) - 2, & \text{if } \circ \in \{\oplus, \equiv\}. \end{cases} \qquad (113)$$

   A particularly interesting family of read-once functions arises when we define

$$\begin{aligned} u_{m+1}(x_1, \ldots, x_{2^{m+1}}) &= v_m(x_1, \ldots, x_{2^m}) \wedge v_m(x_{2^m+1}, \ldots, x_{2^{m+1}}), \\ v_{m+1}(x_1, \ldots, x_{2^{m+1}}) &= u_m(x_1, \ldots, x_{2^m}) \oplus u_m(x_{2^m+1}, \ldots, x_{2^{m+1}}), \end{aligned} \qquad (114)$$

and $u_0(x_1) = v_0(x_1) = x_1$; for example, $u_3(x_1, \ldots, x_8) = ((x_1 \wedge x_2) \oplus (x_3 \wedge x_4)) \wedge ((x_5 \wedge x_6) \oplus (x_7 \wedge x_8))$. Exercise 165 shows that the BDD sizes for these functions, calculated via (112) and (113), involve Fibonacci numbers:

$$\begin{aligned} B(u_{2m}) &= 2^m F_{2m+2} + 2, & B(u_{2m+1}) &= 2^{m+1} F_{2m+2} + 2; \\ B(v_{2m}) &= 2^m F_{2m+2} + 2, & B(v_{2m+1}) &= 2^m F_{2m+4} + 2. \end{aligned} \qquad (115)$$

Thus u_m and v_m are functions of $n = 2^m$ variables whose BDD sizes grow as

$$\Theta(2^{m/2} \phi^m) = \Theta(n^\beta), \qquad \text{where } \beta = 1/2 + \lg \phi \approx 1.19424. \qquad (116)$$

   In fact, the BDD sizes in (115) are optimum for the u and v functions, under all permutations of the variables, because of a fundamental result due to M. Sauerhoff, I. Wegener, and R. Werchner:

__Theorem W.__ *If* $f(x_1, \ldots, x_n) = g(x_1, \ldots, x_k) \circ h(x_{k+1}, \ldots, x_n)$ *is a read-once function, there is a permutation* π *that minimizes* $B(f^\pi)$ *and* $B(f^\pi, \bar{f}^\pi)$ *simultaneously, and in which the variables* $\{x_1, \ldots, x_k\}$ *occur either first or last.*

Proof. Any permutation $(1\pi, \ldots, n\pi)$ leads naturally to an "unshuffled" permutation $(1\sigma, \ldots, n\sigma)$ in which the first k elements are $\{1, \ldots, k\}$ and the last $n - k$ elements are $\{k + 1, \ldots, n\}$, retaining the π order within each group. For example, if $k = 7$, $n = 9$, and $(1\pi, \ldots, 9\pi) = (3, 1, 4, 5, 9, 2, 6, 8, 7)$, we have $(1\sigma, \ldots, 9\sigma) = (3, 1, 4, 5, 2, 6, 7, 9, 8)$. Exercise 166 proves that, in appropriate circumstances, we have $B(f^\sigma) \leq B(f^\pi)$ and $B(f^\sigma, \bar{f}^\sigma) \leq B(f^\pi, \bar{f}^\pi)$. ∎

Using this theorem together with (112) and (113), we can readily optimize the ordering of variables for the BDD of any given read-once function. Consider, for example, $(x_1 \vee x_2) \oplus (x_3 \wedge x_4 \wedge x_5) = g(x_1, x_2) \oplus h(x_3, x_4, x_5)$. We have $B(g) = 4$ and $B(g, \bar{g}) = 6$; $B(h) = 5$ and $B(h, \bar{h}) = 8$. For the overall formula $f = g \oplus h$, Theorem W says that there are two candidates for a best ordering $(1\pi, \ldots, 5\pi)$, namely $(1, 2, 3, 4, 5)$ and $(4, 5, 1, 2, 3)$. The first of these gives $B(f^\pi) = B(g) + B(h, \bar{h}) - 2 = 10$; the other one excels, with $B(f^\pi) = B(h) + B(g, \bar{g}) - 2 = 9$.

The algorithm in exercise 167 finds an optimum π for any read-once function $f(x_1, \ldots, x_n)$ in $O(n)$ steps. Moreover, a careful analysis proves that $B(f^\pi) = O(n^\beta)$ in the best ordering, where β is the constant in (116). (See exercise 168.)

*Multiplication. Some of the most interesting Boolean functions, from a mathematical standpoint, are the $m + n$ bits that arise when an m-bit number is multiplied by an n-bit number:

$$(x_m \ldots x_2 x_1)_2 \times (y_n \ldots y_2 y_1)_2 = (z_{m+n} \ldots z_2 z_1)_2. \tag{117}$$

In particular, the "leading bit" z_{m+n}, and the "middle bit" z_n when $m = n$, are especially noteworthy. To remove the dependence of this notation on m and n, we can imagine that $m = n = \infty$ by letting $x_i = y_j = 0$ for all $i > m$ and $j > n$; then each z_k is a function of $2k$ variables, $z_k = Z_k(x_1, \ldots, x_k; y_1, \ldots, y_k)$, namely the middle bit of the product $(x_k \ldots x_1)_2 \times (y_k \ldots y_1)_2$.

The middle bit turns out to be difficult, BDDwise, even when y is constant. Let $Z_{n,a}(x_1, \ldots, x_n) = Z_n(x_1, \ldots, x_n; a_1, \ldots, a_n)$, where $a = (a_n \ldots a_1)_2$.

Theorem X. *There is a constant a such that $B_{\min}(Z_{n,a}) > \frac{5}{288} \cdot 2^{\lfloor n/2 \rfloor} - 2$.*

Proof. [P. Woelfel, *J. Computer and System Sci.* **71** (2005), 520–534.] We may assume that $n = 2t$ is even, since $Z_{2t+1,2a} = Z_{2t,a}$. Let $x = (x_n \ldots x_1)_2$ and $m = (\lfloor n\pi \leq t \rfloor \ldots \lfloor 1\pi \leq t \rfloor)_2$. Then $x = p + q$, where $q = x \& m$ represents the "known" bits of x after t branches have been taken in a BDD for $Z_{n,a}$ with the ordering π, and $p = x \& \bar{m}$ represents the bits yet unknown. Let

$$P = \{x \& \bar{m} \mid 0 \leq x < 2^n\} \quad \text{and} \quad Q = \{x \& m \mid 0 \leq x < 2^n\}. \tag{118}$$

For any fixed a, the function $Z_{n,a}$ has 2^t subfunctions

$$f_q(p) = ((pa + qa) \gg (n - 1)) \& 1, \qquad q \in Q. \tag{119}$$

We want to show that some n-bit number a will make many of these subfunctions differ; in other words we want to find a large subset $Q^* \subseteq Q$ such that

$$q \in Q^* \text{ and } q' \in Q^* \text{ and } q \neq q' \text{ implies } f_q(p) \neq f_{q'}(p) \text{ for some } p \in P. \tag{120}$$

Exercise 176 shows in detail how this can be done. ∎

Table 1
BEST AND WORST ORDERINGS FOR THE MIDDLE BIT z_n OF MULTIPLICATION

$$x_{11}x_{10}x_9x_7x_8x_6x_{13}x_{15}$$
$$\times\; x_{16}x_{14}x_{12}x_5x_4x_3x_2x_1$$
$$B_{\min}(Z_8) = 756$$

$$x_{10}x_{11}x_9x_8x_7x_{16}x_6x_{15}$$
$$\times\; x_5x_4x_3x_{12}x_{13}x_2x_1x_{14}$$
$$B_{\max}(Z_8) = 6791$$

$$x_{24}x_{20}x_{18}x_{16}x_9x_8x_{10}x_{11}x_7x_{12}x_{14}x_{21}$$
$$\times\; x_{22}x_{19}x_{17}x_{15}x_6x_5x_4x_3x_2x_1x_{13}x_{23}$$
$$B_{\min}(Z_{12}) = 21931$$

$$x_{16}x_{17}x_{15}x_{14}x_{24}x_{13}x_{12}x_{11}x_{20}x_{10}x_9x_{23}$$
$$\times\; x_8x_7x_6x_5x_{18}x_4x_{22}x_3x_2x_{19}x_1x_{21}$$
$$B_{\max}(Z_{12}) = 866283$$

Table 2
BEST AND WORST ORDERINGS FOR ALL BITS $\{z_1, \ldots, z_{m+n}\}$ OF MULTIPLICATION

$$x_{11}x_{16}x_{15}x_{14}x_{13}x_{12}x_{10}x_9$$
$$\times\; x_8x_7x_6x_5x_4x_3x_2x_1$$
$$B_{\min}(Z_{8,8}^{(1)}, \ldots, Z_{8,8}^{(16)}) = 9700$$

$$x_{10}x_8x_9x_{13}x_2x_1x_{11}x_7$$
$$\times\; x_{16}x_5x_{15}x_6x_4x_{14}x_3x_{12}$$
$$B_{\max}(Z_{8,8}^{(1)}, \ldots, Z_{8,8}^{(16)}) = 28678$$

$$x_{15}x_{17}x_{24}x_{23}x_{22}x_{21}x_{20}x_{19}x_{18}x_{16}x_{14}x_{13}$$
$$\times\; x_1x_2x_3x_4x_5x_6x_7x_8x_9x_{10}x_{11}x_{12}$$
$$B_{\min}(Z_{12,12}^{(1)}, \ldots, Z_{12,12}^{(24)}) = 648957$$

$$x_{17}x_{22}x_{14}x_{13}x_{16}x_{10}x_{20}x_3x_2x_1x_{19}x_{12}$$
$$\times\; x_{24}x_{15}x_9x_8x_{21}x_7x_6x_{11}x_{23}x_5x_4x_{18}$$
$$B_{\max}(Z_{12,12}^{(1)}, \ldots, Z_{12,12}^{(24)}) = 4224195$$

$$x_{17}x_{16}x_{10}x_9x_{11}x_{12}\ldots x_{15}x_{18}x_{19}x_{24}x_{23}\ldots x_{20}$$
$$\times\; x_1x_2x_3x_4x_5x_6x_7x_8$$
$$B_{\min}(Z_{16,8}^{(1)}, \ldots, Z_{16,8}^{(24)}) = 157061$$

$$x_{13}x_{14}x_{12}x_{15}x_{16}x_{17}x_{22}x_{10}x_8x_7x_{18}x_9x_2x_1x_{19}x$$
$$\times\; x_{24}x_{11}x_{21}x_5x_4x_{23}x_3x_2$$
$$B_{\max}(Z_{16,8}^{(1)}, \ldots, Z_{16,8}^{(24)}) = 1236251$$

A good upper bound for the BDD size of the middle bit function when neither operand is constant has been found by K. Amano and A. Maruoka, *Discrete Applied Math.* **155** (2007), 1224–1232:

Theorem A. *Let* $f(x_1, \ldots, x_{2n}) = Z_n(x_1, x_3, \ldots, x_{2n-1}; x_2, x_4, \ldots, x_{2n})$. *Then*

$$B(f) \le Q(f) < \tfrac{19}{7} 2^{\lceil 6n/5 \rceil}. \tag{121}$$

Proof. Consider two n-bit numbers $x = 2^k x_h + x_l$ and $y = 2^k y_h + y_l$, with $n - k$ unknown bits in each of their high parts (x_h, y_h), while their k-bit low parts (x_l, y_l) are both known. Then the middle bit of xy is determined by adding together three $(n - k)$-bit quantities when $k \ge n/2$, namely $x_h y_l \bmod 2^{n-k}$, $x_l y_h \bmod 2^{n-k}$, and $(x_l y_l \gg k) \bmod 2^{n-k}$. Hence level $2k$ of the QDD needs to "remember" only the least significant $n - k$ bits of each of the prior quantities x_l, y_l, and $x_l y_l \gg k$, a total of $3n - 3k$ bits, and we have $q_{2k} \le 2^{3n-3k}$ in f's quasi-profile. Exercise 177 completes the proof. ∎

Amano and Maruoka also discovered another important upper bound. Let $Z_{m,n}^{(p)}(x_1, \ldots, x_m; y_1, \ldots, y_n)$ denote the pth bit z_p of the product (117).

Theorem Y. *For all constants* $(a_m \ldots a_1)_2$ *and for all* p, *the BDD and QDD for the function* $Z_{m,n}^{(p)}(a_1, \ldots, a_m; x_1, \ldots, x_n)$ *have fewer than* $3 \cdot 2^{n/2}$ *nodes.*

Proof. Exercise 180 proves that $q_k \le 2^{n+1-k}$ for this function. The theorem follows when we combine that result with the obvious upper bound $q_k \le 2^k$. ∎

Theorem Y shows that the lower bound of Theorem X is best possible, except for a constant factor. It also shows that the BDD base for all $m + n$ product functions $Z_{m,n}^{(p)}(x_1, \ldots, x_m; x_{m+1}, \ldots, x_{m+n})$ is not nearly as large as $\Theta(2^{m+n})$, which we get for almost all instances of $m + n$ functions of $m + n$ variables:

Corollary Y. *If* $m \le n$, $B(Z_{m,n}^{(1)}, \ldots, Z_{m,n}^{(m+n)}) < 3(m + n)2^{m+(n+1)/2}$. ∎

The best orderings of variables for the middle-bit function Z_n and for the complete BDD base remain mysterious, but empirical results for small m and n give reason to conjecture that the upper bounds of Theorem A and Corollary Y are not far from the truth; see Tables 1 and 2. Here, for example, are the optimum results of Z_n when $n \le 12$:

$$
\begin{array}{rccccccccccc}
n = & 1 & 2 & 3 & 4 & 5 & 6 & 7 & 8 & 9 & 10 & 11 & 12 \\
B_{\min}(Z_n) = & 4 & 8 & 14 & 31 & 63 & 136 & 315 & 756 & 1717 & 4026 & 9654 & 21931 \\
2^{6n/5} \approx & 2 & 5 & 12 & 28 & 64 & 147 & 338 & 776 & 1783 & 4096 & 9410 & 21619
\end{array}
$$

The ratios $B_{\max}/B_{\min}$ with respect to the full BDD base $\{Z_{m,n}^{(1)}, \ldots, Z_{m,n}^{(m+n)}\}$ are surprisingly small in Table 2. Therefore all orderings for that problem might turn out to be roughly equivalent.

Zero-suppressed BDDs: A combinatorial alternative. When BDDs are applied to combinatorial problems, a glance at the data in memory often reveals that most of the HI fields simply point to $\boxed{\bot}$. In such cases, we're better off using a variant data structure called a *zero-suppressed binary decision diagram*, or "ZDD" for short, introduced by Shin-ichi Minato [*ACM/IEEE Design Automation Conf.* **30** (1993), 272–277]. A ZDD has nodes like a BDD, but its nodes are interpreted differently: When an (i) node branches to a (j) node for $j > i+1$, it means that the Boolean function is false unless $x_{i+1} = \cdots = x_{j-1} = 0$.

For example, the BDDs for independent sets and kernels in (12) have many nodes with HI $= \boxed{\bot}$. Those nodes go away in the corresponding ZDDs, although a few new nodes must also be added:

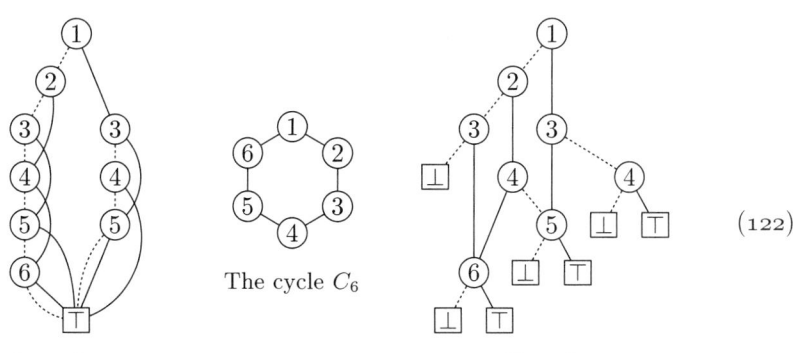

Independent sets   The cycle C_6 Kernels   (122)

Notice that we might have LO = HI in a ZDD, because of the new conventions. Furthermore, the example on the left shows that a ZDD need not contain $\boxed{\bot}$ at all! About 40% of the nodes in (12) have been eliminated from each diagram.

One good way to understand a ZDD is to regard it as a condensed representation of a *family of sets*. Indeed, the ZDDs in (122) represent respectively the families of all independent sets and all kernels of C_6. The root node of a ZDD names the smallest element that appears in at least one of the sets; its HI and LO branches represent the residual subfamilies that do and don't contain that element; and so on. At the bottom, $\boxed{\perp}$ represents the empty family '$\emptyset$', and $\boxed{\top}$ represents '$\{\emptyset\}$'. For example, the rightmost ZDD in (122) represents the family $\{\{1,3,5\}, \{1,4\}, \{2,4,6\}, \{2,5\}, \{3,6\}\}$, because the HI branch of the root represents $\{\{3,5\}, \{4\}\}$ and the LO branch represents $\{\{2,4,6\}, \{2,5\}, \{3,6\}\}$.

Every Boolean function $f(x_1, \ldots, x_n)$ is, of course, equivalent to a family of subsets of $\{1, \ldots, n\}$, and vice versa. But the family concept gives us a different perspective from the function concept. For example, the family $\{\{1,3\}, \{2\}, \{2,5\}\}$ has the same ZDD for all $n \geq 5$; but if, say, $n = 7$, the BDD for the function $f(x_1, \ldots, x_7)$ that defines this family needs additional nodes to ensure that $x_4 = x_6 = x_7 = 0$ when $f(x) = 1$.

Almost every notion that we've discussed for BDDs has a counterpart in the theory of ZDDs, although the actual data structures are often strikingly different. We can, for example, take the truth table for any given function $f(x_1, \ldots, x_n)$ and construct its unique ZDD in a straightforward way, analogous to the construction of its BDD as illustrated in (5). We know that the BDD nodes for f correspond to the "beads" of f's truth table; the ZDD nodes, similarly, correspond to *zeads*, which are binary strings of the form $\alpha\beta$ with $|\alpha| = |\beta|$ and $\beta \neq 0 \ldots 0$, or with $|\alpha| = |\beta| - 1$. Any binary string corresponds to a unique zead, obtained by lopping off the right half repeatedly, if necessary, until the string either has odd length or its right half is nonzero.

Dear reader, please take a moment now to work exercise 187. (Really.)

The *z-profile* of $f(x_1, \ldots, x_n)$ is $(z_0, \ldots, z_n)$, where z_k is the number of zeads of order $n-k$ in f's truth table, for $0 \leq k < n$, namely the number of $\boxed{k+1}$ nodes in the ZDD; also z_n is the number of sinks. We write $Z(f) = z_0 + \cdots + z_n$ for the total number of nodes. For example, the functions in (122) have z-profiles $(1,1,2,2,2,1,1)$ and $(1,1,2,2,1,1,2)$, respectively, so $Z(f) = 10$ in each case.

The basic relations (83)–(85) between profiles and quasi-profiles hold true also for z-profiles, but with q'_k counting only *nonzero* subtables of order $n-k$:

$$q'_k \geq z_k, \qquad \text{for } 0 \leq k < n; \tag{123}$$
$$q'_k \leq 1 + z_0 + \cdots + z_{k-1} \text{ and } q'_k \leq z_k + \cdots + z_n, \quad \text{for } 0 \leq k \leq n; \tag{124}$$
$$Z(f) \geq 2q'_k - 1, \qquad \text{for } 0 \leq k \leq n. \tag{125}$$

Consequently the BDD size and the ZDD size can never be wildly different:

$$Z(f) \leq \frac{n}{2}\big(B(f) + 1\big) + 1 \qquad \text{and} \qquad B(f) \leq \frac{n}{2}\big(Z(f) + 1\big) + 2. \tag{126}$$

On the other hand, a factor of 50 when $n = 100$ is nothing to sneeze at.

When ZDDs are used to find independent sets and kernels of the contiguous USA, using the original order of (17), the BDD sizes of 428 and 780 go down to 177 and 385, respectively. Sifting reduces these ZDD sizes to 160 and 335. Is anybody sneezing? That's amazingly good, for complicated functions of 49 variables.

When we know the ZDDs for f and g, we can synthesize them to obtain the ZDDs for $f \wedge g$, $f \vee g$, $f \oplus g$, etc., using algorithms that are very much like the methods we've used for BDDs. Furthermore we can count and/or optimize the solutions of f, with analogs of Algorithms C and B; in fact, ZDD-based techniques for counting and optimization turn out to be a bit easier than the corresponding BDD-based algorithms are. With slight modifications of BDD methods, we can also do dynamic variable reordering via sifting. Exercises 197–209 discuss the nuts and bolts of all the basic ZDD procedures.

In general, a ZDD tends to be better than a BDD when we're dealing with functions whose solutions are *sparse*, in the sense that νx tends to be small when $f(x) = 1$. And if $f(x)$ itself happens to be sparse, in the sense that it has comparatively few solutions, so much the better.

For example, ZDDs are well suited to *exact cover problems*, defined by an $m \times n$ matrix of 0s and 1s: We want to find all ways to choose rows that sum to $(1, 1, \ldots, 1)$. Our goal might be, say, to cover a chessboard with 32 dominoes, like

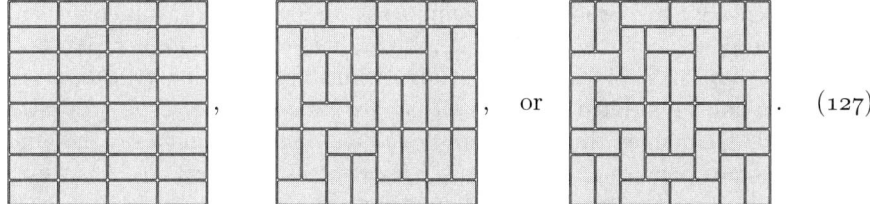

$$\text{, } \qquad \text{, or} \qquad . \qquad (127)$$

This is an exact cover problem whose matrix has $8 \times 8 = 64$ columns, one for each cell; there are $2 \times 7 \times 8 = 112$ rows, one for each pair of adjacent cells:

$$
\begin{pmatrix}
1\,1\,0\,0\,0\,0\,0\,0\,0\,0\,0\,0\ldots 0\,0\,0\,0\,0\,0\,0\,0\,0\,0 \\
1\,0\,0\,0\,0\,0\,0\,0\,1\,0\,0\,0\ldots 0\,0\,0\,0\,0\,0\,0\,0\,0\,0 \\
0\,1\,1\,0\,0\,0\,0\,0\,0\,0\,0\,0\ldots 0\,0\,0\,0\,0\,0\,0\,0\,0\,0 \\
0\,1\,0\,0\,0\,0\,0\,0\,0\,1\,0\,0\ldots 0\,0\,0\,0\,0\,0\,0\,0\,0\,0 \\
\vdots \qquad\qquad \vdots \\
0\,0\,0\,0\,0\,0\,0\,0\,0\,0\,0\,0\ldots 0\,0\,0\,0\,0\,0\,1\,1\,0\,0 \\
0\,0\,0\,0\,0\,0\,0\,0\,0\,0\,0\,0\ldots 0\,0\,0\,0\,0\,0\,0\,1\,1\,0 \\
0\,0\,0\,0\,0\,0\,0\,0\,0\,0\,0\,0\ldots 0\,0\,0\,0\,0\,0\,0\,0\,1\,1
\end{pmatrix} . \qquad (128)
$$

Let variable x_j represent the choice (or not) of row j. Thus the three solutions in (127) have $(x_1, x_2, x_3, x_4, \ldots, x_{110}, x_{111}, x_{112}) = (1, 0, 0, 0, \ldots, 1, 0, 1)$, $(1, 0, 0, 0, \ldots, 1, 0, 1)$, and $(0, 1, 0, 1, \ldots, 1, 0, 0)$, respectively. In general, the solutions to an exact cover problem are represented by the function

$$f(x_1, \ldots, x_m) = \bigwedge_{j=1}^{n} S_1(X_j) = \bigwedge_{j=1}^{n} [\nu X_j = 1], \qquad (129)$$

where $X_j = \{x_i \mid a_{ij} = 1\}$ and (a_{ij}) is the given matrix.

The dominoes-on-a-chessboard ZDD turns out to have only $Z(f) = 2300$ nodes, even though f has $m = 112$ variables in this case. We can use it to prove that there are exactly 12,988,816 coverings such as (127).

Similarly, we can investigate more exotic kinds of covering. In

(130)

for instance, a chessboard has been covered with monominoes, dominoes, and/or trominoes — that is, with rookwise-connected pieces that each have either one, two, or three cells. There are exactly 92,109,458,286,284,989,468,604 ways to do this(!); and we can compute that number almost instantly, doing only about 75 megamems of calculation, by forming a ZDD of size 512,227 on 468 variables.

A special algorithm could be devised to find the ZDD for any given exact cover problem; or we can synthesize the result using (129). See exercise 212.

Incidentally, the problem of domino covering as in (127) is equivalent to finding the perfect matchings of the grid graph $P_8 \square P_8$, which is bipartite. We will see in Section 7.5.1 that efficient algorithms are available by which perfect matchings can be studied on graphs that are far too large to be treated with BDD/ZDD techniques. In fact, there's even an explicit formula for the number of domino coverings of an $m \times n$ grid. By contrast, general coverings such as (130) fall into a wider category of hypergraph problems for which polynomial-time methods are unlikely to exist as $m, n \to \infty$.

An amusing variant of domino covering called the "mutilated chessboard" was considered by Max Black in his book *Critical Thinking* (1946), pages 142 and 394: Suppose we remove opposite corners of the chessboard, and try to cover the remaining cells with 31 dominoes. It's easy to place 30 of them, for example as shown here; but then we're stuck. Indeed, if we consider the corresponding 108×62 exact cover problem, but leave out the last two constraints of (129), we obtain a ZDD with 1224 nodes from which we can deduce that there are 324,480 ways to choose rows that sum to $(1, 1, \ldots, 1, 1, *, *)$. But each of those solutions has at least two 1s in column 61; therefore the ZDD reduces to $\boxed{\bot}$ after we AND in the constraint $[\nu X_{61} = 1]$. ("Critical thinking" explains why; see exercise 213.) This example reminds us that (i) the size of the final ZDD or BDD in a calculation can be much smaller than the time needed to compute it; and (ii) using our brains can save oodles of computer cycles.

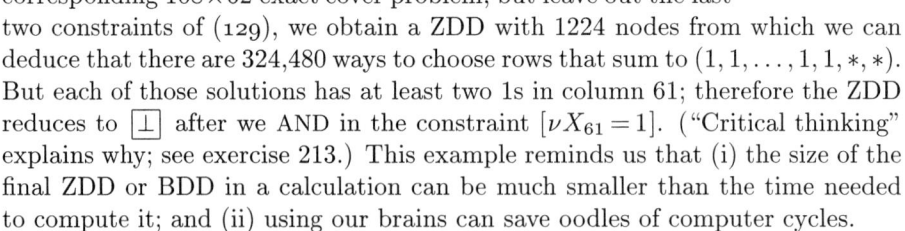

ZDDs as dictionaries. Let's switch gears now, to note that ZDDs are advantageous also in applications that have an entirely different flavor. We can use them, for instance, to represent the *five-letter words of English*, the set WORDS(5757) from the Stanford GraphBase that is discussed near the beginning of this chapter. One way to do this is to consider the function $f(x_1, \ldots, x_{25})$ that is defined to be 1 if and only if the five numbers $(x_1 \ldots x_5)_2$, $(x_6 \ldots x_{10})_2$, $\ldots$, $(x_{21} \ldots x_{25})_2$ encode the letters of an English word, where $\mathtt{a} = (00001)_2$, $\ldots$, $\mathtt{z} = (11010)_2$.

For example, $f(0,0,1,1,1,0,1,1,1,1,0,1,1,1,1,0,0,1,1,0,1,1,0,0,x_{25}) = x_{25}$. This function of 25 variables has $Z(f) = 6233$ nodes—which isn't bad, since it represents 5757 words.

Of course we've studied many other ways to represent 5757 words, in Chapter 6. The ZDD approach is no match for binary trees or tries or hash tables, when we merely want to do simple searches. But with ZDDs we can also retrieve data that is only partially specified, or data that is only supposed to match a key approximately; many complex queries can be handled with ease.

Furthermore, we don't need to worry very much about having lots of variables when ZDDs are being used. Instead of working with the 25 variables x_j considered above, we can also represent those five-letter words as a sparse function $F(a_1,\ldots,z_1,a_2,\ldots,z_2,\ldots,a_5,\ldots,z_5)$ that has $26\times5 = 130$ variables, where variable a_2 (for example) controls whether the second letter is 'a'. To indicate that crazy is a word, we make F true when $c_1 = r_2 = a_3 = z_4 = y_5 = 1$ and all other variables are 0. Equivalently, we consider F to be a family consisting of the 5757 subsets $\{w_1, h_2, i_3, c_4, h_5\}$, $\{t_1, h_2, e_3, r_4, e_5\}$, etc. With these 130 variables the ZDD size $Z(F)$ turns out to be only 5020 instead of 6233.

Incidentally, $B(F)$ is 46,189—more than nine times as large as $Z(F)$. But $B(f)/Z(f)$ is only $8870/6233 \approx 1.4$ in the 25-variable case. The ZDD world is different from the BDD world in many ways, in spite of having similar algorithms and a similar theory.

One consequence of this difference is a need for new primitive operations by which complex families of subsets can readily be constructed from elementary families. Notice that the simple subset $\{f_1, u_2, n_3, n_4, y_5\}$ is actually an extremely long-winded Boolean function:

$$\bar{a}_1 \wedge \cdots \wedge \bar{e}_1 \wedge f_1 \wedge \bar{g}_1 \wedge \cdots \wedge \bar{t}_2 \wedge u_2 \wedge \bar{v}_2 \wedge \cdots \wedge \bar{x}_5 \wedge y_5 \wedge \bar{z}_5, \qquad (131)$$

a minterm of 130 Boolean variables. Exercise 203 discusses an important *family algebra*, by which that subset is expressed more naturally as '$f_1 \sqcup u_2 \sqcup n_3 \sqcup n_4 \sqcup y_5$'. With family algebra we can readily describe and compute many interesting collections of words and word fragments (see exercise 222).

ZDDs to represent simple paths. An important connection between arbitrary directed, acyclic graphs (dags) and a special class of ZDDs is illustrated in Fig. 28. When every source vertex of the dag has out-degree 1 and every sink vertex has in-degree 1, the ZDD for all oriented paths from a source to a sink has essentially the same "shape" as the original dag. The variables in this ZDD are the *arcs* of the dag, in a suitable topological order. (See exercise 224.)

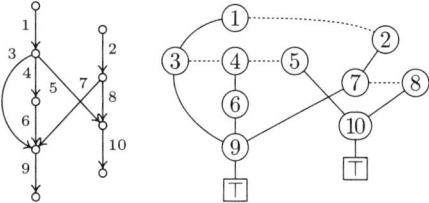

Fig. 28. A dag, and the ZDD for its source-to-sink paths. Arcs of the dag correspond to vertices of the ZDD. All branches to $\boxed{\perp}$ have been omitted from the ZDD in order to show the structural similarities more clearly.

We can also use ZDDs to represent simple paths in an *undirected* graph.
For example, there are 12 ways to go from the upper left corner of a 3×3
grid to the lower right corner, without visiting any point twice:

(132)

These paths can be represented by the ZDD shown at the right, which characterizes all sets of suitable edges. For example, we get the first path by taking
the HI branches at ⑬, ㊱, ⑱, and ⑧⑨ of the ZDD. (As in Fig. 28,
this diagram has been simplified by omitting all of the uninteresting
LO branches that merely go to ⊥.) Of course this ZDD isn't a truly
great way to represent (132), because that family of paths has only 12
members. But on the larger grid $P_8 \square P_8$, the number of simple paths
from corner to corner turns out to be 789,360,053,252; and they can all
be represented by a ZDD that has at most 33580 nodes. Exercise 225
explains how to construct such a ZDD quickly.

A similar algorithm, discussed in exercise 226, constructs a ZDD
that represents all *cycles* of a given graph. With a ZDD of size 22275,
we can deduce that $P_8 \square P_8$ has exactly 603,841,648,931 simple cycles.
This ZDD may well provide the best way to represent all of those cycles within
a computer, and the best way to generate them systematically if desired.

The same ideas work well with graphs from the "real world" that don't
have a neat mathematical structure. For example, we can use them to answer
a question posed to the author in 2008 by Randal Bryant: "Suppose I wanted
to take a driving tour of the Continental U.S., visiting all of the state capitols,
and passing through each state only once. What route should I take to minimize
the total distance?" The following diagram shows the shortest distances between
neighboring capital cities, when restricted to local itineraries that each cross only
one state boundary:

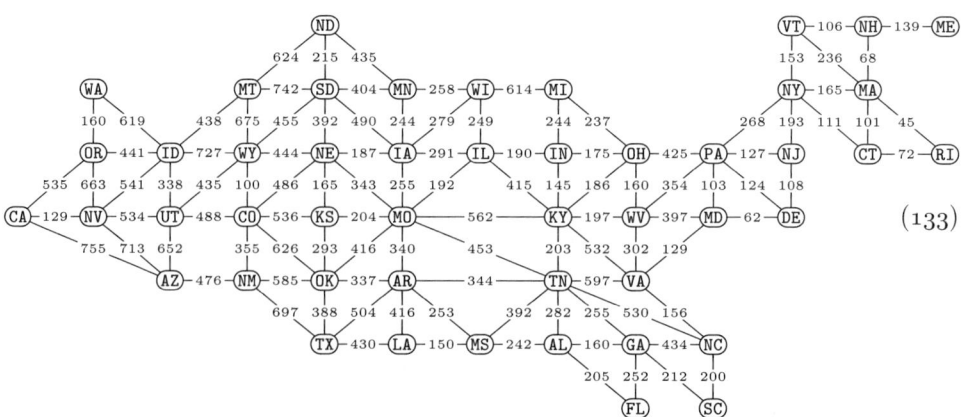

(133)

The problem is to choose a subset of these edges that form a Hamiltonian path
of smallest total length.

Every Hamiltonian path in this graph must clearly either start or end at Augusta, Maine (ME). Suppose we start in Sacramento, California (CA). Proceeding as above, we can find a ZDD that characterizes all paths from CA to ME; this ZDD turns out to have only 7850 nodes, and it quickly tells us that exactly 437,525,772,584 simple paths from CA to ME are possible. In fact, the generating function by number of edges turns out to be

$$4z^{11} + 124z^{12} + 1539z^{13} + \cdots + 33385461z^{46} + 2707075z^{47}; \qquad (134)$$

so the longest such paths are Hamiltonian, and there are exactly 2,707,075 of them. Furthermore, exercise 227 shows how to construct a smaller ZDD, of size 4726, which describes just the Hamiltonian paths from CA to ME.

We could repeat this experiment for each of the states in place of California. (Well, the starting point had better be outside of New England, if we are going to get past New York, which is an articulation point of this graph.) For example, there are 483,194 Hamiltonian paths from NJ to ME. But exercise 228 shows how to construct a *single* ZDD of size 28808 for the family of all Hamiltonian paths from ME to *any* other final state — of which there are 68,656,026. The answer to Bryant's problem now pops out immediately, via Algorithm B. (The reader may like to try finding a minimum route by hand, before turning to exercise 230 and discovering the absolutely optimum answer.)

*ZDDs and prime implicants. Finally, let's look at an instructive application in which BDDs and ZDDs are both used simultaneously.

According to Theorem 7.1.1Q, every monotone Boolean function f has a unique shortest two-level representation as an OR of ANDs, called its "disjunctive prime form" — the disjunction of all of its prime implicants. The prime implicants correspond to the minimal points where $f(x) = 1$, namely the binary vectors x for which we have $f(x') = 1$ and $x' \subseteq x$ if and only if $x' = x$. If

$$f(x_1, x_2, x_3) = x_1 \vee (x_2 \wedge x_3), \qquad (135)$$

for example, the prime implicants of f are x_1 and $x_2 \wedge x_3$, while the minimal solutions are $x_1 x_2 x_3 = 100$ and 011. These minimal solutions can also be expressed conveniently as e_1 and $e_2 \sqcup e_3$, using family algebra (see exercise 203).

In general, $x_{i_1} \wedge \cdots \wedge x_{i_s}$ is a prime implicant of a monotone function f if and only if $e_{i_1} \sqcup \cdots \sqcup e_{i_s}$ is a minimal solution of f. Thus we can consider f's prime implicants PI(f) to be its family of minimal solutions. Notice, however, that $x_{i_1} \wedge \cdots \wedge x_{i_s} \subseteq x_{j_1} \wedge \cdots \wedge x_{j_t}$ if and only if $e_{i_1} \sqcup \cdots \sqcup e_{i_s} \supseteq e_{j_1} \sqcup \cdots \sqcup e_{j_t}$; so it's confusing to say that one prime implicant "contains" another. Instead, we say that the shorter one "absorbs" the longer one.

A curious phenomenon shows up in example (135): The diagram is not only the BDD for f, it's also the ZDD for PI(f)! Similarly, Fig. 21 at the beginning of this section illustrates not only the BDD for $\langle x_1 x_2 x_3 \rangle$ but also the ZDD for PI($\langle x_1 x_2 x_3 \rangle$). On the other hand, let $g = (x_1 \wedge x_3) \vee x_2$. Then the BDD for g is but the ZDD for PI(g) is . What's going on here?

The key to resolving this mystery lies in the recursive structure on which BDDs and ZDDs are based. Every Boolean function can be represented as

$$f(x_1, \ldots, x_n) = (\bar{x}_1?\ f_0\colon f_1) = (\bar{x}_1 \wedge f_0) \vee (x_1 \wedge f_1), \qquad (136)$$

where f_c is the value of f when x_1 is replaced by c. When f is monotone we also have $f = f_0 \vee (x_1 \wedge f_1)$, because $f_0 \subseteq f_1$. If $f_0 \neq f_1$, the BDD for f is obtained by creating a node $\textcircled{1}$ whose LO and HI branches point to the BDDs for f_0 and f_1. Similarly, it's not difficult to see that the prime implicants of f are

$$\mathrm{PI}(f) = \mathrm{PI}(f_0) \cup \left(e_1 \sqcup (\mathrm{PI}(f_1) \setminus \mathrm{PI}(f_0))\right). \qquad (137)$$

(See exercise 253.) This is the recursion that defines the ZDD for $\mathrm{PI}(f)$, when we add the termination conditions for constant functions: The ZDDs for $\mathrm{PI}(0)$ and $\mathrm{PI}(1)$ are $\boxed{\bot}$ and $\boxed{\top}$.

Let's say that a Boolean function f is *sweet* if it is monotone and if the ZDD for $\mathrm{PI}(f)$ is exactly the same as the BDD for f. Constant functions are clearly sweet. And nonconstant sweetness is easily characterized:

Theorem S. *A Boolean function that depends on x_1 is sweet if and only if its prime implicants are $P \cup (x_1 \sqcup Q)$, where P and Q are sweet and independent of x_1, and every member of P is absorbed by some member of Q.*

Proof. See exercise 246. (To say that "P and Q are sweet" means that they each are families of prime implicants that define a sweet Boolean function.) $\blacksquare$

Corollary S. *The connectedness function of any graph is sweet.*

Proof. The prime implicants of the connectedness function f are the spanning trees of the graph. Every spanning tree that does not include arc x_1 has at least one subtree that will be spanning when arc x_1 is added to it. Furthermore, all subfunctions of f are the connectedness functions of smaller graphs. $\blacksquare$

Thus, for example, the BDD in Fig. 22, which defines all 431 of the connected subgraphs of $P_3 \square P_3$, also is the ZDD that defines all 192 of its spanning trees.

Whether f is sweet or not, we can use (137) to compute the ZDD for $\mathrm{PI}(f)$ whenever f is monotone. When we do this we can actually let the BDD nodes and the ZDD nodes *coexist* in the same big base of data: Two nodes with identical (V, LO, HI) fields might as well appear only once in memory, even though they might have complete different meanings in different contexts. We use one routine to synthesize $f \wedge \bar{g}$ when f and g point to BDDs, and another routine to form $f \setminus g$ when f and g point to ZDDs; no trouble will arise if these routines happen to share nodes, as long as the variables aren't being reordered. (Of course the cache memos must distinguish BDD facts from ZDD facts when we do this.)

For example, exercise 7.1.1–67 defines an interesting class of self-dual functions called the Y functions, and the BDD for Y_{12} (which is a function of 91 variables) has 748,416 nodes. This function has 2,178,889,774 prime implicants; yet $Z(\mathrm{PI}(Y_{12}))$ is only 217,388. (We can find this ZDD with a computational cost of about 13 gigamems and 660 megabytes.)

A brief history. The seeds of binary decision diagrams were implicitly planted by Claude Shannon [*Trans. Amer. Inst. Electrical Engineers* **57** (1938), 713–723], in his illustrations of relay-contact networks. Section 4 of that paper showed that any symmetric Boolean function of n variables has a BDD with at most $\binom{n+1}{2}$ branch nodes. Shannon preferred to work with Boolean algebra; but C. Y. Lee, in *Bell System Tech. J.* **38** (1959), 985–999, pointed out several advantages of what he called "binary-decision programs," because any n-variable function could be evaluated by executing at most n branch instructions in such a program.

S. Akers coined the name "binary decision diagrams" and pursued the ideas further in *IEEE Trans.* **C-27** (1978), 509–516. He showed how to obtain a BDD from a truth table by working bottom-up, or from algebraic subfunctions by working top-down. He explained how to count the paths from a root to $\boxed{\top}$ or $\boxed{\bot}$, and observed that these paths partition the n-cube into disjoint subcubes.

Meanwhile a very similar model of Boolean computation arose in theoretical studies of automata. For example, A. Cobham [*FOCS* **7** (1966), 78–87] related the minimum sizes of branching programs for a sequence of functions $f_n(x_1,\ldots,x_n)$ to the space complexity of nonuniform Turing machines that compute this sequence. More significantly, S. Fortune, J. Hopcroft, and E. M. Schmidt [*Lecture Notes in Comp. Sci.* **62** (1978), 227–240] considered "free B-schemes," now known as FBDDs, in which no Boolean variable is tested twice on any path (see exercise 35). Among other results, they gave a polynomial-time algorithm to test whether $f = g$, given FBDDs for f and g, provided that at least one of those FBDDs is ordered consistently as in a BDD. The theory of finite-state automata, which has intimate connections to BDD structure, was also being developed; thus several researchers worked on problems that are equivalent to analyzing the size, $B(f)$, for various functions f. (See exercise 261.)

All of this work was conceptual, not implemented in computer programs, although programmers had found good uses for binary tries and Patrician trees — which are similar to BDDs except that they are trees instead of dags (see Section 6.3). But then Randal E. Bryant discovered that binary decision diagrams are significantly important in practice when they are required to be both *reduced* and *ordered*. His introduction to the subject [*IEEE Trans.* **C-35** (1986), 677–691] became for many years the most cited paper in all of computer science, because it revolutionized the data structures used to represent Boolean functions.

In his paper, Bryant pointed out that the BDD for any function is essentially unique under his conventions, and that most of the functions encountered in practice had BDDs of reasonable size. He presented efficient algorithms to synthesize the BDDs for $f \wedge g$ and $f \oplus g$, etc., from the BDDs for f and g. He also showed how to compute the lexicographically least x such that $f(x) = 1$, etc.

Lee, Akers, and Bryant all noted that many functions can profitably coexist in a BDD base, sharing their common subfunctions. A high-performance "package" for BDD base operations, developed by K. S. Brace, R. L. Rudell, and R. E. Bryant [*ACM/IEEE Design Automation Conf.* **27** (1990), 40–45], has strongly influenced all subsequent implementations of BDD toolkits. Bryant summarized the early uses of BDDs in *Computing Surveys* **24** (1992), 293–318.

Shin-ichi Minato introduced ZDDs in 1993, as noted above, to improve performance in combinatorial work. He gave a retrospective account of early ZDD applications in *Software Tools for Technology Transfer* **3** (2001), 156–170.

The use of Boolean methods in graph theory was pioneered by K. Maghout [*Comptes Rendus Acad. Sci.* **248** (Paris, 1959), 3522–3523], who showed how to express the maximal independent sets and the minimal dominating sets of any graph or digraph as the prime implicants of a monotone function. Then R. Fortet [*Cahiers du Centre d'Etudes Recherche Operationelle* **1**, 4 (1959), 5–36] considered Boolean approaches to a variety of other problems; for example, he introduced the idea of 4-coloring a graph by assigning two Boolean variables to each vertex, as we have done in (73). P. Camion, in that same journal [**2** (1960), 234–289], transformed integer programming problems into equivalent problems in Boolean algebra, hoping to resolve them via techniques of symbolic logic. This work was extended by others, notably P. L. Hammer and S. Rudeanu, whose book *Boolean Methods in Operations Research* (Springer, 1968) summarized the ideas. Unfortunately, however, their approach foundered, because no good techniques for Boolean calculation were available at the time. The proponents of Boolean methods had to wait until the advent of BDDs before the general Boolean programming problem (7) could be resolved, thanks to Algorithm B. The special case of Algorithm B in which all weights are nonnegative was introduced by B. Lin and F. Somenzi [*International Conf. Computer-Aided Design* **CAD-90** (IEEE, 1990), 88–91]. S. Minato [*Formal Methods in System Design* **10** (1997), 221–242] developed software that automatically converts linear inequalities between integer variables into BDDs that can be manipulated conveniently, somewhat as the researchers of the 1960s had hoped would be possible.

The classic problem of finding a minimum size DNF for a given function also became spectacularly simpler when BDD methods became understood. The latest techniques for that problem are beyond the scope of this book, but Olivier Coudert has given an excellent overview in *Integration* **17** (1994), 97–140.

A fine book by Ingo Wegener, *Branching Programs and Binary Decision Diagrams* (SIAM, 2000), surveys the vast literature of the subject, develops the mathematical foundations carefully, and discusses many ways in which the basic ideas have been generalized and extended.

Caveat. We've seen dozens of examples in which the use of BDDs and/or ZDDs has made it possible to solve a wide variety of combinatorial problems with amazing efficiency, and the exercises below contain dozens of additional examples where such methods shine. But BDD and ZDD structures are by no means a panacea; they're only two of the weapons in our arsenal. They apply chiefly to problems that have more solutions than can readily be examined one by one, problems whose solutions have a local structure that allows our algorithms to deal with only relatively few subproblems at a time. In later sections of *The Art of Computer Programming* we shall be studying additional techniques by which other kinds of combinatorial problems can be tamed.

EXERCISES

▶ **1.** [*20*] Draw the BDDs for all 16 Boolean functions $f(x_1, x_2)$. What are their sizes?

▶ **2.** [*21*] Draw a planar dag with sixteen vertices, each of which is the root of one of the 16 BDDs in exercise 1.

3. [*16*] How many Boolean functions $f(x_1, \ldots, x_n)$ have BDD size 3 or less?

4. [*21*] Suppose three fields | V | LO | HI | have been packed into a 64-bit word x, where V occupies 8 bits and the other two fields occupy 28 bits each. Show that five bitwise instructions will transform $x \mapsto x'$, where x' is equal to x except that a LO or HI value of 0 is changed to 1 and vice versa. (Repeating this operation on every branch node x of a BDD for f will produce the BDD for the complementary function, $\bar{f}$.)

5. [*20*] If you take the BDD for $f(x_1, \ldots, x_n)$ and interchange the LO and HI pointers of every node, and if you also swap the two sinks $\boxed{\bot} \leftrightarrow \boxed{\top}$, what do you get?

6. [*10*] Let $g(x_1, x_2, x_3, x_4) = f(x_4, x_3, x_2, x_1)$, where f has the BDD in (6). What is the truth table of g, and what are its beads?

7. [*21*] Given a Boolean function $f(x_1, \ldots, x_n)$, let

$$g_k(x_0, x_1, \ldots, x_n) = f(x_0, \ldots, x_{k-2}, x_{k-1} \vee x_k, x_{k+1}, \ldots, x_n) \qquad \text{for } 1 \le k \le n.$$

Find a simple relation between (a) the truth tables and (b) the BDDs of f and g_k.

8. [*22*] Solve exercise 7 with $x_{k-1} \oplus x_k$ in place of $x_{k-1} \vee x_k$.

9. [*16*] Given the BDD for a function $f(x) = f(x_1, \ldots, x_n)$, represented sequentially as in (8), explain how to determine the lexicographically largest x such that $f(x) = 0$.

▶ **10.** [*21*] Given two BDDs that define Boolean functions f and f', represented sequentially as in (8) and (10), design an algorithm that tests $f = f'$.

11. [*20*] Does Algorithm C give the correct answer if it is applied to a binary decision diagram that is (a) ordered but not reduced? (b) reduced but not ordered?

▶ **12.** [*M21*] A *kernel* of a digraph is a set of vertices K such that

$$v \in K \quad \text{implies} \quad v \not\rightarrow u \text{ for all } u \in K;$$
$$v \notin K \quad \text{implies} \quad v \longrightarrow u \text{ for some } u \in K.$$

a) Show that when the digraph is an ordinary graph (that is, when $u \longrightarrow v$ if and only if $v \longrightarrow u$), a kernel is the same as a maximal independent set.
b) Describe the kernels of the *oriented* cycle $\vec{C_n}$.
c) Prove that an acyclic digraph has a *unique* kernel.

13. [*M15*] How is the concept of a graph kernel related to the concept of (a) a maximal clique? (b) a minimal vertex cover?

14. [*M24*] How big, exactly, are the BDDs for (a) all independent sets of the cycle graph C_n, and (b) all kernels of C_n, when $n \ge 3$? (Number the vertices as in (12).)

15. [*M23*] How many (a) independent sets and (b) kernels does C_n have, when $n \ge 3$?

▶ **16.** [*22*] Design an algorithm that successively generates all vectors $x_1 \ldots x_n$ for which $f(x_1, \ldots, x_n) = 1$, when a BDD for f is given.

17. [*32*] If possible, improve the algorithm of exercise 16 so that its running time is $O(B(f)) + O(N)$ when there are N solutions.

18. [*13*] Play through Algorithm B with the BDD (8) and $(w_1, \ldots, w_4) = (1, -2, -3, 4)$.

19. [*20*] What are the largest and smallest possible values of variable m_k in Algorithm B, based only on the weights $(w_1, \ldots, w_n)$, not on any details of the function f?

20. [*15*] Devise a fast way to compute the Thue–Morse weights (15) for $1 \leq j \leq n$.

21. [*05*] Can Algorithm B *minimize* $w_1 x_1 + \cdots + w_n x_n$, instead of maximizing it?

▶ **22.** [*M21*] Suppose step B3 has been simplified so that '$W_{v+1} - W_{v_l}$' and '$W_{v+1} - W_{v_h}$' are eliminated from the formulas. Prove that the algorithm will still work, when applied to BDDs that represent kernels of graphs.

▶ **23.** [*M20*] All paths from the root of the BDD in Fig. 22 to $\boxed{\top}$ have exactly eight solid arcs. Why is this not a coincidence?

24. [*M22*] Suppose twelve weights $(w_{12}, w_{13}, \ldots, w_{89})$ have been assigned to the edges of the grid in Fig. 22. Explain how to find a minimum spanning tree in that graph (namely, a spanning tree whose edges have minimum total weight), by applying Algorithm B to the BDD shown there.

25. [*M20*] Modify Algorithm C so that it computes the generating function for the solutions to $f(x_1, \ldots, x_n) = 1$, namely $G(z) = \sum_{x_1=0}^{1} \cdots \sum_{x_n=0}^{1} z^{x_1 + \cdots + x_n} f(x_1, \ldots, x_n)$.

26. [*M20*] Modify Algorithm C so that it computes the reliability polynomial for given probabilities, namely

$$F(p_1, \ldots, p_n) = \sum_{x_1=0}^{1} \cdots \sum_{x_n=0}^{1} (1 - p_1)^{1-x_1} p_1^{x_1} \ldots (1 - p_n)^{1-x_n} p_n^{x_n} f(x_1, \ldots, x_n).$$

▶ **27.** [*M26*] Suppose $F(p_1, \ldots, p_n)$ and $G(p_1, \ldots, p_n)$ are the reliability polynomials for Boolean functions $f(x_1, \ldots, x_n)$ and $g(x_1, \ldots, x_n)$, where $f \neq g$. Let q be a prime number, and choose independent random integers $q_1, \ldots, q_n$, uniformly distributed in the range $0 \leq q_k < q$. Prove that $F(q_1, \ldots, q_n) \bmod q \neq G(q_1, \ldots, q_n) \bmod q$ with probability $\geq (1 - 1/q)^n$. (In particular, if $n = 1000$ and $q = 2^{31} - 1$, different functions lead to different "hash values" under this scheme with probability at least 0.9999995.)

28. [*M16*] Let $F(p)$ be the value of the reliability polynomial $F(p_1, \ldots, p_n)$ when $p_1 = \cdots = p_n = p$. Show that it's easy to compute $F(p)$ from the generating function $G(z)$.

29. [*HM20*] Modify Algorithm C so that it computes the reliability polynomial $F(p)$ of exercise 28 and also its derivative $F'(p)$, given p and the BDD for f.

▶ **30.** [*M21*] The reliability polynomial is the sum, over all solutions to $f(x_1, \ldots, x_n) = 1$, of contributions from all "minterms" $(1 - p_1)^{1-x_1} p_1^{x_1} \ldots (1 - p_n)^{1-x_n} p_n^{x_n}$. Explain how to find a solution $x_1 \ldots x_n$ whose contribution to the total reliability is maximum, given a BDD for f and a sequence of probabilities $(p_1, \ldots, p_n)$.

31. [*M21*] Modify Algorithm C so that it computes the fully elaborated truth table of f, formalizing the procedure by which (24) was obtained from Fig. 21.

▶ **32.** [*M20*] What interpretations of 'o', '•', '⊥', '⊤', '$\bar{x}_j$', and 'x_j' will make the general algorithm of exercise 31 specialize to the algorithms of exercises 25, 26, 29, and 30?

▶ **33.** [*M22*] Specialize exercise 31 so that we can efficiently compute

$$\sum_{f(x)=1} (w_1 x_1 + \cdots + w_n x_n) \quad \text{and} \quad \sum_{f(x)=1} (w_1 x_1 + \cdots + w_n x_n)^2$$

from the BDD of a Boolean function $f(x) = f(x_1, \ldots, x_n)$.

34. [*M25*] Specialize exercise 31 so that we can efficiently compute

$$\max\Bigl\{\max_{1\le k\le n}\bigl(w_1x_1+\cdots+w_{k-1}x_{k-1}+w'_kx_k+w_{k+1}x_{k+1}+\cdots+w_nx_n+w''_k\bigr)\mid f(x)=1\Bigr\}$$

from the BDD of f, given $3n$ arbitrary weights $(w_1,\ldots,w_n,w'_1,\ldots,w'_n,w''_1,\ldots,w''_n)$.

▸ **35.** [*22*] A *free binary decision diagram* (FBDD) is a binary decision diagram such as

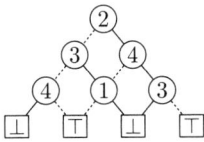

where the branch variables needn't appear in any particular order, but no variable is allowed to occur more than once on any downward path from the root. (An FBDD is "free" in the sense that every path in the dag is possible: No branch constrains another.)

a) Design an algorithm to verify that a supposed FBDD is really free.

b) Show that it's easy to compute the reliability polynomial $F(p_1,\ldots,p_n)$ of a Boolean function $f(x_1,\ldots,x_n)$, given $(p_1,\ldots,p_n)$ and an FBDD that defines f, and to compute the number of solutions to $f(x_1,\ldots,x_n)=1$.

36. [*25*] By extending exercise 31, explain how to compute the elaborated truth table for any given FBDD, if the abstract operators $\circ$ and $\bullet$ are commutative as well as distributive and associative. (Thus we can find optimum solutions as in Algorithm B, or solve problems such as those in exercises 30 and 33, with FBDDs as well as with BDDs.)

37. [*M20*] (R. L. Rivest and J. Vuillemin, 1976.) A Boolean function $f(x_1,\ldots,x_n)$ is called *evasive* if every FBDD for f contains a downward path of length n. Let $G(z)$ be the generating function for f, as in exercise 25. Prove that f is evasive if $G(-1)\ne 0$.

▸ **38.** [*27*] Let $I_{s-1},\ldots,I_0$ be branch instructions that define a nonconstant Boolean function $f(x_1,\ldots,x_n)$ as in (8) and (10). Design an algorithm that computes the status variables $t_1\ldots t_n$, where

$$t_j=\begin{cases}+1, & \text{if } f(x_1,\ldots,x_n)=1 \text{ whenever } x_j=1;\\ -1, & \text{if } f(x_1,\ldots,x_n)=1 \text{ whenever } x_j=0;\\ 0, & \text{otherwise.}\end{cases}$$

(If $t_1\ldots t_n\ne 0\ldots 0$, the function f is therefore *canalizing* as defined in Section 7.1.1.) The running time of your algorithm should be $O(n+s)$.

39. [*M20*] What is the size of the BDD for the threshold function $[x_1+\cdots+x_n\ge k]$?

▸ **40.** [*22*] Let g be the "condensation" of f obtained by setting $x_{k+1}\leftarrow x_k$ as in (27).

a) Prove that $B(g)\le B(f)$. [*Hint:* Consider subtables and beads.]

b) Suppose h is obtained from f by setting $x_{k+2}\leftarrow x_k$. Is $B(h)\le B(f)$?

41. [*M25*] Assuming that $n\ge 4$, find the BDD size of the Fibonacci threshold functions (a) $\langle x_1^{F_1}x_2^{F_2}\ldots x_{n-2}^{F_{n-2}}x_{n-1}^{F_{n-1}}x_n^{F_{n-2}}\rangle$ and (b) $\langle x_n^{F_1}x_{n-1}^{F_2}\ldots x_3^{F_{n-2}}x_2^{F_{n-1}}x_1^{F_{n-2}}\rangle$.

42. [*22*] Draw the BDD base for all symmetric Boolean functions of 3 variables.

▸ **43.** [*22*] What is $B(f)$ when (a) $f(x_1,\ldots,x_{2n})=[x_1+\cdots+x_n=x_{n+1}+\cdots+x_{2n}]$?
(b) $f(x_1,\ldots,x_{2n})=[x_1+x_3+\cdots+x_{2n-1}=x_2+x_4+\cdots+x_{2n}]$?

▸ **44.** [*M32*] Determine the maximum possible size, Σ_n, of $B(f)$ when f is a symmetric Boolean function of n variables.

45. [*22*] Give precise specifications for the Boolean modules that compute the three-in-a-row function as in (33) and (34), and show that the network is well defined.

46. [*M23*] What is the true BDD size of the three-in-a-row function?

47. [*M21*] Devise and prove a *converse* of Theorem M: Every Boolean function f with a small BDD can be implemented by an efficient network of modules.

48. [*M22*] Implement the hidden weighted bit function with a network of modules like Fig. 23, using $a_k = 2 + \lambda k$ and $b_k = 1 + \lambda(n - k)$ connecting wires for $1 \le k < n$. Conclude from Theorem B that the upper bound in Theorem M cannot be improved to $\sum_{k=0}^{n} 2^{p(a_k, b_k)}$ for any polynomial p.

49. [*20*] Draw the BDD base for the following sets of symmetric Boolean functions: (a) $\{S_{\ge k}(x_1, x_2, x_3, x_4) \mid 1 \le k \le 4\}$; (b) $\{S_k(x_1, x_2, x_3, x_4) \mid 0 \le k \le 4\}$.

50. [*22*] Draw the BDD base for the functions of the ⊓-segment display $(7.1.2–(42))$.

51. [*22*] Describe the BDD base for binary addition when the input bits are numbered from right to left, namely $(f_{n+1} f_n f_{n-1} \ldots f_1)_2 = (x_{2n-1} \ldots x_3 x_1)_2 + (x_{2n} \ldots x_4 x_2)_2$, instead of from left to right as in (35) and (36).

52. [*20*] There's a sense in which the BDD base for m functions $\{f_1, \ldots, f_m\}$ isn't really very different from a BDD with just one root: Consider the *junction function* $J(u_1, \ldots, u_n; v_1, \ldots, v_n) = (u_1?\ v_1:\ u_2?\ v_2:\ \cdots u_n?\ v_n:\ 0)$, and let

$$f(t_1, \ldots, t_{m+1}, x_1, \ldots, x_n) = J(t_1, \ldots, t_{m+1}; f_1(x_1, \ldots, x_n), \ldots, f_m(x_1, \ldots, x_n), 1),$$

where $(t_1, \ldots, t_{m+1})$ are new "dummy" variables, placed ahead of $(x_1, \ldots, x_n)$ in the ordering. Show that $B(f)$ is almost the same as the size of the BDD base for $\{f_1, \ldots, f_m\}$.

▸ **53.** [*23*] Play through Algorithm R, when it is applied to the binary decision diagram with seven branch nodes in (2).

54. [*17*] Construct the BDD of $f(x_1, \ldots, x_n)$ from f's truth table, in $O(2^n)$ steps.

55. [*M30*] Explain how to construct the "connectedness BDD" of a graph (like Fig. 22).

56. [*20*] Modify Algorithm R so that, instead of pushing any unnecessary nodes onto an `AVAIL` stack, it creates a brand new BDD, consisting of consecutive instructions $I_{s-1}, \ldots, I_1, I_0$ that have the compact form $(\bar{v}_k?\ l_k:\ h_k)$ assumed in Algorithms B and C. (The original nodes input to the algorithm can then all be recycled en masse.)

57. [*25*] Specify additional actions to be taken between steps R1 and R2 when Algorithm R is extended to compute the restriction of a function. Assume that `FIX`$[v] = t \in \{0, 1\}$ if variable v is to be given the fixed value t; otherwise `FIX`$[v] < 0$.

58. [*20*] Prove that the "melded" diagram defined by recursive use of (37) is reduced.

▸ **59.** [*M28*] Let $h(x_1, \ldots, x_n)$ be a Boolean function. Describe the melded BDD $f \diamond g$ in terms of the BDD for h, when (a) $f(x_1, \ldots, x_{2n}) = h(x_1, \ldots, x_n)$ and $g(x_1, \ldots, x_{2n}) = h(x_{n+1}, \ldots, x_{2n})$; (b) $f(x_1, x_2, \ldots, x_{2n}) = h(x_1, x_3, \ldots, x_{2n-1})$ and $g(x_1, x_2, \ldots, x_{2n}) = h(x_2, x_4, \ldots, x_{2n})$. [In both cases we obviously have $B(f) = B(g) = B(h)$.]

60. [*M22*] Suppose $f(x_1, \ldots, x_n)$ and $g(x_1, \ldots, x_n)$ have the profiles $(b_0, \ldots, b_n)$ and $(b'_0, \ldots, b'_n)$, respectively, and let their respective quasi-profiles be $(q_0, \ldots, q_n)$ and $(q'_0, \ldots, q'_n)$. Show that their meld $f \diamond g$ has $B(f \diamond g) \le \sum_{j=0}^{n}(q_j b'_j + b_j q'_j - b_j b'_j)$ nodes.

▸ **61.** [*M27*] If α and β are nodes of the respective BDDs for f and g, prove that

$$\text{in-degree}(\alpha \diamond \beta) \le \text{in-degree}(\alpha) \cdot \text{in-degree}(\beta)$$

in the melded BDD $f \diamond g$. (Imagine that the root of a BDD has in-degree 1.)

▶ **62.** [*M21*] If $f(x) = \bigvee_{j=1}^{\lfloor n/2 \rfloor}(x_{2j-1} \wedge x_{2j})$ and $g(x) = (x_1 \wedge x_n) \vee \bigvee_{j=1}^{\lceil n/2 \rceil - 1}(x_{2j} \wedge x_{2j+1})$, what are the asymptotic values of $B(f)$, $B(g)$, $B(f \diamond g)$, and $B(f \vee g)$ as $n \to \infty$?

63. [*M27*] Let $f(x_1, \ldots, x_n) = M_m(x_1 \oplus x_2, x_3 \oplus x_4, \ldots, x_{2m-1} \oplus x_{2m}; x_{2m+1}, \ldots, x_n)$ and $g(x_1, \ldots, x_n) = M_m(x_2 \oplus x_3, \ldots, x_{2m-2} \oplus x_{2m-1}, x_{2m}; \bar{x}_{2m+1}, \ldots, \bar{x}_n)$, where $n = 2m + 2^m$. What are $B(f)$, $B(g)$, and $B(f \wedge g)$?

64. [*M21*] We can compute the median $\langle f_1 f_2 f_3 \rangle$ of three Boolean functions by forming

$$f_4 = f_1 \vee f_2, \quad f_5 = f_1 \wedge f_2, \quad f_6 = f_3 \wedge f_4, \quad f_7 = f_5 \vee f_6.$$

Then $B(f_4) = O(B(f_1)B(f_2))$, $B(f_5) = O(B(f_1)B(f_2))$, $B(f_6) = O(B(f_3)B(f_4)) = O(B(f_1)B(f_2)B(f_3))$; therefore $B(f_7) = O(B(f_5)B(f_6)) = O(B(f_1)^2 B(f_2)^2 B(f_3))$. Prove, however, that $B(f_7)$ is actually only $O(B(f_1)B(f_2)B(f_3))$, and the running time to compute it from f_5 and f_6 is also $O(B(f_1)B(f_2)B(f_3))$.

▶ **65.** [*M25*] If $h(x_1, \ldots, x_n) = f(x_1, \ldots, x_{j-1}, g(x_1, \ldots, x_n), x_{j+1}, \ldots, x_n)$, prove that $B(h) = O(B(f)^2 B(g))$. Can this upper bound be improved to $O(B(f)B(g))$ in general?

66. [*20*] Complete Algorithm S by explaining what to do in step S1 if $f \circ g$ turns out to be trivially constant.

67. [*24*] Sketch the actions of Algorithm S when (41) defines f and g, and $op = 1$.

68. [*20*] Speed up step S10 by streamlining the common case when $\text{LEFT}(t) < 0$.

69. [*21*] Algorithm S ought to have one or more precautionary instructions such as "if $\text{NTOP} > \text{TBOT}$, terminate the algorithm unsuccessfully," in case it runs out of room. Where are the best places to insert them?

70. [*21*] Discuss setting b to $\lfloor \lg \text{LCOUNT}[l] \rfloor$ instead of $\lceil \lg \text{LCOUNT}[l] \rceil$ in step S4.

71. [*20*] Discuss how to extend Algorithm S to ternary operators.

72. [*25*] Explain how to eliminate hashing from Algorithm S.

▶ **73.** [*25*] Discuss the use of "virtual addresses" instead of actual addresses as the links of a BDD: Each pointer p has the form $\pi(p)2^e + \sigma(p)$, where $\pi(p) = p \gg e$ is p's "page" and $\sigma(p) = p \bmod 2^e$ is p's "slot"; the parameter e can be chosen for convenience. Show that, with this approach, only two fields (LO, HI) are needed in BDD nodes, because the variable identifier $V(p)$ can be deduced from the virtual address p itself.

▶ **74.** [*M23*] Explain how to count the number of *self-dual* monotone Boolean functions of n variables, by modifying (49).

75. [*M20*] Let $\rho_n(x_1, \ldots, x_{2^n})$ be the Boolean function that is true if and only if $x_1 \ldots x_{2^n}$ is the truth table of a *regular* function (see exercise 7.1.1–110). Show that the BDD for ρ_n can be computed by a procedure similar to that of μ_n in (49).

▶ **76.** [*M22*] A "clutter" is a family S of mutually incomparable sets; in other words, $S \not\subseteq S'$ whenever S and S' are distinct members of S. Every set $S \subseteq \{0, 1, \ldots, n-1\}$ can be represented as an n-bit integer $s = \sum\{2^e \mid e \in S\}$; so every family of such sets corresponds to a binary vector $x_0 x_1 \ldots x_{2^n - 1}$, with $x_s = 1$ if and only if s represents a set of the family.

Show that the BDD for the function '$[x_0 x_1 \ldots x_{2^n - 1}$ corresponds to a clutter]' has a simple relation to the BDD for the monotone-function function $\mu_n(x_1, \ldots, x_{2^n})$.

▶ **77.** [*M30*] Show that there's an infinite sequence $(b_0, b_1, b_2, \ldots) = (1, 2, 3, 5, 6, \ldots)$ such that the profile of the BDD for μ_n is $(b_0, b_1, \ldots, b_{2^{n-1}-1}, b_{2^{n-1}-1}, \ldots, b_1, b_0, 2)$. (See Fig. 25.) How many branch nodes of that BDD have $\text{LO} = \boxed{\bot}$?

▶ **78.** [*25*] Use BDDs to determine the number of graphs on 12 labeled vertices for which the maximum vertex degree is d, for $0 \le d \le 11$.

79. [*20*] For $0 \le d \le 11$, compute the probability that a graph on vertices $\{1, \ldots, 12\}$ has maximum degree d, if each edge is present with probability $1/3$.

80. [*23*] The recursive algorithm (55) computes $f \wedge g$ in a depth-first manner, while Algorithm S does its computation breadth-first. Do both algorithms encounter the same subproblems $f' \wedge g'$ as they proceed (but in a different order), or does one algorithm consider fewer cases than the other?

▶ **81.** [*20*] By modifying (55), explain how to compute $f \oplus g$ in a BDD base.

▶ **82.** [*25*] When the nodes of a BDD base have been endowed with REF fields, explain how those fields should be adjusted within (55) and within Algorithm U.

83. [*M20*] Prove that if f and g both have reference count 1, we needn't consult the memo cache when computing $\text{AND}(f, g)$ by (55).

84. [*24*] Suggest strategies for choosing the size of the memo cache and the sizes of the unique tables, when implementing algorithms for BDD bases. What is a good way to schedule periodic garbage collections?

85. [*16*] Compare the size of a BDD base for the 32 functions of 16×16-bit binary multiplication with the alternative of just storing a complete table of all possible products.

▶ **86.** [*21*] The routine MUX in (62) refers to "obvious" values. What are they?

87. [*20*] If the median operator $\langle fgh \rangle$ is implemented with a recursive subroutine analogous to (62), what are its "obvious" values?

▶ **88.** [*M25*] Find functions f, g, and h for which the recursive ternary computation of $f \wedge g \wedge h$ outperforms any of the binary computations $(f \wedge g) \wedge h$, $(g \wedge h) \wedge f$, $(h \wedge f) \wedge g$.

89. [*15*] Are the following quantified formulas true or false? (a) $\exists x_1 \exists x_2 f = \exists x_2 \exists x_1 f$. (b) $\forall x_1 \forall x_2 f = \forall x_2 \forall x_1 f$. (c) $\forall x_1 \exists x_2 f \le \exists x_2 \forall x_1 f$. (d) $\forall x_1 \exists x_2 f \ge \exists x_2 \forall x_1 f$.

90. [*M20*] When $l = m = n = 3$, Eq. (64) corresponds to the MOR operation of MMIX. Is there an analogous formula that corresponds to MXOR (matrix multiplication mod 2)?

▶ **91.** [*26*] In practice we often want to simplify a Boolean function f with respect to a "care set" g, by finding a function $\hat{f}$ with small $B(\hat{f})$ such that

$$f(x) \wedge g(x) \le \hat{f}(x) \le f(x) \vee \bar{g}(x) \qquad \text{for all } x.$$

In other words, $\hat{f}(x)$ must agree with $f(x)$ whenever x satisfies $g(x) = 1$, but we don't care what value $\hat{f}(x)$ assumes when $g(x) = 0$. An appealing candidate for such an $\hat{f}$ is provided by the function $f \downarrow g$, "f constrained by g," defined as follows: If $g(x)$ is identically 0, $f \downarrow g = 0$. Otherwise $(f \downarrow g)(x) = f(y)$, where y is the first element of the sequence x, $x \oplus 1$, $x \oplus 2$, $\ldots$, such that $g(y) = 1$. (Here we think of x and y as n-bit numbers $(x_1 \ldots x_n)_2$ and $(y_1 \ldots y_n)_2$. Thus $x \oplus 1 = x \oplus 0 \ldots 01 = x_1 \ldots x_{n-1} \bar{x}_n$; $x \oplus 2 = x \oplus 0 \ldots 010 = x_1 \ldots x_{n-2} \bar{x}_{n-1} x_n$; etc.)

a) What are $f \downarrow 1$, $f \downarrow x_j$, and $f \downarrow \bar{x}_j$?
b) Prove that $(f \wedge f') \downarrow g = (f \downarrow g) \wedge (f' \downarrow g)$.
c) True or false: $\bar{f} \downarrow g = \overline{f \downarrow g}$.
d) Simplify the formula $f(x_1, \ldots, x_n) \downarrow (x_2 \wedge \bar{x}_3 \wedge \bar{x}_5 \wedge x_6)$.
e) Simplify the formula $f(x_1, \ldots, x_n) \downarrow (x_1 \oplus x_2 \oplus \cdots \oplus x_n)$.
f) Simplify the formula $f(x_1, \ldots, x_n) \downarrow ((x_1 \wedge \cdots \wedge x_n) \vee (\bar{x}_1 \wedge \cdots \wedge \bar{x}_n))$.
g) Simplify the formula $f(x_1, \ldots, x_n) \downarrow (x_1 \wedge g(x_2, \ldots, x_n))$.

h) Find functions $f(x_1, x_2)$ and $g(x_1, x_2)$ such that $B(f \downarrow g) > B(f)$.

i) Devise a recursive way to compute $f \downarrow g$, analogous to (55).

92. [*M27*] The operation $f \downarrow g$ in exercise 91 sometimes depends on the ordering of the variables. Given $g = g(x_1, \ldots, x_n)$, prove that $(f^\pi \downarrow g^\pi) = (f \downarrow g)^\pi$ for all permutations π of $\{1, \ldots, n\}$ and for all functions $f = f(x_1, \ldots, x_n)$ if and only if $g = 0$ or g is a subcube (a conjunction of literals).

93. [*36*] Given a graph G on the vertices $\{1, \ldots, n\}$, construct Boolean functions f and g with the property that an approximating function $\hat{f}$ exists as in exercise 91 with small $B(\hat{f})$ if and only if G can be 3-colored. (Hence the task of minimizing $B(\hat{f})$ is NP-complete.)

94. [*21*] Explain why (65) performs existential quantification correctly.

▶ **95.** [*20*] Improve on (65) by testing if $r_l = 1$ before computing r_h.

96. [*20*] Show how to achieve (a) universal quantification $\forall x_{j_1} \ldots \forall x_{j_m} f = f \wedge g$, and (b) differential quantification $\mathbb{Q} x_{j_1} \ldots \mathbb{Q} x_{j_m} f = f \, D \, g$, by modifying (65).

97. [*M20*] Prove that it's possible to compute arbitrary bottom-of-the-BDD quantifications such as $\exists x_{n-5} \forall x_{n-4} \mathbb{Q} x_{n-3} \exists x_{n-2} \wedge x_{n-1} \forall x_n f(x_1, \ldots, x_n)$ in $O(B(f))$ steps.

▶ **98.** [*22*] In addition to (70), explain how to define the vertices $\mathrm{ENDPT}(x)$ of $\mathcal{G}$ that have degree ≤ 1. Also characterize $\mathrm{PAIR}(x, y)$, the components of size 2.

99. [*20*] (R. E. Bryant, 1984.) Every 4-coloring of the US map considered in the text corresponds to 24 solutions of the COLOR function (73), under permutation of colors. What's a good way to remove this redundancy?

▶ **100.** [*24*] In how many ways is it possible to 4-color the contiguous USA with exactly 12 states of each color? (Eliminate DC from the graph.)

101. [*20*] Continuing exercise 100, with colors $\{1, 2, 3, 4\}$, find such a coloring that maximizes $\sum$ (state weight) $\times$ (state color), where states are weighted as in (18).

102. [*23*] Design a method to cache the results of functional composition using the following conventions: The system maintains at all times an array of functions $[g_1, \ldots, g_n]$, one for each variable x_j. Initially g_j is simply the projection function x_j, for $1 \leq j \leq n$. This array can be changed only by the subroutine $\mathrm{NEWG}(j, g)$, which replaces g_j by g. The subroutine $\mathrm{COMPOSE}(f)$ always performs functional composition with respect to the current array of replacement functions.

▶ **103.** [*20*] Mr. B. C. Dull wanted to evaluate the formula

$$\exists y_1 \ldots \exists y_m ((y_1 = f_1(x_1, \ldots, x_n)) \wedge \cdots \wedge (y_m = f_m(x_1, \ldots, x_n)) \wedge g(y_1, \ldots, y_m)),$$

for certain functions $f_1, \ldots, f_m$, and g. But his fellow student, J. H. Quick, found a much simpler formula for the same problem. What was Quick's idea?

▶ **104.** [*21*] Devise an efficient way to decide whether $f \leq g$ or $f \geq g$ or $f \parallel g$, where $f \parallel g$ means that f and g are incomparable, given the BDDs for f and g.

105. [*25*] A Boolean function $f(x_1, \ldots, x_n)$ is called *unate* with polarities $(y_1, \ldots, y_n)$ if the function $h(x_1, \ldots, x_n) = f(x_1 \oplus y_1, \ldots, x_n \oplus y_n)$ is monotone.

a) Show that f can be tested for unateness by using the $\wedge$ and N quantifiers.

b) Design a recursive algorithm to test unateness in at most $O(B(f)^2)$ steps, given the BDD for f. If f is unate, your algorithm should also find appropriate polarities.

106. [*25*] Let $f\$g\$h$ denote the relation "$f(x) = g(y) = 1$ implies $h(x \wedge y) = 1$, for all x and y." Show that this relation can be evaluated in at most $O(B(f)B(g)B(h))$ steps. [*Motivation:* Theorem 7.1.1H states that f is a Horn function if and only if $f\$f\$f$; thus we can test Horn-ness in $O(B(f)^3)$ steps.]

107. [*26*] Continuing exercise 106, show that it's possible to determine whether or not f is a Krom function in $O(B(f)^4)$ steps. [*Hint:* See Theorem 7.1.1S.]

108. [*HM24*] Let $b(n, s)$ be the number of n-variable Boolean functions with $B(f) \leq s$. Prove that $(s - 3)!\,b(n, s) \leq (n(s - 1)^2)^{s-2}$ when $s \geq 3$, and explore the ramifications of this inequality when $s = \lfloor 2^n/(n + 1/\ln 2)\rfloor$. *Hint:* See the proof of Theorem 7.1.2S.

▶ **109.** [*HM17*] Continuing exercise 108, show that almost all Boolean functions of n variables have $B(f^\pi) > 2^n/(n + 1/\ln 2)$, for all permutations π of $\{1, \ldots, n\}$, as $n \to \infty$.

110. [*25*] Construct explicit worst-case functions f_n with $B(f_n) = U_n$ in Theorem U.

111. [*M21*] Verify the summation formula (79) in Theorem U.

112. [*HM23*] Prove that $\min(2^k, 2^{2^{n-k}} - 2^{2^{n-k-1}}) - \hat{b}_k$ is very small, where $\hat{b}_k$ is the number defined in (80), except when $n - \lg n - 1 < k < n - \lg n + 1$.

113. [*20*] Instead of having two sink nodes, one for each Boolean constant, we could have 2^{16} sinks, one for each Boolean function of four variables. Then a BDD could stop four levels earlier, after branching on x_{n-4}. Would this be a good idea?

114. [*20*] Is there a function with profile $(1, 1, 1, 1, 1, 2)$ and quasi-profile $(1, 2, 3, 4, 3, 2)$?

▶ **115.** [*M22*] Prove the quasi-profile inequalities (84) and (124).

116. [*M21*] What is the (a) worst case (b) average case of a random quasi-profile?

117. [*M20*] Compare $Q(f)$ to $B(f)$ when $f = M_m(x_1, \ldots, x_m; x_{m+1}, \ldots, x_{m+2^m})$.

118. [*M23*] Show that, from the perspective of Section 7.1.2, the hidden weighted bit function has cost $C(h_n) = O(n)$. What is the exact value of $C(h_4)$?

119. [*20*] True or false: Every symmetric Boolean function of n variables is a special case of h_{2n+1}. (For example, $x_1 \oplus x_2 = h_5(0, 1, 0, x_1, x_2)$.)

120. [*18*] Explain the hidden-permuted-weighted-bit formula (94).

▶ **121.** [*M22*] If $f(x_1, \ldots, x_n)$ is any Boolean function, its *dual* f^D is $\bar{f}(\bar{x}_1, \ldots, \bar{x}_n)$, and its *reflection* f^R is $f(x_n \ldots, x_1)$. Notice that $f^{DD} = f^{RR} = f$ and $f^{DR} = f^{RD}$.

a) Show that $h_n^{DR}(x_1, \ldots, x_n) = h_n(x_2, \ldots, x_n, x_1)$.

b) Furthermore, the hidden weighted bit function satisfies the recurrence

$$h_1(x_1) = x_1, \quad h_{n+1}(x_1, \ldots, x_{n+1}) = (x_{n+1}?\ h_n(x_2, \ldots, x_n, x_1): h_n(x_1, \ldots, x_n)).$$

c) Define $x\psi$, a permutation on the set of all binary strings x, by the recursive rules

$$\epsilon\psi = \epsilon, \quad (x_1 \ldots x_n 0)\psi = (x_1 \ldots x_n\psi)0, \quad (x_1 \ldots x_n 1)\psi = (x_2 \ldots x_n x_1)\psi 1.$$

For example, $1101\psi = (101\psi)1 = (01\psi)11 = (0\psi)111 = (\psi)0111 = 0111$; and we also have $0111\psi = 1101$. Is ψ an involution?

d) Show that $h_n(x) = \hat{h}_n(x\psi)$, where the function $\hat{h}_n$ has a very small BDD.

122. [*27*] Construct an FBDD for h_n that has fewer than n^2 nodes, when $n > 1$.

123. [*M20*] Prove formula (97), which enumerates all slates of offset s.

▶ **124.** [*27*] Design an efficient algorithm to compute the profile and quasi-profile of h_n^π, given a permutation π. *Hint:* When does the slate $[r_0, \ldots, r_{n-k}]$ correspond to a bead?

▶ **125.** [*HM34*] Prove that $B(h_n)$ can be expressed exactly in terms of the sequences

$$A_n = \sum_{k=0}^{n} \binom{n-k}{2k}, \qquad B_n = \sum_{k=0}^{n} \binom{n-k}{2k+1}.$$

126. [*HM42*] Analyze $B(h_n^\pi)$ for the organ-pipe permutation $\pi = (2, 4, \ldots, n, \ldots, 3, 1)$.

127. [*46*] Find a permutation π that minimizes $B(h_{100}^\pi)$.

▶ **128.** [*25*] Given a permutation π of $\{1, \ldots, m + 2^m\}$, explain how to compute the profile and quasi-profile of the permuted 2^m-way multiplexer

$$M_m^\pi(x_1, \ldots, x_m; x_{m+1}, \ldots, x_{m+2^m}) = M_m(x_{1\pi}, \ldots, x_{m\pi}; x_{(m+1)\pi}, \ldots, x_{(m+2^m)\pi}).$$

129. [*M25*] Define $Q_m(x_1, \ldots, x_{m^2})$ to be 1 if and only if the 0–1 matrix $(x_{(i-1)m+j})$ has no all-zero row and no all-zero column. Prove that $B(Q_m^\pi) = \Omega(2^m/m^2)$ for all π.

130. [*HM31*] The adjacency matrix of an undirected graph G on vertices $\{1, \ldots, m\}$ consists of $\binom{m}{2}$ variable entries $x_{uv} = [u \text{ --- } v \text{ in } G]$, for $1 \le u < v \le m$. Let $C_{m,k}$ be the Boolean function $[G$ has a k-clique$]$, for some ordering of those $\binom{m}{2}$ variables.
  a) If $1 < k \le \sqrt{m}$, prove that $B(C_{m,k}) \ge \binom{s+t}{s}$, where $s = \binom{k}{2} - 1$ and $t = m + 2 - k^2$.
  b) Consequently $B(C_{m,\lceil m/2 \rceil}) = \Omega(2^{m/3}/\sqrt{m})$, regardless of the variable ordering.

131. [*M28*] (*The covering function.*) The Boolean function

$$C(x_1, x_2, \ldots, x_p; y_{11}, y_{12}, \ldots, y_{1q}, y_{21}, \ldots, y_{2q}, \ldots, y_{p1}, y_{p2}, \ldots, y_{pq})$$
$$= ((x_1 \wedge y_{11}) \vee (x_2 \wedge y_{21}) \vee \cdots \vee (x_p \wedge y_{p1})) \wedge \cdots \wedge ((x_1 \wedge y_{1q}) \vee (x_2 \wedge y_{2q}) \vee \cdots \vee (x_p \wedge y_{pq}))$$

is true if and only if all columns of the matrix product

$$x \cdot Y = (x_1 x_2 \ldots x_p) \begin{pmatrix} y_{11} & y_{12} & \cdots & y_{1q} \\ y_{21} & y_{22} & \cdots & y_{2q} \\ \vdots & \vdots & \ddots & \vdots \\ y_{p1} & y_{p2} & \cdots & y_{pq} \end{pmatrix}$$

are positive, i.e., when the rows of Y selected by x "cover" every column of that matrix. The reliability polynomial of C is important in the analysis of fault-tolerant systems.
  a) When a BDD for C tests the variables in the order

$$x_1, y_{11}, y_{12}, \ldots, y_{1q}, x_2, y_{21}, y_{22}, \ldots, y_{2q}, \ldots, x_p, y_{p1}, y_{p2}, \ldots, y_{pq},$$

  show that the number of nodes is asymptotically $pq2^{q-1}$ for fixed q as $p \to \infty$.
  b) Find an ordering for which the size is asymptotically $pq2^{p-1}$ for fixed p as $q \to \infty$.
  c) Prove that $B_{\min}(C) = \Omega(2^{\min(p,q)/2})$ in general.

132. [*32*] What Boolean functions $f(x_1, x_2, x_3, x_4, x_5)$ have the largest $B_{\min}(f)$?

133. [*20*] Explain how to compute $B_{\min}(f)$ and $B_{\max}(f)$ from f's master profile chart.

134. [*24*] Construct the master profile chart, analogous to (102), for the Boolean function $x_1 \oplus ((x_2 \oplus (x_1 \vee (\bar{x}_2 \wedge x_3))) \wedge (x_3 \oplus x_4))$. What are $B_{\min}(f)$ and $B_{\max}(f)$? *Hint:* The identity $f(x_1, x_2, x_3, x_4) = f(x_1, x_2, \bar{x}_4, \bar{x}_3)$ saves about half the work.

135. [*M27*] For all $n \ge 4$, find a Boolean function $\theta_n(x_1, \ldots, x_n)$ that is *uniquely thin*, in the sense that $B(\theta_n^\pi) = n + 2$ for exactly one permutation π. (See (93) and (102).)

▶ **136.** [*M34*] What is the master profile chart of the median-of-medians function

$$\langle\langle x_{11}x_{12}\ldots x_{1n}\rangle\langle x_{21}x_{22}\ldots x_{2n}\rangle\ldots\langle x_{m1}x_{m2}\ldots x_{mn}\rangle\rangle,$$

when m and n are odd integers? What is the best ordering? (There are mn variables.)

137. [*M38*] Given a graph, the *optimum linear arrangement problem* asks for a permutation π of the vertices that minimizes $\sum_{u\,-\,v}|u\pi-v\pi|$. Construct a Boolean function f for which this minimum value is characterized by the optimum BDD size $B_{\min}(f)$.

▶ **138.** [*M36*] The purpose of this exercise is to develop an attractive algorithm that computes the master profile chart for a function f, given f's QDD (not its BDD).

  a) Explain how to find $\binom{n+1}{2}$ weights of the master profile chart from a single QDD.
  b) Show that the jump-up operation can be performed easily in a QDD, without garbage collection or hashing. *Hint:* See the "bucket sort" in Algorithm R.
  c) Consider the 2^{n-1} orderings of variables in which the $(i+1)$st is obtained from the ith by a jump-up from depth $\rho i + \nu i$ to depth $\nu i - 1$. For example, we get

12345 21345 32145 31245 43125 41325 42135 42315 54231 52431 53241 53421 51342 51432 51243 51234

  when $n = 5$. Show that every k-element subset of $\{1,\ldots,n\}$ occurs at the top k levels of one of these orderings.
  d) Combine these ideas to design the desired chart-construction algorithm.
  e) Analyze the space and time requirements of your algorithm.

139. [*22*] Generalize the algorithm of exercise 138 so that (i) it computes a common profile chart for all functions of a BDD base, instead of a single function; and (ii) it restricts the chart to variables $\{x_a, x_{a+1},\ldots,x_b\}$, preserving $\{x_1,\ldots,x_{a-1}\}$ at the top and $\{x_{b+1},\ldots,x_n\}$ at the bottom.

140. [*27*] Explain how to find $B_{\min}(f)$ without knowing all of f's master profile chart.

141. [*30*] True or false: If $X_1, X_2, \ldots, X_m$ are disjoint sets of variables, then an optimum BDD ordering for the variables of $g(h_1(X_1), h_2(X_2),\ldots,h_m(X_m))$ can be found by restricting consideration to cases where the variables of each X_j are consecutive.

▶ **142.** [*HM32*] The representation of threshold functions by BDDs is surprisingly mysterious. Consider the self-dual function $f(x) = \langle x_1^{w_1}\ldots x_n^{w_n}\rangle$, where each w_j is a positive integer and $w_1+\cdots+w_n$ is odd. We observed in (28) that $B(f) = O(w_1+\cdots+w_n)^2$; and $B(f)$ is often $O(n)$ even when the weights grow exponentially, as in (29) or exercise 41.

  a) Prove that when $w_1 = 1$, $w_k = 2^{k-2}$ for $1 < k \le m$, and $w_k = 2^m - 2^{n-k}$ for $m < k \le 2m = n$, $B(f)$ grows exponentially as $n \to \infty$, but $B_{\min}(f) = O(n^2)$.
  b) Find weights $\{w_1,\ldots,w_n\}$ for which $B_{\min}(f) = \Omega(2^{\sqrt{n}/2})$.

143. [*24*] Continuing exercise 142(a), find an optimum ordering of variables for the function $\langle x_1 x_2 x_3^2 x_4^4 x_5^8 x_6^{16} x_7^{32} x_8^{64} x_9^{128} x_{10}^{256} x_{11}^{512} x_{12}^{768} x_{13}^{896} x_{14}^{960} x_{15}^{992} x_{16}^{1008} x_{17}^{1016} x_{18}^{1020} x_{19}^{1022} x_{20}^{1023}\rangle$.

144. [*16*] What is the quasi-profile of the addition functions $\{f_1, f_2, f_3, f_4, f_5\}$ in (36)?

145. [*24*] Find $B_{\min}(f_1, f_2, f_3, f_4, f_5)$ and $B_{\max}(f_1, f_2, f_3, f_4, f_5)$ of those functions.

▶ **146.** [*M22*] Let $(b_0,\ldots,b_n)$ and $(q_0,\ldots,q_n)$ be a BDD base profile and quasi-profile.
  a) Prove that $b_0 \le \min(q_0, (b_1 + q_2)(b_1 + q_2 - 1))$, $b_1 \le \min(b_0 + q_0, q_2(q_2 - 1))$, and $b_0 + b_1 \ge q_0 - q_2$.
  b) Conversely, if b_0, b_1, q_0, and q_2 are nonnegative integers that satisfy those inequalities, there is a BDD base with such a profile and quasi-profile.

▶ **147.** [*27*] Flesh out the details of Rudell's swap-in-place algorithm, using the conventions of Algorithm U and the reference counters of exercise 82.

148. [*M21*] True or false: $B(f_1^\pi, \ldots, f_m^\pi) \le 2B(f_1, \ldots, f_m)$, after swapping ① ↔ ②.

149. [*M20*] (Bollig, Löbbing, and Wegener.) Show that, in addition to Theorem J$^-$, we also have $B(f_1^\pi, \ldots, f_m^\pi) \le (2^k - 2)b_0 + B(f_1, \ldots, f_m)$ after a jump-down operation of $k-1$ levels, when $(b_0, \ldots, b_n)$ is the profile of $\{f_1, \ldots, f_m\}$.

150. [*30*] When repeated swaps are used to implement jump-up or jump-down, the intermediate results might be much larger than the initial or final BDD. Show that variable jumps can actually be done more directly, with a method whose worst-case running time is $O(B(f_1, \ldots, f_m) + B(f_1^\pi, \ldots, f_m^\pi))$.

151. [*20*] Suggest a way to invoke Algorithm J so that each variable is sifted just once.

152. [*25*] The hidden weighted bit function h_{100} has more than 17.5 trillion nodes in its BDD. By how much does sifting reduce this number? *Hint:* Use exercise 124, instead of actually constructing the diagrams.

153. [*30*] Put the tic-tac-toe functions $\{y_1, \ldots, y_9\}$ of exercise 7.1.2–65 into a BDD base. How many nodes are present when variables are tested in the order $x_1, x_2, \ldots, x_9$, $o_1, o_2, \ldots, o_9$, from top to bottom? What is $B_{\min}(y_1, \ldots, y_9)$?

154. [*20*] By comparing (104) to (106), can you tell how far each state was moved when it was sifted?

▶ **155.** [*25*] Let f_1 be the independent-set function (105) of the contiguous USA, and let f_2 be the corresponding kernel function (see (68)). Find orderings π of the states so that (a) $B(f_2^\pi)$ and (b) $B(f_1^\pi, f_2^\pi)$ are as small as you can make them. (Note that the ordering (110) gives $B(f_1^\pi) = 339$, $B(f_2^\pi) = 795$, and $B(f_1^\pi, f_2^\pi) = 1129$.)

156. [*30*] Theorems J$^+$ and J$^-$ suggest that we could save reordering time by only jumping up when sifting, not bothering to jump down. Then we could eliminate steps J3, J5, J6, and J7 of Algorithm J. Would that be wise?

157. [*M24*] Show that if the $m + 2^m$ variables of the 2^m-way multiplexer M_m are arranged in any order such that $B(M_m^\pi) > 2^{m+1} + 1$, then sifting will reduce the BDD size.

158. [*M24*] When a Boolean function $f(x_1, \ldots, x_n)$ is symmetrical in the variables $\{x_1, \ldots, x_p\}$, it's natural to expect that those variables will appear consecutively in at least one of the reorderings $f^\pi(x_1, \ldots, x_n)$ that minimize $B(f^\pi)$. Show, however, that if

$$f(x_1, \ldots, x_n) = [x_1 + \cdots + x_p = \lfloor p/3 \rfloor] + [x_1 + \cdots + x_p = \lceil 2p/3 \rceil] g(x_{p+1}, \ldots, x_{p+m}),$$

where $p = n - m$ and $g(y_1, \ldots, y_m)$ is any nonconstant Boolean function, then $B(f^\pi) = \frac{1}{3}n^2 + O(n)$ as $n \to \infty$ when $\{x_1, \ldots, x_p\}$ are consecutive in π, but $B(f^\pi) = \frac{1}{4}n^2 + O(n)$ when π places about half of those variables at the beginning and half at the end.

159. [*20*] John Conway's basic rule for Life, exercise 7.1.3–167, is a Boolean function $L(x_{\text{NW}}, x_{\text{N}}, x_{\text{NE}}, x_{\text{W}}, x, x_{\text{E}}, x_{\text{SW}}, x_{\text{S}}, x_{\text{SE}})$. What ordering of those nine variables will make the BDD as small as possible?

▶ **160.** [*24*] (*Chess Life.*) Consider an 8×8 matrix $X = (x_{ij})$ of 0s and 1s, bordered by infinitely many 0s on all sides. Let $L_{ij}(X) = L(x_{(i-1)(j-1)}, \ldots, x_{ij}, \ldots, x_{(i+1)(j+1)})$ be Conway's basic rule at position (i, j). Call X "tame" if $L_{ij}(X) = 0$ whenever $i \notin [1\,..\,8]$ or $j \notin [1\,..\,8]$; otherwise X is "wild," because it activates cells outside the matrix.

    a) How many tame configurations X vanish in one Life step, making all $L_{ij}(X) = 0$?

    b) What is the maximum weight $\sum_{i=1}^{8} \sum_{j=1}^{8} x_{ij}$ among all such solutions?

    c) How many wild configurations vanish *within* the matrix after one Life step?

    d) What are the minimum and maximum weight, among all such solutions?

    e) How many configurations X make $L_{ij}(X) = 1$ for $1 \le i, j \le 8$?

f) Investigate the tame 8×8 predecessors of the following patterns:

(1) 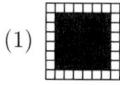   (2) 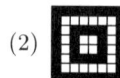   (3) 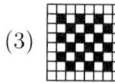   (4) 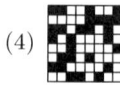   (5)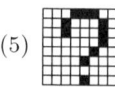

(Here, as in Section 7.1.3, black cells denote 1s in the matrix.)

161. [*28*] Continuing exercise 160, write $L(X) = Y = (y_{ij})$ if X is a tame matrix such that $L_{ij}(X) = y_{ij}$ for $1 \leq i, j \leq 8$.

a) How many X's satisfy $L(X) = X$ ("still Life")?

b) Find an 8×8 still Life with weight 35.

c) A "flip-flop" is a pair of distinct matrices with $L(X)=Y$, $L(Y)=X$. Count them.

d) Find a flip-flop for which X and Y both have weight 28.

▸ **162.** [*30*] (*Caged Life.*) If X and $L(X)$ are tame but $L(L(X))$ is wild, we say that X "escapes" its cage after three steps. How many 6×6 matrices escape their 6×6 cage after exactly k steps, for $k = 1, 2, \ldots$?

163. [*23*] Prove formulas (112) and (113) for the BDD sizes of read-once functions.

▸ **164.** [*M27*] What is the maximum of $B(f)$, over all read-once functions $f(x_1, \ldots, x_n)$?

165. [*M21*] Verify the Fibonacci-based formulas (115) for $B(u_m)$ and $B(v_m)$.

166. [*M29*] Complete the proof of Theorem W.

167. [*21*] Design an efficient algorithm that computes a permutation π for which both $B(f^\pi)$ and $B(f^\pi, \bar{f}^\pi)$ are minimized, given any read-once function $f(x_1, \ldots, x_n)$.

▸ **168.** [*HM40*] Consider the following binary operations on ordered pairs $z = (x, y)$:

$$z \circ z' = (x, y) \circ (x', y') = (x + x', \min(x + y', x' + y));$$
$$z \bullet z' = (x, y) \bullet (x', y') = (x + x' + \min(y, y'), \max(y, y')).$$

(These operations are associative and commutative.) Let $S_1 = \{(1, 0)\}$, and

$$S_n = \bigcup_{k=1}^{n-1} \{z \circ z' \mid z \in S_k,\ z' \in S_{n-k}\} \cup \bigcup_{k=1}^{n-1} \{z \bullet z' \mid z \in S_k,\ z' \in S_{n-k}\} \text{ for } n > 1.$$

Thus $S_2 = \{(2, 0), (2, 1)\}$; $S_3 = \{(3, 0), (3, 1), (3, 2)\}$; $S_4 = \{(4, 0), \ldots, (4, 3), (5, 1)\}$; etc.

a) Prove that there exists a read-once function $f(x_1, \ldots, x_n)$ for which we have $\min_\pi B(f^\pi) = c$ and $\min_\pi B(f^\pi, \bar{f}^\pi) = c'$ if and only if $(\frac{1}{2}c' - 1, c - \frac{1}{2}c' - 1) \in S_n$.

b) True or false: $0 \leq y < x$ for all $(x, y) \in S_n$.

c) If $z^T = (x + y, x - y)/\sqrt{2}$, show that $z^T \circ z'^T = (z \bullet z')^T$ and $z^T \bullet z'^T = (z \circ z')^T$.

d) Prove that $x^2 + y^2 \leq n^{2\beta}$ for all $(x, y) \in S_n$, if β is the constant in (116). *Hints:* Let $|z|^2 = x^2 + y^2$; it suffices to prove that $|z \bullet z'| \leq 2^\beta = \sqrt{2}\phi$ whenever $0 \leq y \leq x$, $0 \leq y' \leq x'$, $|z| = r = (1-\delta)^\beta$, $|z'| = r' = (1+\delta)^\beta$, and $0 \leq \delta \leq 1$. If also $y = y'$, $z \bullet z'$ lies inside the ellipse $(a \cos \theta + b \sin \theta, b \sin \theta)$, where $a = r + r'$ and $b = \sqrt{rr'}$.

169. [*M46*] Is $\min_\pi B(f^\pi) \leq B(v_{2m+1})$ for every read-once function f of 2^{2m+1} variables?

▸ **170.** [*M25*] Let's say that a Boolean function is "skinny" if its BDD involves all the variables in the simplest possible way: A skinny BDD has exactly one branch node (j) for each variable x_j, and either LO or HI is a sink node at every branch.

a) How many Boolean functions $f(x_1, \ldots, x_n)$ are skinny in this sense?

b) How many of them are monotone?

c) Show that $f_t(x_1, \ldots, x_n) = [(x_1 \ldots x_n)_2 \geq t]$ is skinny when $0 < t < 2^n$ and t is odd.

d) What is the *dual* of the function f_t in part (c)?

e) Explain how to find the shortest CNF and DNF formulas for f_t, given t.

171. [*M26*] Continuing exercise 170, show that a function is *read-once* and *regular* if and only if it is skinny and monotone.

172. [*M27*] How many skinny functions $f(x_1, \ldots, x_n)$ are also Horn functions? How many of them have the property that f and $\bar{f}$ *both* satisfy Horn's condition?

▶ **173.** [*HM28*] Exactly how many Boolean functions $f(x_1, \ldots, x_n)$ are skinny after some reordering of the variables, $f(x_{1\pi}, \ldots, x_{n\pi})$?

▶ **174.** [*M39*] Let S_n be the number of Boolean functions $f(x_1, \ldots, x_n)$ whose BDD is "thin" in the sense that it has exactly one node labeled ⓙ for $1 \leq j \leq n$. Show that S_n is also the number of combinatorial objects of the following types:

a) *Dellac permutations of order* $2n$ (namely, permutations $p_1 p_2 \ldots p_{2n}$ such that $\lceil k/2 \rceil \leq p_k \leq n + \lceil k/2 \rceil$ for $1 \leq k \leq 2n$).

b) *Genocchi derangements of order* $2n+2$ (namely, permutations $q_1 q_2 \ldots q_{2n+2}$ such that $q_k > k$ if and only if k is odd, for $1 \leq k \leq 2n+2$; also $q_k \neq k$ in a derangement).

c) *Irreducible Dumont pistols of order* $2n+2$ (namely, sequences $r_1 r_2 \ldots r_{2n+2}$ such that $k \leq r_k \leq 2n+2$ for $1 \leq k \leq 2n+2$ and $\{r_1, r_2, \ldots, r_{2n+2}\} = \{2, 4, 6, \ldots, 2n, 2n+2\}$, with the special property that $2k \in \{r_1, \ldots, r_{2k-1}\}$ for $1 \leq k \leq n$).

d) Paths from $(1, 0)$ to $(2n+2, 0)$ in the directed graph

$$
\begin{array}{ccccccccc}
 & & & & & & (7,3) \rightarrow (8,3) \rightarrow & \cdots \\
 & & & & & & \uparrow \qquad\quad \downarrow \\
 & & (5,2) \rightarrow (6,2) \rightarrow (7,2) \rightarrow (8,2) \rightarrow & \cdots \\
 & & \uparrow \qquad\quad \downarrow \qquad\quad \uparrow \qquad\quad \downarrow \\
(3,1) \rightarrow (4,1) \rightarrow (5,1) \rightarrow (6,1) \rightarrow (7,1) \rightarrow (8,1) \rightarrow & \cdots \\
\uparrow \qquad\quad \downarrow \qquad\quad \uparrow \qquad\quad \downarrow \qquad\quad \uparrow \qquad\quad \downarrow \\
(1,0) \rightarrow (2,0) \rightarrow (3,0) \rightarrow (4,0) \rightarrow (5,0) \rightarrow (6,0) \rightarrow (7,0) \rightarrow (8,0) \rightarrow & \cdots
\end{array}
$$

(Notice that objects of type (d) are very easy to count.)

175. [*M30*] Continuing exercise 174, find a way to enumerate the Boolean functions whose BDD contains exactly b_{j-1} nodes labeled ⓙ, given a profile $(b_0, \ldots, b_{n-1}, b_n)$.

176. [*M35*] To complete the proof of Theorem X, we will use exercise 6.4–78, which states that $\{h_{a,b} \mid a \in A \text{ and } b \in B\}$ is a universal family of hash functions from n bits to l bits, when $h_{a,b}(x) = ((ax+b) \gg (n-l)) \bmod 2^l$, $A = \{a \mid 0 < a < 2^n, a \text{ odd}\}$, $B = \{b \mid 0 \leq b < 2^{n-l}\}$, and $0 \leq l \leq n$. Let $I = \{h_{a,b}(p) \mid p \in P\}$ and $J = \{h_{a,b}(q) \mid q \in Q\}$.

a) Show that if $2^l - 1 \leq 2^{l-1}\epsilon/(1-\epsilon)$, there are constants $a \in A$ and $b \in B$ for which $|I| \geq (1-\epsilon)2^l$ and $|J| \geq (1-\epsilon)2^l$.

b) Given such an a, let $J = \{j_1, \ldots, j_{|J|}\}$ where $0 = j_1 < \cdots < j_{|J|}$, and choose $Q' = \{q_1, \ldots, q_{|J|}\} \subseteq Q$ so that $h_{a,b}(q_k) = j_k$ for $1 \leq k \leq |J|$. Let $g(q)$ denote the middle $l-1$ bits of aq, namely $(aq \gg (n-l+1)) \bmod 2^{l-1}$. Prove that $g(q) \neq g(q')$ whenever q and q' are distinct elements of the set $Q'' = \{q_1, q_3, \ldots, q_{2\lceil |J|/2 \rceil - 1}\}$.

c) Prove that the following set Q^* satisfies condition (120), when $l \geq 3$ and $y = a$:

$$Q^* = \{q \mid q \in Q'', g(q) \text{ is even, and } g(p) + g(q) = 2^{l-1} \text{ for some } p \in P\}.$$

d) Finally, show that $|Q^*|$ is large enough to prove Theorem X.

177. [*M22*] Complete the proof of Theorem A by bounding the entire quasi-profile.

178. [*M24*] (Amano and Maruoka.) Improve the constant in (121) by using a better variable ordering: $Z_n(x_{2n-1}, x_1, x_3, \ldots, x_{2n-3}; x_{2n}, x_2, x_4, \ldots, x_{2n-2})$.

179. [*M47*] Does the middle bit of multiplication satisfy $B_{\min}(Z_n) = \Theta(2^{6n/5})$?

180. [*M27*] Prove Theorem Y, using the hint given in the text.

181. [*M21*] Let $L_{m,n}$ be the *leading bit function* $Z_{m,n}^{(m+n)}(x_1, \ldots, x_m; y_1, \ldots, y_n)$. Prove that $B_{\min}(L_{m,n}) = O(2^m n)$ when $m \le n$.

182. [*M38*] (I. Wegener.) Does $B_{\min}(L_{n,n})$ grow exponentially as $n \to \infty$?

▸ **183.** [*M25*] Draw the first few levels of the BDD for the "limiting leading bit function"

$$[(.x_1 x_3 x_5 \ldots)_2 \cdot (.x_2 x_4 x_6 \ldots)_2 \ge \tfrac{1}{2}],$$

which has infinitely many Boolean variables. How many nodes b_k are there on level k? (We don't allow $(.x_1 x_3 x_5 \ldots)_2$ or $(.x_2 x_4 x_6 \ldots)_2$ to end with infinitely many 1s.)

184. [*M23*] What are the BDD and ZDD profiles of the permutation function P_m?

185. [*M25*] How large can $Z(f)$ be, when f is a symmetric Boolean function of n variables? (See exercise 44.)

186. [*10*] What Boolean function of $\{x_1, x_2, x_3, x_4, x_5, x_6\}$ has the ZDD '⟨③⟩'?

▸ **187.** [*20*] Draw the ZDDs for all 16 Boolean functions $f(x_1, x_2)$ of two variables.

188. [*16*] Express the 16 Boolean functions $f(x_1, x_2)$ as families of subsets of $\{1, 2\}$.

189. [*18*] What functions $f(x_1, \ldots, x_n)$ have a ZDD equal to their BDD?

190. [*20*] Describe all functions f for which (a) $Q(f) = B(f)$; (b) $Q(f) = Z(f)$.

▸ **191.** [*HM25*] How many functions $f(x_1, \ldots, x_n)$ have no ⊥ in their ZDD?

192. [*M20*] Define the *Z-transform* of binary strings as follows: $\epsilon^Z = \epsilon$, $0^Z = 0$, $1^Z = 1$, and

$$(\alpha\beta)^Z = \begin{cases} \alpha^Z \alpha^Z, & \text{if } |\alpha| = n \text{ and } \beta = 0^n; \\ \alpha^Z 0^n, & \text{if } |\alpha| = n \text{ and } \beta = \alpha; \\ \alpha^Z \beta^Z, & \text{if } |\alpha| = |\beta| - 1, \text{ or if } |\alpha| = |\beta| = n \text{ and } \alpha \ne \beta \ne 0^n. \end{cases}$$

a) What is 11001001000011111^Z?
b) True or false: $(\tau^Z)^Z = \tau$ for all binary strings τ.
c) If $f(x_1, \ldots, x_n)$ is a Boolean function with truth table τ, let $f^Z(x_1, \ldots, x_n)$ be the Boolean function whose truth table is τ^Z. Show that the profile of f is almost identical to the z-profile of f^Z, and vice versa. (Therefore Theorem U holds for ZDDs as well as for BDDs, and statistics such as (80) are valid also for z-profiles.)

193. [*M21*] Continuing exercise 192, what is $S_k^Z(x_1, \ldots, x_n)$ when $0 \le k \le n$?

194. [*M25*] How many $f(x_1, \ldots, x_n)$ have the z-profile $(1, \ldots, 1)$? (See exercise 174.)

195. [*24*] Find $Z(M_2)$, $Z_{\min}(M_2)$, and $Z_{\max}(M_2)$, where M_2 is the 4-way multiplexer.

196. [*M21*] Find a function $f(x_1, \ldots, x_n)$ for which $Z(f) = O(n)$ and $Z(\bar{f}) = \Omega(n^2)$.

197. [*25*] Modify the algorithm of exercise 138 so that it computes the "master z-profile chart" of f. (Then $Z_{\min}(f)$ and $Z_{\max}(f)$ can be found as in exercise 133.)

▸ **198.** [*23*] Explain how to compute AND(f, g) with ZDDs instead of BDDs (see (55)).

199. [*21*] Similarly, implement (a) OR(f, g), (b) XOR(f, g), (c) BUTNOT(f, g).

200. [*21*] And similarly, implement MUX(f, g, h) for ZDDs (see (62)).

201. [*22*] The projection functions x_j each have a simple 3-node BDD, but their ZDD representations are more complicated. What's a good way to implement these functions in a general-purpose ZDD toolkit?

202. [*24*] What changes are needed to the swap-in-place algorithm of exercise 147, when levels $(u) \leftrightarrow (v)$ are being interchanged in a ZDD base instead of a BDD base?

▸ **203.** [*M24*] (*Family algebra.*) The following algebraic conventions are useful for dealing with finite families of finite subsets of positive integers, and with their representation as ZDDs. The simplest such families are the *empty family*, denoted by $\emptyset$ and represented by $\boxed{\perp}$; the *unit family* $\{\emptyset\}$, denoted by ϵ and represented by $\boxed{\top}$; and the *elementary families* $\{\{j\}\}$ for $j \geq 1$, denoted by e_j and represented by a branch node (j) with LO $= \boxed{\perp}$ and HI $= \boxed{\top}$. (Exercise 186 illustrates the ZDD for e_3.)

Two families f and g can be combined with the usual set operations:
- The *union* $f \cup g = \{\alpha \mid \alpha \in f \text{ or } \alpha \in g\}$ is implemented by OR(f, g);
- The *intersection* $f \cap g = \{\alpha \mid \alpha \in f \text{ and } \alpha \in g\}$ is implemented by AND(f, g);
- The *difference* $f \setminus g = \{\alpha \mid \alpha \in f \text{ and } \alpha \notin g\}$ is implemented by BUTNOT(f, g);
- The *symmetric difference* $f \oplus g = (f \setminus g) \cup (g \setminus f)$ is implemented by XOR(f, g).

And we also define three new ways to construct families of subsets:
- The *join* $f \sqcup g = \{\alpha \cup \beta \mid \alpha \in f \text{ and } \beta \in g\}$, sometimes written just fg;
- The *meet* $f \sqcap g = \{\alpha \cap \beta \mid \alpha \in f \text{ and } \beta \in g\}$;
- The *delta* $f \boxplus g = \{\alpha \oplus \beta \mid \alpha \in f \text{ and } \beta \in g\}$.

All three are commutative and associative: $f \sqcup g = g \sqcup f$, $f \sqcup (g \sqcup h) = (f \sqcup g) \sqcup h$, etc.

a) Suppose $f = \{\emptyset, \{1, 2\}, \{1, 3\}\} = \epsilon \cup (e_1 \sqcup (e_2 \cup e_3))$ and $g = \{\{1, 2\}, \{3\}\} = (e_1 \sqcup e_2) \cup e_3$. What are $f \sqcup g$ and $(f \sqcap g) \setminus (f \boxplus e_1)$?

b) Any family f can also be regarded as a Boolean function $f(x_1, x_2, \dots)$, where $\alpha \in f \Longleftrightarrow f([1 \in \alpha], [2 \in \alpha], \dots) = 1$. Describe the operations $\sqcup$, $\sqcap$, and $\boxplus$ in terms of Boolean logical formulas.

c) Which of the following formulas hold for all families f, g, and h? (i) $f \sqcup (g \cup h) = (f \sqcup g) \cup (f \sqcup h)$; (ii) $f \sqcap (g \cup h) = (f \sqcap g) \cup (f \sqcap h)$; (iii) $f \sqcup (g \sqcap h) = (f \sqcup g) \sqcap (f \sqcup h)$; (iv) $f \cup (g \sqcup h) = (f \cup g) \sqcup (f \cup h)$; (v) $f \boxplus \emptyset = \emptyset \sqcap g = h \sqcup \emptyset$; (vi) $f \sqcap \epsilon = \epsilon$.

d) We say that f and g are *orthogonal*, written $f \perp g$, if $\alpha \cap \beta = \emptyset$ for all $\alpha \in f$ and all $\beta \in g$. Which of the following statements is true for all families f and g? (i) $f \perp g \Longleftrightarrow f \sqcap g = \epsilon$; (ii) $f \perp g \Longrightarrow |f \sqcup g| = |f||g|$; (iii) $|f \sqcup g| = |f||g| \Longrightarrow f \perp g$; (iv) $f \perp g \Longleftrightarrow f \sqcup g = f \boxplus g$.

e) Describe all families f for which the following statements hold: (i) $f \cup g = g$ for all g; (ii) $f \sqcup g = g$ for all g; (iii) $f \sqcap g = g$ for all g; (iv) $f \sqcup (e_1 \sqcup e_2) = f$; (v) $f \sqcup (e_1 \cup e_2) = f$; (vi) $f \boxplus ((e_1 \sqcup e_2) \cup e_3) = f$; (vii) $f \boxplus f = \epsilon$; (viii) $f \sqcap f = f$.

▸ **204.** [*M25*] Continuing exercise 203, two further operations are also important:
- the *quotient* $f / g = \{\alpha \mid \alpha \cup \beta \in f \text{ and } \alpha \cap \beta = \emptyset, \text{ for all } \beta \in g\}$.
- the *remainder* $f \bmod g = f \setminus (g \sqcup (f/g))$.

The quotient is sometimes also called the "cofactor" of f with respect to g.

a) Prove that $f/(g \cup h) = (f/g) \cap (f/h)$.

b) Suppose $f = \{\{1, 2\}, \{1, 3\}, \{2\}, \{3\}, \{4\}\}$. What are f/e_2 and $f/(f/e_2)$?

c) Simplify the expressions $f/\emptyset$, f/ϵ, f/f, and $(f \bmod g)/g$, for arbitrary f and g.

d) Show that $f/g = f/(f/(f/g))$. *Hint:* Start with the relation $g \subseteq f/(f/g)$.

e) Prove that f/g can also be defined as $\bigcup \{h \mid g \sqcup h \subseteq f \text{ and } g \perp h\}$.

f) Given f and j, show that f has a unique representation $(e_j \sqcup g) \cup h$ with $e_j \perp (g \cup h)$.

g) True or false: $(f \sqcup g) \bmod e_j = (f \bmod e_j) \sqcup (g \bmod e_j)$; $(f \sqcap g)/e_j = (f/e_j) \sqcap (g/e_j)$.

205. [*M25*] Implement the five basic operations of family algebra, namely (a) $f \sqcup g$, (b) $f \sqcap g$, (c) $f \boxplus g$, (d) f/g, and (e) $f \bmod g$, using the conventions of exercise 198.

206. [*M46*] What are the worst-case running times of the algorithms in exercise 205?

▶ **207.** [*M25*] When one or more projection functions x_j are needed in applications, as in exercise 201, the following "symmetrizing" operation turns out to be very handy:

$$(e_{i_1} \cup e_{i_2} \cup \cdots \cup e_{i_l}) \S k = S_k(x_{i_1}, x_{i_2}, \dots, x_{i_l}), \qquad \text{integer } k \geq 0.$$

For example, $e_j \S 1 = x_j$; $e_j \S 0 = \bar{x}_j$; $(e_i \cup e_j) \S 1 = x_i \oplus x_j$; $(e_2 \cup e_3 \cup e_5) \S 2 = (x_2 \wedge x_3 \wedge \bar{x}_5) \vee (x_2 \wedge \bar{x}_3 \wedge x_5) \vee (\bar{x}_2 \wedge x_3 \wedge x_5)$. Show that it's easy to implement this operation. (Notice that $e_{i_1} \cup \cdots \cup e_{i_l}$ has a very simple ZDD of size $l + 2$, when $l > 0$.)

▶ **208.** [*16*] By modifying Algorithm C, show that all solutions of a Boolean function can readily be counted when its ZDD is given instead of its BDD.

209. [*M21*] Explain how to compute the fully elaborated truth table of a Boolean function from its ZDD representation. (See exercise 31.)

▶ **210.** [*23*] Given the ZDD for f, show how to construct the ZDD for the function

$$g(x) = [f(x) = 1 \text{ and } \nu x = \max\{\nu y \mid f(y) = 1\}].$$

211. [*M20*] When f describes the solutions to an exact cover problem, is $Z(f) \leq B(f)$?

▶ **212.** [*25*] What's a good way to compute the ZDD for an exact cover problem?

213. [*16*] Why can't the mutilated chessboard be perfectly covered with dominoes?

▶ **214.** [*21*] When some shape is covered by dominoes, we say that the covering is *faultfree* if every straight line that passes through the interior of the shape also passes through the interior of some domino. For example, the right-hand covering in (127) is faultfree, but the middle one isn't; and the left-hand one has faults galore.

How many domino coverings of a chessboard are faultfree?

215. [*21*] Japanese tatami mats are 1×2 rectangles that are traditionally used to cover rectangular floors in such a way that no four mats meet at any corner. For example, Fig. 29(a) shows a 6×5 pattern from the 1641 edition of Mitsuyoshi Yoshida's *Jinkōki*, a book first published in 1627.

Find all domino coverings of a chessboard that are also tatami tilings.

Fig. 29. Two nice examples:
(a) A 17th-century tatami tiling;   (a)
(b) a tricolored domino covering.

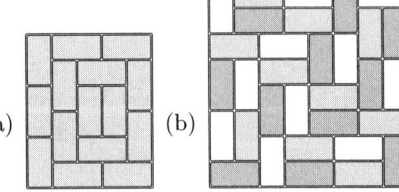

(b)

▶ **216.** [*30*] Figure 29(b) shows a chessboard covered with red, white, and blue dominoes, in such a way that no two dominoes of the same color are next to each other.

  a) In how many ways can this be done?
  b) How many of the 12,988,816 domino coverings are 3-colorable?

217. [*29*] The monomino/domino/tromino covering illustrated in (130) happens to satisfy an additional constraint: *No two congruent pieces are adjacent.* How many of the 92 sextillion coverings mentioned in the text are "separated," in this sense?

▶ **218.** [*24*] Apply BDD and ZDD techniques to the problem of Langford pairs, discussed at the beginning of this chapter.

219. [20] What is $Z(F)$ when F is the family (a) WORDS(1000); ...; (e) WORDS(5000)?

▶ **220.** [21] The z-profile of the 5757 SGB words, represented with 130 variables $a_1 .. z_5$ as discussed in (131), is (1, 1, 1, ..., 1, 1, 1, 23, 3, ..., 6, 2, 0, 3, 2, 1, 1, 2).
    a) Explain the entries 23 and 3, which correspond to the variables a_2 and b_2.
    b) Explain the final entries 0, 3, 2, 1, 1, 2, which correspond to v_5, w_5, x_5, etc.

▶ **221.** [M27] Only 5020 nodes are needed to represent the 5757 most common five-letter words of English, using the 130-variable representation, because of special linguistic properties. But there are $26^5 = 11,881,376$ possible five-letter words. Suppose we choose 5757 of them at random; how big will the ZDD be then, on average?

▶ **222.** [27] When family algebra is applied to five-letter words as in (131), the 130 variables are called a_1, b_1, ..., z_5 instead of x_1, x_2, ..., x_{130}; and the corresponding elementary families are denoted by the symbols a_1, b_1, ..., z_5 instead of $e_1, e_2, ..., e_{130}$. Thus the family $F = \text{WORDS}(5757)$ can be constructed by synthesizing the formula

$$F = (\mathbf{w}_1 \sqcup \mathbf{h}_2 \sqcup \mathbf{i}_3 \sqcup \mathbf{c}_4 \sqcup \mathbf{h}_5) \cup \cdots \cup (\mathbf{f}_1 \sqcup \mathbf{u}_2 \sqcup \mathbf{n}_3 \sqcup \mathbf{n}_4 \sqcup \mathbf{y}_5) \cup \cdots \cup (\mathbf{p}_1 \sqcup \mathbf{u}_2 \sqcup \mathbf{p}_3 \sqcup \mathbf{a}_4 \sqcup \mathbf{l}_5).$$

    a) Let $\wp$ denote the *universal family* of all subsets of $\{a_1, ..., z_5\}$, also called the "power set." What does the formula $F \sqcap \wp$ signify?
    b) Let $X = X_1 \sqcup \cdots \sqcup X_5$, where $X_j = \{a_j, b_j, ..., z_j\}$. Interpret the formula $F \sqcap X$.
    c) Find a simple formula for all words of F that match the pattern t*u*h.
    d) Find a formula for all SGB words that contain exactly k vowels, for $0 \le k \le 5$ (considering only a, e, i, o, and u to be vowels). Let $V_j = a_j \cup e_j \cup i_j \cup o_j \cup u_j$.
    e) How many patterns in which exactly three letters are specified are matched by at least one SGB word? (For example, m*tc* is such a pattern.) Give a formula.
    f) How many of those patterns are matched at least twice (e.g., *atc*)?
    g) Express all words that remain words when a 'b' is changed to 'o'.
    h) What's the significance of the formula F/V_2?
    i) Contrast $(X_1 \sqcup V_2 \sqcup V_3 \sqcup V_4 \sqcup X_5) \cap F$ with $(X_1 \sqcup X_5) \setminus ((\wp \setminus F)/(V_2 \sqcup V_3 \sqcup V_4))$.

223. [28] A "median word" is a five-letter word $\mu = \mu_1 \ldots \mu_5$ that can be obtained from three words $\alpha = \alpha_1 \ldots \alpha_5$, $\beta = \beta_1 \ldots \beta_5$, $\gamma = \gamma_1 \ldots \gamma_5$ by the rule $[\alpha_i = \mu_i] + [\beta_i = \mu_i] + [\gamma_i = \mu_i] = 2$ for $1 \le i \le 5$. For example, mixed is a median of the words {fixed, mixer, mound}, and also of {mated, mixup, nixed}. But noted is not a median of {notes, voted, naked}, because each of those words has e in position 4.
    a) Show that $\{d(\alpha, \mu), d(\beta, \mu), d(\gamma, \mu)\}$ is either $\{1, 1, 3\}$ or $\{1, 2, 2\}$ whenever μ is a median of $\{\alpha, \beta, \gamma\}$. (Here d denotes Hamming distance.)
    b) How many medians can be obtained from WORDS(n), when $n = 100$? 1000? 5757?
    c) How many of those medians belong to WORDS(m), when $m = 100$? 1000? 5757?

▶ **224.** [20] Suppose we form the ZDD for all source-to-sink paths in a dag, as in Fig. 28, when the dag happens to be a forest; that is, assume that every non-source vertex of the dag has in-degree 1. Show that the corresponding ZDD is essentially the same as the binary tree that represents the forest under the "natural correspondence between forests and binary trees," Eqs. 2.3.2–(1) through 2.3.2–(3).

▶ **225.** [30] Design an algorithm that will produce a ZDD for all sets of edges that form a simple path from s to t, given a graph and two distinct vertices $\{s, t\}$ of the graph.

▶ **226.** [20] Modify the algorithm of exercise 225 so that it yields a ZDD for all of the simple *cycles* in a given graph.

227. [20] Similarly, modify it so that it considers only *Hamiltonian paths* from s to t.

228. [*21*] And mutate it once more, for Hamiltonian paths from s to *any* other vertex.

229. [*15*] There are 587,218,421,488 paths from CA to ME in the graphs (18), but only 437,525,772,584 such paths in (133). Explain the discrepancy.

230. [*25*] Find the Hamiltonian paths of (133) that have minimum and maximum total length. What is the *average* length, if all Hamiltonian paths are equally likely?

231. [*23*] In how many ways can a king travel from one corner of a chessboard to the opposite corner, never occupying the same cell twice? (These are the simple paths from corner to corner of the graph $P_8 \boxtimes P_8$.)

▶ **232.** [*23*] Continuing exercise 231, a *king's tour* of the chessboard is an oriented Hamiltonian cycle of $P_8 \boxtimes P_8$. Determine the exact number of king's tours. What is the longest possible king's tour, in terms of Euclidean distance traveled?

▶ **233.** [*25*] Design an algorithm that builds a ZDD for the family of all *oriented cycles* of a given digraph. (See exercise 226.)

234. [*22*] Apply the algorithm of exercise 233 to the directed graph on the 49 postal codes AL, AR, ..., WY of (18), with XY $\longrightarrow$ YZ as in exercise 7–54(b). For example, one such oriented cycle is NC $\longrightarrow$ CT $\longrightarrow$ TN $\longrightarrow$ NC. How many oriented cycles are possible? What are the minimum and maximum cycle lengths?

235. [*22*] Form a digraph on the five-letter words of English by saying that $x \longrightarrow y$ when the last three letters of x match the first three letters of y (e.g., crown $\longrightarrow$ owner). How many oriented cycles does this digraph have? What are the longest and shortest?

▶ **236.** [*M25*] Many extensions to the family algebra of exercise 203 suggest themselves when ZDDs are applied to combinatorial problems, including the following five operations on families of sets:

- The *maximal elements* $f^\uparrow = \{\alpha \in f \mid \beta \in f \text{ and } \alpha \subseteq \beta \text{ implies } \alpha = \beta\}$;
- The *minimal elements* $f^\downarrow = \{\alpha \in f \mid \beta \in f \text{ and } \alpha \supseteq \beta \text{ implies } \alpha = \beta\}$;
- The *nonsubsets* $f \nearrow g = \{\alpha \in f \mid \beta \in g \text{ implies } \alpha \not\subseteq \beta\}$;
- The *nonsupersets* $f \searrow g = \{\alpha \in f \mid \beta \in g \text{ implies } \alpha \not\supseteq \beta\}$;
- The *minimal hitting sets* $f^\sharp = \{\alpha \mid \beta \in f \text{ implies } \alpha \cap \beta \neq \emptyset\}^\downarrow$.

For example, when f and g are the families of exercise 203(a) we have $f^\uparrow = e_1 \sqcup (e_2 \cup e_3)$, $f^\downarrow = \epsilon$, $f^\sharp = \emptyset$, $g^\uparrow = g^\downarrow = g$, $g^\sharp = (e_1 \cup e_2) \sqcup e_3$, $f \nearrow g = e_1 \sqcup e_3$, $f \searrow g = \epsilon$, $g \nearrow f = g \searrow f = \emptyset$.

a) Prove that $f \nearrow g = f \setminus (f \sqcap g)$, and give a similar formula for $f \searrow g$.

b) Let $f^C = \{\overline{\alpha} \mid \alpha \in f\} = f \boxplus U$, where $U = e_1 \sqcup e_2 \sqcup \cdots$ is the "universal set." Clearly $f^{CC} = f$, $(f \cup g)^C = f^C \cup g^C$, $(f \cap g)^C = f^C \cap g^C$, $(f \setminus g)^C = f^C \setminus g^C$. Show that we also have the duality laws $f^{\uparrow C} = f^{C\downarrow}$, $f^{\downarrow C} = f^{C\uparrow}$; $(f \sqcup g)^C = f^C \sqcap g^C$, $(f \sqcap g)^C = f^C \sqcup g^C$; $(f \nearrow g)^C = f^C \searrow g^C$, $(f \searrow g)^C = f^C \nearrow g^C$; $f^\sharp = (\wp \nearrow f^C)^\downarrow$.

c) True or false? (i) $x_1^\downarrow = e_1$; (ii) $x_1^\uparrow = e_1$; (iii) $x_1^\sharp = e_1$; (iv) $(x_1 \vee x_2)^\downarrow = e_1 \cup e_2$; (v) $(x_1 \wedge x_2)^\downarrow = e_1 \sqcup e_2$.

d) Which of the following formulas hold for all families f, g, and h? (i) $f^{\uparrow\uparrow} = f^\uparrow$; (ii) $f^{\uparrow\downarrow} = f^\downarrow$; (iii) $f^{\uparrow\downarrow} = f^\uparrow$; (iv) $f^{\downarrow\uparrow} = f^\downarrow$; (v) $f^{\sharp\downarrow} = f^\sharp$; (vi) $f^{\sharp\uparrow} = f^\sharp$; (vii) $f^{\downarrow\sharp} = f^\sharp$; (viii) $f^{\uparrow\sharp} = f^\sharp$; (ix) $f^{\sharp\sharp} = f^\sharp$; (x) $f \nearrow (g \cup h) = (f \nearrow g) \cap (f \nearrow h)$; (xi) $f \searrow (g \cup h) = (f \searrow g) \cap (f \searrow h)$; (xii) $f \searrow (g \cup h) = (f \searrow g) \searrow h$; (xiii) $f \nearrow g^\uparrow = f \nearrow g$; (xiv) $f \searrow g^\uparrow = f \searrow g$; (xv) $(f \sqcup g)^\sharp = (f^\sharp \sqcup g^\sharp)^\downarrow$; (xvi) $(f \cup g)^\sharp = (f^\sharp \sqcup g^\sharp)^\downarrow$.

e) Suppose $g = \bigcup_{u-v} (e_u \sqcup e_v)$ is the family of all edges in a graph, and let f be the family of all the independent sets. Using the operations of extended family algebra, find simple formulas that express (i) f in terms of g; (ii) g in terms of f.

237. [*25*] Implement the five operations of exercise 236, in the style of exercise 205.

▶ **238.** [*22*] Use ZDDs to compute the *maximal induced bipartite subgraphs* of the contiguous-USA graph G in (18), namely the maximal subsets U such that $G \mid U$ has no cycles of odd length. How many such sets U exist? Give examples of the smallest and largest. Consider also the maximal induced *tripartite* (3-colorable) subgraphs.

▶ **239.** [*21*] Explain how to compute the *maximal cliques* of a graph G using family algebra, when G is specified by its edges g as in exercise 236(e). Find the maximal sets of vertices that can be covered by k cliques, for $k = 1, 2, \ldots$, when G is the graph (18).

▶ **240.** [*22*] A set of vertices U is called a *dominating set* of a graph if every vertex is at most one step away from U.
    a) Prove that every kernel of a graph is a minimal dominating set.
    b) How many minimal dominating sets does the USA graph (18) have?
    c) Find seven vertices of (18) that dominate 36 of the others.

▶ **241.** [*28*] The *queen graph* Q_8 consists of the 64 squares of a chessboard, with $u \mathrel{\text{---}} v$ when squares u and v lie in the same row, column, or diagonal. How large are the ZDDs for its (a) kernels? (b) maximal cliques? (c) minimal dominating sets? (d) minimal dominating sets that are also cliques? (e) maximal induced bipartite subgraphs?
    Illustrate each of these five categories by exhibiting smallest and largest examples.

242. [*24*] Find all of the maximal ways to choose points on an 8×8 grid so that no three points lie on a straight line of any slope.

243. [*M23*] The *closure* $f^\cap$ of a family f of sets is the family of all sets that can be obtained by intersecting one or more members of f.
    a) Prove that $f^\cap = \{\alpha \mid \alpha = \bigcap\{\beta \mid \beta \in f \text{ and } \beta \supseteq \alpha\}\}$.
    b) What's a good way to compute the ZDD for $f^\cap$, given the ZDD for f?
    c) Find the generating function for $F^\cap$ when $F = \texttt{WORDS}(5757)$ as in exercise 222.

244. [*25*] What is the ZDD for the connectedness function of $P_3 \mathbin{\square} P_3$ (Fig. 22)? What is the BDD for the spanning tree function of the same graph? (See Corollary S.)

▶ **245.** [*M22*] Show that the *prime clauses* of a monotone function f are $\mathrm{PI}(f)^{\natural}$.

246. [*M21*] Prove Theorem S, assuming that (137) is true.

▶ **247.** [*M27*] Determine the number of sweet Boolean functions of n variables for $n \le 7$.

248. [*M22*] True or false: If f and g are sweet, so is $f(x_1, \ldots, x_n) \wedge g(x_1, \ldots, x_n)$.

249. [*HM31*] The connectedness function of a graph is "ultrasweet," in the sense that it is sweet under all permutations of its variables. Is there a nice way to characterize ultrasweet Boolean functions?

250. [*28*] There are 7581 monotone Boolean functions $f(x_1, x_2, x_3, x_4, x_5)$. What are the average values of $B(f)$ and $Z(\mathrm{PI}(f))$ when one of them is chosen at random? What is the probability that $Z(\mathrm{PI}(f)) > B(f)$? What is the maximum of $Z(\mathrm{PI}(f))/B(f)$?

251. [*M46*] Is $Z(\mathrm{PI}(f)) = O(B(f))$ for all monotone Boolean functions f?

252. [*M30*] When a Boolean function isn't monotone, its prime implicants involve negative literals; for example, the prime implicants of $(x_1? \, x_2 : x_3)$ are $x_1 \wedge x_2$, $\bar{x}_1 \wedge x_3$, and $x_2 \wedge x_3$. In such cases we can conveniently represent them with ZDDs if we consider them to be words in the $2n$-letter alphabet $\{e_1, e_1', \ldots, e_n, e_n'\}$. A "subcube" such as $01{*}0{*}$ is then $e_1' \sqcup e_2 \sqcup e_4'$ in family algebra (see 7.1.1–(29)); and $\mathrm{PI}(x_1? \, x_2 : x_3) = (e_1 \sqcup e_2) \cup (e_1' \sqcup e_3) \cup (e_2 \sqcup e_3)$.

Exercise 7.1.1–116 shows that symmetric functions of n variables might have $\Omega(3^n/n)$ prime implicants. How large can $Z(\mathrm{PI}(f))$ be when f is symmetric?

▶ **253.** [*M26*] Continuing exercise 252, prove that if $f = (\bar{x}_1 \wedge f_0) \vee (x_1 \wedge f_1)$ we have $\mathrm{PI}(f) = A \cup (e'_1 \sqcup B) \cup (e_1 \sqcup C)$, where $A = \mathrm{PI}(f_0 \wedge f_1)$, $B = \mathrm{PI}(f_0) \setminus A$, and $C = \mathrm{PI}(f_1) \setminus A$. (Equation (137) is the special case when f is monotone.)

▶ **254.** [*M23*] Let the functions f and g of (52) be monotone, with $f \subseteq g$. Prove that

$$\mathrm{PI}(g) \setminus \mathrm{PI}(f) = (\mathrm{PI}(g_l) \setminus \mathrm{PI}(f_l)) \cup (\mathrm{PI}(g_h) \setminus \mathrm{PI}(f_h \cup g_l)).$$

▶ **255.** [*25*] A *multifamily* of sets, in which members of f are allowed to occur more than once, can be represented as a sequence of ZDDs $(f_0, f_1, f_2, \dots)$ in which f_k is the family of sets that occur $(\dots a_2 a_1 a_0)_2$ times in f where $a_k = 1$. For example, if α appears exactly $9 = (1001)_2$ times in the multifamily, α would be in f_3 and f_0.

a) Explain how to insert and delete items from this representation of a multifamily.

b) Implement the multiset union $h = f \uplus g$ for multifamilies.

256. [*M32*] Any nonnegative integer x can be represented as a family of subsets of the binary powers $U = \{2^{2^k} \mid k \geq 0\} = \{2^1, 2^2, 2^4, 2^8, \dots\}$, in the following way: If $x = 2^{e_1} + \dots + 2^{e_t}$, where $e_1 > \dots > e_t \geq 0$ and $t \geq 0$, the corresponding family has t sets $E_j \subseteq U$, where $2^{e_j} = \prod\{u \mid u \in E_j\}$. Conversely, every finite family of finite subsets of U corresponds in this way to a nonnegative integer x. For example, the number $41 = 2^5 + 2^3 + 1$ corresponds to the family $\{\{2^1, 2^4\}, \{2^1, 2^2\}, \emptyset\}$.

a) Find a simple connection between the binary representation of x and the truth table of the Boolean function that corresponds to the family for x.

b) Let $Z(x)$ be the size of the ZDD for the family that represents x, when the elements of U are tested in reverse order $\dots, 2^4, 2^2, 2^1$ (with highest exponents nearest to the root); for example, $Z(41) = 5$. Show that $Z(x) = O(\log x/\log \log x)$.

c) The integer x is called "sparse" if $Z(x)$ is substantially smaller than the upper bound in (b). Prove that the sum of sparse integers is sparse, in the sense that $Z(x + y) = O(Z(x)Z(y))$.

d) Is the saturating difference of sparse integers, $x \dot{-} y$, always sparse?

e) Is the product of sparse integers always sparse?

257. [*40*] (S. Minato.) Explore the use of ZDDs to represent polynomials with nonnegative integer coefficients. *Hint:* Any such polynomial in x, y, and z can be regarded as a family of subsets of $\{2, 2^2, 2^4, \dots, x, x^2, x^4, \dots, y, y^2, y^4, \dots, z, z^2, z^4, \dots\}$; for example, $x^3 + 3xy + 2z$ corresponds naturally to the family $\{\{x, x^2\}, \{x, y\}, \{2, x, y\}, \{2, z\}\}$.

▶ **258.** [*25*] Given a positive integer n, what is the minimum size of a BDD that has exactly n solutions? Answer this question also for a ZDD of minimum size.

▶ **259.** [*25*] A sequence of *parentheses* can be encoded as a binary string by letting 0 represent '(' and 1 represent ')'. For example, ())(() is encoded as 011001.

Every forest of n nodes corresponds to a sequence of $2n$ parentheses that are properly *nested*, in the sense that left and right parentheses match in the normal way. (See, for example, 2.3.3–(1) or 7.2.1.6–(1).) Let

$$N_n(x_1, \dots, x_{2n}) = [x_1 \dots x_{2n} \text{ represents properly nested parentheses}].$$

For example, $N_3(0, 1, 1, 0, 0, 1) = 0$ and $N_3(0, 0, 1, 0, 1, 1) = 1$; in general, N_n has $C_n \approx 4^n/(\sqrt{\pi} n^{3/2})$ solutions, where C_n is a Catalan number. What are $B(N_n)$ and $Z(N_n)$?

▶ **260.** [*M27*] We will see in Section 7.2.1.5 that every partition of $\{1, \ldots, n\}$ into disjoint subsets corresponds to a "restricted growth string" $a_1 \ldots a_n$, which is a sequence of nonnegative integers with

$$a_1 = 0 \quad \text{and} \quad a_{j+1} \leq 1 + \max(a_1, \ldots, a_j) \text{ for } 1 \leq j < n.$$

Elements j and k belong to the same subset of the partition if and only if $a_j = a_k$.

a) Let $x_{j,k} = [a_j = k]$ for $0 \leq k < j \leq n$, and let R_n be the function of these $\binom{n+1}{2}$ variables that is true if and only if $a_1 \ldots a_n$ is a restricted growth string. (By studying this Boolean function we can study the family of all set partitions, and by placing further restrictions on R_n we can study set partitions with special properties. There are $\varpi_{100} \approx 5 \times 10^{115}$ set partitions when $n = 100$.) Calculate $B(R_{100})$ and $Z(R_{100})$. Approximately how large are $B(R_n)$ and $Z(R_n)$ as $n \to \infty$?

b) Show that, with a proper ordering of the variables $x_{j,k}$, the BDD base for $\{R_1, \ldots, R_n\}$ has the same number of nodes as the BDD for R_n alone.

c) We can also use fewer variables, approximately $n \lg n$ instead of $\binom{n+1}{2}$, if we represent each a_k as a binary integer with $\lceil \lg k \rceil$ bits. How large are the BDD and ZDD bases in *this* representation of set partitions?

261. [*HM21*] "The deterministic finite-state automaton with fewest states that accepts any given regular language is unique." What is the connection between this famous theorem of automata theory and the theory of binary decision diagrams?

262. [*M26*] The determination of optimum Boolean chains in Section 7.1.2 was greatly accelerated by restricting consideration to Boolean functions that are *normal*, in the sense that $f(0, \ldots, 0) = 0$. (See Eq. 7.1.2–(10).) Similarly, we could restrict BDDs so that each of their nodes denotes a normal function.

a) Explain how to do this by introducing "complement links," which point to the complement of a subfunction instead of to the subfunction itself.

b) Show that every Boolean function has a unique normalized BDD.

c) Draw the normalized BDDs for the 16 functions in exercise 1.

d) Let $B^0(f)$ be the size of the normalized BDD for f. Find the average and worst case of $B^0(f)$, and compare $B^0(f)$ to $B(f)$. (See (80) and Theorem U.)

e) The BDD base for 3×3 multiplication in (58) has $B(F_1, \ldots, F_6) = 52$ nodes. What is $B^0(F_1, \ldots, F_6)$?

f) How do (54) and (55) change, when AND is implemented with complement links?

263. [*HM25*] A *linear block code* is the set of binary column vectors $x = (x_1, \ldots, x_n)^T$ such that $Hx = 0$, where H is a given $m \times n$ "parity check matrix."

a) The linear block code with $n = 2^m - 1$, whose columns are the nonzero binary m-tuples from $(0, \ldots, 0, 1)^T$ to $(1, \ldots, 1, 1)^T$, is called the *Hamming code*. Prove that the Hamming code is 1-error correcting in the sense of exercise 7–23.

b) Let $f(x) = [Hx = 0]$, where H is an $m \times n$ matrix with no all-zero columns. Show that the BDD profile of f has a simple relation to the ranks of submatrices of H mod 2, and compute $B(f)$ for the Hamming code.

c) In general we can let $f(x) = [x$ is a codeword$]$ define *any* block code. Suppose some codeword $x = x_1 \ldots x_n$ has been transmitted through a possibly noisy channel, and that we've received the bits $y = y_1 \ldots y_n$, where the channel delivers $y_k = x_k$ with probability p_k for each k independently. Explain how to determine the most likely codeword x, given y, p_1, $\ldots$, p_n, and the BDD for f.

264. [*M46*] The text's "sweeping generalization" of Algorithms B and C, based on (22), embraces many important applications; but it does not appear to include quantities such as

$$\max_{f(x)=1} \left(\sum_{k=1}^{n} w_k x_k + \sum_{k=1}^{n-1} w_k' x_k x_{k+1} \right) \qquad \text{or} \qquad \max_{f(x)=1} \sum_{j=0}^{n-1} \left(w_j \sum_{k=1}^{n-j} x_k \dots x_{k+j} \right),$$

which also can be computed efficiently from the BDD or ZDD for f.

Develop a generalization that is even more sweeping.

▶ **265.** [*21*] Devise an algorithm that finds the mth smallest solution to $f(x) = 1$ in lexicographic order of $x_1 \dots x_n$, given m and the BDD for a Boolean function f of n variables. Your algorithm should take $O(nB(f) + n^2)$ steps.

▶ **266.** [*20*] Every forest F whose nodes are numbered $\{1, \dots, n\}$ in preorder defines two families of sets

$$a(F) = \{\text{anc}(1), \dots, \text{anc}(n)\} \quad \text{and} \quad d(F) = \{\text{dec}(1), \dots, \text{dec}(n)\},$$

where $\text{anc}(k)$ and $\text{dec}(k)$ are the inclusive ancestors and descendants of node k. For example, if F is

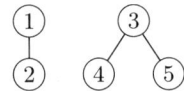

then $a(F) = \{\{1\}, \{1,2\}, \{3\}, \{3,4\}, \{3,5\}\}$ and $d(F) = \{\{1,2\}, \{2\}, \{3,4,5\}, \{4\}, \{5\}\}$. Conversely, F can be reconstructed from either $a(F)$ or $d(F)$.

Prove that the ZDD for the family $a(F)$ has exactly $n + 2$ nodes.

267. [*HM32*] Continuing exercise 266, find the minimum, maximum, and average size of the ZDD for the family $d(F)$, as F ranges over all forests on n nodes.

We dare not lengthen this book much more,
lest it be out of due proportion,
and repel men by its size.
— ÆLFRIC, *Catholic Homilies II* (c. 1000)

There are a thousand hacking at the branches of evil
to one who is striking at the root.
— HENRY D. THOREAU, *Walden; or, Life in the Woods* (1854)

7.2. GENERATING ALL POSSIBILITIES

> *All present or accounted for, sir.*
> — Traditional American military saying

> *All present and correct, sir.*
> — Traditional British military saying

7.2.1. Generating Basic Combinatorial Patterns

OUR GOAL in this section is to study methods for running through all of the possibilities in some combinatorial universe, because we often face problems in which an exhaustive examination of all cases is necessary or desirable. For example, we might want to look at all permutations of a given set.

Some authors call this the task of *enumerating* all of the possibilities; but that's not quite the right word, because "enumeration" most often means that we merely want to *count* the total number of cases, not that we actually want to look at them all. If somebody asks you to enumerate the permutations of $\{1, 2, 3\}$, you are quite justified in replying that the answer is $3! = 6$; you needn't give the more complete answer $\{123, 132, 213, 231, 312, 321\}$.

Other authors speak of *listing* all the possibilities; but that's not such a great word either. No sensible person would want to make a list of the $10! = 3,628,800$ permutations of $\{0, 1, 2, 3, 4, 5, 6, 7, 8, 9\}$ by printing them out on thousands of sheets of paper, nor even by writing them all in a computer file. All we really want is to have them present momentarily in some data structure, so that a program can examine each permutation one at a time.

So we will speak of *generating* all of the combinatorial objects that we need, and *visiting* each object in turn. Just as we studied algorithms for tree traversal in Section 2.3.1, where the goal was to visit every node of a tree, we turn now to algorithms that systematically traverse a combinatorial space of possibilities.

> *He's got 'em on the list —*
> *he's got 'em on the list;*
> *And they'll none of 'em be missed —*
> *they'll none of 'em be missed.*
> — WILLIAM S. GILBERT, *The Mikado* (1885)

7.2.1.1. Generating all n-tuples. Let's start small, by considering how to run through all 2^n strings that consist of n binary digits. Equivalently, we want to visit all n-tuples $(a_1, \ldots, a_n)$ where each a_j is either 0 or 1. This task is also, in essence, equivalent to examining all subsets of a given set $\{x_1, \ldots, x_n\}$, because we can say that x_j is in the subset if and only if $a_j = 1$.

Of course such a problem has an absurdly simple solution. All we need to do is start with the binary number $(0 \ldots 00)_2 = 0$ and repeatedly add 1 until we reach $(1 \ldots 11)_2 = 2^n - 1$. We will see, however, that even this utterly trivial problem has astonishing points of interest when we look into it more deeply. And our study of n-tuples will pay off later when we turn to the generation of more difficult kinds of patterns.

In the first place, we can see that the binary-notation trick extends to other kinds of n-tuples. If we want, for example, to generate all $(a_1, \ldots, a_n)$ in which each a_j is one of the decimal digits $\{0, 1, 2, 3, 4, 5, 6, 7, 8, 9\}$, we can simply count from $(0 \ldots 00)_{10} = 0$ to $(9 \ldots 99)_{10} = 10^n - 1$ in the decimal number system. And if we want more generally to run through all cases in which

$$0 \le a_j < m_j \qquad \text{for } 1 \le j \le n, \tag{1}$$

where the upper limits m_j might be different in different components of the vector $(a_1, \ldots, a_n)$, the task is essentially the same as repeatedly adding unity to the number

$$\begin{bmatrix} a_1, & a_2, & \ldots, & a_n \\ m_1, & m_2, & \ldots, & m_n \end{bmatrix} \tag{2}$$

in a mixed-radix number system; see Eq. 4.1–(9) and exercise 4.3.1–9.

We might as well pause to describe the process more formally:

Algorithm M (*Mixed-radix generation*). This algorithm visits all n-tuples that satisfy (1), by repeatedly adding 1 to the mixed-radix number in (2) until overflow occurs. Auxiliary variables a_0 and m_0 are introduced for convenience.

M1. [Initialize.] Set $a_j \leftarrow 0$ for $0 \le j \le n$, and set $m_0 \leftarrow 2$.

M2. [Visit.] Visit the n-tuple $(a_1, \ldots, a_n)$. (The program that wants to examine all n-tuples now does its thing.)

M3. [Prepare to add one.] Set $j \leftarrow n$.

M4. [Carry if necessary.] If $a_j = m_j - 1$, set $a_j \leftarrow 0$, $j \leftarrow j - 1$, and repeat this step.

M5. [Increase, unless done.] If $j = 0$, terminate the algorithm. Otherwise set $a_j \leftarrow a_j + 1$ and go back to step M2. ▮

Algorithm M is simple and straightforward, but we shouldn't forget that nested loops are even simpler, when n is a fairly small constant. When $n = 4$, we could for example write out the following instructions:

> For $a_1 = 0, 1, \ldots, m_1 - 1$ (in this order) do the following:
> > For $a_2 = 0, 1, \ldots, m_2 - 1$ (in this order) do the following:
> > > For $a_3 = 0, 1, \ldots, m_3 - 1$ (in this order) do the following: $\qquad$ (3)
> > > > For $a_4 = 0, 1, \ldots, m_4 - 1$ (in this order) do the following:
> > > > > Visit (a_1, a_2, a_3, a_4).

These instructions are equivalent to Algorithm M, and they are easily expressed in any programming language.

Gray binary code. Algorithm M runs through all $(a_1, \ldots, a_n)$ in lexicographic order, as in a dictionary. But there are many situations in which we prefer to visit those n-tuples in some other order. The most famous alternative arrangement is the so-called Gray binary code, which lists all 2^n strings of n bits in such a way

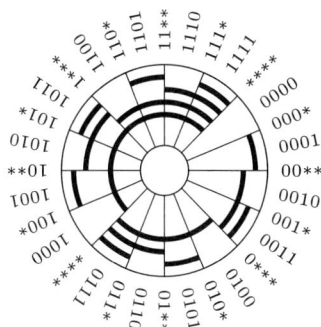 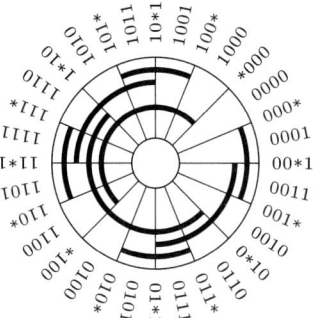

Fig. 30. (a) Lexicographic binary code.   (b) Gray binary code.

that only one bit changes each time, in a simple and regular way. For example, the Gray binary code for $n = 4$ is

$$0000, 0001, 0011, 0010, 0110, 0111, 0101, 0100,$$

$$1100, 1101, 1111, 1110, 1010, 1011, 1001, 1000. \qquad (4)$$

Such codes are especially important in applications where analog information is being converted to digital or vice versa. For example, suppose we want to identify our current position on a rotating disk that has been divided into 16 sectors, using four sensors that each distinguish black from white. If we use lexicographic order to mark the tracks from 0000 to 1111, as in Fig. 30(a), wildly inaccurate measurements can occur at the boundaries between sectors; but the code in Fig. 30(b) never gives a bad reading.

Gray binary code can be defined in many equivalent ways. For example, if Γ_n stands for the Gray binary sequence of n-bit strings, we can define Γ_n recursively by the two rules

$$\Gamma_0 = \epsilon;$$
$$\Gamma_{n+1} = 0\Gamma_n, \; 1\Gamma_n^R. \qquad (5)$$

Here ϵ denotes the empty string, $0\Gamma_n$ denotes the sequence Γ_n with 0 prefixed to each string, and $1\Gamma_n^R$ denotes the sequence Γ_n in *reverse order* with 1 prefixed to each string. Since the last string of Γ_n equals the first string of Γ_n^R, it is clear from (5) that exactly one bit changes in every step of Γ_{n+1} if Γ_n enjoys the same property.

Another way to define the sequence $\Gamma_n = g(0), g(1), \ldots, g(2^n - 1)$ is to give an explicit formula for its individual elements $g(k)$. Indeed, since Γ_{n+1} begins with $0\Gamma_n$, the infinite sequence

$$\Gamma_\infty = g(0), g(1), g(2), g(3), g(4), \ldots$$
$$= (0)_2, (1)_2, (11)_2, (10)_2, (110)_2, \ldots \qquad (6)$$

is a permutation of all the nonnegative integers, if we regard each string of 0s and 1s as a binary integer with optional leading 0s. Then Γ_n consists of the first 2^n elements of (6), converted to n-bit strings by inserting 0s at the left if needed.

When $k = 2^n + r$, where $0 \le r < 2^n$, relation (5) tells us that $g(k)$ is equal to $2^n + g(2^n - 1 - r)$. Therefore we can prove by induction on n that the integer k whose binary representation is $(\ldots b_2 b_1 b_0)_2$ has a Gray binary equivalent $g(k)$ with the representation $(\ldots a_2 a_1 a_0)_2$, where

$$a_j = b_j \oplus b_{j+1}, \qquad \text{for } j \ge 0. \tag{7}$$

(See exercise 6.) For example, $g((111001000011)_2) = (100101100010)_2$. Conversely, if $g(k) = (\ldots a_2 a_1 a_0)_2$ is given, we can find $k = (\ldots b_2 b_1 b_0)_2$ by inverting the system of equations (7), obtaining

$$b_j = a_j \oplus a_{j+1} \oplus a_{j+2} \oplus \cdots, \qquad \text{for } j \ge 0; \tag{8}$$

this infinite sum is really finite because $a_{j+t} = 0$ for all large t.

One of the many pleasant consequences of Eq. (7) is that $g(k)$ can be computed very easily with bitwise arithmetic:

$$g(k) = k \oplus \lfloor k/2 \rfloor. \tag{9}$$

Similarly, the inverse function in (8) satisfies

$$g^{[-1]}(l) = l \oplus \lfloor l/2 \rfloor \oplus \lfloor l/4 \rfloor \oplus \cdots; \tag{10}$$

this function, however, requires more computation (see exercise 7.1.3–117). We can also deduce from (7) that, if k and k' are any nonnegative integers,

$$g(k \oplus k') = g(k) \oplus g(k'). \tag{11}$$

Yet another consequence is that the $(n+1)$-bit Gray binary code can be written

$$\Gamma_{n+1} = 0\Gamma_n, (0\Gamma_n)\oplus110\ldots0;$$

this pattern is evident, for example, in (4). Comparing with (5), we see that reversing the order of Gray binary code is equivalent to complementing the first bit:

$$\Gamma_n^R = \Gamma_n \oplus 1\overbrace{0\ldots0}^{n-1}, \text{ also written } \Gamma_n \oplus 10^{n-1}. \tag{12}$$

The exercises below show that the function $g(k)$ defined in (7), and its inverse $g^{[-1]}$ defined in (8), have many further properties and applications of interest. Sometimes we think of these as functions taking binary strings to binary strings; at other times we regard them as functions from integers to integers, via binary notation, with leading zeros irrelevant.

Gray binary code is named after Frank Gray, a physicist who became famous for helping to devise the method long used for compatible color television broadcasting [*Bell System Tech. J.* **13** (1934), 464–515]. He invented Γ_n for applications to pulse code modulation, a method for analog transmission of digital signals [see *Bell System Tech. J.* **30** (1951), 38–40; *U.S. Patent 2632058* (17 March 1953); W. R. Bennett, *Introduction to Signal Transmission* (1971), 238–240]. But the idea of "Gray binary code" was known long before he worked on it; for example, it appeared in *U.S. Patent 2307868* by George Stibitz (12 January 1943). More significantly, Γ_5 was used in a telegraph machine demonstrated in 1878 by Émile Baudot, after whom the term "baud" was later named. At about the same time, a similar but less systematic code for telegraphy was independently devised by Otto Schäffler [see *Journal Télégraphique* **4** (1878), 252–253; *Annales Télégraphiques* **6** (1879), 361, 382–383].*

In fact, Gray binary code is implicitly present in a classic toy that has fascinated people for centuries, now generally known as the "Chinese ring puzzle" in English, although Englishmen used to call it the "tiring irons." Figure 31 shows a seven-ring example. The challenge is to remove the rings from the bar, and the rings are interlocked in such a way that only two basic types of move are possible (although this may not be immediately apparent from the illustration):

a) The rightmost ring can be removed or replaced at any time;
b) Any other ring can be removed or replaced if and only if the ring to its right is on the bar and all rings to the right of that one are off.

We can represent the current state of the puzzle in binary notation, writing 1 if a ring is on the bar and 0 if it is off; thus Fig. 31 shows the rings in state 1011000. (The second ring from the left is encoded as 0, because it lies entirely above the bar.)

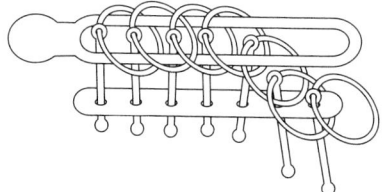

Fig. 31.
The Chinese ring puzzle.

A French magistrate named Louis Gros demonstrated an explicit connection between Chinese rings and binary numbers, in a booklet called *Théorie du Baguenodier* [sic] (Lyon: Aimé Vingtrinier, 1872) that was published anonymously. If the rings are in state $a_{n-1} \ldots a_0$, and if we define the binary number $k = (b_{n-1} \ldots b_0)_2$ by Eq. (8), he showed that exactly k more steps are necessary and sufficient to solve the puzzle. Thus Gros is the true inventor of Gray binary code.

> *Certainly no home should be without*
> *this fascinating, historic, and instructive puzzle.*
> — HENRY E. DUDENEY (1901)

When the rings are in any state other than $00\ldots0$ or $10\ldots0$, exactly two moves are possible, one of type (a) and one of type (b). Only one of these moves advances toward the desired goal; the other is a step backward that will need to be undone. A type (a) move changes k to $k \oplus 1$; thus we want to do it when k is odd, since this will decrease k. A type (b) move from a position that ends in $(10^{j-1})_2$ for $1 \le j < n$ changes k to $k \oplus (1^{j+1})_2 = k \oplus (2^{j+1} - 1)$. [In this formula '$1^{j+1}$' stands for $j+1$ repetitions of '1', but '2^{j+1}' denotes a power of 2.] When

---

* Some authors have asserted that Gray code was invented by Elisha Gray, who developed a printing telegraph machine at the same time as Baudot and Schäffler. Such claims are untrue, although Elisha did get a raw deal with respect to priority for inventing the telephone [see L. W. Taylor, *Amer. Physics Teacher* **5** (1937), 243–251].

k is even, we want $k \oplus (2^{j+1} - 1)$ to equal $k - 1$, which means that k must be a multiple of 2^j but not a multiple of 2^{j+1}; in other words,

$$j = \rho(k), \tag{13}$$

where ρ is the "ruler function" of Eq. 7.1.3–(44). Therefore the rings follow a nice pattern when the puzzle is solved properly: If we number them $0, 1, \ldots, n-1$ (starting at the free end), the sequence of ring moves on or off the bar is the sequence of numbers that ends with $\ldots, \rho(4), \rho(3), \rho(2), \rho(1)$.

Going backwards, starting with $00\ldots0$ and successively putting rings on or off until we reach the ultimate state $10\ldots0$ (which, as John Wallis observed in 1693, is more difficult to reach than the supposedly harder state $11\ldots1$), yields an algorithm for counting in Gray binary code:

Algorithm G (*Gray binary generation*). This algorithm visits all binary n-tuples $(a_{n-1}, \ldots, a_1, a_0)$ by starting with $(0, \ldots, 0, 0)$ and changing only one bit at a time, also maintaining a parity bit a_∞ such that

$$a_\infty = a_{n-1} \oplus \cdots \oplus a_1 \oplus a_0. \tag{14}$$

It successively complements bits $\rho(1), \rho(2), \rho(3), \ldots, \rho(2^n - 1)$ and then stops.

G1. [Initialize.] Set $a_j \leftarrow 0$ for $0 \le j < n$; also set $a_\infty \leftarrow 0$.

G2. [Visit.] Visit the n-tuple $(a_{n-1}, \ldots, a_1, a_0)$.

G3. [Change parity.] Set $a_\infty \leftarrow 1 - a_\infty$.

G4. [Choose j.] If $a_\infty = 1$, set $j \leftarrow 0$. Otherwise let $j \ge 1$ be minimum such that $a_{j-1} = 1$. (After the kth time we have performed this step, $j = \rho(k)$.)

G5. [Complement coordinate j.] Terminate if $j = n$; otherwise set $a_j \leftarrow 1 - a_j$ and return to G2. ▮

The parity bit a_∞ comes in handy if we are computing a sum like

$$X_{000} - X_{001} - X_{010} + X_{011} - X_{100} + X_{101} + X_{110} - X_{111}$$

or

$$X_\emptyset - X_a - X_b + X_{ab} - X_c + X_{ac} + X_{bc} - X_{abc},$$

where the sign depends on the parity of a binary string or the number of elements in a subset. Such sums arise frequently in "inclusion-exclusion" formulas such as Eq. 1.3.3–(29). The parity bit is also necessary, for efficiency: Without it we could not easily choose between the two ways of determining j, which correspond to performing a type (a) or type (b) move in the Chinese ring puzzle. But the most important feature of Algorithm G is that step G5 makes only a single coordinate change. Therefore only a simple change is usually needed to the terms X that we are summing, or to whatever other structures we are concerned with as we visit each n-tuple.

> It is impossible, of course, to remove all ambiguity in the lowest-order digit
> except by a scheme like one the Irish railways are said to have used
> of removing the last car of every train
> because it is too susceptible to collision damage.
> — G. R. STIBITZ and J. A. LARRIVEE, *Mathematics and Computers* (1957)

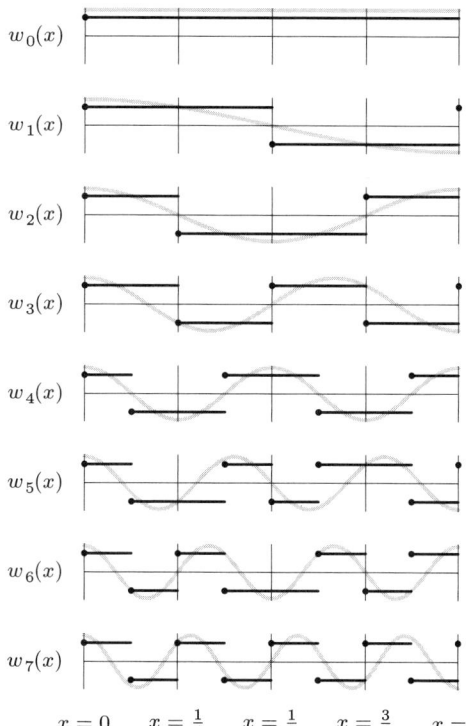

Fig. 32. Walsh functions $w_k(x)$ for $0 \le k < 8$, with the analogous trigonometric functions $\sqrt{2}\cos k\pi x$ shown in gray for comparison.

Another key property of Gray binary code was discovered by J. L. Walsh in connection with an important sequence of functions now known as *Walsh functions* [see *Amer. J. Math.* **45** (1923), 5–24]. Let $w_0(x) = 1$ for all real numbers x, and

$$w_k(x) = (-1)^{\lfloor 2x \rfloor \lceil k/2 \rceil} w_{\lfloor k/2 \rfloor}(2x), \qquad \text{for } k > 0. \tag{15}$$

For example, $w_1(x) = (-1)^{\lfloor 2x \rfloor}$ changes sign whenever x is an integer or an integer plus $\frac{1}{2}$. It follows that $w_k(x) = w_k(x+1)$ for all k, and that $w_k(x) = \pm 1$ for all x. More significantly, $w_k(0) = 1$ and $w_k(x)$ has *exactly* k *sign changes in the interval* $(0 \mathinner{\ldotp\ldotp} 1)$, so that it approaches $(-1)^k$ as x approaches 1 from the left. Therefore $w_k(x)$ behaves rather like a trigonometric function $\cos k\pi x$ or $\sin k\pi x$, and we can represent other functions as a linear combination of Walsh functions in much the same way as they are traditionally represented as Fourier series. This fact, together with the simple discrete nature of $w_k(x)$, makes Walsh functions extremely useful in computer calculations related to information transmission, image processing, and many other applications.

Figure 32 shows the first eight Walsh functions together with their trigonometric cousins. Engineers commonly call $w_k(x)$ the Walsh function of *sequency* k, by analogy with the fact that $\cos k\pi x$ and $\sin k\pi x$ have *frequency* $k/2$. [See, for example, the book *Sequency Theory: Foundations and Applications* (New York: Academic Press, 1977), by H. F. Harmuth.]

Although Eq. (15) may look formidable at first glance, it actually provides an easy way to see by induction why $w_k(x)$ has exactly k sign changes as claimed. If k is even, say $k = 2l$, we have $w_{2l}(x) = w_l(2x)$ for $0 \le x < \frac{1}{2}$; the effect is simply to compress the function $w_l(x)$ into half the space, so $w_{2l}(x)$ has accumulated l sign changes so far. Then $w_{2l}(x) = (-1)^l w_l(2x) = (-1)^l w_l(2x - 1)$ in the range $\frac{1}{2} \le x < 1$; this concatenates another copy of $w_l(2x)$, flipping the sign if necessary to avoid a sign change at $x = \frac{1}{2}$. The function $w_{2l+1}(x)$ is similar, but it *forces* a sign change when $x = \frac{1}{2}$.

What does this have to do with Gray binary code? Walsh discovered that his functions could all be expressed neatly in terms of simpler functions called *Rademacher functions* [Hans Rademacher, *Math. Annalen* **87** (1922), 112–138],

$$r_k(x) = (-1)^{\lfloor 2^k x \rfloor}, \tag{16}$$

which take the value $(-1)^{c-k}$ when $(\ldots c_2 c_1 c_0 . c_{-1} c_{-2} \ldots)_2$ is the binary representation of x. Indeed, we have $w_1(x) = r_1(x)$, $w_2(x) = r_1(x) r_2(x)$, $w_3(x) = r_2(x)$, and in general

$$w_k(x) = \prod_{j \ge 0} r_{j+1}(x)^{b_j \oplus b_{j+1}} \qquad \text{when } k = (\ldots b_2 b_1 b_0)_2. \tag{17}$$

(See exercise 33.) Thus the exponent of $r_{j+1}(x)$ in $w_k(x)$ is the jth bit of the Gray binary number $g(k)$, according to (7), and we have

$$w_k(x) = r_{\rho(k)+1}(x) w_{k-1}(x), \qquad \text{for } k > 0. \tag{18}$$

Equation (17) implies the handy formula

$$w_k(x) w_{k'}(x) = w_{k \oplus k'}(x), \tag{19}$$

which is much simpler than the corresponding product formulas for sines and cosines. This identity follows easily because $r_j(x)^2 = 1$ for all j and x, hence $r_j(x)^{a \oplus b} = r_j(x)^{a+b}$. It implies in particular that $w_k(x)$ is *orthogonal* to $w_{k'}(x)$ when $k \ne k'$, in the sense that the average value of $w_k(x) w_{k'}(x)$ is zero. We also can use (17) to define $w_k(x)$ for fractional values of k like $1/2$ or $13/8$.

The *Walsh transform* of 2^n numbers $(X_0, \ldots, X_{2^n-1})$ is the vector defined by the equation $(x_0, \ldots, x_{2^n-1})^T = W_n (X_0, \ldots, X_{2^n-1})^T$, where W_n is the $2^n \times 2^n$ matrix having $w_j(k/2^n)$ in row j and column k, for $0 \le j, k < 2^n$. For example, Fig. 32 tells us that the Walsh transform when $n = 3$ is

$$
\begin{pmatrix} x_{000} \\ x_{001} \\ x_{010} \\ x_{011} \\ x_{100} \\ x_{101} \\ x_{110} \\ x_{111} \end{pmatrix}
=
\begin{pmatrix}
1 & 1 & 1 & 1 & 1 & 1 & 1 & 1 \\
1 & 1 & 1 & 1 & \bar{1} & \bar{1} & \bar{1} & \bar{1} \\
1 & 1 & \bar{1} & \bar{1} & \bar{1} & \bar{1} & 1 & 1 \\
1 & 1 & \bar{1} & \bar{1} & 1 & 1 & \bar{1} & \bar{1} \\
1 & \bar{1} & \bar{1} & 1 & 1 & \bar{1} & \bar{1} & 1 \\
1 & \bar{1} & \bar{1} & 1 & \bar{1} & 1 & 1 & \bar{1} \\
1 & \bar{1} & 1 & \bar{1} & \bar{1} & 1 & \bar{1} & 1 \\
1 & \bar{1} & 1 & \bar{1} & 1 & \bar{1} & 1 & \bar{1}
\end{pmatrix}
\begin{pmatrix} X_{000} \\ X_{001} \\ X_{010} \\ X_{011} \\ X_{100} \\ X_{101} \\ X_{110} \\ X_{111} \end{pmatrix}.
\tag{20}
$$

(Here $\bar{1}$ stands for -1, and the subscripts are conveniently regarded as binary strings 000–111 instead of as the integers 0–7.) The *Hadamard transform* is defined similarly, but with the matrix H_n in place of W_n, where H_n has $(-1)^{j \cdot k}$ in row j and column k; here '$j \cdot k$' denotes the dot product $a_{n-1}b_{n-1} + \cdots + a_0 b_0$ of the binary representations $j = (a_{n-1} \ldots a_0)_2$ and $k = (b_{n-1} \ldots b_0)_2$. For example, the Hadamard transform for $n = 3$ is

$$
\begin{pmatrix} x'_{000} \\ x'_{001} \\ x'_{010} \\ x'_{011} \\ x'_{100} \\ x'_{101} \\ x'_{110} \\ x'_{111} \end{pmatrix} = \begin{pmatrix} 1 & 1 & 1 & 1 & 1 & 1 & 1 & 1 \\ 1 & \bar{1} & 1 & \bar{1} & 1 & \bar{1} & 1 & \bar{1} \\ 1 & 1 & \bar{1} & \bar{1} & 1 & 1 & \bar{1} & \bar{1} \\ 1 & \bar{1} & \bar{1} & 1 & 1 & \bar{1} & \bar{1} & 1 \\ 1 & 1 & 1 & 1 & \bar{1} & \bar{1} & \bar{1} & \bar{1} \\ 1 & \bar{1} & 1 & \bar{1} & \bar{1} & 1 & \bar{1} & 1 \\ 1 & 1 & \bar{1} & \bar{1} & \bar{1} & \bar{1} & 1 & 1 \\ 1 & \bar{1} & \bar{1} & 1 & \bar{1} & 1 & 1 & \bar{1} \end{pmatrix} \begin{pmatrix} X_{000} \\ X_{001} \\ X_{010} \\ X_{011} \\ X_{100} \\ X_{101} \\ X_{110} \\ X_{111} \end{pmatrix}. \tag{21}
$$

This is the same as the discrete Fourier transform on an n-dimensional cube, Eq. 4.6.4–(38), and we can evaluate it quickly "in place" by adapting the method of Yates discussed in Section 4.6.4:

Given	First step	Second step	Third step
X_{000}	$X_{000}+X_{001}$	$X_{000}+X_{001}+X_{010}+X_{011}$	$X_{000}+X_{001}+X_{010}+X_{011}+X_{100}+X_{101}+X_{110}+X_{111}$
X_{001}	$X_{000}-X_{001}$	$X_{000}-X_{001}+X_{010}-X_{011}$	$X_{000}-X_{001}+X_{010}-X_{011}+X_{100}-X_{101}+X_{110}-X_{111}$
X_{010}	$X_{010}+X_{011}$	$X_{000}+X_{001}-X_{010}-X_{011}$	$X_{000}+X_{001}-X_{010}-X_{011}+X_{100}+X_{101}-X_{110}-X_{111}$
X_{011}	$X_{010}-X_{011}$	$X_{000}-X_{001}-X_{010}+X_{011}$	$X_{000}-X_{001}-X_{010}+X_{011}+X_{100}-X_{101}-X_{110}+X_{111}$
X_{100}	$X_{100}+X_{101}$	$X_{100}+X_{101}+X_{110}+X_{111}$	$X_{000}+X_{001}+X_{010}+X_{011}-X_{100}-X_{101}-X_{110}-X_{111}$
X_{101}	$X_{100}-X_{101}$	$X_{100}-X_{101}+X_{110}-X_{111}$	$X_{000}-X_{001}+X_{010}-X_{011}-X_{100}+X_{101}-X_{110}+X_{111}$
X_{110}	$X_{110}+X_{111}$	$X_{100}+X_{101}-X_{110}-X_{111}$	$X_{000}+X_{001}-X_{010}-X_{011}-X_{100}-X_{101}+X_{110}+X_{111}$
X_{111}	$X_{110}-X_{111}$	$X_{100}-X_{101}-X_{110}+X_{111}$	$X_{000}-X_{001}-X_{010}+X_{011}-X_{100}+X_{101}+X_{110}-X_{111}$

Notice that the rows of H_3 are a permutation of the rows of W_3. This is true in general, so we can obtain the Walsh transform by permuting the elements of the Hadamard transform. Exercise 36 discusses the details.

Going faster. When we're running through 2^n possibilities, we usually want to reduce the computation time as much as possible. Algorithm G needs to complement only one bit a_j per visit to $(a_{n-1}, \ldots, a_0)$, but it loops in step G4 while choosing an appropriate value of j. Another approach has been suggested by Gideon Ehrlich [*JACM* **20** (1973), 500–513], who introduced the notion of *loopless* combinatorial generation: With a loopless algorithm, the number of operations performed between successive visits is required to be bounded in advance, so there never is a long wait before a new pattern has been generated.

We learned some tricks in Section 7.1.3 about quick ways to determine the number of leading or trailing 0s in a binary number. Those methods could be used in step G4 to make Algorithm G loopless, assuming that n isn't unreasonably large. But Ehrlich's method is quite different, and much more versatile, so it provides us with a new weapon in our arsenal of techniques for efficient computation. Here is how his approach can be used to generate binary n-tuples [see Bitner, Ehrlich, and Reingold, *CACM* **19** (1976), 517–521]:

Algorithm L (*Loopless Gray binary generation*). This algorithm, like Algorithm G, visits all binary n-tuples $(a_{n-1}, \ldots, a_0)$ in the order of the Gray binary code. But instead of maintaining a parity bit, it uses an array of "focus pointers" $(f_n, \ldots, f_0)$, whose significance is discussed below.

L1. [Initialize.] Set $a_j \leftarrow 0$ and $f_j \leftarrow j$ for $0 \le j < n$; also set $f_n \leftarrow n$. (A loopless algorithm is allowed to have loops in its initialization step, as long as the initial setup is reasonably efficient; after all, every program needs to be loaded and launched.)

L2. [Visit.] Visit the n-tuple $(a_{n-1}, \ldots, a_1, a_0)$.

L3. [Choose j.] Set $j \leftarrow f_0$, $f_0 \leftarrow 0$. (If this is the kth time we are performing the present step, j is now equal to $\rho(k)$.) Terminate if $j = n$; otherwise set $f_j \leftarrow f_{j+1}$ and $f_{j+1} \leftarrow j + 1$.

L4. [Complement coordinate j.] Set $a_j \leftarrow 1 - a_j$ and return to L2. ∎

For example, the computation proceeds as follows when $n = 4$. Elements a_j have been underlined in this table if the corresponding bit b_j is 1 in the binary string $b_3 b_2 b_1 b_0$ such that $a_3 a_2 a_1 a_0 = g(b_3 b_2 b_1 b_0)$:

a_3	0	0	0	0	0	0	0	0	1	1	1	1	1	1	1	1
a_2	0	0	0	0	1	1	1	1	1	1	1	1	0	0	0	0
a_1	0	0	1	1	1	1	0	0	0	0	1	1	1	1	0	0
a_0	0	1	1	0	0	1	1	0	0	1	1	0	0	1	1	0
f_3	3	3	3	3	3	3	3	3	4	4	4	4	3	3	3	3
f_2	2	2	2	2	3	3	2	2	2	2	2	2	4	4	2	2
f_1	1	1	2	1	1	1	3	1	1	1	2	1	1	1	4	1
f_0	0	1	0	2	0	1	0	3	0	1	0	2	0	1	0	4

Although the binary number $k = (b_{n-1} \ldots b_0)_2$ never appears explicitly in Algorithm L, the focus pointers f_j represent it implicitly in a clever way, so that we can repeatedly form $g(k) = (a_{n-1} \ldots a_0)_2$ by complementing bit $a_{\rho(k)}$ as we should. Let's say that a_j is *passive* when it is underlined, *active* otherwise. Then the focus pointers satisfy the following invariant relations:

1) If a_j is passive and a_{j-1} is active, then f_j is the smallest index $j' > j$ such that $a_{j'}$ is active. (Bits a_n and a_{-1} are considered to be active for purposes of this rule, although they aren't really present in the algorithm.)
2) Otherwise $f_j = j$.

Thus, the rightmost element a_j of a block of passive elements $a_{i-1} \ldots a_{j+1} a_j$, with decreasing subscripts, has a focus f_j that points to the element a_i just to the left of that block. All other elements a_j have f_j pointing to themselves.

In these terms, the first two operations '$j \leftarrow f_0$, $f_0 \leftarrow 0$' in step L3 are equivalent to saying, "Set j to the index of the rightmost active element, and activate all elements to the right of a_j." Notice that if $f_0 = 0$, the operation $f_0 \leftarrow 0$ is redundant; but it doesn't do any harm. The other two operations of L3, '$f_j \leftarrow f_{j+1}$, $f_{j+1} \leftarrow j + 1$', are equivalent to saying, "Make a_j passive," because we know that a_j and a_{j-1} are both active at this point in the computation.

(Again the operation $f_{j+1} \leftarrow j + 1$ might be harmlessly redundant.) The net effect of activation and passivation is therefore equivalent to counting in binary notation, as in Algorithm M, with 1-bits passive and 0-bits active.

Algorithm L is almost blindingly fast, because it does only five assignment operations and one test for termination between each visit to a generated n-tuple. But we can do even better. In order to see how, let's consider an application to recreational linguistics: Rudolph Castown, in *Word Ways* **1** (1968), 165–169, noted that all 16 of the ways to intermix the letters of `sins` with the corresponding letters of `fate` produce words that are found in a sufficiently large dictionary of English: `sine`, `sits`, `site`, etc.; and all but three of those words (namely `fane`, `fite`, and `sats`) are sufficiently common as to be unquestionably part of standard English. Therefore it is natural to ask the analogous question for five-letter words: What two strings of five letters will produce the maximum number of words in the Stanford GraphBase, when letters in corresponding positions are swapped in all 32 possible ways?

To answer this question, we need not examine all $\binom{26}{2}^5 = 3{,}625{,}908{,}203{,}125$ essentially different pairs of strings; it suffices to look at all $\binom{5757}{2} = 16{,}568{,}646$ pairs of words in the GraphBase, provided that at least one of those pairs produces at least 17 words, because every set of 17 or more five-letter words obtainable from two five-letter strings must contain two that are "antipodal" (with no corresponding letters in common). For every antipodal pair, we want to determine as rapidly as possible whether the 32 possible subset-swaps produce a significant number of English words.

Every 5-letter word can be represented as a 25-bit number using 5 bits per letter, from `"a"` $= 00000$ to `"z"` $= 11001$. A table of 2^{25} bits or bytes will then determine quickly whether a given five-letter string is a word. So the problem is reduced to generating the bit patterns of the 32 potential words obtainable by mixing the letters of two given words, and looking those patterns up in the table. We can proceed as follows, for each pair of 25-bit words w and w':

W1. [Check the difference.] Set $z \leftarrow w \oplus w'$. Reject the word pair (w, w') if $m' \mathbin{\&} (z - m) \mathbin{\&} \bar{m} \neq 0$, where $m = 2^{20} + 2^{15} + 2^{10} + 2^5 + 1$ and $m' = 2^5 m$; this test eliminates cases where w and w' have a common letter in some position. (See 7.1.3–(90). It turns out that 10,614,085 of the 16,568,646 word pairs have no such common letters.)

W2. [Form individual masks.] Set $m_0 \leftarrow z \mathbin{\&} (2^5 - 1)$, $m_1 \leftarrow z \mathbin{\&} (2^{10} - 2^5)$, $m_2 \leftarrow z \mathbin{\&} (2^{15} - 2^{10})$, $m_3 \leftarrow z \mathbin{\&} (2^{20} - 2^{15})$, and $m_4 \leftarrow z \mathbin{\&} (2^{25} - 2^{20})$, in preparation for the next step.

W3. [Count words.] Set $l \leftarrow 1$ and $A_0 \leftarrow w$; the variable l will count how many words starting with w we have found so far. Then perform the operations $swap(4)$ defined below.

W4. [Print a record-setting solution.] If l exceeds or equals the current maximum, print A_j for $0 \leq j < l$. ∎

The heart of this high-speed method is the sequence of operations $swap(4)$, which should be expanded inline (for example with a macro-processor) to eliminate all unnecessary overhead. It is defined in terms of the basic operation

$sw(j)$: Set $w \leftarrow w \oplus m_j$. Then if w is a word, set $A_l \leftarrow w$ and $l \leftarrow l + 1$.

Given $sw(j)$, which flips the letters in position j, we define

$$\begin{aligned}
swap(0) &= sw(0); \\
swap(1) &= swap(0), sw(1), swap(0); \\
swap(2) &= swap(1), sw(2), swap(1); \\
swap(3) &= swap(2), sw(3), swap(2); \\
swap(4) &= swap(3), sw(4), swap(3).
\end{aligned}$$
(22)

Thus $swap(4)$ expands into a sequence of 31 steps $sw(0)$, $sw(1)$, $sw(0)$, $sw(2)$, $\ldots$, $sw(0) = sw(\rho(1))$, $sw(\rho(2))$, $\ldots$, $sw(\rho(31))$; these steps will be used 10 million times. We clearly gain speed by embedding the ruler function values $\rho(k)$ directly into our program, instead of recomputing them repeatedly for each word pair via Algorithm M, G, or L.

The winning pair of words generates a set of 21, namely

$$\begin{aligned}
&\texttt{ducks,\quad ducky,\quad duces,\quad dunes,\quad dunks,\quad dinks,\quad dinky,} \\
&\texttt{dines,\quad dices,\quad dicey,\quad dicky,\quad dicks,\quad picks,\quad picky,} \\
&\texttt{pines,\quad piney,\quad pinky,\quad pinks,\quad punks,\quad punky,\quad pucks.}
\end{aligned}$$
(23)

If, for example, $w = \texttt{ducks}$ and $w' = \texttt{piney}$, then $m_0 = \texttt{s} \oplus \texttt{y}$, so the first operation $sw(0)$ changes $\texttt{ducks}$ to $\texttt{ducky}$, which is seen to be a word. The next operation $sw(1)$ applies m_1, which is $\texttt{k} \oplus \texttt{e}$ in the next-to-last letter position, so it produces the nonword $\texttt{ducey}$. Another application of $sw(0)$ changes $\texttt{ducey}$ to $\texttt{duces}$ (a legal term generally followed by the word $\texttt{tecum}$). And so on. All word pairs can be processed by this method in at most a few seconds.

Further streamlining is also possible. For example, once we have found a pair that yields k words, we can reject later pairs as soon as they generate $33 - k$ nonwords. But the method we've discussed is already quite fast, and it demonstrates the fact that even the loopless Algorithm L can be beaten.

Fans of Algorithm L may, of course, complain that we have speeded up the process only in the small special case $n = 5$, while Algorithm L solves the generation problem for n in general. A similar idea does, however, work also for general values of $n > 5$: We can expand out a program so that it rapidly generates all 32 settings of the rightmost bits $a_4 a_3 a_2 a_1 a_0$, as above; then we can apply Algorithm L after every 32 steps, using it to generate successive changes to the other bits $a_{n-1} \ldots a_5$. This approach reduces the amount of unnecessary work done by Algorithm L by nearly a factor of 32.

Other binary Gray codes. The Gray binary code $g(0)$, $g(1)$, $\ldots$, $g(2^n - 1)$ is only one of many ways to traverse all possible n-bit strings while changing only a single bit at each step. Let us say that, in general, a "Gray cycle" on binary n-tuples is *any* sequence $(v_0, v_1, \ldots, v_{2^n-1})$ that includes every n-tuple and has the property that v_k differs from $v_{(k+1) \bmod 2^n}$ in just one bit position. Thus, in the terminology of graph theory, a Gray cycle is an oriented Hamiltonian

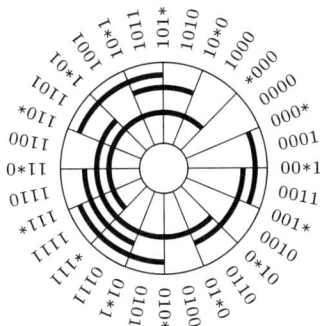

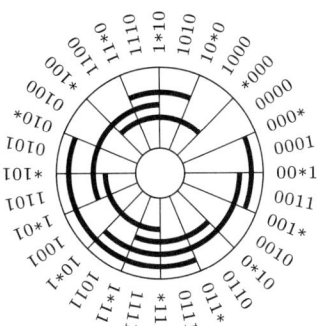

Fig. 33. (a) Complementary Gray code.   (b) Balanced Gray code.

cycle on the n-cube. We can assume that subscripts have been chosen so that $v_0 = 0 \ldots 0$.

If we think of the v's as binary numbers, there are integers $\delta_0 \ldots \delta_{2^n-1}$ such that

$$v_{(k+1) \bmod 2^n} = v_k \oplus 2^{\delta_k}, \qquad \text{for } 0 \le k < 2^n; \tag{24}$$

this so-called "delta sequence" is another way to describe a Gray cycle. For example, the delta sequence for standard Gray binary when $n = 3$ is 01020102; it is essentially the ruler function $\delta_k = \rho(k+1)$ of (13), but the final value δ_{2^n-1} is $n-1$ instead of n, so that the cycle closes. The individual elements δ_k always lie in the range $0 \le \delta_k < n$, and they are called "coordinates."

Let $d(n)$ be the number of different delta sequences that define an n-bit Gray cycle, and let $c(n)$ be the number of "canonical" delta sequences in which each coordinate k appears before the first appearance of $k+1$. Then $d(n) = n!\, c(n)$, because every permutation of the coordinate numbers in a delta sequence obviously produces another delta sequence. The only possible canonical delta sequences for $n \le 3$ are easily seen to be

$$00; \qquad 0101; \qquad 01020102 \quad \text{and} \quad 01210121. \tag{25}$$

Therefore $c(1) = c(2) = 1$, $c(3) = 2$; $d(1) = 1$, $d(2) = 2$, and $d(3) = 12$. A straightforward computer calculation, using techniques for the enumeration of Hamiltonian cycles that we will study later, establishes the next values,

$$\begin{aligned} c(4) &= 112; & d(4) &= 2688; \\ c(5) &= 15{,}109{,}096; & d(5) &= 1{,}813{,}091{,}520. \end{aligned} \tag{26}$$

No simple pattern is evident, and the numbers grow quite rapidly (see exercise 47); therefore it's a fairly safe bet that nobody will ever know the exact values of $c(8)$ and $d(8)$.

Since the number of possibilities is so huge, people have been encouraged to look for Gray cycles that have additional useful properties. For example, Fig. 33(a) shows a 4-bit Gray cycle in which every string $a_3a_2a_1a_0$ is diametrically opposite to its complement $\bar{a}_3\bar{a}_2\bar{a}_1\bar{a}_0$. Such coding schemes are possible whenever the number of bits is even (see exercise 49).

An even more interesting Gray cycle, found by G. C. Tootill [*Proc. IEE* **103**, Part B Supplement (1956), 435], is shown in Fig. 33(b). This one has the same number of changes in each of the four coordinate tracks, hence all coordinates share equally in the activities. Gray cycles that are balanced in a similar way can in fact be constructed for all larger values of n, by using the following versatile method to extend a cycle from n bits to $n + 2$ bits:

Theorem D. *Let* $\alpha_1 j_1 \alpha_2 j_2 \ldots \alpha_l j_l$ *be a delta sequence for an n-bit Gray cycle, where each j_k is a single coordinate, each α_k is a possibly empty sequence of coordinates, and l is odd. Then*

$$\alpha_1 (n+1) \alpha_1^R n \alpha_1$$
$$j_1 \alpha_2 n \alpha_2^R (n+1) \alpha_2 \ j_2 \alpha_3 (n+1) \alpha_3^R n \alpha_3 \ \ldots \ j_{l-1} \alpha_l (n+1) \alpha_l^R n \alpha_l \qquad (27)$$
$$(n+1) \alpha_l^R j_{l-1} \alpha_{l-1}^R \ldots \alpha_2^R j_1 \alpha_1^R n$$

is the delta sequence of an $(n + 2)$-bit Gray cycle.

For example, if we start with the sequence $01\underline{0}20\underline{1}0\underline{2}$ for $n = 3$ and let the three underlined elements be j_1, j_2, j_3, the new sequence (27) for a 5-bit cycle is

$$01410301020131024201043401020103. \qquad (28)$$

Proof. Let α_k have length m_k and let v_{kt} be the vertex reached if we start at $0 \ldots 0$ and apply the coordinate changes $\alpha_1 j_1 \ldots \alpha_{k-1} j_{k-1}$ and the first t of α_k. We need to prove that all vertices $00v_{kt}$, $01v_{kt}$, $10v_{kt}$, and $11v_{kt}$ occur when (27) is used, for $1 \le k \le l$ and $0 \le t \le m_k$. (The leftmost coordinate is $n+1$.)

Starting with $000 \ldots 0 = 00v_{10}$, we proceed to obtain the vertices

$$00v_{11}, \ldots, 00v_{1m_1}, \ 10v_{1m_1}, \ldots, 10v_{10}, 11v_{10}, \ldots, 11v_{1m_1};$$

then j_1 yields $11v_{20}$, which is followed by

$$11v_{21}, \ldots, 11v_{2m_2}, \ 10v_{2m_2}, \ldots, 10v_{20}, 00v_{20}, \ldots, 00v_{2m_2};$$

then comes $00v_{30}$, etc., and we eventually reach $11v_{lm_l}$. The glorious finale then uses the third line of (27) to generate all the missing vertices $01v_{lm_l}, \ldots, 01v_{10}$ and take us back to $000 \ldots 0$. $\blacksquare$

The *transition counts* $(c_0, \ldots, c_{n-1})$ of a delta sequence are defined by letting c_j be the number of times $\delta_k = j$. For example, (28) has transition counts $(12, 8, 4, 4, 4)$, and it arose from a sequence with transition counts $(4, 2, 2)$. If we choose the original delta sequence carefully and underline appropriate elements j_k, we can obtain transition counts that are as equal as possible:

Corollary B. *For all $n \ge 1$, there is an n-bit Gray cycle with transition counts $(c_0, c_1, \ldots, c_{n-1})$ that satisfy the condition*

$$|c_j - c_k| \ \le \ 2 \qquad \text{for } 0 \le j < k < n. \qquad (29)$$

(This is the best possible balance condition, because each c_j must be an even number, and we must have $c_0 + c_1 + \cdots + c_{n-1} = 2^n$. Indeed, condition (29) holds if and only if $n - r$ of the counts are equal to $2q$ and r are equal to $2q + 2$, where $q = \lfloor 2^{n-1}/n \rfloor$ and $r = 2^{n-1} \bmod n$.)

Proof. Given a delta sequence for an n-bit Gray cycle with transition counts $(c_0, \ldots, c_{n-1})$, the counts for cycle (27) are obtained by starting with the values $(c'_0, \ldots, c'_{n-1}, c'_n, c'_{n+1}) = (4c_0, \ldots, 4c_{n-1}, l+1, l+1)$, then subtracting 2 from c'_{j_k} for $1 \le k < l$ and subtracting 4 from c'_{j_l}. For example, when $n = 3$ we can obtain a balanced 5-bit Gray cycle having transition counts $(8 - 2, 16 - 10, 8, 6, 6) = (6, 6, 8, 6, 6)$ if we apply Theorem D to the delta sequence $\underline{01}\underline{2}\underline{10}\underline{1}\underline{21}$. Exercise 51 works out the details for other values of n. $\blacksquare$

Another important class of n-bit Gray cycles in which each of the coordinate tracks has equal responsibility arises when we consider *run lengths*, namely the distances between consecutive appearances of the same δ value. Standard Gray binary code has run length 2 in the least significant position, and this can lead to a loss of accuracy when precise measurements need to be made [see, for example, the discussion by G. M. Lawrence and W. E. McClintock, *Proc. SPIE* **2831** (1996), 104–111]. But all runs have length 4 or more in the remarkable 5-bit Gray cycle whose delta sequence is

$$(0123042103210423)^2. \tag{30}$$

Let $r(n)$ be the maximum value r such that an n-bit Gray cycle can be found in which all runs have length $\ge r$. Clearly $r(1) = 1$, and $r(2) = r(3) = r(4) = 2$; and it is easy to see that $r(n)$ must be less than n when $n > 2$, hence (30) proves that $r(5) = 4$. Exhaustive computer searches establish the values $r(6) = 4$ and $r(7) = 5$. Indeed, a fairly straightforward backtrack calculation for the case $n = 7$ needs a tree of only about 60 million nodes to determine that $r(7) < 6$, and exercise 61(a) constructs a 7-bit cycle with no run shorter than 5. The exact values of $r(n)$ are unknown for $n \ge 8$; but $r(10)$ is almost certainly 8, and interesting constructions are known by which we can prove that $r(n) = n - O(\log n)$ as $n \to \infty$. (See exercises 60–64.)

*Binary Gray paths. We have defined an n-bit Gray cycle as a way to arrange all binary n-tuples into a sequence $(v_0, v_1, \ldots, v_{2^n-1})$ with the property that v_k is adjacent to v_{k+1} in the n-cube for $0 \le k < 2^n - 1$, and such that v_{2^n-1} is also adjacent to v_0. The cyclic property is nice, but not always essential; sometimes we can do better without it. Therefore we say that an n-bit *Gray path*, also commonly called a *Gray code*, is any sequence that satisfies the conditions of a Gray cycle except that the last element need not be adjacent to the first. In other words, a Gray cycle is a Hamiltonian *cycle* on the vertices of the n-cube, but a Gray code is simply a Hamiltonian *path* on that graph.

The most important binary Gray paths that are not also Gray cycles are n-bit sequences $(v_0, v_1, \ldots, v_{2^n-1})$ that are *monotonic*, in the sense that

$$\nu(v_k) \le \nu(v_{k+2}) \qquad \text{for } 0 \le k < 2^n - 2. \tag{31}$$

(Here, as elsewhere, we use ν to denote the "weight" or the "sideways sum" of a binary string, namely the number of 1s that it has.) Trial and error shows that

Fig. 34. Examples of
8-bit Gray codes:

    a) standard;
    b) balanced;
    c) complementary;
    d) long-run;
    e) nonlocal;
    f) monotonic;
    g) trend-free.

(a)   (b)   (c)   (d)   (e)   (f)   (g)

there are essentially only two monotonic n-bit Gray codes for each $n \leq 4$, one starting with 0^n and the other starting with $0^{n-1}1$. The two for $n = 3$ are

$$000, 001, 011, 010, 110, 100, 101, 111; \qquad (32)$$

$$001, 000, 010, 110, 100, 101, 111, 011. \qquad (33)$$

The two for $n = 4$ are slightly less obvious, but not really difficult to discover.

Since $\nu(v_{k+1}) = \nu(v_k) \pm 1$ whenever v_k is adjacent to v_{k+1}, we obviously can't strengthen (31) to the requirement that all n-tuples be strictly sorted by weight. But relation (31) is strong enough to determine the weight of each v_k, given k and the weight of v_0, because we know that exactly $\binom{n}{j}$ of the n-tuples have weight j.

Figure 34 summarizes our discussions so far, by illustrating seven of the zillions of Gray codes that make a grand tour through all 256 of the possible 8-bit bytes. Black squares represent ones and white squares represent zeros. Figure 34(a) is the standard Gray binary code, while Fig. 34(b) is balanced with exactly $256/8 = 32$ transitions in each coordinate position. Figure 34(c) is a Gray code analogous to Fig. 33(a), in which the bottom 128 codes are complements of the top 128. In Fig. 34(d), the transitions in each coordinate position never occur closer than five steps apart; in other words, all run lengths are at least 5. The cycle in Fig. 34(e) is *nonlocal* in the sense of exercise 59. A monotonic path for $n = 8$ appears in Fig. 34(f); notice how black it gets near the bottom. Finally, Fig. 34(g) illustrates a Gray code that is totally nonmonotonic, in the sense that the center of gravity of the black squares lies exactly at the halfway point in each column. Standard Gray binary code has this property in seven of the coordinate positions, but Fig. 34(g) achieves perfect black-white weight balance in all eight. Such codes are called *trend-free*; they are important in the design of agricultural and other experiments (see exercises 75 and 76).

Carla Savage and Peter Winkler [*J. Combinatorial Theory* **A70** (1995), 230–248] found an elegant way to construct monotonic binary Gray codes for all $n > 0$. Such paths are necessarily built from subpaths P_{nj} in which all transitions are between n-tuples of weights j and $j + 1$. Savage and Winkler defined suitable subpaths recursively by letting $P_{10} = 0, 1$ and, for all $n > 0$,

$$P_{(n+1)j} = 1P_{n(j-1)}^{\pi_n}, \; 0P_{nj}; \qquad (34)$$

$$P_{nj} = \emptyset \quad \text{if } j < 0 \text{ or } j \geq n. \qquad (35)$$

Here π_n is a permutation of the coordinates that we will specify later, and the notation P^π means that every element $a_{n-1} \ldots a_1 a_0$ of the sequence P is replaced by $b_{n-1} \ldots b_1 b_0$, where $b_{j\pi} = a_j$. (We don't define P^π by letting $b_j = a_{j\pi}$, because we want $(2^j)^\pi$ to be $2^{j\pi}$.) It follows, for example, that

$$P_{20} = 0P_{10} = 00, \; 01 \qquad (36)$$

because $P_{1(-1)}$ is vacuous; also

$$P_{21} = 1P_{10}^{\pi_1} = 10, \; 11 \qquad (37)$$

because P_{11} is vacuous and π_1 must be the identity permutation. In general, P_{nj} is a sequence of n-bit strings containing exactly $\binom{n-1}{j}$ strings of weight j interleaved with $\binom{n-1}{j}$ strings of weight $j+1$.

Let α_{nj} and ω_{nj} be the first and last elements of P_{nj}. Then we easily find

$$\omega_{nj} = 0^{n-j-1}1^{j+1}, \qquad \text{for } 0 \le j < n; \tag{38}$$

$$\alpha_{n0} = 0^n, \qquad \text{for } n > 0; \tag{39}$$

$$\alpha_{nj} = 1\alpha_{(n-1)(j-1)}^{\pi_{n-1}}, \qquad \text{for } 1 \le j < n. \tag{40}$$

In particular, α_{nj} always has weight j, and ω_{nj} always has weight $j+1$. We will define permutations π_n of $\{0, 1, \ldots, n-1\}$ so that both of the sequences

$$P_{n0}, \; P_{n1}^R, \; P_{n2}, \; P_{n3}^R, \; \ldots \tag{41}$$

$$\text{and } P_{n0}^R, \; P_{n1}, \; P_{n2}^R, \; P_{n3}, \; \ldots \tag{42}$$

are monotonic binary Gray paths for $n = 1, 2, 3, \ldots$. In fact, the monotonicity is clear, so only the Grayness is in doubt; and the sequences (41), (42) link up nicely because the adjacencies

$$\alpha_{n0} \text{—} \alpha_{n1} \text{—} \cdots \text{—} \alpha_{n(n-1)}, \qquad \omega_{n0} \text{—} \omega_{n1} \text{—} \cdots \text{—} \omega_{n(n-1)} \tag{43}$$

follow immediately from (34), regardless of the permutations π_n. Thus the crucial point is the transition at the comma in formula (34), which makes $P_{(n+1)j}$ a Gray subpath if and only if

$$\omega_{n(j-1)}^{\pi_n} = \alpha_{nj} \qquad \text{for } 0 < j < n. \tag{44}$$

For example, when $n = 2$ and $j = 1$ we need $(01)^{\pi_2} = \alpha_{21} = 10$, by (38)–(40); hence π_2 must transpose coordinates 0 and 1. The general formula (see exercise 71) turns out to be

$$\pi_n = \sigma_n \pi_{n-1}^2, \tag{45}$$

where σ_n is the n-cycle $(n-1 \; \ldots \; 1\,0)$. The first few cases are therefore

$$\pi_1 = (0), \qquad\qquad \pi_4 = (0\,3),$$
$$\pi_2 = (0\,1), \qquad\qquad \pi_5 = (0\,4\,3\,2\,1),$$
$$\pi_3 = (0\,2\,1), \qquad\qquad \pi_6 = (0\,5\,2\,4\,1\,3);$$

no simple "closed form" for the magic permutations π_n is apparent. Exercise 73 shows that the Savage–Winkler codes can be generated efficiently.

Nonbinary Gray codes. We have studied the case of binary n-tuples in great detail, because it is the simplest, most classical, most applicable, and most thoroughly explored part of the subject. But of course there are numerous applications in which we want to generate $(a_1, \ldots, a_n)$ with integer components in the more general ranges $0 \le a_j < m_j$, as in Algorithm M. Gray codes apply nicely to this case as well.

Consider, for example, decimal digits, where we want $0 \le a_j < 10$ for each j. Is there a decimal way to count that is analogous to the Gray binary code, changing only one digit at a time? Yes; in fact, *two* natural schemes are available. In the first, called *reflected Gray decimal*, the sequence for counting up to a thousand with 3-digit strings has the form

$$000, 001, \ldots, 009, 019, 018, \ldots, 011, 010, 020, 021, \ldots, 091, 090, 190, 191, \ldots, 900,$$

with each component moving alternately from 0 up to 9 and then back down from 9 to 0. In the second, called *modular Gray decimal*, the digits always increase by 1 mod 10, therefore they "wrap around" from 9 to 0:

$$000, 001, \ldots, 009, 019, 010, \ldots, 017, 018, 028, 029, \ldots, 099, 090, 190, 191, \ldots, 900.$$

In both cases the digit that changes on step k is determined by the radix-ten ruler function $\rho_{10}(k)$, the largest power of 10 that divides k. Therefore each n-tuple of digits occurs exactly once: We generate 10^j different settings of the rightmost j digits before changing any of the others, for $1 \le j \le n$.

In general, the reflected Gray code in any mixed-radix system can be regarded as a permutation of the nonnegative integers, a function that maps an ordinary mixed-radix number

$$k = \begin{bmatrix} b_{n-1}, & \ldots, & b_1, & b_0 \\ m_{n-1}, & \ldots, & m_1, & m_0 \end{bmatrix} = b_{n-1}m_{n-2}\ldots m_1 m_0 + \cdots + b_1 m_0 + b_0 \qquad (46)$$

into its reflected-Gray equivalent

$$\hat{g}(k) = \begin{bmatrix} a_{n-1}, & \ldots, & a_1, & a_0 \\ m_{n-1}, & \ldots, & m_1, & m_0 \end{bmatrix} = a_{n-1}m_{n-2}\ldots m_1 m_0 + \cdots + a_1 m_0 + a_0, \qquad (47)$$

just as (7) does this in the special case of binary numbers. Let

$$A_j = \begin{bmatrix} a_{n-1}, & \ldots, & a_j \\ m_{n-1}, & \ldots, & m_j \end{bmatrix}, \qquad B_j = \begin{bmatrix} b_{n-1}, & \ldots, & b_j \\ m_{n-1}, & \ldots, & m_j \end{bmatrix}, \qquad (48)$$

with $A_n = B_n = 0$, so that when $0 \le j < n$ we have

$$A_j = m_j A_{j+1} + a_j \qquad \text{and} \qquad B_j = m_j B_{j+1} + b_j. \qquad (49)$$

The rule connecting the a's and b's is not difficult to derive by induction on $n-j$:

$$a_j = \begin{cases} b_j, & \text{if } B_{j+1} \text{ is even;} \\ m_j - 1 - b_j, & \text{if } B_{j+1} \text{ is odd.} \end{cases} \qquad (50)$$

(Here we are numbering the coordinates of the n-tuples $(a_{n-1}, \ldots, a_1, a_0)$ and $(b_{n-1}, \ldots, b_1, b_0)$ from right to left, for consistency with (7) and the conventions of mixed-radix notation in Eq. 4.1–(9). Readers who prefer notations like $(a_1, \ldots, a_n)$ can change j to $n - j$ in all the formulas if they wish.) Going the other way, we have

$$b_j = \begin{cases} a_j, & \text{if } a_{j+1} + a_{j+2} + \cdots \text{ is even;} \\ m_j - 1 - a_j, & \text{if } a_{j+1} + a_{j+2} + \cdots \text{ is odd.} \end{cases} \qquad (51)$$

Curiously, rule (50) and its inverse in (51) are exactly the same when all of the radices m_j are odd. In Gray ternary code, for example, when $m_0 = m_1 = \cdots = 3$, we have $\hat{g}\big((10010211012)_3\big) = (12210211010)_3$ and also $\hat{g}\big((12210211010)_3\big) =$

$(10010211012)_3$. Exercise 78 proves (50) and (51), and discusses similar formulas that hold in the modular case.

We can in fact generate such Gray sequences looplessly, generalizing Algorithms M and L:

Algorithm H (*Loopless reflected mixed-radix Gray generation*). This algorithm visits all n-tuples $(a_{n-1}, \ldots, a_0)$ such that $0 \le a_j < m_j$ for $0 \le j < n$, changing only one component by ± 1 at each step. It maintains an array of focus pointers $(f_n, \ldots, f_0)$ to control the actions as in Algorithm L, together with an array of directions $(o_{n-1}, \ldots, o_0)$. We assume that each radix m_j is ≥ 2.

H1. [Initialize.] Set $a_j \leftarrow 0$, $f_j \leftarrow j$, and $o_j \leftarrow 1$, for $0 \le j < n$; also set $f_n \leftarrow n$.

H2. [Visit.] Visit the n-tuple $(a_{n-1}, \ldots, a_1, a_0)$.

H3. [Choose j.] Set $j \leftarrow f_0$ and $f_0 \leftarrow 0$. (As in Algorithm L, j was the rightmost active coordinate; all elements to its right have now been reactivated.)

H4. [Change coordinate j.] Terminate if $j = n$; otherwise set $a_j \leftarrow a_j + o_j$.

H5. [Reflect?] If $a_j = 0$ or $a_j = m_j - 1$, set $o_j \leftarrow -o_j$, $f_j \leftarrow f_{j+1}$, and $f_{j+1} \leftarrow j + 1$. (Coordinate j has thus become passive.) Return to H2. $\blacksquare$

A similar algorithm generates the modular variation (see exercise 77).

*Subforests. An interesting and instructive generalization of Algorithm H, discovered by Y. Koda and F. Ruskey [*J. Algorithms* **15** (1993), 324–340], sheds further light on the subject of Gray codes and loopless generation. Suppose we have a forest of n nodes, and we want to visit all of its "principal subforests," namely all subsets of nodes S such that if x is in S and x is not a root, the parent of x is also in S. For example, the 7-node forest ⁸⅄ has 33 such subsets, corresponding to the black nodes in the following 33 diagrams:

$$\text{[33 forest diagrams]} \tag{52}$$

Notice that if we read the top row from left to right, the middle row from right to left, and the bottom row from left to right, the status of exactly one node changes at each step.

If the given forest consists of degenerate nonbranching trees, the principal subforests are equivalent to mixed-radix numbers. For example, a forest like

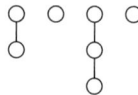

has $3 \times 2 \times 4 \times 2$ principal subforests, corresponding to 4-tuples (x_1, x_2, x_3, x_4) such that $0 \le x_1 < 3$, $0 \le x_2 < 2$, $0 \le x_3 < 4$, and $0 \le x_4 < 2$; the value of x_j is the number of nodes selected in the jth tree. When the algorithm of Koda and

Ruskey is applied to such a forest, it will visit the subforests in the same order
as the reflected Gray code on radices $(3, 2, 4, 2)$.

Algorithm K (*Loopless reflected subforest generation*). Given a forest whose
nodes are $(1, \ldots, n)$ when arranged in postorder, this algorithm visits all binary
n-tuples $(a_1, \ldots, a_n)$ such that $a_p \geq a_q$ whenever p is a parent of q. (Thus,
$a_p = 1$ means that p is a node in the current subforest.) Exactly one bit a_j
changes between one visit and the next. Focus pointers $(f_0, f_1, \ldots, f_n)$ analogous
to those of Algorithm L are used together with additional arrays of pointers
$(l_0, l_1, \ldots, l_n)$ and $(r_0, r_1, \ldots, r_n)$, which represent a doubly linked list called the
"current fringe." The current fringe contains all nodes of the current subforest
and their children; r_0 points to its leftmost node and l_0 to its rightmost.

An auxiliary array $(c_0, c_1, \ldots, c_n)$ defines the forest as follows: If p has no
children, $c_p = 0$; otherwise c_p is the leftmost (smallest) child of p. Also c_0 is the
leftmost root of the forest itself. When the algorithm begins, we assume that
$r_p = q$ and $l_q = p$ whenever p and q are consecutive children of the same family.
Thus, for example, the forest in (52) has the postorder numbering

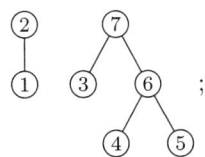

therefore we should have $(c_0, \ldots, c_7) = (2, 0, 1, 0, 0, 0, 4, 3)$ and $r_2 = 7$, $l_7 = 2$,
$r_3 = 6$, $l_6 = 3$, $r_4 = 5$, and $l_5 = 4$ at the beginning of step K1 in this case.

K1. [Initialize.] Set $a_j \leftarrow 0$ and $f_j \leftarrow j$ for $1 \leq j \leq n$, thereby making the initial
subforest empty and all nodes active. Set $f_0 \leftarrow 0$, $l_0 \leftarrow n$, $r_n \leftarrow 0$, $r_0 \leftarrow c_0$,
and $l_{c_0} \leftarrow 0$, thereby putting all roots into the current fringe.

K2. [Visit.] Visit the subforest defined by $(a_1, \ldots, a_n)$.

K3. [Choose p.] Set $q \leftarrow l_0$, $p \leftarrow f_q$. (Now p is the rightmost active node of the
fringe.) Also set $f_q \leftarrow q$ (thereby activating all nodes to p's right).

K4. [Check a_p.] Terminate the algorithm if $p = 0$. Otherwise go to K6 if $a_p = 1$.

K5. [Insert p's children.] Set $a_p \leftarrow 1$. Then, if $c_p \neq 0$, set $q \leftarrow r_p$, $l_q \leftarrow p - 1$,
$r_{p-1} \leftarrow q$, $r_p \leftarrow c_p$, $l_{c_p} \leftarrow p$ (thereby putting p's children to the right of p
in the fringe). Go to K7.

K6. [Delete p's children.] Set $a_p \leftarrow 0$. Then, if $c_p \neq 0$, set $q \leftarrow r_{p-1}$, $r_p \leftarrow q$,
$l_q \leftarrow p$ (thereby removing p's children from the fringe).

K7. [Make p passive.] (At this point we know that p is active.) Set $f_p \leftarrow f_{l_p}$
and $f_{l_p} \leftarrow l_p$. Return to K2. ∎

The reader is encouraged to play through this algorithm on examples like (52),
in order to understand the beautiful mechanism by which the fringe grows and
shrinks at just the right times.

*Shift register sequences. A completely different way to generate all n-tuples of m-ary digits is also possible: We can generate one digit at a time, and repeatedly work with the n most recently generated digits, thus passing from one n-tuple $(x_0, x_1, \ldots, x_{n-1})$ to another one $(x_1, \ldots, x_{n-1}, x_n)$ by shifting an appropriate new digit in at the right. For example, Fig. 35 shows how all 5-bit numbers can be obtained as blocks of 5 consecutive bits in a certain cyclic pattern of length 32. This general idea has already been discussed in some of the exercises of Sections 2.3.4.2 and 3.2.2, and we now are ready to explore it further.

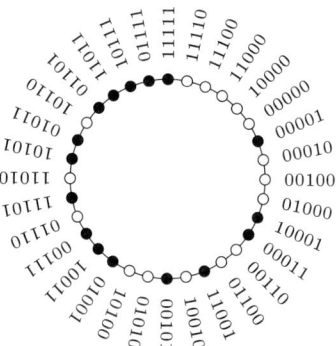

Fig. 35.

A de Bruijn cycle
for 5-bit numbers.

Algorithm S (*Generic shift register generation*). This algorithm visits all n-tuples $(a_1, \ldots, a_n)$ such that $0 \le a_j < m$ for $1 \le j \le n$, provided that a suitable function f is used in step S3.

S1. [Initialize.] Set $a_j \leftarrow 0$ for $-n < j \le 0$ and $k \leftarrow 1$.

S2. [Visit.] Visit the n-tuple $(a_{k-n}, \ldots, a_{k-1})$. Terminate if $k = m^n$.

S3. [Advance.] Set $a_k \leftarrow f(a_{k-n}, \ldots, a_{k-1})$, $k \leftarrow k + 1$, and return to S2. ∎

Every function f that makes Algorithm S valid corresponds to a cycle of m^n radix-m digits such that every combination of n digits occurs consecutively in the cycle. For example, the case $m = 2$ and $n = 5$ illustrated in Fig. 35 corresponds to the binary cycle

$$00000100011001010011101011011111; \tag{53}$$

and the first m^2 digits of the infinite sequence

$$00110212203132133041424344\ldots \tag{54}$$

yield an appropriate cycle for $n = 2$ and arbitrary m. Such cycles are commonly called m-ary *de Bruijn cycles*, because N. G. de Bruijn treated the binary case for arbitrary n in *Indagationes Mathematicæ* **8** (1946), 461–467.

Exercise 2.3.4.2–23 proves that exactly $m!^{m^{n-1}}/m^n$ functions f have the required properties. That's a huge number, but only a few of those functions are known to be efficiently computable. We will discuss three kinds of f that appear to be the most useful.

Table 1

PARAMETERS FOR ALGORITHM A

$3:1$	$8:1,5$	$13:1,3$	$18:7$	$23:5$	$28:3$
$4:1$	$9:4$	$14:1,11$	$19:1,5$	$24:1,3$	$29:2$
$5:2$	$10:3$	$15:1$	$20:3$	$25:3$	$30:1,15$
$6:1$	$11:2$	$16:2,3$	$21:2$	$26:1,7$	$31:3$
$7:1$	$12:3,4$	$17:3$	$22:1$	$27:1,7$	$32:1,27$

The entries '$n:s$' or '$n:s,t$' mean that the polynomials $x^n + x^s + 1$ or $x^n + (x^s+1)(x^t+1)$ are primitive modulo 2. Additional values up to $n = 168$ have been tabulated by W. Stahnke, *Math. Comp.* **27** (1973), 977–980.

The first important case occurs when m is a prime number, and f is the almost linear recurrence

$$f(x_1,\ldots,x_n) = \begin{cases} c_1, & \text{if } (x_1,x_2,\ldots,x_n) = (0,0,\ldots,0); \\ 0, & \text{if } (x_1,x_2,\ldots,x_n) = (1,0,\ldots,0); \\ (c_1x_1 + c_2x_2 + \cdots + c_nx_n) \bmod m, & \text{otherwise.} \end{cases} \quad (55)$$

Here the coefficients $(c_1,\ldots,c_n)$ must be such that

$$x^n - c_n x^{n-1} - \cdots - c_2 x - c_1 \quad (56)$$

is a primitive polynomial modulo m, in the sense discussed following Eq. 3.2.2–(9). The number of such polynomials is $\varphi(m^n - 1)/n$, large enough to allow us to find one in which only a few of the c's are nonzero. [This construction goes back to a pioneering paper of Willem Mantel, *Nieuw Archief voor Wiskunde* (2) **1** (1897), 172–184.]

For example, suppose $m = 2$. We can generate binary n-tuples with a very simple loopless procedure:

Algorithm A (*Almost linear bit-shift generation*). This algorithm visits all n-bit vectors, by using either a special offset s [Case 1] or two special offsets s and t [Case 2], as found in Table 1.

A1. [Initialize.] Set $(x_0, x_1, \ldots, x_{n-1}) \leftarrow (1, 0, \ldots, 0)$ and $k \leftarrow 0$, $j \leftarrow s$. In Case 2, also set $i \leftarrow t$ and $h \leftarrow s + t$.

A2. [Visit.] Visit the n-tuple $(x_{k-1}, \ldots, x_0, x_{n-1}, \ldots, x_{k+1}, x_k)$.

A3. [Test for end.] If $x_k \neq 0$, set $r \leftarrow 0$; otherwise set $r \leftarrow r + 1$, and go to A6 if $r = n - 1$. (We have just seen r consecutive zeros.)

A4. [Shift.] Set $k \leftarrow (k-1) \bmod n$ and $j \leftarrow (j-1) \bmod n$. In Case 2 also set $i \leftarrow (i-1) \bmod n$ and $h \leftarrow (h-1) \bmod n$.

A5. [Compute a new bit.] Set $x_k \leftarrow x_k \oplus x_j$ [Case 1] or $x_k \leftarrow x_k \oplus x_j \oplus x_i \oplus x_h$ [Case 2]. Return to A2.

A6. [Finish.] Visit $(0, \ldots, 0)$ and terminate. ∎

Appropriate offset parameters s and possibly t almost certainly exist for all n, because primitive polynomials are so abundant; for example, eight different choices of (s, t) would work when $n = 32$, and Table 1 merely lists the smallest.

However, a rigorous proof of existence in all cases lies well beyond the present state of mathematical knowledge.

Our first construction of de Bruijn cycles, in (55), was algebraic, relying for its validity on the theory of finite fields. A similar method that works when m is not a prime number appears in exercise 3.2.2–21. Our next construction, by contrast, will be purely combinatorial. In fact, it is strongly related to the idea of modular Gray m-ary codes.

Algorithm R (*Recursive de Bruijn cycle generation*). Suppose $f()$ is a coroutine that will output the successive digits of an m-ary de Bruijn cycle of length m^n, beginning with n zeros, when it is invoked repeatedly. This algorithm is a similar coroutine that outputs a cycle of length m^{n+1}, provided that $n \geq 2$. It maintains three private variables x, y, and t; variable x should initially be zero.

R1. [Output.] Output x. Go to R3 if $x \neq 0$ and $t \geq n$.

R2. [Invoke f.] Set $y \leftarrow f()$.

R3. [Count ones.] If $y = 1$, set $t \leftarrow t + 1$; otherwise set $t \leftarrow 0$.

R4. [Skip one?] If $t = n$ and $x \neq 0$, go back to R2.

R5. [Adjust x.] Set $x \leftarrow (x + y) \bmod m$ and return to R1. ▮

For example, let $m = 3$ and $n = 2$. If $f()$ produces the infinite 9-cycle

$$001102122\ 001102122\ 0\ldots, \tag{57}$$

then Algorithm R will produce the following infinite 27-cycle at step R1:

$$y = \quad 001021220011110212200102122\ 001\ldots$$
$$t = \quad 001001000012340010000100100\ 001\ldots$$
$$x = 000110102220120020211122121\ 0001\ldots$$

The proof that Algorithm R works correctly is interesting and instructive (see exercise 93). And the proof of the next algorithm, which *doubles* the window size n, is even more so (see exercise 95).

Algorithm D (*Doubly recursive de Bruijn cycle generation*). Suppose $f()$ and $f'()$ are coroutines that each will output the successive digits of an m-ary de Bruijn cycle of length m^n when invoked repeatedly, beginning with n zeros. (The two cycles may be identical, but they must be generated by independent coroutines, because we will consume their values at different rates.) This algorithm is a similar coroutine that outputs a cycle of length m^{2n}. It maintains six private variables x, y, t, x', y', and t'; variables x and x' should initially be m.

The special parameter r must be set to a constant value such that

$$0 \leq r \leq m \quad \text{and} \quad \gcd(m^n - r, m^n + r) = 2. \tag{58}$$

The best choice is usually $r = 1$ when m is odd and $r = 2$ when m is even.

D1. [Possibly invoke f.] If $t \neq n$ or $x \geq r$, set $y \leftarrow f()$.

D2. [Count repeats.] If $x \neq y$, set $x \leftarrow y$ and $t \leftarrow 1$. Otherwise set $t \leftarrow t + 1$.

D3. [Output from f.] Output the current value of x.

D4. [Invoke f'.] Set $y' \leftarrow f'()$.

D5. [Count repeats.] If $x' \neq y'$, set $x' \leftarrow y'$ and $t' \leftarrow 1$. Otherwise set $t' \leftarrow t'+1$.

D6. [Possibly reject f'.] If $t' = n$ and $x' < r$ and either $t < n$ or $x' < x$, go to D4. If $t' = n$ and $x' < r$ and $x' = x$, go to D3.

D7. [Output from f'.] Output the current value of x'. Return to D3 if $t' = n$ and $x' < r$; otherwise return to D1. ▮

The basic idea of Algorithm D is to output from $f()$ and $f'()$ alternately, making special adjustments when either sequence generates n consecutive x's for $x < r$. For example, when $f()$ and $f'()$ produce the 9-cycle (57), we take $r = 1$ and get

t in step D2: 12 31211112 12312111 12123121 11121231 21111212 …
x in step D3: 00001102122 00011021 22000110 21220001 102122000 …
t' **in step D5: 121211112121211112121211112121211112121211112121** …
x' **in step D7:** 0 11021220 11021220 11021220 11021220 11021220 1 …;

so the 81-cycle produced in steps D3 and **D7** is $00001011012\ldots2222\,00001\ldots$.

The case $m = 2$ of Algorithm R was discovered by Abraham Lempel [*IEEE Trans.* **C-19** (1970), 1204–1209]; Algorithm D was not discovered until more than 25 years later [C. J. Mitchell, T. Etzion, and K. G. Paterson, *IEEE Trans.* **IT-42** (1996), 1472–1478]. By using them together, starting with simple coroutines for $n = 2$ based on (54), we can build up an interesting family of cooperating coroutines that will generate a de Bruijn cycle of length m^n for any desired $m \geq 2$ and $n \geq 2$, using only $O(\log n)$ simple computations for each digit of output. (See exercise 96.) Furthermore, in the simplest case $m = 2$, this combination "R&D method" has the property that its kth output can be computed directly, as a function of k, by doing $O(n \log n)$ simple operations on n-bit numbers. Conversely, given any n-bit pattern β, the position of β in the cycle can also be computed in $O(n \log n)$ steps. (See exercises 97–99.) No other family of binary de Bruijn cycles is presently known to have the latter property.

Our third construction of de Bruijn cycles is based on the theory of prime strings, which will be of great importance to us when we study pattern matching in Chapter 9. Suppose $\gamma = \alpha\beta$ is the concatenation of two strings; we say that α is a *prefix* of γ and β is a *suffix*. A prefix or suffix of γ is called *proper* if its length is positive but less than the length of γ. Thus β is a proper suffix of $\alpha\beta$ if and only if $\alpha \neq \epsilon$ and $\beta \neq \epsilon$.

Definition P. *A string is* prime *if it is nonempty and (lexicographically) less than all of its proper suffixes.* ▮

For example, 01101 is not prime, because it is greater than 01; but 01102 is prime, because it is less than 1102, 102, 02, and 2. (We assume that strings are composed of letters, digits, or other symbols from a linearly ordered alphabet. Lexicographic or dictionary order is the normal way to compare strings, so we write $\alpha < \beta$ and say that α is less than β when α is lexicographically less than β. In particular, we always have $\alpha \leq \alpha\beta$, and $\alpha < \alpha\beta$ if and only if $\beta \neq \epsilon$.)

Prime strings have often been called *Lyndon words*, because they were introduced by R. C. Lyndon [*Trans. Amer. Math. Soc.* **77** (1954), 202–215]; Lyndon called them "standard sequences." The simpler term "prime" is justified because of the fundamental factorization theorem in exercise 101. We will, however, continue to pay respect to Lyndon implicitly by often using the letter λ to denote strings that are prime.

Several of the most important properties of prime strings were derived by Chen, Fox, and Lyndon in an important paper on group theory [*Annals of Math.* (2) **68** (1958), 81–95], including the following easy but basic result:

Theorem P. *A nonempty string that is less than all its cyclic shifts is prime.*

(The cyclic shifts of $a_1 \ldots a_n$ are $a_2 \ldots a_n a_1$, $a_3 \ldots a_n a_1 a_2$, $\ldots$, $a_n a_1 \ldots a_{n-1}$.)

Proof. Suppose $\gamma = \alpha\beta$ is not prime, because $\alpha \neq \epsilon$ and $\gamma \geq \beta \neq \epsilon$; but suppose γ is also less than its cyclic shift $\beta\alpha$. Then the conditions $\beta \leq \gamma < \beta\alpha$ imply that $\gamma = \beta\theta$ for some string $\theta < \alpha$. Therefore, if γ is also less than its cyclic shift $\theta\beta$, we have $\theta < \alpha < \alpha\beta < \theta\beta$. But that is impossible, because α and θ have the same length. ∎

Let $L_m(n)$ be the number of m-ary primes of length n. Every string $a_1 \ldots a_n$, together with its cyclic shifts, yields d distinct strings for some divisor d of n, corresponding to exactly one prime of length d. For example, from 010010 we get also 100100 and 001001 by cyclic shifting, and the smallest of the periodic parts $\{010, 100, 001\}$ is the prime 001. Therefore we must have

$$\sum_{d \backslash n} d L_m(d) = m^n, \qquad \text{for all } m, n \geq 1. \tag{59}$$

This family of equations can be solved for $L_m(n)$ using exercise 4.5.3–28(a), and we obtain

$$L_m(n) = \frac{1}{n} \sum_{d \backslash n} \mu(d) m^{n/d}. \tag{60}$$

During the 1970s, Harold Fredricksen and James Maiorana discovered a beautifully simple way to generate all of the m-ary primes of length n or less, in increasing order [*Discrete Math.* **23** (1978), 207–210]. Before we are ready to understand their algorithm, we need to consider the *n-extension* of a nonempty string λ, namely the first n characters of the infinite string $\lambda\lambda\lambda \ldots$. For example, the 10-extension of 123 is 1231231231. In general if $|\lambda| = k$, its n-extension is $\lambda^{\lfloor n/k \rfloor} \lambda'$, where λ' is the prefix of λ whose length is $n \bmod k$.

Definition Q. *A string is preprime if it is a nonempty prefix of a prime, on some alphabet.* ∎

Theorem Q. *A string of length $n > 0$ is preprime if and only if it is the n-extension of a prime string λ of length $k \leq n$. This prime string is uniquely determined.*

Proof. See exercise 105. ∎

Theorem Q states, in essence, that there is a one-to-one correspondence between primes of length $\leq n$ and preprimes of length n. The following algorithm generates all of the m-ary instances, in increasing order.

Algorithm F (*Prime and preprime string generation*). This algorithm visits all m-ary n-tuples $(a_1, \ldots, a_n)$ such that the string $a_1 \ldots a_n$ is preprime. It also identifies the index j such that $a_1 \ldots a_n$ is the n-extension of the prime $a_1 \ldots a_j$.

F1. [Initialize.] Set $a_1 \leftarrow \cdots \leftarrow a_n \leftarrow 0$ and $j \leftarrow 1$; also set $a_0 \leftarrow -1$.

F2. [Visit.] Visit $(a_1, \ldots, a_n)$ with index j.

F3. [Prepare to increase.] Set $j \leftarrow n$. Then if $a_j = m - 1$, decrease j until finding $a_j < m - 1$.

F4. [Add one.] Terminate if $j = 0$. Otherwise set $a_j \leftarrow a_j + 1$. (Now $a_1 \ldots a_j$ is prime, by exercise 105(a).)

F5. [Make n-extension.] For $k \leftarrow j + 1$, ..., n (in this order) set $a_k \leftarrow a_{k-j}$. Return to F2. ∎

For example, Algorithm F visits 32 ternary preprimes when $m = 3$ and $n = 4$:

$$
\begin{array}{llllllll}
0000 & 0011 & 0022 & 0111 & 0122 & 0212 & 1111 & 1212 \\
0001 & 0012 & 0101 & 0112 & 0202 & 0220 & 1112 & 1221 \\
0002 & 0020 & 0102 & 0120 & 0210 & 0221 & 1121 & 1222 \\
0010 & 0021 & 0110 & 0121 & 0211 & 0222 & 1122 & 2222
\end{array}
\qquad (61)
$$

(The digits preceding '$_\wedge$' are the prime strings 0, 0001, 0002, 001, 0011, ..., 2.)

Theorem Q explains why this algorithm is correct, because steps F3 and F4 obviously find the smallest m-ary prime of length $\leq n$ that exceeds the previous preprime $a_1 \ldots a_n$. Notice that after a_1 increases from 0 to 1, the algorithm proceeds to visit all the $(m - 1)$-ary primes and preprimes, increased by $1 \ldots 1$.

Algorithm F is quite beautiful, but what does it have to do with de Bruijn cycles? Here now comes the punch line: If we output the digits $a_1, \ldots, a_j$ in step F2 whenever j is a divisor of n, the sequence of all such digits forms a de Bruijn cycle! For example, in the case $m = 3$ and $n = 4$, the following 81 digits are output:

0 0001 0002 0011 0012 0021 0022 01 0102 0111 0112

0121 0122 02 0211 0212 0221 0222 1 1112 1122 12 1222 2.   (62)

(We omit the primes 001, 002, 011, ..., 122 of (61) because their length does not divide 4.) The reasons underlying this almost magical property are explored in exercise 108. Notice that the cycle has the correct length, by (59).

There is a sense in which the outputs of this procedure are actually equivalent to the "granddaddy" of all de Bruijn cycle constructions that work for all m and n, namely the construction first published by M. H. Martin in *Bull. Amer. Math. Soc.* **40** (1934), 859–864: Martin's original cycle for $m = 3$ and $n = 4$ was $2222122202211 \ldots 10000$, the twos' complement of (62). In fact, Fredricksen and Maiorana discovered Algorithm F almost by accident while looking for a simple way to generate Martin's sequence. The explicit connection between their algorithm and preprime strings was not noticed until many years later, when Ruskey, Savage, and Wang carried out a careful analysis of the running time [*J. Algorithms* **13** (1992), 414–430]. The principal results of that analysis appear in exercise 107, namely

  i) The average value of $n - j$ in steps F3 and F5 is approximately $1/(m - 1)$.

 ii) The total running time to produce a de Bruijn cycle like (62) is $O(m^n)$.

EXERCISES

1. [*10*] Explain how to generate all n-tuples $(a_1, \ldots, a_n)$ in which $l_j \leq a_j \leq u_j$, given lower bounds l_j and upper bounds u_j for each component. (Assume that $l_j \leq u_j$.)

2. [*15*] What is the 1000000th n-tuple visited by Algorithm M if $n = 10$ and $m_j = j$ for $1 \leq j \leq n$? *Hint:* $\begin{bmatrix} 0, & 0, & 1, & 2, & 3, & 0, & 2, & 7, & 1, & 0 \\ 1, & 2, & 3, & 4, & 5, & 6, & 7, & 8, & 9, & 10 \end{bmatrix} = 1000000$.

▶ **3.** [*M20*] How many times does Algorithm M perform step M4?

▶ **4.** [*18*] On most computers it is faster to count down to 0 rather than up to m. Revise Algorithm M so that it visits all n-tuples in the opposite order, starting with $(m_1 - 1, \ldots, m_n - 1)$ and finishing with $(0, \ldots, 0)$.

▶ **5.** [*20*] Algorithms such as the "fast Fourier transform" (exercise 4.6.4–14) often end with an array of answers in bit-reflected order, having $A[(b_0 \ldots b_{n-1})_2]$ in the place where $A[(b_{n-1} \ldots b_0)_2]$ is desired. What is a good way to rearrange the answers into proper order? [*Hint:* Reflect Algorithm M.]

6. [*M17*] Prove (7), the basic formula for Gray binary code.

7. [*20*] Figure 30(b) shows the Gray binary code for a disk that is divided into 16 sectors. What would be a good Gray-like code to use if the number of sectors were 12 or 60 (for hours or minutes on a clock), or 360 (for degrees in a circle)?

8. [*15*] What's an easy way to run through all n-bit strings of even parity, changing only two bits at each step?

9. [*16*] What move should follow Fig. 31, when solving the Chinese ring puzzle?

▶ **10.** [*M21*] Find a simple formula for the total number of steps A_n or B_n in which a ring is (a) removed or (b) replaced, in the shortest procedure for removing n Chinese rings. For example, $A_3 = 4$ and $B_3 = 1$.

11. [*M22*] (H. J. Purkiss, 1865.) The two smallest rings of the Chinese ring puzzle can actually be taken on or off the bar simultaneously. How many steps does the puzzle require when such accelerated moves are permitted?

▶ **12.** [*25*] The *compositions* of n are the sequences of positive integers that sum to n. For example, the compositions of 4 are 1111, 112, 121, 13, 211, 22, 31, and 4. An integer n has exactly 2^{n-1} compositions, corresponding to all subsets of the points $\{1, \ldots, n-1\}$ that might be used to break the interval $(0 .. n)$ into integer-sized subintervals.

  a) Design a loopless algorithm to generate all compositions of n, representing each composition as a sequential array of integers $s_1 s_2 \ldots s_j$.

  b) Similarly, design a loopless algorithm that represents the compositions implicitly in an array of pointers $q_0 q_1 \ldots q_t$, where the elements of the composition are $(q_0 - q_1)(q_1 - q_2) \ldots (q_{t-1} - q_t)$ and we have $q_0 = n$, $q_t = 0$. For example, the composition 211 would be represented under this scheme by the pointers $q_0 = 4$, $q_1 = 2$, $q_2 = 1$, $q_3 = 0$, and with $t = 3$.

13. [*21*] Continuing the previous exercise, compute also the multinomial coefficient $C = \binom{n}{s_1,\dots,s_j}$ for use as the composition $s_1 \dots s_j$ is being visited.

14. [*20*] Design an algorithm to generate all strings $a_1 \dots a_j$ such that $0 \le j \le n$ and $0 \le a_i < m_i$ for $1 \le i \le j$, in lexicographic order. For example, if $m_1 = m_2 = n = 2$, your algorithm should successively visit ϵ, 0, 00, 01, 1, 10, 11.

▶ **15.** [*25*] Design a *loopless* algorithm to generate the strings of the previous exercise. All strings of the same length should be visited in lexicographic order as before, but strings of different lengths can be intermixed in any convenient way. For example, 0, 00, 01, ϵ, 10, 11, 1 is an acceptable order when $m_1 = m_2 = n = 2$.

16. [*23*] A loopless algorithm obviously cannot generate all binary vectors $(a_1, \dots, a_n)$ in lexicographic order, because the number of components a_j that need to change between successive visits is not bounded. Show, however, that loopless lexicographic generation does become possible if a *linked* representation is used instead of a sequential one: Suppose there are $2n + 1$ nodes $\{0, 1, \dots, 2n\}$, each containing a LINK field. The binary n-tuple $(a_1, \dots, a_n)$ is represented by letting

> LINK$(0) = 1 + na_1$;
> LINK$(j - 1 + na_{j-1}) = j + na_j$,   for $1 < j \le n$;
> LINK$(n + na_n) = 0$;

the other n LINK fields can have any convenient values.

17. [*20*] A well-known construction called the *Karnaugh map* [M. Karnaugh, *Amer. Inst. Elect. Eng. Trans.* **72**, part I (1953), 593–599] uses Gray binary code in two dimensions to display all 4-bit numbers in a 4×4 torus:

$$
\begin{array}{cccc}
0000 & 0001 & 0011 & 0010 \\
0100 & 0101 & 0111 & 0110 \\
1100 & 1101 & 1111 & 1110 \\
1000 & 1001 & 1011 & 1010
\end{array}
$$

(The entries of a torus "wrap around" at the left and right and also at the top and bottom — just as if they were tiles, replicated infinitely often in a plane.) Show that, similarly, all 6-bit numbers can be arranged in an 8×8 torus so that only one coordinate position changes when we move north, south, east, or west from any point.

▶ **18.** [*20*] The *Lee weight* of a vector $u = (u_1, \dots, u_n)$, where each component satisfies $0 \le u_j < m_j$, is defined to be

$$
\nu_L(u) = \sum_{j=1}^{n} \min(u_j, m_j - u_j);
$$

and the *Lee distance* between two such vectors u and v is

$$
d_L(u, v) = \nu_L(u - v), \qquad \text{where } u - v = ((u_1 - v_1) \bmod m_1, \dots, (u_n - v_n) \bmod m_n).
$$

(This is the minimum number of steps needed to change u to v if we adjust some component u_j by ± 1 (modulo m_j) in each step.)

A quaternary vector has $m_j = 4$ for $1 \le j \le n$, and a binary vector has all $m_j = 2$. Find a simple one-to-one correspondence between quaternary vectors $u = (u_1, \dots, u_n)$ and binary vectors $u' = (u'_1, \dots, u'_{2n})$, with the property that $\nu_L(u) = \nu(u')$ and $d_L(u, v) = \nu(u' \oplus v')$.

19. [*23*] (*The octacode.*) Let $g(x) = x^3 + 2x^2 + x - 1$.

a) Use one of the algorithms in this section to evaluate $\sum z_{u_0} z_{u_1} z_{u_2} z_{u_3} z_{u_4} z_{u_5} z_{u_6} z_{u_\infty}$, a polynomial in the variables z_0, z_1, z_2, and z_3, summed over all 256 polynomials

$$(v_0 + v_1 x + v_2 x^2 + v_3 x^3) g(x) \bmod 4 = u_0 + u_1 x + u_2 x^2 + u_3 x^3 + u_4 x^4 + u_5 x^5 + u_6 x^6$$

for $0 \le v_0, v_1, v_2, v_3 < 4$, where u_∞ is chosen so that $0 \le u_\infty < 4$ and $(u_0 + u_1 + u_2 + u_3 + u_4 + u_5 + u_6 + u_\infty) \bmod 4 = 0$.

b) Construct a set of 256 16-bit numbers that differ from each other in at least six different bit positions. (Such a set, first discovered by Nordstrom and Robinson [*Information and Control* **11** (1967), 613–616], is essentially unique.)

20. [*M36*] The 16-bit codewords in the previous exercise can be used to transmit 8 bits of information, allowing transmission errors to be corrected if any one or two bits are corrupted; furthermore, mistakes will be detected (but not necessarily correctable) if any three bits are received incorrectly. Devise an algorithm that either finds the nearest codeword to a given 16-bit number u' or determines that at least three bits of u' are erroneous. How does your algorithm decode the number $(1100100100001111)_2$? [*Hint:* Use the facts that $x^7 \equiv 1$ (modulo $g(x)$ and 4), and that every quaternary polynomial of degree < 3 is congruent to $x^j + 2x^k$ (modulo $g(x)$ and 4) for some $j, k \in \{0, 1, 2, 3, 4, 5, 6, \infty\}$, where $x^\infty = 0$.]

21. [*M30*] A *t*-subcube of an *n*-cube can be represented by a string like $**10**0*$, containing t asterisks and $n - t$ specified bits. If all 2^n binary n-tuples are written in lexicographic order, the elements belonging to such a subcube appear in $2^{t'}$ clusters of consecutive entries, where t' is the number of asterisks that lie to the left of the rightmost specified bit. (In the example given, $n = 8$, $t = 5$, and $t' = 4$.) But if the n-tuples are written in Gray binary order, the number of clusters might be reduced. For example, the $(n-1)$-subcubes $* \ldots *0$ and $* \ldots *1$ occur in only $2^{n-2} + 1$ and 2^{n-2} clusters, respectively, when Gray binary order is used, not in 2^{n-1} of them.

a) Explain how to compute $C(\alpha)$, the number of Gray binary clusters of the subcube defined by a given string α of asterisks, 0s, and 1s. What is $C(**10**0*)$?

b) Prove that $C(\alpha)$ always lies between $2^{t'-1}$ and $2^{t'}$, inclusive.

c) What is the average value of $C(\alpha)$, over all $2^{n-t} \binom{n}{t}$ possible t-subcubes?

▶ **22.** [*22*] A "right subcube" is a subcube such as $0110**$ in which all the asterisks appear after all the specified digits. Any binary trie (Section 6.3) can be regarded as a way to partition a cube into disjoint right subcubes, as in Fig. 36(a). If we interchange the left and right subtries of every right subtrie, proceeding downward from the root, we obtain a *Gray binary trie*, as in Fig. 36(b).

Prove that if the "lieves" of a Gray binary trie are traversed in order, from left to right, consecutive lieves correspond to adjacent subcubes. (Subcubes are adjacent if they contain adjacent vertices. For example, $00**$ is adjacent to $011*$ because the first contains 0010 and the second contains 0110; but $011*$ is not adjacent to $10**$.)

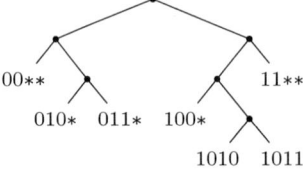   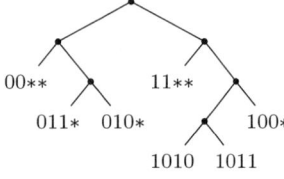

Fig. 36.   (a) Normal binary trie.   (b) Gray binary trie.

23. [20] Suppose $g(k) \oplus 2^j = g(l)$. What is a simple way to find l, given j and k?

24. [M21] Consider extending the Gray binary function g to all 2-adic integers (see Section 7.1.3). What is the corresponding inverse function $g^{[-1]}$?

▶ **25.** [M25] Prove that if $g(k)$ and $g(l)$ differ in $t > 0$ bits, and if $0 \le k, l < 2^n$, then $\lceil 2^t/3 \rceil \le |k - l| \le 2^n - \lceil 2^t/3 \rceil$.

26. [25] (Frank Ruskey.) For which integers N is it possible to generate all of the nonnegative integers less than N in such a way that only one bit of the binary representation changes at each step?

▶ **27.** [20] Let $S_0 = \{1\}$ and $S_{n+1} = 1/(2 + S_n) \cup 1/(2 - S_n)$; thus, for example,

$$S_2 = \left\{ \cfrac{1}{2 + \cfrac{1}{2+1}}, \cfrac{1}{2 + \cfrac{1}{2-1}}, \cfrac{1}{2 - \cfrac{1}{2+1}}, \cfrac{1}{2 - \cfrac{1}{2-1}} \right\} = \left\{ \frac{3}{7}, \frac{1}{3}, \frac{3}{5}, 1 \right\},$$

and S_n has 2^n elements that lie between $\frac{1}{3}$ and 1. Compute the 10^{10}th smallest element of S_{100}.

28. [M27] A *median* of n-bit strings $\{\alpha_1, \ldots, \alpha_t\}$, where α_k has the binary representation $\alpha_k = a_{k(n-1)} \ldots a_{k0}$, is a string $\hat{\alpha} = a_{n-1} \ldots a_0$ whose bits a_j for $0 \le j < n$ agree with the majority of the bits a_{kj} for $1 \le k \le t$. (If t is even and the bits α_{kj} are half 0 and half 1, the median bit a_j can be either 0 or 1.) For example, the strings $\{0010, 0100, 0101, 1110\}$ have two medians, 0100 and 0110, which we can denote by $01*0$.

a) Find a simple way to describe the medians of $G_t = \{g(0), \ldots, g(t-1)\}$, the first t Gray binary strings, when $0 < t \le 2^n$.

b) Prove that if $\alpha = a_{n-1} \ldots a_0$ is such a median, and if $2^{n-1} < t < 2^n$, then the string β obtained from α by complementing any bit a_j is also an element of G_t.

29. [M24] If integer values k are transmitted as n-bit Gray binary codes $g(k)$ and received with errors described by a bit pattern $p = (p_{n-1} \ldots p_0)_2$, the average numerical error is

$$\frac{1}{2^n} \sum_{k=0}^{2^n-1} \left| g^{[-1]}(g(k) \oplus p) - k \right|,$$

assuming that all values of k are equally likely. Show that this sum is equal to $\sum_{k=0}^{2^n-1} |(k \oplus p) - k|/2^n$, just as if Gray binary code were not used, and evaluate it explicitly.

▶ **30.** [M27] (*Gray permutation.*) Design a one-pass algorithm to replace the array elements $(X_0, X_1, X_2, \ldots, X_{2^n-1})$ by $(X_{g(0)}, X_{g(1)}, X_{g(2)}, \ldots, X_{g(2^n-1)})$, using only a constant amount of auxiliary storage. *Hint:* Considering the function $g(n)$ as a permutation of all nonnegative integers, show that the set

$$L = \left\{ 0, 1, (10)_2, (100)_2, (100*)_2, (100*0)_2, (100*0*)_2, \ldots \right\}$$

is the set of *cycle leaders* (the smallest elements of the cycles).

31. [HM35] (*Gray fields.*) Let $f_n(x) = g(r_n(x))$ denote the operation of reflecting the bits of an n-bit binary string as in exercise 5 and then converting to Gray binary code. For example, the operation $f_3(x)$ takes $(001)_2 \mapsto (110)_2 \mapsto (010)_2 \mapsto (011)_2 \mapsto (101)_2 \mapsto (111)_2 \mapsto (100)_2 \mapsto (001)_2$, hence all of the nonzero possibilities appear in a single cycle. Therefore we can use f_3 to define a field of 8 elements, with $\oplus$ as the addition operator and with multiplication defined by the rule

$$f_3^{[j]}(1) \times f_3^{[k]}(1) = f_3^{[j+k]}(1) = f_3^{[j]}(f_3^{[k]}(1)).$$

The functions f_2, f_5, and f_6 have the same nice property. But f_4 does not, because $f_4((1011)_2) = (1011)_2$.

Find all $n \leq 100$ for which f_n defines a field of 2^n elements.

32. [*M20*] True or false: Walsh functions satisfy $w_k(-x) = (-1)^k w_k(x)$.

▶ **33.** [*M20*] Prove the Rademacher-to-Walsh law (17).

34. [*M21*] The *Paley functions* $p_k(x)$ are defined by

$$p_0(x) = 1 \qquad \text{and} \qquad p_k(x) = (-1)^{\lfloor 2x \rfloor k} p_{\lfloor k/2 \rfloor}(2x).$$

Show that $p_k(x)$ has a simple expression in terms of Rademacher functions, analogous to (17), and relate Paley functions to Walsh functions.

35. [*HM23*] The $2^n \times 2^n$ Paley matrix P_n is obtained from Paley functions just as the Walsh matrix W_n is obtained from Walsh functions. (See (20).) Find interesting relations between P_n, W_n, and the Hadamard matrix H_n. Prove that all three matrices are symmetric.

36. [*21*] Spell out the details of an efficient algorithm to compute the Walsh transform $(x_0, \ldots, x_{2^n-1})$ of a given vector $(X_0, \ldots, X_{2^n-1})$.

37. [*HM23*] Let z_{kl} be the location of the lth sign change in $w_k(x)$, for $1 \leq l \leq k$ and $0 < z_{kl} < 1$. Prove that $|z_{kl} - l/(k+1)| = O((\log k)/k)$.

▶ **38.** [*M25*] Devise a ternary generalization of Walsh functions.

▶ **39.** [*HM30*] (J. J. Sylvester.) The rows of $\left(\begin{smallmatrix} a & b \\ b & -a \end{smallmatrix}\right)$ are orthogonal to each other and have the same magnitude; therefore the matrix identity

$$(A\ B) \begin{pmatrix} a^2+b^2 & 0 \\ 0 & a^2+b^2 \end{pmatrix} \begin{pmatrix} A \\ B \end{pmatrix} = (A\ B) \begin{pmatrix} a & b \\ b & -a \end{pmatrix} \begin{pmatrix} a & b \\ b & -a \end{pmatrix} \begin{pmatrix} A \\ B \end{pmatrix}$$

$$= (Aa+Bb\ \ Ab-Ba) \begin{pmatrix} aA+bB \\ bA-aB \end{pmatrix}$$

implies the sum-of-two-squares identity $(a^2+b^2)(A^2+B^2) = (aA+bB)^2 + (bA-aB)^2$. Similarly, the matrix

$$\begin{pmatrix} a & b & c & d \\ b & -a & d & -c \\ d & c & -b & -a \\ c & -d & -a & b \end{pmatrix}$$

leads to the sum-of-four-squares identity

$$(a^2+b^2+c^2+d^2)(A^2+B^2+C^2+D^2) = (aA+bB+cC+dD)^2 + (bA-aB+dC-cD)^2$$
$$+ (dA+cB-bC-aD)^2 + (cA-dB-aC+bD)^2.$$

a) Attach the signs of the matrix H_3 in (21) to the symbols $\{a, b, c, d, e, f, g, h\}$, obtaining a matrix with orthogonal rows and a sum-of-eight-squares identity.

b) Generalize to H_4 and higher-order matrices.

▶ **40.** [*21*] Would the text's five-letter word computation scheme produce correct answers also if the masks in step W2 were computed as $m_j = z \ \& \ (2^{5j} - 1)$ for $0 \leq j < 5$?

41. [*25*] If we use only the 3000 most common five-letter words — thereby omitting ducky, duces, dunks, dinks, dinky, dices, dicey, dicky, dicks, picky, pinky, punky, and pucks from (23) — how many valid words can still be generated from a single pair?

42. [*35*] (M. L. Fredman.) Algorithm L uses $\Theta(n \log n)$ bits of auxiliary memory for focus pointers as it chooses the Gray binary bit a_j to complement next. Step L3 examines $\Theta(\log n)$ of the auxiliary bits, and it occasionally changes $\Omega(\log n)$ of them.

Show that, from a theoretical standpoint, we can do better: The n-bit Gray binary code can be generated by changing at most 2 auxiliary bits between visits. (We still allow ourselves to examine $O(\log n)$ of the auxiliary bits on each step, so that we know which of them should be changed.)

43. [*41*] Determine $d(6)$, the number of 6-bit Gray cycles. (See (26).)

44. [*M20*] Show that $d(n) \leq \binom{M(n)}{2}$, if the n-cube has $M(n)$ perfect matchings.

45. [*M40*] (T. Feder and C. Subi, 2009.) This exercise constructs a large number of Gray cycles in the $(4r+2)$-cube $G = G_4 \square G_3 \square G_2 \square G_1 \square G_0 \square G_{-1}$, where G_i is an r-cube for $i > 0$ and $G_0 = G_{-1} = P_2$. The vertices v are $(4r+2)$-bit strings $v_4 \ldots v_0 v_{-1}$, where v_i has r bits for $i > 0$ and 1 bit for $i \leq 0$. The "signature" of v is the 4-bit string $\sigma(v) = s_4 s_3 s_2 (s_1 \oplus v_0)$, where s_i is the parity of v_i. We treat bit strings as binary numbers.

For $1 \leq l \leq 4$, let $\mathcal{M}_l(v)$ be a perfect matching in G with $v \longrightarrow v' = v_4' \ldots v_0' v_{-1}'$ and $v_i' = v_i$ for $i \neq l$. (Note that $\mathcal{M}_l(v') = v$.) Also define $\mathcal{M}_0(v) = v \oplus 2$. Consider the cycles formed by the edges $v \longrightarrow \mathcal{M}_{l(v)}(v)$, where $l(v)$ depends on v's signature:

$$\sigma(v) = \text{0000 0001 0011 0010 0110 0111 0101 0100 1100 1101 1111 1110 1010 1011 1001 1000}$$
$$l(v) = \quad\; 0 \quad\; 2 \quad\; 0 \quad\; 3 \quad\; 1 \quad\; 2 \quad\; 0 \quad\; 4 \quad\; 1 \quad\; 2 \quad\; 1 \quad\; 3 \quad\; 1 \quad\; 2 \quad\; 0 \quad\; 4$$

a) Suppose $r = 2$ and $\mathcal{M}_l(v) = v \oplus 2^{2l+s_{l-1}}$ for $l > 1$ and $\mathcal{M}_1(v) = v \oplus 2^{2+(v_0 \oplus v_{-1})}$. What cycle contains vertex $0 \ldots 0$ in this case?

b) A vertex whose signature is a power of 2 is called a "ground vertex." Four vertices with the same $v_4 \ldots v_1$ are called "siblings." Define $u \equiv v$ if u and v are in the same cycle, or if u and v are sibling ground vertices, or if a chain of such equivalences leads from u to v. Explain how to construct cycles in G for each equivalence class.

c) Furthermore, if u and v are sibling ground vertices, there is such a cycle that retains the edges $\{u \oplus 2 \longrightarrow u, v \oplus 2 \longrightarrow v\}$ of the original cycles.

d) Finally, show how to convert the cycles of (b) and (c) into a single cycle.

e) When $\mathcal{M}_1, \ldots, \mathcal{M}_4$ vary, how many different Hamiltonian cycles do we get?

46. [*M23*] Extend exercise 45 to the $(kr+2)$-cube, for k even.

47. [*HM24*] What asymptotic estimates do exercises 44 and 46 give for $d(n)^{1/2^n}$?

48. [*HM48*] Determine the asymptotic behavior of $d(n)^{1/2^n}$ as $n \to \infty$.

49. [*20*] Prove that for all $n \geq 1$ there is a $2n$-bit Gray cycle in which $v_{k+2^{2n-1}}$ is the complement of v_k, for all $k \geq 0$.

▶ **50.** [*21*] Find a construction like that of Theorem D but with l even.

51. [*M24*] (*Balanced Gray cycles.*) Complete the proof of Corollary B to Theorem D.

52. [*M20*] Prove that if the transition counts of an n-bit Gray cycle satisfy $c_0 \leq c_1 \leq \cdots \leq c_{n-1}$, we must have $c_0 + \cdots + c_{j-1} \geq 2^j$, with equality when $j = n$.

53. [*M46*] If the numbers $(c_0, \ldots, c_{n-1})$ are even and satisfy the condition of the previous exercise, is there always an n-bit Gray cycle with these transition counts?

54. [*M20*] (H. S. Shapiro, 1953.) Show that if a sequence of integers $(a_1, \ldots, a_{2^n})$ contains only n distinct values, then there is a subsequence whose product $a_{k+1} a_{k+2} \ldots a_l$ is a perfect square, for some $0 \leq k < l \leq 2^n$. However, this conclusion might not be true if we disallow the case $l = 2^n$.

▶ **55.** [*35*] (F. Ruskey and C. Savage, 1993.) If $(v_0, \ldots, v_{2^n-1})$ is an n-bit Gray cycle, the pairs $\{\{v_{2k}, v_{2k+1}\} \mid 0 \leq k < 2^{n-1}\}$ form a perfect matching between the vertices of even and odd parity in the n-cube. Conversely, does every such perfect matching arise as "half" of some n-bit Gray cycle?

56. [*M30*] (E. N. Gilbert, 1958.) Say that two Gray cycles are equivalent if their delta sequences can be made equal by permuting the coordinate names, or by reversing the cycle and/or starting the cycle at a different place. Show that the 2688 different 4-bit Gray cycles fall into just 9 equivalence classes.

57. [*32*] Consider a graph whose vertices are the 2688 possible 4-bit Gray cycles, where two such cycles are adjacent if they are related by one of the following simple transformations:

Before   After Type 1   After Type 2   After Type 3   After Type 4

(Type 1 changes arise when the cycle can be broken into two parts and reassembled with one part reversed. Types 2, 3, and 4 arise when the cycle can be broken into three parts and reassembled after reversing 0, 1, or 2 of the parts. The parts need not have equal size. Such transformations of Hamiltonian cycles are often possible.)

Write a program to discover which 4-bit Gray cycles are transformable into each other, by finding the connected components of the graph; restrict consideration to only one of the four types at a time.

▶ **58.** [*21*] Let α be the delta sequence of an n-bit Gray cycle, and obtain β from α by changing q occurrences of 0 to n, where q is odd. Prove that $\beta\beta$ is the delta sequence of an $(n+1)$-bit Gray cycle.

59. [*22*] The 5-bit Gray cycle of (30) is *nonlocal* in the sense that no 2^t consecutive elements belong to a single t-subcube, for $1 < t < n$. Prove that nonlocal n-bit Gray cycles exist for all $n \geq 5$. [*Hint:* See the previous exercise.]

60. [*20*] Show that the run-length-bound function satisfies $r(n+1) \geq r(n)$.

61. [*M30*] Show that $r(m+n) \geq r(m) + r(n) - 1$ if (a) $m = 2$ and $2 < r(n) < 8$; or (b) $m \leq n$ and $r(n) \leq 2^{m-3}$.

62. [*46*] Does $r(8) = 6$?

63. [*30*] (Luis Goddyn.) Prove that $r(10) \geq 8$.

▶ **64.** [*HM35*] (L. Goddyn and P. Gvozdjak.) An n-bit *Gray stream* is a sequence of permutations $(\sigma_0, \sigma_1, \ldots, \sigma_{l-1})$ where each σ_k is a permutation of the vertices of the n-cube, taking every vertex to one of its neighbors.

  a) Suppose $(u_0, \ldots, u_{2^m-1})$ is an m-bit Gray cycle and $(\sigma_0, \sigma_1, \ldots, \sigma_{2^m-1})$ is an n-bit Gray stream. Let $v_0 = 0\ldots 0$ and $v_{k+1} = v_k\sigma_k$, where $\sigma_k = \sigma_{k \bmod 2^m}$ if $k \geq 2^m$. Under what conditions is the sequence

$$W = (u_0 v_0,\ u_0 v_1,\ u_1 v_1,\ u_1 v_2,\ \ldots,\ u_{2^{m+n-1}-1} v_{2^{m+n-1}-1},\ u_{2^{m+n-1}-1} v_{2^{m+n-1}})$$

an $(m+n)$-bit Gray cycle?

  b) Show that if m is sufficiently large, there is an n-bit Gray stream satisfying the conditions of (a) for which all run lengths of the sequence $(v_0, v_1, \ldots)$ are $\geq n-2$.

  c) Apply these results to prove that $r(n) \geq n - O(\log n)$.

65. [*30*] (Brett Stevens.) In Samuel Beckett's play *Quad*, the stage begins and ends empty; n actors enter and exit one at a time, running through all 2^n possible subsets, and the actor who leaves is always the one whose previous entrance was earliest. When

$n = 4$, as in the actual play, some subsets are necessarily repeated. Show, however, that there is a perfect pattern with exactly 2^n entrances and exits when $n = 5$.

66. [40] Is there a perfect Beckett–Gray pattern for 8 actors?

67. [20] Sometimes it is desirable to run through all n-bit binary strings by changing as *many* bits as possible from one step to the next, for example when testing a physical circuit for reliable behavior in worst-case conditions. Explain how to traverse all binary n-tuples in such a way that each step changes n or $n - 1$ bits, alternately.

68. [21] Rufus Q. Perverse decided to construct an *anti-Gray* ternary code, in which each n-trit number differs from its neighbors in *every* digit position. Is such a code possible for all n?

▶ **69.** [M25] Modify the definition of Gray binary code (7) by letting

$$h(k) = (\ldots (b_6 \oplus b_5)(b_5 \oplus b_4)(b_4 \oplus b_3 \oplus b_2 \oplus b_0)(b_3 \oplus b_0)(b_2 \oplus b_1 \oplus b_0)b_1)_2,$$

when $k = (\ldots b_5 b_4 b_3 b_2 b_1 b_0)_2$.

a) Show that the sequence $h(0)$, $h(1)$, $\ldots$, $h(2^n - 1)$ runs through all n-bit numbers in such a way that exactly 3 bits change each time, when $n > 3$.

b) Generalize this rule to obtain sequences in which exactly t bits change at each step, when t is odd and $n > t$.

70. [21] How many monotonic n-bit Gray codes exist for $n = 5$ and $n = 6$?

71. [M22] Derive (45), the recurrence that defines the Savage–Winkler permutations.

72. [20] What is the Savage–Winkler code from 00000 to 11111?

▶ **73.** [32] Design an efficient algorithm to construct the delta sequence of an n-bit monotonic Gray code.

74. [M25] (Savage and Winkler.) How far apart can adjacent vertices of the n-cube be, in a monotonic Gray code?

75. [32] Find all 5-bit Gray paths v_0, $\ldots$, v_{31} that are *trend-free*, in the sense that $\sum_{k=0}^{31} k(-1)^{v_{kj}} = 0$ in each coordinate position j.

76. [M25] Prove that trend-free n-bit Gray codes exist for all $n \geq 5$.

77. [21] Modify Algorithm H in order to visit mixed-radix n-tuples in *modular* Gray order.

78. [M26] Prove the conversion formulas (50) and (51) for reflected mixed-radix Gray codes, and derive analogous formulas for the modular case.

▶ **79.** [M22] When is the last n-tuple of the (a) reflected (b) modular mixed-radix Gray code adjacent to the first?

80. [M20] Explain how to run through all divisors of a number, given its prime factorization $p_1^{e_1} \ldots p_t^{e_t}$, repeatedly multiplying or dividing by a single prime at each step.

81. [M21] Let (a_0, b_0), (a_1, b_1), $\ldots$, (a_{m^2-1}, b_{m^2-1}) be the 2-digit m-ary modular Gray code. Show that, if $m > 2$, every edge (x, y) — $(x, (y + 1) \bmod m)$ and (x, y) — $((x + 1) \bmod m, y)$ occurs in one of the two cycles

$$(a_0, b_0) \text{ — } (a_1, b_1) \text{ — } \cdots \text{ — } (a_{m^2-1}, b_{m^2-1}) \text{ — } (a_0, b_0),$$
$$(b_0, a_0) \text{ — } (b_1, a_1) \text{ — } \cdots \text{ — } (b_{m^2-1}, a_{m^2-1}) \text{ — } (b_0, a_0).$$

▶ **82.** [M25] (G. Ringel, 1956.) Use the previous exercise to deduce that there exist four 8-bit Gray cycles that, together, cover all edges of the 8-cube.

83. [41] Can four *balanced* 8-bit Gray cycles cover all edges of the 8-cube?

▶ **84.** [*25*] (Howard L. Dyckman.) Figure 37 shows a fascinating puzzle called Loony Loop or the Gordian Knot, in which the object is to remove a flexible cord from the rigid loops that surround it. Show that the solution to this puzzle is inherently related to the reflected Gray ternary code.

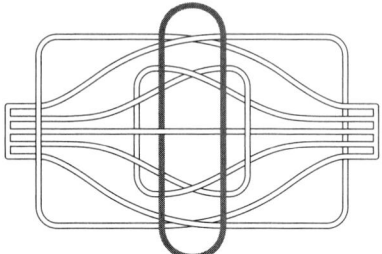

Fig. 37. The Loony Loop puzzle.

▶ **85.** [*M25*] (Dana Richards.) If $\Gamma = (\alpha_0, \dots, \alpha_{t-1})$ is any sequence of t strings and $\Gamma' = (\alpha'_0, \dots, \alpha'_{t'-1})$ is any sequence of t' strings, the *boustrophedon product* $\Gamma \wr \Gamma'$ is the sequence of tt' strings that begins

$$(\alpha_0\alpha'_0, \dots, \alpha_0\alpha'_{t'-1}, \alpha_1\alpha'_{t'-1}, \dots, \alpha_1\alpha'_0, \alpha_2\alpha'_0, \dots, \alpha_2\alpha'_{t'-1}, \alpha_3\alpha'_{t'-1}, \dots)$$

and ends with $\alpha_{t-1}\alpha'_0$ if t is even, $\alpha_{t-1}\alpha'_{t'-1}$ if t is odd. For example, the basic definition of Gray binary code in (5) can be expressed in this notation as $\Gamma_n = (0,1) \wr \Gamma_{n-1}$ when $n > 0$. Prove that the operation $\wr$ is associative, hence $\Gamma_{m+n} = \Gamma_m \wr \Gamma_n$.

▶ **86.** [*26*] Define an infinite Gray code that runs through all possible nonnegative integer n-tuples $(a_1, \dots, a_n)$ in such a way that $\max(a_1, \dots, a_n) \leq \max(a'_1, \dots, a'_n)$ when $(a_1, \dots, a_n)$ is followed by $(a'_1, \dots, a'_n)$.

87. [*27*] Continuing the previous exercise, define an infinite Gray code that runs through *all* integer n-tuples $(a_1, \dots, a_n)$, in such a way that $\max(|a_1|, \dots, |a_n|) \leq \max(|a'_1|, \dots, |a'_n|)$ when $(a_1, \dots, a_n)$ is followed by $(a'_1, \dots, a'_n)$.

▶ **88.** [*25*] After Algorithm K has terminated in step K4, what would happen if we immediately restarted it in step K2?

▶ **89.** [*25*] (*Gray code for Morse code.*) The Morse code words of length n (exercise 4.5.3–32) are strings of dots and dashes, where n is the number of dots plus twice the number of dashes.

   a) Show that it is possible to generate all Morse code words of length n by successively changing a dash to two dots or vice versa. For example, the path for $n = 3$ must be •—, •••, —• or its reverse.

   b) What string follows •——••—••• in your sequence for $n = 15$?

90. [*26*] For what values of n can the Morse code words be arranged in a *cycle*, under the ground rules of exercise 89? [*Hint:* The number of code words is F_{n+1}.]

▶ **91.** [*34*] Design a loopless algorithm to visit all binary n-tuples $(a_1, \dots, a_n)$ such that $a_1 \leq a_2 \geq a_3 \leq a_4 \geq \cdots$. [The number of such n-tuples is F_{n+2}.]

92. [*M30*] Is there an infinite sequence Φ_n whose first m^n elements form an m-ary de Bruijn cycle, for all m? [The case $n = 2$ is solved in (54).]

▶ **93.** [*M28*] Prove that Algorithm R outputs a de Bruijn cycle as advertised.

94. [*22*] What is the output of Algorithm D when $m = 5$, $n = 1$, and $r = 3$, if the coroutines $f()$ and $f'()$ generate the trivial cycles 01234 01234 01...?

▸ **95.** [*M23*] Suppose an infinite sequence $a_0 a_1 a_2 \ldots$ of period p is interleaved with an infinite sequence $b_0 b_1 b_2 \ldots$ of period q to form the infinite cyclic sequence

$$c_0 c_1 c_2 c_3 c_4 c_5 \ldots = a_0 b_0 a_1 b_1 a_2 b_2 \ldots .$$

a) Under what circumstances does $c_0 c_1 c_2 \ldots$ have period pq? (The "period" of a sequence $a_0 a_1 a_2 \ldots$, for the purposes of this exercise, is the smallest integer $p > 0$ such that $a_k = a_{k+p}$ for all $k \geq 0$.)

b) Which $2n$-tuples would occur as consecutive outputs of Algorithm D if step D6 were changed to say simply "If $t' = n$ and $x' < r$, go to D4"?

c) Prove that Algorithm D outputs a de Bruijn cycle as advertised.

▸ **96.** [*M28*] Suppose a family of coroutines has been set up to generate a de Bruijn cycle of length m^n using Algorithms R and D, based recursively on simple coroutines like Algorithm S for the base case $n = 2$, and using Algorithm D when $n > 2$ is even.

a) How many coroutines (R_n, D_n, S_n) of each type will there be?

b) What is the maximum number of coroutine activations needed to get one top-level digit of output?

97. [*M29*] The purpose of this exercise is to analyze the de Bruijn cycles constructed by Algorithms R and D in the important special case $m = 2$. Let $f_n(k)$ be the $(k+1)$st bit of the 2^n-cycle, so that $f_n(k) = 0$ for $0 \leq k < n$. Also let j_n be the index such that $0 \leq j_n < 2^n$ and $f_n(k) = 1$ for $j_n \leq k < j_n + n$.

a) Write out the cycles $\big(f_n(0) \ldots f_n(2^n - 1)\big)$ for $n = 2$, 3, 4, and 5.

b) Prove that, for all even values of n, there is a number $\delta_n = \pm 1$ such that we have

$$f_{n+1}(k) \equiv \begin{cases} \Sigma f_n(k), & \text{if } 0 < k \leq j_n \text{ or } 2^n + j_n < k \leq 2^{n+1}, \\ 1 + \Sigma f_n(k + \delta_n), & \text{if } j_n < k \leq 2^n + j_n, \end{cases}$$

where the congruence is modulo 2. (In this formula Σf stands for the summation function $\Sigma f(k) = \sum_{j=0}^{k-1} f(j)$.) Hence $j_{n+1} = 2^n - \delta_n$ when n is even.

c) Let $\big(c_n(0) c_n(1) \ldots c_n(2^{2n} - 5)\big)$ be the cycle produced when the simplified version of Algorithm D in exercise 95(b) is applied to $f_n()$. Where do the $(2n - 1)$-tuples 1^{2n-1} and $(01)^{n-1}0$ occur in this cycle?

d) Use the results of (c) to express $f_{2n}(k)$ in terms of $f_n()$.

e) Find a (somewhat) simple formula for j_n as a function of n.

98. [*M34*] Continuing the previous exercise, design an efficient algorithm to compute $f_n(k)$, given $n \geq 2$ and $k \geq 0$.

▸ **99.** [*M23*] Exploit the technology of the previous exercises to design an efficient algorithm that locates any given n-bit string in the cycle $\big(f_n(0) f_n(1) \ldots f_n(2^n - 1)\big)$.

100. [*40*] Do the de Bruijn cycles of exercise 97 provide a useful source of pseudo-random bits when n is large?

▸ **101.** [*M30*] (*Unique factorization of strings into nonincreasing primes.*)

a) Prove that if λ and λ' are prime, then $\lambda \lambda'$ is prime if $\lambda < \lambda'$.

b) Consequently every string α can be written in the form

$$\alpha = \lambda_1 \lambda_2 \ldots \lambda_t, \qquad \lambda_1 \geq \lambda_2 \geq \cdots \geq \lambda_t, \qquad \text{where each } \lambda_j \text{ is prime.}$$

c) In fact, only one such factorization is possible. *Hint:* Show that λ_t must be the lexicographically smallest nonempty suffix of α.

d) True or false: λ_1 is the longest prime prefix of α.

e) What are the prime factors of 31415926535897932384626433832795028841 97?

102. [*HM28*] Deduce the number of m-ary primes of length n from the unique factorization theorem in the previous exercise.

103. [*M20*] Use Eq. (59) to prove Fermat's theorem that $m^p \equiv m$ (modulo p).

104. [*17*] According to formula (60), about $1/n$ of all n-letter words are prime. How many of the 5757 five-letter GraphBase words are prime? Which of them is the smallest nonprime? The largest prime?

105. [*M31*] Let α be a preprime string of length n on an infinite alphabet.
  a) Show that if the final letter of α is increased, the resulting string is prime.
  b) If α has been factored as in exercise 101, show that it is the n-extension of λ_1.
  c) Furthermore α cannot be the n-extension of two different primes.

▶ **106.** [*M30*] By reverse-engineering Algorithm F, design an algorithm that visits all m-ary primes and preprimes in *decreasing* order.

107. [*HM30*] Analyze the running time of Algorithm F, for fixed m as $n \to \infty$.

108. [*M35*] Let $\lambda_1 < \cdots < \lambda_t$ be the m-ary prime strings whose lengths divide n, and let $a_1 \ldots a_n$ be any m-ary string. The object of this exercise is to prove that $a_1 \ldots a_n$ appears in $\lambda_1 \ldots \lambda_t \lambda_1 \lambda_2$; hence $\lambda_1 \ldots \lambda_t$ is a de Bruijn cycle (since it has length m^n). For convenience we may assume that $m = 10$ and that strings correspond to decimal numbers; the same arguments will apply for arbitrary $m \geq 2$.
  a) Show that if $a_1 \ldots a_n = \alpha\beta$ is distinct from all its cyclic shifts, and if $\beta\alpha = \lambda_k$ is prime, then $\alpha\beta$ is a substring of $\lambda_k \lambda_{k+1}$, unless $\alpha = 9^j$ for some $j \geq 1$.
  b) Where does $\alpha\beta$ appear in $\lambda_1 \ldots \lambda_t$ if $\beta\alpha$ is prime and α consists of all 9s? *Hint:* Show that if $a_{n+1-l} \ldots a_n = 9^l$ in step F2 for some $l > 0$, and if j is not a divisor of n, the previous step F2 had $a_{n-l} \ldots a_n = 9^{l+1}$.
  c) Now consider n-tuples of the form $(\alpha\beta)^d$, where $d > 1$ is a divisor of n and $\beta\alpha = \lambda_k$ is prime.
  d) Where do 899135, 997879, 913131, 090909, 909090, and 911911 occur when $n=6$?
  e) Is $\lambda_1 \ldots \lambda_t$ the lexicographically least m-ary de Bruijn cycle of length m^n?

109. [*M22*] An m-ary de Bruijn torus of size $m^2 \times m^2$ for 2×2 windows is a matrix of m-ary digits d_{ij} such that each of the m^4 submatrices

$$\begin{pmatrix} d_{ij} & d_{i(j+1)} \\ d_{(i+1)j} & d_{(i+1)(j+1)} \end{pmatrix}, \qquad 0 \leq i, j < m^2$$

is different, where subscripts wrap around modulo m^2. Thus every possible m-ary 2×2 submatrix occurs exactly once; Ian Stewart [*Game, Set, and Math* (Oxford: Blackwell, 1989), Chapter 4] has therefore called it an m-ary *ourotorus*. For example,

$$\begin{pmatrix} 0 & 0 & 1 & 0 \\ 0 & 0 & 0 & 1 \\ 0 & 1 & 1 & 1 \\ 1 & 0 & 1 & 1 \end{pmatrix}$$

is a binary ourotorus; indeed, it is essentially the only such matrix when $m = 2$, except for shifting and/or transposition.

Consider the infinite matrix D whose entry in row $i = (\ldots a_2 a_1 a_0)_2$ and column $j = (\ldots b_2 b_1 b_0)_2$ is $d_{ij} = (\ldots c_2 c_1 c_0)_2$, where

$$c_0 = (a_0 \oplus b_0)(a_1 \oplus b_1) \oplus b_1;$$
$$c_k = (a_{2k} a_0 \oplus b_{2k}) b_0 \oplus (a_{2k+1} a_0 \oplus b_{2k+1})(b_0 \oplus 1), \quad \text{for } k > 0.$$

Show that the upper left $2^{2n} \times 2^{2n}$ submatrix of D is a 2^n-ary ourotorus for all $n \geq 0$.

110. [*M25*] Continuing the previous exercise, construct m-ary ourotoruses for all m.

111. [*20*] We can obtain the number 100 in twelve ways by inserting $+$ and $-$ signs into the sequence 123456789; for example, $100 = 1 + 23 - 4 + 5 + 6 + 78 - 9 = 123 - 45 - 67 + 89 = -1 + 2 - 3 + 4 + 5 + 6 + 78 + 9$.

    a) What is the smallest positive integer that cannot be represented in such a way?

    b) Consider also inserting signs into the 10-digit sequence 9876543210.

▶ **112.** [*25*] Continuing the previous exercise, how far can we go by inserting signs into 12345678987654321? For example, $100 = -1234 - 5 - 6 + 7898 - 7 - 6543 - 2 - 1$.

7.2.1.2. Generating all permutations.

After n-tuples, the next most important item on nearly everybody's wish list for combinatorial generation is the task of visiting all *permutations* of some given set or multiset. Many different ways have been devised to solve this problem. In fact, almost as many different algorithms have been published for unsorting as for sorting! We will study the most important permutation generators in this section, beginning with a classical method that is both simple and flexible:

Algorithm L (*Lexicographic permutation generation*). Given a sequence of n elements $a_1 a_2 \ldots a_n$, initially sorted so that

$$a_1 \leq a_2 \leq \cdots \leq a_n, \tag{1}$$

this algorithm generates all permutations of $\{a_1, a_2, \ldots, a_n\}$, visiting them in lexicographic order. (For example, the permutations of $\{1, 2, 2, 3\}$ are

$$1223, \ 1232, \ 1322, \ 2123, \ 2132, \ 2213, \ 2231, \ 2312, \ 2321, \ 3122, \ 3212, \ 3221,$$

ordered lexicographically.) An auxiliary element a_0 is assumed to be present for convenience; a_0 must be strictly less than the largest element a_n.

L1. [Visit.] Visit the permutation $a_1 a_2 \ldots a_n$.

L2. [Find j.] Set $j \leftarrow n - 1$. If $a_j \geq a_{j+1}$, decrease j by 1 repeatedly until $a_j < a_{j+1}$. Terminate the algorithm if $j = 0$. (At this point j is the smallest subscript such that we've already visited all permutations beginning with $a_1 \ldots a_j$. So the lexicographically next permutation will make a_j larger.)

L3. [Increase a_j.] Set $l \leftarrow n$. If $a_j \geq a_l$, decrease l by 1 repeatedly until $a_j < a_l$. Then interchange $a_j \leftrightarrow a_l$. (Since $a_{j+1} \geq \cdots \geq a_n$, element a_l is the smallest element greater than a_j that can legitimately follow $a_1 \ldots a_{j-1}$ in a permutation. Before the interchange we had $a_{j+1} \geq \cdots \geq a_{l-1} \geq a_l > a_j \geq a_{l+1} \geq \cdots \geq a_n$; after the interchange, we have $a_{j+1} \geq \cdots \geq a_{l-1} \geq a_j > a_l \geq a_{l+1} \geq \cdots \geq a_n$.)

L4. [Reverse $a_{j+1} \ldots a_n$.] Set $k \leftarrow j + 1$ and $l \leftarrow n$. Then, while $k < l$, interchange $a_k \leftrightarrow a_l$ and set $k \leftarrow k + 1$, $l \leftarrow l - 1$. Return to L1. ∎

This algorithm goes back to Nārāyaṇa Paṇḍita in 14th-century India (see Section 7.2.1.7); it also appeared in C. F. Hindenburg's preface to *Specimen Analyticum de Lineis Curvis Secundi Ordinis* by C. F. Rüdiger (Leipzig: 1784), xlvi–xlvii, and it has been frequently rediscovered ever since. The parenthetical remarks in steps L2 and L3 explain why it works.

> *Tin tan din dan bim bam bom bo —*
> *tan tin din dan bam bim bo bom —*
> *tin tan dan din bim bam bom bo —*
> *tan tin dan din bam bim bo bom —*
> *tan dan tin bam din bo bim bom —*
> *.... Tin tan din dan bim bam bom bo.*
> — DOROTHY L. SAYERS, *The Nine Tailors* (1934)

> *A permutation on the ten decimal digits is simply a 10 digit decimal number*
> *in which all digits are distinct. Hence all we need to do is to produce*
> *all 10 digit numbers and select only those whose digits are distinct.*
> *Isn't it wonderful how high speed computing saves us from*
> *the drudgery of thinking! We simply program $k + 1 \rightarrow k$*
> *and examine the digits of k for undesirable equalities.*
> *This gives us the permutations in dictionary order too!*
> *On second sober thought ... we do need to think of something else.*
> — D. H. LEHMER (1957)

In general, the lexicographic successor of any combinatorial pattern $a_1 \ldots a_n$ is obtainable by a three-step procedure:

1) Find the largest j such that a_j can be increased.
2) Increase a_j by the smallest feasible amount.
3) Find the lexicographically least way to extend the new $a_1 \ldots a_j$ to a complete pattern.

Algorithm L follows this general procedure in the case of permutation generation, just as Algorithm 7.2.1.1M followed it in the case of n-tuple generation; we will see numerous further instances later, as we consider other kinds of combinatorial patterns. Notice that we have $a_{j+1} \geq \cdots \geq a_n$ at the beginning of step L4. Therefore the first permutation beginning with the current prefix $a_1 \ldots a_j$ is $a_1 \ldots a_j a_n \ldots a_{j+1}$, and step L4 produces it by doing $\lfloor (n - j)/2 \rfloor$ interchanges.

In practice, step L2 finds $j = n - 1$ half of the time when the elements are distinct, because exactly $n!/2$ of the $n!$ permutations have $a_{n-1} < a_n$. Therefore Algorithm L can be speeded up by recognizing this special case, without making it significantly more complicated. (See exercise 1.) Similarly, the probability that $j \leq n - t$ is only $1/t!$ when the a's are distinct; hence the loops in steps L2–L4 usually go very fast. Exercise 6 analyzes the running time in general, showing that Algorithm L is reasonably efficient even when equal elements are present, unless some values appear much more often than others do in the multiset $\{a_1, a_2, \ldots, a_n\}$.

Adjacent interchanges. We saw in Section 7.2.1.1 that Gray codes are advantageous for generating n-tuples, and similar considerations apply when we want to generate permutations. The simplest possible change to a permutation is to interchange adjacent elements, and we know from Chapter 5 that any permutation can be sorted into order if we make a suitable sequence of such interchanges. (For example, Algorithm 5.2.2B works in this way.) Hence we can go backward and obtain any desired permutation, by starting with all elements in order and then exchanging appropriate pairs of adjacent elements.

A natural question now arises: Is it possible to run through *all* permutations of a given multiset in such a way that only two adjacent elements change places at every step? If so, the overall program that is examining all permutations will often be simpler and faster, because it will only need to calculate the effect of an exchange instead of to reprocess an entirely new array $a_1 \ldots a_n$ each time.

Alas, when the multiset has repeated elements, we can't always find such a Gray-like sequence. For example, the six permutations of $\{1, 1, 2, 2\}$ are connected to each other in the following way by adjacent interchanges:

$$1122 \ \underline{\quad} \ 1212 \ \overset{\textstyle 2112}{\underset{\textstyle 1221}{<\quad>}} \ 2121 \ \underline{\quad} \ 2211; \qquad (2)$$

this graph has no Hamiltonian path.

But most applications deal with permutations of *distinct* elements, and for this case there is good news: A simple algorithm makes it possible to generate all $n!$ permutations by making just $n! - 1$ adjacent interchanges. Furthermore, another such interchange returns to the starting point, so we have a Hamiltonian cycle analogous to Gray binary code.

The idea is to take such a sequence for $\{1, \ldots, n - 1\}$ and to insert the number n into each permutation in all ways. For example, if $n = 4$ the sequence $(123, 132, 312, 321, 231, 213)$ leads to the columns of the array

$$\begin{array}{cccccc}
1234 & 1324 & 3124 & 3214 & 2314 & 2134 \\
1243 & 1342 & 3142 & 3241 & 2341 & 2143 \\
1423 & 1432 & 3412 & 3421 & 2431 & 2413 \\
4123 & 4132 & 4312 & 4321 & 4231 & 4213
\end{array} \qquad (3)$$

when 4 is inserted in all four possible positions. Now we obtain the desired sequence by reading downwards in the first column, upwards in the second, downwards in the third, $\ldots$, upwards in the last: $(1234, 1243, 1423, 4123, 4132, 1432, 1342, 1324, 3124, 3142, \ldots, 2143, 2134)$.

In Section 5.1.1 we studied the inversions of a permutation, namely the pairs of elements (not necessarily adjacent) that are out of order. Every interchange of adjacent elements changes the total number of inversions by ± 1. In fact, when we consider the so-called inversion table $c_1 \ldots c_n$ of exercise 5.1.1–7, where c_j is the number of elements lying to the right of j that are less than j, we find that the permutations in (3) have the following inversion tables:

$$\begin{array}{cccccc}
0000 & 0010 & 0020 & 0120 & 0110 & 0100 \\
0001 & 0011 & 0021 & 0121 & 0111 & 0101 \\
0002 & 0012 & 0022 & 0122 & 0112 & 0102 \\
0003 & 0013 & 0023 & 0123 & 0113 & 0103
\end{array} \qquad (4)$$

And if we read these columns alternately down and up as before, we obtain precisely the reflected Gray code for mixed radices $(1, 2, 3, 4)$, as in Eqs. (46)–(51)

of Section 7.2.1.1. The same property holds for all n, as noticed by E. W. Dijkstra [*Acta Informatica* **6** (1976), 357–359], and it leads us to the following formulation:

Algorithm P (*Plain changes*). Given a sequence $a_1 a_2 \ldots a_n$ of n distinct elements, this algorithm generates all of their permutations by repeatedly interchanging adjacent pairs. It uses an auxiliary array $c_1 c_2 \ldots c_n$, which represents inversions as described above, running through all sequences of integers such that

$$0 \le c_j < j \qquad \text{for } 1 \le j \le n. \tag{5}$$

Another array $o_1 o_2 \ldots o_n$ governs the directions by which the entries c_j change.

P1. [Initialize.] Set $c_j \leftarrow 0$ and $o_j \leftarrow 1$ for $1 \le j \le n$.

P2. [Visit.] Visit the permutation $a_1 a_2 \ldots a_n$.

P3. [Prepare for change.] Set $j \leftarrow n$ and $s \leftarrow 0$. (The following steps determine the coordinate j for which c_j is about to change, preserving (5); variable s is the number of indices $k > j$ such that $c_k = k - 1$.)

P4. [Ready to change?] Set $q \leftarrow c_j + o_j$. If $q < 0$, go to P7; if $q = j$, go to P6.

P5. [Change.] Interchange $a_{j-c_j+s} \leftrightarrow a_{j-q+s}$. Then set $c_j \leftarrow q$ and return to P2.

P6. [Increase s.] Terminate if $j = 1$; otherwise set $s \leftarrow s + 1$.

P7. [Switch direction.] Set $o_j \leftarrow -o_j$, $j \leftarrow j - 1$, and go back to P4. ∎

This procedure, which clearly works for all $n \ge 1$, originated in 17th-century England, when bell ringers began the delightful custom of ringing a set of bells in all possible permutations. They called Algorithm P the method of *plain changes*. Figure 38(a) illustrates the "Cambridge Forty-Eight," an irregular and ad hoc sequence of 48 permutations on 5 bells that had been used in the early 1600s, before the plain-change principle revealed how to achieve all $5! = 120$ possibilities. The venerable history of Algorithm P has been traced to a manuscript by Peter Mundy now in the Bodleian Library, written about 1653 and transcribed by Ernest Morris in *The History and Art of Change Ringing* (1931), 29–30. Shortly afterwards, a famous book called *Tintinnalogia*, published anonymously in 1668 but now known to have been written by Richard Duckworth and Fabian Stedman, devoted its first 60 pages to a detailed description of plain changes, working up from $n = 3$ to the case of arbitrarily large n.

> Cambridge Forty-eight, *for many years,*
> *was the greatest* Peal *that was* Rang *or invented; but now,*
> *neither* Forty-eight, *nor a* Hundred, *nor* Seven-hundred and twenty,
> *nor any* Number *can confine us; for we can* Ring Changes, Ad infinitum.
> *... On four Bells, there are* Twenty four *several Changes,*
> *in* Ringing *of which, there is one Bell called the* Hunt,
> *and the other three are Extream Bells;*
> *the* Hunt *moves, and hunts up and down continually ... ;*
> *two of the* Extream *Bells makes a Change*
> *every time the* Hunt *comes before or behind them.*
> — R. DUCKWORTH and F. STEDMAN, *Tintinnalogia* (1668)

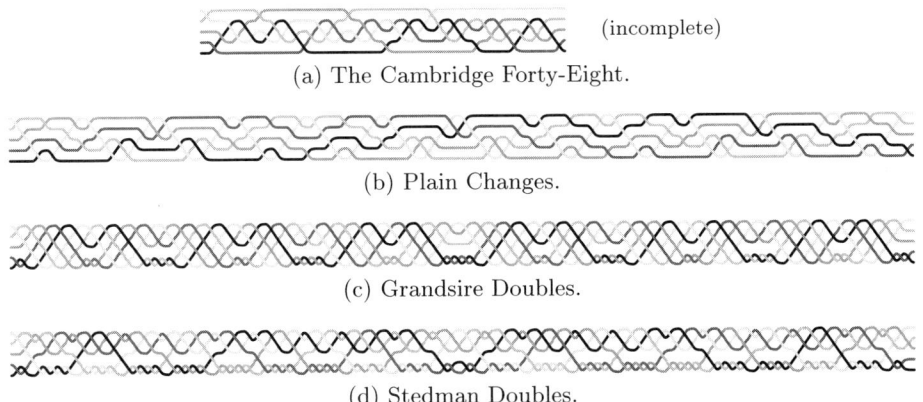

(incomplete)

(a) The Cambridge Forty-Eight.

(b) Plain Changes.

(c) Grandsire Doubles.

(d) Stedman Doubles.

Fig. 38. Four patterns that were used in 17th-century England to ring permutations of five different church-bells. Pattern (b) corresponds to Algorithm P.

British bellringing enthusiasts soon went on to develop more complicated schemes in which two or more pairs of bells change places simultaneously. For example, they devised the pattern in Fig. 38(c) known as Grandsire Doubles, "the best and most ingenious Peal that ever was composed, to be rang on five bells" [*Tintinnalogia*, page 95]. Such fancier methods are more interesting than Algorithm P from a musical standpoint, but they are less useful in computer applications, so we shall not dwell on them here. Interested readers can learn more by reading W. G. Wilson's book, *Change Ringing* (1965); see also A. T. White, *AMM* **103** (1996), 771–778.

H. F. Trotter published the first computer implementation of plain changes in *CACM* **5** (1962), 434–435. The algorithm is quite efficient, especially when it is streamlined as in exercise 16, because $n - 1$ out of every n permutations are generated without using steps P6 and P7. By contrast, Algorithm L enjoys its best case only about half of the time.

The fact that Algorithm P does exactly one interchange per visit means that the permutations it generates are alternately even and odd (see exercise 5.1.1–13). Therefore we can generate all the even permutations by simply bypassing the odd ones. In fact, the c and o tables make it easy to keep track of the current total number of inversions, $c_1 + \cdots + c_n$, as we go.

Many programs need to generate the same permutations repeatedly, and in such cases we needn't run through the steps of Algorithm P each time. We can simply prepare a list of suitable transitions, using the following method:

Algorithm T (*Plain change transitions*). This algorithm computes a table $t[1]$, $t[2]$, ..., $t[n! - 1]$ such that the actions of Algorithm P are equivalent to the successive interchanges $a_{t[k]} \leftrightarrow a_{t[k]+1}$ for $1 \le k < n!$. We assume that $n \ge 2$.

T1. [Initialize.] Set $N \leftarrow n!$, $d \leftarrow N/2$, $t[d] \leftarrow 1$, and $m \leftarrow 2$.

T2. [Loop on m.] Terminate if $m = n$. Otherwise set $m \leftarrow m + 1$, $d \leftarrow d/m$, and $k \leftarrow 0$. (We maintain the condition $d = n!/m!$.)

T3. [Hunt down.] Set $k \leftarrow k + d$ and $j \leftarrow m - 1$. Then while $j > 0$, set $t[k] \leftarrow j$, $k \leftarrow k + d$, and $j \leftarrow j - 1$.

T4. [Offset.] Set $t[k] \leftarrow t[k] + 1$.

T5. [Hunt up.] Set $k \leftarrow k + d$, $j \leftarrow 1$. While $j < m$, set $t[k] \leftarrow j$, $k \leftarrow k + d$, $j \leftarrow j + 1$. Then return to T3 if $k < N$, otherwise return to T2. ∎

For example, if $n = 4$ we get the table $(t[1], t[2], \ldots, t[23]) = (3, 2, 1, 3, 1, 2, 3, 1, 3, 2, 1, 3, 1, 2, 3, 1, 3, 2, 1, 3, 1, 2, 3)$.

Alphametics. Now let's consider a simple kind of puzzle in which permutations are useful: How can the pattern

$$
\begin{array}{r}
\texttt{SEND} \\
+\ \texttt{MORE} \\
\hline
\texttt{MONEY}
\end{array}
\tag{6}
$$

represent a correct sum, if every letter stands for a different decimal digit? [H. E. Dudeney, *Strand* **68** (1924), 97, 214.] Such puzzles are often called "alphametics," a word coined by J. A. H. Hunter [*Globe and Mail* (Toronto: 27 October 1955), 27]; another term, "cryptarithm," has also been suggested by S. Vatriquant [*Sphinx* **1** (May 1931), 50].

The classic alphametic (6) can easily be solved by hand (see exercise 21). But let's suppose we want to deal with a large set of complicated alphametics, some of which may be unsolvable while others may have dozens of solutions. Then we can save time by programming a computer to try out all permutations of digits that match a given pattern, seeing which permutations yield a correct sum. [A computer program for solving alphametics was published by John Beidler in *Creative Computing* **4**, 6 (November–December 1978), 110–113.]

We might as well raise our sights slightly and consider additive alphametics in general, dealing not only with simple sums like (6) but also with examples like

$$\texttt{VIOLIN} + \texttt{VIOLIN} + \texttt{VIOLA} = \texttt{TRIO} + \texttt{SONATA}.$$

Equivalently, we want to solve puzzles such as

$$2(\texttt{VIOLIN}) + \texttt{VIOLA} - \texttt{TRIO} - \texttt{SONATA} = 0, \tag{7}$$

where a sum of terms with integer coefficients is given and the goal is to obtain zero by substituting distinct decimal digits for the different letters. Each letter in such a problem has a "signature" obtained by substituting 1 for that letter and 0 for the others; for example, the signature for $\texttt{I}$ in (7) is

$$2(010010) + 01000 - 0010 - 000000,$$

namely 21010. If we arbitrarily assign the codes $(1, 2, \ldots, 10)$ to the letters $(\texttt{V}, \texttt{I}, \texttt{O}, \texttt{L}, \texttt{N}, \texttt{A}, \texttt{T}, \texttt{R}, \texttt{S}, \texttt{X})$, the respective signatures corresponding to (7) are

$$
\begin{aligned}
&s_1 = 210000, \quad s_2 = 21010, \quad s_3 = -7901, \quad s_4 = 210, \quad s_5 = -998, \\
&s_6 = -100, \quad s_7 = -1010, \quad s_8 = -100, \quad s_9 = -100000, \quad s_{10} = 0.
\end{aligned}
\tag{8}
$$

(An additional letter, X, has been added because we need ten of them.) The problem now is to find all permutations $a_1 \ldots a_{10}$ of $\{0, 1, \ldots, 9\}$ such that

$$a \cdot s = \sum_{j=1}^{10} a_j s_j = 0. \tag{9}$$

There also is a side condition, because the numbers in alphametics should not have zero as a leading digit. For example, the sums

$$
\begin{array}{cccc}
7316 & 5731 & 6524 & 2817 \\
+\,0823 & +\,0647 & +\,0735 & +\,0368 \\
\hline
08139 & 06378 & 07259 & 03185
\end{array}
$$

and   and   and

and numerous others are *not* considered to be valid solutions of (6). In general there is a set F of first letters such that we must have

$$a_j \neq 0 \qquad \text{for all } j \in F; \tag{10}$$

the set F corresponding to (7) and (8) is $\{1, 7, 9\}$.

One way to tackle a family of additive alphametics is to start by using Algorithm T to prepare a table of $10! - 1$ transitions $t[k]$. Then, for each problem defined by a signature sequence $(s_1, \ldots, s_{10})$ and a first-letter set F, we can exhaustively look for solutions as follows:

A1. [Initialize.] Set $a_1 a_2 \ldots a_{10} \leftarrow 01 \ldots 9$, $v \leftarrow \sum_{j=1}^{10} (j-1)s_j$, $k \leftarrow 1$, and $\delta_j \leftarrow s_{j+1} - s_j$ for $1 \leq j < 10$.

A2. [Test.] If $v = 0$ and if (10) holds, output the solution $a_1 \ldots a_{10}$.

A3. [Swap.] Stop if $k = 10!$. Otherwise set $j \leftarrow t[k]$, $v \leftarrow v - (a_{j+1} - a_j)\delta_j$, $a_{j+1} \leftrightarrow a_j$, $k \leftarrow k + 1$, and return to A2. ∎

Step A3 is justified by the fact that swapping a_j with a_{j+1} simply decreases $a \cdot s$ by $(a_{j+1} - a_j)(s_{j+1} - s_j)$. Even though 10! is 3,628,800, a fairly large number, the operations in step A3 are so simple that the whole job takes only a fraction of a second on a modern computer.

An alphametic is said to be *pure* if it has a unique solution. Unfortunately (7) is not pure; the permutations 1764802539 and 3546281970 both solve (9) and (10), hence we have both

$$176478 + 176478 + 17640 = 2576 + 368020$$

and

$$354652 + 354652 + 35468 = 1954 + 742818.$$

Furthermore $s_6 = s_8$ in (8), so we can obtain two more solutions by interchanging the digits assigned to A and R.

On the other hand (6) *is* pure, yet the method we have described will find two different permutations that solve it. The reason is that (6) involves only eight distinct letters, hence we will set it up for solution by using two dummy signatures $s_9 = s_{10} = 0$. In general, an alphametic with m distinct letters will have $10 - m$ dummy signatures $s_{m+1} = \cdots = s_{10} = 0$, and each of its solutions will be found $(10 - m)!$ times unless we insist that, say, $a_{m+1} < \cdots < a_{10}$.

A general framework. A great many algorithms have been proposed for generating permutations of distinct objects, and the best way to understand them is to apply the multiplicative properties of permutations that we studied in Section 1.3.3. For this purpose we will change our notation slightly, by using 0-origin indexing and writing $a_0 a_1 \ldots a_{n-1}$ for permutations of $\{0, 1, \ldots, n-1\}$ instead of writing $a_1 a_2 \ldots a_n$ for permutations of $\{1, 2, \ldots, n\}$. More importantly, we will consider schemes for generating permutations in which most of the action takes place at the *left*, so that all permutations of $\{0, 1, \ldots, k-1\}$ will be generated during the first $k!$ steps, for $1 \le k \le n$. For example, one such scheme for $n = 4$ is

$$0123, 1023, 0213, 2013, 1203, 2103, 0132, 1032, 0312, 3012, 1302, 3102,$$
$$0231, 2031, 0321, 3021, 2301, 3201, 1230, 2130, 1320, 3120, 2310, 3210; \quad (11)$$

this is called "reverse colex order," because if we reflect the strings from right to left we get 3210, 3201, 3120, ..., 0123, the reverse of lexicographic order. Another way to think of (11) is to view the entries as $(n-a_n) \ldots (n-a_2)(n-a_1)$, where $a_1 a_2 \ldots a_n$ runs lexicographically through the permutations of $\{1, 2, \ldots, n\}$.

Let's recall from Section 1.3.3 that a permutation like $\alpha = 250143$ can be written either in the two-line form

$$\alpha = \begin{pmatrix} 012345 \\ 250143 \end{pmatrix}$$

or in the more compact cycle form

$$\alpha = (0\ 2)(1\ 5\ 3),$$

with the meaning that α takes $0 \mapsto 2$, $1 \mapsto 5$, $2 \mapsto 0$, $3 \mapsto 1$, $4 \mapsto 4$, and $5 \mapsto 3$; a 1-cycle like '(4)' need not be indicated. Since 4 is a fixed point of this permutation we say that "α fixes 4." We also write $0\alpha = 2$, $1\alpha = 5$, and so on, saying that "$j\alpha$ is the image of j under α." Multiplication of permutations, like α times β where $\beta = 543210$, is readily carried out either in the two-line form

$$\alpha\beta = \begin{pmatrix} 012345 \\ 250143 \end{pmatrix}\begin{pmatrix} 012345 \\ 543210 \end{pmatrix} = \begin{pmatrix} 012345 \\ 250143 \end{pmatrix}\begin{pmatrix} 250143 \\ 305412 \end{pmatrix} = \begin{pmatrix} 012345 \\ 305412 \end{pmatrix}$$

or in the cycle form

$$\alpha\beta = (0\ 2)(1\ 5\ 3) \cdot (0\ 5)(1\ 4)(2\ 3) = (0\ 3\ 4\ 1)(2\ 5).$$

Notice that the image of 1 under $\alpha\beta$ is $1(\alpha\beta) = (1\alpha)\beta = 5\beta = 0$, etc. *Warning:* About half of all books that deal with permutations multiply them the other way (from right to left), imagining that $\alpha\beta$ means that β should be applied before α. The reason is that traditional functional notation, in which one writes $\alpha(1) = 5$, makes it natural to think that $\alpha\beta(1)$ should mean $\alpha(\beta(1)) = \alpha(4) = 4$. However, the present book subscribes to the other philosophy, and we shall always multiply permutations from left to right.

The order of multiplication needs to be understood carefully when permutations are represented by arrays of numbers. For example, if we "apply" the reflection $\beta = 543210$ to the permutation $\alpha = 250143$, the result 341052 is not $\alpha\beta$

but $\beta\alpha$. In general, the operation of replacing a permutation $\alpha = a_0 a_1 \ldots a_{n-1}$ by some rearrangement $a_{0\beta} a_{1\beta} \ldots a_{(n-1)\beta}$ takes $k \mapsto a_{k\beta} = k\beta\alpha$. Permuting the *positions* by β corresponds to *premultiplication* by β, changing α to $\beta\alpha$; permuting the *values* by β corresponds to *postmultiplication* by β, changing α to $\alpha\beta$. Thus, for example, a permutation generator that interchanges $a_1 \leftrightarrow a_2$ is premultiplying the current permutation by $(1\ 2)$, postmultiplying it by $(a_1\ a_2)$.

Following a proposal made by Évariste Galois in 1830, a nonempty set G of permutations is said to form a *group* if it is closed under multiplication, that is, if the product $\alpha\beta$ is in G whenever α and β are elements of G [see *Écrits et Mémoires Mathématiques d'Évariste Galois* (Paris: 1962), 47]. Consider, for example, the 4-cube represented as a 4×4 torus

$$
\begin{array}{cccc}
0 & 1 & 3 & 2 \\
4 & 5 & 7 & 6 \\
c & d & f & e \\
8 & 9 & b & a
\end{array}
\tag{12}
$$

as in exercise 7.2.1.1–17, and let G be the set of all permutations of the vertices $\{0, 1, \ldots, \mathrm{f}\}$ that preserve adjacency: A permutation α is in G if and only if $u - v$ implies $u\alpha - v\alpha$ in the 4-cube. (Here we are using hexadecimal digits $(0, 1, \ldots, \mathrm{f})$ to stand for the integers $(0, 1, \ldots, 15)$. The labels in (12) are chosen so that $u - v$ if and only if u and v differ in only one bit position.) This set G is obviously a group, and its elements are called the symmetries or "automorphisms" of the 4-cube.

Groups of permutations G are conveniently represented inside a computer by means of a *Sims table*, introduced by Charles C. Sims [*Computational Methods in Abstract Algebra* (Oxford: Pergamon, 1970), 169–183], which is a family of subsets S_1, S_2, ... of G having the following property: S_k contains exactly one permutation σ_{kj} that takes $k \mapsto j$ and fixes the values of all elements greater than k, whenever G contains such a permutation. We let σ_{kk} be the identity permutation, which is always present in G; but when $0 \le j < k$, any suitable permutation can be selected to play the role of σ_{kj}. The main advantage of a Sims table is that it provides a convenient representation of the entire group:

Lemma S. *Let S_1, S_2, ..., S_{n-1} be a Sims table for a group G of permutations on $\{0, 1, \ldots, n-1\}$. Then every element α of G has a unique representation*

$$
\alpha = \sigma_1 \sigma_2 \ldots \sigma_{n-1}, \qquad \text{where } \sigma_k \in S_k \text{ for } 1 \le k < n. \tag{13}
$$

Proof. If α has such a representation and if σ_{n-1} is the permutation $\sigma_{(n-1)j} \in S_{n-1}$, then α takes $n - 1 \mapsto j$, because all elements of $S_1 \cup \cdots \cup S_{n-2}$ fix the value of $n - 1$. Conversely, if α takes $n - 1 \mapsto j$ we have $\alpha = \alpha' \sigma_{(n-1)j}$, where

$$
\alpha' = \alpha \sigma_{(n-1)j}^-
$$

is a permutation of G that fixes $n - 1$. (As in Section 1.3.3, σ^- denotes the inverse of σ.) The set G' of all such permutations is a group, and S_1, ..., S_{n-2} is a Sims table for G'; therefore the result follows by induction on n. ∎

For example, a bit of calculation shows that one possible Sims table for the automorphism group of the 4-cube is

$$S_{\mathsf{f}} = \{(), (01)(23)(45)(67)(89)(\mathsf{ab})(\mathsf{cd})(\mathsf{ef}), \ldots,$$
$$(0\mathsf{f})(1\mathsf{e})(2\mathsf{d})(3\mathsf{c})(4\mathsf{b})(5\mathsf{a})(69)(78)\};$$
$$S_{\mathsf{e}} = \{(), (12)(56)(9\mathsf{a})(\mathsf{de}), (14)(36)(9\mathsf{c})(\mathsf{be}), (18)(3\mathsf{a})(5\mathsf{c})(7\mathsf{e})\};$$
$$S_{\mathsf{d}} = \{(), (24)(35)(\mathsf{ac})(\mathsf{bd}), (28)(39)(6\mathsf{c})(7\mathsf{d})\}; \qquad (14)$$
$$S_{\mathsf{c}} = \{()\};$$
$$S_{\mathsf{b}} = \{(), (48)(59)(6\mathsf{a})(7\mathsf{b})\};$$
$$S_{\mathsf{a}} = S_{9} = \cdots = S_{1} = \{()\};$$

here S_{f} contains 16 permutations $\sigma_{\mathsf{f}j}$ for $0 \le j \le 15$, which respectively take $i \mapsto i \oplus (15 - j)$ for $0 \le i \le 15$. The set S_{e} contains only four permutations, because an automorphism that fixes f must take e into a neighbor of f; thus the image of e must be either e or d or b or 7. The set S_{c} contains only the identity permutation, because an automorphism that fixes f, e, and d must also fix c. Most groups have $S_k = \{()\}$ for all small values of k, as in this example; hence a Sims table usually needs to contain only a fairly small number of permutations although the group itself might be quite large.

The Sims representation (13) makes it easy to test if a given permutation α lies in G: First we determine $\sigma_{n-1} = \sigma_{(n-1)j}$, where α takes $n - 1 \mapsto j$, and we let $\alpha' = \alpha\sigma_{n-1}^-$; then we determine $\sigma_{n-2} = \sigma_{(n-2)j'}$, where α' takes $n - 2 \mapsto j'$, and we let $\alpha'' = \alpha'\sigma_{n-2}^-$; and so on. If at any stage the required σ_{kj} does not exist in S_k, the original permutation α does not belong to G. In the case of (14), this process must reduce α to the identity after finding σ_{f}, σ_{e}, σ_{d}, σ_{c}, and σ_{b}.

For example, let α be the permutation $(14)(28)(3\mathsf{c})(69)(7\mathsf{d})(\mathsf{be})$, which corresponds to transposing (12) about its main diagonal $\{0, 5, \mathsf{f}, \mathsf{a}\}$. Since α fixes f, σ_{f} will be the identity permutation (), and $\alpha' = \alpha$. Then σ_{e} is the member of S_{e} that takes $\mathsf{e} \mapsto \mathsf{b}$, namely $(14)(36)(9\mathsf{c})(\mathsf{be})$, and we find $\alpha'' = (28)(39)(6\mathsf{c})(7\mathsf{d})$. This permutation belongs to S_{d}, so α is indeed an automorphism of the 4-cube.

Conversely, (13) also makes it easy to generate all elements of the corresponding group. We simply run through all permutations of the form

$$\sigma(1, c_1)\sigma(2, c_2) \ldots \sigma(n - 1, c_{n-1}),$$

where $\sigma(k, c_k)$ is the $(c_k + 1)$st element of S_k for $0 \le c_k < s_k = |S_k|$ and $1 \le k < n$, using any algorithm of Section 7.2.1.1 that runs through all $(n - 1)$-tuples $(c_1, \ldots, c_{n-1})$ for the respective radices $(s_1, \ldots, s_{n-1})$.

Using the general framework. Our chief concern is the group of *all* permutations on $\{0, 1, \ldots, n-1\}$, and in this case every set S_k of a Sims table will contain $k+1$ elements $\{\sigma(k, 0), \sigma(k, 1), \ldots, \sigma(k, k)\}$, where $\sigma(k, 0)$ is the identity and the others take k to the values $\{0, \ldots, k-1\}$ in some order. (The permutation $\sigma(k, j)$ need not be the same as σ_{kj}, and it usually is different.) Every such Sims table leads to a permutation generator, according to the following outline:

Algorithm G (*General permutation generator*). Given a Sims table $(S_1, S_2, \ldots, S_{n-1})$ where each S_k has $k+1$ elements $\sigma(k, j)$ as just described, this algorithm generates all permutations $a_0 a_1 \ldots a_{n-1}$ of $\{0, 1, \ldots, n-1\}$, using an auxiliary control table $c_n \ldots c_2 c_1$.

G1. [Initialize.] Set $a_j \leftarrow j$ and $c_{j+1} \leftarrow 0$ for $0 \le j < n$.

G2. [Visit.] (At this point the mixed-radix number $\left[\begin{smallmatrix} c_{n-1}, & \ldots, & c_2, & c_1 \\ n, & \ldots, & 3, & 2 \end{smallmatrix}\right]$ is the number of permutations visited so far.) Visit the permutation $a_0 a_1 \ldots a_{n-1}$.

G3. [Add 1 to $c_n \ldots c_2 c_1$.] Set $k \leftarrow 1$. While $c_k = k$, set $c_k \leftarrow 0$ and $k \leftarrow k+1$. Terminate the algorithm if $k = n$; otherwise set $c_k \leftarrow c_k + 1$.

G4. [Permute.] Apply the permutation $\tau(k, c_k) \omega(k-1)^-$ to $a_0 a_1 \ldots a_{n-1}$, as explained below, and return to G2. ∎

Applying a permutation π to $a_0 a_1 \ldots a_{n-1}$ means replacing a_j by $a_{j\pi}$ for $0 \le j < n$; this corresponds to premultiplication by π as explained earlier. Let us define

$$\tau(k, j) = \sigma(k, j) \sigma(k, j-1)^-, \qquad \text{for } 1 \le j \le k; \tag{15}$$
$$\omega(k) = \sigma(1, 1) \ldots \sigma(k, k). \tag{16}$$

Then steps G3 and G4 maintain the property that

$$a_0 a_1 \ldots a_{n-1} \text{ is the permutation } \sigma(1, c_1) \sigma(2, c_2) \ldots \sigma(n-1, c_{n-1}), \tag{17}$$

and Lemma S proves that every permutation is visited exactly once.

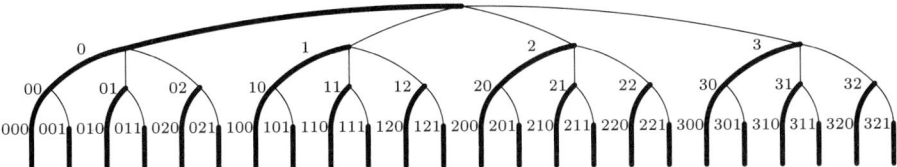

Fig. 39. Algorithm G implicitly traverses this tree when $n = 4$.

The tree in Fig. 39 illustrates Algorithm G in the case $n = 4$. According to (17), every permutation $a_0 a_1 a_2 a_3$ of $\{0, 1, 2, 3\}$ corresponds to a three-digit control string $c_3 c_2 c_1$, with $0 \le c_3 \le 3$, $0 \le c_2 \le 2$, and $0 \le c_1 \le 1$. Some nodes of the tree are labeled by a single digit c_3; these correspond to the permutations $\sigma(3, c_3)$ of the Sims table being used. Other nodes, labeled with two digits $c_3 c_2$, correspond to the permutations $\sigma(2, c_2) \sigma(3, c_3)$. A heavy line connects node c_3 to node $c_3 0$ and node $c_3 c_2$ to node $c_3 c_2 0$, because $\sigma(2, 0)$ and $\sigma(1, 0)$ are the identity permutation and these nodes are essentially equivalent. Adding 1 to the mixed-radix number $c_3 c_2 c_1$ in step G3 corresponds to moving from one node of Fig. 39 to its successor in preorder, and the transformation in step G4 changes the permutations accordingly. For example, when $c_3 c_2 c_1$ changes from 121 to 200, step G4 premultiplies the current permutation by

$$\tau(3, 2) \omega(2)^- = \tau(3, 2) \sigma(2, 2)^- \sigma(1, 1)^-;$$

premultiplying by $\sigma(1,1)^-$ takes us from node 121 to node 12, premultiplying by $\sigma(2,2)^-$ takes us from node 12 to node 1, and premultiplying by $\tau(3,2) = \sigma(3,2)\sigma(3,1)^-$ takes us from node 1 to node $2 \equiv 200$, which is the preorder successor of node 121. Stating this another way, premultiplication by $\tau(3,2)\omega(2)^-$ is exactly what is needed to change $\sigma(1,1)\sigma(2,2)\sigma(3,1)$ to $\sigma(1,0)\sigma(2,0)\sigma(3,2)$, preserving (17).

Algorithm G defines a huge number of permutation generators (see exercise 37), so it is no wonder that many of its special cases have appeared in the literature. Of course some of its variants are much more efficient than others, and we want to find examples where the operations are particularly well suited to the computer we are using.

We can, for instance, obtain permutations in reverse colex order as a special case of Algorithm G (see (11)), by letting $\sigma(k,j)$ be the $(j+1)$-cycle

$$\sigma(k,j) \;=\; (k{-}j \;\; k{-}j{+}1 \;\; \ldots \;\; k).\qquad(18)$$

The reason is that $\sigma(k,j)$ should be the permutation that corresponds to $c_n \ldots c_1$ in reverse colex order when $c_k = j$ and $c_i = 0$ for $i \neq k$, and this permutation $a_0 a_1 \ldots a_{n-1}$ is $01 \ldots (k{-}j{-}1)(k{-}j{+}1)\ldots(k)(k{-}j)(k{+}1)\ldots(n{-}1)$. For example, when $n = 8$ and $c_n \ldots c_1 = 00030000$ the corresponding reverse colex permutation is 01345267, which is $(2\,3\,4\,5)$ in cycle form. When $\sigma(k,j)$ is given by (18), Eqs. (15) and (16) lead to the formulas

$$\tau(k,j) = (k{-}j \;\; k);\qquad(19)$$

$$\omega(k) = (0\,1)(0\,1\,2)\ldots(0\,1\,\ldots\,k) = (0\,k)(1\,k{-}1)(2\,k{-}2)\ldots = \phi(k);\quad(20)$$

here $\phi(k)$ is the "$(k{+}1)$-flip" that changes $a_0 \ldots a_k$ to $a_k \ldots a_0$. In this case $\omega(k)$ turns out to be the same as $\omega(k)^-$, because $\phi(k)^2 = ()$.

Equations (19) and (20) are implicitly present behind the scenes in Algorithm L and in its reverse colex equivalent (exercise 2), where step L3 essentially applies a transposition and step L4 does a flip. Step G4 actually does the flip first; but the identity

$$(k{-}j \;\; k)\phi(k-1) \;=\; \phi(k-1)(j{-}1 \;\; k)\qquad(21)$$

shows that a flip followed by a transposition is the same as a (different) transposition followed by the flip.

In fact, equation (21) is a special case of the important identity

$$\pi^-\,(j_1 \;\; j_2 \;\; \ldots \;\; j_t)\,\pi \;=\; (j_1\pi \;\; j_2\pi \;\; \ldots \;\; j_t\pi),\qquad(22)$$

which is valid for *any* permutation π and any t-cycle $(j_1 \;\; j_2 \;\; \ldots \;\; j_t)$. On the left of (22) we have, for example, $j_1\pi \mapsto j_1 \mapsto j_2 \mapsto j_2\pi$, in agreement with the cycle on the right. Therefore if α and π are any permutations whatsoever, the permutation $\pi^-\alpha\pi$ (called the *conjugate* of α by π) has exactly the same cycle structure as α; we simply replace each element j in each cycle by $j\pi$.

Another significant special case of Algorithm G was introduced by R. J. Ord-Smith [*CACM* **10** (1967), 452; **12** (1969), 638; see also *Comp. J.* **14** (1971),

136–139], whose algorithm is obtained by setting

$$\sigma(k, j) = (k \ \ldots \ 1 \ 0)^j. \tag{23}$$

Now it is clear from (15) that

$$\tau(k, j) = (k \ \ldots \ 1 \ 0); \tag{24}$$

and once again we have

$$\omega(k) = (0 \ k)(1 \ k{-}1)(2 \ k{-}2) \ldots = \phi(k), \tag{25}$$

because $\sigma(k, k) = (0 \ 1 \ \ldots \ k)$ is the same as before. The nice thing about this method is that the permutation needed in step G4, namely $\tau(k, c_k)\omega(k-1)^-$, does not depend on c_k:

$$\tau(k, j)\omega(k-1)^- = (k \ \ldots \ 1 \ 0)\phi(k-1)^- = \phi(k). \tag{26}$$

Thus, Ord-Smith's algorithm is the special case of Algorithm G in which step G4 simply interchanges $a_0 \leftrightarrow a_k$, $a_1 \leftrightarrow a_{k-1}$, ...; this operation is usually quick, because k is small, and it saves some of the work of Algorithm L. (See exercise 38 and the reference to G. S. Klügel in Section 7.2.1.7.)

We can do even better by rigging things so that step G4 needs to do only a single transposition each time, somewhat as in Algorithm P but not necessarily on adjacent elements. Many such schemes are possible. The best is probably to let

$$\tau(k, j)\omega(k-1)^- = \begin{cases} (k \ 0), & \text{if } k \text{ is even,} \\ (k \ j{-}1), & \text{if } k \text{ is odd,} \end{cases} \tag{27}$$

as suggested by B. R. Heap [*Comp. J.* **6** (1963), 293–294]. Notice that Heap's method always transposes $a_k \leftrightarrow a_0$ except when $k = 3, 5, \ldots$; and the value of k, in 5 of every 6 steps, is either 1 or 2. Exercise 40 proves that Heap's method does indeed generate all permutations.

Bypassing unwanted blocks. One noteworthy advantage of Algorithm G is that it runs through all permutations of $a_0 \ldots a_{k-1}$ before touching a_k; then it performs another $k!$ cycles before changing a_k again, and so on. Therefore if at any time we reach a setting of the final elements $a_k \ldots a_{n-1}$ that is unimportant to the problem we're working on, we can skip quickly over all permutations that end with the undesirable suffix. More precisely, we could replace step G2 by the following substeps:

G2.0. [Acceptable?] If $a_k \ldots a_{n-1}$ is not an acceptable suffix, go to G2.1. Otherwise set $k \leftarrow k - 1$. Then if $k > 0$, repeat this step; if $k = 0$, proceed to step G2.2.

G2.1. [Skip this suffix.] While $c_k = k$, apply $\sigma(k, k)^-$ to $a_0 \ldots a_{n-1}$ and set $c_k \leftarrow 0$, $k \leftarrow k + 1$. Terminate if $k = n$; otherwise set $c_k \leftarrow c_k + 1$, apply $\tau(k, c_k)$ to $a_0 \ldots a_{n-1}$, and return to G2.0.

G2.2. [Visit.] Visit the permutation $a_0 \ldots a_{n-1}$. ∎

Step G1 should also set $k \leftarrow n - 1$. Notice that the new steps are careful to preserve condition (17). The algorithm has become more complicated, because we need to know the permutations $\tau(k, j)$ and $\sigma(k, k)$ in addition to the permutations $\tau(k, j)\omega(k - 1)^-$ that appear in G4. But the additional complications are often worth the effort, because the resulting program might run significantly faster.

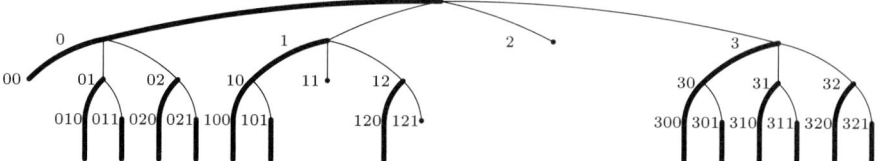

Fig. 40. Unwanted branches can be pruned from the tree of Fig. 39, if Algorithm G is suitably extended.

For example, Fig. 40 shows what happens to the tree of Fig. 39 when the suffixes of $a_0 a_1 a_2 a_3$ that correspond to nodes 00, 11, 121, and 2 are not acceptable. (Each suffix $a_k \ldots a_{n-1}$ of the permutation $a_0 \ldots a_{n-1}$ corresponds to a *prefix* $c_n \ldots c_k$ of the control string $c_n \ldots c_1$, because the permutations $\sigma(1, c_1) \ldots \sigma(k - 1, c_{k-1})$ do not affect $a_k \ldots a_{n-1}$.) Step G2.1 premultiplies by $\tau(k, j)$ to move from node $c_{n-1} \ldots c_{k+1}(j-1)$ to its right sibling $c_{n-1} \ldots c_{k+1}j$, and it premultiplies by $\sigma(k, k)^-$ to move up from node $c_{n-1} \ldots c_{k+1}k$ to its parent $c_{n-1} \ldots c_{k+1}$. Thus, to get from the rejected prefix 121 to its preorder successor, the algorithm premultiplies by $\sigma(1, 1)^-$, $\sigma(2, 2)^-$, and $\tau(3, 2)$, thereby moving from node 121 to 12 to 1 to 2. (This is a somewhat exceptional case, because a prefix with $k = 1$ is rejected only if we don't want to visit the unique permutation $a_0 a_1 \ldots a_{n-1}$ that has suffix $a_1 \ldots a_{n-1}$.) After node 2 is rejected, $\tau(3, 3)$ takes us to node 3, etc.

Notice, incidentally, that bypassing a suffix $a_k \ldots a_{n-1}$ in this extension of Algorithm G is essentially the same as bypassing a prefix $a_1 \ldots a_j$ in our original notation, if we go back to the idea of generating permutations $a_1 \ldots a_n$ of $\{1, \ldots, n\}$ and doing most of the work at the right-hand end. Our original notation corresponds to choosing a_1 first, then a_2, $\ldots$, then a_n; the notation in Algorithm G essentially chooses a_{n-1} first, then a_{n-2}, $\ldots$, then a_0. Algorithm G's conventions may seem backward, but they make the formulas for Sims table manipulation a lot simpler. A good programmer soon learns to switch without difficulty from one viewpoint to another.

We can apply these ideas to alphametics, because it is clear for example that most choices of the values for the letters D, E, and Y will make it impossible for SEND plus MORE to equal MONEY: We need to have $(D + E - Y) \bmod 10 = 0$ in that problem. Therefore many permutations can be eliminated from consideration.

In general, if r_k is the maximum power of 10 that divides the signature value s_k, we can sort the letters and assign codes $\{0, 1, \ldots, 9\}$ so that $r_0 \geq r_1 \geq \cdots \geq r_9$. For example, to solve the trio sonata problem (7), we could use $(0, 1, \ldots, 9)$ respectively for $(\mathtt{X}, \mathtt{S}, \mathtt{V}, \mathtt{A}, \mathtt{R}, \mathtt{I}, \mathtt{L}, \mathtt{T}, \mathtt{O}, \mathtt{N})$, obtaining the signatures

$$s_0 = 0, \quad s_1 = -100000, \quad s_2 = 210000, \quad s_3 = -100, \quad s_4 = -100,$$
$$s_5 = 21010, \quad s_6 = 210, \quad s_7 = -1010, \quad s_8 = -7901, \quad s_9 = -998;$$

hence $(r_0, \ldots, r_9) = (\infty, 5, 4, 2, 2, 1, 1, 1, 0, 0)$. Now if we get to step G2.0 for a value of k with $r_{k-1} \neq r_k$, we can say that the suffix $a_k \ldots a_9$ is unacceptable unless $a_k s_k + \cdots + a_9 s_9$ is a multiple of $10^{r_{k-1}}$. Also, (10) tells us that $a_k \ldots a_9$ is unacceptable if $a_k = 0$ and $k \in F$; the first-letter set F is now $\{1, 2, 7\}$.

Our previous approach to alphametics with steps A1–A3 above used brute force to run through 10! possibilities. It operated rather fast under the circumstances, since the adjacent-transposition method allowed it to get by with only 6 memory references per permutation; but still, 10! is 3,628,800, so the entire process cost almost 22 megamems, regardless of the alphametic being solved. By contrast, the extended Algorithm G with Heap's method and the cutoffs just described will find all four solutions to (7) with fewer than 128 *kilo*mems! Thus the suffix-skipping technique runs more than 170 times faster than the previous method, which simply blasted away blindly.

Most of the 128 kilomems in the new approach are spent applying $\tau(k, c_k)$ in step G2.1. The other memory references come primarily from applications of $\sigma(k, k)^-$ in that step, but τ is needed 7812 times while σ^- is needed only 2162 times. The reason is easy to understand from Fig. 40, because the "shortcut move" $\tau(k, c_k)\omega(k-1)^-$ in step G4 hardly ever applies; in this case it is used only four times, once for each solution. Thus, preorder traversal of the tree is accomplished almost entirely by τ steps that move to the right and σ^- steps that move upward. The τ steps dominate in a problem like this, where very few complete permutations are actually visited, because each step $\sigma(k, k)^-$ is preceded by k steps $\tau(k, 1), \tau(k, 2), \ldots, \tau(k, k)$.

This analysis reveals that Heap's method—which goes to great lengths to optimize the permutations $\tau(k, j)\omega(k-1)^-$ so that each transition in step G4 is a simple transposition—is *not* especially good for the extended Algorithm G unless comparatively few suffixes are rejected in step G2.0. The simpler reverse colex order, for which $\tau(k, j)$ itself is always a simple transposition, is now much more attractive (see (19)). Indeed, Algorithm G with reverse colex order solves the alphametic (7) with only 97 kilomems.

Similar results occur with respect to other alphametic problems. For example, if we apply the extended Algorithm G to the alphametics in exercise 24, parts (a) through (h), the computations involve respectively

$$(551, 110, 14, 8, 350, 84, 153, 1598) \text{ kilomems with Heap's method;}$$
$$(429, 84, 10, 5, 256, 63, 117, 1189) \text{ kilomems with reverse colex.} \tag{28}$$

The speedup factor for reverse colex in these examples, compared to brute force with Algorithm T, ranges from 18 in case (h) to 4200 in case (d), and it is about 80 on the average; Heap's method gives an average speedup of about 60.

We know from Algorithm L, however, that lexicographic order is easily handled *without* the complication of the control table $c_n \ldots c_1$ used by Algorithm G. And a closer look at Algorithm L shows that we can improve its behavior when permutations are frequently being skipped, by using a linked list instead of a sequential array. The improved algorithm is well-suited to a wide variety of algorithms that wish to generate restricted classes of permutations:

Algorithm X (*Lexicographic permutations with restricted prefixes*). This algorithm generates all permutations $a_1 a_2 \ldots a_n$ of $\{1, 2, \ldots, n\}$ that pass a given sequence of tests

$$t_1(a_1), \quad t_2(a_1, a_2), \quad \ldots, \quad t_n(a_1, a_2, \ldots, a_n),$$

visiting them in lexicographic order. It uses an auxiliary table of links l_0, l_1, $\ldots$, l_n to maintain a cyclic list of unused elements, so that if the currently available elements are

$$\{1, \ldots, n\} \setminus \{a_1, \ldots, a_k\} = \{b_1, \ldots, b_{n-k}\}, \qquad \text{where } b_1 < \cdots < b_{n-k}, \quad (29)$$

then we have

$$l_0 = b_1, \quad l_{b_j} = b_{j+1} \quad \text{for } 1 \le j < n - k, \quad \text{and} \quad l_{b_{n-k}} = 0. \quad (30)$$

It also uses an auxiliary table $u_1 \ldots u_n$ to undo operations that have been performed on the l array.

X1. [Initialize.] Set $l_k \leftarrow k + 1$ for $0 \le k < n$, and $l_n \leftarrow 0$. Then set $k \leftarrow 1$.

X2. [Enter level k.] Set $p \leftarrow 0$, $q \leftarrow l_0$.

X3. [Test $a_1 \ldots a_k$.] Set $a_k \leftarrow q$. If $t_k(a_1, \ldots, a_k)$ is false, go to X5. Otherwise, if $k = n$, visit $a_1 \ldots a_n$ and go to X6.

X4. [Increase k.] Set $u_k \leftarrow p$, $l_p \leftarrow l_q$, $k \leftarrow k + 1$, and return to X2.

X5. [Increase a_k.] Set $p \leftarrow q$, $q \leftarrow l_p$. If $q \ne 0$ return to X3.

X6. [Decrease k.] Set $k \leftarrow k - 1$, and terminate if $k = 0$. Otherwise set $p \leftarrow u_k$, $q \leftarrow a_k$, $l_p \leftarrow q$, and go to X5. ∎

The basic idea of this elegant algorithm is due to M. C. Er [*Comp. J.* **30** (1987), 282]. We can apply it to alphametics by changing notation slightly, obtaining permutations $a_0 \ldots a_9$ of $\{0, \ldots, 9\}$ and letting l_{10} play the former role of l_0. The resulting algorithm needs only 49 kilomems to solve the trio-sonata problem (7), and it solves the alphametics of exercise 24(a)–(h) in

$$(248, 38, 4, 3, 122, 30, 55, 553) \text{ kilomems}, \qquad (31)$$

respectively. Thus it runs about 165 times faster than the brute-force approach.

Another way to apply Algorithm X to alphametics is often faster yet (see exercise 49).

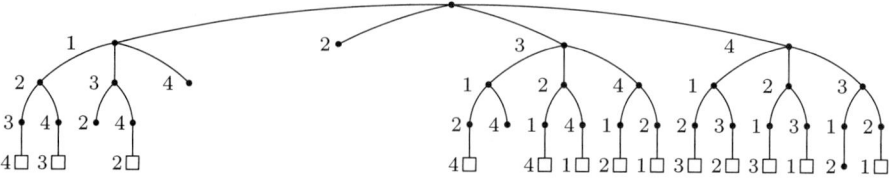

Fig. 41. The tree implicitly traversed by Algorithm X when $n = 4$, if all permutations are visited except those beginning with 132, 14, 2, 314, or 4312.

*Dual methods.** If $S_1, \ldots, S_{n-1}$ is a Sims table for a permutation group G, we learned in Lemma S that every element of G can be expressed uniquely as a product $\sigma_1 \ldots \sigma_{n-1}$, where $\sigma_k \in S_k$; see (13). Exercise 50 shows that every element α can also be expressed uniquely in the dual form

$$\alpha = \sigma_{n-1}^- \ldots \sigma_2^- \sigma_1^-, \qquad \text{where } \sigma_k \in S_k \text{ for } 1 \leq k < n, \tag{32}$$

and this fact leads to another large family of permutation generators. In particular, when G is the group of all $n!$ permutations, every permutation can be written

$$\sigma(n-1, c_{n-1})^- \ldots \sigma(2, c_2)^- \sigma(1, c_1)^-, \tag{33}$$

where $0 \leq c_k \leq k$ for $1 \leq k < n$ and the permutations $\sigma(k, j)$ are the same as in Algorithm G. Now, however, we want to vary c_{n-1} most rapidly and c_1 least rapidly, so we arrive at an algorithm of a different kind:

Algorithm H (*Dual permutation generator*). Given a Sims table as in Algorithm G, this algorithm generates all permutations $a_0 \ldots a_{n-1}$ of $\{0, \ldots, n-1\}$, using an auxiliary table $c_0 \ldots c_{n-1}$.

H1. [Initialize.] Set $a_j \leftarrow j$ and $c_j \leftarrow 0$ for $0 \leq j < n$.

H2. [Visit.] (At this point the mixed-radix number $\left[\begin{smallmatrix} c_1, & c_2, & \ldots, & c_{n-1} \\ 2, & 3, & \ldots, & n \end{smallmatrix} \right]$ is the number of permutations visited so far.) Visit the permutation $a_0 a_1 \ldots a_{n-1}$.

H3. [Add 1 to $c_0 c_1 \ldots c_{n-1}$.] Set $k \leftarrow n-1$. If $c_k = k$, set $c_k \leftarrow 0$, $k \leftarrow k-1$, and repeat until $k = 0$ or $c_k < k$. Terminate the algorithm if $k = 0$; otherwise set $c_k \leftarrow c_k + 1$.

H4. [Permute.] Apply the permutation $\tau(k, c_k) \omega(k+1)^-$ to $a_0 a_1 \ldots a_{n-1}$, as explained below, and return to H2. ∎

Although this algorithm looks almost identical to Algorithm G, the permutations τ and ω that it needs in step H4 are quite different from those needed in step G4. The new rules, which replace (15) and (16), are

$$\tau(k, j) = \sigma(k, j)^- \sigma(k, j-1), \qquad \text{for } 1 \leq j \leq k; \tag{34}$$
$$\omega(k) = \sigma(n-1, n-1)^- \sigma(n-2, n-2)^- \ldots \sigma(k, k)^-. \tag{35}$$

The number of possibilities is just as vast as it was for Algorithm G, so we will confine our attention to a few cases that have special merit. One natural case to try is, of course, the Sims table that makes Algorithm G produce reverse colex order, namely

$$\sigma(k, j) = (k-j \quad k-j+1 \quad \ldots \quad k) \tag{36}$$

as in (18). The resulting permutation generator turns out to be very nearly the same as the method of plain changes; so we can say that Algorithms L and P are essentially dual to each other. (See exercise 52.)

Another natural idea is to construct a Sims table for which step H4 always makes a single transposition of two elements, by analogy with the construction of (27) that achieves maximum efficiency in step G4. But such a mission now turns out to be impossible: We cannot achieve it even when $n = 4$. For if we start with the identity permutation $a_0 a_1 a_2 a_3 = 0123$, the transitions that take us from control table $c_0 c_1 c_2 c_3 = 0000$ to 0001 to 0002 to 0003 must move the 3; so, if they are transpositions, they must be $(3\,a)$, $(a\,b)$, and $(b\,c)$ for some permutation abc of $\{0,1,2\}$. The permutation corresponding to $c_0 c_1 c_2 c_3 = 0003$ is now $\sigma(3,3)^- = (b\,c)(a\,b)(3\,a) = (3\,a\,b\,c)$; and the next permutation, which corresponds to $c_0 c_1 c_2 c_3 = 0010$, will be $\sigma(2,1)^-$, which must fix the element 3. The only suitable transposition is $(3\,c)$, hence $\sigma(2,1)^-$ must be $(3\,c)(3\,a\,b\,c) = (a\,b\,c)$. Similarly we find that $\sigma(2,2)^-$ must be $(a\,c\,b)$, and the permutation corresponding to $c_0 c_1 c_2 c_3 = 0023$ will be $(3\,a\,b\,c)(a\,c\,b) = (3\,c)$. Step H4 is now supposed to convert this to the permutation $\sigma(1,1)^-$, which corresponds to the control table 0100 that follows 0023. But the only transposition that will convert $(3\,c)$ into a permutation that fixes 2 and 3 is $(3\,c)$; and the resulting permutation also fixes 1, so it cannot be $\sigma(1,1)^-$.

The proof in the preceding paragraph shows that we cannot use Algorithm H to generate all permutations with the minimum number of transpositions. But it also suggests a simple generation scheme that comes very close to the minimum, and the resulting algorithm is quite attractive because it needs to do extra work only once per $n(n-1)$ steps. (See exercise 53.)

Finally, let's consider the dual of Ord-Smith's method, when

$$\sigma(k,j) = (k\ \ldots\ 1\ 0)^j \tag{37}$$

as in (23). Once again the value of $\tau(k,j)$ is independent of j,

$$\tau(k,j) = (0\ 1\ \ldots\ k), \tag{38}$$

and this fact is particularly advantageous in Algorithm H because it allows us to dispense with the control table $c_0 c_1 \ldots c_{n-1}$. The reason is that $c_{n-1} = 0$ in step H3 if and only if $a_{n-1} = n-1$, because of (32); and indeed, when $c_j = 0$ for $k < j < n$ in step H3 we have $c_k = 0$ if and only if $a_k = k$. Therefore we can reformulate this variant of Algorithm H as follows.

Algorithm C (*Permutation generation by cyclic shifts*). This algorithm visits all permutations $a_1 \ldots a_n$ of the distinct elements $\{x_1, \ldots, x_n\}$.

C1. [Initialize.] Set $a_j \leftarrow x_j$ for $1 \le j \le n$.

C2. [Visit.] Visit the permutation $a_1 \ldots a_n$, and set $k \leftarrow n$.

C3. [Shift.] Replace $a_1 a_2 \ldots a_k$ by the cyclic shift $a_2 \ldots a_k a_1$, and return to C2 if $a_k \neq x_k$.

C4. [Decrease k.] Set $k \leftarrow k - 1$, and go back to C3 if $k > 1$. ∎

For example, the successive permutations of $\{1,2,3,4\}$ generated when $n = 4$ are

$$1234,\ 2341,\ 3412,\ 4123,\ (1234),$$
$$2314,\ 3142,\ 1423,\ 4231,\ (2314),$$
$$3124,\ 1243,\ 2431,\ 4312,\ (3124),\ (1234),$$
$$2134,\ 1342,\ 3421,\ 4213,\ (2134),$$
$$1324,\ 3241,\ 2413,\ 4132,\ (1324),$$
$$3214,\ 2143,\ 1432,\ 4321,\ (3214),\ (2134),\ (1234),$$

with unvisited intermediate permutations shown in parentheses. This algorithm may well be the simplest permutation generator of all, in terms of minimum program length. It is due to G. G. Langdon, Jr. [*CACM* **10** (1967), 298–299; **11** (1968), 392]; similar methods had been published previously by C. Tompkins [*Proc. Symp. Applied Math.* **6** (1956), 202–205] and, more explicitly, by R. Seitz [*Unternehmensforschung* **6** (1962), 2–15]. The procedure is particularly well suited to applications in which cyclic shifting is efficient, for example when successive permutations are being kept in a machine register instead of in an array.

The main disadvantage of dual methods is that they usually do not adapt well to situations where large blocks of permutations need to be skipped, because the set of all permutations with a given value of the first control entries $c_0 c_1 \ldots c_{k-1}$ is usually not of importance. The special case (36) is, however, sometimes an exception, because the $n!/k!$ permutations with $c_0 c_1 \ldots c_{k-1} = 00 \ldots 0$ in that case are precisely those $a_0 a_1 \ldots a_{n-1}$ in which 0 precedes 1, 1 precedes 2, $\ldots$, and $k - 2$ precedes $k - 1$.

*Ehrlich's swap method. Gideon Ehrlich has discovered a completely different approach to permutation generation, based on yet another way to use a control table $c_1 \ldots c_{n-1}$. His method obtains each permutation from its predecessor by interchanging the leftmost element with another:

Algorithm E (*Ehrlich swaps*). This algorithm generates all permutations of the distinct elements $a_0 \ldots a_{n-1}$ by using auxiliary tables $b_0 \ldots b_{n-1}$ and $c_1 \ldots c_n$.

E1. [Initialize.] Set $b_j \leftarrow j$ and $c_{j+1} \leftarrow 0$ for $0 \le j < n$.

E2. [Visit.] Visit the permutation $a_0 \ldots a_{n-1}$.

E3. [Find k.] Set $k \leftarrow 1$. Then while $c_k = k$, set $c_k \leftarrow 0$ and $k \leftarrow k + 1$. Terminate if $k = n$, otherwise set $c_k \leftarrow c_k + 1$.

E4. [Swap.] Interchange $a_0 \leftrightarrow a_{b_k}$.

E5. [Flip.] Set $j \leftarrow 1$, $k \leftarrow k - 1$. While $j < k$, interchange $b_j \leftrightarrow b_k$ and set $j \leftarrow j + 1$, $k \leftarrow k - 1$. Return to E2. ∎

Notice that steps E2 and E3 are identical to steps G2 and G3 of Algorithm G. The most amazing thing about this algorithm, which Ehrlich communicated to Martin Gardner in 1987, is that it works; exercise 55 contains a proof. A similar method, which simplifies the operations of step E5, can be validated in the same way (see exercise 56). The average number of interchanges performed in step E5 is less than 0.18 (see exercise 57).

As it stands, Algorithm E isn't faster than other methods we have seen. But it has the nice property that it changes each permutation in a minimal way, using only $n - 1$ different kinds of transpositions. Whereas Algorithm P used adjacent interchanges, $a_{t-1} \leftrightarrow a_t$, Algorithm E uses first-element swaps, $a_0 \leftrightarrow a_t$, also called *star transpositions*, for some well-chosen sequence of indices $t[1]$, $t[2]$, $\ldots$, $t[n! - 1]$. And if we are generating permutations repeatedly for the same fairly small value of n, we can precompute this sequence, as we did in Algorithm T for the index sequence of Algorithm P. Notice that star transpositions have an advantage over adjacent interchanges, because we always know the value of a_0 from the previous swap; we need not read it from memory.

Let E_n be the sequence of $n! - 1$ indices t such that Algorithm E swaps a_0 with a_t in step E4. Since E_{n+1} begins with E_n, we can regard E_n as the first $n! - 1$ elements of an infinite sequence

$$E_\infty = 121213212123121213212124313132131312\ldots. \tag{39}$$

For example, if $n = 4$ and $a_0 a_1 a_2 a_3 = 1234$, the permutations visited by Algorithm E are

$$
\begin{array}{l}
1234,\ 2134,\ 3124,\ 1324,\ 2314,\ 3214, \\
4213,\ 1243,\ 2143,\ 4123,\ 1423,\ 2413, \\
3412,\ 4312,\ 1342,\ 3142,\ 4132,\ 1432, \\
2431,\ 3421,\ 4321,\ 2341,\ 3241,\ 4231.
\end{array}
\tag{40}
$$

*Using fewer generators. After seeing Algorithms P and E, we might naturally ask whether all permutations can be obtained by using just *two* basic operations, instead of $n - 1$. For example, Nijenhuis and Wilf [*Combinatorial Algorithms* (1975), Exercise 6] noticed that all permutations can be generated for $n = 4$ if we replace $a_1 a_2 a_3 \ldots a_n$ at each step by either $a_2 a_3 \ldots a_n a_1$ or $a_2 a_1 a_3 \ldots a_n$, and they wondered whether such a method exists for all n.

In general, if G is any group of permutations and if α_1, ..., α_k are elements of G, the *Cayley graph* for G with generators $(\alpha_1, \ldots, \alpha_k)$ is the directed graph whose vertices are the permutations π of G and whose arcs go from π to $\alpha_1 \pi$, ..., $\alpha_k \pi$. [Arthur Cayley, *American J. Math.* **1** (1878), 174–176.] The question of Nijenhuis and Wilf is equivalent to asking whether the Cayley graph for all permutations of $\{1, 2, \ldots, n\}$, with generators σ and τ where σ is the cyclic permutation $(1\ 2\ \ldots\ n)$ and τ is the transposition $(1\ 2)$, has a Hamiltonian path.

A basic theorem due to R. A. Rankin [*Proc. Cambridge Philos. Soc.* **44** (1948), 17–25] allows us to conclude in many cases that Cayley graphs with two generators do not have a Hamiltonian cycle:

Theorem R. *Let G be a group consisting of g permutations. If the Cayley graph for G with generators (α, β) has a Hamiltonian cycle, and if the permutations $(\alpha, \beta, \alpha\beta^-)$ are respectively of order (a, b, c), then either c is even or g/a and g/b are odd.*

(The *order* of a permutation α is the least positive integer a such that α^a is the identity.)

Proof. See exercise 73. ▮

In particular, when $\alpha = \sigma$ and $\beta = \tau$ as above, we have $g = n!$, $a = n$, $b = 2$, and $c = n-1$, because $\sigma\tau^- = (2\ \ldots\ n)$. Therefore we conclude that no Hamiltonian cycle is possible when $n \geq 4$ is even. However, a Hamiltonian *path* is easy to construct when $n = 4$, because we can join up the 12-cycles

$$1234 \to 2341 \to 3412 \to 4312 \to 3124 \to 1243 \to 2431$$
$$\to 4231 \to 2314 \to 3142 \to 1423 \to 4123 \to 1234,$$
$$2134 \to 1342 \to 3421 \to 4321 \to 3214 \to 2143 \to 1432 \tag{41}$$
$$\to 4132 \to 1324 \to 3241 \to 2413 \to 4213 \to 2134,$$

by starting at 2341 and jumping from 1234 to 2134, ending at 4213.

Ruskey, Jiang, and Weston [*Discrete Applied Math.* **57** (1995), 75–83] undertook an exhaustive search in the σ–τ graph for $n = 5$ and discovered that it has five essentially distinct Hamiltonian cycles, one of which (the "most beautiful") is illustrated in Fig. 42(a). They also found a Hamiltonian path for $n = 6$; this was a difficult feat, because it is the outcome of a 720-stage binary decision tree. Unfortunately the solution they discovered has no apparent logical structure. A somewhat less complex path is described in exercise 70, but even that path cannot be called simple. Therefore a σ–τ approach will probably not be of practical interest for larger values of n unless a new construction is discovered. R. C. Compton and S. G. Williamson [*Linear and Multilinear Algebra* **35** (1993), 237–293] have proved that Hamiltonian cycles exist for all n if the three generators σ, σ^-, and τ are allowed instead of just σ and τ; their cycles have the interesting property that every nth transformation is τ, and the intervening $n - 1$ transformations are either all σ or all σ^-. But their method is too complicated to explain in a short space.

Exercise 69 describes a general permutation algorithm that is reasonably simple and needs only three generators, each of order 2. Figure 42(b) illustrates the case $n = 5$ of this method, which was motivated by examples of bell-ringing.

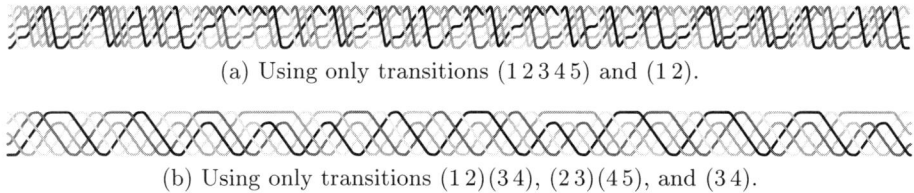

(a) Using only transitions $(1\,2\,3\,4\,5)$ and $(1\,2)$.

(b) Using only transitions $(1\,2)(3\,4)$, $(2\,3)(4\,5)$, and $(3\,4)$.

Fig. 42. Hamiltonian cycles for 5! permutations.

Faster, faster. What is the fastest way to generate permutations? This question has often been raised in computer publications, because people who examine $n!$ possibilities want to keep the running time as small as possible. But the answers have generally been contradictory, because there are many different ways to formulate the question. Let's try to understand the related issues by studying how permutations might be generated most rapidly on the MMIX computer.

Suppose first that our goal is to produce permutations in an array of n consecutive memory words (octabytes). The fastest way to do this, of all those we've seen in this section, is to streamline Heap's method (27), as suggested by R. Sedgewick [*Computing Surveys* **9** (1977), 157–160].

The key idea is to optimize the code for the most common cases of steps G2 and G3, namely the cases in which all activity occurs at the beginning of the array. If registers u, v, and w contain the contents of the first three words, and if the next six permutations to be generated involve permuting those words in all six possible ways, we can clearly do the job as follows:

$$
\begin{array}{lll}
\texttt{PUSHJ 0,Visit} & & \\
\texttt{STO v,A0;} & \texttt{STO u,A1;} & \texttt{PUSHJ 0,Visit} \\
\texttt{STO w,A0;} & \texttt{STO v,A2;} & \texttt{PUSHJ 0,Visit} \\
\texttt{STO u,A0;} & \texttt{STO w,A1;} & \texttt{PUSHJ 0,Visit} \\
\texttt{STO v,A0;} & \texttt{STO u,A2;} & \texttt{PUSHJ 0,Visit} \\
\texttt{STO w,A0;} & \texttt{STO v,A1;} & \texttt{PUSHJ 0,Visit}
\end{array}
\tag{42}
$$

(Here A0 is the address of octabyte a_0, etc.) A complete permutation program, which takes care of getting the right things into u, v, and w, appears in exercise 77, but the other instructions are less important because they need to be performed only $\frac{1}{6}$ of the time. The total cost per permutation, not counting the $4v$ needed for PUSHJ and POP on each call to Visit, comes to approximately $2.77\mu + 5.69v$ with this approach. If we use four registers u, v, w, x, and if we expand (42) to 24 calls on Visit, the running time per permutation drops to about $2.19\mu + 3.07v$. And with r registers and $r!$ Visits, exercise 78 shows that the cost is $(2 + O(1/r!))(\mu + v)$, which is very nearly the cost of two STO instructions.

The latter is, of course, the minimum possible time for any method that generates all permutations in a sequential array. ... Or is it? We have assumed that the visiting routine wants to see permutations in consecutive locations, but perhaps that routine is able to read the permutations from different starting points. Then we can arrange to keep a_{n-1} fixed and to keep two copies of the other elements in its vicinity:

$$
a_0 a_1 \ldots a_{n-2} a_{n-1} a_0 a_1 \ldots a_{n-2}.
\tag{43}
$$

If we now let $a_0 a_1 \ldots a_{n-2}$ run through $(n-1)!$ permutations, always changing both copies simultaneously by doing two STO commands instead of one, we can let every call to Visit look at the n permutations

$$
a_0 a_1 \ldots a_{n-1}, \quad a_1 \ldots a_{n-1} a_0, \quad \ldots, \quad a_{n-1} a_0 \ldots a_{n-2},
\tag{44}
$$

which all appear consecutively. The cost per permutation is now reduced to the cost of three simple instructions like ADD, CMP, PBNZ, plus $O(1/n)$. [See Varol and Rotem, *Comp. J.* **24** (1981), 173–176.]

Furthermore, we might not want to waste time storing permutations into memory at all. Suppose, for example, that our goal is to generate all permutations of $\{0, 1, \ldots, n-1\}$. The value of n will probably be at most 16, because $16! = 20{,}922{,}789{,}888{,}000$ and $17! = 355{,}687{,}428{,}096{,}000$. Therefore an entire permutation will fit in the 16 nybbles of an octabyte, and we can keep it in a single register. This will be advantageous only if the visiting routine doesn't need to unpack the individual nybbles; but let's suppose that it doesn't. How fast can we generate permutations in the nybbles of a 64-bit register?

One idea, suggested by a technique due to A. J. Goldstein [*U. S. Patent 3383661* (14 May 1968)], is to precompute the table $(t[1], \ldots, t[5039])$ of plain-change transitions for seven elements, using Algorithm T. These numbers $t[k]$ lie between 1 and 6, so we can pack 20 of them into a 64-bit word. It is convenient to put the number $\sum_{k=1}^{20} 2^{3k-1} t[20j + k]$ into word j of an auxiliary table, for $0 \le j < 252$, with $t[5040] = 1$; for example, the table begins with the codeword

00|001|010|011|100|101|110|100|110|101|100|011|010|001|110|001|010|011|100|101|110|00.

The following program reads such codes efficiently:

```
Perm   ⟨Set register a to the first permutation⟩
0H     LDA   p,T       p ← address of first codeword.
       JMP   3F
1H     ⟨Visit the permutation in register a⟩
       ⟨Swap the nybbles of a that lie t bits from the right⟩
       SRU   c,c,3     c ← c ≫ 3.
2H     AND   t,c,#1c   t ← c & (11100)₂.
       PBNZ  t,1B      Branch if t ≠ 0.
       ADD   p,p,8
3H     LDO   c,p,0     c ← next codeword.
       PBNZ  c,2B      (The final codeword is followed by 0.)
       ⟨If not done, advance the leading n − 7 nybbles and return to 0B⟩
```
$$(45)$$

Exercise 79 shows how to ⟨Swap the nybbles ...⟩ with seven instructions, using bit manipulation operations that are found on most computers. Therefore the cost per permutation is just a bit more than 10υ. (The instructions that fetch new codewords cost only $(\mu + 5\upsilon)/20$; and the instructions that advance the leading $n-7$ nybbles are even more negligible since their cost is divided by 5040.) Notice that there is now no need for PUSHJ and POP as there was with (42); we ignored those instructions before, but they did cost 4υ.

We can, however, do even better by adapting Langdon's cyclic-shift method, Algorithm C. Suppose we start with the lexicographically largest permutation and operate as follows:

```
       GREG  @
0H     OCTA  #fedcba9876543210&(1<<(4*N)-1)
Perm   LDOU  a,0B                             Set a ← # ...3210.
       JMP   2F
1H     SRU   a,a,4*(16-N)                     a ← ⌊a/16^(16−n)⌋.
       OR    a,a,t                            a ← a | t.
2H     ⟨Visit the permutation in register a⟩
       SRU   t,a,4*(N-1)                      t ← ⌊a/16^(n−1)⌋.
       SLU   a,a,4*(17-N)                     a ← 16^(17−n) a mod 16^16.
       PBNZ  t,1B                             To 1B if t ≠ 0.
       ⟨Continue with Langdon's method⟩
```
$$(46)$$

The running time per permutation is now only $5\upsilon + O(1/n)$, again without the need for PUSHJ and POP. See exercise 81 for an interesting way to extend (46) to a complete program, obtaining a remarkably short and fast routine.

Fast permutation generators are amusing, but in practice we can usually save more time by streamlining the visiting routine than by speeding up the generator.

Topological sorting. Instead of working with all $n!$ permutations of $\{1, \ldots, n\}$, we often want to look only at permutations that obey certain restrictions. For example, we might be interested only in permutations for which 1 precedes 3, 2 precedes 3, and 2 precedes 4; there are five such permutations of $\{1, 2, 3, 4\}$, namely

$$1234, \quad 1243, \quad 2134, \quad 2143, \quad 2413. \qquad (47)$$

The problem of *topological sorting*, which we studied in Section 2.2.3 as a first example of nontrivial data structures, is the general problem of finding a permutation that satisfies m such conditions $x_1 \prec y_1, \ldots, x_m \prec y_m$, where $x \prec y$ means that x should precede y in the permutation. This problem arises frequently in practice, so it has several different names; for example, it is often called the *linear embedding* problem, because we want to arrange objects in a line while preserving certain order relationships. It is also the problem of extending a partial ordering to a total ordering (see exercise 2.2.3–14).

Our goal in Section 2.2.3 was to find a *single* permutation that satisfies all the relations. But now we want rather to find *all* such permutations, all topological sorts. Indeed, we will assume in the present section that the elements x and y on which the relations are defined are integers between 1 and n, and that we have $x < y$ whenever $x \prec y$. Consequently the permutation $12 \ldots n$ will always be topologically correct. (If this simplifying assumption is not met, we can preprocess the data by using Algorithm 2.2.3T to rename the objects appropriately.)

Many important classes of permutations are special cases of this topological ordering problem. For example, the permutations of $\{1, \ldots, 8\}$ such that

$$1 \prec 2, \quad 2 \prec 3, \quad 3 \prec 4, \quad 6 \prec 7, \quad 7 \prec 8$$

are equivalent to permutations of the multiset $\{1, 1, 1, 1, 2, 3, 3, 3\}$, because we can map $\{1, 2, 3, 4\} \mapsto 1$, $5 \mapsto 2$, and $\{6, 7, 8\} \mapsto 3$. We know how to generate permutations of a multiset using Algorithm L, but now we will learn another way.

Notice that x precedes y in a permutation $a_1 \ldots a_n$ if and only if $a'_x < a'_y$ in the inverse permutation $a'_1 \ldots a'_n$. Therefore the algorithm we are about to study will also find all permutations $a'_1 \ldots a'_n$ such that $a'_j < a'_k$ whenever $j \prec k$. For example, we learned in Section 5.1.4 that a Young tableau is an arrangement of $\{1, \ldots, n\}$ in rows and columns so that each row is increasing from left to right and each column is increasing from top to bottom. The problem of generating all 3×3 Young tableaux is therefore equivalent to generating all $a'_1 \ldots a'_9$ such that

$$\begin{aligned} a'_1 < a'_2 < a'_3, \quad a'_4 < a'_5 < a'_6, \quad a'_7 < a'_8 < a'_9, \\ a'_1 < a'_4 < a'_7, \quad a'_2 < a'_5 < a'_8, \quad a'_3 < a'_6 < a'_9, \end{aligned} \qquad (48)$$

and this is a special kind of topological sorting.

We might also want to find all *perfect matchings* of $2n$ elements, namely all ways to partition $\{1,\ldots,2n\}$ into n pairs. There are $(2n-1)(2n-3)\ldots(1) = (2n)!/(2^n n!)$ ways to do this, and they correspond to permutations that satisfy

$$a_1' < a_2', \quad a_3' < a_4', \quad \ldots, \quad a_{2n-1}' < a_{2n}', \quad a_1' < a_3' < \cdots < a_{2n-1}'. \tag{49}$$

An elegant algorithm for exhaustive topological sorting was discovered by Y. L. Varol and D. Rotem [*Comp. J.* **24** (1981), 83–84], who realized that a method analogous to plain changes (Algorithm P) can be used. Suppose we have found a way to arrange $\{1,\ldots,n-1\}$ topologically, so that $a_1\ldots a_{n-1}$ satisfies all the conditions that do not involve n. Then we can easily write down all the allowable ways to insert the final element n without changing the relative order of $a_1\ldots a_{n-1}$: We simply start with $a_1\ldots a_{n-1}n$, then shift n left one step at a time, until it cannot move further. Applying this idea recursively yields the following straightforward procedure.

Algorithm V (*All topological sorts*). Given a relation $\prec$ on $\{1,\ldots,n\}$ with the property that $x \prec y$ implies $x < y$, this algorithm generates all permutations $a_1\ldots a_n$ and their inverses $a_1'\ldots a_n'$ with the property that $a_j' < a_k'$ whenever $j \prec k$. We assume for convenience that $a_0 = a_0' = 0$ and that $0 \prec k$ for $1 \le k \le n$.

V1. [Initialize.] Set $a_j \leftarrow j$ and $a_j' \leftarrow j$ for $0 \le j \le n$.

V2. [Visit.] Visit the permutation $a_1\ldots a_n$ and its inverse $a_1'\ldots a_n'$. Then set $k \leftarrow n$.

V3. [Can k move left?] Set $j \leftarrow a_k'$ and $l \leftarrow a_{j-1}$. If $l \prec k$, go to V5.

V4. [Yes, move it.] Set $a_{j-1} \leftarrow k$, $a_j \leftarrow l$, $a_k' \leftarrow j-1$, and $a_l' \leftarrow j$. Go to V2.

V5. [No, put k back.] While $j < k$, set $l \leftarrow a_{j+1}$, $a_j \leftarrow l$, $a_l' \leftarrow j$, and $j \leftarrow j+1$. Then set $a_k \leftarrow a_k' \leftarrow k$. Decrease k by 1 and return to V3 if $k > 0$. ∎

For example, Theorem 5.1.4H tells us that there are exactly 42 Young tableaux of size 3×3. If we apply Algorithm V to the relations (48) and write the inverse permutation in array form

$$\boxed{\begin{array}{ccc} a_1' & a_2' & a_3' \\ a_4' & a_5' & a_6' \\ a_7' & a_8' & a_9' \end{array}}, \tag{50}$$

we get the following 42 results:

123	123	123	123	123	124	124	124	124	124	125	125	125	125
456	457	458	467	468	356	357	358	367	368	367	368	346	347
789	689	679	589	579	789	689	679	589	579	489	479	789	689

125	126	126	127	126	126	127	134	134	134	134	134	135	135
348	347	348	348	357	358	358	256	257	258	267	268	267	268
679	589	579	569	489	479	469	789	689	679	589	579	489	479

145	145	135	135	135	136	136	137	136	136	137	146	146	147
267	268	246	247	248	247	248	248	257	258	258	257	258	258
389	379	789	689	679	589	579	569	489	479	469	389	379	369

Let t_r be the number of topological sorts for which the final $n - r$ elements are in their initial position $a_j = j$ for $r < j \leq n$. Equivalently, t_r is the number of topological sorts $a_1 \ldots a_r$ of $\{1, \ldots, r\}$, when we ignore the relations involving elements greater than r. Then the recursive mechanism underlying Algorithm V shows that step V2 is performed N times and step V3 is performed M times, where

$$M = t_n + \cdots + t_1 \qquad \text{and} \qquad N = t_n. \tag{51}$$

Also, step V4 and the loop operations of V5 are performed $N - 1$ times; the rest of step V5 is done $M - N + 1$ times. Therefore the total running time of the algorithm is a linear combination of M, N, and n.

If the element labels are chosen poorly, M might be much larger than N. For example, if the constraints input to Algorithm V are

$$2 \prec 3, \quad 3 \prec 4, \quad \ldots, \quad n - 1 \prec n, \tag{52}$$

then $t_j = j$ for $1 \leq j \leq n$ and we have $M = \frac{1}{2}(n^2 + n)$, $N = n$. But those constraints are also equivalent to

$$1 \prec 2, \quad 2 \prec 3, \quad \ldots, \quad n - 2 \prec n - 1, \tag{53}$$

under renaming of the elements; then M is reduced to $2n - 1 = 2N - 1$.

Exercise 89 shows that a simple preprocessing step will find element labels so that a slight modification of Algorithm V is able to generate all topological sorts in $O(N + n)$ steps. Thus topological sorting can always be done efficiently.

Think twice before you permute. We have seen several attractive algorithms for permutation generation in this section, but many algorithms are known by which permutations that are optimum for particular purposes can be found *without* running through all possibilities. For example, Theorem 6.1S showed that we can find the best way to arrange records on a sequential storage simply by sorting them with respect to a certain cost criterion, and this process takes only $O(n \log n)$ steps. In Section 7.5.2 we will study the *assignment problem*, which asks how to permute the columns of a square matrix so that the sum of the diagonal elements is maximized. That problem can be solved in at most $O(n^3)$ operations, so it would be foolish to use a method of order $n!$ unless n is extremely small. Even in cases like the traveling salesrep problem, when no efficient algorithm is known, we can usually find a much better approach than to examine every possible solution. Permutation generation is best used when there is good reason to look at each permutation individually.

EXERCISES

▶ **1.** [*20*] Explain how to make Algorithm L run faster, by streamlining its operations when the value of j is near n.

2. [*20*] Rewrite Algorithm L so that it produces all permutations of $a_1 \ldots a_n$ in reverse colex order. (In other words, the values of the reflections $a_n \ldots a_1$ should be lexicographically decreasing, as in (11). This form of the algorithm is often simpler and faster than the original, because fewer calculations depend on the value of n.)

▶ **3.** [*M21*] The *rank* of a combinatorial arrangement X with respect to a generation algorithm is the number of other arrangements that the algorithm visits prior to X. Explain how to compute the rank of a given permutation $a_1 \ldots a_n$ with respect to Algorithm L, if $\{a_1, \ldots, a_n\} = \{1, \ldots, n\}$. What is the rank of 314592687?

4. [*M23*] Generalizing exercise 3, explain how to compute the rank of $a_1 \ldots a_n$ with respect to Algorithm L when $\{a_1, \ldots, a_n\}$ is the multiset $\{n_1 \cdot x_1, \ldots, n_t \cdot x_t\}$; here $n_1 + \cdots + n_t = n$ and $x_1 < \cdots < x_t$. (The total number of permutations is, of course, the multinomial coefficient

$$\binom{n}{n_1, \ldots, n_t} = \frac{n!}{n_1! \ldots n_t!};$$

see Eq. 5.1.2–(3).) What is the rank of 314159265?

5. [*HM25*] Compute the mean and variance of the number of comparisons made by Algorithm L in (a) step L2, (b) step L3, when the elements $\{a_1, \ldots, a_n\}$ are distinct.

6. [*HM34*] Derive generating functions for the mean number of comparisons made by Algorithm L in (a) step L2, (b) step L3, when $\{a_1, \ldots, a_n\}$ is a general multiset as in exercise 4. Also give the results in closed form when $\{a_1, \ldots, a_n\}$ is the binary multiset $\{s \cdot 0, (n - s) \cdot 1\}$.

7. [*HM35*] What is the limit as $t \to \infty$ of the average number of comparisons made per permutation in step L2 when Algorithm L is being applied to the multiset (a) $\{2 \cdot 1, \ 2 \cdot 2, \ \ldots, \ 2 \cdot t\}$? (b) $\{1 \cdot 1, \ 2 \cdot 2, \ \ldots, \ t \cdot t\}$? (c) $\{2 \cdot 1, \ 4 \cdot 2, \ \ldots, \ 2^t \cdot t\}$?

▶ **8.** [*21*] The *variations* of a multiset are the permutations of all its submultisets. For example, the variations of $\{1, 2, 2, 3\}$ are

ϵ, 1, 12, 122, 1223, 123, 1232, 13, 132, 1322,

  2, 21, 212, 2123, 213, 2132, 22, 221, 2213, 223, 2231, 23, 231, 2312, 232, 2321,

  3, 31, 312, 3122, 32, 321, 3212, 322, 3221.

Show that simple changes to Algorithm L will generate all variations of a given multiset $\{a_1, a_2, \ldots, a_n\}$.

9. [*22*] Continuing the previous exercise, design an algorithm to generate all r-variations of a given multiset $\{a_1, a_2, \ldots, a_n\}$, also called its r-permutations, namely all permutations of its r-element submultisets. (For example, the solution to an alphametic with r distinct letters is an r-variation of $\{0, 1, \ldots, 9\}$.)

10. [*20*] What are the values of $a_1 a_2 \ldots a_n$, $c_1 c_2 \ldots c_n$, and $o_1 o_2 \ldots o_n$ at the end of Algorithm P, if $a_1 a_2 \ldots a_n = 12 \ldots n$ at the beginning?

11. [*M22*] How many times is each step of Algorithm P performed? (Assume that $n \geq 2$.)

▶ **12.** [*M23*] What is the 1000000th permutation visited by (a) Algorithm L, (b) Algorithm P, (c) Algorithm C, if $\{a_1, \ldots, a_n\} = \{0, \ldots, 9\}$? *Hint:* In mixed-radix notation we have $1000000 = \begin{bmatrix} 2, & 6, & 6, & 2, & 5, & 1, & 2, & 2, & 0, & 0 \\ 10, & 9, & 8, & 7, & 6, & 5, & 4, & 3, & 2, & 1 \end{bmatrix} = \begin{bmatrix} 0, & 0, & 1, & 2, & 3, & 0, & 2, & 7, & 1, & 0 \\ 1, & 2, & 3, & 4, & 5, & 6, & 7, & 8, & 9, & 10 \end{bmatrix}$.

13. [*M21*] (Martin Gardner, 1974.) True or false: If $a_1 a_2 \ldots a_n$ is initially $12 \ldots n$, Algorithm P begins by visiting all $n!/2$ permutations in which 1 precedes 2; then the next permutation is $n \ldots 21$.

14. [*M22*] True or false: If $a_1 a_2 \ldots a_n$ is initially $x_1 x_2 \ldots x_n$ in Algorithm P, we always have $a_{j-c_j+s} = x_j$ at the beginning of step P5.

15. [*M23*] (Selmer Johnson, 1963.) Show that the offset variable s never exceeds 2 in Algorithm P.

16. [*21*] Explain how to make Algorithm P run faster, by streamlining its operations when the value of j is near n. (This problem is analogous to exercise 1.)

▶ **17.** [*20*] Extend Algorithm P so that the *inverse permutation* $a'_1 \dots a'_n$ is available for processing when $a_1 \dots a_n$ is visited in step P2. (The inverse satisfies $a'_k = j$ if and only if $a_j = k$.)

18. [*21*] (*Rosary permutations.*) Devise an efficient way to generate $(n-1)!/2$ permutations that represent all possible undirected cycles on the vertices $\{1, \dots, n\}$; that is, no cyclic shift of $a_1 \dots a_n$ or $a_n \dots a_1$ will be generated if $a_1 \dots a_n$ is generated. The permutations (1234, 1324, 3124) could, for example, be used when $n = 4$.

19. [*25*] Construct an algorithm that generates all permutations of n distinct elements *looplessly* in the spirit of Algorithm 7.2.1.1L.

▶ **20.** [*20*] The n-cube has $2^n n!$ symmetries, one for each way to permute and/or complement the coordinates. Such a symmetry is conveniently represented as a *signed permutation*, namely a permutation with optional signs attached to the elements. For example, $23\bar{1}$ is a signed permutation that transforms the vertices of the 3-cube by changing $x_1 x_2 x_3$ to $x_2 x_3 \bar{x}_1$, so that $000 \mapsto 001$, $001 \mapsto 011$, $\dots$, $111 \mapsto 110$. Design a simple algorithm that generates all signed permutations of $\{1, 2, \dots, n\}$, where each step either interchanges two adjacent elements or negates the first element.

21. [*M21*] (E. P. McCravy, 1971.) How many solutions does the alphametic (6) have in radix b?

22. [*M15*] True or false: If an alphametic has a solution in radix b, it has a solution in radix $b+1$.

23. [*M20*] True or false: A pure alphametic cannot have two identical signatures $s_j = s_k \neq 0$ when $j \neq k$.

24. [*25*] Solve the following alphametics by hand or by computer:
  a) SEND + A + TAD + MORE = MONEY.
  b) ZEROES + ONES = BINARY.   (Peter MacDonald, 1977)
  c) DCLIX + DLXVI = MCCXXV.   (Willy Enggren, 1972)
  d) COUPLE + COUPLE = QUARTET.   (Michael R. W. Buckley, 1977)
  e) FISH + N + CHIPS = SUPPER.   (Bob Vinnicombe, 1978)
  f) SATURN + URANUS + NEPTUNE + PLUTO = PLANETS.   (Willy Enggren, 1968)
  g) EARTH + AIR + FIRE + WATER = NATURE.   (Herman Nijon, 1977)
  h) AN + ACCELERATING + INFERENTIAL + ENGINEERING + TALE + ELITE + GRANT + FEE + ET + CETERA = ARTIFICIAL + INTELLIGENCE.
  i) HARDY + NESTS = NASTY + HERDS.

▶ **25.** [*M21*] Devise a fast way to compute $\min(a \cdot s)$ and $\max(a \cdot s)$ over all valid permutations $a_1 \dots a_{10}$ of $\{0, \dots, 9\}$, given the signature vector $s = (s_1, \dots, s_{10})$ and the first-letter set F of an alphametic problem. (Such a procedure makes it possible to rule out many cases quickly when a large family of alphametics is being considered, as in several of the exercises that follow, because a solution can exist only when $\min(a \cdot s) \leq 0 \leq \max(a \cdot s)$.)

26. [*25*] What is the unique alphametic solution to

$$\text{NIIHAU} \pm \text{KAUAI} \pm \text{OAHU} \pm \text{MOLOKAI} \pm \text{LANAI} \pm \text{MAUI} \pm \text{HAWAII} = 0?$$

27. [*30*] Construct pure additive alphametics in which all words have five letters.

28. [*M25*] A *partition* of the integer n is an expression of the form $n = n_1 + \cdots + n_t$ with $n_1 \geq \cdots \geq n_t > 0$. Such a partition is called *doubly true* if $\alpha(n) = \alpha(n_1) + \cdots + \alpha(n_t)$ is also a pure alphametic, where $\alpha(n)$ is the "name" of n in some language. Doubly true partitions were introduced by Alan Wayne in *AMM* **54** (1947), 38, 412–414, where he suggested solving TWENTY = SEVEN + SEVEN + SIX and a few others.

a) Find all partitions that are doubly true in English when $1 \leq n \leq 20$.

b) Wayne also gave the example EIGHTY = FIFTY + TWENTY + NINE + ONE. Find all doubly true partitions for $1 \leq n \leq 100$ in which the parts are *distinct*, using the names ONE, TWO, ..., NINETYNINE, ONEHUNDRED.

▶ **29.** [*M25*] Continuing the previous exercise, find all equations of the form $n_1 + \cdots + n_t = n_1' + \cdots + n_{t'}'$ that are both mathematically and alphametically true in English, when $\{n_1, \ldots, n_t, n_1', \ldots, n_{t'}'\}$ are distinct positive integers less than 20. For example,

$$\text{TWELVE} + \text{NINE} + \text{TWO} = \text{ELEVEN} + \text{SEVEN} + \text{FIVE};$$

the alphametics should all be pure.

30. [*25*] Solve these multiplicative alphametics by hand or by computer:

a) TWO × TWO = SQUARE.   (H. E. Dudeney, 1929)

b) HIP × HIP = HURRAY.   (Willy Enggren, 1970)

c) PI × R × R = AREA.   (Brian Barwell, 1981)

d) NORTH/SOUTH = EAST/WEST.   (Nob Yoshigahara, 1995)

e) NAUGHT × NAUGHT = ZERO × ZERO × ZERO.   (Alan Wayne, 2003)

31. [*M22*] (Nob Yoshigahara.) (a) What is the unique solution to A/BC+D/EF+G/HI = 1, when $\{\text{A}, \ldots, \text{I}\} = \{1, \ldots, 9\}$? (b) Similarly, make AB mod 2 = 0, ABC mod 3 = 0, etc.

32. [*M25*] (H. E. Dudeney, 1901.) Find all ways to represent 100 by inserting a plus sign and a slash into a permutation of the digits $\{1, \ldots, 9\}$. For example, $100 = 91 + 5742/638$. The plus sign should precede the slash.

33. [*25*] Continuing the previous exercise, find all positive integers less than 150 that (a) cannot be represented in such a fashion; (b) have a unique representation.

34. [*M26*] Make the equation EVEN + ODD + PRIME = x doubly true when (a) x is a perfect 5th power; (b) x is a perfect 7th power.

▶ **35.** [*M20*] The automorphisms of a 4-cube have many different Sims tables, only one of which is shown in (14). How many different Sims tables are possible for that group, when the vertices are numbered as in (12)?

36. [*M23*] Find a Sims table for the group of all automorphisms of the 4×4 tic-tac-toe board

$$
\begin{array}{|cccc|}
\hline
0 & 1 & 2 & 3 \\
4 & 5 & 6 & 7 \\
8 & 9 & \text{a} & \text{b} \\
\text{c} & \text{d} & \text{e} & \text{f} \\
\hline
\end{array},
$$

namely the permutations that take lines into lines, where a "line" is a set of four elements that belong to a row, column, or diagonal.

▶ **37.** [*HM22*] How many Sims tables can be used with Algorithms G or H? Estimate the logarithm of this number as $n \to \infty$.

38. [*HM21*] Prove that the average number of transpositions per permutation when using Ord-Smith's algorithm (26) is approximately $\sinh 1 \approx 1.175$.

39. [*16*] Write down the 24 permutations generated for $n = 4$ by (a) Ord-Smith's method (26); (b) Heap's method (27).

40. [*M23*] Show that Heap's method (27) corresponds to a valid Sims table.

▸ **41.** [*M33*] Design an algorithm that generates all r-variations of $\{0, 1, \ldots, n-1\}$ by interchanging just two elements when going from one variation to the next. (See exercise 9.) *Hint:* Generalize Heap's method (27), obtaining the results in positions $a_{n-r} \ldots a_{n-1}$ of an array $a_0 \ldots a_{n-1}$. For example, one solution when $n = 5$ and $r = 2$ uses the final two elements of the respective permutations 01234, 31204, 30214, 30124, 40123, 20143, 24103, 24013, 34012, 14032, 13042, 13402, 23401, 03421, 02431, 02341, 12340, 42310, 41320, 41230.

42. [*M20*] Construct a Sims table for all permutations in which every $\sigma(k, j)$ and every $\tau(k, j)$ for $1 \leq j \leq k$ is a cycle of length ≤ 3.

43. [*M24*] Construct a Sims table for all permutations in which every $\sigma(k, k)$, $\omega(k)$, and $\tau(k, j)\omega(k - 1)^-$ for $1 \leq j \leq k$ is a cycle of length ≤ 3.

44. [*20*] When blocks of unwanted permutations are being skipped by the extended Algorithm G, is the Sims table of Ord-Smith's method (23) superior to the Sims table of the reverse colex method (18)?

45. [*20*] (a) What are the indices $u_1 \ldots u_9$ when Algorithm X visits the permutation 314592687? (b) What permutation is visited when $u_1 \ldots u_9 = 161800000$?

46. [*20*] True or false: When Algorithm X visits $a_1 \ldots a_n$, we have $u_k > u_{k+1}$ if and only if $a_k > a_{k+1}$, for $1 \leq k < n$.

▸ **47.** [*M21*] Express the number of times that each step of Algorithm X is performed in terms of the numbers $N_0, N_1, \ldots, N_n$, where N_k is the number of prefixes $a_1 \ldots a_k$ that satisfy $t_j(a_1, \ldots, a_j)$ for $1 \leq j \leq k$.

▸ **48.** [*M25*] Compare the running times of Algorithm X and Algorithm L, in the case when the tests $t_1(a_1)$, $t_2(a_1, a_2)$, $\ldots$, $t_n(a_1, a_2, \ldots, a_n)$ always are true.

▸ **49.** [*28*] The text's suggested method for solving additive alphametics with Algorithm X essentially chooses digits from right to left; in other words, it assigns tentative values to the least significant digits before considering digits that correspond to higher powers of 10.

Explore an alternative approach that chooses digits from left to right. For example, such a method will deduce immediately that M = 1 when SEND + MORE = MONEY. *Hint:* See exercise 25.

50. [*M15*] Explain why the dual formula (32) follows from (13).

51. [*M16*] True or false: If the sets $S_k = \{\sigma(k, 0), \ldots, \sigma(k, k)\}$ form a Sims table for the group of all permutations, so also do the sets $S_k^- = \{\sigma(k, 0)^-, \ldots, \sigma(k, k)^-\}$.

▸ **52.** [*M22*] What permutations $\tau(k, j)$ and $\omega(k)$ arise when Algorithm H is used with the Sims table (36)? Compare the resulting generator with Algorithm P.

▸ **53.** [*M26*] (F. M. Ives.) Construct a Sims table for which Algorithm H will generate all permutations by making only $n! + O((n - 2)!)$ transpositions.

54. [*20*] Would Algorithm C work properly if step C3 did a right-cyclic shift, setting $a_1 \ldots a_{k-1}a_k \leftarrow a_k a_1 \ldots a_{k-1}$, instead of a left-cyclic shift?

55. [*M27*] Consider the *factorial ruler function*

$$\rho_!(m) = \max\{k \mid m \bmod k! = 0\}.$$

Let σ_k and τ_k be permutations of the nonnegative integers such that $\sigma_j \tau_k = \tau_k \sigma_j$ whenever $j \leq k$. Let α_0 and β_0 be the identity permutation, and for $m > 0$ define

$$\alpha_m = \beta_{m-1}^- \tau_{\rho_!(m)} \beta_{m-1} \alpha_{m-1}, \qquad \beta_m = \sigma_{\rho_!(m)} \beta_{m-1}.$$

For example, if σ_k is the flip operation $(1\ k{-}1)(2\ k{-}2)\ldots = (0\ k)\phi(k)$ and if $\tau_k = (0\ k)$, and if Algorithm E is started with $a_j = j$ for $0 \leq j < n$, then α_m and β_m are the contents of $a_0 \ldots a_{n-1}$ and $b_0 \ldots b_{n-1}$ after step E5 has been performed m times.

   a) Prove that $\beta_{(n+1)!} \alpha_{(n+1)!} = \sigma_{n+1} \sigma_n^- \tau_{n+1} \tau_n^- (\beta_{n!} \alpha_{n!})^{n+1}$.

   b) Use the result of (a) to establish the validity of Algorithm E.

56. [*M22*] Prove that Algorithm E remains valid if step E5 is replaced by

   E5′. [Transpose pairs.] If $k > 2$, interchange $b_{j+1} \leftrightarrow b_j$ for $j = k-2,\ k-4,\ \ldots,$ (2 or 1). Return to E2. ∎

57. [*HM22*] What is the average number of interchanges made in step E5?

58. [*M21*] True or false: If Algorithm E begins with $a_0 \ldots a_{n-1} = x_1 \ldots x_n$ then the final permutation visited begins with $a_0 = x_n$.

59. [*M20*] Some authors define the arcs of a Cayley graph as running from π to $\pi \alpha_j$ instead of from π to $\alpha_j \pi$. Are the two definitions essentially different?

▶ **60.** [*21*] A *Gray cycle for permutations* is a cycle $(\pi_0, \pi_1, \ldots, \pi_{n!-1})$ that includes every permutation of $\{1, 2, \ldots, n\}$ and has the property that π_k differs from $\pi_{(k+1) \bmod n!}$ by an adjacent transposition. It can also be described as a Hamiltonian cycle on the Cayley graph for the group of all permutations on $\{1, 2, \ldots, n\}$, with the $n-1$ generators $((1\ 2), (2\ 3), \ldots, (n{-}1\ n))$. The *delta sequence* of such a Gray cycle is the sequence of integers $\delta_0 \delta_1 \ldots \delta_{n!-1}$ such that

$$\pi_{(k+1) \bmod n!} = (\delta_k\ \delta_k{+}1)\, \pi_k.$$

(See 7.2.1.1–(24), which describes the analogous situation for binary n-tuples.) For example, Fig. 43 illustrates the Gray cycle defined by plain changes when $n = 4$; its delta sequence is $(32131231)^3$.

   a) Find all Gray cycles for permutations of $\{1, 2, 3, 4\}$.

   b) Two Gray cycles are considered to be equivalent if their delta sequences can be obtained from each other by cyclic shifting ($\delta_k \ldots \delta_{n!-1} \delta_0 \ldots \delta_{k-1}$) and/or reversal ($\delta_{n!-1} \ldots \delta_1 \delta_0$) and/or complementation ($(n{-}\delta_0)(n{-}\delta_1)\ldots(n{-}\delta_{n!-1})$). Which of the Gray cycles in (a) are equivalent?

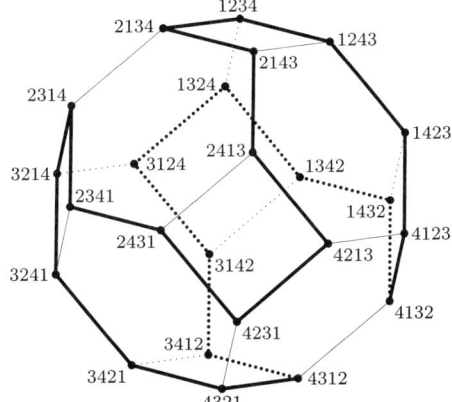

Fig. 43. Algorithm P traces out this Hamiltonian cycle on the truncated octahedron of Fig. 5–1.

61. [*21*] Continuing the previous exercise, a *Gray code for permutations* is like a Gray cycle except that the final permutation $\pi_{n!-1}$ is not required to be adjacent to the initial permutation π_0. Study the set of all Gray codes for $n = 4$ that start with 1234.

▸ **62.** [*M23*] What permutations can be reached as the final element of a Gray code that starts at $12\ldots n$?

63. [*M25*] Estimate the total number of Gray cycles for permutations of $\{1, 2, 3, 4, 5\}$.

64. [*23*] A "doubly Gray" code for permutations is a Gray cycle with the additional property that $\delta_{k+1} = \delta_k \pm 1$ for all k. Compton and Williamson have proved that such codes exist for all $n \geq 3$. How many doubly Gray codes exist for $n = 5$?

65. [*M25*] For which integers N is there a Gray path through the N lexicographically smallest permutations of $\{1, \ldots, n\}$? (Exercise 7.2.1.1–26 solves the analogous problem for binary n-tuples.)

66. [*22*] Ehrlich's swap method suggests another type of Gray cycle for permutations, in which the $n - 1$ generators are the star transpositions $(1\,2)$, $(1\,3)$, $\ldots$, $(1\,n)$. For example, Fig. 44 shows the relevant graph when $n = 4$. Analyze the Hamiltonian cycles of this graph.

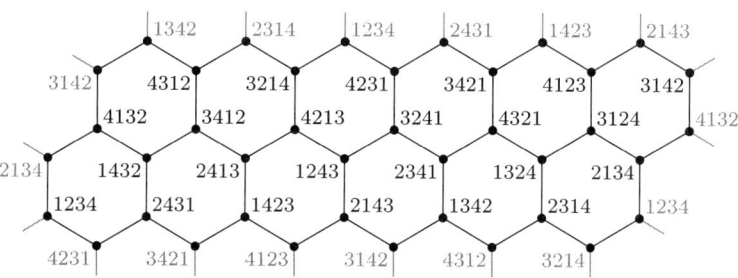

Fig. 44. The Cayley graph for permutations of $\{1, 2, 3, 4\}$, generated by the star transpositions $(1\,2)$, $(1\,3)$, and $(1\,4)$, drawn as a twisted torus.

67. [*26*] Continuing the previous exercise, find a first-element-swap Gray cycle for $n = 5$ in which each star transposition $(1\,j)$ occurs 30 times, for $2 \leq j \leq 5$.

68. [*M30*] (V. L. Kompel'makher and V. A. Liskovets, 1975.) Let G be the Cayley graph for all permutations of $\{1, \ldots, n\}$, with generators $(\alpha_1, \ldots, \alpha_k)$ where each α_j is a transposition $(u_j\,v_j)$; also let A be the graph with vertices $\{1, \ldots, n\}$ and edges $u_j \,—\, v_j$ for $1 \leq j \leq k$. Prove that G has a Hamiltonian cycle if and only if A is connected. (Figure 43 is the special case when A is a path; Figure 44 is the special case when A is a "star.")

▸ **69.** [*28*] If $n \geq 4$, the following algorithm generates all permutations $A_1 A_2 A_3 \ldots A_n$ of $\{1, 2, 3, \ldots, n\}$ using only three transformations,

$$\rho = (1\,2)(3\,4)(5\,6)\ldots, \qquad \sigma = (2\,3)(4\,5)(6\,7)\ldots, \qquad \tau = (3\,4)(5\,6)(7\,8)\ldots,$$

never applying ρ and τ next to each other. Explain why it works.

    Z1. [Initialize.] Set $A_j \leftarrow j$ for $1 \leq j \leq n$. Also set $a_j \leftarrow 2j$ for $1 \leq j \leq n/2$ and $a_{n-j} \leftarrow 2j+1$ for $1 \leq j < n/2$. Then invoke Algorithm P, but with parameter $n - 1$ instead of n. We will treat that algorithm as a coroutine, which should return control to us whenever it "visits" $a_1 \ldots a_{n-1}$ in step P2. We will also share its variables (except n).

Z2. [Set x and y.] Invoke Algorithm P again, obtaining a new permutation $a_1 \ldots a_{n-1}$ and a new value of j. If $j = 2$, interchange $a_{1+s} \leftrightarrow a_{2+s}$ (thereby undoing the effect of step P5) and repeat this step; in such a case we are at the halfway point of Algorithm P. If $j = 1$ (so that Algorithm P has terminated), set $x \leftarrow y \leftarrow 0$ and go to Z3. Otherwise set

$$x \leftarrow a_{j-c_j+s+[o_j=+1]}, \qquad y \leftarrow a_{j-c_j+s-[o_j=-1]};$$

these are the two elements most recently interchanged in step P5.

Z3. [Visit.] Visit the permutation $A_1 \ldots A_n$. Then go to Z5 if $A_1 = x$ and $A_2 = y$.

Z4. [Apply ρ, then σ.] Interchange $A_1 \leftrightarrow A_2$, $A_3 \leftrightarrow A_4$, $A_5 \leftrightarrow A_6$, ... Visit $A_1 \ldots A_n$. Then interchange $A_2 \leftrightarrow A_3$, $A_4 \leftrightarrow A_5$, $A_6 \leftrightarrow A_7$, ... Terminate if $A_1 \ldots A_n = 1 \ldots n$, otherwise return to Z3.

Z5. [Apply τ, then σ.] Interchange $A_3 \leftrightarrow A_4$, $A_5 \leftrightarrow A_6$, $A_7 \leftrightarrow A_8$, ... Visit $A_1 \ldots A_n$. Then interchange $A_2 \leftrightarrow A_3$, $A_4 \leftrightarrow A_5$, $A_6 \leftrightarrow A_7$, ..., and return to Z2. ∎

Hint: Show first that the algorithm works if modified so that $A_j \leftarrow n + 1 - j$ and $a_j \leftarrow j$ in step Z1, and if the "flip" permutations

$$\rho' = (1 \ n)(2 \ n{-}1) \ldots, \qquad \sigma' = (2 \ n)(3 \ n{-}1) \ldots, \qquad \tau' = (2 \ n{-}1)(3 \ n{-}2) \ldots$$

are used instead of ρ, σ, τ in steps Z4 and Z5. In this modification, step Z3 should go to Z5 if $A_1 = x$ and $A_n = y$; step Z4 should terminate when $A_1 \ldots A_n = n \ldots 1$.

▶ **70.** [*M33*] The two 12-cycles (41) can be regarded as σ–τ cycles for the twelve permutations of $\{1, 1, 3, 4\}$:

$$1134 \rightarrow 1341 \rightarrow 3411 \rightarrow 4311 \rightarrow 3114 \rightarrow 1143 \rightarrow 1431$$
$$\rightarrow 4131 \rightarrow 1314 \rightarrow 3141 \rightarrow 1413 \rightarrow 4113 \rightarrow 1134.$$

Replacing $\{1, 1\}$ by $\{1, 2\}$ yields disjoint cycles, and we obtained a Hamiltonian path by jumping from one to the other. Can a σ–τ path for all permutations of 6 elements be formed in a similar way, based on a 360-cycle for the permutations of $\{1, 1, 3, 4, 5, 6\}$?

71. [*48*] Does the Cayley graph with generators $\sigma = (1 \, 2 \, \ldots \, n)$ and $\tau = (1 \, 2)$ have a Hamiltonian cycle whenever $n \geq 3$ is odd?

72. [*M21*] Given a Cayley graph with generators $(\alpha_1, \ldots, \alpha_k)$, assume that each α_j takes $x \mapsto y$. (For example, both σ and τ in exercise 71 take $1 \mapsto 2$.) Prove that any Hamiltonian path starting at $12 \ldots n$ in G must end at a permutation that takes $y \mapsto x$.

▶ **73.** [*M30*] Let α, β, and σ be permutations of a set X, where $X = A \cup B$. Assume that $x\sigma = x\alpha$ when $x \in A$ and $x\sigma = x\beta$ when $x \in B$, and that the order of $\alpha\beta^-$ is odd.
  a) Prove that all three permutations α, β, σ have the same sign; that is, they are all even or all odd. *Hint:* A permutation has odd order if and only if its cycles all have odd length.
  b) Derive Theorem R from part (a).

74. [*M30*] (R. A. Rankin.) Assuming that $\alpha\beta = \beta\alpha$ in Theorem R, prove that a Hamiltonian cycle exists in the Cayley graph for G if and only if there is a number k such that $0 \leq k \leq g/c$ and $t + k \perp c$, where $\beta^{g/c} = \gamma^t$, $\gamma = \alpha\beta^-$. *Hint:* Represent elements of the group in the form $\beta^j \gamma^k$.

75. [*M26*] The directed torus $C_{\vec{m}} \times C_{\vec{n}}$ has mn vertices (x, y) for $0 \le x < m$, $0 \le y < n$, and arcs $(x, y) \longrightarrow (x, y)\alpha = ((x + 1) \bmod m, y)$, $(x, y) \longrightarrow (x, y)\beta = (x, (y + 1) \bmod n)$. Prove that, if $m > 1$ and $n > 1$, the number of Hamiltonian cycles of this digraph is

$$\sum_{k=1}^{d-1} \binom{d}{k} \big[\gcd((d - k)m, kn) = d \big], \qquad d = \gcd(m, n).$$

76. [*M31*] The cells numbered $0, 1, \ldots, 63$ in Fig. 45 illustrate a *northeasterly knight's tour* on an 8×8 torus: If k appears in cell (x_k, y_k), then $(x_{k+1}, y_{k+1}) \equiv (x_k + 2, y_k + 1)$ or $(x_k + 1, y_k + 2)$, modulo 8, and $(x_{64}, y_{64}) = (x_0, y_0)$. How many such tours are possible on an $m \times n$ torus, when $m, n \ge 3$?

29	24	19	14	49	44	39	34
58	53	48	43	38	9	4	63
23	18	13	8	3	62	33	28
52	47	42	37	32	27	22	57
17	12	7	2	61	56	51	46
6	41	36	31	26	21	16	11
35	30	1	60	55	50	45	40
0	59	54	25	20	15	10	5

Fig. 45. A northeasterly knight's tour.

▶ **77.** [*22*] Complete the MMIX program whose inner loop appears in (42), using Heap's method (27).

78. [*M23*] Analyze the running time of the program in exercise 77, generalizing it so that the inner loop does $r!$ visits (with $a_0 \ldots a_{r-1}$ in global registers).

79. [*20*] What seven MMIX instructions will ⟨ Swap the nybbles ... ⟩ as (45) requires? For example, if register t contains the value 4 and register a contains the nybbles #12345678, register a should change to #12345687.

80. [*21*] Solve the previous exercise with only five MMIX instructions. *Hint:* Use MXOR.

▶ **81.** [*22*] Complete the MMIX program (46) by specifying how to ⟨ Continue with Langdon's method ⟩.

82. [*M21*] Analyze the running time of the program in exercise 81.

83. [*22*] Use the σ–τ path of exercise 70 to design an MMIX routine analogous to (42) that generates all permutations of #123456 in register a.

84. [*20*] Suggest a good way to generate all $n!$ permutations of $\{1, \ldots, n\}$ on p processors that are running in parallel.

▶ **85.** [*25*] Assume that n is small enough that $n!$ fits in a computer word. What's a good way to convert a given permutation $\alpha = a_1 \ldots a_n$ of $\{1, \ldots, n\}$ into an integer $k = r(\alpha)$ in the range $0 \le k < n!$? Both functions $k = r(\alpha)$ and $\alpha = r^{[-1]}(k)$ should be computable in only $O(n)$ steps.

86. [*20*] A partial order relation is supposed to be transitive; that is, $x \prec y$ and $y \prec z$ should imply $x \prec z$. But Algorithm V does not require its input relation to satisfy this condition.

Show that if $x \prec y$ and $y \prec z$, Algorithm V will produce identical results whether or not $x \prec z$.

87. [*20*] (F. Ruskey.) Consider the inversion tables $c_1 \ldots c_n$ of the permutations visited by Algorithm V. What noteworthy property do they have? (Compare with the inversion tables (4) in Algorithm P.)

88. [*21*] Show that Algorithm V can be used to generate all ways to partition the digits $\{0, 1, \ldots, 9\}$ into two 3-element sets and two 2-element sets.

▶ **89.** [*M30*] Consider the numbers $t_0, t_1, \ldots, t_n$ defined before (51). Clearly $t_0 = t_1 = 1$.
   a) Say that index j is "trivial" if $t_j = t_{j-1}$. For example, 9 is trivial with respect to the Young tableau relations (48). Explain how to modify Algorithm V so that the variable k takes on only nontrivial values.
   b) Analyze the running time of the modified algorithm. What formulas replace (51)?
   c) Say that the interval $[j \mathinner{\ldotp\ldotp} k]$ is not a chain if there is an index l such that $j \leq l < k$ and we do not have $l \prec l + 1$. Prove that in such a case $t_k \geq 2t_{j-1}$.
   d) Every inverse topological sort $a_1' \ldots a_n'$ defines a labeling that corresponds to relations $a_{j_1}' \prec a_{k_1}', \ldots, a_{j_m}' \prec a_{k_m}'$, which are equivalent to the original relations $j_1 \prec k_1, \ldots, j_m \prec k_m$. Explain how to find a labeling such that $[j \mathinner{\ldotp\ldotp} k]$ is not a chain when j and k are consecutive nontrivial indices.
   e) Prove that with such a labeling, $M < 4N$ in the formulas of part (b).

90. [*M21*] Algorithm V can be used to produce all permutations that are h-ordered for all h in a given set, namely all $a_1' \ldots a_n'$ such that $a_j' < a_{j+h}'$ for $1 \leq j \leq n - h$ (see Section 5.2.1). Analyze the running time of Algorithm V when it generates all permutations that are both 2-ordered and 3-ordered.

91. [*HM21*] Analyze the running time of Algorithm V when it is used with the relations (49) to find perfect matchings.

92. [*M18*] How many permutations is Algorithm V likely to visit, in a "random" case? Let P_n be the number of partial orderings on $\{1, \ldots, n\}$, namely the number of relations that are reflexive, antisymmetric, and transitive. Let Q_n be the number of such relations with the additional property that $j < k$ whenever $j \prec k$. Express the expected number of ways to sort n elements topologically, averaged over all partial orderings, in terms of P_n and Q_n.

93. [*35*] Prove that all topological sorts can be generated in such a way that only one or two adjacent transpositions are made at each step. (The example $1 \prec 2, 3 \prec 4$ shows that a single transposition per step cannot always be achieved, even if we allow nonadjacent swaps, because only two of the six relevant permutations are odd.)

▶ **94.** [*25*] Show that in the case of perfect matchings, using the relations in (49), all topological sorts can be generated with just one transposition per step.

95. [*21*] Discuss how to generate all *up-down permutations* of $\{1, \ldots, n\}$, namely those $a_1 \ldots a_n$ such that $a_1 < a_2 > a_3 < a_4 > \cdots$.

96. [*21*] Discuss how to generate all *cyclic permutations* of $\{1, \ldots, n\}$, namely those $a_1 \ldots a_n$ whose cycle representation consists of a single n-cycle.

97. [*21*] Discuss how to generate all *derangements* of $\{1, \ldots, n\}$, namely those $a_1 \ldots a_n$ such that $a_1 \neq 1$, $a_2 \neq 2$, $a_3 \neq 3$, ...

98. [*HM23*] Analyze the asymptotic running time of the method in the previous exercise.

99. [*M30*] Given $n \geq 3$, show that all derangements of $\{1, \ldots, n\}$ can be generated by making at most two transpositions between visits.

100. [*21*] Discuss how to generate all of the *indecomposable* permutations of $\{1, \ldots, n\}$, namely those $a_1 \ldots a_n$ such that $\{a_1, \ldots, a_j\} \neq \{1, \ldots, j\}$ for $1 \leq j < n$.

101. [*21*] Discuss how to generate all *involutions* of $\{1, \ldots, n\}$, namely those permutations $a_1 \ldots a_n$ with $a_{a_1} \ldots a_{a_n} = 1 \ldots n$.

102. [*M30*] Show that all involutions of $\{1, \ldots, n\}$ can be generated by making at most two transpositions between visits.

103. [*M32*] Show that all even permutations of $\{1, \ldots, n\}$ can be generated by successive *rotations of three consecutive elements*.

▸ **104.** [*M22*] A permutation $a_1 \ldots a_n$ of $\{1, \ldots, n\}$ is *well-balanced* if

$$\sum_{k=1}^{n} k a_k = \sum_{k=1}^{n} (n+1-k) a_k.$$

For example, 3142 is well-balanced when $n = 4$.

    a) Prove that no permutation is well-balanced when $n \bmod 4 = 2$.

    b) Prove that if $a_1 \ldots a_n$ is well-balanced, so are its reversal $a_n \ldots a_1$, its complement $(n+1-a_1) \ldots (n+1-a_n)$, and its inverse $a_1' \ldots a_n'$.

    c) Determine the number of well-balanced permutations for small values of n.

▸ **105.** [*26*] A *weak order* is a relation $\preceq$ that is transitive ($x \preceq y$ and $y \preceq z$ implies $x \preceq z$) and complete ($x \preceq y$ or $y \preceq x$ always holds). We can write $x \equiv y$ if $x \preceq y$ and $y \preceq x$; $x \prec y$ if $x \preceq y$ and $y \not\preceq x$. There are thirteen weak orders on three elements $\{1, 2, 3\}$, namely

$$1 \equiv 2 \equiv 3, \quad 1 \equiv 2 \prec 3, \quad 1 \prec 2 \equiv 3, \quad 1 \prec 2 \prec 3, \quad 1 \equiv 3 \prec 2, \quad 1 \prec 3 \prec 2,$$

$$2 \prec 1 \equiv 3, \quad 2 \prec 1 \prec 3, \quad 2 \equiv 3 \prec 1, \quad 2 \prec 3 \prec 1, \quad 3 \prec 1 \equiv 2, \quad 3 \prec 1 \prec 2, \quad 3 \prec 2 \prec 1.$$

    a) Explain how to generate all weak orders of $\{1, \ldots, n\}$ systematically, as sequences of digits separated by the symbols $\equiv$ or $\prec$.

    b) A weak order can also be represented as a sequence $a_1 \ldots a_n$ where $a_j = k$ if j is preceded by $k \prec$ signs. For example, the thirteen weak orders on $\{1, 2, 3\}$ are respectively 000, 001, 011, 012, 010, 021, 101, 102, 100, 201, 110, 120, 210 in this form. Find a simple way to generate all such sequences of length n.

106. [*M40*] Can exercise 105(b) be solved with a Gray-like code?

▸ **107.** [*30*] (John H. Conway, 1973.) To play the solitaire game of "topswops," start by shuffling a pack of n cards labeled $\{1, \ldots, n\}$ and place them face up in a pile. Then if the top card is $k > 1$, deal out the top k cards and put them back on top of the pile, thereby changing the permutation from $a_1 \ldots a_n$ to $a_k \ldots a_1 a_{k+1} \ldots a_n$. Continue until the top card is 1. For example, the 7-step sequence

$$31452 \to 41352 \to 53142 \to 24135 \to 42135 \to 31245 \to 21345 \to 12345$$

might occur when $n = 5$. What is the longest sequence possible when $n = 13$?

108. [*M27*] If the longest n-card game of topswops has length $f(n)$, prove that $f(n) \leq F_{n+1} - 1$.

109. [*M47*] Find good upper and lower bounds on the topswops function $f(n)$.

▸ **110.** [*25*] Find all permutations $a_0 \ldots a_9$ of $\{0, \ldots, 9\}$ such that

$$\{a_0, a_2, a_3, a_7\} = \{2, 5, 7, 8\}, \qquad \{a_1, a_4, a_5\} = \{0, 3, 6\},$$

$$\{a_1, a_3, a_7, a_8\} = \{3, 4, 5, 7\}, \qquad \{a_0, a_3, a_4\} = \{0, 7, 8\}.$$

Also suggest an algorithm for solving large problems of this type.

▸ **111.** [*M25*] Several permutation-oriented analogs of de Bruijn cycles have been proposed. The simplest and nicest of these is the notion of a *universal cycle of permutations*, introduced by B. W. Jackson in *Discrete Math.* **117** (1993), 141–150, namely a cycle of $n!$ digits such that each permutation of $\{1, \ldots, n\}$ occurs exactly once as a block of $n-1$ consecutive digits (with its redundant final element suppressed). For example, (121323) is a universal cycle of permutations for $n = 3$, and it is essentially unique.

Prove that universal cycles of permutations exist for all $n \geq 2$. What is the lexicographically smallest one when $n = 4$?

▶ **112.** [*M30*] (A. Williams, 2007.) Continuing exercise 111, construct *explicit* cycles:
  a) Show that a universal cycle of permutations is equivalent to a Hamiltonian cycle on the Cayley graph with two generators $\rho = (1\ 2\ \ldots\ n{-}1)$ and $\sigma = (1\ 2\ \ldots\ n)$.
  b) Prove that any Hamiltonian path in that graph is actually a Hamiltonian cycle.
  c) Find such a path of the form $\sigma^2\rho^{n-3}\alpha_1\ldots\sigma^2\rho^{n-3}\alpha_{(n-1)!}$, $\alpha_j \in \{\rho,\sigma\}$, for $n \geq 3$.

113. [*HM43*] Exactly how many universal cycles exist, for permutations of ≤ 9 objects?

7.2.1.3. Generating all combinations.
Combinatorial mathematics is often described as "the study of permutations, combinations, etc.," so we turn our attention now to combinations. A *combination of n things, taken t at a time*, often called simply a *t-combination of n things*, is a way to select a subset of size t from a given set of size n. We know from Eq. 1.2.6–(2) that there are exactly $\binom{n}{t}$ ways to do this; and we learned in Section 3.4.2 how to choose t-combinations at random.

Selecting t of n objects is equivalent to choosing the $n - t$ elements not selected. We will emphasize this symmetry by letting

$$n = s + t \tag{1}$$

throughout our discussion, and we will often refer to a t-combination of n things as an "(s,t)-combination." Thus, an (s,t)-combination is a way to subdivide $s + t$ objects into two collections of sizes s and t.

> *If I ask how many combinations of 21 can be taken out of 25,*
> *I do in effect ask how many combinations of 4 may be taken.*
> *For there are just as many ways of taking 21 as there are of leaving 4.*
> — AUGUSTUS DE MORGAN, *An Essay on Probabilities* (1838)

There are two main ways to represent (s,t)-combinations: We can list the elements $c_t \ldots c_2 c_1$ that have been selected, or we can work with binary strings $a_{n-1} \ldots a_1 a_0$ for which

$$a_{n-1} + \cdots + a_1 + a_0 = t. \tag{2}$$

The string representation has s 0s and t 1s, corresponding to elements that are unselected or selected. The list representation $c_t \ldots c_2 c_1$ tends to work out best if we let the elements be members of the set $\{0, 1, \ldots, n - 1\}$ and if we list them in *decreasing* order:

$$n > c_t > \cdots > c_2 > c_1 \geq 0. \tag{3}$$

Binary notation connects these two representations nicely, because the item list $c_t \ldots c_2 c_1$ corresponds to the sum

$$2^{c_t} + \cdots + 2^{c_2} + 2^{c_1} = \sum_{k=0}^{n-1} a_k 2^k = (a_{n-1} \ldots a_1 a_0)_2. \tag{4}$$

Of course we could also list the positions $b_s \ldots b_2 b_1$ of the 0s in $a_{n-1} \ldots a_1 a_0$, where

$$n > b_s > \cdots > b_2 > b_1 \geq 0. \tag{5}$$

Combinations are important not only because subsets are omnipresent in mathematics but also because they are equivalent to many other configurations. For example, every (s,t)-combination corresponds to a combination of $s + 1$ things taken t at a time *with repetitions permitted*, also called a *multicombination* of $s + 1$ things, namely a sequence of integers $d_t \ldots d_2 d_1$ with

$$s \geq d_t \geq \cdots \geq d_2 \geq d_1 \geq 0. \tag{6}$$

One reason is that $d_t \ldots d_2 d_1$ solves (6) if and only if $c_t \ldots c_2 c_1$ solves (3), where

$$c_t = d_t + t - 1, \quad \ldots, \quad c_2 = d_2 + 1, \quad c_1 = d_1 \tag{7}$$

(see exercise 1.2.6–60). And there is another useful way to relate combinations with repetition to ordinary combinations, suggested by Solomon Golomb [*AMM* **75** (1968), 530–531], namely to define

$$e_j = \begin{cases} c_j, & \text{if } c_j \leq s; \\ e_{c_j - s}, & \text{if } c_j > s. \end{cases} \tag{8}$$

In this form the numbers $e_t \ldots e_1$ don't necessarily appear in descending order, but the multiset $\{e_1, e_2, \ldots, e_t\}$ is equal to $\{c_1, c_2, \ldots, c_t\}$ if and only if $\{e_1, e_2, \ldots, e_t\}$ is a set. (See Table 1 and exercise 1.)

An (s,t)-combination is also equivalent to a *composition* of $n + 1$ into $t + 1$ parts, namely an ordered sum

$$n + 1 = p_t + \cdots + p_1 + p_0, \quad \text{where } p_t, \ldots, p_1, p_0 \geq 1. \tag{9}$$

The connection with (3) is now

$$p_t = n - c_t, \quad p_{t-1} = c_t - c_{t-1}, \quad \ldots, \quad p_1 = c_2 - c_1, \quad p_0 = c_1 + 1. \tag{10}$$

Equivalently, if $q_j = p_j - 1$, we have

$$s = q_t + \cdots + q_1 + q_0, \quad \text{where } q_t, \ldots, q_1, q_0 \geq 0, \tag{11}$$

a composition of s into $t + 1$ *nonnegative* parts, related to (6) by setting

$$q_t = s - d_t, \quad q_{t-1} = d_t - d_{t-1}, \quad \ldots, \quad q_1 = d_2 - d_1, \quad q_0 = d_1. \tag{12}$$

Furthermore it is easy to see that an (s,t)-combination is equivalent to a path of length $s + t$ from corner to corner of an $s \times t$ grid, because such a path contains s vertical steps and t horizontal steps.

Thus, combinations can be studied in at least eight different guises. Table 1 illustrates all $\binom{6}{3} = 20$ possibilities in the case $s = t = 3$.

These cousins of combinations might seem rather bewildering at first glance, but most of them can be understood directly from the binary representation $a_{n-1} \ldots a_1 a_0$. Consider, for example, the "random" bit string

$$a_{23} \ldots a_1 a_0 = 011001001000011111101101, \tag{13}$$

Table 1

THE $(3,3)$-COMBINATIONS AND THEIR EQUIVALENTS

$a_5a_4a_3a_2a_1a_0$	$b_3b_2b_1$	$c_3c_2c_1$	$d_3d_2d_1$	$e_3e_2e_1$	$p_3p_2p_1p_0$	$q_3q_2q_1q_0$	path
000111	543	210	000	210	4111	3000	
001011	542	310	100	310	3211	2100	
001101	541	320	110	320	3121	2010	
001110	540	321	111	321	3112	2001	
010011	532	410	200	010	2311	1200	
010101	531	420	210	020	2221	1110	
010110	530	421	211	121	2212	1101	
011001	521	430	220	030	2131	1020	
011010	520	431	221	131	2122	1011	
011100	510	432	222	232	2113	1002	
100011	432	510	300	110	1411	0300	
100101	431	520	310	220	1321	0210	
100110	430	521	311	221	1312	0201	
101001	421	530	320	330	1231	0120	
101010	420	531	321	331	1222	0111	
101100	410	532	322	332	1213	0102	
110001	321	540	330	000	1141	0030	
110010	320	541	331	111	1132	0021	
110100	310	542	332	222	1123	0012	
111000	210	543	333	333	1114	0003	

which has $s = 11$ zeros and $t = 13$ ones, hence $n = 24$. The dual combination $b_s \ldots b_1$ lists the positions of the zeros, namely

$$23\ 20\ 19\ 17\ 16\ 14\ 13\ 12\ 11\ 4\ 1,$$

because the leftmost position is $n - 1$ and the rightmost is 0. The primal combination $c_t \ldots c_1$ lists the positions of the ones, namely

$$22\ 21\ 18\ 15\ 10\ 9\ 8\ 7\ 6\ 5\ 3\ 2\ 0.$$

The corresponding multicombination $d_t \ldots d_1$ lists the number of 0s to the right of each 1:

$$10\ 10\ 8\ 6\ 2\ 2\ 2\ 2\ 2\ 2\ 1\ 1\ 0.$$

The composition $p_t \ldots p_0$ lists the distances between consecutive 1s, if we imagine additional 1s at the left and the right:

$$2\ 1\ 3\ 3\ 5\ 1\ 1\ 1\ 1\ 2\ 1\ 2\ 1\ 1.$$

And the nonnegative composition $q_t \ldots q_0$ counts how many 0s appear between "fenceposts" represented by 1s:

$$1\ 0\ 2\ 2\ 4\ 0\ 0\ 0\ 0\ 1\ 0\ 1\ 0;$$

thus we have

$$a_{n-1} \ldots a_1 a_0 = 0^{q_t} 10^{q_{t-1}} 1 \ldots 10^{q_1} 10^{q_0}. \tag{14}$$

The paths in Table 1 also have a simple interpretation (see exercise 2).

Lexicographic generation. Table 1 shows combinations $a_{n-1} \ldots a_1 a_0$ and $c_t \ldots c_1$ in lexicographic order, which is also the lexicographic order of $d_t \ldots d_1$. Notice that the dual combinations $b_s \ldots b_1$ and the corresponding compositions $p_t \ldots p_0$, $q_t \ldots q_0$ then appear in *reverse* lexicographic order.

Lexicographic order usually suggests the most convenient way to generate combinatorial configurations. Indeed, Algorithm 7.2.1.2L already solves the problem for combinations in the form $a_{n-1} \ldots a_1 a_0$, since (s,t)-combinations in bitstring form are the same as permutations of the multiset $\{s \cdot 0, t \cdot 1\}$. That general-purpose algorithm can be streamlined in obvious ways when it is applied to this special case. (See also exercise 7.1.3–20, which presents a remarkable sequence of seven bitwise operations that will convert any given binary number $(a_{n-1} \ldots a_1 a_0)_2$ to the lexicographically next t-combination, assuming that n does not exceed the computer's word length.)

Let's focus, however, on generating combinations in the other principal form $c_t \ldots c_2 c_1$, which is more directly relevant to the ways in which combinations are often needed, and which is more compact than the bit strings when t is small compared to n. In the first place we should keep in mind that a simple sequence of nested loops will do the job nicely when t is very small. For example, when $t = 3$ the following instructions suffice:

$$\begin{aligned} &\text{For } c_3 = 2, 3, \ldots, n-1 \text{ (in this order) do the following:} \\ &\quad \text{For } c_2 = 1, 2, \ldots, c_3 - 1 \text{ (in this order) do the following:} \\ &\qquad \text{For } c_1 = 0, 1, \ldots, c_2 - 1 \text{ (in this order) do the following:} \\ &\qquad\quad \text{Visit the combination } c_3 c_2 c_1. \end{aligned} \qquad (15)$$

(See the analogous situation in 7.2.1.1–(3).)

On the other hand when t is variable or not so small, we can generate combinations lexicographically by following the general recipe discussed after Algorithm 7.2.1.2L, namely to find the rightmost element c_j that can be increased and then to set the subsequent elements $c_{j-1} \ldots c_1$ to their smallest possible values:

Algorithm L (*Lexicographic combinations*). This algorithm generates all t-combinations $c_t \ldots c_2 c_1$ of the n numbers $\{0, 1, \ldots, n-1\}$, given $n \geq t \geq 0$. Additional variables c_{t+1} and c_{t+2} are used as sentinels.

L1. [Initialize.] Set $c_j \leftarrow j - 1$ for $1 \leq j \leq t$; also set $c_{t+1} \leftarrow n$ and $c_{t+2} \leftarrow 0$.

L2. [Visit.] Visit the combination $c_t \ldots c_2 c_1$.

L3. [Find j.] Set $j \leftarrow 1$. Then, while $c_j + 1 = c_{j+1}$, set $c_j \leftarrow j - 1$ and $j \leftarrow j+1$; eventually the condition $c_j + 1 \neq c_{j+1}$ will occur.

L4. [Done?] Terminate the algorithm if $j > t$.

L5. [Increase c_j.] Set $c_j \leftarrow c_j + 1$ and return to L2. ∎

The running time of this algorithm is not difficult to analyze. Step L3 sets $c_j \leftarrow j - 1$ just after visiting a combination for which $c_{j+1} = c_1 + j$, and the number of such combinations is the number of solutions to the inequalities

$$n > c_t > \cdots > c_{j+1} \geq j; \qquad (16)$$

but this formula is equivalent to a $(t - j)$-combination of the $n - j$ objects $\{n-1, \ldots, j\}$, so the assignment $c_j \leftarrow j-1$ occurs exactly $\binom{n-j}{t-j}$ times. Summing for $1 \leq j \leq t$ tells us that the loop in step L3 is performed

$$\binom{n-1}{t-1} + \binom{n-2}{t-2} + \cdots + \binom{n-t}{0} = \binom{n-1}{s} + \binom{n-2}{s} + \cdots + \binom{s}{s} = \binom{n}{s+1} \quad (17)$$

times altogether, or an average of

$$\binom{n}{s+1} \bigg/ \binom{n}{t} = \frac{n!}{(s+1)!\,(t-1)!} \bigg/ \frac{n!}{s!\,t!} = \frac{t}{s+1} \quad (18)$$

times per visit. This ratio is less than 1 when $t \leq s$, so Algorithm L is quite efficient in such cases.

But the quantity $t/(s + 1)$ can be embarrassingly large when t is near n and s is small. Indeed, Algorithm L occasionally sets $c_j \leftarrow j - 1$ needlessly, at times when c_j already equals $j - 1$. Further scrutiny reveals that we need not always search for the index j that is needed in steps L4 and L5, since the correct value of j can often be predicted from the actions just taken. For example, after we have increased c_4 and reset $c_3 c_2 c_1$ to their starting values 210, the next combination will inevitably increase c_3. These observations lead to a tuned-up version of the algorithm:

Algorithm T (*Lexicographic combinations*). This algorithm is like Algorithm L, but faster. It also assumes, for convenience, that $0 < t < n$.

T1. [Initialize.] Set $c_j \leftarrow j - 1$ for $1 \leq j \leq t$; then set $c_{t+1} \leftarrow n$, $c_{t+2} \leftarrow 0$, and $j \leftarrow t$.

T2. [Visit.] (At this point j is the smallest index such that $c_{j+1} > j$.) Visit the combination $c_t \ldots c_2 c_1$. Then, if $j > 0$, set $x \leftarrow j$ and go to step T6.

T3. [Easy case?] If $c_1 + 1 < c_2$, set $c_1 \leftarrow c_1 + 1$ and return to T2. Otherwise set $j \leftarrow 2$.

T4. [Find j.] Set $c_{j-1} \leftarrow j - 2$ and $x \leftarrow c_j + 1$. If $x = c_{j+1}$, set $j \leftarrow j + 1$ and repeat step T4.

T5. [Done?] Terminate the algorithm if $j > t$.

T6. [Increase c_j.] Set $c_j \leftarrow x$, $j \leftarrow j - 1$, and return to T2. ∎

Now $j = 0$ in step T2 if and only if $c_1 > 0$, so the assignments in step T4 are never redundant. Exercise 6 carries out a complete analysis of Algorithm T.

Notice that the parameter n appears only in the initialization steps L1 and T1, not in the principal parts of Algorithms L and T. Thus we can think of the process as generating the first $\binom{n}{t}$ combinations of an *infinite* list, which depends only on t. This simplification arises because the list of t-combinations for $n + 1$ things begins with the list for n things, under our conventions; we have been using lexicographic order on the decreasing sequences $c_t \ldots c_1$ for this very reason, instead of working with the increasing sequences $c_1 \ldots c_t$.

Derrick Lehmer noticed another pleasant property of Algorithms L and T [*Applied Combinatorial Mathematics*, edited by E. F. Beckenbach (1964), 27–30]:

Theorem L. *The combination $c_t \ldots c_2 c_1$ is visited after exactly*

$$\binom{c_t}{t} + \cdots + \binom{c_2}{2} + \binom{c_1}{1} \tag{19}$$

other combinations have been visited.

Proof. There are $\binom{c_k}{k}$ combinations $c'_t \ldots c'_2 c'_1$ with $c'_j = c_j$ for $t \geq j > k$ and $c'_k < c_k$, namely $c_t \ldots c_{k+1}$ followed by the k-combinations of $\{0, \ldots, c_k - 1\}$. ∎

When $t = 3$, for example, the numbers

$$\binom{2}{3} + \binom{1}{2} + \binom{0}{1}, \ \ \binom{3}{3} + \binom{1}{2} + \binom{0}{1}, \ \ \binom{3}{3} + \binom{2}{2} + \binom{0}{1}, \ \ \ldots, \ \ \binom{5}{3} + \binom{4}{2} + \binom{3}{1}$$

that correspond to the combinations $c_3 c_2 c_1$ in Table 1 simply run through the sequence 0, 1, 2, ..., 19. Theorem L gives us a nice way to understand the *combinatorial number system* of degree t, which represents every nonnegative integer N uniquely in the form

$$N = \binom{n_t}{t} + \cdots + \binom{n_2}{2} + \binom{n_1}{1}, \qquad n_t > \cdots > n_2 > n_1 \geq 0. \tag{20}$$

[See Ernesto Pascal, *Giornale di Matematiche* **25** (1887), 45–49.]

Binomial trees. The family of trees T_n defined by

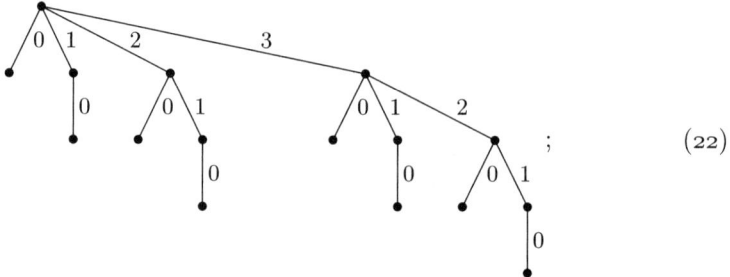

$$T_0 = \bullet \, , \qquad T_n = \quad \overset{0 \quad \ 1 \qquad\qquad\qquad n-1}{\underset{T_0 \quad \ T_1 \quad \cdots \quad T_{n-1}}{\bigwedge}} \qquad \text{for } n > 0, \tag{21}$$

arises in several important contexts and sheds further light on combination generation. For example, T_4 is

$$\tag{22}$$

and T_5, rendered more artistically, appears as the frontispiece to Volume 1 of this series of books.

Notice that T_n is like T_{n-1}, except for an additional copy of T_{n-1}; therefore T_n has 2^n nodes altogether. Furthermore, the number of nodes on level t is the binomial coefficient $\binom{n}{t}$; this fact accounts for the name "binomial tree." Indeed, the sequence of labels encountered on the path from the root to each node on level t defines a combination $c_t \ldots c_1$, and all combinations occur in lexicographic order from left to right. Thus, Algorithms L and T can be regarded as procedures to traverse the nodes on level t of the binomial tree T_n.

The infinite binomial tree T_∞ is obtained by letting $n \to \infty$ in (21). The root of this tree has infinitely many branches, but every node except for the overall root at level 0 is the root of a finite binomial subtree. All possible t-combinations appear in lexicographic order on level t of T_∞.

Let's get more familiar with binomial trees by considering all possible ways to pack a rucksack. More precisely, suppose we have n items that take up respectively $w_{n-1}, \ldots, w_1, w_0$ units of capacity, where

$$w_{n-1} \geq \cdots \geq w_1 \geq w_0 \geq 0; \tag{23}$$

we want to generate all binary vectors $a_{n-1} \ldots a_1 a_0$ such that

$$a \cdot w = a_{n-1} w_{n-1} + \cdots + a_1 w_1 + a_0 w_0 \leq N, \tag{24}$$

where N is the total capacity of a rucksack. Equivalently, we want to find all subsets C of $\{0, 1, \ldots, n-1\}$ such that $w(C) = \sum_{c \in C} w_c \leq N$; such subsets will be called *feasible*. We will write a feasible subset as $c_1 \ldots c_t$, where $c_1 > \cdots > c_t \geq 0$, numbering the subscripts differently from the convention of (3) above because t is variable in this problem.

Every feasible subset corresponds to a node of T_n, and our goal is to visit each feasible node. Clearly the parent of every feasible node is feasible, and so is the left sibling, if any; therefore a simple tree exploration procedure works well:

Algorithm F (*Filling a rucksack*). This algorithm generates all feasible ways $c_1 \ldots c_t$ to fill a rucksack, given $w_{n-1}, \ldots, w_1, w_0$, and N. We let $\delta_j = w_j - w_{j-1}$ for $1 \leq j < n$.

F1. [Initialize.] Set $t \leftarrow 0$, $c_0 \leftarrow n$, and $r \leftarrow N$.

F2. [Visit.] Visit the combination $c_1 \ldots c_t$, which uses $N - r$ units of capacity.

F3. [Try to add w_0.] If $c_t > 0$ and $r \geq w_0$, set $t \leftarrow t + 1$, $c_t \leftarrow 0$, $r \leftarrow r - w_0$, and return to F2.

F4. [Try to increase c_t.] Terminate if $t = 0$. Otherwise, if $c_{t-1} > c_t + 1$ and $r \geq \delta_{c_t+1}$, set $c_t \leftarrow c_t + 1$, $r \leftarrow r - \delta_{c_t}$, and return to F2.

F5. [Remove c_t.] Set $r \leftarrow r + w_{c_t}$, $t \leftarrow t - 1$, and return to F4. ▮

Notice that the algorithm implicitly visits nodes of T_n in preorder, skipping over unfeasible subtrees. An element $c > 0$ is placed in the rucksack, if it fits, just after the procedure has explored all possibilities using element $c - 1$ in its place. The running time is proportional to the number of feasible combinations visited (see exercise 20).

Incidentally, the classical "knapsack problem" of operations research is different: It asks for a feasible subset C such that $v(C) = \sum_{c \in C} v(c)$ is maximum, where each item c has been assigned a value $v(c)$. Algorithm F is not a particularly good way to solve that problem, because it often considers cases that could be ruled out. For example, if C and C' are subsets of $\{1, \ldots, n-1\}$ with $w(C) \leq w(C') \leq N - w_0$ and $v(C) \geq v(C')$, Algorithm F will examine both $C \cup 0$ and $C' \cup 0$, but the latter subset will never improve the maximum. We will consider methods for the classical knapsack problem later; Algorithm F is intended only for situations when *all* of the feasible possibilities are potentially relevant.

Gray codes for combinations. Instead of merely generating all combinations, we often prefer to visit them in such a way that each one is obtained by making only a small change to its predecessor.

For example, we can ask for what Nijenhuis and Wilf have called a "revolving door algorithm": Imagine two rooms that contain respectively s and t people, with a revolving door between them. Whenever a person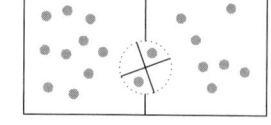
goes into the opposite room, somebody else comes out. Can we devise a sequence of moves so that each (s, t)-combination occurs exactly once?

The answer is yes, and in fact a huge number of such patterns exist. For example, it turns out that if we examine all n-bit strings $a_{n-1} \ldots a_1 a_0$ in the well-known order of Gray binary code (Section 7.2.1.1), but select only those that have exactly s 0s and t 1s, the resulting strings form a revolving-door code.

Here's the proof: Gray binary code is defined by the recurrence $\Gamma_n = 0\Gamma_{n-1}$, $1\Gamma_{n-1}^R$ of 7.2.1.1–(5), so its (s, t) subsequence satisfies the recurrence

$$\Gamma_{st} = 0\Gamma_{(s-1)t}, \ 1\Gamma_{s(t-1)}^R \qquad (25)$$

when $st > 0$. We also have $\Gamma_{s0} = 0^s$ and $\Gamma_{0t} = 1^t$. Therefore it is clear by induction that Γ_{st} begins with $0^s 1^t$ and ends with $10^s 1^{t-1}$ when $st > 0$. The transition at the comma in (25) is from the last element of $0\Gamma_{(s-1)t}$ to the last element of $1\Gamma_{s(t-1)}$, namely from $010^{s-1}1^{t-1} = 010^{s-1}11^{t-2}$ to $110^s 1^{t-2} = 110^{s-1}01^{t-2}$ when $t \geq 2$, and this satisfies the revolving-door constraint. The case $t = 1$ also checks out. For example, Γ_{33} is given by the columns of

$$
\begin{array}{llll}
000111 & 011010 & 110001 & 101010 \\
001101 & 011100 & 110010 & 101100 \\
001110 & 010101 & 110100 & 100101 \qquad (26) \\
001011 & 010110 & 111000 & 100110 \\
011001 & 010011 & 101001 & 100011
\end{array}
$$

and Γ_{23} can be found in the first two columns of this array. One more turn of the door takes the last element into the first. [These properties of Γ_{st} were discovered by J. E. Miller in her Ph.D. thesis (Columbia University, 1971), then independently by D. T. Tang and C. N. Liu, *IEEE Trans.* **C-22** (1973), 176–180. A loopless implementation was presented by J. R. Bitner, G. Ehrlich, and E. M. Reingold, *CACM* **19** (1976), 517–521.]

When we convert the bit strings $a_5 a_4 a_3 a_2 a_1 a_0$ in (26) to the corresponding index-list forms $c_3 c_2 c_1$, a striking pattern becomes evident:

$$
\begin{array}{llll}
210 & 431 & 540 & 531 \\
320 & 432 & 541 & 532 \\
321 & 420 & 542 & 520 \qquad (27) \\
310 & 421 & 543 & 521 \\
430 & 410 & 530 & 510
\end{array}
$$

The first components c_3 occur in nondecreasing order; but for each fixed value of c_3, the values of c_2 occur in non*increasing* order. And for fixed $c_3 c_2$, the values of c_1 are again nondecreasing. The same is true in general: *All combinations*

$c_t \ldots c_2 c_1$ *appear in lexicographic order of*

$$(c_t, -c_{t-1}, c_{t-2}, \ldots, (-1)^{t-1} c_1) \tag{28}$$

in the revolving-door Gray code Γ_{st}. This property follows by induction, because (25) becomes

$$\Gamma_{st} = \Gamma_{(s-1)t}, \ (s+t-1)\Gamma^R_{s(t-1)} \tag{29}$$

for $st > 0$ when we use index-list notation instead of bitstring notation. Consequently the sequence can be generated efficiently by the following algorithm due to W. H. Payne [see *ACM Trans. Math. Software* **5** (1979), 163–172]:

Algorithm R (*Revolving-door combinations*). This algorithm generates all t-combinations $c_t \ldots c_2 c_1$ of $\{0, 1, \ldots, n-1\}$ in lexicographic order of the alternating sequence (28), assuming that $n \geq t > 1$. An auxiliary variable c_{t+1} is used. Step R3 has two variants, depending on whether t is even or odd.

R1. [Initialize.] Set $c_j \leftarrow j - 1$ for $t \geq j \geq 1$, and $c_{t+1} \leftarrow n$.

R2. [Visit.] Visit the combination $c_t \ldots c_2 c_1$.

R3. [Easy case?] If t is odd: If $c_1 + 1 < c_2$, increase c_1 by 1 and return to R2, otherwise set $j \leftarrow 2$ and go to R4. If t is even: If $c_1 > 0$, decrease c_1 by 1 and return to R2, otherwise set $j \leftarrow 2$ and go to R5.

R4. [Try to decrease c_j.] (At this point $c_j = c_{j-1} + 1$.) If $c_j \geq j$, set $c_j \leftarrow c_{j-1}$, $c_{j-1} \leftarrow j - 2$, and return to R2. Otherwise increase j by 1.

R5. [Try to increase c_j.] (At this point $c_{j-1} = j - 2$.) If $c_j + 1 < c_{j+1}$, set $c_{j-1} \leftarrow c_j$, $c_j \leftarrow c_j + 1$, and return to R2. Otherwise increase j by 1, and go to R4 if $j \leq t$. Otherwise the algorithm terminates. ∎

Exercises 21–25 explore further properties of this interesting sequence. One of them is a nice companion to Theorem L: *The combination $c_t c_{t-1} \ldots c_2 c_1$ is visited by Algorithm R after exactly*

$$N = \binom{c_t+1}{t} - \binom{c_{t-1}+1}{t-1} + \cdots + (-1)^t \binom{c_2+1}{2} - (-1)^t \binom{c_1+1}{1} - [t \text{ odd}] \tag{30}$$

other combinations have been visited. We may call this the representation of N in the "alternating combinatorial number system" of degree t; one consequence, for example, is that every positive integer has a unique representation of the form $N = \binom{a}{3} - \binom{b}{2} + \binom{c}{1}$ with $a > b > c > 0$. Algorithm R tells us how to add 1 to N in this system.

Although the strings of (26) and (27) are not in lexicographic order, they are examples of a more general concept called *genlex order*, a name coined by Timothy Walsh. A sequence of strings $\alpha_1, \ldots, \alpha_N$ is said to be in genlex order when all strings with a common prefix occur consecutively. For example, all 3-combinations that begin with 53 appear together in (27).

Genlex order means that the strings can be arranged in a trie structure, as in Fig. 31 of Section 6.3, but with the children of each node ordered arbitrarily. When a trie is traversed in any order such that each node is visited just before or just after its descendants, all nodes with a common prefix—that is, all nodes of

a subtrie — appear consecutively. This principle corresponds to recursive generation schemes, so it makes genlex order convenient. Many of the algorithms we've
seen for generating n-tuples have therefore produced their results in some version
of genlex order; similarly, the method of "plain changes" (Algorithm 7.2.1.2P)
visits permutations in a genlex order of the corresponding inversion tables.

The revolving-door method of Algorithm R is a genlex routine that changes
only one element of the combination at each step. But it isn't totally satisfactory,
because it frequently must change two of the indices c_j simultaneously, in order
to preserve the condition $c_t > \cdots > c_2 > c_1$. For example, Algorithm R changes
210 into 320, and (27) includes nine such "crossing" moves.

The source of this defect can be traced to our proof that (25) satisfies the
revolving-door property: We observed that the string $010^{s-1}11^{t-2}$ is followed
by $110^{s-1}01^{t-2}$ when $t \geq 2$. Hence the recursive construction Γ_{st} involves
transitions of the form $110^a0 \leftrightarrow 010^a1$, when a substring like 11000 is changed
to 01001 or vice versa; the two 1s cross each other.

A Gray path for combinations is said to be *homogeneous* if it changes only
one of the indices c_j at each step. A homogeneous scheme is characterized
in bitstring form by having only transitions of the forms $10^a \leftrightarrow 0^a1$ within
strings, for $a \geq 1$, when we pass from one string
to the next. With a homogeneous scheme we can,
for example, play all t-note chords on an n-note
keyboard by moving only one finger at a time.

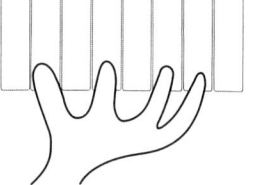

A slight modification of (25) yields a genlex
scheme for (s, t)-combinations that is pleasantly
homogeneous. The basic idea is to construct a
sequence that begins with 0^s1^t and ends with 1^t0^s, and the following recursion
suggests itself almost immediately: Let $K_{s0} = 0^s$, $K_{0t} = 1^t$, $K_{s(-1)} = \emptyset$, and

$$K_{st} = 0K_{(s-1)t}, \ 10K_{(s-1)(t-1)}^R, \ 11K_{s(t-2)} \quad \text{for } st > 0. \tag{31}$$

At the commas of this sequence we have 01^t0^{s-1} followed by $101^{t-1}0^{s-1}$, and
10^s1^{t-1} followed by 110^s1^{t-2}; both of these transitions are homogeneous, although the second one requires the 1 to jump across s 0s. The combinations K_{33}
for $s = t = 3$ are

000111	010101	101100	100011
001011	010011	101001	110001
001101	011001	101010	110010
001110	011010	100110	110100
010110	011100	100101	111000

$$(32)$$

in bitstring form, and the corresponding "finger patterns" are

210	420	532	510
310	410	530	540
320	430	531	541
321	431	521	542
421	432	520	543.

$$(33)$$

When a homogeneous scheme for ordinary combinations $c_t \ldots c_1$ is converted to the corresponding scheme (6) for combinations with repetitions $d_t \ldots d_1$, it retains the property that only one of the indices d_j changes at each step. And when it is converted to the corresponding schemes (9) or (11) for compositions $p_t \ldots p_0$ or $q_t \ldots q_0$, only two (adjacent) parts change when c_j changes.

Near-perfect schemes. But we can do even better! All (s,t)-combinations can be generated by a sequence of strongly homogeneous transitions that are either $01 \leftrightarrow 10$ or $001 \leftrightarrow 100$. In other words, we can insist that each step causes a single index c_j to change by at most 2. Let's call such generation schemes *near-perfect*.

Imposing such strong conditions actually makes it fairly easy to discover near-perfect schemes, because comparatively few choices are available. Indeed, if we restrict ourselves to genlex methods that are near-perfect on n-bit strings, T. A. Jenkyns and D. McCarthy observed that all such methods can be easily characterized [*Ars Combinatoria* **40** (1995), 153–159]:

Theorem N. *If $st > 0$, there are exactly $2s$ near-perfect ways to list all (s,t)-combinations in a genlex order. In fact, when $1 \leq a \leq s$, there is exactly one such listing, N_{sta}, that begins with $1^t 0^s$ and ends with $0^a 1^t 0^{s-a}$; the other s possibilities are the reverse lists, N_{sta}^R.*

Proof. The result certainly holds when $s = t = 1$; otherwise we use induction on $s+t$. The listing N_{sta}, if it exists, must have the form $1 X_{s(t-1)}, 0 Y_{(s-1)t}$ for some near-perfect genlex listings $X_{s(t-1)}$ and $Y_{(s-1)t}$. If $t = 1$, $X_{s(t-1)}$ is the single string 0^s; hence $Y_{(s-1)t}$ must be $N_{(s-1)1(a-1)}$ if $a > 1$, and it must be $N_{(s-1)11}^R$ if $a = 1$. On the other hand if $t > 1$, the near-perfect condition implies that the last string of $X_{s(t-1)}$ cannot begin with 1; hence $X_{s(t-1)} = N_{s(t-1)b}$ for some b. If $a > 1$, $Y_{(s-1)t}$ must be $N_{(s-1)t(a-1)}$, hence b must be 1; similarly, b must be 1 if $s = 1$. Otherwise we have $a = 1 < s$, and this forces $Y_{(s-1)t} = N_{(s-1)tc}^R$ for some c. The transition from $10^b 1^{t-1} 0^{s-b}$ to $0^{c+1} 1^t 0^{s-1-c}$ is near-perfect only if $c = 1$ and $b = 2$. ∎

The proof of Theorem N yields the following recursive formulas when $st > 0$:

$$N_{sta} = \begin{cases} 1 N_{s(t-1)1}, \ 0 N_{(s-1)t(a-1)}, & \text{if } 1 < a \leq s; \\ 1 N_{s(t-1)2}, \ 0 N_{(s-1)t1}^R, & \text{if } 1 = a < s; \\ 1 N_{1(t-1)1}, \ 01^t, & \text{if } 1 = a = s. \end{cases} \qquad (34)$$

Also, of course, $N_{s0a} = 0^s$.

Let us set $A_{st} = N_{st1}$ and $B_{st} = N_{st2}$. These near-perfect listings, discovered by Phillip J. Chase in 1976, have the net effect of shifting a leftmost block of 1s to the right by one or two positions, respectively, and they satisfy the following mutual recursions:

$$A_{st} = 1 B_{s(t-1)}, \ 0 A_{(s-1)t}^R; \qquad\qquad B_{st} = 1 A_{s(t-1)}, \ 0 A_{(s-1)t}. \qquad (35)$$

"To take one step forward, take two steps forward, then one step backward; to take two steps forward, take one step forward, then another." These equations

Table 2

CHASE'S SEQUENCES FOR $(3,3)$-COMBINATIONS

$A_{33} = \widehat{C}_{33}^{R}$				$B_{33} = C_{33}$			
543	531	321	420	543	520	432	410
541	530	320	421	542	510	430	210
540	510	310	431	540	530	431	310
542	520	210	430	541	531	421	320
532	521	410	432	521	532	420	321

hold for all integer values of s and t, if we define A_{st} and B_{st} to be $\emptyset$ when s or t is negative, except that $A_{00} = B_{00} = \epsilon$ (the empty string). Thus A_{st} actually takes $\min(s,1)$ forward steps, and B_{st} actually takes $\min(s,2)$. For example, Table 2 shows the relevant listings for $s = t = 3$, using an equivalent index-list form $c_3c_2c_1$ instead of the bit strings $a_5a_4a_3a_2a_1a_0$.

Chase noticed that a computer implementation of these sequences becomes simpler if we define

$$C_{st} = \begin{cases} A_{st}, & \text{if } s+t \text{ is odd}; \\ B_{st}, & \text{if } s+t \text{ is even}; \end{cases} \qquad \widehat{C}_{st} = \begin{cases} A_{st}^{R}, & \text{if } s+t \text{ is even}; \\ B_{st}^{R}, & \text{if } s+t \text{ is odd}. \end{cases} \qquad (36)$$

[See *Congressus Numerantium* **69** (1989), 215–242.] Then we have

$$C_{st} = \begin{cases} 1C_{s(t-1)}, \ 0\widehat{C}_{(s-1)t}, & \text{if } s+t \text{ is odd}; \\ 1C_{s(t-1)}, \ 0C_{(s-1)t}, & \text{if } s+t \text{ is even}; \end{cases} \qquad (37)$$

$$\widehat{C}_{st} = \begin{cases} 0C_{(s-1)t}, \ 1\widehat{C}_{s(t-1)}, & \text{if } s+t \text{ is even}; \\ 0\widehat{C}_{(s-1)t}, \ 1\widehat{C}_{s(t-1)}, & \text{if } s+t \text{ is odd}. \end{cases} \qquad (38)$$

When bit a_j is ready to change, we can tell where we are in the recursion by testing whether j is even or odd.

Indeed, the sequence C_{st} can be generated by a surprisingly simple algorithm, based on general ideas that apply to *any* genlex scheme. Let us say that bit a_j is *active* in a genlex algorithm if it is supposed to change before anything to its left is altered. (In other words, the node for an active bit in the corresponding trie is not the rightmost child of its parent.) Suppose we have an auxiliary table $w_n \ldots w_1 w_0$, where $w_j = 1$ if and only if either a_j is active or $j < r$, where r is the least subscript such that $a_r \neq a_0$; we also let $w_n = 1$. Then the following method will find the successor of $a_{n-1} \ldots a_1 a_0$:

> Set $j \leftarrow r$. If $w_j = 0$, set $w_j \leftarrow 1$, $j \leftarrow j + 1$, and repeat until $w_j = 1$. Terminate if $j = n$; otherwise set $w_j \leftarrow 0$. Change a_j to $1 - a_j$, and make any other changes to $a_{j-1} \ldots a_0$ and r that apply to the particular genlex scheme being used. $\qquad (39)$

The beauty of this approach comes from the fact that the loop is guaranteed to be efficient: We can prove that the operation $j \leftarrow j + 1$ will be performed less than once per generation step, on the average (see exercise 36).

By analyzing the transitions that occur when bits change in (37) and (38), we can readily flesh out the remaining details:

Algorithm C (*Chase's sequence*). This algorithm visits all (s, t)-combinations $a_{n-1} \ldots a_1 a_0$, where $n = s + t$, in the near-perfect order of Chase's sequence C_{st}.

C1. [Initialize.] Set $a_j \leftarrow 0$ for $0 \le j < s$, $a_j \leftarrow 1$ for $s \le j < n$, and $w_j \leftarrow 1$ for $0 \le j \le n$. If $s > 0$, set $r \leftarrow s$; otherwise set $r \leftarrow t$.

C2. [Visit.] Visit the combination $a_{n-1} \ldots a_1 a_0$.

C3. [Find j and branch.] Set $j \leftarrow r$. While $w_j = 0$, set $w_j \leftarrow 1$ and $j \leftarrow j + 1$. Terminate if $j = n$; otherwise set $w_j \leftarrow 0$ and make a four-way branch: Go to C4 if j is odd and $a_j \ne 0$, to C5 if j is even and $a_j \ne 0$, to C6 if j is even and $a_j = 0$, to C7 if j is odd and $a_j = 0$.

C4. [Move right one.] Set $a_{j-1} \leftarrow 1$, $a_j \leftarrow 0$. If $r = j$ and $j > 1$, set $r \leftarrow j - 1$; otherwise if $r = j - 1$ set $r \leftarrow j$. Return to C2.

C5. [Move right two.] If $a_{j-2} \ne 0$, go to C4. Otherwise set $a_{j-2} \leftarrow 1$, $a_j \leftarrow 0$. If $r = j$, set $r \leftarrow \max(j - 2, 1)$; otherwise if $r = j - 2$, set $r \leftarrow j - 1$. Return to C2.

C6. [Move left one.] Set $a_j \leftarrow 1$, $a_{j-1} \leftarrow 0$. If $r = j$ and $j > 1$, set $r \leftarrow j - 1$; otherwise if $r = j - 1$ set $r \leftarrow j$. Return to C2.

C7. [Move left two.] If $a_{j-1} \ne 0$, go to C6. Otherwise set $a_j \leftarrow 1$, $a_{j-2} \leftarrow 0$. If $r = j - 2$, set $r \leftarrow j$; otherwise if $r = j - 1$, set $r \leftarrow j - 2$. Return to C2. ∎

*Analysis of Chase's sequence. The magical properties of Algorithm C cry out for further exploration, and a closer look turns out to be quite instructive. Given a bit string $a_{n-1} \ldots a_1 a_0$, let us define $a_n = 1$, $u_n = n \bmod 2$, and

$$u_j = (1 - u_{j+1}) a_{j+1}, \quad v_j = (u_j + j) \bmod 2, \quad w_j = (v_j + a_j) \bmod 2, \quad (40)$$

for $n > j \ge 0$. For example, we might have $n = 26$ and

$$
\begin{aligned}
a_{25} \ldots a_1 a_0 &= 11001001000011111101101010, \\
u_{25} \ldots u_1 u_0 &= 10100100100001010100100101, \\
v_{25} \ldots v_1 v_0 &= 00001110001011111110001111, \\
w_{25} \ldots w_1 w_0 &= 11000111001000000011100101.
\end{aligned}
\quad (41)
$$

With these definitions we can prove by induction that $v_j = 0$ if and only if bit a_j is being "controlled" by C rather than by $\widehat{C}$ in the recursions (37)–(38) that generate $a_{n-1} \ldots a_1 a_0$, except when a_j is part of the final run of 0s or 1s at the right end. Therefore w_j agrees with the value computed by Algorithm C at the moment when $a_{n-1} \ldots a_1 a_0$ is visited, for $r \le j < n$. These formulas can be used to determine exactly where a given combination appears in Chase's sequence (see exercise 39).

If we want to work with the index-list form $c_t \ldots c_2 c_1$ instead of the bit strings $a_{n-1} \ldots a_1 a_0$, it is convenient to change the notation slightly, writing

$C_t(n)$ for C_{st} and $\widehat{C}_t(n)$ for $\widehat{C}_{st}$ when $s + t = n$. Then $C_0(n) = \widehat{C}_0(n) = \epsilon$, and the recursions for $t \geq 0$ take the form

$$C_{t+1}(n+1) = \begin{cases} nC_t(n), \ \widehat{C}_{t+1}(n), & \text{if } n \text{ is even;} \\ nC_t(n), \ C_{t+1}(n), & \text{if } n \text{ is odd;} \end{cases} \tag{42}$$

$$\widehat{C}_{t+1}(n+1) = \begin{cases} C_{t+1}(n), \ n\widehat{C}_t(n), & \text{if } n \text{ is odd;} \\ \widehat{C}_{t+1}(n), \ n\widehat{C}_t(n), & \text{if } n \text{ is even.} \end{cases} \tag{43}$$

These new equations can be expanded to tell us, for example, that

$$
\begin{aligned}
C_{t+1}(9) &= 8C_t(8), \ 6C_t(6), \ 4C_t(4), \ \ldots, \ 3\widehat{C}_t(3), \ 5\widehat{C}_t(5), \ 7\widehat{C}_t(7); \\
C_{t+1}(8) &= 7C_t(7), \ 6C_t(6), \ 4C_t(4), \ \ldots, \ 3\widehat{C}_t(3), \ 5\widehat{C}_t(5); \\
\widehat{C}_{t+1}(9) &= \qquad\quad 6C_t(6), \ 4C_t(4), \ \ldots, \ 3\widehat{C}_t(3), \ 5\widehat{C}_t(5), \ 7\widehat{C}_t(7), \ 8\widehat{C}_t(8); \\
\widehat{C}_{t+1}(8) &= \qquad\quad 6C_t(6), \ 4C_t(4), \ \ldots, \ 3\widehat{C}_t(3), \ 5\widehat{C}_t(5), \ 7\widehat{C}_t(7);
\end{aligned}
\tag{44}
$$

notice that the same pattern predominates in all four sequences. The meaning of "$\ldots$" in the middle depends on the value of t: We simply omit all terms $nC_t(n)$ and $n\widehat{C}_t(n)$ where $n < t$.

Except for edge effects at the very beginning or end, all of the expansions in (44) are based on the infinite progression

$$\ldots, \ 10, \ 8, \ 6, \ 4, \ 2, \ 0, \ 1, \ 3, \ 5, \ 7, \ 9, \ \ldots, \tag{45}$$

which is a natural way to arrange the nonnegative integers into a doubly infinite sequence. If we omit all terms of (45) that are $< t$, given any integer $t \geq 0$, the remaining terms retain the property that adjacent elements differ by either 1 or 2. Richard Stanley has suggested the name *endo-order* for this sequence, because we can remember it by thinking "even numbers decreasing, odd $\ldots$". (Notice that if we retain only the terms less than N and complement with respect to N, endo-order becomes organ-pipe order; see exercise 6.1–18.)

We could program the recursions of (42) and (43) directly, but it is interesting to unwind them using (44), thus obtaining an iterative algorithm analogous to Algorithm C. The result needs only $O(t)$ memory locations, and it is especially efficient when t is relatively small compared to n. Exercise 45 contains the details.

*Near-perfect multiset permutations. Chase's sequences lead in a natural way to an algorithm that will generate permutations of any desired multiset $\{s_0 \cdot 0, s_1 \cdot 1, \ldots, s_d \cdot d\}$ in a *near-perfect* manner, meaning that

i) every transition is either $a_{j+1}a_j \leftrightarrow a_j a_{j+1}$ or $a_{j+1}a_j a_{j-1} \leftrightarrow a_{j-1}a_j a_{j+1}$;
ii) transitions of the second kind have $a_j = \min(a_{j-1}, a_{j+1})$.

Algorithm C tells us how to do this when $d = 1$, and we can extend it to larger values of d by the following recursive construction [*CACM* **13** (1970), 368–369, 376]: Suppose

$$\alpha_0, \ \alpha_1, \ \ldots, \ \alpha_{N-1}$$

is any near-perfect listing of the permutations of $\{s_1 \cdot 1, \ldots, s_d \cdot d\}$. Then Algorithm C, with $s = s_0$ and $t = s_1 + \cdots + s_d$, tells us how to generate a listing

$$\Lambda_j = \alpha_j 0^s, \ \ldots, \ 0^a \alpha_j 0^{s-a} \tag{46}$$

in which all transitions are $0x \leftrightarrow x0$ or $00x \leftrightarrow x00$; the final entry has $a = 1$ or 2 leading zeros, depending on s and t. Therefore all transitions of the sequence

$$\Lambda_0, \ \Lambda_1^R, \ \Lambda_2, \ \ldots, \ (\Lambda_{N-1} \text{ or } \Lambda_{N-1}^R) \tag{47}$$

are near-perfect; and this list clearly contains all the permutations.

For example, the permutations of $\{0, 0, 0, 1, 1, 2\}$ generated in this way are

211000, 210100, 210001, 210010, 200110, 200101, 200011, 201001, 201010, 201100,
021100, 021001, 021010, 020110, 020101, 020011, 000211, 002011, 002101, 002110,
001120, 001102, 001012, 000112, 010012, 010102, 010120, 011020, 011002, 011200,
101200, 101020, 101002, 100012, 100102, 100120, 110020, 110002, 110200, 112000,
121000, 120100, 120001, 120010, 100210, 100201, 100021, 102001, 102010, 102100,
012100, 012001, 012010, 010210, 010201, 010021, 000121, 001021, 001201, 001210.

Perfect schemes. Why should we settle for a near-perfect generator like C_{st}, instead of insisting that all transitions have the simplest possible form $01 \leftrightarrow 10$?

One reason is that perfect schemes don't always exist. For example, we observed in 7.2.1.2–(2) that there is no way to generate all six permutations of $\{1, 1, 2, 2\}$ with adjacent interchanges; thus there is no perfect scheme for $(2, 2)$-combinations. In fact, our chances of achieving perfection are only about 1 in 4:

Theorem P. *The generation of all (s, t)-combinations $a_{s+t-1} \ldots a_1 a_0$ by adjacent interchanges $01 \leftrightarrow 10$ is possible if and only if $s \leq 1$ or $t \leq 1$ or st is odd.*

Proof. Consider all permutations of the multiset $\{s \cdot 0, t \cdot 1\}$. We learned in exercise 5.1.2–16 that the number m_k of such permutations having k inversions is the coefficient of z^k in the z-nomial coefficient

$$\binom{s+t}{t}_z = \prod_{k=s+1}^{s+t} (1 + z + \cdots + z^{k-1}) \Big/ \prod_{k=1}^{t} (1 + z + \cdots + z^{k-1}). \tag{48}$$

Every adjacent interchange changes the number of inversions by ± 1, so a perfect generation scheme is possible only if approximately half of all the permutations have an odd number of inversions. More precisely, the value of $\binom{s+t}{t}_{-1} = m_0 - m_1 + m_2 - \cdots$ must be 0 or ± 1. But exercise 49 shows that

$$\binom{s+t}{t}_{-1} = \binom{\lfloor (s+t)/2 \rfloor}{\lfloor t/2 \rfloor} [st \text{ is even}], \tag{49}$$

and this quantity exceeds 1 unless $s \leq 1$ or $t \leq 1$ or st is odd.

Conversely, perfect schemes are easy with $s \leq 1$ or $t \leq 1$, and they turn out to be possible also whenever st is odd. The first nontrivial case occurs for $s = t = 3$, when there are four essentially different solutions; the most symmetrical of these is

$$210 - 310 - 410 - 510 - 520 - 521 - 531 - 532 - 432 - 431 -$$
$$421 - 321 - 320 - 420 - 430 - 530 - 540 - 541 - 542 - 543 \tag{50}$$

(see exercise 51). Several authors have constructed Hamiltonian paths in the relevant graph for arbitrary odd numbers s and t; for example, the method of Eades, Hickey, and Read [*JACM* **31** (1984), 19–29] makes an interesting exercise in programming with recursive coroutines. Unfortunately, however, none of the known constructions are sufficiently simple to describe in a short space, or to implement with reasonable efficiency. Perfect combination generators have therefore not yet proved to be of practical importance. ▮

In summary, then, we have seen that the study of (s,t)-combinations leads to many fascinating patterns, some of which are of great practical importance and some of which are merely elegant and/or beautiful. Figure 46 illustrates the principal options that are available in the case $s = t = 5$, when $\binom{10}{5} = 252$ combinations arise. Lexicographic order (Algorithm L), the revolving-door Gray code (Algorithm R), the homogeneous scheme K_{55} of (31), and Chase's near-perfect scheme (Algorithm C) are shown in parts (a), (b), (c), and (d) of the illustration. Part (e) shows the near-perfect scheme that is as close to perfection as possible while still being in genlex order of the c array (see exercise 34), while part (f) is the perfect scheme of Eades, Hickey, and Read. Finally, Figs. 46(g) and 46(h) are listings that proceed by rotating $a_j a_{j-1} \dots a_0 \leftarrow a_{j-1} \dots a_0 a_j$ or by swapping $a_j \leftrightarrow a_0$, akin to Algorithms 7.2.1.2C and 7.2.1.2E (see exercises 55 and 56).

*Combinations of a multiset. If multisets can have permutations, they can have combinations too. For example, consider the multiset $\{b, b, b, b, g, g, g, r, r, r, w, w\}$, representing a sack that contains four blue balls and three that are green, three red, two white. There are 37 ways to choose five balls from this sack; in lexicographic order (but descending in each combination) they are

> *gbbbb, ggbbb, gggbb, rbbbb, rgbbb, rggbb, rgggb, rrbbb, rrgbb, rrggb,*
> *rrggg, rrrbb, rrrgb, rrrgg, wbbbb, wgbbb, wggbb, wgggb, wrbbb, wrgbb,*
> *wrggb, wrggg, wrrbb, wrrgb, wrrgg, wrrrb, wrrrg, wwbbb, wwgbb, wwggb,*
> *wwggg, wwrbb, wwrgb, wwrgg, wwrrb, wwrrg, wwrrr.*   (51)

This fact might seem frivolous and/or esoteric, yet we will see in Theorem W below that the lexicographic generation of multiset combinations yields optimal solutions to significant combinatorial problems.

James Bernoulli observed in his *Ars Conjectandi* (1713), 119–123, that we can enumerate such combinations by looking at the coefficient of z^5 in the product $(1+z+z^2)(1+z+z^2+z^3)^2(1+z+z^2+z^3+z^4)$. Indeed, his observation is easy to understand, because we get all possible selections from the sack if we multiply out the polynomials

$$(1 + w + ww)(1 + r + rr + rrr)(1 + g + gg + ggg)(1 + b + bb + bbb + bbbb).$$

Multiset combinations are also equivalent to *bounded compositions*, namely to compositions in which the individual parts are bounded. For example, the 37 multicombinations listed in (51) correspond to 37 solutions of

$$5 = r_3 + r_2 + r_1 + r_0, \quad 0 \le r_3 \le 2, \quad 0 \le r_2, r_1 \le 3, \quad 0 \le r_0 \le 4,$$

namely $5 = 0{+}0{+}1{+}4 = 0{+}0{+}2{+}3 = 0{+}0{+}3{+}2 = 0{+}1{+}0{+}4 = \cdots = 2{+}3{+}0{+}0$.

Fig. 46. Examples of $(5,5)$-combinations:

a) lexicographic;
b) revolving-door;
c) homogeneous;
d) near-perfect;
e) nearer-perfect;
f) perfect;
g) suffix-rotated;
h) right-swapped.

(a)   (b)   (c)   (d)   (e)   (f)   (g)   (h)

Bounded compositions, in turn, are special cases of *contingency tables*, which are of great importance in statistics. And all of these combinatorial configurations can be generated with Gray-like codes as well as in lexicographic order. Exercises 60–63 explore some of the basic ideas involved.

*Shadows. Sets of combinations appear frequently in mathematics. For example, a set of 2-combinations (namely a set of pairs) is essentially a graph, and a set of t-combinations for general t is called a uniform hypergraph. If the vertices of a convex polyhedron are perturbed slightly, so that no three are collinear, no four lie in a plane, and in general no $t + 1$ lie in a $(t - 1)$-dimensional hyperplane, the resulting $(t - 1)$-dimensional faces are "simplexes" whose vertices have great significance in computer applications. Researchers have learned that such sets of combinations have important properties related to lexicographic generation.

If α is any t-combination $c_t \ldots c_2 c_1$, its *shadow* $\partial \alpha$ is the set of all its $(t - 1)$-element subsets $c_{t-1} \ldots c_2 c_1,\ \ldots,\ c_t \ldots c_3 c_1,\ c_t \ldots c_3 c_2$. For example, $\partial 5310 = \{310, 510, 530, 531\}$. We can also represent a t-combination as a bit string $a_{n-1} \ldots a_1 a_0$, in which case $\partial \alpha$ is the set of all strings obtained by changing a 1 to a 0: $\partial 101011 = \{001011, 100011, 101001, 101010\}$. If A is any set of t-combinations, we define its shadow

$$\partial A = \bigcup \{ \partial \alpha \mid \alpha \in A \} \tag{52}$$

to be the set of all $(t - 1)$-combinations in the shadows of its members. For example, $\partial \partial 5310 = \{10, 30, 31, 50, 51, 53\}$.

These definitions apply also to combinations with repetitions, namely to multicombinations: $\partial 5330 = \{330, 530, 533\}$ and $\partial \partial 5330 = \{30, 33, 50, 53\}$. In general, when A is a set of t-element multisets, ∂A is a set of $(t - 1)$-element multisets. Notice, however, that ∂A never has repeated elements itself.

The *upper shadow* $\varrho \alpha$ with respect to a universe U is defined similarly, but it goes from t-combinations to $(t + 1)$-combinations:

$$\varrho \alpha = \{ \beta \subseteq U \mid \alpha \in \partial \beta \}, \qquad \text{for } \alpha \in U; \tag{53}$$

$$\varrho A = \bigcup \{ \varrho \alpha \mid \alpha \in A \}, \qquad \text{for } A \subseteq U. \tag{54}$$

If, for example, $U = \{0, 1, 2, 3, 4, 5, 6\}$, we have $\varrho 5310 = \{53210, 54310, 65310\}$; on the other hand, if $U = \{\infty \cdot 0, \infty \cdot 1, \ldots, \infty \cdot 6\}$, we have $\varrho 5310 = \{53100, 53110, 53210, 53310, 54310, 55310, 65310\}$.

The following fundamental theorems, which have many applications in various branches of mathematics and computer science, tell us how small a set's shadows can be:

Theorem K. *If A is a set of N t-combinations contained in $U = \{0, 1, \ldots, n-1\}$, then*

$$|\partial A| \geq |\partial P_{Nt}| \qquad \text{and} \qquad |\varrho A| \geq |\varrho Q_{Nnt}|, \tag{55}$$

where P_{Nt} denotes the first N combinations generated by Algorithm L, namely the N lexicographically smallest combinations $c_t \ldots c_2 c_1$ that satisfy (3), and Q_{Nnt} denotes the N lexicographically largest. ∎

Theorem M. *If A is a set of N t-multicombinations contained in the multiset $U = \{\infty \cdot 0, \infty \cdot 1, \ldots, \infty \cdot s\}$, then*

$$|\partial A| \geq |\partial \widehat{P}_{Nt}| \qquad \text{and} \qquad |\varrho A| \geq |\varrho \widehat{Q}_{Nst}|, \tag{56}$$

where $\widehat{P}_{Nt}$ denotes the N lexicographically smallest multicombinations $d_t \ldots d_2 d_1$ that satisfy (6), and $\widehat{Q}_{Nst}$ denotes the N lexicographically largest. ∎

Both of these theorems are consequences of a stronger result that we shall prove later. Theorem K is generally called the Kruskal–Katona theorem, because it was discovered by J. B. Kruskal [*Math. Optimization Techniques*, edited by R. Bellman (1963), 251–278] and rediscovered by G. Katona [*Theory of Graphs*, Tihany 1966, edited by Erdős and Katona (Academic Press, 1968), 187–207]; M. P. Schützenberger had previously stated it in a less-well-known publication, with incomplete proof [*RLE Quarterly Progress Report* **55** (1959), 117–118]. Theorem M goes back to F. S. Macaulay, many years earlier [*Proc. London Math. Soc.* (2) **26** (1927), 531–555].

Before proving (55) and (56), let's take a closer look at what those formulas mean. We know from Theorem L that the first N of all t-combinations visited by Algorithm L are those that precede $n_t \ldots n_2 n_1$, where

$$N = \binom{n_t}{t} + \cdots + \binom{n_2}{2} + \binom{n_1}{1}, \qquad n_t > \cdots > n_2 > n_1 \geq 0$$

is the degree-t combinatorial representation of N. Sometimes this representation has fewer than t nonzero terms, because n_j can be equal to $j-1$; let's suppress the zeros, and write

$$N = \binom{n_t}{t} + \binom{n_{t-1}}{t-1} + \cdots + \binom{n_v}{v}, \qquad n_t > n_{t-1} > \cdots > n_v \geq v \geq 1. \tag{57}$$

Now the first $\binom{n_t}{t}$ combinations $c_t \ldots c_1$ are the t-combinations of $\{0, \ldots, n_t-1\}$; the next $\binom{n_{t-1}}{t-1}$ are those in which $c_t = n_t$ and $c_{t-1} \ldots c_1$ is a $(t-1)$-combination of $\{0, \ldots, n_{t-1}-1\}$; and so on. For example, if $t = 5$ and $N = \binom{9}{5} + \binom{7}{4} + \binom{4}{3}$, the first N combinations are

$$P_{N5} = \{43210, \ldots, 87654\} \cup \{93210, \ldots, 96543\} \cup \{97210, \ldots, 97321\}. \tag{58}$$

The shadow of this set P_{N5} is, fortunately, easy to understand: It is

$$\partial P_{N5} = \{3210, \ldots, 8765\} \cup \{9210, \ldots, 9654\} \cup \{9710, \ldots, 9732\}, \tag{59}$$

namely the first $\binom{9}{4} + \binom{7}{3} + \binom{4}{2}$ combinations in lexicographic order when $t = 4$.

In other words, if we define Kruskal's function κ_t by the formula

$$\kappa_t N = \binom{n_t}{t-1} + \binom{n_{t-1}}{t-2} + \cdots + \binom{n_v}{v-1} \tag{60}$$

when N has the unique representation (57), with $\kappa_t 0 = 0$, we have

$$\partial P_{Nt} = P_{(\kappa_t N)(t-1)}. \tag{61}$$

Theorem K tells us, for example, that a graph with a million edges can contain at most

$$\binom{1414}{3} + \binom{1009}{2} \;=\; 470{,}700{,}300$$

triangles, that is, at most 470,700,300 sets of vertices $\{u,v,w\}$ with $u \!-\! v \!-\! w \!-\! u$. The reason is that $1000000 = \binom{1414}{2} + \binom{1009}{1}$ by exercise 17, and the edges $P_{(1000000)2}$ do support $\binom{1414}{3} + \binom{1009}{2}$ triangles; but if there were more, the graph would necessarily have at least $\kappa_3\,470700301 = \binom{1414}{2} + \binom{1009}{1} + \binom{1}{0} = 1000001$ edges in their shadow.

Kruskal defined the companion function

$$\lambda_t N = \binom{n_t}{t+1} + \binom{n_{t-1}}{t} + \cdots + \binom{n_v}{v+1} \tag{62}$$

to deal with questions such as this. The κ and λ functions are related by an interesting law proved in exercise 72:

$$M + N = \binom{s+t}{t} \quad \text{implies} \quad \kappa_s M + \lambda_t N = \binom{s+t}{t+1}, \quad \text{if } st > 0. \tag{63}$$

Turning to Theorem M, the sizes of $\partial \widehat{P}_{Nt}$ and $\varrho \widehat{Q}_{Nst}$ turn out to be

$$|\partial \widehat{P}_{Nt}| = \mu_t N \quad \text{and} \quad |\varrho \widehat{Q}_{Nst}| = N + \kappa_s N \tag{64}$$

(see exercise 81), where the function μ_t satisfies

$$\mu_t N = \binom{n_t - 1}{t - 1} + \binom{n_{t-1} - 1}{t - 2} + \cdots + \binom{n_v - 1}{v - 1} \tag{65}$$

when N has the combinatorial representation (57).

Table 3 shows how these functions $\kappa_t N$, $\lambda_t N$, and $\mu_t N$ behave for small values of t and N. When t and N are large, they can be well approximated in terms of a remarkable function $\tau(x)$ introduced by Teiji Takagi in 1903; see Fig. 47 and exercises 82–85.

Theorems K and M are corollaries of a much more general theorem of discrete geometry, discovered by Da-Lun Wang and Ping Wang [*SIAM J. Applied Math.* **33** (1977), 55–59], which we shall now proceed to investigate. Consider the *discrete n-dimensional torus* $T(m_1, \ldots, m_n)$ whose elements are integer vectors $x = (x_1, \ldots, x_n)$ with $0 \le x_1 < m_1$, $\ldots$, $0 \le x_n < m_n$. We define the sum and difference of two such vectors x and y as in Eqs. 4.3.2–(2) and 4.3.2–(3):

$$x + y = \big((x_1 + y_1)\bmod m_1, \ldots, (x_n + y_n)\bmod m_n\big), \tag{66}$$

$$x - y = \big((x_1 - y_1)\bmod m_1, \ldots, (x_n - y_n)\bmod m_n\big). \tag{67}$$

We also define the so-called *cross order* on such vectors by saying that $x \preceq y$ if and only if

$$\nu x < \nu y \quad \text{or} \quad (\nu x = \nu y \text{ and } x \ge y \text{ lexicographically}); \tag{68}$$

here, as usual, $\nu(x_1, \ldots, x_n) = x_1 + \cdots + x_n$. For example, when $m_1 = m_2 = 2$ and $m_3 = 3$, the 12 vectors $x_1 x_2 x_3$ in increasing cross order are

$$000,\ 100,\ 010,\ 001,\ 110,\ 101,\ 011,\ 002,\ 111,\ 102,\ 012,\ 112, \tag{69}$$

Table 3
EXAMPLES OF THE KRUSKAL–MACAULAY FUNCTIONS κ, λ, AND μ

$N =$	0	1	2	3	4	5	6	7	8	9	10	11	12	13	14	15	16	17	18	19	20
$\kappa_1 N =$	0	1	1	1	1	1	1	1	1	1	1	1	1	1	1	1	1	1	1	1	1
$\kappa_2 N =$	0	2	3	3	4	4	4	5	5	5	5	6	6	6	6	6	7	7	7	7	7
$\kappa_3 N =$	0	3	5	6	6	8	9	9	10	10	10	12	13	13	14	14	14	15	15	15	15
$\kappa_4 N =$	0	4	7	9	10	10	13	15	16	16	18	19	19	20	20	20	23	25	26	26	28
$\kappa_5 N =$	0	5	9	12	14	15	15	19	22	24	25	25	28	30	31	31	33	34	34	35	35
$\lambda_1 N =$	0	0	1	3	6	10	15	21	28	36	45	55	66	78	91	105	120	136	153	171	190
$\lambda_2 N =$	0	0	0	1	1	2	4	4	5	7	10	10	11	13	16	20	20	21	23	26	30
$\lambda_3 N =$	0	0	0	1	1	1	2	2	3	5	5	5	6	6	7	9	9	9	10	12	15
$\lambda_4 N =$	0	0	0	0	0	1	1	1	1	2	2	2	3	3	4	6	6	6	6	7	7
$\lambda_5 N =$	0	0	0	0	0	0	1	1	1	1	1	2	2	2	2	3	3	3	4	4	5
$\mu_1 N =$	0	1	1	1	1	1	1	1	1	1	1	1	1	1	1	1	1	1	1	1	1
$\mu_2 N =$	0	1	2	2	3	3	3	4	4	4	4	5	5	5	5	5	6	6	6	6	6
$\mu_3 N =$	0	1	2	3	3	4	5	5	6	6	6	7	8	8	9	9	9	10	10	10	10
$\mu_4 N =$	0	1	2	3	4	4	5	6	7	7	8	9	9	10	10	10	11	12	13	13	14
$\mu_5 N =$	0	1	2	3	4	5	5	6	7	8	9	9	10	11	12	12	13	14	14	15	15

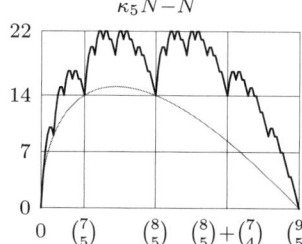
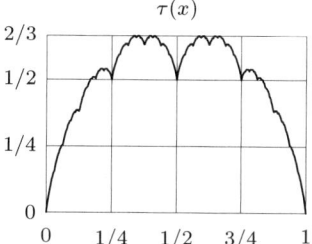

Fig. 47. Approximating a Kruskal function with the Takagi function. (The smooth curve in the left-hand graph is the lower bound $\underline{\kappa}_5 N - N$ of exercise 80.)

omitting parentheses and commas for convenience. The *complement* of a vector in $T(m_1, \ldots, m_n)$ is

$$\bar{x} = (m_1 - 1 - x_1, \ldots, m_n - 1 - x_n). \tag{70}$$

Notice that $x \preceq y$ holds if and only if $\bar{x} \succeq \bar{y}$. Therefore we have

$$\text{rank}(x) + \text{rank}(\bar{x}) = T - 1, \qquad \text{where } T = m_1 \ldots m_n, \tag{71}$$

if $\text{rank}(x)$ denotes the number of vectors that precede x in cross order.

We will find it convenient to call the vectors "points" and to name the points $e_0, e_1, \ldots, e_{T-1}$ in increasing cross order. Thus we have $e_7 = 002$ in (69), and $\bar{e}_r = e_{T-1-r}$ in general. Notice that

$$e_1 = 100\ldots00, \quad e_2 = 010\ldots00, \quad \ldots, \quad e_n = 000\ldots01; \tag{72}$$

these are the so-called *unit vectors*. The set

$$S_N = \{e_0, e_1, \ldots, e_{N-1}\} \qquad (73)$$

consisting of the smallest N points is called a *standard set*, and in the special case $N = n + 1$ we write

$$E = \{e_0, e_1, \ldots, e_n\} = \{000\ldots00, 100\ldots00, 010\ldots00, \ldots, 000\ldots01\}. \qquad (74)$$

Any set of points X has a *spread* X^+, a *core* X°, and a *dual* $X^\sim$, defined by the rules

$$X^+ = \{\, x \in S_T \mid x \in X \text{ or } x - e_1 \in X \text{ or } \cdots \text{ or } x - e_n \in X \,\}; \qquad (75)$$
$$X^\circ = \{\, x \in S_T \mid x \in X \text{ and } x + e_1 \in X \text{ and } \cdots \text{ and } x + e_n \in X \,\}; \qquad (76)$$
$$X^\sim = \{\, x \in S_T \mid \overline{x} \notin X \,\}. \qquad (77)$$

We can also define the spread of X algebraically, writing

$$X^+ = X + E, \qquad (78)$$

where $X + Y$ denotes $\{\, x + y \mid x \in X \text{ and } y \in Y \,\}$. Clearly

$$X^+ \subseteq Y \qquad \text{if and only if} \qquad X \subseteq Y^\circ. \qquad (79)$$

These notions can be illustrated in the two-dimensional case $m_1 = 4$, $m_2 = 6$, by the more-or-less random toroidal arrangement $X = \{00, 12, 13, 14, 15, 21, 22, 25\}$ for which we have, pictorially,

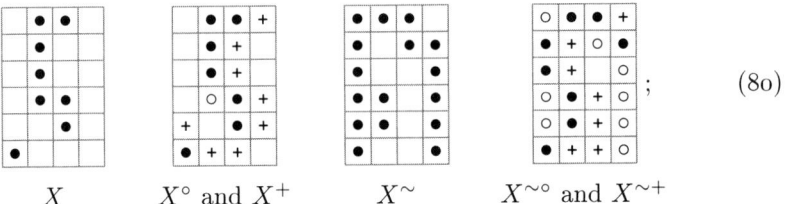

$$\qquad\qquad (80)$$

$$X \qquad\qquad X^\circ \text{ and } X^+ \qquad\qquad X^\sim \qquad\qquad X^{\sim\circ} \text{ and } X^{\sim+}$$

here X in the first two diagrams consists of points marked $\bullet$ or $\circ$, X° comprises just the $\circ$s, and X^+ consists of $+$s plus $\bullet$s plus $\circ$s. Notice that if we rotate the diagram for $X^{\sim\circ}$ and $X^{\sim+}$ by $180°$, we obtain the diagram for X° and X^+, but with $(\bullet, \circ, +, \ )$ respectively changed to $(+, \ , \bullet, \circ)$; and in fact the identities

$$X^\circ = X^{\sim+\sim}, \qquad X^+ = X^{\sim\circ\sim} \qquad (81)$$

hold in general (see exercise 86).

Now we are ready to state the theorem of Wang and Wang:

Theorem W. *Let X be any set of N points in the discrete torus $T(m_1, \ldots, m_n)$, where $m_1 \le \cdots \le m_n$. Then $|X^+| \ge |S_N^+|$ and $|X^\circ| \le |S_N^\circ|$.*

Proof. In other words, the standard sets S_N have the smallest spread and largest core, among all N-point sets. We will prove this result by following a general approach first used by F. W. J. Whipple to prove Theorem M [*Proc. London Math. Soc.* (2) **28** (1928), 431–437]. The first step is to prove that the spread and the core of standard sets are standard:

Lemma S. *There are functions α and β such that $S_N^+ = S_{\alpha N}$ and $S_N^\circ = S_{\beta N}$.*

Proof. We may assume that $N > 0$. Let r be maximum with $e_r \in S_N^+$, and let $\alpha N = r + 1$; we must prove that $e_q \in S_N^+$ for $0 \le q < r$. Suppose $e_q = x = (x_1, \ldots, x_n)$ and $e_r = y = (y_1, \ldots, y_n)$, and let k be the largest subscript with $x_k > 0$. Since $y \in S_N^+$, there is a subscript j such that $y - e_j \in S_N$. It suffices to prove that $x - e_k \preceq y - e_j$, and exercise 88 does this.

The second part follows from (81), with $\beta N = T - \alpha(T - N)$, because $S_N^\sim = S_{T-N}$. ∎

Theorem W is obviously true when $n = 1$, so we assume by induction that it has been proved in $n - 1$ dimensions. The next step is to *compress* the given set X in the kth coordinate position, by partitioning it into disjoint sets

$$X_k(a) = \{ x \in X \mid x_k = a \} \tag{82}$$

for $0 \le a < m_k$ and replacing each $X_k(a)$ by

$$X_k'(a) = \{ (s_1, \ldots, s_{k-1}, a, s_k, \ldots, s_{n-1}) \mid (s_1, \ldots, s_{n-1}) \in S_{|X_k(a)|} \}, \tag{83}$$

a set with the same number of elements. The sets S used in (83) are standard in the $(n-1)$-dimensional torus $T(m_1, \ldots, m_{k-1}, m_{k+1}, \ldots, m_n)$. Notice that we have $(x_1, \ldots, x_{k-1}, a, x_{k+1}, \ldots, x_n) \preceq (y_1, \ldots, y_{k-1}, a, y_{k+1}, \ldots, y_n)$ if and only if $(x_1, \ldots, x_{k-1}, x_{k+1}, \ldots, x_n) \preceq (y_1, \ldots, y_{k-1}, y_{k+1}, \ldots, y_n)$; therefore $X_k'(a) = X_k(a)$ if and only if the $(n-1)$-dimensional points $(x_1, \ldots, x_{k-1}, x_{k+1}, \ldots, x_n)$ with $(x_1, \ldots, x_{k-1}, a, x_{k+1}, \ldots, x_n) \in X$ are as small as possible when projected onto the $(n-1)$-dimensional torus. We let

$$C_k X = X_k'(0) \cup X_k'(1) \cup \cdots \cup X_k'(m_k - 1) \tag{84}$$

be the compression of X in position k. Exercise 90 proves the basic fact that compression does not increase the size of the spread:

$$|X^+| \ge |(C_k X)^+|, \qquad \text{for } 1 \le k \le n. \tag{85}$$

Furthermore, if compression changes X, it replaces some of the elements by other elements of lower rank. Therefore we need to prove Theorem W only for sets X that are totally compressed, having $X = C_k X$ for all k.

Consider, for example, the case $n = 2$. A totally compressed set in two dimensions has all points moved to the left of their rows and the bottom of their columns, as in the eleven-point sets

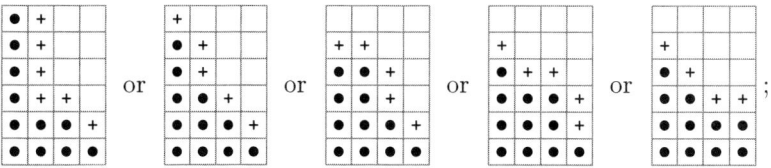

the rightmost of these is standard, and has the smallest spread. Exercise 91 completes the proof of Theorem W in two dimensions.

When $n > 2$, suppose $x = (x_1, \ldots, x_n) \in X$ and $x_j > 0$. The condition
$C_k X = X$ implies that, if $0 \le i < j$ and $i \ne k \ne j$, we have $x + e_i - e_j \in X$.
Applying this fact for three values of k tells us that $x + e_i - e_j \in X$ whenever
$0 \le i < j$. Consequently

$$X_n(a) + E_n(0) \subseteq X_n(a-1) + e_n \quad \text{for } 0 < a < m, \tag{86}$$

where $m = m_n$ and $E_n(0)$ is a clever abbreviation for the set $\{e_0, \ldots, e_{n-1}\}$.

Let $X_n(a)$ have N_a elements, so that $N = |X| = N_0 + N_1 + \cdots + N_{m-1}$, and
let $Y = X^+$. Then

$$Y_n(a) = \left(X_n((a-1) \bmod m) + e_n\right) \cup \left(X_n(a) + E_n(0)\right)$$

is standard in $n - 1$ dimensions, and (86) tells us that

$$N_{m-1} \le \beta N_{m-2} \le N_{m-2} \le \cdots \le N_1 \le \beta N_0 \le N_0 \le \alpha N_0,$$

where α and β refer to coordinates 1 through $n - 1$. Therefore

$$|Y| = |Y_n(0)| + |Y_n(1)| + |Y_n(2)| + \cdots + |Y_n(m-1)|$$
$$= \alpha N_0 + N_0 + N_1 + \cdots + N_{m-2} = \alpha N_0 + N - N_{m-1}.$$

The proof of Theorem W now has a beautiful conclusion. Let $Z = S_N$, and
suppose $|Z_n(a)| = M_a$. We want to prove that $|X^+| \ge |Z^+|$, namely that

$$\alpha N_0 + N - N_{m-1} \ge \alpha M_0 + N - M_{m-1}, \tag{87}$$

because the arguments of the previous paragraph apply to Z as well as to X.
We will prove (87) by showing that $N_{m-1} \le M_{m-1}$ and $N_0 \ge M_0$.

Using the $(n-1)$-dimensional α and β functions, let us define

$$N'_{m-1} = N_{m-1}, \; N'_{m-2} = \alpha N'_{m-1}, \; \ldots, \; N'_1 = \alpha N'_2, \; N'_0 = \alpha N'_1; \tag{88}$$
$$N''_0 = N_0, \; N''_1 = \beta N''_0, \; N''_2 = \beta N''_1, \; \ldots, \; N''_{m-1} = \beta N''_{m-2}. \tag{89}$$

Then we have $N'_a \le N_a \le N''_a$ for $0 \le a < m$, and it follows that

$$N' = N'_0 + N'_1 + \cdots + N'_{m-1} \le N \le N'' = N''_0 + N''_1 + \cdots + N''_{m-1}. \tag{90}$$

Exercise 92 proves that the standard set $Z' = S_{N'}$ has exactly N'_a elements with
nth coordinate equal to a, for each a; and by the duality between α and β, the
standard set $Z'' = S_{N''}$ likewise has exactly N''_a elements with nth coordinate a.
Finally, therefore,

$$M_{m-1} = |Z_n(m-1)| \ge |Z'_n(m-1)| = N_{m-1},$$
$$M_0 = |Z_n(0)| \le |Z''_n(0)| = N_0,$$

because $Z' \subseteq Z \subseteq Z''$ by (90). By (81) we also have $|X^\circ| \le |Z^\circ|$. ∎

Now we are ready to prove Theorems K and M, which are in fact special
cases of a substantially more general theorem of Clements and Lindström that
applies to arbitrary multisets [*J. Combinatorial Theory* **7** (1969), 230–238]:

Corollary C. *If A is a set of N t-multicombinations contained in the multiset $U = \{s_0 \cdot 0, s_1 \cdot 1, \ldots, s_d \cdot d\}$, where $s_0 \geq s_1 \geq \cdots \geq s_d$, then*

$$|\partial A| \geq |\partial P_{Nt}| \quad \text{and} \quad |\varrho A| \geq |\varrho Q_{Nt}|, \tag{91}$$

where P_{Nt} denotes the N lexicographically smallest multicombinations $d_t \ldots d_2 d_1$ of U, and Q_{Nt} denotes the N lexicographically largest.

Proof. Multicombinations of U can be represented as points $x_1 \ldots x_n$ of the torus $T(m_1, \ldots, m_n)$, where $n = d + 1$ and $m_j = s_{n-j} + 1$; we let x_j be the number of occurrences of $n - j$. This correspondence preserves lexicographic order. For example, if $U = \{0, 0, 0, 1, 1, 2, 3\}$, its 3-multicombinations are

$$000, \ 100, \ 110, \ 200, \ 210, \ 211, \ 300, \ 310, \ 311, \ 320, \ 321, \tag{92}$$

in lexicographic order, and the corresponding points $x_1 x_2 x_3 x_4$ are

$$0003, 0012, 0021, 0102, 0111, 0120, 1002, 1011, 1020, 1101, 1110. \tag{93}$$

Let T_w be the points of the torus that have weight $x_1 + \cdots + x_n = w$. Then every allowable set A of t-multicombinations is a subset of T_t. Furthermore — and this is the main point — the spread of $T_0 \cup T_1 \cup \cdots \cup T_{t-1} \cup A$ is

$$\begin{aligned} (T_0 \cup T_1 \cup \cdots \cup T_{t-1} \cup A)^+ &= T_0^+ \cup T_1^+ \cup \cdots \cup T_{t-1}^+ \cup A^+ \\ &= T_0 \cup T_1 \cup \cdots \cup T_t \cup \varrho A. \end{aligned} \tag{94}$$

Thus the upper shadow ϱA is simply $(T_0 \cup T_1 \cup \cdots \cup T_{t-1} \cup A)^+ \cap T_{t+1}$, and Theorem W tells us in essence that $|A| = N$ implies $|\varrho A| \geq |\varrho(S_{M+N} \cap T_t)|$, where $M = |T_0 \cup \cdots \cup T_{t-1}|$. Hence, by the definition of cross order, $S_{M+N} \cap T_t$ consists of the lexicographically largest N t-multicombinations, namely Q_{Nt}.

The proof that $|\partial A| \geq |\partial P_{Nt}|$ now follows by complementation (see exercise 94). ∎

EXERCISES

1. [*M23*] Explain why Golomb's rule (8) makes all sets $\{c_1, \ldots, c_t\} \subseteq \{0, \ldots, n-1\}$ correspond uniquely to multisets $\{e_1, \ldots, e_t\} \subseteq \{\infty \cdot 0, \ldots, \infty \cdot n - t\}$.

2. [*16*] What path in an 11×13 grid corresponds to the bit string (13)?

▸ **3.** [*21*] (R. R. Fenichel, 1968.) Show that the compositions $q_t + \cdots + q_1 + q_0$ of s into $t + 1$ nonnegative parts can be generated in lexicographic order by a simple loopless algorithm.

4. [*16*] Show that every composition $q_t \ldots q_0$ of s into $t + 1$ nonnegative parts corresponds to a composition $r_s \ldots r_0$ of t into $s + 1$ nonnegative parts. What composition corresponds to 10224000001010 under this correspondence?

▸ **5.** [*20*] What is a good way to generate all of the integer solutions to the following systems of inequalities?

a) $n > x_t \geq x_{t-1} > x_{t-2} \geq x_{t-3} > \cdots > x_1 \geq 0$, when t is odd.

b) $n \gg x_t \gg x_{t-1} \gg \cdots \gg x_2 \gg x_1 \gg 0$, where $a \gg b$ means $a \geq b + 2$.

6. [*M22*] How often is each step of Algorithm T performed?

380 COMBINATORIAL SEARCHING 7.2.1.3

7. [22] Design an algorithm that runs through the "dual" combinations $b_s \ldots b_2 b_1$ in *decreasing* lexicographic order (see (5) and Table 1). Like Algorithm T, your algorithm should avoid redundant assignments and unnecessary searching.

8. [M23] Design an algorithm that generates all (s,t)-combinations $a_{n-1} \ldots a_1 a_0$ lexicographically in bitstring form. The total running time should be $O\left(\binom{n}{t}\right)$, assuming that $st > 0$.

9. [M26] When all (s,t)-combinations $a_{n-1} \ldots a_1 a_0$ are listed in lexicographic order, let $2A_{st}$ be the total number of bit changes between adjacent strings. For example, $A_{33} = 25$ because there are respectively

$$2 + 2 + 2 + 4 + 2 + 2 + 4 + 2 + 2 + 6 + 2 + 2 + 4 + 2 + 2 + 4 + 2 + 2 + 2 = 50$$

bit changes between the 20 strings in Table 1.

a) Show that $A_{st} = \min(s,t) + A_{(s-1)t} + A_{s(t-1)}$ when $st > 0$; $A_{st} = 0$ when $st = 0$.

b) Prove that $A_{st} < 2\binom{s+t}{t}$.

▶ **10.** [21] The "World Series" of baseball is traditionally a competition in which the American League champion (A) plays the National League champion (N) until one of them has beaten the other four times. What is a good way to list all possible scenarios AAAA, AAANA, AAANNA, ..., NNNN? What is a simple way to assign consecutive integers to those scenarios?

11. [19] Which of the scenarios in exercise 10 occurred most often during the 1900s? Which of them never occurred? [*Hint:* World Series scores are easily found on the Internet.]

12. [HM32] A set V of n-bit vectors that is closed under addition modulo 2 is called a *binary vector space*.

a) Prove that every such V contains 2^t elements, for some integer t, and can be represented as the set $\{x_1 \alpha_1 \oplus \cdots \oplus x_t \alpha_t \mid 0 \le x_1, \ldots, x_t \le 1\}$ where the vectors $\alpha_1, \ldots, \alpha_t$ form a "canonical basis" with the following property: There is a t-combination $c_t \ldots c_2 c_1$ of $\{0, 1, \ldots, n-1\}$ such that, if α_k is the binary vector $a_{k(n-1)} \ldots a_{k1} a_{k0}$, we have

$$a_{kc_j} = [j = k] \quad \text{for } 1 \le j, k \le t; \qquad a_{kl} = 0 \quad \text{for } 0 \le l < c_k, 1 \le k \le t.$$

For example, the canonical bases with $n = 9$, $t = 4$, and $c_4 c_3 c_2 c_1 = 7641$ have the general form

$$\begin{aligned}
\alpha_1 &= * \, 0 \, 0 \, * \, 0 \, * \, * \, 1 \, 0, \\
\alpha_2 &= * \, 0 \, 0 \, * \, 1 \, 0 \, 0 \, 0 \, 0, \\
\alpha_3 &= * \, 0 \, 1 \, 0 \, 0 \, 0 \, 0 \, 0 \, 0, \\
\alpha_4 &= * \, 1 \, 0 \, 0 \, 0 \, 0 \, 0 \, 0 \, 0;
\end{aligned}$$

there are 2^8 ways to replace the eight asterisks by 0s and/or 1s, and each of these defines a canonical basis. We call t the dimension of V.

b) How many t-dimensional spaces are possible with n-bit vectors?

c) Design an algorithm to generate all canonical bases $(\alpha_1, \ldots, \alpha_t)$ of dimension t. *Hint:* Let the associated combinations $c_t \ldots c_1$ increase lexicographically as in Algorithm L.

d) What is the 1000000th basis visited by your algorithm when $n = 9$ and $t = 4$?

13. [25] A one-dimensional *Ising configuration* of length n, weight t, and energy r, is a binary string $a_{n-1} \ldots a_0$ such that $\sum_{j=0}^{n-1} a_j = t$ and $\sum_{j=1}^{n-1} b_j = r$, where $b_j =$

$a_j \oplus a_{j-1}$. For example, $a_{12} \dots a_0 = 1100100100011$ has weight 6 and energy 6, since $b_{12} \dots b_1 = 010110110010$.

Design an algorithm to generate all such configurations, given n, t, and r.

14. [*26*] When the binary strings $a_{n-1} \dots a_1 a_0$ of (s,t)-combinations are generated in lexicographic order, we sometimes need to change $2\min(s,t)$ bits to get from one combination to the next. For example, 011100 is followed by 100011 in Table 1. Therefore we apparently cannot hope to generate all combinations with a loopless algorithm unless we visit them in some other order.

Show, however, that there actually is a way to compute the lexicographic successor of a given combination in $O(1)$ steps, if each combination is represented indirectly in a doubly linked list as follows: There are arrays $l[0], \dots, l[n]$ and $r[0], \dots, r[n]$ such that $l[r[j]] = j$ for $0 \le j \le n$. If $x_0 = l[0]$ and $x_j = l[x_{j-1}]$ for $0 < j < n$, then $a_j = [x_j > s]$ for $0 \le j < n$.

15. [*M22*] Use the fact that dual combinations $b_s \dots b_2 b_1$ occur in reverse lexicographic order to prove that the sum $\binom{b_s}{s} + \dots + \binom{b_2}{2} + \binom{b_1}{1}$ has a simple relation to the sum $\binom{c_t}{t} + \dots + \binom{c_2}{2} + \binom{c_1}{1}$.

16. [*M21*] What is the millionth combination generated by Algorithm L when t is (a) 2? (b) 3? (c) 4? (d) 5? (e) 1000000?

17. [*HM25*] Given N and t, what is a good way to compute the combinatorial representation (20)?

▶ **18.** [*20*] What binary tree do we get when the binomial tree T_n is represented by "right child" and "left sibling" pointers as in exercise 2.3.2–5?

19. [*21*] Instead of labeling the branches of the binomial tree T_4 as shown in (22), we could label each node with the bit string of its corresponding combination:

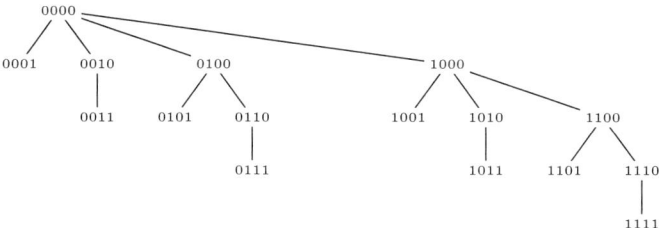

If T_∞ has been labeled in this way, suppressing leading zeros, preorder is the same as the ordinary increasing order of binary notation; so the millionth node turns out to be 11110100001000111111. But what is the millionth node of T_∞ in *postorder*?

20. [*M20*] Devise generating functions g and h such that Algorithm F finds exactly $[z^N] g(z)$ feasible combinations and sets $t \leftarrow t+1$ exactly $[z^N] h(z)$ times.

21. [*M22*] (Joan E. Miller, 1971.) Prove the alternating combination law (30).

22. [*M23*] What is the millionth revolving-door combination visited by Algorithm R when t is (a) 2? (b) 3? (c) 4? (d) 5? (e) 1000000?

23. [*M23*] Suppose we augment Algorithm R by setting $j \leftarrow t+1$ in step R1, and $j \leftarrow 1$ if R3 goes directly to R2. Find the probability distribution of j, and its average value. What does this imply about the running time of the algorithm?

▶ **24.** [*M25*] (W. H. Payne, 1974.) Continuing the previous exercise, let j_k be the value of j on the kth visit by Algorithm R. Show that $|j_{k+1} - j_k| \le 2$, and explain how to make the algorithm loopless by exploiting this property.

25. [*M35*] Let $c_t \ldots c_2 c_1$ and $c'_t \ldots c'_2 c'_1$ be the Nth and N'th combinations generated by the revolving-door method, Algorithm R. If the set $C = \{c_t, \ldots, c_2, c_1\}$ has $m > 0$ elements not in $C' = \{c'_t, \ldots, c'_2, c'_1\}$, prove that $|N - N'| > \sum_{k=1}^{m-1} \binom{2k}{k-1}$.

26. [*26*] Do elements of the *ternary* reflected Gray code have properties similar to the revolving-door Gray code Γ_{st}, if we extract only the n-tuples $a_{n-1} \ldots a_1 a_0$ such that (a) $a_{n-1} + \cdots + a_1 + a_0 = t$? (b) $\{a_{n-1}, \ldots, a_1, a_0\} = \{r \cdot 0, s \cdot 1, t \cdot 2\}$?

▶ **27.** [*25*] Show that there is a simple way to generate all combinations of *at most* t elements of $\{0, 1, \ldots, n-1\}$, using only Gray-code-like transitions $0 \leftrightarrow 1$ and $01 \leftrightarrow 10$. (In other words, each step should either insert a new element, delete an element, or shift an element by ± 1.) For example,

$$0000, \ 0001, \ 0011, \ 0010, \ 0110, \ 0101, \ 0100, \ 1100, \ 1010, \ 1001, \ 1000$$

is one such sequence when $n = 4$ and $t = 2$. *Hint:* Think of Chinese rings.

28. [*M21*] True or false: A listing of (s, t)-combinations $a_{n-1} \ldots a_1 a_0$ in bitstring form is in genlex order if and only if the corresponding index-form listings $b_s \ldots b_2 b_1$ (for the 0s) and $c_t \ldots c_2 c_1$ (for the 1s) are both in genlex order.

▶ **29.** [*M28*] (P. J. Chase.) Given a string on the symbols +, -, and 0, say that an *R-block* is a substring of the form $-^{k+1}$ that is preceded by 0 and not followed by -; an *L-block* is a substring of the form $+-^k$ that is followed by 0; in both cases $k \ge 0$. For example, the string ⌐+00++-++⌐-000⌐ has two L-blocks and one R-block, shown in gray. Notice that blocks cannot overlap.

We form the *successor* of such a string as follows, whenever at least one block is present: Replace the rightmost $0-^{k+1}$ by $-+^k 0$, if the rightmost block is an R-block; otherwise replace the rightmost $+-^k 0$ by $0+^{k+1}$. Also negate the first sign, if any, that appears to the right of the block that has been changed. For example,

$$-⌐+⌐00++- \to -0⌐+⌐0-+- \to -0+-⌐0⌐-- \to -0+--⌐+⌐0 \to -0⌐+⌐--0+ \to -00+++-,$$

where the notation $\alpha \to \beta$ means that β is the successor of α.

   a) What strings have no blocks (and therefore no successor)?

   b) Can there be a cycle of strings with $\alpha_0 \to \alpha_1 \to \cdots \to \alpha_{k-1} \to \alpha_0$?

   c) Prove that if $\alpha \to \beta$ then $-\beta \to -\alpha$, where "$-$" means "negate all the signs." (Therefore every string has at most one predecessor.)

   d) Show that if $\alpha_0 \to \alpha_1 \to \cdots \to \alpha_k$ and $k > 0$, the strings α_0 and α_k do not have all their 0s in the same positions. (Therefore, if α_0 has s signs and t zeros, k must be less than $\binom{s+t}{t}$.)

   e) Prove that every string α with s signs and t zeros belongs to exactly one chain $\alpha_0 \to \alpha_1 \to \cdots \to \alpha_{\binom{s+t}{t}-1}$.

30. [*M32*] The previous exercise defines 2^s ways to generate all combinations of s 0s and t 1s, via the mapping $+ \mapsto 0$, $- \mapsto 0$, and $0 \mapsto 1$. Show that each of these ways is a homogeneous genlex sequence, definable by an appropriate recurrence. Is Chase's sequence (37) a special case of this general construction?

31. [*M23*] How many genlex listings of (s, t)-combinations are possible in (a) bitstring form $a_{n-1} \ldots a_1 a_0$? (b) index-list form $c_t \ldots c_2 c_1$?

▶ **32.** [*M32*] How many of the genlex listings of (s,t)-combination strings $a_{n-1}\ldots a_1 a_0$
(a) have the revolving-door property? (b) are homogeneous?

33. [*HM33*] How many of the genlex listings in exercise 31(b) are near-perfect?

34. [*M32*] Continuing exercise 33, explain how to find such schemes that are as near
as possible to perfection, in the sense that the number of "imperfect" transitions $c_j \leftarrow$
$c_j \pm 2$ is minimized, when s and t are not too large.

35. [*M26*] How many steps of Chase's sequence C_{st} use an imperfect transition?

▶ **36.** [*M21*] Prove that method (39) performs the operation $j \leftarrow j+1$ a total of exactly
$\binom{s+t}{t} - 1$ times as it generates all (s,t)-combinations $a_{n-1}\ldots a_1 a_0$, given any genlex
scheme for combinations in bitstring form.

▶ **37.** [*27*] What algorithm results when the general genlex method (39) is used to
produce (s,t)-combinations $a_{n-1}\ldots a_1 a_0$ in (a) lexicographic order? (b) the revolving-
door order of Algorithm R? (c) the homogeneous order of (31)?

38. [*26*] Design a genlex algorithm like Algorithm C for the *reverse* sequence C_{st}^R.

39. [*M21*] When $s = 12$ and $t = 14$, how many combinations precede the bit string
11001001000011111101101010 in Chase's sequence C_{st}? (See (41).)

40. [*M22*] What is the millionth combination in Chase's sequence C_{st}, when $s = 12$
and $t = 14$?

41. [*M27*] Show that there is a permutation $c(0)$, $c(1)$, $c(2)$, ... of the nonnegative
integers such that the elements of Chase's sequence C_{st} are obtained by complementing
the least significant $s + t$ bits of the elements $c(k)$ for $0 \le k < 2^{s+t}$ that have weight
$\nu(c(k)) = s$. (Thus the sequence $\bar{c}(0)$, ..., $\bar{c}(2^n - 1)$ contains, as subsequences, all of
the C_{st} for which $s + t = n$, just as Gray binary code $g(0)$, ..., $g(2^n - 1)$ contains all
the revolving-door sequences Γ_{st}.) Explain how to compute the binary representation
$c(k) = (\ldots a_2 a_1 a_0)_2$ from the binary representation $k = (\ldots b_2 b_1 b_0)_2$.

42. [*HM34*] Use generating functions of the form $\sum_{s,t} g_{st} w^s z^t$ to analyze each step of
Algorithm C.

43. [*20*] Prove or disprove: If $s(x)$ and $p(x)$ denote respectively the successor and
predecessor of x in endo-order, then $s(x+1) = p(x) + 1$.

▶ **44.** [*M21*] Let $C_t(n) - 1$ denote the sequence obtained from $C_t(n)$ by striking out
all combinations with $c_1 = 0$, then replacing $c_t \ldots c_1$ by $(c_t - 1) \ldots (c_1 - 1)$ in the
combinations that remain. Show that $C_t(n) - 1$ is near-perfect.

45. [*32*] Exploit endo-order and the expansions sketched in (44) to generate the
combinations $c_t \ldots c_2 c_1$ of Chase's sequence $C_t(n)$ with a nonrecursive procedure.

▶ **46.** [*33*] Construct a nonrecursive algorithm for the dual combinations $b_s \ldots b_2 b_1$ of
Chase's sequence C_{st}, namely for the positions of the zeros in $a_{n-1}\ldots a_1 a_0$.

47. [*26*] Implement the near-perfect multiset permutation method of (46) and (47).

48. [*M21*] Suppose $\alpha_0, \alpha_1, \ldots, \alpha_{N-1}$ is any listing of the permutations of the multiset
$\{s_1 \cdot 1, \ldots, s_d \cdot d\}$, where α_k differs from α_{k+1} by the interchange of two elements. Let
$\beta_0, \ldots, \beta_{M-1}$ be any revolving-door listing for (s,t)-combinations, where $s = s_0$, $t = s_1 + \cdots + s_d$, and $M = \binom{s+t}{t}$. Then let Λ_j be the list of M elements obtained by starting
with $\alpha_j \uparrow \beta_0$ and applying the revolving-door exchanges; here $\alpha \uparrow \beta$ denotes the string
obtained by substituting the elements of α for the 1s in β, preserving left-right order.
For example, if $\beta_0, \ldots, \beta_{M-1}$ is 0110, 0101, 1100, 1001, 0011, 1010, and if $\alpha_j = 12$,
then Λ_j is 0120, 0102, 1200, 1002, 0012, 1020. (The revolving-door listing need *not* be
homogeneous.)

384   COMBINATORIAL SEARCHING   7.2.1.3

Prove that the list (47) contains all permutations of $\{s_0 \cdot 0, s_1 \cdot 1, \ldots, s_d \cdot d\}$, and that adjacent permutations differ from each other by the interchange of two elements.

49. [*HM23*] If q is a primitive mth root of unity, such as $e^{2\pi i/m}$, show that

$$\binom{n}{k}_q = \binom{\lfloor n/m \rfloor}{\lfloor k/m \rfloor}\binom{n \bmod m}{k \bmod m}_q.$$

▸ **50.** [*HM25*] Extend the formula of the previous exercise to *q-multinomial* coefficients

$$\binom{n_1 + \cdots + n_t}{n_1, \ldots, n_t}_q.$$

51. [*25*] Find all Hamiltonian paths in the graph whose vertices are permutations of $\{0, 0, 0, 1, 1, 1\}$ related by adjacent transposition. Which of those paths are equivalent under the operations of interchanging 0s with 1s and/or left-right reflection?

52. [*M37*] Generalizing Theorem P, find a necessary and sufficient condition that all permutations of the multiset $\{s_0 \cdot 0, \ldots, s_d \cdot d\}$ can be generated by adjacent transpositions $a_j a_{j-1} \leftrightarrow a_{j-1} a_j$.

53. [*M46*] (D. H. Lehmer, 1965.) Suppose the N permutations of $\{s_0 \cdot 0, \ldots, s_d \cdot d\}$ cannot be generated by a perfect scheme, because $(N + x)/2$ of them have an even number of inversions, where $x \geq 2$. Is it possible to generate them all with a sequence of $N + x - 2$ adjacent interchanges $a_{\delta_k} \leftrightarrow a_{\delta_k - 1}$ for $1 \leq k < N + x - 1$, where $x - 1$ cases are "spurs" with $\delta_k = \delta_{k-1}$ that take us back to the permutation we've just seen? For example, a suitable sequence $\delta_1 \ldots \delta_{94}$ for the 90 permutations of $\{0, 0, 1, 1, 2, 2\}$, where $x = \binom{2+2+2}{2,2,2}_{-1} = 6$, is $234535432523451\alpha42\alpha^R51\alpha42\alpha^R51\alpha4$, where $\alpha = 45352542345355$, if we start with $a_5 a_4 a_3 a_2 a_1 a_0 = 221100$.

54. [*M40*] For what values of s and t can all (s, t)-combinations be generated if we allow end-around swaps $a_{n-1} \leftrightarrow a_0$ in addition to adjacent interchanges $a_j \leftrightarrow a_{j-1}$?

▸ **55.** [*33*] (Frank Ruskey, 2004.) (a) Show that all (s, t)-combinations $a_{s+t-1} \ldots a_1 a_0$ can be generated efficiently by doing successive rotations $a_j a_{j-1} \ldots a_0 \leftarrow a_{j-1} \ldots a_0 a_j$. (b) What MMIX instructions will take $(a_{s+t-1} \ldots a_1 a_0)_2$ to its successor, when $s+t < 64$?

56. [*M49*] (Buck and Wiedemann, 1984.) Can all (t, t)-combinations $a_{2t-1} \ldots a_1 a_0$ be generated by repeatedly swapping a_0 with some other element?

▸ **57.** [*22*] (Frank Ruskey.) Can a piano player run through all possible 4-note chords that span at most one octave, changing only one finger at a time? This is the problem of generating all combinations $c_t \ldots c_1$ such that $n > c_t > \cdots > c_1 \geq 0$ and $c_t - c_1 < m$, where $t = 4$ and (a) $m = 8$, $n = 52$ if we consider only the white notes of a piano keyboard; (b) $m = 13$, $n = 88$ if we consider also the black notes.

58. [*20*] Consider the piano player's problem of exercise 57 with the additional condition that the chords don't involve adjacent notes. (In other words, $c_{j+1} > c_j + 1$ for $t > j \geq 1$. Such chords tend to be more harmonious.)

59. [*M25*] Is there a *perfect* solution to the 4-note piano player's problem, in which each step moves a finger to an *adjacent* key?

60. [*23*] Design an algorithm to generate all *bounded* compositions

$$t = r_s + \cdots + r_1 + r_0, \qquad \text{where } 0 \leq r_j \leq m_j \text{ for } s \geq j \geq 0.$$

61. [*32*] Show that all bounded compositions can be generated by changing only two of the parts at each step.

▶ **62.** [*M27*] A *contingency table* is an $m \times n$ matrix of nonnegative integers (a_{ij}) having given row sums $r_i = \sum_{j=1}^{n} a_{ij}$ and column sums $c_j = \sum_{i=1}^{m} a_{ij}$, where $r_1 + \cdots + r_m = c_1 + \cdots + c_n$.

a) Show that $2 \times n$ contingency tables are equivalent to bounded compositions.

b) What is the lexicographically largest contingency table for $(r_1, \ldots, r_m; c_1, \ldots, c_n)$, when matrix entries are read row-wise from left to right and top to bottom, namely in the order $(a_{11}, a_{12}, \ldots, a_{1n}, a_{21}, a_{22}, \ldots, a_{2n}, \ldots, a_{m1}, a_{m2}, \ldots, a_{mn})$?

c) What is the lexicographically largest contingency table for $(r_1, \ldots, r_m; c_1, \ldots, c_n)$, when matrix entries are read column-wise from top to bottom and left to right, namely in the order $(a_{11}, a_{21}, \ldots, a_{m1}, a_{12}, a_{22}, \ldots, a_{m2}, \ldots, a_{1n}, a_{2n}, \ldots, a_{mn})$?

d) What is the lexicographically smallest contingency table for $(r_1, \ldots, r_m; c_1, \ldots, c_n)$, in the row-wise and column-wise senses?

e) Explain how to generate all contingency tables for $(r_1, \ldots, r_m; c_1, \ldots, c_n)$ in lexicographic order.

63. [*M41*] Show that all contingency tables for $(r_1, \ldots, r_m; c_1, \ldots, c_n)$ can be generated by changing exactly four entries of the matrix at each step.

▶ **64.** [*M30*] Construct a genlex Gray cycle for all of the $2^s \binom{s+t}{t}$ subcubes that have s digits and t asterisks, using only the transformations $*0 \leftrightarrow 0*$, $*1 \leftrightarrow 1*$, $0 \leftrightarrow 1$. For example, one such cycle when $s = t = 2$ is

$$(00**, 01**, 0*1*, 0**1, 0**0, 0*0*, *00*, *01*, *0*1, *0*0, **00, **01,$$
$$**11, **10, *1*0, *1*1, *11*, *10*, 1*0*, 1**0, 1**1, 1*1*, 11**, 10**).$$

65. [*M40*] Enumerate the total number of genlex Gray paths on subcubes that use only the transformations allowed in exercise 64. How many of those paths are cycles?

▶ **66.** [*22*] Given $n \geq t \geq 0$, show that there is a Gray path through all of the canonical bases $(\alpha_1, \ldots, \alpha_t)$ of exercise 12, changing just one bit at each step. For example, one such path when $n = 3$ and $t = 2$ is

$$\frac{001}{010}, \frac{101}{010}, \frac{101}{110}, \frac{001}{110}, \frac{001}{100}, \frac{011}{100}, \frac{010}{100}.$$

67. [*46*] Consider the Ising configurations of exercise 13 for which $a_0 = 0$. Given n, t, and r, is there a Gray cycle for these configurations in which all transitions have the forms $0^k1 \leftrightarrow 10^k$ or $01^k \leftrightarrow 1^k0$? For example, in the case $n = 9$, $t = 5$, $r = 6$, there is a unique cycle

$$(010101110, 010110110, 011010110, 011011010, 011101010, 010111010).$$

68. [*M01*] If α is a t-combination, what is (a) $\partial^t \alpha$? (b) $\partial^{t+1} \alpha$?

▶ **69.** [*M22*] How large is the smallest set A of t-combinations for which $|\partial A| < |A|$?

70. [*M25*] What is the maximum value of $\kappa_t N - N$, for $N \geq 0$?

71. [*M20*] How many t-cliques can a million-edge graph have?

▶ **72.** [*M22*] Show that if N has the degree-t combinatorial representation (57), there is an easy way to find the degree-s combinatorial representation of the complementary number $M = \binom{s+t}{t} - N$, whenever $N < \binom{s+t}{t}$. Derive (63) as a consequence.

73. [*M23*] (A. J. W. Hilton, 1976.) Let A be a set of s-combinations and B a set of t-combinations, both contained in $U = \{0, \ldots, n-1\}$ where $n \geq s+t$. Show that if A and B are *cross-intersecting*, in the sense that $\alpha \cap \beta \neq \emptyset$ for all $\alpha \in A$ and $\beta \in B$, then so are the sets Q_{Mns} and Q_{Nnt} defined in Theorem K, where $M = |A|$ and $N = |B|$.

74. [*M21*] What are $|\varrho P_{Nt}|$ and $|\varrho Q_{Nnt}|$ in Theorem K?

75. [*M20*] The right-hand side of (60) is not always the degree-$(t-1)$ combinatorial representation of $\kappa_t N$, because $v-1$ might be zero. Show, however, that a positive integer N has at most two representations if we allow $v=0$ in (57), and both of them yield the same value $\kappa_t N$ according to (60). Therefore

$$\kappa_k \kappa_{k+1} \ldots \kappa_t N = \binom{n_t}{k-1} + \binom{n_{t-1}}{k-2} + \cdots + \binom{n_v}{k-1+v-t} \qquad \text{for } 1 \le k \le t.$$

76. [*M20*] Find a simple formula for $\kappa_t(N+1) - \kappa_t N$.

▸ **77.** [*M26*] Prove the following properties of the κ functions by manipulating binomial coefficients, without assuming Theorem K:
 a) $\kappa_t(M+N) \le \kappa_t M + \kappa_t N$.
 b) $\kappa_t(M+N) \le \max(\kappa_t M, N) + \kappa_{t-1} N$.
Hint: $\binom{m_t}{t} + \cdots + \binom{m_1}{1} + \binom{n_t}{t} + \cdots + \binom{n_1}{1}$ is equal to $\binom{m_t \vee n_t}{t} + \cdots + \binom{m_1 \vee n_1}{1} + \binom{m_t \wedge n_t}{t} + \cdots + \binom{m_1 \wedge n_1}{1}$, where $\vee$ and $\wedge$ denote max and min.

78. [*M22*] Show that Theorem K follows easily from inequality (b) in the previous exercise. Conversely, both inequalities are simple consequences of Theorem K. *Hint:* Any set A of t-combinations can be written $A = A_1 + A_0 0$, where $A_1 = \{\alpha \in A \mid 0 \notin \alpha\}$.

79. [*M23*] Prove that if $t \ge 2$, we have $M \ge \mu_t N$ if and only if $M + \lambda_{t-1} M \ge N$.

80. [*HM26*] (L. Lovász, 1979.) The function $\binom{x}{t}$ increases monotonically from 0 to ∞ as x increases from $t-1$ to ∞; hence we can define

$$\underline{\kappa}_t N = \binom{x}{t-1}, \qquad \text{if } N = \binom{x}{t} \text{ and } x \ge t-1.$$

Prove that $\kappa_t N \ge \underline{\kappa}_t N$ for all integers $t \ge 1$ and $N \ge 0$. *Hint:* Equality holds when x is an integer.

▸ **81.** [*M27*] Show that the minimum shadow sizes in Theorem M are given by (64).

82. [*HM31*] The Takagi function of Fig. 47 is defined for $0 \le x \le 1$ by the formula

$$\tau(x) = \sum_{k=1}^{\infty} \int_0^x r_k(t)\,dt,$$

where $r_k(t) = (-1)^{\lfloor 2^k t \rfloor}$ is the Rademacher function of Eq. 7.2.1.1–(16).
 a) Prove that $\tau(x)$ is continuous in the interval $[0..1]$, but its derivative does not exist at any point.
 b) Show that $\tau(x)$ is the only continuous function that satisfies

$$\tau(\tfrac{1}{2}x) = \tau(1-\tfrac{1}{2}x) = \tfrac{1}{2}x + \tfrac{1}{2}\tau(x) \qquad \text{for } 0 \le x \le 1.$$

 c) What is the asymptotic value of $\tau(\epsilon)$ when ϵ is small?
 d) Prove that $\tau(x)$ is rational when x is rational.
 e) Find all roots of the equation $\tau(x) = 1/2$.
 f) Find all roots of the equation $\tau(x) = \max_{0 \le x \le 1} \tau(x)$.

83. [*HM46*] Determine the set R of all rational numbers r such that the equation $\tau(x) = r$ has uncountably many solutions. If $\tau(x)$ is rational and x is irrational, is it true that $\tau(x) \in R$? (*Warning:* This problem can be addictive.)

84. [*HM27*] If $T = \binom{2t-1}{t}$, prove the asymptotic formula

$$\kappa_t N - N = \frac{T}{t}\left(\tau\left(\frac{N}{T}\right) + O\left(\frac{(\log t)^3}{t}\right)\right) \qquad \text{for } 0 \le N \le T.$$

85. [*HM21*] Relate the functions $\lambda_t N$ and $\mu_t N$ to the Takagi function $\tau(x)$.

86. [*M20*] Prove the law of spread/core duality, $X^{\sim+} = X^{\circ\sim}$.

87. [*M21*] True or false: (a) $X \subseteq Y^\circ$ if and only if $Y^\sim \subseteq X^{\sim\circ}$; (b) $X^{\circ+\circ} = X^\circ$; (c) $\alpha M \leq N$ if and only if $M \leq \beta N$.

88. [*M20*] Explain why cross order is useful, by completing the proof of Lemma S.

89. [*16*] Compute the α and β functions for the $2 \times 2 \times 3$ torus (69).

90. [*M22*] Prove the basic compression lemma, (85).

91. [*M24*] Prove Theorem W for two-dimensional toruses $T(l, m)$, $l \leq m$.

92. [*M28*] Let $x = x_1 \ldots x_{n-1}$ be the Nth element of the torus $T(m_1, \ldots, m_{n-1})$, and let S be the set of all elements of $T(m_1, \ldots, m_{n-1}, m)$ that are $\preceq x_1 \ldots x_{n-1}(m-1)$ in cross order. If N_a elements of S have final component a, for $0 \leq a < m$, prove that $N_{m-1} = N$ and $N_{a-1} = \alpha N_a$ for $1 \leq a < m$, where α is the spread function for standard sets in $T(m_1, \ldots, m_{n-1})$.

93. [*M25*] (a) Find an N for which the conclusion of Theorem W is false when the parameters $m_1, m_2, \ldots, m_n$ have not been sorted into nondecreasing order. (b) Where does the proof of that theorem use the hypothesis that $m_1 \leq m_2 \leq \cdots \leq m_n$?

94. [*M20*] Show that the ∂ half of Corollary C follows from the ϱ half. *Hint:* The complements of the multicombinations (92) with respect to U are 3211, 3210, 3200, 3110, 3100, 3000, 2110, 2100, 2000, 1100, 1000.

95. [*17*] Explain why Theorems K and M follow from Corollary C.

▶ **96.** [*M22*] If S is an infinite sequence $(s_0, s_1, s_2, \ldots)$ of positive integers, let

$$\binom{S(n)}{k} = [z^k] \prod_{j=0}^{n-1} (1 + z + \cdots + z^{s_j});$$

thus $\binom{S(n)}{k}$ is the ordinary binomial coefficient $\binom{n}{k}$ if $s_0 = s_1 = s_2 = \cdots = 1$.

Generalizing the combinatorial number system, show that every nonnegative integer N has a unique representation

$$N = \binom{S(n_t)}{t} + \binom{S(n_{t-1})}{t-1} + \cdots + \binom{S(n_1)}{1}$$

where $n_t \geq n_{t-1} \geq \cdots \geq n_1 \geq 0$ and $\{n_t, n_{t-1}, \ldots, n_1\} \subseteq \{s_0 \cdot 0, s_1 \cdot 1, s_2 \cdot 2, \ldots\}$. Use this representation to give a simple formula for the numbers $|\partial P_{Nt}|$ in Corollary C.

▶ **97.** [*M26*] The text remarked that the vertices of a convex polyhedron can be perturbed slightly so that all of its faces are simplexes. In general, any set of combinations that contains the shadows of all its elements is called a *simplicial complex*; thus C is a simplicial complex if and only if $\alpha \subseteq \beta$ and $\beta \in C$ implies that $\alpha \in C$, if and only if C is an order ideal with respect to set inclusion.

The *size vector* of a simplicial complex C on n vertices is $(N_0, N_1, \ldots, N_n)$ when C contains exactly N_t combinations of size t.

  a) What are the size vectors of the five regular solids (the tetrahedron, cube, octahedron, dodecahedron, and icosahedron), when their vertices are slightly tweaked?

  b) Construct a simplicial complex with size vector $(1, 4, 5, 2, 0)$.

  c) Find a necessary and sufficient condition that a given size vector $(N_0, N_1, \ldots, N_n)$ is feasible.

  d) Prove that $(N_0, \ldots, N_n)$ is feasible if and only its "dual" vector $(\overline{N}_0, \ldots, \overline{N}_n)$ is feasible, where we define $\overline{N}_t = \binom{n}{t} - N_{n-t}$.

e) List all feasible size vectors $(N_0, N_1, N_2, N_3, N_4)$ and their duals. Which of them are self-dual?

98. [*30*] Continuing exercise 97, find an efficient way to count the feasible size vectors $(N_0, N_1, \ldots, N_n)$ when $n \leq 100$.

99. [*M25*] A *clutter* is a set C of combinations that are incomparable, in the sense that $\alpha \subseteq \beta$ and $\alpha, \beta \in C$ implies $\alpha = \beta$. The size vector of a clutter is defined as in exercise 97.

a) Find a necessary and sufficient condition that $(M_0, M_1, \ldots, M_n)$ is the size vector of a clutter.

b) List all such size vectors in the case $n = 4$.

▶ **100.** [*M30*] (Clements and Lindström.) Let A be a "simplicial multicomplex," a set of submultisets of the multiset U in Corollary C with the property that $\partial A \subseteq A$. How large can the total weight $\nu A = \sum \{|\alpha| \mid \alpha \in A\}$ be when $|A| = N$?

101. [*M25*] If $f(x_1, \ldots, x_n)$ is a Boolean formula, let $F(p)$ be the probability that $f(x_1, \ldots, x_n) = 1$ when each variable x_j independently is 1 with probability p.

a) Calculate $G(p)$ and $H(p)$ for the Boolean formulas $g(w, x, y, z) = wxz \vee wyz \vee xy\bar{z}$, $h(w, x, y, z) = \bar{w}yz \vee xyz$.

b) Show that there is a *monotone* Boolean function $f(w, x, y, z)$ such that $F(p) = G(p)$, but there is no such function with $F(p) = H(p)$. Explain how to test this condition in general.

102. [*HM35*] (F. S. Macaulay, 1927.) A *polynomial ideal* I in the variables $\{x_1 \ldots, x_s\}$ is a set of polynomials closed under the operations of addition, multiplication by a constant, and multiplication by any of the variables. It is called *homogeneous* if it consists of all linear combinations of a set of homogeneous polynomials, namely of polynomials like $xy + z^2$ whose terms all have the same degree. Let N_t be the maximum number of linearly independent elements of degree t in I. For example, if $s = 2$, the set of all $\alpha(x_0, x_1, x_2)(x_0 x_1^2 - 2x_1 x_2^2) + \beta(x_0, x_1, x_2)x_0 x_1 x_2^2$, where α and β run through all possible polynomials in $\{x_0, x_1, x_2\}$, is a homogeneous polynomial ideal with $N_0 = N_1 = N_2 = 0$, $N_3 = 1$, $N_4 = 4$, $N_5 = 9$, $N_6 = 15$, ...

a) Prove that for any such ideal I there is another ideal I' in which all homogeneous polynomials of degree t are linear combinations of N_t independent *monomials*. (A monomial is a product of variables, like $x_1^3 x_2 x_5^4$.)

b) Use Theorem M and (64) to prove that $N_{t+1} \geq N_t + \kappa_s N_t$ for all $t \geq 0$.

c) Show that $N_{t+1} > N_t + \kappa_s N_t$ occurs for only finitely many t. (This statement is equivalent to "Hilbert's basis theorem," proved by David Hilbert in *Göttinger Nachrichten* (1888), 450–457; *Math. Annalen* **36** (1890), 473–534.)

▶ **103.** [*M38*] The shadow of a subcube $a_1 \ldots a_n$, where each a_j is either 0 or 1 or *, is obtained by replacing some * by 0 or 1. For example,

$$\partial 0*11*0 = \{0011*0, 0111*0, 0*1100, 0*1110\}.$$

Find a set P_{Nst} such that, if A is any set of N subcubes $a_1 \ldots a_n$ having s digits and t asterisks, $|\partial A| \geq |P_{Nst}|$.

104. [*M41*] The shadow of a binary string $a_1 \ldots a_n$ is obtained by deleting one of its bits. For example,

$$\partial 110010010 = \{10010010, 11010010, 11000010, 11001000, 11001010, 11001001\}.$$

Find a set P_{Nn} such that, if A is any set of N binary strings $a_1 \ldots a_n$, $|\partial A| \geq |P_{Nn}|$.

105. [*M20*] A *universal cycle of t-combinations* for $\{0, 1, \ldots, n-1\}$ is a cycle of $\binom{n}{t}$ numbers whose blocks of t consecutive elements run through every t-combination $\{c_1, \ldots, c_t\}$. For example,

$$(0214506132051624315263042536410354 6)$$

is a universal cycle when $t = 3$ and $n = 7$.

Prove that no such cycle is possible unless $\binom{n}{t}$ is a multiple of n.

106. [*M21*] (L. Poinsot, 1809.) Find a "nice" universal cycle of 2-combinations for $\{0, 1, \ldots, 2m\}$. *Hint:* Consider the differences of consecutive elements, mod $(2m+1)$.

107. [*22*] (O. Terquem, 1849.) Poinsot's theorem implies that all 28 dominoes of a traditional "double-six" set can be arranged in a cycle so that the spots of adjacent dominoes match each other:

How many such cycles are possible?

108. [*M31*] Find universal cycles of 3-combinations for the sets $\{0, \ldots, n-1\}$ when $n \bmod 3 \neq 0$.

109. [*M31*] Find universal cycles of 3-*multicombinations* for $\{0, 1, \ldots, n-1\}$ when $n \bmod 3 \neq 0$ (namely for combinations $d_1 d_2 d_3$ with repetitions permitted). For example,

$$(00012241112330222344133340024440113)$$

is such a cycle when $n = 5$.

▶ **110.** [*26*] *Cribbage* is a game played with 52 cards, where each card has a suit ($\clubsuit$, $\diamondsuit$, $\heartsuit$, or $\spadesuit$) and a face value (A, 2, 3, 4, 5, 6, 7, 8, 9, 10, J, Q, or K). Its players must become adept at computing the score of a 5-card combination $C = \{c_1, c_2, c_3, c_4, c_5\}$, where one card c_k is called the *starter*. The score is the sum of points computed as follows, for each subset S of C and each choice of k: Let $|S| = s$.

   i) Fifteens: If $\sum\{v(c) \mid c \in S\} = 15$, where $(v(\mathtt{A}), v(2), v(3), \ldots, v(9), v(10), v(\mathtt{J}), v(\mathtt{Q}), v(\mathtt{K})) = (1, 2, 3, \ldots, 9, 10, 10, 10, 10)$, score two points.
   ii) Pairs: If $s = 2$ and both cards have the same face value, score two points.
   iii) Runs: If $s \geq 3$ and the face values are consecutive, and if C does not contain a run of length $s + 1$, score s points.
   iv) Flushes: If $s = 4$ and all cards of S have the same suit, and if $c_k \notin S$, score $4 + [c_k$ has the same suit as the others].
   v) Nobs: If $s = 1$ and $c_k \notin S$, score 1 if the card is J of the same suit as c_k.

For example, if you hold $\{\mathtt{J}\clubsuit, 5\clubsuit, 5\diamondsuit, 6\heartsuit\}$ and if $4\clubsuit$ is the starter, you score 4×2 for fifteens, 2 for a pair, 2×3 for runs, plus 1 for nobs, totalling 17.

Exactly how many combinations and starter choices lead to a score of x points, for $x = 0, 1, 2, \ldots$?

▶ **111.** [*M26*] (P. Erdős, C. Ko, and R. Rado.) Suppose A is a set of r-combinations of an n-set, with $\alpha \cap \beta \neq \emptyset$ whenever $\alpha, \beta \in A$. Show that $|A| \leq \binom{n-1}{r-1}$, if $r \leq n/2$. *Hint:* Consider $\partial^{n-2r} B$, where B is the set of complements of A.

7.2.1.4. Generating all partitions. Richard Stanley's magnificent book *Enumerative Combinatorics* (1986) begins by discussing The Twelvefold Way, a $2 \times 2 \times 3$ array of basic combinatorial problems that arise frequently in practice (see Table 1), based on a series of lectures by Gian-Carlo Rota. All twelve of these basic problems can be described in terms of the ways that a given number of balls can be placed into a given number of urns. For example, there are nine ways to put 2 balls into 3 urns if the balls and urns are labeled:

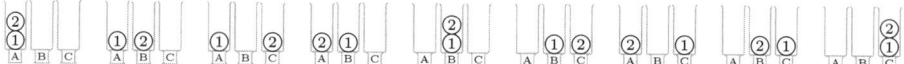

(The order of balls *within* an urn is ignored.) But if the balls are unlabeled, some of these arrangements are indistinguishable, so only six different ways are possible:

$$ \tag{1} $$

If the urns are unlabeled, arrangements like and are essentially the same, hence only two of the original nine arrangements are distinguishable. And if we have three labeled balls, the only distinct ways to place them into three unlabeled urns are

$$ \tag{2} $$

Finally, if neither balls nor urns are labeled, these five possibilities reduce to only three:

$$ \tag{3} $$

The Twelvefold Way considers all arrangements that are possible when balls and urns are labeled or unlabeled, and when the urns may optionally be required to contain at least one ball or at most one ball.

Table 1

THE TWELVEFOLD WAY

balls per urn	unrestricted	≤ 1	≥ 1
n labeled balls, m labeled urns	n-tuples of m things	n-permutations of m things	partitions of $\{1, \ldots, n\}$ into m ordered parts
n unlabeled balls, m labeled urns	n-multicombinations of m things	n-combinations of m things	compositions of n into m parts
n labeled balls, m unlabeled urns	partitions of $\{1, \ldots, n\}$ into $\leq m$ parts	n pigeons into m holes	partitions of $\{1, \ldots, n\}$ into m parts
n unlabeled balls, m unlabeled urns	partitions of n into $\leq m$ parts	n pigeons into m holes	partitions of n into m parts

We've learned about n-tuples, permutations, combinations, and composi-tions in previous sections of this chapter; and two of the twelve entries in Table 1 are trivial (namely the ones related to "pigeons"). So we can complete our study of classical combinatorial mathematics by learning about the remaining five entries in the table, which all involve *partitions*.

> *Let us begin by acknowledging that the word "partition"*
> *has numerous meanings in mathematics.*
> *Any time a division of some object into subobjects is undertaken,*
> *the word partition is likely to pop up.*
> — GEORGE ANDREWS, *The Theory of Partitions* (1976)

Two quite different concepts share the same name: The *partitions of a set* are the ways to subdivide it into nonempty, disjoint subsets; thus (2) illustrates the five partitions of $\{1, 2, 3\}$, namely

$$\{1,2,3\}, \qquad \{1,2\}\{3\}, \qquad \{1,3\}\{2\}, \qquad \{1\}\{2,3\}, \qquad \{1\}\{2\}\{3\}. \qquad (4)$$

And the *partitions of an integer* are the ways to write it as a sum of positive integers, disregarding order; thus (3) illustrates the three partitions of 3, namely

$$3, \qquad\qquad 2+1, \qquad\qquad 1+1+1. \qquad (5)$$

We shall follow the common practice of referring to integer partitions as simply "partitions," without any qualifying adjective; the other kind will be called "set partitions" in what follows, to make the distinction clear. Both kinds of partitions are important, so we'll study each of them in turn.

Generating all partitions of an integer. A partition of n can be defined formally as a sequence of nonnegative integers $a_1 \geq a_2 \geq \cdots$ such that $n = a_1 + a_2 + \cdots$; for example, one partition of 7 has $a_1 = a_2 = 3$, $a_3 = 1$, and $a_4 = a_5 = \cdots = 0$. The number of nonzero terms is called the number of *parts*, and the zero terms are usually suppressed. Thus we write $7 = 3 + 3 + 1$, or simply 331 to save space when the context is clear.

The simplest way to generate all partitions, and one of the fastest, is to visit them in reverse lexicographic order, starting with 'n' and ending with '$11\ldots1$'. For example, the partitions of 8 are

$$8, 71, 62, 611, 53, 521, 5111, 44, 431, 422, 4211, 41111, 332, 3311, \qquad (6)$$
$$3221, 32111, 311111, 2222, 22211, 221111, 2111111, 11111111,$$

when listed in this order.

If a partition isn't all 1s, it ends with $(x{+}1)$ followed by zero or more 1s, for some $x \geq 1$; therefore the next smallest partition in lexicographic order is obtained by replacing the suffix $(x{+}1)1\ldots1$ by $x\ldots xr$ for some appropri-ate remainder $r \leq x$. The process is quite efficient if we keep track of the largest subscript q such that $a_q \neq 1$, as suggested by J. K. S. McKay [*CACM* **13** (1970), 52], and pad the array with 1s as suggested by A. Zoghbi and I. Stojmenović [*International Journal of Computer Math.* **70** (1998), 319–332]:

Algorithm P (*Partitions of n in reverse lexicographic order*). Given an integer $n \geq 1$, this algorithm generates all partitions $a_1 \geq a_2 \geq \cdots \geq a_m \geq 1$ with $a_1 + a_2 + \cdots + a_m = n$ and $1 \leq m \leq n$. The value of a_0 is also set to zero.

P1. [Initialize.] Set $a_m \leftarrow 1$ for $n \geq m > 1$. Then set $m \leftarrow 1$ and $a_0 \leftarrow 0$.

P2. [Store the final part.] Set $a_m \leftarrow n$ and $q \leftarrow m - [n=1]$.

P3. [Visit.] Visit the partition $a_1 a_2 \ldots a_m$. Then go to P5 if $a_q \neq 2$.

P4. [Change 2 to 1+1.] Set $a_q \leftarrow 1$, $q \leftarrow q - 1$, $m \leftarrow m + 1$, and return to P3. (At this point we have $a_k = 1$ for $q < k \leq n$.)

P5. [Decrease a_q.] Terminate the algorithm if $q = 0$. Otherwise set $x \leftarrow a_q - 1$, $a_q \leftarrow x$, $n \leftarrow m - q + 1$, and $m \leftarrow q + 1$.

P6. [Copy x if necessary.] If $n \leq x$, return to step P2. Otherwise set $a_m \leftarrow x$, $m \leftarrow m + 1$, $n \leftarrow n - x$, and repeat this step. ∎

Notice that the operation of going from one partition to the next is particularly easy if a 2 is present; then step P4 simply changes the rightmost 2 to a 1 and appends another 1 at the right. This happy situation is, fortunately, the most common case. For example, nearly 79% of all partitions contain a 2 when $n = 100$.

Another simple algorithm is available when we want to generate all partitions of n into a fixed number of parts. The following method, which was featured in C. F. Hindenburg's 18th-century dissertation [*Infinitinomii Dignitatum Exponentis Indeterminati* (Göttingen, 1779), 73–91], visits the partitions in *colex* order, namely in lexicographic order of the reflected sequence $a_m \ldots a_2 a_1$:

Algorithm H (*Partitions of n into m parts*). Given integers $n \geq m \geq 2$, this algorithm generates all integer m-tuples $a_1 \ldots a_m$ such that $a_1 \geq \cdots \geq a_m \geq 1$ and $a_1 + \cdots + a_m = n$. A sentinel value is stored in a_{m+1}.

H1. [Initialize.] Set $a_1 \leftarrow n - m + 1$ and $a_j \leftarrow 1$ for $1 < j \leq m$. Also set $a_{m+1} \leftarrow -1$.

H2. [Visit.] Visit the partition $a_1 \ldots a_m$. Then go to H4 if $a_2 \geq a_1 - 1$.

H3. [Tweak a_1 and a_2.] Set $a_1 \leftarrow a_1 - 1$, $a_2 \leftarrow a_2 + 1$, and return to H2.

H4. [Find j.] Set $j \leftarrow 3$ and $s \leftarrow a_1 + a_2 - 1$. Then, while $a_j \geq a_1 - 1$, set $s \leftarrow s + a_j$ and $j \leftarrow j + 1$. (Now $s = a_1 + \cdots + a_{j-1} - 1$ and $a_j < a_1 - 1$.)

H5. [Increase a_j.] Terminate if $j > m$. Otherwise set $x \leftarrow a_j + 1$, $a_j \leftarrow x$, $j \leftarrow j - 1$.

H6. [Tweak $a_1 \ldots a_j$.] While $j > 1$, set $a_j \leftarrow x$, $s \leftarrow s - x$, and $j \leftarrow j - 1$. Finally set $a_1 \leftarrow s$ and return to H2. ∎

For example, when $n = 11$ and $m = 4$ the successive partitions visited are

$$8111, \ 7211, \ 6311, \ 5411, \ 6221, \ 5321, \ 4421, \ 4331, \ 5222, \ 4322, \ 3332. \qquad (7)$$

The basic idea is that colex order goes from one partition $a_1 \ldots a_m$ to the next by finding the smallest j such that a_j can be increased without changing $a_{j+1} \ldots a_m$. The new partition $a_1' \ldots a_m'$ will have $a_1' \geq \cdots \geq a_j' = a_j + 1$ and $a_1' + \cdots + a_j' =$

$a_1 + \cdots + a_j$, and these conditions are achievable if and only if $a_j < a_1 - 1$. Furthermore, the smallest such partition $a'_1 \ldots a'_m$ in colex order has $a'_2 = \cdots = a'_j = a_j + 1$.

Step H3 handles the simple case $j = 2$, which is by far the most common. And indeed, the value of j almost always turns out to be quite small; we will prove later that the total running time of Algorithm H is at most a small constant times the number of partitions visited, plus $O(m)$.

Other representations of partitions. We've defined a partition as a sequence of nonnegative integers $a_1 a_2 \ldots$ with $a_1 \geq a_2 \geq \cdots$ and $a_1 + a_2 + \cdots = n$, but we can also regard it as an n-tuple of nonnegative integers $c_1 c_2 \ldots c_n$ such that

$$c_1 + 2c_2 + \cdots + nc_n = n. \tag{8}$$

Here c_j is the number of times the integer j appears in the sequence $a_1 a_2 \ldots$; for example, the partition 331 corresponds to the counts $c_1 = 1$, $c_2 = 0$, $c_3 = 2$, $c_4 = c_5 = c_6 = c_7 = 0$. The number of parts is then $c_1 + c_2 + \cdots + c_n$. A procedure analogous to Algorithm P can readily be devised to generate partitions in part-count form; see exercise 5.

We have already seen the part-count representation implicitly in formulas like Eq. 1.2.9–(38), which expresses the symmetric function

$$h_n = \sum_{N \geq d_n \geq \cdots \geq d_2 \geq d_1 \geq 1} x_{d_1} x_{d_2} \ldots x_{d_n} \tag{9}$$

as

$$\sum_{\substack{c_1, c_2, \ldots, c_n \geq 0 \\ c_1 + 2c_2 + \cdots + nc_n = n}} \frac{S_1^{c_1}}{1^{c_1} c_1!} \frac{S_2^{c_2}}{2^{c_2} c_2!} \cdots \frac{S_n^{c_n}}{n^{c_n} c_n!}, \tag{10}$$

where S_j is the symmetric function $x_1^j + x_2^j + \cdots + x_N^j$. The sum in (9) is essentially taken over all n-multicombinations of N things, while the sum in (10) is taken over all partitions of n. Thus, for example, $h_3 = \frac{1}{6}S_1^3 + \frac{1}{2}S_1 S_2 + \frac{1}{3}S_3$, and when $N = 2$ we have

$$x^3 + x^2 y + xy^2 + y^3 = \tfrac{1}{6}(x+y)^3 + \tfrac{1}{2}(x+y)(x^2 + y^2) + \tfrac{1}{3}(x^3 + y^3).$$

Other sums over partitions appear in exercises 1.2.5–21, 1.2.9–10, 1.2.9–11, 1.2.10–12, etc.; for this reason partitions are of central importance in the study of symmetric functions, a class of functions that pervades mathematics in general. [Chapter 7 of Richard Stanley's *Enumerative Combinatorics 2* (1999) is an excellent introduction to advanced aspects of symmetric function theory.]

Partitions can be visualized in an appealing way by considering an array of n dots, having a_1 dots in the top row and a_2 in the next row, etc. Such an arrangement of dots is called the *Ferrers diagram* of the partition, in honor of N. M. Ferrers [see *Philosophical Mag.* **5** (1853), 199–202]; and the largest square subarray of dots that it contains is called the *Durfee square*, after W. P. Durfee [see *Johns Hopkins Univ. Circular* **2** (December 1882), 23]. For example, the Ferrers diagram of 8887211 is shown with its 4×4 Durfee square in Fig. 48(a).

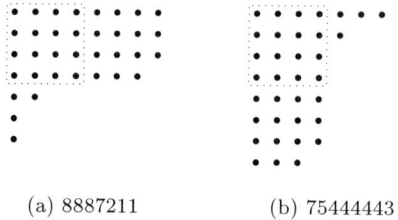

Fig. 48. The Ferrers diagrams and Durfee squares of two conjugate partitions.

(a) 8887211   (b) 75444443

The Durfee square contains k^2 dots when k is the largest subscript such that $a_k \geq k$; we may call k the *trace* of the partition.

If α is any partition $a_1 a_2 \ldots$, its *conjugate* $\alpha^T = b_1 b_2 \ldots$ is obtained by transposing its Ferrers diagram — that is, by reflecting the diagram about the main diagonal. For example, Fig. 48(b) shows that $(8887211)^T = 75444443$. When $\beta = \alpha^T$ we obviously have $\alpha = \beta^T$; the partition β has a_1 parts and α has b_1 parts. Indeed, there's a simple relation between the part-count representation $c_1 \ldots c_n$ of α and the conjugate partition $b_1 b_2 \ldots$, namely

$$b_j - b_{j+1} = c_j \qquad \text{for all } j \geq 1. \tag{11}$$

This relation makes it easy to compute the conjugate of a given partition, or to write it down by inspection (see exercise 6).

The notion of conjugation often explains properties of partitions that would otherwise be quite mysterious. For example, now that we know the definition of α^T, we can easily see that the value of $j - 1$ in step H5 of Algorithm H is just the second-smallest part of the conjugate partition $(a_1 \ldots a_m)^T$, if $m < n$. Therefore the average amount of work that needs to be done in steps H4 and H6 is essentially proportional to the average size of the second-smallest part of a random partition whose largest part is m. And we will see below that the second-smallest part is almost always quite small.

Moreover, *Algorithm H produces partitions in lexicographic order of their conjugates.* For example, the respective conjugates of (7) are

$$41111111,\ 4211111,\ 422111,\ 42221,\ 431111,$$
$$43211,\ 4322,\ 4331,\ 44111,\ 4421,\ 443; \tag{12}$$

these are the partitions of $n = 11$ with largest part 4. One way to generate all partitions of n is to start with the trivial partition 'n', then run Algorithm H for $m = 2, 3, \ldots, n$ in turn; this process yields all α in lexicographic order of α^T (see exercise 7). Thus Algorithm H can be regarded as a dual of Algorithm P.

There is at least one more useful way to represent partitions, called the *rim representation* [see S. Comét, *Numer. Math.* **1** (1959), 90–109]. Suppose we replace the dots of a Ferrers diagram by boxes, thereby obtaining a tableau shape as we did in Section 5.1.4; for example, the partition 8887211 of Fig. 48(a) becomes

$$\tag{13}$$

The right-hand boundary of this shape can be regarded as a path of length $2n$ from the lower left corner to the upper right corner of an $n \times n$ square, and we know from Table 7.2.1.3–1 that such a path corresponds to an (n, n)-combination.

For example, (13) corresponds to the 70-bit string

$$0 \ldots 0 1001011111010001 \ldots 1 \; = \; 0^{28}1^10^21^10^11^50^11^10^31^{27}, \qquad (14)$$

where we place enough 0s at the beginning and 1s at the end to make exactly n of each. The 0s represent upward steps of the path, and the 1s represent rightward steps. It is easy to see that the bit string defined in this way has exactly n inversions; conversely, every permutation of the multiset $\{n \cdot 0, \; n \cdot 1\}$ that has exactly n inversions corresponds to a partition of n. When the number of distinct parts of a partition is equal to t, its bit string can be written in the form

$$0^{n-q_1-q_2-\cdots-q_t}1^{p_1}0^{q_1}1^{p_2}0^{q_2} \ldots 1^{p_t}0^{q_t}1^{n-p_1-p_2-\cdots-p_t}, \qquad (15)$$

where the exponents p_j and q_j are positive integers. Then the partition's standard representation is

$$a_1 a_2 \ldots \; = \; (p_1 + \cdots + p_t)^{q_t} (p_1 + \cdots + p_{t-1})^{q_{t-1}} \ldots (p_1)^{q_1}, \qquad (16)$$

namely $(1+1+5+1)^3(1+1+5)^1(1+1)^1(1)^2 = 8887211$ in our example.

The number of partitions. Inspired by a question that was posed to him by Philippe Naudé in 1740, Leonhard Euler wrote two fundamental papers in which he counted partitions of various kinds by studying their generating functions [*Commentarii Academiæ Scientiarum Petropolitanæ* **13** (1741), 64–93; *Novi Comment. Acad. Sci. Pet.* **3** (1750), 125–169]. He observed that the coefficient of z^n in the infinite product

$$(1+z+z^2+\cdots+z^j+\cdots)(1+z^2+z^4+\cdots+z^{2k}+\cdots)(1+z^3+z^6+\cdots+z^{3l}+\cdots)\ldots$$

is the number of nonnegative integer solutions to the equation $j+2k+3l+\cdots = n$; and $1 + z^m + z^{2m} + \cdots$ is $1/(1 - z^m)$. Therefore if we write

$$P(z) \; = \; \prod_{m=1}^{\infty} \frac{1}{1 - z^m} \; = \; \sum_{n=0}^{\infty} p(n) z^n, \qquad (17)$$

the number of partitions of n is $p(n)$. This function $P(z)$ turns out to have an amazing number of subtle mathematical properties.

For example, Euler discovered that massive cancellation occurs when the denominator of $P(z)$ is multiplied out:

$$(1-z)(1-z^2)(1-z^3)\ldots \; = \; 1 - z - z^2 + z^5 + z^7 - z^{12} - z^{15} + z^{22} + z^{26} - \cdots$$

$$= \; \sum_{-\infty < n < \infty} (-1)^n z^{(3n^2+n)/2}. \qquad (18)$$

A combinatorial proof of this remarkable identity, based on Ferrers diagrams, appears in exercise 5.1.1–14; we can also prove it by setting $u = z$ and $v = z^2$ in

396 COMBINATORIAL SEARCHING 7.2.1.4

the even more remarkable identity that Jacobi published in 1829,

$$\prod_{k=1}^{\infty}(1 - u^k v^{k-1})(1 - u^{k-1}v^k)(1 - u^k v^k) = \sum_{n=-\infty}^{\infty}(-1)^n u^{\binom{n}{2}} v^{\binom{-n}{2}}, \quad (19)$$

because the left-hand side becomes $\prod_{k=1}^{\infty}(1 - z^{3k-2})(1 - z^{3k-1})(1 - z^{3k})$; see exercise 5.1.1–20. Euler pointed out that, because of (18), the partition numbers for $n > 0$ satisfy the unusual recurrence

$$p(n) = p(n-1) + p(n-2) - p(n-5) - p(n-7) + p(n-12) + p(n-15) - \cdots, \quad (20)$$

with $p(k) = 0$ when $k < 0$; this recurrence allows us to compute their values more rapidly than by performing the power series calculations in (17):

$n =$	0	1	2	3	4	5	6	7	8	9	10	11	12	13	14	15
$p(n) =$	1	1	2	3	5	7	11	15	22	30	42	56	77	101	135	176

We know from Section 1.2.8 that solutions to the Fibonacci recurrence $f(n) = f(n-1) + f(n-2)$ grow exponentially, with $f(n) = \Theta(\phi^n)$ when $f(0)$ and $f(1)$ are positive. The additional terms '$- p(n-5) - p(n-7)$' in (20) have a dampening effect on partition numbers, however; in fact, if we were to stop the recurrence there, the resulting sequence would oscillate between positive and negative values. Further terms '$+p(n-12)+p(n-15)$' reinstate exponential growth.

The actual growth rate of $p(n)$ turns out to be of order $A^{\sqrt{n}}/n$ for a certain constant A. For example, exercise 33 proves directly that $p(n)$ grows at least as fast as $e^{2\sqrt{n}}/n$. And one fairly easy way to obtain a decent *upper* bound is to take logarithms in (17),

$$\ln P(z) = \sum_{m=1}^{\infty}\ln\frac{1}{1 - z^m} = \sum_{m=1}^{\infty}\sum_{n=1}^{\infty}\frac{z^{mn}}{n}, \quad (21)$$

and then to look at the behavior near $z = 1$ by setting $z = e^{-t}$ with $t > 0$:

$$\ln P(e^{-t}) = \sum_{m,n\geq 1}\frac{e^{-mnt}}{n} = \sum_{n\geq 1}\frac{1}{n}\frac{1}{e^{tn}-1} < \sum_{n\geq 1}\frac{1}{n^2 t} = \frac{\zeta(2)}{t}. \quad (22)$$

Consequently, since $p(n) \leq p(n+1) < p(n+2) < \cdots$ and $e^t > 1$, we have

$$\frac{p(n)}{1 - e^{-t}} = \sum_{k=n}^{\infty}p(n)e^{(n-k)t} < \sum_{k=0}^{\infty}p(k)e^{(n-k)t} = e^{nt}P(e^{-t}) < e^{nt+\zeta(2)/t} \quad (23)$$

for all $t > 0$. Setting $t = \sqrt{\zeta(2)/n}$ gives

$$p(n) < Ce^{2C\sqrt{n}}/\sqrt{n}, \qquad \text{where } C = \sqrt{\zeta(2)} = \pi/\sqrt{6}. \quad (24)$$

We can obtain more accurate information about the size of $\ln P(e^{-t})$ by using Euler's summation formula (Section 1.2.11.2) or Mellin transforms (Section 5.2.2); see exercise 25. But the methods we have seen so far aren't powerful enough to deduce the precise behavior of $P(e^{-t})$, so it is time for us to add a new weapon to our arsenal of techniques.

Euler's generating function $P(z)$ is ideally suited to the *Poisson summation formula* [*J. École Royale Polytechnique* **12** (1823), 404–509, §63], according to which

$$\sum_{n=-\infty}^{\infty} f(n+\theta) = \lim_{M\to\infty} \sum_{m=-M}^{M} e^{2\pi m i \theta} \int_{-\infty}^{\infty} e^{-2\pi m i y} f(y)\, dy, \qquad (25)$$

whenever f is a "well-behaved" function. This formula is based on the fact that the left-hand side is a periodic function of θ, and the right-hand side is the expansion of that function as a Fourier series. The function f is sufficiently nice if, for example, $\int_{-\infty}^{\infty} |f(y)|\, dy < \infty$ and either

i) $f(n+\theta)$ is an analytic function of the complex variable θ in the region $|\Im\theta| \le \epsilon$ for some $\epsilon > 0$ and $0 \le \Re\theta \le 1$ and every n, and the left-hand side of (25) converges uniformly for $|\Im\theta| \le \epsilon$; or

ii) $f(\theta) = \frac12 \lim_{\epsilon\to 0}\big(f(\theta-\epsilon) + f(\theta+\epsilon)\big) = g(\theta) - h(\theta)$ for all real numbers θ, where g and h are monotone increasing and $g(\pm\infty)$, $h(\pm\infty)$ are finite.

[See Peter Henrici, *Applied and Computational Complex Analysis* **2** (New York: Wiley, 1977), Theorem 10.6e.] Poisson's formula is not a panacea for summation problems of every kind; but when it does apply the results can be spectacular, as we will see.

Let us multiply Euler's formula (18) by $z^{1/24}$ in order to "complete the square":

$$\frac{z^{1/24}}{P(z)} = \sum_{n=-\infty}^{\infty} (-1)^n z^{\frac32(n+\frac16)^2}. \qquad (26)$$

Then for all $t > 0$ we have $e^{-t/24}/P(e^{-t}) = \sum_{n=-\infty}^{\infty} f(n)$, where

$$f(y) = e^{-\frac32 t(y+\frac16)^2 + \pi i y}; \qquad (27)$$

and this function f qualifies for Poisson's summation formula under both of the criteria (i) and (ii) stated above. Therefore we try to integrate $e^{-2\pi m i y} f(y)$, and that integral turns out to be easy for all m (see exercise 27):

$$\int_{-\infty}^{\infty} e^{-a(y+b)^2 + 2ciy}\, dy = \sqrt{\frac{\pi}{a}} e^{-c^2/a - 2bci} \qquad \text{when } a > 0. \qquad (28)$$

Plugging in to (25), with $\theta = 0$, $a = \frac32 t$, $b = \frac16$, and $c = (\frac12 - m)\pi$, yields

$$\sum_{n=-\infty}^{\infty} f(n) = \sum_{m=-\infty}^{\infty} g(m), \qquad g(m) = \sqrt{\frac{2\pi}{3t}} e^{-2(m-\frac12)^2\pi^2/(3t) + \frac{1-2m}{6}\pi i}. \qquad (29)$$

These terms combine and cancel beautifully, as shown in exercise 27, giving

$$\frac{e^{-t/24}}{P(e^{-t})} = \sqrt{\frac{2\pi}{t}} \sum_{n=-\infty}^{\infty} (-1)^n e^{-6\pi^2(n+\frac16)^2/t} = \sqrt{\frac{2\pi}{t}} \frac{e^{-\zeta(2)/t}}{P(e^{-4\pi^2/t})}. \qquad (30)$$

Surprise! We have proved another remarkable fact about $P(z)$:

Theorem D. *The generating function* (17) *for partitions satisfies the functional relation*

$$\ln P(e^{-t}) = \frac{\zeta(2)}{t} + \frac{1}{2}\ln\frac{t}{2\pi} - \frac{t}{24} + \ln P(e^{-4\pi^2/t}) \qquad (31)$$

when $\Re t > 0$. ∎

This theorem was discovered by Richard Dedekind [*Crelle* **83** (1877), 265–292, §6], who wrote $\eta(\tau)$ for the function $z^{1/24}/P(z)$ when $z = e^{2\pi i\tau}$; his proof was based on a much more complicated theory of elliptic functions. Notice that when t is a small positive number, $\ln P(e^{-4\pi^2/t})$ is *extremely* tiny; for example, when $t = 0.1$ we have $\exp(-4\pi^2/t) \approx 3.5 \times 10^{-172}$. Therefore Theorem D tells us essentially everything we need to know about the value of $P(z)$ when z is near 1.

G. H. Hardy and S. Ramanujan used this knowledge to deduce the asymptotic behavior of $p(n)$ for large n, and their work was extended many years later by Hans Rademacher, who discovered a series that is not only asymptotic but convergent [*Proc. London Math. Soc.* (2) **17** (1918), 75–115; **43** (1937), 241–254]. The Hardy–Ramanujan–Rademacher formula for $p(n)$ is surely one of the most astonishing identities ever discovered; it states that

$$p(n) = \frac{\pi}{2^{5/4}3^{3/4}(n-1/24)^{3/4}}\sum_{k=1}^{\infty}\frac{A_k(n)}{k}I_{3/2}\left(\sqrt{\frac{2}{3}}\frac{\pi}{k}\sqrt{n-1/24}\right). \qquad (32)$$

Here $I_{3/2}$ denotes the modified spherical Bessel function

$$I_{3/2}(z) = \left(\frac{z}{2}\right)^{3/2}\sum_{k=0}^{\infty}\frac{1}{\Gamma(k+5/2)}\frac{(z^2/4)^k}{k!} = \sqrt{\frac{2z}{\pi}}\left(\frac{\cosh z}{z} - \frac{\sinh z}{z^2}\right); \qquad (33)$$

and the coefficient $A_k(n)$ is defined by the formula

$$A_k(n) = \sum_{h=0}^{k-1}[h \perp k]\exp\left(2\pi i\left(\frac{\sigma(h,k,0)}{24} - \frac{nh}{k}\right)\right) \qquad (34)$$

where $\sigma(h,k,0)$ is the Dedekind sum defined in Eq. 3.3.3–(16). We have

$$A_1(n) = 1, \qquad A_2(n) = (-1)^n, \qquad A_3(n) = 2\cos\frac{(24n+1)\pi}{18}, \qquad (35)$$

and in general $A_k(n)$ lies between $-k$ and k.

A proof of (32) would take us far afield, but the basic idea is to use the "saddle point method" discussed in Section 7.2.1.5. The term for $k = 1$ is derived from the behavior of $P(z)$ when z is near 1; and the next term is derived from the behavior when z is near -1, where a transformation similar to (31) can be applied. In general, the kth term of (32) takes account of the way $P(z)$ behaves when z approaches $e^{2\pi ih/k}$ for irreducible fractions h/k with denominator k; every kth root of unity is a pole of each of the factors $1/(1 - z^k)$, $1/(1 - z^{2k})$, $1/(1 - z^{3k})$, ... in the infinite product for $P(z)$.

The leading term of (32) can be simplified greatly, if we merely want a rough approximation:

$$p(n) = \frac{e^{\pi\sqrt{2n/3}}}{4n\sqrt{3}}\left(1 + O(n^{-1/2})\right). \tag{36}$$

Or, if we choose to retain a few more details,

$$p(n) = \frac{e^{\pi\sqrt{2n'/3}}}{4n'\sqrt{3}}\left(1 - \frac{1}{\pi}\sqrt{\frac{3}{2n'}}\right)\left(1 + O\left(e^{-\pi\sqrt{n/6}}\right)\right), \quad n' = n - \frac{1}{24}. \tag{37}$$

For example, $p(100)$ has the exact value 190,569,292; formula (36) tells us that $p(100) \approx 1.993 \times 10^8$, while (37) gives the far better estimate 190,568,944.783.

Andrew Odlyzko has observed that, when n is large, the Hardy–Ramanujan–Rademacher formula actually gives a near-optimum way to compute the precise value of $p(n)$, because the arithmetic operations can be carried out in nearly $O\left(\log p(n)\right) = O(n^{1/2})$ steps. [See *Handbook of Combinatorics* **2** (MIT Press, 1995), 1068–1069.] The first few terms of (32) give the main contribution; then the series settles down to terms that are of order $k^{-3/2}$ and usually of order k^{-2}. Furthermore, about half of the coefficients $A_k(n)$ turn out to be zero (see exercise 28). For example, when $n = 10^6$, the terms for $k = 1$, 2, and 3 are $\approx 1.47 \times 10^{1107}$, 1.23×10^{550}, and -1.23×10^{364}, respectively. The sum of the first 250 terms is $\approx 1471684986\ldots73818.01$, while the true value is $1471684986\ldots73818$; and 123 of those 250 terms are zero.

The number of parts. It is convenient to introduce the notation

$$\left|\begin{matrix} n \\ m \end{matrix}\right| \tag{38}$$

for the number of partitions of n that have exactly m parts. Then the recurrence

$$\left|\begin{matrix} n \\ m \end{matrix}\right| = \left|\begin{matrix} n-1 \\ m-1 \end{matrix}\right| + \left|\begin{matrix} n-m \\ m \end{matrix}\right| \tag{39}$$

holds for all integers m and n, because $\left|\begin{smallmatrix} n-1 \\ m-1 \end{smallmatrix}\right|$ counts the partitions whose smallest part is 1 and $\left|\begin{smallmatrix} n-m \\ m \end{smallmatrix}\right|$ counts the others. (If the smallest part is 2 or more, we can subtract 1 from each part and get a partition of $n - m$ into m parts.) By similar reasoning we can conclude that $\left|\begin{smallmatrix} m+n \\ m \end{smallmatrix}\right|$ is the number of partitions of n into *at most* m parts, namely into m nonnegative summands. We also know, by transposing Ferrers diagrams, that $\left|\begin{smallmatrix} n \\ m \end{smallmatrix}\right|$ is the number of partitions of n whose *largest* part is m. Thus $\left|\begin{smallmatrix} n \\ m \end{smallmatrix}\right|$ is a good number to know. The boundary conditions

$$\left|\begin{matrix} n \\ 0 \end{matrix}\right| = \delta_{n0} \quad \text{and} \quad \left|\begin{matrix} n \\ m \end{matrix}\right| = 0 \quad \text{for } m < 0 \text{ or } n < 0 \tag{40}$$

make it easy to tabulate $\left|\begin{smallmatrix} n \\ m \end{smallmatrix}\right|$ for small values of the parameters, and we obtain an array of numbers analogous to the familiar triangles for $\binom{n}{m}$, $\left[\begin{smallmatrix} n \\ m \end{smallmatrix}\right]$, $\left\{\begin{smallmatrix} n \\ m \end{smallmatrix}\right\}$, and $\left\langle\begin{smallmatrix} n \\ m \end{smallmatrix}\right\rangle$ that we've seen before; see Table 2. The generating function is

$$\sum_n \left|\begin{matrix} n \\ m \end{matrix}\right| z^n = \frac{z^m}{(1-z)(1-z^2)\ldots(1-z^m)}. \tag{41}$$

Table 2

PARTITION NUMBERS

n	$\left\lvert{n\atop0}\right\rvert$	$\left\lvert{n\atop1}\right\rvert$	$\left\lvert{n\atop2}\right\rvert$	$\left\lvert{n\atop3}\right\rvert$	$\left\lvert{n\atop4}\right\rvert$	$\left\lvert{n\atop5}\right\rvert$	$\left\lvert{n\atop6}\right\rvert$	$\left\lvert{n\atop7}\right\rvert$	$\left\lvert{n\atop8}\right\rvert$	$\left\lvert{n\atop9}\right\rvert$	$\left\lvert{n\atop10}\right\rvert$	$\left\lvert{n\atop11}\right\rvert$
0	1	0	0	0	0	0	0	0	0	0	0	0
1	0	1	0	0	0	0	0	0	0	0	0	0
2	0	1	1	0	0	0	0	0	0	0	0	0
3	0	1	1	1	0	0	0	0	0	0	0	0
4	0	1	2	1	1	0	0	0	0	0	0	0
5	0	1	2	2	1	1	0	0	0	0	0	0
6	0	1	3	3	2	1	1	0	0	0	0	0
7	0	1	3	4	3	2	1	1	0	0	0	0
8	0	1	4	5	5	3	2	1	1	0	0	0
9	0	1	4	7	6	5	3	2	1	1	0	0
10	0	1	5	8	9	7	5	3	2	1	1	0
11	0	1	5	10	11	10	7	5	3	2	1	1

Almost all partitions of n have $\Theta(\sqrt{n}\log n)$ parts. This fact, discovered by P. Erdős and J. Lehner [*Duke Math. J.* **8** (1941), 335–345], has a very instructive proof:

Theorem E. *Let $C = \pi/\sqrt{6}$ and $m = \frac{1}{2C}\sqrt{n}\ln n + x\sqrt{n} + O(1)$. Then*

$$\frac{1}{p(n)}\left\lvert{m+n\atop m}\right\rvert = F(x)\bigl(1 + O(n^{-1/2+\epsilon})\bigr) \qquad (42)$$

for all $\epsilon > 0$ and all fixed x as $n \to \infty$, where

$$F(x) = e^{-e^{-Cx}/C}. \qquad (43)$$

The function $F(x)$ in (43) approaches 0 quite rapidly when $x \to -\infty$, and it rapidly increases to 1 when $x \to +\infty$; so it is a probability distribution function. Figure 49(b) shows that the corresponding density function $f(x) = F'(x)$ is largely concentrated in the region $-2 \le x \le 4$. (See exercise 35.)

The values of $\left\lvert{n\atop m}\right\rvert = \left\lvert{m+n\atop m}\right\rvert - \left\lvert{m-1+n\atop m-1}\right\rvert$ are shown in Fig. 49(a) for comparison when $n = 100$; in this case $\frac{1}{2C}\sqrt{n}\ln n \approx 18$.

Proof. We will use the fact that $\left\lvert{m+n\atop m}\right\rvert$ is the number of partitions of n whose largest part is $\le m$. Then, by the principle of inclusion and exclusion, Eq. 1.3.3–(29), we have

$$\left\lvert{m+n\atop m}\right\rvert = p(n) - \sum_{j>m} p(n-j) + \sum_{j_2>j_1>m} p(n-j_1-j_2) - \sum_{j_3>j_2>j_1>m} p(n-j_1-j_2-j_3) + \cdots,$$

because $p(n - j_1 - \cdots - j_r)$ is the number of partitions of n that use each of the parts $\{j_1,\ldots,j_r\}$ at least once. Let us write this as

$$\frac{1}{p(n)}\left\lvert{m+n\atop m}\right\rvert = 1 - \Sigma_1 + \Sigma_2 - \Sigma_3 + \cdots, \qquad \Sigma_r = \sum_{j_r > \cdots > j_1 > m} \frac{p(n-j_1- \cdots -j_r)}{p(n)}. \qquad (44)$$

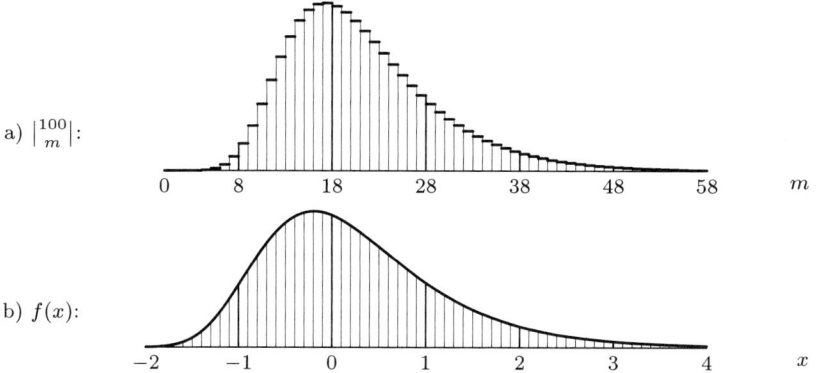

a) $\left|{}^{100}_{\ m}\right|$:

b) $f(x)$:

Fig. 49. Partitions of n with m parts, when (a) $n = 100$; (b) $n \to \infty$. (See Theorem E.)

In order to evaluate Σ_r we need to have a good estimate of the ratio $p(n-t)/p(n)$. And we're in luck, because Eq. (36) implies that

$$\frac{p(n-t)}{p(n)} = \exp\left(2C\sqrt{n-t} - \ln(n-t) + O\left((n-t)^{-1/2}\right) - 2C\sqrt{n} + \ln n\right)$$

$$= \exp\left(-Ctn^{-1/2} + O(n^{-1/2+2\epsilon})\right) \qquad \text{if } 0 \le t \le n^{1/2+\epsilon}. \tag{45}$$

Furthermore, if $t \ge n^{1/2+\epsilon}$ we have $p(n-t)/p(n) \le p(n - n^{1/2+\epsilon})/p(n) \approx \exp(-Cn^\epsilon)$, a value that is asymptotically smaller than any power of n. Therefore we may safely use the approximation

$$\frac{p(n-t)}{p(n)} \approx \alpha^t, \qquad \alpha = \exp(-Cn^{-1/2}), \tag{46}$$

for all values of $t \ge 0$. For example, we have

$$\Sigma_1 = \sum_{j>m} \frac{p(n-j)}{p(n)} = \frac{\alpha^{m+1}}{1-\alpha}\left(1 + O(n^{-1/2+2\epsilon})\right) + \sum_{n \ge j > n^{1/2+\epsilon}} \frac{p(n-j)}{p(n)}$$

$$= \frac{e^{-Cx}}{C}\left(1 + O(n^{-1/2+2\epsilon})\right) + O(ne^{-Cn^\epsilon}),$$

because $\alpha/(1-\alpha) = n^{1/2}/C + O(1)$ and $\alpha^m = n^{-1/2}e^{-Cx} + O(n^{-1})$. A similar argument (see exercise 36) proves that, if $r = O(\log n)$,

$$\Sigma_r = \frac{e^{-Crx}}{C^r r!}\left(1 + O(n^{-1/2+2\epsilon})\right) + O(e^{-n^{\epsilon/2}}). \tag{47}$$

Finally — and this is a wonderful property of the inclusion-exclusion principle in general — the partial sums of (44) always "bracket" the true value, in the sense that

$$1 - \Sigma_1 + \Sigma_2 - \cdots - \Sigma_{2r-1} \le \frac{1}{p(n)}\left|{}^{m+n}_{\ \ m}\right| \le 1 - \Sigma_1 + \Sigma_2 - \cdots - \Sigma_{2r-1} + \Sigma_{2r} \tag{48}$$

for all r. (See exercise 37.) When $2r$ is near $\ln n$ and n is large, the term Σ_{2r} is extremely tiny; therefore we obtain (42), except with 2ϵ in place of ϵ. ∎

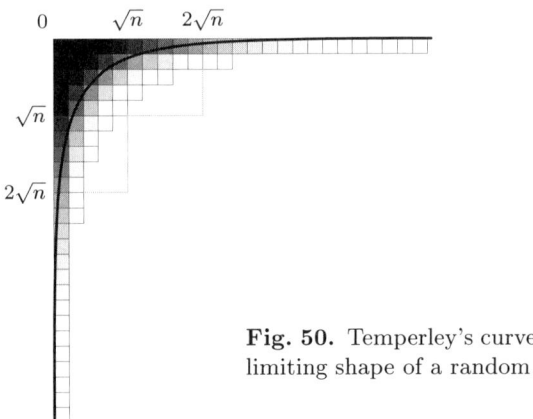

Fig. 50. Temperley's curve (49) for the limiting shape of a random partition.

Theorem E tells us that the largest part of a random partition almost always is $\frac{1}{2C}\sqrt{n}\ln n + O(\sqrt{n}\log\log\log n)$, and when n is reasonably large the other parts tend to be predictable as well. Suppose, for example, that we take all the partitions of 25 and superimpose their Ferrers diagrams, changing dots to boxes as in the rim representation. Which cells are occupied most often? Figure 50 shows the result: A random partition tends to have a typical shape that approaches a limiting curve as $n \to \infty$.

H. N. V. Temperley [*Proc. Cambridge Philos. Soc.* **48** (1952), 683–697] gave heuristic reasons to believe that most parts a_k of a large random partition $a_1 \dots a_m$ will satisfy the approximate law

$$e^{-Ck/\sqrt{n}} + e^{-Ca_k/\sqrt{n}} \;\approx\; 1, \tag{49}$$

and his formula has subsequently been verified in a strong form. For example, a theorem of Boris Pittel [*Advances in Applied Math.* **18** (1997), 432–488] allows us to conclude that the trace of a random partition is almost always $\frac{\ln 2}{C}\sqrt{n} \approx 0.54\sqrt{n}$, in accordance with (49), with an error of at most $O(\sqrt{n}\ln n)^{1/2}$; thus about 29% of all the Ferrers dots tend to lie in the Durfee square.

If, on the other hand, we look only at partitions of n with m parts, where m is fixed, the limiting shape is rather different: Almost all such partitions have

$$a_k \;\approx\; \frac{n}{m}\ln\frac{m}{k}, \tag{50}$$

if m and n are reasonably large. Figure 51 illustrates the case $n = 50$, $m = 5$. In fact, the same limit holds when m grows with n, but at a slower rate than $\sqrt{n}$ [see Vershik and Yakubovich, *Moscow Math. J.* **1** (2001), 457–468].

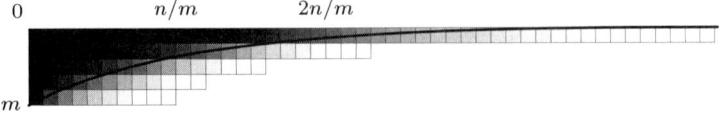

Fig. 51. The limiting shape (50) when there are m parts.

The rim representation of partitions gives us further information about partitions that are *doubly* bounded, in the sense that we not only restrict the number of parts but also the size of each part. A partition that has at most m parts, each of size at most l, fits inside an $m \times l$ box. All such partitions correspond to permutations of the multiset $\{m \cdot 0, l \cdot 1\}$ that have exactly n inversions, and we have studied the inversions of multiset permutations in exercise 5.1.2–16. In particular, that exercise derives a nonobvious formula for the number of ways n inversions can happen:

Theorem C. *The number of partitions of n that have no more than m parts and no part larger than l is*

$$[z^n] \binom{l+m}{m}_z = [z^n] \frac{(1-z^{l+1})}{(1-z)} \frac{(1-z^{l+2})}{(1-z^2)} \cdots \frac{(1-z^{l+m})}{(1-z^m)}. \tag{51}$$

This result is due to A. Cauchy, *Comptes Rendus Acad. Sci.* **17** (Paris, 1843), 523–531. Notice that when $l \to \infty$ the numerator becomes simply 1. An interesting combinatorial proof of a more general result appears in exercise 40 below. ∎

Analysis of the algorithms. Now we know more than enough about the quantitative aspects of partitions to deduce the behavior of Algorithm P quite precisely. Suppose steps P1, ..., P6 of that algorithm are executed respectively $T_1(n), \ldots, T_6(n)$ times. We obviously have $T_1(n) = 1$ and $T_3(n) = p(n)$; furthermore Kirchhoff's law tells us that $T_2(n) = T_5(n)$ and $T_4(n) + T_5(n) = T_3(n)$. We get to step P4 once for each partition that contains a 2; and this is clearly $p(n-2)$.

Thus the only possible mystery about the running time of Algorithm P is the number of times we must perform step P6, which loops back to itself. A moment's thought, however, reveals that the algorithm stores a value ≥ 2 into the array $a_1 a_2 \ldots$ only in step P2 or when we'll soon test $n \leq x$ in P6; and every such value is eventually decreased by 1, either in step P4 or step P5. Therefore

$$T_2''(n) + T_6(n) = p(n) - 1, \tag{52}$$

where $T_2''(n)$ is the number of times step P2 sets a_m to a value ≥ 2. Let $T_2(n) = T_2'(n) + T_2''(n)$, so that $T_2'(n)$ is the number of times step P2 sets $a_m \leftarrow 1$. Then $T_2'(n) + T_4(n)$ is the number of partitions that end in 1, hence

$$T_2'(n) + T_4(n) = p(n-1). \tag{53}$$

Aha! We've found enough equations to determine all of the required quantities:

$$\begin{aligned}
&\big(T_1(n), \ldots, T_6(n)\big) = \\
&\quad \big(1,\ p(n) - p(n-2),\ p(n),\ p(n-2),\ p(n) - p(n-2),\ p(n-1) - 1\big). \tag{54}
\end{aligned}$$

And from the asymptotics of $p(n)$ we also know the average amount of computation per partition:

$$\left(\frac{T_1(n)}{p(n)}, \ldots, \frac{T_6(n)}{p(n)}\right) = \left(0,\ \frac{2C}{\sqrt{n}},\ 1,\ 1 - \frac{2C}{\sqrt{n}},\ \frac{2C}{\sqrt{n}},\ 1 - \frac{C}{\sqrt{n}}\right) + O\left(\frac{1}{n}\right), \tag{55}$$

where $C = \pi/\sqrt{6} \approx 1.283$. (See exercise 45.) The total number of memory accesses per partition therefore comes to only $3 + C/\sqrt{n} + O(1/n)$.

> *Whoever wants to go about generating all partitions*
> *not only immerses himself in immense labor,*
> *but also must take pains to keep fully attentive,*
> *so as not to be grossly deceived.*
> — LEONHARD EULER, *De Partitione Numerorum* (1750)

Algorithm H is more difficult to analyze, but we can at least prove a decent upper bound on its running time. The key quantity is the value of j, the smallest subscript for which $a_j < a_1 - 1$. The successive values of j when $m = 4$ and $n = 11$ are $(2, 2, 2, 3, 2, 2, 3, 4, 2, 3, 5)$, and we have observed that $j = b_{l-1} + 1$ when $b_1 \ldots b_l$ is the conjugate partition $(a_1 \ldots a_m)^T$ and $m < n$. (See (7) and (12).) Step H3 singles out the case $j = 2$, because this case is not only the most common, it is also especially easy to handle.

Let $c_m(n)$ be the accumulated total value of $j - 1$, summed over all of the $\left|{n \atop m}\right|$ partitions generated by Algorithm H. For example, $c_4(11) = 1 + 1 + 1 + 2 + 1 + 1 + 2 + 3 + 1 + 2 + 4 = 19$. We can regard $c_m(n)/\left|{n \atop m}\right|$ as a good indication of the running time per partition, because the time to perform the most costly steps, H4 and H6, is roughly proportional to $j - 2$. This ratio $c_m(n)/\left|{n \atop m}\right|$ is *not* bounded, because $c_m(m) = m$ while $\left|{m \atop m}\right| = 1$. But the following theorem shows that Algorithm H is efficient nonetheless:

Theorem H. *The cost measure $c_m(n)$ for Algorithm H is at most $3\left|{n \atop m}\right| + m$.*

Proof. We can readily verify that $c_m(n)$ satisfies the same recurrence as $\left|{n \atop m}\right|$, namely

$$c_m(n) = c_{m-1}(n-1) + c_m(n-m), \qquad \text{for } m, n \geq 1, \tag{56}$$

if we artificially define $c_m(n) = 1$ when $1 \leq n < m$; see (39). But the boundary conditions are now different:

$$c_m(0) = [m > 0]; \qquad c_0(n) = 0. \tag{57}$$

Table 3 shows how $c_m(n)$ behaves when m and n are small.

To prove the theorem, we will actually prove a stronger result,

$$c_m(n) \leq 3\left|{n \atop m}\right| + 2m - n - 1 \qquad \text{for } n \geq m \geq 2. \tag{58}$$

Exercise 50 shows that this inequality holds when $m \leq n \leq 2m$, so the proof will be complete if we can prove it when $n > 2m$. In the latter case we have

$$
\begin{aligned}
c_m(n) &= c_1(n-m) + c_2(n-m) + c_3(n-m) + \cdots + c_m(n-m) \\
&\leq 1 + \left(3\left|{n-m \atop 2}\right| + 3 - n + m\right) + \left(3\left|{n-m \atop 3}\right| + 5 - n + m\right) + \cdots \\
&\qquad\qquad\qquad + \left(3\left|{n-m \atop m}\right| + 2m - 1 - n + m\right) \\
&= 3\left|{n-m \atop 1}\right| + 3\left|{n-m \atop 2}\right| + \cdots + 3\left|{n-m \atop m}\right| - 3 + m^2 - (m-1)(n-m) \\
&= 3\left|{n \atop m}\right| + 2m^2 - m - (m-1)n - 3
\end{aligned}
$$

by induction; and $2m^2 - m - (m-1)n - 3 \leq 2m - n - 1$ because $n \geq 2m + 1$. ∎

Table 3

COSTS IN ALGORITHM H

n	$c_0(n)$	$c_1(n)$	$c_2(n)$	$c_3(n)$	$c_4(n)$	$c_5(n)$	$c_6(n)$	$c_7(n)$	$c_8(n)$	$c_9(n)$	$c_{10}(n)$	$c_{11}(n)$
0	0	1	1	1	1	1	1	1	1	1	1	1
1	0	1	1	1	1	1	1	1	1	1	1	1
2	0	1	2	1	1	1	1	1	1	1	1	1
3	0	1	2	3	1	1	1	1	1	1	1	1
4	0	1	3	3	4	1	1	1	1	1	1	1
5	0	1	3	4	4	5	1	1	1	1	1	1
6	0	1	4	6	5	5	6	1	1	1	1	1
7	0	1	4	7	7	6	6	7	1	1	1	1
8	0	1	5	8	11	8	7	7	8	1	1	1
9	0	1	5	11	12	12	9	8	8	9	1	1
10	0	1	6	12	16	17	13	10	9	9	10	1
11	0	1	6	14	19	21	18	14	11	10	10	11

*A Gray code for partitions. When partitions are generated in part-count form $c_1 \ldots c_n$ as in exercise 5, at most four of the c_j values change at each step. But we might prefer to minimize the changes to the individual parts, generating partitions in such a way that the successor of $a_1 a_2 \ldots$ is always obtained by simply setting $a_j \leftarrow a_j + 1$ and $a_k \leftarrow a_k - 1$ for some j and k, as in the "revolving door" algorithms of Section 7.2.1.3. It turns out that this is always possible; in fact, there is a unique way to do it when $n = 6$:

$$111111, \; 21111, \; 3111, \; 2211, \; 222, \; 321, \; 33, \; 42, \; 411, \; 51, \; 6. \tag{59}$$

And in general, the $\left| \begin{smallmatrix} m+n \\ m \end{smallmatrix} \right|$ partitions of n into at most m parts can always be generated by a suitable Gray path.

Notice that $\alpha \to \beta$ is an allowable transition from one partition to another if and only if we get the Ferrers diagram for β by moving just one dot in the Ferrers diagram for α. Therefore $\alpha^T \to \beta^T$ is also an allowable transition. It follows that every Gray code for partitions into at most m parts corresponds to a Gray code for partitions into parts that do not exceed m. We shall work with the latter constraint.

The total number of Gray codes for partitions is vast: There are 52 when $n = 7$, and 652 when $n = 8$; there are 298,896 when $n = 9$, and 2,291,100,484 when $n = 10$. But no really simple construction is known. The reason is probably that a few partitions have only two neighbors, namely the partitions $d^{n/d}$ when $1 < d < n$ and d is a divisor of n. Such partitions must be preceded and followed by $\{(d+1)d^{n/d-2}(d-1), \; d^{n/d-1}(d-1)1\}$, and this requirement seems to rule out any simple recursive approach.

Carla D. Savage [*J. Algorithms* **10** (1989), 577–595] found a way to surmount the difficulties with only a modest amount of complexity. Let

$$\mu(m,n) = \overbrace{m \; m \; \ldots \; m}^{\lfloor n/m \rfloor} \; (n \bmod m) \tag{60}$$

be the lexicographically largest partition of n with parts $\leq m$; our goal will be to construct recursively defined Gray paths $L(m,n)$ and $M(m,n)$ from the partition 1^n to $\mu(m,n)$, where $L(m,n)$ runs through all partitions whose parts are bounded by m while $M(m,n)$ runs through those partitions and a few more: $M(m,n)$ also includes partitions whose largest part is $m+1$, provided that the other parts are all strictly less than m. For example, $L(3,8)$ is 11111111, 2111111, 311111, 22211, 2222, 3221, 32111, 3311, 332, while $M(3,8)$ is

$$11111111,\ 2111111,\ 221111,\ 22211,\ 2222,\ 3221,$$
$$3311,\ 32111,\ 311111,\ 41111,\ 4211,\ 422,\ 332; \tag{61}$$

the additional partitions starting with 4 will give us "wiggle room" in other parts of the recursion. We will define $L(m,n)$ for all $n \geq 0$, but $M(m,n)$ only for $n > 2m$.

The following construction, illustrated for $m = 5$ to simplify the notation, *almost* works:

$$L(5) = \begin{Bmatrix} L(3) \\ 4L(\infty)^R \\ 5L(\infty) \end{Bmatrix} \text{ if } n \leq 7; \quad \begin{Bmatrix} L(3) \\ 4L(2)^R \\ 5L(2) \\ 431 \\ 44 \\ 53 \end{Bmatrix} \text{ if } n = 8; \quad \begin{Bmatrix} M(4) \\ 54L(4)^R \\ 55L(5) \end{Bmatrix} \text{ if } n \geq 9; \tag{62}$$

$$M(5) = \begin{Bmatrix} L(4) \\ 5L(4)^R \\ 6L(3) \\ 64L(\infty)^R \\ 55L(\infty) \end{Bmatrix} \text{ if } 11 \leq n \leq 13; \quad \begin{Bmatrix} L(4) \\ 5M(4)^R \\ 6L(4) \\ 554L(4)^R \\ 555L(5) \end{Bmatrix} \text{ if } n \geq 14. \tag{63}$$

Here the parameter n in $L(m,n)$ and $M(m,n)$ has been omitted because it can be deduced from the context; each L or M is supposed to generate partitions of whatever amount remains after previous parts have been subtracted. Thus, for example, (63) specifies that

$$M(5,14) = L(4,14),\ 5M(4,9)^R,\ 6L(4,8),\ 554L(4,0)^R,\ 555L(5,-1);$$

the sequence $L(5,-1)$ is actually empty, and $L(4,0)$ is the empty string, so the final partition of $M(5,14)$ is $554 = \mu(5,14)$ as it should be. The notation $L(\infty)$ stands for $L(\infty,n) = L(n,n)$, the Gray path of all partitions of n, starting with 1^n and ending with n^1.

In general, $L(m)$ and $M(m)$ are defined for all $m \geq 3$ by essentially the same rules, if we replace the digits 2, 3, 4, 5, and 6 in (62) and (63) by $m-3$, $m-2$, $m-1$, m, and $m+1$, respectively. The ranges $n \leq 7$, $n = 8$, $n \geq 9$ become $n \leq 2m-3$, $n = 2m-2$, $n \geq 2m-1$; the ranges $11 \leq n \leq 13$ and $n \geq 14$ become $2m+1 \leq n \leq 3m-2$ and $n \geq 3m-1$. The sequences $L(0)$, $L(1)$, $L(2)$ have obvious definitions because the paths are unique when $m \leq 2$. The sequence $M(2)$ is 1^n, 21^{n-2}, 31^{n-3}, 221^{n-4}, 2221^{n-6}, ..., $\mu(2,n)$ for $n \geq 5$.

Theorem S. *Gray paths $L'(m, n)$ for $m, n \geq 0$ and $M'(m, n)$ for $n \geq 2m+1 \geq 5$ exist for all partitions with the properties described above, except in the case $L'(4, 6)$. Furthermore, L' and M' obey the mutual recursions (62) and (63) except in a few cases.*

Proof. We noted above that (62) and (63) *almost* work; the reader may verify that the only glitch occurs in the case $L(4, 6)$, when (62) gives

$$L(4, 6) = L(2, 6), \; 3L(1, 3)^R, \; 4L(1, 2), \; 321, \; 33, \; 42$$
$$= 111111, \; 21111, \; 2211, \; 222, \; 3111, \; 411, \; 321, \; 33, \; 42. \tag{64}$$

If $m > 4$, we're OK because the transition from the end of $L(m-2, 2m-2)$ to the beginning of $(m-1)L(m-3, m-1)^R$ is from $(m-2)(m-2)2$ to $(m-1)(m-3)2$. There is no satisfactory path $L(4, 6)$, because all Gray codes through those nine partitions must end with either 411, 33, 3111, 222, or 2211.

In order to neutralize this anomaly we need to patch the definitions of $L(m, n)$ and $M(m, n)$ at eight places where the "buggy subroutine" $L(4, 6)$ is invoked. One simple way is to make the following definitions:

$$L'(4, 6) = 111111, 21111, 3111, 411, 321, 33, 42;$$
$$L'(3, 5) = 11111, 2111, 221, 311, 32. \tag{65}$$

Thus, we omit 222 and 2211 from $L(4, 6)$; we also reprogram $L(3, 5)$ so that 2111 is adjacent to 221. Then exercise 60 shows that it is always easy to "splice in" the two partitions that are missing from $L(4, 6)$. ∎

EXERCISES

▶ **1.** [*M21*] Give formulas for the total number of possibilities in each problem of The Twelvefold Way. For example, the number of n-tuples of m things is m^n. (Use the notation (38) when appropriate, and be careful to make your formulas correct even when $m = 0$ or $n = 0$.)

▶ **2.** [*20*] Show that a small change to step H1 yields an algorithm that will generate all partitions of n into *at most* m parts.

3. [*M17*] A partition $a_1 + \cdots + a_m$ of n into m parts $a_1 \geq \cdots \geq a_m$ is *optimally balanced* if $|a_i - a_j| \leq 1$ for $1 \leq i, j \leq m$. Prove that there is exactly one such partition, whenever $n \geq m \geq 1$, and give a simple formula that expresses the jth part a_j as a function of j, m, and n.

4. [*M22*] (Gideon Ehrlich, 1974.) What is the lexicographically smallest partition of n in which all parts are $\geq r$? For example, when $n = 19$ and $r = 5$ the answer is 766.

▶ **5.** [*23*] Design an algorithm that generates all partitions of n in the part-count form $c_1 \ldots c_n$ of (8). Generate them in colex order, namely in the lexicographic order of $c_n \ldots c_1$, which is equivalent to lexicographic order of the corresponding partitions $a_1 a_2 \ldots$. For efficiency, maintain also a table of links $l_0 l_1 \ldots l_n$ so that, if the distinct values of k for which $c_k > 0$ are $k_1 < \cdots < k_t$, we have

$$l_0 = k_1, \quad l_{k_1} = k_2, \quad \ldots, \quad l_{k_{t-1}} = k_t, \quad l_{k_t} = 0.$$

(Thus the partition 331 would be represented by $c_1 \ldots c_7 = 1020000$, $l_0 = 1$, $l_1 = 3$, and $l_3 = 0$; the other links l_2, l_4, l_5, l_6, l_7 can be set to any convenient values.)

6. [*20*] Design an algorithm to compute $b_1 b_2 \ldots = (a_1 a_2 \ldots)^T$, given $a_1 a_2 \ldots$.

7. [*M20*] Suppose $a_1 \ldots a_n$ and $a_1' \ldots a_n'$ are partitions of n with $a_1 \geq \cdots \geq a_n \geq 0$ and $a_1' \geq \cdots \geq a_n' \geq 0$, and let their respective conjugates be $b_1 \ldots b_n = (a_1 \ldots a_n)^T$, $b_1' \ldots b_n' = (a_1' \ldots a_n')^T$. Show that $b_1 \ldots b_n < b_1' \ldots b_n'$ if and only if $a_n \ldots a_1 < a_n' \ldots a_1'$.

8. [*15*] When $(p_1 \ldots p_t, q_1 \ldots q_t)$ yields the rim representation of a partition $a_1 a_2 \ldots$ as in (15) and (16), what's the rim representation of the conjugate partition $(a_1 a_2 \ldots)^T$?

9. [*22*] If $a_1 a_2 \ldots a_m$ and $b_1 b_2 \ldots b_m = (a_1 a_2 \ldots a_m)^T$ are conjugate partitions, show that the multisets $\{a_1 + 1, a_2 + 2, \ldots, a_m + m\}$ and $\{b_1 + 1, b_2 + 2, \ldots, b_m + m\}$ are equal.

10. [*21*] Two simple kinds of binary trees are sometimes helpful for reasoning about partitions: (a) a tree that includes all partitions of all integers, and (b) a tree that includes all partitions of a given integer n, illustrated here for $n = 8$:

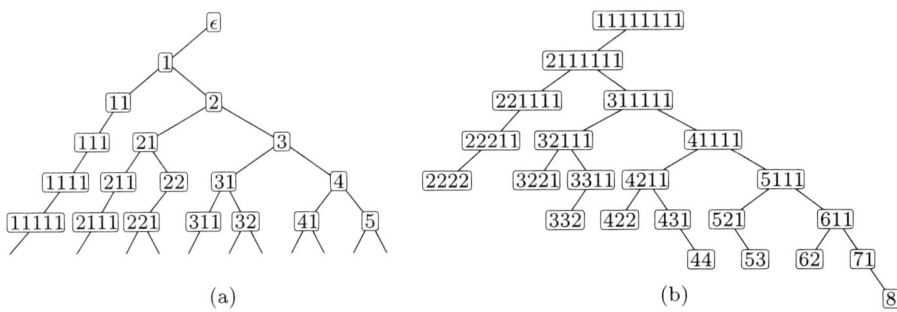

(a)   (b)

Deduce the general rules underlying these constructions. What order of tree traversal corresponds to lexicographic order of the partitions?

11. [*M22*] How many ways are there to pay one euro, using coins worth 1, 2, 5, 10, 20, 50, and/or 100 cents? What if you are allowed to use at most two of each coin?

▶ **12.** [*M21*] (L. Euler, 1750.) Use generating functions to prove that the number of ways to partition n into *distinct* parts is the number of ways to partition n into *odd* parts. For example, $5 = 4 + 1 = 3 + 2$; $5 = 3 + 1 + 1 = 1 + 1 + 1 + 1 + 1$.

[*Note:* The next two exercises use combinatorial techniques to prove extensions of this famous theorem.]

▶ **13.** [*M23*] (F. Franklin, 1882.) Find a one-to-one correspondence $\alpha \leftrightarrow \beta$ between partitions of n such that α has exactly k parts repeated more than once if and only if β has exactly k even parts. (For example, the partition 64421111 has two repeated parts $\{4, 1\}$ and three even parts $\{6, 4, 2\}$. The case $k = 0$ corresponds to Euler's result.)

▶ **14.** [*M28*] (J. J. Sylvester, 1882.) Find a one-to-one correspondence between partitions of n into distinct parts $a_1 > a_2 > \cdots > a_m$ that have exactly k "gaps" where $a_j > a_{j+1} + 1$, and partitions of n into odd parts that have exactly $k + 1$ different values. (For example, when $k = 0$ this construction proves that the number of ways to write n as a sum of consecutive integers is the number of odd divisors of n.)

15. [*M20*] (J. J. Sylvester.) Find a generating function for the number of partitions that are *self-conjugate* (namely, partitions such that $\alpha = \alpha^T$).

16. [*M21*] Find a formula for $\sum_{m,n} p(k, m, n) w^m z^n$, where $p(k, m, n)$ is the number of partitions of n that have m parts and trace k. Sum it on k to obtain a nontrivial identity.

17. [*M26*] A *joint partition* of n is a pair of sequences $(a_1, \ldots, a_r; \; b_1, \ldots, b_s)$ of positive integers for which we have

$$a_1 \geq \cdots \geq a_r, \quad b_1 > \cdots > b_s, \quad \text{and} \quad a_1 + \cdots + a_r + b_1 + \cdots + b_s = n.$$

Thus it is an ordinary partition if $s = 0$, and a partition into distinct parts if $r = 0$.

a) Find a simple formula for the generating function $\sum u^{r+s} v^s z^n$, summed over all joint partitions of n with r ordinary parts a_i and s distinct parts b_j.

b) Similarly, find a simple formula for $\sum v^s z^n$ when the sum is over all joint partitions that have exactly $r+s = t$ total parts, given the value of t. For example, the answer when $t = 2$ is $(1+v)(1+vz)z^2/((1-z)(1-z^2))$.

c) What identity do you deduce?

▶ **18.** [*M23*] (Doron Zeilberger.) Show that there is a one-to-one correspondence between pairs of integer sequences $(a_1, a_2, \ldots, a_r; \; b_1, b_2, \ldots, b_s)$ such that

$$a_1 \geq a_2 \geq \cdots \geq a_r, \quad b_1 > b_2 > \cdots > b_s,$$

and pairs of integer sequences $(c_1, c_2, \ldots, c_{r+s}; \; d_1, d_2, \ldots, d_{r+s})$ such that

$$c_1 \geq c_2 \geq \cdots \geq c_{r+s}, \quad d_j \in \{0, 1\} \quad \text{for } 1 \leq j \leq r+s,$$

related by the multiset equations

$$\{a_1, a_2, \ldots, a_r\} = \{c_j \mid d_j = 0\} \quad \text{and} \quad \{b_1, b_2, \ldots, b_s\} = \{c_j + r + s - j \mid d_j = 1\}.$$

Consequently we obtain the interesting identity

$$\sum_{\substack{a_1 \geq \cdots \geq a_r > 0, \, r \geq 0 \\ b_1 > \cdots > b_s > 0, \, s \geq 0}} u^{r+s} v^s z^{a_1 + \cdots + a_r + b_1 + \cdots + b_s} \;=\; \sum_{\substack{c_1 \geq \cdots \geq c_t > 0, \, t \geq 0 \\ d_1, \ldots, d_t \in \{0,1\}}} u^t v^{d_1 + \cdots + d_t} z^{c_1 + \cdots + c_t + (t-1)d_1 + \cdots + d_{t-1}}.$$

19. [*M22*] (E. Heine, 1847.) Prove the four-parameter identity

$$\prod_{m=1}^{\infty} \frac{(1 - wxz^m)(1 - wyz^m)}{(1 - wz^m)(1 - wxyz^m)} = \sum_{k=0}^{\infty} \frac{w^k (x-1)(x-z) \ldots (x - z^{k-1})(y-1)(y-z) \ldots (y - z^{k-1}) z^k}{(1-z)(1-z^2) \ldots (1-z^k)(1-wz)(1-wz^2) \ldots (1-wz^k)}.$$

Hint: Carry out the sum over either k or l in the formula

$$\sum_{k,l \geq 0} u^k v^l z^{kl} \frac{(z-az)(z-az^2) \ldots (z - az^k)}{(1-z)(1-z^2) \ldots (1-z^k)} \frac{(z-bz)(z-bz^2) \ldots (z - bz^l)}{(1-z)(1-z^2) \ldots (1-z^l)}$$

and consider the simplifications that occur when $b = auz$.

▶ **20.** [*M21*] Approximately how long does it take to compute a table of the partition numbers $p(n)$ for $1 \leq n \leq N$, using Euler's recurrence (20)?

21. [*M21*] (L. Euler.) Let $q(n)$ be the number of partitions of n into distinct parts. What is a good way to compute $q(n)$ if you already know the values of $p(1), \ldots, p(n)$?

22. [*HM21*] (L. Euler.) Let $\sigma(n)$ be the sum of all positive divisors of the positive integer n. Thus, $\sigma(n) = n + 1$ when n is prime, and $\sigma(n)$ can be significantly larger than n when n is highly composite. Prove that, in spite of this rather chaotic behavior, $\sigma(n)$ satisfies almost the same recurrence (20) as the partition numbers:

$$\sigma(n) = \sigma(n-1) + \sigma(n-2) - \sigma(n-5) - \sigma(n-7) + \sigma(n-12) + \sigma(n-15) - \cdots$$

for $n \geq 1$, except that when a term on the right is '$\sigma(0)$' the value 'n' is used instead. For example, $\sigma(11) = 1 + 11 = \sigma(10) + \sigma(9) - \sigma(6) - \sigma(4) = 18 + 13 - 12 - 7$; $\sigma(12) = 1 + 2 + 3 + 4 + 6 + 12 = \sigma(11) + \sigma(10) - \sigma(7) - \sigma(5) + 12 = 12 + 18 - 8 - 6 + 12$.

23. [*HM25*] Use Jacobi's triple product identity (19) to prove another formula that he discovered:

$$\prod_{k=1}^{\infty}(1-z^k)^3 \;=\; 1-3z+5z^3-7z^6+9z^{10}-\cdots \;=\; \sum_{n=0}^{\infty}(-1)^n(2n+1)z^{\binom{n+1}{2}}.$$

24. [*M26*] (S. Ramanujan, 1919.) Let $A(z)=\prod_{k=1}^{\infty}(1-z^k)^4$.

a) Prove that $[z^n]A(z)$ is a multiple of 5 when $n \bmod 5 = 4$.

b) Prove that $[z^n]A(z)B(z)^5$ has the same property, if B is any power series with integer coefficients.

c) Therefore $p(n)$ is a multiple of 5 when $n \bmod 5 = 4$.

25. [*HM27*] Improve on (22) by using (a) Euler's summation formula and (b) Mellin transforms to estimate $\ln P(e^{-t})$. *Hint:* The dilogarithm function $\mathrm{Li}_2(x) = x/1^2 + x^2/2^2 + x^3/3^2 + \cdots$ satisfies $\mathrm{Li}_2(x) + \mathrm{Li}_2(1-x) = \zeta(2) - (\ln x)\ln(1-x)$.

26. [*HM22*] In exercises 5.2.2–44 and 5.2.2–51 we studied two ways to prove that

$$\sum_{k=1}^{\infty}e^{-k^2/n} = \frac{1}{2}(\sqrt{\pi n}-1)+O(n^{-M}) \qquad \text{for all } M>0.$$

Show that Poisson's summation formula gives a much stronger result.

27. [*HM21*] Prove (28) and complete the calculations leading to Theorem D.

28. [*HM42*] (D. H. Lehmer.) Show that the Hardy–Ramanujan–Rademacher coefficients $A_k(n)$ defined in (34) have the following remarkable properties:

a) If k is odd, then $A_{2k}(km+4n+(k^2-1)/8) = A_2(m)A_k(n)$.

b) If p is prime, $p^e > 2$, and $k \perp 2p$, then

$$A_{p^ek}(k^2m+p^{2e}n-(k^2+p^{2e}-1)/24) \;=\; (-1)^{[p^e=4]}A_{p^e}(m)A_k(n).$$

In this formula $k^2+p^{2e}-1$ is a multiple of 24 if p or k is divisible by 2 or 3; otherwise division by 24 should be done modulo p^ek.

c) If p is prime, $|A_{p^e}(n)| < 2^{[p>2]}p^{e/2}$.

d) If p is prime, $A_{p^e}(n) \neq 0$ if and only if $1-24n$ is a quadratic residue modulo p and either $e=1$ or $24n \bmod p \neq 1$.

e) The probability that $A_k(n)=0$, when k is divisible by exactly t primes ≥ 5 and n is a random integer, is approximately $1-2^{-t}$.

▶ **29.** [*M16*] Generalizing (41), evaluate the sum $\sum_{a_1\geq a_2\geq\cdots\geq a_m\geq 1} z_1^{a_1}z_2^{a_2}\ldots z_m^{a_m}$.

30. [*M17*] Find closed forms for the sums

$$\text{(a)} \sum_{k\geq 0}\left|{n-km \atop m-1}\right| \qquad \text{and} \qquad \text{(b)} \sum_{k\geq 0}\left|{n \atop m-k}\right|$$

(which are finite, because the terms being summed are zero when k is large).

31. [*M24*] (A. De Morgan, 1843.) Show that $\left|{n\atop 2}\right| = \lfloor n/2\rfloor$ and $\left|{n\atop 3}\right| = \lfloor(n^2+6)/12\rfloor$; find a similar formula for $\left|{n\atop 4}\right|$.

32. [*M15*] Prove that $\left|{n\atop m}\right| \leq p(n-m)$ for all $m,n \geq 0$. When does equality hold?

33. [*HM20*] Use the fact that there are exactly $\binom{n-1}{m-1}$ *compositions* of n into m parts, Eq. 7.2.1.3–(9), to prove a lower bound on $\left|{n\atop m}\right|$. Then set $m=\lfloor\sqrt{n}\rfloor$ to obtain an elementary lower bound on $p(n)$.

▶ **34.** [*HM21*] Show that $\left|{n - m(m-1)/2 \atop m}\right|$ is the number of partitions of n into m distinct parts. Consequently

$$\left|{n \atop m}\right| = \frac{n^{m-1}}{m!\,(m-1)!}\left(1 + O\left(\frac{m^3}{n}\right)\right) \qquad \text{when } m \le n^{1/3}.$$

35. [*HM21*] In the Erdős–Lehner probability distribution (43), what value of x is (a) most probable? (b) the median? (c) the mean? (d) What is the standard deviation?

36. [*HM24*] Prove the key estimate (47) that is needed in Theorem E.

37. [*M22*] Prove the inclusion-exclusion bracketing lemma (48), by analyzing how many times a partition that has exactly q different parts exceeding m is counted in the rth partial sum.

38. [*M20*] Given positive integers l and m, what generating function enumerates partitions that have exactly m parts, and largest part l? (See Eq. (51).)

39. [*M20*] (A. Cauchy.) Continuing exercise 38, what is the generating function for the number of partitions into m parts, all *distinct* and less than l?

▶ **40.** [*M25*] (F. Franklin.) Generalizing Theorem C, show that, for $0 \le k \le m$,

$$[z^n]\, \frac{(1 - z^{l+1}) \ldots (1 - z^{l+k})}{(1 - z)(1 - z^2) \ldots (1 - z^m)}$$

is the number of partitions $a_1 a_2 \ldots$ of n into m or fewer parts with the property that $a_1 \le a_{k+1} + l$.

41. [*HM42*] Extend the Hardy–Ramanujan–Rademacher formula (32) to obtain a convergent series for partitions of n into at most m parts, with no part exceeding l.

42. [*HM42*] Find the limiting shape, analogous to (49), for random partitions of n into at most $\theta\sqrt{n}$ parts, with no part exceeding $\varphi\sqrt{n}$, assuming that $\theta\varphi > 1$.

43. [*M18*] Given n and k, how many partitions of n have $a_1 > a_2 > \cdots > a_k$?

▶ **44.** [*M22*] How many partitions of n have their two smallest parts equal?

45. [*HM21*] Compute the asymptotic value of $p(n-1)/p(n)$, with relative error $O(n^{-2})$.

46. [*M20*] In the text's analysis of Algorithm P, which is larger, $T_2'(n)$ or $T_2''(n)$?

▶ **47.** [*HM22*] (A. Nijenhuis and H. S. Wilf, 1975.) The following simple algorithm, based on a table of the partition numbers $p(0)$, $p(1)$, ..., $p(n)$, generates a random partition of n using the part-count representation $c_1 \ldots c_n$ of (8). Prove that it produces each partition with equal probability.

N1. [Initialize.] Set $m \leftarrow n$ and $c_1 \ldots c_n \leftarrow 0 \ldots 0$.

N2. [Done?] Terminate if $m = 0$.

N3. [Generate.] Generate a random integer M in the range $0 \le M < mp(m)$.

N4. [Choose parts.] Set $s \leftarrow 0$. Then for $j = 1, 2, \ldots$, and for $k = 1, 2, \ldots, \lfloor m/j \rfloor$, repeatedly set $s \leftarrow s + kp(m - jk)$ until $s > M$.

N5. [Update.] Set $c_k \leftarrow c_k + j$, $m \leftarrow m - jk$, and return to N2. ▮

Hint: Step N4, which is based on the identity

$$\sum_{j=1}^{\infty} \sum_{k=1}^{\lfloor m/j \rfloor} kp(m - jk) = mp(m),$$

chooses each particular pair of values (j, k) with probability $kp(m - jk)/(mp(m))$.

48. [*HM40*] Analyze the running time of the algorithm in the previous exercise.

▶ **49.** [*HM26*] (a) What is the generating function $F(z)$ for the sum of the smallest parts of all partitions of n? (The series begins $z + 3z^2 + 5z^3 + 9z^4 + 12z^5 + \cdots$.)

(b) Find the asymptotic value of $[z^n] F(z)$, with relative error $O(n^{-1})$.

50. [*HM33*] Let $c(m) = c_m(2m)$ in the recurrence (56), (57).

a) Prove that $c_m(m + k) = m - k + c(k)$ for $0 \le k \le m$.

b) Consequently (58) holds for $m \le n \le 2m$, if $c(m) < 3p(m)$ for all $m \ge 0$.

c) Show that $c(m) - m$ is the sum of the second-smallest parts of all partitions of m.

d) Find a one-to-one correspondence between all partitions of n with second-smallest part k and all partitions of numbers $\le n$ with smallest part $k + 1$.

e) Describe the generating function $\sum_{m \ge 0} c(m) z^m$.

f) Conclude that $c(m) < 3p(m)$ for all $m \ge 0$.

51. [*M46*] Make a detailed analysis of Algorithm H.

▶ **52.** [*M21*] What is the millionth partition generated by Algorithm P when $n = 64$? *Hint:* $p(64) = 1741630 = 1000000 + \left|{77 \atop 13}\right| + \left|{60 \atop 10}\right| + \left|{47 \atop 8}\right| + \left|{35 \atop 5}\right| + \left|{27 \atop 3}\right| + \left|{22 \atop 2}\right| + \left|{18 \atop 1}\right| + \left|{15 \atop 0}\right|$.

▶ **53.** [*M21*] What is the millionth partition generated by Algorithm H when $m = 32$ and $n = 100$? *Hint:* $999999 = \left|{80 \atop 12}\right| + \left|{66 \atop 11}\right| + \left|{50 \atop 7}\right| + \left|{41 \atop 6}\right| + \left|{33 \atop 4}\right| + \left|{26 \atop 4}\right| + \left|{21 \atop 4}\right|$.

▶ **54.** [*M30*] Let $\alpha = a_1 a_2 \ldots$ and $\beta = b_1 b_2 \ldots$ be partitions of n. We say that α *majorizes* β, written $\alpha \succeq \beta$ or $\beta \preceq \alpha$, if $a_1 + \cdots + a_k \ge b_1 + \cdots + b_k$ for all $k \ge 0$.

a) True or false: $\alpha \succeq \beta$ implies $\alpha \ge \beta$ (lexicographically).

b) True or false: $\alpha \succeq \beta$ implies $\beta^T \succeq \alpha^T$.

c) Show that any two partitions of n have a greatest lower bound $\alpha \wedge \beta$ such that $\alpha \succeq \gamma$ and $\beta \succeq \gamma$ if and only if $\alpha \wedge \beta \succeq \gamma$. Explain how to compute $\alpha \wedge \beta$.

d) Similarly, explain how to compute a least upper bound $\alpha \vee \beta$ such that $\gamma \succeq \alpha$ and $\gamma \succeq \beta$ if and only if $\gamma \succeq \alpha \vee \beta$.

e) If α has l parts and β has m parts, how many parts do $\alpha \wedge \beta$ and $\alpha \vee \beta$ have?

f) True or false: If α has distinct parts and β has distinct parts, then so do $\alpha \wedge \beta$ and $\alpha \vee \beta$.

▶ **55.** [*M37*] Continuing the previous exercise, say that α *covers* β if $\alpha \succeq \beta$ and $\alpha \ne \beta$, and if $\alpha \succeq \gamma \succeq \beta$ implies that $\gamma = \alpha$ or $\gamma = \beta$. For example, Fig. 52 illustrates the covering relations between partitions of the number 12.

a) Let us write $\alpha \rhd \beta$ if $\alpha = a_1 a_2 \ldots$ and $\beta = b_1 b_2 \ldots$ are partitions for which $b_k = a_k - [k = l] + [k = l + 1]$ for all $k \ge 1$ and some $l \ge 1$. Prove that α covers β if and only if $\alpha \rhd \beta$ or $\beta^T \rhd \alpha^T$.

b) Show that there is an easy way to tell if α covers β by looking at the rim representations of α and β.

c) Let $n = \binom{n_2}{2} + \binom{n_1}{1}$ where $n_2 > n_1 \ge 0$ and $n_2 > 2$. Show that no partition of n covers more than $n_2 - 2$ partitions.

d) Say that the partition μ is *minimal* if there is no partition λ with $\mu \rhd \lambda$. Prove that μ is minimal if and only if μ^T has distinct parts.

e) Suppose $\alpha = \alpha_0 \rhd \alpha_1 \rhd \cdots \rhd \alpha_k$ and $\alpha = \alpha'_0 \rhd \alpha'_1 \rhd \cdots \rhd \alpha'_{k'}$, where α_k and $\alpha'_{k'}$ are minimal partitions. Prove that $k = k'$ and $\alpha_k = \alpha'_{k'}$.

f) Explain how to compute the lexicographically smallest partition into distinct parts that majorizes a given partition α.

g) Describe λ_n, the lexicographically smallest partition of n into distinct parts. What is the length of all paths $n^1 = \alpha_0 \rhd \alpha_1 \rhd \cdots \rhd \lambda_n^T$?

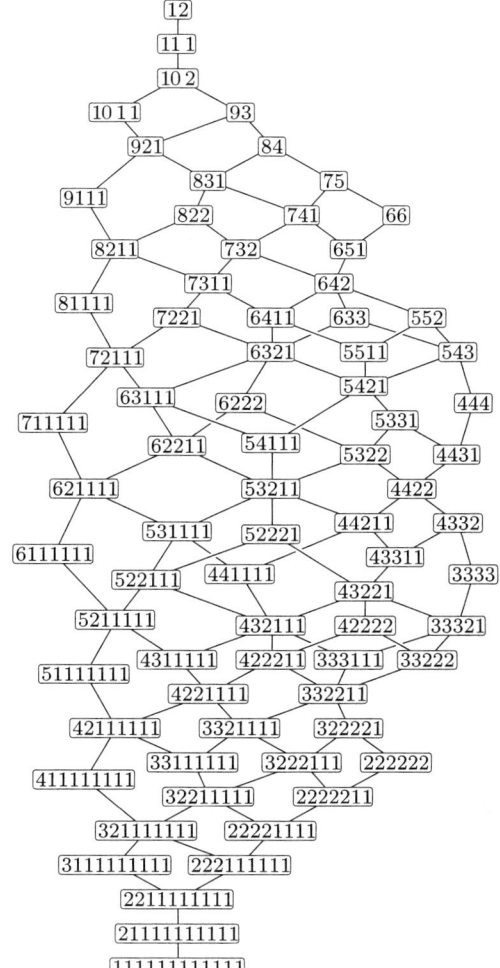

Fig. 52. The majorization lattice for partitions of 12. (See exercises 54–58.)

h) What are the lengths of the longest and shortest paths of the form $n^1 = \alpha_0, \alpha_1, \ldots, \alpha_l = 1^n$, where α_j covers α_{j+1} for $0 \le j < l$?

▶ **56.** [*M32*] Design an algorithm to generate all partitions α such that $\lambda \preceq \alpha \preceq \mu$, given partitions λ and μ with $\lambda \preceq \mu$.

Note: Such an algorithm has numerous applications. For example, to generate all partitions that have m parts and no part exceeding l, we can let λ be the smallest such partition, namely $\lceil n/m \rceil \ldots \lfloor n/m \rfloor$ as in exercise 3, and let μ be the largest, namely $\left((n-m+1)1^{m-1}\right) \wedge \left(l^{\lfloor n/l \rfloor}(n \bmod l)\right)$. Similarly, according to a well-known theorem of H. G. Landau [*Bull. Math. Biophysics* **15** (1953), 143–148], the partitions of $\binom{m}{2}$ such that

$$\left\lfloor \frac{m}{2} \right\rfloor^{\lfloor m/2 \rfloor} \left\lfloor \frac{m-1}{2} \right\rfloor^{\lceil m/2 \rceil} \preceq \alpha \preceq (m-1)(m-2)\ldots21$$

are the possible "score vectors" of a round-robin tournament, namely the partitions $a_1 \ldots a_m$ such that the jth strongest player wins a_j games.

57. [*M22*] Suppose a matrix (a_{ij}) of 0s and 1s has row sums $r_i = \sum_j a_{ij}$ and column sums $c_j = \sum_i a_{ij}$. By permuting rows and columns we can assume that $r_1 \geq r_2 \geq \cdots$ and $c_1 \geq c_2 \geq \cdots$. Then $\lambda = r_1 r_2 \ldots$ and $\mu = c_1 c_2 \ldots$ are partitions of $n = \sum_{i,j} a_{ij}$. Prove that such a matrix exists if and only if $\lambda \preceq \mu^T$.

58. [*M23*] (*Symmetrical means.*) Let $\alpha = a_1 \ldots a_m$ and $\beta = b_1 \ldots b_m$ be partitions of n. Prove that the inequality

$$\frac{1}{m!} \sum x_{p_1}^{a_1} \ldots x_{p_m}^{a_m} \geq \frac{1}{m!} \sum x_{p_1}^{b_1} \ldots x_{p_m}^{b_m}$$

holds for all nonnegative values of the variables $(x_1, \ldots, x_m)$, where the sums range over all $m!$ permutations of $\{1, \ldots, m\}$, if and only if $\alpha \succeq \beta$. (For example, this inequality reduces to $(y_1 + \cdots + y_n)/n \geq (y_1 \ldots y_n)^{1/n}$ in the special case $m = n$, $\alpha = n0 \ldots 0$, $\beta = 11 \ldots 1$, $x_j = y_j^{1/n}$.)

59. [*M22*] The Gray path (59) is symmetrical in the sense that the reversed sequence $6, 51, \ldots, 111111$ is the same as the conjugate sequence $(111111)^T, (21111)^T, \ldots, (6)^T$. Find all Gray paths $\alpha_1, \ldots, \alpha_{p(n)}$ that are symmetrical in this way.

60. [*23*] Complete the proof of Theorem S by modifying the definitions of $L(m, n)$ and $M(m, n)$ in all places where $L(4, 6)$ is called in (62) and (63).

61. [*26*] Implement a partition-generation scheme based on Theorem S, always specifying the two parts that have changed between visits.

62. [*46*] Prove or disprove: For all sufficiently large integers n and $3 \leq m < n$ such that $n \bmod m \neq 0$, and for all partitions α of n with $a_1 \leq m$, there is a Gray path for all partitions with parts $\leq m$, beginning at 1^n and ending at α, unless $\alpha = 1^n$ or $\alpha = 21^{n-2}$.

63. [*47*] For which partitions λ and μ is there a Gray code through all partitions α such that $\lambda \preceq \alpha \preceq \mu$?

▶ **64.** [*32*] (*Binary partitions.*) Design a loopless algorithm that visits all partitions of n into powers of 2, where each step replaces $2^k + 2^k$ by 2^{k+1} or vice versa.

65. [*23*] It is well known that every commutative group of m elements can be represented as a discrete torus $T(m_1, \ldots, m_n)$ with the addition operation of 7.2.1.3–(66), where $m = m_1 \ldots m_n$ and m_j is a multiple of m_{j+1} for $1 \leq j < n$. For example, when $m = 360 = 2^3 \cdot 3^2 \cdot 5^1$ there are six such groups, corresponding to the factorizations $(m_1, m_2, m_3) = (30, 6, 2), (60, 6, 1), (90, 2, 2), (120, 3, 1), (180, 2, 1),$ and $(360, 1, 1)$.

Explain how to generate all such factorizations systematically with an algorithm that changes exactly two of the factors m_j at each step.

▶ **66.** [*M25*] (*P-partitions.*) Instead of insisting that $a_1 \geq a_2 \geq \cdots$, suppose we want to consider all nonnegative compositions of n that satisfy a given *partial* order. For example, P. A. MacMahon observed that all solutions to the "up-down" inequalities $a_4 \leq a_2 \geq a_3 \leq a_1$ can be divided into five nonoverlapping types:

$$a_1 \geq a_2 \geq a_3 \geq a_4; \quad a_1 \geq a_2 \geq a_4 > a_3;$$

$$a_2 > a_1 \geq a_3 \geq a_4; \quad a_2 > a_1 \geq a_4 > a_3; \quad a_2 \geq a_4 > a_1 \geq a_3.$$

Each of these types is easily enumerated since, for example, $a_2 > a_1 \geq a_4 > a_3$ is equivalent to $a_2 - 2 \geq a_1 - 1 \geq a_4 - 1 \geq a_3$; the number of solutions with $a_3 \geq 0$ and $a_1 + a_2 + a_3 + a_4 = n$ is the number of partitions of $n - 1 - 2 - 0 - 1$ into at most four parts.

Explain how to solve a general problem of this kind: Given any partial order relation $\prec$ on m elements, consider all m-tuples $a_1 \ldots a_m$ with the property that $a_j \geq a_k$

when $j \prec k$. Assuming that the subscripts have been chosen so that $j \prec k$ implies $j \leq k$, show that all of the desired m-tuples fall into exactly N classes, one for each of the outputs of the topological sorting algorithm 7.2.1.2V. What is the generating function for all such $a_1 \ldots a_m$ that are nonnegative and sum to n? How could you generate them all?

67. [*M25*] (P. A. MacMahon, 1886.) A *perfect partition* of n is a multiset that has exactly $n+1$ submultisets, and these multisets are partitions of the integers $0, 1, \ldots, n$. For example, the multisets $\{1,1,1,1,1\}$, $\{2,2,1\}$, and $\{3,1,1\}$ are perfect partitions of 5.

Explain how to construct the perfect partitions of n that have fewest elements.

68. [*M23*] What partition of n into m parts has the largest product $a_1 \ldots a_m$, when (a) m is given; (b) m is arbitrary?

69. [*M30*] Find all $n < 10^9$ such that the equation $x_1 + x_2 + \cdots + x_n = x_1 x_2 \ldots x_n$ has only one solution in positive integers $x_1 \geq x_2 \geq \cdots \geq x_n$. (There is, for example, only one solution when $n = 2$, 3, or 4; but $5 + 2 + 1 + 1 + 1 = 5 \cdot 2 \cdot 1 \cdot 1 \cdot 1$ and $3 + 3 + 1 + 1 + 1 = 3 \cdot 3 \cdot 1 \cdot 1 \cdot 1$ and $2 + 2 + 2 + 1 + 1 = 2 \cdot 2 \cdot 2 \cdot 1 \cdot 1$.)

70. [*M30*] ("Bulgarian solitaire.") Take n cards and divide them arbitrarily into one or more piles. Then repeatedly remove one card from each pile and form a new pile.

Show that if $n = 1 + 2 + \cdots + m$, this process always reaches a self-repeating state with piles of sizes $\{m, m-1, \ldots, 1\}$. For example, if $n = 10$ and if we start with piles whose sizes are $\{3, 3, 2, 2\}$, we get the sequence of partitions

$$3322 \to 42211 \to 5311 \to 442 \to 3331 \to 4222 \to 43111 \to 532 \to 4321 \to 4321 \to \cdots.$$

What cycles of states are possible for other values of n?

71. [*M46*] Continuing the previous problem, what is the maximum number of steps that can occur before n-card Bulgarian solitaire reaches a cyclic state?

72. [*M30*] How many partitions of n have no predecessor in Bulgarian solitaire?

73. [*M25*] Suppose we write down all partitions of n, for example

$$6, \ 51, \ 42, \ 411, \ 33, \ 321, \ 3111, \ 222, \ 2211, \ 21111, \ 111111$$

when $n = 6$, and change each jth occurrence of k to j in each one:

$$1, \ 11, \ 11, \ 112, \ 12, \ 111, \ 1123, \ 123, \ 1212, \ 11234, \ 123456.$$

a) Prove that this operation yields a permutation of the individual elements.
b) How many times does the element k appear altogether?

7.2.1.5. Generating all set partitions.

Now let's shift gears and concentrate on a rather different kind of partition. The *partitions of a set* are the ways to regard that set as a union of nonempty, disjoint subsets called *blocks*. For example, we listed the five essentially different partitions of $\{1, 2, 3\}$ at the beginning of the previous section, in 7.2.1.4–(2) and 7.2.1.4–(4). Those five partitions can also be written more compactly in the form

$$123, \quad 12|3, \quad 13|2, \quad 1|23, \quad 1|2|3, \tag{1}$$

using a vertical line to separate one block from another. In this list the elements of each block could have been written in any order, and so could the blocks themselves, because '13|2' and '31|2' and '2|13' and '2|31' all represent the same partition. But we can standardize the representation by agreeing, for example, to list the elements of each block in increasing order, and to arrange the blocks in increasing order of their smallest elements. With this convention the partitions of $\{1, 2, 3, 4\}$ are

$$1234,\ 123|4,\ 124|3,\ 12|34,\ 12|3|4,\ 134|2,\ 13|24,\ 13|2|4,$$
$$14|23,\ 1|234,\ 1|23|4,\ 14|2|3,\ 1|24|3,\ 1|2|34,\ 1|2|3|4, \tag{2}$$

obtained by placing 4 among the blocks of (1) in all possible ways.

Set partitions arise in many different contexts. Political scientists and economists, for example, often see them as "coalitions"; computer system designers may consider them to be "cache hit patterns" for memory accesses; poets know them as "rhyme schemes" (see exercises 34–37). We saw in Section 2.3.3 that any *equivalence relation* between objects — namely any binary relation that is reflexive, symmetric, and transitive — defines a partition of those objects into so-called "equivalence classes." Conversely, every set partition defines an equivalence relation: If Π is a partition of $\{1, 2, \ldots, n\}$ we can write

$$j \equiv k \quad (\text{modulo } \Pi) \tag{3}$$

whenever j and k belong to the same block of Π.

One of the most convenient ways to represent a set partition inside a computer is to encode it as a *restricted growth string*, namely as a string $a_1 a_2 \ldots a_n$ of nonnegative integers in which we have

$$a_1 = 0 \quad \text{and} \quad a_{j+1} \leq 1 + \max(a_1, \ldots, a_j) \text{ for } 1 \leq j < n. \tag{4}$$

The idea is to set $a_j = a_k$ if and only if $j \equiv k$, and to choose the smallest available number for a_j whenever j is smallest in its block. For example, the restricted growth strings for the fifteen partitions in (2) are respectively

$$0000,\ 0001,\ 0010,\ 0011,\ 0012,\ 0100,\ 0101,\ 0102,$$
$$0110,\ 0111,\ 0112,\ 0120,\ 0121,\ 0122,\ 0123. \tag{5}$$

This convention suggests the following simple generation scheme, due to George Hutchinson [*CACM* **6** (1963), 613–614]:

Algorithm H (*Restricted growth strings in lexicographic order*). Given $n \geq 2$, this algorithm generates all partitions of $\{1, 2, \ldots, n\}$ by visiting all strings $a_1 a_2 \ldots a_n$ that satisfy the restricted growth condition (4). We maintain an auxiliary array $b_1 b_2 \ldots b_n$, where $b_{j+1} = 1 + \max(a_1, \ldots, a_j)$; the value of b_n is actually kept in a separate variable, m, for efficiency.

H1. [Initialize.] Set $a_1 \ldots a_n \leftarrow 0 \ldots 0$, $b_1 \ldots b_{n-1} \leftarrow 1 \ldots 1$, and $m \leftarrow 1$.

H2. [Visit.] Visit the restricted growth string $a_1 \ldots a_n$, which represents a partition into $m + [a_n = m]$ blocks. Then go to H4 if $a_n = m$.

H3. [Increase a_n.] Set $a_n \leftarrow a_n + 1$ and return to H2.

H4. [Find j.] Set $j \leftarrow n - 1$; then, while $a_j = b_j$, set $j \leftarrow j - 1$.

H5. [Increase a_j.] Terminate if $j = 1$. Otherwise set $a_j \leftarrow a_j + 1$.

H6. [Zero out $a_{j+1} \ldots a_n$.] Set $m \leftarrow b_j + [a_j = b_j]$ and $j \leftarrow j + 1$. Then, while $j < n$, set $a_j \leftarrow 0$, $b_j \leftarrow m$, and $j \leftarrow j + 1$. Finally set $a_n \leftarrow 0$ and go back to H2. ∎

Exercise 47 proves that steps H4–H6 are rarely necessary, and that the loops in H4 and H6 are almost always short. A linked-list variant of this algorithm appears in exercise 2.

Gray codes for set partitions. One way to pass quickly through all set partitions is to change just one digit of the restricted growth string $a_1 \ldots a_n$ at each step, because a change to a_j simply means that element j moves from one block to another. An elegant way to arrange such a list was proposed by Gideon Ehrlich [*JACM* **20** (1973), 507–508]: We can successively append the digits

$$0, \ m, \ m-1, \ \ldots, \ 1 \qquad \text{or} \qquad 1, \ \ldots, \ m-1, \ m, \ 0 \qquad (6)$$

to each string $a_1 \ldots a_{n-1}$ in the list for partitions of $n - 1$ elements, where $m = 1 + \max(a_1, \ldots, a_{n-1})$, alternating between the two cases. Thus the list '00, 01' for $n = 2$ becomes '000, 001, 011, 012, 010' for $n = 3$; and that list becomes

$$\begin{aligned} & 0000, \ 0001, \ 0011, \ 0012, \ 0010, \ 0110, \ 0112, \ 0111, \\ & 0121, \ 0122, \ 0123, \ 0120, \ 0100, \ 0102, \ 0101 \end{aligned} \qquad (7)$$

when we extend it to the case $n = 4$. Exercise 14 shows that Ehrlich's scheme leads to a simple algorithm that achieves this Gray-code order without doing much more work than Algorithm H.

Suppose, however, that we aren't interested in *all* of the partitions; we might want only the ones that have exactly m blocks. Can we run through this smaller collection of restricted growth strings, still changing only one digit at a time? Yes; a very pretty way to generate such a list has been discovered by Frank Ruskey [*Lecture Notes in Comp. Sci.* **762** (1993), 205–206]. He defined two such sequences, A_{mn} and A'_{mn}, both of which start with the lexicographically smallest m-block string $0^{n-m}01 \ldots (m-1)$. The difference between them, if $n > m + 1$, is that A_{mn} ends with $01 \ldots (m-1)0^{n-m}$ while A'_{mn} ends with $0^{n-m-1}01 \ldots (m-1)0$. Here are Ruskey's recursive rules, when $1 < m < n$:

$$A_{m(n+1)} = \begin{cases} A_{(m-1)n}(m-1), A^R_{mn}(m-1), \ldots, A^R_{mn}1, A_{mn}0, & \text{if } m \text{ is even}; \\ A'_{(m-1)n}(m-1), A_{mn}(m-1), \ldots, A^R_{mn}1, A_{mn}0, & \text{if } m \text{ is odd}; \end{cases} \qquad (8)$$

$$A'_{m(n+1)} = \begin{cases} A'_{(m-1)n}(m-1), A_{mn}(m-1), \ldots, A_{mn}1, A^R_{mn}0, & \text{if } m \text{ is even}; \\ A_{(m-1)n}(m-1), A^R_{mn}(m-1), \ldots, A_{mn}1, A^R_{mn}0, & \text{if } m \text{ is odd}. \end{cases} \qquad (9)$$

(In other words, we begin with either $A_{(m-1)n}(m-1)$ or $A'_{(m-1)n}(m-1)$ and then use either $A^R_{mn}j$ or $A_{mn}j$, alternately, as j decreases from $m - 1$ to 0.) Of course the base cases are simply one-element lists,

$$A_{1n} = A'_{1n} = \{0^n\} \qquad \text{and} \qquad A_{nn} = \{01 \ldots (n-1)\}. \qquad (10)$$

With these definitions the $\{^5_3\} = 25$ partitions of $\{1, 2, 3, 4, 5\}$ into three blocks are

$$00012,\ 00112,\ 01112,\ 01012,\ 01002,\ 01102,\ 00102,$$
$$00122,\ 01122,\ 01022,\ 01222,\ 01212,\ 01202,$$
$$01201,\ 01211,\ 01221,\ 01021,\ 01121,\ 00121, \qquad (11)$$
$$00120,\ 01120,\ 01020,\ 01220,\ 01210,\ 01200.$$

(See exercise 17 for an efficient implementation.)

In Ehrlich's scheme (7) the rightmost digits of $a_1 \ldots a_n$ vary most rapidly, but in Ruskey's scheme most of the changes occur near the left. In both cases, however, each step affects just one digit a_j, and the changes are quite simple: Either a_j changes by ± 1, or it jumps between the two extreme values 0 and $1 + \max(a_1, \ldots, a_{j-1})$. Under the same constraints, the sequence A'_{1n}, A'_{2n}, ..., A'_{nn} runs through *all* partitions, in increasing order of the number of blocks.

The number of set partitions. We've seen that there are 5 partitions of $\{1, 2, 3\}$ and 15 of $\{1, 2, 3, 4\}$. A quick way to compute these counts was discovered by C. S. Peirce, who presented the following triangle of numbers in the *American Journal of Mathematics* **3** (1880), page 48:

$$
\begin{array}{cccccc}
1 \\
2 & 1 \\
5 & 3 & 2 \\
15 & 10 & 7 & 5 \\
52 & 37 & 27 & 20 & 15 \\
203 & 151 & 114 & 87 & 67 & 52
\end{array}
\qquad (12)
$$

Here the entries ϖ_{n1}, ϖ_{n2}, ..., ϖ_{nn} of the nth row obey the simple recurrence

$$\varpi_{nk} = \varpi_{(n-1)k} + \varpi_{n(k+1)} \text{ if } 1 \le k < n; \qquad \varpi_{nn} = \varpi_{(n-1)1} \text{ if } n > 1; \qquad (13)$$

and $\varpi_{11} = 1$. Peirce's triangle has many remarkable properties, some of which are surveyed in exercises 26–31. For example, ϖ_{nk} is the number of partitions of $\{1, 2, \ldots, n\}$ in which k is the smallest of its block.

The entries on the diagonal and in the first column of Peirce's triangle, which tell us the total number of set partitions, are commonly known as *Bell numbers*, because E. T. Bell wrote several influential papers about them [*AMM* **41** (1934), 411–419; *Annals of Math.* (2) **35** (1934), 258–277; **39** (1938), 539–557]. We shall denote Bell numbers by ϖ_n, following the lead of Louis Comtet, in order to avoid confusion with the Bernoulli numbers B_n. The first few cases are

$$
\begin{array}{rccccccccccccc}
n = & 0 & 1 & 2 & 3 & 4 & 5 & 6 & 7 & 8 & 9 & 10 & 11 & 12 \\
\varpi_n = & 1 & 1 & 2 & 5 & 15 & 52 & 203 & 877 & 4140 & 21147 & 115975 & 678570 & 4213597
\end{array}
$$

Notice that this sequence grows rapidly, but not as fast as $n!$; we will prove below that $\varpi_n = \Theta(n/\log n)^n$.

The Bell numbers $\varpi_n = \varpi_{n1}$ for $n \ge 0$ must satisfy the recurrence formula

$$\varpi_{n+1} = \varpi_n + \binom{n}{1}\varpi_{n-1} + \binom{n}{2}\varpi_{n-2} + \cdots = \sum_k \binom{n}{k}\varpi_{n-k}, \qquad (14)$$

because every partition of $\{1, \ldots, n + 1\}$ is obtained by choosing k elements of $\{1, \ldots, n\}$ to put in the block containing $n+1$ and by partitioning the remaining elements in ϖ_{n-k} ways, for some k. This recurrence, found by Yoshisuke Matsunaga in the 18th century (see Section 7.2.1.7), leads to a nice generating function,

$$\Pi(z) = \sum_{n=0}^{\infty} \varpi_n \frac{z^n}{n!} = e^{e^z - 1}, \tag{15}$$

discovered by W. A. Whitworth [*Choice and Chance*, 3rd edition (1878), 3.XXIV]. For if we multiply both sides of (14) by $z^n/n!$ and sum on n we get

$$\Pi'(z) = \sum_{n=0}^{\infty} \varpi_{n+1} \frac{z^n}{n!} = \left(\sum_{k=0}^{\infty} \frac{z^k}{k!}\right)\left(\sum_{m=0}^{\infty} \varpi_m \frac{z^m}{m!}\right) = e^z \Pi(z),$$

and (15) is the solution to this differential equation with $\Pi(0) = 1$.

The numbers ϖ_n had been studied for many years because of their curious properties related to this formula, long before Whitworth pointed out their combinatorial connection with set partitions. For example, we have

$$\varpi_n = \frac{n!}{e}[z^n]e^{e^z} = \frac{n!}{e}[z^n]\sum_{k=0}^{\infty}\frac{e^{kz}}{k!} = \frac{1}{e}\sum_{k=0}^{\infty}\frac{k^n}{k!} \tag{16}$$

[*Mat. Sbornik* **3** (1868), 62; **4** (1869), 39; G. Dobiński, *Archiv der Math. und Physik* **61** (1877), 333–336; **63** (1879), 108–110]. Christian Kramp discussed the expansion of e^{e^z} in *Der polynomische Lehrsatz*, ed. by C. F. Hindenburg (Leipzig: 1796), 112–113; he mentioned two ways to compute the coefficients, namely either to use (14) or to use a summation of $p(n)$ terms, one for each ordinary partition of n. (See Arbogast's formula, exercise 1.2.5–21. Kramp, who came close to discovering that formula, seemed to prefer his partition-based method, not realizing that it would require more than polynomial time as n got larger and larger; and he computed 116015, not 115975, for the coefficient of z^{10}.)

*Asymptotic estimates. We can learn how fast ϖ_n grows by using one of the most basic principles of complex residue theory: If the power series $\sum_{k=0}^{\infty} a_k z^k$ converges whenever $|z| < r$, then

$$a_{n-1} = \frac{1}{2\pi i}\oint \frac{a_0 + a_1 z + a_2 z^2 + \cdots}{z^n}\,dz, \tag{17}$$

if the integral is taken along a simple closed path that goes counterclockwise around the origin and stays inside the circle $|z| = r$. Let $f(z) = \sum_{k=0}^{\infty} a_k z^{k-n}$ be the integrand. We're free to choose any such path, but special techniques often apply when the path goes through a point z_0 at which the derivative $f'(z_0)$ is zero, because we have

$$f(z_0 + \epsilon e^{i\theta}) = f(z_0) + \frac{f''(z_0)}{2}\epsilon^2 e^{2i\theta} + O(\epsilon^3) \tag{18}$$

in the vicinity of such a point. If, for example, $f(z_0)$ and $f''(z_0)$ are real and positive, say $f(z_0) = u$ and $f''(z_0) = 2v$, this formula says that the value of

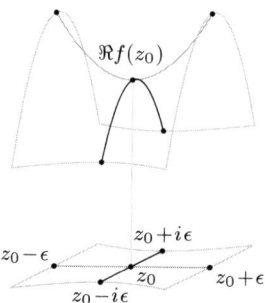

Fig. 53. The behavior of an analytic function near a saddle point.

$f(z_0 \pm \epsilon)$ is approximately $u + v\epsilon^2$ while $f(z_0 \pm i\epsilon)$ is approximately $u - v\epsilon^2$. If z moves from $z_0 - i\epsilon$ to $z_0 + i\epsilon$, the value of $f(z)$ rises to a maximum value u, then falls again; but the larger value $u + v\epsilon^2$ occurs both to the left and to the right of this path. In other words, a mountaineer who goes hiking on the complex plane, when the altitude at point z is $\Re f(z)$, encounters a "pass" at z_0; the terrain looks like a saddle at that point. The overall integral of $f(z)$ will be the same if taken around any path, but a path that doesn't go through the pass won't be as nice because it will have to cancel out some higher values of $f(z)$ that could have been avoided. Therefore we tend to get best results by choosing a path that goes through z_0, in the direction of increasing imaginary part. This important technique, due to P. Debye [*Math. Annalen* **67** (1909), 535–558], is called the "saddle point method."

Let's get familiar with the saddle point method by starting with an example for which we already know the answer:

$$\frac{1}{(n-1)!} = \frac{1}{2\pi i} \oint \frac{e^z}{z^n}\, dz. \tag{19}$$

Our goal is to find a good approximation for the value of the integral on the right when n is large. It will be convenient to deal with $f(z) = e^z/z^n$ by writing it as $e^{g(z)}$ where $g(z) = z - n \ln z$; then the saddle point occurs where $g'(z_0) = 1 - n/z_0$ is zero, namely at $z_0 = n$. If $z = n + it$ we have

$$g(z) = g(n) + \sum_{k=2}^{\infty} \frac{g^{(k)}(n)}{k!}(it)^k$$

$$= n - n \ln n - \frac{t^2}{2n} + \frac{it^3}{3n^2} + \frac{t^4}{4n^3} - \frac{it^5}{5n^4} + \cdots$$

because $g^{(k)}(z) = (-1)^k (k-1)!\, n/z^k$ when $k \geq 2$. Let's integrate $f(z)$ on a rectangular path from $n - im$ to $n + im$ to $-n + im$ to $-n - im$ to $n - im$:

$$\frac{1}{2\pi i} \oint \frac{e^z}{z^n}\, dz = \frac{1}{2\pi} \int_{-m}^{m} f(n + it)\, dt + \frac{1}{2\pi i} \int_{n}^{-n} f(t + im)\, dt$$

$$+ \frac{1}{2\pi} \int_{m}^{-m} f(-n + it)\, dt + \frac{1}{2\pi i} \int_{-n}^{n} f(t - im)\, dt.$$

Clearly $|f(z)| \le 2^{-n} f(n)$ on the last three sides of this path if we choose $m = 2n$, because $|e^z| = e^{\Re z}$ and $|z| \ge \max(|\Re z|, |\Im z|)$; so we're left with

$$\frac{1}{2\pi i} \oint \frac{e^z}{z^n}\, dz = \frac{1}{2\pi} \int_{-m}^{m} e^{g(n+it)}\, dt + O\left(\frac{ne^n}{2^n n^n}\right).$$

Now we fall back on a technique that we've used several times before — for example to derive Eq. 5.1.4–(53): If $\hat{f}(t)$ is a good approximation to $f(t)$ when $t \in A$, and if the sums $\sum_{t \in B} |f(t)|$ and $\sum_{t \in C} |\hat{f}(t)|$ are both small, then $\sum_{t \in A \cup C} \hat{f}(t)$ is a good approximation to $\sum_{t \in A \cup B} f(t)$. The same idea applies to integrals as well as sums. [This general method, introduced by Laplace in 1782, is often called "trading tails"; see *CMath* §9.4.] If $|t| \le n^{1/2+\epsilon}$ we have

$$\begin{aligned}
e^{g(n+it)} &= \exp\left(g(n) - \frac{t^2}{2n} + \frac{it^3}{3n^2} + \cdots\right) \\
&= \frac{e^n}{n^n} \exp\left(-\frac{t^2}{2n} + \frac{it^3}{3n^2} + \frac{t^4}{4n^3} + O(n^{5\epsilon - 3/2})\right) \\
&= \frac{e^n}{n^n} e^{-t^2/(2n)} \left(1 + \frac{it^3}{3n^2} + \frac{t^4}{4n^3} - \frac{t^6}{18n^4} + O(n^{9\epsilon - 3/2})\right).
\end{aligned}$$

And when $|t| > n^{1/2+\epsilon}$ we have

$$\left|e^{g(n+it)}\right| < \left|f(n + in^{1/2+\epsilon})\right| = \frac{e^n}{n^n} \exp\left(-\frac{n}{2}\ln(1 + n^{2\epsilon - 1})\right) = O\left(\frac{e^{n - n^{2\epsilon}/2}}{n^n}\right).$$

Furthermore the incomplete gamma function

$$\int_{n^{1/2+\epsilon}}^{\infty} e^{-t^2/(2n)} t^k\, dt = 2^{(k-1)/2} n^{(k+1)/2} \Gamma\left(\frac{k+1}{2}, \frac{n^{2\epsilon}}{2}\right) = O(n^{O(1)} e^{-n^{2\epsilon}/2})$$

is negligible. Thus we can trade tails and obtain the approximation

$$\begin{aligned}
\frac{1}{2\pi i} \oint \frac{e^z}{z^n}\, dz &= \frac{e^n}{2\pi n^n} \int_{-\infty}^{\infty} e^{-t^2/(2n)} \left(1 + \frac{it^3}{3n^2} + \frac{t^4}{4n^3} - \frac{t^6}{18n^4} + O(n^{9\epsilon - 3/2})\right) dt \\
&= \frac{e^n}{2\pi n^n}\left(I_0 + \frac{i}{3n^2} I_3 + \frac{1}{4n^3} I_4 - \frac{1}{18n^4} I_6 + O(n^{9\epsilon - 3/2})\right),
\end{aligned}$$

where $I_k = \int_{-\infty}^{\infty} e^{-t^2/(2n)} t^k\, dt$. Of course $I_k = 0$ when k is odd. Otherwise we can evaluate I_k by using the well-known fact that

$$\int_{-\infty}^{\infty} e^{-at^2} t^{2l}\, dt = \frac{\Gamma((2l+1)/2)}{a^{(2l+1)/2}} = \frac{\sqrt{2\pi}}{(2a)^{(2l+1)/2}} \prod_{j=1}^{l} (2j-1) \qquad (20)$$

when $a > 0$; see exercise 39. Putting everything together gives us, for all $\epsilon > 0$, the asymptotic estimate

$$\frac{1}{(n-1)!} = \frac{e^n}{\sqrt{2\pi}\, n^{n-1/2}} \left(1 + 0 + \frac{3}{4n} - \frac{15}{18n} + O(n^{9\epsilon - 2})\right); \qquad (21)$$

this result agrees perfectly with Stirling's approximation, which we derived by quite different methods in 1.2.11.2–(19). Further terms in the expansion of

$g(n + it)$ would allow us to prove that the true error in (21) is only $O(n^{-2})$, because the same procedure yields an asymptotic series of the general form $e^n/(\sqrt{2\pi}\,n^{n-1/2})\big(1 + c_1/n + c_2/n^2 + \cdots + c_m/n^m + O(n^{-m-1})\big)$ for all m.

Our derivation of this result has glossed over an important technicality: The function $\ln z$ is not single-valued along the path of integration, because it grows by $2\pi i$ when we loop around the origin. Indeed, this fact underlies the basic mechanism that makes the residue theorem work. But our reasoning was valid because the ambiguity of the logarithm does not affect the integrand $f(z) = e^z/z^n$ when n is an integer. Furthermore, if n were not an integer, we could have adapted the argument and kept it rigorous by choosing to carry out the integral (19) along a path that starts at $-\infty$, circles the origin counterclockwise and returns to $-\infty$. That would have given us Hankel's integral for the gamma function, Eq. 1.2.5–(17); we could thereby have derived the asymptotic formula

$$\frac{1}{\Gamma(x)} = \frac{1}{2\pi i}\oint \frac{e^z}{z^x}\,dz = \frac{e^x}{\sqrt{2\pi}\,x^{x-1/2}}\left(1 - \frac{1}{12x} + O(x^{-2})\right), \qquad (22)$$

valid for all real x as $x \to \infty$.

So the saddle point method seems to work — although it isn't the simplest way to get this particular result. Let's apply it now to deduce the approximate size of the Bell numbers:

$$\frac{\varpi_{n-1}}{(n-1)!} = \frac{1}{2\pi i e}\oint e^{g(z)}\,dz, \qquad g(z) = e^z - n\ln z. \qquad (23)$$

A saddle point for the new integrand occurs at the point $z_0 = \xi > 0$, where

$$\xi e^\xi = n. \qquad (24)$$

(We should actually write $\xi(n)$ to indicate that ξ depends on n; but that would clutter up the formulas below.) Let's assume for the moment that a little bird has told us the value of ξ. Then we want to integrate on a path where $z = \xi + it$, and we have

$$g(\xi + it) = e^\xi - n\left(\ln \xi - \frac{(it)^2}{2!}\frac{\xi + 1}{\xi^2} - \frac{(it)^3}{3!}\frac{\xi^2 - 2!}{\xi^3} - \frac{(it)^4}{4!}\frac{\xi^3 + 3!}{\xi^4} + \cdots\right).$$

By integrating on a suitable rectangular path, we can prove as above that the integral in (23) is well approximated by

$$\int_{-n^{\epsilon-1/2}}^{n^{\epsilon-1/2}} e^{g(\xi) - na_2 t^2 - nia_3 t^3 + na_4 t^4 + \cdots}\,dt, \qquad a_k = \frac{\xi^{k-1} + (-1)^k(k-1)!}{k!\,\xi^k}; \qquad (25)$$

see exercise 43. Noting that $a_k t^k$ is $O(n^{k\epsilon - k/2})$ inside this integral, we obtain an asymptotic expansion of the form

$$\varpi_{n-1} = \frac{e^{e^\xi - 1}(n-1)!}{\xi^{n-1}\sqrt{2\pi n(\xi + 1)}}\left(1 + \frac{b_1}{n} + \frac{b_2}{n^2} + \cdots + \frac{b_m}{n^m} + O\left(\frac{\log n}{n}\right)^{m+1}\right), \qquad (26)$$

where $(\xi+1)^{3k}b_k$ is a polynomial of degree $4k$ in ξ. (See exercise 44.) For example,

$$b_1 = -\frac{2\xi^4-3\xi^3-20\xi^2-18\xi+2}{24(\xi+1)^3}; \qquad (27)$$

$$b_2 = \frac{4\xi^8-156\xi^7-695\xi^6-696\xi^5+1092\xi^4+2916\xi^3+1972\xi^2-72\xi+4}{1152(\xi+1)^6}. \qquad (28)$$

Stirling's approximation (21) can be used in (26) to prove that

$$\varpi_{n-1} = \exp\left(n\left(\xi-1+\frac{1}{\xi}\right)-\xi-\frac{1}{2}\ln(\xi+1)-1-\frac{\xi}{12n}+O\left(\frac{\log n}{n}\right)^2\right); \quad (29)$$

and exercise 45 proves the similar formula

$$\varpi_n = \exp\left(n\left(\xi-1+\frac{1}{\xi}\right)-\frac{1}{2}\ln(\xi+1)-1-\frac{\xi}{12n}+O\left(\frac{\log n}{n}\right)^2\right). \qquad (30)$$

Consequently we have $\varpi_n/\varpi_{n-1} \approx e^\xi = n/\xi$. More precisely,

$$\frac{\varpi_{n-1}}{\varpi_n} = \frac{\xi}{n}\left(1+O\left(\frac{1}{n}\right)\right). \qquad (31)$$

But what is the asymptotic value of ξ? The definition (24) implies that

$$\xi = \ln n - \ln \xi = \ln n - \ln(\ln n - \ln \xi)$$

$$= \ln n - \ln\ln n + O\left(\frac{\log\log n}{\log n}\right); \qquad (32)$$

and we can go on in this vein, as shown in exercise 49. But the asymptotic series for ξ developed in this way never gives better accuracy than $O(1/(\log n)^m)$ for larger and larger m; so it is hugely inaccurate when multiplied by n in formula (29) for ϖ_{n-1} or formula (30) for ϖ_n.

Thus if we want to use (29) or (30) to calculate good numerical approximations to Bell numbers, our best strategy is to start by computing a good numerical value for ξ, without using a slowly convergent series. Newton's rootfinding method, discussed in the remarks preceding Algorithm 4.7N, yields the efficient iterative scheme

$$\xi_0 = \ln n, \qquad \xi_{k+1} = \frac{\xi_k}{\xi_k+1}(1+\xi_0-\ln\xi_k), \qquad (33)$$

which converges rapidly to the correct value. For example, when $n = 100$ the fifth iterate

$$\xi_5 = 3.38563\,01402\,90050\,18488\,82443\,64529\,72686\,74917- \qquad (34)$$

is already correct to 40 decimal places. Using this value in (29) gives us successive approximations

$$(1.6176088053\ldots, 1.6187421339\ldots, 1.6187065391\ldots, 1.6187060254\ldots) \times 10^{114}$$

when we take terms up to 1, b_1/n, b_2/n^2, b_3/n^3 into account; the true value of ϖ_{99} is the 115-digit integer $16187060274460\ldots20741$.

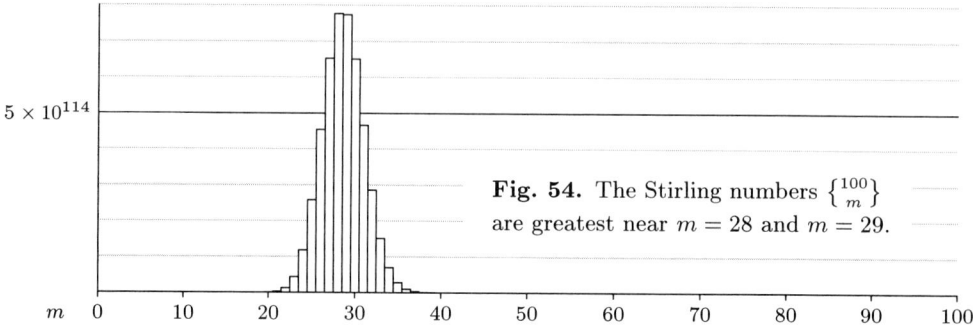

Fig. 54. The Stirling numbers $\left\{{100 \atop m}\right\}$ are greatest near $m = 28$ and $m = 29$.

Now that we know the number of set partitions ϖ_n, let's try to figure out how many of them have exactly m blocks. It turns out that nearly all partitions of $\{1, \ldots, n\}$ have roughly $n/\xi = e^\xi$ blocks, with about ξ elements per block. For example, Fig. 54 shows a histogram of the Stirling numbers $\left\{{n \atop m}\right\}$ when $n = 100$; in that case $e^\xi \approx 29.54$.

We can investigate the size of $\left\{{n \atop m}\right\}$ by applying the saddle point method to formula 1.2.9–(23), which states that

$$\left\{{n \atop m}\right\} = \frac{n!}{m!}[z^n](e^z - 1)^m = \frac{n!}{m!}\frac{1}{2\pi i}\oint e^{m\ln(e^z-1)-(n+1)\ln z}\,dz. \qquad (35)$$

Let $\alpha = (n+1)/m$. The function $g(z) = \alpha^{-1}\ln(e^z - 1) - \ln z$ has a saddle point at $\sigma > 0$ when

$$\frac{\sigma}{1 - e^{-\sigma}} = \alpha. \qquad (36)$$

Notice that $\alpha > 1$ for $1 \leq m \leq n$. This special value σ is given by

$$\sigma = \alpha - \beta, \qquad \beta = T(\alpha e^{-\alpha}), \qquad (37)$$

where T is the tree function of Eq. 2.3.4.4–(30). Indeed, β is the value between 0 and 1 for which we have

$$\beta e^{-\beta} = \alpha e^{-\alpha}; \qquad (38)$$

the function xe^{-x} increases from 0 to e^{-1} when x increases from 0 to 1, then it decreases to 0 again. Therefore β is uniquely defined, and we have

$$e^\sigma = \frac{\alpha}{\beta}. \qquad (39)$$

All such pairs α and β are obtainable by using the inverse formulas

$$\alpha = \frac{\sigma e^\sigma}{e^\sigma - 1}, \qquad \beta = \frac{\sigma}{e^\sigma - 1}; \qquad (40)$$

for example, the values $\alpha = \ln 4$ and $\beta = \ln 2$ correspond to $\sigma = \ln 2$.

We can show as above that the integral in (35) is asymptotically equivalent to an integral of $e^{(n+1)g(z)}\,dz$ over the path $z = \sigma + it$. (See exercise 58.) Exercise 56 proves that the Taylor series about $z = \sigma$,

$$g(\sigma + it) = g(\sigma) - \frac{t^2(1 - \beta)}{2\sigma^2} - \sum_{k=3}^{\infty} \frac{(it)^k}{k!} g^{(k)}(\sigma), \qquad (41)$$

has the property that

$$|g^{(k)}(\sigma)| < 2(k-1)!\,(1-\beta)/\sigma^k \qquad \text{for all } k > 0. \qquad (42)$$

Therefore we can conveniently remove a factor of $N = (n+1)(1-\beta)$ from the power series $(n+1)g(z)$, and the saddle point method leads to the formula

$$\left\{ {n \atop m} \right\} = \frac{n!}{m!}\frac{1}{(\alpha - \beta)^{n-m}\beta^m\sqrt{2\pi N}}\left(1 + \frac{b_1}{N} + \frac{b_2}{N^2} + \cdots + \frac{b_l}{N^l} + O\!\left(\frac{1}{N^{l+1}}\right)\right) \quad (43)$$

as $N \to \infty$, where $(1 - \beta)^{2k}b_k$ is a polynomial in α and β. (The quantity $(\alpha - \beta)^{n-m}\beta^m$ in the denominator comes from the fact that $(e^\sigma - 1)^m/\sigma^n = (\alpha/\beta - 1)^m/(\alpha - \beta)^n$, by (37) and (39).) For example,

$$b_1 = \frac{6 - \beta^3 - 4\alpha\beta^2 - \alpha^2\beta}{8(1 - \beta)} - \frac{5(2 - \beta^2 - \alpha\beta)^2}{24(1 - \beta)^2}. \qquad (44)$$

Exercise 57 proves that $N \to \infty$ if and only if $n - m \to \infty$. An asymptotic expansion for $\left\{{n \atop m}\right\}$ similar to (43), but somewhat more complicated, was first obtained by Leo Moser and Max Wyman, *Duke Math. J.* **25** (1957), 29–43.

Formula (43) looks a bit scary because it is designed to apply over the entire range of block counts m. Significant simplifications are possible when m is relatively small or relatively large (see exercises 60 and 61); but the simplified formulas don't give accurate results in the important cases when $\left\{{n \atop m}\right\}$ is largest. Let's look at those crucial cases more closely now, so that we can account for the sharp peak illustrated in Fig. 54.

Let $\xi e^\xi = n$ as in (24), and suppose $m = \exp(\xi + r/\sqrt{n}) = ne^{r/\sqrt{n}}/\xi$; we will assume that $|r| \le n^\epsilon$, so that m is near e^ξ. The leading term of (43) can be rewritten

$$\frac{n!}{m!}\frac{1}{(\alpha - \beta)^{n-m}\beta^m\sqrt{2\pi(n+1)(1-\beta)}} =$$

$$\frac{m^n}{m!}\frac{(n+1)!}{(n+1)^{n+1}}\frac{e^{n+1}}{\sqrt{2\pi(n+1)}}\left(1 - \frac{\beta}{\alpha}\right)^{m-n}\frac{e^{-\beta m}}{\sqrt{1-\beta}}, \qquad (45)$$

and Stirling's approximation for $(n+1)!$ is evidently ripe for cancellation in the midst of this expression. With the help of computer algebra we find

$$\frac{m^n}{m!} = \frac{1}{\sqrt{2\pi}}\exp\left(n\!\left(\xi - 1 + \frac{1}{\xi}\right) - \frac{1}{2}\!\left(\xi + r^2 + \frac{r^2}{\xi}\right)\right.$$

$$\left. - \left(\frac{r}{2} + \frac{r^3}{6} + \frac{r^3}{3\xi}\right)\frac{1}{\sqrt{n}} + O(n^{4\epsilon-1})\right);$$

and the relevant quantities related to α and β are

$$\frac{\beta}{\alpha} = \frac{\xi}{n} + \frac{r\xi^2}{n\sqrt{n}} + O(\xi^3 n^{2\epsilon-2});$$

$$e^{-\beta m} = \exp\left(-\xi - \frac{r\xi^2}{\sqrt{n}} + O(\xi^3 n^{2\epsilon-1})\right);$$

$$\left(1 - \frac{\beta}{\alpha}\right)^{m-n} = \exp\left(\xi - 1 + \frac{r(\xi^2 - \xi - 1)}{\sqrt{n}} + O(\xi^3 n^{2\epsilon-1})\right).$$

Therefore the overall result is

$$\left\{\begin{matrix} n \\ e^{\xi+r/\sqrt{n}} \end{matrix}\right\} = \frac{1}{\sqrt{2\pi}} \exp\left(n\left(\xi - 1 + \frac{1}{\xi}\right) - \frac{\xi}{2} - 1\right.$$
$$\left. - \frac{\xi+1}{2\xi}\left(r + \frac{3\xi(2\xi+3)+(\xi+2)r^2}{6(\xi+1)\sqrt{n}}\right)^2 + O(\xi^3 n^{4\epsilon-1})\right). \quad (46)$$

The squared expression on the last line is zero when

$$r = -\frac{\xi(2\xi+3)}{2(\xi+1)\sqrt{n}} + O(\xi^2 n^{-3/2});$$

thus the maximum occurs when the number of blocks is

$$m = \frac{n}{\xi} - \frac{3+2\xi}{2+2\xi} + O\left(\frac{\xi}{n}\right). \quad (47)$$

By comparing (46) to (30) we see that the largest Stirling number $\left\{\begin{matrix} n \\ m \end{matrix}\right\}$ for a given value of n is approximately equal to $\xi\varpi_n/\sqrt{2\pi n}$.

The saddle point method applies to problems that are considerably more difficult than the ones we have considered here. Excellent expositions of advanced techniques can be found in several books: N. G. de Bruijn, *Asymptotic Methods in Analysis* (1958), Chapters 5 and 6; F. W. J. Olver, *Asymptotics and Special Functions* (1974), Chapter 4; R. Wong, *Asymptotic Approximations of Integrals* (2001), Chapters 2 and 7.

*Random set partitions. The sizes of blocks in a partition of $\{1, \ldots, n\}$ constitute by themselves an ordinary partition of the number n. Therefore we might wonder what sort of partition they are likely to be. Figure 50 in Section 7.2.1.4 showed the result of superimposing the Ferrers diagrams of all $p(25) = 1958$ partitions of 25; those partitions tended to follow the symmetrical curve of Eq. 7.2.1.4–(49). By contrast, Fig. 55 shows what happens when we superimpose the corresponding diagrams of all $\varpi_{25} \approx 4.6386 \times 10^{18}$ partitions of the set $\{1, \ldots, 25\}$. Evidently the "shape" of a random set partition is quite different from the shape of a random integer partition.

This change is due to the fact that some integer partitions occur only a few times as block sizes of set partitions, while others are extremely common. For example, the partition $n = 1 + 1 + \cdots + 1$ arises in only one way, but if n is

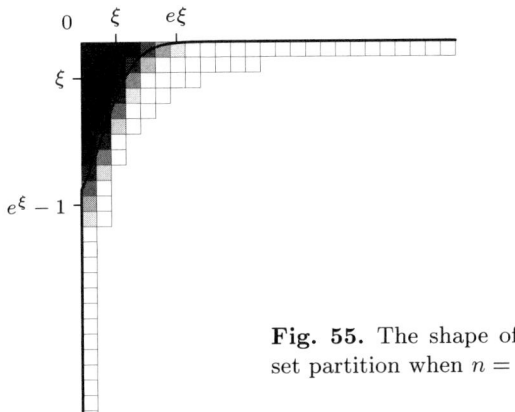

0   ξ $e\xi$

ξ —

$e^\xi - 1$ —

Fig. 55. The shape of a random set partition when $n = 25$.

even the partition $n = 2 + 2 + \cdots + 2$ arises in $(n-1)(n-3)\ldots(1)$ ways. When $n = 25$, the integer partition

$$25 = 4 + 4 + 3 + 3 + 3 + 2 + 2 + 2 + 1 + 1$$

actually occurs in more than 2% of all possible set partitions. (This particular partition turns out to be most common in the case $n = 25$. The answer to exercise 1.2.5–21 explains that exactly

$$\frac{n!}{c_1! \, 1!^{c_1} \, c_2! \, 2!^{c_2} \ldots c_n! \, n!^{c_n}} \tag{48}$$

set partitions correspond to the integer partition $n = c_1 \cdot 1 + c_2 \cdot 2 + \cdots + c_n \cdot n$.)

We can easily determine the average number of k-blocks in a random partition of $\{1, \ldots, n\}$: If we write out all ϖ_n of the possibilities, every particular k-element block occurs exactly ϖ_{n-k} times. Therefore the average number is

$$\binom{n}{k} \frac{\varpi_{n-k}}{\varpi_n}. \tag{49}$$

An extension of Eq. (31) above, proved in exercise 64, shows moreover that

$$\frac{\varpi_{n-k}}{\varpi_n} = \left(\frac{\xi}{n}\right)^k \left(1 + \frac{k\xi(k\xi + k + 1)}{2(\xi + 1)^2 n} + O\left(\frac{k^3}{n^2}\right)\right) \qquad \text{if } k \le n^{2/3}, \tag{50}$$

where ξ is defined in (24). Therefore if, say, $k \le n^\epsilon$, formula (49) simplifies to

$$\frac{n^k}{k!} \left(\frac{\xi}{n}\right)^k \left(1 + O\left(\frac{1}{n}\right)\right) = \frac{\xi^k}{k!} \left(1 + O(n^{2\epsilon - 1})\right). \tag{51}$$

There are, on average, about ξ blocks of size 1, and $\xi^2/2!$ blocks of size 2, etc.

The variance of these quantities is small (see exercise 65), and it turns out that a random partition behaves essentially as if the number of k-blocks were a Poisson deviate with mean $\xi^k/k!$. The smooth curve shown in Fig. 55 runs through the points $(f(k), k)$ in Ferrers-like coordinates, where

$$f(k) = \xi^{k+1}/(k+1)! + \xi^{k+2}/(k+2)! + \xi^{k+3}/(k+3)! + \cdots \tag{52}$$

is the approximate distance from the top line corresponding to block size $k \geq 0$. (This curve becomes more nearly vertical when n is larger.)

The largest block tends to contain approximately $e\xi$ elements. Furthermore, the probability that the block containing element 1 has size less than $\xi + a\sqrt{\xi}$ approaches the probability that a normal deviate is less than a. [See John Haigh, *J. Combinatorial Theory* **A13** (1972), 287–295; V. N. Sachkov, *Probabilistic Methods in Combinatorial Analysis* (1997), Chapter 4, translated from a Russian book published in 1978; Yu. Yakubovich, *J. Mathematical Sciences* **87** (1997), 4124–4137, translated from a Russian paper published in 1995; B. Pittel, *J. Combinatorial Theory* **A79** (1997), 326–359.]

A nice way to generate random partitions of $\{1, 2, \ldots, n\}$ was introduced by A. J. Stam in the *Journal of Combinatorial Theory* **A35** (1983), 231–240: Let M be a random integer that takes the value m with probability

$$p_m = \frac{m^n}{e\,m!\,\varpi_n}; \qquad (53)$$

these probabilities sum to 1 because of (16). Once M has been chosen, generate a random n-tuple $X_1 X_2 \ldots X_n$, where each X_j is uniformly and independently distributed between 0 and $M - 1$. Then let $i \equiv j$ in the partition if and only if $X_i = X_j$. This procedure works because each set partition that has k blocks is obtained with probability $\sum_{m \geq 0} (m^{\underline{k}}/m^n) p_m = 1/\varpi_n$.

For example, if $n = 25$ we have

$p_4 \approx .00000372$	$p_9 \approx .15689865$	$p_{14} \approx .04093663$	$p_{19} \approx .00006068$
$p_5 \approx .00019696$	$p_{10} \approx .21855285$	$p_{15} \approx .01531445$	$p_{20} \approx .00001094$
$p_6 \approx .00313161$	$p_{11} \approx .21526871$	$p_{16} \approx .00480507$	$p_{21} \approx .00000176$
$p_7 \approx .02110279$	$p_{12} \approx .15794784$	$p_{17} \approx .00128669$	$p_{22} \approx .00000026$
$p_8 \approx .07431024$	$p_{13} \approx .08987171$	$p_{18} \approx .00029839$	$p_{23} \approx .00000003$

and the other probabilities are negligible. So we can usually get a random partition of 25 elements by looking at a random 25-digit integer in radix 9, 10, 11, or 12. The number M can be generated using 3.4.1–(3); it tends to be approximately $n/\xi = e^\xi$ (see exercise 67).

*Partitions of a multiset. The partitions of an integer and the partitions of a set are just the extreme cases of a far more general problem, the partitions of a multiset. Indeed, the partitions of n are essentially the same as the partitions of $\{1, 1, \ldots, 1\}$, where there are n 1s.

From this standpoint there are essentially $p(n)$ types of multisets with n elements. For example, five different cases of multiset partitions arise when $n = 4$:

$$1234,\ 123|4,\ 124|3,\ 12|34,\ 12|3|4,\ 134|2,\ 13|24,\ 13|2|4,$$
$$14|23,\ 14|2|3,\ 1|234,\ 1|23|4,\ 1|24|3,\ 1|2|34,\ 1|2|3|4;$$
$$1123,\ 112|3,\ 113|2,\ 11|23,\ 11|2|3,\ 123|1,\ 12|13,\ 12|1|3,\ 13|1|2,\ 1|1|23,\ 1|1|2|3;$$
$$1122,\ 112|2,\ 11|22,\ 11|2|2,\ 122|1,\ 12|12,\ 12|1|2,\ 1|1|22,\ 1|1|2|2;$$
$$1112,\ 111|2,\ 112|1,\ 11|12,\ 11|1|2,\ 12|1|1,\ 1|1|1|2;$$
$$1111,\ 111|1,\ 11|11,\ 11|1|1,\ 1|1|1|1. \qquad (54)$$

When the multiset contains m distinct elements, with n_1 of one kind, n_2 of another, ..., and n_m of the last, we write $p(n_1, n_2, \ldots, n_m)$ for the total number of partitions. Thus the examples in (54) show that

$$p(1,1,1,1) = 15, \quad p(2,1,1) = 11, \quad p(2,2) = 9, \quad p(3,1) = 7, \quad p(4) = 5. \quad (55)$$

Partitions with $m = 2$ are often called "bipartitions"; those with $m = 3$ are "tripartitions"; and in general these combinatorial objects are known as *multi-partitions*. The study of multipartitions was inaugurated long ago by P. A. MacMahon [*Philosophical Transactions* **181** (1890), 481–536; **217** (1917), 81–113; *Proc. Cambridge Philos. Soc.* **22** (1925), 951–963]; but the subject is so vast that many unsolved problems remain. In the remainder of this section and in the exercises below we shall take a glimpse at some of the most interesting and instructive aspects of the theory that have been discovered so far.

In the first place it is important to notice that multipartitions are essentially the partitions of *vectors* with nonnegative integer components, namely the ways to decompose such a vector as a sum of such vectors. For example, the nine partitions of $\{1,1,2,2\}$ listed in (54) are the same as the nine partitions of the bipartite column vector $\frac{2}{2}$, namely

$$\frac{2}{2}, \quad \frac{2\,0}{1\,1}, \quad \frac{2\,0}{0\,2}, \quad \frac{2\,0\,0}{0\,1\,1}, \quad \frac{1\,1}{2\,0}, \quad \frac{1\,1}{1\,1}, \quad \frac{1\,1\,0}{1\,0\,1}, \quad \frac{1\,1\,0}{0\,0\,2}, \quad \frac{1\,1\,0\,0}{0\,0\,1\,1}. \quad (56)$$

(We drop the $+$ signs for brevity, as in the case of one-dimensional integer partitions.) Each partition can be written in canonical form if we list its parts in nonincreasing lexicographic order.

A fairly simple algorithm suffices to generate the partitions of any given multiset. In the following procedure we represent partitions on a stack that contains triples of elements (c, u, v), where c denotes a component number, $u > 0$ denotes the yet-unpartitioned amount remaining in component c, and v denotes the c component of the current part, where $0 \le v \le u$. Triples are actually kept in three arrays $(c_0, c_1, \ldots)$, $(u_0, u_1, \ldots)$, and $(v_0, v_1, \ldots)$ for convenience, and a "stack frame" array $(f_0, f_1, \ldots)$ is also maintained so that the $(l+1)$st vector of the partition consists of elements f_l through $f_{l+1} - 1$ in the c, u, and v arrays. For example, the following arrays would represent the bipartition $\frac{3221100}{1201131}$:

j	0	1	2	3	4	5	6	7	8	9	10	11
c_j	1	2	1	2	1	2	1	2	1	2	2	2
u_j	9	9	6	8	4	6	2	6	1	5	4	1
v_j	3	1	2	2	2	0	1	1	1	1	3	1

$$\begin{array}{cccccccc} f_0 = 0 & f_1 = 2 & f_2 = 4 & f_3 = 6 & f_4 = 8 & f_5 = 10 & f_6 = 11 & f_7 = 12 \end{array} \quad (57)$$

Algorithm M (*Multipartitions in decreasing lexicographic order*). Given a multiset $\{n_1 \cdot 1, \ldots, n_m \cdot m\}$, this algorithm visits all of its partitions using arrays $f_0 f_1 \ldots f_n$, $c_0 c_1 \ldots c_{mn}$, $u_0 u_1 \ldots u_{mn}$, and $v_0 v_1 \ldots v_{mn}$ as described above, where $n = n_1 + \cdots + n_m$. We assume that $m > 0$ and $n_1, \ldots, n_m > 0$.

M1. [Initialize.] Set $c_j \leftarrow j+1$ and $u_j \leftarrow v_j \leftarrow n_{j+1}$ for $0 \leq j < m$; also set $f_0 \leftarrow a \leftarrow l \leftarrow 0$ and $f_1 \leftarrow b \leftarrow m$. (In the following steps, the current stack frame runs from a to $b-1$, inclusive.)

M2. [Subtract v from u.] (At this point we want to find all partitions of the vector u in the current frame, into parts that are lexicographically $\leq v$. First we will use v itself.) Set $j \leftarrow a$, $k \leftarrow b$, and $x \leftarrow 0$. Then while $j < b$ do the following: Set $u_k \leftarrow u_j - v_j$. If $u_k = 0$, just set $x \leftarrow 1$ and $j \leftarrow j+1$. Otherwise if $x = 0$, set $c_k \leftarrow c_j$, $v_k \leftarrow \min(v_j, u_k)$, $x \leftarrow [u_k < v_j]$, $k \leftarrow k+1$, $j \leftarrow j+1$. Otherwise set $c_k \leftarrow c_j$, $v_k \leftarrow u_k$, $k \leftarrow k+1$, $j \leftarrow j+1$. (Notice that $x = [v$ has changed$]$.)

M3. [Push if nonzero.] If $k > b$, set $a \leftarrow b$, $b \leftarrow k$, $l \leftarrow l+1$, $f_{l+1} \leftarrow b$, and return to M2.

M4. [Visit a partition.] Visit the partition represented by the $l+1$ vectors currently in the stack. (For $0 \leq k \leq l$, the vector has v_j in component c_j, for $f_k \leq j < f_{k+1}$.)

M5. [Decrease v.] Set $j \leftarrow b-1$; while $v_j = 0$, set $j \leftarrow j-1$. Then if $j = a$ and $v_j = 1$, go to M6. Otherwise set $v_j \leftarrow v_j - 1$, and $v_k \leftarrow u_k$ for $j < k < b$. Return to M2.

M6. [Backtrack.] Terminate if $l = 0$. Otherwise set $l \leftarrow l-1$, $b \leftarrow a$, $a \leftarrow f_l$, and return to M5. ▮

The key to this algorithm is step M2, which decreases the current residual vector, u, by the largest permissible part, v; that step also decreases v, if necessary, to the lexicographically largest vector $\leq v$ that is less than or equal to the new residual amount in every component. (See exercise 68.)

Let us conclude this section by discussing an amusing connection between multipartitions and the least-significant-digit-first procedure for radix sorting (Algorithm 5.2.5R). The idea is best understood by considering an example. See Table 1, where Step (0) shows nine 4-partite column vectors in lexicographic order. Serial numbers ①–⑨ have been attached at the bottom for identification. Step (1) performs a stable sort of the vectors, bringing their fourth (least significant) entries into decreasing order; similarly, Steps (2), (3), and (4) do a stable sort on the third, second, and top rows. The theory of radix sorting tells us that the original lexicographic order is thereby restored.

Suppose the serial number sequences after these stable sorting operations are respectively α_4, $\alpha_3\alpha_4$, $\alpha_2\alpha_3\alpha_4$, and $\alpha_1\alpha_2\alpha_3\alpha_4$, where the α's are permutations; Table 1 shows the values of α_4, α_3, α_2, and α_1 in parentheses. And now comes the point: Wherever the permutation α_j has a descent, the numbers in row j after sorting must also have a descent, because the sorting is stable. (These descents are indicated by caret marks in the table.) For example, where α_3 has 8 followed by 7, we have 5 followed by 3 in row 3. Therefore the entries $a_1 \ldots a_9$ in row 3 after Step (2) are not an arbitrary partition of their sum; they must satisfy

$$a_1 \geq a_2 \geq a_3 \geq a_4 > a_5 \geq a_6 > a_7 \geq a_8 \geq a_9. \tag{58}$$

Table 1
RADIX SORTING AND MULTIPARTITIONS

Step (0): Original partition	Step (1): Sort row 4	Step (2): Sort row 3
6 5 5 4 3 2 1 0 0	0 6 4 3 5 0 5 2 1	0 6 5 2 5 1 4 3 0
3 2 1 0 4 5 6 4 2	2 3 0 4 2 4 1 5 6	2 3 2 5 1 6 0 4 4
6 6 3 1 1 5 2 0 7	7 6 1 1 6 0 3 5 2	7 6 6 5∧3 2∧1 1 0
4 2 1 3 3 1 1 2 5	5∧4 3 3∧2 2∧1 1 1	5 4 2 1 1 1 3 3 2
① ② ③ ④ ⑤ ⑥ ⑦ ⑧ ⑨	⑨ ① ④ ⑤ ② ⑧ ③ ⑥ ⑦	⑨ ① ② ⑥ ③ ⑦ ④ ⑤ ⑧
	$\alpha_4 = (9{\scriptstyle\wedge}1\ 4\ 5{\scriptstyle\wedge}2\ 8{\scriptstyle\wedge}3\ 6\ 7)$	$\alpha_3 = (1\ 2\ 5\ 8{\scriptstyle\wedge}7\ 9{\scriptstyle\wedge}3\ 4\ 6)$

Step (3): Sort row 2	Step (4): Sort row 1
1 2 3 0 6 0 5 5 4	6 5 5 4∧3∧2∧1 0 0
6∧5 4 4∧3∧2 2 1 0	3 2 1 0 4 5 6 4 2
2 5 1 0 6 7 6 3 1	6 6 3 1 1 5 2 0 7
1 1 3 2 4 5 2 1 3	4 2 1 3 3 1 1 2 5
⑦ ⑥ ⑤ ⑧ ① ⑨ ② ③ ④	① ② ③ ④ ⑤ ⑥ ⑦ ⑧ ⑨
$\alpha_2 = (6{\scriptstyle\wedge}4\ 8\ 9{\scriptstyle\wedge}2{\scriptstyle\wedge}1\ 3\ 5\ 7)$	$\alpha_1 = (5\ 7\ 8\ 9{\scriptstyle\wedge}3{\scriptstyle\wedge}2{\scriptstyle\wedge}1\ 4\ 6)$

But the numbers $(a_1-2, a_2-2, a_3-2, a_4-2, a_5-1, a_6-1, a_7, a_8, a_9)$ do form an essentially arbitrary partition of the original sum, minus $(4+6)$. The amount of decrease, $4+6$, is the sum of the indices where descents occur; this number is what we called $\operatorname{ind}\alpha_3$, the "index" of α_3, in Section 5.1.1.

Thus we see that any given partition of an m-partite number into at most r parts, with extra zeros added so that the number of columns is exactly r, can be encoded as a sequence of permutations $\alpha_1, \ldots, \alpha_m$ of $\{1, \ldots, r\}$ such that the product $\alpha_1 \ldots \alpha_m$ is the identity, together with a sequence of ordinary one-dimensional partitions of the numbers $(n_1 - \operatorname{ind}\alpha_1, \ldots, n_m - \operatorname{ind}\alpha_m)$ into at most r parts. For example, the vectors in Table 1 represent a partition of $(26, 27, 31, 22)$ into 9 parts; the permutations $\alpha_1, \ldots, \alpha_4$ appear in the table, and we have $(\operatorname{ind}\alpha_1, \ldots, \operatorname{ind}\alpha_4) = (15, 10, 10, 11)$; the partitions are respectively

$$26-15 = (322111100), \qquad 27-10 = (332222210),$$
$$31-10 = (544321110), \qquad 22-11 = (221111111).$$

Conversely, any such permutations and partitions will yield a multipartition of $(n_1, \ldots, n_m)$. If r and m are small, it can be helpful to consider these $r!^{m-1}$ sequences of one-dimensional partitions when listing or reasoning about multipartitions, especially in the bipartite case. [This construction is due to Basil Gordon, *J. London Math. Soc.* **38** (1963), 459–464.]

A good summary of early work on multipartitions, including studies of partitions into distinct parts and/or strictly positive parts, appears in a paper by M. S. Cheema and T. S. Motzkin, *Proc. Symp. Pure Math.* **19** (Amer. Math. Soc., 1971), 39–70.

EXERCISES

1. [20] (G. Hutchinson.) Show that a simple modification to Algorithm H will generate all partitions of $\{1, \ldots, n\}$ into *at most* r blocks, given n and $r \geq 2$.

▶ **2.** [*22*] When set partitions are used in practice, we often want to link the elements of each block together. Thus it is convenient to have an array of links $l_1 \ldots l_n$ and an array of headers $h_1 \ldots h_t$ so that the elements of the jth block of a t-block partition are $i_1 > \cdots > i_k$, where

$$i_1 = h_j, \quad i_2 = l_{i_1}, \quad \ldots, \quad i_k = l_{i_{k-1}}, \quad \text{and} \quad l_{i_k} = 0.$$

For example, the representation of 137|25|489|6 would have $t = 4$, $l_1 \ldots l_9 = 001020348$, and $h_1 \ldots h_4 = 7596$.

Design a variant of Algorithm H that generates partitions using this representation.

3. [*M23*] What is the millionth partition of $\{1, \ldots, 12\}$ generated by Algorithm H?

▶ **4.** [*21*] If $x_1 \ldots x_n$ is any string, let $\rho(x_1 \ldots x_n)$ be the restricted growth string that corresponds to the equivalence relation $j \equiv k \iff x_j = x_k$. Classify each of the five-letter English words in the Stanford GraphBase by applying this ρ function; for example, $\rho(\texttt{tooth}) = 01102$. How many of the 52 set partitions of five elements are representable by English words in this way? What's the most common word of each type?

5. [*22*] Guess the next elements of the following two sequences: (a) 0, 1, 1, 1, 12, 12, 12, 12, 12, 12, 100, 121, 122, 123, 123, . . . ; (b) 0, 1, 12, 100, 112, 121, 122, 123, ...

▶ **6.** [*25*] Suggest an algorithm to generate all partitions of $\{1, \ldots, n\}$ in which there are exactly c_1 blocks of size 1, c_2 blocks of size 2, etc.

7. [*M20*] How many permutations $a_1 \ldots a_n$ of $\{1, \ldots, n\}$ have the property that $a_{k-1} > a_k > a_j$ implies $j > k$?

8. [*20*] Suggest a way to generate all permutations of $\{1, \ldots, n\}$ that have exactly m left-to-right minima.

9. [*M20*] How many restricted growth strings $a_1 \ldots a_n$ contain exactly k_j occurrences of j, given the integers k_0, k_1, $\ldots$, k_{n-1}?

10. [*25*] A *semilabeled tree* is an oriented tree in which the leaves are labeled with the integers $\{1, \ldots, k\}$, but the other nodes are unlabeled. Thus there are 15 semilabeled trees with 5 vertices:

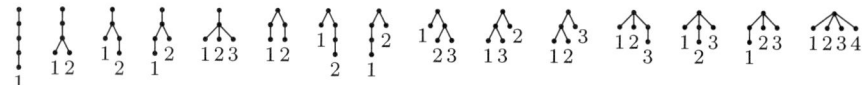

Find a one-to-one correspondence between partitions of $\{1, \ldots, n\}$ and semilabeled trees with $n + 1$ vertices.

▶ **11.** [*28*] We observed in Section 7.2.1.2 that Dudeney's famous problem `send+more = money` is a "pure" alphametic, namely an alphametic with a unique solution. His puzzle corresponds to a set partition on 13 digit positions, for which the restricted growth string $\rho(\texttt{sendmoremoney})$ is 0123456145217; and we might wonder how lucky he had to be in order to come up with such a construction. How many restricted growth strings of length 13 define pure alphametics of the form $a_1a_2a_3a_4 + a_5a_6a_7a_8 = a_9a_{10}a_{11}a_{12}a_{13}$?

12. [*M31*] (*The partition lattice.*) If Π and Π' are partitions of the same set, we write $\Pi \preceq \Pi'$ if $x \equiv y$ (modulo Π) whenever $x \equiv y$ (modulo Π'). In other words, $\Pi \preceq \Pi'$ means that Π' is a "refinement" of Π, obtained by partitioning zero or more of the latter's blocks; and Π is a "crudification" or *coalescence* of Π', obtained by merging zero or more blocks together. This partial ordering is easily seen to be a lattice, with

$\Pi \vee \Pi'$ the greatest common refinement of Π and Π', and with $\Pi \wedge \Pi'$ their least common coalescence. For example, the lattice of partitions of $\{1, 2, 3, 4\}$ is

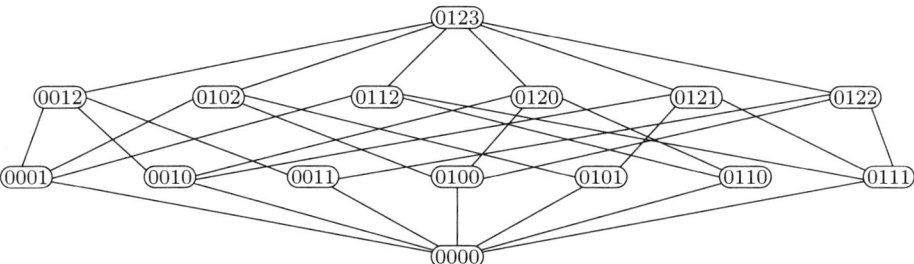

if we represent partitions by restricted growth strings $a_1 a_2 a_3 a_4$; upward paths in this diagram take each partition into its refinements. Partitions with t blocks appear on level t from the bottom, and their descendants form the partition lattice of $\{1, \ldots, t\}$.

a) Explain how to compute $\Pi \vee \Pi'$, given $a_1 \ldots a_n$ and $a_1' \ldots a_n'$.

b) Explain how to compute $\Pi \wedge \Pi'$, given $a_1 \ldots a_n$ and $a_1' \ldots a_n'$.

c) When does Π' cover Π in this lattice? (See exercise 7.2.1.4–55.)

d) If Π has t blocks of sizes $s_1, \ldots, s_t$, how many partitions does it cover?

e) If Π has t blocks of sizes $s_1, \ldots, s_t$, how many partitions cover it?

f) True or false: If $\Pi \vee \Pi'$ covers Π, then Π' covers $\Pi \wedge \Pi'$.

g) True or false: If Π' covers $\Pi \wedge \Pi'$, then $\Pi \vee \Pi'$ covers Π.

h) Let $b(\Pi)$ denote the number of blocks of Π. Prove that

$$b(\Pi) + b(\Pi') \ \leq \ b(\Pi \vee \Pi') + b(\Pi \wedge \Pi').$$

13. [*M28*] (Stephen C. Milne, 1977.) If A is a set of partitions of $\{1, \ldots, n\}$, its *shadow* ∂A is the set of all partitions Π' such that Π covers Π' for some $\Pi \in A$. (We considered the analogous concept for the subset lattice in 7.2.1.3–(54).)

Let $\Pi_1, \Pi_2, \ldots$ be the partitions of $\{1, \ldots, n\}$ into t blocks, in lexicographic order of their restricted growth strings; and let $\Pi_1', \Pi_2', \ldots$ be the $(t-1)$-block partitions, also in lexicographic order. Prove that there is a function $f_{nt}(N)$ such that

$$\partial\{\Pi_1, \ldots, \Pi_N\} = \{\Pi_1', \ldots, \Pi_{f_{nt}(N)}'\} \qquad \text{for } 0 \leq N \leq \begin{Bmatrix} n \\ t \end{Bmatrix}.$$

Hint: The diagram in exercise 12 shows that $(f_{43}(0), \ldots, f_{43}(6)) = (0, 3, 5, 7, 7, 7, 7)$.

14. [*23*] Design an algorithm to generate set partitions in Gray-code order like (7).

15. [*M21*] What is the final partition generated by the algorithm of exercise 14?

16. [*16*] The list (11) is Ruskey's A_{35}; what is A_{35}'?

17. [*26*] Implement Ruskey's Gray code (8) for all m-block partitions of $\{1, \ldots, n\}$.

18. [*M46*] For which n is it possible to generate all restricted growth strings $a_1 \ldots a_n$ in such a way that some a_j changes by ± 1 at each step?

19. [*28*] Prove that there's a Gray code for restricted growth strings in which, at each step, some a_j changes by either ± 1 or ± 2, when (a) we want to generate all ϖ_n strings $a_1 \ldots a_n$; or (b) we want to generate only the $\begin{Bmatrix} n \\ m \end{Bmatrix}$ cases with $\max(a_1, \ldots, a_n) = m - 1$.

20. [*17*] If Π is a partition of $\{1, \ldots, n\}$, its conjugate Π^T is defined by the rule

$$j \equiv k \quad (\text{modulo } \Pi^T) \qquad \Longleftrightarrow \qquad n + 1 - j \equiv n + 1 - k \quad (\text{modulo } \Pi).$$

Suppose Π has the restricted growth string 001010202013; what is the restricted growth string of Π^T?

21. [*M27*] How many partitions of $\{1, \ldots, n\}$ are self-conjugate?

22. [*M23*] If X is a random variable with a given distribution, the expected value of X^n is called the nth *moment* of that distribution. What is the nth moment when X is (a) a Poisson deviate with mean 1 (Eq. 3.4.1–(40))? (b) the number of fixed points of a random permutation of $\{1, \ldots, m\}$, when $m \geq n$ (Eq. 1.3.3–(27))?

23. [*HM30*] If $f(x) = \sum a_k x^k$ is a polynomial, let $f(\varpi)$ stand for $\sum a_k \varpi_k$.

a) Prove the symbolic formula $f(\varpi + 1) = \varpi f(\varpi)$. (For example, if $f(x)$ is the polynomial x^2, this formula states that $\varpi_2 + 2\varpi_1 + \varpi_0 = \varpi_3$.)

b) Similarly, prove that $f(\varpi + k) = \varpi^k f(\varpi)$ for all positive integers k.

c) If p is prime, prove that $\varpi_{n+p} \equiv \varpi_n + \varpi_{n+1}$ (modulo p). *Hint:* Show first that $x^{\underline{p}} \equiv x^p - x$.

d) Consequently $\varpi_{n+N} \equiv \varpi_n$ (modulo p) when $N = p^{p-1} + p^{p-2} + \cdots + p + 1$.

24. [*HM35*] Continuing the previous exercise, prove that the Bell numbers satisfy the periodic law $\varpi_{n+p^{e-1}N} \equiv \varpi_n$ (modulo p^e), if p is an odd prime. *Hint:* Show that

$$x^{\underline{p^e}} \equiv g_e(x) + 1 \ (\text{modulo } p^e, \ p^{e-1}g_1(x), \ \ldots, \text{ and } pg_{e-1}(x)), \text{ where } g_j(x) = (x^p - x - 1)^{p^j}.$$

25. [*M27*] Prove that $\varpi_n / \varpi_{n-1} \leq \varpi_{n+1} / \varpi_n \leq \varpi_n / \varpi_{n-1} + 1$.

▶ **26.** [*M22*] According to the recurrence equations (13), the numbers ϖ_{nk} in Peirce's triangle count the paths from $\widehat{nk}$ to $\textcircled{11}$ in the infinite directed graph

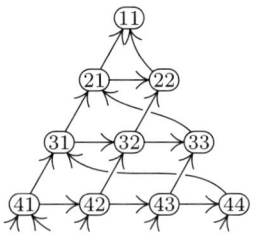

Explain why each path from $\widehat{n1}$ to $\textcircled{11}$ corresponds to a partition of $\{1, \ldots, n\}$.

▶ **27.** [*M35*] A "vacillating tableau loop" of order n is a sequence of integer partitions $\lambda_k = a_{k1} a_{k2} a_{k3} \ldots$ with $a_{k1} \geq a_{k2} \geq a_{k3} \geq \cdots$ for $0 \leq k \leq 2n$, such that $\lambda_0 = \lambda_{2n} = e_0$ and $\lambda_k = \lambda_{k-1} + (-1)^k e_{t_k}$ for $1 \leq k \leq 2n$ and for some t_k with $0 \leq t_k \leq n$; here e_t denotes the unit vector $0^{t-1}10^{n-t}$ when $0 < t \leq n$, and e_0 is all zeros.

a) List all the vacillating tableau loops of order 4. [*Hint:* There are 15 altogether.]

b) Prove that exactly ϖ_{nk} vacillating tableau loops of order n have $t_{2k-1} = 0$.

▶ **28.** [*M25*] (*Generalized rook polynomials.*) Consider an arrangement of $a_1 + \cdots + a_m$ square cells in rows and columns, where row k contains cells in columns $1, \ldots, a_k$. Place zero or more "rooks" into the cells, with at most one rook in each row and at most one in each column. An empty cell is called "free" if there is no rook to its right and no rook below. For example, Fig. 56 shows two such placements, one with four rooks in rows of lengths (3,1,4,1,5,9,2,6,5), and another with nine on a 9×9 square board. Rooks are indicated by solid circles; hollow circles have been placed above and to the left of each rook, thereby leaving the free cells blank.

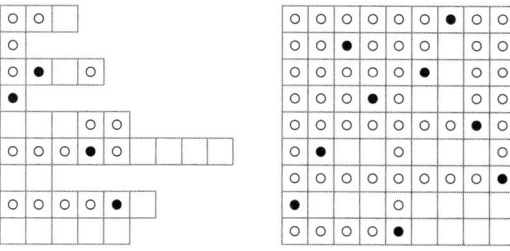

Fig. 56. Rook placements and free cells.

Let $R(a_1, \ldots, a_m)$ be the polynomial in x and y obtained by summing $x^r y^f$ over all legal rook placements, where r is the number of rooks and f is the number of free cells; for example, the left-hand placement in Fig. 56 contributes $x^4 y^{17}$ to the polynomial $R(3, 1, 4, 1, 5, 9, 2, 6, 5)$.

a) Prove that we have $R(a_1, \ldots, a_m) = R(a_1, \ldots, a_{j-1}, a_{j+1}, a_j, a_{j+2}, \ldots, a_m)$; in other words, the order of the row lengths is irrelevant, and we can assume that $a_1 \geq \cdots \geq a_m$ as in a tableau shape like 7.2.1.4–(13).

b) If $a_1 \geq \cdots \geq a_m$ and if $b_1 \ldots b_n = (a_1 \ldots a_m)^T$ is the conjugate partition, prove that $R(a_1, \ldots, a_m) = R(b_1, \ldots, b_n)$.

c) Find a recurrence for evaluating $R(a_1, \ldots, a_m)$ and use it to compute $R(3, 2, 1)$.

d) Generalize Peirce's triangle (12) by changing the addition rule (13) to

$$\varpi_{nk}(x, y) = x\varpi_{(n-1)k}(x, y) + y\varpi_{n(k+1)}(x, y), \qquad 1 \leq k < n.$$

Thus $\varpi_{21}(x, y) = x+y$, $\varpi_{32}(x, y) = x+xy+y^2$, $\varpi_{31}(x, y) = x^2+2xy+xy^2+y^3$, etc. Prove that the resulting quantity $\varpi_{nk}(x, y)$ is the rook polynomial $R(a_1, \ldots, a_{n-1})$ where $a_j = n - j - [j < k]$.

e) The polynomial $\varpi_{n1}(x, y)$ in part (d) can be regarded as a generalized Bell number $\varpi_n(x, y)$, representing paths from $\textcircled{n1}$ to $\textcircled{11}$ in the digraph of exercise 26 that have a given number of "x steps" to the northeast and a given number of "y steps" to the east. Prove that

$$\varpi_n(x, y) = \sum_{a_1 \ldots a_n} x^{n-1-\max(a_1, \ldots, a_n)} y^{a_1 + \cdots + a_n}$$

summed over all restricted growth strings $a_1 \ldots a_n$ of length n.

29. [*M26*] Continuing the previous exercise, let $R_r(a_1, \ldots, a_m) = [x^r] R(a_1, \ldots, a_m)$ be the polynomial in y that enumerates free cells when r rooks are placed.

a) Show that the number of ways to place n rooks on an $n \times n$ board, leaving f cells free, is the number of permutations of $\{1, \ldots, n\}$ that have f inversions. Thus, by Eq. 5.1.1–(8) and exercise 5.1.2–16, we have

$$R_n(\overbrace{n, \ldots, n}^{n}) = n!_y = \prod_{k=1}^{n} (1 + y + \cdots + y^{k-1}).$$

b) What is $R_r(\overbrace{n, \ldots, n}^{m})$, the generating function for r rooks on an $m \times n$ board?

c) If $a_1 \geq \cdots \geq a_m \geq 0$ and t is a nonnegative integer, prove the general formula

$$\prod_{j=1}^{m} \frac{1 - y^{a_j+j-m+t}}{1-y} = \sum_{k=0}^{m} \frac{t!_y}{(t-k)!_y} R_{m-k}(a_1, \ldots, a_m).$$

[*Note:* The quantity $t!_y/(t-k)!_y = \prod_{j=0}^{k-1}((1-y^{t-j})/(1-y))$ is zero when $k > t \geq 0$. Thus, for example, when $t = 0$ the right-hand side reduces to $R_m(a_1, \ldots, a_m)$. We can compute $R_m, R_{m-1}, \ldots, R_0$ by successively setting $t = 0, 1, \ldots, m$.]

d) If $a_1 \geq a_2 \geq \cdots \geq a_m \geq 0$ and $a_1' \geq a_2' \geq \cdots \geq a_m' \geq 0$, show that we have $R(a_1, a_2 \ldots, a_m) = R(a_1', a_2', \ldots, a_m')$ if and only if the associated multisets $\{a_1+1, a_2+2, \ldots, a_m+m\}$ and $\{a_1'+1, a_2'+2, \ldots, a_m'+m\}$ are the same.

30. [*HM30*] The generalized Stirling number ${\scriptstyle \left\{ {n \atop m} \right\}_q}$ is defined by the recurrence

$$\left\{ {n+1 \atop m} \right\}_q = (1+q+\cdots+q^{m-1})\left\{ {n \atop m} \right\}_q + \left\{ {n \atop m-1} \right\}_q; \qquad \left\{ {0 \atop m} \right\}_q = \delta_{m0}.$$

Thus ${\left\{ {n \atop m} \right\}_q}$ is a polynomial in q; and ${\left\{ {n \atop m} \right\}_1}$ is the ordinary Stirling number ${\left\{ {n \atop m} \right\}}$, because it satisfies the recurrence relation in Eq. 1.2.6–(46).

a) Prove that the generalized Bell number $\varpi_n(x,y) = R(n-1, \ldots, 1)$ of exercise 28(e) has the explicit form

$$\varpi_n(x,y) = \sum_{m=0}^{n} x^{n-m} y^{\binom{m}{2}} \left\{ {n \atop m} \right\}_y.$$

b) Show that generalized Stirling numbers also obey the recurrence

$$q^m \left\{ {n+1 \atop m+1} \right\}_q = q^n \left\{ {n \atop m} \right\}_q + \binom{n}{1} q^{n-1} \left\{ {n-1 \atop m} \right\}_q + \cdots = \sum_k \binom{n}{k} q^k \left\{ {k \atop m} \right\}_q.$$

c) Find generating functions for ${\left\{ {n \atop m} \right\}_q}$, generalizing 1.2.9–(23) and 1.2.9–(28).

31. [*HM23*] Generalizing (15), show that the elements of Peirce's triangle have a simple generating function, if we compute the sum

$$\sum_{n,k} \varpi_{nk} \frac{w^{n-k}}{(n-k)!} \frac{z^{k-1}}{(k-1)!}.$$

32. [*M22*] Let δ_n be the number of restricted growth strings $a_1 \ldots a_n$ for which the sum $a_1 + \cdots + a_n$ is even minus the number for which $a_1 + \cdots + a_n$ is odd. Prove that

$$\delta_n = (1, 0, -1, -1, 0, 1) \qquad \text{when} \qquad n \bmod 6 = (1, 2, 3, 4, 5, 0).$$

Hint: See exercise 28(e).

33. [*M21*] How many partitions of $\{1, 2, \ldots, n\}$ have $1 \not\equiv 2$, $2 \not\equiv 3$, $\ldots$, $k-1 \not\equiv k$?

34. [*14*] Many poetic forms involve *rhyme schemes*, which are partitions of the lines of a stanza with the property that $j \equiv k$ if and only if line j rhymes with line k. For example, a "limerick" is generally a 5-line poem with certain rhythmic constraints and with a rhyme scheme described by the restricted growth string 00110.

What rhyme schemes were used in the classical *sonnets* by (a) Guittone d'Arezzo (c. 1270)? (b) Petrarch (c. 1350)? (c) Spenser (1595)? (d) Shakespeare (1609)? (e) Elizabeth Barrett Browning (1850)?

35. [*M21*] Let ϖ_n' be the number of schemes for n-line poems that are "completely rhymed," in the sense that every line rhymes with at least one other. Thus we have $\langle \varpi_0', \varpi_1', \varpi_2', \ldots \rangle = \langle 1, 0, 1, 1, 4, 11, 41, \ldots \rangle$. Give a combinatorial proof of the fact that $\varpi_n' + \varpi_{n+1}' = \varpi_n$.

36. [*M22*] Continuing exercise 35, what is the generating function $\sum_n \varpi_n' z^n/n!$?

37. [*M18*] Alexander Pushkin adopted an elaborate structure in his poetic novel *Eugene Onegin* (1833), based not only on "masculine" rhymes in which the sounds of accented final syllables agree with each other (pain–gain, form–warm, pun–fun, bucks–crux), but also on "feminine" rhymes in which one or two unstressed syllables also participate (humor–tumor, tetrameter–pentameter, lecture–conjecture, iguana–piranha). Every stanza of *Eugene Onegin* is a sonnet with the strict scheme 01012233455477, where the rhyme is feminine or masculine according as the digit is even or odd. Several modern translators of Pushkin's novel have also succeeded in retaining the same form in English and German.

> *How do I justify this stanza? / These feminine rhymes? My wrinkled muse?*
> *This whole passé extravaganza? / How can I (careless of time) use*
> *The dusty bread molds of Onegin / In the brave bakery of Reagan?*
> *The loaves will surely fail to rise / Or else go stale before my eyes.*
> *The truth is, I can't justify it. / But as no shroud of critical terms*
> *Can save my corpse from boring worms, / I may as well have fun and try it.*
> *If it works, good; and if not, well, / A theory won't postpone its knell.*
>
> — VIKRAM SETH, *The Golden Gate* (1986)

A 14-line poem might have any of $\varpi'_{14} = 24{,}011{,}157$ complete rhyme schemes, according to exercise 35. But how many schemes are possible if we are allowed to specify, for each block, whether its rhyme is to be feminine or masculine?

▶ **38.** [*M30*] Let σ_k be the cyclic permutation $(1, 2, \ldots, k)$. The object of this exercise is to study the sequences $k_1 k_2 \ldots k_n$, called σ-*cycles*, for which $\sigma_{k_1} \sigma_{k_2} \ldots \sigma_{k_n}$ is the identity permutation. For example, when $n = 4$ there are exactly 15 σ-cycles, namely

$$1111, 1122, 1212, 1221, 1333, 2112, 2121, 2211, 2222, 2323, 3133, 3232, 3313, 3331, 4444.$$

a) Find a one-to-one correspondence between partitions of $\{1, 2, \ldots, n\}$ and σ-cycles of length n.
b) How many σ-cycles of length n have $1 \le k_1, \ldots, k_n \le m$, given m and n?
c) How many σ-cycles of length n have $k_i = j$, given i, j, and n?
d) How many σ-cycles of length n have $k_1, \ldots, k_n \ge 2$?
e) How many partitions of $\{1, \ldots, n\}$ have $1 \not\equiv 2$, $2 \not\equiv 3$, $\ldots$, $n - 1 \not\equiv n$, and $n \not\equiv 1$?

39. [*HM16*] Evaluate $\int_0^\infty e^{-t^{p+1}} t^q \, dt$ when p and q are nonnegative integers. *Hint:* See exercise 1.2.5–20.

40. [*HM20*] Suppose the saddle point method is used to estimate $[z^{n-1}] e^{cz}$. The text's derivation of (21) from (19) deals with the case $c = 1$; how should that derivation change if c is an arbitrary positive constant?

41. [*HM21*] Solve the previous exercise when $c = -1$.

42. [*HM23*] Use the saddle point method to estimate $[z^{n-1}] e^{z^2}$ with relative error $O(1/n^2)$.

43. [*HM22*] Justify replacing the integral in (23) by (25).

44. [*HM22*] Explain how to compute b_1, b_2, $\ldots$ in (26) from a_2, a_3, $\ldots$ in (25).

▶ **45.** [*HM23*] Show that, in addition to (26), we also have the expansion

$$\varpi_n = \frac{e^{e^\xi - 1} n!}{\xi^n \sqrt{2\pi n(\xi + 1)}} \left(1 + \frac{b'_1}{n} + \frac{b'_2}{n^2} + \cdots + \frac{b'_m}{n^m} + O\left(\frac{1}{n^{m+1}}\right)\right),$$

where $b'_1 = -(2\xi^4 + 9\xi^3 + 16\xi^2 + 6\xi + 2)/(24(\xi + 1)^3)$.

46. [*HM25*] Estimate the value of ϖ_{nk} in Peirce's triangle when $n \to \infty$.

47. [*M21*] Analyze the running time of Algorithm H.

48. [*HM25*] If n is not an integer, the integral in (23) can be taken over a Hankel contour to define a generalized Bell number ϖ_x for all real $x > 0$. Show that, as in (16),

$$\varpi_x = \frac{1}{e} \sum_{k=0}^{\infty} \frac{k^x}{k!}.$$

▶ **49.** [*HM35*] Prove that, for large n, the number ξ defined in Eq. (24) is equal to

$$\ln n - \ln\ln n + \sum_{j,k\geq 0} \begin{bmatrix} j+k \\ j+1 \end{bmatrix} \alpha^j \frac{\beta^k}{k!}, \qquad \alpha = -\frac{1}{\ln n}, \qquad \beta = \frac{\ln\ln n}{\ln n}.$$

▶ **50.** [*HM21*] If $\xi(n) e^{\xi(n)} = n$ and $\xi(n) > 0$, how does $\xi(n+k)$ relate to $\xi(n)$?

51. [*HM27*] Use the saddle point method to estimate $t_n = n!\,[z^n]\,e^{z+z^2/2}$, the number of *involutions* on n elements (aka partitions of $\{1,\ldots,n\}$ into blocks of sizes ≤ 2).

52. [*HM22*] The *cumulants* of a probability distribution are defined in Eq. 1.2.10–(23). What are the cumulants, when the probability that a random integer equals k is (a) $e^{1-e^\xi}\varpi_k \xi^k/k!$? (b) $\sum_j \left\{{k \atop j}\right\} e\, e^{-1}-1-j/k!$?

▶ **53.** [*HM30*] Let $G(z) = \sum_{k=0}^{\infty} p_k z^k$ be the generating function for a discrete probability distribution, converging for $|z| < 1 + \delta$; thus the coefficients p_k are nonnegative, $G(1) = 1$, and the mean and variance are respectively $\mu = G'(1)$ and $\sigma^2 = G''(1) + G'(1) - G'(1)^2$. If $X_1, \ldots, X_n$ are independent random variables having this distribution, the probability that $X_1 + \cdots + X_n = m$ is $[z^m]\,G(z)^n$, and we often want to estimate this probability when m is near the mean value μn.

Assume that $p_0 \neq 0$ and that no integer $d > 1$ is a common divisor of all subscripts k with $p_k \neq 0$; this assumption means that m does not have to satisfy any special congruence conditions mod d when n is large. Prove that

$$[z^{\mu n + r}]\,G(z)^n = \frac{e^{-r^2/(2\sigma^2 n)}}{\sigma\sqrt{2\pi n}} + O\!\left(\frac{1}{n}\right) \qquad \text{as } n \to \infty,$$

when $\mu n + r$ is an integer. *Hint:* Integrate $G(z)^n/z^{\mu n + r}$ on the circle $|z| = 1$.

54. [*HM20*] If α and β are defined by (40), show that their arithmetic and geometric means are respectively $\frac{\alpha + \beta}{2} = s \coth s$ and $\sqrt{\alpha\beta} = s \operatorname{csch} s$, where $s = \sigma/2$.

55. [*HM20*] Suggest a good way to compute the number β needed in (43).

▶ **56.** [*HM26*] Let $g(z) = \alpha^{-1}\ln(e^z - 1) - \ln z$ and $\sigma = \alpha - \beta$ as in (37).

a) Prove that $(-\sigma)^{n+1} g^{(n+1)}(\sigma) = n! - \sum_{k=0}^{n} \binom{n}{k} \alpha^k \beta^{n-k}$, where the Eulerian numbers $\left\langle {n \atop k} \right\rangle$ are defined in Section 5.1.3.

b) Prove that $\frac{\beta}{\alpha} n! < \sum_{k=0}^{n} \binom{n}{k} \alpha^k \beta^{n-k} < n!$ for all $\sigma > 0$. *Hint:* See exercise 5.1.3–25.

c) Now verify the inequality (42).

57. [*HM22*] In the notation of (43), prove that (a) $n+1-m < 2N$; (b) $N < 2(n+1-m)$.

58. [*HM31*] Complete the proof of (43) as follows.

a) Show that for all $\sigma > 0$ there is a number $\tau \geq 2\sigma$ such that τ is a multiple of 2π and $|e^{\sigma+it} - 1|/|\sigma + it|$ is monotone decreasing for $0 \leq t \leq \tau$.

b) Prove that $\int_{-\tau}^{\tau} \exp((n+1)g(\sigma + it))\,dt$ leads to (43).

c) Show that the corresponding integrals over the straight-line paths $z = t \pm i\tau$ for $-n \leq t \leq \sigma$ and $z = -n \pm it$ for $-\tau \leq t \leq \tau$ are negligible.

▶ **59.** [*HM23*] What does (43) predict for the approximate value of $\left\{{n \atop n}\right\}$?

60. [*HM25*] (a) Show that the partial sums in the identity

$$\left\{{n \atop m}\right\} = \frac{m^n}{m!} - \frac{(m-1)^n}{1!\,(m-1)!} + \frac{(m-2)^n}{2!\,(m-2)!} - \cdots + (-1)^m \frac{0^n}{m!\,0!}$$

alternately overestimate and underestimate the final value. (b) Conclude that

$$\left\{{n \atop m}\right\} = \frac{m^n}{m!}\left(1 - O(ne^{-n^\epsilon})\right) \qquad \text{when } m \le n^{1-\epsilon}.$$

(c) Derive a similar result from (43).

61. [*HM26*] Prove that if $m = n - r$ where $r \le n^\epsilon$ and $\epsilon \le n^{1/2}$, Eq. (43) yields

$$\left\{{n \atop n-r}\right\} = \frac{n^{2r}}{2^r r!}\left(1 + O(n^{2\epsilon - 1}) + O\left(\frac{1}{r}\right)\right).$$

62. [*HM40*] Prove rigorously that if $\xi e^\xi = n$, the maximum $\left\{{n \atop m}\right\}$ occurs either when $m = \lfloor e^\xi - 1 \rfloor$ or when $m = \lceil e^\xi - 1 \rceil$.

▶ **63.** [*M35*] (J. Pitman.) Prove that there is an elementary way to locate the maximum Stirling numbers, and many similar quantities, as follows: Suppose $0 \le p_j \le 1$.

a) Let $f(z) = (1 + p_1(z-1)) \ldots (1 + p_n(z-1))$ and $a_k = [z^k]\,f(z)$; thus a_k is the probability that k heads turn up after n independent coin flips with the respective probabilities $p_1, \ldots, p_n$. Prove that $a_{k-1} < a_k$ whenever $k \le \mu = p_1 + \cdots + p_n$, $a_k \ne 0$.

b) Similarly, prove that $a_{k+1} < a_k$ whenever $k \ge \mu$ and $a_k \ne 0$.

c) If $f(x) = a_0 + a_1 x + \cdots + a_n x^n$ is any nonzero polynomial with nonnegative coefficients and with n real roots, prove that $a_{k-1} < a_k$ when $k \le \mu$ and $a_{k+1} < a_k$ when $k \ge \mu$, where $\mu = f'(1)/f(1)$. Therefore if $a_m = \max(a_0, \ldots, a_n)$ we must have either $m = \lfloor \mu \rfloor$ or $m = \lceil \mu \rceil$.

d) Under the hypotheses of (c), and with $a_j = 0$ when $j < 0$ or $j > n$, show that there are indices $s \le t$, such that $a_{k+1} - a_k < a_k - a_{k-1}$ if and only if $s \le k \le t$. (Thus, a histogram of the sequence $(a_0, a_1, \ldots, a_n)$ is always "bell-shaped.")

e) What do these results tell us about Stirling numbers?

64. [*HM21*] Prove the approximate ratio (50), using (30) and exercise 50.

▶ **65.** [*HM22*] What is the variance of the number of blocks of size k in a random partition of $\{1, \ldots, n\}$?

66. [*M46*] What partition of n leads to the most partitions of $\{1, \ldots, n\}$?

67. [*HM20*] What are the mean and variance of M in Stam's method (53)?

68. [*21*] How large can variables l and b get in Algorithm M, when that algorithm is generating all $p(n_1, \ldots, n_m)$ partitions of $\{n_1 \cdot 1, \ldots, n_m \cdot m\}$?

▶ **69.** [*22*] Modify Algorithm M so that it produces only partitions into at most r parts.

▶ **70.** [*M22*] Analyze the number of r-block partitions possible in the n-element multisets (a) $\{0, \ldots, 0, 1\}$; (b) $\{1, 2, \ldots, n-1, n-1\}$. What is the total, summed over r?

71. [*M20*] How many partitions of $\{n_1 \cdot 1, \ldots, n_m \cdot m\}$ have exactly 2 parts?

72. [*M26*] Can $p(n, n)$ be evaluated in polynomial time?

▶ **73.** [*M32*] Can $p(2, \ldots, 2)$ be evaluated in polynomial time when there are n 2s?

74. [*M46*] Can $p(n, \ldots, n)$ be evaluated in polynomial time when there are n ns?

75. [*HM41*] Find the asymptotic value of $p(n, n)$.

76. [*HM36*] Find the asymptotic value of $p(2, \ldots, 2)$ when there are n 2s.

77. [*HM46*] Find the asymptotic value of $p(n, \ldots, n)$ when there are n ns.

78. [*20*] What partition of $(15, 10, 10, 11)$ leads to the permutations α_1, α_2, α_3, and α_4 shown in Table 1?

79. [*22*] A sequence u_1, u_2, u_3, ... is called *universal* for partitions of $\{1, \ldots, n\}$ if its subsequences $(u_{m+1}, u_{m+2}, \ldots, u_{m+n})$ for $0 \le m < \varpi_n$ represent all possible set partitions under the convention "$j \equiv k$ if and only if $u_{m+j} = u_{m+k}$." For example, $(0, 0, 0, 1, 0, 2, 2)$ is a universal sequence for partitions of $\{1, 2, 3\}$.

Write a program to find all universal sequences for partitions of $\{1, 2, 3, 4\}$ with the properties that (i) $u_1 = u_2 = u_3 = u_4 = 0$; (ii) the sequence has restricted growth; (iii) $0 \le u_j \le 3$; and (iv) $u_{16} = u_{17} = u_{18} = 0$ (hence the sequence is essentially *cyclic*).

80. [*M28*] Prove that universal cycles for partitions of $\{1, 2, \ldots, n\}$ exist in the sense of the previous exercise whenever $n \ge 4$.

81. [*29*] Find a way to arrange an ordinary deck of 52 playing cards so that the following trick is possible: Five players each cut the deck (applying a cyclic permutation) as often as they like. Then each player takes a card from the top. A magician tells them to look at their cards and to form affinity groups, joining with others who hold the same suit: Everybody with clubs gets together, everybody with diamonds forms another group, and so on. (The Jack of Spades is, however, considered to be a "joker"; its holder, if any, should remain aloof.)

Observing the affinity groups, but not being told any of the suits, the magician can name all five cards, if the cards were suitably arranged in the first place.

82. [*22*] In how many ways can the following 15 dominoes, optionally rotated, be partitioned into three sets of five having the same sum when regarded as fractions?

> *Just as in a single body there are pairs of individual members,*
> *called by the same name but distinguished as right and left,*
> *so when my speeches had postulated the notion of madness,*
> *as a single generic aspect of human nature,*
> *the speech that divided the left-hand portion*
> *repeatedly broke it down into smaller and smaller parts.*
> — SOCRATES, *Phædrus* 266A (c. 370 B.C.)

7.2.1.6. Generating all trees.

We've now completed our study of the classical concepts of combinatorics: tuples, permutations, combinations, and partitions. But computer scientists have added another fundamental class of patterns to the traditional repertoire, namely the hierarchical arrangements known as trees. Trees sprout up just about everywhere in computer science, as we've seen in Section 2.3 and in nearly every subsequent section of *The Art of Computer Programming*. Therefore we turn now to the study of simple algorithms by which trees of various species can be explored exhaustively.

First let's review the basic connection between nested parentheses and forests of trees. For example,

$$(( )) ((( )) ((( ) (( ))) ( )) (( ) (( )))) \tag{1}$$

illustrates a string containing fifteen left parens '(' labeled 1, 2, ..., f, and fifteen right parens ')' also labeled 1 through f; gray lines beneath the string show how the parentheses match up to form fifteen pairs 12, 21, 3f, 44, 53, 6a, 78, 85, 97, a6, b9, ce, db, ed, and fc. This string corresponds to the forest

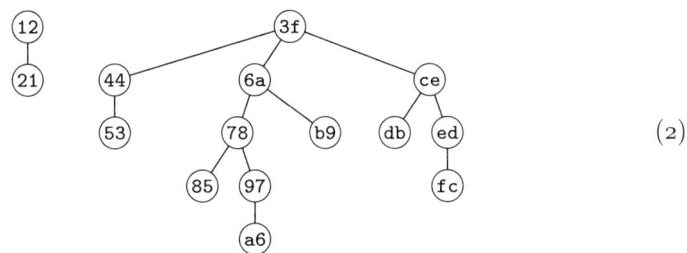

(2)

in which the nodes are ⓐ12, ②1, ③f, ..., ⓕc in preorder (sorted by first coordinates) and ②1, ①2, ⑤3, ..., ③f in postorder (sorted by second coordinates). If we imagine a worm that crawls around the periphery of the forest,

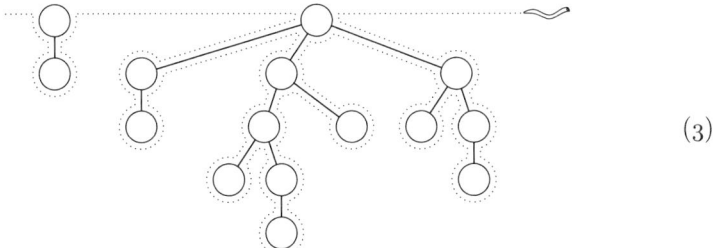

(3)

seeing a '(' whenever it passes the left edge of a node and a ')' whenever it passes a node's right edge, that worm will have reconstructed the original string (1).

The forest in (2) corresponds, in turn, to the binary tree

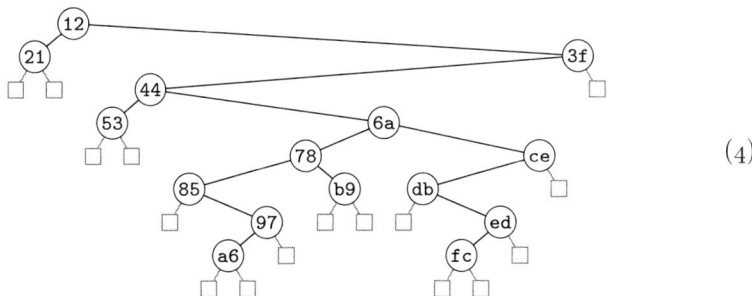

(4)

via the "natural correspondence" discussed in Section 2.3.2; here the nodes are ②1, ①2, ⑤3, ..., ③f in *symmetric* order, also known as inorder. The left subtree of node $\textcircled{x}$ in the binary tree is the leftmost child of $\textcircled{x}$ in the forest, or it is an "external node" □ if $\textcircled{x}$ is childless. The right subtree of node $\textcircled{x}$ in the binary tree is its right sibling in the forest, or □ if $\textcircled{x}$ is the rightmost child in its family. Roots of the trees in the forest are considered to be siblings, and the leftmost root of the forest is the root of the binary tree.

Table 1

NESTED PARENTHESES AND RELATED OBJECTS WHEN $n = 4$

$a_1a_2\ldots a_8$	forest	binary tree	$d_1d_2d_3d_4$	$z_1z_2z_3z_4$	$p_1p_2p_3p_4$	$c_1c_2c_3c_4$	matching
()()()()			1111	1357	1234	0000	
()()(())			1102	1356	1243	0001	
()(())()			1021	1347	1324	0010	
()(()())			1012	1346	1342	0011	
()((()))			1003	1345	1432	0012	
(())()()			0211	1257	2134	0100	
(())(())			0202	1256	2143	0101	
(()())()			0121	1247	2314	0110	
(()()())			0112	1246	2341	0111	
(()(()))			0103	1245	2431	0112	
((()))()			0031	1237	3214	0120	
((())())			0022	1236	3241	0121	
((()()))			0013	1235	3421	0122	
(((())))			0004	1234	4321	0123	

A string $a_1a_2\ldots a_{2n}$ of parentheses is properly nested if and only if it contains n occurrences of '(' and n occurrences of ')', where the kth '(' precedes the kth ')' for $1 \le k \le n$. The easiest way to explore all strings of nested parentheses is to visit them in lexicographic order. The following algorithm, which considers ')' to be lexicographically smaller than '(', includes some refinements for efficiency suggested by I. Semba [*Inf. Processing Letters* **12** (1981), 188–192]:

Algorithm P (*Nested parentheses in lexicographic order*). Given an integer $n \geq 2$, this algorithm generates all strings $a_1 a_2 \ldots a_{2n}$ of nested parentheses.

P1. [Initialize.] Set $a_{2k-1} \leftarrow$ '(' and $a_{2k} \leftarrow$ ')' for $1 \leq k \leq n$; also set $a_0 \leftarrow$ ')' and $m \leftarrow 2n - 1$. (We use a_0 as a sentinel in step P4.)

P2. [Visit.] Visit the nested string $a_1 a_2 \ldots a_{2n}$. (At this point $a_m =$ '(', and $a_k =$ ')' for $m < k \leq 2n$.)

P3. [Easy case?] Set $a_m \leftarrow$ ')'. Then if $a_{m-1} =$ ')', set $a_{m-1} \leftarrow$ '(', $m \leftarrow m - 1$, and return to P2.

P4. [Find j.] Set $j \leftarrow m - 1$ and $k \leftarrow 2n - 1$. While $a_j =$ '(', set $a_j \leftarrow$ ')', $a_k \leftarrow$ '(', $j \leftarrow j - 1$, and $k \leftarrow k - 2$.

P5. [Increase a_j.] Terminate the algorithm if $j = 0$. Otherwise set $a_j \leftarrow$ '(', $m \leftarrow 2n - 1$, and go back to P2. ∎

We will see later that the loop in step P4 is almost always short: The operation $a_j \leftarrow$ ')' is performed only about $\frac{1}{3}$ times per nested string visited, on the average.

Why does Algorithm P work? Let A_{pq} be the sequence of all strings α that contain p left parentheses and $q \geq p$ right parentheses, where $({}^{q-p}\alpha$ is properly nested, listed in lexicographic order. Then Algorithm P is supposed to generate A_{nn}, where it is easy to see that A_{pq} obeys the recursive rules

$$A_{pq} = \,) A_{p(q-1)}, \, (A_{(p-1)q}, \quad \text{if } 0 \leq p \leq q \neq 0; \qquad A_{00} = \epsilon; \qquad (5)$$

also A_{pq} is empty if $p < 0$ or $p > q$. The first element of A_{pq} is $)^{q-p}()\ldots()$, where there are p pairs '()'; the last element is $(^p)^q$. Thus the lexicographic generation process consists of scanning from the right until finding a trailing string of the form $a_j \ldots a_{2n} = \,)(^{p+1})^q$ and replacing it by $()^{q+1-p}()\ldots()$. Steps P4 and P5 do this efficiently, while step P3 handles the simple case $p = 0$.

Table 1 illustrates the output of Algorithm P when $n = 4$, together with the corresponding forest and binary tree as in (2) and (4). Several other equivalent combinatorial objects also appear in Table 1: For example, a string of nested parentheses can be run-length encoded as

$$()^{d_1} \, ()^{d_2} \ldots ()^{d_n}, \qquad (6)$$

where the nonnegative integers $d_1 d_2 \ldots d_n$ are characterized by the constraints

$$d_1 + d_2 + \cdots + d_k \leq k \quad \text{for } 1 \leq k < n; \qquad d_1 + d_2 + \cdots + d_n = n. \qquad (7)$$

We can also represent nested parentheses by the sequence $z_1 z_2 \ldots z_n$, which specifies the indices where the left parentheses appear. In essence, $z_1 z_2 \ldots z_n$ is one of the $\binom{2n}{n}$ combinations of n things from the set $\{1, 2, \ldots, 2n\}$, subject to the special constraints

$$z_{k-1} < z_k < 2k \qquad \text{for } 1 \leq k \leq n, \qquad (8)$$

if we assume that $z_0 = 0$. The z's are of course related to the d's:

$$d_k = z_{k+1} - z_k - 1 \qquad \text{for } 1 \leq k < n. \qquad (9)$$

Algorithm P becomes particularly simple when it is rewritten to generate the combinations $z_1 z_2 \ldots z_n$ instead of the strings $a_1 a_2 \ldots a_{2n}$. (See exercise 2.)

A parenthesis string can also be represented by the permutation $p_1 p_2 \ldots p_n$, where the kth right parenthesis matches the p_kth left parenthesis; in other words, the kth node of the associated forest in postorder is the p_kth node in preorder. By exercise 2.3.2–20, node j is a (proper) descendant of node k in the forest if and only if $j < k$ and $p_j > p_k$, when we label the nodes in postorder. The inversion table $c_1 c_2 \ldots c_n$ characterizes this permutation by the rule that exactly c_k elements to the right of k are less than k (see exercise 5.1.1–7); allowable inversion tables have $c_1 = 0$ and

$$0 \le c_{k+1} \le c_k + 1 \qquad \text{for } 1 \le k < n. \tag{10}$$

Moreover, exercise 3 proves that c_k is the level of the forest's kth node in preorder (the depth of the kth left parenthesis), a fact that is equivalent to the formula

$$c_k = 2k - 1 - z_k. \tag{11}$$

Table 1 and exercise 6 also illustrate a special kind of *matching*, by which $2n$ people at a circular table can simultaneously shake hands without interference.

Thus Algorithm P can be useful indeed. But if our goal is to generate all binary trees, represented by left links $l_1 l_2 \ldots l_n$ and right links $r_1 r_2 \ldots r_n$, the lexicographic sequence in Table 1 is rather awkward; the data we need to get from one tree to its successor is not readily available. Fortunately, an ingenious alternative scheme for direct generation of all linked binary trees is also available:

Algorithm B (*Binary trees*). Given $n \ge 1$, this algorithm generates all binary trees with n internal nodes, representing them via left links $l_1 l_2 \ldots l_n$ and right links $r_1 r_2 \ldots r_n$, with nodes labeled in preorder. (Thus, for example, node 1 is always the root, and l_k is either $k + 1$ or 0; if $l_1 = 0$ and $n > 1$ then $r_1 = 2$.)

B1. [Initialize.] Set $l_k \leftarrow k + 1$ and $r_k \leftarrow 0$ for $1 \le k < n$; also set $l_n \leftarrow r_n \leftarrow 0$, and set $l_{n+1} \leftarrow 1$ (for convenience in step B3).

B2. [Visit.] Visit the binary tree represented by $l_1 l_2 \ldots l_n$ and $r_1 r_2 \ldots r_n$.

B3. [Find j.] Set $j \leftarrow 1$. While $l_j = 0$, set $r_j \leftarrow 0$, $l_j \leftarrow j + 1$, and $j \leftarrow j + 1$. Then terminate the algorithm if $j > n$.

B4. [Find k and y.] Set $y \leftarrow l_j$ and $k \leftarrow 0$. While $r_y > 0$, set $k \leftarrow y$ and $y \leftarrow r_y$.

B5. [Promote y.] If $k > 0$, set $r_k \leftarrow 0$; otherwise set $l_j \leftarrow 0$. Then set $r_y \leftarrow r_j$, $r_j \leftarrow y$, and return to B2. ∎

[See W. Skarbek, *Theoretical Computer Science* **57** (1988), 153–159; step B3 uses an idea of J. Korsh.] Exercise 44 proves that the loops in steps B3 and B4 both tend to be very short. Indeed, fewer than 9 memory references are needed, on the average, to transform a linked binary tree into its successor.

Table 2 shows the fourteen binary trees that are generated when $n = 4$, together with their corresponding forests and with two related sequences: Arrays $e_1 e_2 \ldots e_n$ and $s_1 s_2 \ldots s_n$ are defined by the property that node k in preorder has e_k children and s_k descendants in the associated forest. (Thus s_k is the size of k's left subtree in the binary tree; also, $s_k + 1$ is the length of the SCOPE link in the sense of 2.3.3–(5).) The next column repeats the fourteen forests of Table 1 in the lexicographic ordering of Algorithm P, but mirror-reversed from left to right.

Table 2

LINKED BINARY TREES AND RELATED OBJECTS WHEN $n = 4$

$l_1l_2l_3l_4$	$r_1r_2r_3r_4$	binary tree	forest	$e_1e_2e_3e_4$	$s_1s_2s_3s_4$	colex forest	lsib/rchild
2340	0000			1110	3210		
0340	2000			0110	0210		
2040	0300			2010	3010		
2040	3000			1010	1010		
0040	2300			0010	0010		
2300	0040			1200	3200		
0300	2040			0200	0200		
2300	0400			2100	3100		
2300	4000			1100	2100		
0300	2400			0100	0100		
2000	0340			3000	3000		
2000	4300			2000	2000		
2000	3040			1000	1000		
0000	2340			0000	0000		

And the final column shows the binary tree that represents the colex forest; it also happens to represent the forest in column 4, but by links to left sibling and right child instead of to left child and right sibling. This final column provides an interesting connection between nested parentheses and binary trees, so it gives us some insight into why Algorithm B is valid (see exercise 19).

Gray codes for trees. Our previous experiences with other combinatorial patterns suggest that we can probably generate parentheses and trees by making only small perturbations to get from one instance to another. And indeed, there are at least three very nice ways to achieve this goal.

Consider first the case of nested parentheses, which we can represent by the sequences $z_1 z_2 \ldots z_n$ that satisfy condition (8). A "near-perfect" way to generate all such combinations, in the sense of Section 7.2.1.3, is one in which we run through all possibilities in such a way that some component z_j changes by ± 1 or ± 2 at each step; this means that we get from each string of parentheses to its successor by simply changing either () $\leftrightarrow$)(or ()) $\leftrightarrow$))(in the vicinity of the jth left parenthesis. Here's one way to do the job when $n = 4$:

$$1357, 1356, 1346, 1345, 1347, 1247, 1245, 1246, 1236, 1234, 1235, 1237, 1257, 1256.$$

And we can extend any solution for $n - 1$ to a solution for n, by taking each pattern $z_1 z_2 \ldots z_{n-1}$ and letting z_n run through all of its legal values using *endo-order* or its reverse as in 7.2.1.3–(45), proceeding downward from $2n-2$ and then up to $2n - 1$ or vice versa, and omitting all elements that are $\leq z_{n-1}$.

Algorithm N (*Near-perfect nested parentheses*). This algorithm visits all n-combinations $z_1 \ldots z_n$ of $\{1, \ldots, 2n\}$ that represent the indices of left parentheses in a nested string, changing only one index at a time. The process is controlled by an auxiliary array $g_1 \ldots g_n$ that represents temporary goals.

N1. [Initialize.] Set $z_j \leftarrow 2j - 1$ and $g_j \leftarrow 2j - 2$ for $1 \leq j \leq n$.

N2. [Visit.] Visit the n-combination $z_1 \ldots z_n$. Then set $j \leftarrow n$.

N3. [Find j.] If $z_j = g_j$, set $g_j \leftarrow g_j \oplus 1$ (thereby complementing the least significant bit), $j \leftarrow j - 1$, and repeat this step.

N4. [Home stretch?] If $g_j - z_j$ is even, set $z_j \leftarrow z_j + 2$ and return to N2.

N5. [Decrease or turn.] Set $t \leftarrow z_j - 2$. If $t < 0$, terminate the algorithm. Otherwise, if $t \leq z_{j-1}$, set $t \leftarrow t + 2[t < z_{j-1}] + 1$. Finally set $z_j \leftarrow t$ and go back to N2. ∎

[A somewhat similar algorithm was introduced by D. Rœlants van Baronaigien in *J. Algorithms* **35** (2000), 100–107; see also Xiang, Ushijima, and Tang, *Inf. Proc. Letters* **76** (2000), 169–174. F. Ruskey and A. Proskurowski, in *J. Algorithms* **11** (1990), 68–84, had previously shown how to construct *perfect* Gray codes for all tables $z_1 \ldots z_n$ when $n \geq 4$ is even, thus changing some z_j by only ± 1 at every step; but their construction was quite complex, and no known perfect scheme is simple enough to be of practical use. Exercise 48 shows that perfection is impossible when $n \geq 5$ is odd.]

If our goal is to generate linked tree structures instead of strings of parentheses, perfection of the z-index changes is not good enough, because simple swaps like () $\leftrightarrow$)(don't necessarily correspond to simple link manipulations. A far better approach can be based on the "rotation" algorithms by which we were able to keep search trees balanced in Section 6.2.3. *Rotation to the left* changes a binary tree

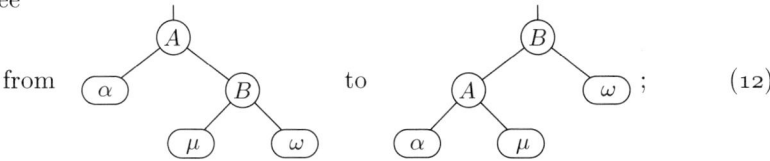

from   to   ;   (12)

thus the corresponding forest is changed

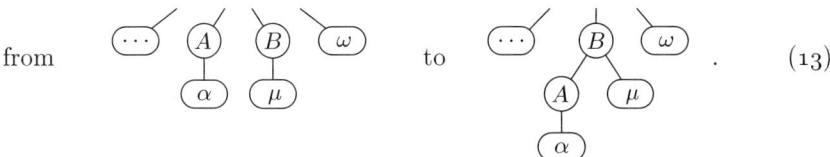

from   to   .   (13)

"Node A becomes the leftmost child of its right sibling." *Rotation to the right* is, of course, the opposite transformation: "The leftmost child of B becomes its left sibling." The vertical line in (12) stands for a connection to the overall context, either a left link or a right link or the pointer to the root. Any or all of the subtrees α, μ, or ω may be empty. The '$\cdots$' in (13), which represents additional siblings at the left of the family containing B, might also be empty.

The nice thing about rotations is that only three links change: The right link from A, the left link from B, and the pointer from above. Rotations preserve inorder of the binary tree and postorder of the forest. (Notice also that the binary-tree form of a rotation corresponds in a natural way to an application of the *associative law*

$$(\alpha\mu)\omega \;=\; \alpha(\mu\omega) \tag{14}$$

in the midst of an algebraic formula.)

A simple scheme very much like the classical reflected Gray code for n-tuples (Algorithm 7.2.1.1H) and the method of plain changes for permutations (Algorithm 7.2.1.2P) can be used to generate all binary trees or forests via rotations. Consider any forest on $n - 1$ nodes, with k roots A_1, ..., A_k. Then there are $k + 1$ forests on n nodes that have the same postorder sequence on the first $n - 1$ nodes but with node n last; for example, when $k = 3$ they are

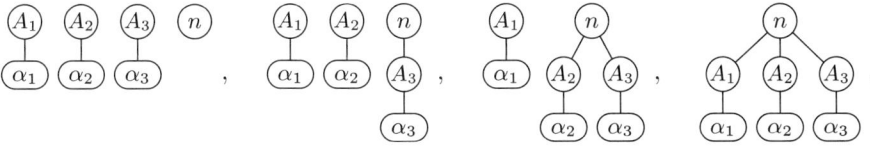

obtained by successively rotating A_3, A_2, and A_1 to the left. Moreover, at the extremes when n is either at the right or at the top, we can perform any desired rotation on the other $n - 1$ nodes, because node n isn't in the way. Therefore, as observed by J. M. Lucas, D. Rœlants van Baronaigien, and F. Ruskey [*J. Algorithms* **15** (1993), 343–366], we can extend any list of the $(n - 1)$-node trees to a list of all n-node trees by simply letting node n roam

back and forth. A careful attention to low-level details makes it possible in fact
to do the job with remarkable efficiency:

Algorithm L (*Linked binary trees by rotations*). This algorithm generates all
pairs of arrays $l_0 l_1 \ldots l_n$ and $r_1 \ldots r_n$ that represent left links and right links of
n-node binary trees, where l_0 is the root of the tree and the links (l_k, r_k) point
respectively to the left and right subtrees of the kth node in symmetric order.
Equivalently, it generates all n-node forests, where l_k and r_k denote the left child
and right sibling of the kth node in postorder. Each tree is obtained from its predecessor by doing a single rotation. Two auxiliary arrays $k_1 \ldots k_n$ and $o_0 o_1 \ldots o_n$,
representing backpointers and directions, are used to control the process.

L1. [Initialize.] Set $l_j \leftarrow 0$, $r_j \leftarrow j + 1$, $k_j \leftarrow j - 1$, and $o_j \leftarrow -1$ for $1 \le j < n$;
also set $l_0 \leftarrow o_0 \leftarrow 1$, $l_n \leftarrow r_n \leftarrow 0$, $k_n \leftarrow n - 1$, and $o_n \leftarrow -1$.

L2. [Visit.] Visit the binary tree or forest represented by $l_0 l_1 \ldots l_n$ and $r_1 \ldots r_n$.
Then set $j \leftarrow n$ and $p \leftarrow 0$.

L3. [Find j.] If $o_j > 0$, set $m \leftarrow l_j$ and go to L5 if $m \ne 0$. If $o_j < 0$, set $m \leftarrow k_j$;
then go to L4 if $m \ne 0$, otherwise set $p \leftarrow j$. If $m = 0$ in either case, set
$o_j \leftarrow -o_j$, $j \leftarrow j - 1$, and repeat this step.

L4. [Rotate left.] Set $r_m \leftarrow l_j$, $l_j \leftarrow m$, $x \leftarrow k_m$, and $k_j \leftarrow x$. If $x = 0$, set
$l_p \leftarrow j$, otherwise set $r_x \leftarrow j$. Return to L2.

L5. [Rotate right.] Terminate if $j = 0$. Otherwise set $l_j \leftarrow r_m$, $r_m \leftarrow j$, $k_j \leftarrow m$,
$x \leftarrow k_m$. If $x = 0$, set $l_p \leftarrow m$, otherwise set $r_x \leftarrow m$. Go back to L2. ∎

Exercise 38 proves that Algorithm L needs only about 9 memory references per
tree generated; thus it is almost as fast as Algorithm B. (In fact, two memory
references per step could be saved by keeping the three quantities o_n, l_n, and k_n
in registers. But of course Algorithm B can be speeded up too.)

Table 3 shows the sequence of binary trees and forests visited by Algorithm L
when $n = 4$, with some auxiliary tables that shed further light on the process.
The permutation $q_1 q_2 q_3 q_4$ lists the nodes in preorder, when they have been
numbered in postorder of the forest (symmetric order of the binary tree); it
is the inverse of the permutation $p_1 p_2 p_3 p_4$ in Table 1. The "coforest" is the
conjugate (right-to-left reflection) of the forest; and the numbers $u_1 u_2 u_3 u_4$ are
its scope coordinates, analogous to $s_1 s_2 s_3 s_4$ in Table 2. A final column shows
the so-called "dual forest." The significance of these associated quantities is
explored in exercises 11–13, 19, 24, 26, and 27.

The links $l_0 l_1 \ldots l_n$ and $r_1 \ldots r_n$ in Algorithm L and Table 3 are *not* comparable to the links $l_1 \ldots l_n$ and $r_1 \ldots r_n$ in Algorithm B and Table 2, because
Algorithm L preserves inorder/postorder while Algorithm B preserves preorder.
Node k in Algorithm L is the kth node from left to right in the binary tree, so
l_0 is needed to identify the root; but node k in Algorithm B is the kth node in
preorder, so the root is always node 1 in that case.

Algorithm L has the desired property that only three links change per step;
but we can actually do even better in this respect if we stick to the preorder
convention of Algorithm B. Exercise 25 presents an algorithm that generates

Table 3

BINARY TREES AND FORESTS GENERATED BY ROTATIONS WHEN $n = 4$

$l_0l_1l_2l_3l_4$	$r_1r_2r_3r_4$	$k_1k_2k_3k_4$	binary tree	forest	$q_1q_2q_3q_4$	coforest	$u_1u_2u_3u_4$	dual
10000	2340	0123			1234		0000	
10003	2400	0122			1243		1000	
10002	4300	0121			1423		2000	
40001	2300	0120			4123		3000	
40021	3000	0110			4132		3100	
10023	4000	0111			1432		2100	
10020	3040	0113			1324		0100	
30010	2040	0103			3124		0200	
40013	2000	0100			4312		3200	
40123	0000	0000			4321		3210	
30120	0040	0003			3214		0210	
20100	0340	0023			2134		0010	
20103	0400	0022			2143		1010	
40102	0300	0020			4213		3010	

all linked binary trees or forests by changing just two links per step, preserving preorder. One link becomes zero while another becomes nonzero. This prune-and-graft algorithm, which is the third of the three "very nice Gray codes for trees" promised above, has only one downside: Its controlling mechanism is a bit trickier than that of Algorithm L, so it needs about 40% more time to do the calculations when we include the cost of deciding what links to change at each step.

The number of trees. There's a simple formula for the total number of outputs that are generated by Algorithms P, B, N, and L, namely

$$C_n = \frac{1}{n+1}\binom{2n}{n} = \binom{2n}{n} - \binom{2n}{n-1}; \qquad (15)$$

we proved this fact in Eq. 2.3.4.4–(14). The first few values are

$n =$	0	1	2	3	4	5	6	7	8	9	10	11	12	13
$C_n =$	1	1	2	5	14	42	132	429	1430	4862	16796	58786	208012	742900

and they are called *Catalan numbers* because of some influential papers written by Eugène Catalan [*Journal de math.* **3** (1838), 508–516; **4** (1839), 95–99]. Stirling's approximation tells us the asymptotic value,

$$C_n = \frac{4^n}{\sqrt{\pi}\, n^{3/2}}\left(1 - \frac{9}{8n} + \frac{145}{128n^2} - \frac{1155}{1024n^3} + \frac{36939}{32768n^4} + O(n^{-5})\right); \qquad (16)$$

in particular we can conclude that

$$\frac{C_{n-k}}{C_n} = \frac{1}{4^k}\left(1 + \frac{3k}{2n} + O\left(\frac{k^2}{n^2}\right)\right) \qquad \text{when } |k| \le \frac{n}{2}. \qquad (17)$$

(And of course C_{n-1}/C_n is equal to $(n+1)/(4n-2)$, exactly, by (15).) In Section 2.3.4.4 we also derived the generating function

$$C(z) = C_0 + C_1 z + C_2 z^2 + C_3 z^3 + \cdots = \frac{1 - \sqrt{1-4z}}{2z} \qquad (18)$$

and proved the important formula

$$[z^n]\, C(z)^r = \frac{r}{n+r}\binom{2n+r-1}{n} = \binom{2n+r-1}{n} - \binom{2n+r-1}{n-1}; \qquad (19)$$

see the answer to exercise 2.3.4.4–33, and *CMath* equation (5.70).

These facts give us more than enough information to analyze Algorithm P, our algorithm for lexicographic generation of nested parentheses. Step P2 is obviously performed C_n times; then P3 usually makes a simple change and goes back to P2. How often do we need to go on to step P4? Easy: It's the number of times that step P2 finds $m = 2n - 1$. And m is the location of the rightmost '(', so we have $m = 2n - 1$ in exactly C_{n-1} cases. Thus the probability that P3 sets $m \leftarrow m - 1$ and returns immediately to P2 is $(C_n - C_{n-1})/C_n \approx 3/4$, by (17). On the other hand when we do get to step P4, suppose we need to set $a_j \leftarrow$ ')' and $a_k \leftarrow$ '(' exactly $h - 1$ times in that step. The number of cases with $h > x$ is the number of nested strings of length $2n$ that end with x trivial pairs () ... (), namely C_{n-x}. Therefore the total number of times the algorithm changes a_j and a_k in step P4 is

$$C_{n-1} + C_{n-2} + \cdots + C_1 = C_n\left(\frac{C_{n-1}}{C_n} + \frac{C_{n-2}}{C_n} + \cdots + \frac{C_1}{C_n}\right)$$

$$= \frac{1}{3}C_n\left(1 + \frac{2}{n} + O\left(\frac{1}{n^2}\right)\right), \qquad (20)$$

by (17); we have proved the claim for efficiency made earlier.

For a deeper understanding it is helpful to study the recursive structure underlying Algorithm P, as expressed in (5). The sequences A_{pq} in that formula have C_{pq} elements, where

$$C_{pq} = C_{p(q-1)} + C_{(p-1)q}, \quad \text{if } 0 \le p \le q \ne 0; \qquad C_{00} = 1; \qquad (21)$$

and $C_{pq} = 0$ if $p < 0$ or $p > q$. Thus we can form the triangular array

$$
\begin{array}{llllll}
C_{00} & & & & & \\
C_{01} & C_{11} & & & & \\
C_{02} & C_{12} & C_{22} & & & \\
C_{03} & C_{13} & C_{23} & C_{33} & & \\
C_{04} & C_{14} & C_{24} & C_{34} & C_{44} & \\
C_{05} & C_{15} & C_{25} & C_{35} & C_{45} & C_{55} \\
C_{06} & C_{16} & C_{26} & C_{36} & C_{46} & C_{56} & C_{66}
\end{array}
=
\begin{array}{lllllll}
1 & & & & & & \\
1 & 1 & & & & & \\
1 & 2 & 2 & & & & \\
1 & 3 & 5 & 5 & & & \\
1 & 4 & 9 & 14 & 14 & & \\
1 & 5 & 14 & 28 & 42 & 42 & \\
1 & 6 & 20 & 48 & 90 & 132 & 132
\end{array}
\qquad (22)
$$

in which every entry is the sum of its nearest neighbors above and to the left; the Catalan numbers $C_n = C_{nn}$ appear on the diagonal. The elements of this triangle, which themselves have a venerable pedigree going back to de Moivre in 1711, are called "ballot numbers," because they represent sequences of $p + q$ ballots for which a running tabulation never favors a candidate with p votes over an opponent who receives q votes. The general formula

$$C_{pq} = \frac{q-p+1}{q+1}\binom{p+q}{p} = \binom{p+q}{p} - \binom{p+q}{p-1} \qquad (23)$$

can be proved by induction or in a variety of more interesting ways; see exercise 39 and the answer to exercise 2.2.1–4. Notice that, because of (19), we have

$$C_{pq} = [z^p] C(z)^{q-p+1}. \qquad (24)$$

When $n = 4$, Algorithm P essentially describes the recursion tree

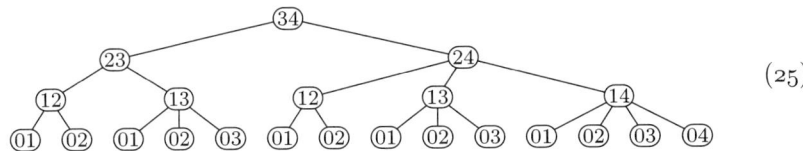

$$(25)$$

because the specification (5) implies that $A_{nn} = (\,A_{(n-1)n}$ and that

$$A_{pq} =)^{q-p}(\,A_{(p-1)p}, \;\;)^{q-p-1}(\,A_{(p-1)(p+1)}, \;\;)^{q-p-2}(\,A_{(p-1)(p+2)},$$
$$\ldots, \;\; (\,A_{(p-1)q} \qquad \text{when } 0 \le p < q. \quad (26)$$

The number of leaves below node $\textcircled{pq}$ in this recursion tree is C_{pq}, and node $\textcircled{pq}$ appears exactly $C_{(n-q)(n-1-p)}$ times on level $n - 1 - p$; therefore we must have

$$\sum_q C_{(n-q)(n-1-p)} C_{pq} = C_n, \qquad \text{for } 0 \le p < n. \qquad (27)$$

The fourteen leaves of (25), from left to right, correspond to the fourteen rows of Table 1, from top to bottom. Notice that the entries in column $c_1 c_2 c_3 c_4$ of that table assign the respective numbers $0000, 0001, 0010, \ldots, 0123$ to the leaves of (25), in accord with "Dewey decimal notation" for tree nodes (but with indices starting at 0 instead of 1, and with an extra 0 tacked on at the beginning).

A worm that crawls from one leaf to the next, around the bottom of the recursion tree, will ascend and descend h levels when h of the coordinates $c_1 \ldots c_n$ are changed, namely when Algorithm P resets the values of h (s and h)s. This observation makes it easy to understand our previous conclusion that the condition $h > x$ occurs exactly C_{n-x} times during a complete crawl.

Yet another way to understand Algorithm P arises when we contemplate an infinite directed graph that is suggested by the recursion (21):

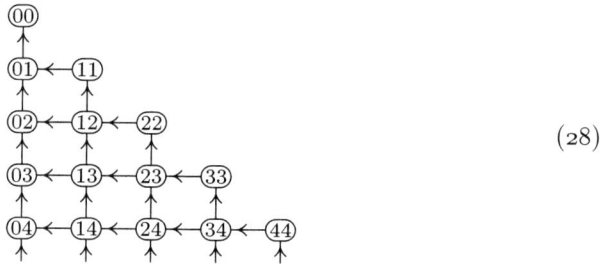

$$(28)$$

Clearly C_{pq} is the number of paths from $\textcircled{pq}$ to $\textcircled{00}$ in this digraph, because of (21). And indeed, every string of parentheses in A_{pq} corresponds directly to such a path, with '(' signifying a step to the left and ')' signifying a step upward. Algorithm P explores all such paths systematically by trying first to go upward when extending a partial path.

Therefore it is easy to determine the Nth string of nested parentheses that is visited by Algorithm P, by starting at node $\textcircled{nn}$ and doing the following calculation when at node $\textcircled{pq}$: If $p = q = 0$, stop; otherwise, if $N \leq C_{p(q-1)}$, emit ')', set $q \leftarrow q - 1$, and continue; otherwise set $N \leftarrow N - C_{p(q-1)}$, emit '(', set $p \leftarrow p - 1$, and continue. The following algorithm [Frank Ruskey, Ph.D. thesis (University of California at San Diego, 1978), 16–24] avoids the need to precompute the Catalan triangle by evaluating C_{pq} on the fly as it goes:

Algorithm U (*Unrank a string of nested parentheses*). Given n and N, where $1 \leq N \leq C_n$, this algorithm computes the Nth output $a_1 \ldots a_{2n}$ of Algorithm P.

U1. [Initialize.] Set $q \leftarrow n$ and $m \leftarrow p \leftarrow c \leftarrow 1$. While $p < n$, set $p \leftarrow p + 1$ and $c \leftarrow ((4p - 2)c)/(p + 1)$.

U2. [Done?] Terminate the algorithm if $q = 0$.

U3. [Go up?] Set $c' \leftarrow ((q + 1)(q - p)c)/((q + p)(q - p + 1))$. (At this point we have $1 \leq N \leq c = C_{pq}$ and $c' = C_{p(q-1)}$.) If $N \leq c'$, set $q \leftarrow q - 1$, $c \leftarrow c'$, $a_m \leftarrow$ ')', $m \leftarrow m + 1$, and return to U2.

U4. [Go left.] Set $p \leftarrow p - 1$, $c \leftarrow c - c'$, $N \leftarrow N - c'$, $a_m \leftarrow$ '(', $m \leftarrow m + 1$, and return to U3. ∎

Random trees. We could choose a string $a_1 a_2 \ldots a_{2n}$ of nested parentheses at random by simply applying Algorithm U to a random integer N between 1 and C_n. But that idea isn't really very good, when n is bigger than 32 or so, because C_n can be quite large. A simpler and better way, proposed by D. B. Arnold and M. R. Sleep [*ACM Trans. Prog. Languages and Systems* **2** (1980), 122–128], is to generate a random "worm walk" by starting at ⓝⓝ in (28) and repeatedly taking leftward or upward branches with the appropriate probabilities. The resulting algorithm is almost the same as Algorithm U, but it deals only with nonnegative integers less than $n^2 + n + 1$:

Algorithm W (*Uniformly random strings of nested parentheses*). This algorithm generates a random string $a_1 a_2 \ldots a_{2n}$ of properly nested (s and)s.

W1. [Initialize.] Set $p \leftarrow q \leftarrow n$ and $m \leftarrow 1$.

W2. [Done?] Terminate the algorithm if $q = 0$.

W3. [Go up?] Let X be a random integer in the range $0 \le X < (q+p)(q-p+1)$. If $X < (q+1)(q-p)$, set $q \leftarrow q - 1$, $a_m \leftarrow$ ')', $m \leftarrow m + 1$, and return to W2.

W4. [Go left.] Set $p \leftarrow p - 1$, $a_m \leftarrow$ '(', $m \leftarrow m + 1$, and return to W3. ∎

A worm's walk can be regarded as a sequence $w_0 w_1 \ldots w_{2n}$, where w_m is the worm's current depth after m steps. Thus, $w_0 = 0$; $w_m = w_{m-1} + 1$ when $a_m =$ '('; $w_m = w_{m-1} - 1$ when $a_m =$ ')'; and we have $w_m \ge 0$, $w_{2n} = 0$. The sequence $w_0 w_1 \ldots w_{30}$ corresponding to (1) and (2) is 012101232123434543232123234343210. At step W3 of Algorithm W we have $q + p = 2n + 1 - m$ and $q - p = w_{m-1}$.

Let's say that the *outline* of a forest is the path that runs through the points $(m, -w_m)$ in the plane, for $0 \le m \le 2n$, where $w_0 w_1 \ldots w_{2n}$ is the worm walk corresponding to the associated string $a_1 \ldots a_{2n}$ of nested parentheses. Figure 57 shows what happens if we plot the outlines of all 50-node forests and darken each point according to the number of forests that lie above it. For example, w_1 is always 1, so the triangular region at the upper left of Fig. 57 is solid black. But w_2 is either 0 or 2, and 0 occurs in $C_{49} \approx C_{50}/4$ cases; so the adjacent diamond-shaped area is a 75% shade of gray. Thus Fig. 57 illustrates the shape of a random forest, analogous to the shapes of random partitions that we've seen in Figs. 50, 51, and 55 of Sections 7.2.1.4 and 7.2.1.5.

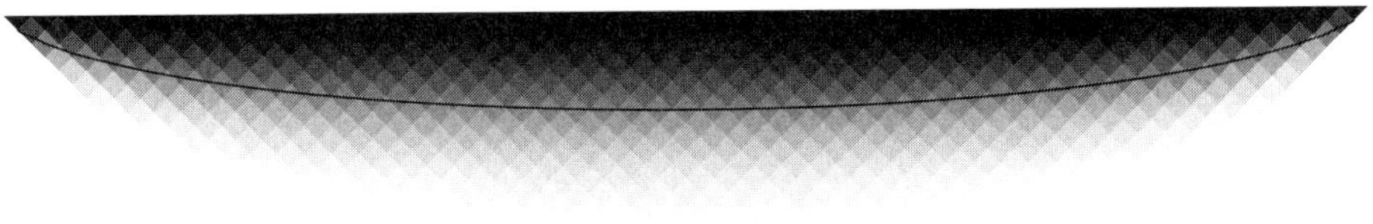

Fig. 57. The shape of a random 50-node forest.

Of course we can't really draw the outlines of all those forests, since there are $C_{50} = 1{,}978{,}261{,}657{,}756{,}160{,}653{,}623{,}774{,}456$ of them. But with the help of mathematics we can pretend that we've done so. The probability that $w_{2m} = 2k$ is $C_{(m-k)(m+k)} C_{(n-m-k)(n-m+k)}/C_n$, because there are $C_{(m-k)(m+k)}$ ways to start with $m + k$ (s and $m - k$)s, and $C_{(n-m-k)(n-m+k)}$ ways to finish with

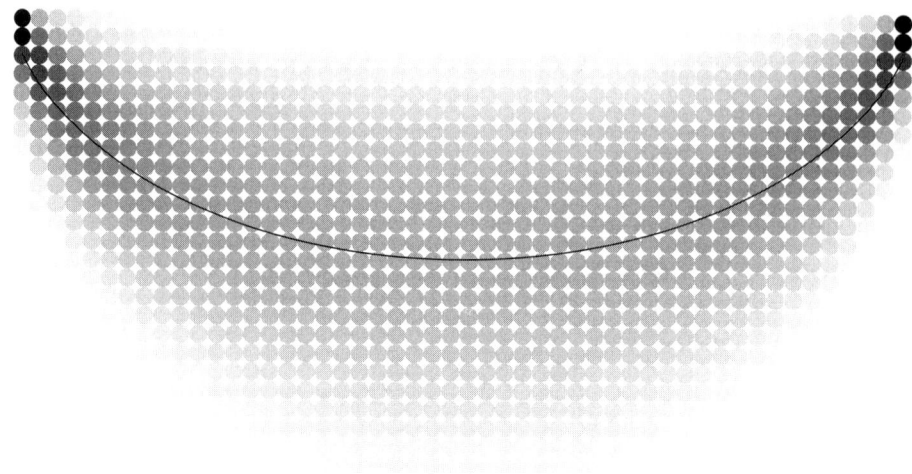

Fig. 58. Locations of the internal nodes in a random 50-node binary tree.

$n - (m + k)$ (s and $n - (m - k)$)s. By (23) and Stirling's approximation, this probability is

$$\frac{(2k+1)^2(n+1)}{(m+k+1)(n-m+k+1)} \binom{2m}{m-k}\binom{2n-2m}{n-m+k}\bigg/\binom{2n}{n}$$

$$= \frac{(2k+1)^2}{\sqrt{\pi}\,\big(\theta(1-\theta)n\big)^{3/2}}\, e^{-k^2/(\theta(1-\theta)n)}\left(1 + O\Big(\frac{k+1}{n}\Big) + O\Big(\frac{k^3}{n^2}\Big)\right) \qquad (29)$$

when $m = \theta n$ and $n \to \infty$, for $0 < \theta < 1$. The average value of w_{2m} is worked out in exercise 57; it comes to

$$\frac{(4m(n-m)+n)\binom{2m}{m}\binom{2n-2m}{n-m}}{n\binom{2n}{n}} - 1 \;=\; 4\sqrt{\frac{\theta(1-\theta)n}{\pi}} - 1 + O\Big(\frac{1}{\sqrt{n}}\Big), \quad (30)$$

and it is illustrated for $n = 50$ as a curved line in Fig. 57.

When n is large, worm walks approach the so-called "Brownian excursion," which is an important concept in probability theory. See, for example, Paul Lévy, *Processus Stochastiques et Mouvement Brownien* (1948), 225–237; Guy Louchard, *J. Applied Prob.* **21** (1984), 479–499, and *BIT* **26** (1986), 17–34; David Aldous, *Electronic Communications in Probability* **3** (1998), 79–90; Jon Warren, *Electronic Communications in Probability* **4** (1999), 25–29; J.-F. Marckert, *Random Structures & Algorithms* **24** (2004), 118–132.

What is the shape of a random *binary* tree? This question was investigated by Frank Ruskey in *SIAM J. Algebraic and Discrete Methods* **1** (1980), 43–50, and the answer turns out to be quite interesting. Suppose we draw a binary tree

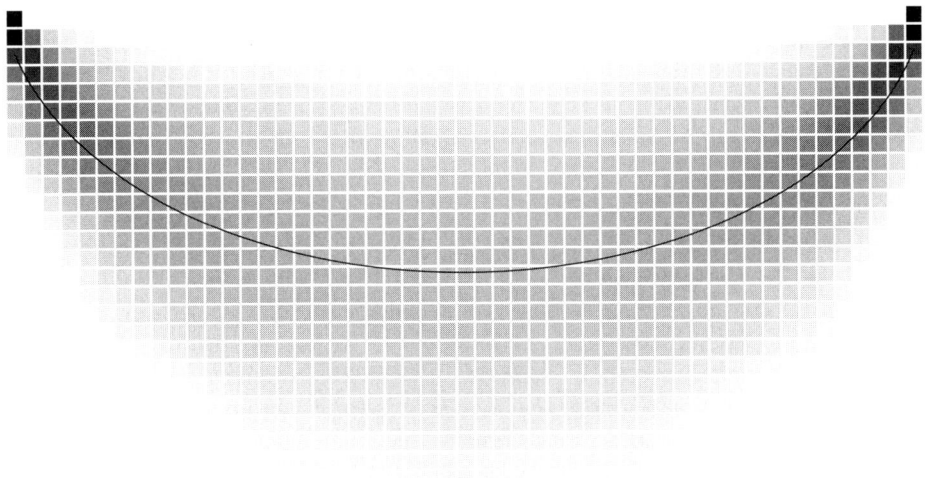

Fig. 59. Locations of the external nodes in a random 50-node binary tree.

as in (4), with the mth internal node at horizontal position m when the nodes
are numbered in symmetric order. If all of the 50-node binary trees are drawn
in this way and superimposed on each other, we get the distribution of node
positions shown in Fig. 58. Similarly, if we number the *external* nodes from 0
to n in symmetric order and place them at horizontal positions $.5, 1.5, \ldots, n+.5$,
the "fringes" of all 50-node binary trees form the distribution shown in Fig. 59.
Notice that the root node is most likely to be either number 1 or number n, at
the extreme left or right; it is least likely to be either $\lfloor (n+1)/2 \rfloor$ or $\lceil (n+1)/2 \rceil$,
in the middle.

As in Fig. 57, the smooth curves in Figs. 58 and 59 show the average node
depths; exact formulas are derived in exercises 58 and 59. Asymptotically, the
average depth of external node m is

$$8\sqrt{\frac{\theta(1-\theta)n}{\pi}} - 1 + O\left(\frac{1}{\sqrt{n}}\right), \qquad \text{when } m = \theta n \text{ and } n \to \infty, \qquad (31)$$

for all fixed ratios θ with $0 < \theta < 1$, curiously like (30); and the average depth
of *internal* node m is asymptotically the same, but with '-1' replaced by '-3'.
Thus we can say that *the average shape of a random binary tree is approximately
the lower half of an ellipse, n units wide and $4\sqrt{n/\pi}$ levels deep.*

Three other noteworthy ways to generate random encodings of forests are
discussed in exercises 60, 61, and 62. They are less direct than Algorithm W,
yet they have substantial combinatorial interest. The first one begins with an
arbitrary random string containing n (s and n)s, not necessarily nested; each
of the $\binom{2n}{n}$ possibilities is equally likely. It then proceeds to convert every such
string into a sequence that is properly nested, in such a way that exactly $n+1$

strings map into each final outcome. The second method is similar, but it starts with a sequence of $n+1$ 0s and n 2s, mapping them in such a way that exactly $2n+1$ original strings produce each possible result. And the third method produces each output from exactly n of the bit strings that contain exactly $n-1$ 1s and $n+1$ 0s. In other words, the three methods provide combinatorial proofs of the fact that C_n is simultaneously equal to $\binom{2n}{n}/(n+1)$, $\binom{2n+1}{n}/(2n+1)$, and $\binom{2n}{n-1}/n$. For example, when $n=4$ we have $14 = 70/5 = 126/9 = 56/4$.

If we want to generate random binary trees directly in linked form, we can use a beautiful method suggested by J. L. Rémy [*RAIRO Informatique Théorique* **19** (1985), 179–195]. His approach is particularly instructive because it shows how random Catalan trees might actually occur "in nature," using a deliciously simple mechanism based on a classical idea of Olinde Rodrigues [*J. de Math.* **3** (1838), 549]. Let us suppose that our goal is to obtain not only an ordinary n-node binary tree, but a *decorated* binary tree, namely an extended binary tree in which the external nodes have been labeled with the numbers 0 to n in some order. There are $(n+1)!$ ways to decorate any given binary tree; so the total number of decorated binary trees with n internal nodes is

$$D_n = (n+1)!\,C_n = \frac{(2n)!}{n!} = (4n-2)D_{n-1}. \tag{32}$$

Rémy observed that there are $4n-2$ easy ways to build a decorated tree of order n from a given decorated tree of order $n-1$: We simply choose any one of the $2n-1$ nodes (internal or external) in the given tree, say x, and replace it by either

$$\text{or} \tag{33}$$

thus inserting a new internal node and a new leaf while moving x and its descendants (if any) down one level.

For example, here's one way to construct a decorated tree of order 6:

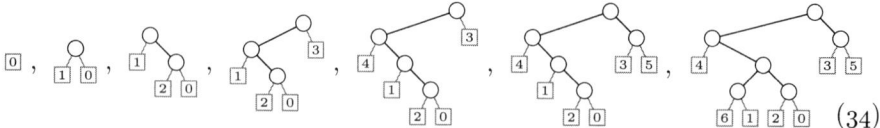

$$(34)$$

Notice that every decorated tree is obtained by this process in exactly one way, because the predecessor of each tree must be the tree we get by striking out the highest-numbered leaf. Therefore Rémy's construction produces decorated trees that are uniformly random; and if we ignore the external nodes, we get random binary trees of the ordinary, undecorated variety.

One appealing way to implement Rémy's procedure is to maintain a table of links $L_0L_1\ldots L_{2n}$ where external (leaf) nodes have even numbers and internal (branch) nodes have odd numbers. The root is node L_0; the left and right children of branch node $2k-1$ are respectively L_{2k-1} and L_{2k}, for $1 \le k \le n$. Then the program is short and sweet:

Algorithm R (*Growing a random binary tree*). This algorithm constructs the linked representation $L_0 L_1 \ldots L_{2N}$ of a uniformly random binary tree with N internal nodes, using the conventions explained above.

R1. [Initialize.] Set $n \leftarrow 0$ and $L_0 \leftarrow 0$.

R2. [Done?] (At this point the links $L_0 L_1 \ldots L_{2n}$ represent a random n-node binary tree.) Terminate the algorithm if $n = N$.

R3. [Advance n.] Let X be a random integer between 0 and $4n + 1$, inclusive. Set $n \leftarrow n + 1$, $b \leftarrow X \bmod 2$, $k \leftarrow \lfloor X/2 \rfloor$, $L_{2n-b} \leftarrow 2n$, $L_{2n-1+b} \leftarrow L_k$, $L_k \leftarrow 2n - 1$, and return to R2. ∎

*Chains of subsets. Now that we've got trees and parentheses firmly in mind, it's a good time to discuss the *Christmas tree pattern*,* which is a remarkable way to arrange the set of all 2^n bit strings of length n into $\binom{n}{\lfloor n/2 \rfloor}$ rows and $n+1$ columns, discovered by de Bruijn, van Ebbenhorst Tengbergen, and Kruyswijk [*Nieuw Archief voor Wiskunde* (2) **23** (1951), 191–193].

The Christmas tree pattern of order 1 is the single row '0 1'; and the pattern of order 2 is

$$
\begin{array}{ccc}
 & 10 & \\
00 & 01 & 11
\end{array}
\qquad (35)
$$

In general we get the Christmas tree pattern of order $n + 1$ by taking every row '$\sigma_1 \sigma_2 \ldots \sigma_s$' of the order-$n$ pattern and replacing it by the two rows

$$
\begin{array}{cccc}
\sigma_2 0 & \ldots & \sigma_s 0 & \\
\sigma_1 0 & \sigma_1 1 & \ldots & \sigma_{s-1} 1 \quad \sigma_s 1
\end{array}
\qquad (36)
$$

(The first of these rows is omitted when $s = 1$.)

Proceeding in this way, we obtain for example the pattern of order 8 that appears in Table 4 on the next page. It is easy to verify by induction that

 i) Each of the 2^n bit strings appears exactly once in the pattern.
 ii) The bit strings with k 1s all appear in the same column.
 iii) Within each row, consecutive bit strings differ by changing a 0 to a 1.

If we think of the bit strings as representing subsets of $\{1, \ldots, n\}$, with 1-bits to indicate the members of a set, property (iii) says that each row represents a *chain* in which each subset is covered by its successor. In symbols, using the notation of Section 7.1.3, every row $\sigma_1 \sigma_2 \ldots \sigma_s$ has the property that $\sigma_j \subseteq \sigma_{j+1}$ and $\nu(\sigma_{j+1}) = \nu(\sigma_j) + 1$ for $1 \le j < s$.

Properties (i) and (ii) tell us that there are exactly $\binom{n}{k}$ elements in column k, if we number the columns from 0 to n. This observation, together with the fact that each row is centered among the columns, proves that the total number of rows is $\max_{0 \le k \le n} \binom{n}{k} = \binom{n}{\lfloor n/2 \rfloor}$, as claimed. Let us call this number M_n.

---

* This name was chosen for sentimental reasons, because the pattern has a general shape not unlike that of a festive tree, and because it was the subject of the author's ninth annual "Christmas Tree Lecture" at Stanford University in December 2002.

Table 4

THE CHRISTMAS TREE PATTERN OF ORDER 8

				10101010				
			10101000	10101001	10101011			
				10101100				
			10100100	10100101	10101101			
			10100010	10100110	10101110			
		10100000	10100001	10100011	10100111	10101111		
				10110010				
			10110000	10110001	10110011			
				10110100				
			10010100	10010101	10110101			
			10010010	10010110	10110110			
		10010000	10010001	10010011	10010111	10110111		
				10111000				
			10011000	10011001	10111001			
			10001010	10011010	10111010			
		10001000	10001001	10001011	10011011	10111011		
			10001100	10011100	10111100			
		10000100	10000101	10001101	10011101	10111101		
		10000010	10000110	10001110	10011110	10111110		
	10000000	10000001	10000011	10000111	10001111	10011111	10111111	
				11001010				
			11001000	11001001	11001011			
				11001100				
			11000100	11000101	11001101			
			11000010	11000110	11001110			
		11000000	11000001	11000011	11000111	11001111		
				11010010				
			11010000	11010001	11010011			
				11010100				
			01010100	01010101	11010101			
			01010010	01010110	11010110			
		01010000	01010001	01010011	01010111	11010111		
				11011000				
			01011000	01011001	11011001			
			01001010	01011010	11011010			
		01001000	01001001	01001011	01011011	11011011		
			01001100	01011100	11011100			
		01000100	01000101	01001101	01011101	11011101		
		01000010	01000110	01001110	01011110	11011110		
	01000000	01000001	01000011	01000111	01001111	01011111	11011111	
				11100010				
			11100000	11100001	11100011			
				11100100				
			01100100	01100101	11100101			
			01100010	01100110	11100110			
		01100000	01100001	01100011	01100111	11100111		
				11101000				
			01101000	01101001	11101001			
			00101010	01101010	11101010			
		00101000	00101001	00101011	01101011	11101011		
			00101100	01101100	11101100			
		00100100	00100101	00101101	01101101	11101101		
		00100010	00100110	00101110	01101110	11101110		
	00100000	00100001	00100011	00100111	00101111	01101111	11101111	
				11110000				
			01110000	01110001	11110001			
			00110010	01110010	11110010			
		00110000	00110001	00110011	01110011	11110011		
			00110100	01110100	11110100			
		00010100	00010101	00110101	01110101	11110101		
		00010010	00010110	00110110	01110110	11110110		
	00010000	00010001	00010011	00010111	00110111	01110111	11110111	
			00111000	01111000	11111000			
		00011000	00011001	00111001	01111001	11111001		
		00001010	00011010	00111010	01111010	11111010		
	00001000	00001001	00011011	00111011	01111011	11111011		
			00011100	00111100	01111100	11111100		
	00000100	00000101	00001101	00011101	00111101	01111101	11111101	
	00000010	00000110	00001110	00011110	00111110	01111110	11111110	
00000000	00000001	00000011	00000111	00001111	00011111	00111111	01111111	11111111

A set C of bit strings is called a *clutter*, or an "antichain of subsets," if its bit strings are incomparable in the sense that $\sigma \not\subseteq \tau$ whenever σ and τ are distinct elements of C. A famous theorem of Emanuel Sperner [*Math. Zeitschrift* **27** (1928), 544–548] asserts that no clutter on $\{1, \ldots, n\}$ can have more than M_n elements; and the Christmas tree pattern provides a simple proof, because no clutter can contain more than one element of each row.

Indeed, the Christmas tree pattern can be used to show that much more is true. Let's note first that exactly $\binom{n}{k} - \binom{n}{k-1}$ rows of length $n + 1 - 2k$ are present, for $0 \le k \le n/2$, because there are exactly $\binom{n}{k}$ elements in column k. For example, Table 4 has one row of length 9, namely the bottom row; it also has $\binom{8}{1} - \binom{8}{0} = 7$ rows of length 7, $\binom{8}{2} - \binom{8}{1} = 20$ rows of length 5, $\binom{8}{3} - \binom{8}{2} = 28$ of length 3, and $\binom{8}{4} - \binom{8}{3} = 14$ of length 1. Moreover, these numbers $\binom{n}{k} - \binom{n}{k-1}$ appear in the Catalan triangle (22), because they're equal to $C_{k(n-k)}$ according to Eq. (23).

Further study reveals that this Catalan connection is not simply a coincidence; nested parentheses are, in fact, the key to a deeper understanding of the Christmas tree pattern, because the theory of parentheses tells us where an arbitrary bit string fits into the array. Suppose we use the symbols (and) instead of 1 and 0, respectively. Any string of parentheses, nested or not, can be written uniquely in the form

$$\alpha_0) \ldots \alpha_{p-1}) \alpha_p (\alpha_{p+1} \ldots (\alpha_q \qquad (37)$$

for some p and q with $0 \le p \le q$, where the substrings $\alpha_0, \ldots, \alpha_q$ are properly nested and possibly empty; exactly p of the right parentheses and $q - p$ of the left parentheses are "free" in the sense that they have no mate. For example, the string

$$) (( )) ( )) ( )))) (((((( ) (( ) ( ) ((( )) \qquad (38)$$

has $p = 5$, $q = 12$, $\alpha_0 = \epsilon$, $\alpha_1 = (())()$, $\alpha_2 = ()$, $\alpha_3 = \epsilon$, $\ldots$, $\alpha_{12} = (())$. In general, the string (37) is part of a chain of length $q + 1$,

$$\alpha_0) \ldots \alpha_{q-1}) \alpha_q, \quad \alpha_0) \ldots \alpha_{q-2}) \alpha_{q-1} (\alpha_q, \quad \ldots, \quad \alpha_0 (\alpha_1 \ldots (\alpha_q, \qquad (39)$$

in which we start with q free)s and change them one by one into free (s. Every row of the Christmas tree pattern is obtained in exactly this manner, but using 1 and 0 instead of (and); for if the chain $\sigma_1 \ldots \sigma_s$ corresponds to the nested strings $\alpha_0, \ldots, \alpha_{s-1}$, its successor chains in (36) correspond respectively to $\alpha_0, \ldots, \alpha_{s-3}, \alpha_{s-2}(\alpha_{s-1})$ and to $\alpha_0, \ldots, \alpha_{s-3}, \alpha_{s-2}, \alpha_{s-1}, \epsilon$. [See Curtis Greene and Daniel J. Kleitman, *J. Combinatorial Theory* **A20** (1976), 80–88.]

Notice furthermore that the rightmost elements in each row of the pattern — such as 10101010, 10101011, 10101100, 10101101, $\ldots$, 11111110, 11111111 in the case $n = 8$ — are in lexicographic order. Thus, for example, the fourteen rows of length 1 in Table 4 correspond precisely to the fourteen strings of nested parentheses in Table 1. This observation makes it easy to generate the rows of Table 4 sequentially from bottom to top, with a method analogous to Algorithm P; see exercise 77.

Let $f(x_1, \ldots, x_n)$ be any monotone Boolean function of n variables. If $\sigma = a_1 \ldots a_n$ is any bit string of length n, we can write $f(\sigma) = f(a_1, \ldots, a_n)$ for convenience. Any row $\sigma_1 \ \ldots \ \sigma_s$ of the Christmas tree pattern forms a chain, so we have

$$0 \leq f(\sigma_1) \leq \cdots \leq f(\sigma_s) \leq 1. \tag{40}$$

In other words, there is an index t such that $f(\sigma_j) = 0$ for $j < t$ and $f(\sigma_j) = 1$ for $j \geq t$; we will know the value of $f(\sigma)$ for all 2^n bit strings σ if we know the indices t for each row of the pattern.

Georges Hansel [*Comptes Rendus Acad. Sci.* (A) **262** (Paris, 1966), 1088–1090] noticed that the Christmas tree pattern has another important property: If σ_{j-1}, σ_j, and σ_{j+1} are three consecutive entries of any row, the bit string

$$\sigma_j' \ = \ \sigma_{j-1} \oplus \sigma_j \oplus \sigma_{j+1} \tag{41}$$

lies in a *previous* row. In fact, σ_j' lies in the same column as σ_j, and it satisfies

$$\sigma_{j-1} \subseteq \sigma_j' \subseteq \sigma_{j+1}; \tag{42}$$

it is called the relative complement of σ_j in the interval $(\sigma_{j-1} \ . . \ \sigma_{j+1})$. Hansel's observation is easy to prove by induction, because of the recursive rule (36) that defines the Christmas tree pattern. He used it to show that we can deduce the values of $f(\sigma)$ for all σ by actually evaluating the function at relatively few well-chosen places; for if we know the value of $f(\sigma_j')$, we will know either $f(\sigma_{j-1})$ or $f(\sigma_{j+1})$ because of relation (42).

Algorithm H (*Learning a monotone Boolean function*). Let $f(x_1, \ldots, x_n)$ be a Boolean function that is nondecreasing in each Boolean variable, but otherwise unknown. Given a bit string σ of length n, let $r(\sigma)$ be the number of the row in which σ appears in the Christmas tree pattern, where $1 \leq r(\sigma) \leq M_n$. If $1 \leq m \leq M_n$, let $s(m)$ be the number of bit strings in row m; also let $\chi(m, k)$ be the bit string in column k of that row, for $(n+1-s(m))/2 \leq k \leq (n-1+s(m))/2$. This algorithm determines the sequence of threshold values $t(1), t(2), \ldots, t(M_n)$ such that

$$f(\sigma) = 1 \quad \Longleftrightarrow \quad \nu(\sigma) \geq t\big(r(\sigma)\big), \tag{43}$$

by evaluating f at no more than two points per row.

H1. [Loop on m.] Perform steps H2 through H4 for $m = 1, \ldots, M_n$; then stop.

H2. [Begin row m.] Set $a \leftarrow (n+1-s(m))/2$ and $z \leftarrow (n-1+s(m))/2$.

H3. [Do a binary search.] If $z \leq a+1$, go to H4. Otherwise set $k \leftarrow \lfloor (a+z)/2 \rfloor$, and

$$\sigma \leftarrow \chi(m, k-1) \oplus \chi(m, k) \oplus \chi(m, k+1). \tag{44}$$

If $k \geq t\big(r(\sigma)\big)$, set $z \leftarrow k$; otherwise set $a \leftarrow k$. Repeat step H3.

H4. [Evaluate.] If $f(\chi(m, a)) = 1$, set $t(m) \leftarrow a$; otherwise, if $a = z$, set $t(m) \leftarrow a+1$; otherwise set $t(m) \leftarrow z+1-f(\chi(m, z))$. ∎

Hansel's algorithm is *optimum*, in the sense that it evaluates f at the fewest possible points in the worst case. For if f happens to be the threshold function

$$f(\sigma) = \big[\nu(\sigma) > n/2\big], \tag{45}$$

any valid algorithm that learns f on the first m rows of the Christmas tree pattern must evaluate $f(\sigma)$ in column $\lfloor n/2 \rfloor$ of each row, and in column $\lfloor n/2 \rfloor + 1$ of each row that has size greater than 1. Otherwise we could not distinguish f from a function that differs from it only at an unexamined point. [See V. K. Korobkov, *Problemy Kibernetiki* **13** (1965), 5–28, Theorem 5.]

Oriented trees and forests. Let's turn now to another kind of tree, in which the parent-child relationship is important but the order of children in each family is not. An *oriented forest* of n nodes can be defined by a sequence of pointers $p_1 \ldots p_n$, where p_j is the parent of node j (or $p_j = 0$ if j is a root); the directed graph on vertices $\{0, 1, \ldots, n\}$ with arcs $\{j \to p_j \mid 1 \le j \le n\}$ will have no oriented cycles. An *oriented tree* is an oriented forest with exactly one root. (See Section 2.3.4.2.) Every n-node oriented forest is equivalent to an $(n+1)$-node oriented tree, because the root of that tree can be regarded as the parent of all the roots of the forest. We saw in Section 2.3.4.4 that there are A_n oriented trees with n nodes, where the first few values are

$$
\begin{array}{cccccccccccccc}
n = & 1 & 2 & 3 & 4 & 5 & 6 & 7 & 8 & 9 & 10 & 11 & 12 & 13 & 14 \\
A_n = & 1 & 1 & 2 & 4 & 9 & 20 & 48 & 115 & 286 & 719 & 1842 & 4766 & 12486 & 32973
\end{array} \ ; \tag{46}
$$

asymptotically, $A_n = c\alpha^n n^{-3/2} + O(\alpha^n n^{-5/2})$ where $\alpha \approx 2.9558$ and $c \approx 0.4399$. Thus, for example, only 9 of the 14 forests in Table 1 are distinct when we ignore the horizontal left-to-right ordering and consider only the vertical orientation.

Every oriented forest corresponds to a unique ordered forest if we sort the members of each family appropriately, using an ordering on trees introduced by H. I. Scoins [*Machine Intelligence* **3** (1968), 43–60]: Recall from (11) that ordered forests can be characterized by their level codes $c_1 \ldots c_n$, where node j in preorder appears on level c_j. An ordered forest is called *canonical* if the level code sequences for the subtrees in each family are in nonincreasing lexicographic order. For example, the canonical forests in Table 1 are those whose level codes $c_1 c_2 c_3 c_4$ are 0000, 0100, 0101, 0110, 0111, 0120, 0121, 0122, and 0123. The level sequence 0112 is not canonical, because the subtrees of the root have respective level codes 1 and 12; the string 1 is lexicographically less than 12. We can readily verify by induction that *the canonical level codes are lexicographically largest, among all ways of reordering the subtrees of a given oriented forest.*

T. Beyer and S. M. Hedetniemi [*SICOMP* **9** (1980), 706–712] noticed that there is a remarkably simple way to generate oriented forests if we visit them in *decreasing* lexicographic order of the canonical level codes. Suppose $c_1 \ldots c_n$ is canonical, where $c_k > 0$ and $c_{k+1} = \cdots = c_n = 0$. The next smallest sequence is obtained by decreasing c_k, then increasing $c_{k+1} \ldots c_n$ to the largest levels consistent with canonicity; and those levels are easy to compute. For if $j = p_k$ is the parent of node k, we have $c_j = c_k - 1 < c_l$ for $j < l \le k$, hence the levels $c_j \ldots c_k$

represent the subtree currently rooted at node j. To get the largest sequence of levels less than $c_1 \ldots c_n$ we therefore replace $c_k \ldots c_n$ by the first $n+1-k$ elements of the infinite sequence $(c_j \ldots c_{k-1})^\infty = c_j \ldots c_{k-1} c_j \ldots c_{k-1} c_j \ldots$. (The effect is to remove k from its current position as the rightmost child of j, then to append new subtrees that are siblings of j, by cloning j and its descendants as often as possible. This cloning process may terminate in the midst of the sequence $c_j \ldots c_{k-1}$, but that causes no difficulty because every prefix of a canonical level sequence is canonical.) For example, to obtain the successor of any sequence of canonical codes that ends with 23443433000000000, we replace the final 3000000000 by 2344343234.

Algorithm O (*Oriented forests*). This algorithm generates all oriented forests on n nodes, by visiting all canonical n-node forests in decreasing lexicographic order of their level codes $c_1 \ldots c_n$. The level codes are not computed explicitly, however; each canonical forest is represented directly by its sequence of parent pointers $p_1 \ldots p_n$, in preorder of the nodes. To generate all oriented trees on $n+1$ nodes, we can imagine that node 0 is the root.

O1. [Initialize.] Set $p_k \leftarrow k - 1$ for $0 \leq k \leq n$. (In particular, this step makes p_0 nonzero, for use in termination testing; see step O4.)

O2. [Visit.] Visit the forest represented by parent pointers $p_1 \ldots p_n$.

O3. [Easy case?] If $p_n > 0$, set $p_n \leftarrow p_{p_n}$ and return to step O2.

O4. [Find j and k.] Find the largest $k < n$ such that $p_k \neq 0$. Terminate the algorithm if $k = 0$; otherwise set $j \leftarrow p_k$ and $d \leftarrow k - j$.

O5. [Clone.] If $p_{k-d} = p_j$, set $p_k \leftarrow p_j$; otherwise set $p_k \leftarrow p_{k-d} + d$. Return to step O2 if $k = n$; otherwise set $k \leftarrow k + 1$ and repeat this step. ∎

As in other algorithms we've been seeing, the loops in steps O4 and O5 tend to be quite short; see exercise 88. Exercise 90 proves that slight changes to this algorithm suffice to generate all arrangements of edges that form *free* trees.

Spanning trees. Now let's consider the minimal subgraphs that "span" a given graph. If G is a connected graph on n vertices, the *spanning trees* of G are the subsets of $n-1$ edges that contain no cycles; equivalently, they are the subsets of edges that form a free tree connecting all the vertices. Spanning trees are important in many applications, especially in the study of networks, so the problem of generating all spanning trees has been treated by many authors. In fact, systematic ways to list them all were developed early in the 20th century by Wilhelm Feussner [*Annalen der Physik* (4) **9** (1902), 1304–1329], long before anybody thought about generating other kinds of trees.

In the following discussion we will allow graphs to have any number of edges between two vertices; but we disallow loops from a vertex to itself, because self-loops cannot be part of a tree. Feussner's basic idea was very simple, yet eminently suited for calculation: If e is any edge of G, a spanning tree either contains e or it doesn't. Suppose e joins vertex u to vertex v, and suppose it is part of a spanning tree; then the other $n-2$ edges of that tree span the graph

G / e that we obtain by regarding u and v as identical. In other words, the spanning trees that contain e are essentially the same as the spanning trees of the contracted graph G / e that results when we shrink e down to a single point. On the other hand the spanning trees that do *not* contain e are spanning trees of the reduced graph $G \setminus e$ that results when we eliminate edge e. Symbolically, therefore, the set $S(G)$ of all spanning trees of G satisfies

$$S(G) \;=\; e\, S(G / e) \;\cup\; S(G \setminus e). \tag{47}$$

Malcolm J. Smith, in his Master's thesis at the University of Victoria (1997), introduced a nice way to carry out the recursion (47) by finding all spanning trees in a "revolving-door Gray code" order: Each tree in his scheme is obtained from its predecessor by simply removing one edge and substituting another. Such orderings are not difficult to find, but the trick is to do the job efficiently.

The basic idea of Smith's algorithm is to generate $S(G)$ in such a way that the first spanning tree includes a given *near tree*, namely a set of $n - 2$ edges containing no cycle. This task is trivial if $n = 2$; we simply list all the edges. If $n > 2$ and if the given near tree is $\{e_1, \ldots, e_{n-2}\}$, we proceed as follows: Assume that G is connected; otherwise there are no spanning trees. Form G / e_1 and append e_1 to each of its spanning trees, beginning with one that contains $\{e_2, \ldots, e_{n-2}\}$; notice that $\{e_2, \ldots, e_{n-2}\}$ is a near tree of G/e_1, so this recursion makes sense. If the last spanning tree found in this way for G / e_1 is $f_1 \ldots f_{n-2}$, complete the task by listing all spanning trees for $G \setminus e_1$, beginning with one that contains the near tree $\{f_1, \ldots, f_{n-2}\}$.

For example, suppose G is the graph

$$G = \quad \tag{48}$$

with four vertices and five edges $\{p, q, r, s, t\}$. Starting with the near tree $\{p, q\}$, Smith's procedure first forms the contracted graph

$$G / p = \quad \tag{49}$$

and lists its spanning trees, beginning with one that contains $\{q\}$. This list might be qs, qt, ts, tr, rs; thus the trees pqs, pqt, pts, ptr, and prs span G. The remaining task is to list the spanning trees of

$$G \setminus p = \quad , \tag{50}$$

starting with one that contains $\{r, s\}$; they are rsq, rqt, qts.

A detailed implementation of Smith's algorithm turns out to be quite instructive. As usual we represent the graph by letting two arcs $u \longrightarrow v$ and $v \longrightarrow u$ correspond to each edge $u \longrightarrow v$, and we maintain lists of "arc nodes" to represent the arcs that leave each vertex. We'll need to shrink and unshrink the graph's edges, so we will make these lists doubly linked. If a points to an arc node that represents $u \longrightarrow v$, then

$a \oplus 1$ points to the "mate" of a, which represents $v \longrightarrow u$;

$\quad t_a$ is the "tip" of a, namely v (hence $t_{a \oplus 1} = u$);

$\quad i_a$ is an optional name that identifies this edge (and equals $i_{a \oplus 1}$);

$\quad n_a$ points to the next element of u's arc list;

$\quad p_a$ points to the previous element of u's arc list;

and l_a is a link used for undeleting arcs as explained below.

The vertices are represented by integers $\{1, \ldots, n\}$; and arc number $v - 1$ is a header node for vertex v's doubly linked arc list. A header node a is recognizable by the fact that its tip, t_a, is 0. We let d_v be the degree of vertex v. Thus, for example, the graph (48) might be represented by $(d_1, d_2, d_3, d_4) = (2, 3, 3, 2)$ and by the following fourteen nodes of arc data:

$$
\begin{array}{rccccccccccccccc}
a = & 0 & 1 & 2 & 3 & 4 & 5 & 6 & 7 & 8 & 9 & 10 & 11 & 12 & 13 \\
t_a = & 0 & 0 & 0 & 0 & 1 & 2 & 1 & 3 & 2 & 3 & 2 & 4 & 3 & 4 \\
i_a = & & & & & p & p & q & q & r & r & s & s & t & t \\
n_a = & 5 & 4 & 6 & 10 & 9 & 7 & 8 & 0 & 13 & 11 & 12 & 1 & 3 & 2 \\
p_a = & 7 & 11 & 13 & 12 & 1 & 0 & 2 & 5 & 6 & 4 & 3 & 9 & 10 & 8
\end{array}
$$

The implicit recursion of Smith's algorithm can be controlled conveniently by using an array of arc pointers $a_1 \ldots a_{n-1}$. At level l of the process, arcs $a_1 \ldots a_{l-1}$ denote edges that have been included in the current spanning tree; a_l is ignored; and arcs $a_{l+1} \ldots a_{n-1}$ denote edges of a near tree on the contracted graph $(\ldots (G/a_1) \ldots)/a_{l-1}$ that should be part of the next spanning tree visited.

There's also another array of arc pointers $s_1 \ldots s_{n-2}$, representing stacks of arcs that have been temporarily removed from the current graph. The top element of the stack for level l is s_l, and each arc a links to its successor, l_a (which is 0 at the bottom of the stack).

An edge whose removal would disconnect a connected graph is called a *bridge*. One of the key points in the algorithm that follows is the fact that we want to keep the current graph connected; therefore we don't set $G \leftarrow G \setminus e$ when e is a bridge.

Algorithm S (*All spanning trees*). Given a connected graph represented with the data structures explained above, this algorithm visits all of its spanning trees.

A technique called "dancing links," which we will discuss extensively in Section 7.2.2.1, is used here to remove and restore items from and to doubly linked lists. The abbreviation "delete(a)" in the steps below is shorthand for the pair of operations

$$n_{p_a} \leftarrow n_a, \quad p_{n_a} \leftarrow p_a; \tag{51}$$

similarly, "undelete(a)" stands for

$$p_{n_a} \leftarrow a, \quad n_{p_a} \leftarrow a. \tag{52}$$

S1. [Initialize.] Set $a_1 \ldots a_{n-1}$ to a spanning tree of the graph. (See exercise 94.) Also set $x \leftarrow 0$, $l \leftarrow 1$, and $s_1 \leftarrow 0$. If $n = 2$, set $v \leftarrow 1$, $e \leftarrow n_0$, and go to S5.

S2. [Enter level l.] Set $e \leftarrow a_{l+1}$, $u \leftarrow t_e$, and $v \leftarrow t_{e \oplus 1}$. If $d_u > d_v$, interchange $v \leftrightarrow u$ and set $e \leftarrow e \oplus 1$.

S3. [Shrink e.] (Now we will make u identical to v by inserting u's adjacency list into v's. We also must delete all former edges between u and v, including e itself, because such edges would otherwise become loops. Deleted edges are linked together so that we can restore them later in step S7.) Set $k \leftarrow d_u + d_v$, $f \leftarrow n_{u-1}$, and $g \leftarrow 0$. While $t_f \neq 0$, do the following: If $t_f = v$, delete(f), delete$(f \oplus 1)$, and set $k \leftarrow k - 2$, $l_f \leftarrow g$, $g \leftarrow f$; otherwise set $t_{f \oplus 1} \leftarrow v$. Then set $f \leftarrow n_f$ and repeat these operations until $t_f = 0$. Finally set $l_e \leftarrow g$, $d_v \leftarrow k$, $g \leftarrow v - 1$, $n_{p_f} \leftarrow n_g$, $p_{n_g} \leftarrow p_f$, $p_{n_f} \leftarrow g$, $n_g \leftarrow n_f$, and $a_l \leftarrow e$.

S4. [Advance l.] Set $l \leftarrow l + 1$. If $l < n - 1$, set $s_l \leftarrow 0$ and return to S2. Otherwise set $e \leftarrow n_{v-1}$.

S5. [Visit.] (The current graph now has only two vertices, one of which is v.) Set $a_{n-1} \leftarrow e$ and visit the spanning tree $a_1 \ldots a_{n-1}$. (If $x = 0$, this is the first spanning tree to be visited; otherwise it differs from its predecessor by deleting x and inserting e.) Set $x \leftarrow e$ and $e \leftarrow n_e$. Repeat step S5 if $t_e \neq 0$.

S6. [Decrease l.] Set $l \leftarrow l - 1$. Terminate the algorithm if $l = 0$; otherwise set $e \leftarrow a_l$, $u \leftarrow t_e$, and $v \leftarrow t_{e \oplus 1}$.

S7. [Unshrink e.] Set $f \leftarrow u - 1$, $g \leftarrow v - 1$, $n_g \leftarrow n_{p_f}$, $p_{n_g} \leftarrow g$, $n_{p_f} \leftarrow f$, $p_{n_f} \leftarrow f$, and $f \leftarrow p_f$. While $t_f \neq 0$, set $t_{f \oplus 1} \leftarrow u$ and $f \leftarrow p_f$. Then set $f \leftarrow l_e$, $k \leftarrow d_v$; while $f \neq 0$ set $k \leftarrow k + 2$, undelete$(f \oplus 1)$, undelete(f), and set $f \leftarrow l_f$. Finally set $d_v \leftarrow k - d_u$.

S8. [Test for bridge.] If e is a bridge, go to S9. (See exercise 95 for one way to perform this test.) Otherwise set $x \leftarrow e$, $l_e \leftarrow s_l$, $s_l \leftarrow e$; delete(e) and delete$(e \oplus 1)$. Set $d_u \leftarrow d_u - 1$, $d_v \leftarrow d_v - 1$, and go to S2.

S9. [Undo level l deletions.] Set $e \leftarrow s_l$. While $e \neq 0$, set $u \leftarrow t_e$, $v \leftarrow t_{e \oplus 1}$, $d_u \leftarrow d_u + 1$, $d_v \leftarrow d_v + 1$, undelete$(e \oplus 1)$, undelete(e), and $e \leftarrow l_e$. Return to S6. ∎

The reader is encouraged to play through the steps of this algorithm on a small graph such as (48). Notice that a subtle case arises in steps S3 and S7, if u's adjacency list happens to become empty. Notice also that several shortcuts would be possible, at the expense of a more complicated algorithm; we will discuss such improvements later in this section.

*Series-parallel graphs. The task of finding all spanning trees becomes especially simple when the given graph has a serial and/or parallel decomposition. A *series-parallel graph between s and t* is a graph G with two designated vertices, s and t, whose edges can be built up recursively as follows: Either G consists of a single edge, $s \!-\! t$; or G is a *serial superedge* consisting of $k \geq 2$ series-parallel subgraphs G_j between s_j and t_j, joined in series with $s = s_1$ and $t_j = s_{j+1}$ for

$1 \leq j < k$ and $t_k = t$; or G is a *parallel superedge* consisting of $k \geq 2$ series-parallel subgraphs G_j between s and t joined in parallel. This decomposition is essentially unique, given s and t, if we require that the subgraphs G_j for serial superedges are not themselves serial superedges, and that the subgraphs G_j for parallel superedges are not themselves parallel.

Any series-parallel graph can be represented conveniently as a tree, with no nodes of degree 1. The leaf nodes of this tree represent edges, and the branch nodes represent superedges, alternating between serial and parallel from level to level. For example, the tree

$$\text{(tree diagram)} \tag{53}$$

corresponds to the series-parallel graphs and subgraphs

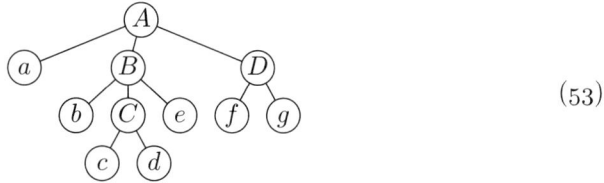

$$A = \quad , \quad B = \quad , \quad C = \quad , \quad D = \quad , \tag{54}$$

if the top node A is taken to be parallel. Edges are named in (54), but not vertices, because edges are of prime importance with respect to spanning trees.

Let's say that a *near tree* of a series-parallel graph between s and t is a set of $n - 2$ cycle-free edges that do not connect s to t. The spanning trees and near trees of a series-parallel graph are easy to describe recursively, as follows: (1) A spanning tree of a serial superedge corresponds to spanning trees of all its principal subgraphs G_j; a near tree corresponds to spanning trees in all but one of the G_j, and a near tree in the other. (2) A near tree of a parallel superedge corresponds to near trees of all its principal subgraphs G_j; a spanning tree corresponds to near trees in all but one of the G_j, and a spanning tree in the other.

Rules (1) and (2) suggest the following data structures for listing the spanning trees and/or near trees of series-parallel graphs. Let p point to a node in a tree like (53). Then we define

$\quad t_p = 1$ for serial superedges, 0 otherwise (the "type" of p);
$\quad v_p = 1$ if we have a spanning tree for p, 0 if we have a near tree;
$\quad l_p = $ pointer to p's leftmost child, or 0 if p is a leaf;
$\quad r_p = $ pointer to p's right sibling, wrapping around cyclically;
$\quad d_p = $ pointer to a designated child of p, or 0 if p is a leaf.

If q points to the rightmost child of p, its "right sibling" r_q equals l_p. And if q points to *any* child of p, rules (1) and (2) state that

$$v_q = \begin{cases} v_p, & \text{if } q = d_p; \\ t_p, & \text{if } q \neq d_p. \end{cases} \tag{55}$$

(For example, if p is a branch node that represents a serial superedge, we must have $v_q = 1$ for all but one of p's children; the only exception is the designated child d_p. Thus we must have a spanning tree for all of the subgraphs that were joined serially to form p, except for one designated subgraph in the case that we have a near tree for p.)

Given any setting of the designated-child pointers d_p, and given any value 0 or 1 for v_p at the root of the tree, Eq. (55) tells us how to propagate values down to all of the leaves. For example, if we set $v_A \leftarrow 1$ in the tree (53), and if we designate the leftmost child of each branch node (so that $d_A = a$, $d_B = b$, $d_C = c$, and $d_D = f$), we find successively

$$v_a = 1, \ v_B = 0, \ v_b = 0, \ v_C = 1, \ v_c = 1, \ v_d = 0, \ v_e = 1, \ v_D = 0, \ v_f = 0, \ v_g = 1. \quad (56)$$

A leaf node q is present in the spanning tree if and only if $v_q = 1$; hence (56) specifies the spanning tree $aceg$ of the series-parallel graph A in (54).

For convenience, let's say that the *configs* of p are its spanning trees if $v_p = 1$, its near trees if $v_p = 0$. We would like to generate all configs of the root. A branch node p is called "easy" if $v_p = t_p$; that is, a serial node is easy if its configs are spanning trees, and a parallel node is easy if its configs are near trees. If p is easy, its configs are the Cartesian product of the configs of its children, namely all k-tuples of the children's configs, varying independently; the designated child d_p is immaterial in the easy case. But if p is uneasy, its configs are the union of such Cartesian k-tuples, taken over all possible choices of d_p.

As luck would have it, easy nodes are relatively rare: At most one child of an uneasy node (namely the designated child) can be easy, and all children of an easy node are uneasy unless they are leaves.

Even so, the tree representation of a series-parallel graph makes the recursive generation of all its spanning trees and/or near trees quite straightforward and efficient. The operations of Algorithm S — shrinking and unshrinking, deleting and undeleting, bridge detection — are not needed when we deal with series-parallel graphs. Furthermore, exercise 99 shows that there is a pleasant way to obtain the spanning trees or near trees in a revolving-door Gray code order, by using focus pointers as in several algorithms that we've seen earlier.

*Refinements of Algorithm S.** Although Algorithm S provides us with a simple and reasonably effective way to visit all spanning trees of a general graph, its author Malcolm Smith realized that the properties of series-parallel graphs can be used to make it even better. For example, if a graph has two or more edges that run between the same vertices u and v, we can combine them into a superedge; the spanning trees of the original graph can then be obtained readily from those of the simpler, reduced graph. And if a graph has a vertex v of degree 2, so that the only edges touching v are $u \longrightarrow v$ and $v \longrightarrow w$, we can eliminate v and replace those edges by a single superedge between u and w. Furthermore, any vertex of degree 1 can effectively be eliminated, together with its adjacent edge, by simply including that edge in every spanning tree.

After the reductions in the preceding paragraph have been applied to a given graph G, we obtain a reduced graph $\hat{G}$ having no parallel edges and no vertices of degrees 1 or 2, together with a set of $m \geq 0$ series-parallel graphs $S_1, \ldots, S_m$, representing edges (or superedges) that must be included in all spanning trees of G. Every remaining edge $u \mathop{—} v$ of $\hat{G}$ corresponds, in fact, to a series-parallel graph S_{uv} between vertices u and v. *The spanning trees of G are then obtained as the union, taken over all spanning trees T of $\hat{G}$, of the Cartesian product of the spanning trees of $S_1, \ldots, S_m$ and the spanning trees of all S_{uv} for edges $u \mathop{—} v$ in T, together with the near trees of all S_{uv} for edges $u \mathop{—} v$ that are in $\hat{G}$ but not in T.* And all spanning trees T of $\hat{G}$ can be obtained by using the strategy of Algorithm S.

In fact, when Algorithm S is extended in this way, its operations of replacing the current graph G by $G \mathbin{/} e$ or $G \setminus e$ typically trigger further reductions, as new parallel edges appear or as the degree of a vertex drops below 3. Therefore it turns out that the "stopping state" of the implicit recursion in Algorithm S, namely the case when only two vertices are left (step S5), never actually arises: A reduced graph $\hat{G}$ either has only a single vertex and no edges, or it has at least four vertices and six edges.

The resulting algorithm retains the desirable revolving-door property of Algorithm S, and it is quite pretty (although about four times as long as the original); see exercise 100. Smith proved that it has the best possible asymptotic running time: If G has n vertices, m edges, and N spanning trees, the algorithm visits them all in $O(m + n + N)$ steps.

The performance of Algorithm S and of its souped-up version Algorithm S′ can best be appreciated by considering the number of memory accesses that those algorithms actually make when they generate the spanning trees of typical graphs, as shown in Table 5. The bottom line of that table corresponds to the graph *plane_miles*(16, 0, 0, 1, 0, 0, 0) from the Stanford GraphBase, which serves as an "organic" antidote to the purely mathematical examples on the previous lines. The random multigraph on the penultimate line, also from the Stanford GraphBase, can be described more precisely by its official name *random_graph*(16, 37, 1, 0, 0, 0, 0, 0, 0, 0). Although the 4×4 torus is isomorphic to the 4-cube (see exercise 7.2.1.1–17), those isomorphic graphs yield slightly different running times because their vertices and edges are encountered differently when the algorithms are run.

In general we can say that Algorithm S is not too bad on small examples, except when the graph is quite sparse; but Algorithm S′ begins to shine when many spanning trees are present. Once Algorithm S′ gets warmed up, it tends to crank out a new tree after every 18 or 19 mems go by.

Table 5 also indicates that a mathematically-defined graph often has a surprisingly "round" number of spanning trees. For example, D. M. Cvetković [*Srpska Akademija Nauka, Matematicheski Institut* **11** (Belgrade: 1971), 135–141] discovered, among other things, that the n-cube has exactly

$$2^{2^n - n - 1} \, 1^{\binom{n}{1}} \, 2^{\binom{n}{2}} \ldots n^{\binom{n}{n}} \tag{57}$$

of them. Exercises 104–109 explore some of the reasons why that happens.

Table 5

RUNNING TIME IN MEMS NEEDED TO GENERATE ALL SPANNING TREES

	m	n	N	Algorithm S	Algorithm S$'$	μ per tree	
path P_{10}	9	10	1	794 μ	473 μ	794.0	473.0
path P_{100}	99	100	1	9,974 μ	5,063 μ	9974.0	5063.0
cycle C_{10}	10	10	10	3,480 μ	998 μ	348.0	99.8
cycle C_{100}	100	100	100	355,605 μ	10,538 μ	3556.1	105.4
complete graph K_4	6	4	16	1,213 μ	1,336 μ	75.8	83.5
complete graph K_{10}	45	10	100,000,000	3,759.58 Mμ	1,860.95 Mμ	37.6	18.6
complete bigraph $K_{5,5}$	25	10	390,625	23.43 Mμ	8.88 Mμ	60.0	22.7
4×4 grid $P_4\square P_4$	24	16	100,352	12.01 Mμ	1.87 Mμ	119.7	18.7
5×5 grid $P_5\square P_5$	40	25	557,568,000	54.68 Gμ	10.20 Gμ	98.1	18.3
4×4 cylinder $P_4\square C_4$	28	16	2,558,976	230.96 Mμ	49.09 Mμ	90.3	19.2
5×5 cylinder $P_5\square C_5$	45	25	38,720,000,000	3,165.31 Gμ	711.69 Gμ	81.7	18.4
4×4 torus $C_4\square C_4$	32	16	42,467,328	3,168.15 Mμ	823.08 Mμ	74.6	19.4
4-cube $P_2\square P_2\square P_2\square P_2$	32	16	42,467,328	3,172.19 Mμ	823.38 Mμ	74.7	19.4
random multigraph	37	16	59,933,756	3,818.19 Mμ	995.91 Mμ	63.7	16.6
16 cities	37	16	179,678,881	11,772.11 Mμ	3,267.43 Mμ	65.5	18.2

A general quasi-Gray code. Let's close this section by discussing something completely different, yet still related to trees. Consider the following hybrid variants of the two standard ways to traverse a nonempty forest:

Prepostorder traversal	Postpreorder traversal
Visit the root of the first tree	Traverse the subtrees of the first
Traverse the subtrees of the first	tree, in prepostorder
tree, in postpreorder	Visit the root of the first tree
Traverse the remaining trees,	Traverse the remaining trees,
in prepostorder	in postpreorder

In the first case, every tree of the forest is traversed in prepostorder, with its root first; but the subtrees of those roots are traversed in postpreorder, with roots coming last. The second variant is similar but with 'pre' and 'post' interchanged. And in general, prepostorder visits roots first on every even-numbered level of the forest, but visits them last on the odd-numbered levels. For example, the forest in (2) becomes

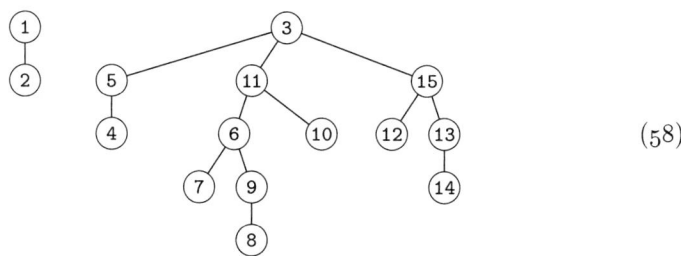   (58)

when we label its nodes in prepostorder.

Prepostorder and postpreorder are not merely curiosities; they're actually useful. The reason is that adjacent nodes, in either of these orders, are always near each other in the forest. For example, nodes k and $k+1$ are adjacent in (58) for $k = 1$, 4, 6, 8, 10, 13; they are separated by only one node when $k = 3$, 12, 14; and they're three steps apart when $k = 2$, 5, 7, 9, 11 (if we imagine an invisible super-parent at the top of the forest). A moment's thought proves inductively that at most two nodes can possibly intervene between prepostorder neighbors or postpreorder neighbors — because postpreorder(F) always begins with the root of the first tree or its leftmost child, and prepostorder(F) always ends with the root of the last tree or its rightmost child.

Suppose we want to generate all combinatorial patterns of some kind, and we want to visit them in a Gray-code-like manner so that consecutive patterns are always "close" to each other. We can form, at least conceptually, the graph of all possible patterns p, with edges $p - q$ for all pairs of patterns that are close to each other. The following theorem, due to Milan Sekanina [*Spisy Přírodovědecké Fakulty University v Brně*, No. 412 (1960), 137–140], proves that a pretty good Gray code is always possible, provided only that we can get from any pattern to any other in a sequence of short steps:

Theorem S. *The vertices of any connected graph can be listed in a cyclic order* $(v_0, v_1, \ldots, v_{n-1})$ *so that the distance between* v_k *and* $v_{(k+1) \bmod n}$ *is at most* 3, *for* $0 \le k < n$.

Proof. Find a spanning tree in the graph, and traverse it in prepostorder. ▮

Graph theorists traditionally say that the kth power of a graph G is the graph G^k whose vertices are those of G, with $u - v$ in G^k if and only if there's a path of length k or less from u to v in G. Thus they can state Theorem S much more succinctly, when $n > 2$: *The cube of a connected graph is Hamiltonian.*

Prepostorder traversal is also useful when we want to visit the nodes of a tree in loopless fashion, with a bounded number of steps between stops:

Algorithm Q (*Prepostorder successor in a triply linked forest*). If P points to a node in a forest represented by links PARENT, CHILD, and SIB, corresponding to each node's parent, leftmost child, and right sibling, this algorithm computes P's successor node, Q, in prepostorder. We assume that we know the level L at which P appears in the forest; the value of L is updated to be the level of Q. If P happens to be the final node in prepostorder, the algorithm sets Q ← Λ and L ← −1.

Q1. [Pre or post?] If L is even, go to step Q4.

Q2. [Continue postpreorder.] Set Q ← SIB(P). Go to Q6 if Q ≠ Λ.

Q3. [Move up.] Set P ← PARENT(P) and L ← L − 1. Go to Q7.

Q4. [Continue prepostorder.] If CHILD(P) = Λ, go to Q7.

Q5. [Move down.] Set Q ← CHILD(P) and L ← L + 1.

Q6. [Move down if possible.] If CHILD(Q) ≠ Λ, set Q ← CHILD(Q) and L ← L + 1. Terminate the algorithm.

Q7. [Move right or up.] If $\texttt{SIB(P)} \neq \Lambda$, set $\texttt{Q} \leftarrow \texttt{SIB(P)}$; otherwise set $\texttt{Q} \leftarrow$ $\texttt{PARENT(P)}$ and $\texttt{L} \leftarrow \texttt{L} - 1$. Terminate the algorithm. ∎

Notice that, as in Algorithm 2.4C, the link $\texttt{PARENT(P)}$ is examined only if $\texttt{SIB(P)} = \Lambda$. A complete traversal is really a worm walk around the forest, like (3): The worm "sees" the nodes on even-numbered levels when it passes them on the left, and it sees the odd-level nodes when it passes them on the right.

EXERCISES

1. [15] If a worm crawls around the binary tree (4), how could it easily reconstruct the parentheses of (1)?

2. [20] (S. Zaks, 1980.) Modify Algorithm P so that it produces the combinations $z_1 z_2 \ldots z_n$ of (8) instead of the parenthesis strings $a_1 a_2 \ldots a_{2n}$.

▶ **3.** [23] Prove that (11) converts $z_1 z_2 \ldots z_n$ to the inversion table $c_1 c_2 \ldots c_n$.

4. [20] True or false: If the strings $a_1 \ldots a_{2n}$ are generated in lexicographic order, so are the corresponding strings $d_1 \ldots d_n$, $z_1 \ldots z_n$, $p_1 \ldots p_n$, and $c_1 \ldots c_n$.

5. [15] What tables $d_1 \ldots d_n$, $z_1 \ldots z_n$, $p_1 \ldots p_n$, and $c_1 \ldots c_n$ correspond to the nested parenthesis string (1)?

▶ **6.** [20] What *matching* corresponds to (1)? (See the final column of Table 1.)

7. [16] (a) What is the state of the string $a_1 a_2 \ldots a_{2n}$ when Algorithm P terminates? (b) What do the arrays $l_1 l_2 \ldots l_n$ and $r_1 r_2 \ldots r_n$ contain when Algorithm B terminates?

8. [15] What tables $l_1 \ldots l_n$, $r_1 \ldots r_n$, $e_1 \ldots e_n$, and $s_1 \ldots s_n$ correspond to the example forest (2)?

9. [M20] Show that the tables $c_1 \ldots c_n$ and $s_1 \ldots s_n$ are related by the law

$$c_k = [s_1 \geq k - 1] + [s_2 \geq k - 2] + \cdots + [s_{k-1} \geq 1].$$

10. [M20] (*Worm walks.*) Given a string of nested parentheses $a_1 a_2 \ldots a_{2n}$, let w_j be the excess of left parentheses over right parentheses in $a_1 a_2 \ldots a_j$, for $0 \leq j \leq 2n$. Prove that $w_0 + w_1 + \cdots + w_{2n} = 2(c_1 + \cdots + c_n) + n$.

11. [11] If F is a forest, its *conjugate* F^R is obtained by left-to-right mirror reflection. For example, the fourteen forests in Table 1 are

•••• , •• ⁞ , • ⁞ • , • ⋀ , • ⁞ , ⁞ •• , ⁞ ⁞ , ⋀ • , ⋀ , ⋀ , ⁞ • , ⋀ , ⋋ , ⁞

and their conjugates are respectively

•••• , ⁞ •• , • ⁞ • , ⋀ • , ⁞ • , •• ⁞ , ⁞ ⁞ , • ⋀ , ⋀ , ⋀ , • ⁞ , ⋀ , ⋋ , ⁞

as in the colex forests of Table 2. If F corresponds to the nested parentheses $a_1 a_2 \ldots a_{2n}$, what string of parentheses corresponds to F^R?

12. [15] If F is a forest, its *transpose* F^T is the forest whose binary tree is obtained by interchanging left and right links in the binary tree representing F. For example, the transposes of the fourteen forests in Table 1 are respectively

⁞ , ⋋ , ⋀ , ⋀ , ⋀ , ⁞ • , ⋀ • , ⁞ ⁞ , • ⁞ , • ⋀ , ⁞ •• , •• ⁞ , •• ⁞ , •••• .

What is the transpose of the forest (2)?

13. [20] Continuing exercises 11 and 12, how do the preorder and postorder of a labeled forest F relate to the preorder and postorder of (a) F^R? (b) F^T?

▶ **14.** [*21*] Find all labeled forests F such that $F^{RT} = F^{TR}$.

15. [*20*] Suppose B is the binary tree obtained from a forest F by linking each node to its left sibling and its rightmost child, as in exercise 2.3.2–5 and the last column of Table 2. Let F' be the forest that corresponds to B in the normal way, via left-child and right-sibling links. Prove that $F' = F^{RT}$, in the notation of exercises 11 and 12.

16. [*20*] If F and G are forests, let FG be the forest obtained by placing the trees of F to the left of the trees of G; also let $F \mid G = (G^T F^T)^T$. Give an intuitive explanation of the operator $\mid$, and prove that it is associative.

17. [*M46*] Characterize all *unlabeled* forests F such that $F^{RT} = F^{TR}$. (See exercise 14.)

18. [*30*] Two forests are said to be *cognate* if one can be obtained from the other by repeated operations of taking the conjugate and/or the transpose. The examples in exercises 11 and 12 show that all forests on 4 nodes belong to one of three cognate classes:

Study the set of all forests with 15 nodes. How many equivalence classes of cognate forests do they form? What is the largest class? What is the smallest class? What is the size of the class containing (2)?

19. [*28*] Let F_1, F_2, ..., F_N be the sequence of unlabeled forests that correspond to the nested parentheses generated by Algorithm P, and let G_1, G_2, ..., G_N be the sequence of unlabeled forests that correspond to the binary trees generated by Algorithm B. Prove that $G_k = F_k^{RTR}$, in the notation of exercises 11 and 12. (The forest F^{RTR} is called the *dual* of F; it is denoted by F^D in several exercises below.)

20. [*25*] Recall from Section 2.3 that the *degree* of a node in a tree is the number of children it has, and that an extended binary tree is characterized by the property that every node has degree either 0 or 2. In the extended binary tree (4), the sequence of node degrees is 22002220022202200020022022200000 in preorder; this string of 0s and 2s is identical to the sequence of parentheses in (1), except that each '(' has been replaced by 2, each ')' has been replaced by 0, and an additional 0 has been appended.

   a) Prove that a sequence of nonnegative integers $b_1 b_2 \ldots b_N$ is the preorder degree sequence of a forest if and only if it satisfies the following property for $1 \le k \le N$:

$$b_1 + b_2 + \cdots + b_k + f \; > \; k \qquad \text{if and only if} \qquad k < N.$$

   Here $f = N - b_1 - b_2 - \cdots - b_N$ is the number of trees in the forest.

   b) Recall from exercise 2.3.4.5–6 that an *extended ternary tree* is characterized by the property that every node has degree 0 or 3; an extended ternary tree with n internal nodes has $2n + 1$ external nodes, hence $N = 3n + 1$ nodes altogether. Design an algorithm to generate all ternary trees with n internal nodes, by generating the associated sequences $b_1 b_2 \ldots b_N$ in lexicographic order.

▶ **21.** [*26*] (S. Zaks and D. Richards, 1979.) Continuing exercise 20, explain how to generate the preorder degree sequences of all forests that have $N = n_0 + \cdots + n_t$ nodes, with exactly n_j nodes of degree j. *Example:* When $n_0 = 4$, $n_1 = n_2 = n_3 = 1$, and $t = 3$, and the valid sequences $b_1 b_2 b_3 b_4 b_5 b_6 b_7$ are

1203000, 1230000, 1300200, 1302000, 1320000, 2013000, 2030010, 2030100, 2031000, 2103000,
2130000, 2300010, 2300100, 2301000, 2310000, 3001200, 3002010, 3002100, 3010200, 3012000,
3020010, 3020100, 3021000, 3100200, 3102000, 3120000, 3200010, 3200100, 3201000, 3210000.

▸ **22.** [*30*] (J. Korsh, 2004.) As an alternative to Algorithm B, show that binary trees can also be generated directly and efficiently in linked form if we produce them in *colex* order of the numbers $d_1 \ldots d_{n-1}$ defined in (9). (The actual values of $d_1 \ldots d_{n-1}$ should not be computed explicitly; but the links $l_1 \ldots l_n$ and $r_1 \ldots r_n$ should be manipulated in such a way that we get the binary trees corresponding successively to $d_1 d_2 \ldots d_{n-1} =$ $000\ldots0$, $100\ldots0$, $010\ldots0$, $110\ldots0$, $020\ldots0$, $001\ldots0$, $\ldots$, $000\ldots(n-1)$.)

▸ **23.** [*25*] (a) What is the last string visited by Algorithm N? (b) What is the last binary tree or forest visited by Algorithm L? *Hint:* See exercise 40 below.

24. [*22*] Using the notation of Table 3, what sequences $l_0 l_1 \ldots l_{15}$, $r_1 \ldots r_{15}$, $k_1 \ldots k_{15}$, $q_1 \ldots q_{15}$, and $u_1 \ldots u_{15}$ correspond to the binary tree (4) and the forest (2)?

▸ **25.** [*30*] (*Pruning and grafting.*) Representing binary trees as in Algorithm B, design an algorithm that visits all link tables $l_1 \ldots l_n$ and $r_1 \ldots r_n$ in such a way that, between visits, exactly one link changes from j to 0 and another from 0 to j, for some index j. (In other words, every step removes some subtree j from the binary tree and places it elsewhere, preserving preorder.)

26. [*M31*] (*The Kreweras lattice.*) Let F and F' be n-node forests with their nodes numbered 1 to n in preorder. We write $F \Kutimes F'$ ("F coalesces F'") if j and k are siblings in F whenever they are siblings in F', for $1 \le j < k \le n$. Figure 60 illustrates this partial ordering in the case $n = 4$; each forest is encoded by the sequence $c_1 \ldots c_n$ of (10) and (11), which specifies the depth of each node. (With this encoding, j and k are siblings if and only if $c_j = c_k \le c_{j+1}, \ldots, c_{k-1}$.)

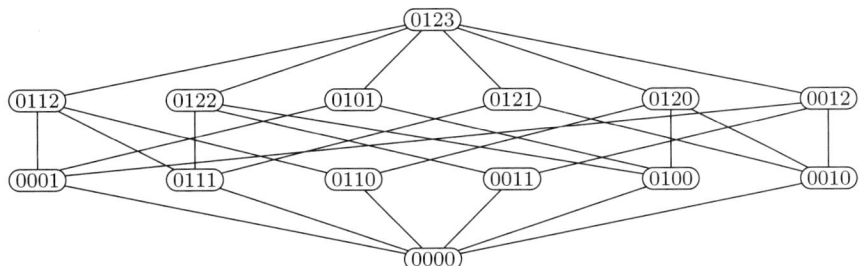

Fig. 60. The Kreweras lattice of order 4. Each forest is represented by its sequence of node depths $c_1 c_2 c_3 c_4$ in preorder. (See exercises 26–28.)

a) Let Π be a partition of $\{1, \ldots, n\}$. Show that there exists a forest F, with nodes labeled $(1, \ldots, n)$ in preorder and with

$$j \equiv k \pmod{\Pi} \iff j \text{ is a sibling of } k \text{ in } F,$$

if and only if Π satisfies the *noncrossing* property

$$i < j < k < l \text{ and } i \equiv k \text{ and } j \equiv l \pmod{\Pi} \quad \text{implies} \quad i \equiv j \equiv k \equiv l \pmod{\Pi}.$$

b) Given any two n-node forests F and F', explain how to compute their least upper bound $F \vee F'$, the element such that $F \Kutimes G$ and $F' \Kutimes G$ if and only if $F \vee F' \Kutimes G$.

c) When does F' cover F with respect to the relation $\Kutimes$? (See exercise 7.2.1.4–55.)

d) Show that if F' covers F, it has exactly one less leaf than F.

e) How many forests cover F, when node k has e_k children for $1 \le k \le n$?

f) Using the definition of duality in exercise 19, what is the dual of the forest (2)?

g) Prove that $F \mathrel{\text{K}} F'$ holds if and only if $F'^D \mathrel{\text{K}} F^D$. (Because of this property, dual elements have been placed symmetrically about the center of Fig. 60.)

h) Given any two n-node forests F and F', explain how to compute their greatest lower bound $F \wedge F'$; that is, $G \mathrel{\text{K}} F$ and $G \mathrel{\text{K}} F'$ if and only if $G \mathrel{\text{K}} F \wedge F'$.

i) Does this lattice satisfy a semimodular law analogous to exercise 7.2.1.5–12(f)?

▸ **27.** [*M33*] (*The Tamari lattice.*) Continuing exercise 26, let us write $F \dashv F'$ if the jth node in preorder has at least as many descendants in F' as it does in F, for all j. In other words, if F and F' are characterized by their scope sequences $s_1 \ldots s_n$ and $s'_1 \ldots s'_n$ as in Table 2, we have $F \dashv F'$ if and only if $s_j \le s'_j$ for $1 \le j \le n$. (See Fig. 61.)

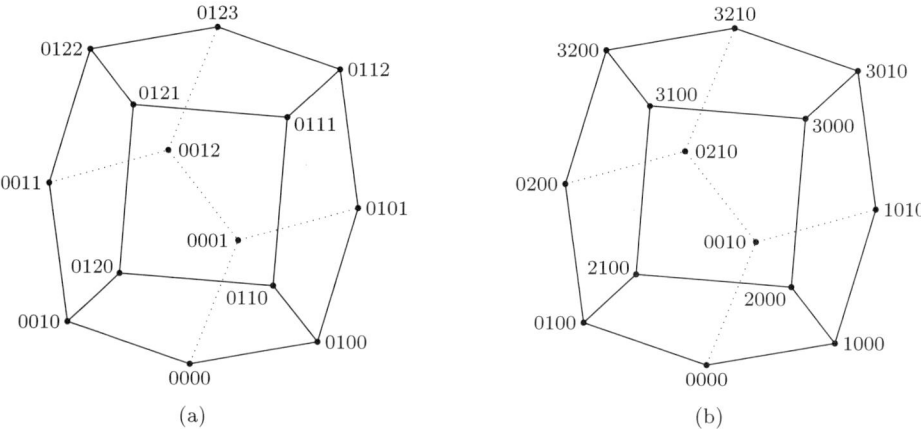

Fig. 61. The Tamari lattice of order 4. Each forest is represented by its sequences of (a) node depths and (b) descendant counts, in preorder. (See exercises 26–28.)

a) Show that the scope coordinates $\min(s_1, s'_1) \min(s_2, s'_2) \ldots \min(s_n, s'_n)$ define a forest that is the greatest lower bound of F and F'. (We denote it by $F \perp F'$.) *Hint:* Prove that $s_1 \ldots s_n$ corresponds to a forest if and only if $0 \le k \le s_j$ implies $s_{j+k} + k \le s_j$, for $0 \le j \le n$, if we define $s_0 = n$.

b) When does F' cover F in this partial ordering?

c) Prove that $F \dashv F'$ if and only if $F'^D \dashv F^D$. (Compare with exercise 26(g).)

d) Explain how to compute a least upper bound, $F \top F'$, given F and F'.

e) Prove that $F \mathrel{\text{K}} F'$ in the Kreweras lattice implies $F \dashv F'$ in the Tamari lattice.

f) True or false: $F \wedge F' \dashv F \perp F'$.

g) True or false: $F \vee F' \mathrel{\text{K}} F \top F'$.

h) What are the longest and shortest paths from the top of the Tamari lattice to the bottom, when each forest of the path covers its successor? (Such paths are called *maximal chains* in the lattice; compare with exercise 7.2.1.4–55(h).)

28. [*M26*] (*The Stanley lattice.*) Continuing exercises 26 and 27, let us define yet another partial ordering on n-node forests, saying that $F \subseteq F'$ whenever the depth coordinates $c_1 \ldots c_n$ and $c'_1 \ldots c'_n$ satisfy $c_j \le c'_j$ for $1 \le j \le n$. (See Fig. 62.)

a) Prove that this partial ordering is a lattice, by explaining how to compute the greatest lower bound $F \cap F'$ and least upper bound $F \cup F'$ of any two given forests.

b) Show that Stanley's lattice satisfies the distributive laws

$$F \cap (G \cup H) = (F \cap G) \cup (F \cap H), \qquad F \cup (G \cap H) = (F \cup G) \cap (F \cup H).$$

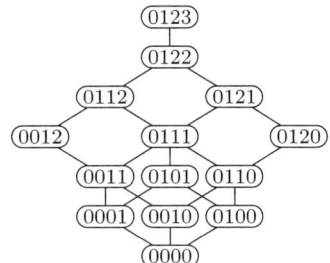

Fig. 62. The Stanley lattice of order 4. Each forest is represented by its sequence of node depths in preorder. (See exercises 26–28.)

c) When does F' cover F in this lattice?

d) True or false: $F \subseteq G$ if and only if $F^R \subseteq G^R$.

e) Prove that $F \subseteq F'$ in the Stanley lattice whenever $F \dashv F'$ in the Tamari lattice.

29. [*HM31*] The covering graph of a Tamari lattice is sometimes known as an "associahedron," because of its connection with the associative law (14), proved in exercise 27(b). The associahedron of order 4, depicted in Fig. 61, looks like it has three square faces and six faces that are regular pentagons. (Compare with Fig. 43 in exercise 7.2.1.2–60, which shows the "permutahedron" of order 4, a well-known Archimedean solid.) Why doesn't Fig. 61 show up in classical lists of uniform polyhedra?

30. [*M26*] The *footprint* of a forest is the bit string $f_1 \ldots f_n$ defined by

$$f_j = [\text{node } j \text{ in preorder is not a leaf}].$$

a) If F has footprint $f_1 \ldots f_n$, what is the footprint of F^D? (See exercise 27.)

b) How many forests have the footprint 101011011111110000101010001011000?

c) Prove that $f_j = [d_j = 0]$, for $1 \le j < n$, in the notation of (6).

d) Two elements of a lattice are called *complementary* if their greatest lower bound is the bottom element while their least upper bound is the top element. Show that F and F' are complementary in the Tamari lattice if and only if their footprints are complementary, in the sense that $f'_1 \ldots f'_{n-1} = \bar{f}_1 \ldots \bar{f}_{n-1}$.

▶ **31.** [*M28*] A binary tree with n internal nodes is called *degenerate* if it has height n.

a) How many n-node binary trees are degenerate?

b) We've seen in Tables 1, 2, and 3 that binary trees and forests can be encoded by various n-tuples of numbers. For each of the encodings $c_1 \ldots c_n$, $d_1 \ldots d_n$, $e_1 \ldots e_n$, $k_1 \ldots k_n$, $p_1 \ldots p_n$, $s_1 \ldots s_n$, $u_1 \ldots u_n$, and $z_1 \ldots z_n$, explain how to see at a glance if the corresponding binary tree is degenerate.

c) True or false: If F is degenerate, so is F^D.

d) Prove that if F and F' are degenerate, so are $F \barwedge F' = F \perp F'$ and $F \veebar F' = F \top F'$.

▶ **32.** [*M30*] Prove that if $F \dashv F'$, there is a forest F'' such that for all G we have

$$F' \perp G = F \quad \text{if and only if} \quad F \dashv G \dashv F''.$$

Consequently the *semidistributive laws* hold in the Tamari lattice:

$$F \perp G = F \perp H \quad \text{implies} \quad F \perp (G \top H) = F \perp G;$$
$$F \top G = F \top H \quad \text{implies} \quad F \top (G \perp H) = F \top G.$$

▸ **33.** [*M27*] (*Permutation representation of trees.*) Let σ be the cycle $(1\ 2\ \ldots\ n)$.

a) Given any binary tree whose nodes are numbered 1 to n in symmetric order, prove that there is a unique permutation λ of $\{1, \ldots, n\}$ such that, for $1 \le k \le n$,

$$\text{LLINK}[k] = \begin{cases} k\lambda, & \text{if } k\lambda < k; \\ 0, & \text{otherwise;} \end{cases} \qquad \text{RLINK}[k] = \begin{cases} k\sigma\lambda, & \text{if } k\sigma\lambda > k; \\ 0, & \text{otherwise.} \end{cases}$$

Thus λ neatly packs $2n$ link fields into a single n-element array.

b) Show that this permutation λ is particularly easy to describe in cycle form when the binary tree is the left-sibling/right-child representation of a forest F. What is the cycle form of $\lambda(F)$ when F is the forest in (2)?

c) Find a simple relation between $\lambda(F)$ and the dual permutation $\lambda(F^D)$.

d) Prove that, in exercise 26, F' covers F if and only if $\lambda(F') = (j\ k)\,\lambda(F)$, where j and k are siblings in F.

e) Consequently the number of maximal chains in the Kreweras lattice of order n is the number of ways to factor an n-cycle as a product of $n-1$ transpositions. Evaluate this number. *Hint:* See Eq. 1.2.6–(16).

34. [*M25*] (R. P. Stanley.) Show that the number of maximal chains in the Stanley lattice of order n is $(n(n-1)/2)!/(1^{n-1}3^{n-2}\ldots(2n-5)^2(2n-3)^1)$.

35. [*HM37*] (D. B. Tyler and D. R. Hickerson.) Explain why the denominators of the asymptotic formula (16) are all powers of 2.

▸ **36.** [*M25*] Analyze the ternary tree generation algorithm of exercise 20(b). *Hint:* There are $(2n+1)^{-1}\binom{3n}{n}$ ternary trees with n internal nodes, by exercise 2.3.4.4–11.

▸ **37.** [*M40*] Analyze the Zaks–Richards algorithm for generating all trees with a given distribution $n_0, n_1, n_2, \ldots, n_t$ of degrees (exercise 21). *Hint:* See exercise 2.3.4.4–32.

38. [*M22*] What is the total number of memory references performed by Algorithm L, as a function of n?

39. [*22*] Prove formula (23) by showing that the elements of A_{pq} in (5) correspond to Young tableaux with two rows.

40. [*M22*] (a) Prove that C_{pq} is odd if and only if $p\ \&\ (q+1) = 0$, in the sense that the binary representations of p and $q+1$ have no bits in common. (b) Therefore C_n is odd if and only if $n+1$ is a power of 2.

41. [*M21*] Show that the ballot numbers have a simple generating function $\sum C_{pq}w^p z^q$.

▸ **42.** [*M22*] How many unlabeled forests with n nodes are (a) self-conjugate? (b) self-transpose? (c) self-dual? (See exercises 11, 12, 19, and 26.)

43. [*M21*] Express C_{pq} in terms of the Catalan numbers $\langle C_0, C_1, C_2, \ldots \rangle$, aiming for a formula that is simple when $q-p$ is small. (For example, $C_{(q-2)q} = C_q - C_{q-1}$.)

▸ **44.** [*M27*] Prove that Algorithm B makes only $8\frac{2}{3} + O(n^{-1})$ references to memory per binary tree visited.

45. [*M26*] Analyze the memory references made by the algorithm in exercise 22. How does it compare to Algorithm B?

46. [*M30*] (*Generalized Catalan numbers.*) Generalize (21) by defining

$$C_{pq}(x) = C_{p(q-1)}(x) + x^{q-p}C_{(p-1)q}(x), \quad \text{if } 0 \le p \le q \ne 0; \qquad C_{00}(x) = 1;$$

and $C_{pq}(x) = 0$ if $p < 0$ or $p > q$; thus $C_{pq} = C_{pq}(1)$. Also let $C_n(x) = C_{nn}(x)$, so that

$$\langle C_0(x), C_1(x), \ldots \rangle = \langle 1, 1, 1+x, 1+2x+x^2+x^3, 1+3x+3x^2+3x^3+2x^4+x^5+x^6, \ldots \rangle.$$

a) Show that $[x^k] C_{pq}(x)$ is the number of paths from $\textcircled{pq}$ to $\textcircled{00}$ in (28) that have area k, where the "area" of a path is the number of rectangular cells above it. (Thus an L-shaped path has the maximum possible area, $p(q - p) + \binom{p}{2}$.)

b) Prove that $C_n(x) = \sum_F x^{c_1 + \cdots + c_n} = \sum_F x^{\text{internal path length}(F)}$, summed over all n-node forests F.

c) If $C(x, z) = \sum_{n=0}^{\infty} C_n(x) z^n$, show that $C(x, z) = 1 + zC(x, z)C(x, xz)$.

d) Furthermore, $C(x, z)C(x, xz)\ldots C(x, x^r z) = \sum_{p=0}^{\infty} C_{p(p+r)}(x) z^p$.

47. [*M27*] Continuing the previous exercise, generalize the identity (27).

48. [*M28*] (F. Ruskey and A. Proskurowski.) Evaluate $C_{pq}(x)$ when $x = -1$, and use this result to show that no "perfect" Gray code for nested parentheses is possible when $n \geq 5$ is odd.

49. [*17*] What is the lexicographically millionth string of 15 nested parenthesis pairs?

50. [*20*] Design the inverse of Algorithm U: Given a string $a_1 \ldots a_{2n}$ of nested parentheses, determine its rank $N - 1$ in lexicographic order. What is the rank of (1)?

51. [*M22*] Let $\bar{z}_1 \bar{z}_2 \ldots \bar{z}_n$ be the complement of $z_1 z_2 \ldots z_n$ with respect to $2n$; in other words, $\bar{z}_j = 2n - z_j$, where z_j is defined in (8). Show that if $\bar{z}_1 \bar{z}_2 \ldots \bar{z}_n$ is the $(N + 1)$st n-combination of $\{0, 1, \ldots, 2n - 1\}$ generated by Algorithm 7.2.1.3L, then $z_1 z_2 \ldots z_n$ is the $(N - \kappa_n N + 1)$st n-combination of $\{1, 2, \ldots, 2n\}$ generated by the algorithm of exercise 2. (Here κ_n denotes the nth Kruskal function, defined in 7.2.1.3–(60).)

52. [*M23*] Find the mean and variance of the quantity d_n in Table 1, when nested parentheses $a_1 \ldots a_{2n}$ are chosen at random.

53. [*M28*] Let X be the distance from the root of an extended binary tree to the leftmost external node. (a) What is the expected value of X, when all binary trees with n nodes are equally likely? (b) What is the expected value of X in a random *binary search tree*, constructed by Algorithm 6.2.2T from a random permutation $K_1 \ldots K_n$? (c) What is the expected value of X in a random *degenerate* binary tree, in the sense of exercise 31? (d) What is the expected value of 2^X in all three cases?

54. [*HM29*] What are the mean and variance of $c_1 + \cdots + c_n$? (See exercise 46.)

55. [*HM33*] Evaluate $C'_{pq}(1)$, the total area of all the paths in exercise 46(a).

56. [*M23*] (Renzo Sprugnoli, 1990.) Prove the summation formula

$$\sum_{k=0}^{m-1} C_k C_{n-1-k} = \frac{1}{2} C_n + \frac{2m - n}{2n(n+1)} \binom{2m}{m} \binom{2n - 2m}{n - m}, \qquad \text{for } 0 \leq m \leq n.$$

57. [*M28*] Express the sums $S_p(a, b) = \sum_{k \geq 0} \binom{2a}{a-k} \binom{2b}{b-k} k^p$ in closed form for $p = 0$, 1, 2, 3, and use these formulas to prove (30).

58. [*HM34*] Let t_{lmn} be the number of n-node binary trees in which external node m appears at level l when the external nodes are numbered from 0 to n in symmetric order. Also let $t_{mn} = \sum_{l=1}^{n} l t_{lmn}$, so that t_{mn}/C_n is the average level of external node m; and let $t(w, z)$ be the super generating function

$$\sum_{m,n} t_{mn} w^m z^n = (1+w)z + (3+4w+3w^2)z^2 + (9+13w+13w^2+9w^3)z^3 + \cdots.$$

Prove that $t(w, z) = \big(C(z) - wC(wz)\big)/(1 - w) - 1 + zC(z)t(w, z) + wzC(wz)t(w, z)$, and deduce a simple formula for the numbers t_{mn}.

59. [*HM29*] Similarly, let T_{lmn} count all n-node binary trees in which *internal* node m appears at level l. Find a simple formula for $T_{mn} = \sum_{l=1}^{n} l T_{lmn}$.

▶ **60.** [*M26*] (*Balanced strings.*) A string α of nested parentheses is *atomic* if it has the form (α') where α' is nested; every nested string can be represented uniquely as a product of atoms $\alpha_1 \ldots \alpha_r$. A string with equal numbers of left and right parentheses is called *balanced*; every balanced string can be represented uniquely as $\beta_1 \ldots \beta_r$ where each β_j is either an atom or a *co-atom* (the reverse of an atom). The *defect* of a balanced string is half the length of its co-atoms. For example, the balanced string

$$(\, (\,) \,) \,) \, (\, (\, (\,) \,) \,) \,) \,) \,) \, (\, (\,) \, (\, (\, (\,) \,) \, (\, (\, (\,) \,) \, (\, (\,)$$

has the factored form $\beta_1 \beta_2 \beta_3 \beta_4 \beta_5 \beta_6 \beta_7 \beta_8 = \alpha_1 \alpha_2^R \alpha_3 \alpha_4^R \alpha_5^R \alpha_6 \alpha_7^R \alpha_8$, with four atoms and four co-atoms; its defect is $|\alpha_2 \alpha_4 \alpha_5 \alpha_7|/2 = 9$.

a) Prove that the defect of a balanced string is the number of indices k for which the kth right parenthesis *precedes* the kth left parenthesis.

b) If $\beta_1 \ldots \beta_r$ is balanced, we can map it into a nested string by simply reversing its co-atoms. But the following mapping is more interesting, because it produces unbiased (uniformly random) nested strings from unbiased balanced strings: Let there be s co-atoms $\beta_{i_1} = \alpha_{i_1}^R$, $\ldots$, $\beta_{i_s} = \alpha_{i_s}^R$. Replace each co-atom by (; then append the string $)\alpha'_{i_s} \ldots)\alpha'_{i_1}$, where $\alpha_j = (\alpha'_j)$. For example, the string above is mapped into $\alpha_1 (\alpha_3 ((\alpha_6 (\alpha_8) \alpha_7') \alpha_5') \alpha_4') \alpha_2'$, which just happens to equal the string (1) illustrated at the beginning of this section.

Design an algorithm that applies this mapping to a given balanced string $b_1 \ldots b_{2n}$.

c) Also design an algorithm for the inverse mapping: Given a nested string $\alpha = a_1 \ldots a_{2n}$ and an integer l with $0 \le l \le n$, compute a balanced string $\beta = b_1 \ldots b_{2n}$ of defect l for which $\beta \mapsto \alpha$. What balanced string of defect 11 maps into (1)?

▶ **61.** [*M26*] (*Raney's Cycle Lemma.*) Let $b_1 b_2 \ldots b_N$ be a string of nonnegative integers such that $f = N - b_1 - b_2 - \cdots - b_N > 0$.

a) Prove that exactly f of the cyclic shifts $b_{j+1} \ldots b_N b_1 \ldots b_j$ for $1 \le j \le N$ satisfy the preorder degree sequence property in exercise 20.

b) Design an efficient algorithm to determine all such j, given $b_1 b_2 \ldots b_N$.

c) Explain how to generate a random forest that has $N = n_0 + \cdots + n_t$ nodes, with exactly n_j nodes of degree j. (For example, we obtain random n-node t-ary trees as a special case of this general procedure when $N = tn + 1$, $n_0 = (t-1)n + 1$, $n_1 = \cdots = n_{t-1} = 0$, and $n_t = n$.)

62. [*22*] A binary tree can also be represented by bit strings $(l_1 \ldots l_n, r_1 \ldots r_n)$, where l_j and r_j tell whether the left and right subtrees of node j in preorder are nonempty. (See Theorem 2.3.1A.) Prove that if $l_1 \ldots l_n$ and $r_1 \ldots r_n$ are arbitrary bit strings with $l_1 + \cdots + l_n + r_1 + \cdots + r_n = n - 1$, exactly one cyclic shift $(l_{j+1} \ldots l_n l_1 \ldots l_j, r_{j+1} \ldots r_n r_1 \ldots r_j)$ yields a valid binary tree representation, and explain how to find it.

63. [*16*] If the first two iterations of Rémy's algorithm have produced , what decorated binary trees are possible after the next iteration?

64. [*20*] What sequence of X values in Algorithm R corresponds to the decorated trees of (34), and what are the final values of $L_0 L_1 \ldots L_{12}$?

65. [*38*] Generalize Rémy's algorithm (Algorithm R) to t-ary trees.

66. [*21*] A *Schröder tree* is a binary tree in which every nonnull right link is colored either white or black. The number S_n of n-node Schröder trees is

n	=	0	1	2	3	4	5	6	7	8	9	10	11	12
S_n	=	1	1	3	11	45	197	903	4279	20793	103049	518859	2646723	13648869

for small n. For example, $S_3 = 11$ because the possibilities are

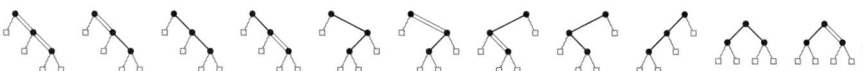

(White links are "hollow"; external nodes have also been attached.)

a) Find a simple correspondence between Schröder trees with n internal nodes and ordinary trees with $n + 1$ leaves and no nodes of degree one.

b) Devise a Gray code for Schröder trees.

67. [*M22*] What is the generating function $S(z) = \sum_n S_n z^n$ for Schröder numbers?

68. [*10*] What is the Christmas tree pattern of order 0?

69. [*20*] Are the Christmas tree patterns of orders 6 and 7 visible in Table 4, possibly in slight disguise?

▶ **70.** [*20*] Find a simple rule that defines, for every bit string σ, another bit string σ' called its *mate*, with the following properties: (i) $\sigma'' = \sigma$; (ii) $|\sigma'| = |\sigma|$; (iii) either $\sigma \subseteq \sigma'$ or $\sigma' \subseteq \sigma$; (iv) $\nu(\sigma) + \nu(\sigma') = |\sigma|$.

71. [*M21*] Let M_{tn} be the size of the largest possible set S of n-bit strings with the property that, if σ and τ are members of S with $\sigma \subseteq \tau$, then $\nu(\tau) < \nu(\sigma) + t$. (Thus, for example, $M_{1n} = M_n$ by Sperner's theorem.) Find a formula for M_{tn}.

▶ **72.** [*M28*] If you start with a single row $\sigma_1 \sigma_2 \ldots \sigma_s$ of length s and apply the growth rule (36) repeatedly n times, how many rows do you obtain?

73. [*15*] In the Christmas tree pattern of order 30, what are the first and last elements of the row that contains the bit string 011001001000011111101101011100?

74. [*M26*] Continuing the previous exercise, how many rows precede that row?

▶ **75.** [*HM23*] Let $(r_1^{(n)}, r_2^{(n)}, \ldots, r_{n-1}^{(n)})$ be the row numbers in which the Christmas tree pattern of order n has $n - 1$ entries; for example, Table 4 tells us that $(r_1^{(8)}, \ldots, r_7^{(8)}) = (20, 40, 54, 62, 66, 68, 69)$. Find formulas for $r_{j+1}^{(n)} - r_j^{(n)}$ and for $\lim_{n \to \infty} r_j^{(n)}/M_n$.

76. [*HM46*] Study the limiting shape of the Christmas tree patterns as $n \to \infty$. Does it, for example, have a fractal dimension under some appropriate scaling?

77. [*21*] Design an algorithm to generate the sequence of rightmost elements $a_1 \ldots a_n$ in the rows of the Christmas tree pattern, given n. *Hint:* These bit strings are characterized by the property that $a_1 + \cdots + a_k \geq k/2$ for $0 \leq k \leq n$.

78. [*20*] True or false: If $\sigma_1 \ldots \sigma_s$ is a row of the Christmas tree pattern, so is $\bar{\sigma}_s^R \ldots \bar{\sigma}_1^R$ (the reverse sequence of reverse complements).

79. [*M26*] The number of permutations $p_1 \ldots p_n$ that have exactly one "descent" where $p_k > p_{k+1}$ is the Eulerian number $\left\langle {n \atop 1} \right\rangle = 2^n - n - 1$, according to Eq. 5.1.3–(12). The number of entries in the Christmas tree pattern, above the bottom row, is the same.

a) Find a combinatorial explanation of this coincidence, by giving a one-to-one correspondence between one-descent permutations and unsorted bit strings.

b) Show that two unsorted bit strings belong to the same row of the Christmas tree pattern if and only if they correspond to permutations that define the same P tableau under the Robinson–Schensted correspondence (Theorem 5.1.4A).

80. [*30*] Say that two bit strings are *concordant* if we can obtain one from the other via the transformations $010 \leftrightarrow 100$ or $101 \leftrightarrow 110$ on substrings. For example, the strings

$$011100 \leftrightarrow 011010 \leftrightarrow 010110 \leftrightarrow 010101 \leftrightarrow 011001$$
$$\updownarrow \qquad\quad \updownarrow$$
$$100110 \leftrightarrow 100101 \leftrightarrow 101001 \leftrightarrow 110001$$

are mutually concordant, but no other string is concordant with any of them.

Prove that strings are concordant if and only if they belong to the same column of the Christmas tree pattern and to rows of the same length in that pattern.

81. [*M30*] A *biclutter* of order (n, n') is a family S of bit string pairs (σ, σ'), where $|\sigma| = n$ and $|\sigma'| = n'$, with the property that distinct members (σ, σ') and (τ, τ') of S are allowed to satisfy $\sigma \subseteq \tau$ and $\sigma' \subseteq \tau'$ only if $\sigma \neq \tau$ and $\sigma' \neq \tau'$.

Use Christmas tree patterns to prove that S contains at most $M_{n+n'}$ string pairs.

▶ **82.** [*M26*] Let $E(f)$ be the number of times Algorithm H evaluates the function f.

  a) Show that $M_n \leq E(f) \leq M_{n+1}$, with equality when f is constant.

  b) Among all f such that $E(f) = M_n$, which one minimizes $\sum_\sigma f(\sigma)$?

  c) Among all f such that $E(f) = M_{n+1}$, which one maximizes $\sum_\sigma f(\sigma)$?

83. [*M20*] (G. Hansel.) Show that there are at most 3^{M_n} monotone Boolean functions $f(x_1, \ldots, x_n)$ of n Boolean variables.

▶ **84.** [*HM27*] (D. Kleitman.) Let A be an $m \times n$ matrix of real numbers in which every column v has length $\|v\| \geq 1$, and let b be an m-dimensional column vector. Prove that at most M_n column vectors $x = (a_1, \ldots, a_n)^T$, with components $a_j = 0$ or 1, satisfy $\|Ax - b\| < \frac{1}{2}$. *Hint:* Use a construction analogous to the Christmas tree pattern.

85. [*HM35*] (Philippe Golle.) Let V be any vector space contained in the set of all real n-dimensional vectors, but containing none of the unit vectors $(1, 0, \ldots, 0)$, $(0, 1, 0, \ldots, 0)$, $\ldots$, $(0, \ldots, 0, 1)$. Prove that V contains at most M_n vectors whose components are all 0 or 1; furthermore the upper bound M_n is achievable.

86. [*15*] If (2) is regarded as an *oriented forest* instead of an ordered forest, what canonical forest corresponds to it? Specify that forest both by its level codes $c_1 \ldots c_{15}$ and its parent pointers $p_1 \ldots p_{15}$.

87. [*M20*] Let F be an ordered forest in which the kth node in preorder appears on level c_k and has parent p_k, where $p_k = 0$ if that node is a root.

  a) How many forests satisfy the condition $c_k = p_k$ for $1 \leq k \leq n$?

  b) Suppose F and F' have level codes $c_1 \ldots c_n$ and $c'_1 \ldots c'_n$, respectively, as well as parent links $p_1 \ldots p_n$ and $p'_1 \ldots p'_n$. Prove that, lexicographically, $c_1 \ldots c_n \leq c'_1 \ldots c'_n$ if and only if $p_1 \ldots p_n \leq p'_1 \ldots p'_n$.

88. [*M20*] Analyze Algorithm O: How often is step O4 performed? What is the total number of times p_k is changed in step O5?

89. [*M46*] How often does step O5 set $p_k \leftarrow p_j$?

▶ **90.** [*M27*] If $p_1 \ldots p_n$ is a canonical sequence of parent pointers for an oriented forest, the graph with vertices $\{0, 1, \ldots, n\}$ and edges $\{k \text{ --- } p_k \mid 1 \leq k \leq n\}$ is a *free tree*, namely a connected graph with no cycles. (See Theorem 2.3.4.1A.) Conversely, every free tree corresponds to at least one oriented forest in this way. But the parent pointers 011 and 000 both yield the same free tree $\succ$; similarly, 012 and 010 both yield $\cdots$.

The purpose of this exercise is to restrict the sequences $p_1 \ldots p_n$ further so that each free tree is obtained exactly once. We proved in 2.3.4.4–(9) that the number of structurally different free trees on $n+1$ vertices has a fairly simple generating function, by showing that a free tree always has at least one *centroid*.

a) Show that a canonical n-node forest corresponds to a free tree with a single centroid if and only if no tree in the forest has more than $\lfloor n/2 \rfloor$ nodes.

b) Modify Algorithm O so that it generates all sequences $p_1 \ldots p_n$ that satisfy (a).

c) Explain how to find all $p_1 \ldots p_n$ for free trees that have *two* centroids.

91. [*M37*] (Nijenhuis and Wilf.) Show that a random oriented tree can be generated with a procedure analogous to the random partition algorithm of exercise 7.2.1.4–47.

92. [*15*] Are the first and last spanning trees visited by Algorithm S adjacent, in the sense that they have $n-2$ edges in common?

93. [*20*] When Algorithm S terminates, has it restored the graph to its original state?

94. [*22*] Algorithm S needs to "prime the pump" by finding an initial spanning tree in step S1. Explain how to do that task.

95. [*26*] Complete Algorithm S by implementing the bridge test in step S8.

▶ **96.** [*28*] Analyze the approximate running time of Algorithm S when the given graph is simply (a) a path P_n of length $n-1$; (b) a cycle C_n of length n.

97. [*15*] Is (48) a series-parallel graph?

98. [*16*] What series-parallel graph corresponds to (53) if A is taken to be *serial*?

▶ **99.** [*30*] Consider a series-parallel graph represented by a tree as in (53), together with node values that satisfy (55). These values define a spanning tree or a near tree, according as v_p is 1 or 0 at the root p. Show that the following method will generate all of the other configs of the root:

i) Begin with all uneasy nodes active, other nodes passive.

ii) Select the rightmost active node, p, in preorder; but terminate if all nodes are passive.

iii) Change $d_p \leftarrow r_{d_p}$, update all values in the tree, and visit the new config.

iv) Activate all uneasy nodes to the right of p.

v) If d_p has run through all children of p since p last became active, make node p passive. Return to (ii).

Also explain how to perform these steps efficiently. *Hints:* To implement step (v), introduce a pointer z_p; make node p passive when d_p becomes equal to z_p, and at such times also reset z_p to the previous value of d_p. To implement steps (ii) and (iv), use focus pointers f_p analogous to those in Algorithms 7.2.1.1L and 7.2.1.1K.

100. [*40*] Implement the text's "Algorithm S'" for revolving-door generation of all spanning trees, by combining Algorithm S with the ideas of exercise 99.

101. [*46*] Is there a simple revolving-door way to list all n^{n-2} spanning trees of the complete graph K_n? (The order produced by Algorithm S is quite complicated.)

102. [*46*] An *oriented spanning tree* of a directed graph D on n vertices, also known as a "spanning arborescence," is an oriented subtree of D containing $n-1$ arcs. The matrix tree theorem (exercise 2.3.4.2–19) tells us that the oriented subtrees having a given root can readily be counted by evaluating an $(n-1) \times (n-1)$ determinant.

Can those oriented subtrees be listed in a revolving-door order, always removing one arc and replacing it with another?

▶ **103.** [*HM39*] (*Sandpiles.*) Consider any digraph D on vertices V_0, V_1, ..., V_n with e_{ij} arcs from V_i to V_j, where $e_{ii} = 0$. Assume that D has at least one oriented spanning tree rooted at V_0; this assumption means that, if we number the vertices appropriately, we have $e_{i0} + \cdots + e_{i(i-1)} > 0$ for $1 \le i \le n$. Let $d_i = e_{i0} + \cdots + e_{in}$ be the total out-degree of V_i. Put x_i grains of sand on vertex V_i for $0 \le i \le n$, and play the following game: If $x_i \ge d_i$ for any $i \ge 1$, decrease x_i by d_i and set $x_j \leftarrow x_j + e_{ij}$ for all $j \ne i$. (In other words, pass one grain of sand from V_i through each of its outgoing arcs, whenever possible, except when $i = 0$. This operation is called "toppling" V_i, and a sequence of topplings is called an "avalanche." Vertex V_0 is special; instead of toppling, it collects particles of sand that essentially leave the system.) Continue until $x_i < d_i$ for $1 \le i \le n$. Such a state $x = (x_1, \ldots, x_n)$ is called *stable*.

a) Prove that every avalanche terminates in a stable state after a finite number of topplings. Furthermore, the final state depends only on the initial state, not on the order in which toppling is performed.

b) Let $\sigma(x)$ be the stable state that results from initial state x. A stable state is called *recurrent* if it is $\sigma(x)$ for some x with $x_i \ge d_i$ for $1 \le i \le n$. (Recurrent states correspond to sandpiles that have evolved over a long period of time, after new grains of sand are repeatedly introduced at random.) Find the recurrent states in the special case when $n = 4$ and when the only arcs of D are

$$V_1 \to V_0,\; V_1 \to V_2,\; V_2 \to V_0,\; V_2 \to V_1,\; V_3 \to V_0,\; V_3 \to V_4,\; V_4 \to V_0,\; V_4 \to V_3.$$

c) Let $d = (d_1, \ldots, d_n)$. Prove that x is recurrent if and only if $x = \sigma(x + t)$, where t is the vector $d - \sigma(d)$.

d) Let a_i be the vector $(-e_{i1}, \ldots, -e_{i(i-1)}, d_i, -e_{i(i+1)}, \ldots, -e_{in})$, for $1 \le i \le n$; thus, toppling V_i corresponds to changing the state vector $x = (x_1, \ldots, x_n)$ to $x - a_i$. Say that two states x and x' are *congruent*, written $x \equiv x'$, if $x - x' = m_1 a_1 + \cdots + m_n a_n$ for some integers m_1, ..., m_n. Prove that there are exactly as many equivalence classes of congruent states as there are oriented spanning trees in D, rooted at V_0. *Hint:* See the matrix tree theorem, exercise 2.3.4.2–19.

e) If $x \equiv x'$ and if both x and x' are recurrent, prove that $x = x'$.

f) Prove that every congruence class contains a unique recurrent state.

g) If D is *balanced*, in the sense that the in-degree of each vertex equals its out-degree, prove that x is recurrent if and only if $x = \sigma(x + a)$, where $a = (e_{01}, \ldots, e_{0n})$.

h) Illustrate these concepts when D is a "wheel" with n spokes: Let there be $3n$ arcs, $V_j \to V_0$ and $V_j \leftrightarrow V_{j+1}$ for $1 \le j \le n$, regarding V_{n+1} as identical to V_1. Find a one-to-one correspondence between the oriented spanning trees of this digraph and the recurrent states of its sandpiles.

i) Similarly, analyze the recurrent sandpiles when D is the *complete* graph on $n+1$ vertices, namely when $e_{ij} = [i \ne j]$ for $0 \le i, j \le n$. *Hint:* See exercise 6.4–31.

▶ **104.** [*HM21*] If G is a graph on n vertices $\{V_1, \ldots, V_n\}$, with e_{ij} edges between V_i and V_j, let $C(G)$ be the matrix with entries $c_{ij} = -e_{ij} + \delta_{ij} d_i$, where $d_i = e_{i1} + \cdots + e_{in}$ is the degree of V_i. Let us say that the *aspects* of G are the eigenvalues of $C(G)$, namely the roots α_0, ..., α_{n-1} of the equation $\det(\alpha I - C(G)) = 0$. Since $C(G)$ is a symmetric matrix, its eigenvalues are real numbers, and we can assume that $\alpha_0 \le \alpha_1 \le \cdots \le \alpha_{n-1}$.

a) Prove that $\alpha_0 = 0$.

b) Prove that G has exactly $c(G) = \alpha_1 \ldots \alpha_{n-1}/n$ spanning trees.

c) What are the aspects of the complete graph K_n?

105. [*HM38*] Continuing exercise 104, we wish to prove that there is often an easy way to determine the aspects of G when G has been constructed from other graphs whose aspects are known. Suppose G' has aspects $\alpha'_0, \ldots, \alpha'_{n'-1}$ and G'' has aspects $\alpha''_0, \ldots, \alpha''_{n''-1}$; what are the aspects of G in the following cases?

  a) $G = \overline{G'}$ is the complement of G'. (Assume that $e'_{ij} \leq [i \neq j]$ in this case.)
  b) $G = G' \oplus G''$ is the direct sum (juxtaposition) of G' and G''.
  c) $G = G' \!-\! G''$ is the join of G' and G''.
  d) $G = G' \square G''$ is the Cartesian product of G' and G''.
  e) $G = L(G')$ is the line graph of G', when G' is a regular graph of degree d' (namely when all vertices of G' have exactly d' neighbors, and there are no self-loops).
  f) $G = G' \otimes G''$ is the direct product (conjunction) of G' and G'', when G' is regular of degree d' and G'' is regular of degree d''.
  g) $G = G' \boxtimes G''$ is the strong product of regular graphs G' and G''.
  h) $G = G' \triangle G''$ is the odd product of regular graphs G' and G''.
  i) $G = G' \circ G''$ is the lexicographic product of regular graphs G' and G''.

▶ **106.** [*HM37*] Find the total number of spanning trees in (a) an $m \times n$ grid $P_m \square P_n$; (b) an $m \times n$ cylinder $P_m \square C_n$; (c) an $m \times n$ torus $C_m \square C_n$. Why do these numbers tend to have only small prime factors? *Hint:* Show that the aspects of P_n and C_n can be expressed in terms of the numbers $\sigma_{kn} = 4 \sin^2 \frac{k\pi}{2n}$.

107. [*M24*] Determine the aspects of all connected graphs that have $n \leq 5$ vertices and no self-loops or parallel edges.

108. [*HM40*] Extend the results of exercises 104–106 to directed graphs.

109. [*M46*] Find a combinatorial explanation for the fact that (57) is the number of spanning trees in the n-cube.

▶ **110.** [*M27*] Prove that if G is any connected multigraph without self-loops, it has

$$c(G) > \sqrt{(d_1 - 1) \ldots (d_n - 1)}$$

spanning trees, where d_j is the degree of vertex j.

111. [*05*] List the nodes of the tree (58) in postpreorder.

112. [*15*] If node p of a forest precedes node q in prepostorder and follows it in postpreorder, what can you say about p and q?

▶ **113.** [*20*] How do prepostorder and postpreorder of a forest F relate to prepostorder and postpreorder of the conjugate forest F^R? (See exercise 13.)

114. [*15*] If we want to traverse an entire forest in prepostorder using Algorithm Q, how should we begin the process?

115. [*20*] Analyze Algorithm Q: How often is each step performed, during the complete traversal of a forest?

▶ **116.** [*28*] If the nodes of a forest F are labeled 1 to n in prepostorder, say that node k is *lucky* if it is adjacent to node $k + 1$ in F, *unlucky* if it is three steps away, and *ordinary* otherwise, for $1 \leq k \leq n$; in this definition, node $n + 1$ is an imaginary super-root considered to be the parent of each root.

  a) Prove that lucky nodes occur only on even-numbered levels; unlucky nodes occur only on odd-numbered levels.
  b) Show that the number of lucky nodes is exactly one greater than the number of unlucky nodes, unless $n = 0$.

117. [21] Continuing exercise 116, how many n-node forests contain no unlucky nodes?

118. [M28] How many lucky nodes are present in (a) the complete t-ary tree with $(t^k - 1)/(t-1)$ internal nodes? (b) the Fibonacci tree of order k, with $F_{k+1} - 1$ internal nodes? (See 2.3.4.5–(6) and Fig. 8 in Section 6.2.1.)

119. [21] The *twisted binomial tree* $\tilde{T}_n$ of order n is defined recursively by the rules

$$\tilde{T}_0 = \bullet \,, \qquad \tilde{T}_n = \overset{\displaystyle 0 \quad 1 \qquad\qquad n-1}{\underset{\displaystyle \tilde{T}_0^R \quad \tilde{T}_1^R \quad \cdots \quad \tilde{T}_{n-1}^R}{\bigwedge}} \qquad \text{for } n > 0.$$

(Compare with 7.2.1.3–(21); we reverse the order of children on alternate levels.) Show that prepostorder traversal of $\tilde{T}_n$ has a simple connection with Gray binary code.

120. [22] True or false: The square of a graph is Hamiltonian if the graph is connected and has no bridges.

121. [M34] (F. Neuman, 1964.) The *derivative* of a graph G is the graph $G^{(\prime)}$ obtained by removing all vertices of degree 1 and the edges touching them. Prove that, when T is a free tree, its square T^2 contains a Hamiltonian path if and only if its derivative has no vertex of degree greater than 4 and the following two additional conditions hold:

  i) All vertices of degree 3 or 4 in $T^{(\prime)}$ lie on a single path.

  ii) Between any two vertices of degree 4 in $T^{(\prime)}$, there is at least one vertex that has degree 2 in T.

▶ **122.** [31] (*Dudeney's Digital Century puzzle.*) There are many curious ways to obtain the number 100 by inserting arithmetical operators and possibly also parentheses into the sequence 123456789. For example,

$$100 = 1 + 2 \times 3 + 4 \times 5 - 6 + 7 + 8 \times 9 = (1 + 2 - 3 - 4) \times (5 - 6 - 7 - 8 - 9)$$
$$= ((1/((2+3)/4 - 5 + 6)) \times 7 + 8) \times 9 \,.$$

a) How many such representations of 100 are possible? To make this question precise, in view of the associative law and other algebraic properties, assume that expressions are written in canonical form according to the following syntax:

$\langle\, \text{expression}\, \rangle \to \langle\, \text{number}\, \rangle \mid \langle\, \text{sum}\, \rangle \mid \langle\, \text{product}\, \rangle \mid \langle\, \text{quotient}\, \rangle$

$\langle\, \text{sum}\, \rangle \to \langle\, \text{term}\, \rangle + \langle\, \text{term}\, \rangle \mid \langle\, \text{term}\, \rangle - \langle\, \text{term}\, \rangle \mid \langle\, \text{sum}\, \rangle + \langle\, \text{term}\, \rangle \mid \langle\, \text{sum}\, \rangle - \langle\, \text{term}\, \rangle$

$\langle\, \text{term}\, \rangle \to \langle\, \text{number}\, \rangle \mid \langle\, \text{product}\, \rangle \mid \langle\, \text{quotient}\, \rangle$

$\langle\, \text{product}\, \rangle \to \langle\, \text{factor}\, \rangle \times \langle\, \text{factor}\, \rangle \mid \langle\, \text{product}\, \rangle \times \langle\, \text{factor}\, \rangle \mid (\langle\, \text{quotient}\, \rangle) \times \langle\, \text{factor}\, \rangle$

$\langle\, \text{quotient}\, \rangle \to \langle\, \text{factor}\, \rangle / \langle\, \text{factor}\, \rangle \mid \langle\, \text{product}\, \rangle / \langle\, \text{factor}\, \rangle \mid (\langle\, \text{quotient}\, \rangle) / \langle\, \text{factor}\, \rangle$

$\langle\, \text{factor}\, \rangle \to \langle\, \text{number}\, \rangle \mid (\langle\, \text{sum}\, \rangle)$

$\langle\, \text{number}\, \rangle \to \langle\, \text{digit}\, \rangle$

  The digits used must be 1 through 9, in that order.

b) Extend problem (a) by allowing multidigit numbers, with the syntax

$$\langle\, \text{number}\, \rangle \to \langle\, \text{digit}\, \rangle \mid \langle\, \text{number}\, \rangle \langle\, \text{digit}\, \rangle$$

For example, $100 = (1/(2 - 3 + 4)) \times 567 - 89$. What is the shortest such representation? What is the longest?

c) Extend problem (b) by also allowing decimal points:

$$\langle\, \text{number}\, \rangle \to \langle\, \text{digit string}\, \rangle \mid .\langle\, \text{digit string}\, \rangle$$
$$\langle\, \text{digit string}\, \rangle \to \langle\, \text{digit}\, \rangle \mid \langle\, \text{digit string}\, \rangle \langle\, \text{digit}\, \rangle$$

For example, $100 = (.1 - 2 - 34 \times .5)/(.6 - .789)$, amazingly enough.

123. [*21*] Continuing the previous exercise, what are the smallest positive integers that *cannot* be represented using conventions (a), (b), (c)?

Fig. 63. "Organic" illustrations of binary trees.

▶ **124.** [*40*] Experiment with methods for drawing extended binary trees that are inspired by simple models from nature. For example, we can assign a value $v(x)$ to each node x, called its *Horton–Strahler number*, as follows: Each external (leaf) node has $v(x) = 0$; an internal node with children (l, r) has $v(x) = \max(v(l), v(r)) + [v(l) = v(r)]$. The edge from internal node x to its parent can be drawn as a rectangle with height $h(v(x))$ and width $w(v(x))$, and the edge rectangles with children (l, r) can be offset by angles $\theta(v(l(x)), v(r(x)))$, $-\theta(v(r(x)), v(l(x)))$, for certain functions h, w, and θ. The examples in Fig. 63 show typical results when we choose $w(k) = 3 + k$, $h(k) = 18k$, $\theta(k, k) = 30°$, $\theta(j, k) = ((k + 1)/j) \times 20°$ for $0 \le k < j$, and $\theta(j, k) = ((k - j)/k) \times 30°$ for $0 \le j < k$; the roots appear at the bottom. Part (a) of Fig. 63 is the binary tree (4); part (b) is a random 100-node tree generated by Algorithm R; part (c) is the Fibonacci tree of order 11, which has 143 nodes; and part (d) is a random 100-node binary search tree. (The trees in parts (b), (c), and (d) clearly belong to different species.)

> *[This subject] has a relation*
> *to almost every species of useful knowledge*
> *that the mind of man can be employed upon.*
> — JAMES BERNOULLI, *Ars Conjectandi* (1713)

7.2.1.7. History and further references. Early work on the generation of combinatorial patterns began as civilization itself was taking shape. The story is quite fascinating, and we will see that it spans many cultures in many parts of the world, with ties to poetry, music, and religion. There is space here to discuss only some of the principal highlights; but perhaps a few glimpses into the past will stimulate the reader to dig deeper into the roots of the subject, as the world gets ever smaller and as global scholarship continues to advance.

Lists of binary n-tuples can be traced back thousands of years to ancient China, India, and Greece. The most notable source — because it still is a best-selling book in modern translations — is the Chinese *I Ching* or *Yijing*, whose name means "the Bible of Changes." This book, which is one of the five classics of Confucian wisdom, consists essentially of $2^6 = 64$ chapters; and each chapter is symbolized by a hexagram formed from six lines, each of which is either -- ("yin") or — ("yang"). For example, hexagram 1 is pure yang, ☰; hexagram 2 is pure yin, ☷; and hexagram 64 intermixes yin and yang, with yang on top: ䷿. Here is the complete list:

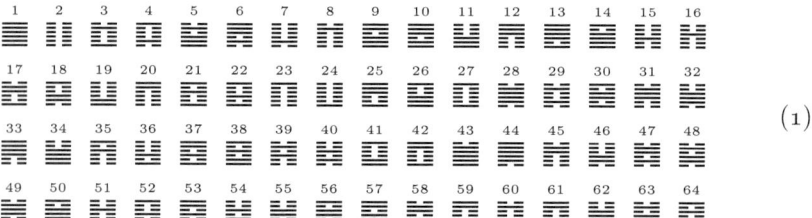

$$(1)$$

This arrangement of the 64 possibilities is called King Wen's ordering, because the basic text of the *I Ching* has traditionally been ascribed to King Wen (c. 1100 B.C.), the legendary progenitor of the Chou dynasty. Ancient texts are, however, notoriously difficult to date reliably, and modern historians have found no solid evidence that anyone actually compiled such a list of hexagrams before the third century B.C.

Notice that the hexagrams of (1) occur in pairs: Those with odd numbers are immediately followed by their top-to-bottom reflections, except when reflection would make no change; and the eight symmetrical diagrams are paired with their complements ($1 = \overline{2}$, $27 = \overline{28}$, $29 = \overline{30}$, $61 = \overline{62}$). Hexagrams that are composed from two trigrams that represent the four basic elements heaven (☰), earth (☷), fire (☲), and water (☵) have also been placed judiciously. Otherwise the arrangement appears to be essentially random, as if a person untrained in mathematics kept listing different possibilities until being unable to come up with any more. A few intriguing patterns do exist between the pairs, but no more than are present by coincidence in the digits of π (see 3.3–(1)).

Yin and yang represent complementary aspects of the elementary forces of nature, always in tension, always changing. The *I Ching* is somewhat analogous to a thesaurus in which the hexagrams serve as an index to accumulated wisdom about fundamental concepts like giving (☰̿), receiving (☷̿), modesty (䷎), joy (䷹), fellowship (䷌), withdrawal (䷠), peace (䷊), conflict (䷅), organization (䷇), corruption (䷑), immaturity (䷃), elegance (䷕), etc. One can choose a pair of hexagrams at random, obtaining the second from the first by, say, independently changing each yin to yang (or vice versa) with probability 1/4; this technique yields 4096 ways to ponder existential mysteries, as well as a Markov process by which change itself might perhaps give meaning to life.

A strictly logical way to arrange the hexagrams was eventually introduced about A.D. 1060 by Shao Yung. His ordering, which proceeded lexicographically from ䷁ to ䷖ to ䷇ to ䷓ to ䷏ to ⋯ to ䷪ to ䷀ (reading each hexagram from bottom to top), was much more user-friendly than the King Wen order, because a random pattern could now be found quickly. When G. W. Leibniz learned about this sequence of hexagrams in 1702, he jumped to the erroneous conclusion that Chinese mathematicians had once been familiar with binary arithmetic. [See Frank Swetz, *Mathematics Magazine* **76** (2003), 276–291. Further details about the *I Ching* can be found, for example, in Joseph Needham's *Science and Civilisation in China* **2** (Cambridge University Press, 1956), 304–345; R. J. Lynn, *The Classic of Changes* (New York: Columbia University Press, 1994).]

Another ancient Chinese philosopher, Yang Hsiung, proposed a system based on 81 ternary tetragrams instead of 64 binary hexagrams. His *Canon of Supreme Mystery*, written c. 2 B.C., has recently been translated into English by Michael Nylan (Albany, New York: 1993). Yang described a complete, hierarchical ternary tree structure in which there are 3 regions, with 3 provinces in each region, 3 departments in each province, 3 families in each department, and 9 short poems called "appraisals" for each family, hence 729 appraisals in all — making almost exactly 2 appraisals for every day in the year. His tetragrams were arranged in strict lexicographic order when read top-to-bottom: ䷀, ䷁, ䷂, ䷃, ䷄, ䷅, ䷆, ..., ䷿. In fact, as explained on page 28 of Nylan's book, Yang presented a simple way to compute the rank of each tetragram, as if using a radix-3 number system. Thus he would not have been surprised or impressed by Shao Yung's systematic ordering of binary hexagrams, although Shao lived more than 1000 years later.

Indian prosody. Binary n-tuples were studied in a completely different context by pundits in ancient India, who investigated the poetic meters of sacred Vedic chants. Syllables in Sanskrit are either short (ı) or long (ട), and the study of syllable patterns is called "prosody." Modern writers use the symbols ⌣ and — instead of ı and ട. A typical Vedic verse consists of four lines with n syllables per line, for some $n \geq 8$; prosodists therefore sought a way to classify all 2^n possibilities. The classic work *Chandaḥśāstra* by Piṅgala, written before A.D. 400 and probably much earlier (the exact date is quite uncertain), described procedures by which one could readily find the index k of any given pattern of ⌣s and —s, as well as to find the kth pattern, given k. In other words, Piṅgala explained how to *rank* any given pattern as well as to *unrank* any given index;

thus he went beyond the work of Yang Hsiung, who had considered ranking but not unranking. Piṅgala's methods were also related to exponentiation, as we have noted earlier in connection with Algorithm 4.6.3A.

The next important step was taken by a prosodist named Kedāra in his work *Vṛttaratnākara*, thought to have been written in the 8th century. Kedāra gave a step-by-step procedure for listing all the n-tuples from $---\ldots-$ to $\smile--\ldots-$ to $-\smile-\ldots-$ to $\smile\smile-\ldots-$ to $--\smile\ldots-$ to $\smile-\smile\ldots-$ to $\cdots$ to $\smile\smile\smile\ldots\smile$, essentially Algorithm 7.2.1.1M in the case of radix 2. His method may well have been the first-ever explicit algorithm for combinatorial sequence generation. [See B. van Nooten, *J. Indian Philos.* **21** (1993), 31–50.]

Poetic meters can also be regarded as rhythms, with one beat for each $\smile$ and two beats for each $-$. An n-syllable pattern can involve between n and $2n$ beats, but musical rhythms suitable for marching or dancing generally are based on a fixed number of beats. Therefore it was natural to consider the set of all sequences of $\smile$s and $-$s that have exactly m beats, for fixed m. Such patterns are now called Morse code sequences of length m, and we know from exercise 4.5.3–32 that there are exactly F_{m+1} of them. For example, the 21 sequences when $m = 7$ are

$$
\begin{array}{l}
\smile---,\ -\smile--,\ \smile\smile\smile--,\ --\smile-,\ \smile\smile-\smile-,\\
\smile-\smile\smile-,\ -\smile\smile\smile-,\ \smile\smile\smile\smile\smile-,\ ---\smile,\\
\smile\smile--\smile,\ \smile-\smile-\smile,\ -\smile\smile-\smile,\ \smile\smile\smile\smile-\smile,\\
\smile--\smile\smile,\ -\smile-\smile\smile,\ \smile\smile\smile-\smile\smile,\ --\smile\smile\smile,\\
\smile\smile-\smile\smile\smile,\ \smile-\smile\smile\smile\smile,\ -\smile\smile\smile\smile\smile,\ \smile\smile\smile\smile\smile\smile\smile.
\end{array}
\tag{2}
$$

In this way Indian prosodists were led to discover the Fibonacci sequence, as we have observed in Section 1.2.8.

Moreover, the anonymous author of *Prākṛta Paiṅgala* (c. 1320) discovered elegant algorithms for ranking and unranking with respect to m-beat rhythms. To find the kth pattern, one starts by writing down m $\smile$s, then expresses the difference $d = F_{m+1} - k$ as a sum of Fibonacci numbers $F_{j_1} + \cdots + F_{j_t}$; here F_{j_1} is the largest Fibonacci number that is $\leq d$ and F_{j_2} is the largest $\leq d - F_{j_1}$, etc., continuing until the remainder is zero. Then beats $j - 1$ and j are to be changed from $\smile\smile$ to $-$, for $j = j_1, \ldots, j_t$. For example, to get the 5th element of (2) we compute $21 - 5 = 16 = 13 + 3 = F_7 + F_4$; the answer is $\smile\smile-\smile-$.

A few years later, Nārāyaṇa Paṇḍita treated the more general problem of finding all compositions of m whose parts are $\leq q$, where q is *any* given positive integer. As a consequence he discovered the qth-order Fibonacci sequence 5.4.2–(4), which was destined to be used 600 years later in polyphase sorting; he also developed the corresponding ranking and unranking algorithms. [See Parmanand Singh, *Historia Mathematica* **12** (1985), 229–244, and exercise 16.]

Piṅgala gave special code names to all the three-syllable meters,

$$
\begin{array}{llll}
--- = \text{म (m)}, &\qquad& --\smile = \text{त (t)}, \\
\smile-- = \text{य (y)}, && \smile-\smile = \text{ज (j)}, \\
-\smile- = \text{र (r)}, && -\smile\smile = \text{भ (bh)}, \\
\smile\smile- = \text{स (s)}, && \smile\smile\smile = \text{न (n)},
\end{array}
\tag{3}
$$

and students of Sanskrit have been expected to memorize them ever since. Somebody long ago devised a clever way to recall these codes, by inventing the nonsense word *yamātārājabhānasalagām* (यमाताराजभानसलगाम्); the point is that the ten syllables of this word can be written

$$\text{ya mā tā rā ja bhā na sa la gām} \quad \smile - - - \smile - \smile \smile \smile - \tag{4}$$

and each three-syllable pattern occurs just after its code name. The origin of yamā...lagām is obscure, but Subhash Kak [*Indian J. History of Science* **35** (2000), 123–127] has traced it back at least to C. P. Brown's *Sanskrit Prosody* (1869), page 28; thus it qualifies as the earliest known appearance of a "de Bruijn cycle" that encodes binary n-tuples.

Meanwhile, in Europe. In a similar way, classic Greek poetry was based on groups of short and/or long syllables called "metrical feet," analogous to bars of music. Each basic type of foot acquired a Greek name; for example, two short syllables '$\smile\smile$' were called a *pyrrhic*, and two long syllables '$--$' were called a *spondee*, because those rhythms were used respectively in a song of war (πυρρίχη) or a song of peace (σπονδαί). Greek names for metric feet were soon assimilated into Latin and eventually into modern languages, including English:

$\smile$	arsis	$\smile\smile\smile\smile$	proceleusmatic
$-$	thesis	$\smile\smile\smile-$	fourth pæon
		$\smile\smile-\smile$	third pæon
$\smile\smile$	pyrrhic	$\smile\smile--$	minor ionic
$\smile-$	iambus	$\smile-\smile\smile$	second pæon
$-\smile$	trochee	$\smile-\smile-$	diiambus
$--$	spondee	$\smile--\smile$	antispast
		$\smile---$	first epitrite
$\smile\smile\smile$	tribrach	$-\smile\smile\smile$	first pæon
$\smile\smile-$	anapest	$-\smile\smile-$	choriambus
$\smile-\smile$	amphibrach	$-\smile-\smile$	ditrochee
$\smile--$	bacchius	$-\smile--$	second epitrite
$-\smile\smile$	dactyl	$--\smile\smile$	major ionic
$-\smile-$	amphimacer	$--\smile-$	third epitrite
$--\smile$	palimbacchius	$---\smile$	fourth epitrite
$---$	molossus	$----$	dispondee

$$\tag{5}$$

Alternative names, like "choree" instead of "trochee," or "cretic" instead of "amphimacer," were also in common use. Moreover, by the time Diomedes wrote his Latin grammar (approximately A.D. 375), each of the 32 *five*-syllable feet had acquired at least one name. Diomedes also pointed out the relation between complementary patterns; he stated for example that tribrach and molossus are "*contrarius*," as are amphibrach and amphimacer. But he also regarded dactyl as the contrary of anapest, and bacchius as the contrary of palimbacchius, although the literal meaning of *palimbacchius* is actually "reverse bacchius." Greek prosodists had no standard order in which to list the individual possibilities, and the form of the names makes it clear that no connection to a radix-two number system was contemplated. [See H. Keil, *Grammatici Latini* **1** (1857), 474–482; W. von Christ, *Metrik der Griechen und Römer* (1879), 78–79.]

Surviving fragments of a work by Aristoxenus called *Elements of Rhythm* (c. 325 B.C.) show that the same terminology was applied also to music. And indeed, the same traditions lived on after the Renaissance; for example, we find

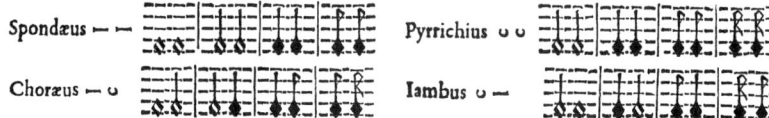

on page 32 of Athanasius Kircher's *Musurgia Universalis* **2** (Rome: 1650), and Kircher went on to describe all of the three-note and four-note rhythms of (5).

Early lists of permutations. We've traced the history of formulas for counting permutations in Section 5.1.2; but nontrivial *lists* of permutations were not published until hundreds of years after the formula $n!$ was discovered. The first such tabulation currently known was compiled by the Italian physician Shabbetai Donnolo in his commentary on the kabbalistic *Sefer Yetzirah*, written in A.D. 946. Table 1 shows his list for $n = 5$ as it was subsequently printed in Warsaw (1884). (The Hebrew letters in this table are typeset in a rabbinical font traditionally used for commentaries; notice that the letter מ changes its shape to ס when it appears at the left end of a word.) Donnolo went on to list 120 permutations of the six-letter word שכתבנו, all beginning with shin (ס); then he noted that 120 more could be obtained with each of the other five letters in front, making 720 in all. His lists involved groupings of six permutations, but in a haphazard fashion that led him into error (see exercise 4). Although he knew how many permutations there were supposed to be, and how many should start with a given letter, he evidently didn't have an algorithm for generating them.

Table 1
A MEDIEVAL LIST OF PERMUTATIONS

דברים , דבירס , דבימר, דבמיר, דבמרי, דברמי, דרבים , דרימב , דרימי, דרבמי, דרימב, דרמבי, דרמיב,

דיברס, דירבס , דירמב , דיבמר, דיבמר, דימרב , דימבר, דימברי, דמביר, דמברי, דמירב, דמיבר, דמירב,

בדימר, בדירס , בדרמי, בדלמי, בדלים , בדמיר , בדמרי , בדמיר, בילמר, בילדס, בילדס, בימדל , בימדר , בידמר,

במדרי , במדיר, במריד , במרדי , במריד , במידר , במילד , בדמיר , בדרמי , בדרים , בדריס , בדימר , בדילס,

רימדב , רימבד , רידבס, רידמב , רידמב , רידמי , ריבדס, ריבמד , רדבמי, רדמבי, רדימב , רדבים , רדמיב,

רבמדי , רבדמי , רבדיס , רבדים , רביס , רבימד , רבמיד , רבמיד , רמידב , רמיבד , רמביד , רמבדי , רמדבי,

ימדרב , ימרדב , ימבדר, ימברד , ימרבד , ימרבד , ידמבר, ידבמר, ידרבס, ידרבס, ידמבר, ידלמב , ידמרב,

יבדרס, יבדמר, יבדרס , יברדס, יבדמר, יבמדר, יבמרד, יברמד , ירמבד , ירמבד , ירבמד , ירבדס, ידרמב,

מדברי , מדרבי, מדביר , מדביר, מדיבר , מדירב , מדריב , מדביר, מביד , מבירד , מבדיר , מבדרי , מבדלי,

מרדבי , מרבדי , מרדיב , מרביד , מרביד , מריבד , מרידב , מרדיב , מיברד , מידרב , מידבר, מירדב , מירבד

A complete list of all 720 permutations of $\{a, b, c, d, e, f\}$ appeared on pages 668–671 of Jeremias Drexel's *Orbis Phaëthon* (Munich: 1629; also on pages 526–531 of the Cologne edition in 1631). He offered it as proof that a man with six guests could seat them differently at lunch and dinner every day for a year—

altogether 360 days, because there were five days of fasting during Holy Week. Shortly afterwards, Marin Mersenne exhibited all 720 permutations of the six tones {ut, re, mi, fa, sol, la}, on pages 111–115 of his *Traitez de la Voix et des Chants* (Volume 2 of *Harmonie Universelle*, 1636); then on pages 117–128 he presented the same data in musical notation:

Drexel's table was organized lexicographically by columns; Mersenne's tables were lexicographic with respect to the order ut < re < mi < fa < sol < la, beginning with "ut,re,mi,fa,sol,la" and ending with "la,sol,fa,mi,re,ut." Mersenne also prepared a "grand et immense" manuscript that listed all 40,320 permutations of *eight* notes on 672 folio pages, followed by ranking and unranking algorithms [Bibliothèque nationale de France, Fonds Français, no. 24256].

We saw in Section 7.2.1.2 that the important idea of plain changes, Algorithm 7.2.1.2P, was invented in England a few years later.

Methods for listing all permutations of a multiset with *repeated* elements were often misunderstood by early authors. For example, when Bhāskara exhibited the permutations of {4, 5, 5, 5, 8} in section 271 of his *Līlāvatī* (c. 1150), he gave them in the following order:

$$
\begin{array}{ccccc}
\text{४५५५४} & \text{५४५५४} & \text{४५४५५} & \text{४५४५५} & \text{४५५४५} \\
\text{४५५४४} & \text{४५५५४} & \text{४५५५४} & \text{४४५५५} & \text{४५५४५} \\
\text{४४५५५} & \text{५४५४५} & \text{५४५५४} & \text{५४५५४} & \text{४५४५५} \\
\text{४५४५४} & \text{४४५४५} & \text{४५५४४} & \text{४४४५५} & \text{४५५४४}
\end{array}
\tag{6}
$$

Mersenne used a slightly more sensible but not completely systematic order on page 131 of his book when he listed sixty anagrams of the Latin name IESVS. When Athanasius Kircher wanted to illustrate the 30 permutations of a five-note melody on pages 10 and 11 of *Musurgia Universalis* **2** (1650), this lack of a system got him into trouble (see exercise 5):

$$
\tag{7}
$$

But John Wallis knew better. On page 117 of his *Discourse of Combinations* (1685) he correctly listed the 60 anagrams of "messes" in lexicographic order, if we let m < e < s; and on page 126 he recommended respecting alphabetic order "that we may be the more sure, not to miss any."

We will see later that the Indian pundits Śārṅgadeva and Nārāyaṇa had already developed a theory of permutation generation in the 13th and 14th centuries, although their work was ahead of its time and remained obscure.

Seki's list. Takakazu Seki (1642–1708) was a charismatic teacher and researcher who revolutionized the study of mathematics in 17th-century Japan. While he was studying the elimination of variables from simultaneous homogeneous equations, he was led to expressions such as $a_1b_2 - a_2b_1$ and $a_1b_2c_3 - a_1b_3c_2 + a_2b_3c_1 - a_2b_1c_3 + a_3b_1c_2 - a_3b_2c_1$, which we now recognize as *determinants*. In 1683 he published a booklet about this discovery, introducing an ingenious scheme for listing all permutations in such a way that half of them were "alive" (even) and the other half were "dead" (odd). Starting with the case $n = 2$, when '12' was alive and '21' was dead, he formulated the following rules for $n > 2$:

1) Take every live permutation for $n-1$, increase all its elements by 1, and insert 1 in front. This rule produces $(n-1)!/2$ "basic permutations" of $\{1, \ldots, n\}$.

2) From each basic permutation, form $2n$ others by rotation and reflection:

$$a_1 a_2 \ldots a_{n-1} a_n, \quad a_2 \ldots a_{n-1} a_n a_1, \quad \ldots, \quad a_n a_1 a_2 \ldots a_{n-1}; \tag{8}$$

$$a_n a_{n-1} \ldots a_2 a_1, \quad a_1 a_n a_{n-1} \ldots a_2, \quad \ldots, \quad a_{n-1} \ldots a_2 a_1 a_n. \tag{9}$$

If n is odd, those in the first row are alive and those in the second are dead; if n is even, those in each row are alternatively alive, dead, ..., alive, dead. For example, when $n = 3$ the only basic permutation is 123. Thus 123, 231, 312 are alive while 321, 132, 213 are dead, and we've successfully generated the six terms of a 3×3 determinant. The basic permutations for $n = 4$ are 1234, 1342, 1423; and from, say, 1342 we get a set of eight, namely

$$+ 1342 - 3421 + 4213 - 2134 + 2431 - 1243 + 3124 - 4312, \tag{10}$$

alternately alive $(+)$ and dead $(-)$. A 4×4 determinant therefore includes the terms $a_1b_3c_4d_2 - a_3b_4c_2d_1 + \cdots - a_4b_3c_1d_2$ and sixteen others.

Seki's rule for permutation generation is quite pretty, but unfortunately it has a serious problem: It doesn't work when $n > 4$. His error seems to have gone unrecognized for hundreds of years. [See Y. Mikami, *The Development of Mathematics in China and Japan* (1913), 191–199; *Takakazu Seki's Collected Works* (Osaka: 1974), 18–20, 八五－－－四一; and exercises 7–8.]

Lists of combinations. The earliest exhaustive list of *combinations* known to have survived the ravages of time appears in the last book of Suśruta's well-known Sanskrit treatise on medicine, Chapter 63, written before A.D. 600 and perhaps much earlier. Noting that medicine can be sweet, sour, salty, peppery, bitter, and/or astringent, Suśruta's book diligently listed the $(15, 20, 15, 6, 1, 6)$ cases that arise when those qualities occur two, three, four, five, six, and one at a time.

Bhāskara repeated this example in sections 110–114 of *Līlāvatī*, and observed that the same reasoning applies to six-syllable poetic meters with a given number of long syllables. But he simply mentioned the totals, $(6, 15, 20, 15, 6, 1)$, without listing the combinations themselves. In sections 274 and 275, he observed that the numbers $(n(n-1) \ldots (n-k+1))/(k(k-1) \ldots (1))$ enumerate *compositions* (that is, ordered partitions) as well as combinations; again he gave no list.

To avoid prolixity this is treated in a brief manner;
for the science of calculation is an ocean without bounds.
— BHĀSKARA (c. 1150)

An isolated but interesting list of combinations appeared in the remarkable algebra text *Al-Bāhir fi'l-ḥisāb* (*The Shining Book of Calculation*), written by al-Samaw'al of Baghdad when he was only 19 years old (1144). In the closing part of that work he presented a list of $\binom{10}{6} = 210$ simultaneous linear equations in 10 unknowns:

Al-Samaw'al's Arabic original			Equivalent modern notation	
٦٥	٦٥٤٣٢١	ا	(1)　$x_1 + x_2 + x_3 + x_4 + x_5 + x_6 = 65$	
٧٠	٧٠٥٤٣٢١	ب	(2)　$x_1 + x_2 + x_3 + x_4 + x_5 + x_7 = 70$	
٧٥	٨٥٤٣٢١	ج	(3)　$x_1 + x_2 + x_3 + x_4 + x_5 + x_8 = 75$	(11)
⋮			⋮	
٩١	١٠٩٨٧٦٤	طر	(209)　$x_4 + x_6 + x_7 + x_8 + x_9 + x_{10} = 91$	
١٠٠	١٠٩٨٧٦٥	ري	(210)　$x_5 + x_6 + x_7 + x_8 + x_9 + x_{10} = 100$	

Each combination of ten things taken six at a time yielded one of his equations. His purpose was evidently to demonstrate that over-determined equations can still have a unique solution — which in this case was $(x_1, x_2, \ldots, x_{10}) = (1, 4, 9, 16, 25, 10, 15, 20, 25, 5)$. [Salah Ahmad and Roshdi Rashed, *Al-Bāhir en Algèbre d'As-Samaw'al* (Damascus: 1972), 77–82, ٢٤٨–٢٣١.]

Rolling dice. Some glimmerings of elementary combinatorics arose also in medieval Europe, especially in connection with the question of listing all possible outcomes when three dice are thrown. There are, of course, $\binom{8}{3} = 56$ ways to choose 3 things from 6 when repetitions are allowed. Gambling was officially prohibited; yet these 56 ways became rather well known. In about A.D. 965, Bishop Wibold of Cambrai in northern France devised a game called Ludus Clericalis, so that members of the clergy could enjoy rolling dice while remaining pious. His idea was to associate each possible roll with one of 56 virtues, according to the following table:

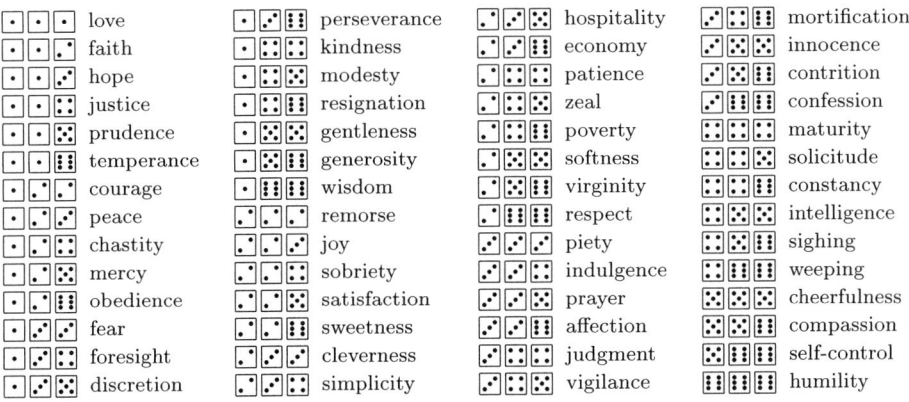

love	perseverance	hospitality	mortification
faith	kindness	economy	innocence
hope	modesty	patience	contrition
justice	resignation	zeal	confession
prudence	gentleness	poverty	maturity
temperance	generosity	softness	solicitude
courage	wisdom	virginity	constancy
peace	remorse	respect	intelligence
chastity	joy	piety	sighing
mercy	sobriety	indulgence	weeping
obedience	satisfaction	prayer	cheerfulness
fear	sweetness	affection	compassion
foresight	cleverness	judgment	self-control
discretion	simplicity	vigilance	humility

Players took turns, and the first to roll each virtue acquired it. After all possibilities had arisen, the most virtuous player won. Wibold noted that love (*caritas*) is the best virtue of all. He gave a complicated scoring system by which two virtues could be combined if the sum of pips on all six of their dice was 21; for example, love + humility or chastity + intelligence could be paired in this way, and such combinations ranked above any individual virtue. He also considered more complex variants of the game in which vowels appeared on the dice instead of spots, so that virtues could be claimed if their vowels were thrown.

Wibold's table of virtues was presented in lexicographic order, as above, when it was first described by Baldéric in his *Chronicon Cameracense*, about 150 years later. [*Patrologia Latina* **134** (Paris: 1884), 1007–1016.] But another medieval manuscript presented the possible dice rolls in quite a different order:

$$\text{(dice roll table)} \tag{12}$$

In this case the author knew how to deal with repeated values, but had a very complicated, ad hoc way to handle the cases in which all dice were different. [See D. R. Bellhouse, *International Statistical Review* **68** (2000), 123–136.]

An amusing poem entitled "Chaunce of the Dyse," attributed to John Lydgate, was written in the early 1400s for use at parties. Its opening verses invite each person to throw three dice; then the remaining verses, which are indexed in decreasing lexicographic order from ⚅⚅⚅ to ⚅⚅⚄ to ··· to ⚀⚀⚀, give 56 character sketches that light-heartedly describe the thrower. [The full text was published by E. P. Hammond in *Englische Studien* **59** (1925), 1–16; a translation into modern English would be desirable.]

> *I pray to god that euery wight may caste*
> *Vpon three dyse ryght as is in hys herte*
> *Whether he be rechelesse or stedfaste*
> *So moote he lawghen outher elles smerte*
> *He that is gilty his lyfe to converte*
> *They that in trouthe haue suffred many a throwe*
> *Moote ther chaunce fal as they moote be knowe.*
>
> *— The Chaunce of the Dyse* (c. 1410)

Ramon Llull. Significant ripples of combinatorial concepts also emanated from an energetic and quixotic Catalan poet, novelist, encyclopedist, educator, mystic, and missionary named Ramon Llull (c. 1232–1316). Llull's approach to knowledge was essentially to identify basic principles and then to contemplate combining them in all possible ways.

For example, one chapter in his *Ars Compendiosa Inveniendi Veritatem* (c. 1274) began by enumerating sixteen attributes of God: Goodness, greatness, eternity, power, wisdom, love, virtue, truth, glory, perfection, justice, generosity, mercy, humility, sovereignty, and patience. Then Llull wrote $\binom{16}{2} = 120$ short essays of about 80 words each, considering God's goodness as related to greatness,

God's goodness as related to eternity, and so on, ending with God's sovereignty as related to patience. In another chapter he considered seven virtues (faith, hope, charity, justice, prudence, fortitude, temperance) and seven vices (gluttony, lust, greed, sloth, pride, envy, anger), with $\binom{14}{2} = 91$ subchapters to deal with each pair in turn. Other chapters were systematically divided in a similar way, into $\binom{8}{2} = 28$, $\binom{15}{2} = 105$, $\binom{4}{2} = 6$, and $\binom{16}{2} = 120$ subsections. (One wonders what might have happened if he had been familiar with Wibold's list of 56 virtues; would he have produced commentaries on all $\binom{56}{2} = 1540$ of their pairs?)

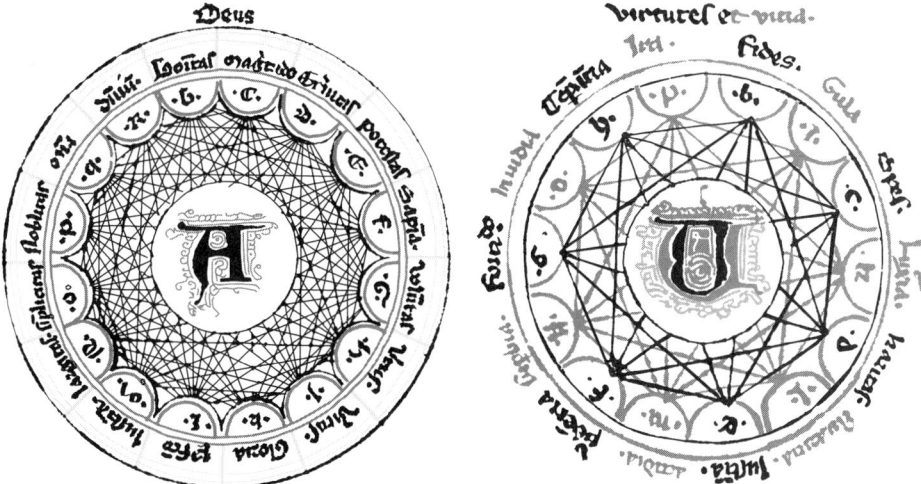

Fig. 64. Illustrations in a manuscript presented by Ramon Llull to the doge of Venice in 1280. [From his *Ars Demonstrativa*, Biblioteca Marciana, VI 200, folio 3ᵛ.]

Llull illustrated his methodology by drawing circular diagrams like those in Figure 64. The left-hand circle in this illustration, *Deus*, names sixteen divine attributes — essentially the same sixteen listed earlier, except that love (*amor*) was now called will (*voluntas*), and the final four were now respectively simplicity, rank, mercy, and sovereignty. Each attribute is assigned a code letter, and the illustration depicts their interrelations as the complete graph K_{16} on vertices (B, C, D, E, F, G, H, I, K, L, M, N, O, P, Q, R). The right-hand figure, *virtutes et vitia*, shows the seven virtues (b, c, d, e, f, g, h) interleaved with the seven vices (i, k, l, m, n, o, p); in the original manuscript virtues appeared in blue ink while vices appeared in red. Notice that in this case his illustration depicted two independent complete graphs K_7, one of each color. (He no longer bothered to compare each individual virtue with each individual vice, since every virtue was clearly better than every vice.)

Llull used the same approach to write about medicine: Instead of juxtaposing theological concepts, his *Liber Principiorum Medicinæ* (c. 1275) considered combinations of symptoms and treatments. And he also wrote books

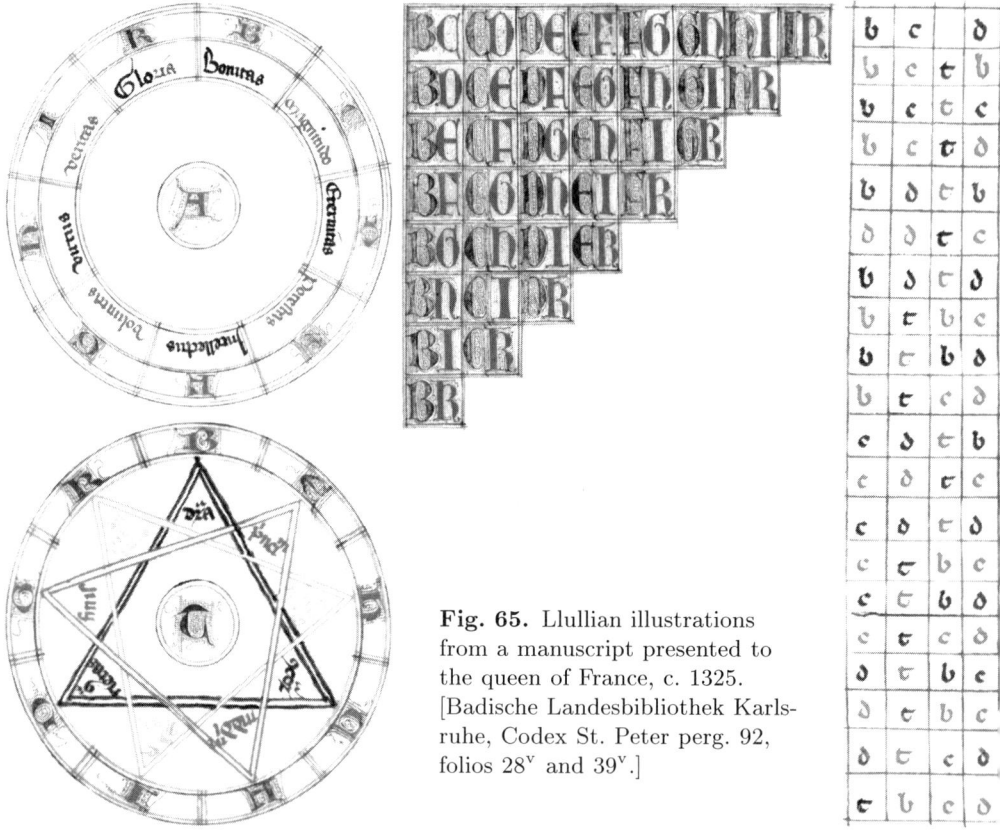

Fig. 65. Llullian illustrations from a manuscript presented to the queen of France, c. 1325. [Badische Landesbibliothek Karlsruhe, Codex St. Peter perg. 92, folios 28ᵛ and 39ᵛ.]

on philosophy, logic, jurisprudence, astrology, zoology, geometry, rhetoric, and chivalry — more than 200 works in all. It must be admitted, however, that much of this material was highly repetitive; modern data compression techniques would probably reduce Llull's output to a size much less than that of, say, Aristotle.

He eventually decided to simplify his system by working primarily with groups of nine things. See, for example, Fig. 65, where circle A now lists only the first nine of God's attributes (B, C, D, E, F, G, H, I, K). The $\binom{9}{2} = 36$ associated pairs (BC, BD, . . . , IK) appear in the stairstep chart at the right of that circle. By adding two more virtues, namely patience and compassion — as well as two more vices, namely lying and inconsistency — he could treat virtues vis-à-vis virtues and vices vis-à-vis vices with the same chart. He also proposed using the same chart to carry out an interesting scheme for voting, in an election with nine candidates [see I. McLean and J. London, *Studia Lulliana* **32** (1992), 21–37].

The encircled triangles at the lower left of Fig. 65 illustrate another key aspect of Llull's approach. Triangle (B, C, D) stands for (difference, concordance, contrariness); triangle (E, F, G) stands for (beginning, middle, ending); and triangle (H, I, K) stands for (greater, equal, less). These three interleaved appearances of K_3 represent three kinds of three-valued logic. Llull had experimented earlier with other such triplets, notably '(true, unknown, false)'. We can get an idea of how he used the triangles by considering how he dealt with combinations of the four basic elements (earth, air, fire, water): All four elements are different; earth is concordant with fire, which concords with air, which concords with water, which concords with earth; earth is contrary to air, and fire is contrary to water; these considerations complete an analysis with respect to triangle (B, C, D). Turning to triangle (E, F, G), he noted that various processes in nature begin with one element dominating another; then a transition or middle state occurs, until a goal is reached, like air becoming warm. For triangle (H, I, K) he said that in general we have fire > air > water > earth with respect to their "spheres," their "velocities," and their "nobilities"; nevertheless we also have, for example, air > fire with respect to supporting life, while air and fire have equal value when they are working together.

Llull provided the vertical table at the right of Fig. 65 as a further aid. (See exercise 11 below.) He also introduced movable concentric wheels, labeled with the letters (B, C, D, E, F, G, H, I, K) and with other names, so that many things could be contemplated simultaneously. In this way a faithful practitioner of the Llullian art could be sure to have all the bases covered. [Llull may have seen similar wheels that were used in nearby Jewish communities; see M. Idel, *J. Warburg and Courtauld Institutes* **51** (1988), 170–174 and plates 16–17.]

Several centuries later, Athanasius Kircher published an extension of Llull's system as part of a large tome entitled *Ars Magna Sciendi sive Combinatoria* (Amsterdam: 1669), with five movable wheels accompanying page 173 of that book. Kircher also extended Llull's repertoire of complete graphs K_n by providing illustrations of complete *bipartite* graphs $K_{m,n}$; for example, Fig. 66 is taken from page 171 of Kircher's book, and his page 170 contains a glorious picture of $K_{18,18}$.

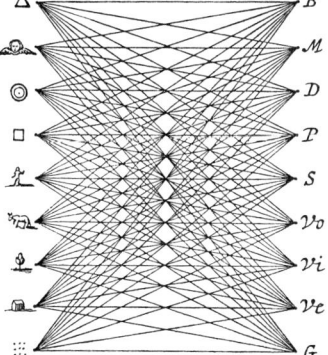

Fig. 66. $K_{9,9}$ as presented by Athanasius Kircher in 1669.

> *It is an investigative and inventive art.*
> *When ideas are combined in all possible ways,*
> *the new combinations start the mind thinking along novel channels*
> *and one is led to discover fresh truths and arguments.*
> — MARTIN GARDNER, *Logic Machines and Diagrams* (1958)

The most extensive modern development of Llull-like methods is perhaps *The Schillinger System of Musical Composition* by Joseph Schillinger (New York:

Carl Fischer, 1946), a remarkable two-volume work that presents theories of rhythm, melody, harmony, counterpoint, composition, orchestration, etc., from a combinatorial perspective. On page 56, for example, Schillinger lists the 24 permutations of $\{a, b, c, d\}$ in the Gray-code order of plain changes (Algorithm 7.2.1.2P); then on page 57 he applies them not to pitches but rather to rhythms, to the durations of notes. On page 364 he exhibits the symmetrical cycle

$$(2, 0, 3, 4, 2, 5, 6, 4, 0, 1, 6, 2, 3, 1, 4, 5, 3, 6, 0, 5, 1), \qquad (13)$$

a universal cycle of 2-combinations for the seven objects $\{0, 1, 2, 3, 4, 5, 6\}$; in other words, (13) is an Eulerian trail in K_7: All $\binom{7}{2} = 21$ pairs of digits occur exactly once. Such patterns are grist for a composer's mill. But we can be grateful that Schillinger's better students (like George Gershwin) did not commit themselves entirely to a strictly mathematical sense of aesthetics.

Tacquet, van Schooten, and Izquierdo. Three additional books related to our story were published during the 1650s. André Tacquet wrote a popular text, *Arithmeticæ Theoria et Praxis* (Louvain: 1656), that was reprinted and revised often during the next fifty years. Near the end, on pages 376 and 377, he gave a procedure for listing combinations two at a time, then three at a time, etc.

Frans van Schooten's *Exercitationes Mathematicæ* (Leiden: 1657) was more advanced. On page 373 he listed all combinations in an appealing layout

$$\frac{\begin{array}{c} a \\ \hline b.\ ab \\ \hline c.\ ac.\ bc.\ abc \\ \hline d.\ ad.\ bd.\ abd.\ cd.\ acd.\ bcd.\ abcd \end{array}}{} \qquad (14)$$

and he proceeded on the next few pages to extend this pattern to the letters e, f, g, h, i, k, "et sic in infinitum." On page 376 he observed that one can replace (a, b, c, d) by $(2, 3, 5, 7)$ in (14) to get the divisors of 210 that exceed unity:

$$\frac{\begin{array}{c} 2 \\ \hline 3\ \ 6 \\ \hline 5\ \ 10\ \ 15\ \ 30 \\ \hline 7\ \ 14\ \ 21\ \ 42\ \ 35\ \ 70\ \ 105\ \ 210 \end{array}}{} \qquad (15)$$

And on the following page he extended the idea to

$$\frac{\begin{array}{c} a \\ \hline a.\ aa \\ \hline b.\ ab.\ aab \\ \hline c.\ ac.\ aac.\ bc.\ abc.\ aabc \end{array}}{} \qquad (16)$$

thereby allowing two a's. He didn't really understand this extension, though; his next example

$$\frac{\begin{array}{c} a \\ \hline a.\ aa \\ \hline a.\ aaa \\ \hline b.\ ab.\ aab.\ aaab \\ \hline b.\ bb.\ abb.\ aabb.\ aaabb \end{array}}{} \qquad (17)$$

was botched, indicating the limits of his knowledge at the time. (See exercise 13.)

On page 411 van Schooten observed that the weights $(a, b, c, d) = (1, 2, 4, 8)$ could be assigned in (14), leading to

$$\begin{array}{c} \dfrac{\begin{array}{c} 1 \\ \overline{2\ \ 3} \\ \overline{4\ \ 5\ \ 6\ \ 7} \end{array}}{8\ \ 9\ \ 10\ \ 11\ \ 12\ \ 13\ \ 14\ \ 15} \end{array} \tag{18}$$

after addition. But he didn't see the connection with radix-2 numbers.

Sebastián Izquierdo's two-volume work *Pharus Scientiarum* (Lyon: 1659), "The Lighthouse of Science," included a nicely organized discussion of combinatorics entitled Disputatio 29, *De Combinatione*. He gave a detailed discussion of four key parts of Stanley's Twelvefold Way, namely the n-tuples, n-variations, n-multicombinations, and n-combinations of m objects that appear in the first two rows and the first two columns of Table 7.2.1.4–1.

In Sections 81–84 of *De Combinatione* he listed all combinations of m letters taken n at a time, for $2 \leq n \leq 5$ and $n \leq m \leq 9$, always in lexicographic order; he also tabulated them for $m = 10$ and 20 in the cases $n = 2$ and 3. But when he listed the $m^{\underline{n}}$ *variations* of m things taken n at a time, he chose a more complicated ordering (see exercise 14).

Izquierdo was first to discover the formula $\binom{m+n-1}{n}$ for combinations of m things taken n at a time with unlimited repetition; this rule appeared in §48–§51 of his work. But in §105, when he attempted to list all such combinations in the case $n = 3$, he didn't know that there was a simple way to do it. In fact, his listing of the 56 cases for $m = 6$ was rather like the old, awkward ordering of (12).

Combinations with repetition were not well understood until James Bernoulli's *Ars Conjectandi*, "The Art of Guessing," came out in 1713. In Part 2, Chapter 5, Bernoulli simply listed the possibilities in lexicographic order, and showed that the formula $\binom{m+n-1}{n}$ follows by induction as an easy consequence. [Niccolò Tartaglia had, incidentally, come close to discovering this formula in his *General trattato di numeri, et misure* **2** (Venice: 1556), 17^{r} and 69^{v}; so had the Maghrebi mathematician Ibn Mun'im in his 13th-century *Fiqh al-Ḥisāb*.]

The null case. Before we conclude our discussion of early work on combinations, we should not forget a small yet noble step taken by John Wallis on page 110 of his *Discourse of Combinations* (1685), where he specifically considered the combination of m things taken 0 at a time: "It is manifest, That, if we would *take None*, that is, if we would *leave All*; there can be but one case thereof, what ever be the Number of things exposed." Furthermore, on page 113, he knew that $\binom{0}{0} = 1$: "(for, here, to take all, or to leave all, is but one and the same case)."

However, when he gave a table of $n!$ for $n \leq 24$, he did not go so far as to point out that $0! = 1$, or that there is exactly one permutation of the empty set.

The work of Nārāyaṇa. A remarkable monograph entitled *Gaṇita Kaumudī* ("Lotus Delight of Calculation"), written by Nārāyaṇa Paṇḍita in 1356, has recently become known in detail to scholars outside of India for the first time, thanks to an English translation by Parmanand Singh [*Gaṇita Bhāratī* **20** (1998), 25–82; **21** (1999), 10–73; **22** (2000), 19–85; **23** (2001), 18–82; **24** (2002), 35–98];

see also the Ph.D. thesis of Takanori Kusuba, Brown University (1993). Chapter 13 of Nārāyaṇa's work, subtitled *Aṅka Pāśa* ("Concatenation of Numbers"), was devoted to combinatorial generation. Indeed, although the 97 "sutras" of this chapter were rather cryptic, they presented a comprehensive theory of the subject that anticipated developments in the rest of the world by several hundred years.

For example, Nārāyaṇa dealt with permutation generation in sutras 49–55a, where he gave algorithms to list all permutations of a set in decreasing colex order, together with algorithms to rank a given permutation and to unrank a given serial number. These algorithms had appeared more than a century earlier in the well-known work *Saṅgītaratnākara* ("Jewel-Mine of Music") by Śārṅgadeva, §1.4.60–71, who thereby had essentially discovered the factorial representation of positive integers. Nārāyaṇa went on in sutras 57–60 to extend Śārṅgadeva's algorithms so that general multisets could readily be permuted; for example, he listed the permutations of $\{1, 1, 2, 4\}$ as

$$1124, 1214, 2114, 1142, 1412, 4112, 1241, 2141, 1421, 4121, 2411, 4211,$$

again in decreasing colex order.

Nārāyaṇa's sutras 88–92 dealt with systematic generation of combinations. Besides illustrating the combinations of $\{1, \ldots, 8\}$ taken 3 at a time, namely

$$(678, 578, 478, \ldots, 134, 124, 123),$$

he also considered a bit-string representation of these combinations in the reverse order (*increasing* colex), extending a 10th-century method of Bhaṭṭotpala:

$$(11100000, 11010000, 10110000, \ldots, 00010011, 00001011, 00000111).$$

He almost, but not quite, discovered Theorem 7.2.1.3L.

Permutable poetry. Let's turn now to a curious question that attracted the attention of several prominent mathematicians in the seventeenth century, because it sheds considerable light on the state of combinatorial knowledge in Europe at that time. A Jesuit priest named Bernard Bauhuis had composed a famous one-line tribute to the Virgin Mary, in Latin hexameter:

$$\text{Tot tibi sunt dotes, Virgo, quot sidera cælo.} \qquad (19)$$

["Thou hast as many virtues, O Virgin, as there are stars in heaven"; see his *Epigrammatum Libri V* (Cologne: 1615), 49.] His verse inspired Erycius Puteanus, a professor at the University of Louvain, to write a book entitled *Pietatis Thaumata* (Antwerp: 1617), presenting 1022 permutations of Bauhuis's words. For example, Puteanus wrote

107	Tot dotes tibi, quot cælo sunt sidera, Virgo.
270	Dotes tot, cælo sunt sidera quot, tibi Virgo.
329	Dotes, cælo sunt quot sidera, Virgo tibi tot.
384	Sidera quot cælo, tot sunt Virgo tibi dotes.
725	Quot cælo sunt sidera, tot Virgo tibi dotes.
949	Sunt dotes Virgo, quot sidera, tot tibi cælo.
1022	Sunt cælo tot Virgo tibi, quot sidera, dotes.

(20)

He stopped at 1022, because 1022 was the number of visible stars in Ptolemy's well-known catalog of the heavens.

The idea of permuting words in this way was well known at the time; such wordplay was what Julius Scaliger had called "Proteus verses" in his *Poetices Libri Septem* (Lyon: 1561), Book 2, Chapter 30. The Latin language lends itself to permutations like (20), because Latin word endings tend to define the function of each noun, making the relative word order much less important to the meaning of a sentence than it is in English. Puteanus did state, however, that he had specifically avoided unsuitable permutations such as

$$\text{Sidera tot cælo, Virgo, quot sunt tibi dotes,} \qquad (21)$$

because they would place an *upper* bound on the Virgin's virtues rather than a lower bound. [See pages 12 and 103 of his book.]

Of course there are $8! = 40{,}320$ ways to permute the words of (19). But that wasn't the point; most of those ways don't "scan." Each of Puteanus's 1022 verses obeyed the strict rules of classical *hexameter*, the rules that had been followed by Greek and Latin poets since the days of Homer and Vergil, namely:

i) Each word consists of syllables that are either long ($-$) or short ($\smile$).

ii) The syllables of each line belong to one of 32 patterns,

$$\left\{ \begin{array}{c} - \smile\smile \\ -- \end{array} \right\} \left\{ \begin{array}{c} - \smile\smile \\ -- \end{array} \right\} \left\{ \begin{array}{c} - \smile\smile \\ -- \end{array} \right\} \left\{ \begin{array}{c} - \smile\smile \\ -- \end{array} \right\} - \smile\smile \left\{ \begin{array}{c} - \smile \\ -- \end{array} \right\}. \qquad (22)$$

In other words there are six metrical feet, where each of the first four is either a dactyl or a spondee in the terminology of (5); the fifth foot should be a dactyl, and the last is either trochee or spondee.

The rules for long versus short syllables in Latin poetry are somewhat tricky in general, but the eight words of Bauhuis's verse can be characterized by the following patterns:

$$\text{tot} = -, \quad \text{tibi} = \left\{ \begin{array}{c} \smile\smile \\ \smile - \end{array} \right\}, \quad \text{sunt} = -, \quad \text{dotes} = --,$$

$$\text{Virgo} = \left\{ \begin{array}{c} - \smile \\ -- \end{array} \right\}, \quad \text{quot} = -, \quad \text{sidera} = - \smile\smile, \quad \text{cælo} = --. \qquad (23)$$

Notice that poets had two choices when they used the words 'tibi' or 'Virgo'. Thus, for example, (19) fits the hexameter pattern

$$\underset{\text{Tot ti-bi}}{- \,\, \smile\smile} \quad \underset{\text{sunt do-}}{- \,\, -} \quad \underset{\text{tes, Vir-}}{- \,\, -} \quad \underset{\text{go, quot}}{- \,\, -} \quad \underset{\text{si-de-ra}}{- \,\, \smile\smile} \quad \underset{\text{cæ-lo.}}{- \,\, -} \qquad (24)$$

(Dactyl, spondee, spondee, spondee, dactyl, spondee; "dum-diddy dum-dum dum-dum dum-dum dum-diddy dum-dum." The commas represent slight pauses, called "cæsuras," when the words are read; they don't concern us here, although Puteanus inserted them carefully into each of his 1022 permutations.)

A natural question now arises: If we permute Bauhuis's words at random, what are the odds that they scan? In other words, how many of the permutations obey rules (i) and (ii), given the syllable patterns in (23)? G. W. Leibniz raised this question, among others, in his *Dissertatio de Arte Combinatoria* (1666), a work published when he was applying for a position at the University of Leipzig. At this time Leibniz was just 19 years old, largely self-taught, and his understanding of combinatorics was quite limited; for example, he believed that there are 600 permutations of $\{ut, ut, re, mi, fa, sol\}$ and 480 of $\{ut, ut, re, re, mi, fa\}$, and he even stated that (22) represents 76 possibilities instead of 32. [See §5 and §8 in his Problem 6.]

But Leibniz did realize that it would be worthwhile to develop general methods for counting all permutations that are "useful," in situations when many permutations are "useless." He considered several examples of Proteus verses, enumerating some of the simpler ones correctly but making many errors when the words were complicated. Although he mentioned Puteanus's work, he didn't attempt to enumerate the scannable permutations of (19).

A much more successful approach was introduced a few years later by Jean Prestet in his *Élémens des Mathématiques* (Paris: 1675), 342–438. Prestet gave a clear exposition leading to the conclusion that exactly 2196 permutations of Bauhuis's verse would yield a proper hexameter. However, he soon realized that he had forgotten to count quite a few cases — including those numbered 270, 384, and 725 in (20). So he completely rewrote this material when he published *Nouveaux Élémens des Mathématiques* in 1689. Pages 127–133 of Prestet's new book were devoted to showing that the true number of scannable permutations was 3276, almost 50% larger than his previous total.

Meanwhile John Wallis had treated the problem in his *Discourse of Combinations* (London: 1685), 118–119, published as a supplement to his *Treatise of Algebra*. After explaining why he believed the correct number to be 3096, Wallis admitted that he may have overlooked some possibilities and/or counted some cases more than once; "but I do not, at present, discern either the one and other."

An anonymous reviewer of Wallis's work remarked that the true number of metrically correct permutations was actually 2580 — but he gave no proof [*Acta Eruditorum* **5** (1686), 289]. The reviewer was almost certainly G. W. Leibniz himself, although no clue to the reasoning behind the number 2580 has been found among Leibniz's voluminous unpublished notes.

Finally James Bernoulli entered the picture. In his inaugural lecture as Dean of Philosophy at the University of Basel, 1692, he mentioned the tottibi enumeration problem and stated that a careful analysis is necessary to obtain the correct answer — which, he said, was 3312(!). His proof appeared posthumously in the first edition of his *Ars Conjectandi* (1713), 79–81. [Those pages were, incidentally, omitted from later editions of that famous book, and from his collected works, because he didn't actually intend them for publication; a proofreader had inserted them by mistake. See *Die Werke von Jakob Bernoulli* **3** (Basel: Birkhäuser, 1975), 78, 98–106, 108, 154–155.]

So who was right? Are there 2196 scannable permutations, or 3276, or 3096, or 2580, or 3312? W. A. Whitworth and W. E. Hartley considered the question anew in *The Mathematical Gazette* **2** (1902), 227–228, where they each presented elegant arguments and concluded that the true total was in fact none of the above. Their joint answer, 2880, represented the first time that any two math-ematicians had independently come to the same conclusion about this problem.

But exercises 21 and 22, below, reveal the truth: Bernoulli is vindicated, and everybody else was wrong. Moreover, a study of Bernoulli's systematic and carefully indented 3-page derivation indicates that he was successful chiefly because he adhered faithfully to a discipline that we now call the *backtrack method*. We shall study the backtrack method thoroughly in Section 7.2.2, where we will also see that the tot-tibi question is readily solved as a special case of the *exact cover problem*.

> *Even the wisest and most prudent people often suffer from*
> *what Logicians call* insufficient enumeration of cases.
>
> — JAMES BERNOULLI (1692)

Set partitions. The partitions of a set seem to have been studied first in Japan, where a parlor game called *genji-ko* ("Genji incense") became popular among upperclass people about A.D. 1500. The host of a gathering would secretly select five packets of incense, some of which might be identical, and he would burn them one at a time. The guests would try to discern which of the scents were the same and which were different; in other words, they would try to guess which of the $\varpi_5 = 52$ partitions of $\{1, 2, 3, 4, 5\}$ had been chosen by their host.

Fig. 67. Diagrams used to represent set partitions in 16th century Japan. [From a copy in the collection of Tamaki Yano at Saitama University.]

Soon it became customary to represent the 52 possible outcomes by diagrams like those in Fig. 67. For example, the uppermost diagram of that illustration, when read from right to left, would indicate that the first two scents are identical and so are the last three; thus the partition is $12\,|\,345$. The other two diagrams, similarly, are pictorial ways to represent the respective partitions $124\,|\,35$ and $1\,|\,24\,|\,35$. As an aid to memory, each of the 52 patterns was named after a chapter of Lady Murasaki's famous 11th-century *Tale of Genji*, according to the following sequence [*Encyclopedia Japonicæ* (Tokyo: Sanseido, 1910), 1299]:

$$(25)$$

(Once again, as we've seen in many other examples, the possibilities were not arranged in any particularly logical order.)

The appealing nature of these genji-ko patterns led many families to adopt them as heraldic crests. For example, the following stylized variants of (25) were found in standard catalogs of kimono patterns early in the 20th century:

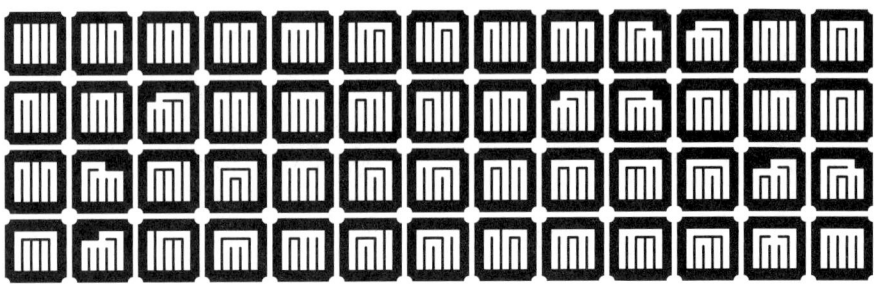

[See Fumie Adachi, *Japanese Design Motifs* (New York: Dover, 1972), 150–153.]

Early in the 1700s, Takakazu Seki and his students began to investigate the number of set partitions ϖ_n for arbitrary n, inspired by the known result that $\varpi_5 = 52$. Yoshisuke Matsunaga found formulas for the number of set partitions when there are k_j subsets of size n_j for $1 \le j \le t$, with $k_1 n_1 + \cdots + k_t n_t = n$ (see the answer to exercise 1.2.5–21). He also discovered the basic recurrence relation 7.2.1.5–(14), namely

$$\varpi_{n+1} = \binom{n}{0}\varpi_n + \binom{n}{1}\varpi_{n-1} + \binom{n}{2}\varpi_{n-2} + \cdots + \binom{n}{n}\varpi_0, \qquad (26)$$

by which the values of ϖ_n can readily be computed.

Matsunaga's discoveries remained unpublished until Yoriyuki Arima's book *Shūki Sanpō* came out in 1769. Problem 56 of that book asked the reader to solve the equation "$\varpi_n = 678570$" for n; and Arima's answer, worked out in detail (with credit duly given to Matsunaga), was $n = 11$.

Shortly afterwards, Masanobu Saka studied the number $\left\{{n \atop k}\right\}$ of ways that an n-set can be partitioned into k subsets, in his work *Sanpō-Gakkai* (1782). He discovered the recurrence formula

$$\left\{{n+1 \atop k}\right\} = k\left\{{n \atop k}\right\} + \left\{{n \atop k-1}\right\}, \qquad (27)$$

and tabulated the results for $n \le 11$. James Stirling, in his *Methodus Differentialis* (1730), had discovered the numbers $\left\{{n \atop k}\right\}$ in a purely algebraic context; thus Saka was the first person to realize their combinatorial significance.

An interesting algorithm for listing set partitions was subsequently devised by Toshiaki Honda (see exercise 24). Further details about genji-ko and its relation to the history of mathematics can be found in Japanese articles by Tamaki Yano, *Sugaku Seminar* **34**, 11 (Nov. 1995), 58–61; **34**, 12 (Dec. 1995), 56–60.

Set partitions remained virtually unknown in Europe until much later, except for three isolated incidents. First, George and/or Richard Puttenham published *The Arte of English Poesie* in 1589, and pages 70–72 of that book contain diagrams similar to those of genji-ko. For example, the seven diagrams

(28)

were used to illustrate possible rhyme schemes for 5-line poems, "whereof some of them be harsher and unpleasaunter to the eare then other some be." But this visually appealing list was incomplete (see exercise 25).

Second, an unpublished manuscript of G. W. Leibniz from the late 1600s shows that he had tried to count the number of ways to partition $\{1, \ldots, n\}$ into three or four subsets, but with almost no success. He enumerated $\left\{{n \atop 2}\right\}$ by a very cumbersome method, which would not have led him to see readily that $\left\{{n \atop 2}\right\} = 2^{n-1} - 1$. He attempted to compute $\left\{{n \atop 3}\right\}$ and $\left\{{n \atop 4}\right\}$ only for $n \leq 5$, and made several numerical slips leading to incorrect answers. [See E. Knobloch, *Studia Leibnitiana Supplementa* **11** (1973), 229–233; **16** (1976), 316–321.]

The third European appearance of set partitions had a completely different character. John Wallis devoted the third chapter of his *Discourse of Combinations* (1685) to questions about "aliquot parts," the proper divisors of numbers, and in particular he studied the set of all ways to factorize a given integer. This question is equivalent to the study of *multiset* partitions; for example, the factorizations of $p^3 q^2 r$ are essentially the same as the partitions of $\{p, p, p, q, q, r\}$, when p, q, and r are prime numbers. Wallis devised an excellent algorithm for listing all factorizations of a given integer n, essentially anticipating Algorithm 7.2.1.5M (see exercise 28). But he didn't investigate the important special cases that arise when n is the power of a prime (equivalent to integer partitions) or when n is squarefree (equivalent to set partitions). Thus, although Wallis was able to solve the more general problem, its complexities paradoxically deflected him from discovering partition numbers, Bell numbers, or Stirling subset numbers, or from devising simple algorithms that would generate integer partitions or set partitions.

Integer partitions. Partitions of integers arrived on the scene even more slowly. We saw above that Bishop Wibold (c. 965) knew the partitions of n into exactly three parts ≤ 6. So did Galileo, who wrote a memo about them (c. 1627) and also studied their frequency of occurrence as rolls of three dice. ["Sopra le scoperte de i dadi," in Galileo's *Opere*, Volume 8, 591–594; he listed partitions in decreasing lexicographic order.] Thomas Harriot, in unpublished work a few years earlier, had considered up to six dice [see J. Stedall, *Historia Math.* **34** (2007), 398].

Mersenne listed the partitions of 9 into any number of parts, on page 130 of his *Traitez de la Voix et des Chants* (1636). With each partition $9 = a_1 + \cdots + a_k$ he also computed the multinomial coefficient $9!/(a_1! \ldots a_k!)$; as we've seen earlier, he was interested in counting various melodies, and he knew for example that there are $9!/(3!\,3!\,3!) = 1680$ melodies on the nine notes $\{a, a, a, b, b, b, c, c, c\}$. But he failed to mention the cases $8 + 1$ and $3 + 2 + 1 + 1 + 1 + 1$, probably because he hadn't listed the possibilities in any systematic way.

Leibniz considered two-part partitions in Problem 3 of his *Dissertatio de Arte Combinatoria* (1666), and his unpublished notes show that he subsequently

spent considerable time trying to enumerate the partitions that have three or
more summands. He called them "discerptions," or (less frequently) "divul-
sions" — in Latin of course — or sometimes "sections" or "dispersions" or even
"partitions." He was interested in them primarily because of their connection
with the monomial symmetric functions $\sum x_{i_1}^{a_1} x_{i_2}^{a_2} \dots$. But his many attempts
led to almost total failure, except in the case of three summands, when he almost
(but not quite) discovered the formula for $\left|{n \atop 3}\right|$ in exercise 7.2.1.4–31. For example,
he carelessly counted only 21 partitions of 8, forgetting the case $2+2+2+1+1$;
and he got only 26 for $p(9)$, after missing $3 + 2 + 2 + 2$, $3 + 2 + 2 + 1 + 1$,
$2 + 2 + 2 + 1 + 1 + 1$, and $2 + 2 + 1 + 1 + 1 + 1 + 1$ — in spite of the fact that
he was trying to list partitions systematically in decreasing lexicographic order.
[See E. Knobloch, *Studia Leibnitiana Supplementa* **11** (1973), 91–258; **16** (1976),
255–337; *Historia Mathematica* **1** (1974), 409–430.]

Abraham de Moivre had the first real success with partitions, in his paper
"A Method of Raising an infinite Multinomial to any given Power, or Extracting
any given Root of the same" [*Philosophical Transactions* **19** (1697), 619–625 and
Fig. 5]. He proved that the coefficient of z^{m+n} in $(az + bz^2 + cz^3 + \cdots)^m$ has
one term for each partition of n; for example, the coefficient of z^{m+6} is

$$\binom{m}{6} a^{m-6} b^6 + 5\binom{m}{5} a^{m-5} b^4 c + 4\binom{m}{4} a^{m-4} b^3 d + 6\binom{m}{4} a^{m-4} b^2 c^2$$
$$+ 3\binom{m}{3} a^{m-3} b^2 e + 6\binom{m}{3} a^{m-3} bcd + 2\binom{m}{2} a^{m-2} bf + \binom{m}{3} a^{m-3} c^3$$
$$+ 2\binom{m}{2} a^{m-2} ce + \binom{m}{2} a^{m-2} d^2 + \binom{m}{1} a^{m-1} g. \qquad (29)$$

If we set $a = 1$, the term with exponents $b^i c^j d^k e^l \dots$ corresponds to the partition
with i 1s, j 2s, k 3s, l 4s, etc. Thus, for example, when $n = 6$ he essentially
presented the partitions in the order

$$111111, \quad 11112, \quad 1113, \quad 1122, \quad 114, \quad 123, \quad 15, \quad 222, \quad 24, \quad 33, \quad 6. \qquad (30)$$

He explained how to list the partitions recursively, as follows (but in different
language related to his own notation): For $k = 1, 2, \dots, n$, start with k and
append the (previously listed) partitions of $n - k$ whose smallest part is $\geq k$.

> *[My solution] was ordered to be published in the Transactions,*
> *not so much as a matter relating to Play,*
> *but as containing some general Speculations*
> *not unworthy to be considered by the Lovers of Truth.*
> — ABRAHAM DE MOIVRE (1717)

P. R. de Montmort tabulated all partitions of numbers ≤ 9 into ≤ 6 parts
in his *Essay d'Analyse sur les Jeux de Hazard* (1708), in connection with dice
problems. His partitions were listed in a different order from (30); for example,

$$111111, \quad 21111, \quad 2211, \quad 222, \quad 3111, \quad 321, \quad 33, \quad 411, \quad 42, \quad 51, \quad 6. \qquad (31)$$

He probably was unaware of de Moivre's prior work.

So far almost none of the authors we've been discussing actually bothered
to describe the procedures by which they generated combinatorial patterns. We
can only infer their methods, or lack thereof, by studying the lists that they
actually published. Furthermore, in rare cases such as de Moivre's paper where a

tabulation method *was* explicitly described, the author assumed that all patterns for the first cases 1, 2, ..., $n - 1$ had been listed before it was time to tackle the case of order n. No method for generating patterns "on the fly," moving directly from one pattern to its successor without looking at auxiliary tables, was actually explained by any of the authors we have encountered, except for Kedāra and Nārāyaṇa. Today's computer programmers naturally prefer methods that are more direct and need little memory.

Roger Joseph Boscovich published the first direct algorithm for partition generation in *Giornale de' Letterati* (Rome, 1747), on pages 393–404 together with two foldout tables facing page 404. His method, which produces for $n = 6$ the respective outputs

$$111111, \ 11112, \ 1122, \ 222, \ 1113, \ 123, \ 33, \ 114, \ 24, \ 15, \ 6, \qquad (32)$$

generates partitions in precisely the reverse order from which they are visited by Algorithm 7.2.1.4P; and his method would indeed have been featured in Section 7.2.1.4, except for the fact that the reverse order turns out to be slightly easier and faster than the order that he had chosen.

Boscovich published sequels in *Giornale de' Letterati* (Rome, 1748), 12–27 and 84–99, extending his algorithm in two ways. First, he considered generating only partitions whose parts belong to a given set S, so that symbolic multinomials with sparse coefficients could be raised to the mth power. (He said that the gcd of all elements of S should be 1; in fact, however, his method could fail if $1 \notin S$.) Second, he introduced an algorithm for generating partitions of n into m parts, given m and n. Again he was unlucky: A slightly better way to do that task, Algorithm 7.2.1.4H, was found subsequently, diminishing his chances for fame.

Hindenburg's hype. The inventor of Algorithm 7.2.1.4H was Carl Friedrich Hindenburg, who also rediscovered Nārāyaṇa's Algorithm 7.2.1.2L, a winning technique for generating multiset permutations. Unfortunately, these small successes led him to believe that he had made revolutionary advances in mathematics — although he did condescend to remark that other people such as de Moivre, Euler, and Lambert had come close to making similar discoveries.

Hindenburg was a prototypical overachiever, extremely energetic if not inspired. He founded or cofounded Germany's first professional journals of mathematics (published 1786–1789 and 1794–1800), and contributed long articles to each. He served several times as academic dean at the University of Leipzig, where he was also the Rector in 1792. If he had been a better mathematician, German mathematics might well have flourished more in Leipzig than in Berlin or Göttingen.

But his first mathematical work, *Beschreibung einer ganz neuen Art, nach einem bekannten Gesetze fortgehende Zahlen durch Abzählen oder Abmessen bequem und sicher zu finden* (Leipzig: 1776), amply foreshadowed what was to come: His "ganz neue" (completely new) idea in that booklet was simply to give combinatorial significance to the digits of numbers written in decimal notation. Incredibly, he concluded his monograph with large foldout sheets that contained a table of the numbers 0000 through 9999 — followed by two other tables that listed the even numbers and odd numbers separately(!).

Hindenburg published letters from people who praised his work, and invited them to contribute to his journals. In 1796 he edited *Sammlung combinatorisch-analytischer Abhandlungen*, whose subtitle stated (in German) that de Moivre's multinomial theorem was "the most important proposition in all of mathematical analysis." About a dozen people joined forces to form what became known as Hindenburg's Combinatorial School, and they published thousands of pages filled with esoteric symbolism that must have impressed many nonmathematicians.

The work of this School was not completely trivial from the standpoint of computer science. For example, H. A. Rothe, who was Hindenburg's best student, noticed that there is a simple way to go from a Morse code sequence to its lexicographic successor or predecessor. Another student, J. K. Burckhardt, observed that Morse code sequences of length n could also be generated easily by first considering those with no dashes, then one dash, then two, etc. Their motivation was not to tabulate poetic meters of n beats, as it had been in India, but rather to list the terms of the continuant polynomials $K(x_1, x_2, \ldots, x_n)$, Eq. 4.5.3–(4). [See *Archiv der reinen und angewandten Mathematik* **1** (1794), 154–195.] Furthermore, on page 53 of Hindenburg's 1796 *Sammlung* cited above, G. S. Klügel introduced a way to list all permutations that has subsequently become known as Ord-Smith's algorithm; see Eqs. (23)–(26) in Section 7.2.1.2.

Hindenburg believed that his methods deserved equal time with algebra, geometry, and calculus in the standard curriculum. But he and his disciples were combinatorialists who only made combinatorial lists. Burying themselves in formulas and formalisms, they rarely discovered any new mathematics of real interest. Eugen Netto has admirably summarized their work in M. Cantor's *Geschichte der Mathematik* **4** (1908), 201–219: "For a while they controlled the German market; however, most of what they dug up soon sank into a not-entirely-deserved oblivion."

The sad outcome was that combinatorial studies in general got a bad name. Gösta Mittag-Leffler, who assembled a magnificent library of mathematical literature about 100 years after Hindenburg's death, decided to place all such work on a special shelf marked "Dekadenter." And this category still persists in the library of Sweden's Institut Mittag-Leffler today, even as that institute attracts world-class combinatorial mathematicians whose research is anything but decadent.

Looking on the bright side, we may note that at least one good book did emerge from all of this activity. Andreas von Ettingshausen's *Die combinatorische Analysis* (Vienna: 1826) is noteworthy as the first text to discuss combinatorial generation methods in a perspicuous way. He discussed the general principles of lexicographic generation in §8, and applied them to construct good ways to list all permutations (§11), combinations (§30), and partitions (§41–§44).

Where were the trees? We've now seen that lists of tuples, permutations, combinations, and partitions were compiled rather early in human history, by interested and interesting researchers. Thus we've accounted for the evolution of the topics studied in Sections 7.2.1.1 through 7.2.1.5, and our story will be complete if we can trace the origins of tree generation, Section 7.2.1.6.

But the historical record of that topic before the advent of computers is virtually a blank page, with the exception of a few 19th-century papers by Arthur Cayley. Cayley's major work on trees, originally published in 1875 and reprinted on pages 427–460 of his *Collected Mathematical Papers*, Volume 4, was climaxed by a large foldout illustration that exhibited all the free trees with 9 or fewer unlabeled vertices. Earlier in that paper he had also illustrated the nine *oriented* trees with 5 vertices. The methods he used to produce those lists were quite complicated, completely different from Algorithm 7.2.1.6O and exercise 7.2.1.6–90. All free trees with up to 10 vertices were listed many years later by F. Harary and G. Prins [*Acta Math.* **101** (1958), 158–162], who also went up to $n = 12$ in the cases of free trees with no nodes of degree 2 or with no symmetries.

The trees most dearly beloved by computer scientists — binary trees or the equivalent ordered forests or nested parentheses — are however strangely absent from the literature. We saw in Section 2.3.4.5 that many mathematicians of the 1700s and 1800s had learned how to count binary trees, and we also know that the Catalan numbers C_n enumerate dozens of different kinds of combinatorial objects. Yet nobody seems to have published an actual *list* of the $C_4 = 14$ objects of order 4 in *any* of these guises, much less the $C_5 = 42$ objects of order 5, before 1950. (Except indirectly: The 42 genji-ko diagrams in (25) that have no intersecting lines turn out to be equivalent to the 5-node binary trees and forests. But this fact was not learned until the 20th century.)

There are a few isolated instances where authors of yore did prepare lists of $C_3 = 5$ Catalan-related objects. Cayley, again, was first; he illustrated the binary trees with 3 internal nodes and 4 leaves as follows in *Philosophical Magazine* **18** (1859), 374–378:

$$\text{\Large 🜸🜸🜸🜸🜸} \tag{33}$$

(That same paper also illustrated another species of tree, equivalent to so-called weak orderings.) Then, in 1901, E. Netto listed the five ways to insert parentheses into the expression '$a + b + c + d$':

$$(a+b)+(c+d), \quad [(a+b)+c]+d, \quad [a+(b+c)]+d, \quad a+[(b+c)+d], \quad a+[b+(c+d)]. \tag{34}$$

[*Lehrbuch der Combinatorik*, §122.] And the five permutations of $\{+1, +1, +1, -1, -1, -1\}$ whose partial sums are nonnegative were listed in the following way by Paul Erdős and Irving Kaplansky [*Scripta Math.* **12** (1946), 73–75]:

$$1+1+1-1-1-1, \quad 1+1-1+1-1-1, \quad 1+1-1-1+1-1,$$
$$1-1+1+1-1-1, \quad 1-1+1-1+1-1. \tag{35}$$

Even though only five objects are involved, we can see that the orderings in (33) and (34) were basically catch-as-catch-can; only (35), which matches Algorithm 7.2.1.6P, was systematic and lexicographic.

We should also note briefly the work of Walther von Dyck, since many recent papers use the term "Dyck words" to refer to strings of nested parentheses. Dyck was an educator known for co-founding the Deutsches Museum in Munich, among other things. He wrote two pioneering papers about the theory of free groups [*Math. Annalen* **20** (1882), 1–44; **22** (1883), 70–108]. Yet the so-called Dyck words have at best a tenuous connection to his actual research: He studied the words on $\{x_1, x_1^{-1}, \ldots, x_k, x_k^{-1}\}$ that reduce to the empty string after repeatedly erasing adjacent letter-pairs of the forms $x_i x_i^{-1}$ or $x_i^{-1} x_i$; the connection with parentheses and trees arises only when we limit erasures to the first case, $x_i x_i^{-1}$.

Thus we may conclude that, although an explosion of interest in binary trees and their cousins occurred after 1950, such trees represent the only aspect of our story whose historical roots are rather shallow.

After 1950. Of course the arrival of electronic computers changed everything. The first computer-oriented publication about combinatorial generation methods was a note by C. B. Tompkins, "Machine attacks on problems whose variables are permutations" [*Proc. Symp. Applied Math.* **6** (1956), 202–205]. Thousands more were destined to follow.

Several articles by D. H. Lehmer, especially his "Teaching combinatorial tricks to a computer" in *Proc. Symp. Applied Math.* **10** (1960), 179–193, proved to be extremely influential in the early days. [See also *Proc. 1957 Canadian Math. Congress* (1959), 160–173; *Proc. IBM Scientific Computing Symposium on Combinatorial Problems* (1964), 23–30; and Chapter 1 of *Applied Combinatorial Mathematics*, edited by E. F. Beckenbach (Wiley, 1964), 5–31.] Lehmer represented an important link to previous generations. For example, Stanford's library records show that he had checked out Netto's *Lehrbuch der Combinatorik* in January of 1932.

The main publications relevant to particular algorithms that we've studied have already been cited in previous sections, so there is no need to repeat them here. But textbooks and monographs that first put pieces of the subject together in a coherent framework were also of great importance. Three books, in particular, were especially noteworthy with respect to establishing general principles:

- *Elements of Combinatorial Computing* by Mark B. Wells (Pergamon Press, 1971), especially Chapter 5.

- *Combinatorial Algorithms* by Albert Nijenhuis and Herbert S. Wilf (Academic Press, 1975). A second edition was published in 1978, containing additional material, and Wilf subsequently wrote *Combinatorial Algorithms: An Update* (Philadelphia: SIAM, 1989).

- *Combinatorial Algorithms: Theory and Practice* by Edward M. Reingold, Jurg Nievergelt, and Narsingh Deo (Prentice–Hall, 1977), especially the material in Chapter 5.

Robert Sedgewick compiled the first extensive survey of permutation generation methods in *Computing Surveys* **9** (1977), 137–164, 314. Carla Savage's survey article about Gray codes in *SIAM Review* **39** (1997), 605–629, was another milestone.

We noted above that algorithms to generate Catalan-counted objects were not invented until computer programmers developed an appetite for them. The first such algorithms to be published were not cited in Section 7.2.1.6 because they have been superseded by better techniques; but it is appropriate to list them here. First, H. I. Scoins gave two recursive algorithms for ordered tree generation, in the same paper we have cited with respect to the generation of *oriented* trees [*Machine Intelligence* **3** (1968), 43–60]. His algorithms dealt with binary trees represented as bit strings that were essentially equivalent to Polish prefix notation or to nested parentheses. Then Mark Wells, in Section 5.5.4 of his book cited above, generated binary trees by representing them as noncrossing set partitions. And Gary Knott [*CACM* **20** (1977), 113–115] gave recursive ranking and unranking algorithms for binary trees, representing them via the inorder-to-preorder permutations $q_1 \dots q_n$ of Table 7.2.1.6–3.

Algorithms to generate all spanning trees of a given graph have been published by numerous authors ever since the 1950s, motivated originally by the study of electrical networks. Among the earliest such papers were works of N. Nakagawa, *IRE Trans.* **CT-5** (1958), 122–127; W. Mayeda, *IRE Trans.* **CT-6** (1959), 136–137, 394; H. Watanabe, *IRE Trans.* **CT-7** (1960), 296–302; S. Hakimi, *J. Franklin Institute* **272** (1961), 347–359.

A recent introduction to the entire subject can be found in Chapters 2 and 3 of *Combinatorial Algorithms: Generation, Enumeration, and Search* by Donald L. Kreher and Douglas R. Stinson (CRC Press, 1999).

Frank Ruskey is preparing a book entitled *Combinatorial Generation* that will contain a thorough treatment and a comprehensive bibliography. He has made working drafts of several chapters available on the Internet.

EXERCISES

Many of the exercises below ask a modern reader to find and/or to correct errors in the literature of bygone days. The point is not to gloat over how smart we are in the 21st century; the point is rather to understand that even the pioneers of a subject can stumble. One good way to learn that a set of ideas is not really as simple as it might seem to today's computer scientists and mathematicians is to observe that some of the world's leading thinkers had to struggle with the concepts when they were new.

   1. [*15*] Does the notion of "computing" arise in the *I Ching*?

▶ **2.** [*M30*] (*The genetic code.*) DNA molecules are strings of "nucleotides" on the 4-letter alphabet $\{T, C, A, G\}$, and most protein molecules are strings of "amino acids" on the 20-letter alphabet $\{A, C, D, E, F, G, H, I, K, L, M, N, P, Q, R, S, T, V, W, Y\}$. Three consecutive nucleotides xyz form a "codon," and a strand $x_1 y_1 z_1 x_2 y_2 z_2 \dots$ of DNA specifies the protein $f(x_1, y_1, z_1) f(x_2, y_2, z_2) \dots$, where $f(x, y, z)$ is the element in row z and column y of matrix x in the array

$$\begin{pmatrix} F & S & Y & C \\ F & S & Y & C \\ L & S & - & - \\ L & S & - & W \end{pmatrix} \begin{pmatrix} L & P & H & R \\ L & P & H & R \\ L & P & Q & R \\ L & P & Q & R \end{pmatrix} \begin{pmatrix} I & T & N & S \\ I & T & N & S \\ I & T & K & R \\ M & T & K & R \end{pmatrix} \begin{pmatrix} V & A & D & G \\ V & A & D & G \\ V & A & E & G \\ V & A & E & G \end{pmatrix}.$$

(Here $(T, C, A, G) = (1, 2, 3, 4)$; for example, $f(\texttt{CAT})$ is the element in row 1 and column 3 of matrix 2, namely H.) Encoding proceeds until a codon leads to the stopper '$-$'.

a) Show that there is a simple way to map each codon into a hexagram of the *I Ching*, with the property that the 21 possible outcomes $\{A, C, D, \ldots, W, Y, -\}$ correspond to 21 *consecutive* hexagrams of the King Wen ordering (1).

b) Is that a sensational discovery?

3. [*20*] What is the millionth meter that has 30 beats, in colex ordering analogous to (2)? What is the rank of ⏑⏑⏑—⏑——⏑⏑⏑⏑——⏑⏑⏑⏑⏑⏑—⏑—?

4. [*19*] Analyze the imperfections of Donnolo's list of permutations in Table 1.

5. [*16*] What's wrong with Kircher's list of five-note permutations in (7)?

6. [*25*] Mersenne published a table of the first 64 factorials on pages 108–110 of his *Traitez de la Voix et des Chants* (1636). His value for 64! was $\approx 2.2 \times 10^{89}$; but it should have been $\approx 1.3 \times 10^{89}$. Find a copy of his book and try to figure out where he erred.

7. [*20*] What permutations of $\{1, 2, 3, 4, 5\}$ are "alive" and "dead" according to Seki's rules (8) and (9)?

▶ **8.** [*M27*] Make a patch to (9) so that Seki's procedure will be correct.

9. [*15*] From (11), deduce the Arabic way to write the Arabic numerals $(0, 1, \ldots, 9)$.

▶ **10.** [*HM27*] In Ludus Clericalis, what is the expected number of times the three dice are rolled before all possible virtues are acquired?

11. [*21*] Decipher Llull's vertical table at the right of Fig. 65. What 20 combinatorial objects does it represent? *Hint:* Don't be misled by typographic errors.

12. [*M20*] Relate Schillinger's universal cycle (13) to the universal cycle of Poinsot in exercise 7.2.1.3–106.

13. [*21*] What should van Schooten have written, instead of (17)? Give also the corresponding tableau for combinations of the multiset $\{a, a, a, b, b, c\}$.

▶ **14.** [*20*] Complete the following sequence, from §95 of Izquierdo's *De Combinatione*:

ABC ABD ABE ACD ACE ACB ADE ADB ADC AEB ....

15. [*15*] If all n-combinations $x_1 \ldots x_n$ of $\{1, \ldots, m\}$ with repetition are listed in lexicographic order, with $x_1 \leq \cdots \leq x_n$, how many of them begin with the number j?

16. [*20*] (Nārāyaṇa Paṇḍita, 1356.) Design an algorithm to generate all compositions of n into parts $\leq q$, namely all ordered partitions $n = a_1 + \cdots + a_t$, where $1 \leq a_j \leq q$ for $1 \leq j \leq t$ and t is arbitrary. Illustrate your method when $n = 7$ and $q = 3$.

17. [*HM27*] Analyze the algorithm of exercise 16.

18. [*10*] Trick question: Leibniz published his *Dissertatio de Arte Combinatoria* in 1666. Why was that a particularly auspicious year, permutationwise?

19. [*17*] In which of Puteanus's verses (20) is 'tibi' treated as ⏑— instead of ⏑⏑?

20. [*M25*] To commemorate the visit of three illustrious noblemen to Dresden in 1617, a poet published 1617 permutations of the hexameter verse

Dant tria jam Dresdæ, ceu sol dat, lumina lucem.

"Three give now to Dresden, as the sun gives, lights to light." [Gregor Kleppis, *Proteus Poeticus* (Leipzig: 1617).] How many permutations of those words would actually scan properly? *Hint:* The verse has dactyls in the first and fifth feet, spondees elsewhere.

21. [*HM30*] Let $f(p, q, r; s, t)$ be the number of ways to make (o^p, o^q, o^r) by concatenating the strings $\{s \cdot o, t \cdot oo\}$, when $p + q + r = s + 2t$. For example, $f(2, 3, 2; 3, 2) = 5$ because the five ways are

$$(o|o, o|oo, oo), \quad (o|o, oo|o, oo), \quad (oo, o|o|o, oo), \quad (oo, o|oo, o|o), \quad (oo, oo|o, o|o).$$

a) Show that $f(p, q, r; s, t) = [u^p v^q w^r z^s] 1/((1 - zu - u^2)(1 - zv - v^2)(1 - zw - w^2))$.
b) Use the function f to enumerate the scannable permutations of (19), subject to the additional condition that the fifth foot doesn't begin in the middle of a word.
c) Now enumerate the remaining cases.

▸ **22.** [*M40*] Look up the original discussions of the tot-tibi problem that were published by Prestet, Wallis, Whitworth, and Hartley. What errors did they make?

23. [*20*] What order of the 52 genji-ko diagrams corresponds to Algorithm 7.2.1.5H?

▸ **24.** [*23*] Early in the 1800s, Toshiaki Honda gave a recursive rule for generating all partitions of $\{1, \ldots, n\}$. His algorithm produced them in the following order when $n = 4$:

Can you guess the corresponding order for $n = 5$? *Hint:* See (26).

25. [*15*] The 16th-century author of *The Arte of English Poesie* was interested only in rhyme schemes that are "complete" in the sense of exercise 7.2.1.5–35; in other words, every line should rhyme with at least one other. Furthermore, the scheme should be "indecomposable" in the sense of exercise 7.2.1.2–100: A partition like $12|345$ decomposes into a 2-line poem followed by a 3-line poem. And the scheme shouldn't consist trivially of lines that all rhyme with each other. Under these conditions, is (28) a complete list of 5-line rhyme schemes?

▸ **26.** [*HM25*] How many n-line rhyme schemes satisfy the constraints of exercise 25?

▸ **27.** [*HM31*] The set partition $14|25|36$ can be represented by a genji-ko diagram such as ; but every such diagram for this partition must have at least three places where lines cross, and crossings are sometimes considered undesirable. How many partitions of $\{1, \ldots, n\}$ have a genji-ko diagram in which the lines cross at most once?

▸ **28.** [*25*] Let a, b, and c be prime numbers. John Wallis listed all possible factorizations of $a^3 b^2 c$ as follows: $cbbaaa$, $cbbaa \cdot a$, $cbaaa \cdot b$, $bbaaa \cdot c$, $cbba \cdot aa$, $cbba \cdot a \cdot a$, $cbaa \cdot ba$, $cbaa \cdot b \cdot a$, $bbaa \cdot ca$, $bbaa \cdot c \cdot a$, $caaa \cdot bb$, $caaa \cdot b \cdot b$, $baaa \cdot cb$, $baaa \cdot c \cdot b$, $cbb \cdot aaa$, $cbb \cdot aa \cdot a$, $cbb \cdot a \cdot a \cdot a$, $cba \cdot baa$, $cba \cdot ba \cdot a$, $cba \cdot aa \cdot b$, $cba \cdot b \cdot a \cdot a$, $bba \cdot caa$, $bba \cdot ca \cdot a$, $bba \cdot aa \cdot c$, $bba \cdot c \cdot a \cdot a$, $caa \cdot bb \cdot a$, $caa \cdot ba \cdot b$, $caa \cdot b \cdot b \cdot a$, $baa \cdot cb \cdot a$, $baa \cdot ca \cdot b$, $baa \cdot ba \cdot c$, $baa \cdot c \cdot b \cdot a$, $aaa \cdot cb \cdot b$, $aaa \cdot bb \cdot c$, $aaa \cdot c \cdot b \cdot b$, $cb \cdot ba \cdot aa$, $cb \cdot ba \cdot a \cdot a$, $cb \cdot aa \cdot b \cdot a$, $cb \cdot b \cdot a \cdot a \cdot a$, $bb \cdot ca \cdot aa$, $bb \cdot ca \cdot a \cdot a$, $bb \cdot aa \cdot c \cdot a$, $bb \cdot c \cdot a \cdot a \cdot a$, $ca \cdot ba \cdot ba$, $ca \cdot ba \cdot b \cdot a$, $ca \cdot aa \cdot b \cdot b$, $ca \cdot b \cdot b \cdot a \cdot a$, $ba \cdot ba \cdot c \cdot a$, $ba \cdot aa \cdot c \cdot b$, $ba \cdot c \cdot b \cdot a \cdot a$, $aa \cdot c \cdot b \cdot b \cdot a$, $c \cdot b \cdot b \cdot a \cdot a \cdot a$. What algorithm did he use to generate them in this order?

▸ **29.** [*24*] In what order would Wallis have generated all factorizations of the number $abcde = 5 \cdot 7 \cdot 11 \cdot 13 \cdot 17$? Give your answer as a sequence of genji-ko diagrams.

30. [*M20*] What is the coefficient of $a_1^{i_1} a_2^{i_2} \ldots z^{m+n}$ in $(a_0 z + a_1 z^2 + a_2 z^3 + \cdots)^m$? (See (29).)

31. [*20*] Compare de Moivre's and de Montmort's orders for partitions, (30) and (31), with Algorithm 7.2.1.4P.

32. [*21*] (R. J. Boscovich, 1748.) List all partitions of 20 for which all parts are 1, 7, or 10. Also design an algorithm that lists all such partitions of any given integer $n > 0$.

ANSWERS TO EXERCISES

Answer not a fool according to his folly,
lest thou also be like unto him.

— Proverbs 26:4

NOTES ON THE EXERCISES

1. A moderately easy problem for a mathematically inclined reader.

2. The author will reward you if you are first to report an error in the statement of an exercise or in its answer, assuming that he or she is suitably sagacious.

3. See H. Poincaré, *Rendiconti Circ. Mat. Palermo* **18** (1904), 45–110; R. H. Bing, *Annals of Math.* (2) **68** (1958), 17–37; G. Perelman, arXiv:math.DG/0211159, 0303109, 0307245.

SECTION 7

1. Following the hint, we'll want the second '$4m-4$' to be immediately followed by the first '$2m-1$'. The desired arrangements can be deduced from the first four examples, given in hexadecimal notation: 231213, 46171435623725, 86a31b1368597a425b2479, ca8e531f1358ac7db9e6427f2469bd. [R. O. Davies, *Math. Gazette* **43** (1959), 253–255.]

2. Such arrangements exist if and only if $n \bmod 4 = 0$ or 1. This condition is necessary because there must be an even number of odd items. And it is sufficient because we can place '00' in front of the solutions in the previous exercise.

Notes: This question was first raised by Marshall Hall in 1951, and solved the following year by F. T. Leahy, Jr., in unpublished work [Armed Forces Security Agency report 343 (28 January 1952)]. It was independently posed and resolved by T. Skolem and T. Bang, *Math. Scandinavica* **5** (1957), 57–58. For other intervals of numbers, see the complete solution by J. E. Simpson, *Discrete Math.* **44** (1983), 97–104.

3. Yes. For example, the cycle (0072362435714165) can't be broken up.

4. The kth occurrence of b is in position $\lfloor k\phi \rfloor$ from the left, and the kth occurrence of a is in position $\lfloor k\phi^2 \rfloor$. Clearly $\lfloor k\phi^2 \rfloor - \lfloor k\phi \rfloor = k$, because $\phi^2 = \phi + 1$. (The integers $\lfloor k\phi \rfloor$ form the "spectrum" of ϕ; see exercise 3.13 of *CMath*.)

5. $2n - k - 1$ of the $\binom{2n}{2}$ equally likely pairs of positions satisfy the stated condition. If these probabilities were independent (but they aren't), the value of $2L_n$ would be

$$\binom{2n}{2, 2, \ldots, 2} \prod_{k=1}^{n} ((2n - 1 - k)/\binom{2n}{2})) = \frac{(2n)!^2 n(n-1)}{n!\,(2n)^{n+1}(2n-1)^{n+1}}$$

$$= \exp\left(n \ln \frac{4n}{e^3} + \ln \sqrt{\frac{\pi e n}{2}} + O(n^{-1}) \right).$$

514

6. (a) When the products are expanded, we obtain a polynomial of $(2n-2)!/(n-2)!$ terms, each of degree $4n$. There's a term $x_1^2 \ldots x_{2n}^2$ for each Langford pairing; every other term has at least one variable of degree 1. Summing over $x_1, \ldots, x_{2n} \in \{-1, +1\}$ therefore cancels out all the bad terms, but gives 2^{2n} for the good terms. An extra factor of 2 arises because there are $2L_n$ Langford pairings (including left-right reversals).

(b) Let $f_k = \sum_{j=1}^{2n-k-1} x_j x_{j+k+1}$ be the main part of the kth factor. We can run through all 4^n cases $x_1, \ldots, x_{2n} \in \{-1, +1\}$ in Gray-code order (Algorithm 7.2.1.1L), negating only one of the x_j each time. A change in x_j causes at most two adjustments to each f_k; so each Gray-code step costs $O(n)$.

We needn't compute the sum exactly; it suffices to work mod 2^N, where 2^N comfortably exceeds $2^{2n+1}L_n$. Even better, when $n = 24$, would be to do the computations mod $2^{60} - 1$, or mod both $2^{30} - 1$ and $2^{30} + 1$. One can also save $\lceil n/2 \rceil$ bits of precision by exploiting the fact that $f_k \equiv k + 1$ (modulo 2).

(c) The third equality is actually valid only when $n \bmod 4 = 0$ or 3; but those are the interesting n's. The sum can be carried out in n phases, where phase p for $p < n$ involves the cases where $x_{n-1} = x_{n+2}$, $x_{n-2} = x_{n+3}$, $\ldots$, $x_{n-p+1} = x_{n+p}$, $x_{n-p} = x_n = x_{n+1} = +1$, and $x_{n+p+1} = -1$; it has an outer loop that chooses $(x_{n-p+1}, \ldots, x_{n-1})$ in all 2^{p-1} ways, and an inner loop that chooses $(x_1, \ldots, x_{n-p-1}, x_{n+p+2}, \ldots, x_{2n})$ in all $2^{2n-2p-2}$ ways. (The inner loop uses Gray binary code, preferably with "organ-pipe order" to prioritize the subscripts so that x_1 and x_{2n} vary most rapidly. The outer loop need not be especially efficient.) Phase n covers the 2^{n-1} palindromic cases with $x_j = x_{2n+1-j}$ for $1 \le j < n$ and $x_n = x_{n+1} = +1$. If s_p denotes the sum in phase p, then $s_1 + \cdots + s_{n-1} + \frac{1}{2}s_n = 2^{2n-2}L_n$.

A substantial fraction of the terms turn out be zero. For example, when $n = 16$, zeros appear about 76% of the time (in 408,838,754 cases out of $2^{29} + 2^{14}$). This fact can be used to avoid many multiplications in the inner loop. (Only f_1, f_3, $\ldots$ can be zero.)

7. Let d_k be the number of incomplete pairs after k characters have been read; thus $d_0 = d_{2n} = 0$, and $d_k = d_{k-1} \pm 1$ for $1 \le k \le 2n$. The largest such sequence in which d_k never exceeds 6 is $(d_0, d_1, \ldots, d_{2n}) = (0, 1, 2, 3, 4, 5, 6, 5, 6, \ldots, 5, 6, 5, 4, 3, 2, 1, 0)$, which has $\sum_{k=1}^{2n} d_k = 11n - 30$. But $\sum_{k=1}^{2n} d_k = \sum_{k=1}^{n}(k+1) = \binom{n+1}{2} + n$ in any Langford pairing. Hence $\binom{n+1}{2} + n \le 11n - 30$, and $n \le 15$. (In fact, width 6 is also impossible when $n = 15$. The largest and smallest possible width are unknown in general.)

8. There are no solutions when $n = 4$ or $n = 7$. When $n = 8$ there are four:

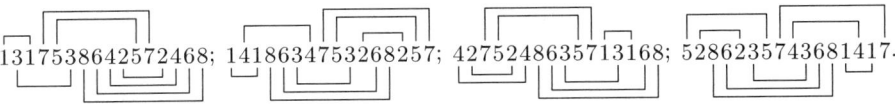

1317538642572468; 1418634753268257; 4275248635713168; 5286235743681417.

(This problem makes a pleasant mechanical puzzle, using gadgets of width $k + 1$ and height $\lceil k/2 \rceil$ for piece k. In his original note [*Math. Gazette* **42** (1958), 228], C. Dudley Langford illustrated similar pieces, and exhibited a planar solution for $n = 12$. The question can be cast as an exact cover problem, with nonprimary columns representing places where two gadgets are not allowed to intersect; see exercise 7.2.2.1–00. Jean Brette has devised a somewhat similar puzzle, based on Skolem's variant of the problem and using width instead of planarity; he gave a copy to David Singmaster in 1992.)

9. Just three ways: 18191526727285296475384639743, 19121824627945863475396835 7, 19161825726925847635493874 3 (and their reversals). [First found in 1969 by G. Baron; see *Combinatorial Theory and Its Applications* (Budapest: 1970), 81–92. The "dancing links" method of Section 7.2.2.1 resolves this question by traversing a search tree that has only 360 nodes, given an exact cover problem with 132 rows.]

10. For example, let $A = 12$, $K = 8$, $Q = 4$, $J = 0$, $\spadesuit = 4$, $\heartsuit = 3$, $\diamondsuit = 2$, $\clubsuit = 1$; add.

[In this connection, orthogonal latin squares equivalent to Fig. 1 were implicitly present already in medieval Islamic talismans illustrated by Ibn al-Hajj in his *Kitab Shumus al-Anwar* (Cairo: 1322); he also gave a 5×5 example. See E. Doutté, *Magie et Religion dans l'Afrique du Nord* (Algiers: 1909), 193–194, 214, 247; W. Ahrens, *Der Islam* **7** (1917), 228–238. See also an article on the history of latin squares being prepared by Lars D. Andersen.]

11. $\begin{pmatrix} d\gamma\aleph & a\delta\beth & b\beta\gimel & c\alpha\daleth \\ c\beta\gimel & b\alpha\aleph & a\gamma\daleth & d\delta\beth \\ a\alpha\beth & d\beta\daleth & c\delta\aleph & b\gamma\gimel \\ b\delta\daleth & c\gamma\gimel & d\alpha\beth & a\beta\aleph \end{pmatrix}$. [Joseph Sauveur presented the earliest known example of such squares in *Mémoires de l'Académie Royale des Sciences* (Paris, 1710), 92–138, §83.]

12. If n is odd, we can let $M_{ij} = (i - j) \bmod n$. But if n is even, there are no transversals: For if $\{(t_0 + 0) \bmod n, \ldots, (t_{n-1} + n - 1) \bmod n\}$ is a transversal, we have $\sum_{k=0}^{n-1} t_k \equiv \sum_{k=0}^{n-1} (t_k + k)$ (modulo n), hence $\sum_{k=0}^{n-1} k = \frac{1}{2}n(n-1)$ is a multiple of n.

13. Replace each element l by $\lfloor l/5 \rfloor$ to get a matrix of 0s and 1s. Let the four quarters be named $\left(\begin{smallmatrix} A & B \\ C & D \end{smallmatrix}\right)$; then A and D each contain exactly k 1s, while B and C each contain exactly k 0s. Suppose the original matrix has ten disjoint transversals. If $k \le 2$, at most four of them go through a 1 in A or D, and at most four go through a 0 in B or C. Thus at least two of them hit only 0s in A and D, only 1s in B and C. But such a transversal has an even number of 0s (not five), because it intersects A and D equally often.

Similarly, a latin square of order $4m + 2$ with an orthogonal mate must have more than m intruders in each of its $(2m + 1) \times (2m + 1)$ submatrices, under all renamings of the elements. [H. B. Mann, *Bull. Amer. Math. Soc.* (2) **50** (1944), 249–257.]

14. Cases (b) and (d) have no mates. Cases (a), (c), and (e) have respectively 2, 6, and 12265168(!), of which the lexicographically first and last are

(a)	(a)	(c)	(c)	(e)	(e)
0456987213	0691534782	0362498571	0986271435	0214365897	0987645321
1305629847	1308257964	1408327695	1354068792	1025973468	1795402638
2043798165	2169340578	2673519408	2741853960	2690587143	2506913874
3289176504	3250879416	3521970846	3572690814	3857694201	3154067289
4518263790	4587902631	4890253167	4630789251	4168730925	4231850967
5167432089	5412763890	5736841920	5218947306	5473829016	5348276190
6894015372	6945081327	6259784013	6095324178	6942158730	6820394715
7920341658	7836425109	7915602384	7869512043	7309216584	7069128543
8731504926	8723196045	8147036259	8407136529	8531402679	8412739056
9672850431	9074618253	9084165732	9123405687	9786041352	9673581402

Notes: Squares (a), (b), (c), and (d) were obtained from the decimal digits of π, e, γ, and ϕ, by discarding each digit that is inconsistent with a completed latin square. Although they aren't truly random, they're probably typical of 10×10 latin squares in general, roughly half of which appear to have orthogonal mates. Parker constructed square (e) in order to obtain an unusually large number of transversals; it has 5504 of them. (Euler had studied a similar example of order 6, therefore "just missing" the discovery of a 10×10 pair.)

15. Parker was dismayed to discover that none of the mates of square 14(e) are orthogonal to each other. With J. W. Brown and A. S. Hedayat [*J. Combinatorics, Inf. and System Sci.* **18** (1993), 113–115], he later found two 10×10s that have four disjoint common transversals (but not ten). [See also B. Ganter, R. Mathon, and A. Rosa,

Congressus Numerantium **20** (1978), 383–398; **22** (1979), 181–204.] While pursuing an idea of L. Weisner [*Canadian Math. Bull.* **6** (1963), 61–63], the author accidentally noticed some squares that come even closer to a mutually orthogonal trio: The square below is orthogonal to its transpose; and it has five diagonally symmetric transversals, in cells $(0, p_0)$, ..., $(9, p_9)$ for $p_0 \ldots p_9 = $ 0132674598, 2301457689, 3210896745, 4897065312, and 6528410937, which are *almost* disjoint: They cover 49 cells.

$$
L = \begin{pmatrix}
0234567891 \\
3192708546 \\
6528139407 \\
8753241960 \\
1689473025 \\
4970852613 \\
5047986132 \\
9416320758 \\
7361095284 \\
2805614379
\end{pmatrix}
\perp
\begin{pmatrix}
0368145972 \\
2157690438 \\
3925874160 \\
4283907615 \\
5712489306 \\
6034758291 \\
7891326054 \\
8549061723 \\
9406213587 \\
1670532849
\end{pmatrix}
= L^T.
$$

Extensive computations by B. D. McKay, A. Meynert, and W. Myrvold [*J. Comb. Designs* **15** (2007), 98–119] prove that no 10×10 latin square with nontrivial symmetry has two mates orthogonal to each other. Three mutually orthogonal latin squares are known to exist for all orders $n > 10$ [see S. M. P. Wang and R. M. Wilson, *Congressus Numerantium* **21** (1978), 688; D. T. Todorov, *Ars Combinatoria* **20** (1985), 45–47].

16. See R. A. Brualdi and H. J. Ryser, *Combinatorial Matrix Theory* (Cambridge University Press, 1991), §8.2.

17. (a) Let there be $3n$ columns r_j, c_j, v_j for $0 \le j < n$, and n^2 rows; row (i, j) has 1 in columns r_i, c_j, and v_l, where $l = L_{ij}$, for $0 \le i, j < n$.

(b) Let there be $4n^2$ columns r_{ij}, c_{ij}, x_{ij}, y_{ij} for $0 \le i, j < n$, and $n^3 - n^2 + n$ rows; row (i, j, k) has 1 in columns r_{ik}, c_{jk}, x_{ij}, and y_{lk}, where $l = L_{ij}$, for $0 \le i, j, k < n$ and ($i = k$ or $j > 0$).

18. Given an orthogonal array A with rows A_i for $1 \le i \le m$, define latin square $L_i = (L_{ijk})$ for $1 \le i \le m - 2$ by setting $L_{ijk} = A_{iq}$ when $A_{(m-1)q} = j$ and $A_{mq} = k$, for $0 \le j, k < n$. (The value of q is uniquely determined by the values of j and k.) Permuting the columns of the array does not change the corresponding latin squares.

This construction can also be reversed, to produce orthogonal arrays of order n from mutually orthogonal latin squares of order n. In exercise 11, for example, we can let $a = \alpha = \aleph = 0$, $b = \beta = \beth = 1$, $c = \gamma = \gimel = 2$, and $d = \delta = \daleth = 3$, obtaining

$$
A = \begin{pmatrix}
3012210303211230 \\
2310102301323201 \\
0123103223013210 \\
0000111122223333 \\
0123012301230123
\end{pmatrix}.
$$

(The concept of an orthogonal array is mathematically "cleaner" than the concept of orthogonal latin squares, because it accounts better for the underlying symmetries. Notice, for example, that an $n \times n$ matrix L with entries in $\{1, 2, \ldots, n\}$ is a latin square if and only if it is orthogonal to two particular non-latin squares, namely

$$
L \perp \begin{pmatrix}
1 & 1 & \cdots & 1 \\
2 & 2 & \cdots & 2 \\
\vdots & \vdots & \ddots & \vdots \\
n & n & \cdots & n
\end{pmatrix}
\quad \text{and} \quad
L \perp \begin{pmatrix}
1 & 2 & \cdots & n \\
1 & 2 & \cdots & n \\
\vdots & \vdots & \ddots & \vdots \\
1 & 2 & \cdots & n
\end{pmatrix}.
$$

Therefore Latin squares, Græco-Latin squares, Hebraic-Græco-Latin squares, etc., are equivalent to orthogonal arrays of depth 3, 4, 5, ... Moreover, the orthogonal arrays considered here are merely the special case $t = 2$ and $\lambda = 1$ of a more general concept of n-ary $m \times \lambda n^t$ arrays having "strength t" and "index λ," introduced by C. R. Rao in *Proc. Edinburgh Math. Soc.* **8** (1949), 119–125; see the book *Orthogonal Arrays* by A. S. Hedayat, N. J. A. Sloane, and J. Stufken (Springer, 1999).)

19. We can rearrange the columns so that the first row is $0^n 1^n \ldots (n-1)^n$. Then we can renumber the elements of the other rows so that they begin with $01 \ldots (n-1)$. The elements in each remaining column must then be distinct, in all rows but the first.

To achieve the upper bound when $n = p$, let each column be indexed by two numbers x and y, where $0 \le x, y < p$, and put the numbers y, x, $(x + y) \bmod p$, $(x + 2y) \bmod p$, ..., $(x + (p-1)y) \bmod p$ into that column. For example, when $p = 5$ we get the following orthogonal array, equivalent to four mutually orthogonal latin squares:

$$
\begin{pmatrix}
0\,0\,0\,0\,0\,1\,1\,1\,1\,1\,2\,2\,2\,2\,2\,3\,3\,3\,3\,3\,4\,4\,4\,4\,4 \\
0\,1\,2\,3\,4\,0\,1\,2\,3\,4\,0\,1\,2\,3\,4\,0\,1\,2\,3\,4\,0\,1\,2\,3\,4 \\
0\,1\,2\,3\,4\,1\,2\,3\,4\,0\,2\,3\,4\,0\,1\,3\,4\,0\,1\,2\,4\,0\,1\,2\,3 \\
0\,1\,2\,3\,4\,2\,3\,4\,0\,1\,4\,0\,1\,2\,3\,1\,2\,3\,4\,0\,3\,4\,0\,1\,2 \\
0\,1\,2\,3\,4\,3\,4\,0\,1\,2\,1\,2\,3\,4\,0\,4\,0\,1\,2\,3\,2\,3\,4\,0\,1 \\
0\,1\,2\,3\,4\,4\,0\,1\,2\,3\,3\,4\,0\,1\,2\,2\,3\,4\,0\,1\,1\,2\,3\,4\,0
\end{pmatrix}.
$$

[Essentially the same idea works when n is a prime power, using the finite field $\mathrm{GF}(p^e)$; see E. H. Moore, *American Journal of Mathematics* **18** (1896), 264–303, §15(1). These arrays are equivalent to finite *projective planes*; see Marshall Hall, Jr., *Combinatorial Theory* (Blaisdell, 1967), Chapters 12 and 13.]

20. Let $\omega = e^{2\pi i/n}$, and suppose $a_1 \ldots a_{n^2}$ and $b_1 \ldots b_{n^2}$ are the vectors in different rows. Then $a_1 b_1 + \cdots + a_{n^2} b_{n^2} = \sum_{0 \le j,k < n} \omega^{j+k} = 0$ because $\sum_{k=0}^{n-1} \omega^k = 0$.

21. (a) To show that equality-or-parallelism is an equivalence relation, we need to verify the transitive law: If $L \parallel M$ and $M \parallel N$ and $L \ne N$, then we must have $L \parallel N$. Otherwise there would be a point p with $L \cap N = \{p\}$, by (ii); and p would lie on two different lines parallel to M, contradicting (iii).

(b) Let $\{L_1, \ldots, L_n\}$ be a class of parallel lines, and assume that M is a line of another class. Then each L_j intersects M in a unique point p_j; and every point of M is encountered in this way, because every point of the geometry lies on exactly one line of each class, by (iii). Thus M contains exactly n points.

(c) We've already observed that every point belongs to m lines when there are m classes. If lines L, M, and N belong to three different classes, then M and N have the same number of points as the number of lines in L's class. So there's a common line size n, and in fact the total number of points is n^2. (Of course n might be infinite.)

22. Given an orthogonal array A of order n and depth m, define a geometric net with n^2 points and m classes of parallel lines by regarding the columns of A as points; line j of class k is the set of columns where symbol j appears in row k of A.

All finite geometric nets with $m \ge 3$ classes arise in this way. But a geometric net with only one class is trivially a partition of the points into disjoint subsets. A geometric net with $m = 2$ classes has nn' points (x, x'), where there are n lines '$x = $ constant' in one class and n' lines '$x' = $ constant' in the other. [For further information, see R. H. Bruck, *Canadian J. Math.* **3** (1951), 94–107; *Pacific J. Math.* **13** (1963), 421–457.]

23. (a) If $d(x, y) \le t$ and $d(x', y) \le t$ and $x \ne x'$, then $d(x, x') \le 2t$. Thus a code with distance $> 2t$ between codewords allows the correction of up to t errors — at least in principle, although the computations might be complex. Conversely, if $d(x, x') \leq 2t$ and $x \neq x'$, there's an element y with $d(x, y) \leq t$ and $d(x', y) \leq t$; hence we can't reconstruct x uniquely when y is received.

(b, c) Let $m = r + 2$, and observe that a set of b^2 b-ary m-tuples has Hamming distance $\geq m - 1$ between all pairs of elements if and only if it forms the columns of a b-ary orthogonal array of depth m. [See S. W. Golomb and E. C. Posner, *IEEE Trans.* **IT-10** (1964), 196–208. The literature of coding theory often denotes a code $C(b, n, r)$ of distance d by the symbol $(n + r, b^n, d)_b$. Thus, a b-ary orthogonal array of depth m is essentially an $(m, b^2, m - 1)_b$ code.]

24. (a) Suppose $x_j \neq x'_j$ for $1 \leq j \leq l$ and $x_j = x'_j$ for $l < j \leq N$. We have $x = x'$ if $l = 0$. Otherwise consider the parity bits that correspond to the m lines through point 1. At most $l - 1$ of those bits correspond to lines that touch the points $\{2, \ldots, l\}$. Hence x' has at least $m - (l-1)$ parity changes, and $d(x, x') \geq l + (m - (l-1)) = m + 1$.

(b) Let $l_{p1}, \ldots, l_{pm}$ be the index numbers of the lines through point p. After receiving a message $y_1 \ldots y_{N+R}$, compute x_p for $1 \leq p \leq N$ by taking the majority value of the $m + 1$ "witness bits" $\{y_{p0}, \ldots, y_{pm}\}$, where $y_{p0} = y_p$ and

$$y_{pk} = \left(y_{N+l_{pk}} + \sum \{y_j \mid j \neq p \text{ and point } j \text{ lies on line } l_{pk}\}\right) \bmod 2, \quad \text{for } 1 \leq k \leq m.$$

This method works because each received bit y_j affects at most one of the witness bits.

For example, in the 25-point geometry of exercise 19, suppose the parity bit $x_{26+5i+j}$ of each codeword corresponds to line j of row i, for $0 \leq i \leq 5$ and $0 \leq j < 5$; thus $x_{26} = x_1 \oplus x_2 \oplus x_3 \oplus x_4 \oplus x_5$, $x_{27} = x_6 \oplus x_7 \oplus x_8 \oplus x_9 \oplus x_{10}$, $\ldots$, $x_{55} = x_5 \oplus x_6 \oplus x_{12} \oplus x_{18} \oplus x_{24}$. Given message $y_1 \ldots y_{55}$, we decode bit x_1 (say) by computing the majority of the seven bits y_1, $y_{26} \oplus y_2 \oplus y_3 \oplus y_4 \oplus y_5$, $y_{31} \oplus y_6 \oplus y_{11} \oplus y_{16} \oplus y_{21}$, $y_{36} \oplus y_{10} \oplus y_{14} \oplus y_{18} \oplus y_{22}$, $y_{41} \oplus y_9 \oplus y_{12} \oplus y_{20} \oplus y_{23}$, $y_{46} \oplus y_8 \oplus y_{15} \oplus y_{17} \oplus y_{24}$, $y_{51} \oplus y_7 \oplus y_{13} \oplus y_{19} \oplus y_{25}$. [Section 7.1.2 explains how to calculate majority functions efficiently. Notice that we can eliminate the last 10 bits if we only wish to correct up to two errors, and the last 20 if single-error correction is sufficient. See M. Y. Hsiao, D. C. Bossen, and R. T. Chien, *IBM J. Research and Development* **14** (1970), 390–394.]

25. By considering anagrams of $\{1, e, a, s, t\}$ (see exercise 5–21), we're led to the square

```
stela
telas
elast ,
laste
astel
```

and the cyclic rotations of its rows. Here `telas` are Spanish fabrics; `elast` is a prefix meaning flexible; and `laste` is an imperative Chaucerian verb. (Of course just about every pronounceable combination of five letters has been used to spell or misspell something somewhere, at some point in history.)

26. "`every night, young video buffs catch rerun fever forty years after those great shows first aired.`" [Robert Leighton, *GAMES* **16**, 6 (December 1992), 34, 47.]

27. $(0, 4, 163, 1756, 3834)$ for $k = (1, 2, 3, 4, 5)$; `mamma` and `esses` give a "full house."

28. Yes, 38 pairs altogether. The "most common" solution is `needs` (rank 180) and `offer` (rank 384). Only three cases differ consistently by $+1$ (`adder beefs`, `sheer tiffs`, `sneer toffs`). Other memorable examples are `ghost hints` and `strut rusts`. One word of the pair ends with the letter `s` except in four cases, such as `robed spade`. [See Leonard J. Gordon, *Word Ways* **23** (1990), 59–61.]

29. There are 18 palindromes, from `level` (rank 184) to `dewed` (rank 5688). Some of the 34 mirror pairs are 'devil lived', 'knits stink', 'smart trams', 'faced decaf'.

30. Among 105 such words in the SGB, `first`, `below`, `floor`, `begin`, `cells`, `empty`, and `hills` are the most common; `abbey` and `pssst` are lexicographically first and last. (If you don't like `pssst`, the next-to-last is `mossy`.) Only 37 words, from `mecca` to `zoned`, have their letters in *reverse* order; but they are, of course, `wrong` answers.

31. The middle word is the average of the other two, so the extreme words must be congruent mod 2; this observation reduces the number of dictionary lookups by a factor of about 32. There are 119 such triples in WORDS(5757), but only two in WORDS(2000): `marry`, `photo`, `solve`; `risky`, `tempo`, `vague`. [*Word Ways* **25** (1992), 13–15.]

32. The only reasonably common example seems to be `peopleless`.

33. `chief`, `fight`, `right`, `which`, `ouija`, `jokes`, `ankle`, `films`, `hymns`, `known`, `crops`, `pique`, `quart`, `first`, `first`, `study`, `mauve`, `vowel`, `waxes`, `proxy`, `crazy`, `pizza`. (The idea is to find the most common word in which x is followed by $(x + 1) \bmod 26$, for $x = $ `a` (0), $x = $ `b` (1), ..., $x = $ `z` (25). We also minimize the intervening distance, thus preferring `bacon` to the more common word `black`. In the one case where no such word exists, `crazy` seems most rational. See *OMNI* **16**, 8 (May 1994), 94.)

34. The top two (and total number) in each category are: `pssst` and `pffft` (2), `schwa` and `schmo` (2), `threw` and `throw` (36), `three` and `spree` (5), `which` and `think` (709), `there` and `these` (234), `their` and `great` (291), `whooo` and `wheee` (3), `words` and `first` (628), `large` and `since` (376), `water` and `never` (1313), `value` and `radio` (84), `would` and `could` (460), `house` and `voice` (101), `quiet` and `queen` (25), `queue` only (1), `ahhhh` and `ankhs` (4), `angle` and `extra` (20), `other` and `after` (227), `agree` and `issue` (20), `along` and `using` (124), `above` and `alone` (92), `about` and `again` (58), `adieu` and `aquae` (2), `earth` and `eight` (16), `eagle` and `ounce` (8), `outer` and `eaten` (42), `eerie` and `audio` (4), (0), `ouija` and `aioli` (2), (0), (0); `years` and `every` are the most common of the 868 omitted words. [To fill the three holes, Internet usage suggests `ooops`, `ooooh`, and `ooooo`. See P. M. Cohen, *Word Ways* **10** (1977), 221–223.]

35. Consider the collection WORDS(n) for $n = 1, 2, \ldots, 5757$. The illustrated trie, rooted at `s`, first becomes possible when n reaches 978 (the rank of `stalk`). The next root letter to support such a trie is `c`, which acquires enough branching in its descendants when $n = 2503$ (the rank of `craze`). Subsequent breakthroughs occur when $n = 2730$ (`bulks`), 3999 (`ducky`), 4230 (`panty`), 4459 (`minis`), 4709 (`whooo`), 4782 (`lardy`), 4824 (`herem`), 4840 (`firma`), 4924 (`ridgy`), 5343 (`taxol`).

(A breakthrough occurs when a top-level trie acquires Horton–Strahler number 4; see exercise 7.2.1.6–124. Amusing sets of words, suggestive of a new kind of poetry, arise also when the branching is right-to-left instead of left-to-right: `black`, `slack`, `crack`, `track`, `click`, `slick`, `brick`, `trick`, `blank`, `plank`, `crank`, `drank`, `blink`, `clink`, `brink`, `drink`. In fact, right-to-left branching yields a complete *ternary* trie with 81 leaves: `males`, `sales`, `tales`, `files`, `miles`, `piles`, `holes`, ..., `tests`, `costs`, `hosts`, `posts`.)

36. Denoting the elements of the cube by a_{ijk} for $1 \leq i, j, k \leq 5$, the symmetry condition is $a_{ijk} = a_{ikj} = a_{jik} = a_{jki} = a_{kij} = a_{kji}$. In general an $n \times n \times n$ cube has $3n^2$ words, obtained by fixing two coordinates and letting the third range from 1 to n; but the symmetry condition means that we need only $\binom{n+1}{2}$ words. Hence when $n = 5$ the number of necessary words is reduced from 75 to 15. [Jeff Grant was able to find 75 suitable words in the *Oxford English Dictionary*; see *Word Ways* **11** (1978), 156–157.]

Changing (`stove`, `event`) to (`store`, `erect`) or (`stole`, `elect`) gives two more.

37. The densest part of the graph, which we might call its "bare core," contains the vertices named `bares` and `cores`, which each have degree 25.

38. `tears` → `raise` → `aisle` → `smile`; the second word might also be `reals`. [Going from `tears` to `smile` as in (11) was one of Lewis Carroll's first five-letter examples. He would have been delighted to learn that the directed rule makes it more difficult to go from `smile` to `tears`, because *four* steps are needed in that direction.]

39. Always spanning, never induced.

40. (a) 2^e, (b) 2^n, one for each subset of E or V.

41. (a) $n = 1$ and $n = 2$; P_0 is undefined. (b) $n = 0$ and $n = 3$.

42. G has $65/2$ edges (hence it doesn't exist).

43. Yes: The first three are isomorphic to Fig. 2(e). [The left-hand diagram is, in fact, identical to the earliest known appearance of the Petersen graph in print: See A. B. Kempe, *Philosophical Transactions* **177** (1886), 1–70, especially Fig. 13 in §59.] But the right-hand graph is definitely different; it is planar, Hamiltonian, and has girth 3.

44. Any automorphism must take a corner point into a corner point, because three distinct paths of length 2 can be found only between certain pairs of non-corner points. Therefore the graph has only the eight symmetries of C_4.

45. All edges of this graph connect vertices of the same row or adjacent rows. Therefore we can use the colors 0 and 2 alternately in even-numbered rows, 1 and 3 alternately in odd-numbered rows. The neighbors of `NV` form a 5-cycle, hence four colors are necessary.

46. (a) Every vertex has degree ≥ 2, and its neighbors have a well-defined cyclic order corresponding to the incoming lines. If $u - v$ and $u - w$, where v and w are cyclically consecutive neighbors of u, we must have $v - w$. Thus all points in the vicinity of any vertex u belong to a unique triangular region.

(b) The formula holds when $n = 3$. If $n > 3$, shrink any edge to a point; this transformation removes one vertex and three edges. (If $u - v$ shrinks, suppose it was part of the triangles $x - u - v - x$ and $y - u - v - y$. We lose vertex v and edges $\{x - v, u - v, y - v\}$; all other edges of the form $w - v$ become $w - u$.)

47. A planar diagram would divide the plane into regions, with either 4 or 6 vertices in the boundary of each region (because $K_{3,3}$ has no odd cycles). If there are f_4 and f_6 of each kind, we must have $4f_4 + 6f_6 = 18$, since there are 9 edges; hence $(f_4, f_6) = (3, 1)$ or $(0, 3)$. We could also triangulate the graph by adding $f_4 + 3f_6$ more edges; but then it would have at least 15 edges, contradicting exercise 46.

[The fact that $K_{3,3}$ is nonplanar goes back to a puzzle about connecting three houses to three utilities (water, gas, and electricity), without crossing pipes. Its origin is unknown; H. E. Dudeney called it "ancient" in *Strand* **46** (1913), 110.]

48. If u, v, w are vertices and $u - v$, we must have $d(w, u) \not\equiv d(w, v)$ (modulo 2); otherwise shortest paths from w to u and from w to v would yield an odd cycle. After w is colored 0, the procedure therefore assigns the color $d(w, v) \bmod 2$ to each new uncolored vertex v that is adjacent to a colored vertex u; and every vertex v with $d(w, v) < \infty$ is colored before a new w is chosen.

49. There are only three: K_4, $K_{3,3}$, and ▢ (which is $\overline{C_6}$).

50. The graph must be connected, because the number of 3-colorings is divisible by 3^r when there are r components. It must also be contained in a complete bipartite graph $K_{m,n}$, which can be 3-colored in $3(2^m + 2^n - 2)$ ways. Deleting edges from

$K_{m,n}$ does not decrease the number of colorings; hence $2^m + 2^n - 2 \leq 8$, and we have $\{m,n\} = \{1,1\}, \{1,2\}, \{1,3\}$, or $\{2,2\}$. So the only possibilities are the claw $K_{1,3}$ and the path P_4.

51. A 4-cycle $p_1 - L_1 - p_2 - L_2 - p_1$ would correspond to two distinct lines $\{L_1, L_2\}$ with two common points $\{p_1, p_2\}$, contradicting (ii). So the girth is at least 6.

If there's only one class of parallel lines, the girth is ∞; if there are two classes, with $n \leq n'$ members, it is 8, or ∞ if $n = 1$. (See answer 22.) Otherwise we can find a 6-cycle by making a triangle from three lines that are chosen from different classes.

52. If the diameter is d and the girth is g, then $d \geq \lfloor g/2 \rfloor$, unless $g = \infty$.

53. happy (which is connected to tears and sweat, but not to world).

54. (a) It's a single, highly connected component. (Incidentally, this graph is the *line graph* of the bipartite graph in which one part corresponds to the initial letters $\{A, C, D, F, G, \ldots, W\}$ and the other to the final letters $\{A, C, D, E, H, \ldots, Z\}$.)

(b) Vertex WY is isolated. The other vertices with in-degree zero, namely FL, GA, PA, UT, WA, WI, and WV, form strong components by themselves; they all precede a giant strong component, which is followed by each of the remaining single-vertex strong components with out-degree zero: AZ, DE, KY, ME, NE, NH, NJ, NY, OH, TX.

(c) Now the strong component $\{$GU$\}$ precedes $\{$UT$\}$; NH, OH, PA, WA, WI, and WV join the giant strong component; $\{$FM$\}$ precedes it; $\{$AE$\}$ and $\{$WY$\}$ follow it.

55. $\binom{N}{2} - \binom{n_1}{2} - \cdots - \binom{n_k}{2}$, where $N = n_1 + \cdots + n_k$.

56. True. Note that J_n is simple, but it doesn't correspond to any multigraph.

57. False, in the connected digraph $u \longrightarrow w \longleftarrow v$. (But u and v are in the same *strongly connected* component if and only if $d(u,v) < \infty$ and $d(v,u) < \infty$; see Section 2.3.4.2.)

58. Each component is a cycle whose order is at least (a) 3 (b) 1.

59. (a) By induction on n, we can use straight insertion sorting: Suppose $v_1 \longrightarrow \cdots \longrightarrow v_{n-1}$. Then either $v_n \longrightarrow v_1$ or $v_{n-1} \longrightarrow v_n$ or $v_{k-1} \longrightarrow v_n \longrightarrow v_k$, where k is minimum such that $v_n \longrightarrow v_k$. [L. Rédei, *Acta litterarum ac scientiarum* **7** (Szeged, 1934), 39–43.]

(b) 15: 01234, 02341, 02413, and their cyclic shifts. [The number of such oriented paths is always odd; see T. Szele, *Matematikai és Fizikai Lapok* **50** (1943), 223–256.]

(c) Yes. (By induction: If there's only one place to insert v_n as in part (a), the tournament is transitive.)

60. Let $A = \{x \mid u \longrightarrow x\}$, $B = \{x \mid x \longrightarrow v\}$, $C = \{x \mid v \longrightarrow x\}$. If $v \notin A$ and $A \cap B = \emptyset$ we have $|A| + |B| = |A \cup B| \leq n - 2$, because $u \notin A \cup B$ and $v \notin A \cup B$. But $|B| + |C| = n - 1$; hence $|A| < |C|$. [H. G. Landau, *Bull. Math. Biophysics* **15** (1953), 148.]

61. $1 \longrightarrow 1$, $1 \longrightarrow 2$, $2 \longrightarrow 2$; then $A = \begin{pmatrix} 1 & 1 \\ 0 & 1 \end{pmatrix}$ and $A^k = \begin{pmatrix} 1 & k \\ 0 & 1 \end{pmatrix}$ for all integers k.

62. (a) Suppose the vertices are $\{1, \ldots, n\}$. Each of the $n!$ terms $a_{1p_1} \ldots a_{np_n}$ in the expansion of the permanent is the number of spanning permutation digraphs that have arcs $j \longrightarrow p_j$. (b) A similar argument shows that $\det A$ is the number of even spanning permutation digraphs minus the number of odd ones. [See F. Harary, *SIAM Review* **4** (1962), 202–210, where permutation digraphs are called "linear subgraphs."]

63. Let v be any vertex. If $g = 2t+1$, at least $d(d-1)^{k-1}$ vertices x satisfy $d(v,x) = k$, for $1 \leq k \leq t$. If $g = 2t + 2$ and v' is any neighbor of v, there also are at least $(d-1)^t$ vertices x for which $d(v,x) = t + 1$ and $d(v',x) = t$.

64. To achieve the lower bound in answer 63, *every* vertex v must have degree d, and the d neighbors of v must all be adjacent to the remaining $d - 1$ vertices. This graph is, in fact, $K_{d,d}$.

65. (a) By answer 63, G must be regular of degree d, and there must be exactly one path of length ≤ 2 between any two distinct vertices.

(b) We may take $\lambda_1 = d$, with $x_1 = (1\ldots1)^T$. All other eigenvectors satisfy $Jx_j = (0\ldots0)^T$; hence $\lambda_j^2 + \lambda_j = d - 1$ for $1 < j \leq N$.

(c) If $\lambda_2 = \cdots = \lambda_m = (-1+\sqrt{4d-3})/2$ and $\lambda_{m+1} = \cdots = \lambda_N = (-1-\sqrt{4d-3})/2$, we must have $m - 1 = N - m$. With this value we find $\lambda_1 + \cdots + \lambda_N = d - d^2/2$.

(d) If $4d - 3 = s^2$ and m is as in (c), the eigenvalues sum to

$$\frac{s^2+3}{4} + (m-1)\frac{s-1}{2} - \left(\frac{(s^2+3)^2}{16} + 1 - m\right)\frac{s+1}{2},$$

which is $15/32$ plus a multiple of s. Hence s must be a divisor of 15.

[These results are due to A. J. Hoffman and R. R. Singleton, *IBM J. Research and Development* **4** (1960), 497–504, who also proved that the graph for $d = 7$ is unique.]

66. Denote the 50 vertices by $[a, b]$ and (a, b) for $0 \leq a, b < 5$, and define three kinds of edges, using arithmetic mod 5:

$$[a, b] \longrightarrow [a+1, b]; \qquad (a, b) \longrightarrow (a+2, b); \qquad (a, b) \longrightarrow [a+bc, c] \quad \text{for } 0 \leq a, b, c < 5.$$

[See W. G. Brown, *Canadian J. Math.* **19** (1967), 644–648; *J. London Math. Soc.* **42** (1967), 514–520. Without the edges of the first two kinds, the graph has girth 6 and corresponds to a geometric net as in exercise 51, using the orthogonal array in answer 19.]

67. Certain possibilities have been ruled out by Michael Aschbacher in *Journal of Algebra* **19** (1971), 538–540.

68. If G has s automorphisms, it has $n!/s$ adjacency matrices, because there are s permutation matrices P such that $P^-AP = A$.

69. First set $\text{IDEG}(v) \leftarrow 0$ for all vertices v. Then perform (31) for all v, also setting $u \leftarrow \text{TIP}(a)$ and $\text{IDEG}(u) \leftarrow \text{IDEG}(u) + 1$ in the second line of that mini-algorithm.

To do something "for all v" using the SGB format, first set $v \leftarrow \text{VERTICES}(g)$; then while $v < \text{VERTICES}(g) + \text{N}(g)$, do the operation and set $v \leftarrow v + 1$.

70. Step B1 is performed once (but it takes $O(n)$ units of time). Steps (B2, B3, ..., B8) are performed respectively $(n+1, n, n, m+n, m, m, n)$ times, each with $O(1)$ cost.

71. Many choices are possible. Here we use 32-bit pointers, all relative to a symbolic address Pool, which lies in the Data_Segment. The following declarations provide one way to establish conventions for dealing with basic SGB data structures.

```
VSIZE IS 32 ;ASIZE IS 20          Node sizes in bytes
ARCS IS 0 ;COLOR IS 8 ;LINK IS 12 Offsets of vertex fields
TIP IS 0 ;NEXT IS 4               Offsets of arc fields

arcs GREG Pool+ARCS ;color GREG Pool+COLOR ;link GREG Pool+LINK
tip GREG Pool+TIP ;next GREG Pool+NEXT
u GREG ;v GREG ;w GREG ;s GREG ;a GREG ;mone GREG -1
```

AlgB	BZ	n,Success	Exit if the graph is null.
	MUL	$0,n,VSIZE	*B1. Initialize.*
	ADDU	v,v0,$0	$v \leftarrow v_0 + n$.
	SET	w,v0	$w \leftarrow v_0$.
1H	STT	mone,color,w	$\text{COLOR}(w) \leftarrow -1$.
	ADDU	w,w,VSIZE	$w \leftarrow w + 1$.
	CMP	$0,w,v	
	PBNZ	$0,1B	Repeat until $w = v$.

```
OH        SUBU    w,w,VSIZE       w ← w − 1.
3H        LDT     $0,color,w      B3. Color w if necessary.
          PBNN    $0,2F           To B2 if COLOR(w) ≥ 0.
          STCO    0,link,w        COLOR(w) ← 0, LINK(w) ← Λ.
          SET     s,w             s ← w.
4H        SET     u,s             B4. Stack ⇒ u. Set u ← s.
          LDTU    s,link,s        s ← LINK(s).
          LDT     $1,color,u
          NEG     $1,1,$1         $1 ← 1 − COLOR(u).
          LDTU    a,arcs,u        a ← ARCS(u).
5H        BZ      a,8F            B5. Done with u? To B8 if a = Λ.
5H        LDTU    v,tip,a         v ← TIP(a).
6H        LDT     $0,color,v      B6. Process v.
          CMP     $2,$0,$1        (Here the program is slightly clever)
          PBZ     $2,7F           To B7 if COLOR(v) = 1 − COLOR(u).
          BNN     $0,Failure      Fail if COLOR(v) = COLOR(u).
          STT     $1,color,v      COLOR(v) ← 1 − COLOR(u).
          STTU    s,link,v        LINK(v) ← s.
          SET     s,v             s ← v.
7H        LDTU    a,next,a        B7. Loop on a. Set a ← NEXT(a).
          PBNZ    a,5B            To B5 if a ≠ Λ.
8H        PBNZ    s,4B            B8. Stack nonempty? To B4 if s ≠ Λ.
2H        CMP     $0,w,v0         B2. Done?
          PBNZ    $0,0B           If w ≠ v0, decrease w and go to B3.
Success LOC      @                (Successful termination)  ▌
```

72. (a) This condition clearly remains invariant as vertices enter or leave the stack.

(b) Vertex v has been colored but not yet explored, because the neighbors of every explored vertex have the proper color.

(c) Just before setting $s \leftarrow v$ in step B6, set $\texttt{PARENT}(v) \leftarrow u$, where $\texttt{PARENT}$ is a new utility field. And just before terminating unsuccessfully in that step, do the following: "Repeatedly output $\texttt{NAME}(u)$ and set $u \leftarrow \texttt{PARENT}(u)$, until $u = \texttt{PARENT}(v)$; then output $\texttt{NAME}(u)$ and $\texttt{NAME}(v)$."

73. K_{10}. (And $random\_graph(10,100,0,1,1,0,0,0,0,0)$ is J_{10}.)

74. badness has out-degree 22; no other vertices have out-degree > 20.

75. Let the parameters $(n_1, n_2, n_3, n_4, p, w, o)$ be respectively (a) $(n,0,0,0,-1,0,0)$; (b) $(n,0,0,0,1,0,0)$; (c) $(n,0,0,0,1,1,0)$; (d) $(n,0,0,0,-1,0,1)$; (e) $(n,0,0,0,1,0,1)$; (f) $(n,0,0,0,1,1,1)$; (g) $(m,n,0,0,1,0,0)$; (h) $(m,n,0,0,1,2,0)$; (i) $(m,n,0,0,1,3,0)$; (j) $(m,n,0,0,-1,0,0)$; (k) $(m,n,0,0,1,3,1)$; (l) $(n,0,0,0,2,0,0)$; (m) $(2,-n,0,0,1,0,0)$.

76. Yes, for example from C_1 and C_2 in answer 75(c). (But no self-loops can occur when $p < 0$, because arcs $x \longrightarrow y = x + k\delta$ are generated for $k = 1, 2, \ldots$ until y is out of range or $y = x$.)

77. Suppose x and y are vertices with $d(x,y) > 2$. Thus $x \not\!\!- y$; and if v is any other vertex we must have either $v \not\!\!- x$ or $v \not\!\!- y$. These facts yield a path of length at most 3 in $\overline{G}$ between any two vertices u and v.

78. (a) The number of edges, $\binom{n}{2}/2$, must be an integer. The smallest examples are K_0, K_1, P_4, C_5, and $\mathcal{W}$.

(b) If q is any odd number, we have $u \!-\! v$ if and only if $\varphi^q(u) \not\!\!-\, \varphi^q(v)$. Therefore φ^q cannot have two fixed points, nor can it contain a 2-cycle.

(c) Such a permutation of V also defines a permutation $\widehat{\varphi}$ of the edges of K_n, taking $\{u, v\} \mapsto \widehat{\varphi}(\{u, v\}) = \{\varphi(u), \varphi(v)\}$, and it's easy to see that the cycle lengths of $\widehat{\varphi}$ are all even. If $\widehat{\varphi}$ has t cycles, we obtain 2^t self-complementary graphs by painting the edges of each cycle with alternating colors.

(d) In this case φ has a unique fixed point v, and $G' = G \setminus v$ is self-complementary. Suppose φ has r cycles in addition to (v); then $\widehat{\varphi}$ has r cycles involving the edges that touch vertex v, and there are 2^r ways to extend G' to a graph G.

[*References:* H. Sachs, *Publicationes Mathematicæ* **9** (Debrecen, 1962), 270–288; G. Ringel, *Archiv der Mathematik* **14** (1963), 354–358.]

79. Solution 1, by H. Sachs, with $\varphi = (1\,2\,\ldots\,4k)$: Let $u \!-\! v$ when $u > v > 0$ and $u + v \bmod 4 \leq 1$; also $0 \!-\! v$ when $v \bmod 2 = 0$.

Solution 2, with $\varphi = (a_1\,b_1\,c_1\,d_1)\ldots(a_k\,b_k\,c_k\,d_k)$, where $a_j = 4j - 3$, $b_j = 4j - 2$, $c_j = 4j - 1$, and $d_j = 4j$: Let $0 \!-\! b_j \!-\! a_j \!-\! c_j \!-\! d_j \!-\! 0$ for $1 \leq j \leq k$, and $a_i \!-\! a_j \!-\! b_i \!-\! d_j \!-\! c_i \!-\! c_j \!-\! d_i \!-\! b_j \!-\! a_i$, for $1 \leq i < j \leq k$.

80. (Solution by G. Ringel.) Let φ be as in answer 79, solution 2. Let E_0 be the $3k$ edges $b_j \!-\! a_j \!-\! c_j \!-\! d_j$ for $1 \leq j \leq k$; let E_1 be the $8\binom{k}{2}$ edges between $\{a_i, b_i, c_i, d_i\}$ and $\{b_j, d_j\}$ for $1 \leq i < j \leq k$; let E_2 be the $8\binom{k}{2}$ edges between $\{a_i, b_i, c_i, d_i\}$ and $\{a_j, c_j\}$ for $1 \leq i < j \leq k$. In case (a), $E_0 \cup E_1$ gives diameter 2; $E_0 \cup E_2$ gives diameter 3. Case (b) is similar, but we add $2k$ edges $b_j \!-\! 0 \!-\! d_j$ to E_1, $a_j \!-\! 0 \!-\! c_j$ to E_2.

81. $\vec{C_3}$, $\vec{K_3}$, $D = \text{o}\!\!-\!\!\!\!\rightarrow\!\!\!\text{o}\!\!\!\text{⊃o}$, and $D^T = \text{o}\!\!\leftarrow\!\!\!\text{o}\!\!\!\text{⊂o}$. (The *converse* D^T of a digraph D is obtained by reversing the direction of its arcs. There are 16 nonisomorphic simple digraphs of order 3 without loops, 10 of which are self-converse, including $\vec{C_3}$ and $\vec{K_3}$.)

82. (a) True, by definition. (b) True: If every vertex has d neighbors, every edge $u \!-\! v$ has $d - 1$ neighbors $u \!-\! w$ and $d - 1$ neighbors $w \!-\! v$. (c) True: $\{a_i, b_j\}$ has $m + n - 2$ neighbors, for $0 \leq i < m$ and $0 \leq j < n$. (d) False: $L(K_{1,1,2})$ has 5 vertices and 8 edges. (e) True. (f) True: The only nonadjacent edges are $\{0, 1\} \not\!\!-\, \{2, 3\}$, $\{0, 2\} \not\!\!-\, \{1, 3\}$, $\{0, 3\} \not\!\!-\, \{1, 2\}$. (g) True, for all $n > 0$. (h) False, unless G has no isolated vertices.

83. It is the Petersen graph. [A. Kowalewski, *Sitzungsberichte der Akademie der Wissenschaften in Wien*, Mathematisch-Nat. Klasse, Abteilung IIa, **126** (1917), 67–90.]

84. Yes: Let $\varphi(\{a_u, b_v\}) = \{a_{(u+v) \bmod 3}, b_{(u-v) \bmod 3}\}$ for $0 \leq u, v < 3$.

85. Let the vertex degrees be $\{d_1, \ldots, d_n\}$. Then G has $\frac{1}{2}(d_1 + \cdots + d_n)$ edges, and $L(G)$ has $\frac{1}{2}(d_1(d_1 - 1) + \cdots + d_n(d_n - 1))$. Thus G and $L(G)$ both have exactly n edges if and only if $(d_1 - 2)^2 + \cdots + (d_n - 2)^2 = 0$. Consequently exercise 58 gives the answer. [See V. V. Menon, *Canadian Math. Bull.* **8** (1965), 7–15.]

86. If $G = \text{⟋⟍}$ then $\overline{G} = \text{△} = L(G)$.

87. (a) Yes, easily. [In fact, R. L. Brooks has proved that *every* connected graph with maximum vertex degree $d > 2$ is d-colorable, except for the complete graph K_{d+1}; see *Proc. Cambridge Phil. Soc.* **37** (1941), 194–197.]

(b) No. There's essentially only one way to 3-color the edges of the outer 5-cycle in Fig. 2(e); this forces a conflict on the inner 5-cycle. [Petersen proved this in 1898.]

88. One cycle doesn't use the center vertex, and there are $(n-1)(n-2)$ cycles that do (namely, one for every ordered pair of distinct vertices on the rim). We don't count C_0.

89. Both sides equal $\begin{pmatrix} A & O & O \\ O & B & O \\ O & O & C \end{pmatrix}$, $\begin{pmatrix} A & J & J \\ J & B & J \\ J & J & C \end{pmatrix}$, $\begin{pmatrix} A & J & J \\ O & B & J \\ O & O & C \end{pmatrix}$, $\begin{pmatrix} A & O & O \\ J & B & O \\ J & J & C \end{pmatrix}$, respectively.

90. K_4 and $\overline{K_4}$; $K_{1,1,2}$ and $\overline{K_{1,1,2}}$; $K_{2,2} = C_4$ and $\overline{K_{2,2}}$; $K_{1,3}$ and $\overline{K_{1,3}}$; $K_1 \oplus K_{1,2}$ and its complement; all graphs K_α are cographs by (39). Missing is $P_4 = \overline{P_4}$. (All connected subgraphs of a cograph have diameter ≤ 2; W_5 is a cograph, but not W_6.)

91. (a) ⬜; (b) ✕; (c) ⊠; (d) ⬜; (e) ⊠; (f) | |; (g) ✕.   (In general we have $K_2 \bigtriangleup H = (K_2 \square H) \cup (K_2 \otimes \overline{H})$, and $K_2 \circ H = H \,\text{---}\, H$. Thus the coincidences $K_2 \bigtriangleup H = K_2 \square H$ and $K_2 \circ H = K_2 \boxtimes H$ occur if and only if H is a complete graph.)

Mnemonics: Our notations $G \square H$ and $G \boxtimes H$ nicely match diagrams (a) and (c), as suggested by J. Nešetřil, *Lecture Notes in Comp. Sci.* **118** (1981), 94–102. His analogous recommendation to write $G \times H$ for (b) is also tempting; but it wasn't adopted here, because hundreds of authors have used $G \times H$ to denote $G \square H$.

92. (a) ⬜; (b) ⁄; (c) ⊠; (d) ⊠; (e) ⊠.

93. $K_m \boxtimes K_n = K_m \circ K_n \cong K_{mn}$.

94. No; they're induced subgraphs of $K_{26} \square K_{26} \square K_{26} \square K_{26} \square K_{26}$.

95. (a) $d_u + d_v$. (b) $d_u d_v$. (c) $d_u d_v + d_u + d_v$. (d) $d_u(n - d_v) + (m - d_u)d_v$. (e) $d_u n + d_v$.

96. (a) $A \square B = A \otimes I + I \otimes B$. (b) $A \boxtimes B = A \square B + A \otimes B$. (c) $A \bigtriangleup B = A \otimes J + J \otimes B - 2A \otimes B$. (d) $A \circ B = A \otimes J + I \otimes B$. (Formulas (a), (b), and (d) define graph products of arbitrary digraphs and multigraphs. Formula (c) is valid in general for simple digraphs; but negative entries can occur when A and B contain values > 1.)

Historical notes: The direct product of matrices is often called the Kronecker product, because K. Hensel [*Crelle* **105** (1889), 329–344] said he had heard it in Kronecker's lectures; however, Kronecker never actually published anything about it. Its first known appearance was in a paper by J. G. Zehfuss [*Zeitschrift für Math. und Physik* **3** (1858), 298–301], who proved that $\det(A \otimes B) = (\det A)^n (\det B)^m$ when $m = m'$ and $n = n'$. The basic formulas $(A \otimes B)^T = A^T \otimes B^T$, $(A \otimes B)(A' \otimes B') = AA' \otimes BB'$, and $(A \otimes B)^{-1} = A^{-1} \otimes B^{-1}$ are due to A. Hurwitz [*Math. Annalen* **45** (1894), 381–404].

97. Operations on adjacency matrices prove that $(G \oplus G') \square H = (G \square H) \oplus (G' \square H)$; $(G \oplus G') \boxtimes H = (G \boxtimes H) \oplus (G' \boxtimes H)$; $(G \oplus G') \circ H = (G \circ H) \oplus (G' \circ H)$. Since $G \square H \cong H \square G$, $G \otimes H \cong H \otimes G$, and $G \boxtimes H \cong H \boxtimes G$, we also have right-distributive laws $G \square (H \oplus H') \cong (G \square H) \oplus (G \square H')$; $G \otimes (H \oplus H') \cong (G \otimes H) \oplus (G \otimes H')$; $G \boxtimes (H \oplus H') \cong (G \boxtimes H) \oplus (G \boxtimes H')$. The lexicographic product satisfies $\overline{G \circ H} = \overline{G} \circ \overline{H}$; also $K_m \circ H = H \,\text{---}\, \cdots \,\text{---}\, H$, hence $K_m \circ \overline{K_n} = K_{n,\dots,n}$. Furthermore $G \circ K_n = G \boxtimes K_n$; $K_m \square K_n = \overline{K_m \otimes K_n} = L(K_{m,n})$.

98. There are kl components (because of the distributive laws in the previous exercise, and the facts that $G \square H$ and $G \boxtimes H$ are connected when G and H are connected).

99. Every path from (u, v) to (u', v') in $G \square H$ must use at least $d_G(u, u')$ "G-steps" and at least $d_H(v, v')$ "H-steps"; and that minimum is achievable. Similar reasoning shows that $d_{G \boxtimes H}((u, v), (u', v')) = \max(d_G(u, u'), d_H(v, v'))$.

100. If G and H are connected, and if each of them has at least two vertices, $G \otimes H$ is disconnected if and only if G and H are bipartite. The "if" part is easy; conversely, if there's an odd cycle in G, we can get from (u, v) to (u', v') as follows: First go to (u'', v'), where u'' is any vertex of G that happens to be expedient. Then walk an even number of steps in G from u'' to u', while alternating in H between v' and one of its neighbors. [P. M. Weichsel, *Proc. Amer. Math. Soc.* **13** (1962), 47–52.]

101. Choose vertices u and v with maximum degree. Then $d_u + d_v = d_u d_v$ by exercise 95; so either $G = H = K_1$, or $d_u = d_v = 2$. In the latter case, $G = P_m$ or C_m, and $H = P_n$ or C_n. But $G \square H$ is connected, so G or H must be nonbipartite, say G. Then $G \square H$ is nonbipartite, so H must also be nonbipartite; thus $G = C_m$ and $H = C_n$, with m and n both odd. The shortest odd cycle in $C_m \square C_n$ has length $\min(m,n)$; in $C_m \otimes C_n$ it has length $\max(m,n)$; hence $m = n$. Conversely, if $n \geq 3$ is odd, we have $C_n \square C_n \cong C_n \otimes C_n$, under the isomorphism that takes $(u,v) \mapsto ((u+v) \bmod n, (u-v) \bmod n)$ for $0 \leq u, v < n$. [D. J. Miller, *Canadian J. Math.* **20** (1968), 1511–1521.]

102. $P_m \boxtimes P_n$. (It is planar only when $\min(m,n) \leq 2$ or $m = n = 3$.)

103.

1	2	3	4	5	7
2	1	3	4	6	8
3	1	2	5	6	8
4	1	2	5	6	
5	3	4	1	7	
6	2	3	4		
7	5	1			
8	2	3			

1	2	3	4	5	6	7	8	9
2	1	3	4	6	8	9		
3	1	2	5	6	8	9		
4	1	2	5	7				
5	3	4	1	7				
6	2	3	1	7				
7	4	5	6	1				
8	2	3	1	9				
9	8	2	3	1				

104. Edges must be created in a somewhat circuitous order, to maintain the tableau shape. Variables i and r delimit the available rows in column t. For example, the second part of exercise 103 begins with $i \leftarrow 1$, $t \leftarrow 8$, $r \leftarrow 1$; then $9 — 1$, $i \leftarrow 2$, $t \leftarrow 6$, $r \leftarrow 3$; then $9 — 3$, $9 — 2$, $i \leftarrow 4$, $t \leftarrow 4$, $r \leftarrow 8$; then $9 — 8$.

105. Notice that $d_k \geq k$ if and only if $c_k \geq k$. When $d_k \geq k$ we have

$$c_1 + \cdots + c_k = k^2 + \min(k, d_{k+1}) + \min(k, d_{k+2}) + \cdots + \min(k, d_n);$$

therefore the condition $d_1 + \cdots + d_k \leq c_1 + \cdots + c_k - k$ is equivalent to

$$d_1 + \cdots + d_k \leq f(k), \quad \text{where } f(k) = k(k-1) + \min(k, d_{k+1}) + \cdots + \min(k, d_n). \quad (*)$$

If $k \geq s$ we have $f(k+1) - f(k) = 2k - d_{k+1} \geq d_{k+1}$; hence $(*)$ holds for $1 \leq k \leq n$ if and only if it holds for $1 \leq k \leq s$. Condition $(*)$ was discovered by P. Erdős and T. Gallai [*Matematikai Lapok* **11** (1960), 264–274]. It is obviously necessary, if we consider the edges between $\{1, \ldots, k\}$ and $\{k+1, \ldots, n\}$.

Let $a_k = d_1 + \cdots + d_k - c_1 - \cdots - c_k + k$, and suppose that we reach $a_k > 0$ in step H2 for some $k \leq s$. Let A_j, C_j, D_j, N, and S be the numbers that correspond to a_j, c_j, d_j, n, and s *before* steps H3 and H4; thus $N = n + 1$, $D_j = d_j + (0 \text{ or } 1)$, etc. We want to prove that $A_K > 0$ for some $K \leq S$.

Steps H3 and H4 have removed row N and the bottommost remaining q cells in column t, for some $t \geq S$ and $q > 0$, together with the rightmost cells in rows 1 through p. If $p > 0$ we have $C_{t+1} = p$. Let $r = D_N = p + q$, and $u = C_t$. Notice that $D_j = t$ for $p < j \leq u$, and $C_j = N$ for $1 \leq j \leq r$; also $A_j = a_j$ for $1 \leq j \leq p$.

If k is minimal we have $1 \leq a_k \leq d_k - c_k + 1$, hence $c_k \leq d_k$. If $D_k > t$ then $k \leq p$ and $A_k = a_k$. If $D_k < t$ it follows that $A_k = a_k + r - \min(k, r) \geq a_k$, because $k \leq D_k$. Thus we may assume that $D_k = t$.

Suppose $t > S$; hence $u \leq S$. For $k < j \leq u$ we have $d_j \geq D_j - 1 = t - 1 \geq d_k - 1 \geq c_k - 1 \geq c_j - 1$. Thus $a_u \geq a_k > 0$. But $A_u = a_u$, because $r \leq u \leq S < t$. We may therefore assume that $t = S$. Suppose $k < t$; then $c_k = d_k = t$, because $S \leq c_k \leq d_k \leq t$. But $r = t$ leads to $c_k = N - 1$ and a contradiction; and $r < t$ leads to $u = t$, from which it follows that $A_t > A_{t-1} = a_{t-1} - 1 \geq 0$.

(Deep breath.) OK; we've reduced the problem to cases with $k = t = S$. Hence $t = s \leq c_t \leq d_t \leq D_t = t$, and we have $a_t = a_{t-1} + 1$. Consequently $a_{t-1} = 0$.

In fact we can show by induction on $t - j$ that $a_j = 0$ for $p \leq j < t$: If $a_{j+1} = 0$ then $0 \geq a_j = c_{j+1} - t - 1 \geq q - 1 \geq 0$, because $c_{j+1} \geq t + q$ when $p \leq j < t - 1$.

If $p < t - 1$, this argument proves that $q = 1$ and $c_r = N - 1 = t + 1$. We conclude that, regardless of p, we must have $q = 1$, $N = t + 2$, $D_j = t + 1$ for $1 \leq j \leq p$, $D_j = t$ for $p < j \leq t + 1$, and $D_N = p + 1$. Algorithm H does actually change this "good" sequence into a "bad" one; but $D_1 + \cdots + D_N = 2p + t(t+1) + 1$ is odd.

106. False in the trivial cases when $d \leq 1$ and $n \geq d + 2$. Otherwise true: In fact, the first $n - 1$ edges generated in step H4 contain no cycles, so they form a spanning tree.

107. The permutation φ of exercise 78 takes a vertex of degree d into a vertex of degree $n - 1 - d$. And φ^2 is an automorphism that pairs up two vertices of equal degree, except for a possible fixed point of degree $(n-1)/2$.

(Conversely, a somewhat intricate extension of Algorithm H will construct a self-complementary graph from every graphical sequence that satisfies these conditions, provided that $d_{(n-1)/2} = (n-1)/2$ when n is odd. See C. R. J. Clapham and D. J. Kleitman, *J. Combinatorial Theory* **B20** (1976), 67–74.)

108. We may assume that $d_1^+ \geq \cdots \geq d_n^+$; the in-degrees d_k^- need not be in any particular order. Apply Algorithm H to the sequence $d_1 \ldots d_n = d_1^+ \ldots d_n^+$, but with the following changes: Step H2 becomes "[Done?] Terminate successfully if $d_1 = n = 0$; terminate unsuccessfully if $d_1 > n$." In step H3, change "$j \leftarrow d_n$" to "$j \leftarrow d_n^-$," and terminate unsuccessfully if $j > c_1$. In step H4, change "Set ... and set" to "If $j > 0$, set $m \leftarrow c_t$, create the arc $m \longrightarrow n$, and set"; and set $n \leftarrow n - 1$ just before returning to H2. An argument like Lemma M and Corollary H justifies this approach.

(Exercise 7.2.1.4–57 proves that such digraphs exist if and only if $d_1^- + \cdots + d_n^- = d_1^+ + \cdots + d_n^+$ and $d_1^- \ldots d_n^- = \{d_1', \ldots, d_n'\}$, where $d_1' \geq \cdots \geq d_n'$ and $d_1' \ldots d_n'$ is majorized by the conjugate partition $c_1 \ldots c_n = (d_1^+ \ldots d_n^+)^T$. The variant where loops $v \longrightarrow v$ are forbidden is harder; see D. R. Fulkerson, *Pacific J. Math.* **10** (1960), 831–836.)

109. It's the same as exercise 108, if we put $d_k^+ = d_k[k \leq m]$ and $d_k^- = d_k[k > m]$.

110. There are p vertices of degree $d = d_1$ and q vertices of degree $d - 1$, where $p + q = n$.

Case 1, $d = 2k + 1$. Make $u \text{ --- } v$ whenever $(u - v) \bmod n \in \{2, 3, \ldots, k+1, n-k-1, \ldots, n-3, n-2\}$; also add the $p/2$ edges $1 \text{ --- } 2$, $3 \text{ --- } 4$, $\ldots$, $(p-1) \text{ --- } p$.

Case 2, $d = 2k > 0$. Make $u \text{ --- } v$ whenever $(u - v) \bmod n \in \{2, 3, \ldots, k, n-k, \ldots, n-3, n-2\}$; also add the edges $1 \text{ --- } 2$, $\ldots$, $(q-1) \text{ --- } q$, as well as the path or cycle $(q = 0? \ n: q) \text{ --- } (q+1) \text{ --- } \cdots \text{ --- } (n-1) \text{ --- } n$. [D. L. Wang and D. J. Kleitman, in *Networks* **3** (1973), 225–239, have proved that such graphs are highly connected.]

111. Suppose $N = n + n'$ and $V' = \{n+1, \ldots, N\}$. We want to construct $e_k = d - d_k$ edges between k and V', and additional edges within V', so that each vertex of V' has degree d. Let $s = e_1 + \cdots + e_n$. This task is possible only if (i) $n' \geq \max(e_1, \ldots, e_n)$; (ii) $n'd \geq s$; (iii) $n'd \leq s + n'(n' - 1)$; and (iv) $(n + n')d$ is even.

Such edges do exist whenever n' satisfies (i)–(iv): First, s suitable edges between V and V' can be created by cyclically choosing endpoints $(n+1, n+2, \ldots, n+n', n+1, \ldots)$, because of (i). This process assigns either $\lfloor s/n' \rfloor$ or $\lceil s/n' \rceil$ edges to each vertex of V'; we have $\lceil s/n' \rceil \leq d$ by (ii), and $d - \lfloor s/n' \rfloor \leq n' - 1$ by (iii). Therefore the additional edges needed inside V' are constructible by exercise 110 and (iv).

The choice $n' = n$ always works. Conversely, if $G = K_n(V) \setminus \{1 \text{ --- } 2\}$, condition (iii) requires $n' \geq n$ when $n \geq 4$. [P. Erdős and P. Kelly, *AMM* **70** (1963), 1074–1075.]

112. The uniquely best triangle in the *miles* data is

Saint Louis, MO $\overset{748}{—\!—}$ Toronto, ON $\overset{746}{—\!—}$ Winston-Salem, NC $\overset{748}{—\!—}$ Saint Louis, MO.

113. By Murphy's Law, it has n rows and m columns; so it's $n \times m$, not $m \times n$.

114. A loop in a multigraph is an edge $\{a, a\}$ with repeated vertices, and a multigraph is a 2-uniform hypergraph. Thus we should allow the incidence matrix of a general hypergraph to have entries greater than 1 when an edge contains a vertex more than once. (A pedant would probably call this a "multihypergraph.") With these considerations in mind, the incidence matrix and bipartite multigraph corresponding to (26) are

$$\begin{pmatrix} 210000 \\ 011100 \\ 001122 \end{pmatrix};$$

115. The element in row e and column f of $B^T B$ is $\sum_v b_{ve} b_{vf}$; so $B^T B$ is $2I$ plus the adjacency matrix of $L(G)$. Similarly, BB^T is D plus the adjacency matrix of G, where D is the diagonal matrix with $d_{vv} =$ degree of v. (See exercises 2.3.4.2–18, 19, and 20.)

116. $\overline{K_{m,n}^{(r)}} = K_m^{(r)} \oplus K_n^{(r)}$, generalizing (38), for all $r \geq 1$.

117. The nonisomorphic multisets of singleton edges for $m = 4$ and $V = \{0, 1, 2\}$ are $\{\{0\}, \{0\}, \{0\}, \{0\}\}$, $\{\{0\}, \{0\}, \{0\}, \{1\}\}$, $\{\{0\}, \{0\}, \{1\}, \{1\}\}$, and $\{\{0\}, \{0\}, \{1\}, \{2\}\}$. The answer in general is the number of partitions of m into at most n parts, namely $\left| \begin{smallmatrix} m+n \\ n \end{smallmatrix} \right|$, using the notation explained in Section 7.2.1.4. (Of course, there's little reason to think of partitions as 1-uniform hypergraphs, except when answering strange exercises.)

118. Let d be the sum of the vertex degrees. The corresponding bipartite graph is a forest with $m + n$ vertices, d edges, and p components. Hence $d = m + n - p$, by Theorem 2.3.4.1A.

119. Then there's an additional edge, containing all seven vertices.

120. We could say that (hyper)arcs are arbitrary sequences of vertices, or sequences of distinct vertices. But most authors seem to define hyperarcs to be $A \longrightarrow v$, where A is an unordered set of vertices. When the best definition is found, it will probably be the one that has the most important practical applications.

121. $\chi(H) = |F| - \alpha(I(H)^T)$ is the size of a minimum cover of V by sets of F.

122. (a) One can verify that there are just seven 3-element covers, namely the vertices of an edge; so there are seven 4-element independent sets, namely the complements of an edge. We can't two-color the hypergraph, because one color would need to be used 4 times and the other three vertices would be an edge. (Hypergraph (56) is essentially the projective plane with seven points and seven lines.)

(b) Since we're dualizing, let's call the vertices and edges of the Petersen graph "points" and "lines"; then the vertices and edges of the dual are lines and points, respectively. Color red the five lines that join an outer point to an inner point. The other ten lines are independent (they don't contain all three of the lines touching any point); so they can be colored green. No set of eleven lines can be independent, because no four lines can touch all ten points. (Thus the Petersen dual is a bipartite hypergraph, in spite of the fact that it contains cycles of length 5.)

123. They correspond to $n \times n$ latin squares, whose entries are the vertex colors.

124. Four colors easily suffice. If it were 3-colorable, there must be four vertices of each color, since no five vertices are independent. Then two opposite corners must have the same color, and a contradiction arises quickly.

125. The Chvátal graph is the smallest such graph with $g = 4$. G. Brinkmann found the smallest with $g = 5$: It has 21 vertices a_j, b_j, c_j for $0 \leq j < 7$, with edges $a_j \!-\! a_{j+2}$, $a_j \!-\! b_j$, $a_j \!-\! b_{j+1}$, $b_j \!-\! c_j$, $b_j \!-\! c_{j+2}$, $c_j \!-\! c_{j+3}$ and subscripts mod 7. M. Meringer showed that there must be at least 35 vertices if $g > 5$. B. Grünbaum conjectured that g can be arbitrarily large; but no further constructions are known. [See *AMM* **77** (1970), 1088–1092; *Graph Theory Notes of New York* **32** (1997), 40–41.]

126. When m and n are even, both C_m and C_n are bipartite, and 4-coloring is easy. Otherwise a 4-coloring is impossible. When $m = n = 3$, a 9-coloring is optimum by exercise 93. When $m = 3$ and $n = 4$ or 5, at most two vertices are independent; it's easy to find an optimum 6- or 8-coloring. Otherwise we obtain a 5-coloring by painting vertex (j, k) with $(a_j + 2b_k) \bmod 5$, where periodic sequences $\langle a_j \rangle$ and $\langle b_k \rangle$ exist with period lengths m and n, respectively, such that $a_j - a_{j+1} \equiv \pm 1$ and $b_k - b_{k+1} \equiv \pm 1$ for all j and k. [K. Vesztergombi, *Acta Cybernetica* **4** (1979), 207–212.]

127. (a) The result is true when $n = 1$. Otherwise let $H = G \backslash v$, where v is any vertex. Then $\overline{H} = \overline{G} \backslash v$, and we have $\chi(H) + \chi(\overline{H}) \leq n$ by induction. Clearly $\chi(G) \leq \chi(H) + 1$ and $\chi(\overline{G}) \leq \chi(\overline{H}) + 1$; so there's no problem unless equality holds in all three cases. But that can't happen; it implies that $\chi(H) \leq d$ and $\chi(\overline{H}) \leq n - 1 - d$, where d is the degree of v in G. [E. A. Nordhaus and J. W. Gaddum, *AMM* **63** (1956), 175–177.]

To get equality, let $G = K_a \oplus \overline{K_b}$, where $ab > 0$ and $a + b = n$. Then we have $\overline{G} = \overline{K_a} \!-\! K_b$, $\chi(G) = a$, and $\chi(\overline{G}) = b + 1$. [All graphs for which equality holds have been found by H.-J. Finck, *Wiss. Zeit. der Tech. Hochschule Ilmenau* **12** (1966), 243–246.]

(b) A k-coloring of G has at least $\lceil n/k \rceil$ vertices of some color; those vertices form a clique in $\overline{G}$. Hence $\chi(G)\chi(\overline{G}) \geq \chi(G)\lceil n/\chi(G) \rceil \geq n$. Equality holds when $G = K_n$.

(From (a) and (b) we deduce that $\chi(G) + \chi(\overline{G}) \geq 2\sqrt{n}$ and $\chi(G)\chi(\overline{G}) \leq \frac{1}{4}(n+1)^2$.)

128. $\chi(G \square H) = \max(\chi(G), \chi(H))$. This many colors is clearly necessary. And if the functions $a(u)$ and $b(v)$ color G and H with the colors $\{0, 1, \ldots, k-1\}$, we can color $G \square H$ with $c(u, v) = (a(u) + b(v)) \bmod k$.

129. A complete row or column (16 cases); a complete diagonal of length 4 or more (18 cases); a 5-cell pattern $\{(x,y), (x-a, y-a), (x-a, y+a), (x+a, y-a), (x+a, y+a)\}$ for $a \in \{1, 2, 3\}$ (36 + 16 + 4 cases); a 5-cell pattern $\{(x,y), (x-a, y), (x+a, y), (x, y-a),$ $(x, y+a)\}$ for $a \in \{1, 2, 3\}$ (36 + 16 + 4 cases); a pattern containing four of those five cells, when the fifth lies off the board (24 + 32 + 24 cases); or a 4-cell pattern $\{(x,y), (x+a, y), (x, y+a), (x+a, y+a)\}$ for $a \in \{1, 3, 5, 7\}$ (49 + 25 + 9 + 1 cases). Altogether 310 maximal cliques, with respectively $(168, 116, 4, 4, 18)$ of size $(4, 5, 6, 7, 8)$.

130. If graph G has p maximal cliques and graph H has q, then the join $G \!-\! H$ has pq, because the cliques of $G \!-\! H$ are simply the unions of cliques from G and H. Furthermore, the empty graph $\overline{K_n}$ has n maximal cliques (namely its singleton sets).

Thus the complete k-partite graph with part sizes $\{n_1, \ldots, n_k\}$, being the join of empty graphs of those sizes, has $n_1 \ldots n_k$ maximal cliques.

131. Assume that $n > 1$. In a complete k-partite graph, the number $n_1 \ldots n_k$ is maximized when each part has size 3, except perhaps for one or two parts of size 2. (See exercise 7.2.1.4–68(a).) So we must prove that $N(n)$ cannot be larger than this in *any* graph.

Let $m(v)$ be the number of maximal cliques that contain vertex v. If $u \not\!\!-\! v$ and $m(u) \leq m(v)$, construct the graph G' that is like G except that u is now adjacent to all the neighbors of v instead of to its former neighbors. Every maximal clique U in either graph belongs to one of three classes:

    i) $u \in U$; there are $m(u)$ of these in G and $m(v)$ of them in G'.

ii) $v \in U$; there are $m(v)$ of these in G and also in G'.

iii) $u \notin U$ and $v \notin U$; such maximal cliques in G are also maximal in G'.

Therefore G' has at least as many maximal cliques as G. And we can obtain a complete k-partite graph by appropriately repeating the process.

[This argument, due to Paul Erdős, was presented by J. W. Moon and L. Moser in *Israel J. Math.* **3** (1965), 23–25.]

132. The strong product of cliques in G and H is a clique in $G \boxtimes H$, by exercise 93; hence $\omega(G \boxtimes H) \geq \omega(G)\omega(H) = \chi(G)\chi(H)$. On the other hand, colorings $a(u)$ and $b(v)$ of G and H lead to the coloring $c(u,v) = (a(u), b(v))$ of $G \boxtimes H$; hence $\chi(G \boxtimes H) \leq \chi(G)\chi(H)$. And $\omega(G \boxtimes H) \leq \chi(G \boxtimes H)$.

133. (a) 24; (b) 60; (c) 3; (d) 6; (e) 6; (f) 4; (g) 5; (h) 4; (i) $K_2 \boxtimes C_{12}$; (j) 18; (k) 12. (l) Yes, of degree 5. (m) No. [In fact, Markus Chimani used branch-and-cut methods in 2009 to prove that it cannot be drawn with fewer than 12 crossings.] (n) Yes; in fact, it is 4-connected (see Section 7.4.1). (o) Yes; we consider *every* graph to be directed, with two arcs for each edge. (p) Of course not. (q) Yes, easily.

[The musical graph represents simple modulations between key signatures. It appears on page 73 of *Graphs* by R. J. Wilson and J. J. Watkins (1990).]

134. By rotating and/or swapping the inner and outer vertices, we can find an automorphism that takes any vertex into C. If C is fixed, we can interchange the inner and outer vertices of any subset of the remaining 11 pairs, and/or do a left-right reflection. Therefore there are $24 \times 2^{11} \times 2 = 98{,}304$ automorphisms altogether.

135. Let $\omega = e^{2\pi i/12}$, and define the matrices $Q = (q_{ij})$, $S = (s_{ij})$, where $q_{ij} = [j = (i+1) \bmod 12]$ and $s_{ij} = \omega^{ij}$, for $0 \leq i, j < 12$. By exercise 96(b), the adjacency matrix of the musical graph $K_2 \boxtimes C_{12}$ is $A = \binom{1\,1}{1\,1} \otimes (I + Q + Q^-) - I$. Let T be the matrix $\binom{1\ \ 1}{1\ -1} \otimes S$; then $T^- A T$ is a diagonal matrix D whose first 12 entries are $1 + 4\cos\frac{j\pi}{6}$ for $0 \leq j < 12$, and whose other 12 entries are -1. Therefore $A^{2m} = T D^{2m} T^-$, and it follows that the number of $2m$-step walks from C to (C, G, D, A, E, B, F$^\sharp$) respectively is

$$C_m = \tfrac{1}{24}(25^m + 2(13 + 4\sqrt{3})^m + 3^{2m+1} + 2(13 - 4\sqrt{3})^m + 16);$$

$$G_m = \tfrac{1}{24}(25^m + \sqrt{3}(13 + 4\sqrt{3})^m - \sqrt{3}(13 - 4\sqrt{3})^m - 1);$$

$$D_m = \tfrac{1}{24}(25^m + (13 + 4\sqrt{3})^m + (13 - 4\sqrt{3})^m - 3);$$

$$A_m = \tfrac{1}{24}(25^m - 3^{2m+1} + 2);$$

$$E_m = \tfrac{1}{24}(25^m - (13 + 4\sqrt{3})^m - (13 - 4\sqrt{3})^m + 1);$$

$$B_m = \tfrac{1}{24}(25^m - \sqrt{3}(13 + 4\sqrt{3})^m + \sqrt{3}(13 - 4\sqrt{3})^m - 1);$$

$$F_m^\sharp = \tfrac{1}{24}(25^m - 2(13 + 4\sqrt{3})^m + 3^{2m+1} - 2(13 - 4\sqrt{3})^m);$$

also $a_m = C_m - 1$, $d_m = F_m = e_m = G_m$, etc. In particular, $(C_6, G_6, D_6, A_6, E_6, B_6, F_6^\sharp) = (15462617, 14689116, 12784356, 10106096, 7560696, 5655936, 5015296)$, so the desired probability is $15462617/5^{12} \approx 6.33\%$. As $m \to \infty$, the probabilities are all $\tfrac{1}{24} + O(0.8^m)$.

136. No. Only two Cayley graphs of order 10 are cubic, namely $K_2 \square C_5$ (whose vertices can be written $\{e, \alpha, \alpha^2, \alpha^3, \alpha^4, \beta, \beta\alpha, \beta\alpha^2, \beta\alpha^3, \beta\alpha^4\}$ where $\alpha^5 = \beta^2 = (\alpha\beta)^2 = e$) and the graph with vertices $\{0, 1, \ldots, 9\}$ and arcs $v \to (v \pm 1) \bmod 10$, $v \to (v+5) \bmod 10$. [See D. A. Holton and J. Sheehan, *The Petersen Graph* (1993), exercise 9.10. Incidentally, the SGB graphs *raman*$(p, q, t, 0)$ are Cayley graphs.]

137. Let $[x, y]$ denote the label of (x, y); we want $[x, y] = [x + a, y + b] = [x + c, y + d]$ for all x and y. If A is the matrix $\left(\begin{smallmatrix} a & b \\ c & d \end{smallmatrix}\right)$, the operation of adding t times the bottom row of A to the top row changes A to the matrix $A' = \left(\begin{smallmatrix} 1 & t \\ 0 & 1 \end{smallmatrix}\right)A = \left(\begin{smallmatrix} a' & b' \\ c' & d' \end{smallmatrix}\right)$, where $a' = a + tc$, $b' = b + td$, $c' = c$, $d' = d$. The new condition $[x, y] = [x + a', y + b'] = [x + c', y + d']$ is equivalent to the old; and $\gcd(a', b', c', d') = \gcd(a, b, c, d)$. Similarly we can premultiply A by $\left(\begin{smallmatrix} 1 & 0 \\ t & 1 \end{smallmatrix}\right)$ without really changing the problem.

We can also operate on columns, replacing A by $A'' = A\left(\begin{smallmatrix} 1 & t \\ 0 & 1 \end{smallmatrix}\right) = \left(\begin{smallmatrix} a'' & b'' \\ c'' & d'' \end{smallmatrix}\right)$, where $a'' = a$, $b'' = ta + b$, $c'' = c$, $d'' = tc + d$. This operation does alter the problem, but only slightly: If we find a labeling that satisfies $[\![x, y]\!] = [\![x + a'', y + b'']\!] = [\![x + c'', y + d'']\!]$ for all x and y, then we'll have $[x, y] = [x + a, y + b] = [x + c, x + d]$ if $[x, y] = [\![x, y + tx]\!]$. Similarly we can postmultiply A by $\left(\begin{smallmatrix} 1 & 0 \\ t & 1 \end{smallmatrix}\right)$; the problem remains almost the same.

A series of such row and column operations will reduce A to the simple form $UAV = \left(\begin{smallmatrix} 1 & 0 \\ 0 & n \end{smallmatrix}\right)$, where U and V are integer matrices with $\det U = \det V = 1$. Furthermore, if we have $V = \left(\begin{smallmatrix} \alpha & \beta \\ \gamma & \delta \end{smallmatrix}\right)$, a labeling for the reduced problem that satisfies the simple conditions $[\![x, y]\!] = [\![x + 1, y]\!] = [\![x, y + n]\!]$ will provide a solution to the original labeling problem if we define $[x, y] = [\![\alpha x + \gamma y, \beta x + \delta y]\!]$.

Finally, the reduced labeling problem is easy: We let $[\![x, y]\!] = y \bmod n$. Thus the desired answer is to set $p = \beta$, $q = \delta$.

138. Proceeding as before, but with a $k \times k$ matrix A, row and column operations will reduce the problem to a diagonal matrix UAV. The diagonal entries $(d_1, \ldots, d_k)$ are characterized by the condition that $d_1 \ldots d_j$ is the greatest common divisor of the determinants of all $j \times j$ submatrices of A. [This is "Smith normal form"; see H. J. S. Smith, *Philosophical Transactions* **151** (1861), 293–326, §14.] If the labeling $[\![x]\!]$ satisfies the reduced problem, the original problem is satisfied by $[x] = [\![xV]\!]$. The number of elements in the generalized torus is $n = \det A = d_1 \ldots d_k$.

The reduced problem has a simple solution as before if $d_1 = \cdots = d_{k-1} = 1$. But in general the reduced labeling will be an r-dimensional ordinary torus of dimensions $(d_{k-r+1}, \ldots, d_k)$, where $d_{k-r+1} > d_{k-r} = 1$. (Here $d_0 = 1$; we might have $r = k$.)

In the requested example, we find $d_1 = 1$, $d_2 = 2$, $d_3 = 10$, $n = 20$; indeed,

$$UAV = \begin{pmatrix} 1 & -2 & 0 \\ 0 & 1 & -1 \\ -1 & -1 & 4 \end{pmatrix}\begin{pmatrix} 3 & 1 & 1 \\ 1 & 3 & 1 \\ 1 & 1 & 3 \end{pmatrix}\begin{pmatrix} 1 & 5 & 6 \\ 0 & 1 & 1 \\ 0 & 0 & 1 \end{pmatrix} = \begin{pmatrix} 1 & 0 & 0 \\ 0 & 2 & 0 \\ 0 & 0 & 10 \end{pmatrix}.$$

Each point (x, y, z) now receives a two-dimensional label $(u, v) = ((5x + y) \bmod 2, (6x + y + z) \bmod 10)$. The six neighbors of (u, v) are $((u \pm 1) \bmod 2, v)$, $((u \pm 1) \bmod 2, (v \pm 1) \bmod 10)$, $(u, (v \pm 1) \bmod 10)$. It's a multigraph, since the first two neighbors are identical; but it's not the same as the multigraph $C_2 \boxtimes C_{10}$, which has degree 8.

[Generalized toruses are essentially the Cayley graphs of Abelian groups; see exercise 136. They have been proposed as convenient interconnection networks, in which case it is desirable to minimize the diameter when k and n are given. See C. K. Wong and D. Coppersmith, *JACM* **21** (1974), 392–402; C. M. Fiduccia, R. W. Forcade, and J. S. Zito, *SIAM J. Discrete Math.* **11** (1998), 157–167.]

139. (This exercise helps clarify the distinction between labeled graphs G, in which the vertices have definite names, and unlabeled graphs H such as those in Fig. 2.) If N_H is the number of labeled graphs on $\{1, 2, \ldots, h\}$ that are isomorphic to H, and if U is any h-element subset of V, the probability that $G \mid U$ is isomorphic to H is $N_H / 2^{h(h-1)/2}$. Therefore the answer is $\binom{n}{h} N_H / 2^{h(h-1)/2}$. We need only figure out the value of N_H, which is: (a) 1; (b) $h!/2$; (c) $(h-1)!/2$; (d) $h!/a$, where H has a automorphisms.

140. (a) $\#(K_3{:}W_n) = n-1$ and $\#(P_3{:}W_n) = \binom{n-1}{2}$ for $n \geq 5$; also $\#(\overline{K_3}{:}W_8) = 7$.

(b) G is proportional if and only if $\#(K_3{:}G) = \#(\overline{K_3}{:}G) = \frac{1}{8}\binom{n}{3}$ and $\#(P_3{:}G) = \#(\overline{P_3}{:}G) = \frac{3}{8}\binom{n}{3}$. If G has e edges, we have $(n-2)e = 3\#(K_3{:}G)+2\#(P_3{:}G)+\#(\overline{P_3}{:}G)$, because every pair of vertices appears in $n-2$ induced subgraphs. If G has degree sequence $d_1 \ldots d_n$, we have $d_1 + \cdots + d_n = 2e$, $\binom{d_1}{2} + \cdots + \binom{d_n}{2} = 3\#(K_3{:}G)+\#(P_3{:}G)$, and $d_1(n-1-d_1)+\cdots+d_n(n-1-d_n) = 2\#(P_3{:}G)+2\#(\overline{P_3}{:}G)$. Therefore a proportional graph satisfies $(*)$ — unless $n = 2$. (The exercise should have excluded that case.)

Conversely, if G satisfies $(*)$ and has the correct $\#(K_3{:}G)$, it also has the correct $\#(P_3{:}G)$, $\#(\overline{P_3}{:}G)$, and $\#(\overline{K_3}{:}G)$.

[*References:* S. Janson and J. Kratochvíl, *Random Structures & Algorithms* **2** (1991), 209–224. In *J. Combinatorial Theory* **B47** (1989), 125–145, A. D. Barbour, M. Karoński, and A. Ruciński had shown that the variance of $\#(H{:}G)$ is proportional to either n^{2h-2}, n^{2h-3}, or n^{2h-4}, where the first case occurs when H does not have $\frac{1}{2}\binom{h}{2}$ edges, and the third case occurs when H is a proportional graph.]

141. Only 8 degree sequences $d_1 \ldots d_8$ satisfy $(*)$: $73333333 \, (1/2)$, $65433322 \, (26/64)$, $64444222 \, (2/10)$, $64443331 \, (8/22)$, $55543222 \, (8/20)$, $55533331 \, (2/10)$, $55444321 \, (26/64)$, and $44444440 \, (1/2)$. Each degree sequence is shown here with statistics (N_1/N), where N nonisomorphic graphs have that sequence and N_1 of them are proportional. The last three cases are complements of the first three. No graph of order 8 is both proportional and self-complementary. Maximally symmetric examples of the first five cases are W_8,

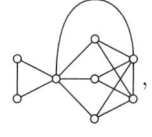 , 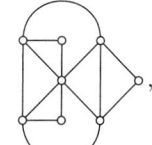 , 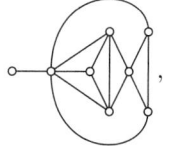 , and 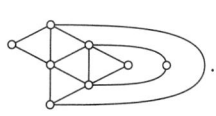 .

142. The hint follows as in answer 140; $(n - 3)\#(\overline{K_3}{:}G)$ and $(n - 3)\#(P_3{:}G)$ can also be expressed in terms of four-vertex counts. Furthermore, a graph with e edges has $\binom{e}{2} = \#(P_3 \subseteq G)+\#(K_2 \oplus K_2 \subseteq G)$, because any two edges form either P_3 or $K_2 \oplus K_2$; in this formula, $\#(P_3 \subseteq G)$ counts not-necessarily-induced subgraphs.

We have $\#(P_3 \subseteq G) = \#(P_3{:}G) + 3\#(K_3{:}G)$, and a similar formula expresses $\#(K_2 \oplus K_2 \subseteq G)$ in terms of induced counts. Thus an extraproportional graph must be proportional and satisfy $e = \frac{1}{2}\binom{n}{2}$, $\#(P_3 \subseteq G) = \frac{3}{4}\binom{n}{3}$, $\#(K_2 \oplus K_2 \subseteq G) = \frac{3}{4}\binom{n}{4}$. But these values contradict the formula for $\binom{e}{2}$.

143. Consider the graph whose vertices are the rows of A, and whose edges $u - v$ signify that rows u and v agree except in one column, j. Label such an edge j.

If the graph contains a cycle, delete any edge of the cycle, and repeat the process until no cycles remain. Notice that the label on every deleted edge appears elsewhere in its cycle; hence the deletions don't affect the set of edge labels. But we're left with fewer than $m \leq n$ edges, by Theorem 2.3.4.1A; so there are fewer than n different labels. [See J. A. Bondy, *J. Combinatorial Theory* **B12** (1972), 201–202.]

144. Let G be the graph on vertices $\{1,\ldots,m\}$, with edges $i - j$ if and only if $* \neq x_{il} \neq x_{jl} \neq *$ for some l. This graph is k-colorable if and only if there is a completion with at most k distinct rows. Conversely, if G is a graph on vertices $\{1,\ldots,n\}$, with adjacency matrix A, the $n \times n$ matrix $X = A + *(J - I - A)$ has the property that $i - j$ if and only if $* \neq x_{il} \neq x_{jl} \neq *$ for some l. [See M. Sauerhoff and I. Wegener, *IEEE Trans.* **CAD-15** (1996), 1435–1437.]

145. Set $c \leftarrow 0$ and repeat the following operations for $1 \leq j \leq n$: If $c = 0$, set $x \leftarrow a_j$ and $c \leftarrow 1$; otherwise if $x = a_j$, set $c \leftarrow c + 1$; otherwise set $c \leftarrow c - 1$. Then x is the answer. The idea is to keep track of a possible majority element x, which occurs c times in nondiscarded elements; we discard a_j and one x whenever finding $x \neq a_j$. [See *Automated Reasoning* (Kluwer, 1991), 105–117. Extensions to find all elements that occur more than n/k times, in $O(n \log k)$ steps, have been discussed by J. Misra and D. Gries, *Science of Computer Programming* **2** (1982), 143–152.]

SECTION 7.1.1

1. (Solution by C. Sartena.) He was describing the implication $x \Rightarrow y$, with "it" standing respectively for y, x, x, y, y, x. (Other solutions are possible.)

2. The Earth operation corresponding to the Pincusian $x \circ y$ is $\overline{\bar{x} \circ \bar{y}}$; its truth table is therefore the reverse of the complement of the truth table for $\circ$. Hence the respective answers are $\top$, $\vee$, $\subset$, $\llcorner$, $\supset$, R, $\equiv$, $\wedge$, $\bar{\wedge}$, $\oplus$, $\bar{\mathsf{R}}$, $\bar{\supset}$, $\bar{\llcorner}$, $\bar{\subset}$, $\bar{\vee}$, $\bot$. (Any identity involving the 16 operations of Table 1 implies a corresponding dual identity obtained by substituting the Pincusian equivalents. For example, each of De Morgan's laws (11) and (12) is the dual of the other, as are the identities (3), (4) relating $\equiv$ and $\oplus$. In this sense $\equiv$ can be considered to be just as useful as its dual, $\oplus$.)

3. (a) $\vee$; (b) $\wedge$; (c) $\bar{\llcorner}$; (d) $\equiv$. [Many formulas actually work out better if we use -1 for truth and $+1$ for falsehood, even though this convention seems a bit immoral; then $x \cdot y$ corresponds to $\oplus$. Notice that $\langle xyz \rangle = \text{sign}(x + y + z)$, with either convention.]

4. [*Trans. Amer. Math. Soc.* **14** (1913), 481–488.] (a) Start with the truth tables for $\llcorner$ and R; then compute truth table $\alpha \bar{\wedge} \beta$ bitwise from each known pair of truth tables α and β, generating the results in order of the length of each formula and writing down a shortest formula that leads to each new 4-bit table:

$\bot$: $(x \bar{\wedge} (x \bar{\wedge} x)) \bar{\wedge} (x \bar{\wedge} (x \bar{\wedge} x))$ $\bar{\vee}$: $(x \bar{\wedge} (x \bar{\wedge} x)) \bar{\wedge} ((y \bar{\wedge} y) \bar{\wedge} (x \bar{\wedge} x))$

$\wedge$: $(x \bar{\wedge} y) \bar{\wedge} (x \bar{\wedge} y)$ $\equiv$: $(x \bar{\wedge} y) \bar{\wedge} ((y \bar{\wedge} y) \bar{\wedge} (x \bar{\wedge} x))$

$\bar{\supset}$: $(x \bar{\wedge} (x \bar{\wedge} y)) \bar{\wedge} (x \bar{\wedge} (x \bar{\wedge} y))$ $\bar{\mathsf{R}}$: $y \bar{\wedge} y$

$\llcorner$: x $\subset$: $y \bar{\wedge} (x \bar{\wedge} x)$

$\bar{\subset}$: $(y \bar{\wedge} (x \bar{\wedge} x)) \bar{\wedge} (y \bar{\wedge} (x \bar{\wedge} x))$ $\bar{\llcorner}$: $x \bar{\wedge} x$

R: y $\supset$: $x \bar{\wedge} (x \bar{\wedge} y)$

$\oplus$: $(y \bar{\wedge} (x \bar{\wedge} x)) \bar{\wedge} (x \bar{\wedge} (x \bar{\wedge} y))$ $\bar{\wedge}$: $x \bar{\wedge} y$

$\vee$: $(y \bar{\wedge} y) \bar{\wedge} (x \bar{\wedge} x)$ $\top$: $x \bar{\wedge} (x \bar{\wedge} x)$

(b) In this case we start with four tables $\bot$, $\top$, $\llcorner$, R, and we prefer formulas with fewer occurrences of variables whenever there's a choice between formulas of a given length:

$\bot$: 0 $\bar{\vee}$: $1 \bar{\wedge} ((y \bar{\wedge} 1) \bar{\wedge} (x \bar{\wedge} 1))$

$\wedge$: $(x \bar{\wedge} y) \bar{\wedge} 1$ $\equiv$: $(x \bar{\wedge} y) \bar{\wedge} ((y \bar{\wedge} 1) \bar{\wedge} (x \bar{\wedge} 1))$

$\bar{\supset}$: $((y \bar{\wedge} 1) \bar{\wedge} x) \bar{\wedge} 1$ $\bar{\mathsf{R}}$: $y \bar{\wedge} 1$

$\llcorner$: x $\subset$: $y \bar{\wedge} (x \bar{\wedge} 1)$

$\bar{\subset}$: $(y \bar{\wedge} (x \bar{\wedge} 1)) \bar{\wedge} 1$ $\bar{\llcorner}$: $x \bar{\wedge} 1$

R: y $\supset$: $(y \bar{\wedge} 1) \bar{\wedge} x$

$\oplus$: $(y \bar{\wedge} (x \bar{\wedge} 1)) \bar{\wedge} ((y \bar{\wedge} 1) \bar{\wedge} x)$ $\bar{\wedge}$: $x \bar{\wedge} y$

$\vee$: $(y \bar{\wedge} 1) \bar{\wedge} (x \bar{\wedge} 1)$ $\top$: 1

5. (a) $\perp$: $x\,\overline{C}\,x$; $\wedge$: $(x\,\overline{C}\,y)\,\overline{C}\,y$; $\overline{\supset}$: $y\,\overline{C}\,x$;   L: x; $\overline{C}$: $x\,\overline{C}\,y$;   R: y;   the other 10 cannot be expressed.   (b) With constants, however, all 16 are possible:

$\perp$: 0

$\wedge$: $(y\,\overline{C}\,1)\,\overline{C}\,x$

$\overline{\supset}$: $y\,\overline{C}\,x$

L: x

$\overline{C}$: $x\,\overline{C}\,y$

R: y

$\oplus$: $((y\,\overline{C}\,x)\,\overline{C}\,((x\,\overline{C}\,y)\,\overline{C}\,1))\,\overline{C}\,1$

$\vee$: $(y\,\overline{C}\,(x\,\overline{C}\,1))\,\overline{C}\,1$

$\overline{\vee}$: $y\,\overline{C}\,(x\,\overline{C}\,1)$

$\equiv$: $(y\,\overline{C}\,x)\,\overline{C}\,((x\,\overline{C}\,y)\,\overline{C}\,1)$

$\overline{R}$: $y\,\overline{C}\,1$

C: $(x\,\overline{C}\,y)\,\overline{C}\,1$

$\overline{L}$: $x\,\overline{C}\,1$

$\supset$: $(y\,\overline{C}\,x)\,\overline{C}\,1$

$\overline{\wedge}$: $((y\,\overline{C}\,1)\,\overline{C}\,x)\,\overline{C}\,1$

$\top$: 1

[B. A. Bernstein, *University of California Publications in Mathematics* **1** (1914), 87–96.]

6. (a) $\perp$, $\wedge$, L, R, $\oplus$, $\vee$, $\equiv$, $\top$. (b) $\perp$, L, R, $\oplus$, $\equiv$, $\top$. [Notice that all of these operators are associative. In fact, the stated identity implies the associative law in general: First we have (i) $(x \circ y) \circ ((z \circ y) \circ w) = ((x \circ z) \circ (z \circ y)) \circ ((z \circ y) \circ w) = (x \circ z) \circ w$, and similarly (ii) $(x \circ (y \circ z)) \circ (y \circ w) = x \circ (z \circ w)$. Furthermore (iii) $(x \circ y) \circ (z \circ w) = (x \circ y) \circ ((z \circ y) \circ (y \circ w)) = (x \circ z) \circ (y \circ w)$ by (i). Thus $(x \circ z) \circ w = (x \circ z) \circ ((z \circ z) \circ w) = (x \circ (z \circ z)) \circ (z \circ w) = x \circ (z \circ w)$ by (i), (iii), (ii). The free system generated by $\{x_1, \ldots, x_n\}$ has exactly $n + 2^n n^2$ distinct elements, namely $\{x_j \mid 1 \le j \le n\}$ and $\{x_i \circ x_{j_1} \circ \cdots \circ x_{j_r} \circ x_k \mid r \ge 0 \text{ and } 1 \le i, k \le n \text{ and } 1 \le j_1 < \cdots < j_r \le n\}$.]

7. Equivalently, we want the identity $y \circ (x \circ y) = x$, which holds only for $\oplus$ and $\equiv$. [Jevons noticed this property of $\oplus$ in *Pure Logic* §151, but he did not pursue the matter. We will investigate general systems of this nature, called "gropes," in Section 7.2.3.]

8. $(\{\perp, \wedge, \overline{C}\}, S_0)$, $(\{\top, \vee, \supset\}, S_1)$, $(\{L, \overline{L}\}, S_0 \cap S_1)$, $(\{\oplus, \equiv, \overline{R}\}, S_2)$, $(\{\overline{\supset}, \overline{\vee}\}, S_0 \cap S_2)$, $(\{C, \overline{\wedge}\}, S_1 \cap S_2)$, and (R, any), where $S_0 = \{\square \mid 0 \square 0 = 0\}$, $S_1 = \{\square \mid 1 \square 1 = 1\}$, and $S_2 = \{\square \mid \bar{x} \square \bar{y} = \overline{x \square y}\} = \{L, R, \overline{L}, \overline{R}\}$. Thus 92 of the 256 pairs are left-distributive. [This problem and those of exercise 6 were first treated by E. Schröder in §55 of his posthumously published *Vorlesungen über die Algebra der Logik* **2**, 2 (1905). He expressed the answer by saying in essence that the respective truth tables $(pqrs, wxyz)$ of $(\circ, \square)$ must satisfy the relation $((pq \vee rs) \wedge \bar{z}) \vee ((\bar{p}\bar{q} \vee \bar{r}\bar{s}) \wedge w) \vee ((p\bar{q} \vee r\bar{s}) \wedge ((w \equiv z) \vee (x \equiv y))) = 0$.]

9. (a) False; $(x \oplus y) \vee z = (x \vee z) \oplus (y \vee z) \oplus z$. (b) True, because the identity obviously holds when $z = 0$ and when $z = 1$. (c) True; it's also $(x \oplus y) \vee (x \oplus z) = 1 - [x = y = z]$.

10. The first stage of decomposition (16) yields the functions with truth tables $g = 10100011$ and $h = 10100011 \oplus 10010011 = 00110000$; and the process continues in a similar way, yielding $1 + y + xz + w + wy + wx + wxz$ (modulo 2).

11. The stated term is present if and only if $f(x_1, \ldots, x_n)$ is true an odd number of times when $x_1 = x_4 = x_5 = x_7 = x_9 = x_{10} = \cdots = 0$. (There are 2^k such cases when we set all but k variables to zero.) In other words the multilinear representation can be expressed in a suggestive notation like

$$f(x, y, z) = (f_{000} + f_{00*}z + f_{0*0}y + f_{0**}yz + f_{*00}x + f_{*0*}xz + f_{**0}xy + f_{***}xyz) \bmod 2$$

illustrated here for $n = 3$, where $f_{**0} = f(1, 1, 0) \oplus f(1, 0, 0) \oplus f(0, 1, 0) \oplus f(0, 0, 0)$, etc.

12. (a) Substitute $1 - w$ for $\bar{w}$, etc., in (23), getting $1 - y - xz + 2xyz - w + wy + wx + wxz - 2wxyz$. [Some authors have called this the "Zhegalkin polynomial"; but I. I. Zhegalkin himself always worked modulo 2. Other names in the literature are "availability polynomial," "reliability polynomial," "characteristic polynomial."]

(b) The corresponding coefficients for an arbitrary n-ary function can be as large as 2^{n-1} in absolute value (and this, by induction, is the maximum). For example, the integer multilinear representation of $x_1 \oplus \cdots \oplus x_n$ over the integers turns out to be $e_1 - 2e_2 + 4e_3 - \cdots + (-2)^{n-1}e_n$, where e_k is the kth elementary symmetric function of $\{x_1, \ldots, x_n\}$. The formula in the previous answer becomes

$$f(x, y, z) = f_{000} + f_{00*}z + f_{0*0}y + f_{0**}yz + f_{*00}x + f_{*0*}xz + f_{**0}xy + f_{***}xyz$$

over the integers, where we now have $f_{**0} = f(1, 1, 0) - f(1, 0, 0) - f(0, 1, 0) + f(0, 0, 0)$, etc. This expansion is a disguised form of the Hadamard transform, Eq. 4.6.4–(38).

(c, d) The polynomial is the sum of its minterms like $x_1(1 - x_2)(1 - x_3)x_4$. Each minterm is nonnegative for $0 \leq x_1, \ldots, x_n \leq 1$, and the sum of all minterms is 1.

(e) $\partial f/\partial x_j = h(x) - g(x)$, where $h(x) \geq g(x)$ by (d). (See exercise 21.)

13. In fact, F is precisely the integer multilinear representation (see exercise 12).

14. Let $r_j = p_j/(1 - p_j)$. We want $f(0, 0, 0) = 0$ and $f(1, 1, 1) = 1 \Leftrightarrow r_1 r_2 r_3 > 1$, $f(0, 0, 1) = 0$ and $f(1, 1, 0) = 1 \Leftrightarrow r_1 r_2 > r_3$, $f(0, 1, 0) = 0$ and $f(1, 0, 1) = 1 \Leftrightarrow r_1 r_3 > r_2$, $f(0, 1, 1) = 0$ and $f(1, 0, 0) = 1 \Leftrightarrow r_1 > r_2 r_3$. So we get (a) $\langle x_1 x_2 x_3 \rangle$; (b) x_1; (c) $\bar{x}_3$.

15. Exercise 1.2.6–10 tells us that $\binom{x}{k} \bmod 2 = [x \& k = k]$. Hence, for example, $\binom{x}{11} \equiv x_4 \wedge x_2 \wedge x_1$ (modulo 2) when $x = (x_n \ldots x_1)_2$; and we can obtain every term in a multilinear representation like (19) in this way. Moreover, we needn't work mod 2, because the interpolating polynomial $\binom{x}{11}\binom{15-x}{4}$ represents $x_4 \wedge \bar{x}_3 \wedge x_2 \wedge x_1$ exactly.

16. Yes, or even by $+$, because different minterms can't be simultaneously true. (But we can't do that in ordinary disjunctive normal forms like (25). See exercise 35.)

17. The binary operation $\bar{\wedge}$ is not associative, so an expression like $x \bar{\wedge} y \bar{\wedge} z$ must be interpreted as a *ternary* operation. Quick's notation is fine if one understands NAND to be an n-ary operation, being careful to note that the NAND of a *single* variable x is $\bar{x}$.

18. If not, we could set $u_1 \leftarrow \cdots \leftarrow u_s \leftarrow 1$ and $v_1 \leftarrow \cdots \leftarrow v_t \leftarrow 0$, making f both true and false. (And if we consider applying the distributive law (2) repeatedly to a DNF until it becomes a CNF, we find that the converse is also true: The disjunction $v_1 \vee \cdots \vee v_t$ is implied by f if and only if it has a literal in common with every implicant of f, if and only if it has a literal in common with every prime implicant of f, if and only if it has a literal in common with every implicant of some DNF for f.)

19. The maximal subcubes contained in 0010, 0011, 0101, 0110, 1000, 1001, 1010, and 1011 are 0∗10, 0101, ∗01∗, and 10∗∗; so the answer is $(w \vee \bar{y} \vee z) \wedge (w \vee \bar{x} \vee y \vee \bar{z}) \wedge (x \vee \bar{y}) \wedge (\bar{w} \vee x)$. (This CNF is also shortest.)

20. True. The corresponding maximal subcube is contained in some maximal subcubes f' and g', and their intersection can't be larger. (This observation is due to Samson and Mills, whose paper is cited in answer 31 below.)

21. By Boole's law (20), we see that an n-ary function f is monotone if and only if its $(n-1)$-ary projections g and h are monotone and satisfy $g \leq h$. Therefore

$$f = (g \wedge \bar{x}_n) \vee (h \wedge x_n) = (g \wedge \bar{x}_n) \vee (g \wedge x_n) \vee (h \wedge x_n) = g \vee (h \wedge x_n),$$

so we can do without complementation. The constants 0 and 1 disappear unless the function is identically constant. Conversely, any expression built up from $\wedge$ and $\vee$ is obviously monotone.

Note on terminology: Strictly speaking, we should say "monotone nondecreasing" instead of simply "monotone," if we want to preserve the language of classical mathematics, because a decreasing function of a real variable is also said to be monotonic.

(See, for example, the "run test" in Section 3.3.2G.) But "nondecreasing" is quite a mouthful; so researchers who work extensively on Boolean functions have almost unanimously opted to assume that "monotone" automatically implies nondecreasing, in a Boolean context. Similarly, the mathematical term "positive function" normally refers to a function whose value exceeds zero; but authors who write about "positive Boolean functions" are referring to the functions that we are calling monotone. Since a monotone function is order-preserving, some authors have adopted the term *isotone*; but that word has already been coopted by physicists, chemists, and musicologists.

A Boolean function like $\bar{x} \vee y$, which becomes monotone if some subset of its variables is complemented, is called *unate*. Theorem Q obviously applies to unate functions.

22. Both g and $g \oplus h$ must be monotone, and $g(x) \wedge h(x) = 0$.

23. $x \wedge (v \vee y) \wedge (v \vee z) \wedge (w \vee z)$. (Corollary Q applies also to *conjunctive* prime forms of monotone functions. Therefore, to solve any problem of this kind, we need only apply the distributive law (2) until no $\wedge$ occurs within a $\vee$, then remove any clause that contains all the variables of another.)

24. By induction on k, the similar tree with $\vee$ at the root gives a function with $2^{2^{\lceil k/2 \rceil} - 1}$ prime implicants of length $2^{\lfloor k/2 \rfloor}$, while the tree with $\wedge$ gives $4^{2^{\lfloor k/2 \rfloor} - 1}$ of length $2^{\lceil k/2 \rceil}$. When $k = 6$, for example, the $4^7 = 2^{14}$ prime implicants in the $\wedge$ case have the form

$$x_{(0t_00t_00 0t_{000})_2} \wedge x_{(0t_00t_00 1t_{001})_2} \wedge x_{(0t_01t_01 0t_{010})_2} \wedge x_{(0t_01t_01 1t_{011})_2}$$
$$\wedge x_{(1t_10t_10 0t_{100})_2} \wedge x_{(1t_10t_10 1t_{101})_2} \wedge x_{(1t_11t_11 0t_{110})_2} \wedge x_{(1t_11t_11 1t_{111})_2},$$

with the t's either 0 or 1. [For further information about such Boolean functions, see D. E. Knuth and R. W. Moore, *Artificial Intelligence* **6** (1975), 293–326; V. Gurvich and L. Khachiyan, *Discrete Mathematics* **169** (1997), 245–248.]

25. Let a_n be the answer. Then $a_2 = a_3 = 2$, $a_4 = 3$, and $a_n = a_{n-2} + a_{n-3}$ for $n > 4$, because the prime implicants when $n > 4$ are either $p_{n-2} \wedge x_{n-1}$ or $p_{n-3} \wedge x_{n-2} \wedge x_n$ for some prime implicant p_k in the k-variable case. (These prime implicants correspond to minimal vertex covers of the path graph P_n. They are *shellable*, in the sense of exercise 35, when listed in lexicographic order. We have $a_n = (7P_n + 10P_{n+1} + P_{n+2})/23$ when P_n is the Perrin number of exercise 7.1.4–15.)

26. (a) Let $x_j = [j \in J]$. Then $f(x) = 0$ and $g(x) = 1$. (This fact was exercise 18.)

(b) Suppose, for example, that $k \in J \in \mathcal{G}$ and $k \notin \bigcup_{I \in \mathcal{F}} I$, and assume that test (a) has been passed. Let $x_j = [j \in J$ and $j \neq k]$. Then $f(x) = 1$; and $g(x) = 0$, because every $J' \in \mathcal{G}$ with $J' \neq J$ contains an element $\notin J$.

(c) Again assume that condition (a) has been ruled out. If, say, $|J| > |\mathcal{F}|$, let $x_j = [j$ is the smallest element of $I \cap J$, for some $I \in \mathcal{F}]$. Then $f(x) = 1$, $g(x) = 0$.

(d) Now we assume that $\bigcup_{I \in \mathcal{F}} I = \bigcup_{J \in \mathcal{G}} J$. Each $I \in \mathcal{F}$ stands for $2^{n-|I|}$ vectors where $f(x) = 0$; similarly, each $J \in \mathcal{G}$ stands for $2^{n-|J|}$ vectors where $g(x) = 1$. If the sum s is less than 2^n, we can compute $s = s_0 + s_1$, where s_0 counts the contributions to s when $x_n = 0$. If $s_0 < 2^{n-1}$, set $x_n \leftarrow 0$; otherwise $s_1 < 2^{n-1}$, so we set $x_n \leftarrow 1$. Then we set $n \leftarrow n - 1$; eventually all x_j are known, and $f(x) = 1$, $g(x) = 0$.

27. Let $m = \min(\{|I| \mid I \in \mathcal{F}\} \cup \{|J| \mid J \in \mathcal{G}\})$ be the length of the shortest prime clause or implicant. Then $N \cdot 2^{n-m} \geq \sum_{I \in \mathcal{F}} 2^{n-|I|} + \sum_{J \in \mathcal{G}} 2^{n-|J|} \geq 2^n$; so we have $m \leq \lg N$. If, say, $|I| = m$, some index k must appear in at least $1/m$ of the members $J \in \mathcal{G}$, because each J intersects I. This observation proves the hint.

Now let $A(0) = A(1) = 1$ and $A(v) = 1 + A(v - 1) + A(\lfloor \rho v \rfloor)$ for $v > 1$. Then $A(|\mathcal{F}||\mathcal{G}|)$ is an upper bound on the number of recursive calls (the number of times X1 is performed). Letting $B(v) = A(v) + 1$, we have $B(v) = B(v-1) + B(\lfloor \rho v \rfloor)$ for $v > 1$, hence $B(v) \leq B(v-k) + kB(\lfloor \rho v \rfloor)$ for $v > k$. Taking $k = v - \lfloor \rho v \rfloor$ shows that $B(v) \leq ((1-\rho)v+2)B(\lfloor \rho v \rfloor)$; hence $B(v) = O(((1-\rho)v+2)^t)$ when $\rho^t v \leq 1$, namely when $t \geq \ln v / \ln(1/\rho) = \Theta((\log v)(\log N))$. Consequently $A(|\mathcal{F}||\mathcal{G}|) \leq A(N^2/4) = N^{O(\log N)^2}$.

In practice the algorithm will run much faster than the pessimistic bounds just derived. Since the prime clauses of a function are the prime implicants of its dual, this problem is essentially the same as verifying that one given DNF is the dual of another. Moreover, if we start with $f(x) = 0$ and repeatedly find minimal x's where $f(x) = g(\bar{x}) = 0$, we can "grow" f until we've obtained the dual of g.

The ideas presented here are due to M. L. Fredman and L. Khachiyan, *J. Algorithms* **21** (1996), 618–628, who also presented refinements that reduce the running time to $N^{O(\log N / \log \log N)}$. No polynomial-time algorithm is known; yet the problem is unlikely to be NP-complete, because we can solve it in less-than-exponential time.

28. This result is obvious once understood, but the notations and terminology can make it confusing; so let's consider a concrete example: If, say, $y_1 = y_4 = y_6 = 1$ and the other y_k are zero, the function g is true if and only if the prime implicants p_1, p_4, and p_6 cover all the places where f is true. Thus we see that there is a one-to-one correspondence between every implicant of g and every DNF for f that contains only prime implicants p_j. In this correspondence, the prime implicants of g correspond to the "irredundant" DNFs in which no p_j can be left out.

Numerous refinements of this principle have been discussed by R. B. Cutler and S. Muroga, *IEEE Transactions* **C-36** (1987), 277–292.

29. B1. [Initialize.] Set $k \leftarrow k' \leftarrow 0$. (Similar methods are discussed in exercise 5–19.)

  B2. [Find a zero.] Increase k zero or more times, until either $k = m$ (terminate) or v_k & $2^j = 0$.

  B3. [Make $k' > k$.] If $k' \leq k$, set $k' \leftarrow k + 1$.

  B4. [Advance k'.] Increase k' zero or more times, until either $k' = m$ (terminate) or $v_{k'} \geq v_k + 2^j$.

  B5. [Skip past a big mismatch.] If $v_k \oplus v_{k'} \geq 2^{j+1}$, set $k \leftarrow k'$ and return to B2.

  B6. [Record a match.] If $v_{k'} = v_k + 2^j$, output (k, k').

  B7. [Advance k.] Set $k \leftarrow k + 1$ and return to B2. ∎

(Steps B3 and B5 are optional, but recommended.)

30. The following algorithm keeps variable-length, sorted lists in a stack S whose size will never exceed $2m + n$. When the topmost entry of the stack is $S_t = s$, the topmost list is the ordered set $S_s < S_{s+1} < \cdots < S_{t-1}$. Tag bits are maintained in another stack T, having the same size as S (after the initialization step).

  P1. [Initialize.] Set $T_k \leftarrow 0$ for $0 \leq k < m$. Then for $0 \leq j < n$, apply the j-buddy scan algorithm of exercise 29, and set $T_k \leftarrow T_k + 2^j$, $T_{k'} \leftarrow T_{k'} + 2^j$ for all pairs (k, k') found. Then set $s \leftarrow t \leftarrow 0$ and repeat the following operations until $s = m$: If $T_s = 0$, output the subcube $(0, v_s)$ and set $s \leftarrow s+1$; otherwise set $S_t \leftarrow v_s$, $T_t \leftarrow T_s$, $t \leftarrow t + 1$, $s \leftarrow s + 1$. Finally set $A \leftarrow 0$ and $S_t \leftarrow 0$.

  P2. [Advance A.] (At this point stack S contains $\nu(A) + 1$ lists of subcubes. Namely, if $A = 2^{e_1} + \cdots + 2^{e_r}$ with $e_1 > \cdots > e_r \geq 0$, the stack contains the b-values of all subcubes $(a, b) \subseteq V$ whose a-values are respectively 0, 2^{e_1}, $2^{e_1} + 2^{e_2}, \ldots, A$, except that subcubes whose tags are zero do not appear. All of these lists are nonempty, except possibly the last. We will now increase A to the next relevant value.) Set $j \leftarrow 0$. If $S_t = t$ (that is, if the topmost list is empty), increase j zero or more times until $j \geq n$ or $A \mathbin{\&} 2^j \neq 0$. Then while $j < n$ and $A \mathbin{\&} 2^j \neq 0$, set $t \leftarrow S_t - 1$, $A \leftarrow A - 2^j$, and $j \leftarrow j + 1$. Terminate the algorithm if $j \geq n$; otherwise set $A \leftarrow A + 2^j$.

P3. [Generate list A.] Set $r \leftarrow t$, $s \leftarrow S_t$, and apply the j-buddy scan algorithm of exercise 29 to the $r - s$ numbers $S_s < \cdots < S_{r-1}$. For all pairs (k, k') found, set $x \leftarrow (T_k \mathbin{\&} T_{k'}) - 2^j$; and if $x = 0$, output the subcube (A, S_k), otherwise set $t \leftarrow t + 1$, $S_t \leftarrow S_k$, $T_t \leftarrow x$. Finally set $t \leftarrow t + 1$, $S_t \leftarrow r + 1$, and go back to step P2. $\blacksquare$

This algorithm is based in part on ideas of Eugenio Morreale [*IEEE Trans.* **EC-16** (1967), 611–620; *Proc. ACM Nat. Conf.* **23** (1968), 355–365]. The running time is essentially proportional to mn (for step P1) plus the total number of subcubes contained in V. If $m \leq 2^n(1 - \epsilon)$, and if V is chosen at random with size m, exercise 34 shows that the average total number of subcubes is at most $O(\log \log n / \log \log \log n)$ times the average number of maximal subcubes; hence the average running time in most cases will be nearly proportional to the average amount of output produced. On the other hand, exercises 32 and 116 show that the amount of output might be huge.

31. (a) Let $c = c_{n-1} \ldots c_0$, $c' = c'_{n-1} \ldots c'_0$, $c'' = c''_{n-1} \ldots c''_0$. There must be some j with $c_j \neq *$ and $c_j \neq c''_j$; otherwise $c'' \subseteq c$. Similarly there must be some k with $c'_k \neq *$ and $c'_k \neq c''_k$. If $j \neq k$, there would be a point $x_{n-1} \ldots x_0 \in c''$ that is in neither c nor c', because we could let $x_j = \bar{c}_j$ and $x_k = \bar{c}'_k$. Hence $j = k$, and the value of j is uniquely determined. Furthermore it's easy to see that $c'_j = \bar{c}_j$. And if $i \neq j$, we have either $c_i = *$ or $c_i = c''_i$, and either $c'_i = *$ or $c'_i = c''_i$.

(b) This statement is an obvious consequence of (a).

(c) First we prove that the parenthesized remark in step E2 is true whenever that step is encountered. It's clearly true when $j = 0$. Otherwise, let $c \subseteq V$ be a j-cube, and suppose $c = c_0 \cup c_1$ where c_0 and c_1 are $(j - 1)$-cubes. On the preceding execution of step E2 we had $c_0 \subseteq c'_0 \in C$ and $c_1 \subseteq c'_1 \in C$ for some c'_0 and c'_1; hence either $c \subseteq c'_0 \sqcup c'_1$ or $c \subseteq c'_0$ or $c \subseteq c'_1$. In each case, c is now contained in some element of C.

Secondly, we prove that the outputs in step E3 are precisely the maximal j-cubes contained in V: Let $c \subseteq V$ be any k-cube. If c is maximal, then c will be in C when we reach step E3 with $j = k$, and it will be output. If c isn't maximal, it has a buddy $c' \subseteq V$, which is a k-cube contained in some subcube $c'' \in C$ when we reach E3. Since $c \not\subseteq c''$, the consensus $c \sqcup c''$ will be a $(j + 1)$-cube of C', and c will not be output.

References: The notion of consensus was first defined by Archie Blake in his Ph.D. dissertation at the University of Chicago (1937); see *J. Symbolic Logic* **3** (1938), 93, 112–113. It was independently rediscovered by Edward W. Samson and Burton E. Mills [Air Force Cambridge Research Center Tech. Report 54-21 (Cambridge, Mass.: April 1954), 54 pp.] and by W. V. Quine [*AMM* **62** (1955), 627–631]. The operation is also sometimes called the *resolvent*, since J. A. Robinson used it in a more general form (but with respect to clauses rather than implicants) as the basis of his "resolution principle" for theorem proving [*JACM* **12** (1965), 23–41]. Algorithm E is due to Ann C. Ewing, J. Paul Roth, and Eric G. Wagner, *AIEE Transactions*, Part 1, **80** (1961), 450–458.

32. (a) Change the definition of $\sqcup$ in exercise 31 to the following associative and commutative operation on the four symbols $A = \{0, 1, *, \bullet\}$, for all $a \in A$ and $x \in \{0, 1\}$:

$$* \sqcup a = a \sqcup * = a, \qquad \bullet \sqcup a = a \sqcup \bullet = x \sqcup \bar{x} = \bullet, \qquad \text{and} \qquad x \sqcup x = x.$$

Also let $h(0) = 0$, $h(1) = 1$, $h(*) = *$, and $h(\bullet) = *$. Then $c = h(c_1 \sqcup \cdots \sqcup c_m)$, computed componentwise, is the only subcube that could possibly be a generalized consensus. [See P. Tison, *IEEE Transactions* **EC-16** (1967), 446–456.]

(b) For example, let $c_j = *^{j-1}1*^{m-j}1^{j-1}0*^{m-j}$. [The final component is superfluous. All solutions have been characterized by R. H. Sloan, B. Szörényi, and G. Turán, in *SIAM J. Discrete Math.* **21** (2008), 987–998.]

(c) By (a), every prime implicant corresponds uniquely to the subset of implicants that it "meets." [A. K. Chandra and G. Markowsky, *Discrete Math.* **24** (1978), 7–11.]

(d) For example, $(y_1 \wedge \bar{x}_1) \vee (y_2 \wedge x_1 \wedge \bar{x}_2) \vee \cdots \vee (y_m \wedge x_1 \wedge \cdots \wedge x_{m-1} \wedge \bar{x}_m)$ as in (b). [J.-M. Laborde, *Discrete Math.* **32** (1980), 209–212.]

33. (a) $\binom{2^n - 2^{n-k}}{m - 2^{n-k}} / \binom{2^n}{m}$. (b) We must exclude the cases when $x_1 \wedge \cdots \wedge x_{j-1} \wedge \bar{x}_j \wedge x_{j+1} \wedge \cdots \wedge x_k$ is also an implicant. By the inclusion-exclusion principle, the answer is

$$\sum_l \binom{k}{l} (-1)^l \binom{2^n - (l+1)2^{n-k}}{m - (l+1)2^{n-k}} / \binom{2^n}{m}.$$

It simplifies to $\binom{2^n - n - 1}{m - 1} / \binom{2^n}{m}$ when $k = n$; see, for example, Eq. 1.2.6–(24).

34. (a) We have $c(m, n) = \sum c_j(m, n)$, where $c_j(m, n) = 2^{n-j} \binom{n}{j} \binom{2^n - 2^j}{m - 2^j} / \binom{2^n}{m}$ is the average number of implicants with $n - j$ literals (the average number of subcubes of dimension j in the terminology of exercise 30). Clearly $c_0(m, n) = m$, and

$$c_1(m, n) = \frac{nm(m-1)}{2(2^n - 1)} \le \frac{mn}{2} \left(\frac{m}{2^n} \right) \le \frac{1}{2} m;$$

similarly $c_j(m, n) \le m/(2^j j! n^{2^j - 1 - j})$. Also $p(m, n) = \sum_j p_j(m, n)$, where we have

$$p_0(m, n) = 2^n \binom{2^n - n - 1}{m - 1} / \binom{2^n}{m} = m \frac{(2^n - n - 1)^{\underline{m-1}}}{(2^n - 1)^{\underline{m-1}}} \ge m \frac{(2^n - n - m)^{m-1}}{(2^n - m)^{m-1}}$$

$$\ge m \left(1 - \frac{n}{2^n - m} \right)^m \ge m \left(1 - \frac{n}{2^n - 2^n/n} \right)^{2^n/n} = m \exp \left(\frac{2^n}{n} \ln \left(1 - \frac{n^2}{2^n(n-1)} \right) \right).$$

(b) Notice that $t = \lfloor \lg \lg n - \lg \lg(2^n/m) + \lg(4/3) \rfloor \le \lg \lg n + O(1)$ is quite small. We will repeatedly use the fact that $\binom{2^n - j \cdot 2^t}{m - j \cdot 2^t} / \binom{2^n}{m} < \alpha_{mn}^j$, and indeed that

$$\binom{2^n - j \cdot 2^t}{m - j \cdot 2^t} / \binom{2^n}{m} = \alpha_{mn}^j (1 + O(j^2 2^{2t}/m))$$

is an extremely good approximation when j isn't too large. To establish the hint, note that $\sum_{j<t} c_j(m, n)/c_t(m, n) = O(t c_{t-1}(m, n)/c_t(m, n)) = O(t^2/(n\sqrt{\alpha_{mn}})) = O((\log \log n)^2/n^{1/3})$; and $c_{t+j}(m, n)/c_t(m, n) = O((n/(2t))^j \alpha_{mn}^{2^j - 1})$. Consequently we have $c(m, n)/c_t(m, n) \approx 1 + \frac{1}{2} (\frac{n-t}{t+1}) \alpha_{mn}$, where the second term dominates when α_{mn} is in the upper part of its range. Furthermore

$$\sum_l \binom{n-t}{l} (-1)^l \alpha_{mn}^l \left(1 + O\left(\frac{l^2 2^{2t}}{m} \right) \right) = (1 - \alpha_{mn})^{n-t} + O(n^2 \alpha_{mn}(1 + \alpha_{mn})^n 2^{2t}/m)$$

has an exponentially small error term, because $(1 + \alpha_{mn})^n = O(e^{n^{1/3}}) \ll m$. Therefore $p(m, n)/c_t(m, n)$ is asymptotically $e^{-n\alpha_{mn}} + \frac{1}{2}(\frac{n-t}{t+1})\alpha_{mn} e^{-n\alpha_{mn}^2}$.

(c) Here $\alpha_{mn} = 2^{-2^t} \approx n^{-1}\ln(t/\ln t)$; so $c(m,n)/c_t(m,n) = 1 + O(t^{-1}\log t)$, $p(m,n)/c_t(m,n) = t^{-1}\ln t + \frac{1}{2}t^{-1}\ln t + O(t^{-1}\log\log t)$. We conclude that, in this case,

$$\frac{c(m,n)}{p(m,n)} = \frac{2}{3}\frac{\lg\lg n}{\lg\lg\lg n}\left(1 + O\left(\frac{\log\log\log\log n}{\log\log\log n}\right)\right).$$

(d) If $n\alpha_{mn} \le \ln t - \ln\ln t$, we have $p(m,n)/c(m,n) \ge p_t(m,n)/c(m,n) \ge t^{-1}\ln t + O(t^{-1}\log t)^2$. On the other hand if $n\alpha_{mn} \ge \ln t - \ln\ln t$, we have $p(m,n)/c(m,n) \ge p_{t+1}(m,n)/c(m,n) \ge \frac{1}{2}t^{-1}\ln t + O(t^{-1}\log\log t)$.

[The means $c(m,n)$ and $p(m,n)$, and the variance of $c(m,n)$, were first studied by F. Mileto and G. Putzolu, *IEEE Trans.* **EC-13** (1964), 87–92; *JACM* **12** (1965), 364–375. Detailed asymptotic information about implicants, prime implicants, and irredundant DNFs of random Boolean functions, when each value $f(x_1,\ldots,x_n)$ is independently equal to 1 with probability $p(n)$, has been derived by Karl Weber, *Elektronische Informationsverarbeitung und Kybernetik* **19** (1983), 365–374, 449–458, 529–534.]

35. (a) By rearranging coordinates we can assume that the pth subcube is $0^k 1^u *^v$, so that $B_p = 0^k 1^u 0^v$ and $S_p = 1^k 0^{u+v}$. Then all points of $*^k 1^u *^v$ are still covered, by induction on p, because all points of $*^{j-1}1*^{k-j}1^u *^v$ have been covered for $1 \le j \le k$.

(b) The jth and kth subcubes differ in every coordinate position where B_j & S_k is nonzero. On the other hand if B_j & S_k is zero, the point $\bar{S}_k$ of subcube k lies in a previous subcube, by (a), because we have $\bar{S}_k \supseteq B_j$.

(c) From the list 1100, 1011, 0011 (with the bits of each S_k underlined) we obtain the orthogonal DNF $(x_1 \wedge x_2) \vee (x_1 \wedge \bar{x}_2 \wedge x_3 \wedge x_4) \vee (\bar{x}_1 \wedge x_3 \wedge x_4)$.

(d) There are eight solutions; for example, $(01100, 00110, 00011, 11010, 11000)$.

(e) $(001100, 011000, 000110, 110010, 110000, 010011, 000011)$ is a symmetrical solution. And there are many more possibilities; for example, 42 permutations of the bit codes $\{110000, 011000, 001100, 000110, 000011, 110010, 011010\}$ are shellings.

[The concept of a shelling for monotone Boolean functions was introduced by Michael O. Ball and J. Scott Provan, *Operations Research* **36** (1988), 703–715, who discussed many significant applications.]

36. If $j < k$ we have $B_j = \alpha 1 \beta$ and $B_k = \alpha 0 \gamma$ for some strings α, β, γ. Form the sequence $x_0 = \alpha 1 \gamma$, $x_1 = x_0'$, $\ldots$, $x_l = x_{l-1}'$, where $x_l = \alpha 0 0^{|\gamma|}$. We have $f(x_0) = 1$ since $x_0 \supseteq B_k$, but $f(x_l) = 0$ since $x_l \subseteq B_j'$. So the string x_i, where $f(x_i) = 1$ and $f(x_{i+1}) = \cdots = f(x_l) = 0$, is in B. It precedes B_k and proves that B_j & $S_k \supseteq 0^{|\alpha|}10^{|\beta|}$.

[This construction and parts of exercise 35 are due to E. Boros, Y. Crama, O. Ekin, P. L. Hammer, T. Ibaraki, and A. Kogan, *SIAM J. Discrete Math.* **13** (2000), 212–226.]

37. The shelling order $(000011, 001101, 001100, 110101, 110100, 110001, 110000)$ generalizes to all n. There also are interesting solutions not based on shelling, like the cyclically symmetrical $(110***, 1110**, **110*, **1110, 0***11, 10**11, 111111)$.

For the lower bound, assign the weight $w_x = -\prod_{j=1}^{n}(x_{2j-1} + x_{2j} - 3x_{2j-1}x_{2j})$ to each point x, and notice that the sum of w_x over all x in any subcube is 0 or ± 1. (It suffices to verify this curious fact for each of the nine possible subcubes when $n = 1$.) Now choose a set of disjoint subcubes that partition the set $F = \{x \mid f(x) = 1\}$; we have

$$\sum_{C \text{ chosen}} 1 \ge \sum_{C \text{ chosen}} \sum_{x \in C} w_x = \sum_{x \in F} w_x \sum_{C \text{ chosen}} [x \in C] = \sum_{x \in F} w_x.$$

There are $\binom{n}{k}2^{n-k}$ vectors x with exactly k pairs $x_{2j-1}x_{2j} = 1$ and nonzero weight. Their weight is $(-1)^{k-1}$, and they lie in F except when $k = 0$. Hence $\sum_{x \in F} w_x = \sum_{k>0} \binom{n}{k}2^{n-k}(-1)^{k-1} = 2^n - (2-1)^n$.

[See M. O. Ball and G. L. Nemhauser, *Mathematics of Operations Research* **4** (1979), 132–143.]

38. Certainly not; a DNF is satisfiable if and only if it has at least one implicant. The hard problem for a DNF is to decide whether or not it is a *tautology* (always true).

39. Associate variables $y_1, \ldots, y_N$ with each internal node in preorder, so that every tree node corresponds to exactly one variable of F. For each internal node y, with children (l, r) and labeled with the binary operator $\circ$, construct four 3CNF clauses $c_{00} \wedge c_{01} \wedge c_{10} \wedge c_{11}$, where

$$c_{pq} = (y^{\overline{p \circ q}N} \vee l^{pN} \vee r^{qN})$$

and N denotes complementation (so that $x^{0N} = x$ and $x^{1N} = \bar{x}$). These clauses state in effect that $y = l \circ r$; for example, if $\circ$ is $\wedge$, the four clauses are $(\bar{y} \vee l \vee r) \wedge (\bar{y} \vee l \vee \bar{r}) \wedge (\bar{y} \vee \bar{l} \vee r) \wedge (y \vee \bar{l} \vee \bar{r})$. Finally, add one more clause, $(y_1 \vee y_1 \vee y_1)$, to force $F = 1$.

> *Every higher number can be formed by mere complications of threes.*
> *. . . Take the quadruple fact that A sells B to C for the price D.*
> *This is a compound of two facts:*
> *first, that A makes with C a certain transaction, which we may name E;*
> *and second, that this transaction E is a sale of B for the price D.*
> — CHARLES S. PEIRCE, *A Guess at the Riddle* (1887)

40. Following the hint, A says '$u < v \oplus v < u$' and B says '$u < v \wedge v < w \Rightarrow u < w$'. So $A \wedge B$ says that there's a linear ordering of the vertices, $u_1 < u_2 < \cdots < u_n$. (There are $n!$ ways to satisfy $A \wedge B$.) Now C says that q_{uvw} is equivalent to $u < v < w$; so D says that u and w are not consecutive in the ordering, when $u \not\!\!\!- w$. Thus $A \wedge B \wedge C \wedge D$ is satisfiable if and only if there is a linear ordering in which all nonadjacent vertices are nonconsecutive (that is, in which all consecutive vertices are adjacent).

41. Solution 0: '$[m \le n]$' is such a formula, but it is not in the spirit of this exercise.

Solution 1: Let x_{jk} mean that pigeon j occupies hole k. Then the clauses are $(x_{j1} \vee \cdots \vee x_{jn})$ for $1 \le j \le m$ and $(\bar{x}_{ik} \vee \bar{x}_{jk})$ for $1 \le i < j \le m$ and $1 \le k \le n$. [See S. A. Cook and R. A. Reckhow, *J. Symbolic Logic* **44** (1979), 36–50; A. Haken, *Theoretical Comp. Sci.* **39** (1985), 297–308.]

Solution 2: Assume that $n = 2^t$ and let pigeon j occupy hole $(x_{j1} \ldots x_{jt})_2$. The clauses $((x_{i1} \oplus x_{j1}) \vee \cdots \vee (x_{it} \oplus x_{jt}))$ for $1 \le i < j \le m$ can be put into the CNF form $(y_{ij1} \vee \cdots \vee y_{ijt})$ as in exercise 39, by introducing auxiliary clauses $(\bar{y}_{ijk} \vee x_{ik} \vee x_{jk}) \wedge (y_{ijk} \vee x_{ik} \vee \bar{x}_{jk}) \wedge (y_{ijk} \vee \bar{x}_{ik} \vee x_{jk}) \wedge (\bar{y}_{ijk} \vee \bar{x}_{ik} \vee \bar{x}_{jk})$. The total size of this CNF is $\Theta(m^2 \log n)$, compared to $\Theta(m^2 n)$ in Solution 1. If n is not a power of 2, $O(m \log n)$ additional clauses of size $O(\log n)$ will rule out inappropriate values.

42. $(\bar{x} \vee y) \wedge (\bar{z} \vee x) \wedge (\bar{y} \vee z) \wedge (z \vee z)$.

43. Probably not, because every 3SAT problem can be converted to this form. For example, the clause $(x_1 \vee x_2 \vee \bar{x}_3)$ can be replaced by $(x_1 \vee \bar{y} \vee \bar{x}_3) \wedge (\bar{y} \vee \bar{x}_2) \wedge (y \vee x_2)$, where y is a new variable (essentially equivalent to $\bar{x}_2$).

44. Suppose $f(x) = f(y) = 1$ implies $f(x\&y) = 1$ and also that, say, $c = x_1 \lor x_2 \lor \bar{x}_3 \lor \bar{x}_4$ is a prime clause of f. Then $c' = \bar{x}_1 \lor x_2 \lor \bar{x}_3 \lor \bar{x}_4$ is *not* a clause; otherwise $c \land c' = x_2 \lor \bar{x}_3 \lor \bar{x}_4$ would also be a clause, contradicting primality. So there's a vector y with $f(y) = 1$ and $y_1 = 1$, $y_2 = 0$, $y_3 = y_4 = 1$. Similarly, there's a z with $f(z) = 1$ and $z_1 = 0$, $z_2 = 1$, $z_3 = z_4 = 1$. But then $f(y \& z) = 1$, and c isn't a clause. The same argument works for a clause c that has a different number of literals, as long as at least two of the literals aren't complemented.

45. (a) A Horn function $f(x_1, \ldots, x_n)$ is indefinite if and only if it is unequal to the definite Horn function $g(x_1, \ldots, x_n) = f(x_1, \ldots, x_n) \lor (x_1 \land \cdots \land x_n)$. So $f \leftrightarrow g$ is a one-to-one correspondence between indefinite and definite Horn functions. (b) If f is monotone, its complement $\bar{f}$ is either identically 1 or an indefinite Horn function.

46. Algorithm C puts 88 pairs xy in the core: When x = a, b, c, 0, or 1, the following character y can be anything but (. When x = (, *, /, +, -, we can have y = (, a, b, c, 0, 1; also y = - when x = (, +, or -. Finally, the legitimate pairs beginning with x =) are)+,)-,)*,)/,)).

47. The order in which Algorithm C brings vertices into the core is a topological sort, since all predecessors of k are asserted before the algorithm sets TRUTH$(x_k) \leftarrow 1$. But Algorithm 2.2.3T uses a queue instead of a stack, so the ordering it actually produces is usually different from that of Algorithm C.

48. Let $\bot$ be a new variable, and change every indefinite Horn clause to a definite one by ORing in this new variable. (For example, '$\bar{w} \lor \bar{y}$' becomes '$\bar{w} \lor \bar{y} \lor \bot$', namely '$w \land y \Rightarrow \bot$'; definite Horn clauses stay unchanged.) Then apply Algorithm C. The original clauses are unsatisfiable if and only if $\bot$ is in the core of the new clauses. The algorithm can therefore be terminated as soon as it is about to set TRUTH$(\bot) \leftarrow 1$.

(J. H. Quick thought of another solution: We could apply Algorithm C to the function g constructed in the answer to exercise 45(a), because f is unsatisfiable if and only if *every* variable x_j is in the core of g. However, indefinite clauses of f such as $\bar{w} \lor \bar{y}$ become many different clauses $(\bar{w} \lor \bar{y} \lor z) \land (\bar{w} \lor \bar{y} \lor x) \land (\bar{w} \lor \bar{y} \lor v) \land (\bar{w} \lor \bar{y} \lor u) \land \cdots$ of g, one for each variable not in the original clause. So Quick's suggestion, which might sound elegant at first blush, could increase the number of clauses by a factor of $\Omega(n)$.)

49. We have $f \leq g$ if and only if $f \land \bar{g}$ is unsatisfiable, if and only if $f \land \bar{c}$ is unsatisfiable for every clause c of g. But $\bar{c}$ is an AND of literals, so we can apply exercise 48. [See H. Kleine Büning and T. Lettmann, *Aussagenlogik: Deduktion und Algorithmen* (1994), §5.6, for further results including an efficient way to test if g is a "renaming" of f, namely to determine whether or not there exist constants $(y_1, \ldots, y_n)$ such that $f(x_1, \ldots, x_n) = g(x_1 \oplus y_1, \ldots, x_n \oplus y_n)$.]

50. See Gabriel Istrate, *Random Structures & Algorithms* **20** (2002), 483–506.

51. If vertex v is marked A, introduce the clauses $\Rightarrow A^+(v)$ and $\Rightarrow B^-(v)$; if it is marked B, introduce $\Rightarrow A^-(v)$ and $\Rightarrow B^+(v)$. Otherwise let v have k outgoing arcs $v \to u_1, \ldots, v \to u_k$. Introduce the clauses $A^-(u_j) \Rightarrow B^+(v)$ and $B^-(u_j) \Rightarrow A^+(v)$ for $1 \leq j \leq k$. Also, if v is not marked C, introduce the clauses $A^+(u_1) \land \cdots \land A^+(u_k) \Rightarrow B^-(v)$ and $B^+(u_1) \land \cdots \land B^+(u_k) \Rightarrow A^-(v)$. All forcing strategies are consequences of these clauses. Exercise 2.2.3–28 and its answer provide further information.

Notice that, in principle, Algorithm C can therefore be used to decide whether or not the game of chess is a forced victory for the white pieces — except for the annoying detail that the corresponding digraph is larger than the physical universe.

52. With best play, the results (see exercise 51) are:

n	(a)	(b)	(c)	(d)
2	0 wins	second player wins	1 wins	second player wins
3	0 wins	first player wins	first player wins	first player wins
4	first player wins	first player wins	first player wins	first player wins
5	second player wins	draw	draw	1 loses if first
6	second player wins	second player wins	1 loses if first	1 loses if first
7	1 loses if first	second player wins	1 loses if first	1 loses if first
8	draw	draw	draw	1 loses if first
9	draw	draw	draw	1 loses if first

(Here "1 loses if first" means that the game is a draw if player 0 plays first, otherwise 0 can win.) *Comments:* In (a), player 1 has a slight disadvantage, because $f(x) = 0$ when $x_1 \ldots x_n$ is a palindrome. This small difference affects the result even when $n = 7$. Although player 1 would seem to be better off playing 0s in the left half of the board, it turns out that his/her first move when $n = 4$ must be to $*1**$; the alternative, $*0**$, draws. Game (b) is essentially a race to see who can eliminate the last $*$. In game (c), a random choice of $x_1 \ldots x_n$ makes $f(x) = 1$ with probability $F_{n+2}/2^n = \Theta((\phi/2)^n)$; in game (d), this probability approaches zero more slowly, as $\Theta(1/\log n)$. Still, player 1 does better in (c) than in (d) when $n = 2$, 5, 8, and 9; no worse in the other cases.

53. (a) She should switch either day 1 or day 2 to day 3.

(b, f) Several possibilities; for example, change day 2 to day 3.

(c) This case is illustrated in Fig. 6; change either Desert or Excalibur to Aladdin.

(d) Change either Caesars or Excalibur to Aladdin.

(e) Change either Bellagio or Desert to Aladdin.

Of course Williams, who doesn't appear in the cycle (42), bears no responsibility whatever for the conflicts.

54. If x and $\bar{x}$ are both in S, then $u \in S \iff \bar{u} \in S$, because the existence of paths from x to $\bar{x}$ and $\bar{x}$ to x and x to u and u to x implies the existence of paths from $\bar{u}$ to $\bar{x}$ and $\bar{x}$ to $\bar{u}$, hence from u to $\bar{u}$ and $\bar{u}$ to u.

55. (a) Necessary and sufficient conditions for successfully renaming a clause such as $x_1 \lor \bar{x}_2 \lor x_3 \lor \bar{x}_4$ are $(y_1 \lor \bar{y}_2) \land (y_1 \lor y_3) \land (y_1 \lor \bar{y}_4) \land (\bar{y}_2 \lor y_3) \land (\bar{y}_2 \lor \bar{y}_4) \land (y_3 \lor \bar{y}_4)$. A similar set of $\binom{k}{2}$ clauses of length 2 in the variables $\{y_1, \ldots, y_n\}$ corresponds to any clause of length k in $\{x_1, \ldots, x_n\}$. [H. R. Lewis, *JACM* **25** (1978), 134–135.]

(b) A given clause of length $k > 3$ in $\{x_1, \ldots, x_n\}$ can be converted into $3(k-2)$ clauses of length 2, instead of the $\binom{k}{2}$ clauses above, by introducing $k-3$ new variables $\{t_2, \ldots, t_{k-2}\}$, illustrated here for the clause $x_1 \lor x_2 \lor x_3 \lor x_4 \lor x_5$:

$$(y_1 \lor y_2) \land (y_1 \lor t_2) \land (y_2 \lor t_2) \land (\bar{t}_2 \lor y_3) \land (\bar{t}_2 \lor t_3) \land (y_3 \lor t_3) \land (\bar{t}_3 \lor y_4) \land (\bar{t}_3 \lor y_5) \land (y_4 \lor y_5).$$

In general, the clauses from $x_1 \lor \cdots \lor x_k$ are $(\bar{t}_{j-1} \lor y_j) \land (\bar{t}_{j-1} \lor t_j) \land (y_j \lor t_j)$ for $1 < j < k$, but with t_1 replaced by $\bar{y}_1$ and t_{k-1} replaced by y_k; change y_j to $\bar{y}_j$ if $\bar{x}_j$ appears instead of x_j. Do this for each given clause, using different auxiliary variables t_j for different clauses; the result is a formula in 2CNF that has length $< 3m$ and is satisfiable if and only if Horn renaming is possible. Now apply Theorem K.

[See B. Aspvall, *J. Algorithms* **1** (1980), 97–103. One consequence, noted by H. Kleine Büning and T. Lettmann in *Aussagenlogik: Deduktion und Algorithmen* (1994), Theorem 5.24, is that any satisfiable formula in 2CNF can be renamed to Horn clauses. Notice that two CNFs for the same function may give different outcomes; for example, $(x \lor y \lor z) \land (\bar{x} \lor \bar{y} \lor \bar{z}) \land (\bar{x} \lor z) \land (\bar{y} \lor z)$ is actually a Horn function, but the clauses in this representation cannot be converted to Horn form by complementation.]

56. Here $f(x, y, z)$ corresponds to the digraph shown below (analogous to Fig. 6), and it can also be simplified to $y \land (\bar{x} \lor z)$. Each vertex is a strong component. So the formula is true with respect to the quantifiers $\exists\exists\exists$, $\exists\exists\forall$, $\forall\exists\exists$; false in the other cases $\forall\exists\forall$, (any)$\forall$(any). In general the eight possibilities can be arranged at the corners of a cube, with each change from $\exists$ to $\forall$ making the formula more likely to be false.

57. Forming the digraph as in Theorem K, we can prove that the quantified formula holds if and only if (i) no strong component contains both x and $\bar{x}$; (ii) there is no path from one universal variable x to another universal variable y or to its complement $\bar{y}$; (iii) no strong component containing a universal variable x also contains an existential variable v or its complement $\bar{v}$, when '$\exists v$' appears to the left of '$\forall x$'. These three conditions are clearly necessary, and they are readily tested as the strong components are being found.

To show that they are sufficient, notice first that if S is a strong component with only existential literals, condition (i) allows us to set them all equal as in Theorem K. Otherwise S has exactly one universal literal, $u_j = x_j$ or $u_j = \bar{x}_j$; all other literals in S are existential and declared to the right of x_j, so we can equate them to u_j. And all paths into S in such a case come from purely existential strong components, whose value can be set to 0 because the complements of such strong components cannot also lead into S; for if v and $\bar{v}$ imply u_j, then $\bar{u}_j$ implies $\bar{v}$ and v.

[*Information Proc. Letters* **8** (1979), 121–123. By contrast, M. Krom had proved in *J. Symbolic Logic* **35** (1970), 210–216, that an analogous problem in first-order predicate calculus (where parameterized predicates take the place of simple Boolean variables, and quantification is over the parameters) is actually unsolvable in general.]

58. We can assume that each clause is definite, by introducing '$\bot$' as in exercise 48 and placing '$\forall\bot$' at the left. Call the universal variables $x_0, x_1, \ldots, x_m$ (where x_0 is $\bot$) and call the existential variables $y_1, \ldots, y_n$. Let '$u \prec v$' mean that variable u appears to the left of variable v in the list of quantifiers. Remove $\bar{x}_j$ from any clause whose unbarred literal is y_k when $y_k \prec x_j$. Then, for $0 \leq j \leq m$, let C_j be the core of the Horn clauses when the additional clauses $(x_0) \land \cdots \land (x_{j-1}) \land (x_{j+1}) \land \cdots \land (x_m) \land \bigwedge\{(y_k) \mid y_k \prec x_j$ and $y_k \in C_0\}$ are appended. (In other words, C_j tells us what can be deduced when all the x's except x_j are assumed to be true.) We claim that the given formula is true if and only if $x_j \notin C_j$, for $0 \leq j \leq m$.

To prove this claim, note first that the formula is certainly false if $x_j \in C_j$ for some j. (When $y_k \in C_0$ and $y_k \prec x_j$ and $x_i = 1$ for $i \neq j$ we must set $y_k \leftarrow 1$.) Otherwise we can choose each y_k to make the formula true, as follows: If $y_k \notin C_0$, set $y_k \leftarrow 0$; otherwise set $y_k \leftarrow \bigwedge\{x_j \mid y_k \notin C_j\}$. Notice that y_k depends on x_j only when $x_j \prec y_k$. Each clause c with unbarred literal x_j is now true: For if $x_j = 0$, some $\bar{y}_k$ appears in c for which $y_k \notin C_j$, because $x_j \notin C_j$; hence $y_k = 0$. And each clause c with unbarred literal y_k is also true: If $y_k = 0$, we either have $y_k \notin C_0$, in which case some $\bar{y}_l$ in c is $\notin C_0$, hence $y_l = 0$; or $y_k \in C_0 \setminus C_j$ for some j, in which case some $x_j = 0$ and either $\bar{x}_j$ appears in c or some $\bar{y}_l$ appears in c where $y_l \notin C_j$, making $y_l = 0$.

[This solution is due to T. Dahlheimer. See M. Karpinski, H. Kleine Büning, and P. H. Schmitt, *Lecture Notes in Comp. Sci.* **329** (1988), 129–137; H. Kleine Büning, K. Subramani, and X. Zhao, *Lecture Notes in Comp. Sci.* **2919** (2004), 93–104.]

59. By induction on n: Suppose $f(0, x_2, \ldots, x_n)$ leads to the quantified results $y_1, \ldots, y_{2^{n-1}}$, while $f(1, x_2, \ldots, x_n)$ leads similarly to $z_1, \ldots, z_{2^{n-1}}$. Then $\exists x_1 f(x_1, x_2, \ldots, x_n)$ leads to $y_1 \vee z_1, \ldots, y_{2^{n-1}} \vee z_{2^{n-1}}$, and $\forall x_1 f(x_1, x_2, \ldots, x_n)$ leads to $y_1 \wedge z_1, \ldots, y_{2^{n-1}} \wedge z_{2^{n-1}}$. Now use the fact that $(y \vee z) + (y \wedge z) = y + z$. [See *Proc. Mini-Workshop on Quantified Boolean Formulas 2* (QBF-02) (Cincinnati: May 2002), 1–16.]

60. Both (a) and (b). But (c) is always 0; (d) is always 1; (e) is $\overline{\langle xyz \rangle}$; (f) is $\bar{x} \vee \bar{y} \vee \bar{z}$.

61. True — indeed obviously so, when $w = 0$, and when $w = 1$.

62. Since $\{x_1, x_2, x_3\} \subseteq \{0, 1\}$, we can assume by symmetry that x_1 equals x_2. Then either $f(x_1, x_1, x_3, x_4, \ldots, x_n) = f(x_1, x_1, x_1, x_4, \ldots, x_n)$ or $f(x_1, x_1, x_3, x_4, \ldots, x_n) = f(x_3, x_1, x_3, x_4, \ldots, x_n)$, assuming only that f is monotone in its first three variables.

63. $\langle xyz \rangle = \langle xxyyz \rangle$. *Note:* Emil Post proved, in fact, that a single subroutine for *any* nontrivial monotone self-dual function will suffice to compute them all. (By induction on n, at least one appropriate way to call such an n-ary subroutine will yield $\langle xyz \rangle$.)

64. [*FOCS* **3** (1962), 149–157.] (a) If f is monotone and self-dual, Theorem P says that $f(x) = x_k$ or $f(x) = \langle f_1(x) f_2(x) f_3(x) \rangle$. The condition therefore holds either immediately or by induction. Conversely, if the condition holds it implies that f is monotone (when x and y differ in just one bit) and self-dual (when they differ in all bits).

(b) We merely need to show that it is possible to define f at one new point without introducing a conflict. Let x be the lexicographically smallest point where $f(x)$ is undefined. If $f(\bar{x})$ is defined, set $f(x) = \overline{f(\bar{x})}$. Otherwise if $f(x') = 1$ for some $x' \subseteq x$, set $f(x) = 1$; otherwise set $f(x) = 0$. Then the condition still holds.

65. If $\mathcal{F}$ is maximal intersecting, we have (i) $X \in \mathcal{F} \implies \overline{X} \notin \mathcal{F}$, where $\overline{X}$ is the complementary set $\{1, 2, \ldots, n\} \setminus X$; (ii) $X \in \mathcal{F}$ and $X \subseteq Y \implies Y \in \mathcal{F}$, because $\mathcal{F} \cup \{Y\}$ is intersecting; and (iii) $X \notin \mathcal{F} \implies \overline{X} \in \mathcal{F}$, because $\mathcal{F} \cup \{X\}$ must contain an element $Y \subseteq \overline{X}$. Conversely, one can prove without difficulty that any family $\mathcal{F}$ satisfying (i) and (ii) is intersecting, and maximal if it also satisfies (iii).

Punch line: All three statements are simple, in the language of Boolean functions: (i) $f(x) = 1 \implies f(\bar{x}) = 0$; (ii) $x \subseteq y \implies f(x) \leq f(y)$; (iii) $f(x) = 0 \implies f(\bar{x}) = 1$.

66. [T. Ibaraki and T. Kameda, *IEEE Transactions on Parallel and Distributed Systems* **4** (1993), 779–794.] Every family with the property that $Q \subseteq Q'$ implies $Q = Q'$ clearly corresponds to the prime implicants of a monotone Boolean function f. The further condition that $Q \cap Q' \neq \emptyset$ corresponds to the further relation $f(\bar{x}) \leq \overline{f(x)}$, because $f(\bar{x}) = f(x) = 1$ holds if and only if x and $\bar{x}$ both make prime implicants true.

If coteries $\mathcal{C}$ and $\mathcal{C}'$ correspond in this way to functions f and f', then $\mathcal{C}$ dominates $\mathcal{C}'$ if and only if $f \neq f'$ and $f'(x) \leq f(x)$ for all x. Then f' is not self-dual, because there is an x with $f'(\bar{x}) = 0$, $f(\bar{x}) = 1$; and we have $f(x) = 0$, hence $f'(x) = 0$.

Conversely, if f' is not self-dual, there's a y with $f'(y) = f'(\bar{y}) = 0$. If $y = 0 \ldots 0$, coterie $\mathcal{C}'$ is empty, and dominated by every other coterie. Otherwise define $f(x) = f'(x) \vee [x \supseteq y]$. Then f is monotone, and $f(\bar{x}) \leq \overline{f(x)}$ for all x; so it corresponds to a coterie that dominates $\mathcal{C}'$.

67. (a) A black Y in t forces a black Y in t^*, because adjacent black stones $a - b - c$ in t yield two adjacent black stones in t^*. Similarly, a black Y in t^* forces a black Y in t.

(b) This formula follows from (a) and the fact that $(t_{abc})_{def} = t_{(a+d)(b+e)(c+f)} = (t_{def})_{abc}$. [Schensted stated the results of this exercise, and those of exercises 62 and 69, in a 28-page letter sent to Martin Gardner on 21 January 1979. Milnor had written to Gardner on 26 March 1957 about a corresponding game called "Triangle."]

68. Here is one of the 258,594 solutions for $n = 15$ that has 59 black stones: (The answers for $1 \le n \le 15$ are respectively 2, 3, 4, 6, 8, 11, 14, 18, 23, 27, 33, 39, 45, 52, 59. The prime implicants for these functions can be represented by fairly small ZDDs; see Section 7.1.4.)

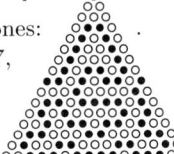

69. The proof of Theorem P shows that we need only prove $Y(T) \le f(x)$. A Y in T means that we've got at least one variable in each p_j. Therefore $f(\bar{x}_1, \dots, \bar{x}_n) = 0$, and $f(x_1, \dots, x_n) = 1$.

70. Self-duality of g is obvious for arbitrary t when f is self-dual: $\overline{g(\bar{x})} = \overline{(\overline{f(\bar{x})} \vee [\bar{x}=t])} \wedge [\bar{x} \ne \bar{t}] = (f(x) \vee [x=\bar{t}]) \wedge [x \ne t] = (f(x) \wedge [x \ne t]) \vee ([x=\bar{t}] \wedge [x \ne t]) = g(x)$.

Let $x = x_1 \dots x_{j-1} 0 x_{j+1} \dots x_n$ and $y = x_1 \dots x_{j-1} 1 x_{j+1} \dots x_n$; for monotonicity we must prove that $g(x) \le g(y)$. If $x = t$ or $y = \bar{t}$, we have $g(x) = 0$; if $x = \bar{t}$ or $y = t$, we have $g(y) = 1$; otherwise $g(x) = f(x) \le f(y) = g(y)$. [*European J. Combinatorics* **16** (1995), 491–501; discovered independently by J. C. Bioch and T. Ibaraki, *IEEE Transactions on Parallel and Distributed Systems* **6** (1995), 905–914.]

71. $\langle\langle xyz\rangle uv\rangle = \langle\langle\langle xyz\rangle uv\rangle uv\rangle = \langle\langle\langle yuv\rangle x\langle zuv\rangle\rangle uv\rangle = \langle\langle yuv\rangle\langle xuv\rangle\langle\langle zuv\rangle uv\rangle\rangle = \langle\langle xuv\rangle\langle yuv\rangle\langle zuv\rangle\rangle$.

72. For (58), $v = \langle uvu\rangle = u$. For (59), $\langle uyv\rangle = \langle vu\langle xuy\rangle\rangle = \langle\langle vux\rangle uy\rangle = \langle xuy\rangle = y$. And for (60), $\langle xyz\rangle = \langle\langle xuv\rangle yz\rangle = \langle x\langle uyz\rangle\langle vyz\rangle\rangle = \langle xyy\rangle = y$.

73. (a) If $d(u,v) = d(u,x) + d(x,v)$, we obviously obtain a shortest path of the form $u - \cdots - x - \cdots - v$. Conversely, if $[uxv]$, let $u - \cdots - x - \cdots - v$ be a shortest path, with l steps to x followed by m steps to v. Then $d(u,v) = l + m \ge d(u,x) + d(x,v) \ge d(u,v)$.

(b) For all z, $\langle zxu\rangle = \langle z\langle vux\rangle\langle yux\rangle\rangle = \langle\langle zvy\rangle ux\rangle \in \{\langle yux\rangle, \langle vux\rangle\} = \{u, x\}$.

(c) We can assume that $d(x,u) \ge d(x,v) > 0$. Let $u - \cdots - y - v$ be a shortest path, and let $w = \langle xuy\rangle$. Then $\langle vxw\rangle = \langle v\langle vux\rangle\langle wux\rangle\rangle = \langle\langle vvw\rangle ux\rangle = \langle vux\rangle = x$, so $x \in [w..v]$. We have $[uwy]$, because $d(u,y) < d(u,v)$ and $w \in [u..y]$. If $w \ne u$ we have $d(w,v) < d(u,v)$; hence $[wxv]$, hence $[uxv]$. If $w = u$ we have $x - u$ by (b). But $d(x,u) \ge d(x,v)$; therefore $x - v$, and $[uxv]$.

(d) Let $y = \langle uxv\rangle$. Since $y \in [u..x]$, we have $d(u,x) = d(u,y) + d(y,x)$ by (a) and (c). Similarly, $d(u,v) = d(u,y) + d(y,v)$ and $d(x,v) = d(x,y) + d(y,v)$. But these three equations, together with $d(u,v) = d(u,x) + d(x,v)$, yield $d(x,y) = 0$. [*Proc. Amer. Math. Soc.* **12** (1961), 407–414.]

74. $w = \langle yxw\rangle = \langle yx\langle zxw\rangle\rangle = \langle yx\langle zx\langle yzw\rangle\rangle\rangle = \langle\langle yxz\rangle x\langle yzw\rangle\rangle = \langle x\langle xyz\rangle\langle wyz\rangle\rangle = \langle\langle xxw\rangle yz\rangle = \langle xyz\rangle$ by (55), (55), (55), (52), (51), (53), and (50).

75. (a) If $w = \langle xxy\rangle$ we have $[xwx]$ by (iii), hence $w = x$ by (i).

(b) Axiom (iii) and part (a) tell us that $[xxy]$ is always true. So we can set $x = y$ in (ii) to conclude that $[uxv] \iff [vxu]$. The definition of $\langle xyz\rangle$ in (iii) is therefore perfectly symmetrical between x, y, and z.

(c) By the definition of $\langle uxv\rangle$ in (iii), we have $x = \langle uxv\rangle$ if and only if $[uxx]$, $[uxv]$, and $[xxv]$. But we know that $[uxx]$ and $[xxv]$ are always true.

(d) In this step and subsequent steps, we will construct one or more auxiliary points of M and then use Algorithm C to derive every consequence of the betweenness relations that are known. (The axioms have the convenient form of Horn clauses.) For example, here we define $z = \langle xyv \rangle$, so that we know $[uxy]$, $[uyv]$, $[xzy]$, $[xzv]$, and $[yzv]$. From these hypotheses we deduce $[uzy]$ and $[uzv]$. So $z = \langle uyv \rangle = y$.

(e) The hinted construction implies, among other things, $[utv]$, $[utz]$, $[vtz]$, $[uwv]$, $[uwz]$, $[vwz]$; hence $t = w$. (A computer program is helpful here.) Adding the hypotheses $[rws]$, $[rwz]$, $[swz]$ now yields $[xyz]$ as desired; it also turns out that $r = p$ and $s = q$.

(f) Let $r = \langle yuv \rangle$, $s = \langle zuv \rangle$, $t = \langle xyz \rangle$, $p = \langle xrs \rangle$, $q = \langle tuv \rangle$; then $[pqp]$ flows out. [*Proc. Amer. Math. Soc.* **5** (1954), 801–807. For early studies of betweenness axioms, see E. V. Huntington and J. R. Kline, *Trans. Amer. Math. Soc.* **18** (1917), 301–325.]

76. Axiom (i) obviously holds, and axiom (ii) follows from commutativity and (52). The answer to exercise 74 derives (iii) from the identity $\langle xyz \rangle = \langle x\langle xyz\rangle\langle wyz\rangle\rangle$; so we need only verify that formula: $\langle x\langle xyz\rangle\langle wyz\rangle\rangle = \langle\langle yxz\rangle x\langle wyz\rangle\rangle = \langle\langle\langle yxz\rangle xz\rangle x\langle wyz\rangle\rangle = \langle\langle yxz\rangle x\langle zx\langle wyz\rangle\rangle\rangle = \langle x\langle xyz\rangle\langle z\langle xyz\rangle w\rangle\rangle = \langle\langle x\langle xyz\rangle z\rangle\langle xyz\rangle w\rangle = \langle\langle xyz\rangle\langle xyz\rangle w\rangle$.

Notes: The original treatment of median algebra by Birkhoff and Kiss in *Bull. Amer. Math. Soc.* **53** (1947), 749–752, assumed (50), (51), and the short distributive law (53). The fact that associativity (52) actually implies distributivity was not realized until many years later; M. Kolibiar and T. Marcisová, *Matematický Časopis* **24** (1974), 179–185, proved it via Sholander's axioms as in this exercise. A mechanical derivation of (53) from (50)–(52) was found in 2005 by R. Veroff and W. McCune, using an extension of the Otter theorem prover.

77. (a) In coordinate $r — s$ of the labels, suppose $l(r)$ has a 0 and $l(s)$ has a 1; then the left vertices have 0 in that coordinate. If $u — v — u'$, where u and u' are on the left but v is on the right, $\langle uu'v \rangle$ lies on the left. But $[u \mathbin{..} v] \cap [u' \mathbin{..} v] = \{v\}$, unless $u = u'$.

(b) This statement is obvious, by Corollary C.

(c) Suppose $u — v$ and $u' — v'$, where u and u' are on the left, v and v' are on the right. Let $v = v_0 — \cdots — v_k = v'$ be a shortest path, and let $u_0 = u$, $u_k = u'$. All vertices v_j lie on the right, by (b). The left vertex $u_1 = \langle u_0 v_1 u_k \rangle$ must be a common neighbor of u_0 and v_1, since the distance $d(u_0, v_1) = 2$. (We cannot have $u_1 = u_0$, because that would imply the existence of a shortest path from v to v' going through the left vertex u.) Therefore v_1 has rank 1; and so do v_2, ..., v_{k-1}, by the same argument. [L. Nebeský, *Commentationes Mathematicæ Universitatis Carolinæ* **12** (1971), 317–325; M. Mulder, *Discrete Math.* **24** (1978), 197–204.]

(d) These steps visit all vertices v of rank 1 in order of their distance $d(v, s)$ from s. If such a v has a late neighbor u not yet seen, the rank of u must be 1 or 2. If the rank is 1, u will have at least two early neighbors, namely v and the future MATE(u). Step I8 bases its decision on an arbitrary early neighbor w of u such that $w \neq v$. The vertex $x = \langle svw \rangle$ has rank 1 by (c). If $x = v$, then u has rank 2 unless w has rank 0. Otherwise $d(x, s) < d(v, s)$, and the rank of w was correctly determined when x was visited. If w has rank 1, u lies on a shortest path from v to w; if w has rank 2, w lies on a shortest path from u to s. In both cases u and w have the same rank, by (c).

(e) The algorithm removes all edges equivalent to $r — s$, by (a) and (d). Their removal clearly disconnects the graph; the two pieces that remain are convex by (b), so they are connected and in fact they are median graphs. Step I7 records all of the relevant relations between the two pieces, because all 4-cycles that disappear are examined there. By induction on the number of vertices, each piece is properly labeled.

78. Every time v appears in step I4, it loses one of its neighbors u_j. Each of these edges $v \relbar\joinrel\relbar u_j$ corresponds to a different coordinate of the labels, so we can assume that $l(v)$ has the form $\alpha 1^k$ for some binary string α. The labels for $u_1, u_2, \ldots, u_k$ are then $\alpha 01^{k-1}$, $\alpha 101^{k-2}$, $\ldots$, $\alpha 1^{k-1}0$. By taking componentwise medians, we can now prove that all 2^k labels of the form $\alpha\beta$ occur for vertices in the graph, since $\langle(\alpha\beta)(\alpha\beta')(0\ldots0)\rangle$ is the bit string $\alpha(\beta \,\&\, \beta')$.

79. (a) If $l(v) = k$, exactly $\nu(k)$ smaller vertices are neighbors of v.

(b) At most $\lfloor n/2 \rfloor$ 1s appear in bit position j, for $0 \le j < \lceil \lg n \rceil$.

(c) Suppose exactly k vertices have labels beginning with 0. At most $\min(k, n-k)$ edges correspond to that bit position, and at most $f(k) + f(n-k)$ other edges are present. But

$$f(n) = \max_{0 \le k \le n} \big(\min(k, n-k) + f(k) + f(n-k)\big),$$

because the function $g(m, n) = f(m+n) - m - f(m) - f(n)$ satisfies the recurrence

$$g(2m+a, 2n+b) = ab + g(m+a, n) + g(m, n+b) \qquad \text{for } 0 \le a, b \le 1.$$

It follows by induction that $g(m, m) = g(m, m+1) = 0$, and that $g(m, n) \ge 0$ when $m \le n$. [*Annals of the New York Academy of Sciences* **175** (1970), 170–186; D. E. Knuth, *Proc. IFIP Congress 1971* (1972), 24.]

80. (a) (Solution by W. Imrich.) The graph with vertex labels 0000, 0001, 0010, 0011, 0100, 0110, 0111, 1100, 1101, 1110, 1111 cannot be labeled in any essentially different way; but the distance from 0001 to 1101 is 4, not 2.

(b) The cycle C_{2m} is a partial cube, because its vertices can be labeled $l(k) = 1^k 0^{m-k}$, $l(m+k) = 0^k 1^{m-k}$ for $0 \le k < m$. But the bitwise median of $l(0)$, $l(m-1)$, and $l(m+1)$ is $01^{m-2}0$; and indeed those vertices don't have a median, when $m > 2$.

81. Yes. A median graph is an induced subgraph of a hypercube, which is bipartite.

82. The general case reduces to the simple case where G has only two vertices $\{0, 1\}$, because we can operate componentwise on the median labels, and because $d(u, v)$ is the Hamming distance between $l(u)$ and $l(v)$.

In the simple case, the stated rule sets $u_k \leftarrow v_k$ except when $u_{k-1} = v_{k-1} = v_{k+1} \ne v_k$, and it is readily proved optimum. (Other optimum possibilities do exist, however; for example, if $v_0 v_1 v_2 v_3 = 0110$, we could set $u_0 u_1 u_2 u_3 = 0000$.)

[This problem was motivated by the study of self-organizing data structures. F. R. K. Chung, R. L. Graham, and M. E. Saks, in *Discrete Algorithms and Complexity* (Academic Press, 1987), 351–387, have proved that median graphs are the *only* graphs for which u_k can always be chosen optimally as a function of $(v_0, v_1, \ldots, v_{k+1})$, regardless of the subsequent values $(v_{k+2}, \ldots, v_t)$. They have also characterized all cases for which a given finite amount of lookahead will suffice, in *Combinatorica* **9** (1989), 111–131.]

83. Consider first the Boolean (two-vertex) case, and let an optimum solution be obtainable by the recursive rules $u_0 \leftarrow v_0$ and $u_j \leftarrow f_{t+2-j}(u_{j-1}, v_j, \ldots, v_t)$ for $1 \le j \le t$, where each f_k is a suitable Boolean function of k variables. The first function $f_{t+1}(v_0, v_1, \ldots, v_t)$ actually depends on its "most remote" variable v_t, because we must have $f_{2k+1}(0, 1, 1, 0, 1, 0, 1, \ldots, 0, 1, 0, x) = x$ when $\rho = 1 - \epsilon$ and $k \ge 2$.

One suitable function f_{t+1} can be obtained as follows: Let $f_{t+1}(0, v_1, \ldots, v_t) = 0$ if $v_1 = 0$. Otherwise let the "runs" of the input sequence be

$$v_0 v_1 \ldots v_t = 01^{a_k} 0^{a_{k-1}} \ldots 1^{a_2} 0^{a_1} \qquad \text{or} \qquad 01^{a_k} 0^{a_{k-1}} \ldots 1^{a_3} 0^{a_2} 1^{a_1},$$

where $a_k, \ldots, a_1 \geq 1$, and let $\alpha_j = 2 \mathbin{\dot-} a_j\rho = \max(0, 2 - a_j\rho)$ for $1 \leq j \leq k$. Then

$$f_{t+1}(0, v_1, \ldots, v_t) = [\alpha_k \mathbin{\dot-} (\alpha_{k-1} \mathbin{\dot-} (\cdots \mathbin{\dot-} (\alpha_2 \mathbin{\dot-} (1 \mathbin{\dot-} a_1\rho))\cdots)) = 0].$$

Also let $f_{t+1}(1, v_1, \ldots, v_t) = \bar{f}_{t+1}(0, \bar{v}_1, \ldots, \bar{v}_t)$, so that f_{t+1} is self-dual.

With a somewhat delicate proof one can show that f_{t+1} is also monotone.

Therefore, by Theorem P, we can apply f_{t+1} componentwise to the labels of an arbitrary median graph, always staying within the graph.

84. There are 81 such functions, each of which can be represented as the median of an odd number of elements. Seven types of vertices occur:

Type	Typical vertex	Cases	Adjacent to	Degree
1	$\langle z\rangle$	5	$\langle vwxyzzz\rangle$	1
2	$\langle vwxyzzz\rangle$	5	$\langle z\rangle, \langle wxyzz\rangle$	5
3	$\langle wxyzz\rangle$	20	$\langle vwxyzzz\rangle, \langle vwxxyyzzz\rangle$	4
4	$\langle vwxxyyzzz\rangle$	30	$\langle xyz\rangle, \langle wxyzz\rangle, \langle vwxyyzz\rangle$	5
5	$\langle vwxyyzz\rangle$	10	$\langle vwxxyyzzz\rangle, \langle vwxyz\rangle$	7
6	$\langle vwxyz\rangle$	1	$\langle vwxyyzz\rangle$	10
7	$\langle xyz\rangle$	10	$\langle vwxxyyzzz\rangle$	3

[Von Neumann and Morgenstern enumerated these seven types in their book *Theory of Games and Economic Behavior* (1944), §52.5, in connection with the study of an equivalent problem about systems of winning coalitions that they called *simple games*. The graph for six-variable functions, which has 2646 vertices of 30 types, appears in the paper by Meyerowitz cited in exercise 70. Only 21 of those types can be represented as a simple median-of-odd; a vertex like $\langle\langle abd\rangle\langle ace\rangle\langle bcf\rangle\rangle$, for example, has no such representation. Let the corresponding graph for n variables have M_n vertices; P. Erdős and N. Hindman, in *Discrete Math.* **48** (1984), 61–65, showed that $\lg M_n$ is asymptotic to $\binom{n-1}{\lfloor n/2\rfloor}$. D. Kleitman, in *J. Combin. Theory* **1** (1966), 153–155, showed that the vertices for distinct projection functions like x and y are always furthest apart in this graph.]

85. Every strong component must consist of a single vertex; otherwise two coordinates would always be equal, or always complementary. Thus the digraph must be acyclic.

Furthermore, there must be no path from a vertex to its complement; otherwise a coordinate would be constant.

When these two conditions are satisfied, we can prove that no vertex x is redundant, by assigning the value 0 to all vertices that precede x or $\bar{x}$, assigning 1 to all vertices that follow, and giving appropriate values to all other vertices.

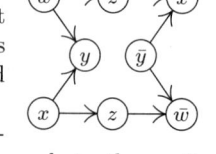

(Consequently we obtain a completely different way to represent a median graph. For example, the digraph shown corresponds to the median graph whose labels are $\{0000, 0001, 0010, 0011, 0111, 1010\}$.)

86. Yes. By Theorem P, *any* monotone self-dual function maps elements of X into X.

87. Here the topological ordering $7\,6\,5\,4\,3\,2\,1\,\bar1\,\bar2\,\bar3\,\bar4\,\bar5\,\bar6\,\bar7$ can replace (72); we get

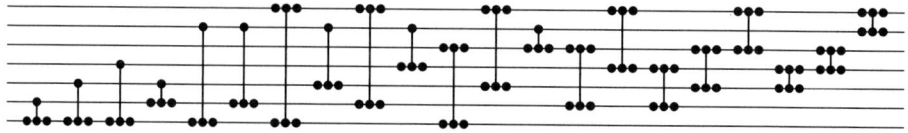

(Consecutive inverters on the same line can, of course, be canceled out.)

88. A given value of d contributes at most $6\lceil t/d\rceil$ units of delay (for $2\lceil t/d\rceil$ clusters).

89. Suppose first that the new condition is $i \to j$ while the old was $i' \to j'$, where $i < j$ and $i' < j'$ and there are no complemented literals. The new module changes $x_1 \dots x_t$ to $y_1 \dots y_t$, where $y_i = x_i \wedge x_j$, $y_j = x_i \vee x_j$, and $y_k = x_k$ otherwise. We certainly have $y_{i'} \le y_{j'}$ when $\{i', j'\} \cap \{i, j\} = \emptyset$. And there is no problem if $i = i'$, since $y_{i'} = y_i \le x_i = x_{i'} \le x_{j'} = y_{j'}$. But the case $i = j'$ is trickier: Here the relations $i' \to i$ and $i \to j$ imply also $i' \to j$; and this relation has been enforced by *previous* modules, because modules have been appended in order of decreasing distance d in the topological ordering $u_1 \dots u_{2t}$. Therefore $y_{i'} = x_{i'} \le x_j$ and $y_{i'} \le x_{j'} = x_i$, hence $y_{i'} \le x_i \wedge x_j = y_i = y_{j'}$. A similar proof works when $j = i'$ or $j = j'$.

Finally, with complemented literals, the construction cleverly reduces the general case to the uncomplemented case by inverting and un-inverting the bits.

90. When $t = 2$, ⊥⊥⊥ does the job. The general case follows recursively from this building block by reducing t to $\lceil t/2\rceil$.

[The study of CI-nets, and other networks of greater generality, was initiated by E. W. Mayr and A. Subramanian, *J. Computer and System Sci.* **44** (1992), 302–323.]

91. The answer does not yet seem to be known even in the special case when the median graph is a free tree (with $t + 1$ vertices), or in the monotone case when it is a distributive lattice as in Corollary F. In the latter case, inverters may be unnecessary.

93. Let $d_X(u, v)$ be the number of edges on a shortest path between u and v, when the path lies entirely within X. Clearly $d_X(u, v) \ge d_G(u, v)$. And if $u = u_0 \mathbin{-\!\!-} u_1 \mathbin{-\!\!-} \cdots \mathbin{-\!\!-} u_k = v$ is a shortest path in G, the path $u = f(u_0) \mathbin{-\!\!-} f(u_1) \mathbin{-\!\!-} \cdots \mathbin{-\!\!-} f(u_k) = v$ lies in X when f is a retraction from G to X; hence $d_X(u, v) \le d_G(u, v)$.

94. If f is a retraction of the t-cube onto X, two different coordinate positions cannot always be equal or always complementary for all $x \in X$, unless they are constant. For if, say, all elements of X have the forms $00*\dots*$ or $11*\dots*$, there would be no path between vertices of those two types, contradicting the fact that X is an isometric subgraph (hence connected).

Given $x, y, z \in X$, let $w = \langle xyz\rangle$ be their median in the t-cube. Then $f(w) \in [x \mathbin{..} y] \cap [x \mathbin{..} z] \cap [y \mathbin{..} z]$, because (for example) $f(w)$ lies on a shortest path from x to y in X. So $f(w) = w$, and we have proved that $w \in X$. [This result and its considerably more subtle converse are due to H. J. Bandelt, *J. Graph Theory* **8** (1984), 501–510.]

95. False (although the author was hoping otherwise); the network at the right takes $0001 \mapsto 0000$, $0010 \mapsto 0011$, $1101 \mapsto 0110$, but nothing $\mapsto 0010$. 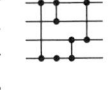 (The set of all possible outputs appears to have no easy characterization, even when no inverters are used. For example, the pure-comparator network at the left, constructed by Tomás Feder, takes $000000 \mapsto 000000$, $010101 \mapsto 010101$, and $101010 \mapsto 011001$, but nothing $\mapsto 010001$. See also exercises 5.3.4–50, 5.3.4–52.)

96. No. If f is a threshold function based on real parameters $w = (w_1, \dots, w_n)$ and t, let $\max\{w \cdot x \mid f(x) = 0\} = t - \epsilon$. Then $\epsilon > 0$, and f is defined by the 2^n inequalities $w \cdot x - t \ge 0$ when $f(x) = 1$, $t - w \cdot x - \epsilon \ge 0$ when $f(x) = 0$. If A is any $M \times N$ matrix of integers for which the system of linear inequalities $Av \ge (0, \dots, 0)^T$ has a real-valued solution $v = (v_1, \dots, v_N)^T$ with $v_N > 0$, there also is such a solution in integers. (Proof by induction on N.) So we can assume that $w_1, \dots, w_n, t$, and ϵ are integers.

[A closer analysis using Hadamard's inequality (see Eq. 4.6.1–(25)) proves in fact that integer weights of magnitude at most $(n + 1)^{(n+1)/2}/2^n$ will suffice; see

S. Muroga, I. Toda, and S. Takasu, *J. Franklin Inst.* **271** (1961), 376–418, Theorem 16. Furthermore, exercise 112 shows that weights nearly that large are sometimes needed.]

97. $\langle 11111 x_1 x_2 \rangle$, $\langle 111 x_1 x_2 \rangle$, $\langle 1 x_1 x_2 \rangle$, $\langle 0 x_1 x_2 \rangle$, $\langle 000 x_1 x_2 \rangle$, $\langle 00000 x_1 x_2 \rangle$.

98. We may assume that $f(x_1, \ldots, x_n) = \langle y_1^{w_1} \ldots y_n^{w_n} \rangle$, with positive integer weights w_j and with $w_1 + \cdots + w_n$ odd. Let δ be the minimum positive value of the 2^n sums $\pm w_1 \pm \cdots \pm w_n$, with n independently varying signs. Renumber all subscripts so that $w_1 + \cdots + w_k - w_{k+1} - \cdots - w_n = \delta$. Then $w_1 y_1 + \cdots + w_n y_n > \frac{1}{2}(w_1 + \cdots + w_n) \iff w_1(y_1 - \frac{1}{2}) + \cdots + w_n(y_n - \frac{1}{2}) > 0 \iff w_1(y_1 - \frac{1}{2}) + \cdots + w_n(y_n - \frac{1}{2}) > -\delta/2 \iff w_1 y_1 + \cdots + w_n y_n > \frac{1}{2}(w_1 + \cdots + w_n - (w_1 + \cdots + w_k - w_{k+1} - \cdots - w_n)) = w_{k+1} + \cdots + w_n \iff w_1 y_1 + \cdots + w_k y_k - w_{k+1} \bar{y}_{k+1} - \cdots - w_n \bar{y}_n > 0$.

99. We have $\lceil x_1 + \cdots + x_{2s-1} + s(y_1 + \cdots + y_{2t-2}) \geq st \rceil = \lceil \lfloor (x_1 + \cdots + x_{2s-1})/s \rfloor + y_1 + \cdots + y_{2t-2} \geq t \rceil$; and $\lfloor (x_1 + \cdots + x_{2s-1})/s \rfloor = \lceil x_1 + \cdots + x_{2s-1} \geq s \rceil$.

(For example, $\langle\langle xyz \rangle uv \rangle = \langle xyzu^2 v^2 \rangle$, a quantity that we also know is equal to $\langle x \langle yuv \rangle \langle zuv \rangle\rangle$ and $\langle\langle xuv \rangle \langle yuv \rangle \langle zuv \rangle\rangle$ by Eqs. (53) and (54). *Reference:* C. C. Elgot, *FOCS* **2** (1961), 238.)

100. True, because of the preceding exercise and (45).

101. (a) When $n = 7$ they are $x_7 \wedge x_6$, $x_6 \wedge x_5$, $x_7 \wedge x_5 \wedge x_4$, $x_6 \wedge x_4 \wedge x_3$, $x_7 \wedge x_5 \wedge x_3 \wedge x_2$, $x_6 \wedge x_4 \wedge x_2 \wedge x_1$, $x_7 \wedge x_5 \wedge x_3 \wedge x_1$; and in general there are n prime implicants, forming a similar pattern. (We have either $x_n = x_{n-1}$ or $x_n = \bar{x}_{n-1}$. In the first case, $x_n \wedge x_{n-1}$ is obviously a prime implicant. In the second case, $F_n(x_1, \ldots, x_{n-1}, \bar{x}_{n-1}) = F_{n-1}(x_1, \ldots, x_{n-1})$; so we use the prime implicants of the latter, and insert x_n when x_{n-1} does not appear.)

(b) The shelling pattern (0000011, $000011\underline{0}$, $00011\underline{0}1$, $0011\underline{0}1\underline{0}$, $011\underline{0}1\underline{0}1$, $11\underline{0}1\underline{0}1\underline{0}$, $1\underline{0}1\underline{0}1\underline{0}1$) for $n = 7$ works for all n.

(c) Two of several possibilities for $n = 7$ illustrate the general case:

$$F_7(x_1, \ldots, x_7) = Y \begin{pmatrix} x_6 \\ x_7 \ x_5 \\ x_6 \ x_6 \ x_4 \\ x_7 \ x_5 \ x_7 \ x_3 \\ x_6 \ x_6 \ x_4 \ x_6 \ x_2 \\ x_7 \ x_5 \ x_7 \ x_3 \ x_7 \ x_1 \end{pmatrix} = Y \begin{pmatrix} x_6 \\ x_7 \ x_5 \\ x_6 \ x_6 \ x_4 \\ x_7 \ x_5 \ x_5 \ x_3 \\ x_6 \ x_6 \ x_4 \ x_4 \ x_2 \\ x_7 \ x_5 \ x_5 \ x_3 \ x_3 \ x_1 \end{pmatrix}.$$

[The Fibonacci threshold functions were introduced by S. Muroga, who also discovered the optimality result in exercise 105; see *IEEE Transactions* **EC-14** (1965), 136–148.]

102. (a) By (11) and (12), $\hat{f}(\bar{x}_0, \bar{x}_1, \ldots, \bar{x}_n)$ is the complement of $\hat{f}(x_0, x_1, \ldots, x_n)$.

(b) If f is given by (75), $\hat{f}$ is $[(w + 1 - 2t)x_0 + w_1 x_1 + \cdots + w_n x_n \geq w + 1 - t]$, where $w = w_1 + \cdots + w_n$. Conversely, if $\hat{f}$ is a threshold function, so is $f(x_1, \ldots, x_n) = \hat{f}(1, x_1, \ldots, x_n)$. [E. Goto and H. Takahasi, *Proc. IFIP Congress* (1962), 747–752.]

103. [See R. C. Minnick, *IRE Transactions* **EC-10** (1961), 6–16.] We want to minimize $w_1 + \cdots + w_n$ subject to the constraints $w_j \geq 0$ for $1 \leq j \leq n$ and $(2e_1 - 1)w_1 + \cdots + (2e_n - 1)w_n \geq 1$ for each prime implicant $x_1^{e_1} \wedge \cdots \wedge x_n^{e_n}$. For example, if $n = 6$, the prime implicant $x_2 \wedge x_5 \wedge x_6$ would lead to the constraint $-w_1 + w_2 - w_3 - w_4 + w_5 + w_6 \geq 1$. If the minimum is $+\infty$, the given function is not a threshold function. (The answer to exercise 84 gives one of the simplest examples of such a case.) Otherwise, if the solution $(w_1, \ldots, w_n)$ involves only integers, it minimizes the desired size. When noninteger solutions arise, additional constraints must be added until the best solution is found, as in part (c) of the following exercise.

104. First we need an algorithm to generate the prime implicants $x_1^{e_1} \wedge \cdots \wedge x_n^{e_n}$ of a given majority function $\langle x_1^{w_1} \ldots x_n^{w_n} \rangle$, when $w_1 \geq \cdots \geq w_n$ and $w_1 + \cdots + w_n$ is odd:

K1. [Initialize.] Set $t \leftarrow 0$. Then for $j = n, n-1, \ldots, 1$ (in this order), set $a_j \leftarrow t$, $t \leftarrow t + w_j$, $e_j \leftarrow 0$. Finally set $t \leftarrow (t+1)/2$, $s_1 \leftarrow 0$, and $l \leftarrow 0$.

K2. [Enter level l.] Set $l \leftarrow l+1$, $e_l \leftarrow 1$, $s_{l+1} \leftarrow s_l + w_l$.

K3. [Below threshold?] If $s_{l+1} < t$, return to K2.

K4. [Visit a prime implicant.] Visit the exponents $(e_1, \ldots, e_n)$.

K5. [Downsize.] Set $e_l \leftarrow 0$. Then if $s_l + a_l \geq t$, set $s_{l+1} \leftarrow s_l$ and go to K2.

K6. [Backtrack.] Set $l \leftarrow l-1$. Terminate if $l = 0$; otherwise go to K5 if $e_l = 1$; otherwise repeat this step. ∎

(a) $\langle x_1 x_2^2 x_3^3 x_4^5 x_5^6 x_6^8 x_7^{10} x_8^{12} \rangle$ (21 prime implicants).

(b) The optimum weights for $\langle x_0^{16-2t} x_1^8 x_2^4 x_3^2 x_4 \rangle$ are $w_0 w_1 w_2 w_3 w_4 = 10000, 31111,$ $21110, 32211, 11100, 23211, 12110, 13111, 01000$, for $0 \leq t \leq 8$; the other cases are dual.

(c) Here the optimum weights $(w_1, \ldots, w_{10})$ are $(29, 25, 19, 15, 12, 8, 8, 3, 3, 0)/2$; so we learn that x_{10} is irrelevant, and we must deal with fractional weights. Constraining $w_8 \geq 2$ gives integer weights $(15, 13, 10, 8, 6, 4, 4, 2, 1, 0)$, which must be optimum because their sum exceeds the previous sum by 2. (Only two of the 175,428 self-dual threshold functions on nine variables have nonintegral weights minimizing $w_1 + \cdots + w_n$; the other one is $\langle x_1^{17} x_2^{15} x_3^{11} x_4^9 x_5^7 x_6^5 x_7^4 x_8^2 x_9 \rangle$. The largest w_1 in a minimum representation occurs in $\langle x_1^{42} x_2^{22} x_3^{18} x_4^{15} x_5^{10} x_6^8 x_7^4 x_8^4 x_9^3 \rangle$; the largest $w_1 + \cdots + w_9$ occurs uniquely in $\langle x_1^{34} x_2^{32} x_3^{28} x_4^{27} x_5^{24} x_6^{20} x_7^{18} x_8^{15} x_9^{11} \rangle$, which is also an example of the largest w_9. See S. Muroga, T. Tsuboi, and C. R. Baugh, *IEEE Transactions* **C-19** (1970), 818–825.)

105. When $n = 7$, the inequalities generated in exercise 103 are $w_7 + w_6 - w_5 - w_4 - w_3 - w_2 - w_1 \geq 1$, $-w_7 + w_6 + w_5 - w_4 - w_3 - w_2 - w_1 \geq 1$, $w_7 - w_6 + w_5 + w_4 - w_3 - w_2 - w_1 \geq 1$, $-w_7 + w_6 - w_5 + w_4 + w_3 - w_2 - w_1 \geq 1$, $w_7 - w_6 + w_5 - w_4 + w_3 + w_2 - w_1 \geq 1$, $-w_7 + w_6 - w_5 + w_4 - w_3 + w_2 + w_1 \geq 1$, $w_7 - w_6 + w_5 - w_4 + w_3 - w_2 + w_1 \geq 1$. Multiply them respectively by $1, 1, 2, 3, 5, 8, 5$ to get $w_1 + \cdots + w_7 \geq 1 + 1 + 2 + 3 + 5 + 8 + 5$. The same idea works for all $n \geq 3$.

106. (a) $\langle x_1^{2^{n-1}} x_2^{2^{n-2}} \ldots x_n \, \bar{y}_1^{2^{n-1}} \bar{y}_2^{2^{n-2}} \ldots \bar{y}_n \bar{z} \rangle$. (By exercise 99, we could also perform n medians-of-three: $\langle\langle \ldots \langle x_n \bar{y}_n \bar{z} \rangle \ldots x_2 \bar{y}_2 \rangle x_1 \bar{y}_1 \rangle$.)

(b) If $\langle x_1^{u_1} x_2^{u_2} \ldots x_n^{u_n} \bar{y}_1^{v_1} \bar{y}_2^{v_2} \ldots \bar{y}_n^{v_n} \bar{z}^w \rangle$ solves the problem, $2^{n+1} - 1$ basic inequalities need to hold; for example, when $n = 2$ they are $u_1 + u_2 - v_1 + v_2 - w \geq 1$, $u_1 + u_2 - v_1 - v_2 + w \geq 1$, $u_1 - u_2 + v_1 - v_2 - w \geq 1$, $u_1 - u_2 - v_1 + v_2 + w \geq 1$, $-u_1 + u_2 + v_1 + v_2 - w \geq 1$, $-u_1 + u_2 + v_1 - v_2 + w \geq 1$. Add them all up to get $u_1 + u_2 + \cdots + u_n + v_1 + v_2 + \cdots + v_n + w \geq 2^{n+1} - 1$.

107.

f	$N(f)$	$\Sigma(f)$	f	$N(f)$	$\Sigma(f)$	f	$N(f)$	$\Sigma(f)$	f	$N(f)$	$\Sigma(f)$
$\bot$	0	$(0,0)$	$\bar{C}$	1	$(0,1)$	$\bar{\vee}$	1	$(0,0)$	$\bar{L}$	2	$(0,1)$
$\wedge$	1	$(1,1)$	R	2	$(1,2)$	$\equiv$	2	$(1,1)$	$\supset$	3	$(1,2)$
$\bar{\supset}$	1	$(1,0)$	$\oplus$	2	$(1,1)$	$\bar{R}$	2	$(1,0)$	$\bar{\wedge}$	3	$(1,1)$
L	2	$(2,1)$	$\vee$	3	$(2,2)$	C	3	$(2,1)$	$\top$	4	$(2,2)$

Notice that $\oplus$ and $\equiv$ have the same parameters $N(f)$ and $\Sigma(f)$; they are the only Boolean binary operations that aren't threshold functions.

108. If $\Sigma(g) = (s_0, s_1, \ldots, s_n)$, the value of g is 1 in s_0 cases when $x_0 = 1$ and in $2^n - s_0$ cases when $x_0 = 0$. We also have $\Sigma(f_0) + \Sigma(f_1) = (s_1, \ldots, s_n)$, and

$$\Sigma(f_0) = \sum_{x_1=0}^{1} \cdots \sum_{x_n=0}^{1} (\bar{x}_1, \ldots, \bar{x}_n) g(0, \bar{x}_1, \ldots, \bar{x}_n)$$

$$= \sum_{x_1=0}^{1} \cdots \sum_{x_n=0}^{1} \big((1, \ldots, 1) - (x_1, \ldots, x_n)\big)\big(1 - g(1, x_1, \ldots, x_n)\big)$$

$$= (2^{n-1} - s_0, \ldots, 2^{n-1} - s_0) + \Sigma(f_1).$$

So the answers, for $n > 0$, are (a) $N(f_0) = 2^n - s_0$, $\Sigma(f_0) = \frac{1}{2}(s_1 - s_0 + 2^{n-1}, \ldots, s_n - s_0 + 2^{n-1})$; (b) $N(f_1) = s_0$, $\Sigma(f_1) = \frac{1}{2}(s_1 + s_0 - 2^{n-1}, \ldots, s_n + s_0 - 2^{n-1})$. [Equivalent results were presented by E. Goto in lectures at MIT in 1963.]

109. (a) $a_1 + \cdots + a_k \geq b_1 + \cdots + b_k$ if and only if $k - a_1 - \cdots - a_k \leq k - b_1 - \cdots - b_k$.

(b) Let $\alpha^+ = (a_1, a_1 + a_2, \ldots, a_1 + \cdots + a_n)$. Then the vector $(c_1, \ldots, c_n)$ obtained by componentwise minimization of α^+ and β^+ is $(\alpha \wedge \beta)^+$. (Clearly $c_j = c_{j-1} + a_j$ or b_j.)

(c) Proceed as in (b) but with componentwise *maximization*; or take $\overline{\bar{\alpha} \wedge \bar{\beta}}$.

(d) True, because max and min satisfy these distributive laws. (In fact, we obtain a distributive *mixed-radix majorization lattice* in a similar way from the set of all n-tuples $a_1 \ldots a_n$ with $0 \leq a_j < m_j$ for $1 \leq j \leq n$. R. P. Stanley has observed that Fig. 8 is also the lattice of order ideals of the triangular grid shown here.)

(e) $\alpha 1$ covers $\alpha 0$ and $\alpha 10\beta$ covers $\alpha 01\beta$. [This characterization is due to R. O. Winder, *IEEE Trans.* **EC-14** (1965), 315–325, but he didn't prove the lattice property. The lattice is often called $M(n)$; see B. Lindström, *Nordisk Mat. Tidskrift* **17** (1969), 61–70; R. P. Stanley, *SIAM J. Algebraic and Discrete Methods* **1** (1980), 177–179.]

(f) Because of (e) we have $r(\alpha) = na_1 + (n-1)a_2 + \cdots + a_n$.

(g) The point is that $0\beta \succeq 0\alpha$ if and only if $\beta \succeq \alpha$ and that $1\beta \succeq 0\alpha$ if and only if $1\beta \succeq 10 \ldots 0 \vee 0\alpha = 1\alpha'$.

(h) That is, how many $a_1 \ldots a_n$ have the property that $a_1 \ldots a_k$ contains no more 1s than 0s? The answer is $\binom{n}{\lfloor n/2 \rfloor}$; see, for example, exercise 2.2.1–4 or 7.2.1.6–42(a).

110. (a) If $x \subseteq y$ then $x \preceq y$, hence $f(x) \leq f(y)$; QED.

(b) No; a threshold function need not be monotone (see (79)). But we *can* show that f is regular if we also require $w_n \geq 0$: For if $f(x) = 1$ and y covers x we then have $w \cdot y \geq w \cdot x$.

(c) Whenever $f(x) = 1$ and $x_j < x_{j+1}$, we have $f(y) = 1$ when y covers x with $x_j \leftrightarrow x_{j+1}$; hence $s_j \geq s_{j+1}$. (This argument holds even when $w_n < 0$.)

(d) No; consider, for example, $\langle x_1 x_2^2 x_3^2 \rangle$, which equals $\langle x_1 x_2 x_3 \rangle$. Counterexamples can arise even when the weights minimize $w_1 + \cdots + w_n$, because the solution to the linear program in exercise 103 is not always unique. One such case, found by Muroga, Tsuboi, and Baugh, is $\langle x_1^{17} x_2^9 x_3^8 x_4^6 x_5^7 x_6^5 x_7^3 x_8^2 x_9^2 \rangle$, a function that is actually symmetric in x_4 and x_5. But if $s_j > s_{j+1}$ we must have $w_j > w_{j+1}$, because of (c).

111. (a) Find an optimum self-dual function f pointwise as in exercise 14; in case of ties, choose $f(x_1, \ldots, x_n) = x_1$. Thus $f(x_1, \ldots, x_n) = [r_1^{x_1} \ldots r_n^{x_n} \geq \sqrt{r_1 \ldots r_n}]$, except that '$\geq$' becomes '$>$' when $x_1 = 0$. This function is regular when $r_1 \geq \cdots \geq r_n \geq 1$.

(b) Let g be the regular, self-dual function constructed in (a). If f is a given regular, self-dual function, we want to verify that $f(x) \leq g(x)$ for all vectors x; this will imply that $f = g$, because both functions are self-dual.

Suppose $f(x) = 1$, and let $y \preceq x$ be minimal such that $f(y) = 1$. If we have verified that $g(y) = 1$, then indeed $g(x) = 1$, as desired. [See K. Makino and T. Kameda, *SIAM Journal on Discrete Mathematics* **14** (2001), 381–407.]

For example, there are only seven self-dual regular Boolean functions when $n = 5$, generated by the following minimal elements in Fig. 8: 10000; 01111, 10001; 01110, 10010; 01101, 10011, 10100; 01100; 01011, 11000; 00111. So an optimum coterie can be found by examining only a few function values.

(c) Suppose $1 > p_1 \ge \cdots \ge p_r \ge \frac{1}{2} > p_{r+1} \ge \cdots \ge p_n > 0$. Let $f_k(x_1, \ldots, x_n)$ be the kth monotone, self-dual function and $F_k(x_1, \ldots, x_n)$ its integer multilinear representation. We want to find the optimum availability $G(p_1, \ldots, p_n) = \max_k F_k(p_1, \ldots, p_n)$. If $p_1 \le p_1', \ldots, p_n \le p_n'$, we have $F_k(p_1, \ldots, p_n) \le F_k(p_1', \ldots, p_n')$ by exercise 12(e); hence $G(p_1, \ldots, p_n) \le G(p_1', \ldots, p_n')$.

Therefore if $0 < r < n$ we have

$$G(p_1, \ldots, p_n) \le G(p_1, \ldots, p_r, \tfrac{1}{2}, \ldots, \tfrac{1}{2}).$$

And the latter is $F(p_1, \ldots, p_r, \frac{1}{2}, \ldots, \frac{1}{2})$, derived from these larger probabilities as in part (a). This function does not depend on $(x_{r+1}, \ldots, x_n)$, so it gives the optimum.

If $r = 0$ the problem seems to be deeper. We have $G(p_1, \ldots, p_n) \le G(p_1, \ldots, p_1)$; so we can conclude that the optimum coterie is $f(x_1, \ldots, x_n) = x_1$ in this case if we can show that $F_k(p, \ldots, p) \le p$ for all k whenever $p < \frac{1}{2}$. In general $F_k(p, \ldots, p) = \sum_m c_m p^m (1-p)^{n-m}$, where c_m is the number of vectors x such that $f_k(x) = 1$ and $\nu x = m$. Exercise 70 tells us that $c_m + c_{n-m} = \binom{n}{m}$, for all k. And the Erdős–Ko–Rado theorem (exercise 7.2.1.3–111) tells us that we have $c_m \le \binom{n-1}{m-1}$ for any intersecting family of m-sets when $m \le n/2$. The result follows.

[See Y. Amir and A. Wool, *Information Processing Letters* **65** (1998), 223–228.]

112. (a) The leading terms are respectively $0, +xy, -xy, +x, -xy, +y, -2xy, -xy, +xy, +2xy, -y, +xy, -x, +xy, -xy, 1$; so $F(f) = 1$ when f is $\wedge, \mathsf{L}, \mathsf{R}, \overline{\vee}, \equiv, \subset, \supset, \top$.

(b) The coefficient corresponding to exponents 01101, say, is f_{0**0*} in the notation of answer 12; it is a linear combination of truth table entries, always lying in the range $\lceil -2^{k-1} \rceil \le f_{0**0*} \le \lceil 2^{k-1} \rceil$ when there are k asterisks. Thus the leading coefficient is positive if and only if the mixed-radix number

$$\begin{bmatrix} f_{**\ldots*}, & f_{0*\ldots*}, & \ldots, & f_{*0\ldots0}, & f_{00\ldots0} \\ 2^m+1, & 2^{m-1}+1, & \ldots, & 2^1+1, & 2^0+1 \end{bmatrix}$$

is positive, where the f's are arranged in reverse order of Chase's sequence and the radix $2^k + 1$ corresponds to an f with k asterisks. For example, when $m = 2$ we have $F(f) = 1$ if and only if the sum $18f_{**} + 6f_{0*} + 2f_{*0} + f_{00} = 18(f_{11} - f_{01} - f_{10} + f_{00}) + 6(f_{01} - f_{00}) + 2(f_{10} - f_{00}) + f_{00} = 18f_{11} - 12f_{01} - 16f_{10} + 11f_{00}$ is positive; so the threshold function can be written $\langle f_{11}^{18} \bar{f}_{01}^{12} \bar{f}_{10}^{16} f_{00}^{11} \rangle$.

(In this particular case the much simpler expression $\langle f_{11} f_{11} \bar{f}_{01} \bar{f}_{10} f_{00} \rangle$ is actually valid. But part (c) will show that when m is large we can't do a great deal better.)

(c) Suppose $F(f) = [\sum_\alpha v_\alpha (f_\alpha - \frac{1}{2}) > 0]$, where the sum is over all 2^m binary strings α of length m and where each v_α is an integer weight. Define

$$w_\alpha = \sum_\beta (-1)^{\nu(\alpha \,\dot-\, \beta)} v_\beta \qquad \text{and} \qquad F_\alpha = \sum_\beta (-1)^{\nu(\alpha \,\dot-\, \beta)} f_\beta - 2^{m-1}[\alpha = 00\ldots0];$$

thus, for example, $w_{01} = -v_{00} + v_{01} - v_{10} + v_{11}$ and $F_{11} = f_{00} - f_{01} - f_{10} + f_{11}$. One can show that $F_{1^k0^l} = 2^l f_{*^k0^l}$, if $F_\alpha = 0$ whenever $\nu(\alpha) > k > 0$; therefore the signs of the transformed truth coefficients F_α determine the sign of the leading coefficient in the multilinear representation. Furthermore, we now have $F(f) = [\sum_\alpha w_\alpha F_\alpha > 0]$.

The general idea of the proof is to choose test functions f from which we can derive properties of the transformed weights w_α. For example, if $f(x_1, \ldots, x_m) = x_1 \oplus \cdots \oplus x_k$, we find $F_\alpha = 0$ for all α except that $F_{1^k 0^{m-k}} = (-1)^{k-1} 2^{m-1}$. The multilinear representation of $x_1 \oplus \cdots \oplus x_k$ has leading term $\lceil (-2)^{k-1} \rceil x_1 \ldots x_k$; hence we can conclude that $w_{1^k 0^{m-k}} > 0$, and in a similar way that $w_\alpha > 0$ for all α. In general if m changes to $m+1$ but f does not depend on x_{m+1}, we have $F_{\alpha 0} = 2 F_\alpha$ and $F_{\alpha 1} = 0$.

The test function $x_2 \oplus \cdots \oplus x_m \oplus x_1 \bar{x}_2 \ldots \bar{x}_m$ proves that

$$w_{1^m} > (2^{m-1}-1)w_{01^{m-1}} + \sum_{k=1}^{m-1} w_{1^k 01^{m-1-k}} + \text{smaller terms},$$

where the smaller terms involve only w_α with $\nu(\alpha) \leq m - 2$. In particular, $w_{11} > w_{01} + w_{10} + w_{00}$. The test function $x_1 \oplus \cdots \oplus x_{m-1} \oplus \bar{x}_1 \ldots \bar{x}_{m-2}(x_{m-1} \oplus \bar{x}_m)$ proves

$$w_{1^{m-2}01} > (2^{m-2}-1)w_{1^{m-2}10} + \sum_{k=0}^{m-3}(w_{1^k 01^{m-3-k}10} + w_{1^k 01^{m-3-k}01}) + \text{smaller terms},$$

where the smaller terms this time have $\nu(\alpha) \leq m - 3$. In particular, $w_{101} > w_{110} + w_{010} + w_{001}$. By permuting subscripts, we obtain similar inequalities leading to

$$w_{\alpha_j} > (2^{\nu(\alpha_j)-1} - 1)w_{\alpha_{j-1}} \qquad \text{for } 0 < j < 2^m,$$

because the w's begin to grow rapidly. But we have $v_\alpha = \sum_\beta (-1)^{\nu(\beta \dot{-} \alpha)} w_\beta / n$; hence $|v_\alpha| = w_{11\ldots 1}/n + O(w_{11\ldots 1}/n^2)$. [*SIAM J. Discrete Math.* **7** (1994), 484–492. Important generalizations of this result have been obtained by N. Alon and V. H. Vũ, *J. Combinatorial Theory* **A79** (1997), 133–160.]

113. The stated g_3 is $S_{2,3,6,8,9}$ because the stated g_2 is $S_{2,3,4,5,8,9,10,11,12}$.

For the more difficult function $S_{1,3,5,8}$, let $g_1 = [\nu x \geq 6]$; $g_2 = [\nu x \geq 3]$; $g_3 = [\nu x - 5g_1 - 2g_2 \geq 2] = S_{2,4,5,9,10,11,12}$; $g_4 = [2\nu x - 15g_1 - 9g_3 \geq 1] = S_{1,3,5,8}$. [See M. A. Fischler and M. Tannenbaum, *IEEE Transactions* **C-17** (1968), 273–279.]

114. $[4x + 2y + z \in \{3,6\}] = (\bar{x} \wedge y \wedge z) \vee (x \wedge y \wedge \bar{z})$. In the same way, *any* Boolean function of n variables is a special case of a symmetric function of $2^n - 1$ variables. [See W. H. Kautz, *IRE Transactions* **EC-10** (1961), 378.]

115. Both sides are self-dual, so we may assume that $x_0 = 0$. Then

$$s_j = [x_j + \cdots + x_{j+m-1} > x_{j+m} + \cdots + x_{j+2m-1}].$$

If $x_1 + \cdots + x_{2m}$ is odd, we have $s_j = \bar{s}_{j+m}$; hence $s_1 + \cdots + s_{2m} = m$ and the result is 1. But if $x_1 + \cdots + x_{2m}$ is even, the difference $x_j + \cdots + x_{j+m-1} - x_{j+m} - \cdots - x_{j+2m-1}$ will be zero for at least one $j \leq m$; that makes $s_j = s_{j+m} = 0$, so we will have $s_1 + \cdots + s_{2m} < m$.

116. (a) It's an implicant if and only if $f(x) = 1$ whenever $j \leq \nu x \leq n - k + j$. It's a prime implicant if and only if we also have $f(x) = 0$ when $\nu x = j-1$ or $\nu x = n-k+j+1$.

(b) Consider the string $v = v_0 v_1 \ldots v_n$ such that $f(x) = v_{\nu x}$. By part (a), there are $\binom{a+b+c}{a,b,c}$ prime implicants when $v = 0^a 1^{b+1} 0^c$. In the stated case, $a = b = c = 3$, so there are 1680 prime implicants.

(c) For a general symmetric function, we add together the prime implicants for each run of 1s in v. Clearly there are more for $v = 0^{a+1}1^{b+1}0^{c-1}$ than for $v = 0^a1^b0^c$ when $a < c - 1$; so v contains no two consecutive 0s when the maximum is reached.

Let $\hat{b}(m, n)$ be the maximum number of prime implicants possible when $v_m = 1$ and $v_j = 0$ for $m < j \le n$. Then when $m \le \frac{1}{2}n$ we have

$$\hat{b}(m, n) = \max_{0 \le k \le m}\left(\binom{n}{k, m-k, n-m} + \hat{b}(k-2, n)\right)$$
$$= \binom{n}{\lceil m/2 \rceil, \lfloor m/2 \rfloor, n-m} + \hat{b}(\lceil m/2 \rceil - 2, n),$$

with $\hat{b}(-2, n) = \hat{b}(-1, n) = 0$. And the overall maximum is

$$\hat{b}(n) = \binom{n}{n_0, n_1, n_2} + \hat{b}(n_1 - 2, n) + \hat{b}(n_2 - 2, n), \qquad n_j = \left\lfloor \frac{n+j}{3} \right\rfloor.$$

In particular we have $\hat{b}(9) = 1698$, with the maximum occurring for $v = 1101111011$.

(d) By Stirling's approximation, $\hat{b}(n) = 3^{n+3/2}/(2\pi n) + O(3^n/n^2)$.

(e) In this case the appropriate recurrence for $m < \lceil n/2 \rceil$ is

$$\tilde{b}(m, n) = \max_{0 \le k \le m}\left(\binom{n}{k, m-k, n-m} + \binom{n}{k-1, 0, n-k+1} + \tilde{b}(k-2, n)\right)$$
$$= \binom{n}{\lceil m/2 \rceil, \lfloor m/2 \rfloor, n-m} + \binom{n}{\lceil m/2 \rceil - 1} + \tilde{b}(\lceil m/2 \rceil - 2, n)$$

and $\tilde{b}(n) = \tilde{b}(\lceil n/2 \rceil - 1, n)$ maximizes $\min(\text{prime implicants}(f), \text{prime implicants}(\bar{f}))$. We have $(\tilde{b}(1), \tilde{b}(2), \dots) = (1, 1, 4, 5, 21, 31, 113, 177, 766, 1271, 4687, 7999, 34412, \dots)$; for example, $\tilde{b}(9) = 766$ corresponds to $S_{0,2,3,4,8}(x_1, \dots, x_9)$. Asymptotically, $\tilde{b}(n) = 2^{(3n+3+(n \bmod 2))/2}/(2\pi n) + O(2^{3n/2}/n^2)$.

References: Summaries, Summer Inst. for Symbolic Logic (Dept. of Math., Cornell Univ., 1957), 211–212; B. Dunham and R. Fridshal, *J. Symbolic Logic* **24** (1959), 17–19; A. P. Vikulin, *Problemy Kibernetiki* **29** (1974), 151–166, which reports on work done in 1960; Y. Igarashi, *Transactions of the IEICE of Japan* **E62** (1979), 389–394.

117. The maximum number of subcubes of the n-cube, with none contained in another, is obtained when we choose all subcubes of dimension $\lfloor n/3 \rfloor$. (It is also obtained by choosing all subcubes of dimension $\lfloor (n+1)/3 \rfloor$; for example, when $n = 2$ we can choose either $\{0*, 1*, *0, *1\}$ or $\{00, 01, 10, 11\}$.) Hence $b^*(n) = \binom{n}{\lfloor n/3 \rfloor}2^{n-\lfloor n/3 \rfloor} = 3^{n+1}/\sqrt{4\pi n} + O(3^n/n^{3/2})$. [See the paper of Vikulin in the previous answer, pages 164–166; A. K. Chandra and G. Markowsky, *Discrete Math.* **24** (1978), 7–11; N. Metropolis and G. C. Rota, *SIAM J. Applied Math.* **35** (1978), 689–694.]

118. Consider two functions equivalent if we can obtain one from the other by complementing and/or permuting variables, but not complementing the function value itself. Such functions clearly have the same number of prime implicants; this equivalence relation is studied further in answer 125 below. A computer program based on exercise 30 produces the following results:

m	Classes	Functions	m	Classes	Functions	m	Classes	Functions
0	1	1	5	87	17472	10	7	632
1	5	81	6	70	12696	11	1	96
2	18	1324	7	43	7408	12	2	24
3	46	6608	8	24	3346	13	1	16
4	87	14536	9	10	1296	14	0	0

And here are the corresponding statistics for functions of five variables:

m	Classes	Functions	m	Classes	Functions	m	Classes	Functions
0	1	1	11	186447	666555696	22	338	608240
1	6	243	12	165460	590192224	23	130	197440
2	37	14516	13	129381	459299440	24	71	75720
3	244	318520	14	91026	319496560	25	37	28800
4	1527	3319580	15	57612	199792832	26	15	10560
5	6997	19627904	16	33590	113183894	27	6	2880
6	23434	73795768	17	17948	58653984	28	4	1040
7	57048	190814016	18	8880	27429320	29	2	640
8	105207	362973410	19	3986	11597760	30	2	48
9	152763	538238660	20	1795	4548568	31	2	64
10	183441	652555480	21	720	1633472	32	1	16

119. Several authors have conjectured that $b(n) = \hat{b}(n)$; M. M. Gadzhiev has proved that equality holds for $n \le 6$ [*Diskretnyĭ Analiz* **18** (1971), 3–24].

120. (a) Every prime implicant is a minterm, since no adjacent points of the n-cube have the same parity. So the full disjunctive form is the only decent DNF in this case.

(b) Now all prime implicants consist of two adjacent points. We must include the 14 subcubes 0^j*0^{6-j} and 1^j*1^{6-j} for $0 \le j \le 6$, in order to cover the points with $\nu x = 1$ and $\nu x = 6$. The other $\binom{7}{3} + \binom{7}{4} = 70$ points can be covered by 35 well-chosen prime implicants (see, for example, exercise 6.5–1, or the "Christmas tree pattern" in Section 7.2.1.6). Thus the shortest DNF has length 49. [An ingeniously plausible but fallacious argument that 70 prime implicants are necessary was presented by S. B. Yablonsky in *Problemy Kibernetiki* **7** (1962), 229–230.]

(c) For each of 2^{n-1} choices of $(x_1, \ldots, x_{n-1})$ we need at most one implicant to account for the behavior of the function with respect to x_n.

[Asymptotically, almost all Boolean functions of n variables have a shortest DNF with $\Theta(2^n/(\log n \log \log n))$ prime implicants. See R. G. Nigmatullin, *Diskretnyĭ Analiz* **10** (1967), 69–89; V. V. Glagolev, *Problemy Kibernetiki* **19** (1967), 75–94; A. D. Korshunov, *Metody Diskretnogo Analiza* **37** (1981), 9–41; N. Pippenger, *Random Structures & Algorithms* **22** (2003), 161–186.]

121. (a) Let $x = x_1 \ldots x_m$ and $y = y_1 \ldots y_n$. Since f is a function of $(\nu x, \nu y)$, there are altogether $2^{(m+1)(n+1)}$ possibilities.

(b) In this case $\nu x \le \nu x'$ and $\nu y \le \nu y'$ implies $f(x, y) \le f(x', y')$. Every such function corresponds to a zigzag path from $a_0 = (-\frac{1}{2}, n + \frac{1}{2})$ to $a_{m+n+2} = (m + \frac{1}{2}, -\frac{1}{2})$, with $a_j = a_{j-1} + (1, 0)$ or $a_j = a_{j-1} - (0, 1)$ for $1 \le j \le m + n + 2$; we have $f(x, y) = 1$ if and only if the point $(\nu x, \nu y)$ lies above the path. So the number of possibilities is the number of such paths, namely $\binom{m+n+2}{m+1}$.

(c) Complementing x and y changes νx to $m - \nu x$ and νy to $n - \nu y$. So there are no such functions when m and n are both even; otherwise there are $2^{(m+1)(n+1)/2}$.

(d) The path in (b) must now satisfy $a_j + a_{m+n+2-j} = (m, n)$ for $0 \le j \le m+n+2$. Hence there are $\binom{\lceil m/2 \rceil + \lceil n/2 \rceil}{\lceil m/2 \rceil}$ [m odd or n odd] such functions. For example, the following ten cases arise when $m = 3$ and $n = 6$:

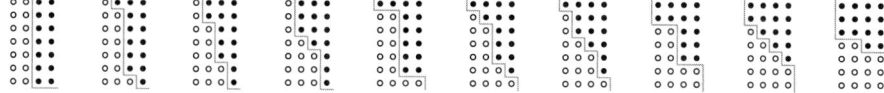

122. A function of this kind is regular with the x's to the left of the y's if and only if the zigzag path does not contain two points (x, y) and $(x + 2, y)$ with $0 < y < n$; it is regular with the y's left of the x's if and only if the zigzag path does not contain both $(x, y + 2)$ and (x, y) with $0 < x < m$. It is a threshold function if and only if there is a straight line through the point $(m/2, n/2)$ with the property that (s, t) is above the line if and only if (s, t) is above the path, for $0 \le s \le m$ and $0 \le t \le n$. So cases 5 and 8, illustrated in the previous answer, fail to be regular; cases 1, 2, 3, 7, 9, and 10 are threshold functions. The regular non-threshold functions that remain can also be expressed as follows: $((x_1 \vee x_2 \vee x_3) \wedge \langle x_1 x_2 x_3 y_1 y_2 y_3 y_4 y_5 y_6 \rangle) \vee (x_1 \wedge x_2 \wedge x_3)$ (case 4); $\langle 00 x_1 x_2 x_3 y_1 y_2 y_3 y_4 y_5 y_6 \rangle \vee (\langle x_1 x_2 x_3 \rangle \wedge \langle 11 x_1 x_2 x_3 y_1 y_2 y_3 y_4 y_5 y_6 \rangle)$ (case 6).

123. Self-dual *regular* functions are relatively easy to list, for small n, but the numbers grow rapidly: When $n = 9$ there are 319,124 of them, found by Muroga, Tsuboi, and Baugh in 1967, and when $n = 10$ there are 1,214,554,343 (see exercise 7.1.4–75). The corresponding numbers for $n \le 6$ appear in Table 5, because all such functions are threshold functions when $n < 9$; there are 135 when $n = 7$, and 2470 when $n = 8$.

The threshold condition can be tested quickly for any such function by improving on the method of exercise 103, because constraints are needed only for the *minimal* vectors x (with respect to majorization) such that $f(x) = 1$.

The number θ_n of n-variable threshold functions is known to satisfy $\lg \theta_n = n^2 - O(n^2/\log n)$; see Yu. A. Zuev, *Matematicheskie Voprosy Kibernetiki* **5** (1994), 5–61.

124. The 222 equivalence classes listed in Table 5 include 24 classes of size $2^{n+1} n! = 768$; so there are $24 \times 768 = 18432$ answers to this problem. One of them is the function $(w \wedge (x \vee (y \wedge z))) \oplus z$.

125. 0; x; $x \wedge y$; $x \wedge y \wedge z$; $x \wedge (y \vee z)$; $x \wedge (y \oplus z)$. (These functions are $x \wedge f(y, z)$, where f runs through the equivalence classes of two-variable functions under permutation and/or complementation of variables but *not* of the function values. In general, let $f \simeq g$ mean that f is equivalent to g in that weaker sense, but write $f \cong g$ if they are equivalent in the sense of Table 5. Then $x \wedge f \cong x \wedge g$ if and only if $f \simeq g$, assuming that f and g are independent of the variable x. For it's easy to see that $(x \wedge f) \simeq (\bar{x} \vee \bar{g})$ is impossible. And if $(x \wedge f) \simeq (x \wedge g)$, we can prove that $f \simeq g$ by showing that, if σ is a signed permutation of $\{x_0, \dots, x_n\}$ and if $x = x_1 \dots x_n$, then the identity $x_0 \wedge f(x) = (x_0 \sigma) \wedge g(x \sigma)$ implies $f(x) = g(x \sigma \tau)$, where τ interchanges $x_0 \leftrightarrow x_0 \sigma$. Consequently the bottom line of Table 5 enumerates equivalence classes under $\simeq$, but with n increased by 1; there are, for example, 402 such classes of 4-variable functions.)

126. (a) The function is canalizing if and only if it has a prime implicant with at most one literal, or a prime clause with at most one literal.

(b) The function is canalizing if and only if at least one of the components of $\Sigma(f)$ is equal to 0, 2^{n-1}, $N(f)$, or $N(f) - 2^{n-1}$. [See I. Shmulevich, H. Lähdesmäki, and K. Egiazarian, *IEEE Signal Processing Letters* **11** (2004), 289–292, Proposition 6.]

(c) If, say, $\vee(f) = y_1 \dots y_n$ with $y_j = 0$, then $f(x) = 0$ whenever $x_j = 1$. Therefore f is canalizing if and only if we don't have $\vee(f) = \vee(\bar{f}) = 1 \dots 1$ and $\wedge(f) = \wedge(\bar{f}) = 0 \dots 0$. With this test one can prove that many functions are noncanalizing when their value is known at only a few points.

127. (a) Since a self-dual function $f(x_1, \dots, x_n)$ is true at exactly 2^{n-1} points, it is canalizing with respect to the variable x_j if and only if $f(x_1, \dots, x_n) = x_j$ or $\bar{x}_j$.

(b) A definite Horn function is clearly canalizing if (i) it contains any clause with a single literal, or (ii) some literal occurs in every clause. Otherwise it is not canalizing. For we have $f(0, \dots, 0) = f(1, \dots, 1) = 1$, because (i) is false; and if x_j is any variable, there is a clause C_0 not containing $\bar{x}_j$ and a clause C_1 not containing x_j, because (ii) is false. By choosing appropriate values of the other variables, we can make $C_0 \wedge C_1$ false when $x_j = 0$ and also when $x_j = 1$.

128. For example, $(x_1 \wedge \cdots \wedge x_n) \vee (\bar{x}_1 \wedge \cdots \wedge \bar{x}_n)$.

129. $\sum_{k=1}^{n} (-1)^{k+1} \binom{n}{k} 2^{2^{n-k}+k+1} - 2(n-1) - 4(n \bmod 2) = n 2^{2^{n-1}+2} + O(n^2 2^{2^{n-2}})$. [See W. Just, I. Shmulevich, and J. Konvalina, *Physica* **D197** (2004), 211–221.]

130. (a) If there are a_n functions of n or fewer variables, but b_n functions of exactly n variables, we have $a_n = \sum_k \binom{n}{k} b_k$. Therefore $b_n = \sum_k (-1)^{n-k} \binom{n}{k} a_k$. (This rule, noted by C. E. Shannon in *Trans. Amer. Inst. Electrical Engineers* **57** (1938), 713–723, §4, applies to all rows of Table 3, *except* for the case of symmetric functions.) In particular, the answer sought here is $168 - 4 \cdot 20 + 6 \cdot 6 - 4 \cdot 3 + 2 = 114$.

(b) If there are a_n' essentially distinct functions of n or fewer variables, and b_n' of exactly n variables, we have $a_n' = \sum_{k=0}^{n} b_k'$. Hence $b_n' = a_n' - a_{n-1}'$, and the answer in this case is $30 - 10 = 20$.

131. Let there be $h(n)$ Horn functions and $k(n)$ Krom functions. Clearly $\lg h(n) \geq \binom{n}{\lfloor n/2 \rfloor}$ and $\lg k(n) \geq \binom{n}{2}$. V. B. Alekseyev [*Diskretnaĭa Matematika* **1** (1989), 129–136] has proved that $\lg h(n) = \binom{n}{\lfloor n/2 \rfloor}(1 + O(n^{-1/4} \log n))$. B. Bollobás, G. Brightwell, and I. Leader [*Israel J. Math.* **133** (2003), 45–60] have proved that $\lg k(n) \sim \frac{1}{2}n^2$.

132. (a) The hint is true because $\sum_y s(y) s(y \oplus z) = \sum_{w,x,y} (-1)^{f(w)+w \cdot y + f(x) + x \cdot (y+z)} = 2^n \sum_{w,x} (-1)^{f(w)+f(x)+x \cdot z} [x = w]$. Now suppose that $f(x) = g(x)$ for $2^{n-1} + k$ values of x; then $f(x) = g(x) \oplus 1$ for $2^{n-1} - k$ values of x. But if $|k| < 2^{n/2-1}$ for all affine g, we would have $|s(y)| < 2^{n/2}$ for all y, contradicting the hint when $z = 0$.

(b) Given $y_0, y_1, \ldots, y_n$, there are exactly $2^{n/2}((y_1 y_2 + y_3 y_4 + \cdots + y_{n-1} y_n + 1 + y_0 + h(y_1, y_3, \ldots, y_{n-1})) \bmod 2)$ solutions to $f(x) = (y_0 + x \cdot y) \bmod 2$ when $x_{2k} = y_{2k-1}$ for $1 \leq k \leq n/2$, and there are $2^{n/2-1}$ solutions for each of the other $2^{n/2} - 1$ values of $(x_2, x_4, \ldots, x_n)$. So there are $2^{n-1} \pm 2^{n/2-1}$ solutions altogether. (This argument proves, in fact, that $(g(x_1, x_3, \ldots, x_{2n-1}) \cdot (x_2, x_4, \ldots, x_{2n}) + h(x_2, x_4, \ldots, x_{2n})) \bmod 2$ is bent whenever $g(x_1, x_3, \ldots, x_{2n-1})$ is a permutation of all $2^{n/2}$-bit vectors.)

(c) The argument in part (a) proves that $f(x)$ is bent if and only if $s(y) = 2^{n/2}(-1)^{g(y)}$ for some Boolean function $g(y)$. This function g, the Fourier/Hadamard transform of f, is also bent, because $\sum_y (-1)^{g(y)+w \cdot y} = 2^{-n/2} \sum_{x,y} (-1)^{f(x)+x \cdot y + w \cdot y} = 2^{n/2} \sum_x (-1)^{f(x)} [x = w] = 2^{n/2} (-1)^{f(w)}$ for all w. The hint now tells us that we have $\sum_y (-1)^{g(y)+g(y \oplus z)} = 0$ for all nonzero z, and the same holds for f.

Conversely, assume that $f(x)$ satisfies the stated condition. Then we have

$$s(y)^2 = \sum_{x,t} (-1)^{f(x)+x \cdot y + f(x \oplus t) + (x \oplus t) \cdot y} = \sum_t (-1)^{t \cdot y} \sum_x (-1)^{f(x)+f(x \oplus t)} = 2^n$$

for all y.

(d) By exercise 11, the term $x_1 \ldots x_r$ is present if and only if the equation $f(x_1, \ldots, x_r, 0, \ldots, 0) = 1$ has an odd number of solutions, and an equivalent condition is $(\sum_{x_1, \ldots, x_r} (-1)^{f(x_1, \ldots, x_r, 0, \ldots, 0)}) \bmod 4 = 2$. We've seen in part (c) that this sum is

$$2^{-n} \sum_{x_1, \ldots, x_r, y} s(y) (-1)^{x_1 y_1 + \cdots + x_r y_r} = 2^{r-n} \sum_{y_{r+1}, \ldots, y_n} s(0, \ldots, 0, y_{r+1}, \ldots, y_n).$$

If $r = n$, the latter sum is $\pm 2^{n/2}$; otherwise it contains an even number of summands, each of which is $\pm 2^{r-n/2}$. So the result is a multiple of 4.

[Bent functions were introduced by O. S. Rothaus in 1966; his privately circulated paper was eventually published in *J. Combinatorial Theory* **A20** (1976), 300–305. J. F. Dillon, *Congressus Numerantium* **14** (1975), 237–249, discovered additional families of bent functions, and many other examples have subsequently been found when $n \geq 8$ and n is even. Bent functions don't exist when n is odd, but a function like $g(x_1, \ldots, x_{n-1}) \oplus x_n \wedge h(x_1, \ldots, x_{n-1})$ has distance $2^{n-1} - 2^{(n-1)/2}$ from all affine functions when g and $g \oplus h$ are bent. A better construction for the case $n = 15$ was found by N. J. Patterson and D. H. Wiedemann, *IEEE Transactions* **IT-29** (1983), 354–356, **IT-36** (1990), 443, achieving distance $2^{14} - 108$. S. Kavut and M. Diker Yücel, *Information and Computation* **208** (2010), 341–350, have achieved distance $2^8 - 14$ when $n = 9$.]

133. Let $p_k = 1/(2^{2^{n-k}}+1)$, so that $\bar{p}_k = 2^{2^{n-k}}/(2^{2^{n-k}}+1)$. [Ph.D. thesis (MIT, 1994).]

SECTION 7.1.2

1. $((x_1 \vee x_4) \wedge x_2) \equiv (x_1 \vee x_3)$.

2. (a) $(w \oplus (x \wedge y)) \oplus ((x \oplus y) \wedge z)$; (b) $(w \wedge (x \vee y)) \wedge ((x \wedge y) \vee z)$.

3. [*Doklady Akademii Nauk SSSR* **115** (1957), 247–248.] Construct a $k \times n$ matrix whose rows are the vectors x where $f(x) = 1$. By permuting and/or complementing variables, we may assume that the top row is $1 \ldots 1$ and that the columns are sorted. Suppose there are l distinct columns. Then $f = g \wedge h$, where g is the AND of the expressions $(x_{j-1} \equiv x_j)$ over all $1 < j \leq n$ such that column $j - 1$ equals column j, and h is the OR of k minterms of length l, using one variable from each group of equal columns. For example, if $n = 8$ and if f is 1 at the $k = 3$ points 11111111, 00001111, 00110111, then $l = 4$ and $f(x)$ equals $(x_1 \equiv x_2) \wedge (x_3 \equiv x_4) \wedge (x_6 \equiv x_7) \wedge (x_7 \equiv x_8) \wedge ((x_1 \wedge x_3 \wedge x_5 \wedge x_6) \vee (\bar{x}_1 \wedge \bar{x}_3 \wedge x_5 \wedge x_6) \vee (\bar{x}_1 \wedge x_3 \wedge \bar{x}_5 \wedge x_6))$. The length of this formula in general is $2n + (k - 2)l - 1$, and we have $l \leq 2^{k-1}$.

Notice that, if k is large, we get shorter formulas by writing $f(x)$ as a disjunction $f_1(x) \vee \cdots \vee f_r(x)$, where each f_j has at most $\lceil k/r \rceil$ 1s. Thus

$$L(f) \leq \min_{r \geq 1}\left(r - 1 + (2n + \lceil k/r - 2\rceil 2^{\lceil k/r-1\rceil})r\right).$$

4. The first inequality is obvious, because a binary tree of depth d has at most $1 + 2 + \cdots + 2^{d-1} = 2^d - 1$ internal nodes.

The hint follows when we let f_t be the formula of size $L(f) - L(g) - 1$ that arises when g is replaced by t. For $1 \leq k < L(f)$ let g_k be a minimal subformula of size $\geq k$. Then g_k? f_{k1}: f_{k0} is obtained from a tree that has g_k, f_{k1}, and f_{k0} on level 2.

Let $d_r = \max\{D(f) \mid L(f) = r\}$. Since the children of g_k appear on level 3 and have size $< k$, we have $d_r \leq \min_{k=1}^{r-1} \max(3 + d_{k-1}, 2 + d_{r-k-1})$ for $r \geq 3$. By induction on r it follows that $d_r \leq l$ when $r \leq b_l$, where $b_l = l$ for $0 \leq l \leq 2$ and $b_l = b_{l-2}+b_{l-3}+2$ for $l \geq 3$. We also have $b_l + 2 = (8P_l + 18P_{l+1} + 11P_{l+2})/23 = c\chi^l + O(0.87^l)$ in terms of the Perrin numbers of exercise 7.1.4–15, where $c = (2 + 4\chi + 3\chi^2)/(3 + 2\chi) \approx 2.224$. Hence $d_r < \alpha \lg r$ when $r > 1$. [See P. M. Spira, *Hawaii Int. Conf. Syst. Sci.* **4** (1971), 525–527; R. Brent, D. Kuck, and K. Maruyama, *IEEE* **C-22** (1973), 532–534. In *JACM* **23** (1976), 534–543, D. E. Muller and F. P. Preparata proved that $D(f) \leq \beta \lg L(f) + O(1)$, where $\beta = 1/\lg z \approx 2.0807$, $z^4 = 2z + 1$. Is β optimum?]

5. Let $g_0 = 0$, $g_1 = x_1$, and $g_j = x_j \wedge (x_{j-1} \vee g_{j-2})$ for $j \geq 2$. Then $F_n = g_n \vee g_{n-1}$, with cost $2n - 2$ and depth n. [These functions g_j also play a prominent role in binary addition; see exercises 42 and 44 for ways to compute them with depth $O(\log n)$.]

6. True: Consider the cases $y = 0$ and $y = 1$.

7. $\hat{x}_5 = x_1 \vee x_4$, $\hat{x}_6 = x_2 \wedge \hat{x}_5$, $\hat{x}_7 = x_1 \vee x_3$, $\hat{x}_8 = \hat{x}_6 \oplus \hat{x}_7$. (The original chain computes the "random" function (6); see exercise 1. The new chain computes the normalization of that function, namely its complement.)

8. The desired truth table consists of blocks of 2^{n-k} 0s alternating with blocks of 2^{n-k} 1s, as in (7). Therefore, if we multiply by $2^{2^{n-k}} + 1$ we get $x_k + (x_k \ll 2^{n-k})$, which is all 1s.

9. When finding $L(f) = \infty$ in step L6, we can store g and h in a record associated with f. Then a recursive procedure will be able to construct a minimum-length formula for f from the respective formulas for g and h.

10. In step L3, use $k = r - 1$ instead of $k = r - 1 - j$. Also change L to D everywhere.

11. The only subtle point is that j should *decrease* in step U3; then we'll never have $\phi(g) \,\&\, \phi(h) \neq 0$ when $j = 0$, so all cases of cost $r - 1$ will be discovered before we begin to look at list $r - 1$.

> **U1.** [Initialize.] Set $U(0) \leftarrow \phi(0) \leftarrow 0$ and $U(f) \leftarrow \infty$ for $1 \le f < 2^{2^n - 1}$. Then set $U(x_k) \leftarrow \phi(x_k) \leftarrow 0$ and put x_k into list 0, as in step L1. Also set $U(x_j \circ x_k) \leftarrow 1$, set $\phi(x_j \circ x_k)$ to its unique footprint vector (which contains exactly one 1), and put $x_j \circ x_k$ into list 1, for $1 \le j < k \le n$ and all five normal operators $\circ$. Finally set $c \leftarrow 2^{2^n - 1} - 5\binom{n}{2} - n - 1$.
>
> **U2.** [Loop on r.] Do step U3 for $r = 2, 3, \ldots$, while $c > 0$.
>
> **U3.** [Loop on j and k.] Do step U4 for $j = \lfloor (r - 1)/2 \rfloor$, $\lfloor (r - 1)/2 \rfloor - 1, \ldots$, and $k = r - 1 - j$, while $j \ge 0$.
>
> **U4.** [Loop on g and h.] Do step U5 for all g in list j and all h in list k; if $j = k$, restrict h to functions that *follow* g in list k.
>
> **U5.** [Loop on f.] If $\phi(g) \,\&\, \phi(h) \neq 0$, set $u \leftarrow r - 1$ and $v \leftarrow \phi(g) \,\&\, \phi(h)$; otherwise set $u \leftarrow r$ and $v \leftarrow \phi(g) \mid \phi(h)$. Then do step U6 for $f = g \,\&\, h$, $f = \bar{g} \,\&\, h$, $f = g \,\&\, \bar{h}$, $f = g \mid h$, and $f = g \oplus h$.
>
> **U6.** [Update $U(f)$ and $\phi(f)$.] If $U(f) = \infty$, set $c \leftarrow c - 1$, $\phi(f) \leftarrow v$, $U(f) \leftarrow u$, and put f into list u. Otherwise if $U(f) > u$, move f from list $U(f)$ to list u and set $\phi(f) \leftarrow v$, $U(f) \leftarrow u$. Otherwise if $U(f) = u$, set $\phi(f) \leftarrow \phi(f) \mid v$. ∎

12. $x_4 = x_1 \oplus x_2$, $x_5 = x_3 \wedge x_4$, $x_6 = x_2 \wedge \bar{x}_4$, $x_7 = x_5 \vee x_6$.

13. $f_5 = 01010101$ (x_3); $f_4 = 01110111$ $(x_2 \vee x_3)$; $f_3 = 01110101$ $((\bar{x}_1 \wedge x_2) \vee x_3)$; $f_2 = 00110101$ $(x_1? \; x_3 \colon x_2)$; $f_1 = 00010111$ $(\langle x_1 x_2 x_3 \rangle)$.

14. For $1 \le j \le n$, first compute $t \leftarrow (g \oplus (g \gg 2^{n-j})) \,\&\, x_j$, $t \leftarrow t \oplus (t \ll 2^{n-j})$, where x_j is the truth table (11); then for $1 \le k \le n$ and $k \neq j$, the desired truth table corresponding to $x_j \leftarrow x_j \circ x_k$ is $g \oplus (t \,\&\, ((x_j \circ x_k) \oplus x_j))$.

(The $5n(n - 1)$ masks $(x_j \circ x_k) \oplus x_j$ are independent of g and can be computed in advance. The same idea applies if we allow more general computations of the form $x_{j(i)} \leftarrow x_{k(i)} \circ_i x_{l(i)}$, with $5n^2(n - 1)$ masks $(x_k \circ x_l) \oplus x_j$.)

15. Remarkably asymmetrical ways to compute symmetrical functions:

(a) $x_1 \leftarrow x_1 \oplus x_2$,
$x_1 \leftarrow x_1 \oplus x_3$,
$x_2 \leftarrow x_2 \wedge x_3$,
$x_1 \leftarrow x_1 \wedge \bar{x}_2$.

(b) $x_1 \leftarrow x_1 \oplus x_2$,
$x_3 \leftarrow x_3 \oplus x_4$,
$x_1 \leftarrow x_1 \oplus x_3$,
$x_2 \leftarrow x_2 \oplus x_4$,
$x_3 \leftarrow x_3 \vee x_2$,
$x_3 \leftarrow x_3 \wedge \bar{x}_1$.

(c) $x_1 \leftarrow x_1 \oplus x_2$,
$x_2 \leftarrow x_2 \wedge \bar{x}_1$,
$x_3 \leftarrow x_3 \oplus x_4$,
$x_4 \leftarrow x_4 \wedge x_1$,
$x_2 \leftarrow \bar{x}_2 \wedge x_3$,
$x_2 \leftarrow x_2 \oplus x_1$,
$x_2 \leftarrow x_2 \wedge \bar{x}_4$.

(d) $x_1 \leftarrow x_1 \oplus x_2$,
$x_2 \leftarrow x_2 \oplus x_3$,
$x_2 \leftarrow x_2 \vee x_1$,
$x_1 \leftarrow x_1 \oplus x_4$,
$x_1 \leftarrow x_1 \wedge x_3$,
$x_2 \leftarrow x_2 \wedge \bar{x}_1$,
$x_2 \leftarrow x_2 \oplus x_4$.

23. We need only consider the 32 normal cases, as in Fig. 9, since the complement of a symmetric function is symmetric. Then we can use reflection, like $S_{1,2}(x) = S_{3,4}(\bar{x})$, possibly together with complementation, like $S_{2,3,4,5}(x) = \bar{S}_{0,1}(x) = \bar{S}_{4,5}(\bar{x})$, to deduce most of the remaining cases. Of course S_1, $S_{1,3,5}$, and $S_{1,2,3,4,5}$ trivially have cost 4. That leaves only $S_{1,2,3,4}(x_1, x_2, x_3, x_4, x_5) = (x_1 \oplus x_2) \vee (x_2 \oplus x_3) \vee (x_3 \oplus x_4) \vee (x_4 \oplus x_5)$, which is discussed for general n in exercise 79.

24. As noted in the text, this conjecture holds for $n \le 5$.

25. It is $2^{2^n-1} - n - 1$, the number of nontrivial normal functions. (In any normal chain of length r that doesn't include all of these functions, $x_j \circ x_k$ will be a new function for some j and k in the range $1 \le j, k \le n + r$ and some normal binary operator $\circ$; so we can compute a new function with every new step, until we've got them all.)

26. False. For example, if $g = S_{1,3}(x_1, x_2, x_3)$ and $h = S_{2,3}(x_1, x_2, x_3)$, then $C(gh) = 5$ is the cost of a full adder; but $f = S_{2,3}(x_0, x_1, x_2, x_3)$ has cost 6 by Fig. 9.

27. Yes: The operations '$x_2 \leftarrow x_2 \oplus x_1$, $x_1 \leftarrow x_1 \oplus x_3$, $x_1 \leftarrow x_1 \wedge \bar{x}_2$, $x_1 \leftarrow x_1 \oplus x_3$, $x_2 \leftarrow x_2 \oplus x_3$' transform (x_1, x_2, x_3) into (z_1, z_0, x_3).

28. Let $v' = v'' = v \oplus (x \oplus y)$; $u' = ((v \oplus y) \overline{\subset} (x \oplus y)) \oplus u$, $u'' = ((v \oplus y) \vee (x \oplus y)) \oplus u$. Thus we can set $u_0 \leftarrow 0$, $v_0 \leftarrow x_1$, $u_j \leftarrow ((v_{j-1} \oplus x_{2j+1}) \vee (x_{2j} \oplus x_{2j+1})) \oplus u_{j-1}$ if j is odd, $u_j \leftarrow ((v_{j-1} \oplus x_{2j+1}) \overline{\subset} (x_{2j} \oplus x_{2j+1})) \oplus u_{j-1}$ if j is even, and $v_j \leftarrow v_{j-1} \oplus (x_{2j} \oplus x_{2j+1})$, obtaining $(u_j v_j)_2 = (x_1 + \cdots + x_{2j+1}) \bmod 4$ for $1 \le j \le \lfloor n/2 \rfloor$. Set $x_{n+1} \leftarrow 0$ if n is even. Thus $[(x_1 + \cdots + x_n) \bmod 4 = 0] = \bar{u}_{\lfloor n/2 \rfloor} \wedge \bar{v}_{\lfloor n/2 \rfloor}$ is computed in $\lfloor 5n/2 \rfloor - 2$ steps.

This construction is due to L. J. Stockmeyer, who proved that it is nearly optimal. In fact, the result of exercise 80 together with Figs. 9 and 10 shows that it is at most one step longer than a best possible chain, for all $n \ge 5$.

Incidentally, the analogous formula $u''' = ((v \oplus y) \wedge (x \oplus y)) \oplus u$ yields $(u''' v')_2 = ((uv) + x - y) \bmod 4$. The simpler-looking function $((uv)_2 + x + y) \bmod 4$ costs 6, not 5.

29. To get an upper bound, assume that each full adder or half adder increases the depth by 3. If there are a_{jd} bits of weight 2^j and depth $3d$, we schedule at most $\lceil a_{jd}/3 \rceil$ subsequent bits of weights $\{2^j, 2^{j+1}\}$ and depth $3(d + 1)$. It follows by induction that $a_{jd} \le \binom{d}{j} 3^{-d} n + 4$. Hence $a_{jd} \le 5$ when $d \ge \log_{3/2} n$, and the overall depth is at most $3 \log_{3/2} n + 3$. (Curiously, the actual depth turns out to be exactly 100 when $n = 10^7$.)

30. As usual, let νn denote the sideways addition of the bits in the binary representation of n itself. Then $s(n) = 5n - 2\nu n - 3 \lfloor \lg n \rfloor - 3$.

31. After sideways addition in $s(n) < 5n$ steps, an arbitrary function of $(z_{\lfloor \lg n \rfloor}, \dots, z_0)$ can be evaluated in $\sim 2n/\lg n$ steps at most, by Theorem L. [See O. B. Lupanov, *Doklady Akademii Nauk SSSR* **140** (1961), 322–325.]

32. Bootstrap: First prove by induction on n that $t(n) \le 2^{n+1}$.

33. False, on a technicality: If, say, $N = \sqrt{n}$, at least n steps are needed. A correct asymptotic formula $N + O(\sqrt{N}) + O(n)$ can, however, be proved by first noting that the text's method gives $N + O(\sqrt{N})$ when $N \ge 2^{n-1}$; otherwise, if $\lfloor \lg N \rfloor = n - k - 1$, we can use $O(n)$ operations to AND the quantity $\bar{x}_1 \wedge \cdots \wedge \bar{x}_k$ to the other variables $x_{k+1}, \dots, x_n$, then proceed with n reduced by k.

(One consequence is that we can compute the symmetric functions $\{S_1, S_2, \dots, S_n\}$ with cost $s(n) + n + O(\sqrt{n}) = 6n + O(\sqrt{n})$ and depth $O(\log n)$.)

34. Say that an *extended* priority encoder has $n + 1 = 2^m$ inputs $x_0 x_1 \dots x_n$ and $m + 1$ outputs $y_0 y_1 \dots y_m$, where $y_0 = x_0 \vee x_1 \vee \cdots \vee x_n$. If Q'_m and Q''_m are extended encoders for $x'_0 \dots x'_n$ and $x''_0 \dots x''_n$, then Q_{m+1} works for $x'_0 \dots x'_n x''_0 \dots x''_n$ if we define

$y_0 = y_0' \vee y_0''$, $y_1 = y_0''$, $y_2 = y_1?\ y_1'': y_1'$, ..., $y_{m+1} = y_1?\ y_m'': y_m'$. If P_m' is an ordinary priority encoder for $x_1' \ldots x_n'$, we get P_{m+1} for $x_1' \ldots x_n' x_0'' \ldots x_n''$ in a similar way.

Starting with $m = 2$ and $y_2 = x_3 \vee (x_1 \wedge \bar{x}_2)$, $y_1 = x_2 \vee x_3$, $y_0 = x_0 \vee x_1 \vee y_1$, this construction yields P_m and Q_m of costs p_m and q_m, where $p_2 = 3$, $q_2 = 5$, and $p_{m+1} = 3m + p_m + q_m$, $q_{m+1} = 3m + 1 + 2q_m$ for $m \geq 2$. Consequently $p_m = q_m - m$ and $q_m = 15 \cdot 2^{m-2} - 3m - 4 \approx 3.75n$.

35. If $n = 2m$, compute $x_1 \wedge x_2$, ..., $x_{n-1} \wedge x_n$, then recursively form $x_1 \wedge \cdots \wedge x_{2k-2} \wedge x_{2k+1} \wedge \cdots \wedge x_n$ for $1 \leq k \leq m$, and finish in n more steps. If $n = 2m - 1$, use this chain for $n + 1$ elements; three steps can be eliminated by setting $x_{n+1} \leftarrow 1$. [I. Wegener, *The Complexity of Boolean Functions* (1987), exercise 3.25. The same idea can be used with *any* associative and commutative operator in place of $\wedge$.]

36. Recursively construct $P_n(x_1, \ldots, x_n)$ and $Q_n(x_1, \ldots, x_n)$ as follows, where P_n has $D(y_j) \leq \lceil \lg n \rceil$ for $1 \leq j \leq n$ and Q_n has $D(y_j) \leq \lceil \lg n \rceil + [j \neq n]$: The case $n = 1$ is trivial; otherwise P_n is obtained from $Q_r'(x_1, \ldots, x_r)$ and $P_s''(x_{r+1}, \ldots, x_n)$, where $r = \lceil n/2 \rceil$ and $s = \lfloor n/2 \rfloor$, by setting $y_j \leftarrow y_j'$ for $1 \leq j \leq r$, $y_j \leftarrow y_r' \wedge y_{j-r}''$ for $r < j \leq n$. And Q_n is obtained from either $P_r'(x_1 \wedge x_2, \ldots, x_{n-1} \wedge x_n)$ or $P_r'(x_1 \wedge x_2, \ldots, x_{n-2} \wedge x_{n-1}, x_n)$ by setting $y_1 \leftarrow x_1$, $y_{2j} \leftarrow y_j'$, $y_{2j+1} \leftarrow y_j' \wedge x_{2j+1}$ for $1 \leq j < s$, and $y_{2s} \leftarrow y_s'$, $y_n \leftarrow y_r'$.

These calculations can be performed in *minimum memory*, setting $x_{k(i)} \leftarrow x_{j(i)} \wedge x_{k(i)}$ at step i for some indices $j(i) < k(i)$. Thus we can illustrate the construction with diagrams analogous to the diagrams for sorting networks. For example,

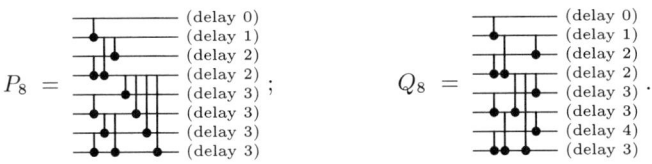

$$P_8 = \qquad ; \qquad Q_8 = \qquad .$$

The costs p_n and q_n satisfy $p_n = \lfloor n/2 \rfloor + q_{\lceil n/2 \rceil} + p_{\lfloor n/2 \rfloor}$, $q_n = 2\lfloor n/2 \rfloor - 1 + p_{\lceil n/2 \rceil}$ when $n > 1$; for example, $(p_1, \ldots, p_7) = (q_1, \ldots, q_7) = (0, 1, 2, 4, 5, 7, 9)$. Setting $\bar{p}_n = 4n - p_n$ and $\bar{q}_n = 3n - q_n$ leads to simpler formulas, which prove that $p_n < 4n$ and $q_n < 3n$: $\bar{q}_n = \bar{p}_{\lceil n/2 \rceil} + [n \text{ even}]$; $\bar{p}_{4n} = \bar{p}_{2n} + \bar{p}_n + 1$, $\bar{p}_{4n+1} = \bar{p}_{2n} + \bar{p}_{n+1} + 1$, $\bar{p}_{4n+2} = \bar{p}_{2n+1} + \bar{p}_{n+1}$, $\bar{p}_{4n+3} = \bar{p}_{4n+2} + 2$. In particular, $1 + \bar{p}_{2^m} = F_{m+5}$ is a Fibonacci number. [See *JACM* **27** (1980), 831–834. Slightly better chains are obtained if we replace Q_{2n+1} by (Q_{2n} and $y_{2n+1} = y_{2n} \wedge x_{2n+1}$) when n is a power of 2, if we replace P_5 and P_6 by Q_5 and Q_6, and if we then replace $(P_9, P_{10}, P_{11}, P_{17})$ by $(Q_9, Q_{10}, Q_{11}, Q_{17})$.]

Notice that this construction works in general if we replace '$\wedge$' by *any* associative operator. In particular, the sequence of prefixes $x_1 \oplus \cdots \oplus x_k$ for $1 \leq k \leq n$ defines the conversion from Gray binary code to radix-2 integers, Eq. 7.2.1.1–(10).

37. The case $m = 15$, $n = 16$ is illustrated at the right.

(a) Let $x_{i..j}$ denote the original value of $x_i \wedge \cdots \wedge x_j$. Whenever the algorithm sets $x_k \leftarrow x_j \wedge x_k$, one can show that the previous value of x_k was $x_{j+1..k}$. After step S1, x_k is $x_{f(k)+1..k}$ where $f(k) = k \ \& \ (k - 1)$ for $1 \leq k < m$ and $f(m) = 0$. After step S2, x_k is $x_{1..k}$ for $1 \leq k \leq m$.

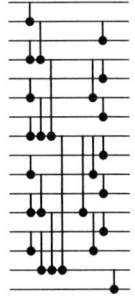

(b) The cost of S1 is $m - 1$, the cost of S2 is $m - 1 - \lceil \lg m \rceil$, and the cost of S3 is $n - m$. The final delay of x_k is $\lfloor \lg k \rfloor + \nu k - 1$ for $1 \leq k < m$, and it is $\lceil \lg m \rceil + k - m$ for $m \leq k \leq n$. So the maximum delay for $\{x_1, \ldots, x_{m-1}\}$ turns out to be $g(m) = m - 1$ for $m < 4$, $g(m) = \lfloor \lg m \rfloor + \lfloor \lg \frac{m}{3} \rfloor$ for $m \geq 4$. We have $c(m, n) = m + n - 2 - \lceil \lg m \rceil$, $d(m, n) = \max(g(m), \lceil \lg m \rceil + n - m)$. Hence $c(m, n) + d(m, n) = 2n - 2$

23. We need only consider the 32 normal cases, as in Fig. 9, since the complement of a symmetric function is symmetric. Then we can use reflection, like $S_{1,2}(x) = S_{3,4}(\bar{x})$, possibly together with complementation, like $S_{2,3,4,5}(x) = \bar{S}_{0,1}(x) = \bar{S}_{4,5}(\bar{x})$, to deduce most of the remaining cases. Of course S_1, $S_{1,3,5}$, and $S_{1,2,3,4,5}$ trivially have cost 4. That leaves only $S_{1,2,3,4}(x_1, x_2, x_3, x_4, x_5) = (x_1 \oplus x_2) \vee (x_2 \oplus x_3) \vee (x_3 \oplus x_4) \vee (x_4 \oplus x_5)$, which is discussed for general n in exercise 79.

24. As noted in the text, this conjecture holds for $n \le 5$.

25. It is $2^{2^n-1} - n - 1$, the number of nontrivial normal functions. (In any normal chain of length r that doesn't include all of these functions, $x_j \circ x_k$ will be a new function for some j and k in the range $1 \le j, k \le n + r$ and some normal binary operator $\circ$; so we can compute a new function with every new step, until we've got them all.)

26. False. For example, if $g = S_{1,3}(x_1, x_2, x_3)$ and $h = S_{2,3}(x_1, x_2, x_3)$, then $C(gh) = 5$ is the cost of a full adder; but $f = S_{2,3}(x_0, x_1, x_2, x_3)$ has cost 6 by Fig. 9.

27. Yes: The operations '$x_2 \leftarrow x_2 \oplus x_1$, $x_1 \leftarrow x_1 \oplus x_3$, $x_1 \leftarrow x_1 \wedge \bar{x}_2$, $x_1 \leftarrow x_1 \oplus x_3$, $x_2 \leftarrow x_2 \oplus x_3$' transform (x_1, x_2, x_3) into (z_1, z_0, x_3).

28. Let $v' = v'' = v \oplus (x \oplus y)$; $u' = ((v \oplus y) \overline{\subset} (x \oplus y)) \oplus u$, $u'' = ((v \oplus y) \vee (x \oplus y)) \oplus u$. Thus we can set $u_0 = 0$, $v_0 = x_1$, $u_j = ((v_{j-1} \oplus x_{2j+1}) \vee (x_{2j} \oplus x_{2j+1})) \oplus u_{j-1}$ if j is odd, $u_j = ((v_{j-1} \oplus x_{2j+1}) \overline{\subset} (x_{2j} \oplus x_{2j+1})) \oplus u_{j-1}$ if j is even, and $v_j = v_{j-1} \oplus (x_{2j} \oplus x_{2j+1})$, obtaining $(u_j v_j)_2 = (x_1 + \cdots + x_{2j+1}) \bmod 4$ for $1 \le j \le \lfloor n/2 \rfloor$. Set $x_{n+1} = 0$ if n is even. Thus $[(x_1 + \cdots + x_n) \bmod 4 = 0] = \bar{u}_{\lfloor n/2 \rfloor} \wedge \bar{v}_{\lfloor n/2 \rfloor}$ is computed in $\lfloor 5n/2 \rfloor - 2$ steps.

This construction is due to L. J. Stockmeyer, who proved that it is nearly optimal. In fact, the result of exercise 80 together with Figs. 9 and 10 shows that it is at most one step longer than a best possible chain, for all $n \ge 5$.

Incidentally, the analogous formula $u''' = ((v \oplus y) \wedge (x \oplus y)) \oplus u$ yields $(u''' v')_2 = ((uv)_2 + x - y) \bmod 4$. The simpler-looking function $((uv)_2 + x + y) \bmod 4$ costs 6, not 5.

29. To get an upper bound, assume that each full adder or half adder increases the depth by 3. If there are a_{jd} bits of weight 2^j and depth $3d$, we schedule at most $\lceil a_{jd}/3 \rceil$ subsequent bits of weights $\{2^j, 2^{j+1}\}$ and depth $3(d+1)$. It follows by induction that $a_{jd} \le \binom{d}{j} 3^{-d} n + 4$. Hence $a_{jd} \le 5$ when $d \ge \log_{3/2} n$, and the overall depth is at most $3 \log_{3/2} n + 3$. (Curiously, the actual depth turns out to be exactly 100 when $n = 10^7$.)

30. As usual, let νn denote the sideways addition of the bits in the binary representation of n itself. Then $s(n) = 5n - 2\nu n - 3\lfloor \lg n \rfloor - 3$.

31. After sideways addition in $s(n) < 5n$ steps, an arbitrary function of $(z_{\lfloor \lg n \rfloor}, \dots, z_0)$ can be evaluated in $\sim 2n/\lg n$ steps at most, by Theorem L. [See O. B. Lupanov, *Doklady Akademii Nauk SSSR* **140** (1961), 322–325.]

32. Bootstrap: First prove by induction on n that $t(n) \le 2^{n+1}$.

33. False, on a technicality: If, say, $N = \sqrt{n}$, at least n steps are needed. A correct asymptotic formula $N + O(\sqrt{N}) + O(n)$ can, however, be proved by first noting that the text's method gives $N + O(\sqrt{N})$ when $N \ge 2^{n-1}$; otherwise, if $\lfloor \lg N \rfloor = n - k - 1$, we can use $O(n)$ operations to AND the quantity $\bar{x}_1 \wedge \cdots \wedge \bar{x}_k$ to the other variables $x_{k+1}, \dots, x_n$, then proceed with n reduced by k.

(One consequence is that we can compute the symmetric functions $\{S_1, S_2, \dots, S_n\}$ with cost $s(n) + n + O(\sqrt{n}) = 6n + O(\sqrt{n})$ and depth $O(\log n)$.)

34. Say that an *extended* priority encoder has $n + 1 = 2^m$ inputs $x_0 x_1 \dots x_n$ and $m + 1$ outputs $y_0 y_1 \dots y_m$, where $y_0 = x_0 \vee x_1 \vee \cdots \vee x_n$. If Q'_m and Q''_m are extended encoders for $x'_0 \dots x'_n$ and $x''_0 \dots x''_n$, then Q_{m+1} works for $x'_0 \dots x'_n x''_0 \dots x''_n$ if we define

$y_0 = y_0' \lor y_0''$, $y_1 = y_0''$, $y_2 = y_1$? y_1'': y_1', ..., $y_{m+1} = y_1$? y_m'': y_m'. If P_m' is an ordinary priority encoder for $x_1' \ldots x_n'$, we get P_{m+1} for $x_1' \ldots x_n' x_0'' \ldots x_n''$ in a similar way.

Starting with $m = 2$ and $y_2 = x_3 \lor (x_1 \land \bar{x}_2)$, $y_1 = x_2 \lor x_3$, $y_0 = x_0 \lor x_1 \lor y_1$, this construction yields P_m and Q_m of costs p_m and q_m, where $p_2 = 3$, $q_2 = 5$, and $p_{m+1} = 3m + p_m + q_m$, $q_{m+1} = 3m + 1 + 2q_m$ for $m \geq 2$. Consequently $p_m = q_m - m$ and $q_m = 15 \cdot 2^{m-2} - 3m - 4 \approx 3.75n$.

35. If $n = 2m$, compute $x_1 \land x_2$, ..., $x_{n-1} \land x_n$, then recursively form $x_1 \land \cdots \land x_{2k-2} \land x_{2k+1} \land \cdots \land x_n$ for $1 \leq k \leq m$, and finish in n more steps. If $n = 2m - 1$, use this chain for $n + 1$ elements; three steps can be eliminated by setting $x_{n+1} \leftarrow 1$. [I. Wegener, *The Complexity of Boolean Functions* (1987), exercise 3.25. The same idea can be used with *any* associative and commutative operator in place of $\land$.]

36. Recursively construct $P_n(x_1, \ldots, x_n)$ and $Q_n(x_1, \ldots, x_n)$ as follows, where P_n has $D(y_j) \leq \lceil \lg n \rceil$ for $1 \leq j \leq n$ and Q_n has $D(y_j) \leq \lceil \lg n \rceil + [j \neq n]$: The case $n = 1$ is trivial; otherwise P_n is obtained from $Q_r'(x_1, \ldots, x_r)$ and $P_s''(x_{r+1}, \ldots, x_n)$, where $r = \lceil n/2 \rceil$ and $s = \lfloor n/2 \rfloor$, by setting $y_j = y_j'$ for $1 \leq j \leq r$, $y_j = y_r' \land y_{j-r}''$ for $r < j \leq n$. And Q_n is obtained from either $P_r'(x_1 \land x_2, \ldots, x_{n-1} \land x_n)$ or $P_r'(x_1 \land x_2, \ldots, x_{n-2} \land x_{n-1}, x_n)$ by setting $y_1 = x_1$, $y_{2j} = y_j'$, $y_{2j+1} = y_j' \land x_{2j+1}$ for $1 \leq j < s$, and $y_{2s} = y_s'$, $y_n = y_r'$.

These calculations can be performed in *minimum memory*, setting $x_{k(i)} \leftarrow x_{j(i)} \land x_{k(i)}$ at step i for some indices $j(i) < k(i)$. Thus we can illustrate the construction with diagrams analogous to the diagrams for sorting networks. For example,

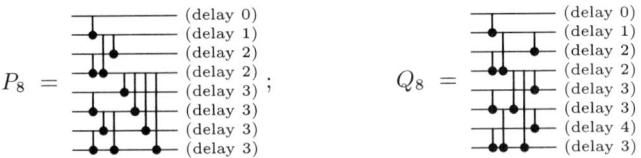

$$P_8 = \qquad ; \qquad Q_8 = \qquad .$$

The costs p_n and q_n satisfy $p_n = \lfloor n/2 \rfloor + q_{\lceil n/2 \rceil} + p_{\lfloor n/2 \rfloor}$, $q_n = 2\lfloor n/2 \rfloor - 1 + p_{\lceil n/2 \rceil}$ when $n > 1$; for example, $(p_1, \ldots, p_7) = (q_1, \ldots, q_7) = (0, 1, 2, 4, 5, 7, 9)$. Setting $\bar{p}_n = 4n - p_n$ and $\bar{q}_n = 3n - q_n$ leads to simpler formulas, which prove that $p_n < 4n$ and $q_n < 3n$: $\bar{q}_n = \bar{p}_{\lceil n/2 \rceil} + [n \text{ even}]$; $\bar{p}_{4n} = \bar{p}_{2n} + \bar{p}_n + 1$, $\bar{p}_{4n+1} = \bar{p}_{2n} + \bar{p}_{n+1} + 1$, $\bar{p}_{4n+2} = \bar{p}_{2n+1} + \bar{p}_{n+1}$, $\bar{p}_{4n+3} = \bar{p}_{4n+2} + 2$. In particular, $1 + \bar{p}_{2m} = F_{m+5}$ is a Fibonacci number. [See *JACM* **27** (1980), 831–834. Slightly better chains are obtained if we replace Q_{2n+1} by (Q_{2n} and $y_{2n+1} = y_{2n} \land x_{2n+1}$) when n is a power of 2, if we replace P_5 and P_6 by Q_5 and Q_6, and if we then replace $(P_9, P_{10}, P_{11}, P_{17})$ by $(Q_9, Q_{10}, Q_{11}, Q_{17})$.]

Notice that this construction works in general if we replace '$\land$' by *any* associative operator. In particular, the sequence of prefixes $x_1 \oplus \cdots \oplus x_k$ for $1 \leq k \leq n$ defines the conversion from Gray binary code to radix-2 integers, Eq. 7.2.1.1–(10).

37. The case $m = 15$, $n = 16$ is illustrated at the right.

(a) Let $x_{i..j}$ denote the original value of $x_i \land \cdots \land x_j$. Whenever the algorithm sets $x_k \leftarrow x_j \land x_k$, one can show that the previous value of x_k was $x_{j+1..k}$. After step S1, x_k is $x_{f(k)+1..k}$ where $f(k) = k \,\&\, (k-1)$ for $1 \leq k < m$ and $f(m) = 0$. After step S2, x_k is $x_{1..k}$ for $1 \leq k \leq m$.

(b) The cost of S1 is $m - 1$, the cost of S2 is $m - 1 - \lceil \lg m \rceil$, and the cost of S3 is $n - m$. The final delay of x_k is $\lfloor \lg k \rfloor + \nu k - 1$ for $1 \leq k < m$, and it is $\lceil \lg m \rceil + k - m$ for $m \leq k \leq n$. So the maximum delay for $\{x_1, \ldots, x_{m-1}\}$ turns out to be $g(m) = m - 1$ for $m < 4$, $g(m) = \lfloor \lg m \rfloor + \lfloor \lg \frac{m}{3} \rfloor$ for $m \geq 4$. We have $c(m, n) = m + n - 2 - \lceil \lg m \rceil$, $d(m, n) = \max(g(m), \lceil \lg m \rceil + n - m)$. Hence $c(m, n) + d(m, n) = 2n - 2$

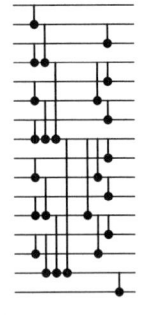

whenever $n \geq m + g(m) - \lceil \lg m \rceil$.

(c) A table of values reveals that $d(n) = \lceil \lg n \rceil$ for $n < 8$, and $d(n) = \lfloor \lg(n - \lfloor \lg n \rfloor + 3) \rfloor + \lfloor \lg \frac{2}{3}(n - \lfloor \lg n \rfloor + 3) \rfloor - 1$ for $n \geq 8$. Stating this another way, we have $d(n) > d(n-1)$ and $n > 2$ if and only if $n = 2^k + k - 3$ or $2^k + 2^{k-1} + k - 3$ for some $k > 1$. The minimum with minimal cost occurs for $m = n$ when $n < 8$; otherwise it occurs for $m = n - \lfloor \lg \frac{2}{3}(n - \lfloor \lg n \rfloor + 3) \rfloor + 2 - [n = 2^k + k - 3$ for some $k]$.

(d) Set $m \leftarrow m(n,d)$, where $m(n, d(n))$ is defined in the previous sentence and $m(n,d) = m(n-1, d-1)$ when $d > d(n)$. [See *J. Algorithms* **7** (1986), 185–201.]

38. (a) From top to bottom, $f_k(x_1, \ldots, x_n)$ is an elementary symmetric function also called the threshold function $S_{\geq k}(x_1, \ldots, x_n)$. (See exercise 5.3.4–28, Eq. 7.1.1–(90).)

(b) After calculating $\{S_1, \ldots, S_n\}$ in $\approx 6n$ steps as in answer 33, we can apply the method of exercise 37 to finish in $2n$ further steps.

But it is more interesting to design a Boolean chain specifically for the computation of the $2^m + 1$ threshold functions $g_k(x_1, \ldots, x_m) = [(x_1 \ldots x_m)_2 \geq k]$ for $0 \leq k \leq 2^m$. Since $[(x'x'')_2 \geq (y'y'')_2] = [(x')_2 \geq (y')_2 + 1] \vee ([(x')_2 \geq (y')_2] \wedge [(x'')_2 \geq (y'')_2])$, a divide-and-conquer construction analogous to a binary decoder solves this problem with a cost at most $2t(m)$.

Furthermore, if $2^{m-1} \leq n < 2^m$, the cost $u(n)$ of computing $\{g_1, \ldots, g_n\}$ by this method turns out to be $2n + O(\sqrt{n})$, and it is quite reasonable when n is small:

$$
\begin{array}{rccccccccccccccccccccc}
n = & 1 & 2 & 3 & 4 & 5 & 6 & 7 & 8 & 9 & 10 & 11 & 12 & 13 & 14 & 15 & 16 & 17 & 18 & 19 & 20 \\
u(n) = & 0 & 1 & 2 & 4 & 7 & 7 & 8 & 12 & 15 & 17 & 19 & 19 & 20 & 21 & 22 & 27 & 32 & 34 & 36 & 36
\end{array}
$$

Starting with sideways addition, we can sort n Boolean values in $s(n) + u(n) \approx 7n$ steps. A sorting network, which costs $2\hat{S}(n)$, is better when $n = 4$ but loses when $n \geq 8$. [See 5.3.4–(11); D. E. Muller and F. P. Preparata, *JACM* **22** (1975), 195–201.]

39. [*IEEE Transactions* **C-29** (1980), 737–738.] The identity

$$M_{r+s}(x_1, \ldots, x_r, x_{r+1}, \ldots, x_{r+s}; y_0, \ldots, y_{2^{r+s}-1}) = M_r(x_1, \ldots, x_r; y'_0, \ldots, y'_{2^r-1}),$$

where $y'_j = \bigvee_{k=0}^{2^s-1}(d_k \wedge y_{2^s j + k})$ and d_k is the kth output of an s-to-2^s decoder applied to $(x_{r+1}, \ldots, x_{r+s})$, shows that $C(M_{r+s}) \leq C(M_r) + 2^{r+s} + 2^r(2^s - 1) + t(s)$, where $t(s)$ is the cost (30) of the decoder. The depth is $D(M_{r+s}) = \max(D_x(M_{r+s}), D_y(M_{r+s}))$, where D_x and D_y denote the maximum depth of the x and y variables; we have $D_x(M_{r+s}) \leq \max(D_x(M_r), 1 + s + \lceil \lg s \rceil + D_y(M_r))$ and $D_y(M_{r+s}) \leq 1 + s + D_y(M_r)$.

Taking $r = \lceil m/2 \rceil$ and $s = \lfloor m/2 \rfloor$ yields $C(M_m) \leq 2^{m+1} + O(2^{m/2})$, $D_y(M_m) \leq m + 1 + \lceil \lg m \rceil$, and $D_x(M_m) \leq D_y(M_m) + \lceil \lg m \rceil$.

40. We can, for example, let $f_{nk}(x) = \bigvee_{j=1}^{n+1-k}(l_j(x) \wedge r_{j+k-1}(x))$, where

$$l_j(x) = \begin{cases} x_j, & \text{if } j \bmod k = 0, \\ x_j \wedge l_{j+1}(x), & \text{if } j \bmod k \neq 0, \end{cases} \quad \text{for } 1 \leq j \leq n - (n \bmod k);$$

$$r_j(x) = \begin{cases} 1, & \text{if } j \bmod k = 0, \\ x_j \wedge r_{j-1}(x), & \text{if } j \bmod k \neq 0, \end{cases} \quad \text{for } k \leq j \leq n.$$

The cost is $4n - 3k - 3\lfloor \frac{n}{k} \rfloor - \lfloor \frac{n-1}{k} \rfloor + 2 - (n \bmod k)$.

A recursive solution is preferable when n is small or k is small: Observe that

$$f_{nk}(x) = \begin{cases} x_{n-k+1} \wedge \cdots \wedge x_k \wedge \\ \quad f_{(2n-2k)(n-k)}(x_1, \ldots, x_{n-k}, x_{k+1}, \ldots, x_n), & \text{for } k < n < 2k; \\ f_{\lfloor (n+k)/2 \rfloor k}(x_1, \ldots, x_{\lfloor (n+k)/2 \rfloor}) \vee \\ \quad f_{\lfloor (n+k-1)/2 \rfloor k}(x_{\lfloor (n-k)/2 \rfloor + 1}, \ldots, x_n), & \text{for } n \geq 2k. \end{cases}$$

The cost of this solution can be shown to equal $n - 1 + \sum_{j=1}^{n-k} \lfloor \lg j \rfloor$ when $k \le n < 2k$, and it lies asymptotically between $(m + \alpha_k - 1)n + O(km)$ and $(m + 2 - 2/\alpha_k)n + O(km)$ as $n \to \infty$, where $m = \lfloor \lg k \rfloor$ and $1 < \alpha_k = (k+1)/2^m \le 2$.

A marriage of these methods is better yet; the optimum cost is unknown.

41. Let $c(m)$ be the cost of computing both $(x)_2 + (y)_2$ and $(x)_2 + (y)_2 + 1$ by the conditional-sum method when x and y have $n = 2^m$ bits, and let $c'(m)$ be the cost of the simpler problem of computing just $(x)_2 + (y)_2$. Then $c(m+1) = 2c(m) + 6 \cdot 2^m + 2$, $c'(m+1) = c(m) + c'(m) + 3 \cdot 2^m + 1$. (Bit z_n of the sum costs 1; but bits z_k for $n < k \le 2n + 1$ cost 3, because they have the form $c? \, a_k : b_k$ where c is a carry bit.) If we start with $n = 1$ and $c(0) = 3$, $c'(0) = 2$, the solution is $c(m) = (3m + 5)2^m - 2$, $c'(m) = (3m + 2)2^m - m$. But improved constructions for the case $n = 2$ allow us to start with $c(1) = 11$ and $c'(1) = 7$; then the solution is $c(m) = (3m + \frac{7}{2})2^m - 2$, $c'(m) = (3m + \frac{1}{2})2^m - m + 1$. In either case the depth is $2m + 1$. [See J. Sklansky, *IRE Transactions* **EC-9** (1960), 226–231.]

42. (a) Since $\langle x_k y_k c_k \rangle = u_k \vee (v_k \wedge c_k)$, we can use (26) and induction.

(b) Notice that $U_k^{k+1} = u_k$ and $V_k^{k+1} = v_k$; use induction on $j - i$. [See A. Weinberger and J. L. Smith, *IRE Transactions* **EC-5** (1956), 65–73; R. P. Brent and H. T. Kung, *IEEE Transactions* **C-31** (1982), 260–264.]

(c) First, for $l = 1, 2, \ldots, m - 1$, and for $1 \le k \le n$, compute V_i^k for all multiples i of $h(l)$ in the range $k_l \ge i \ge k_{l+1}$, where $k_l = h(l) \lfloor (k-1)/h(l) \rfloor$ denotes the largest multiple of $h(l)$ that is less than k. For example, when $l = 3$ and $k = 99$, we compute V_{96}^{99}, $V_{88}^{99} = V_{96}^{99} \wedge V_{88}^{96}$, $V_{80}^{99} = V_{88}^{99} \wedge V_{80}^{88}$, $\ldots$, $V_{64}^{99} = V_{72}^{99} \wedge V_{64}^{72}$; this is a prefix computation using the values V_{96}^{99}, V_{88}^{96}, V_{80}^{88}, $\ldots$, V_{64}^{72} that were computed when $l = 2$. Using the method of exercise 36, step l adds at most l levels to the depth, and it requires a total of $(p_1 + p_2 + \cdots + p_{2^l})n/2^l = O(2^l n)$ gates.

Then, again for $l = 1, 2, \ldots, m - 1$, and for $1 \le k \le n$, compute U_i^k for $i = k_{l+1}$, using the "unrolled" formula

$$U_{k_{l+1}}^k = U_{k_l}^k \vee \bigvee_{\substack{k_l > j \ge k_{l+1} \\ h(l) \backslash j}} (V_{j+h(l)}^k \wedge U_j^{j+h(l)}).$$

For example, the unrolled formula when $l = 3$ and $k = 99$ is

$$U_{64}^{99} = U_{96}^{99} \vee (V_{96}^{99} \wedge U_{88}^{96}) \vee (V_{88}^{99} \wedge U_{80}^{88}) \vee (V_{80}^{99} \wedge U_{72}^{80}) \vee (V_{72}^{99} \wedge U_{64}^{72}).$$

Every such U_i^k is a union of at most 2^l terms, so it can be computed with depth $\le l$ in addition to the depth of each term. The total cost of this phase for $1 \le k \le n$ is $(0 + 2 + 4 + \cdots + (2^l - 2))n/2^l = O(2^l n)$.

The overall cost to compute all necessary U's and V's is therefore $\sum_{l=1}^{m-1} O(2^l n) = O(2^m n)$. (Furthermore the quantities V_0^k aren't actually needed, so we save the cost of $\sum_{l=1}^{m-1} h(l) p_{2^l}$ gates.) For example, when $m = (2, 3, 4, 5)$ we obtain Boolean chains for the addition of $(2, 8, 64, 1024)$-bit numbers, respectively, with overall depths $(3, 7, 11, 16)$ and costs $(7, 64, 1254, 48470)$.

[This construction is due to V. M. Khrapchenko, *Problemy Kibernetiki* **19** (1967), 107–122, who also showed how to combine it with other methods so that the overall cost will be $O(n)$ while still achieving depth $\lg n + O(\sqrt{\log n})$. However, his combined method is purely of theoretical interest, because it requires $n > 2^{64}$ before the depth becomes less than $2 \lg n$. Another way to achieve small depth using the recurrences in (b) can be based on the Fibonacci numbers: The Fibonacci method computes the carries with depth $\log_\phi n + O(1) \approx 1.44 \lg n$ and cost $O(n \log n)$. For example, it yields chains for binary addition with the following characteristics:

$n =$	4	8	16	32	64	128	256	512	1024
depth	6	7	9	10	12	13	15	16	18
cost	24	71	186	467	1125	2648	6102	13775	30861

See D. E. Knuth, *The Stanford GraphBase* (1994), 276–279.

Charles Babbage found an ingenious mechanical solution to the analogous problem for addition in radix 10, claiming that his design would be able to add numbers of arbitrary precision in constant time; for this to work he would have needed idealized, rigid components with vanishing clearances. See H. P. Babbage, *Babbage's Calculating Engines* (1889), 334–335. Curiously, an equivalent idea works fine with physical transistors, although it cannot be expressed in terms of Boolean chains; see P. M. Fenwick, *Comp. J.* **30** (1987), 77–79.]

43. (a) Let $A = B = Q = \{0,1\}$ and $q_0 = 0$. Define $c(q,a) = d(q,a) = \bar{q} \wedge a$.

(b) The key idea is to construct the functions $d_1(q) \ldots d_{n-1}(q)$, where $d_1(q) = d(q, a_1)$ and $d_j(q) = d(d_{j-1}(q), a_j)$. In other words, $d_1 = d^{(a_1)}$ and $d_j = d_{j-1} \circ d^{(a_j)}$, where $d^{(a)}$ is the function that takes $q \mapsto d(q, a)$ and where $\circ$ denotes composition of functions. Each function d_j can be encoded in binary notation, and $\circ$ is an associative operation on these binary representations. Hence the functions $d_1 d_2 \ldots d_{n-1}$ are the prefixes $d^{(a_1)}$, $d^{(a_1)} \circ d^{(a_2)}$, ..., $d^{(a_1)} \circ \cdots \circ d^{(a_{n-1})}$; and $q_1 q_2 \ldots q_n = q_0 d_1(q_0) \ldots d_{n-1}(q_0)$.

(c) Represent a function $f(q)$ by its truth table $f_0 f_1$. Then the composition $f_0 f_1 \circ g_0 g_1$ is $h_0 h_1$, where the functions $h_0 = f_0$? $g_1 : g_0$ and $h_1 = f_1$? $g_1 : g_0$ are muxes that can each be computed with cost 3 and depth 2. (The combined cost $C(h_0 h_1)$ is only 5, but we are trying to keep the depth small.) The truth table for $d^{(a)}$ is $a0$. Using exercise 36, we can therefore compute the truth tables $d_{10} d_{11} d_{20} d_{21} \ldots d_{(n-1)0} d_{(n-1)1}$ with cost $\leq 6p_{n-1} < 24n$ and depth $\leq 2\lceil \lg(n-1) \rceil$; then $b_1 = a_1$, and $b_j = \bar{q}_j \wedge a_j = \bar{d}_{(j-1)0} \wedge a_j$ for $j > 1$. (These cost estimates are quite conservative; substantial simplifications arise because of the 0s in the initial truth tables of $d^{(a_j)}$ and because many of the intermediate values d_{j1} are never used. For example, when $n = 5$ the actual cost is only 10, not $6p_{n-1} + (n-1) = 28$; the actual depth is 4, not $2\lceil \lg(n-1) \rceil + 1 = 5$. Notice that the straightforward chain $b_j = a_j \wedge \bar{b}_{j-1}$ for $1 < j \leq n$ also solves problem (a); it wins on cost, but has depth $n - 1$.)

44. The inputs may be regarded as the string $x_0 y_0 \, x_1 y_1 \, \ldots \, x_{n-1} y_{n-1}$ whose elements belong to the four-letter alphabet $A = \{00, 01, 10, 11\}$; there are two states $Q = \{0,1\}$, representing a possible carry bit, with $q_0 = 0$; the output alphabet is $B = \{0,1\}$; and we have $c(q, xy) = q \oplus x \oplus y$, $d(q, xy) = \langle qxy \rangle$. In this case, therefore, the finite state transducer is essentially described by a full adder.

Only three of the four possible functions of q occur when we compose the mappings $d^{(xy)}$. We can encode them as $u \vee (q \wedge v)$. The initial functions $d^{(xy)}$ have $u = x \wedge y$, $v = x \oplus y$; and the composition $(uv) \circ (u'v')$ is $u''v''$, where $u'' = u' \vee (v' \wedge u)$ and $v'' = v \wedge v'$.

When $n = 4$, for example, the chain has the following form, using the notation of exercise 42: $U_k^{k+1} = x_k \wedge y_k$, $V_k^{k+1} = x_k \oplus y_k$, for $0 \leq k < 4$; $U_0^2 = U_1^2 \vee (V_1^2 \wedge U_0^1)$, $U_2^4 = U_3^4 \vee (V_3^4 \wedge U_2^3)$, $V_2^4 = V_2^3 \wedge V_3^4$; $U_0^3 = U_2^3 \vee (V_2^3 \wedge U_0^2)$, $U_0^4 = U_2^4 \vee (V_2^4 \wedge U_0^2)$; $z_0 = V_0^1$, $z_1 = U_0^1 \oplus V_1^2$, $z_2 = U_0^2 \oplus V_2^3$, $z_3 = U_0^3 \oplus V_3^4$, $z_4 = U_0^4$. The total cost is 20; the maximum depth, 6, occurs in the computation of z_3.

In general the cost will be $2n + 3p_n$ in the notation of exercise 36, because we need $2n$ gates for the initial u's and v's, then $3p_n$ gates for the prefix computation; the $n-1$ additional gates needed to form z_j for $0 < j < n$ are compensated by the fact that we need not compute V_0^j for $1 < j \leq n$. Therefore the total cost is $14 \cdot 2^m - 3F_{m+5} + 3$, superior to the conditional-sum method (which however has depth $2m+1$, not $2m+2$):

$n =$	2	4	8	16	32	64	128	256	512	1024
cost of conditional-sum chain	7	25	74	197	492	1179	2746	6265	14072	31223
cost of Ladner–Fischer chain	7	20	52	125	286	632	1363	2888	6040	12509

[George Boole introduced his Algebra in order to show that logic can be understood in terms of arithmetic. Eventually logic became so well understood, the situation was reversed: People like Shannon and Zuse began in the 1930s to design circuits for arithmetic in terms of logic, and since then many approaches to the problem of parallel addition have been discovered. The first Boolean chains of cost $O(n)$ and depth $O(\log n)$ were devised by Yu. P. Ofman, *Doklady Akademii Nauk SSSR* **145** (1962), 48–51. His chains were similar to the construction above, but the depth was approximately $4m$.]

45. That argument would indeed be simpler, but it wouldn't be strong enough to prove the desired result. (Many chains with steps of fan-out 0 inflate the simpler estimate.) The text's permutation-enhanced proof technique was introduced by J. E. Savage in his book *The Complexity of Computing* (New York: Wiley, 1976), Theorem 3.4.1.

46. When $r = 2^n/n + O(1)$ we have $\ln(2^{2r+1}(n+r-1)^{2r}/(r-1)!) = r \ln r + (1 + \ln 4)r + O(n) = (2^n/n)(n \ln 2 - \ln n + 1 + \ln 4) + O(n)$. So $\alpha(n) \leq (n/(4e))^{-2^n/n + O(n/\log n)}$, which approaches zero quite rapidly indeed when $n > 4e$.
(In fact, (32) gives $\alpha(11) < 7.6 \times 10^7$, $\alpha(12) < 4.2 \times 10^{-6}$, $\alpha(13) < 1.2 \times 10^{-38}$.)

47. Restrict permutations to the $(r - m)!$ cases where $i\pi = i$ for $1 \leq i \leq n$ and $(n+r+1-k)\pi$ is the kth output. Then we get $(r - m)! \, c(m, n, r) \leq 2^{2r+1}(n+r-1)^{2r}$ in place of (32). Hence, as in exercise 46, almost all such functions have cost exceeding $2^n m/(n + \lg m)$ when $m = O(2^n/n^2)$.

48. (a) Not surprisingly, this lower bound on $C(n)$ is rather crude when n is small:

$n =$	1	2	3	4	5	6	7	8	9	10	11	12	13	14	15	16
$r(n) =$	1	1	2	3	5	9	16	29	54	99	184	343	639	1196	2246	4229

(b) The bootstrap method (see *Concrete Mathematics* §9.4) yields

$$r(n) = \frac{2^n}{n}\left(1 + \frac{\lg n - 2 - 1/\ln 2}{n} + O\left(\frac{\log n}{n^2}\right)\right).$$

49. The number of normal Boolean functions that can be represented by a formula of length $\leq r$ is at most $5^r n^{r+1} g_r$, where g_r is the number of oriented binary trees with r internal nodes. Set $r = 2^n/\lg n - 2^{n+2}/(\lg n)^2$ in this formula and divide by $2^{2^n - 1}$ to get an upper bound on the fraction of functions with $L(f) \leq r$. The result rapidly approaches zero, by exercise 2.3.4.4–7, because it is $O((5\alpha/16)^{2^n/\lg n})$ where $\alpha \approx 2.483$.
[J. Riordan and C. E. Shannon obtained a similar lower bound for series-parallel switching networks in *J. Math. and Physics* **21** (1942), 83–93; such networks are equivalent to formulas in which only canalizing operators are used. R. E. Krichevsky obtained more general results in *Problemy Kibernetiki* **2** (1959), 123–138, and O. B. Lupanov gave an asymptotically matching upper bound in *Prob. Kibernetiki* **3** (1960), 61–80.]

50. (a) Using subcube notation as in exercise 7.1.1–30, the prime implicants are $00001*$, $(0001*1)$, $0100*1$, $0111*1$, $1010*1$, $101*11$, $00*011$, $00*101$, $(01*111)$, $11*101$,

(0∗1101), (1∗0101), 1∗1011, 0∗0∗11, ∗00101, (∗01011), (∗11101), where the parenthe-sized subcubes are omitted in a shortest DNF. (b) Similarly, the prime clauses and a shortest CNF are given by 00111∗, 01010∗, 10110∗, 0110∗∗, 00∗00∗, 11∗00∗, 11∗11∗, (0∗100∗), (1∗00∗∗), 1∗0∗1∗, (1∗∗∗∗0), ∗0000∗, (∗1100∗), ∗1∗∗∗0, ∗∗1∗∗0, ∗∗∗1∗0, and (∗∗∗∗00). (Thus the CNF is $(x_1 \lor x_2 \lor \bar{x}_3 \lor \bar{x}_4 \lor \bar{x}_5) \land (x_1 \lor \bar{x}_2 \lor x_3 \lor \bar{x}_4 \lor x_5) \land \cdots \land (\bar{x}_4 \lor x_6)$.)

51. $f = ([x_5 x_6 \in \{01\}] \land [(x_1 x_2 x_3 x_4)_2 \in \{1, 3, 4, 7, 9, 10, 13, 15\}]) \lor ([x_5 x_6 \in \{10, 11\}] \land [x_1 x_2 x_3 x_4 = 0000]) \lor ([x_5 x_6 \in \{11\}] \land [(x_1 x_2 x_3 x_4)_2 \in \{1, 2, 4, 5, 7, 10, 11, 14\}]).$

52. The small-n results are quite different from those that work asymptotically:

n k l (38)	n k l (38)	n k l (38)	n k l (38)
5 2 2 39	8 3 2 175	11 4 4 803	14 5 5 4045
6 2 2 67	9 3 2 279	12 4 3 1329	15 5 5 7141
7 2 1 109	10 4 4 471	13 5 6 2355	16 5 4 12431

(These upper bounds are quite weak when n is small. For example, we know that $C(n) = (0, 1, 4, 7, 12)$ when $n = (1, 2, 3, 4, 5)$; and Eq. 7.1.1–(16) gives $C(n + 1) \leq 2C(n) + 2$, so that $C(6) \leq 26$, $C(7) \leq 54$, etc.)

53. First note that $2^k/l \leq n - 3 \lg n$, hence $m_i \leq n - 3 \lg n + 1$ and $2^{m_i} = O(2^n/n^3)$. Also $l = O(n)$ and $t(n - k) = O(2^n/n^2)$. So (38) reduces to $l \cdot 2^{n-k} + O(2^n/n^2) = 2^n/(n - 3 \lg n) + O(2^n/n^2)$.

54. The greedy-footprint heuristic gives a chain of length 14:

$x_5 = x_1 \oplus x_3,$	$x_{10} = x_4 \land \bar{x}_5,$	$f_3 = x_{15} = \bar{x}_8 \land x_9,$
$x_6 = x_2 \oplus x_3,$	$x_{11} = x_4 \oplus x_5,$	$f_4 = x_{16} = x_4 \land x_8,$
$x_7 = x_1 \land x_2,$	$x_{12} = x_6 \land x_{11},$	$f_5 = x_{17} = x_7 \land x_9,$
$x_8 = x_1 \land \bar{x}_6,$	$f_1 = x_{13} = \bar{x}_7 \land x_{12},$	$f_6 = x_{19} = x_6 \land x_{10}.$
$x_9 = x_4 \land x_5,$	$f_2 = x_{14} = \bar{x}_6 \land x_{10},$	

The minterm-first method corresponds to a chain of length 22, after we remove steps that are never used:

$x_5 = \bar{x}_1 \land \bar{x}_2,$	$x_{13} = x_5 \land x_{10},$	$x_{20} = x_8 \land x_{11},$
$x_6 = \bar{x}_1 \land x_2,$	$x_{14} = x_5 \land x_{11},$	$f_6 = x_{21} = x_{15} \lor x_{18},$
$x_7 = x_1 \land \bar{x}_2,$	$x_{15} = x_6 \land x_9,$	$f_1 = x_{22} = x_{13} \lor x_{21},$
$x_8 = x_1 \land x_2,$	$x_{16} = x_6 \land x_{11},$	$f_2 = x_{23} = x_{12} \lor x_{20},$
$x_9 = \bar{x}_3 \land x_4,$	$x_{17} = x_7 \land x_9,$	$x_{24} = x_{14} \lor x_{16},$
$x_{10} = x_3 \land \bar{x}_4,$	$x_{18} = x_7 \land x_{11},$	$f_3 = x_{25} = x_{24} \lor x_{19},$
$x_{11} = x_3 \land x_4,$	$f_5 = x_{19} = x_8 \land x_9,$	$f_4 = x_{26} = x_{17} \lor x_{20}.$
$x_{12} = x_5 \land x_9,$		

(The distributive law could replace the computation of x_{14}, x_{16}, and x_{24} by two steps.)

Incidentally, the three functions in the answer to exercise 51 can be computed in only ten steps:

$x_5 = x_2 \lor x_4,$	$f_3 = x_9 = x_6 \oplus x_8,$	$x_{12} = x_2 \oplus x_3,$
$x_6 = \bar{x}_1 \land x_5,$	$x_{10} = x_1 \oplus x_8,$	$x_{13} = \bar{x}_{10} \land x_{12},$
$x_7 = x_2 \land x_4,$	$\bar{f}_2 = x_{11} = x_9 \lor x_{10},$	$f_1 = x_{14} = x_4 \oplus x_{13}.$
$x_8 = x_3 \land \bar{x}_7,$		

55. The optimum two-level DNF and CNF representations in answer 50 cost 53 and 43, respectively. Formula (37) costs 29, when optimized as in exercise 54. The alternative in exercise 51 costs only 17. But the catalog of optimum five-variable chains suggests

$$x_7 = \bar{x}_1 \wedge x_2, \qquad x_{11} = x_5 \wedge x_{10}, \qquad x_{15} = x_{13} \oplus x_{14}, \qquad x_{18} = \bar{x}_4 \wedge x_{17},$$
$$x_8 = x_3 \oplus x_7, \qquad x_{12} = x_5 \vee x_{10}, \qquad x_{16} = x_5 \wedge \bar{x}_{10}, \qquad x_{19} = x_6 \wedge x_{15},$$
$$x_9 = x_2 \wedge x_8, \qquad x_{13} = x_4 \wedge \bar{x}_{11}, \qquad x_{17} = \bar{x}_3 \wedge x_{16}, \qquad x_{20} = x_{18} \vee x_{19},$$
$$x_{10} = x_1 \oplus x_9, \qquad x_{14} = x_8 \wedge x_{12},$$

for this six-variable function. Is there a better way?

56. If we care about at most two values, the function can be either constant or x_j or $\bar{x}_j$.

57. The truth tables for x_5 through x_{15}, in hexadecimal notation, are respectively
0fff, 3ccc, 30c0, 75d5, 4919, 7000, 0606, 4808, 2000, 5d5d, 3ece. So we get

$$1010 \mapsto \text{0}, \quad 1011 \mapsto \text{7}, \quad 1100 \mapsto \text{4}, \quad 1101 \mapsto \text{5}, \quad 1110 \mapsto \text{6}, \quad 1111 \mapsto \text{7}.$$

[Corey Plover, believing that it might be better to have a solution in which nondigits never masquerade as digits, has discovered a 12-step chain (with non-greedy x_7)

$$x_5 = x_1 \oplus x_2, \qquad x_9 = x_2 \oplus x_3, \qquad \bar{b} = x_{13} = x_2 \wedge \bar{x}_{11},$$
$$x_6 = x_3 \wedge \bar{x}_4, \qquad g = x_{10} = x_7 \vee x_9, \qquad \bar{c} = x_{14} = x_7 \wedge x_9,$$
$$x_7 = x_1 \oplus x_6, \qquad \bar{d} = x_{11} = x_8 \oplus x_{10}, \qquad \bar{e} = x_{15} = x_4 \vee x_{12},$$
$$x_8 = x_4 \vee x_7, \qquad \bar{a} = x_{12} = \bar{x}_3 \wedge x_{11}, \qquad \bar{f} = x_{16} = \bar{x}_5 \wedge x_8,$$

for which $a, \ldots, g$ have the truth tables b7ff, f9f0, dfe3, b6df, a2aa, 8ff2, 3efd, and

$$1010 \mapsto \text{A}, \quad 1011 \mapsto \text{0}, \quad 1100 \mapsto \text{c}, \quad 1101 \mapsto \text{=}, \quad 1110 \mapsto \text{G}, \quad 1111 \mapsto \text{3}.$$

He has also shown that all 11-step solutions to (44) map the nondigits into either
$(0,7,4,5,6,7)$, $(0,7,6,1,9,3)$, $(0,7,6,1,8,3)$, $(2,3,6,7,6,7)$, $(2,1,6,7,4,5)$, or $(2,4,6,7,4,5)$.]

58. The truth tables of all cost-7 functions with exactly eight 1s in their truth tables are equivalent to either 0779, 169b, or 179a. Combining these in all possible ways yields 9656 solutions that are distinct under permutation and/or complementation of $\{x_1, x_2, x_3, x_4\}$ as well as under permutation and/or complementation of $\{f_1, f_2, f_3, f_4\}$.

59. The greedy-footprint heuristic produces the following 17-step chain:

$$x_5 = x_2 \oplus x_3, \qquad x_{11} = x_2 \vee x_7, \qquad x_{17} = \bar{x}_6 \wedge x_8,$$
$$x_6 = x_1 \oplus x_4, \qquad x_{12} = x_2 \wedge \bar{x}_6, \qquad f_1 = x_{18} = x_{11} \oplus x_{17},$$
$$x_7 = x_1 \oplus x_3, \qquad x_{13} = x_3 \wedge x_4, \qquad f_2 = x_{19} = x_{10} \wedge \bar{x}_{14},$$
$$x_8 = x_4 \vee x_5, \qquad x_{14} = x_4 \wedge x_5, \qquad f_3 = x_{20} = x_9 \oplus x_{16},$$
$$x_9 = x_6 \wedge x_8, \qquad x_{15} = x_5 \wedge x_{10}, \qquad f_4 = x_{21} = x_{12} \oplus x_{15}.$$
$$x_{10} = x_7 \vee x_9, \qquad x_{16} = x_2 \wedge \bar{x}_{13},$$

The initial functions all have large footprints, so we can't achieve $C(f_1 f_2 f_3 f_4) = 28$; but a slightly more difficult S-box probably does exist.

60. One way is $u_1 = x_1 \oplus y_1$, $u_2 = x_2 \oplus y_2$, $v_1 = y_2 \oplus u_1$, $v_2 = y_1 \oplus u_2$, $z_1 = v_1 \wedge \bar{u}_2$, $z_2 = v_2 \wedge \bar{u}_1$.

61. The following 17-gate solution by David Stevenson generalizes to $8m + 1$ gates for addition mod $2^m + 1$: $u_0 = x_0 \wedge y_0$, $v_0 = x_0 \oplus y_0$, $u_1 = x_1 \wedge y_1$, $v_1 = x_1 \oplus y_1$, $t_1 = v_1 \wedge u_0$, $t_2 = v_1 \oplus u_0$, $c_2 = u_1 \vee t_1$; $u_2 = x_2 \wedge y_2$, $t_3 = x_2 \vee y_2$, $t_4 = t_3 \wedge c_2$; $t_5 = t_2 \vee v_0$, $t_6 = t_5 \wedge t_4$, $t_7 = t_6 \vee u_2$; $t_8 = t_7 \wedge \bar{v}_0$, $z_0 = t_7 \oplus v_0$, $z_1 = t_2 \oplus t_8$; $z_2 = t_4 \oplus t_7$. (Notice that $(x_2 x_1 x_0)_2 + (y_2 y_1 y_0)_2 = (u_2 t_4 t_2 v_0)_2 - 4[x = y = 4]$. Gilbert Lee has found another 17-step solution if the inputs are represented by 000, 001, 011, 101, and 111.)

62. There are $\binom{2^n}{2^n d}2^{2^n c}$ such functions, at most $\binom{2^n}{2^n d}c(n,r)$ of which have cost $\leq r$. So we can argue as in exercise 46 to conclude from (32) that the fraction with cost $\leq r = \lfloor 2^n c/n \rfloor$ is at most $2^{2r+1-2^n c}(n+r-1)^{2r}/(r-1)! = 2^{-r\lg n + O(r)}$.

63. [*Problemy Kibernetiki* **21** (1969), 215–226.] Put the truth table in a $2^k \times 2^{n-k}$ array as in Lupanov's method, and suppose there are c_j cares in column j, for $0 \leq j < 2^{n-k}$. Break that column into $\lfloor c_j/m \rfloor$ subcolumns that each have m cares, plus a possibly empty subcolumn at the bottom that contains fewer than m of them. The hint tells us that at most 2^{m+k} column vectors suffice to match the 0s and 1s of every subcolumn that has a specified top row i_0 and bottom row i_1. With $O(m2^{m+3k})$ operations we can therefore construct $O(2^{m+3k})$ functions $g_t(x_1,\ldots,x_k)$ from the minterms of $\{x_1,\ldots,x_k\}$, so that every subcolumn matches some type t. And for every type t we can construct functions $h_t(x_{k+1},\ldots,x_n)$ from the minterms of $\{x_{k+1},\ldots,x_n\}$, specifying the columns that match t; the cost is at most $\sum_j(\lfloor c_j/m \rfloor + 1) \leq 2^n c/m + 2^{n-k}$. Finally, $f = \bigvee_t(g_t \wedge h_t)$ requires $O(2^{m+3k})$ additional steps. Choosing $k = \lfloor 2\lg n \rfloor$ and $m = \lceil n - 9\lg n \rceil$ makes the total cost at most $(2^n c/n)(1 + 9n^{-1}\lg n + O(n^{-1}))$.

Of course we need to prove the hint, which is due to E. I. Nechiporuk [*Doklady Akad. Nauk SSSR* **163** (1965), 40–42]. In fact, $2^m(1+\lceil k\ln 2\rceil)$ vectors suffice (see S. K. Stein, *J. Combinatorial Theory* **A16** (1974), 391–397): If we choose $q = 2^m\lceil k\ln 2\rceil$ vectors at random, not necessarily distinct, the expected number of untouched subcubes is $\binom{k}{m}2^m(1-2^{-m})^q < \binom{k}{m}2^m e^{-q2^{-m}} < 2^m$. (An explicit construction would be nicer.)

For extensive generalizations — tolerating a percentage of errors and specifying the density of 1s — see N. Pippenger, *Mathematical Systems Theory* **10** (1977), 129–167.

64. It's exactly the game of tic-tac-toe, if we number the cells $\begin{smallmatrix}6|1|8\\7|5|3\\2|9|4\end{smallmatrix}$ as in an ancient Chinese magic square. [Berlekamp, Conway, and Guy use this numbering scheme to present a complete analysis of tic-tac-toe in their book *Winning Ways* **3** (2003), 732–736.]

65. One solution is to replace the "defending" moves d_j by "attacking" moves a_j and "counterattacking" moves c_j, and to include them only for corner cells $j \in \{1,3,9,7\}$. Let $j \cdot k = (jk)$ mod 10; then

$$\begin{array}{ccc} j\cdot 1 & j\cdot 2 & j\cdot 3 \\ j\cdot 4 & j\cdot 5 & j\cdot 6 \\ j\cdot 7 & j\cdot 8 & j\cdot 9 \end{array}$$

gives us another way to look at the tic-tac-toe diagram, when j is a corner, because $j \perp 10$. The precise definition of a_j and c_j is then

$$a_j = m_j \wedge \left((x_{j\cdot 3} \wedge \beta_{(j\cdot 8)(j\cdot 9)} \wedge (o_{j\cdot 4}\oplus o_{j\cdot 6})) \vee (x_{j\cdot 7} \wedge \beta_{(j\cdot 6)(j\cdot 9)} \wedge (o_{j\cdot 2}\oplus o_{j\cdot 8}))\right.$$
$$\left.\vee (m_{j\cdot 9} \wedge ((m_{j\cdot 8} \wedge x_{j\cdot 2} \wedge \overline{(o_{j\cdot 3}\oplus o_{j\cdot 6})}) \vee (m_{j\cdot 6} \wedge x_{j\cdot 4} \wedge \overline{(o_{j\cdot 7}\oplus o_{j\cdot 8})})))\right);$$
$$c_j = d_j \wedge \overline{(x_{j\cdot 6} \wedge o_{j\cdot 7})} \wedge \overline{(x_{j\cdot 8} \wedge o_{j\cdot 3})} \wedge \bar{d}_{j\cdot 9};$$

here $d_j = m_j \wedge \beta_{(j\cdot 2)(j\cdot 3)} \wedge \beta_{(j\cdot 4)(j\cdot 7)}$ takes the place of (51). We also define

$$u = (x_1 \oplus x_3) \oplus (x_7 \oplus x_9), \qquad z_j = \begin{cases} m_j \wedge \bar{t}, & \text{if } j = 5, \\ m_j \wedge \bar{d}_{j\cdot 9}, & \text{if } j \in \{1,3,9,7\}, \\ m_j, & \text{if } j \in \{2,6,8,4\}; \end{cases}$$
$$v = (o_1 \oplus o_3) \oplus (o_7 \oplus o_9),$$
$$t = m_2 \wedge m_6 \wedge m_8 \wedge m_4 \wedge (u \vee \bar{v}),$$

in order to cover a few more exceptional cases. Finally the sequence of rank-ordered moves $d_5 d_1 d_3 d_9 d_7 d_2 d_6 d_8 d_4 m_5 m_1 m_3 m_9 m_7 m_2 m_6 m_8 m_4$ in (53) is replaced by the sequence $a_1 a_3 a_9 a_7 c_1 c_3 c_9 c_7 z_5 z_1 z_3 z_9 z_7 z_2 z_6 z_8 z_4$; and we replace $(d_j \wedge \bar{d}'_j)\vee(m_j \wedge \bar{m}'_j)$ in (55) by $(a_j \wedge \bar{a}'_j) \vee (c_j \wedge \bar{c}'_j) \vee (z_j \wedge \bar{z}'_j)$ when j is a corner cell, otherwise simply by $(z_j \wedge \bar{z}'_j)$.

(Notice that this machine is required to move correctly from *all* legal positions, even when those positions couldn't arise after the machine had made X's earlier moves. We essentially allow humans to play the game until they ask the machine for advice. Otherwise great simplifications would be possible. For example, if X always goes first, it could grab the center cell and eliminate a huge number of future possibilities; fewer than $8 \times 6 \times 4 \times 2 = 384$ games could arise. Even if O goes first, there are fewer than $9 \times 7 \times 5 \times 3 = 945$ possible scenarios against a fixed strategy. In fact, the actual number of different games with the strategy defined here turns out to be $76 + 457$, of which $72 + 328$ are won by the machine and the rest belong to the cat.)

66. The Boolean chain in the previous answer fulfills its mission of making correct moves from all 4520 legal positions, where correctness was essentially defined to mean that the worst-case final outcome is maximized. But a truly great tic-tac-toe player would do things differently. For example, from position ⊞ the machine takes the center, ⊞, and O probably draws by playing in a corner. But moving to ⊞ or ⊞ would give O only two chances to avoid defeat. [See Martin Gardner, *Hexaflexagons and Other Mathematical Diversions*, Chapter 4.]

Furthermore the best move from a position like ⊞ is to ⊞ instead of winning immediately; then if the reply is ⊞, move to ⊞. That way you still win, but without humiliating your opponent so badly.

Finally, even the concept of a single "best move" is flawed, because a good player will choose different moves in different games (as Babbage observed).

> *It might be thought that programing a digital computer to play ticktacktoe, or designing special circuits for a ticktacktoe machine, would be simple. This is true unless your aim is to construct a master robot that will win the maximum number of games against inexperienced players.*
>
> — MARTIN GARDNER, *The Scientific American Book of Mathematical Puzzles & Diversions* (1959)

67. The best solution known so far, due to David Stevenson in 2010, uses a total of 818 gates (472 AND, 327 OR, 13 NOR, 6 BUTNOT); see

http://www-cs-faculty.stanford.edu/~knuth/818-gate-solution

for the details. After taking care of moves such as w_j and b_j, and cleverly optimizing don't-cares, Stevenson essentially ORs together about 200 special positions (such as ⊞) that make $c = 1$, about 200 others (such as ⊞) that make $s = 1$, and about 50 (such as ⊞) that make $m = 1$; then he saves gates by finding common subexpressions among the ANDs that define special positions, and by using the distributive law, etc.

[This exercise was inspired by a discussion in John Wakerly's book *Digital Design* (Prentice–Hall, 3rd edition, 2000), §6.2.7. Incidentally, Babbage planned to choose among k possible moves by looking at $N \bmod k$, where N was the number of games won so far; he didn't realize that successive moves would tend to be highly correlated until N changed. Much better would have been to let N be the number of *moves made* so far.]

68. No. That method yields a "uniform" chain with a comprehensible structure, but its cost is $\Omega(n2^n)$. A circuit with approximately $2^n/n$ gates, constructed by Theorem L, exists but is more difficult to fabricate. (Incidentally, $C(\pi_5) = 10$.)

69. (a) One can, for example, verify this result by trying all 64 cases.

(b) If x_m lies in the same row or column as x_i, and also in the same row or column as x_j, we have $\alpha_{111} = \alpha_{101} = \alpha_{011} = 0$, so the pairs are good. Otherwise there are essentially three different possibilities, all bad: If $(i, j, m) = (1, 2, 4)$ then $\alpha_{101} = 0$,

$\alpha_{100} = x_5 x_9 \oplus x_6 x_8$, $\alpha_{011} = x_9$; if $(i,j,m) = (1,2,6)$ then $\alpha_{010} = x_4 x_9$, $\alpha_{011} = x_7$, $\alpha_{100} = x_5 x_9$, $\alpha_{101} = x_8$; if $(i,j,m) = (1,5,9)$ then $\alpha_{111} = 1$, $\alpha_{110} = 0$, $\alpha_{010} = x_3 x_7$.

70. (a) $x_1 \wedge ((x_5 \wedge x_9) \oplus (x_6 \wedge x_8)) \oplus x_2 \wedge ((x_6 \wedge x_7) \oplus (x_4 \wedge x_9)) \oplus x_3 \wedge ((x_4 \wedge x_8) \oplus (x_5 \wedge x_7))$.

(b) $x_1 \wedge ((x_5 \wedge x_9) \vee (x_6 \wedge x_8)) \vee x_2 \wedge ((x_6 \wedge x_7) \vee (x_4 \wedge x_9)) \vee x_3 \wedge ((x_4 \wedge x_8) \vee (x_5 \wedge x_7))$.

(c) Let $y_1 = x_1 \wedge x_5 \wedge x_9$, $y_2 = x_1 \wedge x_6 \wedge x_8$, $y_3 = x_2 \wedge x_6 \wedge x_7$, $y_4 = x_2 \wedge x_4 \wedge x_9$, $y_5 = x_3 \wedge x_4 \wedge x_8$, $y_6 = x_3 \wedge x_5 \wedge x_7$. The function $f(y_1, \ldots, y_6) = [y_1 + y_2 + y_3 > y_4 + y_5 + y_6]$ can be evaluated in 15 further steps with two full adders and a comparator; but there is a 14-step solution: Let $z_1 = (y_1 \oplus y_2) \oplus y_3$, $z_2 = (y_1 \oplus y_2) \vee (y_1 \oplus y_3)$, $z_3 = (y_4 \oplus y_5) \oplus y_6$, $z_4 = (y_4 \oplus y_5) \vee (y_4 \oplus y_6)$. Then $f = (z_1 \oplus (z_2 \wedge (\bar{z}_4 \oplus (z_1 \vee z_3)))) \wedge (\bar{z}_3 \vee z_4)$. Furthermore $y_1 y_2 y_3 = 111 \iff y_4 y_5 y_6 = 111$; so there are don't-cares, leading to an 11-step solution: $f = ((\bar{z}_1 \wedge z_3) \vee \bar{z}_4) \wedge z_2$. The total cost is $12 + 11 = 23$.

(The author knows of no way by which a computer could discover such an efficient chain in a reasonable amount of time, given only the truth table of f. But perhaps an even better chain exists.)

71. (a) $P(p) = 1 - 12p^2 + 24p^3 + 12p^4 - 96p^5 + 144p^6 - 96p^7 + 24p^8$, which is $\frac{11}{32} + \frac{9}{2}\epsilon^2 - 3\epsilon^4 - 24\epsilon^6 + 24\epsilon^8$ when $p = \frac{1}{2} + \epsilon$.

(b) There are $N = 2^{n-3}$ sets of eight values $(f_0, \ldots, f_7)$, each of which yields good pairs with probability $P(p)$. So the answer is $1 - P(p)^N$.

(c) The probability is $\binom{N}{r} P(p)^r (1 - P(p))^{N-r}$ that exactly r sets succeed; and in such a case t trials will find good pairs with probability $(r/N)^t$. The answer is therefore $1 - \sum_{r=0}^{N} \binom{N}{r} P(p)^r (1 - P(p))^{N-r} (r/N)^t = 1 - P(p)^t + O(t^2/N)$.

(d) $\sum_{r=0}^{N} \binom{N}{r} P(p)^r (1 - P(p))^{N-r} \sum_{j=0}^{t-1} (r/N)^j = (1 - P(p)^t)/(1 - P(p)) + O(t^3/N)$.

72. The probability in exercise 71(a) becomes $P(p) + (72p^3 - 264p^4 + 432p^5 - 336p^6 + 96p^7)r + (60p^2 - 240p^3 + 456p^4 - 432p^5 + 144p^6)r^2 + (-48p^2 + 144p^3 - 216p^4 + 96p^5)r^3 + (-36p^2 + 24p^3 + 12p^4)r^4 + (48p^2 - 24p^3)r^5 - 12p^2r^6$. If $p = q = (1 - r)/2$, this is $(11 + 48r + 36r^2 - 144r^3 - 30r^4 + 336r^5 - 348r^6 + 144r^7 - 21r^8)/32$; for example, it's $7739/8192 \approx 0.94$ when $r = 1/2$.

73. Consider the Horn clauses $1 \wedge 2 \Rightarrow 3$, $1 \wedge 3 \Rightarrow 4$, ..., $1 \wedge (n-1) \Rightarrow n$, $1 \wedge n \Rightarrow 2$, and $i \wedge j \Rightarrow 1$ for $1 < i < j \le n$. Suppose $|Z| > 1$ in a decomposition, and let i be minimum such that $x_i \in Z$. Also let j be minimum such that $j > i$ and $x_j \in Z$. We cannot have $i > 1$, since $i \wedge j \Rightarrow 1$ in that case. Thus $i = 1$, and $x_j \in Z$ for $2 \le j \le n$.

74. Suppose we know that no nontrivial decomposition exists with $x_1 \in Z$ or $\cdots$ or $x_{i-1} \in Z$; initially $i = 1$. We hope to rule out $x_i \in Z$ too, by choosing j and m cleverly. The Horn clauses $i \wedge j \Rightarrow m$ reduce to Krom clauses $j \Rightarrow m$ when i is asserted. So we essentially want to use Tarjan's depth-first search for strong components, in a digraph with arcs $j \Rightarrow m$ that may or may not exist.

When exploring from vertex j, first try $m = 1$, ..., $m = i - 1$; if any such implication $i \wedge j \Rightarrow m$ succeeds, we can eliminate j and all its predecessors from the digraph for i. Otherwise, test if $j \Rightarrow m$ for any such eliminated vertex m. Otherwise test unexplored vertices m. Otherwise try vertices m that have already been seen, favoring those near the root of the depth-first tree.

In the example $f(x) = (\det X) \bmod 2$, we would successively find $1 \wedge 2 \not\Rightarrow 3$, $1 \wedge 2 \Rightarrow 4$, $1 \wedge 4 \Rightarrow 3$, $1 \wedge 3 \Rightarrow 5$, $1 \wedge 5 \Rightarrow 6$, $1 \wedge 6 \Rightarrow 7$, $1 \wedge 7 \Rightarrow 8$, $1 \wedge 8 \Rightarrow 9$, $1 \wedge 9 \Rightarrow 2$ (now $i \leftarrow 2$); $2 \wedge 3 \not\Rightarrow 1$, $2 \wedge 3 \Rightarrow 4$, $2 \wedge 4 \not\Rightarrow 1$, $2 \wedge 4 \not\Rightarrow 5$, $2 \wedge 4 \Rightarrow 6$, $2 \wedge 6 \Rightarrow 1$ (now 3, 4, and 6 are eliminated from the digraph for 2), $2 \wedge 5 \Rightarrow 1$ (and 5 is eliminated), $2 \wedge 7 \not\Rightarrow 1$, $2 \wedge 7 \Rightarrow 3$ (7 is eliminated), $2 \wedge 8 \Rightarrow 1$, $2 \wedge 9 \Rightarrow 1$ (now $i \leftarrow 3$); $3 \wedge 4 \not\Rightarrow 1$, $3 \wedge 4 \Rightarrow 2$, $3 \wedge 5 \Rightarrow 1$, etc.

75. This function is 1 at only two points, which are complementary. So it is indecomposable; yet the pairs (58) are *never* bad when $n > 3$. Every partition (Y, Z) will therefore be a candidate for decomposition.

Similarly, if f is decomposable with respect to (Y, Z), the indecomposable function $f(x) \oplus S_{0,n}(x)$ will act essentially like f in the tests. (A method to deal with *approximately decomposable functions* should probably be provided in a general-purpose decomposability tester.)

76. (a) Let $a_l = [i \geq l]$ for $0 \leq l \leq 2^m$. The cost is $\leq 2t(m)$, as observed in answer 38(b); and in fact, the cost can be reduced to $2^{m+1} - 2m - 2$ with $\Theta(m)$ depth. Furthermore the function $[i \leq j] = (\bar{\imath}_1 \wedge j_1) \vee ((i_1 \equiv j_1) \wedge [i_2 \ldots i_m \leq j_2 \ldots j_m])$ can be evaluated with $4m - 3$ gates. After computing $x \oplus y$, each z_l costs $2^{m+1} + 1 = O(n)$.

(b) Here the cost is at most $C(g_0) + \cdots + C(g_{2^m}) \leq (2^m + 1)(2^{2^m}/(2^m - O(m)))$ by Theorem L, because each g_l is a function of 2^m inputs.

(c) If $i \leq j$ we have $z_l = x$ for $l \leq i$ and $z_l = y$ for $l > i$; hence $f_i(x) = c_0 \oplus \cdots \oplus c_i$ and $f_j(y) = c_{j+1} \oplus \cdots \oplus c_{2^m}$. If $i > j$ we have $z_l = y$ for $l \leq i$ and $z_l = x$ for $l > i$; hence $f_j(y) = c_0 \oplus \cdots \oplus c_j$ and $f_i(x) = c_{i+1} \oplus \cdots \oplus c_{2^m}$.

(d) The functions $b_l = [j < l]$ can be computed for $0 \leq l \leq 2^m$ in $O(2^m)$ steps, as in (a). So we can compute F from $(c_0, \ldots, c_{2^m})$ with $O(2^m)$ further gates. Step (b) therefore dominates the cost, for large m.

(e) $a_0 = 1$, $a_1 = i$, $a_2 = 0$; $b_0 = 0$, $b_1 = j$, $b_2 = 1$; $d = [i \leq j] = \bar{\imath} \vee j$; $m_l = a_l \oplus d$, $z_{l0} = x_0 \oplus (m_l \wedge (x_0 \oplus y_0))$, $z_{l1} = x_1 \oplus (m_l \wedge (x_1 \oplus y_1))$, for $l = 0, 1, 2$; $c_0 = z_{01}$; $c_1 = z_{10} \wedge \bar{z}_{11}$; $c_2 = z_{20} \vee z_{21}$; $c'_l = c_l \wedge (d \equiv a_l)$, $c''_l = c_l \wedge (d \equiv b_l)$, for $l = 0, 1, 2$; and finally $F = (c'_0 \oplus c'_1 \oplus c'_2) \vee (c''_0 \oplus c''_1 \oplus c''_2)$.

The net cost (29 after obvious simplifications) is, of course, outrageous in such a small example. But one wonders if a state-of-the-art automatic optimizer would be able to reduce this chain to just 5 gates.

[This result is a special case of more general theorems in *Matematicheskie Zametki* **15** (1974), 937–944; *London Math. Soc. Lecture Note Series* **169** (1992), 165–173.]

77. Given a shortest such chain for f_n or $\bar{f}_n$, let $U_l = \{i \mid l = j(i) \text{ or } l = k(i)\}$ be the "uses" of x_l, and let $u_l = |U_l|$. Let $t_i = 1$ if $x_i = x_{j(i)} \vee x_{k(i)}$, otherwise $t_i = 0$. We will show that there's a chain of length $\leq r - 4$ that computes either f_{n-1} or $\bar{f}_{n-1}$, by using the following idea: If variable x_m is set to 0 or 1, for any m, we can obtain a chain for f_{n-1} or $\bar{f}_{n-1}$ by deleting all steps of U_m and modifying other steps appropriately. Furthermore, if $x_i = x_{j(i)} \circ x_{k(i)}$ and if either $x_{j(i)}$ or $x_{k(i)}$ is known to equal t_i when x_m has been set to 0 or 1, then we can also delete the steps U_i. (Throughout this argument, the letter m will stand for an index in the range $1 \leq m \leq n$.)

Case 1: $u_m = 1$ for some m. This case cannot occur in a shortest chain. For if the only use of x_m is $x_i = \bar{x}_m$, eliminating this step would change $f_n \leftrightarrow \bar{f}_n$; and otherwise we could set the values of $x_1, \ldots, x_{m-1}, x_{m+1}, \ldots, x_n$ to make x_i independent of x_m, contradicting $x_{n+r} = f_n$ or $\bar{f}_n$. Thus every variable must be used at least twice.

Case 2: $x_l = \bar{x}_m$ for some l and m, where $u_m > 1$. Then $x_i = x_l \circ x_k$ for some i and k, and we can set $x_m \leftarrow \bar{t}_i$ to make x_i independent of x_k. Eliminating steps U_m, U_l, and U_i then removes at least 4 steps, except when $u_l = u_i = 1$ and $u_m = 2$ and $x_j = x_m \circ x_i$; but in that case we can also eliminate U_j.

Case 3: $u_m \geq 3$ for some m, and not Case 2. If $i, j, k \in U_m$ and $i < j < k$, set $x_m \leftarrow t_k$ and remove steps i, j, k, U_k.

Case 4: $u_1 = u_2 = \cdots = u_n = 2$, and not Case 2. We may assume that the first step is $x_{n+1} = x_1 \circ x_2$, and that $x_l = x_1 \circ x_k$ for some $k < l$.

Case 4.1: $k > n$. Then $k > n+1$. If $u_k = 1$, set $x_1 \leftarrow t_l$ and remove steps $n+1$, k, l, U_l. Otherwise set $x_2 \leftarrow t_{n+1}$; this forces $x_k = \bar{t}_l$, and we can remove $n+1$, k, l, U_k.

Case 4.2: $x_l = x_1 \circ x_m$. Then we must have $m = 2$; for if $m > 2$ we could set $x_2 \leftarrow t_{n+1}$, $x_m \leftarrow t_l$, and make x_{n+r} independent of x_1. Hence we may assume that $x_{n+1} = x_1 \wedge x_2$, $x_{n+2} = x_1 \vee x_2$. Setting $x_1 \leftarrow 0$ allows us to remove U_1 and U_{n+1}; setting $x_1 \leftarrow 1$ allows us to remove U_1 and U_{n+2}. Thus we're done unless $u_{n+1} = u_{n+2} = 1$.

If $x_p = \bar{x}_{n+1}$, set $x_1 \leftarrow 0$ and remove $n+1$, $n+2$, p, U_p; if $x_q = \bar{x}_{n+2}$, set $x_1 \leftarrow 1$ and remove $n+1$, $n+2$, q, U_q. Otherwise $x_p = x_{n+1} \circ x_u$ and $x_q = x_{n+2} \circ x_v$, where x_u and x_v do not depend on x_1 or x_2. But that's impossible; it would allow us to set x_3, ..., x_n to make $x_u = t_p$, then $x_2 \leftarrow 1$ to make x_{n+r} independent of x_1.

[*Problemy Kibernetiki* **23** (1970), 83–101; **28** (1974), 4. With similar proofs, Red'kin showed that the shortest AND-OR-NOT chains for the functions $[x_1 \ldots x_n < y_1 \ldots y_n]$ and $[x_1 \ldots x_n = y_1 \ldots y_n]$ have lengths $5n-3$ and $5n-1$, respectively.]

78. [*SICOMP* **6** (1977), 427–430.] Say that y_k is *active* if $k \in S$. We may assume that the chain is normal and that $\|S\| > 1$; the proof is like Red'kin's in answer 77:

Case 1: Some active y_k is used more than once. Setting $y_k \leftarrow 0$ saves at least two steps and yields a chain for a function with $\|S\| - 1$ active values.

Case 2: Some active y_k appears only in an AND gate. Setting $y_k \leftarrow 0$ eliminates at least two steps, unless this AND is the final step. But it can't be the final step, because $y_k = 0$ makes the result independent of every other active y_j.

Case 3: Like Case 2 but with an OR or NOTBUT or BUTNOT gate. Setting $y_k \leftarrow c$ for some appropriate constant c has the desired effect.

Case 4: Like Case 2 but with XOR. The gate can't be final, since the result should be independent of y_k when $(x_1 \ldots x_m)_2$ addresses a different active value y_j. So we can eliminate two steps by setting y_k to the function defined by the *other* input to XOR.

79. (a) Suppose the cost is $r < 2n-2$; then $n > 1$. If each variable is used exactly once, two leaves must be mates. Therefore some variable is used at least twice. Pruning it away produces a chain of cost $\le r-2$ on $n-1$ variables, having no mates.

(Incidentally, the cost is at least $2n-1$ if every variable is used at least twice, because at least $2n$ uses of variables must be connected together in the chain.)

(b) Notice that $S_{0,n} = \bigwedge_{u-v}(u \equiv v)$ whenever the edges $u - v$ form a free tree on $\{x_1, \ldots, x_n\}$. So there are many ways to achieve cost $2n-3$.

Any chain of cost $r < 2n-3$ must have $n > 2$ and must contain mates u and v. By renaming and possibly complementing intermediate results, we can assume that $u = 1$, $v = 2$, and that $f(x_1, \ldots, x_n) = g(x_1 \circ h(x_3, \ldots, x_n), x_2, \ldots, x_n)$, where $\circ$ is $\wedge$ or $\oplus$.

Case 1: $\circ$ is AND. We must have $h(0, \ldots, 0) = h(1, \ldots, 1) = 1$, for otherwise $f(x_1, x_2, y, \ldots, y)$ wouldn't depend on x_1. Therefore $f(x_1, \ldots, x_n) = h(x_3, \ldots, x_n) \wedge g(x_1, x_2, \ldots, x_n)$ can be computed by a chain of the same cost in which 1 and 2 are mates and in which the path between them has gotten shorter.

Case 2: $\circ$ is XOR. Then $f = f_0 \vee f_1$, where $f_0(x_1, \ldots, x_n) = (x_1 \equiv h(x_3, \ldots, x_n)) \wedge g(0, x_2, \ldots, x_n)$ and $f_1(x_1, \ldots, x_n) = (x_1 \oplus h(x_3, \ldots, x_n)) \wedge g(1, x_2, \ldots, x_n)$. But $f = S_{0,n}$ has only two prime implicants; so there are only four possibilities:

Case 2a: $f_0 = f$. Then we can replace $x_1 \oplus h$ by 0, to get a chain of cost $\le r-2$ for the function $g(0, x_2, \ldots, x_n) = S_{0,n-1}(x_2, \ldots, x_n)$.

Case 2b: $f_1 = f$. Similar to Case 2a.

Case 2c: $f_0(x) = x_1 \wedge \cdots \wedge x_n$ and $f_1(x) = \bar{x}_1 \wedge \cdots \wedge \bar{x}_n$. In this case we must have $g(0, x_2, \ldots, x_n) = x_2 \wedge \cdots \wedge x_n$ and $g(1, x_2, \ldots, x_n) = \bar{x}_2 \wedge \cdots \wedge \bar{x}_n$. Replacing h by 1 therefore yields a chain that computes f in $< r$ steps.

Case 2d: $f_0(x) = \bar{x}_1 \wedge \cdots \wedge \bar{x}_n$ and $f_1(x) = x_1 \wedge \cdots \wedge x_n$. Similar to Case 2c.

Applying these reductions repeatedly will lead to a contradiction. Similarly, one can show that $C(S_0 S_n) = 2n - 2$. [*Theoretical Computer Science* **1** (1976), 289–295.]

80. (a) Without loss of generality, $a_0 = 0$ and the chain is normal. Define U_l and u_l as in answer 77. We may assume by symmetry that $u_1 = \max(u_1, \ldots, u_n)$.

We must have $u_1 \geq 2$. For if $u_1 = 1$, we could assume further that $x_{n+1} = x_1 \circ x_2$; hence two of the three functions $S_\alpha(0, 0, x_3, \ldots, x_n) = S_{\alpha''}$, $S_\alpha(0, 1, x_3, \ldots, x_n) = S_{'\alpha'}$, $S_\alpha(1, 1, x_3, \ldots, x_n) = S_{''\alpha}$ would be equal. But then S_α would be a parity function, or $S_{'\alpha'}$ would be constant.

Therefore setting $x_1 \leftarrow 0$ allows us to eliminate the gates of U_1, giving a chain for $S_{\alpha'}$ with at least 2 fewer gates. It follows that $C(S_\alpha) \geq C(S_{\alpha'}) + 2$. Similarly, setting $x_1 \leftarrow 1$ proves that $C(S_\alpha) \geq C(S_{'\alpha}) + 2$.

Three cases arise when we explore the situation further:

Case 1: $u_1 \geq 3$. Setting $x_1 \leftarrow 0$ proves that $C(S_\alpha) \geq C(S_{\alpha'}) + 3$.

Case 2: $U_1 = \{i, j\}$ and operator $\circ_j$ is canalizing (namely, AND, BUTNOT, NOTBUT, or OR). Setting x_1 to an appropriate constant forces the value of x_j and allows us to eliminate $U_1 \cup U_j$; notice that $i \notin U_j$ in an optimum chain. So either $C(S_\alpha) \geq C(S_{\alpha'}) + 3$ or $C(S_\alpha) \geq C(S_{'\alpha}) + 3$.

Case 3: $U_1 = \{i, j\}$ and $\circ_i = \circ_j = \oplus$. We may assume that $x_i = x_1 \oplus x_2$ and $x_j = x_1 \oplus x_k$. If $u_j = 1$ and $x_l = x_j \oplus x_p$, we can restructure the chain by letting $x_j = x_k \oplus x_p$, $x_l = x_1 \oplus x_j$; therefore we can assume that either $u_j \neq 1$ or $x_l = x_j \circ x_p$ for some canalizing operator $\circ$. If $U_2 = \{i, j'\}$, we can assume similarly that $x_{j'} = x_2 \oplus x_{k'}$ and that either $u_{j'} \neq 1$ or $x_{l'} = x_{j'} \circ' x_{p'}$ for some canalizing operator $\circ'$. Furthermore we can assume by symmetry that x_j does not depend on $x_{j'}$.

If x_k does not depend on x_i, let $f(x_3, \ldots, x_n) = x_k$; otherwise let $f(x_3, \ldots, x_n)$ be the value of x_k when $x_i = 1$. By setting $x_1 \leftarrow f(x_3, \ldots, x_n)$ and $x_2 \leftarrow \bar{f}(x_3, \ldots, x_n)$, or vice versa, we make x_i and x_j constant, and we obtain a chain for the nonconstant function $S_{\alpha'}$. We can, in fact, ensure that x_l is constant in the case $u_j = 1$. We claim that at least five gates of this chain (including x_i and x_j) can be eliminated; hence $C(S_\alpha) \geq C(S_{\alpha'}) + 5$. The claim is clearly true if $|U_i \cup U_j| \geq 3$.

We must have $|U_i \cup U_j| > 1$. Otherwise we'd have $p = i$, and x_k would not depend on x_i, so S_α would be independent of x_1 with our choice of x_2. Therefore $|U_i \cup U_j| = 2$.

Case 3a: $U_j = \{l\}$. Then x_l is constant; we can eliminate x_i, x_j, and $U_i \cup U_j \cup U_l$. If the latter set contains only two elements, then $x_q = x_i \circ x_l$ is also constant and we eliminate U_q. Since $S_{\alpha'}$ isn't constant, we won't eliminate the output gate.

Case 3b: $U_i \subseteq U_j$, $|U_j| = 2$. Then $x_q = x_i \circ x_j$ for some q; we can eliminate x_i, x_j, and $U_j \cup U_q$. The claim has been proved.

(b) By induction, $C(S_k) \geq 2n + \min(k, n - k) - 3 - [n = 2k]$, for $0 < k < n$; $C(S_{\geq k}) \geq 2n + \min(k, n + 1 - k) - 4$, for $1 < k < n$. The easy cases are $C(S_0) = C(S_n) = C(S_{\geq 1}) = C(S_{\geq n}) = n - 1$; $C(S_{\geq 0}) = 0$. (According to Figs. 9 and 10, these bounds are optimum when $n = 4$ except for S_1, S_3, $S_{\geq 2}$, and $S_{\geq 3}$, and optimum when $n = 5$ except for S_1, S_4, $S_{\geq 2}$, and $S_{\geq 4}$. All known results are consistent with the conjecture that $C(S_k) = C(S_{\geq k})$ for $k > n/2$.)

Reference: Mathematical Systems Theory **10** (1977), 323–336.

81. If some variable is used more than once, we can set it to a constant, decreasing n by 1 and decreasing c by ≥ 2. Otherwise the first operation must involve x_1, because $y_1 = x_1$ is the only output that doesn't need computation; making x_1 constant decreases n by 1, c by ≥ 1, and d by ≥ 1. [*J. Algorithms* **7** (1986), 185–201.]

82. (62) is false.

(63) reads, "For all numbers m there's a number n such that $m < n + 1$"; it is true because we can take $m = n$.

(64) fails when $n = 0$ or $n = 1$, because the numbers in these formulas are required to be nonnegative integers.

(65) says that, if b exceeds a by 2 or more, there's a number ab between them. Of course it's true, because we can let $ab = a + 1$.

(66) was explained in the text, and it too is true. Notice that '$\wedge$' takes precedence over '$\vee$' and '$\equiv$' takes precedence over '$\Leftrightarrow$', just as '$+$' takes precedence over '$\geq$' and '$<$' over '$\wedge$' in (65); these conventions reduce the need for parentheses in sentences of L.

(67) says that, if A contains at least one element n, it must contain a minimum element m (an element that's less than or equal to all of its elements). True.

(68) is similar, but m is now a maximum element. Again true, because all sets are assumed to be finite.

(69) asks for a set P with the property that $[0 \in P] = [3 \notin P]$, $[1 \in P] = [4 \notin P]$, ..., $[999 \in P] = [1002 \notin P]$, $[1000 \in P] \neq [1003 \notin P]$, $[1001 \in P] \neq [1004 \notin P]$, etc. It's true if (and only if) $P = \{x \mid x \bmod 6 \in \{1, 2, 3\}$ and $0 \leq x < 1000\}$.

Finally, the subformula $\forall n \, (n \in C \Leftrightarrow n + 1 \in C)$ in (70) is another way of saying that $C = \emptyset$, because C is finite. Hence the parenthesized formula after $\forall A \, \forall B$ is a tricky way to say that $A = \emptyset$ and $B \neq \emptyset$. (Stockmeyer and Meyer used this trick to abbreviate statements in L that involve long subformulas more than once.) Statement (70) is true because an empty set doesn't equal a nonempty set.

83. We can assume that the chain is normal. Let the canalizing steps be $y_1, \ldots, y_p$. Then $y_k = \alpha_k \circ \beta_k$ and $f = \alpha_{p+1}$, where α_k and β_k are $\oplus$'s of some subsets of $\{x_1, \ldots, x_n, y_1, \ldots, y_{k-1}\}$; at most $n + k - 2$ $\oplus$'s are needed to compute them, combining common terms first. Hence $C(f) \leq p + \sum_{k=1}^{p+1} (n + k - 2) = (p + 1)(n + p/2) - 1$.

84. Argue as in the previous answer, with $\vee$ or $\wedge$ in place of $\oplus$. [N. Alon and R. B. Boppana, *Combinatorica* **7** (1987), 15–16.]

85. (a) A simple computer program shows that 13744 are legitimate and 19024 aren't. (An illegitimate family of this kind has at least 8 members; one such is $\{00, 0f, 33, 55, ff, 15, 3f, 77\}$. Indeed, if the functions $x_1 \vee x_2$ (3f), $x_2 \vee x_3$ (77), and $(x_1 \vee x_2) \wedge x_3$ (15) are present in a legitimate family L, then $x_2 \sqcup 15 = 33 \mid 15 = 37$ must also be in L.)

(b) The projection and constant functions are obviously present. Define $A^* = \bigcap \{B \mid B \supseteq A$ and $B \in \mathcal{A}\}$, or $A^* = \infty$ if no such set B exists. Then we have $\lceil A \rceil \sqcap \lceil B \rceil = \lceil A \cap B \rceil$ and $\lceil A \rceil \sqcup \lceil B \rceil = \lceil (A \cup B)^* \rceil$.

(c) Abbreviate the formulas as $\hat{x}_l \subseteq x_l \vee \bigvee_{i=n+1}^{l} \delta_i$, $x_l \subseteq \hat{x}_l \vee \bigvee_{i=n+1}^{l} \epsilon_i$, and argue by induction: If step l is an AND step, $\hat{x}_l = \hat{x}_j \sqcap \hat{x}_k \subseteq \hat{x}_j \wedge \hat{x}_k \subseteq (x_j \vee \bigvee_{i=n+1}^{l} \delta_i) \wedge (x_k \vee \bigvee_{i=n+1}^{l} \delta_i) = x_l \vee \bigvee_{i=n+1}^{l} \delta_i$; $x_l = x_j \wedge x_k \subseteq (\hat{x}_j \vee \bigvee_{i=n+1}^{l-1} \epsilon_i) \wedge (\hat{x}_k \vee \bigvee_{i=n+1}^{l-1} \epsilon_i) = (\hat{x}_j \wedge \hat{x}_k) \vee \bigvee_{i=n+1}^{l-1} \epsilon_i$, and $\hat{x}_j \wedge \hat{x}_k = \hat{x}_l \vee \epsilon_l$. Argue similarly if step l is an OR step.

86. (a) If S is an r-family contained in the $(r + 1)$-family S', clearly $\Delta(S) \subseteq \Delta(S')$.

(b) By the pigeonhole principle, $\Delta(S)$ contains elements u and v of each part, whenever S is an r-family. And if $\Delta(S) = \{u, v\}$, we certainly have $u \mathbin{\text{—}} v$.

(c) The result is obvious when $r = 1$. There are at most $r - 1$ edges containing any given vertex u, by the "strong" property. And if $u \mathbin{\text{—}} v$, the edges *disjoint* from $\{u, v\}$ are strongly $(r - 1)$-closed; so there are at most $(r - 2)^2$ of them, by induction. Thus there are at most $1 + 2(r - 2) + (r - 2)^2$ edges altogether.

(d) Yes, by exercise 85(b), if $r > 1$, because strongly r-closed graphs are closed under intersection. All graphs with ≤ 1 edges are strongly r-closed when $r > 1$, because they have no r-families containing distinct edges.

(e) There are $\binom{n}{3}$ triangles $x_{ij} \wedge x_{ik} \wedge x_{jk}$, only $n - 2$ of which are contained in any term x_{uv} of $\hat{f}$. Hence the minterms for at most $(r-1)^2(n-2)$ triangles are contained in $\hat{f}$, and the others must be contained in the union of the terms $\epsilon_i = \hat{x}_i \oplus (\hat{x}_{j(i)} \wedge \hat{x}_{k(i)})$ for the p AND steps. Such a term has the form

$$T = (\lceil G \rceil \sqcap \lceil H \rceil) \oplus (\lceil G \rceil \wedge \lceil H \rceil) = (\lceil G \rceil \wedge \lceil H \rceil) \wedge \overline{\lceil G \sqcap H \rceil},$$

where G and H are strongly r-closed; but T contains at most $2(r-1)^3$ triangles.

Why? Because a triangle $x_{ij} \wedge x_{ik} \wedge x_{jk}$ in T must involve some variable (say x_{ij}) of $\lceil G \rceil$ and some variable (say x_{ik}) of $\lceil H \rceil$, but no variable of $\lceil G \sqcap H \rceil$. There are at most $(r-1)^2$ choices for ij; and then there are at most $2(r-1)$ choices for k, since H has at most $r - 1$ edges touching i and at most $r - 1$ edges touching j.

(f) There are 2^{n-1} complete bigraphs obtained by coloring 1 red, coloring other vertices either red or blue, and letting $u \text{---} v$ if and only if u and v have opposite colors. By the first formula in exercise 85(c), every such graph's minterms B must be contained within the terms

$$T = \delta_i = \hat{x}_i \oplus (\hat{x}_{j(i)} \vee \hat{x}_{k(i)}) = \lceil (G \cup H)^* \rceil \wedge \overline{\lceil G \cup H \rceil}.$$

(For example, if $n = 4$ and if vertices $(2, 3, 4)$ are (red, blue, blue), then $B = \bar{x}_{12} \wedge x_{13} \wedge x_{14} \wedge x_{23} \wedge x_{24} \wedge \bar{x}_{34}$.) A minterm B is contained in T if and only if, in the coloring for B, some edge of $(G \cup H)^*$ has vertices of opposite colors, but all edges of $G \cup H$ are monochromatic. We will prove that each term T includes at most $2^{n-2-r}r^2$ such B, hence $2^{n-2-r}r^2 q \geq 2^{n-1}$.

We can compute $G^* = G_t$ from any given graph G by the following (inefficient) algorithm: Set $G_0 \leftarrow G$, $t \leftarrow 0$. If G_t has an r-family S with $|\Delta(S)| < 2$, set $t \leftarrow t + 1$, $G_t \leftarrow \infty$, and stop. Otherwise, if $\Delta(S) = \{u, v\}$ and $u \neq\!\!\!- v$, set $t \leftarrow t + 1$, $G_t \leftarrow (G_{t-1}$ plus the edge $u \text{---} v)$ and repeat. Otherwise stop.

There are 2^{n-1-r} bipartite minterms B with monochromatic $\{u_j, v_j\}$ for $1 \leq j \leq r$ when $|\Delta(S)| < 2$. And when $\Delta(S) = \{u, v\}$ there are 2^{n-2-r} with monochromatic $\{u_j, v_j\}$ and bichromatic $\{u, v\}$. Hence

$$T = \lceil G^* \rceil \setminus \lceil G \rceil = (\lceil G_t \rceil \setminus \lceil G_{t-1} \rceil) \vee \cdots \vee (\lceil G_1 \rceil \setminus \lceil G_0 \rceil)$$

contains $2^{n-2-r}(t + [G^* = \infty])$ minterms B. And the algorithm stops with $t \leq (r-1)^2$.

(g) Exercise 84 tells us that $q < \binom{p}{2} + (p+1)\binom{n}{2}$. Thus we have either $2(r-1)^3 p \geq \binom{n}{3} - (r-1)^2(n-2)$ or $\binom{p}{2} + (p+1)\binom{n}{2} > 2^{r+1}/r^2$. Both lower bounds for p are

$$\geq \frac{1}{6}\left(\frac{n}{6\lg n}\right)^3 \left(1 + O\left(\frac{\log\log n}{\log n}\right)\right) \quad \text{when} \quad r = \left\lceil \lg\left(\frac{n^6}{746496(\lg n)^4}\right)\right\rceil.$$

[Noga Alon and Ravi B. Boppana, *Combinatorica* **7** (1987), 1–22, proceeded in this way to prove, among other things, the lower bound $\Omega(n/\log n)^s$ for the number of $\wedge$'s in any monotone chain that decides whether or not G has a clique of fixed size $s \geq 3$.]

87. The entries of X^3 are at most n^2 when X is a 0–1 matrix. A Boolean chain with $O(n^{\lg 7}(\log n)^2)$ gates can implement Strassen's matrix multiplication algorithm 4.6.4–(36), on integers modulo $2^{\lfloor \lg n^2 \rfloor + 1}$.

88. There are 1,422,564 such functions, in 716 classes with respect to permutation of variables. Algorithm L and the other methods of this section extend readily to ternary operations, and we obtain the following results for optimum median-only computation:

$C(f)$	Classes	Functions	$C_m(f)$	Classes	Functions	$L(f)$	Classes	Functions	$D(f)$	Classes	Functions
0	1	7	0	1	7	0	1	7	0	1	7
1	1	35	1	1	35	1	1	35	1	1	35
2	2	350	2	2	350	2	2	350	2	13	5670
3	9	3885	3	9	3885	3	8	3745	3	700	1416822
4	48	42483	4	48	42483	4	38	35203	4	1	30
5	201	406945	5	188	391384	5	139	270830	5	0	0
6	353	798686	6	253	622909	6	313	699377	6	0	0
7	99	169891	7	69	134337	7	176	367542	7	0	0
8	2	282	8	2	2520	8	34	43135	8	0	0
9	0	0	9	0	0	9	3	2310	9	0	0
10	0	0	10	0	0	10	0	0	10	0	0
11	0	0	∞	143	224654	11	1	30	11	0	0

S. Amarel, G. E. Cooke, and R. O. Winder [*IEEE Trans.* **EC-13** (1964), 4–13, Fig. 5b] conjectured that the 9-operation formula

$$\langle x_1 x_2 x_3 x_4 x_5 x_6 x_7 \rangle = \langle x_1 \langle\langle x_2 x_3 x_5 \rangle \langle x_2 x_4 x_6 \rangle \langle x_3 x_4 x_7 \rangle\rangle \langle\langle x_2 x_5 x_6 \rangle \langle x_3 x_5 x_7 \rangle \langle x_4 x_6 x_7 \rangle\rangle\rangle$$

is the best way to compute medians-of-7 via medians-of-3. But the "magic" formula

$$\langle x_1 \langle x_2 \langle x_3 x_4 x_5 \rangle \langle x_3 x_6 x_7 \rangle\rangle \langle x_4 \langle x_2 x_6 x_7 \rangle \langle x_3 x_5 \langle x_5 x_6 x_7 \rangle\rangle\rangle\rangle$$

needs only 8 operations; and in fact the shortest chain needs just seven steps:

$$\langle x_1 x_2 x_3 x_4 x_5 x_6 x_7 \rangle = \langle x_1 \langle x_2 \langle x_5 x_6 x_7 \rangle \langle x_3 \langle x_5 x_6 x_7 \rangle x_4 \rangle\rangle \langle x_5 \langle x_2 x_3 x_4 \rangle \langle x_6 \langle x_2 x_3 x_4 \rangle x_7 \rangle\rangle\rangle.$$

The interesting function $f(x_1,\ldots,x_7) = (x_1 \wedge x_2 \wedge x_4) \vee (x_2 \wedge x_3 \wedge x_5) \vee (x_3 \wedge x_4 \wedge x_6) \vee (x_4 \wedge x_5 \wedge x_7) \vee (x_5 \wedge x_6 \wedge x_1) \vee (x_6 \wedge x_7 \wedge x_2) \vee (x_7 \wedge x_1 \wedge x_3)$, whose prime implicants correspond to the projective plane with 7 points, is the toughest of all: Its minimum length $L(f) = 11$ and minimum depth $D(f) = 4$ are achieved by the remarkable formula

$$\langle\langle\langle x_1 x_4 \langle x_4 x_5 x_6 \rangle\rangle \langle x_3 x_6 \langle x_1 \langle x_2 x_3 x_7 \rangle \langle x_2 x_5 x_6 \rangle\rangle\rangle \langle x_2 x_7 \langle x_1 \langle x_5 x_2 x_4 \rangle \langle x_5 x_3 x_7 \rangle\rangle\rangle\rangle.$$

And the following even more astonishing chain computes it optimally:

$$x_8 = \langle x_1 x_2 x_3 \rangle, \quad x_9 = \langle x_1 x_4 x_6 \rangle, \quad x_{10} = \langle x_1 x_5 x_8 \rangle, \quad x_{11} = \langle x_2 x_7 x_8 \rangle,$$
$$x_{12} = \langle x_3 x_9 x_{10} \rangle, \quad x_{13} = \langle x_4 x_5 x_{12} \rangle, \quad x_{14} = \langle x_6 x_{11} x_{12} \rangle, \quad x_{15} = \langle x_7 x_{13} x_{14} \rangle.$$

SECTION 7.1.3

1. These operations interchange the bits of x and y in positions where m is 1. (In particular, if $m = -1$, the step '$y \leftarrow y \oplus (x \mathbin{\&} m)$' becomes just '$y \leftarrow y \oplus x$', and the three assignments will swap $x \leftrightarrow y$ without needing an auxiliary register. H. S. Warren, Jr., has located this trick in vintage-1961 IBM programming course notes.)

2. All three hold when x and y are nonnegative, or if we regard x and y as "unsigned 2-adic integers" in which $0 < 1 < 2 < \cdots < -3 < -2 < -1$. But if negative integers are less than nonnegative integers, (i) fails if and only if $x < 0$ and $y < 0$; (ii) and (iii) fail if and only if $x \oplus y < 0$, namely, if and only if $x < 0$ and $y \geq 0$ or $x \geq 0$ and $y < 0$.

3. Note that $x - y = (x \oplus y) - 2(\bar{x} \mathbin{\&} y)$ (see exercise 93). By removing bits common to x and y at the left, we may assume that $x_{n-1} = 1$ and $y_{n-1} = 0$. Then $2(\bar{x} \mathbin{\&} y) \leq 2((x \oplus y) - 2^{n-1}) = (x \oplus y) - (x \oplus y)^M - 1$.

4. $x^{CN} = x + 1 = x^S$, by (16). Hence $x^{NC} = x^{NCSP} = x^{NCCNP} = x^{NNP} = x^P$.

5. (a) Disproof: Let $x = (\dots x_2x_1x_0)_2$. Then bit l of $x \ll k$ is $x_{l-k}[l \geq k]$. So bit l of the left-hand side is $x_{l-k-j}[l \geq k][l - k \geq j]$, while bit l of the right-hand side is $x_{l-j-k}[l \geq j + k]$. These expressions agree if $j \geq 0$ or $k \leq 0$. But if $j < 0 < k$, they differ when $l = \max(0, j + k)$ and $x_{l-j-k} = 1$.

(We do, however, have $(x \ll j) \ll k \subseteq x \ll (j + k)$ in all cases.)

(b) Proof: Bit l in all three formulas is $x_{l+j}[l \geq -j] \wedge y_{l-k}[l \geq k]$.

6. Since $x \ll y \geq 0$ if and only if $x \geq 0$, we must have $x \geq 0$ if and only if $y \geq 0$. Obviously $x = y$ is always a solution. The solutions with $x > y$ are (a) $x = -1$ and $y = -2$, or $2^y > x > y > 0$; (b) $x = 2$ and $y = 1$, or $2^{-x} \geq -y > -x > 0$.

7. Set $x' \leftarrow (x + \bar{\mu}_0) \oplus \bar{\mu}_0$, where μ_0 is the constant in (47). Then $x' = (\dots x_2'x_1'x_0')_2$, since $(x' \oplus \bar{\mu}_0) - \bar{\mu}_0 = (\dots \bar{x}_3'x_2'\bar{x}_1'x_0')_2 - (\dots 1010)_2 = (\dots 0x_2'0x_0')_2 - (\dots x_3'0x_1'0)_2 = x$.

[This is Hack 128 in HAKMEM; see answer 20 below. An alternative formula, $x' \leftarrow (\mu_0 - x) \oplus \mu_0$, has also been suggested by D. P. Agrawal, *IEEE Trans.* **C-29** (1980), 1032–1035. The results are correct modulo 2^n for all n, but overflow or underflow can occur. For example, two's complement binary numbers in an n-bit register range from -2^{n-1} to $2^{n-1} - 1$, inclusive, but negabinary numbers range from $-\frac{2}{3}(2^n - 1)$ to $\frac{1}{3}(2^n - 1)$ when n is even. In general the formula $x' \leftarrow (x + \mu) \oplus \mu$ converts from binary notation to the general number system with binary basis $\langle 2^n(-1)^{m_n} \rangle$ discussed in exercise 4.1–30(c), when $\mu = (\dots m_2m_1m_0)_2$.]

8. First, $x \oplus y \notin (S \oplus y) \cup (x \oplus T)$. Second, suppose that $0 \leq k < x \oplus y$, and let $x \oplus y = (\alpha 1\alpha')_2$, $k = (\alpha 0\alpha'')_2$, where α, α', and α'' are strings of 0s and 1s with $|\alpha'| = |\alpha''|$. Assume by symmetry that $x = (\beta 1\beta')_2$ and $y = (\gamma 0\gamma')_2$, where $|\alpha'| = |\beta'| = |\gamma'|$. Then $k \oplus y = (\beta 0\gamma'')_2$ is less than x. Hence $k \oplus y \in S$, and $k = (k \oplus y) \oplus y \in S \oplus y$. [See R. P. Sprague, *Tôhoku Math. J.* **41** (1936), 438–444; P. M. Grundy, *Eureka* **2** (1939), 6–8.]

9. The Sprague–Grundy theorem in the previous exercise shows that two piles of x and y sticks are equivalent in play to a single pile of $x \oplus y$ sticks. (There is a nonnegative integer $k < x \oplus y$ if and only if there either is a nonnegative $i < x$ with $i \oplus y < x \oplus y$ or a nonnegative $j < y$ with $x \oplus j < x \oplus y$.) So the k piles are equivalent to a single pile of size $a_1 \oplus \cdots \oplus a_k$. [See C. L. Bouton, *Annals of Math.* (2) **3** (1901–1902), 35–39.]

10. For clarity and brevity we shall write simply xy for $x \otimes y$ and $x + y$ for $x \oplus y$, *in parts (i) through (iv) of this answer only.*

(i) Clearly $0y = 0$ and $x + y = y + x$ and $xy = yx$. Also $1y = y$, by induction on y.

(ii) If $x \neq x'$ and $y \neq y'$ then $xy + xy' + x'y + x'y' \neq 0$, because the definition of xy says that $xy' + x'y + x'y' \neq xy$ when $0 \leq x' < x$ and $0 \leq y' < y$. In particular, if $x \neq 0$ and $y \neq 0$ then $xy \neq 0$. Another consequence is that, if $x = \text{mex}(S)$ and $y = \text{mex}(T)$ for arbitrary finite sets S and T, we have $xy = \text{mex}\{xj + iy + ij \mid i \in S, j \in T\}$.

(iii) Consequently, by induction on the (ordinary) sum of x, y, and z, $(x + y)z$ is

$$\text{mex}\{(x + y)z' + (x' + y)z + (x' + y)z', (x + y)z' + (x + y')z + (x + y')z'$$
$$\mid 0 \leq x' < x, \ 0 \leq y' < y, \ 0 \leq z' < z\},$$

which is $\text{mex}\{xz' + x'z + x'z' + yz, xz + yz' + y'z + y'z'\} = xz + yz$. In particular, there's a cancellation law: If $xz = yz$ then $(x + y)z = 0$, so $x = y$ or $z = 0$.

(iv) By a similar induction, $(xy)z = \text{mex}\{(xy)z' + (xy' + x'y + x'y')(z + z')\} = \text{mex}\{(xy)z' + (xy')z + (xy')z' + \cdots\} = \text{mex}\{x(yz') + x(y'z) + x(y'z') + \cdots\} = \text{mex}\{(x + x')(yz' + y'z + y'z') + x'(yz)\} = x(yz)$.

(v) If $0 \leq x, y < 2^{2^n}$ we shall prove that $x \otimes y < 2^{2^n}$, $2^{2^n} \otimes y = 2^{2^n}y$, and $2^{2^n} \otimes 2^{2^n} = \frac{3}{2}2^{2^n}$. By the distributive law (iii) it suffices to consider the case $x = 2^a$

and $y = 2^b$ for $0 \le a, b < 2^n$. Let $a = 2^p + a'$ and $b = 2^q + b'$, where $0 \le a' < 2^p$ and $0 \le b' < 2^q$; then $x = 2^{2^p} \otimes 2^{a'}$ and $y = 2^{2^q} \otimes 2^{b'}$, by induction on n.

If $p < n-1$ and $q < n-1$ we've already proved that $x \otimes y < 2^{2^{n-1}}$. If $p < q = n-1$, then $x \otimes 2^{b'} < 2^{2^q}$, hence $x \otimes y < 2^{2^n}$. And if $p = q = n-1$, we have $x \otimes y = 2^{2^p} \otimes 2^{2^p} \otimes 2^{a'} \otimes 2^{b'} = (\frac{3}{2}2^{2^p}) \otimes z$, where $z < 2^{2^p}$. Thus $x \otimes y < 2^{2^n}$ in all cases.

By the cancellation law, the nonnegative integers less than 2^{2^n} form a subfield. Hence in the formula

$$2^{2^n} \otimes y = \operatorname{mex}\{2^{2^n}y' \oplus x'(y \oplus y') \mid 0 \le x' < 2^{2^n}, 0 \le y' < y\}$$

we can choose x' for each y' to exclude all numbers between $2^{2^n}y'$ and $2^{2^n}(y'+1) - 1$; but $2^{2^n}y$ is never excluded.

Finally in $2^{2^n} \otimes 2^{2^n} = \operatorname{mex}\{2^{2^n}(x' \oplus y') \oplus (x' \otimes y') \mid 0 \le x', y' < 2^{2^n}\}$, choosing $x' = y'$ will exclude all numbers up to and including $2^{2^n} - 1$, since $x \otimes x = y \otimes y$ implies that $(x \oplus y) \otimes (x \oplus y) = 0$, hence $x = y$. Choosing $x' = y' \oplus 1$ excludes numbers from 2^{2^n} to $\frac{3}{2}2^{2^n} - 1$, since $(x \otimes x) \oplus x = (y \otimes y) \oplus y$ implies that $x = y$ or $x = y \oplus 1$, and since the most significant bit of $x \otimes x$ is the same as that of x. This same observation shows that $\frac{3}{2}2^{2^n}$ is *not* excluded. QED.

Consider, for example, the subfield $\{0, 1, \ldots, 15\}$. By the distributive law we can reduce $x \otimes y$ to a sum of $x \otimes 1$, $x \otimes 2$, $x \otimes 4$, and/or $x \otimes 8$. We have $2 \otimes 2 = 3$, $2 \otimes 4 = 8$, $4 \otimes 4 = 6$; and multiplication by 8 can be done by multiplying first by 2 and then by 4 or vice versa, because $8 = 2 \otimes 4$. Thus $2 \otimes 8 = 12$, $4 \otimes 8 = 11$, $8 \otimes 8 = 13$.

In general, for $n > 0$, let $n = 2^m + r$ where $0 \le r < 2^m$. There is a $2^{m+1} \times 2^{m+1}$ matrix Q_n such that multiplication by 2^n is equivalent to applying Q_n to blocks of 2^{m+1} bits and working mod 2. For example, $Q_1 = \binom{1\,1}{1\,0}$, and $(\ldots x_4x_3x_2x_1x_0)_2 \otimes 2^1 = (\ldots y_4y_3y_2y_1y_0)_2$, where $y_0 = x_1$, $y_1 = x_1 \oplus x_0$, $y_2 = x_3$, $y_3 = x_3 \oplus x_2$, $y_4 = x_5$, etc. The matrices are formed recursively as follows: Let $Q_0 = R_0 = (1)$ and

$$Q_{2^m + r} = \begin{pmatrix} I & R_m \\ I & 0 \end{pmatrix} \begin{pmatrix} Q_r & & 0 \\ & \ddots & \\ 0 & & Q_r \end{pmatrix}, \qquad R_{m+1} = \begin{pmatrix} R_m & R_m^2 \\ R_m & 0 \end{pmatrix} = Q_{2^{m+1} - 1},$$

where Q_r is replicated enough times to make 2^{m+1} rows and columns. For example,

$$Q_2 = \begin{pmatrix} 1 & 0 & 1 & 1 \\ 0 & 1 & 1 & 0 \\ 1 & 0 & 0 & 0 \\ 0 & 1 & 0 & 0 \end{pmatrix}; \qquad Q_3 = Q_2 \begin{pmatrix} Q_1 & 0 \\ 0 & Q_1 \end{pmatrix} = \begin{pmatrix} 1 & 1 & 0 & 1 \\ 1 & 0 & 1 & 1 \\ 1 & 1 & 0 & 0 \\ 1 & 0 & 0 & 0 \end{pmatrix} = R_2.$$

If register x holds any 64-bit number, and if $0 \le j \le 7$, the MMIX instruction MXOR y,q$_j$,x will compute $y = x \otimes 2^j$, given the hexadecimal matrix constants

$q_0 = 8040201008040201$, $\quad q_3 = \text{d0b0c0800d0b0c08}$,

$q_1 = \text{c08030200c080302}$, $\quad q_4 = 8\text{d4b2c1880402010}$, $\qquad q_6 = \text{b9678d4bb0608040}$,

$q_2 = \text{b06080400b060804}$, $\quad q_5 = \text{c68d342cc0803020}$, $\qquad q_7 = \text{deb9c68dd0b0c080}$.

[J. H. Conway, *On Numbers and Games* (1976), Chapter 6, shows that these definitions actually yield an algebraically closed field over the ordinal numbers.]

11. Let $m = 2^{a_s} + \cdots + 2^{a_1}$ with $a_s > \cdots > a_1 \ge 0$ and $n = 2^{b_t} + \cdots + 2^{b_1}$ with $b_t > \cdots > b_1 \ge 0$. Then $m \otimes n = mn$ if and only if $(a_s \mid \cdots \mid a_1) \,\&\, (b_t \mid \cdots \mid b_1) = 0$.

12. If $x = 2^{2^n}a + b$ where $0 \le a, b < 2^{2^n}$, let $x' = x \otimes (x \oplus a)$. Then

$$x' = ((2^{2^n} \otimes a) \oplus b) \otimes ((2^{2^n} \otimes a) \oplus a \oplus b) = (2^{2^{n-1}} \otimes a \otimes a) \oplus (b \otimes (a \oplus b)) < 2^{2^n}.$$

To nim-divide by x we can therefore nim-divide by x' and multiply by $x \oplus a$. [This algorithm is due to H. W. Lenstra, Jr.; see *Séminaire de Théorie des Nombres* (Université de Bordeaux, 1977–1978), exposé 11, exercise 5.]

13. If $a_2 \oplus \cdots \oplus a_k = a_1 \oplus a_3 \oplus \cdots \oplus ((k-2) \otimes a_k) = 0$, every move breaks this condition; we can't have $(a \otimes x) \oplus (b \otimes y) = (a \otimes x') \oplus (b \otimes y')$ when $x \oplus y = x' \oplus y'$ and $a \neq b$ unless $(x, y) = (x', y')$.

Conversely, if $a_2 \oplus \cdots \oplus a_k \neq 0$ we can reduce some a_j with $j \geq 2$ to make this sum zero; then a_1 can be set to $a_3 \oplus \cdots \oplus ((k-2) \otimes a_k)$. If $a_2 \oplus \cdots \oplus a_k = 0$ and $a_1 \neq a_3 \oplus \cdots \oplus ((k-2) \otimes a_k)$, we simply reduce a_1 if it is too large. Otherwise there's a $j \geq 3$ such that equality will occur if $(j-2) \otimes a_j$ is replaced by an appropriate smaller value $((j-2) \otimes a'_j) \oplus ((i-2) \otimes (a_j \oplus a'_j))$, for some $2 \leq i < j$ and $0 \leq a'_j < a_j$, because of the definition of nim multiplication; hence both of the desired equalities are achieved by setting $a_j \leftarrow a'_j$ and $a_i \leftarrow a_i \oplus a_j \oplus a'_j$. [This game was introduced in *Winning Ways* by Berlekamp, Conway, and Guy, at the end of Chapter 14.]

14. (a) Each $y = (\ldots y_2 y_1 y_0)_2 = x^T$ determines $x = (\ldots x_2 x_1 x_0)_2$ uniquely, since $x_0 = y_0 \oplus t$ and $\lfloor y/2 \rfloor = \lfloor x/2 \rfloor^{T_{x_0}}$.

(b) When $k > 0$, it is a branching function with labels $t_{\alpha a \beta} = a$ for $|\beta| = k-1$, and $t_\alpha = 0$ for $|\alpha| < k$. But when $k \leq 0$, the mapping is not a permutation; in fact, it sends 2^{-k} different 2-adic integers into 0, when $k < 0$.

[The case $k = 1$ is particularly interesting: Then x^T takes nonnegative integers into nonnegative integers of even parity, negative integers into nonnegative integers of odd parity, and $-1/3 \mapsto -1$. Furthermore $\lfloor x^T/2 \rfloor$ is "Gray binary code," 7.2.1.1–(9).]

(c) If $\rho(x \oplus y) = k$ we have $T(x) \equiv T(y)$ and $x \equiv y + 2^k$ (modulo 2^{k+1}). Hence $\rho(x^T \oplus y^T) = \rho(x \oplus y \oplus T(x) \oplus T(y)) = k$. Conversely, if $\rho(x^T \oplus y^T) = k$ whenever $y = x + 2^k$, we obtain a suitable bit labeling by letting $t_\alpha = (x^T \gg |\alpha|) \bmod 2$ when $x = (\alpha^R)_2$.

(d) This statement follows immediately from (a) and (c). For if we always have $\rho(x \oplus y) = \rho(x^U \oplus y^U) = \rho(x^V \oplus y^V)$, then $\rho(x \oplus y) = \rho(x^U \oplus y^U) = \rho(x^{UV} \oplus y^{UV})$. And if $x^{TU} = x$ for all x, $\rho(x^U \oplus y^U) = \rho(x \oplus y)$ is equivalent to $\rho(x \oplus y) = \rho(x^T \oplus y^T)$.

We can also construct the labelings explicitly: If $W = UV$, note that when $a, b, c \in \{0, 1\}$ we have $W_a = U_a V_{a'}$, $W_{ab} = U_{ab} V_{a'b'}$, and $W_{abc} = U_{abc} V_{a'b'c'}$, where $a' = a \oplus u$, $b' = b \oplus u_a$, $c' = c \oplus u_{ab}$, and so on; hence $w = u \oplus v$, $w_a = u_a \oplus v_{a'}$, $w_{ab} = u_{ab} \oplus v_{a'b'}$, etc. The labeling T inverse to U is obtained by swapping left and right subtrees of all nodes labeled 1; thus $t = u$, $t_{a'} = u_a$, $t_{a'b'} = u_{ab}$, etc.

(e) The explicit constructions in (d) demonstrate that the balance condition is preserved by compositions and inverses, because $\{0', 1'\} = \{0, 1\}$ at each level.

Notes: Hendrik Lenstra observes that branching functions can profitably be viewed as the *isometries* (distance-preserving permutations) of the 2-adic integers, when we use the formula $1/2^{\rho(x \oplus y)}$ to define the "distance" between 2-adic integers x and y. Moreover, the branching functions mod 2^d turn out to be the Sylow 2-subgroup of the group of all permutations of $\{0, 1, \ldots, 2^d - 1\}$, namely the unique (up to isomorphism) subgroup that has maximum power-of-2 order among all subgroups of that group. They also are equivalent to the automorphisms of the complete binary tree with 2^d leaves.

15. Equivalently, $(x + 2a) \oplus b = (x \oplus b) + 2a$; so we might as well find all b and c such that $(x \oplus b) + c = (x + c) \oplus b$. Setting $x = 0$ and $x = -c$ implies that $b + c = b \oplus c$ and $b - c = b \oplus (-c)$; hence $b \& c = b \& (-c) = 0$ by (89), and we have $b < 2^{\rho c}$. This condition is also sufficient. Thus $0 \leq b < 2^{\rho a + 1}$ is necessary and sufficient for the original problem.

16. (a) If $\rho(x \oplus y) = k$ we have $x \equiv y + 2^k$ (modulo 2^{k+1}); hence $x + a \equiv y + a + 2^k$ and $\rho((x + a) \oplus (y + a)) = k$. And $\rho((x \oplus b) \oplus (y \oplus b))$ is obviously k.

(b) The hinted labeling, call it $P(c)$, has 1s on the path corresponding to c, and 0s elsewhere; thus it is balanced. The general animating function can be written

$$x^{P(c_0)^{-a_1}P(c_1)^{-a_2}\ldots P(c_{m-1})^{-a_m}} \oplus c_m, \qquad \text{where } c_j = b_1 \oplus \cdots \oplus b_j;$$

so it is balanced if and only if $c_m = 0$.

[Incidentally, the set $S = \{P(0)\} \cup \{P(k) \oplus P(k+2^e) \mid k \geq 0 \text{ and } 2^e > k\}$ provides an interesting *basis* for all possible balanced labelings: A labeling is balanced if and only if it is $\bigoplus\{q \mid q \in Q\}$ for some $Q \subseteq S$. This exclusive-or operation is well defined even though Q might be infinite, because only finitely many 1s appear at each node.]

(c) The function $P(c)$ in (b) has this form, because $x^{P(c)} = x \oplus \lfloor x \oplus c \rfloor$. Its inverse, $x^{S(c)} = ((x \oplus c) + 1) \oplus c$, is $x \oplus \lfloor x \oplus \bar{c} \rfloor = x^{P(\bar{c})}$. Furthermore we have $x^{P(c)P(d)} = x^{P(c)} \oplus \lfloor x^{P(c)} \oplus d \rfloor = x \oplus \lfloor x \oplus c \rfloor \oplus \lfloor x \oplus d^{S(c)} \rfloor$, because $\lfloor x \oplus y \rfloor = \lfloor x^T \oplus y^T \rfloor$ for any branching function x^T. Similarly $x^{P(c)P(d)P(e)} = x \oplus \lfloor x \oplus c \rfloor \oplus \lfloor x \oplus d^{S(c)} \rfloor \oplus \lfloor x \oplus e^{S(d)S(c)} \rfloor$, etc. After discarding equal terms we obtain the desired form. The resulting numbers p_j are unique because they are the only values of x at which the function changes sign.

(d) We have, for example, $x \oplus \lfloor x \oplus a \rfloor \oplus \lfloor x \oplus b \rfloor \oplus \lfloor x \oplus c \rfloor = x^{P(a')P(b')P(c')}$ where $a' = a$, $b' = b^{P(a')}$, and $c' = c^{P(a')P(b')}$.

[The theory of animating functions was developed by J. H. Conway in Chapter 13 of his book *On Numbers and Games* (1976), inspired by previous work of C. P. Welter in *Indagationes Math.* **14** (1952), 304–314; **16** (1954), 194–200.]

17. (Solution by M. Slanina.) Such equations are decidable even if we also allow operations such as $x \& y$, $\bar{x}$, $x \ll 1$, $x \gg 1$, $2^{\rho x}$, and $2^{\lambda x}$, and even if we allow Boolean combinations of statements and quantifications over integer variables, by translating them into formulas of second-order monadic logic with one successor (S1S). Each 2-adic variable $x = (\ldots x_2 x_1 x_0)_2$ corresponds to an S1S set variable X, where $j \in X$ means $x_j = 1$:

$$
\begin{aligned}
z = \bar{x} && \text{becomes} && \forall t(t \in Z \Leftrightarrow t \notin X); \\
z = x \& y && \text{becomes} && \forall t(t \in Z \Leftrightarrow (t \in X \wedge t \in Y)); \\
z = 2^{\rho x} && \text{becomes} && \forall t(t \in Z \Leftrightarrow (t \in X \wedge \forall s(s < t \Rightarrow s \notin X))); \\
z = x + y && \text{becomes} && \exists C \forall t (0 \notin C \ \wedge \ (t \in Z \Leftrightarrow (t \in X) \oplus (t \in Y) \oplus (t \in C)) \\
&& && \wedge \ (t{+}1 \in C \Leftrightarrow \langle(t \in X)(t \in Y)(t \in C)\rangle)).
\end{aligned}
$$

An identity such as $x \& (-x) = 2^{\rho x}$ is equivalent to the translation of

$$\forall X \forall Y \forall Z((\text{integer}(X) \ \wedge \ 0 = x + y \ \wedge \ z = x \& y) \ \Rightarrow \ z = 2^{\rho x}),$$

where $\text{integer}(X)$ stands for $\exists t \forall s(s > t \Rightarrow (s \in X \Leftrightarrow t \in X))$. We can also include 2-adic constants if they are, say, ratios of integers; for example, $z = \mu_0$ is equivalent to the formula $0 \in Z \wedge \forall t(t \in Z \Leftrightarrow t + 1 \notin Z)$. But of course we cannot include arbitrary (uncomputable) constants.

J. R. Büchi proved that all formulas of S1S are decidable, in *Logic, Methodology, and Philosophy of Science: Proceedings* (Stanford, 1960), 1–11. If we restrict attention to equations, one can show in fact that exponential time suffices.

On the other hand M. Hamburg has shown that the problem would be unsolvable if ρx, λx, or $1 \ll x$ were added to the repertoire; multiplication could then be encoded.

Incidentally, many nontrivial identities exist, even if we use only the operations $x \oplus y$ and $x + 1$. For example, C. P. Welter noticed in 1952 that

$$((x \oplus (y + 1)) + 1) \oplus (x + 1) \ = \ ((((x + 1) \oplus y) + 1) \oplus x) + 1.$$

18. Of course row x is entirely blank when x is a multiple of 64. The fine details of this image are apparently "chaotic" and complex, but there is a fairly easy way to understand what happens near the points where the straight lines $x = 64\sqrt{j}$ intersect the hyperbolas $xy = 2^{11}k$, for integers $j, k \geq 1$ that aren't too large.

Indeed, when x and y are integers, the value of $x^2 y \gg 11$ is odd if and only if $x^2 y/2^{12} \bmod 1 \geq \frac{1}{2}$. Thus, if $x = 64\sqrt{j} + \delta$ and $xy = 2^{11}(k + \epsilon)$ we have

$$\frac{x^2 y}{2^{12}} \bmod 1 = \left(\frac{128\sqrt{j}\delta + \delta^2}{4096}\right)y \bmod 1 = \left(\frac{2\delta x - \delta^2}{4096}\right)y \bmod 1 = \left((k + \epsilon)\delta - \frac{\delta^2 y}{4096}\right) \bmod 1,$$

and this quantity has a known relation to $\frac{1}{2}$ when, say, δ is close to a small integer. [See C. A. Pickover and A. Lakhtakia, *J. Recreational Math.* **21** (1989), 166–169.]

19. (a) When $n = 1$, $f(A, B, C)$ has the same value under all arrangements except when $a_0 \neq a_1$, $b_0 \neq b_1$, and $c_0 \neq c_1$; and then it cannot exceed 1. For larger values of n we argue by induction, assuming that $n = 3$ in order to avoid cumbersome notation. Let $A_0 = (a_0, a_1, a_2, a_3)$, $A_1 = (a_4, a_5, a_6, a_7)$, ..., $C_1 = (c_4, c_5, c_6, c_7)$. Then $f(A, B, C) = \sum_{j \oplus k \oplus l = 0} f(A_j, B_k, C_l) \leq \sum_{j \oplus k \oplus l = 0} f(A_j^*, B_k^*, C_l^*)$ by induction. Thus we can assume that $a_0 \geq a_1 \geq a_2 \geq a_3$, $a_4 \geq a_5 \geq a_6 \geq a_7$, ..., $c_4 \geq c_5 \geq c_6 \geq c_7$. We can also sort the subvectors $A_0' = (a_0, a_1, a_4, a_5)$, $A_1' = (a_2, a_3, a_6, a_7)$, ..., $C_1' = (c_2, c_3, c_6, c_7)$ in a similar way. Finally, we can sort $A_0'' = (a_0, a_1, a_6, a_7)$, $A_1'' = (a_2, a_3, a_4, a_5)$, ..., $C_1'' = (c_2, c_3, c_4, c_5)$, because in each term $a_j b_k c_l$ the number of subscripts $\{j, k, l\}$ with leading bits 01, 10, and 11 must satisfy $s_{01} \equiv s_{10} \equiv s_{11}$ (modulo 2). And these three sorting operations leave A, B, C fully sorted, by exercise 5.3.4–48. (Exactly three sorts on subvectors of length 2^{n-1} are needed, for all $n \geq 2$.)

(b) Suppose $A = A^*$, $B = B^*$, and $C = C^*$. Then we have $a_j = \sum_{t=0}^{2^n - 1} \alpha_t [j \leq t]$, where $\alpha_j = a_j - a_{j+1} \geq 0$ and we set $a_{2^n} = 0$; similar formulas hold for b_k and c_l. Let $A_{(p)}$ denote the vector $(a_{p(0)}, \ldots, a_{p(2^n - 1)})$ when p is a permutation of $\{0, 1, \ldots, 2^n - 1\}$. Then by part (a) we have

$$f(A_{(p)}, B_{(q)}, C_{(r)}) = \sum_{j \oplus k \oplus l = 0} \sum_{t, u, v} \alpha_t \beta_u \gamma_v [p(j) \leq t][q(k) \leq u][r(l) \leq v]$$
$$\leq \sum_{j \oplus k \oplus l = 0} \sum_{t, u, v} \alpha_t \beta_u \gamma_v [j \leq t][k \leq u][l \leq v] = f(A, B, C).$$

[This proof is due to Hardy, Littlewood, and Pólya, *Inequalities* (1934), §10.3.]

(c) The same proof technique extends to any number of vectors. [R. E. A. C. Paley, *Proc. London Math. Soc.* (2) **34** (1932), 265–279, Theorem 15.]

20. The given steps compute the least integer y greater than x such that $\nu y = \nu x$. They're useful for generating all combinations of n objects, taken m at a time (that is, all m-element subsets of an n-element set, with elements represented by 1 bits). [This tidbit is Hack 175 in HAKMEM, Massachusetts Institute of Technology Artificial Intelligence Laboratory Memo No. 239 (29 February 1972).]

21. Set $t \leftarrow y + 1$, $u \leftarrow t \oplus y$, $v \leftarrow t \& y$, $x \leftarrow v - (v \& -v)/(u + 1)$. If $y = 2^m - 1$ is the *first* m-combination, these eight operations set x to zero. (The fact that $x = \overline{f(\bar{y})}$ does not seem to yield any shorter scheme.)

22. Sideways addition avoids the division: `SUBU t,x,1; ANDN u,x,t; SADD k,t,x; ADDU v,x,u; XOR t,v,x; ADDU k,k,2; SRU t,t,k; ADDU y,v,t`. But we can actually save a step by judiciously using the constant `mone = -1`: `SUBU t,x,1; XOR u,x,t; ADDU y,x,u; SADD k,t,y; ANDN y,y,u; SLU t,mone,k; ORN y,y,t`.

23. (a) $(0\ldots01\ldots1)_2 = 2^m - 1$ and $(0101\ldots01)_2 = (2^{2m} - 1)/3$.

(b) This solution uses the 2-adic constant $\mu_0 = (\ldots 010101)_2 = -1/3$:

$$t \leftarrow x \oplus \mu_0, \quad u \leftarrow (t-1) \oplus t, \quad v \leftarrow x \mid u, \quad w \leftarrow v+1, \quad y \leftarrow w + \left\lfloor \frac{v \,\&\, \overline{w}}{\sqrt{u+1}} \right\rfloor.$$

If $x = (2^{2m} - 1)/3$, the operations produce a strange result because $u = 2^{2m+1} - 1$.

(c) XOR t,x,m0; SUBU u,t,1; XOR u,t,u; OR v,x,u; SADD y,u,m0; ADDU w,v,1;
ANDN t,v,w; SRU y,t,y; ADDU y,w,y. [This exercise was inspired by Jörg Arndt.]

24. It's expedient to "prime the pump" by initializing the array to the state that it should have after all multiples of 3, 5, 7, and 11 have been sieved out. We can combine 3 with 11 and 5 with 7, as suggested by E. Wada:

```
        LOC Data_Segment
qbase GREG @ ;N IS 3584 ;n GREG N ;one GREG 1
Q       OCTA #816d129a64b4cb6e                     Q0 (little-endian)
        LOC Q+N/16
qtop GREG @                                        End of the Q table
Init OCTA #9249249249249249|#4008010020040080      Multiples of 3 or 11 in [129..255]
        OCTA #8421084210842108|#0408102040810204   Multiples of 5 or 7
t IS $255 ;x33 IS $0 ;x35 IS $1 ;j IS $4
        LOC #100
Main LDOU x33,Init; LDOU x35,Init+8
        LDA j,qbase,8; SUB j,j,qtop                Prepare to set Q1.
1H      NOR t,x33,x33; ANDN t,t,x35; STOU t,qtop,j Initialize 64 sieve bits.
        SLU t,x33,2; SRU x33,x33,31; OR x33,x33,t  Prepare for the next 64 values.
        SLU t,x35,6; SRU x35,x35,29; OR x35,x35,t
        ADD j,j,8; PBN j,1B                        Repeat until reaching qtop.  ∎
```

Then we cast out nonprimes p^2, $p^2 + 2p$, ..., for $p = 13, 17, \ldots$, until $p^2 > N$:

```
p IS $0 ;pp IS $1 ;m IS $2 ;mm IS $3 ;q IS $4 ;s IS $5
        LDOU q,qbase,0; LDA pp,qbase,8
        SET p,13; NEG m,13*13,n; SRU q,q,6         Begin with p = 13.
1H      SR m,m,1                                    m ← ⌊(p² − N)/2⌋.
2H      SR mm,m,3; LDOU s,qtop,mm; AND t,m,#3f;
        SLU t,one,t; ANDN s,s,t; STOU s,qtop,mm    Zero out a bit.
        ADD m,m,p; PBN m,2B                        Advance by p bits.
        SRU q,q,1; PBNZ q,3F                       Move to next potential prime.
2H      LDOU q,pp,0; INCL pp,8                      Read in another batch
        OR p,p,#7f; PBNZ q,3F                          of potential primes.
        ADD p,p,2; JMP 2B                          Skip past 128 nonprimes.
2H      SRU q,q,1
3H      ADD p,p,2; PBEV q,2B                       Set p ← p + 2 until p is prime.
        MUL m,p,p; SUB m,m,n; PBN m,1B             Repeat until p² > N.  ∎
```

The running time, $1172\mu + 5166\upsilon$, is of course much less than the time needed for steps P1–P8 of Program 1.3.2′P, namely $10037\mu + 641543\upsilon$ (improved to $10096\mu + 215351\upsilon$ in exercise 1.3.2′–14). [See P. Pritchard, *Science of Computer Programming* **9** (1987), 17–35, for several instructive variations. In practice, a program like this one tends to slow down dramatically when the sieve is too big for the computer's cache. Better results are obtained by working with a segmented sieve, which contains bits for numbers between $N_0 + k\delta$ and $N_0 + (k+1)\delta$, as suggested by L. J. Lander and T. R. Parkin,

Math. Comp. **21** (1967), 483–488; C. Bays and R. H. Hudson, *BIT* **17** (1977), 121–127. Here N_0 can be quite large, but δ is limited by the cache size; calculations are done separately for $k = 0, 1, \ldots$. Segmented sieves have become highly developed; see, for example, T. R. Nicely, *Math. Comp.* **68** (1999), 1311–1315, and the references cited there. The author used such a program in 2006 to discover an unusually large gap of length 1370 between 418032645936712127 and the next larger prime.]

25. $(1 + 1 + 25 + 1 + 1 + 25 + 1 + 1 = 56)$ mm; the worm never sees pages 2–500 of Volume 1 or 1–499 of Volume 4. (Unless the books have been placed in little-endian fashion on the bookshelf; then the answer would be 106 mm.) This classic brain-teaser can be found in Sam Loyd's *Cyclopedia* (New York: 1914), pages 327 and 383.

26. We could multiply by $^\#$aa...ab instead of dividing by 12 (see exercise 1.3.1′–17); but multiplication is slow too. Or we could deal with a "flat" sequence of 12000000×5 consecutive bits ($= 7.5$ megabytes), ignoring the boundaries between words. Another possibility is to use a scheme that is neither big-endian nor little-endian but *transposed*: Put item k into octabyte $8(k \bmod 2^{20})$, where it is shifted left by $5\lfloor k/2^{20}\rfloor$. Since $k < 12000000$, the amount of shift is always less than 60. The MMIX code to put item k into register $1 is AND $0,k,[#fffff]; SLU $0,$0,3; LDOU $1,base,$0; SRU $0,k,20; 4ADDU $0,$0,$0; SRU $1,$1,$0; AND $1,$1,#1f.

[This solution uses 8 large megabytes (2^{23} bytes). *Any* convenient scheme for converting item numbers to octabyte addresses and shift amounts will work, as long as the same method is used consistently. Of course, just 'LDBU $1,base,k' would be faster.]

27. (a) $((x-1) \oplus x) + x$. [This exercise is based on an idea of Luther Woodrum, who noticed that $((x-1)\,|\,x) + 1 = (x \mathbin{\&} -x) + x$.]

  (b) $(y + x)\,|\,y$, where $y = (x-1) \oplus x$.

  (c, d, e) $((z \oplus x) + x) \mathbin{\&} z$, $((z \oplus x) + x) \oplus z$, and $\overline{((z \oplus x) + x)} \mathbin{\&} z$, where $z = x-1$.

  (f) $x \oplus (a)$; alternatively, $t \oplus (t+1)$, where $t = x\,|\,(x-1)$. [The number $(0^\infty 01^a 11^b)_2$ looks simpler, but it apparently requires *five* operations: $((t+1) \mathbin{\&} \bar{t}) - 1$.]

  These constructions all give sensible results in the exceptional cases when $x = -2^b$.

28. A 1 bit indicates x's rightmost 0 (for example, $(101011)_2 \mapsto (000100)_2$); $-1 \mapsto 0$.

29. $\mu_k = \mu_{k+1} \oplus (\mu_{k+1} \ll 2^k)$ [see *STOC* **6** (1974), 125]. This relation holds also for the constants $\mu_{d,k}$ of (48), when $0 \le k < d$, if we start with $\mu_{d,d} = 2^{2^d} - 1$. (There is, however, no easy way to go from μ_k to μ_{k+1}, unless we use the "zip" operation; see (77).)

30. Append 'CSZ rho,x,64' to (50), thereby adding 1υ to its execution time; or replace the last two lines by SRU t,y,rho; SLU t,t,2; SRU t,[#300020104],t; AND t,t,#f; ADD rho,rho,t, saving 1υ. For (51), we simply need to make sure that $rhotab[0] = 8$.

31. In the first place, his code loops forever when $x = 0$. But even after that bug is patched, his assumption that x is a random integer is highly questionable. In many applications when we want to compute ρx for a nonzero 64-bit number x, a more reasonable assumption would be that each of the outcomes $\{0, 1, \ldots, 63\}$ is equally likely. The average and standard deviation then become 31.5 and ≈ 18.5.

32. 'NEGU y,x; AND y,x,y; MULU y,debruijn,y; SRU y,y,58; LDB rho,decode,y' has estimated cost $\mu + 14\upsilon$, although multiplication by a power of 2 might well be faster than a typical multiplication. Add 1υ for the correction in answer 30.

33. In fact, an exhaustive calculation shows that exactly 94727 suitable constants a yield a "perfect hash function" for this problem, 90970 of which also identify the power-of-two cases $y = 2^j$; 90918 of those also distinguish the case $y = 0$. The multiplier

$^\#$208b2430c8c82129 is uniquely best, in the sense that it doesn't need to refer to table entries above $decode[32400]$ when y is known to be a valid input.

34. Identity (a) fails when $x = 5$, $y = 6$; but (b) is true, also when $xy = 0$. Proof of (c): If $x \neq y$ and $\rho x = \rho y = k$ we have $x = \alpha 10^k$ and $y = \beta 10^k$; hence $x \oplus y = (\alpha \oplus \beta)00^k = (x-1) \oplus (y-1)$. If $\rho x > \rho y = k$ we have $(x \oplus y) \bmod 2^{k+2} \neq ((x-1) \oplus (y-1)) \bmod 2^{k+2}$.

35. Let $f(x) = x \oplus 3x$. Clearly $f(2x) = 2f(x)$, and $f(4x + 1) = 4f(x) + 2$. We also have $f(4x - 1) = 4f(x) + 2$, by exercise 34(c). The hinted identity follows.

Given n, set $u \leftarrow n \gg 1$, $v \leftarrow u + n$, $t \leftarrow u \oplus v$, $n^+ \leftarrow v \mathbin{\&} t$, and $n^- \leftarrow u \mathbin{\&} t$. Clearly $u = \lfloor n/2 \rfloor$ and $v = \lfloor 3n/2 \rfloor$, so $n^+ - n^- = v - u = n$. And this is Reitwiesner's representation, because $n^+ \mid n^-$ has no consecutive 1s. [H. Prodinger, *Integers* **0** (2000), A08:1–A08:14. Incidentally we also have $f(-x) = f(x)$.]

36. (i) The commands $x \leftarrow x \oplus (x \ll 1)$, $x \leftarrow x \oplus (x \ll 2)$, $x \leftarrow x \oplus (x \ll 4)$, $x \leftarrow x \oplus (x \ll 8)$, $x \leftarrow x \oplus (x \ll 16)$, $x \leftarrow x \oplus (x \ll 32)$ change x to $x^\oplus$. (ii) $x^\& = x \mathbin{\&} \sim(x+1)$.
(See exercises 66 and 70 for applications of $x^\oplus$; see also exercises 128 and 209.)

37. Insert 'CSZ y,x,half' after the FLOTU in (55), where $\mathtt{half} = {}^\#\mathtt{3fe0000000000000}$; note that (55) says 'SR' (not 'SRU'). No change is needed to (56), if $lamtab[0] = -1$.

38. 'SRU t,x,1; OR y,x,t; SRU t,y,2; OR y,y,t; SRU t,y,4; OR y,y,t; $\ldots$; SRU t,y,32; OR y,y,t; SRU t,y,1; SUBU y,y,t' takes $14v$.

39. (Solution by H. S. Warren, Jr.) Let $\sigma(x)$ denote the result of smearing x to the right, as in the first line of (57). Compute $x \mathbin{\&} \sigma((x \gg 1) \mathbin{\&} \bar{x})$.

40. Suppose $\lambda x = \lambda y = k$. If $x = y = 0$, (58) certainly holds, regardless of how we define $\lambda 0$. Otherwise $x = (1\alpha)_2$ and $y = (1\beta)_2$, for some binary strings α and β with $|\alpha| = |\beta| = k$; and $x \oplus y < 2^k \leq x \mathbin{\&} y$. On the other hand if $\lambda x < \lambda y = k$, we have $x \oplus y \geq 2^k > x \mathbin{\&} y$. And H. S. Warren, Jr., notes that $\lambda x < \lambda y$ if and only if $x < y \mathbin{\&} \bar{x}$.

41. (a) $\sum_{n=1}^{\infty} (\rho n) z^n = \sum_{k=1}^{\infty} z^{2^k}/(1 - z^{2^k}) = z/(1-z) - \sum_{k=0}^{\infty} z^{2^k}/(1 + z^{2^k})$. The Dirichlet generating function is simpler: $\sum_{n=1}^{\infty} (\rho n)/n^z = \zeta(z)/(2^z - 1)$.
(b) $\sum_{n=1}^{\infty} (\lambda n) z^n = \sum_{k=1}^{\infty} z^{2^k}/(1 - z)$.
(c) $\sum_{n=1}^{\infty} (\nu n) z^n = \sum_{k=0}^{\infty} z^{2^k}/((1 - z)(1 + z^{2^k})) = \sum_{k=0}^{\infty} z^{2^k} \mu_k(z)$, where $\mu_k(z) = (1 + z + \cdots + z^{2^k - 1})/(1 - z^{2^{k+1}})$. (The "magic masks" of (47) correspond to $\mu_k(2)$.)
[See *Automatic Sequences* by J.-P. Allouche and J. Shallit (2003), Chapter 3, for further information about the functions ρ and ν, which they denote by ν_2 and s_2.]

42. $e_1 2^{e_1 - 1} + (e_2 + 2)2^{e_2 - 1} + \cdots + (e_r + 2r - 2)2^{e_r - 1}$, by induction on r. [D. E. Knuth, *Proc. IFIP Congress* (1971), **1**, 19–27. The fractal aspects of this sum are illustrated in Figs. 3.1 and 3.2 of the book by Allouche and Shallit.] Consider also $S_n'(1)$ where

$$S_n(z) = \sum_{k=0}^{n-1} z^{\nu k} = (1 + z)^{e_1} + z(1 + z)^{e_2} + \cdots + z^{r-1}(1 + z)^{e_r}.$$

43. The straightforward implementation of (63), 'SET nu,0; SET y,x; BZ y,Done; 1H ADD nu,nu,1; SUBU t,y,1; AND y,y,t; PBNZ y,1B' costs $(5 + 4\nu x)v$; it beats the implementation of (62) when $\nu x < 4$, ties when $\nu x = 4$, and loses when $\nu x > 4$.

But we can save $4v$ from the implementation of (62) if we replace the final multiplication-and-shift by '$y \leftarrow y + (y \gg 8)$, $y \leftarrow y + (y \gg 16)$, $y \leftarrow y + (y \gg 32)$, $\nu \leftarrow y \mathbin{\&} {}^\#\mathtt{ff}$'. [Of course, MMIX's single instruction 'SADD nu,x,0' is much better.]

44. Let this sum be $\nu^{(2)}x$. If we can solve the problem for 2^d-bit numbers, we can solve it for 2^{d+1}-bit numbers, because $\nu^{(2)}(2^{2^d}x + x') = \nu^{(2)}x + \nu^{(2)}x' + 2^d \nu x$. Therefore a solution analogous to (62) suggests itself, on a 64-bit machine:

Set $z \leftarrow (x \gg 1)\ \&\ \mu_0$ and $y \leftarrow x - z$.
Set $z \leftarrow ((z + (z \gg 2))\ \&\ \mu_1) + ((y\ \&\ \bar{\mu}_1) \gg 1)$ and $y \leftarrow (y\ \&\ \mu_1) + ((y \gg 2)\ \&\ \mu_1)$.
Set $z \leftarrow ((z + (z \gg 4))\ \&\ \mu_2) + ((y\ \&\ \bar{\mu}_2) \gg 2)$ and $y \leftarrow (y + (y \gg 4))\ \&\ \mu_2$.
Finally $\nu^{(2)} \leftarrow (((Az) \bmod 2^{64}) \gg 56) + ((((By) \bmod 2^{64}) \gg 56) \ll 3)$,
    where $A = (11111111)_{256}$ and $B = (01234567)_{256}$.

But on MMIX, which has sideways addition built in, there's a better solution by J. Dallos:

```
SADD  nu2,x,m5      SADD  t,x,m3        2ADDU nu2,nu2,t     SADD  t,x,m0
SADD  t,x,m4        2ADDU nu2,nu2,t     SADD  t,x,m1        2ADDU nu2,nu2,t ▌
2ADDU nu2,nu2,t     SADD  t,x,m2        2ADDU nu2,nu2,t
```

[In general, $\nu^{(2)}x = \sum_k 2^k \nu(x\ \&\ \bar{\mu}_k)$. See *Dr. Dobb's Journal* **8**, 4 (April 1983), 24–37.]

45. Let $d = (x - y)\ \&\ (y - x)$; test if $d\ \&\ y \neq 0$. [Rokicki found that this idea, which is called *colex ordering*, can be used with node addresses to near-randomize binary search trees or Cartesian trees as if they were treaps, without needing an additional random "priority key" in each node. See *U.S. Patent 6347318* (12 February 2002).]

46. SADD t,x,m; NXOR y,x,m; CSOD x,t,y; the mask m is ~(1<<i|1<<j). (In general, these instructions complement the bits specified by $\bar{m}$ if those bits have odd parity.)

47. $y \leftarrow (x \gg \delta)\ \&\ \theta$, $z \leftarrow (x\ \&\ \theta) \ll \delta$, $x \leftarrow (x\ \&\ m)\ |\ y\ |\ z$, where $\bar{m} = \theta\ |\ (\theta \ll \delta)$.

48. Given δ, there are $s_\delta = \prod_{j=0}^{\delta-1} F_{\lfloor(n+j)/\delta\rfloor+1}$ different δ-swaps, including the identity permutation. (See exercise 4.5.3–32.) Summing over δ gives $1 + \sum_{\delta=1}^{n-1}(s_\delta - 1)$ altogether.

49. (a) The set $S = \{a_1\delta_1 + \cdots + a_m\delta_m\ |\ \{a_1, \ldots, a_m\} \subseteq \{-1, 0, +1\}\}$ for displacements $\delta_1, \ldots, \delta_m$ must contain $\{n-1, n-3, \ldots, 1-n\}$, because the kth bit must be exchanged with the $(n+1-k)$th bit for $1 \leq k \leq n$. Hence $|S| \geq n$. And S contains at most 3^m numbers, at most $2 \cdot 3^{m-1}$ of which are odd.

(b) Clearly $s(mn) \leq s(m) + s(n)$, because we can reverse m fields of n bits each. Thus $s(3^m) \leq m$ and $s(2 \cdot 3^m) \leq m + 1$. Furthermore the reversal of 3^m bits uses only δ-swaps with even values of δ; the corresponding $(\delta/2)$-swaps prove that we have $s((3^m \pm 1)/2) \leq m$. These upper bounds match the lower bounds of (a) when $m > 1$.

(c) The string $\alpha a \beta \theta \psi z \omega$ with $|\alpha| = |\beta| = |\theta| = |\psi| = |\omega| = n$ can be changed to $\omega z \psi \theta \beta a \alpha$ with a $(3n+1)$-swap followed by an $(n+1)$-swap. Then $s(n)$ further swaps reverse all. Hence $s(32) \leq s(6) + 2 = 4$, and $s(64) \leq 5$. Again, equality holds by (a).

Incidentally, $s(63) = 4$ because $s(7) = s(9) = 2$. The lower bound in (a) turns out to be the exact value of $s(n)$ for $1 \leq n \leq 22$, except that $s(16) = 4$.

50. Express $n = (t_m \ldots t_1 t_0)_3$ in balanced ternary notation. Let $n_j = (t_m \ldots t_j)_3$ and $\delta_j = 2n_j + t_{j-1}$, so that $n_{j-1} - \delta_j = n_j$ and $2\delta_j - n_{j-1} = n_j + t_{j-1}$ for $1 \leq j \leq m$. Let $E_0 = \{0\}$ and $E_{j+1} = E_j \cup \{t_j - x\ |\ x \in E_j\}$ for $0 \leq j < m$. (Thus, for example, $E_1 = \{0, t_0\}$ and $E_2 = \{0, t_0, t_1, t_1 - t_0\}$.) Notice that $\varepsilon \in E_j$ implies $|\varepsilon| \leq j$.

Assume by induction on j that δ-swaps for $\delta = \delta_1, \ldots, \delta_j$ have changed the n-bit word $\alpha_1 \ldots \alpha_{3^j}$ to $\alpha_{3^j} \ldots \alpha_1$, where each subword α_k has length $n_j + \varepsilon_k$ for some $\varepsilon_k \in E_j$. If $n_{j+1} > j$, a δ_{j+1}-swap within each subword will preserve this assumption. Otherwise each subword α_k has $|\alpha_k| \leq n_j + j \leq 3n_{j+1} + 1 + j \leq 4j + 1 < 4m$. Therefore 2^k-swaps for $\lfloor \lg 4m \rfloor \geq k \geq 0$ will reverse them all. (Note that a 2^k-swap on a subword of size t, where $2^k < t \leq 2^{k+1}$, reduces it to three subwords of sizes $t - 2^k$, $2^{k+1} - t$, $t - 2^k$.)

51. (a) If $c = (c_{d-1} \ldots c_0)_2$, we must have $\theta_{d-1} = c_{d-1}\mu_{d,d-1}$. But for $0 \le k < d-1$ we can take $\theta_k = c_k\mu_{d,k} \oplus \hat{\theta}_k$, where $\hat{\theta}_k$ is *any* mask $\subseteq \mu_{d,k}$.

(b) Let $\Theta(d,c)$ be the set of all such mask sequences. Clearly $\Theta(1,c) = \{c\}$. When $d > 1$ we will have, recursively,

$$\Theta(d,c) = \{(\theta_0, \ldots, \theta_{d-2}, \theta_{d-1}, \hat{\theta}_{d-2}, \ldots, \hat{\theta}_0) \mid \theta_k = \theta'_{k-1} \ddagger \theta''_{k-1}, \ \hat{\theta}_k = \hat{\theta}'_{k-1} \ddagger \hat{\theta}''_{k-1}\},$$

by "zipping together" two sequences $(\theta'_0, \ldots, \theta'_{d-3}, \theta'_{d-2}, \hat{\theta}'_{d-3}, \ldots, \hat{\theta}'_0) \in \Theta(d-1,c')$ and $(\theta''_0, \ldots, \theta''_{d-3}, \theta''_{d-2}, \hat{\theta}''_{d-3}, \ldots, \hat{\theta}''_0) \in \Theta(d-1,c'')$ for some appropriate θ_0, $\hat{\theta}_0$, c', and c''.

When c is odd, the bigraph corresponding to (75) has only one cycle; so $(\theta_0, \hat{\theta}_0, c', c'')$ is either $(\mu_{d,0}, 0, \lceil c/2 \rceil, \lfloor c/2 \rfloor)$ or $(0, \mu_{d,0}, \lfloor c/2 \rfloor, \lceil c/2 \rceil)$. But when c is even, the bigraph has 2^{d-1} double bonds; so $\theta_0 = \hat{\theta}_0$ is any mask $\subseteq \mu_{d,0}$, and $c' = c'' = c/2$. [Incidentally, $\lg |\Theta(d,c)| = 2^{d-1}(d-1) - \sum_{k=1}^{d-1}(2^{d-k}-1)(2^{k-1} - |2^{k-1} - c \bmod 2^k|)$.]

In both cases we can therefore let $\hat{\theta}_{d-2} = \cdots = \hat{\theta}_0 = 0$ and omit the second half of (71) entirely. Of course in case (b) we would do the cyclic shift directly, instead of using (71) at all. But exercise 58 proves that many other useful permutations, such as selective reversal followed by cyclic shift, can also be handled by (71) with $\hat{\theta}_k = 0$ for all k. The *inverses* of those permutations can be handled with $\theta_k = 0$ for $0 \le k < d-1$.

52. The following solutions make $\hat{\theta}_j = 0$ whenever possible. We shall express the θ masks in terms of the μ's, for example by writing $\mu_{6,5} \ \& \ \mu_0$ instead of stating the requested hexadecimal form $^\#\mathtt{55555555}$; the μ form is shorter and more instructive.

(a) $\theta_k = \mu_{6,k} \ \& \ \mu_5$ and $\hat{\theta}_k = \mu_{6,k} \ \& \ (\mu_{k+1} \oplus \mu_{k-1})$ for $0 \le k < 5$; $\theta_5 = \theta_4$. (Here $\mu_{-1} = 0$. To get the "other" perfect shuffle, $(x_{31}x_{63} \ldots x_1x_{33}x_0x_{32})_2$, let $\hat{\theta}_0 = \mu_{6,0} \& \bar{\mu}_1$.)

(b) $\theta_0 = \theta_3 = \hat{\theta}_0 = \mu_{6,0} \ \& \ \mu_3$; $\theta_1 = \theta_4 = \hat{\theta}_1 = \mu_{6,1} \ \& \ \mu_4$; $\theta_2 = \theta_5 = \hat{\theta}_2 = \mu_{6,2} \ \& \ \mu_5$; $\hat{\theta}_3 = \hat{\theta}_4 = 0$. [See J. Lenfant, *IEEE Trans.* **C-27** (1978), 637–647, for a general theory.]

(c) $\theta_0 = \mu_{6,0} \ \& \ \mu_4$; $\theta_1 = \mu_{6,1} \ \& \ \mu_5$; $\theta_2 = \theta_4 = \mu_{6,2} \ \& \ \mu_4$; $\theta_3 = \theta_5 = \mu_{6,3} \ \& \ \mu_5$; $\hat{\theta}_0 = \mu_{6,0} \ \& \ \mu_2$; $\hat{\theta}_1 = \mu_{6,1} \ \& \ \mu_3$; $\hat{\theta}_2 = \hat{\theta}_0 \oplus \theta_2$; $\hat{\theta}_3 = \hat{\theta}_1 \oplus \theta_3$; $\hat{\theta}_4 = 0$.

(d) $\theta_k = \mu_{6,k} \ \& \ \mu_{5-k}$ for $0 \le k \le 5$; $\hat{\theta}_k = \theta_k$ for $0 \le k \le 2$; $\hat{\theta}_3 = \hat{\theta}_4 = 0$.

53. We can write ψ as a product of $d - t$ transpositions, $(u_1v_1) \ldots (u_{d-t}v_{d-t})$ (see exercise 5.2.2–2). The permutation induced by a single transposition (uv) on the index digits, when $u < v$, corresponds to a $(2^v - 2^u)$-swap with mask $\mu_{d,v} \ \& \ \bar{\mu}_u$. We should do such a swap for (u_1v_1) first, $\ldots$, $(u_{d-t}v_{d-t})$ last.

In particular, the perfect shuffle in a 2^d-bit register corresponds to the case where $\psi = (01 \ldots (d-1))$ is a one-cycle; so it can be achieved by doing such $(2^v - 2^u)$-swaps for $(u, v) = (0, 1)$, $\ldots$, $(0, d-1)$. For example, when $d = 3$ the two-step procedure is $12345678 \mapsto 13245768 \mapsto 15263748$. [Guy Steele suggests an alternative $(d-1)$-step procedure: We can do a 2^k-swap with mask $\mu_{d,k+1} \ \& \ \bar{\mu}_k$ for $d-1 > k \ge 0$. When $d = 3$ his method takes $12345678 \mapsto 12563478 \mapsto 15263748$.]

The matrix transposition in exercise 52(b) corresponds to $d = 6$ and $(u, v) = (0, 3)$, $(1, 4)$, $(2, 5)$. These operations are the 7-swap, 14-swap, and 28-swap steps for 8×8 matrix transposition illustrated in the text; they can be done in any order.

For exercise 52(c), use $d = 6$ and $(u, v) = (0, 2)$, $(1, 3)$, $(0, 4)$, $(1, 5)$. Exercise 52(d) is as easy as 52(b), with $(u, v) = (0, 5)$, $(1, 4)$, $(2, 3)$.

54. Transposition amounts to reversing the bits of the minor diagonals. Successive elements of those diagonals are $m - 1$ apart in the register. Simultaneous reversal of all diagonals corresponds to simultaneous reversal of subwords of sizes $1, \ldots, m$, which can be done with 2^k-swaps for $0 \le k < \lceil \lg m \rceil$ (because such transposition is easy when m is a power of 2, as illustrated in the text). Here's the procedure for $m = 7$:

Given	6-swap	12-swap	24-swap
00 01 02 03 04 05 06	00 **10** 02 **12** 04 **14** 06	00 10 **20 30** 04 14 **24**	00 10 20 30 **40 50 60**
10 11 12 13 14 15 16	**01** 11 **03** 13 **05** 15 25	01 11 **21 31** 05 15 25	01 11 21 31 **41 51 61**
20 21 22 23 24 25 26	20 **30** 22 **32** 24 16 26	**02 12** 22 32 **06** 16 26	02 12 22 32 **42 52 62**
30 31 32 33 34 35 36	**21** 31 **23** 33 **43** 35 **45**	**03 13** 23 33 43 **53 63**	03 13 23 33 43 53 63
40 41 42 43 44 45 46	40 **50** 42 **34** 44 **36** 46	40 50 **60** 34 44 **54 64**	**04 14 24** 34 44 54 64
50 51 52 53 54 55 56	**41** 51 **61** 53 **63** 55 **65**	41 51 61 **35 45** 55 65	**05 15 25** 35 45 55 65
60 61 62 63 64 65 66	60 **52** 62 **54** 64 **56** 66	**42** 52 62 **36 46** 56 66	**06 16 26** 36 46 56 66

55. Given x and y, first set $x \leftarrow x \mid (x \ll 2^k)$ and $y \leftarrow y \mid (y \ll 2^k)$ for $2d \leq k < 3d$. Then set $x \leftarrow (2^{2d+k} - 2^k)$-swap of x with mask $\mu_{2d+k} \& \bar{\mu}_k$ and $y \leftarrow (2^{2d+k} - 2^{d+k})$-swap of y with mask $\mu_{2d+k} \& \bar{\mu}_{d+k}$ for $0 \leq k < d$. Finally set $z \leftarrow x \& y$, then either $z \leftarrow z \mid (z \gg 2^k)$ or $z \leftarrow z \oplus (z \gg 2^k)$ for $2d \leq k < 3d$, and $z \leftarrow z \& (2^{n^2} - 1)$. [The idea is to form two $n \times n \times n$ arrays $x = (x_{000} \ldots x_{(n-1)(n-1)(n-1)})_2$ and $y = (y_{000} \ldots y_{(n-1)(n-1)(n-1)})_2$ with $x_{ijk} = a_{jk}$ and $y_{ijk} = b_{jk}$, then transpose coordinates so that $x_{ijk} = a_{ji}$ and $y_{ijk} = b_{ik}$; now $x \& y$ does all n^3 bitwise multiplications at once. This method is due to V. R. Pratt and L. J. Stockmeyer, *J. Computer and System Sci.* **12** (1976), 210–213.]

56. Use (71) with $\theta_0 = \hat{\theta}_0 = 0$, $\theta_1 = {}^\#0010201122113231$, $\theta_2 = {}^\#00080e0400080c06$, $\theta_3 = {}^\#00000092008100a2$, $\theta_4 = {}^\#0000000000000f16$, $\theta_5 = {}^\#0000000003199c26$, $\hat{\theta}_4 = {}^\#00000c9f0000901a$, $\hat{\theta}_3 = {}^\#003a00b50015002b$, $\hat{\theta}_2 = {}^\#000103080c0d0f0c$, and $\hat{\theta}_1 = {}^\#0020032033233333$.

57. The two choices for each cycle when $d > 1$ have complementary settings. So we can choose a setting in which at least half of the crossbars are inactive, except in the middle column. (See exercise 5.3.4–55 for more about permutation networks.)

58. (a) Every different setting of the crossbars gives a different permutation, because there is exactly one path from input line i to output line j for all $0 \leq i, j < N$. (A network with that property is called a "banyan.") The unique such path carries input i on line $l(i, j, k) = ((i \gg k) \ll k) + (j \bmod 2^k)$ after k swapping steps have been made.

(b) We have $l(i\varphi, i, k) = l(j\varphi, j, k)$ if and only if $i \bmod 2^k = j \bmod 2^k$ and $i\varphi \gg k = j\varphi \gg k$; so $(*)$ is necessary. And it is also sufficient, because a mapping φ that satisfies $(*)$ can always be routed in such a way that $j\varphi$ appears on line $l = l(j\varphi, j, k)$ after k steps: If $k > 1$, $j\varphi$ will appear on line $l(j\varphi, j, k - 1)$, which is one of the inputs to l. Condition $(*)$ says that we can route it to l without conflict, even if l is $l(i\varphi, i, k)$. [In *IEEE Transactions* **C-24** (1975), 1145–1155, Duncan Lawrie proved that condition $(*)$ is necessary and sufficient for an arbitrary *mapping* φ of the set $\{0, 1, \ldots, N-1\}$ into itself, when the crossbar modules are allowed to be general 2×2 mapping modules as in exercise 75. Furthermore the mapping φ might be only partially specified, with $j\varphi = *$ ("wild card" or "don't-care") for some values of j. The proof that appears in the previous paragraph actually demonstrates Lawrie's more general theorem.]

(c) $i \bmod 2^k = j \bmod 2^k$ if and only if $k \leq \rho(i \oplus j)$; $i \gg k = j \gg k$ if and only if $k > \lambda(i \oplus j)$; and $i\varphi = j\varphi$ if and only if $i = j$, when φ is a permutation.

(d) $\lambda(i\varphi \oplus j\varphi) \geq \rho(i \oplus j)$ for all $i \neq j$ if and only if $\lambda(i\tau\varphi \oplus j\tau\varphi) \geq \rho(i\tau \oplus j\tau) = \rho(i \oplus j)$ for all $i \neq j$, because τ is a permutation. [Note that the notation can be confusing: Bit $j\tau\varphi$ appears in bit position j if permutation φ is applied first, *then* τ. The Sylow group T includes many interesting and important permutations, including bit reversal and cyclic shifts. It corresponds to settings of the Omega network where crossbars of length 2^j that are congruent mod 2^{j+1} all switch or all pass, as a unit.]

(e) Since $l(j, j, k) = j$ for $0 \leq k \leq d$, a permutation of Ω fixes j if and only if each of its swaps fixes j. Thus the swaps performed by φ and by ψ operate on disjoint elements. The union of these swaps gives $\varphi\psi$.

(f) Any setting of the crossbars corresponds to a permutation that makes Batcher's comparator modules do the equivalent switching.

59. It is $2^{M_d(a,b)}$, where $M_d(a, b)$ is the number of crossbars that have both endpoints in $[a \mathinner{.\,.} b]$. To count them, let $k = \lambda(a \oplus b)$, $a' = a \bmod 2^k$, and $b' = b \bmod 2^k$; notice that $b - a = 2^k + b' - a'$, and $M_d(a, b) = M_{k+1}(a', 2^k + b')$. Counting the crossbars in the top half and bottom half, plus those that jump between halves, gives $M_{k+1}(a', 2^k + b') = M_k(a', 2^k - 1) + M_k(0, b') + ((b' + 1) \mathbin{\dot-} a')$. Finally, we have $M_k(0, b') = S(b' + 1)$; and $M_k(a', 2^k - 1) = M_k(0, 2^k - 1 - a') = S(2^k - a') = k2^{k-1} - ka' + S(a')$, where $S(n)$ is evaluated in exercise 42.

60. A cycle of length $2l$ corresponds to a pattern $u_0 \leftarrow v_0 \leftrightarrow v_1 \rightarrow u_1 \leftrightarrow u_2 \leftarrow v_2 \leftrightarrow \cdots \leftrightarrow v_{2l-1} \rightarrow u_{2l-1} \leftrightarrow u_{2l}$, where $u_{2l} = u_0$ and '$u \leftarrow v$' or '$v \rightarrow u$' means that the permutation sends u to v, '$x \leftrightarrow y$' means that $x = y \oplus 1$.

We can generate a random permutation as follows: Given u_0, there are $2n$ choices for v_0, then $2n - 1$ choices for u_1 only one of which causes $u_2 = u_0$, then $2n - 2$ choices for v_2, then $2n - 3$ choices for u_3 only one of which closes a cycle, etc.

Consequently the generating function is $G(z) = \prod_{j=1}^{n} \frac{2n-2j+z}{2n-2j+1}$. The expected number of cycles, k, is $G'(1) = H_{2n} - \frac{1}{2}H_n = \frac{1}{2}\ln n + \ln 2 + \frac{1}{2}\gamma + O(n^{-1})$. The mean of 2^k is

$$G(2) = (2^n n!)^2 / (2n)! = \sqrt{\pi n} + O(n^{-1/2});$$

and the variance is $G(4) - G(2)^2 = (n + 1 - G(2))G(2) = \sqrt{\pi} n^{3/2} + O(n)$.

62. The crossbar settings in $P(2^d)$ can be stored in $(2d-1)2^{d-1} = Nd - \frac{1}{2}N$ bits. To get the inverse permutation proceed from right to left. [See P. Heckel and R. Schroeppel, *Electronic Design* **28**, 8 (12 April 1980), 148–152. Note that *any* way to represent an arbitrary permutation requires at least $\lg N! > Nd - N/\ln 2$ bits of memory; so this representation is nearly optimum, spacewise.]

63. (i) $x = y$. (ii) Either z is even or $x \oplus y < 2^{\max(0,(z-1)/2)}$. (When z is odd we have $(x \ddagger y) \gg z = (y \gg \lceil z/2 \rceil) \ddagger (x \gg \lfloor z/2 \rfloor)$, even when $z < 0$.) (iii) This identity holds for all w, x, y, and z (and also with any other bitwise Boolean operator in place of &).

64. $(((z \mathbin{\&} \mu_0) + (z' \mid \bar{\mu}_0)) \mathbin{\&} \mu_0) \mid (((z \mathbin{\&} \bar{\mu}_0) + (z' \mid \mu_0)) \mathbin{\&} \bar{\mu}_0)$. (See (86).)

65. $x u(x^2) + v(x^2) = x u(x)^2 + v(x)^2$.

66. (a) $v(x) = (u(x)/(1+x^\delta)) \bmod x^n$; it's the unique polynomial of degree less than n such that $(1+x^\delta)v(x) \equiv u(x)$ (modulo x^n). (Equivalently, v is the unique n-bit integer such that $(v \oplus (v \ll \delta)) \bmod 2^n = u$.)

(b) We may as well assume that $n = 64m$, and that $u = (u_{m-1} \ldots u_1 u_0)_{2^{64}}$, $v = (v_{m-1} \ldots v_1 v_0)_{2^{64}}$. Set $c \leftarrow 0$; then, using exercise 36, set $v_j \leftarrow u_j^\oplus \oplus (-c)$ and $c \leftarrow v_j \gg 63$ for $j = 0, 1, \ldots, m - 1$.

(c) Set $c \leftarrow v_0 \leftarrow u_0$; then $v_j \leftarrow u_j \oplus c$ and $c \leftarrow v_j$, for $j = 1, 2, \ldots, m - 1$.

(d) Start with $c \leftarrow 0$ and do the following for $j = 0, 1, \ldots, m - 1$: Set $t \leftarrow u_j$, $t \leftarrow t \oplus (t \ll 3)$, $t \leftarrow t \oplus (t \ll 6)$, $t \leftarrow t \oplus (t \ll 12)$, $t \leftarrow t \oplus (t \ll 24)$, $t \leftarrow t \oplus (t \ll 48)$, $v_j \leftarrow t \oplus c$, $c \leftarrow (t \gg 61) \times {}^\#\mathtt{9249249249249249}$.

(e) Start with $v \leftarrow u$. Then, for $j = 1, 2, \ldots, m - 1$, set $v_j \leftarrow v_j \oplus (v_{j-1} \ll 3)$ and (if $j < m - 1$) $v_{j+1} \leftarrow v_{j+1} \oplus (v_{j-1} \gg 61)$.

67. Let $n = 2l - 1$ and $m = n - 2d$. If $\frac{1}{2}n < k < n$ we have $x^{2k} \equiv x^{m+t} + x^t$ (modulo $x^n + x^m + 1$), where $t = 2k - n$ is odd. Consequently, if $v = (v_{n-1} \dots v_1 v_0)_2$, the number

$$w = u \oplus (((u \gg d) \oplus (u \gg 2d) \oplus (u \gg 3d) \oplus \cdots) \,\&\, -2^{l-d})$$

turns out to equal $(v_{n-2} \dots v_3 v_1 v_{n-1} \dots v_2 v_0)_2$. For example, when $l = 4$ and $d = 2$, the square of $u_6 x^6 + \cdots + u_1 x + u_0$ modulo $(x^7 + x^3 + 1)$ is $u_6 x^5 + u_5 x^3 + (u_6 \oplus u_4) x^1 + (u_5 \oplus u_3) x^6 + (u_6 \oplus u_4 \oplus u_2) x^4 + u_1 x^2 + u_0$. To compute v, we therefore do a perfect shuffle, $v = \lfloor w/2^l \rfloor \ddagger (w \bmod 2^l)$. The number w can be calculated by methods like those of the previous exercise. [See R. P. Brent, S. Larvala, and P. Zimmermann, *Math. Comp.* **72** (2003), 1443–1452; **74** (2005), 1001–1002.]

68. `SRU t,x,delta; PUT rM,theta; MUX x,t,x.`

69. Notice that the procedure might fail if we attempt to do the 2^{d-1}-shift first instead of last. The key to proving that a small-shift-first strategy works correctly is to watch the spaces *between* selected bits; we will prove that the lengths of these spaces are multiples of 2^{k+1} after the 2^k-shift.

Consider the infinite string $\chi_k = \dots 1^{t_4} 0^{2^k} 1^{t_3} 0^{2^k} 1^{t_2} 0^{2^k} 1^{t_1} 0^{2^k} 1^{t_0}$, which represents the situation where $t_l \geq 0$ items need to move $2^k l$ places to the right. A 2^k-shift with any mask of the form $\theta_k = \dots 0^{t_4} *^{2^{k+1}} 1^{t_3} 0^{t_2} *^{2^{k+1}} 1^{t_1} 0^{t_0}$ leaves us with the situation represented by the string $\chi_{k+1} = \dots 1^{T_2} 0^{2^{k+1}} 1^{T_1} 0^{2^{k+1}} 1^{T_0}$, where exactly $T_l = t_{2l} + t_{2l+1}$ items need to move right $2^{k+1} l$ places. So the claim holds by induction on k.

70. Let $\psi_k = \theta_k \oplus (\theta_k \ll 1)$, so that $\theta_k = \psi_k^\oplus$ in the notation of exercise 36. If we take $*^{2^{k+1}} = 0^{2^k} 1^{2^k}$ in the previous answer, we have $\psi_0 = \bar{\chi}$ and $\psi_{k+1} = (\psi_k \,\&\, \bar{\theta}_k) \gg 2^k$. Therefore we can proceed as follows:

Set $\psi \leftarrow \bar{\chi}$, $k \leftarrow 0$, and repeat the following steps while $\psi \neq 0$: Set $x \leftarrow \psi$, then $x \leftarrow x \oplus (x \ll 2^l)$ for $0 \leq l < d$, then $\theta_k \leftarrow x$, $\psi \leftarrow (\psi \,\&\, \bar{x}) \gg 2^k$, and $k \leftarrow k + 1$.

The computation ends with $k = \lambda \nu \bar{\chi} + 1$; the remaining masks $\theta_k, \dots, \theta_{d-1}$, if any, are zero and those steps can be omitted from (80). "Minimal" masks, for which $*^{2^{k+1}} = 0^{2^{k+1}}$ in answer 69, are obtained if the operations '$\theta_k \leftarrow x$, $\psi \leftarrow (\psi \,\&\, \bar{x}) \gg 2^k$' are replaced by '$\psi \leftarrow (\psi \,\&\, \bar{x}) \gg 2^k$, $\theta_k \leftarrow x \,\&\, (x + \psi)$' in the loop above.

[See *compress* in H. S. Warren, Jr., *Hacker's Delight* (Addison–Wesley, 2002), §7–4; also G. L. Steele Jr., *U.S. Patent 6715066* (30 March 2004). The BESM-6 computer, designed in 1965, implemented *compress* under the name «сборка» ("gather" or "pack"). Its «разборка» command ("scatter" or "unpack") went the other way.]

71. Start with $x \leftarrow y$. Do a (-2^k)-shift of x with mask θ_k, for $k = d-1, \dots, 1, 0$, using the masks of exercise 70. Finally set $z \leftarrow x$ (or $z \leftarrow x \,\&\, \chi$, if you want a "clean" result).

72. Assume that the leftmost mask bit, χ_{N-1}, is zero, since it is immaterial. Then the result $(z_{(N-1)\varphi} \dots z_{1\varphi} z_{0\varphi})_2$ of any gather-flip corresponds to a permutation with $0\varphi < \cdots < k\varphi > \cdots > (N-1)\varphi$, where $k = \nu \chi$. For example, if $N = 8$ and $\chi = (00101100)_2$, the result is $(z_0 z_1 z_4 z_6 z_7 z_5 z_3 z_2)_2$. So φ is a cyclic shift of a bitonic permutation, and $\varphi \in \Omega$ by exercises 58(d) and 58(f).

Moreover, the masks $\theta_0, \theta_1, \dots, \theta_{d-1}$ for the 1-swap, 2-swap, $\dots$, 2^{d-1}-swap can be computed as follows: The permutation $\psi = \varphi^-$ satisfies $j\psi = (N-1-j)\bar{\chi}_j + s_j$, where $s_j = \chi_{j-1} + \cdots + \chi_1 + \chi_0$ counts the 1s following mask bit χ_j. Let $\psi_0 = \psi$ and $\theta_k = (\lfloor \psi_k/2^k \rfloor \bmod 2) \,\&\, \mu_k$, where ψ_{k+1} is the 2^k-swap of ψ_k with mask θ_k. (In our example, $s_7 \dots s_1 s_0 = 33221000$ and $(0\bar{\chi}_7) \dots (6\bar{\chi}_1)(7\bar{\chi}_0) = 01030067$; hence $\psi_0 = (7\psi) \dots (1\psi)(0\psi) = 33221000 + 01030067 = 34251067$. Then $\theta_0 = (10011001)_2 \,\&\, \mu_0 = (00010001)_2$; $\psi_1 = 34521076$; $\theta_1 = (10010010)_2 \,\&\, \mu_1 = (00010011)_2$; $\psi_2 = 32547610$;

$\theta_2 = (00111100)_2$ & $\mu_2 = (00001100)_2$. In general $j\psi_k \equiv j$ (modulo 2^k).) Represent each permutation ψ_k as a set of d bit vectors, namely as the "bit slices" $\psi_k \bmod 2$, $\lfloor \psi_k/2 \rfloor \bmod 2$, etc. Then $O(d^2)$ bitwise operations suffice for this computation.

The *scatter-flip* operation, which undoes the effect of gather-flip, is obtained via the same crossbar network but from right to left (first a 2^{d-1}-swap, ending with a 1-swap).
[See *Journal of Signal Processing Systems* **53** (2008), 145–169.]

73. (a) Equivalently, d sheep-and-goats operations must be able to transform the word $x^\pi = (x_{(2^d-1)\pi} \ldots x_{1\pi}x_{0\pi})_2$ into $(x_{2^d-1} \ldots x_1 x_0)_2$, for any permutation π of $\{0, 1, \ldots, 2^d-1\}$. And this can be done by radix-2 sorting (Algorithm 5.2.5R): First bring the odd numbered bits to the left, then bring the bits j for odd $\lfloor j/2 \rfloor$ left, and so on. For example, when $d = 3$ and $x^\pi = (x_3 x_1 x_0 x_7 x_5 x_2 x_6 x_4)_2$, the three operations yield successively $(x_3 x_1 x_7 x_5 x_0 x_2 x_6 x_4)_2$, $(x_3 x_7 x_2 x_6 x_1 x_5 x_0 x_4)_2$, $(x_7 x_6 x_5 x_4 x_3 x_2 x_1 x_0)_2$. [See Z. Shi and R. Lee, *Proc. IEEE Conf. ASAP'00* (IEEE CS Press, 2000), 138–148.]

(b) With gather-flip, the same strategy always yields $(x_{g(2^d-1)} \ldots x_{g(1)} x_{g(0)})_2$, where $g(k)$ is Gray binary code, 7.2.1.1–(9). For instance, the example of (a) is now $(x_5 x_7 x_1 x_3 x_0 x_2 x_6 x_4)_2$, $(x_6 x_2 x_3 x_7 x_5 x_1 x_0 x_4)_2$, $(x_4 x_5 x_7 x_6 x_2 x_3 x_1 x_0)_2$.

74. If $|\sum c_{2l} - \sum c_{2l+1}| = 2\Delta > 0$, we must rob Δ from the rich half and give it to the poor. There's a position l in the poor half with $c_l = 0$; otherwise that half would sum to at least 2^{d-1}. A cyclic 1-shift that modifies positions l through $(l+t) \bmod 2^d$ makes $c'_{l+k} = c_{l+k+1}$ for $0 \le k < t$, $c'_{l+t} = c_{l+t+1} - \delta$, $c'_{l+t+1} = \delta$, and $c'_{l+k} = c_{l+k}$ for all other k; here δ can be any desired value in the range $0 \le \delta \le c_{l+t+1}$. (We've treated all subscripts modulo 2^d in these formulas.) So we can use the smallest even t such that $c_{l+1} + c_{l+3} + \cdots + c_{l+t+1} = c_l + c_{l+2} + \cdots + c_{l+t} + \Delta + \delta$ for some $\delta \ge 0$.

(The 1-shift need not be cyclic, if we allow ourselves to shift left instead of right. But the cyclic property may be needed in subsequent steps.)

75. Equivalently, given indices $0 \le i_0 < i_1 < \cdots < i_{s-1} < i_s = 2^d$ and $0 = j_0 < j_1 < \cdots < j_{s-1} < j_s = 2^d$, we want to map $(x_{2^d-1} \ldots x_1 x_0)_2 \mapsto (x_{(2^d-1)\varphi} \ldots x_{1\varphi} x_{0\varphi})_2$, where $j\varphi = i_r$ for $j_r \le j < j_{r+1}$ and $0 \le r < s$. If $d = 1$, a mapping module does this.

When $d > 1$, we can set the left-hand crossbars so that they route input i_r to line $i_r \oplus ((i_r + r) \bmod 2)$. If s is even, we recursively ask one of the networks $P(2^{d-1})$ inside $P(2^d)$ to solve the problem for indices $\lfloor \{i_0, i_2, \ldots, i_s\}/2 \rfloor$ and $\lfloor \{j_0, j_2, \ldots, j_s\}/2 \rfloor$, while the other solves it for $\lfloor \{i_1, i_3, \ldots, i_{s-1}, 2^d\}/2 \rfloor$ and $\lceil \{j_0, j_2, \ldots, j_s\}/2 \rceil$. At the right of $P(2^d)$, one can now check that when $j_r \le j < j_{r+1}$, the mapping module for lines j and $j \oplus 1$ has input i_r on line j if $j \equiv r$ (modulo 2), otherwise i_r is on line $j \oplus 1$. A similar proof works when s is odd. For example, if $(i_0, \ldots, i_5) = (j_0, \ldots, j_5) = (0, 1, 3, 5, 7, 8)$, the subproblems have $i = j = (0, 1, 3, 4)$ and $(0, 2, 4)$; $x_7 \ldots x_0 \mapsto x_6 x_7 x_5 x_4 x_2 x_3 x_1 x_0 \mapsto \cdots \mapsto x_5 x_7 x_5 x_3 x_1 x_3 x_1 x_0 \mapsto x_7 x_5 x_5 x_3 x_1 x_1 x_0$.

Notes: This network is a slight improvement over a construction by Yu. P. Ofman, *Trudy Mosk. Mat. Obshchestva* **14** (1965), 186–199. We can implement the corresponding network by substituting a "δ-map" for a δ-swap; instead of (69), we use two masks and do seven operations instead of six: $y \leftarrow x \oplus (x \gg \delta)$, $x \leftarrow x \oplus (y \& \theta) \oplus ((y \& \theta') \ll \delta)$. This extension of (71) therefore takes only d additional units of time.

76. When a mapping network realizes a permutation, all of its modules must act as crossbars; hence $G(n) \ge \lg n!$. Ofman proved that $G(n) \le 2.5n \lg n$, and remarked in a footnote that the constant 2.5 could be improved (without giving any details). We have seen that in fact $G(n) \le 2n \lg n$. Note that $G(3) = 3$.

77. Represent an n-network by $(x_{2^n-1} \ldots x_1 x_0)_2$, where $x_k = $ [the binary representation of k is a possible configuration of 0s and 1s when the network has been applied to all 2^n sequences of 0s and 1s], for $0 \le k < 2^n$. Thus the empty network is represented by $2^{2^n} - 1$, and a sorting network for $n = 3$ is represented by $(10001011)_2$. In general, x represents a sorting network for n elements if and only if it represents an n-network and $\nu x = n + 1$, if and only if $x = 2^0 + 2^1 + 2^3 + 2^7 + \cdots + 2^{2^n - 1}$.

If x represents α according to these conventions, the representation of $\alpha[i:j]$ is $(x \oplus y) \mid (y \gg (2^{n-i} - 2^{n-j}))$, where $y = x \,\&\, \bar{\mu}_{n-i} \,\&\, \mu_{n-j}$.
[See V. R. Pratt, M. O. Rabin, and L. J. Stockmeyer, *STOC* **6** (1974), 122–126.]

78. If $k \ge \lg(m-1)$ the test is valid, because we always have $x_1 + x_2 + \cdots + x_m \ge x_1 \mid x_2 \mid \cdots \mid x_m$, with equality if and only if the sets are disjoint. Moreover, we have $(x_1 + \cdots + x_m) - (x_1 \mid \cdots \mid x_m) \le (m-1)(2^{n-k-1} + \cdots + 1) < (m-1)2^{n-k} \le 2^n$.

Conversely, if $m \ge 2^k + 2$ and $n > 2k$, the test is invalid. We might have, for example, $x_1 + \cdots + x_m = (2^k + 1)(2^{n-k} - 2^{n-2k-1}) + 2^{n-k-1} = 2^n + (2^{n-k} - 2^{n-2k-1})$.

But if $n \le 2k$ the test is still valid when $m = 2^k + 2$, because our proof shows that $x_1 + \cdots + x_m - (x_1 \mid \cdots \mid x_m) \le (2^k + 1)(2^{n-k} - 1) < 2^n$ in that case.

79. $x_{\prime} = (x - 1) \,\&\, \chi$. (And the formula $x_{\prime} = ((x - b - 1) \,\&\, a) + b$ corresponds to (85).) These recipes for x' and $x_{\prime}$ are part of Jörg Arndt's "bit wizardry" routines (2001); their origin is unknown.

80. Perhaps the nicest way is to start with $x \leftarrow \chi - 1$ as a signed number; then while $x \ge 0$, set $x \leftarrow x \,\&\, \chi$, visit x, and set $x \leftarrow 2x - \chi$. (The operation $2x - \chi$ can in fact be performed with a single MMIX instruction, '2ADDU x,x,minuschi'.)

But that trick fails if χ is so large as to be *already* "negative." A slightly slower but more general method starts with $x \leftarrow \chi$ and does the following while $x \ne 0$: Set $t \leftarrow x \,\&\, -x$, visit $\chi - t$, and set $x \leftarrow x - t$.

81. $((z \,\&\, \chi) - (z' \,\&\, \chi)) \,\&\, \chi$. (One way to verify this formula is to use (18).)

82. Yes, by letting $z = z'$ in (86): $w \mid (z \,\&\, \bar{\chi})$, where $w = ((z \,\&\, \chi) + (z \mid \bar{\chi})) \,\&\, \chi$.

83. (The following iteration propagates bits of y to the right, in the gaps of a scattered accumulator t. Auxiliary variables u and v respectively mark the left and right of each gap; they double in size until being wiped out by w.) Set $t \leftarrow z \,\&\, \chi$, $u' \leftarrow (\chi \gg 1) \,\&\, \bar{\chi}$, $v \leftarrow ((\chi \ll 1) + 1) \,\&\, \bar{\chi}$, $w \leftarrow 3(u' \,\&\, v)$, $u \leftarrow 3u'$, $v \leftarrow 3v$, and $k \leftarrow 1$. Then, while $u \ne 0$, do the following steps: $t \leftarrow t \mid ((t \gg k) \,\&\, u')$, $k \leftarrow k \ll 1$, $u \leftarrow u \,\&\, \overline{w}$, $v \leftarrow v \,\&\, \overline{w}$, $w \leftarrow ((v \,\&\, (u \gg 1) \,\&\, \bar{u}) \ll (k+1)) - ((u \,\&\, (v \ll 1) \,\&\, \bar{v}) \gg k)$, $u' \leftarrow (u \,\&\, \bar{v}) \gg k$, $v \leftarrow v + ((v \,\&\, \bar{u}) \ll k)$, $u \leftarrow u + u'$. Finally return the answer $((t \gg 1) \,\&\, \chi) \mid (z \,\&\, \bar{\chi})$.

84. $z \leftarrow \chi = w - (z \,\&\, \chi)$, where $w = (((z \,\&\, \chi) \ll 1) + \bar{\chi}) \,\&\, \chi$ appears in answer 82; $z \rightarrow \chi$ is the quantity t computed (with more difficulty) in the answer to exercise 83.

85. (a) If $x = \text{LOC}(a[i,j,k])$ is the drum location corresponding to interleaved bits as stated, then $\text{LOC}(a[i+1,j,k]) = x \oplus ((x \oplus ((x \,\&\, \chi) - \chi)) \,\&\, \chi)$ and $\text{LOC}(a[i-1,j,k]) = x \oplus ((x \oplus ((x \,\&\, \chi) - 1)) \,\&\, \chi)$, where $\chi = (11111)_8$, by (84) and answer 79. The formulas for $\text{LOC}(a[i, j \pm 1, k])$ and $\text{LOC}(a[i,j,k \pm 1])$ are similar, with masks 2χ and 4χ.

(b) For random access, let's hope there is room for a table of length 32 giving $f[(i_4 i_3 i_2 i_1 i_0)_2] = (i_4 i_3 i_2 i_1 i_0)_8$. Then $\text{LOC}(a[i,j,k]) = (((f[k] \ll 1) + f[j]) \ll 1) + f[i]$. (On a vintage machine, bitwise computation of f would be much worse than table lookup, because register operations used to be as slow as fetches from memory.)

(c) Let p be the location of the page currently in fast memory, and let $z = -128$. When accessing location x, if $x \,\&\, z \ne p$ it is necessary to read 128 words from drum location $x \,\&\, z$ (after saving the current data to drum location p if it has changed); then set $p \leftarrow x \,\&\, z$. [See *J. Royal Stat. Soc.* **B-16** (1954), 53–55. This scheme of array allocation for external storage was devised independently by E. W. Dijkstra, circa 1960, who called it the "zip-fastener" method. It has often been rediscovered, for example in 1966 by G. M. Morton and later by developers of quadtrees; see Hanan Samet, *Applications of Spatial Data Structures* (Addison–Wesley, 1990). See also R. Raman and D. S. Wise, *IEEE Trans.* **C57** (2008), 567–573, for a contemporary perspective. Georg Cantor had considered interleaving the digits of decimal fractions in *Crelle* **84** (1878), 242–258, §7; but he observed that this idea does *not* lead to an easy one-to-one correspondence between the unit interval $[0 . . 1]$ and the unit square $[0 . . 1] \times [0 . . 1]$.]

86. If (p', q', r') rightmost bits and (p'', q'', r'') other bits of (i, j, k) are in the part of the address that does not affect the page number, the total number of page faults is $2((2^{p-p'} - 1)2^{q+r} + (2^{q-q'} - 1)2^{p+r} + (2^{r-r'} - 1)2^{p+q})$. Hence we want to minimize $2^{-p'} + 2^{-q'} + 2^{-r'}$ over nonnegative integers $(p', q', r', p'', q'', r'')$ with $p' + p'' \leq p$, $q' + q'' \leq q$, $r' + r'' \leq r$, $p' + q' + r' + p'' + q'' + r'' = s$. Since $2^a + 2^b > 2^{a-1} + 2^{b+1}$ when a and b are integers with $a > b+1$, the minimum (for all s) occurs when we select bits from right to left cyclically until running out. For example, when $(p, q, r) = (2, 6, 3)$ the addressing function would be $(j_5 j_4 j_3 k_2 j_2 k_1 j_1 i_1 k_0 j_0 i_0)_2$. In particular, Tocher's scheme is optimal.

[But such a mapping is not necessarily best when the page size isn't a power of 2. For example, consider a 16×16 matrix; the addressing function $(j_3 i_3 i_2 i_1 i_0 j_2 j_1 j_0)_2$ is better than $(j_3 i_3 j_2 i_2 j_1 i_1 j_0 i_0)_2$ for all page sizes from 17 to 62, except for size 32 when they are equally good.]

87. Set $x \leftarrow x \& \sim((x \& \text{"@@@@@@@@"}) \gg 1)$; each byte $(a_7 \ldots a_0)_2$ is thereby changed to $(a_7 a_6 (a_5 \wedge \bar{a}_6) a_4 \ldots a_0)_2$. The same transformation works also on 30 additional letters in the Latin-1 supplement to ASCII (for example, æ $\mapsto$ Æ); but there's one glitch, ÿ $\mapsto$ ß.

[Don Woods used this trick in his original program for the game of Adventure (1976), uppercasing the user's input words before looking them up in a dictionary.]

88. Set $z \leftarrow (x \oplus \bar{y}) \& h$, then $z \leftarrow ((x \mid h) - (y \& \bar{h})) \oplus z$.

89. $t \leftarrow x \mid \bar{y}$, $t \leftarrow t \& (t \gg 1)$, $z \leftarrow (x \& \bar{y} \& \bar{\mu}_0) \mid (t \& \mu_0)$. [From the "nasty" test program for H. G. Dietz and R. J. Fisher's SWARC compiler (1998), optimized by T. Dahlheimer.]

90. Insert '$z \leftarrow z \mid ((x \oplus y) \& l)$' either before or after '$z \leftarrow (x \& y) + z$'. (The ordering makes no difference, because $x + y \equiv x \oplus y$ (modulo 4) when $x + y$ is odd. Therefore MMIX can round to odd at no additional cost, using MOR. Rounding to even in the ambiguous cases is more difficult, and with fixed point arithmetic it is not advantageous.)

91. If $\frac{1}{2}[x, y]$ denotes the average as in (88), the desired result is obtained by repeating the following operations seven times, then concluding with $z \leftarrow \frac{1}{2}[x, y]$ once more:

$$z \leftarrow \frac{1}{2}[x, y], \quad t \leftarrow \alpha \& h, \quad m \leftarrow (t \ll 1) - (t \gg 7),$$
$$x \leftarrow (m \& z) \mid (\overline{m} \& x), \quad y \leftarrow (\overline{m} \& z) \mid (m \& y), \quad \alpha \leftarrow \alpha \ll 1.$$

Although rounding errors accumulate through eight levels, the resulting absolute error never exceeds $807/255$. Moreover, it is ≈ 1.13 if we average over all 256^3 cases, and it is less than 2 with probability $\approx 94.2\%$. If we round to odd as in exercise 90, the maximum and average error are reduced to $616/255$ and ≈ 0.58; the probability of error < 2 rises to $\approx 99.9\%$. Therefore the following MMIX code uses such unbiased rounding:

```
x GREG ;y GREG ;z GREG              ⎛ XOR  t,x,y      MOR  m,ffhi,alf ⎞
alf GREG ;m GREG ;t IS $255         ⎜ MOR  z,rodd,t   PUT  rM,m       ⎜
                 repeat seven times: ⎨ AND  t,x,y      MUX  x,z,x       ⎬
rodd GREG #4020100804020101         ⎜ ADDU z,z,t      MUX  y,y,z       ⎜
ffhi GREG -1<<56                    ⎝                 SLU  alf,alf,1   ⎠
```

but omit the final SLU, then repeat the first four instructions again. The total time for eight α-blends ($66v$) is less than the cost of eight multiplications.

92. We get $z_j = \lceil (x_j + y_j)/2 \rceil$ for each j. (This fact, noticed by H. S. Warren, Jr., follows from the identity $x + y = ((x \mid y) \ll 1) - (x \oplus y)$. See also the next exercise.)

93. $x - y = (x \oplus y) - ((\bar{x} \& y) \ll 1)$. ("Borrows" instead of "carries.")

94. $(x - l)_j = (x_j - 1 - b_j) \bmod 256$, where b_j is the "borrow" from fields to the right. So t_j is nonzero if and only if $(x_j \ldots x_0)_{256} < (1 \ldots 1)_{256} = (256^{j+1} - 1)/255$. (The answers to the stated questions are therefore "yes" and "no.")

In general if the constant l is allowed to have *any* value $(l_7 \ldots l_1 l_0)_{256}$, operation (90) makes $t_j \neq 0$ if and only if $(x_j \ldots x_0)_{256} < (l_j \ldots l_0)_{256}$ and $x_j < 128$.

95. Use (90): Test if $h \& (t(x \oplus ((x \gg 8) + (x \ll 56))) \mid t(x \oplus ((x \gg 16) + (x \ll 48))) \mid t(x \oplus ((x \gg 24) + (x \ll 40))) \mid t(x \oplus ((x \gg 32) + (x \ll 32)))) = 0$, where $t(x) = (x - l) \& \bar{x}$. (These 28 steps reduce to 20 if cyclic shift is available, or to 11 with MXOR and BDIF.)

96. Suppose $0 \le x, y < 256$, $x_h = \lfloor x/128 \rfloor$, $x_l = x \bmod 128$, $y_h = \lfloor y/128 \rfloor$, $y_l = y \bmod 128$. Then $[x < y] = \langle \bar{x}_h y_h [x_l < y_l] \rangle$; see exercise 7.1.1–106. And $[x_l < y_l] = [y_l + 127 - x_l \ge 128]$. Hence $[x < y] = \lfloor \langle \bar{x} y z \rangle/128 \rfloor$, where $z = (\bar{x} \& 127) + (y \& 127)$.

It follows that $t = h \& \langle \bar{x} y z \rangle$ has the desired properties, when $z = (\bar{x} \& \bar{h}) + (y \& \bar{h})$. This formula can also be written $t = h \& \sim \langle x \bar{y} \bar{z} \rangle$, where $\bar{z} = \sim ((\bar{x} \& \bar{h}) + (y \& \bar{h})) = (x \mid h) - (y \& \bar{h})$ by (18).

To get a similar test function for $[x_j \le y_j] = 1 - [y_j < x_j]$, we just interchange $x \leftrightarrow y$ and take the complement: $t \leftarrow h \& \sim \langle x \bar{y} z \rangle = h \& \langle \bar{x} y \bar{z} \rangle$, where $z = (x \& \bar{h}) + (\bar{y} \& \bar{h})$.

97. Set $x' \leftarrow x \oplus \texttt{"********"}$, $y' \leftarrow x \oplus y$, $t \leftarrow h \& (x \mid ((x \mid h) - l)) \& (y' \mid ((y' \mid h) - l))$, $m \leftarrow (t \ll 1) - (t \gg 7)$, $t \leftarrow t \& (x' \mid ((x' \mid h) - l))$, $z \leftarrow (m \& \texttt{"********"}) \mid (\overline{m} \& y)$. (20 steps.)

98. Set $u \leftarrow x \oplus y$, $z \leftarrow (\bar{x} \& \bar{h}) + (y \& \bar{h})$, $t \leftarrow h \& (x \oplus (u \mid (x \oplus z)))$, $v \leftarrow ((t \ll 1) - (t \gg 7)) \& u$, $z \leftarrow x \oplus v$, $w \leftarrow y \oplus v$. [This 14-step procedure invokes answer 96 to compute $t = h \& \langle \bar{x} y z \rangle$, using the footprint method of Section 7.1.2 to evaluate the median in only three steps when $x \oplus y$ is known. Of course the MMIX solution is much quicker, if available: BDIF t,x,y; ADDU z,y,t; SUBU w,x,t.]

99. In this potpourri, each of the eight bytes appears to be solving a different kind of problem; we must recast the conditions so that they fit into a common framework: $f_0 = [x_0 \oplus \texttt{'!'} \le 0]$, $f_1 = [x_1 \oplus \texttt{'*'} > 0]$, $f_2 = [x_2 \le \texttt{'A'} - 1]$, $f_3 = [x_3 > \texttt{'z'}]$, $f_4 = [x_4 > \texttt{'a'} - 1]$, $f_5 = [x_5 \oplus \texttt{'0'} \le 9]$, $f_6 = [x_6 \oplus 255 > 86]$, $f_7 = [x_7 \oplus \texttt{'?'} \le 3]$. Aha! We can use the formulas in answer 96, adjusting d to switch between $\le$ and $>$ as needed: $a = (\texttt{'?'}(255)\texttt{'0'}000\texttt{'*'}\texttt{'!'})_{256} = {}^\#\texttt{3fff300000002a21}$; $b = \bar{h} = {}^\#\texttt{7f7f7f7f7f7f7f7f}$; $c = \bar{h} \& \sim (3(86)9(\texttt{'a'} - 1)\texttt{'z'}(\texttt{'A'} - 1)00)_{256} = {}^\#\texttt{7c29761f053f7f7f}$ (the hardest one); $d = {}^\#\texttt{8000800000800080}$; and $e = h = {}^\#\texttt{8080808080808080}$.

100. We want $u_j = x_j + y_j + c_j - 10 c_{j+1}$ and $v_j = x_j - y_j - b_j + 10 b_{j+1}$, where c_j and b_j are the "carry" and "borrow" into digit position j. Set $u' \leftarrow (x + y + (6 \ldots 66)_{16}) \bmod 2^{64}$ and $v' \leftarrow (x - y) \bmod 2^{64}$. Then we find $u'_j = x_j + y_j + c_j + 6 - 16 c_{j+1}$ and $v'_j = x_j - y_j - b_j + 16 b_{j+1}$ for $0 \le j < 16$, by induction on j. Hence u' and v' have the same pattern of carries and borrows as if we were working in radix 10, and we have $u = u' - 6(\bar{c}_{16} \ldots \bar{c}_2 \bar{c}_1)_{16}$, $v = v' - 6(b_{16} \ldots b_2 b_1)_{16}$. The following computation schemes therefore provide the desired results (10 operations for addition, 9 for subtraction):

$$y' \leftarrow y + (6 \ldots 66)_{16}, \quad u' \leftarrow x + y', \qquad\qquad v' \leftarrow x - y,$$
$$t \leftarrow \langle \bar{x} \bar{y}' u' \rangle \& (8 \ldots 88)_{16}, \qquad\qquad t \leftarrow \langle \bar{x} y v' \rangle \& (8 \ldots 88)_{16},$$
$$u \leftarrow u' - t + (t \gg 2); \qquad\qquad v \leftarrow v' - t + (t \gg 2).$$

101. For subtraction, set $z \leftarrow x - y$; for addition, set $z \leftarrow x + y + {}^{\#}\texttt{e8c4c4fc18}$, where this constant is built from $256 - 24 = {}^{\#}\texttt{e8}$, $256 - 60 = {}^{\#}\texttt{c4}$, and $65536 - 1000 = {}^{\#}\texttt{fc18}$. Borrows and carries will occur between fields as if mixed-radix subtraction or addition were being performed. The remaining task is to correct for cases in which borrows occurred or carries did not; we can do this easily by inspecting individual digits, because the radices are less than half of the field sizes: Set $t \leftarrow z \mathbin{\&} {}^{\#}\texttt{8080808000}$, $t \leftarrow (t \ll 1) - (t \gg 7) - ((t \gg 15) \mathbin{\&} 1)$, $z \leftarrow z - (t \mathbin{\&} {}^{\#}\texttt{e8c4c4fc18})$. [See Stephen Soule, *CACM* **18** (1975), 344–346. We're lucky that the 'c' in 'fc18' is even.]

102. (a) We assume that $x = (x_{15} \dots x_0)_{16}$ and $y = (y_{15} \dots y_0)_{16}$, with $0 \leq x_j, y_j < 5$; the goal is to compute $u = (u_{15} \dots u_0)_{16}$ and $v = (v_{15} \dots v_0)_{16}$, with components $u_j = (x_j + y_j) \bmod 5$ and $v_j = (x_j - y_j) \bmod 5$. Here's how:

$$u \leftarrow x + y, \qquad\qquad\qquad v \leftarrow x - y + 5l,$$
$$t \leftarrow (u + 3l) \mathbin{\&} h, \qquad\qquad t \leftarrow (v + 3l) \mathbin{\&} h,$$
$$u \leftarrow u - ((t - (t \gg 3)) \mathbin{\&} 5l); \qquad v \leftarrow v - ((t - (t \gg 3)) \mathbin{\&} 5l).$$

Here $l = (1 \dots 1)_{16} = (2^{64} - 1)/15$, $h = 8l$. (Addition in 7 operations, subtraction in 8.)

(b) Now $x = (x_{20} \dots x_0)_8$, etc., and we must be more careful to confine carries:

$$t \leftarrow x + \bar{h}, \qquad\qquad\qquad\qquad z \leftarrow (x \mid h) - (y \mathbin{\&} \bar{h}),$$
$$z \leftarrow (t \mathbin{\&} \bar{h}) + (y \mathbin{\&} \bar{h}), \qquad\qquad t \leftarrow (y \mid \bar{z}) \mathbin{\&} \bar{x} \mathbin{\&} h,$$
$$t \leftarrow (y \mid z) \mathbin{\&} t \mathbin{\&} h, \qquad\qquad\quad v \leftarrow x - y + t + (t \gg 2).$$
$$u \leftarrow x + y - (t + (t \gg 2));$$

Here $h = (4 \dots 4)_8 = (2^{65} - 4)/7$. (Addition in 11 operations, subtraction in 10.)

Similar procedures work, of course, for other moduli. In fact we can do multibyte arithmetic on the coordinates of toruses in general, with different moduli in each component (see 7.2.1.3–(66)).

103. Let h and l be the constants in (87) and (88). Addition is easy: $u \leftarrow x \mid ((x \mathbin{\&} \bar{h}) + y)$. For subtraction, take away 1 and add $x_j \mathbin{\&} (1 - y_j)$: $t \leftarrow (x \mathbin{\&} \bar{l}) \gg 1$, $v \leftarrow t \mid (t + (x \mathbin{\&} (y \oplus l)))$.

104. Yes, in 19: Let $a = (((1901 \ll 4) + 1) \ll 5) + 1$, $b = (((2099 \ll 4) + 12) \ll 5) + 28$. Set $m \leftarrow (x \gg 5) \mathbin{\&} {}^{\#}\texttt{f}$ (the month), $c \leftarrow {}^{\#}\texttt{10} \mathbin{\&} \sim((x \mid (x \gg 1)) \gg 5)$ (the leap year correction), $u \leftarrow b + {}^{\#}\texttt{3} \mathbin{\&} (({}^{\#}\texttt{3bbeecc} + c) \gg (m + m))$ (the *max_day* adjustment), and $t \leftarrow ((x \oplus a \oplus (x - a)) \mid (x \oplus u \oplus (u - x))) \mathbin{\&} {}^{\#}\texttt{1000220}$ (the test for unwanted carries).

105. Exercise 98 explains how to compute bytewise min and max; a simple modification will compute min in some byte positions and max in others. Thus we can "sort by perfect shuffles" as in Section 5.3.4, Fig. 57, if we can permute bytes between x and y appropriately. And such permutation is easy, by exercise 1. [Of course there are much simpler and faster ways to sort 16 bytes. But see S. Albers and T. Hagerup, *Inf. and Computation* **136** (1997), 25–51, and M. Thorup, *J. Algorithms* **42** (2002), 205–230, for asymptotic implications of this approach.]

106. The n bits are regarded as g fields of g bits each. First the nonzero fields are detected (t_1), and we form a word y that has $(y_{g-1} \dots y_0)_2$ in each g-bit field, where $y_j = [\text{field } j \text{ of } x \text{ is nonzero}]$. Then we compare each field with the constants 2^{g-1}, $\dots, 2^0$ (t_2), and form a mask m that identifies the most significant nonzero field of x. After putting g copies of that field into z, we test z as we tested y (t_3). Finally an appropriate sideways addition of t_2 and t_3 (g-bit-wise) yields λ. (Try the case $g = 4$, $n = 16$.)

To compute 2^λ without shifting left, replace '$t_2 \ll 1$' by '$t_2 + t_2$', and replace the final line by $w \leftarrow (((a \cdot (t_3 \oplus (t_3 \gg g)))) \bmod 2^n) \gg (n - g)) \cdot l$; then $w \mathbin{\&} m$ is $2^{\lambda x}$.

107. h `GREG #8000800080008000`   `SLU q,t,16`   `OR  t,t,y`
   ms `GREG #00ff0f0f33335555`   `ADDU t,t,q`   `AND  t,t,h`
  1H `SRU  q,x,32`   `SLU  q,t,32` **5H** `SLU q,t,15`
     `ZSNZ lam,q,32`   `ADDU t,t,q`   `ADDU t,t,q`
     `ADD  t,lam,16`   **3H** `ANDN y,t,ms`   `SLU  q,t,30`
     `SRU  q,x,t`   **4H** `XOR  t,t,y`   `ADDU t,t,q`
     `CSNZ lam,q,t`   `OR   q,y,h` **6H** `SRU q,t,60`
  2H `SRU  t,x,lam`   `SUBU t,q,t`   `ADDU lam,lam,q` ∎

The total time is 22υ (and no mems). [There's also a mem-less version of (56), costing only 16υ, if its last line is replaced by `ADD t,lam,4; SRU y,x,t; CSNZ lam,y,t; SRU y,x,lam; SLU t,y,1; SRU t,[#ffffaa50],t; AND t,t,3; ADD lam,lam,t.`]

108. For example, let e be minimum so that $n \le 2^e \cdot 2^{2^e}$. If n is a multiple of 2^e, we can use 2^e fields of size $n/2^e$, with e reductions in step B1; otherwise we can use 2^e fields of size $2^{\lceil \lg n \rceil - e - 1}$, with $e+1$ reductions in step B1. In either case there are e iterations in steps B2 and B5, so the total running time is $O(e) = O(\log \log n)$.

109. Start with $x \leftarrow x \,\&\, -x$ and apply Algorithm B. (Step B4 of that algorithm can be slightly simplified in this special case, using a constant l instead of $x \oplus y$.)

110. Let $s = 2^d$ where $d = 2^e - e$. We will use s-bit fields in n-bit words.

K1. [Stretch $x \bmod s$.] Set $y \leftarrow x \,\&\, (s-1)$. Then set $t \leftarrow y \,\&\, \bar{\mu}_j$ and $y \leftarrow y \oplus t \oplus (t \ll 2^j (s-1))$ for $e > j \ge 0$. Finally set $y \leftarrow (y \ll s) - y$. [If $x = (x_{2^e - 1} \dots x_0)_2$ we now have $y = (y_{2^e - 1} \dots y_0)_{2^s}$, where $y_j = (2^s - 1) x_j [j < d]$.]

K2. [Set up minterms.] Set $y \leftarrow y \oplus (a_{2^e - 1} \dots a_0)_{2^s}$, where $a_j = \mu_{d,j}$ for $0 \le j < d$ and $a_j = 2^s - 1$ for $d \le j < 2^e$.

K3. [Compress.] Set $y \leftarrow y \,\&\, (y \gg 2^j s)$ for $e > j \ge 0$. [Now $y = 1 \ll (x \bmod s)$. This is the key point that makes the algorithm work.]

K4. [Finish.] Set $y \leftarrow y \,|\, (y \ll 2^j s)$ for $0 \le j < e$. Finally set $y \leftarrow y \,\&\, (\mu_{2^e, j} \oplus -((x \gg j) \,\&\, 1))$ for $d \le j < 2^e$. ∎

111. The n bits are divided into fields of s bits each, although the leftmost field might be shorter. First y is set to flag the all-1 fields. Then $t = (\dots t_1 t_0)_{2^s}$ contains candidate bits for q, including "false drops" for certain patterns 01^k with $s \le k < r$. We always have $\upsilon t_j \le 1$, and $t_j \ne 0$ implies $t_{j-1} = 0$. The bits of u and v subdivide t into two parts so that we can safely compute $m = (t \gg 1) \,|\, (t \gg 2) \,|\, \cdots \,|\, (t \gg r)$, before making a final test to eliminate the false drops.

112. Notice that if $q = x \,\&\, (x \ll 1) \,\&\, \cdots \,\&\, (x \ll (r-1)) \,\&\, \sim(x \ll r)$ then we have $x \,\&\, \overline{x+q} = x \,\&\, (x \ll 1) \,\&\, \cdots \,\&\, (x \ll (r-1))$.

If we can solve the stated problem in $O(1)$ steps, we can also extract the most significant bit of an r-bit number in $O(1)$ steps: Apply the case $n = 2r$ to the number $2^n - 1 - x$. Conversely, a solution to the extraction problem can be shown to yield a solution to the $1^r 0$ problem. Exercise 110 therefore implies a solution in $O(\log \log r)$ steps.

113. Let $0' = 0$, $x'_0 = x_0$, and construct $x'_{i'} = x_i$ for $1 \le i \le r$ as follows: If $x_i = a \circ_i b$ and $\circ_i \notin \{+, -, \ll\}$, let $i' = (i-1)' + 1$ and $x'_{i'} = a' \circ_i b'$, where $a' = x'_{j'}$ if $a = x_j$ and $a' = a$ if $a = c_i$. If $x_i = a \ll c$, let $i' = (i-1)' + 2$ and $(x'_{i'-1}, x'_{i'}) = (a' \,\&\, (\lceil 2^{n-c} \rceil - 1), x'_{i'-1} \ll c)$. If $x_i = a + b$, let $i' = (i-1)' + 6$ and let $(x'_{(i-1)'+1}, \dots, x'_{i'})$ compute $((a' \,\&\, \bar{h}) + (b' \,\&\, \bar{h})) \oplus ((a' \oplus b') \,\&\, h)$, where $h = 2^{n-1}$. And if $x_i = a - b$, do the similar computation $((a' \,|\, h) - (b' \,\&\, \bar{h})) \oplus ((a' \equiv b') \,\&\, h)$. Clearly $r' \le 6r$.

114. Simply let $X_i = X_{j(i)} \circ_i X_{k(i)}$ when $x_i = x_{j(i)} \circ_i x_{k(i)}$, $X_i = C_i \circ_i X_{k(i)}$ when $x_i = c_i \circ_i x_{k(i)}$, and $X_i = X_{j(i)} \circ_i C_i$ when $x_i = x_{j(i)} \circ_i c_i$, where $C_i = c_i$ when c_i is a shift amount, otherwise $C_i = (c_i \ldots c_i)_{2^n} = (2^{mn} - 1)c_i/(2^n - 1)$. This construction is possible thanks to the fact that variable-length shifts are prohibited.

[Notice that if $m = 2^d$, we can use this idea to simulate 2^d instances of $f(x, y_i)$; then $O(d)$ further operations allow "quantification."]

115. (a) $z \leftarrow (\bar{x} \ll 1) \& (x \ll 2)$, $y \leftarrow x \& (x + z)$. [This problem was posed to the author by Vaughan Pratt in 1977.]

(b) First find $x_l \leftarrow (x \ll 1) \& \bar{x}$ and $x_r \leftarrow x \& (\bar{x} \ll 1)$, the left and right ends of x's blocks; and set $x_r' \leftarrow x_r \& (x_r - 1)$. Then $z_e \leftarrow x_r' \& (x_r' - (x_l \& \mu_0))$ and $z_o \leftarrow x_r' \& (x_r' - (x_l \& \mu_0))$ are the right ends that are followed by a left end in even or odd position, respectively. The answer is $y \leftarrow x \& (x + (z_e \& \bar{\mu}_0) + (z_o \& \mu_0))$; it can be simplified to $y \leftarrow x \& (x + (z_e \oplus (x_r' \& \mu_0)))$.

(c) This case is impossible, by Corollary I.

116. The language L is well defined, by Lemma A (except that the presence or absence of the empty string is irrelevant). A language is regular if and only if it can be defined by a finite-state automaton, and a 2-adic integer is rational if and only if it can be defined by a finite-state automaton that ignores its inputs. The identity function corresponds to the language $L = 1(0 \cup 1)^*$, and a simple construction will define an automaton that corresponds to the sum, difference, or Boolean combination of the numbers defined by any two given automata acting on the sequence $x_0 x_1 x_2 \ldots$. Hence L is regular.

In exercise 115, L is (a) $11^*(000^*1(0 \cup 1)^* \cup 0^*)$; (b) $11^*(00(00)^*1(0 \cup 1)^* \cup 0^*)$.

117. Incidentally, the stated language L corresponds to an inverse Gray binary code: It defines a function with the property that $f(2x) = \sim f(2x + 1)$, and $g(f(2x)) = g(f(2x + 1)) = x$, where $g(x) = x \oplus (x \gg 1)$ (see Eq. 7.2.1.1–(9)).

118. If $x = (x_{n-1} \ldots x_1 x_0)_2$ and $0 \le a_j \le 2^j$ for $0 \le j < n$, we have $\sum_{j=0}^{n-1} a_j x_j = \sum_{j=0}^{n-1} (a_j \dotdiv (\bar{x} \& 2^j))$. Take $a_j = \lfloor 2^{j-1} \rfloor$ to get $x \gg 1$.

Conversely, the following argument by M. S. Paterson proves that monus must be used at least $n - 1$ times: Consider any chain for $f(x)$ that uses addition, subtraction, bitwise Booleans, and k occurrences of the "underflow" operation $y \lhd z = (2^n - 1)[y < z]$. If $k < n - 1$ there must be two n-bit numbers x' and x'' such that $x' \bmod 2 = x'' \bmod 2 = 0$ and such that all k of the $\lhd$'s yield the same result for both x' and x''. Then $f(x') \bmod 2^j = f(x'') \bmod 2^j$ when $j = \rho(x' \oplus x'')$. So $f(x)$ is not the function $x \gg 1$.

119. $z \leftarrow x \oplus y$, $f \leftarrow 2^p \& \bar{z} \& (z - 1)$. (See (90).)

120. Generalizing Corollary W, these are the functions such that $f(x_1, \ldots, x_m) \equiv f(y_1, \ldots, y_m)$ (modulo 2^k) whenever $x_j \equiv y_j$ (modulo 2^k) for $1 \le j \le m$, for $0 \le k \le n$. The least significant bit is a binary function of m variables, so it has 2^{2^m} possibilities. The next-to-least is a binary function of $2m$ variables, namely the bits of $(x_1 \bmod 4, \ldots, x_m \bmod 4)$, so it has $2^{2^{2m}}$; and so on. Thus the answer is $2^{2^m + 2^{2m} + \cdots + 2^{nm}}$.

121. (a) If f has a period of length pq, where $q > 1$ is odd, its p-fold iteration $f^{[p]}$ has a period of length q, say $y_0 \mapsto y_1 \mapsto \cdots \mapsto y_q = y_0$ where $y_{j+1} = f^{[p]}(y_j)$ and $y_1 \ne y_0$. But then, by Corollary W, we must have $y_0 \bmod 2^{n-1} \mapsto y_1 \bmod 2^{n-1} \mapsto \cdots \mapsto y_q \bmod 2^{n-1}$ in the corresponding $(n - 1)$-bit chain. Consequently $y_1 \equiv y_0$ (modulo 2^{n-1}), by induction on n. Hence $y_1 = y_0 \oplus 2^{n-1}$, and $y_2 = y_0$, etc., a contradiction.

(b) $x_1 = x_0 + x_0$, $x_2 = x_0 \gg (p - 1)$, $x_3 = x_1 \mid x_2$; a period of length p starts with the value $x_0 = (1 + 2^p + 2^{2p} + \cdots) \bmod 2^n$.

122. Subtraction is analogous to addition; Boolean operations are even simpler; and constants have only one bit pattern. The only remaining case is $x_r = x_j \gg c$, where we have $S_r = S_j + c$; the shift goes left when $c < 0$. Then $V_{pqr} = V_{(p+c)(q+c)j}$, and

$$x_r \mathbin{\&} \lfloor 2^p - 2^q \rfloor = \bigl((x_j \mathbin{\&} \lfloor 2^{p+c} - 2^{q+c} \rfloor) \gg c\bigr) \mathbin{\&} (2^n - 1).$$

Hence $|X_{pqr}| \leq |X_{(p+c)(q+c)j}| \leq B_j = B_r$ by induction.

123. If $x = (x_{g-1} \ldots x_0)_2$, note first that $t = 2^{g-1}(x_0 \ldots x_{g-1})_{2^g}$ in (104); hence $y = (x_0 \ldots x_{g-1})_2$ as claimed. Theorem P now implies that $\lfloor \frac{1}{3} \lg g \rfloor$ broadword steps are needed to multiply by a_{g+1} and by a_{g-1}. At least one of those multiplications must require $\lfloor \frac{1}{6} \lg g \rfloor$ or more steps.

124. Initially $t \leftarrow 0$, $x_0 = x$, $U_0 = \{2^0, 2^1, \ldots, 2^{n-1}\}$, and $1' \leftarrow 0$. When advancing $t \leftarrow t+1$, if the current instruction is $r_i \leftarrow r_j \pm r_k$ we simply define $x_t = x_{j'} \pm x_{k'}$ and $i' \leftarrow t$. The cases $r_i \leftarrow r_j \circ r_k$ and $r_i \leftarrow c$ are similar.

If the current instruction branches when $r_i \leq r_j$, define $x_t = x_{t-1}$ and let $V_1 = \{x \in U_{t-1} \mid x_{i'} \leq x_{j'}\}$, $V_0 = U_{t-1} \setminus V_1$. Let U_t be the larger of V_0 and V_1; branch if $U_t = V_1$. Notice that $|U_t| \geq |U_{t-1}|/2$ in this case.

If the current instruction is $r_i \leftarrow r_j \gg r_k$, let $W = \{x \in U_{t-1} \mid x \mathbin{\&} \lfloor 2^{\lg n + s} - 2^s \rfloor \neq 0$ for some $s \in S_{k'}\}$, and note that $|W| \leq |S_{k'}| \lg n \leq 2^{t-1+e+f}$. Let $V_c = \{x \in U_{t-1} \setminus W \mid x_{k'} = c\}$ for $|c| < n$, and $V_n = U_{t-1} \setminus W \setminus \bigcup_{|c|<n} V_c$. Lemma B tells us that at most $B_{k'} + 1 \leq 2^{2^{t-1}-1} + 1$ of the sets V_c are nonempty. Let U_t be the largest; and if it is V_c, define $x_t = x_{j'} \gg c$, $i' \leftarrow t$. In this case $|U_t| \geq (|U_{t-1}| - 2^{t-1+e+f})/(2^{2^{t-1}-1} + 1)$.

Similarly for $r_i \leftarrow M[r_j \bmod 2^m]$ or $M[r_j \bmod 2^m] \leftarrow r_i$, let $W = \{x \in U_{t-1} \mid x \mathbin{\&} \lfloor 2^{m+s} - 2^s \rfloor \neq 0$ for some $s \in S_{j'}\}$, and $V_z = \{x \in U_{t-1} \setminus W \mid x_{j'} \bmod 2^m = z\}$, for $0 \leq z < 2^m$. By Lemma B, at most $B_{j'} \leq 2^{2^{t-1}-1}$ of the sets V_z are nonempty; let $U_t = V_z$ be the largest. To write r_i in $M[z]$, define $x_t = x_{t-1}$, $z'' \leftarrow i'$; to read r_i from $M[z]$, set $i' \leftarrow t$ and put $x_t = x_{z''}$ if z'' is defined, otherwise let x_t be the precomputed constant $M[z]$. In both cases $|U_t| \geq (|U_{t-1}| - 2^{t-1}m)/2^{2^{t-1}-1}$ is sufficiently large.

If $t < f$ we cannot be sure that $r_1 = \rho x$. The reason is that the set $W = \{x \in U_t \mid x \mathbin{\&} \lfloor 2^{\lg n + s} - 2^s \rfloor \neq 0$ for some $s \in S_{1'}\}$ has size $|W| \leq |S_{1'}| \lg n \leq 2^{t+e+f}$, and $|U_t \setminus W| \geq 2^{2^{e+f}-2^t+1} - 2^{t+e+f} > 2^{2^t-1} \geq |\{x_{1'} \mathbin{\&} \lfloor 2^{\lg n} - 1 \rfloor \mid x_0 \in U_t \setminus W\}|$. Two elements of $U_t \setminus W$ cannot have the same value of $\rho x = x_{1'} \mathbin{\&} \lfloor 2^{\lg n} - 1 \rfloor$.

[The same lower bound applies even if we allow the RAM to make arbitrary $2^{2^{t-1}}$-way branches based on the contents of $(r_1, \ldots, r_l)$ at time t.]

125. Start as in answer 124, but with $U_0 = [0 .. 2^g)$. Simplifying that argument by eliminating the sets W will yield sets such that $|U_t| \geq 2^g / \max(2^m, 2n)^t$; for example, at most $2n$ different shift instructions can occur.

Suppose we can stop at time t with $t < \lfloor \lg(h+1) \rfloor$. The proof of Theorem P yields p and q with $x^R \mathbin{\&} \lfloor 2^p - 2^q \rfloor$ independent of $x \mathbin{\&} \lfloor 2^{p+s} - 2^{q+s} \rfloor$. Hence the hinted extension of Lemma B shows that x^R takes on at most $2^{2^t-1} \leq 2^{(h-1)/2}$ different values, for every setting of the other bits $\{x \mathbin{\&} \lfloor 2^{p+s} - 2^{q+s} \rfloor \mid s \in S_t\}$. Consequently $r_1 = x_{1'}$ can be the correct value of x^R for at most $2^{(h-1)/2+g-h}$ values of x. But $2^{(h-1)/2+g-h}$ is less than $|U_t|$, by (106).

126. M. S. Paterson has proposed a related (but different) conjecture: For every 2-adic chain with k addition-subtraction operations, there is a (possibly huge) integer x with $\nu x = k + 1$ such that the chain does not calculate $2^{\lambda x}$.

127. Johan Håstad [*Advances in Computing Research* **5** (1989), 143–170] has shown that every polynomial-size circuit that computes the parity function from the inputs

$\{x_1, \ldots, x_n, \bar{x}_1, \ldots, \bar{x}_n\}$ with AND and OR gates of unlimited fanin must have depth $\Omega(\log n / \log \log n)$.

128. (Note also that the suffix parity function $x^\oplus$ is considered in exercises 36 and 66.)

130. If the answer is "no," the analogous question with *variable a* suggests itself.

131. This program does a typical "breadth-first search," keeping LINK(q) = r. Register u is the vertex currently being examined; v is one of its successors.

OH	LDOU r,q,link	1	r ← LINK(q).	STOU v,q,link	$\|R\|-\|Q\|$	LINK(q) ← v.
	SET u,r	1	u ← r.	STOU r,v,link	$\|R\|-\|Q\|$	LINK(v) ← r.
1H	LDOU a,u,arcs	$\|R\|$	a ← ARCS(u).	SET q,v	$\|R\|-\|Q\|$	q ← v.
	BZ a,4F	$\|R\|$	Is $S[u] = \emptyset$?	3H PBNZ a,2B	S	Loop on a.
2H	LDOU v,a,tip	S	v ← TIP(a).	4H LDOU u,u,link	$\|R\|$	u ← LINK(u).
	LDOU a,a,next	S	a ← NEXT(a).	CMPU t,u,r	$\|R\|$	Is u ≠ r?
	LDOU t,v,link	S	t ← LINK(v).	PBNZ t,1B	$\|R\|$	If so, continue.
	PBNZ t,3F	S	Is v ∈ R?			∎

132. (a) We always have $\tau(U) \subseteq \&_{u \notin U} \delta_u = \sigma(U)$. And equality holds if and only if $2^u \subseteq \rho(u')$ for all $u \in U$ and $u' \in U$.

(b) We've proved that $\tau(U) \subseteq \sigma(U)$; hence $T \subseteq U$. And if $t \in T$ we have $2^t \subseteq \rho_u$ for all $u \in U$. Therefore $\sigma(T) \subseteq \tau(T)$.

(c) Parts (a) and (b) prove that the elements of C_n represent the cliques.

(d) If $u \subseteq v$ then $u \& \rho_k \subseteq v \& \rho_k$ and $u \& \delta_k \subseteq v \& \delta_k$; so we can work entirely with maximal entries. The following algorithm uses cache-friendly sequential (rather than linked) allocation, in a manner analogous to radix exchange sort (Algorithm 5.2.2R).

We assume that $w_1 \ldots w_s$ is a workspace of s unsigned words, bounded by $w_0 = 0$ and $w_{s+1} = 2^n - 1$. The elements of C_{k-1}^+ appear initially in positions $w_1 \ldots w_m$, and our goal is to replace them by the elements of C_k^+.

M1. [Initialize.] Terminate if $\rho_k = 2^n - 1$. Otherwise set $v \leftarrow 2^k$, $i \leftarrow 1$, $j \leftarrow m$.

M2. [Partition on v.] While $w_i \& v = 0$, set $i \leftarrow i + 1$. While $w_j \& v \neq 0$, set $j \leftarrow j - 1$. Then if $i > j$, go to M3; otherwise swap $w_i \leftrightarrow w_j$, set $i \leftarrow i + 1$, $j \leftarrow j - 1$, and repeat this step.

M3. [Split $w_i \ldots w_m$.] Set $l \leftarrow j$, $p \leftarrow s + 1$. While $i \leq m$, do subroutine Q with $u = w_i$ and set $i \leftarrow i + 1$.

M4. [Combine maximal elements.] Set $m \leftarrow l$. While $p \leq s$, set $m \leftarrow m + 1$, $w_m \leftarrow w_p$, and $p \leftarrow p + 1$. ∎

Subroutine Q uses global variables j, k, l, p, and v. It essentially replaces the word u by $u' = u \& \rho_k$ and $u'' = u \& \delta_k$, retaining them if they are still maximal. If so, u' goes into the upper workspace $w_p \ldots w_s$ but u'' stays below.

Q1. [Examine u'.] Set $w \leftarrow u \& \rho_k$ and $q \leftarrow s$. If $w = u$, go to Q4.

Q2. [Is it comparable?] If $q < p$, go to Q3. Otherwise if $w \& w_q = w$, go to Q7. Otherwise if $w \& w_q = w_q$, go to Q4. Otherwise set $q \leftarrow q - 1$ and repeat Q2.

Q3. [Tentatively accept u'.] Set $p \leftarrow p - 1$ and $w_p \leftarrow w$. Memory overflow occurs if $p \leq m + 1$. Otherwise go to Q7.

Q4. [Prepare for loop.] Set $r \leftarrow p$ and $w_{p-1} \leftarrow 0$.

Q5. [Remove nonmaximals.] While $w \mid w_q \neq w$, set $q \leftarrow q - 1$. While $w \mid w_r = w$, set $r \leftarrow r + 1$. Then if $q < r$, go to Q6; otherwise set $w_q \leftarrow w_r$, $w_r \leftarrow 0$, $q \leftarrow q - 1$, $r \leftarrow r + 1$, and repeat this step.

604 ANSWERS TO EXERCISES 7.1.3

Q6. [Reset p.] Set $w_q \leftarrow w$ and $p \leftarrow q$. Terminate the subroutine if $w = u$.

Q7. [Examine u''.] Set $w \leftarrow u$ & $\bar{v}$. If $w = w_q$ for some q in the range $1 \le q \le j$, do nothing. Otherwise set $l \leftarrow l + 1$ and $w_l \leftarrow w$. ∎

In practice this algorithm performs reasonably well; for example, when it is applied to the 8×8 queen graph (exercise 7–129), it finds the 310 maximal cliques after 306,513 mems of computation, using 397 words of workspace. It finds the 10188 maximal independent sets of that same graph after about 310 megamems, using 15090 words; there are respectively $(728, 6912, 2456, 92)$ such sets of sizes $(5, 6, 7, 8)$, including the 92 famous solutions to the eight queens problem.

Reference: N. Jardine and R. Sibson, *Mathematical Taxonomy* (Wiley, 1971), Appendix 5. Many other algorithms for listing maximal cliques have also been published. See, for example, W. Knödel, *Computing* **3** (1968), 239–240, **4** (1969), 75; C. Bron and J. Kerbosch, *CACM* **16** (1973), 575–577; S. Tsukiyama, M. Ide, H. Ariyoshi, and I. Shirakawa, *SICOMP* **6** (1977), 505–517; E. Loukakis, *Computers and Math. with Appl.* **9** (1983), 583–589; D. S. Johnson, M. Yannakakis, and C. H. Papadimitriou, *Inf. Proc. Letters* **27** (1988), 119–123. See also exercise 5–23.

133. (a) An independent set is a clique of $\overline{G}$; so complement G. (b) A vertex cover is the complement of an independent set; so complement G, then complement the outputs.

134. $a \mapsto 00$, $b \mapsto 01$, $c \mapsto 11$ is the first mapping of class II.

135. The unary operators are simple: $\neg(x_l x_r) = \bar{x}_r \bar{x}_l$; $\diamond(x_l x_r) = x_r x_r$; $\square(x_l x_r) = x_l x_l$. And $x_l x_r \Leftrightarrow y_l y_r = (z_l \wedge z_r)(z_l \vee z_r)$, where $z_l = (x_l \equiv y_l)$ and $z_r = (x_r \equiv y_r)$.

136. (a) Classes II, III, IV$_a$, and IV$_c$ all have the optimum cost 4. Curiously the functions $z_l = x_l \vee y_l \vee (x_r \wedge y_r)$, $z_r = x_r \vee y_r$ work for the mapping $(a, b, c) \mapsto (00, 01, 11)$ of class II as well as for the mapping $(a, b, c) \mapsto (00, 01, 1*)$ of class IV$_c$. [This operation is equivalent to saturating addition, when $a = 0$, $b = 1$, and c stands for "more than 1."]

(b) The symmetry between a, b, and c implies that we need only try classes I, IV$_a$, and V$_a$; and those classes turn out to cost 6, 7, and 8. One winner for class I, with $(a, b, c) \mapsto (00, 01, 10)$, is $z_l = v_r \wedge \bar{u}_l$, $z_r = v_l \wedge \bar{u}_r$, where $u_l = x_l \oplus y_l$, $u_r = x_r \oplus y_r$, $v_l = y_r \oplus u_l$, and $v_r = y_l \oplus u_r$. [See exercise 7.1.2–60, which gives the same answer but with $z_l \leftrightarrow z_r$. The reason is that we have $(x + y + z) \bmod 3 = 0$ in this problem but $(x + y - z) \bmod 3 = 0$ in that one; and $z_l \leftrightarrow z_r$ is equivalent to negation. The binary operation $z = x \circ y$ in this case can also be characterized by the fact that the elements (x, y, z) are all the same or all different; thus it is familiar to people who play the game of SET. It is the only binary operation on n-element sets that has $n!$ automorphisms and differs from the trivial examples $x \circ y = x$ or $x \circ y = y$.]

(c) Cost 3 is achieved only with class I: Let $(a, b, c) \mapsto (00, 01, 10)$ and $z_l = (x_l \vee x_r) \wedge y_l$, $z_r = \bar{x}_r \wedge y_r$.

137. In fact, $z = (x + 1)$ & y when $(a, b, c) \mapsto (00, 01, 10)$. [It's a contrived example.]

138. The simplest case known to the author requires the calculation of *two* binary operations, such as

$$\begin{pmatrix} a & b & b \\ a & b & b \\ c & a & a \end{pmatrix} \quad \text{and} \quad \begin{pmatrix} a & b & a \\ a & b & a \\ c & a & c \end{pmatrix};$$

each has cost 2 in class V$_a$, but the costs are $(3, 2)$ and $(2, 3)$ in classes I and II.

139. The calculation of z_2 is essentially equivalent to exercise 136(b); so the natural representation (111) wins. Fortunately this representation also is good for z_1, with $z_{1l} = x_l \wedge y_l$, $z_{1r} = x_r \wedge y_r$.

140. With representation (111), first use full binary adders to compute $(a_1 a_0)_2 = x_l + y_l + z_l$ and $(b_1 b_0)_2 = x_r + y_r + z_r$ in $5 + 5 = 10$ steps. Now the "greedy footprint" method shows how to compute the four desired functions of (a_1, a_0, b_1, b_0) in eight further steps: $u_l = a_1 \wedge \bar{b}_0$, $u_r = a_0 \wedge \bar{b}_1$; $t_1 = a_1 \oplus b_0$, $t_2 = a_0 \oplus b_1$, $t_3 = a_1 \oplus t_2$, $t_4 = a_0 \oplus t_1$, $v_l = t_3 \wedge \bar{t}_1$, $v_r = t_4 \wedge \bar{t}_2$. [Is this method optimum?]

141. Suppose we've computed bits $a = a_0 a_1 \dots a_{2m-1}$ and $b = b_0 b_1 \dots b_{2m-1}$ such that

$a_s = [s = 1$ or $s = 2$ or s is a sum of distinct Ulam numbers $\le m$ in exactly one way],

$b_s = [s$ is a sum of distinct Ulam numbers $\le m$ in more than one way],

for some integer $m = U_n \ge 2$. For example, when $m = n = 2$ we have $a = 0111$ and $b = 0000$. Then $\{s \mid s \le m$ and $a_s = 1\} = \{U_1, \dots, U_n\}$; and $U_{n+1} = \min\{s \mid s > m$ and $a_s = 1\}$. (Notice that $a_s = 1$ when $s = U_{n-1} + U_n$.) The following simple bitwise operations preserve these conditions: $n \leftarrow n + 1$, $m \leftarrow U_n$, and

$$(a_m \dots a_{2m-1}, b_m \dots b_{2m-1}) \leftarrow ((a_m \dots a_{2m-1} \oplus a_0 \dots a_{m-1}) \,\&\, \overline{b_m \dots b_{2m-1}},$$
$$(a_m \dots a_{2m-1} \,\&\, a_0 \dots a_{m-1}) \mid b_m \dots b_{2m-1}),$$

where $a_s = b_s = 0$ for $2U_{n-1} \le s < 2U_n$ on the right side of this assignment.

[See M. C. Wunderlich, *BIT* **11** (1971), 217–224; *Computers in Number Theory* (1971), 249–257. These mysterious numbers, which were first defined by S. Ulam in *SIAM Review* **6** (1964), 348, have baffled number theorists for many years. The ratio U_n/n appears to converge to a constant, ≈ 13.52; for example, $U_{20000000} = 270371127$ and $U_{40000000} = 540752349$. Furthermore, D. W. Wilson has observed empirically that the numbers form quasi-periodic "clusters" whose centers differ by multiples of another constant, ≈ 21.6016. Calculations by Jud McCranie and the author for $U_n < 640000000$ indicate that the largest gap $U_n - U_{n-1}$ may occur between $U_{24576523} = 332250401$ and $U_{24576524} = 332251032$; the smallest gap $U_n - U_{n-1} = 1$ apparently occurs only when $U_n \in \{2, 3, 4, 48\}$. Certain small gaps like 6, 11, 14, and 16 have never been observed.]

142. Algorithm E in that exercise performs the following operations on subcubes: (i) Count the $*$s in a given subcube c. (ii) Given c and c', test if $c \subseteq c'$. (iii) Given c and c', compute $c \sqcup c'$ (if it exists). Operation (i) is simple with sideways addition; let's see which of the nine classes of two-bit encodings (119), (123), (124) works best for (ii) and (iii). Suppose $a = 0$, $b = 1$, $c = *$; the symmetry between 0 and 1 means that we need only examine classes I, III, IV$_c$, IV$_c$, V$_a$, and V$_c$.

For the asterisks-and-bits mapping $(0, 1, *) \mapsto (00, 01, 10)$, which belongs to class I, the truth table for $c \not\subseteq c'$ is $010*100*110*****$ in each component. (For example, $0 \subseteq *$ and $* \not\subseteq 1$. The $*$s in this truth table are don't-cares for the unused codes 11.) The methods of Section 7.1.2 tell us that the cheapest such functions have cost 3; for example, $c \subseteq c'$ if and only if $((b \oplus b') \mid a) \,\&\, \bar{a}' = 0$. Furthermore the consensus $c \sqcup c' = c''$ exists if and only if $\nu z = 1$, where $z = (b \oplus b') \,\&\, {\sim}(a \oplus a')$. And in that case, $a'' = (a \oplus b \oplus b') \,\&\, {\sim}(a \oplus a')$, $b'' = (b \mid b') \,\&\, \bar{z}$. [The asterisk and bit codes were used for this purpose by M. A. Breuer in *Proc. ACM Nat. Conf.* **23** (1968), 241–250.]

But class III works out better, with $(0, 1, *) \mapsto (01, 10, 00)$. Then $c \subseteq c'$ if and only if $(\bar{c}_l \,\&\, c'_l) \mid (\bar{c}_r \,\&\, c'_r) = 0$; $c \sqcup c' = c''$ exists if and only if $\nu z = 1$ where $z = x \,\&\, y$, $x = c_l \mid c'_l$, $y = c_r \mid c'_r$; and $c''_l = x \oplus z$, $c''_r = y \oplus z$. We save two operations for each consensus, with respect to class I, compensating for an extra step when counting asterisks.

Classes IV$_a$, V$_a$, and V$_c$ turn out to be far inferior. Class IV$_c$ has some merit, but class III is best.

143. $f(x) = ((x \& m_1) \ll 17) | ((x \gg 17) \& m_1) | ((x \& m_2) \ll 15) | ((x \gg 15) \& m_2) | ((x \& m_3) \ll$ $10) | ((x \gg 10) \& m_3) | ((x \& m_4) \ll 6) | ((x \gg 6) \& m_4)$, where $m_1 = {}^\#\texttt{7f7f7f7f7f7f7f7f}$, $m_2 = {}^\#\texttt{fefefefefe}$, $m_3 = {}^\#\texttt{3f3f3f3f3f3f3f}$, $m_4 = {}^\#\texttt{fcfcfcfcfcfcfc}$. [See, for example, *Chess Skill in Man and Machine*, edited by Peter W. Frey (1977), page 59. Five steps suffice to compute $f(x)$ on MMIX (four MOR operations and one OR), since $f(x) = q \cdot x \cdot q' | q' \cdot x \cdot q$ with $q = {}^\#\texttt{40a05028140a0502}$ and $q' = {}^\#\texttt{2010884422110804}$.]

144. Node $j \oplus (k \ll 1)$, where $k = j \& -j$.

145. It names the ancestor of the leaf node $j | 1$ at height h.

146. By (136) we want to show that $\lambda(j \& -i) = \rho l$ when $l - 2^{\rho l} < i \le l \le j < l + 2^{\rho l}$. The desired result follows from (35) because $-l \le -i < -l + 2^{\rho l}$.

147. (a) $\pi v_j = \beta v_j = j$, $\alpha v_j = 1 \ll \rho j$, and $\tau j = \Lambda$, for $1 \le j \le n$.

(b) Suppose $n = 2^{e_1} + \cdots + 2^{e_t}$ where $e_1 > \cdots > e_t \ge 0$, and let $n_k = 2^{e_1} + \cdots + 2^{e_k}$ for $0 \le k \le t$. Then $\pi v_j = j$ and $\beta v_j = \alpha v_j = n_k$ for $n_{k-1} < j \le n_k$. Also $\tau n_k = v_{n_{k-1}}$ for $1 \le k \le t$, where $v_0 = \Lambda$; all other $\tau j = \Lambda$.

148. Yes, if $\pi y_1 = 010000$, $\pi y_2 = 010100$, $\pi x_1 = 010101$, $\pi x_2 = 010110$, $\pi x_3 = 010111$, $\beta x_3 = 010111$, $\beta y_2 = 010100$, $\beta x_2 = 011000$, $\beta y_1 = 010000$, and $\beta x_1 = 100000$.

149. We assume that $\texttt{CHILD}(v) = \texttt{SIB}(v) = \texttt{PARENT}(v) = \Lambda$ initially for all vertices v (including $v = \Lambda$), and that there is at least one nonnull vertex.

S1. [Make triply linked tree.] For each of the n arcs $u \longrightarrow v$ (perhaps $v = \Lambda$), set $\texttt{SIB}(u) \leftarrow \texttt{CHILD}(v)$, $\texttt{CHILD}(v) \leftarrow u$, $\texttt{PARENT}(u) \leftarrow v$. (See exercise 2.3.3–6.)

S2. [Begin first traversal.] Set $p \leftarrow \texttt{CHILD}(\Lambda)$, $n \leftarrow 0$, and $\lambda 0 \leftarrow -1$.

S3. [Compute β in the easy case.] Set $n \leftarrow n + 1$, $\pi p \leftarrow n$, $\tau n \leftarrow \Lambda$, and $\lambda n \leftarrow 1 + \lambda(n \gg 1)$. If $\texttt{CHILD}(p) \ne \Lambda$, set $p \leftarrow \texttt{CHILD}(p)$ and repeat this step; otherwise set $\beta p \leftarrow n$.

S4. [Compute τ, bottom-up.] Set $\tau \beta p \leftarrow \texttt{PARENT}(p)$. Then if $\texttt{SIB}(p) \ne \Lambda$, set $p \leftarrow \texttt{SIB}(p)$ and return to S3; otherwise set $p \leftarrow \texttt{PARENT}(p)$.

S5. [Compute β in the hard case.] If $p \ne \Lambda$, set $h \leftarrow \lambda(n \& -\pi p)$, then $\beta p \leftarrow ((n \gg h) | 1) \ll h$, and go back to S4.

S6. [Begin second traversal.] Set $p \leftarrow \texttt{CHILD}(\Lambda)$, $\lambda 0 \leftarrow \lambda n$, $\pi \Lambda \leftarrow \beta \Lambda \leftarrow \alpha \Lambda \leftarrow 0$.

S7. [Compute α, top-down.] Set $\alpha p \leftarrow \alpha(\texttt{PARENT}(p)) | (\beta p \& -\beta p)$. Then if $\texttt{CHILD}(p) \ne \Lambda$, set $p \leftarrow \texttt{CHILD}(p)$ and repeat this step.

S8. [Continue to traverse.] If $\texttt{SIB}(p) \ne \Lambda$, set $p \leftarrow \texttt{SIB}(p)$ and go to S7. Otherwise set $p \leftarrow \texttt{PARENT}(p)$, and repeat step S8 if $p \ne \Lambda$. ∎

150. We may assume that the elements A_j are distinct, by regarding them as ordered pairs (A_j, j). The hinted binary search tree, which is a special case of the "Cartesian trees" introduced by Jean Vuillemin [*CACM* **23** (1980), 229–239], has the property that $k(i, j)$ is the nearest common ancestor of i and j. Indeed, the ancestors of any given node j are precisely the nodes k such that A_k is a right-to-left minimum of $A_1 \ldots A_j$ or A_k is a left-to-right minimum of $A_j \ldots A_n$.

The algorithm of the preceding answer does the desired preprocessing, except that we need to set up a triply linked tree differently on the nodes $\{0, 1, \ldots, n\}$. Start as before with $\texttt{CHILD}(v) = \texttt{SIB}(v) = \texttt{PARENT}(v) = 0$ for $0 \le v \le n$, and let $\Lambda = 0$. Assume that $A_0 \le A_j$ for $1 \le j \le n$. Set $t \leftarrow 0$ and do the following steps for $v = n$, $n - 1$, $\ldots$, 1: Set $u \leftarrow 0$; then while $A_v < A_t$ set $u \leftarrow t$ and $t \leftarrow \texttt{PARENT}(t)$. If $u \ne 0$, set SIB(v) ← SIB(u), SIB(u) ← 0, PARENT(u) ← v, CHILD(v) ← u; otherwise simply set SIB(v) ← CHILD(t). Also set CHILD(t) ← v, PARENT(v) ← t, t ← v.

Continue with step S2 after the tree has been built. The running time is $O(n)$, because the operation t ← PARENT(t) is performed at most once for each node t. [This beautiful way to reduce the range minimum query problem to the nearest common ancestor problem was discovered by H. N. Gabow, J. L. Bentley, and R. E. Tarjan, *STOC* **16** (1984), 137–138, who also suggested the following exercise.]

151. For node v with k children $u_1, \ldots, u_k$, define the node sequence $S(v) = v$ if $k = 0$; $S(v) = vS(u_1)$ if $k = 1$; and $S(v) = S(u_1)v \ldots vS(u_k)$ if $k > 1$. (Consequently v appears exactly $\max(k-1, 1)$ times in $S(v)$.) If there are k trees in the forest, rooted at $u_1, \ldots, u_k$, write down the node sequence $S(u_1)\Lambda \ldots \Lambda S(u_k) = V_1 \ldots V_N$. (The length of this sequence will satisfy $n \le N < 2n$.) Let A_j be the depth of node V_j, for $1 \le j \le N$, where Λ has depth 0. (For example, consider the forest (141), but add another child $K \longrightarrow D$ and an isolated node L. Then $V_1 \ldots V_{15} = CFAGJDHDK\Lambda BEI\Lambda L$ and $A_1 \ldots A_{15} = 231342323012301$.) The nearest common ancestor of u and v, when $u = V_i$ and $v = V_j$, is then $V_{k(i,j)}$ in the range minimum query problem. [See J. Fischer and V. Heun, *Lecture Notes in Comp. Sci.* **4009** (2006), 36–48.]

152. Step V1 finds the level above which αx and αy have bits that apply to both of their ancestors. (See exercise 148.) Step V2 increases h, if necessary, to the level where they have a common ancestor, or to the top level λn if they don't (namely if $k = 0$). If $\beta x \ne \beta z$, step V4 finds the topmost level among x's ancestors that leads to level h; hence it knows the lowest ancestor $\hat{x}$ for which $\beta \hat{x} = \beta z$ (or $\hat{x} = \Lambda$). Finally in V5, preorder tells us which of $\hat{x}$ or $\hat{y}$ is an ancestor of the other.

153. That pointer has ρj bits, so it ends after $\rho 1 + \rho 2 + \cdots + \rho j = j - \nu j$ bits of the packed string, by (61). [Here j is even. Navigation piles were introduced in *Nordic Journal of Computing* **10** (2003), 238–262.]

154. The gray lines define 36°-36°-90° triangles, ten of which make a pentagon with 72° angles at each vertex. These pentagons tile the hyperbolic plane in such a way that *five* of them meet at each vertex.

155. Observe first that $0 \le (\alpha 0)_{1/\phi} < \phi^{-1} + \phi^{-3} + \phi^{-5} + \cdots = 1$, since there are no consecutive 1s. Observe next that $F_{-n}\phi \equiv \phi^{-n}$ (modulo 1), by exercise 1.2.8–11. Now add $F_{k_1}\phi + \cdots + F_{k_r}\phi$. For example, $(4\phi) \bmod 1 = \phi^{-5} + \phi^{-2}$; $(-2\phi) \bmod 1 = \phi^{-4} + \phi^{-1}$. This argument also proves the interesting formula $\lfloor N(\alpha)\phi \rfloor = -N(\alpha 0)$.

156. (a) Start with y ← 0, and with k large enough that $|x| < F_{k+1}$. If $x < 0$, set k ← $(k-1) \mid 1$, and while $x + F_k > 0$ set k ← $k - 2$; then set y ← $y + (1 \ll k)$, x ← $x + F_{k+1}$; repeat. Otherwise if $x > 1$, set k ← k &–2, and while $x - F_k \le 0$ set k ← $k - 2$; then set y ← $y + (1 \ll k)$, x ← $x - F_{k+1}$; repeat. Otherwise set y ← $y + x$ and terminate with $y = (\alpha)_2$.

(b) The operations x_1 ← a_1, y_1 ← $-a_1$, x_k ← $y_{k-1} + a_k$, y_k ← $x_{k-1} - x_k$ compute $x_k = N(a_1 \ldots a_k)$ and $y_k = N(a_1 \ldots a_k 0)$. [Does *every* broadword chain for $N(a_1 \ldots a_n)$ require $\Omega(n)$ steps?]

157. The laws are obvious except for the two cases involving $(\alpha-)$. For those we have $N((\alpha-)0^k) = N(\alpha 0^k) + F_{-k-2}$ for all $k \ge 0$, because decrementation never "borrows" at the right. (But the analogous formula $N((\alpha+)0^k) = N(\alpha 0^k) + F_{-k-1}$ does *not* hold.)

158. Incrementation satisfies the rules $(\alpha 00)+ = \alpha 01$, $(\alpha 10)+ = (\alpha+)00$, $(\alpha 1)+ = (\alpha+)0$. It can be achieved with six 2-adic operations on the integer $x = (\alpha)_2$ by setting y ← $x \mid (x \gg 1)$, z ← y & $\sim(y + 1)$, x ← $(x \mid z) + 1$.

Decrementation of a nonzero codeword is more difficult. It satisfies $(\alpha 10^{2k})- = \alpha 0(10)^k$, $(\alpha 10^{2k+1})- = \alpha(01)^{k+1}$; hence by Corollary I it cannot be computed by a 2-adic chain. Yet six operations suffice, if we allow monus: $y \leftarrow x - 1$, $z \leftarrow y \,\&\, \bar{x}$, $w \leftarrow z \,\&\, \mu_0$, $x \leftarrow y - w + (w \doteq (z - w))$.

159. Besides the Fibonacci number system (146) and the negaFibonacci number system (147), there's also an *odd Fibonacci number system*: Every positive integer x can be written uniquely in the form

$$x = F_{l_1} + F_{l_2} + \cdots + F_{l_s}, \qquad \text{where } l_1 \ggg l_2 \ggg \cdots \ggg l_s > 0 \text{ and } l_s \text{ is odd.}$$

Given a negaFibonacci code α, the following 20-step 2-adic chain converts $x = (\alpha)_2$ to $y = (\beta)_2$ to $z = (\gamma)_2$, where β is the odd codeword with $N(\alpha) = F(\beta)$ and γ is the standard codeword with $F(\beta) = F(\gamma 0)$: $x^+ \leftarrow x \,\&\, \mu_0$, $x^- \leftarrow x \oplus x^+$; $d \leftarrow x^+ - x^-$; $t \leftarrow d \mid x^-$, $t \leftarrow t \,\&\, \sim(t \ll 1)$; $y \leftarrow (d \,\&\, \bar{\mu}_0) \oplus t \oplus ((t \,\&\, x^-) \gg 1)$; $z \leftarrow (y + 1) \gg 1$; $w \leftarrow z \oplus (4\mu_0)$; $t \leftarrow w \,\&\, \sim(w+1)$; $z \leftarrow z \oplus (t \,\&\, (z \oplus ((w+1) \gg 1)))$.

Corresponding negaFibonacci and odd representations satisfy the remarkable law

$$F_{k_1+m} + \cdots + F_{k_r+m} = (-1)^m (F_{l_1-m} + \cdots + F_{l_s-m}), \qquad \text{for all integers } m.$$

For example, if $N(\alpha) < 0$ the steps above will convert $x = (\alpha 0)_2$ to $y = (\beta)_2$, where $F((\beta \gg 2)0) = -N(\alpha)$. Furthermore β is the odd code for negaFibonacci α if and only if α^R is the odd code for negaFibonacci β^R, when $|\alpha| = |\beta|$ is odd and $N(\alpha) > 0$.

No finite 2-adic chain will go the other way, by Corollary I, because the Fibonacci code 10^k corresponds to negaFibonacci 10^{k+1} when k is odd, $(10)^{k/2}1$ when k is even. But if γ is a standard Fibonacci codeword we can compute $y = (\beta)_2$ from $z = (\gamma)_2$ by setting $y \leftarrow z \ll 1$, $t \leftarrow y \,\&\, (y - 1) \,\&\, \bar{\mu}_0$, $y \leftarrow y - t + [t \neq 0]((t - 1) \,\&\, \mu_0)$. And then the method above will compute α^R from β^R. The overall running time for conversion to negaFibonacci form will then be of order $\log |\gamma|$, for two string reversals.

160. The text's rules are actually incomplete: They should also define the orientation of each neighbor. Let us stipulate that $\alpha_{sn} = \alpha$; $\alpha_{en} = \alpha$; $(\alpha 0)_{wn} = \alpha 0$, $(\alpha 1)_{wo} = \alpha 1$; $(\alpha 00)_{ns} = \alpha 00$, $(\alpha 10)_{nw} = \alpha 10$, $(\alpha 1)_{ne} = \alpha 1$; $(\alpha 0)_{oo} = \alpha 0$, $(\alpha 101)_{oo} = \alpha 101$, $(\alpha 1001)_{oo} = \alpha 1001$, $(\alpha 0001)_{ow} = \alpha 0001$. Then a case analysis proves that all cells within d steps of the starting cell have a consistent labeling and orientation, by induction on the graph distance d. (Note the identity $\alpha+ = ((\alpha 0)-) \gg 1$.) Furthermore the labeling remains consistent when we attach y coordinates and move when necessary from one strip to another via the δ-rules of (153).

161. Yes, it is bipartite, because all of its edges are defined by the set of boundary lines. (The hyperbolic *cylinder* cannot be bicolored; but two adjacent strips can.)

162. It's convenient to view the hyperbolic plane through another lens, by mapping its points to the upper halfplane $\Im z > 0$. Then the "straight lines" become semicircles centered on the x-axis, together with vertical halflines as a limiting case. In this representation, the edges $|z - 1| = \sqrt{2}$, $|z| = r$, and $\Re z = 0$ define a 36°-45°-90° triangle if $r^2 = \phi + \sqrt{\phi}$. Every triangle ABC has three neighbors CBA', ACB', and BAC', obtained by "reflecting" two of its edges about the third, where the reflection of $|z - c'| = r'$ about $|z - c| = r$ is $|z - c - \frac{1}{2}(x_1 + x_2)| = \frac{1}{2}|x_1 - x_2|$, $x_j = r^2/(c' \pm r' - c)$.

The mapping $z \mapsto (z - z_0)/(z - \bar{z}_0)$ takes the upper halfplane into the unit circle; when $z_0 = \frac{1}{2}(\sqrt{\phi} - 1/\phi)(1 + 5^{1/4}i)$ the central pentagon will be symmetric. Repeated reflections of the initial triangle, using breadth-first search until reaching triangles that are invisible, will lead to Fig. 14. To get just the pentagons (without the gray lines), one can begin with just the central cell and perform reflections about *its* edges, etc.

163. (This figure can be drawn as in exercise 162, starting with vertices that project to the three points ir, $ir\omega$, and $ir\omega^2$, where $r^2 = \frac{1}{2}(1+\sqrt{2})(4-\sqrt{2}-\sqrt{6})$ and $\omega = e^{2\pi i/3}$. Using a notation devised by L. Schläfli in 1852, it can be described as the infinite tiling with parameters $\{3,8\}$, meaning that eight triangles meet at every vertex; see Schläfli's *Gesammelte Mathematische Abhandlungen* **1** (1950), 212. Similarly, the pentagrid and the tiling of exercise 154 have Schläfli symbols $\{5,4\}$ and $\{5,5\}$, respectively.)

164. The original definition requires more computation, even though it can be factored:

$$\text{custer}'(X) = X \ \& \sim(Y_{\rm N} \ \& \ Y \ \& \ Y_{\rm S}), \qquad Y = X_{\rm W} \ \& \ X \ \& \ X_{\rm E}.$$

But the main reason for preferring (157) is that it produces a thinner, kingwise connected border. The rookwise connected border that results from the 1957 definition is less attractive, because it's noticeably darker when the border travels diagonally than when it travels horizontally or vertically. (Try some experiments and you'll see.)

165. The first image $X^{(1)}$ is the "outer" border of the original black pixels. Fingerprint-like whorls are formed thereafter. For example, starting with Fig. 15(a) we get

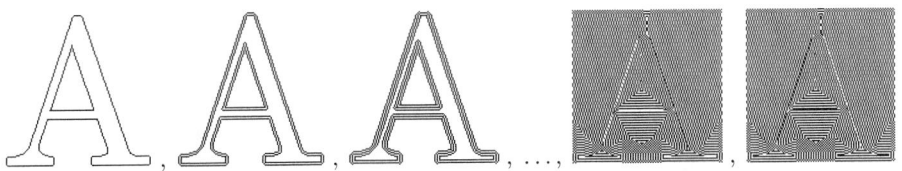

in a 120×120 bitmap, eventually alternating endlessly between two bizarre patterns. (Does *every* nonempty $M \times N$ bitmap lead to such a 2-cycle?)

166. If $X = \text{custer}(X)$, the sum of the elements of $X + (X \mathbin{\wedge} 1) + (X \ll 1) + (X \gg 1) + (X \mathbin{\vee} 1)$ is at most $4MN + 2M + 2N$, since it is at most 4 in each cell of the rectangle and at most 1 in the adjacent cells. This sum is also five times the number of black pixels. Hence $f(M,N) \le \frac{4}{5}MN + \frac{2}{5}M + \frac{2}{5}N$. Conversely we get $f(M,N) \ge \frac{4}{5}MN - \frac{2}{5}$ by letting the pixel in row i and column j be black unless $(i + 2j) \bmod 5 = 2$. (This problem is equivalent to finding a minimum dominating set of the $M \times N$ grid.)

167. (a) With 17 steps we can construct a half adder and three full adders (see 7.1.2–(23)) so that $(z_1 z_2)_2 = x_{\rm NW} + x_{\rm W} + x_{\rm SW}$, $(z_3 z_4)_2 = x_{\rm N} + x_{\rm S}$, $(z_5 z_6)_2 = x_{\rm NE} + x_{\rm E} + x_{\rm SE}$, and $(z_7 z_8)_2 = z_2 + z_4 + z_6$. Then $f = S_1(z_1, z_3, z_5, z_7) \wedge (x \vee z_8)$, where the symmetric function S_1 needs seven operations by Fig. 9 in Section 7.1.2. [This solution is based on ideas of W. F. Mann and D. Sleator.]

(b) Given $x^- = X_{j-1}^{(t)}$, $x = X_j^{(t)}$, and $x^+ = X_{j+1}^{(t)}$, compute $a \leftarrow x^- \ \& \ x^+ \ (= z_3)$, $b \leftarrow x^- \oplus x^+ \ (= z_4)$, $c \leftarrow x \oplus b \ (= z_6)$, $c \leftarrow c \gg 1 \ (= z_2)$, $e \leftarrow c \oplus d$, $c \leftarrow c \ \& \ d$, $f \leftarrow b \ \& \ e$, $f \leftarrow f \mid c \ (= z_7)$, $e \leftarrow b \oplus e \ (= z_8)$, $c \leftarrow x \ \& \ b$, $c \leftarrow c \mid a$, $b \leftarrow c \ll 1 \ (= z_5)$, $c \leftarrow c \gg 1 \ (= z_1)$, $d \leftarrow b \ \& \ c$, $c \leftarrow b \mid c$, $b \leftarrow a \ \& \ f$, $f \leftarrow a \mid f$, $f \leftarrow d \mid f$, $c \leftarrow b \mid c$, $f \leftarrow f \oplus c \ (= S_1(z_1, z_3, z_5, z_7))$, $e \leftarrow e \mid x$, $f \leftarrow f \ \& \ e$.

[For excellent summaries of the joys and passions of Life, including a proof that any Turing machine can be simulated, see Martin Gardner, *Wheels, Life and Other Mathematical Amusements* (1983), Chapters 20–22; E. R. Berlekamp, J. H. Conway, and R. K. Guy, *Winning Ways* **4** (A. K. Peters, 2004), Chapter 25.]

At last I've got what I wanted — an apparently unpredictable law of genetics.
. . . Overpopulation, like underpopulation, tends to kill.
A healthy society is neither too dense nor too sparse.
— JOHN H. CONWAY, *letter to Martin Gardner* (March 1970)

168. The following algorithm, which uses four n-bit registers x^-, x, x^+, and y, works properly even when $M = 1$ or $N = 1$. It needs only about two reads and two writes per raster word to transform $X^{(t)}$ to $X^{(t+1)}$ in (158):

C1. [Loop on k.] Do step C2 for $k = 1, 2, \ldots, N'$; then go to C5.

C2. [Loop on j.] Set $x \leftarrow A_{(M-1)k}$, $x^+ \leftarrow A_{0k}$, and $A_{Mk} \leftarrow x^+$. Then perform steps C3 and C4 for $j = 0, 1, \ldots, M - 1$.

C3. [Move down.] Set $x^- \leftarrow x$, $x \leftarrow x^+$, and $x^+ \leftarrow A_{(j+1)k}$. (Now $x = A_{jk}$, and x^- holds the former value of $A_{(j-1)k}$.) Compute the bitwise function values $y \leftarrow f(x^- \gg 1, x^-, x^- \ll 1, x \gg 1, x, x \ll 1, x^+ \gg 1, x^+, x^+ \ll 1)$.

C4. [Update A_{jk}.] Set $x^- \leftarrow A_{j(k-1)}$ & -2, $y \leftarrow y$ & $(2^{n-1} - 1)$, $A_{j(k-1)} \leftarrow x^- + (y \gg (n-2))$, $A_{jk} \leftarrow y + (x^- \ll (n-2))$.

C5. [Wrap around.] For $0 \leq j < M$, set $x \leftarrow A_{jN'}$ & -2^{n-1-d}, $A_{jN'} \leftarrow x + (A_{j1} \gg d)$, and $A_{j1} \leftarrow A_{j1} + (x \ll d)$, where $d = 1 + (N-1) \bmod (n-2)$. ∎

[An $M \times N$ torus is equivalent to an $(M-1) \times (N-1)$ array surrounded by zeros, in many cases like (157) and (159) and even (161). For exercise 173 we can clean an $(M-2) \times (N-2)$ array that is bordered by two rows and columns of zeros. But Life images (exercise 167) can grow without bound; they can't safely be confined to a torus.]

169. It quickly morphs into a rabbit, which proceeds to explode. Beginning at time 278, all activity stabilizes to a two-cycle formed from a set of traffic lights and three additional blinkers, together with three still lifes (tub, boat, and bee hive).

170. If $M \geq 2$ and $N \geq 2$, the first step blanks out the top row and the rightmost column. Then if $M \geq 3$ and $N \geq 3$, the next step blanks out the bottom row and the leftmost column. So in general we're left after $t = \min(M, N) - 1$ steps with a single row or column of black pixels: The first $\lceil t/2 \rceil$ rows, the last $\lceil t/2 \rceil$ columns, the last $\lfloor t/2 \rfloor$ rows, and the first $\lfloor t/2 \rfloor$ columns have been set to zero. The automaton will stop after making two more (nonproductive) cycles.

171. Without (160): $x_1 \leftarrow x_{\text{SE}}$ & $\bar{x}_{\text{N}}$, $x_2 \leftarrow x_{\text{N}}$ & $\bar{x}_{\text{SE}}$, $x_3 \leftarrow x_{\text{E}}$ & $\bar{x}_1$, $x_4 \leftarrow x_{\text{NE}}$ & $\bar{x}_2$, $x_5 \leftarrow x_3 \mid x_4$, $x_6 \leftarrow x_{\text{W}}$ & $\bar{x}_5$, $x_7 \leftarrow x_1$ & $\bar{x}_{\text{NE}}$, $x_8 \leftarrow x_7$ & $\bar{x}_{\text{NW}}$, $x_9 \leftarrow x_{\text{E}} \mid x_{\text{SW}}$, $x_{10} \leftarrow x_8$ & x_9, $x_{11} \leftarrow x_{10} \mid x_6$, $x_{12} \leftarrow x_{\text{S}}$ & x_{11}, $x_{13} \leftarrow x_2$ & $\bar{x}_{\text{E}}$, $x_{14} \leftarrow x_{13}$ & x_{W}, $x_{15} \leftarrow x_{\text{N}}$ & x_{NE}, $x_{16} \leftarrow x_{\text{SW}}$ & x_{W}, $x_{17} \leftarrow x_{15} \mid x_{16}$, $x_{18} \leftarrow x_{\text{NE}}$ & x_{SW}, $x_{19} \leftarrow x_{17}$ & $\bar{x}_{18}$, $x_{20} \leftarrow x_{\text{E}} \mid x_{\text{SE}}$, $x_{21} \leftarrow x_{20} \mid x_{\text{S}}$, $x_{22} \leftarrow x_{\text{NW}}$ & $\bar{x}_{21}$, $x_{23} \leftarrow x_{22}$ & x_{19}, $x_{24} \leftarrow x_{12} \mid x_{14}$, $g \leftarrow x_{23} \mid x_{24}$. With (160), set $x_4 \leftarrow x_{\text{NE}}$ & $\bar{x}_{\text{N}}$ and leave everything else the same.

172. The statement isn't quite true; consider the following examples:

The 'I' and 'H' at the left show that pixels are sometimes left intact where paths join, and that rotating by $90°$ can make a difference. The next two examples illustrate a quirky influence of left-right reflection. The diamond example demonstrates that very thick images can be unthinnable; none of its black pixels can be removed without changing the number of holes. The final examples, one of which was inspired by the answer to exercise 166, were processed first without (160), in which case they are unchanged by the transformation. But with (160) they're thinned dramatically.

173. (a) The hint is readily verified. Notice that if X and Y are closed, $X \& Y$ is closed; if X and Y are open, $X \mid Y$ is open. Thus X^D is closed and X^L is open; $X^{DD} = X^D$ and $X^{LL} = X^L$. (In fact we have $X^L = {\sim}({\sim}X)^D$, because the definitions are dual, obtained by swapping black with white.) Now $X^{DL} \subseteq X^D$, so $X^{DLD} \subseteq X^{DD} = X^D$. And dually, $X^L \subseteq X^{LDL}$. We conclude that there's no reason to launder a clean picture: $X^{DLDL} = (X^{DLD})^L \subseteq X^{DL} \subseteq (X^D)^{LDL} = X^{DLDL}$.

(b) We have $X^D = (X \mid X_W \mid X_{NW} \mid X_N) \& (X \mid X_N \mid X_{NE} \mid X_E) \& (X \mid X_E \mid X_{SE} \mid X_S) \& (X \mid X_S \mid X_{SW} \mid X_W)$. Furthermore, in analogy with answer 167(b), this function can be computed from x^-, x, and x^+ in ten broadword steps: $f \leftarrow x \mid (x \gg 1) \mid ((x^- \mid (x^- \gg 1)) \& (x^+ \mid (x^+ \gg 1)))$, $f \leftarrow f \& (f \ll 1)$. [This answer incorporates ideas of D. R. Fuchs.]

To get X^L, just interchange $\mid$ and $\&$. [For further discussion, see C. Van Wyk and D. E. Knuth, Report STAN-CS-79-707 (Stanford Univ., 1979), 15–36.]

174. Three-dimensional digital topology has been studied by R. Malgouyres, *Theoretical Computer Science* **186** (1997), 1–41.

175. There are 25 in the outline, $2 + 3$ in the eyes, $1 + 1$ in the ears, 4 in the nose, and 1 in the smile, totalling 37. (All white pixels are connected kingwise to the background.)

176. (a) If v isn't isolated, there are eight easy cases to consider, depending on what kind of neighbor v has in G.

(b) There's a vertex of G' adjacent to each vertex of $(N_u \cup N_v) \setminus G'$. (Four cases.)

(c) Yes. In fact, by definition (161), we always have $|S'(v')| \geq 2$.

(d) Let $N'_{v'} = \{v \mid v' \in N_v\}$. If v' is the east neighbor of u', call it u'_E, either $u' \in G$ or $u'_S \in G$; this element is equal-or-adjacent to every vertex of $N'_{u'} \cup N'_{v'}$. A similar argument applies when $v' = u'_N$. If $v' = u'_{NE}$, there's no problem if $u' \in G$. Otherwise $u'_W \in G$, $u'_S \in G$, and either $u'_N \in G$ or $u'_E \in G$; hence $N'_{u'} \cup N'_{v'}$ is connected in G. Finally if $v' = u'_{SE}$, the proof is easy if $u'_S \in G$; otherwise $u' \in G$ and $v' \in G$.

(e) Given a nontrivial component C of G, with $v \in C$ and $v' \in S(v)$, let C' be the component of G' that contains v'. This component C' is well defined, by (a) and (b). Given a component C' of G', with $v' \in C'$ and $v \in S'(v')$, let C be the component of G that contains v. This component C is nontrivial and well defined, by (c) and (d). Finally, the correspondence $C \leftrightarrow C'$ is one-to-one.

177. Now the vertices of G are the *white* pixels, adjacent when they are *rook*-neighbors. So we define $N_{(i,j)} = \{(i,j), (i-1,j), (i,j+1)\}$. Arguments like those of answer 176, but simpler, establish a one-to-one correspondence between the nontrivial components of G and the components of G'.

178. Observe that in adjacent rows of X^*, two pixels of the same value are kingwise neighbors only if they are rookwise connected.

179. The pixels $x_1 \ldots x_N$ of each row can be "runlength encoded" as a sequence of integers $0 = c_0 < c_1 < \cdots < c_{2m+1} = N+2$ so that $x_j = 0$ for $j \in [c_0 \ldots c_1) \cup [c_2 \ldots c_3) \cup \cdots \cup [c_{2m} \ldots c_{2m+1})$ and $x_j = 1$ for $j \in [c_1 \ldots c_2) \cup \cdots \cup [c_{2m-1} \ldots c_{2m})$. (The number of runs per row tends to be reasonably small in most images. Notice that the background condition $x_0 = x_{N+1} = 0$ is implicitly assumed.)

The algorithm below uses a modified encoding with $a_j = 2c_j - (j \bmod 2)$ for $0 \leq j \leq 2m+1$. For example, the second row of the Cheshire cat has $(c_1, c_2, c_3, c_4, c_5) = (5, 8, 23, 25, 32)$; we will use $(a_1, a_2, a_3, a_4, a_5) = (9, 16, 45, 50, 63)$ instead. The reason is that white runs of adjacent rows are rookwise adjacent if and only if the corresponding intervals $[a_j .. a_{j+1})$ and $[b_k .. b_{k+1})$ overlap, and exactly the same condition characterizes when black runs of adjacent rows are kingwise adjacent. Thus the modified encoding nicely unifies both cases (see exercise 178).

We construct a triply linked tree of current components, where each node has several fields: CHILD, SIB, and PARENT (tree links); DORMANT (a circular list, via SIB links, of all former children that aren't connected to the current row); HEIR (a node that has absorbed this one); ROW and COL (location of the first pixel); and AREA (the total number of pixels in the component).

The algorithm traverses the tree in *double order* (see exercise 2.3.1–18), using pairs of pointers (P, P'), where $P' = P$ when P is traversed the first time, $P' = \text{PARENT}(P)$ when P is traversed the second time. The successor of (P, P') is $(Q, Q') = \text{next}(P, P')$, determined as follows: If $P = P'$ and $\text{CHILD}(P) \neq \Lambda$, then $Q \leftarrow Q' \leftarrow \text{CHILD}(P)$; otherwise $Q \leftarrow P$ and $Q' \leftarrow \text{PARENT}(Q)$. If $P \neq P'$ and $\text{SIB}(P) \neq \Lambda$, then $Q \leftarrow Q' \leftarrow \text{SIB}(P)$; otherwise $Q \leftarrow \text{PARENT}(P)$ and $Q' \leftarrow \text{PARENT}(Q)$.

When there are m black runs, the tree will have $m+1$ nodes, not counting nodes that are dormant or have been absorbed. Moreover, the primed pointers $P'_1, \ldots, P'_{2m+1}$ of the double traversal $(P_1, P'_1), \ldots, (P_{2m+1}, P'_{2m+1})$ are precisely the components of the current row, in left-to-right order. For example, in (163) we have $m = 5$; and $(P'_1, \ldots, P'_{11})$ point respectively to ⓪, ❸, ①, ❸, ⓪, ❸, ⓪, ❹, ②, ❹, ⓪.

I1. [Initialize.] Set $t \leftarrow 1$, $\text{ROOT} \leftarrow \text{LOC}(\text{NODE}(0))$, $\text{CHILD}(\text{ROOT}) \leftarrow \text{SIB}(\text{ROOT}) \leftarrow$ $\text{PARENT}(\text{ROOT}) \leftarrow \text{DORMANT}(\text{ROOT}) \leftarrow \text{HEIR}(\text{ROOT}) \leftarrow \Lambda$; also $\text{ROW}(\text{ROOT}) \leftarrow$ $\text{COL}(\text{ROOT}) \leftarrow 0$, $\text{AREA}(\text{ROOT}) \leftarrow N + 2$, $s \leftarrow 0$, $a_0 \leftarrow b_0 \leftarrow 0$, $a_1 \leftarrow 2N + 3$.

I2. [Input a new row.] Terminate if $s > M$. Otherwise set $b_k \leftarrow a_k$ for $k = 1, 2,$ $\ldots$, until $b_k = 2N+3$; then set $b_{k+1} \leftarrow b_k$ as a "stopper." Set $s \leftarrow s+1$. If $s >$ M, set $a_1 \leftarrow 2N + 3$; otherwise let $a_1, \ldots, a_{2m+1}$ be the modified runlength encoding of row s as discussed above. (This encoding can be obtained with the help of the ρ function; see (43).) Set $j \leftarrow k \leftarrow 1$ and $P \leftarrow P' \leftarrow \text{ROOT}$.

I3. [Gobble up short b's.] If $b_{k+1} \geq a_j$, go to I9. Otherwise set $(Q, Q') \leftarrow$ $\text{next}(P, P')$, $(R, R') \leftarrow \text{next}(Q, Q')$, and do a four-way branch to (I4, I5, I6, I7) according as $2[Q \neq Q'] + [R \neq R'] = (0, 1, 2, 3)$.

I4. [Case 0.] (Now $Q = Q'$ is a child of P', and $R = R'$ is the first child of Q'. Node Q will remain a child of P', but it will be preceded by any children of R.) Absorb R into P' (see below). Set $\text{CHILD}(Q) \leftarrow \text{SIB}(R)$ and $Q' \leftarrow \text{CHILD}(R)$. If $Q' \neq \Lambda$, set $R \leftarrow Q'$, and while $R \neq \Lambda$ set $\text{PARENT}(R) \leftarrow P'$, $R' \leftarrow R$, $R \leftarrow \text{SIB}(R)$; then $\text{SIB}(R') \leftarrow Q$, $Q \leftarrow Q'$. Set $\text{CHILD}(P) \leftarrow Q$ if $P = P'$, $\text{SIB}(P) \leftarrow Q$ if $P \neq P'$. Go to I8.

I5. [Case 1.] (Now component $Q = R$ is surrounded by $P' = R'$.) If $P = P'$, set $\text{CHILD}(P) \leftarrow \text{SIB}(Q)$; otherwise set $\text{SIB}(P) \leftarrow \text{SIB}(Q)$. Set $R \leftarrow \text{DORMANT}(R')$. Then if $R = \Lambda$, set $\text{DORMANT}(R') \leftarrow \text{SIB}(Q) \leftarrow Q$; otherwise $\text{SIB}(Q) \leftarrow \text{SIB}(R)$ and $\text{SIB}(R) \leftarrow Q$. Go to I8.

I6. [Case 2.] (Now Q' is the parent of both P' and R. Either $P = P'$ is childless, or P is the last child of P'.) Absorb R into P' (see below). Set $\text{SIB}(P') \leftarrow \text{SIB}(R)$ and $R \leftarrow \text{CHILD}(R)$. If $P = P'$, set $\text{CHILD}(P) \leftarrow R$; otherwise $\text{SIB}(P) \leftarrow R$. While $R \neq \Lambda$, set $\text{PARENT}(R) \leftarrow P'$ and $R \leftarrow \text{SIB}(R)$. Go to I8.

I7. [Case 3.] (Node $P' = Q$ is the last child of $Q' = R$, which is a child of R'.) Absorb P' into R' (see below). If $P = P'$, set $P \leftarrow R$. Otherwise set $P' \leftarrow$ $\text{CHILD}(P')$, and while $P' \neq \Lambda$ set $\text{PARENT}(P') \leftarrow R'$, $P' \leftarrow \text{SIB}(P')$; also set $\text{SIB}(P) \leftarrow \text{SIB}(Q')$ and $\text{SIB}(Q') \leftarrow \text{CHILD}(Q)$. If $Q = \text{CHILD}(R)$, set

CHILD(R) ← Λ. Otherwise set R ← CHILD(R), then R ← SIB(R) until SIB(R) = Q, then SIB(R) ← Λ. Finally set P′ ← R′.

I8. [Advance k.] Set $k ← k + 2$ and return to step I3.

I9. [Update the area.] Set AREA(P′) ← AREA(P′) + $\lceil a_j/2 \rceil - \lceil a_{j-1}/2 \rceil$. Then go back to I2 if $a_j = 2N + 3$.

I10. [Gobble up short a.] If $a_{j+1} \geq b_k$, go to I11. Otherwise set Q ← LOC(NODE(t)) and $t ← t + 1$. Set PARENT(Q) ← P′, DORMANT(Q) ← HEIR(Q) ← Λ; also ROW(Q) ← s, COL(Q) ← $\lceil a_j/2 \rceil$, AREA(Q) ← $\lceil a_{j+1}/2 \rceil - \lceil a_j/2 \rceil$. If P = P′, set SIB(Q) ← CHILD(P) and CHILD(P) ← Q; otherwise set SIB(Q) ← SIB(P) and SIB(P) ← Q. Finally set P ← Q, $j ← j + 2$, and return to I3.

I11. [Move on.] Set $j ← j + 1$, $k ← k + 1$, (P, P′) ← next(P, P′), and go to I3. ∎

To "absorb P into Q" means to do the following things: If (ROW(P), COL(P)) is less than (ROW(Q), COL(Q)), set (ROW(Q), COL(Q)) ← (ROW(P), COL(P)). Set AREA(Q) ← AREA(P) + AREA(Q). If DORMANT(Q) = Λ, set DORMANT(Q) ← DORMANT(P); otherwise if DORMANT(P) ≠ Λ, swap SIB(DORMANT(P)) ↔ SIB(DORMANT(Q)). Finally set HEIR(P) ← Q. (The HEIR links could be used on a second pass to identify the final component of each pixel. Notice that the PARENT links of dormant nodes are not kept up to date.)

[A similar algorithm was given by R. K. Lutz in *Comp. J.* **23** (1980), 262–269.]

180. Let $F(x,y) = x^2 - y^2 + 13$ and $Q(x,y) = F(x - \frac{1}{2}, y - \frac{1}{2}) = x^2 - y^2 - x + y + 13$. Apply Algorithm T to digitize the hyperbola from $(\xi, \eta) = (-6, 7)$ to $(\xi', \eta') = (0, \sqrt{13})$; hence $x = -6$, $y = 7$, $x' = 0$, $y' = 4$. The resulting edges are $(-6,7) — (-5,7) — (-5,6) — (-4,6) — (-4,5) — (-3,5) — (-3,4) — \cdots — (0,4)$. Then apply it again with $\xi = 0$, $\eta = \sqrt{13}$, $\xi' = 6$, $\eta' = 7$, $x = 0$, $y = 4$, $x' = 6$, $y' = 7$; the same edges are found (in reverse order), but with negated x coordinates.

181. Subdivide at points (ξ, η) where $F_x(\xi, \eta) = 0$ or $F_y(\xi, \eta) = 0$, namely at the real roots of $\{Q(-(b\eta + d)/(2a), \eta + \frac{1}{2}) = 0, \ \xi = -(b\eta + d)/(2a) - \frac{1}{2}\}$ or the real roots of $\{Q(\xi + \frac{1}{2}, -(b\xi + e)/(2c)) = 0, \ \eta = -(b\xi + e)/(2c) - \frac{1}{2}\}$, if they exist.

182. By induction on $|x' - x| + |y' - y|$. Consider, for example, the case $x > x'$ and $y < y'$. We know from (iii) that (ξ, η) lies in the box $x - \frac{1}{2} \leq \xi < x + \frac{1}{2}$ and $y - \frac{1}{2} \leq \eta < y + \frac{1}{2}$, and from (ii) that the curve travels monotonically as it moves from (ξ, η) to (ξ', η'). It must therefore exit the box at the edge $(x - \frac{1}{2}, y - \frac{1}{2}) — (x - \frac{1}{2}, y + \frac{1}{2})$ or $(x - \frac{1}{2}, y + \frac{1}{2}) — (x + \frac{1}{2}, y + \frac{1}{2})$. The latter holds if and only if $F(x - \frac{1}{2}, y + \frac{1}{2}) < 0$, because the curve can't intersect that edge twice when $x' < x$. And $F(x - \frac{1}{2}, y + \frac{1}{2})$ is the value $Q(x, y + 1)$ that is tested in step T4, because of the initialization in step T1. (We assume that the curve doesn't go *exactly* through $(x - \frac{1}{2}, y + \frac{1}{2})$, by implicitly adding a tiny positive amount to the function F behind the scenes.)

183. Consider, for example, the ellipse defined by $F(x - \frac{1}{2}, y - \frac{1}{2}) = Q(x,y) = 13x^2 + 7xy + y^2 - 2 = 0$; this ellipse is a cigar-shaped curve that extends roughly between $(-2, 5)$ and $(1, -6)$. Suppose we want to digitize its upper right boundary. Hypotheses (i)–(iv) of Algorithm T hold with

$$\xi = \sqrt{\frac{8}{3}} - \frac{1}{2}, \quad \eta = -\sqrt{\frac{98}{3}} - \frac{1}{2}, \quad \xi' = -\sqrt{\frac{98}{39}} - \frac{1}{2}, \quad \eta' = \sqrt{\frac{104}{3}} - \frac{1}{2},$$

$x = 1$, $y = -6$, $x' = -2$, $y' = 5$. Step T1 sets $Q ← Q(1, -5) = 1$, which causes step T4 to move left (L); in fact, the resulting path is L^3U^{11}, while the correct digitization according to (164) is $\text{U}^3\text{LU}^4\text{LU}^3\text{LU}$. Failure occurred because $Q(x,y) = 0$ has two roots on the edge $(1, -5) — (2, -5)$, namely $((35 \pm -\sqrt{29})/26, -5)$, causing $Q(1, -5)$

to have the same sign as $Q(2, -5)$. (One of those roots is on the boundary we are *not* trying to draw, but it's still there.) Similar failure occurs with the parabola defined by $Q(x, y) = 9x^2 + 6xy + y^2 - y = 0$, $\xi = -5/12$, $\eta = -1/4$, $\xi' = -5/2$, $\eta' = -19/2$, $x = 0$, $y = 0$, $x' = -2$, $y' = 9$. Hyperbolas can fail too (consider $6x^2 + 5xy + y^2 = 1$).

Algorithms for discrete geometry are notoriously delicate; unusual cases tend to drive them berserk. Algorithm T works properly for portions of any ellipse or parabola whose maximum curvature is less than 2. The maximum curvature of an ellipse with semiaxes $\alpha \geq \beta$ is α/β^2; the cigar-shaped example has maximum curvature ≈ 42.5. The maximum curvature of the parabola $y = \alpha x^2$ is $\alpha/2$; the anomalous parabola above has maximum curvature ≈ 5.27. "Reasonable" conics don't make such sharp turns.

To make Algorithm T work correctly *without* hypothesis (v), we need to slow it down a bit, by changing the tests '$Q < 0$' to '$Q < 0$ or X', where X is a test on the sign of a derivative. Namely, X is respectively '$S > c$', '$R > a$', '$R < -a$', '$S < -c$', in steps T2, T3, T4, T5.

184. Let $Q'(x, y) = -1 - Q(x, y)$. The key point is that $Q(x, y) < 0$ if and only if $Q'(x, y) \geq 0$. (Curiously the algorithm makes the same decisions, backwards, although it probes the values of Q' and Q in different places.)

185. Find a positive integer h so that $d = (\eta - \eta')h$ and $e = (\xi' - \xi)h$ are integers and $d + e$ is even. Then carry out Algorithm T with $x = \lfloor \xi + \frac{1}{2} \rfloor$, $y = \lfloor \eta + \frac{1}{2} \rfloor$, $x' = \lfloor \xi' + \frac{1}{2} \rfloor$, $y' = \lfloor \eta' + \frac{1}{2} \rfloor$, and $Q(x, y) = d(x - \frac{1}{2}) + e(y - \frac{1}{2}) + f$, where

$$f = \lfloor (\eta'\xi - \xi'\eta)h \rfloor - [d > 0 \text{ and } (\eta'\xi - \xi'\eta)h \text{ is an integer}].$$

(The '$d > 0$' term ensures that the opposite straight line, from (ξ', η') back to (ξ, η), will have precisely the same edges; see exercise 183.) Steps T1 and T6–T9 become much simpler than they were in the general case, because $R = d$ and $S = e$ are constant.

(F. G. Stockton [*CACM* **6** (1963), 161, 450] and J. E. Bresenham [*IBM Systems Journal* **4** (1965), 25–30] gave similar algorithms, but with diagonal edges permitted.)

186. (a) $B(\epsilon) = z_0 + 2\epsilon(z_1 - z_0) + O(\epsilon^2)$; $B(1 - \epsilon) = z_2 - 2\epsilon(z_2 - z_1) + O(\epsilon^2)$.

(b) Every point of $S(z_0, z_1, z_2)$ is a convex combination of z_0, z_1, and z_2.

(c) Obviously true, since $(1 - t)^2 + 2(1 - t)t + t^2 = 1$.

(d) The collinear condition follows from (b). Otherwise, by (c), we need only consider the case $z_0 = 0$ and $z_2 - 2z_1 = 1$, where $z_1 = x_1 + iy_1$ and $y_1 \neq 0$. In that case all points lie on the parabola $4x = (y/y_1)^2 + 4yx_1/y_1$.

(e) Note that $B(u\theta) = (1-u)^2 z_0 + 2u(1-u)((1-\theta)z_0 + \theta z_1) + u^2 B(\theta)$ for $0 \leq u \leq 1$.

[S. N. Bernshteĭn introduced $B_n(z_0, z_1, \ldots, z_n; t) = \sum_k \binom{n}{k}(1 - t)^{n-k} t^k z_k$ in *Soobshcheniiā Khar'kovskoe matematicheskoe obshchestvo* (2) **13** (1912), 1–2.]

187. We can assume that $z_0 = (x_0, y_0)$, $z_1 = (x_1, y_1)$, and $z_2 = (x_2, y_2)$, where the coordinates are (say) fixed-point numbers represented as 16-bit integers divided by 32.

If z_0, z_1, and z_2 are collinear, use the method of exercise 185 to draw a straight line from z_0 to z_2. (If z_1 doesn't lie between z_0 and z_2, the other edges will cancel out, because edges are implicitly XORed by a filling algorithm.) This case occurs if and only if $D = x_0 y_1 + x_1 y_2 + x_2 y_0 - x_1 y_0 - x_2 y_1 - x_0 y_2 = 0$.

Otherwise the points (x, y) of $S(z_0, z_1, z_2)$ satisfy $F(x, y) = 0$, where

$$F(x, y) = ((x - x_0)(y_2 - 2y_1 + y_0) - (y - y_0)(x_2 - 2x_1 + x_0))^2 \\ - 4D((x_1 - x_0)(y - y_0) - (y_1 - y_0)(x - x_0))$$

and D is defined above. We multiply by 32^4 to obtain integer coefficients; then negate this formula and subtract 1, if $D < 0$, to satisfy condition (iv) of Algorithm T and the reverse-order condition. (See exercise 184.)

The monotonicity condition (ii) holds if and only if $(x_1 - x_0)(x_2 - x_1) > 0$ and $(y_1 - y_0)(y_2 - y_1) > 0$. If necessary, we can use the recurrence of exercise 186(e) to break $S(z_0, z_1, z_2)$ into at most three monotonic subsquines; for example, setting $\theta = (x_0 - x_1)/(x_0 - 2x_1 + x_2)$ will achieve monotonicity in x. (A slight rounding error may occur during this fixed point arithmetic, but the recurrence can be performed in such a way that the subsquines are definitely monotonic.)

Notes: When z_0, z_1, and z_2 are near each other, a simpler and faster method based on exercise 186(e) with $\theta = \frac{1}{2}$ is adequate for most practical purposes, if one doesn't care about making the exactly correct choice between local edge sequences like "up-then-left" versus "left-then-up." In the late 1980s, Sampo Kaasila chose to use squines as the basic method of shape specification in the TrueType font format, because they can be digitized so rapidly. The METAFONT system achieves greater flexibility with cubic Bézier splines [see D. E. Knuth, *METAFONT: The Program* (Addison–Wesley, 1986)], but at the cost of extra processing time. A fairly fast "six-register algorithm" for the resulting cubic curves was, however, developed subsequently by John Hobby [*ACM Trans. on Graphics* **9** (1990), 262–277]. Vaughan Pratt introduced *conic splines*, which are sort of midway between squines and Bézier cubics, in *Computer Graphics* **19**, 3 (July 1985), 151–159. Conic spline segments can be elliptical and hyperbolic as well as parabolic, hence they require fewer intermediate points and control points than squines; furthermore, they can be handled by Algorithm T.

188. The following big-endian program assumes that $n \leq 74880$.

```
         LOC  Data_Segment                LDO  k,Initk
BITMAP   LOC  @+M*N/8             OH   SET  s,N/64
base     GREG @                   1H   SET  a,h          A trick (see below)
GRAYMAP  LOC  @+M*N/64                 SET  r,8
GTAB     BYTE 255,252,249,246,243 2H   LDOU t,base,k
         BYTE 240,236,233,230,227      MOR  u,c1,t
         BYTE 224,221,217,214,211      SUBU t,t,u        (Nypwise sums)
         BYTE 208,204,201,198,194      MOR  u,c2,t
         BYTE 191,188,184,181,178      AND  t,t,mu1
         BYTE 174,171,167,164,160      ADDU t,t,u        (Nybblewise sums)
         BYTE 157,153,150,146,142      MOR  u,c3,t
         BYTE 139,135,131,128,124      AND  t,t,mu2
         BYTE 120,116,112,108,104      ADDU t,t,u        (Bytewise sums)
         BYTE 100,96,92,88,84          ADDU a,a,t
         BYTE 79,75,70,66,61           INCL k,N/8        Move to next row.
         BYTE 56,52,46,41,36           SUB  r,r,1
         BYTE 30,24,18,10,0            PBNZ r,2B         Repeat 8 times.
Initk    OCTA BITMAP-GRAYMAP      3H   SRU  t,a,56
corr     GREG N-8                      LDBU t,gtab,t
c1       GREG #4000100004000100        SLU  a,a,8
c2       GREG #2010000002010000        STBU t,z,0
c3       GREG #0804020100000000        INCL z,1
mu1      GREG #3333333333333333        PBN  a,3B         (The trick)
mu2      GREG #0f0f0f0f0f0f0f0f        SUB  k,k,corr
h        GREG #8080808080808080        SUB  s,s,1
gtab     GREG GTAB-#80                 PBNZ s,1B         Loop on columns.
         LOC  #100                     INCL k,7*N/8      Loop on groups
MakeGray LDA  z,GRAYMAP               PBN  k,0B            of 8 rows. ∎
```

[Inspired by Neil Hunt's DVIPAGE, the author used such graymaps extensively when preparing new editions of *The Art of Computer Programming* in 1992–1998.]

189. If the rows of the bitmap are $(X_0, X_1, \ldots, X_{63})$, do the following operations for $k = 0, 1, \ldots, 5$: For all i such that $0 \le i < 64$ and $i \,\&\, 2^k = 0$, let $j = i + 2^k$ and either (a) set $t \leftarrow (X_i \oplus (X_j \gg 2^k)) \,\&\, \mu_{6,k}$, $X_i \leftarrow X_i \oplus t$, $X_j \leftarrow X_j \oplus (t \ll 2^k)$; or (b) set $t \leftarrow X_i \,\&\, \bar{\mu}_{6,k}$, $u \leftarrow X_j \,\&\, \mu_{6,k}$, $X_i \leftarrow ((X_i \ll 2^k) \,\&\, \bar{\mu}_{6,k}) \mid u$, $X_j \leftarrow ((X_j \gg 2^k) \,\&\, \mu_{6,k}) \mid t$.

[The basic idea is to transform $2^k \times 2^k$ submatrices for increasing k, as in exercise 5–12. Speedups are possible with MMIX, using MOR and MUX as in exercise 208, and using LDTU/STTU when $k = 5$. See L. J. Guibas and J. Stolfi, *ACM Transactions on Graphics* **1** (1982), 204–207; M. Thorup, *J. Algorithms* **42** (2002), 217. Incidentally, Theorem P and answer 54 show that $\Omega(n \log n)$ operations on n-bit numbers are needed to transpose an $n \times n$ bit matrix. An application that needs frequent transpositions might therefore be better off using a redundant representation, maintaining its matrices in both normal and transposed form.]

190. (a) We must have $\alpha_{j+1} = f(\alpha_j) \oplus \alpha_{j-1}$ for $j \ge 1$, where $\alpha_0 = 0\ldots0$ and $f(\alpha) = ((\alpha \ll 1) \,\&\, 1\ldots1) \oplus \alpha \oplus (\alpha \gg 1)$. The elements of the bottom row α_m satisfy the parity condition if and only if this rule makes α_{m+1} entirely zero.

(b) True. The parity condition on matrix entries a_{ij} is $a_{ij} = a_{(i-1)j} \oplus a_{i(j-1)} \oplus a_{i(j+1)} \oplus a_{(i+1)j}$, where $a_{ij} = 0$ if $i = 0$ or $i = m + 1$ or $j = 0$ or $j = n + 1$. If two matrices (a_{ij}) and (b_{ij}) satisfy this condition, so does (c_{ij}) when $c_{ij} = a_{ij} \oplus b_{ij}$.

(c) The upper left submatrix consisting of all rows that precede the first all-zero row (if any) and all columns that precede the first all-zero column (if any) is perfect. And this submatrix determines the entire matrix, because the pattern on the other side of a row or column of zeros is the top/bottom or left/right reflection of its neighbor. For example, if $\alpha_{m'+1}$ is zero, then $\alpha_{m'+1+j} = \alpha_{m'+1-j}$ for $1 \le j \le m'$.

(d) Starting with a given vector α_1 and using the rule in (a) will always lead to a row with $\alpha_{m+1} = 0\ldots0$. Proof: We must have $(\alpha_j, \alpha_{j+1}) = (\alpha_k, \alpha_{k+1})$ for some $0 \le j < k \le 2^{2n}$, by the pigeonhole principle. If $j > 0$ we also have $(\alpha_{j-1}, \alpha_j) = (\alpha_{k-1}, \alpha_k)$, because $\alpha_{j-1} = f(\alpha_j) \oplus \alpha_{j+1} = f(\alpha_k) \oplus \alpha_{k+1} = \alpha_{k-1}$. Therefore the first repeated pair begins with a row α_k of zeros. Furthermore we have $\alpha_i = \alpha_{k-i}$ for $0 \le i \le k$; hence the first all-zero row α_{m+1} occurs when m is $k - 1$ or $k/2 - 1$.

Rows $\alpha_1, \ldots, \alpha_m$ will form a perfect pattern unless there is a column of 0s. There are $t > 0$ such columns if and only if $t + 1$ is a divisor of $n + 1$ and α_1 has the form $\alpha 0 \alpha^R 0 \ldots 0 \alpha$ (t even) or $\alpha 0 \alpha^R 0 \ldots 0 \alpha^R$ (t odd), where $|\alpha| + 1 = (n + 1)/(t + 1)$.

(e) This starting vector does not have the form forbidden in (d).

191. (a) The former is $\alpha_1, \alpha_2, \ldots$ if and only if the latter is $0\alpha_1 0\alpha_1^R$, $0\alpha_2 0\alpha_2^R$, $\ldots$.

(b) Let the binary string $a_0 a_1 \ldots a_{N-1}$ correspond to the polynomial $a_0 + a_1 x + \cdots + a_{N-1}x^{N-1}$, and let $y = x^{-1} + 1 + x$. Then $\alpha_0 = 0\ldots0$ corresponds to $F_0(y)$; $\alpha_1 = 10\ldots0$ corresponds to $F_1(y)$; and by induction α_j corresponds to $F_j(y)$, mod $x^N + 1$ and mod 2. For example, when $N = 6$ we have $\alpha_2 = 110001 \leftrightarrow 1 + x + x^5$ because $x^{-1} \bmod (x^6 + 1) = x^5$, etc.

(c) Again, induction on j.

(d) The identity in the hint holds by induction on m, because it is clearly true when $m = 1$ and $m = 2$. Working mod 2, this identity yields the simple equations

$$F_{2k}(y) = yF_k(y)^2; \qquad F_{2k-1}(y) = (F_{k-1}(y) + F_k(y))^2.$$

So we can go from the pair $P_k = (F_{k-1}(y) \bmod (x^N+1), F_k(y) \bmod (x^N+1))$ to the pair P_{k+1} in $O(n)$ steps, and to the pair P_{2k} in $O(n^2)$ steps. We can therefore compute

$F_j(y) \bmod (x^N + 1)$ after $O(\log j)$ iterations. Multiplying by $f_\alpha(x) + f_\alpha(x^{-1})$ and reducing mod $x^N + 1$ then allows us to read off the value of α_j.

Incidentally, $F_{n+1}(x)$ is the special case $K_n(x, x, \ldots, x)$ of a continuant polynomial; see Eq. 4.5.3–(4). We have $F_{n+1}(x) = \sum_{k=0}^{n} \binom{n-k}{k} x^{n-2k} = i^{-n} U_n(ix/2)$, where U_n is the classical Chebyshev polynomial defined by $U_n(\cos\theta) = \sin((n+1)\theta)/\sin\theta$.

192. (a) By exercise 191(c), $c(q)$ is the least $j > 0$ such that $(x + x^{-1})F_j(x^{-1} + 1 + x) \equiv 0$ (modulo $x^{2q} + 1$), using polynomial arithmetic mod 2. Equivalently, it's the smallest positive j for which $F_j(y)$ is a multiple of $(x^{2q} + 1)/(x^2 + 1) = (1 + x + \cdots + x^{q-1})^2$, when $y = x^{-1} + 1 + x$.

(b) Use the method of exercise 191(d) to evaluate $((x + x^{-1})F_j(y)) \bmod (x^{2q} + 1)$ when $j = M/p$, for all prime divisors p of M. If the result is zero, set $M \leftarrow M/p$ and repeat the process. If no such result is zero, $c(q) = M$.

(c) We want to show that $c(2^e)$ is a divisor of $3 \cdot 2^{e-1}$ but not of $3 \cdot 2^{e-2}$ or 2^{e-1}. The latter holds because $F_{2^e-1}(y) = y^{2^{e-1}-1}$ is relatively prime to $x^{2^{e+1}} + 1$. The former holds because

$$F_{3 \cdot 2^e - 1}(y) = y^{2^{e-1}-1} F_3(y)^{2^{e-1}} = y^{2^{e-1}-1}(1+y)^{2^e} = y^{2^{e-1}-1}(x^{-1} + x)^{2^e},$$

which is $\equiv 0$ modulo $x^{2^{e+1}} + 1$ but not modulo $x^{2^{e+2}} + 1$.

(d) $F_{2^e-1}(y) = \sum_{k=1}^{e} y^{2^e - 2^k}$. Since $y = x^{-1}(1 + x + x^2)$ is relatively prime to $x^q + 1$, we have $y^{-1} \equiv a_0 + a_1 x + \cdots + a_{q-1} x^{q-1}$ (modulo $x^q + 1$) for some coefficients a_i; hence

$$y^{-2^k} \equiv a_0 + a_1 x^{2^k} + \cdots + a_{q-1} x^{2^k(q-1)} \equiv a_0 + a_1 x^{2^{k+e}} + \cdots + a_{q-1} x^{2^{k+e}(q-1)} \equiv y^{-2^{k+e}}$$

(modulo $x^q + 1$) for $0 \le k < e$, and it follows that $F_{2^{2e}-1}(y)$ is a multiple of $x^{2q} + 1$.

(e) In this case $c(q)$ divides $4(2^{2e} - 1)$. Proof: Let $x^q + 1 = f_1(x) f_2(x) \ldots f_r(x)$ where $f_1(x) = x + 1$, $f_2(x) = x^2 + x + 1$, and each $f_i(x)$ is irreducible mod 2. Since q is odd, these factors are distinct. Therefore, in the finite field of polynomials mod $f_j(x)$ for $j \ge 3$, we have $y^{-2^k} = y^{-2^{k+e}}$ as in (d). Consequently $F_{2^{2e}-1}(y)$ is a multiple of $f_3(x) \ldots f_r(x) = (x^q + 1)/(x^3 + 1)$. So $F_{2(2^{2e}-1)}(y) = y F_{2^{2e}-1}(y)^2$ is a multiple of $(x^{2q} + 1)/(x^2 + 1)$ as desired.

(f) If $F_{c(q)}(y)$ is a multiple of $x^{2q} + 1$, it's easy to see that $c(2q) = 2c(q)$. Otherwise $F_{3c(q)}(y)$ is a multiple of $F_3(y) = (1 + y)^2 = x^{-2}(1 + x)^4$; hence $F_{6c(q)}(y)$ is a multiple of $x^{4q} + 1$ and $c(2q)$ divides $6c(q)$. The latter case can happen only when q is odd.

Notes: Parity patterns are related to a popular puzzle called "Lights Out," which was invented in the early 1980s by Dario Uri, also invented independently about the same time by László Mérő and called ✗∟☐⧈. [See David Singmaster's *Cubic Circular*, issues 7&8 (Summer 1985), 39–42; Dieter Gebhardt, *Cubism For Fun* **69** (March 2006), 23–25.] Klaus Sutner has pursued further aspects of this theory in *Theoretical Computer Science* **230** (2000), 49–73.

193. Let $b_{(2i)(2j)} = a_{ij}$, $b_{(2i+1)(2j)} = a_{ij} \oplus a_{(i+1)j}$, $b_{(2i)(2j+1)} = a_{ij} \oplus a_{i(j+1)}$, and $b_{(2i+1)(2j+1)} = 0$, for $0 \le i \le m$ and $0 \le j \le n$, where we regard $a_{ij} = 0$ when $i = 0$ or $i = m + 1$ or $j = 0$ or $j = n + 1$. We don't have $(b_{(2i)1}, b_{(2i)2}, \ldots, b_{(2i)(2n+1)}) = (0, 0, \ldots, 0)$ because $(a_{i1}, \ldots, a_{in}) \ne (0, \ldots, 0)$ for $1 \le i \le m$. And we don't have $(b_{(2i+1)1}, b_{(2i+1)2}, \ldots, b_{(2i+1)(2n+1)}) = (0, 0, \ldots, 0)$ because adjacent rows $(a_{i1}, \ldots, a_{in})$ and $(a_{(i+1)1}, \ldots, a_{(i+1)n})$ always differ for $0 \le i \le m$ when m is odd.

194. Set $\beta_i \leftarrow (1 \ll (n-i)) \mid (1 \ll (i-1))$ for $1 \le i \le m$, where $m = \lceil n/2 \rceil$. Also set $\gamma_i \leftarrow (\beta_1 \mathbin{\&} \alpha_{i1}) + (\beta_2 \mathbin{\&} \alpha_{i2}) + \cdots + (\beta_m \mathbin{\&} \alpha_{im})$, where α_{ij} is the jth row of the parity pattern that begins with β_i; vector γ_i records the diagonal elements of such a matrix. Then set $r \leftarrow 0$ and apply subroutine N of answer 195 for $i \leftarrow 1, 2, \ldots, m$. The resulting vectors $\theta_1, \ldots, \theta_r$ are a basis for all $n \times n$ parity patterns with 8-fold symmetry.

To test if any such pattern is perfect, let the pattern starting with θ_i first be zero in row c_i. If any $c_i = n + 1$, the answer is yes. If $\mathrm{lcm}(c_1, \ldots, c_r) < n$, the answer is no. If neither of these conditions decides the matter, we can resort to brute-force examination of $2^r - 1$ nonzero linear combinations of the θ vectors.

For example, when $n = 9$ we find $\gamma_1 = 111101111$, $\gamma_2 = \gamma_3 = 010101010$, $\gamma_4 = 000000000$, $\gamma_5 = 001010100$; then $r = 0$, $\theta_1 = 011000110$, $\theta_2 = 000101000$, $c_1 = c_2 = 5$. So there is no perfect solution.

In the author's experiments for $n \leq 3000$, "brute force" was needed only when $n = 1709$. Then $r = 21$ and the values of c_i were all equal to 171 or 855 except that $c_{21} = 342$. The solution $\theta_1 \oplus \theta_{21}$ was found immediately.

The answers for $1 \leq n \leq 383$ are 4, 5, 11, 16, 23, 29, 30, 32, 47, 59, 62, 64, 65, 84, 95, 101, 119, 125, 126, 128, 131, 154, 164, 170, 185, 191, 203, 204, 239, 251, 254, 256, 257, 263, 314, 329, 340, 341, 371, 383.

[A fractal similar to Fig. 20, called the "mikado pattern," appears in a paper by H. Eriksson, K. Eriksson, and J. Sjöstrand, *Advances in Applied Math.* **27** (2001), 365. See also S. Wolfram, *A New Kind of Science* (2002), rule 150R on page 439.]

195. Set $\beta_i \leftarrow 1 \ll (m - i)$ and $\gamma_i \leftarrow \alpha_i$ for $1 \leq i \leq m$; also set $r \leftarrow 0$. Then perform the following subroutine for $i = 1, 2, \ldots, m$:

N1. [Extract low bit.] Set $x \leftarrow \gamma_i \,\&\, -\gamma_i$. If $x = 0$, go to N4.

N2. [Find j.] Find the smallest $j \geq 1$ such that $\gamma_j \,\&\, x \neq 0$ and $\gamma_j \,\&\, (x - 1) = 0$.

N3. [Dependent?] If $j < i$, set $\gamma_i \leftarrow \gamma_i \oplus \gamma_j$, $\beta_i \leftarrow \beta_i \oplus \beta_j$, and return to N1. (These operations preserve the matrix equation $C = BA$.) Otherwise terminate the subroutine (because γ_i is linearly independent from $\gamma_1, \ldots, \gamma_{i-1}$).

N4. [Record a solution.] Set $r \leftarrow r + 1$ and $\theta_r \leftarrow \beta_i$. ∎

At the conclusion, the $m - r$ nonzero vectors γ_i are a basis for the vector space of all linear combinations of $\alpha_1, \ldots, \alpha_m$; they're characterized by their low bits.

196. (a) $^\#$0a; $^\#$cea3; $^\#$e7ae97; $^\#$f09d8581.

(b) If $\lambda x = \lambda x'$, the result is clear because $l = l'$. Otherwise we have either $\alpha_1 < \alpha_1'$ or $(\alpha_1 = \alpha_1'$ and $\alpha_2 < \alpha_2')$; the latter case can occur only when $x \geq 2^{16}$.

(c) Set $j \leftarrow k$; while $\alpha_j \oplus {^\#}80 < {^\#}40$, set $j \leftarrow j - 1$. Then $\alpha(x^{(i)})$ begins with α_j.

197. (a) $^\#$000a; $^\#$03a3; $^\#$7b97; $^\#$d834dd41.

(b) Lexicographic order is *not* preserved when, say, $x = {^\#}$ffff and $x' = {^\#}$10000.

(c) To answer this question properly one needs to know that the 2048 integers in the range $^\#$d800 $\leq x < {^\#}$e000 are not legal codepoints of UCS; they are called *surrogates*. With this understanding, $\beta(x^{(i)})$ begins at β_k if $\beta_k \oplus {^\#}$dc00 $\geq {^\#}$0400, otherwise it begins at β_{k-1}.

198. $a = {^\#}$e50000, $b = 3$, $c = {^\#}$16. (We could let $b = 0$, but then a would be huge. This trick was suggested by P. Raynaud-Richard in 1997. The stated constants, suggested by R. Pournader in 2008, are the smallest possible.)

199. We want $\alpha_1 > {^\#}$c1; $2^8\alpha_1 + \alpha_2 < {^\#}$f490; and either $(\alpha_1 \,\&\, -\alpha_1) + \alpha_1 < {^\#}$100 or $\alpha_1 + \alpha_2 > {^\#}$17f. These conditions hold if and only if

$$\left({^\#}\mathtt{c1} - \alpha_1\right) \,\&\, \left(2^8\alpha_1 + \alpha_2 - {^\#}\mathtt{f490}\right) \,\&\, \left(\left((\alpha_1 \,\&\, -\alpha_1) + \alpha_1 - {^\#}\mathtt{100}\right) \,|\, \left({^\#}\mathtt{17f} - \alpha_1 - \alpha_2\right)\right) \;<\; 0.$$

Markus Kuhn suggests adding the further clause '& $\left(^{\#}20 - ((2^8\alpha_1 + \alpha_2) \oplus {}^{\#}\texttt{eda0})\right)$', to ensure that $\alpha_1\alpha_2$ doesn't begin the encoding of a surrogate.

200. If $\$0 = (x_7 \ldots x_1 x_0)_{256}$ then $\$3$ is set to the symmetric function $S_2(x_7, x_4, x_2)$.

201. MOR x,c,x, where $\texttt{c} = {}^{\#}\texttt{f0f0f0f00f0f0f0f}$.

202. MOR x,x,c, where $\texttt{c} = {}^{\#}\texttt{c0c030300c0c0303}$; then MOR x,mone,x. (See answer 209.)

203. $\texttt{a} = {}^{\#}\texttt{0008000400020001}$, $\texttt{b} = {}^{\#}\texttt{0f0f0f0f0f0f0f0f}$, $\texttt{c} = {}^{\#}\texttt{0606060606060606}$, $\texttt{d} = {}^{\#}\texttt{0000002700000000}$, $\texttt{e} = {}^{\#}\texttt{2a2a2a2a2a2a2a2a}$. (The ASCII code for 0 is $6 + {}^{\#}\texttt{2a}$; the ASCII code for a is $6 + {}^{\#}\texttt{2a} + 10 + {}^{\#}\texttt{27}$.)

204. $p = {}^{\#}\texttt{8008400420021001}$, $q = {}^{\#}\texttt{8020080240100401}$ (the transpose of p), $r = {}^{\#}\texttt{4080102004080102}$ (a symmetric matrix), and $m = {}^{\#}\texttt{aa55aa55aa55aa55}$.

205. Shuffle, but with $p \leftrightarrow q$, $r = {}^{\#}\texttt{0804020180402010}$, $m = {}^{\#}\texttt{f0f0f0f00f0f0f0f}$.

206. Just change p to ${}^{\#}\texttt{0880044002200110}$. (Incidentally, these shuffles can also be defined as permutations on $z = (z_{63} \ldots z_1 z_0)_2$ in another way: The outshuffle maps $z_j \mapsto z_{(2j) \bmod 63}$, for $0 \le j < 64$, while the inshuffle maps $z_j \mapsto z_{(2j+1) \bmod 65}$.)

207. Do MOR y,p,x; MOR y,y,p; MOR t,y,q; PUT rM,m1; MUX y,y,t; MOR t,t,q; PUT rM,m2; MUX y,y,t. In both cases $p = {}^{\#}\texttt{2004801002400801}$; for triple zip, $q = {}^{\#}\texttt{4020100804020180}$, $m_1 = {}^{\#}\texttt{4949494949494949}$, $m_2 = {}^{\#}\texttt{dbdbdbdbdbdbdbdb}$; for the inverse, $q = {}^{\#}\texttt{0402018040201008}$, $m_1 = {}^{\#}\texttt{0707070707070707}$, $m_2 = {}^{\#}\texttt{3f3f3f3f3f3f3f3f}$.

208. (Solution by H. S. Warren, Jr.) The text's 7-swap, 14-swap, 28-swap method can be implemented with only 12 instructions:

$$\begin{aligned}
&\texttt{MOR t,x,c1;} \quad \texttt{MOR t,c1,t;} \quad \texttt{PUT rM,m1;} \quad \texttt{MUX y,x,t;}\\
&\texttt{MOR t,y,c2;} \quad \texttt{MOR t,c2,t;} \quad \texttt{PUT rM,m2;} \quad \texttt{MUX y,y,t;}\\
&\texttt{MOR t,y,c3;} \quad \texttt{MOR t,c3,t;} \quad \texttt{PUT rM,m3;} \quad \texttt{MUX y,y,t;}
\end{aligned}$$

here $c_1 = {}^{\#}\texttt{4080102004080102}$, $c_2 = {}^{\#}\texttt{2010804002010804}$, $c_3 = {}^{\#}\texttt{0804020180402010}$, $m_1 = {}^{\#}\texttt{aa55aa55aa55aa55}$, $m_2 = {}^{\#}\texttt{cccc3333cccc3333}$, $m_3 = {}^{\#}\texttt{f0f0f0f00f0f0f0f}$.

209. Four instructions suffice: MXOR y,p,x; MXOR x,mone,x; MXOR x,x,q; XOR x,x,y; here $p = {}^{\#}\texttt{80c0e0f0f8fcfeff} = \bar{q}$, and register $\texttt{mone} = -1$.

210. SLU x,one,x; MOR x,b,x; AND x,x,a; MOR x,x,#ff; here register $\texttt{one} = 1$.

211. In general, element ij of the Boolean matrix product AXB is $\bigvee\{x_{kl} \mid a_{ik}b_{lj} = 1\}$. For this problem we choose $a_{ik} = [i \supseteq k]$ and $b_{lj} = [l \subseteq j]$; the answer is 'MOR t,f,a; MOR t,b,t' where $\texttt{a} = {}^{\#}\texttt{80c0a0f088ccaaff}$ and $\texttt{b} = {}^{\#}\texttt{ff5533110f050301} = \texttt{a}^T$.

(Notice that this trick gives a simple test $[f = \hat{f}]$ for monotonicity. Furthermore, the 64-bit result $(t_{63} \ldots t_1 t_0)_2$ gives the coefficients of the multilinear representation

$$f(x_1, \ldots, x_6) = (t_{63} + t_{62}x_6 + \cdots + t_1 x_1 x_2 x_3 x_4 x_5 + t_0 x_1 x_2 x_3 x_4 x_5 x_6) \bmod 2,$$

if we substitute MXOR for MOR, by the result of exercise 7.1.1–11.)

212. If $\cdot$ denotes MXOR as in (183) and $b = (\beta_7 \ldots \beta_1 \beta_0)_{256}$ has bytes β_j, we can evaluate

$$c = (a \cdot B_0^L) \oplus ((a \ll 8) \cdot (B_1^L + B_0^U)) \oplus ((a \ll 16) \cdot (B_2^L + B_1^U)) \oplus \cdots \oplus ((a \ll 56) \cdot (B_7^L + B_6^U)),$$

where $B_j^U = (q\beta_j) \,\&\, m$, $B_j^L = (((q\beta_j) \ll 8) + \beta_j) \,\&\, \overline{m}$, $q = {}^{\#}\texttt{0080402010080402}$, and $m = {}^{\#}\texttt{7f3f1f0f07030100}$. (Here $q\beta_j$ denotes *ordinary* multiplication of integers.)

213. In this big-endian computation, register `nn` holds $-n$, and register `data` points to the octabyte following the given bytes $\alpha_{n-1} \dots \alpha_1 \alpha_0$ in memory (with α_{n-1} first). The constants `aa` = #8381808080402010 and `bb` = #339bcf6530180c06 correspond to matrices A and B, found by computing the remainders $x^k \bmod p(x)$ for $72 \le k < 80$.

	SET	c,0	$c \leftarrow 0$.	LDOU	t,data,nn	$t \leftarrow$ next octa.
	LDOU	t,data,nn	$t \leftarrow$ next octa.	XOR	u,u,c	$u \leftarrow u \oplus c$.
	ADD	nn,nn,8	$n \leftarrow n - 8$.	SLU	c,v,56	$c \leftarrow v \ll 56$.
	BZ	nn,2F	Done if $n = 0$.	SRU	v,v,8	$v \leftarrow v \gg 8$.
1H	MXOR	u,aa,t	$u \leftarrow t \cdot A$.	XOR	u,u,v	$u \leftarrow u \oplus v$.
	MXOR	v,bb,t	$v \leftarrow t \cdot B$.	XOR	t,t,u	$t \leftarrow t \oplus u$.
	ADD	nn,nn,8	$n \leftarrow n - 8$.	PBN	nn,1B	Repeat if $n > 0$. ∎

A similar method finishes the job, with no auxiliary table needed:

2H	SET	nn,8	$n \leftarrow 8$.	SRU	v,v,8	$v \leftarrow v \gg 8$.
3H	AND	x,t,ffooo	$x \leftarrow$ high byte.	XOR	t,t,v	$t \leftarrow t \oplus v$.
	MXOR	u,aaa,x	$u \leftarrow x \cdot A'$.	SUB	nn,nn,1	$n \leftarrow n - 1$.
	MXOR	v,bbb,x	$v \leftarrow x \cdot B'$.	PBP	nn,3B	Repeat if $n > 0$.
	SLU	t,t,8	$t \leftarrow t \ll 8$.	XOR	t,t,c	$t \leftarrow t \oplus c$.
	XOR	t,t,u	$t \leftarrow t \oplus u$.	SRU	crc,t,48	Return $t \gg 48$. ∎

Here `aaa` = #8381808080808080, `bbb` = #0383c363331b0f05, and `ffooo` = #ff00...00.

> *The Books of the* Big-Endians *have been long forbidden.*
> — LEMUEL GULLIVER, *Travels Into Several Remote Nations of the World* (1726)

214. By considering the irreducible factors of the characteristic polynomial of X, we must have $X^n = I$ where $n = 2^3 \cdot 3^2 \cdot 5 \cdot 7 \cdot 17 \cdot 31 \cdot 127 = 168661080$. Neill Clift has shown that $l(n-1) = 33$ and found the following sequence of 33 `MXOR` instructions to compute $Y = X^{-1} = X^{n-1}$: `MXOR t,x,x`; `MXOR $1,t,x`; `MXOR $2,t,$1`; `MXOR $3,$2,$2`; `MXOR t,$3,$3`; S^6; `MXOR t,t,$2`; S^3; `MXOR $1,t,$1`; `MXOR t,$1,$3`; S^{13}; `MXOR t,t,$1`; S; `MXOR y,t,x`; here S stands for '`MXOR t,t,t`'. To test if X is nonsingular, do `MXOR t,y,x` and compare `t` to the identity matrix #8040201008040201.

215. `SADD $0,x,0`; `SADD $1,x,a`; `NEG $0,32,$0`; `2ADDU $1,$1,$0`; `SLU $0,b,$1`; then `BN $0,Yes`; here a = #aaaaaaaaaaaaaaaa and b = #2492492492492492.

216. Start with $s_k \leftarrow 0$ and $t_k \leftarrow -1$ for $0 \le k < m$. Then do the following for $1 \le k \le m$: If $x_k \ne 0$ and $x_k < 2^m$, set $l \leftarrow \lambda x_k$ and $s_l \leftarrow s_l + x_k$; if $t_l < 0$ or $t_l > x_k$, also set $t_l \leftarrow x_k$. Finally, set $y \leftarrow 1$ and $k \leftarrow 0$; while $y \ge t_k$ and $k < m$, set $y \leftarrow y + s_k$ and $k \leftarrow k + 1$. Double-precision n-bit arithmetic is sufficient for y and s_k. [This pleasant algorithm appeared in D. Eppstein's blog, 2008.03.22.]

217. See R. D. Cameron, *U.S. Patent 7400271* (15 July 2008); *Proc. ACM Symp. Principles and Practice of Parallel Programming* **13** (2008), 91–98.

218. Let b be any integer with $b \bmod 8 = 5$. Then $x = b^{L(x)} \bmod 2^d$ for some integer $L(x)$, depending on b, whenever $0 < x < 2^d$ and $x \bmod 4 = 1$ (see Section 3.2.1.2). The following algorithm computes $s = 4L(x)$, given a table of the numbers $t_k = -4L(2^k+1)$ for $1 < k < d$, and assuming that $t_k = 2^k + 1$ for $k \ge d/2$: Set $s \leftarrow 0$, $j \leftarrow 1$; then while $j < d/2 - 1$, set $j \leftarrow j + 1$, and if $x \,\&\, (1 \ll j) \ne 0$ also set $x \leftarrow (x + (x \ll j)) \bmod 2^d$, $s \leftarrow (s + t_j) \bmod 2^d$. Finally set $s \leftarrow (s + 1 - x) \bmod 2^d$.

Now to compute $a \cdot x^y$ we can proceed as follows (with all arithmetic done mod 2^d): If $x \,\&\, 2 \ne 0$, set $x \leftarrow -x$ and $a \leftarrow (-1)^{y \,\&\, 1} a$. (Now $x \bmod 4 = 1$.) Set $s \leftarrow 4L(x) \cdot y$, using the algorithm above, and $j \leftarrow 1$; then while $s \neq 0$, set $j \leftarrow j + 1$, and if $s \mathbin{\&} (1 \ll j) \neq 0$ also set $s \leftarrow s + t_j$, $a \leftarrow a + (a \ll j)$. The desired answer is then a. (With another muliplication we could return $(1 - s)a$ as soon as $j \geq d/2$.)

Suitable numbers t_k can be computed by setting $t_k \leftarrow 1 \ll k$ for $d - 1 \geq k \geq d/2$ and proceeding as follows for the remaining ks, in decreasing order: Set $x \leftarrow 1 + (1 \ll k)$, $x \leftarrow x + (x \ll k)$, $s \leftarrow 0$, $j \leftarrow k$; then while $j < d/2 - 1$ set $j \leftarrow j + 1$, and if $x \mathbin{\&} (1 \ll j) \neq 0$ also set $x \leftarrow x + (x \ll j)$, $s \leftarrow s - t_j$; finally $t_k \leftarrow (s + x - 1) \gg 1$. For example, when $d = 32$ we get $t_{15} = {}^\#20008000$, $t_{14} = {}^\#18004000$, $t_{13} = {}^\#0e002000$, $t_{12} = {}^\#07801000$, $t_{11} = {}^\#03e00800$, $t_{10} = {}^\#41f80400$, $t_9 = {}^\#18fe0200$, $t_8 = {}^\#0b7f8100$, $t_7 = {}^\#319fe080$, $t_6 = {}^\#5e8bf840$, $t_5 = {}^\#4a617e20$, $t_4 = {}^\#17c26f90$, $t_3 = {}^\#6119d1e8$, $t_2 = {}^\#2c30267c$. (This procedure finds the L's for *some* integer b, without revealing the actual value of b itself!)

[The methods of this exercise have interesting connections to the algorithms of Briggs and Feynman for *real*-valued logarithm and exponential in exercises 1.2.2–25 and 1.2.2–28. Our broadword procedure for x^y works also for calculating the inverse of x, modulo 2^d, when $y = -1$; but there's a direct algorithm available for that: Set $z \leftarrow 1$, $j \leftarrow 0$; while $x \neq 1$ set $j \leftarrow j + 1$, and if $x \mathbin{\&} (1 \ll j) \neq 0$, also set $z \leftarrow (z + (z \ll j)) \bmod 2^d$, $x \leftarrow (x + (x \ll j)) \bmod 2^d$. The final z is the inverse of the original odd number x.]

SECTION 7.1.4

1. Here are the BDDs for truth tables 0000, 0001, ..., 1111, showing the sizes below:

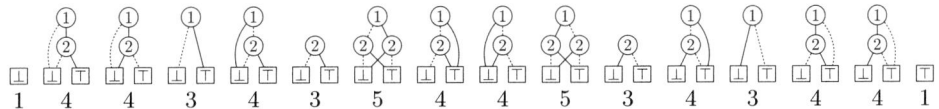

  1   4   4   3   4   3   5   4   4   5   3   4   3   4   4   1

2. (The ordering property determines the direction of each arc.)

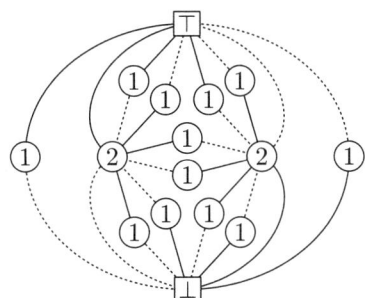

3. There are two with size 1 (namely the two constant functions); none with size 2 (because two sinks cannot both be reachable unless there's also a branch node); and $2n$ with size 3 (namely x_j and $\bar{x}_j$ for $1 \leq j \leq n$).

4. Set $y \leftarrow {}^\#0fffffff\mathtt{effffffe} \mathbin{\&} \bar{x} + {}^\#20000002$, $y \leftarrow (y \gg 28) \mathbin{\&} {}^\#10000001$, $x' \leftarrow x \oplus y$. (See 7.1.3–(93).)

5. You get $\overline{f(\bar{x}_1, \ldots, \bar{x}_n)} = f^D(x_1, \ldots, x_n)$, the *dual* of f (see exercise 7.1.1–2).

6. The largest subtables of 1011000110010011, namely 10110001, 10010011, 1011, 0001, 1001, 0011, are all distinct beads; squares and duplicates don't appear until we look at the subtables $\{10, 11, 00, 01\}$ of length 2. So g has size 11.

7. (a) If the truth table of f is $\alpha_0 \alpha_1 \ldots \alpha_{2^k - 1}$, where each α_j is a binary string of length 2^{n-k}, the truth table of g_k is $\beta_0 \beta_2 \ldots \beta_{2^k - 2}$, where $\beta_{2j} = \alpha_{2j} \alpha_{2j+1} \alpha_{2j+1} \alpha_{2j+1}$.

(b) Thus the beads of f and g_k are closely related. We get the BDD for g_k from the BDD for f by changing $\widehat{j}$ to $\widehat{j-1}$ for $1 \le j < k$, and replacing $\widehat{k}$ by $\widehat{k-1}$.

8. (a) Now $\beta_{2j} = \alpha_{2j}\alpha_{2j+1}\alpha_{2j+1}\alpha_{2j}$. (b) Again change $\widehat{j}$ to $\widehat{j-1}$ for $1 \le j < k$. If $\widehat{k}$ is present in f but not $\widehat{k}$, replace $\widehat{k}$ by $\widehat{k-1}$; otherwise replace $\widehat{k}$ $\widehat{k}$ by

. [E. Dubrova and L. Macchiarulo, *IEEE Trans.* **C-49** (2000), 1290–1292.]

9. There is no solution if $s = 1$. Otherwise set $k \leftarrow s-1$, $j \leftarrow 1$, and do the following steps repeatedly: (i) While $j < v_k$, set $x_j \leftarrow 1$ and $j \leftarrow j+1$; (ii) stop if $k = 0$; (iii) if $h_k \ne 1$, set $x_j \leftarrow 1$ and $k \leftarrow h_k$, otherwise set $x_j \leftarrow 0$ and $k \leftarrow l_k$; (iv) set $j \leftarrow j+1$.

10. Let $I_k = (\bar{v}_k ? l_k : h_k)$ for $0 \le k < s$ and $I_k' = (\bar{v}_k' ? l_k' : h_k')$ for $0 \le k < s'$. We may assume that $s = s'$; otherwise $f \ne f'$. The following algorithm either finds indices $(t_0, \dots, t_{s-1})$ such that I_k corresponds to I_{t_k}', or concludes that $f \ne f'$:

> **I1.** [Initialize and loop.] Set $t_{s-1} \leftarrow s-1$, $t_1 \leftarrow 1$, $t_0 \leftarrow 0$, and $t_k \leftarrow -1$ for $2 \le k \le s-2$. Do steps I2–I4 for $k = s-1, s-2, \dots, 2$ (in this order). If those steps "quit" at any point, we have $f \ne f'$; otherwise $f = f'$.
>
> **I2.** [Test v_k.] Set $t \leftarrow t_k$. (Now $t \ge 0$; otherwise I_k would have no predecessor.) Quit if $v_t' \ne v_k$.
>
> **I3.** [Test l_k.] Set $l \leftarrow l_k$. If $t_l < 0$, set $t_l \leftarrow l_t'$; otherwise quit if $l_t' \ne t_l$.
>
> **I4.** [Test h_k.] Set $h \leftarrow h_k$. If $t_h < 0$, set $t_h \leftarrow h_t'$; otherwise quit if $h_t' \ne t_h$. ∎

11. (a) Yes, since c_k correctly counts the number of settings of $x_{v_k} \dots x_n$ that lead from node k to node 1. (In fact, many BDD algorithms will run correctly — but more slowly — in the presence of equivalent nodes or redundant branches. But reduction is important when, say, we want to test quickly if $f = f'$ as in exercise 10.)

(b) No. For example, suppose $I_3 = (\bar{1}? 2:1)$, $I_2 = (\bar{1}? 0:1)$, $I_1 = (\bar{2}? 1:1)$, $I_0 = (\bar{2}? 0:0)$; then the algorithm sets $c_2 \leftarrow 1$, $c_3 \leftarrow \frac{3}{2}$. (But see exercise 35(b).)

12. (a) The first condition makes K independent; the second makes it maximally so.

(b) None when n is odd; otherwise there are two sets of alternate vertices.

(c) A vertex is in the kernel if and only if it is a sink vertex or in the kernel of the graph obtained by deleting all sink vertices and their immediate predecessors.

[Kernels represent winning positions in nim-like games, and they also arise in n-person games. See J. von Neumann and O. Morgenstern, *Theory of Games and Economic Behavior* (1944), §30.1; C. Berge, *Graphs and Hypergraphs* (1973), Chapter 14.]

13. (a) A maximal clique of G is a kernel of $\overline{G}$, and vice versa. (b) A minimal vertex cover U is the complement $V \setminus W$ of a kernel W, and vice versa (see 7–(6₁)).

14. (a) The size is $4(n-2) + 2[n\,{=}\,3]$. When $n \ge 6$ these BDDs form a pattern in which there are four branch nodes for variables $4, 5, \dots, n-2$, together with a fixed pattern at the top and bottom. The four branches are essentially

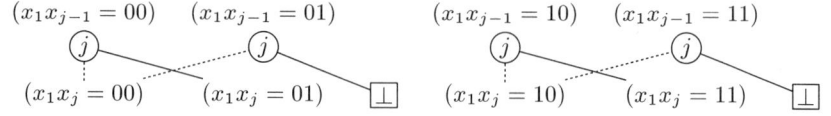

(b) Here the numbers for $3 \le n \le 10$ are $(7, 9, 14, 17, 22, 30, 37, 45)$; then a fixed pattern at the top and bottom develops as in (a), with nine branch nodes for each variable in the middle, and the total size comes to $9(n-5)$. The nine nodes on each middle level fall into three groups of three,

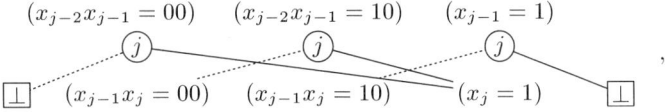

with one group for $x_1 x_2 = 00$, one for $x_1 x_2 = 01$, and one for $x_1 = 1$.

15. Both cases lead by induction to well known sequences of numbers: (a) The Lucas numbers $L_n = F_{n+1} + F_{n-1} = \phi^n + \hat\phi^n$ [see E. Lucas, *Théorie des Nombres* (1891), Chapter 18]. (b) The Perrin numbers, defined by $P_3 = 3$, $P_4 = 2$, $P_5 = 5$, $P_n = P_{n-2} + P_{n-3} = \chi^n + \hat\chi^n + \bar{\hat\chi}^n$. [See E. Lucas, *Association Française pour l'Avancement des Sciences*, Compte-rendu **5** (1876), 62; R. Perrin, *L'Intermédiaire des Mathématiciens* **6** (1899), 76–77; Z. Füredi, *Journal of Graph Theory* **11** (1987), 463.]

16. When the BDD isn't $\boxed{\bot}$, all solutions are generated by calling $List(1, \text{root})$, where $List(j, p)$ is the following recursive procedure: If $v(p) > j$, set $x_j \leftarrow 0$, call $List(j+1, p)$, set $x_j \leftarrow 1$, and call $List(j+1, p)$. Otherwise if p is the sink node $\boxed{\top}$, visit the solution $x_1 \ldots x_n$. (The idea of "visiting" a combinatorial object while generating them all is discussed at the beginning of Section 7.2.1.) Otherwise set $x_j \leftarrow 0$; call $List(j+1, \text{LO}(p))$ if $\text{LO}(p) \ne \boxed{\bot}$; set $x_j \leftarrow 1$; and call $List(j+1, \text{HI}(p))$ if $\text{HI}(p) \ne \boxed{\bot}$.

The solutions are generated in lexicographic order. Suppose there are N of them. If the kth solution agrees with the $(k-1)$st solution in positions $x_1 \ldots x_{j-1}$ but not in x_j, let $c(k) = n - j$; and let $c(1) = n$. Then the running time is proportional to $\sum_{k=1}^{N} c(k)$, which is $O(nN)$ in general. (This bound holds because every branch node of a BDD leads to at least one solution. In fact, the running time is usually $O(N)$ in practice.)

17. That mission is impossible, because there's a function with $N = 2^{2^k}$ and $B(f) = O(2^{2^k})$ for which every two solutions differ in more than 2^{k-1} bit positions. The running time for any algorithm that generates all solutions for such a function must be $\Omega(2^{3k})$, because $\Omega(2^k)$ operations are needed between solutions. To construct f, first let

$$g(x_1, \ldots, x_k, y_0, \ldots, y_{2^k-1}) = [y_{(t_1 \ldots t_k)_2} = x_1 t_1 \oplus \cdots \oplus x_k t_k \text{ for } 0 \le t_1, \ldots, t_k \le 1].$$

(In other words, g asserts that $y_0 \ldots y_{2^k-1}$ is row $(x_1 \ldots x_k)_2$ of an Hadamard matrix; see Eq. 4.6.4–(38).) Now we let $f(x_1, \ldots, x_k, y_0, \ldots, y_{2^k-1}, x'_1, \ldots, x'_k, y'_0, \ldots, y'_{2^k-1}) = g(x_1, \ldots, x_k, y_0, \ldots, y_{2^k-1}) \wedge g(x'_1, \ldots, x'_k, y'_0, \ldots, y'_{2^k-1})$. Clearly $B(f) = O(2^{2^k})$ when the variables are ordered in this way. Indeed, T. Dahlheimer observes that $B(f) = 2B(g) - 2$, where $B(g) = 2^k + 1 + \sum_{j=1}^{2^k} 2^{\min(k, 1 + \lceil \lg j \rceil)} = \frac{5}{3} 2^{2k-1} + 2^k + \frac{5}{3}$.

18. First, $(W_1, \ldots, W_5) = (5, 4, 4, 4, 0)$. Then $m_2 = w_4 = 4$ and $t_2 = 1$; $m_3 = t_3 = 0$; $m_4 = \max(m_3, m_2 + w_3) = 1$, $t_4 = 1$; $m_5 = W_4 - W_5 = 4$, $t_5 = 0$; $m_6 = w_2 + W_3 - W_5 = 2$, $t_6 = 1$; $m_7 = \max(m_5, m_4 + w_2) = 4$, $t_7 = 0$; $m_8 = \max(m_7, m_6 + w_1) = 4$, $t_8 = 0$. Solution $x_1 x_2 x_3 x_4 = 0001$.

19. $\sum_{j=1}^{n} \min(w_j, 0) \le \sum_{j=v_k}^{n} \min(w_j, 0) \le m_k \le \sum_{j=v_k}^{n} \max(w_j, 0) = W_{v_k} \le W_1$.

20. Set $w_1 \leftarrow -1$, then $w_{2j} \leftarrow w_j$ and $w_{2j+1} \leftarrow -w_j$ for $1 \le j \le n/2$. [This method may also compute w_{n+1}. The sequence is named for works of A. Thue, *Skrifter udgivne af Videnskabs-Selskabet i Christiania*, Mathematisk-Naturvidenskabelig Klasse (1912), No. 1, §7, and H. M. Morse, *Trans. Amer. Math. Soc.* **22** (1921), 84–100, §14.]

21. Yes; we just have to change the sign of each weight w_j. (Or we could reverse the roles of LO and HI at each vertex.)

22. If $f(x) = f(x') = 1$ when f represents a graph kernel, the Hamming distance $\nu(x \oplus x')$ cannot be 1. In such cases $v_l = v + 1$ when $l \neq 0$ and $v_h = v + 1$ when $h \neq 0$.

23. The BDD for the connectedness function of any connected graph will have exactly $n - 1$ solid arcs on every root-to-$\boxed{\top}$ path, because that many edges are needed to connect n vertices, and because a BDD has no redundant branches. (See also Theorem S.)

24. Apply Algorithm B with weights $(w'_{12}, \ldots, w'_{89}) = (-w_{12} - x, \ldots, -w_{89} - x)$, where x is large enough to make all of these new weights w'_{uv} negative. The maximum of $\sum w'_{uv} x_{uv}$ will then occur with $\sum x_{uv} = 8$, and those edges will form a spanning tree with minimum $\sum w_{uv} x_{uv}$. (We've seen a better algorithm for minimum spanning trees in exercise 2.3.4.1–11, and other methods will be studied in Section 7.5.4. However, this exercise indicates that a BDD can compactly represent the set of *all* spanning trees.)

25. The answer in step C1 becomes $(1 + z)^{v_s - 1 - 1} c_{s-1}$; the value of c_k in step C2 becomes $(1 + z)^{v_l - v_k - 1} c_l + (1 + z)^{v_h - v_k - 1} z c_h$.

26. In this case the answer in step C1 is simply c_{s-1}; and the value of c_k in step C2 is simply $(1 - p_{v_k}) c_l + p_{v_k} c_h$.

27. The multilinear polynomial $H(x_1, \ldots, x_n) = F(x_1, \ldots, x_n) - G(x_1, \ldots, x_n)$ is nonzero modulo q, because it is ± 1 for some choice of integers with each $x_k \in \{0, 1\}$. If it has degree d (modulo q), we can prove that there are at least $(q - 1)^d q^{n-d}$ sets of values $(q_1, \ldots, q_n)$ with $0 \leq q_k < q$ such that $H(q_1, \ldots, q_n) \bmod q \neq 0$. This statement is clear when $d = 0$. And if x_k is a variable that appears in a term of degree $d > 0$, the coefficient of x_k is a polynomial of degree $d - 1$, which by induction on d is nonzero for at least $(q - 1)^{d-1} q^{n-d}$ choices of $(q_1, \ldots, q_{k-1}, q_{k+1}, \ldots, q_n)$; for each of those choices there are $q - 1$ values of q_k such that $H(q_1, \ldots, q_n) \bmod q \neq 0$.

Hence the stated probability is $\geq (1 - 1/q)^d \geq (1 - 1/q)^n$. [See M. Blum, A. K. Chandra, and M. N. Wegman, *Information Processing Letters* **10** (1980), 80–82.]

28. $F(p) = (1 - p)^n G(p/(1 - p))$. Similarly, $G(z) = (1 + z)^n F(z/(1 + z))$.

29. In step C1, also set $c'_0 \leftarrow 0$, $c'_1 \leftarrow 0$; return c_{s-1} and c'_{s-1}. In step C2, set $c_k \leftarrow (1 - p) c_l + p c_h$ and $c'_k \leftarrow (1 - p) c'_l - c_l + p c'_h + c_h$.

30. The following analog of Algorithm B does the job (assuming exact arithmetic):

A1. [Initialize.] Set $P_{n+1} \leftarrow 1$ and $P_j \leftarrow P_{j+1} \max(1 - p_j, p_j)$ for $n \geq j \geq 1$.

A2. [Loop on k.] Set $m_1 \leftarrow 1$ and do step A3 for $2 \leq k < s$. Then do step A4.

A3. [Process I_k.] Set $v \leftarrow v_k$, $l \leftarrow l_k$, $h \leftarrow h_k$, $t_k \leftarrow 0$. If $l \neq 0$, set $m_k \leftarrow m_l (1 - p_v) P_{v+1} / P_{v_l}$. Then if $h \neq 0$, compute $m \leftarrow m_h p_v P_{v+1} / P_{v_h}$; and if $l = 0$ or $m > m_k$, set $m_k \leftarrow m$ and $t_k \leftarrow 1$.

A4. [Compute the x's.] Set $j \leftarrow 0$, $k \leftarrow s - 1$, and do the following operations until $j = n$: While $j < v_k - 1$, set $j \leftarrow j + 1$ and $x_j \leftarrow [p_j > \frac{1}{2}]$; if $k > 1$, set $j \leftarrow j + 1$ and $x_j \leftarrow t_k$ and $k \leftarrow (t_k = 0?\ l_k : h_k)$. ∎

31. **C1′.** [Loop over k.] Set $\alpha_0 \leftarrow \bot$, $\alpha_1 \leftarrow \top$, and do step C2′ for $k = 2, 3, \ldots, s - 1$. Then go to C3′.

C2′. [Compute α_k.] Set $v \leftarrow v_k$, $l \leftarrow l_k$, and $h \leftarrow h_k$. Set $\beta \leftarrow \alpha_l$ and $j \leftarrow v_l - 1$; then while $j > v$ set $\beta \leftarrow (\bar{x}_j \circ x_j) \bullet \beta$ and $j \leftarrow j - 1$. Set $\gamma \leftarrow \alpha_h$ and $j \leftarrow v_h - 1$; then while $j > v$ set $\gamma \leftarrow (\bar{x}_j \circ x_j) \bullet \gamma$ and $j \leftarrow j - 1$. Finally set $\alpha_k \leftarrow (\bar{x}_v \bullet \beta) \circ (x_v \bullet \gamma)$.

C3′. [Finish.] Set $\alpha \leftarrow \alpha_{s-1}$ and $j \leftarrow v_{s-1}-1$; then while $j > 0$ set $\alpha \leftarrow (\bar{x}_j \circ x_j) \bullet \alpha$ and $j \leftarrow j - 1$. Return the answer α. ∎

This algorithm performs $\circ$ and $\bullet$ operations at most $O(nB(f))$ times. The upper bound can often be lowered to $O(n) + O(B(f))$; but shortcuts like the calculation of W_k in step B1 aren't always available. [See O. Coudert and J. C. Madre, *Proc. Reliability and Maint. Conf.* (IEEE, 1993), 240–245, §4; O. Coudert, *Integration* **17** (1994), 126–127.]

32. For exercise 25, '$\circ$' is addition, '$\bullet$' is multiplication, '$\perp$' is 0, '$\top$' is 1, '$\bar{x}_j$' is 1, 'x_j' is z. Exercise 26 is similar, but '$\bar{x}_j$' is $1 - p_j$ and 'x_j' is p_j.

In exercise 29 the objects of the algebra are pairs (c, c'), and we have $(a, a') \circ (b, b') = (a + b, a' + b')$, $(a, a') \bullet (b, b') = (ab, ab' + a'b)$. Also '$\perp$' is $(0, 0)$, '$\top$' is $(1, 0)$, '$\bar{x}_j$' is $(1-p, -1)$, and 'x_j' is $(p, 1)$.

In exercise 30, '$\circ$' is max, '$\bullet$' is multiplication, '$\perp$' is $-\infty$, '$\top$' is 1, '$\bar{x}_j$' is $1 - p_j$, 'x_j' is p_j. Multiplication distributes over max in this case because the quantities are either nonnegative or $-\infty$; we must define $0 \bullet (-\infty) = -\infty$ in order to satisfy (22).

(Additional possibilities abound, because associative and distributive operators are ubiquitous in mathematics. The algebraic objects need not be numbers or polynomials or pairs; they can be strings, matrices, functions, sets of numbers, sets of strings, sets or multisets of matrices of pairs of functions of strings, etc., etc. We will see many further examples in Section 7.3. The min-plus algebra, with $\circ = \min$ and $\bullet = +$, is particularly important, and we could have used it in exercise 21 or 24. It is often called *tropical*, implicitly honoring the Brazilian mathematician Imre Simon.)

33. Operate on triples (c, c', c''), with $(a, a', a'') \circ (b, b', b'') = (a + b, a' + b', a'' + b'')$ and $(a, a', a'') \bullet (b, b', b'') = (ab, a'b + b'a, a''b + 2a'b' + ab'')$. Interpret '$\perp$' as $(0, 0, 0)$, '$\top$' as $(1, 0, 0)$, '$\bar{x}_j$' as $(1, 0, 0)$, and 'x_j' as $(1, w_j, w_j^2)$.

34. Let $x \vee y = \max(x, y)$. Operate on pairs (c, c'), with $(a, a') \circ (b, b') = (a \vee b, a' \vee b')$ and $(a, a') \bullet (b, b') = (a + b, (a' + b) \vee (a + b'))$. Interpret '$\perp$' as $(-\infty, -\infty)$, '$\top$' as $(0, -\infty)$, '$\bar{x}_j$' as $(0, w_j'')$, and 'x_j' as $(w_j, w_j' + w_j'')$. The first component of the result will agree with Algorithm B; the second component is the desired maximum.

35. (a) The supposed FBDD can be represented by instructions $I_{s-1}, \ldots, I_0$ as in Algorithm C. Start with $R_0 \leftarrow R_1 \leftarrow \emptyset$, then do the following for $k = 2, \ldots, s - 1$: Report failure if $v_k \in R_{l_k} \cup R_{h_k}$; otherwise set $R_k \leftarrow \{v_k\} \cup R_{l_k} \cup R_{h_k}$. (The set R_k identifies all variables that are reachable from I_k.)

(b) The reliability polynomial can be calculated just as in answer 26. To count solutions, we essentially set $p_1 = \cdots = p_n = \frac{1}{2}$ and multiply by 2^n: Start with $c_0 \leftarrow 0$ and $c_1 \leftarrow 2^n$, then set $c_k \leftarrow (c_{l_k} + c_{h_k})/2$ for $1 < k < s$. The answer is c_{s-1}.

36. Compute the sets R_k as in answer 35(a). Instead of looping on j as stated in step C2′ of answer 31, set $\beta \leftarrow \alpha_l$ and then $\beta \leftarrow (\bar{x}_j \circ x_j) \bullet \beta$ for all $j \in R_k \setminus R_l \setminus \{v\}$; treat γ in the same manner. Similarly, in step C3′ set $\alpha \leftarrow (\bar{x}_j \circ x_j) \bullet \alpha$ for all $j \notin R_{s-1}$.

37. Given any FBDD for f, the function $G(z)$ is the sum of $(1+z)^{n-\text{length } P} z^{\text{solid arcs in } P}$ over all paths P from the root to $\boxed{\top}$. [See *Theoretical Comp. Sci.* **3** (1976), 371–384.]

38. The key fact is that $x_j = 1$ forces $f = 1$ if and only if we have (i) $h_k = 1$ whenever $v_k = j$; (ii) $v_k = j$ in at least one step k; (iii) there are no steps with $(v_k < j < v_{l_k}$ and $l_k \neq 1)$ or $(v_k < j < v_{h_k}$ and $h_k \neq 1)$.

K1. [Initialize.] Set $t_j \leftarrow 2$ and $p_j \leftarrow 0$ for $1 \leq j \leq n$.

K2. [Examine all branches.] Do the following operations for $2 \leq k < s$: Set $j \leftarrow v_k$ and $q \leftarrow 0$. If $l_k = 1$, set $q \leftarrow -1$; otherwise set $p_j \leftarrow \max(p_j, v_{l_k})$. If $h_k = 1$, set $q \leftarrow +1$; otherwise set $p_j \leftarrow \max(p_j, v_{h_k})$. If $t_j = 2$, set $t_j \leftarrow q$; otherwise if $t_j \neq q$ set $t_j \leftarrow 0$.

K3. [Finish up.] Set $m \leftarrow v_{s-1}$, and do the following for $j = 1, 2, \ldots, n$: If $j < m$, set $t_j \leftarrow 0$; then if $p_j > m$, set $m \leftarrow p_j$. ∎

[See S.-W. Jeong and F. Somenzi, in *Logic Synthesis and Optimization* (1993), 154–156.]

39. $k(n+1-k)+2$, for $1 \leq k \leq n$. (See (26).)

40. (a) Suppose the BDDs for f and g have respectively a_j and b_j branch nodes ⓙ, for $1 \leq j \leq n$. Each subtable of f of order $n+1-k$ has the form $\alpha\beta\gamma\delta$, where α, β, γ, and δ are subtables of order $n-1-k$. The corresponding subtables of g are $\alpha\alpha\delta\delta$; hence they are beads if and only if $\alpha \neq \delta$, in which case either $\alpha\beta\gamma\delta$ is a bead or $\alpha\beta = \gamma\delta$ is a bead. Consequently $b_k \leq a_k + a_{k+1}$, and $b_{k+1} = 0$. We also have $b_j \leq a_j$ for $1 \leq j < k$, because every bead of g of order $> n+1-k$ is "condensed" from at least one such bead of f. And $b_j \leq a_j$ for $j > k+1$, because the subtables on $(x_{k+2}, \ldots, x_n)$ are identical although they might not appear in g.

(b) Not always, although $B(h) < 2B(f)$. The simplest counterexample is $f(x_1, x_2, x_3, x_4) = x_2 \wedge (x_3 \vee x_4)$, $h(x_1, x_2, x_1, x_4) = x_2 \wedge (x_1 \vee x_4)$, when $B(f) = 5$ and $B(h) = 6$.

41. (a) $3n - 3$; (b) $2n$. (The general patterns are illustrated here for $n = 6$. One can also show that the "organ-pipe ordering" $\langle x_n^{F_1} x_1^{F_2} x_{n-1}^{F_3} x_2^{F_4} \cdots x_{\lfloor n/2 \rfloor + [n \text{ even}]}^{F_{n-1}} x_{\lceil n/2 \rceil}^{F_{n-2}} \rangle$ produces the profile $1, 2, 4, \ldots, 2\lceil n/2 \rceil - 2$, $2\lfloor n/2 \rfloor - 1, \ldots, 5, 3, 1, 2$, giving the total BDD size $\binom{n}{2} + 3$; this ordering appears to be the worst for the Fibonacci weights.)

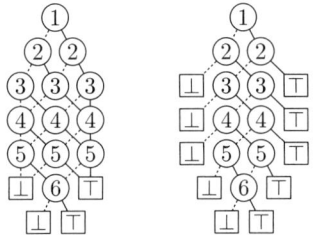

The functions $[F_n x_1 + \cdots + F_1 x_n \geq t]$ have been studied by J. T. Butler and T. Sasao, *Fibonacci Quart.* **34** (1996), 413–422.

42. (Compare with exercise 2.) The sixteen roots are the ① nodes and the two sinks:

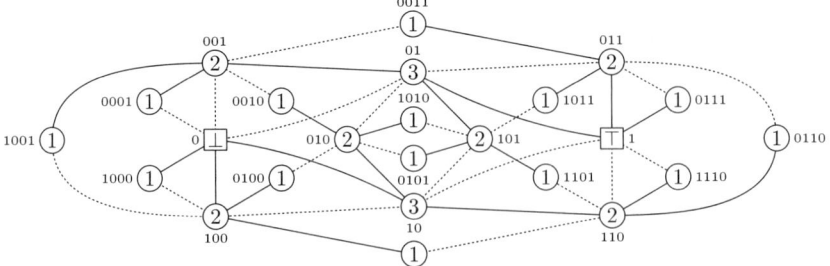

43. (a) Since $f(x_1, \ldots, x_{2n})$ is the symmetric function $S_n(x_1, \ldots, x_n, \bar{x}_{n+1}, \ldots, \bar{x}_{2n})$, we have $B(f) = 1 + 2 + \cdots + (n+1) + \cdots + 3 + 2 + 2 = n^2 + 2n + 2$.

(b) By symmetry, the size is the same for $[\sum\{x_i \mid i \in I\} = \sum\{x_i \mid i \notin I\}]$, $|I| = n$.

44. There are at most $\min(k, 2^{n+2-k} - 2)$ nodes labeled ⓚ, for $1 \leq k \leq n$, because there are $2^{n+2-k} - 2$ symmetric functions of $(x_k, \ldots, x_n)$ that aren't constant. Thus Σ_n is at most $2 + \sum_{k=1}^{n} \min(k, 2^{n+2-k} - 2)$, which can be expressed in closed form as $(n+2-b_n)(n+1-b_n)/2 + 2(2^{b_n} - b_n)$, where $b_n = \lambda(n+4-\lambda(n+4))$ and $\lambda n = \lfloor \lg n \rfloor$.

A symmetric function that attains this worst-case bound can be constructed in the following way (related to the de Bruijn cycles constructed in exercise 3.2.2–7): Let $p(x) = x^d + a_1 x^{d-1} + \cdots + a_d$ be a primitive polynomial modulo 2. Set $t_k \leftarrow 1$

for $0 \le k < d$; $t_k \leftarrow (a_1 t_{k-1} + \cdots + a_d t_{k-d}) \bmod 2$ for $d \le k < 2^d + d - 2$; $t_k \leftarrow (1 + a_1 t_{k-1} + \cdots + a_d t_{k-d}) \bmod 2$ for $2^d + d - 2 \le k < 2^{d+1} + d - 3$; and $t_{2^{d+1}+d-3} \leftarrow 1$. For example, when $p(x) = x^3 + x + 1$ we get $t_0 \ldots t_{16} = 11100101101000111$.

Then (i) the sequence $t_1 \ldots t_{2^d + d - 3}$ contains all d-tuples except 0^d and 1^d as substrings; (ii) the sequence $t_{2^d + d - 2} \ldots t_{2^{d+1} + d - 4}$ is a cyclic shift of $\bar{t}_0 \ldots \bar{t}_{2^d - 2}$; and (iii) $t_k = 1$ for $2^d - 1 \le k \le 2^d + d - 3$ and $2^{d+1} - 2 \le k \le 2^{d+1} + d - 3$. Consequently the sequence $t_0 \ldots t_{2^{d+1} + d - 3}$ contains all $(d+1)$-tuples except 0^{d+1} and 1^{d+1} as substrings. Set $f(x) = t_{\nu x}$ to maximize $B(f)$ when $2^d + d - 4 < n \le 2^{d+1} + d - 3$.

Asymptotically, $\Sigma_n = \frac{1}{2} n^2 - n \lg n + O(n)$. [See I. Wegener, *Information and Control* **62** (1984), 129–143; M. Heap, *J. Electronic Testing* **4** (1993), 191–195.]

45. Module M_1 has only three inputs (x_1, y_1, z_1), and only three outputs $u_2 = x_1$, $v_2 = y_1 x_1$, $w_2 = z_1 x_1$. Module M_{n-1} is almost normal, but it has no input port for z_{n-1}, and it doesn't output u_n; it sets $z_{n-2} = x_{n-1} y_{n-1}$. Module M_n has only three inputs (v_n, w_n, x_n), and one output $y_{n-1} = x_n$ together with the main output, $w_n \vee v_n x_n$. With these definitions the dependencies between ports form an acyclic digraph.

(Modules could be constructed with all $b_k = 0$ and $a_k \le 5$, or even with $a_k \le 4$ as we'll see in exercise 47. But (33) and (34) are intended to illustrate backward signals in a simple example, not to demonstrate the tightest possible construction.)

46. For $6 \le k \le n - 3$ there are nine branches on $\textcircled{k}$, corresponding to three cases $(\bar{x}_1, x_1 \bar{x}_2, x_1 x_2)$ times three cases $(\bar{x}_{k-1}, \bar{x}_{k-2} x_{k-1}, \bar{x}_{k-3} x_{k-2} x_{k-1})$. The total BDD size turns out to be exactly $9n - 38$, if $n \ge 6$.

47. Suppose f has q_k subtables of order $n-k$, so that its QDD has q_k nodes that branch on x_{k+1}. We can encode them in $a_k = \lceil \lg q_k \rceil$ bits, and construct a module M_{k+1} with $b_k = b_{k+1} = 0$ that mimics the behavior of those q_k branch nodes. Thus by (86),

$$\sum_{k=0}^{n} 2^{a_k 2^{b_k}} = \sum_{k=0}^{n} 2^{\lceil \lg q_k \rceil} \le \sum_{k=0}^{n} (2q_k - 1) = 2Q(f) - (n+1) \le (n+1)B(f).$$

(The 2^m-way multiplexer shows that the additional factor of $(n+1)$ is necessary; indeed, Theorem M actually gives an upper bound on $Q(f)$.)

48. The sums $u_k = x_1 + \cdots + x_k$ and $v_k = x_{k+1} + \cdots + x_n$ can be represented on $1 + \lambda k$ and $1 + \lambda(n-k)$ wires, respectively. Let $t_k = x_k \wedge [u_k + v_k = k]$ and $w_k = t_1 \vee \cdots \vee t_k$. We can construct modules M_k having inputs u_{k-1} and w_{k-1} from M_{k-1} together with inputs v_k from M_{k+1}; module M_k outputs $u_k = u_{k-1} + x_k$ and $w_k = w_{k-1} \vee t_k$ to M_{k+1} as well as $v_{k-1} = v_k + x_k$ to M_{k-1}.

If p is a polynomial, $\sum_{k=0}^{n} 2^{p(a_k, b_k)} = 2^{(\log n)^{O(1)}}$ is asymptotically less than $2^{\Omega(n)}$. [See K. L. McMillan, *Symbolic Model Checking* (1993), §3.5, where Theorem M was introduced, with extensions to nonlinear layouts. The special case $b_1 = \cdots = b_n = 0$ had been noted previously by C. L. Berman, *IEEE Trans.* **CAD-10** (1991), 1059–1066.]

49.

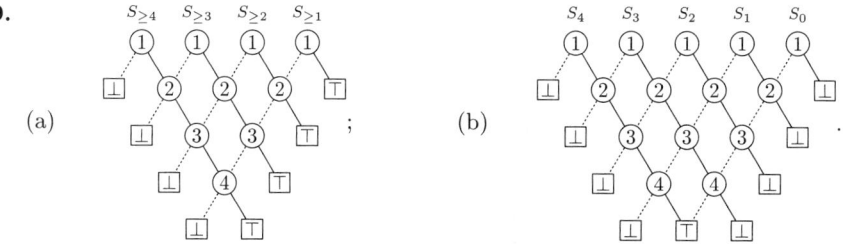

[See I. Semba and S. Yajima, *Trans. Inf. Proc. Soc. Japan* **35** (1994), 1663–1665.]

50.

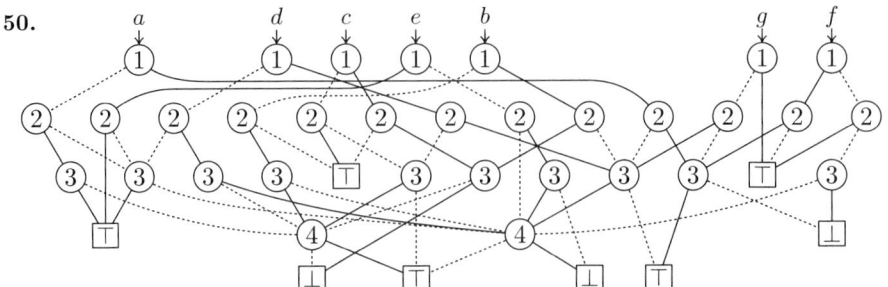

51. In this case $B(f_j) = 3j + 2$ for $1 \le j \le n$, and $B(f_{n+1}) = 3n + 1$; so the individual BDDs are only about $1/3$ as big as they are within (36). But almost no nodes are shared — only the sinks and one branch. So the total BDD size comes to $(3n^2 + 9n)/2$.

52. If the BDD base for $\{f_1, \ldots, f_m\}$ has s nodes, then $B(f) = s + m + 1 + [s = 1]$.

53. Call the branch nodes a, b, c, d, e, f, g, with ROOT $= a$. After step R1 we have HEAD$[1] = {\sim}a$, AUX$(a) = {\sim}0$; HEAD$[2] = {\sim}b$, AUX$(b) = {\sim}c$, AUX$(c) = {\sim}0$; HEAD$[3] = {\sim}d$, AUX$(d) = {\sim}e$, AUX$(e) = {\sim}f$, AUX$(f) = {\sim}g$, AUX$(g) = {\sim}0$.

After R3 with $v = 3$ we have $s = {\sim}0$, AUX$(0) = {\sim}e$, AUX$(e) = f$, AUX$(f) = 0$; also AVAIL $= g$, LO$(g) = {\sim}1$, HI$(g) = d$, LO$(d) = {\sim}0$, and HI$(d) = \alpha$, where α was the initial value of AVAIL. (Nodes g and d have been recycled in favor of 1 and 0.) Then R4 sets $s \leftarrow e$ and AUX$(0) \leftarrow 0$. (The remaining nodes with V $= v$ start at s, linked via AUX.)

Now R7, starting with $p = q = e$ and $s = 0$, sets AUX$(1) \leftarrow {\sim}e$, LO$(f) \leftarrow {\sim}e$, HI$(f) \leftarrow g$, AVAIL $\leftarrow f$; and R8 resets AUX$(1) \leftarrow 0$.

Then step R3 with $v = 2$ sets LO$(b) \leftarrow 0$, LO$(c) \leftarrow e$, and HI$(c) \leftarrow 1$. No further changes of importance take place, although some AUX fields temporarily become negative. We end up with Fig. 21.

54. Create nodes j for $1 < j \le 2^{n-1}$ by setting V$(j) \leftarrow \lceil \lg j \rceil$, LO$(j) \leftarrow 2j - 1$, and HI$(j) \leftarrow 2j$; also for $2^{n-1} < j \le 2^n$ by setting V$(j) \leftarrow n$, LO$(j) \leftarrow f(x_1, \ldots, x_{n-1}, 0)$, and HI$(j) \leftarrow f(x_1, \ldots, x_{n-1}, 1)$ when $j = (1x_1 \ldots x_{n-1})_2 + 1$. Then apply Algorithm R with ROOT $= 2$. (We can bypass step R1 by first setting AUX$(j) \leftarrow -j$ for $4 \le j \le 2^n$, then HEAD$[k] \leftarrow {\sim}(2^k)$ and AUX$(2^{k-1} + 1) \leftarrow -1$ for $1 \le k \le n$.)

55. It suffices to construct an unreduced diagram, since Algorithm R will then finish the job. Number the vertices $1, \ldots, n$ in such a way that no vertex except 1 appears before all of its neighbors. Represent the edges by arcs $a_1, \ldots, a_e$, where a_k is $u_k \longrightarrow v_k$ for some $u_k < v_k$, and where the arcs having $u_k = j$ are consecutive, with $s_j \le k < s_{j+1}$ and $1 = s_1 \le \cdots \le s_n = s_{n+1} = e + 1$. Define the "frontier" $V_k = \{1, v_1, \ldots, v_k\} \cap \{u_k, \ldots, n\}$ for $1 \le k \le e$, and let $V_0 = \{1\}$. The unreduced decision diagram will have branches on arc a_k for all partitions of V_{k-1} that correspond to connectedness relations that have arisen because of previous branches.

For example, consider $P_3 \square P_3$, where $(s_1, \ldots, s_{10}) = (1, 3, 5, 7, 8, 10, 11, 12, 13, 13)$ and $V_0 = \{1\}$, $V_1 = \{1, 2\}$, $V_2 = \{1, 2, 3\}$, $V_3 = \{2, 3, 4\}$, $\ldots$, $V_{12} = \{8, 9\}$. The branch on a_1 goes from the trivial partition 1 of V_0 to the partition 1|2 of V_1 if $1 \not\!\!- 2$, or to the partition 12 if $1 - 2$. (The notation '1|2' stands for the set partition $\{1\} \cup \{2\}$, as in Section 7.2.1.5.) From 1|2, the branch on a_2 goes to the partition 1|2|3 of V_2 if $1 \not\!\!- 3$, otherwise to 13|2; from 12, the branches go respectively to partitions 12|3 and 123. Then from 1|2|3, both branches on a_3 go to $\boxed{\bot}$, because vertex 1 can no longer be connected to the others. And so on. Eventually the partitions of $V_e = V_{12}$ are all identified with $\boxed{\bot}$, except for the trivial one-set partition, which corresponds to $\boxed{\top}$.

56. Start with $m \leftarrow 2$ in step R1, and $v_0 \leftarrow v_1 \leftarrow v_{\max} + 1$, $l_0 \leftarrow h_0 \leftarrow 0$, $l_1 \leftarrow h_1 \leftarrow 1$ as in (8). Assume that $\mathtt{HI}(0) = 0$ and $\mathtt{HI}(1) = 1$. Omit the assignments that involve AVAIL in steps R3 and R7. After setting $\mathtt{AUX}(\mathtt{HI}(p)) \leftarrow 0$ in step R8, also set $v_m \leftarrow v$, $l_m \leftarrow \mathtt{HI}(\mathtt{LO}(p))$, $h_m \leftarrow \mathtt{HI}(\mathtt{HI}(p))$, $\mathtt{HI}(p) \leftarrow m$, and $m \leftarrow m + 1$. At the end of step R9, set $s \leftarrow m - [\mathtt{ROOT}{=}0]$.

57. Set $\mathtt{LO}(\mathtt{ROOT}) \leftarrow {\sim}\mathtt{LO}(\mathtt{ROOT})$. (We briefly complement the LO field of nodes that are still accessible after restriction.) Then for $v = \mathtt{V}(\mathtt{ROOT})$, ..., $v_{\max}$, set $p \leftarrow {\sim}\mathtt{HEAD}[v]$, $\mathtt{HEAD}[v] \leftarrow {\sim}0$, and do the following while $p \neq 0$: (i) Set $p' \leftarrow {\sim}\mathtt{AUX}(p)$. (ii) If $\mathtt{LO}(p) \geq 0$, set $\mathtt{HI}(p) \leftarrow \mathtt{AVAIL}$, $\mathtt{AUX}(p) \leftarrow 0$, and $\mathtt{AVAIL} \leftarrow p$ (node p can no longer be reached). Otherwise set $\mathtt{LO}(p) \leftarrow {\sim}\mathtt{LO}(p)$; if $\mathtt{FIX}[v] = 0$, set $\mathtt{HI}(p) \leftarrow \mathtt{LO}(p)$; if $\mathtt{FIX}[v] = 1$, set $\mathtt{LO}(p) \leftarrow \mathtt{HI}(p)$; if $\mathtt{LO}(\mathtt{LO}(p)) \geq 0$, set $\mathtt{LO}(\mathtt{LO}(p)) \leftarrow {\sim}\mathtt{LO}(\mathtt{LO}(p))$; if $\mathtt{LO}(\mathtt{HI}(p)) \geq 0$, set $\mathtt{LO}(\mathtt{HI}(p)) \leftarrow {\sim}\mathtt{LO}(\mathtt{HI}(p))$; and set $\mathtt{AUX}(p) \leftarrow \mathtt{HEAD}[v]$, $\mathtt{HEAD}[v] \leftarrow {\sim}p$. (iii) Set $p \leftarrow p'$. Finally, after finishing the loop on v, restore $\mathtt{LO}(0) \leftarrow 0$, $\mathtt{LO}(1) \leftarrow 1$.

58. Since $l \neq h$ and $l' \neq h'$, we have $l \diamond l' \neq h \diamond h'$, $l \diamond \alpha' \neq h \diamond \alpha'$, and $\alpha \diamond l' \neq \alpha \diamond h'$.

Suppose $\alpha \diamond \alpha' = \beta \diamond \beta'$, where $\beta = (v'', l'', h'')$ and $\beta' = (v''', l''', h''')$. If $v'' = v'''$ we have $v = v''$, $l \diamond l' = l'' \diamond l'''$, and $h \diamond h' = h'' \diamond h'''$. If $v'' < v'''$ we have $v = v''$, $l \diamond \alpha' = l'' \diamond \beta'$, and $h \diamond \alpha' = h'' \diamond \beta'$. Otherwise we have $v' = v'''$, $\alpha \diamond l' = \beta \diamond l'''$, and $\alpha \diamond h' = \beta \diamond h'''$. By induction, therefore, we have $\alpha = \beta$ and $\alpha' = \beta'$ in all cases.

59. (a) If h isn't constant we have $B(f \diamond g) = 3B(h) - 2$, essentially obtained by taking a copy of the BDD for h and replacing its sink nodes by two other copies.

(b) Suppose the profile and quasi-profile of h are $(b_0, \ldots, b_n)$ and $(q_0, \ldots, q_n)$, where $b_n = q_n = 2$. Then there are $b_k q_k$ branches on x_{2k+1} in $f \diamond g$, and $q_k b_{k-1}$ branches on x_{2k}, corresponding to ordered pairs of beads and subtables of h. When the BDD for h contains a branch from α to β and from α' to β', where $\mathtt{V}(\alpha) = j$, $\mathtt{V}(\beta) = k$, $\mathtt{V}(\alpha') = j'$, and $\mathtt{V}(\beta') = k'$, the BDD for $f \diamond g$ contains a corresponding branch with $\mathtt{V}(\alpha \diamond \alpha') = 2j - 1$ from $\alpha \diamond \alpha'$ to $\beta \diamond \alpha'$ when $j \leq j' < k$, and with $\mathtt{V}(\alpha \diamond \alpha') = 2j'$ from $\alpha \diamond \alpha'$ to $\alpha \diamond \beta'$ when $j' < j \leq k'$.

60. Every bead of order $n - j$ of the ordered pair (f, g) is either one of the $b_j b_j'$ ordered pairs of beads of f and g, or one of the $b_j(q_j' - b_j') + (q_j - b_j)b_j'$ ordered pairs that have the form (bead, nonbead) or (nonbead, bead). [This upper bound is achieved in the examples of exercises 59(b) and 63.]

61. Assume that $v = V(\alpha) \leq V(\beta)$. Let $\alpha_1, \ldots, \alpha_k$ be the nodes that point to α, and let $\beta_1, \ldots, \beta_l$ be the nodes with $V(\beta_j) < v$ that point to β; an imaginary node is assumed to point to each root. (Thus $k = $ in-degree(α) and $l \leq $ in-degree(β).) Then the melded nodes that point to $\alpha \diamond \beta$ are of three types: (i) $\alpha_i \diamond \beta_j$, where $V(\alpha_i) = V(\beta_j)$ and either $(\mathtt{LO}(\alpha_i) = \alpha$ and $\mathtt{LO}(\beta_j) = \beta)$ or $(\mathtt{HI}(\alpha_i) = \alpha$ and $\mathtt{HI}(\beta_j) = \beta)$; (ii) $\alpha \diamond \beta_j$, where $V(\alpha_i) < V(\beta_j)$ for some i; or (iii) $\alpha_i \diamond \beta$, where $V(\alpha_i) > V(\beta_j)$ for some j.

62. The BDD for f has one node on each level, and the BDD for g has two, except at the top and bottom. The BDD for $f \vee g$ has four nodes on nearly every level, by exercise 14(a). The BDD for $f \diamond g$ has seven nodes (j) when $5 \leq j \leq n - 3$, corresponding to ordered pairs of subtables of (f, g) that depend on x_j when $(x_1, \ldots, x_{j-1})$ have fixed values. Thus $B(f) = n + O(1)$, $B(g) = 2n + O(1)$, $B(f \diamond g) = 7n + O(1)$, and $B(f \vee g) = 4n + O(1)$. (Also $B(f \wedge g) = 7n + O(1)$, $B(f \oplus g) = 7n + O(1)$.)

63. The profiles of f and g are respectively $(1, 2, 2, \ldots, 2^{m-1}, 2^{m-1}, 2^m, 1, 1, \ldots, 1, 2)$ and $(0, 1, 2, 2, \ldots, 2^{m-1}, 2^{m-1}, 1, 1, \ldots, 1, 2)$; so $B(f) = 2^{m+2} - 1 \approx 4n$ and $B(g) = 2^{m+1} + 2^m - 1 \approx 3n$. The profile of $f \wedge g$ begins with $(1, 2, 4, \ldots, 2^{2m-2}, 2^{2m-1} - 2^{m-1})$, because there's a unique solution $x_1 \ldots x_{2m}$ to the equations

$$((x_1 \oplus x_2)(x_3 \oplus x_4) \ldots (x_{2m-1} \oplus x_{2m}))_2 = p, ((x_2 \oplus x_3) \ldots (x_{2m-2} \oplus x_{2m-1})x_{2m})_2 = q$$

for $0 \le p, q < 2^m$, and $p = q$ if and only if $x_1 = x_3 = \cdots = x_{2m-1} = 0$. After that the profile continues $(2^{m+1} - 2, 2^{m+1} - 2, 2^{m+1} - 4, 2^{m+1} - 6, \ldots, 4, 2, 2)$; the subfunctions are $x_{2m+j} \wedge \bar{x}_{2m+k}$ or $\bar{x}_{2m+j} \wedge x_{2m+k}$ for $1 \le j < k \le 2^m$, together with x_{2m+j} and $\bar{x}_{2m+j}$ for $2 \le j \le 2^m$. All in all, we have $B(f \wedge g) = 2^{2m+1} + 2^{m-1} - 1 \approx 2n^2$.

64. The BDD for *any* Boolean combination of f_1, f_2, and f_3 is contained in the meld $f_1 \diamond f_2 \diamond f_3$, whose size is at most $B(f_1)B(f_2)B(f_3)$.

65. $h = g$? f_1: f_0, where f_c is the restriction of f obtained by setting $x_j \leftarrow c$. The first upper bound follows as in answer 64, because $B(f_c) \le B(f)$. The second bound fails when, for example, $n = 2^m + 3m$ and $h = M_m(x; y)$? $M_m(x'; y)$: $M_m(x''; y)$, where $x = (x_1, \ldots, x_m)$, $x' = (x_1', \ldots, x_m')$, $x'' = (x_1'', \ldots, x_m'')$, and $y = (y_0, \ldots, y_{2^m-1})$; but such failures appear to be rare. [See R. E. Bryant, *IEEE Trans.* **C-35** (1986), 685; J. Jain, K. Mohanram, D. Moundanos, I. Wegener, and Y. Lu, *ACM/IEEE Design Automation Conf.* **37** (2000), 681–686.]

66. Set NTOP $\leftarrow f_0 + 1 - l$ and terminate the algorithm.

67. Let t_k denote template location POOLSIZE $- 2k$. Step S1 sets LEFT$(t_1) \leftarrow 5$, RIGHT$(t_1) \leftarrow 7$, $l \leftarrow 1$. Step S2 for $l = 1$ puts t_1 into both LLIST[2] and HLIST[2]. Step S5 for $l = 2$ sets LEFT$(t_2) \leftarrow 4$, RIGHT$(t_2) \leftarrow 5$, L$(t_1) \leftarrow t_2$; LEFT$(t_3) \leftarrow 3$, RIGHT$(t_3) \leftarrow 6$, H$(t_1) \leftarrow t_3$. Step S2 for $l = 2$ sets L$(t_2) \leftarrow 0$ and puts t_2 in HLIST[3]; then it puts t_3 into LLIST[3] and HLIST[3]. And so on. Phase 1 ends with (LSTART[0], ..., LSTART[4]) $= (t_0, t_1, t_3, t_5, t_8)$ and

k	LEFT(t_k)	RIGHT(t_k)	L(t_k)	H(t_k)	k	LEFT(t_k)	RIGHT(t_k)	L(t_k)	H(t_k)
1	5 $[\alpha]$	7 $[\omega]$	t_2	t_3	5	3 $[\gamma]$	4 $[\varphi]$	t_6	t_8
2	4 $[\beta]$	5 $[\chi]$	0	t_4	6	2 $[\delta]$	2 $[\tau]$	0	1
3	3 $[\gamma]$	6 $[\psi]$	t_4	t_5	7	2 $[\delta]$	1 $[\top]$	0	1
4	3 $[\gamma]$	1 $[\top]$	t_7	1	8	1 $[\top]$	3 $[\upsilon]$	1	0

representing the meld $\alpha \diamond \omega$ in Fig. 24 but with $\bot \diamond x = x \diamond \bot = \bot$ and $\top \diamond \top = \top$.

Let $f_k = f_0 + k$. In phase 2, step S7 for $l = 4$ sets LEFT$(t_6) \leftarrow {\sim}0$, LEFT$(t_7) \leftarrow t_6$, LEFT$(t_8) \leftarrow {\sim}1$, and RIGHT$(t_6) \leftarrow$ RIGHT$(t_7) \leftarrow$ RIGHT$(t_8) \leftarrow -1$. Step S8 undoes the changes made to LEFT(0) and LEFT(1). Step S11 with $s = t_8$ sets LEFT$(t_8) \leftarrow {\sim}2$, RIGHT$(t_8) \leftarrow t_8$, V$(f_2) \leftarrow 4$, LO$(f_2) \leftarrow 1$, HI$(f_2) \leftarrow 0$. With $s = t_7$ that step sets LEFT$(t_7) \leftarrow {\sim}3$, RIGHT$(t_7) \leftarrow t_7$, V$(f_3) \leftarrow 4$, LO$(f_3) \leftarrow 0$, HI$(f_3) \leftarrow 1$; meanwhile step S10 has set RIGHT$(t_6) \leftarrow t_7$. Eventually the templates will be transformed to

k	LEFT(t_k)	RIGHT(t_k)	L(t_k)	H(t_k)	k	LEFT(t_k)	RIGHT(t_k)	L(t_k)	H(t_k)
1	${\sim}8$	t_1	t_2	t_3	5	${\sim}4$	t_5	t_7	t_8
2	${\sim}7$	t_2	0	t_4	6	${\sim}0$	t_7	0	1
3	${\sim}6$	t_3	t_4	t_5	7	${\sim}3$	t_7	0	1
4	${\sim}5$	t_4	t_7	1	8	${\sim}2$	t_8	1	0

(but they can then be discarded). The resulting BDD for $f \wedge g$ is

k	V(f_k)	LO(f_k)	HI(f_k)	k	V(f_k)	LO(f_k)	HI(f_k)
2	4	1	0	6	2	5	4
3	4	0	1	7	2	0	5
4	3	3	2	8	1	7	6.
5	3	3	1				

68. If $\text{LEFT}(t) < 0$ at the beginning of step S10, set $\text{RIGHT}(t) \leftarrow t$, $q \leftarrow \text{NTOP}$, $\text{NTOP} \leftarrow q + 1$, $\text{LEFT}(t) \leftarrow {\sim}(q - f_0)$, $\text{LO}(q) \leftarrow {\sim}\text{LEFT}(\text{L}(t))$, $\text{HI}(q) \leftarrow {\sim}\text{LEFT}(\text{H}(t))$, $\text{V}(q) \leftarrow l$, and return to S9.

69. Make sure that $\text{NTOP} \leq \text{TBOT}$ at the end of step S1 and when going from S11 to S9. (It's *not* necessary to make this test inside the loop of S11.) Also make sure that $\text{NTOP} \leq \text{HBASE}$ just after setting HBASE in step S4.

70. This choice would make the hash table a bit smaller; memory overflow would therefore be slightly less likely, at the expense of slightly more collisions. But it also would slow down the action, because *make_template* would have to check that $\text{NTOP} \leq \text{TBOT}$ whenever TBOT decreases.

71. Add a new field, $\text{EXTRA}(t) = \alpha''$, to each template t (see (43)).

72. In place of steps S4 and S5, use the approach of Algorithm R to bucket-sort the elements of the linked lists that begin at $\text{LLIST}[l]$ and $\text{HLIST}[l]$. This is possible if an extra one-bit hint is used within the pointers to distinguish links in the L fields from links in the H fields, because we can then determine the LO and HI parameters of t's descendants as a function of t and its "parity."

73. If the BDD profile is $(b_0, \ldots, b_n)$, we can assign $p_j = \lceil b_{j-1}/2^e \rceil$ pages to branches on x_j. Auxiliary tables of $p_1 + \cdots + p_{n+1} \leq \lceil B(f)/2^e \rceil + n$ short integers allow us to compute $V(p) = T[\pi(p)]$, $\text{LO}(p) = \text{LO}(M[\pi(p)] + \sigma(p))$, $\text{HI}(p) = \text{HI}(M[\pi(p)] + \sigma(p))$.

For example, if $e = 12$ and $n < 2^{16}$, we can represent arbitrary BDDs of up to $2^{32} - 2^{28} + 2^{16} + 2^{12}$ nodes with 32-bit virtual LO and HI pointers. Each BDD requires appropriate auxiliary T and M tables of size $\leq 2^{20}$, constructible from its profile.

[This method can significantly improve caching behavior. It was inspired by the paper of P. Ashar and M. Cheong, *IEEE/ACM Internat. Conf. Computer-Aided Design* **CAD-94** (1994), 622–627, which also introduced algorithms similar to Algorithm S.]

74. The required condition is now $\mu_n(x_1, \ldots, x_{2^n}) \wedge [\bar{x}_1 = x_{2^n}] \wedge \cdots \wedge [\bar{x}_{2^{n-1}} = x_{2^{n-1}+1}]$. If we set $y_1 = x_1$, $y_2 = x_3$, ..., $y_{2^{n-2}} = x_{2^{n-1}-1}$, $y_{2^{n-2}+1} = \bar{x}_{2^{n-1}}$, $y_{2^{n-2}+2} = \bar{x}_{2^{n-1}-2}$, ..., $y_{2^{n-1}} = \bar{x}_2$, (49) yields the equivalent condition $\mu_{n-1}(y_1, \ldots, y_{2^{n-1}}) \wedge [y_{2^{n-2}} \leq \bar{y}_{2^{n-2}+1}] \wedge [y_{2^{n-2}-1} \leq \bar{y}_{2^{n-2}+2}] \wedge \cdots \wedge [y_1 \leq \bar{y}_{2^{n-1}}]$, which is eminently suitable for evaluation by Algorithm S. (The evaluation should be from left to right; right-to-left would generate enormous intermediate results.)

With this approach we find that there are respectively 1, 2, 4, 12, 81, 2646, 1422564, 229809982112 monotone self-dual functions of 1, 2, ..., 8 variables. (See Table 7.1.1–3 and answer 7.1.2–88.) The 8-variable functions are characterized by a BDD of 130,305,082 nodes; Algorithm S needs about 204 gigamems to compute it.

75. Begin with $\rho_1(x_1, x_2) = [x_1 \leq x_2]$, and replace $G_{2^n}(x_1, \ldots, x_{2^n})$ in (49) by the function $H_{2^n}(x_1, \ldots, x_{2^n}) = [x_1 \leq x_2 \leq x_3 \leq x_4] \wedge \cdots \wedge [x_{2^n-3} \leq x_{2^n-2} \leq x_{2^n-1} \leq x_{2^n}]$.

(It turns out that $B(\rho_9) = 3{,}683{,}424$; about 170 megamems suffice to compute that BDD, and ρ_{10} is almost within reach. Algorithm C now quickly yields the exact numbers of regular n-variable Boolean functions for $1 \leq n \leq 9$, namely 3, 5, 10, 27, 119, 1173, 44315, 16175190, 284432730176. Similarly, we can count the self-dual ones, as in exercise 74; those numbers, whose early history is discussed in answer 7.1.1–123, are 1, 1, 2, 3, 7, 21, 135, 2470, 319124, 1214554343, for $1 \leq n \leq 10$.)

76. Say that $x_0 \ldots x_{j-1}$ *forces* x_j if $x_i = 1$ for some $i \subseteq j$ with $0 \leq i < j$. Then $x_0 x_1 \ldots x_{2^n-1}$ corresponds to a clutter if and only if $x_j = 0$ whenever $x_0 \ldots x_{j-1}$ forces x_j, for $0 \leq j < 2^n$. And $\mu_n(x_0, \ldots, x_{2^n-1}) = 1$ if and only if $x_j = 1$ whenever $x_0 \ldots x_{j-1}$ forces x_j. So we get the desired BDD from that of $\mu_n(x_1, \ldots, x_{2^n})$ by (i) changing each branch (j) to $(j-1)$, and (ii) interchanging the LO and HI branches at every branch node that has LO = $\boxed{\perp}$. (Notice that, by Corollary 7.1.1Q, the prime implicants of every monotone Boolean function correspond to clutters.)

77. Continuing the previous answer, say that the bit vector $x_0 \ldots x_{k-1}$ is *consistent* if we have $x_j = 1$ whenever $x_0 \ldots x_{j-1}$ forces x_j, for $0 < j < k$. Let b_k be the number of consistent vectors of length k. For example, $b_4 = 6$ because of the vectors $\{0000, 0001, 0011, 0101, 0111, 1111\}$. Notice that exactly $c_k = b_{k+1} - b_k$ clutters S have the property that k represents their "largest" set, $\max\{s \mid s$ represents a set of $S\}$.

The BDD for $\mu_n(x_1, \ldots, x_{2^n})$ has b_{k-1} branch nodes (k) when $1 \le k \le 2^{n-1}$. Proof: Every subfunction defined by $x_1, \ldots, x_{k-1}$ is either identically false or defines a consistent vector $x_1 \ldots x_{k-1}$. In the latter case the subfunction is a bead, because it takes different values under certain settings of $x_{k+1}, \ldots, x_{2^n}$. Indeed, if $x_1 \ldots x_{k-1}$ forces x_k, we set $x_{k+1} \leftarrow \cdots \leftarrow x_{2^n} \leftarrow 1$; otherwise we set $x_j \leftarrow y_j$ for $k < j \le 2^n$, where

$$y_{j+1} = [x_{i+1} = 1 \text{ for some } i \subseteq j \text{ with } i + 1 < k],$$

noting that $y_{2^n+k} = 0$.

On the other hand there are $b_{k'}$ branches (k) when $k = 2^n - k'$ and $0 \le k' < 2^{n-1}$. In this case the nonconstant subfunctions arising from $x_1, \ldots, x_{k-1}$ lead to values y_j as above, where the vector $\bar{y}_{0'} \bar{y}_{1'} \ldots \bar{y}_{k'}$ is consistent. (Here $0' = 2^n$, $1' = 2^n - 1$, etc.) Conversely, every such consistent vector describes such a subfunction; we can, for example, set $x_j \leftarrow 0$ when $j < k - 2^{n-1}$ or $2^{n-1} \le j < k$, otherwise $x_j \leftarrow y_{2^{n-1}+j}$. This subfunction is a bead if and only if $y_{k'} = 1$ or $\bar{y}_{0'} \ldots \bar{y}_{(k-1)'}$ forces $\bar{y}_{k'}$. Thus the beads correspond to consistent vectors of length k'; and different vectors define different beads.

This argument shows that there are $b_{k-1} - c_{k-1}$ branches (k) with LO = $\boxed{\perp}$ when $1 \le k \le 2^{n-1}$ and c_{2^n-k} such branches when $2^{n-1} < k \le 2^n$. Hence exactly half of the $B(\mu_n) - 2$ branch nodes have LO = $\boxed{\perp}$.

78. To count graphs on n labeled vertices with maximum degree $\le d$, construct the Boolean function of the $\binom{n}{2}$ variables in its adjacency matrix, namely $\bigwedge_{k=1}^n S_{\le d}(X_k)$, where X_k is the set of variables in row k of the matrix. For example, when $n = 5$ there are 10 variables, and the function is $S_{\le d}(x_1, x_2, x_3, x_4) \wedge S_{\le d}(x_1, x_5, x_6, x_7) \wedge S_{\le d}(x_2, x_5, x_8, x_9) \wedge S_{\le d}(x_3, x_6, x_8, x_{10}) \wedge S_{\le d}(x_4, x_7, x_9, x_{10})$. When $n = 12$ the BDDs for $d = (1, 2, \ldots, 10)$ have respectively (5960, 137477, 1255813, 5295204, 10159484, 11885884, 9190884, 4117151, 771673, 28666) nodes, so they are readily computed with Algorithm S. To count solutions with maximum degree d, subtract the number of solutions for degree $\le d-1$ from the number for degree $\le d$; the answers for $0 \le d \le 11$ are:

1	3038643940889754	29271277569846191555
140151	211677202624318662	17880057008325613629
3568119351	3617003021179405538	4489497643961740521
8616774658305	17884378201906645374	430038382710483623

[In general there are $t_n - 1$ graphs on n labeled vertices with maximum degree 1, where t_n is the number of involutions, Eq. 5.1.4–(40).]

The methods of Section 7.2.3 are superior to BDDs for enumerations such as these, when n is large, because labeled graphs have $n!$ symmetries. But when n has a moderate size, BDDs produce answers quickly, and nicely characterize all the solutions.

79. In the following counts, obtained from the BDDs in the previous answer, each graph with k edges is weighted by 2^{66-k}. Divide by 3^{66} to get probabilities.

73786976294838206464	11646725483430295546484263747584
55315674993080529074112	77677416878709243055475188039968
59853550286831523654847692	25144575345589759186086686888384
68379835220584550117167595520	45273361563608993921819340390
13803589275645776834792332984	45968637738881805341545676736
70240963762983970769690815365	20931955804803138182922949855

80. If the original functions f and g have no BDD nodes in common, both algorithms encounter almost exactly the same subproblems: Algorithm S deals with all nodes of $f \diamond g$ that aren't descended from nodes of the forms $\alpha \diamond \boxed{\perp}$ or $\boxed{\perp} \diamond \beta$, while (55) also avoids nodes that descend from the forms $\alpha \diamond \boxed{\top}$ or $\boxed{\top} \diamond \beta$. Furthermore, (55) takes shortcuts when it meets nontrivial subproblems AND(f', g') with $f' = g'$; Algorithm S cannot recognize the fact that such cases are easy. And (55) can also win if it happens to stumble across a relevant memo left over from a previous computation.

81. Just change 'AND' to 'XOR' and '$\wedge$' to '$\oplus$' throughout. The simple cases are now $f \oplus 0 = f$, $0 \oplus g = g$, and $f \oplus g = 0$ if $f = g$. We should also swap $f \leftrightarrow g$ if $f > g \neq 0$.

Notes: The author experimentally inserted further memos '$f \oplus r = g$' and '$g \oplus r = f$' in the bottom line; but these additional cache entries seemed to do more harm than good. Considering other binary operators, there's no need to implement both BUTNOT$(f, g) = f \wedge \bar{g}$ and NOTBUT$(f, g) = \bar{f} \wedge g$, since the latter is BUTNOT(g, f). Also, XOR$(1, \text{OR}(f, g))$ may be better than an implementation of NOR$(f, g) = \neg(f \vee g)$.

82. A top-level computation of $F \leftarrow \text{AND}(f, g)$ begins with f and g in computer registers, but REF(f) and REF(g) do not include "references" such as those. (We do, however, assume that f and g are both alive.)

If (55) discovers that $f \wedge g$ is obviously r, it increases REF(r) by 1.

If (55) finds $f \wedge g = r$ in the memo cache, it increases REF(r), and recursively increases REF(LO(r)) and REF(HI(r)) in the same way if r was dead.

If step U1 finds $p = q$, it *decreases* REF(p) by 1 (believe it or not); this won't kill p.

If step U2 finds r, there are two cases: If r was alive, it sets REF$(r) \leftarrow$ REF$(r) + 1$, REF$(p) \leftarrow$ REF$(p) - 1$, REF$(q) \leftarrow$ REF$(q) - 1$. Otherwise it simply sets REF$(r) \leftarrow 1$.

When step U3 creates a new node r, it sets REF$(r) \leftarrow 1$.

Finally, after the top-level AND returns a value r that we wish to assign to F, we must first *dereference* F, if $F \neq \Lambda$; this means setting REF$(F) \leftarrow$ REF$(F) - 1$, and recursively dereferencing LO(F) and HI(F) if REF(F) has become 0. Then we set $F \leftarrow r$ (without adjusting REF(r)).

[Furthermore, in a quantification routine such as (65) or in the composition routine (72), both r_l and r_h should be dereferenced after the OR or MUX has computed r.]

83. Exercise 61 shows that the subproblem $f \wedge g$ occurs at most once per top-level call, when REF$(f) = $ REF$(g) = 1$. [This idea is due to F. Somenzi; see the paper cited in answer 84. Many nodes have reference count 1, because the average count is approximately 2, and because the sinks usually have large counts. However, such cache-avoidance did not improve the overall performance in the author's experiments, possibly because of the examples investigated, or possibly because "accidental" cache hits in other top-level operations can be useful.]

84. Many possibilities exist, and no simple technique appears to be a clear winner. The cache and table sizes should be powers of 2, to facilitate calculating the hash functions. The size of the unique table for x_v should be roughly proportional to the number of nodes that currently branch on x_v (alive or dead). It's necessary to rehash everything when a table is downsized or upsized.

In the author's experiments while writing this section, the cache size was doubled whenever the number of insertions since the beginning of the most recent top-level command exceeded ln 2 times the current cache size. (At that point a random hash function will have filled about half of the slots.) After garbage collection, the cache was downsized, if necessary, so that it either had 256 slots or was at least 1/4 full.

It's easy to keep track of the current number of dead nodes; hence we know at all times how much memory a garbage collection will reclaim. The author obtained satisfactory results by inserting a new step U2$\frac{1}{2}$ between U2 and U3: "Increase C by 1, where C is a global counter. If C mod $1024 = 0$, and if at least 1/8 of all current nodes are dead, collect garbage."

[See F. Somenzi, *Software Tools for Technology Transfer* **3** (2001), 171–181 for numerous further suggestions based on extensive experience.]

85. The complete table would have 2^{32} entries of 32 bits each, for a total of 2^{34} bytes ($\approx$ 17.2 gigabytes). The BDD base discussed after (58), with about 136 million nodes using zip-ordered bits, can be stored in about 1.1 gigabyte; the one discussed in Corollary Y, which ranks all of the multiplier bits first, needs only about 400 megabytes.

86. If $f = 0$ or $g = h$, return g. If $f = 1$, return h. If $g = 0$ or $f = g$, return AND(f, h). If $h = 1$ or $f = h$, return OR(f, g). If $g = 1$, return IMPLIES(f, h); if $h = 0$, return BUTNOT(g, f). (If binary IMPLIES and/or BUTNOT aren't implemented directly, it's OK to let the corresponding cases propagate in ternary guise.)

87. Sort the given pointer values f, g, h so that $f \leq g \leq h$. If $f = 0$, return AND(g, h). If $f = 1$, return OR(g, h). If $f = g$ or $g = h$, return g.

88. The trio of functions $(f, g, h) = (R_0, R_1, R_2)$ makes an amusing example, when

$$R_a(x_1, \ldots, x_n) = [(x_n \ldots x_1)_2 \bmod 3 \neq a] = R_{(2a+x_1) \bmod 3}(x_2, \ldots, x_n).$$

Thanks to the memos, the ternary recursion finds $f \wedge g \wedge h = 0$ by examining only one case at each level; the binary computation of, say, $f \wedge g = \bar{h}$ definitely takes longer.

More dramatically, let $f = x_1 \wedge (x_2? \ F: G)$, $g = x_2 \wedge (x_1? \ G: F)$, and $h = x_1? \ \bar{x}_2 \wedge F: x_2 \wedge G$, where F and G are functions of $(x_3, \ldots, x_n)$ such that $B(F \wedge G) = \Theta(B(F)B(G))$ as in exercise 63. Then $f \wedge g$, $g \wedge h$, and $h \wedge f$ all have large BDDs, but the ternary recursion immediately discovers that $f \wedge g \wedge h = 0$.

89. (a) True; the left side is $(f_{00} \vee f_{01}) \vee (f_{10} \vee f_{11})$, the right side is $(f_{00} \vee f_{10}) \vee (f_{01} \vee f_{11})$.
(b) Similarly true. (And ⊓'s are commutative too.)
(c) Usually false; see part (d).
(d) $\forall x_1 \exists x_2 f = (f_{00} \vee f_{01}) \wedge (f_{10} \vee f_{11}) = (\exists x_2 \forall x_1 f) \vee (f_{00} \wedge f_{11}) \vee (f_{01} \wedge f_{10})$.

90. Change $\exists j_1 \ldots \exists j_m$ to ⊓$j_1 \ldots$⊓j_m.

91. (a) $f \downarrow 1 = f$, $f \downarrow x_j = f_1$, and $f \downarrow \bar{x}_j = f_0$, in the notation of (63).
(b) This distributive law is obvious, by the definition of $\downarrow$. (Also true for $\vee$, $\oplus$, etc.)
(c) True if and only if g is not identically zero. (Consequently the value of $f(x_1, \ldots, x_n) \downarrow g$ for $g \neq 0$ is determined solely by the values of $x_j \downarrow g$ for $1 \leq j \leq n$.)
(d) $f(x_1, 1, 0, x_4, 0, 1, x_7, \ldots, x_n)$. This is the restriction of f with respect to $x_2 = 1$, $x_3 = 0$, $x_5 = 0$, $x_6 = 1$ (see exercise 57), also called the *cofactor* of f with respect to the subcube g. (A similar result holds when g is any product of literals.)
(e) $f(x_1, \ldots, x_{n-1}, x_1 \oplus \cdots \oplus x_{n-1} \oplus 1)$. (Consider the case $f = x_j$, for $1 \leq j \leq n$.)
(f) $x_1? \ f(1, \ldots, 1): f(0, \ldots, 0)$.
(g) $f(1, x_2, \ldots, x_n) \downarrow g(x_2, \ldots, x_n)$.
(h) If $f = x_2$ and $g = x_1 \vee x_2$ we have $f \downarrow g = \bar{x}_1 \vee x_2$.

(i) CONSTRAIN(f, g) = "If $f \downarrow g$ has an obvious value, return it. Otherwise, if $f \downarrow g = r$ is in the memo cache, return r. Otherwise represent f and g as in (52); set $r \leftarrow$ CONSTRAIN(f_h, g_h) if $g_l = 0$, $r \leftarrow$ CONSTRAIN(f_l, g_l) if $g_h = 0$, otherwise $r \leftarrow$ UNIQUE$(v,$ CONSTRAIN$(f_l, g_l),$ CONSTRAIN$(f_h, g_h))$; put '$f \downarrow g = r$' into the memo cache, and return r." Here the obvious values are $f \downarrow 0 = 0 \downarrow g = 0$; $f \downarrow 1 = f$; $1 \downarrow g = g \downarrow g = [g \neq 0]$.

[The operator $f \downarrow g$ was introduced in 1989 by O. Coudert, C. Berthet, and J. C. Madre. Examples such as the functions in (h) led them to propose also the modified operator $f \Downarrow g$, "f restricted to g," which has a similar recursion except that it uses $f \Downarrow (\exists x_v g)$ instead of $(\bar{x}_v? f_l \Downarrow g_l: f_h \Downarrow g_h)$ when $f_l = f_h$. See *Lecture Notes in Computer Science* **407** (1989), 365–373.]

92. See answer 91(d) for the "if" part. Notice also that (i) $x_1 \downarrow g = x_1$ if and only if $g_0 \neq 0$ and $g_1 \neq 0$, where $g_c = g(c, x_2, \ldots, x_n)$; (ii) $x_n \downarrow g = x_n$ if and only if $\exists x_n g = 0$ and $g \neq 0$.

Suppose $f^\pi \downarrow g^\pi = (f \downarrow g)^\pi$ for all f and π. If $g \neq 0$ isn't a subcube, there's an index j such that $g_0 \neq 0$ and $g_1 \neq 0$ and $\exists x_j g \neq 0$, where $g_c = g(x_1, \ldots, x_{j-1}, c, x_{j+1}, \ldots, x_n)$. By the previous paragraph, we have (i) $x_j \downarrow g = x_j$ and (ii) $x_j \downarrow g \neq x_j$, a contradiction.

93. Let $f = J(x_1, \ldots, x_n; f_1, \ldots, f_n)$ and $g = J(x_1, \ldots, x_n; g_1, \ldots, g_n)$, where

$$f_v = x_{n+1} \vee \cdots \vee x_{5n} \vee J(x_{5n+1}, \ldots, x_{6n}; [v-1], \ldots, [v-n]),$$
$$g_v = x_{n+1} \vee \cdots \vee x_{5n} \vee J(x_{5n+1}, \ldots, x_{6n}; [v=1]+[v-1], \ldots, [v=n]+[v-n]),$$

and J is the junction function of exercise 52.

If G can be 3-colored, let $\hat{f} = J(x_1, \ldots, x_n; \hat{f}_1, \ldots, \hat{f}_n)$, where

$$\hat{f}_v = x_{n+1} \vee \cdots \vee x_{5n} \vee J(x_{5n+1}, \ldots, x_{6n}; \hat{f}_{v1}, \ldots, \hat{f}_{vn}),$$

and $\hat{f}_{vw} = [v$ and w have different colors$]$. Then $B(\hat{f}) < n + 3(5n) + 2$.

Conversely, suppose there's an approximating $\hat{f}$ such that $B(\hat{f}) < 16n + 2$, and let $\hat{f}_v$ be the subfunction with $x_1 = [v=1]$, $\ldots$, $x_n = [v=n]$. At most three of these subfunctions are distinct, because every distinct $\hat{f}_v$ must branch on each of x_{n+1}, $\ldots$, x_{5n}. Color the vertices so that u and v get the same color if and only if $\hat{f}_u = \hat{f}_v$; this can happen only if $u \not\!-\!\!\!- v$, so the coloring is legitimate.

[M. Sauerhoff and I. Wegener, *IEEE Transactions* **CAD-15** (1996), 1435–1437.]

94. *Case 1: $v \neq g_v$.* Then we aren't quantifying over x_v; hence $g = g_h$, and $f \, \mathrm{E} \, g = \bar{x}_v? \, f_l \, \mathrm{E} \, g: f_h \, \mathrm{E} \, g$.

Case 2: $v = g_v$. Then $g = x_v \wedge g_h$ and $f \, \mathrm{E} \, g = (f_l \, \mathrm{E} \, g_h) \vee (f_h \, \mathrm{E} \, g_h) = r_l \vee r_h$. In the subcase $v \neq f_v$, we have $f_l = f_h = f$; hence $r_l = r_h$, and we can directly reduce $f \, \mathrm{E} \, g$ to $f \, \mathrm{E} \, g_h$ (an instance of "tail recursion").

[Rudell observes that the order of quantification in (65) corresponds to bottom-up order of the variables. That order is convenient, but not always best; sometimes it's better to remove the ∃s one by one in another order, based on knowledge of the functions involved.]

95. If $r_l = 1$ and $v = g_v$, we can set $r \leftarrow 1$ and forget about r_h. (This change led to a 100-fold speedup in some of the author's experiments.)

96. For ∀, just change E to A and OR to AND. For ∃, change E to D and OR to XOR; also, if $v \neq f_v$, return 0. [Routines for the yes/no quantifiers A and N are analogous to ∃. Yes/no quantifiers should be used only when $m = 1$; otherwise they make little sense.]

97. Proceeding bottom-up, the amount of work on each level is at worst proportional to the number of nodes on that level.

98. The function $\text{NOTEND}(x) = \exists y \exists z (\text{ADJ}(x, y) \wedge \text{ADJ}(x, z) \wedge [y \neq z])$ identifies all vertices of degree ≥ 2. Hence $\text{ENDPT}(x) = \text{KER}(x) \wedge \neg\text{NOTEND}(x)$. And $\text{PAIR}(x, y) = \text{ENDPT}(x) \wedge \text{ENDPT}(y) \wedge \text{ADJ}(x, y)$.

[For example, when G is the contiguous-USA graph, with the states ordered as in (104), we have $B(\text{NOTEND}) = 992$, $B(\text{ENDPT}) = 264$, and $B(\text{PAIR}) = 203$. Before applying $\exists y \exists z$ the BDD size is 50511. There are exactly 49 kernels of degree 1. The nine components of size 2 are obtained by mixing the following three solutions:

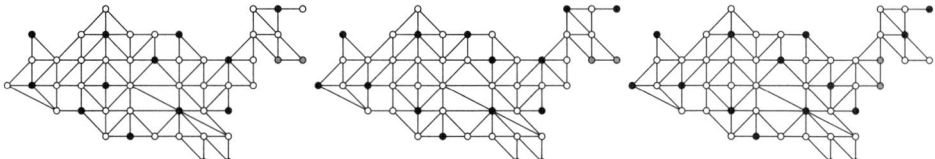

The total cost of this calculation, using the stated algorithms, is about 14 megamems, in 6.3 megabytes of memory — only about 52 memory references per kernel.]

99. Find a triangle of mutually adjacent states, and fix their colors. The BDD size also decreases substantially if we choose states of high degree in the "middle" levels. For example, by setting $a_{\text{MO}} = b_{\text{MO}} = a_{\text{TN}} = \bar{b}_{\text{TN}} = \bar{a}_{\text{AR}} = b_{\text{AR}} = 1$ we reduce the 25579 nodes to only 4642 (and the total execution time also drops below 2 megamems).

[Bryant's original manuscript about BDDs discussed graph coloring in detail, but he decided to substitute other material when his paper was published in 1986.]

100. Replace $\text{IND}(x_{\text{ME}}, \ldots, x_{\text{CA}})$ by $\text{IND}(x_{\text{ME}}, \ldots, x_{\text{CA}}) \wedge S_{12}(x_{\text{ME}}, \ldots, x_{\text{CA}})$, to get the 12-node independent sets; this BDD has size 1964. Then use (73) as before, and the trick of answer 99, getting a COLOR function with 184,260 nodes and 12,554,677,864 solutions. (The running time is approximately 26 megamems.)

101. If a state's weight is w, assign $2w$ and w as the respective weights of its a and b variables, and use Algorithm B. (For example, variable a_{WY} gets weight $2(23 + 25) = 96$.) The solution, shown here with color codes ①②❸❹, is unique.

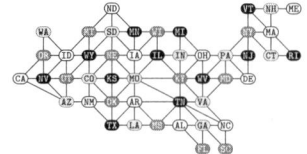

102. The main idea is that, when g_j changes, all results in the cache for functions with $f_v > j$ remain valid. To exploit this principle we can maintain an array of "time stamps" $G_1 \geq G_2 \geq \cdots \geq G_n \geq 0$, one for each variable. There's a master clock time $G \geq G_1$, representing the number of distinct compositions done or prepared; another variable G' records whether G has changed since COMPOSE was last invoked. Initially $G = G' = G_1 = \cdots = G_n = 0$. The subroutine $\text{NEWG}(j, g)$ is implemented as follows:

N1. [Easy case?] If $g_j = g$, exit the subroutine. Otherwise set $g_j \leftarrow g$.

N2. [Can we reset?] If $g \neq x_j$, or if $j < n$ and $G_{j+1} > 0$, go to N4.

N3. [Reset stamps.] While $j > 0$ and $g_j = x_j$, set $G_j \leftarrow 0$ and $j \leftarrow j - 1$. Then if $j = 0$, set $G \leftarrow G - G'$, $G' \leftarrow 0$, and exit.

N4. [Update G?] If $G' = 0$, set $G \leftarrow G + 1$ and $G' \leftarrow 1$.

N5. [New stamps.] While $j > 0$ and $G_j \neq G$, set $G_j \leftarrow G$ and $j \leftarrow j - 1$. Exit. ∎

(Reference counts also need to be maintained appropriately.) Before launching a top-level call of COMPOSE, set $G' \leftarrow 0$. Change the COMPOSE routine (72) to use $f[G_v]$ in references to the cache, where $v = f_v$; the test '$v > m$' becomes '$G_v = 0$'.

103. The equivalent formula $g(f_1(x_1, \ldots, x_n), \ldots, f_m(x_1, \ldots, x_n))$ can be implemented with the COMPOSE operation (72). (However, Dull was vindicated when it turned out that his formula could be evaluated more than a hundred times faster than Quick's, in spite of the fact that it uses twice as many variables! In his application, the computation of $(y_1 = f_1(x_1, \ldots, x_n)) \wedge \cdots \wedge (y_m = f_m(x_1, \ldots, x_n)) \wedge g(y_1, \ldots, y_m)$ turned out to be much easier than COMPOSE's computation of $g_j(f_1, \ldots, f_m)$ for every subfunction g_j of g; see, for example, exercise 162.)

104. The following recursive algorithm COMPARE(f, g) needs at most $O(B(f)B(g))$ steps when used with a memo cache: If $f = g$, return '$=$'. Otherwise, if $f = 0$ or $g = 1$, return '$<$'; if $f = 1$ or $g = 0$, return '$>$'. Otherwise represent f and g as in (52); compute $r_l \leftarrow$ COMPARE(f_l, g_l). If r_l is '$\|$', return '$\|$'; otherwise compute $r_h \leftarrow$ COMPARE(f_h, g_h). If r_h is '$\|$', return '$\|$'. Otherwise if r_l is '$=$', return r_h; if r_h is '$=$', return r_l; if $r_l = r_h$, return r_l. Otherwise return '$\|$'.

105. (a) A unate function with polarities $(y_1, \ldots, y_n)$ has $\wedge x_j f = 0$ when $y_j = 1$ and $\mathsf{N}x_j f = 0$ when $y_j = 0$, for $1 \le j \le n$. Conversely, f is unate if these conditions hold for all j. (Notice that $\wedge x_j f = \mathsf{N}x_j f = 0$ if and only if $\Box x_j f = 0$, if and only if f doesn't depend on x_j. In such cases y_j is irrelevant; otherwise y_j is uniquely determined.)

(b) The following algorithm maintains global variables $(p_1, \ldots, p_n)$, initially zero, with the property that $p_j = +1$ if y_j must be 0 and $p_j = -1$ if y_j must be 1; p_j will remain zero if f doesn't depend on x_j. With this understanding, UNATE(f) is defined as follows: If f is constant, return *true*. Otherwise represent f as in (50). Return *false* if either UNATE(f_l) or UNATE(f_h) is *false*; otherwise set $r \leftarrow$ COMPARE(f_l, f_h) using exercise 104. If r is '$\|$', return *false*. If r is '$<$', return *false* if $p_v < 0$, otherwise set $p_v \leftarrow +1$ and return *true*. If r is '$>$', return *false* if $p_v > 0$, otherwise set $p_v \leftarrow -1$ and return *true*.

This algorithm often terminates quickly. It relies on the fact that $f(x) \le g(x)$ for all x if and only if $f(x \oplus y) \le g(x \oplus y)$ for all x, when y is fixed. If we simply want to test whether or not f is monotone, the p variables should be initialized to $+1$ instead of 0.

106. Define HORN(f, g, h) thus: If $f > g$, interchange $f \leftrightarrow g$. Then if $f = 0$ or $h = 1$, return *true*. Otherwise if $g = 1$ or $h = 0$, return *false*. Otherwise represent f, g, and h as in (59). Return *true* if HORN(f_l, g_l, h_l), HORN(f_l, g_h, h_l), HORN(f_h, g_l, h_l), and HORN(f_h, g_h, h_h) are all *true*; otherwise return *false*. [This algorithm is due to T. Horiyama and T. Ibaraki, *Artificial Intelligence* **136** (2002), 189–213, who also introduced an algorithm similar to that of answer 105(b).]

107. Let $e\$f\$g\$h$ mean that $e(x) = f(y) = g(z) = 1$ implies $h(\langle xyz \rangle) = 1$. Then f is a Krom function if and only if $f\$f\$f\$f$, and we can use the following recursive algorithm KROM(e, f, g, h): Rearrange $\{e, f, g\}$ so that $e \le f \le g$. Then if $e = 0$ or $h = 1$, return *true*. Otherwise if $f = 1$ or $h = 0$, return *false*. Otherwise represent e, f, g, h with the quaternary analog of (59). Return *true* if KROM(e_l, f_l, g_l, h_l), KROM(e_l, f_l, g_h, h_l), KROM(e_l, f_h, g_l, h_l), KROM(e_l, f_h, g_h, h_h), KROM(e_h, f_l, g_l, h_l), KROM(e_h, f_l, g_h, h_h), KROM(e_h, f_h, g_l, h_h), and KROM(e_h, f_h, g_h, h_h) are all *true*; otherwise return *false*.

108. Label the nodes $\{1, \ldots, s\}$ with root 1 and sinks $\{s-1, s\}$; then $(s-3)!$ permutations of the other labels give different dags for the same function. The stated inequality follows because each instruction $(\bar{v}_k? \ l_k : h_k)$ has at most $n(s-1)^2$ possibilities, for $1 \le k \le s-2$. (In fact, it holds also for arbitrary *branching programs*, namely for binary decision diagrams in general, whether or not they are ordered and/or reduced.)

Since $1/(s-3)! < (s-1)^3/s!$ and $s! > (s/e)^s$, we have (generously) $b(n,s) <$ $(nse)^s$. Let $s_n = 2^n/(n+\theta)$, where $\theta = \lg e = 1/\ln 2$; then $\lg b(n, s_n) < s_n \lg(nsne) =$ $2^n(1 - (\lg(1+\theta/n))/(n+\theta)) = 2^n - \Omega(2^n/n^2)$. So the probability that a random n-variable Boolean function has $B(f) \le s_n$ is at most $1/2^{\Omega(2^n/n^2)}$. And that is really tiny.

109. $1/2^{\Omega(2^n/n^2)}$ is really tiny even when multiplied by $n!$.

110. Let $f_n = M_m(x_{n-m+1}, \dots, x_n; 0, \dots, 0, x_1, \dots, x_{n-m}) \vee (\bar{x}_{n-m+1} \wedge \cdots \wedge \bar{x}_n \wedge [0 \dots 0x_1 \dots x_{n-m}$ is a square]), when $2^{m-1} + m - 1 < n < 2^m + m$. Each term of this formula has $2^m + m - n$ zeros; the second term destroys all of the 2^m-bit squares. [See H.-T. Liaw and C.-S. Lin, *IEEE Transactions* **C-41** (1992), 661–664; Y. Breitbart, H. Hunt III, and D. Rosenkrantz, *Theoretical Comp. Sci.* **145** (1995), 45–69.]

111. Let $\mu n = \lambda(n - \lambda n)$, and notice that $\mu n = m$ if and only if $2^m + m \le n < 2^{m+1} + m + 1$. The sum for $0 \le k < n - \mu n$ is $2^{n-\mu n} - 1$; the other terms sum to $2^{2^{\mu n}}$.

112. Suppose $k = n - \lg n + \lg \alpha$. Then

$$\frac{(2^{2^{n-k}} - 1)^{2^k}}{2^{2^n}} = \exp\left(\frac{2^n \alpha}{n} \ln\left(1 - \frac{1}{2^{n/\alpha}}\right)\right) = \exp\left(-\frac{2^{n-n/\alpha}\alpha}{n}\left(1 + O\left(\frac{1}{2^{n/\alpha}}\right)\right)\right).$$

If $\alpha \le \frac{1}{2}$ we have $2^{n-n/\alpha}\alpha/n \le 1/(n2^{n+1})$; hence $\hat{b}_k = (2^{n/\alpha} - 2^{n/(2\alpha)})(2^{n-n/\alpha}\alpha/n) \times$ $(1 + O(2^{-n/\alpha})) = 2^k(1 - O(2^{-n/(2\alpha)}))$. And if $\alpha \ge 2$ we have $2^{n-n/\alpha}\alpha/n \ge 2^{n/2+1}/n$; thus $\hat{b}_k = (2^{2^{n-k}} - 2^{2^{n-k-1}})(1 + O(\exp(-2^{n/2}/n)))$.

[For the variance of b_k, see I. Wegener, *IEEE Trans.* **C-43** (1994), 1262–1269.]

113. The idea looks attractive at first glance, but loses its luster when examined closely. Comparatively few nodes of a BDD base appear on the lower levels, by Theorem U; and algorithms like Algorithm S spend comparatively little of their time dealing with those levels. Furthermore, nonconstant sink nodes would make several algorithms more complicated, especially those for reordering.

114. For example, the truth table might be 01010101 00110011 00001111 00001111.

115. Let $N_k = b_0 + \cdots + b_{k-1}$ be the number of nodes (j) of the BDD for which $j \le k$. The sum of the in-degrees of those nodes is at least N_k; the sum of the out-degrees is $2N_k$; and there's an external pointer to the root. Thus at most $N_k + 1$ branches can cross from the upper k levels to lower levels. Every subtable of order $n - k$ corresponds to some such branch. Therefore $q_k \le N_k + 1$.

Moreover, we must have $q_k \le b_k + \cdots + b_n$, because every subtable of order $n - k$ corresponds to a unique bead of order $\le n - k$.

For (124), change 'BDD' to 'ZDD', 'b_k' to 'z_k', 'bead' to 'zead', and 'q_k' to 'q'_k'.

116. (a) Let $v_k = 2^{2^k} + 2^{2^{k-1}} + \cdots + 2^{2^0}$. Then $Q(f) \le \sum_{k=1}^{n+1} \min(2^{k-1}, 2^{2^{n+1-k}}) = U_n + v_{\lambda(n-\lambda n)-1}$. Examples like (78) show that this upper bound cannot be improved.
(b) $\hat{q}_k/\hat{b}_k = 2^{2^{n-k}}/(2^{2^{n-k}} - 2^{2^{n-k-1}})$ for $0 \le k < n$; $\hat{q}_n = \hat{b}_n$.

117. $q_k = 2^k$ for $0 \le k \le m$, and $q_{m+k} = 2^m + 2 - k$ for $1 \le k \le 2^m$. Hence $Q(f) = 2^{2m-1} + 7 \cdot 2^{m-1} - 1 \approx B(f)^2/8$. (Such f's make QDDs unattractive in practice.)

118. If $n = 2^m - 1$ we have $h_n(x_1, \dots, x_n) = M_m(z_{m-1}, \dots, z_0; 0, x_1, \dots, x_n)$, where $(z_{m-1} \dots z_0)_2 = x_1 + \cdots + x_n$ is computable in $5n - 5m$ steps by exercise 7.1.2–30, and M_m takes another $2n + O(\sqrt{n})$ by exercise 7.1.2–39. Since $h_n(x_1, \dots, x_n) =$ $h_{n+k}(x_1, \dots, x_n, 0, \dots, 0)$, we have $C(h_n) \le 14n + O(\sqrt{n})$ for all n. (A little more work will bring this down to $7n + O(\sqrt{n} \log n)$; can the reader do better?)

The cost of h_4 is $6 = L(h_4)$, and $x_2 \oplus ((x_1 \oplus (x_2 \wedge \bar{x}_4)) \wedge (\bar{x}_3 \oplus (\bar{x}_2 \wedge x_4)))$ is a formula of shortest length. (Also $C(h_5) = 10$ and $L(h_5) = 11$.)

119. True. For example, $S_{2,3,5}(x_1, \ldots, x_6) = h_{13}(x_1, x_2, 0, 0, 1, 1, 0, 1, 0, x_3, x_4, x_5, x_6)$.

120. We have $h_n^\pi(x_1, \ldots, x_n) = h_n(y_1, \ldots, y_n)$, where $y_j = x_{j\pi}$ for $1 \le j \le n$. And $h_n(y_1, \ldots, y_n) = y_{y_1 + \cdots + y_n} = y_{x_1 + \cdots + x_n} = x_{(x_1 + \cdots + x_n)\pi}$.

121. (a) If $y_k = \bar{x}_{n+1-k}$ we have $h_n(y_1, \ldots, y_n) = y_{\nu y} = y_{n-\nu x} = \bar{x}_{n+1-(n-\nu x)} = \bar{x}_{\nu x+1}$.

(b) If $x = (x_1, \ldots, x_n)$ and $t \in \{0, 1\}$ we have $h_{n+1}(x, t) = (t?\ x_{\nu x+1}\colon x_{\nu x})$.

(c) No. For example, ψ sends $0^k 11 \mapsto 0^{k-1} 101 \mapsto 0^{k-2} 10^2 1 \mapsto \cdots \mapsto 10^k 1 \mapsto 0^k 11$. (In spite of its simple definition, ψ has remarkable properties, including fixed points such as $100110100001010110001110010 11$ and $111011110110010111011110110 1111$.)

(d) In fact, $\hat{h}_n(x_1 \ldots x_n) = x_1(!)$, by induction using recurrence (b).

(If $f(x_1, \ldots, x_n)$ is *any* Boolean function and τ is *any* permutation of the binary vectors $x_1 \ldots x_n$, we can write $f(x) = \hat{f}(x\tau)$, and the transformed function $\hat{f}$ may well be much easier to work with. Since $f(x) \wedge g(x) = \hat{f}(x\tau) \wedge \hat{g}(x\tau)$, the transform of the AND of two functions is the AND of their transforms, etc. The vector permutations $(x_1 \ldots x_n)\pi = x_{1\pi} \ldots x_{n\pi}$ that merely transform the indices, as considered in the text, are a simple special case of this general principle. But the principle is, in a sense, *too* general, because every function f trivially has at least one τ for which $\hat{f}$ is skinny in the sense of exercise 170; all the complexity of f can be transferred to τ. Even simple transformations like ψ have limited utility, because they don't compose well; for example, $\psi\psi$ is not a transformation of the same type. But linear transformations, which take $x \mapsto xT$ for some nonsingular binary matrix T, have proved to be useful ways to simplify BDDs. [See S. Aborhey, *IEEE Trans.* **C-37** (1988), 1461–1465; J. Bern, C. Meinel, and A. Slobodová, *ACM/IEEE Design Automation Conf.* **32** (1995), 408–413; C. Meinel, F. Somenzi, and T. Theobald, *IEEE Trans.* **CAD-19** (2000), 521–533.])

122. For example, when $n = 7$ the recurrence in answer 121(b) gives

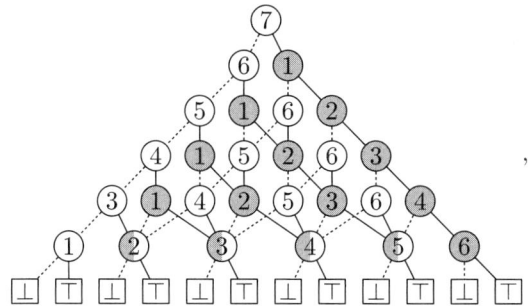

,

where shaded nodes compute the subfunction h^{DR} on the variables that haven't yet been tested. Simplifications occur at the bottom, because $h_2(x_1, x_2) = x_1$ and $h_2^{DR}(x_1, x_2) = x_2$. [See D. Sieling and I. Wegener, *Theoretical Comp. Sci.* **141** (1995), 283–310.]

123. Let $t = k - s = \bar{x}_1 + \cdots + \bar{x}_k$. There's a slate for every combination of s' 1s and t' 0s such that $s' + t' = w$, $s' \le s$, and $t' \le t$. The sum of $\binom{w}{s'} = \binom{w}{t'}$ over all such (s', t') is $\binom{w}{97}$. (Notice furthermore that it equals 2^w if and only if $w \le \min(s, t)$.)

124. Let $m = n - k$. Each slate $[r_0, \ldots, r_m]$ corresponds to a function of $(x_{k+1}, \ldots, x_n)$, whose truth table is a bead except in four cases: (i) $[0, \ldots, 0] = 0$; (ii) $[1, \ldots, 1] = 1$; (iii) $[0, x_n, 1] = x_n$ (which doesn't depend on x_{n-1}); (iv) $[1, \ldots, 1, x_{k+1}, 0, \ldots, 0]$, where there are p 1s so that $x_{k+1} = r_p$, is $S_{<p}(x_{k+2}, \ldots, x_n)$.

The following polynomial-time algorithm computes $q_k = q$ and $b_k = q - q'$ by counting all slates. A subtle aspect arises when the entries of $[r_0, \ldots, r_m]$ are all 0 or 1, because such slates can occur for different values of s; we don't want to count them twice. The solution is to maintain four sets

$$C_{ab} = \{r_1 + \cdots + r_{m-1} \mid r_0 = a \text{ and } r_m = b \text{ in some slate}\}.$$

The value of 0π should be artificially set to $n+1$, not 0. Assume that $0 \le k < n$.

H1. [Initialize.] Set $m \leftarrow n - k$, $q \leftarrow q' \leftarrow s \leftarrow 0$, $C_{00} \leftarrow C_{01} \leftarrow C_{10} \leftarrow C_{11} \leftarrow \emptyset$.

H2. [Find v and w.] Set $v \leftarrow \sum_{j=1}^{m-1}[(s+j)\pi \le k]$ and $w \leftarrow v + [s\pi \le k] + [(s+m)\pi \le k]$. If $v = m - 1$, go to step H5.

H3. [Check for nonbeads.] Set $p \leftarrow -1$. If $v \ne m - 2$, go to H4. Otherwise, if $m = 2$ and $(s+1)\pi = n$, set $p \leftarrow [(s+2)\pi \le k]$. Otherwise, if $w = m$ and $(s+j)\pi = k+1$ for some $j \in [1 .. m-1]$, set $p \leftarrow j$.

H4. [Add binomials.] For all s' and t' such that $s' + t' = w$, $0 \le s' \le s$, and $0 \le t' \le k - s$, set $q \leftarrow q + \binom{w}{s'}$ and $q' \leftarrow q' + [s' = p]$. Then go to H6.

H5. [Remember 0–1 slates.] Do the following for all s' and t' as in step H4: If $(s+m)\pi \le k$, set $C_{00} \leftarrow C_{00} \cup s'$ and $C_{01} \leftarrow C_{01} \cup (s'-1)$; otherwise set $C_{01} \leftarrow C_{01} \cup s'$. If $s\pi \le k$ and $(s+m)\pi \le k$, set $C_{10} \leftarrow C_{10} \cup (s'-1)$ and $C_{11} \leftarrow C_{11} \cup (s'-2)$. If $s\pi \le k$ and $(s+m)\pi > k$, set $C_{11} \leftarrow C_{11} \cup (s'-1)$.

H6. [Loop on s.] If $s < k$, set $s \leftarrow s + 1$ and return to H2.

H7. [Finish.] For $ab = 00, 01, 10,$ and 11, set $q \leftarrow q + \binom{m-1}{r}$ for all $r \in C_{ab}$. Also set $q' \leftarrow q' + [0 \in C_{00}] + [m-1 \in C_{11}]$. ∎

125. Let $S(n, m) = \binom{n}{0} + \cdots + \binom{n}{m}$. There are $S(k+1-s, s) - 1$ nonconstant slates when $0 < s \le k$ and $s \ge 2k - n + 2$. The only other nonconstant slates, one each, arise when $s = 0$ and $k < (n-1)/2$. The constant slates are trickier to count, but there usually are $S(n+1-k, 2k+1-n)$ of them, appearing when $s = 2k - n$ or $s = 2k+1-n$. Taking account of nitpicky boundary conditions and nonbeads, we find

$$b_k = S(n-k, 2k-n) + \sum_{s=0}^{n-k} S(n-k-s,\, 2k+1-n+s)$$
$$- \min(k, n-k) - [n = 2k] - [3k \ge 2n - 1] - 1$$

for $0 \le k < n$. Although $S(n, m)$ has no simple form, we can express $\sum_{k=0}^{n-1} b_k$ as $B_{n/2} + \sum_{0 \le m \le n - 2k \le n}(n + 3 - m - 2k)\binom{k}{m} + \text{(small change)}$ when n is even, and the same expression works when n is odd if we replace $B_{n/2}$ by $A_{(n+1)/2}$. The double sum can be reduced by summing first on k, since $(k+1)\binom{k}{m} = (m+1)\binom{k+1}{m+1}$:

$$\sum_{m=0}^{n}\left((n+5-m)\binom{\lfloor(n-m+2)/2\rfloor}{m+1} - (2m+2)\binom{\lfloor(n-m+4)/2\rfloor}{m+2}\right).$$

And the remaining sum can be tackled by breaking it into four parts, depending on whether m and/or n is odd. Generating functions are helpful: Let $A(z) = \sum_{k \le n}\binom{n-k}{2k}z^n$ and $B(z) = \sum_{k \le n}\binom{n-k}{2k+1}z^n$. Then $A(z) = 1 + \sum_{k<n}\binom{n-k-1}{2k}z^n + \sum_{k<n}\binom{n-k-1}{2k-1}z^n = 1 + \sum_{k \le n}\binom{n-k}{2k}z^{n+1} + \sum_{k \le n}\binom{n-k}{2k+1}z^{n+2} = 1 + zA(z) + z^2 B(z)$. A similar derivation proves that $B(z) = zB(z) + zA(z)$. Consequently

$$A(z) = \frac{1-z}{1-2z+z^2-z^3} = \frac{1-z^2}{1-z-z^2-z^4}, \quad B(z) = \frac{z}{1-2z+z^2-z^3} = \frac{z+z^2}{1-z-z^2-z^4}.$$

Thus $A_n = 2A_{n-1} - A_{n-2} + A_{n-3} = A_{n-1} + A_{n-2} + A_{n-4}$ for $n \geq 4$, and B_n satisfies the same recurrences. In fact, we have $A_n = (3P_{2n+1} + 7P_{2n} - 2P_{2n-1})/23$ and $B_n = (3P_{2n+2} + 7P_{2n+1} - 2P_{2n})/23$, using the Perrin numbers of exercise 15.

Furthermore, setting $A^*(z) = \sum_{k \leq n} k \binom{n-k}{2k} z^n$ and $B^*(z) = \sum_{k \leq n} k \binom{n-k}{2k+1} z^n$, we find $A^*(z) = z^2 A(z) B(z)$ and $B^*(z) = z^2 B(z)^2$. Putting it all together now yields the remarkable exact formula

$$B(h_n) = \frac{56P_{n+2} + 77P_{n+1} + 47P_n}{23} - \left\lfloor \frac{n^2}{4} \right\rfloor - \left\lfloor \frac{7n+1}{3} \right\rfloor + (n \bmod 2) - 10.$$

Historical notes: The sequence $\langle A_n \rangle$ was apparently first studied by R. Austin and R. K. Guy, *Fibonacci Quarterly* **16** (1978), 84–86; it counts binary $x_1 \ldots x_{n-1}$ with each 1 next to another. The plastic constant χ was shown by C. L. Siegel to be the smallest "Pisot number," namely the smallest algebraic integer > 1 whose conjugates all lie inside the unit circle; see *Duke Math. J.* **11** (1944), 597–602.

126. When $n \geq 6$, we have $b_k = F_{\lfloor (k+7)/2 \rfloor} + F_{\lceil (k+7)/2 \rceil} - 4$ for $1 \leq k < 2n/3$, and $b_k = 2^{n-k+2} - 6 - [k = n - 2]$ for $4n/5 \leq k < n$. But the main contributions to $B(h_n^\pi)$ come from the $2n/15$ profile elements between those two regions, and the methods of answer 125 can be extended to deal with them. The interesting sequences

$$A_n = \sum_{k=0}^{\lfloor n/2 \rfloor} \binom{n-2k}{3k}, \qquad B_n = \sum_{k=0}^{\lfloor n/2 \rfloor} \binom{n-2k}{3k+1}, \qquad C_n = \sum_{k=0}^{\lfloor n/2 \rfloor} \binom{n-2k}{3k+2}$$

have respective generating functions $(1-z)^2/p(z)$, $(1-z)z/p(z)$, $z^2/p(z)$, where $p(z) = (1-z)^3 - z^5$. These sequences arise in this problem because $\sum_{k=0}^{n} \binom{n-2k/3}{k} = A_n + B_{n-1} + C_{n-2}$. They grow as α^n, where $\alpha \approx 1.7016$ is the real root of $(\alpha-1)^3 \alpha^2 = 1$.

The BDD size can't be expressed in closed form, but there is a closed form in terms of $A_{\lfloor n/3 \rfloor}$ through $A_{\lfloor n/3 \rfloor + 4}$ that is accurate to $O(2^{n/4}/\sqrt{n})$. Thus $B(h_n^\pi) = \Theta(\alpha^{n/3})$.

127. (The permutation $\pi = (3, 5, 7, \ldots, 2n' - 1, n, n - 1, n - 2, \ldots, 2n', 2n' - 2, \ldots, 4, 2, 1)$, $n' = \lfloor 2n/5 \rfloor$, turns out to be optimum for h_n when $12 < n \leq 24$; but it gives $B(h_{100}^\pi) = 1{,}366{,}282{,}025$. Sifting does much better, as shown in answer 152; but still better permutations almost surely exist.)

128. Consider, for example, $M_3(x_4, x_2, x_7; x_6, x_1, x_8, x_3, x_9, x_{11}, x_5, x_{10})$. The first m variables $\{x_4, x_2, x_7\}$ are called "address bits"; the other 2^m are called "targets." The subfunctions corresponding to $x_1 = c_1, \ldots, x_k = c_k$ can be described by slates of options analogous to (96). For example, when $k = 2$ there are three slates $[x_6, 0, x_9, x_{11}]$, $[x_6, 1, x_9, x_{11}]$, $[x_8, x_3, x_5, x_{10}]$, where the result is obtained by using $(x_4 x_7)_2$ to select the appropriate component. Only the third of these depends on x_3; hence $q_2 = 3$ and $b_2 = 1$. When $k = 6$ the slates are $[0, 0]$, $[0, 1]$, $[1, 0]$, $[1, 1]$, $[x_8, 0]$, $[x_8, 1]$, $[x_9, x_{11}]$, $[0, x_{10}]$, and $[1, x_{10}]$, with components selected by x_7; hence $q_6 = 9$ and $b_6 = 7$.

In general, if the variables $\{x_1, \ldots, x_k\}$ include a address bits and t targets, the slates will have $A = 2^{m-a}$ entries. Divide the set of all 2^m targets into 2^a subsets, depending on the known address bits, and suppose s_j of those subsets contain j known targets. (Thus $s_0 + s_1 + \cdots + s_A = 2^a$ and $s_1 + 2s_2 + \cdots + As_A = t$. We have $(s_0, \ldots, s_4) = (1, 1, 0, 0, 0)$ when $k = 2$ and $a = t = 1$ in the example above; and $(s_0, s_1, s_2) = (1, 2, 1)$ when $k = 6$, $a = 2$, $t = 4$.) Then the total number of slates, q_k, is $2^0 s_0 + 2^1 s_1 + \cdots + 2^{A-1} s_{A-1} + 2^A [s_A > 0]$. If x_{k+1} is an address bit, the number b_k of slates that depend on x_{k+1} is $q_k - 2^{A/2} [s_A > 0]$. Otherwise $b_k = 2^c$, where c is the number of constants that appear in the slates containing target x_{k+1}.

129. (Solution by M. Sauerhoff; see I. Wegener, *Branching Programs* (2000), Theorem 6.2.13.) Since $P_m(x_1, \ldots, x_{m^2}) = Q_m(x_1, \ldots, x_{m^2}) \wedge S_m(x_1, \ldots, x_{m^2})$ and $B(S_m) = m^3 + 2$, we have $B(P_m^\pi) \le (m^3 + 2)B(Q_m^\pi)$. Apply Theorem K.

(A stronger lower bound should be possible, because Q_m seems to have *larger* BDDs than P_m. For example, when $m = 5$ the permutation $(1\pi, \ldots, 25\pi) = (3, 1, 5, 7, 9, 2, 4, 6, 8, 10, 11, 12, 13, 14, 15, 16, 20, 23, 17, 21, 19, 18, 22, 24, 25)$ is optimum for Q_5; but $B(Q_5^\pi) = 535$, while $B(P_5) = 229$.)

130. (a) Each path that starts at the root of the BDD and takes s HI branches and t LO branches defines a subfunction that corresponds to graphs in which s adjacencies are forced and t are forbidden. We shall show that these $\binom{s+t}{s}$ subfunctions are distinct.

If subfunctions g and h correspond to different paths, we can find k vertices W with the following properties: (i) W contains vertices w and w' with $w - w'$ forced in g and forbidden in h. (ii) No adjacencies between vertices of W are forced in h or forbidden in g. (iii) If $u \in W$ and $v \notin W$ and $u - v$ is forced in h, then $u = w$ or $u = w'$. (These conditions make at most $2s + t = m - k$ vertices ineligible to be in W.) We can set the remaining variables so that $u - v$ if and only if $\{u, v\} \subseteq W$, whenever adjacency is neither forced nor forbidden. This assignment makes $g = 1$, $h = 0$.

(b) Consider the subfunction of $C_{m, \lceil m/2 \rceil}$ in which vertices $\{1, \ldots, k\}$ are required to be isolated, but $u - v$ whenever $k < u \le \lceil m/2 \rceil < v \le m$. Then a k-clique on the $\lfloor m/2 \rfloor$ vertices $\{\lceil m/2 \rceil + 1, \ldots, m\}$ is equivalent to an $\lceil m/2 \rceil$-clique on $\{1, \ldots, m\}$. In other words, this subfunction of $C_{m, \lceil m/2 \rceil}$ is $C_{\lfloor m/2 \rfloor, k}$.

Now chose $k \approx \sqrt{m/3}$ and apply (a). [I. Wegener, *JACM* **35** (1988), 461–471.]

131. (a) The profile can be shown to be $(1, 1, 2, 4, \ldots, 2^{q-1}, (p-2) \times (2^q - 1, q \times 2^{q-1}), 2^q - 1, 2^{q-1}, \ldots, 4, 2, 1, 2)$, where $r \times b$ denotes the r-fold repetition of b. Hence the total size is $(pq + 2p - 2q + 2)2^{q-1} - p + 2$.

(b) With the ordering $x_1, x_2, \ldots, x_p, y_{11}, y_{21}, \ldots, y_{p1}, \ldots, y_{1q}, y_{2q}, \ldots, y_{pq}$, the profile comes to $(1, 2, 4, \ldots, 2^{p-1}, (q-1)p \times (2^{p-1}), 2^{p-1}, \ldots, 4, 2, 1, 2)$, making the total size $(pq - p + 4)2^{p-1}$.

(c) Suppose exactly $m = \lfloor \min(p, q)/2 \rfloor$ x's occur among the first k variables in some ordering; we may assume that they are $\{x_1, \ldots, x_m\}$. Consider the 2^m paths in the QDD for C such that $x_j = \bar{x}_{m+j}$ for $1 \le j \le p - m$ and $y_{ij} = [i = j$ or $i = j + m$ or $j > m]$. These paths must pass through distinct nodes on level k. Hence $q_k \ge 2^m$; use (85). [See M. Nikolskaia and L. Nikolskaia, *Theor. Comp. Sci.* **255** (2001), 615–625.]

Optimum orderings for $(p, q) = (4, 4)$, $(4, 5)$, and $(5, 4)$, via exercise 138, are:

$$x_1 y_{11} x_2 y_{21} x_3 y_{31} y_{41} y_{12} y_{22} y_{32} y_{42} y_{13} y_{23} y_{33} y_{43} y_{14} y_{24} y_{34} y_{44} x_4 \text{ (size 108);}$$
$$x_1 y_{11} x_2 y_{21} x_3 y_{31} y_{41} y_{12} y_{22} y_{32} y_{42} y_{13} y_{23} y_{33} y_{43} y_{14} y_{24} y_{34} y_{44} y_{15} y_{25} y_{35} y_{45} x_4 \text{ (size 140);}$$
$$x_1 y_{11} x_2 y_{21} y_{12} y_{22} y_{13} y_{23} y_{14} y_{24} x_3 y_{31} y_{32} y_{33} y_{34} x_4 y_{41} y_{42} y_{51} y_{52} y_{43} y_{53} y_{44} y_{54} x_5 \text{ (size 167).}$$

132. There are 616,126 essentially different classes of 5-variable functions, by Table 7.1.1–5. The maximum $B_{\min}(f)$, 17, is attained by 38 of those classes. Three classes have the property that $B(f^\pi) = 17$ for *all* permutations π; one such example, $((x_2 \oplus x_4 \oplus (x_1 \wedge (x_3 \vee \bar{x}_4))) \wedge ((x_2 \oplus x_5) \vee (x_3 \oplus x_4))) \oplus (x_5 \wedge (x_3 \oplus (x_1 \vee \bar{x}_2)))$, has the interesting symmetries $f(x_1, x_2, x_3, x_4, x_5) = f(\bar{x}_2, \bar{x}_3, \bar{x}_4, \bar{x}_1, \bar{x}_5) = f(x_2, \bar{x}_5, x_1, x_3, \bar{x}_4)$.

Incidentally, the maximum difference $B_{\max}(f) - B_{\min}(f) = 10$ occurs only in the "junction function" class $x_1? x_2: x_3? x_4: x_5$, when $B_{\min} = 7$ and $B_{\max} = 17$.

(When $n = 4$ there are 222 classes; and $B_{\min}(f) = 10$ in 25 of them, including S_2 and $S_{2,4}$. The class exemplified by truth table `16ad` is uniquely hardest, in the sense that $B_{\min}(f) = 10$ and most of the 24 permutations give $B(f^\pi) = 11$.)

133. Represent each subset $X \subseteq \{1, \ldots, n\}$ by the n-bit integer $i(X) = \sum_{x \in X} 2^{x-1}$, and let $b_{i(X),x}$ be the weight of the edge between X and $X \cup x$. Set $c_0 \leftarrow 0$, and for $1 \le i < 2^n$ set $c_i \leftarrow \min\{c_{i \oplus j} + b_{i \oplus j, x} \mid j = 2^{x-1}$ and $i \,\&\, j \ne 0\}$. Then $B_{\min}(f) = c_{2^n - 1} + 2$, and an optimum ordering can be found by remembering which $x = x(i)$ minimizes each c_i. For $B_{\max}$, replace 'min' by 'max' in this recipe.

134.

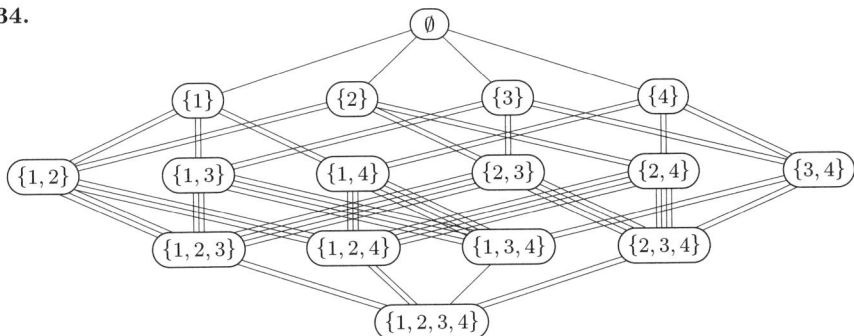

The maximum profile, $(1, 2, 4, 2, 2)$, occurs on paths such as $\emptyset \to \{2\} \to \{2, 3\} \to \{2, 3, 4\} \to \{1, 2, 3, 4\}$. The minimum profile, $(1, 2, 2, 1, 2)$, occurs only on the paths $\emptyset \to (\{3\}$ or $\{4\}) \to \{3, 4\} \to \{1, 3, 4\} \to \{1, 2, 3, 4\}$. (Five of the 24 possible paths have the profile $(1, 2, 3, 2, 2)$ and are unimprovable by sifting on any variable.)

135. Let $\theta_0 = 1$, $\theta_1 = x_1$, $\theta_2 = x_1 \wedge x_2$, and $\theta_n = x_n? \,\theta_{n-1} : \theta_{n-3}$ for $n \ge 3$. One can prove that, when $n \ge 4$, $B(\theta_n^\pi) = n + 2$ if and only if $(n\pi, \ldots, 1\pi) = (1, \ldots, n)$. The key fact is that if $k < n$ and $n \ge 5$, the subfunctions obtained by setting $x_k \leftarrow 0$ or $x_k \leftarrow 1$ are distinct, and they both depend on the variables $\{x_1, \ldots, x_{k-1}, x_{k+1}, \ldots, x_n\}$, except that the subfunction for $x_{n-1} \leftarrow 0$ does not depend on x_{n-2}. Thus the weights $\{x_k\} \to \{x_k, x_l\}$ in the master profile chart are 2 except when $k = n$ or $(k, l) = (n-1, n-2)$. Below $\{x_{n-1}, x_{n-2}\}$ there are three subfunctions, namely $x_n? \,\theta_{n-4} : \theta_{n-3}$, $x_n? \,\theta_{n-5} : \theta_{n-3}$, and θ_{n-3}; all of them depend on $\{x_1, \ldots, x_{n-3}\}$, and two of them on x_n.

136. Let $n = 2n' - 1$ and $m = 2m' - 1$. The inputs form an $m \times n$ matrix, and we're computing the median of m row-medians. Let V_i be the variables in row i. If X is a subset of the mn variables, let $X_i = X \cap V_i$ and $r_i = |X_i|$. Subfunctions of type $(s_1, \ldots, s_m)$ arise when exactly s_i elements of X_i are set to 1; these subfunctions are

$$\langle S_1 S_2 \ldots S_m \rangle, \qquad \text{where } S_i = S_{\ge n' - s_i}(V_i \setminus X_i) \text{ and } 0 \le s_i \le r_i \text{ for } 1 \le i \le m.$$

When $x \notin X$, we want to count how many of these subfunctions depend on x. By symmetry we may assume that $x = x_{mn}$. Notice that the symmetric threshold function $S_{\ge t}(x_1, \ldots, x_n)$ equals 0 if $t > n$, or 1 if $t \le 0$; it depends on all n variables if $1 \le t \le n$. In particular, S_m depends on x for exactly $r_m \$ n = \min(r_m + 1, n - r_m)$ choices of s_m.

Let $a_j = \sum_{i=1}^{m-1}[r_i = j]$ for $0 \le j \le n$. Then a_n of the functions $\{S_1, \ldots, S_{m-1}\}$ are constant, and $a_{n-1} + \cdots + a_{n'}$ of them might or might not be constant. Choosing c_i to be nonconstant gives us $(r_m \$ n)((a_n + a_{n-1} + \cdots + a_{n'} - c_{n-1} - \cdots - c_{n'})\$ m)$ times

$$\binom{a_{n-1}}{c_{n-1}} \cdots \binom{a_{n'}}{c_{n'}} 1^{a_0} 2^{a_1} \ldots (n')^{a_{n'-1}} (n'-1)^{c_{n'}} (n'-2)^{c_{n'+1}} \ldots 1^{c_{n-1}}$$

distinct subfunctions that depend on x. Summing over $\{c_{n-1}, \ldots, c_{n'}\}$ gives the answer.

When variables have the natural row-by-row order, these formulas apply with $r_m = k \bmod n$, $a_n = \lfloor k/n \rfloor$, $a_0 = m - 1 - a_n$. The profile element b_k for $0 \le k < mn$ is therefore $(\lfloor k/n \rfloor \$ m)((k \bmod n)\$ n)$, and we have $\sum_{k=0}^{mn} b_k = (m'n')^2 + 2$. This ordering is optimum, although no easy proof is apparent; for example, some orderings can decrease b_{n+2} or b_{2n-2} from 4 to 3 while increasing b_k for other k.

Every path from top to bottom of the master chart can be represented as $\alpha_0 \to \alpha_1 \to \cdots \to \alpha_{mn}$, where each α_j is a string $r_{j1} \ldots r_{jm}$ with $0 \le r_{j1} \le \cdots \le r_{jm} \le n$, $r_{j1} + \cdots + r_{jm} = j$, one coordinate increasing at each step. For example, one path when $m = 5$ and $n = 3$ is $00000 \to 00001 \to 00011 \to 00111 \to 00112 \to 00122 \to 00123 \to 01123 \to 11123 \to 11223 \to 12223 \to 12233 \to 12333 \to 22333 \to 23333 \to 33333$. We can convert this path to the "natural" path by a series of steps that don't increase the total edge weight, as follows: In the initial segment up to the first time $r_{jm} = n$, do all transitions on the rightmost coordinate first. (Thus the first steps of the example path would become $00000 \to 00001 \to 00002 \to 00003 \to 00013 \to 00123$.) Then in the final segment after the last time $r_{j1} = 0$, do all transitions on the leftmost coordinate last. (The final steps would thereby become $01123 \to 01223 \to 02223 \to 02233 \to 02333 \to 03333 \to 13333 \to 23333 \to 33333$.) Then, after the first n steps, normalize the second-last coordinates in a similar fashion ($00003 \to 00013 \to 00023 \to 00033 \to 00133 \to 01133 \to 01233 \to 02233$); and before the last n steps, normalize the second coordinates ($00133 \to 00233 \to 00333 \to 01333 \to 02333 \to 03333$). Et cetera.

[This back-and-forth proof technique was inspired by the paper of Bollig and Wegener cited below. Can every nonoptimal ordering be improved by merely sifting?]

137. If we add a clique of c new vertices and $\binom{c}{2}$ new edges, the cost of the optimum arrangement increases by $\binom{c+1}{3}$. So we may assume that the given graph has m edges and n vertices $\{1, \ldots, n\}$, where m and n are odd and sufficiently large. The corresponding function f, which depends on $mn + m + 1$ variables x_{ij} and s_k for $1 \le i \le m$, $1 \le j \le n$, and $0 \le k \le m$, is $J(s_0, s_1, \ldots, s_m; h, g_1, \ldots, g_m)$, where $g_i = (x_{iu_i} \oplus x_{iv_i}) \wedge \bigwedge \{x_{iw} \mid w \notin \{u_i, v_i\}\}$ when the ith edge is $u_i \!\!-\!\! v_i$, and where $h = \langle\langle x_{11} \ldots x_{m1}\rangle \ldots \langle x_{1n} \ldots x_{mn}\rangle\rangle$ is the transpose of the function in exercise 136.

One can show that $B_{\min}(f) = \min_\pi \sum_{u-v} |u\pi - v\pi| + (\frac{m+1}{2})^2 (\frac{n+1}{2})^2 + mn + m + 2$; the optimum ordering uses $(\frac{m+1}{2})^2(\frac{n+1}{2})^2$ nodes for h, $n + |u_i\pi - v_i\pi|$ nodes for g_i, one node for each s_k, and two sink nodes, minus one node that is shared between h and some g_i. [See B. Bollig and I. Wegener, *IEEE Trans.* **C-45** (1996), 993–1002.]

138. (a) Let $X_k = \{x_1, \ldots, x_k\}$. The QDD nodes at depth k represent the subfunctions that can arise when constants replace the variables of X_k. We can add an n-bit field DEP to each node, to specify exactly which variables of $X_n \setminus X_k$ it depends on. For example, the QDD for f in (92) has the following subfunctions and DEPs:

depth 0: 0011001001110010 [1111];

depth 1: 00110010 [0111], 01110010 [0111];

depth 2: 0010 [0011], 0011 [0010], 0111 [0011];

depth 3: 00 [0000], 01 [0001], 10 [0001], 11 [0000].

An examination of all DEP fields at depth k tells us the master profile weights between X_k and $X_k \cup x_l$, for $0 \le k < l \le n$.

(b) Represent the nodes at depth k as triples $N_{kp} = (l_{kp}, h_{kp}, d_{kp})$ for $0 \le p < q_k$, where (l_{kp}, h_{kp}) are the (LO, HI) pointers and d_{kp} records the DEP bits. If $k < n$, these nodes branch on x_{k+1}, so we have $0 \le l_{kp}, h_{kp} < q_{k+1}$; but if $k = n$, we have

$l_{n0} = h_{n0} = 0$ and $l_{n1} = h_{n1} = 1$ to represent $\boxed{\perp}$ and $\boxed{\top}$. We define

$$d_{kp} = \sum \{2^{t-k-1} \mid N_{kp} \text{ depends on } x_t\};$$

hence $0 \le d_{kp} < 2^{n-k}$. For example, the QDD (82) is equivalent to $N_{00} = (0,1,7)$; $N_{10} = (0,1,3)$, $N_{11} = (1,2,3)$; $N_{20} = (0,0,0)$, $N_{21} = (0,1,1)$, $N_{22} = (1,1,0)$; $N_{30} = (0,0,0)$, $N_{31} = (1,1,0)$.

To jump up from depth b to depth a, we essentially make two copies of the nodes at depths $b-1$, $b-2$, ..., a, one for the case $x_{b+1} = 0$ and one for the case $x_{b+1} = 1$. Those copies are moved down to depths b, $b-1$, ..., $a+1$, and reduced to eliminate duplicates. Then every original node at depth a is replaced by a node that branches on x_{b+1}; its LO and HI fields point respectively to the 0-copy and the 1-copy of the original.

This process involves some simple (but cool) list processing to update DEPs while bucket sorting: Nodes are unpacked into a work area consisting of auxiliary arrays r, s, t, u, and v, initially zero. Instead of using l_{kp} and h_{kp} for LO and HI, we store HI in cell u_p of the work area, and we let v_p link to the previous node (if any) with the same LO field; furthermore we make s_l point to the last node (if any) for which LO = l. The algorithm below uses UNPACK(p,l,h) as an abbreviation for "$u_p \leftarrow h$, $v_p \leftarrow s_l$, $s_l \leftarrow p+1$."

When nodes of depth k have been unpacked in this way to arrays s, u, and v, the following subroutine ELIM(k) packs them back into the main QDD structure with duplicates eliminated. It also sets r_p to the new address of node p.

E1. [Loop on l.] Set $q \leftarrow 0$ and $t_h \leftarrow 0$ for $0 \le h < q_{k+1}$. Do step E2 for $0 \le l < q_{k+1}$. Then set $q_k \leftarrow q$ and terminate.

E2. [Loop on p.] Set $p \leftarrow s_l$ and $s_l \leftarrow 0$. While $p > 0$, do step E3 and set $p \leftarrow v_{p-1}$. Then resume step E1.

E3. [Pack node $p-1$.] Set $h \leftarrow u_{p-1}$. (The unpacked node has (LO, HI) = (l,h).) If $t_h \ne 0$ and $l_{k(t_h-1)} = l$, set $r_{p-1} \leftarrow t_h - 1$. Otherwise set $l_{kq} \leftarrow l$, $h_{kq} \leftarrow h$, $d_{kq} \leftarrow ((d_{(k+1)l} \mid d_{(k+1)h}) \ll 1) + [l \ne h]$, $r_{p-1} \leftarrow q$, $q \leftarrow q+1$, $t_h \leftarrow q$. Resume step E2. ∎

We can now use ELIM to jump up from b to a. (i) For $k = b-1$, $b-2$, ..., a, do the following steps: For $0 \le p < q_k$, set $l \leftarrow l_{kp}$, $h \leftarrow h_{kp}$; if $k = b-1$, UNPACK$(2p, l_{bl}, h_{bl})$ and UNPACK$(2p+1, l_{bh}, h_{bh})$, otherwise UNPACK$(2p, r_{2l}, r_{2h})$ and UNPACK$(2p+1, r_{2l+1}, r_{2h+1})$ (thereby making two copies of N_{kp} in the work area). Then ELIM$(k+1)$. (ii) For $0 \le p < q_a$, UNPACK(p, r_{2p}, r_{2p+1}). Then ELIM(a). (iii) If $a > 0$, set $l \leftarrow l_{(a-1)p}$, $h \leftarrow h_{(a-1)p}$, $l_{(a-1)p} \leftarrow r_l$, $h_{(a-1)p} \leftarrow r_h$, for $0 \le p < q_{a-1}$.

This jump-up procedure garbles the DEP fields above depth a, because the variables have been reordered. But we'll use it only when those fields are no longer needed.

(c) By induction, the first 2^{n-2} steps account for all subsets that do not contain n; then comes a jump-up from $n-1$ to 0, and the remaining steps account for all subsets that do contain n.

(d) Start by setting $y_k \leftarrow k$ and $w_k \leftarrow 2^k - 1$ for $0 \le k < n$. In the following algorithm, the y array represents the current variable ordering, and the bitmap $w_k = \sum \{2^{y_j} \mid 0 \le j < k\}$ represents the set of variables on the top k levels.

We augment the subroutine ELIM(k) so that it also computes the desired edge weights of the master profile: Counters c_j are initially 0 for $0 \le j < n-k$; after setting d_{kq} in step E3, we set $c_j \leftarrow c_j + 1$ for each j such that $2^j \subseteq d_{kq}$; finally we set $b_{w_k, y_{k+j}+1} \leftarrow c_j$ for $0 \le j < n-k$, using the notation of answer 133. [To speed this up, we could count bytes not bits, increasing $c_{j,(d_{kq} \gg 8j) \& \#\text{ff}}$ by 1 for $0 \le j < (n-k)/8$.]

We initialize the DEP fields by doing the following for $k = n - 1, n - 2, \ldots, 0$: UNPACK$(p, l_{kp}, h_{kp})$ for $0 \le p < q_k$; ELIM(k); if $k > 0$, set $l \leftarrow l_{(k-1)p}$, $h \leftarrow h_{(k-1)p}$, $l_{(k-1)p} \leftarrow r_l$, and $h_{(k-1)p} \leftarrow r_h$, for $0 \le p < q_{k-1}$.

The main loop of the algorithm now does the following for $1 \le i < 2^{n-1}$: Set $a \leftarrow \nu i - 1$ and $b \leftarrow \nu i + \rho i$. Set $(y_a, \ldots, y_b) \leftarrow (y_b, y_a, \ldots, y_{b-1})$ and $(w_{a+1}, \ldots, w_b) \leftarrow (2^{y_b} + w_a, \ldots, 2^{y_b} + w_{b-1})$. Jump up from b to a with the procedure of part (b); but use the original (non-augmented) ELIM routine for ELIM(a) in step (ii).

(e) The space required for nodes at depth k is at most $Q_k = \min(2^k, 2^{2^{n-k}})$; we also need space for $2\max(Q_1, \ldots, Q_n)$ elements in arrays r, u, v, plus $\max(Q_1, \ldots, Q_n)$ elements in arrays s and t. So the total is dominated by $O(2^n n)$ for the outputs $b_{w,x}$.

Subroutine ELIM(k) is called $\binom{n}{k}$ times in augmented form, for $0 \le k < n$, and $\binom{n-1}{k+1}$ times non-augmented. Its running time in either case is $O(q_k(n-k))$. Thus the total comes to $O(\sum_k \binom{n}{k} 2^k (n-k)) = O(3^n n)$, and it will be substantially less if the QDD never gets large. (For example, it's $O((1 + \sqrt{2})^n n)$ for the function h_n.)

[The first exact algorithm to determine optimum variable ordering in a BDD was introduced by S. J. Friedman and K. J. Supowit, *IEEE Trans.* **C-39** (1990), 710–713. They used extended truth tables instead of QDDs, obtaining a method for $m = 1$ that required $\Theta(3^n/\sqrt{n})$ space and $\Theta(3^n n^2)$ time, improvable to $\Theta(3^n n)$.]

139. The same algorithm applies, almost unchanged: Consider all QDD nodes that branch on x_a to be at level 0, and all nodes that branch on x_{b+1} to be sinks. Thus we do 2^{b-a} jump-ups, not 2^{n-1}. (The algorithm doesn't rely on the assumptions that $q_0 = 1$ and $q_n = 2$, except in the space and time analyses of part (e).)

140. We can find shortest paths in a network without knowing the network in advance, by generating vertices and arcs "on the fly" as needed. Section 7.3 points out that the distance $d(X, Y)$ of each arc $X \to Y$ can be changed to $d'(X, Y) = d(X, Y) - l(X) + l(Y)$ for any function $l(X)$, without changing the shortest paths. If the revised distances d' are nonnegative, $l(X)$ is a lower bound on the distance from X to the goal; the trick is to find a good lower bound that focuses the search yet isn't difficult to compute.

If $|X| = l$, and if a QDD for f with X on its top l levels has q nonconstant nodes on the next level, then $l(X) = \max(q, n - l)$ is a suitable lower bound for the $B_{\min}$ problem. [See R. Drechsler, N. Drechsler, and W. Günther, *ACM/IEEE Design Automation Conf.* **35** (1998), 200–205.] However, a stronger lower bound is needed to make this approach competitive with the algorithm of exercise 138, unless f has a relatively short BDD that cannot be attained in very many ways.

141. False. Consider $g(x_1 \vee \cdots \vee x_6, x_7 \vee \cdots \vee x_{12}, (x_{13} \vee \cdots \vee x_{16}) \oplus x_{18}, x_{17}, x_{19} \vee \cdots \vee x_{22})$, where $g(y_1, \ldots, y_5) = ((((\bar{y}_1 \vee y_5) \wedge y_4) \oplus y_3) \wedge ((y_1 \wedge y_2) \oplus y_4 \oplus y_5)) \oplus y_5$. Then $B(g) = 40 = B_{\min}(g)$ can't be achieved with $\{x_{13}, \ldots, x_{16}, x_{18}\}$ consecutive. [M. Teslenko, A. Martinelli, and E. Dubrova, *IEEE Trans.* **C-54** (2005), 236–237.]

142. (a) Suppose m is odd. The subfunctions that arise after $(x_1, \ldots, x_{m+1})$ are known are $[w_{m+2} x_{m+2} + \cdots + w_n x_n > 2^{m-1} m - 2^{m-2} - t]$, where $0 \le t \le 2^m$. The subcases $x_{m+2} + \cdots + x_n = (m-1)/2$ show that at least $\binom{m-1}{(m-1)/2}$ of these subfunctions differ.

But organ-pipe order, $\langle x_1 x_2^{2^m-1} x_3^1 x_4^{2^m-2} x_5^2 \ldots x_{n-2}^{2^m-2^{m-2}} x_{n-1}^{2^{m-2}} x_n^{2^m-1} \rangle$, is much better: Let $t_k = x_1 + (2^m - 1)x_2 + x_3 + \cdots + (2^m - 2^{k-1})x_{2k} + 2^{k-1} x_{2k+1}$, for $1 \le k < m-1$. The remaining subfunction depends on at most $2k + 2$ different values, $\lceil t_k/2^k \rceil$.

(b) Let $n = 1 + 4m^2$. The variables are x_0 and x_{ij} for $0 \le i, j < 2m$; the weights are $w_0 = 1$ and $w_{ij} = 2^i + 2^{2m+1+j} m$. Let X_l be the first l variables in some ordering, and suppose X_l includes elements in i_l rows and j_l columns of the matrix (x_{ij}). If $\max(i_l, j_l) = m$, we will prove that $q_l \geq 2^m$; hence $B(f) > 2^m$ by (85).

Let I and J be subsets of $\{1, \ldots, 2m\}$ with $|I| = |J| = m$ and $X_l \subseteq x_0 \cup \{x_{ij} \mid i \in I, j \in J\}$; let I' and J' be the complementary subsets. Choose m elements $X' \subseteq X_l \setminus x_0$, in different rows (or, if $i_l < m$, in different columns). Consider 2^m paths in the QDD defined as follows: $x_0 = 0$, and $x_{ij} = 0$ if $x_{ij} \in X_l \setminus X'$; also $x_{i'j} = x_{ij'} = \bar{x}_{i'j'} = \bar{x}_{ij}$ for $i \in I$, $j \in J$, where $i \leftrightarrow i'$ and $j \leftrightarrow j'$ are matchings between $I \leftrightarrow I'$ and $J \leftrightarrow J'$. Then there are 2^m distinct values $t = \sum_{i \in I, j \in J} w_{ij} x_{ij}$; but $\sum_{0 \leq i, j < 2m} w_{ij} x_{ij} = (2^{2m} - 1)(1 + 2^{2m+1} m)$ on each path. The paths must pass through distinct nodes on level l. Otherwise, if $t \neq t'$, one of the lower subpaths would lead to $\boxed{\bot}$, the other to $\boxed{\top}$.

[These results are due to K. Hosaka, Y. Takenaga, T. Kaneda, and S. Yajima, *Theoretical Comp. Sci.* **180** (1997), 47–60, who also proved that $|Q(f) - Q(f^R)| < n$. Do self-dual threshold functions always satisfy also $|B(f) - B(f^R)| < n$?]

143. In fact, the algorithm of exercises 133 and 138 proves that organ-pipe order is best for these weights: (1, 1023, 1, 1022, 2, 1020, 4, 1016, 8, 1008, 16, 992, 32, 960, 64, 896, 128, 768, 256, 512) gives the profile (1, 2, 2, 4, 3, 6, 4, 8, 5, 10, 4, 8, 3, 6, 2, 4, 1, 2, 2, 1, 2) and $B(f) = 80$. The worst ordering, (1022, 896, 512, 64, 8, 1, 4, 32, 1008, 1020, 768, 992, 1016, 1023, 960, 256, 128, 16, 2, 1), makes $B(f) = 1913$.

(One might think that properties of binary notation are crucial to this example. But $\langle x_1 x_2 x_3^2 x_4^4 x_5^8 x_6^{16} x_7^{31} x_8^{60} x_9^{116} x_{10}^{224} x_{11}^{224} x_{12}^{448} x_{13}^{564} x_{14}^{620} x_{15}^{649} x_{16}^{664} x_{17}^{672} x_{18}^{676} x_{19}^{678} x_{20}^{679} \rangle$ is actually the same function, by exercise 7.1.1–103(!).)

144. (5, 7, 7, 10, 6, 9, 5, 4, 2); the QDD-not-BDD nodes correspond to f_1, f_2, f_3, 0, 1.

145. $B_{\min} = 31$ is attained in (36). The worst ordering for $(x_3 x_2 x_1 x_0)_2 + (y_3 y_2 y_1 y_0)_2$ is y_0, y_1, y_2, y_3, x_2, x_1, x_0, x_3, making $B_{\max} = 107$. Incidentally, the worst ordering for the 24 inputs of 12-bit addition, $(x_{11} \ldots x_0)_2 + (y_{11} \ldots y_0)_2$, turns out to be y_0, y_1, $\ldots$, y_{11}, x_{10}, x_8, x_6, x_4, x_3, x_5, x_2, x_7, x_1, x_9, x_0, x_{11}, yielding $B_{\max} = 39111$.

[B. Bollig, N. Range, and I. Wegener, *Lecture Notes in Comp. Sci.* **4910** (2008), 174–185, have proved that $B_{\min} = 9n - 5$ for addition of two n-bit numbers whenever $n > 1$, and also that $B_{\min}(M_m) = 2n - 2m + 1$ for the 2^m-way multiplexer.]

146. (a) Obviously $b_0 \leq q_0$; and if $q_0 = b_0 + a_0$, then $b_1 \leq 2b_0 + a_0 = b_0 + q_0$. Also $q_0 - b_0 = a_0 \leq b_1 + q_2 \leq q_2^2$, the number of strings of length 2 on a q_2-letter alphabet; similarly $b_0 + b_1 + q_2 \leq (b_1 + q_2)^2$. (The same relations hold between q_k, q_{k+2}, b_k, and b_{k+1}.)

(b) Let the subfunctions at level 2 have truth tables α_j for $1 \leq j \leq q_2$, and use them to construct beads $\beta_1, \ldots, \beta_{b_1}$ at level 1. Let $(\gamma_1, \ldots, \gamma_{q_2+b_1})$ be the truth tables $(\alpha_1 \alpha_1, \ldots, \alpha_{q_2} \alpha_{q_2}, \beta_1, \ldots, \beta_{b_1})$. If $b_0 \leq b_1/2$, let the functions at level 0 have truth tables $\{\beta_{2i-1} \beta_{2i} \mid 1 \leq i \leq b_0\} \cup \{\beta_j \beta_j \mid 2b_0 < j \leq b_1\} \cup \{\gamma_j \gamma_j \mid 1 \leq j \leq b_0 + q_0 - b_1\}$. Otherwise it's not difficult to define b_0 beads that include all the β's, and use them at level 0 together with the nonbeads $\{\gamma_j \gamma_j \mid 1 \leq j \leq q_0 - b_0\}$.

147. Before doing any reordering, we clear the cache and collect all garbage. The following algorithm interchanges levels $\textcircled{u} \leftrightarrow \textcircled{v}$ when $v = u + 1$. It works by creating linked lists of solitary, tangled, and hidden nodes, pointed to by variables S, T, and H (initially Λ), using auxiliary LINK fields that can be borrowed temporarily from the hash-table algorithm of the unique lists as they are being rebuilt.

T1. [Build S and T.] For each $\textcircled{u}$-node p, set $q \leftarrow \text{LO}(p)$, $r \leftarrow \text{HI}(p)$, and delete p from its hash table. If $\text{V}(q) \neq v$ and $\text{V}(r) \neq v$ (p is solitary), set $\text{LINK}(p) \leftarrow S$ and

$S \leftarrow p$. Otherwise (p is tangled), set $\mathtt{REF}(q) \leftarrow \mathtt{REF}(q) - 1$, $\mathtt{REF}(r) \leftarrow \mathtt{REF}(r) - 1$, $\mathtt{LINK}(p) \leftarrow T$, and $T \leftarrow p$.

T2. [Build H and move the visible nodes.] For each (v)-node p, set $q \leftarrow \mathtt{LO}(p)$, $r \leftarrow \mathtt{HI}(p)$, and delete p from its hash table. If $\mathtt{REF}(p) = 0$ (p is hidden), set $\mathtt{REF}(q) \leftarrow \mathtt{REF}(q) - 1$, $\mathtt{REF}(r) \leftarrow \mathtt{REF}(r) - 1$, $\mathtt{LINK}(p) \leftarrow H$, and $H \leftarrow p$; otherwise (p is visible) set $\mathtt{V}(p) \leftarrow u$ and $\mathrm{INSERT}(u, p)$.

T3. [Move the solitary nodes.] While $S \neq \Lambda$, set $p \leftarrow S$, $S \leftarrow \mathtt{LINK}(p)$, $\mathtt{V}(p) \leftarrow v$, and $\mathrm{INSERT}(v, p)$.

T4. [Transmogrify the tangled nodes.] While $T \neq \Lambda$, set $p \leftarrow T$, $T \leftarrow \mathtt{LINK}(p)$, and do the following: Set $q \leftarrow \mathtt{LO}(p)$, $r \leftarrow \mathtt{HI}(p)$. If $\mathtt{V}(q) > v$, set $q_0 \leftarrow q_1 \leftarrow q$; otherwise set $q_0 \leftarrow \mathtt{LO}(q)$ and $q_1 \leftarrow \mathtt{HI}(q)$. If $\mathtt{V}(r) > v$, set $r_0 \leftarrow r_1 \leftarrow r$; otherwise set $r_0 \leftarrow \mathtt{LO}(r)$ and $r_1 \leftarrow \mathtt{HI}(r)$. Then set $\mathtt{LO}(p) \leftarrow \mathrm{UNIQUE}(v, q_0, r_0)$, $\mathtt{HI}(p) \leftarrow \mathrm{UNIQUE}(v, q_1, r_1)$, and $\mathrm{INSERT}(u, p)$.

T5. [Kill the hidden nodes.] While $H \neq \Lambda$, set $p \leftarrow H$, $H \leftarrow \mathtt{LINK}(p)$, and recycle node p. (All of the remaining nodes are alive.) ∎

The subroutine $\mathrm{INSERT}(v, p)$ simply puts node p into x_v's unique table, using the key $(\mathtt{LO}(p), \mathtt{HI}(p))$; this key will not already be present. The subroutine UNIQUE in step T4 is like Algorithm U, but instead of using answer 82 it treats reference counts quite differently in steps U1 and U2: If U1 finds $p = q$, it *increases* $\mathtt{REF}(p)$ by 1; if U2 finds r, it simply sets $\mathtt{REF}(r) \leftarrow \mathtt{REF}(r) + 1$.

Internally, the branch variables retain their natural order $1, 2, \ldots, n$ from top to bottom. Mapping tables ρ and π represent the current permutation from the external user's point of view, with $\rho = \pi^-$; thus the user's variable x_v appears on level $v\pi - 1$, and node $\mathrm{UNIQUE}(v, p, q)$ on level $v - 1$ represents the user's function $(\bar{x}_{v\rho}? \ p: q)$. To maintain these mappings, set $j \leftarrow u\rho$, $k \leftarrow v\rho$, $u\rho \leftarrow k$, $v\rho \leftarrow j$, $j\pi \leftarrow v$, $k\pi \leftarrow u$.

148. False. For example, consider six sinks and nine source functions, with extended truth tables 1156, 2256, 3356, 4456, 5611, 5622, 5633, 5644, 5656. Eight of the nodes are tangled and one is visible, but none are hidden or solitary. There are 16 newbies: 15, 16, 25, 26, 35, 36, 45, 46, 51, 61, 52, 62, 53, 63, 54, 64. So the swap takes 15 nodes into 31. (We can use the nodes of $B(x_3 \oplus x_4, x_3 \oplus \bar{x}_4)$ for the sinks.)

149. The successive profiles are bounded by $(b_0, b_1, \ldots, b_n)$, $(b_0 + b_1, 2b_0, b_2, \ldots, b_n)$, $(b_0 + b_1, 2b_0 + b_2, 4b_0, b_3, \ldots, b_n)$, $\ldots$, $(2^0 b_0 + b_1, \ldots, 2^{k-2} b_0 + b_{k-1}, 2^{k-1} b_0, b_k, \ldots, b_n)$.

Similarly, we also have $B(f_1^\pi, \ldots, f_m^\pi) \leq B(f_1, \ldots, f_m) + 2(b_0 + \cdots + b_{k-1})$ in addition to Theorem J$^+$, because swaps contribute at most $2b_{k-1}, 2b_{k-2}, \ldots, 2b_0$ new nodes.

150. We may assume that $m = 1$, as in exercise 52. Suppose we want to jump x_k to the position that is jth in the ordering, where $j \neq k$. First compute the restrictions of f when $x_k = 0$ and $x_k = 1$ (see exercise 57); call them g and h. Then renumber the remaining variables: If $j < k$, change $(x_j, \ldots, x_{k-1})$ to $(x_{j+1}, \ldots, x_k)$; otherwise change $(x_{k+1}, \ldots, x_j)$ to $(x_k, \ldots, x_{j-1})$. Then compute $f \leftarrow (\bar{x}_j \wedge g) \vee (x_j \wedge h)$, using the linear-time variant of Algorithm S in exercise 72.

To show that this method has the desired running time, it suffices to prove the following: *Let $g(x_1, \ldots, x_n)$ and $h(x_1, \ldots, x_n)$ be functions such that $g(x) = 1$ implies $x_j = 0$ and $h(x) = 1$ implies $x_j = 1$. Then the meld $g \diamond h$ has at most twice as many nodes as $g \vee h$.* But this is almost obvious, when truth tables are considered: For example, if $n = 3$ and $j = 2$, the truth tables for g and h have the respective forms $ab00cd00$ and $00st00uv$. The beads β of $g \vee h$ on levels $< j$ correspond uniquely to the beads $\beta' \diamond \beta''$ of $g \diamond h$ on those levels, because $\beta = \beta' \vee \beta''$ can be "factored" in only one way by putting 0s in the appropriate places. And the beads β of $g \vee h$ on levels $\geq j$ correspond to at most two beads of $g \diamond h$, namely to $\beta \diamond \boxed{\perp}$ and/or $\boxed{\perp} \diamond \beta$.

[See P. Savický and I. Wegener, *Acta Informatica* **34** (1997), 245–256, Theorem 1.]

151. Set $t_k \leftarrow 0$ for $1 \leq k \leq n$, and make the swapping operation $x_{j-1} \leftrightarrow x_j$ also swap $t_{j-1} \leftrightarrow t_j$. Then set $k \leftarrow 1$ and do the following until $k > n$: If $t_k = 1$ set $k \leftarrow k+1$; otherwise set $t_k \leftarrow 1$ and sift x_k.

(This method repeatedly sifts on the topmost variable that hasn't yet been sifted. Researchers have tried fancier strategies, such as to sift the largest level first; but no such method has turned out to dominate the simple-minded approach proposed here.)

152. Applying Algorithm J as in answer 151 yields $B(h_{100}^\pi) = 1{,}382{,}685{,}050$ after 17,179 swaps, which is almost as good as the result of the "hand-tuned" permutation (95). Another sift brings the size down to 300,451,396; and further repetitions converge down to just 231,376,264 nodes, after a total of 232,951 swaps.

If the loops of steps J2 and J5 are aborted when $S > 1.05s$, the results are even better(!), although fewer swaps are made: 1,342,191,700 nodes after one sift reduce eventually to 208,478,228 after 139,245 total swaps. Moreover, Filip Stappers used sifting together with random swapping in September 2010 to get the value of $B(h_{100}^\pi)$ down to only 198,961,868, with the following "current champion" permutation π:

```
 3  4  6  8 10 12 14 16 18 20 22 24 27 28 30 32 35 37 39 41
43 45 47 49 51 53 54 83 85 98 99 100 79 77 81 75 73 95 71 97
69 96 57 91 67 59 65 60 63 62 64 61 66 87 58 68 56 94 93 70
92 72 90 74 76 78 80 89 88 86 84 82 55 52 50 48 46 44 42 40
38 36 34 33 31 29 26 25 23 21 19 17 15 13 11  9  7  5  1  2
```

Incidentally, if we sift the variables of h_{100} in order of profile size, so that x_{60} is sifted first, then x_{59}, x_{61}, x_{58}, x_{57}, x_{62}, x_{56}, etc. (wherever they currently happen to be), the resulting BDD turns out to have 2,196,768,534 nodes.

Simple "downhill swapping" instead of full sifting is of no use whatever for h_{100}: The $\binom{100}{2}$ swaps $x_1 \leftrightarrow x_2$, $x_3 \leftrightarrow x_1$, $x_3 \leftrightarrow x_2$, ..., $x_{100} \leftrightarrow x_1$, ..., $x_{100} \leftrightarrow x_{99}$ completely reverse the order of all variables without changing the BDD size at any step.

153. Each gate is easily synthesized using recursions like (55). About 1 megabyte of memory and 3.5 megamems of computation suffice to construct the entire BDD base of 8242 nodes. Using exercise 138 we may conclude that the ordering x_7, x_3, x_9, x_1, o_9, o_1, o_3, o_7, x_4, x_6, o_6, o_4, o_2, o_8, x_2, x_8, o_5, x_5 is optimum, and that $B_{\min}(y_1, \ldots, y_9) = 5308$.

Reordering of variables is *not* advisable for a problem such as this, since there are only 18 variables. For example, autosifting whenever the size doubles would require more than 100 megamems of work, just to reduce 8242 nodes to about 6400.

154. Yes: CA was moved between ID and OR at the last sifting step, and we can work backwards all the way to deduce that the first sift moved ME between MA and RI.

155. The author's best attempt for (a) is

```
ME NH VT MA CT RI NY DE NJ MD PA DC VA OH WV KY NC SC GA FL AL IN MI IA
IL MO TN AR MS TX LA CO WI KS SD ND NE OK WY MN ID MT NM AZ OR CA WA UT NV
```

giving $B(f_1^\pi) = 403$, $B(f_2^\pi) = 677$, $B(f_1^\pi, f_2^\pi) = 1073$; and for (b) the ordering

```
NH ME MA VT CT RI NY DE NJ MD PA VA DC OH WV KY TN NC SC GA FL AL IN MI
IL IA AR MO MS TX LA CO KS OK WI SD NE ND MN WY ID MT AZ NM UT OR CA WA NV
```

gives $B(f_1^\pi) = 352$, $B(f_2^\pi) = 702$, $B(f_1^\pi, f_2^\pi) = 1046$.

156. One might expect two "siftups" to be at least as good as a single sifting process that goes both up and down. But in fact, benchmark tests by R. Rudell show that siftup alone is definitely unsatisfactory. Occasional jump-downs are needed to compensate for variables that temporarily jump up, although their optimum final position lies below.

157. A careful study of answer 128 shows that we always improve the size when the first address bit that follows a target bit is jumped up past all targets. [But simple swaps are too weak. For example, $M_2(x_1, x_6; x_2, x_3, x_4, x_5)$ and $M_3(x_1, x_{10}, x_{11}; x_2, x_3, \ldots, x_9)$ are locally optimal under the swapping of $x_{j-1} \leftrightarrow x_j$ for any j.]

158. Consider first the case when $m = 1$ and $n = 3t - 1 \geq 5$. Then if $n\pi = k$, the number of nodes that branch on j is a_j if $j\pi < k$, b_j if $j\pi = k$, and a_{n+2-j} if $j\pi > k$, where

$$ a_j = j - 3 \max(j - 2t, 0), \qquad b_j = \min(j, t, n + 1 - j). $$

The cases with $\{x_1, \ldots, x_{n-1}\}$ consecutive are $k = 1$ and $B(f^\pi) = 3t^2 + 2$; $k = n$ and $B(f^\pi) = 3t^2 + 1$. But when $k = \lceil n/2 \rceil$ we have $B(f^\pi) = \lfloor 3t/2 \rfloor (\lceil 3t/2 \rceil - 1) + n - \lfloor t/2 \rfloor + 2$.

Similar calculations apply when $m > 1$: We have $B(f^\pi) > 6\binom{p/3}{2} + B(g^\pi)$ when π makes $\{x_1, \ldots, x_p\}$ consecutive, but

$$ B(f^\pi) \approx 2\binom{p/2}{2} + \tfrac{p}{3} B(g^\pi) $$

when π puts $\{x_{p+1}, \ldots, x_{p+m}\}$ in the middle. Since g is fixed, $pB(g^\pi) = O(n)$ as $n \to \infty$.

[If g is a function of the same kind, we obtain examples where symmetric variables within g are best split up, and so on. But no Boolean functions are known for which the optimum $B(f^\pi)$ is less than 3/4 of the best that is obtainable under the constraint that no blocks of symmetric variables are split. See D. Sieling, *Random Structures & Algorithms* **13** (1998), 49–70.]

159. The function is almost symmetric, so there are only nine possibilities. When the center element x is placed in position $(1, 2, \ldots, 9)$ from the top, the BDD size is respectively $(43, 43, 42, 39, 36, 33, 30, 28, 28)$.

160. (a) Compute $\bigwedge_{i=0}^{9} \bigwedge_{j=0}^{9} (\neg L_{ij}(X))$, a Boolean function of 64 variables — for example, by applying COMPOSE to the relatively simple L function of exercise 159, 100 times. With the author's experimental programs, about 320 megamems and 35 megabytes are needed to find this BDD, which has 251,873 nodes with the normal ordering. Then Algorithm C quickly finds the desired answer: 21,929,490,122. (The number of 11×11 solutions, 5,530,201,631,127,973,447, can be found in the same way.)

(b) The generating function is $1 + 64z + 2016z^2 + 39740z^3 + \cdots + 80z^{45} + 8z^{46}$, and Algorithm B rapidly finds the eight solutions of weight 46. Three of them are distinct under chessboard symmetry; the most symmetric solution is shown as (A0) below.

(c) The BDD for $\bigwedge_{i=1}^{8} \bigwedge_{j=1}^{8} (\neg L_{ij}(X))$ has 305,507 nodes and 21,942,036,750 solutions. So there must be 12,546,628 wild ones.

(d) Now the generating function is $40z^{14} + 936z^{15} + 10500z^{16} + \cdots + 16z^{55} + z^{56}$; examples of weight 14 and 56 appear below as (A1) and (A2).

(e) Exactly 28 of weight 27 and 54 of weight 28, all tame; see (A3).

(f) There are respectively $(26260, 5, 347, 0, 122216)$ solutions, found with about $(228, 3, 32, 1, 283)$ megamems of calculation. Among the lightest and heaviest solutions to (1) are (A4) and (A5); the nicest solution to (2) is (A6); (A7) and (A9) solve (3) lightly and (5) heavily. Pattern (4), which is based on the binary representation of π, has no 8×8 predecessor; but it does, for example, have the 9×10 in (A8):

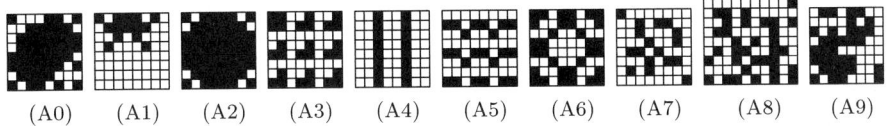

(A0) (A1) (A2) (A3) (A4) (A5) (A6) (A7) (A8) (A9)

161. (a) With the normal row-by-row ordering $(x_{11}, x_{12}, \ldots, x_{n(n-1)}, x_{nn})$, the BDD has 380,727 nodes and characterizes 4,782,725 solutions. The computational cost is about 2 gigamems, in 100 megabytes. (Similarly, the 29,305,144,137 still Lifes of size 10×10 can be enumerated with 14,492,923 nodes, after fewer than 50 gigamems.)

(b) This solution is essentially unique; see (B1) below. There's also a unique (and obvious) solution of weight 36.

(c) Now the BDD has 128 variables, with the ordering $(x_{11}, y_{11}, \ldots, x_{nn}, y_{nn})$. We could first set up BDDs for $[L(X) = Y]$ and $[L(Y) = X]$, then intersect them; but that turns out to be a bad idea, requiring some 36 million nodes even in the 7×7 case. Much better is to apply the constraints $L_{ij}(X) = y_{ij}$ and $L_{ij}(Y) = x_{ij}$ row by row, and also to add the lexicographic constraint $X < Y$ so that still Lifes are ruled out early. The computation can then be completed with about 20 gigamems and 1.6 gigabytes; there are 978,563 nodes and 582,769 solutions.

(d) Again the solution is unique, up to rotation; see the "spark plug" (B2) $\leftrightarrow$ (B3). (And (B4) $\leftrightarrow$ (B5) is the unique 7×7 flip-flop of constant weight 26. Life is astonishing.)

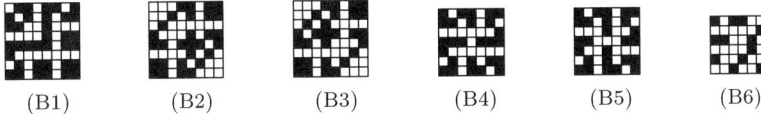

(B1)   (B2)   (B3)   (B4)   (B5)   (B6)

162. Let $T(X) = [X \text{ is tame}]$ and $E_k(X) = [X \text{ escapes after } k \text{ steps}]$. We can compute the BDD for each E_k by using the recurrence

$$E_1(X) = \neg T(X); \qquad E_{k+1}(X) = \exists Y (T(X) \wedge [L(X) = Y] \wedge E_k(Y)).$$

(Here $\exists Y$ stands for $\exists y_{11} \exists y_{12} \cdots \exists y_{66}$. As noted in answer 103, this recurrence turns out to be much more efficient than the rule $E_{k+1} = T(X) \wedge E_k(L_{11}(X), \ldots, L_{66}(X))$, although the latter looks more "elegant.") The number of solutions, $|E_k|$, is found to be $(806544 \cdot 2^{16}, 657527179 \cdot 2^4, 2105885159, 763710262, 331054880, 201618308, 126169394, 86820176, 63027572, 41338572, 30298840, 17474640, 9797472, 5258660, 3058696, 1416132, 523776, 204192, 176520, 62456, 13648, 2776, 2256, 440, 104, 0)$ for $k = (1, 2, \ldots, 26)$; thus $\sum_{k=1}^{25} |E_k| = 67,166,017,379$ of the $2^{36} = 68,719,476,736$ possible configurations eventually escape from the 6×6 cage. (One of the 104 procrastinators in E_{25} is shown in (B6) above.)

BDD techniques are excellent for this problem when k is small; for example, $B(E_1) = 101$ and $B(E_2) = 14441$. But E_k eventually becomes a complicated "nonlocal" function: The size peaks at $B(E_6) = 28,696,866$, after which the number of solutions gets small enough to keep the size down. More than 80 million nodes are present in the formula $T(X) \wedge [L(X) = Y] \wedge E_5(Y)$ before quantification; this stretches memory limits. Indeed, the BDD for $\bigvee_{k=1}^{25} E_k(X)$ takes up more space than its 2^{33}-byte truth table. Therefore a "forward" method for this exercise would be preferable to the use of BDDs.

(Cages larger than 6×6 appear to be impossibly difficult, by *any* known method.)

163. Suppose first that $\circ$ is $\wedge$. We obtain the BDD for $f = g \wedge h$ by taking the BDD for g and replacing its $\boxed{\top}$ sink by the root of the BDD for h. To represent also $\bar{f}$, make a separate copy of the BDD for g, and use a BDD base for both h and $\bar{h}$; replace the $\boxed{\perp}$ in the copy by $\boxed{\top}$, and replace the $\boxed{\top}$ in the copy by the root of the BDD for $\bar{h}$. This decision diagram is reduced because h isn't constant.

Similarly, if $\circ$ is $\oplus$, we obtain a BDD for $f = g \oplus h$ (and possibly $\bar{f}$) from the BDD for g (and possibly $\bar{g}$) after replacing $\boxed{\perp}$ and $\boxed{\top}$ by the roots of BDDs for h and $\bar{h}$.

The other binary operations $\circ$ are essentially the same, because $B(f) = B(\bar{f})$. For example, if $f = g \supset h = \overline{g \wedge \bar{h}}$, we have $B(f) = B(\bar{f}) = B(g) + B(\bar{h}) - 2 = B(g) + B(h) - 2$.

164. Let $U_1(x_1) = V_1(x_1) = x_1$, $U_{n+1}(x_1, \ldots, x_{n+1}) = x_1 \oplus V_n(x_2, \ldots, x_{n+1})$, and $V_{n+1}(x_1, \ldots, x_{n+1}) = U_n(x_1, \ldots, x_n) \wedge x_{n+1}$. Then one can show by induction that $B(f) \le B(U_n) = 2^{\lceil (n+1)/2 \rceil} + 2^{\lfloor (n+1)/2 \rfloor} - 1$ for all read-once f, and also that we always have $B(f, \bar{f}) \le B(V_n, \overline{V_n}) = 2^{\lceil n/2 \rceil + 1} + 2^{\lfloor n/2 \rfloor + 1} - 2$. (But an optimum ordering reduces these sizes dramatically, to $B(U_n^\pi) = \lfloor \frac{3}{2} n + 2 \rfloor$ and $B(V_n^\pi, \overline{V_n^\pi}) = 2n + 2$.)

165. By induction, we prove also that $B(u_{2m}, \bar{u}_{2m}) = 2^m F_{2m+3} + 2$, $B(u_{2m+1}, \bar{u}_{2m+1}) = 2^{m+1} F_{2m+3} + 2$, $B(v_{2m}, \bar{v}_{2m}) = 2^{m+1} F_{2m+1} + 2$, $B(v_{2m+1}, \bar{v}_{2m+1}) = 2^{m+1} F_{2m+3} + 2$.

166. We may assume as in answer 163 that $\circ$ is either $\wedge$ or $\oplus$. By renumbering, we can also assume that $j\sigma = j$ for $1 \le j \le n$, hence $f^\sigma = f$. Let $(b_0, \ldots, b_n)$ be the profile of f, and $(b'_0, \ldots, b'_n)$ the profile of $(f, \bar{f})$; let $(c_{1\pi}, \ldots, c_{(n+1)\pi})$ and $(c'_{1\pi}, \ldots, c'_{(n+1)\pi})$ be the profiles of f^π and $(f^\pi, \bar{f}^\pi)$, where $(n+1)\pi = n + 1$. Then $c_{j\pi}$ is the number of subfunctions of $f^\pi = g^\pi \circ h^\pi$ that depend on $x_{j\pi}$ after setting the variables $\{x_{1\pi}, \ldots, x_{(j-1)\pi}\}$ to fixed values. Similarly, $c'_{j\pi}$ is the number of such subfunctions of f^π or $\bar{f}^\pi$. We will try to prove that $b_{j\pi-1} \le c_{j\pi}$ and $b'_{j\pi-1} \le c'_{j\pi}$ for all j.

Case 1: $\circ$ is $\wedge$. We may assume that $n\pi = n$, since $\wedge$ is commutative. *Case 1a:* $1 \le j\pi \le k$. Then $b_{j\pi-1}$ and $b'_{j\pi-1}$ count subfunctions in which only the variables $x_{i\pi}$ with $1 \le i < j$ and $1 \le i\pi \le k$ are specified. These subfunctions of $g \wedge h$ or $\bar{g} \vee \bar{h}$ have counterparts that are counted in $c_{j\pi}$ and $c'_{j\pi}$, because h^π is not constant in any subfunction when $n\pi = n$. *Case 1b:* $k < j\pi \le n$. Then $b_{j\pi-1}$ and $b'_{j\pi-1}$ count subfunctions of h or $\bar{h}$, which have counterparts counted in $c_{j\pi}$ and $c'_{j\pi}$.

Case 2: $\circ$ is $\oplus$. We may assume that $1\pi = 1$, since $\oplus$ is commutative. Then an argument analogous to Case 1 applies. [*Discrete Applied Math.* **103** (2000), 237–258.]

167. Let $f = f_{1n}$; proceed recursively to compute $c_{ij} = B_{\min}(f_{ij})$, $c'_{ij} = B_{\min}(f_{ij}, \bar{f}_{ij})$, and a permutation π_{ij} of $\{i, \ldots, j\}$ for each subfunction $f_{ij}(x_i, \ldots, x_j)$ as follows: If $i = j$, we have $f_{ij}(x_i) = x_i$; let $c_{ij} = 3$, $c'_{ij} = 4$, $\pi_{ij} = i$. Otherwise $i < j$, and we have $f_{ij}(x_i, \ldots, x_j) = f_{ik}(x_i, \ldots, x_k) \circ f_{(k+1)j}(x_{k+1}, \ldots, x_j)$ for some k and some operator $\circ$. If $\circ$ is like $\wedge$, let $c_{ij} = c_{ik} + c_{(k+1)j} - 2$, and either $(c'_{ij} = 2c_{ik} + c'_{(k+1)j} - 4$, $\pi_{ij} = \pi_{ik}\pi_{(k+1)j})$ or $(c'_{ij} = 2c_{(k+1)j} + c'_{ik} - 4$, $\pi_{ij} = \pi_{(k+1)j}\pi_{ik})$, whichever minimizes c'_{ij}. If $\circ$ is like $\oplus$, let $c'_{ij} = c'_{ik} + c'_{(k+1)j} - 2$, and either $(c_{ij} = c_{ik} + c'_{(k+1)j} - 2$, $\pi_{ij} = \pi_{ik}\pi_{(k+1)j})$ or $(c_{ij} = c_{(k+1)j} + c'_{ik} - 2$, $\pi_{ij} = \pi_{(k+1)j}\pi_{ik})$, whichever minimizes c_{ij}.

(The permutations π_{ij} represented as strings in this description would be represented as linked lists inside a computer. We could also construct an optimum BDD for f recursively in $O(B_{\min}(f))$ steps, using answer 163.)

168. (a) This statement transforms and simplifies the recurrences (112) and (113).

(b) True by induction; also $x \ge n$.

(c) Easily verified. Notice that T is a reflection about the $22\frac{1}{2}°$ line $y = (\sqrt{2} - 1)x$.

(d) If $z \in S_k$ and $z' \in S_{n-k}$ we have $|z| = q^\beta$ and $|z'| = q'^\beta$, where $q \le k$ and $q' \le n - k$ by induction. By symmetry we may let $q = (1 - \delta)t$ and $q' = (1 + \delta)t$, where $t = \frac{1}{2}(q + q') \le \frac{1}{2} n$. Then if the first hint is true, we have $|z \bullet z'| \le (2t)^\beta \le n^\beta$. And we also will have $|z \circ z'| \le n^\beta$, by (c), since $|z^T| = |z|$.

To prove the first hint, we note that the maximum $|z \bullet z'|$ occurs when $y = y'$. For when $y \geq y'$ we have $|z \bullet z'|^2 = (x + x' + y')^2 + y^2 = r^2 + 2(x' + y')x + (x' + y')^2$; the largest value, given z', occurs when $y = y'$. A similar argument applies when $y' \geq y$.

Now when $y = y'$ we have $y = \sqrt{rr'} \sin\theta$ for some θ; and one can show that $x + x' \leq (r + r') \cos\theta$. Thus $z \bullet z' = (x + x' + y, y)$ lies in the ellipse of the second hint. On that ellipse we have $(a\cos\theta + b\sin\theta)^2 + (b\sin\theta)^2 = a^2/2 + b^2 + u\sin 2\theta + v\cos 2\theta = a^2/2 + b^2 + w\sin(2\theta + \tau)$, where $u = ab$, $v = \frac{1}{2}a^2 - b^2$, $w^2 = u^2 + v^2$, and $\cos\tau = u/w$. Hence $|z \bullet z'|^2 \leq \frac{1}{2}a^2 + b^2 + w$. And $4w^2 = (r + r')^4 + 4(rr')^2 \leq (r^2 + (2\sqrt{5} - 2)rr' + r'^2)^2$, so

$$|z \bullet z'|^2 \leq r^2 + (\sqrt{5} + 1)rr' + r'^2, \qquad r = (1 - \delta)^\beta, \; r' = (1 + \delta)^\beta.$$

The remaining task is to prove that this quantity is at most $2^{2\beta} = 2\phi^2$; equivalently, $f_t(2) \leq f_t(2\beta)$, where $f_t(\alpha) = (e^{t/\alpha} + e^{-t/\alpha})^\alpha - 2^\alpha$ and $t = \beta\ln((1 - \delta)/(1 + \delta))$. One can show, in fact, that f_t is an increasing function of α when $\alpha \geq 2$. [See G. Bennett, *AMM* **117** (2010), 334–351. The $O(n^\beta)$ bound on S_n seems to require a delicate analysis; an earlier attempt by Sauerhoff, Wegener, and Werchner was flawed. The proof given here is due to A. X. Chang and V. I. Spitkovsky in 2007.]

169. This conjecture has been verified for $m \leq 7$. [Many other curious properties also remain unexplained. A paper that describes what is known so far is currently being prepared by members of the "curious research group."]

170. (a) 2^{2n-1}. There are four choices at (j) when $1 \leq j < n$, namely LO $= \boxed{\perp}$ or LO $= \boxed{\top}$ or HI $= \boxed{\perp}$ or HI $= \boxed{\top}$; and there are two choices for (n).

(b) 2^{n-1}, since half the choices at each branch are ruled out.

(c) Indeed, if $t = (t_1 \dots t_n)_2$ we have LO $= \boxed{\perp}$ at (j) when $t_j = 1$ and HI $= \boxed{\top}$ at (j) when $t_j = 0$. (This idea was applied to random bit generation in exercise 3.4.1–25. Since there are 2^{n-1} such values of t, we've shown that every monotone, skinny function is a threshold function, with weights $\{2^{n-1}, \dots, 2, 1\}$. The other skinny functions are obtained by complementing individual variables.)

(d) $\bar{f}_t(\bar{x}) = [(\bar{x})_2 < t] = [(x)_2 > \bar{t}] = [(x)_2 > 2^n - 1 - t] = f_{2^n - t}(x)$.

(e) By Theorem 7.1.1Q, the shortest DNF is the OR of the prime implicants, and its general pattern is exhibited by the case $n = 10$ and $t = (1100010111)_2$: $(x_1 \wedge x_2 \wedge x_3) \vee (x_1 \wedge x_2 \wedge x_4) \vee (x_1 \wedge x_2 \wedge x_5) \vee (x_1 \wedge x_2 \wedge x_6 \wedge x_7) \vee (x_1 \wedge x_2 \wedge x_6 \wedge x_8 \wedge x_9 \wedge x_{10})$. (One term for each 0 in t, and one more.) The shortest CNF is the dual of the shortest DNF of the dual, which corresponds to $2^n - t = (0011101001)_2$: $(x_1) \wedge (x_2) \wedge (x_3 \vee x_4 \vee x_5 \vee x_6) \wedge (x_3 \vee x_4 \vee x_5 \vee x_7 \vee x_8) \wedge (x_3 \vee x_4 \vee x_5 \vee x_7 \vee x_9) \wedge (x_3 \vee x_4 \vee x_5 \vee x_7 \vee x_{10})$.

171. Note that the classes of read-once, regular, skinny, and monotone functions are each closed under the operations of taking duals and restrictions. A skinny function is clearly read-once; a monotone threshold function with $w_1 \geq \dots \geq w_n$ is regular; and a regular function is monotone. We must show that a regular read-once function is skinny.

Suppose $f(x_1, \dots, x_n) = g(x_{i_1}, \dots, x_{i_k}) \circ h(x_{j_1}, \dots, x_{j_l})$, where $\circ$ is a nontrivial binary operator and we have $i_1 < \dots < i_k$, $j_1 < \dots < j_l$, $k + l = n$, and $\{i_1, \dots, i_k, j_1, \dots, j_l\} = \{1, \dots, n\}$. (This condition is weaker than being "read-once.") We can assume that $i_1 = 1$. By taking restrictions and using induction, both g and h are skinny and monotone; thus their prime implicants have the special form in exercise 170(e). The operator $\circ$ must be monotone, so it is either $\vee$ or $\wedge$. By duality we can assume that $\circ$ is $\vee$.

Case 1: f has a prime implicant of length 1. Then x_1 is a prime implicant of f, by regularity. Hence $f(x_1, \dots, x_n) = x_1 \vee f(0, x_2, \dots, x_n)$, and we can use induction.

Case 2: All prime implicants of g and h have length > 1. Then $x_{j_1} \wedge \cdots \wedge x_{j_p}$ is a prime implicant, for some $p \geq 2$, but $x_{j_1-1} \wedge x_{j_2} \wedge \cdots \wedge x_{j_p}$ is not, contradicting regularity. [See T. Eiter, T. Ibaraki, and K. Makino, *Theor. Comp. Sci.* **270** (2002), 493–524.]

172. By examining the CNF for f_t in exercise 170(e), we see that when $t = (t_1 \ldots t_n)_2$ the number of Horn functions obtainable by complementing variables is one more than the number for $(t_2 \ldots t_n)_2$ when $t_1 = 0$, but twice that number when $t_1 = 1$. Thus the example $t = (1100010111)_2$ corresponds to $2 \times (2 \times (1 + (1 + (1 + (2 \times (1 + (2 \times (2 \times 2)))))))))$ Horn functions. Summing over all t gives s_n where $s_n = (2^{n-2} + s_{n-1}) + 2s_{n-1}$, where $s_1 = 2$; and the solution to this recurrence is $3^n - 2^{n-1}$.

To make both f and $\bar{f}$ Horn functions, assume (by duality) that $t \bmod 4 = 3$. Then we must complement x_j if and only if $t_j = 0$, except for the string of 1s at the right of t. For example, when $t = (1100010111)_2$, we should complement x_3, x_4, x_5, x_7, and then at most one of $\{x_8, x_9, x_{10}\}$. This gives $\rho(t+1) + 1 \geq 3$ choices related to f_t. Summing over all t with $t \bmod 4 = 3$ gives $2^n - 1$; so the answer is $2^{n+1} - 2$.

173. Consider monotone functions first. We can write $t = (0^{a_1} 1^{a_2} \ldots 0^{a_{2k-1}} 1^{a_{2k}})_2$, where $a_1 + \cdots + a_{2k} = n$, $a_1 \geq 0$, $a_j \geq 1$ for $1 < j < 2k$, and $a_{2k} \geq 2$ when $t \bmod 4 = 3$. When $t \bmod 4 = 1$, $2^n - t$ has this form. Then f_t has $a_1! a_2! \ldots a_{2k}!$ automorphisms, so it is equivalent to $n!/(a_1! a_2! \ldots a_{2k}!) - 1$ others, none of which are skinny. Summing over all t gives $2(P_n - nP_{n-1})$ monotone Boolean functions that are reorderable to skinny form, when $n \geq 2$, where P_n is the number of weak orderings (exercise 5.3.1–3). [See J. S. Beissinger and U. N. Peled, *Graphs and Combinatorics* **3** (1987), 213–219.]

Every such monotone function corresponds to 2^n different unate functions that are equally skinny, when variables are complemented. (These are the functions with the property that all of their restrictions are canalizing, known also as "unate cascades," "1-decision list functions," or "generalized read-once threshold functions.")

174. (a) Assign the numbers $0, \ldots, n-1, n, n+1$ to nodes $①, \ldots, ⓝ, \boxed{\top}, \boxed{\bot}$; and let the (LO, HI) branches from node k go to nodes (a_{2k+1}, a_{2k+2}) for $0 \leq k < n$. Then define p_k as follows, for $1 \leq k \leq 2n$: Let $l = \lfloor (k-1)/2 \rfloor$ and $P_l = \{p_1, \ldots, p_{2l}\}$. Set $p_k \leftarrow a_k$ if $a_k \notin P_l$; otherwise, if a_k is the mth smallest element of $P_l \cap \{l+1, \ldots, n+1\}$, set p_k to the mth smallest element of $\{n+2, \ldots, n+l+1\} \setminus P_l$. (This construction is due to T. Dahlheimer.)

(b) The inverse $p_1^{-1} \ldots p_{2n}^{-1}$ of a Dellac permutation satisfies $2(k-n) - 1 \leq p_k^{-1} \leq 2k$. It corresponds to a Genocchi derangement $q_1 \ldots q_{2n+2}$ when $q_2 = 1$, $q_{2n+1} = 2n+2$, and $q_{2k+2} = 1 + p_k^{-1}$, $q_{2k-1} = 1 + p_{k+n}^{-1}$ for $1 \leq k \leq n$.

(c) Given a permutation $q_1 \ldots q_{2n+2}$, let r_k be the first element of the sequence q_k^{-1}, $q_{q_k^{-1}}^{-1}$, $\ldots$ that is $\geq k$. This transformation takes Genocchi permutations into Dumont pistols, and has the property that $q_k = k$ if and only if $r_k = k \notin \{r_1, \ldots, r_{k-1}\}$.

(d) Each node (j, k) represents a set of strings $r_1 \ldots r_j$, where $(1, 0) = \{1\}$ and the other sets are defined by the following transition rules: Suppose $r_1 \ldots r_j \in (j, k)$, and let $l = 2k$. If $k = 0$ then $(j+1, k)$ contains $1r_1^+ \ldots r_j^+$ when j is even, $2r_1^+ \ldots r_j^+$ when j is odd, where r^+ denotes $r+1$. If $k > 0$ then $(j+1, k)$ contains $r_1^+ \ldots r_l^+ (l+1) r_{l+1}^+ \ldots r_j^+$ when j is even, $r_1^\pm \ldots r_{l-1}^\pm (l) r_l^\pm \ldots r_j^\pm$ when j is odd, where $r^\pm$ denotes $r + 1$ when $r \geq l$, $r - 1$ when $r < l$. Going vertically, if $l \leq j - 3$ and j is odd, $(j, k+1)$ contains $r_1 \ldots r_l r_{l+2} r_{l+3} (l+3) r_{l+4} \ldots r_j$. On the other hand if $k = 1$ and j is even, $(j, 0)$ contains $r_2 r_1 r_3 \ldots r_j$. Finally if $k > 1$ and j is even, $(j, k-1)$ contains the string $r_1' \ldots r_{l-3}' (l-2) r_{l-2}' r_{l-1}' r_{l+1}' \ldots r_j'$, where r' denotes l when $r = l - 2$, otherwise $r' = r$. (One can show that the elements of $(2j, k)$ are the Dumont pistols for Genocchi permutations of order $2j$ whose largest fixed point is $2k$.)

All of these constructions are invertible. For example, the path $(1,0) \to (2,0) \to (3,0) \to (3,1) \to (4,1) \to (5,1) \to (6,1) \to (7,1) \to (7,2) \to (7,3) \to (8,3) \to (8,2) \to (8,1) \to (8,0)$ corresponds to the pistols $1 \to 22 \to 133 \to 333 \to 4244 \to 53355 \to 624466 \to 7335577 \to 7355577 \to 7355777 \to 82448688 \to 82646888 \to 82466888 \to 28466888$. The latter pistol, which can be represented by the diagram ⟨diagram⟩, corresponds to the Genocchi derangement $q_1 \ldots q_8 = 61537482$. And this derangement corresponds to $p_1^{-1} \ldots p_6^{-1} = 231546$ and the Dellac permutation $p_1 \ldots p_6 = 312546$. That permutation, in turn, corresponds to $a_1 \ldots a_6 = 312343$, which stands for the thin BDD

$$\boxed{1}\!-\!\boxed{2}\cdots\!\boxed{3}\!-\!\boxed{\top}\ \ \boxed{\bot}.$$

Let d_{jk} be the number of pistols in (j,k), which is also the number of directed paths from $(1,0)$ to (j,k). These numbers are readily found by addition, beginning with

									38227	38227	$\cdots$
							2073	2073	38227	76454	$\cdots$
					155	155	2073	4146	36154	112608	$\cdots$
			17	17	155	310	1918	6064	32008	144616	$\cdots$
	3	3	17	34	138	448	1608	7672	25944	170560	$\cdots$
1	1	3	6	14	48	104	552	1160	8832	18272	188832	$\cdots$
1	1	1	2	2	8	8	56	56	608	608	9440	9440	198272	$\cdots$;

and the column totals $D_j = \sum_k d_{jk}$ are $(D_1, D_2, \ldots) = (1, 1, 2, 3, 8, 17, 56, 155, 608, 2073, 9440, 38227, 198272, 929569, \ldots)$. The even-numbered elements of this sequence, D_{2n}, have long been known as the Genocchi numbers G_{2n+2}. The odd-numbered elements, D_{2n+1}, have therefore been called "median Genocchi numbers." The number S_n of thin BDDs is $d_{(2n+2)0} = D_{2n+1}$.

References: L. Euler discussed the Genocchi numbers in the second volume of his *Institutiones Calculi Differentialis* (1755), Chapter 7, where he showed that the odd integers G_{2n} are expressible in terms of the Bernoulli numbers: In fact, $G_{2n} = (2^{2n+1} - 2)|B_{2n}|$, and $z \tan \frac{z}{2} = \sum_{n=1}^{\infty} G_{2n} z^{2n}/(2n)!$. A. Genocchi examined these numbers further in *Annali di Scienze Matematiche e Fisiche* **3** (1852), 395–405; and L. Seidel, in *Sitzungsberichte math.-phys. Classe, Akademie Wissen. München* **7** (1877), 157–187, discovered that they could be computed additively via the numbers d_{jk}. Their combinatorial significance was not discovered until much later; see D. Dumont, *Duke Math. J.* **41** (1974), 305–318; D. Dumont and A. Randrianarivony, *Discrete Math.* **132** (1994), 37–49. Meanwhile H. Dellac had proposed an apparently unrelated problem, equivalent to enumerating what we have called Dellac permutations; see *L'Intermédiaire des Math.* **7** (1900), 9–10, 328; *Annales de la Faculté sci. Marseille* **11** (1901), 141–164.

There's also a *direct* connection between thin BDDs and the paths of (d), discovered in 2007 by Thorsten Dahlheimer. Notice first that unrestricted Dumont pistols of order $2n + 2$ correspond to thin BDDs that are ordered but not necessarily reduced, because we can let $r_1 \ldots r_{2n}r_{2n+1}r_{2n+2} = (2a_1) \ldots (2a_{2n})(2n+2)(2n+2)$. The number of such pistols in which $\min\{i \mid r_{2i-1} = r_{2i}\} = l$ turns out to be $d_{(2n+2)(n+1-l)}$.

To prove this, we can use new transition rules instead of those in answer (d): Suppose $r_1 \ldots r_j \in (j,k)$, and let $l = j - 2k$. Then $(j+1, k)$ contains $r_1^+ \ldots r_l^+ r_l^+ \ldots r_j^+$ when j is odd, $r_1^{\pm} \ldots r_{l-1}^{\pm}(l-1)r_l^{\pm} \ldots r_j^{\pm}$ when j is even. If j is odd, $(j, k+1)$ contains $1r_1r_3 \ldots r_j$ when $l = 3$, and when $l > 3$ it contains $r_1' \ldots r_{l-4}'(l-4)r_{l-3}'r_{l-2}'r_l' \ldots r_j'$, where $r' = r + 2[r = l-4]$. Finally, if j is even and $k > 0$, $(j, k-1)$ contains $r_1 \ldots r_{l-1}qr_{l+2}r_{l+2} \ldots r_j$, where $q = l$ if $r_l = r_{l+1}$, otherwise $q = r_{l+1}$.

With these magic transitions the path above corresponds to $1 \to 22 \to 313 \to 133 \to 2244 \to 31355 \to 424466 \to 5153577 \to 5135577 \to 1535577 \to 22646688 \to 26446688 \to 26466688 \to 26466888$; so $a_1 \ldots a_6 = 132334$.

175. This problem seems to require a different approach from the methods that worked when $b_0 = \cdots = b_{n-1} = 1$. Suppose we have a BDD base of N nodes including the two sinks $\boxed{\bot}$ and $\boxed{\top}$ together with various branches labeled $\textcircled{2}, \ldots, \textcircled{n}$, and assume that exactly s of the nodes are sources (having in-degree zero). Let $c(b, s, t, N)$ be the number of ways to introduce b additional nodes labeled $\textcircled{1}$, in such a way that exactly $s+b-t$ source nodes remain. (Thus $0 \le t \le 2b$; exactly t of the old source nodes are now reachable from a $\textcircled{1}$ branch.) Then the number of nonconstant Boolean functions $f(x_1, \ldots, x_n)$ having the BDD profile $(b_0, \ldots, b_n)$ is equal to $T(b_0, \ldots, b_{n-1}; 1)$, where

$$T(b_0; s) = 2[s = b_0 = 1] + [s = 2][b_0 = 0] + [s = 2][b_0 = 2];$$

$$T(b_0, \ldots, b_{n-1}; s) = \sum_{t=\max(0, b_0 - s)}^{2b_0} c(b_0, s+t-b_0, t, b_1 + \cdots + b_{n-1} + 2) \, T(b_1, \ldots, b_{n-1}; s+t-b_0).$$

One can show that $c(b, s, t, N) = \sum_{r=0}^{2b} a_{rb} p_{tr}(s, N)/b!$, where we have $(N(N-1))^b = \sum_{r=0}^{2b} a_{rb} N^r$ and $p_{tr}(s, N) = \sum_k \binom{r}{k} \left\{ \begin{smallmatrix} k \\ t \end{smallmatrix} \right\} s^t (N-s)^{r-k} = \sum_k \left\{ \begin{smallmatrix} r \\ k \end{smallmatrix} \right\} \binom{k}{t} s^t (N-s)^{\underline{k-t}} = r! \, [w^t z^r] \, e^{(N-s)z} (we^z - w + 1)^s$.

176. (a) If $p \ne p'$ we have $\sum_{a \in A, b \in B} [h_{a,b}(p) = h_{a,b}(p')] \le |A||B|/2^l$, by the definition of universal hashing. Let $r_i(a, b)$ be the number of $p \in P$ such that $h_{a,b}(p) = i$. Then

$$\sum_{a \in A, b \in B} \sum_{0 \le i < 2^l} r_i(a, b)^2 = \sum_{a \in A, b \in B} \sum_{p \in P} \sum_{p' \in P} [h_{a,b}(p) = h_{a,b}(p')]$$

$$\le |P||A||B| + \sum_{p \in P} \sum_{p' \in P} [p \ne p'] \frac{|A||B|}{2^l} = 2^t |A||B| \left(1 + \frac{2^t - 1}{2^l} \right).$$

On the other hand $\sum_{i=0}^{2^l - 1} r_i(a, b)^2 = \sum_{i=0}^{2^l - 1} \left(r_i(a, b) - 2^t/|I| \right)^2 + 2^{2t}/|I| \ge 2^{2t}/|I|$, for any a and b. Similar formulas apply when there are $s_j(a, b)$ solutions to $h_{a,b}(q) = j$. So there must be $a \in A$ and $b \in B$ such that

$$\frac{2^{2t}}{|I|} + \frac{2^{2t}}{|J|} \le \sum_{i \in I} r_i(a, b)^2 + \sum_{j \in J} s_j(a, b)^2 \le 2^{t+1} \left(1 + \frac{2^t - 1}{2^l} \right) \le \frac{2^{2t}}{2^l} + \frac{2^{2t}}{(1 - \epsilon) 2^l}.$$

(b) The middle l bits of $aq_k + b$ and $aq_{k+2} + b$ differ by at least 2, so the middle $l - 1$ bits of aq_k and aq_{k+2} must be different.

(c) Let q and q' be different elements of Q^* with $(g(q') - g(q)) \bmod 2^{l-1} \ge 2^{l-2}$. (Otherwise we can swap $q \leftrightarrow q'$.) If $l \ge 3$, the condition $g(p) + g(q) = 2^{l-1}$ implies that $f_q(p) = 0$. Now we have $(g(p) + g(q')) \bmod 2^{l-1} = (g(q') - g(q)) \bmod 2^{l-1}$; furthermore $g(q')$ and $g(p)$ are both even. Therefore no carry can propagate to change the middle bit, and we have $f_{q'}(p) = 1$.

(d) The set Q'' has at least $(1 - \epsilon) 2^{l-1}$ elements, and so does the analogous set P''. At most 2^{l-2} elements of Q'' have $g(q)$ odd; and at most $2^{l-1} + 1 - |P''|$ of the elements with $g(q)$ even are not in Q^*. Thus $|Q^*| \ge (1 - \epsilon) 2^{l-1} - 2^{l-2} - 2^{l-1} - 1 + (1 - \epsilon) 2^{l-1} = (1 - 4\epsilon) 2^{l-2} - 1$, and we have $B_{\min}(Z_{n,a}) \ge (1 - 4\epsilon) 2^{l-1} - 2$ by (85).

Finally, choose $l = t - 4$ and $\epsilon = 1/9$. The theorem is obvious when $n < 14$.

177. Suppose $k \ge n/2$ and $x = 2^{k+1} x_h + x_l$, $y = 2^k y_h + y_l$. Then $(xy \gg k) \bmod 2^{n-k}$ depends on $2x_h y_l$, $x_l y_h$, and $x_l y_l \gg k$, modulo 2^{n-k}, so $q_{2k+1} \le 2^{n-k-1+n-k+n-k}$.

Summing up, we get $\sum_{k=0}^{2n} q_k \le \sum_{0 \le k \le 6n/5} 2^k + \sum_{6n/5 < k \le 2n} 2^{3n - 2\lfloor k/2 \rfloor - \lceil k/2 \rceil}$.

If $n = 5t + (0, 1, 2, 3, 4)$ the total comes to exactly $(2^{\lceil 6n/5 \rceil} \cdot (19, 10, 12, 13, 17) - 12)/7$. [M. Sauerhoff, in *Discrete Applied Math.* **158** (2010), 1195–1204, has proved the lower bound $\Omega(2^{6n/5})$ for this ordering.]

178. We can write $x = 2^k x_h + x_l$ as in the proof of Theorem A; but now $x_l = \hat{x}_l + (x \bmod 2)$, where $\hat{x}_l$ is even and $x \bmod 2$ is not yet known. Similarly $y = 2^k y_h + y_l = 2^k y_h + \hat{y}_l + (y \bmod 2)$. Let $\hat{z}_l = \hat{x}_l \hat{y}_l \bmod 2^k$. At level $2k - 2$, for $n/2 \le k < n$, we need only "remember" three $(n - k)$-bit numbers $\hat{x}_l \bmod 2^{n-k}$, $\hat{y}_l \bmod 2^{n-k}$, $(\hat{x}_l \hat{y}_l \gg k) \bmod 2^{n-k}$, and three "carries" $c_1 = (\hat{x}_l + \hat{z}_l) \gg k$, $c_2 = (\hat{y}_l + \hat{z}_l) \gg k$, $c_3 = (\hat{x}_l + \hat{y}_l + \hat{z}_l) \gg k$. These six quantities tell us the middle bit, once x_h, y_h, $x \bmod 2$, and $y \bmod 2$ are known.

There are only six possibilities for the carries: $c_1 c_2 c_3 = 000$, 001, 011, 101, 111, or 112. Thus $q_{2k-2} \le 6 \cdot 2^{(n-k-1)+(n-k-1)+(n-k)}$. Similarly, when $n/2 \le k < n - 1$, we have $q_{2k-1} \le 6 \cdot 2^{(n-k-2)+(n-k-1)+(n-k)}$. With these estimates, together with $q_k \le 2^k$, we get $\sum_{k=0}^{2n-4} q_k \le (2^{6t} \cdot (37, 86, 184, 464, 1024) - 268)/28$ when $n = 5t + (0, 1, 2, 3, 4)$.

The actual BDD sizes, for the function f of Theorem A and the function g of this exercise, are $B(f) = (169, 381, 928, 2188, 5248, 12373, 29400, 68777, 162768, 377359, 879709)$ and $B(g) = (165, 352, 806, 1802, 4195, 9774, 22454, 52714, 121198, 278223, 650188)$ for $6 \le n \le 16$; so this variant appears to save about 25%. A slightly better ordering is obtained by testing $(\text{lo-bit}(x), \text{hi-bit}(y), \text{hi-bit}(x), \text{lo-bit}(y))$ on the last four levels, giving $B(h) = B(g) - 20$ for $n \ge 6$. Then $B(h)/B_{\min}(f) \approx (1.07, 1.05, 1.04, 1.04, 1.04, 1.01, 1.02)$ for $6 \le n \le 12$, so this ordering may be close to optimal as $n \to \infty$.

180. By letting $a_{m+1} = a_{m+2} = \cdots = 0$, we may assume that $m \ge p$. Let $a = (a_p \ldots a_1)_2$, and write $x = 2^k x_h + x_l$ as in the proof of Theorem A. If $p \le n$, we have $q_k \le 2^{p-k}$ for $0 \le k < p$, because the given function $f = Z_{m,n}^{(p)}(a; x)$ depends only on a, x_h, and $(ax_l \gg k) \bmod 2^{p-k}$. We may therefore assume that $p > n$.

Consider the multiset $A = \{2^k x_h a \bmod 2^{p-1} \mid 0 \le x_h < 2^{n-k}\}$. Write $A = \{2^{p-1} - \alpha_1, \ldots, 2^{p-1} - \alpha_s\}$, where $s = 2^{n-k}$ and $0 < \alpha_1 \le \cdots \le \alpha_s = 2^{p-1}$, and let $\alpha_{s+i} = \alpha_i + 2^{p-1}$ for $0 \le i \le s$. Then $q_k \le 2s$, because f depends only on a, x_h, and the index $i \in [0 \mathinner{..} 2s]$ such that $\alpha_i \le ax_l \bmod 2^p < \alpha_{i+1}$.

Consequently $\sum_{k=0}^n q_k \le \sum_{k=0}^n \min(2^k, 2^{n+1-k}) = 2^{\lfloor n/2 \rfloor + 1} + 2^{\lceil n/2 \rceil + 1} - 3$.

181. For every $(x_1, \ldots, x_m)$ only $O(n)$ further nodes are needed, by exercise 170.

182. Yes; B. Bollig [*Lecture Notes in Comp. Sci.* **4978** (2008), 306–317] has shown that it is $\Omega(2^{n/432})$. Incidentally, $B_{\min}(L_{12,12}) = 1158$ is obtained with the strange ordering $L_{12,12}(x_{18}, x_{17}, x_{16}, x_{15}, x_{14}, x_{12}, x_{10}, x_8, x_6, x_4, x_2, x_1; x_{19}, x_{20}, x_{21}, x_{22}, x_{23}, x_{13}, x_{11}, x_9, x_7, x_5, x_3, x_{24})$; and $B_{\max}(L_{12,12}) = 9302$ arises with $L_{12,12}(x_{24}, x_{23}, x_{20}, x_{19}, x_{22}, x_{11}, x_6, x_7, x_8, x_9, x_{10}, x_{13}; x_1, x_2, x_3, x_4, x_5, x_{21}, x_{18}, x_{17}, x_{16}, x_{15}, x_{14}, x_{12})$. Similarly $B_{\min}(L_{8,16}) = 606$ and $B_{\max}(L_{8,16}) = 3415$ aren't terribly far apart. Could $B_{\min}(L_{m,n})$ and $B_{\max}(L_{m,n})$ both conceivably be $\Theta(2^{\min(m,n)})$?

183. The profile $(b_0, b_1, \ldots)$ begins (1, 1, 1, 2, 3, 5, 7, 11, 15, 23, 31, 47, 63, 95, ...). When $k > 0$ there's a node on level $2k$ for every pair of integers (a, b) such that $2^{k-1} \le a, b < 2^k$ and $ab < 2^{2k-1} < (a+1)(b+1)$; this node represents the function $[((a + x)/2^k)((b + y)/2^k) \ge \frac{1}{2}]$. When b is given, in the appropriate range, there are $\lceil 2^{2k-1}/b \rceil - \lfloor 2^{2k-1}/(b+1) \rfloor$ choices for a; hence $b_{2k} = \sum_{2^{k-1} \le b < 2^k} (\lceil 2^{2k-1}/b \rceil - \lfloor 2^{2k-1}/(b+1) \rfloor)$,

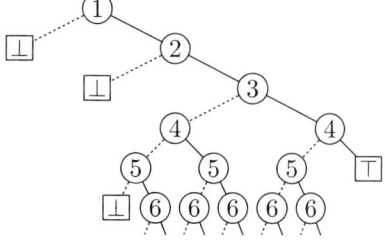

which telescopes to $2^k - 1$. A similar argument shows that $b_{2k+1} = 2^k + 2^{k-1} - 1$.

184. Two kinds of beads contribute to $b_{m(i-1)+j-1}$: One for every choice of i columns, at least one of which is $< j$; and one for every choice of $i-1$ columns, missing at least one element $\geq j$. Thus $b_{m(i-1)+j-1} = \left(\binom{m}{i} - \binom{m+1-j}{i}\right) + \left(\binom{m}{i-1} - \binom{j-1}{m+1-i}\right)$. Summing over $1 \leq i, j \leq m$ gives $B(P_m) = (2m-3)2^m + 5$. (Incidentally, $q_k = b_k + 1$ for $2 \leq k < m^2$.)

The ZDD has simply $z_{m(i-1)+j-1} = \binom{m-1}{i-1}$ for $1 \leq i, j \leq m$, one for every choice of $i-1$ columns $\neq j$; hence $Z(P_m) = m2^{m-1} + 2 \approx \frac{1}{4}B(P_m)$. (The lower bound of Theorem K applies also to ZDD nodes, because only such nodes get tickets; therefore the natural ordering of variables is optimum for ZDDs. The natural ordering might be optimum also for BDDs; this conjecture is known to be true for $m \leq 5$.)

185. Suppose $f(x) = t_{\nu x}$ for some binary vector $t_0 \ldots t_n$. Then the subfunctions of order $d > 0$ correspond to the distinct substrings $t_i \ldots t_{i+d}$. Such substrings τ correspond to beads if and only if $\tau \neq 0^{d+1}$ and $\tau \neq 1^{d+1}$; they correspond to zeads if and only if $\tau \neq 0^{d+1}$ and $\tau \neq 10^d$.

Thus the maximum $Z(f)$ is the function S_n of answer 44. To attain this worst case we need a binary vector of length $2^{d+1} + d - 2$ that contains all $(d+1)$-tuples except 0^{d+1} and 10^d as substrings; such vectors can be characterized as the first $2^{d+1} + d - 2$ elements of any de Bruijn cycle of period 2^{d+1}, beginning with $0^d 1$.

186. $\bar{x}_1 \wedge \bar{x}_2 \wedge x_3 \wedge \bar{x}_4 \wedge \bar{x}_5 \wedge \bar{x}_6$.

187. (These diagrams should be compared with the answer to exercise 1.)

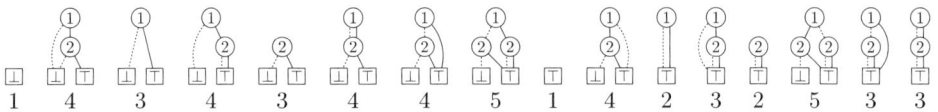

1	4	3	4	3	4	4	5	1	4	2	3	2	5	3	3

188. To avoid nested braces, let ϵ, a, b, and ab stand for the subsets $\emptyset$, $\{1\}$, $\{2\}$, and $\{1,2\}$. The families are then $\emptyset$, $\{ab\}$, $\{a\}$, $\{a, ab\}$, $\{b\}$, $\{b, ab\}$, $\{a, b\}$, $\{a, b, ab\}$, $\{\epsilon\}$, $\{\epsilon, ab\}$, $\{\epsilon, a\}$, $\{\epsilon, a, ab\}$, $\{\epsilon, b\}$, $\{\epsilon, b, ab\}$, $\{\epsilon, a, b\}$, $\{\epsilon, a, b, ab\}$, in truth-table order.

189. When $n = 0$, only the constant functions; when $n > 0$, only 0 and $x_1 \wedge \cdots \wedge x_n$. (But there are many functions, such as $x_2 \wedge (x_1 \vee \bar{x}_3)$, with $(b_0, \ldots, b_n) = (z_0, \ldots, z_n)$.)

190. (a) Only $x_1 \oplus \cdots \oplus x_n$ and $1 \oplus x_1 \oplus \cdots \oplus x_n$, for $n \geq 0$. (b) This condition holds if and only if all subtables of order 1 are either 01 or 11. So there are $2^{2^{n-1}}$ solutions when $n > 0$, namely all functions such that $f(x_1, \ldots, x_{n-1}, 1) = 1$.

191. The language L_n of truth tables for all such functions has the context-free grammar $L_0 \to 1$; $L_{n+1} \to L_n L_n \mid L_n 0^{2^n}$. The desired number $l_n = |L_n|$ therefore satisfies $l_0 = 1$, $l_{n+1} = l_n(l_n + 1)$; so $(l_0, l_1, l_2, \ldots)$ is the sequence (1, 2, 6, 42, 1806, 3263442, 10650056950806, ...). Asymptotically, $l_n = \theta^{2^n} - \frac{1}{2} - \epsilon$, where $0 < \epsilon < \theta^{-2^n}/8$ and

$$\theta = 1.59791\,02180\,31873\,17833\,80701\,18157\,45531\,23622+.$$

[See *CMath* exercises 4.37 and 4.59, where $l_n + 1$ is called e_{n+1} (a "Euclid number") and θ is called E^2. The numbers $l_n + 1$ were introduced by J. J. Sylvester in connection with his study of Egyptian fractions, *Amer. J. Math.* **3** (1880), 388. Notice that a monotone decreasing function, like a function representing independent sets, always has $z_n = 1$.]

192. (a) 10101101000010110.

(b) True, by induction on $|\tau|$, because $\alpha \neq \beta \neq 0^n$ if and only if $\alpha^Z \neq \beta^Z \neq 0^n$.

(c) The beads of f of order k are the zeads of f^Z of order k, for $0 < k \leq n$. Hence the beads of f^Z are also the zeads of $(f^Z)^Z = f$. Therefore, if $(b_0, \ldots, b_n)$ and

$(z_0, \ldots, z_n)$ are the profile and z-profile of f while $(b'_0, \ldots, b'_n)$ and $(z'_0, \ldots, z'_n)$ are the profile and z-profile of f^Z, we have $b_k = z'_k$ and $z_k = b'_k$ for $0 \le k < n$.

(We also have $z_n = z'_n$, but they might both be 1 instead of 2. The *quasi-profiles* of f and f^Z may differ, but only by at most 1 at each level, because of all-0 subtables.)

193. $S_{\ge k}(x_1, \ldots, x_n)$, by induction on n. (Hence we also have $S^Z_{\ge k}(x_1, \ldots, x_n) = S_k(x_1, \ldots, x_n)$. Exercise 249 gives similar examples.)

194. Define $a_1 \ldots a_{2n}$ as in answer 174, but use the ZDD instead of the BDD. Then $(1, \ldots, 1)$ is the z-profile if and only if $(2a_1) \ldots (2a_{2n})$ is an unrestricted Dumont pistol of order $2n$. So the answer is the Genocchi number G_{2n+2}.

195. The z-profile is $(1, 2, 4, 4, 3, 2, 2)$. We get an optimum z-profile $(1, 2, 3, 2, 3, 2, 2)$ from $M_2(x_4, x_2; x_5, x_6, x_3, x_1)$, and a pessimum z-profile $(1, 2, 4, 8, 12, 2, 2)$ comes from $M_2(x_5, x_6; x_1, x_2, x_3, x_4)$ as in (78). (Incidentally, the algorithm of exercise 197 can be used to show that $Z_{\min}(M_4) = 116$ is obtained with the strikingly peculiar ordering $M_4(x_8, x_5, x_{17}, x_2; x_{20}, x_{19}, x_{18}, x_{16}, x_{15}, x_{13}, x_{14}, x_{12}, x_{11}, x_9, x_{10}, x_4, x_7, x_6, x_3, x_1)!$)

196. For example, $M_m(x_1, \ldots, x_m; e_{m+1}, \ldots, e_n)$, where $n = m + 2^m$ and e_j is the elementary function of exercise 203. Then we have $Z(f) = 2(n - m) + 1$ and $Z(\bar{f}) = (n - m + 7)(n - m)/2 - 2$.

197. The key idea is to change the significance of the DEP fields so that d_{kp} is now $\sum \{2^{t-k-1} \mid N_{kp} \text{ supports } x_t\}$, where we say that $g(x_1, \ldots, x_m)$ *supports* x_j if there is a solution to $g(x_1, \ldots, x_m) = 1$ with $x_j = 1$.

To implement this change, we introduce an auxiliary array $(\zeta_0, \ldots, \zeta_n)$, where we will have $\zeta_k = q$ if N_{kq} denotes the subfunction 0 and $\zeta_k = -1$ if that subfunction does not appear on level k. Initially $\zeta_n \leftarrow 0$, and we set $\zeta_k \leftarrow -1$ at the beginning of step E1. In step E3, the operation of setting d_{kq} should become the following: "If $d_{(k+1)h} \ne \zeta_{k+1}$, set $d_{kq} \leftarrow ((d_{(k+1)l} \mid d_{(k+1)h}) \ll 1) + 1$; otherwise set $d_{kq} \leftarrow d_{(k+1)l} \ll 1$. Also set $\zeta_k \leftarrow q$ if $d_{(k+1)l} = d_{(k+1)h} = \zeta_{k+1}$."

(The master z-profile chart can be used as before to minimize $z_0 + \cdots + z_{n-1}$; but additional work is needed to consider z_n if the *absolute* minimum is important.)

198. Reinterpreting (50), we represent an arbitrary family of sets f as $(\bar{x}_v? \ f_l: f_h)$, where $v = f_v$ indexes the first variable that f *supports*; see answer 197. Thus f_l is the subfamily of f that doesn't support x_v, and f_h is the subfamily that does (but with x_v deleted). We also let $f_v = \infty$ if f has no support (i.e., if f is either $\emptyset$ or $\{\emptyset\}$, represented internally by $\boxed{\perp}$ or $\boxed{\top}$; see answer 200). In (52), $v = \min(f_v, g_v)$ now indexes the first variable *supported* by either f or g; thus $f_h = \emptyset$ if $f_v > g_v$, and $g_h = \emptyset$ if $f_v < g_v$.

Subroutine AND(f, g), ZDD-style, is now the following instead of (55): "Represent f and g as in (52). While $f_v \ne g_v$, return $\emptyset$ if either $f = \emptyset$ or $g = \emptyset$; otherwise set $f \leftarrow f_l$ if $f_v < g_v$, set $g \leftarrow g_l$ if $f_v > g_v$. Swap $f \leftrightarrow g$ if $f > g$. Return f if $f = g$ or $f = \emptyset$. Otherwise, if $f \wedge g = r$ is in the memo cache, return r. Otherwise compute $r_l \leftarrow$ AND(f_l, g_l) and $r_h \leftarrow$ AND(f_h, g_h); set $r \leftarrow$ ZUNIQUE(v, r_l, r_h), using an algorithm like Algorithm U except that the first step returns p when $q = \emptyset$ instead of when $q = p$; put '$f \wedge g = r$' into the memo cache, and return r." (See also the suggestion in answer 200.)

Reference counts are updated as in exercise 82, with slight changes; for example, step U1 will now decrease the reference count of $\boxed{\perp}$ (and only of this node), when $q = \emptyset$. It is important to write a "sanity check" routine that double-checks all reference counts and other redundancies in the entire BDD/ZDD base, so that subtle errors are nipped in the bud. The sanity checker should be invoked frequently until all subroutines have been thoroughly tested.

199. (a) If $f = g$, return f. If $f > g$, swap $f \leftrightarrow g$. If $f = \emptyset$, return g. If $f \vee g = r$ is in the memo cache, return r. Otherwise

$$\begin{aligned}
&\text{set } v \leftarrow f_v,\ r_l \leftarrow \text{OR}(f_l, g_l),\ r_h \leftarrow \text{OR}(f_h, g_h), &&\text{if } f_v = g_v; \\
&\text{set } v \leftarrow f_v,\ r_l \leftarrow \text{OR}(f_l, g),\ r_h \leftarrow f_h,\ \text{increase REF}(f_h) \text{ by } 1, &&\text{if } f_v < g_v; \\
&\text{set } v \leftarrow g_v,\ r_l \leftarrow \text{OR}(f, g_l),\ r_h \leftarrow g_h,\ \text{increase REF}(g_h) \text{ by } 1, &&\text{if } f_v > g_v.
\end{aligned}$$

Then set $r \leftarrow \text{ZUNIQUE}(v, r_l, r_h)$; cache it and return it as in answer 198.

(b) If $f = g$, return $\emptyset$. Otherwise proceed as in (a), but use $(\oplus, \text{XOR})$ not $(\vee, \text{OR})$.

(c) If $f = \emptyset$ or $f = g$, return $\emptyset$. If $g = \emptyset$, return f. Otherwise, if $g_v < f_v$, set $g \leftarrow g_l$ and begin again. Otherwise

$$\begin{aligned}
&\text{set } r_l \leftarrow \text{BUTNOT}(f_l, g_l),\ r_h \leftarrow \text{BUTNOT}(f_h, g_h), &&\text{if } f_v = g_v; \\
&\text{set } r_l \leftarrow \text{BUTNOT}(f_l, g),\ r_h \leftarrow f_h,\ \text{increase REF}(f_h) \text{ by } 1, &&\text{if } f_v < g_v.
\end{aligned}$$

Then set $r \leftarrow \text{ZUNIQUE}(f_v, r_l, r_h)$ and finish as usual.

200. If $f = \emptyset$, return g. If $f = h$, return $\text{OR}(f, g)$. If $g = h$, return g. If $g = \emptyset$ or $f = g$, return $\text{AND}(f, h)$. If $h = \emptyset$, return $\text{BUTNOT}(g, f)$. If $f_v < g_v$ and $f_v < h_v$, set $f \leftarrow f_l$ and start over. If $h_v < f_v$ and $h_v < g_v$, set $h \leftarrow h_l$ and start over. Otherwise check the cache and proceed recursively as usual.

201. In applications of ZDDs where projection functions and/or the complementation operation are permitted, it's best to fix the set of Boolean variables at the beginning, when everything is being initialized. Otherwise, *every* external function in a ZDD base must change whenever a new variable enters the fray.

Suppose therefore that we've decided to deal with functions of $(x_1, \ldots, x_N)$, where N is prespecified. In answer 198, we let $f_v = N + 1$, not ∞, when $f = \emptyset$ or $f = \{\emptyset\}$. Then the tautology function $1 = \wp$ has the $(N+1)$-node ZDD $①\!-\!②\cdots\!\fbox{N}\!-\!\boxed{\top}$, which we construct as soon as N is known. Let t_j be node $⨐$ of this structure, with $t_{N+1} = \boxed{\top}$. The ZDD for x_j is now $①\cdots\!⨐\!-t_{j+1}\boxed{\bot}$; thus the ZDD base for the set of all x_j will occupy $\binom{N+1}{2}$ nodes in addition to the representations of $\emptyset$ and $\wp$.

If N is small, all N projection functions can be prepared in advance. But N is large in many applications of ZDDs; and projection functions are rarely needed when "family algebra" is used to build the structures as in exercises 203–207. So it's generally best to wait until a projection function is actually required, before creating it.

Incidentally, the partial-tautology functions t_j can be used to speed up the synthesis operations of exercises 198–199: If $v = f_v \le g_v$ and $f = t_v$, we have $\text{AND}(f, g) = g$, $\text{OR}(f, g) = f$, and (if $v \le h_v$) also $\text{MUX}(f, g, h) = h$, $\text{MUX}(g, h, f) = \text{OR}(g, h)$.

202. In the transmogrification step T4, change '$q_0 \leftarrow q_1 \leftarrow q$' to '$q_0 \leftarrow q$, $q_1 \leftarrow \emptyset$' and '$r_0 \leftarrow r_1 \leftarrow r$' to '$r_0 \leftarrow r$, $r_1 \leftarrow \emptyset$'. Also use ZUNIQUE instead of UNIQUE; within T4, this subroutine increases REF(p) by 1 if step U1 finds $q = \emptyset$.

A subtler change is needed to keep the partial-tautology functions of answer 201 up to date, because of their special meaning. Correct behavior is to keep t_u unchanged and set $t_v \leftarrow \text{LO}(t_u)$.

203. (a) $f \sqcup g = \{\{1,2\}, \{1,3\}, \{1,2,3\}, \{3\}\} = (e_1 \sqcup ((e_2 \sqcup (e_3 \cup \epsilon)) \cup e_3)) \cup e_3$; the other is $(e_1 \sqcup e_2) \cup \epsilon$, because $f \sqcap g = (e_1 \sqcup (e_2 \cup \epsilon)) \cup e_3 \cup \epsilon$ and $f \boxplus e_1 = e_1 \cup e_2 \cup e_3$.

(b) $(f \sqcup g)(z) = \exists x \exists y (f(x) \wedge g(y) \wedge (z \equiv x \vee y))$; $(f \sqcap g)(z) = \exists x \exists y (f(x) \wedge g(y) \wedge (z \equiv x \wedge y))$; $(f \boxplus g)(z) = \exists x \exists y (f(x) \wedge g(y) \wedge (z \equiv x \oplus y))$. Another formula is $(f \boxplus g)(z) = \bigvee \{f(z \oplus y) \mid g(y) = 1\} = \bigvee \{g(z \oplus x) \mid f(x) = 1\}$.

(c) Both (i) and (ii) are true; also $f \boxplus (g \cup h) = (f \boxplus g) \cup (f \boxplus h)$. Formula (iii) fails in general, although we do have $f \sqcup (g \sqcap h) \subseteq (f \sqcup g) \sqcap (f \sqcup h)$. Formula (iv) makes little sense; the right-hand side is $(f \sqcup f) \cup (f \sqcup h) \cup (g \sqcup f) \cup (g \sqcup h)$, by (i). Formula (v) is true because all three parts are $\emptyset$. And (vi) is true if and only if $f \neq \emptyset$.

(d) Only (ii) is always true. For (i), the condition should be $f \sqcap g \subseteq \epsilon$, since $f \sqcap g = \emptyset$ implies $f \perp g$. For (iii), notice that $|f \sqcup g| = |f \sqcap g| = |f \boxplus g| = 1$ whenever $|f| = |g| = 1$. Finally, in statement (iv), we do have $f \perp g \implies f \sqcup g = f \boxplus g$; but the converse fails when, say, $f = g = e_1 \cup \epsilon$.

(e) $f = \emptyset$ in (i) and $f = \epsilon$ in (ii); also $\epsilon \boxplus g = g$ for all g. There's no solution to (iii), because f would have to be $\{\{1, 2, 3, \dots\}\}$ and we are considering only finite sets. But in the finite universe of answer 201 we have $f = \{\{1, \dots, N\}\}$. (This family U has the property that $(f \boxplus U) \sqcup (g \boxplus U) = (f \sqcap g) \boxplus U$.) The general solution to (iv) is $f = e_1 \sqcup e_2 \sqcup f'$, where f' is an arbitrary family; similarly, the general solution to (v) is $f = (e_1 \sqcup f') \cup (e_2 \sqcup f'') \cup (e_1 \sqcup e_2 \sqcup (f' \cup f'' \cup f'''))$, where f', f'', and f''' are arbitrary. In (vi), $f = (((e_1 \sqcup e_2) \cup \epsilon) \sqcup f') \cup ((e_1 \cup e_2) \sqcup f'')) \sqcup (e_3 \cup \epsilon)$, where $f' \cup f'' \perp e_1 \cup e_2 \cup e_3$; this representation follows from exercise 204(f). In (vii), $|f| = 1$. Finally, (viii) characterizes Horn functions (Theorem 7.1.1H).

204. (a) This relation is obvious from the definition. (Also $(f \cup g)/h \supseteq (f/h) \cup (g/h)$.)

(b) $f/e_2 = \{\{1\}, \emptyset\} = e_1 \cup \epsilon$; $f/e_1 = e_2 \cup e_3$; $f/\epsilon = f$; hence $f/(e_1 \cup \epsilon) = e_2 \cup e_3$.

(c) Division by $\emptyset$ gives trouble, because *all* sets α belong to $f/\emptyset$. (But if we restrict consideration to families of subsets of $\{1, \dots, N\}$, as in exercises 201 and 207, we have $f/\emptyset = \wp$; also $\wp/\wp = \epsilon$, and $f/\wp = \emptyset$ when $f \neq \wp$.) Clearly $f/\epsilon = f$. And $f/f = \epsilon$ when $f \neq \emptyset$. Finally, $(f \bmod g)/g = \emptyset$ when $g \neq \emptyset$, because $\alpha \in (f \bmod g)/g$ and $\beta \in g$ implies $\alpha \cup \beta \in f$, $\alpha \in f/g$, and $\alpha \cup \beta \notin (f/g) \sqcup g$ — a contradiction.

(d) If $\beta \in g$, we have $\beta \cup \alpha \in f$ and $\beta \cap \alpha = \emptyset$ for all $\alpha \in f/g$; this proves the hint. Hence $f/g \subseteq f/(f/(f/g))$. Also $f/h \subseteq f/g$ when $h \supseteq g$, by (a); let $h = f/(f/g)$.

(e) Let $f/\!/g$ be the family in the new definition. Then $f/g \subseteq f/\!/g$, because $g \sqcup (f/g) \subseteq f$ and $g \perp (f/g)$. Conversely, if $\alpha \in f/\!/g$ and $\beta \in g$, we have $\alpha \in h$ for some h with $g \sqcup h \subseteq f$ and $g \perp h$; consequently $\alpha \cup \beta \in f$ and $\alpha \cap \beta = \emptyset$.

(f) If f has such a representation, we must have $g = f/e_j$ and $h = f \bmod e_j$. Conversely, those families satisfy $e_j \perp g \cup h$. (This law is the fundamental recursive principle underlying ZDDs — just as the unique representation $f = (x_j? \, g: h)$, with g and h independent of x_j, underlies BDDs.)

(g) Both true. (To prove them, represent f and g as in part (f).)

[R. K. Brayton and C. McMullen introduced the quotient and remainder operations in *Proc. Int. Symp. Circuits and Systems* (IEEE, 1982), 49–54, but in a slightly different context: They dealt with families of incomparable sets of subcubes.]

205. In all cases we construct a recursion based on exercise 204(f). For example, if $f_v = g_v = v$, we have $f \sqcup g = (\bar{v}? \, f_l \sqcup g_l: (f_l \sqcup g_h) \cup (f_h \sqcup g_l) \cup (f_h \sqcup g_h))$; $f \sqcap g = (\bar{v}? \, (f_l \sqcap g_l) \cup (f_l \sqcap g_h) \cup (f_h \sqcap g_l): f_h \sqcap g_h)$; $f \boxplus g = (\bar{v}? \, (f_l \boxplus g_l) \cup (f_h \boxplus g_h): (f_h \boxplus g_l) \cup (f_l \boxplus g_h))$.

(a) If $f_v < g_v$ or ($f_v = g_v$ and $f > g$), swap $f \leftrightarrow g$. If $f = \emptyset$, return f; if $f = \epsilon$, return g. If $f \sqcup g = r$ is in the memo cache, return r. If $f_v > g_v$, set $r_l \leftarrow \text{JOIN}(f, g_l)$ and $r_h \leftarrow \text{JOIN}(f, g_h)$; otherwise set $r_l \leftarrow \text{JOIN}(f_l, g_l)$, $r_{lh} \leftarrow \text{JOIN}(f_l, g_h)$, $r_{hl} \leftarrow \text{JOIN}(f_h, g_l)$, $r_{hh} \leftarrow \text{JOIN}(f_h, g_h)$, $r_h \leftarrow \text{OROR}(r_{lh}, r_{hl}, r_{hh})$, and dereference r_{lh}, r_{hl}, r_{hh}. Finish with $r \leftarrow \text{ZUNIQUE}(g_v, r_l, r_h)$; cache it and return it as in exercise 198.

(We could also compute r_h via the formula $\text{OR}(r_{lh}, \text{JOIN}(f_h, \text{OR}(g_l, g_h)))$, or via $\text{OR}(r_{hl}, \text{JOIN}(\text{OR}(f_l, f_h), g_h))$. Sometimes one way is much better than the other two.)

The DISJOIN operation, which produces the family of *disjoint* unions $\{\alpha \cup \beta \mid \alpha \in f, \, \beta \in g, \, \alpha \cap \beta = \emptyset\}$, is similar but with r_{hh} omitted.

(b) If $f_v < g_v$ or ($f_v = g_v$ and $f > g$), swap $f \leftrightarrow g$. If $f \leq \epsilon$, return f. (We consider $\emptyset < \epsilon$ and $\epsilon <$ all others.) Otherwise, if $\text{MEET}(f, g)$ hasn't been cached, there are two cases. If $f_v > g_v$, set $r_h \leftarrow \text{OR}(g_l, g_h)$, $r \leftarrow \text{MEET}(f, r_h)$, and dereference r_h; otherwise proceed analogously to (a) but with $l \leftrightarrow h$. Cache and return r as usual.

(c) This operation is similar to (a), but $r_l \leftarrow \text{OR}(r_{ll}, r_{hh})$ and $r_h \leftarrow \text{OR}(r_{lh}, r_{hl})$.

(d) First we implement the important simple cases f/e_v and $f \bmod e_v$:

$$\text{EZDIV}(f, v) = \begin{cases} \text{If } f_v = v, \text{ return } f_h; \text{ if } f_v > v, \text{ return } \emptyset. \text{ Otherwise look for} \\ f/e_v = r \text{ in the cache; if it isn't present, compute it via} \\ r \leftarrow \text{ZUNIQUE}(f_v, \text{EZDIV}(f_l, v), \text{EZDIV}(f_h, v)). \end{cases}$$

$$\text{EZMOD}(f, v) = \begin{cases} \text{If } f_v = v, \text{ return } f_l; \text{ if } f_v > v, \text{ return } f. \text{ Otherwise look for} \\ f \bmod e_v = r \text{ in the cache; if it isn't present, compute it via} \\ r \leftarrow \text{ZUNIQUE}(f_v, \text{EZMOD}(f_l, v), \text{EZMOD}(f_h, v)). \end{cases}$$

Now $\text{DIV}(f, g) = $ "If $g = \emptyset$, see below; if $g = \epsilon$, return f. Otherwise, if $f \leq \epsilon$, return $\emptyset$; if $f = g$, return ϵ. If $g_l = \emptyset$ and $g_h = \epsilon$, return $\text{EZDIV}(f, g_v)$. Otherwise, if $f/g = r$ is in the memo cache, return r. Otherwise set $r_l \leftarrow \text{EZDIV}(f, g_v)$, $r \leftarrow \text{DIV}(r_l, g_h)$, and dereference r_l. If $r \neq \emptyset$ and $g_l \neq \emptyset$, set $r_h \leftarrow \text{EZMOD}(f, g_v)$ and $r_l \leftarrow \text{DIV}(r_h, g_l)$, dereference r_h, set $r_h \leftarrow r$ and $r \leftarrow \text{AND}(r_l, r_h)$, dereference r_l and r_h. Insert '$f/g = r$' in the memo cache and return r." Division by $\emptyset$ returns $\wp$ if there is a fixed universe $\{1, \ldots, N\}$ as in exercise 201. Otherwise it's an error (because the universal family $\wp$ doesn't exist).

(e) If $g = \emptyset$, return f. If $g = \epsilon$, return $\emptyset$. If $(g_l, g_h) = (\emptyset, \epsilon)$, return $\text{EZMOD}(f, g_v)$. If $f \bmod g = r$ is cached, return it. Otherwise set $r \leftarrow \text{DIV}(f, g)$ and $r_h \leftarrow \text{JOIN}(r, g)$, dereference r, set $r \leftarrow \text{BUTNOT}(f, r_h)$, and dereference r_h. Cache and return r.

[S. Minato gave $\text{EZDIV}(f, v)$, $\text{EZREM}(f, v)$, and $\text{DELTA}(f, e_v)$ in his original paper on ZDDs. His algorithms for $\text{JOIN}(f, g)$ and $\text{DIV}(f, g)$ appeared in the sequel, *ACM/IEEE Design Automation Conf.* **31** (1994), 420–424.]

206. The upper bound $O(Z(f)^3 Z(g)^3)$ is not difficult to prove for cases (a) and (b), as well as $O(Z(f)^2 Z(g)^2)$ for case (c). But are there examples that take such a long time? And can the running time for (d) be exponential? All five routines seem to be reasonably fast in practice.

207. If $f = e_{i_1} \cup \cdots \cup e_{i_l}$ and $k \geq 0$, let $\text{SYM}(f, v, k)$ be the Boolean function that is true if and only if exactly k of the variables $\{x_{i_1}, \ldots, x_{i_l}\} \cap \{x_v, x_{v+1}, \ldots\}$ are 1 and $x_1 = \cdots = x_{v-1} = 0$. We compute $(e_{i_1} \cup \cdots \cup e_{i_l}) \S k$ by calling $\text{SYM}(f, 1, k)$.

$\text{SYM}(f, v, k) = $ "While $f_v < v$, set $f \leftarrow f_l$. If $f_v = N + 1$ and $k > 0$, return $\emptyset$. If $f_v = N + 1$ and $k = 0$, return the partial-tautology function t_v (see answer 201). If $f \S v \S k = r$ is in the cache, return r. Otherwise set $r \leftarrow \text{SYM}(f, f_v + 1, k)$. If $k > 0$, set $q \leftarrow \text{SYM}(f_l, f_v + 1, k - 1)$ and $r \leftarrow \text{ZUNIQUE}(f_v, r, q)$. While $f_v > v$, set $f_v \leftarrow f_v - 1$, increase $\text{REF}(r)$ by 1, and set $r \leftarrow \text{ZUNIQUE}(f_v, r, r)$. Put '$f \S v \S k = r$' in the cache, and return r." The running time is $O((k+1)N)$. Notice that $\emptyset \S 0 = \wp$.

208. Just omit the factors $2^{v_s - 1 - 1}$, $2^{v_l - v_k - 1}$, and $2^{v_h - v_k - 1}$ from steps C1 and C2. (And we get the generating function by setting $c_k \leftarrow c_l + z c_h$ in step C2; see exercise 25.) *The number of solutions equals the number of paths in the ZDD from the root to $\boxed{\top}$.*

209. Initially compute $\delta_n \leftarrow \bot$ and $\delta_j \leftarrow (\bar{x}_{j+1} \circ x_{j+1}) \bullet \delta_{j+1}$ for $n > j \geq 1$. Then, where answer 31 says '$\alpha \leftarrow (\bar{x}_j \circ x_j) \bullet \alpha$', change it to '$\alpha \leftarrow (\bar{x}_j \bullet \alpha) \circ (x_j \bullet \delta_j)$'. Also make the analogous changes with β and γ in place of α.

210. In fact, when $x = x_1 \ldots x_n$ we can replace νx in the definition of g by any linear function $c(x) = c_1 x_1 + \cdots + c_n x_n$, thus characterizing all of the optimal solutions to the general Boolean programming problem treated by Algorithm B.

For each branch node x of the ZDD, with fields $\mathtt{V}(x)$, $\mathtt{LO}(x)$, $\mathtt{HI}(x)$, we can compute its optimum value $\mathtt{M}(x)$ and new links $\mathtt{L}(x)$, $\mathtt{H}(x)$ as follows: Let $m_l = \mathtt{M}(\mathtt{LO}(x))$ and $m_h = c_{\mathtt{V}(x)} + \mathtt{M}(\mathtt{HI}(x))$, where $\mathtt{M}(\boxed{\perp}) = -\infty$ and $\mathtt{M}(\boxed{\top}) = 0$. Then $\mathtt{L}(x) \leftarrow \mathtt{LO}(x)$ if $m_l \geq m_h$, otherwise $\mathtt{L}(x) \leftarrow \boxed{\perp}$; $\mathtt{H}(x) \leftarrow \mathtt{HI}(x)$ if $m_l \leq m_h$, otherwise $\mathtt{H}(x) \leftarrow \boxed{\perp}$. The ZDD for g is obtained by reducing the $\mathtt{L}$ and $\mathtt{H}$ links accessible from the root. Notice that $Z(g) \leq Z(f)$, and the entire computation takes $O(Z(f))$ steps. (This nice property of ZDDs was pointed out by O. Coudert; see answer 237.)

211. Yes, unless the matrix has all-zero rows. Without such rows, in fact, the profile and z-profile of f satisfy $b_k \geq q_k - 1 \geq z_k$ for $0 \leq k < n$, because the only level-k subfunction independent of x_{k+1} is the constant 0.

212. The best alternative in the author's experiments was to make ZDDs for each term $T_j = S_1(X_j)$ in (129), using the algorithm of exercise 207, and then to AND them together. For example, in problem (128) we have $X_1 = \{x_1, x_2\}$, $X_2 = \{x_1, x_3, x_4\}$, $\ldots$, $X_{64} = \{x_{105}, x_{112}\}$; to make the term $S_1(X_2) = S_1(x_1, x_3, x_4)$, whose ZDD has 115 nodes, just form the 5-node ZDD for $e_1 \cup (e_3 \cup e_4)$ and compute $T_2 \leftarrow (e_1 \cup e_3 \cup e_4) \,\S\, 1$.

But in what order should the ANDs be done, after we've got the individual terms $T_1, \ldots, T_n$ of (129)? Consider problem (128). *Method 1:* $T_1 \leftarrow T_1 \wedge T_2$, $T_1 \leftarrow T_1 \wedge T_3$, $\ldots$, $T_1 \leftarrow T_1 \wedge T_{64}$. This "top-down" method fills in the upper levels first, and takes about 6.2 megamems. *Method 2:* $T_{64} \leftarrow T_{64} \wedge T_{63}$, $T_{64} \leftarrow T_{64} \wedge T_{62}$, $\ldots$, $T_{64} \leftarrow T_{64} \wedge T_1$. By filling in the lower levels first ("bottom-up"), the time goes down to about 1.75 megamems. *Method 3:* $T_2 \leftarrow T_2 \wedge T_1$, $T_4 \leftarrow T_4 \wedge T_3$, $\ldots$, $T_{64} \leftarrow T_{64} \wedge T_{63}$; $T_4 \leftarrow T_4 \wedge T_2$, $T_8 \leftarrow T_8 \wedge T_6$, $\ldots$, $T_{64} \leftarrow T_{64} \wedge T_{62}$; $T_8 \leftarrow T_8 \wedge T_4$, $T_{16} \leftarrow T_{16} \wedge T_{12}$, $\ldots$, $T_{64} \leftarrow T_{64} \wedge T_{60}$; $\ldots$; $T_{64} \leftarrow T_{64} \wedge T_{32}$. This "balanced" approach also takes about 1.75 megamems. *Method 4:* $T_{33} \leftarrow T_{33} \wedge T_1$, $T_{34} \leftarrow T_{34} \wedge T_2$, $\ldots$, $T_{64} \leftarrow T_{64} \wedge T_{32}$; $T_{49} \leftarrow T_{49} \wedge T_{33}$, $T_{50} \leftarrow T_{50} \wedge T_{34}$, $\ldots$, $T_{64} \leftarrow T_{64} \wedge T_{48}$; $T_{57} \leftarrow T_{57} \wedge T_{49}$, $T_{58} \leftarrow T_{58} \wedge T_{50}$, $\ldots$, $T_{64} \leftarrow T_{64} \wedge T_{56}$; $\ldots$; $T_{64} \leftarrow T_{64} \wedge T_{63}$. This is a much better way to balance the work, needing only about 850 kilomems. *Method 5:* An analogous balancing strategy that uses the ternary ANDAND operation turns out to be still better, costing just 675 kilomems. (In all five cases, add 190 kilomems for the time to form the 64 initial terms T_j.)

Incidentally, we can reduce the ZDD size from 2300 to 1995 by insisting that $x_1 = 0$ and $x_2 = 1$ in (128) and (129), because the "transpose" of every covering is another covering. This idea does not, however, reduce the running time substantially.

The rows of (128) appear in decreasing lexicographic order, and that may not be ideal. But dynamic variable ordering is unhelpful when so many variables are present. (Sifting reduces the size from 2300 to 1887, but takes a *long* time.)

Further study, with a variety of exact cover problems, would clearly be desirable.

213. It is a bipartite graph with 30 vertices in one part and 32 in the other. (Think of a chessboard as a *checkerboard*: Every domino joins a white square to a black square, and we've removed two black squares.) A row sum of $(1, \ldots, 1, 1, *, *)$ has 1s in at least 31 "white" positions, so its last two coordinates must be either $(2, 1)$ or $(3, 2)$.

214. Add further constraints to the covering condition (128), namely $\bigwedge_{j=1}^{14} S_{\geq 1}(Y_j)$, where Y_j is the set of x_i that cross the jth potential fault line. (For example, $Y_1 = \{x_2, x_4, x_6, x_8, x_{10}, x_{12}, x_{14}, x_{15}\}$ is the set of ways to place a domino vertically in the top two rows of the board; each $|Y_j| = 8$.) The resulting ZDD has 9812 nodes, and characterizes 25,506 solutions. Incidentally, the BDD size is 26,622. [Faultfree domino tilings of $m \times n$ boards exist if and only if mn is even, $m \geq 5$, $n \geq 5$, and $(m, n) \neq$ (6, 6); see R. L. Graham, *The Mathematical Gardner* (Wadsworth International, 1981), 120–126. The solution in (127) is the only 8×8 example that is symmetric under both horizontal and vertical reflection; see Fig. 29(b) for symmetry under 90° rotation.]

215. This time we add the constraints $\bigwedge_{j=1}^{49} S_{\geq 1}(Z_j)$, where Z_j is the set of four place-ments x_i that surround an internal corner point. (For example, $Z_1 = \{x_1, x_2, x_4, x_{16}\}$.) These constraints reduce the ZDD size to 66. There are just two solutions, one the transpose of the other, and they can readily be found by hand. [See Y. Kotani, *Puzzlers' Tribute* (A. K. Peters, 2002), 413–420. The set of all tatami tilings has been characterized by Dean Hickerson; the corresponding generating functions have been obtained by Frank Ruskey and Jennifer Woodcock, *Electronic J. Combinatorics* **16**, 1 (2009), #R126.]

216. (a) Assign three variables (a_i, b_i, c_i) to each row of (128), corresponding to the domino's color if row i is chosen. Every branch node of the ZDD for f in (129) now becomes three branch nodes. We can take advantage of symmetry under transposition by replacing f by $f \wedge x_2$; this reduces the ZDD size from 2300 to 1995, which grows to 5981 when each branch node is triplicated.

Now we AND in the adjacency constraints, for all 682 cases $\{i, i'\}$ where rows i and i' are adjacent domino positions. Such constraints have the form $\neg((a_i \wedge a_{i'}) \vee (b_i \wedge b_{i'}) \vee (c_i \wedge c_{i'}))$, and we apply them bottom-up as in Method 2 of answer 212. This computation inflates the ZDD until it reaches more than 800 thousand nodes; but eventually it settles down and ends up with size 584,205.

The desired answer turns out to be 13,343,246,232 (which, of course, is a multiple of $3! = 6$, because each permutation of the three colors yields a different solution).

(b) This question is distinct from part (a), because many coverings (including Fig. 29(b)) can be 3-colored in several ways; we want to count them only once.

Suppose $f(a_1, b_1, c_1, \ldots, a_m, b_m, c_m) = f(x_1, \ldots, x_{3m})$ is a function with $a_i = x_{3i-2}$, $b_i = x_{3i-1}$, and $c_i = x_{3i}$, such that $f(x_1, \ldots, x_{3m}) = 1$ implies $a_i + b_i + c_i \leq 1$ for $1 \leq i \leq m$. Let's define the *uncoloring* $\$f$ of f to be

$$\$f(x_1, \ldots, x_m) = \exists y_1 \cdots \exists y_{3m} \left(f(y_1, \ldots, y_{3m}) \right.$$
$$\left. \wedge \, (x_1 = y_1 + y_2 + y_3) \wedge \cdots \wedge (x_m = y_{3m-2} + y_{3m-1} + y_{3m}) \right).$$

A straightforward recursive subroutine will compute the ZDD for $\$f$ from the ZDD for f. This process transforms the 584,205 nodes obtained in part (a) into a ZDD of size 33,731, from which we deduce the answer: 3,272,232.

(The running time is 1.2 gigamems for part (a), plus 1.3 gigamems to uncolor; the total memory requirement is about 44 megabytes. A similar computation based on BDDs instead of ZDDs cost $13.6 + 1.5$ gigamems and occupied 185 megabytes.)

217. The separation condition adds 4198 further constraints of the form $\neg(x_i \wedge x_{i'})$, where rows i and i' specify adjacent placements of congruent pieces. Applying these constraints while also evaluating the conjunction $\bigwedge_{j=1}^{468} S_1(X_j)$ turned out to be a bad idea, in the author's experiments; even worse was an attempt to construct a separate ZDD for the new constraints alone. Much better was to build the 512,227-node ZDD as before, then to incorporate the new constraints one by one, first constraining the variables at the lowest levels. The resulting ZDD of size 31,300,699 was finally completed after 286 gigamems of work, proving that exactly 7,099,053,234,102 separated solutions exist.

We might also ask for *strongly* separated solutions, where congruent pieces are not allowed to touch even at their corners; this requirement adds 1948 more constraints. There are 554,626,216 strongly separated coverings, findable after 245 gigamems with a ZDD of size 4,785,236. (But standard backtracking finds them faster and with neglible memory.)

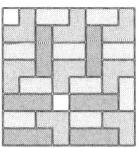

218. This is an exact cover problem. For example, the matrix when $n = 3$ is

$$\begin{array}{ll} 001001010 & (--2--2) \\ 010001001 & (-3---3) \\ 010010010 & (-2--2-) \\ 010100100 & (-1-1--) \\ 100010001 & (3---3-) \\ 100100010 & (2--2--) \\ 101000100 & (1-1---) \end{array}$$

and in general there are $3n$ columns and $\binom{2n-1}{2} - \binom{n}{2}$ rows. Consider the case $n = 12$: The ZDD on 187 variables has 192,636 nodes. It can be found with a cost of 300 megamems, using Method 4 of answer 212 (binary balancing); Method 5 turns out to be 25% slower than Method 4 in this case. The BDD is much larger (2,198,195 nodes) and it costs more than 900 megamems.

Thus the ZDD is clearly preferable to the BDD for this problem, and it identifies the $L_{12} = 108,144$ solutions with reasonable efficiency. (However, the "dancing links" technique of Section 7.2.2 is about four times faster, and it needs far less memory.)

219. (a) 1267; (b) 2174; (c) 2958; (d) 3721; (e) 4502. (To form the ZDD for WORDS(n) we do $n - 1$ ORs of the 7-node ZDDs for $w_1 \sqcup h_2 \sqcup i_3 \sqcup c_4 \sqcup h_5$, $t_1 \sqcup h_2 \sqcup e_3 \sqcup r_4 \sqcup e_5$, etc.)

220. (a) There is one a_2 node for the descendants of each initial letter that can be followed by a in the second position (aargh, babel, ..., zappy); 23 letters qualify, all except q, u, and x. And there's one b_2 node for each initial letter that can be followed by b (abbey, ebony, oboes). However, the actual rule isn't so simple; for example, there are three z_2 nodes, not four, because of sharing between czars and tzars.

(b) There's no v_5 because no five-letter word ends with v. (The SGB collection doesn't include arxiv or webtv.) The three nodes for w_5 arise because one stands for cases where the letters $< w_5$ must be followed by w (aglo and many others); another node stands for cases where either w or y must follow (stra, or resa, or when we've seen allo but not allot); and there's also a w_5 node for the case when unse is not followed by e or t, because it must then be followed by either w or x. Similarly, the two nodes for x_5 represent the cases where x is forced, or where the last letter must be either x or y (following rela). There's only one y_5 node, because no four letters can be followed by both y and z. Of course there's just one z_5 node, and two sinks.

221. We compute, for every possible zead ζ, the probability that ζ will occur, and sum over all ζ. For definiteness, consider a zead that corresponds to branching on r_3, and suppose it represents a subfamily of 10 three-letter suffixes. There are exactly $\binom{6084}{10} - \binom{5408}{10} \approx 1.3 \times 10^{31}$ such zeads, and by the principle of inclusion and exclusion they each arise with probability $\sum_{k \geq 1} \binom{676}{k}(-1)^{k+1}\binom{11881376-6084k}{5757-10k}/\binom{11881376}{5757} \approx 2.5 \times 10^{-32}$. [*Hint:* $|\{r, s, t, u, v, w, x, y, z\}| = 9$, $676 = 26^2$, and $6084 = 9 \times 26^2$.] Thus such zeads contribute about 0.33 to the total. The r_3-zeads for subfamilies of sizes 1, 2, 3, 4, 5, ..., contribute approximately 11.5, 32.3, 45.1, 41.9, 29.3, ..., by a similar analysis;

so we expect about 188.8 branches on r_3 altogether, on average. The grand total

$$\sum_{l=1}^{5}\sum_{j=1}^{26}\sum_{s=1}^{5757}\left(\binom{26^{5-l}(27-j)}{s}-\binom{26^{5-l}(26-j)}{s}\right)$$
$$\times\sum_{k=1}^{\infty}\binom{26^{l-1}}{k}(-1)^{k+1}\binom{26^5-26^{5-l}(27-j)k}{5757-sk}\Big/\binom{26^5}{5757},$$

plus 2 for the sinks, comes to ≈ 7151.986. The average z-profile is $\approx (1.00, \ldots, 1.00;$ $25.99, \ldots, 25.99; 188.86, \ldots, 171.43; 86.31, \ldots, 27.32; 3.53, \ldots, 1.00; 2.00)$.

222. (a) It's the set of all subsets of the words of F. (There are 50,569 such subwords, out of $27^5 = 14{,}348{,}907$ possibilities. They are described by a ZDD of size 18,784, constructed from F and $\wp$ via answer 205(b) at a cost of about 15 megamems.)

(b) This formula gives the same result as $F \sqcap \wp$, because every member of F contains exactly one element of each X_j. But the computation turns out to be much slower — about 370 megamems — in spite of the fact that $Z(X) = 132$ is almost as small as $Z(\wp) = 131$. (Notice that $|\wp| = 2^{130}$ while $|X| = 26^5 \approx 2^{23.5}$.)

(c) $(F/P) \sqcup P$, where $P = t_1 \sqcup u_3 \sqcup h_5$ is the pattern. (The words are touch, tough, truth. This computation costs about 3000 mems with the algorithms of answer 205.) Other contenders for simple formulas are $F \cap Q$, where Q describes the admissible words. If we set $Q = t_1 \sqcup X_2 \sqcup u_3 \sqcup X_4 \sqcup h_5$, we have $Z(Q) = 57$ and the cost once again is $\approx 3000\mu$. With $Q = (t_1 \cup u_3 \cup h_5)\,\S\,3$, on the other hand, we have $Z(Q) = 132$ and the cost rises to about 9000 mems. (Here $|Q|$ is 26^2 in the first case, but 2^{127} in the second — *reversing* any intuition gained from (a) and (b)! Go figure.)

(d) $F \cap ((V_1 \cup \cdots \cup V_5)\,\S\,k)$. The number of such words is $(24, 1974, 3307, 443, 9, 0)$ for $k = (0, \ldots, 5)$, respectively, from ZDDs of sizes $(70, 1888, 3048, 686, 34, 1)$. ("See exercise 7–34 for the words F mod y_1 mod y_2 mod $\cdots$ mod y_5," said the author wryly.)

(e) The desired patterns satisfy $P = (F \sqcap \wp) \cap Q$, where $Q = ((X_1 \cup \cdots \cup X_5)\,\S\,3)$. We have $Z(Q) = 386$, $Z(P) = 14221$, and $|P| = 19907$.

(f) The formula for this case is trickier. First, $P_2 = F \sqcap F$ gives F together with all patterns satisfied by two distinct words; we have $Z(P_2) = 11289$, $|P_2| = 21234$, and $|P_2 \cap Q| = 7753$. But $P_2 \cap Q$ is *not* the answer; for example, it omits the pattern *atc*, which occurs eight times but only in the context *atch. The correct answer is given by $P_2' \cap Q$, where $P_2' = (P_2 \backslash F) \sqcap \wp$. Then $Z(P_2') = 8947$, $Z(P_2' \cap Q) = 7525$, $|P_2' \cap Q| = 10472$.

(g) $G_1 \cup \cdots \cup G_5$, where $G_j = (F/(b_j \cup o_j)) \sqcup b_j$. The answers are bared, bases, basis, baths, bobby, bring, busts, herbs, limbs, tribs.

(h) Patterns that admit all vowels in second place: b*lls, b*nds, m*tes, p*cks.

(i) The first gives all words whose middle three letters are vowels. The second gives all patterns with first and last letter specified, for which there's at least one match with three vowels inserted. There are 30 solutions to the first, but only 27 to the second (because, e.g., louis and luaus yield the same pattern). Incidentally, the complementary family $\wp \backslash F$ has $2^{130} - 5757$ members, and 46316 nodes in its ZDD.

223. (a) $d(\alpha, \mu) + d(\beta, \mu) + d(\gamma, \mu) = 5$, since $d(\alpha, \mu) = [\alpha_1 \neq \mu_1] + \cdots + [\alpha_5 \neq \mu_5]$.

(b) Given families f, g, h, the family $\{\mu \mid \mu = \langle\alpha\beta\gamma\rangle$ for some $\alpha \in f$, $\beta \in g$, $\gamma \in h$ with $\alpha \neq \mu$, $\beta \neq \mu$, $\gamma \neq \mu$, and $\alpha \cap \beta \cap \gamma = \emptyset\}$ can be defined recursively to allow ZDD computation, if we consider eight variants in which subsets of the inequality constraints are relaxed. In the author's experimental system, the ZDDs for medians of WORDS(n) for $n = (100, 1000, 5757)$ have respectively $(595, 14389, 71261)$ nodes and characterize $(47, 7310, 86153)$ five-letter solutions. Among the 86153 medians

when $n = 5757$ are chads, stent, blogs, ditzy, phish, bling, and tetch; in fact,
tetch = ⟨fetch teach total⟩ arises already when $n = 1000$. (The running times of
about $(.01, 2, 700)$ gigamems, respectively, were not especially impressive; ZDDs are
probably not the best tool for this problem. Still, the programming was instructive.)

(c) When $n = 100$, exactly $(1, 14, 47)$ medians of WORDS(n) belong to WORDS(100),
WORDS(1000), WORDS(5757), respectively; the solution with most common words is
while = ⟨white whole still⟩. When $n = 1000$, the corresponding numbers are $(38,$
$365, 1276)$; and when $n = 5757$ they are $(78, 655, 4480)$. The most common English
words that *aren't* medians of three other English words are their, first, and right.

224. Every arc $u \longrightarrow v$ of the dag corresponds to a vertex v of the forest. The ZDD
has exactly one branch node for every arc. The LO pointer of that node leads to the
right sibling of the corresponding vertex v, or to ⊥ if v has no right sibling. The HI
pointer leads to the left child of v, or to ⊤ if v is a leaf. The arcs can be ordered in
many ways (e.g., preorder, postorder, level order), without changing this ZDD.

225. As in exercise 55, we try to number the vertices in such a way that the "frontier"
between early and late vertices remains fairly small; then we needn't remember too
much about what decisions were made on the early vertices. In the present case we
also want the source vertex s to be number 1.

In answer 55, the relevant state from previous branches corresponded to an
equivalence relation (a set partition); but now we express it by a table $mate[i]$ for
$j \le i \le l$, where $j = u_k$ is the smaller vertex of the current edge u_k — v_k and where
$l = \max\{v_1, \ldots, v_{k-1}\}$. Let $mate[i] = i$ if vertex i is untouched so far; let $mate[i] = 0$
if vertex i has been touched twice already. Otherwise $mate[i] = r$ and $mate[r] = i$, if
previous edges form a simple path with endpoints $\{i, r\}$. Initially we set $mate[i] \leftarrow i$ for
$1 \le i \le n$, except that $mate[1] \leftarrow t$ and $mate[t] \leftarrow 1$. (If $t > l$, the value of $mate[t]$ need
not be stored, because it can be determined from the values of $mate[i]$ for $j \le i \le l$.)

Let $j' = u_{k+1}$ and $l' = \max\{v_1, \ldots, v_k\}$ be the values of j and l after edge k
has been considered; and suppose $u_k = j$, $v_k = m$, $mate[j] = \hat{\jmath}$, $mate[m] = \hat{m}$. We
cannot choose edge j — m if $\hat{\jmath} = 0$ or $\hat{m} = 0$. Otherwise, if $\hat{\jmath} \ne m$, the new $mate$ table
after choosing edge j — m can be computed by doing the assignments $mate[j] \leftarrow 0$,
$mate[m] \leftarrow 0$, $mate[\hat{\jmath}] \leftarrow \hat{m}$, $mate[\hat{m}] \leftarrow \hat{\jmath}$ (in that order).

Otherwise we have $\hat{\jmath} = m$ and $\hat{m} = j$; we must contemplate the endgame. Let
i be the smallest integer such that $i > j$, $i \ne m$, and either $i > l'$ or $mate[i] \ne 0$ and
$mate[i] \ne i$. The new state after choosing edge j — m is $\emptyset$ if $i \le l'$, otherwise it is ϵ.

Whether or not the edge is chosen, the new state will be $\emptyset$ if $mate[i] \ne 0$ and
$mate[i] \ne i$ for some i in the range $j \le i < j'$.

For example, here are the first steps for paths from 1 to 9 in a 3×3 grid (see (132)):

k	j	l	m	$mate[1] \ldots mate[9]$	$\hat{\jmath}$	$\hat{m}$	$mate'[1] \ldots mate'[9]$
1	1	1	2	9 2 3 4 5 6 7 8 1	9	2	0 9 3 4 5 6 7 8 2
2	1	2	3	9 2 3 4 5 6 7 8 1	9	3	0 2 9 4 5 6 7 8 3
2	1	2	3	0 9 3 4 5 6 7 8 2	0	3	—
3	2	3	4	0 2 9 4 5 6 7 8 3	2	4	0 4 9 2 5 6 7 8 3
3	2	3	4	0 9 3 4 5 6 7 8 2	9	4	0 0 3 9 5 6 7 8 4

where $mate'$ describes the next state if edge j — m is chosen. The state transitions
$mate_{j..l} \mapsto mate'_{j'..l'}$ are $9 \mapsto (\overline{12}? \; 92: 09)$; $92 \mapsto (\overline{13}? \; \emptyset: 29)$; $09 \mapsto (\overline{13}? \; 93: \emptyset)$;
$29 \mapsto (\overline{24}? \; 294: 492)$; $93 \mapsto (\overline{24}? \; 934: 039)$.

After all reachable states have been found, the ZDD can be obtained by reducing
equivalent states, using a procedure like Algorithm R. (In the 3×3 grid problem,

57 branch nodes are reduced to 28, plus two sinks. The 22-branch ZDD illustrated in the text was obtained by subsequently optimizing with exercise 197.)

226. Just omit the initial assignments '$mate[1] \leftarrow t$, $mate[t] \leftarrow 1$.'

227. Change the test '$mate[i] \neq 0$ and $mate[i] \neq i$' to just '$mate[i] \neq 0$' in two places. Also, change '$i \leq l'$' to '$i \leq n$'.

228. Use the previous answer with the following further changes: Add a dummy vertex $d = n + 1$, with new edges $v - d$ for all $v \neq s$; accepting this new edge will mean "end at v." Initialize the $mate$ table with $mate[1] \leftarrow d$, $mate[d] \leftarrow 1$. Leave d out of the maximization when calculating l and l'. When beginning to examine a stored $mate$ table, start with $mate[d] \leftarrow 0$ and then, if encountering $mate[i] = d$, set $mate[d] \leftarrow i$.

229. 149,692,648,904 of the latter paths go from VA to MD; graph (133) omits DC. (However, the graphs of (18) have fewer *Hamiltonian* paths than (133), because (133) has 1,782,199 Hamiltonian paths from CA to ME that do not go from VA to MD.)

230. The unique minimum and maximum routes from ME both end at WA:

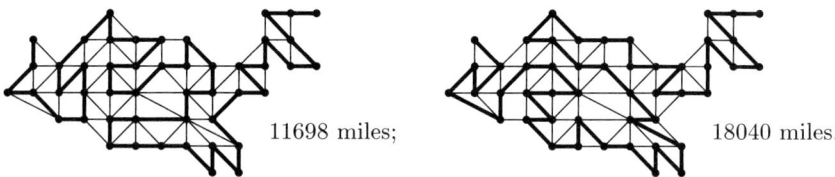

11698 miles;   18040 miles.

Let $g(z) = \sum z^{\text{miles}(r)}$, summed over all routes r. The average cost, $g'(1)/g(1) = 1022014257375/68656026 \approx 14886.01$, can be computed rapidly as in answer 29.

(Similarly, $g''(1) = 15243164303013274$, so the standard deviation is ≈ 666.2.)

231. The algorithm of answer 225 gives a proto-ZDD with 8,062,831 branch nodes; it reduces to a ZDD with 3,024,214 branches. The number of solutions, via answer 208, is 50,819,542,770,311,581,606,906,543.

232. With answer 227 we find $h = 721,613,446,615,109,970,767$ Hamiltonian paths from a corner to its horizontal neighbor, and $d = 480,257,285,722,344,701,834$ of them to its diagonal neighbor; in both cases the relevant ZDD has about 1.3 million nodes. The number of oriented Hamiltonian cycles is $2h + d = 1,923,484,178,952,564,643,368$. (Divide by 2 to get the number of *undirected* Hamiltonian cycles.)

Essentially only two king's tours achieve the maximal length $8 + 56\sqrt{2}$:

 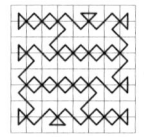

233. A similar procedure can be used but with $mate[i] = r$ and $mate[r] = -i$ when the previous choices define an oriented path from i to r. Process all arcs $u_k \longrightarrow v_k$ and $u_k \longleftarrow v_k$ consecutively when $u_k = j < v_k = m$. Define $\hat{\jmath} = -j$ if $mate[j] = j$, otherwise $\hat{\jmath} = mate[j]$. Choosing $j \longrightarrow m$ is illegal if $\hat{\jmath} \geq 0$ or $\hat{m} \leq 0$. The updating rule for that choice, when legal, is: $mate[j] \leftarrow 0$, $mate[m] \leftarrow 0$, $mate[-\hat{\jmath}] \leftarrow \hat{m}$, $mate[\hat{m}] \leftarrow \hat{\jmath}$.

234. The 437 oriented cycles can be represented by a ZDD of ≈ 800 nodes. The shortest are, of course, AL $\longrightarrow$ LA $\longrightarrow$ AL and MN $\longrightarrow$ NM $\longrightarrow$ MN. There are 37 of length 17 (the maximum), such as (ALARINVTNMIDCOKSC) — i.e., AL $\longrightarrow$ LA $\longrightarrow \cdots \longrightarrow$ SC $\longrightarrow$ CA $\longrightarrow$ AL.

Incidentally, the directed graph in question is the arc digraph D^* of the digraph D on 26 vertices $\{\texttt{A}, \texttt{B}, \ldots, \texttt{Z}\}$ whose 49 arcs are $\texttt{A} \longrightarrow \texttt{L}$, $\texttt{A} \longrightarrow \texttt{R}$, ..., $\texttt{W} \longrightarrow \texttt{Y}$. Every oriented walk of D^* is an oriented walk of D, and conversely (see exercise 2.3.4.2–21); but the oriented *cycles* of D^* are not necessarily simple in D. In fact, D has only 37 oriented cycles, the longest of which is unique: (`ARINMOKSDC`).

If we extend consideration to the 62 postal codes in exercise 7–54(c), the number of oriented cycles rises to 38336, including the unique 1-cycle (`A`), as well as 192 that have length 23, such as (`APRIALASCTNMMNVINCOKSDCA`). About 17000 ZDD nodes suffice to characterize the entire family of oriented cycles in this case.

235. The digraph has 7912 arcs; but we can prune them dramatically by removing arcs from vertices of in-degree zero, or arcs to vertices of out-degree zero. For example, `owner` $\longrightarrow$ `nerdy` goes away, because `nerdy` is a dead end; in fact, all successors of `owner` are likewise eliminated, so `crown` is out too. Eventually we're left with only 112 arcs among 85 words, and the problem can basically be done by hand.

There are just 74 oriented cycles. The unique shortest one, `slant` $\longrightarrow$ `antes` $\longrightarrow$ `tesla` $\longrightarrow$ `slant`, can be abbreviated to '(slante)' as in the previous answer. The two longest are $(\alpha\omega)$ and $(\beta\omega)$, where $\alpha = $ `picastepsomaso`, $\beta = $ `pointrotherema`, and $\omega = $ `nicadrearedidoserumorelicitesslabsitaresetuplenactoricedarerunichesto`.

236. (a) Suppose $\alpha \in f$ and $\beta \in g$. If $\alpha \subseteq \beta$, then $\alpha \in f \sqcap g$. If $\alpha \cap \beta \in f$, then $\alpha \cap \beta \notin f \nearrow g$. A similar argument, or the use of part (b), shows that $f \searrow g = f \setminus (f \sqcup g)$.

Notes: The complementary operations "$f \nwarrow g = f \setminus (f \searrow g) = \{\alpha \in f \mid \alpha \supseteq \beta$ for some $\beta \in g\}$" for supersets, and "$f \swarrow g = f \setminus (f \nearrow g) = \{\alpha \in f \mid \alpha \subseteq \beta$ for some $\beta \in g\}$" for subsets, are also important in applications. They were omitted from this exercise only because five operations are already rather intimidating. The superset operation was introduced by O. Coudert, J. C. Madre, and H. Fraisse [*ACM/IEEE Design Automation Conference* **30** (1993), 625–630]. The identity $f \nwarrow g = f \cap (f \sqcup g)$ was noted by H. G. Okuno, S. Minato, and H. Isozaki [*Information Processing Letters* **66** (1998), 195–199], who also listed several of the laws in (d).

(b) Elementary set theory suffices. (The first six identities appear in pairs, each of which is equivalent to its mate. Strictly speaking, f^C involves infinite sets, and U is the AND of infinitely many variables; but the formulas hold in any finite universe. Notice that, when cast in the language of Boolean functions, $f^C(x) = f(\bar{x})$ is the complement of f^D, the Boolean dual; see exercise 7.1.1–2. Is there any use for the dual of $f^\sharp$, namely $\{\alpha \mid \beta \in f$ implies $\alpha \cup \beta \neq U\}^\uparrow$? If so, we might denote it by $f^\flat$.)

(c) All true except (ii), which should have said that $x_1^\uparrow = x_1^{C\downarrow C} = \bar{x}_1^{\downarrow C} = \epsilon^C = U$.

(d) The "identities" to cross out here are (ii), (viii), (ix), (xiv), and (xvi); the others are worth remembering. Regarding (ii)–(vi), notice that $f = f^\uparrow$ if and only if $f = f^\downarrow$, if and only if f is a clutter. Formula (xiv) should be $f \searrow g^\downarrow = f \searrow g$, the dual of (xiii). Formula (xvi) is almost right; it fails only when $f = \emptyset$ or $g = \emptyset$. Formula (ix) is perhaps the most interesting: We actually have $f^{\sharp\sharp} = f$ if and only if f is a clutter.

(e) Assuming that the universe of all vertices is finite, we have (i) $f = \wp \searrow g$ and (ii) $g = (\wp \setminus f)^\downarrow$, where $\wp$ is the universal family of exercises 201 and 222, because g is the family of minimal dependent sets. (Purists should substitute $\wp_V = \bigsqcup_{v \in V} (\epsilon \cup e_v)$ for $\wp$ in these formulas. The same relations hold in any hypergraph for which no edge is contained in another.)

237. MAXMAL$(f) = $ "If $f = \emptyset$ or $f = \epsilon$, return f. If $f^\uparrow = r$ is cached, return r. Otherwise set $r \leftarrow $ MAXMAL(f_l), $r_h \leftarrow $ MAXMAL(f_h), $r_l \leftarrow $ NONSUB(r, r_h), dereference r, and $r \leftarrow $ ZUNIQUE(f_v, r_l, r_h); cache and return r."

MINMAL(f) = "If $f = \emptyset$ or $f = \epsilon$, return f. If $f^{\downarrow} = r$ is cached, return r. Otherwise set $r_l \leftarrow$ MINMAL(f_l), $r \leftarrow$ MINMAL(f_h), $r_h \leftarrow$ NONSUP(r, r_l), dereference r, and $r \leftarrow$ ZUNIQUE(f_v, r_l, r_h); cache and return r."

NONSUB(f, g) = "If $g = \emptyset$, return f. If $f = \emptyset$ or $f = \epsilon$ or $f = g$, return $\emptyset$. If $f \nearrow g = r$ is cached, return r. Otherwise represent f and g as in (52). If $v < g_v$, set $r_l \leftarrow$ NONSUB(f_l, g), $r_h \leftarrow f_h$, and increase REF(f_h) by 1; otherwise set $r_h \leftarrow$ NONSUB(f_l, g_l), $r \leftarrow$ NONSUB(f_l, g_h), $r_l \leftarrow$ AND(r, r_h), dereference r and r_h, and set $r_h \leftarrow$ NONSUB(f_h, g_h). Finally $r \leftarrow$ ZUNIQUE(v, r_l, r_h); cache and return r."

NONSUP(f, g) = "If $g = \emptyset$, return f. If $f = \emptyset$ or $g = \epsilon$ or $f = g$, return $\emptyset$. If $f_v > g_v$, return NONSUP(f, g_l). If $f \searrow g = r$ is cached, return r. Otherwise set $v = f_v$. If $v < g_v$, set $r_l \leftarrow$ NONSUP(f_l, g) and $r_h \leftarrow$ NONSUP(f_h, g); otherwise set $r_l \leftarrow$ NONSUP(f_h, g_h), $r \leftarrow$ NONSUP(f_h, g_l), $r_h \leftarrow$ AND(r, r_l), dereference r and r_l, and set $r_l \leftarrow$ NONSUP(f_l, g_l). Finally $r \leftarrow$ ZUNIQUE(v, r_l, r_h); cache and return r."

MINHIT(f) = "If $f = \emptyset$, return ϵ. If $f = \epsilon$, return $\emptyset$. If $f^{\sharp} = r$ is cached, return r. Otherwise set $r \leftarrow$ OR(f_l, f_h), $r_l \leftarrow$ MINHIT(r), dereference r, $r \leftarrow$ MINHIT(f_l), $r_h \leftarrow$ NONSUP(r, r_l), dereference r, and $r \leftarrow$ ZUNIQUE(f_v, r_l, r_h); cache and return r."

As in exercise 206, the worst-case running times of these routines are unknown. Although NONSUB and NONSUP can be computed via JOIN or MEET and BUTNOT, by exercise 236(a), this direct implementation tends to be faster. It may be preferable to replace '$f = \epsilon$' by '$\epsilon \in f$' in MINMAL and MINHIT; also '$g = \epsilon$' by '$\epsilon \in g$' in NONSUP.

[Olivier Coudert introduced and implemented the operators $f^{\uparrow}$, $f \nearrow g$, and $f \searrow g$ in *Proc. Europ. Design and Test Conf.* (IEEE, 1997), 224–228. He also gave a recursive implementation of the interesting operator $f \odot g = (f \sqcup g)^{\uparrow}$; however, in the author's experiments, much better results have been obtained without it. For example, if f is the 177-node ZDD for the independent sets of the contiguous USA, the operation $g \leftarrow$ JOIN(f, f) costs about 350 kilomems and $h \leftarrow$ MAXMAL(g) costs about 3.6 megamems; but more than 69 *gigamems* are needed to compute $h \leftarrow$ MAXJOIN(f, f) all at once. Improved caching and garbage-collection strategies may, of course, change the picture.]

238. We can compute the 177-node ZDD for the family f of independent sets, using the ordering (104), in two ways: With Boolean algebra (67), $f = \neg \bigvee_{u - v}(x_u \wedge x_v)$; the cost is about 1.1 megamems with the algorithms of answers 198–201. With family algebra, on the other hand, we have $f = \wp \searrow \bigcup_{u-v}(e_u \sqcup e_v)$ by exercise 236(e); the cost, via answer 237, is less than 175 kilomems.

The subsets that give 2-colorable and 3-colorable subgraphs are $g = f \sqcup f$ and $h = g \sqcup f$, respectively; the maximal ones are $g^{\uparrow}$ and $h^{\uparrow}$. We have $Z(g) = 1009$, $Z(g^{\uparrow}) = 3040$, $Z(h) = 179$, $Z(h^{\uparrow}) = 183$, $|g| = 9{,}028{,}058{,}789{,}780$, $|g^{\uparrow}| = 2{,}949{,}441$, $|h| = 543{,}871{,}144{,}820{,}736$, and $|h^{\uparrow}| = 384$. The successive costs of computing g, $g^{\uparrow}$, h, and $h^{\uparrow}$ are approximately 350 Kμ (kilomems), 3.6 Mμ, 1.1 Mμ, and 230 Kμ. (We could compute $h^{\uparrow}$ by, say, $(g^{\uparrow} \sqcup f)^{\uparrow}$; but that turns out to be a bad idea.)

The maximal induced bipartite and tripartite subgraphs have the respective generating functions $7654z^{25} + \cdots + 9040z^{33} + 689z^{34}$ and $128z^{43} + 84z^{44} + 112z^{45} + 36z^{46} + 24z^{47}$. Here are typical examples of the smallest and largest:

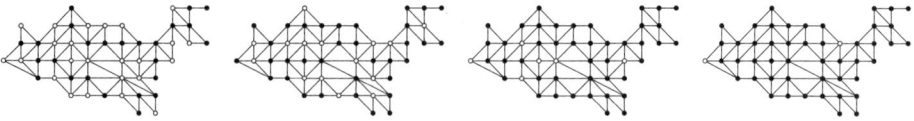

(Compare with the smallest and largest "1-partite" subgraphs in 7–(61) and 7–(62).)

Notice that the families g and h tell us exactly which induced subgraphs can be 2-colored and 3-colored, but they *don't* tell us how to color them.

239. Since $h = ((e_1 \cup \cdots \cup e_{49}) \S 2) \setminus g$ is the set of nonedges of G, the cliques are $f = \wp \setminus h$, and the maximal cliques are $f^\uparrow$. For example, we have $Z(f) = 144$ for the 214 cliques of the USA graph, and $Z(f^\uparrow) = 130$ for the 60 maximal ones. In this case the maximal cliques consist of 57 triangles (which are easily visible in (18)), together with three edges that aren't part of any triangle: AZ — NM, WI — MI, NH — ME.

Let f_k describe the sets coverable by k cliques. Then $f_1 = f$, and $f_{k+1} = f_k \sqcup f$ for $k \geq 1$. (It's not a good idea to compute f_{16} as $f_8 \sqcup f_8$; much faster is to do each join separately, even if the intermediate results are not of interest.)

The maxim*um* elements of f_k in the USA graph have sizes 3, 6, 9, ..., 36, 39, 41, 43, 45, 47, 48, 49 for $1 \leq k \leq 19$; these maxima can readily be determined by hand, in a small graph such as this. But the question of maxim*al* elements is much more subtle, and ZDDs are probably the best tool for investigating them. The ZDDs for $f_1, \ldots, f_{19}$ are quickly found after about 30 megamems of calculation, and they aren't large: $\max Z(f_k) = Z(f_{11}) = 9547$. Another 400 megamems produces the ZDDs for $f_1^\uparrow, \ldots, f_{19}^\uparrow$, which likewise are small: $\max Z(f_k^\uparrow) = Z(f_{11}^\uparrow) = 9458$.

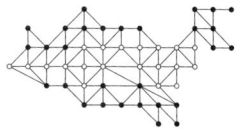

We find, for example, that the generating function for $f_{18}^\uparrow$ is $12z^{47} + 13z^{48}$; eighteen cliques suffice to cover all but one of the 49 vertices, if we leave out CA, DC, FL, IL, LA, MI, MN, MT, SC, TN, UT, WA, or WV. There also are twelve cases where we can maximally cover 47 vertices; for example, if all but NE and NM are covered by 18 cliques, then neither of those states are covered. An unusual example of maximal clique covering is illustrated here: If the 29 "black" states are covered by 12 cliques, none of the "white" states will also be covered.

240. (a) In fact, the subformula $f(x) = \bigwedge_v (x_v \vee \bigvee_{u-v} x_u)$ of (68) precisely characterizes the dominating sets x. And if any element of a kernel is removed, it isn't dominated by the others. [C. Berge, *Théorie des graphes et ses applications* (1958), 44.]

(b) The Boolean formula of part (a) yields a ZDD with $Z(f) = 888$ after about 1.5 Mμ of computation; then another 1.5 Mμ with the MINMAL algorithm of answer 237 gives the minimal elements, with $Z(f^\downarrow) = 2082$.

A more clever way is to start with $h = \bigcup_v (e_v \sqcup \bigsqcup_{u-v} e_u)$, and then to compute $h^\sharp$, because $h^\sharp = f^\downarrow$. However, cleverness doesn't pay in this case: About 80 Kμ suffice to compute h, but the computation of $h^\sharp$ by the MINHIT algorithm costs about 350 Mμ.

Either way, we deduce that there are exactly 7,798,658 minimal dominating sets. More precisely, the generating function has the form $192z^{11} + 58855z^{12} + \cdots + 4170z^{18} + 40z^{19}$ (which can be compared to $80z^{11} + 7851z^{12} + \cdots + 441z^{18} + 18z^{19}$ for kernels).

(c) Proceeding as in answer 239, we can determine the sets of vertices d_k that are dominated by subsets of size $k = 1, 2, 3, \ldots$, because $d_{k+1} = d_k \sqcup d_1$. Here it's much faster to start with $d_1 = \wp \sqcap h$ instead of $d_1 = h$, even though $Z(\wp \sqcap h) = 313$ while $Z(h) = 213$, because we aren't interested in details about the small-cardinality members of d_k. Using the fact that the generating function for d_7 is $\cdots + 61z^{42} + z^{43}$, one can verify that the illustrated solution is unique. (Total cost $\approx$ 300 Mμ.)

241. Let g be the family of all 728 edges. Then, as in previous exercises, $f = \wp \setminus g$ is the family of independent sets, and the cliques are $c = \wp \setminus (((\bigcup_v e_v) \S 2) \setminus g)$. We have $Z(g) = 699$, $Z(f) = 20244$, $Z(c) = 1882$.

(a) Among $|f| = 118969$ independent sets, there are $|f^{\uparrow}| = 10188$ kernels, with $Z(f^{\uparrow}) = 8577$ and generating function $728z^5 + 6912z^6 + 2456z^7 + 92z^8$. The 92 maximum independent sets are the famous solutions to the classic 8-queens problem, which we shall study in Section 7.2.2; example (C1) is the only solution with no three queens in a straight line, as noted by Sam Loyd in the *Brooklyn Daily Eagle* (20 December 1896). The $728 = 91 \times 8$ minimum kernels were first listed by C. F. de Jaenisch, *Traité des applications de l'analyse math. au jeu des échecs* **3** (1863), 255–259, who ascribed them to "M^r de R∗∗∗." The upper left queen in (C0) can be replaced by king, bishop, or pawn, still dominating every open square [H. E. Dudeney, *The Weekly Dispatch* (3 Dec 1899)].

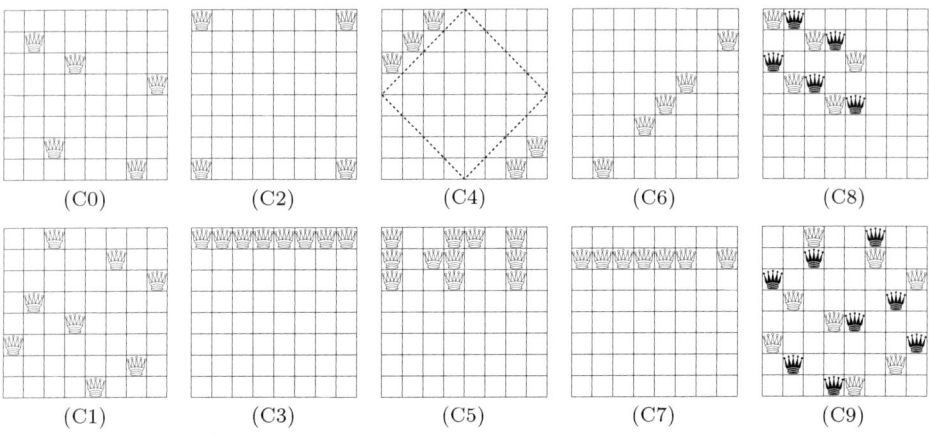

(C0)   (C2)   (C4)   (C6)   (C8)

(C1)   (C3)   (C5)   (C7)   (C9)

(b) Here $Z(c^{\uparrow}) = 866$; the 310 maximal cliques are described in exercise 7–129.

(c) These subsets are computationally more difficult: The ZDD for all dominating sets d has $Z(d) = 12,663,505$, $|d| = 18,446,595,708,474,987,957$; the minimal ones have $Z(d^{\downarrow}) = 11,363,849$, $|d^{\downarrow}| = 28,281,838$, and generating function $4860z^5 + 1075580z^6 + 14338028z^7 + 11978518z^8 + 873200z^9 + 11616z^{10} + 36z^{11}$. One can compute the ZDD for d in 1.5 Gμ by Boolean algebra, and then the ZDD for $d^{\downarrow}$ in another 680 Gμ; alternatively, the "clever" approach of answer 240 obtains $d^{\downarrow}$ in 775 Gμ without computing d. The 11-queen arrangement in (C5) is the only such minimal dominating set that is confined to three rows. H. E. Dudeney presented (C4), the only 5-queen solution that avoids the central diamond, in *Tit Bits* (1 Jan 1898), 257. The set of all 4860 minimum solutions was first enumerated by K. von Szily [*Deutsche Schachzeitung* **57** (1902), 199]; his complete list appears in W. Ahrens, *Math. Unterhaltungen und Spiele* **1** (1910), 313–318.

(d) Here it suffices to compute $(c \cap d)^{\downarrow}$ instead of $c \cap (d^{\downarrow})$, if we don't already know $d^{\downarrow}$, because $c \sqcap \wp = c$. We have $Z(c \cap d^{\downarrow}) = 342$ and $|c \cap d^{\downarrow}| = 92$, with generating function $20z^5 + 56z^6 + 16z^7$. Once again, Dudeney was first to discover all 20 of the 5-queen solutions [*The Weekly Dispatch* (30 July 1899)].

(e) We have $Z(f \sqcup f) = 91,780,989$ at a cost of 24 Gμ; then $Z((f \sqcup f)^{\uparrow}) = 11,808,436$ after another 290 Gμ. There are 27,567,390 maximal induced bipartite subgraphs, with generating function $109894z^{10} + 2561492z^{11} + 13833474z^{12} + 9162232z^{13} + 1799264z^{14} + 99408z^{15} + 1626z^{16}$. Any 8 independent queens can be combined with their mirror reflection to obtain a 16-queen solution, as (C1) yields (C9). But the disjoint union of minimum kernels is not always a maximal induced bipartite subgraph; for example, consider the union of (C0) with its reflection:

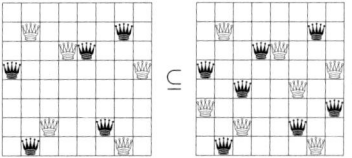

Parts (a), (b), (d), and possibly (c) can be solved just as well without the use of ZDDs; see, for example, exercise 7.1.3–132 for (a) and (b). But the ZDD approach seems best for (e). And the computation of all the maximal *tripartite* subgraphs of Q_8 may be beyond the reach of *any* feasible algorithm.

[In larger queen graphs Q_n, the smallest kernels and the minimum dominating sets are each known to have sizes either $\lceil n/2 \rceil$ or $\lceil n/2 \rceil + 1$ for $12 \le n \le 120$. See P. R. J. Östergård and W. D. Weakley, *Electronic J. Combinatorics* **8** (2001), #R29; D. Finozhenok and W. D. Weakley, *Australasian J. Combinatorics* **37** (2007), 295–300. The largest minimal dominating sets have been investigated by A. P. Burger, E. J. Cockayne, and C. M. Mynhardt, *Discrete Mathematics* **163** (1997), 47–66.]

242. These are the kernels of an interesting 3-regular hypergraph with 1544 edges. Its 4,113,975,079 independent subsets f (that is, its subsets with no three collinear points) have $Z(f) = 52{,}322{,}105$, computable with about 12 gigamems using family algebra as in answer 236(e). Another 575 Gμ will compute the kernels $f^\uparrow$, for which we have $Z(f^\uparrow) = 31{,}438{,}750$ and $|f^\uparrow| = 66{,}509{,}584$; the generating function is $228z^8 + 8240z^9 + 728956z^{10} + 9888900z^{11} + 32215908z^{12} + 20739920z^{13} + 2853164z^{14} + 73888z^{15} + 380z^{16}$.

[The problem of finding an independent set of size 16 was first posed by H. E. Dudeney in *The Weekly Dispatch* (29 Apr 1900 and 13 May 1900), where he gave the leftmost pattern shown above. Later, in the London *Tribune* (7 Nov 1906), Dudeney asked puzzlists to find the second pattern, which has two points in the center. The full set of maximum kernels, including 57 that are distinct under symmetry, was found by M. A. Adena, D. A. Holton, and P. A. Kelly, *Lecture Notes in Math.* **403** (1974), 6–17, who also noted the existence of an 8-point kernel. The middle pattern above is the only such kernel with all points in the central 4×4. The other two patterns yield kernels that have respectively $(8, 8, 10, 10, 12, 12, 12)$ points in $n \times n$ grids for $n = (8, 9, \ldots, 14)$; they were found by S. Ainley and described in a letter to Martin Gardner, 27 Oct 1976.]

243. (a) This result is readily verified even for infinite sets. (Notice that, as a Boolean function, $f^\cap$ is the least Horn function that is $\supseteq f$, by Theorem 7.1.1H.)

(b) We could form $f^{(2)} = f \sqcap f$, then $f^{(4)} = f^{(2)} \sqcap f^{(2)}$, $\ldots$, until $f^{(2^{k+1})} = f^{(2^k)}$, using exercise 205. But it's faster to devise a recurrence that goes to the limit all at once. If $f = f_0 \cup (e_1 \sqcup f_1)$ we have $f^\cap = f' \cup (e_1 \sqcup f_1^\cap)$, where $f' = f_0^\cap \cup (f_0^\cap \sqcap f_1^\cap)$. [An alternative formula is $f' = (f_0 \cup f_1)^\cap \setminus (f_1^\cap \nearrow f_0)$; see S. Minato and H. Arimura, *Transactions of the Japanese Society for Artificial Intelligence* **22** (2007), 165–172.]

(c) With the first suggestion of (b), the computation of $F^{(2)}$, $F^{(4)}$, and $F^{(8)} = F^{(4)}$ costs about $(610 + 450 + 460)$ megamems. In this example it turns out that $F^{(4)} = F^{(3)}$, and that just three patterns belong to $F^{(3)} \setminus F^{(2)}$, namely `c***f`, `*k*t*`, and `***sp`. (The words that match `***sp` are `clasp`, `crisp`, and `grasp`.) A direct computation of $F^\cap$ using the recurrence based on $f_0^\cap \sqcap f_1^\cap$ costs only 320 Mμ; and in this example the alternative recurrence based on $(f_0 \cup f_1)^\cap$ costs 470 Mμ. The generating function is $1 + 124z + 2782z^2 + 7753z^3 + 4820z^4 + 5757z^5$.

244. To convert Fig. 22 from a BDD to a ZDD, we add appropriate nodes with LO = HI where links jump levels, obtaining the z-profile $(1, 2, 2, 4, 4, 5, 5, 5, 5, 5, 2, 2, 2)$.

To convert it from a ZDD to a BDD, we add nodes in the same places, but with HI = $\boxed{\perp}$, obtaining the profile (1, 2, 2, 4, 4, 5, 5, 5, 5, 5, 2, 2, 2). (In fact, the connectedness function and the spanning tree function are Z-transforms of each other; see exercise 192.)

245. See exercise 7.1.1–26. (It should be interesting to compare the performance of the Fredman–Khachiyan algorithm in exercise 7.1.1–27 with the ZDD-based algorithm MINHIT in answer 237, on a variety of different functions.)

246. If a nonconstant function doesn't depend on x_1, we can replace x_1 in the formulas by x_v, as in (50). Let P and Q be the prime implicants of functions p and q. (For example, if $P = e_2 \cup (e_3 \sqcup e_4)$ then $p = x_2 \vee (x_3 \wedge x_4)$.) By (137) and induction on $|f|$, the function f described in the theorem is sweet if and only if p and q are sweet and $\mathrm{PI}(f_0) \cap \mathrm{PI}(f_1) = \emptyset$. The latter equality holds if and only if $p \subseteq q$.

247. We can characterize them with BDDs as in (49) and exercise 75; but this time

$$\sigma_n(x_1, \ldots, x_{2^n}) = \sigma_{n-1}(x_1, \ldots, x_{2^n-1}) \wedge$$
$$\left((\bar{x}_2 \wedge \cdots \wedge \bar{x}_{2^n}) \vee \left(\sigma_{n-1}(x_2, \ldots, x_{2^n}) \wedge \bigwedge_{j=0}^{2^{k-1}} \left(\bar{x}_{2j+1} \vee \bigvee_{i \subset j} x_{2i+2} \right) \right) \right).$$

The answers $|\sigma_n|$ for $0 \leq n \leq 7$ are (2, 3, 6, 18, 106, 2102, 456774, 7108935325). (This computation builds a BDD of size $B(\sigma_7) = 7{,}701{,}683$, using about 900 megamems and 725 megabytes altogether.)

248. False; for example, $(x_1 \vee x_2) \wedge (x_2 \vee x_3)$ isn't sweet. (But the conjunction *is* sweet if f and g depend on disjoint sets of variables, or if x_1 is the only variable on which they both depend.)

249. (Solution by Shaddin Dughmi and Ian Post.) A nonzero monotone Boolean function is ultrasweet if and only if its prime implicants are the bases of a matroid; see Section 7.6.1. By extending answer 247 we can determine the number of ultrasweet functions $f(x_1, \ldots, x_n)$ for $0 \leq n \leq 7$: (2, 3, 6, 17, 69, 407, 3808, 75165).

250. Exhaustive analysis shows that ave $B(f) = 76726/7581 \approx 10.1$; ave $Z(\mathrm{PI}(f)) = 71513/7581 \approx 9.4$; $\Pr(Z(\mathrm{PI}(f)) > B(f)) = 151/7581 \approx .02$; and max $Z(\mathrm{PI}(f))/B(f) = 8/7$ occurs uniquely when f is $(x_1 \wedge x_4) \vee (x_1 \wedge x_5) \vee (x_2 \wedge x_3 \wedge x_4) \vee (x_2 \wedge x_5)$.

251. More strongly, could it be that $\limsup Z(\mathrm{PI}(f))/B(f) = 1$?

252. The ZDD should describe all words on $\{e_1, e_1', \ldots, e_n, e_n'\}$ that have exactly j unprimed letters and $k - j$ primed letters, and no occurrences of both e_i and e_i' in the same word, for some set of pairs (j, k). For example, if $n = 9$ and $f(x) = v_{\nu x}$, where $v = 110111011$, the pairs are $(0, 8)$, $(3, 6)$, and $(8, 8)$. Regardless of the set of pairs, the z-profile elements will all be $O(n^2)$, hence $Z(\mathrm{PI}(f)) = O(n^3)$. (We order the variables so that x_i and x_i' are adjacent.) And $f(x) = S_{\lfloor n/3 \rfloor, \ldots, \lfloor 2n/3 \rfloor}(x)$ has $Z(\mathrm{PI}(f)) = \Omega(n^3)$.

253. Let $\mathrm{I}(f)$ be the family of all *implicants* of f; then $\mathrm{PI}(f) = \mathrm{I}(f)^\downarrow$. The formula $\mathrm{I}(f) = \mathrm{I}(f_0 \wedge f_1) \cup (e_1' \sqcup \mathrm{I}(f_0)) \cup (e_1 \sqcup \mathrm{I}(f_1))$ is easy to verify. Thus $\mathrm{I}(f)^\downarrow = A \cup (e_1' \sqcup (\mathrm{PI}(f_0) \searrow A)) \cup (e_1 \sqcup (\mathrm{PI}(f_1) \searrow A))$, as in exercise 237. But $\mathrm{PI}(f_0) \searrow A = \mathrm{PI}(f_0) \setminus A$, since $A \subseteq \mathrm{I}(f)$.

[This recurrence for prime implicants is due to O. Coudert and J. C. Madre, *ACM/IEEE Design Automation Conf.* **29** (1992), 36–39. Partial results had previously been formulated by B. Reusch, *IEEE Trans.* **C-24** (1975), 924–930.]

254. By (53) and (137), we need to show that $\mathrm{PI}(g_h) \setminus \mathrm{PI}(f_h \cup g_l) = (\mathrm{PI}(g_h) \backslash \mathrm{PI}(g_l)) \setminus (\mathrm{PI}(f_h) \backslash \mathrm{PI}(f_l))$. But both of these are equal to $\mathrm{PI}(g_h) \setminus (\mathrm{PI}(f_h) \cup \mathrm{PI}(g_l))$, because $f_l \subseteq f_h \subseteq g_h$ and $f_l \subseteq g_l \subseteq g_h$.

[This recurrence produces a ZDD directly from the BDDs for f and g, and it yields $\mathrm{PI}(g)$ when $f = 0$. Thus it is easier to implement than (137), which requires also the set-difference operator on ZDDs. And it sometimes runs much faster in practice.]

255. (a) A typical item α like $e_2 \sqcup e_5 \sqcup e_6$ has a very simple ZDD. We can readily devise a BUMP routine that sets $g \leftarrow g \oplus \alpha$ and returns $[\alpha \in g]$, given ZDDs g and α.

To insert α into the multifamily f, start with $k \leftarrow c \leftarrow 0$; then while $c = 0$, set $c \leftarrow \mathrm{BUMP}(f_k)$ and $k \leftarrow k + 1$. To delete α, assuming that it is present, start with $k \leftarrow 0$ and $c \leftarrow 1$; while $c = 1$, set $c \leftarrow \mathrm{BUMP}(f_k)$ and $k \leftarrow k + 1$.

(b) Suppose f_k and g_k are $\emptyset$ for $k \geq m$. Set $k \leftarrow 0$ and $t \leftarrow \emptyset$ (the ZDD $\boxed{\perp}$). While $k < m$, set $h_k \leftarrow f_k \oplus g_k \oplus t$ and $t \leftarrow \langle f_k g_k t \rangle$. Finally set $h_m \leftarrow t$.

[This representation and its insertion algorithm are due to S. Minato and H. Arimura, *Proc. Workshop, Web Information Retrieval and Integration* (IEEE, 2005), 4–11.]

256. (a) Reflect the binary representation from left to right, and append 0s until the number of bits is 2^n for some n. The result is the truth table of the corresponding Boolean function $f(x_1, \ldots, x_n)$, with x_k corresponding to $2^{2^{n-k}} \in U$. When $x = 41$, for example, 10010100 is the truth table of $(x_1 \wedge \bar{x}_2 \wedge x_3) \vee (\bar{x}_1 \wedge x_2 \wedge x_3) \vee (\bar{x}_1 \wedge \bar{x}_2 \wedge x_3)$.

(b) If $x < 2^{2^n}$, we have $Z(x) \leq U_n = O(2^n/n)$, by (79) and exercise 192.

(c) There's a simple recursive routine $\mathrm{ADD}(x, y, c)$, which takes a "carry bit" c and pointers to the ZDDs for x and y and returns a pointer to the ZDD for $x + y + c$. This routine is invoked at most $4Z(x)Z(y)$ times.

(d) We cannot claim that $Z(x \mathbin{\dot-} y) = O(Z(x)Z(y))$, because $Z(x \mathbin{\dot-} y) = n + 1$ and $Z(x) = 3$ and $Z(y) = 1$ when $x = 2^{2^n}$ and $y = 1$. But by computing $x \mathbin{\dot-} y = (x + 1 + ((2^{2^n} - 1) \oplus y)) - 2^{2^n}$ when $y \leq x < 2^{2^n}$, we can show that $Z(x \mathbin{\dot-} y) = O(Z(x)Z(y) \log \log x)$. (See the ZDD nodes t_j in answer 201.) So the answer is "yes."

(e) No. For example, if $x = (2^{2^{2^k+k}} - 1)/(2^{2^k} - 1)$, we have $Z(x) = 2^k + 1$ but $Z(x^2) = 3 \cdot (2^{2^k} - 1) = U_{2^k+k+1} - 2$, where U_{2^k+k+1} is the largest possible ZDD size for numbers with $\lg \lg x^2 < 2^k + k + 1$ (see part (b)).

[This exercise was inspired by Jean Vuillemin, who began to experiment with such sparse integers about 1993. Unfortunately the numbers that are of greatest importance in combinatorial calculations, such as Fibonacci numbers, factorials, binomial coefficients, etc., rarely turn out to be sparse in practice.]

257. See *Proc. Europ. Design and Test Conf.* (IEEE, 1995), 449–454. With signed coefficients one can use $\{-2, 4, -8, \ldots\}$ instead of $\{2, 4, 8, \ldots\}$, as in negabinary arithmetic.

[In the special case where the degree is at most 1 in each variable and where addition is done modulo 2, the polynomials of this exercise are equivalent to the multilinear representations of Boolean functions (see 7.1.1–(19)), and the ZDDs are equivalent to "binary moment diagrams" (BMDs). See R. E. Bryant and Y.-A. Chen, *ACM/IEEE Design Automation Conf.* **32** (1995), 535–541.]

258. If n is odd, the BDD must depend on all its variables, and there must be at least $\lceil \lg n \rceil$ of them. Thus $B(f) \geq \lceil \lg n \rceil + 2$ when $n > 1$, and the skinny functions of exercise 170(c) achieve this bound. If n is even, add an unused variable to the solution for $n/2$.

The ZDD question is easily seen to be equivalent to finding a shortest addition chain, as in Section 4.6.3. Thus the smallest $Z(f)$ for $|f| = n$ is $l(n) + 1$, including $\boxed{\top}$.

259. The theory of nested parentheses (see, for example, exercise 2.2.1–3) tells us that $N_n(x) = 1$ if and only if $\bar{x}_1 + \cdots + \bar{x}_k \geq x_1 + \cdots + x_k$ for $0 \leq k \leq 2n$, with equality when $k = 2n$. Equivalently, $k - n \leq x_1 + \cdots + x_k \leq k/2$ for $0 \leq k \leq 2n$. So the BDD for N_n is rather like the BDD for $S_n(x)$, but simpler; in fact, the profile elements are $b_k = \lfloor k/2 \rfloor + 1$ for $0 \leq k \leq n$ and $b_k = n + 1 - \lceil k/2 \rceil$ for $n \leq k < 2n$. Hence $B(N_n) = b_0 + \cdots + b_{2n-1} + 2 = \binom{n+2}{2} + 1$. The z-profile has $z_k = b_k - [k \text{ even}]$ for $0 \leq k < 2n$, because of HI branches to $\boxed{\bot}$ on even levels; hence $Z(N_n) = B(N_n) - n$.

[An interesting BDD base for the $n+1$ Boolean functions that correspond to C_{nn}, $C_{(n-1)(n+1)}, \ldots, C_{0(2n)}$ in 7.2.1.6–(21) can be constructed by analogy with exercise 49.]

260. (a, b) Arrange the variables $x_{n,0}$, $x_{n,1}$, $\ldots$, $x_{n,n-1}$, $x_{n-1,0}$, $\ldots$, $x_{1,0}$, from top to bottom. Then the HI branch from the ZDD root of R_n is the ZDD root of R_{n-1}. (This ordering actually turns out to minimize $Z(R_n)$ for $n \leq 6$, probably also for all n.) The z-profile is $1, \ldots, 1$; $n - 2, \ldots, 2, 1, 1$; $n - 3, \ldots, 2, 1, 1$; $\ldots$; hence $Z(R_n) = \binom{n}{3} + 2n + 1 \approx \frac{1}{6}n^3$ and $Z(R_{100}) = 161{,}901$. The ordinary profile is $1, 2, 2,$ $3, 4, \ldots, n-1$; $n-1, 2n-4, 2n-5, \ldots, n-1$; $n-2, 2n-6, \ldots, n-2$; $\ldots$; altogether $B(R_n) = 3\binom{n}{3} + \binom{n+1}{2} + 3$ for $n \geq 2$, and $B(R_{100}) = 490{,}153$.

[See I. Semba and S. Yajima, *Trans. Inf. Proc. Soc. Japan* **35** (1994), 1666–1667. Incidentally, the method of exercise 7.2.1.5–26 leads to a ZDD for set partitions that has only $\binom{n}{2}$ variables and $\binom{n}{2} + 1$ nodes. But the connection between that representation and the partitions themselves is less direct, thus harder to restrict in a natural way.]

(c) Now there are 573 variables instead of 5050 when $n = 100$; the number of variables in general is $nl - 2^l + 1$, where $l = \lceil \lg n \rceil$, by Eq. 5.3.1–(3). We examine the bits of $a_n, a_{n-1}, \ldots$, with the most significant bit first. Then $B(R'_{100}) = 31{,}861$, and one can show that $B(R'_n) = \binom{n}{2}l - \frac{1}{6}4^l - \frac{1}{2}2^l - \nu(n-1) + l + \frac{8}{3}$ for $n > 2$. The ZDD size is more complicated, and appears to be roughly 60% larger; we have $Z(R'_{100}) = 50{,}154$.

261. Given a Boolean function $f(x_1, \ldots, x_n)$, the set of all binary strings $x_1 \ldots x_n$ such that $f(x_1, \ldots, x_n) = 1$ is a finite language, so it is regular. The minimum-state deterministic automaton $\mathcal{A}$ for this language is the QDD for f. (In general, when L is regular, the state of $\mathcal{A}$ after reading $x_1 \ldots x_k$ accepts the language $\{\alpha \mid x_1 \ldots x_k \alpha \in L\}$.)

[The quoted theorem was discovered in a more general context by D. A. Huffman, *Journal of the Franklin Institute* **257** (1954), 161–190, and independently by E. F. Moore, *Annals of Mathematics Studies* **34** (1956), 129–153.]

An interesting example of the connection between this theory and the theory of BDDs can be found in early work by Yuri Breitbart that is summarized in *Doklady Akad. Nauk SSSR* **180** (1968), 1053–1055. Lemma 7 of Breitbart's paper states, in essence, that $B_{\min}(\psi) = \Omega(2^{n/4})$, where ψ is the function of $2n$ variables $x = (x_1, \ldots, x_n)$ and $y = (y_1, \ldots, y_n)$ defined by $\psi(x, y) = x_{\nu y} \oplus y_{\nu x}$, with the understanding that $x_0 = y_0 = 0$. (Notice that ψ is sort of a "two-sided" hidden weighted bit function.)

262. (a) If a denotes the function or subfunction f, we can for example let $C(a) = a \oplus 1$ denote $\bar{f}$, assuming that each node occupies an even number of bytes. Then $C(C(a)) = a$, and a link to a denotes a nonnormal function if and only if a is odd; $a \,\&\, -2$ always points to a node, which always represents a normal function.

The LO pointer of every node is even, because a normal function remains normal when we replace any variable by 0. But the HI pointer of any node might be complemented, and an external root pointer to any function of a normalized BDD base might also be complemented. Notice that the $\boxed{\top}$ sink is now impossible.

(b) Uniqueness is obvious because of the relation to truth tables: A bead is either normal (i.e., begins with 0) or the complement of a normal bead.

(c) In diagrams, each complement link is conveniently indicated by a dot:

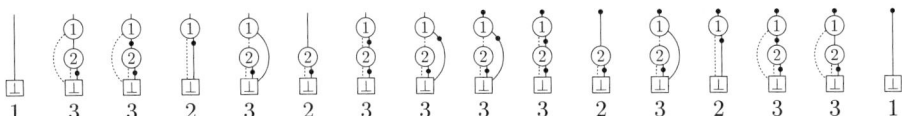

1   3   3   2   3   2   3   3   3   3   2   3   2   3   3   1

(d) There are $2^{2^m-1} - 2^{2^{m-1}-1}$ normal beads of order m. The worst case, $B^0(f) \le B^0(f_n) = 1 + \sum_{k=0}^{n-1} \min(2^k, 2^{2^{n-k}-1} - 2^{2^{n-k-1}-1}) = (U_{n+1} - 1)/2$, occurs with the functions of answer 110. For the average normalized profile, change $2^{2^{n-k}} - 1$ in (80) to $2^{2^{n-k}} - 2$, and divide the whole formula by 2; again the average case is very close to the worst case. For example, instead of (81) we have

$$(1.0, 2.0, 4.0, 8.0, 16.0, 32.0, 64.0, 127.3, 103.9, 6.0, 1.0, 1.0).$$

(e) We save $\boxed{\top}$, one $\textcircled{6}$, two $\textcircled{5}$s, and three $\textcircled{4}$s, leaving 45 normalized nodes.

(f) It's probably best to have subroutines AND, OR, BUTNOT for the case where f and g are known to be normal, together with a subroutine GAND for the general case. The routine $\mathrm{GAND}(f, g)$ returns $\mathrm{AND}(f, g)$ if f and g are even, $\mathrm{BUTNOT}(f, C(g))$ if f is even but g is odd, $\mathrm{BUTNOT}(g, C(f))$ if g is even but f is odd, $C(\mathrm{OR}(C(f), C(g)))$ if f and g are odd. The routine $\mathrm{AND}(f, g)$ is like (55) except that $r_h \leftarrow \mathrm{GAND}(f_h, g_h)$; only the cases $f = 0$, $g = 0$, and $f = g$ need be tested as "obvious" values.

Notes: Complement links were proposed by S. Akers in 1978, and independently by J. P. Billon in 1987. Although such links are used by all the major BDD packages, they are hard to recommend because the computer programs become much more complicated. The memory saving is usually negligible, and never better than a factor of 2; furthermore, the author's experiments show little gain in running time.

With ZDDs instead of BDDs, a "normal family" of functions is a family that doesn't contain the empty set. Shin-ichi Minato has suggested using $C(a)$ to denote the family $f \oplus \epsilon$, instead of $\bar{f}$, in ZDD work.

263. (a) If $Hx = 0$ and $x \ne 0$, we can't have $\nu x = 1$ or 2 because the columns of H are nonzero and distinct. [R. W. Hamming, *Bell System Tech. J.* **29** (1950), 147–160.]

(b) Let r_k be the rank of the first k columns of H, and s_k the rank of the last k columns. Then $b_k = 2^{r_k + s_{n-k} - r_n}$ for $0 \le k < n$, because this is the number of elements in the intersection of the vector spaces spanned by the first k and last $n - k$ columns. In the Hamming code, $r_k = 1 + \lambda k$ and $s_k = \min(m, 2 + \lambda(k-1))$ for $k > 1$; so we find $B(f) = (n^2 + 5)/2$. [See G. D. Forney, Jr., *IEEE Trans.* **IT-34** (1988), 1184–1187.]

(c) Let $q_k = 1 - p_k$. Maximizing $\prod_{k=1}^n p_k^{[x_k = y_k]} q_k^{[x_k \ne y_k]}$ is the same as maximizing $\sum_{k=1}^n w_k x_k$, where $w_k = (2y_k - 1)\log(p_k/q_k)$, so we can use Algorithm B.

Notes: Coding theorists, beginning with unpublished work of Forney in 1967, have developed the idea of a code's so-called *trellis*. In the binary case, the trellis is the same as the QDD for f, but with all nodes for the constant subfunction 0 eliminated. (Useful codes have distance > 1; then the trellis is also the BDD for f, but with $\boxed{\perp}$ eliminated.) Forney's original motivation was to show that the decoding algorithm of A. Viterbi [*IEEE Trans.* **IT-13** (1967), 260–269] is optimum for convolutional codes. A few years later, L. R. Bahl, J. Cocke, F. Jelinek, and J. Raviv [*IEEE Trans.* **IT-20** (1974), 284–287] extended trellis structure to linear block codes and presented further optimization algorithms. See also the papers of G. B. Horn and F. R. Kschischang [*IEEE Trans.* **IT-42** (1996), 2042–2048]; J. Lafferty and A. Vardy [*IEEE Trans.* **C-48** (1999), 971–986].

264. Procedures that combine the "bottom-up" methods of Algorithm B with "top-down" methods that optimize over predecessors of a node might be more efficient than methods that go strictly in one direction.

265. Compute counts c_j bottom-up as in Algorithm C, using n-bit arithmetic. Then proceed top-down, by starting with $k \leftarrow s-1$, $j \leftarrow 1$, $m \leftarrow m-1$, and repeating the following steps (during which we will have $0 \leq m < 2^{v_k-j}c_k$): If $v_k > j$, set $x_j \leftarrow \lfloor m/2^{v_k-j-1}c_k \rfloor$, $m \leftarrow m \bmod 2^{v_k-j-1}c_k$, $j \leftarrow j+1$; otherwise if $k=1$, terminate; otherwise set $l \leftarrow l_k$, $h \leftarrow h_k$, and if $m < 2^{v_l-v_k-1}c_l$ set $x_j \leftarrow 0$, $k \leftarrow l$, $j \leftarrow j+1$; otherwise set $x_j \leftarrow 1$, $m \leftarrow m - 2^{v_l-v_k-1}c_l$, $k \leftarrow h$, $j \leftarrow j+1$.

266. In fact, the ZDD is obtained directly from the standard "left child, right sibling" binary tree for F (see 7.2.1.6–(4)) if we use the left child link for HI and the right sibling link for LO; null links are changed to point to $\boxed{\top}$, except that the LO link of the root of the rightmost tree (the final node in postorder) should point to $\boxed{\bot}$.

267. The ZDD size of $d(F)$ can be computed as follows, using an auxiliary function $\zeta(T)$ defined recursively on trees: If $|T|=1$ (that is, if T has only one node), $\zeta(T)=1$. Otherwise T consists of a root together with $k \geq 1$ subtrees, $T_1, \ldots, T_k$, and we define $\zeta(T) = 1 + \zeta(T_1) + \cdots + \zeta(T_k) + |T| - |T_k|$. Then if F consists of $k \geq 1$ trees $T_1, \ldots, T_k$, we have $Z(d(F)) = 1 + \zeta(T_1) + \cdots + \zeta(T_k) + [|T_k| = 1]$.

The minimum size, n, clearly occurs when F consists of n one-node trees. The maximum size, $\lfloor n^2/4 \rfloor + 2n + 1$, occurs for $n = 2m-1$ in a tree for which node k has two children, $k+1$ and $k+m$ for $1 \leq k < m$; the case $n = 2m$ is similar.

For the average size, consider the generating function $Z(w,z) = \sum w^{\zeta(T)} z^{|T|}$, summed over all trees T. The definition of ζ yields the functional equation $Z(w,z) = wz + w^2 z Z(w,z)/(1-Z(w,wz))$. Differentiation with respect to w and to z, then setting $w=1$, tells us that $Z(1,z) = (1-s)/2$, $Z_w(1,z) = z/s + z/s^2$, and $Z_z(1,z) = 1/s$, where $s = \sqrt{1-4z}$. The generating function $\sum_F w^{Z(d(F))} z^{|F|}$, summed over all nonempty forests F, is $(wZ(w,z) + w^3 z - w^2 z)/(1 - Z(w,z))$. Differentiating with respect to w and setting $w \leftarrow 1$, we obtain $z/(1-4z) + 2z/\sqrt{1-4z}$; hence the average of $Z(d(F))$ is

$$(4^{n-1} + 2nC_{n-1})/C_n = \tfrac{1}{4}\sqrt{\pi} n^{3/2} + \tfrac{n}{2} + O(n^{1/2}),$$

where C_n is the Catalan number 7.2.1.6–(15).

SECTION 7.2.1.1

1. Let $m_j = u_j - l_j + 1$, and visit $(a_1 + l_1, \ldots, a_n + l_n)$ instead of visiting $(a_1, \ldots, a_n)$ in Algorithm M. Or, change '$a_j \leftarrow 0$' to '$a_j \leftarrow l_j$' and '$a_j = m_j - 1$' to '$a_j = u_j$' in that algorithm, and set $l_0 \leftarrow 0$, $u_0 \leftarrow 1$ in step M1.

2. $(0,0,1,2,3,0,2,7,0,9)$.

3. Step M4 is performed $m_1 m_2 \ldots m_k$ times when $j = k$; therefore the total is $\sum_{k=0}^{n} \prod_{j=1}^{k} m_j = m_1 \ldots m_n (1 + 1/m_n + 1/m_n m_{n-1} + \cdots + 1/m_n \ldots m_1)$. If all m_j are 2 or more, this is less than $2m_1 \ldots m_n$. [Thus, we should keep in mind that fancy Gray-code methods, which change only one digit per visit, actually reduce the total number of digit changes by at most a factor of 2.]

4. N1. [Initialize.] Set $a_j \leftarrow m_j - 1$ for $0 \leq j \leq n$, where $m_0 = 2$.

N2. [Visit.] Visit the n-tuple $(a_1, \ldots, a_n)$.

N3. [Prepare to subtract one.] Set $j \leftarrow n$.

N4. [Borrow if necessary.] If $a_j = 0$, set $a_j \leftarrow m_j - 1$, $j \leftarrow j - 1$, and repeat this step.

N5. [Decrease, unless done.] If $j = 0$, terminate the algorithm. Otherwise set $a_j \leftarrow a_j - 1$ and go back to step N2. ∎

5. Bit reflection is easy on a machine like MMIX, but on other computers we can proceed as follows:

Z1. [Initialize.] Set $j \leftarrow k \leftarrow 0$.

Z2. [Swap.] Interchange $A[j+1] \leftrightarrow A[k + 2^{n-1}]$. Also, if $j < k$, interchange $A[j] \leftrightarrow A[k]$ and $A[j + 2^{n-1} + 1] \leftrightarrow A[k + 2^{n-1} + 1]$.

Z3. [Advance k.] Set $k \leftarrow k + 2$, and terminate if $k \geq 2^{n-1}$.

Z4. [Advance j.] Set $h \leftarrow 2^{n-2}$. If $j \geq h$, repeatedly set $j \leftarrow j - h$ and $h \leftarrow h/2$ until $j < h$. Then set $j \leftarrow j + h$. (Now $j = (b_0 \ldots b_{n-1})_2$ if $k = (b_{n-1} \ldots b_0)_2$.) Return to Z2. ∎

6. If $g((0 b_{n-1} \ldots b_1 b_0)_2) = (0 (b_{n-1}) \ldots (b_2 \oplus b_1)(b_1 \oplus b_0))_2$ then $g((1 b_{n-1} \ldots b_1 b_0)_2) = 2^n + g((0 \bar{b}_{n-1} \ldots \bar{b}_1 \bar{b}_0)_2) = (1(\bar{b}_{n-1}) \ldots (\bar{b}_2 \oplus \bar{b}_1)(\bar{b}_1 \oplus \bar{b}_0))_2$, where $\bar{b} = b \oplus 1$.

7. To accommodate $2r$ sectors one can use $g(k)$ for $2^n - r \leq k < 2^n + r$, where $n = \lceil \lg r \rceil$, because $g(2^n - r) \oplus g(2^n + r - 1) = 2^n$ by (5). [G. C. Tootill, *Proc. IEE* **103**, Part B Supplement (1956), 434.] See also exercise 26.

8. Use Algorithm G with $n \leftarrow n - 1$ and include the parity bit a_∞ at the right. (This yields $g(0), g(2), g(4), \ldots$.)

9. Replace the rightmost ring, since $\nu(1011000)$ is odd.

10. $A_n + B_n = g^{[-1]}(2^n - 1) = \lfloor 2^{n+1}/3 \rfloor$ and $A_n = B_n + n$. Hence $A_n = \lfloor 2^n/3 + n/2 \rfloor$ and $B_n = \lfloor 2^n/3 - n/2 \rfloor$.

Historical notes: The early Japanese mathematician Yoriyuki Arima (1714–1783) treated this problem in his *Shūki Sanpō* (1769), Problem 44, observing that the n-ring puzzle reduces to an $(n-1)$-ring puzzle after a certain number of steps. Let $C_n = A_n - A_{n-1} = B_n - B_{n-1} + 1$ be the number of rings removed during this reduction. Arima noticed that $C_n = 2C_{n-1} - [n \text{ even}]$; thus he could compute $A_n = C_1 + C_2 + \cdots + C_n$ for $n = 9$ without actually knowing the formula $C_n = \lceil 2^{n-1}/3 \rceil$.

More than two centuries earlier, Cardano had already mentioned the "complicati annuli" in his *De Subtilitate Libri XXI* (Nuremberg: 1550), Book 15. He wrote that they are "useless yet admirably subtle," stating erroneously that 95 moves are needed to remove seven rings and 95 more to put them back. John Wallis devoted seven pages to this puzzle in the Latin edition of his *Algebra* **2** (Oxford: 1693), Chapter 111, presenting detailed but nonoptimum methods for the nine-ring case. He included the operation of sliding a ring through the bar as well as putting it on or off, and he hinted that shortcuts were available, but he did not attempt to find a shortest solution.

11. The solution to $S_n = S_{n-2} + 1 + S_{n-2} + S_{n-1}$ when $S_1 = S_2 = 1$ is $S_n = 2^{n-1} - [n \text{ even}]$. [*Math. Quest. Educational Times* **3** (1865), 66–67.]

12. (a) The theory of $n - 1$ Chinese rings proves that Gray binary code yields the compositions in a convenient order (4, 31, 211, 22, 112, 1111, 121, 13):

C1. [Initialize.] Set $t \leftarrow 0$, $j \leftarrow 1$, $s_1 \leftarrow n$. (We assume that $n > 1$.)

C2. [Visit.] Visit $s_1 \ldots s_j$. Then set $t \leftarrow 1 - t$, and go to C4 if $t = 0$.

C3. [Odd step.] If $s_j > 1$, set $s_j \leftarrow s_j - 1$, $s_{j+1} \leftarrow 1$, $j \leftarrow j + 1$; otherwise set $j \leftarrow j - 1$ and $s_j \leftarrow s_j + 1$. Return to C2.

C4. [Even step.] If $s_{j-1} > 1$, set $s_{j-1} \leftarrow s_{j-1} - 1$, $s_{j+1} \leftarrow s_j$, $s_j \leftarrow 1$, $j \leftarrow j + 1$; otherwise set $j \leftarrow j - 1$, $s_j \leftarrow s_{j+1}$, $s_{j-1} \leftarrow s_{j-1} + 1$ (but terminate if $j - 1 = 0$). Return to C2. ∎

(b) Now $q_1, \ldots, q_{t-1}$ represent rings on the bar:

B1. [Initialize.] Set $t \leftarrow 1$, $q_0 \leftarrow n$. (We assume that $n > 1$.)

B2. [Visit.] Set $q_t \leftarrow 0$ and visit $(q_0 - q_1) \ldots (q_{t-1} - q_t)$. Go to B4 if t is even.

B3. [Odd step.] If $q_{t-1} = 1$, set $t \leftarrow t - 1$; otherwise set $q_t \leftarrow 1$ and $t \leftarrow t + 1$. Return to step B2.

B4. [Even step.] If $q_{t-2} = q_{t-1} + 1$, set $q_{t-2} \leftarrow q_{t-1}$ and $t \leftarrow t - 1$ (but terminate if $t = 2$); otherwise set $q_t \leftarrow q_{t-1}$, $q_{t-1} \leftarrow q_t + 1$, $t \leftarrow t + 1$. Return to B2. ∎

These algorithms [see J. Misra, *ACM Trans. Math. Software* **1** (1975), 285] are loopless even in their initialization steps.

13. In step C1, also set $C \leftarrow 1$. In step C3, set $C \leftarrow s_j C$ if $s_j > 1$, otherwise $C \leftarrow C/(s_{j-1}+1)$. In step C4, set $C \leftarrow s_{j-1}C$ if $s_{j-1} > 1$, otherwise $C \leftarrow C/(s_{j-2}+1)$. Similar modifications apply to steps B1, B3, B4. Sufficient precision is needed to accommodate the value $C = n!$ for the composition $1 \ldots 1$; we are stretching the definition of looplessness by assuming that arithmetic operations take unit time.

14. V1. [Initialize.] Set $j \leftarrow 0$.

   V2. [Visit.] Visit the string $a_1 \ldots a_j$.

   V3. [Lengthen.] If $j < n$, set $j \leftarrow j + 1$, $a_j \leftarrow 0$, and return to V2.

   V4. [Increase.] If $a_j < m_j - 1$, set $a_j \leftarrow a_j + 1$ and return to V2.

   V5. [Shorten.] Set $j \leftarrow j - 1$, and return to V4 if $j > 0$. ∎

15. J1. [Initialize.] Set $j \leftarrow 0$.

   J2. [Even visit.] If j is even, visit the string $a_1 \ldots a_j$.

   J3. [Lengthen.] If $j < n$, set $j \leftarrow j + 1$, $a_j \leftarrow 0$, and return to J2.

   J4. [Odd visit.] If j is odd, visit the string $a_1 \ldots a_j$.

   J5. [Increase.] If $a_j < m_j - 1$, set $a_j \leftarrow a_j + 1$ and return to J2.

   J6. [Shorten.] Set $j \leftarrow j - 1$, and return to J4 if $j > 0$. ∎

This algorithm is loopless, although it may appear at first glance to contain loops; at most four steps separate consecutive visits. The basic idea is related to exercise 2.3.1–5 and to "prepostorder" traversal (Algorithm 7.2.1.6Q).

16. Suppose $\text{LINK}(j - 1) = j + nb_j$ for $1 \leq j \leq n$ and $\text{LINK}(j - 1 + n) = j + n(1 - b_j)$ for $1 < j \leq n$. These links represent $(a_1, \ldots, a_n)$ if and only if $g(a_1 \ldots a_n) = b_1 \ldots b_n$, so we can use a loopless Gray binary generator to achieve the desired result.

17. Put the concatenation of 3-bit codes $(g(j), g(k))$ in row j and column k, for $0 \leq j, k < 8$. [It is not difficult to prove that this is essentially the *only* solution, except for permuting and/or complementing coordinate positions and/or rotating rows, because the coordinate that changes when moving north or south depends only on the row, and a similar statement applies to columns. Karnaugh's isomorphism between the 4-cube and the 4×4 torus can be traced back to *The Design of Switching Circuits* by W. Keister, A. E. Ritchie, and S. H. Washburn (1951), page 174. Incidentally, Keister went on to design an ingenious variant of Chinese rings called SpinOut, and a generalization called The Hexadecimal Puzzle, *U.S. Patents 3637215–3637216* (1972).]

18. Use 2-bit Gray code to represent the digits $u_j = (0, 1, 2, 3)$ respectively as the bit pairs $u'_{2j-1}u'_{2j} = (00, 01, 11, 10)$. [C. Y. Lee introduced his metric in *IRE Trans.* **IT-4** (1958), 77–82. A similar $m/2$-bit encoding works for even values of m; for example, when $m = 8$ we can represent $(0, 1, 2, 3, 4, 5, 6, 7)$ by $(0000, 0001, 0011, 0111, 1111, 1110,$ $1100, 1000)$. But such a scheme leaves out some of the binary patterns when $m > 4$.]

19. (a) A modular Gray quaternary algorithm needs slightly less computation than Algorithm M, but it doesn't matter because 256 is so small. The result is $z_0^8 + z_1^8 + z_2^8 + z_3^8 + 14(z_0^4 z_2^4 + z_1^4 z_3^4) + 56 z_0 z_1 z_2 z_3 (z_0^2 + z_2^2)(z_1^2 + z_3^2)$.

(b) Replacing (z_0, z_1, z_2, z_3) by $(1, z, z^2, z)$ gives $1 + 112 z^6 + 30 z^8 + 112 z^{10} + z^{16}$; thus all of the nonzero Lee weights are ≥ 6. Now use the construction in the previous exercise to convert each $(u_0, u_1, u_2, u_3, u_4, u_5, u_6, u_\infty)$ into a 16-bit number.

20. Recover the quaternary vector $(u_0, u_1, u_2, u_3, u_4, u_5, u_6, u_\infty)$ from u', and use Algorithm 4.6.1D to find the remainder of $u_0 + u_1 x + \cdots + u_6 x^6$ divided by $g(x)$, mod 4; that algorithm can be used in spite of the fact that the coefficients do not belong to a field, because $g(x)$ is monic. Express the remainder as $x^j + 2x^k$ (modulo $g(x)$ and 4), and let $d = (k - j) \bmod 7$, $s = (u_0 + \cdots + u_6 + u_\infty) \bmod 4$.

Case 1: $s = 1$. If $k = \infty$, the error was x^j (in other words, the correct vector has $u_j \leftarrow (u_j - 1) \bmod 4$); otherwise there were three or more errors.

Case 2: $s = 3$. If $j = k$ the error was $-x^j$; otherwise ≥ 3 errors occurred.

Case 3: $s = 0$. If $j = k = \infty$, no errors were made; if $j = \infty$ and $k < \infty$, at least four errors were made. Otherwise the errors were $x^a - x^b$, where $a = (j + (\infty, 6, 5, 2, 3, 1, 4, 0)) \bmod 7$ according as $d = (0, 1, 2, 3, 4, 5, 6, \infty)$, and $b = (j + 2d) \bmod 7$.

Case 4: $s = 2$. If $j = \infty$ the errors were $2x^k$. Otherwise the errors were

$$x^j + x^\infty, \text{ if } k = \infty;$$
$$-x^j - x^\infty, \text{ if } d = 0;$$
$$x^a + x^b, \text{ if } d \in \{1, 2, 4\}, \ a = (j - 3d) \bmod 7, \ b = (j - 2d) \bmod 7;$$
$$-x^a - x^b, \text{ if } d \in \{3, 5, 6\}, \ a = (j - 3d) \bmod 7, \ b = (j - d) \bmod 7.$$

Given $u' = (1100100100001111)_2$, we have $u = (2, 0, 3, 1, 0, 0, 2, 2)$ and $2 + 3x^2 + x^3 + 2x^6 \equiv 1 + 3x + 3x^2 \equiv x^5 + 2x^6$; also $s = 2$. Thus the errors are $x^2 + x^3$, and the nearest errorfree codeword is $(2, 0, 2, 0, 0, 0, 2, 2)$. Algorithm 4.6.1D tells us that $2 + 2x^2 + 2x^6 \equiv (2 + 2x + 2x^3) g(x)$ (modulo 4); so the eight information bits correspond to $(v_0, v_1, v_2, v_3) = (2, 2, 0, 2)$. [A more intelligent algorithm would also say, "Aha: The first 16 bits of π."]

For generalizations to other efficient coding schemes based on quaternary vectors, see the classic paper by Hammons, Kumar, Calderbank, Sloane, and Solé, *IEEE Trans.* **IT-40** (1994), 301–319.

21. (a) $C(\epsilon) = 1$, $C(0\alpha) = C(1\alpha) = C(\alpha)$, and $C(*\alpha) = 2C(\alpha) - [10\ldots0 \in \alpha]$. Iterating this recurrence gives $C(\alpha) = 2^t - 2^{t-1} e_t - 2^{t-2} e_{t-1} - \cdots - 2^0 e_1$, where $e_j = [10\ldots0 \in \alpha_j]$ and α_j is the suffix of α following the jth asterisk. In the example we have $\alpha_1 = *10**0*$, $\alpha_2 = 10**0*$, $\ldots$, $\alpha_5 = \epsilon$; thus $e_1 = 0$, $e_2 = 1$, $e_3 = 1$, $e_4 = 0$, and $e_5 = 1$ (by convention), hence $C(**10**0*) = 2^5 - 2^4 - 2^2 - 2^1 = 10$.

(b) We may remove trailing asterisks so that $t = t'$. Then $e_t = 1$ implies $e_{t-1} = \cdots = e_1 = 0$. [The case $C(\alpha) = 2^{t'-1}$ occurs if and only if α ends in $10^j *^k$.]

(c) To compute the sum of $C(\alpha)$ over all t-subcubes, note that $\binom{n}{t}$ clusters begin at the n-tuple $0\ldots0$, and $\binom{n-1}{t}$ begin at each succeeding n-tuple (namely one cluster for each t-subcube containing that n-tuple and specifying the bit that changed). Thus the average is $(\binom{n}{t} + (2^n - 1)\binom{n-1}{t})/2^{n-t}\binom{n}{t} = 2^t(1 - t/n) + 2^{t-n}(t/n)$. [The formula in (c) holds for *any* n-bit Gray path, but (a) and (b) are specific to the reflected Gray binary code. These results are due to C. Faloutsos, *IEEE Trans.* **SE-14** (1988), 1381–1393.]

22. Let $\alpha*^j$ and $\beta*^k$ be consecutive lieves of a Gray binary trie, where α and β are binary strings and $j \le k$. Then the last $k - j$ bits of α are a string α' such that α and $\beta\alpha'$ are consecutive elements of Gray binary code, hence adjacent. [Interesting applications of this property to cube-connected message-passing concurrent computers are discussed in *A VLSI Architecture for Concurrent Data Structures* by William J. Dally (Kluwer, 1987), Chapter 3.]

23. $2^j = g(k) \oplus g(l) = g(k \oplus l)$ implies that $l = k \oplus g^{[-1]}(2^j) = k \oplus (2^{j+1} - 1)$. In other words, if $k = (b_{n-1} \ldots b_0)_2$ we have $l = (b_{n-1} \ldots b_{j+1}\bar{b}_j \ldots \bar{b}_0)_2$.

24. Defining $g(k) = k \oplus \lfloor k/2 \rfloor$ as usual, we find $g(k) = g(-1-k)$; hence there are *two* 2-adic integers k such that $g(k)$ has a given 2-adic value l. One of them is even, the other is odd. We can conveniently define $g^{[-1]}$ to be the solution that is even; then (8) is replaced by $b_j = a_{j-1} \oplus \cdots \oplus a_0$, for $j \ge 0$. For example, $g^{[-1]}(1) = -2$ by this definition; when l is a normal integer, the "sign" of $g^{[-1]}(l)$ is the parity of l.

25. Let $p = k \oplus l$; exercise 7.1.3–3 tells us that $2^{\lfloor \lg p \rfloor + 1} - p \le |k - l| \le p$. We have $\nu(g(p)) = \nu(g(k) \oplus g(l)) = t$ if and only if there are positive integers $j_1, \ldots, j_t$ such that $p = (1^{j_1}0^{j_2}1^{j_3} \ldots (0 \text{ or } 1)^{j_t})_2$. The largest possible $p < 2^n$ occurs when $j_1 = n + 1 - t$ and $j_2 = \cdots = j_t = 1$, yielding $p = 2^n - \lceil 2^t/3 \rceil$. The smallest possible $q = 2^{\lfloor \lg p \rfloor + 1} - p = (1^{j_2}0^{j_3} \ldots (1 \text{ or } 0)^{j_t})_2 + 1$ occurs when $j_2 = \cdots = j_t = 1$, yielding $q = \lceil 2^t/3 \rceil$. [C. K. Yuen, *IEEE Trans.* **IT-20** (1974), 668; S. R. Cavior, *IEEE Trans.* **IT-21** (1975), 596. The analogous bound for the modular m-ary Gray code is $\lceil m^t/(m^2 - 1) \rceil$, and this formula holds also for the reflected m-ary Gray code when m is even; see van Zanten and Suparta, *IEEE Trans.* **IT-49** (2003), 485–487; *Proc. South East Asian Math. Soc. Conf.* (Yogyakarta: Gadjah Mada University, 2003), 98–105.]

26. Let $N = 2^{n_t} + \cdots + 2^{n_1}$ where $n_t > \cdots > n_1 \ge 0$; also, let Γ_n be any Gray code for $\{0, 1, \ldots, 2^n - 1\}$ that begins at 0 and ends at 1, except that Γ_0 is simply 0. Use

$$\Gamma_{n_t}^R, \ 2^{n_t} + \Gamma_{n_{t-1}}, \ \ldots, \ 2^{n_t} + \cdots + 2^{n_3} + \Gamma_{n_2}^R, \ 2^{n_t} + \cdots + 2^{n_2} + \Gamma_{n_1}, \ \text{if } t \text{ is even};$$

$$\Gamma_{n_t}, \ 2^{n_t} + \Gamma_{n_{t-1}}^R, \ \ldots, \ 2^{n_t} + \cdots + 2^{n_3} + \Gamma_{n_2}^R, \ 2^{n_t} + \cdots + 2^{n_2} + \Gamma_{n_1}, \ \text{if } t \text{ is odd}.$$

27. In general, if $k = (b_{n-1} \ldots b_0)_2$, the $(k+1)$st largest element of S_n is equal to

$$1/(2 - (-1)^{a_{n-1}}/(2 - \cdots /(2 - (-1)^{a_1}/(2 - (-1)^{a_0}))\ldots)),$$

corresponding to the sign pattern $g(k) = (a_{n-1} \ldots a_0)_2$. Thus we can compute any element of S_n in $O(n)$ steps, given its rank. Setting $k = 2^{100} - 10^{10}$ and $n = 100$ yields the answer $373065177/1113604409$. [Whenever $f(x)$ is a positive and monotonic function, the 2^n elements $f(\pm f(\ldots \pm f(\pm x)\ldots))$ are ordered according to Gray binary code, as observed by H. E. Salzer, *CACM* **16** (1973), 180. In this particular case there is, however, another way to get the answer, because we also have

$$S_n = /\!/2, \pm 2, \ldots, \pm 2, \pm 1/\!/$$

using the notation of Section 4.5.3; continued fractions in this form are ordered by complementing alternate bits of k.]

28. (a) As $t = 1, 2, \ldots$, bit a_j of median(G_t) runs through the periodic sequence

$$0, \ldots, 0, *, 1, \ldots, 1, *, 0, \ldots, 0, *, \ldots$$

with asterisks at every 2^{1+j}th step. Thus the strings that correspond to the binary representations of $\lfloor (t-1)/2 \rfloor$ and $\lfloor t/2 \rfloor$ are medians. And those strings are in fact "extreme" cases, in the sense that all medians agree with the common bits of $\lfloor (t-1)/2 \rfloor$

and $\lfloor t/2 \rfloor$, hence asterisks appear where they disagree. For example, when $t = 100 = (01100100)_2$ and $n = 8$, we have $\text{median}(G_{100}) = 001100**$.

(b) Since $G_{2t} = 2G_t \cup (2G_t + 1)$, we may assume that $t = (a_{n-2} \ldots a_1 a_0 1)_2$ is odd. If α is $g(p)$ and β is $g(q)$ in Gray binary, we have $p = (p_{n-1} \ldots p_0)_2$ and $q = (p_{n-1} \ldots p_{j+1} \bar{p}_j \ldots \bar{p}_0)_2$; and $a_{n-1} a_{n-2} = 01 = p_{n-1} p_{n-2}$. We cannot have $p < t \leq q$, because this would imply that $j = n - 1$ and $p_{n-3} = p_{n-4} = \cdots = p_0 = 1$. [See A. J. Bernstein, K. Steiglitz, and J. E. Hopcroft, *IEEE Trans.* **IT-12** (1966), 425–430.]

29. Assuming that $p \neq 0$, let $l = \lfloor \lg p \rfloor$ and $S_a = \{s \mid 2^l a \leq s < 2^l(a+1)\}$ for $0 \leq a < 2^{n-l}$. Then $(k \oplus p) - k$ has a constant sign for all $k \in S_a$, and

$$\sum_{k \in S_a} \left| (k \oplus p) - k \right| = 2^l |S_a| = 2^{2l}.$$

Also $g^{[-1]}(g(k) \oplus p) = k \oplus g^{[-1]}(p)$, and $\lfloor \lg g^{[-1]}(p) \rfloor = \lfloor \lg p \rfloor$. Therefore

$$\frac{1}{2^n} \sum_{k=0}^{2^n-1} \left| g^{[-1]}(g(k) \oplus p) - k \right| = \frac{1}{2^n} \sum_{a=0}^{2^{n-l}-1} \sum_{k \in S_a} \left| (k \oplus g^{[-1]}(p)) - k \right| = \frac{1}{2^n} \sum_{a=0}^{2^{n-l}-1} 2^{2l} = 2^l.$$

[See Morgan M. Buchner, Jr., *Bell System Tech. J.* **48** (1969), 3113–3130.]

30. The cycle containing $k > 1$ has length $2^{\lfloor \lg \lg k \rfloor + 1}$, because it is easy to show from Eq. (7) that if $k = (b_{n-1} \ldots b_0)_2$ we have

$$g^{[2^l]}(k) = (c_{n-1} \ldots c_0)_2, \qquad \text{where } c_j = b_j \oplus b_{j+2^l}.$$

To permute all elements k such that $\lfloor \lg k \rfloor = t$, there are two cases: If t is a power of 2, the cycle containing $2 \lfloor k/2 \rfloor$ also contains $2 \lfloor k/2 \rfloor + 1$, so we must double the cycle leaders for $t - 1$. Otherwise the cycle containing $2 \lfloor k/2 \rfloor$ is disjoint from the cycle containing $2 \lfloor k/2 \rfloor + 1$, so $L_t = (2L_{t-1}) \cup (2L_{t-1} + 1) = (L_{t-1}*)_2$. This argument, discovered by Jörg Arndt in 2001, establishes the hint and yields the following algorithm:

P1. [Initialize.] Set $t \leftarrow 1$, $m \leftarrow 0$. (We may assume that $n \geq 2$.)

P2. [Loop through leaders.] Set $r \leftarrow m$. Perform Algorithm Q with $k = 2^t + r$; then if $r > 0$, set $r \leftarrow (r-1) \,\&\, m$ and repeat until $r = 0$. [See exercise 7.1.3–79.]

P3. [Increase $\lg k$.] Set $t \leftarrow t + 1$. Terminate if t is now equal to n; otherwise set $m \leftarrow 2m + [t \,\&\, (t-1) \neq 0]$ and return to P2. ∎

Q1. [Begin a cycle.] Set $s \leftarrow X_k$, $l \leftarrow k$, $j \leftarrow l \oplus \lfloor l/2 \rfloor$.

Q2. [Follow the cycle.] While $j \neq k$, set $X_l \leftarrow X_j$, $l \leftarrow j$, and $j \leftarrow l \oplus \lfloor l/2 \rfloor$. Then set $X_l \leftarrow s$. ∎

31. We get a field from f_n if and only if we get one from $f_n^{[2]}$, which takes $(a_{n-1} \ldots a_0)_2$ to $((a_{n-1} \oplus a_{n-2})(a_{n-1} \oplus a_{n-3})(a_{n-2} \oplus a_{n-4}) \ldots (a_2 \oplus a_0)(a_1))_2$. Let $c_n(x)$ be the characteristic polynomial of the matrix A defining this transformation, mod 2; then $c_1(x) = x + 1$, $c_2(x) = x^2 + x + 1$, and $c_{j+1}(x) = x c_j(x) + c_{j-1}(x)$. Since $c_n(A)$ is the zero matrix, by the Cayley–Hamilton theorem, a field is obtained if and only if $c_n(x)$ is a primitive polynomial, and this condition can be tested as in Section 3.2.2. The first such values of n are 1, 2, 3, 5, 6, 9, 11, 14, 23, 26, 29, 30, 33, 35, 39, 41, 51, 53, 65, 69, 74, 81, 83, 86, 89, 90, 95.

[Running the recurrence backwards shows that $c_{-j-1}(x) = c_j(x)$, hence $c_j(x)$ divides $c_{(2j+1)k+j}(x)$; for example, $c_{3k+1}(x)$ is always a multiple of $x+1$. All numbers n of the form $2jk + j + k$ are therefore excluded when $j > 0$ and $k > 0$. The polynomials $c_{18}(x)$, $c_{50}(x)$, $c_{98}(x)$, and $c_{99}(x)$ are irreducible but not primitive.]

32. Mostly true, but false at the points where $w_k(x)$ changes sign. (Walsh originally suggested that $w_k(x)$ should be zero at such points; but the convention adopted here is better, because it makes simple formulas like (15)–(19) valid for all x.)

33. By induction on k, we have

$$w_k(x) = w_{\lfloor k/2 \rfloor}(2x) = r_1(2x)^{b_1+b_2} r_2(2x)^{b_2+b_3} \ldots = r_1(x)^{b_0+b_1} r_2(x)^{b_1+b_2} r_3(x)^{b_2+b_3} \ldots$$

for $0 \le x < \frac{1}{2}$, because $r_j(2x) = r_{j+1}(x)$ and $r_1(x) = 1$ in this range. And when $\frac{1}{2} \le x < 1$,

$$w_k(x) = (-1)^{\lceil k/2 \rceil} w_{\lfloor k/2 \rfloor}(2x - 1) = r_1(x)^{b_0+b_1} r_1(2x-1)^{b_1+b_2} r_2(2x-1)^{b_2+b_3} \ldots$$
$$= r_1(x)^{b_0+b_1} r_2(x)^{b_1+b_2} r_3(x)^{b_2+b_3} \ldots$$

because $\lceil k/2 \rceil \equiv b_0 + b_1$ (modulo 2) and $r_j(2x - 1) = r_{j+1}(x - \frac{1}{2}) = r_{j+1}(x)$ for $j \ge 1$.

34. $p_k(x) = \prod_{j \ge 0} r_{j+1}^{b_j}(x)$; hence $w_k(x) = p_k(x)p_{\lfloor k/2 \rfloor}(x) = p_{g(k)}(x)$. [R. E. A. C. Paley, *Proc. London Math. Soc.* (2) **34** (1932), 241–279.]

35. If $j = (a_{n-1} \ldots a_0)_2$ and $k = (b_{n-1} \ldots b_0)_2$, the element in row j and column k is $(-1)^{f(j,k)}$, where $f(j, k)$ is the sum of all $a_r b_s$ such that: $r = s$ (Hadamard); $r+s = n-1$ (Paley); $r + s = n$ or $n - 1$ (Walsh).

Let R_n, F_n, and G_n be permutation matrices for the permutations that take $j = (a_{n-1} \ldots a_0)_2$ to $k = (a_0 \ldots a_{n-1})_2$, $k = 2^n - 1 - j = (\bar{a}_{n-1} \ldots \bar{a}_0)_2$, and $k = g^{[-1]}(j) = ((a_{n-1}) \ldots (a_{n-1} \oplus \cdots \oplus a_0))_2$, respectively. Then, using the direct product of matrices, we have the recursive formulas

$$R_{n+1} = \begin{pmatrix} R_n \otimes (1\ 0) \\ R_n \otimes (0\ 1) \end{pmatrix}, \qquad F_{n+1} = F_n \otimes \begin{pmatrix} 0 & 1 \\ 1 & 0 \end{pmatrix}, \qquad G_{n+1} = \begin{pmatrix} G_n & 0 \\ 0 & G_n F_n \end{pmatrix},$$

$$H_{n+1} = H_n \otimes \begin{pmatrix} 1 & 1 \\ 1 & \bar{1} \end{pmatrix}, \qquad P_{n+1} = \begin{pmatrix} P_n \otimes (1\ 1) \\ P_n \otimes (1\ \bar{1}) \end{pmatrix}, \qquad W_{n+1} = \begin{pmatrix} W_n \otimes (1\ 1) \\ F_n W_n \otimes (1\ \bar{1}) \end{pmatrix}.$$

Thus $W_n = G_n^T P_n = P_n G_n$; $H_n = P_n R_n = R_n P_n$; and $P_n = W_n G_n^T = G_n W_n = H_n R_n = R_n H_n$.

36. T1. [Hadamard transform.] For $k = 0, 1, \ldots, n - 1$, replace the pair (X_j, X_{j+2^k}) by $(X_j + X_{j+2^k}, X_j - X_{j+2^k})$ for all j with $\lfloor j/2^k \rfloor$ even, $0 \le j < 2^n$. (These operations effectively set $X^T \leftarrow H_n X^T$.)

T2. [Bit reversal.] Apply the algorithm of exercise 5 to the vector X. (These operations effectively set $X^T \leftarrow R_n X^T$, in the notation of exercise 35.)

T3. [Gray binary permutation.] Apply the algorithm of exercise 30 to the vector X. (These operations effectively set $X^T \leftarrow G_n^T X^T$.) ∎

If n has one of the special values in exercise 31, it may be faster to combine steps T2 and T3 into a single permutation step.

37. If $k = 2^{e_1} + \cdots + 2^{e_t}$ with $e_1 > \cdots > e_t \ge 0$, the sign changes occur at $S_{e_1} \cup \cdots \cup S_{e_t}$, where

$$S_0 = \left\{ \frac{1}{2} \right\}, \qquad S_1 = \left\{ \frac{1}{4}, \frac{3}{4} \right\}, \qquad \ldots, \qquad S_e = \left\{ \frac{2j+1}{2^{e+1}} \ \middle|\ 0 \le j < 2^e \right\}.$$

Therefore the number of sign changes in $(0 .. x)$ is $\sum_{j=1}^{t} \lfloor 2^{e_j} x + \frac{1}{2} \rfloor$. Setting $x = l/(k+1)$ gives $l + O(t)$ changes; so the lth is at a distance of at most $O(\nu(k))/2^{\lfloor \lg k \rfloor}$ from $l/(k+1)$.

[This argument makes it plausible that infinitely many pairs (k, l) exist with $|z_{kl} - l/(k+1)| = \Omega((\log k)/k)$. But no explicit construction of such "bad" pairs is immediately apparent.]

38. Let $t_0(x) = 1$ and $t_k(x) = \omega^{\lfloor 3x \rfloor \lceil 2k/3 \rceil} t_{\lfloor k/3 \rfloor}(3x)$, where $\omega = e^{2\pi i/3}$. Then $t_k(x)$ winds around the origin $\frac{2}{3}k$ times as x increases from 0 to 1. If $s_k(x) = \omega^{\lfloor 3^k x \rfloor}$ is the ternary analog of the Rademacher function $r_k(x)$, we have $t_k(x) = \prod_{j \geq 0} s_{j+1}(x)^{b_j - b_{j+1}}$ when $k = (b_{n-1} \ldots b_0)_3$, as in the modular ternary Gray code.

39. (a) Let's call the symbols $\{x_0, x_1, \ldots, x_7\}$ instead of $\{a, b, c, d, e, f, g, h\}$. We want to find a permutation p of $\{0, 1, \ldots, 7\}$ such that the matrix with $(-1)^{j \cdot k} x_{p(j) \oplus k}$ in row j and column k has orthogonal rows; this condition is equivalent to requiring that

$$(j \oplus j') \cdot (p(j) \oplus p(j')) \equiv 1 \pmod{2}, \quad \text{for } 0 \leq j < j' < 8.$$

One solution is $p(0) \ldots p(7) = 0\,1\,7\,2\,5\,6\,3\,4$, yielding the identity $(a^2 + b^2 + c^2 + d^2 + e^2 + f^2 + g^2 + h^2)(A^2 + B^2 + C^2 + D^2 + E^2 + F^2 + G^2 + H^2) = \mathcal{A}^2 + \mathcal{B}^2 + \mathcal{C}^2 + \mathcal{D}^2 + \mathcal{E}^2 + \mathcal{F}^2 + \mathcal{G}^2 + \mathcal{H}^2$, where

$$
\begin{pmatrix} \mathcal{A} \\ \mathcal{B} \\ \mathcal{C} \\ \mathcal{D} \\ \mathcal{E} \\ \mathcal{F} \\ \mathcal{G} \\ \mathcal{H} \end{pmatrix} =
\begin{pmatrix}
a & b & c & d & e & f & g & h \\
b & -a & d & -c & f & -e & h & -g \\
h & g & -f & -e & d & c & -b & -a \\
c & -d & -a & b & g & -h & -e & f \\
f & e & h & g & -b & -a & -d & -c \\
g & -h & e & -f & -c & d & -a & b \\
d & c & -b & -a & -h & -g & f & e \\
e & -f & -g & h & -a & b & c & -d
\end{pmatrix}
\begin{pmatrix} A \\ B \\ C \\ D \\ E \\ F \\ G \\ H \end{pmatrix}.
$$

[This identity was discovered by C. F. Degen, *Mémoires de l'Acad. Sci. St. Petersbourg* (5) **8** (1818), 207–219. The related octonions are discussed in an interesting survey by J. C. Baez, *Bull. Amer. Math. Soc.* **39** (2002), 145–205; **42** (2005), 213, 229–243. See also J. H. Conway and D. A. Smith, *On Quaternions and Octonions* (2003).]

(b) There *is* no 16×16 solution. The closest one can come is

$$p(0) \ldots p(15) = 0\ 1\ 11\ 2\ 14\ 15\ 13\ 4\ 9\ 10\ 7\ 12\ 5\ 6\ 3\ 8,$$

which fails if and only if $j \oplus j' = 5$. (See *Philos. Mag.* **34** (1867), 461–475. In §9, §10, §11, and §13 of this paper, Sylvester stated and proved the basic results about what has somehow come to be known as the Hadamard transform — although Hadamard himself gave credit to Sylvester [*Bull. des Sciences Mathématiques* (2) **17** (1893), 240–246]. Moreover, Sylvester introduced transforms of m^n elements in §14, using mth roots of unity.)

40. Yes; this change would in fact run through the swapped subsets in lexicographic binary order rather than in Gray binary order. (Any 5×5 matrix of 0s and 1s that is nonsingular mod 2 will generate all 32 possibilities when we run through all linear combinations of its rows.) The most important thing is the appearance of the ruler function, or some other Gray code delta sequence, not the fact that only one a_j changes per step, in cases like this where any number of the a_j can be changed simultaneously at the same cost.

41. At most 16; for example, `fired`, `fires`, `finds`, `fines`, `fined`, `fares`, `fared`, `wares`, `wards`, `wands`, `wanes`, `waned`, `wines`, `winds`, `wires`, `wired`. We also get 16 from `paced`/`links` and `paled`/`mints`; perhaps also from a word mixed with an antipodal nonword.

42. Suppose $n \le 2^{2^r} + r + 1$, and let $s = 2^r$. We use an auxiliary table of 2^{r+s} bits f_{jk} for $0 \le j < 2^s$ and $0 \le k < s$, representing focus pointers as in Algorithm L, together with an auxiliary s-bit "register" $j = (j_{s-1} \ldots j_0)_2$ and an $(r+2)$-bit "program counter" $p = (p_{r+1} \ldots p_0)_2$. At each step we examine the program counter and possibly the j register and one of the f bits; then, based on the bits seen, we complement a bit of the Gray code, complement a bit of the program counter, and possibly change a j or f bit, thereby emulating step L3 with respect to the most significant $n - r - 2$ bits.

For example, here is the construction when $r = 1$:

$p_2 p_1 p_0$	Change	Set		$p_2 p_1 p_0$	Change	Set
0 0 0	a_0, p_0	$j_0 \leftarrow f_{00}$	$\left.\begin{array}{l}\\\\\end{array}\right\} j \leftarrow f_0$	1 1 0	a_0, p_0	$f_{j0} \leftarrow f_{(j+1)0}$	$\left.\begin{array}{l}\\\\\end{array}\right\} f_j \leftarrow f_{j+1}$
0 0 1	a_1, p_1	$j_1 \leftarrow f_{01}$		1 1 1	a_1, p_1	$f_{j1} \leftarrow f_{(j+1)1}$	
0 1 1	a_0, p_0	$f_{00} \leftarrow 0$	$\left.\begin{array}{l}\\\\\end{array}\right\} f_0 \leftarrow 0$	1 0 1	a_0, p_0	$f_{(j+1)0} \leftarrow (j+1)_0$	$\left.\begin{array}{l}\\\\\end{array}\right\} f_{j+1} \leftarrow j+1$
0 1 0	a_2, p_2	$f_{01} \leftarrow 0$		1 0 0	a_{j+3}, p_2	$f_{(j+1)1} \leftarrow (j+1)_1$	

The process stops when it attempts to change bit a_n.

[In fact, we need change only *one* auxiliary bit per step if we allow ourselves to examine some Gray binary bits as well as the auxiliary bits, because $p_r \ldots p_0 = a_r \ldots a_0$, and we can set $f_0 \leftarrow 0$ in a more clever way when j doesn't have its final value $2^s - 1$. This construction, suggested by Fredman in 2001, improves on another that he had published in *SICOMP* **7** (1978), 134–146. With a more elaborate construction it is possible to reduce the number of auxiliary bits to $O(n)$.]

43. This number was estimated by Silverman, Vickers, and Sampson [*IEEE Trans.* **IT-29** (1983), 894–901] to be about 7×10^{22}. And indeed, H. Haanpää and P. R. J. Östergård found the exact value $d(6) = 71{,}676{,}427{,}445{,}141{,}767{,}741{,}440$ in 2011, by using symmetry and "gluing together" disjoint paths whose endpoints x have $\nu x = 3$ and whose interior vertices have $\nu x \le 3$. [To appear.]

44. Every n-bit Gray cycle defines a pair of perfect matchings (see exercise 55).

45. (a) (000 002 012 010 090 094 0b4 ... 112 102 100), in hexadecimal, 32 elements in all. Notice that the signatures of elements in each cycle run through the Gray code Γ_4.

(b) A ground vertex v is preceded in its cycle by its sibling $v \oplus 2$. If v is a ground vertex in a different cycle from its sibling $u = v \oplus 1$, we can join the cycles by deleting $\{u \oplus 2 - u, \, v \oplus 2 - v\}$ and inserting $\{u - v, \, u \oplus 2 - v \oplus 2\}$. Repeat for all ground v.

(c) Consider the multigraph G' whose vertices are the cycles and whose edges go from the cycle of v to the cycle of $v + 1$ for all even ground vertices v. Every vertex of G' has even degree, so the edges are a union of cycles in G'. Thus any edge of G' can be deleted without changing the connected components.

(d) It's not difficult to construct a path $P = v^{(0)} \!-\! v^{(1)} \!-\! v^{(2)} \!-\! \cdots$ through vertices of G with $v_0 = v_{-1} = 0$ that passes through all such v with $\sigma(v) \le 1$, and such that $\sigma(v^{(i)}) \in \{0, 1, 2, 4, 8\}$ for all i. Take the cycle from (b) that contains $v^{(0)}$ and call it the "working cycle" W; then do the following for $i = 1, 2, \ldots$, until W includes all vertices: If $v = v^{(i)} \notin W$, suppose $u = v^{(i-1)}$ has $u_l \ne v_l$. *Case 1:* $u \oplus c - u$ is an edge of W, for $c = 1$ or $c = 2$. Take a cycle for the equivalence class of v that has the edge $v \oplus c - v$. Delete those edges and insert $\{u - v, \, u \oplus c - v \oplus c\}$. *Case 2:* Otherwise Case 1 must have applied to $w = v^{(i-2)}$ and u on the previous step. If $c = 1$ then W contains the edge $u \oplus 2 - u \oplus 3$. We can find a cycle with $v \oplus 2 - v \oplus 3$, and replace those edges by $\{u \oplus 2 - v \oplus 3, \, u \oplus 3 - v \oplus 3\}$. A similar edge-swap works when $c = 2$.

(e) The final cycle W allows us to reconstruct $\mathcal{M}_{l(v)}(v)$. When $l(v) \ne 0$ the function $\mathcal{M}_{l(v)}$ is equivalent to $t = 2^{3^{r-1}}$ independent matchings of the r-cube, because there are t ways to choose the v_i for $i \neq l$ having the correct signature. So the number of different cycles is at least $M(r)^{12t}$ (see exercise 44).

46. There are k-bit signatures $\sigma(v)$. When $\sigma(v) = g(j)$ in Gray binary code, $l(v) = (\rho(j+1) + [j \neq 2^k - 1])[j + 2$ is not a power of 2]. At least $M(r)^{(2^k-k)t}$ cycles arise, where $t = 2^{(k-1)(r-1)+2}$. [*Information Processing Letters* **109** (2009), 267–272.]

47. The bounds $\left(\frac{r}{e}\right)^{2^{r-1}} < 2^{r-1}!/(2^{r-1}/r)^{2^{r-1}} \leq M(r) \leq r!^{2^{r-1}/r} = \left(\frac{r}{e} + O(\log r)\right)^{2^{r-1}}$ are proved in Section 7.5.1. Hence $d(n)^{1/2^n} \leq n/e + O(\log n)$ by exercise 44.

The lower bound from exercise 46, if we let G_j be an r_j-cube, is

$$\left(M(r_1)^{2^{n-r_1-k+1}}\right)^{2^{k-1}-k} \cdot \left(M(r_2)^{2^{n-r_2-k+1}}\right)^{2^{k-2}} \cdot \left(M(r_3)^{2^{n-r_3-k+1}}\right)^{2^{k-3}}$$
$$\cdots \cdot \left(M(r_{k-1})^{2^{n-r_{k-1}-k+1}}\right)^2 \cdot \left(M(r_k)^{2^{n-r_k-k+1}}\right)^2 ;$$

and it's better to choose $r_j \approx (n-2)/2^{j-[j=k]}$ for $1 \leq j \leq k$ instead of using cubes of roughly the same size. Let $\alpha_j = r_j/e$ be a lower bound on $M(r_j)^{2^{1-r_j}}$. The lower bound on $d(n)^{1/2^n}$ simplifies to

$$\alpha_1^{1/2 - k/2^k} \alpha_2^{1/4} \alpha_3^{1/8} \cdots \alpha_{k-1}^{1/2^{k-1}} \alpha_k^{1/2^{k-1}} = 2^{-2+(k-4)/2^k} \left(\frac{n-2}{e}\right)^{1-k/2^k} \left(1 + O\left(\frac{k}{n}\right)\right),$$

and this is $n/(4e) + O(\log n)^2$ when $k = \lg n + O(1)$.

49. Take any Hamiltonian path P from $0\ldots0$ to $1\ldots1$ in the $(2n-1)$-cube, such as the Savage–Winkler code, and use $0P$, $1\overline{P}$. (All such cycles are obtained by this construction when $n = 1$ or $n = 2$, but many more possibilities exist when $n > 2$.)

50. $\alpha_1(n+1)\alpha_1^R n \alpha_1 j_1 \alpha_2 n \alpha_2^R (n+1)\alpha_2 \ldots j_{l-1}\alpha_l n \alpha_l^R (n+1)\alpha_l n \alpha_l^R j_{l-1} \ldots j_1 \alpha_1^R n$.

51. Let $c_j = 2\lfloor(2^{n-1}+j)/n\rfloor$ and $c_j' = 2\lfloor(2^{n+1}+j)/(n+2)\rfloor$. If $n \neq 3$, it is not difficult to verify that $4c_j \geq 8\lfloor 2^{n-1}/n \rfloor > 2\lceil 2^{n+1}/(n+2)\rceil \geq c_k'$ for $0 \leq j < n$ and $0 \leq k < n+2$. Therefore we can apply Theorem D to any n-bit Gray cycle with transition counts c_j, underlining b_j copies of j and putting an underlined digit 0 last, where $b_j = 2c_j - \frac{1}{2}c_{(j+2+d) \bmod (n+2)}' - [j=0]$ and d is chosen so that $c_d' = c_{d+1}'$. This construction works because $l = b_0 + \cdots + b_{n-1} = 2(c_0 + \cdots + c_{n-1}) - \frac{1}{2}(c_0' + \cdots + c_{n+1}' - c_d' - c_{d+1}') - 1 = c_d' - 1$ is odd. [Corollary B was discovered by T. Bakos in the 1950s, and proved in detail by A. Ádám in *Truth Functions* (Budapest: 1968), 28–37. Ádám's book also presents a proof by G. Pollák that, in fact, $c_0' = c_1'$ for all n; hence we may take $d = 0$. See also J. P. Robinson and M. Cohn, *IEEE Trans.* **C-30** (1981), 17–23.]

52. The number of different code patterns in the smallest j coordinate positions is at most $c_0 + \cdots + c_{j-1}$.

53. Theorem D produces only cycles with $c_j = c_{j+1}$ for some j, so it can't produce the counts $(2, 4, 6, 8, 12)$. The extension in exercise 50 gives also $c_j = c_{j+1} - 2$, but it can't produce $(6, 10, 14, 18, 22, 26, 32)$. The sets of numbers satisfying the conditions of exercise 52 are precisely those obtainable by starting with $\{2, 2, 4, \ldots, 2^{n-1}\}$ and repeatedly replacing some pair $\{c_j, c_k\}$ for which $c_j < c_k$ by the pair $\{c_j + 2, c_k - 2\}$.

54. Suppose the values are $\{p_1, \ldots, p_n\}$, and let x_{jk} be the number of times p_j occurs in $(a_1, \ldots, a_k)$. We must have $(x_{1k}, \ldots, x_{nk}) \equiv (x_{1l}, \ldots, x_{nl})$ (modulo 2) for some $k < l$. But if the p's are prime numbers, varying as the delta sequence of an n-bit Gray cycle, the only solution is $k = 0$ and $l = 2^n$. [*AMM* **60** (1953), 418; **83** (1976), 54.]

55. In fact, given any perfect matching Q of K_{2^n}, one can find in $O(2^n)$ steps a perfect matching R of the n-cube such that $Q \cup R$ is a Hamiltonian cycle of K_{2^n}. [See J. Fink, *J. Comb. Theory* **B97** (2007), 1074–1076; *Elect. Notes Disc. Math.* **29** (2007), 345–351.]

56. [*Bell System Tech. J.* **37** (1958), 815–826.] The 112 canonical delta sequences yield

Class	Example	t	Class	Example	t	Class	Example	t
A	0102101302012023	2	D	0102013201020132	4	G	0102030201020302	8
B	0102303132101232	2	E	0102032021202302	4	H	0102101301021013	8
C	0102030130321013	2	F	0102013102010232	4	I	0102013121012132	1

Here B is the balanced code (Fig. 33(b)), G is standard Gray binary (Fig. 30(b)), and H is the complementary code (Fig. 33(a)). Class H is also equivalent to the modular $(4,4)$ Gray code under the correspondence of exercise 18. A class with t automorphisms corresponds to $32 \times 24/t$ of the 2688 different delta sequences $\delta_0 \delta_1 \ldots \delta_{15}$.

Similarly (see exercise 7.2.3–00), the 5-bit Gray cycles fall into 237,675 different equivalence classes.

57. With Type 1 only, 480 vertices are isolated, namely those of classes D, F, G in the previous answer. With Type 2 only, the graph has 384 components, 288 of which are isolated vertices of classes F and G. There are 64 components of size 9, each containing 3 vertices from E and 6 from A; 16 components of size 30, each with 6 from H and 24 from C; and 16 components of size 84, each with 12 from D, 24 from B, 48 from I. With Type 3 (or Type 4) only, the entire graph is connected. [Similarly, all 91,392 of the 4-bit Gray *paths* are connected if path $\alpha\beta$ is considered adjacent to path $\alpha^R\beta$. Vickers and Silverman, *IEEE Trans.* **C-29** (1980), 329–331, have conjectured that Type 3 changes will suffice to connect the graph of n-bit Gray cycles for all $n \geq 3$.]

58. If some nonempty substring of $\beta\beta$ involves each coordinate an even number of times, that substring cannot have length $|\beta|$, so some cyclic shift of β has a prefix γ with the same evenness property. But then α doesn't define a Gray cycle, because we could change each n of γ back to 0.

59. If α is nonlocal in exercise 58, so is $\beta\beta$, provided that $q > 1$ and that 0 occurs more than $q + 1$ times in α. Therefore, starting with the α of (30) but with 0 and 1 interchanged, we obtain nonlocal cycles for $n \geq 5$ in which coordinate 0 changes exactly 6 times. [Mark Ramras, *Discrete Math.* **85** (1990), 329–331.] On the other hand, a 4-bit Gray cycle cannot be nonlocal because it always has a run of length 2; if $\delta_k = \delta_{k+2}$, elements $\{v_k, v_{k+1}, v_{k+2}, v_{k+3}\}$ form a 2-subcube.

60. Use the construction of exercise 58 with $q = 1$.

61. The idea is to interleave an m-bit cycle $U = (u_0, u_1, u_2, \ldots)$ with an n-bit cycle $V = (v_0, v_1, v_2, \ldots)$, by forming concatenations

$$W = (u_{i_0}v_{j_0},\ u_{i_1}v_{j_1},\ u_{i_2}v_{j_2},\ \ldots), \qquad i_k = \bar{a}_0 + \cdots + \bar{a}_{k-1}, \quad j_k = a_0 + \cdots + a_{k-1},$$

where $a_0 a_1 a_2 \ldots$ is a periodic string of control bits $\alpha\alpha\alpha\ldots$; we advance to the next element of U when $a_k = 0$, otherwise to the next element of V.

If α is any string of length $2^m \leq 2^n$, containing s bits that are 0 and $t = 2^m - s$ bits that are 1, W will be an $(m + n)$-bit Gray cycle if s and t are odd. For we have $i_{k+l} \equiv i_k$ (modulo 2^m) and $j_{k+l} \equiv j_k$ (modulo 2^n) only if l is a multiple of 2^m, since $i_k + j_k = k$. Suppose $l = 2^m c$; then $j_{k+l} = j_k + tc$, so c is a multiple of 2^n.

(a) Let $\alpha = 0111$; then runs of length 8 occur in the left 2 bits and runs of length $\geq \lfloor \frac{4}{3} r(n) \rfloor$ occur in the right n bits.

(b) Let s be the largest odd number $\leq 2^m r(m)/(r(m)+r(n))$. Also let $t = 2^m - s$ and $a_k = \lfloor (k + 1)t/2^m \rfloor - \lfloor kt/2^m \rfloor$, so that $i_k = \lceil ks/2^m \rceil$ and $j_k = \lfloor kt/2^m \rfloor$. If a run of length l occurs in the left m bits, we have $i_{k+l+1} \geq i_k + r(m) + 1$, hence

$l+1 > 2^m r(m)/s \geq r(m)+r(n)$. And if it occurs in the right n bits we have $j_{k+l+1} \geq j_k + r(n) + 1$, hence

$$l+1 > 2^m r(n)/t > 2^m r(n)/(2^m r(n)/(r(m)+r(n)) + 2)$$

$$= r(m) + r(n) - \frac{2(r(m)+r(n))^2}{2^m r(n) + 2(r(m)+r(n))} > r(m) + r(n) - 1$$

because $r(m) \leq r(n)$.

The construction often works also in less restricted cases. See the paper that introduced the study of Gray-code runs: L. Goddyn, G. M. Lawrence, and E. Nemeth, *Utilitas Math.* **34** (1988), 179–192.

63. Set $a_k \leftarrow k \bmod 4$ for $0 \leq k < 2^{10}$, except that $a_k = 4$ when $k \bmod 16 = 15$ or $k \bmod 64 = 42$ or $k \bmod 256 = 133$. Also set $(j_0, j_1, j_2, j_3, j_4) \leftarrow (0, 2, 4, 6, 8)$. Then for $k = 0, 1, \ldots, 1023$, set $\delta_k \leftarrow j_{a_k}$ and $j_{a_k} \leftarrow 1 + 4a_k - j_{a_k}$. (This construction generalizes the method of exercise 61.)

64. (a) Each element u_k appears together with $\{v_k, v_{k+2^m}, \ldots, v_{k+2^m(2^{n-1}-1)}\}$ and $\{v_{k+1}, v_{k+1+2^m}, \ldots, v_{k+1+2^m(2^{n-1}-1)}\}$. Thus the permutation $\sigma_0 \ldots \sigma_{2^m-1}$ must be a 2^{n-1}-cycle containing the n-bit vertices of even parity, times an arbitrary permutation of the other vertices. This condition is also sufficient.

(b) Let τ_j be the permutation that takes $v \mapsto v \oplus 2^j$, and let $\pi_j(u, w)$ be the permutation $(uw)\tau_j$. If $u \oplus w = 2^i + 2^j$ then $\pi_j(u, w)$ takes $u \mapsto u \oplus 2^i$ and $w \mapsto w \oplus 2^i$, while $v \mapsto v \oplus 2^j$ for all other vertices v, so it takes each vertex to a neighbor.

If S is any set $\subseteq \{0, \ldots, n-1\}$, let $\sigma(S)$ be the stream of all permutations τ_j for all $j \in \{0, \ldots, n-1\} \setminus S$, in increasing order of j, repeated twice; for example, if $n = 5$ we have $\sigma(\{1, 2\}) = \tau_0 \tau_3 \tau_4 \tau_0 \tau_3 \tau_4$. Then the Gray stream

$$\Sigma(i, j, u) = \sigma(\{i, j\}) \pi_j(u, u \oplus 2^i \oplus 2^j) \sigma(\{i, j\}) \tau_j \sigma(\{j\})$$

consists of $6n - 8$ permutations whose product is the transposition $(u \; u \oplus 2^i \oplus 2^j)$. Moreover, when this stream is applied to any n-bit vertex v, its runs all have length $n-2$ or more.

We may assume that $n \geq 5$. Let $\delta_0 \ldots \delta_{2^n-1}$ be the delta sequence for an n-bit Gray cycle $(v_0, v_1, \ldots, v_{2^n-1})$ with all runs of length 3 or more. Then the product of all permutations in

$$\Sigma = \prod_{k=1}^{2^{n-1}-1} \left(\Sigma(\delta_{2k-1}, \delta_{2k}, v_{2k-1}) \Sigma(\delta_{2k}, \delta_{2k+1}, v_{2k}) \right)$$

is $(v_1 \, v_3)(v_2 \, v_4) \ldots (v_{2^n-3} \, v_{2^n-1})(v_{2^n-2} \, v_0) = (v_{2^n-1} \ldots v_1)(v_{2^n-2} \ldots v_0)$, so it satisfies the cycle condition of (a).

Moreover, all powers $(\sigma(\emptyset)\Sigma)^t$ produce runs of length $\geq n-2$ when applied to any vertex v. By repeating individual factors $\sigma(\{i, j\})$ or $\sigma(\{j\})$ in Σ as many times as we wish, we can adjust the length of $\sigma(\emptyset)\Sigma$, obtaining $2n + (2^{n-1}-1)(12n-16) + 2(n-2)a + 2(n-1)b$ for any integers $a, b \geq 0$; thus we can increase its length to exactly 2^m, provided that $2^m \geq 2n + (2^{n-1}-1)(12n-16) + 2(n^2-5n+6)$, by exercise 5.2.1–21.

(c) The bound $r(n) \geq n - 4 \lg n + 8$ can be proved for $n \geq 5$ as follows. First we observe that it holds for $5 \leq n < 33$ by the methods of exercises 60–63. Then we observe that every integer $N \geq 33$ can be written as $N = m + n$ or $N = m + n + 1$, for some $m \geq 20$, where

$$n = m - \lfloor 4 \lg m \rfloor + 10.$$

If $m \geq 20$, 2^m is sufficiently large for the construction in part (b) to be valid; hence

$$r(N) \geq r(m + n) \geq 2\min(r(m), n - 2) \geq 2(m - \lfloor 4\lg m\rfloor + 8)$$
$$= m + n + 1 - \lfloor 4\lg N - 1 + \epsilon\rfloor + 8$$
$$\geq N - 4\lg N + 8$$

where $\epsilon = 4\lg(2m/N) < 1 + [N = m + n]$. [*Electronic Journal of Combinatorics* **10** (2003), #R27, 1–10.] Recursive use of (b) gives, in fact, $r(1024) \geq 1000$.

65. A computer search reveals that eight essentially different patterns (and their reverses) are possible. One of them has the delta sequence 01020314203024041234 214103234103, and it is close to two of the others.

66. (Solution by Mark Cooke.) One suitable delta sequence is 012345607012132435 65760710213534626701537412362567017314262065701342146560573102464537 57102043537614073630464273703564027132750541210275641502403654250136 02541615604312576032572043157624321760452041751635476703564757062543 724213262416152341751436714316431434. (Solutions for $n > 8$ are still unknown.)

67. Let $v_{2k+1} = \bar{v}_{2k}$ and $v_{2k} = 0u_k$, where $(u_0, u_1, \ldots, u_{2^{n-1}-1})$ is any $(n-1)$-bit Gray cycle. [See Robinson and Cohn, *IEEE Trans.* **C-30** (1981), 17–23.]

68. Yes. The simplest way is probably to take $(n - 1)$-trit modular Gray ternary code and add $0\ldots0$, $1\ldots1$, $2\ldots2$ to each string (modulo 3). For example, when $n = 3$ the code is 000, 111, 222, 001, 112, 220, 002, 110, 221, 012, 120, 201, $\ldots$, 020, 101, 212.

69. (a) We need only verify the change in h when bits $b_{j-1}\ldots b_0$ are simultaneously complemented, for $j = 1, 2, \ldots$; and these changes are respectively $(1110)_2$, $(1101)_2$, $(0111)_2$, $(1011)_2$, $(10011)_2$, $(100011)_2$, $\ldots$. To prove that every n-tuple occurs, note that $0 \leq h(k) < 2^n$ when $0 \leq k < 2^n$ and $n > 3$; also $h^{[-1]}((a_{n-1}\ldots a_0)_2) = (b_{n-1}\ldots b_0)_2$, where $b_0 = a_0 \oplus a_1 \oplus a_2 \oplus \cdots$, $b_1 = a_0$, $b_2 = a_2 \oplus a_3 \oplus a_4 \oplus \cdots$, $b_3 = a_0 \oplus a_1 \oplus a_3 \oplus \cdots$, and $b_j = a_j \oplus a_{j+1} \oplus \cdots$ for $j \geq 4$.
   (b) Let $h(k) = (\ldots a_2 a_1 a_0)_2$ where $a_j = b_j \oplus b_{j+1} \oplus b_0[j \leq t] \oplus b_{t-1}[t - 1 \leq j \leq t]$.

70. As in (32) and (33), we can remove a factor of $n!$ by assuming that the strings of weight 1 occur in order. Then there are 14 solutions for $n = 5$ starting with 00000, and 21 starting with 00001. When $n = 6$ there are 46,935 of each type (related by reversal and complementation). When $n = 7$ the number is much, much larger, yet very small by comparison with the total number of 7-bit Gray codes.

71. Suppose that $\alpha_{n(j+1)}$ differs from α_{nj} in coordinate t_j, for $0 \leq j < n - 1$. Then $t_j = j\pi_n$, by (44) and (38). Now Eq. (34) tells us that $t_0 = n - 1$; and if $0 < j < n - 1$ we have $t_j = ((j - 1)\pi_{n-1})\pi_{n-1}$ by (40). Thus $t_j = j\sigma_n\pi_{n-1}^2$ for $0 \leq j < n - 1$, and the value of $(n - 1)\pi_n$ is whatever is left. (Notations for permutations are notoriously confusing, so it is always wise to check a few small cases carefully.)

72. The delta sequence is 0102132432020123401231304102132.

73. Let $Q_{nj} = P_{nj}^R$ and denote the sequences (41), (42) by S_n and T_n. Thus $S_n = P_{n0}Q_{n1}P_{n2}\ldots$ and $T_n = Q_{n0}P_{n1}Q_{n2}\ldots$, if we omit the commas; and we have

$$S_{n+1} = 0P_{n0}\ 0Q_{n1}\ 1Q_{n0}^\pi\ 1P_{n1}^\pi\ 0P_{n2}\ 0Q_{n3}\ 1Q_{n2}^\pi\ 1P_{n3}^\pi\ 0P_{n4}\ \cdots,$$
$$T_{n+1} = 0Q_{n0}\ 1P_{n0}^\pi\ 0P_{n1}\ 0Q_{n2}\ 1Q_{n1}^\pi\ 1P_{n2}^\pi\ 0P_{n3}\ 0Q_{n4}\ 1Q_{n3}^\pi\ \cdots,$$

where $\pi = \pi_n$, revealing a reasonably simple joint recursion between the delta sequences Δ_n and E_n of S_n and T_n. Namely, if we write

$$\Delta_n = \phi_1\, a_1\, \phi_2\, a_2 \ldots \phi_{n-1}\, a_{n-1}\, \phi_n, \qquad E_n = \psi_1\, b_1\, \psi_2\, b_2 \ldots \psi_{n-1}\, b_{n-1}\, \psi_n,$$

where each ϕ_j and ψ_j is a string of length $2\binom{n-1}{j-1} - 1$, the next sequences are

$$\Delta_{n+1} = \phi_1\ a_1\ \phi_2\ n\ \psi_1\pi\ b_1\pi\ \psi_2\pi\ n\ \phi_3\ a_3\ \phi_4\ n\ \psi_3\pi\ b_3\pi\ \psi_4\pi\ n\ \dots$$
$$E_{n+1} = \psi_1\ n\ \phi_1\pi\ n\ \psi_2\ b_2\ \psi_3\ n\ \phi_2\pi\ a_2\pi\ \phi_3\pi\ n\ \psi_4\ b_4\ \psi_5\ n\ \phi_4\pi\ a_4\pi\ \phi_5\pi\ n\ \dots$$

For example, we have $\Delta_3 = 01\underline{0}210\underline{1}$ and $E_3 = 02\underline{1}202\underline{1}$, if we underline the a's and b's to distinguish them from the ϕ's and ψ's; and

$$\Delta_4 = 0\ 1\ 0\ 2\ 1\ 3\ 0\pi\ 2\pi\ 1\pi\ 2\pi\ 0\pi\ 3\ 1\ 3\ 1\pi = 0\ \underline{1}\ 0\ 2\ 1\ 3\ 2\ \underline{1}\ 0\ 1\ 2\ 3\ 1\ \underline{3}\ 0,$$
$$E_4 = 0\ 3\ 0\pi\ 3\ 1\ 2\ 0\ 2\ 1\ 3\ 0\pi\ 2\pi\ 1\pi\ 0\pi\ 1\pi = 0\ \underline{3}\ 2\ 3\ 1\ 2\ 0\ 2\ 1\ 3\ 2\ 1\ 0\ \underline{2}\ 0;$$

here $a_3\phi_4$ and $b_3\psi_4$ are empty. Elements have been underlined for the next step.

Thus we can compute the delta sequences in memory as follows. Here $p[j] = j\pi_n$ for $1 \le j < n$; $s_k = \delta_k$, $t_k = \varepsilon_k$, and $u_k = [\delta_k$ and ε_k are underlined], for $0 \le k < 2^n - 1$.

X1. [Initialize.] Set $n \leftarrow 1$, $p[0] \leftarrow 0$, $s_0 \leftarrow t_0 \leftarrow u_0 \leftarrow 0$.

X2. [Advance n.] Perform Algorithm Y below, which computes the arrays s', t', and u' for the next value of n; then set $n \leftarrow n + 1$.

X3. [Ready?] If n is sufficiently large, the desired delta sequence Δ_n is in array s'; terminate. Otherwise keep going.

X4. [Compute π_n.] Set $p'[0] = n - 1$, and $p'[j] = p[p[j-1]]$ for $1 \le j < n$.

X5. [Prepare to advance.] Set $p[j] \leftarrow p'[j]$ for $0 \le j < n$; set $s_k \leftarrow s'_k$, $t_k \leftarrow t'_k$, and $u_k \leftarrow u'_k$ for $0 \le k < 2^n - 1$. Return to X2. ∎

In the following steps, "Transmit stuff(l, j) while $u_j = 0$" is an abbreviation for "If $u_j = 0$, repeatedly stuff(l, j), $l \leftarrow l + 1$, $j \leftarrow j + 1$, until $u_j \ne 0$."

Y1. [Prepare to compute Δ_{n+1}.] Set $j \leftarrow k \leftarrow l \leftarrow 0$ and $u_{2^n-1} \leftarrow -1$.

Y2. [Advance j.] Transmit $s'_l \leftarrow s_j$ and $u'_l \leftarrow 0$ while $u_j = 0$. Then go to Y5 if $u_j < 0$.

Y3. [Advance j and k.] Set $s'_l \leftarrow s_j$, $u'_l \leftarrow 1$, $l \leftarrow l + 1$, $j \leftarrow j + 1$. Then transmit $s'_l \leftarrow s_j$ and $u'_l \leftarrow 0$ while $u_j = 0$. Then set $s'_l \leftarrow n$, $u'_l \leftarrow 0$, $l \leftarrow l + 1$. Then transmit $s'_l \leftarrow p[t_k]$ and $u'_l \leftarrow 0$ while $u_k = 0$. Then set $s'_l \leftarrow p[t_k]$, $u'_l \leftarrow 1$, $l \leftarrow l + 1$, $k \leftarrow k + 1$. And once again transmit $s'_l \leftarrow p[t_k]$ and $u'_l \leftarrow 0$ while $u_k = 0$.

Y4. [Done with Δ_{n+1}?] If $u_k < 0$, go to Y6. Otherwise set $s'_l \leftarrow n$, $u'_l \leftarrow 0$, $l \leftarrow l + 1$, $j \leftarrow j + 1$, $k \leftarrow k + 1$, and return to Y2.

Y5. [Finish Δ_{n+1}.] Set $s'_l \leftarrow n$, $u'_l \leftarrow 1$, $l \leftarrow l + 1$. Then transmit $s'_l \leftarrow p[t[k]]$ and $u'_l \leftarrow 0$ while $u_k = 0$.

Y6. [Prepare to compute E_{n+1}.] Set $j \leftarrow k \leftarrow l \leftarrow 0$. Transmit $t'_l \leftarrow t_k$ while $u_k = 0$. Then set $t'_l \leftarrow n$, $l \leftarrow l + 1$.

Y7. [Advance j.] Transmit $t'_l \leftarrow p[s_j]$ while $u_j = 0$. Then terminate if $u_j < 0$; otherwise set $t'_l \leftarrow n$, $l \leftarrow l + 1$, $j \leftarrow j + 1$, $k \leftarrow k + 1$.

Y8. [Advance k.] Transmit $t'_l \leftarrow t_k$ while $u_k = 0$. Then go to Y10 if $u_k < 0$.

Y9. [Advance k and j.] Set $t'_l \leftarrow t_k$, $l \leftarrow l + 1$, $k \leftarrow k + 1$. Then transmit $t'_l \leftarrow t_k$ while $u_k = 0$. Then set $t'_l \leftarrow n$, $l \leftarrow l + 1$. Then transmit $t'_l \leftarrow p[s_j]$ while $u_j = 0$. Then set $t'_l \leftarrow p[s_j]$, $l \leftarrow l + 1$, $j \leftarrow j + 1$. Return to Y7.

Y10. [Finish E_{n+1}.] Set $t'_l \leftarrow n$, $l \leftarrow l + 1$. Then transmit $t'_l \leftarrow p[s_j]$ while $u_j = 0$. ∎

To generate the monotonic Savage–Winkler code for fairly large n, one can first generate Δ_{10} and E_{10}, say, or even Δ_{20} and E_{20}. Using these tables, a suitable recursive procedure will then be able to reach higher values of n with very little computational overhead per step, on the average.

74. If the monotonic path is $v_0, \ldots, v_{2^n-1}$ and if v_k has weight j, we have

$$2 \sum_{t>0} \binom{n}{j-2t} + ((j + \nu(v_0)) \bmod 2) \le k \le 2 \sum_{t \ge 0} \binom{n}{j-2t} + ((j + \nu(v_0)) \bmod 2) - 2.$$

Therefore the maximum distance between vertices of respective weights j and $j+1$ is $2(\binom{n-1}{j-1} + \binom{n-1}{j} + \binom{n-1}{j+1}) - 1$. The maximum value, approximately $3 \cdot 2^{n+1}/\sqrt{2\pi n}$, occurs when j is approximately $n/2$. [This is only about three times the smallest value achievable in *any* ordering of the vertices, which is $\sum_{j=0}^{n-1} \binom{j}{\lfloor j/2 \rfloor}$ by exercise 7.10–00.]

75. The trend-free canonical delta sequences all turn out to yield Gray *cycles*:

$$0\,1\,2\,3\,0\,1\,2\,4\,2\,1\,0\,3\,2\,1\,0\,1\,2\,1\,0\,3\,2\,1\,0\,4\,0\,1\,2\,3\,0\,1\,2\,(1)$$
$$0\,1\,2\,3\,0\,1\,2\,4\,2\,1\,0\,3\,2\,1\,0\,1\,3\,0\,1\,2\,3\,0\,1\,4\,1\,0\,3\,2\,1\,0\,3\,(1)$$
$$0\,1\,2\,3\,0\,1\,2\,4\,2\,1\,0\,3\,2\,1\,0\,2\,0\,3\,2\,1\,0\,3\,2\,4\,2\,3\,0\,1\,2\,3\,0\,(2)$$
$$0\,1\,2\,3\,0\,1\,2\,4\,2\,1\,0\,3\,2\,1\,0\,2\,1\,2\,3\,0\,1\,2\,3\,4\,3\,2\,1\,0\,3\,2\,1\,(2)$$
$$0\,1\,2\,3\,0\,1\,2\,4\,2\,3\,0\,1\,2\,3\,0\,2\,0\,1\,2\,3\,0\,1\,2\,4\,2\,3\,0\,1\,2\,3\,0\,(2)$$
$$0\,1\,2\,3\,4\,1\,0\,1\,2\,1\,0\,3\,0\,1\,4\,3\,2\,1\,0\,3\,0\,1\,4\,1\,0\,1\,2\,3\,4\,1\,0\,(3)$$

(The second and fourth of these are cyclically equivalent.)

76. If $v_0, \ldots, v_{2^n-1}$ is trend-free, so is the $(n+1)$-bit cycle $0v_0, 1v_0, 1v_1, 0v_1, 0v_2, 1v_2,$ $\ldots, 1v_{2^n-1}, 0v_{2^n-1}$. Figure 34(g) shows a somewhat more interesting construction, which generalizes the first solution of exercise 75 to an $(n+2)$-bit cycle

$$00\Gamma''^R, \; 01\Gamma'^R, \; 11\Gamma', \; 10\Gamma'', \; 10\Gamma, \; 11\Gamma''', \; 01\Gamma'''^R, \; 00\Gamma^R$$

where Γ is the n-bit sequence $g(1), \ldots, g(2^n-1)$ and $\Gamma' = \Gamma \oplus g(1)$, $\Gamma'' = \Gamma \oplus g(2^{n-1})$, $\Gamma''' = \Gamma \oplus g(2^{n-1} + 1)$. [An n-bit trend-free design that is *almost* a Gray code, having just four steps in which $\nu(v_k \oplus v_{k+1}) = 2$, was found for all $n \ge 3$ by C. S. Cheng, *Proc. Berkeley Conf. Neyman and Kiefer* **2** (Hayward, Calif.: Inst. of Math. Statistics, 1985), 619–633.]

77. Replace the array $(o_{n-1}, \ldots, o_0)$ by an array of sentinel values $(s_{n-1}, \ldots, s_0)$, with $s_j \leftarrow m_j - 1$ in step H1. Set $a_j \leftarrow (a_j + 1) \bmod m_j$ in step H4. If $a_j = s_j$ in step H5, set $s_j \leftarrow (s_j - 1) \bmod m_j$, $f_j \leftarrow f_{j+1}$, $f_{j+1} \leftarrow j+1$.

78. For (50), notice that B_{j+1} is the number of times reflection has occurred in coordinate j, because we bypass coordinate j on steps that are multiples of $m_j \ldots m_0$. Hence, if $b_j < m_j - 1$, an increase of b_j by 1 causes a_j to increase or decrease by 1 as appropriate. Furthermore, if $b_i = m_i - 1$ for $0 \le i < j$, changing all these b_i to 0 when incrementing b_j will increase each of $B_0, \ldots, B_j$ by 1, thereby leaving the values $a_0, \ldots, a_{j-1}$ unchanged in (50).

For (51), note that $B_j = m_j B_{j+1} + b_j \equiv m_j B_{j+1} + a_j + (m_j - 1)B_{j+1} \equiv a_j + B_{j+1}$ (modulo 2); hence $B_j \equiv a_j + a_{j+1} + \cdots$, and (51) is obviously equivalent to (50).

In the modular Gray code for general radices $(m_{n-1}, \ldots, m_0)$, let

$$\bar{g}(k) = \begin{bmatrix} a_{n-1}, & \ldots, & a_2, & a_1, & a_0 \\ m_{n-1}, & \ldots, & m_2, & m_1, & m_0 \end{bmatrix}$$

when k is given by (46). Then $a_j = (b_j - B_{j+1}) \bmod m_j$, because coordinate j has increased modulo m_j exactly $B_j - B_{j+1}$ times if we start at $(0, \ldots, 0)$. The inverse function, which determines the b's from the modular Gray a's, is $b_j = (a_j + a_{j+1} + a_{j+2} + \cdots) \bmod m_j$ in the special case that each m_j is a divisor of m_{j+1} (for example, if all m_j are equal). But the inverse has no simple form in general; it can be computed by using the recurrences $b_j = (a_j + B_{j+1}) \bmod m_j$, $B_j = m_j B_{j+1} + b_j$ for $j = n - 1$, $\ldots$, 0, starting with $B_n = 0$.

[Reflected Gray codes for radix $m > 2$ were introduced by Ivan Flores in *IRE Trans.* **EC-5** (1956), 79–82; he derived (50) and (51) in the case that all m_j are equal. Modular Gray codes with general mixed radices were implicitly discussed by Joseph Rosenbaum in *AMM* **45** (1938), 694–696, but without the conversion formulas; conversion formulas when all m_j have a common value m were published by Martin Cohn, *Information and Control* **6** (1963), 70–78.]

79. (a) The last n-tuple always has $a_{n-1} = m_{n-1} - 1$, so it is one step from $(0, \ldots, 0)$ only if $m_{n-1} = 2$. And this condition suffices to make the final n-tuple $(1, 0, \ldots, 0)$. [Similarly, the final subforest output by Algorithm K is adjacent to the initial one if and only if the leftmost tree is an isolated vertex.]

(b) The last n-tuple is $(m_{n-1} - 1, 0, \ldots, 0)$ if and only if $m_{n-1} \ldots m_{j+1} \bmod m_j = 0$ for $0 \le j < n - 1$, because $b_j = m_j - 1$ and $B_j = m_{n-1} \ldots m_j - 1$.

80. Run through $p_1^{a_1} \ldots p_t^{a_t}$ using reflected Gray code with radices $m_j = e_j + 1$.

81. The first cycle contains the edge from (x, y) to $(x, (y + 1) \bmod m)$ if and only if $(x + y) \bmod m \ne m - 1$ if and only if the second cycle contains the edge from (x, y) to $((x + 1) \bmod m, y)$.

82. There are two 4-bit Gray cycles $(u_0, \ldots, u_{15})$ and $(v_0, \ldots, v_{15})$ that cover all edges of the 4-cube. (Indeed, the non-edges of classes A, B, D, H, and I in exercise 56 form Gray cycles, in the same classes as their complements.) Therefore with 16-ary modular Gray code we can form the four desired cycles $(u_0 u_0, u_0 u_1, \ldots, u_0 u_{15}, u_1 u_{15}, \ldots, u_{15} u_0)$, $(u_0 u_0, u_1 u_0, \ldots, u_{15} u_0, u_{15} u_1, \ldots, u_0 u_{15})$, $(v_0 v_0, \ldots, v_{15} v_0)$, $(v_0 v_0, \ldots, v_0 v_{15})$.

In a similar way we can show that $n/2$ edge-disjoint n-bit Gray cycles exist when n is 16, 32, 64, etc. [*Abhandlungen Math. Sem. Hamburg* **20** (1956), 13–16.] J. Aubert and B. Schneider [*Discrete Math.* **38** (1982), 7–16] have proved that the same property holds for *all* even values of $n \ge 4$, but no simple construction is known.

83. Mark Cooke found the following totally unsymmetric solution in December, 2002:

(1) 2737465057320265612316546743610525106052042416314372145101421737
2506246064173213107351607103156205713172463452102434643207054702
4147356146737625047350745130620656415073123731427376432561240264
3016735467532402524637475217640270736065105215106073575463253105;

(2) 0616713417232175171671540460247164742473202531621673531632736052
6710141503047313570615453627623241426465272021632075363710750740
3157674761545652756510451024023107353424651230406545306213710537
2620501752453406703437343531502602463045627674152752406021610434;

(3) 3701063751507131236243765735103012042353747207410473621617247324
6505132565057121565024570473247421427640231034362703262764130574
0560620341745613151756314702721725205613212604053506260460173642
6717641743513401245360241730636545061563027414535676432625745051;

(4) 6706546435672147236210405432054510737405170532145431636430504673
4560621206416201320742373627204506473140171020514126107452343672
1320452752353410515426370601363567307105420163151210535061731236
4272537165617217542510760215462375452674257037346403647376271657.

(Each of these delta sequences should start from the same vertex of the cube.) Is there a symmetrical way to do the job?

84. Calling the initial position $(2, 2)$, the 8-step solution in Fig. A–1 shows how the sequence progresses down to $(0, 0)$. In the first move, for example, the front half of the cord passes around and behind the right comb, then through the large right loop. The middle line should be read from right to left. The generalization to n pairs of loops would, similarly, take $3^n - 1$ steps.

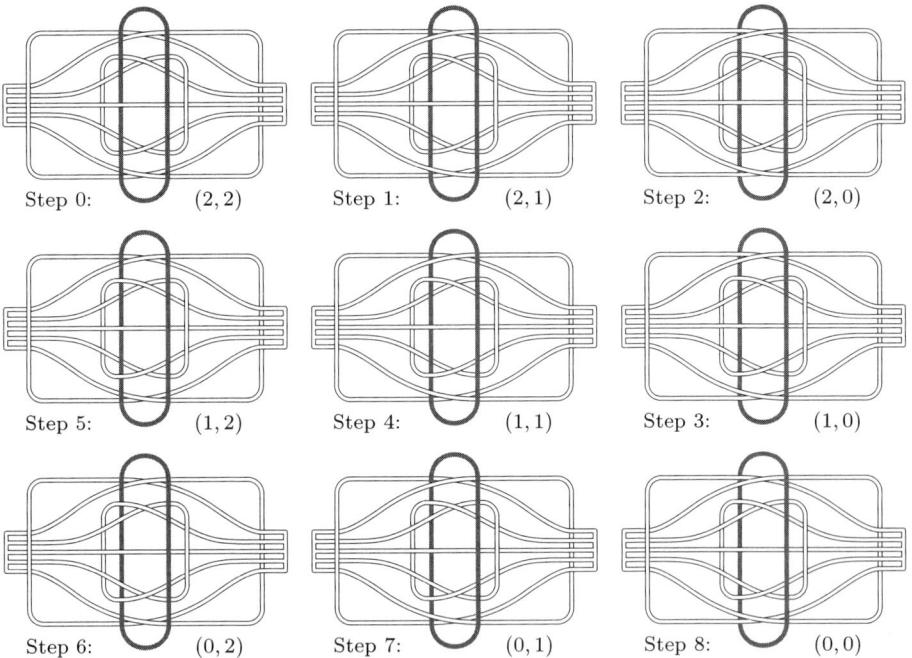

Fig. A–1. Freeing the Loony Loop.

[The origin of this delightful puzzle is obscure. *The Book of Ingenious & Diabolical Puzzles* by Jerry Slocum and Jack Botermans (1994) shows a 2-loop version carved from horn, probably made in China about 1850 [page 101], and a modern 6-loop version made in Malaysia about 1988 [page 93]. Slocum also owns a 4-loop version made from bamboo in England about 1884. He has found it listed in Henry Novra's *Catalogue of Conjuring Tricks and Puzzles* (1858 or 1859) and W. H. Cremer's *Games, Amusements, Pastimes and Magic* (1867), as well as in Hamley's catalog of 1895, under the name "Marvellous Canoe Puzzle." See also *U.S. Patents 2091191* (1937), *D172310* (1954), *3758114* (1973), *D406866* (1999). Dyckman noted its connection to reflected Gray ternary in a letter to Martin Gardner, dated 2 August 1972.]

85. By (50), element $\left[\begin{smallmatrix} b, & b' \\ t, & t' \end{smallmatrix}\right]$ of $\Gamma \wr \Gamma'$ is $\alpha_a \alpha'_{a'}$ if $\hat{g}(\left[\begin{smallmatrix} b, & b' \\ t, & t' \end{smallmatrix}\right]) = \left[\begin{smallmatrix} a, & a' \\ t, & t' \end{smallmatrix}\right]$ in the reflected Gray code for radices (t, t'). We can now show that element $\left[\begin{smallmatrix} b, & b', & b'' \\ t, & t', & t'' \end{smallmatrix}\right]$ of both $(\Gamma \wr \Gamma') \wr \Gamma''$

and $\Gamma \wr (\Gamma' \wr \Gamma'')$ is $\alpha_a \alpha'_{a'} \alpha''_{a''}$ if $\hat{g}([\begin{smallmatrix} b, & b', & b'' \\ t, & t', & t'' \end{smallmatrix}]) = [\begin{smallmatrix} a, & a', & a'' \\ t, & t', & t'' \end{smallmatrix}]$ in the reflected Gray code for radices (t, t', t''). See exercise 4.1–10, and note also the mixed-radix law

$$m_1 \dots m_n - 1 - \begin{bmatrix} x_1, & \dots, & x_n \\ m_1, & \dots, & m_n \end{bmatrix} = \begin{bmatrix} m_1 - 1 - x_1, & \dots, & m_n - 1 - x_n \\ m_1, & \dots, & m_n \end{bmatrix}.$$

In general, the reflected Gray code for radices $(m_1, \dots, m_n)$ is $(0, \dots, m_1 - 1) \wr \dots \wr (0, \dots, m_n - 1)$. [*Information Processing Letters* **22** (1986), 201–205.]

86. Let Γ_{mn} be the reflected m-ary Gray code, which can be defined by $\Gamma_{m0} = \epsilon$ and

$$\Gamma_{m(n+1)} = (0, 1, \dots, m - 1) \wr \Gamma_{mn}, \qquad n \geq 0.$$

This path runs from $(0, 0, \dots, 0)$ to $(m - 1, 0, \dots, 0)$ when m is even. Consider the Gray path Π_{mn} defined by $\Pi_{m0} = \emptyset$ and

$$\Pi_{m(n+1)} = \begin{cases} (0, 1, \dots, m - 1) \wr \Pi_{mn}, \; m\Gamma^R_{(m+1)n}, & \text{if } m \text{ is odd;} \\ (0, 1, \dots, m) \wr \Pi_{mn}, \; m\Gamma^R_{mn}, & \text{if } m \text{ is even.} \end{cases}$$

This path traverses all of the $(m + 1)^n - m^n$ nonnegative integer n-tuples for which $\max(a_1, \dots, a_n) = m$, starting with $(0, \dots, 0, m)$ and ending with $(m, 0, \dots, 0)$. The desired infinite Gray path is $\Pi_{0n}, \Pi^R_{1n}, \Pi_{2n}, \Pi^R_{3n}, \dots$.

87. This is impossible when n is odd, because the n-tuples with $\max(|a_1|, \dots, |a_n|) = 1$ include $\frac{1}{2}(3^n + 1)$ with odd parity and $\frac{1}{2}(3^n - 3)$ with even parity. When $n = 2$ we can use a spiral $\Sigma_0, \Sigma_1, \Sigma_2, \dots$, where Σ_m winds counterclockwise from $(m, 1 - m)$ to $(m, -m)$ when $m > 0$. For even values of $n \geq 2$, if T_m is a path of n-tuples from $(m, 1 - m, m - 1, 1 - m, \dots, m - 1, 1 - m)$ to $(m, -m, m, -m, \dots, m, -m)$, we can use $\Sigma_m \wr (T_0, \dots, T_{m-1})^R, (\Sigma_0, \dots, \Sigma_m)^R \wr \bar{T}_m$ for $(n + 2)$-tuples with the same property, where $\bar{\wr}$ is the dual operation

$$\Gamma \bar{\wr} \Gamma' = (\alpha_0 \alpha'_0, \dots, \alpha_{t-1} \alpha'_0, \alpha_{t-1} \alpha'_1, \dots, \alpha_0 \alpha'_1, \alpha_0 \alpha'_2, \dots, \alpha_{t-1} \alpha'_2, \alpha_{t-1} \alpha'_3, \dots).$$

[Infinite n-dimensional Gray codes *without* the magnitude constraint were first constructed by E. Vázsonyi, *Acta Litterarum ac Scientiarum*, sectio Scientiarum Mathematicarum **9** (Szeged: 1938), 163–173.]

88. It would visit all the subforests again, but in reverse order, ending with $(0, \dots, 0)$ and returning to the state it had after the initialization step K1. (This reflection principle is, in fact, the key to understanding how Algorithm K works.)

89. (a) Let $M_0 = \epsilon$, $M_1 = \cdot$, and $M_{n+2} = \cdot M^R_{n+1}, \; - M^R_n$. This construction works because the last element of M^R_{n+1} is the first element of M_{n+1}, namely a dot followed by the first element of M^R_n.

(b) Given a string $d_1 \dots d_l$ where each d_j is $\cdot$ or $-$, we can find its successor by letting $k = l - [d_l = \cdot]$ and proceeding as follows: If k is odd and $d_k = \cdot$, change $d_k d_{k+1}$ to $-$; if k is even and $d_k = -$, change d_k to $\cdot\cdot$; otherwise decrease k by 1 and repeat until either making a change or reaching $k = 0$. The successor of the given word is $\cdot - - \cdot \cdot \cdot - \cdot - \cdot$.

90. A cycle can exist only when the number of code words is even, since the number of dashes changes by ± 1 at each step. Thus we must have $n \bmod 3 = 2$. The Gray paths M_n of exercise 89 are not suitable; they begin with $(\cdot -)^{\lfloor n/3 \rfloor} \cdot^{n \bmod 3}$ and end with $(- \cdot)^{\lfloor n/3 \rfloor} \cdot^{[n \bmod 3 = 1]} -^{[n \bmod 3 = 2]}$. But $M_{3k+1} \cdot, M^R_{3k} -$ is a Hamiltonian cycle in the Morse code graph when $n = 3k + 2$.

91. Equivalently, the n-tuples $a_1\bar{a}_2 a_3 \bar{a}_4 \ldots$ have no two consecutive 1s. Such n-tuples correspond to Morse code sequences of length $n + 1$, if we append 0 and then represent • and — respectively by 0 and 10. Under this correspondence we can convert the path M_{n+1} of exercise 89 into a procedure like Algorithm K, with the fringe containing the indices where each dot or dash begins (except for a final dot):

> **U1.** [Initialize.] Set $a_j \leftarrow \lfloor ((j-1) \bmod 6)/3 \rfloor$ and $f_j \leftarrow j$ for $1 \leq j \leq n$. Also set $f_0 \leftarrow 0$, $r_0 \leftarrow 1$, $l_1 \leftarrow 0$, $r_j \leftarrow j + (j \bmod 3)$ and $l_{j+(j \bmod 3)} \leftarrow j$ for $1 \leq j \leq n$, except if $j + (j \bmod 3) > n$ set $r_j \leftarrow 0$ and $l_0 \leftarrow j$. (The "fringe" now contains 1, 2, 4, 5, 7, 8, ...)
>
> **U2.** [Visit.] Visit the n-tuple $(a_1, \ldots, a_n)$.
>
> **U3.** [Choose p.] Set $q \leftarrow l_0$, $p \leftarrow f_q$, $f_q \leftarrow q$.
>
> **U4.** [Check a_p.] Terminate the algorithm if $p = 0$. Otherwise set $a_p \leftarrow 1 - a_p$ and go to U6 if $a_p + p$ is now even.
>
> **U5.** [Insert $p+1$.] If $p < n$, set $q \leftarrow r_p$, $l_q \leftarrow p+1$, $r_{p+1} \leftarrow q$, $r_p \leftarrow p+1$, $l_{p+1} \leftarrow p$. Go to U7.
>
> **U6.** [Delete $p+1$.] If $p < n$, set $q \leftarrow r_{p+1}$, $r_p \leftarrow q$, $l_q \leftarrow p$.
>
> **U7.** [Make p passive.] Set $f_p \leftarrow f_{l_p}$ and $f_{l_p} \leftarrow l_p$. Return to U2. ∎

This algorithm can also be derived as a special case of a considerably more general method due to Gang Li, Frank Ruskey, and D. E. Knuth, which extends Algorithm K by allowing the user to specify either $a_p \geq a_q$ or $a_p \leq a_q$ for each (parent, child) pair (p, q). [See Knuth and Ruskey, *Lecture Notes in Computer Science* **2635** (2004), 183–204.] A generalization in another direction, which produces all strings of length n that do not contain certain substrings, has been discovered by M. B. Squire, *Electronic J. Combinatorics* **3** (1996), #R17, 1–29.

Incidentally, it is amusing to note that the mapping $k \mapsto g(k)/2$ is a one-to-one correspondence between all binary n-tuples with no odd-length runs of 1s and all binary n-tuples with no two consecutive 1s.

92. Yes, because the digraph of all $(n-1)$-tuples $(x_1, \ldots, x_{n-1})$ with $x_1, \ldots, x_{n-1} \leq m$ and with arcs $(x_1, \ldots, x_{n-1}) \to (x_2, \ldots, x_n)$ whenever $\max(x_1, \ldots, x_n) = m$ is connected and balanced; see Theorem 2.3.4.2G. Indeed, we get such a sequence from Algorithm F if we note that the final k^n elements of the prime strings of length dividing n, when subtracted from $m - 1$, are the same for all $m \geq k$. When $n = 4$, for example, the first 81 digits of the sequence Φ_4 are $2 - \alpha^R = 0\,0001\,010\,0011\ldots$, where α is the string (62). [There also are infinite m-ary sequences whose first m^n elements are de Bruijn cycles for all n, given any fixed $m \geq 3$. See L. J. Cummings and D. Wiedemann, *Cong. Numerantium* **53** (1986), 155–160.]

93. The cycle generated by $f()$ is a cyclic permutation of $\alpha 1$, where α has length $m^n - 1$ and ends with 1^{n-1}. The cycle generated by Algorithm R is a cyclic permutation of $\gamma = c_0 \ldots c_{m^{n+1}-1}$, where $c_k = (c_0 + b_0 + \cdots + b_{k-1}) \bmod m$ and $b_0 \ldots b_{m^{n+1}-1} = \beta = \alpha^m 1^m$.

If $x_0 \ldots x_n$ occurs in γ, say $x_j = c_{k+j}$ for $0 \leq j \leq n$, then $y_j = b_{k+j}$ for $0 \leq j < n$, where $y_j = (x_{j+1} - x_j) \bmod m$. [This is the connection with modular m-ary Gray code; see exercise 78.] Now if $y_0 \ldots y_{n-1} = 1^n$ we have $m^{n+1} - m - n < k \leq m^{n+1} - n$; otherwise there is an index k' such that $-n < k' < m^n - n$ and $y_0 \ldots y_{n-1}$ occurs in β at positions $k = (k' + r(m^n - 1)) \bmod m^{n+1}$ for $0 \leq r < m$. In both cases the m choices of k have different values of x_0, because the sum of all elements in α is $m - 1$ (modulo m) when $n \geq 2$. [Algorithm R is valid also for $n = 1$ if $m \bmod 4 \neq 2$, because $m \perp \sum \alpha$ in that case.]

94. $\underline{00}1\underline{02}03\underline{04}11\underline{2}13\underline{14}2\underline{23}24\underline{33}44$. (The underlined digits are effectively inserted into the interleaving of 00112234 with 34. Algorithm D can be used in general when $n = 1$ and $r = m - 2 \geq 0$; but it is pointless to do so, in view of (54).)

95. (a) Let $c_0 c_1 c_2 \ldots$ have period r. If r is odd we have $p = q = r$, so $r = pq$ only in the trivial case when $p = q = 1$ and $a_0 = b_0$. Otherwise $r/2 = \mathrm{lcm}(p, q) = pq/\gcd(p, q)$ by 4.5.2–(10), hence $\gcd(p, q) = 2$. In the latter case the $2n$-tuples $c_l c_{l+1} \ldots c_{l+2n-1}$ that occur are $a_j b_k \ldots a_{j+n-1} b_{k+n-1}$ for $0 \leq j < p$, $0 \leq k < q$, $j \equiv k$ (modulo 2), and $b_k a_j \ldots b_{k+n-1} a_{j+n-1}$ for $0 \leq j < p$, $0 \leq k < q$, $j \not\equiv k$ (modulo 2).

(b) The output would interleave two sequences $a_0 a_1 \ldots$ and $b_0 b_1 \ldots$ whose periods are respectively $m^n + r$ and $m^n - r$; the a's are the cycle of $f()$ with x^n changed to x^{n+1} and the b's are the cycle of $f'()$ with x^n changed to x^{n-1}, for $0 \leq x < r$. By (58) and part (a), the period length is $m^{2n} - r^2$, and every $2n$-tuple occurs with the exception of $(xy)^n$ for $0 \leq x, y < r$.

(c) The real step D6 alters the behavior of (b) by going to D3 when $t \geq n$, $t' = n$, and $0 \leq x' = x < r$; this change emits an extra x at the time when x^{2n-1} has just been output and b is about to be emitted, where b is the digit following x^n in the cycle. D6 also allows control to pass to D7 and then D3 with $t' = n$ in the case that $t \geq n$ and $x < x' < r$; this behavior emits an extra $x'x$ at the time when $(xx')^{n-1}x$ has just been output and b will be next. These r^2 extra digits provide the r^2 missing $2n$-tuples of (b).

96. (a) For example, when $n = 5$ the top-level coroutine of type R invokes a coroutine of type D for $n = 4$, which invokes two of type S for $n = 2$; hence $R_5 = D_5 = 1$ and $S_5 = 2$. The recurrences $R_2 = 0$, $R_{2n+1} = 1 + R_{2n}$, $R_{2n} = 2R_n$, $D_2 = 0$, $D_{2n+1} = D_{2n} = 1 + 2D_n$, $S_2 = 1$, $S_{2n+1} = S_{2n} = 2S_n$ have the solution $R_n = n - 2S_n$, $D_n = S_n - 1$, $S_n = 2^{\lfloor \lg n \rfloor - 1}$. Thus $R_n + D_n + S_n = n - 1$.

(b) Each top-level output usually involves $\lfloor \lg n \rfloor - 1$ D-activations and $\nu(n) - 1$ R-activations, plus one basic activation at the bottom level. But there are exceptions: Algorithm R might invoke its $f()$ twice, if the first activation completed a sequence 1^n; and sometimes Algorithm R doesn't need to invoke $f()$ at all. Algorithm D might invoke its $f'()$ twice, if the first activation completed a sequence $(x')^n$ for $x' < r$; but sometimes Algorithm D doesn't need to invoke either $f()$ or $f'()$.

Algorithm R completes a sequence x^{n+1} if and only if its child $f()$ has just completed a sequence 0^n. Algorithm D completes a sequence x^{2n} for $x < r$ if and only if it has just jumped from D6 to D3 without invoking any child.

From these observations we can conclude that no exceptions arise at any level when the coroutine for an m^n-cycle produces the final digit of a run x^n, or the first digit following such a run. Hence the worst case occurs when the top-level coroutine activates a subcoroutine twice, making $2\lfloor \lg n \rfloor + 2\nu(n) - 3$ activations altogether.

97. (a) (0011), (00011101), (0000101001111011), and $(00000110001011011111$ $001110101001)$. Thus $j_2 = 2$, $j_3 = 3$, $j_4 = 9$, $j_5 = 15$.

(b) We obviously have $f_{n+1}(k) = \Sigma f_n(k) \bmod 2$ for $0 \leq k < j_n + n$. The next value, $f_{n+1}(j_n + n)$, depends on whether step R4 jumps to R2 after computing $y = f_n(j_n + n - 1)$. If it does (namely, if $f_{n+1}(j_n + n - 1) \neq 0$), we have $f_{n+1}(k) \equiv 1 + \Sigma f_n(k+1)$ for $j_n + n \leq k < 2^n + j_n + n$; otherwise we have $f_{n+1}(k) \equiv 1 + \Sigma f_n(k-1)$ for those values of k. In particular, $f_{n+1}(k) = 1$ when $2^n \leq k + \delta_n \leq 2^n + n$. The stated formula, which has simpler ranges for the index k, holds because $1 + \Sigma f_n(k \pm 1) \equiv \Sigma f_n(k)$ when $j_n < k < j_n + n$ or $2^n + j_n < k < 2^n + j_n + n$.

(c) The interleaved cycle has $c_n(2k) = f_n^+(k)$ and $c_n(2k+1) = f_n^-(k)$, where

$$f_n^+(k) = \begin{cases} f_n(k-1), & \text{if } 0 < k \le j_n+1; \\ f_n(k-2), & \text{if } j_n+1 < k \le 2^n+2; \end{cases} \qquad f_n^-(k) = \begin{cases} f_n(k+1), & \text{if } 0 \le k < j_n; \\ f_n(k+2), & \text{if } j_n \le k < 2^n-2; \end{cases}$$

$f_n^+(k) = f_n^+(k \bmod (2^n+2))$, $f_n^-(k) = f_n^-(k \bmod (2^n-2))$. Therefore the subsequence 1^{2n-1} begins at position $k_n = (2^{n-1}-2)(2^n+2) + 2j_n + 2$ in the c_n cycle; this will make j_{2n} odd. The subsequence $(01)^{n-1}0$ begins at position $l_n = (2^{n-1}+1)(j_n-1)$ if $j_n \bmod 4 = 1$, at $l_n = (2^{n-1}+1)(2^n+j_n-3)$ if $j_n \bmod 4 = 3$. Also $k_2 = 6$, $l_2 = 2$.

(d) Algorithm D inserts four elements into the c_n cycle; hence

when $j_n \bmod 4 < 3$ ($l_n < k_n$):   when $j_n \bmod 4 = 3$ ($k_n < l_n$):

$$f_{2n}(k) = \begin{cases} c_n(k-1), & \text{if } 0 < k \le l_n+2; \\ c_n(k-3), & \text{if } l_n+2 < k \le k_n+3; \\ c_n(k-4), & \text{if } k_n+3 < k \le 2^{2n}; \end{cases} = \begin{cases} c_n(k-1), & \text{if } 0 < k \le k_n+1; \\ c_n(k-2), & \text{if } k_n+1 < k \le l_n+3; \\ c_n(k-4), & \text{if } l_n+3 < k \le 2^{2n}. \end{cases}$$

(e) Consequently $j_{2n} = k_n + 1 + 2[j_n \bmod 4 < 3]$. Indeed, the elements preceding 1^{2n} consist of $2^{n-2}-1$ complete periods of $f_n^+()$ interleaved with 2^{n-2} complete periods of $f_n^-()$, with one 0 inserted and also with 10 inserted if $l_n < k_n$, followed by $f_n(1)f_n(1)f_n(2)f_n(2)\dots f_n(j_n-1)f_n(j_n-1)$. The sum of all these elements is odd, unless $l_n < k_n$; therefore $\delta_{2n} = 1 - 2[j_n \bmod 4 = 3]$.

Let $n = 2^t q$, where q is odd and $n > 2$. The recurrences imply that, if $q = 1$, we have $j_n = 2^{n-1} + b_t$ where $b_t = 2^t/3 - (-1)^t/3$. And if $q > 1$ we have $j_n = 2^{n-1} \pm b_{t+2}$, where the $+$ sign is chosen if and only if $\lfloor \lg q \rfloor + \lfloor \lfloor 4q/2^{\lfloor \lg q \rfloor} \rfloor = 5 \rfloor$ is even.

98. If $f(k) = g(k)$ when k lies in a certain range, there's a constant C such that $\Sigma f(k) = C + \Sigma g(k)$ for k in that range. We can therefore continue almost mindlessly to derive additional recurrences: If $n > 1$ we have

$\Sigma f_{2n}(k)$, when $j_n \bmod 4 < 3$ ($l_n < k_n$):   when $j_n \bmod 4 = 3$ ($k_n < l_n$):

$$\equiv \begin{cases} \Sigma c_n(k-1), & \text{if } 0 < k \le l_n+2; \\ 1 + \Sigma c_n(k-3), & \text{if } l_n+2 < k \le k_n+3; \\ \Sigma c_n(k-4), & \text{if } k_n+3 < k \le 2^{2n}; \end{cases} \equiv \begin{cases} \Sigma c_n(k-1), & \text{if } 0 < k \le k_n+1; \\ 1 + \Sigma c_n(k-2), & \text{if } k_n+1 < k \le l_n+3; \\ \Sigma c_n(k-4), & \text{if } l_n+3 < k \le 2^{2n}. \end{cases}$$

$$\Sigma c_n(k) \equiv \Sigma f_n^+(\lceil k/2 \rceil) + \Sigma f_n^-(\lfloor k/2 \rfloor).$$

$$\Sigma f_n^+(k) \equiv \begin{cases} \Sigma f_n(k-1), & \text{if } 0 < k \le j_n+1; \\ 1 + \Sigma f_n(k-2), & \text{if } j_n+1 < k \le 2^n+2; \end{cases} \qquad \Sigma f_n^-(k) \equiv \begin{cases} \Sigma f_n(k+1), & \text{if } 0 \le k < j_n; \\ 1 + \Sigma f_n(k+2), & \text{if } j_n \le k < 2^n-2; \end{cases}$$

$$\Sigma f_n^\pm(k) \equiv \lfloor k/(2^n \pm 2) \rfloor + \Sigma f_n^\pm(k \bmod (2^n \pm 2)); \qquad \Sigma f_n(k) \equiv \Sigma f_n(k \bmod 2^n).$$

$$\Sigma f_{2n+1}(k) \equiv \begin{cases} \Sigma \Sigma f_{2n}(k), & \text{if } 0 < k \le j_{2n} \text{ or } 2^{2n} + j_{2n} < k \le 2^{2n+1}; \\ 1 + k + \Sigma \Sigma f_{2n}(k + \delta_{2n}), & \text{if } j_{2n} < k \le 2^{2n} + j_{2n}. \end{cases}$$

$\Sigma\Sigma f_{2n}(k)$, when $j_n \bmod 4 < 3$ ($l_n < k_n$):   when $j_n \bmod 4 = 3$ ($k_n < l_n$):

$$\equiv \begin{cases} \Sigma\Sigma c_n(k-1), & \text{if } 0 < k \le l_n+2; \\ 1 + k + \Sigma\Sigma c_n(k-3), & \text{if } l_n+2 < k \le k_n+3; \\ \Sigma\Sigma c_n(k-4), & \text{if } k_n+3 < k \le 2^{2n}; \end{cases} \equiv \begin{cases} \Sigma\Sigma c_n(k-1), & \text{if } 0 < k \le k_n+1; \\ 1 + k + \Sigma\Sigma c_n(k-2), & \text{if } k_n+1 < k \le l_n+3; \\ 1 + \Sigma\Sigma c_n(k-4), & \text{if } l_n+3 < k \le 2^{2n}. \end{cases}$$

$$\Sigma\Sigma f_{2n}(k) \equiv [j_n \bmod 4 < 3] \lfloor k/2^{2n} \rfloor + \Sigma\Sigma f_{2n}(k \bmod 2^{2n}).$$

And then, aha, there is closure:

$$\Sigma\Sigma c_n(2k) = \Sigma f_n^+(k), \qquad \Sigma\Sigma c_n(2k+1) = \Sigma f_n^-(k).$$

If $n = 2^t q$ where q is odd, the running time to evaluate $f_n(k)$ by this system of recursive formulas is $O(t + S(q))$, where $S(1) = 1$, $S(2k) = 1 + 2S(k)$, and $S(2k+1) = 1 + S(k)$. Clearly $S(k) < 2k$, so the evaluations involve at most $O(n)$ simple operations on n-bit numbers. In fact, the method is often significantly faster: If we average $S(k)$ over all k with $\lfloor \lg k \rfloor = s$ we get $(3^{s+1} - 2^{s+1})/2^s$, which is less than $3k^{\lg(3/2)} < 3k^{0.59}$. (Incidentally, if $k = 2^{s+1} - 1 - (2^{s-e_1} + 2^{s-e_2} + \cdots + 2^{s-e_t})$ where $0 < e_1 < \cdots < e_t$, we have $S(k) = s + 1 + e_t + 2e_{t-1} + 4e_{t-2} + \cdots + 2^{t-1}e_1$.)

99. A string that starts at position k in $f_n()$ starts at position $k^+ = k + 1 + [k > j_n]$ in $f_n^+()$ and at position $k^- = k - 1 - [k > j_n]$ in $f_n^-()$, except that 0^n and 1^n occur twice in $f_n^+()$ but not at all in $f_n^-()$.

To find $\gamma = a_0 b_0 \ldots a_{n-1} b_{n-1}$ in the cycle $f_{2n}()$, let $\alpha = a_0 \ldots a_{n-1}$ and $\beta = b_0 \ldots b_{n-1}$. Suppose α starts at position j and β at position k in $f_n()$, and assume that neither α nor β is 0^n or 1^n. If $j^+ \equiv k^+$ (modulo 2), let $l/2$ be a solution to the equation $j^+ + (2^n + 2)x = k^- + (2^n - 2)y$; we may take $l/2 = k + (2^n - 2)(2^{n-3}(j - k) \bmod (2^{n-1} + 1))$ if $j \ge k$, otherwise $l/2 = j + (2^n + 2)(2^{n-3}(k - j) \bmod (2^{n-1} - 1))$. Otherwise let $(l-1)/2 = k^+ + (2^n + 2)x = j^- + (2^n - 2)y$. Then γ starts at position l in the cycle $c_n()$; hence it starts at position $l + 1 + [l \ge k_n] + 2[l \ge l_n]$ in the cycle $f_{2n}()$. Similar formulas hold when $\alpha \in \{0^n, 1^n\}$ or $\beta \in \{0^n, 1^n\}$ (but not both). Finally, 0^{2n}, 1^{2n}, $(01)^n$, and $(10)^n$ start respectively in positions 0, j_{2n}, $l_n + 1 + [k_n < l_n]$, and $l_n + 2 + [k_n < l_n]$.

To find $\beta = b_0 b_1 \ldots b_n$ in $f_{n+1}()$ when n is even, suppose that the n-bit string $(b_0 \oplus b_1) \ldots (b_{n-1} \oplus b_n)$ starts at position j in $f_n()$. Then β starts at position $k = j - \delta_n[j \ge j_n] + 2^n[j = j_n][\delta_n = 1]$ if $f_{n+1}(k) = b_0$, otherwise at position $k + (2^n - \delta_n, \delta_n, 2^n + \delta_n)$ according as $(j < j_n, j = j_n, j > j_n)$.

The running time of this recursion satisfies $T(n) = O(n) + 2T(\lfloor n/2 \rfloor)$, so it is $O(n \log n)$. [Exercises 97–99 are based on the work of J. Tuliani, who also has developed methods for certain larger values of m; see *Discrete Math.* **226** (2001), 313–336.]

100. No obvious defects are apparent, but extensive testing should be done before any sequence can be recommended. By contrast, the de Bruijn cycle produced implicitly by Algorithm F is a terrible source of supposedly random bits, even though it is n-distributed in the sense of Definition 3.5D, because 0s predominate at the beginning. Indeed, when n is prime, bits $tn + 1$ of that sequence are zero for $0 \le t < (2^n - 2)/n$.

101. (a) Let β be a proper suffix of $\lambda\lambda'$ with $\beta \le \lambda\lambda'$. Either β is a suffix of λ', whence $\lambda < \lambda' \le \beta$, or $\beta = \alpha\lambda'$ and we have $\lambda < \alpha < \beta$.

Now $\lambda < \beta \le \lambda\lambda'$ implies that $\beta = \lambda\gamma$ for some $\gamma \le \lambda'$. But γ is a suffix of β with $1 \le |\gamma| = |\beta| - |\lambda| < |\lambda'|$; hence γ is a proper suffix of λ', and $\lambda' < \gamma$. Contradiction.

(b) Any string of length 1 is prime. Combine adjacent primes by (a), in any order, until no further combination is possible. [See the more general results of M. P. Schützenberger, *Proc. Amer. Math. Soc.* **16** (1965), 21–24.]

(c) If $t \ne 0$, let λ be the smallest suffix of $\lambda_1 \ldots \lambda_t$. Then λ is prime by definition, and it has the form $\beta\gamma$ where β is a nonempty suffix of some λ_j. Therefore $\lambda_t \le \lambda_j \le \beta \le \beta\gamma = \lambda \le \lambda_t$, so we must have $\lambda = \lambda_t$. Remove λ_t and repeat until $t = 0$.

(d) True. For if we had $\alpha = \lambda\beta$ for some prime λ with $|\lambda| > |\lambda_1|$, we could append the factors of β to obtain another factorization of α.

(e) $3 \cdot 14159265358979323846264433832795 \cdot 02884197$. (An efficient algorithm appears in exercise 106. Knowing more digits of π would not change the first two factors. The infinite decimal expansion of any number that is "normal" in the sense of Borel (see Section 3.5) factors into primes of finite length.)

102. We must have $1/(1 - mz) = 1/\prod_{n=1}^{\infty}(1 - z^n)^{L_m(n)}$. This implies (60) as in exercise 4.6.2–4.

103. When $n = p$ is prime, (59) tells us that $L_m(1) + pL_m(p) = m^p$, and we also have $L_m(1) = m$. [This combinatorial proof provides an interesting contrast to the traditional algebraic proof of Theorem 1.2.4F.]

104. The 4483 nonprimes are `abaca`, `agora`, `ahead`, ...; the 1274 primes are ..., `rusts`, `rusty`, `rutty`. (Since `prime` isn't prime, we should perhaps call prime strings `lowly`.)

105. (a) Let α' be α with its last letter increased, and suppose $\alpha' = \beta\gamma'$ where $\alpha = \beta\gamma$ and $\beta \neq \epsilon$, $\gamma \neq \epsilon$. Let θ be the prefix of α with $|\theta| = |\gamma|$. By hypothesis there is a string ω such that $\alpha\omega$ is prime; hence $\theta \leq \alpha\omega < \gamma\omega$, so we must have $\theta \leq \gamma$. Consequently $\theta < \gamma'$, and we have $\alpha' < \gamma'$.

(b) Let $\alpha = \lambda_1\beta = a_1 \ldots a_n$ where $\lambda_1\beta\omega$ is prime. The condition $\lambda_1\beta\omega < \beta\omega$ implies that $a_j \leq a_{j+r}$ for $1 \leq j \leq n-r$, where $r = |\lambda_1|$. But we cannot have $a_j < a_{j+r}$; otherwise α would begin with a prime longer than λ_1, contradicting exercise 101(d).

(c) If α is the n-extension of both λ and λ', where $|\lambda| > |\lambda'|$, we must have $\lambda = (\lambda')^q\theta$ where θ is a nonempty prefix of λ'. But then $\theta \leq \lambda' < \lambda < \theta$.

106. E1. [Initialize.] Set $a_1 \leftarrow \cdots \leftarrow a_n \leftarrow m - 1$, $a_{n+1} \leftarrow -1$, and $j \leftarrow 1$.

E2. [Visit.] Visit $(a_1, \ldots, a_n)$ with index j.

E3. [Subtract one.] Terminate if $a_j = 0$. Otherwise set $a_j \leftarrow a_j - 1$, and $a_k \leftarrow m - 1$ for $j < k \leq n$.

E4. [Prepare to factor.] (According to exercise 105(b), we now want to find the first prime factor λ_1 of $a_1 \ldots a_n$.) Set $j \leftarrow 1$ and $k \leftarrow 2$.

E5. [Find the new j.] (Now $a_1 \ldots a_{k-1}$ is the $(k-1)$-extension of the prime $a_1 \ldots a_j$.) If $a_{k-j} > a_k$, return to E2. Otherwise, if $a_{k-j} < a_k$, set $j \leftarrow k$. Then increase k by 1 and repeat this step. ▌

The efficient factoring algorithm in steps E4 and E5 is due to J. P. Duval, *J. Algorithms* **4** (1983), 363–381. For further information, see Cattell, Ruskey, Sawada, Serra, and Miers, *J. Algorithms* **37** (2000), 267–282.

107. The number of n-tuples visited is $P_m(n) = \sum_{j=1}^{n} L_m(j)$. Since $L_m(n) = \frac{1}{n}m^n + O(m^{n/2}/n)$, we have $P_m(n) = Q(m,n) + O(Q(\sqrt{m},n))$, where

$$Q(m,n) = \sum_{k=1}^{n} \frac{m^k}{k} = \frac{m^n}{n} R(m,n);$$

$$R(m,n) = \sum_{k=0}^{n-1} \frac{m^{-k}}{1 - k/n} = \sum_{k=0}^{n/2} \frac{m^{-k}}{1 - k/n} + O(nm^{-n/2})$$

$$= \frac{m}{m-1} \sum_{j=0}^{t-1} \frac{1}{n^j} \sum_l \left\{ {j \atop l} \right\} \frac{l!}{(m-1)^l} + O(n^{-t}), \quad \text{for all } t.$$

Thus $P_m(n) \sim m^{n+1}/((m-1)n)$. The main contributions to the running time come from the loops in steps F3 and F5, which cost $n - j$ for each prime of length j, hence a total of $nP_m(n) - \sum_{j=1}^{n} jL_m(j) = m^{n+1}(1/((m-1)^2 n) + O(1/(mn^2)))$. This is less than the time needed to output the m^n individual digits of the de Bruijn cycle.

108. (a) If $\alpha \neq 9\ldots9$, we have $\lambda_{k+1} \leq \beta 9^{|\alpha|}$, because the latter is prime.

(b) We can assume that β is not all 0s, since $9^j 0^{n-j}$ is a substring of $\lambda_{t-1}\lambda_t\lambda_1\lambda_2 = 89^n 0^n 1$. Let k be minimal with $\beta \leq \lambda_k$; then $\lambda_k \leq \beta\alpha$, so β is a prefix of λ_k. Since β is a preprime, it is the $|\beta|$-extension of some prime $\beta' \leq \beta$. The preprime visited by Algorithm F just before β' is $(\beta'-1)9^{n-|\beta'|}$, by exercise 106, where $\beta' - 1$ denotes the decimal number that is one less than β'. Thus, if β' is not λ_{k-1}, the hint (which also follows from exercise 106) implies that λ_{k-1} ends with at least $n - |\beta'| \geq n - |\beta|$ 9s, and α is a suffix of λ_{k-1}. On the other hand if $\beta' = \lambda_{k-1}$, α is a suffix of λ_{k-2}, and β is a prefix of $\lambda_{k-1}\lambda_k$.

(c) If $\alpha \neq 9\ldots9$, we have $\lambda_{k+1} \leq (\beta\alpha)^{d-1}\beta 9^{|\alpha|}$, because the latter is prime. Otherwise λ_{k-1} ends with at least $(d-1)|\beta\alpha|$ 9s, and $\lambda_{k+1} \leq (\beta\alpha)^{d-1}9^{|\beta\alpha|}$, so $(\alpha\beta)^d$ is a substring of $\lambda_{k-1}\lambda_k\lambda_{k+1}$.

(d) Within the primes $135899\,135914$, $787899\,787979$, $129999\,13\,131314$, $09\,090911$, $089999\,09\,090911$, $118999\,119\,119122$.

(e) Yes: In all cases, the position of $a_1\ldots a_n$ precedes the position of the substring $a_1\ldots a_{n-1}(a_n + 1)$, if $0 \leq a_n < 9$ (and if we assume that strings like $9^j 0^{n-j}$ occur at the beginning). Furthermore $9^j 0^{n-j-1}$ occurs only after $9^{j-1}0^{n-j}a$ has appeared for $1 \leq a \leq 9$, so we must not place 0 after $9^j 0^{n-j-1}$.

109. Suppose we want to locate the submatrix

$$\begin{pmatrix} (w_{n-1}\ldots w_1 w_0)_2 & (x_{n-1}\ldots x_1 x_0)_2 \\ (y_{n-1}\ldots y_1 y_0)_2 & (z_{n-1}\ldots z_1 z_0)_2 \end{pmatrix}.$$

The binary case $n = 1$ is the given example, and if $n > 1$ we can assume by induction that we only need to determine the leading bits a_{2n-1}, a_{2n-2}, b_{2n-1}, and b_{2n-2}. The case $n = 3$ is typical: We must solve

$$
\begin{array}{llll}
b_5 = w_2, & b_4 = x_2, & a_5 \oplus b_5 = y_2, & a_4 \oplus b_4 = z_2, \quad \text{if } a_0 = 0, b_0 = 0; \\
b_4 = w_2, & b'_5 = x_2, & a_4 \oplus b_4 = y_2, & a_5 \oplus b'_5 = z_2, \quad \text{if } a_0 = 0, b_0 = 1; \\
a_5 \oplus b_5 = w_2, & a_4 \oplus b_4 = x_2, & b_5 = y_2, & b_4 = z_2, \quad \text{if } a_0 = 1, b_0 = 0; \\
a_4 \oplus b_4 = w_2, & a_5 \oplus b'_5 = x_2, & b_4 = y_2, & b'_5 = z_2, \quad \text{if } a_0 = 1, b_0 = 1;
\end{array}
$$

here $b'_5 = b_5 \oplus b_4 b_3 b_2 b_1$ takes account of carrying when j becomes $j + 1$.

110. Let $a_0 a_1 \ldots a_{m^2-1}$ be an m-ary de Bruijn cycle, such as the first m^2 elements of (54). If m is odd, let $d_{ij} = a_j$ when i is even, $d_{ij} = a_{(j+(i-1)/2) \bmod m^2}$ when i is odd. [The first of many people to discover this construction seems to have been John C. Cock, who also constructed de Bruijn toruses of other shapes and sizes in *Discrete Math.* **70** (1988), 209–210.]

If $m = m'm''$ where $m' \perp m''$, we use the Chinese remainder algorithm to define

$$d_{ij} \equiv d'_{ij} \;(\text{modulo } m') \qquad \text{and} \qquad d_{ij} \equiv d''_{ij} \;(\text{modulo } m'')$$

in terms of matrices that solve the problem for m' and m''. Thus the previous exercise leads to a solution for arbitrary m.

Another interesting solution for even values of m was found by Antal Iványi and Zoltán Tóth [*2nd Conf. Automata, Languages, and Programming Systems* (1988), 165–172; see also Hurlbert and Isaak, *Contemp. Math.* **178** (1994), 153–160]. The first m^2 elements a_j of the infinite sequence

$$0011\,021331203223\,0415243553425\,1405445\,0617263746577564\ldots0766708\ldots$$

define a de Bruijn cycle with the property that the distance between the appearances of ab and ba is always even. Then we can let $d_{ij} = a_j$ if $i + j$ is even, $d_{ij} = a_i$ if $i + j$ is odd. For example, when $m = 4$ we have

$$\begin{pmatrix} 0\,0\,1\,0\,0\,2\,1\,2\,2\,0\,3\,0\,2\,2\,3\,2 \\ 0\,0\,0\,1\,0\,2\,0\,3\,2\,0\,2\,1\,2\,2\,2\,3 \\ 0\,1\,1\,1\,0\,3\,1\,3\,2\,1\,3\,1\,2\,3\,3\,3 \\ 1\,0\,1\,1\,1\,2\,1\,3\,3\,0\,3\,1\,3\,2\,3\,3 \\ 0\,0\,1\,0\,0\,2\,1\,2\,2\,0\,3\,0\,2\,2\,3\,2 \\ 0\,2\,0\,3\,0\,0\,0\,1\,2\,2\,2\,3\,2\,0\,2\,1 \\ 0\,1\,1\,1\,0\,3\,1\,3\,2\,1\,3\,1\,2\,3\,3\,3 \\ 1\,2\,1\,3\,1\,0\,1\,1\,3\,2\,3\,3\,3\,0\,3\,1 \\ 0\,0\,1\,0\,0\,2\,1\,2\,2\,0\,3\,0\,2\,2\,3\,2 \\ 2\,0\,2\,1\,2\,2\,2\,3\,0\,0\,0\,1\,0\,2\,0\,3 \\ 0\,1\,1\,1\,0\,3\,1\,3\,2\,1\,3\,1\,2\,3\,3\,3 \\ 3\,0\,3\,1\,3\,2\,3\,3\,1\,0\,1\,1\,1\,2\,1\,3 \\ 0\,0\,1\,0\,0\,2\,1\,2\,2\,0\,3\,0\,2\,2\,3\,2 \\ 2\,2\,2\,3\,2\,0\,2\,1\,0\,2\,0\,3\,0\,0\,0\,1 \\ 0\,1\,1\,1\,0\,3\,1\,3\,2\,1\,3\,1\,2\,3\,3\,3 \\ 3\,2\,3\,3\,3\,0\,3\,1\,1\,2\,1\,3\,1\,0\,1\,1 \end{pmatrix} \text{ (exercise 109);}$$

$$\begin{pmatrix} 0\,0\,1\,0\,0\,0\,1\,0\,3\,0\,2\,0\,3\,0\,2\,0 \\ 0\,0\,0\,1\,0\,2\,0\,3\,0\,1\,0\,0\,0\,2\,0\,3 \\ 0\,1\,1\,1\,0\,1\,1\,1\,3\,1\,2\,1\,3\,1\,2\,1 \\ 1\,0\,1\,1\,1\,2\,1\,3\,1\,1\,1\,0\,1\,2\,1\,3 \\ 0\,0\,1\,0\,0\,0\,1\,0\,3\,0\,2\,0\,3\,0\,2\,0 \\ 2\,0\,2\,1\,2\,2\,2\,3\,2\,1\,2\,0\,2\,2\,2\,3 \\ 0\,1\,1\,1\,0\,1\,1\,1\,3\,1\,2\,1\,3\,1\,2\,1 \\ 3\,0\,3\,1\,3\,2\,3\,3\,3\,1\,3\,0\,3\,2\,3\,3 \\ 0\,3\,1\,3\,0\,3\,1\,3\,3\,3\,2\,3\,3\,3\,2\,3 \\ 1\,0\,1\,1\,1\,2\,1\,3\,1\,1\,1\,0\,1\,2\,1\,3 \\ 0\,2\,1\,2\,0\,2\,1\,2\,3\,2\,2\,2\,3\,2\,2\,2 \\ 0\,0\,0\,1\,0\,2\,0\,3\,0\,1\,0\,0\,0\,2\,0\,3 \\ 0\,3\,1\,3\,0\,3\,1\,3\,3\,3\,2\,3\,3\,3\,2\,3 \\ 2\,0\,2\,1\,2\,2\,2\,3\,2\,1\,2\,0\,2\,2\,2\,3 \\ 0\,2\,1\,2\,0\,2\,1\,2\,3\,2\,2\,2\,3\,2\,2\,2 \\ 3\,0\,3\,1\,3\,2\,3\,3\,3\,1\,3\,0\,3\,2\,3\,3 \end{pmatrix} \text{ (Tóth).}$$

111. (a) Let $d_j = j$ and $0 \leq a_j < 3$ for $1 \leq j \leq 9$, $a_9 \neq 0$. Form sequences s_j, t_j by the rules $s_1 = 0$, $t_1 = d_1$; $t_{j+1} = d_{j+1} + 10t_j[a_j = 0]$ for $1 \leq j < 9$; $s_{j+1} = s_j + (0, t_j, -t_j)$ for $a_j = (0, 1, 2)$ and $1 \leq j \leq 9$. Then s_{10} is a possible result; we need only remember the smallish values that occur. More than half the work is saved by disallowing $a_k = 2$ when $s_k = 0$, then using $|s_{10}|$ instead of s_{10}. Since fewer than $3^8 = 6561$ possibilities need to be tried, brute force via the ternary version of Algorithm M works well; fewer than 24,000 mems and 1600 multiplications are needed to deduce that all integers less than 211 are representable, but 211 is not.

Another approach, using Gray code to vary the signs after breaking the digits into blocks in 2^8 possible ways, reduces the number of multiplications to 255, but at the cost of about 500 additional mems. Therefore Gray code is not advantageous in this application.

(b) Now (with 73,000 mems and 4900 multiplications) we can reach all numbers less than 241, but not 241. There are 46 ways to represent 100, including the remarkable $9 - 87 + 6 + 5 - 43 + 210$.

[H. E. Dudeney introduced his "century" problem in *The Weekly Dispatch* (4 and 18 June 1899). See also *The Numerology of Dr. Matrix* by Martin Gardner, Chapter 6; Steven Kahan, *J. Recreational Math.* **23** (1991), 19–25; and exercise 7.2.1.6–122.]

112. The method of exercise 111 now needs more than 167 million mems and 10 million multiplications, because 3^{16} is so much larger than 3^8. We can do much better (10.4 million mems, 1100 mults) by first tabulating the possibilities obtainable from the first k and last k digits, for $1 \leq k < 9$, then considering all blocks of digits that use the 9. There are 60,318 ways to represent 100, and the first unreachable number is 16,040.

SECTION 7.2.1.2

1. [J. P. N. Phillips, *Comp. J.* **10** (1967), 311.] Assuming that $n \geq 3$, we can replace steps L2–L4 by:

L2′. [Easiest case?] Set $y \leftarrow a_{n-1}$ and $z \leftarrow a_n$. If $y < z$, set $a_{n-1} \leftarrow z$, $a_n \leftarrow y$, and return to L1.

L2.1′. [Next easiest case?] Set $x \leftarrow a_{n-2}$. If $x \geq y$, go on to step L2.2′. Otherwise set $(a_{n-2}, a_{n-1}, a_n) \leftarrow (z, x, y)$ if $x < z$, (y, z, x) if $x \geq z$. Return to L1.

L2.2′. [Find j.] Set $j \leftarrow n - 3$ and $y \leftarrow a_j$. While $y \geq x$, set $j \leftarrow j - 1$, $x \leftarrow y$, and $y \leftarrow a_j$. Terminate if $j = 0$.

L3′. [Easy increase?] If $y < z$, set $a_j \leftarrow z$, $a_{j+1} \leftarrow y$, $a_n \leftarrow x$, and go to L4.1′.

L3.1′. [Increase a_j.] Set $l \leftarrow n - 1$; if $y \geq a_l$, repeatedly decrease l by 1 until $y < a_l$. Then set $a_j \leftarrow a_l$ and $a_l \leftarrow y$.

L4′. [Begin to reverse.] Set $a_n \leftarrow a_{j+1}$ and $a_{j+1} \leftarrow z$.

L4.1′. [Reverse $a_{j+2} \ldots a_{n-1}$.] Set $k \leftarrow j + 2$ and $l \leftarrow n - 1$. Then, while $k < l$, interchange $a_k \leftrightarrow a_l$ and set $k \leftarrow k + 1$, $l \leftarrow l - 1$. Return to L1. ∎

The program might run still faster if a_t is stored in memory location $\texttt{A}[n - t]$ for $0 \leq t \leq n$, or if reverse colex order is used as in the following exercise.

2. Again we assume that $a_1 \leq a_2 \leq \cdots \leq a_n$ initially; the permutations generated from $\{1, 2, 2, 3\}$ will, however, be 1223, 2123, 2213, ..., 2321, 3221. Let a_{n+1} be an auxiliary element, *larger* than a_n.

M1. [Visit.] Visit the permutation $a_1 a_2 \ldots a_n$.

M2. [Find j.] Set $j \leftarrow 2$. If $a_{j-1} \geq a_j$, increase j by 1 until $a_{j-1} < a_j$. Terminate if $j > n$.

M3. [Decrease a_j.] Set $l \leftarrow 1$. If $a_l \geq a_j$, increase l until $a_l < a_j$. Then swap $a_l \leftrightarrow a_j$.

M4. [Reverse $a_1 \ldots a_{j-1}$.] Set $k \leftarrow 1$ and $l \leftarrow j - 1$. Then, if $k < l$, swap $a_k \leftrightarrow a_l$, set $k \leftarrow k + 1$, $l \leftarrow l - 1$, and repeat until $k \geq l$. Return to M1. ∎

3. Let $C_1 \ldots C_n = c_{a_1} \ldots c_{a_n}$ be the inversion table, as in exercise 5.1.1–7. Then $\mathrm{rank}(a_1 \ldots a_n)$ is the mixed-radix number $\left[\begin{smallmatrix} C_1, & \ldots, & C_{n-1}, & C_n \\ n, & \ldots, & 2, & 1 \end{smallmatrix} \right]$. [See H. A. Rothe, *Sammlung combinatorisch-analytischer Abhandlungen* **2** (1800), 263–264; and see also the pioneering work of Śārṅgadeva and Nārāyaṇa cited in Section 7.2.1.7.] For example, 314592687 has rank $\left[\begin{smallmatrix} 2, & 0, & 1, & 1, & 4, & 0, & 0, & 1, & 0 \\ 9, & 8, & 7, & 6, & 5, & 4, & 3, & 2, & 1 \end{smallmatrix} \right] = 2 \cdot 8! + 6! + 5! + 4 \cdot 4! + 1! = 81577$; this is the factorial number system featured in Eq. 4.1–(10).

4. Use the recurrence $\mathrm{rank}(a_1 \ldots a_n) = \frac{1}{n} \sum_{j=1}^{t} n_j [x_j < a_1] \binom{n}{n_1, \ldots, n_t} + \mathrm{rank}(a_2 \ldots a_n)$. For example, $\mathrm{rank}(314159265)$ is

$$\tfrac{3}{9} \binom{9}{2,1,1,1,2,1,1} + 0 + \tfrac{2}{7} \binom{7}{1,1,1,2,1,1} + 0 + \tfrac{1}{5} \binom{5}{1,2,1,1} + \tfrac{3}{4} \binom{4}{1,1,1,1} + 0 + \tfrac{1}{2} \binom{2}{1,1} = 30991.$$

5. (a) Step L2 is performed $n!$ times. The probability that exactly k comparisons are made is $q_k - q_{k+1}$, where q_t is the probability that $a_{n-t+1} > \cdots > a_n$, namely $\lfloor t \leq n \rfloor / t!$. Therefore the mean is $\sum k(q_k - q_{k+1}) = q_1 + \cdots + q_n = \lfloor n! \, e \rfloor / n! - 1 \approx e - 1 \approx 1.718$, and the variance is

$$\sum k^2 (q_k - q_{k+1}) - \mathrm{mean}^2 = q_1 + 3q_2 + \cdots + (2n-1)q_n - (q_1 + \cdots + q_n)^2 \approx e(3-e) \approx 0.766.$$

[For higher moments, see R. Kemp, *Acta Informatica* **35** (1998), 17–89, Theorem 4.]

Incidentally, the average number of interchange operations in step L4 is therefore $\sum \lfloor k/2 \rfloor (q_k - q_{k+1}) = q_2 + q_4 + \cdots \approx \cosh 1 - 1 = (e + e^{-1} - 2)/2 \approx 0.543$, a result due to R. J. Ord-Smith [*Comp. J.* **13** (1970), 152–155].

(b) Step L3 is performed only $n! - 1$ times, but we will assume for convenience that it occurs once more (with 0 comparisons). Then the probability that exactly k

comparisons are made is $\sum_{j=k+1}^{n} 1/j!$ for $1 \leq k < n$ and $1/n!$ for $k = 0$. Hence the mean is $\frac{1}{2}\sum_{j=0}^{n-2} 1/j! \approx e/2 \approx 1.359$; exercise 1 reduces this number by $\frac{2}{3}$. The variance is $\frac{1}{3}\sum_{j=0}^{n-3} 1/j! + \frac{1}{2}\sum_{j=0}^{n-2} 1/j! - \text{mean}^2 \approx \frac{5}{6}e - \frac{1}{4}e^2 \approx 0.418$.

6. (a) Let $e_n(z) = \sum_{k=0}^{n} z^k/k!$; then the number of different prefixes $a_1 \ldots a_j$ is $j! [z^j] e_{n_1}(z) \ldots e_{n_t}(z)$. This is $N = \binom{n}{n_1, \ldots, n_t}$ times the probability q_{n-j} that at least $n-j$ comparisons are made in step L2. Therefore the mean is $\frac{1}{N}w(e_{n_1}(z) \ldots e_{n_t}(z)) - 1$, where $w(\sum x_k z^k/k!) = \sum x_k$. In the binary case the mean is $M/\binom{n}{s} - 1$, where $M = \sum_{l=0}^{s}\sum_{k=l}^{n-s+l} \binom{k}{l} = \sum_{l=0}^{s}\binom{n-s+l+1}{l+1} = \binom{n+2}{s+1} - 1 = \binom{n}{s}(2 + \frac{s}{n-s+1} + \frac{n-s}{s+1}) - 1$.

(b) If $\{a_1, \ldots, a_j\} = \{n'_1 \cdot x_1, \ldots, n'_t \cdot x_t\}$, the prefix $a_1 \ldots a_j$ contributes altogether $\sum_{1 \leq k < l \leq t}(n_k - n'_k)[n_l > n'_l]$ to the total number of comparisons made in step L3. Thus the mean is $\frac{1}{N}\sum_{1 \leq k < l \leq t} w(f_{kl}(z))$, where

$$f_{kl}(z) = \left(\prod_{\substack{1 \leq m \leq t \\ m \neq k,\, m \neq l}} e_{n_m}(z)\right)\left(\sum_{r=0}^{n_k}(n_k - r)\frac{z^r}{r!}\right)e_{n_l-1}(z)$$

$$= e_{n_1}(z) \ldots e_{n_t}(z)(n_k - z\, r_k(z))r_l(z), \qquad \text{where } r_k(z) = \frac{e_{n_k-1}(z)}{e_{n_k}(z)}.$$

In the two-valued case this formula reduces to $\frac{1}{N}w((se_s(z) - ze_{s-1}(z))e_{n-s-1}(z)) = \frac{s}{N}(\binom{n+1}{s+1} - 1) - \frac{1}{N}(\binom{n+1}{s+1}(s - \frac{s+1}{n-s+1}) + 1) = \frac{1}{N}(-s - 1 + \binom{n+1}{s}) = \frac{n+1}{n-s+1} - \frac{s+1}{N}$.

7. In the notation of the previous answer, the quantity $\frac{1}{N}w(e_{n_1}(z) \ldots e_{n_t}(z)) - 1$ is

$$\frac{n_1 + \cdots + n_t}{n} + \frac{(n_1 n_2 + n_1 n_3 + \cdots + n_{t-1}n_t) + n_1(n_1-1) + \cdots + n_t(n_t-1)}{n(n-1)} + \cdots .$$

One can show using Eq. 1.2.9–(38) that the limit is $-1 + \exp\sum_{k \geq 1} r_k/k$, where $r_k = \lim_{t \to \infty}(n_1^k + \cdots + n_t^k)/(n_1 + \cdots + n_t)^k$. In cases (a) and (b) we have $r_k = [k=1]$, so the limit is $e - 1 \approx 1.71828$. In case (c) we have $r_k = 1/(2^k - 1)$, so the limit is $-1 + \exp\sum_{k \geq 1} 1/(k(2^k - 1)) \approx 2.46275$.

8. Assume that j is initially zero, and change step L1 to

L1'. [Visit.] Visit the variation $a_1 \ldots a_j$. If $j < n$, set $j \leftarrow j + 1$ and repeat this step. ∎

This algorithm is due to L. J. Fischer and K. C. Krause, *Lehrbuch der Combinationslehre und der Arithmetik* (Dresden: 1812), 55–57.

Incidentally, the total number of variations is $w(e_{n_1}(z) \ldots e_{n_t}(z))$ in the notation of answer 6. This counting problem was first treated by James Bernoulli in *Ars Conjectandi* (1713), Part 2, Chapter 9.

9. Assume that $r > 0$ and that we begin with $a_0 < a_1 \leq a_2 \leq \cdots \leq a_n$.

R1. [Visit.] Visit the variation $a_1 \ldots a_r$. (At this point $a_{r+1} \leq \cdots \leq a_n$.)

R2. [Easy case?] If $a_r < a_n$, interchange $a_r \leftrightarrow a_j$ where j is the smallest subscript such that $j > r$ and $a_j > a_r$, and return to R1.

R3. [Reverse.] Set $(a_{r+1}, \ldots, a_n) \leftarrow (a_n, \ldots, a_{r+1})$ as in step L4.

R4. [Find j.] Set $j \leftarrow r - 1$. If $a_j \geq a_{j+1}$, decrease j by 1 repeatedly until $a_j < a_{j+1}$. Terminate if $j = 0$.

R5. [Increase a_j.] Set $l \leftarrow n$. If $a_j \geq a_l$, decrease l by 1 repeatedly until $a_j < a_l$. Then interchange $a_j \leftrightarrow a_l$.

R6. [Reverse again.] Set $(a_{j+1}, \ldots, a_n) \leftarrow (a_n, \ldots, a_{j+1})$ as in step L4, and return to R1. ∎

The number of outputs is $r! \, [z^r] \, e_{n_1}(z) \ldots e_{n_t}(z)$; this is, of course, n^r when the elements are distinct.

10. $a_1 a_2 \ldots a_n = 213 \ldots n$, $c_1 c_2 \ldots c_n = 010 \ldots 0$, $o_1 o_2 \ldots o_n = 1(-1)1 \ldots 1$, if $n \geq 2$.

11. Step (P1, ..., P7) is performed $(1, n!, n!, n! + x_n, n! - 1, (x_n + 3)/2, x_n)$ times, where $x_n = \sum_{k=1}^{n-1} k!$, because P7 is performed $(j-1)!$ times when $2 \leq j \leq n$.

12. We want the permutation of rank 999999. The answers are (a) 2783915460, by exercise 3; (b) 8750426319, because the reflected mixed-radix number corresponding to $\begin{bmatrix} 0, & 0, & 1, & 2, & 3, & 0, & 2, & 7, & 0, & 9 \\ 1, & 2, & 3, & 4, & 5, & 6, & 7, & 8, & 9, & 10 \end{bmatrix}$ is $\begin{bmatrix} 0, & 0, & 1, & 3-2, & 3, & 5-0, & 2, & 7, & 8-0, & 9-9 \\ 1, & 2, & 3, & 4, & 5, & 6, & 7, & 8, & 9, & 10 \end{bmatrix}$ by 7.2.1.1–(50); (c) the product $(0\, 1 \ldots 9)^9 (0\, 1 \ldots 8)^0 (0\, 1 \ldots 7)^7 (0\, 1 \ldots 6)^2 \ldots (0\, 1\, 2)^1$, namely 9703156248.

13. The first statement is true for all $n \geq 2$. But when 2 crosses 1, namely when c_2 changes from 0 to 1, we have $c_3 = 2$, $c_4 = 3$, $c_5 = \cdots = c_n = 0$, and the next permutation when $n \geq 5$ is $432156 \ldots n$. [See *Time Travel* (1988), page 74.]

14. True at the beginning of steps P4, P5, and P6, because exactly $j - 1 - c_j + s$ elements lie to the left of x_j, namely $j - 1 - c_j$ from $\{x_1, \ldots, x_{j-1}\}$ and s from $\{x_{j+1}, \ldots, x_n\}$. (In a sense, this formula is the main point of Algorithm P.)

15. If $\begin{bmatrix} b_{n-1}, & \ldots, & b_0 \\ 1, & \ldots, & n \end{bmatrix}$ corresponds to the reflected Gray code $\begin{bmatrix} c_1, & \ldots, & c_n \\ 1, & \ldots, & n \end{bmatrix}$, we get to step P6 if and only if $b_{n-k} = k - 1$ for $j \leq k \leq n$ and B_{n-j+1} is even, by 7.2.1.1–(50). But $b_{n-k} = k - 1$ for $j \leq k \leq n$ implies that B_{n-k} is odd for $j < k \leq n$. Therefore $s = [c_{j+1} = j] + [c_{j+2} = j + 1] = [o_{j+1} < 0] + [o_{j+2} < 0]$ in step P5. [See *Math. Comp.* **17** (1963), 282–285.]

16. P1'. [Initialize.] Set $c_j \leftarrow j$ and $o_j \leftarrow -1$ for $1 \leq j < n$; also set $z \leftarrow a_n$.

   P2'. [Visit.] Visit $a_1 \ldots a_n$. Then go to P3.5' if $a_1 = z$.

   P3'. [Hunt down.] For $j \leftarrow n - 1, n - 2, \ldots, 1$ (in this order), set $a_{j+1} \leftarrow a_j$, $a_j \leftarrow z$, and visit $a_1 \ldots a_n$. Then set $j \leftarrow n - 1$, $s \leftarrow 1$, and go to P4'.

   P3.5'. [Hunt up.] For $j \leftarrow 1, 2, \ldots, n - 1$ (in this order), set $a_j \leftarrow a_{j+1}$, $a_{j+1} \leftarrow z$, and visit $a_1 \ldots a_n$. Then set $j \leftarrow n - 1$, $s \leftarrow 0$.

   P4'. [Ready to change?] Set $q \leftarrow c_j + o_j$. If $q = 0$, go to P6'; if $q > j$, go to P7'.

   P5'. [Change.] Interchange $a_{c_j + s} \leftrightarrow a_{q+s}$. Then set $c_j \leftarrow q$ and return to P2'.

   P6'. [Increase s.] Terminate if $j = 1$; otherwise set $s \leftarrow s + 1$.

   P7'. [Switch direction.] Set $o_j \leftarrow -o_j$, $j \leftarrow j - 1$, and go back to P4'. ∎

17. Initially $a_j \leftarrow a'_j \leftarrow j$ for $1 \leq j \leq n$. Step P5 should now set $t \leftarrow j - c_j + s$, $u \leftarrow j - q + s$, $v \leftarrow a_u$, $a_t \leftarrow v$, $a'_v \leftarrow t$, $a_u \leftarrow j$, $a'_j \leftarrow u$, $c_j \leftarrow q$. (See exercise 14.)

But with the inverse required and available we can actually simplify the algorithm significantly, avoiding the offset variable s and letting the control table $c_1 \ldots c_n$ count only downwards, as noted by G. Ehrlich [*JACM* **20** (1973), 505–506]:

   Q1. [Initialize.] Set $a_j \leftarrow a'_j \leftarrow j$, $c_j \leftarrow j - 1$, and $o_j \leftarrow -1$ for $1 \leq j \leq n$. Also set $c_0 = -1$.

   Q2. [Visit.] Visit the permutation $a_1 \ldots a_n$ and its inverse $a'_1 \ldots a'_n$.

   Q3. [Find k.] Set $k \leftarrow n$. Then, while $c_k = 0$, set $c_k \leftarrow k - 1$, $o_k \leftarrow -o_k$, and $k \leftarrow k - 1$. Terminate if $k = 0$.

   Q4. [Change.] Set $c_k \leftarrow c_k - 1$, $j \leftarrow a'_k$, and $i = j + o_k$. Then set $t \leftarrow a_i$, $a_i \leftarrow k$, $a_j \leftarrow t$, $a'_t \leftarrow j$, $a'_k \leftarrow i$, and return to Q2. ∎

18. Set $a_n \leftarrow n$, and use $(n-1)!/2$ iterations of Algorithm P to generate all permutations of $\{1, \ldots, n-1\}$ such that 1 precedes 2. [M. K. Roy, *CACM* **16** (1973), 312–313; see also exercise 13.]

19. For example, we can use the idea of Algorithm P, with the n-tuples $c_1 \ldots c_n$ changing as in Algorithm 7.2.1.1H with respect to the radices $(1, 2, \ldots, n)$. That algorithm maintains the directions correctly, although it numbers subscripts differently. The offset s needed by Algorithm P can be computed as in the answer to exercise 15, or the inverse permutation can be maintained as in exercise 17. [See G. Ehrlich, *CACM* **16** (1973), 690–691.] Other algorithms, like that of Heap, can also be implemented looplessly.

(*Note:* In most applications of permutation generation we are interested in minimizing the *total* running time, not the maximum time between successive visits; from this standpoint looplessness is usually undesirable, except on a parallel computer. Yet there's something intellectually satisfying about the fact that a loopless algorithm exists, whether practical or not.)

20. For example, when $n = 3$ we can begin 123, 132, 312, $\bar{3}12$, $1\bar{3}2$, $12\bar{3}$, $21\bar{3}$, ..., $21\bar{3}$, $\bar{2}13$, ... If the delta sequence for n is $(\delta_1 \delta_2 \ldots \delta_{2^n n!})$, the corresponding sequence for $n+1$ is $(\Delta_n \delta_1 \Delta_n \delta_2 \ldots \Delta_n \delta_{2^n n!})$, where Δ_n is the sequence of $2n+1$ operations $n \ n{-}1 \ \ldots \ 1 \ - \ 1 \ \ldots \ n{-}1 \ n$; here $\delta_k = j$ means $a_j \leftrightarrow a_{j+1}$ and $\delta_k = -$ means $a_1 \leftarrow -a_1$.

(Signed permutations appear in another guise in exercises 5.1.4–43 and 44. The set of all signed permutations is called the octahedral group.)

21. Clearly $M = 1$, hence O must be 0 and S must be $b - 1$. Then $N = E + 1$, $R = b - 2$, and $D + E = b + Y$. This leaves exactly $\max(0, b - 7 - k)$ choices for E when $Y = k \geq 2$, hence a total of $\sum_{k=2}^{b-7}(b - 7 - k) = \binom{b-8}{2}$ solutions when $b \geq 8$. [*Math. Mag.* **45** (1972), 48–49. Incidentally, D. Eppstein has proved that the task of solving alphametics with a given radix is NP-complete; see *SIGACT News* **18**, 3 (1987), 38–40.]

22. $(X)_b + (X)_b = (XY)_b$ is solvable only when $b = 2$.

23. Almost true, because the number of solutions will be even, *unless* $[j \in F] \neq [k \in F]$. (Consider the ternary alphametic $X + (XX)_3 + (YY)_3 + (XZ)_3 = (XYX)_3$.)

24. (a) $9283 + 7 + 473 + 1062 = 10825$. (b) $698392 + 3192 = 701584$. (c) $63952 + 69275 = 133227$. (d) $653924 + 653924 = 1307848$. (e) $5718 + 3 + 98741 = 104462$. (f) $127503 + 502351 + 3947539 + 46578 = 4623971$. (g) $67432 + 704 + 8046 + 97364 = 173546$. (h) $59 + 577404251698 + 69342491650 + 49869442698 + 1504 + 40614 + 82591 + 344 + 41 + 741425 = 5216367650 + 691400684974$. [All solutions are unique. References for (b)–(g): *J. Recreational Math.* **10** (1977), 115; **5** (1972), 296; **10** (1977), 41; **10** (1978), 274; **12** (1979), 133–134; **9** (1977), 207.]

(i) In this case there are $\frac{8}{10}10! = 2903040$ solutions, because *every* permutation of $\{0, 1, \ldots, 9\}$ works except those that assign H or N to 0. (A well-written general additive alphametic solver will be careful to reduce the amount of output in such cases.)

25. We may assume that $s_1 \leq \cdots \leq s_{10}$. Let i be the least index $\notin F$, and set $a_i \leftarrow 0$; then set the remaining elements a_j in order of increasing j. A proof like that of Theorem 6.1S shows that this procedure maximizes $a \cdot s$. A similar procedure yields the minimum, because $\min(a \cdot s) = -\max(a \cdot (-s))$.

26. $400739 + 63930 - 2379 - 1252630 + 53430 - 1390 + 738300$.

27. Readers can probably improve upon the following examples: BLOOD + SWEAT + TEARS = LATER; EARTH + WATER + WRATH = HELLO + WORLD; AWAIT + ROBOT + ERROR =

SOBER + WORDS; CHILD + THEME + PEACE + ETHIC = IDEAL + ALPHA + METIC. (This exercise was inspired by WHERE + SEDGE + GRASS + GROWS = MARSH [A. W. Johnson, Jr., *J. Recr. Math.* **15** (1982), 51], which would be marvelously pure except that D and O have the same signature.) J. A. Brown, J. Szabó, and T. J. Trowbridge suggest GREAT + GREAT = LARGE and GREAT + GREAT = SMALL.

28. (a) $11 = 3 + 3 + 2 + 2 + 1$, $20 = 11 + 3 + 3 + 3$, $20 = 11 + 3 + 3 + 2 + 1$, $20 = 11 + 3 + 3 + 1 + 1 + 1$, $20 = 8 + 8 + 2 + 1 + 1$, $20 = 7 + 7 + 6$, $20 = 7 + 7 + 2 + 2 + 2$, $20 = 7 + 7 + 2 + 1 + 1 + 1 + 1$, $20 = 7 + 5 + 5 + 2 + 1$, $20 = 7 + 5 + 2 + 2 + 2 + 1 + 1$, $20 = 7 + 5 + 2 + 2 + 1 + 1 + 1 + 1$, $20 = 7 + 3 + 3 + 2 + 2 + 1 + 1 + 1$, $20 = 7 + 3 + 3 + 1 + 1 + 1 + 1 + 1 + 1 + 1$, $20 = 5 + 3 + 3 + 3 + 3 + 3$. [These fourteen solutions were first computed by Roy Childs in 1999. The next doubly partitionable values of n are 30 (in 20 ways), then 40 (in 94 ways), 41 (in 67), 42 (in 57), 50 (in 190 ways, including $50 = 2 + 2 + \cdots + 2$), etc.]

(b) $51 = 20 + 15 + 14 + 2$, $51 = 15 + 14 + 10 + 9 + 3$, $61 = 19 + 16 + 11 + 9 + 6$, $65 = 17 + 16 + 15 + 9 + 7 + 1$, $66 = 20 + 19 + 16 + 6 + 5$, $69 = 18 + 17 + 16 + 10 + 8$, $70 = 30 + 20 + 10 + 7 + 3$, $70 = 20 + 16 + 12 + 9 + 7 + 6$, $70 = 20 + 15 + 12 + 11 + 7 + 5$, $80 = 50 + 20 + 9 + 1$, $90 = 50 + 12 + 11 + 9 + 5 + 2 + 1$, $91 = 45 + 19 + 11 + 10 + 5 + 1$. [The two 51s are due to Steven Kahan; see his book *Have Some Sums To Solve* (Farmingdale, New York: Baywood, 1978), 36–37, 84, 112. Amazing examples with seventeen distinct terms in Italian and fifty-eight distinct terms in Roman numerals have been found by Giulio Cesare, *J. Recr. Math.* **30** (1999), 63.]

Notes: The beautiful example THREE = TWO+ONE+ZERO [Richard L. Breisch, *Recreational Math. Magazine* **12** (December 1962), 24] is unfortunately ruled out by our conventions. The total number of doubly true partitions into distinct parts is probably finite, in English, although nomenclature for arbitrarily large integers is not standard. Is there an example bigger than NINETYNINENONILLIONNINETYNINESEXTILLIONSIXTYONE = NINETYNINENONILLIONNINETYNINESEXTILLIONNINETEEN+SIXTEEN+ELEVEN+NINE+SIX (suggested by G. González-Morris)?

29. $10 + 7 + 1 = 9 + 6 + 3$, $11 + 10 = 8 + 7 + 6$, $12 + 7 + 6 + 5 = 11 + 10 + 9$, $\ldots$, $19 + 10 + 3 = 14 + 13 + 4 + 1$ (31 examples in all).

30. (a) $567^2 = 321489$, $807^2 = 651249$, or $854^2 = 729316$. (b) $958^2 = 917764$. (c) $96 \times 7^2 = 4704$. (d) $51304/61904 = 7260/8760$. (e) $328509^2 = 4761^3$. [*Strand* **78** (1929), 91, 208; *J. Recr. Math* **3** (1970), 43; **13** (1981), 212; **27** (1995), 137; **31** (2003), 133. The solutions to (b), (c), (d), and (e) are unique. With a right-to-left approach based on Algorithm X, the answers are found in (14, 13, 11, 3423, 42) kilomems, respectively. Nob also noticed that NORTH/SOUTH = WEST/EAST has the unique solution $67104/27504 = 9320/3820$.]

31. (a) $5/34 + 7/68 + 9/12(!)$. One can verify uniqueness with Algorithm X using the side condition A < D < G, in about 265 Kμ. [*Quark Visual Science Magazine*, No. 136 (Tokyo: Kodansha, October 1993).] Curiously, a similar puzzle also has a unique solution: $1/(3 \times 6) + 5/(8 \times 9) + 7/(2 \times 4) = 1$ [Scot Morris, *Omni* **17**, 4 (January 1995), 97].

(b) ABCDEFGHI = 381654729, via Algorithm X in 10 Kμ.

32. There are eleven ways, of which the most surprising is $3 + 69258/714$. [See *The Weekly Dispatch* (9 and 23 June 1901); *Amusements in Mathematics* (1917), 158–159.]

33. (a) 1, 2, 3, 4, 15, 18, 118, 146. (b) 6, 9, 16, 20, 27, 126, 127, 129, 136, 145. [*The Weekly Dispatch* (11 and 30 November, 1902); *Amusements in Math.* (1917), 159.]

In this case one suitable strategy is to find all variations where $a_k \ldots a_{l-1}/a_l \ldots a_9$ is an integer, then to record solutions for all permutations of $a_1 \ldots a_{k-1}$. There are exactly 164959 integers with a unique solution, the largest being 9876533. There are solutions for all years in the 21st century except 2091. The most solutions (389) occur when $n = 12221$; the longest stretch of representable n's is $5109 < n < 7060$. Dudeney was able to get the correct answers by hand for small n by "casting out nines."

34. (a) $x = 10^5$, $7378 + 155 + 92467 = 7178 + 355 + 92467 = 1016 + 733 + 98251 = 1014 + 255 + 98731 = 100000$.

(b) $x = 4^7$, $3036 + 455 + 12893 = 16384$ is unique. The fastest way to resolve this problem is probably to start with a list of the 2529 primes that consist of five distinct digits (namely 10243, 10247, ..., 98731) and to permute the five remaining digits.

Incidentally, the unrestricted alphametic EVEN + ODD = PRIME has ten solutions; both ODD and PRIME are prime in just one of them. [See M. Arisawa, *J. Recr. Math.* **8** (1975), 153.]

35. In general, if $s_k = |S_k|$ for $1 \le k < n$, there are $s_1 \dots s_{k-1}$ ways to choose each of the nonidentity elements of S_k. Hence the answer is $\prod_{k=1}^{n-1} (\prod_{j=1}^{k-1} s_j^{s_k-1})$, which in this case is $2^2 \cdot 6^3 \cdot 24^{15} = 4361966924740238366123136$.

(But if the vertices are renumbered, the s_k values may change. For example, if vertices (0, 3, 5) of (12) are interchanged with (e, d, c), we have $s_{14} = 1$, $s_{13} = 6$, $s_{12} = 4$, $s_{11} = 1$, and $4^5 \cdot 24^{15}$ Sims tables.)

36. Since each of $\{0, 3, 5, 6, 9, a, c, f\}$ lies on three lines, but every other element lies on only two, it is clear that we may let $S_f = \{(), \sigma, \sigma^2, \sigma^3, \alpha, \alpha\sigma, \alpha\sigma^2, \alpha\sigma^3\}$, where $\sigma = (03fc)(17e8)(2bd4)(56a9)$ is a 90° rotation and $\alpha = (05)(14)(27)(36)(8d)(9c)(af)(be)$ is an inside-out twist. Also $S_e = \{(), \beta, \gamma, \beta\gamma\}$, where $\beta = (14)(28)(3c)(69)(7d)(be)$ is a transposition and $\gamma = (12)(48)(5a)(69)(7b)(de)$ is another twist; $S_d = \dots = S_1 = \{()\}$. (There are $4^7 - 1$ alternative answers.)

37. The set S_k can be chosen in $k!^k$ ways (see exercise 35), and its nonidentity elements can be assigned to $\sigma(k, 1)$, ..., $\sigma(k, k)$ in $k!$ further ways. So the answer is $A_n = \prod_{k=1}^{n-1} k!^{k+1} = n!^{\binom{n+1}{2}} / \prod_{k=1}^{n} k^{\binom{k+1}{2}}$. For example, $A_{10} \approx 1.148 \times 10^{170}$. We have

$$\sum_{k=1}^{n-1} \binom{k}{2} \ln k = \frac{1}{2} \int_1^n x(x-1) \ln x \, dx + O(n^2 \log n) = \frac{1}{6} n^3 \ln n + O(n^3)$$

by Euler's summation formula; thus $\ln A_n = \frac{1}{3} n^3 \ln n + O(n^3)$.

38. The probability that $\phi(k)$ is needed in step G4 is $1/k! - 1/(k+1)!$, for $1 \le k < n$; the probability is $1/n!$ that we don't get to step G4 at all. Since $\phi(k)$ does $\lceil k/2 \rceil$ transpositions, the average is $\sum_{k=1}^{n-1} (1/k! - 1/(k+1)!) \lceil k/2 \rceil = \sum_{k=1}^{n-1} (\lceil k/2 \rceil - \lceil (k-1)/2 \rceil)/k! - \lceil (n-1)/2 \rceil/n! = \sum_{k \text{ odd}} 1/k! + O(1/(n-1)!)$.

39. (a) 0123, 1023, 2013, 0213, 1203, 2103, 3012, 0312, 1302, 3102, 0132, 1032, 2301, 3201, 0231, 2031, 3021, 0321, 1230, 2130, 3120, 1320, 2310, 3210; (b) 0123, 1023, 2013, 0213, 1203, 2103, 3102, 1302, 0312, 3012, 1032, 0132, 0231, 2031, 3021, 0321, 2301, 3201, 3210, 2310, 1320, 3120, 2130, 1230.

40. By induction we find $\sigma(1, 1) = (0\ 1)$, $\sigma(2, 2) = (0\ 1\ 2)$,

$$\sigma(k, k) = \begin{cases} (0\ k)(k{-}1\ k{-}2\ \dots\ 1), & \text{if } k \ge 3 \text{ is odd,} \\ (0\ k{-}1\ k{-}2\ 1\ \dots\ k{-}3\ k), & \text{if } k \ge 4 \text{ is even;} \end{cases}$$

also $\omega(k) = (0\ k)$ when k is even, $\omega(k) = (0\ k{-}2\ \dots\ 1\ k{-}1\ k)$ when $k \ge 3$ is odd. Thus when $k \ge 3$ is odd, $\sigma(k, 1) = (k\ k{-}1\ 0)$ and $\sigma(k, j)$ takes $k \mapsto j - 1$ for $1 < j < k$; when $k \ge 4$ is even, $\sigma(k, j) = (0\ k\ k{-}3\ \dots\ 1\ k{-}2\ k{-}1)^j$ for $1 \le j \le k$.

Notes: The first scheme that causes Algorithm G to generate all permutations by single transpositions was devised by Mark Wells [*Math. Comp.* **15** (1961), 192–195], but it was considerably more complicated. W. Lipski, Jr., studied such schemes in general and found a variety of additional methods [*Computing* **23** (1979), 357–365].

41. We may assume that $r < n$. Algorithm G will generate r-variations for any Sims table if we simply change '$k \leftarrow 1$' to '$k \leftarrow n - r$' in step G3, provided that we redefine $\omega(k)$ to be $\sigma(n - r, n - r) \ldots \sigma(k, k)$ instead of using (16).

If $n - r$ is odd, the method of (27) is still valid, although the formulas in answer 40 need to be revised when $k < n - r + 2$. The new formulas are $\sigma(k, j) = (k\ j{-}1\ \ldots\ 1\ 0)$ and $\omega(k) = (k\ \ldots\ 1\ 0)$ when $k = n - r$; $\sigma(k, j) = (k\ \ldots\ 1\ 0)^j$ when $k = n - r + 1$.

If $n - r$ is even, we can use (27) with even and odd reversed, if $r \leq 3$. But when $r \geq 4$ a more complex scheme is needed, because a fixed transposition like $(k\ 0)$ can be used for odd k only if $\omega(k - 1)$ is a k-cycle, which means that $\omega(k - 1)$ must be an even permutation; but $\omega(k)$ is odd for $k \geq n - r + 2$.

The following scheme works when $n - r$ is even: Let $\tau(k, j)\omega(k - 1)^- = (k\ k{-}j)$ for $1 \leq j \leq k = n - r$, and use (27) when $k > n - r$. Then, when $k = n - r + 1$, we have $\omega(k - 1) = (0\ 1\ \ldots\ k{-}1)$, hence $\sigma(k, j)$ takes $k \mapsto (2j - 1) \bmod k$ for $1 \leq j \leq k$, and $\sigma(k, k) = (k\ k{-}1\ k{-}3\ \ldots\ 0\ k{-}2\ \ldots\ 1)$, $\omega(k) = (k\ \ldots\ 1\ 0)$, $\sigma(k{+}1, j) = (k{+}1\ \ldots\ 0)^j$.

42. If $\sigma(k, j) = (k\ j{-}1)$ we have $\tau(k, 1) = (k\ 0)$ and $\tau(k, j) = (k\ j{-}1)(k\ j{-}2) = (k\ j{-}1\ j{-}2)$ for $2 \leq j \leq k$.

43. Of course $\omega(1) = \sigma(1, 1) = \tau(1, 1) = (0\ 1)$. The following construction makes $\omega(k) = (k{-}2\ k{-}1\ k)$ for all $k \geq 2$: Let $\alpha(k, j) = \tau(k, j)\omega(k - 1)^-$, where $\alpha(2, 1) = (2\ 0)$, $\alpha(2, 2) = (2\ 0\ 1)$, $\alpha(3, 1) = \alpha(3, 3) = (3\ 1)$, $\alpha(3, 2) = (3\ 1\ 0)$; this makes $\sigma(2, 2) = (0\ 2)$, $\sigma(3, 3) = (0\ 3\ 1)$. Then for $k \geq 4$, let $\alpha(k, 1) = (k\ k{-}4)$, $\alpha(k, j) = (k\ k{-}3{-}j\ k{-}2{-}j)$ for $1 < j < k - 2$, and

	$k \bmod 3 = 0$		$k \bmod 3 = 1$		$k \bmod 3 = 2$
$\alpha(k, k{-}2) =$	$(k\ k{-}2\ 0)$	or	$(k\ k{-}3\ 0)$	or	$(k\ k{-}1\ 0)$,
$\alpha(k, k{-}1) =$	$(k\ k{-}2\ k{-}3)$	or	$(k\ k{-}3)$	or	$(k\ k{-}1\ k{-}3)$,
$\alpha(k, k) =$	$(k\ k{-}2)$	or	$(k\ k{-}3\ k{-}2)$	or	$(k\ k{-}2)$;

this makes $\sigma(k, k) = (k{-}3\ k\ k{-}2)$ as required.

44. No, because $\tau(k, j)$ is a $(k + 1)$-cycle, not a transposition. (See (19) and (24).)

45. (a) 202280070, since $u_k = \max(\{0, 1, \ldots, a_k - 1\} \setminus \{a_1, \ldots, a_{k-1}\})$. (Actually u_n is never set by the algorithm, but we can assume that it is zero.) (b) 273914568.

46. True (assuming that $u_n = 0$). If either $u_k > u_{k+1}$ or $a_k > a_{k+1}$ we must have $a_k > u_k \geq a_{k+1} > u_{k+1}$.

47. Steps $(X1, X2, \ldots, X6)$ are performed respectively $(1, A, B, A - 1, B - N_n, A)$ times, where $A = N_0 + \cdots + N_{n-1}$ and $B = nN_0 + (n - 1)N_1 + \cdots + 1N_{n-1}$.

48. Steps $(X2, X3, X4, X5, X6)$ are performed respectively $A_n + (1, n!, 0, 0, 1)$ times, where $A_n = \sum_{k=1}^{n-1} n^{\underline{k}} = n! \sum_{k=1}^{n-1} 1/k! \approx n!\,(e - 1)$. Assuming that they cost respectively $(1, 1, 3, 1, 3)$ mems, for operations involving a_j, l_j, or u_j, the total cost is about $9e - 8 \approx 16.46$ mems per permutation.

Algorithm L uses approximately $(e, 2 + e/2, 2e + 2e^{-1} - 4)$ mems per permutation in steps $(L2, L3, L4)$, for a total of $3.5e + 2e^{-1} - 2 \approx 8.25$ (see exercise 5).

Algorithm X could be tuned up for this case by streamlining the code when k is near n. But so can Algorithm L, as shown in exercise 1.

49. Order the signatures so that $|s_0| \geq \cdots \geq |s_9|$; also prepare tables $w_0 \ldots w_9$, $x_0 \ldots x_9$, $y_0 \ldots y_9$, so that the signatures $\{s_k, \ldots, s_9\}$ are $w_{x_k} \leq \cdots \leq w_{y_k}$. For example, when SEND + MORE = MONEY we have $(s_0, \ldots, s_9) = (-9000, 1000, -900, 91,$ $-90, 10, 1, -1, 0, 0)$ for the respective letters (M, S, O, E, N, R, D, Y, A, B); also $(w_0, \ldots, w_9) =$ $(-9000, -900, -90, -1, 0, 0, 1, 10, 91, 1000)$, and $x_0 \ldots x_9 = 0112233344$, $y_0 \ldots y_9 =$ 9988776554. Yet another table $f_0 \ldots f_9$ has $f_j = 1$ if the digit corresponding to w_j cannot be zero; in this case $f_0 \ldots f_9 = 1000000001$. These tables make it easy to compute the largest and smallest values of

$$s_k a_k + \cdots + s_9 a_9$$

over all choices $a_k \ldots a_9$ of the remaining digits, using the method of exercise 25, since the links l_j tell us those digits in increasing order.

This method requires a rather expensive computation at each node of the search tree, but it often succeeds in keeping that tree small. For example, it solves the first eight alphametics of exercise 24 with costs of only 7, 13, 7, 9, 5, 343, 44, and 89 kilomems; this is a substantial improvement in cases (a), (b), (e), and (h), although case (f) comes out significantly worse. Another bad case is the 'CHILD' example of answer 27, where left-to-right needs 2947 kilomems compared to 588 for the right-to-left approach. Left-to-right does, however, fare better on BLOOD + SWEAT + TEARS (73 versus 360) and HELLO + WORLD (340 versus 410).

50. If α is in a permutation group, so are all its powers α^2, α^3, $\ldots$, including $\alpha^{m-1} = \alpha^-$, where m is the order of α (the least common multiple of its cycle lengths). And (32) is equivalent to $\alpha^- = \sigma_1 \sigma_2 \ldots \sigma_{n-1}$.

51. False. For example, $\sigma(k, i)^-$ and $\sigma(k, j)^-$ might both take $k \mapsto 0$.

52. $\tau(k, j) = (k{-}j \ \ k{-}j{+}1)$ is an adjacent interchange, and

$$\omega(k) = (n{-}1 \ \ldots \ 0)(n{-}2 \ \ldots \ 0) \ldots (k \ \ldots \ 0) = \phi(n-1)\phi(k-1)$$

is a k-flip followed by an n-flip. The permutation corresponding to control table $c_0 \ldots c_{n-1}$ in Algorithm H has c_j elements to the right of j that are less than j, for $0 \leq j < n$; so it is the same as the permutation corresponding to $c_1 \ldots c_n$ in Algorithm P, except that subscripts are shifted by 1.

The only essential difference between Algorithm P and this version of Algorithm H is that Algorithm P uses a reflected Gray code to run through all possibilities of its control table, while Algorithm H runs through those mixed-radix numbers in ascending (lexicographic) order.

Indeed, Gray code can be used with any Sims table, by modifying either Algorithm G or Algorithm H. Then all transitions are by $\tau(k, j)$ or by $\tau(k, j)^-$, and the permutations $\omega(k)$ are irrelevant.

53. The text's proof that $n! - 1$ transpositions cannot be achieved for $n = 4$ also shows that we can reduce the problem from n to $n - 2$ at the cost of a single transposition $(n{-}1 \ n{-}2)$, which was called '$(3\,c)$' in the notation of that proof.

Thus we can generate all permutations by making the following transformation in step H4: If $k = n - 1$ or $k = n - 2$, transpose $a_{j \bmod n} \leftrightarrow a_{(j-1) \bmod n}$, where $j = c_{n-1} - 1$. If $k = n - 3$ or $k = n - 4$, transpose $a_{n-1} \leftrightarrow a_{n-2}$ and also $a_{j \bmod (n-2)} \leftrightarrow a_{(j-1) \bmod (n-2)}$, where $j = c_{n-3} - 1$. And in general if $k = n - 2t - 1$ or $k = n - 2t - 2$, transpose $a_{n-2i+1} \leftrightarrow a_{n-2i}$ for $1 \leq i \leq t$ and also $a_{j \bmod (n-2t)} \leftrightarrow a_{(j-1) \bmod (n-2t)}$, where $j = c_{n-2t-1} - 1$. [See *CACM* **19** (1976), 68–72.]

The corresponding Sims table permutations can be written down as follows, although they don't appear explicitly in the algorithm itself:

$$\sigma(k,j)^- = \begin{cases} (0\ 1\ \ldots\ j{-}1\ k), & \text{if } n-k \text{ is odd}; \\ (0\ 1\ \ldots\ k)^j, & \text{if } n-k \text{ is even}. \end{cases}$$

The value of $a_{j \bmod (n-2t)}$ will be $n - 2t - 1$ after the interchange. For efficiency we can also use the fact that k usually equals $n - 1$. The total number of transpositions is $\sum_{t=0}^{\lfloor n/2 \rfloor} (n - 2t)! - \lfloor n/2 \rfloor - 1$.

54. Yes; the transformation can be any k-cycle on positions $\{1, \ldots, k\}$.

55. (a) Since $\rho_!(m) = \rho_!(m \bmod n!)$ when $n > \rho_!(m)$, we have $\rho_!(n! + m) = \rho_!(m)$ for $0 < m < n \cdot n! = (n+1)! - n!$. Therefore $\beta_{n!+m} = \sigma_{\rho_!(n!+m)} \cdots \sigma_{\rho_!(n!+1)} \beta_{n!} = \sigma_{\rho_!(m)} \cdots \sigma_{\rho_!(1)} \beta_{n!} = \beta_m \beta_{n!}$ for $0 \le m < n \cdot n!$, and we have in particular

$$\beta_{(n+1)!} = \sigma_{n+1} \beta_{(n+1)!-1} = \sigma_{n+1} \beta_{n!-1} \beta_{n!}^n = \sigma_{n+1} \sigma_n^- \beta_{n!}^{n+1}.$$

Similarly $\alpha_{n!+m} = \beta_{n!}^- \alpha_m \beta_{n!} \alpha_{n!}$ for $0 \le m < n \cdot n!$.

Since $\beta_{n!}$ commutes with τ_n and τ_{n+1} we find $\alpha_{n!} = \tau_n \alpha_{n!-1}$, and

$$\begin{aligned} \alpha_{(n+1)!} &= \tau_{n+1} \alpha_{(n+1)!-1} = \tau_{n+1} \beta_{n!}^- \alpha_{(n+1)!-1-n!} \beta_{n!} \alpha_{n!} = \cdots \\ &= \tau_{n+1} \beta_{n!}^{-n} \alpha_{n!-1} (\beta_{n!} \alpha_{n!})^n \\ &= \beta_{n!}^{-n-1} \tau_{n+1} \tau_n^- (\beta_{n!} \alpha_{n!})^{n+1} \\ &= \beta_{(n+1)!}^- \sigma_{n+1} \sigma_n^- \tau_{n+1} \tau_n^- (\beta_{n!} \alpha_{n!})^{n+1}. \end{aligned}$$

(b) In this case $\sigma_{n+1} \sigma_n^- = (n\ n{-}1\ \ldots\ 1)$ and $\tau_{n+1} \tau_n^- = (n{+}1\ n\ 0)$, and we have $\beta_{(n+1)!} \alpha_{(n+1)!} = (n{+}1\ n\ \ldots\ 0)$ by induction. Therefore $\alpha_{jn!+m} = \beta_{n!}^{-j} \alpha_m (n\ \ldots\ 0)^j$ for $0 \le j \le n$ and $0 \le m < n!$. All permutations of $\{0, \ldots, n\}$ are achieved because $\beta_{n!}^{-j} \alpha_m$ fixes n and $(n\ \ldots\ 0)^j$ takes $n \mapsto n - j$.

56. If we set $\sigma_k = (k{-}1\ k{-}2)(k{-}3\ k{-}4) \ldots$ in the previous exercise, we find by induction that $\beta_{n!} \alpha_{n!}$ is the $(n+1)$-cycle $(0\ n\ n{-}1\ n{-}3\ \ldots\ (2\text{ or }1)\ (1\text{ or }2)\ \ldots\ n{-}4\ n{-}2)$.

57. Arguing as in answer 5, we obtain $\sum_{k=2}^{n-1} [k\ \text{odd}]/k! - (\lfloor n/2 \rfloor - 1)/n! = \sinh 1 - 1 - O(1/(n-1)!)$.

58. True. By the formulas of exercise 55 we have $\alpha_{n!-1} = (0\ n) \beta_{n!}^- (n\ \ldots\ 0)$, and this takes $0 \mapsto n - 1$ because $\beta_{n!}$ fixes n. (Consequently Algorithm E will define a Hamiltonian *cycle* on the graph of exercise 66 if and only if $\beta_{n!} = (n{-}1\ \ldots\ 2\ 1)$, and this holds if and only if the length of every cycle of $\beta_{(n-1)!}$ is a divisor of n. The latter is true for $n = 2, 3, 4, 6, 12, 20$, and 40, but for no other $n \le 250,000$.)

59. The Cayley graph with generators $(\alpha_1, \ldots, \alpha_k)$ in the text's definition is isomorphic to the Cayley graph with generators $(\alpha_1^-, \ldots, \alpha_k^-)$ in the alternative definition, since $\pi \to \alpha_j \pi$ in the former if and only if $\pi^- \to \pi^- \alpha_j^-$ in the latter.

60. (a, b) There are 88 delta sequences, which reduce to four classes: $P = (32131231)^3$ (plain changes, represented by 8 different delta sequences); $Q = (32121232)^3$ (a doubly Gray variant of plain changes, with 8 representatives); $R = (121232321232)^2$ (a doubly Gray code with 24 representatives); $S = 2\alpha3\alpha^R$, $\alpha = 12321312121$ (48 representatives). Classes P and Q are cyclic shifts of their complements; classes P, Q, and S are shifts of their reversals; class R is a shifted reversal of its complement. [See A. L. Leigh Silver, *Math. Gazette* **48** (1964), 1–16.]

61. There are respectively $(26, 36, 20, 26, 28, 40, 40, 20, 26, 28, 28, 26)$ such paths ending at $(1243, 1324, 1432, 2134, 2341, 2413, 3142, 3214, 3421, 4123, 4231, 4312)$.

62. There are only two paths when $n = 3$, ending respectively at 132 and 213. But when $n \geq 4$ there are Gray codes leading from $12\ldots n$ to any odd permutation $a_1 a_2 \ldots a_n$. Exercise 61 establishes this when $n = 4$, and we can prove it by induction for $n > 4$ as follows.

Let $A(j)$ be the set of all permutations that begin with j, and let $A(j,k)$ be those that begin with jk. If $(\alpha_0, \alpha_1, \ldots, \alpha_n)$ are any odd permutations such that $\alpha_j \in A(x_j, x_{j+1})$, then $(1\,2)\alpha_j$ is an even permutation in $A(x_{j+1}, x_j)$. Consequently, if $x_1 x_2 \ldots x_n$ is a permutation of $\{1, 2, \ldots, n\}$, there is at least one Hamiltonian path of the form

$$(1\,2)\alpha_0 - \cdots - \alpha_1 - (1\,2)\alpha_1 - \cdots - \alpha_2 - \cdots - (1\,2)\alpha_{n-1} - \cdots - \alpha_n;$$

the subpath from $(1\,2)\alpha_{j-1}$ to α_j includes all elements of $A(x_j)$.

This construction solves the problem in at least $(n-2)!^n / 2^{n-1}$ distinct ways when $a_1 \neq 1$, because we can take $\alpha_0 = 2\,1\ldots n$ and $\alpha_n = a_1 a_2 \ldots a_n$; there are $(n-2)!$ ways to choose $x_2 \ldots x_{n-1}$, and $(n-2)!/2$ ways to choose each of $\alpha_1, \ldots, \alpha_{n-1}$.

Finally, if $a_1 = 1$, take any path $12\ldots n - \cdots - a_1 a_2 \ldots a_n$ that runs through all of $A(1)$, and choose any step $\alpha - \alpha'$ with $\alpha \in A(1, j)$ and $\alpha' \in A(1, j')$ for some $j \neq j'$. Replace that step by

$$\alpha - (1\,2)\alpha_1 - \cdots - \alpha_2 - \cdots - (1\,2)\alpha_{n-1} - \cdots - \alpha_n - \alpha',$$

using a construction like the Hamiltonian path above but now with $\alpha_1 = \alpha$, $\alpha_n = (1\,2)\alpha'$, $x_1 = 1$, $x_2 = j$, $x_n = j'$, and $x_{n+1} = 1$. (In this case the permutations $\alpha_1, \ldots, \alpha_n$ might all be even.)

63. Monte Carlo estimates using the techniques of Section 7.2.3 suggest that the total number of equivalence classes will be roughly 1.2×10^{21}; most of those classes will contain 480 Gray cycles.

64. Exactly 2,005,200 delta sequences have the doubly Gray property; they belong to 4206 equivalence classes under cyclic shift, reversal, and/or complementation. Nine classes, such as the code $2\alpha 2\alpha^R$ where

$$\alpha = 12343234321232121232321232121234343212123432123432121232321,$$

are shifts of their reversal; 48 classes are composed of repeated 60-cycles. One of the most interesting of the latter type is $\alpha\alpha$ where

$$\alpha = \beta 2\beta 4\beta 4\beta 4\beta 4, \qquad \beta = 32121232123.$$

65. Such a path exists for any given $N \leq n!$: Let the Nth permutation be $\alpha = a_1 \ldots a_n$, and let $j = a_1$. Also let Π_k be the set of all permutations $\beta = b_1 \ldots b_n$ for which $b_1 = k$ and $\beta \leq \alpha$. By induction on N there is a Gray path P_1 for Π_j. We can then construct Gray paths P_k for $\Pi_j \cup \Pi_1 \cup \cdots \cup \Pi_{k-1}$ for $2 \leq k \leq j$, successively combining P_{k-1} with a Gray cycle for Π_{k-1}. (See the "absorption" construction of answer 62. In fact, P_j will be a Gray *cycle* when N is a multiple of 6.)

66. Defining the delta sequence by the rule $\pi_{(k+1) \bmod n!} = (1\,\delta_k)\pi_k$, we find exactly 36 such sequences, all of which are cyclic shifts of a pattern like $(xyzyzyxzyzyz)^2$. (The next case, $n = 5$, probably has about 10^{18} solutions that are inequivalent with respect to cyclic shifting, reversal, and permutation of coordinates, thus about 6×10^{21} different delta sequences.) Incidentally, Igor Pak has shown that the Cayley graph generated by star transpositions is an $(n-2)$-dimensional torus in general.

67. If we let π be equivalent to $\pi(12345)$, we get a reduced graph on 24 vertices that has 40768 Hamiltonian cycles, 240 of which lead to delta sequences of the form α^5 in which α uses each transposition 6 times (for example, $\alpha = 354232534234532454352452$). The total number of solutions to this problem is probably about 10^{16}.

68. If A isn't connected, neither is G. If A is connected, we can assume that it is a free tree. Moreover, in this case we can prove a generalization of the result in exercise 62: For $n \geq 4$ there is a Hamiltonian path in G from the identity permutation to any odd permutation. For we can assume without loss of generality that A contains the edge $1 \!-\!\!-\! 2$ where 1 is a leaf of the tree, and a proof like that of exercise 62 applies.

[This elegant construction is due to M. Tchuente, *Ars Combinatoria* **14** (1982), 115–122. Extensive generalizations have been discussed by Ruskey and Savage in *SIAM J. Discrete Math.* **6** (1993), 152–166. See also the original Russian publication in *Kibernetika* **11**, 3 (1975), 17–21; English translation, *Cybernetics* **11** (1975), 362–366.]

69. Following the hint, the modified algorithm behaves like this when $n = 5$:

1234	1243	1423	4123	4132	1432	1342	1324	3124	3142	3412	4312
↓	↑	↓	↑	↓	↑	↓	↑	↓	↑	↓	↑
54321	24351	24153	54123	14523	14325	24315	24513	54213	14253	14352	54312
12345	15342	35142	32145	32541	52341	51342	31542	31245	35241	25341	21345
15432	12435	32415	35412←31452	51432	52431	32451←35421	31425	21435	25431
23451	53421	51423	21453→25413	23415	13425	15423→12453	52413	53412	13452
21543	51243	53241	23541	23145	25143	15243	13245	13542	53142	52143	12543
34512	34215	14235	14532	54132	34152	34251	54231	24531	24135	34125	34521
32154→35124	15324→12354	52314	32514←31524	51324	21354→25314	35214→31254
45123←42153	42351←45321	41325	41523→42513	42315	45312←41352	41253←45213
43215	43512←41532	41235	45231→43251	43152→45132	42135	42531←43521	43125
51234	21534→23514	53214	13254←15234	25134←23154	53124	13524→12534	52134
↓	↑	↓	↑	↓	↑	↓	↑	↓	↑	↓	↑

Here the columns represent sets of permutations that are cyclically rotated and/or reflected in all $2n$ ways; therefore each column contains exactly one "rosary permutation" (exercise 18). We can use Algorithm P to run through the rosary permutations systematically, knowing that the pair xy will occur before yx in its column, at which time τ' instead of ρ' will move us to the right or to the left. Step Z2 omits the interchange $a_1 \leftrightarrow a_2$, thereby causing the permutations $a_1 \ldots a_{n-1}$ to repeat themselves going backwards. (We implicitly use the fact that $t[k] = t[n! - k]$ in the output of Algorithm T.)

Now if we replace $1 \ldots n$ by $24 \ldots 31$ and change $A_1 \ldots A_n$ to $A_1 A_n A_2 A_{n-1} \ldots$, we get the unmodified algorithm whose results are shown in Fig. 42(b).

This method was inspired by a (nonconstructive) theorem of E. S. Rapaport, *Scripta Math.* **24** (1959), 51–58. It illustrates a more general fact observed by Carla Savage in 1989, namely that the Cayley graph for *any* group generated by three involutions ρ, σ, τ has a Hamiltonian cycle when $\rho\tau = \tau\rho$. [See I. Pak and R. Radoičić, *Discrete Math.* **309** (2009), 5501–5508.]

70. No; the longest cycle in that digraph has length 358. But there do exist pairs of disjoint 180-cycles from which a Hamiltonian path of length 720 can be derived. For example, consider the cycles $\alpha\sigma\beta\sigma$ and $\gamma\sigma\sigma$ where

$$\alpha = \tau\sigma^5\tau\sigma^5\tau\sigma^3\tau\sigma^3\tau\sigma^2\tau\sigma^5\tau\sigma^3\tau\sigma^2\tau\sigma^5\tau\sigma^5\tau\sigma^2\tau\sigma^3\tau\sigma^1\tau\sigma^5\tau\sigma^5\tau\sigma^3\tau\sigma^3\tau\sigma^1\tau\sigma^1\tau\sigma^3\tau\sigma^2\tau\sigma^1\tau\sigma^1;$$

$$\beta = \sigma^3\tau\sigma^5\tau\sigma^2\tau\sigma^2\tau\sigma^5\tau\sigma^2\tau\sigma^3\tau\sigma^1\tau\sigma^1\tau\sigma^5\tau\sigma^1\tau\sigma^3\tau\sigma^5\tau\sigma^5\tau\sigma^3\tau\sigma^2\tau\sigma^1\tau\sigma^2\tau\sigma^3\tau\sigma^1\tau\sigma^1\tau\sigma^3\tau\sigma^3\tau\sigma^2\tau\sigma^4;$$

$$\gamma = \sigma\tau\sigma^5\tau\sigma^5\tau\sigma^3\tau\sigma^1\tau\sigma^1\tau\sigma^3\tau\sigma^3\tau\sigma^2\tau\sigma^5\tau\sigma^2\tau\sigma^3\tau\sigma^5\tau\sigma^5\tau\sigma^1\tau\sigma^5\tau\sigma^3\tau\sigma^3\tau\sigma^2\tau\sigma^1\tau\sigma^2\tau\sigma^3\tau\sigma^3\tau\sigma^1\tau\sigma^1\tau\sigma^3\tau\sigma^2$$
$$\tau\sigma^5\tau\sigma^5\tau\sigma^5\tau\sigma^3\tau\sigma^3\tau\sigma^2\tau\sigma^5\tau\sigma^2\tau\sigma^3\tau\sigma^1\tau\sigma^1\tau\sigma^5\tau\sigma^1\tau\sigma^3\tau\sigma^3\tau\sigma^5\tau\sigma^5\tau\sigma^1\tau\sigma^5\tau\sigma^2\tau\sigma^3\tau\sigma^3\tau\sigma^1\tau\sigma^2.$$

If we start with 134526 and follow $\alpha\sigma\beta\tau$ we reach 163452; then follow $\gamma\sigma\tau$ and reach 126345; then follow $\sigma\gamma\tau$ and reach 152634; then follow $\beta\sigma\alpha$, ending at 415263.

71. Brendan McKay and Frank Ruskey have found such cycles by computer when $n = 7$, 9, and 11, but no nice structure was apparent.

72. Any Hamiltonian path includes $(n-1)!$ vertices that take $y \mapsto x$, each of which (if not the last) is followed by a vertex that takes $x \mapsto x$. So one must be last; otherwise $(n-1)! + 1$ vertices would take $x \mapsto x$.

73. (a) Assume first that β is the identity permutation (). Then every cycle of α that contains an element of A lies entirely within A. Hence the cycles of σ are obtained by omitting all cycles of α that contain no element of A. All remaining cycles have odd length, so σ is an even permutation.

If β is not the identity, we apply this argument to $\alpha' = \alpha\beta^-$, $\beta' = ()$, and $\sigma' = \sigma\beta^-$, concluding that σ' is an even permutation; thus σ and β have the same sign.

Similarly, σ and α have the same sign, because $\beta\alpha^- = (\alpha\beta^-)^-$ has the same order as $\alpha\beta^-$.

(b) Let X be the vertices of the Cayley graph in Theorem R, and let $\hat\alpha$ be the permutation of X that takes a vertex π into $\alpha\pi$; this permutation has g/a cycles of length a. Define the permutation $\hat\beta$ similarly. Then $\hat\alpha\hat\beta^-$ has g/c cycles of length c. If c is odd, any Hamiltonian cycle in the graph defines a cycle $\hat\sigma$ that contains all the vertices and satisfies the hypotheses of (a). Therefore $\hat\alpha$ and $\hat\beta$ have an odd number of cycles, because the sign of a permutation on n elements with r cycles is $(-1)^{n-r}$ (see exercise 5.2.2–2).

[This proof, which shows that X cannot be the union of any odd number of cycles, was presented by Rankin in *Proc. Cambridge Phil. Soc.* **62** (1966), 15–16.]

74. The representation $\beta^j\gamma^k$ is unique if we require $0 \le j < g/c$ and $0 \le k < c$. For if we had $\beta^j = \gamma^k$ for some j with $0 < j < g/c$, the group would have at most jc elements. It follows that $\beta^{g/c} = \gamma^t$ for some t.

Let $\hat\sigma$ be a Hamiltonian cycle, as in the previous answer, and let $\hat\gamma = \hat\alpha\hat\beta^-$. If $\pi\hat\sigma = \pi\hat\alpha$ then $\pi\hat\gamma\hat\sigma$ must be $\pi\hat\gamma\hat\alpha$, because $\pi\hat\gamma\hat\beta = \pi\hat\alpha$. And if $\pi\hat\sigma = \pi\hat\beta$ then $\pi\hat\gamma\hat\sigma$ cannot be $\pi\hat\gamma\hat\alpha$, because that would imply $\pi\hat\gamma^2\hat\sigma = \pi\hat\gamma^2\hat\alpha$, ..., $\pi\hat\gamma^c\hat\sigma = \pi\hat\gamma^c\hat\alpha$. Thus the elements π, $\pi\hat\gamma$, $\pi\hat\gamma^2$, ..., all have equivalent behavior with respect to their successors in $\hat\sigma$.

When the path $\pi \longrightarrow \pi\hat\sigma \longrightarrow \cdots \longrightarrow \pi\hat\sigma^j$ has $k(j)$ steps of type $\hat\alpha$, we have $\pi\hat\sigma^j = \pi\hat\beta^j\hat\gamma^{k(j)}$. Thus $\pi\hat\sigma^{g/c} = \pi\hat\gamma^{t+k(g/c)}$, and we have $k(j + g/c) = k(j)$ for $j \ge 0$. The path returns to π for the first time in g steps if and only if $t + k(g/c)$ is relatively prime to c.

75. Apply the previous exercise with $g = mn$, $a = m$, $b = n$, $c = mn/d$. The number t satisfies $t \equiv 0$ (modulo m), $t + d \equiv 0$ (modulo n); and it follows that $k + t \perp c$ if and only if $(d-k)m/d \perp kn/d$.

Notes: The modular Gray code of exercise 7.2.1.1–78 is a Hamiltonian path from $(0,0)$ to $(m-1, (-m) \bmod n)$, so it is a Hamiltonian cycle if and only if m is a multiple of n. It is natural to conjecture (falsely) that at least one Hamiltonian cycle exists whenever $d > 1$. But P. Erdős and W. T. Trotter have observed [*J. Graph Theory* **2**

(1978), 137–142] that if p and $2p+1$ are odd prime numbers, no suitable k exists when $m = p(2p+1)(3p+1)$ and $n = (3p+1)\prod_{q=1}^{3p} q^{[q \text{ is prime}][q\neq p][q\neq 2p+1]}$.

See J. A. Gallian, *Mathematical Intelligencer* **13**,3 (Summer 1991), 40–43, for interesting facts about other kinds of cycles in $\vec{C_m} \times \vec{C_n}$.

76. We may assume that the tour begins in the lower left corner. There are no solutions when m and n are both divisible by 3, because $2/3$ of the cells are unreachable in that case. Otherwise, letting $d = \gcd(m,n)$ and arguing as in the previous exercise but with $(x,y)\alpha = ((x+2) \bmod m, (y+1) \bmod n)$ and $(x,y)\beta = ((x+1) \bmod m, (y+2) \bmod n)$, we find the answer

$$\sum_{k=0}^{d} \binom{d}{k}[\gcd((2d-k)m, (k+d)n) = d \text{ or } (mn \perp 3 \text{ and } \gcd((2d-k)m, (k+d)n) = 3d)].$$

77.

```
01  * Permutation generator \'a la Heap
02  N    IS    10              The value of n (3 or more, not large)
03  t    IS    $255
04  j    IS    $0              8j
05  k    IS    $1              8k
06  ak   IS    $2
07  aj   IS    $3
08       LOC   Data_Segment
09  a    GREG  @               Base address for a_0 ... a_{n-1}
10  A0   IS    @
11  A1   IS    @+8
12  A2   IS    @+16
13       LOC   @+8*N           Space for a_0 ... a_{n-1}
14  c    GREG  @-8*3           Location of 8c_0
15       LOC   @-8*3+8*N       8c_3 ... 8c_{n-1}, initially zero
16       OCTA  -1              8c_n = -1, a convenient sentinel
17  u    GREG  0               Contents of a_0, except in inner loop
18  v    GREG  0               Contents of a_1, except in inner loop
19  w    GREG  0               Contents of a_2, except in inner loop
20       LOC   #100
21  1H   STCO  0,c,k       B - A   c_k <- 0.
22       INCL  k,8         B - A   k <- k+1.
23  0H   LDO   j,c,k       B       j <- c_k.
24       CMP   t,j,k       B
25       BZ    t,1B        B       Loop if c_k = k.
26       BN    j,Done      A       Terminate if c_k < 0 (k = n).
27       LDO   ak,a,k      A - 1   Fetch a_k.
28       ADD   t,j,8       A - 1
29       STO   t,c,k       A - 1   c_k <- j+1.
30       AND   t,k,#8      A - 1
31       CSZ   j,t,0       A - 1   Set j <- 0 if k is even.
32       LDO   aj,a,j      A - 1   Fetch a_j.
33       STO   ak,a,j      A - 1   Replace it by a_k.
34       CSZ   u,j,ak      A - 1   Set u <- a_k if j = 0.
35       SUB   j,j,8       A - 1   j <- j-1.
36       CSZ   v,j,ak      A - 1   Set v <- a_k if j = 0.
```

37		SUB	j,j,8	$A-1$	$j \leftarrow j - 1$.
38		CSZ	w,j,ak	$A-1$	Set $w \leftarrow a_k$ if $j = 0$.
39		STO	aj,a,k	$A-1$	Replace a_k by what was a_j.
40	Inner	PUSHJ	0,Visit	A	
		...			(See (42))
55		PUSHJ	0,Visit	A	
56		SET	t,u	A	Swap $u \leftrightarrow w$.
57		SET	u,w	A	
58		SET	w,t	A	
59		SET	k,8*3	A	$k \leftarrow 3$.
60		JMP	0B	A	
61	Main	LDO	u,A0	1	
62		LDO	v,A1	1	
63		LDO	w,A2	1	
64		JMP	Inner	1	∎

78. Lines 31–38 become $2r - 1$ instructions, lines 61–63 become r, and lines 56–58 become $3 + (r-2)[r \text{ even}]$ instructions (see $\omega(r-1)$ in answer 40). The total running time is therefore $\big((2r!+2)A+2B+r-5\big)\mu+\big((2r!+2r+7+(r-2)[r \text{ even}])A+7B-r-4\big)\upsilon$, where $A = n!/r!$ and $B = n!(1/r! + \cdots + 1/n!)$.

79. SLU u,[#f],t; SLU t,a,4; XOR t,t,a; AND t,t,u; SRU u,t,4; OR t,t,u; XOR a,a,t; here, as in the answer to exercise 1.3.1′–34, the notation '[#f]' denotes a register that contains the constant value $^\#$f. (See the similar code in 7.1.3–(69).)

80. SLU u,a,t; MXOR u,[#8844221188442211],u; AND u,u,[#ff000000]; SRU u,u,t; XOR a,a,u. This cheats, since it transforms $^\#$12345678 to $^\#$13245678 when $t = 4$, but (45) still works.

Even faster and trickier would be a routine analogous to (42): Consider

PUSHJ 0,Visit; MXOR a,a,c1; PUSHJ 0,Visit; ... MXOR a,a,c5; PUSHJ 0,Visit

where c1, ..., c5 are constants that would cause $^\#$12345678 to become successively $^\#$12783456, $^\#$12567834, $^\#$12563478, $^\#$12785634, $^\#$12347856. Other instructions, executed only 1/6 or 1/24 as often, can take care of shuffling nybbles within and between bytes. Very clever, but it doesn't beat (46) in view of the PUSHJ/POP overhead.

81.

```
k   IS   $0 ;kk IS $1 ;c IS $2 ;d IS $3
    SET  k,1      k ← 1.
3H  SRU  d,a,60   d ← leftmost nybble.
    SLU  a,a,4    a ← 16a mod 16^16.
    CMP  c,d,k
    SLU  kk,k,2
    SLU  d,d,kk
    OR   t,t,d    t ← t + 16^k d.
    PBNZ c,1B     Return to main loop if d ≠ k.
    INCL k,1      k ← k + 1.
    PBNZ a,3B     Return to second loop if k < n.  ∎
```

82. $\mu + \big(5n! + 11A - (n-1)! + 6\big)\upsilon = \big((5 + 10/n)\upsilon + O(n^{-2})\big)n!$, plus the visiting time, where $A = \sum_{k=1}^{n-1} k!$ is the number of times the loop at 3H is used.

83. With suitable initialization and a 13-octabyte table, only about a dozen MMIX instructions are needed:

```
magic   GREG  #8844221188442211
OH      ⟨Visit register a⟩
        PBN   c,Sigma
Tau     MXOR  t,magic,a; ANDNL t,#ffff; JMP 1F
Sigma   SRU   t,a,20; SLU a,a,4; ANDNML a,#f00
1H      XOR   a,a,t; SLU c,c,1
2H      PBNZ  c,0B; INCL p,8
3H      LDOU  c,p,0; PBNZ c,0B                          ▌
```

84. Assuming that the processors all have essentially the same speed, we can let the kth processor generate all permutations of rank r for $(k-1)n!/p \le r < kn!/p$, using any method based on control tables $c_1 \ldots c_n$. The starting and ending control tables are easily computed by converting their ranks to mixed-radix notation (exercise 12).

85. We can use a technique like that of Algorithm 3.4.2P: To compute $k = r(\alpha)$, first set $a'_{a_j} \leftarrow j$ for $1 \le j \le n$ (the inverse permutation). Then set $k \leftarrow 0$, and for $j = n$, $n-1$, ..., 2 (in this order) set $t \leftarrow a'_j$, $k \leftarrow kj + t - 1$, $a_t \leftarrow a_j$, $a'_{a_j} \leftarrow t$. To compute $r^{[-1]}(k)$, start with $a_1 \leftarrow 1$. Then for $j = 2$, ..., $n-1$, n (in this order) set $t \leftarrow (k \bmod j) + 1$, $a_j \leftarrow a_t$, $a_t \leftarrow j$, $k \leftarrow \lfloor k/j \rfloor$. [See S. Pleszczyński, *Inf. Proc. Letters* **3** (1975), 180–183; W. Myrvold and F. Ruskey, *Inf. Proc. Letters* **79** (2001), 281–284.]

Another method is preferable if we want to rank and unrank only the $n^{\underline{m}}$ *variations* $a_1 \ldots a_m$ of $\{1, \ldots, n\}$: To compute $k = r(a_1 \ldots a_m)$, start with $b_1 \ldots b_n \leftarrow b'_1 \ldots b'_n \leftarrow 1 \ldots n$; then for $j = 1$, ..., m (in this order) set $t \leftarrow b'_{a_j}$, $b_t \leftarrow b_{n+1-j}$, and $b'_{b_t} \leftarrow t$; finally set $k \leftarrow 0$ and for $j = m$, ..., 1 (in this order) set $k \leftarrow k \times (n+1-j) + b'_{a_j} - 1$. To compute $r^{[-1]}(k)$, start with $b_1 \ldots b_n \leftarrow 1 \ldots n$; then for $j = 1, \ldots, m$ (in this order) set $t \leftarrow (k \bmod (n+1-j)) + 1$, $a_j \leftarrow b_t$, $b_t \leftarrow b_{n+1-j}$, $k \leftarrow \lfloor k/(n+1-j) \rfloor$. (See exercise 3.4.2–15 for cases with large n and small m.)

86. If $x \prec y$ and $y \prec z$, the algorithm will never move y to the left of x, nor z to the left of y, so it will never test x versus z.

87. They appear in lexicographic order; Algorithm P used a reflected Gray order.

88. Generate inverse permutations with $a'_0 < a'_1 < a'_2$, $a'_3 < a'_4 < a'_5$, $a'_6 < a'_7$, $a'_8 < a'_9$, $a'_0 < a'_3$, $a'_6 < a'_8$.

89. (a) Let $d_k = \max\{j \mid 0 \le j \le k$ and j is nontrivial$\}$, where 0 is considered nontrivial. This table is easily precomputed, because j is trivial if and only if it must follow $\{1, \ldots, j-1\}$. Set $k \leftarrow d_n$ in step V2 and $k \leftarrow d_{k-1}$ in step V5. (Assume $d_n > 0$.)

(b) Now $M = \sum_{j=1}^{n} t_j [j$ is nontrivial$]$.

(c) There are at least two topological sorts $a_j \ldots a_k$ of the set $\{j, \ldots, k\}$, and either of them can be placed after any topological sort $a_1 \ldots a_{j-1}$ of $\{1, \ldots, j-1\}$.

(d) Algorithm 2.2.3T repeatedly outputs minimal elements (elements with no predecessors), removing them from the relation graph. We use it in reverse, repeatedly removing and giving the highest labels to *maximal* elements (elements with no successors). If only one maximal element exists, it is trivial. If k and l are both maximal, they both are output before any element x with $x \prec k$ or $x \prec l$, because steps T5 and T7 keep maximal elements in a queue (not a stack). Thus if k is nontrivial and output first, element l might become trivial, but the next nontrivial element j will not be output before l; and k is unrelated to l.

(e) Let the nontrivial t's be $s_1 < s_2 < \cdots < s_r = N$. Then we have $s_j \ge 2s_{j-2}$, by (c). Consequently $M = s_2 + \cdots + s_r \le s_r(1 + \frac{1}{2} + \frac{1}{4} + \cdots) + s_{r-1}(1 + \frac{1}{2} + \frac{1}{4} + \cdots) < 4s_r$.

(A sharper estimate is in fact true, as observed by M. Peczarski: Let $s_0 = 1$, let the nontrivial indices be $0 = k_1 < k_2 < \cdots < k_r$, and let $k'_j = \max\{k \mid 1 \leq k < k_j,\ k \not\prec k_j\}$ for $j > 1$. Then $k'_{j+1} \geq k_j$. There are s_j topological sorts of $\{1, \ldots, k_{j+1}\}$ that end with k_{j+1}; and there are at least s_{j-1} that end with k'_{j+1}, since each of the s_{j-1} topological sorts of $\{1, \ldots, k_j - 1\}$ can be extended. Hence

$$s_{j+1} \geq s_j + s_{j-1} \qquad \text{for } 1 \leq j < r.$$

Now let $y_0 = 0$, $y_1 = F_2 + \cdots + F_r$, and $y_j = y_{j-2} + y_{j-1} - F_{r+1}$ for $1 < j < r$. Then

$$F_{r+1}(s_1 + \cdots + s_r) + \sum_{j=1}^{r-1} y_j\left(s_{r+1-j} - s_{r-j} - s_{r-1-j}\right) = (F_2 + \cdots + F_{r+1})s_r,$$

and each $y_j = F_{r+1} - 2F_j - (-1)^j F_{r+1-j}$ is nonnegative. Hence $s_1 + \cdots + s_r \leq ((F_2 + \cdots + F_{r+1})/F_{r+1})s_r \approx 2.6 s_r$. The following exercise shows that this bound is best possible.)

90. The number N of such permutations is F_{n+1} by exercise 5.2.1–25. Therefore $M = F_{n+1} + \cdots + F_2 = F_{n+3} - 2 \approx \phi^2 N$. Notice incidentally that all such permutations satisfy $a_1 \ldots a_n = a'_1 \ldots a'_n$. They can be arranged in a Gray path (exercise 7.2.1.1–89).

91. Since $t_j = (j-1)(j-3) \ldots (2 \text{ or } 1)$, we find $M = \left(1 + 2/\sqrt{\pi n} + O(1/n)\right)N$.

Note: The inversion tables $c_1 \ldots c_{2n}$ for permutations satisfying (49) are characterized by the conditions $c_1 = 0$, $0 \leq c_{2k} \leq c_{2k-1}$, $0 \leq c_{2k+1} \leq c_{2k-1} + 1$.

92. The total number of pairs (R, S), where R is a partial ordering and S is a linear ordering that includes R, is equal to P_n times the expected number of topological sorts; it is also Q_n times $n!$. So the answer is $n!\, Q_n/P_n$.

We will discuss the computation of P_n and Q_n in Section 7.2.3. For $1 \leq n \leq 12$ the expectation turns out to be approximately

$$(1,\ 1.33,\ 2.21,\ 4.38,\ 10.1,\ 26.7,\ 79.3,\ 262,\ 950,\ 3760,\ 16200,\ 74800).$$

Asymptotic values as $n \to \infty$ have been deduced by Brightwell, Prömel, and Steger [*J. Combinatorial Theory* **A73** (1996), 193–206], but the limiting behavior is quite different from what happens when n is in a practical range. The values of Q_n were first determined for $n \leq 5$ by S. P. Avann [*Æquationes Math.* **8** (1972), 95–102].

93. The basic idea is to introduce dummy elements $n+1$ and $n+2$ with $j \prec n+1$ and $j \prec n+2$ for $1 \leq j \leq n$, and to find all topological sorts of such an extended relation via adjacent interchanges; then take every *second* permutation, suppressing the dummy elements. An algorithm similar to Algorithm V can be used, but with a recursion that reduces n to $n-2$ by inserting $n-1$ and n among $a_1 \ldots a_{n-2}$ in all possible ways, assuming that $n-1 \not\prec n$, occasionally swapping $n+1$ with $n+2$. [See G. Pruesse and F. Ruskey, *SICOMP* **23** (1994), 373–386. A loopless implementation has been described by Canfield and Williamson, *Order* **12** (1995), 57–75.]

94. The case $n = 3$ illustrates the general idea of a pattern that begins with $1 \ldots (2n)$ and ends with $1(2n)2(2n-1) \ldots n(n+1)$: 123456, 123546, 123645, 132645, 132546, 132456, 142356, 142536, 142635, 152634, 152436, 152346, 162345, 162435, 162534.

Perfect matchings can also be regarded as involutions of $\{1, \ldots, 2n\}$ that have n cycles. With that representation this pattern involves two transpositions per step.

Notice that the C inversion tables of the permutations just listed are respectively 000000, 000100, 000200, 010200, 010100, 010000, 020000, 020100, 020200, 030200, 030100, 030000, 040000, 040100, 040200. In general, $C_1 = C_3 = \cdots = C_{2n-1} = 0$

and the n-tuples $(C_2, C_4, \ldots, C_{2n})$ run through a reflected Gray code on the radices $(2n - 1, 2n - 3, \ldots, 1)$. Thus the generation process can easily be made loopless if desired. [See Timothy Walsh, *J. Combinatorial Math. and Combinatorial Computing* **36** (2001), 95–118, Section 1.]

Note: Algorithms to generate all perfect matchings go back to J. F. Pfaff [*Abhandlungen Akad. Wissenschaften* (Berlin: 1814–1815), 124–125], who described two such procedures: His first method was lexicographic, which also corresponds to lexicographic order of the C inversion tables; his second method corresponds to *colex* order of those tables. Even and odd permutations alternate in both cases.

95. Generate inverse permutations with $a_1' < a_n' > a_2' < a_{n-1}' > \cdots$, using Algorithm V. (See exercise 5.1.4–23 for the number of solutions.)

96. For example, we can start with $a_1 \ldots a_{n-1} a_n = 2 \ldots n1$ and $b_1 b_2 \ldots b_n b_{n+1} = 12 \ldots n1$, and use Algorithm P to generate the $(n - 1)!$ permutations $b_2 \ldots b_n$ of $\{2, \ldots, n\}$. Just after that algorithm swaps $b_i \leftrightarrow b_{i+1}$, we set $a_{b_{i-1}} \leftarrow b_i$, $a_{b_i} \leftarrow b_{i+1}$, $a_{b_{i+1}} \leftarrow b_{i+2}$, and visit $a_1 \ldots a_n$.

97. Use Algorithm X, with $t_k(a_1, \ldots, a_k) = \text{'}a_k \neq k\text{'}$.

98. Using the notation of exercise 47, we have $N_k = \sum \binom{k}{j}(-1)^j(n - j)^{\underline{k-j}}$ by the method of inclusion and exclusion (exercise 1.3.3–26). If $k = O(\log n)$ then $N_{n-k} = (n!\,e^{-1}/k!)(1 + O(\log n)^2/n)$; hence $A/n! \approx (e - 1)/e$ and $B/n! \approx 1$. The number of memory references, under the assumptions of answer 48, is therefore $\approx A + B + 3A + B - N_n + 3A \approx n!\,(9 - \frac{8}{e}) \approx 6.06n!$, about 16.5 per derangement. [See S. G. Akl, *BIT* **20** (1980), 2–7, for a similar method.]

99. Suppose L_n generates $D_n \cup D_{n-1}$, beginning with $(1\ 2\ \ldots\ n)$, then $(2\ 1\ \ldots\ n)$, and ending with $(1\ \ldots\ n{-}1)$; for example, $L_3 = (1\ 2\ 3)$, $(2\ 1\ 3)$, $(1\ 2)$. Then we can generate D_{n+1} as K_{nn}, $\ldots$, K_{n2}, K_{n1}, where $K_{nk} = (1\ 2\ \ldots\ n)^{-k}(n\ n{+}1)L_n(1\ 2\ \ldots\ n)^k$; for example, D_4 is

$$(1\,2\,3\,4),\ (2\,1\,3\,4),\ (1\,2)(3\,4),\ (3\,1\,2\,4),\ (1\,3\,2\,4),\ (3\,1)(2\,4),\ (2\,3\,1\,4),\ (3\,2\,1\,4),\ (2\,3)(1\,4).$$

Notice that K_{nk} begins with the cycle $(k{+}1\ \ldots\ n\ 1\ \ldots\ k\ n{+}1)$ and ends with $(k{+}1\ \ldots\ n\ 1\ \ldots\ k{-}1)(k\ n{+}1)$; so premultiplication by $(k{-}1\ k)$ takes us from K_{nk} to $K_{n(k-1)}$. Also, premultiplication by $(1\ n)$ will return from the last element of D_{n+1} to the first. Premultiplication by $(1\ 2\ n{+}1)$ takes us from the last element of D_{n+1} to $(2\ 1\ 3\ \ldots\ n)$, from which we can return to $(1\ 2\ \ldots\ n)$ by following the cycle for D_n backwards, thereby completing the list L_{n+1} as desired.

100. Use Algorithm X, with $t_k(a_1, \ldots, a_k) = \text{'}p > 0$ or $l[q] \neq k + 1\text{'}$.

Notes: The number of indecomposable permutations is $[z^n]\,\bigl(1 - 1/\sum_{k=0}^{\infty} k!\,z^k\bigr)$; see L. Comtet, *Comptes Rendus Acad. Sci.* **A275** (Paris, 1972), 569–572.

A. D. King [*Discrete Math.* **306** (2006), 508–516] has shown that indecomposable permutations can be generated efficiently by making only a single transposition at each step. In fact, *adjacent* transpositions may well suffice; for example, when $n = 4$ the indecomposable permutations are 3142, 3412, 3421, 3241, 2341, 2431, 4231, 4321, 4312, 4132, 4123, 4213, 2413.

101. Here is a lexicographic involution generator analogous to Algorithm X.

> **Y1.** [Initialize.] Set $a_k \leftarrow k$ and $l_{k-1} \leftarrow k$ for $1 \leq k \leq n$. Then set $l_n \leftarrow 0$, $k \leftarrow 1$.
>
> **Y2.** [Enter level k.] If $k > n$, visit $a_1 \ldots a_n$ and go to Y3. Otherwise set $p \leftarrow l_0$, $u_k \leftarrow p$, $l_0 \leftarrow l_p$, $k \leftarrow k + 1$, and repeat this step. (We have decided to let $a_p = p$.)

Y3. [Decrease k.] Set $k \leftarrow k - 1$, and terminate if $k = 0$. Otherwise set $q \leftarrow u_k$ and $p \leftarrow a_q$. If $p = q$, set $l_0 \leftarrow q$, $q \leftarrow 0$, $r \leftarrow l_p$, and $k \leftarrow k + 1$ (preparing to make $a_p > p$). Otherwise set $l_{u_{k-1}} \leftarrow q$, $r \leftarrow l_q$ (preparing to make $a_p > q$).

Y4. [Increase a_p.] If $r = 0$ go to Y5. Otherwise set $l_q \leftarrow l_r$, $u_{k-1} \leftarrow q$, $u_k \leftarrow r$, $a_p \leftarrow r$, $a_q \leftarrow q$, $a_r \leftarrow p$, $k \leftarrow k + 1$, and go to Y2.

Y5. [Restore a_p.] Set $l_0 \leftarrow p$, $a_p \leftarrow p$, $a_q \leftarrow q$, $k \leftarrow k - 1$, and return to Y3. ▐

Let $t_{n+1} = t_n + n t_{n-1}$, $a_{n+1} = 1 + a_n + n a_{n-1}$, $t_0 = t_1 = 1$, $a_0 = 0$, $a_1 = 1$. (See Eq. 5.1.4–(40).) Step Y2 is performed t_n times with $k > n$ and a_n times with $k \leq n$. Step Y3 is performed a_n times with $p = q$ and $a_n + t_n$ times altogether. Step Y4 is performed $t_n - 1$ times; step Y5, a_n times. The total number of mems for all t_n outputs is therefore approximately $11 a_n + 12 t_n$, where $a_n < 1.25331414 t_n$. (Optimizations are clearly possible if speed is essential.)

102. We construct a list L_n that begins with () and ends with $(n-1\ n)$, starting with $L_3 = ()$, $(1\ 2)$, $(1\ 3)$, $(2\ 3)$. If n is odd, L_{n+1} is L_n, K_{n1}^R, K_{n2}, $\ldots$, K_{nn}^R, where $K_{nk} = (k\ \ldots\ n)^- L_{n-1}(k\ \ldots n)(k\ n+1)$. For example,

$$L_4 \;=\; (),\, (1\ 2),\, (1\ 3),\, (2\ 3),\, (2\ 3)(1\ 4),\, (1\ 4),\, (2\ 4),\, (1\ 3)(2\ 4),\, (1\ 2)(3\ 4),\, (3\ 4).$$

If n is even, L_{n+1} is L_n, $K_{n(n-1)}$, $K_{n(n-2)}^R$, $\ldots$, K_{n1}, $(1\ n-2)L_{n-1}^R(1\ n-2)(n\ n+1)$.

For further developments, see the article by Walsh cited in answer 94.

103. The following elegant solution by Carla Savage needs only $n - 2$ different operations ρ_j, for $1 < j < n$, where ρ_j replaces $a_{j-1} a_j a_{j+1}$ by $a_{j+1} a_{j-1} a_j$ when j is even, $a_j a_{j+1} a_{j-1}$ when j is odd. We may assume that $n \geq 4$; let $A_4 = (\rho_3 \rho_2 \rho_2 \rho_3)^3$. In general A_n will begin and end with ρ_{n-1}, and it will contain $2n - 2$ occurrences of ρ_{n-1} altogether. To get A_{n+1}, replace the kth ρ_{n-1} of A_n by $\rho_n A_n' \rho_n$, where $k = 1, 2, 4, \ldots, 2n - 2$ if n is even and $k = 1, 3, \ldots, 2n - 3, 2n - 2$ if n is odd, and where A_n' is A_n with its first or last element deleted. Then, if we begin with $a_1 \ldots a_n = 1 \ldots n$, the operations ρ_{n-1} of A_n will cause position a_n to run through the successive values $n \to p_1 \to n \to p_2 \to \cdots \to p_{n-1} \to n$, where $p_1 \ldots p_{n-1} = (n-1 - [n\,\text{even}]) \ldots 4213 \ldots (n-1 - [n\,\text{odd}])$; the final permutation will again be $1 \ldots n$.

104. (a) A well-balanced permutation has $\sum_{k=1}^{n} k a_k = n(n+1)^2/4$, an integer.

(b) Replace k by a_k when summing over k.

(c) A fairly fast way to count, when n is not too large, can be based on the streamlined plain-change algorithm of exercise 16, because the quantity $\sum k a_k$ changes in a simple way with each adjacent interchange, and because $n - 1$ of every n steps are "hunts" that can be done rapidly. We can save half the work by considering only permutations in which 1 precedes 2. The values for $1 \leq n \leq 15$ are 0, 0, 0, 2, 6, 0, 184, 936, 6688, 0, 420480, 4298664, 44405142, 0, 6732621476.

105. (a) For each permutation $a_1 \ldots a_n$, insert $\prec$ between a_j and a_{j+1} if $a_j > a_{j+1}$; insert either $\equiv$ or $\prec$ between them if $a_j < a_{j+1}$. (A permutation with k "ascents" therefore yields 2^k weak orders. Weak orders are sometimes called "preferential arrangements"; exercise 5.3.1–4 shows that there are approximately $n!/(2(\ln 2)^{n+1})$ of them. A Gray code for weak orders, in which each step changes $\prec \leftrightarrow \equiv$ and/or $a_j \leftrightarrow a_{j+1}$, can be obtained by combining Algorithm P with Gray binary code at the ascents.

(b) Start with $a_1 \ldots a_n a_{n+1} = 0 \ldots 00$ and $a_0 = -1$. Perform Algorithm L until it stops with $j = 0$. Find k such that $a_1 > \cdots > a_k = a_{k+1}$, and terminate if $k = n$. Otherwise set $a_l \leftarrow a_{k+1} + 1$ for $1 \leq l \leq k$ and go to step L4. [See M. Mor and A. S. Fraenkel, *Discrete Math.* **48** (1984), 101–112. Weak ordering sequences are characterized by the property that, if k appears and $k > 0$, then $k - 1$ also appears.]

106. All weak ordering sequences can be obtained by a sequence of elementary operations $a_i \leftrightarrow a_j$ or $a_i \leftarrow a_j$. (Perhaps one could actually restrict the transformations further, allowing only $a_j \leftrightarrow a_{j+1}$ or $a_j \leftarrow a_{j+1}$ for $1 \le j < n$.)

107. Every step increases the quantity $\sum_{k=1}^{n} 2^k [a_k = k]$, as noted by H. S. Wilf, so the game must terminate. At least three approaches to the solution are plausible: one bad, one good, and one better.

The bad one is to play the game on all 13! shuffles and to record the longest. This method does produce the correct answer; but 13! is 6,227,020,800, and the average game lasts ≈ 8.728 steps.

The good one [A. Pepperdine, *Math. Gazette* **73** (1989), 131–133] is to play backwards, starting with the final position $1*\ldots*$ where $*$ denotes a card that is face down; we will turn a card up only when its value becomes relevant. To move backward from a given position $a_1 \ldots a_n$, consider all $k > 1$ such that either $a_k = k$ or $a_k = *$ and k has not yet turned up. Thus the next-to-last positions are $21*\ldots*$, $3*1*\ldots*$, $\ldots$, $n*\ldots*1$. Some positions (like $6**213$ for $n = 6$) have no predecessors, even though we haven't turned all the cards up. It is easy to explore the tree of potential backwards games systematically, and one can in fact show that the number of nodes with t $*$'s is exactly $(n-1)!/t!$. Hence the total number of nodes considered is exactly $\lfloor (n-1)!\, e \rfloor$. When $n = 13$ this is 1,302,061,345.

The better one is to play forwards, starting with initial position $*\ldots*$ and turning over the top card when it is face down, running through all $(n-1)!$ permutations of $\{2, \ldots, n\}$ as cards are turned. If the bottom $n - m$ cards are known to be equal to $(m+1)(m+2)\ldots n$, in that order, at most $f(m)$ further moves are possible; thus we need not pursue a line of play any further if it cannot last long enough to be interesting. A permutation generator like Algorithm X allows us to share the computation for all permutations with the same prefix and to reject unimportant prefixes. The card in position j need not take the value j when it is turned. When $n = 13$ this method needs to consider only respectively $(1, 11, 940, 6960, 44745, 245083, 1118216, 4112676, 11798207, 26541611, 44380227, 37417359)$ branches at levels $(1, 2, \ldots, 12)$ and to make a total of only 482,663,902 forward moves. Although it repeats some lines of play, the early cutoffs of unprofitable branches make it run more than 11 times faster than the backward method when $n = 13$.

The unique way to attain length 80 is to start with 2 9 4 5 11 12 10 1 8 13 3 6 7.

108. This result holds for any game in which

$$a_1 \ldots a_n \to a_k a_{p(k,2)} \cdots a_{p(k,k-1)} a_1 a_{k+1} \ldots a_n$$

when $a_1 = k$, where $p(k,2)\ldots p(k,k-1)$ is an arbitrary permutation of $\{2, \ldots, k-1\}$. Suppose a_1 takes on exactly m distinct values $d(1) < \cdots < d(m)$ during a play of the game; we will prove that at most F_{m+1} permutations occur, including the initial shuffle. This assertion is obvious when $m = 1$.

Let $d(j)$ be the initial value of $a_{d(m)}$, where $j < m$, and suppose $a_{d(m)}$ changes on step r. If $d(j) = 1$, the number of permutations is $r + 1 \le F_m + 1 \le F_{m+1}$. Otherwise $r \le F_{m-1}$, and at most F_m further permutations follow step r. [*SIAM Review* **19** (1977), 739–741.]

The values of $f(n)$ for $1 \le n \le 16$ are $(0, 1, 2, 4, 7, 10, 16, 22, 30, 38, 51, 65, 80, 101, 113, 139)$, and they are attainable in respectively $(1, 1, 2, 2, 1, 5, 2, 1, 1, 1, 1, 1,$

1, 4, 6, 1) ways. The unique longest-winded permutation for $n = 16$ is

$$9\ 12\ 6\ 7\ 2\ 14\ 8\ 1\ 11\ 13\ 5\ 4\ 15\ 16\ 10\ 3.$$

109. An ingenious construction by I. H. Sudborough and L. Morales [*Theoretical Comp. Sci.* **411** (2010), 3965–3970] proves that $f(n) \geq \frac{19}{128}n^2 + O(1)$.

110. For $0 \leq j \leq 9$ construct the bit vectors $A_j = [a_j \in S_1] \ldots [a_j \in S_m]$ and $B_j = [j \in S_1] \ldots [j \in S_m]$. Then the number of j such that $A_j = v$ must equal the number of k such that $B_k = v$, for all bit vectors v. And if so, the values $\{a_j \mid A_j = v\}$ should be assigned to permutations of $\{k \mid B_k = v\}$ in all possible ways.

For example, the bit vectors in the given problem are

$$(A_0, \ldots, A_9) = (9, 6, 8, \mathsf{b}, 5, 4, 0, \mathsf{a}, 2, 0), \qquad (B_0, \ldots, B_9) = (5, 0, 8, 6, 2, \mathsf{a}, 4, \mathsf{b}, 9, 0),$$

in hexadecimal notation; hence $a_0 \ldots a_9 = 8327061549$ or 8327069541.

In a larger problem we would keep the bit vectors in a hash table. It would be better to give the answer in terms of equivalence classes, not permutations; indeed, this problem has comparatively little to do with permutations.

111. In the directed graph with $n!/2$ vertices $a_1 \ldots a_{n-2}$ and $n!$ arcs $a_1 \ldots a_{n-2} \rightarrow a_2 \ldots a_{n-1}$ (one for each permutation $a_1 \ldots a_n$), each vertex has in-degree 2 and out-degree 2. Furthermore, from paths like $a_1 \ldots a_{n-2} \rightarrow a_2 \ldots a_{n-1} \rightarrow a_3 \ldots a_n \rightarrow a_4 \ldots a_n a_2 \rightarrow a_5 \ldots a_n a_2 a_1 \rightarrow \cdots \rightarrow a_2 a_1 a_3 \ldots a_{n-2}$, we can see that any vertex is reachable from any other. Therefore an Eulerian trail exists by Theorem 2.3.4.2G, and such a trail clearly is equivalent to a universal cycle of permutations. The lexicographically smallest example when $n = 4$ is $(123124132134214324314234)$.

[G. Hurlbert and G. Isaak, in *Discrete Math.* **149** (1996), 123–129, have suggested another appealing approach: Let's say that a *modular universal cycle of permutations* is a cycle of $n!$ digits $\{0, \ldots, n\}$ with the property that each permutation $a_1 \ldots a_n$ of $\{1, \ldots, n\}$ arises from consecutive digits $u_1 \ldots u_n$ by letting $a_j = (u_j - c) \bmod (n+1)$, where c is the "missing" digit in $\{u_1, \ldots, u_n\}$. For example, the modular universal cycle (012032) is essentially unique for $n = 3$; and the lexicographically smallest for $n = 4$ is $(012301420132014321430243)$. If vertices $a_1 \ldots a_{n-2}$ and $a'_1 \ldots a'_{n-2}$ in the digraph of the previous paragraph are considered equivalent when $a_1 - a'_1 \equiv \cdots \equiv a_{n-2} - a'_{n-2}$ (modulo n), we get a digraph of $(n-1)!/2$ vertices whose Eulerian trails correspond to the modular universal cycles of permutations for $\{1, \ldots, n-1\}$.]

112. (a) If the cycle is $a_1 a_2 \ldots$, use σ at step j if the subsequence $a_j a_{j+1} \ldots a_{j+n-1}$ is a permutation; otherwise use ρ.

(b) This statement follows immediately from exercise 72.

(c) Let $\Omega_2 = \sigma^2$, and obtain Ω_{n+1} from Ω_n by substituting $\sigma \mapsto \sigma^2 \rho^{n-1}$ and $\rho \mapsto \sigma^2 \rho^{n-2} \sigma$. For example, $\Omega_3 = (\sigma^2 \rho)^2$ and $\Omega_4 = ((\sigma^2 \rho^2)^2 \sigma^2 \rho \sigma)^2$. Generate permutations by starting with $n \ldots 21$ and applying the successive elements of Ω_n; for example, the sequence when $n = 4$ is

$$4321, 3214, 2143, 1423, 4213, 2134, 1342, 3412, 4132, 1324, 3241, 2431,$$

$$4312, 3124, 1243, 2413, 4123, 1234, 2341, 3421, 4231, 2314, 3142, 1432,$$

and the corresponding universal cycle is $(432142134132431241234231)$. Notice that n moves cyclically in this sequence of permutations; and the permutations that begin with n correspond to the sequence obtained from Ω_{n-1}.

[See F. Ruskey and A. Williams, *ACM Trans. on Algorithms* **6** (2010), 45:1–45:12. Similar methods are said to be known to bell-ringers. Universal cycles can also be constructed explicitly for permutations of an arbitrary *multiset*, with a method analogous to 7.2.1.1–(62); see A. Williams, Ph.D. thesis (Univ. of Victoria, 2009).]

113. By exercise 2.3.4.2–22 it suffices to count the oriented trees rooted at $12\ldots(n-2)$, in the digraph of the preceding answer; and those trees can be counted by exercise 2.3.4.2–19. For $n \le 6$ the numbers U_n turn out to be tantalizingly simple: $U_2 = 1$, $U_3 = 3$, $U_4 = 2^7 \cdot 3$, $U_5 = 2^{33} \cdot 3^8 \cdot 5^3$, $U_6 = 2^{190} \cdot 3^{49} \cdot 5^{33}$. (Here we consider (121323) to be the same cycle as (213231), but different from (131232).)

Mark Cooke has discovered the following instructive way to compute these values efficiently: Consider the $n! \times n!$ matrix $M = 2I - R - S$, where $R_{\pi\pi'} = [\pi' = \pi\rho]$ and $S_{\pi\pi'} = [\pi' = \pi\sigma]$. There is a matrix H such that H^-RH and H^-SH each have block diagonal form consisting of k_λ copies of $k_\lambda \times k_\lambda$ matrices R_λ and S_λ, for each partition λ of n, where k_λ is $n!$ divided by the product of the hook lengths of shape λ (Theorem 5.1.4H), and where R_λ and S_λ are matrix representations of ρ and σ based on Young tableaux. [A proof can be found in Bruce Sagan, *The Symmetric Group* (Pacific Grove, Calif.: Wadsworth & Brooks/Cole, 1991).] For example, when $n = 3$ we have

$$R = \begin{pmatrix} 0 & 0 & 0 & 1 & 0 & 0 \\ 0 & 0 & 0 & 0 & 0 & 1 \\ 0 & 0 & 0 & 0 & 1 & 0 \\ 1 & 0 & 0 & 0 & 0 & 0 \\ 0 & 0 & 1 & 0 & 0 & 0 \\ 0 & 1 & 0 & 0 & 0 & 0 \end{pmatrix}, \quad S = \begin{pmatrix} 0 & 1 & 0 & 0 & 0 & 0 \\ 0 & 0 & 1 & 0 & 0 & 0 \\ 1 & 0 & 0 & 0 & 0 & 0 \\ 0 & 0 & 0 & 0 & 1 & 0 \\ 0 & 0 & 0 & 0 & 0 & 1 \\ 0 & 0 & 0 & 1 & 0 & 0 \end{pmatrix}, \quad H = \begin{pmatrix} 1 & 1 & 1 & -1 & 1 & 0 \\ 1 & 1 & -1 & 0 & 0 & -1 \\ 1 & 1 & 0 & 1 & -1 & 1 \\ 1 & -1 & -1 & 1 & 0 & 1 \\ 1 & -1 & 1 & 0 & 1 & -1 \\ 1 & -1 & 0 & -1 & -1 & 0 \end{pmatrix},$$

$$H^-RH = \begin{pmatrix} 1 & 0 & 0 & 0 & 0 & 0 \\ 0 & -1 & 0 & 0 & 0 & 0 \\ 0 & 0 & 0 & 1 & 0 & 0 \\ 0 & 0 & 1 & 0 & 0 & 0 \\ 0 & 0 & 0 & 0 & 0 & 1 \\ 0 & 0 & 0 & 0 & 1 & 0 \end{pmatrix}, \quad H^-SH = \begin{pmatrix} 1 & 0 & 0 & 0 & 0 & 0 \\ 0 & 1 & 0 & 0 & 0 & 0 \\ 0 & 0 & 0 & -1 & 0 & 0 \\ 0 & 0 & 1 & -1 & 0 & 0 \\ 0 & 0 & 0 & 0 & 0 & -1 \\ 0 & 0 & 0 & 0 & 1 & -1 \end{pmatrix}$$

when rows and columns are indexed by the respective permutations 1, σ, σ^2, ρ, $\rho\sigma$, $\rho\sigma^2$; here $k_3 = k_{111} = 1$ and $k_{21} = 2$. Therefore the eigenvalues of M are the union, over λ, of k_λ-fold repeated eigenvalues of the $k_\lambda \times k_\lambda$ matrices $2I - R_\lambda - S_\lambda$. In the example, the eigenvalues of (0), (2), and $\left(\begin{smallmatrix} 2 & 0 \\ -2 & 3 \end{smallmatrix}\right)$ twice are $\{0\}$, $\{2\}$, and $\{2, 3\}$ twice.

The eigenvalues of M are directly related to those of the matrix A in exercise 2.3.4.2–19. Indeed, each eigenvector of A yields an eigenvector of M, if we equate the components for permutations π and $\pi\rho\sigma^-$, because rows π and $\pi\rho\sigma^-$ of $R + S$ are equal. For example,

$$A = \begin{pmatrix} 2 & -1 & -1 \\ -1 & 2 & -1 \\ -1 & -1 & 2 \end{pmatrix} \text{ has eigenvectors } \begin{pmatrix} 1 \\ 1 \\ 1 \end{pmatrix}, \begin{pmatrix} 1 \\ -1 \\ 0 \end{pmatrix}, \begin{pmatrix} 1 \\ 0 \\ -1 \end{pmatrix} \text{ for eigenvalues } 0, 3, 3,$$

yielding the eigenvectors $(1, 1, 1, 1, 1, 1)^T$, $(1, -1, 0, 0, -1, 1)^T$, $(1, 0, -1, -1, 0, 1)^T$ of M for the same eigenvalues. And M has $n!/2$ additional eigenvectors, with all components zero except those indexed by π and $\pi\sigma^-\rho$ for some π, because only rows $\pi\rho^-$ and $\pi\sigma^-$ of $R+S$ have nonzero entries in columns π and $\pi\sigma^-\rho$; such vectors yield $n!/2$ additional eigenvalues, all equal to 2.

Therefore U_n, which is $2/n!$ times the product of the nonzero eigenvalues of A, is $2^{1-n!/2}/n!$ times the product of the nonzero eigenvalues of M.

Unfortunately the small-prime-factor phenomenon does not continue; U_7 equals $2^{1217} 3^{123} 5^{119} 7^5 11^{28} 43^{35} 73^{20} 79^{21} 109^{35}$, and U_9 is divisible by 59229013196333^{168}.

SECTION 7.2.1.3

1. Given a multiset, form the sequence $e_t \ldots e_2 e_1$ from right to left by listing the distinct elements first, then those that appear twice, then those that appear thrice, etc. Let us set $e_{-j} \leftarrow s - j$ for $0 \le j \le s = n - t$, so that every element e_j for $1 \le j \le t$ is equal to some element to its right in the sequence $e_t \ldots e_1 e_0 \ldots e_{-s}$. If the first such element is $e_{c_j - s}$, we obtain a solution to (3). Conversely, every solution to (3) yields a unique multiset $\{e_1, \ldots, e_t\}$, because $c_j < s + j$ for $1 \le j \le t$.

[A similar correspondence was proposed by E. Catalan: If $0 \le e_1 \le \cdots \le e_t \le s$, let

$$\{c_1, \ldots, c_t\} = \{e_1, \ldots, e_t\} \cup \{s + j \mid 1 \le j < t \text{ and } e_j = e_{j+1}\}.$$

See *Mémoires de la Soc. roy. des Sciences de Liège* (2) **12** (1885), *Mélanges Math.*, 3.]

2. Start at the bottom left corner; then go up for each 0, go right for each 1. The result is . Conversely, we can easily "read off" the representations a_i, b_i, c_i, d_i, p_i, or q_i of (2)–(11) from any given path from $(0, 0)$ to (s, t).

3. In this algorithm, variable r is the least positive index such that $q_r > 0$.

N1. [Initialize.] Set $q_j \leftarrow 0$ for $1 \le j \le t$, and $q_0 \leftarrow s$. (We assume that $st > 0$.)

N2. [Visit.] Visit the composition $q_t \ldots q_0$. Go to N4 if $q_0 = 0$.

N3. [Easy case.] Set $q_0 \leftarrow q_0 - 1$, $r \leftarrow 1$, and go to N5.

N4. [Tricky case.] Terminate if $r = t$. Otherwise set $q_0 \leftarrow q_r - 1$, $q_r \leftarrow 0$, $r \leftarrow r + 1$.

N5. [Increase q_r.] Set $q_r \leftarrow q_r + 1$ and return to N2. ∎

[See *CACM* **11** (1968), 430; **12** (1969), 187. The task of generating such compositions in *decreasing* lexicographic order is more difficult.]

4. We can reverse the roles of 0 and 1 in (14), so that $0^{q_t} 10^{q_t - 1} 1 \ldots 10^{q_1} 10^{q_0} = 1^{r_s} 01^{r_s - 1} 0 \ldots 01^{r_1} 01^{r_0}$. This gives $0^1 10^0 10^2 10^2 10^4 10^0 10^0 10^0 10^0 10^0 10^1 10^0 10^1 10^0 = 1^0 01^2 01^0 01^1 01^0 01^1 01^0 01^0 01^0 01^6 01^2 01^1$. Lexicographic order of $a_{n-1} \ldots a_1 a_0$ corresponds to lexicographic order of $r_s \ldots r_1 r_0$.

Incidentally, there's also a multiset connection: $\{d_t, \ldots, d_1\} = \{r_s \cdot s, \ldots, r_0 \cdot 0\}$. For example, $\{10, 10, 8, 6, 2, 2, 2, 2, 2, 2, 1, 1, 0\} = \{0 \cdot 11, 2 \cdot 10, 0 \cdot 9, 1 \cdot 8, 0 \cdot 7, 1 \cdot 6, 0 \cdot 5, 0 \cdot 4, 0 \cdot 3, 6 \cdot 2, 2 \cdot 1, 1 \cdot 0\}$.

5. (a) Set $x_j = c_j - \lfloor (j-1)/2 \rfloor$ in each t-combination of $n + \lfloor t/2 \rfloor$. (b) Set $x_j = c_j + j + 1$ in each t-combination of $n - t - 2$.

(A similar approach finds all solutions $(x_t, \ldots, x_1)$ to the inequalities $x_{j+1} \ge x_j + \delta_j$ for $0 \le j \le t$, given the values of x_{t+1}, $(\delta_t, \ldots, \delta_0)$, and x_0.)

6. Assume that $t > 0$. We get to T3 when $c_1 > 0$; to T5 when $c_2 = c_1 + 1 > 1$; to T4 for $2 \le j \le t+1$ when $c_j = c_1 + j - 1 \ge j$. So the counts are: T1, 1; T2, $\binom{n}{t}$; T3, $\binom{n-1}{t}$; T4, $\binom{n-2}{t-1} + \binom{n-3}{t-2} + \cdots + \binom{n-t-1}{0} = \binom{n-1}{t-1}$; T5, $\binom{n-2}{t-1}$; T6, $\binom{n-1}{t-1} + \binom{n-2}{t-1} - 1$.

7. A procedure slightly simpler than Algorithm T suffices: Assume that $s < n$.

S1. [Initialize.] Set $b_j \leftarrow j + n - s - 1$ for $1 \le j \le s$; then set $j \leftarrow 1$.

S2. [Visit.] Visit the combination $b_s \ldots b_2 b_1$. Terminate if $j > s$.

S3. [Decrease b_j.] Set $b_j \leftarrow b_j - 1$. If $b_j < j$, set $j \leftarrow j + 1$ and return to S2.

S4. [Reset $b_{j-1} \ldots b_1$.] While $j > 1$, set $b_{j-1} \leftarrow b_j - 1$ and $j \leftarrow j - 1$. Go to S2. ∎

(See S. Dvořák, *Comp. J.* **33** (1990), 188. Notice that if $x_k = n - b_k$ for $1 \le k \le s$, this algorithm runs through all combinations $x_s \ldots x_2 x_1$ of $\{1, 2, \ldots, n\}$ with $1 \le x_s < \cdots < x_2 < x_1 \le n$, in *increasing* lexicographic order.)

8. A1. [Initialize.] Set $a_n \ldots a_0 \leftarrow 0^{s+1} 1^t$, $q \leftarrow t$, $r \leftarrow 0$. (We assume that $0 < t < n$.)

   A2. [Visit.] Visit the combination $a_{n-1} \ldots a_1 a_0$. Go to A4 if $q = 0$.

   A3. [Replace $\ldots 01^q$ by $\ldots 101^{q-1}$.] Set $a_q \leftarrow 1$, $a_{q-1} \leftarrow 0$, $q \leftarrow q - 1$; then if $q = 0$, set $r \leftarrow 1$. Return to A2.

   A4. [Shift block of 1s.] Set $a_r \leftarrow 0$ and $r \leftarrow r + 1$. Then if $a_r = 1$, set $a_q \leftarrow 1$, $q \leftarrow q + 1$, and repeat step A4.

   A5. [Carry to left.] Terminate if $r = n$; otherwise set $a_r \leftarrow 1$.

   A6. [Odd?] If $q > 0$, set $r \leftarrow 0$. Return to A2. ∎

In step A2, q and r point respectively to the rightmost 0 and 1 in $a_{n-1} \ldots a_0$. Steps A1, $\ldots$, A6 are executed with frequency 1, $\binom{n}{t}$, $\binom{n-1}{t-1}$, $\binom{n}{t} - 1$, $\binom{n-1}{t}$, $\binom{n-1}{t} - 1$.

9. (a) The first $\binom{n-1}{t}$ strings begin with 0 and have $2A_{(s-1)t}$ bit changes; the other $\binom{n-1}{t-1}$ begin with 1 and have $2A_{s(t-1)}$. And $\nu(01^t 0^{s-1} \oplus 10^s 1^{t-1}) = 2 \min(s, t)$.

(b) Solution 1 (direct): Let $B_{st} = A_{st} + \min(s, t) + 1$. Then

$$B_{st} = B_{(s-1)t} + B_{s(t-1)} + [s = t] \quad \text{when } st > 0; \qquad B_{st} = 1 \quad \text{when } st = 0.$$

Consequently $B_{st} = \sum_{k=0}^{\min(s,t)} \binom{s+t-2k}{s-k}$. If $s \le t$ this is $\le \sum_{k=0}^{s} \binom{s+t-k}{s-k} = \binom{s+t+1}{s} = \binom{s+t}{s} \frac{s+t+1}{t+1} < 2\binom{s+t}{t}$.

Solution 2 (indirect): The algorithm in answer 8 makes $2(x + y)$ bit changes when steps (A3, A4) are executed (x, y) times. Thus $A_{st} \le \binom{n-1}{t-1} + \binom{n}{t} - 1 < 2\binom{n}{t}$.

[The comment in answer 7.2.1.1–3 therefore applies to combinations as well.]

10. Each scenario corresponds to a $(4, 4)$-combination $b_4 b_3 b_2 b_1$ or $c_4 c_3 c_2 c_1$ in which A wins games $\{8 - b_4, 8 - b_3, 8 - b_2, 8 - b_1\}$ and N wins games $\{8 - c_4, 8 - c_3, 8 - c_2, 8 - c_1\}$, because we can assume that the losing team wins the remaining games in a series of 8. (Equivalently, we can generate all permutations of $\{A, A, A, A, N, N, N, N\}$ and omit the trailing run of As or Ns.) The American League wins if and only if $b_1 \ne 0$, if and only if $c_1 = 0$. The formula $\binom{c_4}{4} + \binom{c_3}{3} + \binom{c_2}{2} + \binom{c_1}{1}$ assigns a unique integer between 0 and 69 to each scenario.

For example, ANANAA $\iff a_7 \ldots a_1 a_0 = 01010011 \iff b_4 b_3 b_2 b_1 = 7532 \iff c_4 c_3 c_2 c_1 = 6410$, and this is the scenario of rank $\binom{6}{4} + \binom{4}{3} + \binom{1}{2} + \binom{0}{1} = 19$ in lexicographic order. (The term $\binom{c_j}{j}$ will be zero if and only if it corresponds to a trailing N.)

11. AAAA (9 times), NNNN (8), and ANAAA (7) were most common. Exactly 27 of the 70 failed to occur, including all four beginning with NNNA. (We disregard the games that were tied because of darkness, in 1907, 1912, and 1922. The case ANNAAAA should perhaps be excluded too, because it occurred only in 1920 as part of ANNAAAAA in a best-of-nine series. The scenario NNAAANN occurred for the first time in 2001.)

12. (a) Let V_j be the subspace $\{a_{n-1} \ldots a_0 \in V \mid a_k = 0 \text{ for } 0 \le k < j\}$, so that $\{0 \ldots 0\} = V_n \subseteq V_{n-1} \subseteq \cdots \subseteq V_0 = V$. Then $\{c_1, \ldots, c_t\} = \{c \mid V_c \ne V_{c+1}\}$, and α_k is the unique element $a_{n-1} \ldots a_0$ of V with $a_{c_j} = [j = k]$ for $1 \le j \le t$.

Incidentally, the $t \times n$ matrix corresponding to a canonical basis is said to be in *reduced row-echelon form*. It can be found by a standard "triangulation" algorithm (see exercise 4.6.1–19 and Algorithm 4.6.2N).

(b) The 2-nomial coefficient $\binom{n}{t}_2 = 2^t \binom{n-1}{t}_2 + \binom{n-1}{t-1}_2$ of exercise 1.2.6–58 has the right properties, because $2^t \binom{n-1}{t}_2$ binary vector spaces have $c_t < n-1$ and $\binom{n-1}{t-1}_2$ have $c_t = n - 1$. [In general the number of canonical bases with r asterisks is the number of partitions of r into at most t parts, with no part exceeding $n - t$, and this is $[z^r] \binom{n}{t}_z$ by Eq. 7.2.1.4–(51). See D. E. Knuth, *J. Combinatorial Theory* **A10** (1971), 178–180.]

(c) The following algorithm assumes that $n > t > 0$ and that $a_{(t+1)j} = 0$ for $t \leq j \leq n$.

V1. [Initialize.] Set $a_{kj} \leftarrow [j = k - 1]$ for $1 \leq k \leq t$ and $0 \leq j < n$. Also set $q \leftarrow t$, $r \leftarrow 0$.

V2. [Visit.] (At this point we have $a_{k(k-1)} = 1$ for $1 \leq k \leq q$, $a_{(q+1)q} = 0$, and $a_{1r} = 1$.) Visit the canonical basis $(a_{1(n-1)} \ldots a_{11}a_{10}, \ldots, a_{t(n-1)} \ldots a_{t1}a_{t0})$. Go to V4 if $q > 0$.

V3. [Find block of 1s.] Set $q \leftarrow 1, 2, \ldots$, until $a_{(q+1)(q+r)} = 0$. Terminate if $q + r = n$.

V4. [Add 1 to column $q + r$.] Set $k \leftarrow 1$. While $a_{k(q+r)} = 1$, set $a_{k(q+r)} \leftarrow 0$ and $k \leftarrow k + 1$. Then if $k \leq q$, set $a_{k(q+r)} \leftarrow 1$; otherwise set $a_{q(q+r)} \leftarrow 1$, $a_{q(q+r-1)} \leftarrow 0$, $q \leftarrow q - 1$.

V5. [Shift block right.] If $q = 0$, set $r \leftarrow r+1$. Otherwise, if $r > 0$, set $a_{k(k-1)} \leftarrow 1$ and $a_{k(r+k-1)} \leftarrow 0$ for $1 \leq k \leq q$, then set $r \leftarrow 0$. Go to V2. ∎

Step V2 finds $q > 0$ with probability $1 - (2^{n-t} - 1)/(2^n - 1) \approx 1 - 2^{-t}$, so we could save time by treating this case separately.

(d) Since $999999 = 4\binom{8}{4}_2 + 16\binom{7}{4}_2 + 5\binom{6}{3}_2 + 5\binom{5}{3}_2 + 8\binom{4}{3}_2 + 0\binom{3}{2}_2 + 4\binom{2}{2}_2 + 1\binom{1}{1}_2 + 2\binom{0}{1}_2$, the millionth output has binary columns 4, 16/2, 5, 5, 8/2, 0, 4/2, 1, 2/2, namely

$$\alpha_1 = 0\,0\,1\,1\,0\,0\,0\,1\,1,$$
$$\alpha_2 = 0\,0\,0\,0\,0\,0\,1\,0\,0,$$
$$\alpha_3 = 1\,0\,1\,1\,1\,0\,0\,0\,0,$$
$$\alpha_4 = 0\,1\,0\,0\,0\,0\,0\,0\,0.$$

[*Reference:* E. Calabi and H. S. Wilf, *J. Combinatorial Theory* **A22** (1977), 107–109.]

13. Let $n = s + t$. There are $\binom{s-1}{\lceil(r-1)/2\rceil}\binom{t-1}{\lfloor(r-1)/2\rfloor}$ configurations beginning with 0 and $\binom{s-1}{\lfloor(r-1)/2\rfloor}\binom{t-1}{\lceil(r-1)/2\rceil}$ beginning with 1, because an Ising configuration that begins with 0 corresponds to a composition of s 0s into $\lceil(r+1)/2\rceil$ parts and a composition of t 1s into $\lfloor(r+1)/2\rfloor$ parts. We can generate all such pairs of compositions and weave them into configurations. [See E. Ising, *Zeitschrift für Physik* **31** (1925), 253–258; J. M. S. Simões Pereira, *CACM* **12** (1969), 562.]

14. Start with $l[j] \leftarrow j - 1$ and $r[j - 1] \leftarrow j$ for $1 \leq j \leq n$; $l[0] \leftarrow n$, $r[n] \leftarrow 0$. To get the next combination, assuming that $t > 0$, set $p \leftarrow s$ if $l[0] > s$, otherwise $p \leftarrow r[n] - 1$. Terminate if $p \leq 0$; otherwise set $q \leftarrow r[p]$, $l[q] \leftarrow l[p]$, and $r[l[p]] \leftarrow q$. Then if $r[q] > s$ and $p < s$, set $r[p] \leftarrow r[n]$, $l[r[n]] \leftarrow p$, $r[s] \leftarrow r[q]$, $l[r[q]] \leftarrow s$, $r[n] \leftarrow 0$, $l[0] \leftarrow n$; otherwise set $r[p] \leftarrow r[q]$, $l[r[q]] \leftarrow p$. Finally set $r[q] \leftarrow p$ and $l[p] \leftarrow q$.

[See Korsh and Lipschutz, *J. Algorithms* **25** (1997), 321–335, where the idea is extended to a loopless algorithm for multiset permutations. *Caution:* This exercise, like exercise 7.2.1.1–16, is more academic than practical, because the routine that visits the linked list might need a loop that nullifies any advantage of loopless generation.]

15. (The stated fact is true because lexicographic order of $c_t \ldots c_1$ corresponds to lexicographic order of $a_{n-1} \ldots a_0$, which is reverse lexicographic order of the complementary sequence $1 \ldots 1 \oplus a_{n-1} \ldots a_0$.) By Theorem L, the combination $c_t \ldots c_1$ is visited *before* exactly $\binom{b_s}{s} + \cdots + \binom{b_2}{2} + \binom{b_1}{1}$ others have been visited, and we must have

$$\binom{b_s}{s} + \cdots + \binom{b_1}{1} + \binom{c_t}{t} + \cdots + \binom{c_1}{1} = \binom{s+t}{t} - 1.$$

This general identity can be written

$$\sum_{j=0}^{n-1} x_j \binom{j}{x_0 + \cdots + x_j} + \sum_{j=0}^{n-1} \bar{x}_j \binom{j}{\bar{x}_0 + \cdots + \bar{x}_j} = \binom{n}{x_0 + \cdots + x_{n-1}} - 1$$

when each x_j is 0 or 1, and $\bar{x}_j = 1 - x_j$; it follows also from the equation

$$x_n \binom{n}{x_0 + \cdots + x_n} + \bar{x}_n \binom{n}{\bar{x}_0 + \cdots + \bar{x}_n} = \binom{n+1}{x_0 + \cdots + x_n} - \binom{n}{x_0 + \cdots + x_{n-1}}.$$

16. Since $999999 = \binom{1414}{2} + \binom{1008}{1} = \binom{182}{3} + \binom{153}{2} + \binom{111}{1} = \binom{71}{4} + \binom{56}{3} + \binom{36}{2} + \binom{14}{1} = \binom{43}{5} + \binom{32}{4} + \binom{21}{3} + \binom{15}{2} + \binom{6}{1}$, the answers are (a) 1414 1008; (b) 182 153 111; (c) 71 56 36 14; (d) 43 32 21 15 6; (e) 1000000 999999 ... 2 0.

17. By Theorem L, n_t is the largest integer such that $N \geq \binom{n_t}{t}$; the remaining terms are the degree-$(t-1)$ representation of $N - \binom{n_t}{t}$.

A simple sequential method for $t > 1$ starts with $x = 1$, $c = t$, and sets $c \leftarrow c + 1$, $x \leftarrow xc/(c-t)$ zero or more times until $x > N$; then we complete the first phase by setting $x \leftarrow x(c-t)/c$, $c \leftarrow c - 1$, at which point we have $x = \binom{c}{t} \leq N < \binom{c+1}{t}$. Set $n_t \leftarrow c$, $N \leftarrow N - x$; terminate with $n_1 \leftarrow N$ if $t = 2$; otherwise set $x \leftarrow xt/c$, $t \leftarrow t - 1$, $c \leftarrow c - 1$; while $x > N$ set $x \leftarrow x(c-t)/c$, $c \leftarrow c - 1$; repeat. This method requires $O(n)$ arithmetic operations if $N < \binom{n}{t}$, so it is suitable unless t is small and N is large.

When $t = 2$, exercise 1.2.4–41 tells us that $n_2 = \lfloor \sqrt{2N+2} + \frac{1}{2} \rfloor$. In general, n_t is $\lfloor x \rfloor$ where x is the largest root of $x^{\underline{t}} = t! \, N$; this root can be approximated by reverting the series $y = (x^{\underline{t}})^{1/t} = x - \frac{1}{2}(t-1) + \frac{1}{24}(t^2-1)x^{-1} + \cdots$ to get $x = y + \frac{1}{2}(t-1) + \frac{1}{24}(t^2-1)/y + O(y^{-3})$. Setting $y = (t! \, N)^{1/t}$ in this formula gives a good approximation, after which we can check that $\binom{\lfloor x \rfloor}{t} \leq N < \binom{\lfloor x \rfloor + 1}{t}$ or make a final adjustment. [See A. S. Fraenkel and M. Mor, *Comp. J.* **26** (1983), 336–343.]

18. A complete binary tree of $2^n - 1$ nodes is obtained, with an extra node at the top, like the "tree of losers" in replacement selection sorting (Fig. 63 in Section 5.4.1). Therefore explicit links aren't necessary; the right child of node k is node $2k + 1$, and the left sibling is node $2k$, for $1 \leq k < 2^{n-1}$.

This representation of a binomial tree has the curious property that node $k = (0^a 1 \alpha)_2$ corresponds to the combination whose binary string is $0^a 1 \alpha^R$.

19. It is 11110100001001000100, the binary representation of post(1000000), where post$(2^{k+1} - 1) = 2^k$, and post$(n) = 2^k + $post$(n - 2^k + 1)$ if $2^k \leq n < 2^{k+1} - 1$, for $k \geq 0$. [Incidentally, the left-child/right-sibling representation of T_∞ is the sideways heap.]

20. $f(z) = (1 + z^{w_{n-1}}) \ldots (1 + z^{w_1})/(1 - z)$, $g(z) = (1 + z^{w_0})f(z)$, $h(z) = z^{w_0} f(z)$.

21. The rank of $c_t \ldots c_2 c_1$ is $\binom{c_t + 1}{t} - 1$ minus the rank of $c_{t-1} \ldots c_2 c_1$. [Page 40 of Miller's thesis; see also H. Lüneburg, *Abh. Math. Sem. Hamburg* **52** (1982), 208–227.]

22. Since $999999 = \binom{1415}{2} - \binom{406}{1} = \binom{183}{3} - \binom{98}{2} + \binom{21}{1} = \binom{72}{4} - \binom{57}{3} + \binom{32}{2} - \binom{27}{1} = \binom{44}{5} - \binom{40}{4} + \binom{33}{3} - \binom{13}{2} + \binom{3}{1}$, the answers are (a) 1414 405; (b) 182 97 21; (c) 71 56 31 26; (d) 43 39 32 12 3; (e) 1000000 999999 999998 999996 ... 0.

23. There are $\binom{n-r}{t-r}$ combinations with $j > r$, for $r = 1, 2, \ldots, t$. (If $r = 1$ we have $c_2 = c_1 + 1$; if $r = 2$ we have $c_1 = 0$, $c_2 = 1$; if $r = 3$ we have $c_1 = 0$, $c_2 = 1$, $c_4 = c_3 + 1$; etc.) Thus the mean is $(\binom{n}{t} + \binom{n-1}{t-1} + \cdots + \binom{n-t}{0}) / \binom{n}{t} = \binom{n+1}{t} / \binom{n}{t} = (n+1)/(n+1-t)$. The average running time per step is approximately proportional to this quantity; thus the algorithm is quite fast when t is small, but slow if t is near n.

24. In fact $j_k - 2 \leq j_{k+1} \leq j_k + 1$ when $j_k \equiv t$ (modulo 2) and $j_k - 1 \leq j_{k+1} \leq j_k + 2$ when $j_k \not\equiv t$, because R5 is performed only when $c_i = i - 1$ for $1 \leq i < j$.

Thus we could say, "If $j \geq 4$, set $j \leftarrow j-1-[j \text{ odd}]$ and go to R5" at the end of R2, if t is odd; "If $j \geq 3$, set $j \leftarrow j - 1 - [j \text{ even}]$ and go to R5" if t is even. The algorithm will then be loopless, since R4 and R5 will be performed at most twice per visit.

25. Assume that $N > N'$ and $N - N'$ is minimum; furthermore let t and c_t be minimum, subject to those assumptions. Then $c_t > c'_t$.

If there is an element $x \notin C \cup C'$ with $0 \leq x < c_t$, map each t-combination of $C \cup C'$ by changing $j \mapsto j-1$ for $j > x$; or, if there is an element $x \in C \cap C'$, map each t-combination that contains x into a $(t-1)$-combination by omitting x and changing $j \mapsto x - j$ for $j < x$. In either case the mapping preserves alternating lexicographic order; hence $N - N'$ must exceed the number of combinations between the images of C and C'. But c_t is minimum, so no such x can exist. Consequently $t = m$ and $c_t = 2m - 1$.

Now if $c'_m < c_m - 1$, we could decrease $N - N'$ by increasing c'_m. Therefore $c'_m = 2m-2$, and the problem has been reduced to finding the *maximum* of $\text{rank}(c_{m-1} \ldots c_1) - \text{rank}(c'_{m-1} \ldots c'_1)$, where rank is calculated as in (30).

Let $f(s,t) = \max(\text{rank}(b_s \ldots b_1) - \text{rank}(c_t \ldots c_1))$ over all $\{b_s, \ldots, b_1, c_t, \ldots, c_1\} = \{0, \ldots, s+t-1\}$. Then $f(s,t)$ satisfies the curious recurrence

$$f(s,0) = f(0,t) = 0; \qquad f(1,t) = t;$$
$$f(s,t) = \binom{s+t-1}{s} + \max(f(t-1, s-1), f(s-2, t)) \quad \text{if } st > 0 \text{ and } s > 1.$$

When $s + t = 2u + 2$ the solution turns out to be

$$f(s,t) = \binom{2u+1}{t-1} + \sum_{j=1}^{u-r} \binom{2u+1-2j}{r} + \sum_{j=0}^{r-1} \binom{2j+1}{j}, \qquad r = \min(s-2, t-1),$$

with the maximum occurring at $f(t-1, s-1)$ when $s \leq t$ and at $f(s-2, t)$ when $s \geq t+2$. Therefore the minimum $N - N'$ occurs for

$$C = \{2m-1\} \cup \{2m - 2 - x \mid 1 \leq x \leq 2m - 2, \ x \bmod 4 \leq 1\},$$
$$C' = \{2m-2\} \cup \{2m - 2 - x \mid 1 \leq x \leq 2m - 2, \ x \bmod 4 \geq 2\};$$

and it equals $\binom{2m-1}{m-1} - \sum_{k=0}^{m-2} \binom{2k+1}{k} = 1 + \sum_{k=1}^{m-1} \binom{2k}{k-1}$. [See A. J. van Zanten, *IEEE Trans.* **IT-37** (1991), 1229–1233.]

26. (a) Yes: The first is $0^{n-\lceil t/2 \rceil} 1^{t \bmod 2} 2^{\lfloor t/2 \rfloor}$ and the last is $2^{\lfloor t/2 \rfloor} 1^{t \bmod 2} 0^{n - \lceil t/2 \rceil}$; transitions are substrings of the forms $02^a 1 \leftrightarrow 12^a 0$, $02^a 2 \leftrightarrow 12^a 1$, $10^a 1 \leftrightarrow 20^a 0$, $10^a 2 \leftrightarrow 20^a 1$.

(b) No: If $s = 0$ there is a big jump from $02^t 0^{r-1}$ to $20^r 2^{t-1}$.

27. The following procedure extracts all combinations $c_1 \ldots c_k$ of Γ_n that have weight $\leq t$: Begin with $k \leftarrow 0$ and $c_0 \leftarrow n$. Visit $c_1 \ldots c_k$. If k is even and $c_k = 0$, set $k \leftarrow k - 1$; if k is even and $c_k > 0$, set $c_k \leftarrow c_k - 1$ if $k = t$, otherwise $k \leftarrow k + 1$ and $c_k \leftarrow 0$. On the other hand if k is odd and $c_k + 1 = c_{k-1}$, set $k \leftarrow k - 1$ and

$c_k \leftarrow c_{k+1}$ (but terminate if $k = 0$); if k is odd and $c_k + 1 < c_{k-1}$, set $c_k \leftarrow c_k + 1$ if $k = t$, otherwise $k \leftarrow k + 1$, $c_k \leftarrow c_{k-1}$, $c_{k-1} \leftarrow c_k + 1$. Repeat.

(This loopless algorithm reduces to that of exercise 7.2.1.1–12(b) when $t = n$, with slight changes of notation.)

28. True. Bit strings $a_{n-1} \ldots a_0 = \alpha\beta$ and $a'_{n-1} \ldots a'_0 = \alpha\beta'$ correspond to index lists $(b_s \ldots b_1 = \theta\chi, c_t \ldots c_1 = \phi\psi)$ and $(b'_s \ldots b'_1 = \theta\chi', c'_t \ldots c'_1 = \phi\psi')$ such that everything between $\alpha\beta$ and $\alpha\beta'$ begins with α if and only if everything between $\theta\chi$ and $\theta\chi'$ begins with θ and everything between $\phi\psi$ and $\phi\psi'$ begins with ϕ. For example, if $n = 10$, the prefix $\alpha = 01101$ corresponds to prefixes $\theta = 96$ and $\phi = 875$.

(But just having $c_t \ldots c_1$ in genlex order is a much weaker condition. For example, *every* such sequence is genlex when $t = 1$.)

29. (a) $-^k 0^{l+1}$ or $-^k 0^{l+1} + \pm^m$ or $\pm^k$, for $k, l, m \geq 0$.

(b) No; the successor is always smaller in balanced ternary notation.

(c) For all α and all $k, l, m \geq 0$ we have $\alpha 0 -^{k+1} 0^l + \pm^m \to \alpha -+^k 0^{l+1} - \pm^m$ and $\alpha +-^k 0^{l+1} + \pm^m \to \alpha 0 +^{k+1} 0^l - \pm^m$; also $\alpha 0 -^{k+1} 0^l \to \alpha -+^k 0^{l+1}$ and $\alpha +-^k 0^{l+1} \to \alpha 0 +^{k+1} 0^l$.

(d) Let the jth sign of α_i be $(-1)^{a_{ij}}$, and let it be in position b_{ij}. Then we have $(-1)^{a_{ij} + b_{i(j-1)}} = (-1)^{a_{(i+1)j} + b_{(i+1)(j-1)}}$ for $0 \leq i < k$ and $1 \leq j \leq s$, if we let $b_{i0} = 0$.

(e) By parts (a), (b), and (c), α belongs to some chain $\alpha_0 \to \cdots \to \alpha_k$, where α_k is final (has no successor) and α_0 is initial (has no predecessor). By part (d), every such chain has at most $\binom{s+t}{t}$ elements. But there are 2^s final strings, by (a), and there are $2^s \binom{s+t}{t}$ strings with s signs and t zeros; so k must be $\binom{s+t}{t} - 1$.

Reference: SICOMP **2** (1973), 128–133.

30. Assume that $t > 0$. Initial strings are the negatives of final strings. Let σ_j be the initial string $0^t -\tau_j$ for $0 \leq j < 2^{s-1}$, where the kth character of τ_j for $1 \leq k < s$ is the sign of $(-1)^{a_k}$ when j is the binary number $(a_{s-1} \ldots a_1)_2$; thus $\sigma_0 = 0^t -++\ldots +$, $\sigma_1 = 0^t --+\ldots +$, $\ldots$, $\sigma_{2^{s-1}-1} = 0^t ---\ldots -$. Let ρ_j be the final string obtained by inserting -0^t after the first (possibly empty) run of minus signs in τ_j; thus $\rho_0 = -0^t ++\ldots +$, $\rho_1 = --0^t + \ldots +$, $\ldots$, $\rho_{2^{s-1}-1} = --\ldots -0^t$. We also let $\sigma_{2^s-1} = \sigma_0$ and $\rho_{2^s-1} = \rho_0$. Then we can prove by induction that the chain beginning with σ_j ends with ρ_j when t is even, with ρ_{j-1} when t is odd, for $1 \leq j \leq 2^{s-1}$. Therefore the chain beginning with $-\rho_j$ ends with $-\sigma_j$ or $-\sigma_{j+1}$.

Let $A_j(s, t)$ be the sequence of (s, t)-combinations derived by mapping the chain that starts with σ_j, and let $B_j(s, t)$ be the analogous sequence derived from $-\rho_j$. Then, for $1 \leq j \leq 2^{s-1}$, the reverse sequence $A_j(s, t)^R$ is $B_j(s, t)$ when t is even, $B_{j-1}(s, t)$ when t is odd. The corresponding recurrences when $st > 0$ are

$$A_j(s, t) = \begin{cases} 1A_j(s, t-1),\ 0A_{\lfloor (2^{s-1}-1-j)/2 \rfloor}(s-1, t)^R, & \text{if } j + t \text{ is even}; \\ 1A_j(s, t-1),\ 0A_{\lfloor j/2 \rfloor}(s-1, t), & \text{if } j + t \text{ is odd}; \end{cases}$$

and when $st > 0$ all 2^{s-1} of these sequences are distinct.

Chase's sequence C_{st} is $A_{\lfloor 2^s/3 \rfloor}(s, t)$, and $\widehat{C}_{st}$ is $A_{\lfloor 2^s-1/3 \rfloor}(s, t)^R$. Incidentally, the homogeneous sequence K_{st} of (31) is $A_{2^{s-1}-[t \text{ even}]}(s, t)^R$.

31. (a) $2^{\binom{s+t}{t}-1}$ solves the recurrence $f(s, t) = 2f(s-1, t)f(s, t-1)$ when $f(s, 0) = f(0, t) = 1$. (b) Now $f(s, t) = (s+1)! f(s, t-1) \ldots f(0, t-1)$ has the solution

$$(s+1)!^t s!^{\binom{t}{2}} (s-1)!^{\binom{t+1}{3}} \ldots 2!^{\binom{s+t-2}{s}} = \prod_{r=1}^{s} (r+1)!^{\binom{s+t-1-r}{t-2} + [r=s]}.$$

32. (a) No simple formula seems to exist, but the listings can be counted for small s and t by systematically computing the number of genlex paths that run through all weight-t strings from a given starting point to a given ending point via revolving-door moves. The totals for $s + t \leq 6$ are

$$
\begin{array}{ccccccccccccc}
 & & & & & & 1 & & & & & & \\
 & & & & & 1 & & 1 & & & & & \\
 & & & & 1 & & 2 & & 1 & & & & \\
 & & & 1 & & 4 & & 4 & & 1 & & & \\
 & & 1 & & 8 & & 20 & & 8 & & 1 & & \\
 & 1 & & 16 & & 160 & & 160 & & 16 & & 1 & \\
1 & & 32 & & 2264 & & 17152 & & 2264 & & 32 & & 1
\end{array}
$$

and $f(4,4) = 95{,}304{,}112{,}865{,}280$; $f(5,5) \approx 5.92646 \times 10^{48}$. [This class of combination generators was first studied by G. Ehrlich, *JACM* **20** (1973), 500–513, but he did not attempt to enumerate them.]

(b) By extending the proof of Theorem N, one can show that all such listings or their reversals must run from $1^t 0^s$ to $0^a 1^t 0^{s-a}$ for some a, $1 \leq a \leq s$. Moreover, the number n_{sta} of possibilities, given s, t, and a with $st > 0$, satisfies $n_{1t1} = 1$ and

$$
n_{sta} = \begin{cases}
n_{s(t-1)1} n_{(s-1)t(a-1)}, & \text{if } a > 1; \\
n_{s(t-1)2} n_{(s-1)t1} + \cdots + n_{s(t-1)s} n_{(s-1)t(s-1)}, & \text{if } a = 1 < s.
\end{cases}
$$

This recurrence has the remarkable solution $n_{sta} = 2^{m(s,t,a)}$, where

$$
m(s,t,a) = \begin{cases}
\binom{s+t-3}{t} + \binom{s+t-5}{t-2} + \cdots + \binom{s-1}{2}, & \text{if } t \text{ is even}; \\
\binom{s+t-3}{t} + \binom{s+t-5}{t-2} + \cdots + \binom{s}{3} + s - a - [a < s], & \text{if } t \text{ is odd}.
\end{cases}
$$

33. Consider first the case $t = 1$: The number of near-perfect paths from i to $j > i$ is $f(j - i - [i > 0] - [j < n - 1])$, where $\sum_j f(j) z^j = 1/(1 - z - z^3)$. (By coincidence, the same sequence $f(j)$ arises in Caron's polyphase merge on 6 tapes, Table 5.4.2–2.) The sum over $0 \leq i < j < n$ is $3f(n) + f(n-1) + f(n-2) + 2 - n$; and we must double this, to cover cases with $j > i$.

When $t > 1$ we can construct $\binom{n}{t} \times \binom{n}{t}$ matrices that tell how many genlex listings begin and end with particular combinations. The entries of these matrices are sums of products of matrices for the case $t - 1$, summed over all paths of the type considered for $t = 1$. The totals for $s + t \leq 6$ turn out to be

$$
\begin{array}{ccccccccccccc}
 & & & & & 1 & & & & & & \quad & 1 \\
 & & & & 1 & & 1 & & & & & & 1\ 1 \\
 & & & 1 & & 2 & & 1 & & & & & 1\ 2\ 1 \\
 & & 1 & & 6 & & 2 & & 1 & & & & 1\ 2\ 0\ 1 \\
 & 1 & & 12 & & 10 & & 2 & & 1 & & & 1\ 2\ 2\ 0\ 1 \\
1 & & 20 & & 44 & & 10 & & 2 & & 1 & & 1\ 2\ 0\ 0\ 0\ 1 \\
1 & & 34 & & 238 & & 68 & & 10 & & 2 & 1 & 1\ 2\ 6\ 0\ 0\ 0\ 1
\end{array}
$$

where the right-hand triangle shows the number of *cycles*, $g(s,t)$. Further values include $f(4,4) = 17736$; $f(5,5) = 9{,}900{,}888{,}879{,}984$; $g(4,4) = 96$; $g(5,5) = 30{,}961{,}456{,}320$.

There are exactly 10 such schemes when $s = 2$ and $n \geq 4$. For example, when $n = 7$ they run from 43210 to 65431 or 65432, or from 54321 to 65420 or 65430 or 65432, or the reverse.

34. The minimum can be computed as in the previous answer, but using min-plus matrix multiplication $c_{ij} = \min_k(a_{ik} + b_{kj})$ instead of ordinary matrix multiplication $c_{ij} = \sum_k a_{ik} b_{kj}$. (When $s = t = 5$, the genlex path in Fig. 46(e) with only 49 imperfect transitions is essentially unique. There is a genlex cycle for $s = t = 5$ that has only 55 imperfections.)

35. From the recurrences (35) we have $a_{st} = b_{s(t-1)} + [s>1][t>0] + a_{(s-1)t}$, $b_{st} = a_{s(t-1)} + a_{(s-1)t}$; consequently $a_{st} = b_{st} + [s>1][t\,\text{odd}]$ and $a_{st} = a_{s(t-1)} + a_{(s-1)t} + [s>1][t\,\text{odd}]$. The solution is

$$a_{st} = \sum_{k=0}^{t/2} \binom{s+t-2-2k}{s-2} - [s>1][t\,\text{even}];$$

this sum is approximately $s/(s+2t)$ times $\binom{s+t}{t}$.

36. Consider the binary tree with root node (s,t) and with recursively defined subtrees rooted at $(s-1,t)$ and $(s,t-1)$ whenever $st > 0$; the node (s,t) is a leaf if $st = 0$. Then the subtree rooted at (s,t) has $\binom{s+t}{t}$ leaves, corresponding to all (s,t)-combinations $a_{n-1} \ldots a_1 a_0$. Nodes on level l correspond to prefixes $a_{n-1} \ldots a_{n-l}$, and leaves on level l are combinations with $r = n - l$.

Any genlex algorithm for combinations $a_{n-1} \ldots a_1 a_0$ corresponds to preorder traversal of such a tree, after the children of the $\binom{s+t}{t} - 1$ branch nodes have been ordered in any desired way; that, in fact, is why there are $2^{\binom{s+t}{t}-1}$ such genlex schemes (exercise 31(a)). And the operation $j \leftarrow j + 1$ is performed exactly once per branch node, namely after both children have been processed.

Incidentally, exercise 7.2.1.2–6(a) implies that the average value of r is $s/(t+1) + t/(s+1)$, which can be $\Omega(n)$; thus the extra time needed to keep track of r is worthwhile.

37. (a) In the lexicographic case we needn't maintain the w_j table, since a_j is active for $j \geq r$ if and only if $a_j = 0$. After setting $a_j \leftarrow 1$ and $a_{j-1} \leftarrow 0$ there are two cases to consider if $j > 1$: If $r = j$, set $r \leftarrow j - 1$; otherwise set $a_{j-2} \ldots a_0 \leftarrow 0^r 1^{j-1-r}$ and $r \leftarrow j - 1 - r$ (or $r \leftarrow j$ if r was $j - 1$).

(b) Now the transitions to be handled when $j > 1$ are to change $a_j \ldots a_0$ as follows: $01^r \to 1101^{r-2}$, $010^r \to 10^{r+1}$, $010^a 1^r \to 110^{a+1} 1^{r-1}$, $10^r \to 010^{r-1}$, $110^r \to 010^{r-1} 1$, $10^a 1^r \to 0^a 1^{r+1}$; these six cases are easily distinguished. The value of r should change appropriately.

(c) Again the case $j = 1$ is trivial. Otherwise $01^a 0^r \to 101^{a-1} 0^r$; $0^a 1^r \to 10^a 1^{r-1}$; $101^a 0^r \to 01^{a+1} 0^r$; $10^a 1^r \to 0^a 1^{r+1}$; and there is also an ambiguous case, which can occur only if $a_{n-1} \ldots a_{j+1}$ contains at least one 0: Let $k > j$ be minimal with $a_k = 0$. Then $10^r \to 010^{r-1}$ if k is odd, $10^r \to 0^r 1$ if k is even.

38. The same algorithm works, except that (i) step C1 sets $a_{n-1} \ldots a_0 \leftarrow 01^t 0^{s-1}$ if n is odd or $s = 1$, $a_{n-1} \ldots a_0 \leftarrow 001^t 0^{s-2}$ if n is even and $s > 1$, with an appropriate value of r; (ii) step C3 interchanges the roles of even and odd; (iii) step C5 goes to C4 also if $j = 1$.

39. In general, start with $r \leftarrow 0$, $j \leftarrow s + t - 1$, and repeat the following steps until $st = 0$:

$$r \leftarrow r + [w_j = 0]\binom{j}{s - a_j}, \quad s \leftarrow s - [a_j = 0], \quad t \leftarrow t - [a_j = 1], \quad j \leftarrow j - 1.$$

Then r is the rank of $a_{n-1} \ldots a_1 a_0$. So the rank of $110010010000111111101101010$ is $\binom{23}{12} + \binom{22}{11} + \binom{21}{9} + \binom{17}{8} + \binom{16}{7} + \binom{14}{5} + \binom{13}{3} + \binom{12}{3} + \binom{11}{3} + \binom{10}{3} + \binom{9}{3} + \binom{8}{3} + \binom{4}{1} + \binom{3}{1} + \binom{1}{0} = 2390131$.

40. We start with $N \leftarrow 999999$, $v \leftarrow 0$, and repeat the following steps until $st = 0$: If $v = 0$, set $t \leftarrow t - 1$ and $a_{s+t} \leftarrow 1$ if $N < \binom{s+t-1}{s}$, otherwise set $N \leftarrow N - \binom{s+t-1}{s}$, $v \leftarrow (s+t) \bmod 2$, $s \leftarrow s - 1$, $a_{s+t} \leftarrow 0$. If $v = 1$, set $v \leftarrow (s+t) \bmod 2$, $s \leftarrow s - 1$, and $a_{s+t} \leftarrow 0$ if $N < \binom{s+t-1}{t}$, otherwise set $N \leftarrow N - \binom{s+t-1}{t}$, $t \leftarrow t - 1$, $a_{s+t} \leftarrow 1$. Finally if $s = 0$, set $a_{t-1} \ldots a_0 \leftarrow 1^t$; if $t = 0$, set $a_{s-1} \ldots a_0 \leftarrow 0^s$. The answer is $a_{25} \ldots a_0 = 11101001111110101001000001$.

41. Let $c(0), \ldots, c(2^n - 1) = C_n$ where $C_{2n} = 0 C_{2n-1}, 1 C_{2n-1}$; $C_{2n+1} = 0 \widehat{C}_{2n}$, $1 \widehat{C}_{2n}$; $\widehat{C}_{2n} = 1 C_{2n-1}, 0 \widehat{C}_{2n-1}$; $\widehat{C}_{2n+1} = 1 \widehat{C}_{2n}, 0 \widehat{C}_{2n}$; $C_0 = \widehat{C}_0 = \epsilon$. Then $a_j \oplus b_j = b_{j+1} \& (b_{j+2} | (b_{j+3} \& (b_{j+4} | \cdots)))$ if j is even, $b_{j+1} | (b_{j+2} \& (b_{j+3} | (b_{j+4} \& \cdots)))$ if j is odd. Curiously we also have the inverse relation $c((\ldots a_4 \bar{a}_3 a_2 \bar{a}_1 a_0)_2) = (\ldots b_4 \bar{b}_3 b_2 \bar{b}_1 b_0)_2$.

42. Equation (40) shows that the left context $a_{n-1} \ldots a_{l+1}$ does not affect the behavior of the algorithm on $a_{l-1} \ldots a_0$ if $a_l = 0$ and $l > r$. Therefore we can analyze Algorithm C by counting combinations that end with certain bit patterns, and it follows that the number of times each operation is performed can be represented as $[w^s z^t] p(w, z)/(1 - w^2)^2 (1 - z^2)^2 (1 - w - z)$ for an appropriate polynomial $p(w, z)$.

For example, the algorithm goes from C5 to C4 once for each combination that ends with $01^{2a+1}01^{2b+1}$ or has the form $1^{a+1}01^{2b+1}$, for integers $a, b \geq 0$; the corresponding generating functions are $w^2 z^2/(1 - z^2)^2 (1 - w - z)$ and $w(z^2 + z^3)/(1 - z^2)^2$.

Here are the polynomials $p(w, z)$ for key operations. Let $W = 1 - w^2$, $Z = 1 - z^2$.

C3 → C4:	$wzW(1+wz)(1-w-z^2)$;	C5$(r \leftarrow 1)$:	$w^2 z W^2 Z(1-wz-z^2)$;
C3 → C5:	$wzW(w+z)(1-wz-z^2)$;	C5$(r \leftarrow j-1)$:	$w^2 z^3 W^2(1-wz-z^2)$;
C3 → C6:	$w^2 z^2 W(w+z)$;	C6$(j = 1)$:	$w^2 z W^2 Z$;
C3 → C7:	$w^2 z W(1+wz)$;	C6$(r \leftarrow j-1)$:	$w^2 z^3 W^2$;
C4$(j = 1)$:	$wzW^2 Z(1-w-z^2)$;	C6$(r \leftarrow j)$:	$w^3 z^2 W Z$;
C4$(r \leftarrow j-1)$:	$w^3 zWZ(1-w-z^2)$;	C7 → C6:	$w^2 z W^2$;
C4$(r \leftarrow j)$:	$wz^2 W^2(1+z-2wz-z^2-z^3)$;	C7$(r \leftarrow j)$:	$w^4 zWZ$;
C5 → C4:	$wz^2 W^2(1-wz-z^2)$;	C7$(r \leftarrow j-2)$:	$w^3 z^2 W^2$.
C5$(r \leftarrow j-2)$:	$w^4 zWZ(1-wz-z^2)$;		

The asymptotic value is $\binom{s+t}{t}(p(1 - x, x)/(2x - x^2)^2 (1 - x^2)^2 + O(n^{-1}))$, for fixed $0 < x < 1$, if $t = xn + O(1)$ as $n \to \infty$. Thus we find, for example, that the four-way branching in step C3 takes place with relative frequencies $x + x^2 - x^3 : 1 : x : 1 + x - x^2$.

Incidentally, the number of cases with j odd exceeds the number of cases with j even by

$$\sum_{k,l \geq 1} \binom{s + t - 2k - 2l}{s - 2k} [2k + 2l \leq s + t] + [s \text{ odd}][t \text{ odd}],$$

in *any* genlex scheme that uses (39). This quantity has the interesting generating function $wz/(1 + w)(1 + z)(1 - w - z)$.

43. The identity is true for all nonnegative integers x, except when $x = 1$. (Incidentally, $s(x) = f(x) \oplus 1$ and $p(x) = f(x \oplus 1)$, where $f(x) = (x \dot{-} 1) + ((x \,\&\, 1) \ll 1)$.)

44. In fact, $C_t(n) - 1 = \widehat{C}_t(n - 1)^R$, and $\widehat{C}_t(n) - 1 = C_t(n - 1)^R$. (Hence $C_t(n) - 2 = C_t(n - 2)$, etc.)

45. In the following algorithm, r is the least subscript with $c_r \geq r$.

    CC1. [Initialize.] Set $c_j \leftarrow n - t - 1 + j$ and $z_j \leftarrow 0$ for $1 \leq j \leq t + 1$. Also set $r \leftarrow 1$. (We assume that $0 < t < n$.)

    CC2. [Visit.] Visit the combination $c_t \ldots c_2 c_1$. Then set $j \leftarrow r$.

    CC3. [Branch.] Go to CC5 if $z_j \neq 0$.

CC4. [Try to decrease c_j.] Set $x \leftarrow c_j + (c_j \bmod 2) - 2$. If $x \geq j$, set $c_j \leftarrow x$, $r \leftarrow 1$; otherwise if $c_j = j$, set $c_j \leftarrow j - 1$, $z_j \leftarrow c_{j+1} - ((c_{j+1} + 1) \bmod 2)$, $r \leftarrow j$; otherwise if $c_j < j$, set $c_j \leftarrow j$, $z_j \leftarrow c_{j+1} - ((c_{j+1} + 1) \bmod 2)$, $r \leftarrow \max(1, j - 1)$; otherwise set $c_j \leftarrow x$, $r \leftarrow j$. Return to CC2.

CC5. [Try to increase c_j.] Set $x \leftarrow c_j + 2$. If $x < z_j$, set $c_j \leftarrow x$; otherwise if $x = z_j$ and $z_{j+1} \neq 0$, set $c_j \leftarrow x - (c_{j+1} \bmod 2)$; otherwise set $z_j \leftarrow 0$, $j \leftarrow j + 1$, and go to CC3 (but terminate if $j > t$). If $c_1 > 0$, set $r \leftarrow 1$; otherwise set $r \leftarrow j - 1$. Return to CC2. ▮

46. Equation (40) implies that $u_k = (b_j + k + 1) \bmod 2$ when j is minimal with $b_j > k$. Then (37) and (38) yield the following algorithm, where we assume for convenience that $3 \leq s < n$.

CB1. [Initialize.] Set $b_j \leftarrow j - 1$ for $1 \leq j \leq s$; also set $z \leftarrow s + 1$, $b_z \leftarrow 1$. (When subsequent steps examine the value of z, it is the smallest index such that $b_z \neq z - 1$.)

CB2. [Visit.] Visit the dual combination $b_s \ldots b_2 b_1$.

CB3. [Branch.] If b_2 is odd: Go to CB4 if $b_2 \neq b_1 + 1$, otherwise to CB5 if $b_1 > 0$, otherwise to CB6 if b_z is odd. Go to CB9 if b_2 is even and $b_1 > 0$. Otherwise go to CB8 if $b_{z+1} = b_z + 1$, otherwise to CB7.

CB4. [Increase b_1.] Set $b_1 \leftarrow b_1 + 1$ and return to CB2.

CB5. [Slide b_1 and b_2.] If b_3 is odd, set $b_1 \leftarrow b_1 + 1$ and $b_2 \leftarrow b_2 + 1$; otherwise set $b_1 \leftarrow b_1 - 1$, $b_2 \leftarrow b_2 - 1$, $z \leftarrow 3$. Go to CB2.

CB6. [Slide left.] If z is odd, set $z \leftarrow z - 2$, $b_{z+1} \leftarrow z + 1$, $b_z \leftarrow z$; otherwise set $z \leftarrow z - 1$, $b_z \leftarrow z$. Go to CB2.

CB7. [Slide b_z.] If b_{z+1} is odd, set $b_z \leftarrow b_z + 1$ and terminate if $b_z \geq n$; otherwise set $b_z \leftarrow b_z - 1$, then if $b_z < z$ set $z \leftarrow z + 1$. Go to CB2.

CB8. [Slide b_z and b_{z+1}.] If b_{z+2} is odd, set $b_z \leftarrow b_{z+1}$, $b_{z+1} \leftarrow b_z + 1$, and terminate if $b_{z+1} \geq n$. Otherwise set $b_{z+1} \leftarrow b_z$, $b_z \leftarrow b_z - 1$, then if $b_z < z$ set $z \leftarrow z + 2$. Go to CB2.

CB9. [Decrease b_1.] Set $b_1 \leftarrow b_1 - 1$, $z \leftarrow 2$, and return to CB2. ▮

Notice that this algorithm is *loopless*. Chase gave a similar procedure for the sequence $\widehat{C}^R_{st}$ in *Cong. Num.* **69** (1989), 233–237. It is truly amazing that this algorithm defines precisely the complements of the indices $c_t \ldots c_1$ produced by the algorithm in the previous exercise.

47. We can, for example, use Algorithm C and its reverse (exercise 38), with w_j replaced by a d-bit number whose bits represent activity at different levels of the recursion. Separate pointers $r_0, r_1, \ldots, r_{d-1}$ are needed to keep track of the r-values on each level. (Many other solutions are possible.)

48. There are permutations $\pi_1, \ldots, \pi_M$ such that the kth element of Λ_j is $\pi_k \alpha_j \uparrow \beta_{k-1}$. And $\pi_k \alpha_j$ runs through all permutations of $\{s_1 \cdot 1, \ldots, s_d \cdot d\}$ as j varies from 0 to $N-1$.

Historical note: The first publication of a homogeneous revolving-door scheme for (s, t)-combinations was by Éva Török, *Matematikai Lapok* **19** (1968), 143–146, who was motivated by the generation of multiset permutations. Many authors have subsequently relied on the homogeneity condition for similar constructions, but this exercise shows that homogeneity is not necessary.

49. We have $\lim_{z \to q}(z^{km+r} - 1)/(z^{lm+r} - 1) = 1$ when $0 < r < m$, and the limit is $\lim_{z \to q}(kmz^{km-1})/(lmz^{lm-1}) = k/l$ when $r = 0$. So we can pair up factors of the numerator $\prod_{n-k < a \le n}(z^a - 1)$ with factors of the denominator $\prod_{0 < b \le k}(z^b - 1)$ when $a \equiv b$ (modulo m).

Notes: This formula was discovered by G. Olive, *AMM* **72** (1965), 619. In the special case $m = 2$, $q = -1$, the second factor vanishes only when n is even and k is odd.

The formula $\binom{n}{k}_q = \binom{n}{n-k}_q$ holds for all $n \ge 0$, but $\binom{\lfloor n/m \rfloor}{\lfloor k/m \rfloor}$ is *not* always equal to $\binom{\lfloor n/m \rfloor}{\lfloor (n-k)/m \rfloor}$. The reason is that the second factor is zero unless $n \bmod m \ge k \bmod m$, and in that case we do have $\lfloor k/m \rfloor + \lfloor (n-k)/m \rfloor = \lfloor n/m \rfloor$.

50. The stated coefficient is zero when $n_1 \bmod m + \cdots + n_t \bmod m \ge m$. Otherwise it equals

$$\binom{\lfloor (n_1 + \cdots + n_t)/m \rfloor}{\lfloor n_1/m \rfloor, \ldots, \lfloor n_t/m \rfloor} \binom{(n_1 + \cdots + n_t) \bmod m}{n_1 \bmod m, \ldots, n_t \bmod m}_q,$$

by Eq. 1.2.6–(43); here each upper index is the sum of the lower indices.

51. All paths clearly run between 000111 and 111000, since those vertices have degree 1. Fourteen total paths reduce to four under the stated equivalences. The path in (50), which is equivalent to itself under reflection-and-reversal, can be described by the delta sequence $A = 3452132523414354123$; the other three classes are $B = 3452541453414512543$, $C = 3452541453252154123$, $D = 3452134145341432543$. D. H. Lehmer found path C [*AMM* **72** (1965), Part II, 36–46]; D is essentially the path constructed by Eades, Hickey, and Read.

(Incidentally, perfect schemes aren't really rare, although they seem to be difficult to construct systematically. The case $(s,t) = (3,5)$ has 4,050,046 of them.)

52. We may assume that each s_j is nonzero and that $d > 1$. Then the difference between permutations with an even and odd number of inversions is $\binom{\lfloor (s_0 + \cdots + s_d)/2 \rfloor}{\lfloor s_0/2 \rfloor, \ldots, \lfloor s_d/2 \rfloor} \ge 2$, by exercise 50, unless at least two of the multiplicities s_j are odd.

Conversely, if at least two multiplicities are odd, a general construction by G. Stachowiak [*SIAM J. Discrete Math.* **5** (1992), 199–206] shows that a perfect scheme exists. Indeed, his construction applies to a variety of topological sorting problems; in the special case of multisets it gives a Hamiltonian cycle in all cases with $d > 1$ and $s_0 s_1$ odd, except when $d = 2$, $s_0 = s_1 = 1$, and s_2 is even.

53. See *AMM* **72** (1965), Part II, 36–46.

54. Assuming that $st \ne 0$, a Hamiltonian path exists if and only if s and t are not both even; a Hamiltonian cycle exists if and only if, in addition, ($s \ne 2$ and $t \ne 2$) or $n = 5$. [T. C. Enns, *Discrete Math.* **122** (1993), 153–165.]

55. (a) [Solution by Aaron Williams.] The sequence $0^s 1^t$, W_{st} has the right properties if

$$W_{st} = 0W_{(s-1)t}, \; 1W_{s(t-1)}, \; 10^s 1^{t-1}, \quad \text{for } st > 0; \qquad W_{0t} = W_{s0} = \emptyset.$$

And there is an amazingly efficient, *loopless* implementation: Assume that $t > 0$.

W1. [Initialize.] Set $n \leftarrow s + t$, $a_j \leftarrow 1$ for $0 \le j < t$, and $a_j \leftarrow 0$ for $t \le j \le n$. Then set $j \leftarrow k \leftarrow t - 1$. (This is tricky, but it works.)

W2. [Visit.] Visit the (s,t)-combination $a_{n-1} \ldots a_1 a_0$.

W3. [Zero out a_j.] Set $a_j \leftarrow 0$ and $j \leftarrow j + 1$.

W4. [Easy case?] If $a_j = 1$, set $a_k \leftarrow 1$, $k \leftarrow k + 1$, and return to W2.

W5. [Wrap around.] Terminate if $j = n$. Otherwise set $a_j \leftarrow 1$. Then if $k > 0$, set $a_k \leftarrow 1$, $a_0 \leftarrow 0$, $j \leftarrow 1$, and $k \leftarrow 0$. Return to W2. ∎

After the second visit, j is the smallest index with $a_j a_{j-1} = 10$, and k is smallest with $a_k = 0$. The easy case occurs exactly $\binom{s+t-1}{s} - 1$ times; the condition $k = 0$ occurs in step W5 exactly $\binom{s+t-2}{t} + \delta_{t1}$ times. Curiously, if N has the combinatorial representation (57), the combination of rank N in Algorithm L has rank $N - t + \binom{n_v}{v-1} + v - 1$ in Algorithm W. [*Lecture Notes in Comp. Sci.* **3595** (2005), 570–576; see also A. Williams, *SODA* **20** (2009), 987–996, for a significant generalization by which the permutations of an arbitrary multiset can be generated looplessly by prefix rotations.]

> (b) `SET bits,(1<<t)-1`   (This program assumes that $s > 0$ and $t > 0$.)
> `1H PUSHJ $0,Visit`   Visit $\text{bits} = (a_{s+t-1} \ldots a_1 a_0)_2$.
> `   ADDU $0,bits,1; AND $0,$0,bits`   Set $\$0 \leftarrow \text{bits} \,\&\, (\text{bits} + 1)$.
> `   SUBU $1,$0,1; XOR $1,$0,$1`   Set $\$1 \leftarrow \$0 \oplus (\$0 - 1)$.
> `   ADDU $0,$1,1; AND $1,$1,bits`   Set $\$0 \leftarrow \$1 + 1$, $\$1 \leftarrow \$1 \,\&\, \text{bits}$.
> `   AND $0,$0,bits; ODIF $0,$0,1`   Set $\$0 \leftarrow (\$0 \,\&\, \text{bits}) \mathbin{\dot-} 1$.
> `   SUBU $1,$1,$0; ADDU bits,bits,$1`   Set $\text{bits} \leftarrow \text{bits} + \$1 - \$0$.
> `   SRU $0,bits,s+t; PBZ $0,1B`   Repeat unless $a_{s+t} = 1$. ∎

56. [*Discrete Math.* **48** (1984), 163–171.] This problem is equivalent to the "middle levels conjecture," which states that there is a Gray path through all binary strings of length $2t - 1$ and weights $\{t - 1, t\}$. In fact, such strings can almost certainly be generated by a delta sequence of the special form $\alpha_0 \alpha_1 \ldots \alpha_{2t-2}$ where the elements of α_k are those of α_0 shifted by k, modulo $2t - 1$. For example, when $t = 3$ we can start with $a_5 a_4 a_3 a_2 a_1 a_0 = 000111$ and repeatedly swap $a_0 \leftrightarrow a_\delta$, where δ runs through the cycle (4134 5245 1351 2412 3523). The middle levels conjecture is known to be true for $t \leq 15$ [see I. Shields and C. D. Savage, *Cong. Num.* **140** (1999), 161–178].

57. Yes; there is a near-perfect genlex solution for all m, n, and t when $n \geq m > t$. One such scheme, in bitstring notation, is $1 A_{(m-t)(t-1)} 0^{n-m}$, $01 A_{(m-t)(t-1)} 0^{n-m-1}$, $\ldots, 0^{n-m} 1 A_{(m-t)(t-1)}$, $0^{n-m+1} 1 A_{(m-1-t)(t-1)}$, $\ldots, 0^{n-t} 1 A_{0(t-1)}$, using the sequences A_{st} of (35).

58. Solve the previous problem with m and n reduced by $t - 1$, then add $j - 1$ to each c_j. (Case (a), which is particularly simple, was probably known to Czerny.)

59. The generating function $G_{mnt}(z) = \sum g_{mntk} z^k$ for the number g_{mntk} of chords reachable in k steps from $0^{n-t} 1^t$ satisfies $G_{mmt}(z) = \binom{m}{t}_z$ and $G_{m(n+1)t}(z) = G_{mnt}(z) + z^{tn-(t-1)m} \binom{m-1}{t-1}_z$, because the latter term accounts for cases with $c_t = n$ and $c_1 > n - m$. A perfect scheme is possible only if $|G_{mnt}(-1)| \leq 1$. But if $n \geq m > t \geq 2$, this condition holds only when $m = t + 1$ or $(n - t)t$ is odd, by (49). So there is no perfect solution when $t = 4$ and $m > 5$. (Many chords have only two neighbors when $n = t + 2$, so one can easily rule out that case. All cases with $n \geq m > 5$ and $t = 3$ apparently do have perfect paths when n is even.)

60. The following solution uses lexicographic order, taking care to ensure that the average amount of computation per visit is bounded. We may assume that $s t m_s \ldots m_0 \neq 0$ and $t \leq m_s + \cdots + m_1 + m_0$.

> **Q1.** [Initialize.] Set $q_j \leftarrow 0$ for $s \geq j \geq 1$, and $x \leftarrow t$.
>
> **Q2.** [Distribute.] Set $j \leftarrow 0$. Then while $x > m_j$, set $q_j \leftarrow m_j$, $x \leftarrow x - m_j$, and $j \leftarrow j + 1$. Finally set $q_j \leftarrow x$.
>
> **Q3.** [Visit.] Visit the bounded composition $q_s + \cdots + q_1 + q_0$.
>
> **Q4.** [Pick up the rightmost units.] If $j = 0$, set $x \leftarrow q_0 - 1$, $j \leftarrow 1$. Otherwise if $q_0 = 0$, set $x \leftarrow q_j - 1$, $q_j \leftarrow 0$, and $j \leftarrow j + 1$. Otherwise go to Q7.

Q5. [Full?] Terminate if $j > s$. Otherwise if $q_j = m_j$, set $x \leftarrow x + m_j$, $q_j \leftarrow 0$, $j \leftarrow j + 1$, and repeat this step.

Q6. [Increase q_j.] Set $q_j \leftarrow q_j + 1$. Then if $x = 0$, set $q_0 \leftarrow 0$ and return to Q3. (In that case $q_{j-1} = \cdots = q_0 = 0$.) Otherwise go to Q2.

Q7. [Increase and decrease.] (Now $q_i = m_i$ for $j > i \geq 0$.) While $q_j = m_j$, set $j \leftarrow j + 1$ and repeat until $q_j < m_j$ (but terminate if $j > s$). Then set $q_j \leftarrow q_j + 1$, $j \leftarrow j - 1$, $q_j \leftarrow q_j - 1$. If $q_0 = 0$, set $j \leftarrow 1$. Return to Q3. ∎

For example, if $m_s = \cdots = m_0 = 9$, the successors of the composition $3+9+9+7+0+0$ are $4+0+0+6+9+9$, $4+0+0+7+8+9$, $4+0+0+7+9+8$, $4+0+0+8+7+9$, ...

61. Let $F_s(t) = \emptyset$ if $t < 0$ or $t > m_s + \cdots + m_0$; otherwise let $F_0(t) = t$, and

$$F_s(t) = 0 + F_{s-1}(t), \ 1 + F_{s-1}(t-1)^R, \ 2 + F_{s-1}(t-2), \ \ldots, \ m_s + F_{s-1}(t-m_s)^{R^{m_s}}$$

when $s > 0$. This sequence can be shown to have the required properties; it is, in fact, equivalent to the compositions defined by the homogeneous sequence K_{st} of (31) under the correspondence of exercise 4, when restricted to the subsequence defined by the bounds $m_s, \ldots, m_0$. [See T. Walsh, *J. Combinatorial Math. and Combinatorial Computing* **33** (2000), 323–345, who has implemented it looplessly.]

62. (a) A $2 \times n$ contingency table with row sums r and $c_1 + \cdots + c_n - r$ is equivalent to solving $r = a_1 + \cdots + a_n$ with $0 \leq a_1 \leq c_1, \ldots, 0 \leq a_n \leq c_n$.

(b) We can compute it sequentially by setting $a_{ij} \leftarrow \min(r_i - a_{i1} - \cdots - a_{i(j-1)}, c_j - a_{1j} - \cdots - a_{(i-1)j})$ for $j = 1, \ldots, n$, for $i = 1, \ldots, m$. Alternatively, if $r_1 \leq c_1$, set $a_{11} \leftarrow r_1$, $a_{12} \leftarrow \cdots \leftarrow a_{1n} \leftarrow 0$, and do the remaining rows with c_1 decreased by r_1; if $r_1 > c_1$, set $a_{11} \leftarrow c_1$, $a_{21} \leftarrow \cdots \leftarrow a_{m1} \leftarrow 0$, and do the remaining columns with r_1 decreased by c_1. The second approach shows that at most $m + n - 1$ of the entries are nonzero. We can also write down the explicit formula

$$a_{ij} = \max(0, \min(r_i, c_j, r_1 + \cdots + r_i - c_1 - \cdots - c_{j-1}, c_1 + \cdots + c_j - r_1 - \cdots - r_{i-1})).$$

(c) The same matrix is obtained as in (b).

(d) Reverse left and right in (b) and (c); in both cases the answer is

$$a_{ij} = \max(0, \min(r_i, c_j, r_1 + \cdots + r_i - c_{j+1} - \cdots - c_n, c_j + \cdots + c_n - r_1 - \cdots - r_{i-1})).$$

(e) Here we choose, say, row-wise order: Generate the first row just as for bounded compositions of r_1, with bounds $(c_1, \ldots, c_n)$; and for each row $(a_{11}, \ldots, a_{1n})$, generate the remaining rows recursively in the same way, but with the column sums $(c_1 - a_{11}, \ldots, c_n - a_{1n})$. Most of the action takes place on the bottom two rows, but when a change is made to an earlier row the later rows must be re-initialized.

63. If a_{ij} and a_{kl} are positive, we obtain another contingency table by setting $a_{ij} \leftarrow a_{ij} - 1$, $a_{il} \leftarrow a_{il} + 1$, $a_{kj} \leftarrow a_{kj} + 1$, $a_{kl} \leftarrow a_{kl} - 1$. We want to show that the graph G whose vertices are the contingency tables for $(r_1, \ldots, r_m; c_1, \ldots, c_n)$, adjacent if they can be obtained from each other by such a transformation, has a Hamiltonian path.

When $m = n = 2$, G is a simple path. When $m = 2$ and $n = 3$, G has a two-dimensional structure from which we can see that every vertex is the starting point of at least two Hamiltonian paths, having distinct endpoints. When $m = 2$ and $n \geq 4$ we can show, inductively, that G actually has Hamiltonian paths from any vertex to any other.

When $m \geq 3$ and $n \geq 3$, we can reduce the problem from m to $m-1$ as in answer 62(e), if we are careful not to "paint ourselves into a corner." Namely, we must avoid reaching a state where the nonzero entries of the bottom two rows have the form $\left(\begin{smallmatrix} 1 & a & 0 \\ 0 & b & c \end{smallmatrix}\right)$

for some a, b, $c > 0$ and a change to row $m - 2$ forces this to become $\left(\begin{smallmatrix} 0 & a & 1 \\ 0 & b & c \end{smallmatrix}\right)$. The previous round of changes to rows $m - 1$ and m can avoid such a trap unless $c = 1$ and it begins with $\left(\begin{smallmatrix} 0 & a+1 & 0 \\ 1 & b-1 & 1 \end{smallmatrix}\right)$ or $\left(\begin{smallmatrix} 1 & a-1 & 1 \\ 0 & b+1 & 0 \end{smallmatrix}\right)$. But that situation can be avoided too.

(A genlex method based on exercise 61 would be considerably simpler, and it almost always would make only four changes per step. But it would occasionally need to update $2 \min(m, n)$ entries at a time.)

64. When $x_1 \ldots x_s$ is a binary string and A is a list of subcubes, let $A \oplus x_1 \ldots x_s$ denote replacing the digits $(a_1, \ldots, a_s)$ in each subcube of A by $(a_1 \oplus x_1, \ldots, a_s \oplus x_s)$, from left to right. For example, $0*1**10 \oplus 1010 = 1*1**00$. Then the following mutual recursions define a Gray cycle, because A_{st} gives a Gray path from $0^s *^t$ to $10^{s-1} *^t$ and B_{st} gives a Gray path from $0^s *^t$ to $*01^{s-1} *^{t-1}$, when $st > 0$:

$$A_{st} = 0B_{(s-1)t}, \; *A_{s(t-1)} \oplus 001^{s-2}, \; 1B_{(s-1)t}^R;$$

$$B_{st} = 0A_{(s-1)t}, \; 1B_{(s-1)t} \oplus 010^{s-2}, \; *A_{s(t-1)} \oplus 1^s.$$

The strings 001^{s-2} and 010^{s-2} are simply 0^s when $s < 2$; A_{s0} is Gray binary code; $A_{0t} = B_{0t} = *^t$. (Incidentally, the somewhat simpler construction

$$G_{st} = *G_{s(t-1)}, \; a_t G_{(s-1)t}, \; a_{t-1} G_{(s-1)t}^R, \qquad a_t = t \bmod 2,$$

defines a pleasant Gray *path* from $*^t 0^s$ to $a_{t-1} *^t 0^{s-1}$.)

65. If a path P is considered equivalent to P^R and to $P \oplus x_1 \ldots x_s$, the total number can be computed systematically as in exercise 33, with the following results for $s + t \leq 6$:

paths							cycles						
1							1						
1	1						1	1					
1	2	1					1	1	1				
1	3	3	1				1	1	1	1			
1	5	10	4	1			1	2	1	1	1		
1	6	36	35	5	1		1	2	3	1	1	1	
1	9	310	4630	218	6	1	1	3	46	4	1	1	1

In general there are $t + 1$ paths when $s = 1$ and $\binom{\lceil s/2 \rceil + 2}{2} - (s \bmod 2)$ when $t = 1$. The cycles for $s \leq 2$ are unique. When $s = t = 5$ there are approximately 6.869×10^{170} paths and 2.495×10^{70} cycles.

66. Let $G(n, 0) = \epsilon$; $G(n, t) = \emptyset$ when $n < t$; and for $1 \leq t \leq n$, let $G(n, t)$ be

$$\hat{g}(0)G(n - 1, t), \; \hat{g}(1)G(n - 1, t)^R, \; \ldots, \; \hat{g}(2^t - 1)G(n - 1, t)^R, \; \hat{g}(2^t - 1)G(n - 1, t - 1),$$

where $\hat{g}(k)$ is a t-bit column containing the Gray binary number $g(k)$ with its least significant bit at the top. In this general formula we implicitly add a row of zeros below the bases of $G(n - 1, t - 1)$.

This remarkable rule gives ordinary Gray binary code when $t = 1$, omitting $0 \ldots 00$. A cyclic Gray code is impossible because $\binom{n}{t}_2$ is odd.

67. A Gray path for compositions corresponding to Algorithm C implies that there is a path in which all transitions are $0^k 1^l \leftrightarrow 1^l 0^k$ with $\min(k, l) \leq 2$. Perhaps there is, in fact, a cycle with $\min(k, l) = 1$ in each transition.

68. (a) $\{\emptyset\}$; (b) $\emptyset$.

69. The least N with $\kappa_t N < N$ is $\binom{2t-1}{t} + \binom{2t-3}{t-1} + \cdots + \binom{1}{1} + 1 = \frac{1}{2}(\binom{2t}{t} + \binom{2t-2}{t-1} + \cdots + \binom{0}{0} + 1)$, because $\binom{n}{t-1} \leq \binom{n}{t}$ if and only if $n \geq 2t - 1$.

70. Using the facts that $t \geq 3$ implies

$$\kappa_t\left(\binom{2t-3}{t}+N'\right)-\left(\binom{2t-3}{t}+N'\right) = \kappa_t\left(\binom{2t-2}{t}+N'\right)-\left(\binom{2t-2}{t}+N'\right) = \binom{2t-2}{t}\frac{1}{t-1}+\kappa_{t-1}N'-N'$$

when $N' < \binom{2t-3}{t}$, we conclude that the maximum is $\binom{2t-2}{t}\frac{1}{t-1}+\binom{2t-4}{t-1}\frac{1}{t-2}+\cdots+\binom{2}{2}\frac{1}{1}$, and it occurs at 2^{t-1} values of N when $t > 1$.

71. Let C_t be the t-cliques. The first $\binom{1414}{t} + \binom{1009}{t-1}$ t-combinations visited by Algorithm L define a graph on 1415 vertices with 1000000 edges. If $|C_t|$ were larger, $|\partial^{t-2}C_t|$ would exceed 1000000. Thus the single graph defined by $P_{(1000000)2}$ has the maximum number of t-cliques for all $t \geq 2$.

72. $M = \binom{m_s}{s} + \cdots + \binom{m_u}{u}$ for $m_s > \cdots > m_u \geq u \geq 1$, where $\{m_s, \ldots, m_u\} = \{s+t-1, \ldots, n_v\}\setminus\{n_t, \ldots, n_{v+1}\}$. (Compare with exercise 15, which gives $\binom{s+t}{t}-1-N$.)

If $\alpha = a_{n-1}\ldots a_0$ is the bit string corresponding to the combination $n_t\ldots n_1$, then v is 1 plus the number of trailing 1s in α, and u is the length of the rightmost run of 0s. For example, when $\alpha = 1010001111$ we have $s = 4$, $t = 6$, $M = \binom{8}{4} + \binom{7}{3}$, $u = 3$, $N = \binom{9}{6} + \binom{7}{5}$, $v = 5$.

73. A and B are cross-intersecting $\iff \alpha \not\subseteq U \setminus \beta$ for all $\alpha \in A$ and $\beta \in B \iff A \cap \partial^{n-s-t}B^- = \emptyset$, where $B^- = \{U\setminus\beta \mid \beta \in B\}$ is a set of $(n-t)$-combinations. Since $Q_{Nnt}^- = P_{N(n-t)}$, we have $|\partial^{n-s-t}B^-| \geq |\partial^{n-s-t}P_{N(n-t)}|$, and $\partial^{n-s-t}P_{N(n-t)} = P_{N's}$ where $N' = \kappa_{s+1}\ldots\kappa_{n-t}N$. Thus if A and B are cross-intersecting we have $M + N' \leq |A| + |\partial^{n-s-t}B^-| \leq \binom{n}{s}$, and $Q_{Mns} \cap P_{N's} = \emptyset$.

Conversely, if $Q_{Mns} \cap P_{N's} \neq \emptyset$ we have $\binom{n}{s} < M + N' \leq |A| + |\partial^{n-s-t}B^-|$, so A and B cannot be cross-intersecting.

74. $|\varrho Q_{Nnt}| = \kappa_{n-t}N$ (see exercise 94). Also, arguing as in (58) and (59), we find $\varrho P_{N5} = (n-1)P_{N5} \cup \cdots \cup 10P_{N5} \cup \{543210, \ldots, 987654\}$ in that particular case; and $|\varrho P_{Nt}| = (n+1-n_t)N + \binom{n_t+1}{t+1}$ in general.

75. The identity $\binom{n+1}{k} = \binom{n}{k} + \binom{n-1}{k-1} + \cdots + \binom{n-k}{0}$, Eq. 1.2.6–(10), gives another representation if $n_v > v$. But (60) is unaffected, since we have $\binom{n+1}{k-1} = \binom{n}{k-1} + \binom{n-1}{k-2} + \cdots + \binom{n-k+1}{0}$.

76. Represent $N+1$ by adding $\binom{v-1}{v-1}$ to (57); then use the previous exercise to deduce that $\kappa_t(N+1) - \kappa_t N = \binom{v-1}{v-2} = v - 1$.

77. [D. E. Daykin, *Nanta Math.* **8**, 2 (1975), 78–83.] We work with extended representations $M = \binom{m_t}{t} + \cdots + \binom{m_u}{u}$ and $N = \binom{n_t}{t} + \cdots + \binom{n_v}{v}$ as in exercise 75, calling them *improper* if the final index u or v is zero. Call N *flexible* if it has both proper and improper representations, that is, if $n_v > v > 0$.

(a) Given an integer S, find $M + N$ such that $M + N = S$ and $\kappa_t M + \kappa_t N$ is minimum, with M as large as possible. If $N = 0$, we're done. Otherwise the max-min operation preserves both $M + N$ and $\kappa_t M + \kappa_t N$, so we can assume that $v \geq u \geq 1$ in the proper representations of M and N. If N is inflexible, $\kappa_t(M + 1) + \kappa_t(N - 1) = (\kappa_t M + u - 1) + (\kappa_t N - v) < \kappa_t M + \kappa_t N$, by exercise 76; therefore N must be flexible. But then we can apply the max-min operation to M and the improper representation of N, increasing M: Contradiction.

This proof shows that equality holds if and only if $MN = 0$, a fact that was noted in 1927 by F. S. Macaulay.

(b) Now we try to minimize $\max(\kappa_t M, N) + \kappa_{t-1}N$ when $M + N = S$, this time representing N as $\binom{n_{t-1}}{t-1} + \cdots + \binom{n_v}{v}$. The max-min operation can still be used if $n_{t-1} < m_t$; leaving m_t unchanged, it preserves $M + N$ and $\kappa_t M + \kappa_{t-1}N$ as well as the relation $\kappa_t M > N$. We arrive at a contradiction as in (a) if $N \neq 0$, so we can assume that $n_{t-1} \geq m_t$.

If $n_{t-1} > m_t$ we have $N > \kappa_t M$ and also $\lambda_t N > M$; hence $M + N < \lambda_t N + N = \binom{n_{t-1}+1}{t} + \cdots + \binom{n_v+1}{v+1}$, and we have $\kappa_t(M+N) \leq \kappa_t(\lambda_t N + N) = N + \kappa_{t-1}N$.

Finally if $n_{t-1} = m_t = a$, let $M = \binom{a}{t} + M'$ and $N = \binom{a}{t-1} + N'$. Then $\kappa_t(M+N) = \binom{a+1}{t-1} + \kappa_{t-1}(M' + N')$, $\kappa_t M = \binom{a}{t-1} + \kappa_{t-1}M'$, and $\kappa_{t-1}N = \binom{a}{t-2} + \kappa_{t-2}N'$; the result follows by induction on t.

78. [J. Eckhoff and G. Wegner, *Periodica Math. Hung.* **6** (1975), 137–142; A. J. W. Hilton, *Periodica Math. Hung.* **10** (1979), 25–30.] Let $M = |A_1|$ and $N = |A_0|$; we can assume that $t > 0$ and $N > 0$. Then $|\partial A| = |\partial A_1 \cup A_0| + |\partial A_0| \geq \max(|\partial A_1|, |A_0|) + |\partial A_0| \geq \max(\kappa_t M, N) + \kappa_{t-1}N \geq \kappa_t(M+N) = |P_{|A|t}|$, by induction on $m + n + t$.

Conversely, let $A_1 = P_{Mt} + 1$ and $A_0 = P_{N(t-1)} + 1$; this notation means, for example, that $\{210, 320\} + 1 = \{321, 431\}$. Then $\kappa_t(M + N) \leq |\partial A| = |\partial A_1 \cup A_0| + |(\partial A_0)0| = \max(\kappa_t M, N) + \kappa_{t-1}N$, because $\partial A_1 = P_{(\kappa_t M)(t-1)} + 1$. [Schützenberger observed in 1959 that $\kappa_t(M + N) \leq \kappa_t M + \kappa_{t-1}N$ if and only if $\kappa_t M \geq N$.]

For the first inequality, let A and B be disjoint sets of t-combinations with $|A| = M$, $|\partial A| = \kappa_t M$, $|B| = N$, $|\partial B| = \kappa_t N$. Then $\kappa_t(M + N) = \kappa_t|A \cup B| \leq |\partial(A \cup B)| = |\partial A \cup \partial B| = |\partial A| + |\partial B| = \kappa_t M + \kappa_t N$.

79. In fact, $\mu_t(M + \lambda_{t-1}M) = M$, and $\mu_t N + \lambda_{t-1}\mu_t N = N + (n_2 - n_1)[v=1]$ when N is given by (57).

80. If $N > 0$ and $t > 1$, represent N as in (57) and let $N = N_0 + N_1$, where

$$N_0 = \binom{n_t - 1}{t} + \cdots + \binom{n_v - 1}{v}, \qquad N_1 = \binom{n_t - 1}{t - 1} + \cdots + \binom{n_v - 1}{v - 1}.$$

Let $N_0 = \binom{y}{t}$ and $N_1 = \binom{z}{t-1}$. Then, by induction on t and $\lfloor x \rfloor$, we have $\binom{x}{t} = N_0 + \kappa_t N_0 \geq \binom{y}{t} + \binom{y}{t-1} = \binom{y+1}{t}$; $N_1 = \binom{x}{t} - \binom{y}{t} \geq \binom{x}{t} - \binom{x-1}{t} = \binom{x-1}{t-1}$; and $\kappa_t N = N_1 + \kappa_{t-1}N_1 \geq \binom{z}{t-1} + \binom{z}{t-2} = \binom{z+1}{t-1} \geq \binom{x}{t-1}$.

[Lovász actually proved a stronger result; see exercise 1.2.6–66. We have, similarly, $\mu_t N \geq \binom{x-1}{t-1}$; see Björner, Frankl, and Stanley, *Combinatorica* **7** (1987), 27–28.]

81. For example, if the largest element of $\widehat{P}_{N5}$ is 66433, we have

$$\widehat{P}_{N5} = \{00000, \dots, 55555\} \cup \{60000, \dots, 65555\} \cup \{66000, \dots, 66333\} \cup \{66400, \dots, 66433\}$$

so $N = \binom{10}{5} + \binom{9}{4} + \binom{6}{3} + \binom{5}{2}$. Its lower shadow is

$$\partial\widehat{P}_{N5} = \{0000, \dots, 5555\} \cup \{6000, \dots, 6555\} \cup \{6600, \dots, 6633\} \cup \{6640, \dots, 6643\},$$

of size $\binom{9}{4} + \binom{8}{3} + \binom{5}{2} + \binom{4}{1}$.

If the smallest element of Q_{N95} is 66433, we have

$$\widehat{Q}_{N95} = \{99999, \dots, 70000\} \cup \{66666, \dots, 66500\} \cup \{66444, \dots, 66440\} \cup \{66433\}$$

so $N = (\binom{13}{9} + \binom{12}{8} + \binom{11}{7}) + (\binom{8}{6} + \binom{7}{5}) + \binom{5}{4} + \binom{3}{3}$. Its upper shadow is

$$\varrho\widehat{Q}_{N95} = \{999999, \dots, 700000\} \cup \{666666, \dots, 665000\}$$
$$\cup \{664444, \dots, 664400\} \cup \{664333, \dots, 664330\},$$

of size $(\binom{14}{9} + \binom{13}{8} + \binom{12}{7}) + (\binom{9}{6} + \binom{8}{5}) + \binom{6}{4} + \binom{4}{3} = N + \kappa_9 N$. The size, t, of each combination is essentially irrelevant, as long as $N \leq \binom{s+t}{t}$; for example, the smallest element of $\widehat{Q}_{N98}$ is 99966433 in the case we have considered.

82. (a) The derivative would have to be $\sum_{k>0} r_k(x)$, but that series diverges.

[Informally, the graph of $\tau(x)$ shows "pits" of relative magnitude 2^{-k} at all odd multiples of 2^{-k}. Takagi's original publication, in *Proc. Physico-Math. Soc. Japan* (2) **1** (1903), 176–177, has been translated into English in his *Collected Papers* (Iwanami Shoten, 1973).]

(b) Since $r_k(1-t) = (-1)^{\lceil 2^k t\rceil}$ when $k > 0$, we have $\int_0^{1-x} r_k(t)\,dt = \int_x^1 r_k(1-u)\,du = -\int_x^1 r_k(u)\,du = \int_0^x r_k(u)\,du$. The second equation follows from the fact that $r_k(\frac{1}{2}t) = r_{k-1}(t)$. Part (d) shows that these two equations suffice to define $\tau(x)$ when x is rational.

(c) Since $\tau(2^{-a}x) = a2^{-a}x + 2^{-a}\tau(x)$ for $0 \le x \le 1$, we have $\tau(\epsilon) = a\epsilon + O(\epsilon)$ when $2^{-a-1} \le \epsilon \le 2^{-a}$. Therefore $\tau(\epsilon) = \epsilon\lg\frac{1}{\epsilon} + O(\epsilon)$ for $0 < \epsilon \le 1$.

(d) Suppose $0 \le p/q \le 1$. If $p/q \le 1/2$ we have $\tau(p/q) = p/q + \tau(2p/q)/2$; otherwise $\tau(p/q) = (q-p)/q + \tau(2(q-p)/q)/2$. Therefore we can assume that q is odd. When q is odd, let $p' = p/2$ when p is even, $p' = (q-p)/2$ when p is odd. Then $\tau(p/q) = 2\tau(p'/q) - 2p'/q$ for $0 < p < q$; this system of $q-1$ equations has a unique solution. For example, the values for $q = 3, 4, 5, 6, 7$ are $2/3, 2/3$; $1/2, 1/2, 1/2$; $8/15, 2/3, 2/3, 8/15$; $1/2, 2/3, 1/2, 2/3, 1/2$; $22/49, 30/49, 32/49, 32/49, 30/49, 22/49$.

(e) The solutions $< \frac{1}{2}$ are $x = \frac{1}{4}, \frac{1}{4} - \frac{1}{16}, \frac{1}{4} - \frac{1}{16} - \frac{1}{64}, \frac{1}{4} - \frac{1}{16} - \frac{1}{64} - \frac{1}{256}, \dots, \frac{1}{6}$.

(f) The value $\frac{2}{3}$ is achieved for $x = \frac{1}{2} \pm \frac{1}{8} \pm \frac{1}{32} \pm \frac{1}{128} \pm \cdots$, an uncountable set.

83. Given any integers $q > p > 0$, consider paths starting from 0 in the digraph

$$0 \leftarrow 1 \leftarrow 2 \leftarrow 3 \leftarrow 4 \leftarrow 5 \leftarrow \cdots$$
$$\updownarrow \quad \updownarrow \quad \updownarrow \quad \updownarrow \quad \updownarrow \quad \updownarrow$$
$$1 \rightarrow 2 \rightarrow 3 \rightarrow 4 \rightarrow 5 \rightarrow 6 \rightarrow \cdots$$

Compute an associated value v, starting with $v \leftarrow -p$; horizontal moves change $v \leftarrow 2v$, vertical moves from node a change $v \leftarrow 2(qa - v)$. The path stops if we reach a node twice with the same value v. Transitions are not allowed to upper node a if $v \le -q$ or $v \ge qa$ at that node; they are not allowed to lower node a with $v \le 0$ or $v \ge q(a + 1)$. These restrictions force most steps of the path. (Node a in the upper row means, "Solve $\tau(x) = ax - v/q$"; in the lower row it means, "Solve $\tau(x) = v/q - ax$.") Empirical tests suggest that all such paths are finite. The equation $\tau(x) = p/q$ then has solutions $x = x_0$ defined by the sequence $x_0, x_1, x_2, \dots$ where $x_k = \frac{1}{2}x_{k+1}$ on a horizontal step and $x_k = 1 - \frac{1}{2}x_{k+1}$ on a vertical step; eventually $x_k = x_j$ for some $j < k$. If $j > 0$ and if q is not a power of 2, these are all the solutions to $\tau(x) = p/q$ when $x > 1/2$.

For example, this procedure establishes that $\tau(x) = 1/5$ and $x > 1/2$ only when x is $83581/87040$; the only path yields $x_0 = 1 - \frac{1}{2}x_1$, $x_1 = \frac{1}{2}x_2$, $\dots$, $x_{18} = \frac{1}{2}x_{19}$, and $x_{19} = x_{11}$. There are, similarly, just two values $x > 1/2$ with $\tau(x) = 3/5$, having denominator $2^{46}(2^{56} - 1)/3$.

Moreover, it appears that all cycles in the digraph that pass through node 0 define values of p and q such that $\tau(x) = p/q$ has uncountably many solutions. Such values are, for example, $2/3, 8/15, 8/21$, corresponding to the cycles $(01), (0121), (012321)$. The value $32/63$ corresponds to (012121) and also to (012101234545454321), as well as to two other paths that do not return to 0.

84. [Frankl, Matsumoto, Ruzsa, and Tokushige, *J. Combinatorial Theory* **A69** (1995), 125–148.] If $a \le b$ we have

$$\binom{2t-1-b}{t-a} \bigg/ T = t^a(t-1)^{b-a}/(2t-1)^b = 2^{-b}(1 + f(a,b)t^{-1} + O(b^4/t^2)),$$

where $f(a,b) = a(1+b) - a^2 - b(1+b)/4 = f(a+1,b) - b + 2a$. Therefore if N has the combinatorial representation (57), and if we set $n_j = 2t - 1 - b_j$, we have

$$\frac{t}{T}\left(\kappa_t N - N\right) = \frac{b_t}{2^{b_t}} + \frac{b_{t-1} - 2}{2^{b_{t-1}}} + \frac{b_{t-2} - 4}{2^{b_{t-2}}} + \cdots + \frac{O(\log t)^3}{t},$$

the terms being negligible when b_j exceeds $2 \lg t$. And one can show that

$$\tau\left(\sum_{j=0}^{l} 2^{-e_j}\right) = \sum_{j=0}^{l}(e_j - 2j)2^{-e_j}.$$

85. $N - \lambda_{t-1}N$ has the same asymptotic form as $\kappa_t N - N$, by (63), since $\tau(x) = \tau(1-x)$. So does $2\mu_t N - N$, up to $O(T(\log t)^3/t^2)$, because $\binom{2t-1-b}{t-a} = 2\binom{2t-2-b}{t-a}(1 + O(\log t)/t)$ when $b < 2\lg t$.

86. $x \in X^{\circ\sim} \iff \bar{x} \notin X^{\circ} \iff \bar{x} \notin X$ or $\bar{x} \notin X + e_1$ or $\cdots$ or $\bar{x} \notin X + e_n \iff x \in X^{\sim}$ or $x \in X^{\sim} - e_1$ or $\cdots$ or $x \in X^{\sim} - e_n \iff x \in X^{\sim+}$.

87. All three are true, using the fact that $X \subseteq Y^{\circ}$ if and only if $X^+ \subseteq Y$: (a) $X \subseteq Y^{\circ} \iff X^{\sim} \supseteq Y^{\circ\sim} = Y^{\sim+} \iff Y^{\sim} \subseteq X^{\sim\circ}$. (b) $X^+ \subseteq X^+ \implies X \subseteq X^{+\circ}$; hence $X^{\circ} \subseteq X^{\circ+\circ}$. Also $X^{\circ} \subseteq X^{\circ} \implies X^{\circ+} \subseteq X$; hence $X^{\circ+\circ} \subseteq X^{\circ}$. (c) $\alpha M \leq N \iff S_M^+ \subseteq S_N \iff S_M \subseteq S_N^{\circ} \iff M \leq \beta N$.

88. If $\nu x < \nu y$ then $\nu(x - e_k) < \nu(y - e_j)$, so we can assume that $\nu x = \nu y$ and that $x > y$ in lexicographic order. We must have $y_j > 0$; otherwise $\nu(y - e_j)$ would exceed $\nu(x - e_k)$. If $x_i = y_i$ for $1 \leq i \leq j$, clearly $k > j$ and $x - e_k \prec y - e_j$. Otherwise $x_i > y_i$ for some $i \leq j$; again we have $x - e_k \prec y - e_j$, unless $x - e_k = y - e_j$.

89. From the table

$j =$	0	1	2	3	4	5	6	7	8	9	10	11
$e_j + e_1 =$	e_1	e_0	e_4	e_5	e_2	e_3	e_8	e_9	e_6	e_7	e_{11}	e_{10}
$e_j + e_2 =$	e_2	e_4	e_0	e_6	e_1	e_8	e_3	e_{10}	e_5	e_{11}	e_7	e_9
$e_j + e_3 =$	e_3	e_5	e_6	e_7	e_8	e_9	e_{10}	e_0	e_{11}	e_1	e_2	e_4

we find $(\alpha 0, \alpha 1, \ldots, \alpha 12) = (0, 4, 6, 7, 8, 9, 10, 11, 11, 12, 12, 12, 12)$; $(\beta 0, \beta 1, \ldots, \beta 12) = (0, 0, 0, 0, 1, 1, 2, 3, 4, 5, 6, 8, 12)$.

90. Let $Y = X^+$ and $Z = C_k X$, and let $N_a = |X_k(a)|$ for $0 \leq a < m_k$. Then

$$|Y| = \sum_{a=0}^{m_k-1} |Y_k(a)| = \sum_{a=0}^{m_k-1} |(X_k(a-1) + e_k) \cup (X_k(a) + E_k(0))|$$
$$\geq \sum_{a=0}^{m_k-1} \max(N_{a-1}, \alpha N_a),$$

where $a - 1$ stands for $(a - 1) \bmod m_k$ and the α function comes from the $(n-1)$-dimensional torus, because $|X_k(a) + E_k(0)| \geq \alpha N_a$ by induction. Also

$$|Z^+| = \sum_{a=0}^{m_k-1} |Z_k^+(a)| = \sum_{a=0}^{m_k-1} |(Z_k(a-1) + e_k) \cup (Z_k(a) + E_k(0))|$$
$$= \sum_{a=0}^{m_k-1} \max(N_{a-1}, \alpha N_a),$$

because both $Z_k(a-1) + e_k$ and $Z_k(a) + E_k(0)$ are standard in $n - 1$ dimensions.

91. Let there be N_a points in row a of a totally compressed array, where row 0 is at the bottom; thus $l = N_{-1} \geq N_0 \geq \cdots \geq N_{m-1} \geq N_m = 0$. We show first that there is an optimum X for which the "bad" condition $N_a = N_{a+1}$ never occurs except when $N_a = 0$ or $N_a = l$. For if a is the smallest bad subscript, suppose $N_{a-1} > N_a = N_{a+1} = \cdots = N_{a+k} > N_{a+k+1}$. Then we can always decrease N_{a+k} by 1 and add 1 to some N_b for $b \leq a$ without increasing $|X^+|$, except in cases where $k = 1$ and $N_{a+2} = N_{a+1} - 1$ and $N_b = N_a + a - b < l$ for $0 \leq b \leq a$. Exploring such cases further, if $N_{c+1} < N_c = N_{c-1}$ for some $c > a + 1$, we can set $N_c \leftarrow N_c - 1$ and $N_a \leftarrow N_a + 1$, thereby either decreasing a or increasing N_0. Otherwise we can find a subscript d such that $N_c = N_{a+1} + a + 1 - c > 0$ for $a < c < d$, and either $N_d = 0$ or $N_d < N_{d-1} - 1$. Then it is OK to decrease N_c by 1 for $a < c < d$ and subsequently to increase N_b by 1 for $0 \leq b < d - a - 1$. (It is important to note that if $N_d = 0$ we have $N_0 \geq d - 1$; hence $d = m$ implies $l = m$.)

Repeating such transformations until $N_a > N_{a+1}$ whenever $N_a \neq l$ and $N_{a+1} \neq 0$, we reach situation (86), and the proof can be completed as in the text.

92. Let $x + k$ denote the lexicographically smallest element of $T(m_1, \ldots, m_{n-1})$ that exceeds x and has weight $\nu x + k$, if any such element exists. For example, if $m_1 = m_2 = m_3 = 4$ and $x = 211$, we have $x+1 = 212$, $x+2 = 213$, $x+3 = 223$, $x+4 = 233$, $x+5 = 333$, and $x+6$ does not exist; in general, $x + k + 1$ is obtained from $x + k$ by increasing the rightmost component that can be increased. If $x + k = (m_1 - 1, \ldots, m_{n-1} - 1)$, let us set $x + k + 1 = x + k$. Then if $S(k)$ is the set of all elements of $T(m_1, \ldots, m_{n-1})$ that are $\preceq x + k$, we have $S(k+1) = S(k)^+$. Furthermore, the elements of S that end in a are those whose first $n - 1$ components are in $S(m - 1 - a)$.

The result of this exercise can be stated more intuitively: As we generate n-dimensional standard sets S_1, S_2, $\ldots$, the $(n - 1)$-dimensional standard sets on each layer become spreads of each other just after each point is added to layer $m - 1$. Similarly, they become cores of each other just before each point is added to layer 0.

93. (a) Suppose the parameters are $2 \leq m_1' \leq m_2' \leq \cdots \leq m_n'$ when sorted properly, and let k be minimal with $m_k \neq m_k'$. Then take $N = 1 + \text{rank}(0, \ldots, 0, m_k' - 1, 0, \ldots, 0)$. (We must assume that $\min(m_1, \ldots, m_n) \geq 2$, since parameters equal to 1 can be placed anywhere.)

(b) Only in the proof for $n = 2$, buried inside the answer to exercise 91. That proof is incorporated by induction when n is larger.

94. Complementation reverses lexicographic order and changes ϱ to ∂.

95. For Theorem K, let $d = n - 1$ and $s_0 = \cdots = s_d = 1$. For Theorem M, let $d = s$ and $s_0 = \cdots = s_d = t + 1$.

96. In such a representation, N is the number of t-multicombinations of $\{s_0 \cdot 0, s_1 \cdot 1, s_2 \cdot 2, \ldots\}$ that precede $n_t n_{t-1} \ldots n_1$ in lexicographic order, because the generalized coefficient $\binom{S(n)}{t}$ counts the multicombinations whose leftmost component is $< n$.

If we truncate the representation by stopping at the rightmost nonzero term $\binom{S(n_v)}{v}$, we obtain a nice generalization of (60):

$$|\partial P_{Nt}| = \binom{S(n_t)}{t-1} + \binom{S(n_{t-1})}{t-2} + \cdots + \binom{S(n_v)}{v-1}.$$

[See G. F. Clements, *J. Combinatorial Theory* **A37** (1984), 91–97. The inequalities $s_0 \geq s_1 \geq \cdots \geq s_d$ are needed for the validity of Corollary C, but not for the calculation of $|\partial P_{Nt}|$. Some terms $\binom{S(n_k)}{k}$ for $t \geq k > v$ may be zero. For example, when $N = 1$, $t = 4$, $s_0 = 3$, and $s_1 = 2$, we have $N = \binom{S(1)}{4} + \binom{S(1)}{3} = 0 + 1$.]

97. (a) The tetrahedron has four vertices, six edges, four faces: $(N_0, \ldots, N_4) = (1, 4, 6, 4, 1)$. The octahedron, similarly, has $(N_0, \ldots, N_6) = (1, 6, 8, 8, 0, 0, 0)$, and the icosahedron has $(N_0, \ldots, N_{12}) = (1, 12, 30, 20, 0, \ldots, 0)$. The hexahedron, aka the 3-cube, has eight vertices, 12 edges, and six square faces; perturbation breaks each square face into two triangles and introduces new edges, so we have $(N_0, \ldots, N_8) = (1, 8, 18, 12, 0, \ldots, 0)$. Finally, the perturbed pentagonal faces of the dodecahedron lead to $(N_0, \ldots, N_{20}) = (1, 20, 54, 36, 0, \ldots, 0)$.

(b) $\{210, 310\} \cup \{10, 20, 21, 30, 31\} \cup \{0, 1, 2, 3\} \cup \{\epsilon\}$.

(c) $0 \le N_t \le \binom{n}{t}$ for $0 \le t \le n$ and $N_{t-1} \ge \kappa_t N_t$ for $1 \le t \le n$. The second condition is equivalent to $\lambda_{t-1} N_{t-1} \ge N_t$ for $1 \le t \le n$, if we define $\lambda_0 1 = \infty$. These conditions are necessary for Theorem K, and sufficient if $A = \bigcup P_{N_t t}$.

(d) The complements of the elements not in a simplicial complex, namely the sets $\{\, \{0, \ldots, n-1\} \setminus \alpha \mid \alpha \notin C \,\}$, form a simplicial complex. (We can also verify that the necessary and sufficient condition holds: $N_{t-1} \ge \kappa_t N_t \iff \lambda_{t-1} N_{t-1} \ge N_t \iff \kappa_{n-t+1} \overline{N}_{n-t+1} \le \overline{N}_{n-t}$, because $\kappa_{n-t} \overline{N}_{n-t+1} = \binom{n}{t} - \lambda_{t-1} N_{t-1}$ by exercise 94.)

(e) $00000 \leftrightarrow 14641$; $10000 \leftrightarrow 14640$; $11000 \leftrightarrow 14630$; $12000 \leftrightarrow 14620$; $13000 \leftrightarrow 14610$; $14000 \leftrightarrow 14600$; $12100 \leftrightarrow 14520$; $13100 \leftrightarrow 14510$; $14100 \leftrightarrow 14500$; $13200 \leftrightarrow 14410$; $14200 \leftrightarrow 14400$; $13300 \leftrightarrow 14310$; and the self-dual cases 14300, 13310.

98. The following procedure by S. Linusson [*Combinatorica* **19** (1999), 255–266], who considered also the more general problem for multisets, is considerably faster than a more obvious approach. Let $L(n, h, l)$ count feasible vectors with $N_t = \binom{n}{t}$ for $0 \le t \le l$, $N_{t+1} < \binom{n}{t+1}$, and $N_t = 0$ for $t > h$. Then $L(n, h, l) = 0$ unless $-1 \le l \le h \le n$; also $L(n, h, h) = L(n, h, -1) = 1$, and $L(n, n, l) = L(n, n-1, l)$ for $l < n$. When $n > h \ge l \ge 0$ we can compute $L(n, h, l) = \sum_{j=l}^{h} L(n-1, h, j) L(n-1, j-1, l-1)$, a recurrence that follows from Theorem K. (Each size vector corresponds to the complex $\bigcup P_{N_t t}$, with $L(n-1, h, j)$ representing combinations that do not contain the maximum element $n-1$ and $L(n-1, j-1, l-1)$ representing those that do.) Finally the grand total is $L(n) = \sum_{l=1}^{n} L(n, n, l)$.

We have $L(0), L(1), L(2), \ldots$ = 2, 3, 5, 10, 26, 96, 553, 5461, 100709, 3718354, 289725509, $\ldots$; $L(100) \approx 3.2299 \times 10^{1842}$.

99. The maximal elements of a simplicial complex form a clutter; conversely, the combinations contained in elements of a clutter form a simplicial complex. Thus the two concepts are essentially equivalent.

(a) If $(M_0, M_1, \ldots, M_n)$ is the size vector of a clutter, then $(N_0, N_1, \ldots, N_n)$ is the size vector of a simplicial complex if $N_n = M_n$ and $N_t = M_t + \kappa_{t+1} N_{t+1}$ for $0 \le t < n$. Conversely, every such $(N_0, \ldots, N_n)$ yields an $(M_0, \ldots, M_n)$ if we use the lexicographically first N_t t-combinations. [G. F. Clements extended this result to general multisets in *Discrete Math.* **4** (1973), 123–128.]

(b) In the order of answer 97(e) they are 00000, 00001, 10000, 00040, 01000, 00030, 02000, 00120, 03000, 00310, 04000, 00600, 00100, 00020, 01100, 00210, 02100, 00500, 00200, 00110, 01200, 00400, 00300, 01010, 01300, 00010. Notice that $(M_0, \ldots, M_n)$ is feasible if and only if $(M_n, \ldots, M_0)$ is feasible, so we have a different sort of duality in this interpretation.

100. Represent A as a subset of $T(m_1, \ldots, m_n)$ as in the proof of Corollary C. Then the maximum value of νA is obtained when A consists of the N lexicographically smallest points $x_1 \ldots x_n$.

The proof starts by reducing to the case that A is compressed, in the sense that its t-multicombinations are $P_{|A \cap T_t| t}$ for each t. Then if y is the largest element $\in A$

and if x is the smallest element $\notin A$, we prove that $x < y$ implies $\nu x > \nu y$, hence $\nu(A \setminus y \cup x) > \nu A$. For if $\nu x = \nu y - k$ we could find an element of $\partial^k y$ that is greater than x, contradicting the assumption that A is compressed.

101. (a) In general, $F(p) = N_0 p^n + N_1 p^{n-1}(1-p) + \cdots + N_n(1-p)^n$ when $f(x_1, \ldots, x_n)$ is satisfied by exactly N_t binary strings $x_1 \ldots x_n$ of weight t. Thus we find $G(p) = p^4 + 3p^3(1-p) + p^2(1-p)^2$; $H(p) = p^4 + p^3(1-p) + p^2(1-p)^2$.

(b) A monotone formula f is equivalent to a simplicial complex C under the correspondence $f(x_1, \ldots, x_n) = 1 \iff \{j - 1 \mid x_j = 0\} \in C$. Therefore the functions $f(p)$ of monotone Boolean functions are those that satisfy the condition of exercise 97(c), and we obtain a suitable function by choosing the lexicographically last N_{n-t} t-combinations (which are complements of the first N_s s-combinations): $\{3210\}$, $\{321, 320, 310\}$, $\{32\}$ gives $f(w, x, y, z) = wxyz \lor xyz \lor wyz \lor wxz \lor yz = wxz \lor yz$.

M. P. Schützenberger observed that we can find the parameters N_t easily from $f(p)$ by noting that $f(1/(1+u)) = (N_0 + N_1 u + \cdots + N_n u^n)/(1+u)^n$. One can show that $H(p)$ is not equivalent to a monotone formula in any number of variables, because $(1 + u + u^2)/(1+u)^4 = (N_0 + N_1 u + \cdots + N_n u^n)/(1+u)^n$ implies that $N_1 = n - 3$, $N_2 = \binom{n-3}{2} + 1$, and $\kappa_2 N_2 = n - 2$.

But the task of deciding this question is not so simple in general. For example, the function $(1 + 5u + 5u^2 + 5u^3)/(1+u)^5$ does not match any monotone formula in five variables, because $\kappa_3 5 = 7$; but it equals $(1 + 6u + 10u^2 + 10u^3 + 5u^4)/(1+u)^6$, which works fine with six.

102. (a) Choose N_t linearly independent polynomials of degree t in I; order their terms lexicographically, and take linear combinations so that the lexicographically smallest terms are distinct monomials. Let I' consist of all multiples of those monomials.

(b) Each monomial of degree t in I' is essentially a t-multicombination; for example, $x_1^3 x_2 x_5^4$ corresponds to 55552111. If M_t is the set of independent monomials for degree t, the ideal property is equivalent to saying that $M_{t+1} \supseteq \varrho M_t$.

In the given example, $M_3 = \{x_0 x_1^2\}$; $M_4 = \varrho M_3 \cup \{x_0 x_1 x_2^2\}$; $M_5 = \varrho M_4 \cup \{x_1 x_2^4\}$, since $x_2^2(x_0 x_1^2 - 2x_1 x_2^2) - x_1(x_0 x_1 x_2^2) = -2x_1 x_2^4$; and $M_{t+1} = \varrho M_t$ thereafter.

(c) By Theorem M we can assume that $M_t = \widehat{Q}_{Mst}$. Let $N_t = \binom{n_{ts}}{s} + \cdots + \binom{n_{t2}}{2} + \binom{n_{t1}}{1}$, where $s + t \geq n_{ts} > \cdots > n_{t2} > n_{t1} \geq 0$; then $n_{ts} = s + t$ if and only if $n_{t(s-1)} = s - 2$, $\ldots$, $n_{t1} = 0$. Furthermore we have

$$N_{t+1} \geq N_t + \kappa_s N_t = \binom{n_{ts} + [n_{ts} \geq s]}{s} + \cdots + \binom{n_{t2} + [n_{t2} \geq 2]}{2} + \binom{n_{t1} + [n_{t1} \geq 1]}{1}.$$

Therefore the sequence $(n_{ts} - t - \infty[n_{ts} < s], \ldots, n_{t2} - t - \infty[n_{t2} < 2], n_{t1} - t - \infty[n_{t1} < 1])$ is lexicographically nondecreasing as t increases, where we insert '$-\infty$' in components that have $n_{tj} = j - 1$. Such a sequence cannot increase infinitely many times without exceeding the maximum value $(s, -\infty, \ldots, -\infty)$, by exercise 1.2.1–15(d).

103. Let P_{Nst} be the first N elements of a sequence determined as follows: For each binary string $x = x_{s+t-1} \ldots x_0$, in lexicographic order, write down $\binom{\nu x}{t}$ subcubes by changing t of the 1s to *s in all possible ways, in lexicographic order (considering $1 < *$). For example, if $x = 0101101$ and $t = 2$, we generate the subcubes $0101*0*$, $010*10*$, $010**01$, $0*0110*$, $0*01*01$, $0*0*101$.

[See B. Lindström, *Arkiv för Mat.* **8** (1971), 245–257; a generalization analogous to Corollary C appears in K. Engel, *Sperner Theory* (Cambridge Univ. Press, 1997), Theorem 8.1.1.]

104. The first N strings in cross order have the desired property. [T. N. Danh and D. E. Daykin, *J. London Math. Soc.* (2) **55** (1997), 417–426.]

Notes: Beginning with the observation that the "1-shadow" of the N lexicographically first strings of weight t (namely the strings obtained by deleting 1 bits only) consists of the first $\mu_t N$ strings of weight t, R. Ahlswede and N. Cai extended the Danh–Daykin theorem to allow insertion, deletion, and/or transposition of bits [*Combinatorica* **17** (1997), 11–29; *Applied Math. Letters* **11**, 5 (1998), 121–126]. Uwe Leck has proved that no total ordering of *ternary strings* has the analogous minimum-shadow property [Preprint 98/6 (Univ. Rostock, 1998), 6 pages].

105. Every number must occur the same number of times in the cycle. Equivalently, $\binom{n-1}{t-1}$ must be a multiple of t. This necessary condition appears to be sufficient as well, provided that n is not too small with respect to t; but such a result may well be true yet impossible to prove. [See Chung, Graham, and Diaconis, *Discrete Math.* **110** (1992), 55–57.]

The next few exercises consider the cases $t = 2$ and $t = 3$, for which elegant results are known. Similar but more complicated results have been derived for $t = 4$ and $t = 5$, and the case $t = 6$ has been partially resolved. The case $(n, t) = (12, 6)$ is currently the smallest for which the existence of a universal cycle is unknown.

106. Let the differences mod $(2m+1)$ be $1, 2, \ldots, m, 1, 2, \ldots, m, \ldots$, repeated $2m+1$ times; for example, the cycle for $m = 3$ is $(01360256145034623512 4)$. This works because $1 + \cdots + m = \binom{m+1}{2}$ is relatively prime to $2m + 1$. [*J. École Polytechnique* **4**, Cahier 10 (1810), 16–48.]

107. The seven doubles ▮▮▮, ▮ ▮▮, $\ldots$, ▤▤▤ can be inserted in 3^7 ways into any universal cycle of 2-combinations for $\{0, 1, 2, 3, 4, 5, 6\}$. The number of such universal cycles is the number of Eulerian trails of the complete graph K_7, which can be shown to be 129,976,320 if we regard $(a_0 a_1 \ldots a_{20})$ as equivalent to $(a_1 \ldots a_{20} a_0)$ but not to the reverse-order cycle $(a_{20} \ldots a_1 a_0)$. So the answer is 284,258,211,840.

[This problem was first solved in 1859 by M. Reiss, whose method was so complicated that people doubted the result; see *Nouvelles Annales de Mathématiques* **8** (1849), 74; **11** (1852), 115; *Annali di Matematica Pura ed Applicata* (2) **5** (1871–1873), 63–120. A considerably simpler solution, confirming Reiss's claim, was found by P. Jolivald and G. Tarry, who also enumerated the Eulerian trails of K_9; see *Comptes Rendus Association Française pour l'Avancement des Sciences* **15**, part 2 (1886), 49–53; É. Lucas, *Récréations Mathématiques* **4** (1894), 123–151. Brendan D. McKay and Robert W. Robinson found an approach that is better still, enabling them to continue the enumeration through K_{21} by using the fact that the number of trails is

$$(m - 1)!^{2m+1} \, [z_0^{2m} z_1^{2m-2} \ldots z_{2m}^{2m-2}] \, \det(a_{jk}) \prod_{1 \le j < k \le 2m} (z_j^2 + z_k^2),$$

where $a_{jk} = -1/(z_j^2 + z_k^2)$ when $j \ne k$; $a_{jj} = -1/(2z_j^2) + \sum_{0 \le k \le 2m} 1/(z_j^2 + z_k^2)$; see *Combinatorics, Probability, and Computing* **7** (1998), 437–449.]

C. Flye Sainte-Marie, in L'*Intermédiaire des Mathématiciens* **1** (1894), 164–165, noted that the Eulerian trails of K_7 include 2×720 that have 7-fold symmetry under permutation of $\{0, 1, \ldots, 6\}$ (namely Poinsot's cycle and its reverse), plus 32×1680 with 3-fold symmetry, plus 25778×5040 cycles that are asymmetric.

108. No solution is possible for $n < 7$, except in the trivial case $n = 4$. When $n = 7$ there are $12,255,208 \times 7!$ universal cycles, not considering $(a_0 a_1 \ldots a_{34})$ to be the same as $(a_1 \ldots a_{34} a_0)$, including cases with 5-fold symmetry like the example cycle in exercise 105.

When $n \geq 8$ we can proceed systematically as suggested by B. Jackson in *Discrete Math.* **117** (1993), 141–150; see also G. Hurlbert, *SIAM J. Disc. Math.* **7** (1994), 598–604: Put each 3-combination into the "standard cyclic order" $c_1 c_2 c_3$ where $c_2 = (c_1 + \delta) \bmod n$, $c_3 = (c_2 + \delta') \bmod n$, $0 < \delta, \delta' < n/2$, and either $\delta = \delta'$ or $\max(\delta, \delta') < n - \delta - \delta' \neq (n-1)/2$ or $(1 < \delta < n/4$ and $\delta' = (n-1)/2)$ or $(\delta = (n-1)/2$ and $1 < \delta' < n/4)$. For example, when $n = 8$ the allowable values of (δ, δ') are $(1,1)$, $(1,2)$, $(1,3)$, $(2,1)$, $(2,2)$, $(3,1)$, $(3,3)$; when $n = 11$ they are $(1,1)$, $(1,2)$, $(1,3)$, $(1,4)$, $(2,1)$, $(2,2)$, $(2,3)$, $(2,5)$, $(3,1)$, $(3,2)$, $(3,3)$, $(4,1)$, $(4,4)$, $(5,2)$, $(5,5)$. Then construct the digraph with vertices (c, δ) for $0 \leq c < n$ and $1 \leq \delta < n/2$, and with arcs $(c_1, \delta) \to (c_2, \delta')$ for every combination $c_1 c_2 c_3$ in standard cyclic order. This digraph is connected and balanced, so it has an Eulerian trail by Theorem 2.3.4.2D. (The peculiar rules about $(n-1)/2$ make the digraph connected when n is odd. The Eulerian trail can be chosen to have n-fold symmetry when $n = 8$, but not when $n = 12$.)

109. When $n = 1$ the cycle (000) is trivial; when $n = 2$ there is no cycle; and there are essentially only two when $n = 4$, namely

$$(00011122233302021313) \quad \text{and} (00011120203332221313).$$

When $n \geq 5$, let the multicombination $d_1 d_2 d_3$ be in standard cyclic order if $d_2 = (d_1 + \delta - 1) \bmod n$, $d_3 = (d_2 + \delta' - 1) \bmod n$, and (δ, δ') is allowable for $n + 3$ in the previous answer. Construct the digraph with vertices (d, δ) for $0 \leq d < n$ and $1 \leq \delta < (n+3)/2$, and with arcs $(d_1, \delta) \to (d_2, \delta')$ for every multicombination $d_1 d_2 d_3$ in standard cyclic order; then find an Eulerian trail.

Perhaps a universal cycle of t-multicombinations exists for $\{0, 1, \ldots, n-1\}$ if and only if a universal cycle of t-combinations exists for $\{0, 1, \ldots, n + t - 1\}$.

110. A nice way to check for runs is to compute the numbers

$$b(S) = \sum \{2^{p(c)} \mid c \in S\}$$

where $(p(\mathtt{A}), \ldots, p(\mathtt{K})) = (1, \ldots, 13)$; then set $l \leftarrow b(S) \mathbin{\&} -b(S)$ and check that $b(S) + l = l \ll s$, and also that $((l \ll s) \mid (l \gg 1)) \mathbin{\&} a = 0$, where $a = 2^{p(c_1)} \mid \cdots \mid 2^{p(c_5)}$. The values of $b(S)$ and $\sum \{v(c) \mid c \in S\}$ are easily maintained as S runs through all 31 nonempty subsets in Gray-code order. The answers are $(1009008,\ 99792,\ 2813796,\ 505008,\ 2855676,\ 697508,\ 1800268,\ 751324,\ 1137236,\ 361224,\ 388740,\ 51680,\ 317340,\ 19656,\ 90100,\ 9168,\ 58248,\ 11196,\ 2708,\ 0,\ 8068,\ 2496,\ 444,\ 356,\ 3680,\ 0,\ 0,\ 0,\ 76,\ 4)$ for $x = (0, \ldots, 29)$; thus the mean score is ≈ 4.769 and the variance is ≈ 9.768.

> *Hands without points are sometimes facetiously called nineteen,*
> *as that number cannot be made by the cards.*
> — G. H. DAVIDSON, *Dee's Hand-Book of Cribbage* (1839)

Note: A four-card flush is not allowed in the "crib." Then the distribution is a bit easier to compute, and it turns out to be $(1022208,\ 99792,\ 2839800,\ 508908,\ 2868960,\ 703496,\ 1787176,\ 755320,\ 1118336,\ 358368,\ 378240,\ 43880,\ 310956,\ 16548,\ 88132,\ 9072,\ 57288,\ 11196,\ 2264,\ 0,\ 7828,\ 2472,\ 444,\ 356,\ 3680,\ 0,\ 0,\ 0,\ 76,\ 4)$; the mean and variance decrease to approximately 4.735 and 9.667.

111. $\partial^{n-2r} B$ is the set of all r-subsets of B; these subsets must not be in A. If $|A| = |B| = \binom{x}{n-r}$ for some real $x > n-1$, we would have $\binom{n}{r} \geq |A| + |\partial^{n-2r} B| \geq \binom{x}{n-r} + \binom{x}{r} > \binom{n-1}{n-r} + \binom{n-1}{r} = \binom{n}{r}$, by exercise 80. [See *Quart. J. Math. Oxford* **12** (1961), 313–320.]

SECTION 7.2.1.4

1.

m^n	$m^{\underline{n}}$	$m!\left\{{n \atop m}\right\}$
$\binom{m+n-1}{n}$	$\binom{m}{n}$	$\binom{n-1}{n-m}$
$\left\{{n \atop 0}\right\} + \cdots + \left\{{n \atop m}\right\}$	$[m \geq n]$	$\left\{{n \atop m}\right\}$
$\left\lfloor{m+n \atop m}\right\rfloor$	$[m \geq n]$	$\left\lfloor{n \atop m}\right\rfloor$

2. In general, given any integers $x_1 \geq \cdots \geq x_m$, we obtain all integer m-tuples $a_1 \ldots a_m$ such that $a_1 \geq \cdots \geq a_m$, $a_1 + \cdots + a_m = x_1 + \cdots + x_m$, and $a_m \ldots a_1 \geq x_m \ldots x_1$ by initializing $a_1 \ldots a_m \leftarrow x_1 \ldots x_m$ and $a_{m+1} \leftarrow x_m - 2$. In particular, if c is any integer constant, we obtain all integer m-tuples such that $a_1 \geq \cdots \geq a_m \geq c$ and $a_1 + \cdots + a_m = n$ by initializing $a_1 \leftarrow n - mc + c$, $a_j \leftarrow c$ for $1 < j \leq m$, and $a_{m+1} \leftarrow c - 2$, assuming that $n \geq cm$.

3. $a_j = \lfloor (n + m - j)/m \rfloor = \lceil (n+1-j)/m \rceil$, for $1 \leq j \leq m$; see *CMath* §3.4.

4. Assume that $1 \leq r \leq n$. We must have $a_m \geq a_1 - 1$; therefore $a_j = \lfloor (n+m-j)/m \rfloor$ for $1 \leq j \leq m$, where m is the largest integer with $\lfloor n/m \rfloor \geq r$, namely $m = \lfloor n/r \rfloor$.

5. [See Eugene M. Klimko, *BIT* **13** (1973), 38–49.]

C1. [Initialize.] Set $c_0 \leftarrow 1$, $c_1 \leftarrow n$, $c_2 \ldots c_n \leftarrow 0 \ldots 0$, $l_0 \leftarrow 1$, $l_1 \leftarrow 0$. (We assume that $n > 0$.)

C2. [Visit.] Visit the partition represented by part counts $c_1 \ldots c_n$ and links $l_0 l_1 \ldots l_n$.

C3. [Branch.] Set $j \leftarrow l_0$ and $k \leftarrow l_j$. If $c_j = 1$, go to C6; otherwise, if $j > 1$, go to C5.

C4. [Change 1+1 to 2.] Set $c_1 \leftarrow c_1 - 2$, $c_2 \leftarrow c_2 + 1$, and $l_{[c_1 > 0]} \leftarrow 2$. If $k \neq 2$, also set $l_2 \leftarrow k$. Return to C2.

C5. [Change $j \cdot c_j$ to $(j+1) + 1 + \cdots + 1$.] Set $c_1 \leftarrow j(c_j - 1) - 1$ and go to C7.

C6. [Change $k \cdot c_k + j$ to $(k+1) + 1 + \cdots + 1$.] Terminate if $k = 0$. Otherwise set $c_j \leftarrow 0$; then set $c_1 \leftarrow k(c_k - 1) + j - 1$, $j \leftarrow k$, and $k \leftarrow l_k$.

C7. [Adjust links.] If $c_1 > 0$, set $l_0 \leftarrow 1$, $l_1 \leftarrow j + 1$; otherwise set $l_0 \leftarrow j + 1$. Then set $c_j \leftarrow 0$ and $c_{j+1} \leftarrow c_{j+1} + 1$. If $k \neq j + 1$, set $l_{j+1} \leftarrow k$. Return to C2. ▮

Notice that this algorithm is *loopless*; but it isn't really faster than Algorithm P. Steps C4, C5, and C6 are performed respectively $p(n - 2)$, $2p(n) - p(n + 1) - p(n - 2)$, and $p(n + 1) - p(n)$ times; thus step C4 is most important when n is large. (See exercise 45 and the detailed analysis by Fenner and Loizou in *Acta Inf.* **16** (1981), 237–252.)

6. Assume that each partition is followed by 0. Set $j \leftarrow 0$, $k \leftarrow a_1$, and $b_{k+1} \leftarrow 0$. Then, while $k > 0$, set $j \leftarrow j + 1$ and, while $k > a_{j+1}$, set $b_k \leftarrow j$ and $k \leftarrow k - 1$. (We have used (11) in the dual form $a_j - a_{j+1} = d_j$, where $d_1 \ldots d_n$ is the part-count representation of $b_1 b_2 \ldots$. This algorithm essentially walks along the rim of the Ferrers diagram; so its running time is roughly proportional to $a_1 + b_1$, the number of parts in the output plus the number of parts in the input.)

7. We have $b_1 \ldots b_n = n^{a_n} (n-1)^{a_{n-1} - a_n} \ldots 1^{a_1 - a_2} 0^{n - a_1}$, by the dual of (11).

8. Transposing the Ferrers diagram corresponds to reflecting and complementing the bit string (15). So we simply interchange and reverse the p's and q's, getting the partition $(a_1 a_2 \ldots)^T = (q_t + \cdots + q_1)^{p_1} (q_t + \cdots + q_2)^{p_2} \ldots (q_t)^{p_t}$.

9. By induction: If $a_k = l - 1$ and $b_l = k - 1$, increasing a_k and b_l preserves equality.

10. (a) The left child of each node is obtained by appending '1'. The right child is obtained by increasing the rightmost digit; this child exists if and only if the parent node ends with unequal digits. All partitions of n appear on level n in lexicographic order.

(b) The left child is obtained by changing '11' to '2'; it exists if and only if the parent node contains at least two 1s. The right child is obtained by deleting a 1 and increasing the smallest part that exceeds 1; it exists if and only if there is at least one 1 and the smallest larger part appears exactly once. All partitions of n into m parts appear on level $n - m$ in lexicographic order; preorder of the entire tree gives lexicographic order of the whole. [T. I. Fenner and G. Loizou, *Comp. J.* **23** (1980), 332–337.]

11. $[z^{100}] 1/((1-z)(1-z^2)(1-z^5)(1-z^{10})(1-z^{20})(1-z^{50})(1-z^{100})) = 4563$; and $[z^{100}](1+z+z^2)(1+z^2+z^4)\ldots(1+z^{100}+z^{200}) = 7$. [See G. Pólya, *AMM* **63** (1956), 689–697.] In the infinite product $\prod_{k\geq 0}\prod_{r\in\{10^k,2\cdot 10^k,5\cdot 10^k\}}(1+z^r+z^{2r})$, the coefficient of z^{10^n} is $2^{n+1} - 1$, and the coefficient of z^{10^n-1} is 2^n.

12. To prove that $(1+z)(1+z^2)(1+z^3)\ldots = 1/((1-z)(1-z^3)(1-z^5)\ldots)$, write the left-hand side as

$$\frac{(1-z^2)}{(1-z)}\frac{(1-z^4)}{(1-z^2)}\frac{(1-z^6)}{(1-z^3)}\ldots$$

and cancel common factors from numerator and denominator. Alternatively, replace z by z^1, z^3, z^5, $\ldots$ in the identity $(1+z)(1+z^2)(1+z^4)(1+z^8)\ldots = 1/(1-z)$ and multiply the results together. [*Novi Comment. Acad. Sci. Pet.* **3** (1750), 125–169, §47.]

13. Map the partition $c_1\cdot 1 + c_2\cdot 2 + c_3\cdot 3 + \cdots$ into $r_1\cdot 1 + \lfloor c_1/2\rfloor\cdot 2 + r_3\cdot 3 + \lfloor c_2/2\rfloor\cdot 4 + r_5\cdot 5 + \lfloor c_3/2\rfloor\cdot 6 + \cdots$, where $r_m = (c_m \bmod 2) + 2(c_{2m}\bmod 2) + 4(c_{4m}\bmod 2) + 8(c_{8m}\bmod 2) + \cdots$; $433222211 \mapsto 64421111 \mapsto 8332211$. [*Johns Hopkins Univ. Circular* **2** (1882), 72.]

14. Sylvester's correspondence is best understood as a diagram in which the dots of the odd parts are centered and the partition is divided into disjoint hooks. For example, the partition $17 + 15 + 15 + 9 + 9 + 9 + 9 + 5 + 5 + 3 + 3$, having five different odd parts, corresponds via the diagram

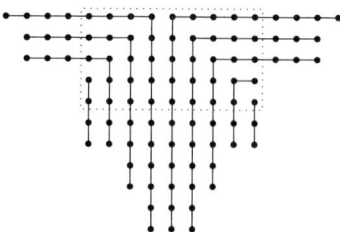

to the all-distinct partition $19 + 18 + 16 + 13 + 12 + 9 + 5 + 4 + 3$ with four gaps.

In general, when the "Durfee rectangle" (shown in the diagram) has t rows, suppose there are $a_1, \ldots, a_t$ extra dots at the right and $b_t, \ldots, b_1, \ldots, b_t$ extra dots below, where $a_1 \geq \cdots \geq a_t \geq 0$ and $b_1 \geq \cdots \geq b_t \geq 0$. Then the distinct parts obtained are $2t - 1 + a_1 + b_1, 2t - 2 + a_1 + b_2, \ldots, 2 + a_{t-1} + b_t, 1 + a_t + b_t$, and (if it's nonzero) $0 + a_t$. Conversely, any partition with $2t$ distinct nonnegative parts can uniquely be written in this form.

The relevant odd-parts partitions when $n = 10$ are $9 + 1, 7 + 3, 7 + 1 + 1 + 1, 5 + 5, 5 + 3 + 1 + 1, 5 + 1 + 1 + 1 + 1 + 1, 3 + 3 + 3 + 1, 3 + 3 + 1 + 1 + 1 + 1, 3 + 1 + \cdots + 1, 1 + \cdots + 1$, corresponding respectively to the distinct-parts partitions $6 + 4, 5 + 4 + 1,$

$7 + 3$, $4 + 3 + 2 + 1$, $6 + 3 + 1$, $8 + 2$, $5 + 3 + 2$, $7 + 2 + 1$, $9 + 1$, 10. [See Sylvester's remarkable paper in *Amer. J. Math.* **5** (1882), 251–330; **6** (1883), 334–336.]

15. Every self-conjugate partition of trace k corresponds to a partition of n into k distinct odd parts ("hooks"). Therefore we can write the generating function either as the product $(1+z)(1+z^3)(1+z^5)\dots$ or as the sum $1 + z^1/(1-z^2) + z^4/((1-z^2)(1-z^4)) + z^9/((1-z^2)(1-z^4)(1-z^6)) + \cdots$. [*Johns Hopkins Univ. Circular* **3** (1883), 42–43.]

16. The Durfee square contains k^2 dots, and the remaining dots correspond to two independent partitions with largest part $\le k$. Thus, if we use w to count parts and z to count dots, we find

$$\prod_{m=1}^{\infty} \frac{1}{1 - wz^m} = \sum_{k=0}^{\infty} \frac{w^k z^{k^2}}{(1-z)(1-z^2)\dots(1-z^k)(1-wz)(1-wz^2)\dots(1-wz^k)}.$$

[This impressive-looking formula turns out to be just the special case $x = y = 0$ of the even more impressive identity of exercise 19.]

17. (a) $((1+uvz)(1+uvz^2)(1+uvz^3)\dots)/((1-uz)(1-uz^2)(1-uz^3)\dots)$.

(b) A joint partition can be represented by a generalized Ferrers diagram in which all of the parts are merged together, with a_i above b_j if $a_i \ge b_j$, and with a mark on the rightmost dot of each b_j. For example, the joint partition $(8,8,5;\ 9,7,5,2)$ has the diagram illustrated here, with marked dots shown as '♦'. Marks appear only in corners; thus the transposed diagram corresponds to another joint partition, which in this case is $(7,6,6,4,3;\ 7,6,4,1)$. [See J. T. Joichi and D. Stanton, *Pacific J. Math.* **127** (1987), 103–120; S. Corteel and J. Lovejoy, *Trans. Amer. Math. Soc.* **356** (2004), 1623–1635; Igor Pak, *The Ramanujan Journal* **12** (2006), 5–75.]

Every joint partition with $t > 0$ parts corresponds in this way to a "conjugate" in which the largest part is t. And the generating function for such joint partitions is $((1+vz)\dots(1+vz^{t-1}))/((1-z)\dots(1-z^t))$ times $(vz^t + z^t)$, where vz^t corresponds to the case that $b_1 = t$, and z^t corresponds to the case that $s = 0$ or $b_1 < t$.

(c) Thus we obtain a form of the general z-nomial theorem in answer 1.2.6–58:

$$\frac{(1+uvz)}{(1-uz)}\frac{(1+uvz^2)}{(1-uz^2)}\frac{(1+uvz^3)}{(1-uz^3)} \cdots = \sum_{t=0}^{\infty} \frac{(1+v)}{(1-z)}\frac{(1+vz)}{(1-z^2)} \cdots \frac{(1+vz^{t-1})}{(1-z^t)} u^t z^t.$$

18. The equations obviously determine the a's and b's when the c's and d's are given, so we want to show that the c's and d's are uniquely determined from the a's and b's. The following algorithm determines the c's and d's from right to left:

A1. [Initialize.] Set $i \leftarrow r$, $j \leftarrow s$, $k \leftarrow 0$, and $a_0 \leftarrow b_0 \leftarrow \infty$.

A2. [Branch.] Stop if $i + j = 0$. Otherwise go to A4 if $a_i \ge b_j - k$.

A3. [Absorb a_i.] Set $c_{i+j} \leftarrow a_i$, $d_{i+j} \leftarrow 0$, $i \leftarrow i-1$, $k \leftarrow k+1$, and return to A2.

A4. [Absorb b_j.] Set $c_{i+j} \leftarrow b_j - k$, $d_{i+j} \leftarrow 1$, $j \leftarrow j-1$, $k \leftarrow k+1$, and return to A2. ∎

There's also a left-to-right method:

B1. [Initialize.] Set $i \leftarrow 1$, $j \leftarrow 1$, $k \leftarrow r + s$, and $a_{r+1} \leftarrow b_{s+1} \leftarrow -\infty$.

B2. [Branch.] Stop if $k = 0$. Otherwise set $k \leftarrow k-1$, then go to B4 if $a_i \le b_j - k$.

B3. [Absorb a_i.] Set $c_{i+j-1} \leftarrow a_i$, $d_{i+j-1} \leftarrow 0$, $i \leftarrow i+1$, and return to B2.

B4. [Absorb b_j.] Set $c_{i+j-1} \leftarrow b_j - k$, $d_{i+j-1} \leftarrow 1$, $j \leftarrow j+1$, and return to B2. ∎

In both cases the branching is forced and the resulting sequence satisfies $c_1 \geq \cdots \geq c_{r+s}$. Notice that $c_{r+s} = \min(a_r, b_s)$ and $c_1 = \max(a_1, b_1 - r - s + 1)$.

We have thereby proved the identity of exercise 17(c) in a different way. Extensions of this idea lead to a combinatorial proof of Ramanujan's "remarkable formula with many parameters,"

$$\sum_{n=-\infty}^{\infty} w^n \prod_{k=0}^{\infty} \frac{1 - bz^{k+n}}{1 - az^{k+n}} = \prod_{k=0}^{\infty} \frac{(1-a^{-1}bz^k)(1-a^{-1}w^{-1}z^{k+1})(1-awz^k)(1-z^{k+1})}{(1-a^{-1}bw^{-1}z^k)(1-a^{-1}z^{k+1})(1-az^k)(1-wz^k)}.$$

[*References:* G. H. Hardy, *Ramanujan* (1940), Eq. (12.12.2); D. Zeilberger, *Europ. J. Combinatorics* **8** (1987), 461–463; A. J. Yee, *J. Comb. Theory* **A105** (2004), 63–77.]

19. [*Crelle* **34** (1847), 285–328.] By exercise 17(c), the hinted sum over k is

$$\left(\sum_{l \geq 0} v^l \frac{(z - bz) \ldots (z - bz^l)}{(1 - z) \ldots (1 - z^l)} \frac{(1 - uz) \ldots (1 - uz^l)}{(1 - auz) \ldots (1 - auz^l)} \right) \cdot \prod_{m=1}^{\infty} \frac{1 - auz^m}{1 - uz^m};$$

and the sum over l is similar but with $u \leftrightarrow v$, $a \leftrightarrow b$, $k \leftrightarrow l$. Furthermore the sum over both k and l reduces to

$$\prod_{m=1}^{\infty} \frac{(1 - uvz^{m+1})(1 - auz^m)}{(1 - uz^m)(1 - vz^m)}$$

when $b = auz$. Now let $u = wxy$, $v = 1/(yz)$, $a = 1/x$, and $b = wyz$; equate this infinite product to the sum over l.

20. To get $p(n)$ we need to add or subtract approximately $\sqrt{8n/3}$ of the previous entries, and most of those entries are $\Theta(\sqrt{n})$ bits long. Therefore $p(n)$ is computed in $\Theta(n)$ steps and the total time is $\Theta(n^2)$.

(A straightforward use of (17) would take $\Theta(n^{5/2})$ steps.)

21. Since $\sum_{n=0}^{\infty} q(n) z^n = (1 + z)(1 + z^2) \ldots$ is equal to $(1 - z^2)(1 - z^4) \ldots P(z) = (1 - z^2 - z^4 + z^{10} + z^{14} - z^{24} - \cdots) P(z)$, we have

$$q(n) = p(n) - p(n - 2) - p(n - 4) + p(n - 10) + p(n - 14) - p(n - 24) - \cdots.$$

[There is also a "pure recurrence" in the q's alone, analogous to the recurrence for $\sigma(n)$ in the next exercise.]

22. From (21) we have $\sum_{n=1}^{\infty} \sigma(n) z^n = \sum_{m,n \geq 1} m z^{mn} = z \frac{d}{dz} \ln P(z) = (z + 2z^2 - 5z^5 - 7z^7 + \cdots)/(1 - z - z^2 + z^5 + z^7 + \cdots)$. [*Bibliothèque Impartiale* **3** (1751), 10–31.]

23. (Solution by Marc van Leeuwen.) Divide (19) by $1 - v$, to get

$$\prod_{k=1}^{\infty} (1 - u^k v^{k-1})(1 - u^k v^k)(1 - u^k v^{k+1}) = \sum_{n=0}^{\infty} (-1)^n u^{\binom{n+1}{2}} \left(\frac{v^{\binom{n}{2}} - v^{\binom{n+2}{2}}}{1 - v} \right)$$

$$= \sum_{n=0}^{\infty} (-1)^n u^{\binom{n+1}{2}} \sum_{k=0}^{2n} v^k;$$

now set $u = z$ and $v = 1$.

[See §57 of Sylvester's paper cited in answer 14. Jacobi's proof is in §66 of his monograph *Fundamenta Nova Theoriæ Functionum Ellipticarum* (1829).]

24. (a) By (18) and exercise 23, $[z^n] A(z) = \sum (-1)^{j+k}(2k+1)[3j^2 + j + k^2 + k = 2n]$, summed over all integers j and all nonnegative integers k. When $n \bmod 5 = 4$, the contributions all have $j \bmod 5 = 4$ and $k \bmod 5 = 2$; but then $(2k + 1) \bmod 5 = 0$.

(b) $B(z)^p \equiv B(z^p)$ (modulo p) when p is prime, by Eq. 4.6.2–(5).

(c) Take $B(z) = P(z)$, since $A(z) = P(z)^{-4}$. [*Proc. Cambridge Philos. Soc.* **19** (1919), 207–210. A similar proof shows that $p(n)$ is a multiple of 7 when $n \bmod 7 = 5$. Ramanujan went on to obtain the beautiful formulas $p(5n + 4)/5 = [z^n] P(z)^6/P(z^5)^5$; $p(7n + 5)/7 = [z^n] (P(z)^4/P(z^7)^3 + 7zP(z)^8/P(z^7)^7)$. Atkin and Swinnerton-Dyer, in *Proc. London Math. Soc.* (3) **4** (1953), 84–106, showed that the partitions of $5n + 4$ and $7n + 5$ can be divided into equal-size classes according to the respective values of (largest part – number of parts) mod 5 or mod 7, as conjectured by F. Dyson. A slightly more complicated combinatorial statistic proves also that $p(n) \bmod 11 = 0$ when $n \bmod 11 = 6$; see F. G. Garvan, *Trans. Amer. Math. Soc.* **305** (1988), 47–77.]

25. [The hint can be proved by differentiating both sides of the stated identity. It is the special case $y = 1 - x$ of a beautiful formula discovered by N. H. Abel in 1826:

$$\mathrm{Li}_2(x) + \mathrm{Li}_2(y) = \mathrm{Li}_2\left(\frac{x}{1-y}\right) + \mathrm{Li}_2\left(\frac{y}{1-x}\right) - \mathrm{Li}_2\left(\frac{xy}{(1-x)(1-y)}\right) - \ln(1-x)\ln(1-y).$$

See Abel's *Œuvres Complètes* **2** (Christiania: Grøndahl, 1881), 189–193.]

(a) Let $f(x) = \ln(1/(1 - e^{-xt}))$. Then $\int_1^x f(x)\,dx = -\mathrm{Li}_2(e^{-tx})/t$ and $f^{(n)}(x) = (-t)^n e^{tx} \sum_k \binom{n-1}{k} e^{ktx}/(e^{tx} - 1)^n$, so Euler's summation formula gives $\mathrm{Li}_2(e^{-t})/t + \frac{1}{2}\ln(1/(1 - e^{-t})) + O(1) = (\zeta(2) + t\ln(1 - e^{-t}) - \mathrm{Li}_2(1 - e^{-t}))/t - \frac{1}{2}\ln t + O(1) = \zeta(2)/t + \frac{1}{2}\ln t + O(1)$, as $t \to 0$.

(b) We have $\sum_{m,n\geq 1} e^{-mnt}/n = \frac{1}{2\pi i} \sum_{m,n\geq 1} \int_{1-i\infty}^{1+i\infty} (mnt)^{-z}\Gamma(z)\,dz/n$, which sums to $\frac{1}{2\pi i} \int_{1-i\infty}^{1+i\infty} \zeta(z + 1)\zeta(z)t^{-z}\Gamma(z)\,dz$. The pole at $z = 1$ gives $\zeta(2)/t$; the double pole at $z = 0$ gives $-\zeta(0)\ln t + \zeta'(0) = \frac{1}{2}\ln t - \frac{1}{2}\ln 2\pi$; the pole at $z = -1$ gives $-\zeta(-1)\zeta(0)t = B_2 B_1 t = -t/24$. Zeros of $\zeta(z + 1)\zeta(z)$ cancel the other poles of $\Gamma(z)$, so the result is $\ln P(e^{-t}) = \zeta(2)/t + \frac{1}{2}\ln(t/2\pi) - t/24 + O(t^M)$ for arbitrarily large M.

26. Let $F(n) = \sum_{k=1}^{\infty} e^{-k^2/n}$. We can use (25) either with $f(x) = e^{-x^2/n}[x > 0] + \frac{1}{2}\delta_{x0}$, or with $f(x) = e^{-x^2/n}$ for all x because $2F(n) + 1 = \sum_{k=-\infty}^{\infty} e^{-k^2/n}$. Let's choose the latter alternative; then the right-hand side of (25), for $\theta = 0$, is the rapidly convergent

$$\lim_{M\to\infty} \sum_{m=-M}^{M} \int_{-\infty}^{\infty} e^{-2\pi miy - y^2/n}\,dy = \sum_{m=-\infty}^{\infty} e^{-\pi^2 m^2 n} \int_{-\infty}^{\infty} e^{-u^2/n}\,du$$

if we substitute $u = y + \pi mni$; and the integral is $\sqrt{\pi n}$. [This result is formula (15) on page 420 of Poisson's original paper.]

27. First, $\int_{-\infty}^{\infty} e^{-a(y+b)^2 + 2ciy}\,dy = e^{-c^2/a - 2bci} \int_{-\infty}^{\infty} e^{-au^2}\,du$, by the substitution $u = y + b - ci/a$. And $\int_{-\infty}^{\infty} e^{-au^2}\,du = \int_0^{\infty} e^{-t}\,dt/\sqrt{at} = \Gamma(\frac{1}{2})/\sqrt{a} = \sqrt{\pi/a}$, by the substitution $t = au^2$ and exercises 1.2.5–20, 1.2.6–43.

Now (30) follows from (29) because we have, for all integers m,

$$g(3m + 1) + g(-3m) = \sqrt{\frac{2\pi}{t}}(-1)^m e^{-6\pi^2(m+\frac{1}{6})^2/t}; \quad g(3m + 2) + g(-3m - 1) = 0.$$

[See M. I. Knopp, *Modular Functions in Analytic Number Theory* (1970), Chapter 3.]

28. (a, b, c, d) See *Trans. Amer. Math. Soc.* **43** (1938), 271–295. In fact, Lehmer found explicit formulas for $A_{p^e}(n)$, in terms of the Jacobi symbol of exercise 4.5.4–23:

$$A_{2^e}(n) = (-1)^e \left(\frac{-1}{m}\right) 2^{e/2} \sin\frac{4\pi m}{2^{e+3}}, \qquad \text{if } (3m)^2 \equiv 1 - 24n \ (\text{modulo } 2^{e+3});$$

$$A_{3^e}(n) = (-1)^{e+1} \left(\frac{m}{3}\right) \frac{2}{\sqrt{3}} 3^{e/2} \sin\frac{4\pi m}{3^{e+1}}, \quad \text{if } (8m)^2 \equiv 1 - 24n \ (\text{modulo } 3^{e+1});$$

$$A_{p^e}(n) = \begin{cases} 2\left(\frac{3}{p^e}\right) p^{e/2} \cos\frac{4\pi m}{p^e}, & \text{if } (24m)^2 \equiv 1 - 24n \ (\text{modulo } p^e), p \geq 5, \\ & \text{and } 24n \bmod p \neq 1; \\ \left(\frac{3}{p^e}\right) p^{e/2} [e=1], & \text{if } 24n \bmod p = 1 \text{ and } p \geq 5. \end{cases}$$

(e) If $k = 2^a 3^b p_1^{e_1} \ldots p_t^{e_t}$ for $3 < p_1 < \cdots < p_t$ and $e_1 \ldots e_t \neq 0$, the probability that $A_k(n) \neq 0$ is $2^{-t}(1 + (-1)^{[e_1>1]}/p_1)\ldots(1 + (-1)^{[e_t>1]}/p_t)$.

29. $z_1 z_2 \ldots z_m/((1 - z_1)(1 - z_1 z_2)\ldots(1 - z_1 z_2 \ldots z_m))$.

30. (a) $\left|{n+1 \atop m}\right|$ and (b) $\left|{m+n \atop m}\right|$, by (39).

31. *First solution* [Marshall Hall, Jr., *Combinatorial Theory* (1967), §4.1]: From the recurrence (39), we can show directly that, for $0 \leq r < k!$, there is a polynomial $f_{k,r}(n) = n^{k-1}/(k!(k-1)!) + O(n^{k-2})$ such that $\left|{n \atop k}\right| = f_{n,n \bmod k!}(n)$.

Second solution: Since $(1 - z)\ldots(1 - z^m) = \prod_{p\perp q}(1 - e^{2\pi ip/q}z)^{\lfloor m/q\rfloor}$, where the product is over all reduced fractions p/q with $0 \leq p < q$, the coefficient of z^n in (41) can be expressed as a sum of roots of unity times polynomials in n, namely as $\sum_{p\perp q} e^{2\pi ipn/q} f_{p,q}(n)$ where $f_{p,q}(n)$ is a polynomial of degree less than $\lfloor m/q \rfloor$. Thus there exist constants such that $\left|{n \atop 2}\right| = a_1 n + a_2 + (-1)^n a_3$; $\left|{n \atop 3}\right| = b_1 n^2 + b_2 n + b_3 + (-1)^n b_4 + \omega^n b_5 + \omega^{-n} b_6$, where $\omega = e^{2\pi i/3}$; etc. The constants are determined by the values for small n, and the first two cases are

$$\left|{n \atop 2}\right| = \frac{1}{2}n - \frac{1}{4} + \frac{1}{4}(-1)^n; \qquad \left|{n \atop 3}\right| = \frac{1}{12}n^2 - \frac{7}{72} - \frac{1}{8}(-1)^n + \frac{1}{9}\omega^n + \frac{1}{9}\omega^{-n}.$$

It follows that $\left|{n \atop 3}\right|$ is the nearest integer to $n^2/12$. Similarly, $\left|{n \atop 4}\right|$ is the nearest integer to $(n^3 + 3n^2 - 9n\,[n\,\text{odd}])/144$.

[Exact formulas for $\left|{n \atop 2}\right|$, $\left|{n \atop 3}\right|$, and $\left|{n \atop 4}\right|$, without the simplification of floor functions, were first found by G. F. Malfatti, *Memorie di Mat. e Fis. Società Italiana* **3** (1786), 571–663. W. J. A. Colman, in *Fibonacci Quarterly* **21** (1983), 272–284, showed that $\left|{n \atop 5}\right|$ is the nearest integer to $(n^4 + 10n^3 + 10n^2 - 75n - 45n(-1)^n)/2880$, and gave similar formulas for $\left|{n \atop 6}\right|$ and $\left|{n \atop 7}\right|$.]

32. Since $\left|{m+n \atop m}\right| \leq p(n)$, with equality if and only if $m \geq n$, we have $\left|{n \atop m}\right| \leq p(n - m)$ with equality if and only if $2m \geq n$.

33. A partition into m parts corresponds to at most $m!$ compositions; hence $\binom{n-1}{m-1} \leq m!\left|{n \atop m}\right|$. Consequently $p(n) \geq (n - 1)!/((n - m)!\,m!\,(m - 1)!)$, and when $m = \lfloor\sqrt{n}\rfloor$ Stirling's approximation proves that $\ln p(n) \geq 2\sqrt{n} - \ln n - \frac{1}{2} - \ln 2\pi$.

34. $a_1 > a_2 > \cdots > a_m > 0$ if and only if $a_1 - m + 1 \geq a_2 - m + 2 \geq \cdots \geq a_m \geq 1$. And partitions into m distinct parts correspond to $m!$ compositions. Thus, by the previous answer, we have

$$\frac{1}{m!}\binom{n-1}{m-1} \leq \left|{n \atop m}\right| \leq \frac{1}{m!}\binom{n + m(m-1)/2}{m-1}.$$

[See H. Gupta, *Proc. Indian Acad. Sci.* **A16** (1942), 101–102. A detailed asymptotic formula for $\left|\begin{smallmatrix} n \\ m \end{smallmatrix}\right|$ when $n = \Theta(m^3)$ appears in exercise 3.3.2–30.]

35. (a) $x = \frac{1}{C}\ln\frac{1}{C} \approx -0.194$.

(b) $x = \frac{1}{C}\ln\frac{1}{C} - \frac{1}{C}\ln\ln 2 \approx 0.092$; in general we have $x = \frac{1}{C}\left(\ln\frac{1}{C} - \ln\ln\frac{1}{F(x)}\right)$.

(c) $\int_{-\infty}^{\infty} x\,dF(x) = \int_0^\infty (Cu)^{-2}(\ln u)e^{-1/(Cu)}\,du = -\frac{1}{C}\int_0^\infty (\ln C + \ln v)e^{-v}\,dv = (\gamma - \ln C)/C \approx 0.256$.

(d) Similarly, $\int_{-\infty}^{\infty} x^2 e^{-Cx}\exp(-e^{-Cx}/C)\,dx = (\gamma^2 + \zeta(2) - 2\gamma\ln C + (\ln C)^2)/C^2 \approx 1.0656$. So the variance is $\zeta(2)/C^2 = 1$, exactly(!).

[The probability distribution $e^{-e^{(a-x)/b}}$ is commonly called the Fisher–Tippett distribution; see *Proc. Cambridge Phil. Soc.* **24** (1928), 180–190.]

36. The sum over $j_r - (m+r-1) \geq \cdots \geq j_2 - (m+1) \geq j_1 - m \geq 1$ gives

$$\Sigma_r = \sum_t \left|\begin{matrix} t - rm - r(r-1)/2 \\ r \end{matrix}\right| \frac{p(n-t)}{p(n)}$$

$$= \frac{\alpha}{1-\alpha}\frac{\alpha^2}{1-\alpha^2}\cdots\frac{\alpha^r}{1-\alpha^r}\alpha^{rm}\left(1+O(n^{-1/2+2\epsilon})\right) + E$$

$$= \frac{n^{-1/2}}{\alpha^{-1}-1}\frac{n^{-1/2}}{\alpha^{-2}-1}\cdots\frac{n^{-1/2}}{\alpha^{-r}-1}\exp\left(-Crx + O(rn^{-1/2+2\epsilon})\right) + E,$$

where E is an error term that accounts for the cases $t > n^{1/2+\epsilon}$. The leading factor $n^{-1/2}/(\alpha^{-j}-1)$ is $\frac{1}{jC}(1+O(jn^{-1/2}))$. And it is easy to verify that $E = O(n^{\log n}e^{-Cn^\epsilon})$, even if we use the crude upper bound $\left|\begin{smallmatrix} t-rm-r(r-1)/2 \\ r \end{smallmatrix}\right| \leq t^r$, because

$$\sum_{t \geq xN} t^r e^{-t/N} = O\left(\int_{xN}^\infty t^r e^{-t/N}\,dt\right) = O\left(N^{r+1}x^r e^{-x}/(1-r/x)\right),$$

where $N = \Theta(\sqrt{n})$, $x = \Theta(n^\epsilon)$, $r = O(\log n)$.

37. Such a partition is counted once in Σ_0, q times in Σ_1, $\binom{q}{2}$ times in Σ_2, ...; so it is counted exactly $\sum_{j=0}^r (-1)^j\binom{q}{j} = (-1)^r\binom{q-1}{r}$ times in the partial sum that ends with $(-1)^r\Sigma_r$. This count is at most δ_{q0} when r is odd, at least δ_{q0} when r is even. [A similar argument shows that the generalized principle of exercise 1.3.3–26 also has this bracketing property. *Reference:* C. Bonferroni, *Pubblicazioni del Reale Istituto Superiore di Scienze Economiche e Commerciali di Firenze* **8** (1936), 3–62.]

38. $z^{l+m-1}\binom{l+m-2}{m-1}_z = z^{l+m-1}(1-z^l)\ldots(1-z^{l+m-2})/((1-z)\ldots(1-z^{m-1}))$.

39. $[x^m](1+zx)(1+z^2x)\ldots(1+z^{l-1}x) = z^{m(m+1)/2}\binom{l-1}{m}_z$, by exercise 1.2.6–58; this is $(z-z^l)(z^2-z^l)\ldots(z^m-z^l)/((1-z)(1-z^2)\ldots(1-z^m))$. The answer also follows from Theorem C: Replacing $a_1\ldots a_m$ by $(a_1-m)\ldots(a_m-1)$ gives an equivalent partition of $n - m(m+1)/2$ into at most m parts, not exceeding $l-1-m$.

40. If $\alpha = a_1\ldots a_m$ is a partition with at most m parts, let $f(\alpha) = \infty$ if $a_1 \leq l$, otherwise $f(\alpha) = \min\{j \mid a_1 > l + a_{j+1}\}$. Let g_k be the generating function for partitions with $f(\alpha) > k$. Partitions with $f(\alpha) = k < \infty$ are characterized by the inequalities

$$a_1 \geq a_2 \geq \cdots \geq a_k \geq a_1 - l > a_{k+1} \geq \cdots \geq a_{m+1} = 0.$$

Thus $a_1 a_2 \ldots a_m = (b_k+l+1)(b_1+1)\ldots(b_{k-1}+1)b_{k+1}\ldots b_m$, where $f(b_1\ldots b_m) \geq k$; and the converse is also true. It follows that $g_k = g_{k-1} - z^{l+k}g_{k-1}$.

[See *American J. Math.* **5** (1882), 254–257.]

41. See G. Almkvist and G. E. Andrews, *J. Number Theory* **38** (1991), 135–144.

42. A. Vershik [*Functional Anal. Applic.* **30** (1996), 90–105, Theorem 4.7] has stated the formula

$$\frac{1 - e^{-c\varphi}}{1 - e^{-c(\theta+\varphi)}} e^{-ck/\sqrt{n}} + \frac{1 - e^{-c\theta}}{1 - e^{-c(\theta+\varphi)}} e^{-ca_k/\sqrt{n}} \approx 1,$$

where the constant c must be chosen as a function of θ and φ so that the area of the shape is n. This constant c is negative if $\theta\varphi < 2$, positive if $\theta\varphi > 2$; the shape reduces to a straight line

$$\frac{k}{\theta\sqrt{n}} + \frac{a_k}{\varphi\sqrt{n}} \approx 1$$

when $\theta\varphi = 2$. If $\varphi = \infty$ we have $c = \sqrt{\text{Li}_2(t)}$ where t satisfies $\theta = (\ln \frac{1}{1-t})/\sqrt{\text{Li}_2(t)}$.

43. $p(n - k(k-1)/2)$. (Change $a_1 a_2 \ldots a_k$ to $(a_1 - k + 1)(a_2 - k + 2) \ldots a_k$ to get an equivalent partition of $n - k(k-1)/2$.)

44. Assume that $n > 0$. The number with smallest parts *unequal* (or with only one part) is $p(n+1) - p(n)$, the number of partitions of $n+1$ that don't end in 1, because we get the former from the latter by changing the smallest part. Therefore the answer is $2p(n) - p(n+1)$. [See R. J. Boscovich, *Giornale de' Letterati* (Rome, 1748), 15. The number of partitions whose smallest *three* parts are equal is $3p(n) - p(n+1) - 2p(n+2) + p(n+3)$; similar formulas can be derived for other constraints on the smallest parts.]

45. By Eq. (37) we have $p(n-j)/p(n) = 1 - Cjn^{-1/2} + (C^2 j^2 + 2j)/(2n) - (8C^3 j^3 + 60Cj^2 + Cj + 12C^{-1}j)/(48n^{3/2}) + O(j^4 n^{-2})$.

46. If $n > 1$, $T_2'(n) = p(n-1) - p(n-2) \le p(n) - p(n-1) = T_2''(n)$, because $p(n) - p(n-1)$ is the number of partitions of n that don't end in 1; every such partition of $n-1$ yields one for n if we increase the largest part. But the difference is rather small: $(T_2''(n) - T_2'(n))/p(n) = C^2/n + O(n^{-3/2})$.

47. The identity in the hint follows by differentiating (21); see exercise 22. The probability of obtaining the part-counts $c_1 \ldots c_n$ when $c_1 + 2c_2 + \cdots + nc_n = n$ is

$$\Pr(c_1 \ldots c_n) = \sum_{k=1}^{n} \sum_{j=1}^{c_k} \frac{kp(n-jk)}{np(n)} \Pr(c_1 \ldots c_{k-1}(c_k-j)c_{k+1} \ldots c_n)$$

$$= \sum_{k=1}^{n} \sum_{j=1}^{c_k} \frac{k}{np(n)} = \frac{1}{p(n)},$$

by induction on n. [*Combinatorial Algorithms* (Academic Press, 1975), Chapter 10.]

48. The probability that j has a particular fixed value in step N5 is $6/(\pi^2 j^2) + O(n^{-1/2})$, and the average value of jk is order $\sqrt{n}$. The average time spent in step N4 is $\Theta(n)$, so the average running time is of order $n^{3/2}$. (A more precise analysis would be desirable.)

49. (a) We have $F(z) = \sum_{k=1}^{\infty} F_k(z)$, where $F_k(z)$ is the generating function for all partitions whose smallest part is $\ge k$, namely $1/((1 - z^k)(1 - z^{k+1}) \ldots) - 1$.

(b) Let $f_k(n) = [z^n] F_k(z)/p(n)$. Then $f_1(n) = 1$; $f_2(n) = 1 - p(n-1)/p(n) = Cn^{-1/2} + O(n^{-1})$; $f_3(n) = (p(n) - p(n-1) - p(n-2) + p(n-3))/p(n) = 2C^2 n^{-1} + O(n^{-3/2})$; and $f_4(n) = 6C^3 n^{-3/2} + O(n^{-2})$. (See exercise 45.) It turns out that $f_{k+1}(n) = k! C^k n^{-k/2} + O(n^{-(k+1)/2})$; in particular, $f_5(n) = O(n^{-2})$. Hence $f_5(n) + \cdots + f_n(n) = O(n^{-1})$, because $f_{k+1}(n) \le f_k(n)$.

Adding everything up yields $[z^n] F(z) = p(n)(1 + C/\sqrt{n} + O(n^{-1}))$.

50. (a) $c_m(m+k) = c_{m-1}(m-1+k) + c_m(k) = m-1-k+c(k)+1$ by induction when $0 \le k < m$.

(b) Because $\left|{m+k \atop m}\right| = p(k)$ for $0 \le k \le m$.

(c) When $n = 2m$, Algorithm H essentially generates the partitions of m, and we know that $j-1$ is the second-smallest part in the conjugate of the partition just generated — except when $j-1 = m$, just after the partition $1\ldots1$ whose conjugate has only one part.

(d) If all parts of α exceed k, let $\alpha k^{q+1}j$ correspond to $\alpha(k+1)$.

(e) Continuing the previous exercise and its answer, the generating function $G_k(z)$ for all partitions whose second-smallest part is $\ge k$ is $F_{k+1}(z)/(1-z)$ by (d). Consequently $C(z) = (F(z) - F_1(z))/(1-z) + z/(1-z)^2$.

(f) We can show as in the previous exercise that $[z^n]G_k(n)/p(n) = O(n^{-k/2})$ for $k \le 5$; hence $c(m)/p(m) = 1 + O(m^{-1/2})$. The ratios $(c(m)+1)/p(m)$, which are readily computed for small m, reach a maximum of 2.6 at $m = 7$ and decrease steadily thereafter. So a rigorous attention to asymptotic error bounds will complete the proof.

Note: B. Fristedt [*Trans. Amer. Math. Soc.* **337** (1993), 703–735] has proved, among other things, that the number of k's in a random partition of n is greater than $Cx\sqrt{n}$ with asymptotic probability e^{-x}.

52. In lexicographic order, $\left|{64+13 \atop 13}\right|$ partitions of 64 have $a_1 \le 13$; $\left|{50+10 \atop 10}\right|$ of them have $a_1 = 14$ and $a_2 \le 10$; etc. Therefore, by the hint, the partition $14\ 11\ 9\ 6\ 4\ 3\ 2\ 1^{15}$ is preceded by exactly $p(64) - 1000000$ partitions in lexicographic order, making it the millionth in *reverse* lexicographic order.

53. As in the previous answer, $\left|{80 \atop 12}\right|$ partitions of 100 have $a_1 = 32$ and $a_2 \le 12$, etc.; so the lexicographically millionth partition in which $a_1 = 32$ is $32\ 13\ 12\ 8\ 7\ 6\ 5\ 5\ 1^{12}$. Algorithm H produces its conjugate, namely $20\ 8\ 8\ 8\ 8\ 6\ 5\ 4\ 3\ 3\ 3\ 3\ 2\ 1^{19}$.

54. (a) Obviously true. This question was just a warmup.

(b) True, but not so obvious. If $\alpha^T = a'_1 a'_2 \ldots$ we have
$$a_1 + \cdots + a_k + a'_1 + \cdots + a'_l \le n + kl \qquad \text{for } 1 \le k \le a'_l$$
by considering the Ferrers diagram, with equality when $k = a'_l$. Thus if $\alpha \succeq \beta$ and $a'_1 + \cdots + a'_l > b'_1 + \cdots + b'_l$ for some l, with l minimum, we have $n + kl = b_1 + \cdots + b_k + b'_1 + \cdots + b'_l < a_1 + \cdots + a_k + a'_1 + \cdots + a'_l \le n + kl$ when $k = b'_l$, a contradiction.

(c) The recurrence $c_k = \min(a_1 + \cdots + a_k, b_1 + \cdots + b_k) - (c_1 + \cdots + c_{k-1})$ clearly defines a greatest lower bound, if $c_1 c_2 \ldots$ is a partition. And it is; for if $c_1 + \cdots + c_k = a_1 + \cdots + a_k$ we have $0 \le \min(a_{k+1}, b_{k+1}) \le \min(a_{k+1}, b_{k+1} + b_1 + \cdots + b_k - a_1 - \cdots - a_k) = c_{k+1} \le a_{k+1} \le a_k = c_k + (c_1 + \cdots + c_{k-1}) - (a_1 + \cdots + a_{k-1}) \le c_k$.

(d) $\alpha \vee \beta = (\alpha^T \wedge \beta^T)^T$. (Double conjugation is needed because a max-oriented recurrence analogous to the one in part (c) can fail.)

(e) $\alpha \wedge \beta$ has $\max(l, m)$ parts and $\alpha \vee \beta$ has $\min(l, m)$ parts. (Consider the first components of their conjugates.)

(f) True for $\alpha \wedge \beta$, by the derivation in part (c). False for $\alpha \vee \beta$; for example, $6321 \vee 543 = 633$ in Fig. 52.

Reference: T. Brylawski, *Discrete Mathematics* **6** (1973), 201–219.

55. (a) If $\alpha \vdash \beta$ and $\alpha \succeq \gamma \succeq \beta$, where $\gamma = c_1 c_2 \ldots$, we have $a_1 + \cdots + a_k = c_1 + \cdots + c_k = b_1 + \cdots + b_k$ for all k except $k = l$ and $k = l+1$; thus α covers β. Therefore β^T covers α^T.

Conversely, if $\alpha \succeq \beta$ and $\alpha \ne \beta$ we can find $\gamma \succeq \beta$ such that $\alpha \vdash \gamma$ or $\gamma^T \vdash \alpha^T$, as follows: Find the smallest k with $a_k > b_k$, the smallest l with $a_k > a_{l+1}$, and the smallest m with $a_k - 1 > a_{m+1}$. (Note that $b_k > 0$.) If $a_m > a_{m+1} + 1$, define $\gamma = c_1 c_2 \ldots$ by $c_k = a_k - [k = m] + [k = m+1]$. Otherwise let $c_k = a_k - [k = l] + [k = m+1]$.

(b) Consider α and β to be strings of n 0s and n 1s, as in (15). Then $\alpha \vdash \beta$ if and only if $\alpha \to \beta$, and $\beta^T \vdash \alpha^T$ if and only if $\alpha \Rightarrow \beta$, where '$\to$' denotes replacing a substring of the form $011^q 10$ by $101^q 01$ and '$\Rightarrow$' denotes replacing a substring of the form $010^q 10$ by $100^q 01$, for some $q \geq 0$.

(c) A partition covers at most $[a_1 > a_2] + \cdots + [a_{m-1} > a_m] + [a_m \geq 2]$ others. The partition $\alpha = (n_2 + n_1 - 1)(n_2 - 2)(n_2 - 3) \ldots 21$ maximizes this quantity in the case $a_m = 1$; cases with $a_m \geq 2$ give no improvement. (The conjugate partition, namely $(n_2 - 1)(n_2 - 2) \ldots 21^{n_1 + 1}$, is just as good. Therefore both α and α^T are also *covered by* the maximum number of others.)

(d) Equivalently, consecutive parts of μ differ by at most 1, and the smallest part is 1; the rim representation has no consecutive 1s.

(e) Use rim representations and replace $\vdash$ by the relation $\to$. If $\alpha \to \alpha_1$ and $\alpha \to \alpha_1'$ we can easily show the existence of a string β such that $\alpha_1 \to \beta$ and $\alpha_1' \to \beta$; for example,

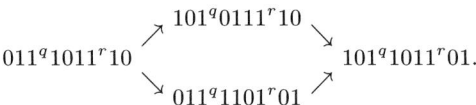

Let $\beta = \beta_2 \vdash \cdots \vdash \beta_m$ where β_m is minimal. Then, by induction on $\max(k, k')$, we have $k = m$ and $\alpha_k = \beta_m$; also $k' = m$ and $\alpha_{k'}' = \beta_m$.

(f) Set $\beta \leftarrow \alpha^T$; then repeatedly set $\beta \leftarrow \beta'$ until β is minimal, using any convenient partition β' such that $\beta \vdash \beta'$. The desired partition is β^T.

Proof: Let $\mu(\alpha)$ be the common value $\alpha_k = \alpha_{k'}'$ in part (e); we must prove that $\alpha \succeq \beta$ implies $\mu(\alpha) \succeq \mu(\beta)$. There is a sequence $\alpha = \alpha_0, \ldots, \alpha_k = \beta$ where $\alpha_j \to \alpha_{j+1}$ or $\alpha_j \Rightarrow \alpha_{j+1}$ for $0 \leq j < k$. If $\alpha_0 \to \alpha_1$ we have $\mu(\alpha) = \mu(\alpha_1)$; thus it suffices to prove that $\alpha \Rightarrow \beta$ and $\alpha \to \alpha'$ implies $\alpha' \succeq \mu(\beta)$. But we have, for example,

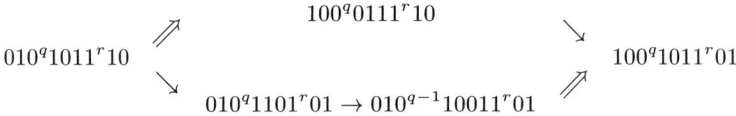

because we may assume that $q > 0$; and the other cases are similar.

(g) The parts of λ_n are $a_k = n_2 + [k \leq n_1] - k$ for $1 \leq k < n_2$; the parts of λ_n^T are $b_k = n_2 - k + [n_2 - k < n_1]$ for $1 \leq k \leq n_2$. The algorithm of (f) reaches λ_n^T from n^1 after $\binom{n_2 + 1}{3} - \binom{n_2 - n_1}{2}$ steps, because each step increases $\sum k b_k = \sum \binom{a_k + 1}{2}$ by 1.

(h) The path n, $(n-1)1$, $(n-2)2$, $(n-2)11$, $(n-3)21$, $\ldots$, 321^{n-5}, 31^{n-3}, 221^{n-4}, 21^{n-2}, 1^n, of length $2n - 4$ when $n \geq 3$, is shortest.

It can be shown that the longest path has $m = 2\binom{n_2}{3} + n_1(n_2 - 1)$ steps. One such path has the form $\alpha_0, \ldots, \alpha_k, \ldots, \alpha_l, \ldots, \alpha_m$ where $\alpha_0 = n^1$; $\alpha_k = \lambda_n$; $\alpha_l = \lambda_n^T$; $\alpha_j \vdash \alpha_{j+1}$ for $0 \leq j < l$; and $\alpha_{j+1}^T \vdash \alpha_j^T$ for $k \leq j < m$.

Reference: C. Greene and D. J. Kleitman, *Europ. J. Combinatorics* **7** (1986), 1–10.

56. Suppose $\lambda = u_1 \ldots u_m$ and $\mu = v_1 \ldots v_m$. The following (unoptimized) algorithm applies the theory of exercise 54 to generate the partitions in colex order, maintaining $\alpha = a_1 a_2 \ldots a_m \preceq \mu$ as well as $\alpha^T = b_1 b_2 \ldots b_l \preceq \lambda^T$. To find the successor of α, we first find the largest j such that b_j can be increased. Then we have $\beta = b_1 \ldots b_{j-1}(b_j + 1)1 \ldots 1 \preceq \lambda^T$, hence the desired successor is $\beta^T \wedge \mu$. The algorithm maintains auxiliary tables $r_j = b_j + \cdots + b_l$, $s_j = v_1 + \cdots + v_j$, and $t_j = w_j + w_{j+1} + \cdots$, where $\lambda^T = w_1 w_2 \dots$.

M1. [Initialize.] Set $q \leftarrow 0$, $k \leftarrow u_1$. For $j = 1, \dots, m$, while $u_{j+1} < k$ set $t_k \leftarrow q \leftarrow q + j$ and $k \leftarrow k - 1$. Then set $q \leftarrow 0$ again, and for $j = 1, \dots, m$ set $a_j \leftarrow v_j$, $s_j \leftarrow q \leftarrow q + a_j$. Then set $q \leftarrow 0$ yet again, and $k \leftarrow l \leftarrow a_1$. For $j = 1, \dots, m$, while $a_{j+1} < k$ set $b_k \leftarrow j$, $r_k \leftarrow q \leftarrow q + j$, and $k \leftarrow k - 1$. Finally, set $t_1 \leftarrow 0$, $b_0 \leftarrow 0$, $b_{-1} \leftarrow -1$.

M2. [Visit.] Visit the partition $a_1 \dots a_m$ and/or its conjugate $b_1 \dots b_l$.

M3. [Find j.] Let j be the largest integer $< l$ such that $r_{j+1} > t_{j+1}$ and $b_j \neq b_{j-1}$. Terminate the algorithm if $j = 0$.

M4. [Increase b_j.] Set $x \leftarrow r_{j+1} - 1$, $k \leftarrow b_j$, $b_j \leftarrow k + 1$, and $a_{k+1} \leftarrow j$. (The previous value of a_{k+1} was $j - 1$. Now we're going to update $a_1 \dots a_k$ using essentially the method of exercise 54(c) to distribute x dots into columns $j+1, j+2, \dots$.)

M5. [Majorize.] Set $z \leftarrow 0$ and then do the following for $i = 1, \dots, k$: Set $x \leftarrow x + j$, $y \leftarrow \min(x, s_i)$, $a_i \leftarrow y - z$, $z \leftarrow y$; if $i = 1$, set $l \leftarrow p \leftarrow a_1$ and $q \leftarrow 0$; if $i > 1$, while $p > a_i$ set $b_p \leftarrow i - 1$, $r_p \leftarrow q \leftarrow q + i - 1$, $p \leftarrow p - 1$. Finally, while $p > j$ set $b_p \leftarrow k$, $r_p \leftarrow q \leftarrow q + k$, $p \leftarrow p - 1$. Return to M2. ∎

57. If $\lambda = \mu^T$ there obviously is only one such matrix, essentially the Ferrers diagram of λ. And the condition $\lambda \preceq \mu^T$ is necessary, for if $\mu^T = b_1 b_2 \dots$ we have $b_1 + \cdots + b_k = \min(c_1, k) + \min(c_2, k) + \cdots$, and this quantity must not be less than the number of 1s in the first k rows. Finally, if there is a matrix for λ and μ and if λ covers α, we can readily construct a matrix for α and μ by moving a 1 from any specified row to another that has fewer 1s.

Notes: This result is often called the Gale–Ryser theorem, because of well-known papers by D. Gale [*Pacific J. Math.* **7** (1957), 1073–1082] and H. J. Ryser [*Canadian J. Math.* **9** (1957), 371–377]. But the number of 0–1 matrices with row sums λ and column sums μ is the coefficient of the monomial symmetric function $\sum x_{i_1}^{c_1} x_{i_2}^{c_2} \dots$ in the product of elementary symmetric functions $e_{r_1} e_{r_2} \dots$, where

$$e_r = [z^r](1 + x_1 z)(1 + x_2 z)(1 + x_3 z) \dots.$$

In this context the result has been known at least since the 1930s; see D. E. Littlewood's formula for $\prod_{m,n \geq 0}(1 + x_m y_n)$ in *Proc. London Math. Soc.* (2) **40** (1936), 49–70. [Cayley had shown much earlier, in *Philosophical Trans.* **147** (1857), 489–499, that the lexicographic condition $\lambda \leq \mu^T$ is necessary.] See also the algorithm in exercise 7–108.

58. [R. F. Muirhead, *Proc. Edinburgh Math. Soc.* **21** (1903), 144–157.] The condition $\alpha \succeq \beta$ is necessary, because we can set $x_1 = \cdots = x_k = x$ and $x_{k+1} = \cdots = x_n = 1$ and let $x \to \infty$. It is sufficient because we need only prove it when α covers β. Then if, say, parts (a_1, a_2) become $(a_1 - 1, a_2 + 1)$, the left-hand side is the right-hand side plus the nonnegative quantity

$$\frac{1}{2m!} \sum x_{p_1}^{a_2} x_{p_2}^{a_2} \dots x_{p_m}^{a_m} (x_{p_1}^{a_1 - a_2 - 1} - x_{p_2}^{a_1 - a_2 - 1})(x_{p_1} - x_{p_2}).$$

[*Historical notes:* Muirhead's paper is the earliest known appearance of the concept now known as majorization; shortly afterward, an equivalent definition was given by M. O. Lorenz, *Quarterly Publ. Amer. Stat. Assoc.* **9** (1905), 209–219, who was interested in measuring nonuniform distribution of wealth. Yet another equivalent

concept was formulated by I. Schur in *Sitzungsberichte Berliner Math. Gesellschaft*
22 (1923), 9–20. "Majorization" was named by Hardy, Littlewood, and Pólya, who
established its most basic properties in *Messenger of Math.* **58** (1929), 145–152; see
exercise 2.3.4.5–17. An excellent book, *Inequalities* by A. W. Marshall and I. Olkin
(Academic Press, 1979), is entirely devoted to the subject.]

59. The unique paths for $n = 0$, 1, 2, 3, 4, and 6 must have the stated symmetry.
There is one such path for $n = 5$, namely 11111, 2111, 221, 311, 32, 41, 5. And there
are four for $n = 7$:

   1111111, 211111, 22111, 2221, 322, 3211, 31111, 4111, 511, 421, 331, 43, 52, 61, 7;

   1111111, 211111, 22111, 2221, 322, 421, 511, 4111, 31111, 3211, 331, 43, 52, 61, 7;

   1111111, 211111, 31111, 22111, 2221, 322, 3211, 4111, 421, 331, 43, 52, 511, 61, 7;

   1111111, 211111, 31111, 22111, 2221, 322, 421, 4111, 3211, 331, 43, 52, 511, 61, 7.

There are no others, because at least two self-conjugate partitions exist for all $n \geq 8$
(see exercise 15).

60. For $L(6,6)$, use (59); otherwise use $L'(4,6)$ and $L'(3,5)$ everywhere.
   In $M(4, 18)$, insert 444222, 4442211 between 443322 and 4432221.
   In $M(5, 11)$, insert 52211, 5222 between 62111 and 6221.
   In $M(5, 20)$, insert 5542211, 554222 between 5552111 and 555221.
   In $M(6, 13)$, insert 72211, 7222 between 62221 and 6322.
   In $L(4, 14)$, insert 44222, 442211 between 43322 and 432221.
   In $L(5, 15)$, insert 542211, 54222 between 552111 and 55221.
   In $L(7, 12)$, insert 62211, 6222 between 72111 and 7221.

62. The statement holds for $n = 7$, 8, and 9, except in two cases: $n = 8$, $m = 3$,
$\alpha = 3221$; $n = 9$, $m = 4$, $\alpha = 432$.

64. If $n = 2^k q$ where q is odd, let ω_n denote the partition $(2^k)^q$, namely q parts equal
to 2^k. The recursive rule

$$B(n) = B(n-1)^R 1, \ 2 \times B(n/2)$$

for $n > 0$, where $2 \times B(n/2)$ denotes doubling all parts of $B(n/2)$ (or the empty sequence
if n is odd), defines a pleasant Gray path that begins with $\omega_{n-1}1$ and ends with ω_n, if
we let $B(0)$ be the unique partition of 0. Thus,

$$B(1) = 1; \quad B(2) = 11, 2; \quad B(3) = 21, 111; \quad B(4) = 1111, 211, 22, 4.$$

Among the remarkable properties satisfied by this sequence is the fact that

$$B(n) = \left(2 \times B(0)\right)1^n, \ \left(2 \times B(1)\right)1^{n-2}, \ \left(2 \times B(2)\right)1^{n-4}, \ \ldots, \ \left(2 \times B(n/2)\right)1^0,$$

when n is even; for example,

$$B(8) = 11111111, 2111111, 221111, 41111, 4211, 22211, 2222, 422, 44, 8.$$

The following algorithm generates $B(n)$ looplessly when $n \geq 2$:

   K1. [Initialize.] Set $c_0 \leftarrow p_0 \leftarrow 0$, $p_1 \leftarrow 1$. If n is even, set $c_1 \leftarrow n$, $t \leftarrow 1$; other-
       wise let $n - 1 = 2^k q$ where q is odd and set $c_1 \leftarrow 1$, $c_2 \leftarrow q$, $p_2 \leftarrow 2^k$, $t \leftarrow 2$.

   K2. [Even visit.] Visit the partition $p_t^{c_t} \ldots p_1^{c_1}$. (Now $c_t + \cdots + c_1$ is even.)

   K3. [Change the largest part.] If $c_t = 1$, split the largest part: If $p_t \neq 2p_{t-1}$, set
       $c_t \leftarrow 2$, $p_t \leftarrow p_t/2$, otherwise set $c_{t-1} \leftarrow c_{t-1} + 2$, $t \leftarrow t - 1$. But if $c_t > 1$,
       merge two of the largest parts: If $c_t = 2$, set $c_t \leftarrow 1$, $p_t \leftarrow 2p_t$, otherwise set
       $c_t \leftarrow c_t - 2$, $c_{t+1} \leftarrow 1$, $p_{t+1} \leftarrow 2p_t$, $t \leftarrow t + 1$.

K4. [Odd visit.] Visit the partition $p_t^{c_t} \ldots p_1^{c_1}$. (Now $c_t + \cdots + c_1$ is odd.)

K5. [Change the next-largest part.] Now we wish to apply the following transformation: "Remove $c_t - [t \text{ is even}]$ of the largest parts temporarily, then apply step K3, then restore the removed parts." More precisely, there are nine cases: (1a) If c_t is odd and $t = 1$, terminate. (1b1) If c_t is odd, $c_{t-1} = 1$, and $p_{t-1} = 2p_{t-2}$, set $c_{t-2} \leftarrow c_{t-2} + 2$, $c_{t-1} \leftarrow c_t$, $p_{t-1} \leftarrow p_t$, $t \leftarrow t - 1$. (1b2) If c_t is odd, $c_{t-1} = 1$, and $p_{t-1} \neq 2p_{t-2}$, set $c_{t-1} \leftarrow 2$, $p_{t-1} \leftarrow p_{t-1}/2$. (1c1) If c_t is odd, $c_{t-1} = 2$, and $p_t = 2p_{t-1}$, set $c_{t-1} \leftarrow c_t + 1$, $p_{t-1} \leftarrow p_t$, $t \leftarrow t - 1$. (1c2) If c_t is odd, $c_{t-1} = 2$, and $p_t \neq 2p_{t-1}$, set $c_{t-1} \leftarrow 1$, $p_{t-1} \leftarrow 2p_{t-1}$. (1d1) If c_t is odd, $c_{t-1} > 2$, and $p_t = 2p_{t-1}$, set $c_{t-1} \leftarrow c_{t-1} - 2$, $c_t \leftarrow c_t + 1$. (1d2) If c_t is odd, $c_{t-1} > 2$, and $p_t \neq 2p_{t-1}$, set $c_{t+1} \leftarrow c_t$, $p_{t+1} \leftarrow p_t$, $c_t \leftarrow 1$, $p_t \leftarrow 2p_{t-1}$, $c_{t-1} \leftarrow c_{t-1} - 2$, $t \leftarrow t + 1$. (2a) If c_t is even and $p_t = 2p_{t-1}$, set $c_t \leftarrow c_t - 1$, $c_{t-1} \leftarrow c_{t-1} + 2$. (2b) If c_t is even and $p_t \neq 2p_{t-1}$, set $c_{t+1} \leftarrow c_t - 1$, $p_{t+1} \leftarrow p_t$, $c_t \leftarrow 2$, $p_t \leftarrow p_t/2$, $t \leftarrow t + 1$. Return to K2. ∎

[The transformations in K3 and K5 undo themselves when performed twice in a row. This construction is due to T. Colthurst and M. Kleber, "A Gray path on binary partitions," http://arxiv.org/abs/0907.3873. Euler considered the number of such partitions in §50 of his paper in 1750.]

65. If $p_1^{e_1} \ldots p_r^{e_r}$ is the prime factorization of m, the number of such factorizations is $p(e_1) \ldots p(e_r)$, and we can let $n = \max(e_1, \ldots, e_r)$. Indeed, for each r-tuple $(x_1, \ldots, x_r)$ with $0 \le x_k < p(e_k)$ we can let $m_j = p_1^{a_{1j}} \ldots p_r^{a_{rj}}$, where $a_{k1} \ldots a_{kn}$ is the $(x_k + 1)$st partition of e_k. Thus we can use a reflected Gray code for r-tuples together with a Gray code for partitions.

66. Let $a_1 \ldots a_m$ be an m-tuple that satisfies the specified inequalities. We can sort it into nonincreasing order $a_{x_1} \ge \cdots \ge a_{x_m}$, where the permutation $x_1 \ldots x_m$ is uniquely determined if we require the sorting to be *stable*; see Eq. 5–(2).

If $j \prec k$, we have $a_j \ge a_k$, hence j appears to the left of k in the permutation $x_1 \ldots x_m$. Therefore $x_1 \ldots x_m$ is one of the permutations output by Algorithm 7.2.1.2V. Moreover, j will be left of k also when $a_j = a_k$ and $j < k$, by stability. Hence a_{x_i} is strictly greater than $a_{x_{i+1}}$ when $x_i > x_{i+1}$ is a "descent."

To generate all the relevant partitions of n, take each topological permutation $x_1 \ldots x_m$ and generate the partitions $y_1 \ldots y_m$ of $n - t$ where t is the *index* of $x_1 \ldots x_m$ (see Section 5.1.1). For $1 \le j \le m$ set $a_{x_j} \leftarrow y_j + t_j$, where t_j is the number of descents to the right of x_j in $x_1 \ldots x_m$.

For example, if $x_1 \ldots x_m = 314592687$ we want to generate all cases with $a_3 > a_1 \ge a_4 \ge a_5 \ge a_9 > a_2 \ge a_6 \ge a_8 > a_7$. In this case $t = 1 + 5 + 8 = 14$; so we set $a_1 \leftarrow y_2 + 2$, $a_2 \leftarrow y_6 + 1$, $a_3 \leftarrow y_1 + 3$, $a_4 \leftarrow y_3 + 2$, $a_5 \leftarrow y_4 + 2$, $a_6 \leftarrow y_7 + 1$, $a_7 \leftarrow y_9$, $a_8 \leftarrow y_8 + 1$, and $a_9 \leftarrow y_5 + 2$. The generalized generating function $\sum z_1^{a_1} \ldots z_9^{a_9}$ in the sense of exercise 29 is

$$\frac{z_1^2 z_2 z_3^3 z_4^2 z_5^2 z_6 z_8 z_9^2}{(1 - z_3)(1 - z_3 z_1)(1 - z_3 z_1 z_4)(1 - z_3 z_1 z_4 z_5) \ldots (1 - z_3 z_1 z_4 z_5 z_9 z_2 z_6 z_8 z_7)}.$$

When $\prec$ is any given partial ordering, the ordinary generating function for the number of all such partitions of n is therefore $\sum z^{\text{ind }\alpha}/((1 - z)(1 - z^2) \ldots (1 - z^m))$, where the sum is over all outputs α of Algorithm 7.2.1.2V.

[See R. P. Stanley, *Memoirs Amer. Math. Soc.* **119** (1972), for significant extensions and applications of these ideas. See also L. Carlitz, *Studies in Foundations and Combinatorics* (New York: Academic Press, 1978), 101–129, for information about up-down partitions.]

67. If $n + 1 = q_1 \ldots q_r$, where the factors q_1, ..., q_r are all ≥ 2, we get a perfect partition $\{(q_1-1) \cdot 1, (q_2-1) \cdot q_1, (q_3-1) \cdot q_1 q_2, \ldots, (q_r-1) \cdot q_1 \ldots q_{r-1}\}$ that corresponds in an obvious way to mixed radix notation. (The order of the factors q_j is significant.)

Conversely, all perfect partitions arise in this way. Suppose the multiset $M = \{k_1 \cdot p_1, \ldots, k_m \cdot p_m\}$ is a perfect partition, where $p_1 < \cdots < p_m$; then we must have $p_j = (k_1+1) \ldots (k_{j-1}+1)$ for $1 \leq j \leq m$, because p_j is the smallest sum of a submultiset of M that is not a submultiset of $\{k_1 \cdot p_1, \ldots, k_{j-1} \cdot p_{j-1}\}$.

The perfect partitions of n with fewest elements occur if and only if the q_j are all prime, because $pq - 1 > (p-1) + (q-1)$ whenever $p > 1$ and $q > 1$. Thus, for example, the minimal perfect partitions of 11 correspond to the ordered factorizations $2 \cdot 2 \cdot 3$, $2 \cdot 3 \cdot 2$, and $3 \cdot 2 \cdot 2$. *Reference: Quarterly Journal of Mathematics* **21** (1886), 367–373.

68. (a) If $a_i + 1 \leq a_j - 1$ for some i and j we can change $\{a_i, a_j\}$ to $\{a_i+1, a_j-1\}$, thereby increasing the product by $a_j - a_i - 1 > 0$. Thus the optimum occurs only in the optimally balanced partition of exercise 3. [L. Oettinger and J. Derbès, *Nouv. Ann. Math.* **18** (1859), 442; **19** (1860), 117–118.]

(b) Assume that $n > 1$. Then no part is 1; and if $a_j \geq 4$ we can change it to $2 + (a_j-2)$ without decreasing the product. Thus we can assume that all parts are 2 or 3. We get an improvement by changing $2 + 2 + 2$ to $3 + 3$, hence there are at most two 2s. The optimum therefore is $3^{n/3}$ when $n \bmod 3$ is 0; $4 \cdot 3^{(n-4)/3} = 3^{(n-4)/3} \cdot 2 \cdot 2 = (4/3^{4/3}) 3^{n/3}$ when $n \bmod 3$ is 1; $3^{(n-2)/3} \cdot 2 = (2/3^{2/3}) 3^{n/3}$ when $n \bmod 3$ is 2. [O. Meißner, *Mathematisch-naturwissenschaftliche Blätter* **4** (1907), 85.]

69. All $n > 2$ have the solution $(n, 2, 1, \ldots, 1)$. We can "sieve out" the other cases $\leq N$ by starting with $s_2 \ldots s_N \leftarrow 1 \ldots 1$ and then setting $s_{ak-b} \leftarrow 0$ whenever $ak - b \leq N$, where $a = x_1 \ldots x_t - 1$, $b = x_1 + \cdots + x_t - t - 1$, $k \geq x_1 \geq \cdots \geq x_t$, and $a > 1$, because $k + x_1 + \cdots + x_t + (ak - b - t - 1) = kx_1 \ldots x_t$. The sequence $(x_1, \ldots, x_t)$ needs to be considered only when $(x_1 \ldots x_t - 1)x_1 - (x_1 + \cdots + x_t) < N - t$; we can also continue to decrease N so that $s_N = 1$. In this way only $(32766, 1486539, 254887, 1511, 937, 478, 4)$ sequences $(x_1, \ldots, x_t)$ need to be tried when N is initially 2^{30}, and the only survivors turn out to be 2, 3, 4, 6, 24, 114, 174, and 444. [See E. Trost, *Elemente der Math.* **11** (1956), 135; M. Misiurewicz, *Elemente der Math.* **21** (1966), 90.]

Notes: No new survivors are likely as $N \to \infty$, but a new idea will be needed to rule them out. The simplest sequences $(x_1, \ldots, x_t) = (3)$ and $(2, 2)$ already exclude all $n > 5$ with $n \bmod 6 \neq 0$; this fact can be used to speed up the computation by a factor of 6. The sequences (6) and $(3, 2)$ exclude 40% of the remainder (namely all n of the forms $5k - 4$ and $5k - 2$); the sequences (8), $(4, 2)$, and $(2, 2, 2)$ exclude 3/7 of the remainder; the sequences with $t = 1$ imply that $n - 1$ must be prime; the sequences in which $x_1 \ldots x_t = 2^r$ exclude about $p(r)$ residues of $n \bmod (2^r - 1)$; sequences in which $x_1 \ldots x_t$ is the product of r distinct primes will exclude about ϖ_r residues of $n \bmod (x_1 \ldots x_t - 1)$.

70. Each step takes one partition of n into another, so we must eventually reach a repeating cycle. Many partitions simply perform a cyclic shift on each northeast-to-southwest diagonal of the Ferrers diagram, changing it

from
$$
\begin{matrix}
x_1 & x_2 & x_4 & x_7 & x_{11} & x_{16} \cdots \\
x_3 & x_5 & x_8 & x_{12} & x_{17} & x_{23} \cdots \\
x_6 & x_9 & x_{13} & x_{18} & x_{24} & x_{31} \cdots \\
x_{10} & x_{14} & x_{19} & x_{25} & x_{32} & x_{40} \cdots \\
x_{15} & x_{20} & x_{26} & x_{33} & x_{41} & x_{50} \cdots \\
x_{21} & x_{27} & x_{34} & x_{42} & x_{51} & x_{61} \cdots \\
\vdots & \vdots & \vdots & \vdots & \vdots & \vdots
\end{matrix}
$$
to
$$
\begin{matrix}
x_1 & x_3 & x_6 & x_{10} & x_{15} & x_{21} \cdots \\
x_2 & x_4 & x_7 & x_{11} & x_{16} & x_{22} \cdots \\
x_5 & x_8 & x_{12} & x_{17} & x_{23} & x_{30} \cdots \\
x_9 & x_{13} & x_{18} & x_{24} & x_{31} & x_{39} \cdots ; \\
x_{14} & x_{19} & x_{25} & x_{32} & x_{40} & x_{49} \cdots \\
x_{20} & x_{26} & x_{33} & x_{41} & x_{50} & x_{60} \cdots \\
\vdots & \vdots & \vdots & \vdots & \vdots & \vdots
\end{matrix}
$$

in other words, they apply the permutation $\rho = (1)(2\,3)(4\,5\,6)(7\,8\,9\,10)\ldots$ to the cells. Exceptions occur only when ρ introduces an empty cell above a dot; for example, x_{10} might be empty when x_{11} isn't. But we can get the correct new diagram by moving the top row down, sorting it into its proper place after applying ρ in such cases. Such a move always reduces the number of occupied diagonals, so it cannot be part of a cycle. Thus every cycle consists entirely of permutations by ρ.

If any element of a diagonal is empty in a cyclic partition, all elements of the next diagonal must be empty. For if, say, x_5 is empty, repeated application of ρ will make x_5 adjacent to each of the cells x_7, x_8, x_9, x_{10} of the next diagonal. Therefore if $n = \binom{n_2}{2} + \binom{n_1}{1}$ with $n_2 > n_1 \geq 0$ the cyclic states are precisely those with $n_2 - 1$ completely filled diagonals and n_1 dots in the next. [This result is due to J. Brandt, *Proc. Amer. Math. Soc.* **85** (1982), 483–486. The problem reportedly stems from Russia via Bulgaria and Sweden. See also Martin Gardner, *The Last Recreations* (1997), Chapter 2.]

71. When $n = 1 + \cdots + m > 1$, the starting partition $(m-1)(m-1)(m-2)\ldots 211$ has distance $m(m-1)$ from the cyclic state, and this is maximum. [K. Igusa, *Math. Magazine* **58** (1985), 259–271; G. Etienne, *J. Combin. Theory* **A58** (1991), 181–197.] In the general case, Griggs and Ho [*Advances in Appl. Math.* **21** (1998), 205–227] have conjectured that the maximum distance to a cycle is $\max(2n+2-n_1(n_2+1), n+n_2+1, n_1(n_2+1)) - 2n_2$ for all $n > 1$; their conjecture has been verified for $n \leq 100$. Moreover, the worst-case starting partition appears to be unique when $n_2 = 2n_1 + \{-1, 0, 2\}$.

72. Equivalently, $a_1 < m-1$ [B. Hopkins and J. A. Sellers, *Integers* **7**, 2 (2007), #A19].

73. (a) [R. Stanley, 1972 (unpublished).] Swap the jth occurrence of k in the partition $n = j \cdot k + \alpha$ with the kth occurrence of j in $k \cdot j + \alpha$, for every partition α of $n - jk$. For example, when $n = 6$ the swaps are

$$6, \quad 51, \quad 42, \quad 411, \quad 33, \quad 321, \quad 3111, \quad 222, \quad 2211, \quad 21111, \quad 111111.$$
$$\texttt{a} \quad \texttt{bl} \quad \texttt{fg} \quad \texttt{clg} \quad \texttt{hi} \quad \texttt{jkl} \quad \texttt{dlkh} \quad \texttt{n2i} \quad \texttt{m2ln} \quad \texttt{elmjf} \quad \texttt{ledcba}$$

(b) $p(n-k) + p(n-2k) + p(n-3k) + \cdots$. [A. H. M. Hoare, *AMM* **93** (1986), 475–476.]

SECTION 7.2.1.5

1. Whenever m is set equal to r in step H6, change it back to $r-1$.

2. **L1.** [Initialize.] Set $l_j \leftarrow j - 1$ and $a_j \leftarrow 0$ for $1 \leq j \leq n$. Also set $h_1 \leftarrow n$, $t \leftarrow 1$, and set l_0 to any convenient nonzero value.

    L2. [Visit.] Visit the t-block partition represented by $l_1 \ldots l_n$ and $h_1 \ldots h_t$. (The restricted growth string corresponding to this partition is $a_1 \ldots a_n$.)

    L3. [Find j.] Set $j \leftarrow n$; then, while $l_j = 0$, set $j \leftarrow j - 1$ and $t \leftarrow t - 1$.

    L4. [Move j to the next block.] Terminate if $j = 0$. Otherwise set $k \leftarrow a_j + 1$, $h_k \leftarrow l_j$, $a_j \leftarrow k$. If $k = t$, set $t \leftarrow t + 1$ and $l_j \leftarrow 0$; otherwise set $l_j \leftarrow h_{k+1}$. Finally set $h_{k+1} \leftarrow j$.

    L5. [Move $j + 1, \ldots, n$ to block 1.] While $j < n$, set $j \leftarrow j + 1$, $l_j \leftarrow h_1$, $a_j \leftarrow 0$, and $h_1 \leftarrow j$. Return to L2. ∎

3. Let $\tau(k, n)$ be the number of strings $a_1 \ldots a_n$ that satisfy the condition $0 \leq a_j \leq 1 + \max(k-1, a_1, \ldots, a_{j-1})$ for $1 \leq j \leq n$; thus $\tau(k, 0) = 1$, $\tau(0, n) = \varpi_n$, and $\tau(k, n) = k\tau(k, n-1) + \tau(k+1, n-1)$. [S. G. Williamson has called $\tau(k, n)$ a "tail coefficient"; see *SICOMP* **5** (1976), 602–617.] The number of strings that are generated by Algorithm H before a given restricted growth string $a_1 \ldots a_n$ is $\sum_{j=1}^{n} a_j \tau(b_j, n - j)$, where $b_j = 1 + \max(a_1, \ldots, a_{j-1})$. Working backwards with the help of a precomputed table of the tail coefficients, we find that this formula yields 999999 when $a_1 \ldots a_{12} = 010220345041$.

4. The most common representatives of each type, subscripted by the number of corresponding occurrences in the GraphBase, are zzzzz_0, ooooh_0, xxxix_0, xxxii_0, ooops_0, llull_0, llala_0, eeler_0, iitti_0, xxiii_0, ccxxv_0, eerie_1, llama_1, xxvii_0, oozed_5, uhuuu_0, mamma_1, puppy_{28}, anana_0, hehee_0, vivid_{15}, rarer_3, etext_1, amass_2, again_{137}, ahhaa_0, esses_1, teeth_{25}, yaaay_0, ahhhh_2, pssst_2, seems_7, added_6, lxxii_0, books_{184}, swiss_3, sense_{10}, ended_3, check_{160}, level_{18}, tepee_4, slyly_5, never_{154}, sells_6, motto_{21}, whooo_2, trees_{384}, going_{307}, which_{151}, there_{174}, three_{100}, their_{3834}. (See S. Golomb, *Math. Mag.* **53** (1980), 219–221. Words with only two distinct letters are, of course, rare. The 18 representatives listed here with subscript 0 can be found in larger dictionaries or in English-language pages of the Internet.)

5. (a) $112 = \rho(0225)$. The sequence is $r(0)$, $r(1)$, $r(4)$, $r(9)$, $r(16)$, ..., where $r(n)$ is obtained by expressing n in decimal notation (with one or more leading zeros), applying the ρ function of exercise 4, then deleting the leading zeros. Notice that $n/9 \leq r(n) \leq n$.

(b) $1012 = r(45^2)$. The sequence is the same as (a), but sorted into order and with duplicates removed. (Who knew that $88^2 = 7744$, $212^2 = 44944$, and $264^2 = 69696$?)

6. Use the topological sorting approach of Algorithm 7.2.1.2V, with an appropriate partial ordering: Include c_j chains of length j, with their least elements ordered. For example, if $n = 20$, $c_2 = 3$, and $c_3 = c_4 = 2$, we use that algorithm to find all permutations $a_1 \ldots a_{20}$ of $\{1, \ldots, 20\}$ such that $1 \prec 2$, $3 \prec 4$, $5 \prec 6$, $1 \prec 3 \prec 5$, $7 \prec 8 \prec 9$, $10 \prec 11 \prec 12$, $7 \prec 10$, $13 \prec 14 \prec 15 \prec 16$, $17 \prec 18 \prec 19 \prec 20$, $13 \prec 17$, forming the restricted growth strings $\rho(f(a_1) \ldots f(a_{20}))$, where ρ is defined in exercise 4 and $(f(1), \ldots, f(20)) = (1, 1, 2, 2, 3, 3, 4, 4, 4, 5, 5, 5, 6, 6, 6, 6, 7, 7, 7, 7)$. The total number of outputs is, of course, given by (48).

7. Exactly ϖ_n. They are the permutations we get by reversing the left-right order of the blocks in (2) and dropping the '|' symbols: 1234, 4123, 3124, 3412, ..., 4321. [See A. Claesson, *European J. Combinatorics* **22** (2001), 961–971. S. Kitaev, in *Discrete Math.* **298** (2005), 212–229, has discovered a far-reaching generalization: Let π be a permutation of $\{0, \ldots, r\}$, let g_n be the number of permutations $a_1 \ldots a_n$ of $\{1, \ldots, n\}$ such that $a_{k-0\pi} > a_{k-1\pi} > \cdots > a_{k-r\pi} > a_j$ implies $j > k$, and let f_n be the number of permutations $a_1 \ldots a_n$ for which the pattern $a_{k-0\pi} > a_{k-1\pi} > \cdots > a_{k-r\pi}$ is avoided altogether for $r < k \leq n$. Then $\sum_{n \geq 0} g_n z^n / n! = \exp(\sum_{n \geq 1} f_{n-1} z^n / n!)$.]

8. For each partition of $\{1, \ldots, n\}$ into m blocks, arrange the blocks in decreasing order of their smallest elements, and permute the non-smallest block elements in all possible ways. If $n = 9$ and $m = 3$, for example, the partition 126|38|4579 would yield 457938126 and eleven other cases obtained by permuting $\{5, 7, 9\}$ and $\{2, 6\}$ among themselves. (Essentially the same method generates all permutations that have exactly k cycles; see the "unusual correspondence" of Section 1.3.3.)

9. Among the permutations of the multiset $\{k_0 \cdot 0, k_1 \cdot 1, \ldots, k_{n-1} \cdot (n-1)\}$, exactly

$$\binom{k_0 + k_1 + \cdots + k_{n-1}}{k_0, k_1, \ldots, k_{n-1}} \frac{k_0}{(k_0 + k_1 + \cdots + k_{n-1})} \frac{k_1}{(k_1 + \cdots + k_{n-1})} \cdots \frac{k_{n-1}}{k_{n-1}}$$

have restricted growth, since $k_j / (k_j + \cdots + k_{n-1})$ is the probability that j precedes $\{j + 1, \ldots, n - 1\}$.

The average number of 0s, if $n > 0$, is $1 + (n - 1)\varpi_{n-1} / \varpi_n = \Theta(\log n)$, because the total number of 0s among all ϖ_n cases is $\sum_{k=1}^{n} k \binom{n-1}{k-1} \varpi_{n-k} = \varpi_n + (n - 1)\varpi_{n-1}$.

10. Given a partition of $\{1, \ldots, n\}$, construct an oriented tree on $\{0, 1, \ldots, n\}$ by letting $j - 1$ be the parent of all members of a block whose least member is j. Then relabel the leaves, preserving order, and erase the other labels. For example, the 15 partitions in (2) correspond respectively to

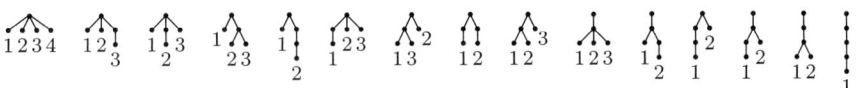

To reverse the process, take a semilabeled tree and assign new numbers to its nodes by considering the nodes first encountered on the path from the root to the smallest leaf, then on the path from the root to the second-smallest leaf, etc. The number of leaves is $n + 1$ minus the number of blocks. [This construction is closely related to exercise 2.3.4.4–18 and to many enumerations in that section. See P. L. Erdős and L. A. Székely, *Advances in Applied Math.* **10** (1989), 488–496.]

11. We get pure alphametics from 900 of the 64855 set partitions into at most 10 blocks for which $\rho(a_1 \ldots a_{13}) = \rho(a_5 \ldots a_8 a_1 \ldots a_4 a_9 \ldots a_{13})$, and from 563,527 of the 13,788,536 for which $\rho(a_1 \ldots a_{13}) < \rho(a_5 \ldots a_8 a_1 \ldots a_4 a_9 \ldots a_{13})$. The first examples are aaaa + aaaa = baaac, aaaa + aaaa = bbbbc, and aaaa + aaab = baaac; the last are abcd + efgd = dceab (goat + newt = tango) and abcd + efgd = dceaf (clad + nerd = dance). [The idea of hooking a partition generator to an alphametic solver is due to Alan Sutcliffe.]

12. (a) Form $\rho((a_1 a'_1) \ldots (a_n a'_n))$, where ρ is defined in exercise 4, since we have $x \equiv y$ (modulo $\Pi \vee \Pi'$) if and only if $x \equiv y$ (modulo Π) and $x \equiv y$ (modulo Π').

    (b) Represent Π by links as in exercise 2; represent Π' as in Algorithm 2.3.3E; and use that algorithm to make $j \equiv l_j$ whenever $l_j \neq 0$. (For efficiency, we can assume that Π has at least as many blocks as Π'.)

    (c) When one block of Π has been split into two parts; that is, when two blocks of Π' have been merged together.

    (d) $\binom{t}{2}$; (e) $(2^{s_1 - 1} - 1) + \cdots + (2^{s_t - 1} - 1)$.

    (f) True: Let $\Pi \vee \Pi'$ have blocks $B_1 | B_2 | \cdots | B_t$, where $\Pi = B_1 B_2 | B_3 | \cdots | B_t$. Then Π' is essentially a partition of $\{B_1, \ldots, B_t\}$ with $B_1 \not\equiv B_2$, and $\Pi \wedge \Pi'$ is obtained by merging the block of Π' that contains B_1 with the block that contains B_2. [A finite lattice that satisfies this condition is called *lower semimodular*; see G. Birkhoff, *Lattice Theory* (1940), §I.8. The majorization lattice of exercise 7.2.1.4–54 does not have this property when, for example, $\alpha = 4111$ and $\alpha' = 331$.]

    (g) False: For example, let $\Pi = 0011$, $\Pi' = 0101$.

    (h) The blocks of Π and Π' are unions of the blocks of $\Pi \vee \Pi'$, so we can assume that $\Pi \vee \Pi' = \{1, \ldots, t\}$. As in part (b), merge j with l_j to get Π in r steps, when Π has $t - r$ blocks. These merges applied to Π' will each reduce the number of blocks by 0 or 1. Hence $b(\Pi') - b(\Pi \wedge \Pi') \leq r = b(\Pi \vee \Pi') - b(\Pi)$.

    [In *Algebra Universalis* **10** (1980), 74–95, P. Pudlák and J. Tůma proved that *every* finite lattice is a sublattice of the partition lattice of $\{1, \ldots, n\}$, for suitably large n.]

13. [See *Advances in Math.* **26** (1977), 290–305.] If the j largest elements of a t-block partition appear in singleton blocks, but the next element $n - j$ does not, let us say that the partition has order $t - j$. Define the "Stirling string" Σ_{nt} to be the sequence of orders of the t-block partitions Π_1, Π_2, $\ldots$; for example, $\Sigma_{43} = 122333$. Then $\Sigma_{tt} = 0$, and we get $\Sigma_{(n+1)t}$ from Σ_{nt} by replacing each digit d in the latter by the string $d^d (d+1)^{d+1} \ldots t^t$ of length $\binom{t+1}{2} - \binom{d}{2}$; for example,

$$\Sigma_{53} = 122333223332233333333333.$$

The basic idea is to consider the lexicographic generation process of Algorithm H. Suppose $\Pi = a_1 \ldots a_n$ is a t-block partition of order j; then it is the lexicographically smallest t-block partition whose restricted growth string begins with $a_1 \ldots a_{n-t+j}$. The partitions covered by Π are, in lexicographic order, Π_{12}, Π_{13}, Π_{23}, Π_{14}, Π_{24}, Π_{34}, ..., $\Pi_{(t-1)t}$, where Π_{rs} means "coalesce blocks r and s of Π" (that is, "change all occurrences of $s-1$ to $r-1$ and then apply ρ to get a restricted growth string"). If Π' is any of the last $\binom{t}{2} - \binom{j}{2}$ of these, from $\Pi_{1(j+1)}$ onwards, then Π is the smallest t-block partition following Π'. For example, if $\Pi = 001012034$, then $n = 9$, $t = 5$, $j = 3$, and the relevant partitions Π' are $\rho(001012004)$, $\rho(001012014)$, $\rho(001012024)$, $\rho(001012030)$, $\rho(001012031)$, $\rho(001012032)$, $\rho(001012033)$.

Therefore $f_{nt}(N) = f_{nt}(N-1) + \binom{t}{2} - \binom{j}{2}$, where j is the Nth digit of Σ_{nt}.

14. E1. [Initialize.] Set $a_j \leftarrow 0$ and $b_j \leftarrow d_j \leftarrow 1$ for $1 \leq j \leq n$.

  E2. [Visit.] Visit the restricted growth string $a_1 \ldots a_n$.

  E3. [Find j.] Set $j \leftarrow n$; then, while $a_j = d_j$, set $d_j \leftarrow 1 - d_j$ and $j \leftarrow j - 1$.

  E4. [Done?] Terminate if $j = 1$. Otherwise go to E6 if $d_j = 0$.

  E5. [Move down.] If $a_j = 0$, set $a_j \leftarrow b_j$, $m \leftarrow a_j + 1$, and go to E7. Otherwise if $a_j = b_j$, set $a_j \leftarrow b_j - 1$, $m \leftarrow b_j$, and go to E7. Otherwise set $a_j \leftarrow a_j - 1$ and return to E2.

  E6. [Move up.] If $a_j = b_j - 1$, set $a_j \leftarrow b_j$, $m \leftarrow a_j + 1$, and go to E7. Otherwise if $a_j = b_j$, set $a_j \leftarrow 0$, $m \leftarrow b_j$, and go to E7. Otherwise set $a_j \leftarrow a_j + 1$ and return to E2.

  E7. [Fix $b_{j+1} \ldots b_n$.] Set $b_k \leftarrow m$ for $k = j + 1, \ldots, n$. Return to E2. ∎

[This algorithm can be extensively optimized because, as in Algorithm H, j is almost always equal to n.]

15. It corresponds to the first n digits of the infinite binary string $01011011011\ldots$, because ϖ_{n-1} is even if and only if $n \bmod 3 = 0$ (see exercise 23).

16. 00012, 01012, 01112, 00112, 00102, 01102, 01002, 01202, 01212, 01222, 01022, 01122, 00122, 00121, 01121, 01021, 01221, 01211, 01201, 01200, 01210, 01220, 01020, 01120, 00120.

17. The following solution uses two mutually recursive procedures, $f(\mu, \nu, \sigma)$ and $b(\mu, \nu, \sigma)$, for "forward" and "backward" generation of $A_{\mu\nu}$ when $\sigma = 0$ and of $A'_{\mu\nu}$ when $\sigma = 1$. To start the process, assuming that $1 < m < n$, first set $a_j \leftarrow 0$ for $1 \leq j \leq n - m$ and $a_{n-m+j} \leftarrow j - 1$ for $1 \leq j \leq m$, then call $f(m, n, 0)$.

Procedure $f(\mu, \nu, \sigma)$: If $\mu = 2$, visit $a_1 \ldots a_n$; otherwise call $f(\mu - 1, \nu - 1, (\mu+\sigma) \bmod 2)$. Then, if $\nu = \mu + 1$, do the following: Change a_μ from 0 to $\mu - 1$, and visit $a_1 \ldots a_n$; repeatedly set $a_\nu \leftarrow a_\nu - 1$ and visit $a_1 \ldots a_n$, until $a_\nu = 0$. But if $\nu > \mu + 1$, change $a_{\nu-1}$ (if $\mu+\sigma$ is odd) or a_μ (if $\mu+\sigma$ is even) from 0 to $\mu - 1$; then call $b(\mu, \nu-1, 0)$ if $a_\nu + \sigma$ is odd, $f(\mu, \nu-1, 0)$ if $a_\nu + \sigma$ is even; and while $a_\nu > 0$, set $a_\nu \leftarrow a_\nu - 1$ and call $b(\mu, \nu-1, 0)$ or $f(\mu, \nu-1, 0)$ again in the same way until $a_\nu = 0$.

Procedure $b(\mu, \nu, \sigma)$: If $\nu = \mu + 1$, first do the following: Repeatedly visit $a_1 \ldots a_n$ and set $a_\nu \leftarrow a_\nu + 1$, until $a_\nu = \mu - 1$; then visit $a_1 \ldots a_n$ and change a_μ from $\mu - 1$ to 0. But if $\nu > \mu + 1$, call $f(\mu, \nu-1, 0)$ if $a_\nu + \sigma$ is odd, $b(\mu, \nu-1, 0)$ if $a_\nu + \sigma$ is even; then while $a_\nu < \mu - 1$, set $a_\nu \leftarrow a_\nu + 1$ and call $f(\mu, \nu-1, 0)$ or $b(\mu, \nu-1, 0)$ again in the same way until $a_\nu = \mu - 1$; finally change $a_{\nu-1}$ (if $\mu+\sigma$ is odd) or a_μ (if $\mu+\sigma$ is even) from $\mu - 1$ to 0. And finally, in both cases, if $\mu = 2$ visit $a_1 \ldots a_n$, otherwise call $b(\mu - 1, \nu - 1, (\mu+\sigma) \bmod 2)$.

Most of the running time is actually spent handing the case $\mu = 2$; faster routines based on Gray binary code (and deviating from Ruskey's actual sequences) could be substituted for this case. A streamlined procedure could also be used when $\mu = \nu - 1$.

18. The sequence must begin (or end) with $01 \ldots (n-1)$. By exercise 32, no such Gray code can exist when $0 \neq \delta_n \neq (1)^{0+1+\cdots+(n-1)}$, namely when $n \bmod 12$ is 4, 6, 7, or 9.

The cases $n = 1, 2, 3$, are easily solved; and 1,927,683,326 solutions exist when $n = 5$. Thus there probably are zillions of solutions for all $n \geq 8$ except for the cases already excluded. Indeed, we can probably find such a Gray path through all ϖ_{nk} of the strings considered in answer 28(e) below, except when $n \equiv 2k + (2, 4, 5, 7)$ (modulo 12).

Note: The generalized Stirling number $\left\{ {n \atop m} \right\}_{-1}$ in exercise 30 exceeds 1 for $2 < m < n$, so there can be no such Gray code for the partitions of $\{1, \ldots, n\}$ into m blocks.

19. (a) Change (6) to the pattern $0, 2, \ldots, m, \ldots, 3, 1$ or its reverse, as in endo-order $(7.2.1.3-(45))$.

(b) We can generalize (8) and (9) to obtain sequences $A_{mn\alpha}$ and $A'_{mn\alpha}$ that begin with $0^{n-m}01 \ldots (m-1)$ and end with $01 \ldots (m-1)\alpha$ and $0^{n-m-1}01 \ldots (m-1)a$, respectively, where $0 \leq a \leq m-2$ and α is any string $a_1 \ldots a_{n-m}$ with $0 \leq a_j \leq m-2$. When $2 < m < n$ the new rules are

$$A_{m(n+1)(\alpha a)} = \begin{cases} A_{(m-1)n(b\beta)} x_1, A^R_{mn\beta} x_1, A_{mn\alpha} x_2, \ldots, A_{mn\alpha} x_m, & \text{if } m \text{ is even;} \\ A'_{(m-1)nb} x_1, A_{mn\alpha} x_1, A^R_{mn\alpha} x_2, \ldots, A_{mn\alpha} x_m, & \text{if } m \text{ is odd;} \end{cases}$$

$$A'_{m(n+1)a} = \begin{cases} A'_{(m-1)nb} x_1, A_{mn\beta} x_1, A^R_{mn\beta} x_2, \ldots, A^R_{mn\beta} x_m, & \text{if } m \text{ is even;} \\ A_{(m-1)n(b\beta)} x_1, A^R_{mn\beta} x_1, A_{mn\beta} x_2, \ldots, A^R_{mn\beta} x_m, & \text{if } m \text{ is odd;} \end{cases}$$

here $b = m - 3$, $\beta = b^{n-m}$, and $(x_1, \ldots, x_m)$ is a path from $x_1 = m - 1$ to $x_m = a$.

20. 012323212122; in general $(a_1 \ldots a_n)^T = \rho(a_n \ldots a_1)$, in the notation of exercise 4.

21. The numbers $\langle s_0, s_1, s_2, \ldots \rangle = \langle 1, 1, 2, 3, 7, 12, 31, 59, 164, 339, 999, \ldots \rangle$ satisfy the recurrences $s_{2n+1} = \sum_k \binom{n}{k} s_{2n-2k}$, $s_{2n+2} = \sum_k \binom{n}{k} (2^k + 1) s_{2n-2k}$, because of the way the middle elements relate to the others. Therefore $s_{2n} = n! [z^n] \exp((e^{2z}-1)/2 + e^z - 1)$ and $s_{2n+1} = n! [z^n] \exp((e^{2z} - 1)/2 + e^z + z - 1)$. By considering set partitions on the first half we also have $s_{2n} = \sum_k \left\{ {n \atop k} \right\} x_k$ and $s_{2n+1} = \sum_k \left\{ {n+1 \atop k} \right\} x_{k-1}$, where $x_n = 2x_{n-1} + (n-1)x_{n-2} = n! [z^n] \exp(2z + z^2/2)$. [T. S. Motzkin considered the sequence $\langle s_{2n} \rangle$ in *Proc. Symp. Pure Math.* **19** (1971), 173.]

22. (a) $\sum_{k=0}^{\infty} k^n \Pr(X=k) = e^{-1} \sum_{k=0}^{\infty} k^n/k! = \varpi_n$ by (16). (b) $\sum_{k=0}^{\infty} k^n \Pr(X=k) = \sum_{k=0}^{\infty} k^n \sum_{j=0}^{m} \binom{j}{k} (-1)^{j-k}/j!$, and we can extend the inner sum to $j = \infty$ because $\sum_k \binom{j}{k} (-1)^k k^n = 0$ when $j > n$. Thus we get $\sum_{k=0}^{\infty} (k^n/k!) \sum_{l=0}^{\infty} (-1)^l/l! = \varpi_n$. [See J. O. Irwin, *J. Royal Stat. Soc.* **A118** (1955), 389–404; J. Pitman, *AMM* **104** (1997), 201–209.]

23. (a) The formula holds whenever $f(x) = x^n$, by (14), so it holds in general. (Thus we also have $\sum_{k=0}^{\infty} f(k)/k! = e f(\varpi)$, by (16).)

(b) Suppose we have proved the relation for k, and let $h(x) = (x-1)^k f(x)$, $g(x) = f(x+1)$. Then $f(\varpi + k + 1) = g(\varpi + k) = \varpi^k g(\varpi) = h(\varpi + 1) = \varpi h(\varpi) = \varpi^{k+1} f(\varpi)$. [See J. Touchard, *Ann. Soc. Sci. Bruxelles* **53** (1933), 21–31. This symbolic "umbral calculus," invented by John Blissard in *Quart. J. Pure and Applied Math.* **4** (1861),

279–305, is quite useful; but it must be handled carefully because $f(\varpi) = g(\varpi)$ does not imply that $f(\varpi)h(\varpi) = g(\varpi)h(\varpi)$.]

(c) The hint is a special case of exercise 4.6.2–16(c). Setting $f(x) = x^n$ and $k = p$ in (b) then yields $\varpi_n \equiv \varpi_{p+n} - \varpi_{1+n}$.

(d) Modulo p, the polynomial $x^N - 1$ is divisible by $g(x) = x^p - x - 1$, because $x^{p^k} \equiv x + k$ and $x^N \equiv x^{\bar{p}} \equiv x^{\underline{p}} \equiv x^p - x \equiv 1$ (modulo $g(x)$ and p). Thus if $h(x) = (x^N - 1)x^n/g(x)$ we have $h(\varpi) \equiv h(\varpi + p) \equiv \varpi^p h(\varpi) \equiv (\varpi^p - \varpi)h(\varpi)$; and $0 \equiv g(\varpi)h(\varpi) = \varpi^{N+n} - \varpi^n$ (modulo p).

24. The hint follows by induction on e, because $x^{\underline{p^e}} = \prod_{k=0}^{p-1}(x - kp^{e-1})^{\underline{p^{e-1}}}$. We can also prove by induction on n that $x^n \equiv r_n(x)$ (modulo $g_1(x)$ and p) implies

$$x^{p^{e-1}n} \equiv r_n(x)^{p^{e-1}} \pmod{g_e(x),\ pg_{e-1}(x),\ \ldots,\ p^{e-1}g_1(x),\ \text{and } p^e}.$$

Hence $x^{p^{e-1}N} = 1 + h_0(x)g_e(x) + ph_1(x)g_{e-1}(x) + \cdots + p^{e-1}h_{e-1}(x)g_1(x) + p^e h_e(x)$ for certain polynomials $h_k(x)$ with integer coefficients. Modulo p^e we have $h_0(\varpi)\varpi^n \equiv h_0(\varpi + p^e)(\varpi + p^e)^n = \varpi^{\underline{p^e}}h_0(\varpi)\varpi^n \equiv (g_e(\varpi) + 1)h_0(\varpi)\varpi^n$; hence

$$\varpi^{p^{e-1}N+n} = \varpi^n + h_0(\varpi)g_e(\varpi)\varpi^n + ph_1(\varpi)g_{e-1}(\varpi)\varpi^n + \cdots \equiv \varpi^n.$$

[A similar derivation applies when $p = 2$, but we let $g_{j+1}(x) = g_j(x)^2 + 2[j = 2]$, and we obtain $\varpi_n \equiv \varpi_{n+3\cdot2^e}$ (modulo 2^e). These results are due to Marshall Hall; see *Bull. Amer. Math. Soc.* **40** (1934), 387; *Amer. J. Math.* **70** (1948), 387–388. For further information see W. F. Lunnon, P. A. B. Pleasants, and N. M. Stephens, *Acta Arith.* **35** (1979), 1–16.]

25. The first inequality follows by applying a much more general principle to the tree of restricted growth strings: In any tree for which $\deg(p) \geq \deg(\text{parent}(p))$ for all non-root nodes p, we have $w_k/w_{k-1} \leq w_{k+1}/w_k$ when w_k is the total number of nodes on level k. For if the $m = w_{k-1}$ nodes on level $k-1$ have respectively $a_1, \ldots, a_m$ children, they have at least $a_1^2 + \cdots + a_m^2$ grandchildren; hence $w_{k-1}w_{k+1} \geq m(a_1^2 + \cdots + a_m^2) \geq (a_1 + \cdots + a_m)^2 = w_k^2$.

For the second inequality, note that $\varpi_{n+1} - \varpi_n = \sum_{k=0}^{n}\left(\binom{n}{k} - \binom{n-1}{k-1}\right)\varpi_{n-k}$; thus

$$\frac{\varpi_{n+1}}{\varpi_n} - 1 = \sum_{k=0}^{n-1}\binom{n-1}{k}\frac{\varpi_{n-k}}{\varpi_n} \leq \sum_{k=0}^{n-1}\binom{n-1}{k}\frac{\varpi_{n-k-1}}{\varpi_{n-1}} = \frac{\varpi_n}{\varpi_{n-1}}$$

because, for example, $\varpi_{n-3}/\varpi_n = (\varpi_{n-3}/\varpi_{n-2})(\varpi_{n-2}/\varpi_{n-1})(\varpi_{n-1}/\varpi_n)$ is less than or equal to $(\varpi_{n-4}/\varpi_{n-3})(\varpi_{n-3}/\varpi_{n-2})(\varpi_{n-2}/\varpi_{n-1}) = \varpi_{n-4}/\varpi_{n-1}$.

26. There are $\binom{n-1}{n-t}$ rightward paths from $\widehat{n1}$ to $\widehat{tt}$; we can represent them by 0s and 1s, where 0 means "go right," 1 means "go up," and the positions of the 1s tell us which $n-t$ of the elements are in the block with 1. The next step, if $t > 1$, is to another vertex at the far left; so we continue with a path that defines a partition on the remaining $t-1$ elements. For example, the partition $14|2|3$ corresponds to the path 0010 under these conventions, where the respective bits mean that $1 \not\equiv 2$, $1 \not\equiv 3$, $1 \equiv 4$, $2 \not\equiv 3$. [Many other interpretations are possible. The convention suggested here shows that ϖ_{nk} enumerates partitions with $1 \not\equiv 2, \ldots, 1 \not\equiv k$, a combinatorial property discovered by H. W. Becker; see *AMM* **51** (1944), 47, and *Mathematics Magazine* **22** (1948), 23–26.]

27. (a) In general, $\lambda_0 = \lambda_1 = \lambda_{2n-1} = \lambda_{2n} = 0$. The following list shows also the restricted growth strings that correspond to each loop via the algorithm of part (b):

0,0,0,0,0,0,0,0,0 0123	0,0,1,0,0,0,0,0,0 0012	0,0,1,1,1,0,0,0,0 0102
0,0,0,0,0,0,1,0,0 0122	0,0,1,0,0,0,1,0,0 0011	0,0,1,1,1,0,1,0,0 0100
0,0,0,0,1,0,0,0,0 0112	0,0,1,0,1,0,0,0,0 0001	0,0,1,1,1,1,1,0,0 0120
0,0,0,0,1,0,1,0,0 0111	0,0,1,0,1,0,1,0,0 0000	0,0,1,1,11,1,1,0,0 0101
0,0,0,0,1,1,1,0,0 0121	0,0,1,0,1,1,1,0,0 0010	0,0,1,1,2,1,1,0,0 0110

(b) The name "tableau" suggests a connection to Section 5.1.4, and indeed the theory developed there leads to an interesting one-to-one correspondence. We can represent set partitions on a triangular chessboard by putting a rook in column l_j of row $n + 1 - j$ whenever $l_j \neq 0$ in the linked list representation of exercise 2 (see the answer to exercise 5.1.3–19). For example, the rook representation of $135|27|489|6$ is shown here. Equivalently, the nonzero links can be specified in a two-line array, such as $\binom{1\,2\,3\,4\,8}{3\,7\,5\,8\,9}$; see 5.1.4–(11).

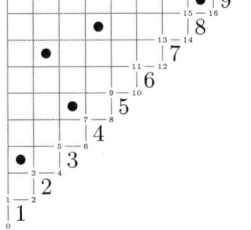

Consider the path of length $2n$ that begins at the lower left corner of this triangular diagram and follows the right boundary edges, ending at the upper right corner: The points of this path are $z_k = (\lfloor k/2 \rfloor, \lceil k/2 \rceil)$ for $0 \leq k \leq 2n$. Moreover, the rectangle above and to the left of z_k contains precisely the rooks that contribute coordinate pairs $\frac{i}{j}$ to the two-line array when $i \leq \lfloor k/2 \rfloor$ and $j > \lceil k/2 \rceil$; in our example, there are just two such rooks when $9 \leq k \leq 12$, namely $\binom{2\,4}{7\,8}$. Theorem 5.1.4A tells us that such two-line arrays are equivalent to tableaux (P_k, Q_k), where the elements of P_k come from the lower line and the elements of Q_k come from the upper line, and where both P_k and Q_k have the same shape. It is advantageous to use decreasing order in the P tableaux but increasing order in the Q tableaux, so that in our example they are respectively

k	P_k	Q_k	k	P_k	Q_k	k	P_k	Q_k
2	3	1	7	7 5	2 3	12	8 / 7	2 / 4
3	3	1	8	8 5 / 7	2 3 / 4	13	8	4
4	7 / 3	1 / 2	9	8 / 7	2 / 4	14	8	4
5	7	2	10	8 / 7	2 / 4	15	.	.
6	7 5	2 3	11	8 / 7	2 / 4	16	9	8

while P_k and Q_k are empty for $k = 0$, 1, 17, and 18.

In this way every set partition leads to a vacillating tableau loop $\lambda_0, \lambda_1, \ldots, \lambda_{2n}$, if we let λ_k be the integer partition that specifies the common shape of P_k and Q_k. (The loop is 0, 0, 1, 1, 11, 1, 2, 2, 21, 11, 11, 11, 11, 1, 1, 0, 1, 0, 0 in our example.) Moreover, $t_{2k-1} = 0$ if and only if row $n + 1 - k$ contains no rook, if and only if k is smallest in its block.

Conversely, the elements of P_k and Q_k can be uniquely reconstructed from the sequence of shapes λ_k. Namely, $Q_k = Q_{k-1}$ if $t_k = 0$. Otherwise, if k is even, Q_k is Q_{k-1} with the number $k/2$ placed in a new cell at the right of row t_k; if k is odd, Q_k is obtained from Q_{k-1} by using Algorithm 5.1.4D to delete the rightmost entry of row t_k. A similar procedure defines P_k from the values of P_{k+1} and t_{k+1}, so we can work back from P_{2n} to P_0. Thus the sequence of shapes λ_k is enough to tell us where to place the rooks.

Vacillating tableau loops were introduced in a paper by W. Y. C. Chen, E. Y. P. Deng, R. R. X. Du, R. P. Stanley, and C. H. Yan [*Transactions of the Amer. Math. Soc.* **359** (2007), 1555–1575], who showed that the construction has significant (and surprising) consequences. For example, if the set partition Π corresponds to the vacillating tableau loop $\lambda_0, \lambda_1, \ldots, \lambda_{2n}$, let's say that its *dual* Π^D is the set partition that corresponds to the sequence of transposed shapes $\lambda_0^T, \lambda_1^T, \ldots, \lambda_{2n}^T$. Then, by exercise 5.1.4–7, Π contains a "k-crossing at l," namely a sequence of indices with $i_1 < \cdots < i_k \le l < j_1 < \cdots < j_k$ and $i_1 \equiv j_1, \ldots, i_k \equiv j_k$ (modulo Π), if and only if Π^D contains a "k-nesting at l," which is a sequence of indices with $i_1' < \cdots < i_k' \le l < j_k' < \cdots < j_1'$ and $i_1' \equiv j_1', \ldots, i_k' \equiv j_k'$ (modulo Π^D). Notice also that an involution is essentially a set partition in which all blocks have size 1 or 2; the dual of an involution is an involution having the same singleton sets. In particular, the dual of a perfect matching (when there are no singleton sets) is a perfect matching.

Furthermore, an analogous construction applies to rook placements in *any* Ferrers diagram, not only in the stairstep shapes that correspond to set partitions. Given a Ferrers diagram that has at most m parts, all of size $\le n$, we simply consider the path $z_0 = (0,0), z_1, \ldots, z_{m+n} = (n,m)$ that hugs the right edge of the diagram, and stipulate that $\lambda_k = \lambda_{k-1} + e_{t_k}$ when $z_k = z_{k-1} + (1,0)$, $\lambda_k = \lambda_{k-1} - e_{t_k}$ when $z_k = z_{k-1} + (0,1)$. The proof we gave for stairstep shapes shows also that every placement of rooks in the Ferrers diagram, with at most one rook in each row and at most one in each column, corresponds to a unique tableau loop of this kind.

[And much more is true, besides! See A. Berele, *J. Combinatorial Theory* **A43** (1986), 320–328; S. Fomin, *J. Combinatorial Theory* **A72** (1995), 277–292; M. van Leeuwen, *Electronic J. Combinatorics* **3**, 2 (1996), paper #R15.]

28. (a) Define a one-to-one correspondence between rook placements, by interchanging the positions of rooks in rows j and $j+1$ if and only if there's a rook in the "panhandle" of the longer row:

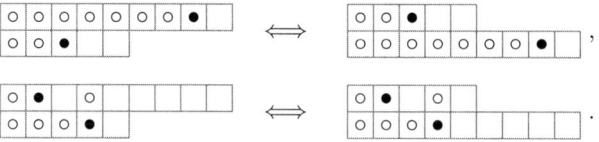

(b) This relation is obvious from the definition, by transposing all the rooks.

(c) Suppose $a_1 \ge a_2 \ge \cdots$ and $a_k > a_{k+1}$. Then we have

$$R(a_1, a_2, \ldots) = x R(a_1 - 1, \ldots, a_{k-1} - 1, a_{k+1}, \ldots) + y R(a_1, \ldots, a_{k-1}, a_k - 1, a_{k+1}, \ldots)$$

because the first term counts cases where a rook is in row k and column a_k. Also $R(0) = 1$ because of the empty placement. From these recurrences we find

$$R(1) = x + y; \quad R(2) = R(1,1) = x + xy + y^2; \quad R(3) = R(1,1,1) = x + xy + xy^2 + y^3;$$

$$R(2,1) = x^2 + 2xy + xy^2 + y^3;$$

$$R(3,1) = R(2,2) = R(2,1,1) = x^2 + x^2 y + xy + 2xy^2 + xy^3 + y^4;$$

$$R(3,1,1) = R(3,2) = R(2,2,1) = x^2 + 2x^2 y + x^2 y^2 + 2xy^2 + 2xy^3 + xy^4 + y^5;$$

$$R(3,2,1) = x^3 + 3x^2 y + 3x^2 y^2 + x^2 y^3 + 3xy^3 + 2xy^4 + xy^5 + y^6.$$

(d) For example, the formula $\varpi_{73}(x, y) = x\varpi_{63}(x, y) + y\varpi_{74}(x, y)$ is equivalent to $R(5, 4, 4, 3, 2, 1) = xR(4, 3, 3, 2, 1) + yR(5, 4, 3, 3, 2, 1)$, a special case of (c); and $\varpi_{nn}(x, y) = R(n - 2, \ldots, 0)$ is obviously equal to $\varpi_{(n-1)1}(x, y) = R(n - 2, \ldots, 1)$.

(e) In fact $y^{k-1}\varpi_{nk}(x, y)$ is the stated sum over all restricted growth strings $a_1 \ldots a_n$ for which $a_2 > 0, \ldots, a_k > 0$.

29. (a) If the rooks are respectively in columns $(c_1, \ldots, c_n)$, the number of free cells is the number of inversions of the permutation $(n+1-c_1) \ldots (n+1-c_n)$. [Rotate the right-hand example of Fig. 56 by $180°$ and compare the result to the illustration that follows Eq. 5.1.1–(5).]

(b) Each $r \times r$ configuration can be placed in, say, rows $i_1 < \cdots < i_r$ and columns $j_1 < \cdots < j_r$, yielding $(m - r)(n - r)$ free cells in the unchosen rows and columns; there are $(i_2-i_1+1) + 2(i_3-i_2-1) + \cdots + (r-1)(i_r-i_{r-1}-1) + r(m-i_r)$ in the unchosen rows and chosen columns, and a similar number in the chosen rows and unchosen columns. Furthermore

$$\sum_{1 \leq i_1 < \cdots < i_r \leq m} y^{(i_2-i_1+1)+2(i_3-i_2-1)+\cdots+(r-1)(i_r-i_{r-1}-1)+r(m-i_r)}$$

may be regarded as the sum of $y^{a_1+a_2+\cdots+a_{m-r}}$ over all partitions $r \geq a_1 \geq a_2 \geq \cdots \geq a_{m-r} \geq 0$, so it is $\binom{m}{r}_y$ by Theorem C. The polynomial $r!_y$ generates free cells for the chosen rows and columns, by (a). Therefore the answer is $y^{(m-r)(n-r)}\binom{m}{r}_y\binom{n}{r}_y r!_y = y^{(m-r)(n-r)}m!_y n!_y / ((m - r)!_y (n - r)!_y r!_y)$.

(c) The left-hand side is the generating function $R_m(t + a_1, \ldots, t + a_m)$ for the Ferrers diagram with t additional columns of height m. For there are $t + a_m$ ways to put a rook in row m, yielding $1 + y + \cdots + y^{t+a_m-1} = (1 - y^{t+a_m})/(1 - y)$ free cells with respect to those choices; then there are $t + a_{m-1} - 1$ available cells in row $m - 1$, etc.

The right-hand side, likewise, equals $R_m(t + a_1, \ldots, t + a_m)$. For if $m - k$ rooks are placed into columns $> t$, we must put k rooks into columns $\leq t$ of the k unused rows; and we have seen that $t!_y/(t - k)!_y$ is the generating function for free cells when k rooks are placed on a $k \times t$ board.

Notes: The formula proved here can be regarded as a polynomial identity in the variables y and y^t; therefore it is valid for arbitrary t, although our proof assumed that t is a nonnegative integer. This result was discovered in the case $y = 1$ by J. Goldman, J. Joichi, and D. White, *Proc. Amer. Math. Soc.* **52** (1975), 485–492. The general case was established by A. M. Garsia and J. B. Remmel, *J. Combinatorial Theory* **A41** (1986), 246–275, who used a similar argument to prove the additional formula

$$\sum_{t=0}^{\infty} z^t \prod_{j=1}^{m} \frac{1 - y^{a_j+m-j+t}}{1 - y} = \sum_{k=0}^{n} k!_y \left(\frac{z}{1 - yz}\right) \cdots \left(\frac{z}{1 - y^k z}\right) R_{m-k}(a_1, \ldots, a_m).$$

(d) This statement, which follows immediately from (c), also implies that we have $R(a_1, \ldots, a_m) = R(a'_1, \ldots, a'_m)$ if and only if equality holds for all x and for any nonzero value of y. The Peirce polynomial $\varpi_{nk}(x, y)$ of exercise 28(d) is the rook polynomial for $\binom{n-1}{k-1}$ different Ferrers diagrams; for example, $\varpi_{63}(x, y)$ enumerates rook placements for the shapes 43321, 44221, 44311, 4432, 53221, 53311, 5332, 54211, 5422, and 5431.

30. (a) We have $\varpi_n(x, y) = \sum_m x^{n-m} A_{mn}$, where $A_{mn} = R_{n-m}(n-1, \ldots, 1)$ satisfies a simple law: If we don't place a rook in row 1 of the shape $(n - 1, \ldots, 1)$, that row has $m - 1$ free cells because of the $n - m$ rooks in other rows. But if we do put a rook there, we leave 0 or 1 or $\cdots$ or $m-1$ of its cells free. Hence $A_{mn} = y^{m-1}A_{(m-1)(n-1)} + (1 + y + \cdots + y^{m-1})A_{m(n-1)}$, and it follows by induction that $A_{mn} = y^{m(m-1)/2}{n \brace m}_y$.

(b) The formula $\varpi_{n+1}(x, y) = \sum_k \binom{n}{k} x^{n-k} y^k \varpi_k(x, y)$ yields

$$A_{m(n+1)} = \sum_k \binom{n}{k} y^k A_{(m-1)k}.$$

(c) From (a) and (b) we have

$$\frac{z^n}{(1 - z)(1 - (1+q)z)\ldots(1 - (1+q+\cdots+q^{n-1})z)} = \sum_k {k \brace n}_q z^k;$$

$$\sum_k \binom{n}{k}_q (-1)^k q^{\binom{k}{2}} e^{(1+q+\cdots+q^{n-k-1})z} = q^{\binom{n}{2}} n!_q \sum_k {k \brace n}_q \frac{z^k}{k!}.$$

[The second formula is proved by induction on n, because both sides satisfy the differential equation $G'_{n+1}(z) = (1 + q + \cdots + q^n)e^z G_n(qz)$; exercise 1.2.6–58 proves equality when $z = 0$.]

Historical note: Leonard Carlitz introduced q-Stirling numbers in *Transactions of the Amer. Math. Soc.* **33** (1933), 127–129. Then in *Duke Math. J.* **15** (1948), 987–1000, he derived (among other things) an appropriate generalization of Eq. 1.2.6–(45):

$$(1 + q + \cdots + q^{m-1})^n = \sum_k {n \brace k}_q q^{\binom{k}{2}} \frac{m!_q}{(m - k)!_q}.$$

31. $\exp(e^{w+z} + w - 1)$; therefore $\varpi_{nk} = (\varpi + 1)^{n-k}\varpi^{k-1} = \varpi^{n+1-k}(\varpi - 1)^{k-1}$ in the umbral notation of exercise 23. [L. Moser and M. Wyman, *Trans. Royal Soc. Canada* (3) **43** (1954), Section 3, 31–37.] In fact, the numbers $\varpi_{nk}(x, 1)$ of exercise 28(d) are generated by $\exp((e^{xw+xz} - 1)/x + xw)$.

32. We have $\delta_n = \varpi_n(1, -1)$, and a simple pattern is easily perceived in the generalized Peirce triangle of exercise 28(d) when $x = 1$ and $y = -1$: We have $|\varpi_{nk}(1, -1)| \leq 1$ and $\varpi_{n(k+1)}(1, -1) \equiv \varpi_{nk}(1, -1) + (-1)^n$ (modulo 3) for $1 \leq k < n$. [In *JACM* **20** (1973), 512–513, Gideon Ehrlich gave a combinatorial proof of an equivalent result.]

33. Representing set partitions by rook placements as in answer 27 leads to the answer ϖ_{nk}, by setting $x = y = 1$ in exercise 28(d). [The case $k = n$ was discovered by H. Prodinger, *Fibonacci Quarterly* **19** (1981), 463–465.]

34. (a) Guittone's *Sonetti* included 149 of scheme 01010101232323, 64 of scheme 01010101234234, two of scheme 01010101234342, seven with schemes used only once (like 01100110234432), and 29 poems that we would no longer consider to be sonnets because they do not have 14 lines.

(b) Petrarch's *Canzoniere* included 115 sonnets of scheme 01100110234234, 109 of scheme 01100110232323, 66 of scheme 01100110234324, 7 of scheme 01100110232232, and 20 others of schemes like 01010101232323 used at most four times each.

(c) In Spenser's *Amoretti*, 88 of 89 sonnets used the scheme 01011212232344; the exception (number 8) was "Shakespearean."

(d) Shakespeare's 154 sonnets all used coalescences of the rather easy scheme 01012323454566, except that two of them (99 and 126) didn't have 14 lines.

(e) Browning's 44 *Sonnets From the Portuguese* obeyed the Petrarchan scheme 01100110232323.

Sometimes the lines would rhyme (by chance?) even when they didn't need to; for example, Browning's final sonnet actually had the scheme 01100110121212.

Incidentally, the lengthy cantos in Dante's *Divine Comedy* used an interlocking scheme of rhymes in which $1 \equiv 3$ and $3n - 1 \equiv 3n + 1 \equiv 3n + 3$ for $n = 1, 2, \ldots$.

35. Every incomplete n-line rhyme scheme Π corresponds to a singleton-free partition of $\{1, \ldots, n+1\}$ in which $(n+1)$ is grouped with all of Π's singletons. [H. W. Becker gave an algebraic proof in *AMM* **48** (1941), 702. Notice that $\varpi'_n = \sum_k \binom{n}{k}(-1)^{n-k}\varpi_k$, by the principle of inclusion and exclusion, and $\varpi_n = \sum_k \binom{n}{k}\varpi'_k$; we can in fact write $\varpi' = \varpi - 1$ in the umbral notation of exercise 23. J. O. Shallit has suggested extending Peirce's triangle by setting $\varpi_{n(n+1)} = \varpi'_n$; see exercises 38(e) and 33. In fact, ϖ_{nk} is the number of partitions of $\{1, \ldots, n\}$ with the property that $1, \ldots, k-1$ are not singletons; see H. W. Becker, *Bull. Amer. Math. Soc.* **58** (1952), 63.]

36. $\exp(e^z - 1 - z)$. (In general, if ϑ_n is the number of partitions of $\{1, \ldots, n\}$ into subsets of allowable sizes $s_1 < s_2 < \cdots$, the exponential generating function $\sum_n \vartheta_n z^n/n!$ is $\exp(z^{s_1}/s_1! + z^{s_2}/s_2! + \cdots)$, because $(z^{s_1}/s_1! + z^{s_2}/s_2! + \cdots)^k$ is the exponential generating function for partitions into exactly k parts.)

37. There are $\sum_k \binom{n}{k}\varpi'_k \varpi'_{n-k}$ possibilities of length n, hence 784,071,966 when $n = 14$. (But Pushkin's scheme is hard to beat.)

38. (a) Imagine starting with $x_1 x_2 \ldots x_n = 01 \ldots (n-1)$, then successively removing some element b_j and placing it at the left, for $j = 1, 2, \ldots, n$. Then x_k will be the kth most recently moved element, for $1 \le k \le |\{b_1, \ldots, b_n\}|$; see exercise 5.2.3–36. Consequently the array $x_1 \ldots x_n$ will return to its original state if and only if $b_n \ldots b_1$ is a restricted growth string. [Robbins and Bolker, *Æquat. Math.* **22** (1981), 281–282.]

In other words, let $a_1 \ldots a_n$ be a restricted growth string. Set $b_{-j} \leftarrow j$ and $b_{j+1} \leftarrow a_{n-j}$ for $0 \le j < n$. Then for $1 \le j \le n$, define k_j by the rule that b_j is the k_jth distinct element of the sequence $b_{j-1}, b_{j-2}, \ldots$. For example, the string $a_1 \ldots a_{16} = 0123032303456745$ corresponds in this way to the σ-cycle 6688448628232384.

(b) Such paths correspond to restricted growth strings with $\max(a_1, \ldots, a_n) \le m$, so the answer is $\left\{ {n \atop 0} \right\} + \left\{ {n \atop 1} \right\} + \cdots + \left\{ {n \atop m} \right\}$.

(c) We may assume that $i = 1$, because the sequence $k_2 \ldots k_n k_1$ is a σ-cycle whenever $k_1 k_2 \ldots k_n$ is. Thus the answer is the number of restricted growth strings with $a_n = j - 1$, namely $\left\{ {n-1 \atop j-1} \right\} + \left\{ {n-1 \atop j} \right\} + \left\{ {n-1 \atop j+1} \right\} + \cdots$.

(d) If the answer is f_n we must have $\sum_k \binom{n}{k} f_k = \varpi_n$, since σ_1 is the identity permutation. Therefore $f_n = \varpi'_n$, the number of set partitions without singletons (exercise 35).

(e) Again ϖ'_n, by (a) and (d). [Consequently $\varpi'_p \bmod p = 1$ when p is prime.]

39. Set $u = t^{p+1}$ to obtain $\frac{1}{p+1} \int_0^\infty e^{-u} u^{(q-p)/(p+1)}\, du = \frac{1}{p+1}\Gamma\left(\frac{q+1}{p+1}\right)$.

40. We have $g(z) = cz - n \ln z$, so the saddle point occurs at n/c. The rectangular path now has corners at $\pm n/c \pm mi/c$; and $\exp g(n/c + it) = (e^n c^n/n^n)\exp(-t^2 c^2/(2n) + it^3 c^3/(3n^2) + \cdots)$. The final result is $e^n (c/n)^{n-1}/\sqrt{2\pi n}$ times $1 + n/12 + O(n^{-2})$.

(Of course we could have obtained this result more quickly by letting $w = cz$ in the integral. But the answer given here applies the saddle point method mechanically, without attempting to be clever.)

41. Again the net result is just to multiply (21) by c^{n-1}; but in this case the *left* edge of the rectangular path is significant instead of the right edge. (Incidentally, when $c = -1$ we cannot derive an analog of (22) using Hankel's contour when x is real and positive, because the integral on that path diverges. But with the usual definition of z^x, a suitable path of integration does yield the formula $-(\cos \pi x)/\Gamma(x)$ when $n = x > 0$.)

42. We have $\oint e^{z^2} dz/z^n = 0$ when n is even. Otherwise both left and right edges of the rectangle with corners $\pm\sqrt{n/2} \pm in$ contribute approximately

$$\frac{e^{n/2}}{2\pi(n/2)^{n/2}} \int_{-\infty}^{\infty} \exp\left(-2t^2 - \frac{(-it)^3}{3}\frac{2^{3/2}}{n^{1/2}} + \frac{(it)^4}{n} - \cdots\right) dt,$$

when n is large. We can restrict $|t| \le n^\epsilon$ to show that this integral is $I_0 + (I_4 - \frac{4}{9}I_6)/n$ with relative error $O(n^{9\epsilon - 3/2})$, where $I_k = \int_{-\infty}^{\infty} e^{-2t^2} t^k \, dt$. As before, the relative error is actually $O(n^{-2})$; we deduce the answer

$$\frac{1}{((n-1)/2)!} = \frac{e^{n/2}}{\sqrt{2\pi}(n/2)^{n/2}}\left(1 + \frac{1}{12n} + O\left(\frac{1}{n^2}\right)\right), \qquad n \text{ odd}.$$

(The analog of (22) is $(\sin\frac{\pi x}{2})^2/\Gamma((x-1)/2)$ when $n = x > 0$.)

43. Let $f(z) = e^{e^z}/z^n$. When $z = -n + it$ we have $|f(z)| < en^{-n}$; when $z = t + 2\pi in + i\pi/2$ we have $|f(z)| = |z|^{-n} < (2\pi n)^{-n}$. So the integral is negligible except on a path $z = \xi + it$; and on that path $|f|$ decreases as $|t|$ increases from 0 to π. Already when $t = n^{\epsilon - 1/2}$ we have $|f(z)|/f(\xi) = O(\exp(-n^{2\epsilon}/(\log n)^2))$. And when $|t| > \pi$ we have $|f(z)|/f(\xi) < 1/|1 + i\pi/\xi|^n = \exp(-\frac{n}{2}\ln(1 + \pi^2/\xi^2))$.

44. Set $u = na_2 t^2$ in (25) to obtain $\Re \int_0^\infty e^{-u} \exp(n^{-1/2}c_3(-u)^{3/2} + n^{-1}c_4(-u)^2 + n^{-3/2}c_5(-u)^{5/2} + \cdots) \, du/\sqrt{na_2 u}$ where $c_k = (2/(\xi+1))^{k/2}(\xi^{k-1} + (-1)^k(k-1)!)/k! = a_k/a_2^{k/2}$. This expression leads to

$$b_l = \sum_{\substack{k_1 + 2k_2 + 3k_3 + \cdots = 2l \\ k_1 + k_2 + k_3 + \cdots = m \\ k_1, k_2, k_3, \ldots \ge 0}} \left(-\frac{1}{2}\right)^{l+m} \frac{c_3^{k_1}}{k_1!}\frac{c_4^{k_2}}{k_2!}\frac{c_5^{k_3}}{k_3!}\cdots,$$

a sum over partitions of $2l$. For example, $b_1 = \frac{3}{4}c_4 - \frac{15}{16}c_3^2$.

45. To get $\varpi_n/n!$ we replace $g(z)$ by $e^z - (n+1)\ln z$ in the derivation of (26). This change multiplies the integrand in the previous answer by $1/(1 + it/\xi)$, which is $1/(1 - n^{-1/2}a(-u)^{1/2})$ where $a = -\sqrt{2/(\xi+1)}$. Thus we get

$$b_l' = \sum_{\substack{k + k_1 + 2k_2 + 3k_3 + \cdots = 2l \\ k_1 + k_2 + k_3 + \cdots = m \\ k, k_1, k_2, k_3, \ldots \ge 0}} \left(-\frac{1}{2}\right)^{l+m} a^k \frac{c_3^{k_1}}{k_1!}\frac{c_4^{k_2}}{k_2!}\frac{c_5^{k_3}}{k_3!}\cdots,$$

a sum of $p(2l) + p(2l - 1) + \cdots + p(0)$ terms; $b_1' = \frac{3}{4}c_4 - \frac{15}{16}c_3^2 + \frac{3}{4}ac_3 - \frac{1}{2}a^2$. [The coefficient b_1' was obtained in a different way by L. Moser and M. Wyman, *Trans. Royal Soc. Canada* (3) **49**, Section 3 (1955), 49–54, who were the first to deduce an asymptotic series for ϖ_n. Their approximation is slightly less accurate than the result of (26) with n changed to $n + 1$, because it doesn't pass exactly through the saddle point. Formula (26) is due to I. J. Good, *Iranian J. Science and Tech.* **4** (1975), 77–83.]

46. Equations (13) and (31) show that $\varpi_{nk} = (1 - \xi/n)^k \varpi_n(1 + O(n^{-1}))$ for fixed k as $n \to \infty$. And this approximation also holds when $k = n$, but with relative error $O((\log n)^2/n)$.

47. Steps $(H1, H2, \ldots, H6)$ are performed respectively $(1, \varpi_n, \varpi_n - \varpi_{n-1}, \varpi_{n-1}, \varpi_{n-1}, \varpi_{n-1} - 1)$ times. The loop in H4 sets $j \leftarrow j - 1$ a total of $\varpi_{n-2} + \varpi_{n-3} + \cdots + \varpi_1$ times; the loop in H6 sets $b_j \leftarrow m$ a total of $(\varpi_{n-2} - 1) + \cdots + (\varpi_1 - 1)$ times. The ratio ϖ_{n-1}/ϖ_n is approximately $(\ln n)/n$, and $(\varpi_{n-2} + \cdots + \varpi_1)/\varpi_n \approx (\ln n)^2/n^2$.

48. We can easily verify the interchange of summation and integration in

$$\frac{e\varpi_x}{\Gamma(x+1)} = \frac{1}{2\pi i} \oint \frac{e^{e^z}}{z^{x+1}} \, dz = \frac{1}{2\pi i} \oint \sum_{k=0}^{\infty} \frac{e^{kx}}{k! \, z^{x+1}} \, dz$$

$$= \sum_{k=0}^{\infty} \frac{1}{k!} \frac{1}{2\pi i} \oint \frac{e^{kz}}{z^{x+1}} \, dz = \sum_{k=0}^{\infty} \frac{1}{k!} \frac{k^x}{\Gamma(x+1)}.$$

49. If $\xi = \ln n - \ln \ln n + x$, we have $\beta = 1 - e^{-x} - \alpha x$. Therefore by Lagrange's inversion formula (exercise 4.7–8),

$$x = \sum_{k=1}^{\infty} \frac{\beta^k}{k} [t^{k-1}] \left(\frac{f(t)}{1 - \alpha f(t)}\right)^k = \sum_{k=1}^{\infty} \sum_{j=0}^{\infty} \frac{\beta^k}{k} \alpha^j \binom{k+j-1}{j} [t^{k-1}] f(t)^{j+k},$$

where $f(t) = t/(1 - e^{-t})$. So the result follows from the handy identity

$$\left(\frac{z}{1-e^{-z}}\right)^m = \sum_{n=0}^{\infty} \left[\begin{matrix} m \\ m-n \end{matrix}\right] \frac{z^n}{(m-1)(m-2)\ldots(m-n)}.$$

(This identity should be interpreted carefully when $n \geq m$; the coefficient of z^n is a polynomial in m of degree n, as explained in *CMath* equation (7.59).)

The formula in this exercise is due to L. Comtet, *Comptes Rendus Acad. Sci.* (A) **270** (Paris, 1970), 1085–1088, who identified the coefficients previously computed by N. G. de Bruijn, *Asymptotic Methods in Analysis* (1958), 25–28. Convergence for $n \geq e$ was shown by Jeffrey, Corless, Hare, and Knuth, *Comptes Rendus Acad. Sci.* (I) **320** (1995), 1449–1452, who also derived a formula that converges somewhat faster.

(The equation $\xi e^\xi = n$ has complex roots as well. We can obtain them all by using $\ln n + 2\pi i m$ in place of $\ln n$ in the formula of this exercise; the sum converges rapidly when $m \neq 0$. See Corless, Gonnet, Hare, Jeffrey, and Knuth, *Advances in Computational Math.* **5** (1996), 347–350.)

50. Let $\xi = \xi(n)$. Then $\xi'(n) = \xi/((\xi+1)n)$, and the Taylor series

$$\xi(n+k) = \xi + k\xi'(n) + \frac{k^2}{2}\xi''(n) + \cdots$$

can be shown to converge for $|k| < n + 1/e$.

Indeed, much more is true, because the function $\xi(n) = -T(-n)$ is obtained from the tree function $T(z)$ by analytic continuation to the negative real axis. (The tree function has a quadratic singularity at $z = e^{-1}$; after going around this singularity we encounter a logarithmic singularity at $z = 0$, as part of an interesting multi-level Riemann surface on which the quadratic singularity appears only at level 0.) The derivatives of the tree function satisfy $z^k T^{(k)}(z) = R(z)^k p_k(R(z))$, where $R(z) = T(z)/(1 - T(z))$ and $p_k(x)$ is the polynomial of degree $k - 1$ defined by $p_{k+1}(x) = (1+x)^2 p_k'(x) + k(2+x)p_k(x)$. For example,

$$p_1(x) = 1, \quad p_2(x) = 2 + x, \quad p_3(x) = 9 + 10x + 3x^2, \quad p_4(x) = 64 + 113x + 70x^2 + 15x^3.$$

(The coefficients of $p_k(x)$, incidentally, enumerate certain phylogenetic trees called Greg trees: $[x^j]\,p_k(x)$ is the number of oriented trees with j unlabeled nodes and k labeled nodes, where leaves must be labeled and unlabeled nodes must have at least two children. See J. Felsenstein, *Systematic Zoology* **27** (1978), 27–33; L. R. Foulds and R. W. Robinson, *Lecture Notes in Math.* **829** (1980), 110–126; C. Flight, *Manuscripta* **34** (1990), 122–128.) If $q_k(x) = p_k(-x)$, we can prove by induction that $(-1)^m q_k^{(m)}(x) \ge 0$ for $0 \le x \le 1$. Therefore $q_k(x)$ decreases monotonically from k^{k-1} to $(k-1)!$ as x goes from 0 to 1, for all $k, m \ge 1$. It follows that

$$\xi(n+k) = \xi + \frac{kx}{n} - \left(\frac{kx}{n}\right)^2 \frac{q_2(x)}{2!} + \left(\frac{kx}{n}\right)^3 \frac{q_3(x)}{3!} - \cdots, \qquad x = \frac{\xi}{\xi+1},$$

where the partial sums alternately overshoot and undershoot the correct value if $k > 0$.

51. There are two saddle points, $\sigma = \sqrt{n+5/4} - 1/2$ and $\sigma' = -1 - \sigma$. Integration on a rectangular path with corners at $\sigma \pm im$ and $\sigma' \pm im$ shows that only σ is relevant as $n \to \infty$ (although σ' contributes a relative error of roughly $e^{-\sqrt{n}}$, which can be significant when n is small). Arguing almost as in (25), but with $g(z) = z + z^2/2 - (n+1)\ln z$, we find that t_n is well approximated by

$$\frac{n!}{2\pi} \int_{-n^\epsilon}^{n^\epsilon} e^{g(\sigma) - a_2 t^2 + a_3 it^3 + \cdots + a_l(-it)^l + O(n^{(l+1)\epsilon - (l-1)/2})}\,dt, \qquad a_k = \frac{\sigma+1}{k\sigma^{k-1}} + \frac{[k=2]}{2}.$$

The integral expands as in exercise 44 to

$$\frac{n!\,e^{(n+\sigma)/2}}{2\sigma^{n+1}\sqrt{\pi a_2}}\big(1 + b_1 + b_2 + \cdots + b_m + O(n^{-m-1})\big).$$

This time $c_k = (\sigma+1)\sigma^{1-k}(1 + 1/(2\sigma))^{-k/2}/k$ for $k \ge 3$, hence $(2\sigma+1)^{3k}\sigma^k b_k$ is a polynomial in σ of degree $2k$; for example,

$$b_1 = \frac{3}{4}c_4 - \frac{15}{16}c_3^2 = \frac{8\sigma^2 + 7\sigma - 1}{12\sigma(2\sigma+1)^3}.$$

In particular, Stirling's approximation and the b_1 term yield

$$t_n = \frac{1}{\sqrt{2}}n^{n/2}e^{-n/2+\sqrt{n}-1/4}\left(1 + \frac{7}{24}n^{-1/2} - \frac{119}{1152}n^{-1} - \frac{7933}{414720}n^{-3/2} + O(n^{-2})\right)$$

after we plug in the formula for σ — a result substantially more accurate than equation 5.1.4–(53), and obtained with considerably less labor.

52. Let $G(z) = \sum_k \Pr(X = k)z^k$, so that the jth cumulant κ_j is $j!\,[t^j]\ln G(e^t)$. In case (a) we have $G(z) = e^{e^{\xi z} - e^\xi}$; hence

$$\ln G(e^t) = e^{\xi e^t} - e^\xi = e^\xi(e^{\xi(e^t-1)} - 1) = e^\xi \sum_{k=1}^{\infty}(e^t-1)^k \frac{\xi^k}{k!}, \qquad \kappa_j = e^\xi \sum_k \left\{{k \atop j}\right\}\xi^k[j \ne 0].$$

Case (b) is sort of a dual situation: Here $\kappa = j = \varpi_j\,[j \ne 0]$ because

$$G(z) = e^{e^{-1}-1}\sum_{j,k}\left\{{k \atop j}\right\}e^{-j}\frac{z^k}{k!} = e^{e^{-1}-1}\sum_j \frac{(e^{z-1} - e^{-1})^j}{j!} = e^{e^{z-1}-1}.$$

[If $\xi e^\xi = 1$ in case (a) we have $\kappa_j = e\varpi\,[j \ne 0]$. But if $\xi e^\xi = n$ in that case, the mean is $\kappa_1 = n$ and the variance σ^2 is $(\xi+1)n$. Thus, the formula in exercise 45 states that the mean value n occurs with approximate probability $1/\sqrt{2\pi\sigma}$ and relative error $O(1/n)$. This observation leads to another way to prove that formula.]

53. We can write $\ln G(e^t) = \mu t + \sigma^2 t^2/2 + \kappa_3 t^3/3! + \cdots$ as in Eq. 1.2.10–(23), and there is a positive constant δ such that $\sum_{j=3}^{\infty} |\kappa_j||t|^j/j! < \sigma^2 t^2/6$ when $|t| \leq \delta$. Hence, if $0 < \epsilon < 1/2$, we can prove that

$$[z^{\mu n+r}] G(z)^n = \frac{1}{2\pi} \int_{-\pi}^{\pi} \frac{G(e^{it})^n \, dt}{e^{it(\mu n+r)}}$$

$$= \frac{1}{2\pi} \int_{-n^{\epsilon-1/2}}^{n^{\epsilon-1/2}} \exp\left(-irt - \frac{\sigma^2 t^2 n}{2} + O(n^{3\epsilon-1/2})\right) dt + O(e^{-cn^{2\epsilon}})$$

as $n \to \infty$, for some constant $c > 0$: The integrand for $n^{\epsilon-1/2} \leq |t| \leq \delta$ is bounded in absolute value by $\exp(-\sigma^2 n^{2\epsilon}/3)$; and when $\delta \leq |t| \leq \pi$ its magnitude is at most α^n, where $\alpha = \max |G(e^{it})|$ is less than 1 because the individual terms $p_k e^{kit}$ don't all lie on a straight line by our assumption. Thus

$$[z^{\mu n+r}] G(z)^n = \frac{1}{2\pi} \int_{-\infty}^{\infty} \exp\left(-irt - \frac{\sigma^2 t^2 n}{2} + O(n^{3\epsilon-1/2})\right) dt + O(e^{-cn^{2\epsilon}})$$

$$= \frac{1}{2\pi} \int_{-\infty}^{\infty} \exp\left(-\frac{\sigma^2 n}{2}\left(t + \frac{ir}{\sigma^2 n}\right)^2 - \frac{r^2}{2\sigma^2 n} + O(n^{3\epsilon-1/2})\right) dt + O(e^{-cn^{2\epsilon}})$$

$$= \frac{e^{-r^2/(2\sigma^2 n)}}{\sigma\sqrt{2\pi n}} + O(n^{3\epsilon-1}).$$

By taking account of $\kappa_3, \kappa_4, \ldots$ in a similar way we can refine the estimate to $O(n^{-m})$ for arbitrarily large m; thus the result is valid also for $\epsilon = 0$. [In fact, such refinements lead to the "Edgeworth expansion," according to which $[z^{\mu n+r}] G(z)^n$ is asymptotic to

$$\frac{e^{-r^2/(2\sigma^2 n)}}{\sigma\sqrt{2\pi n}} \sum_{\substack{k_1+2k_2+3k_3+\cdots=m \\ k_1+k_2+k_3+\cdots=l \\ k_1,k_2,k_3,\ldots \geq 0 \\ 0 \leq s \leq l+m/2}} \frac{(-1)^s (2l+m)^{\underline{2s}}}{\sigma^{4l+2m-2s} 2^s s!} \frac{r^{2l+m-2s}}{n^{l+m-s}} \frac{1}{k_1! k_2! \ldots} \left(\frac{\kappa_3}{3!}\right)^{k_1} \left(\frac{\kappa_4}{4!}\right)^{k_2} \cdots ;$$

the absolute error is $O(n^{-p/2})$, where the constant hidden in the O depends only on p and G but not on r or n, if we restrict the sum to cases with $m < p - 1$. For example, when $p = 3$ we get

$$[z^{\mu n+r}] G(z)^n = \frac{e^{-r^2/(2\sigma^2 n)}}{\sigma\sqrt{2\pi n}}\left(1 - \frac{\kappa_3}{2\sigma^4}\left(\frac{r}{n}\right) + \frac{\kappa_3}{6\sigma^6}\left(\frac{r^3}{n^2}\right)\right) + O\left(\frac{1}{n^{3/2}}\right),$$

and there are seven more terms when $p = 4$. See P. L. Chebyshev, *Zapiski Imp. Akad. Nauk* **55** (1887), No. 6, 1–16; *Acta Math.* **14** (1890), 305–315; F. Y. Edgeworth, *Trans. Cambridge Phil. Soc.* **20** (1905), 36–65, 113–141; H. Cramér, *Skandinavisk Aktuarietidsskrift* **11** (1928), 13–74, 141–180.]

54. Formula (40) is equivalent to $\alpha = s \coth s + s$, $\beta = s \coth s - s$.

55. Let $c = \alpha e^{-\alpha}$. The Newtonian iteration $\beta_0 = c$, $\beta_{k+1} = (1 - \beta_k) c e^{\beta_k}/(1 - c e^{-\beta_k})$ rises rapidly to the correct value, unless α is extremely close to 1. For example, β_7 differs from $\ln 2$ by less than 10^{-75} when $\alpha = \ln 4$.

56. (a) By induction on n, $g^{(n+1)}(z) = (-1)^n \left(\dfrac{\sum_{k=0}^{n} \langle {n \atop k} \rangle e^{(n-k)z}}{\alpha(e^z - 1)^{n+1}} - \dfrac{n!}{z^{n+1}}\right).$

(b) $\sum_{k=0}^{n} \binom{n}{k} e^{k\sigma}/n! = \int_0^1 \cdots \int_0^1 \exp(\lfloor u_1 + \cdots + u_n \rfloor \sigma)\, du_1 \ldots du_n$

$< \int_0^1 \cdots \int_0^1 \exp((u_1 + \cdots + u_n)\sigma)\, du_1 \ldots du_n = (e^{\sigma} - 1)^n/\sigma^n.$

The lower bound is similar, since $\lfloor u_1 + \cdots + u_n \rfloor > u_1 + \cdots + u_n - 1$.

(c) Thus $n!\,(1 - \beta/\alpha) < (-\sigma)^n g^{(n+1)}(\sigma) < 0$, and we need only verify that $1 - \beta/\alpha < 2(1 - \beta)$, namely that $2\alpha\beta < \alpha + \beta$. But $\alpha\beta < 1$ and $\alpha + \beta > 2$, by exercise 54.

57. (a) $n + 1 - m = (n+1)(1 - 1/\alpha) < (n+1)(1 - \beta/\alpha) = (n+1)\sigma/\alpha \le 2N$ as in answer 56(c). (b) The quantity $\alpha + \alpha\beta$ increases as α increases, because its derivative with respect to α is $1 + \beta + \beta(1 - \alpha)/(1 - \beta) = (1 - \alpha\beta)/(1 - \beta) + \beta > 0$. Therefore $1 - \beta < 2(1 - 1/\alpha)$.

58. (a) The derivative of $|e^{\sigma+it} - 1|^2/|\sigma + it|^2 = (e^{\sigma+it} - 1)(e^{\sigma-it} - 1)/(\sigma^2 + t^2)$ with respect to t is $(\sigma^2 + t^2)\sin t - t(2\sin\frac{t}{2})^2 - (2\sinh\frac{\sigma}{2})^2 t$ times a positive function. This derivative is always negative for $0 < t \le 2\pi$, because it is less than $t^2 \sin t - t(2\sin\frac{t}{2})^2 = 8u \sin u \cos u(u - \tan u)$ where $t = 2u$.

Let $s = 2\sinh\frac{\sigma}{2}$. When $\sigma \ge \pi$ and $2\pi \le t \le 4\pi$, the derivative is still negative, because we have $t \le 4\pi \le s^2 - \sigma^2/(2\pi) \le s^2 - \sigma^2/t$. Similarly, when $\sigma \ge 2\pi$ the derivative remains negative for $4\pi \le t \le 168\pi$; the proof gets easier and easier.

(b) Let $t = u\sigma/\sqrt{N}$. Then (41) and (42) prove that

$$\int_{-\tau}^{\tau} e^{(n+1)g(\sigma+it)}\, dt =$$

$$\frac{(e^{\sigma} - 1)^m}{\sigma^n \sqrt{N}} \int_{-N^{\epsilon}}^{N^{\epsilon}} \exp\left(-\frac{u^2}{2} + \frac{(-iu)^3 a_3}{N^{1/2}} + \cdots + \frac{(-iu)^l a_l}{N^{l/2-1}} + O(N^{(l+1)\epsilon - (l-1)/2})\right) du,$$

where $(1 - \beta)a_k$ is a polynomial of degree $k - 1$ in α and β, with $0 \le a_k \le 2/k$. (For example, $6a_3 = (2 - \beta(\alpha + \beta))/(1 - \beta)$ and $24a_4 = (6 - \beta(\alpha^2 + 4\alpha\beta + \beta^2))/(1 - \beta)$.) The monotonicity of the integrand shows that the integral over the rest of the range is negligible. Now trade tails, extend the integral over $-\infty < u < \infty$, and use the formula of answer 44 with $c_k = 2^{k/2} a_k$ to define $b_1, b_2, \ldots$.

(c) We will prove that $|e^z - 1|^m \sigma^{n+1}/((e^{\sigma} - 1)^m |z|^{n+1})$ is exponentially small on those three paths. If $\sigma \le 1$, this quantity is less than $1/(2\pi)^{n+1}$ (because, for example, $e^{\sigma} - 1 > \sigma$). If $\sigma > 1$, we have $\sigma < 2|z|$ and $|e^z - 1| \le e^{\sigma} - 1$.

59. In this extreme case, $\alpha = 1 + n^{-1}$ and $\beta = 1 - n^{-1} + \frac{2}{3}n^{-2} + O(n^{-3})$; hence $N = 1 + \frac{1}{3}n^{-1} + O(n^{-2})$. The leading term $\beta^{-n}/\sqrt{2\pi N}$ is $e/\sqrt{2\pi}$ times $1 - \frac{1}{3}n^{-1} + O(n^{-2})$. (Notice that $e/\sqrt{2\pi} \approx 1.0844$.) The quantity a_k in answer 58(b) turns out to be $1/k + O(n^{-1})$. So the correction terms, to first order, are

$$\frac{b_j}{N^j} = [z^j] \exp\left(-\sum_{k=1}^{\infty} \frac{B_{2k} z^{2k-1}}{2k(2k-1)}\right) + O\left(\frac{1}{n}\right),$$

namely the terms in the (divergent) series corresponding to Stirling's approximation

$$\frac{1}{1!} \sim \frac{e}{\sqrt{2\pi}}\left(1 - \frac{1}{12} + \frac{1}{288} + \frac{139}{51840} - \frac{571}{2488320} - \cdots\right).$$

60. (a) The number of m-ary strings of length n in which all m digits appear is $m!\,{n \brace m}$, and the inclusion-exclusion principle expresses this quantity as $\binom{m}{0}m^n - \binom{m}{1}(m-1)^n + \cdots$. Now see exercise 7.2.1.4–37.

(b) We have $(m-1)^n/(m-1)! = (m^n/m!)m\exp(n\ln(1-1/m))$, and $\ln(1-1/m)$ is less than $-n\epsilon^{-1}$.

(c) In this case $\alpha > n^\epsilon$ and $\beta = \alpha e^{-\alpha}e^\beta < \alpha e^{1-\alpha}$. Therefore $1 < (1-\beta/\alpha)^{m-n} < \exp(nO(e^{-\alpha}))$; and $1 > e^{-\beta m} = e^{-(n+1)\beta/\alpha} > \exp(-nO(e^{-\alpha}))$. So (45) becomes $(m^n/m!)(1+O(n^{-1})+O(ne^{-n^\epsilon}))$.

61. Now $\alpha = 1 + \frac{r}{n} + O(n^{2\epsilon-2})$ and $\beta = 1 - \frac{r}{n} + O(n^{2\epsilon-2})$. Thus $N = r + O(n^{2\epsilon-1})$, and the case $l = 0$ of Eq. (43) reduces to

$$n^r \left(\frac{n}{2}\right)^r \frac{e^r}{r^r \sqrt{2\pi r}} \left(1 + O(n^{2\epsilon-1}) + O\left(\frac{1}{r}\right)\right).$$

(This approximation meshes well with identities such as $\left\{{n \atop n-1}\right\} = \binom{n}{2}$ and $\left\{{n \atop n-2}\right\} = 2\binom{n}{4} + \binom{n+1}{4}$; indeed, we have

$$\left\{{n \atop n-r}\right\} = \frac{n^{2r}}{2^r r!}\left(1 + O\left(\frac{1}{n}\right)\right) \qquad \text{as } n \to \infty$$

when r is constant, according to formulas (6.42) and (6.43) of *CMath*.)

62. The assertion is true for $1 \le n \le 10000$ (with $m = \lfloor e^\xi - 1\rfloor$ in 5648 of those cases). E. R. Canfield and C. Pomerance, in a paper that nicely surveys previous work on related problems, have shown that the statement holds for all sufficiently large n, and that the maximum occurs in *both* cases only if $e^\xi \bmod 1$ is extremely close to $\frac{1}{2}$. [*Integers* **2** (2002), A1, 1–13.]

63. (a) The result holds when $p_1 = \cdots = p_n = p$, because $a_{k-1}/a_k = (k/(n+1-k)) \times ((n-\mu)/\mu) \le (n-\mu)/(n+1-\mu) < 1$. It is also true by induction when $p_n = 0$ or 1. For the general case, consider the minimum of $a_k - a_{k-1}$ over all choices of $(p_1, \ldots, p_n)$ with $p_1 + \cdots + p_n = \mu$: If $0 < p_1 < p_2 < 1$, let $p_1' = p_1 - \delta$ and $p_2' = p_2 + \delta$, and notice that $a_k' - a_{k-1}' = a_k - a_{k-1} + \delta(p_1 - p_2 - \delta)\alpha$ for some α depending only on $p_3, \ldots, p_n$. At a minimum point we must have $\alpha = 0$; thus we can choose δ so that either $p_1' = 0$ or $p_2' = 1$. The minimum can therefore be achieved when all p_j have one of three values $\{0, 1, p\}$. But we have proved that $a_k - a_{k-1} > 0$ in such cases.

(b) Changing each p_j to $1 - p_j$ changes μ to $n - \mu$ and a_k to a_{n-k}.

(c) No roots of $f(x)$ are positive. Hence $f(z)/f(1)$ has the form in (a) and (b).

(d) Let $C(f)$ be the number of sign changes in the sequence of coefficients of f; we want to show that $C((1-x)^2 f) = 2$. In fact, $C((1-x)^m f) = m$ for all $m \ge 0$. For $C((1-x)^m) = m$, and $C((a+bx)f) \le C(f)$ when a and b are positive; hence $C((1-x)^m f) \le m$. And if $f(x)$ is any nonzero polynomial whatsoever, $C((1-x)f) > C(f)$; hence $C((1-x)^m f) \ge m$.

(e) Since $\sum_k \left[{n \atop k}\right] x^k = x(x+1)\ldots(x+n-1)$, part (c) applies directly with $\mu = H_n$. And for the polynomials $f_n(x) = \sum_k \left\{{n \atop k}\right\} x^k$, we can use part (c) with $\mu = \varpi_{n+1}/\varpi_n - 1$, if $f_n(x)$ has n real roots. The latter statement follows by induction because $f_{n+1}(x) = x(f_n(x) + f_n'(x))$: If $a > 0$ and if $f(x)$ has n real roots, so does the function $g(x) = e^{ax}f(x)$. And $g(x) \to 0$ as $x \to -\infty$; hence $g'(x) = e^{ax}(af(x) + f'(x))$ also has n real roots (namely, one at the far left, and $n - 1$ between the roots of $g(x)$).

[See E. Laguerre, *J. de Math.* (3) **9** (1883), 99–146; W. Hoeffding, *Annals Math. Stat.* **27** (1956), 713–721; J. N. Darroch, *Annals Math. Stat.* **35** (1964), 1317–1321; J. Pitman, *J. Combinatorial Theory* **A77** (1997), 297–303.]

64. We need only use computer algebra to subtract $\ln \varpi_n$ from $\ln \varpi_{n-k}$.

65. It is ϖ_n^{-1} times the number of occurrences of k-blocks plus the number of occurrences of ordered pairs of k-blocks in the list of all set partitions, namely $\left(\binom{n}{k}\varpi_{n-k} + \binom{n}{k}\binom{n-k}{k}\varpi_{n-2k}\right)/\varpi_n$, minus the square of (49). Asymptotically, $(\xi^k/k!)(1+O(n^{4\epsilon-1}))$.

66. (The maximum of (48) when $n = 100$ is achieved for the partitions $7^1 6^2 5^4 4^6 3^7 2^6 1^4$ and $7^1 6^2 5^4 4^6 3^8 2^5 1^3$.)

67. The expected value of M^k is ϖ_{n+k}/ϖ_n. By (50), the mean is therefore $\varpi_{n+1}/\varpi_n = n/\xi + \xi/(2(\xi+1)^2) + O(n^{-1})$, and the variance is

$$\frac{\varpi_{n+2}}{\varpi_n} - \frac{\varpi_{n+1}^2}{\varpi_n^2} = \left(\frac{n}{\xi}\right)^2\left(1 + \frac{\xi(2\xi+1)}{(\xi+1)^2 n} - 1 - \frac{\xi^2}{(\xi+1)^2 n} + O\left(\frac{1}{n^2}\right)\right) = \frac{n}{\xi(\xi+1)} + O(1).$$

68. The maximum number of nonzero components in all parts of a partition is $n = n_1 + \cdots + n_m$; it occurs if and only if all component parts are 0 or 1. Then the values of $l+1 = n$ and $b = mn_1 + (m-1)n_2 + \cdots + n_m$ reach their maximum. [Thus it's best to choose names of the multiset elements so that $n_1 \le n_2 \le \cdots \le n_m$.]

69. At the beginning of step M3, if $k > b$ and $l = r - 1$, go to M5. In step M5, if $j = a$ and $(v_j - 1)(r - l) < u_j$, go to M6 instead of decreasing v_j.

70. (a) $\left|{n-1 \atop r-1}\right| + \left|{n-2 \atop r-1}\right| + \cdots + \left|{r-1 \atop r-1}\right|$, since $\left|{n-k \atop r-1}\right|$ contain the block $\{0, \ldots, 0, 1\}$ with k 0s. The total, also known as $p(n-1, 1)$, is $p(n-1) + \cdots + p(1) + p(0)$.

(b) Exactly $N = \left\{{n-1 \atop r}\right\} + \left\{{n-2 \atop r-2}\right\}$ of the r-block partitions of $\{1, \ldots, n-1, n\}$ are the same if we interchange $n-1 \leftrightarrow n$. So the answer is $N + \frac{1}{2}\left(\left\{{n \atop r}\right\} - N\right) = \frac{1}{2}\left(\left\{{n \atop r}\right\} + N\right)$, which is also the number of restricted growth strings $a_1 \ldots a_n$ with $\max(a_1, \ldots, a_n) = r - 1$ and $a_{n-1} \le a_n$. And the total is $\frac{1}{2}(\varpi_n + \varpi_{n-1} + \varpi_{n-2})$.

71. $\lfloor\frac{1}{2}(n_1+1)\ldots(n_m+1) - \frac{1}{2}\rfloor$, because there are $(n_1+1)\ldots(n_m+1) - 2$ *compositions* into two parts, and half of those compositions fail to be in lexicographic order unless all n_j are even. (See exercise 7.2.1.4–31. Formulas for up to 5 parts have been worked out by E. M. Wright, *Proc. London Math. Soc.* (3) **11** (1961), 499–510.)

72. Yes. The following algorithm computes $a_{jk} = p(j,k)$ for $0 \le j, k \le n$ in $\Theta(n^4)$ steps: Start with $a_{jk} \leftarrow 1$ for all j and k. Then for $l = 0, 1, \ldots, n$ and $m = 0, 1, \ldots, n$ (in any order), if $l + m > 1$ set $a_{jk} \leftarrow a_{jk} + a_{(j-l)(k-m)}$ for $j = l, \ldots, n$ and $k = m, \ldots, n$ (in increasing order).

(See Table A–1. A similar method computes $p(n_1, \ldots, n_m)$ in $O(n_1 \ldots n_m)^2$ steps. Cheema and Motzkin, in the cited paper, have derived the recurrence relation

$$n_1 p(n_1, \ldots, n_m) = \sum_{l=1}^{\infty} \sum_{k_1, \ldots, k_m \ge 0} k_1 p(n_1 - k_1 l, \ldots, n_m - k_m l),$$

but this interesting formula is helpful for computation only in certain cases.)

Table A–1

MULTIPARTITION NUMBERS

n	0	1	2	3	4	5	6	n	0	1	2	3	4	5
$p(0,n)$	1	1	2	3	5	7	11	$P(0,n)$	1	2	9	66	712	10457
$p(1,n)$	1	2	4	7	12	19	30	$P(1,n)$	1	4	26	249	3274	56135
$p(2,n)$	2	4	9	16	29	47	77	$P(2,n)$	2	11	92	1075	16601	325269
$p(3,n)$	3	7	16	31	57	97	162	$P(3,n)$	5	36	371	5133	91226	2014321
$p(4,n)$	5	12	29	57	109	189	323	$P(4,n)$	15	135	1663	26683	537813	13241402
$p(5,n)$	7	19	47	97	189	339	589	$P(5,n)$	52	566	8155	149410	3376696	91914202

73. Yes. Let $P(m, n) = p(1, \ldots, 1, 2, \ldots, 2)$ when there are m 1s and n 2s; then $P(m, 0) = \varpi_m$, and we can use the recurrence

$$2P(m, n + 1) = P(m + 2, n) + P(m + 1, n) + \sum_k \binom{n}{k} P(m, k).$$

This recurrence can be proved by considering what happens when we replace a pair of x's in the multiset for $P(m, n + 1)$ by two distinct elements x and x'. We get $2P(m, n + 1)$ partitions, representing $P(m + 2, n)$, except in the $P(m + 1, n)$ cases where x and x' belong to the same block, or in $\binom{n}{k} P(m, n - k)$ cases where the blocks containing x and x' are identical and have k additional elements.

Notes: See Table A–1. Another recurrence, less useful for computation, is

$$P(m + 1, n) = \sum_{j,k} \binom{n}{k} \binom{n - k + m}{j} P(j, k).$$

The sequence $P(0, n)$ was first investigated by E. K. Lloyd, *Proc. Cambridge Philos. Soc.* **103** (1988), 277–284, and by G. Labelle, *Discrete Math.* **217** (2000), 237–248, who computed it by completely different methods. Exercise 70(b) showed that $P(m, 1) = (\varpi_m + \varpi_{m+1} + \varpi_{m+2})/2$; in general $P(m, n)$ can be written in the umbral notation $\varpi^m q_n(\varpi)$, where $q_n(x)$ is a polynomial of degree $2n$ defined by the generating function $\sum_{n=0}^{\infty} q_n(x) z^n/n! = \exp((e^z + (x + x^2)z - 1)/2)$. Thus, by exercise 31,

$$\sum_{n=0}^{\infty} P(m, n) \frac{z^n}{n!} = e^{(e^z - 1)/2} \sum_{k=0}^{\infty} \frac{\varpi_{(2k+m+1)(k+m+1)}}{2^k} \frac{z^k}{k!}.$$

Labelle proved, as a special case of much more general results, that the number of partitions of $\{1, 1, \ldots, n, n\}$ into exactly r blocks is

$$n! \, [x^r z^n] \, e^{-x + x^2(e^z - 1)/2} \sum_{k=0}^{\infty} e^{zk(k+1)/2} \frac{x^k}{k!}.$$

75. The saddle point method yields $C e^{An^{2/3} + Bn^{1/3}}/n^{55/36}$, where $A = 3\zeta(3)^{1/3}$, $B = \pi^2 \zeta(3)^{-1/3}/2$, and $C = \zeta(3)^{19/36}(2\pi)^{-5/6} 3^{-1/2} \exp(1/3 + B^2/4 + \zeta'(2)/(2\pi^2) - \gamma/12)$. [F. C. Auluck, *Proc. Cambridge Philos. Soc.* **49** (1953), 72–83; E. M. Wright, *American J. Math.* **80** (1958), 643–658.]

76. Using the fact that $p(n_1, n_2, n_3, \ldots) \geq p(n_1 + n_2, n_3, \ldots)$, hence $P(m + 2, n) \geq P(m, n + 1)$, one can prove by induction that $P(m, n + 1) \geq (m + n + 1)P(m, n)$. Thus

$$2P(m, n) \leq P(m + 2, n - 1) + P(m + 1, n - 1) + eP(m, n - 1).$$

Iterating this inequality shows that $2^n P(0, n) = (\varpi^2 + \varpi)^n + O(n(\varpi^2 + \varpi)^{n-1}) = (n\varpi_{2n-1} + \varpi_{2n})(1 + O((\log n)^3/n))$. (A more precise asymptotic formula can be obtained from the generating function in the answer to exercise 73.)

78. 3 3 3 3 2 1 0 0 0
  1 0 0 0 2 2 3 2 0   (because the encoded partitions
  2 2 1 0 0 2 1 0 2   must all be (000000000))
  2 1 0 2 2 0 0 1 3

79. There are 432 such cycles. But they yield only 304 different cycles of set partitions, since different cycles might describe the same sequence of partitions. For example, (000012022332321) and (000012022112123) are partitionwise equivalent.

80. [See F. Chung, P. Diaconis, and R. Graham, *Discrete Mathematics* **110** (1992), 52–55.] Construct a digraph with ϖ_{n-1} vertices and ϖ_n arcs; each restricted growth string $a_1 \ldots a_n$ defines an arc from vertex $a_1 \ldots a_{n-1}$ to vertex $\rho(a_2 \ldots a_n)$, where ρ is the function of exercise 4. (For example, arc 01001213 runs from 0100121 to 0110203.) Every universal cycle defines an Eulerian trail in this digraph; conversely, every Eulerian trail can be used to define one or more universal sequences of restricted growth on the elements $\{0, 1, \ldots, n-1\}$.

An Eulerian trail exists by the method of Section 2.3.4.2, if we let the last exit from every nonzero vertex $a_1 \ldots a_{n-1}$ be through arc $a_1 \ldots a_{n-1}a_{n-1}$. The sequence might not be cyclic, however. For example, no universal cycle exists when $n < 4$; and when $n = 4$ the universal sequence 000012030110100222 defines a cycle of set partitions that does not correspond to any universal cycle.

The existence of a cycle can be proved for $n \geq 6$ if we start with an Eulerian trail that begins $0^n xyx^{n-3} u(uv)^{\lfloor (n-2)/2 \rfloor} u^{[n\text{ odd}]}$ for some distinct elements $\{u, v, x, y\}$. This pattern is possible if we alter the last exit of $0^k 121^{n-3-k}$ from $0^{k-1}121^{n-2-k}$ to $0^{k-1}121^{n-3-k}2$ for $2 \leq k \leq n-4$, and let the last exits of 0121^{n-4} and $01^{n-3}2$ be respectively $010^{n-4}1$ and $0^{n-3}10$. Now if we choose numbers of the cycle *backwards*, thereby determining u and v, we can let x and y be the smallest elements distinct from $\{0, u, v\}$.

We can conclude in fact that the number of universal cycles having this extremely special type is huge — at least

$$\left(\prod_{k=2}^{n-1} (k!\,(n-k))^{\left\{ {n-1 \atop k} \right\}} \right) \Big/ \left((n-1)!\,(n-2)^3 3^{2n-5} 2^2 \right), \qquad \text{when } n \geq 6.$$

Yet none of them are known to be readily decodable. See below for the case $n = 5$.

81. Noting that $\varpi_5 = 52$, we use a universal cycle for $\{1, 2, 3, 4, 5\}$ in which the elements are 13 clubs, 13 diamonds, 13 hearts, 12 spades, and a joker. One such cycle, found by trial and error using Eulerian trails as in the previous answer, is

$$(\spadesuit\spadesuit\spadesuit\spadesuit\spadesuit\spadesuit\diamondsuit\heartsuit\text{J}\clubsuit\heartsuit\diamondsuit\heartsuit\spadesuit\clubsuit\heartsuit\diamondsuit\heartsuit\spadesuit\heartsuit\diamondsuit\diamondsuit\heartsuit\clubsuit\heartsuit\diamondsuit\clubsuit\heartsuit\clubsuit\spadesuit\clubsuit\clubsuit\diamondsuit\heartsuit\clubsuit\diamondsuit\diamondsuit\heartsuit\clubsuit\spadesuit\spadesuit\heartsuit\diamondsuit\diamondsuit\heartsuit\heartsuit\spadesuit\diamondsuit\heartsuit\heartsuit\spadesuit\spadesuit\diamondsuit\diamondsuit).$$

(In fact, there are essentially 114,056 such cycles if we branch to $a_k = a_{k-1}$ as a last resort and if we introduce the joker as soon as possible.) The trick still works with probability $\frac{47}{52}$ if we call the joker a spade.

82. There are 13644 solutions, although this number reduces to 1981 if we regard

$$\blacksquare \equiv \blacksquare \equiv \blacksquare, \quad \blacksquare \equiv \blacksquare, \quad \blacksquare \equiv \blacksquare.$$

The smallest common sum is 5/2, and the largest is 25/2; the remarkable solution

$$\blacksquare + \blacksquare + \blacksquare + \blacksquare + \blacksquare = \blacksquare + \blacksquare + \blacksquare + \blacksquare + \blacksquare = \blacksquare + \blacksquare + \blacksquare + \blacksquare + \blacksquare$$

is one of only two essentially distinct ways to get the common sum 118/15. [This exercise was problem 78 in B. A. Kordemsky's *Matematicheskaĭa Smekalka* (1954), translated into English as *The Moscow Puzzles* (1972).]

SECTION 7.2.1.6

1. It could "see" a left parenthesis at the left of every internal node and a right parenthesis at the bottom of every internal node. Alternatively, it could associate right parentheses with the *external* nodes that it encounters — except for the very last $\square$; see exercise 20.

2. Z1. [Initialize.] Set $z_k \leftarrow 2k - 1$ for $0 \leq k \leq n$. (Assume that $n \geq 2$.)

　　Z2. [Visit.] Visit the tree-combination $z_1 z_2 \ldots z_n$.

　　Z3. [Easy case?] If $z_{n-1} < z_n - 1$, set $z_n \leftarrow z_n - 1$ and return to Z2.

　　Z4. [Find j.] Set $j \leftarrow n - 1$ and $z_n \leftarrow 2n - 1$. While $z_{j-1} = z_j - 1$, set $z_j \leftarrow 2j - 1$ and $j \leftarrow j - 1$.

　　Z5. [Decrease z_j.] Terminate the algorithm if $j = 1$. Otherwise set $z_j \leftarrow z_j - 1$ and go back to Z2. ∎

3. Label the nodes of the forest in preorder. The first $z_k - 1$ elements of $a_1 \ldots a_{2n}$ contain $k - 1$ left parentheses and $z_k - k$ right parentheses. So there is an excess of $2k - 1 - z_k$ left parentheses over right parentheses when the "worm" first reaches node k; and $2k - 1 - z_k$ is the level (or depth) of that node.

　　Let $q_1 \ldots q_n$ be the inverse of $p_1 \ldots p_n$, so that node k is the q_kth node in postorder. Since k occurs to the left of j in $p_1 \ldots p_n$ if and only if $q_k < q_j$, we see that c_k is the number of nodes j that precede k in preorder but follow it in postorder, namely the number of proper ancestors of k; again, this is the level of k.

　　Alternative proof: We can also show that both sequences $z_1 \ldots z_n$ and $c_1 \ldots c_n$ have essentially the same recursive structure as (5): $Z_{pq} = (Z_{p(q-1)} + 1^p), 1(Z_{(p-1)q} + 1^{p-1})$ when $0 \leq p \leq q$; and $C_{pq} = C_{p(q-1)}, (q-p)C_{(p-1)q}$. (Consider the mate of the last, next-to-last, etc., left parenthesis.)

　　Incidentally, the formula '$c_{k+1} + d_k = c_k + 1$' is equivalent to (11).

4. Almost true; but $d_1 \ldots d_n$ and $z_1 \ldots z_n$ occur in *decreasing* order, while $p_1 \ldots p_n$ and $c_1 \ldots c_n$ are increasing. (This lexicographic property for a sequence of permutations $p_1 \ldots p_n$ is not automatically inherited from lexicographic order of the corresponding inversion tables $c_1 \ldots c_n$; but the result does hold for this particular class of $p_1 \ldots p_n$.)

5. $d_1 \ldots d_{15} = 0\,2\,0\,0\,2\,0\,0\,1\,0\,3\,2\,0\,1\,0\,4$; $z_1 \ldots z_{15} = 1\,2\,5\,6\,7\,10\,11\,12\,14\,15\,19\,22\,23\,25\,26$; $p_1 \ldots p_{15} = 2\,1\,5\,4\,8\,10\,9\,7\,11\,6\,13\,15\,14\,12\,3$; $c_1 \ldots c_{15} = 0\,1\,0\,1\,2\,1\,2\,3\,3\,4\,2\,1\,2\,2\,3$.

6. Match up the parentheses as usual; then simply curl the string up and around until a_{2n} becomes adjacent to a_1, and notice that the distinction between left and right parentheses can be reconstructed from the context. Letting a_1 correspond to the bottom of the circle, as in Table 1, yields the diagram shown. [A. Errera, *Mémoires de la Classe Sci. 8°, Acad. Royale de Belgique* (2) **11**, 6 (1931), 26 pp.]

7. (a) It equals $)\,)\,(\,)\,\ldots\,(\,)$; setting $a_1 \leftarrow$ '(' will restore the initial string. (b) The initial binary tree (from step B1) will have been restored, except that $l_n = n + 1$.

8. $l_1 \ldots l_{15} = 2\,0\,4\,5\,0\,7\,8\,0\,10\,0\,0\,13\,0\,15\,0$; $r_1 \ldots r_{15} = 3\,0\,0\,6\,0\,12\,11\,9\,0\,0\,0\,0\,14\,0\,0$; $e_1 \ldots e_{15} = 1\,0\,3\,1\,0\,2\,2\,0\,1\,0\,0\,2\,0\,1\,0$; $s_1 \ldots s_{15} = 1\,0\,12\,1\,0\,5\,3\,0\,1\,0\,0\,3\,0\,1\,0$.

9. Node j is a (proper) ancestor of node k if and only if $j < k$ and $s_j + j \geq k$. (As a consequence, we have $c_1 + \cdots + c_n = s_1 + \cdots + s_n$.)

10. If j is the index z_k of the kth left parenthesis, we have $w_j = c_k + 1$ and $w_{j'} = c_k$, where j' is the index of the matching right parenthesis.

11. Swap left and right parentheses in $a_{2n} \ldots a_1$ to get the mirror image of $a_1 \ldots a_{2n}$.

12. The mirror reflection of (4) corresponds to the forest

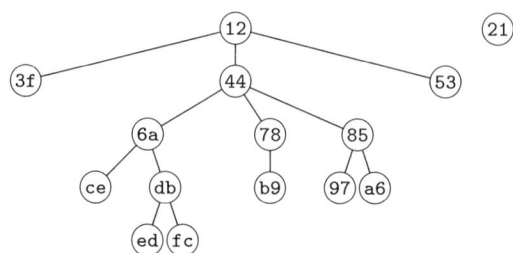

;

but the significance of transposition is clearer, forest-wise, if we draw right-sibling and left-child links horizontally and vertically, then do a matrix-like transposition:

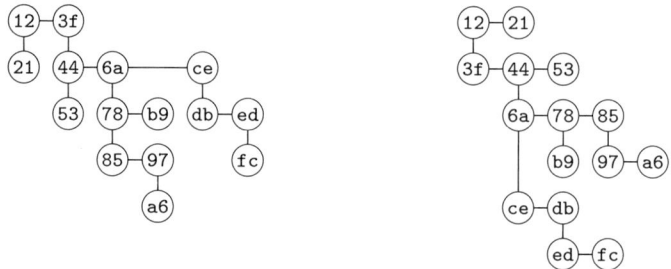

13. (a) By induction on the number of nodes, we have $\mathrm{preorder}(F^R) = \mathrm{postorder}(F)^R$ and $\mathrm{postorder}(F^R) = \mathrm{preorder}(F)^R$.

(b) Let F correspond to the binary tree B; then $\mathrm{preorder}(F) = \mathrm{preorder}(B)$ and $\mathrm{postorder}(F) = \mathrm{inorder}(B)$, as noted after 2.3.2–(6). Therefore $\mathrm{preorder}(F^T) = \mathrm{preorder}(B^R) = \mathrm{postorder}(B)^R$ has no simple relationship to either $\mathrm{preorder}(F)$ or $\mathrm{postorder}(F)$. But $\mathrm{postorder}(F^T) = \mathrm{inorder}(B^R) = \mathrm{inorder}(B)^R = \mathrm{postorder}(F)^R$.

14. According to answer 13, $\mathrm{postorder}(F^{RT}) = \mathrm{preorder}(F) = \mathrm{preorder}(B)$ when F corresponds naturally to B; and $\mathrm{postorder}(F^{TR}) = \mathrm{preorder}(F^T)^R = \mathrm{postorder}(B)$. Therefore the equation $F^{RT} = F^{TR}$ holds if and only if F has at most one node.

15. If F^R corresponds naturally to the binary tree B', the root of B' is the root of F's rightmost tree. The left link of node x in B' is to the leftmost child of x in F^R, which is the rightmost child of x in F; similarly, the right link is to x's left sibling in F.

Note: Since B corresponds naturally to F^{RT}, answer 13 tells us that $\mathrm{inorder}(B) = \mathrm{postorder}(F^{RT}) = \mathrm{postorder}(F^R)^R = \mathrm{preorder}(F)$.

16. The forest $F \mid G$ is obtained by placing the trees of F below the first node of G in postorder. Associativity follows because $F \mid (G \mid H) = (H^T G^T F^T)^T = (F \mid G) \mid H$. Notice, incidentally, that $\mathrm{postorder}(F \mid G) = \mathrm{postorder}(F)\,\mathrm{postorder}(G)$, and that $F \mid (GH) = (F \mid G)H$ when G is nonnull.

17. Any nonnull forest can be written $F = (G \mid \cdot)H$, where $\cdot$ denotes the 1-node forest; then $F^R = H^R(G^R \mid \cdot)$ and $F^T = (H^T \mid \cdot)G^T$. In particular we cannot have $F^R = F^T$ unless H is the null forest Λ, since the first tree of H^R can't be $H^T \mid \cdot$; and G must then also be Λ. Furthermore $F = F^T$ if and only if $G = H^T$. In that case we cannot also have $F^R = F^{RT}$ unless $G = \Lambda$; the first tree of G^{TR} would otherwise have more nodes than G itself.

It appears to be true that we cannot have $F^{RT} = F^{TR}$ unless $F = F^R$. Under that assumption, $F^{RT} = F^{TR}$ if and only if F and F^T are both self-conjugate. David Callan has discovered two infinite families of such forests, with parameters $i, j, k \geq 0$:

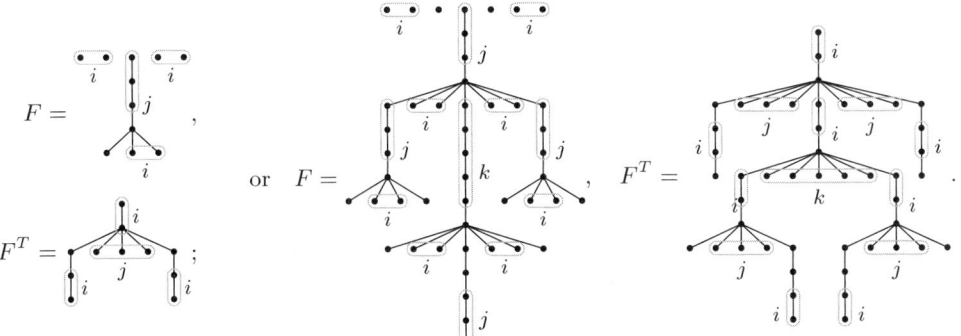

(In these examples, $i = 2$, $j = 3$, and $k = 5$.) Are there any other cases?

18. The $C_{15} = 9{,}694{,}845$ forests are partitioned into 20,982 classes. The largest is a cycle of length 58,968, one of whose elements is $((()(()))())()(((()(())())())()$. The shortest are six two-element classes (corresponding to exercise 17), consisting of

$()()()()()()()()()()()()()()$,　　　$()()()()(((()()()()()))()()()()$,

$()()()((((((()()()()())))))()()()$,　　　$()()(((((((((()()()())))))))))()()$,

$()(((()())((()(())()))(()()))()$,　　　$()((((((((((()()))))))))))()$,

and their transposes. The somewhat strange strings $((((((((()))))))()()()()()()()$, $()()()()()()(((((((())))))))$, and $((((((()()()()()()()()(())))))))$ each have wedge-shaped binary trees and form a unique class of size 3. The path that runs from $()(((()())))()()((()()())())()$ to $(((()())((()()))(()))(()())(()()))$ has 3120 elements, one of which is (2). According to the conjecture in answer 19, the shortest possible cycle has length 6; when $n = 15$ there are 66 such cycles. (The next-shortest cycle, which is unique, has length 10 and includes $()(()()())()(((()())))((())))$.)

19. The transformation from F_j to F_{j+1} by Algorithm P can be paraphrased as follows: "Find the last node in preorder, say x, that has a left sibling, say y. Remove x from its family and make it the new rightmost child of y. And if $x < n$, change all of x's descendants $x + 1$, ..., n into trivial one-node trees."

The transformation that takes F_j^R into F_{j+1}^R can therefore be stated as follows, if we recall that the kth node of F_j in preorder is the kth-from-last node of F_j^R in postorder: "Find the first node in postorder, say x, that has a right sibling, say y. Remove x from its family and make it the new leftmost child of y. And if $x > 1$, change all of x's descendants $x - 1$, ..., 1 into trivial one-node trees."

Similarly, we can paraphrase the transformation from G_j to G_{j+1} that is specified by Algorithm B: "Find j, the root of the leftmost nontrivial tree; then find k, its rightmost child. Remove k and its descendants from j's family, and insert them between j and j's right sibling. Finally, if $j > 1$, make j and its right siblings all children of $j - 1$, and $j - 1$ a child of $j - 2$, etc."

When this transformation changes the left-sibling/right-child representation from G_j^{RT} to G_{j+1}^{RT} (see exercise 15), it turns out to be identical to the transformation that takes F_j^R to F_{j+1}^R in the left-child/right-sibling representation. Therefore $G_j^{RT} = F_j^R$, because this identity clearly holds when $j = 1$.

(It follows that the sequence of tables $e_1 \ldots e_{n-1}$ for the binary trees generated by Algorithm B is exactly the sequence of tables $d_{n-1} \ldots d_1$ for the parenthesis strings generated by Algorithm P; this phenomenon is illustrated in Tables 1 and 2.)

Several symmetries between lists of forests have been explored by M. C. Er in *Comp. J.* **32** (1989), 76–85.

20. (a) This assertion, which generalizes Lemma 2.3.1P, is readily proved by induction.
(b) The following procedure is, in fact, almost identical to Algorithm P:

T1. [Initialize.] Set $b_{3k-2} \leftarrow 3$ and $b_{3k-1} \leftarrow b_{3k} \leftarrow 0$ for $1 \leq k \leq n$; also set $b_0 \leftarrow b_N \leftarrow 0$ and $m \leftarrow N - 3$, where $N = 3n + 1$.

T2. [Visit.] Visit $b_1 \ldots b_N$. (Now $b_m = 3$ and $b_{m+1} \ldots b_N = 0 \ldots 0$.)

T3. [Easy case?] Set $b_m \leftarrow 0$. If $b_{m-1} = 0$, set $b_{m-1} \leftarrow 3$, $m \leftarrow m - 1$, and go to T2.

T4. [Find j.] Set $j \leftarrow m - 1$ and $k \leftarrow N - 3$. While $b_j = 3$, set $b_j \leftarrow 0$, $b_k \leftarrow 3$, $j \leftarrow j - 1$, and $k \leftarrow k - 3$.

T5. [Increase b_j.] Terminate the algorithm if $j = 0$. Otherwise set $b_j \leftarrow 3$, $m \leftarrow N - 3$, and return to T2. ∎

[See S. Zaks, *Theoretical Comp. Sci.* **10** (1980), 63–82. In that article, Zaks pointed out that it is even easier to generate the sequence $z_1 \ldots z_n$ of indices j such that $b_j = 3$, using an algorithm virtually identical to the answer to exercise 2, because a valid ternary tree combination $z_1 \ldots z_n$ is characterized by the inequalities $z_{k-1} < z_k \leq 3k - 2$.]

21. For this problem we can essentially combine Algorithm P with Algorithm 7.2.1.2L. We shall assume for convenience that $n_t > 0$ and $n_1 + \cdots + n_t > 1$.

G1. [Initialize.] Set $l \leftarrow N$. Then for $j = t, \ldots, 2, 1$ (in this order), do the following operations n_j times: Set $b_{l-j} \leftarrow j$, $b_{l-j+1} \leftarrow \cdots \leftarrow b_{l-1} \leftarrow 0$, and $l \leftarrow l - j$. Finally set $b_0 \leftarrow b_N \leftarrow c_0 \leftarrow 0$ and $m \leftarrow N - t$.

G2. [Visit.] Visit $b_1 \ldots b_N$. (At this point $b_m > 0$ and $b_{m+1} = \cdots = b_N = 0$.)

G3. [Easy case?] If $b_{m-1} = 0$, set $b_{m-1} \leftarrow b_m$, $b_m \leftarrow 0$, $m \leftarrow m - 1$, and return to G2.

G4. [Find j.] Set $c_1 \leftarrow b_m$, $b_m \leftarrow 0$, $j \leftarrow m - 1$, and $k \leftarrow 1$. While $b_j \geq c_k$, set $k \leftarrow k + 1$, $c_k \leftarrow b_j$, $b_j \leftarrow 0$, and $j \leftarrow j - 1$.

G5. [Increase b_j.] If $b_j > 0$, find the smallest $l \geq 1$ such that $b_j < c_l$, and interchange $b_j \leftrightarrow c_l$. Otherwise, if $j > 0$, set $b_j \leftarrow c_1$ and $c_1 \leftarrow 0$. Otherwise terminate.

G6. [Reverse and spread out.] Set $j \leftarrow k$ and $l \leftarrow N$. While $c_j > 0$, set $b_{l-c_j} \leftarrow c_j$, $l \leftarrow l - c_j$, and $j \leftarrow j - 1$. Then set $m \leftarrow N - c_k$ and go back to G2. ∎

This algorithm assumes that $N > n_1 + 2n_2 + \cdots + tn_t$. [See *SICOMP* **8** (1979), 73–81.]

22. Note first that d_1 can be increased if and only if $r_1 = 0$ in the linked representation. Otherwise the successor of $d_1 \ldots d_{n-1}$ is obtained by finding the smallest j with $d_j > 0$ and setting $d_j \leftarrow 0$, $d_{j+1} \leftarrow d_{j+1} + 1$. We may assume that $n > 2$.

K1. [Initialize.] Set $l_k \leftarrow k + 1$ and $r_k \leftarrow 0$ for $1 \leq k < n$; also set $l_n \leftarrow r_n \leftarrow 0$.

K2. [Visit.] Visit the binary tree represented by $l_1 l_2 \ldots l_n$ and $r_1 r_2 \ldots r_n$.

K3. [Easy cases?] Set $y \leftarrow r_1$. If $y = 0$, set $r_1 \leftarrow 2$, $l_1 \leftarrow 0$, and return to K2. Otherwise if $l_1 = 0$, set $l_1 \leftarrow 2$, $r_1 \leftarrow r_2$, $r_2 \leftarrow l_2$, $l_2 \leftarrow 0$, and return to K2. Otherwise set $j \leftarrow 2$ and $k \leftarrow 1$.

K4. [Find j and k.] If $r_j > 0$, set $k \leftarrow j$ and $y \leftarrow r_j$. Then if $j \neq y - 1$, set $j \leftarrow j + 1$ and repeat this step.

K5. [Shuffle subtrees.] Set $l_j \leftarrow y$, $r_j \leftarrow r_y$, $r_y \leftarrow l_y$, and $l_y \leftarrow 0$. If $j = k$, go to K2.

K6. [Shift subtrees.] Terminate if $y = n$. Otherwise, while $k > 1$, set $k \leftarrow k - 1$, $j \leftarrow j - 1$, and $r_j \leftarrow r_k$. Then while $j > 1$, set $j \leftarrow j - 1$ and $r_j \leftarrow 0$. Return to K2. ∎

(See the analysis in exercise 45. Korsh [*Comp. J.* **48** (2005), 488–497; **49** (2006), 351–357; **54** (2011), 776–785] has shown that this algorithm, Algorithm P, and Algorithm B can all be extended to t-ary trees in interesting ways.)

23. (a) Since z_n begins at $2n - 1$ and goes back and forth C_{n-1} times, it ends at $2n - 1 - (C_{n-1} \bmod 2)$, when $n > 1$. Furthermore the final value of z_j is constant for all $n \geq j$. Thus the final string $z_1 z_2 \ldots$ is $1\ 2\ 5\ 6\ 9\ 11\ 13\ 14\ 17\ 19\ \ldots$, containing all odd numbers $< 2n$ except 3, 7, 15, 31, ...

(b) Similarly, the preorder permutation that characterizes the final tree is $2^k\ 2^{k-1}$ $\ldots\ 1\ 3\ 5\ 6\ 7\ 9\ 10\ \ldots$, where $k = \lfloor \lg n \rfloor$. Forestwise, node 2^j is the parent of 2^{j-1} nodes $\{2^{j-1}, 2^{j-1} + 1, \ldots, 2^j - 1\}$, for $1 < j \leq k$, and the trees $\{2^k + 1, \ldots, n\}$ are trivial.

Note: If Algorithm N is restarted at step N2 after it has terminated, it will generate the same sequence, but backwards. Algorithm L has the same property.

24. $l_0 l_1 \ldots l_{15} = 2\ 0\ 1\ 0\ 3\ 0\ 0\ 6\ 5\ 0\ 8\ 0\ 0\ 12\ 11\ 4$; $r_1 \ldots r_{15} = 0\ 15\ 0\ 10\ 7\ 0\ 0\ 9\ 0\ 14\ 13\ 0\ 0\ 0\ 0$; $k_1 \ldots k_{15} = 0\ 0\ 2\ 2\ 4\ 5\ 5\ 4\ 8\ 4\ 10\ 11\ 11\ 10\ 2$; $q_1 \ldots q_{15} = 2\ 1\ 15\ 4\ 3\ 10\ 8\ 5\ 7\ 6\ 9\ 14\ 11\ 13\ 12$; and $u_1 \ldots u_{15} = 1\ 2\ 3\ 1\ 0\ 0\ 5\ 0\ 3\ 1\ 0\ 0\ 1\ 0\ 1\ 0$. (If nodes of the forest F are numbered in postorder, k_j is the left sibling of j; or, if j is the leftmost child of p, $k_j = k_p$. Stated another way, k_j is the parent of j in the forest F^{TR}. And k_j is also $j - 1 - u_{n+1-j}$, the number of elements to the left of j in $q_1 \ldots q_n$ that are less than j.)

25. Taking a cue from Algorithms N and L, we want to extend each $(n - 1)$-node tree to a list of two or more n-node trees. The idea in this case is to make n a child of $n - 1$ in the binary tree at the beginning and the end of every such list. The following algorithm uses additional link fields p_j and s_j, where p_j points to the parent of j in the forest, and s_j points to j's left sibling or to j's rightmost sibling if j is the leftmost in its family. (These pointers p_j and s_j are, of course, not the same as the permutations $p_1 \ldots p_n$ in Table 1 or the scope coordinates $s_1 \ldots s_n$ in Table 2. In fact $s_1 \ldots s_n$ is the permutation λ of exercise 33 below.)

M1. [Initialize.] Set $l_j \leftarrow j+1$, $r_j \leftarrow 0$, $s_j \leftarrow j$, $p_j \leftarrow j-1$, and $o_j \leftarrow -1$ for $1 \leq j \leq n$, except that $l_n \leftarrow 0$.

M2. [Visit.] Visit $l_1 \ldots l_n$ and $r_1 \ldots r_n$. Then set $j \leftarrow n$.

M3. [Find j.] If $o_j > 0$, set $k \leftarrow p_j$ and go to M5 if $k \neq j - 1$. If $o_j < 0$, set $k \leftarrow s_j$ and go to M4 if $k \neq j - 1$. If $k = j - 1$ in either case, set $o_j \leftarrow -o_j$, $j \leftarrow j - 1$, and repeat this step.

M4. [Transfer down.] (At this point k is j's left sibling, or the rightmost member of j's family.) If $k \geq j$, terminate if $j = 1$, otherwise set $x \leftarrow p_j$, $l_x \leftarrow 0$, $z \leftarrow k$, and $k \leftarrow 0$ (thereby detaching node j from its parent and heading for the top level). But if $k < j$, set $x \leftarrow p_j + 1$, $z \leftarrow s_x$, $r_k \leftarrow 0$, and $s_x \leftarrow k$ (thereby detaching node j from k and going down a level). Then set $x \leftarrow k + 1$, $y \leftarrow s_x$, $s_x \leftarrow z$, $s_j \leftarrow y$, $r_y \leftarrow j$, and $x \leftarrow j$. While $x \neq 0$, set $p_x \leftarrow k$ and $x \leftarrow r_x$. Return to M2.

M5. [Transfer up.] (At this point k is j's parent.) Set $x \leftarrow k + 1$, $y \leftarrow s_j$, $z \leftarrow s_x$, $s_x \leftarrow y$, and $r_y \leftarrow 0$. If $k \neq 0$, set $y \leftarrow p_k$, $r_k \leftarrow j$, $s_j \leftarrow k$, $s_{y+1} \leftarrow z$, and $x \leftarrow j$; otherwise set $y \leftarrow j - 1$, $l_y \leftarrow j$, $s_j \leftarrow z$, and $x \leftarrow j$. While $x \neq 0$, set $p_x \leftarrow y$ and $x \leftarrow r_x$. Return to M2. ∎

Running time notes: We can argue as in exercise 44 that step M3 costs $2C_n + 3(C_{n-1} + \cdots + C_1)$ mems, and that steps M4 and M5 together cost $8C_n - 2(C_{n-1} + \cdots + C_1)$, plus twice the number of times $x \leftarrow r_x$. The latter quantity is difficult to analyze precisely; for example, when $n = 15$ and $j = 6$, the algorithm sets $x \leftarrow r_x$ exactly $(1, 2, 3, 4, 5, 6)$ times in respectively $(45, 23, 7, 9, 2, 4)$ cases. But heuristically the average number of times $x \leftarrow r_x$ should be approximately $2 - 2^{j-n}$ when j is given, therefore about $(2C_n - (C_n - C_{n-1}) - (C_{n-1} - C_{n-2})/2 - (C_{n-2} - C_{n-3})/4 - \cdots)/C_n \approx 8/7$ overall. Empirical tests confirm this predicted behavior, showing that the total cost per tree approaches $265/21 \approx 12.6$ mems as $n \to \infty$.

26. (a) The condition is clearly necessary. And if it holds, we can uniquely construct F: Node 1 and its siblings are the roots of the forest, and their descendants are defined inductively by noncrossing partitions. (In fact, we can compute the depth coordinates $c_1 \ldots c_n$ directly from Π's restricted growth string $a_1 \ldots a_n$: Set $c_1 \leftarrow 0$ and $i_0 \leftarrow 0$. For $2 \leq j \leq n$, if $a_j > \max(a_1, \ldots, a_{j-1})$, set $c_j \leftarrow c_{j-1} + 1$ and $i_{a_j} \leftarrow c_j$, otherwise set $c_j \leftarrow i_{a_j}$.)

(b) If Π and Π' satisfy the noncrossing condition, so does their greatest common refinement $\Pi \vee \Pi'$, so we can proceed as in exercise 7.2.1.5–12(a).

(c) Let x_1, ..., x_m be the children of some node in F, and let $1 \leq j < k \leq m$. Form F' by removing x_{j+1}, ..., x_k from their family and reattaching them as children of $x_{j+1} - 1$, the rightmost descendant of x_j.

(d) Obvious, by (c). Thus the forests are ranked from bottom to top by the number of nonleaf nodes they contain (which is one less than the number of blocks in Π).

(e) Exactly $\sum_{k=0}^{n} e_k(e_k - 1)/2$, where $e_0 = n - e_1 - \cdots - e_n$ is the number of roots.

(f) Dualization is similar to the transposition operation in exercise 12, but we use left-sibling and right-child links instead of left-child and right-sibling, and we transpose about the *minor* diagonal:

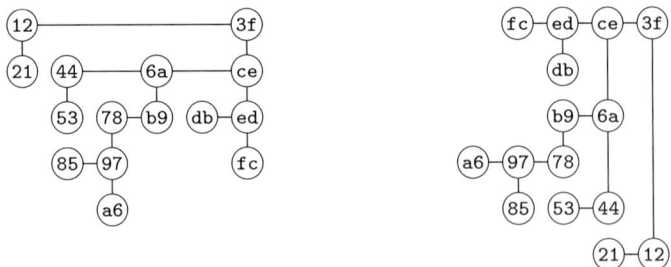

("Right" links now point downward. Notice that j is the rightmost child of k in F if and only if j is the left sibling of k in F^D. Preorder of F^D reverses the preorder of F, just as postorder of F^T reverses postorder of F.)

(g) From (f) we can see that F' covers F if and only if F^D covers F'^D. (Therefore F^D has $n + 1 - k$ leaves if F has k.)

(h) $F \barwedge F' = (F^D \vee F'^D)^D$.

(i) No. If it did, equality would necessarily hold, by duality. But, for example, $0101 \barwedge 0121 = 0000$ and $0101 \vee 0121 = 0123$, while leaves(0101) + leaves(0121) $\neq$ leaves(0000) + leaves(0123).

[Noncrossing partitions were first considered by H. W. Becker in *Math. Mag.* **22** (1948), 23–26. G. Kreweras proved in 1971 that they form a lattice; see the references in answer 2.3.4.6–3.]

27. (a) This assertion is equivalent to exercise 2.3.3–19.

(b) If we represent a forest by right-child and left-sibling links, preorder corresponds to inorder of the binary tree (see exercise 2.3.2–5), and s_j is the size of node j's right subtree. Rotation to the left at any nonleaf of this binary tree decreases exactly one of the scope coordinates, and the amount of decrease is as small as possible consistent with a valid table $s_1 \ldots s_n$. Therefore F' covers F if and only if F is obtained from F' by such a rotation. (Rotation in the left-child/right-sibling representation is similar, but with respect to postorder.)

(c) Dualization preserves the covering relation but exchanges left with right.

(d) $F \top F' = (F^D \perp F'^D)^D$. Equivalently, as noted in exercise 6.2.3–32, we can independently minimize the left-subtree sizes.

(e) The covering transformation in answer 26(c) obviously makes $s_j \le s'_j$ for all j.

(f) True, because $F \wedge F' \mathbin{\scriptstyle\kappa} F \dashv F \perp F'$ and $F \wedge F' \mathbin{\scriptstyle\kappa} F' \dashv F \perp F'$.

(g) False; for example, $0121 \vee 0122 = 0123$ and $0121 \top 0122 = 0122$. (But we do have $F \top F' \dashv F \vee F'$, by taking duals in (f).)

(h) The longest path, of length $\binom{n}{2}$, repeatedly decreases the rightmost nonzero s_j by 1. The shortest, of length $n-1$, repeatedly sets the leftmost nonzero s_j to 0.

Answer 6.2.3–32 gives many references to the literature of Tamari lattices.

28. (a) Just compute $\min(c_1, c'_1) \ldots \min(c_n, c'_n)$ and $\max(c_1, c'_1) \ldots \max(c_n, c'_n)$, because $c_1 \ldots c_n$ is a valid sequence if and only if $c_1 = 0$ and $c_j \le c_{j-1} + 1$ for $1 < j \le n$.

(b) Obvious because of (a). *Note:* The elements of any distributive lattice can be represented as the order ideals of some partial ordering. In the case of Fig. 62, that partial ordering is shown at the right, and a similar triangular grid with sides of length $n-2$ yields Stanley's lattice of order n.

(c) Take a node k of F that has a left sibling, j. Remove k from its family and place it as a new right child of j, followed by its former children as new children of j; the former children of k retain their own descendants. (This operation corresponds to changing)(to () in a nested parenthesis string. Thus a "perfect" Gray code for parentheses corresponds to a Hamiltonian path in the cover graph of Stanley's lattice. Exactly 38 such paths exist when $n = 4$, namely $(8, 6, 6, 8, 4, 6)$ from 0123 to $(0001, 0010, 0012, 0100, 0111, 0120)$ respectively.)

(d) True, because the cover relation in (c) is left-right symmetric. (We have $F \subseteq F'$ if and only if $w_j \le w'_j$ for $0 \le j \le 2n$, where the worm depths w_j are defined in exercise 10. If $w_0 \ldots w_{2n}$ is the worm walk of F, its reverse $w_{2n} \ldots w_0$ is the worm walk of F^R. Notice that the cover relation changes just one coordinate w_j. One can compute $F \cap F'$ and $F \cup F'$ by taking min and max of the w's instead of the c's.)

(e) See exercise 9. (Thus $F \perp F' \subseteq F \cap F'$, etc., as in exercise 27(f).)

Notes: Stanley introduced this lattice in *Fibonacci Quarterly* **13** (1975), 222–223. Since three important lattices are defined on the same elements, we need three notations for the different orderings; the symbols $\mathbin{\scriptstyle\kappa}$, $\dashv$, and $\subseteq$ adopted here are intended to be reminiscent of the names of Kreweras, Tamari, and Stanley (who is Стенли in Russia).

29. If we paste six regular pentagons together, we get 14 vertices whose coordinates after suitable rotation and scaling are respectively

$$p_{1010} = p_{\overline{0000}}^* = p_{3000}^* = p_{2\overline{1}00}^{*-} = (-1, \sqrt{3}, 2/\phi);$$
$$p_{0010} = p_{3100}^* = (\phi^{-2}, \sqrt{3}\,\phi, 0); \quad p_{3010} = p_{0\overline{1}00}^- = (0, 0, 2); \quad p_{3210} = p_{0\overline{2}00}^- = (2, 0, 2/\phi);$$
$$p_{0210} = p_{3200}^* = (\sqrt{5}, \sqrt{3}, 0); \quad p_{1000} = p_{2000}^* = (-\phi^2, \sqrt{3}/\phi, 0);$$

here $(x, y, z)^*$ means $(x, -y, z)$ and $(x, y, z)^-$ means $(x, y, -z)$. But then the three 4-edged "faces" are not squares; in fact, they don't even lie in a plane.

(One can however get a similar-looking solid, with true squares but irregular pentagons, by gluing together two suitable tetrahedra and lopping off the three glued-together corners. Alternative sets of coordinates for the associahedron, of substantial mathematical interest but less appealing to the eye, are discussed by Günter Ziegler in his *Lectures on Polytopes* (New York: Springer, 1995), example 9.11.)

30. (a) $\bar{f}_{n-1} \dots \bar{f}_1 0$, because internal node j in symmetric order has a nonempty right subtree if and only if internal node $j+1$ in symmetric order has an empty left subtree.

(b) In general if the footprint were $1^{p_1} 0^{q_1+1} 1^{p_2+1} 0^{q_2+1} \dots 1^{p_k+1} 0^{q_k+1}$, we would want to count all binary trees whose nodes in symmetric order have the specification $R^{p_1} N L^{q_1} B R^{p_2} N L^{q_2} B \dots R^{p_k} N L^{q_k}$, where B means "both subtrees are nonempty," R means "the right subtree is nonempty but not the left," L means "the left subtree is nonempty but not the right," and N means "neither subtree is nonempty." This number in general is

$$\binom{p_1 + q_1}{p_1} \binom{p_2 + q_2}{p_2} \dots \binom{p_k + q_k}{p_k} C_{k-1},$$

and in particular it is $\binom{1+0}{1} \binom{0+0}{0} \binom{1+0}{1} \binom{5+3}{5} \binom{0+0}{0} \binom{0+0}{0} \binom{0+2}{0} \binom{0+0}{0} \binom{1+2}{1} C_8 = 240240$.

(c) $d_j = 0$ if and only if $c_{j+1} > c_j$, by exercise 3.

(d) In general, the footprint of $F \perp F'$ is $f_1 \dots f_n \wedge f'_1 \dots f'_n$, by exercise 27(a); the footprint of $F \top F'$ is $f_1 \dots f_n \vee f'_1 \dots f'_n$, by (a) and exercise 27(d).

[The fact that complements always exist in the Tamari lattice is due to H. Lakser; see G. Grätzer, *General Lattice Theory* (1978), exercise I.6.30.]

31. (a) 2^{n-1}; see exercise 6.2.2–5.

(b) $c_1 \leq \dots \leq c_n$; $d_1, \dots, d_{n-1} \leq 1$; $e_j > 0$ implies $e_j + \dots + e_n = n - j$; $k_{j+1} \leq k_j + 1$; $p_1 \leq \dots \leq p_j \geq \dots \geq p_n$ for some j; $s_j > 0$ implies $s_j = n - j$; $u_1 \geq \dots \geq u_n$; $z_{j+1} \leq z_j + 2$. (Other constraints, which apply in general, whittle down the number of possibilities to 2^{n-1} in each case. For example, $u_1 \dots u_n$ must be a valid sequence of scope coordinates.)

(c) True in only n cases out of 2^{n-1}. (But F^T *is* degenerate.)

(d) The degenerate forest with footprint $f_1 \dots f_n$ has $c_{j+1} = c_j + f_j$. Elements $j < k$ are siblings if and only if $f_j = f_{j+1} = \dots = f_{k-1} = 0$. Thus if F'' is the degenerate forest with footprint $f_1 \dots f_n \wedge f'_1 \dots f'_n$, then $F'' \preceq F$ and $F'' \preceq F'$; hence $F'' \preceq F \wedge F' \dashv F \perp F'$. And we also have $F \perp F' \dashv F''$ by (b). A similar argument proves that $F \vee F' = F \top F'$ is the degenerate forest with footprint $f_1 \dots f_n \vee f'_1 \dots f'_n$.

Thus, when the Kreweras and Tamari lattices are restricted to degenerate forests, they become identical to the Boolean lattice of subsets of $\{1, \dots, n-1\}$. [This result, in the case of Tamari lattices, is due to George Markowsky, *Order* **9** (1992), 265–290, whose paper also shows that Tamari lattices enjoy many further properties.]

32. Suppose F and F' have scope coordinates $s_1 \dots s_n$ and $s'_1 \dots s'_n$. Call index j *frozen* if $s_j < s'_j$ or $j = 0$. We want to specify the values of the frozen coordinates and maximize the others. Let $s_0 = n$, and for $0 \leq k \leq n$ let

$$s''_k = s_j - k + j, \quad \text{where } j = \max\{i \mid 0 \leq i \leq k, i \text{ is frozen, and } i + s_i \geq k\}.$$

Since $s_k \leq s_j - (k - j)$ whenever $0 \leq k - j \leq s_j$, we have $s''_k \geq s_k$, with equality when k is frozen.

The scopes $s_0'' s_1'' \ldots s_n''$ correspond to a valid forest according to the condition of exercise 27(a). For if $k \geq 0$ and $0 \leq l \leq s_k'' = s_j - k + j$ and $s_{k+l}'' = s_{j'} - k - l + j'$, we have $s_{k+l}'' + l \leq s_k''$ if $0 \leq j' - j \leq s_j$, because $s_{j'} + j' - j \leq s_j$ in that case. And we can't have $j > j'$ or $j' > j + s_j$, because $j + s_j \geq k + l \geq j'$.

Let F''' be a forest with scopes satisfying $s_k \leq s_k''' \leq s_k''$. Then $\min(s_k', s_k''') = s_k$, because $s_k = s_k''$ when k is frozen, otherwise $s_k = s_k'$.

Conversely, if F''' is a forest with $F' \perp F''' = F$, we must have $s_k \leq s_k''' \leq s_k''$. For $s_k''' < s_k$ would imply $s_k''' < s_k'$. And if k is minimal with $s_k''' > s_k''$, we have $s_k'' = s_j - k + j$ for some frozen j with $0 \leq j \leq k$ and $j + s_j \geq k$. Then $s_j''' \geq s_j$ implies $k - j \leq s_j'''$, hence $s_k''' + k - j \leq s_j'''$. If $j < k$ we have $s_j''' \leq s_j'' = s_j$, a contradiction. But $j = k$ implies $\min(s_k''', s_k') > s_k$.

To get the first semidistributive law, apply this principle with F replaced by $F \perp G$ and F' replaced by F; then the hypotheses $F \dashv G \dashv F''$ and $F \dashv H \dashv F''$ imply that $F \dashv G \top H \dashv F''$. The second semidistributive law follows by taking duals in the first.

(Ralph Freese suggests calling F'' the *pseudo-complement* of F' over F.)

33. (a) Let $k\lambda = \text{LLINK}[k]$ if $\text{LLINK}[k] \neq 0$, otherwise $\text{RLINK}[k-1]$ if $k \neq 1$, otherwise the root of the binary tree. This rule defines a permutation because $k\lambda = j$ if and only if $k = \text{parent}(j) + [j$ is a right child$]$, or $k = 1$ and j is the root. Also $k\lambda \geq k$ when $\text{LLINK}[k] = 0$ and $k\sigma\lambda \leq k$ when $\text{RLINK}[k] = 0$. [For a generalization to t-ary trees, see P. H. Edelman, *Discrete Math.* **40** (1982), 171–179.]

(b) Using the representation of (2) in answer 26(f), we see that $\lambda(F)$ is $(3\,1)(2)$ $(12\,6\,4)(5)(11\,7)(14\,13)(9\,8)(15)(10)$ in that case. In general the cycles are the families of the forest, in decreasing order within each cycle; nodes are numbered in preorder. [See Dershowitz and Zaks, *Discrete Math.* **62** (1986), 215–218.]

(c) $\lambda(F^D) = \rho\sigma\lambda(F)\rho$, where ρ is the "flip" permutation $(1\,n)(2\,n-1)\ldots$, because the dual forest interchanges $\text{LLINK} \leftrightarrow \text{RLINK}$ and flips the preorder numbering.

(d) The cycle breakup $(x_j\,x_k)(x_1 \ldots x_m) = (x_1 \ldots x_j x_{k+1} \ldots x_m)(x_{j+1} \ldots x_k)$ corresponds to answer 26(c).

(e) By (d), each covering path corresponds to a factorization of $(n \ldots 2\,1)$. Let q_n denote the number of such factorizations. Then we have the recurrence $q_1 = 1$ and $q_n = \sum_{l=1}^{n-1}(n-l)\binom{n-2}{l-1}q_l q_{n-l}$, because there are $n-l$ choices with $k-j = l$ by which the first transposition breaks the cycle into parts of sizes l and $n-l$, then $\binom{n-2}{l-1}$ ways to interleave the subsequent factors. The solution is $q_n = n^{n-2}$, because

$$\sum_{l=1}^{n-1}\binom{n-1}{l}l^{l-1}(y-l)^{n-1-l} = \lim_{x\to 0}\sum_{l=1}^{n-1}\binom{n-1}{l}(x+l)^{l-1}(y-l)^{n-1-l}$$
$$= \lim_{x\to 0}\frac{(x+y)^{n-1}-y^{n-1}}{x} = (n-1)y^{n-1}.$$

[See J. Dénes, *Magyar Tudományos Akadémia Matematikai Kutató Intézetének Közleményei* **4** (1959), 63–70. It is natural to seek a correspondence between factorizations and labeled free trees, since there also happen to be n^{n-2} of the latter. Perhaps the simplest is the following, given $(1\,2\ldots n) = (x_1\,y_1)\ldots(x_{n-1}\,y_{n-1})$ where $x_j < y_j$: Suppose the cycle containing x_j and y_j in $(x_j\,y_j)\ldots(x_{n-1}\,y_{n-1})$ is $(z_1 \ldots z_m)$, where $z_1 < \cdots < z_m$. If $y_j = z_m$, let $a_j = z_1$, otherwise let $a_j = \min\{z_i \mid z_i > x_j\}$. Then one can show that $a_1 \ldots a_{n-1}$ is a "wake-up sequence" for parking $n-1$ cars, and exercise 6.4–31 connects it to free trees.]

34. Each covering path from bottom to top is equivalent to a Young tableau of shape $(n-1, n-2, \ldots, 1)$, so we can use Theorem 5.1.4H. (See exercise 5.3.4–38.)

[The enumeration of such paths in Tamari lattices remains mysterious; the relevant sequence is 1, 1, 2, 9, 98, 2981, 340549, ...]

35. Multiply by $n+1$, then see *AMM* **97** (1990), 626–630.

36. We might as well generalize to t-ary trees for arbitrary $t \geq 1$, by making obvious amendments to steps T1–T5. Let $C_n^{(t)}$ be the number of t-ary trees with n internal nodes; thus $C_n = C_n^{(2)}$ and $C_n^{(t)} = ((t-1)n+1)^{-1}\binom{tn}{n}$. If h of the degrees b_j are changed between visits, we have $h \geq x$ in $C_{n-x}^{(t)}$ cases. So the easy case occurs with probability $1 - C_{n-1}^{(t)}/C_n^{(t)} \approx 1 - (t-1)^{t-1}/t^t$, and the average number of times $b_j \leftarrow 0$ in step T4 is $(C_{n-1}^{(t)} + \cdots + C_1^{(t)})/C_n^{(t)} \approx (t-1)^{t-1}/(t^t - (t-1)^{t-1})$, or 4/23 when $t = 3$.

Indeed, we can also study the t-ary recursive structure $A_{pq}^{(t)} = 0\,A_{p(q-1)}^{(t)},\ t\,A_{(p-1)q}^{(t)}$ when $0 \leq (t-1)p \leq q \neq 0$, generalizing (5). The number of such degree sequences, $C_{pq}^{(t)}$, satisfies the recurrence (21) except that $C_{pq}^{(t)} = 0$ when $p < 0$ or $(t-1)p > q$. The general solution is

$$C_{pq}^{(t)} = \frac{q - (t-1)p + 1}{q+1}\binom{p+q}{p} = \binom{p+q}{p} - (t-1)\binom{p+q}{p-1},$$

and we have $C_n^{(t)} = C_{n((t-1)n)}^{(t)}$. The triangle for $t = 3$ begins as shown at the right.

37. The basic lexicographic recursion for all such forests is

$$A(n_0, n_1, \ldots, n_t) = 0\,A(n_0 - 1, n_1, \ldots, n_t),$$
$$1\,A(n_0, n_1 - 1, \ldots, n_t), \quad \ldots, \quad t\,A(n_0, n_1, \ldots, n_t - 1)$$

1			
1			
1	1		
1	2		
1	3	3	
1	4	7	
1	5	12	12
1	6	18	30
1	7	25	55	55
1	8	33	88	143

when $n_0 > n_2 + 2n_3 + \cdots + (t-1)n_t$ and $n_1, \ldots, n_t \geq 0$; otherwise $A(n_0, n_1, \ldots, n_t)$ is empty, except that $A(0, \ldots, 0) = \epsilon$ is the sequence consisting of the empty string alone. Step G1 computes the first entry of $A(n_0, \ldots, n_t)$. We want to analyze five quantities:

C, the number of times G2 is executed (the total number of forests);
E, the number of times G3 goes to G2 (the number of easy cases);
K, the number of times G4 moves some b_i into list c;
L, the number of times G5 compares b_j with some c_i;
Z, the number of times G5 sets $c_1 \leftarrow 0$.

Then the loop in step G6 sets $b_{l-c_j} \leftarrow c_j$ a total of $K - Z - n_1 - \cdots - n_t$ times.

Let n be the vector $(n_0, n_1, \ldots, n_t)$, and let e_j be the unit vector with 1 in coordinate position j. Let $|n| = n_0 + n_1 + \cdots + n_t$ and $\|n\| = n_1 + 2n_2 + \cdots + tn_t$. Using this notation we can rewrite the basic recurrence above in the convenient form

$$A(n) = 0\,A(n - e_0),\ 1\,A(n - e_1),\ \ldots,\ t\,A(n - e_t) \qquad \text{when } |n| > \|n\|.$$

Consider the general recurrence relation

$$F(n) = f(n) + \left(\sum_{j=0}^{t} F(n - e_j)\right)[|n| > \|n\|],$$

with $F(n) = 0$ whenever the vector n has a negative component. If $f(n) = [|n| = 0]$, then $F(n) = C(n)$ is the total number of forests. Answer 2.3.4.4–32 tells us that

$$C(n) = \frac{(|n| - 1)!\,(|n| - \|n\|)}{n_0!\,n_1!\dots n_t!} = \sum_{j=0}^{t}(1-j)\binom{|n| - 1}{n_0, \dots, n_{j-1}, n_j - 1, n_{j+1}, \dots, n_t},$$

generalizing the formula for $C_{pq}^{(t)}$ in answer 36 (which is the case $n_0 = (t-1)q + 1$ and $n_t = p$). Similarly, we obtain recurrences for the other quantities $E(n)$, $K(n)$, $L(n)$, and $Z(n)$ needed in our analysis by choosing other kernel functions $f(n)$:

$f(n) = [|n| = n_0 + 1 \text{ and } n_0 > \|n\|]$	yields	$F(n) = E(n);$
$f(n) = [|n| > n_0]$	yields	$F(n) = E(n) + K(n);$
$f(n) = [|n| = \|n\| + 1]$	yields	$F(n) = C(n) + K(n) - Z(n);$
$f(n) = \sum_{1 \le j < k \le t} n_j [n_k > 0]$	yields	$F(n) = L(n).$

The symbolic methods of exercise 2.3.4.4–32 do not seem to yield quick solutions to these more general recurrences, but we can readily establish the value of $C - E$ by noting that $b_m + m < N$ in step G2 if and only if the previous step was G3. Therefore

$$C(n) - E(n) = \sum_{j=1}^{t} C(n - f_j), \qquad \text{where } f_j = e_j - (j-1)e_0;$$

this sum counts the subforests in which $n_1 + \cdots + n_t$, the number of internal (nonleaf) nodes, has decreased by 1. Similarly we can let

$$C^{(x)}(n) = \sum \{C(n - i_1 f_1 - \cdots - i_t f_t) \mid i_1 + \cdots + i_t = x\}$$

be the number of subforests having $n_1 + \cdots + n_t - x$ internal nodes. Then we have

$$K(n) - Z(n) = \sum_{x=1}^{|n|} C^{(x)}(n),$$

a formula analogous to (20), because $k - [b_j = 0] \ge x \ge 1$ in step G5 if and only if $b_{m-x} > 0$ and $b_{m-x+1} \ge \cdots \ge b_m$. Such preorder degree strings are in one-to-one correspondence with the forests of $C^{(x)}(n)$ if we remove $b_{m-x+1} \dots b_m$ and an appropriate number of trailing 0s from the string $b_1 \dots b_N$.

From these formulas we can conclude that the Zaks–Richards algorithm needs only $O(1)$ operations per forest visited, whenever $n_1 = n_2 + \cdots + n_t + O(1)$, because $C(n - f_j)/C(n) = n_j n_0^{j-1}/(|n| - 1)^{\underline{j}} \le 1/4 + O(|n|^{-1})$ when $j > 1$. Indeed, the value of K is quite small in nearly all cases of practical interest. However, the algorithm can be slow when n_1 is large. For example, if $t = 1$, $n_0 = m + r + 1$, and $n_1 = m$, the algorithm essentially computes all r-combinations of $m + r$ things; then $C(n) = \binom{m+r}{r}$ and $K(n) - Z(n) = \binom{m+r}{r+1} = \Omega(mC(n))$ when r is fixed. [To ensure efficiency in all cases, we can keep track of trailing 1s; see Ruskey and Rœlants van Baronaigien, *Congressus Numerantium* **41** (1984), 53–62.]

Exact formulas for K, Z, and (especially) L do not seem to be simple, but we can compute those quantities as follows. Say that the "active block" of a forest is the rightmost substring of nonzero degrees; for example, the active block of 302102021230000000 is 2123. All permutations of the active block occur equally often. Indeed, let $D(n)$ denote the sum of "trailing zeros(β) − 1" over all preorder degree strings β for forests of specification n. Then a block with n'_j occurrences of j for $1 \le j \le t$ is active in exactly $D(n - n'_1 f_1 - \cdots - n'_t f_t) + [n'_1 + \cdots + n'_t = n_1 + \cdots + n_t]$ cases. For example, given the string 3021020000, we can insert 21230000 in three places to obtain a forest with active block 2123. The contributions to K and L when the active block is flush left (not preceded by any 0s) can be computed as in exercise 7.2.1.2–6, namely

$$k(n) = w\big(e_{n_1}(z) \ldots e_{n_t}(z)\big), \qquad l(n) = w\Big(e_{n_1}(z) \ldots e_{n_t}(z) \sum_{1 \le i < j \le t} (n_i - z r_i(z)) r_j(z)\Big)$$

in the notation of that answer. Analogous contributions occur in general; therefore

$$K(n) = k(n) + \sum D(n - n') k(n'), \quad L(n) = l(n) + \sum D(n - n') l(n'), \quad Z(n) = \sum D(n - n'),$$

summed over all vectors n' such that $n'_j \le n_j$ for $1 \le j \le t$ and $|n'| - \|n'\| = |n| - \|n\|$ and $n'_1 + \cdots + n'_t \le n_1 + \cdots + n_t - 2$.

It remains to determine $D(n)$. Let $C(n; j)$ be the number of forests of specification $n = (n_0, \ldots, n_t)$ in which the last internal node in preorder has degree j. Then we have

$$C(n) = \sum_{j=1}^{t} C(n; j) \text{ and } C(n + e_1; 1) = C(n + e_2; 2) = \cdots = C(n + e_t; t) = C(n) + D(n).$$

From this infinite system of linear equations we can deduce that $C(n) + D(n)$ is

$$\sum_{i_2=0}^{n_2} \cdots \sum_{i_t=0}^{n_t} (-1)^{i_2 + \cdots + i_t} \binom{i_2 + \cdots + i_t}{i_2, \ldots, i_t} C(n + (1 + i_2 + \cdots + i_t) e_1 - i_2 f_2 - \cdots - i_t f_t).$$

Simpler expressions would of course be desirable, if they exist.

38. Step L1 obviously uses $4n + 2$ mems. Step L3 exits to L4 or L5 exactly $C_j - C_{j-1}$ times with a particular value of j; therefore it costs $2C_n + 3 \sum_{j=0}^{n} (n - j)(C_j - C_{j-1}) = 2C_n + 3(C_{n-1} + \cdots + C_1 + C_0)$ mems. Steps L4 and L5 jointly cost a total of $6C_n - 6$. Therefore the entire process involves $9 + O(n^{-1/2})$ mems per visit.

39. A Young tableau of shape (q, p) and entries y_{ij} corresponds to an element of A_{pq} that has left parens in positions $p + q + 1 - y_{21}, \ldots, p + q + 1 - y_{2p}$ and right parens in positions $p + q + 1 - y_{11}, \ldots, p + q + 1 - y_{1q}$. The hook lengths are $\{q + 1, q, \ldots, 1, p, p - 1, \ldots, 1\} \setminus \{q - p + 1\}$; so $C_{pq} = (p + q)!(q - p + 1)/(p!(q + 1)!)$ by Theorem 5.1.4H.

40. (a) $C_{pq} = \binom{p+q}{p} - \binom{p+q}{p-1} \equiv \binom{p+q}{p} + \binom{p+q}{p-1} = \binom{p+q+1}{p}$ (modulo 2); now use exercise 1.2.6–11. (b) By Eq. 7.1.3–(36) we know that $\nu(n \,\&\, (n + 1)) = \nu(n + 1) - 1$.

41. It equals $C(wz)/(1 - zC(wz)) = 1/(1 - z - wzC(wz)) = (1 - wC(wz))/(1 - w - z)$, where $C(z)$ is the Catalan generating function (18). The first of these formulas, $C(wz) + zC(wz)^2 + z^2 C(wz)^3 + \cdots$, is easily seen to be equivalent to (24). [See P. A. MacMahon, *Combinatory Analysis* **1** (Cambridge Univ. Press, 1915), 128–130.]

42. (a) Elements $a_1 \ldots a_n$ determine an entire self-conjugate nested string $a_1 \ldots a_{2n}$, and there are $C_{q(n-q)}$ possibilities for $a_1 \ldots a_n$ having exactly q right parentheses. So the answer is

$$\sum_{q=0}^{\lfloor n/2 \rfloor} C_{q(n-q)} = \sum_{q=0}^{\lfloor n/2 \rfloor} \left(\binom{n}{q} - \binom{n}{q-1} \right) = \binom{n}{\lfloor n/2 \rfloor}.$$

(b) Exactly $C_{(n-1)/2}$ [n odd], because a self-transpose binary tree is determined by its left subtree. And (c) has the same answer, because F is self-dual if and only if F^R is self-transpose.

43. $C_{pq} = C_q - \binom{q-p-1}{1}C_{q-1} + \cdots = \sum_{r=0}^{q-p}(-1)^r\binom{q-p-r}{r}C_{q-r}$, by induction on $q - p$.

44. The number of mems between visits is $3j - 2$ in step B3, $h + 1$ in step B4, and 4 in step B5, where h is the number of times $y \leftarrow r_y$. The number of binary trees with $h \geq x$, given j and x, is $[z^{n-j-x-1}]C(z)^{x+3}$ when $j < n$, because we get such trees by attaching $x+3$ subtrees below $j+x+1$ internal nodes. Setting $x = 0$ tells us that a given value of j occurs $C_{(n-j-1)(n-j+1)} = C_{n+1-j} - C_{n-j}$ times, using (24) and exercise 43. Thus $\sum j$ over all binary trees is $n + \sum_{j=1}^{n}(C_{n+1-j} - C_{n-j})j = C_n + C_{n-1} + \cdots + C_1$. Similarly, $\sum(h + 1)$ is $\sum_{j=1}^{n-1}\sum_{x=0}^{n-j-1}C_{(n-j-x-1)(n-j+1)} = \sum_{j=1}^{n-1}C_{(n-j-1)(n-j+2)} = \sum_{j=1}^{n}(C_{n-j+2} - 2C_{n-j+1}) = C_{n+1} - (C_n + C_{n-1} + \cdots + C_0)$. So overall, the algorithm costs $C_{n+1} + 4C_n + 2(C_{n-1} + \cdots + C_1) + O(n) = (26/3 - 10/(3n) + O(n^{-2}))C_n$ mems.

45. Each of the easy cases in step K3 occurs C_{n-1} times, so the total cost of that step is $3C_{n-1} + 8C_{n-1} + 2(C_n - 2C_{n-1})$ mems. Step K4 fetches r_i a total of $[z^{n-i-1}]C(z)^{i+2} = C_{(n-i-1)n}$ times; summing for $i \geq 2$ gives $C_{(n-3)(n+1)} = C_{n+1} - 3C_n + C_{n-1}$ mems altogether in that loop. Step K5 costs $6C_n - 12C_{n-1}$. Step K6 is a bit more complicated, but one can show that the operation $r_j \leftarrow r_k$ is performed $C_n - 3C_{n-1} + 1$ times when $n > 2$, while the operation $r_j \leftarrow 0$ is performed $C_{n-1} - n + 1$ times. The total number of mems therefore comes to $C_{n+1} + 7C_n - 9C_{n-1} + n + 3 = (8.75 - 9.375/n + O(n^{-2}))C_n$.

Although this total is asymptotically worse than that of Algorithm B in answer 44, the large negative coefficient of n^{-1} means that Algorithm B actually wins only when $n \geq 58$; and n won't ever be that big.

Skarbek has, however, improved Algorithm B to the following Algorithm B*, which generates the trees in reverse order and uses an auxiliary table $c_1 \ldots c_n$:

B1*. [Initialize.] Set $l_k \leftarrow c_k \leftarrow 0$ and $r_k \leftarrow k+1$ for $1 \leq k < n$; also set $l_n \leftarrow r_n \leftarrow 0$, and set $r_{n+1} \leftarrow 1$ (for convenience in step B3*).

B2*. [Visit.] Visit the binary tree represented by $l_1l_2\ldots l_n$ and $r_1r_2\ldots r_n$.

B3*. [Find j.] Set $j \leftarrow 1$. While $r_j = 0$, set $l_j \leftarrow c_j \leftarrow 0$, $r_j \leftarrow j+1$, and $j \leftarrow j+1$. Then terminate the algorithm if $j > n$.

B4*. [Demote r_j.] Set $x \leftarrow r_j$, $r_j \leftarrow r_x$, $r_x \leftarrow 0$, $z \leftarrow c_j$, $c_j \leftarrow x$. If $z > 0$, set $r_z \leftarrow x$; otherwise set $l_j \leftarrow x$. Return to B2*. ∎

If the values of r_1 and c_1 are maintained in registers, this algorithm needs only $4C_n + C_{n-1} + 4(C_{n-1} + C_{n-2} + \cdots + C_0) + 3n - 6 = (67/12 + 73/(24n) + O(n^{-2}))C_n$ mems to generate all C_n trees. [See W. Skarbek, *Fundamenta Informaticæ* **75** (2007), 505–536.]

46. (a) Going to the left from $\widehat{pq}$ increases the area by $q - p$.

(b) The leftward steps on a path from $\widehat{nn}$ to $\widehat{00}$ correspond to the left parentheses in $a_1 \ldots a_{2n}$, and we have $q - p = c_k$ at the kth such step.

(c) Equivalently, $C_{n+1}(x) = \sum_{k=0}^{n} x^k C_k(x) C_{n-k}(x)$. This recurrence holds because an $(n + 1)$-node forest F consists of the root of the leftmost tree together with a k-node forest F_l (the descendants of that root) and an $(n - k)$-node forest F_r (the remaining trees), and because we have

internal path length(F) $=$ k + internal path length(F_l) + internal path length(F_r).

(d) The strings of $A_{p(p+r)}$ have the form $\alpha_0)\alpha_1)\ldots\alpha_{r-1})\alpha_r$ where each α_j is properly nested. The area of such a string is the sum over j of the area of α_j plus $r - j$ times the number of left parens in α_j.

Notes: The polynomials $C_{pq}(x)$ were introduced by L. Carlitz and J. Riordan in *Duke Math. J.* **31** (1964), 371–388; the identity in part (d) is equivalent to their formula

(10.12). They also proved that

$$C_{pq}(x) = \sum_r (-1)^r x^{r(r-1)-\binom{q-p}{2}} \binom{q-p-r}{r}_x C_{q-r}(x),$$

generalizing the result of exercise 43. From part (c) we have the infinite continued fraction $C(x,z) = 1/(1 - z/(1 - xz/(1 - x^2 z/(1 - \cdots))))$, which G. N. Watson proved is equal to $F(x,z)/F(x,z/x)$, where

$$F(x,z) = \sum_{n=0}^{\infty} \frac{(-1)^n x^{n^2} z^n}{(1-x)(1-x^2)\dots(1-x^n)};$$

see *J. London Math. Soc.* **4** (1929), 39–48. We have already encountered the same generating function, slightly disguised, in exercise 5.2.1–15.

The internal path length of a forest is the "left path length" of the corresponding binary tree, namely the sum over all internal nodes of the number of left branches on the path from the root. The more general polynomial

$$C_n(x,y) = \sum x^{\text{left path length}(T)} y^{\text{right path length}(T)},$$

summed over all n-node binary trees T, seems to obey no simple additive recurrence like the one for $C_{nn}(x) = C_n(x,1)$ studied in this exercise; but we do have $C_{n+1}(x,y) = \sum_k x^k C_k(x,y) y^{n-k} C_{n-k}(x,y)$. Therefore the super generating function $C(x,y,z) = \sum_n C_n(x,y)z^n$ satisfies the functional equation $C(x,y,z) = 1 + zC(x,y,xz)C(x,y,yz)$. (The case $x = y$ was considered in exercise 2.3.4.5–5.)

47. $C_n(x) = \sum_q x^{\binom{q-p}{2}} C_{pq}(x) C_{(n-q)(n-1-p)}(x)$ for $0 \le p < n$.

48. Let $\bar{C}(z) = C(-1, z)$ in the notation of exercise 46, and let $\bar{C}(z)\bar{C}(-z) = F(z^2)$. Then $\bar{C}(z) = 1 + zF(z^2)$ and $\bar{C}(-z) = 1 - zF(z^2)$; so $F(z) = 1 - zF(z)^2$, and $F(z) = C(-z)$. It follows that $C_{pq}(-1) = [z^p] C(-z^2)^{\lceil (q-p)/2 \rceil} (1 + zC(-z^2))^{[q-p \text{ even}]}$, which is $(-1)^{(p/2)} C_{(p/2)(q/2-1)} [p \text{ even}]$ when q is even, $(-1)^{\lfloor p/2 \rfloor} C_{\lfloor p/2 \rfloor \lfloor q/2 \rfloor}$ when q is odd. A perfect Gray code through the strings of A_{pq} can exist only if $|C_{pq}(-1)| \le 1$, because the associated graph is bipartite (see Fig. 62); $|C_{pq}(-1)|$ is the difference between the sizes of the parts, because each perfect transposition changes $c_1 + \cdots + c_n$ by ± 1.

49. By Algorithm U with $n = 15$ and $N = 10^6$, it is ()(()())((((())))(((()())()))).

50. Make the following changes to Algorithm U: In step U1, also set $r \leftarrow 0$. In step U3, test if $a_m = $ ')' instead of testing if $N \le c'$. In step U4, set $r \leftarrow r + c'$ instead of $N \leftarrow N - c'$. And omit the assignments to a_m in steps U3 and U4.

The string in (1) turns out to have rank 3141592. (Who knew?)

51. By Theorem 7.2.1.3L, $N = \binom{\bar{z}_1}{n} + \binom{\bar{z}_2}{n-1} + \cdots + \binom{\bar{z}_n}{1}$; hence $\kappa_n N = \binom{\bar{z}_1}{n-1} + \binom{\bar{z}_2}{n-2} + \cdots + \binom{\bar{z}_n}{0}$, since $\bar{z}_n \ge 1$. Now note that $N - \kappa_n N$ is the rank of $z_1 z_2 \dots z_n$, because of (23) and exercise 50. (For example, let $z_1 \dots z_4 = 1256$, which has rank 6 in Table 1. Then $\bar{z}_1 \dots \bar{z}_4 = 7632$, $N = 60$, and $\kappa_4 60 = 54$. Notice that N is fairly large, because $\bar{z}_1 = 2n - 1$; Fig. 47 shows that $\kappa_n N$ usually *exceeds* N when N is smaller.)

52. The number of trailing right parentheses has the same distribution as the number of leading left parentheses, and the sequence of nested strings that begin with '$(^k)$' is

$(^k)A_{(n-k)(n-1)}$. Therefore the probability that $d_n = k$ is $C_{(n-k)(n-1)}/C_n$. We find

$$\sum_{k=0}^{n} \binom{k}{t} C_{(n-k)(n-1)} = \sum_{k=0}^{n} \left(\binom{2n-1-k}{n-1} - \binom{2n-1-k}{n} \right) \binom{k}{t}$$

$$= \binom{2n}{n+t} - \binom{2n}{n+t+1} = C_{(n-t)(n+t)}$$

using Eq. 1.2.6–(25), and it follows that the mean and variance are respectively equal to $3n/(n+2) = 3 - 6/(n+2)$ and $2n(2n^2 - n - 1)/((n+2)^2(n+3)) = 4 + O(n^{-1})$. [The moments of this distribution were first calculated by R. Kemp in *Acta Informatica* **35** (1998), 17–89, Theorem 9. Notice that $c_n = d_n - 1$ has essentially the same behavior.]

53. (a) $3n/(n+2)$, by exercise 52. (b) H_n, by exercise 6.2.2–7. (c) $2-2^{-n}$, by induction.

(d) Any particular (but fixed) sequence of left or right branches has the same distribution of steps before a leaf is encountered. (In other words, the probability that a node with Dewey binary notation 01101 occurs is the same as the probability that 00000 occurs.) Thus if $X = k$ with probability p_k, each of the 2^k potential nodes on level k is external with probability p_k. The expected value $\sum_k 2^k p_k$ is therefore the expected number of external nodes, namely $n+1$ in all three cases. (One can of course also verify this result directly, with $p_k = C_{(n-k)(n-1)}/C_n$ in case (a), $p_k = \begin{bmatrix} n \\ k \end{bmatrix}/n!$ in case (b), and $p_k = 2^{-k+[k=n]}$ in case (c).)

Notes: The average level of a leaf turns out to be $\Theta(\sqrt{n})$, $\Theta(\log n)$, and $\Theta(n)$ in these three cases; thus it is longer when the expected time to hit the leftmost leaf is shorter! The reason is that ubiquitous "holes" near the root force other paths to be long. Case (a) has an interesting generalization to t-ary trees, when $p_k = C^{(t)}_{(n-k)((t-1)n-1)}/C^{(t)}_n$ in the notation of answer 36. Then the mean distance to the leftmost leaf is $(t+1)n/((t-1)n+2)$, and it is instructive to prove via telescoping series that

$$\sum_k t^k C^{(t)}_{(n-k)((t-1)n-1)} = \binom{tn}{n}.$$

54. Differentiating with respect to x we have

$$C'(x,z) = zC'(x,z)C(x,xz) + zC(x,z)(C'(x,xz) + zC_I(x,xz)),$$

where $C_I(x,z)$ denotes the derivative of $C(x,z)$ with respect to z. Thus $C'(1,z) = 2zC'(1,z)C(z) + z^2C(z)C'(z)$; and since $C'(z) = C(z)^2 + 2zC(z)C'(z)$ we can solve for $C'(1,z)$, obtaining $z^2C(z)^3/(1-2zC(z))^2$. Therefore $\sum(c_1 + \cdots + c_n) = [z^n]C'(1,z) = 2^{2n-1} - \frac{1}{2}(3n+1)C_n$, in agreement with exercise 2.3.4.5–5. Similarly we find

$$\sum(c_1 + \cdots + c_n)^2 = [z^n]C''(1,z) = \left(\frac{5n^2 + 19n + 6}{6}\right)\binom{2n}{n} - \left(1 + \frac{3n}{2}\right)4^n.$$

Thus the mean and variance are $\frac{1}{2}\sqrt{\pi}n^{3/2} + O(n)$ and $(\frac{5}{6} - \frac{\pi}{4})n^{3/2} + O(n)$, respectively.

55. Differentiating as in answer 54, and using the formulas of exercises 46(d) and 5.2.1–14 together with $[z^n]C(z)^r/(1-4z) = 2^{2n+r} - \sum_{j=1}^{r} 2^{r-j}\binom{2n+j}{n}$, yields

$$C'_{p(p+r)}(1) = [z^p]\left((r+1)\frac{z^2C(z)^{r+3}}{1-4z} + \binom{r+1}{2}\frac{zC(z)^{r+2}}{\sqrt{1-4z}}\right)$$

$$= [z^p]\left((r+1)\frac{C(z)^{r+1} - 2C(z)^r + C(z)^{r-1}}{1-4z} + \binom{r+1}{2}\frac{C(z)^{r+1} - C(z)^r}{\sqrt{1-4z}}\right)$$

$$= (r+1)\left(2^{2p+r-1} - \binom{2p+r+1}{p} - \sum_{j=1}^{r-1} 2^{r-1-j}\binom{2p+j}{p}\right) + \binom{r+1}{2}\binom{2p+r}{p-1}.$$

56. Use 1.2.6–53(b). [See *BIT* **30** (1990), 67–68.]

57. $2S_0(a,b) = \binom{2a}{a}\binom{2b}{b} + \binom{2a+2b}{a+b}$ by 1.2.6–(21). Exercise 1.2.6–53 tells us that

$$\sum_{k=a-m}^{a}\binom{2a}{a-k}\binom{2b}{b-k}k = (m+1)(a+b-m)\binom{2a}{m+1}\binom{2b}{a+b-m};$$

therefore $2S_1(a,b) = \binom{2a}{a}\binom{2b}{b}\frac{ab}{a+b}$. And since $b^2S_p(a,b) - S_{p+2}(a,b) = S_p(a,b-1)$, we find $2S_2(a,b) = \binom{2a+2b}{a+b}\frac{ab}{2a+2b-1}$; $2S_3(a,b) = \binom{2a}{a}\binom{2b}{b}a^2b^2/(a+b)^2$. Formula (30) follows by setting $a = m$, $b = n - m$, and $C_{(x-k)(x+k)} = \binom{2x}{x-k} - \binom{2x}{x-k-1}$.

Similarly, the average of w_{2m-1} is $\sum_{k\geq0}(2k-1)C_{(m-k)(m+k-1)}C_{(n-m-k+1)(n-m+k)}$ divided by C_n, namely

$$\frac{2S_3(m,n+1-m) - S_2(m,n+1-m)}{m(n+1-m)C_n} = \frac{m(n+1-m)}{n}\binom{2m}{m}\binom{2n+2-2m}{n+1-m}\bigg/\binom{2n}{n} - 1.$$

[R. Kemp, *BIT* **20** (1980), 157–163; H. Prodinger, *Soochow J. Math.* **9** (1983), 193–196.]

58. Summing over cases in which the left subtree has k internal nodes, we have

$$t_{lmn} = [l=m=n=0] + \sum_{k=0}^{m-1} C_k t_{(l-1)(m-k-1)(n-k-1)} + \sum_{k=m}^{n-1} C_{n-1-k}t_{(l-1)mk}.$$

Thus the triple generating function $t(v,w,z) = \sum_{l,m,n} t_{lmn}v^l w^m z^n$ satisfies

$$t(v,w,z) = 1 + vwzC(wz)t(v,w,z) + vzC(z)t(v,w,z);$$

and the analogous linear relation for $t(w,z) = \partial t(v,w,z)/\partial v\,|_{v=1}$ follows, because $t(1,w,z) = \sum_{n=0}^{\infty}\sum_{m=0}^{n} C_n w^m z^n = (C(z) - wC(wz))/(1-w)$ and $zC(z)^2 = C(z) - 1$. Algebraic manipulation now yields

$$t(w,z) = \frac{C(z) + wC(wz) - (1+w)}{(1-w)^2 z} - \frac{2wC(z)C(wz)}{(1-w)^2} - \frac{C(z) - wC(wz)}{1-w},$$

and we obtain the formula $t_{mn} = (m+1)C_{n+1} - 2\sum_{k=0}^{m}(m-k)C_k C_{n-k} - C_n$. Now

$$\sum_{k=0}^{m-1}(k+1)C_k C_{n-1-k} = \frac{m}{2n}\binom{2m}{m}\binom{2n-2m}{n-m}$$

can be proved as in exercise 56, and it follows that

$$t_{mn} = 2\binom{2m}{m}\binom{2n-2m}{n-m}\frac{(2m+1)(2n-2m+1)}{(n+1)(n+2)} - C_n, \qquad \text{for } 0 \leq m \leq n.$$

[P. Kirschenhofer, *J. Combinatorics, Information and System Sciences* **8** (1983), 44–60. For higher moments and generalizations, see W. J. Gutjahr, *Random Structures & Algorithms* **3** (1992), 361–374; A. Panholzer and H. Prodinger, *J. Statistical Planning and Inference* **101** (2002), 267–279. Note that the generating function $t(v,w,z)$ yields

$$t_{lmn} = \sum_k \binom{l}{k}C_{(m-k)(m-1)}C_{(n-m-l+k)(n-m-1)}.$$

Using the fact that $\sum_k \binom{k}{r}C_{(n-k)(m-1)} = C_{(n-r)(m+r)}$ when $m \geq 1$, we obtain the formula $t_{mn}+C_n = \sum_k (k+1)C_{(m-k)(m-1)}C_{(n-m)(n-m+k+1)}$, a sum that can therefore (surprisingly) be expressed in closed form.]

59. $T(w, z) = \dfrac{w(C(z) - C(wz))}{(1-w)} - wzC(z)C(wz) + zC(z)T(w, z) + wzC(wz)T(wz)$

$\qquad = \dfrac{w((C(z) + C(wz) - 2)/z - (1+w)C(z)C(wz) - (1-w)(C(z) - C(wz)))}{(1-w)^2}.$

Hence $T_{mn} = t_{mn} - \sum_{k=m}^{n} C_k C_{n-k}$. [Is there a combinatorial proof?] And

$$T_{mn} = \binom{2m}{m}\binom{2n+2-2m}{n+1-m}\frac{4m(n+1-m) + n + 1}{2(n+1)(n+2)} - \frac{1}{2}C_{n+1} - C_n, \quad \text{for } 1 \le m \le n.$$

60. (a) It is the number of right parentheses in co-atoms. (Therefore it is also the number of k for which $w_{2k-1} < 0$ in the associated "worm walk.")

(b) For convenience let $d(\text{`('}) = +1$ and $d(\text{`)'}) = -1$.

A1. [Initialize.] Set $i \leftarrow j \leftarrow 1$ and $k \leftarrow 2n$.

A2. [Done?] Terminate the algorithm if $j > k$. Otherwise set $a_j \leftarrow \text{`('}$, $j \leftarrow j + 1$.

A3. [Atom?] If $b_i = \text{`)'}$, set $s \leftarrow -1$, $i \leftarrow i + 1$, and go to A4. Otherwise set $s \leftarrow 1$, $i \leftarrow i + 1$, and while $s > 0$ set $a_j \leftarrow b_i$, $j \leftarrow j + 1$, $s \leftarrow s + d(b_i)$, $i \leftarrow i + 1$. Return to A2.

A4. [Co-atom.] Set $s \leftarrow s + d(b_i)$. Then if $s < 0$, set $a_k \leftarrow b_i$, $k \leftarrow k - 1$, $i \leftarrow i + 1$, and repeat step A4. Otherwise set $a_k \leftarrow \text{`)'}$, $k \leftarrow k - 1$, $i \leftarrow i + 1$, and return to A2. ∎

(c) The defect-11 inverse of (1) is $(( ))) (((())))) () ((()) (())) ((($. In general we find it by locating the subscript m just before the lth-from-last right parenthesis, and the indices $(u_0, v_0), \ldots, (u_{s-1}, v_{s-1})$ of matching parentheses such that $u_j \le m < v_j$.

I1. [Initialize.] Set $c \leftarrow j \leftarrow s \leftarrow 0$, $k \leftarrow m \leftarrow 2n$, and $u_0 \leftarrow 2n + 1$.

I2. [Scan right to left.] If $k = 0$, go to I5; if $a_k = \text{`)'}$, go to I3; if $a_k = \text{`('}$, go to I4.

I3. [Process a `)'.] Set $r_j \leftarrow k$, $j \leftarrow j + 1$, $c \leftarrow c + 1$. If $c = l$, set $m \leftarrow k - 1$, $s \leftarrow j$, and $u_s \leftarrow k$. Then decrease k by 1 and return to I2.

I4. [Process a `('.] (At this point the left parenthesis a_k matches the right parenthesis $a_{r_{j-1}}$.) Set $j \leftarrow j - 1$. If $r_j > m$, set $u_j \leftarrow k$ and $v_j \leftarrow r_j$. Then decrease k by 1 and return to I2.

I5. [Prepare to permute.] Set $i \leftarrow j \leftarrow 1$, $k \leftarrow 2n$, and $c \leftarrow 0$.

I6. [Permute.] While $j \ne u_c$, set $b_i \leftarrow a_j$, $i \leftarrow i + 1$, $j \leftarrow j + 1$. Then terminate if $c = s$; otherwise set $b_i \leftarrow \text{`)'}$, $i \leftarrow i + 1$, $j \leftarrow j + 1$. While $k \ne v_c$, set $b_i \leftarrow a_k$, $i \leftarrow i + 1$, $k \leftarrow k - 1$. Then set $b_i \leftarrow \text{`('}$, $i \leftarrow i + 1$, $k \leftarrow k - 1$, $c \leftarrow c + 1$, and repeat step I6. ∎

Notes: The fact that exactly C_n balanced strings of length $2n$ have defect l, for $0 \le l \le n$, was discovered by P. A. MacMahon [*Philosophical Transactions* **209** (1909), 153–175, §20], then rediscovered by K. L. Chung and W. Feller [*Proc. Nat. Acad. Sci.* **35** (1949), 605–608], using generating functions. A simple combinatorial explanation was found subsequently by J. L. Hodges, Jr. [*Biometrika* **42** (1955), 261–262], who observed that if $\beta_1 \ldots \beta_r$ has defect $l > 0$ and if $\beta_k = \alpha_k^R$ is its rightmost co-atom, the balanced string $\beta_1 \ldots \beta_{k-1}(\beta_{k+1} \ldots \beta_r)\alpha_k'^R$ has defect $l - 1$ (and this transformation is reversible). The efficient mapping in the present exercise is similar to a construction of M. D. Atkinson and J.-R. Sack [*Information Processing Letters* **41** (1992), 21–23].

61. (a) Let $c_j = 1 - b_j$; thus $c_j \le 1$, $c_1 + \cdots + c_N = f$, and we must prove that

$$c_1 + c_2 + \cdots + c_k < f \qquad \text{if and only if} \qquad k < N$$

holds for exactly f cyclic shifts. We can define c_j for all integers j by letting $c_{j\pm N} = c_j$. Let us also define Σ_j for all j by letting $\Sigma_0 = 0$ and $\Sigma_j = \Sigma_{j-1} + c_j$; then $\Sigma_{j+Nt} = \Sigma_j + ft$, and $\Sigma_{j+1} \le \Sigma_j + 1$. It follows that for each integer x there is a smallest integer $j = j(x)$ such that $\Sigma_j = x$. Moreover, $j(x) < j(x+1)$; and $j(x+f) = j(x) + N$. Thus the desired condition holds if and only if we shift by $j(x) \bmod N$ for $x = 1, 2, \ldots,$ or f. (The history of this important lemma is discussed in answer 2.3.4.4–32.)

(b) Start with $l \leftarrow m \leftarrow s \leftarrow 0$. Then for $k = 1, 2, \ldots, N$ (in this order) do the following: Set $s \leftarrow s + 1 - b_k$; and if $s > m$, set $m \leftarrow s$, $j_l \leftarrow k$, and $l \leftarrow (l+1) \bmod f$. The answers are $j_0, \ldots, j_{f-1}$, by the proof in part (a).

(c) Start with any string $b_1 b_2 \ldots b_N$ containing n_j occurrences of j for $0 \le j \le t$. Apply a random permutation to this string, then apply the algorithm of part (b). Choose randomly between $(j_0, \ldots, j_{f-1})$ and use the resulting cyclic shift as a preorder sequence to define the forest.

[See L. Alonso, J. L. Rémy, and R. Schott, *Algorithmica* **17** (1997), 162–182, for an even more general algorithm.]

62. Bit strings $(l_1 \ldots l_n, r_1 \ldots r_n)$ are valid if and only if $b_1 \ldots b_n$ is valid in exercise 20, where $b_j = l_j + r_j$. Therefore we can use exercise 61. [See J. F. Korsh, *Information Processing Letters* **45** (1993), 291–294.]

63.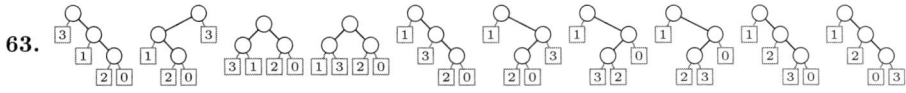

64. $X = 2k + b$ where $(k, b) = (0,1), (2,1), (0,0), (5,1), (6,0), (1,1)$; eventually $L_0 L_1 \ldots L_{12} = 5\ 11\ 3\ 4\ 0\ 7\ 9\ 8\ 1\ 6\ 10\ 12\ 2$.

65. See A. Panholzer and H. Prodinger, *Discrete Mathematics* **250** (2002), 181–195; M. Luczak and P. Winkler, *Random Structures & Algorithms* **24** (2004), 420–443.

66. (a) "Shrink" the white edges, merging the nodes that they connect. For example,

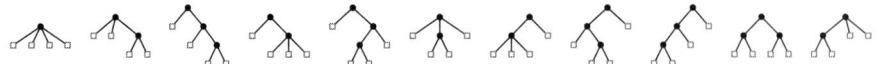

are the ordinary trees that correspond to the eleven Schröder trees depicted for $n = 3$. Under this correspondence a left link means, "here is a child"; a white right link means, "look here for more children"; a black right link means, "here's the last child."

(b) Mimic Algorithm L, but between rotations use an ordinary Gray binary code to run through all color patterns of whatever right links are present. (The case $n = 3$ has, in fact, been illustrated in the example.)

Note that Schröder trees also correspond to series-parallel graphs, as in (53). They do, however, impose an order on the edges and/or superedges that are joined in parallel; so they correspond more precisely to series-parallel graphs *as embedded in the plane* (and with edges and vertices unlabeled, except for s and t).

67. $S(z) = 1 + zS(z)(1 + 2(S(z) - 1))$, because $1 + 2(S(z) - 1)$ enumerates the right subtrees; therefore $S(z) = (1 + z - \sqrt{1 - 6z + z^2})/(4z)$.

Notes: We've seen Schröder numbers in exercise 2.3.4.4–31, where $G(z) = zS(z)$; and in exercise 2.2.1–11, where $b_n = 2S_{n-1}$ for $n \ge 2$ and where we found the recurrence $(n-1)S_n = (6n-3)S_{n-1} - (n-2)S_{n-2}$. They grow asymptotically as explored in exercise 2.2.1–12. A triangle of numbers S_{pq}, analogous to (22), can be used to generate random Schröder trees. These numbers satisfy

$$S_{pq} = S_{p(q-1)} + S_{(p-1)q} + S_{(p-2)q} + \cdots + S_{0q} = S_{p(q-1)} + 2S_{(p-1)q} - S_{(p-1)(q-1)}$$

$$= \frac{q-p+1}{q+1} \sum_{k=0}^{p} \binom{q+1}{p-k}\binom{p-1}{k} 2^k = \sum_{k=0}^{p}\left(\binom{q}{p-k}\binom{p-1}{k} - \binom{q}{p-k-1}\binom{p-1}{k-1}\right) 2^k$$

$$= [w^p z^q]\, S(wz)/(1 - zS(wz));$$

the double generating function on the last line is due to Emeric Deutsch. Many other properties of Schröder trees are discussed in Richard Stanley's *Enumerative Combinatorics* **2** (1999), exercise 6.39.

68. A single row that contains only the empty string ϵ. (The general rule (36) for going from $n-1$ to n converts this row into '0 1', the pattern of order 1.)

69. The first $\binom{6}{3} = 20$ rows are the Christmas tree pattern of order 6, if we ignore the '10' at the beginning of each string. The pattern of order 7 is a bit more difficult to see; but there are $\binom{7}{3} = 35$ rows in which the leftmost entry begins with 0. Disregard the rightmost string in all such rows, and ignore the 0 at the beginning of each remaining string. (Other answers are also possible.)

70. If σ appears in column k of the Christmas tree pattern, let σ' be the string in column $n - k$ of the same row. (If we think of parentheses instead of bits, this rule takes the mirror reflection of the free parentheses in the sense of answer 11, by (39).)

71. M_{tn} is the sum of the t largest binomial coefficients $\binom{n}{k}$, because each row of the Christmas tree pattern can contain at most t elements of S, and because we do get such a set S by choosing all strings σ with $(n-t)/2 \le \nu(\sigma) \le (n+t-1)/2$. (The formula

$$M_{tn} = \sum_{n-t \le 2k \le n+t-1} \binom{n}{k}$$

is about as simple as possible; however, special formulas like $M_{(2)n} = M_{n+1}$ hold for small t, and we also have $M_{tn} = 2^n$ for $t > n$.)

72. You get M_{sn}, the same number as in the previous exercise. In fact, one can prove by induction that there are exactly $\binom{n}{n-k} - \binom{n}{k-s}$ rows of length $s + n - 2k \ge 0$.

73. 011001001000000000100101001100, 11100101101111111101101011100; see (38).

74. By the lexicographic property, we want to count the number of rows whose rightmost elements have the respective forms $0*^{29}$, $10*^{28}$, $110*^{27}$, $111000*^{24}$, $11100100*^{22}$, $111001010*^{21}$, $11100101100*^{19}$, $111001011010*^{18}$, $1110010110110*^{17}$, ..., namely all 30-bit strings that precede $\tau = 11100101101111111101101011100$.

If θ has p more 1s than 0s, the number of Christmas tree rows ending with $\theta*^n$ is the same as the number of rows ending with 1^p*^n; and this is $M_{(p+1)n}$, by exercise 71, because all such rows are the n-step descendants of the starting row '$0^p\, 0^{p-1}1 \ldots 1^p$'.

Consequently the answer is $M_{0(29)} + M_{1(28)} + M_{2(27)} + M_{1(24)} + \cdots + M_{(12)3} +$
$M_{(13)2} = \sum_{k=1}^{21} M_{(2k-1-z_k)(n-z_k)} = 0 + \binom{28}{14} + \binom{27}{14} + \binom{27}{13} + \binom{24}{12} + \cdots + 8 + 4 = 84867708$, where $(z_1, \ldots, z_{21}) = (1, 2, 3, 6, \ldots, 27, 28)$ is the sequence of places where 1s occur in τ.

75. We have $r_1^{(n)} = M_{n-2}$, because row $r_1^{(n)}$ is the bottom descendant of the first row in (33). We also have $r_{j+1}^{(n)} - r_j^{(n)} = M_{j(n-1-j)} - M_{(j-1)(n-2-j)} = M_{(j+1)(n-2-j)}$

by the formula in answer 74, because the relevant sequence $z_1 \ldots z_{n-1}$ for row $r_j^{(n)}$ is $1^j 01^{n-1-j}$. Therefore, since $M_{jn}/M_n \to j$ for fixed j as $n \to \infty$, we have

$$\lim_{n \to \infty} \frac{r_j^{(n)}}{M_n} = \sum_{k=1}^{j} \frac{k}{2^{k+1}} = 1 - \frac{j+2}{2^{j+1}}.$$

And we've also implicitly proved that $\sum_{k=0}^{n} M_{k(n-k)} = M_{n+1} - 1$.

76. The first $\binom{2n}{n}$ elements of the infinite sequence

$Q = 131335131335133535571313351313351335355713133513353557133535573557779 \ldots$

are the row sizes in the pattern of order $2n$; this sequence $Q = q_1 q_2 q_3 \ldots$ is the unique fixed point of the transformation that maps $1 \mapsto 13$ and $n \mapsto (n-2)\,n\,n\,(n+2)$ for odd $n > 1$, representing two steps of (36).

Let $f(x) = \limsup_{n \to \infty} s(\lceil xM_n \rceil)/n$ for $0 < x \le 1$. This function apparently vanishes almost everywhere; but it equals 1 when x has the form $(q_1 + \cdots + q_j)/2^n$, because of answer 72. On the other hand if we define $g(x) = \lim_{n \to \infty} s(\lceil xM_n \rceil)/\sqrt{n}$, the function $g(x)$ appears to be measurable, with $\int_0^1 g(x)\,dx = \sqrt{\pi}$, although $g(x)$ is infinite when $f(x) > 0$. (Rigorous proofs or disproofs of these conjectures are solicited.)

77. The hint follows from (39), by considering worm walks; so we can proceed thus:

X1. [Initialize.] Set $a_j \leftarrow 0$ for $0 \le j \le n$; also set $x \leftarrow 1$. (In the following steps we will have $x = 1 + 2(a_1 + \cdots + a_n)$.)

X2. [Correct the tail.] While $x \le n$, set $a_x \leftarrow 1$ and $x \leftarrow x + 2$.

X3. [Visit.] Visit the bit string $a_1 \ldots a_n$.

X4. [Easy case?] If $a_n = 0$, set $a_n \leftarrow 1$, $x \leftarrow x + 2$, and return to X3.

X5. [Find and advance a_j.] Set $a_n \leftarrow 0$ and $j \leftarrow n - 1$. Then while $a_j = 1$, set $a_j \leftarrow 0$, $x \leftarrow x - 2$, and $j \leftarrow j - 1$. Stop if $j = 0$; otherwise set $a_j \leftarrow 1$ and go back to X2. ∎

78. True, by (39) and exercise 11.

79. (a) List the indices of the 0s, then the indices of the 1s; for instance, the bit string in exercise 73 corresponds to the permutation 1 4 5 7 8 10 11 12 13 20 23 25 29 30 2 3 6 9 14 15 16 17 18 19 21 22 24 26 27 28.

(b) Using the conventions of (39), the P tableau has the indices of left parentheses and free parentheses in its top row, other indices in the second row. Thus, from (38),

$$P = \begin{array}{|c|c|c|c|c|c|c|c|c|c|c|c|c|c|c|c|c|c|c|c|}
\hline
1 & 2 & 3 & 6 & 8 & 9 & 11 & 12 & 13 & 14 & 15 & 16 & 17 & 18 & 19 & 21 & 22 & 24 & 26 & 27 & 28 \\
\hline
4 & 5 & 7 & 10 & 20 & 23 & 25 & 29 & 30 \\
\cline{1-9}
\end{array}$$

[See K.-P. Vo, *SIAM J. Algebraic and Discrete Methods* **2** (1981), 324–332, for a generalization to chains of submultisets.]

80. This curious fact is a consequence of exercise 79 together with Theorem 6 in the author's paper on tableaux; see *Pacific J. Math.* **34** (1970), 709–727.

81. Suppose σ and σ' belong respectively to chains of length s and s' in the Christmas tree patterns of order n and n'. At most $\min(s, s')$ of the ss' pairs of strings in those chains can be in the biclutter. Furthermore, because of (39), those ss' pairs of strings actually constitute exactly $\min(s, s')$ chains in the Christmas tree pattern of order $n + n'$, when they are concatenated. Therefore the sum of $\min(s, s')$ over all pairs of chains is $M_{n+n'}$, and the result follows. We have incidentally proved the nonobvious identity

$$\sum_{j,k} \min(m+1-2j, n+1-2k) \, C_{j(m-j)} C_{k(n-k)} \; = \; M_{m+n}.$$

Notes: This extension of Sperner's theorem was proved independently by G. Katona [*Studia Sci. Math. Hungar.* **1** (1966), 59–63] and D. J. Kleitman [*Math. Zeitschrift* **90** (1965), 251–259]. See Greene and Kleitman, *J. Combinatorial Theory* **A20** (1976), 80–88, for the proof given here and for further results.

82. (a) There is at least one evaluation in each row m; there are two if and only if $s(m) > 1$ and the first evaluation yields 0. Thus if f is identically 1, we get the minimum, M_n; if f is identically 0, we get the maximum, $M_n + \sum_m [s(m) > 1] = M_{n+1}$.

   (b) Let $f(\chi(m, n/2)) = 0$ in the $C_{n/2}$ cases where $s(m) = 1$; otherwise let $f(\chi(m, a)) = 1$, where a is defined by the algorithm. When n is odd, this rule implies that $f(\sigma)$ is always 1; but when n is even, $f(\sigma) = 0$ if and only if σ is first in its row. (To see why, use the fact that the row containing σ'_j in (41) always has size $s - 2$.) This function f is indeed monotonic; for if $\sigma \leq \tau$ and if σ has a free left parenthesis, so does τ. For example, in the case $n = 8$ we have

$$f(x_1, \ldots, x_8) = x_8 \vee x_6 x_7 \vee x_4 x_5 (x_6 \vee x_7) \vee x_2 x_3 (x_4 (x_5 \vee x_6 \vee x_7) \vee x_5 (x_6 \vee x_7)).$$

   (c) In these circumstances (45) is the solution for all n.

83. At most 3 outcomes are possible in step H4 — in fact, at most 2 when $s(m) = 1$. [See exercise 5.3.4–31 for sharper bounds; in the notation of that exercise, there are exactly $\delta_n + 2$ monotone Boolean functions of n Boolean variables.]

84. For this problem we partition the 2^n bit strings into M_n blocks instead of chains, where the strings $\{\sigma_1, \ldots, \sigma_s\}$ of each block satisfy $\|A\sigma_i^T - A\sigma_j^T\| \geq 1$ for $i \neq j$; then at most one bit string per block can satisfy $\|A\sigma^T - b\| < \frac{1}{2}$.

   Let A' denote the first $n-1$ columns of A, and let v be the nth column. Suppose $\{\sigma_1, \ldots, \sigma_s\}$ is a block for A', and number the subscripts so that $v^T A' \sigma_1^T$ is the minimum of $v^T A' \sigma_j^T$. Then rule (36) defines appropriate blocks for A, because we have $\|A(\sigma_i 0)^T - A(\sigma_j 0)^T\| = \|A(\sigma_i 1)^T - A(\sigma_j 1)^T\| = \|A' \sigma_i^T - A' \sigma_j^T\|$ and

$$\|A(\sigma_j 1)^T - A(\sigma_1 0)^T\|^2 = \|A' \sigma_j^T + v - A' \sigma_1^T\|^2$$
$$= \|A'(\sigma_j - \sigma_1)^T\|^2 + \|v\|^2 + 2v^T A'(\sigma_j - \sigma_1)^T \geq \|v\|^2 \geq 1.$$

[And more is true; see *Advances in Math.* **5** (1970), 155–157. This result extends a theorem of J. E. Littlewood and A. C. Offord, *Mat. Sbornik* **54** (1943), 277–285, who considered the case $m = 2$.]

85. If V has dimension $n - m$, we can renumber the coordinates so that

$$\begin{matrix}
(1, & 0, & \ldots, & 0, & x_{11}, & \ldots, & x_{1m}) \\
(0, & 1, & \ldots, & 0, & x_{21}, & \ldots, & x_{2m}) \\
\vdots & \vdots & \ddots & \vdots & \vdots & & \vdots \\
(0, & 0, & \ldots, & 1, & x_{(n-m)1}, & \ldots, & x_{(n-m)m})
\end{matrix}$$

is a basis, with none of the row vectors $v_j = (x_{j1}, \ldots, x_{jm})$ entirely zero. Let $v_{n-m+1} = (-1, 0, \ldots, 0), \ldots, v_n = (0, 0, \ldots, -1)$. Then the number of 0–1 vectors in V is the number of 0–1 solutions to $Ax = 0$, where A is the $m \times n$ matrix with columns $v_1, \ldots, v_n$. But this quantity is at most the number of solutions to $\|Ax\| < \frac{1}{2} \min(\|v_1\|, \ldots, \|v_n\|)$, which is at most M_n by exercise 84.

Conversely, the basis with $m = 1$ and $x_{j1} = (-1)^{j-1}$ yields M_n solutions. [This result has application to electronic voting; see Golle's Ph.D. thesis (Stanford, 2004).]

86. First reorder the 4-node subtrees so that their level codes are 0121 (plus a constant); then sort larger and larger subtrees until everything is canonical. The resulting level codes are 0 1 2 3 4 3 2 1 2 3 2 1 2 0 1, and the parent pointers are 0 1 2 3 4 3 2 1 8 9 8 1 12 0 14.

87. (a) The condition holds if and only if $c_1 < \cdots < c_k \geq c_{k+1} \geq \cdots \geq c_n$ for some k, so the total number of cases is $\sum_k \binom{n-1}{n-k} = 2^{n-1}$.

(b) Note that $c_1 \ldots c_k = c'_1 \ldots c'_k$ if and only if $p_1 \ldots p_k = p'_1 \ldots p'_k$; and in such cases, $c_{k+1} < c'_{k+1}$ if and only if $p_{k+1} < p'_{k+1}$.

88. Exactly A_{n+1} forests are visited, and A_k of them have $p_k = \cdots = p_n = 0$. Therefore O4 is performed A_n times; and p_k is changed $A_{k+1} - 1$ times in step O5, for $1 \leq k < n$. Step O5 also changes p_n a total of $A_n - 1$ times. The average number of mems per visit is therefore only $2 + 3/(\alpha - 1) + O(1/n) \approx 3.534$, if we keep p_n in a register. [See E. Kubicka, *Combinatorics, Probability and Computing* **5** (1996), 403–417.]

89. If step O5 sets $p_n \leftarrow p_j$ exactly Q_n times, it sets $p_k \leftarrow p_j$ exactly $Q_k + A_{k+1} - A_k$ times, for $1 < k < n$, because every prefix of a canonical $p_1 \ldots p_n$ is canonical. We have $(Q_1, Q_2, \ldots) = (0, 0, 1, 2, 5, 9, 22, 48, 118, 288, \ldots)$; and one can show that $Q_n = \sum_{d \geq 1} \sum_{1 \leq c < n/d-1} a_{(n-cd)(n-cd-d)}$, where a_{nk} is the number of canonical parent sequences $p_1 \ldots p_n$ with $p_n = k$. But these numbers a_{nk} remain mysterious.

90. (a) This property is equivalent to 2.3.4.4–(7); vertex 0 is the centroid.

(b) Let $m = \lfloor n/2 \rfloor$. At the end of step O1, set $p_{m+1} \leftarrow 0$, and also $p_{2m+1} \leftarrow 0$ if n is odd. At the end of step O4, set $i \leftarrow j$ and while $p_i \neq 0$ set $i \leftarrow p_i$. (Then i is the root of the tree containing j and k.) At the beginning of step O5, if $k = i + m$ and $i < j$, set $j \leftarrow i$ and $d \leftarrow m$.

(c) If n is even, there are no bicentroidal trees with $n + 1$ vertices. Otherwise find all pairs $(p'_1 \ldots p'_m, p''_1 \ldots p''_m)$ of canonical forests on $m = \lfloor n/2 \rfloor$ nodes, with $p'_1 \ldots p'_m \geq p''_1 \ldots p''_m$; let $p_1 = 0$, $p_{j+1} = p'_j + 1$, and $p_{m+j+1} = (p''_j + m + 1)[p''_j > 0]$ for $1 \leq j \leq m$. (Two incarnations of Algorithm O will generate all such sequences. This algorithm for free trees is due to F. Ruskey and G. Li; see *SODA* **10** (1999), S939–S940.)

91. Use the following recursive procedure $W(n)$: If $n \leq 2$, return the unique n-node oriented tree. Otherwise choose positive integers j and d so that a given pair (j, d) is obtained with probability $dA_dA_{n-jd}/((n-1)A_n)$. Compute random oriented trees $T' \leftarrow W(n - jd)$ and $T'' \leftarrow W(d)$. Return the tree T obtained by linking j clones of T'' to the root of T'. [*Combinatorial Algorithms* (Academic Press, 1975), Chapter 25.]

92. Not always. [R. L. Cummins, in *IEEE Trans.* **CT-13** (1966), 82–90, proved that the graph of $S(G)$ always contains a cycle; see also C. A. Holzmann and F. Harary, *SIAM J. Applied Math.* **22** (1972), 187–193. But their constructions are unsuitable for efficient computation, because they require foreknowledge of the parity of the sizes of intermediate results.]

93. Yes. Step S7 undoes step S3; step S9 undoes the deletions of step S8.

94. For example, we can use depth-first search, with an auxiliary table $b_1 \ldots b_n$:

i) Set $b_1 \ldots b_n \leftarrow 0 \ldots 0$, then $v \leftarrow 1$, $w \leftarrow 1$, $b_1 \leftarrow 1$, and $k \leftarrow n - 1$.

ii) Set $e \leftarrow n_{v-1}$. While $t_e \neq 0$, do the following substeps:

   a) Set $u \leftarrow t_e$. If $b_u \neq 0$, go to substep (c).

   b) Set $b_u \leftarrow w$, $w \leftarrow u$, $a_k \leftarrow e$, $k \leftarrow k - 1$. Terminate if $k = 0$.

   c) Set $e \leftarrow n_e$.

iii) If $w \neq 1$, set $v \leftarrow w$, $w \leftarrow b_w$, and return to (ii). Otherwise report an error: The given graph was not connected.

We could actually terminate as soon as substep (b) reduces k to 1, since Algorithm S never looks at the initial value of a_1. But we might as well test for connectivity.

95. The following steps perform a breadth-first search from u, to see if v is reachable without using edge e. An auxiliary array $b_1 \ldots b_n$ of arc pointers is used, which should be initialized to $0 \ldots 0$ at the end of step S1; we will reset it to $0 \ldots 0$ again.

i) Set $w \leftarrow u$ and $b_w \leftarrow v$.
ii) Set $f \leftarrow n_{u-1}$. While $t_f \neq 0$, do the following substeps:
   a) Set $v' \leftarrow t_f$. If $b_{v'} \neq 0$, go to substep (d).
   b) If $v' \neq v$, set $b_{v'} \leftarrow v$, $b_w \leftarrow v'$, $w \leftarrow v'$, and go to substep (d).
   c) If $f \neq e \oplus 1$, go to step (v).
   d) Set $f \leftarrow n_f$.
iii) Set $u \leftarrow b_u$. If $u \neq v$, return to step (ii).
iv) Set $u \leftarrow t_e$. While $u \neq v$, set $w \leftarrow b_u$, $b_u \leftarrow 0$, $u \leftarrow w$. Go to S9 (e is a bridge).
v) Set $u \leftarrow t_e$. While $u \neq v$, set $w \leftarrow b_u$, $b_u \leftarrow 0$, $u \leftarrow w$. Then set $u \leftarrow t_e$ again and continue step S8 (e is not a bridge).

Two quick heuristics can be used before starting this calculation: If $d_u = 1$, then e is obviously a bridge; and if $l_{l_e} \neq 0$, then e is obviously a nonbridge (because there's another edge between u and v). Such special cases are detected readily by the breadth-first search, yet experiments by the author indicate that both heuristics are definitely worthwhile. For example, the test on l_{l_e} typically saves 3% or so of the total running time.

96. (a) Let e_k be the arc $k - 1 \to k$. The steps in answer 94 set $a_k \leftarrow e_{n+1-k}$ for $n > k \geq 1$. Then at level k we shrink e_{n-k}, for $1 \leq k < n - 1$. After visiting the (unique) spanning tree $e_{n-1} \ldots e_2 e_n$, we unshrink e_{n-k} and discover quickly that it is a bridge, for $n - 1 > k \geq 1$. Thus the running time is linear in n; in the author's implementation it turns out to be exactly $102n - 226$ mems for $n \geq 3$.

However, this result depends critically on the order of the edges in the initial spanning tree. If step S1 had produced "organ-pipe order" such as

$$e_{n/2+1} \, e_{n/2} \, e_{n/2+2} \, e_{n/2-1} \, \cdots \, e_{n-1} \, e_2$$

in positions $a_2 \ldots a_{n-1}$ when n is even, the running time would have been $\Omega(n^2)$, because $\Omega(n)$ of the bridge tests would each have taken $\Omega(n)$ steps.

(b) Now a_k is initially e_{n-k} for $n > k \geq 1$, where e_1 is the arc $n \to 1$. The spanning trees visited, when $n \geq 4$, are respectively $e_{n-2} \ldots e_1 e_n$, $e_{n-2} \ldots e_1 e_{n-1}$, $e_{n-2} \ldots e_2 e_{n-1} e_n$, $e_{n-2} \ldots e_3 e_{n-1} e_n e_1$, $\ldots$, $e_{n-1} e_n e_1 \ldots e_{n-3}$. Following the tree $e_{n-2} \ldots e_{k+2} e_{n-1} e_n e_1 \ldots e_k$ the computations move down to level $n - k - 3$ and up again, for $0 \leq k \leq n - 4$; the bridge tests are all efficient. Thus the total running time is quadratic (in the author's version, exactly $35.5n^2 + 7.5n - 145$ mems, for $n \geq 5$).

Incidentally, P_n is $board(n, 0, 0, 0, 1, 0, 0)$ in the notation of the Stanford GraphBase, and C_n is $board(n, 0, 0, 0, 1, 1, 0)$; the SGB vertices are named 0 through $n - 1$.

97. Yes, when $\{s, t\}$ is $\{1, 2\}$, $\{1, 3\}$, $\{2, 3\}$, $\{2, 4\}$, or $\{3, 4\}$, but not $\{1, 4\}$.

98. $A' = $; this is the "dual planar graph" of the planar graph A.

(The near trees of A' are complements of the spanning trees of A, and vice versa.)

99. The stated method works, by induction on the size of the tree, for essentially the same reasons that it worked for n-tuples in Section 7.2.1.1 — but with the additional proviso that we must successively designate each child of an uneasy node.

   Leaf nodes are always passive, and they are neither easy nor uneasy; so we will assume that the branch nodes are numbered 1 to m in preorder. Let $f_p = p$ for all branch nodes, except when p is a passive uneasy node for which the nearest uneasy node to its right is active; in the latter case, f_p should point to the nearest active uneasy node to its left. (For purposes of this definition, we imagine that artificial nodes 0 and $m+1$ are present at the left and right, both of which are uneasy and active.)

F1. [Initialize.] Set $f_p \leftarrow p$ for $0 \leq p \leq m$; also set $t_0 \leftarrow 1$, $v_0 \leftarrow 0$, and set each z_p so that $r_{z_p} = d_p$.

F2. [Select node p.] Set $q \leftarrow m$; then while $t_q = v_q$ set $q \leftarrow q - 1$. Set $p \leftarrow f_q$ and $f_q \leftarrow q$; terminate the algorithm if $p = 0$.

F3. [Change d_p.] Set $s \leftarrow d_p$, $s' \leftarrow r_s$, $k \leftarrow v_p$, and $d_p \leftarrow s'$. (Now $k = v_s \neq v_{s'}$.)

F4. [Update the values.] Set $q \leftarrow s$ and $v_q \leftarrow k \oplus 1$. While $d_q \neq 0$, set $q \leftarrow d_q$ and $v_q \leftarrow k \oplus 1$. (Now q is a leaf that has entered the config if $k = 0$, left it if $k = 1$.) Similarly, set $q \leftarrow s'$ and $v_q \leftarrow k$. While $d_q \neq 0$, set $q \leftarrow d_q$ and $v_q \leftarrow k$. (Now q is a leaf that has left the config if $k = 0$, entered it if $k = 1$.)

F5. [Visit.] Visit the current config, represented by all the leaf values.

F6. [Passivate p?] (All uneasy nodes to p's right are now active.) If $d_p \neq z_p$, return to step F2. Otherwise set $z_p \leftarrow s$, $q \leftarrow p - 1$; while $t_q = v_q$, set $q \leftarrow q - 1$. (Now q is the first uneasy node to the left of p; we will make p passive.) Set $f_p \leftarrow f_q$, $f_q \leftarrow q$, and return to F2. ▮

Although step F4 may change uneasy nodes to easy nodes and vice versa, the focus pointers need not be updated, because they're still set correctly.

100. A complete program, called GRAYSPSPAN, appears on the author's website. Its asymptotic efficiency can be proved by using the result of exercise 110 below.

102. If so, ordinary spanning trees can be listed in a *strong revolving-door order*, where the edges that enter and leave at each step are adjacent.

   Interesting algorithms to generate all the oriented spanning trees with a given root have been developed by Harold N. Gabow and Eugene W. Myers, *SICOMP* **7** (1978), 280–287; S. Kapoor and H. Ramesh, *Algorithmica* **27** (2000), 120–130.

103. (a) Toppling increases $(x_0, x_1, \ldots, x_n)$ lexicographically, but does not change $x_0 + \cdots + x_n$. If we can topple at both V_i and V_j, either order gives the same result.

   (b) Adding a grain of sand changes the 16 stable states as follows:

Given 0000 0001 0010 0011 0100 0101 0110 0111 1000 1001 1010 1011 1100 1101 1110 1111
+ 0001 0001 0010 0011 0001 0101 0110 0111 0101 1001 1010 1011 1001 1101 1110 1111 1101
+ 0010 0010 0011 0001 0010 0110 0111 0101 0110 1010 1011 1001 1010 1110 1111 1101 1110
+ 0100 0100 0101 0110 0111 1000 1001 1010 1011 1100 1101 1110 1111 0100 0101 0110 0111
+ 1000 1000 1001 1010 1011 1100 1101 1110 1111 0100 0101 0110 0111 1000 1001 1010 1011

The recurrent states are the nine cases with $x_1 + x_2 > 0$ and $x_3 + x_4 > 0$. Notice that repeated addition of 0001 leads to the infinite cycle 0000 → 0001 → 0010 → 0011 → 0001 → 0010 → ⋯; but the states 0001, 0010, and 0011 are *not* recurrent.

   (c) If $x = \sigma(x + t)$ then also $x = \sigma(x + kt)$ for all $k \geq 0$. All components of t are positive; thus $x = \sigma(x + \max(d_1, \ldots, d_n)t)$ is recurrent. Conversely, suppose

$x = \sigma(d + y)$, where all $y_i \geq 0$; then $d + y + t$ topples to $x + t$ and it also topples to $\sigma(d) + y + t = d + y$. Therefore $\sigma(x + t) = \sigma(d + y) = x$.

(d) There are $N = \det(a_{ij})$ classes, because elementary row operations (exercise 4.6.1–19) triangularize the matrix while preserving congruence.

(e) There are nonnegative integers $m_1, \ldots, m_n, m_1', \ldots, m_n'$ such that

$$x + m_1 a_1 + \cdots + m_n a_n = x' + m_1' a_1 + \cdots + m_n' a_n = y, \text{ say.}$$

For sufficiently large k, the vector $y + kt$ topples in $m_1 + \cdots + m_n$ steps to $x + kt$, and in $m_1' + \cdots + m_n'$ steps to $x' + kt$. Therefore $x = \sigma(x + kt) = \sigma(x' + kt) = x'$.

(f) The triangularization in (d) shows that $x \equiv x + Ny$ for arbitrary vectors y. And toppling preserves congruence; hence every class contains a recurrent state.

(g) Since $a = a_1 + \cdots + a_n$ in a balanced digraph, we have $x \equiv x + a$. If x is recurrent, we see in fact that every vertex topples exactly once when $x + a$ reduces to x, because the vectors $\{a_1, \ldots, a_n\}$ are linearly independent.

Conversely, if $\sigma(x + a) = x$ we must prove that x is recurrent. Let $z_m = \sigma(ma)$; there must be some positive k and m with $z_{m+k} = z_m$. Then every vertex topples k times when $z_m + ka$ reduces to z_m; hence there are vectors $y_j = (y_{j1}, \ldots, y_{jn})$ with $y_{jj} \geq d_j$ such that $(m + k)a$ topples to y_j. It follows that $x + n(m + k)a$ topples to $x + y_1 + \cdots + y_n$, and $\sigma(x + y_1 + \cdots + y_n) = \sigma(x + n(m + k)a) = x$.

(h) Treating subscripts cyclically, the spanning trees with arcs $V_j \to V_0$ for $j = i_1$, $\ldots, i_k$ have $n - k$ other arcs: $V_j \to V_{j-1}$ for $i_l < j \leq i_l + q_l$ and $V_j \to V_{j+1}$ for $i_l + q_l < j < i_{l+1}$. The recurrent states, similarly, have $x_j = 2$ for $j = i_1, \ldots, i_k$, and $x_j = 1$ for $i_l < j < i_{l+1}$, except that $x_j = 0$ when $j = i_l + q_l$ and $q_l > 0$.

(i) In this case state $x = (x_1, \ldots, x_n)$ is recurrent if and only if $(n - x_1, \ldots, n - x_n)$ solves the parking problem in the hint, because $t = (1, \ldots, 1)$, and a sequence that doesn't get parked leaves a "hole" that stops $x + t$ from toppling to x.

Notes: This sandpile model, introduced by Deepak Dhar [*Phys. Review Letters* **64** (1990), 1613–1616], has led to many papers in the physics literature. Dhar noted that, if M grains of sand are introduced at random, each recurrent state is equally probable as $M \to \infty$. The present exercise was inspired by the work of R. Cori and D. Rossin, *European J. Combinatorics* **21** (2000), 447–459.

Sandpile theory proves that every digraph D yields an abelian group whose elements correspond somehow to the oriented spanning trees of D with root V_0. In particular, the same is true when D is an ordinary graph, with arcs $u \to v$ and $v \to u$ whenever u and v are adjacent. Thus, for example, we can "add" two spanning trees; and some spanning tree can be regarded as "zero." An elegant correspondence between spanning trees and recurrent states, in the special case when D is an ordinary graph, has been found by R. Cori and Y. Le Borgne, *Advances in Applied Math.* **30** (2003), 44–52. But no simple correspondence is known for general digraphs D. For example, suppose $n = 2$ and $(e_{10}, e_{12}, e_{20}, e_{21}) = (p, q, r, s)$; then there are $pr + ps + qr$ oriented trees, and the recurrent states correspond to generalized two-dimensional toruses as in exercise 7–137. Yet even in the "balanced" case, when $p + q \geq s$ and $r + s \geq q$, no easy mapping between spanning trees and recurrent states is apparent.

104. (a) If $\det(\alpha I - C) = 0$, there is a vector $x = (x_1, \ldots, x_n)^T$ such that $Cx = \alpha x$ and $\max(x_1, \ldots, x_n) = x_m = 1$ for some m. Then $\alpha = \alpha x_m = c_{mm} - \sum_{j \neq m} e_{mj} x_j \geq c_{mm} - \sum_{j \neq m} e_{mj} = 0$. (Incidentally, a real symmetric matrix whose eigenvalues are nonnegative is called *positive semidefinite*. Our proof establishes the well-known fact that any real symmetric matrix with $c_{mm} \geq |\sum_{j \neq m} c_{mj}|$ for $1 \leq m \leq n$ has this property.) Thus $\alpha_0 \geq 0$; and $\alpha_0 = 0$ because $C(1, \ldots, 1)^T = (0, \ldots, 0)^T$.

(b) $\det(xI - C(G)) = x(x - \alpha_1) \ldots (x - \alpha_{n-1})$; and the coefficient of x is $(-1)^{n-1}n$ times the number of spanning trees, by the matrix tree theorem.

(c) $\det(\alpha I - C(K_n)) = \det((\alpha - n)I + J) = (\alpha - n)^{n-1}\alpha$ by exercise 1.2.3–36; here J is the matrix of all 1s. The aspects are therefore $0, n, \ldots, n$.

105. (a) If $e_{ij} = a + be'_{ij}$ we have $C(G) = naI - aJ + bC(G')$. And if C is any matrix whose row sums are zero, the identity

$$\det(xI + yJ - zC) = \frac{x + ny}{x} z^n \det((x/z)I - C)$$

can be proved by adding columns 2 through n to column 1, factoring out $(x + ny)/x$, subtracting y/x times column 1 from columns 2 through n, then subtracting columns 2 through n from column 1. Therefore, by setting $x = \alpha - na$, $y = a$, $z = b$, $a = 1$, and $b = -1$, we find that G has the aspects $0, n - \alpha_{n-1}, \ldots, n - \alpha_1$. (In particular, this result agrees with exercise 104(c) when G' is the empty graph $\overline{K_n}$.)

(b) Sort $\{\alpha'_0, \ldots, \alpha'_{n'-1}, \alpha''_0, \ldots, \alpha''_{n''-1}\}$ into order. (An easy case, for variety.)

(c) Here $\overline{G} = \overline{G'} \oplus \overline{G''}$, so G's aspects are $\{0, n' + n'', n'' + \alpha'_1, \ldots, n'' + \alpha'_{n'-1}, n' + \alpha''_1, \ldots, n' + \alpha''_{n''-1}\}$ by (a) and (b). (In particular, G is $K_{m,n}$ when $G' = \overline{K_m}$ and $G'' = \overline{K_n}$, hence the aspects of $K_{m,n}$ are $\{0, (n-1) \cdot m, (m-1) \cdot n, m+n\}$.)

(d) $C(G) = I_{n'} \otimes C(G'') + C(G') \otimes I_{n''}$, where I_n denotes the $n \times n$ identity matrix and $\otimes$ denotes the direct product of matrices. The aspects of $C(G)$ are $\{\alpha'_j + \alpha''_k \mid 0 \leq j < n', 0 \leq k < n''\}$; for if A and B are arbitrary matrices whose eigenvalues are $\{\lambda_1, \ldots, \lambda_m\}$ and $\{\mu_1, \ldots, \mu_n\}$, respectively, the eigenvalues of $A \otimes I_n + I_m \otimes B$ are the mn sums $\lambda_j + \mu_k$. *Proof:* Choose S and T so that $S^- A S$ and $T^- B T$ are triangular. Then use the matrix identity $(A \otimes B)(C \otimes D) = AC \otimes BD$ to show that $(S \otimes T)^-(A \otimes I_n + I_m \otimes B)(S \otimes T) = (S^- A S) \otimes I_n + I_m \otimes (T^- B T)$. (In particular, repeated use of this formula shows that the aspects of the n-cube are $\{\binom{n}{0} \cdot 0, \binom{n}{1} \cdot 2, \ldots, \binom{n}{n} \cdot 2n\}$, and Eq. (57) follows from exercise 104(b).)

(e) When G is a regular graph of degree d, its aspects are $\alpha_j = d - \lambda_{j+1}$, where $\lambda_1 \geq \cdots \geq \lambda_n$ are the eigenvalues of the adjacency matrix $A = (a_{ij})$. The adjacency matrix of G' is $A' = B^T B - d' I_{n'}$, where $B = (b_{ij})$ is the $n \times n'$ incidence matrix with entries $b_{ij} = [\text{edge } i \text{ touches vertex } j]$, and where $n = n'd'/2$ is the number of edges. The adjacency matrix of G is $A = BB^T - 2I_n$. Now we have

$$x^n \det(xI_{n'} - B^T B) = x^{n'} \det(xI_n - BB^T);$$

this identity follows from the fact that the coefficients of $\det(xI - A)$ can be expressed in terms of $\text{trace}(A^k)$ for $k = 1, 2, \ldots$, via Newton's identities (exercise 1.2.9–10). So the aspects of G are the same as those of G', plus $n - n'$ aspects equal to $2d'$. [This result is due to E. B. Vakhovsky, *Sibirskiĭ Mat. Zhurnal* **6** (1965), 44–49; see also H. Sachs, *Wissenschaftliche Zeitschrift der Technischen Hochschule Ilmenau* **13** (1967), 405–412.]

(f) $A = A' \otimes A''$, so the aspects are $\{d'\alpha'_j + d'\alpha''_k - \alpha'_j\alpha''_k \mid 0 \leq j < n', 0 \leq k < n''\}$.

(g) $A(G) = I_{n'} \otimes A'' + A' \otimes I_{n''} + A' \otimes A'' = (I_{n'} + A') \otimes (I_{n''} + A'') - I_n$ yields the aspects $\{(d'' + 1)\alpha'_j + (d' + 1)\alpha''_k - \alpha'_j\alpha''_k \mid 0 \leq j < n', 0 \leq k < n''\}$.

(h) When G' is regular, we can make $S^- A' S$ a diagonal matrix with entries $d' - \alpha'_j$, while simultaneously $S^- J_{n'} S$ is a diagonal matrix with entries $(n', 0, \ldots, 0)$, because $(1, \ldots, 1)^T$ is an eigenvector of both A' and $J_{n'}$. Thus, by the formula of answer 7–96(c), the aspects turn out to be $\{d + (d' - \alpha'_j n'[j = 0])(d'' - \alpha''_k) + (d' - \alpha'_j)(d'' - \alpha''_k - n''[k = 0]) \mid 0 \leq j < n', 0 \leq k < n''\}$, where $d = d'(n'' - d'') + (n' - d')d''$.

(i) A similar argument yields the scaled aspects $\{n''\alpha'_j \mid 0 \le j < n'\}$ of G', together with n' copies of shifted aspects $\{d'n'' + \alpha''_k \mid 1 \le k < n''\}$ of G''.

106. (a) If α is an aspect of the path P_n, there's a nonzero solution $(x_0, x_1, \ldots, x_{n+1})$ to the equations $\alpha x_k = 2x_k - x_{k-1} - x_{k+1}$ for $1 \le k \le n$, with $x_0 = x_1$ and $x_n = x_{n+1}$. If we set $x_k = \cos(2k-1)\theta$, we find $x_0 = x_1$ and $2x_k - x_{k-1} - x_{k+1} = 2x_k - (2\cos 2\theta)x_k$; hence $2 - 2\cos 2\theta = 4\sin^2\theta$ will be an aspect if we choose θ so that $x_n = x_{n+1}$ and so that the x's are not all zero. Thus the aspects of P_n turn out to be $\sigma_{0n}, \ldots, \sigma_{(n-1)n}$.

We must have $\alpha_1 \ldots \alpha_{n-1} = n$, by exercise 104(b), since $c(P_n) = 1$; therefore

$$c(P_m \,\square\, P_n) = \prod_{j=1}^{m-1} \prod_{k=1}^{n-1} (\sigma_{jm} + \sigma_{kn}).$$

(b, c) Similarly, if α is an aspect of the cycle C_n, there's a nonzero solution to the stated equations with $x_n = x_0$. For this case we try $x_k = \cos 2k\theta$ and find solutions when $\theta = j\pi/n$ for $0 \le j < \lceil n/2 \rceil$. And $x_k = \sin k\theta$ gives further, linearly independent solutions for $\lceil n/2 \rceil \le j < n$. The aspects of C_n are therefore $\sigma_{0n}, \sigma_{2n}, \ldots, \sigma_{(2n-2)n}$; and we have

$$c(P_m \,\square\, C_n) = n \prod_{j=1}^{m-1} \prod_{k=1}^{n-1} (\sigma_{jm} + \sigma_{(2k)n}), \quad c(C_m \,\square\, C_n) = mn \prod_{j=1}^{m-1} \prod_{k=1}^{n-1} (\sigma_{(2j)m} + \sigma_{(2k)n}).$$

Let $f_n(x) = (x + \sigma_{1n}) \ldots (x + \sigma_{(n-1)n})$ and $g_n(x) = (x + \sigma_{2n}) \ldots (x + \sigma_{(2n-2)n})$. These polynomials have integer coefficients; indeed, $f_n(x) = U_{n-1}(x/2+1)$ and $g_n(x) = 2(T_n(x/2 + 1) - 1)/x$, where $T_n(x)$ and $U_n(x)$ are the Chebyshev polynomials defined by $T_n(\cos\theta) = \cos n\theta$ and $U_n(\cos\theta) = (\sin(n+1)\theta)/\sin\theta$. The calculation of $c(P_m \,\square\, P_n)$ can be reduced to the evaluation of an $m \times m$ determinant, because it is the resultant of $f_m(x)$ with $f_n(-x)$; see exercise 4.6.1–12. Similarly, $\frac{1}{n}c(P_m \,\square\, C_n)$ and $\frac{1}{mn}c(C_m \,\square\, C_n)$ are the respective resultants of $f_m(x)$ with $g_n(-x)$ and of $g_m(x)$ with $g_n(-x)$.

Let $\alpha_n(x) = \prod_{d \setminus n} f_d(x)^{\mu(n/d)}$; thus $\alpha_1(x) = 1$, $\alpha_2(x) = x + 2$, $\alpha_3(x) = (x+3) \times (x+1)$, $\alpha_4(x) = x^2 + 4x + 2$, $\alpha_5(x) = (x^2 + 5x + 5)(x^2 + 3x + 1)$, $\alpha_6(x) = x^2 + 4x + 1$, etc. By considering so-called field polynomials one can show that $\alpha_n(x)$ is irreducible over the integers when n is even, otherwise it is the product of two irreducible factors of the same degree. Similarly, if $\beta_n(x) = \prod_{d \setminus n} g_d(x)^{\mu(n/d)}$, it turns out that $\beta_n(x)$ is the square of an irreducible polynomial when $n \ge 3$. These facts account for the presence of fairly small prime factors in the results. For example, the largest prime factor in $c(P_m \,\square\, P_n)$ for $m \le n \le 10$ is 1009; it occurs only in the resultant of $\alpha_6(x)$ with $\alpha_9(-x)$, which is $662913 = 3^2 \cdot 73 \cdot 1009$.

107. There are $(1, 1, 2, 6, 21)$ nonisomorphic graphs for $n = (1, \ldots, 5)$; but we need consider only cases with $\le \frac{1}{2}\binom{n}{2}$ edges, because of exercise 105(a). The surviving cases when $n = 4$ are free trees: The star is the complement of $K_1 \oplus K_3$, with aspects 0, 1, 1, 4; and P_4 has aspects $0, 2 - \sqrt{2}, 2, 2 + \sqrt{2}$ by exercise 106. There are three free trees when $n = 5$: The star has aspects 0, 1, 1, 1, 5; P_5's aspects are $0, 2 - \phi, 3 - \phi, 1 + \phi, 2 + \phi$; and the aspects of ∘–∘–∘–∘ are $0, r_1, 1, r_2, r_3$, where $(r_1, r_2, r_3) \approx (0.52, 2.31, 4.17)$ are the roots of $x^3 - 7x^2 + 13x - 5 = 0$.

Finally, there are five cases with a single cycle: ⋈ is $K_1 — (K_2 \oplus \overline{K_2})$, so its aspects are 0, 1, 1, 3, 5; C_5 has aspects $0, 3 - \phi, 3 - \phi, 2 + \phi, 2 + \phi$; ∘–∘–∘–∘ has aspects $0, r_1, r_2, 3, r_3$; its complement ∘⋈∘–∘ has aspects $0, 5 - r_3, 2, 5 - r_2, 5 - r_1$; and the aspects of ∘–⋈–∘ turn out to be $0, (5 - \sqrt{13})/2, 3 - \phi, 2 + \phi, (5 + \sqrt{13})/2$.

108. Given a digraph D on vertices $\{V_1, \ldots, V_n\}$, let e_{ij} be the number of arcs from V_i to V_j. Define $C(D)$ and its aspects as before. Since $C(D)$ is not necessarily symmetric, the aspects are no longer guaranteed to be real. But if α is an aspect, so is its complex conjugate $\bar{\alpha}$; and if we order the aspects by their real parts, again we find $\alpha_0 = 0$. The formula $c(D) = \alpha_1 \ldots \alpha_{n-1}/n$ remains valid if we now interpret $c(D)$ as the *average* number of *oriented* spanning trees, taken over all n possible roots V_j. The aspects of the transitive tournament $\vec{K_n}$, whose arcs are $V_i \to V_j$ for $1 \le i < j \le n$, are obviously $0, 1, \ldots, n-1$; and those of its subgraphs are equally obvious.

The derivations in parts (a)–(d) of answer 105 carry over without change. For example, consider $K_1\!\!-\!\!\vec{K_3}$, which has aspects $0, 2, 3, 4$; this digraph D has $(2, 4, 6, 12)$ oriented spanning trees with the four possible roots, and $c(D)$ is indeed equal to $2 \cdot 3 \cdot 4 / 4$. Notice also that the digraph $\circ\!\!-\!\!\!\!\leftarrow\!\!\!\bigcirc\!\!\!\circ$ is its own complement, and that it has the same aspects as $\vec{K_3}$.

Directed graphs also admit another family of interesting operations: If D' and D'' are digraphs on disjoint sets of vertices V' and V'', consider adding a arcs $v' \to v''$ and b arcs $v'' \to v'$ whenever $v' \in V'$ and $v'' \in V''$. By manipulating determinants as in answer 105(a), we can show that the resulting digraph has aspects $\{0, an'' + bn', an'' + \alpha'_1, \ldots, an'' + \alpha'_{n'-1}, bn' + \alpha''_1, \ldots, bn' + \alpha''_{n''-1}\}$. In the special case $a = 1$ and $b = 0$, we can conveniently denote the new digraph by $D' \to D''$; thus, for example, $\vec{K_n} = K_1 \to \vec{K_{n-1}}$. The digraph $K_{n_1} \to K_{n_2} \to \cdots \to K_{n_m}$ on $n_1 + n_2 + \cdots + n_m$ vertices has aspects $\{0, n_m \cdot s_m, \ldots, n_2 \cdot s_2, (n_1-1) \cdot s_1\}$, where $s_k = n_k + \cdots + n_m$.

The aspects of the oriented path $\vec{P_n}$ from V_1 to V_n are obviously $0, 1, \ldots, 1$. The oriented cycle $\vec{C_n}$ has aspects $\{0, 1 - \omega, \ldots, 1 - \omega^{n-1}\}$, where $\omega = e^{2\pi i/n}$.

There is also a nice result for arc digraphs: The aspects of D^* are obtained from those of D by simply adding $\tau_k - 1$ copies of the number σ_k, for $1 \le k \le n$, where τ_k is the in-degree of V_k and σ_k is its out-degree. (If $\tau_k = 0$, we *remove* one aspect equal to σ_k.) The proof is similar to, but simpler than, the derivation in answer 2.3.4.2–21.

Historical remarks: The results in exercises 104(b) and 105(a) are due to A. K. Kelmans, *Avtomatika i Telemekhanika* **26** (1965), 2194–2204; **27**, 2 (February 1966), 56–65; English translation in *Automation and Remote Control* **26** (1965), 2118–2129; **27** (1966), 233–241. Miroslav Fiedler [*Czech. Math. J.* **23** (1973), 298–305] introduced exercise 105(d), and proved interesting results about the aspect α_1, which he called the "algebraic connectivity" of G. Germain Kreweras, in *J. Combinatorial Theory* **B24** (1978), 202–212, enumerated spanning trees on grids, cylinders, and toruses, as well as oriented spanning trees on directed toruses such as $\vec{C_m} \,\square\, \vec{C_n}$. An excellent survey of graph aspects was published by Bojan Mohar in *Graph Theory, Combinatorics and Applications* (Wiley, 1991), 871–898; *Discrete Math.* **109** (1992), 171–183. For a thorough discussion of important families of graph eigenvalues and their properties, including a comprehensive bibliography, see *Spectra of Graphs* by D. M. Cvetković, M. Doob, and H. Sachs, third edition (1995).

109. Perhaps there is also a sandpile-related reason; see exercise 103.

110. By induction: Suppose there are $k \ge 1$ parallel edges between u and v. Then $c(G) = kc(G_1) + c(G_2)$, where G_1 is G with u and v identified, and G_2 is G with those k edges removed. Let $d_u = k + a$ and $d_v = k + b$.

Case 1: G_2 is connected. Then $ab > 0$, so we can write $a = x + 1$ and $b = y + 1$. We have $c(G_1) > \alpha\sqrt{x + y + 1}$ and $c(G_2) > \alpha\sqrt{xy}$, where α is a product over the other $n - 2$ vertices; and it is easy to verify that

$$k\sqrt{x + y + 1} + \sqrt{xy} \ge \sqrt{(x + k)(y + k)}.$$

Case 2: There are no such u and v for which G_2 is connected. Then every multi-edge of G is a bridge; in other words, G is a free tree except for parallel edges. In this case the result is trivial if there's a vertex of degree 1. Otherwise suppose u is an endpoint, with $d_u = k$ edges $u \text{ --- } v$. If $d_v > k + 1$, we have $\underline{c(G) = kc(G_1) > \alpha k\sqrt{x}}$ where $d_v = k + 1 + x$, and it is easy to check that $k\sqrt{x} > \sqrt{(k-1)(k+x)}$ when $x > 0$. If $d_v = k$ we have $c(G) = k > \sqrt{(k-1)^2}$. Finally if $d_v = k + 1$, let $v_0 = u$, $v_1 = v$, and consider the unique path $v_1 \text{ --- } v_2 \text{ --- } \cdots \text{ --- } v_r$ where $r > 1$ and v_r has degree greater than 2; only one edge joins v_j to v_{j+1} for $1 \le j < r$. Again the induction goes through.

[Other lower bounds on the number of spanning trees have been derived by A. V. Kostochka, *Random Structures & Algorithms* **6** (1995), 269–274.]

111. 2 1 5 4 11 7 9 8 6 10 15 12 14 13 3.

112. Either p appears on an even level and is an ancestor of q, or q appears on an odd level and is an ancestor of p.

113. prepostorder(F^R)=postpreorder$(F)^R$ and postpreorder(F^R)=prepostorder$(F)^R$.

114. The most elegant approach, considering that the forest might be empty, is to set things up so that CHILD(Λ) points to the root of the leftmost tree, if any. Then initiate the first visit by setting $\text{Q} \leftarrow \Lambda$, $\text{L} \leftarrow -1$, and going to step Q6.

115. Suppose there are n_e nodes on even levels and n_o nodes on odd levels, and that n_e' of the even-level nodes are nonleaves. Then steps (Q1,...,Q7) are performed respectively $(n_e + n_o, n_o, n_e', n_e, n_e', n_o + 1, n_e)$ times, including one execution of Q6 because of answer 114.

116. (a) This result follows from Algorithm Q.

(b) In fact, non-ordinary nodes strictly alternate between lucky and unlucky, beginning and ending with a lucky one. *Proof:* Consider the forest F' obtained by deleting the leftmost leaf of F, and use induction on n.

117. Such forests are precisely those whose left-child/right-sibling representation is a degenerate binary tree (exercise 31). So the answer is 2^{n-1}.

118. (a) t^{k-2}, for $k > 1$; luckiness occurs only near extreme leaves.

(b) An interesting recurrence leads to the solution $(F_k + 1 - (k + 1) \bmod 3)/2$.

119. Label each node x with the value $v(x) = \sum\{\, 2^k \mid k$ is an arc label on the path from the root to $x\}$. Then the node values in prepostorder are exactly the Gray binary code Γ_n, because exercise 113 shows that they satisfy recurrence 7.2.1.1–(5).

(If we apply the same value labeling to the ordinary binomial tree T_n and traverse it in preorder, we simply get the integers $0, 1, \ldots, 2^n - 1$.)

120. False: Only four of the "hollow" vertices in the illustration can appear next to the two "square" vertices, in a Hamiltonian cycle; one hollow pair is therefore out of luck. [See H. Fleischner and H. V. Kronk, *Monatshefte für Mathematik* **76** (1972), 112–117.]

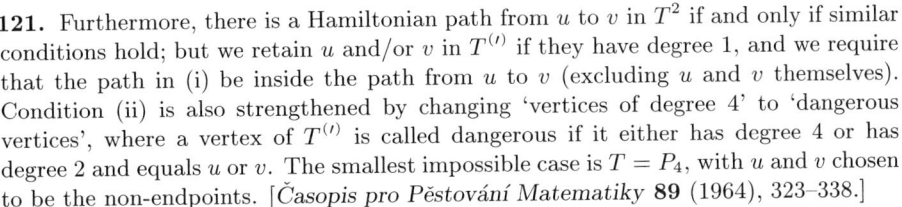

121. Furthermore, there is a Hamiltonian path from u to v in T^2 if and only if similar conditions hold; but we retain u and/or v in $T^{(\prime)}$ if they have degree 1, and we require that the path in (i) be inside the path from u to v (excluding u and v themselves). Condition (ii) is also strengthened by changing 'vertices of degree 4' to 'dangerous vertices', where a vertex of $T^{(\prime)}$ is called dangerous if it either has degree 4 or has degree 2 and equals u or v. The smallest impossible case is $T = P_4$, with u and v chosen to be the non-endpoints. [*Časopis pro Pěstování Matematiky* **89** (1964), 323–338.]

Consequently T^2 contains a Hamiltonian cycle if and only if T is a *caterpillar*, namely a free tree whose derivative is a path. [See Frank Harary and A. J. Schwenk, *Mathematika* **18** (1971), 138–140.]

122. (a) We can represent an expression by a binary tree, with operators at the internal nodes and digits at the external nodes. If binary trees are implemented as in Algorithm B, the essential constraint imposed by the given grammar is that, if $r_j = k > 0$, then the operator at node j is $+$ or $-$ if and only if the operator at node k is $\times$ or $/$. Therefore the total number of possibilities for a tree with n leaves is $2^n S_{n-1}$, where S_n is a Schröder number; namely 10,646,016 when $n = 9$. (See exercise 66, but interchange left with right.) We can rather quickly generate them all, encountering exactly 1641 solutions. Only one expression, namely $1 + 2/((3-4)/(5+6) - (7-8)/9)$, does the job with no multiplications; twenty of them, such as $(((1-2)/((3/4) \times 5 - 6)) \times 7 + 8) \times 9$, require five pairs of parentheses; only 15 require no parentheses whatever.

(b) Now there are $1 + \sum_{k=1}^{8} \binom{8}{k} 2^{k+1} S_k = 23{,}463{,}169$ cases, and 3366 solutions. The shortest, of length 12, was found by Dudeney [*The Weekly Dispatch* (18 June 1899)], namely $123 - 45 - 67 + 89$; but he wasn't sure at the time that it was best. The longest solutions have length 27; there are twenty of them, as mentioned above.

(c) The number of cases rises dramatically to $2 + \sum_{k=1}^{8} \binom{8}{k} 4^{k+1} S_k = 8{,}157{,}017{,}474$, and there now are 97,221 solutions. The longest, which is unique, has length 40: $((((.1/(.2 + .3))/.4)/.5)/(.6 - .7))/(.8 - .9)$. There are five amusing examples such as $.1 + (2 + 3 + 4 + 5) \times 6 + 7 + 8 + .9$, with seven $+$'s; furthermore, there are ten like $(1 - .2 - .3 - 4 - .5 - 6) \times (7 - 8 - 9)$, with seven $-$'s.

> *There is in fact very little principle in the thing,*
> *and there is no certain way of demonstrating*
> *that we have got the best possible solution.*
> — HENRY E. DUDENEY (1899)

Notes: Marie Leske's *Illustriertes Spielbuch für Mädchen*, first published in 1864, contained the earliest known appearance of such a problem; in the eleventh edition (1889), the fact that $100 = 1 + 2 + 3 + 4 + 5 + 6 + 7 + 8 \times 9$ was the solution to puzzle 16 in section 553. See also the references in exercise 7.2.1.1–111.

Richard Bellman explained in *AMM* **69** (1962), 640–643, how to handle the special case of part (a) in which the operators are restricted to be either $+$ and $\times$, without parentheses. His technique of dynamic programming can be used also in this more general problem to reduce the number of cases being considered. The idea is to determine the rational numbers obtainable from every subinterval of the digits $\{1, \ldots, n\}$, having a given operator at the root of the tree. We can also save a good deal of computation by discarding cases for the subintervals $\{1, \ldots, 8\}$ and $\{2, \ldots, 9\}$ that cannot lead to integer solutions. In this way the number of essentially different trees to consider is reduced to (a) 2,735,136 cases; (b) 6,813,760; (c) 739,361,319.

Floating point arithmetic is unreliable in this application. But the exact rational arithmetic routines of Section 4.5.1 do the job nicely, never needing to work with an integer greater than 10^9 in absolute value.

123. (a) 2284; but $2284 = (1 + 2 \times 3) \times (4 + 5 \times 67) - 89$. (b) 6964; but $6964 = (1/.2) \times 34 + 5 + 6789$. (c) 14786; but $14786 = -1 + 2 \times (.3 + 4 + 5) \times (6 + 789)$. [If we allow also a minus sign at the left of the expression, as Dudeney did, we actually obtain 1362, 2759, and 85597 additional solutions to problems 122(a), (b), and (c), including nineteen longer expressions in case (a) such as $-(1-2) \times ((3+4) \times (5 - (6-7) \times 8) + 9$.

With such an extension, the smallest unreachable numbers in the present problem become (a) 3802, (b) 8312, and (c) 17722.] The total number of representable integers (positive, negative, or zero) turns out to be (a) 27,666; (b) 136,607; (c) 200,765.

124. Horton–Strahler numbers originated in studies of river flows: R. E. Horton, *Bull. Geol. Soc. Amer.* **56** (1945), 275–370; A. N. Strahler, *Bull. Geol. Soc. Amer.* **63** (1952), 1117–1142. Many tree-drawing ideas are explored and illustrated in a classic paper by Viennot, Eyrolles, Janey, and Arquès, *Computer Graphics* **23**, 3 (July 1989), 31–40.

SECTION 7.2.1.7

1. Perhaps under hexagram 21, "crunching" (▤); however, the ancient commentators related this hexagram more to law enforcement than to the interaction of electrons.

2. (a) For the first nucleotide in the codon, let $(\mathtt{T},\mathtt{C},\mathtt{A},\mathtt{G})$ be respectively represented by (⚏,⚏,⚏,⚏); represent the second nucleotide, similarly, by (⚎,⚎,⚎,⚎); represent the third by (⚍,⚍,⚍,⚍); and superimpose those three representations. Thus, for example, hexagram number 34 is ▤ = ⚏ + ⚎ + ⚍; it represents the codon TTC, which maps to the amino acid F. Under this correspondence, hexagrams 34 through 54 inclusive map into the respective values $(\mathtt{F},\mathtt{G},\mathtt{L},\mathtt{Q},\mathtt{W},\mathtt{D},\mathtt{S},-,\mathtt{P},\mathtt{Y},\mathtt{K},\mathtt{A},\mathtt{I},\mathtt{T},\mathtt{N},\mathtt{H},\mathtt{M},\mathtt{R},\mathtt{V},\mathtt{E},\mathtt{C})$. Moreover, the three hexagrams that map to '$-$' are numbers 1, 9, and 41, namely ▤, ▤, and ▤, which mean "creation," "taming," and "removal of excess" in the *I Ching* — all quite appropriate for the notion of completing a protein.

(b) Consider the $\binom{64}{6,6,6,4,4,4,4,4,3,3,2,2,2,2,2,2,2,2,2,1,1} \approx 2.3 \times 10^{69}$ ways to permute the elements of the $4 \times 4 \times 4$ genetic code array. Exactly

$$2402880402175789790003993681964551328451668718750185553920000000 \approx 2.4 \times 10^{63}$$

of them contain at least one run of 21 distinct consecutive elements. [Using the principle of inclusion and exclusion one can show that any multiset $\{(n_1+1)\cdot x_1, \ldots, (n_r+1)\cdot x_r\}$ with r distinct elements and $n_r = 0$ has exactly

$$(n+1)\binom{n}{n_1,\ldots,n_r}r! - \sum_{k=1}^{r}(n+1-k)k!(r-k)!\,a_k \sum_{\substack{0 \le d_1,\ldots,d_r \le 1 \\ d_1+\cdots+d_r=k}} \binom{n-k}{n_1-d_1,\ldots,n_r-d_r}$$

such permutations, where $n = n_1 + \cdots + n_r$ and a_k is the number of indecomposable permutations with k elements (exercise 7.2.1.2–100).] Thus only about one out of every million permutations has the stated property.

But there are $4!^3\binom{6}{2,2,2} = 1244160$ ways to represent codons as in part (a), and most of them correspond to different permutations of the amino acids (except for interchanging the representations of T and C in third position).

Empirically, in fact, about 31% of all permutations of the 64 hexagrams turn out to have suitable codon mappings. Thus the construction in part (a) gives no reason to believe that the authors of the *I Ching* anticipated the genetic code in any way.

3. Since $F_{31} - 10^6 = F_{28} + F_{22} + F_{20} + F_{18} + F_{16} + F_{14} + F_9$, the millionth is

⌣⌣⌣⌣⌣⌣⌣ ⎯⌣⌣⌣ ⎯ ⎯ ⎯ ⎯ ⎯⌣⌣⌣ ⎯⌣⌣.

Going the other way is easier: $F_{31} - (F_5 + F_8 + F_{10} + F_{16} + F_{18} + F_{27} + F_{30}) = 314159$.

4. One of the two appearances of במדיר on line 4 should be במידר; similarly, one ירדמב on line 8 should be ירמדב. And the six cases with rightmost letters גכ appear twice, in lines 3 and 4, while the cases with rightmost כב are missing. These glitches are probably typographical and/or scribal errors, not made by Donnolo himself.

5. The last one should have been ⬛, not ⬛.

6. The nth value m_n in Mersenne's list agrees with $n!$ only for $1 \le n \le 13$ and $15 \le n \le 38$. Mersenne knew that $14! = 87178291200 \ne m_{14} = 8778291200$, because he inserted the missing '1' in his personal copy of the book (now owned by the Bibliothèque Nationale; a facsimile was published in 1963). But the other errors in his table were not merely typographical, because they propagated into subsequent entries, except in the case of m_{50}: $m_{39} = 39! + 10^{26} - 10^{10}$; $m_{40} = 40m_{39}$; $m_{41} = 41m_{40} - 4 \cdot 10^{25} - 14 \cdot 10^{11}$; $m_n = nm_{n-1}$ for $n = 42, 43, 44, 46, 47, 48, 49, 55, 60$, and 62; $m_{50} = 50m_{49} + 10^{66}$; $m_{51} = 51 \cdot 50 \cdot m_{49}$. When he computed $m_{45} = 9 \cdot 45 \cdot m_{44} - 10^{40} + 10^{29}$, he apparently decided to take a shortcut, because it's easy to multiply by 5 or by 9; but he multiplied *twice* by 9. Most of his errors indicate an unreliable multiplication technique, which may have depended on an abacus: $m_{52} = 52m_{51} + 5 \cdot 10^{56} - 2 \cdot 10^{47} + 10^{34}$; $m_{53} = 53m_{52} - 4 \cdot 10^{29}$; $m_{54} = 54m_{53} + 10^{16}$; $m_{57} = 57m_{56} + 10^{33} + 10^{24}$; $m_{58} = 58m_{57} + 10^{67} - 10^{35} + 10^{32} + 11 \cdot 10^{26}$; $m_{59} = 59m_{58} + 10^{66} + 10^{49} - 10^{28}$; $m_{61} = 61m_{60} - 5 \cdot 10^{81}$; $m_{63} = 63m_{62} + 10^{82} - 10^{74}$; $m_{64} = 64m_{63} + 3 \cdot 10^{81} + 10^{67} + 2 \cdot 10^{38} - 2 \cdot 10^{33} - 10^{23}$.

The remaining case, $m_{56} \approx 10.912m_{55}$ is baffling; it is $\equiv 56m_{55}$ (modulo 10^{17}), but its other digits seem to satisfy neither rhyme nor reason. Can they be easily explained?

Notes: Athanasius Kircher must have copied from Mersenne when he tabulated $n!$ for $1 \le n \le 50$ on page 157 of his *Ars Magna Sciendi* (1669), because he repeated all of Mersenne's mistakes. Kircher did, however, list the values $10m_{14}$, $m_{45}/10$, and $10m_{49}$ instead of m_{14}, m_{45}, and m_{49}; perhaps he was trying to make the sequence grow more steadily. It is not clear who first calculated the correct value of 39!; exercise 1.2.5–4 tells the story of 1000!.

7. The basic permutations are 12345, 13254, 14523, 15432, 12453, 14235, 15324, 13542, 12534, 15243, 13425, 14352. But then we find that all 60 of the even permutations are both alive and dead, because (9) differs by an even permutation from (8). (Moreover, if we somehow repair the case $n = 5$, half of the live permutations for $n = 6$ will turn out to be odd.)

8. For example, we can replace (9) by

$$a_n a_3 \dots a_{n-1} a_2 a_1, \quad a_1 a_4 \dots a_n a_3 a_2, \quad \dots, \quad a_{n-1} a_2 \dots a_{n-2} a_1 a_n,$$

thus flipping the ends and cyclically shifting the other elements in the permutations of (8). This modification works because all permutations have the correct parity, and because the live and dead ones both have a_1 in every possible position. (We essentially have a dual Sims table for the alternating group, as in Eq. 7.2.1.2–(32); but our elements are named $(n, n-1, \dots, 1)$ instead of $(0, 1, \dots, n-1)$.)

A simpler way to generate permutations with the proper signs was published by É. Bézout [*Mémoires Acad. Royale des Sciences* (Paris, 1764), 292]: Each permutation $\pm a_1 \dots a_{n-1}$ of $\{1, \dots, n-1\}$ yields n others, $\pm a_1 \dots a_{n-1} a_n \mp a_1 \dots a_{n-2} a_n a_{n-1} \pm \dots$.

9. $(\cdot, \backslash, \Upsilon, \Upsilon, \xi, \circ, ٦, \vee, \wedge, ٩)$; or perhaps we should say $(٩, \wedge, \vee, ٦, \circ, \xi, \Upsilon, \Upsilon, \backslash, \cdot)$. *Notes:* A different system was used for the index numbers of the equations; for example, 'ٮ' stood for 200. Moreover, it should be noted that (11) is actually a transcription of al-Samaw'al's work into *modern* Arabic; Ahmad and Rashed based their work on a 14th-century copy that used similar but older forms of the digits: $(\circ, \backslash, \Upsilon, \Upsilon, ۴, ٨, ٦, \vee, \wedge, ٩)$. Al-Samaw'al himself may well have used numerals of an even earlier vintage.

10. If the 56 cases were equally likely, the answer would be $56H_{56} \approx 258.2$, as in the coupon collector's problem (exercise 3.3.2–8). But $(6, 30, 20)$ cases occur with the respective probabilities $(1/216, 1/72, 1/36)$; so the correct answer turns out to be

$$\int_0^\infty \left(1 - (1 - e^{-t/216})^6 (1 - e^{-t/72})^{30} (1 - e^{-t/36})^{20}\right) dt \approx 546.6,$$

about 42% of the upper bound $216H_{216}$. [See P. Flajolet, D. Gardy, and L. Thimonier, *Discrete Applied Math.* **39** (1992), 207–229.]

11. It tabulates the $\binom{6}{3} = 20$ combinations of (b, c, d, B, C, D) taken three at a time; furthermore, they appear in lexicographic order if we regard $b < c < d < B < C < D$. The letter t (𝕥) means "shift from lowercase to uppercase." [See A. Bonner, *Selected Works of Ramon Llull* (Princeton: 1985), 596–597.] There are two typos: 'd' should be 'b' at the beginning of line 6; 'c' should be 'd' at the end of line 18. Line 1 would have been more consistent with the others if Llull had presented it as

but in that line, of course, no case shift was needed.

12. Multiply Poinsot's cycle by 5 and add 2 (mod 7).

13. It's best to have just n lines when there are n different letters:

$$a.\ aa.\ aaa$$
$$\overline{b.\ ab.\ aab.\ aaab.\ bb.\ abb.\ aabb.\ aaabb}$$

Then, assigning the weights $(a, b) = (1, 4)$ gives the numbers 1 through 11 as in (18). (The first line of (16) should also be omitted.) Similarly, for $\{a, a, a, b, b, c\}$ we would implicitly give c the weight 12 and add the additional line

$$c.\ ac.\ aac.\ aaac.\ bc.\ abc.\ aabc.\ aaabc.\ bbc.\ abbc.\ aabbc.\ aaabbc.$$

[J. Bernoulli *almost* did it right in *Ars Conjectandi*, Part 2, Chapter 6.]

14. ABC ABD ABE ACD ACE ACB ADE ADB ADC AEB AEC AED BCD BCE BCA BDE BDA BDC BEA BEC BED BAC BAD BAE CDE CDA CDB CEA CEB CED CAB CAD CAE CBD CBE CBA DEA DEB DEC DAB DAC DAE DBC DBE DBA DCE DCA DCB EAB EAC EAD EBC EBD EBA ECD ECA ECB EDA EDB EDC. It's a genlex ordering (see Algorithm 7.2.1.3R), proceeding cyclically through the letters not yet used.

[A similar ordering had been used to form all 120 permutations of five letters in a kabbalistic work entitled *Sha'ari Tzedeq*, ascribed to the 13th-century author Natan ben Sa'adyah Har'ar of Messina, Sicily; see *Le Porte della Giustizia* (Milan: Adelphi, 2001).]

15. After j we place the $(n-1)$-combinations of $\{j, \ldots, m\}$ with repetition, so the answer is $\binom{(m+1-j)+(n-1)-1}{n-1} = \binom{m+n-j-1}{n-1}$. [Jean Borrel, also known as Buteonis, pointed this out on pages 305–309 of his early book *Logistica* (Lyon: 1560). He tabulated all throws of n dice for $1 \le n \le 4$, then used a sum over j to deduce that there are $56 + 35 + 20 + 10 + 4 + 1 = 252$ distinct throws for $n = 5$, and 462 for $n = 6$.]

16. N1. [Initialize.] Set $r \leftarrow n$, $t \leftarrow 0$, and $a_0 \leftarrow 0$.

    N2. [Advance.] While $r \ge q$, set $t \leftarrow t + 1$, $a_t \leftarrow q$, and $r \leftarrow r - q$. Then if $r > 0$, set $t \leftarrow t + 1$ and $a_t \leftarrow r$.

    N3. [Visit.] Visit the composition $a_1 \ldots a_t$.

    N4. [Find j.] Set $j \leftarrow t, t-1, \ldots$, until $a_j \ne 1$. Terminate the algorithm if $j = 0$.

    N5. [Decrease a_j.] Set $a_j \leftarrow a_j - 1$, $r \leftarrow t - j + 1$, $t \leftarrow j$; return to N2. ∎

For example, the compositions for $n = 7$ and $q = 3$ are 331, 322, 3211, 313, 3121, 3112, 31111, 232, 2311, 223, 2221, 2212, 22111, 2131, 2122, 21211, 2113, 21121, 21112, 211111, 133, 1321, 1312, 13111, 1231, 1222, 12211, 1213, 12121, 12112, 121111, 1132, 11311, 1123, 11221, 11212, 112111, 11131, 11122, 111211, 11113, 111121, 111112, 1111111.

Nārāyaṇa's sutras 79 and 80 gave essentially this procedure, but with the strings reversed (133, 223, 1123, ...), because he preferred decreasing colex order. [Śārṅgadeva, in *Saṅgītaratnākara* §5.316–375, had previously developed an elaborate theory for the set of all compositions (rhythms) that can be formed from the basic parts $\{1, 2, 4, 6\}$.]

17. The number V_n of visits is $F_{n+q-1}^{(q)} = \Theta(\alpha_q^n)$; see exercise 5.4.2–7. The number X_n of times step N4 tests $a_j = 1$ satisfies $X_n = X_{n-1} + \cdots + X_{n-q} + 1$, and we find $X_n = V_0 + \cdots + V_n = (qV_n + (q-1)V_{n-1} + \cdots + V_{n-q+1} - 1)/(q-1) = \Theta(V_n)$. The number Y_n of times step N2 sets $a_t \leftarrow q$ satisfies the same recurrence, and we find $Y_n = X_{n-q}$. And the number of times step N2 finds $r = 0$ turns out to be V_{n-q}.

18. It was MDCLXVI in Roman numerals, where M > D > C > L > X > V > I.

19. Lines 329 and 1022. (Puteanus included 139 such verses among his list of 1022.)

20. With 'tria' preceding 'lumina', there are $5! \times 2! \times (11, 12, 12, 16)$ ways having a dactyl in the (1st, 2nd, 3rd, 4th) foot, respectively; with 'lumina' preceding 'tria' there are $5! \times 2! \times (16, 12, 12, 11)$. So the total is 24480. [Leibniz considered this problem near the end of his *Dissertatio de Arte Combinatoria*, and came up with the answer 45870; but his argument was riddled with errors.]

21. (a) The generating function $1/((1 - zu - yu^2)(1 - zv - yv^2)(1 - zw - yw^2))$ is clearly equal to $\sum_{p,q,r,s,t \geq 0} f(p, q, r; s, t) u^p v^q w^r z^s y^t$.

(b) If 'tibi' is $\smile\smile$ and 'Virgo' is $--$, the number is $3! \, 3!$ times $\sum_{k=0}^{3} (f(2k+1, 6-2k, 2; 3, 3) + f(2k, 6-2k, 2; 2, 3))$, namely $36((7+7) + (9+5) + (10+5) + (14+7)) = 2304$. Otherwise 'tibi' is $\smile-$, 'Virgo' is $-\smile$, and the number is $2! \, 3!$ times $\sum_{k=0}^{3} (f(2k, 5-2k, 2; 3, 2) + f(2k, 6-2k, 1; 3, 2))$, namely $12((7+6) + (5+4) + (4+4) + (0+6)) = 432$.

(c) The fifth foot begins with the second syllable of 'cælo', 'dotes', or 'Virgo'. Hence the additional number is $3! \, 3! \sum_{k=0}^{2} f(2k, 5-2k, 2; 3, 2) = 36(7 + 5 + 4) = 576$, and the grand total is $2304 + 432 + 576 = 3312$.

22. Let $\alpha \in \{\text{quot}, \text{sunt}, \text{tot}\}$, $\beta \in \{\text{cælo}, \text{dotes}, \text{Virgo}\}$, $\sigma = \text{sidera}$, and $\tau = \text{tibi}$. Prestet's analysis was essentially equivalent to that of Bernoulli, but he forgot to include the 36 cases $\alpha\alpha\alpha\tau\beta\beta\sigma\beta$. (In his favor one can say that those cases are poetically sterile; Puteanus found no use for them.) The 1675 edition of Prestet's book had also omitted all permutations that end with $\tau\beta$.

Wallis divided the possibilities into 23 types, $T_1 \cup T_2 \cup \cdots \cup T_{23}$. He claimed that his types 6 and 7 each yielded 324 verses; but actually $|T_6| = |T_7| = 252$, because his variable i should be 7, not 9. He also counted many solutions twice: $|T_3 \cap T_5| = 72$, $|T_2 \cap T_7| = |T_5 \cap T_7| = |T_3 \cap T_6| = |T_6 \cap T_{10}| = 36$, and $|T_{11} \cap T_{12}| = |T_{12} \cap T_{13}| = |T_{14} \cap T_{15}| = 12$. He missed the 36 possibilities $\alpha\beta\beta\alpha\sigma\alpha\tau\beta$ (19 of which were used by Puteanus). And he also missed all the permutations of exercise 21(c); Puteanus had used 250 of those 576. The Latin edition of Wallis's book, published in 1693, corrected several typographic errors in this section, but none of the mathematical mistakes.

Whitworth and Hartley omitted all cases with 'tibi' = $\smile-$ (see exercise 19), possibly because people's knowledge of classical hexameter was beginning to fade.

[Speaking of errors, Puteanus actually published only 1020 distinct permutations, not 1022, because lines 592 and 593 in his list were identical to lines 601 and 602. But he would have had no trouble finding two more cases — for example, by changing 'tot sunt' to 'sunt tot' in lines 252, 345, 511, 548, 659, 663, 678, 693, or 797.]

23. Reading each diagram left-to-right, so that $12\mid345 \leftrightarrow$ ▥, we get

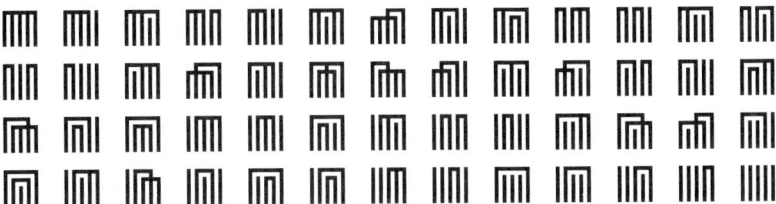

24. His rule was: For $k = 0, 1, \ldots, n-1$, and for each combination $0 < j_1 < \cdots < j_k < n$ of $n-1$ things taken k at a time, visit all partitions of $\{1,\ldots,n-1\}\setminus\{j_1,\ldots,j_k\}$ together with the block $\{j_1,\ldots,j_k,n\}$. His order for $n = 5$ was:

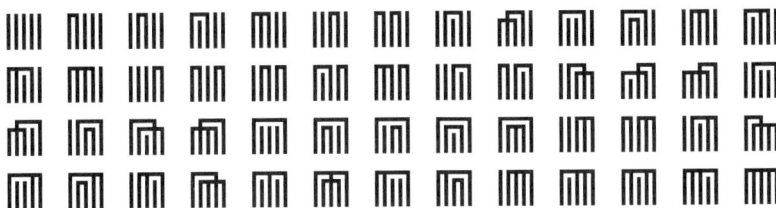

But strictly speaking, the answer to this exercise is "No" — because Honda's rule is not complete until the order of the combinations is specified. He generated combinations in *colex* order (lexicographic on $j_t \ldots j_1$). Lexicographic order on $j_1 \ldots j_t$ would also be consistent with the list given for $n = 4$, but it would put ▥ ▥ before ▥ ▥. *Reference:* T. Hayashi, *Tôhoku Math. J.* **33** (1931), 332–337.

25. No; (28) misses $14\mid235$ (the top-bottom reflection of its second pattern).

26. Let a_n be the number of indecomposable partitions of $\{1,\ldots,n\}$, and let a'_n be the number that are both indecomposable and complete. These sequences begin $\langle a_1, a_2, \ldots \rangle = \langle 1, 1, 2, 6, 22, 92, 426, \ldots \rangle$, $\langle a'_1, a'_2, \ldots \rangle = \langle 0, 1, 1, 3, 9, 33, 135, \ldots \rangle$; and the answer to this exercise is $a'_n - 1$ for $n \geq 2$. It turns out that a_n is also the number of symmetric polynomials of degree n in noncommuting variables. [See M. C. Wolf, *Duke Math. J.* **2** (1936), 626–637, who also tabulated indecomposable partitions into k parts.]

If $A(z) = \sum_n a_n z^n$, and if $B(z) = \sum_n \varpi_n z^n$ is the non-exponential generating function for Bell numbers, we have $A(z) B(z) = B(z) - 1$, hence $A(z) = 1 - 1/B(z)$. And the result of exercise 7.2.1.5–35 implies that $\sum_n a'_n z^n = zA(z)/(1 + z - A(z)) = z(B(z) - 1)/(1 + zB(z))$. Unfortunately $B(z)$ has no especially nice closed form, although it does satisfy the interesting functional relation $1 + zB(z) = B(z/(1 + z))$. Notice that indecomposable set partitions with $n > 1$ correspond to vacillating tableau loops with no three consecutive λs equal to zero (see exercise 7.2.1.5–27).

27. The problem is ambiguous because genji-ko diagrams are not well defined. Let's require all vertical lines of a block to have the same height; then, for example, $145\mid236$ has no single-crossing diagram because ▥ is not allowed.

The number of partitions with no crossing is C_n (see exercise 7.2.1.6–26). For one crossing, the elements of the two blocks that cross must appear within the restricted growth string as either $x^i y x^j y^k$ or $x^i y^{j+1} x y^k$ or $x^i y^j x y^k x^l$, where $i, j, k, l > 0$.

Suppose the pattern is $x^i y x^j y^k$. There are $t = i + j + k + 2$ "slots" between the $i + 1 + j + k$ elements of this pattern, and the number of ways to fill these slots with noncrossing partitions is $\sum_{i_1+\cdots+i_t=n-i-j-k-1} C_{i_1}\ldots C_{i_t}$. We can express this number as

$$[z^{n-i-j-k-1}]\,C(z)^{i+j+k+2} = C_{(n-i-j-k-1)n}$$

by Eq. 7.2.1.6–(24). Summing on k gives $C_{(n-i-j-2)(n+1)}$; then summing on j and i gives $C_{(n-4)(n+3)}$.

Similarly, the other two patterns contribute $C_{(n-5)(n+3)}$ and $C_{(n-5)(n+4)}$. The total number of single-crossing partitions is therefore $C_{(n-5)(n+3)} + C_{(n-4)(n+4)}$.

28. Order the divisors of $cbbaaa$ by their number of prime factors and then colexicographically: $1 \prec a \prec b \prec c \prec aa \prec ba \prec ca \prec bb \prec cb \prec aaa \prec baa \prec caa \prec bba \prec cba \prec cbb \prec baaa \prec caaa \prec bbaa \prec cbaa \prec cbba \prec bbaaa \prec cbaaa \prec cbbaa \prec cbbaaa$. For every such divisor d, in decreasing order, let d be the first factor; recursively append all factorizations of $cbbaaa/d$ whose first factor is $\preceq d$.

If the divisors had been ordered lexicographically (namely $1 < a < aa < aaa < b < ba < \cdots < cbbaa < cbbaaa$), Wallis's algorithm would have been equivalent to Algorithm 7.2.1.5M with $(n_1, n_2, n_3) = (1, 2, 3)$. He probably chose his more complicated ordering of the divisors because it tends to agree more closely with ordinary numerical order when $a \approx b \approx c$; for example, his ordering is precisely numerical when $(a, b, c) = (7, 11, 13)$. By generating the divisors according to his somewhat complex scheme, Wallis was essentially generating multiset combinations, which we noted in Section 7.2.1.3 are equivalent to bounded compositions. [*Reference: A Discourse of Combinations* (1685), 126–128, with two typographic errors corrected.]

29. The factorizations $edcba, edcb\cdot a, edca\cdot b, \ldots, e\cdot d\cdot c\cdot b\cdot a$ correspond respectively to

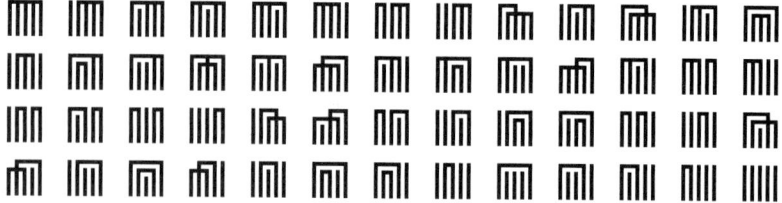

30. The coefficient is zero unless $i_1 + 2i_2 + \cdots = n$; in that case it is $\binom{m}{k}a_0^{m-k}\binom{k}{i_1,i_2,\ldots}$ where $k = i_1 + i_2 + \cdots$. (Consider $(a_0 z)^m$ times $(1 + (a_1/a_0)z + (a_2/a_0)z^2 + \cdots)^m$.)

31. The order produced by that algorithm is decreasing lexicographic, the reverse of (31), if we assume that partitions $a_1 \ldots a_k$ have $a_1 \geq \cdots \geq a_k$; de Moivre's was increasing *colexicographic*.

32. $20 \cdot 1 = 7 + 13 \cdot 1 = 2 \cdot 7 + 6 \cdot 1 = 10 + 10 \cdot 1 = 10 + 7 + 3 \cdot 1 = 2 \cdot 10$. In general, Boscovich suggested starting with $n \cdot 1$ and computing the successor of $a \cdot 10 + b \cdot 7 + c \cdot 1$ as follows: If $c \geq 7$, the successor is $a \cdot 10 + (b+1) \cdot 7 + (c-7) \cdot 1$; otherwise if $c + 7b \geq 10$, the successor is $(a + 1) \cdot 10 + (c + 7b - 10) \cdot 1$; otherwise stop.

"I may," said Poirot in a completely unconvinced tone, *"be wrong."*
— AGATHA CHRISTIE, *After the Funeral* (1953)

— HARPO MARX, *The Cocoanuts* (1925)
— MARCEL MARCEAU, *Baptiste* (1946)

APPENDIX A

TABLES OF NUMERICAL QUANTITIES

Table 1

QUANTITIES THAT ARE FREQUENTLY USED IN STANDARD SUBROUTINES
AND IN ANALYSIS OF COMPUTER PROGRAMS (40 DECIMAL PLACES)

$$\sqrt{2} = 1.41421\ 35623\ 73095\ 04880\ 16887\ 24209\ 69807\ 85697-$$
$$\sqrt{3} = 1.73205\ 08075\ 68877\ 29352\ 74463\ 41505\ 87236\ 69428+$$
$$\sqrt{5} = 2.23606\ 79774\ 99789\ 69640\ 91736\ 68731\ 27623\ 54406+$$
$$\sqrt{10} = 3.16227\ 76601\ 68379\ 33199\ 88935\ 44432\ 71853\ 37196-$$
$$\sqrt[3]{2} = 1.25992\ 10498\ 94873\ 16476\ 72106\ 07278\ 22835\ 05703-$$
$$\sqrt[3]{3} = 1.44224\ 95703\ 07408\ 38232\ 16383\ 10780\ 10958\ 83919-$$
$$\sqrt[4]{2} = 1.18920\ 71150\ 02721\ 06671\ 74999\ 70560\ 47591\ 52930-$$
$$\ln 2 = 0.69314\ 71805\ 59945\ 30941\ 72321\ 21458\ 17656\ 80755+$$
$$\ln 3 = 1.09861\ 22886\ 68109\ 69139\ 52452\ 36922\ 52570\ 46475-$$
$$\ln 10 = 2.30258\ 50929\ 94045\ 68401\ 79914\ 54684\ 36420\ 76011+$$
$$1/\ln 2 = 1.44269\ 50408\ 88963\ 40735\ 99246\ 81001\ 89213\ 74266+$$
$$1/\ln 10 = 0.43429\ 44819\ 03251\ 82765\ 11289\ 18916\ 60508\ 22944-$$
$$\pi = 3.14159\ 26535\ 89793\ 23846\ 26433\ 83279\ 50288\ 41972-$$
$$1° = \pi/180 = 0.01745\ 32925\ 19943\ 29576\ 92369\ 07684\ 88612\ 71344+$$
$$1/\pi = 0.31830\ 98861\ 83790\ 67153\ 77675\ 26745\ 02872\ 40689+$$
$$\pi^2 = 9.86960\ 44010\ 89358\ 61883\ 44909\ 99876\ 15113\ 53137-$$
$$\sqrt{\pi} = \Gamma(1/2) = 1.77245\ 38509\ 05516\ 02729\ 81674\ 83341\ 14518\ 27975+$$
$$\Gamma(1/3) = 2.67893\ 85347\ 07747\ 63365\ 56929\ 40974\ 67764\ 41287-$$
$$\Gamma(2/3) = 1.35411\ 79394\ 26400\ 41694\ 52880\ 28154\ 51378\ 55193+$$
$$e = 2.71828\ 18284\ 59045\ 23536\ 02874\ 71352\ 66249\ 77572+$$
$$1/e = 0.36787\ 94411\ 71442\ 32159\ 55237\ 70161\ 46086\ 74458+$$
$$e^2 = 7.38905\ 60989\ 30650\ 22723\ 04274\ 60575\ 00781\ 31803+$$
$$\gamma = 0.57721\ 56649\ 01532\ 86060\ 65120\ 90082\ 40243\ 10422-$$
$$\ln \pi = 1.14472\ 98858\ 49400\ 17414\ 34273\ 51353\ 05871\ 16473-$$
$$\phi = 1.61803\ 39887\ 49894\ 84820\ 45868\ 34365\ 63811\ 77203+$$
$$e^\gamma = 1.78107\ 24179\ 90197\ 98523\ 65041\ 03107\ 17954\ 91696+$$
$$e^{\pi/4} = 2.19328\ 00507\ 38015\ 45655\ 97696\ 59278\ 73822\ 34616+$$
$$\sin 1 = 0.84147\ 09848\ 07896\ 50665\ 25023\ 21630\ 29899\ 96226-$$
$$\cos 1 = 0.54030\ 23058\ 68139\ 71740\ 09366\ 07442\ 97660\ 37323+$$
$$-\zeta'(2) = 0.93754\ 82543\ 15843\ 75370\ 25740\ 94567\ 86497\ 78979-$$
$$\zeta(3) = 1.20205\ 69031\ 59594\ 28539\ 97381\ 61511\ 44999\ 07650-$$
$$\ln \phi = 0.48121\ 18250\ 59603\ 44749\ 77589\ 13424\ 36842\ 31352-$$
$$1/\ln \phi = 2.07808\ 69212\ 35027\ 53760\ 13226\ 06117\ 79576\ 77422-$$
$$-\ln \ln 2 = 0.36651\ 29205\ 81664\ 32701\ 24391\ 58232\ 66946\ 94543-$$

Table 2

QUANTITIES THAT ARE FREQUENTLY USED IN STANDARD SUBROUTINES
AND IN ANALYSIS OF COMPUTER PROGRAMS (40 HEXADECIMAL PLACES)

The names at the left of the "=" signs are given in decimal notation.

$$0.1 = 0.1999\ 9999\ 9999\ 9999\ 9999\ 9999\ 9999\ 9999\ 9999\ 999A-$$
$$0.01 = 0.028F\ 5C28\ F5C2\ 8F5C\ 28F5\ C28F\ 5C28\ F5C2\ 8F5C\ 28F6-$$
$$0.001 = 0.0041\ 8937\ 4BC6\ A7EF\ 9DB2\ 2D0E\ 5604\ 1893\ 74BC\ 6A7F-$$
$$0.0001 = 0.0006\ 8DB8\ BAC7\ 10CB\ 295E\ 9E1B\ 089A\ 0275\ 2546\ 0AA6+$$
$$0.00001 = 0.0000\ A7C5\ AC47\ 1B47\ 8423\ 0FCF\ 80DC\ 3372\ 1D53\ CDDD+$$
$$0.000001 = 0.0000\ 10C6\ F7A0\ B5ED\ 8D36\ B4C7\ F349\ 3858\ 3621\ FAFD-$$
$$0.0000001 = 0.0000\ 01AD\ 7F29\ ABCA\ F485\ 787A\ 6520\ EC08\ D236\ 9919+$$
$$0.00000001 = 0.0000\ 002A\ F31D\ C461\ 1873\ BF3F\ 7083\ 4ACD\ AE9F\ 0F4F+$$
$$0.000000001 = 0.0000\ 0004\ 4B82\ FA09\ B5A5\ 2CB9\ 8B40\ 5447\ C4A9\ 8188-$$
$$0.0000000001 = 0.0000\ 0000\ 6DF3\ 7F67\ 5EF6\ EADF\ 5AB9\ A207\ 2D44\ 268E-$$
$$\sqrt{2} = 1.6A09\ E667\ F3BC\ C908\ B2FB\ 1366\ EA95\ 7D3E\ 3ADE\ C175+$$
$$\sqrt{3} = 1.BB67\ AE85\ 84CA\ A73B\ 2574\ 2D70\ 78B8\ 3B89\ 25D8\ 34CC+$$
$$\sqrt{5} = 2.3C6E\ F372\ FE94\ F82B\ E739\ 80C0\ B9DB\ 9068\ 2104\ 4ED8-$$
$$\sqrt{10} = 3.298B\ 075B\ 4B6A\ 5240\ 9457\ 9061\ 9B37\ FD4A\ B4E0\ ABB0-$$
$$\sqrt[3]{2} = 1.428A\ 2F98\ D728\ AE22\ 3DDA\ B715\ BE25\ 0D0C\ 288F\ 1029+$$
$$\sqrt[3]{3} = 1.7137\ 4491\ 23EF\ 65CD\ DE7F\ 16C5\ 6E32\ 67C0\ A189\ 4C2B-$$
$$\sqrt[4]{2} = 1.306F\ E0A3\ 1B71\ 52DE\ 8D5A\ 4630\ 5C85\ EDEC\ BC27\ 3436+$$
$$\ln 2 = 0.B172\ 17F7\ D1CF\ 79AB\ C9E3\ B398\ 03F2\ F6AF\ 40F3\ 4326+$$
$$\ln 3 = 1.193E\ A7AA\ D030\ A976\ A419\ 8D55\ 053B\ 7CB5\ BE14\ 42DA-$$
$$\ln 10 = 2.4D76\ 3776\ AAA2\ B05B\ A95B\ 58AE\ 0B4C\ 28A3\ 8A3F\ B3E7+$$
$$1/\ln 2 = 1.7154\ 7652\ B82F\ E177\ 7D0F\ FDA0\ D23A\ 7D11\ D6AE\ F552-$$
$$1/\ln 10 = 0.6F2D\ EC54\ 9B94\ 38CA\ 9AAD\ D557\ D699\ EE19\ 1F71\ A301+$$
$$\pi = 3.243F\ 6A88\ 85A3\ 08D3\ 1319\ 8A2E\ 0370\ 7344\ A409\ 3822+$$
$$1° = \pi/180 = 0.0477\ D1A8\ 94A7\ 4E45\ 7076\ 2FB3\ 74A4\ 2E26\ C805\ BD78-$$
$$1/\pi = 0.517C\ C1B7\ 2722\ 0A94\ FE13\ ABE8\ FA9A\ 6EE0\ 6DB1\ 4ACD-$$
$$\pi^2 = 9.DE9E\ 64DF\ 22EF\ 2D25\ 6E26\ CD98\ 08C1\ AC70\ 8566\ A3FE+$$
$$\sqrt{\pi} = \Gamma(1/2) = 1.C5BF\ 891B\ 4EF6\ AA79\ C3B0\ 520D\ 5DB9\ 383F\ E392\ 1547-$$
$$\Gamma(1/3) = 2.ADCE\ EA72\ 905E\ 2CEE\ C8D3\ E92C\ D580\ 46D8\ 4B46\ A6B3-$$
$$\Gamma(2/3) = 1.5AA7\ 7928\ C367\ 8CAB\ 2F4F\ EB70\ 2B26\ 990A\ 54F7\ EDBC+$$
$$e = 2.B7E1\ 5162\ 8AED\ 2A6A\ BF71\ 5880\ 9CF4\ F3C7\ 62E7\ 160F+$$
$$1/e = 0.5E2D\ 58D8\ B3BC\ DF1A\ BADE\ C782\ 9054\ F90D\ DA98\ 05AB-$$
$$e^2 = 7.6399\ 2E35\ 376B\ 730C\ E8EE\ 881A\ DA2A\ EEA1\ 1EB9\ EBD9+$$
$$\gamma = 0.93C4\ 67E3\ 7DB0\ C7A4\ D1BE\ 3F81\ 0152\ CB56\ A1CE\ CC3B-$$
$$\ln \pi = 1.250D\ 048E\ 7A1B\ D0BD\ 5F95\ 6C6A\ 843F\ 4998\ 5E6D\ DBF4-$$
$$\phi = 1.9E37\ 79B9\ 7F4A\ 7C15\ F39C\ C060\ 5CED\ C834\ 1082\ 276C-$$
$$e^\gamma = 1.C7F4\ 5CAB\ 1356\ BF14\ A7EF\ 5AEB\ 6B9F\ 6C45\ 60A9\ 1932+$$
$$e^{\pi/4} = 2.317A\ CD28\ E395\ 4F87\ 6B04\ B8AB\ AAC8\ C708\ F1C0\ 3C4A+$$
$$\sin 1 = 0.D76A\ A478\ 4867\ 7020\ C6E9\ E909\ C50F\ 3C32\ 89E5\ 1113+$$
$$\cos 1 = 0.8A51\ 407D\ A834\ 5C91\ C246\ 6D97\ 6871\ BD29\ A237\ 3A89+$$
$$-\zeta'(2) = 0.F003\ 2992\ B55C\ 4F28\ 88E9\ BA28\ 1E4C\ 405F\ 8CBE\ 9FEE+$$
$$\zeta(3) = 1.33BA\ 004F\ 0062\ 1383\ 7171\ 5C59\ E690\ 7F1B\ 180B\ 7DB1+$$
$$\ln \phi = 0.7B30\ B2BB\ 1458\ 2652\ F810\ 812A\ 5A31\ C083\ 4C9E\ B233+$$
$$1/\ln \phi = 2.13FD\ 8124\ F324\ 34A2\ 63C7\ 5F40\ 76C7\ 9883\ 5224\ 4685-$$
$$-\ln \ln 2 = 0.5DD3\ CA6F\ 75AE\ 7A83\ E037\ 67D6\ 6E33\ 2DBC\ 09DF\ AA82-$$

Several interesting constants with less common names have arisen in connection with the analyses in the present book. Those constants have been evaluated to 40 decimal places in Eqs. 7.1.4–(90) and 7.2.1.5–(34), and in the answer to exercise 7.1.4–191.

Table 3

VALUES OF HARMONIC NUMBERS, BERNOULLI NUMBERS,
AND FIBONACCI NUMBERS, FOR SMALL VALUES OF n

n	H_n	B_n	F_n	n
0	0	1	0	0
1	1	$-1/2$	1	1
2	3/2	1/6	1	2
3	11/6	0	2	3
4	25/12	$-1/30$	3	4
5	137/60	0	5	5
6	49/20	1/42	8	6
7	363/140	0	13	7
8	761/280	$-1/30$	21	8
9	7129/2520	0	34	9
10	7381/2520	5/66	55	10
11	83711/27720	0	89	11
12	86021/27720	$-691/2730$	144	12
13	1145993/360360	0	233	13
14	1171733/360360	7/6	377	14
15	1195757/360360	0	610	15
16	2436559/720720	$-3617/510$	987	16
17	42142223/12252240	0	1597	17
18	14274301/4084080	43867/798	2584	18
19	275295799/77597520	0	4181	19
20	55835135/15519504	$-174611/330$	6765	20
21	18858053/5173168	0	10946	21
22	19093197/5173168	854513/138	17711	22
23	444316699/118982864	0	28657	23
24	1347822955/356948592	$-236364091/2730$	46368	24
25	34052522467/8923714800	0	75025	25
26	34395742267/8923714800	8553103/6	121393	26
27	312536252003/80313433200	0	196418	27
28	315404588903/80313433200	$-2749461029/870$	317811	28
29	9227046511387/2329089562800	0	514229	29
30	9304682830147/2329089562800	8615841276005/14322	832040	30

For any x, let $H_x = \sum_{n \geq 1} \left(\dfrac{1}{n} - \dfrac{1}{n+x} \right)$. Then

$$H_{1/2} = 2 - 2\ln 2,$$

$$H_{1/3} = 3 - \tfrac{1}{2}\pi/\sqrt{3} - \tfrac{3}{2}\ln 3,$$

$$H_{2/3} = \tfrac{3}{2} + \tfrac{1}{2}\pi/\sqrt{3} - \tfrac{3}{2}\ln 3,$$

$$H_{1/4} = 4 - \tfrac{1}{2}\pi - 3\ln 2,$$

$$H_{3/4} = \tfrac{4}{3} + \tfrac{1}{2}\pi - 3\ln 2,$$

$$H_{1/5} = 5 - \tfrac{1}{2}\pi\phi^{3/2}5^{-1/4} - \tfrac{5}{4}\ln 5 - \tfrac{1}{2}\sqrt{5}\ln\phi,$$

$$H_{2/5} = \tfrac{5}{2} - \tfrac{1}{2}\pi\phi^{-3/2}5^{-1/4} - \tfrac{5}{4}\ln 5 + \tfrac{1}{2}\sqrt{5}\ln\phi,$$

$$H_{3/5} = \tfrac{5}{3} + \tfrac{1}{2}\pi\phi^{-3/2}5^{-1/4} - \tfrac{5}{4}\ln 5 + \tfrac{1}{2}\sqrt{5}\ln\phi,$$

$$H_{4/5} = \tfrac{5}{4} + \tfrac{1}{2}\pi\phi^{3/2}5^{-1/4} - \tfrac{5}{4}\ln 5 - \tfrac{1}{2}\sqrt{5}\ln\phi,$$

$$H_{1/6} = 6 - \tfrac{1}{2}\pi\sqrt{3} - 2\ln 2 - \tfrac{3}{2}\ln 3,$$

$$H_{5/6} = \tfrac{6}{5} + \tfrac{1}{2}\pi\sqrt{3} - 2\ln 2 - \tfrac{3}{2}\ln 3,$$

and, in general, when $0 < p < q$ (see exercise 1.2.9–19),

$$H_{p/q} = \frac{q}{p} - \frac{\pi}{2}\cot\frac{p}{q}\pi - \ln 2q + 2\sum_{1 \leq n < q/2} \cos\frac{2pn}{q}\pi \cdot \ln\sin\frac{n}{q}\pi.$$

> *Reader, if you ever have to start a computing laboratory,*
> *be warned by me and do not take as a computer an accountant,*
> *no matter how honest and efficient. Your computer must work*
> *to so and so many significant figures, whether the significance*
> *of the digits begins six places before or six places after the*
> *decimal point. Your accountant works to cents, and he will work to cents*
> *until hell freezes over. Whatever numbers our accountant computed*
> *he kept at all stages to exactly two places after the decimal point …*
>
> *This was his conscience, that he should be accurate to the last cent;*
> *and he simply could not understand that physical quantities are not*
> *measured in cents but on a sliding scale of values in which*
> *the cents of one problem might be the dollars of another.*
>
> — NORBERT WIENER, *I am a Mathematician* (1956)

APPENDIX B

INDEX TO NOTATIONS

In the following formulas, letters that are not further qualified have the following significance:

j, k	integer-valued arithmetic expression
m, n	nonnegative integer-valued arithmetic expression
p, q	binary-valued arithmetic expression (0 or 1)
x, y	real-valued arithmetic expression
z	complex-valued arithmetic expression
f	integer-valued, real-valued, or complex-valued function
G, H	graph
S, T	set or multiset
$\mathcal{F}, \mathcal{G}$	family of sets
u, v	vertex of a graph
α, β	string of symbols

The place of definition is either a page number in the present volume or a section number in a previous volume. Many other notations, such as K_n for the complete graph on n vertices, appear in the main index at the close of this book.

Formal symbolism	Meaning	Where defined
$V \leftarrow E$	give variable V the value of expression E	§1.1
$U \leftrightarrow V$	interchange the values of variables U and V	§1.1
A_n or $A[n]$	the nth element of linear array A	§1.1
A_{mn} or $A[m, n]$	the element in row m and column n of rectangular array A	§1.1
$(R?\ a{:}\ b)$	conditional expression: denotes a if relation R is true, b if R is false	96
$[R]$	characteristic function of relation R: $(R?\ 1{:}\ 0)$	§1.2.3
δ_{jk}	Kronecker delta: $[j = k]$	§1.2.3
$[z^n]\, f(z)$	coefficient of z^n in power series $f(z)$	§1.2.9
$z_1 + z_2 + \cdots + z_n$	sum of n numbers (even when n is 0 or 1)	§1.2.3
$a_1 a_2 \dots a_n$	product or string or vector of n elements	
$(x_1, \dots, x_n)$	vector of n elements	
$\langle x_1 x_2 \dots x_{2k-1} \rangle$	median value (middle value after sorting)	75

Formal symbolism	Meaning	Where defined
$\sum_{R(k)} f(k)$	sum of all $f(k)$ such that relation $R(k)$ is true	§1.2.3
$\prod_{R(k)} f(k)$	product of all $f(k)$ such that relation $R(k)$ is true	§1.2.3
$\min_{R(k)} f(k)$	minimum of all $f(k)$ such that relation $R(k)$ is true	§1.2.3
$\max_{R(k)} f(k)$	maximum of all $f(k)$ such that relation $R(k)$ is true	§1.2.3
$\bigcup_{R(k)} S(k)$	union of all $S(k)$ such that relation $R(k)$ is true	
$\sum_{k=a}^{b} f(k)$	shorthand for $\sum_{a \leq k \leq b} f(k)$	§1.2.3
$\{a \mid R(a)\}$	set of all a such that relation $R(a)$ is true	
$\sum \{f(k) \mid R(k)\}$	another way to write $\sum_{R(k)} f(k)$	
$\{a_1, a_2, \ldots, a_n\}$	the set or multiset $\{a_k \mid 1 \leq k \leq n\}$	
$[x \mathrel{..} y]$	closed interval: $\{a \mid x \leq a \leq y\}$	§1.2.2
$(x \mathrel{..} y)$	open interval: $\{a \mid x < a < y\}$	§1.2.2
$[x \mathrel{..} y)$	half-open interval: $\{a \mid x \leq a < y\}$	§1.2.2
$(x \mathrel{..} y]$	half-closed interval: $\{a \mid x < a \leq y\}$	§1.2.2
$\lvert S \rvert$	cardinality: the number of elements in S	
$\lvert f \rvert$	number of solutions (when f is Boolean): $\sum_x f(x)$	207
$\lvert x \rvert$	absolute value of x: $(x \geq 0?\ x:\ -x)$	
$\lvert z \rvert$	absolute value of z: $\sqrt{z\bar{z}}$	§1.2.2
$\lvert \alpha \rvert$	length of α: m if $\alpha = a_1 a_2 \ldots a_m$	
$\lfloor x \rfloor$	floor of x, greatest integer function: $\max_{k \leq x} k$	§1.2.4
$\lceil x \rceil$	ceiling of x, least integer function: $\min_{k \geq x} k$	§1.2.4
$x \bmod y$	mod function: $\big(y = 0?\ x:\ x - y\lfloor x/y \rfloor\big)$	§1.2.4
$\{x\}$	fractional part (used in contexts where a real value, not a set, is implied): $x \bmod 1$	§1.2.11.2
$x \equiv x' \pmod{y}$	relation of congruence: $x \bmod y = x' \bmod y$	§1.2.4
$j \backslash k$	j divides k: $k \bmod j = 0$ and $j > 0$	§1.2.4
$S \setminus T$	set difference: $\{s \mid s \text{ in } S \text{ and } s \text{ not in } T\}$	
$S \setminus t$	shorthand for $S \setminus \{t\}$	
$G \setminus v$	G with vertex v removed	13
$G \setminus e$	G with edge e removed	13
G / e	G with edge e shrunk to a point	463
$S \cup t$	shorthand for $S \cup \{t\}$	
$S \uplus T$	multiset sum; e.g., $\{a,b\} \uplus \{a,c\} = \{a,a,b,c\}$	§4.6.3
$\gcd(j,k)$	greatest common divisor: $(j=k=0?\ 0:\ \max_{d \backslash j, d \backslash k} d)$	§1.1
$j \perp k$	j is relatively prime to k: $\gcd(j,k) = 1$	§1.2.4

Formal symbolism	Meaning	Where defined
A^T	transpose of rectangular array A: $A^T[j,k] = A[k,j]$	
α^R	left-right reversal of string α	
α^T	conjugate of partition α	394
x^y	x to the y power (when $x > 0$): $e^{y\ln x}$	§1.2.2
x^k	x to the k power: $\left(k \geq 0?\ \prod_{j=0}^{k-1} x\colon 1/x^{-k}\right)$	§1.2.2
x^-	inverse (or reciprocal) of x: x^{-1}	§1.3.3
$x^{\bar{k}}$	x to the k rising: $\Gamma(x+k)/\Gamma(k) =$ $\left(k \geq 0?\ \prod_{j=0}^{k-1}(x+j)\colon 1/(x+k)^{\overline{-k}}\right)$	§1.2.5
$x^{\underline{k}}$	x to the k falling: $x!/(x-k)! =$ $\left(k \geq 0?\ \prod_{j=0}^{k-1}(x-j)\colon 1/(x-k)^{\underline{-k}}\right)$	§1.2.5
$n!$	n factorial: $\Gamma(n+1) = n^{\underline{n}}$	§1.2.5
$\binom{x}{k}$	binomial coefficient: $(k < 0?\ 0\colon x^{\underline{k}}/k!)$	§1.2.6
$\binom{n}{n_1,\dots,n_m}$	multinomial coefficient (when $n = n_1 + \dots + n_m$)	§1.2.6
$\left[{n \atop m}\right]$	Stirling cycle number: $\sum_{0 < k_1 < \dots < k_{n-m} < n} k_1 \dots k_{n-m}$	§1.2.6
$\left\{{n \atop m}\right\}$	Stirling subset number: $\sum_{1 \leq k_1 \leq \dots \leq k_{n-m} \leq m} k_1 \dots k_{n-m}$	§1.2.6
$\left\langle{n \atop m}\right\rangle$	Eulerian number: $\sum_{k=0}^{m}(-1)^k \binom{n+1}{k}(m+1-k)^n$	§5.1.3
$\left|{n \atop m}\right|$	m-part partitions of n: $\sum_{1 \leq k_1 \leq \dots \leq k_m}[k_1 + \dots + k_m = n]$	399
$(\dots a_1 a_0 . a_{-1} \dots)_b$	radix-b positional notation: $\sum_k a_k b^k$	§4.1
$\Re z$	real part of z	§1.2.2
$\Im z$	imaginary part of z	§1.2.2
$\bar{z}$	complex conjugate: $\Re z - i\,\Im z$	§1.2.2
$\sim p$ or $\bar{p}$	complement: $1 - p$	49
$\sim x$ or $\bar{x}$	bitwise complement	135
$p \wedge q$	Boolean conjunction (and): pq	49
$x \wedge y$	minimum: $\min\{x,y\}$	63
$x \mathbin{\&} y$	bitwise AND	134
$p \vee q$	Boolean disjunction (or): $\overline{\bar{p}\bar{q}}$	49
$x \vee y$	maximum: $\max\{x,y\}$	63
$x \mid y$	bitwise OR	134
$p \oplus q$	Boolean exclusive disjunction (xor): $(p+q) \bmod 2$	50
$x \oplus y$	bitwise XOR	134
$x \mathbin{\dot-} y$	saturated subtraction, x monus y: $\max\{0, x-y\}$	§1.3.1′
$x \ll k$	bitwise left shift: $\lfloor 2^k x \rfloor$	135
$x \gg k$	bitwise right shift: $x \ll (-k)$	135
$x \mathbin{\ddagger} y$	"zipper function" for interleaving bits, x zip y	147

Formal symbolism	Meaning	Where defined
$\log_b x$	logarithm, base b, of x (defined when $x > 0$, $b > 0$, and $b \neq 1$): the y such that $x = b^y$	§1.2.2
$\ln x$	natural logarithm: $\log_e x$	§1.2.2
$\lg x$	binary logarithm: $\log_2 x$	§1.2.2
λn	binary logsize (when $n > 0$): $\lfloor \lg n \rfloor$	142
$\exp x$	exponential of x: $e^x = \sum_{k=0}^{\infty} x^k/k!$	§1.2.9
ρn	ruler function (when $n > 0$): $\max_{2^m \backslash n} m$	140
νn	sideways sum (when $n > 0$): $\sum_{k \geq 0} \big((n \gg k) \mathbin{\&} 1 \big)$	143
$\langle X_n \rangle$	the infinite sequence $X_0, X_1, X_2, \ldots$ (here the letter n is part of the symbolism)	§1.2.9
$f'(x)$	derivative of f at x	§1.2.9
$f''(x)$	second derivative of f at x	§1.2.10
$H_n^{(x)}$	harmonic number of order x: $\sum_{k=1}^{n} 1/k^x$	§1.2.7
H_n	harmonic number: $H_n^{(1)}$	§1.2.7
F_n	Fibonacci number: $(n \leq 1\,?\ n\colon F_{n-1} + F_{n-2})$	§1.2.8
B_n	Bernoulli number: $n!\,[z^n]\,z/(e^z - 1)$	§1.2.11.2
$\det(A)$	determinant of square matrix A	§1.2.3
$\operatorname{sign}(x)$	sign of x: $[x > 0] - [x < 0]$	
$\zeta(x)$	zeta function: $\lim_{n \to \infty} H_n^{(x)}$ (when $x > 1$)	§1.2.7
$\Gamma(x)$	gamma function: $(x-1)! = \gamma(x, \infty)$	§1.2.5
$\gamma(x, y)$	incomplete gamma function: $\int_0^y e^{-t} t^{x-1}\,dt$	§1.2.11.3
γ	Euler's constant: $-\Gamma'(1) = \lim_{n \to \infty}(H_n - \ln n)$	§1.2.7
e	base of natural logarithms: $\sum_{n \geq 0} 1/n!$	§1.2.2
π	circle ratio: $4 \sum_{n \geq 0} (-1)^n/(2n + 1)$	§1.2.2
∞	infinity: larger than any number	
Λ	null link (pointer to no address)	§2.1
$\emptyset$	empty set (set with no elements)	
ϵ	empty string (string of length zero)	
ϵ	unit family: $\{\emptyset\}$	273
ϕ	golden ratio: $(1 + \sqrt{5})/2$	§1.2.8
$\varphi(n)$	Euler's totient function: $\sum_{k=0}^{n-1} [k \perp n]$	§1.2.4
$x \approx y$	x is approximately equal to y	§1.2.5
$G \cong H$	G is isomorphic to H	14
$O\big(f(n)\big)$	big-oh of $f(n)$, as the variable $n \to \infty$	§1.2.11.1
$O\big(f(z)\big)$	big-oh of $f(z)$, as the variable $z \to 0$	§1.2.11.1
$\Omega\big(f(n)\big)$	big-omega of $f(n)$, as the variable $n \to \infty$	§1.2.11.1
$\Theta\big(f(n)\big)$	big-theta of $f(n)$, as the variable $n \to \infty$	§1.2.11.1

Formal symbolism	Meaning	Where defined
$\overline{G}$	complement of graph (or uniform hypergraph) G	26
$G \mid U$	G restricted to the vertices of set U	13
$G \setminus e$	G with edge e removed	13
G / e	G with edge e contracted	463
$u \mathbin{—} v$	u is adjacent to v	13
$u \mathbin{\not\!\!—} v$	u is not adjacent to v	13
$u \longrightarrow v$	there is an arc from u to v	18
$u \longrightarrow^* v$	transitive closure: v is reachable from u	159
$d(u, v)$	distance from u to v	16
$G \cup H$	union of G and H	26
$G \oplus H$	direct sum (juxtaposition) of G and H	26
$G \mathbin{—} H$	join of G and H	26
$G \longrightarrow H$	directed join of G and H	26
$G \,\square\, H$	Cartesian product of G and H	27
$G \otimes H$	direct product (conjunction) of G and H	28
$G \boxtimes H$	strong product of G and H	28
$G \triangle H$	odd product of G and H	28
$G \circ H$	lexicographic product (composition) of G and H	28
e_j	elementary family: $\{\{j\}\}$	273
$\wp$	universal family: all subsets of a given universe	275
$\mathcal{F} \cup \mathcal{G}$	union of families: $\{S \mid S \in \mathcal{F}$ or $S \in \mathcal{G}\}$	273
$\mathcal{F} \cap \mathcal{G}$	intersection of families: $\{S \mid S \in \mathcal{F}$ and $S \in \mathcal{G}\}$	273
$\mathcal{F} \setminus \mathcal{G}$	difference of families: $\{S \mid S \in \mathcal{F}$ and $S \notin \mathcal{G}\}$	273
$\mathcal{F} \oplus \mathcal{G}$	symmetric difference of families: $(\mathcal{F} \setminus \mathcal{G}) \cup (\mathcal{G} \setminus \mathcal{F})$	273
$\mathcal{F} \sqcup \mathcal{G}$	join of families: $\{S \cup T \mid S \in \mathcal{F}, T \in \mathcal{G}\}$	273
$\mathcal{F} \sqcap \mathcal{G}$	meet of families: $\{S \cap T \mid S \in \mathcal{F}, T \in \mathcal{G}\}$	273
$\mathcal{F} \boxplus \mathcal{G}$	delta of families: $\{S \oplus T \mid S \in \mathcal{F}, T \in \mathcal{G}\}$	273
$\mathcal{F}/\mathcal{G}$	quotient (cofactor) of families	273
$\mathcal{F} \bmod \mathcal{G}$	remainder of families: $\mathcal{F} \setminus (\mathcal{G} \sqcup (\mathcal{F}/\mathcal{G}))$	273
$\mathcal{F} \S k$	symmetrized family, if $\mathcal{F} = e_{j_1} \cup e_{j_2} \cup \cdots \cup e_{j_n}$	274
$\mathcal{F}^\uparrow$	maximal elements of $\mathcal{F}$: $\{S \in \mathcal{F} \mid T \in \mathcal{F}$ and $S \subseteq T$ implies $S = T\}$	276
$\mathcal{F}^\uparrow$	minimal elements of $\mathcal{F}$: $\{S \in \mathcal{F} \mid T \in \mathcal{F}$ and $S \supseteq T$ implies $S = T\}$	276
$\mathcal{F} \nearrow \mathcal{G}$	nonsubsets: $\{S \in \mathcal{F} \mid T \in \mathcal{G}$ implies $S \not\subseteq T\}$	276
$\mathcal{F} \searrow \mathcal{G}$	nonsupersets: $\{S \in \mathcal{F} \mid T \in \mathcal{G}$ implies $S \not\supseteq T\}$	276
$\mathcal{F} \swarrow \mathcal{G}$	subsets: $\{S \in \mathcal{F} \mid T \in \mathcal{G}$ implies $S \subseteq T\} = \mathcal{F} \setminus (\mathcal{F} \nearrow \mathcal{G})$	669
$\mathcal{F} \nwarrow \mathcal{G}$	supersets: $\{S \in \mathcal{F} \mid T \in \mathcal{G}$ implies $S \supseteq T\} = \mathcal{F} \setminus (\mathcal{F} \searrow \mathcal{G})$	669

Formal symbolism	Meaning	Where defined
$X \cdot Y$	dot product of vectors: $x_1y_1 + x_2y_2 + \cdots + x_ny_n$, if $X = x_1x_2\ldots x_n$ and $Y = y_1y_2\ldots y_n$	12
$X \subseteq Y$	containment of vectors: $x_k \leq y_k$ for $1 \leq k \leq n$, if $X = x_1x_2\ldots x_n$ and $Y = y_1y_2\ldots y_n$	135
$\alpha \diamond \beta$	melding of truth tables	218
$\alpha(G)$	independence number of G	35
$\gamma(G)$	domination number of G	673
$\kappa(G)$	vertex connectivity of G	§7.4.1
$\lambda(G)$	edge connectivity of G	§7.4.1
$\nu(G)$	matching number of G	§7.5.5
$\chi(G)$	chromatic number of G	35
$\omega(G)$	clique number of G	35
$c(G)$	number of spanning trees of G	482
∎	end of algorithm, program, or proof	§1.1

And to auoide the tediouse repetition of these woordes : is equalle to :
I will sette as I doe often in woorke use, a paire of paralleles,
or Gemowe lines of one lengthe, thus: ====== ,
bicause noe .2. thynges, can be moare equalle.
— ROBERT RECORDE, *The Whetstone of Witte* (1557)

Prof. Le Gendre, in the treatise that we shall often have occasion to cite,
used the same sign for both equality and congruence.
To avoid ambiguity we have made a distinction.
— C. F. GAUSS, *Disquisitiones Arithmeticæ* (1801)

Someone told me that each equation I included in the book
would halve the sales.
— STEPHEN HAWKING, *A Brief History of Time* (1987)

APPENDIX C

INDEX TO ALGORITHMS AND THEOREMS

*[An inverted list] provides duplicate, redundant information
in order to speed up secondary key retrieval.*
— DONALD E. KNUTH, *Sorting and Searching* (1973)

APPENDIX D

INDEX TO COMBINATORIAL PROBLEMS

The purpose of this appendix is to present concise descriptions of the major problems treated in the present book, and to associate each problem description with the name under which it can be found in the main index. Some of these problems can be solved efficiently, while others appear to be very difficult in general although special cases might be easy. No indication of problem complexity is given here.

Combinatorial problems have a chameleon-like tendency to assume many forms. For example, certain properties of graphs and hypergraphs are equivalent to other properties of 0–1 matrices; and an $m \times n$ matrix of 0s and 1s can itself be regarded as a Boolean function of mn Boolean variables, with 0 representing TRUE and 1 representing FALSE. Each problem also has many flavors: We sometimes ask only whether a solution to certain constraints exists at all; but usually we ask to see at least one explicit solution, or we try to count the number of solutions, or to visit them all. Often we require a solution that is optimum in some sense.

In the following list — which is intended to be helpful but by no means complete — each problem is presented in more-or-less formal terms as the task of "finding" some desired objective. This characterization is then followed by an informal paraphrase (in parentheses and quotation marks), and perhaps also by further comments.

Any problem that is stated in terms of directed graphs is automatically applicable also to undirected graphs, unless the digraph must be acyclic, because an undirected edge $u \!-\! v$ is equivalent to the two directed arcs $u \longrightarrow v$ and $v \longrightarrow u$.

• <u>Satisfiability</u>: Given a Boolean function f of n Boolean variables, find Boolean values $x_1, \ldots, x_n$ such that $f(x_1, \ldots, x_n) = 1$. ("If possible, show that f can be true.")

• <u>kSAT</u>: The satisfiability problem when f is the conjunction of clauses, where each clause is a disjunction of at most k literals x_j or $\bar{x}_j$. ("Can all the clauses be true?") The cases 2SAT and 3SAT are most important. Another significant special case arises when f is a conjunction of *Horn clauses*, each having at most one negated literal $\bar{x}_j$.

• <u>Boolean chain</u>: Given one or more Boolean functions of n Boolean values $x_1, \ldots, x_n$, find $x_{n+1}, \ldots, x_N$ such that each x_k for $n < k \le N$ is a Boolean function of x_i and x_j for some $i < k$ and $j < k$, and such that each of the given functions is either constant or equal to x_l for some $l \le N$. ("Construct a straight-line program to evaluate a given set of functions, sharing intermediate values.") ("Build a circuit to compute a given collection of outputs from the inputs 0, 1, $x_1, \ldots, x_n$, using 2-input Boolean gates with unlimited fanout.") The goal is usually to minimize N.

• <u>Broadword chain</u>: Like a Boolean chain, but using bitwise and/or arithmetic operations on integers modulo 2^d instead of Boolean operations on Boolean values; the given value of d can be arbitrarily large. ("Work on several related problems at once.")

• <u>Boolean programming</u>: Given a Boolean function f of n Boolean variables, together with given weights $w_1, \ldots, w_n$, find Boolean values $x_1, \ldots, x_n$ such that $f(x_1, \ldots, x_n) = 1$ and $w_1 x_1 + \cdots + w_n x_n$ is as large as possible. ("How can f be satisfied with maximum payoff?")

• Matching: Given a graph G, find a set of disjoint edges. ("Pair up the vertices so that each vertex has at most one partner.") The goal is usually to find as many edges as possible; a "perfect matching" includes all the vertices. In a bipartite graph with m vertices in one part and n vertices in the other, matching is equivalent to selecting a set of 1s in an $m \times n$ matrix of 0s and 1s, with at most one selected in each row and at most one selected in each column.

• Assignment problem: A generalization of bipartite matching, with weights associated with each edge; the total weight of the matching should be maximized. ("What assignment of people to jobs is best?") Equivalently, we wish to select elements of an $m \times n$ matrix, at most one per row and at most one per column, so that the sum of selected elements is as large as possible.

• Covering: Given a matrix A_{jk} of 0s and 1s, find a set of rows R such that we have $\sum_{j \in R} A_{jk} > 0$ for all k. ("Mark a 1 in each column and select all rows that have been marked.") The goal is usually to minimize $|R|$.

• Exact cover: Given a matrix A_{jk} of 0s and 1s, find a set of rows R such that $\sum_{j \in R} A_{jk} = 1$ for all k. ("Cover with mutually orthogonal rows.") The perfect matching problem is equivalent to finding an exact cover of the transposed incidence matrix.

• Independent set: Given a graph or hypergraph G, find a set of vertices U such that the induced graph $G \mid U$ has no edges. ("Choose unrelated vertices.") The goal is usually to maximize $|U|$. Classical special cases include the 8-queens problem, when G is the graph of queen moves on a chessboard, and the no-three-on-a-line problem.

• Clique: Given a graph G, find a set of vertices U such that the induced graph $G \mid U$ is complete. ("Choose mutually adjacent vertices.") Equivalently, find an independent set in $\sim G$. The goal is usually to maximize $|U|$.

• Vertex cover: Given a graph or hypergraph, find a set of vertices U such that every edge includes at least one vertex of U. ("Mark some vertices so that no edge remains unmarked.") Equivalently, find a covering of the transposed incidence matrix. Equivalently, find U such that $V \setminus U$ is independent, where V is the set of all vertices. The goal is usually to minimize $|U|$.

• Dominating set: Given a graph, find a set of vertices U such that every vertex not in U is adjacent to some vertex of U. ("What vertices are within one step of them all?") The classic 5-queens problem is the special case when G is the graph of queen moves on a chessboard.

• Kernel: Given a directed graph, find an independent set of vertices U such that every vertex not in U is the predecessor of some vertex of U. ("In what independent positions of a 2-player game can your opponent force you to remain?") If the graph is undirected, a kernel is equivalent to a maximal independent set, and to a dominating set that is both minimal and independent.

• Coloring: Given a graph, find a way to partition its vertices into k independent sets. ("Color the vertices with k colors, never giving the same color to adjacent points.") The goal is usually to minimize k.

• Shortest path: Given vertices u and v of a directed graph in which weights are associated with every arc, find the smallest total weight of an oriented path from u to v. ("Determine the best route.")

• Longest path: Given vertices u and v of a directed graph in which weights are associated with every arc, find the largest total weight of a simple oriented path from u to v. ("What route meanders the most?")

• Reachability: Given a set of vertices U in a directed graph G, find all vertices v such that $u \longrightarrow^* v$ for some $u \in U$. ("What vertices occur on paths that start in U?")

• Spanning tree: Given a graph G, find a free tree F on the same vertices, such that every edge of F is an edge of G. ("Choose just enough edges to connect up all the vertices.") If weights are associated with each edge, a *minimum spanning tree* is a spanning tree of smallest total weight.

• Hamiltonian path: Given a graph G, find a path P on the same vertices, such that every edge of P is an edge of G. ("Discover a path that encounters every vertex exactly once.") This is the classic knight's tour problem when G is the graph of knight moves on a chessboard. When the vertices of G are combinatorial objects — for example, tuples, permutations, combinations, partitions, or trees — that are adjacent when they are "close" to each other, a Hamiltonian path is often called a Gray code.

• Hamiltonian cycle: Given a graph G, find a cycle C on the same vertices, such that every edge of C is an edge of G. ("Discover a path that encounters every vertex exactly once and returns to the starting point.")

• Traveling Salesrep Problem: Find a Hamiltonian cycle of smallest total weight, when weights are associated with each edge of the given graph. ("What's the cheapest way to visit everything?") If the graph has no Hamiltonian cycle, we extend it to a complete graph by assigning a very large weight W to every nonexistent edge.

• Topological sorting: Given a directed graph, find a way to label each vertex x with a distinct number $l(x)$ in such a way that $x \longrightarrow y$ implies $l(x) < l(y)$. ("Place the vertices in a row, with each vertex to the left of all its successors.") Such a labeling is possible if and only if the given digraph is acyclic.

• Optimum linear arrangement: Given a graph, find a way to label each vertex x with a distinct integer $l(x)$, such that $\sum_{u \text{—} v} |l(u) - l(v)|$ is as small as possible. ("Place the vertices in a row, minimizing the sum of the resulting edge lengths.")

• Knapsack problem: Given a sequence of weights $w_1, \ldots, w_n$, a threshold W, and a sequence of values $v_1, \ldots, v_n$, find $K \subseteq \{1, \ldots, n\}$ such that $\sum_{k \in K} w_k \le W$ and $\sum_{k \in K} v_k$ is maximum. ("How much value can be carried?")

• Orthogonal array: Given positive integers m and n, find an $m \times n^2$ array with entries $A_{jk} \in \{0, 1, \ldots, n-1\}$ and with the property that $j \ne j'$ and $k \ne k'$ implies $(A_{jk}, A_{j'k}) \ne (A_{jk'}, A_{j'k'})$. ("Construct m different $n \times n$ matrices of n-ary digits in such a way that all n^2 possible digit pairs occur when any two of the matrices are superimposed.") The case $m = 3$ corresponds to a latin square, and the case $m > 3$ corresponds to $m - 2$ mutually orthogonal latin squares.

• Nearest common ancestor: Given nodes u and v of a forest, find w such that every inclusive ancestor of u and of v is also an inclusive ancestor of w. ("Where does the shortest path from u to v change direction?")

• Range minimum query: Given a sequence of numbers $a_1, \ldots, a_n$, find the minimum elements of each subinterval $a_i, \ldots, a_j$ for $1 \le i < j \le n$. ("Solve all possible queries concerning the minimum value in any given range.") Exercises 150 and 151 of Section 7.1.3 show that this problem is equivalent to finding nearest common ancestors.

• Universal cycle: Given b, k, and N, find a cyclic sequence of elements x_0, x_1, $\ldots$, x_{N-1}, x_0, $\ldots$ of b-ary digits $\{0, 1, \ldots, b-1\}$ with the property that all combinatorial arrangements of a particular kind are given by the consecutive k-tuples $x_0 x_1 \ldots x_{k-1}$, $x_1 x_2 \ldots x_k$, $\ldots$, $x_{N-1} x_0 \ldots x_{k-2}$. ("Exhibit all possibilities in a circular fashion.") The result is called a de Bruijn cycle if $N = b^k$ and all possible k-tuples appear; it's a universal cycle of combinations if $N = \binom{b}{k}$ and if all k-combinations of b things appear; and it's a universal cycle of permutations if $N = b!$, $k = b-1$, and if all $(b-1)$-variations appear as k-tuples.

In most cases we have been able to give a set-theoretic definition that describes the problem completely, although the need for conciseness has often led to some obscuring of the intuition behind the problem.

— M. R. GAREY and D. S. JOHNSON, *A List of NP-Complete Problems* (1979)

INDEX AND GLOSSARY

Indexes need not necessarily be dry.
— HENRY B. WHEATLEY, *How to Make an Index* (1902)

When an index entry refers to a page containing a relevant exercise, see also the *answer* to that exercise for further information. An answer page is not indexed here unless it refers to a topic not included in the statement of the exercise.

⌣, *see* smile.
\# (number sign or hash mark), x.
∂ (shadow), 372.
ϱ (upper shadow), 372.

⊥ (FALSE), 202–208, 249, 250, 253–254, 259, 272, 273, 676–677.
⊤ (TRUE), 202–209, 250, 259, 273, 676–677.

−1 (the constant $(\cdots 111)_2$), 135, 140, 141, 182, 581, 586, 619.
0-origin indexing, 326.
0-preserving functions, *see* Normal Boolean functions.
0–1 matrices, *see* Matrices of 0s and 1s.
0–1 principle, 68, 186.
0–1 vectors, 480.
1-decision list functions, 654.
2-adic chains, 155–159, 169, 193, 602, 608.
2-adic fractions, 141, 193, 585, *see also* Magic masks.
2-adic integers: Infinite binary strings $(\ldots x_2 x_1 x_0)_2$ subject to arithmetic and bitwise operations, 134, 140, 147, 153, 185, 187, 193, 311.
  as a metric space, 584.
  with unsigned ordering, 581.
2-bit encoding for 3-state data, 160–163, 195.
2-coloring problem, 17, 22–23, 41.
2-cube equivalence, 161–162.
2-dimensional data allocation, 147–148.
2-level redundancies function, *see* Covering function.
2-monotonic functions, *see* Regular Boolean functions.
2-nomial coefficients, 726.
2-partite graphs (2-colorable graphs), *see* Bipartite graphs.
2-variable functions, 47–50, 79–80, 259, 272, 279.
  table, 49.
2ADDU (times 2 and add unsigned), 590, 596, 620.
2CNF, 57, 72, 86–87, 91, 545, *see also* Krom functions.
2SAT functions, *see* 2CNF, Krom clauses.
2SAT problem, 57, 60–62, 72, 86, 830.

2^m-way multiplexer $(M_m(x; y))$, 109, 127, 131, 214, 243, 263, 266, 272, 627, 630, 638, 647, 659.
  permuted, 235, 239, 267, 269.
3-colorable tilings, 274.
3-colored tilings, 634.
3-coloring problem, 39, 42, 529.
3-cube, 14, 346, 387.
3-partite graphs (3-colorable graphs), 265, 277.
3-regular graphs, 14, 15, 39, 531.
3-state encodings, 160–163, 195.
3-uniform hypergraphs, 32–33, 672.
3-valued logic, 163, 195.
3-variable functions, 63, 99, 104–105, 126.
  table, 78.
3CNF, 56, 85.
3SAT problem, 56, 85, 542, 830.
4-colored graphs, 233, 246, 258, 265.
4-coloring problem, 17, 39, 530.
4-cube, 90, 327–328, 347, 468–469, 680, 693.
4-cycles, 69, 522.
4-neighbors, 172, *see* Rook-neighbors.
4-variable functions, 79, 98–105, 112–114, 122, 126, 129, 641.
5-queens problem, 672, 831.
5-variable functions, 79, 105–106, 126, 267, 277, 572.
8-cube, 297, 315.
8-neighbors, 172, *see* King-neighbors.
8-queens problem, 604, 672, 831.
∞ (infinity), 63, 140, 187.

$\alpha(H)$ (independence number of a graph or hypergraph), 35, 44.
γ (Euler's constant), as source of "random" data, 516, 818–819.
Γ_n, *see* Gray binary code.
δ-maps, 595.
δ-shifts, 148, 189.
  cyclic, 149, 190.
δ-swaps, 145–148, 182, 187–188, 619.
ϵ (the empty string), 266, 272.
ϵ (the unit family $\{\emptyset\}$), 273, 658, 662, 669–670.
$\kappa_t(n)$ (Kruskal's lower function), 373–375, 385–388, 477, 739.
Λ (the null link), 21, 222–223, 647–648.
λx ($\lfloor \lg x \rfloor$), x, *see* Binary logsize function.

THIS BOOK was composed on an HP Compaq 2510p with Computer Modern typefaces, using the TEX and METAFONT software as described in the author's books *Computers & Typesetting* (Reading, Mass.: Addison–Wesley, 1986), Volumes A–E. The illustrations were produced with John Hobby's METAPOST system. Some names in the index were typeset with additional fonts developed by Yannis Haralambous (Greek, Hebrew, Arabic), Olga G. Lapko (Cyrillic), Frans J. Velthuis (Devanagari), Masatoshi Watanabe (Japanese), and Linbo Zhang (Chinese).

ASCII CHARACTERS

	#0	#1	#2	#3	#4	#5	#6	#7	#8	#9	#a	#b	#c	#d	#e	#f	
#2x		!	"	#	$	%	&	'	(	)	*	+	,	-	.	/	#2x
#3x	0	1	2	3	4	5	6	7	8	9	:	;	<	=	>	?	#3x
#4x	@	A	B	C	D	E	F	G	H	I	J	K	L	M	N	O	#4x
#5x	P	Q	R	S	T	U	V	W	X	Y	Z	[	\	]	^	_	#5x
#6x	`	a	b	c	d	e	f	g	h	i	j	k	l	m	n	o	#6x
#7x	p	q	r	s	t	u	v	w	x	y	z	{	|	}	~	■	#7x
	#0	#1	#2	#3	#4	#5	#6	#7	#8	#9	#a	#b	#c	#d	#e	#f	

MMIX OPERATION CODES

	#0	#1	#2	#3	#4	#5	#6	#7	
#0x	TRAP $5v$	FCMP v	FUN v	FEQL v	FADD $4v$	FIX $4v$	FSUB $4v$	FIXU $4v$	#0x
	FLOT[I] $4v$		FLOTU[I] $4v$		SFLOT[I] $4v$		SFLOTU[I] $4v$		
#1x	FMUL $4v$	FCMPE $4v$	FUNE v	FEQLE $4v$	FDIV $40v$	FSQRT $40v$	FREM $4v$	FINT $4v$	#1x
	MUL[I] $10v$		MULU[I] $10v$		DIV[I] $60v$		DIVU[I] $60v$		
#2x	ADD[I] v		ADDU[I] v		SUB[I] v		SUBU[I] v		#2x
	2ADDU[I] v		4ADDU[I] v		8ADDU[I] v		16ADDU[I] v		
#3x	CMP[I] v		CMPU[I] v		NEG[I] v		NEGU[I] v		#3x
	SL[I] v		SLU[I] v		SR[I] v		SRU[I] v		
#4x	BN[B] $v+\pi$		BZ[B] $v+\pi$		BP[B] $v+\pi$		BOD[B] $v+\pi$		#4x
	BNN[B] $v+\pi$		BNZ[B] $v+\pi$		BNP[B] $v+\pi$		BEV[B] $v+\pi$		
#5x	PBN[B] $3v-\pi$		PBZ[B] $3v-\pi$		PBP[B] $3v-\pi$		PBOD[B] $3v-\pi$		#5x
	PBNN[B] $3v-\pi$		PBNZ[B] $3v-\pi$		PBNP[B] $3v-\pi$		PBEV[B] $3v-\pi$		
#6x	CSN[I] v		CSZ[I] v		CSP[I] v		CSOD[I] v		#6x
	CSNN[I] v		CSNZ[I] v		CSNP[I] v		CSEV[I] v		
#7x	ZSN[I] v		ZSZ[I] v		ZSP[I] v		ZSOD[I] v		#7x
	ZSNN[I] v		ZSNZ[I] v		ZSNP[I] v		ZSEV[I] v		
#8x	LDB[I] $\mu+v$		LDBU[I] $\mu+v$		LDW[I] $\mu+v$		LDWU[I] $\mu+v$		#8x
	LDT[I] $\mu+v$		LDTU[I] $\mu+v$		LDO[I] $\mu+v$		LDOU[I] $\mu+v$		
#9x	LDSF[I] $\mu+v$		LDHT[I] $\mu+v$		CSWAP[I] $2\mu+2v$		LDUNC[I] $\mu+v$		#9x
	LDVTS[I] v		PRELD[I] v		PREGO[I] v		GO[I] $3v$		
#Ax	STB[I] $\mu+v$		STBU[I] $\mu+v$		STW[I] $\mu+v$		STWU[I] $\mu+v$		#Ax
	STT[I] $\mu+v$		STTU[I] $\mu+v$		STO[I] $\mu+v$		STOU[I] $\mu+v$		
#Bx	STSF[I] $\mu+v$		STHT[I] $\mu+v$		STCO[I] $\mu+v$		STUNC[I] $\mu+v$		#Bx
	SYNCD[I] v		PREST[I] v		SYNCID[I] v		PUSHGO[I] $3v$		
#Cx	OR[I] v		ORN[I] v		NOR[I] v		XOR[I] v		#Cx
	AND[I] v		ANDN[I] v		NAND[I] v		NXOR[I] v		
#Dx	BDIF[I] v		WDIF[I] v		TDIF[I] v		ODIF[I] v		#Dx
	MUX[I] v		SADD[I] v		MOR[I] v		MXOR[I] v		
#Ex	SETH v	SETMH v	SETML v	SETL v	INCH v	INCMH v	INCML v	INCL v	#Ex
	ORH v	ORMH v	ORML v	ORL v	ANDNH v	ANDNMH v	ANDNML v	ANDNL v	
#Fx	JMP[B] v		PUSHJ[B] v		GETA[B] v		PUT[I] v		#Fx
	POP $3v$	RESUME $5v$	[UN]SAVE $20\mu+v$		SYNC v	SWYM v	GET v	TRIP $5v$	
	#8	#9	#A	#B	#C	#D	#E	#F	

$\pi = 2v$ if the branch is taken, $\pi = 0$ if the branch is not taken